Women's History Sources

WOMEN'S HISTORY SOURCES

A GUIDE TO ARCHIVES AND MANUSCRIPT COLLECTIONS IN THE UNITED STATES

Edited by
ANDREA HINDING

AMES SHELDON BOWER
Associate Editor

CLARKE A. CHAMBERS
Consulting Editor

In association with the University of Minnesota

VOLUME I / COLLECTIONS

R.R. BOWKER COMPANY
NEW YORK & LONDON · 1979

The Women's History Sources Survey
was made possible by a series of grants from
the National Endowment for the Humanities.

Published by R. R. Bowker Company
1180 Avenue of the Americas, New York, N.Y. 10036

Printed and bound in the United States of America

Library of Congress Cataloging in Publication Data
Main entry under title:

Women's history sources.

Vol. 2 edited by Suzanna Moody.
CONTENTS: v. 1. Collections.—v. 2. Index.
1. Women—United States—History—Archival resources—United States. I. Hinding, Andrea. II. Bower, Ames S.
Z7964.U49W64 [HQ1410] 016.30141'2'0973 78-15634

ISBN 0-8352-1103-7 (set)
ISBN 0-8352-1266-1 (Vol. I)

For the archivists, curators of manuscripts, librarians,
and other custodians of historical records
whose intelligent and generous cooperation
has made possible this work.

And for
Alice May Stahl • 1925–1978
cataloger, colleague, and friend,
whose strength and determination was characteristic
of so much of women's experience represented herein.

Women's History Sources Survey Staff

Cecelia Nelson Boone, writer and editor
Ames Sheldon Bower, writer and editor
Mary Jo Dobson, indexing assistant
Anna Bakuzis Glover, project manager
Andrea Hinding, project director and editor
David Klaassen, repository list compiler
Wendy Sue Larson, writer
Jeanne L'Heureux, indexing assistant
Doris Hanson Lunden, writer and fieldwork coordinator
Karen M. Mason, writer
Susan W. A. Mead, writer
Suzanna Moody, indexer
Randall Wallach, project assistant

Women's History Sources Survey Fieldworkers

Cathy F. Abernathy
Michele L. Aldrich
Nancy H. Burkett
Robert Conte
Howard A. Droker
Mathew J. Ferrero
Loretta Hefner
Heather Huyck
Patricia A. Michaelis
Dee Ann Montgomery
Mary Murphy
Ellen Newcombe
Mary Ostling
Cynthia H. Requardt
Kim Lacy Rogers
Darlene Roth-White
Marylynn Salmon
Phyllis Steele
Virginia Stewart
Sandra Van Burkleo

Women's History Sources Survey Advisory Board

Clarke A. Chambers, Professor of History, University of Minnesota
Maxine B. Clapp, University Archivist, University of Minnesota
Carl N. Degler, Professor of History, Stanford University
Lynn Bonfield Donovan, Archivist, California Historical Society
Frank B. Evans, Archivist, National Archives and Records Service
Elsie Freivogel, Archivist, National Archives and Records Service
Janet Wilson James, Professor of History, Boston College
Lucile M. Kane, Minnesota State Archivist, Minnesota Historical Society
Gerda Lerner, Professor of History, Sarah Lawrence College
Dorothy Porter, Librarian Emeritus, Howard University
Anne Firor Scott, Professor of History, Duke University
Joan Hoff Wilson, Professor of History, Arizona State University, Tempe

Contents

Preface

FROM 1975 TO 1979 the Social Welfare History Archives at the University of Minnesota conducted a nationwide survey of 11,000 archives and manuscript repositories for collections of unpublished (or primary) sources pertaining to the history of tens of thousands of women in the United States from the colonial period to the present. *Women's History Sources,* which contains descriptions of 18,026 collections in 1,586 repositories, arranged geographically by state and city, is the result of that survey.

ORIGIN OF THE SURVEY

The "grand manuscripts search," as historian Anne Firor Scott characterized the survey, began in the early 1970s with the interest of a group of historians—Gerda Lerner, Anne Firor Scott, Janet Wilson James, Carl Degler, and Clarke Chambers among them—in identifying little-known archival sources to support the growing field of women's history. To promote that interest, the group sponsored a program session at the 1972 annual convention of the Organization of American Historians in Washington, DC, at which eight archivists and historians discussed archival and manuscript sources for women's history. The enthusiastic response to the session in turn contributed to a decision by the Rockefeller Foundation to convene a conference of scholars and students in the summer of 1972 to discuss priorities for women's history. High among the priorities that emerged from the conference was a project to advance intellectual control over primary sources that serve as a base for research in women's history, women's studies, and other fields in the humanities and the social sciences. The group of historians urged Clarke Chambers and Andrea Hinding, then director and curator, respectively, of the Social Welfare History Archives, to seek a grant to conduct a systematic national survey. Funding for the survey—nearly $600,000 awarded in a series of grants—was eventually provided by the National Endowment for the Humanities and the University of Minnesota. The project was formally titled the Women's History Sources Survey.

SURVEY PROCEDURE

Because no union list of repositories existed when the Women's History Sources Survey began, the staff's first step was to identify, insofar as possible, the "universe" to be surveyed. Staff members used published directories, reference works, and the footnotes of scholarly works. Contributions to the list came from colleagues at the University of Illinois Chicago Circle manuscript division, the Minnesota Historical Society, and the California Historical Society. Major assistance was offered by the *National Union Catalog of Manuscript Collections* repository list, the American Association for State and Local History's directories and mailing lists, and the staff of the National Historical Publication and Records Commission, which was then at work revising Philip Hamer's *Guide to Archives and Manuscripts in the United States.* The list of potential repositories to be surveyed finally included more than 11,000 names, among them state, county, and local historical societies; manuscript divisions and collections within public, college, and university libraries; federal, state, and municipal government archives; and institutional archives of colleges and universities, corporations, labor unions, professional societies, churches, and religious organizations.

The bulk of the work of the Women's History Sources Survey was accomplished by use of a mail questionnaire. In a first mailing in March 1976, Survey staff members explained the purpose of the Survey in a letter and asked the respondents to complete a business reply card indicating whether the repository had primary sources and, if so, the number of collections that pertained to women's history. More than 7,000 repositories eventually responded (the final answer was received three years after the initial mailing), and of these approximately 2,000 indicated that they held pertinent collections. Those repositories that reported holding women's collections were sent questionnaires and accompanying explanatory material (described below) and were asked to report as many collections as possible, using one questionnaire for each collection.

The work accomplished by mail was supplemented by that of 20 fieldworkers who were employed for several months during 1976 and 1977 to conduct on-site surveys of repositories that were, for various reasons, unable to report their own holdings. After an initial training session held at the University of Minnesota, fieldworkers were assigned to the National Archives and the Library of Congress, the two largest repositories in the country, as well as to county historical societies, small museums, and other repositories in every state except Alaska and Hawaii, which was eventually visited by a Survey volunteer. In some instances fieldworkers simply explained the significance of the Survey and encouraged repository staff members to describe their own holdings. In other cases the fieldworkers described holdings on the basis of finding aids or reviewed the collections, some of which were housed in attics, basements, and remote storage areas. In several locations the fieldworkers organized volunteers or students to assist in their work.

After the questionnaires completed by either repository staffs or fieldworkers were submitted, the editorial staff drafted entries based on the questionnaires and returned the drafts to the repositories for reviewing factual accuracy, historical sense, and appropriateness of interpretation. (In some instances entries were drafted by staff members from a repository's published guide to its holdings or to a particular collection; these draft entries were also sent to repositories for review.) When the drafts were returned by repositories they were revised further by the editorial staff before final text was sent to the publisher. The completed text was then indexed.

PREFACE

SCOPE OF THE SURVEY

In the March 1976 initial mailing that introduced the Women's History Sources Survey, staff members explained that collections of family and personal papers and records of organizations and institutions were appropriate for inclusion but that book collections, even those of rare books, were specifically excluded. They also noted that photograph and oral history collections as well as more traditional record types—correspondence, diaries, financial and other organizational records—should be reported.

The questionnaires which were sent to repositories that indicated they held pertinent material were accompanied by instructions for completing the questionnaires and criteria for inclusion of collections in the Survey. In the instructions a collection was defined as a "group of manuscripts with a common source that is treated as a unit by a repository." For purposes of the Survey, archivists, whose terminology frequently differs from that of manuscripts curators and librarians, were asked to treat their archival record groups, subgroups, and similar units as synonymous with "collection."

Criteria for Inclusion

The general criterion for inclusion of collections offered by the Survey staff was that "the collections contain material by or about women's lives or roles." It was also suggested that such collections would typically fall into one of the following seven categories, which proceed from the more to the less obvious:

Papers of a woman:
- Jane Addams
- Maud McLure Kelly
- Sojourner Truth

Records of a women's organization:
- American Nurses' Association
- Miss Porter's School
- Society of Women Geographers

Records of an organization, institution, or movement in which women played a significant but not exclusive part:
- The Butterick Company
- National Association of Social Workers
- The Salvation Army

Records of an organization, institution, or movement that significantly affected women:
- Birth Control Federation of America
- Massachusetts Anti-Suffrage League
- The U.S. Senate

Groups of materials assembled by a collector or repository around a theme or type of record that relates to women (an "artificial" collection):
- International Fiddlers and Fiddling Collection
- Western Diaries and Journals Collection
- Wives of U.S. Presidents Collection

Papers of a family (in which there are papers of female members):
- Holyoke Family
- Pinckney Family
- Ramsey Family

Collections with "hidden" women (collections that contain significant or extensive material about women but whose titles or main emphases do not indicate the presence of such material):
- Survey Associates, Inc.
- Theodore Weld Papers (includes correspondence with Sarah and Angelina Grimké)
- U.S. War Manpower Commission

Finally, archivists were urged in form letters, other correspondence, and conversation to use their own judgment and knowledge of their collections in deciding which to report.

SURVEY LIMITATIONS

Although some limitations and inconsistencies in *Women's History Sources* result from human frailty, others are attributable to the nature of historical records, diversity within the archives profession(s), and the nature of a survey project of this sort. Historical records reflect the language, concepts, and assumptions of a period and place, and collections of historical records and the finding aids prepared to describe them thus mirror changes in society over time. The first and most obvious consequence of these changes is that the researcher must use a variety of terms to locate material. For example, assistance given to dependent members of society in the nineteenth century was termed "charity" and later "philanthropy." In the twentieth century organized philanthropy became social work and social welfare and, more recently, is sometimes considered part of public welfare. Less obvious, perhaps, is that primary sources contain language that contemporary society considers sexist, racist, or condescending, but that earlier generations found acceptable. Where possible, the use of such language was avoided or eliminated, but in some cases use of it was necessary for historical accuracy.

Other limitations grow out of the diversity of repositories and staffs who reported holdings to the Women's History Sources Survey. Experienced professional archivists with custody of massive records of a state government, for example, approach their holdings with a vocabulary, categories, and priorities vastly different from the part-time volunteer in a small local historical society or museum. Many archivists with custody of the records of an ongoing organization or institution tend to think in terms of record groups, measure in cubic feet, and work with single collections (or record groups) as large as the entire holdings of some manuscript repositories. Many curators of manuscripts acquire and organize collections, measure in linear feet or items (occasionally "wallets," "rooms," and "small boxes"), and focus on names and themes in collections of personal papers and organizational records. Archivists usually give first priority to meeting the administrative, fiscal, and legal needs of the institutions whose records they keep, while manuscripts curators tend to emphasize response to the needs of researchers—be they scholars, genealogists, or interested citizens—who seek access to their historical records. Although the contrasts can be drawn too starkly, the differences exist, and they account in part for variations in the quality, focus, and extent of descriptions in the text.

Verification

A guiding principle in compiling *Women's History Sources* was to present as much information as accurately as possible, particularly about the thousands of women whose papers or whose existence is being reported for the first time in a published work. The enormity of the project and the separation of the editorial staff from the sources through physical distance and levels of reporting limited the ability, at times, to verify factual information to the extent desirable. The absence of a tradition in the archives profession of name authority files and the chronic underfunding of archives and manuscript repositories throughout the country made this matter of verification difficult of solution.

RESULTS OF THE SURVEY

The grant proposal submitted to the National Endowment for the Humanities proposed a nationwide survey in order to create a research tool to aid scholars in women's history, other subfields in history, and a variety of fields in the humanities and social sciences, among them American studies, sociology, and literature. It noted that serious scholarly research is absolutely dependent on access to primary sources and that such sources for women's history existed but were not as available to researchers as they should be. The request also stated that a published guide would aid archivists in reinterpreting their holdings and assessing their collections; it would also reinforce a tradition of cooperation between archivists and historians.

The results of the Survey exceeded the expectations of even the most knowledgeable of archivists and historians of women's history, for every aspect of the social history of the American people is represented in *Women's History Sources*. Provided, for example, are descriptions of the archives of 200 congregations of religious women whose records date back to the early nineteenth century and document the achievements of women as leaders and executives as well as their activities serving others. *Women's History Sources* identifies the location of hundreds of collections containing diaries, journals, and other first-person accounts of women from all chronological periods and in all regions of the United States. It gives access to large bodies of public records housed in the National Archives and in small county and municipal agencies; it describes extensive holdings of college and university archives and archives of corporations and professional societies. *Women's History Sources* reports new information about prominent women—more than 125 collections containing material by or about Susan B. Anthony—but it also brings to light hundreds of other women, among them a substantial number of minority women who may not have been considered notable but whose achievements at state and local levels parallel those of women working in a national arena.

In addition to serving as a traditional reference work, however, *Women's History Sources* is also a compendium of women's experience in the United States. It describes women who were arsonists, astronomers, attorneys, botanists, legislators, madams, paleobotanists, physicians, and stagecoach drivers, along with those whose contributions were made as wives, mothers, homemakers, and leaders of or participants in local civic and cultural organizations. It describes women who were conventional and those who were eccentric, those who promoted suffrage while opposing birth control and others who did the reverse. As a record of variety and of achievement and survival, *Women's History Sources* not only is the culmination of a four-year "grand manuscripts search" but the beginning of a new era of research into women's lives.

Acknowledgments

Women's History Sources is the result, to borrow librarian Marcia Pankake's phrase, of a long journey in a short time. That journey could not have been undertaken or completed without the remarkable cooperation and wise counsel of many archivists, historians, editors, and friends of women's history whose contributions far exceeded professional obligations and the requirements of friendship. Although not everyone who assisted us can be noted below, each is remembered in the hearts and the archives of the editors and staff of the Women's History Sources Survey.

The Survey began, as have so many projects in the archives profession, with the interest of historians and other scholars in an emerging area of study. The historians who sponsored the session at the 1972 Organization of American Historians (OAH) convention continued their work on the Survey advisory board: Gerda Lerner, Anne Firor Scott, Janet Wilson James, and Carl Degler were joined by Joan Hoff Wilson to bring their intellectual leadership and passionate commitment to women's history to the project. Without their support and that of Dorothy Rabin Ross, then special assistant to the American Historical Association (AHA), and Paul Ward, then AHA executive director who testified to the energy and significance of this new field in history, the Survey might never have been planned or funded.

A project as large as the Survey requires, in addition to intellectual leadership, the resources of major institutions to conduct and complete it. After the 1972 OAH session, the Rockefeller Foundation, through the efforts of its staff members Peter Wood and Jane Allen, sponsored with dispatch a conference that eventually led to formulation of a grant proposal. The National Endowment for the Humanities (NEH) awarded financial support of more than half a million dollars, but our debt to NEH is far more than a monetary one, for research grants division staff members, particularly Simone Reagor, Margaret Child, and John Borden, also offered perceptive and sympathetic guidance to the occasionally bewildered and often frightened Survey staff. The University of Minnesota contributed extensive matching funding, but the availability of its vast resources was equally important to the Survey staff. The University of Minnesota Libraries, the Office of Research Administration, the University of Minnesota Press, and others mentioned below helped in innumerable ways. Dean of the college of liberal arts Frank J. Sorauf, directors of libraries Ralph H. Hopp and Eldred Smith, and assistant director of libraries Raymond Bohling supported funding proposals and even offered, as a genuine symbol of commitment, that most precious of institutional commodities, the typewriter. Measurement Services assisted in devising the questionnaire and form letters, and the staff of the Wilson Library's Reference/Resources tirelessly sought answers to hundreds of queries that arose during the Survey. Faculty members in numerous departments shared with staff members their expertise on language, style, history, women's studies, and publishing.

The actual work of the Survey—preparing the questionnaire, reviewing draft entries, checking factual accuracy—was undertaken by hundreds of archivists, curators of manuscripts, librarians, and others to whom this work is gratefully dedicated. The most extensive single contribution was made by Betty Falle and Eva Moseley at the Arthur and Elizabeth Schlesinger Library, the richest collection of women's history sources in the country. The Minnesota Historical Society, ever generous in its support of cooperative projects, employed Kathleen O'Brien for six months to survey its vast holdings; her work was scrupulously reviewed and edited by her colleague, Dallas Lindgren Chrislock. Other archivists whose contributions are exceptionally noteworthy are Mary Jo Pugh, the Bentley Library at the University of Michigan; Christine Rongone, the State Historical Society of Wisconsin; Linda Glasgow, the Western Historical Manuscript Collections and State Historical Society of Missouri; Anne P. Diffendal and Jacquelynn S. Haines, Nebraska State Historical Society; and the late Martin Schmitt, University of Oregon, whose wit is remembered as affectionately as his extensive contributions to the archives profession.

We are grateful also to the following colleagues for their assistance in preparing questionnaires, reviewing draft entries, or mustering support for either process. Although the list is long and alphabetical, our appreciation is nevertheless sincere and heartfelt: Judith Austin, Thomas C. Battle, Clark L. Beck, Jr., Maxine Benson, Barbara Blundell, Valerie Gerrard Browne, Phyllis Burnham, Marie Byrne, Ronald Chepesiuk, Charles Colley, Inez Cooper, Miriam Crawford, Amy S. Doherty, Eleanor M. Gehres, Joyce Giaquinta, Margaret Goostray, William Hanna, Dennis Harrison, Jay Haymond, Bruce Henry, Kathleen Jacklin, Charlotte Jacobson, William Joyce, Chester V. Kielman, Karen Klinkenberg, Loreen Ledahl, Robert A. McCown, Phyllis E. McLaughlin, Ellen O. Mark, Elizabeth B. Mason, Thornton W. Mitchell, David Moltke-Hansen, Laura Monti, Archie Motley, Mary-Elizabeth Murdock, Ellen Neal, Clodaugh Neiderheiser, Patricia Palmer, Mary Ritzenthaler, Guy Louis Rocha, Earl M. Rogers, Donald T. Schmidt, Peter E. Shinkel, Richard Shrader, Don C. Skemer, Allen Stokes and the staff of the South Caroliniana Library at the University of South Carolina, John E. Wickman, JoAnn Williamson, Robert M. Willingham, Jr., Karyl Winn, and staff members at the National Archives, the Library of Congress, the American Jewish Archives, and the Henry E. Huntington Library.

For these and for all the unnamed others, we echo Wallace Stegner's prayer for librarians, "God grant them space."

In planning and developing the Survey, the staff incurred numerous and varied professional debts. Simone Reagor, then head of NEH's research grants division, reviewed rigorously a draft of the Survey grant proposal. She and Social Welfare History Archives staff members David Klaassen and William Wallach were responsible for the vastly improved and subsequently funded proposal. Shonnie Finnegan, Edward T. James, Harriet Ostroff, Philip Mason, C. F. W. Coker, Carolyn Hoover Sung,

ACKNOWLEDGMENTS

Mary Jo Kline, Margaret Henson, Elsa Greene, Sister Rita Bergamini, SP, and Reed Whitaker gave invaluable advice and comfort at points during the project. Advisory board members Maxine Clapp and Lucile Kane drew on their own substantial talents as well as those of their staffs at the University of Minnesota and the Minnesota Historical Society in helping to cope with what must have seemed at times an unending series of problems and questions. Endorsement of the project was given by the council of the Society of American Archivists and its executive director, Ann Morgan Campbell; the Society also gave permission to publish excerpts from its journal, *The American Archivist,* as "A Brief Glossary." Other supporters included the Midwest Archives Conference, the OAH Committee of Women Historians, and the Women Historians of the Midwest, whose members never seemed to tire of hearing reports of the Survey's progress.

Women's History Sources grows out of and builds on the tradition and accomplishments of other reference tools in women's history and the archives profession. It is difficult to overstate the importance of both *Notable American Women* and the Library of Congress *National Union Catalog of Manuscript Collections* to the Survey; while providing information available in few other places, they also served as models of thoroughness and precision. Clodaugh Neiderheiser, who may have conducted the first subject survey, that of *Forest History Sources,* drew on her experience in that project and on her formidable intelligence to advise the Survey staff. *On Equal Terms* and *Index to Women,* which may appear as only gray reference works to the outsider, were beacons to the staff in compiling the index and verifying information on women's names, birth and death dates, and occupations.

Other assistance was necessary during the long search for an appropriate publisher and method of publication. Help came from John Ervin, Jr., Paula Ruddy, and the late Jeanne Sinnen of the University of Minnesota Press; from Tom Franklin, Penny Franklin, and Erica Adams of Burt Franklin Publishers; from Aida DiPace Donald and Sue Hayes at Harvard University Press; and from Buck Roach, Bob Anderson and Barbara Preschell. Russell Hobbie, Stephen P. Nachtsheim, and Don Norris, University of Minnesota faculty members, advised on the questions of what role, if any, a computer might play in the Survey and publication of *Women's History Sources.*

The search for a publisher proved ultimately unnecessary, however, for perspicacious Judy Garodnick, editor-in-chief of R. R. Bowker's book division, was among the first to understand the significance of the Women's History Sources Survey; she called the Social Welfare History Archives to express her interest shortly after NEH announced award of the grant in the spring of 1975. Over a period of four years she educated the staff to the problems of producing massive, computerized reference works, cajoled them through troubled periods, and finally insisted, gently and firmly, that the work be concluded. She was assisted throughout, with dedication and skill, by Iris Topel, editing supervisor; and Nancy Volkman, senior editor; members of Bowker's editorial staff responsible for turning manuscript into a reference tool. The quality of their work and the extent to which R. R. Bowker contributed its resources have been essential to completion of the Survey.

Finally, it was the staff of the Women's History Sources Survey who developed mailing lists, elicited 18,000 questionnaires, wrote and edited 10,000 pages of text, and compiled an index that at one point, consisted of more than 200,000 index cards heaped about the Social Welfare History Archives. Staff members labored unselfishly and unstintingly; they were sustained by their joy in the project and by exhilaration at what was being discovered about women's lives in this country. Ames Sheldon Bower organized the editorial effort, created a style manual, trained staff members to write and edit, and contributed her good sense and wise editorial eye to every aspect of the Survey. Her principal associate, Cecelia Nelson Boone, drafted more than 4,000 entries, assisted extensively in editing and resolving questions of style, and shared her poise and calm with others. She and Ames Bower were joined by writers Wendy Larson, Doris Lunden, Karen Mason, and Susan Mead in transforming a mountain of questionnaires into text. Doris Lunden also coordinated the efforts of the fieldworkers, whose adventures themselves would require a separate volume to recount (one arrived late at night in a small motel in a Nebraska town only to find a portrait of Jane Addams under her cot). David Klaassen brought his archives and history training and his systematic intelligence to bear in compiling the repository list and answering myriad questions about both archival practice and American history. Suzanna Moody mastered the elements of indexing, faced the complications of authority files and subject headings, and then braved the task of indexing 18,000 entries, a project of a size unprecedented in the archives profession; she was assisted by Mary Jo Dobson, Jeanne L'Heureaux, Randall Wallach, and others. Lynn McCormick and Cheryl Jensen Peters worked during early stages of the project, and Mary Wrucke helped proofread text. Student assistants Linda Ziemer, Linda Beltrand, Jane Morris, Claudia Tysdale, Nancy Kinney, Cynthia Dyrdahl, Marie Freidrichs, and Elizabeth Schwarz made important contributions as did volunteers William Wallach, Ruth Klaassen, Lisa Glover, Mark Aldrich, and (especially) Mark Peine, who toiled long nights at the thankless task of alphabetizing index cards. In what seems now a heroic feat, Anna Glover compiled the mailing list, managed multiple budgets, supervised part-time staff members, nurtured fieldworkers, typed and edited and photocopied, assisted in compiling the index, and coordinated other aspects of Survey work. No title can fully acknowledge her contributions.

To the many colleagues and professional associates who tolerated missed deadlines, deferred obligations, and diminished attention spans and to families and friends who likewise tolerated absence and distraction, the staff collectively offers its thanks.

Andrea Hinding

How to Use an Archives

RULES GOVERNING USE

Because archives and manuscript collections consist of material that has cultural, legal, financial, or administrative value, repositories establish rules that are deemed necessary to protect them from theft or misuse. Although these rules vary from repository to repository, they usually include a provision that collections must be used on the premises; very few repositories allow original material to circulate, although a number, including many governmental archives, loan material that is available on microfilm. Most repositories require researchers to register, to complete an application to use their collections, or to identify themselves and their purpose in some way; a few require letters of introduction. Most repositories monitor their reading rooms or other areas in which records are used, and they usually prohibit smoking, eating, and drinking in the area. They may also limit the amount of material that will be brought to a researcher at one time and the kinds of writing instruments that may be used (many prohibit the use of fountain pens). In some repositories readers are required to check briefcases, coats, and other belongings before entering the reading room while in others briefcases and other belongings are inspected before researchers leave the reading area.

REFERENCE ASSISTANCE

As part of their activities, most archivists attempt to assist researchers in using the collections in their own repositories and in locating related material in other repositories. Such efforts are limited, however, by the degree of intellectual or bibliographic control a repository has over its collections, by the size of its staff and budget, and by the way in which researchers seek assistance.

It is usually easier, for example, for a repository which has item-by-item control over a valued Revolutionary-era collection to answer an inquiry about correspondence with George Washington than for a state archives to specify precisely which of its holdings contains correspondence with Franklin Roosevelt. Moreover, repositories with small staffs may have to choose among such priorities as improving their finding aids, meeting the needs of genealogists, historians, and filmmakers working on the premises, and responding to requests for information received by mail. (Some repositories with part-time or volunteer staffs may not be able to answer written requests while other, larger repositories have developed policies limiting the amount of research they will do for mail inquiries.) Researchers who are able to define clearly their projects and who give notice of research visits are more likely to receive satisfactory assistance than those who drop in unexpectedly.

PHOTOCOPYING AND OTHER REPRODUCTION OF COLLECTIONS

Photocopying facilities are available in many repositories but the cost of reproduction and the conditions under which photocopying is done vary. Some repositories allow researchers themselves to photocopy material but most require that repository staff members make the copies. Some will copy material only for researchers working on the premises while others will answer written requests for photocopying (especially when the request is specific and limited). Some repositories have facilities to microfilm collections or portions of them and a few may allow researchers to film their own material. Rules governing photocopying and microfilming are affected by copyright law, by the condition of the material to be copied, and occasionally by restrictions imposed by donors. Most repositories are reluctant to allow fragile material to be copied.

Charges for photocopying and microfilming or other forms of reproduction may be limited to the actual cost of copying but are more likely to include a service or handling charge.

A Brief Glossary

Because those unfamiliar with archives and manuscripts may find some terms in *Women's History Sources* confusing, the following brief glossary is offered. The terms given are taken from "A Basic Glossary for Archivists, Manuscript Curators, and Records Managers" (prepared by Frank B. Evans and others and published in *The American Archivist,* July 1974). That there is no standard vocabulary for archivists and their colleagues means that the reader will find the terms used in various ways in finding aids and by repositories.

Archives (1) The noncurrent records of an organization or institution preserved because of their continuing value; also referred to, in this sense, as archival materials or archival holdings. (2) The agency responsible for selecting, preserving, and making available archival materials; also referred to as an archival agency. (3) The building or part of a building where such materials are located.

Collection (1) An artificial accumulation of manuscripts or documents devoted to a single theme, person, event, or type of record. (2) A body of manuscripts of papers, including associated printed or near-print materials, having a common source. If formed by or around an individual or family, such materials are more properly termed *personal papers* or *records*. If the cumulation is that of a corporate entity, it is more properly termed *records*. (3) In singular or plural form, the total holdings—accessions and deposits—of a repository.

Document (1) Recorded information regardless of medium or characteristics. Frequently used interchangeably with *record*. (2) A single record or manuscript item. . . .

Finding aids The descriptive media, published or unpublished, created by an originating office, an archival agency, or a manuscript repository, to establish physical or administrative and intellectual control over records and other holdings. Basic finding aids include guides (general or repository and subject or topical), inventories or registers, location registers, card catalogs, special lists, shelf box lists, indexes, calendars, and, for machine-readable records, software documentation.

Guide At the repository level, a finding aid that briefly describes and indicates the relationships between holdings, with record groups, papers, collections, or comparable bodies of material as the units of entry. Guides may also be limited to the description of the holdings of one or more repositories relating to particular subjects, periods, or geographical areas.

Literary manuscript Manuscripts, including drafts and proofs, or literary compositions, such as novels, essays, plays, and poetry.

Manuscripts Documents of manuscript character usually having historical or literary value or significance. . . . Included in the term are bodies or groups of personal papers with organic unity, artificial collections of documents acquired from various sources. . . and individual documents acquired by a manuscript repository because of their special importance.

Papers (1) A natural accumulation of personal and family materials, as distinct from records. (2) A general term used to designate more than one type of manuscript material.

Personal papers The private documents accumulated by an individual, belonging to him or her. . . .

Records All recorded information, regardless of media or characteristics, made or received and maintained by an organization or institution in pursuance of its legal obligations or in the transaction of its business.

Repository A place where archives, records, or manuscripts are kept. Frequently used as synonymous with depository.

Restricted access A limitation on the use of a body of archives, manuscripts, or records, or on those (records) containing information of a specific kind or of a particular form. The restriction may limit the use for a time to particular persons or classes of persons or may exclude all potential users. Restrictions may be imposed by officials of transferring agencies or by donors and are enforced by the repository. [Restrictions governing access to some collections and regulations governing use of all archives and manuscripts are so varied that the researcher is advised to notify the repository of his or her interest in doing research and to inquire about conditions under which collections may be used.]

How to Use This Book

WOMEN'S HISTORY SOURCES is arranged in two volumes. Volume I consists of descriptions of 18,000 archives and manuscript collections of primary sources relating to women. Entries are arranged alphabetically by state and city, and within cities, by institution and/or repository, and collection title; each entry has been assigned a number. Volume I also includes an alphabetical list, with complete name and address, of each contributing repository whose holdings are represented in the book. Volume II, the index, provides name, subject, and geographic access to information in the collections. For greater ease of use, numbers in the index refer to entry numbers and not to page numbers.

ORGANIZATION OF ENTRIES

The following collection represents a typical entry and indicates the type of information that is included whenever it was available. The standard data elements provided in each entry are an entry number, collection title, statement of the size and inclusive dates of material in the collection, information on whether the collection is open for research and whether finding aids exist, and where the collection is located. In addition, a narrative gives further detailed information about the contents of the collection and persons, organizations, and subjects in it.

Sample Entry

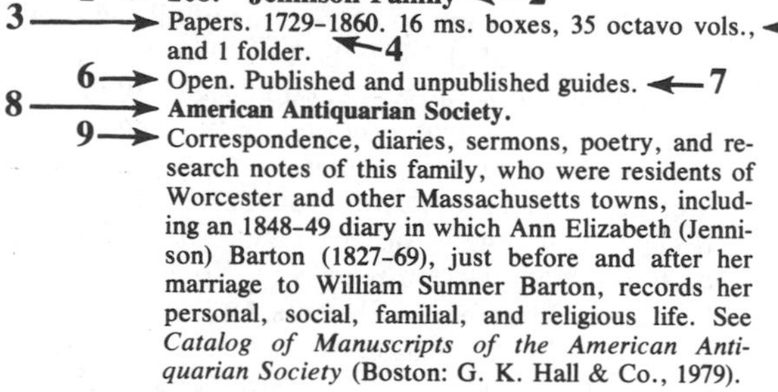

1 → **208. Jennison Family** ← 2
3 → Papers. 1729–1860. 16 ms. boxes, 35 octavo vols., ← 5
and 1 folder. ← 4
6 → Open. Published and unpublished guides. ← 7
8 → **American Antiquarian Society.**
9 → Correspondence, diaries, sermons, poetry, and research notes of this family, who were residents of Worcester and other Massachusetts towns, including an 1848–49 diary in which Ann Elizabeth (Jennison) Barton (1827–69), just before and after her marriage to William Sumner Barton, records her personal, social, familial, and religious life. See *Catalog of Manuscripts of the American Antiquarian Society* (Boston: G. K. Hall & Co., 1979).

Explanation of an Entry

1 **Entry number.**
2 **Collection title.**
3 **Generic record type.**
"Papers" signifies documents generated by or around an individual person, personal documents of an administrator, or documents collected by someone who has a professional interest in doing so.
"Records" signifies documents generated by or around an organization or institution.
"Collection" signifies a fairly uniform group of the same kind of material or artificially assembled kinds of material, which in most cases have been grouped by a collector, not a repository.
"Oral history" signifies tapes, transcripts, and/or related items pertaining to oral history interviews.
"Phonotape" signifies tapes of lectures or other presentations that do not qualify as oral history.
"Finding aid" signifies documents that are simply indexes, catalogs, or the like. Inevitably, some collections do not fit these categories readily.
4 **Inclusive dates** during which the documents were generated. "Nd" is used to indicate that no dates were given; it may also be used in conjunction with dates (e.g., "1850, nd."), indicating the presence of undated material.
5 **Size of collection.** The size of the collection is indicated as reported by the repository, e.g., linear or cubic feet or inches, volumes, folders, items, boxes, reels, tapes, and so forth. "Other material" or "items" can refer to artifacts and other things—flags, crochet hooks, locks of hair, gates, etc.—that are not made out of paper, tape, or phonograph record material.
6 **Access.**
"Access restricted" signifies that any researcher must obtain a special permission or agree to work under certain conditions before he or she will be allowed to look at this particular collection at the repository; the term does not pertain to rules that govern normal use of materials in a repository and are imposed no matter which collection the researcher wishes to peruse.
"Closed" signifies that no researcher can look at the particular collection under any circumstances.
"Partially restricted" or "partially closed" applies the above definitions to portions of the collection. Sometimes a repository has reported that a collection is restricted or closed because, for example, it is being processed; in other words, restrictions on access often change over time, and they usually change in the direction of greater accessibility. In no case, however, does access refer to literary and other property rights, understanding of which is the researcher's responsibility.
"Open" signifies that a collection may be used by any researcher who complies with the regulations governing the use of archival material which are stipulated by the repositories.
7 **Bibliographic control.**
"Unpublished guide" can mean anything from an accession card to a 300-page inventory, including such finding aids as card catalogs, registers, calendars, descriptions, data sheets, and similar terms.
If "published guide" is designated, the guide is cited at the end of the individual entry.
8 **Repository name**, which in some cases is a shortened version of the formal title that is provided in the listing at the end of Volume 1.
9 **Description of contents.** Citations to published guides, which

appear at the end of descriptions of contents, are preceded by the terms "Taken from" or "See." "Taken from" indicates that the entry is based entirely or in substantial part on the repositories publication. "See" refers the reader to supplementary material.

NAME FORMAT

A woman's name can become extraordinarily complex if she has married once or more, adopted a pseudonym or a nickname, or used a professional name that is different from her married name. The format used in this guide is exemplified as follows:

> Anna Mary (Robertson) "Grandma" [Mrs. Thomas Salmon] Moses (1860-1961)

Maiden names are indicated by parentheses as are birth and death dates, brackets denote husbands' names or other marital information, and quotation marks indicate nicknames. It is clear then, that Anna Mary Robertson, who lived from 1860 to 1961, married Thomas Salmon Moses. Her full married name was Anna Mary (Robertson) Moses, but as a painter she was known as Grandma Moses.

If the reader has an interest in a particular name, he or she should consult the index, for there, insofar as they are known, each woman's full name and variants will be listed, as well as referents from maiden names, previous married names, pseudonyms, and the like.

DIRECTORY OF CONTRIBUTING REPOSITORIES

A list of repositories whose holdings are described in *Women's History Sources* appears at the back of this volume. The list is arranged alphabetically by name of repository and includes current addresses; both the official name and address were verified by the repositories themselves.

INDEX

A statement on the procedure used in compiling the index and on using it is included in Volume II.

ABBREVIATIONS

Abbreviations used in the *Women's History Sources* text and index include general abbreviations and U.S. Post Office's two-letter state abbreviations.

References to a number of organizations, many of which have branches throughout the country, appear frequently in entries as follows. The commonly used acronym, e.g., DAR occasionally varies from the formal corporate title of the organization.

Some organizational names may seem inconsistent. Early branches of the WCTU, for example, were called Wom<u>en</u>'s Christian Temperance Union as well as Wom<u>an</u>'s Christian Temperance Union. As these national organizations grew stronger and became better known, greater consistency in the use of names occurred.

AAUP — American Association of University Professors is an organization of college and university teachers, research scholars, and academic librarians, which was founded in 1915 to promote professional and educational interests. The AAUP's national headquarters is in Washington, DC.

AAUW — American Association of University Women, a group of women graduates of regionally accredited colleges, was founded in 1882 to promote education for women. The AAUW's national headquarters is in Washington, DC.

DAR — The National Society of the Daughters of the American Revolution was founded in 1890 to preserve history and to promote educational and patriotic endeavors. The DAR's national headquarters is in Washington, DC.

GFWC — General Federation of Women's Clubs was founded in 1889 to unite and promote throughout the world the common interest of women's clubs in education, industry, philanthropy, literature, art, science, and culture. The GFWC's headquarters is in Washington, DC.

LWV — League of Women Voters of the United States, an organization of women citizens 18 years of age and older, was founded in 1920 to promote political responsibility through the informed and active participation of citizens in every level of government. The LWV's national headquarters is in Washington, DC.

NAACP — National Association for the Advancement of Colored People is a group of persons of all races and religions, founded in 1909 to achieve, through peaceful and lawful means, equal rights of citizenship for all Americans by eliminating segregation and discrimination in housing, employment, voting, schools, the courts, transportation, recreation, prisons, and the military. The NAACP's national headquarters is in New York City.

PTA — National Congress of Parents and Teachers, an educational organization of parents, teachers, administrators, and others, was founded in 1897 to unite the forces of home, school, and community on behalf of children and youth. Originally known as the National Congress of Mothers, the group adopted its current name in 1925. The PTA's national headquarters is in Chicago.

WAC — Women's Army Corps, Army of the United States, was founded in 1942 to provide the army a source of volunteer womanpower trained in noncombatant skills to augment the regular forces. Originally known as the Women's Army Auxiliary Corps, the WAC's name was changed in 1943. The WAC's national headquarters is in Washington, DC.

WAVES Women Accepted for Voluntary Emergency Service is the misnomer by which women who enlisted in the U.S. Navy's Women's Reserve were known. The Women's Reserve was established in 1942 but disbanded when the navy discontinued its separate program for women.

WCTU National Woman's Christian Temperance Union is an organization of Christian women which was founded in 1874 to protect the home, to abolish liquor traffic, and to promote public sentiment for the standard of total abstinence by means of education and legislation. The WCTU's national headquarters is in Evanston, IL.

YMCA National Council of the Young Men's Christian Associations of the United States of America, a worldwide fellowship of persons seeking to improve the spiritual, physical, social, recreational, and other aspects of life of young people, was founded in London, England, in 1844. The first YMCA in the United States was established in 1851. The YMCA's national headquarters is in New York City.

YWCA The Young Women's Christian Associations of the United States of America, an organization of women and girls over 12 years of age who participate in programs, clubs, and classes for their educational, personal, social, and spiritual development, was founded in London, England, in 1855. The first official YWCA in the United States was established in 1866. The YWCA's national headquarters is in New York City.

Standard Abbreviations

AFL-CIO	American Federation of Labor–Congress of Industrial Organizations
BA or AB	bachelor of arts
BS	bachelor of science
Ca.	circa
FBI	Federal Bureau of Investigation
FCC	Federal Communications Commission
HEW	Department of Health, Education and Welfare
LLB	bachelor of laws
MA or AM	master of arts
MS	master of science
MD	medical doctor
PhD	doctor of philosophy
UAW	United Automobile, Aerospace, and Agricultural Implement Workers of America
UN	United Nations
UNESCO	United Nations Educational, Scientific, and Cultural Organization
UNICEF	United Nations International Children's Emergency Fund and United Nations Children's Fund
US	United States
USO	United Service Organizations
USSR	Union of Soviet Socialist Republics
VISTA	Volunteers in Service to America
WPA	Works Progress Administration and Work Projects Administration
WWI	World War I
WWII	World War II

State Abbreviations

Alabama	**AL**	Missouri	**MO**
Alaska	**AK**	Montana	**MT**
Arizona	**AZ**	Nebraska	**NE**
Arkansas	**AR**	Nevada	**NV**
California	**CA**	New Hampshire	**NH**
Canal Zone	**CZ**	New Jersey	**NJ**
Colorado	**CO**	New Mexico	**NM**
Connecticut	**CT**	New York	**NY**
Delaware	**DE**	North Carolina	**NC**
District of Columbia	**DC**	North Dakota	**ND**
		Ohio	**OH**
Florida	**FL**	Oklahoma	**OK**
Georgia	**GA**	Oregon	**OR**
Guam	**GU**	Pennsylvania	**PA**
Hawaii	**HI**	Puerto Rico	**PR**
Idaho	**ID**	Rhode Island	**RI**
Illinois	**IL**	South Carolina	**SC**
Indiana	**IN**	South Dakota	**SD**
Iowa	**IA**	Tennessee	**TN**
Kansas	**KS**	Texas	**TX**
Kentucky	**KY**	Utah	**UT**
Louisiana	**LA**	Vermont	**VT**
Maine	**ME**	Virgin Islands	**VI**
Maryland	**MD**	Virginia	**VA**
Massachusetts	**MA**	Washington	**WA**
Michigan	**MI**	West Virginia	**WV**
Minnesota	**MN**	Wisconsin	**WI**
Mississippi	**MS**	Wyoming	**WY**

Women's History Sources
Collections

ALABAMA

ATHENS

1. Rare Book Room
Collection. 1877-1921. Ca. 1000 items and 11 microfilm reels.
Open. Unpublished guides.
Athens State College Library.
Athens State College, a women's school during the 19th century, was founded in 1840. History of the College, scrapbooks, college catalogs and annuals, and other records. Also includes correspondence, diaries, photos, and newspapers. Now a coeducational institution, the school was the first college in the state to offer classes for juniors and seniors.

AUBURN

2. Alice Carr Trust Fund
Records. 1909-67. 700 items.
Open. Unpublished guide.
Auburn University Archives.
The Fund, which was in operation from 1909 to 1967, provided loans from the Alice Carr estate for women students at Auburn University, formerly Alabama Polytechnic Institute. Correspondence, financial papers, a history of the Fund, rules, and loan application forms.

3. American Association of University Women
Records. 1925-72. 700 items.
Open. Unpublished guide.
Auburn University Archives.
This local affiliate of the national AAUW was founded in 1925. Minutes, committee reports, information on workshops, and publications.

4. Auburn Campus Club
Records. 1948-73. Ca. 200 items.
Open. Unpublished guide.
Auburn University Archives.
The Club, founded in 1948, is an organization of wives of faculty members. Constitution, financial records, reports, membership lists, yearbooks, clippings, and copies of the *Auburn Campus Club Bulletin.*

5. Auburn Equal Suffrage Association
Records. 1915-17. 14 items.
Open. Unpublished guide.
Auburn University Archives.
Constitution, minutes, meeting programs, and clippings of this suffrage group, which was formed in 1915 and disbanded in 1917.

6. Auburn University Newcomers Club
Records. 1948-73. 1 cu.ft.
Open. Unpublished guide.
Auburn University Archives.
Founded in 1948, the Club is an organization for wives of new faculty members. Minutes, budgets, reports, membership records, a scrapbook of clippings, and yearbooks.

7. Business and Professional Women's Club of Auburn
Records. 1928-38. 300 items.
Open. Unpublished guide.
Auburn University Archives.
The local BPWC, founded in 1928, contributed to the John J. Pratt Memorial Fund, which provided loans for men and women who went to business or professional schools. Constitution, minutes, financial records, correspondence, committee reports, and scrapbooks contain some information on the poll tax bill of 1935.

8. Crocheron, Mabel
Papers. 1875-1920. 200 items.
Open. Unpublished guide.
Auburn University Archives.
Correspondence, pamphlets, transport orders, WWI photos, post cards, clippings, memorabilia, and miscellany collected by Crocheron in connection with her work as a YMCA hostess in France during WWI.

9. Daughters of the American Revolution
Records. 1896-1975. 87 items.
Open. Unpublished guide.
Auburn University Archives.
Constitution, minutes, correspondence, speeches, and yearbooks of the local DAR group called the Light Horse Harry Lee Chapter, which was founded in 1896. Includes a scrapbook containing information on the Zebulon Vance Judd family, particularly [Mrs.] Edith R. Judd, and a pamphlet by George Petrie regarding a Mrs. Mell and the early days of the DAR in Auburn.

10. Desteiger, Julia W.
Papers. 1939. 5-page item.
Open. No guide.
Auburn University Archives.
Reminiscences in which [Mrs.] Desteiger (1848-?) describes frontier life in Panola County, TX, during the 1850s and 1860s, women's work managing farms, and other roles they assumed while men were away during the Civil War.

11. Hails, Frances Mathews
Papers. 19th century. 16 Paige boxes.
Access restricted. Unpublished guide.
Auburn University Archives.
Librarian of the Alabama Department of Archives and History, Hails was a professional archivist and genealogist for more than 40 years.
Correspondence, family histories, public records, bibliography, pamphlets, photos, scrapbooks, clippings, newspapers, maps, and other personal papers.

12. League of Women Voters of Alabama
Records. 1915- . 6 drawers and 27 tapes.
Access restricted. Unpublished guide.
Auburn University Archives.
Minutes, financial records, correspondence, speeches, reports, press releases, photos, scrapbooks, clippings, publications, and oral history tapes concern activities of the state LWV, formed in 1915. Copies of the *Alabama Voter* are included.

13. Noble Hall
Records. Nd. 8 vols.
Open. Unpublished guide.
Auburn University Archives.
Scrapbooks of students and student activities in a freshman women's dormitory at Auburn University.

14. Presbyterian Female Institute
Records. 1851-1901. 1 microfilm reel.
Open. Unpublished guide.
Auburn University Archives.
Catalogs and circulars of the Institute, a women's college, in Talladega, AL, 1851-54; of the Synodical Female Institute, 1885-86; and of the Isbell College and Conservatory of Music, 1900-01. Also includes an address regarding religion in the schools delivered in 1851 at the Presbyterian Institute by James Holt, a clergyman.

15. Thursday Club
Records. 1897-1900. 1 vol.
Open. Unpublished guide.
Auburn University Archives.
Secretary's book of this social service women's club, formed in 1897 and disbanded in 1900, which was a member of the Alabama Federation of Women's Clubs. The minutes reflect discussions about art and literature.

16. United Daughters of the Confederacy
Records. 1896-1969. 605 items.
Open. Unpublished guide.
Auburn University Archives.
The local Admiral Semmes Chapter of the UDC was founded in 1896. Minutes, histories, scrapbooks, and pamphlets include local, state, and national material.

17. Women's Music Club, Alabama Polytechnic Institute
Records. Nd. 1 folder.
Open. Unpublished guide.
Auburn University Archives.
Two constitutions of this group which sought "to promote and dignify the musical profession." Alabama Polytechnic is now Auburn University.

18. Women's Recreation Association, Auburn University
Records. 1951-64. 1 folder.
Open. Unpublished guide.
Auburn University Archives.
Constitution, correspondence, and reports of the Association, which was founded in 1951 to promote recreational activities for women students.

19. York, Emily (Smith)
Papers. 1855-1949. 500 items.
Open. Unpublished guide.
Auburn University Archives.
Correspondence of Josephine Noble Smith of Rome, GA, and her daughter Emily York, Civil

War letters from the Army of Virginia, records of the Ladies Memorial Association of Rome, GA, and a Confederate soldier registry from Rome, GA.

BIRMINGHAM

20. Bledsoe and Kelly
Papers. Nd. 47 Hollinger boxes and 55 vols.
Open. Unpublished guide.
Samford University Library, Special Collection Department.
[Miss] Maud McLure Kelly (1887-1973) was Alabama's first woman attorney to enter a law practice. She was admitted to practice before the US Supreme Court in 1914; served on the legal staff of the General Land Office in Washington, DC, from 1918 to 1924; and wrote papers and collected material about genealogy and history. Personal and professional correspondence; genealogical material; census record, public land record, and tax list extracts; marriage records; Civil War soldier roster; maps; scrapbooks; historical books; and data on Alabama, Georgia, North and South Carolina, and Virginia. Also includes information on Alabama counties, officials, historical and professional organizations, and events in the state.

21. Board of Lady Managers
Records. 1884-ca. 1970. 1 folder.
Open. Unpublished guide.
University of Alabama in Birmingham, The Medical Center, Lister Hill Library of the Health Sciences, Alabama Historical Collection.
Established in 1884, the Board of Lady Managers founded Hillman Hospital as a 28-bed charity hospital; the Board directed and funded the Hospital until 1907 when it relinquished control to Jefferson County government. Minutes, treasurers' reports, deeds and other legal documents, correspondence, membership lists, and histories of the Board, which has remained in existence but has no official function.

22. Hillman Hospital Training School for Nurses
Records. 1888- . 4 folders and 1 drawer.
Open. Unpublished guide.
University of Alabama in Birmingham, The Medical Center, Lister Hill Library of the Health Sciences, Alabama Historical Collection.
Founded in 1888, the School became the Jefferson-Hillman Hospital School of Nursing in 1945, the University Hospital School of Nursing in 1955, and the University of Alabama in Birmingham School of Nursing in 1967. Correspondence, schedules, class rosters, photos, diplomas, certificates, licenses, programs, school catalogs, invitations, and clippings.

23. Nightingale, Florence
Papers. 1853-93. 51 items.
Open. Published and unpublished guides.
University of Alabama in Birmingham, The Medical Center, Lister Hill Library of the Health Sciences, Reynolds Historical Library.
Nightingale (1820-1910) founded nursing as a professional practice. Correspondence shows some of her ideas on the organization and practice of medicine and nursing. See *Rare Books and Collections of the Reynolds Historical Library: A Bibliography* (Birmingham: University of Alabama Press, 1968).

CULLMAN

24. Convent Archives
Records. 1881- . Ca. 10 boxes and 9 vols.
Closed. No guide.
Benedictine Sisters, Sacred Heart Convent.
Minutes, financial records, correspondence, diaries, retreat notes, photos, scrapbooks, school and parish yearbooks, commencement programs, school catalogs and regulations, school publications, and other records of the Convent, which was founded in Cullman in 1902. The Sisters are engaged primarily in educational activities. The Convent sponsored Sacred Heart Academy and Junior College and Southern Benedictine College, both located in Cullman.

FLORENCE

25. Foster, Sallie Independence
Papers. 1862-87. 1 item.
Open. No guide.
University of North Alabama, Wesleyan Archives and Museum.
Foster, the daughter of a Florence-area planter, married another plantation owner. Diary includes her chronicle of Civil War events. Foster's father built a house that is located on the University of North Alabama campus.

26. Sannoner, Nannie
Papers. 1856-65. Ca. 40 pp.
Open. No guide.
University of North Alabama, Wesleyan Archives and Museum.
Sannoner, a homemaker, was the daughter of Ferdinand Sannoner (1793-1859), a native of Tuscany in Italy who became a surveyor in the Florence area. Diary in which she chronicles her life at Early Grove, MS, before and during the Civil War.

27. Sloss
Papers. 1840s-1879. 96 items.
Open. No guide.
University of North Alabama, Wesleyan Archives and Museum.
Correspondence of Ann Eliza (Sloss) Coffee, the wife of Colonel A. D. Coffee. She was the daughter of James L. Sloss (?-1844), who was a Presbyterian minister and schoolteacher in Florence from 1830 until his death. A. D. Coffee was a plantation owner.

28. Weakley Family
Papers. 1831-1913. 3 vols. and ca. 280 items.
Open. No guide.
University of North Alabama, Wesleyan Archives and Museum.
Correspondence, diary, photos, local newspapers, and other papers of Samuel Davies Weakley (1812-?), the joint owner of Cypress Creek Cotton Mills and founder of Florence Insurance and Banking Company, and his wife Eliza (Bedford) Weakley, who was the daughter of Lauderdale County's first physician. Her diary, which dates from 1864 to 1873, reflects social and economic conditions in Florence during and after the Civil War. Some of the papers pertain to Florence Wesleyan University and Florence Synodical Female College. Samuel and Eliza Weakley were married in 1836. He served as assistant to his brother James Harvey Weakley, who was surveyor of public lands in Florence, and was influential in affairs of the Memphis and Charleston Railroad, Florence Wesleyan University, and Florence Synodical Female College.

29. Young and Whitten
Papers. 1869-75. Ca. 200 pp.
Open. No guide.
University of North Alabama, Wesleyan Archives and Museum.
Includes two journals that Martha L. Young (?-1902) kept during her college years at Mountain Home School in Alabama and while she was teaching school near Cypress Creek in Lauderdale County, AL. She married Jonathan M. Whitten.

FORT RUCKER

30. WASP Program
Records. 1943-72. 1 folder and 3 microfiche.
Open. Unpublished guide.
United States Army Aviation Museum.
The Women Air Force Service Pilots (WASP), a unit that operated from August 1943 to December 1944, consisted of women pilots who ferried aircraft in non-combat missions, principally in the US and Canada. Records concern the program's inception, recommendations, problems faced, missions, uniforms, and other topics. Also includes correspondence; an article, "I Was a WASP," by Peg Roberts; "The WASP Program: An Historical Synopsis" by Dora Dougherty Strother, a lieutenant colonel in the US Air Force Reserve; and a directory for the 30th memorial reunion in 1972.

31. Whirly-Girls, International Women Helicopter Pilots
Records. 1960. 1 folder and 1 microfiche.
Open. Unpublished guide.
United States Army Aviation Museum.
Newsletter of this organization of women helicopter pilots provides a report of the 6th Annual Hovering, welcomes two new members, and gives news of members. The 6th Annual Hovering was held in Washington, DC, with President Eisenhower's two personal helicopter pilots as guest speakers.

MARION

32. Alabama Women's Hall of Fame
Records. Nd. No size given.
Open. No guide.
Judson College Library.
Nomination forms, biographical summaries, supporting documents, photos, and plaques of members of the Hall of Fame.

33. Archives and Special Collection
Records. 1800s-1900s. No size given.
Open. No guide.
Judson College Library.
Financial records, correspondence, diaries, photos, and scrapbooks pertain to the history of Judson College, its students, and the surrounding area.

MAXWELL AIR FORCE BASE

34. Office of the Director, Women in the Air Force
Records. 1944- . No size given.
Partially restricted. Published guide and card catalog.
Albert F. Simpson Historical Research Center.
Periodic reports, conference reports, staff studies, and miscellaneous records of the director of the Women in the Air Forces (WAFs) and of the WAFs' predecessor, the Air WACs. Includes addresses and other papers of Colonel, later Major General, Jeanne M. Holm, who was director of the WAFs. Also contains annual reports, 1949-68, of the Nurse Corps and Women's Medical Specialist Corps; a list of women officers and nurses; a study concerning recruitment of women during WWII, problems with public opinion, and dissatisfaction with uniforms; a 1951 personnel policy board study of womanpower and career opportunities in the armed services in peace and war; studies concerning the reasons women gave for joining the Air Force; record of a 1970 proceeding concerning Captain Susan R. Struck's attempt to block the Air

Force from discharging her as an Air Force nurse because she was pregnant; report on marriage of WAF personnel at Selfridge Air Force Base, MI; information on the first band composed of Air Force women; statistical reports on women at the Air Force Academy; and reports on the development and problems of women in the Army Corps. Also includes a biographical sketch of Holm, a Portland, OR, native who was the first woman to become a brigadier general and then major general in the Air Force. She assumed the rank of brigadier general in 1971 and of major general in 1973. See Eleanor E. Peets, *USAF History of Women in the Armed Forces: A Selected Bibliography* (Maxwell Air Force Base, AL: Albert F. Simpson Historical Research Center, 1976).

35. Oral History
Oral history. 1960-73. No size given.
Partially restricted. Published guide.
Albert F. Simpson Historical Research Center.
Oral history interviews, including one with Colonel Sara J. Windland concerning the training of women in the US Air Force and one with Sergeant Ruby Johnson concerning women's lives in the Air Force in 1973. See Eleanor E. Peets, *USAF History of Women in the Armed Forces: A Selected Bibliography* (Maxwell Air Force Base, AL: Albert F. Simpson Historical Research Center, 1976).

36. Women Air Force Service Pilots
Records. 1942-45. No size given.
Open. Published guide.
Albert F. Simpson Historical Research Center.
Miscellaneous records of the Women Air Force Service Pilots (WASPs), women who flew military aircraft in noncombat situations during WWII. Includes information about WASPs who trained on B-17s during 1943 at Lockbourne Army Air Base in Columbus, OH; a history of WASP activities in the Army Air Forces Training Command; report of utilization, adaptability, conduct, housing, messing, and other problems of WASPs in 1944; a summary of findings and experiences peculiar to women pilots that contains a medical evaluation of women's adaptability to flying; history and supporting documents from the Women's Auxiliary Ferrying Squadron; reports by Jacqueline Cochran, director of the WASPs; lists of records Cochran established as a pilot between 1939 and 1941; data on WASP uniforms and insignia; regulations; and such public relations material as correspondence, memos, speeches, and news releases. See Eleanor E. Peets, *USAF History of Women in the Armed Forces: A Selected Bibliography* (Maxwell Air Force Base, AL: Albert F. Simpson Historical Research Center, 1976).

37. Women in the Military
Records. 1917-76. No size given.
Partially restricted. Published guide.
Albert F. Simpson Historical Research Center.
Miscellaneous records concerning women in the armed services, particularly the Air Force, including a sketch about the 20 years of service of Colonel Verena M. Zeller, the first chief nurse in the Air Force Nurse Corps; information about Captain Lorraine Potter, a native of Warwick, RI, who was the first woman chaplain in the Air Force; "Ladies First," a report about Joyce Kutsch and Rita Johnson, who in 1973 became the first female paratroopers to jump from a C-141; miscellaneous information concerning the participation of women in WWI; and a list of women buried in France and England during WWI. See Eleanor E. Peets, *USAF History of Women in the Armed Forces: A Selected Bibliography* (Maxwell Air Force Base, AL: Albert F. Simpson Historical Research Center, 1976).

MOBILE

38. Chaudron, Adelaide de Vendel
Papers. Nd. No size given.
Access restricted. No guide.
Museums of the City of Mobile.
[Madame] Chaudron was translator of the Mühlbach novels, an author, and a prominent figure in education in early Alabama. Copies of her publications bearing a Confederate imprint and memorabilia. The Mühlbach novels, which included *Henry VIII and His Court, or Catherine Parr* (1865), were written by Klara Mundt who used the pseudonym Louise Mülbach.

39. Fenollosa, Mary McNeill
Papers. Nd. No size given.
Access restricted. No guide.
Museums of the City of Mobile.
Fenollosa was a popular novelist and woman of letters who used the pseudonym Sidney McCall. Correspondence, diaries, manuscripts of unpublished books, and books.

40. Ladies Memorial Association of Mobile
Records. Nd. 1 vol.
Access restricted. No guide.
Museums of the City of Mobile.
Records and minutes of this patriotic organization formed in March 1865. Bulk of material covers from 1912 to 1922.

41. Le Vert, Octavia Celeste Walton
Papers. Nd. No size given.
Access restricted. No guide.
Museums of the City of Mobile.
Portion of journal kept by [Madame] Le Vert (1810-77), a society woman of the antebellum South, during a tour of Europe. Biographical file is also included.

42. Mobile Equal Suffrage Association
Records. 1915-?. 1 vol.
Access restricted. No guide.
Museums of the City of Mobile.
Minute book describes the group's organizational meeting at Mobile's Cawthorn Hotel in 1915 as well as subsequent meetings and efforts of the ladies of Mobile to obtain suffrage.

43. Sheip, Marie Layette
Papers. Nd. No size given.
Access restricted. No guide.
Museums of the City of Mobile.
Literary correspondence, manuscript of an unpublished novel, and scrapbooks of Sheip, author of the novel *Gulf Stream,* who used the pseudonym Marie Stanley.

44. Stuart, Mary Horton
Papers. Nd. No size given.
Access restricted. No guide.
Museums of the City of Mobile.
Stuart was a Southern Presbyterian Church missionary in China. Family papers and correspondence, including letters of advice that Stuart wrote from China to her son Leighton while he was attending school in Mobile. Leighton Stuart became a missionary and university president in China and was the last US ambassador to mainland China.

45. Thomas, Lillian
Papers. Nd. Ca. 20 items.
Access restricted. No guide.
Museums of the City of Mobile.
Thomas was a black Southern Presbyterian Church missionary to the Congo. Notes about Thomas's life supplied by family members, bibliography, a photo, and artifacts from the Congo that Thomas presented to the city of Mobile.

46. Vanderbilt, Frank Armstrong (Crawford)
Papers. Nd. No size given.
Access restricted. No guide.
Museums of the City of Mobile.
Daughter of Robert Leighton Crawford (1799-1853) and Martha (Everitt) Crawford (ca. 1820-?), Frank Vanderbilt (1839-85) was named for a business partner of her father; she married Cornelius Vanderbilt after emigrating from Mobile to New York as a result of the Civil War. Biographical file, photos, and portrait in oils. Frank Crawford's earlier marriage to John F. Elliott of Mobile ended in divorce or annulment shortly after the honeymoon.

47. Wilson, Augusta Jane Evans
Papers. Nd. No size given.
Access restricted. No guide.
Museums of the City of Mobile.
Biographical file, personal possessions, and copies of novels by Wilson (1835-1909), a popular 19th-century novelist.

MONTGOMERY

48. Owen, Marie Bankhead
Papers. 1920-58. Ca. 35 folders.
Open. No guide.
Alabama Department of Archives and History, Alabama Civil Archives.
Director of the Alabama Department of Archives and History from 1920 to 1958, Owen (1869-1958) was an antisuffragist and an active supporter of the Democratic and Dixiecrat parties. Personal and departmental correspondence, financial records, press releases, handbills, posters, and promotional material. Owen's correspondence reflects her interests in antisuffrage, the national Democratic party and the Democratic National Committee's women's division, and the Dixiecrat or States' Rights Democratic party in Alabama and the South. Her correspondents included state suffrage leader Pattie Jacobs, Franklin Delano Roosevelt, national Democratic leader John J. Rascob, and Strom Thurmond. Collection also contains promotional material, 1928-1940s, of the Democratic party and the women's division, including issues of *The Democratic Digest,* the monthly women's division publication edited by Helen Essary.

49. Woman Suffrage Movement
Collection. 1915-19. 1 box.
Open. No guide.
Alabama Department of Archives and History, Alabama Civil Archives.
Letters to legislators, press releases, handbills, publications, and other material related to Alabama suffrage activity. Despite efforts from 1915 to 1919, the suffrage amendment was not approved in Alabama until ca. 1940. Includes correspondence of the Equal Suffrage Association; the Men's League for Woman's Suffrage of Birmingham, AL; and the Woman's Anti-Amendment League of Alabama. Also contains the original suffrage bill presented to the Alabama legislature in ca. 1919; maps and cartoons linking suffrage with foreign threats, old maidism, and racial take-over; copies of *The Remonstrance Against Woman Suffrage* (Boston: 1919); a 1919 copy of the National Woman's party organ *The Suffragist;* speeches of Anna Howard Shaw; handbills from the National Woman's party Alabama headquarters in Montgomery urging approval of the suffrage amendment; and pamphlets, including one that contended no state with women voters had enacted prohibition before 1914. Antisuffrage forces argued that woman suffrage would mean the end of white supremacy in parts of the South.

50. Alabama Federation of Garden Clubs
Records. 1932-48. Ca. 14 vols.
Open. Card catalog.
Alabama Department of Archives and History, Manuscripts Division.
Minutes, scrapbooks, yearbooks, bulletins, and reports of the Federation. The Federation had special interest in civic projects, beautification, fall and spring flower shows, May Day events, and the development of junior garden clubs. Activities of the Montgomery chapter included efforts to stimulate appreciation and protection of birds, wild flowers, shrubs, and trees.

51. Alabama Federation of Music Clubs
Records. Ca. 1917-77. 6 Paige boxes and 2 ft.
Open. Card catalog.
Alabama Department of Archives and History, Manuscripts Division.
Minutes, cancelled checks, correspondence, reports, scrapbooks, club directories, and handbooks of the Federation, which has had a largely female membership since its founding in ca. 1917. The group supports contests for student musicians, scholarships, student loans, and educational projects in keeping with its goal to promote music appreciation and "through organization and education to make America the musical center of the world." Research conducted in 1941 included collecting spirituals and other folk music through visits to the state's rural churches. Federation interests are revealed by their creation of state-level committees on music in the home, motion pictures, and radio as well as rural music, opera, and composer research.

52. Alabama Federation of Women's Clubs
Records. 1912-47. Ca. 4 in.
Open. Card catalog.
Alabama Department of Archives and History, Manuscripts Division.
Financial statements, memoranda, correspondence, booklets, and clippings show the Federation's interest in community service, child welfare, and improved radio programming. During the 1930s the group sponsored programs to promote public health and a child labor amendment; education programs concerning the problem of crime; founding of day nurseries; provision of free books, clothes, lunches, fuel, and other goods for needy persons; memorial tree- and shrub-planting; and support for the arts in Alabama. In addition, the Federation developed statewide Junior Women's Clubs to provide themselves with experienced leaders. Material of the Montgomery Women's Club is also included.

53. Alabama League of Women Voters Convict Lease System Abolition Activities
Records. 1913-26. 4 folders.
Open. No guide.
Alabama Department of Archives and History, Manuscripts Division.
Meeting records, correspondence, form letters, clippings, and printed material reflect the LWV's efforts opposing the use of leased convicts in Alabama mines. Correspondence refers to related efforts of groups including Seventh-day Adventists, the WCTU, various southern lawyers and officials, ministers, and large landholders. Included are statements from then Governor William Brandon supporting the lease system and a tract by Laura J. Stern of the Montgomery Federation of Women's Clubs opposing it.

54. Alabama Pen Women
Records. 1916-61. Ca. 1.5 ft.
Open. Card catalog.
Alabama Department of Archives and History, Manuscripts Division.
Founded in 1916 in Mobile, AL, for women artists, writers, and musicians, this organization, the first of its kind in the Deep South, was initially the state branch of the National League of American Pen Women. Minutes, manuscripts, records of the Writers Shop Talk Group, music scores, club scrapbooks, biographies of members, and clippings about the national organization include material on Narcissa (Tayloe) Shawhan, an author and lecturer on parliamentary law; author Kate Lea (Gazzam) Donald; author [Mrs.] M. E. Henry-Ruffin; essayist Fanny (Lesesne) Johnstone; social writer Amanda (Moore) Goldthwaite; Mobile artist Emma Langdon Roche; poet-journalist Eugenia Marx; and journalist-writer [Mrs.] Frances Durham and poet Anne Bozeman Lyon, members of the Fugitive writers group, a circle of southern writers who championed an agrarian, anti-industrial way of life. The Pen Women conducted patriotic "sings" in parks as a wartime gesture; organized canning demonstrations, Hoover luncheons out of jars, meatless and wheatless parties, and a war relief bazaar; endorsed Opera-In-Our-Language and the public library movement; planted shrubbery around the statue of Abram J. Ryan, poet-priest of the Confederacy; and promoted beautification and other civic projects.

55. Alabama Woman Suffrage Organizations
Records. 1914-20. 2 Hollinger boxes, 2 vols., and 1 folder.
Open. Card catalog.
Alabama Department of Archives and History, Manuscripts Division.
Pro- and antisuffrage material of the Alabama Equal Suffrage Association and the Alabama Woman's Anti-Ratification League, also called the Southern Woman's League for Rejection of the Susan B. Anthony Amendment. Financial reports, correspondence, other reports, photos, scrapbooks, press releases, bulletins, handbills, clippings, and a copy of the *Woman's Journal and Suffrage News,* a newspaper printed in Boston. Pro-suffrage items include reports on a 1917 suffrage school held in Birmingham, AL, and a speech Florence Kelley made in that city, announcements concerning Anna Howard Shaw's tour of Alabama in 1917 and suffragist reading classes, and lists of National American Woman Suffrage Association goals, which included establishment of women's employment bureaus, agricultural training for women, and Americanization efforts. Antisuffrage items include a leaflet entitled "America When Feminized" and an Anti-Ratification League scrapbook.

56. Alabama Woman's Christian Temperance Union, Frances Willard Centenary Pictorial Review
Records. 1939. 220-page vol.
Open. Card catalog.
Alabama Department of Archives and History, Manuscripts Division.
The Review, a scrapbook containing notes, photos, maps, and clippings, illustrates activities of WCTU members in 1939 and includes accounts of earlier events. Material provides information on Frances Willard; the national WCTU's field secretary Grace Leigh Scott; and various state WCTU leaders including Alabama educator and reformer Julia Tutwiler, who was superintendent for 32 years of the state chapter's department of prison reform. Also contains copies of *Alabama White Ribbon,* the state WCTU's official publication, and items concerning the group's educational projects and work among the Negroes.

57. Alabama Writers Conclave
Records. Ca. 1923-48. 5 vols. (ca. 1 ft.).
Open. Card catalog.
Alabama Department of Archives and History, Manuscripts Division.
The group, which existed from ca. 1923 to 1948 though it held annual conventions only between 1923 and 1928, sought to bring Alabama writers together "to develop craftsmanship and markets and to become a power for good" in the state. Included are material concerning state archivist Marie (Bankhead) Owen and poems and brief biographical material of poets Emily Campbell Adams, Agnes (Ware) Bishop, Mary (Tarver) Carroll, Mary (Chase) Cornelius, Belle (Richardson) Harrison, Anna Bozeman Lyon, and others.

58. American Association of University Women, Alabama Division
Records. 1927-71. 1 Paige box, 1 Hollinger box, and 7 vols.
Open. Card catalog.
Alabama Department of Archives and History, Manuscripts Division.
Organizational records, committee and project reports, membership lists, scrapbooks, conference booklets, and other material of the state and Montgomery AAUW units reflect the members' continuing interest in economic conditions, the status of women's education, international relations, national politics, and a concern for aesthetics, particularly the art and culture of the South. The Montgomery chapter material dates from 1927 while state division records begin in 1963.

59. Andrews, Eliza Frances
Papers. 1864-65. 287-page vol.
Open. Card catalog.
Alabama Department of Archives and History, Manuscripts Division.
Typescript and galley proof of the diary in which Andrews (1840-1931) details her travels and social and family life in Georgia at the end of the Civil War. Diary was published as *War-time Journal of a Georgia Girl* (Appleton & Co., 1908).

60. Bankhead, Tallulah Brockman
Papers. 1910-69. Ca. 4 ft.
Open. Description.
Alabama Department of Archives and History, Manuscripts Division.
Correspondence, bills and accounts, biographical sketches, photos, playbills, magazines, clippings, articles, and other material of Bankhead (1902-68), a stage and motion picture actress born in Huntsville, AL. Her father William Brockman Bankhead (1874-1940) served in the US Congress from 1917 until his death in 1940 and her aunt Marie Bankhead Owen headed the Alabama Department of Archives and History for ca. 35 years. Tallulah Bankhead's correspondence includes many items from Owen as well as material reflecting the actress's work from 1918 to 1922 in a group of unremarked New York plays, her success in England from 1923 to 1930, and her return to the New York stage after a two-year period in Hollywood in the early 1930s. Bankhead's most noted performances were in New York productions of *Rain, Reflected Glory,* and in 1939 of Lillian Hellman's *The Little Foxes.* Other major roles included those in *The Skin of Our Teeth,* the 1943 movie *Lifeboat,* and the 1947 revival of Noel Coward's *Private Lives.*

61. Bankhead, William Brockman
Papers. 1894-1940. 56 boxes, 26 vols., and folders.
Open. Description.
Alabama Department of Archives and History, Manuscripts Division.
Correspondence, diaries, speeches, photos, scrapbooks, clippings, and calling cards of Bankhead (1874-1940), an Alabama politician and US congressman, include material relating to the family life and career of his daughter Tallulah Bankhead (1902-68), a stage and motion picture actress.

62. Brandon, Zillah (Haynie)
Papers. 1855-71. 3 vols.
Open. Description.
Alabama Department of Archives and History, Manuscripts Division.
Diaries of Brandon (1801-post 1871) reflect her life

as a pioneer woman in Georgia and Alabama and as the mother of nine children. Born in Old Pendleton, SC, and orphaned while very young, Zillah Haynie was sent to live with relatives who treated her as a servant. Self-educated, she read widely and "committed herself fervently and wholeheartedly to a Christian life." Her diaries, addressed to her children, relate her parentage, her early life, her faith and philosophical perceptions, her marriage to Francis Lawson Brandon, and their move to Gwinett County, GA. She touches on such topics as relations with Cherokee Indian neighbors, supernatural phenomena including a meteor shower observed in 1833 and mysterious lights hovering over swamps near their home, raising her children, and hardships of life in rural Georgia and, later, Gaylesville in Cherokee County, AL. The diaries also describe the plundering and burning that occurred during General Sherman's occupation of Gaylesville in 1864. Brandon's husband engaged in land dealings, mercantile businesses, and milling.

63. Browne, William Phineas

Papers. 1804-1933. 2 file drawers.
Open. Description.
Alabama Department of Archives and History, Manuscripts Division.
Correspondence of Browne (1804-69), a merchant and pioneer coal operator in Alabama, includes letters exchanged by Browne and Margaret Stevens, whom he married in 1846. Also included is correspondence of his daughter Nina (Browne) DeCottes and her friend Irene M. (Ashby) MacFadyen, an early labor organizer and feminist who agitated for a child labor law and women's rights in the US and England. DeCottes became the first women's editor of the Montgomery *Advertiser* in 1897 and editor of a weekly Montgomery newspaper, *The Social World* in 1908. Her material includes letters MacFadyen wrote from South Africa following her marriage in 1902 to Alfred MacFadyen, a British civil servant. Margaret Browne's papers include letters written in 1836 and 1837 while she was a student at the Alabama Female Athenaeum in Tuscaloosa and later as a young belle in Shelby County, AL. Collection also contains letters from William Browne's Vermont-born niece Jane Burritt while attending Miss Emma Willard's Seminary in Troy, NY, in 1836 and family letters that reflect social life in the South, particularly in Augusta and Atlanta, GA, and Montgomery, between 1870 and 1935.

64. Durr, Clifford Judkins

Papers. 1933-73. Ca. 10 ft.
Open. Description.
Alabama Department of Archives and History, Manuscripts Division.
Business and personal correspondence, speeches, articles, clippings, pamphlets, and other printed material of Durr (1899-1975), an attorney, civil libertarian, counsel for New Deal agencies, and Federal Communications Commission member. After his government career, Durr, the husband of Virginia (Foster) Durr (1903-), entered private law practice and successfully defended individuals brought before the US House of Representatives Un-American Activities Committee and the Loyalty Review Board. Active in the civil rights movement from the 1950s, Durr defended Rosa Parks, the central figure in the Montgomery bus boycott. His correspondents included Presidents Truman and Johnson, Eleanor Roosevelt, Lady Bird Johnson, and US Supreme Court Justices Felix Frankfurter, William O. Douglas, and Hugo Black, who was Virginia Durr's brother-in-law.

65. Durr, Virginia (Foster)

Papers. 1840-1974. Ca. 2.5 ft.
Open. Description.
Alabama Department of Archives and History, Manuscripts Division.
Durr (1903-) worked for the Democratic National Committee women's division and, with her husband Clifford J. Durr (1899-1975) was an active participant in the civil rights movement. Personal, political, and family correspondence; genealogical material; and antebellum and Confederate items. Born in Birmingham, AL, the daughter of a Presbyterian minister, Virginia Heard Foster was educated at the National Cathedral School in Washington, DC, and at Wellesley College. Clifford Durr, an attorney whom she married in 1926, worked in the federal government from 1933 to 1948. During this period Virginia Durr began work with the National Committee women's division, primarily seeking to interest southern women in the party. She became vice-chairman of the National Committee to Abolish the Poll Tax in 1939 and, in 1946, received a National Council of Negro Women, Inc., award. After moving to Montgomery in 1952, the Durrs were active in political affairs and the civil rights movement. They were made Southern Regional Council life fellows in 1973.

66. Espy, Sarah Rodgers (Rousseau)

Papers. 1859-68. 134 pp.
Open. Card catalog.
Alabama Department of Archives and History, Manuscripts Division.
Diary of [Mrs. Thomas] Espy (1815-98), a businessman's wife in Cherokee County, AL, and mother of seven children, contains descriptions of arduous civilian farm life during the Civil War, including the planting of crops, weather, illnesses, and troop movements. Espy was a widow for much of the period covered by the diary.

67. Gould, Eliza Williams (Chotard)

Papers. 1798-1878. 1 folder.
Open. No guide.
Alabama Department of Archives and History, Manuscripts Division.
Autobiography of [Mrs. William Proctor] Gould (1798-1878), a settler in Boligee, AL, and friend of Indian agent John McKee, includes reminiscences about food, housekeeping, social life, travel between Huntsville and Tuscaloosa, and other aspects of Alabama pioneer life.

68. Johnston, Joseph Eggleston

Papers. 1861-63. 1 vol. and 2 copies.
Open. Card catalog.
Alabama Department of Archives and History, Manuscripts Division.
Journal of Johnston (1807-91), a Confederate general, includes his comments on women, their homefront activities during the Civil War, balls and dances, hospital and bandage work, and the strength women displayed. Also contains descriptions of fashion and wartime constrictions and his observation that "under the burthens of the time . . . men led nobler and women more natural lives."

69. Keyes, Jennie Rutledge

Papers. 1867-69. 3 items.
Open. Card catalog.
Alabama Department of Archives and History, Manuscripts Division.
Diaries of Keyes (ca. 1848-?), who left Montgomery with her family and other southerners after the Civil War; the expatriates hoped to establish plantations in Brazil where slavery was legal until ca. 1880. Keyes's diaries record the sights, impressions, and social observations of a teenager introduced into a new culture and environment after difficult years in Alabama. The diaries describe her close friendship with Lizzie Freligh, daughter of another Alabama emigré family, and her feelings of homesickness. Keyes's family returned to the US in 1870. Parts of the diaries have been published in *Alabama Historical Quarterly.*

70. Keyes, Julia Louisa (Hentz)

Papers. 1867-70. 4 folders.
Open. Card catalog.
Alabama Department of Archives and History, Manuscripts Division.
[Mrs. John Washington] Keyes (ca. 1825-?), the mother of Jennie Rutledge Keyes, moved from Montgomery to Brazil in 1867 with her husband and family and, then, repatriated in 1870. Diaries, photos, and sketches contain detailed observations on Brazilian life including descriptions of Rio de Janeiro, local social customs, food, markets, travel, the natural environment, relationships with Brazilians and other southern expatriates, and efforts of the southerners to adapt to the new country. Portions of the diaries have been published in *Alabama Historical Quarterly.*

71. Lowe, Sarah

Papers. 1861-62. 2 items.
Open. Card catalog.
Alabama Department of Archives and History, Manuscripts Division.
The early years of the Civil War provide the focus of the journals of Lowe (1845-1937), a schoolgirl at Huntsville Female College in Huntsville, AL.

72. Lowe, Sophia

Papers. 1843-44. 1 folder.
Open. Unpublished guide.
Alabama Department of Archives and History, Manuscripts Division.
Diary in which Lowe, the daughter of Bartley M. Lowe, recorded a trip to Baltimore, Philadelphia, and on to New York where she spent the winter in school. Lowe later married Nicholas Davis of Huntsville, AL.

73. Mencken, Henry L., and Mencken, Sarah (Haardt)

Papers. 1843-1956. Ca. 2 in.
Open. No guide.
Alabama Department of Archives and History, Manuscripts Division.
H. L. Mencken (1880-1956) was a critic, writer, and editor of *The American Mercury* and the *Baltimore Sun;* Sarah Powell Haardt (1898-1935), whom he married in 1930, was a writer who died of tuberculosis. Correspondence, diary, Sarah Mencken's manuscripts, social announcements, and genealogical material about her Alabama family. Sarah Mencken's manuscripts include the stories "Little Lady" and "Alabama April," which include descriptions and remembrances of childhood and young adulthood in Alabama.

74. Montgomery Mothers' Circle

Records. 1900-60. Ca. 1 Hollinger box.
Open. Card catalog.
Alabama Department of Archives and History, Manuscripts Division.
Known as the Mothers Union, Mothers Club, Mothers Circle and Child Study Club during its 60-year history, this Montgomery group discussed literary topics, international concerns, and civic problems. Minutes, record books, club history, correspondence, reports, and miscellaneous material. In ca. 1958, the Circle had committees on the Children's Home, music, mental health, the Girl Scouts, golden age, hospital, safety, and library extension.

75. No Name Club

Records. 1893-1952. 6 vols.
Open. Card catalog.
Alabama Department of Archives and History, Manuscripts Division.
Founded in 1893, this Montgomery woman's literary group sought to further the education of women and to improve social and mental culture through bi-monthly meetings centering on an

annually selected topic. Record books and scrapbook reflect these topics, which included Europe in the 19th century, "America and Things American," Germany, the literature of self-revelation, the psychology of modernism, and underdeveloped countries.

76. Owen, Marie (Bankhead)
Papers. 1869-1958. 4 file drawers.
Open. No guide.
Alabama Department of Archives and History, Manuscripts Division.
Director of the Alabama Department of Archives and History from ca. 1920 to 1955 and active participant in state women's groups, Owen (1869-1958) lobbied to obtain federal funds to build the current state archives and history department building. Correspondence, diaries, scrapbooks, guest books, clippings, tributes, and printed material. Owen was the widow of Thomas M. Owen, who had headed the archives and history department after its founding in 1901. Lobbying in Washington while one of her brothers William Brockman Bankhead was speaker of the US House of Representatives and another brother John Hollis Bankhead, II, was a US senator, Marie Owen obtained WPA funding and labor for the archives building. She also was a leader in the Southern Commercial Convention women's auxiliary and in the Alabama antisuffrage effort. Her papers include material relating to the Alabama Federation of Women's Clubs, the Pilot Club, the No Name Club, the Business and Professional Women's Club, and the Press and Author Club.

77. Perry, Sally (Randle)
Papers. 1867-83. 1 vol.
Open. Card catalog.
Alabama Department of Archives and History, Manuscripts Division.
Mistress of Ingleside Plantation in Dallas County, AL, Perry wrote for *Godey's Lady's Book* under the pen name of Lee Afton. Her diary from 1867 and 1868 and a letter from a descendant. The widow of John Perry, who had been killed in the battle of Sharpsburg, Sally Perry "was to take the chair of languages at Martha Washington College when she suddenly died at about 33 years."

78. Waring, Mary D.
Papers. 1863-65. 1 vol. and 1 copy.
Open. Card catalog.
Alabama Department of Archives and History, Manuscripts Division.
Diary of Waring, a schoolgirl at Ellen H. Easton Girls High School in Mobile, AL, includes descriptions of the Civil War as well as thoughts about philosophy, religion, the occupation of Mobile, and the behavior of her friends, relatives, and acquaintances.

79. Williamson, Mary Louisa (Mitchell)
Papers. 1861-92. 40 pp.
Open. Card catalog.
Alabama Department of Archives and History, Manuscripts Division.
Mother of nine children, mistress of an antebellum plantation, and relative of the wealthy Fitzpatrick and Toombs families, [Mrs. Samuel Thomas] Williamson (1842-1915) saw her family's fortunes dwindle in the post-Civil War years and then rise again following Reconstruction. Copy of her 1861-63 diary describes social life and family affairs on the eve of the Civil War in Alabama's Montgomery, Macon, and Autauga counties, then hardships civilians encountered during the war, including anxiety over relatives in the army, food, illness, death, and rumors that circulated because of poor communications. Journal entries from 1890 and 1891 deal with family matters.

80. Wilson, Augusta Jane (Evans)
Papers. 1860-1903. 5 items.
Open. Card catalog.
Alabama Department of Archives and History, Manuscripts Division.
Correspondence and copies of other letters of [Mrs. Lorenzo Madison] Wilson (1835-1909), an Alabama woman who had brothers in the Confederate army. Her letters include descriptions of Norfolk, VA, just before the Civil War, of euphoric feelings among Confederate sympathizers at the war's outbreak, and of losses felt in 1866 after the defeat of "our holy precious cause." One 1866 letter, which describes New England as the "synagogue of Satan," was written to a friend whose husband died at the battle of Vicksburg, MS, while another letter of that year, addressed to the mayor of Mobile, pleaded for a monument to honor the Confederate army.

81. Yeatman, Reaia (Chatfield)
Papers. 1834-1953. 1 folder.
Open. No guide.
Alabama Department of Archives and History, Manuscripts Division.
Enrollment lists for the State Teachers College at Livingston, AL (now Livingston State University), clippings, and other material collected by [Mrs. W. E.] Yeatman relate to the history of Livingston, its educational institutions, and social customs. Also included is information on Ruby (Pickens) Tartt, a local artist, folklorist, and author whose short stories featured Alabama Negroes, and on [Miss] Julia S. Tutwiler, president in the late 1800s of Livingston Normal School (later the State Teachers College), who fought to make the University of Alabama coeducational and helped lead the Alabama prison reform movement. Collection also contains reminiscences, printed in 1893 in the *Livingston Journal,* of the Choctaw Indian settlers of the 1830s; descriptions of Alabama schools, including *Historical Sketches, State Teachers College, Livingston, Ala.,* by president emeritus G. W. Brock; translations of Sumter County Choctaw place-names; and grade school student reminiscences of family educational histories (ca. 1953).

82. Brown, Ollie L.
Papers. 1924-72. 1 Hollinger box.
Open. Unpublished guide.
Alabama State University Archives.
Brown (1891-1972) was head librarian at Alabama State University from 1921 to 1961. Professional memoranda and reports; speeches, including one she gave at Lane College in Jackson, TN, when she received the school's alumni award; a library history; photos; awards; and diplomas. Brown was a relative of the family of Harper Council Trenholm, former president of State Normal School.

83. Jennifer, Portia Lee (Evans) Trenholm
Papers. 1958?. 13-page item.
Open. Unpublished guide.
Alabama State University Archives.
An Alabama State University music teacher, Jennifer remarried after the death of her husband Harper Councill Trenholm (1900-62), president of Alabama State University, then called State Normal School, from 1925 to 1962. Her memoirs include information about Montgomery social life from 1922 to about 1954 and comments about racial discrimination.

84. Montgomery Bus Boycott
Collection. 1955-57. 4 vols.
Open. Unpublished guide.
Alabama State University Archives.
Clippings and other papers pertain to the yearlong boycott of Montgomery city buses by local blacks. The boycott began after [Mrs.] Rosa Parks refused to give up her seat in the whites-only section of a segregated city bus. The clippings, from newspapers in Alabama and those in other states, deal with the boycott and its aftermath and provide information about Parks; Martin Luther King, Jr.; his wife Coretta (Scott) King; and other persons involved in the boycott.

85. Trenholm, Harper Councill
Papers. 1921-62. No size given.
Open. Unpublished guide.
Alabama State University Archives.
Personal and official correspondence, speeches, transcripts, photos, and diplomas of Trenholm (1900-62), president of Alabama State University, then called State Normal School, from 1925 to 1962. Includes letters of his wife Portia Lee Trenholm, who taught music at Alabama State, and of his daughters Edwyna and Yvonne. Trenholm entered college at the age of 15 and became president of State Normal School upon the death of his father.

TALLADEGA

86. African Missions
Records. 1839-1962. 213 items.
Open. Unpublished guide.
Talladega College Historical Collections.
Correspondence, photos, serials, and other records reflect the role of women in mission work of the American Board of Commissioners for Foreign Missions in Angola, South Africa, and Rhodesia and of the Southern Presbyterian Board of Missions in the Congo. Includes papers of Negro Women missionaries Maria Fearing, Lillian Thomas DeYampert, and Lucy Gantt Sheppard, all of whom worked in the Congo, and of Bessie Fonvielle McDowell, who worked in Angola.

87. Bunker, Fred R.
Papers. 1891-1970. 12 ft.
Open. Unpublished guide.
Talladega College Historical Collections.
Papers of Bunker, who was involved in mission work in southern Africa, include diaries of his wife Belle H. Bunker regarding her mission experiences from 1892 to 1895 in Natal, Rhodesia, and Mozambique. She worked under the auspices of the American Board of Commissioners for Foreign Missions. Also includes lantern slides and accompanying notes by Fred Bunker on the status of African women.

88. Calhoun School
Records. 1892-1949. 5 microfilm reels.
Open. Unpublished guide.
Talladega College Historical Collections.
The School was founded in 1892 by two white women, Mabel W. Dillingham and Charlotte R. Thorne, who had taught at Hampton Institute and responded to Booker T. Washington's appeal for educational facilities for Negroes in Calhoun, AL. Annual reports, minutes of the board of trustees, endowment records, deeds of the Calhoun Land Trust, correspondence, photos, and other records. The material concerns Negro education and the School's efforts to help persons with tenancy problems through land purchase arrangements and through housing improvement programs. The School became part of the state education system in 1945.

89. Davis, Hilda Andrea
Papers. 1934-70. 5 ft.
Open. Unpublished guide.
Talladega College Historical Collections.
An educator, Davis (1905-) was dean of women at Talladega College from 1937 to 1952. Personal and professional correspondence, speeches, and other papers relating to Talladega College; Negro education; the YWCA; the Alabama Student Conference on Civil Rights; the Southern Negro Youth Congress in 1946; efforts by Negro students to enter the University of Alabama graduate school in 1949; Shaw University in Raleigh, NC; the Association of Deans of Women and Advisers to

Girls in Negro Schools; and the National Association of College Women. Davis served as president of the Association of Deans of Women and of the National Association of College Women.

90. Sharecroppers Union
Oral history. 1971-72. 4 tapes and transcripts.
Open. No guide.
Talladega College Historical Collections.
The Union, active in Alabama in the 1930s, attempted to rectify grievances of sharecroppers and tenants. Interviews with black women around Camp Hill, AL, who were active in organizing the Union, focus on women's roles in the movement and on their efforts to establish a type of women's auxiliary for the Union.

91. Trammell, Mattie Rivers
Papers. 1910-65. 43 items.
Open. Unpublished guide.
Talladega College Historical Collections.
Trammell (1890s-), like her mother before her, has been active in the Alabama Federation of Colored Women's Clubs. Her papers consist almost entirely of minutes and programs of the Federation's annual sessions. The material provides information about the Mount Meigs reformatory in Alabama.

TUSCALOOSA

92. Edmiston, Althea Brown
Papers. 1938. 1 folder.
Open. No guide.
Stillman College Library.
Booklet concerning the work of Edmiston (1874-1937), a Presbyterian missionary to the Congo. The booklet was published in 1938 by the committee on woman's work of the Presbyterian Church in the US. Edmiston was the author of a grammar and dictionary of the Bushonga or Bukuba language.

93. Fearing, Maria
Papers. Nd. 1 folder.
Open. No guide.
Stillman College Library.
Biographical material and a booklet about [Miss] Fearing (1838-1937), a Presbyterian missionary to Africa.

94. Franklin, Samuel
Papers. 1974. 105-page item.
Open. No guide.
Stillman College Library.
Manuscript by Franklin concerns the history of Stillman College, which was established by the Presbyterian Church in the US in 1876 as an institute for training Negro pastors. The school now is a four-year coeducational liberal arts college. Includes biographies of Emily Estes Snedecor, Myrtle Williamson, Hallie Paxson Winsborough, Louise R. McKinney, Margaret M. Davis, [Mrs.] Evelyn E. Nall, [Mrs.] Willierean Jackson Crosley, [Mrs.] Mildred Brown Coleman, [Mrs.] Mae Miller Beck, [Mrs.] Zadie Beford Whisenton, and [Mrs.] Elizabeth Ann Withrow Turner.

95. Sheppard, Lucy Gantt
Papers. Nd. 14 items.
Open. No guide.
Stillman College Library.
Booklet and photos of Sheppard (1867-1955) who served with her husband William Sheppard as a Presbyterian missionary to the Congo. Includes photos of the Sheppards in Europe and Africa. Lucy Sheppard began the first school at the American Presbyterian Congo Mission at Ibanche and founded the first women's society at the Congo Mission.

96. Snedecor, Emily Alston Estes
Papers. Nd. 1 folder.
Open. No guide.
Stillman College Library.
Snedecor (1858-1942) was dean of women at Stillman Institute, now Stillman College, from 1922 to 1930 and a leader in women's auxiliary work of the Presbyterian Church in the US. Biographical sketch and a memoir about her husband James George Snedecor, a minister who held a doctor of laws degree. She wrote the memoir for their children and grandchildren.

97. Williamson, Myrtle
Papers. 1958-67. 1 folder and 1 Hollinger box.
Open. No guide.
Stillman College Library.
Williamson (1898-1958) was director of Christian activities and a teacher of the Bible at Stillman College from 1948 to 1958. Correspondence, prayer notebooks, religious booklets she wrote, and a rough draft of her book *One Out of Four* (1960), which concerns her struggle with cancer. Includes correspondence about the book with John Knox Press. Williamson also was involved in home missionary and Christian education work for the Presbyterian church.

98. Winsborough, Hallie Paxson
Papers. Nd. 1 folder.
Open. No guide.
Stillman College Library.
Winsborough (1865-1940) was an organizer and the first executive of the women's auxiliary of the Presbyterian Church in the US. Biographical sketch about Winsborough and a booklet published by the committee on woman's work of the Presbyterian Church in the US.

99. Alabama Civil War Centennial Commission
Records. 1960-65. Ca. 28 folders.
Open. Index.
University of Alabama, W. S. Hoole Special Collections Library.
Correspondence, speeches, booklets, pamphlets, and articles that relate to the activities of scholars and state institutions commemorating the Civil War centennial. Includes four folders of papers, such as "Celia and Winnie Mae Murphree" and "A Ballad of Emma Sansom," that concern the role of women in centennial activities and the War and correspondence and memoranda pertaining to the National Women's Committee of 100 organized in 1960 to carry out observances marking the Civil War role of women. Committee members included Bertha S. Adkins, undersecretary of HEW; Congresswoman Marguerite Stitt Church of Illinois; Mrs. Spessard Holland of Florida; Mary Elizabeth Massey of Winthrop College in Rock Hill, SC; and National Federation of Business and Professional Women's Clubs official Marguerite Rawalt. Also included are addresses from the United Daughters of the Confederacy and copies of a pamphlet about noted Alabama women of the Civil War, including propagandist Augusta Jane (Evans) Wilson, Emma Sansom, Eliza McLane, hospital founder Juliet Ann (Opie) Hopkins who was called the "angel of the South," nurse Kate Cumming, and Mary Cook Chadick, who was characterized as a "northern-born Confederate patriot."

100. Butler, Nellie
Papers. 1857-1904. 1 scrapbook.
Open. Index.
University of Alabama, W. S. Hoole Special Collections Library.
Scrapbook contains announcements, post cards, clippings, and illustrations focusing on the city of Mobile, AL, which relate to the role and image of women during and after the Civil War. Includes examples of poetry, in particular "The Lost Cause," "The Blue and the Grey," and "Somebody's Darling," printed in newspapers and periodicals; newspaper accounts of Civil War battles; newspaper columns written by women; engagement announcements and invitations of Mobile social organizations; memorabilia of Civil War divisions; and illustrations in which women figure prominently.

101. Davis, Jefferson
Papers. 1823-84. 2 drawers.
Open. Index.
University of Alabama, W. S. Hoole Special Collections Library.
Personal and business correspondence and miscellaneous material of Davis (1808-89), the president of the Confederate States of America, and Varina Anne (Howell) Davis (1826-1906), whom he married in 1844. Includes correspondence between the two extending from their courtship and early married years, through the Mexican and Civil wars, to the period of his postwar imprisonment.

102. Desegregation: University of Alabama, 1963
Records. 1963. 1 folder.
Open. Subject index.
University of Alabama, W. S. Hoole Special Collections Library.
Vivian Malone (1943-) sought entrance to the University of Alabama in 1963. Alabama governor George C. Wallace attempted to block her admission, but US Justice Department officials ordered that she be allowed to register. A copy of Wallace's proclamation at the University campus, University information services releases, articles, and clippings describe the confrontation.

103. Educational Institutions in Alabama
Collection. 1963-64. 15 folders.
Open. No guide.
University of Alabama, W. S. Hoole Special Collections Library.
Correspondence and memoranda accumulated by educational institutions in connection with their commemoration of the Civil War centennial. The schools were to explore all phases of Alabama Civil War history, particularly the role of faculty, students, and the institutions themselves in the War effort. For example, home economics departments were to study "dietary, textiles, and clothing of the period." Henry E. Sterx of Troy State College, who earned a PhD at the University of Alabama, prepared a book commemorating the state's Civil War heroines. Collection contains material concerning women's participation in the centennial and references to chapter activities of the United Daughters of the Confederacy.

104. Farmer, Hallie
Papers. 1924-60. 24 folders.
Open. Index.
University of Alabama, W. S. Hoole Special Collections Library.
A scholar, reformer, and educator, Farmer (1891-ca. 1960) was a department head and professor of history and government at Alabama College at Montevallo, AL, from 1927 to 1952. Correspondence, journals, manuscripts, a vita, biographical material, and clippings. Farmer headed the Alabama College history and government departments from 1927 to 1949 and the social science division from 1949 to 1952. An authority on Alabama state government, she wrote government guidebooks and articles, was elected to the Montevallo town council, and served on the staff of the University of Alabama bureau of public administration from 1941 to 1950. A member of the state AAUW and president of that group from 1937 to 1939, she devoted much time to what she saw as the AAUW's central goal, "raising the social and political consciousness of educated women." Farmer received a doctorate in 1927 from the University of Wisconsin. Her thesis *The Recession of the Frontier* was the basis for later articles on populism, particularly "The Economic Background

of Southern Populism," published in the *Mississippi Valley Historical Review* X, no. 4 (March 1924).

105. Gorgas
Papers. 1821-1920. Ca. 3594 items.
Open. Card catalog and index.
University of Alabama, W. S. Hoole Special Collections Library.
Correspondence, diaries, speeches, scrapbooks, pamphlets, articles, clippings, and miscellaneous material of the Gorgas family, which was influential in Alabama's legal, military, political, and educational affairs. Papers include subgroups centered around Sarah Haynesworth Gayle (ca. 1795-1835), wife of Alabama governor John Gayle, and Amelia (Gayle) [Mrs. Josiah] Gorgas (1826-1913), librarian at the University of Alabama. Other women represented in the family papers include Mary Gorgas; Clarissa Steadman Peck, who was the second wife of Governor John Gayle; Mamie Gorgas; and Elizabeth Haynesworth.

106. Gorgas Papers: Gayle, Sarah Haynesworth
Papers. Ca. 1821-35. No size given.
Open. Card catalog and index.
University of Alabama, W. S. Hoole Special Collections Library.
Gayle (ca. 1795-1835) was the wife of John Gayle, governor of Alabama from 1831 to 1835, and mother of Amelia (Gayle) [Mrs. Josiah] Gorgas (1826-1913), the first woman librarian at the University of Alabama. Correspondence includes letters to her husband, to her Haynesworth relatives in South Carolina, and to women friends. Also includes her journals in which she describes her family's life in frontier Alabama from 1821 to 1835. Sarah Gayle died of lockjaw.

107. Gorgas Papers: Gorgas, Amelia (Gayle)
Papers. 1858-83. 3 drawers and miscellaneous vols.
Open. Card catalog and description.
University of Alabama, W. S. Hoole Special Collections Library.
Correspondence, diaries, records, scrapbooks, and miscellaneous papers of Gorgas (1826-1913), the first female librarian and first female faculty member at the University of Alabama. The wife of General Josiah Gorgas, Amelia Gorgas became postmistress, nurse, and librarian at the University of Alabama in 1883, 10 years before the school admitted its first women students. She served on the faculty until 1907. The Amelia Gayle Gorgas Library, completed in 1925, is the only academic building named for a woman on the University campus. Prior to her University work, Gorgas served as a nurse during the Civil War siege of Richmond; her husband was chief ordnance officer of the Confederate Army. During Reconstruction she formed a Sunday school and assisted workers' families in Briarfield, AL, where her husband ran a foundry. Josiah Gorgas also served as vice-chancellor of the University of the South in Sewanee, TN, and Amelia Gorgas worked with mountain people in that area.

108. Harris, Agnes Ellen
Papers. 1919-60. 40 drawers.
Open. Index.
University of Alabama, W. S. Hoole Special Collections Library.
Harris (1883-ca. 1952) was dean of women and dean of the school of home economics at the University of Alabama. Personal and institutional correspondence; home economics school class records, tests, and student grades; operational records of the dean of women's office and the home economics department; pamphlets from other Alabama state colleges; and items concerning home economics, agriculture, and other subjects. A staunch advocate of the combination of career and family for college-trained women, Harris supported the entry of women into professional, business, and political fields on an equal basis with men. She sent a representative of the dean of women's office to visit seniors in the state's high schools each year to counteract the tendency of wealthy Alabamians to educate their daughters in private colleges outside the state. She also issued women's bulletins from 1940 until 1943 advertising opportunities the University provided for women.

109. Hayden, Bessie Leach
Papers. 1940-66. Ca. 5 in.
Open. Index.
University of Alabama, W. S. Hoole Special Collections Library.
Counselor for women at the University of Alabama from ca. 1939 to 1953, Hayden (1886-post 1966) matriculated at the Tuscaloosa school in 1900, seven years after its first women students were admitted. The collection's principal item is Hayden's manuscript "Then Came the Women," which traces the education of women at the University from 1893 until 1966, but correspondence and a 1940 women's bulletin from the school are included as well. The manuscript concerns the role of educator and reformer Julia Tutwiler in winning approval of coeducation at the University, the conditions of early coeducation, and biographical information about early women students, the first 10 of whom were graduates of Tutwiler's State Normal School at Livingstone, AL. The manuscript also contains information about [Mrs.] Amelia Gayle Gorgas, the first woman faculty member at the University, and her daughters Jessie and Marie, who was called Mamie, as well as descriptions of women students' dress, residence hall life, course work, and attentions received from professors and male students.

110. Heflin, James Thomas
Papers. 1895-1941. Ca. 20,000 items (7 drawers).
Access restricted. Register index.
University of Alabama, W. S. Hoole Special Collections Library.
Personal and business correspondence, speeches, press releases, photos, scrapbooks, campaign material, articles, souvenirs, and other papers of Heflin (1869-1951), a politician who was a US representative from Alabama's 5th district from 1904 to 1920 and a US senator from 1920 to 1931. Heflin's papers provide information about his positions on woman suffrage, segregation, immigration, the League of Nations, the Federal Reserve Board, the World Court, and other issues. Heflin, who introduced the bill calling for establishment of Mother's Day, was known for his participation in the 1928 presidential campaign of Governor Al Smith and for his attitude toward Catholicism.

111. Hentz, Caroline Lee (Whiting)
Papers. 1800-56. 26 items.
Open. Index.
University of Alabama, W. S. Hoole Special Collections Library.
Correspondence, notes, notebooks of biographical information, and a picture of [Mrs. Nicholas Marcellus] Hentz (1800-56), a novelist, teacher, and playwright, who wrote *Lovell's Folly* (1832), *Aunt Patty's Scrap Bag* (1843), *The Mob-Cap* (1848), *Linda* (1850), *Marcus Warland* (1852), *Eoline, or Magnolia Vale* (1852), and *The Planter's Northern Bride.* Hentz lived in Alabama while teaching; her novels depicted "Southern life in its refined aspects."

112. Lucy, Autherine
Papers. 1956. 6 boxes.
Open. Card catalog.
University of Alabama, W. S. Hoole Special Collections Library.
Lucy (1930-) sought to attend the University of Alabama as a library science student, but she was expelled following bitter racial incidents. Alabama newspapers, copies of *Life* and *Punch,* and clippings from *The New York Times* document Lucy's attempt to attend the University. Articles contain descriptions of her family life, riots by white students, the formation of a White Citizens' Council in Tuscaloosa, and the heckling of the University president's wife when she asked a mob of students to disperse. Among the newspapers represented are the *Anniston Star,* the *Birmingham News,* the *Birmingham Post-Herald,* the *Dothan Eagle,* and the *Tuscaloosa News,* all from Alabama; the *Alabama Citizen,* a black newspaper published in Tuscaloosa; and the *Chicago Daily Tribune, South,* and the University's student newspaper *Crimson White.*

113. Mayfield, Sara
Papers. 1910-66. 4 drawers.
Access restricted. Index.
University of Alabama, W. S. Hoole Special Collections Library.
Correspondence, manuscripts, poems, critical articles, notebooks, maps, clippings, and copies of *The Reviewer* of Mayfield (1905-), an author and scholar. A friend of Zelda Fitzgerald and Henry L. Mencken, Mayfield wrote *Exiles from Paradise: Zelda and Scott Fitzgerald* (1971) and *The Constant Circle: H. L. Mencken and His Friends* (1968). Another of her published works is *Mona Lisa, The Woman in the Portrait, a Fictional Biography* (1974). She wrote "The Influence of Dorothy Wordsworth on the Poetry of Samuel Taylor Coleridge" as her English master's thesis at the University of Alabama in 1931. Collection also contains working manuscripts of her poetry and papers from the 1945 Inter-American Conference on Problems of War and Peace.

114. Scott, Alice Keyes
Papers. 1846-1944. Ca. 0.5 drawer and vols.
Open. Description.
University of Alabama, W. S. Hoole Special Collections Library.
Scott's papers are included in those of her family, the Keyeses, an upper-class Alabama family that emigrated to Brazil after the Civil War and repatriated in the 1870s. Correspondence, diaries, biographical notes, photos, scrapbooks, and other papers include material on Scott and her relatives Caroline Lee Hentz and Julia L. Keyes. Includes photos, poems, and literary works of the three women from the 1870s and later years as well as photos and correspondence concerning the family's life in Brazil and notebooks the women filled with poems and artistic efforts. Also contains magazines and catalogs, in particular one dated 1887-88 from the Synodical Female College of Florence, AL, and a 1913-14 volume from the Highland Home College in Highland Home, AL.

115. Spencer, Sue Townsend (McDaniel)
Papers. 1956-64. 1 Hollinger box.
Open. Index.
University of Alabama, W. S. Hoole Special Collections Library.
Correspondence with publishers, letters from Africa, manuscripts, galley proofs, and clippings of Spencer (1919-), an Alabama-born author who lived in Africa and Australia with her husband Robert Spencer, a mining engineer. Born in Northport and educated at Northport Elementary and Tuscaloosa County High School, McDaniel entered the University of Alabama at age 15. After her marriage she lived in Alabama and Florida before moving in 1956 to Sierra Leone where she wrote *African Creeks I Have Been Up* (1963), the manuscript of which is in the collection. The Spencers later moved to Australia.

116. Thompson, Henrietta W.
Papers. Ca. 1930-66. 12 drawers.
Open. Index.
University of Alabama, W. S. Hoole Special Collections Library.
Thompson was a professor and dean of the

University of Alabama school of home economics from the mid-1930s until the mid-1950s. She wrote about consumer activities, the PTA, and 4-H groups. Correspondence, Thompson's home economics publications, official publications of women's groups, conference and club material, and memoranda partially relate to the problems, opportunities, and goals of women's education in the South and the nation. Included are bulletins of the Alabama Federation of Women's Clubs and Alabama College, a women's school; copies of *The Alabama Club Woman* and the *Alabama School Journal;* publications of the state AAUW and the state chapter of the Business and Professional Women's Clubs; and newsletters of the state Delta Kappa Gamma Society chapter.

117. Tutwiler, Julia Strudwick
Papers. 1873-1910. 0.5 drawer.
Open. Index and card catalog.
University of Alabama, W. S. Hoole Special Collections Library.
An educator, author, poet, and reformer, [Miss] Tutwiler (1841-1916) was an exponent of social change in Alabama and a pioneer in women's education. Correspondence, Tutwiler's writings and will, speeches, poems, manuscript about Tutwiler by Anne Gary Pannell, scrapbooks, articles, and clippings. As director of the State Normal College at Livingston, AL, Tutwiler sought scholarships and aid for deserving students. She also waged a 20-year campaign for coeducation that ended in 1893 when the University of Alabama admitted its first two women students. She was active in the state WCTU and advocated prison reform and an end to the state's convict lease system. Largely because of her efforts, male and female prisoners were given separate quarters in Alabama penitentiaries and a women's prison was approved. Included are her writings on standardized examinations for Alabama teachers, education of prisoners, the evils of the convict lease system, her trip to Europe, and women's education.

118. Tutwiler, Julia Strudwick: Tuscaloosa Female Benevolent Society
Records. 1853-68. 2 vols.
Open. Index.
University of Alabama, W. S. Hoole Special Collections Library.
Minutes and roll books of this organization, which helped needy families and citizens, many of them married women. Includes annual information on the amount of aid given per family and the number of recipient families. In 1856, for example, the records listed 12 aid recipients, all of them married women who received amounts ranging from $1.75 to $14.60. Dues of $1 per year helped build the Society's treasury. Records from the Civil War years show a decline in income and expenditures. Accounts for 1862 show Society funds were used to buy candles, potatoes, molasses, meat, shoes, clothes, servants' labor, clothing, wood, and corn. Later records show expenditures to help soldiers' wives.

119. United Daughters of the Confederacy, Alabama Division
Records. 1820-1904. 0.25 drawer.
Open. Index.
University of Alabama, W. S. Hoole Special Collections Library.
Correspondence, typescripts, and biographical information gathered by UDC members center on the Civil War years, principally relating to the activities of Alabama soldiers in the conflict. The collection documents relationships of the UDC members to Confederate soldiers and their families. Includes the "Lost Cause" regional history and genealogy.

120. United Daughters of the Confederacy, Alabama Division, Amelia Gayle Gorgas Chapter
Records. 1942-66. 8 vols.
Open. Card catalog.
University of Alabama, W. S. Hoole Special Collections Library.
Record-minute book and seven scrapbooks of this organization, which is concerned with the genealogy and history of Confederate soldiers, their families, and descendants. Minutes reflect the group's projects including a commemorative plaque in Gorgas Library for Amelia Gayle Gorgas, the first woman faculty member and librarian at the University of Alabama, and a stained glass window on the library's third floor. Also includes items about the Gorgas House on the University campus and biographical material on Amelia Gayle Gorgas, her husband General Josiah Gorgas, and their daughter [Miss] Mary Gorgas, assistant librarian at the University of Alabama.

121. Wilson, Augusta Evans
Papers. Ca. 1862-94. Ca. 24 items.
Open. Index.
University of Alabama, W. S. Hoole Special Collections Library.
Correspondence and clippings of Wilson (1835-1909), a Mobile, AL, woman who supported the Confederate cause. Her letters relating to the Civil War, its effect, and its aftermath include letters to relatives and friends during the war and letters urging the mayor of Mobile to erect a monument to the Confederate army.

TUSKEGEE INSTITUTE

122. Brewster, Juanita Gilmore
Papers. 1800-1970. 17 Hollinger boxes.
Open. Unpublished guide.
Tuskegee Institute Archives.
Correspondence, photos, and scrapbooks of Brewster (1895-1970), an educator, concern black leadership among women in the South, the early history of the Fisk Jubilee Singers, and early Tennessee history.

123. Delaney, Sadie Peterson
Papers. 1923-58. 11 Hollinger boxes.
Open. Unpublished guide.
Tuskegee Institute Archives.
Correspondence, photos, and scrapbooks of Delaney (1889-1958), a librarian, concern bibliotherapy, library science, and medical librarianship.

124. Guzman, Jessie Parkhurst
Papers. 1940-64. 10 Hollinger boxes.
Open. Unpublished guide.
Tuskegee Institute Archives.
Guzman (1898-), an educator, served as editor of the *Negro Year Book.* Correspondence and speeches concern race relations in the South and the Women's International League for Peace and Freedom.

125. National Committee to Abolish the Poll Tax
Records. 1943-48. 24 Hollinger boxes.
Open. Unpublished guide.
Tuskegee Institute Archives.
Correspondence, receipts, press releases, and campaign material of the Committee and of Virginia (Foster) Durr.

126. Shehee, Edith Meriwether Washington
Papers. 1910-64. 8 Hollinger boxes.
Open. Unpublished guide.
Tuskegee Institute Archives.
Correspondence, photos, and scrapbooks of Shehee (1891-1968), an educator, concern the Tuskegee Woman's Club and the role of women in the development of Tuskegee Institute.

127. Southern Conference Educational Fund
Records. 1938-63. 155 Hollinger boxes.
Open. Unpublished guide.
Tuskegee Institute Archives.
Board minutes, correspondence, and photos of the Fund include information about Anne Braden, Mary (McLeod) Bethune, Eleanor Roosevelt, Virginia (Foster) Durr, and Jessie Parkhurst Guzman.

128. Washington, Margaret James Murray
Papers. 1896-1925. 5 Hollinger boxes.
Open. Unpublished guide.
Tuskegee Institute Archives.
Correspondence of Washington (1865-1925), an educator, pertains to the Alabama State Federation of Colored Women's Clubs, the National Association of Colored Women, and the National Federation of Colored Women's Clubs.

ALASKA

ANCHORAGE

129. Burr, A. Regina
Papers. 1898-1904. 86-page vol. and 2 items.
Open. No guide.
Anchorage Historical and Fine Arts Museum Archives.
Diary of the trip [Mrs.] Burr made to the Alaskan gold fields in Klondike contains factual information about the trip, weather, and hardships. Also includes a newspaper narrative Burr wrote after her return and a photo.

EAGLE

130. Manuscripts
Collection. 1898-?. 3 items.
Access restricted. No guide.
Eagle Historical Society.
Contains a booklet by Mrs. William Kirk, a Presbyterian minister's wife, about the frontier gold mining town of Eagle, where she lived from 1899 to 1902, and her experiences there; Rev. and Mrs. Kirk are thought to have been the first Presbyterian couple to come to Alaska. Also includes oral history tapes and transcripts of Borghilde "Ole" (Hendricksen) [Mrs. Burnett] Hansen, who came in 1927 to Eagle, where she taught in an Indian school for 13 years, married a gold miner, and became postmistress and of Anne [Mrs. Fred] Purdy, who arrived in Eagle in 1928, taught school in Eagle and Chicken, and raised 12 Indian or part-Indian children. The novel *Tisha* is about Purdy's life.

FAIRBANKS

131. Clark, Orah Dee
Papers. 1913-62. 5 cu.in.
Open. Unpublished guide.
University of Alaska Archives.
Papers of [Miss] Clark (1875-1965), an educator who helped organize the first Anchorage school and became the first superintendent of the city's schools, include correspondence, articles written by her, a manuscript written by Clara Goss for Clark, and a biographical sketch of Clark.

132. Fairbanks, Lulu M.
Papers. 1897-1965. 12.5 cu.ft.
Open. Unpublished guide.

University of Alaska Archives.
Papers of Fairbanks (1888-1968), a reporter and editor with the *Alaska Weekly* from 1922 to 1956, include business correspondence, post cards, scrapbooks, photos of Alaska and the Yukon Territory from 1886 to the early 1960s, tourist information, material regarding Eskimos, clippings, and other items.

133. Fairbanks Republican Women's Club
Records. 1915- . 1.5 cu.ft.
Open. Unpublished guide.
University of Alaska Archives.
Reports, papers, correspondence, and publications of the Club, which was founded in 1915.

134. Fejes, Claire
Papers. 1959. 11 cu.ft.
Partially closed. Unpublished guide.
University of Alaska Archives.
Papers of Fejes (1920-), an artist, writer, and poet, contain correspondence, drafts and completed copies of her books, etchings and drawings, poems, financial papers, research material, and clippings. Many of her writings, paintings, and drawings portray Eskimo culture.

135. Gibson, Sarah Ellen
Papers. 1884-1918. 2.5 cu.ft.
Open. Unpublished guide.
University of Alaska Archives.
Correspondence, receipts, bills, legal documents, licenses, and other papers of Gibson (?-1908), a pioneer and entrepreneur. She traveled to Dawson in Yukon Territory, Canada, with her husband, a miner, where she purchased and operated the Montana Laundry. Five years later she moved to Fairbanks, where she purchased property and acquired mining claims. Her correspondence contains descriptions of the difficulties of her overland journey.

136. Goddard, Elizabeth Hayes
Papers. 1934. 2.5 in.
Open. Unpublished guide.
University of Alaska Archives.
Diary and photos of [Mrs.] Goddard regarding her travels along the Yukon and Koyukuk rivers.

137. Hadley, Martha
Papers. 1899-1903. 1 cu.ft.
Open. Unpublished guide.
University of Alaska Archives.
Diaries, accounts, and photos of Hadley, a missionary who was sent to Kotzebue, AK, in 1899 by the Society of Friends church, relate to her journey from San Francisco and life in Kotzebue. Includes photos of the village and the natives of Kotzebue.

138. Harrais, Margaret (Keenan)
Papers. 1897-1963. 2.5 cu.ft.
Open. Unpublished guide.
University of Alaska Archives.
Correspondence, school papers, speeches, photos, maps, clippings relating to Alaska, and other papers of Harrais (1872-1964), an educator, US commissioner, and ex-officio probate judge in Valdez, AK, since 1937. Includes correspondence with her husband Martin Harrais, whom she married in 1920; with Alaskan political figures; and with friends. Also includes material relating to her presidency of the Alaska WCTU from 1924 to 1942. Harrais was a graduate of Valparaiso University and a member of the Committee of Fifteen, which in 1931 was concerned with law enforcement and observance. Harrais served on the Committee with Commander Evangeline Booth, [Mrs.] Carrie Chapman Catt, Mrs. Irving Fisher, Alice Hegan Rice, and others.

139. League of Women Voters of Alaska
Records. 1966-72. 3.5 cu.ft.
Open. Unpublished guide.
University of Alaska Archives.
Bylaws, minutes, annual reports, correspondence, printed material, clippings, and other records of the Alaska LWV, which was founded in 1966.

140. McGown, Eva (Montgomery)
Papers. 1914-59. 2.5 cu.ft.
Open. Unpublished guide.
University of Alaska Archives.
Correspondence, photos, pamphlets, menus, clippings, and other papers of McGown (1884-1972), a Fairbanks housing manager who was proclaimed Alaska's official hostess by the governor in 1953. Born in Ireland, McGown was a schoolteacher who came to Alaska in 1914, the same year she married Arthur McGown. She was secretary of the Tanana Valley Fair Association, a member of the Order of the Eastern Star and the Fairbanks Women's Club, and a volunteer worker. She was an Episcopalian and a Republican.

141. Martin, Frederika
Papers. 1941-69. 2.5 cu.ft.
Open. Unpublished guide.
University of Alaska Archives.
Correspondence, a medical log, reference material, and other papers of Martin, an author and public health nurse on the Pribilof Islands. Includes information about the Island, medical records, and WWII evacuation material.

142. Pedersen, Elsa
Papers. 1949-71. 2.5 in.
Open. Unpublished guide.
University of Alaska Archives.
Publications containing short stories, essays, and articles by [Mrs.] Pedersen, an author.

143. Pilgrim, Mariette Shaw
Papers. 1939-52. 7.5 in.
Open. Unpublished guide.
University of Alaska Archives.
Papers of Pilgrim (1898-), an author and schoolteacher, consist of manuscripts for her *Alaska: Its History, Resources, Geography and Government* (1939), the first textbook of Alaskan history for school and popular use. Includes two revisions of the text.

144. Rust, Clara H.
Papers. 1953-78. 1.5 cu.ft.
Open. Unpublished guide.
University of Alaska Archives.
Personal papers of Rust (?-1978) and minutes, enrollment forms, newsletters, and clippings of Pioneer Women of Alaska, for which she served as secretary. Rust was also a member of the Pioneers of Alaska Auxiliary.

145. Strong, J. F. A.
Papers. 1889-1937. 3 cu.ft.
Open. Unpublished guide.
University of Alaska Archives.
Papers of Strong (1859-1929), governor of Alaska from 1913 to 1918, include correspondence, post cards, photos, bylaws, reports, and clippings of his wife Anna Strong, who was president of the Alaska Women's Patriotic League from 1917 to 1918, regarding the League and the activities of a governor's wife.

146. Willoughby, Barrett
Papers. 1870-1956. 2 cu.ft.
Open. Unpublished guide.
University of Alaska Archives.
Papers of Willoughby (1894-1959), a novelist, contain correspondence, drafts of her stories, notes, photos of Alaska from 1900 to 1920, research data, excerpts from other authors' writings, articles, and other papers. Willoughby's given name was Florance Barrett, and her pen name was Barrett Willoughby. Her stepfather's name was Charles P. Willoughby.

HAINES

147. Haines Women's Club
Records. 1929- . 4 vols.
Open. No guide.
Sheldon Museum.
Scrapbooks and photos of this public service group, founded in 1929. The Club sponsored and built the public library and, in addition to other projects, led the drive for establishment of Sheldon Museum.

JUNEAU

148. Juneau Woman's Club
Records. 1917-64?. 2 boxes and 3 vols.
Open. Inventory.
Alaska Division of State Libraries and Museums, Alaska Historical Library.
Constitution, minutes, treasurer's records, committee programs and reports, photos, scrapbooks, clippings, and a history of the Club, which became affiliated with the GFWC in 1916. Also contains information on other Alaska clubs.

ARIZONA

CHANDLER

149. Women's Club
Records. Ca. 1919-?. 2 vols. and other items.
Open. No guide.
Chandler Historical Museum.
Scrapbooks, photos, clippings, and memorabilia of this Chandler club, which was founded in ca. 1919.

FLAGSTAFF

150. American Association of University Women
Records. 1938-62. 12 in.
Open. No guide.
Northern Arizona University Library, Special Collections.
Correspondence, subject files, membership lists, and publications of the Flagstaff branch of the AAUW.

151. Arizona Champion-Coconino Sun Index
Finding aid. 1973-76. Ca. 2000 pp.
Open. No guide.
Northern Arizona University Library, Special Collections.
Newspaper index for the Flagstaff *Arizona Champion-Coconino Sun* was prepared by the Flagstaff Cooperative Newspaper Indexing Project and covers the years 1883 through 1894. Contains the subject heading "women" and lists individual women in the name index.

152. Arizona Federation of Women's Clubs
Records. 1903-65. 6 in.
Open. No guide.
Northern Arizona University Library, Special Collections.
Scrapbooks, programs, yearbooks, and directories include material on the Flagstaff Women's Club and the northern district clubs of the Arizona Federation.

153. Barker, Florence
Papers. 1911-60. 5 in.
Open. Unpublished guide.
Northern Arizona University Library, Special Collections.
Diaries from 1922 to 1927 and photo albums

reflect the career of Barker (1891-?), a Plymouth Brethren missionary-nurse to the Navajo Indians at the Immanuel Mission in Apache County, AZ, from 1922 to 1927. In 1927 she was put in charge of a small government hospital in Valentine, AZ, serving the Hualapai Indians. She was later transferred, first to the nearby Havasupai Indian Reservation and then in 1938 to Acomita, NM, where she worked with the Acoma and Laguna Indians as a public health nurse. She retired in 1952.

154. Birth Control
Collection. 1915-65. 5 in.
Open. No guide.
Northern Arizona University Library, Special Collections.
Correspondence, clippings, pamphlets, and brochures regarding birth control issues in the US.

155. Day, Anna
Papers. 1872-1932. 2 in.
Open. Unpublished guide.
Northern Arizona University Library, Special Collections.
Correspondence of Day, the wife of a trader in the eastern section of Arizona's Navajo Indian Reservation.

156. Flagstaff City-Coconino County Public Library Oral History
Oral history. 1975-76. No size given.
Open. Unpublished guide.
Northern Arizona University Library, Special Collections.
Includes ca. 40 taped interviews with older women in the Flagstaff area. Reminiscences about the careers and lives of educators, musicians, ranchers, housewives, writers, businesswomen, and others during the first half of the 20th century.

157. Horstman, Patrice
Oral history. 1975. 5 tapes.
Open. No guide.
Northern Arizona University Library, Special Collections.
Interviews with women members of the Arizona legislature of 1975: Betty Morrison, Anne Lindeman, Marcia Weeks, Sue James, and Pat Bosch. Concerns women and state politics and includes information on Isabella (Selmes) Greenway, an Arizona congresswoman.

158. Shakespeare Club
Records. 1903-71. 12 in.
Open. No guide.
Northern Arizona University Library, Special Collections.
Minutes and programs of this Flagstaff women's literary group, which was founded in 1903 and is believed to be the oldest active women's organization in Arizona.

159. Sisters of Loretto
Records. 1920s-60s. 10 in.
Open. No guide.
Northern Arizona University Library, Special Collections.
The Sisters of Loretto operated the School of the Nativity in Flagstaff from 1899 to 1966. Correspondence, class records, photos, and publications. Includes material on Sister Mary Imelda, formerly Lorabel Wallace, a Flagstaff native who was an educator and Pulitzer Prize-winning children's author.

160. Tanner, George S.
Collection. 1870s-1972. 6 ft.
Open. Published guide.
Northern Arizona University Library, Special Collections.
Correspondence, diaries, and family histories collected by Tanner, a descendant of Mormon settlers of northern Arizona, include extensive information on Mormon women pioneers of the area. See Margery Ward, ed., *Register of the Records of Mormon Settlement in Arizona,* Register 8 (Salt Lake City: University of Utah Libraries, Special Collections, 1974).

PEORIA

161. American Church
Collection. 1803- . 115 microfilm reels.
Open. Unpublished guide.
Ecumenism Research Agency.
The Ecumenism Research Agency has issued in microfilm records of a variety of churches and religious organizations. This collection consists of annual reports, minutes, statistics, and official yearbooks of the Assemblies of God, 1914-65; the Christian Church (Disciples of Christ), 1848-1964; the Churches of Christ, 1906-63; the Congregational Church, 1854-1961; the Cumberland Presbyterian Church in Tennessee, 1810-1966; the Associate Reformed Presbyterian Church, 1803-1970; the Brethren in Christ (formerly, the River Brethren of Lancaster County, PA), 1871-1970; the Seventh-Day Adventist Church, 1867-1970; the American Baptist Convention, 1814-1969; and the American Baptist Missionary Union, 1814-1906.

PHOENIX

162. Arizona County Records
Records. 1871-1957. 500 cu.ft. and 1000 microfilm reels.
Open. Card catalog.
Arizona Department of Library, Archives, and Public Records.
District and county court records, probate cases, rolls of attorneys, records of estates, insanity proceedings, assessment and tax rolls, sheriffs' actions, registrations of midwives, birth and death indexes, burial records, marriage licenses, naturalization records, school ledgers and censuses, teacher certifications, attendance reports on Indian school children, and military enlistments. Arizona's earliest counties, particularly Pima and Maricopa counties, are most fully represented.

163. Arizona Press Women
Records. 1953-71. 3 cu.ft.
Open. Preliminary inventory.
Arizona Department of Library, Archives, and Public Records.
In 1953 the Arizona branch of the National Federation of Press Women was founded to encourage women journalists to meet and exchange ideas about journalistic trends and techniques. Scrapbooks, national convention information, photos of members, copies of the group's official publication *The Type Rider,* and other periodicals such as *Arizona Highways* and *Writer's Digest.*

164. Church Women United of Arizona
Records. 1954-73. 1.25 cu.ft.
Open. Preliminary inventory.
Arizona Department of Library, Archives, and Public Records.
Bylaws, minutes, official reports, correspondence, programs, photos, and brochures of the Arizona chapter, founded in 1954, of United Church Women, which is a department within the National Council of Churches of Christ in the U.S.A. The group is concerned with family life; children and youth; economic and industrial relations; race relations; civil liberties; refugee placement; Church World Service projects; service to migrants, Indians, and foreign students; and the use of media to promote the organization's objectives. Also includes records of city chapters of the group.

165. Yuma Prison
Records. 1867-1902. Ca. 10 microfilm reels.
Open. Calendar.
Arizona Department of Library, Archives, and Public Records.
Correspondence, reports, personnel records, and data on prisoners of this correctional facility, which housed about 20 women inmates between 1867 and 1902. Material includes names of prisoners, county where they were tried, crime committed, and date of sentence. Founded in 1867, the prison was transferred in 1909 to Florence, AZ.

166. City Directories
Collection. 1884-1969. Ca. 50 vols.
Open. No guide.
Arizona Historical Society, Phoenix Chapter and Museum.
Directories list names, addresses, and telephone numbers of citizens. Includes directories of Phoenix from 1892 to 1969 and of Japanese-Americans and members of the Japanese American Citizens League, greater Phoenix area. Also contains telephone directories of Langford, KS, from 1932 and of Independence, KS, from 1922 to 1930.

167. Miscellaneous Phoenix Records
Collection. Ca. 1870- . No size given.
Open. Accession list.
Arizona Historical Society, Phoenix Chapter and Museum.
Records of organizations, photos, scrapbooks, obituary notices, and clippings, some of which date from 1870 when Phoenix was founded. Includes a 1920 paper on American National Red Cross activities, a 1925 program of the Phoenix Women's Club, and 1947 clippings on prostitution and gambling.

168. Phoenix History and Project Oral Histories
Oral History. Nd. 400 tapes.
Access restricted. Transcripts with tables of contents.
Arizona Historical Society, Phoenix Chapter and Museum.
One hundred and forty of the tapes are interviews of women, while many of the interviews with men contain information on wives, families, and the area's notable women. The tapes include interviews with persons whose families arrived in the area before Phoenix was founded in 1870; with those whose families came before 1912, the end of Arizona's territorial period; and with those who either arrived prior to 1930 or who had resided in the area for up to 30 years. Examples from each period include June Osborn Cook, a member of one of Phoenix's earliest pioneer families; Eleanor B. Sloan, daughter of Arizona's last territorial governor, Richard E. Sloan; and Rose Mofford, former Arizona state treasurer, former assistant secretary of state, former director of revenue, and current secretary of state, who came to Phoenix in 1940. The tapes are also organized by ethnic group, organizational membership, and profession.

169. Phoenix Pioneers
Collection. Ca. 1870- . 6 tapes and other items.
Access restricted. No guide.
Arizona Historical Society, Phoenix Chapter and Museum.
Oral history tapes, correspondence, a manuscript, financial records, photos, and booklets of notable individuals of the Phoenix area.

Oral history tape and family register of Dorothy McLaughlin, a photographer and leading chronicler of Phoenix's past and present through photos. Together with her husband Herb, she organized the Arizona Photographic Associates in 1955 and co-authored *Phoenix 1870-1970: In Photographs.* She is a member and past president of the Phoenix Soroptimist Club.

Manuscript of Mrs. Paul Pierson (ca. 1860s-?), a

teacher at the Phoenix Indian School, chronicles the School's development and teaching and disciplinary methods from 1891 to 1958. Also includes lists of graduates of the School and its Navajo program.

Oral history tape of Robert Creighton (1910-), an editor of the Arizona Newsservice that covered state government activities. His family, which arrived in Phoenix in 1884, was closely associated with the news service.

Oral history tape of Louise (Shoemaker) Stewart (1915-) who with her husband Jack was founder and proprietor of the Camelback Inn, a Phoenix resort.

Oral history and other papers of Eleanor (Alexander) Wiebeck (1905-) deal with her family's history and include letters regarding Theodore Roosevelt and the Phoenix Woman's Roosevelt Memorial Association and a manuscript written by Wiebeck regarding her mother Grace Maye (Forbes) Alexander (1874-1957), known as Mrs. Suffragette, who was active within the Republican party and who ran for office. Also contains correspondence regarding community organization, women's rights, and the education of girls.

[Mrs.] Lucille Wallace (1897-) was president of the Musician's Club of Phoenix, an organization that sought to educate its members about music. Oral history tape, Club yearbooks from 1931 to 1950, and Club programs.

Oral history tape of Marie Steinegger (1896-), whose ancestors arrived in the Phoenix area in 1867, includes details of family financial affairs. Her family became the largest property owners in the area, and her husband operated the Phoenix Coliseum Theater. Also included are family financial records such as bankbooks, checks, and receipts.

Notes by [Mrs.] Agnes G. Miller regarding her family history and early Phoenix life.

170. Yuma Territorial Prison
Records. 1876-1909. 4 vols., ca. 150 items, and 4 microfilm reels.
Open. Unpublished guide.
Yuma Territorial Prison State Historic Park.
Minutes of Prison board meetings, superintendents' reports, official convict records, correspondence, personal accounts, purchasing records, photos, articles, and clippings of this maximum security penitentiary for the Territory of Arizona, which was opened in 1876; 29 women convicts were imprisoned there in the same facility with male convicts. Collection contains information on the national and ethnic origins, religion, education, marital status, occupation, and personal habits of the women as well as limited information about them after their release from prison. In addition, the collection provides a view of the lives many of these women led on the Arizona frontier and the difficulties of housing male and female convicts in the same prison.

PRESCOTT

171. Brown, Angie Mitchell
Papers. Ca. 1880-1903. Ca. 1.5 cu.ft.
Open. Card catalog.
Sharlot Hall Museum.
Correspondence, a diary for 1880 and 1881, historical notes, and music of Brown (ca. 1870s-1909), a pioneer, teacher, musician, and writer who was known for her interest in the history of Arizona and the Southwest.

172. Hall, Sharlot M.
Papers. 1885-1934. Ca. 9 cu.ft.
Open. Unpublished guide.
Sharlot Hall Museum.
The first woman to hold a state office, Hall (1870-1943) was Arizona territorial historian as well as a poet, collector of historical manuscripts and artifacts, and founder of the Museum. Correspondence, journals, notebooks, rough drafts of manuscripts and poems, and business papers and records from her tenure as Arizona historian.

173. Cory, Kate
Papers. 1905-13. No size given.
Access restricted. No guide.
Smoki Museum.
Diary, scrapbooks containing ca. 500 photos, dictionary, and paintings of Cory (1861-1958), who was born in Illinois and moved to Arizona in 1906 to teach school among the Hopi Indians. Diary and photos taken by Cory document her seven years with the Hopis. She compiled the dictionary of English to Hopi and Hopi to English words; the Hopis had had no written language.

TEMPE

174. Smedley, Agnes
Papers. 1894-1950. 8 ft.
Open. Unpublished guide.
Arizona State University Archives.
Correspondence, notes, speeches, articles, book reviews, maps, photos, clippings, and other papers of [Miss] Smedley (1894?-1950), a writer who worked as a correspondent for the German newspaper *Frankfurter Zeitung* and the British *Manchester Guardian* in China from 1928 to 1940. She also was the author of such books as *Daughter of Earth* (1929) and *Battle Hymn of China* (1943). A student at Arizona State University in 1911 and 1912, when it was the Tempe Normal School, Smedley married mining engineer Ernest Brundin, but the marriage did not last because, she believed, "for women marriage is at best an economic investment; at its worst, a relic of human slavery." In 1918 Smedley moved to New York where she worked as a free-lance writer; there she also became involved in the India Independence movement and the birth control movement, which resulted in her being jailed for some time. In China, Smedley marched with Red Army units and guerrilla detachments, often behind the Japanese lines. A fieldworker and fund raiser for the Chinese Red Cross Medical Corps and an organizer of a nurses corps, she also worked to develop a league for civil rights with Madame Sun Yat-Sen and Dr. Lin Yu-Tang. A close friend of Chinese author Lu Hsun and translator of some of his works, Smedley was denounced by officers of the US Army in 1949 as a Communist, at which point she moved to England and died soon thereafter. According to her request, she was buried in Peking. In addition to her other papers, the collection contains Chinese and Japanese propaganda leaflets and Chinese Eighth Route Army newspapers.

175. Fullinwider, Pat
Papers. 1974-76. 14 ft.
Open. Unpublished guide.
Arizona State University Library, Arizona Collection.
Correspondence, statistics, ephemera, and publications of Fullinwider, a politician, relate to campaigns she waged against John Rhodes for the US House of Representatives in 1974 and 1976.

176. Hayden, Carl T.
Papers. 1904-68. 1500 ft.
Open. Computer printout.
Arizona State University Library, Arizona Collection.
Congressional papers of Hayden (1877-1972), a US senator, include correspondence and other items pertaining to women's suffrage in 1916 and 1917, suffrage speeches and issues of *The Suffragist* from 1912 to 1916, a journal of the Women's Suffrage Committee and Democratic Caucus from 1914, correspondence of the Women's Voter's League from 1961, and women's rights correspondence and pamphlets regarding legislation in 1949.

177. Kaufman, Lucile B.
Papers. 1960-75. 3 ft.
Open. No guide.
Arizona State University Library, Arizona Collection.
Papers of Kaufman, an engineering professor, contain her correspondence, clippings, and publications relating to the Equal Rights Amendment and women's rights.

TUCSON

178. Aldrich, Mark A.
Papers. 1969. 2 in.
Open. Published guide.
Arizona Historical Society Library.
Family genealogy of Aldrich (1801-73), an Arizona territorial legislator and the first American to open a store in Tucson, Arizona Territory. He was indicted for alleged participation in the murder of Mormon leader Joseph Smith. See Charles C. Colley, comp., *Documents of Southwestern History: A Guide to the Manuscript Collections of the Arizona Historical Society* (Tucson, AZ: Arizona Historical Society, 1972).

179. Anderson, John B.
Papers. 1870-1910. 10 in.
Open. Published guide.
Arizona Historical Society Library.
Personal correspondence; reminiscences of travels from 1907 to 1910; a description of Greaterville, Arizona Territory; business and mining records; location notices; registers for Greaterville schools; pamphlets; and other papers of Anderson (1845-1925), postmaster and notary public at Greaterville and Helvetia, Arizona Territory, and his wife Mary Emma (Booth) Anderson (1854-1948), who came to Arizona with her husband in 1881 and taught school. See Charles C. Colley, comp., *Documents of Southwestern History: A Guide to the Manuscript Collections of the Arizona Historical Society* (Tucson, AZ: Arizona Historical Society, 1972).

180. Bandel, Eugene
Papers. 1853-57. 1 in.
Open. Published guide.
Arizona Historical Society Library.
Bandel (1835-89), a native of Germany, came to America in 1853; in 1854 he joined the US Army and traveled throughout the Southwest. Letters Bandel wrote in German to his family describing his experiences; his diary; his manuscript "Frontier Life in the Army 1854-1861," a description of his career which was translated by his daughter Olga Bandel; and correspondence between Olga Bandel and the Arthur H. Clarke Company, which published the manuscript in 1932, concerning details of translation and other editorial matters. See Charles C. Colley, comp., *Documents of Southwestern History: A Guide to the Manuscript Collections of the Arizona Historical Society* (Tucson, AZ: Arizona Historical Society, 1972).

181. Becker Family
Papers. 1888-1959. 42 ft.
Open. Published guide.
Arizona Historical Society Library.
Gustav Becker (1856-1959) established Becker Mercantile Company, founded the town of Springerville, AZ, and became a staunch supporter of highway construction throughout Arizona. Correspondence with US Senator Carl T. Hayden of Arizona and President Harry S. Truman, correspondence regarding highway construction, business accounts, ledger books, and tax receipts. Also includes family correspondence, which provides insight into social and business conditions in eastern Arizona. See Charles C. Colley, comp.,

Documents of Southwestern History: A Guide to the Manuscript Collections of the Arizona Historical Society (Tucson, AZ: Arizona Historical Society, 1972).

182. Boyd, E.
Papers. 1952-62. 2 in.
Open. Published guide.
Arizona Historical Society Library.
[Miss] Boyd was curator of the Museum of New Mexico's Spanish Colonial Department and an expert on Spanish colonial art. Collection consists of correspondence with Mrs. James P. Moore and clippings detailing Boyd's activities. See Charles C. Colley, comp., *Documents of Southwestern History: A Guide to the Manuscript Collections of the Arizona Historical Society* (Tucson, AZ: Arizona Historical Society, 1972).

183. Brown, Estelle (Aubrey)
Papers. 1919-52. 4 in.
Open. Published guide.
Arizona Historical Society Library.
Born in New York, [Mrs. H. T.] Brown (1877-?), a writer, came to Arizona in 1904; she became national vice-president of American Pen Women and published *Stubborn Fool* in 1952. Correspondence, notebooks, copies of Brown's articles, reviews, service certificates, membership cards, and booklets on the Southwest. See Charles C. Colley, comp., *Documents of Southwestern History: A Guide to the Manuscript Collections of the Arizona Historical Society* (Tucson, AZ: Arizona Historical Society, 1972).

184. Bush, Nellie (Trent)
Papers. 1931-36. 8 pp.
Open. Catalog cards.
Arizona Historical Society Library.
[Mrs. Joseph E.] Bush (1888-1963) was a teacher, attorney, river pilot in 1920, US commissioner at Parker, AZ, Arizona state legislator for six years, and a member of the US House of Representatives from 1921 to 1932. Letter from Bush to George Kitt soliciting his support for her congressional candidacy and listing her qualifications and beliefs, a letter to Mrs. George Kitt requesting her presence at the dedication of a state monument, an autobiography, and a political pamphlet.

185. Bushman, John
Papers. 1843-1946. 5 in.
Open. Published guide.
Arizona Historical Society Library.
Raised a Mormon near Salt Lake City, Bushman (1843-1946), a farmer and missionary, moved to Arizona in 1876 and settled near the Little Colorado River. Biography summarizing his career and an autobiography describing family life, his relationship with his wives, and Mormon organization and settlement in Utah and Arizona. See Charles C. Colley, comp., *Documents of Southwestern History: A Guide to the Manuscript Collections of the Arizona Historical Society* (Tucson, AZ: Arizona Historical Society, 1972).

186. California Justice Court
Records. 1858-81. 3 in.
Open. Published guide.
Arizona Historical Society Library.
Manuscript volumes of court records describing cases heard in the justice court of Granite Township in Sacramento County, CA. Cases involving women include such examples as a woman filing a complaint against a boarder for refusing to pay rent and cases filed against Chinese women charged with prostitution. See Charles C. Colley, comp., *Documents of Southwestern History: A Guide to the Manuscript Collections of the Arizona Historical Society* (Tucson, AZ: Arizona Historical Society, 1972).

187. Carroll, Elva Haskell
Papers. 1885-1961. 1 in.
Open. Published guide.
Arizona Historical Society Library.
Carroll (1877-?) was a teacher. Reminiscences; a manuscript "The West's Greatest Catastrophe," which describes the decline of Indian civilization around Casa Grande, AZ; a biography concerning Carroll's grandparents' trip to Prescott, Arizona Territory, and their pioneer life there; and an autograph book. See Charles C. Colley, comp., *Documents of Southwestern History: A Guide to the Manuscript Collections of the Arizona Historical Society* (Tucson, AZ: Arizona Historical Society, 1972).

188. Clip Book File
Collection. 1870-1971. 35 ft.
Open. Published guide.
Arizona Historical Society Library.
Clippings, including obituaries on and articles written by such prominent Arizonans as Edith Kitt, Isabella Greenway, and Carl T. Hayden. The clippings contain reminiscences and biographical information. See Charles C. Colley, comp., *Documents of Southwestern History: A Guide to the Manuscript Collections of the Arizona Historical Society* (Tucson, AZ: Arizona Historical Society, 1972).

189. Coleman, Evans P.
Papers. 1887-1954. 4 ft.
Open. Published guide and calendar.
Arizona Historical Society Library.
Coleman (1874-1954) was a cowboy. Personal correspondence; business records; reminiscences, folk tales, and songs relating to cowboy life in Arizona and the Southwest; Coleman's diary for 1897 to 1903 and an autobiography concerning his experiences in Arizona and Mormon settlements; a manuscript history of the Coleman family and a biography of Coleman's wife Emma (Beck) Coleman; photos of Coleman's family and trips; a scrapbook including material on Coleman family genealogy; and notes from "Mrs. Layton." Also includes tall tales, a letter from Coleman to the Arizona Pioneers' Historical Society regarding the tale "The Wild Woman of Galloria [Galiura] Mountains," and historical sketches describing such pioneer incidents as the time Mare Slaughter hired a temporary "hand," only to discover later that the "hand" was a girl. See Charles C. Colley, comp., *Documents of Southwestern History: A Guide to the Manuscript Collections of the Arizona Historical Society* (Tucson, AZ: Arizona Historical Society, 1972).

190. Daniels, Benjamin F.
Papers. 1900-40. 6 in.
Open. Published guide.
Arizona Historical Society Library.
Correspondence, notebooks, business and legal records, and biographical material of Daniels (1852-1923), a miner, cattle raiser, superintendent of Yuma Territorial Prison, marshal of Arizona, and sheriff of Pima County. Includes material on Daniels's wife Annie (Stakebake) Seayrs Daniels (1869-1946), who in 1915 organized the committee that later founded the Arizona Children's Home, helped establish the Tucson YWCA, served as superintendent of Pima County Schools, and was active in Republican politics. Annie Daniels was married to H. J. Seayrs from 1896 to 1906 and to Benjamin Daniels from 1908 to 1923. See Charles C. Colley, comp., *Documents of Southwestern History: A Guide to the Manuscript Collections of the Arizona Historical Society* (Tucson, AZ: Arizona Historical Society, 1972).

191. Dellenbaugh, Frederick Samuel
Papers. 1870-1910. 7 ft.
Open. Published guide and calendar.
Arizona Historical Society Library.
Dellenbaugh (1853-1935) was an artist and topographer on Major John Wesley Powell's second Colorado River expedition in 1871 and 1872 and librarian for the American Geographical Society from 1900 to 1911. Diaries, manuscripts, oil paintings dating from 1870 to 1907 of the Colorado River and Grand Canyon, stereoscopic views of the Colorado River expedition, and clippings. Also included are notebooks compiled by Dellenbaugh on Indian and western US history and personal narratives from 1851 to 1884 of Mormon exploration and settlement in Utah, Arizona, Wyoming, Nevada, and Idaho; these narratives provide information on family and social conditions as well. See Charles C. Colley, comp., *Documents of Southwestern History: A Guide to the Manuscript Collections of the Arizona Historical Society* (Tucson, AZ: Arizona Historical Society, 1972).

192. Dime Novels
Collection. 1881-1950. 2 ft.
Open. Published guide.
Arizona Historical Society Library.
More than 100 dime novels concerning the "wild west." Series include "The Campfire Library," "The Buffalo Bill Stories," and "Beadle's Frontier Series." Also includes "Bibliography of Dime Novels, 1860-1964," "Big Little Books," and various western comic books, some of which are based on Arizona subjects or settings. Dime novels were particularly popular in the East and abroad. See Charles C. Colley, comp., *Documents of Southwestern History: A Guide to the Manuscript Collections of the Arizona Historical Society* (Tucson, AZ: Arizona Historical Society, 1972).

193. Douglass, Andrew Ellicott
Papers. 1856-1962. 10 in.
Open. Published guide.
Arizona Historical Society Library.
Douglass (1867-1962) was a Harvard-trained astronomer who established the Steward Observatory and the Laboratory of Tree Ring Research at the University of Arizona. Manuscripts and typescripts regarding astronomical and tree ring research and higher education in Arizona and a scrapbook of advertisements and clippings. Also includes a typescript journal, which Douglass's sister Mary Carolyn Douglass kept of her travels to Santa Fe, NM, and San Diego, CA, from 1888 to 1889. See Charles C. Colley, comp., *Documents of Southwestern History: A Guide to the Manuscript Collections of the Arizona Historical Society* (Tucson, AZ: Arizona Historical Society, 1972).

194. Greenway, John Campbell, and Greenway, Isabella
Papers. 1860-1936. 100 ft.
Open. Published guide and calendar.
Arizona Historical Society Library.
John Greenway (1872-1926) was a mining engineer and executive who founded the town of Ajo, AZ, and was active in politics, ranching, and real estate. [Mrs.] Isabella Greenway (1886-1953) was a confidante of Eleanor Roosevelt and was the first US congresswoman from Arizona, serving from 1933 to 1936. Correspondence, diaries, business records and political material, including 140 letters from Theodore Roosevelt to John Greenway regarding political and personal matters, letters of Mrs. Theodore Roosevelt and the Roosevelt children, 40 letters from Eleanor Roosevelt and 10 from Franklin D. Roosevelt, and correspondence from General Douglas MacArthur and Minnesota pioneer and author Charles M. Flandrau. Isabella Greenway's papers include personal and business correspondence and state and national political material relating to real estate, taxation, banking, patents, homesteads, the Federal Housing Administration, railroads, veterans' pensions, Arizona Indians, and post offices. See Charles C. Colley, comp., *Documents of Southwestern History: A Guide to the Manuscript Collections of*

the Arizona Historical Society (Tucson, AZ: Arizona Historical Society, 1972).

195. Hall, Sharlot Mabridth
Papers. 1870-1943. 1 in.
Open. Published guide.
Arizona Historical Society Library.
[Miss] Hall (1870-1943) was a territorial historian of Arizona from 1909 to 1912 and an Arizona bibliophile. Correspondence, poetry by Hall, typescript of 1924 interview with Hall, typescript of news items from California, "My Memories of Sharlot Hall" by Ida Davisson, and biographical material. See Charles C. Colley, comp., *Documents of Southwestern History: A Guide to the Manuscript Collections of the Arizona Historical Society* (Tucson, AZ: Arizona Historical Society, 1972).

196. Hockderffer, George
Papers. 1890-1950. 1 ft.
Open. Published guide.
Arizona Historical Society Library.
Hockderffer (1864-1955) was a rancher, Arizona territorial legislator, Flagstaff, AZ, city marshal, and an organizer of the Arizona National Guard. Facsimile records of the founding and operation of the state National Guard and an autobiography concerning his family's Civil War experiences, life in Seneca and Dodge City, KS, travel in New Mexico and California, and the history of northern Arizona, of pioneer families in the region, and of the Babbit family. See Charles C. Colley, comp., *Documents of Southwestern History: A Guide to the Manuscript Collections of the Arizona Historical Society* (Tucson, AZ: Arizona Historical Society, 1972).

197. Hughes, Louis C.
Papers. 1861-1935. 8 in.
Open. Published guide.
Arizona Historical Society Library.
A Pima County, AZ, attorney who established the *Arizona Weekly Star* in 1877 and the *Daily Star* in 1880, Hughes (1842-1915) was appointed Arizona governor in 1893 and removed from office in 1896 for alleged wrongdoing. Correspondence, court records regarding Hughes's removal from office, and clippings. Also included are ca. 15 items, mostly biographical in nature, relating to Hughes's wife Josephine Brawley Hughes (1838-1926), who was the first woman public school teacher in Arizona. She helped establish the first Methodist church in Arizona in 1877, was president of the Arizona WCTU, and was known as the "mother of Arizona." See Charles C. Colley, comp., *Documents of Southwestern History: A Guide to the Manuscript Collections of the Arizona Historical Society* (Tucson, AZ: Arizona Historical Society, 1972).

198. Kitt Family
Papers. 1906-61. 2 ft.
Open. Published guide.
Arizona Historical Society Library.
Family correspondence, manuscripts, speeches, and a genealogy of mercantile businessman William F. Kitt (1842-1904). Contains material relating to his daughter-in-law [Mrs.] Edith Stratton Kitt (1878-1967), who was active in the Arizona Federation of Women's Clubs and was historical secretary of the Arizona Pioneers' Historical Society from 1925 to 1948. Includes correspondence and a ledger containing Edith Kitt's speeches to women's clubs. See Charles C. Colley, comp., *Documents of Southwestern History: A Guide to the Manuscript Collections of the Arizona Historical Society* (Tucson, AZ: Arizona Historical Society, 1972).

199. Lewis, Robert A.
Papers. 1880-1927. 39 pp.
Open. Published guide.
Arizona Historical Society Library.
Manuscript reminiscences of Lewis (1858-?), an Arizona pioneer and merchant, include "Social Life in Tucson in the Early 80's," which contains a description of the city's most notable residents and their daughters; comments on Anglo-Mexican intermarriage, dances, and parties; and the remark that girls never went astray, though they had a good time, and divorce was almost unknown. See Charles C. Colley, comp., *Documents of Southwestern History: A Guide to the Manuscript Collections of the Arizona Historical Society* (Tucson, AZ: Arizona Historical Society, 1972).

200. Mathews, Rena A.
Papers. 1902-45. 5.5 ft.
Open. Published guide and calendar.
Arizona Historical Society Library.
[Mrs. J. D.] Mathews (1874-1962) helped establish the Arizona Children's Home. Personal and business correspondence, a manuscript autobiography "The Claim of Being a Western Pioneer, 1902-1932," biographical information, material pertaining to woman suffrage in Arizona, and clippings and other material relating to southwestern and Mexican history. See Charles C. Colley, comp., *Documents of Southwestern History: A Guide to the Manuscript Collections of the Arizona Historical Society* (Tucson, AZ: Arizona Historical Society, 1972).

201. Mayse, Lola May
Papers. 1929-73. 1 in.
Open. Catalog cards.
Arizona Historical Society Library.
Lola Mayse (1899-) was married to Charles Mayse. Manuscript entitled "Charley Mayse, Pioneer Aviator" and an Arizona Historical Society biographical form and membership certificates for Mr. and Mrs. W. A. Carter.

202. Oral History
Oral history. 1952-71. 3 ft.
Open. Published guide.
Arizona Historical Society Library.
Tapes and transcripts of interviews with Arizona pioneers regarding such subjects as homesteading, settlement of communities, cattle raising, mining, law, politics, business, Indians, missions, Mormons, transportation, and science. Of about 133 individuals interviewed, approximately 40 were women. Also included are tapes of talks by professional and amateur historians and recordings of conventions, dedications, and special historical topics. See Charles C. Colley, comp., *Documents of Southwestern History: A Guide to the Manuscript Collections of the Arizona Historical Society* (Tucson, AZ: Arizona Historical Society, 1972).

203. Organizations
Collection. 1870-1971. 60 ft.
Open. Published guide.
Arizona Historical Society Library.
Minutes, scrapbooks, brochures, and other records of Arizona organizations. Includes records of the following organizations that involved women: the Mariner's Juvenile Band, 1899-1910; the Tucson Little Theater, 1937-51; the Tucson Festival Society, 1951-52; the Arizona Retired Teacher's Association, 1960-70; the Tucson Committee for Interracial Understanding, 1940-45, which includes material on community relations of Japanese, Chinese, and Negroes; the Arizona Federation of Women's Clubs, 1900-63, with material from branches throughout southern Arizona; the Alianza Hispano-Americana, 1921-65; the Arizona Historical Society, formerly known as the Organization of Arizona Pioneers and the Arizona Pioneers' Historical Society, which includes records from 1884 to 1971 of founding members, business documents, correspondence, and publications; the Arizona State Cowbelles, from 1947 to the present, with annual reports of local chapters and scrapbooks from 1954 to the present of the Tucson Cowbelles; the DAR; and the WCTU. See Charles C. Colley, comp., *Documents of Southwestern History: A Guide to the Manuscript Collections of the Arizona Historical Society* (Tucson, AZ: Arizona Historical Society, 1972).

204. Osgood, Dora
Papers. 1901-02. 0.25 in.
Open. Published guide.
Arizona Historical Society Library.
Day-by-day account by Osgood (1886-?), a pioneer, of a 1901 journey from Provo, UT, to Cottonwood, Arizona Territory, by a family of six in two horse drawn wagons. Includes descriptions of dangers along the Virgin River to the Colorado River, becoming lost in the desert near Hackberry, AZ, generous people encountered, and school and life in the Verde Valley. See Charles C. Colley, comp., *Documents of Southwestern History: A Guide to the Manuscript Collections of the Arizona Historical Society* (Tucson, AZ: Arizona Historical Society, 1972).

205. Parsons, Mildred F.
Papers. 1930-59. 10 in.
Open. No guide.
Arizona Historical Society Library.
[Mrs.] Parsons was historian for the Tucson unit of the Women's Overseas Service League, an organization of women who served overseas during wartime and who seek to maintain ties formed during overseas duty, to carry out social service work, and to foster friendship between the US and its allies. Correspondence regarding formation of the Tucson unit of the WOSL in 1935; constitution and bylaws, minutes, records, and membership lists of the Tucson unit; photos of Tucson members and other WOSL members, some of which were taken during WWI and WWII; a 1952 WOSL national membership register; minutes of the National WOSL Conference held in Tucson in 1958; and a list of 4000 women who served in the European, Mediterranean, and African theaters with the American National Red Cross during WWII.

206. Photo Collection
Collection. 1870s- . 300,000 items.
Open. No guide.
Arizona Historical Society Library.
Negatives and prints, 50,000 of which are classified by subject, depict many facets of life and people in the Southwest. Includes photos of women, blacks, Mexicans, and Indians.

207. Pioneer Biographical Files
Collection. 1866-1971. 30 ft.
Open. Published guide.
Arizona Historical Society Library.
Over 3000 biographical files containing correspondence, manuscript biographies, photos, clippings, and other material regarding Arizona pioneers; members of the Organization of Arizona Pioneers, the Arizona Pioneers' Historical Society, and the Arizona Historical Society; and other prominent residents of Arizona and the Southwest. Included are brief biographies of the seven wives of John Conrad Naegle, a Mormon, which contain descriptions of their lives and impressions of polygamy, based in part on their reminiscences. Also included are correspondence, speeches, and reports relating to the work of Eleanor B. Sloan, daughter of Arizona's last territorial governor Richard E. Sloan, in her capacity as historical secretary of the Arizona Pioneers' Historical Society. Many of the collection's files were compiled by Mrs. George F. Kitt while she served as historical secretary of the APHS from 1925 to 1948. See Charles C. Colley, comp., *Documents of Southwestern History: A Guide to the Manuscript Collections of the Arizona Historical Society* (Tucson, AZ: Arizona Historical Society, 1972).

208. Ross, Margaret (Wheeler)
Papers. Ca. 1916. Ca. 10 pp.
Open. Catalog cards.
Arizona Historical Society Library.
[Mrs. Henry D.] Ross (1867-?) was a writer and president of the Arizona Federation of Women's Clubs. Material by Ross includes reminiscences, poetry, lyrics of "Desert Night," a biography, and articles regarding the Monday Club of Prescott, AZ, and the founding, progress, and activities of the Arizona Federation of Women's Clubs.

209. Toohey, Elizabeth
Papers. 1933-36. Ca. 1 in.
Open. Catalog cards.
Arizona Historical Society Library.
Correspondence, most of which was between [Miss] Toohey, a folklorist, in her capacity as state historian and Mrs. George Kitt, reference librarian of the Arizona Pioneers' Historical Society, about questions from researchers. Also includes letters between Toohey and Kitt concerning their efforts to revive publication of the *Arizona Historical Review*, which was discontinued when its funding was cut off by the Arizona state legislature. The Arizona Pioneers' Historical Society was later renamed the Arizona Historical Society.

210. Women in Arizona
Collection. 1912- . Ca. 22 items.
Open. Catalog cards.
Arizona Historical Society Library.
Articles and manuscripts, including a 1971 typescript "History of Arizona Women Lawyers and Judges" by Rosemary D. Gallon; a 1972 seminar paper "Women's Rights and Community Property in Arizona" by Joan F. Shullo; a 1973 historical paper "De-sexing the Ballot Box: The History of Woman Suffrage in Arizona, 1883-1912" by Thomas Lauerman, a 1974 term paper "History of Woman Suffrage of Arizona" by Amanda McGee; a list of notable Arizona women compiled in 1975 by Bert Fireman; a list of women prisoners confined in the Yuma Territorial Prison; proceedings of the Arizona Women's Commission, which concern economic equality, employment, and politics; and a short biography by Margaret W. Ross of Ann D. McClatchie, who was active in founding the Woman's Club of Phoenix and the Arizona Federation of Women's Clubs.

211. Doris Duke American Indian Oral History
Oral history. 1967-75. 577 tapes and other items.
Access restricted. Project description.
Arizona State Museum.
Tapes, transcripts, and field notes of interviews, primarily with Indians. Ninety-nine percent of the interviews are with Indians of 24 different southwestern tribes and with one group of Eskimos. The remaining one percent deal with other nationalities such as Spaniards, Mexicans, and other Americans and also include the recording and analysis of tribal songs. About 25 percent of the interviews are with women. A Yavapai Indian, Nellie Quail, relates her kidnapping by the black troopers of the 10th US Cavalry, who brought her to Colorado where she was placed in a boarding school. After a number of years she "escaped" from the school and returned to her people. Quail, who eventually became a schoolteacher, expressed no animosity toward her abductors or about her experience.

212. Audio Cassette Collection
Oral history. 1960- . Ca. 1000 tapes and ca. 12 transcripts.
Open. Unpublished guide.
Lewis Audiovisual Research and Teaching Archive.
Over 5000 interviews with people in politics, the arts, the sciences, law, journalism, sports, and other areas, including Indians of the Southwest. Interviews of 30 minutes or longer with women include those with Erika Freeman, a psychologist, author, and protégée of Theodore Reich; Colonel and Mrs. Laird Guttersen, concerning his experiences as a prisoner of war in North Vietnam and her experiences at home during his absence; Coral and Leslie Lorenzen, a husband-wife team who have pioneered research into unidentified flying objects; Aden and Marjorie Meinal, pioneer researchers and proponents of solar energy; Mrs. John Steinbeck, discussing her experiences and family life; Margaret Mead, an anthropologist; Ann and Leon Steinberg, who sought healing through psychic surgery in the Philippines; and Juanita Kreps, US secretary of commerce.

213. Austin, Jane (Goodwin)
Papers. Nd. 2 boxes.
Open. Unpublished guide.
University of Arizona Library, Special Collections.
Correspondence, manuscripts of novels and short stories, and notes of Austin (1831-94), an author.

214. Cosulich, Bernice
Papers. 1923-56. 4 boxes and 8 vols.
Open. Unpublished guide.
University of Arizona Library, Special Collections.
Correspondence, notes, photos, publications, clippings, and other papers of Cosulich (1896-1956), a Tucson newspaperwoman, relate primarily to her career with the *Arizona Daily Star* and work as a free-lance writer. Includes letters from various American and English authors and notes for a biography about actress Helena Modjeska.

215. Douglas, Frances
Papers. 1890-1963. 19 boxes.
Open. Unpublished guide.
University of Arizona Library, Special Collections.
Papers of [Miss] Douglas (1870-1969), an author and translator of Spanish literature, include correspondence; diaries; translations, chiefly unpublished, of works by Concha Espina, Vicente Blasco Ibáñez, J. M. Carretero, Rafael Delgado, and others; stories; articles; photos; Mexican and US newspapers from 1911 to 1915 regarding the Mexican Revolution; clippings; and memorabilia. Contains personal papers of Douglas from the period when she was married to Charles Fletcher Lummis and then to Courtenay De Kalb, with whom she operated the Roadside Mine in Pima County, AZ. Papers relating to [Mrs.] Phoebe Hearst, writers Eugene Manlove Rhodes and Henry Herbert Knibbs, and artists Carl Oscar Borg and E. A. Burbank are also included.

216. Gates, Gertrude Edna (Lewis)
Papers. 1903-35. 3 boxes.
Open. Unpublished guide.
University of Arizona Library, Special Collections.
Correspondence, notebooks, financial papers, and cattle records of Gates pertain to the operation and maintenance of the D A Ranch in Cornville, AZ, and of rental property in Flagstaff, AZ. Also includes her personal letters, many of which relate to missionary work among the Indians.

217. Hale Family
Papers. 1913. 1 portfolio.
Open. No guide.
University of Arizona Library, Special Collections.
Correspondence of pharmacist Eugene B. Hale, his wife Lela Hale, and his sister Laura (Hale) Scott with their parents in Mendon, OH, concern their experiences as new arrivals in Arizona and endeavors to settle in Parker, Mesa, and Phoenix. Also includes letters from local citizens regarding positions for pharmacists.

218. Hammer, Angela (Hutchinson)
Papers. 1917-52. 1 box.
Open. Card catalog.
University of Arizona Library, Special Collections.
Papers of Hammer (1870-1955?), a teacher and newspaper editor, include correspondence, a short story, and autobiographical sketches relating to her life in Wickenburg and Casa Grande, AZ.

219. Henderson, Alexander S.
Papers. 1893-1963. 24 boxes and 4 vols.
Open. Unpublished guide.
University of Arizona Library, Special Collections.
Papers of Henderson (1859-1944), a resident of Patagonia in Santa Cruz County, AZ, who engaged in retail trade, politics, and mining. Contains two boxes of papers of his wife Eva (Stevens) Henderson, a registered osteopath, including personal correspondence with pioneer relatives in Oklahoma and material about her educational and professional activities in Oklahoma and Arizona.

220. Milton, Mildred (Taitt)
Papers. 1900-37. 1 box.
Open. Card catalog.
University of Arizona Library, Special Collections.
Papers of Milton (1879-1963) include correspondence with her husband Jefferson Davis Milton (1861-1947) and with her sister Mrs. J. O. Sheldon, photos, a scrapbook Milton kept while she was a student at Vassar College from 1900 to 1901, and a marriage book from 1919.

221. Ownby, Anna
Papers. 1881-88. 1 portfolio.
Open. Card catalog.
University of Arizona Library, Special Collections.
Correspondence, photos, biographical information, and other papers of Ownby, a Lordsburg, NM, pioneer. Includes correspondence with her husband Bramble B. Ownby regarding daily life in Lordsburg.

222. Pollock, Mary (Morton)
Papers. 1910-32. 3 vols.
Open. Card catalog.
University of Arizona Library, Special Collections.
Diaries of Pollock (18??-1941), the wife of T. E. Pollock, a prominent northern Arizona livestock man and businessman, concern daily activities in the Flagstaff, AZ, area and trips to California, New York, and the Midwest.

223. Rak, Mary (Kidder)
Papers. Nd. 2 boxes.
Open. Card catalog.
University of Arizona Library, Special Collections.
Papers of Rak (1879-1958), an author and rancher, contain correspondence from 1934 to 1944 with [Mrs.] Gertrude Hills, manuscripts of stories, notes, photos, and other papers.

224. Roberts, Clara (Fish)
Papers. 1903-04. 8 items.
Open. Card catalog.
University of Arizona Library, Special Collections.
Correspondence, grade books, and other papers of Roberts relate to a teaching position at Northern Arizona Normal School in Flagstaff, AZ.

225. Stevens, Helen (Bradshaw)
Papers. 1906-54. 1 box.
Open. Card catalog.
University of Arizona Library, Special Collections.
Papers of Stevens (1878-1954), wife of Thomas Wood Stevens (1880-1942), who was a playwright, poet, artist, drama director and teacher, and producer of pageants, include correspondence with her daughter Phoebe [Mrs. Fergus] Mera and friend Marguerite [Mrs. Albert S.] Griswold. Also includes correspondence with associates of her husband regarding a projected history of the Globe Theatre.

226. Treadwell, Sophie
Papers. 1905-69. 27 boxes.
Open. Unpublished guide.
University of Arizona Library, Special Collections.
Papers of Treadwell (1890-1970), a playwright and author, include manuscripts of published and

unpublished plays, novels, stories, articles, and television scripts as well as correspondence with producer Arthur Hopkins, literary agents, friends, actors and actresses, and scene designers. Also contains travel diaries, photos, copyright papers, and clippings.

227. University of Arizona Desert Riders
Records. 1931-51. 1 portfolio.
Open. Card catalog.
University of Arizona Library, Special Collections.
Constitution, minutes, membership lists, an historical sketch, and other records of this women's honorary riding club at the University of Arizona.

228. University of Arizona Faculty Women's Club
Records. 1930-71. 3 vols.
Open. Unpublished guide.
University of Arizona Library, Special Collections.
Scrapbooks of the Club contain a record of activities, photos, historical notes, and clippings.

ARKANSAS

CONWAY

229. American Association of University Women
Records. 1925. 1 ft.
Open. No guide.
University of Central Arkansas, Torreyson Library.
History, a clipping file, and other records of this local AAUW group, which was founded in 1925.

230. Atwood, Eva
Oral history. 1970. 1 tape.
Open. Index.
University of Central Arkansas, Torreyson Library.
Tape and transcript of an interview in which [Miss] Atwood (1890-1975) discusses her childhood and family, her nursing training at Little Rock Sanitarium, her experiences as an American National Red Cross nurse during WWI, the effects of the Depression on nursing, and other subjects related to her career. Atwood, a member of the Arkansas State Nurses Association, served on the Arkansas State Board of Nurse Examiners from 1921 to 1925 and from 1928 to 1932. She also worked in various Arkansas hospitals and served with the Department of Agriculture in migrant workers camps in Arkansas and Texas. Also includes documents, photos, a short history of the Board of Nurse Examiners, and clippings.

231. Beauchamp, Linnie
Oral history. 1970. 2 tapes.
Open. Index.
University of Central Arkansas, Torreyson Library.
Tapes and transcript of interviews with Beauchamp (1890-), which include descriptions of her childhood in Forest City, AR, where her father was a country doctor; her early education; her nursing training in Memphis, and her work as a public health nurse and American National Red Cross nurse during and after WWI. Beauchamp served as executive secretary of the Arkansas State Nurses Association. Her description of work in rural areas of Arkansas and Alabama includes the discovery of trachoma in southern Arkansas, the resentment of nurses by local physicians, and securing a traveling clinic of the Children's Bureau of the Department of Labor to examine children and mothers and establish effective registration of births and deaths. Beauchamp speaks of her brief association with [Miss] Mae Sinclair, a pioneer Arkansas psychiatric nurse; of the Emergency Relief Administration and WPA programs for nurses during the Depression; and of the movement to establish a collegiate school of nursing in connection with the University of Arkansas.

232. Belzner, Barbara
Oral history. 1974. 1 tape.
Open. Index.
University of Central Arkansas, Torreyson Library.
Tape and transcript of an interview with Belzner (1902-), a registered nurse, which includes comments on her childhood and family, race relations, her education at the University of Arkansas, and her nursing training at Peabody School and at the Trade School, both in Little Rock, AR. Belzner discusses the accomplishments of the Arkansas State Nurses Association during her presidency and her work in pediatrics, tuberculosis, private duty nursing, home nursing, and in various hospitals. Other topics include social security for nurses, economic security of nurses, employment of nurses during the Depression, patient care, the cost of medical care, socialized medicine, and hospital administrators.

233. Burt, Marguerite
Oral history. 1974. 1 tape.
Open. Index.
University of Central Arkansas, Torreyson Library.
Tape and transcript of an interview in which Burt (1918-), a registered nurse and administrator, speaks of her childhood and family; her education, including studies at George Peabody College; and her nursing training at the Baptist hospital in Memphis. She discusses public health and tuberculosis nursing; her work at the Veterans Administration hospital in Little Rock, AR, and the VA program of continuing nursing care; and working in Gondar, Ethiopia. Other subjects include the Methodist church, politics, the women's liberation movement, continuing education for nurses, a nurse practitioner program, doctor-nurse relationships, economic security for nurses, unions, putting a nurse on a board of health, the public image of professional nursing organizations, the League of Nurses, the Arkansas Joint Commission for the Improvement of Patient Care, and the Arkansas State Nurses Association.

234. Dillon, Margie
Oral history. 1973. 1 tape.
Open. Index.
University of Central Arkansas, Torreyson Library.
Tape and transcript of an interview with Dillon (1926-), an Arkansas folk artist who never received formal instruction in art. She discusses how and when she began to paint and important elements in painting a picture, gives advice on becoming an artist, and mentions displaying her paintings at the Mountain View Folk Festival.

235. Doster, Daphine De Luxe
Oral history. 1969. 1 tape.
Open. Index.
University of Central Arkansas, Torreyson Library.
Tape and transcript of an interview in which [Miss] Doster (1906-), first dean of the University of Arkansas school of nursing, gives a brief account of her early life and career in North Carolina and service with the Johns Hopkins Unit in the army during WWII. Doster worked in Arkansas with the State Public Health Department and the Little Rock Health Department giving in-service instruction to nurses. Interview contains a detailed account of the movement for a collegiate school of nursing and of the formative years of the University's nursing school.

236. Falconer, Marjorie (Ward)
Oral history. 1974. 1 tape.
Open. Index.
University of Central Arkansas, Torreyson Library.
Tape and transcript of an interview in which [Mrs.] Falconer (1898-) talks about her family, childhood in Quitman, AR, nursing training in Little Rock, AR, and her career as a public health nurse. Falconer joined the army in 1917 through the American National Red Cross program, taught home nursing in Faulkner County, AR, was a private duty nurse and a school nurse, and served as president of the Arkansas State Nurses Association. Other subjects include the Visiting Nurses Association, the Texas Nurses Association, the National Organization for Public Health Nursing, an infant welfare station operated with the Junior League, nurse-doctor relationships, doctors' cliques, the sociological attitude toward nursing, the quality of health and patient care, the role of nurses, and women's liberation.

237. Fiveash, Virgie (Hill)
Oral history. 1973. 1 tape.
Open. Index.
University of Central Arkansas, Torreyson Library.
Tape and transcript of an interview in which [Mrs. Wilburn] Fiveash (1915-), an Arkansas folk artist, talks about learning art from a teacher who boarded with her family when she was young, taking art lessons later in life, painting at Dogpatch, AR, the elements of a good picture, subject material for painting, and the difference between artists and nonartists.

238. Funk, Dorothea M. (Johnson)
Oral history. 1974. No size given.
Open. Index.
University of Central Arkansas, Torreyson Library.
Tape and transcript of an interview with [Mrs. Frank] Funk (1916-), a nursing executive who served as president of the Arkansas State Nurses Association. Funk comments on her childhood in Little Rock, AR, nursing training, her marriage, service as an army nurse during WWII, work as an investigator with the Arkansas State Board of Health venereal disease control clinic, and her employment from 1950 to 1962 as a public health nurse in Clark County, AR.

Funk discusses home care for premature babies, supervision of midwives, integration of the ASNA, the ASNA's health manpower recruitment program for inactive persons in the health disciplines, the care of the elderly, welfare programs, the difficulty of securing action by the State Board of Nurse Examiners, nurses practicing without licenses and other unprofessional conduct, and the possible need for national or international licensing of nurses.

239. Knox, Eupha Sue (Hixson)
Oral history. 1974. 1 tape.
Open. Index.
University of Central Arkansas, Torreyson Library.
Tape and transcript of an interview with [Mrs. John] Knox (1906-) concerning her childhood, family, education and nursing training, marriage, and career. Knox served as state director of public health nursing, as director of nursing services at University Hospital, as acting administrator and administrative assistant at Baptist Memorial Hospital in Kansas City, MO, as an administrator at John Knox Med-Center in Lee's Summit, MO, and as president of the Arkansas State Nurses Association. She discusses a pellagra and hookworm survey in Mississippi, the Public Health Certification Program, LPN programs, the National Geriatric Hospital, the League of Nursing, continuing education for nurses, the Nurse Practice Act, religion, and the women's liberation movement.

240. Martin, Jimmy Elizabeth
Oral history. 1973. 1 tape.
Open. Index.
University of Central Arkansas, Torreyson Library.
Tape and transcript of an interview in which Martin (1928-), an Arkansas folk artist, speaks of her early interest in art, being encouraged to paint by friends, exhibiting her art work, giving painting lessons, the similarity between writing and painting, analyzing paintings, and the personal qualities one needs to be a painter.

241. Morgan, Emma
Oral history. 1973. 1 tape.
Open. Index.
University of Central Arkansas, Torreyson Library.
Tape and transcript of an interview in which Morgan (1906-), an Arkansas folk artist, comments on her first exhibition of paintings, influential persons connected with her artistic pursuits, her reasons for painting, and the importance of drawing to painting.

242. Needham, Christine (Edwards)
Oral history. 1974. 2 tapes.
Open. Index.
University of Central Arkansas, Torreyson Library.
Tape and transcript of an interview with [Mrs. James Leland] Needham (1897-) concerning her childhood, family background, husband, education, a nursing program in St. Louis, and her career with the Public Health Service and as a private duty nurse, a nurse supervisor, and teacher at Pine Bluff, AR, Practical Nurse School. She served as president and vice-president of the Arkansas State Nurses Association, as assistant director of nursing services at the University of Arkansas, and as director of nursing services at Cleveland County, AR, Nursing Home. Needham discusses working conditions during the Depression, the first intensive care unit in Arkansas, Negro members of the ASNA, nursing and WWII, the Nurse Practice Act, the economic security of nurses, and the future of nursing.

243. Presley, Ann (Cullen)
Oral history. 1974. 1 tape.
Open. Index.
University of Central Arkansas, Torreyson Library.
Tape and transcript of an interview with [Mrs. Walter] Presley (1913-) concerning her childhood, education, family, marriage, nursing training, and career. Presley served as president and vice-president of the Arkansas State Nurses Association, as community health coordinator at St. Edward School of Nursing in Fort Smith, AR, and as a district nurse supervisor in Oklahoma. She discusses mental health work, the development of rural nurse stations in Oklahoma, integration of the ASNA, nurse licensing, economic security for nurses, nurse practitioner programs, and working with Cherokee Indians in Oklahoma.

244. Reed, Alladean (Holland)
Oral history. 1973. 1 tape.
Open. Index.
University of Central Arkansas, Torreyson Library.
Tape and transcript of an interview in which [Mrs. Eldon] Reed, (1928-), a secretary and folk artist in Arkansas, speaks of her first interest in painting, her art training, the value of painting, her opinion of modern art, advice on becoming an artist, and ideas for paintings.

245. Shank, Florence
Oral history. 1973. 1 tape.
Open. Index.
University of Central Arkansas, Torreyson Library.
Tape and transcript of an interview in which Shank (1901-), an Arkansas folk artist, comments on her interest in painting "little people," her reason for painting pictures, subjects of paintings, and her personal method of painting a picture.

246. Smith, Mary Emma
Oral history. 1970. 3 tapes.
Open. Index.
University of Central Arkansas, Torreyson Library.
Tapes and transcript of interviews with Smith (1891-), a hospital superintendent at Tupelo Hospital in Mississippi in 1921 and state director of public health nursing in New Mexico in 1935. She discusses her childhood and family, education, training, American National Red Cross service in WWI, attending Teachers College in New York, recruiting Spanish American nurses, employment opportunities for women, working conditions for nurses, the exploitation of nurses, midwifery, a maternal and child health demonstration program, and the American Nurses Foundation.

247. Teter, Martha Ann Brown
Oral history. 1970. 1 tape.
Open. Index.
University of Central Arkansas, Torreyson Library.
Tape and transcript of interviews in which [Mrs. Eugene] Teter (1893-) discusses growing up in Oklahoma, a Cherokee school, her nursing training at the Mayo Clinic and St. Paul City Hospital, and her marriage to Eugene Teter, who was in the real estate business in Arkansas. Martha Teter taught home nursing courses for the American National Red Cross and in 1924 became supervisor of nurses at Trinity Hospital in Little Rock, AR. Also contains interviews with [Mrs.] Eleanor Geiser Dennis, a nurse at Trinity Hospital, and [Mrs.] Pattie Compton, a nurse and night supervisor in Little Rock, AR, hospitals.

248. Ward, Essie (Treat)
Oral history. 1973. 1 tape.
Open. Index.
University of Central Arkansas, Torreyson Library.
Tape and transcript of an interview in which Ward (1902-), an Arkansas folk artist, discusses her "Hezekiah and Miranda" series, her paintings being sold all over the world, her lifelong desire to paint, her method of painting, working with clay, and material put in the Smithsonian Institute.

249. Weisenberger, Dorothy (Hamilton)
Oral history. 1973. 1 tape.
Open. Index.
University of Central Arkansas, Torreyson Library.
Tape and transcript of an interview in which Weisenberger (1914-), a retired teacher and an Arkansas folk artist, comments on introducing art to her third-grade students, visits to art museums, attending art school in New Mexico, the importance of drawing, favorite artists and styles of painting, and finishing a painting.

FAYETTEVILLE

250. Arkansas Federation of Women's Clubs
Records. 1913-45. 2 ft. (809 items).
Open. Unpublished guide.
University of Arkansas Library.
Correspondence, speeches, reports, photos, scrapbooks, bulletins, and other records created or received by [Mrs.] Leslie Stringfellow Read of Fayetteville, who served as state publicity chairman for the AFWC, Arkansas editor of the GFWC's *General Federation Magazine,* and as GFWC publicity chairman. Contains material concerning the GFWC's 14th biennial convention in Hot Springs, AR, in 1918 and the activities of the Women's News Service, Inc.; the Authors and Composers Society of Arkansas; the League of American Pen Women; and, particularly, the National American Woman Suffrage Association. Also includes correspondence of Ethel Estes Sure of Fayetteville concerning activities of the International Association of Altrusa Clubs.

251. Beaver, Mary Elizabeth (Brandon)
Papers. 1865. 1 vol.
Open. Published guide.
University of Arkansas Library.
Portion of a diary kept by Beaver (1840-?) during a February to April journey from Texas to Chicago. See Samuel A. Sizer, *A Guide to Selected Manuscript Collections in The University of Arkansas Library* (Fayetteville, AR: University of Arkansas, University Library, 1976).

252. Bonneville, Benjamin Louis Eulalie De
Papers. 1870-1910. 4 items.
Open. Published guide.
University of Arkansas Library.
Papers of Bonneville (1796-1878) include documents dated 1908 to 1910 concerning the pension claim of Mexican War widow Susan Neis Bonneville. See Samuel A. Sizer, *A Guide to Selected Manuscript Collections in The University of Arkansas Library* (Fayetteville, AR: University of Arkansas, University Library, 1976).

253. Brisco, Mary Susan (High) Casey
Papers. 1954. 1 item.
Open. No guide.
University of Arkansas Library.
[Mrs.] Brisco (1875-1958) was a Berryville, AR, folk singer. An autobiographical sketch with introduction by Mary Celestia Parler. Also includes a photo of Brisco, whose recordings are part of the University Folklore Collection.

254. Cantrell, Ellen Maria (Harrell)
Papers. 1895-97, nd. 4 items.
Open. Unpublished guide.
University of Arkansas Library.
An Arkansas author, Cantrell (1833-1909) wrote numerous articles and a book. Manuscripts of speeches and articles, including an article for the woman's edition of the *Arkansas Democrat* in 1895, a paper to be read on Arkansas Day in Nashville in 1897, and a paper on the royal palaces of England.

255. Caraway, Hattie Ophelia (Wyatt)
Papers. Ca. 1884-1950. 82 items.
Access restricted. Published and unpublished guides.
University of Arkansas Library.
Caraway (1878-1950) was a US senator from Arkansas from 1931 to 1945. Correspondence, a journal from 1931 to 1934, photos, scrapbooks, and other papers pertain to political and personal activities of Caraway and her husband Thaddeus Horatius Caraway (1871-1931), who was US senator from Arkansas from 1920 to 1931. Also includes information about Hattie Caraway's work as a federal civil servant from 1945 to 1950, her husband's death, and Caraway family matters. Correspondents include Grace Coolidge, James Aloysius Farley, Lewis Blaine Hershey, Mary Teresa Norton, Claude Denson Pepper, Franklin Delano Roosevelt, and Harry S. Truman. See Samuel A. Sizer, *A Guide to Selected Manuscript Collections in The University of Arkansas Library* (Fayetteville, AR: University of Arkansas, University Library, 1976).

256. Cook, Gertrude (Fallin)
Papers. 1830-78. 24 items.
Open. Published and unpublished guides.
University of Arkansas Library.
Correspondence, land records, and other papers of the Bloyd, Combs, Corum, Fallin, McMurtry, and Tigard families of Arkansas, Missouri, and Texas. Two letters concern the experiences of the Tigard family and other Arkansas emigrants who traveled to Oregon during the 1850s. These letters contain descriptions of the hardships and sufferings encountered en route and discussions of the land, land prices, economic conditions, and political affairs in Oregon Territory. See Samuel A. Sizer, *A Guide to Selected Manuscript Collections in The University of Arkansas Library* (Fayetteville, AR: University of Arkansas, University Library, 1976).

257. Donaghey, George Washington
Papers. 1870-1947. 356 items.
Open. Published and unpublished guides.
University of Arkansas Library.
Correspondence, memoranda, speeches, photos, pamphlets, clippings, and other papers pertain to the personal, political, business, and philanthropic activities of Donaghey (1856-1937), an Arkansas

farmer, architect, educator, banker, and governor from 1909 to 1913, and to the personal and social activities of his wife Martha Louvenia (Wallace) Donaghey (1862-1947). See Samuel A. Sizer, *A Guide to Selected Manuscript Collections in The University of Arkansas Library* (Fayetteville, AR: University of Arkansas, University Library, 1976).

258. Dresbach, Beverley (Githens)
Papers. Ca. 1920-71. 5 ft.
Closed. Published guide.
University of Arkansas Library.
Correspondence, literary manuscripts, photos, scrapbooks, and other papers of poet and essayist Beverley Githens (1903-71), who was the wife of poet Glenn Ward Dresbach. Correspondents include Elizabeth Goudge, Rosa Zagnoni Marinoni, and Jean (Starr) Untermeyer. See Samuel A. Sizer, *A Guide to Selected Manuscript Collections in The University of Arkansas Library* (Fayetteville, AR: University of Arkansas, University Library, 1976).

259. Eno, Clara Bertha
Papers. 1830-1947. 176 items and 1 microfilm reel.
Open. Published and unpublished guides.
University of Arkansas Library.
Eno (1854-1951) was a Van Buren, AR, clubwoman, schoolteacher, and historian. Correspondence, bills of lading, statements and receipts, legal documents, reminiscences, obituaries, and other papers; many of the items relate to Van Buren businesses and to steamboat travel on the Arkansas River during the 1840s and 1850s. Eno was a member of the Arkansas History Commission and vice-president of the Arkansas Historical Society. See Samuel A. Sizer, *A Guide to Selected Manuscript Collections in The University of Arkansas Library* (Fayetteville, AR: University of Arkansas, University Library, 1976).

260. Fletcher, Susan (Bricelin)
Papers. Ca. 1908. 1 item.
Open. Published guide.
University of Arkansas Library.
[Mrs. Henry Lewis] Fletcher (ca. 1838-?) owned a plantation in the Little Rock area at the outbreak of the Civil War. Reminiscences of her experiences at the plantation and in Little Rock during and immediately after the War. See Samuel A. Sizer, *A Guide to Selected Manuscript Collections in The University of Arkansas Library* (Fayetteville, AR: University of Arkansas, University Library, 1976).

261. Gist, Ariel Idella Hottel
Papers. 1892-93. 57 items.
Closed. Published guide.
University of Arkansas Library.
Correspondence, a journal, photos, and other papers of Idella "Della" Gist (1870-1928) during her residence in Fredericksted on St. Croix, Danish West Indies. Gist was governess to the children of US Consul William F. Moore. See Samuel A. Sizer, *A Guide to Selected Manuscript Collections in The University of Arkansas Library* (Fayetteville, AR: University of Arkansas, University Library, 1976).

262. Hudgins, Mary Dengler
Papers. 1847-1974. 16.5 cu.ft.
Closed. No guide.
University of Arkansas Library.
Correspondence, memoranda, literary manuscripts, photos, musical scores, programs, clippings, and other papers gathered by [Miss] Hudgins (1903-), a writer, for her research about the lives and work of composers and authors who were connected with Arkansas.

263. Organized Independent Women
Records. 1947-57. 2 vols.
Open. Published guide.
University of Arkansas Library.
Scrapbooks contain photos, invitations, programs, clippings, and other items of this University organization of women students. See Samuel A. Sizer, *A Guide to Selected Manuscript Collections in The University of Arkansas Library* (Fayetteville, AR: University of Arkansas, University Library, 1976).

264. Price, Florence Beatrice (Smith)
Papers. 1926-75. 1.5 cu.ft.
Closed. No guide.
University of Arkansas Library.
Price (1888-1953) was an Arkansas-born composer. Correspondence, photos, musical scores, programs, and other papers generated by or concerning Price.

265. Purdue, Ida (Pace)
Papers. 1884-1958. 2 items.
Access restricted. No guide.
University of Arkansas Library.
An 1888 graduate of the University of Arkansas, Purdue (1869-1958) was an associate professor of English and modern language at the University from 1895 to 1898. Scrapbook of clippings and other items concerning Purdue's social, religious, literary, and general interests and activities. Also includes an autograph book containing inscriptions from about 62 persons, 46 of them Arkansas Industrial University students. She married geologist Albert Homer Purdue in 1898.

266. Riley, Susan B.
Papers. 1916-63. 43 items.
Open. Published and unpublished guides.
University of Arkansas Library.
Correspondence, photos, and miscellaneous papers that Riley (1896-), a professor at George Peabody College for Teachers from 1928 to 1965, compiled for her PhD dissertation about Albert Pike's life and works and for subsequent research on the topic. See Samuel A. Sizer, *A Guide to Selected Manuscript Collections in The University of Arkansas Library* (Fayetteville, AR: University of Arkansas, University Library, 1976).

267. Swinnerton, Frank Arthur
Papers. 1899-1964. 22 ft.
Open. Published and unpublished guides.
University of Arkansas Library.
Correspondence of Swinnerton (1884-), an English novelist and critic, includes letters from Norah Hoult, Willa Sibert Cather, Ellen Glasgow, Dorothy Leigh Sayers, Rebecca West, and other authors. The 41 items of correspondence with Hoult, an Irish novelist, concern personal, family, and professional matters. See Samuel A. Sizer, *A Guide to Selected Manuscript Collections in The University of Arkansas Library* (Fayetteville, AR: University of Arkansas, University Library, 1976).

268. University Dames
Records. 1945-51. 1 vol.
Open. No guide.
University of Arkansas Library.
Founded in 1921, the organization consisted principally of wives of University students and married women students who sought to promote friendship, provide social activities, and encourage their cultural interests. Scrapbook contains clippings, invitations, programs, photos, and other items. The organization did not receive its charter until 1945.

269. University Infirmary Association
Records. 1895-1908. 1 item.
Access restricted. Published guide.
University of Arkansas Library.
Organized in 1895 by a group of local women, the Association helped on-campus University students who became ill. See Samuel A. Sizer, *A Guide to Selected Manuscript Collections in The University of Arkansas Library* (Fayetteville, AR: University of Arkansas, University Library, 1976).

270. Winslow, Thyra (Samter)
Papers. 1900-70. 76 items.
Open. Unpublished guide.
University of Arkansas Library.
[Mrs.] Winslow (ca. 1885-1961) was an Arkansas-born novelist, short story writer, and scenarist. Correspondence and clippings concerning and an academic transcript of Winslow; the papers were collected by Richard Clarence Winegard in preparation for his PhD dissertation about Winslow. Includes correspondence between Winegard and several former associates of Winslow.

271. Young Womens Christian Association
Records. 1916-23. 1 vol.
Open. Published guide.
University of Arkansas Library.
Scrapbook containing photos, receipts, announcements, programs, clippings, memorabilia, and other items of the YWCA at the University. Also includes a letter from Governor Charles Hillman Brough in Little Rock to [Miss] Gladys Hollabaugh of Fayetteville. The YWCA attempted to apply Christian principles to college life and to prepare young women for religious leadership in their post-collegiate years. See Samuel A. Sizer, *A Guide to Selected Manuscript Collections in The University of Arkansas Library* (Fayetteville, AR: University of Arkansas, University Library, 1976).

FORT SMITH

272. Archives
Records. 1879- . No size given.
Access restricted. No guide.
Benedictine Sisters, St. Scholastica Convent.
Chapter minutes, financial records, correspondence, diaries, histories, files pertaining to deceased members of the community, liturgies, photos, scrapbooks, newsletters of superiors, prayer books, travelogs, and other records of the order, which was founded in Shoal Creek, AR, in 1879.

GILLETT

273. Mothers Club of DeWitt
Records. 1916-66. 1 vol.
Open. No guide.
Grand Prairie Historical Society.
The group, founded in 1916, sought to help children. Membership list, meeting programs and mementos, lists of social projects, and other records.

274. Pioneers of Arkansas County
Records. 1924-74. 5-page item.
Open. No guide.
Grand Prairie Historical Society.
A history of the Arkansas County Federation of Women's Clubs, which included 50 clubs across the state that worked together on art, citizenship, music, education, public welfare, home economics, and conservation programs.

JONESBORO

275. Archives
Records. 1887- . 17 boxes.
Closed. No guide.
Olivetan Benedictine Sisters, Holy Angels Convent.
Minutes, financial records, correspondence, diaries, photos, scrapbooks, and other records of the order, which was founded in 1887 in Pocahontas, AR. Includes papers of the mothers superior and material relating to schools and hospitals staffed by the Sisters.

LITTLE ROCK

276. Aesthetic Club of Little Rock
Records. 1883-1970. 6 microfilm reels.
Open. No guide.
Arkansas History Commission.
Minutes, correspondence, programs, and yearbooks of this fine arts and cultural appreciation organization, which was formed in 1883.

277. Arkansas Federation of Business and Professional Women's Clubs
Records. 1919-75. 9 microfilm reels.
Open. No guide.
Arkansas History Commission.
Bylaws, minutes, records of the loan fund, membership lists, programs, copies of the state organization's official organ *The Arkansas Business Woman,* and other records of the Federation, which sought to encourage cooperative effort among business and professional women, to stimulate interest in civic affairs, to gather information concerning educational and vocational opportunities, and to recognize the universal sisterhood of the world's women.

278. The Arkansas Gardener
Records. 1961-66. 15 items.
Open. No guide.
Arkansas History Commission.
Copies of *The Arkansas Gardener,* a magazine owned and published by the Arkansas Federation of Garden Clubs, Inc.

279. Arkansas Pioneers Association
Records. 1912-70. 7 microfilm reels.
Open. No guide.
Arkansas History Commission.
Speeches, a scrapbook, memorials, publications, and other records of this hereditary and patriotic society.

280. Arkansas Society Colonial Dames of XVII Century
Records. 1961-65. No size given.
Open. No guide.
Arkansas History Commission.
Yearbooks of the John Eliot Chapter of this patriotic and hereditary group. The national Society was founded in 1915 and the Eliot Chapter, in 1961.

281. Daughters of the American Revolution
Records. 1924-75. 18 microfilm reels.
Open. No guide.
Arkansas History Commission.
Arkansas genealogical research records.

282. Donaghey, Martha Louvenia Wallace
Papers. 1897-1951. 23 in.
Open. Unpublished guide.
Arkansas History Commission.
Correspondence, speeches, memoranda, notebooks, financial records, legal papers, photos, a scrapbook, a press release, a life insurance policy, and other papers pertain to the life, philanthropic activities, and business and political careers of George Washington Donaghey (1856-1937), who served as governor of Arkansas from 1909 to 1913; to his nephew Raymond Ruskin Donaghey (1897-); and to the personal and family affairs of his wife Martha Donaghey (1862-1947). Provides information about her widowhood, death, and burial. Also contains material about Hattie (Wyatt) Caraway.

283. Edmonson
Papers. Nd. No size given.
Open. No guide.
Arkansas History Commission.
Diary of Mary Frances (Sale) [Mrs. Albert G.] Edmonson, the wife of a doctor and slave owner, deals with domestic events during the Civil War era.

284. Fariss, Mary Ward
Papers. 1844-1961. 1 microfilm reel.
Open. No guide.
Arkansas History Commission.
Correspondence and papers of Joseph F. Earle, Cynthia Ann Earle Ward, J. E. H. Ward, and others.

285. Fraser and Wyche Families
Papers. 1823-1919. 1 microfilm reel.
Open. No guide.
Arkansas History Commission.
Correspondence and papers of James H. Fraser and his mother Martha Ann Wyche Fraser.

286. Horrocks, Dilla Basham
Papers. 1872-1951. 6 in.
Open. Unpublished guide.
Arkansas History Commission.
Correspondence, notes, speeches, poems, photos, reports, bulletins, certificates, and other papers of the family of Horrocks (?-1954).

287. Lincoln, Eudora "Dora" Percival (Knox), Family
Papers. 1869-90. No size given.
Open. Unpublished guide.
Arkansas History Commission.
Lincoln (1849-1921), the daughter of early Arkansas settlers, was the wife of Charles James Lincoln, a Little Rock physician, and the mother of two children. Includes correspondence between Dora and C. J. Lincoln and letters from Dora Lincoln's mother Eudora (Rose) Knox and her sisters Fannie Rose (Knox) [Mrs. Hugh] Thomason, Georgia Lydia (Knox) [Mrs. W. L.] Faber, and Martha "Mattie" Washington (Knox) [Mrs. Syme] Hayman. Also available on microfilm.

288. McRae, Annie
Papers. 1857. 1 microfilm reel.
Open. No guide.
Arkansas History Commission.
Letter to [Miss] Fannie Fletcher of West Point, AR.

289. Morgan, Mrs. J. D.
Papers. 1930-64. 32 items.
Open. Unpublished guide.
Arkansas History Commission.
Photos, pamphlets, articles, clippings, and books concern Arkansas and its residents. Includes poems by Arkansas poets, members of the Poets' Roundtable, and the state's poet laureate. Several of the poems are by Arkansas women, including Rosa Zagnoni Marinoni, Lorraine Bass, and Fentem Utley.

290. Prestridge, Mary Ann Rebecca Frost
Papers. 1849-1901. 1 microfilm reel.
Open. No guide.
Arkansas History Commission.
Correspondence and papers of Prestridge.

291. Sims, Mary Owen
Papers. 1855-60. 1 microfilm reel.
Open. No guide.
Arkansas History Commission.
Diary of [Mrs. John D.] Sims of Dallas County, AR, who was the wife of a rural doctor and a mother.

292. Stetson, Ellen
Papers. 1821. Partial microfilm reel.
Open. No guide.
Arkansas History Commission.
Journal of a New England woman who was traveling to the Dwight Mission in Arkansas where she was to teach and serve as a missionary to the Indians.

293. Trimble, Margaret Spencer
Papers. 1787-1975. 2077 items.
Open. Unpublished guide.
Arkansas History Commission.
Manuscript material, photos, post cards, pamphlets, sheet music, and books relate to the history of the W. Russell Spencer family of Fayetteville, AR. W. Russell Spencer, a professor of civil engineering at the University of Arkansas, was married to Hallie LaFollette Spencer.

294. Woman's Chronicle
Records. 1888-93. 2 microfilm reels.
Closed. No guide.
Arkansas History Commission.
Copies of the *Chronicle,* a Little Rock suffrage newspaper.

295. Women's Emergency Committee to Open Our Schools
Records. Ca. 1957. No size given.
Closed. No guide.
Arkansas History Commission.
Records relate to civic efforts to reopen Little Rock schools after the 1957 school desegregation crisis.

296. Hanger, Francis Marion (Harrow)
Papers. 1834-1944. 1 ft.
Open. Unpublished guide.
Arkansas Territorial Restoration.
Hanger (1856-1945) was a Little Rock civic and social leader and housewife. Correspondence, diaries, and scrapbooks.

297. Loughborough, Louisa Watkins Wright
Papers. 1938-62. 2 ft.
Open. Unpublished guide.
Arkansas Territorial Restoration.
[Mrs.] Loughborough (1881-1962), a civic leader, was the founder and chairman of the Arkansas Territorial Restoration Commission. Correspondence, building invoices, photos, scrapbooks, and clippings relate to her work for the Commission and for the Mount Vernon Ladies Association, of which she was vice-regent for 30 years. Loughborough's grandfathers were the first Supreme Court justice of Arkansas and the last Arkansas territorial governor.

CALIFORNIA

AUBURN

298. Russell Library
Records. 1857- . No size given.
Closed. No guide.
Our Lady of Mercy Convent.
Correspondence, histories of foundations of the Sisters of Mercy in the US, biographies, photos, scrapbooks, and other records of the Sisters of Mercy, who are involved in education and nursing. The order was established in the US in Sacramento, CA, in 1857. Includes biographies of Mother Catherine McAuley, the foundress.

BELMONT

299. California Province Archives
Records. 1843- . 362 ft. and 2 cabinets.
Open. Preliminary inventory.
Sisters of Notre Dame de Namur, California Province Archives.
The Sisters were established in Oregon in 1844 and moved to San Jose, CA, in 1851. Minutes, accounts, journals, academic records, community annals, microforms, scrapbooks, and clippings relating to the motherhouse in Belgium, the

mothers general, the California Province, and secondary houses. The Sisters are involved in education in Montessori, elementary, and secondary schools and colleges.

BERKELEY

300. Women in Religion
Collection. 1970s. 5 in. and 20 tapes.
Open. Card catalog.
Graduate Theological Union, Library.
Typescripts about the relationship between women and religion, including "Ordained Women and Ministry: An Approach" by Claire-Marie Heesacker Kahn, 1976, and tapes of sermons, speeches, and panels about women, women's liberation and the church, feminism, women in the ministry, and other topics. A number of the tapes were made in Grailville, OH. Includes one entitled "Reclaiming Our Heritage" by Anne Bennett, 1974.

301. Sex Discrimination
Collection. 1961- . 500 legal case files and pamphlets.
Open. No guide.
Meiklejohn Civil Liberties Institute.
Attorneys' working papers, consisting of briefs, complaints, and memos filed in courts, as well as periodicals and pamphlets pertaining to more than 130 cases of sex discrimination since 1965. The sex discrimination cases often involve employment practices.

302. Morgan, Julia
Papers. 1872-1957. Ca. 1000 items.
Open. Unpublished guide.
University of California, Berkeley, College of Environmental Design Documents Collection.
Correspondence, diaries, sketchbooks, school projects, architectural drawings, and photos of Morgan (1872-1957), a California architect who was the first American woman to graduate from the Ecole des Beaux Arts in Paris. Although she is best known for her work on the Hearst Castle in San Simeon, CA, Morgan also designed buildings for the YWCA in Pasadena and the YWCA in Honolulu.

303. Reef Point Gardens
Records. 1877-1959. Ca. 20 Hollinger boxes, 12 vols., and 5000 items.
Open. Unpublished guide.
University of California, Berkeley, College of Environmental Design Documents Collection.
Correspondence, notes, drawings and plans for gardens, photos, scrapbooks, and memorabilia of the Reef Point Gardens, which was founded in 1939. Includes papers of Beatrix Farrand, a landscape architect who was one of the founding members of the American Society of Landscape Architects. Reef Point Gardens included a library specializing in landscape architecture.

304. Women Transportation Workers
Records. Nd. No size given.
Open. Card catalog.
University of California, Berkeley, Institute of Transportation and Traffic Engineering.
Includes a 35-page transcript of a talk that Elizabeth O. Cullen, librarian of the Bureau of Railway Economics Library of the Association of American Railroads, gave to the American Council of Railroad Women in St. Louis in 1955. Cullen spoke about women's progress in the field of transportation since 1900. Her speech also contains a list of women railroad officials and of US postage stamps honoring women.

305. Abernethy, Anne Pope
Papers. 1878. 6-page item.
Open. Published guide.
University of California, Berkeley, The Bancroft Library, Manuscripts Division.
Interview with Abernethy, the widow of George Abernethy who traveled to Oregon in 1839 and 1840 on the ship *Lausanne* and later became provisional governor. She describes Fort Vancouver; Oregon City; the Old Mission, a small settlement ca. 12 miles from Salem where there was a school for Indian children; and the life of a mission family. Also available on microfilm. See Dale L. Morgan and George P. Hammond, eds., *A Guide to the Manuscript Collections of The Bancroft Library,* vol. I (Berkeley, CA: University of California Press, 1963).

306. Ackerman, Rhea Carolyn
Oral history. 1968. 217-page transcript.
Open. No guide.
University of California, Berkeley, The Bancroft Library, Manuscripts Division.
Interview with Ackerman (1896-) concerns her experiences from 1936 to 1943 as assistant superintendent and superintendent of Juvenile Hall, the county detention home for juvenile delinquents in Los Angeles.

307. Adams, Ellen Tompkins
Papers. 1863. 40-page item.
Open. No guide.
University of California, Berkeley, The Bancroft Library, Manuscripts Division.
Diary in which Adams describes her journey from Council Bluffs, IA, to Markleeville, CA.

308. Aiken, Ednah (Robinson)
Papers. Nd. No size given.
Open. No guide.
University of California, Berkeley, The Bancroft Library, Manuscripts Division.
Excerpt notes from a book by Aiken (1872-1960) entitled *The Colorado River.*

309. Alameda County Society for the Prevention of Cruelty to Children
Records. 1914-15. 1 portfolio.
Open. No guide.
University of California, Berkeley, The Bancroft Library, Manuscripts Division.
Correspondence of Susan J. Fenton, president of the Society, and papers of Jessica Peixotto and other members of the Society's board, which was made up primarily of women. The Women's Missionary Society of the First Congregational Church of Oakland helped to found the organization.

310. Alexander, Annie Montague
Papers. Ca. 1904-49. 3 boxes, 3 vols., and 1 portfolio.
Open. Key.
University of California, Berkeley, The Bancroft Library, Manuscripts Division.
[Miss] Alexander (1867-1950), a benefactor of the University, was knowledgeable in the fields of paleontology and zoology, participated in many field trips, and collected specimens. She financed numerous scientific expeditions as well as the establishment of the University's Museum of Paleontology and Museum of Vertebrate Zoology; she also advised the Museums' first director Joseph Grinnell on their operation. Correspondence, a manuscript and other material about the Museum of Vertebrate Zoology, her field trips, and her friendship with Grinnell and Louise Kellogg. Also includes a scrapbook containing photos and letters by Alexander and her father Samuel T. Alexander while on safari in British East Africa in 1904.

311. Alexander, Evaline Throop (Martin)
Papers. 1866-67. 180-page vol.
Open. Published guide.
University of California, Berkeley, The Bancroft Library, Manuscripts Division.
Diary of Alexander, who traveled first from New York to Fort Smith, AR, to join her husband Colonel A. J. Alexander and then to New Mexico and Colorado. She describes her journey; life at military posts, including forts Union, Bascom, and Garland; Ute, Navaho, Pueblo, and other Indians; and people she met, including Kit Carson. Also available on microfilm. See Dale L. Morgan and George P. Hammond, eds., *A Guide to the Manuscript Collections of The Bancroft Library,* vol. I (Berkeley, CA: University of California Press, 1963).

312. Allen, Judith
Papers. Nd. 1 portfolio.
Open. No guide.
University of California, Berkeley, The Bancroft Library, Manuscripts Division.
Correspondence and notes about Allen's research for an MA thesis on [Miss] Nora May French.

313. Allen, Netta Powell
Oral history. 1970-71. 92-page transcript.
Open. No guide.
University of California, Berkeley, The Bancroft Library, Manuscripts Division.
Allen (1890-), a missionary, discusses her experiences in China with her husband, who served as secretary to the YMCA in Nanchung from 1918 to 1931, as a teacher in Boone School in Hankow under the sponsorship of the Episcopal church, and as mission treasurer in Shanghai and West China from 1932 to 1951.

314. Aloysius, Sister Mary
Papers. 1932-36. 21 folders.
Open. No guide.
University of California, Berkeley, The Bancroft Library, Manuscripts Division.
Correspondence, notes, and clippings concerning the Argüello family relate primarily to María de la Concepción Argüello, who became Sister Dominica. Also included are letters by [Mrs.] Ysabel Argüello Den.

315. Altrocchi, Julia (Cooley)
Papers. Ca. 1934-59. 2 boxes, 16 cartons, and 280 pp.
Open. No guide.
University of California, Berkeley, The Bancroft Library, Manuscripts Division.
Correspondence, published and unpublished manuscripts, and other papers of Altrocchi (1893-1972), the author of *Golden Adventures in California History* and *Snow Covered Wagons.* Includes letters about radio broadcasts on California pioneers.

316. Alverson, Rosana Margaret (Kroh) Blake
Papers. Ca. 1902-20. 1 portfolio.
Open. No guide.
University of California, Berkeley, The Bancroft Library, Manuscripts Division.
Papers of Alverson (1836-1923), a singer and voice teacher, include letters to her friend Carrie Laidlaw, an announcement of and the foreword to her book *Sixty Years of California Song,* and programs and clippings concerning her career.

317. American Literary Miscellany
Collection. Nd. 1 box.
Open. Unpublished guide.
University of California, Berkeley, The Bancroft Library, Manuscripts Division.
Includes manuscripts of poems by Genevieve Taggard and Hildegarde Flanner and of the play *A Little Miracle* by Zoë Akins, transcript of an interview with Imogen Cunningham, and letters by Hildegarde Hawthorne, Ruth Comfort Mitchell, Mary Hannah (Bacon) Field, Mary Elizabeth Warren Ledford, Ella May Sexton, Caroline (Howard) Gilman, Marianne Moore, Margaret Fuller, and Amélie (Rives) Troubetzkoy.

318. American National Red Cross, San Francisco Chapter
Records. 1938. 2 pp.
Open. No guide.
University of California, Berkeley, The Bancroft Library, Manuscripts Division.
Illuminated copy of resolutions of appreciation presented to [Miss] Julia George for her gift of her family's home to be used as permanent headquarters of the Chapter.

319. Archivos de las Misiones
Records. 1769-1856. 4 boxes and 1 portfolio.
Open. Unpublished guide.
University of California, Berkeley, The Bancroft Library, Manuscripts Division.
Records of California missions include a book listing marriages for the years 1824 to 1839 from the San Francisco Solano Mission.

320. Armstrong, Jessie
Oral history. 1968. 37-page transcript.
Open. No guide.
University of California, Berkeley, The Bancroft Library, Manuscripts Division.
Interview with Armstrong (1878-?) concerns her life in Virginia City, NV, during the 1870s and 1880s and in Emerald Bay, CA, in the Lake Tahoe area.

321. Arnstein, Lawrence
Oral history. 1961-64. 307-page transcript.
Open. No guide.
University of California, Berkeley, The Bancroft Library, Manuscripts Division.
Tapes and transcripts of interviews with Arnstein (1880-) on community service, public health, and social welfare in California and with his wife Flora (Jacobi) Arnstein on progressive education and the Presidio Open-Air School of San Francisco. Includes letters, articles, photos, and clippings. Also available on microfilm.

322. Artieda, Helen (Swett)
Papers. 1898-1901. 188 folders.
Open. No guide.
University of California, Berkeley, The Bancroft Library, Manuscripts Division.
Letters by Artieda to her fiancé Charles E. Schwartz.

323. Ashburner, William
Papers. 1864-1902. 1 portfolio.
Open. No guide.
University of California, Berkeley, The Bancroft Library, Manuscripts Division.
Letters from Ashburner (1831-87) and his wife Emilia (Field) Ashburner to William H. Brewer.

324. Atherton, CA, Interviews
Oral history. 1972. 1 box.
Open. Shelflist.
University of California, Berkeley, The Bancroft Library, Manuscripts Division.
Includes interviews with librarian Hazel M. Farrell, who recalls the origin in 1931 of Atherton library, which first was housed in the Atherton police department; with Mildred Stolberg, who discusses Irish gardeners who worked on Atherton estates and lived in the boarding house where she lived; and with Eleanor Weir Tilden, who recalls the founding of the Menlo Circus Club in 1920 and life in Atherton and Menlo Park, CA.

325. Atherton, Gertrude Franklin (Horn)
Papers. Ca. 1917-48. 16 boxes and 4 cartons.
Open. Partial unpublished guide.
University of California, Berkeley, The Bancroft Library, Manuscripts Division.
Atherton (1857-1948) was an author whose novels and stories included *Can Women Be Gentlemen?* (1938), *Dido, Queen of Hearts* (1929), and *My San Francisco* (1946). Correspondence with friends and publishers, manuscripts and copies of her works, contracts and accounts with publishers, extensive clippings about her writings, and other items. Repository has an alphabetical list of her numerous correspondents, among them the Authors' League of America, Inc.; Mary (Ritter) [Mrs. Charles] Beard; the Hoover Institution on War, Revolution and Peace at Stanford University; the National League of American Pen Women; *Saturday Home Magazine;* Ida M. Tarbell; Twentieth-Century Fox Film Corporation; Mrs. Henry E. Wallace; and Rebecca West.

326. Atkins Family
Papers. 1796-1909. 5 boxes.
Open. Key.
University of California, Berkeley, The Bancroft Library, Manuscripts Division.
Correspondence and other papers of the Atkins family, who were settlers in Ashtabula, OH, reflect participation in the antislavery movement between 1836 and 1850 and land transactions in Ohio. Mary (Atkins) [Mrs. John] Lynch (1819-82) taught in Ohio and New York before moving to Benicia, CA, where she was principal of the Young Ladies Seminary from 1854 to 1867. Her papers relating to the Seminary include a letter of recommendation for her by evangelist Charles Grandison Finney; accounts; a catalog of pupils; commencement programs; Alumnae Association minutes and records, 1878-83; clippings; and a diary of her voyage to Shanghai via Hawaii and Japan in 1863 and 1864. Other family correspondents include Sarah (Wright) Atkins, Stella M. (Atkins) Gaylord, Sarah Louisa (Atkins) Wade, Flora (Atkins) Wheeler, and Marcia Gaylord Fowler.

327. Atkinson, Sallie Jane (Yeargin)
Papers. 1941?. 1 vol.
Open. No guide.
University of California, Berkeley, The Bancroft Library, Manuscripts Division.
Autobiography by Atkinson (1857-1949) concerns her childhood in the South during the Civil War, her life in the San Joaquin Valley in California from 1870, and her experiences as the wife of a Methodist minister. Also included are other writings by Atkinson and a photo.

328. Austin, Mary (Hunter)
Papers. Ca. 1903-33. 1 box.
Open. No guide.
University of California, Berkeley, The Bancroft Library, Manuscripts Division.
Correspondence of [Mrs. Stafford Wallace] Austin (1868-1934), an author, including letters to Henry Nash Smith and to Mr. and Mrs. Gerald Cassidy, a copy of her play *Fire,* articles about her, and publicity material.

329. Avakian, Anne
Papers. Nd. 1 box.
Open. No guide.
University of California, Berkeley, The Bancroft Library, Manuscripts Division.
Correspondence relating to the Hopi Indians.

330. Avakian, Sarah (Mahdesian)
Papers. Nd. 1 microfilm reel.
Open. No guide.
University of California, Berkeley, The Bancroft Library, Manuscripts Division.
Manuscript songbook in Armenian by Avakian.

331. Ávila, María Inocenta (Pico)
Papers. 1878. 1 item.
Open. No guide.
University of California, Berkeley, The Bancroft Library, Manuscripts Division.
Dictation by Ávila (1811-?), a resident of Monterey, CA, concerns her husband Miguel Ávila, early California governors, missions in 1840, schooling for girls in Monterey, a meeting with Agustín Fernández de San Vicente, and her friendship with José Castro and J. B. Alvarado. Also available on microfilm.

332. Baker, Dorothy (Dodds)
Papers. Nd. 2 boxes.
Open. No guide.
University of California, Berkeley, The Bancroft Library, Manuscripts Division.
Manuscripts of the novels *Our Gifted Son, Trio,* and *Young Man with a Horn* by Baker (1907-), an author.

333. Bale Family
Papers. Ca. 1841-99. 2 boxes.
Open. Key.
University of California, Berkeley, The Bancroft Library, Manuscripts Division.
Personal and business papers of María Ignacia (Soberanes) de Bale, the niece of Mariano G. Vallejo, primarily relate to Carne Humana Rancho in Napa Valley, CA, which she owned with her first husband Edward Turner Bale and managed after his death in 1849. Included are her 1856 marriage contract with Edward T. Peabody, deeds and promissory notes, accounts with a Napa bank, a fire insurance policy, an 1870 statement of release of all demands to her from her son Mariano G. Bale, and the 1870 revocation of her will.

334. Bancroft Family
Papers. 1844-82. 2 microfilm reels.
Open. No guide.
University of California, Berkeley, The Bancroft Library, Manuscripts Division.
Includes letters by Emily (Ketchum) Bancroft and letters and a journal by Kate Bancroft.

335. Bancroft, Matilda Coley (Griffing)
Papers. 1879-92. 3 vols. and 1 item.
Open. Published guide.
University of California, Berkeley, The Bancroft Library, Manuscripts Division.
Bancroft assisted her husband Hubert Howe Bancroft in his historical research. Unpublished manuscript, research notes pertaining to New Mexico, and childhood memory books kept for her son Griffing Bancroft, 1879-92, and her daughter Lucy Bancroft, 1882-92. Manuscript, which includes photos and clippings, concerns the winter she and her family spent in Mexico in 1891; it contains descriptions of life in Mexico City, visits with President Porfirio Díaz, excursions, Christmas festivities, and bullfights. See Dale L. Morgan and George P. Hammond, eds., *A Guide to the Manuscript Collections of The Bancroft Library,* vol. I (Berkeley, CA: University of California Press, 1963).

336. Bancroft, Minnie L. (Smith)
Papers. 1884. 141-page vol.
Open. Published guide.
University of California, Berkeley, The Bancroft Library, Manuscripts Division.
Diary of [Mrs. Edward] Bancroft of Holly, MI, in which she describes her daily life and her experiences as a schoolteacher. Also available on microfilm. See George P. Hammond, ed., *A Guide to the Manuscript Collections of The Bancroft Library,* vol. II (Berkeley, CA: University of California Press, 1972).

337. Barnes, Mary Downing (Sheldon)
Papers. Nd. 1 carton.
Open. No guide.
University of California, Berkeley, The Bancroft Library, Manuscripts Division.
Papers of [Mrs. Earl] Barnes (1850-98), an instructor of history at Stanford University, include correspondence concerning her historical research, notes and manuscripts of her writings on Indians and western history, reports by her students, articles, and clippings.

338. Barstow, Alfred
Papers. 1877. 8-page item.
Open. No guide.
University of California, Berkeley, The Bancroft Library, Manuscripts Division.
Statement by Barstow, a pioneer who arrived in California in 1849, concerns his experiences as a goldminer; the lynching of a Mexican woman in Downieville, CA; Indian customs; and crime in the mines. Also available on microfilm.

339. Barstow, David Pierce
Papers. 1878. 14-page item.
Open. No guide.
University of California, Berkeley, The Bancroft Library, Manuscripts Division.
Statement by Barstow includes discussion of the lynching of a Mexican woman in Downieville, CA. Also available on microfilm.

340. Barton, Clara
Papers. Ca. 1890. 1 item.
Open. No guide.
University of California, Berkeley, The Bancroft Library, Manuscripts Division.
Letter from [Miss] Barton (1821-1912), a nurse and president of the American Association of the Red Cross, to Felix Deutsch of Washington, DC.

341. Bary, Helen Valeska
Oral history. 1972-73. 1 vol. and 1 tape.
Open. No guide.
University of California, Berkeley, The Bancroft Library, Manuscripts Division.
[Miss] Bary (1888-1973) discusses her work for private charities in northern California, the Industrial Welfare Commission, the US War Labor Policies Board, the US Children's Bureau, the California state department of social welfare, the National Recovery Administration, and the Social Security Board; her interest in the suffrage movement; the trial of the McNamara brothers in Los Angeles; and Japanese relocation during WWII. Also includes articles by Bary, a bibliography, and photos.

342. Bashford, Herbert
Papers. 1890-1927. 33 folders.
Open. Shelflist.
University of California, Berkeley, The Bancroft Library, Manuscripts Division.
Bashford (1871-1928) was a literary editor of the San Francisco *Bulletin* and San Jose *Times* and the state librarian of Washington. Correspondence and other papers of contemporary writers and publishers, including Ina Donna Coolbrith, Elizabeth (Bacon) Custer, Ella (Rhoades) Higginson, Emelie Tracy Y. Parkhurst, and Isabel Darling.

343. Batchelder and Nelson Family
Papers. 1835-1956. 2 boxes and 1 portfolio.
Open. No guide.
University of California, Berkeley, The Bancroft Library, Manuscripts Division.
Papers of the family of physician Amos Batchelder and of the Nelson family include diaries and sketchbooks of Emily Serena Nelson.

344. Beattie, Margaret Isabel
Papers. Ca. 1960-70. 1 vol.
Open. No guide.
University of California, Berkeley, The Bancroft Library, Manuscripts Division.
Scrapbook of Beattie (1893-1976) documents her career as a professor in the University's school of public health. Includes reminiscences about her work in the diagnosis of communicable diseases, letters and tributes from colleagues and students, an essay, photos, and clippings.

345. Bell, Catherine Jane (Mills)
Papers. 1859. 1 item.
Open. No guide.
University of California, Berkeley, The Bancroft Library, Manuscripts Division.
Letter from Bell, an early settler of California, to her sister Jane of Oroville, CA, in which she gives an account of her trip from Iowa to California.

346. Bennett, Ella Costillo
Papers. Ca. 1896-1926. 1 carton.
Open. No guide.
University of California, Berkeley, The Bancroft Library, Manuscripts Division.
Papers of Bennett (1865-1932), an author, consist of manuscripts of her stories, plays, and articles; family photos; and scrapbooks containing poems by Bennett and by her son Raphael, clippings of her writings, and notes by her daughter Mary. Additional scrapbooks relate to the Mission Dolores in San Francisco and to woman suffrage.

347. Berkeley, CA, Relief Committee
Records. 1906. 1 carton.
Open. No guide.
University of California, Berkeley, The Bancroft Library, Manuscripts Division.
The Committee provided relief to victims of the 1906 earthquake. Accounts, bills, receipts, data cards on housing and clothing, and letters to the Committee requesting help in locating refugees and securing other kinds of aid.

348. Berkeley Day Nursery
Records. Nd. 8 cartons and 1 portfolio.
Open. No guide.
University of California, Berkeley, The Bancroft Library, Manuscripts Division.
Records of this Berkeley nursery, which was organized in 1908 and incorporated in 1914. It ceased operations in ca. 1965 as a result of labor disputes.

349. Bidwell Family
Papers. 1792-1934. 8 boxes, 3 cartons, and 1 portfolio.
Open. Key and shelflist.
University of California, Berkeley, The Bancroft Library, Manuscripts Division.
Papers of John Bidwell (1819-1900), a California pioneer; his wife Annie Ellicott (Kennedy) Bidwell (1839-1918); and members of families related to Annie Bidwell. Born in Chautauqua County, NY, John Bidwell moved to California in 1841 where he eventually purchased the 20,000-acre Rancho Chico in Butte County. He was a prominent agriculturist, a member of the senate in California's first legislature, and a US congressman who in 1875 ran for governor on an antimonopoly ticket in 1875 and as the Prohibition party candidate in 1890; in 1892 he ran for US President as a Prohibition party candidate. Annie Bidwell, daughter of Joseph Camp Griffith Kennedy, a statistician and superintendent of the 1850 and 1860 censuses, married Bidwell in 1868 and moved to California with him.

Correspondence, financial and other records of Rancho Chico, diaries, poems, obituaries, and other papers. Annie Bidwell's papers reflect her interest in Indian welfare and the Indian village on Rancho Chico, woman suffrage, prohibition, temperance, and the Civil War and include her poems and notes on conservation and on observation of the Sabbath. Correspondents include Mary S. Anthony, who describes her sister Susan B. Anthony; Rachel Foster Avery; Louise Wanda (Strentzel) [Mrs. John] Muir; Anna Howard Shaw; and Frances Elizabeth Caroline Willard. Papers of members of the Kennedy, Ellicott, and Morrison families contain correspondence of Annie Bidwell's mother Catharine (Morrison) [Mrs. Joseph Camp Griffith] Kennedy (1834-97), her sister Sarah Jane (Kennedy) Alexander, and others.

350. Birmingham, J.
Papers. 1920. 4-page item.
Open. No guide.
University of California, Berkeley, The Bancroft Library, Manuscripts Division.
Address which Captain Birmingham gave at a reunion of alumnae of the Benicia Young Ladies Seminary; he reminisces about the early days of the school.

351. Bitner Family
Papers. Ca. 1944. 38 pp.
Open. Published guide.
University of California, Berkeley, The Bancroft Library, Manuscripts Division.
Biographical sketches of members of the Bitner family, including the three wives of Breneman Barr Bitner (1837-1909): Mary Esther (Benedict) Bitner (1847-66), Martina Marjorie (Halseth) Bitner (1847-1912), and Sarah Ann (Osguthorpe) Bitner (1847-1930). Also includes a genealogical chart and a poem by Eliza Roxey Snow on the occasion of Mary Bitner's death. See Dale L. Morgan and George P. Hammond, eds., *A Guide to the Manuscript Collections of The Bancroft Library,* vol. I (Berkeley, CA: University of California Press, 1963).

352. Blackinger, Dorothy (Eaton)
Oral history. 1970. 14-page transcript.
Open. No guide.
University of California, Berkeley, The Bancroft Library, Manuscripts Division.
This interview with Blackinger was conducted as part of a project on people and places in Atherton, CA.

353. Blake Family
Papers. 1881-1962. 4 boxes, 1 carton, and 1 portfolio.
Open. Unpublished guide.
University of California, Berkeley, The Bancroft Library, Manuscripts Division.
Consists primarily of the papers of Anita Day (Symmes) Blake (1872-1962), an 1894 graduate of the University of California, Berkeley, and the wife of Anson Stiles Blake (1870-1959). Her papers include letters to her husband and others, a 1944 diary, a manuscript article she wrote about Henry Correvan, an address book, a genealogy of the Symmes and Blake families, poems about her, and other papers relating to her education and to her interest in horticulture. Correspondents include Julia (Cooley) Altrocchi and Mary Edith (Briggs) Moses.

354. Boggs, Mae Hélène (Bacon)
Papers. 1822-91. 18 vols.
Open. No guide.
University of California, Berkeley, The Bancroft Library, Manuscripts Division.
Papers of [Mrs. Angus] Boggs (1863-?), the author of a book on California history, include manuscript notes for her book *My Playhouse Was a Concord Coach* and an anthology of documents, notes, and clippings about 19th-century California personalities.

355. Bolton, Herbert Eugene
Papers. Ca. 1900-59. 159 boxes and 5 vols.
Open. Partial key and shelflist.
University of California, Berkeley, The Bancroft Library, Manuscripts Division.
Papers of Bolton (1870-1953) include correspondence and a 1959 tribute to him by Irene (Dakin) Paden with recollections of a trip to locate a portion of the Anza Trail. Among the numerous correspondents are his wife Gertrude (Janes) Bolton; his daughter Gertrude (Bolton) [Mrs. Joseph Griswold, III] Coleman; Phoebe (Apperson) Hearst; Eleanor Deming, president of the San Francisco College for Women; and the National Council of Catholic Women.

356. Bolton, Sarah
Papers. 1886. 1 item.
Open. No guide.

University of California, Berkeley, The Bancroft Library, Manuscripts Division.
Letter from [Miss] Bolton, a graduate of the University of California, to Edward S. Holden of San Francisco in which she discusses her teaching experiences and suggests that the University help place alumni in positions in education.

357. Bonney, Mabel Thérèse
Papers. Ca. 1941- . 1 package.
Open. No guide.
University of California, Berkeley, The Bancroft Library, Manuscripts Division.
Papers of Bonney (1895-1978), a photographer, primarily concern her documentation of WWII and other photographic work. Includes letters from Joseph Pulitzer and Edward Alden Jewell, samples of her work, biographical information, scrapbooks of testimonials, and clippings.

358. Booth, Anne (Willson)
Papers. 1849. 250-page item.
Open. No guide.
University of California, Berkeley, The Bancroft Library, Manuscripts Division.
Journal of an 1849 ocean voyage from Baltimore around Cape Horn to San Francisco, where passengers remained on shipboard at anchor for seven weeks. Includes description of life in San Francisco.

359. Bourn and Ingalls Family
Papers. 1865-1958. 1 portfolio.
Open. No guide.
University of California, Berkeley, The Bancroft Library, Manuscripts Division.
Letters in which Hannah (Bourn) Ingalls and her son William describe their voyage to San Francisco in 1865 through Panama, life in San Francisco, and travels in California in 1865 and 1866.

360. Bowen, Mary E.
Papers. 1865-66. 1 vol.
Open. No guide.
University of California, Berkeley, The Bancroft Library, Manuscripts Division.
Diary kept by Bowen, probably in Albany, NY, chiefly relates to her school days.

361. Bowie, Ruth (Boericke) White
Oral history. 1969. 29-page transcript.
Open. No guide.
University of California, Berkeley, The Bancroft Library, Manuscripts Division.
Interview with Bowie (1888-1977) concerns her residence in Mill Valley, CA, since 1904; her marriage to Ralston White; and their estate Garden of Allah. Photos are also included.

362. Boynton and Quitzow Family: "Dance at the Temple of the Wings"
Oral history. 1972. 2 vols. and 1 tape.
Open. No guide.
University of California, Berkeley, The Bancroft Library, Manuscripts Division.
Interviews with Charles and Sülgwynn Quitzow and their children OElóel (Quitzow) Braun and Vol Quitzow contain comments on the Boynton, Treadwell, and Quitzow families; their home Temple of the Wings, located in Berkeley; the 1923 Berkeley fire; their interest and involvement in dance; and their impressions of Isadora Duncan, José Limón, and other dancers. Includes an afterword by Rhea (Boynton) Hildebrand and photos.

363. Boys Aid Society of California, San Francisco
Records. 1874-1929. 210 vols. and 29 cartons.
Open. No guide.
University of California, Berkeley, The Bancroft Library, Manuscripts Division.
Founded in 1874 as the Boys and Girls Aid Society, the organization was renamed in 1920. Accounts, correspondence, and case records, including psychological test data, of the Society as well as records of the Jesse W. Lilienthal School.

364. Bracelin, Nina Floy
Papers. 1938-63. 1 box and 4 card file boxes.
Open. No guide.
University of California, Berkeley, The Bancroft Library, Manuscripts Division.
Papers of [Mrs.] Bracelin include letters from Anita Blake, Nell Haley, and others, some of which relate to Ynés Mexía; charts and other items pertaining to her research on dried and frozen foods for the US Western Regional Laboratory in Albany, CA; card files on garden specimens; and notes and homework for a chemistry course at the University.

365. Braden, Amy (Steinhart)
Oral history. 1960-64. 1 vol.
Open. No guide.
University of California, Berkeley, The Bancroft Library, Manuscripts Division.
Tape and transcript of an interview with [Mrs. Robert] Braden (1879-?) concerning her family and social life in San Francisco, her student days at the University, the 1906 earthquake, her professional career as a children's agent for the State Board of Control from 1913 to 1924, volunteer social service and settlement work, and work with minority groups. Included are photos and documentary material on child welfare. Also available on microfilm.

366. Bradley, Walter Wadsworth
Papers. 1888-1949. 15 cartons.
Open. No guide.
University of California, Berkeley, The Bancroft Library, Manuscripts Division.
Papers of Bradley (1878-1950) include material of the Order of the Eastern Star and Knights Templar.

367. Bradner, Clara (Harwood)
Papers. 1956. 1 portfolio.
Open. No guide.
University of California, Berkeley, The Bancroft Library, Manuscripts Division.
Papers of Bradner (1855-1956), an early resident of Sacramento, CA, include a letter to [Mrs.] Hazel Z. Weller, a biographical note concerning Bradner, and a poem she wrote about Yosemite.

368. Brainard, Clementine H.
Papers. 1853-55. 31-page item.
Open. No guide.
University of California, Berkeley, The Bancroft Library, Manuscripts Division.
Diary in which Brainard, who moved to Columbia, CA, as the bride of merchant B. M. Brainard, records her first few years in that town.

369. Bramer, Electa (Snow)
Papers. 1818-38. 105 items.
Open. Published guide.
University of California, Berkeley, The Bancroft Library, Manuscripts Division.
Letters by Bramer (1796-?) to her family describing her teaching experiences in Massachusetts and New York, letters to Bramer from relatives, and a biographical sketch of Bramer by Achsa Snow Parker. See George P. Hammond, ed., *A Guide to the Manuscript Collections of The Bancroft Library,* vol. II (Berkeley, CA: University of California Press, 1972).

370. Brennan, Arcadia Bandini (Scott)
Papers. Nd. 1 box.
Open. No guide.
University of California, Berkeley, The Bancroft Library, Manuscripts Division.
Reminiscences and photos of Brennan (1885-) relate to the Bandini family, from which she was descended; her childhood on the Guajome Rancho and Indians there; her early memories of San Diego; and recollections of her great aunt Arcadia Bandini Stearns de Baker.

371. Brewer, William Henry
Papers. 1860-84. 5 folders.
Open. Shelflist.
University of California, Berkeley, The Bancroft Library, Manuscripts Division.
Contains five letters to Brewer (1828-1910) from Louise (Goddard) Howe [Mrs. Josiah Dwight] Whitney.

372. Brico, Antonia
Papers. 1948. 1 item.
Open. No guide.
University of California, Berkeley, The Bancroft Library, Manuscripts Division.
Letter from Brico in Helsinki, Finland, to Lucy Ward Stebbins describing her visit with the composer Jean Sibelius.

373. Brode, Bernice Bidwell
Papers. Ca. 1943-60. 1 box.
Open. No guide.
University of California, Berkeley, The Bancroft Library, Manuscripts Division.
Photos and other papers of Brode (1901-) relating to Los Alamos.

374. Brown, Bill
Papers. Nd. 1 box.
Open. No guide.
University of California, Berkeley, The Bancroft Library, Manuscripts Division.
Manuscripts of novels and stories by Brown and poems by his wife Rosalie (Moore) Brown (1910-).

375. Brown, Madie D.
Papers. Nd. 4 cartons.
Open. No guide.
University of California, Berkeley, The Bancroft Library, Manuscripts Division.
Correspondence and other papers of [Mrs. Edmund N.] Brown pertain to her work as a member of the California State Park Commission.

376. Bucknall, Mary (Davis)
Papers. Ca. 1856-1924. 1 portfolio.
Open. No guide.
University of California, Berkeley, The Bancroft Library, Manuscripts Division.
Consists primarily of letters written from [Mrs. George] Bucknall (1845-?) to her father while she was in school at St. Mary's Hall in Sonoma, CA. Includes one letter from Fanny Ver Mehr and a study schedule for Mary and Lizzie Davis.

377. Bum Hill Gazette
Records. 1906. 2 items.
Open. No guide.
University of California, Berkeley, The Bancroft Library, Manuscripts Division.
Issues of the *Bum Hill Gazette,* which was compiled, handwritten, and illustrated by [Miss] Hazel Snell and published by the Prowlers of Ashbarrel Street, New San Francisco.

378. Burgess, Gelett
Papers. Ca. 1873-1951. 5 boxes, 6 cartons, 1 portfolio, and 2 microfilm reels.
Open. Key.
University of California, Berkeley, The Bancroft Library, Manuscripts Division.
Papers of Burgess (1866-1951) include correspondence with Gertrude Franklin (Horn) Atherton, Mary (Hunter) Austin, Willa Cather, Fannie Hurst, Amy Lowell, Eleanor Roosevelt, Cornelia Otis Skinner, Ida M. Tarbell, Edith Wharton, and others. Also includes manuscript reminiscences and poems by Gelett Burgess and manuscript short stories, notes, and clippings of Estelle (Loomis) [Mrs. Gelett] Burgess.

379. Burke, Emma
Papers. Nd. 1 vol.
Open. No guide.
University of California, Berkeley, The Bancroft Library, Manuscripts Division.
Commonplace book of Burke, who perhaps was a student.

380. Burnham, Elizabeth
Oral history. 1967. 1 tape.
Open. Table of contents.
University of California, Berkeley, The Bancroft Library, Manuscripts Division.
Interview with [Miss] Burnham (1894-) concerns her career with the YWCA, her service with the Peace Corps in Peru from 1962 to 1964, and her work for VISTA with migrant labor families around Gilroy, CA. Also includes a written account by Burnham of the VISTA project in Gilroy and a photo.

381. Burt, Clara M.
Papers. 1875-89. 1 vol.
Open. No guide.
University of California, Berkeley, The Bancroft Library, Manuscripts Division.
Papers of Burt (1857-?) include a journal about her experiences as a teacher in San Joaquin, Santa Clara, and Amador counties in California and genealogical information on the Burt family.

382. Burton, Alice Irene
Papers. 1918-19. 2 vols.
Open. No guide.
University of California, Berkeley, The Bancroft Library, Manuscripts Division.
Photo album and scrapbook of Burton (1890-?) relate to her service as an army nurse in France during WWI. Contains letters of appreciation, mementos, and clippings.

383. Byrne, Clarissa (Young)
Oral history. 1968. 22-page transcript.
Open. No guide.
University of California, Berkeley, The Bancroft Library, Manuscripts Division.
Interview with Byrne (1895-?) concerns her arrival in Mill Valley, CA, in 1904 and her life there.

384. California Association of Women Deans and Vice-Principals
Records. 1929-?. 3 boxes.
Open. No guide.
University of California, Berkeley, The Bancroft Library, Manuscripts Division.
Records of the Association begin in 1929 and include reports, newsletters, and programs of state and section meetings.

385. California Biographical Miscellany
Collection. Nd. 1 portfolio and 1 microfilm reel.
Open. Shelflist.
University of California, Berkeley, The Bancroft Library, Manuscripts Division.
Short biographical sketches, reminiscences, and other accounts of Californians contain material on Anna (Hundley) Glud, a "drummer boy" in the Civil War; Ann Elizabeth (Lewis) Peter, who traveled to California in 1853; and others. Also available on microfilm.

386. California Civic League, San Francisco Center, Public Dance Hall Committee
Records. 1918-50. 1 portfolio.
Open. No guide.
University of California, Berkeley, The Bancroft Library, Manuscripts Division.
Minutes, agenda, accounts, correspondence, reports, and other records of the Committee.

387. California Federation for Civic Unity
Records. 1945-56. 6 boxes and 3 cartons.
Open. Shelflist.
University of California, Berkeley, The Bancroft Library, Manuscripts Division.
Minutes, accounts, records relating to various conferences, correspondence, and pamphlets of the Federation, which was concerned with racial discrimination and segregation, immigration, and employment practices. Correspondents include the YWCA, California congresswoman Helen (Gahagan) Douglas, and a number of other women.

388. California Gold Rush Letters
Collection. 1848-1959. 1 box.
Open. Key.
University of California, Berkeley, The Bancroft Library, Manuscripts Division.
Includes a letter by a woman to her husband and one by Mary A. Hill to her brother Jason in East Woodstock, CA; both letters were written in 1853.

389. California League for American Indians
Records. 1918-41. 13 cartons.
Open. Key.
University of California, Berkeley, The Bancroft Library, Manuscripts Division.
Records of the League and of its predecessor the Indian Defense Association include manuscripts, correspondence, photos, scrapbook of clippings, card file, and ephemera relating to various women and to the YWCA, the Camp Fire Girls, the GFWC, the LWV, and other organizations. Also included are bylaws and minutes of the California Committee on Indian Relief Work.

390. California Militia
Records. 1861. 36-page item.
Open. No guide.
University of California, Berkeley, The Bancroft Library, Manuscripts Division.
Subscriptions by the Ladies of San Francisco for regimental colors for the First Regiment of Infantry, California Militia, include a list of regimental field officers, signatures of ladies subscribing, and a list of members and statement of costs of the committee on regimental colors.

391. California Miscellany
Collection. Nd. 3 boxes.
Open. Shelflist.
University of California, Berkeley, The Bancroft Library, Manuscripts Division.
Includes letters, reminiscences, and other writings by a number of women on such subjects as the 1906 San Francisco earthquake and fire, the histories of early California towns and cities, life on Lombard Street in San Francisco, the role of early Mormon settlers in California, and Phoebe (Apperson) Hearst.

392. California Mission Statistics
Records. 1769-1834. 32 folders.
Open. No guide.
University of California, Berkeley, The Bancroft Library, Manuscripts Division.
Lists of births, marriages, deaths, population, livestock, and crops for each mission; the presidios of San Diego, Monterey, San Francisco, and Santa Barbara; the pueblos of San Jose and Los Angeles; and the Villa Branciforte. Includes an analysis by place and summary statistics. Also available on microfilm.

393. California Social Workers Organization, Inc.
Records. 1953-67. 5 cartons.
Open. No guide.
University of California, Berkeley, The Bancroft Library, Manuscripts Division.
Minutes of board meetings; correspondence of the president, vice-president, and regional vice-presidents; treasurer's records; secretary's correspondence; subject files; issues of *Advance*, a publication of the Organization; material on *Parrish v. the Civil Service Commission;* scrapbooks; and other records. Files relate to regional chapters, legislative and social action, public information, social work practice and education, and welfare rights organization. Includes correspondence of the California Foundation for Economic Opportunity.

394. California State Emergency Relief Administration
Records. 1939-40. 1 box.
Open. No guide.
University of California, Berkeley, The Bancroft Library, Manuscripts Division.
Memoranda, circulars, and forms used by the Administration, whose caseworkers were primarily women.

395. Camp, Charles Lewis
Papers. Nd. 7 boxes and 6 cartons.
Open. Key.
University of California, Berkeley, The Bancroft Library, Manuscripts Division.
Camp (1893-1975) was a professor of paleontology and historian of early California and the pioneer West. Letters from Dorothy H. Huggins, his sister Dorothy Nourse, Annie A. Nunns, Margaret Pratt, Ida M. Tarbell, and others.

396. Carden, Georgiana Caroline
Papers. 1920-67. 1 portfolio and 4 tapes.
Open. Partial summary.
University of California, Berkeley, The Bancroft Library, Manuscripts Division.
Correspondence, accounts, records and reports of her activities, and other papers of [Miss] Carden relate primarily to her work with migrant and Indian children for the California department of education; to her Little House experiment, an attempt to provide low-cost housing for working girls in San Francisco; and to regulations she drew up for San Francisco dance halls. Also included is an interview concerning her experiences as supervisor of public dance halls in San Francisco and her work in migrant camps and in schools for migrant children and a letter from Katharine Conway Felton.

397. Carlson, Ruth Elizabeth (Kearney)
Papers. 1944. 16-page item.
Open. Published guide.
University of California, Berkeley, The Bancroft Library, Manuscripts Division.
Notes by Carlson on Baja California relate to a proposed military colony in 1849 and 1850 at Santo Tomás, the Ensenada filibustering scheme of 1889 and 1890, biographies of people associated with colonization ventures in Lower California, and recent economic history. See George P. Hammond, ed., *A Guide to the Manuscript Collections of The Bancroft Library,* vol. II (Berkeley, CA: University of California Press, 1972).

398. Carpenter, Julia M.
Papers. 1882-87. 1 vol.
Open. No guide.
University of California, Berkeley, The Bancroft Library, Manuscripts Division.
Biographical note on [Mrs.] Carpenter (1838-1906) and a manuscript by her about her western travels, including a visit to California; she describes Los Angeles, Santa Barbara, Oakland, and Berkeley and comments on prices, the cost of living, and wages.

399. Carrall, Maria L.
Papers. 1859-71. 1 vol.
Open. No guide.
University of California, Berkeley, The Bancroft Library, Manuscripts Division.
Autograph album of Carrall, a resident of Philadelphia, inscribed by her friends.

400. Carter, Jesse Washington
Papers. Ca. 1912-39. 47 boxes and 91 cartons.
Access restricted. Key.

University of California, Berkeley, The Bancroft Library, Manuscripts Division.
Correspondence, reference material, reports, clippings, and other papers of Judge Carter (1888-1959). Included are reports on an investigation of houses of prostitution and bars conducted from 1920 to 1923 and letters from his wife Tiny (Gish) Carter, his secretary Thelma Brooks, Annette (Abbott) Adams, Mae Helene Bacon Boggs, Esther B. Phillips, and the California Anti-Saloon League.

401. Case, Catherine Norton
Papers. 1905. 7-page item.
Open. No guide.
University of California, Berkeley, The Bancroft Library, Manuscripts Division.
Recollections by Case of a 1905 trip to Yosemite.

402. Cassidy, Rosalind Frances
Oral history. 1967. 354-page transcript.
Open. No guide.
University of California, Berkeley, The Bancroft Library, Manuscripts Division.
Cassidy (1895-?) discusses teaching physical education at Mills College in Oakland, CA; her role in the development of the physical education department at the University of California, Los Angeles; her interest in the modern dance movement; and her activities with the California Youth Authority and other organizations concerned with youth welfare. Also includes a photo.

403. Castle Family
Papers. 1854-77. 1 portfolio.
Open. No guide.
University of California, Berkeley, The Bancroft Library, Manuscripts Division.
Includes letters from 1854 to 1860 by Frances A. (Ferry) Castle (1827-60), a resident of Amador County, CA.

404. Castro, Manuel de Jesús
Papers. 1830-63. 3 boxes.
Open. Calendar.
University of California, Berkeley, The Bancroft Library, Manuscripts Division.
Correspondence and other papers of Castro (1821-?) concerning family and business affairs. Includes a letter by Maria Lorenza Salinas to Castro requesting a ruling on her marital difficulties and letters from several other women.

405. Chesnut, Helen (Van Valkenburgh)
Oral history. 1969. 17-page transcript.
Open. No guide.
University of California, Berkeley, The Bancroft Library, Manuscripts Division.
Chesnut discusses the growth of Mill Valley, CA, from the time of her arrival in 1919 and the 1929 Mt. Tamalpais fire.

406. Child, Maria M. (Eastman)
Papers. 1849-51. 24 folders.
Open. No guide.
University of California, Berkeley, The Bancroft Library, Manuscripts Division.
Includes letters to [Mrs. Isaac] Child from her sister Sophie A. Eastman, who later married Harrison Eastman, about a voyage from Boston on the brig *Colorado* and her experiences in San Francisco, including nursing at the City Hospital.

407. Child, Sarah "Sade" B. (Treat)
Papers. Nd. 1 carton.
Open. No guide.
University of California, Berkeley, The Bancroft Library, Manuscripts Division.
Correspondence of Child with her husband George Child and May Crittenden.

408. Children's Protective Society of San Francisco
Records. 1939-44. 2 vols.
Open. No guide.
University of California, Berkeley, The Bancroft Library, Manuscripts Division.
Annual reports; final report, 1944; and statement regarding the purposes, organization, and history of the Society. [Miss] Julia George of San Francisco was an honorary member of the Society's board.

409. China Missionaries Oral History Project
Oral history. Ca. 1969-72. 1 box.
Open. Shelflist.
University of California, Berkeley, The Bancroft Library, Manuscripts Division.
Includes interviews conducted through the Associated Colleges at Claremont, CA, with Mary Lee Latimer, who describes her experiences in China as the daughter of missionaries and as a teacher in mission and non-mission schools; Agnes (Kelly) Scott, who discusses teaching music and directing choral groups at a high school in Foochow and at Fukien Christian University; and Margaret (Garrett) Smythe, who discusses her childhood in China as the daughter of missionaries, her study of medicine in the US, her return to China in 1928 and service in a mission hospital, the Sino-Japanese War, and life under the Communists until 1951.

410. Clarke, Harriet T. (Buckingham)
Papers. 1878. 12-page item.
Open. Published guide.
University of California, Berkeley, The Bancroft Library, Manuscripts Division.
Interview with Clarke (1832-90), an early settler of Oregon who wintered in Utah in 1851. She discusses her journey, the attitude of Brigham Young toward the US government, and the attitude of Mormon women toward polygamy. Also available on microfilm. See Dale L. Morgan and George P. Hammond, eds., *A Guide to the Manuscript Collections of The Bancroft Library,* vol. I (Berkeley, CA: University of California Press, 1963).

411. Coblentz, Edmond David
Papers. Ca. 1917-60. 16 boxes and 3 vols.
Open. Key.
University of California, Berkeley, The Bancroft Library, Manuscripts Division.
Social, business, and political correspondence of Coblentz (1882-1962) includes letters from many women, among them Millicent [Mrs. William Randolph, Sr.] Hearst, Fannie Hurst, Alice Roosevelt Longworth, and Anna Roosevelt.

412. Cochrane, Adelaide (Griffith)
Oral history. 1969. 1 tape.
Open. No guide.
University of California, Berkeley, The Bancroft Library, Manuscripts Division.
Cochrane reminisces about her grandfather Captain Millen Griffith and his tugboat business in San Francisco, whaling and the Alaska Packers company, her interest in the Empire Mines of Grass Valley, her aunt Alice Griffith and her aunt's association with nurse Elizabeth Ashe, and the founding of the Telegraph Hill Neighborhood Association in San Francisco.

413. Conner, Louisa A.
Papers. 1887. 2-page item.
Open. Published guide.
University of California, Berkeley, The Bancroft Library, Manuscripts Division.
Dictation by Conner, a resident of La Conner, WA, concerns the experiences of her husband J. S. Conner (1838-84) in the hotel and mining businesses and at the trading post in La Conner. Also available on microfilm. See Dale L. Morgan and George P. Hammond, eds., *A Guide to the Manuscript Collections of The Bancroft Library,* vol. I (Berkeley, CA: University of California Press, 1963).

414. Conti, Bianca
Papers. Ca. 1920-38. 3 folders.
Open. No guide.
University of California, Berkeley, The Bancroft Library, Manuscripts Division.
Papers of Conti (1874?-1954) include letters from Carlotta Monterey, Francis McComas, and Isobelle (Sterling) Rounthwaite with explanatory notes.

415. Cooke, Grace (MacGowan)
Papers. 1909-15. 64-page vol.
Open. No guide.
University of California, Berkeley, The Bancroft Library, Manuscripts Division.
Journal in which Cooke (1863-1944) describes her life in Carmel and San Francisco and the writing of her novel *The Joy Bringer.* Also contains revisions of her play *The Sword in the Mountains,* an article about her sister Alice MacGowan, an obituary for Cooke, and a clipping on the MacGowan and Cooke family of Carmel.

416. Cooke, Sarah A.
Papers. 1884. 11-page item.
Open. Published guide.
University of California, Berkeley, The Bancroft Library, Manuscripts Division.
Interview with Cooke, the wife of William Cooke, who was killed in 1858, concerns her conversion to Mormonism in 1852 en route to California, her involvement with theatrical affairs, Brigham Young and his family, teaching music to Young's children, polygamy, and Mormon attitudes toward the government. Also available on microfilm. See Dale L. Morgan and George P. Hammond, eds., *A Guide to the Manuscript Collections of The Bancroft Library,* vol. I (Berkeley, CA: University of California Press, 1963).

417. Cool, Sarah M. (Aram)
Papers. 1883-1913. 1 portfolio.
Open. No guide.
University of California, Berkeley, The Bancroft Library, Manuscripts Division.
Includes a letter to Cool (1836-1912) from a friend in the East, a letter by Cool to her brother concerning life in Los Angeles, a statement relating to property she owned there, and papers concerning the settlement of her estate.

418. Coolidge, Dane
Papers. Ca. 1889-1942. 19 boxes and 1 carton.
Open. Unpublished guide.
University of California, Berkeley, The Bancroft Library, Manuscripts Division.
Correspondence, manuscripts, notes and notebooks, biographical information, clippings, and other papers of Coolidge (1873-1940). Includes letters from Betty (Blake) [Mrs. Will] Rogers, Agnes Wright Spring, and others. Papers of Coolidge's wife Mary (Roberts) Coolidge (1860-1945) pertain primarily to woman suffrage and to her career as a teacher and include correspondence, manuscripts of her articles, notes, lecture outlines, memorandum books, reference material, memorabilia, and clippings.

419. Corson Family
Papers. 1858-93. 117 items.
Open. Published guide.
University of California, Berkeley, The Bancroft Library, Manuscripts Division.
Letters of W. A. and Mary E. Carter to their daughter Ada (Carter) Corson and her husband Joseph K. Corson, an army surgeon in Wyoming, and a few letters by Ada to her parents. See Dale L. Morgan and George P. Hammond, eds., *A Guide to the Manuscript Collections of The Bancroft Library,* vol. I (Berkeley, CA: University of California Press, 1963).

420. Coulter, Edith Margaret
Papers. 1949-50. 125-page item.
Open. No guide.
University of California, Berkeley, The Bancroft Library, Manuscripts Division.
Papers presented to [Miss] Coulter (1880-1963), a librarian, by the class in advanced bibliography of the University of California's school of librarianship contain letters, photos, a biographical sketch of Coulter, a bibliography of her work, and a biobibliography of members of the class of 1905 at Stanford University, the class of 1907 of the New York state library school at Albany, the class of 1924 of the University of California, Berkeley, and of graduates of the University of California's school of librarianship who have published books.

421. Cranston, Mildred (Welch)
Oral history. 1971. 86-page transcript.
Open. No guide.
University of California, Berkeley, The Bancroft Library, Manuscripts Division.
Cranston (1898-?) discusses her work as a missionary in China from 1922 to 1927, teaching in Chengtu under the sponsorship of the Women's Board of the Methodist Church, and her views on missionary activities.

422. Cranstone, Susan (Marsh)
Papers. 1851-59. 2 vols.
Open. Published guide.
University of California, Berkeley, The Bancroft Library, Manuscripts Division.
Journal kept by Cranstone (1829-57) on her trip from St. Joseph, MO, to Oregon in 1851. Also includes letters to Huldah and Reuben Fairchild in Illinois concerning life in Lebanon and Salem, OR, and in Indian Creek, CA. Also available on microfilm. See Dale L. Morgan and George P. Hammond, eds., *A Guide to the Manuscript Collections of The Bancroft Library,* vol. I (Berkeley, CA: University of California Press, 1963).

423. Culbertson, Matthew Simpson
Papers. 1843-60. 1 box.
Open. No guide.
University of California, Berkeley, The Bancroft Library, Manuscripts Division.
Includes letters by Culbertson's daughter Helen (Culbertson) Kip concerning her travels in Europe in 1888.

424. Cumming, Alfred
Papers. 1857-65. 1 microfilm reel.
Open. Published guide.
University of California, Berkeley, The Bancroft Library, Manuscripts Division.
Includes letters by Cumming's wife Elizabeth Wells (Randall) Cumming. See Dale L. Morgan and George P. Hammond, eds., *A Guide to the Manuscript Collections of The Bancroft Library,* vol. I (Berkeley, CA: University of California Press, 1963).

425. Cunningham, Imogen
Oral history. 1959. 1 vol. and 1 tape.
Open. No guide.
University of California, Berkeley, The Bancroft Library, Manuscripts Division.
Tape and transcript of interviews with Cunningham (1883-1976) in which she discusses her family and early life in Seattle, studying in Germany, Alfred Stieglitz, the Photo Secession, her marriage to Roi Partridge, the "f/64" group and other colleagues, her work for *Vanity Fair,* and photographic equipment and literature. Also available on microfilm.

426. Dace, Catherine (Hubbard) Egbert
Oral history. 1960. 59-page transcript.
Open. No guide.
University of California, Berkeley, The Bancroft Library, Manuscripts Division.
Dace (1886-1961) provides recollections of her grandfather Charles Maclay and her father Henry Cutler Hubbard, a pioneer rancher in the San Fernando Valley.

427. Dakin, Susanna (Bryant)
Papers. 1964. 19-page item.
Open. No guide.
University of California, Berkeley, The Bancroft Library, Manuscripts Division.
Manuscript by Dakin (1905-66) concerns an introduction to Carrie Le Conte's *Yosemite* (1878) and includes biographical information on Caroline Eaton Le Conte and other members of the Le Conte family.

428. Dakin, Susanna (Bryant)
Papers. 1966. 1 vol.
Open. No guide.
University of California, Berkeley, The Bancroft Library, Manuscripts Division.
Manuscript of *The Scent of Violets* (1966), a recollection by Dakin (1905-66) of her family and her childhood in Los Angeles and at Rancho Los Alamitos. After her death, the manuscript was prepared for publication by Elizabeth Wecter.

429. Dalton, Lucinda (Lee)
Papers. 1876. 25 pp.
Open. Published guide.
University of California, Berkeley, The Bancroft Library, Manuscripts Division.
Letters by [Mrs. Charles W.] Dalton (1847-1925), a resident of Circle Valley, UT, to [Mrs.] Emmeline B. Wells in which she comments on woman's place in a man's world and on Mormon life. Also available on microfilm. See Dale L. Morgan and George P. Hammond, eds., *A Guide to the Manuscript Collections of The Bancroft Library,* vol. I (Berkeley, CA: University of California Press, 1963).

430. D'Apery, Helen (Burrell)
Papers. Nd. 2 vols.
Open. No guide.
University of California, Berkeley, The Bancroft Library, Manuscripts Division.
Scrapbook of obituaries and memoirs by D'Apery (1842-1915) concerning her family and personal life, her voyage in 1852 from New York to San Francisco around the Horn, and life in Oakland, CA, with her family. The narrative does not cover the period after 1872, when she left California and began her career as a writer. Memoirs also available on microfilm.

431. Daughters of the American Revolution
Records. 1937-58. 3 vols.
Open. No guide.
University of California, Berkeley, The Bancroft Library, Manuscripts Division.
Scrapbooks of the Berkeley Hills, CA, chapter containing photos, programs, and clippings.

432. Daughters of the American Revolution, California
Records. Nd. 8 microfilm reels.
Open. No guide.
University of California, Berkeley, The Bancroft Library, Manuscripts Division.
Vital records abstracted from the *San Francisco Bulletin* for the years 1855 to 1874 and copied from cemeteries in California from 1934 to 1962 by various chapters of the DAR. Data from cemeteries is arranged by county, cemetery, and individual.

433. Davidian, Nectar
Papers. Ca. 1964-69. 1 box.
Open. No guide.
University of California, Berkeley, The Bancroft Library, Manuscripts Division.
Correspondence, scrapbook of reviews, and material used by Davidian, a writer, in the preparation of her booklet *The Seropians* and in the reprinting of Wilson D. Wallis's *Fresno Armenians.*

434. Davidson, George
Papers. Ca. 1845-1911. 64 boxes, 30 cartons, and 7 packages.
Open. Key.
University of California, Berkeley, The Bancroft Library, Manuscripts Division.
Correspondence, diaries, and other papers of Davidson (1825-1911); family correspondence and autobiographical sketches of his wife Ellinor (Fauntleroy) Davidson, including letters describing their travels in 1874 and 1875, which were published in *The Little Monitor and Parish Guide;* and correspondence and an article on California Indian shellmounds by their daughter Ellinor C. Davidson. Papers of Ellinor F. Davidson's mother Jane Dale (Owen) Fauntleroy include correspondence, estate papers, articles by her on German castles, a biographical sketch of her husband, and a passport. Also includes other papers relating to the Owen and Fauntleroy families.

435. Davidson, Mary Blossom
Oral history. 1966. 89-page transcript.
Open. No guide.
University of California, Berkeley, The Bancroft Library, Manuscripts Division.
Davidson (?-1968) recalls her days as a student at the University in the class of 1906, as assistant to the dean of women students, and then as dean of women students at the University.

436. Davies, Mary Carolyn
Papers. Ca. 1913-18. 1 portfolio.
Open. No guide.
University of California, Berkeley, The Bancroft Library, Manuscripts Division.
Includes letters by Davies (1888-?), an author and poet, to Sheldon Cheney, a letter of recommendation written for her by Cheney, manuscripts of her poems and plays, clippings, and a reprint of some poems.

437. Davis, Ethelreda C.
Papers. 1966-67. 1 portfolio.
Open. No guide.
University of California, Berkeley, The Bancroft Library, Manuscripts Division.
Lists compiled by Davis from newspaper sources of women in the suffrage movement between 1869 and 1911, of suffrage conventions, and of men associated with the movement.

438. Day, Emeline (Hubbard)
Papers. 1853-56. 118-page item.
Open. No guide.
University of California, Berkeley, The Bancroft Library, Manuscripts Division.
Journal in which Day describes Panama and Acapulco, which she visited en route to San Francisco; gold mines; and life at Mountain House, an inn near Placerville. Includes stories and articles of a religious nature written by Day; some of these have an antislavery theme. Also available on microfilm.

439. De Witt Family
Papers. Ca. 1848-67. 2 boxes.
Open. No guide.
University of California, Berkeley, The Bancroft Library, Manuscripts Division.
Letters from Alfred De Witt and from his wife Margaret to her family in New York concern their journey to California via the Isthmus of Panama in 1849 and their life in San Francisco.

440. Deane, Martha Blanchard
Oral history. 1966. 221-page transcript.
Open. No guide.
University of California, Berkeley, The Bancroft Library, Manuscripts Division.
Interview with Deane (1896-?), a dance instructor and dancer at the University of California, Los Angeles, concerns her role in the development of dance at UCLA, the establishment of the department of theater arts, and various faculty members.

441. Denman, William
Papers. Ca. 1900-59. 42 boxes, 32 cartons, and 21 vols.
Open. Key.
University of California, Berkeley, The Bancroft Library, Manuscripts Division.
Correspondence and other papers of Denman (1872-1959), a lawyer and assistant professor of law at the Hastings College of Law and the University of California who defended the state's law limiting women's hours of work. Includes letters from Alice (Goldmark) [Mrs. Louis Dembitz] Brandeis, Frances Perkins, Edith (Bolling) Galt [Mrs. Woodrow] Wilson, and others and a subject file on woman suffrage. Papers of his wife Leslie (Van Ness) Denman (1867-1959), who was chairman of social relations for the department of the Pacific area of the 1939 World's Fair, include correspondence, diary entries, minutes, photos, and clippings relating primarily to the Pacific House at the Fair, which was held in San Francisco.

442. Denny, Melcena Burns
Papers. Nd. 1 portfolio.
Open. No guide.
University of California, Berkeley, The Bancroft Library, Manuscripts Division.
Papers of Denny, a writer, consist of manuscripts of her plays *Lola Montez* and *Black Bart.*

443. Derrickson, Frances Ada (Martin)
Papers. Nd. 1 vol.
Open. No guide.
University of California, Berkeley, The Bancroft Library, Manuscripts Division.
Biography of the Azariah Martin family by Derrickson (1865-?) includes photos and genealogical tables.

444. Diaries of Overland Journeys to California
Collection. Nd. 5 microfilm reels.
Open. Shelflist.
University of California, Berkeley, The Bancroft Library, Manuscripts Division.
Includes a diary by Jane Augusta (Holbrook) Gould Tourtillote (1833-1917) describing a trip to California in 1862.

445. Diary
Papers. 1864. 143-page vol.
Open. Published guide.
University of California, Berkeley, The Bancroft Library, Manuscripts Division.
Pocket diary kept by an unidentified young woman who taught school near Canandaigua, NY. See George P. Hammond, ed., *A Guide to the Manuscript Collections of The Bancroft Library,* vol. II (Berkeley, CA: University of California Press, 1972).

446. Disciples of Christ, Woman's Missionary Society, California North
Records. 1914-37. 2 vols.
Open. No guide.
University of California, Berkeley, The Bancroft Library, Manuscripts Division.
Minutes of meetings of the executive and state boards of the Society, which from its founding in 1914 until ca. 1921 was known as the Christian Woman's Board of Missions, California North. The Society built and supported the Chinese Christian Institute in San Francisco.

447. Dizney, Helen
Oral history. 1970. 31-page transcript.
Open. No guide.
University of California, Berkeley, The Bancroft Library, Manuscripts Division.
Dizney (1894-?) discusses her work in China from 1920 to 1938 as a nurse under the sponsorship of the Congregational church and from 1946 to 1950 as a supervisor of public health training and the nursing school at a mission hospital.

448. Dobie, Charles Caldwell
Papers. Ca. 1905-43. 12 boxes, 12 cartons, 1 portfolio, and 1 vol.
Open. Descriptive guide and shelflist.
University of California, Berkeley, The Bancroft Library, Manuscripts Division.
Correspondence and other papers of Dobie (1881-1943), including letters from Gertrude Franklin (Horn) Atherton, Ina Donna Coolbrith, Fannie Hurst, Charmian (Kittredge) London, *Woman's Home Companion,* and others.

449. Donnelly, Ruth (Norton)
Oral history. 1966-69. 141-page transcript.
Open. No guide.
University of California, Berkeley, The Bancroft Library, Manuscripts Division.
Donnelly (1903-) discusses her experiences at the University as a student, as a campus administrative officer in the dean of women's office, as supervisor of housing services, and as dean of University housing. Includes an introduction by Margaret O. Dewell and a photo. Tape also available.

450. Dowd, Margaret (Wosser)
Oral history. 1968. 21-page transcript.
Open. No guide.
University of California, Berkeley, The Bancroft Library, Manuscripts Division.
Dowd (1906-?) reminisces about her life in Mill Valley, CA.

451. Draper, Barbara M.
Papers. 1955. 1 binder.
Open. No guide.
University of California, Berkeley, The Bancroft Library, Manuscripts Division.
Script for a television program about the geological formation and paleontology of the Yampa Canyon, which is part of Dinosaur National Monument in Utah; the early history of the region; and Indians of the area. Includes photos and notes on the history of the Yampa and Green Rivers.

452. Drinkwater, Sarah Bradley (Merrill)
Papers. 1843-68. 24 folders.
Open. No guide.
University of California, Berkeley, The Bancroft Library, Manuscripts Division.
Letters which Drinkwater wrote to her family in Maine while she was on a trip to California in 1865 and 1866, letters to her from her husband Captain Leoline Howell Drinkwater, and an 1898 history of the Drinkwater family by Louis Bond Mason.

453. Drobish, Harry Everett
Papers. 1917-54. 13 boxes, 6 cartons, 3 vols., and 1 microfilm reel.
Open. Key.
University of California, Berkeley, The Bancroft Library, Manuscripts Division.
Correspondence of Drobish (1893-1954), an agricultural extension adviser for the University of California, farm labor chief, and state senator from Butte County from 1947 to 1950, includes letters from Helen (Gahagan) Douglas; the American Temperance Society; the California Council of Republican Women, Southern Division; the LWV of California; the Native Daughters of the Golden West; and others.

454. Duncan, Robert Edward
Papers. Ca. 1938-69. 1 box.
Open. No guide.
University of California, Berkeley, The Bancroft Library, Manuscripts Division.
Includes letters to Duncan from Mary Fabilli, Pauline Kael, Anaïs Nin, and Laura Riding.

455. Dunlap, Katherine
Papers. 1864-65. 48-page item.
Open. Published guide.
University of California, Berkeley, The Bancroft Library, Manuscripts Division.
Journal by Dunlap gives a detailed account of a journey in 1864 from Council Bluffs, IA, to Bannack City, MT, and includes an incomplete letter concerning Montana's resources with a comment added by Dunlap's husband. Also available on microfilm. See Dale L. Morgan and George P. Hammond, eds., *A Guide to the Manuscript Collections of The Bancroft Library,* vol. I (Berkeley, CA: University of California Press, 1963).

456. Dunnell, John Henry
Papers. 1849-58. 1 portfolio.
Open. No guide.
University of California, Berkeley, The Bancroft Library, Manuscripts Division.
Correspondence of Dunnell (1813-1904), including letters from his wife Harriet (Baldwin) Dunnell and family in New York.

457. Durant Family
Papers. 1845-82. 1 portfolio.
Open. No guide.
University of California, Berkeley, The Bancroft Library, Manuscripts Division.
Includes a letter from Mary E. (Buffett) [Mrs. Henry] Durant, an early settler of California, to her cousins in which she describes her trip to California via Panama on board the steamship *Sierra Nevada.*

458. Earl Warren and the State Department of Mental Hygiene
Oral history. 1970-71. 246-page vol.
Open. No guide.
University of California, Berkeley, The Bancroft Library, Manuscripts Division.
Includes an interview with Portia (Bell) Hume concerning her involvement in the development of mental health services, the early days of the Langley Porter Neuropsychiatric Institute, her role as director of community services in the state department of mental hygiene, the political career of her father Theodore Bell, and her husband Samuel James Hume, a faculty member and director of the Greek Theatre at the University of California, Berkeley.

459. Earth's the Right Place for Love: A Portrait of the '60s
Oral history. 1970. 1 tape.
Open. No guide.
University of California, Berkeley, The Bancroft Library, Manuscripts Division.
Recording of dramatic readings selected from poetry, songs, and news commentaries of the 1960s and performed with music. The production, written and directed by Barbara Mertes, who holds a PhD, and presented by the Readers Theatre Group of Chabot College in Hayward, CA, relates to politics, civil rights, the Vietnam War, drugs, sex, and the generation gap.

460. Eastman and Smith Family
Papers. Ca. 1842-1915. 1 portfolio.
Open. No guide.

University of California, Berkeley, The Bancroft Library, Manuscripts Division.
Includes reminiscences of Lucy Ann (Eastman) Smith.

461. Eastman, Sophia A. (Eastman)
Papers. 1854. 1 portfolio.
Open. No guide.
University of California, Berkeley, The Bancroft Library, Manuscripts Division.
Letters from [Mrs. Harrison] Eastman to her family relate primarily to family matters and contain some descriptive comment on San Francisco and on economic conditions.

462. Eaton Family
Papers. 1862-1906. 1 portfolio.
Open. No guide.
University of California, Berkeley, The Bancroft Library, Manuscripts Division.
Includes letters which Vesta Marie (Eaton) Smith Daniels (?-1926), the daughter of Colonel Willard Gould Eaton, wrote her daughter and grandson Elton E. Merrifield in 1906 describing her situation and that of other refugees from San Francisco.

463. The Eddy Breeding Station: Institute of Forest Genetics
Oral history. 1967-68. 174-page item.
Open. No guide.
University of California, Berkeley, The Bancroft Library, Manuscripts Division.
Includes an interview with Gladys Austin, the widow of the Institute's first director Lloyd Austin, as well as letters, photos, and other material.

464. Edwards, Sara K. (Upton)
Papers. 1872. 1 item.
Open. No guide.
University of California, Berkeley, The Bancroft Library, Manuscripts Division.
Letter from Edwards to her sister Louise [Mrs. Kellogg B.] Finley of West Point, NY, in which she describes a visit at the home of Jessie (Benton) [Mrs. John Charles] Frémont in Tarrytown, NY.

465. Egbert, Eliza Ann (McAuley)
Papers. 1852. 58-page item.
Open. No guide.
University of California, Berkeley, The Bancroft Library, Manuscripts Division.
Consists of a diary in which Egbert (1835-?) records her journey across the plains from Iowa to California in 1852. Also available on microfilm.

466. Eggleston, Arthur Dupuy
Papers. 1935-41. 2 boxes and 2 cartons.
Open. Key.
University of California, Berkeley, The Bancroft Library, Manuscripts Division.
Papers of Eggleston (1899-1959) include a letter from Dorothea Lange in 1940 and letters from Mildred Bowen in 1938 and 1939 on behalf of the United Fisherman's Union of the Pacific.

467. Eggleston, William Green
Papers. Ca. 1891-1937. 3 boxes and 5 cartons.
Open. Key.
University of California, Berkeley, The Bancroft Library, Manuscripts Division.
Includes letters to Eggleston (1859-1937) from his wife Blanche (Stokes) Eggleston, his niece Elizabeth, and Margaret Wade (Campbell) [Mrs. Lorin Fuller] Deland.

468. Ehlers, Alice
Oral history. 1965-66. 442-page transcript.
Open. No guide.
University of California, Berkeley, The Bancroft Library, Manuscripts Division.
Ehlers (1887-?), a harpsichordist, discusses her musical career, her association with Albert Schweitzer, teaching at the University of Southern California, and her recollections of Alban Berg, Arnold Schoenberg, Wanda Landowska, Paul Hindemith, and other musicians. Included are translations of some of her correspondence with Schweitzer from 1932 to 1965 and photos.

469. Ehrman, Elizabeth (Bissinger)
Oral history. 1972. 16-page item.
Open. No guide.
University of California, Berkeley, The Bancroft Library, Manuscripts Division.
Ehrman, a resident of Atherton, CA, since 1908, describes the community, its early residents, and her home and comments on the Bissinger family.

470. Erskine, Dorothy (Ward)
Oral history. 1971. 1 tape.
Open. Description.
University of California, Berkeley, The Bancroft Library, Manuscripts Division.
[Mrs.] Erskine comments on the history of the San Francisco Planning and Urban Renewal Association, housing planning, and environmental issues.

471. Evans, Nora
Oral history. 1969. 22-page transcript.
Open. No guide.
University of California, Berkeley, The Bancroft Library, Manuscripts Division.
Evans (1887-?) reminisces about her life in Mill Valley, CA, from 1913 to 1968, first as a weekend resident and later as a permanent resident; she also comments on the 1929 Mt. Tamalpais fire. A photo is included.

472. Fabiola Hospital Association
Records. 1884-1952. 2 boxes and 1 vol.
Open. No guide.
University of California, Berkeley, The Bancroft Library, Manuscripts Division.
Accounts; correspondence; scrapbooks about medical affairs in Oakland, CA; and other material from the estate papers of Catherine (Chabot) [Mrs. J. P. H.] Dunn, the last president of the Association, which was founded in 1884. Records relate chiefly to organization of this Oakland hospital, its property, and its merger in 1938 with the Samuel Merritt Hospital and include some items from the Oakland Homeopathic Hospital and Dispensary Association.

473. Farquhar, Francis Peloubet
Papers. Nd. 5 boxes and 10 cartons.
Open. Key.
University of California, Berkeley, The Bancroft Library, Manuscripts Division.
Papers relate primarily to the National Parks and include letters, notes, articles, clippings, and printed material of Alice Eastwood and Caroline Wenzel and items about women in the Sierra.

474. Ferré, Ella
Papers. Nd. 1 vol.
Open. No guide.
University of California, Berkeley, The Bancroft Library, Manuscripts Division.
Includes manuscript poems by Ferré.

475. Field, Isobel (Osbourne) Strong
Papers. Nd. 1 vol.
Open. No guide.
University of California, Berkeley, The Bancroft Library, Manuscripts Division.
Notes written in a printed book on French grammar.

476. Field, Sara Bard
Papers. 1929-36. 1 portfolio.
Open. No guide.
University of California, Berkeley, The Bancroft Library, Manuscripts Division.
Letters written to Amy Requa Long by Field (1882-1974), an author who was married to Charles Erskine Scott Wood.

477. Fish Family
Papers. 1835-1913. 1 microfilm reel.
Open. No guide.
University of California, Berkeley, The Bancroft Library, Manuscripts Division.
Scrapbook of letters, clippings, and other papers of Charles Fish, his brother Lafayette, his sisters Caroline and Cornelia, and other family members. Much of the material relates to ranching in Contra Costa County, CA, and to bringing large herds of sheep overland in the 1850s.

478. Fish, Mary C.
Papers. 1860. 128-page item.
Open. No guide.
University of California, Berkeley, The Bancroft Library, Manuscripts Division.
Diary of Fish gives an account of a journey from Cedar Grove, IA, to California and includes a description of Salt Lake City, miscellaneous accounts, and recipes. Also available on microfilm.

479. Fisher, Lillian E.
Papers. Nd. 1 box.
Open. No guide.
University of California, Berkeley, The Bancroft Library, Manuscripts Division.
Papers of Fisher, who is a professor of history.

480. Fitch Family
Papers. 1829-86. 6 vols.
Open. Key.
University of California, Berkeley, The Bancroft Library, Manuscripts Division.
Includes correspondence, accounts, and legal papers for the period 1849 to 1886 of Josefa (Carrillo) de Fitch (1810-?), who was the wife of Henry Delano Fitch (1799-1849). Henry Fitch was born in Massachusetts and came to California, where he became a naturalized Mexican citizen; a grantee of Sotoyomi Rancho near San Francisco, he held various municipal positions.

481. Floyd-Jones Family
Papers. 1848-78. 2 portfolios.
Open. Key.
University of California, Berkeley, The Bancroft Library, Manuscripts Division.
Includes letters by Helen Watts (DeLancey) [Mrs. Henry] Floyd-Jones (?-1872), Isabelle (Mizner) [Mrs. Charles] Floyd-Jones, Sarah Floyd-Jones, Julia Clinton Jones, and Mary (Lord) [Mrs. Edward] Floyd-Jones (?-1874), who died of consumption. Mary Floyd-Jones's letters concern her trip from New York to San Francisco via Panama on the steamers *Henry Chauncey* and the *Constitution.*

482. Foote, Mary Anna (Hallock)
Papers. 1868-1915. 5 microfilm reels.
Open. No guide.
University of California, Berkeley, The Bancroft Library, Manuscripts Division.
Letters by [Mrs. Arthur De Wint] Foote (1847-1938), an author, to her friends and family.

483. Fowler, Mrs. Warren R.
Papers. 1884. 8-page item.
Open. Published guide.
University of California, Berkeley, The Bancroft Library, Manuscripts Division.
Dictation by Fowler (ca. 1820-?) concerns her move in 1860 to Cañon City, CO, with her husband. Also available on microfilm. See Dale L. Morgan and George P. Hammond, eds., *A Guide to the Manuscript Collections of The Bancroft Library,* vol. I (Berkeley, CA: University of California Press, 1963).

484. Francis, Myrtle (Shepherd)
Papers. Nd. 1 box.
Open. No guide.

University of California, Berkeley, The Bancroft Library, Manuscripts Division.
Biographical sketch by Francis of her mother Theodosia Burr (Hall) Shepherd (1854-1906) and photos.

485. Frank, Nan, and Sheldon, Irene
Oral history. 1969. 1 portfolio and 1 tape.
Open. No guide.
University of California, Berkeley, The Bancroft Library, Manuscripts Division.
Interview with [Mrs. Ludwig] Frank and [Mrs. Edwin] Sheldon concerns the San Francisco LWV and board of education and includes discussion of the method of appointing members to the board, the work of the Public Education Society in awakening San Francisco to educational needs, Sheldon's efforts as a school board member to prevent "released" time for religious education, and women who worked for the San Francisco Center.

486. Franklin, Lucy A. (Harrison)
Papers. 1856-77. 5 folders.
Open. No guide.
University of California, Berkeley, The Bancroft Library, Manuscripts Division.
Business and personal correspondence of Franklin (?-1882), a resident of Tuolumne County, CA, and a letter from Isa (Franklin) Beaumont.

487. Frederickson, Hansena
Oral history. Ca. 1966. 1 vol.
Access restricted. No guide.
University of California, Berkeley, The Bancroft Library, Manuscripts Division.
Transcript of interview with Frederickson concerns her career as an administrator at the University of California, Los Angeles, from 1936 to 1966.

488. Frémont Family
Papers. Ca. 1839-1927. 5 boxes and 5 vols.
Open. Key.
University of California, Berkeley, The Bancroft Library, Manuscripts Division.
Papers of John Charles Frémont (1813-90), his wife Jessie (Benton) Frémont, and their children Elizabeth, Francis, and John. Includes correspondence, memoirs, notes, a will, legal papers, scrapbooks of clippings, and obituaries of Jessie Frémont; her memoirs concern her father Thomas Hart Benton, her upbringing in Missouri and Washington, DC, and her life with her husband. Also includes correspondence, memoirs, notes, bills, greeting cards, and scrapbooks of clippings of Elizabeth Benton Frémont and a manuscript about the life of John C. Frémont by his wife Jessie Frémont and son Francis Frémont, which was intended as a sequel to his autobiography.

489. Fulkerth, Abby E.
Papers. 1863. 76-page item.
Open. No guide.
University of California, Berkeley, The Bancroft Library, Manuscripts Division.
Diary in which Fulkerth describes her journey from Milton, IA, to Mead Springs, CA, with her husband William Fulkerth.

490. Funk, Helen (Muir)
Papers. 1911-63. 1 portfolio.
Open. No guide.
University of California, Berkeley, The Bancroft Library, Manuscripts Division.
Letters by Funk, the daughter of John Muir, to her childhood friend Hattie Joost contain references to her father, other family members, and the Muir home in Martinez, CA.

491. Gage, Helen Sommer
Oral history. 1973. 43-page item.
Open. No guide.
University of California, Berkeley, The Bancroft Library, Manuscripts Division.
Gage (1888-?) reminisces about Prattville, CA, and Warner Valley, CA; her family and friends, including Annie (Kennedy) Bidwell and her husband John Bidwell; and Indians living in the area.

492. Gallagher, Mary Eleanora
Papers. 1919-55. 1 box, 1 vol., 1 tape, and 1 portfolio.
Open. No guide.
University of California, Berkeley, The Bancroft Library, Manuscripts Division.
Tape and transcript of a 1955 interview with Gallagher (1883-1966) in which she describes her early life, Socialist and International Workers of the World influences on her, her work on behalf of various radicals, the Workers' Defense League, and her husband Douglas Robson. Also included are the manuscript of a play by Gallagher based on the Tom Mooney case and photos, articles, clippings, and other material relating to the IWW, Lena Morrow Lewis, and various labor and Socialist leaders. Part of collection available on microfilm.

493. García, Marcelino
Papers. 1877. 2 items.
Open. No guide.
University of California, Berkeley, The Bancroft Library, Manuscripts Division.
Item removed from a manuscript about General Manuel Micheltoreno consists of Francisca Gómez's description of a ball given in 1836 in Santa Barbara. Also on microfilm.

494. Gattini, Pearl (Heckman)
Oral history. 1970. 8-page item.
Open. No guide.
University of California, Berkeley, The Bancroft Library, Manuscripts Division.
Gattini (1886-?) gives her recollections of Mill Valley, CA. She arrived in the community in 1904.

495. Gatzert and Schwabacher Family
Papers. 1878-1945. 4 vols.
Open. Published guide.
University of California, Berkeley, The Bancroft Library, Manuscripts Division.
Papers of Babette (Schwabacher) Gatzert and her husband Bailey Gatzert, who were residents of Seattle. The Schwabacher family was prominent in Seattle and San Francisco business circles. See Dale L. Morgan and George P. Hammond, eds., *A Guide to the Manuscript Collections of The Bancroft Library,* vol. I (Berkeley, CA: University of California Press, 1963).

496. Gauld, Charles Anderson
Papers. 1958. 1 vol.
Open. No guide.
University of California, Berkeley, The Bancroft Library, Manuscripts Division.
Biographical sketch of [Mrs.] Josephine (Whitney) Duveneck (1891-), a Quaker of Palo Alto, CA, who was involved with civil rights, education, and minority groups; letters by Frank Quinn of the American Friends Service Committee concerning Duveneck's work with California Indians; a report; photos; and clippings.

497. Gay, Theresa
Oral history. 1958. 1 portfolio.
Open. No guide.
University of California, Berkeley, The Bancroft Library, Manuscripts Division.
Interviews with residents of Trinity County, CA, relate to the early history of the county, gold mining, lumbering, bears, and the Chinese and Indians who resided there.

498. Giffen, Helen (Smith)
Papers. 1939-40. 235-page vol.
Open. No guide.
University of California, Berkeley, The Bancroft Library, Manuscripts Division.
Typescript of *The Life of General Mariano Guadalupe Vallejo, the Portrait of a Man of His Times* (Los Angeles, 1940) by Giffen (1893-?), an author.

499. Gillhouse, Eva Olenna
Papers. 1949-52. 1 carton.
Open. Published guide.
University of California, Berkeley, The Bancroft Library, Manuscripts Division.
Papers of Gillhouse, an author, include a manuscript of her book *Pistol Pete, the Autobiography of Frank Eaton* and other material pertaining to the book, including correspondence about her research, correspondence with the publisher, and notes, pictures, and maps of the Cherokee Strip in the last quarter of the 19th century. See Dale L. Morgan and George P. Hammond, eds., *A Guide to the Manuscript Collections of The Bancroft Library,* vol. I (Berkeley, CA: University of California Press, 1963).

500. Gillis Family
Papers. Ca. 1880-1954. 4 cartons and 1 vol.
Open. Unpublished guide.
University of California, Berkeley, The Bancroft Library, Manuscripts Division.
Includes personal papers of Ethel L. [Mrs. Claude E.] Gillis and of her mother-in-law Anna [Mrs. Hudson B.] Gillis, both of whom were residents of Yreka in Siskiyou County, CA, and minutes by Ethel Gillis of the Yreka Elementary School Board, 1941-47.

501. Girls' Club
Records. Ca. 1908-40. 2 boxes.
Open. No guide.
University of California, Berkeley, The Bancroft Library, Manuscripts Division.
Records assembled by Leah Selix, a former member of the Club, which was located in San Francisco, include photos; scrapbook of dance, music, and theater programs and clippings; bulletins of the Club; and clippings and other information about former members. Also includes material of the Mission Neighborhood Centers, Inc., of which the Club became a part in 1942.

502. Gnagi, Elvira (Marsh)
Papers. 1884. 1 microfilm reel.
Open. No guide.
University of California, Berkeley, The Bancroft Library, Manuscripts Division.
Diary with daily entries by Gnagi (1830-1910), a housewife who lived in a vineyard in Mountain Home, CA, near Saratoga.

503. Goodyear Family
Papers. 1830-81. 1 portfolio.
Open. No guide.
University of California, Berkeley, The Bancroft Library, Manuscripts Division.
Includes letters from Andrew Goodyear and his wife Cynthia (Vaughn) Goodyear (1835-1901) to his sister and niece in Connecticut.

504. The Governor and the Public, the Press, and the Legislature
Oral history. 1970-72. 1 vol.
Open. No guide.
University of California, Berkeley, The Bancroft Library, Manuscripts Division.
Interviews with three individuals involved in the operation of the California governor's office during the Earl Warren administration include one with Marguerite Gallagher, who discusses the attorney general's office, her political work during conventions and between campaigns, and

administrative procedures in Warren's office from 1938 to 1953.

505. Grabhorn, Jane Bissell
Oral history. 1965. 2 vols. and 1 tape.
Open. No guide.
University of California, Berkeley, The Bancroft Library, Manuscripts Division.
Interview with Grabhorn (1911-73) concerns her career as a printer, in particular her first imprint the Jumbo Press and founding of the Colt Press in 1938 with William M. Roth. Also included are clippings from San Francisco newspapers on the Grabhorn Press and the catalog of an exhibition of her typographic work.

506. Grace Female Institute
Records. 1864-68. 61-page vol.
Open. No guide.
University of California, Berkeley, The Bancroft Library, Manuscripts Division.
Handwritten roll book recording attendance at this San Francisco school.

507. Graff Family
Papers. 1941-54. 3 cartons.
Open. Key.
University of California, Berkeley, The Bancroft Library, Manuscripts Division.
Consists primarily of papers of Louise (Boepple) [Mrs. Ulrich] Graff relating to her activities in San Francisco women's clubs, especially the California Federation of Women's Clubs. Graff served as secretary, vice-president, and president of the San Francisco city and county branches of the California Federation. Correspondence, diaries, notebooks, financial records, scrapbooks, and other papers of Graff as well as constitution, bylaws, minutes, financial records, and other organizational records of various branches of the Federation. Also includes reports and other records of La Mesa Redonda Club of San Francisco.

508. Grant, Blanche Chloe
Papers. 1922-23. 68-page vol.
Open. Published guide.
University of California, Berkeley, The Bancroft Library, Manuscripts Division.
Biographical sketches of Taos, NM, artists by Grant (1874-?) include one of Burt and Elizabeth Harwood. See Dale L. Morgan and George P. Hammond, eds., *A Guide to the Manuscript Collections of The Bancroft Library,* vol. I (Berkeley, CA: University of California Press, 1963).

509. Graupner Family
Papers. 1886-1962. 3 boxes, 7 cartons, and 5 vols.
Open. Key.
University of California, Berkeley, The Bancroft Library, Manuscripts Division.
Includes papers of Annabel Elise (Wenzelburger) [Mrs. Adolphus Earhart] Graupner, a 1902 graduate of the University of California who was active in the Republican party, the California Civic League, the American Association for Study and Prevention of Infant Mortality, and other civic and charitable organizations. Her papers contain correspondence with the State Anti-Saloon League of Northern and Central California, the AAUW, Lucy (Sprague) Mitchell, Carrie Chapman Catt, and others; notes; scrapbooks of invitations, grade cards, programs, and clippings; financial reports, membership lists, and other records of the California Alumni Association; and subject files on kindergartens, peace, the National Woman's party, and other topics.

510. Gravander, Valborg (Mattson)
Oral history. 1970. 15-page item.
Open. No guide.
University of California, Berkeley, The Bancroft Library, Manuscripts Division.
Gravander (1888-?) comments on the Swedish Center she and her husband established in San Francisco; their move to Mill Valley, CA, in 1945; and her interest in crafts. Photos are included.

511. Gray, Maria (Willey)
Papers. 1927. 1 item.
Open. No guide.
University of California, Berkeley, The Bancroft Library, Manuscripts Division.
Letter from Gray to Herbert I. Priestly in which she reminisces about the early days of Berkeley, the University of California, and her father Samuel Hopkins Willey.

512. Grayson, Andrew Jackson
Papers. 1844-1901. 23 boxes and 2 microfilm reels.
Open. Key.
University of California, Berkeley, The Bancroft Library, Manuscripts Division.
Includes letters by Grayson (1819-69) and his wife Frances Jane (Timmons) Grayson (1823-1908), who married George Belden Crane after Andrew Grayson's death, and an account of an overland trip to California in 1846 by the Graysons and their infant son Edward. Her letters relate to Andrew Grayson's work and to her attempts to publish his portfolio of drawings.

513. Green, Mrs. Will S.
Papers. Nd. 1 vol.
Open. No guide.
University of California, Berkeley, The Bancroft Library, Manuscripts Division.
Scrapbook pertains to the Winnie Davis Chapter of the United Daughters of the Confederacy in Colusa, CA.

514. Green, Sallie B. (Morgan)
Papers. Nd. 1 vol.
Open. No guide.
University of California, Berkeley, The Bancroft Library, Manuscripts Division.
Scrapbook relating to the Civil War contains clippings pasted over ledger entries for the years 1884 to 1888.

515. Greenfield, Margaret
Papers. 1958-63. 1 portfolio.
Open. No guide.
University of California, Berkeley, The Bancroft Library, Manuscripts Division.
Correspondence of Greenfield with Governor Edmund G. Brown concerns the Aid to Dependent Children Program.

516. Greenwood Family
Papers. Nd. 1 portfolio.
Open. No guide.
University of California, Berkeley, The Bancroft Library, Manuscripts Division.
Includes notes on Britton Greenwood and the Donner Party by Mary Antonia (Greenwood) Reinking and her daughter Erma (Reinking) King.

517. Griffith, Alice
Papers. 1936-55. 1 portfolio.
Open. No guide.
University of California, Berkeley, The Bancroft Library, Manuscripts Division.
Papers of [Miss] Griffith, who worked for housing rights in San Francisco, include a letter from James P. Shaw, director of the Hunters Point Project Committee; a letter by Griffith to Catherine (Bauer) [Mrs. William Wilson] Wurster concerning the first Telegraph Hill Neighborhood House in San Francisco; and a speech by Griffith.

518. Grinnell, Joseph
Papers. Nd. 5 cartons.
Open. No guide.
University of California, Berkeley, The Bancroft Library, Manuscripts Division.
Papers of Grinnell (1877-1939) include correspondence of his wife Hilda (Wood) Grinnell relating to her interest in conservation and ornithology.

519. Grover, Sherwood
Oral history. 1970. 1 vol.
Open. No guide.
University of California, Berkeley, The Bancroft Library, Manuscripts Division.
Interviews with Sherwood and Katharine (Carruth) Grover (1911-) concern their work for the Grabhorn Press from 1934 to 1962; the establishment of their own press, the Grace Hoper Press; and the small private press movement. Also includes photos.

520. Grunsky Family
Papers. 1830-1960. 2 boxes, 3 cartons, 1 portfolio, and 6 card files.
Open. Key.
University of California, Berkeley, The Bancroft Library, Manuscripts Division.
Diaries and letters to their families by Charles Grunsky and Josephine Fredericke Clotilde (Camerer) Grunsky (1830-64) edited by their granddaughter Clotilde (Grunsky) Taylor (1891-); correspondence and other papers of Clotilde (Grunsky) Taylor; and correspondence of Charlotte Fredericke Grunsky (1853-1920?).

521. Guenther, Adaline C.
Oral history. 1974. 434-page item.
Open. No guide.
University of California, Berkeley, The Bancroft Library, Manuscripts Division.
Guenther (1897-) discusses her work as executive secretary of the University Religious Conference at the University of California, Los Angeles; projects sponsored by the Conference; formation of the Student Religious Board; former students; and clergymen. Includes photos.

522. Gundlach, Anita (Hinz)
Papers. Nd. 16 cartons.
Partially restricted. Key.
University of California, Berkeley, The Bancroft Library, Manuscripts Division.
Papers of Gundlach (1875-1955) include business and personal correspondence, diaries of a trip to Europe in 1891 and 1892, estate papers, receipts and bills, photos, autograph albums, family history, invitations, Christmas cards, programs, pamphlets, clippings, and a partial translation by her of her father-in-law Jacob Gundlach's diary of his voyage to San Francisco in 1850 and 1851. Also includes correspondence of her husband Heini Gundlach, her father August C. Hinz and stepmother Dora Wieger Hinz, her sister Helene (Hinz) [Mrs. Edwin W.] Davis, her daughter Alexandra Gundlach, and her nieces Dorothy (Davis) Boyich and Jane Buttler.

523. Haas, Elise (Stern)
Papers. Nd. 1 portfolio.
Open. No guide.
University of California, Berkeley, The Bancroft Library, Manuscripts Division.
Includes letters from Alice B. Toklas.

524. Haase, Ynez
Papers. 1956. 17-page item.
Open. Published guide.
University of California, Berkeley, The Bancroft Library, Manuscripts Division.
Daily record kept by Haase during an 11-day trip down the Colorado River rapids from Lees Ferry, AZ, to Temple Bar, AZ. The party of 15 included three women. See Dale L. Morgan and George P. Hammond, eds., *A Guide to the Manuscript Collections of The Bancroft Library,* vol. I (Berkeley, CA: University of California Press, 1963).

525. Hagar, Ella (Barrows)
Oral history. 1972-73. 299-page item.
Open. No guide.
University of California, Berkeley, The Bancroft Library, Manuscripts Division.
Hagar (1898-) reminisces about her childhood in the Philippines; her father David Prescott Barrows; attending the University of California, Berkeley, from 1915 to 1919; her marriage to Gerald Hanna Hagar; her role as the wife of a University regent; and her association with the YWCA and with various other organizations, committees, and volunteer groups. Includes photos.

526. Hall, Harvey Monroe
Papers. 1896-1932. 3 boxes and 1 carton.
Open. No guide.
University of California, Berkeley, The Bancroft Library, Manuscripts Division.
Hall (1874-1932) and his wife Carlotta (Case) Hall (1880-?) were botanists at the University of California and co-authors of *A Yosemite Flora.* Includes correspondence between the Halls and letters from their daughter Martha (Hall) Niccolls (1916-?) and from Katharine Brandegee, Alice Eastwood, Florence Augusta (Merriam) [Mrs. Vernon] Bailey, and Louise Kellogg.

527. Hall, Maggie
Papers. 1853. 14-page item.
Open. No guide.
University of California, Berkeley, The Bancroft Library, Manuscripts Division.
Journal of an overland journey to California from Texas in 1853 when Hall was about 9 years old.

528. Hanna, Esther Belle
Papers. 1852. 34-page item.
Open. Published guide.
University of California, Berkeley, The Bancroft Library, Manuscripts Division.
Diary kept by Hanna on a journey from Pittsburgh to Oregon City, OR, via St. Joseph, the Sublette Cutoff, the south bank of the Snake, and the Barlow Road. See Dale L. Morgan and George P. Hammond, eds., *A Guide to the Manuscript Collections of The Bancroft Library,* vol. I (Berkeley, CA: University of California Press, 1963).

529. Hare, Alice Iola
Papers. 1857-1926. 1 box.
Open. No guide.
University of California, Berkeley, The Bancroft Library, Manuscripts Division.
Papers of Hare include letters pertaining chiefly to education in early Santa Clara, CA; manuscripts of her writings; attendance books for a Santa Clara school for the years 1857 to 1863; and clippings.

530. Harland, Hester (Lambert)
Papers. 1888-1911. 1 box.
Open. No guide.
University of California, Berkeley, The Bancroft Library, Manuscripts Division.
Correspondence, articles, minutes, accounts, handbills, and leaflets relate to woman's suffrage in California from 1888 to 1911. Includes articles by Harland on woman's suffrage and on Lucy Stone; minutes and accounts, 1910-11, of the Berkeley Suffrage Campaign Committee; and letters from May L. Cheney, Anna Scott, Helen M. Wixson, and the California Equal Suffrage Association.

531. Harroun, Margaret
Papers. Ca. 1915-20. 1 vol.
Open. No guide.
University of California, Berkeley, The Bancroft Library, Manuscripts Division.
Scrapbook of Harroun contains photos and clippings relating to early Hollywood movie stars and some answers to fan letters.

532. Hart and Clark
Papers. 1869-1903. 6 boxes.
Open. Key.
University of California, Berkeley, The Bancroft Library, Manuscripts Division.
Letters of Jerome Alfred Hart (1854-1937) and Ann Clark (1871-?) before and after their marriage pertain to Hart's editorship of the *Argonaut* and to San Francisco social life in the 1890s. Also includes letters by Lillie (Hitchcock) Coit, Isabella Duncan Clark, and other members of the Clark family.

533. Harvey, Angelina
Papers. 1863. 1 item.
Open. No guide.
University of California, Berkeley, The Bancroft Library, Manuscripts Division.
Letter from Harvey to her cousin Mary Ann Wheaton in which she describes crossing the Isthmus of Panama on her voyage to California, her arrival in San Francisco, and her trip to Stockton and then Jamestown, CA.

534. Harvey, Eloisa (McLaughlin) Rae
Papers. 1878. 39-page item.
Open. Published guide.
University of California, Berkeley, The Bancroft Library, Manuscripts Division.
Interview with Harvey (1817-84), who was married first to William Glenn Rae and later to Daniel Harvey. She describes life at Fort Vancouver, Stikine, and Yerba Buena, CA, and talks about her father John McLaughlin, who was governor of the Hudson's Bay Company's possessions on the Pacific Slope at Fort Vancouver. Also available on microfilm. See Dale L. Morgan and George P. Hammond, eds., *A Guide to the Manuscript Collections of The Bancroft Library,* vol. I (Berkeley, CA: University of California Press, 1963).

535. Haskell Family
Papers. 1878-1951. 12 boxes and 7 vols.
Open. Key.
University of California, Berkeley, The Bancroft Library, Manuscripts Division.
Includes correspondence of Maria Antoinette (Briggs) Haskell and Edward Wilder Haskell to their children; courtship letters of Jennie Helen Cryer and Edward Prince Haskell; and correspondence, reminiscences, drawings, and school papers of Helen (Haskell) Thomas (1860-1942), including letters to Stephen Seymour Thomas before their marriage. Papers of Anna (Fader) Haskell (1858-1942) include correspondence, teaching certificates, her 1882 marriage contract, photos, a scrapbook, a hymnbook, and 62 volumes of her diaries for the years 1876 to 1942, which concern life in San Francisco and Kaweah, her husband Burnette Gregor Haskell, labor unions such as the Coast Seamen's Union, the International Workmen's Association and other socialist groups, and the Naturalist Club of San Francisco. Also includes correspondence, an autobiographical sketch, manuscripts and poems, a bankbook and canceled checks, notes relating to the Fader and Hayden families, photos, clippings, and other papers of Anne Keith (Hayden) Fader Field (1835-96), who was the mother of Anna (Fader) Haskell.

536. Hastings, John Russel
Papers. 1909-42. 1 carton.
Open. Key.
University of California, Berkeley, The Bancroft Library, Manuscripts Division.
Correspondence of Hastings (1878-1942), a newspaper editor, concerns playwriting and includes items from Minnie Maddern Fiske and Helen Ware.

537. Hawkins, Helen Lyon
Papers. Nd. 1 box.
Open. No guide.
University of California, Berkeley, The Bancroft Library, Manuscripts Division.
Notes for Hawkins's one-act play *The New Idea,* which was based on the life of [Miss] Lotta Crabtree in the 1860s.

538. Hawkins, Helen Lyon
Papers. 1955. 2 vols.
Open. Published guide.
University of California, Berkeley, The Bancroft Library, Manuscripts Division.
Papers of Hawkins, an author, include a manuscript of her novel *Fear Is the Enemy,* material used in its preparation, and notes concerning Fort Simcoe, Indians, and Washington pioneers. Also available on microfilm. See Dale L. Morgan and George P. Hammond, eds., *A Guide to the Manuscript Collections of The Bancroft Library,* vol. I (Berkeley, CA: University of California Press, 1963).

539. Hayler, Guy, Family
Papers. Nd. 1 box and 7 vols.
Open. No guide.
University of California, Berkeley, The Bancroft Library, Manuscripts Division.
Includes a scrapbook of [Mrs.] Mollie B. Hayler pertaining to her involvement with the PTA in San Francisco and with the Women's International League for Peace and Freedom and to her lectures on science of the mind.

540. Hearst, Phoebe (Apperson)
Papers. Ca. 1864-1918. 60 boxes, 19 cartons, and 1 portfolio.
Open. Key.
University of California, Berkeley, The Bancroft Library, Manuscripts Division.
Hearst (1842-1919) was born in Franklin County, MO, and in 1862 married George Hearst (1820-91), a Missourian who had amassed a fortune by speculating in California and Nevada during the gold rush. They moved to California where their only child William Randolph Hearst was born in 1863. George Hearst was elected to the State Assembly in 1865 and 1866 and served in the US Senate from 1886 until his death. While living in Washington, DC, Phoebe Hearst helped to found the National Cathedral School for Girls and was involved in various other philanthropic activities. She returned to California after her husband's death and settled in a home she had built at Pleasanton, the Hacienda del Pozo de Verona.

Correspondence with family, friends, protégés, and organizations with which she was involved; diary fragments; biographical sketches; speeches; accounts; household expenses; subject files; photos; memorabilia; and clippings. Subject files relate to such topics as kindergartens and training schools for kindergarten teachers, free libraries, hospitals, orphanages, woman suffrage, the American Anthropological Association, and other organizations. Among the numerous correspondents are Alice Paul, Elizabeth (Cady) Stanton, Jane Addams, the National Congress of Mothers, and the YWCA.

Phoebe Hearst was a benefactor of the University of California and served on its board of regents from 1897 until her death. She also served on the board of directors of the GFWC and as president of the Century Club of San Francisco.

541. Heinlen Family
Papers. 1865-1916. 1 box.
Open. No guide.
University of California, Berkeley, The Bancroft Library, Manuscripts Division.
Includes diplomas from the University of the Pacific from 1880 and 1882 for Anna J. and Mary E. Heinlen.

542. Henry, Ann
Papers. 1847-82. 2 vols.
Open. No guide.
University of California, Berkeley, The Bancroft Library, Manuscripts Division.
Correspondence and scrapbook containing invitations of Henry, a young woman who lived in Mamaluke Hill in El Dorado County, CA.

543. Heyneman, Julie Helen
Papers. 1886-1942. 7 boxes, 2 cartons, 1 vol., and 1 portfolio.
Open. Key.
University of California, Berkeley, The Bancroft Library, Manuscripts Division.
[Miss] Heyneman (1868-?), an artist and writer, was born in San Francisco, studied art in Paris and London, and wrote and illustrated articles for San Francisco newspapers under the pen name Van Dyck Brown. In 1915 she founded the California House for Belgian soldiers, the first institution to give occupational training to disabled soldiers while they were still in the hospital. She also helped the British Red Cross found the Kitchener Houses for wounded British soldiers in 1917. Correspondence; manuscript short stories, novels, and articles; notes; sketches; photos; and clippings relating primarily to the California House and Kitchener Houses, to her friend and teacher John Singer Sargent, and to her biography of sculptor Arthur Putnam. Heyneman wrote *Woman at the Crossroads,* a survey of woman's position after WWI, in collaboration with Mary S. Allen. Correspondents include Ruth Draper, Una (Call) [Mrs. Robinson] Jeffers, Kathleen (Thompson) [Mrs. Charles Gilman] Norris, Margaret (James) [Mrs. Bruce] Porter, and Alma (de Bretteville) Spreckels.

544. History and Architecture of Berkeley
Oral history. 1968-72. 10 tapes.
Open. No guide.
University of California, Berkeley, The Bancroft Library, Manuscripts Division.
Interviews with Merodine (Keeler) McIntyre, Esther Merrill Fay, Dorothy W. Coblentz, Mrs. Harold P. Kelly, and others on the history and architecture of Berkeley from 1895 to 1941. Includes discussion of Charles A. Keeler, Julia Morgan, and the Berkeley fire of 1923 and notes pertaining to the interviews.

545. Hitchcock Family
Papers. Ca. 1835-85. 1 package and 2 portfolios.
Open. Shelflist.
University of California, Berkeley, The Bancroft Library, Manuscripts Division.
Correspondence, clippings, and other papers of Charles M. Hitchcock (?-1885), a physician, and his wife Martha Taliaferro (Hunter) Hitchcock. Papers of Martha Hitchcock include letters to her sister-in-law in 1851 and 1852 describing life in San Francisco; letters of introduction from 1860 to 1865 for a European tour; a letter from Maria Champe (Garnett) Garnett; and clippings about her daughter Eliza "Lillie" (Hitchcock) Coit (1843-1929). Estate papers of Lillie Coit include a family Bible with genealogical notes.

546. Hittell Family
Papers. Ca. 1855-1916. 1 box, 6 cartons, and 1 vol.
Open. Key.
University of California, Berkeley, The Bancroft Library, Manuscripts Division.
Papers of Elise Christine (Wiehe) [Mrs. Theodore Henry] Hittell (?-1900), who was active in the California Academy of Sciences and helped found the San Francisco Foundling Asylum and the Ladies Silk Culture Society of California, include correspondence, a diary for 1884 to 1888, notebooks, and sketches by her children Charles and Franklin. Also includes letters to her daughter Catherine, papers relating to the estate of Amelia Hittell, and papers of other members of the Hittell family.

547. Hockensmith, Mrs. M. S.
Papers. 1865-66. 55-page item.
Open. No guide.
University of California, Berkeley, The Bancroft Library, Manuscripts Division.
Diary by Hockensmith of an overland trip with her family in 1865 and 1866 from Summit, MS, to California. Includes her introduction, which explains the circumstances of the journey and identifies family members.

548. Hollister Family
Papers. Nd. 2 boxes and 4 vols.
Partially restricted. No guide.
University of California, Berkeley, The Bancroft Library, Manuscripts Division.
Correspondence and other papers of Lottie "Dot" (Steffens) Hollister (1872-1956) and John James Hollister and of their children Jane (Hollister) [Mrs. Joseph Balch] Wheelwright and John James Hollister, Jr.

549. Holmes, Hazel (Snell) Schreiber
Papers. Nd. 2 boxes.
Open. No guide.
University of California, Berkeley, The Bancroft Library, Manuscripts Division.
Correspondence and other papers of Holmes.

550. Holmes, Lulu H.
Oral history. 1966. 2 vols.
Open. No guide.
University of California, Berkeley, The Bancroft Library, Manuscripts Division.
Transcript of interviews with [Miss] Holmes in which she discusses her experiences as adviser from 1946 to 1948 to the Supreme Command of Allied Powers on higher education for women in Japan. Also included are correspondence, articles by Holmes, a report, and clippings.

551. Hooker Family
Papers. Ca. 1785-1950. 4 boxes.
Open. Unpublished guide.
University of California, Berkeley, The Bancroft Library, Manuscripts Division.
Papers of Katharine (Putnam) Hooker (1849-1935) and her daughter Marian Osgood Hooker include correspondence from Margaret (James) Porter, Alice (Gibbens) James, and others; notes and drafts of writings by Katharine Hooker; and items on the 1906 earthquake and fire in San Francisco.

552. Hooker, Katharine (Putnam)
Papers. 1927?. 529-page item.
Open. No guide.
University of California, Berkeley, The Bancroft Library, Manuscripts Division.
Manuscript by Hooker (1849-1935) of *Italian Sketches,* an account of her travels in Italy, with photos and sketches.

553. Hooven, Edna M.
Papers. Nd. 1 item.
Open. No guide.
University of California, Berkeley, The Bancroft Library, Manuscripts Division.
Typescript of an unpublished story by Hooven.

554. Horne, Mary Isabella (Hales)
Papers. 1884. 42-page item.
Open. Published guide.
University of California, Berkeley, The Bancroft Library, Manuscripts Division.
Interview with Horne (1818-1905) concerns her marriage to Joseph Horne; her conversion to Mormonism in 1836; her experiences in Missouri, Illinois, and Iowa; the migration to Utah in 1847; and life in Salt Lake Valley. Also available on microfilm. See Dale L. Morgan and George P. Hammond, eds., *A Guide to the Manuscript Collections of The Bancroft Library,* vol. I (Berkeley, CA: University of California Press, 1963).

555. Houston, Lyda Suydam
Oral history. 1970-71. 89-page item.
Open. No guide.
University of California, Berkeley, The Bancroft Library, Manuscripts Division.
Transcript of interview with Houston in which she discusses her missionary and teaching activities in Fukien province in China from 1924 to 1950 and life there under Japanese occupation and under the Communists.

556. Howard, Sidney Coe
Papers. Ca. 1903-39. 19 boxes and 19 cartons.
Open. Key.
University of California, Berkeley, The Bancroft Library, Manuscripts Division.
Correspondence; manuscript plays, short stories, articles, and motion picture scripts; financial records; contracts; biographical material; photos; clippings; and other papers of Howard (1891-1939), a playwright, author, and Hollywood script writer. Papers of his wife Leopoldine "Polly" Blaine (Damrosch) Howard include correspondence, diaries, plays and stories by her, a photo album, and clippings about the Damrosch family. Also includes correspondence and diaries of Sidney Howard's mother Helen Louise (Coe) [Mrs. John Lawrence] Howard. Correspondents include Sidney Howard's daughter Jennifer (Howard) Goldwyn, his sister Jean (Howard) [Mrs. Duncan] McDuffie, Mary (McLeod) Bethune, Willa Sibert Cather, Edna Ferber, Lillian Hellman, Margaret Mitchell, and Marjorie (Kinnan) Rawlings.

557. Hulme, Kathryn Cavarly
Papers. Nd. 249-page item.
Open. No guide.
University of California, Berkeley, The Bancroft Library, Manuscripts Division.
Typescript by Hulme (1900-), an author, of her novel *The Wild Place.*

558. Hult, Ruby El
Papers. Nd. 1 item.
Open. No guide.
University of California, Berkeley, The Bancroft Library, Manuscripts Division.
Manuscript of Jay Mahoney's reminiscences of his early theatrical experiences with Maud Miller and her father Joaquin Miller, as told to [Mrs.] Hult (1912-).

559. Hume, Emma L.
Papers. 1899-1927. 1 portfolio.
Open. No guide.
University of California, Berkeley, The Bancroft Library, Manuscripts Division.
Correspondence of Hume, including letters from Ninetta Eames Payne and Katherine Boyd concerning Charmian London and Frances (Fuller) Victor.

560. Hunt, Nancy (Zumwalt) Cotton
Papers. Ca. 1916. 1 item.
Open. No guide.
University of California, Berkeley, The Bancroft Library, Manuscripts Division.
Recollections by Hunt, which were published in 1916 in the *Overland Monthly,* concern her 1854 trip from Illinois to California by oxteam with her husband and family.

561. Huntington, Emily Harriett
Oral history. 1969-70. 1 vol.
Open. No guide.
University of California, Berkeley, The Bancroft Library, Manuscripts Division.
Huntington (1895-?) discusses her study of economics at the University of California, Berkeley, in the class of 1917; at the London School of

Economics; and at Radcliffe and Harvard. She also reminisces about teaching economics at the University of California from 1928 to 1961, her research work for the Heller committee, her interest in consumer economics and social insurance, her work during WWII in the wage stabilization division of the National War Labor Board, and the loyalty oath controversy. Includes photos.

562. Hyde, Mary Ann (Price)
Papers. 1880. 6-page item.
Open. Published guide.
University of California, Berkeley, The Bancroft Library, Manuscripts Division.
Autobiography of Hyde (1816-1900) concerns her conversion to Mormonism in England; her move to Nauvoo, IL, ca. 1840; her plural marriage in 1843 to Orson Hyde; the exodus to Utah; and life in Sanpete County, UT. Also available on microfilm. See Dale L. Morgan and George P. Hammond, eds., *A Guide to the Manuscript Collections of The Bancroft Library,* vol. I (Berkeley, CA: University of California Press, 1963).

563. Hylbert, Ethel (Lacey)
Oral history. 1970. 1 vol.
Open. No guide.
University of California, Berkeley, The Bancroft Library, Manuscripts Division.
Transcript of interview with Hylbert (1889-?) concerns her missionary work in China from 1920 to 1943 and 1946 to 1948; she served as treasurer for the Baptist missions in China and assisted her husband Lewis C. Hylbert in his work as secretary of the East China Mission. A photo is also included.

564. Indian Occupation of Alcatraz
Oral history. 1969-70. 4 tapes.
Open. No guide.
University of California, Berkeley, The Bancroft Library, Manuscripts Division.
Panel discussions with Indians of various tribes who participated in the occupation of Alcatraz, including a talk with Marilyn Miracle, a young Mohawk.

565. International Order of Job's Daughters, San Francisco Bethel, No. 3
Records. 1925-28. 1 vol.
Open. No guide.
University of California, Berkeley, The Bancroft Library, Manuscripts Division.
Scrapbook containing photos, invitations, programs, and clippings relating to the organization.

566. Isenberg, Gerda
Papers. 1942-46. 2 boxes.
Open. No guide.
University of California, Berkeley, The Bancroft Library, Manuscripts Division.
[Mrs. R. A.] Isenberg was active on the Committee on American Principles and Fair Play in Palo Alto, CA, and was responsible for the relocation of many evacuees in that area. Correspondence, articles, speeches, photos, reports, pamphlets, clippings, magazines, and other material about the evacuation program and the rights of Japanese as citizens; interviews with and biographical information about Japanese seeking relocation; and a newspaper, bulletins, and pamphlets of the Japanese American Citizens League.

567. Issler, Anne Roller
Papers. Nd. 1 carton and 1 portfolio.
Open. No guide.
University of California, Berkeley, The Bancroft Library, Manuscripts Division.
Papers of Issler, an author, consist of notes, clippings on publications, and galley proofs of her book *Our Mountain Heritage,* which concerns R. L. Stevenson.

568. Jackson, Helen Maria (Fiske) Hunt
Papers. Nd. 1 portfolio.
Open. No guide.
University of California, Berkeley, The Bancroft Library, Manuscripts Division.
Correspondence and other material of Jackson (1830-85), an author who was first married to Edward Bissell Hunt and then to William Sharpless Jackson.

569. Jackson, Joseph Henry
Papers. Ca. 1931-55. 14 boxes, 7 cartons, and 1 portfolio.
Open. Descriptive guide and shelflist.
University of California, Berkeley, The Bancroft Library, Manuscripts Division.
Correspondence and other papers of Jackson (1894-1955), including letters from Gertrude Franklin (Horn) Atherton, Rachel Lyman Field, Frances Perkins, Margaret (Higgins) Sanger, Jessamyn West, Mary Frances (Kennedy) Fisher, Jane Bissell Grabhorn, Shirley Jackson, Phyllis McGinley, Ruth Comfort Mitchell, Lenore (Glen) Offord, Cornelia Otis Skinner, and Lillian Eugenia Smith.

570. Japanese American Evacuation and Resettlement
Records. Ca. 1941-53. 14 boxes, 224 cartons, and 37 card files.
Partially restricted. Published guide.
University of California, Berkeley, The Bancroft Library, Manuscripts Division.
Correspondence, memoranda, staff papers, press releases, case histories, reports, photos, films, and publications of the US War Relocation Authority and records and papers collected or generated by the Japanese-American Evacuation and Resettlement Study at the University of California, Berkeley, under the direction of professor Dorothy Swaine Thomas. Includes evacuee diaries and recollections, staff correspondence, reports, and studies prepared by the staff. See Edward N. Barnhart, *Japanese American Evacuation and Resettlement: Catalog of Material in the General Library* (Berkeley: University of California, 1958).

571. Jatta, Mary (Hall)
Papers. 1869. 10-page item.
Open. No guide.
University of California, Berkeley, The Bancroft Library, Manuscripts Division.
Journal of Jatta (1841-?) records her journey from Nebraska City, NE, to Sacramento, CA.

572. Jeffers, Una (Call)
Papers. Ca. 1930-46. 2 boxes.
Open. No guide.
University of California, Berkeley, The Bancroft Library, Manuscripts Division.
Correspondence, petition, photos, clippings, and other papers of [Mrs. Robinson] Jeffers (1885-1950), an artist and writer. Includes poems and many letters by Mabel Dodge Luhan and letters by Frieda (von Richthofen) [Mrs. D. H.] Lawrence, Dorothy Brett, and Claire Spencer.

573. Jelenko, Therese
Oral history. Ca. 1965. 10-page item.
Open. No guide.
University of California, Berkeley, The Bancroft Library, Manuscripts Division.
Jelenko reminisces about her study of music, her association with Michael and Sarah Stein as music teacher of their son Allen, her life in Paris with the Steins, Leo Stein and Gertrude Stein, the Steins' interest in painting and nature, her friendship with Pablo Casals, and her later life. Also available on microfilm.

574. Jewish Committee for Personal Service
Records. 1931-54. 1 portfolio.
Open. No guide.
University of California, Berkeley, The Bancroft Library, Manuscripts Division.
Records of the northern California district of the Committee include speeches and annual reports written primarily by executive director Elsie (Shirpser) Coggins.

575. Johnson, Hiram Warren
Papers. Ca. 1895-1945. 145 boxes and 49 cartons.
Open. Key.
University of California, Berkeley, The Bancroft Library, Manuscripts Division.
Papers of Johnson (1866-1945) relate primarily to his career as governor of California from 1911 to 1917 and as US senator from California from 1917 to 1945 and to his leadership of the Progressive party and include a subject file on women's suffrage and correspondence from Lillian Gish, Frances Perkins, Eleanor (Roosevelt) Roosevelt, the WCTU, and others. Papers of his wife Minnie L. (McNeal) Johnson (1869-1955) include correspondence, her will, obituaries, and material on the Johnson memorial, Cypress Lawn Memorial Park.

576. Johnson, Lydia
Oral history. 1970-71. 1 vol.
Open. No guide.
University of California, Berkeley, The Bancroft Library, Manuscripts Division.
Transcript of interview with Johnson (1893-?) in which she discusses her work on education projects and training personnel for the YWCA in China from 1926 to 1943 and comments on evangelizing by church missions.

577. Johnson, Robert Underwood
Papers. 1889-1924. 13 boxes.
Open. Key.
University of California, Berkeley, The Bancroft Library, Manuscripts Division.
Correspondence and other papers of Johnson (1853-1937) relate primarily to conservation of the Yosemite area. Includes letters from many women.

578. Johnston, Marguerite Kulp
Oral history. 1967. 62-page item.
Open. No guide.
University of California, Berkeley, The Bancroft Library, Manuscripts Division.
Johnston (1920-) comments on her student days at the University from 1939 to 1943, housing problems, the Welfare Council, the Associated Students of the University of California, and her work as social secretary to Mrs. Clark Kerr, wife of the president of the University.

579. Jones, Ada (Millington)
Papers. 1862. 80-page item.
Open. No guide.
University of California, Berkeley, The Bancroft Library, Manuscripts Division.
Journal kept by Ada Millington (1849-1930) while crossing the plains to California at age 13 contains a note added in 1878. Millington married a Mr. Jones.

580. Jones, Lucile (Williams)
Oral history. 1970. 1 vol.
Open. No guide.
University of California, Berkeley, The Bancroft Library, Manuscripts Division.
Transcript of interview with Jones in which she describes her life as the wife of a missionary in China from 1915 to 1950, teaching in mission schools, and her evacuation from Chengtu during WWII by the US Air Force.

581. Jones, Lucy
Papers. 1874-75. 1 vol.
Open. No guide.
University of California, Berkeley, The Bancroft Library, Manuscripts Division.
Diary of Jones, a resident of San Francisco.

582. Jones, Mary Ann (Smith)
Papers. Nd. 2 portfolios.
Open. No guide.
University of California, Berkeley, The Bancroft Library, Manuscripts Division.
Reminiscences of [Mrs. John M.] Jones (1825-1918) concern an overland journey to California in 1846; the Nathaniel Jones, Elam Brown, and David Allen families, with whom she traveled; spending the winter at the Joseph B. Chiles ranch; and settling at Alamo, CA. Also included is a 1935 letter from Flora M. Jones to a Mrs. Bell, which relates to these recollections.

583. Jones, William Griffith
Papers. 1872-1906. 116 items.
Open. No guide.
University of California, Berkeley, The Bancroft Library, Manuscripts Division.
Correspondence of the family of Jones (?-1906), including some letters in Welsh, and letters from E. H. Griffin and his wife Emily, who were pioneers in Oregon.

584. Joralemon, Mary E. (Beamon)
Papers. 1873. 1 portfolio.
Open. No guide.
University of California, Berkeley, The Bancroft Library, Manuscripts Division.
Consists of letters from Elizabeth Cabot (Cary) Agassiz and from Louis Agassiz concerning Joralemon's application for entrance to the Anderson School of Natural History, a poem, and autographs of people at the School.

585. Jorgensen, Virgil W., Family
Papers. Ca. 1923-54. 1 box.
Open. No guide.
University of California, Berkeley, The Bancroft Library, Manuscripts Division.
Includes letters to Jorgensen's wife Florence (Orr) Jorgensen from her mother Mrs. James Wallace Orr (1854-?), Florence Jorgensen's diary of a 1954 trip to Europe, and other papers.

586. Judd, Harriet (Stewart)
Papers. Ca. 1870. 1 microfilm reel.
Open. No guide.
University of California, Berkeley, The Bancroft Library, Manuscripts Division.
Autobiography of Judd (1822-1907).

587. Kearsing and Díaz Peña Family
Papers. 1846-85. 2 vols.
Open. Shelflist.
University of California, Berkeley, The Bancroft Library, Manuscripts Division.
Letters from Harriet Amelia (Kearsing) Díaz Peña to her family from Independence, MO, while she was on her way to California, and from San Francisco; by Mary Ann (Kearsing) Weston of Jackson, CA, to her nephew; and by Mary H. Díaz Peña to her aunt in Mazatlán, Mexico. Also included is a note on family history by Marguerite Díaz Peña [Mrs. Elliott M.] Smith.

588. Keeler, Charles, Family
Papers. Ca. 1879-1937. 16 cartons.
Open. Unpublished guide.
University of California, Berkeley, The Bancroft Library, Manuscripts Division.
Papers of the Charles Augustus Keeler family include letters and drawings by his first wife Louise Mapes (Bunnell) Keeler (1877-1907), letters and scrapbooks of his sister Sarah I. Keeler, papers of his second wife Ormeida Curtis Harrison Keeler, and correspondence and other papers of his daughters Merodine (Keeler) McIntyre and Eloise Keeler and others.

589. Keith Family
Papers. Nd. 24 boxes, 15 cartons, 1 portfolio, and 3 card files.
Open. Key.
University of California, Berkeley, The Bancroft Library, Manuscripts Division.
Correspondence, writings, and other papers of Barbara Allen (Harris) [Mrs. Asa Baldwin] Metcalfe (1802-91); of her daughters Ellen (Metcalfe) [Mrs. John] McHenry (1827-1922) and Emma (Metcalfe) [Mrs. William Gilbert] Hay (1840-1937); of her granddaughters Emma (McHenry) [Mrs. Charles Fremont] Pond (1857-1934), Mary (McHenry) [Mrs. William] Keith (1855-1947), Elizabeth (McHenry) [Mrs. Emmanuel Benjamin] Lamare (1850-1907), and Emily Parsons Babcock Hay (?-1937); and of her great-granddaughter Elizabeth Keith Pond (1886-1955).

Includes diaries for 1842 and 1846, manuscripts, receipts, a biographical sketch, and published writings of Ellen McHenry; bills, receipts, papers relating to the DAR and the United Daughters of the Confederacy, sketches, and paintings of Emma Pond; autobiographical sketches, speeches, notes, tributes, scrapbooks, clippings, publications, and other papers of Mary Keith relating to her education and to woman suffrage; journals of a 1937 European trip, financial records, photos, artwork, and memorabilia of Elizabeth Pond. Also includes correspondence of Mary Virginia (Pond) [Mrs. Jack Arthur] Culbertson; correspondence, financial records, and other papers of Inez (Henderson) [Mrs. Charles McHenry] Pond (?-1961), of the Lamare family, and of Emmanuel Lamare's mother Caroline (Goddefroy) [Mrs. François Nicolas] Lamare (?-1906); and financial and legal papers, biographical and genealogical information, and scrapbooks of the Hay family. Among the correspondents are Mary Hortense "Tennie" (Keith) [Mrs. Edward N.] Harmon (1868-1948), Susan B. Anthony, Carrie Chapman Catt, John Muir, and the National Woman's party.

590. Kelley, Margaret A.
Papers. 1921-39. 1 portfolio and 1 microfilm reel.
Open. No guide.
University of California, Berkeley, The Bancroft Library, Manuscripts Division.
Includes notes on "Pegleg Smith" as well as "Ballads of Murderer's Bar," a compilation by [Miss] Kelley of lyrics, music, and anecdotes about the ballads, most of which were written by John A. Stone.

591. Kennedy, Helen (Weber)
Oral history. 1965. 1 tape.
Open. No guide.
University of California, Berkeley, The Bancroft Library, Manuscripts Division.
Tape and transcript of interview with Kennedy concerning her grandfather Captain Charles Maria Weber (1814-81), a Stockton, CA, pioneer, and his family and describing life in early Stockton.

592. Kenny, Robert Walker
Papers. 1920-47. 41 boxes and 16 cartons.
Open. Key.
University of California, Berkeley, The Bancroft Library, Manuscripts Division.
Papers of Walker (1901-76) relate primarily to his career as attorney general of California from 1942 to 1946 and as a judge and state senator and concern such subjects as prohibition repeal, minority groups, civil rights, and control of venereal disease. Correspondents include Helen (Gahagan) Douglas, Anna Eleanor (Roosevelt) Roosevelt, Rita Hayworth, the South of Market Girls' Club of San Francisco, and the YWCA.

593. Kerr, William John, Family
Papers. Ca. 1956-75. 1 portfolio.
Open. No guide.
University of California, Berkeley, The Bancroft Library, Manuscripts Division.
Includes poems and paintings by Dorothy (Fish) Kerr (1889-1971), letters by her and her husband William John Kerr, clippings about their activities, and obituaries.

594. Kettlewell, Mrs. Frank
Papers. 1937-68. 35 vols.
Open. No guide.
University of California, Berkeley, The Bancroft Library, Manuscripts Division.
Diaries of Kettlewell (1887-), a Piedmont, CA, housewife.

595. Keyes, McIntire, Voorheis, and Clark Family
Papers. Ca. 1849-1970. 18 cartons, 2 boxes, and 2 vols.
Access restricted. No guide.
University of California, Berkeley, The Bancroft Library, Manuscripts Division.
Papers relate to politics, government, mining, and education in Amador County, CA, and include those of Gertrude (Voorheis) [Mrs. Baylies Coleman] Clark.

596. Kimball, Victoria E. (Stewart)
Papers. Ca. 1902. 1 vol.
Open. No guide.
University of California, Berkeley, The Bancroft Library, Manuscripts Division.
Consists of a sewing book with examples of fine needlework compiled for the Hearst Domestic Industries of Berkeley, a school established by Phoebe (Apperson) Hearst to aid young women.

597. Klenke, Jeannie (Morgan)
Oral history. 1967-69. 85-page vol.
Open. No guide.
University of California, Berkeley, The Bancroft Library, Manuscripts Division.
Transcript of interview with Klenke (?-1970) concerns her recollections of her sister Mary DeNeale Morgan (1868-1948), an artist from Carmel, and other members of her family; of California artists, including William Keith; and of the artist colony in Carmel. Includes an introduction by [Mrs.] Betty Lochrie Hoag, research director of the Carmel Museum of Art, and photos.

598. Knights of Labor
Records. 1886-92. 1 vol. and 1 portfolio.
Open. No guide.
University of California, Berkeley, The Bancroft Library, Manuscripts Division.
Includes a minute book and letters certifying the election of delegates to the state assembly of the Women's Labor League, San Francisco Assembly.

599. Koch, Carlota
Papers. Nd. 1 vol.
Access restricted. No guide.
University of California, Berkeley, The Bancroft Library, Manuscripts Division.
Typescript by Koch concerns early California and her grandparents Gaspar de Oreña and María Antonia de Oreña, who was the daughter of José de la Guerra y Noriega and the widow of Cesáreo Lataillade, the Spanish vice-consul in Monterey.

600. Kofoid, Carrie Prudence (Winter)
Papers. 1915-16. 1 portfolio.
Open. No guide.
University of California, Berkeley, The Bancroft Library, Manuscripts Division.
Letters by Kofoid to her mother relate her observations during a trip to the Orient.

601. Koshland, Lucile (Wolf) Heming
Oral history. 1968. 1 vol.
Open. No guide.
University of California, Berkeley, The Bancroft Library, Manuscripts Division.
Transcript of interview with [Mrs. Daniel Edward] Koshland in which she comments on Jewish communities in San Francisco and New York, her

work with the LWV, her educational interests, and her grandmother Delia Fleishhacker.

602. Kroeber, Theodora (Kracaw) Brown
Papers. Nd. 1 box, 2 cartons, and 1 package.
Access restricted. No guide.
University of California, Berkeley, The Bancroft Library, Manuscripts Division.
Correspondence of Kroeber, a writer who is the widow of anthropologist Alfred Louis Kroeber, relates primarily to the publication of her books.

603. La Harpe, Jacqueline Ellen Violette de
Papers. 1918-62. 1 box.
Open. No guide.
University of California, Berkeley, The Bancroft Library, Manuscripts Division.
Papers of La Harpe (1894-?) consist of lectures on French literature and other subjects, book reviews, and clippings of her articles on travels in the US and South America.

604. Laidlaw Family
Papers. Ca. 1885-1928. 1 box.
Open. No guide.
University of California, Berkeley, The Bancroft Library, Manuscripts Division.
Includes an autograph book, dance programs, and other papers relating to Mrs. Laidlaw's early life in Evanston, WY.

605. Landweer, Lulu Dorothea (Rubke)
Papers. Ca. 1911-12. 1 box and 1 oversize portfolio.
Open. No guide.
University of California, Berkeley, The Bancroft Library, Manuscripts Division.
Pictures, programs, clippings, and other papers of Landweer relate chiefly to the University of California, where she was a student in the class of 1912. Included are clippings about Sarah Bernhardt's performance in 1911 in the San Francisco Bay Area.

606. Lane County Pioneer Historical Association
Records. Ca. 1845-60. 24 vols.
Open. Published guide.
University of California, Berkeley, The Bancroft Library, Manuscripts Division.
Oregon pioneer records include diaries and narratives of Charlotte Emily (Stearns) Pengra, Agnes (Stewart) Warner, Helen Marnie (Stewart) Love, Esther (Brakeman) Lyman Butler, Catherine Amanda (Stansbury) Washburn, Elizabeth Julia (Ellison) Goltra Farrington, and other emigrants who attempted the Elliott Cutoff across southern Oregon in 1853. See Dale L. Morgan and George P. Hammond, eds., *A Guide to the Manuscript Collections of The Bancroft Library,* vol. I (Berkeley, CA: University of California Press, 1963).

607. Lange, Dorothea
Oral history. 1960-61. 1 vol.
Open. No guide.
University of California, Berkeley, The Bancroft Library, Manuscripts Division.
Transcript of interviews with Lange (1895-1965), in which she discusses studying photography with Clarence White; taking, printing, captioning, and exhibiting photos; her marriage to Maynard Dixon; her work with Arnold Genthe; her studio in San Francisco and the Bohemian group there; the beginnings of documentary photography and photojournalism; and her photographic work for the Farm Security Administration, the Office of War Information, and the War Relocation Authority. Also includes her proposal for a photography center, articles about her, tributes to her, and other material.

608. Lawson, Andrew Cowper
Papers. Ca. 1885-1951. 19 boxes, 9 cartons, and 1 portfolio.
Open. Key.
University of California, Berkeley, The Bancroft Library, Manuscripts Division.
Papers of Lawson (1861-1952), a geologist and professor at the University, include letters and a few poems by his sister Katherine Leslie (Lawson) Appleby, letters from his sister Alice (Lawson) [Mrs. John W. S.] McCullough, and letters from Florence R. D. Bascom.

609. Le Conte Family
Papers. 1858-1949. 3 boxes, 2 cartons, and 1 portfolio.
Open. Key.
University of California, Berkeley, The Bancroft Library, Manuscripts Division.
Papers of various members of the Joseph Le Conte family, including letters and a poem by his wife Caroline Elizabeth (Nisbet) Le Conte (ca. 1828-1915) and correspondence, a notebook with pencil sketches and a journal relating to trips to Yosemite in 1878 and 1882, a diploma from the University of California, genealogical notes, and other papers of his daughter Caroline Eaton Le Conte (1863-1945), who lived in California but spent much of her time in Europe. Also includes Emma (Le Conte) Furman's sketch of the Le Conte family of the Nonant line and correspondence of Helen Marion (Gompertz) Le Conte (1865-1924) and her husband Joseph Nisbet Le Conte, Helen Malcolm Le Conte (1904-), and Adelaide Elizabeth (Graham) [Mrs. Joseph Nisbet] Le Conte.

610. League of Women Voters of Berkeley
Records. Ca. 1911-71. 7 cartons and 12 vols.
Open. Unpublished guide.
University of California, Berkeley, The Bancroft Library, Manuscripts Division.
Minutes, financial and administrative records, position papers, and scrapbooks of the LWV.

611. Leary, Mary Ellen
Papers. 1944-1970. 50 cartons, 5 bundles, and 1 box.
Partially restricted. Partial key.
University of California, Berkeley, The Bancroft Library, Manuscripts Division.
Papers of Leary, political editor for the *San Francisco Daily News,* include notes, press releases, pamphlets, and clippings about politics and government in California, labor, pollution, world trade, and Angela Davis.

612. Lees Family
Papers. 1850-1922. 1 box.
Open. No guide.
University of California, Berkeley, The Bancroft Library, Manuscripts Division.
Includes letters to Isaiah W. Lees, who in 1866 was captain of detective police in San Francisco, from his wife Jane A. (Fisher) Lees (1829-97) and a diary of his daughter Ella (Lees) Leigh (1859-?) for the years 1905 to 1907, which contains her account of the San Francisco earthquake and fire and biographical data on her family.

613. Leif Erikson League, Oakland, CA
Records. 1939-48. 1 vol.
Open. No guide.
University of California, Berkeley, The Bancroft Library, Manuscripts Division.
Secretary's record containing minutes kept by [Mrs.] Minnie Kjer.

614. Leighly, John Barger
Papers. 1957. 1 vol.
Open. No guide.
University of California, Berkeley, The Bancroft Library, Manuscripts Division.
Mementos of Leighly's wife Katherine (Edmonds) Leighly (1904-56) include photos and other items.

615. Lenski, Lois
Papers. Nd. 3 cartons and oversize material.
Open. Unpublished guide.
University of California, Berkeley, The Bancroft Library, Manuscripts Division.
Papers of Lenski (1893-1974), an author of children's books, include manuscripts of her writings, galley proofs, original illustrations, photos, background material, and articles by and about her.

616. Leonard, Alexander Thomas
Papers. Nd. 2 boxes.
Open. No guide.
University of California, Berkeley, The Bancroft Library, Manuscripts Division.
Includes letters by authors Ina D. Coolbrith, Emma Frances Dawson, and Ella Sterling (Clark) Mighels and clippings about Gertrude Atherton, Helen Hunt Jackson, Juanita Miller, Kathleen Norris, and others.

617. Leslie, Miriam Florence (Folline)
Papers. 1910-14. 1 portfolio.
Open. No guide.
University of California, Berkeley, The Bancroft Library, Manuscripts Division.
Letters by Leslie (1836-1914) to Mrs. A. B. Games, inscribed calling cards, and clippings about Leslie, who was first married to David Charles Peacock, then to Ephraim George Squier, and then to Frank Leslie.

618. Lester, Anson Wood, Family
Papers. 1853-ca. 1910. 6 folders and 2 vols.
Open. No guide.
University of California, Berkeley, The Bancroft Library, Manuscripts Division.
Papers of Lester (1838?-76) and his wife Addie Lester (1850-?), who were pioneers in California, and of other members of their family. Includes a scrapbook of a 1909 trip to Alaska, theatrical programs, and other papers of Minerva L. and E. B. Powers and an 1853 subscription list of a Mrs. Waller.

619. Levison, Alice (Gerstle)
Oral history. 1966. 151-page item.
Open. No guide.
University of California, Berkeley, The Bancroft Library, Manuscripts Division.
Reminiscences by Levison (1873-?) concern prominent Jewish families in San Francisco, her family life there, social customs, the Alaska Commercial Company, her husband Jacob Bertha Levison (1862-1947), and the 1906 San Francisco earthquake.

620. Levy, Harriet Lane
Papers. Ca. 1914-50. 1 portfolio.
Open. No guide.
University of California, Berkeley, The Bancroft Library, Manuscripts Division.
Papers of Levy (1867-1950) include letters from Alice Babette Toklas and reminiscences concerning her trip to Paris with Toklas, ca. 1906; her friendship with Gertrude Stein, Leo Stein, and Michael and Sarah Stein; the Steins' interest in Picasso, Matisse, and other painters; and her life in Paris.

621. Lewis, Austin
Papers. 1913-44. 1 box and 4 cartons.
Open. Key.
University of California, Berkeley, The Bancroft Library, Manuscripts Division.
Papers of Lewis (1865?-1944) include correspondence, a manuscript by Elizabeth Gurley Flynn, a scrapbook of clippings about civil liberties and world conditions, and pamphlets about equal

rights for women, labor unions, and syndicalism. Among the correspondents are Mary Elizabeth Burroughs (Roberts) Smith Coolidge, Jessica Blanche Peixotto, and other women.

622. Lewis Family
Papers. Ca. 1898-1915. 1 box.
Open. No guide.
University of California, Berkeley, The Bancroft Library, Manuscripts Division.
Includes letters from John M. Lewis to Sophie (Borel) Lewis before and after their marriage, letters by Sophie Lewis, and letters to her, primarily from her parents and sister Alice.

623. Lewis, Ruth (Krandis)
Papers. 1942. 1 portfolio.
Open. No guide.
University of California, Berkeley, The Bancroft Library, Manuscripts Division.
Correspondence of Lewis with officials of the US District Court for the Southern District of California and the Tulare County Board of Trade concerning the Kaweah Cooperative Colony.

624. Liebig, Caroline Louise (Eshman)
Oral history. 1971. 147-page item.
Open. No guide.
University of California, Berkeley, The Bancroft Library, Manuscripts Division.
Liebig (1901-) discusses her association with the Los Angeles County Museum of Art beginning in 1939 and with the art world of southern California. A photo is included.

625. Light, Jerome T.
Papers. 1942-48. 2 boxes.
Open. No guide.
University of California, Berkeley, The Bancroft Library, Manuscripts Division.
Includes papers of Light's wife Dorothy B. Light, a War Relocation Authority relocation adviser.

626. Limantour, José Yves
Papers. 1842-85. 2 boxes and 1 portfolio.
Open. Key.
University of California, Berkeley, The Bancroft Library, Manuscripts Division.
Limantour (?-1885) was a French trader who came to California in 1841 and for his services was given land grants by Governor Manuel Micheltorena. Papers deal primarily with disputed claims to these grants and include letters from Rose Greenhow, Angustias (de la Guerra) [Mrs. James L.] Ord, Julie Perricaudet, Julie Renard, and Ysabelle Renard.

627. Lodge, Carrie Electa
Oral history. 1964. 1 vol.
Open. No guide.
University of California, Berkeley, The Bancroft Library, Manuscripts Division.
Transcript of interview with Lodge (1881-) concerns the family of her grandmother Martina (Castro) Lodge (1807?-90), who was the owner of the largest ranch in Santa Cruz County, CA; ranch life in the Mexican period; division of the land; and life in Santa Cruz. Includes a family tree of the Castro-Lodge family and a map of land owned by the family. Also available on microfilm.

628. London, Charmian (Kittredge)
Papers. 1929-47. 2 portfolios.
Open. No guide.
University of California, Berkeley, The Bancroft Library, Manuscripts Division.
Letters by London (1883-1955), an author, to Cyril Clemens and to Nadia Lavrova Shapiro concern her husband Jack London, publication of and increased interest in his novels abroad, her writing, and news notes for publication in San Francisco newspapers. Also included are clippings and an article by Shapiro, who was then Miss Lavrova.

629. London, Jack
Papers. Ca. 1897-1916. 1 box and 1 vol.
Open. Partial unpublished guide.
University of California, Berkeley, The Bancroft Library, Manuscripts Division.
Papers of London (1876-1916) include an excerpt from his wife Charmian London's 1907 diary and letters by her, primarily to Ralph Kasper.

630. Long, J. M. (Underwood)
Papers. 1887. 4-page item.
Open. No guide.
University of California, Berkeley, The Bancroft Library, Manuscripts Division.
Dictation in which Long (1842-?) describes her early life and her residence at Lakeport, CA, after ca. 1884. Also available on microfilm.

631. Lorenzana, Apolinaria
Papers. 1878. 1 vol.
Open. No guide.
University of California, Berkeley, The Bancroft Library, Manuscripts Division.
Dictation in which Lorenzana describes her work as a teacher and nurse, primarily at the San Diego Mission; the lives of Indians at the Mission and their depredations at Rancho Jamul and elsewhere; and the American occupation of southern California. Also available on microfilm.

632. Lovey, Gertrude
Papers. Nd. 8 vols.
Open. No guide.
University of California, Berkeley, The Bancroft Library, Manuscripts Division.
Autobiography, reminiscences of Lovey (?-1965), and scrapbooks.

633. Lowrie, Mrs. John R.
Papers. 1956. 41-page vol.
Open. Published guide.
University of California, Berkeley, The Bancroft Library, Manuscripts Division.
Tombstone inscriptions from and information concerning the St. Martinville, LA, cemetery compiled by the Attakapas Chapter of the DAR. See George P. Hammond, ed., *A Guide to the Manuscript Collections of The Bancroft Library,* vol. II (Berkeley, CA: University of California Press, 1972).

634. Lufkin and Swain Families
Papers. Nd. 1 portfolio.
Open. No guide.
University of California, Berkeley, The Bancroft Library, Manuscripts Division.
Account by Sarah Carpenter Swain, widow of William C. Swain, of a South Pacific cruise from 1848 to 1852 aboard the whaling bark *George Chamberlain,* of which Swain was master and third owner. Also included is an autobiographical sketch by their daughter Emeline Baker (Swain) Lufkin and genealogical material.

635. Lyman Family
Papers. Ca. 1860-1968. 36 boxes and 5 cartons.
Open. Unpublished guide.
University of California, Berkeley, The Bancroft Library, Manuscripts Division.
Includes correspondence, manuscripts of poems, and other papers of California poet Helen (Hoyt) [Mrs. William Whittingham] Lyman, who published under the name Helen Hoyt. Correspondents include Sara Bard Field, Hildegarde Flanner, Julia (Cooley) Altrocchi, Harriet Monroe, Bertha Pope Damon, Genevieve Taggard, Sara Teasdale, and Ella Young.

636. Lynch, Alice Mary (Kennedy)
Papers. 1857-65. 76-page item.
Open. No guide.
University of California, Berkeley, The Bancroft Library, Manuscripts Division.
Diary in French that Lynch (1833-1911), a resident of San Francisco, kept in a former roll book of North Beach School in San Francisco. Also included are accounts for Tierra Redonda, her husband's sheep ranch in San Luis Obispo County.

637. Lyon, Eleanor (Richards)
Oral history. 1974-75. 1 vol.
Open. No guide.
University of California, Berkeley, The Bancroft Library, Manuscripts Division.
Tape and transcript of interview concerning Lyon's activities as a civic volunteer, clubwoman, and conservationist. Includes photos.

638. McCormick, Sister Mary Colmcille
Oral history. 1971. 35-page item.
Open. No guide.
University of California, Berkeley, The Bancroft Library, Manuscripts Division.
Interview with McCormick (1892-) concerns her experiences from 1929 to 1939 as a missionary in China, primarily teaching Catholic doctrine.

639. McCrackin, Josephine (Wompner) Clifford
Papers. Nd. 1 portfolio.
Open. No guide.
University of California, Berkeley, The Bancroft Library, Manuscripts Division.
Letters to Juanita Goldmann, clippings, and magazines containing articles by [Mrs. Jackson] McCrackin (1838-1920), an author.

640. McCrary, Jim
Papers. 1924-30. 1 portfolio.
Open. No guide.
University of California, Berkeley, The Bancroft Library, Manuscripts Division.
Correspondence and other papers relating to McCrary's activities as a California labor leader and member of the International Labor Defense and the Workers Party of America. Includes letters from Charlotte Anita Whitney and a biographical sketch of McCrary by Joan London.

641. McCulloh Family
Papers. 1852-1936. 4 boxes.
Open. Key.
University of California, Berkeley, The Bancroft Library, Manuscripts Division.
Correspondence, diaries, accounts, land papers, and clippings of Jane E. and John McCulloh and their children Frank, John G., Hiram William, and Frances Jane. Includes letters and diaries, 1885-86 and 1891-1918, of Jane McCulloh; correspondence of Frances Jane (McCulloh) Bartlett and her husband Carleton T. Bartlett, both of whom were elementary school teachers in California; Frances Bartlett's county primary teacher's certificate; and other papers relating to the Bartlett family.

642. McEnerney, Genevieve Green Hamilton
Papers. Nd. 1 box.
Open. No guide.
University of California, Berkeley, The Bancroft Library, Manuscripts Division.
Manuscripts of plays and other writings by McEnerney, of a short story by Zoë Akins, and of a poem by Sara Bard Field. Also includes a marriage certificate of Genevieve and Garrett W. McEnerney.

643. McGettigan, Francisca (Vallejo)
Papers. 1936-37. 1 portfolio.
Open. No guide.
University of California, Berkeley, The Bancroft Library, Manuscripts Division.
Scripts, apparently written by McGettigan, for the radio program "Padres, Gringoes and Gold."

644. McGlashan, Charles Fayette
Papers. 1878-1946. 3 boxes, 2 cartons, and 1 oversize portfolio.
Open. Key.

University of California, Berkeley, The Bancroft Library, Manuscripts Division.
McGlashan (1847-1931), a lawyer and editor of the Truckee, CA, *Republican,* was the author of *History of the Donner Party, A Tragedy of the Sierra* (1879). His papers relate primarily to his work on the Donner party and include correspondence, diaries, and statements by members of the Donner party and rescue parties and their relatives; patents; legal papers; commonplace book containing letters from his sister Ann; maps; scrapbooks; and other material. Correspondents include members of the Donner, Graves, Breen, and Reed families, in particular Eliza Poor (Donner) Houghton, Martha Jane "Patty" (Reed) Lewis, and Virginia Elizabeth Backenstoe (Reed) Murphy.

645. MacGregor, Helen R.
Papers. 1969-72. 4 cartons, 1 box, and 1 vol.
Open. No guide.
University of California, Berkeley, The Bancroft Library, Manuscripts Division.
MacGregor was secretary to Earl Warren from 1935 to 1953 while he served as district attorney of Alameda County, CA, state attorney general, and governor of California. In 1953 she was appointed by Governor Warren to the Youth Authority. Correspondence and other papers of MacGregor relate to her work on the Governor's Advisory Committee on Children and Youth beginning in 1959. Also includes transcript of an interview in which she recalls her work with Warren and her role as liaison to the Youth Authority; to the departments of health, mental hygiene, and education; and to the University of California.

646. McIntyre, Emma Jane
Papers. 1874. 28-page item.
Open. Published guide.
University of California, Berkeley, The Bancroft Library, Manuscripts Division.
Manuscript written by McIntyre (1846?-?) for her mother Mrs. Ashford Baker concerns her daily life and the geography, climate, flora, fauna, and natives of St. Georges Island in the Pribilof Islands of Alaska, where McIntyre's husband Captain William J. McIntyre was resident agent for the Alaska Commercial Company. Includes an explanatory note by the McIntyres' daughter Julia (McIntyre) Merriman and articles about the Islands. Also available on microfilm. See Dale L. Morgan and George P. Hammond, eds., *A Guide to the Manuscript Collections of The Bancroft Library,* vol. I (Berkeley, CA: University of California Press, 1963).

647. McLaughlin, Emma (Moffat)
Papers. 1965-68. 15 cartons, 1 item, and 1 tape.
Open. No guide.
University of California, Berkeley, The Bancroft Library, Manuscripts Division.
Tape and transcript of interviews with McLaughlin (1880-1968) in which she discusses her father's livestock business in California; social life in San Francisco; attending the University of California from 1898 to 1902; her marriage to Alfred McLaughlin, a physician; her volunteer work in civic and social welfare; her service on the state board of social welfare; and her work with the LWV, the World Affairs Council of Northern California, and the Institute of Pacific Relations. Also includes correspondence and other papers relating to her involvement with these and other organizations, including the Community Chest of San Francisco; biographical information on her family and husband; a brief history of the California LWV; and obituaries. Introduction to the interview is by Caroline Moore Charles.

648. McLean Family
Papers. Nd. 12 cartons.
Open. Key.
University of California, Berkeley, The Bancroft Library, Manuscripts Division.
Correspondence of Edward McLean and his wife Sarah E. Chester McLean with each other and with their children Fannie Williams McLean, Agnes Maria McLean, and Francis H. McLean; photos; and other papers. Fannie McLean, who graduated from the University of California, Berkeley, in 1885, was head of the English department and vice-principal at Berkeley High School and was active in the woman suffrage movement. Her papers include correspondence, diaries, manuscripts of short stories and a novel, notebooks, speeches, accounts, income tax returns, scrapbooks of clippings, and material on the College Equal Suffrage League of California, of which she was vice-president. Agnes McLean taught English to adults at Hewitt Street Cottage School and was a social worker; her papers include correspondence, diaries, and bank statements.

649. Maguire, Sarah Edna
Oral history. 1970. 10-page item.
Open. No guide.
University of California, Berkeley, The Bancroft Library, Manuscripts Division.
Maguire (1889-?), a resident of Mill Valley, CA, comments on teaching in the Mill Valley school district from 1920 to 1955.

650. Malozemoff, Elizabeth
Oral history. 1960. 458-page vol.
Open. No guide.
University of California, Berkeley, The Bancroft Library, Manuscripts Division.
Transcript of interview with Malozemoff (1881-?) in which she discusses her life as a teacher in czarist Russia and Siberia; her experiences in Russia during the revolution; her escape through China; her residence in Oakland, CA; Russian emigrant societies; and study and teaching at the University of California, Berkeley. Includes photos and maps.

651. Mann, Henry Rice, and Mann, Olive Lucinda (Trobridge)
Papers. Nd. 1 item.
Open. No guide.
University of California, Berkeley, The Bancroft Library, Manuscripts Division.
Correspondence and diaries of Henry Mann, who came to California in 1849, and of his wife Olive Mann. Also includes genealogical and other information on the Mann and Trobridge families, which was annotated by the donor Mrs. William H. Cox.

652. Manning, Malvina Virginia (Van Lear)
Papers. 1860-62. 2 folders.
Open. No guide.
University of California, Berkeley, The Bancroft Library, Manuscripts Division.
Pocket diary of Manning (1841-1920) records her overland journey in 1861 to California via the Salt Lake. The original destination of the journey was Texas, but it was changed after entering the Indian nation.

653. Marrón, Felipa Osuña de
Papers. 1814-78. 2 vols.
Open. No guide.
University of California, Berkeley, The Bancroft Library, Manuscripts Division.
Family papers and recollections by Marrón (1809-?) of life in California in 1846. Also available on microfilm.

654. Marsh Family
Papers. 1815-1960. 4 boxes, 1 carton, and 1 portfolio.
Open. Key.
University of California, Berkeley, The Bancroft Library, Manuscripts Division.
Correspondence, journals, accounts, a deed for rental of land, calling cards, articles, books, and other papers of California pioneer John Marsh (1798-1856) and his wife Abigail Smith (Tuck) Marsh (1818-57), a schoolteacher. Also contains papers of their daughter Alice Frances (Marsh) Cameron (1852-1927), including a letter from Caroline Thela (Cameron) Brown and other correspondence, diaries of a trip to Europe in 1878 and 1879 and for the years 1879 to 1897, a manuscript about her father, and legal papers; correspondence and a Cameron family genealogy of her husband William Walker Cameron; and papers of their daughter Amy Gertrude Cameron (1872-?), including letters from Julia A. Drake and other correspondence, diaries for 1886 and 1935 to 1943, notes, and papers concerning the estate of Viola J. Cameron. Also includes Tuck family correspondence, manuscripts and notes about the Tuck family, scrapbooks, and clippings.

655. Marshall, Robert Bradford
Papers. 1898-1949. 23 boxes, 5 vols., and 1 portfolio.
Open. Key.
University of California, Berkeley, The Bancroft Library, Manuscripts Division.
Includes correspondence between Marshall (1867-1949) and his wife Myra (Crow) Marshall before and after their marriage, from their daughters Evelyn Bradford (Marshall) [Mrs. Philip] Maddox and Virginia Mann Marshall, from Myra Marshall's sister Evelyn (Crow) Simmons, and from several other women. Also includes invitations to Myra Crow.

656. Martin, Anne Henrietta
Papers. 1892-1951. 16 boxes, 8 cartons, and 17 vols.
Open. Published and unpublished guides.
University of California, Berkeley, The Bancroft Library, Manuscripts Division.
Correspondence, campaign material, manuscripts, notes, bills, receipts, photos, scrapbooks, pamphlets, articles, and clippings of Martin (1875-1951), an educator and suffragist. The daughter of William O'Hara Martin and Louise Stadtmuller Martin, Anne Martin was born in Empire City, NV, and educated at the University of Nevada, Stanford and Columbia universities, and the universities of Leipzig and London. She was head of the history department at the University of Nevada from 1897 to 1899 and again in the 1900s and was a leader in the suffrage movement in Nevada, serving as president of the Nevada Equal Franchise Society from 1911 to 1914 and in various national suffrage organizations. Martin campaigned unsuccessfully for the US Senate in 1918 and 1920 as an independent and later was active in the Women's International League for Peace and Freedom and other pacifist organizations. Among the numerous correspondents are Jane Addams, Alice Paul, Mary (Ritter) Beard, and various suffrage associations. See Dale L. Morgan and George P. Hammond, eds., *A Guide to the Manuscript Collections of The Bancroft Library,* vol. I (Berkeley, CA: University of California Press, 1963).

657. Martinez, Elsie (Whitaker)
Oral history. 1962-63. 290-page item.
Open. No guide.
University of California, Berkeley, The Bancroft Library, Manuscripts Division.
Recollections by Martinez (1890-) of various San Francisco Bay Area artists and writers, including her father Herman Whitaker, her husband Xavier Martinez, Jack London, George Sterling, Ambrose Bierce, and Joaquin Miller; of life in Piedmont and Carmel, CA; of Harriet Dean and the *Little Review;* and of her daughter and son-in-law Micaela and Ralph DuCasse, both of whom are artists. Also included are an article by Elsie Martinez on the Carmel Mission, her correspondence with the interviewer [Mrs.] Willa (Klug) Baum, clippings, and a booklet on Carmel.

658. Matthews, Burnita (Shelton)
Oral history. 1973. 1 vol., 1 portfolio, and 1 tape.
Open. No guide.
University of California, Berkeley, The Bancroft Library, Manuscripts Division.
Tape and transcript of interview with Matthews (1894-) in which she discusses studying law in Washington, DC; her interest in woman suffrage, the Equal Rights Amendment, the National Woman's party, and eliminating discrimination from state laws; and her appointment to the federal judiciary in 1949. Includes an introduction by her law clerk Betty Poston Jones as well as speeches, articles, legal briefs, photos, and other documentary material.

659. Matyas, Jennie
Oral history. 1955. 1 microfilm reel and 1 tape.
Open. Index.
University of California, Berkeley, The Bancroft Library, Manuscripts Division.
Interview with Matyas (1895-?) in which she discusses her early life in Hungary and arrival in New York in 1905, her work in the garment industry in New York beginning in 1911, and her career with the International Ladies' Garment Workers' Union from its inception. She comments on communist infiltration of the Union; Union organization on the West Coast, especially in San Francisco; problems with Negro and Chinese groups; her appointment as vice-president of the Union; the initiation of health, education, retirement, and welfare benefits for members; her activity in and observations about local and national politics; her interest in compulsory health insurance; and her work on the US Manpower Commission.

660. Mauk, Charlotte Ellen
Papers. Ca. 1945-73. 1 box.
Open. Unpublished guide.
University of California, Berkeley, The Bancroft Library, Manuscripts Division.
Correspondence and other papers of Mauk (1907-73) relate primarily to her conservation work in California.

661. May, Bernice (Hubbard)
Papers. Nd. 5 cartons and 2 vols.
Open. No guide.
University of California, Berkeley, The Bancroft Library, Manuscripts Division.
Correspondence and other papers of [Mrs. Samuel Chester] May (1897-1975) relate to her career as a member of the Berkeley city council and to her work with the Association of Bay Area Governments and the San Francisco Bay Conservation and Development Commission. Also includes a tape and transcript of an interview with May concerning her leadership in public affairs as well as photos.

662. Maybeck, Bernard Ralph, Family
Papers. 1900-55. 2 boxes and 1 portfolio.
Open. Key.
University of California, Berkeley, The Bancroft Library, Manuscripts Division.
Includes letters by Annie (White) [Mrs. Bernard Ralph] Maybeck for the most part to her neighbor Charles C. Boynton concerning a property line dispute and others relating to property in Mendocino County, CA.

663. Mellen, Kathleen (Dickenson)
Papers. Ca. 1961-69. 1 vol. and 1 portfolio.
Open. No guide.
University of California, Berkeley, The Bancroft Library, Manuscripts Division.
Consists of letters by Mellen (1895-1969), an author, to her nephew commenting on her books about Hawaii; articles about her and her husband George Mellen; and obituaries.

664. Merrill, Phyllis (Moulton)
Oral history. 1971. 28-page item.
Open. No guide.
University of California, Berkeley, The Bancroft Library, Manuscripts Division.
Merrill (1887-?) describes her home and family life; the formation of Atherton, CA; her experiences during the 1906 earthquake there; and the establishment of the Peninsula School.

665. Metcalfe, Mrs. A. B.
Papers. 1853-55. 1 portfolio.
Open. No guide.
University of California, Berkeley, The Bancroft Library, Manuscripts Division.
Includes letters and reports relating to the education of Metcalfe's daughter at the Academy of the Sisters of Notre Dame in San Jose, CA.

666. Mezquida, Anna (Blake)
Papers. Ca. 1906-65. 4 boxes and 6 cartons.
Open. Unpublished guide.
University of California, Berkeley, The Bancroft Library, Manuscripts Division.
Correspondence and other papers of [Mrs. Mateo M.] Mezquida (?-1965), a writer.

667. Miles, Josephine
Papers. Ca. 1923-52. 3 boxes and 1 carton.
Open. Partial unpublished guide.
University of California, Berkeley, The Bancroft Library, Manuscripts Division.
[Miss] Miles (1911-), a poet and educator, received her BA from the University of California, Los Angeles, in 1932 and taught English at the University of California, Berkeley, beginning in 1940. Includes correspondence with publishers, editors of literary magazines, and poets and manuscripts of her poems.

668. Mill Valley Library Association
Oral history. 1970-72. 1 box.
Open. No guide.
University of California, Berkeley, The Bancroft Library, Manuscripts Division.
Transcripts of interviews with Mill Valley residents, including teacher Rita Abrams; Bella (Fischer) Resek, a voice teacher; Elizabeth (Cooper) Terwilliger, a Bay Area naturalist; Helen (Davis) Clinton, who first came to Mill Valley in 1887 as a summer visitor; Elsie (Maier) Kellers, a summer resident from 1895 to 1900 and permanent resident since 1943; Thelma Fenton, a resident since 1894; and Marjorie (Mills) White, a summer resident from 1898 to 1900.

669. Miller, Katherine Browning (Fischer)
Papers. Nd. 3 cartons.
Open. No guide.
University of California, Berkeley, The Bancroft Library, Manuscripts Division.
Correspondence, manuscripts of plays and novels, and clippings of Miller (1858-1960), an author.

670. Miller, Minnie Lee (Cardwell)
Papers. 1937. 11-page item.
Open. Published guide.
University of California, Berkeley, The Bancroft Library, Manuscripts Division.
Recollections by Miller of a trip by covered wagon in ca. 1885 from Sacramento to Washington Territory, where she subsequently settled. See Dale L. Morgan and George P. Hammond, eds., *A Guide to the Manuscript Collections of The Bancroft Library,* vol. I (Berkeley, CA: University of California Press, 1963).

671. Minto, Martha Ann (Morrison)
Papers. 1878. 26-page item.
Open. Published guide.
University of California, Berkeley, The Bancroft Library, Manuscripts Division.
Interview with Minto (1832?-?), in which she discusses pioneering by women in Oregon, the Indians, and society in the Willamette Valley. Also available on microfilm. See Dale L. Morgan and George P. Hammond, eds., *A Guide to the Manuscript Collections of The Bancroft Library,* vol. I (Berkeley, CA: University of California Press, 1963).

672. Miscellany
Collection. Nd. 1 box.
Open. Published guide.
University of California, Berkeley, The Bancroft Library, Manuscripts Division.
Includes the following writings by women in the 19th century: letters by Ella (Wheeler) Wilcox relating to her books and poems; a letter by Emma Abbott recommending Tillie Ogran as a seamstress; a letter from an unidentified woman to her husband giving family news; a poem by Rose (Terry) [Mrs. Rollin H.] Cooke; and a diary for the years 1861 to 1864 by an unidentified woman. See George P. Hammond, ed., *A Guide to the Manuscript Collections of The Bancroft Library,* vol. II (Berkeley, CA: University of California Press, 1972).

673. Mission Statistics
Records. 1780-1829. 112-page item.
Open. No guide.
University of California, Berkeley, The Bancroft Library, Manuscripts Division.
Statistics on population, baptisms, marriages, deaths, livestock, and agriculture compiled from Baja California mission records. Also available on microfilm.

674. Mitchell, Lucy (Sprague)
Oral history. 1960. 2 vols. and 1 tape.
Open. No guide.
University of California, Berkeley, The Bancroft Library, Manuscripts Division.
Mitchell (1878-1967), an educator, discusses her association with the University of California, Berkeley, as the first dean of women; her friendship with the University's president Benjamin Ide Wheeler and his wife; and the establishment of the Bank Street College of Education in New York City. Includes an introduction by Irma S. Black and Joan W. Blos of the Bank Street College and pamphlets and articles by Mitchell. Also available on microfilm.

675. Mobilized Women of Berkeley
Records. 1917-69. 2 cartons and 4 vols.
Open. No guide.
University of California, Berkeley, The Bancroft Library, Manuscripts Division.
Minutes, 1917-65; cashbook; photos; and scrapbooks containing press releases about the activities of the organization, which was established to do war work and later became a welfare organization.

676. Moede, Helen (Manz)
Oral history. 1965-68. 121-page item.
Open. No guide.
University of California, Berkeley, The Bancroft Library, Manuscripts Division.
Moede (1879-?) comments on her association with the Los Angeles Juvenile Hall from 1926 to 1949.

677. Mooney, Thomas Joseph
Papers. 1906-42. 83 cartons, 121 vols., 14 bundles, and 1 portfolio.
Open. Key and shelflist.
University of California, Berkeley, The Bancroft Library, Manuscripts Division.
Mooney (1882-1942) was tried and convicted of the murder of 10 persons by a bomb explosion during a 1916 preparedness parade in San Francisco. He was sentenced to death, but his sentence was commuted to life imprisonment. He was pardoned in 1939. Mooney's papers relate primarily to the case and include correspondence, legal documents, and testimonies by his wife Rena

Mooney, Sadie Edeau, Dora E. Monroe, and others. Also includes scrapbooks and memorabilia of Rena Mooney. Among the numerous correspondents are Jane Addams, Fannie Hurst, the International Ladies' Garment Workers' Union, the Women's International League for Peace and Freedom, and Margaret (Higgins) Sanger.

678. Morgan, Julia
Papers. Nd. 101 folders, 3 vols., and 1 portfolio.
Open. Partial unpublished guide.
University of California, Berkeley, The Bancroft Library, Manuscripts Division.
Transcript of a 1976 interview about Morgan (1872-1957), an architect, and more than 1000 of her drawings and blueprints for residences and other buildings, primarily in the Berkeley area. Includes drawings from 1927 for the projection room in the San Simeon home of William Randolph Hearst and for a building for the Native Daughters of the Golden West.

679. Morley, Grace Louise (McCann)
Oral history. 1960. 2 vols. and 1 tape.
Open. No guide.
University of California, Berkeley, The Bancroft Library, Manuscripts Division.
Tape and transcript of interview with Morley (1900-) in which she discusses her education, the San Francisco Museum of Art, art and museums in modern society, and her associations with UNESCO, the Guggenheim Museum, the New Delhi National Museum, and various art exhibitions. Also included are letters, photos of paintings, portraits, and clippings.

680. Morton, William James
Papers. 1873-90. 1 box.
Open. Shelflist.
University of California, Berkeley, The Bancroft Library, Manuscripts Division.
Papers of Morton (1845-1920) include letters and notes of introduction for him by Jessie (Benton) Frémont, a letter by her about the electoral commission's decision in the disputed Hayes-Tilden presidential election, and a biographical sketch by her of her father Thomas Hart Benton. Also includes letters by Elizabeth Benton Frémont.

681. Mosher, Clelia Duel
Papers. Ca. 1894-1906. 2 vols.
Open. No guide.
University of California, Berkeley, The Bancroft Library, Manuscripts Division.
Accounts, medical notes, clippings, and other papers of Mosher (1863-?).

682. Murphy, Alyce (Sullivan)
Papers. Ca. 1928-33. 1 box.
Open. No guide.
University of California, Berkeley, The Bancroft Library, Manuscripts Division.
Consists primarily of correspondence of Murphy (1884-1942), who was the daughter of Francis J. Sullivan and niece of Senator James D. Phelan. Correspondents include Gladys (Sullivan) Doyle.

683. Myrick, Elizabeth T.
Papers. 1854. 1 microfilm reel.
Open. No guide.
University of California, Berkeley, The Bancroft Library, Manuscripts Division.
Diary of Myrick in which she recorded an overland journey to California.

684. Naglee, Henry Morris, Family
Papers. 1846-1959. 33 boxes, 6 vols., and 2 portfolios.
Open. Key.
University of California, Berkeley, The Bancroft Library, Manuscripts Division.
Includes letters to Naglee (1815-86) from his sister Mary (Naglee) [Mrs. James Alexander] Burk (?-1911), his daughter Antoinette (Naglee) Burk (1869-1952), and Virginia (Ringgold) Key and letters to Marie Antoinette (Ringgold) [Mrs. Henry Morris] Naglee (ca. 1846-69) from Emily L. [Mrs. Benjamin] Alvord, and her friend Ellen B. Rankin, who worked in the San Francisco mint.

685. Nankervis, Elizabeth Maud (Johnston)
Papers. 1959. 1 portfolio.
Open. No guide.
University of California, Berkeley, The Bancroft Library, Manuscripts Division.
Manuscript account by Nankervis (1873-1961), a resident of San Francisco, of the 1906 earthquake and fire.

686. National Union of Marine Cooks and Stewards
Records. Ca. 1936-65. 21 cartons.
Open. No guide.
University of California, Berkeley, The Bancroft Library, Manuscripts Division.
Records of the Union include items concerning litigation in 1948 that centered around Mary Olson.

687. Nevada, Emma
Papers. 1939. 1 item.
Open. No guide.
University of California, Berkeley, The Bancroft Library, Manuscripts Division.
Letter written from London by Emma Nevada [Mrs. Raymond Spooner] Palmer (1859-1940), an actress, singer, and dancer, to Herbert S. Hamlin in California concerning her title "Empress of Treasure Island." Includes clippings about her 80th birthday from the *London Daily Telegraph* and *Morning Post* and a biographical sketch by the Grass Valley Chamber of Commerce.

688. Newmark, Mrs. Joseph Solomon
Papers. 1900. 1 vol.
Open. No guide.
University of California, Berkeley, The Bancroft Library, Manuscripts Division.
Autobiographical notes by Newmark in German concern her childhood in Germany, her voyage in 1855 to America and then to San Francisco via Panama, and her life and various business enterprises in San Francisco, Sacramento, Berkeley, and Alameda, CA. Also included is a translation of the reminiscences by her daughter.

689. Neylan, John Francis
Papers. Ca. 1911-60. 202 boxes, 12 cartons, and 5 vols.
Partially restricted. Partial unpublished guide.
University of California, Berkeley, The Bancroft Library, Manuscripts Division.
Papers of Neylan (1885-1960), an attorney and regent of the University of California, include correspondence and clippings by and about various individuals, including Alice M. Head, Kathleen and Charles G. Norris, Mrs. Arthur Hays Sulzberger, and [Mrs.] Helen S. Young; stories by Winifred (Sweet) Black, who also was known as Annie Laurie; a manuscript play by Cora Miranda (Baggerly) Older; a subject file on the Mother's Pension Committee; and correspondence, legal documents, bills, pamphlets, and clippings relating to the Charlotte Anita Whitney case and efforts to repeal the criminal syndicalism law in California under which [Miss] Whitney was convicted. Whitney, a social worker and suffragist, was arrested in ca. 1920 because of her membership in the Communist party. Also included is a transcript of a 1954 interview in which Neylan, who defended Whitney without charge, discusses his defense in the case.

690. Nichols, Rowena
Papers. 1879. 31-page item.
Open. Published guide.
University of California, Berkeley, The Bancroft Library, Manuscripts Division.
Manuscript notes on Indian affairs in Oregon include reminiscences by W. P. Breeding and Joseph Joset, a Catholic priest of the Coeur d'Alene Mission. Also available on microfilm. See Dale L. Morgan and George P. Hammond, eds., *A Guide to the Manuscript Collections of The Bancroft Library,* vol. I (Berkeley, CA: University of California Press, 1963).

691. Norris Family
Papers. Nd. 4 cartons and 1 portfolio.
Open. Key.
University of California, Berkeley, The Bancroft Library, Manuscripts Division.
Manuscripts of an autobiography, novels, short stories, and articles by author Kathleen (Thompson) [Mrs. Charles Gilman] Norris (1880-1966) and letters to Charles and Kathleen Norris from Fannie Hurst, Mary (Roberts) Rinehart, Gertrude Franklin (Horn) Atherton, Katharine Brush, Edna Ferber, Margaret (Higgins) Sanger, and Peggy Wood.

692. Norris, Kathleen (Thompson)
Papers. Ca. 1910-57. 1 carton, 2 vols., and 1 tape.
Open. No guide.
University of California, Berkeley, The Bancroft Library, Manuscripts Division.
Manuscripts by Norris (1880-1966), an author, of *Saturday's Child, The Heart of Rachel,* and *Walls of Gold;* notes for her book *The Venables;* verses written by her and set to music; a photo; a bibliography of her magazine contributions for the period 1910 to 1930; a scrapbook of clippings; and bibliographies for her husband Charles Gilman Norris and his brother Frank Norris (?-1902). Also includes an interview in which Norris describes her early life in San Francisco and Mill Valley, CA; the Thompson and Norris families; the literary world of New York and California; and her views on writing. Interview also available on microfilm.

693. Norton, Clementine Ursula
Papers. Ca. 1859-99. 1 box.
Open. No guide.
University of California, Berkeley, The Bancroft Library, Manuscripts Division.
Consists primarily of letters to Norton (1843-1926) from her fiance Seneca R. Flint while he was serving in the cavalry with the Wisconsin volunteers during the Civil War. Flint died in the war in 1864, and Norton never married.

694. Norton, Maria J. (Elliott)
Papers. 1859. 1 microfilm reel.
Open. No guide.
University of California, Berkeley, The Bancroft Library, Manuscripts Division.
Diary in which Norton describes an 1859 overland journey from Illinois to California, recording the progress of the Elliott party to Nevada. The diary stops before their arrival in California.

695. Nuestra Señora de la Soledad Mission
Records. Ca. 1791-1878. 2 folders and 1 item.
Open. No guide.
University of California, Berkeley, The Bancroft Library, Manuscripts Division.
Extracts from mission record books for 1791 to 1840 list baptisms, marriages, confirmations, and burials. Mission records for 1818 to 1834 list boys, girls, widows, widowers, and name, baptismal number, and age of neophytes. Also available on microfilm.

696. Nystrom, Elvira
Papers. 1937-40. 1 portfolio.
Open. No guide.
University of California, Berkeley, The Bancroft Library, Manuscripts Division.
Form letters and notes relating to the Los Angeles Girls' Town, of which [Mrs.] Nystrom was founder

and president, and minutes of the Los Angeles Scientific Psychic Research Society.

697. Oberndorfer, Leonora (Levy)
Papers. Ca. 1880-1900. 2 vols. and 1 envelope.
Open. Published guide.
University of California, Berkeley, The Bancroft Library, Manuscripts Division.
Scrapbooks of Oberndorfer and articles and clippings of short stories, poetry, and news events. See George P. Hammond, ed., *A Guide to the Manuscript Collections of The Bancroft Library,* vol. II (Berkeley, CA: University of California Press, 1972).

698. O'Connor, James Francis Thaddeus
Papers. 1933-47. 21 vols.
Open. Key.
University of California, Berkeley, The Bancroft Library, Manuscripts Division.
Correspondence of O'Connor (1886-1949) relates to his work as comptroller of the currency, to political events, and to his appointment as US district judge in southern California and includes letters from Elizabeth Arden, Helen (Gahagan) Douglas, Hedda Hopper, Maria Jeritza, Florence (Prag) Kahn, Kay Kyser, Elissa Landi, Evalyn Walsh McLean, Louella (Oettinger) Parsons, Frances Perkins, and Grace Tully.

699. Odell, Elizabeth F. (McClench) Thurston
Papers. 1879. 45-page item.
Open. Published guide.
University of California, Berkeley, The Bancroft Library, Manuscripts Division.
Biography of Samuel Royal Thurston (1816-51) by Odell, his widow, concerns Thurston's early life in Maine and Iowa, his overland journey to Oregon in 1847, and his service in the Oregon legislature in 1848 and 1849 and as a delegate to Congress in 1849. Also includes a letter by Odell to H. H. Bancroft. Also available on microfilm. See Dale L. Morgan and George P. Hammond, eds., *A Guide to the Manuscript Collections of The Bancroft Library,* vol. I (Berkeley, CA: University of California Press, 1963).

700. Offord, Lenore (Glen)
Papers. Nd. 1 portfolio.
Open. No guide.
University of California, Berkeley, The Bancroft Library, Manuscripts Division.
Corrected typescript and galley proofs of *Clues to Burn* by Offord (1905-), an author.

701. Older, Cora Miranda (Baggerly)
Papers. 1914-65. 52 vols.
Open. No guide.
University of California, Berkeley, The Bancroft Library, Manuscripts Division.
Diaries in which Older (1876-1968) records her daily activities and comments about her husband Fremont Older.

702. Older, Fremont
Papers. Ca. 1907-41. 7 boxes, 1 vol., and 1 portfolio.
Open. Shelflist.
University of California, Berkeley, The Bancroft Library, Manuscripts Division.
Papers of Older (1856-1935) include correspondence of his wife Cora consisting for the most part of letters of condolence. Among the correspondents are Gertrude Franklin (Horn) Atherton, Winifred (Sweet) Black, Emma Goldman, Millicent Veronica (Willson) Hearst, Mabel Dodge Luhan, and Louella O. Parsons.

703. Olney, Mary (McLean)
Oral history. 1963. 1 vol. and 1 tape.
Open. No guide.
University of California, Berkeley, The Bancroft Library, Manuscripts Division.
Olney (1873-1965) reminisces about her father John Knox McLean, who was pastor of the First Congregational Church of Oakland, CA, and about life in Oakland and Berkeley and as a student at the University of California, Berkeley, from 1891 to 1895. Also included are photos.

704. Oregon Sketches
Papers. 1878. 1 portfolio.
Open. Published guide.
University of California, Berkeley, The Bancroft Library, Manuscripts Division.
Includes a sketch by Elizabeth (Miller) Wilson, who came to Oregon in 1851 as one of Governor Slade's company of teachers, in which she remarks on early Oregon, curiosities of behavior and costume, and Oregon personalities. Also available on microfilm. See Dale L. Morgan and George P. Hammond, eds., *A Guide to the Manuscript Collections of The Bancroft Library,* vol. I (Berkeley, CA: University of California Press, 1963).

705. Pacific Coast Association of Friends
Records. 1931. 1 portfolio.
Open. No guide.
University of California, Berkeley, The Bancroft Library, Manuscripts Division.
Letters addressed to Anna Cox Brinton, Howard Brinton, and Peter Gulbrandsen; completed questionnaires regarding the proposed Association; a summary of replies to the questionnaire; and lists of potential members.

706. Paden, Irene (Dakin)
Papers. Nd. 1 box.
Open. No guide.
University of California, Berkeley, The Bancroft Library, Manuscripts Division.
Papers of Paden (1888-1974), an author, include a partial manuscript, notes, sketch maps, and a design for the dust jacket of her book *Prairie Schooner Detours.*

707. Pardee, George Cooper
Papers. 1890-1941. 117 boxes, 11 cartons, 58 vols., and 1 portfolio.
Open. Key.
University of California, Berkeley, The Bancroft Library, Manuscripts Division.
Papers of Pardee (1857-1941) include telegrams from his wife Helen N. (Penniman) Pardee (?-1945) and letters from the WCTU, the Woman's Relief Corps Home Association, the Native Daughters of the Golden West, Clara Barton, Ina Donna Coolbrith, Phoebe (Apperson) Hearst, and other women.

708. The Parents' View of the University Elementary School, Los Angeles
Oral history. 1960. 1 vol.
Open. No guide.
University of California, Berkeley, The Bancroft Library, Manuscripts Division.
Interviews with Margaret Kiskadden and Jean Trapnell concern the campaign by Los Angeles citizens and parents of pupils to help Corinne Seeds save the School, which was part of the educational program at the University of California, Los Angeles.

709. Parker, Cornelia (Stratton)
Papers. 1954-63. 2 cartons.
Open. No guide.
University of California, Berkeley, The Bancroft Library, Manuscripts Division.
Papers of Parker (1885-1972) consist of research notes on California history and on the Stratton family, in particular her grandfather James T. Stratton; fragments of a manuscript about the family; and correspondence.

710. Parsons Family
Papers. Ca. 1880-1953. 9 boxes, 5 cartons, 2 vols., and 1 portfolio.
Open. Key.
University of California, Berkeley, The Bancroft Library, Manuscripts Division.
Consists primarily of papers of Marion (Randall) Parsons (1878-1953), an author of short stories and novels and self-taught artist in water colors and oils who was active in the Sierra Club; she replaced her husband Edward Taylor Parsons on the Club's board of directors upon his death in 1914 and served until 1936. Her papers include correspondence, manuscripts, notes, publishing contracts and other legal papers, her will, marriage certificate, photos, memorabilia, book reviews, and clippings relating to her service in the American National Red Cross during WWI, her interest in mountaineering, and her writing. Correspondents include Mary (McHenry) [Mrs. William] Keith, Helen Marion (Gompertz) [Mrs. Joseph Nisbet] Le Conte, and [Miss] Josephine Miles. Parsons contributed articles to the *Sierra Club Bulletin, Sunset,* and *Out West;* she also worked with John Muir on his *Travels in Alaska* and prepared it for publication after his death.

711. Parten, Carroll (Borland)
Papers. 1929-34. 3 vols.
Open. No guide.
University of California, Berkeley, The Bancroft Library, Manuscripts Division.
Scrapbooks of photos, programs, and clippings compiled by Parten while a student at Oakland High School and the University of California, Berkeley, concern drama productions at the schools, and sets, plays, actors, and dance on the American stage.

712. Partington, Blanche
Papers. Ca. 1882-1946. 6 boxes and 1 portfolio.
Open. Descriptive guide and shelflist.
University of California, Berkeley, The Bancroft Library, Manuscripts Division.
Consists primarily of correspondence of [Miss] Blanche Partington (?-1951), drama critic for the San Francisco *Call* at the turn of the century and a member of the city's music and literary colony. Also includes correspondence of her father John Herbert Evelyn Partington, an English painter who in 1890 emigrated to the US and established the School of Magazine and Newspaper Illustration in San Francisco, and of her sisters Gertrude, an artist, and Phyllis, an opera singer whose stage name was Frances Peralta, as well as announcements, programs, leaflets, articles, clippings, and books. Correspondents include Ina Donna Coolbrith, Charmian (Kittredge) London, Caroline (Rand) Sterling, Lora Bierce, Helen Ray Bierce, Gertrude Franklin (Horn) Atherton, Mary (Hunter) Austin, Nora May French, and Juanita Miller.

713. Patton, Annaleone Davis
Papers. 1957. 10-page item.
Open. No guide.
University of California, Berkeley, The Bancroft Library, Manuscripts Division.
Scrapbook concerning the first schoolhouses in San Francisco and Alameda County contains photos and clippings by [Mrs.] Patton on schools established by Brooklyn Mormons in 1847 in Yerba Buena and in 1850 in Alameda County.

714. Paul, Alice
Oral history. 1972-73. 1 vol., 1 portfolio, and 22 tapes.
Open. No guide.
University of California, Berkeley, The Bancroft Library, Manuscripts Division.
Tapes and transcript of interview with Paul (1885-1977) in which she discusses her work in the suffrage campaigns in Great Britain and the US, the formation of the National Woman's party, and

the Equal Rights Amendment campaign. Includes letters, suffragist songs, articles, and material relating to the Woman's party. Also includes photos.

715. Pérez, Eulalia
Papers. 1877. 37-page vol.
Open. No guide.
University of California, Berkeley, The Bancroft Library, Manuscripts Division.
Dictation by Pérez (?-1878), who was said to be 139 years old at the time, concerns her life in San Diego and in the vicinity of San Gabriel Mission; her family, associates, and mission priests, including Fathers José Sánchez and Zalvidea; and her recollections of songs and dances. Includes a corroborating statement signed by her daughter María del Rosario (Pérez) de White, photos, and clippings. Also available on microfilm.

716. Perkins Family
Papers. Ca. 1855-60. 3 folders.
Open. No guide.
University of California, Berkeley, The Bancroft Library, Manuscripts Division.
Invitations and programs for cotillions and balls in Todds Valley, Michigan Bluff, and nearby communities in Placer County, CA, addressed primarily to [Miss] Emma Perkins. Also includes *The Todds Valley Gazette* and *School Pioneer,* newspapers handwritten by her younger sister.

717. Pestana, Jean (Kidwell)
Oral history. Ca. 1960s. 1 vol.
Closed. No guide.
University of California, Berkeley, The Bancroft Library, Manuscripts Division.
Interview with Pestana concerns the Jackson freedom ride.

718. Peters Family
Papers. Ca. 1833-1969. 1 portfolio.
Open. No guide.
University of California, Berkeley, The Bancroft Library, Manuscripts Division.
Articles by Lenore (Peters) Job concern her sister Anita (Peters) Wright, a dancer; the establishment of the Peters Wright Creative Dance group; and her recollections of famous dancers in San Francisco. Also includes letters to Peter J. Peters, genealogical material and other papers pertaining to Peters family history, and clippings.

719. Petrov, Ivan
Papers. 1874-90. 1 portfolio.
Open. No guide.
University of California, Berkeley, The Bancroft Library, Manuscripts Division.
Correspondence and other papers of Petrov (1842-96), including letters to his wife about trips to Alaska. Includes papers of his daughter Olga (Petrov) McKibban. Also available on microfilm.

720. Phelan, James Duval
Papers. Ca. 1880-1930. 131 boxes, 29 cartons, and 103 vols.
Open. Key.
University of California, Berkeley, The Bancroft Library, Manuscripts Division.
Correspondence, reports, photo albums, circulars, announcements, programs, clippings, and other material of Phelan (1861-1930), including subject files relating to the California LWV, the League of American Pen Women, the American National Red Cross, the San Francisco Women's City Club, the Western Women's Club, the Woman's Press Association, the YWCA, and such women as Gertrude Franklin (Horn) Atherton, Ina Donna Coolbrith, and Mary Theresa Walsh. Also includes photos of Fannie Hurst, Mary Pickford, Charmian London, and others and correspondence from a number of women, among them Gertrude Atherton, Ella Sterling (Clark) Mighels, Cora Miranda (Baggerly) [Mrs. Fremont] Older, and Phelan's sister Mary Louise Phelan.

721. Phelan, Mary Louise
Papers. Ca. 1896-1930. 2 boxes and 1 vol.
Open. Key.
University of California, Berkeley, The Bancroft Library, Manuscripts Division.
Correspondence and financial papers of Phelan (?-1933), including letters of condolence on the death of her brother Senator James D. Phelan.

722. Pierce Family
Papers. Ca. 1868-1961. 1 carton.
Open. No guide.
University of California, Berkeley, The Bancroft Library, Manuscripts Division.
Includes correspondence and an 1868 diary of Margaret (Cameron) Pierce concerning her early life in San Francisco and her singing career; diaries for 1897 and 1915 to 1917 of her daughter Mary Eugenia concerning her travels in the Orient and social life in the Bay Area, photo albums, scrapbook of clippings, and other material.

723. Pinart, Alphonse Louis
Papers. 1878-80. 1 box (11 folders).
Open. No guide.
University of California, Berkeley, The Bancroft Library, Manuscripts Division.
Lists of Indian names and Indian settlements, or rancherías, compiled and transcribed by Pinart with notes from birth, death, and marriage records of 11 California missions for the period 1771-1844. Also available on microfilm.

724. Pioneer Sketches
Collection. Ca. 1875. No size given.
Open. Unpublished guide.
University of California, Berkeley, The Bancroft Library, Manuscripts Division.
Narratives by pioneers, including a dictation by Josefa (Carrillo) Fitch (1810-?) in which she discusses her elopement with Henry Delano Fitch, her return to California, and her husband's commercial ventures in South America and California. Includes Fitch's 1831 marriage certificate. Also available on microfilm.

725. Pittman Family
Papers. 1798-1873. 15 items.
Open. Published guide.
University of California, Berkeley, The Bancroft Library, Manuscripts Division.
Correspondence and accounts, including letters by Amelia Pittman and by Anna Maria (Pittman) [Mrs. Jason] Lee to her brother George Pittman. See Dale L. Morgan and George P. Hammond, eds., *A Guide to the Manuscript Collections of The Bancroft Library,* vol. I (Berkeley, CA: University of California Press, 1963).

726. Pittman, Tarea Hall
Papers. Ca. 1950-72. 1 box, 171-page transcript, and 1 tape.
Open. No guide.
University of California, Berkeley, The Bancroft Library, Manuscripts Division.
Correspondence, interview transcript, minutes, memoranda, press releases, tape, reports, clippings, and other papers of Pittman pertain primarily to her role in establishing the California Fair Employment Practices Commission. Interview concerns her early life in Bakersfield, CA, and the position of Negroes there; her student days at the University of California, Berkeley, in the 1920s; social work; civil rights campaigns; and her work with the California Association of Negro Women's Clubs, with the California Council of Negro Women, and with the NAACP as field director and acting director of the West Coast region.

727. Pleasant, Mary Ellen
Papers. 1896. 1 portfolio.
Open. No guide.
University of California, Berkeley, The Bancroft Library, Manuscripts Division.
Pleasant, a black resident of San Francisco also known as "Mammy" Pleasant, was sometimes described as the mother of civil rights in California. Letters to James Grases of San Francisco concerning his niece Susie.

728. Porter, Lavinia (Honneyman)
Papers. 1910?. 1 vol.
Open. No guide.
University of California, Berkeley, The Bancroft Library, Manuscripts Division.
Recollections by Porter (1836-1910) of a journey by oxteam in 1859 and 1860 from Hannibal, MO, to California via Denver and Salt Lake City.

729. Poston, Eugenia C.
Papers. 1906. 1 item.
Open. No guide.
University of California, Berkeley, The Bancroft Library, Manuscripts Division.
Typescript by Poston, a resident of San Francisco, concerns her experiences in 1906 and includes a description of the San Francisco earthquake and fire.

730. Powell, Mary (Bennion)
Papers. 1952-53. 332-page item.
Open. Published guide.
University of California, Berkeley, The Bancroft Library, Manuscripts Division.
Manuscript by Powell, originally written as a series of letters to George R. Stewart of the University of California, concerns her experiences as a member of a polygamous family in Utah after the Manifesto of 1890. See Dale L. Morgan and George P. Hammond, eds., *A Guide to the Manuscript Collections of The Bancroft Library,* vol. I (Berkeley, CA: University of California Press, 1963).

731. Prescott, Jessie Kennedy
Oral history. 1962. 1 tape.
Open. No guide.
University of California, Berkeley, The Bancroft Library, Manuscripts Division.
In an interview conducted by her daughter Marion (Prescott) Kimble, Prescott comments on silver mining in Nevada, sheepherding in the San Joaquin Valley of California, ranch life in the 1880s, and summers in Los Banos, CA. Includes notes on the interview.

732. Prevaux, Francis Edward
Papers. 1846-59. 1 box.
Open. No guide.
University of California, Berkeley, The Bancroft Library, Manuscripts Division.
Includes letters to Prevaux (1822-60) from his wife Lydia Dean (Rowell) Prevaux.

733. Purisima Concepción Mission
Records. 1876. 1 vol.
Open. No guide.
University of California, Berkeley, The Bancroft Library, Manuscripts Division.
Information copied from record books in 1876 includes lists of officiating priests, a list of rancherías, an 1836 census of people living at the Mission, lists of baptisms and deaths in the period 1787 to 1851, and a table of baptisms, marriages, and burials. Also available on microfilm.

734. Putnam, Ruth
Papers. Ca. 1917. 1 item.
Open. No guide.
University of California, Berkeley, The Bancroft Library, Manuscripts Division.
Typescript of a book by Putnam (1856-1931),

California—The Name (University of California Press, 1917).

735. Radcliffe College, Schlesinger Library, Schlesinger-Rockefeller History Project
Oral history. 1973-76. 17 vols.
Open. No guide.
University of California, Berkeley, The Bancroft Library, Manuscripts Division.
Transcripts of interviews with women involved in the birth control and maternal health movements.

736. Radcliffe, Mary (Van Wagener)
Papers. 1860-1902. 358-page vol.
Open. Published guide.
University of California, Berkeley, The Bancroft Library, Manuscripts Division.
Journal that Radcliffe kept in a diary, which had belonged to her husband Lewis Radcliffe, a clergyman. Her journal describes their life in the Middle West and includes some of his entries. See George P. Hammond, ed., *A Guide to the Manuscript Collections of The Bancroft Library,* vol. II (Berkeley, CA: University of California Press, 1972).

737. Radcliffe, Zoe (Green)
Papers. Nd. 1 box.
Open. No guide.
University of California, Berkeley, The Bancroft Library, Manuscripts Division.
Contains letters from Charmian London, Ina Coolbrith, and others; photos; and clippings.

738. Rahm, Louisa (Moeller)
Papers. 1862. 75-page item.
Open. No guide.
University of California, Berkeley, The Bancroft Library, Manuscripts Division.
Diary of Rahm records a trip from Fairfield, IL, to California. Also available on microfilm.

739. Ralston, Jackson Harvey
Papers. 1890-1945. 13 cartons.
Open. Unpublished guide.
University of California, Berkeley, The Bancroft Library, Manuscripts Division.
Biographical sketch of Ralston's mother Harriet N. (Jackson) [Mrs. James H.] Ralston, written by his wife.

740. Ramsland, Margaret Alyce Ruth (Chivers)
Papers. 1972-74. 1 vol. and 1 item.
Open. No guide.
University of California, Berkeley, The Bancroft Library, Manuscripts Division.
Two manuscripts by Ramsland, one of which concerns Daniel Bidwell, who settled on Rancho Chico in Butte County in 1854, and his family and descendants. The other is a history with photos and genealogies of the Hawaiian Ke' a' a' la family that arrived in California in 1839 with Sutter and married into the Kon Kau tribe of California; it also concerns the life and work of John and Annie (Kennedy) Bidwell and the background of the Round Valley Reservation.

741. Rankin, Jeannette
Oral history. 1972. 313-page item.
Open. No guide.
University of California, Berkeley, The Bancroft Library, Manuscripts Division.
Rankin (1880-1973) discusses her work for woman suffrage, her campaign for Congress, her stand against American participation in WWI and WWII and in the Vietnam War, her views on political action, and her work for world peace. Includes photos.

742. Reed, Alice Clara
Oral history. 1969. 127-page item.
Open. No guide.
University of California, Berkeley, The Bancroft Library, Manuscripts Division.
Reed (1890-?) discusses her life as an educational missionary from 1916 to 1948 in various Congregational mission settlements in China.

743. Reed, Virginia
Collection. 1847-1912. 1 portfolio.
Open. No guide.
University of California, Berkeley, The Bancroft Library, Manuscripts Division.
Includes an 1847 letter by Reed to her cousin in Springfield, IL, concerning the Donner party; letters by Virginia Reed Murphy to Porter Garnett; and letters, an introduction by Garnett, and other material pertaining to the proposed publication of Reed's 1847 letter by the Academy of Pacific Coast History.

744. Reilly, Jean Burt
Oral history. 1962. 135-page item.
Open. No guide.
University of California, Berkeley, The Bancroft Library, Manuscripts Division.
Reilly discusses her career as a hair stylist in the motion picture industry.

745. Richards, Bessie (Launder)
Oral history. 1967. 1 vol. and 1 tape.
Open. Partial published guide.
University of California, Berkeley, The Bancroft Library, Manuscripts Division.
Tape and transcript of interview with Richards (1885-1969) in which she describes her childhood in the Colorado mining towns of St. Elmo and Buena Vista; her marriage to mining engineer Edwin R. Richards; her life in Mexico at the Pinguico and La Luz silver mines near Guanajuato from 1908 to 1911, at Monterrey from 1923 to 1928, and at La Noria near Sombrerete in 1929; and her contacts with guerrillas and bandits and other experiences during the Mexican revolution. Also includes photos. See George P. Hammond, ed., *A Guide to the Manuscript Collections of The Bancroft Library,* vol. II (Berkeley: University of California Press, 1972).

746. Richards, Jane (Snyder)
Papers. 1880. 2 items.
Open. Published guide.
University of California, Berkeley, The Bancroft Library, Manuscripts Division.
Interviews with Richards (1823-1912), the first wife of polygamist Franklin O. Richards, concern her early life in New York and Canada; her experiences in Nauvoo, IL, and exodus to Salt Lake City; her husband's missions to England; her views on plural marriage; and Indian relations. Also available on microfilm. See Dale L. Morgan and George P. Hammond, eds., *A Guide to the Manuscript Collections of The Bancroft Library,* vol. I (Berkeley, CA: University of California Press, 1963).

747. Richardson, Caroline L.
Papers. 1852-53. 214-page item.
Open. No guide.
University of California, Berkeley, The Bancroft Library, Manuscripts Division.
Diary records an 1852 journey from Illinois to California and contains a letter, poems, and recipes. Also available on microfilm.

748. Ridington, Juana de Dios (Machado) Alipás
Papers. 1878. 44-page item.
Open. No guide.
University of California, Berkeley, The Bancroft Library, Manuscripts Division.
Dictation by Ridington (1814-?) in which she reminisces about her father José Manuel Machado, a soldier who was involved in subduing Indians; Indian depredations at Rancho Jamul and elsewhere; her acquaintance with Apolinaria Lorenzana; her first husband's experiences as a soldier in San Diego, as part of the Solás revolt, and as a member of Echeandía's expedition to Colorado; the Padrés Hijar colony; and the American occupation of southern California. Also available on microfilm.

749. Rinder, Rose (Perlmutter)
Oral history. 1968-69. 1 vol.
Open. No guide.
University of California, Berkeley, The Bancroft Library, Manuscripts Division.
Interview with Rinder in which she discusses her and her husband cantor Reuben Rinder's association from 1913 to 1969 with the Temple Emanu-El in San Francisco; their participation in the musical life of the Bay Area; and their friendship with various musicians, including Ernest Bloch, Yehudi Menuhin, and Isaac Stern. Also includes letters, photos, programs, and other miscellaneous items.

750. Robb, Agnes R.
Oral history. Nd. No size given.
Open. No guide.
University of California, Berkeley, The Bancroft Library, Manuscripts Division.
Transcript of interview with Robb in which she discusses her association with Robert Gordon Sproul and with the University of California. Also includes photos and miscellaneous items.

751. Roberts, Myra
Papers. Nd. 16-page item.
Open. No guide.
University of California, Berkeley, The Bancroft Library, Manuscripts Division.
Manuscript written by [Miss] Roberts for the Missionary Society of The Dalles, OR, concerns her experiences as a missionary in 1857 in Hawaii, with comments on the country, its natives, missions, and missionaries.

752. Rodgers, Viola
Papers. Ca. 1907-32. 2 boxes.
Open. No guide.
University of California, Berkeley, The Bancroft Library, Manuscripts Division.
Papers of Rodgers include letters from George Moore and an autobiographical sketch.

753. Rogers, William King
Papers. 1879-84. 75 folders.
Open. Shelflist.
University of California, Berkeley, The Bancroft Library, Manuscripts Division.
Consists primarily of letters to Rogers (1828-93), private secretary to President Rutherford B. Hayes, from General and Mrs. Frémont relating to Frémont's governorship of Arizona Territory. Includes letters from Jessie (Benton) Frémont.

754. Rosenshine, Annette
Papers. Ca. 1909-60. 1 box, 1 carton, 3 vols., and 1 microfilm reel.
Open. No guide.
University of California, Berkeley, The Bancroft Library, Manuscripts Division.
Letters from Alice B. Toklas and a manuscript by Rosenshine (1880-1971), a sculptor, concerning her childhood in San Francisco, her friendship with Toklas, her early interest in and study of art, a trip to Paris from 1906 to 1908 with Michael and Sarah Stein, her study with Matisse, her friendship with Leo Stein and Gertrude Stein, social service in San Francisco, and psychoanalysis.

755. Rosenshine, Edith H.
Papers. Nd. 1 box.
Open. No guide.
University of California, Berkeley, The Bancroft Library, Manuscripts Division.
Manuscripts by Rosenshine (1895-) relate to such subjects as early life in San Francisco, the 1906

earthquake and fire, a trip to Europe in 1908 with her sister Annette (1880-1971), the Gertrude Stein family, the Community Music School in San Francisco, and her experiences with psychiatrists.

756. Rowell, Chester Harvey
Papers. 1887-1946. 27 boxes and 10 cartons.
Open. Shelflist.
University of California, Berkeley, The Bancroft Library, Manuscripts Division.
Papers of Rowell (1867-1948) include correspondence from the LWV, the YWCA, the WCTU, the Woman's City Club of Los Angeles, and a number of women, among them Ida Minerva Tarbell, Charlotte Anita Whitney, Jane Addams, and Aurelia Isabel (Henry) Reinhardt, president of Mills College in Oakland, CA.

757. Rowell, Joseph Cummings
Papers. 1884-1937. 3 boxes.
Open. Key.
University of California, Berkeley, The Bancroft Library, Manuscripts Division.
Papers of Rowell (1853-1938), a librarian at the University of California, include correspondence from Gertrude Franklin (Horn) Atherton, Ina Donna Coolbrith, and a number of other women.

758. Rowley, Grace May
Oral history. 1970-71. 57-page item.
Open. No guide.
University of California, Berkeley, The Bancroft Library, Manuscripts Division.
Rowley (1887-?) discusses her experiences in China as a teacher and principal of girls' schools in Weihsien from 1910 to 1932 and in Yihsien, Shantung, from 1932 to 1941 under the sponsorship of the Board of Foreign Missions of the Presbyterian Church. Includes a photo.

759. Royce, Sarah Eleanor (Bayliss)
Papers. Ca. 1884-86. 1 vol.
Open. No guide.
University of California, Berkeley, The Bancroft Library, Manuscripts Division.
Reminiscences of [Mrs. Josiah] Royce (1819-91), written at the request of her son Josiah Royce, were based on her "Pilgrimage Diary" and concern her overland journey in 1849 to California with her husband and daughter and her experiences in Sacramento, CA, in San Francisco, and in various mining camps. Her reminiscences were published as *A Frontier Lady* (1932).

760. Russell, Helen (Crocker)
Papers. Ca. 1930s-1960s. 9 cartons.
Open. Unpublished guide.
University of California, Berkeley, The Bancroft Library, Manuscripts Division.
Papers of Russell (?-1966) relate to her involvement with UNESCO, the San Francisco Foundation, the San Francisco Museum of Art, the Children's Hospital Women's Board, the Asia Foundation, the Institute of International Education, the Katharine Branson School, and Mills College. Includes correspondence files on the Garden Club Fellowship, International House, youth councils, human rights, and the Women's Foundation; diaries for 1936 and 1939-66; photos; scrapbooks; and clippings.

761. Ryan, Beatrice Judd
Papers. Nd. 1 item.
Open. No guide.
University of California, Berkeley, The Bancroft Library, Manuscripts Division.
Recollections written by [Mrs.] Ryan (ca. 1880-1966) during the last years of her life concern the establishment of the Galerie Beaux Arts in San Francisco, life on Russian Hill, her work with the Federal Art Project, a trip to Mexico, the Panama Pacific International Exposition, and her association with Diego Rivera, Benjamino Bufano, Robert Boardman Howard, Antonio Sotomayor, Jean Varda, and Louis and Lundy Siegriest. Also included are a letter by Lucille Matthews and obituaries of Ryan.

762. Sagen, Ethel (Ames)
Papers. Nd. 1 portfolio.
Open. No guide.
University of California, Berkeley, The Bancroft Library, Manuscripts Division.
Papers of Sagen relate to her studies on Sir Francis Drake and the Plate of Brass.

763. Saint David's Presbyterian Church, San Francisco, Women's Guild
Records. 1944-63. 2 vols.
Open. No guide.
University of California, Berkeley, The Bancroft Library, Manuscripts Division.
Financial records of the Guild.

764. St. Denis, Ruth
Papers. 1925-65. 2 vols.
Open. No guide.
University of California, Berkeley, The Bancroft Library, Manuscripts Division.
Transcript of interview with St. Denis (1880-1968) includes comments on her career as a dancer; on Ted Shawn, Isadora Duncan, and other dancers; on her interest in metaphysics and Eastern religions; and on her poetry. Also included is a photo album with typed captions depicting her dance tour to the Orient in 1925 and 1926 with Shawn.

765. Salz, Helen (Arnstein)
Oral history. 1973-74. 1 vol. and 1 portfolio.
Open. No guide.
University of California, Berkeley, The Bancroft Library, Manuscripts Division.
Tape and transcript of interview with Salz in which she recalls family life in San Francisco, her friendships with artists, her study of art, her portrait painting and poetry, her marriage to Ansley K. Salz, her part in establishing the Presidio Open Air School in San Francisco, and her role in the formation of the Northern California branch of the American Civil Liberties Union in 1934. Includes letters from artist Ralph Stackpole and photos.

766. San Antonio de Padua Mission
Records. 1878. 49 pp.
Open. No guide.
University of California, Berkeley, The Bancroft Library, Manuscripts Division.
Extracts from Mission record books for the period 1771 to 1878 list baptisms, marriages, confirmations, and burials. Also available on microfilm.

767. San Antonio de Padua Mission
Records. 1803-ca. 1834. 2 folders.
Open. No guide.
University of California, Berkeley, The Bancroft Library, Manuscripts Division.
Consists of a list of neophyte families with name, age, baptismal number, and sponsor for each member and a chronological list of widowers and widows. Also available on microfilm.

768. San Buenaventura Mission
Records. 1878. 2 vols.
Open. No guide.
University of California, Berkeley, The Bancroft Library, Manuscripts Division.
Extracts from Mission record books list baptisms, marriages, and deaths for the period 1782 to 1878. Also available on microfilm.

769. San Diego Mission
Records. 1878. 98 pp.
Open. No guide.
University of California, Berkeley, The Bancroft Library, Manuscripts Division.
Extracts from Mission record books list baptisms, marriages, confirmations, and burials for the period 1769 to 1849. Also available on microfilm.

770. San Francisco de Asis Mission
Records. 1878. 75 pp.
Open. No guide.
University of California, Berkeley, The Bancroft Library, Manuscripts Division.
Extracts from Mission record books list baptisms, marriages, and deaths for the period 1776 to 1856. Also included are similar records from Mission San Jose for the period 1797 to 1859. Also available on microfilm.

771. San Francisco Earthquake and Fire
Oral history. 1971. 1 tape.
Open. No guide.
University of California, Berkeley, The Bancroft Library, Manuscripts Division.
Includes interviews with Mrs. Walter Sharp and Mrs. Samuel W. Haile about their experiences during the 1906 earthquake and fire.

772. San Francisco Interviews
Oral history. 1966. 1 tape.
Open. Summary.
University of California, Berkeley, The Bancroft Library, Manuscripts Division.
Theodora Burton describes life in Chinatown from 1890 to 1900; Hazel Hubbard and Dorothy Clarke reminisce about the 1906 earthquake and fire; and Dorothy Forde discusses the earthquake and fire, her experiences with the Chinese, and biographical data on her grandfather in San Francisco.

773. San Juan Bautista Mission
Records. 1878. 35 pp.
Open. No guide.
University of California, Berkeley, The Bancroft Library, Manuscripts Division.
Extracts from record books of the Mission list baptisms, marriages, and burials for the period 1797 to 1833 and include a list of rancherías belonging to the Mission in 1797. Also available on microfilm.

774. San Juan Capistrano Mission
Records. 1878. 53 pp.
Open. No guide.
University of California, Berkeley, The Bancroft Library, Manuscripts Division.
Extracts from Mission record books list baptisms, deaths, and marriages for the period 1776 to 1850. Also available on microfilm.

775. San Miguel Mission
Records. 1878. 21 pp.
Open. No guide.
University of California, Berkeley, The Bancroft Library, Manuscripts Division.
Extracts from Mission record books list baptisms, marriages, and deaths for the period 1797 to 1850. Also available on microfilm.

776. San Rafael Arcángel Mission
Records. 1878. 12 pp.
Open. No guide.
University of California, Berkeley, The Bancroft Library, Manuscripts Division.
Extracts from Mission records for 1773 to 1875 list baptisms, marriages, and deaths. Also available on microfilm.

777. Sanchez, Nellie (Van de Grift)
Papers. Nd. 1 box.
Open. No guide.
University of California, Berkeley, The Bancroft Library, Manuscripts Division.
Manuscripts of articles, speeches, and other writings by Sanchez (1856-1935), an author, on California history and social life.

778. Santa Barbara Mission
Records. 1878. 47 pp.
Open. No guide.
University of California, Berkeley, The Bancroft Library, Manuscripts Division.
Mission record extracts for the years 1782 to 1852 list baptisms, confirmations, and deaths. Also available on microfilm.

779. Sarría, Vicente Francisco de
Papers. 1830. 2 items.
Open. No guide.
University of California, Berkeley, The Bancroft Library, Manuscripts Division.
Circular letter by Sarría (1767-1835) of La Soledad Mission requests that the mission fathers copy Father Antonio José Rodríguez's treatise on the method of performing cesarean operations. Included is a copy of the treatise. Also available on microfilm.

780. Saunders, Mary
Papers. Nd. 24-page item.
Open. Published guide.
University of California, Berkeley, The Bancroft Library, Manuscripts Division.
Narrative by Saunders in which she describes her journey from Iowa to Oregon in 1847, life at the Whitman Mission in Oregon, and the Whitman massacre. See Dale L. Morgan and George P. Hammond, eds., *A Guide to the Manuscript Collections of The Bancroft Library,* vol. I (Berkeley, CA: University of California Press, 1963).

781. Sawyer, Luella Kenan
Papers. Ca. 1924-72. 1 box and 1 vol.
Open. No guide.
University of California, Berkeley, The Bancroft Library, Manuscripts Division.
Consists of papers relating to her work for the Federation of Western Outdoor Clubs and for the Sierra Club. Genealogical material for the Sawyer family is included also.

782. Sawyer, Mrs. Francis H.
Papers. 1852, nd. 2 items.
Open. No guide.
University of California, Berkeley, The Bancroft Library, Manuscripts Division.
Journal kept by Sawyer during an 1852 journey across the plains from Kentucky to California, along with an explanatory letter from her daughter.

783. Scheffauer, Herman George
Papers. 1893-1926. 1 box and 2 cartons.
Open. No guide.
University of California, Berkeley, The Bancroft Library, Manuscripts Division.
Correspondence; manuscripts of poems, short stories, and novels; articles; and clippings of Scheffauer (1878-1927) and his wife Ethel (Talbot) Scheffauer. Correspondents include Elizabeth Förster-Nietzsche, Charmian London, and Karin Michaëlis.

784. Schultze, Mrs. Theodore
Papers. 1879. 4-page item.
Open. Published guide.
University of California, Berkeley, The Bancroft Library, Manuscripts Division.
Manuscript by Schultze concerns her journey with a pack train from Siskiyou County, CA, to Idaho in 1862; profiteering by ferry and bridge owners; and her experiences as the first woman at the Idaho mining camps of Millersburg and Warrens. Also available on microfilm. See Dale L. Morgan and George P. Hammond, eds., *A Guide to the Manuscript Collections of The Bancroft Library,* vol. I (Berkeley, CA: University of California Press, 1963).

785. Schwesinger, Gladys C.
Papers. Nd. 1 box (12 folders).
Open. No guide.
University of California, Berkeley, The Bancroft Library, Manuscripts Division.
Typescript by Schwesinger concerns the struggle for self-government at Manzanar Relocation Center and her experiences as supervisor of adult and vocational education at this WWII relocation center for Japanese evacuees in Manzanar, Inyo County, CA. Includes related notes and papers.

786. Scott, Flora Murray
Oral history. 1970. 1 vol.
Open. No guide.
University of California, Berkeley, The Bancroft Library, Manuscripts Division.
Interview with Scott (1891-), who was born and educated in Scotland and came to the US in 1922, concerns her career as a teacher and botanist before going to the University of California, Los Angeles; the botany department, faculty, and administrators at UCLA; and her research in plant anatomy.

787. Scott, William Anderson
Papers. Ca. 1830-85. 11 boxes.
Open. Key.
University of California, Berkeley, The Bancroft Library, Manuscripts Division.
Papers of Scott (1813-85) include letters by and to his wife Ann (Nicholson) Scott (1811-88); letters from and between their children; and letters from Phoebe (Apperson) Hearst, Ann M. [Mrs. Alfred] Hennen, and Sarah (York) Jackson.

788. Seeds, Corinne Aldine
Oral history. 1960. 1 vol.
Open. No guide.
University of California, Berkeley, The Bancroft Library, Manuscripts Division.
Seeds (1889-1969) discusses progressive education; Tenney Committee's investigation of her and charges of communism; and her career as a teacher in Los Angeles city and county schools, as principal of an Americanization center and of the University Elementary School, and as a faculty member of the school of education at the University of California, Los Angeles.

789. Serrurier, Zenna Leshing
Oral history. 1962-63. 3 vols.
Open. No guide.
University of California, Berkeley, The Bancroft Library, Manuscripts Division.
Serrurier (1906-) discusses her experiences as principal of Ramona High School, formerly East Los Angeles Girls' Vocational High School, a school for girls who have difficulty adjusting to regular school. Includes a photo.

790. Shane, Mary Lea (Heger)
Oral history. 1966-67. 272-page item.
Open. No guide.
University of California, Berkeley, The Bancroft Library, Manuscripts Division.
Shane discusses her student days at the University of California, Berkeley, in the class of 1919; her work and study at the Lick Observatory in Santa Cruz, CA; living conditions on Mount Hamilton; her marriage to Charles D. Shane; directors, astronomers, and instruments at the Observatory; and her organization of the Lick Archives.

791. Sharon, Frederick William, Family
Papers. Ca. 1882-1915. 37 boxes and 1 carton.
Open. Key.
University of California, Berkeley, The Bancroft Library, Manuscripts Division.
Correspondence and other papers of Sharon (1857-1915) and his wife Louise (Tevis) Breckinridge Sharon (ca. 1858-1938), who was the daughter of financier Lloyd Tevis. Includes numerous letters from female correspondents.

792. Shinn, Milicent Washburn
Papers. Ca. 1882-1906. 1 box and 1 portfolio.
Open. No guide.
University of California, Berkeley, The Bancroft Library, Manuscripts Division.
Papers of Shinn (1858-1940), an educator and editor of the *Overland Monthly,* include correspondence by H. Josephine Shute relating to proposed educational reforms in California and from May Cheney, Jessica Peixotto, Elizabeth N. [Mrs. Edward R.] Sill, Samuel L. Clemens, Marion Talbot, and others; a continuation of Shinn's PhD dissertation on child development, parts of which were published in the University of California Publications in Education; and school compositions by her and her sister.

793. Shirpser, Clara (Garfinkle)
Papers. Ca. 1948-73. 3 boxes, 1 carton, and 2 vols.
Open. Partial key.
University of California, Berkeley, The Bancroft Library, Manuscripts Division.
[Mrs. Adolph J.] Shirpser (1901-), a resident of Berkeley, was active in the Berkeley LWV, the YWCA, the Children's Hospital Association, and other clubs and philanthropic organizations and served as Democratic national committeewoman for California from 1952 to 1956. Correspondence, speeches, interview transcript, press releases, biographical material, photos, subject files, and clippings relate primarily to her political activities, including her work as vice-chairman of the national Estes Kefauver for President Committee in 1955 and 1956 and for the Stevenson-Kefauver campaign in 1956. Interview concerns her involvement in Democratic party politics on the local, state, and national levels. Includes letters from Democratic national committeewomen of other states and a subject file on the 1964 Women for Johnson and Humphrey campaign.

794. Short, Marie
Papers. 1935-66. 1 box.
Access restricted. No guide.
University of California, Berkeley, The Bancroft Library, Manuscripts Division.
Letters to Short from Van Wyck Brooks's first wife Eleanor (Stimson) Brooks and second wife Gladys Brooks and from Una (Call) Jeffers. Many of the letters refer to Carmel, CA, and its inhabitants.

795. Sierra Club Women: Badè, Evans, and Prager
Oral history. 1976. 1 vol.
Open. No guide.
University of California, Berkeley, The Bancroft Library, Manuscripts Division.
Transcripts of interviews with Elizabeth (Marston) [Mrs. William Frederic] Badè, Nora Evans, and Ruth E. Prager, who are active in conservation and the Sierra Club.

796. Simkin, Margaret (Timberlake)
Oral history. 1970-71. 1 vol.
Open. No guide.
University of California, Berkeley, The Bancroft Library, Manuscripts Division.
Transcript of interview with Simkin (1892-?) in which she discusses her life as the wife of a Quaker missionary stationed from 1923 to 1944 at the West China Union University in Chengtu, Szechwan province. Includes a photo.

797. Simon J. Lubin Society
Records. Ca. 1928-40. 15 cartons.
Open. Unpublished guide.
University of California, Berkeley, The Bancroft Library, Manuscripts Division.
Includes studies of households, a settlement survey, information on agricultural unions and organizations in California, and information on migrant housing, education and health of migrant children, and urban groups of migrants.

798. Sketches of California Pioneers
Collection. Ca. 1874. 1 vol.
Open. Unpublished guide.
University of California, Berkeley, The Bancroft Library, Manuscripts Division.
Dictations by California pioneers, including Rosalia (Vallejo) Leese, who talks about the history of the Bear party, the behavior of Frémont and other Americans, and the treatment accorded her husband Jacob Leese in prison. Isidora Filomena Solano talks about her husband, who was an Indian chief, and about Indian customs before and after the coming of white men. Also available on microfilm.

799. Slaughter, Elsie Pynchon
Papers. Nd. 8 vols.
Open. No guide.
University of California, Berkeley, The Bancroft Library, Manuscripts Division.
Typescripts of writings by Slaughter, an author, include *God's Waif,* which concerns her experiences as an actress in Ireland; *I Knew a Lovely Lady,* a history and description of London; *Edwardian Days,* an autobiography of her early years; *Women Who Work;* and other works.

800. Smith, Elizabeth H.
Papers. 1966. 6-page item.
Open. No guide.
University of California, Berkeley, The Bancroft Library, Manuscripts Division.
Essay by Smith concerns Emma Wixom's education at Mills Seminary for Girls and in Europe and her appearance in the West as operatic singer Emma Nevada.

801. Smith, Jedediah, Family
Papers. 1814-1953. 3 boxes, 3 vols., and 6 portfolios
Open. Published guide.
University of California, Berkeley, The Bancroft Library, Manuscripts Division.
Papers of Jedediah Strong Smith (1799-1831), a fur trader and explorer, his brothers Peter Smith (1810-79) and Ira Gilbert Smith (1811-89), his sister Sally (Smith) Shiffer Jones (1791-1871), and other family members and descendants. Includes papers of Peter Smith's wife Juline E. (Babcock) Smith and their daughters Juline (Smith) Thummel and Evelyn (Smith) [Mrs. Walter R.] Bacon; letters of Ira Gilbert Smith and his wife Eliza (Hubbard) Smith to her parents and papers of their daughter Frances Cornelia (Smith) Hubbard, including her account of a voyage from California via the Isthmus of Panama in 1853 and her reminiscences of a journey to New Mexico later in life; an 1859 wedding certificate and other papers of Sally Jones's son Peter S. Jones (1835-65) and his wife Eliza (Prescott) Jones; and correspondence, a family record from a Bible, obituaries, and clippings of Peter and Eliza Jones's granddaughter Stella (Doty) Smith Hare. Includes correspondence by Libbie (Smith) Killpatrick, Lura S. Smith, Mary S. Smith, Sara Eliza (Simons) Spearman, Edna Smith Yeoman, Frances Smith, and other women. See Dale L. Morgan and George P. Hammond, eds., *A Guide to the Manuscript Collections of The Bancroft Library,* vol. I (Berkeley, CA: University of California Press, 1963).

802. Smith, Jennie L.
Papers. 1884. 1 vol.
Open. No guide.
University of California, Berkeley, The Bancroft Library, Manuscripts Division.
Diary in which Smith records her experiences as a teacher in Holly, MI.

803. Smith, Nora Archibald
Papers. Ca. 1925. 345-page item.
Open. No guide.
University of California, Berkeley, The Bancroft Library, Manuscripts Division.
Manuscript by Smith about her sister Kate Douglas Wiggin includes letters from and to [Mrs.] Wiggin.

804. Smith, Pearl (Brown)
Papers. Nd. 1 box.
Open. No guide.
University of California, Berkeley, The Bancroft Library, Manuscripts Division.
Manuscripts, notes, drafts, and clippings of Smith (1879-1957) concern the Modoc Indians and Modoc War and were based primarily on information obtained from her family and other early settlers of Modoc County, CA.

805. Smoot, Margaret Thompson (McMeans)
Papers. 1880. 10-page item.
Open. Published guide.
University of California, Berkeley, The Bancroft Library, Manuscripts Division.
Narrative by Smoot (1809-84) in which she describes her conversion to Mormonism in Tennessee; removal to Missouri in 1837 and expulsion in 1838 and 1839; life in Nauvoo, IL; exodus to and settlement of Great Salt Lake City by the Mormons; her husband Abraham Owen Smoot's mission to England in 1851 and 1852; and her views on polygamy. Also available on microfilm. See Dale L. Morgan and George P. Hammond, eds., *A Guide to the Manuscript Collections of The Bancroft Library,* vol. I (Berkeley, CA: University of California Press, 1963).

806. Snow, Eliza Roxey
Papers. 1880-85. 2 items.
Open. Published guide.
University of California, Berkeley, The Bancroft Library, Manuscripts Division.
Sketches by Snow (1804-87), who was a plural wife of Joseph Smith, Jr., and later of Brigham Young, concern her childhood; her early literary efforts and religious views; her move to Missouri in 1838 and subsequent expulsion with the Saints; life in Nauvoo, IL; plural marriage; the Female Relief Society; the murder of Joseph Smith, Jr., and Hyrum Smith; exodus to and pioneer life in Utah; and various women's auxiliaries of the Church of Jesus Christ of Latter-day Saints she helped to found. Also available on microfilm. See Dale L. Morgan and George P. Hammond, eds., *A Guide to the Manuscript Collections of The Bancroft Library,* vol. I (Berkeley, CA: University of California Press, 1963).

807. Snow, Sallie A.
Papers. 1868. 1 portfolio.
Open. No guide.
University of California, Berkeley, The Bancroft Library, Manuscripts Division.
Letters from Snow to her sister describe her life in San Francisco after her arrival there.

808. Socialist Party, California, Alameda County Campaign Committee
Records. 1912-17. 1 vol. and 1 item.
Open. No guide.
University of California, Berkeley, The Bancroft Library, Manuscripts Division.
Includes minutes, some of which are signed by [Mrs.] Elvina S. Beals; campaign leaflets; and lists of members.

809. Soltysik, Patricia Michelle
Papers. 1971. 49-page item.
Open. No guide.
University of California, Berkeley, The Bancroft Library, Manuscripts Division.
Annotated bibliography of journals, letters, memoirs, biographies, and other writings of western pioneer women compiled for a course at the University of California, Berkeley, by Soltysik (?-1974), who later became known as "Mizmoon," a member of the Symbionese Liberation Army.

810. Southack, Blanche Juliette
Papers. Ca. 1896-1904. 1 vol.
Open. No guide.
University of California, Berkeley, The Bancroft Library, Manuscripts Division.
Scrapbook of Southack contains wedding invitations, theater programs, memorabilia, and clippings pertaining to her social activities while a student at the University of California, Berkeley, in the class of 1904.

811. Sproul, Ida (Wittschen)
Oral history. 1960. 1 vol. and 1 tape.
Open. No guide.
University of California, Berkeley, The Bancroft Library, Manuscripts Division.
Sproul (1891-) discusses her family and childhood; her marriage to Robert G. Sproul and his advancement to the presidency of the University of California, Berkeley; her role as University hostess; distinguished guests; the Los Angeles, Davis, and Santa Barbara campuses of the University; student groups; and the loyalty oath controversy. Photos are included. Also available on microfilm.

812. Stanley, Louise (Hathaway)
Oral history. 1971. 91-page item.
Open. No guide.
University of California, Berkeley, The Bancroft Library, Manuscripts Division.
Stanley (1880-?), the wife of Congregational Board missionary Charles Alfred Stanley, discusses early missionaries and life in Tientsin and Shantung provinces in northern China where she taught English and music from 1904 to 1941. A photo is included.

813. Staples, Mary Pratt (Winslow)
Papers. 1886. 2 folders.
Open. No guide.
University of California, Berkeley, The Bancroft Library, Manuscripts Division.
Correspondence concerning the Lick Old Ladies' Home in San Francisco, David J. Staples as a 49er, Mary Staples's journey to California in 1850 via the Isthmus of Panama, and her subsequent life in California. Also available on microfilm.

814. Stein, Amelia (Keyser)
Papers. 1878-86. 5 vols.
Open. No guide.
University of California, Berkeley, The Bancroft Library, Manuscripts Division.
Diaries kept by Stein, the mother of Gertrude Stein, while living in Vienna, Paris, and Oakland, CA.

815. Stein, Gertrude
Papers. Nd. 1 portfolio.
Open. No guide.
University of California, Berkeley, The Bancroft Library, Manuscripts Division.
Manuscripts of the plays *Not Sightly* and *Old and Old* by [Miss] Stein (1874-1946), an author, and clippings concerning Stein and Alice B. Toklas.

816. Sterling, George
Papers. Ca. 1880-1926. 9 boxes and 1 carton.
Open. Descriptive guide.
University of California, Berkeley, The Bancroft Library, Manuscripts Division.
Includes correspondence of Sterling's sister Alice (Sterling) Gregory with his biographers Jackson Barber and Henry Dumont and with others and correspondence of Sterling's sister Flora (Sterling) Liliencrantz pertaining to settlement of his estate, of which she was executor. Also included are letters to Sterling from Una (Call) Jeffers.

817. Steurt, Marjorie (Rankin)
Oral history. 1970. 1 vol.
Open. No guide.
University of California, Berkeley, The Bancroft Library, Manuscripts Division.
Steurt (1888-?) discusses her career as a teacher in China from 1912 to 1927 under the sponsorship of the Presbyterian Mission Board, her return to China in 1929 and service as director of experimental education at Nankai University until 1932, and her views on education.

818. Stevenson, Matilda "Tilly" Coxe (Evans)
Papers. 1914. 1 portfolio.
Open. Published guide.
University of California, Berkeley, The Bancroft Library, Manuscripts Division.
Letters written from Santa Fe, NM, by [Mrs. James] Stevenson (1849-1915) to George Wharton James concerning charges brought against her for mistreatment of Indian children. See Dale L. Morgan and George P. Hammond, eds., *A Guide to the Manuscript Collections of The Bancroft Library,* vol. I (Berkeley, CA: University of California Press, 1963).

819. Steward, Sam M.
Papers. 1934-71. 1 box.
Open. No guide.
University of California, Berkeley, The Bancroft Library, Manuscripts Division.
Manuscript novel and reminiscences by Steward; letters from [Miss] Gertrude Stein and [Miss] Alice B. Toklas; typescript of Stein's opera libretto *Doctor Faustus Lights the Lights;* manuscript poem written by Stein on Steward's birthday in 1939; manuscript of Steward's *A Love Letter to Gertrude and Alice,* which concerns his friendship with the two women.

820. Stoddard, Charles Warren
Papers. 1867-1918. 3 boxes, 1 carton, and 1 vol.
Open. Descriptive guide and shelflist.
University of California, Berkeley, The Bancroft Library, Manuscripts Division.
Correspondents include Lotta Crabtree, Louise Imogen Guiney, and Carrie (Stevens) Walters, who signed her letters "Ingle." Also included are letters and drawings from Samoa by Isobel (Osbourne) Strong Field.

821. Storer, Tracy Irwin
Oral history. 1975. 1 vol.
Open. No guide.
University of California, Berkeley, The Bancroft Library, Manuscripts Division.
Transcripts of interviews with Storer, a professor, concerning his work at the University's Museum of Vertebrate Zoology and with his wife Ruth (Risdon) Storer (1888-) concerning her career as a physician. Also includes photos.

822. Stoutenburg, Adrien
Papers. Nd. 1 box.
Open. No guide.
University of California, Berkeley, The Bancroft Library, Manuscripts Division.
Manuscript poems and correspondence of Stoutenburg, a poet, with magazine editors.

823. Stratton, Frederick Smith
Papers. 1900-17. 23 boxes, 6 cartons, and 1 portfolio.
Open. Key and shelflist.
University of California, Berkeley, The Bancroft Library, Manuscripts Division.
Papers of Stratton (1859-1915) include letters from his sister Jeanne (Stratton) Good, Georgiana B. Karmandy, Susan Lincoln Mills, and his daughter Cornelia (Stratton) Parker and a scrapbook of his daughter Ann Stratton.

824. Strong, Elizabeth
Papers. Nd. 1 portfolio.
Open. No guide.
University of California, Berkeley, The Bancroft Library, Manuscripts Division.
Autobiographical sketch by Strong in which she recalls her childhood in Hawaii as the daughter of a missionary, her brother Joseph D. Strong, R. L. Stevenson, early days in Monterey, and her career as an artist.

825. Strunsky and Walling
Papers. Ca. 1903-59. 2 boxes.
Open. Unpublished guide.
University of California, Berkeley, The Bancroft Library, Manuscripts Division.
Anna (Strunsky) Walling (1879-1964), an author and lecturer, was a leading figure in the American socialist movement of the early 1900s and a close friend of Jack London, with whom she collaborated on the *Kempton-Wace Letters* (1903). In 1906 she married William English Walling (?-1936), an author and socialist who helped found the NAACP. Correspondence, manuscript of her book *Père Lachaise,* notebooks concerning travels in Europe in 1903, excerpts from the journal of Inez (Haynes) Irwin concerning the Wallings, manuscript speeches and articles, photos, tributes to William Walling, and clippings. Correspondents include Emma Goldman, Charmian (Kittredge) London, and Mary Marvin (Heaton) Vorse.

826. Suffrage in Nevada
Collection. 1914-18. 173 items.
Open. Published guide.
University of California, Berkeley, The Bancroft Library, Manuscripts Division.
Correspondence relating to the suffrage campaign includes letters of Grace Bridges, Bessie Eichelberger, Minnie Flannigan, Maud McCreery, Anne Martin, and Anna Howard Shaw. See Dale L. Morgan and George P. Hammond, eds., *A Guide to the Manuscript Collections of The Bancroft Library,* vol. I (Berkeley, CA: University of California Press, 1963).

827. The Suffragists: From Tea-Parties to Prison
Oral history. 1972-73. 422-page item.
Open. No guide.
University of California, Berkeley, The Bancroft Library, Manuscripts Division.
Interviews with five women concerning their participation in the woman suffrage movement, their ideas on feminism, and their views on the women's liberation movement. Women interviewed were Sylvie Grace (Thompson) Thygeson (1868-1975), who also comments on the birth control movement; Jessie (Haver) Butler (1886-), who comments on Alice Paul and Carrie Chapman Catt and on her work for the Washington, DC, Consumers League; Miriam Allen de Ford (1888-1975), who speaks of her writing and newspaper work; Laura Ellsworth Seiler (1891-); and Ernestine (Hara) Kettler (1896-), who comments on her interest in radical movements.

828. Sullivan, Alice (Phelan)
Papers. Ca. 1904-12. 4 boxes and 1 carton.
Open. Key.
University of California, Berkeley, The Bancroft Library, Manuscripts Division.
Correspondence, financial records, insurance and legal papers, invitations, announcements, and calling cards of Sullivan (1860-1912), who was the wife of attorney Francis John Sullivan and sister of Senator James D. Phelan. Correspondents include Gladys (Sullivan) Doyle, Alyce (Sullivan) Murphy, Mary Louise Phelan, and Mother Agnes of Jesus, whose given name was Ada Sullivan.

829. Sullivan, Francis John
Papers. Ca. 1906-24. 1 carton and 1 box.
Open. No guide.
University of California, Berkeley, The Bancroft Library, Manuscripts Division.
Letters to Sullivan (1852-1930) from Alyce (Sullivan) Murphy, his wife Alice (Phelan) Sullivan, and Mother Agnes of Jesus, whose given name was Ada Sullivan.

830. Sullivan, Joseph Augustine
Papers. 1949-61. 1 portfolio.
Open. No guide.
University of California, Berkeley, The Bancroft Library, Manuscripts Division.
Correspondence of Sullivan (1888-) relates to publications in the California centennial series and includes letters from Helen (Pruitt) Beattie, Helen Smith Giffen, Beryl Hoskin, and Rosena A. Giles.

831. Sullivan, Noël
Papers. Ca. 1911-56. 135 boxes and 8 cartons.
Partially restricted. Key.
University of California, Berkeley, The Bancroft Library, Manuscripts Division.
Sullivan (1890-1956), a patron of the arts who was active in the social and cultural life of San Francisco, supported the establishment of a Carmelite monastery in Berkeley. Correspondence; manuscripts of short stories, poems, and plays by Muriel Gurdon (Sanders) Draper, Sara Bard Field, Lotte Lehmann, Mabel Dodge Luhan, Sister Mary Madeleva, Genevieve Taggard, Marie de Laveaga Welch, Ella Young, Sarah Edwards, and Dora Hagemeyer; and subject files on Gladys (Sullivan) Doyle, Dorothy Maynor, Mary Louise Phelan, and others. Among the numerous correspondents are Lotte Lehmann, Sara Bard Field, Alice Phelan (Doyle) [Mrs. William Patrick] Mahoney, Una (Call) Jeffers, and Dorothy (Ward) [Mrs. Morse] Erskine.

832. Sutro, Adolph Heinrich Joseph
Papers. 1853-1915. 44 boxes, 2 cartons, and 1 portfolio.
Open. Key.
University of California, Berkeley, The Bancroft Library, Manuscripts Division.
Papers of Sutro (1830-98) include correspondence, payrolls and job applications for Sutro Baths and the Sutro Library, estate papers of his wife Leah (Harris) Sutro, and legal documents. Correspondents include Anna (Botsford) Comstock, Phoebe Wilson Couzins, the Florence Crittenton Home in San Francisco, Emma Laura (Sutro) Merritt, and Florence (Clinton) Sutro.

833. Tabor, Augusta (Pierce)
Papers. 1884. 7-page item.
Open. Published guide.
University of California, Berkeley, The Bancroft Library, Manuscripts Division.
Dictation by Tabor (1833?-95) concerns her arrival in Colorado in 1859 from Kansas, her experiences in mining regions, her work with her husband in the post office and express office at California Gulch, and the shipment of gold to Denver. Also available on microfilm. See Dale L. Morgan and George P. Hammond, eds., *A Guide to the Manuscript Collections of The Bancroft Library,* vol. I (Berkeley, CA: University of California Press, 1963).

834. Tanner, Mary Jane (Mount)
Papers. Nd. 1 microfilm reel.
Open. No guide.
University of California, Berkeley, The Bancroft Library, Manuscripts Division.
Journal kept by Tanner (1837-90).

835. Taylor, Paul Schuster
Papers. 1927-30. 1 box.
Open. No guide.
University of California, Berkeley, The Bancroft Library, Manuscripts Division.
Field notes for Taylor's book on Mexican labor in the US include interviews with American and

Mexican government officials, labor contractors and agencies, and laborers pertaining to Mexican, Philippine, Negro, and Japanese laborers; Negroes in Mexico; women in industry; and discrimination.

836. Tevis, Henry Lloyd
Papers. 1907-31. 17 boxes and 1 carton.
Open. Key.
University of California, Berkeley, The Bancroft Library, Manuscripts Division.
Papers of Tevis (1856-1931) consist primarily of family correspondence and requests for financial help and contributions to charitable causes. Includes letters from many women.

837. Thompson, Celia May (Crocker)
Papers. Ca. 1952. 7-page item.
Open. No guide.
University of California, Berkeley, The Bancroft Library, Manuscripts Division.
Typescript by Thompson (1874-?) concerns her parents Henry Robinson Crocker and Ellen May (Hall) Crocker (1848-1935), who operated Crocker's Station in Bronson, CA.

838. Thompson, Ruth S.
Papers. 1928. 10-page item.
Open. Published guide.
University of California, Berkeley, The Bancroft Library, Manuscripts Division.
Narrative by Thompson concerns the experiences of her grandmother Matilda Jane (Jones) Friend (1848-1909), who was the daughter of Britton Jones and the wife of John S. Friend, during an Indian raid in 1868 in Llano County, TX, and her later life in Kansas. See Dale L. Morgan and George P. Hammond, eds., *A Guide to the Manuscript Collections of The Bancroft Library,* vol. I (Berkeley, CA: University of California Press, 1963).

839. Thompson, Sarah Reed
Papers. Ca. 1870s. 1 vol.
Open. No guide.
University of California, Berkeley, The Bancroft Library, Manuscripts Division.
Commonplace book of Thompson consists primarily of compositions she wrote while attending Girls' High School in San Francisco.

840. Toklas, Alice Babette
Papers. 1952-67. 1 box and 1 portfolio.
Open. No guide.
University of California, Berkeley, The Bancroft Library, Manuscripts Division.
Correspondence of [Miss] Toklas (1877-1967), including letters to Wendell Wilcox, and a transcript of interviews with her relating primarily to her family and upbringing in San Francisco, Gertrude Stein's early life, and the Stein family.

841. Tompkins Family
Papers. 1858-1955. 5 folders.
Open. No guide.
University of California, Berkeley, The Bancroft Library, Manuscripts Division.
Includes letters to [Miss] Elizabeth Knight Tompkins and an 1858 diary kept by Sarah Haight, who later married Edward Tompkins, during a trip to Calaveras Big Trees and Yosemite Valley in the wedding party of William C. Ralston and his bride.

842. Tovey, Eloyde
Papers. 1965-66. 1 portfolio.
Open. No guide.
University of California, Berkeley, The Bancroft Library, Manuscripts Division.
Papers of Tovey, a supporter of the United Farm Workers, relate to the Delano, CA, agricultural strike of 1965 and 1966 and include her report on a trip to Delano, a speech she made on behalf of the strikers, and miscellaneous announcements and proclamations of the National Farm Workers Association.

843. Towle, Katherine Amelia
Papers. 1948-68. 2 vols., 1 portfolio, and 1 tape.
Open. No guide.
University of California, Berkeley, The Bancroft Library, Manuscripts Division.
Articles by [Miss] Towle (1898-), memoranda, clippings, and an interview relating to her childhood; student days at the University of California, Berkeley, from 1916 to 1920; teaching at Miss Ransom and Miss Bridges School for Girls in Piedmont, CA; her tours of duty with the US Marine Corps during and after WWII; her career as dean of women and dean of students at the University; and the Free Speech Movement. Interview contains introductions by Eric E. Bellquist and Ruth C. Streeter.

844. Townsend, Susanna (Roberts)
Papers. 1838-68. 1 portfolio.
Open. No guide.
University of California, Berkeley, The Bancroft Library, Manuscripts Division.
Letters from Townsend (1817-?) to her family in the East describing her teaching experiences in Louisville, KY; her life in San Francisco in 1851; farming and education in Placer County and at Clear Lake; and her husband's law practice.

845. Tracy, Nancy N. (Alexander)
Papers. 1880. 36-page item.
Open. Published guide.
University of California, Berkeley, The Bancroft Library, Manuscripts Division.
Narrative by Tracy (1816-?), the widow of polygamist Moses Tracy, discusses her life as a Mormon after 1834, her recollections of Joseph Smith and Brigham Young, living conditions in early Utah, the Utah War of 1858, and plural marriage. Also available on microfilm. See Dale L. Morgan and George P. Hammond, eds., *A Guide to the Manuscript Collections of The Bancroft Library,* vol. I (Berkeley, CA: University of California Press, 1963).

846. Trotter, Ada M.
Papers. 1887-88. 15-page item.
Open. Published guide.
University of California, Berkeley, The Bancroft Library, Manuscripts Division.
Diary of Trotter in which she describes a series of earthquakes in Summerville, SC. See George P. Hammond, ed., *A Guide to the Manuscript Collections of The Bancroft Library,* vol. II (Berkeley, CA: University of California Press, 1972).

847. Turner, Ethel (Duffy)
Oral history. 1966. 67-page vol.
Open. No guide.
University of California, Berkeley, The Bancroft Library, Manuscripts Division.
Turner (1885-1969), an author, reminisces about her childhood in San Quentin, CA; her husband John Kenneth Turner; her residence in Mexico and participation from 1908 to 1911 in the Mexican revolutionary movement; her writing career; Jack and Charmian London; and friends in Carmel, CA.

848. Turner, Ethel (Duffy)
Papers. Ca. 1919-69. 1 box and 2 cartons.
Open. Unpublished guide.
University of California, Berkeley, The Bancroft Library, Manuscripts Division.
Papers of Turner (1885-1969), an author, include correspondence; manuscripts of her novel *The Orange Tree,* her short stories, her history of Mexico, and other books; and clippings about her and her husband John Kenneth Turner. Also includes manuscripts of stories by her daughter Juanita (Turner) Lusk concerning her grandfather and San Quentin.

849. Tusch, Mary
Papers. 1939. 1 item.
Open. No guide.
University of California, Berkeley, The Bancroft Library, Manuscripts Division.
Recollections by Tusch concern the University of California Mother's Club, its WWI work, and the origin of her museum of aviation mementos in Berkeley. Also included are articles from *The Family Circle* about her hobby.

850. Tuthill Family
Papers. 1799-1879. 1 box.
Open. Unpublished guide.
University of California, Berkeley, The Bancroft Library, Manuscripts Division.
Includes Mary E. Tuthill's autograph album with signatures of prominent contemporaries; Sarah J. Tuthill's commonplace book; and letters to Louisa Caroline (Huggins) Tuthill and her husband Cornelius Tuthill from Theodosia (Burr) Alston, Elizabeth Fries Ellet, Caroline Howard Gilman, Eliza (Buckminster) Lee, Lydia (Huntley) Sigourney, and Elizabeth Oakes (Prince) Smith.

851. Tuttle, Charles Albion
Papers. 1849-88. 27 items.
Open. No guide.
University of California, Berkeley, The Bancroft Library, Manuscripts Division.
Includes correspondence between Tuttle (1818-88) and his wife Maria (Batchelder) Tuttle (?-1868) and letters from Maria Tuttle to her sister.

852. Twist, Julia S. (Peck)
Papers. 1861. 55-page item.
Open. No guide.
University of California, Berkeley, The Bancroft Library, Manuscripts Division.
Journal by Twist (1831-?) concerns her voyage in 1861 from New York to San Francisco via Panama with a stop in Acapulco for ship repairs. Also available on microfilm.

853. UCLA Near Eastern Center
Oral history. 1973. 1 item.
Open. No guide.
University of California, Berkeley, The Bancroft Library, Manuscripts Division.
Transcript of interview with Helen A. Dillon and Wolf Leslau, in which Dillon comments on the growth of the Center, the role of Gustave von Grunebaum, publications of the Center, and its affiliations with centers abroad.

854. Uridge, Margaret D.
Papers. 1947-56. 1 portfolio.
Open. No guide.
University of California, Berkeley, The Bancroft Library, Manuscripts Division.
Correspondence, minutes, and an agenda relate primarily to Uridge's activities on the library committee of the World Affairs Council of Northern California.

855. Utah Miscellany
Collection. 1880. 1 vol.
Open. Published guide.
University of California, Berkeley, The Bancroft Library, Manuscripts Division.
Includes a letter by Mary Jane (Mount) Tanner to Matilda [Mrs. H. H.] Bancroft remarking on Mormon society and on her life as a Mormon; a letter by Martha H. (Anderson) Brown to H. H. Bancroft giving a short autobiography, telling that her father was killed in an 1846 battle at Nauvoo, IL, and discussing her life as the third wife of Francis A. Brown; and memoirs by Hannah (Tapfield) King concerning her early Mormon life and her trip to Utah as an English convert to Mormonism in 1853. Also available on microfilm. See Dale L. Morgan and George P. Hammond, eds., *A Guide to the Manuscript Collections of The*

Bancroft Library, vol. I (Berkeley, CA: University of California Press, 1963).

856. Utah Notes
Collection. 1884. 13-page item.
Open. Published guide.
University of California, Berkeley, The Bancroft Library, Manuscripts Division.
Notes by Matilda C. Bancroft and her husband H. H. Bancroft pertain to polygamy, Brigham Young's family, social life, decreasing power of the Mormon Church over its membership after the death of Brigham Young, and other subjects relating to Mormonism. Also available on microfilm. See Dale L. Morgan and George P. Hammond, eds., *A Guide to the Manuscript Colle~tions of The Bancroft Library,* vol. I (Berkeley, CA: University of California Press, 1963).

857. Utah Questionnaires
Collection. 1936-39. 61 items.
Open. Published guide.
University of California, Berkeley, The Bancroft Library, Manuscripts Division.
Personal histories of Utah pioneers, including ca. 42 women, were obtained by interviewers of the Historical Records Survey, Utah Work Projects Administration. See Dale L. Morgan and George P. Hammond, eds., *A Guide to the Manuscript Collections of The Bancroft Library,* vol. I (Berkeley, CA: University of California Press, 1963).

858. Vallejo Family
Papers. Ca. 1834-1932. 1 oversize folder, 16 boxes, and 1 vol.
Open. Key.
University of California, Berkeley, The Bancroft Library, Manuscripts Division.
Correspondence, will, and other papers of Mariano Guadalupe Vallejo (1807-90); correspondence, family papers, will, address books, and calling cards of his wife Francisca Benicia (Carrillo) Vallejo (1815-91); papers of Platón Vallejo, including a scrapbook concerning the death of his wife Lilly Vallejo, letters from his daughter Mary Adelaide (Vallejo) Peters, and estate papers of Adelayde "Adela" (Vallejo) [Mrs. Levi C.] Frisbie (1837-95); and correspondence and other papers of the Empáran family, including an account book of Lachryma Montis. Correspondents include Luisa Eugenia "Lulu" (Vallejo) [Mrs. Ricardo] de Empáran, Maria Ygnacia (Vallejo) [Mrs. James Harry] Cutter, Epifania de Guadalupe "Fannie" (Vallejo) [Mrs. John E.] Frisbie (1835-1905), and other members of the Vallejo family.

859. Vernon, Mabel
Oral history. 1972-73. 2 vols.
Open. No guide.
University of California, Berkeley, The Bancroft Library, Manuscripts Division.
Tape and transcript of interview with Vernon (1883-1975) in which she reminisces about campaigning for woman suffrage; her friendship with Alice Paul, Sara Bard Field, and other women in the movement; Anne Martin's senatorial campaign; organization of the National Woman's party; and campaigning for world peace. Also includes an introduction by Hazel Hunkins-Hallinan, Rebecca Reyher, and Consuelo Reyes-Calderón; an interview with Hunkins-Hallinan; letters; articles; photos; and other material.

860. Vernon, Mabel
Papers. 1914-20. 7 boxes.
Open. Published guide.
University of California, Berkeley, The Bancroft Library, Manuscripts Division.
Correspondence of Vernon (1883-1975), a suffragist who was active in the Nevada suffrage campaign and in the National Woman's party. Vernon served as campaign manager for Anne Martin in her unsuccessful senatorial races in 1918 and 1920 and was associated with the Women's International League for Peace and Freedom and with the People's Mandate to End Wars. Correspondence relates to woman suffrage and to Martin's senatorial campaigns and includes letters from Alice Paul, Charlotte (Perkins) Gilman, and others. See Dale L. Morgan and George P. Hammond, eds., *A Guide to the Manuscript Collections of The Bancroft Library,* vol. I (Berkeley, CA: University of California Press, 1963).

861. Victor, Frances Auretta (Fuller) Barritt
Papers. 1865-ca. 1886. 12 items.
Open. Published guide.
University of California, Berkeley, The Bancroft Library, Manuscripts Division.
Letter by Victor (1826-1902) to H. H. Bancroft, for whom she did historical research; letters to Victor from Louise Lanit; and notes on Oregon history. See Dale L. Morgan and George P. Hammond, eds., *A Guide to the Manuscript Collections of The Bancroft Library,* vol. I (Berkeley, CA: University of California Press, 1963).

862. Victor, Frances Auretta (Fuller) Barritt
Papers. 1863. 3-page item.
Open. No guide.
University of California, Berkeley, The Bancroft Library, Manuscripts Division.
Manuscript poem "Pioneer Anniversary" by Victor (1826-1902). The poem was one of the first pieces she contributed to West Coast periodicals. Turner was first married to Jackson Barritt and then to Henry Clay Victor. Also available on microfilm.

863. Vollmer, August
Papers. Ca. 1918-55. 46 boxes, 7 cartons, and 3 vols.
Open. Key.
University of California, Berkeley, The Bancroft Library, Manuscripts Division.
Correspondence of Vollmer (1876-1955), a criminologist, includes letters by a number of women, among them Annette (Abbott) Adams, Eleanor (Touroff) Glueck, Helen Adams Keller, US representative Ruth (Bryan) Owen, Jessica Blanche Peixotto, and Alida Cynthia Bowler while she was director of the division of public relations of the Los Angeles Police Department and then director of the delinquency unit of the US Children's Bureau.

864. Walsworth Family
Papers. Ca. 1842-1906. 2 boxes and 2 cartons.
Open. Unpublished guide.
University of California, Berkeley, The Bancroft Library, Manuscripts Division.
Correspondence; diaries, manuscript sermons, lectures, and writings; scrapbooks; clippings; and other papers of Presbyterian minister Edward Brown Walsworth (1819-92) and his wife Sarah A. (Pierson) Walsworth (1829-?) relate to their travels and to their association with Oakland Female College of the Pacific, which Edward Walsworth founded. Includes diaries of Sarah Walsworth for 1852 to 1862 concerning their voyage around Cape Horn to California on the *Trade Wind* in 1852 and their life in San Francisco, Marysville, and Oakland as well as her reminiscences, manuscript writings and poems, programs, clippings of her articles and poems, and other papers. Also includes letters, accounts, and other papers of the Gibson and Pierson families and genealogical material relating to the Pierson, Walsworth, and Redington families.

865. Ward, Harriet (Sherrill)
Papers. 1852-53. 132-page item.
Open. No guide.
University of California, Berkeley, The Bancroft Library, Manuscripts Division.
Diary by Ward (1803-65) describes life in Wisconsin and a journey to California. Also included are notes about the diary and biographical information about Ward.

866. Ward, Katherine Bertha Boege
Oral history. 1970-71. 1 vol.
Open. No guide.
University of California, Berkeley, The Bancroft Library, Manuscripts Division.
Transcript of interviews with Ward (1900-?) in which she discusses her experiences as a missionary in China from 1925 to 1939, teaching in Nanking and Chunking, and her life as a bishop's wife in Shanghai and Taiwan from 1948 to 1958.

867. Warner, Mary Eliza
Papers. 1864. 34-page item.
Open. No guide.
University of California, Berkeley, The Bancroft Library, Manuscripts Division.
Diary kept by Warner, the daughter of Alexander L. Warner, during an overland trip to California with her family and her uncle Chester H. Warner when she was 15 years old.

868. Warr, Vernille DeWitt
Papers. Nd. 1 portfolio.
Open. No guide.
University of California, Berkeley, The Bancroft Library, Manuscripts Division.
Clippings and ephemera of Warr relating to her interest in politics and woman suffrage.

869. Warren, James Lloyd LaFayette
Papers. 1846-89. 18 boxes.
Open. Key.
University of California, Berkeley, The Bancroft Library, Manuscripts Division.
Papers of Warren (1805-96), editor of the *California Farmer,* include letters from Eliza Wood Farnham, Sara Jane (Clarke) Lippincott, and other women and manuscripts of articles and poems written for the newspaper by women.

870. Waterman Family
Papers. 1839-1906. 17 boxes, 14 cartons, 4 vols., and 1 portfolio.
Open. Key.
University of California, Berkeley, The Bancroft Library, Manuscripts Division.
Papers of Robert Whitney Waterman (1826-91), who served as governor of California from 1887 to 1891; correspondence, diaries, and other papers of his wife Jane (Gardner) Waterman (1829-1914); and papers of their six children. Includes letters of their daughters Abbie Louisa Waterman (1869-?), Anna Charlotte (Waterman) [Mrs. Irving Murray, Jr.] Scott (1866-?), and Mary Pamelia (Waterman) [Mrs. Hyland Washington] Rice (1850-1925), who writes about the family ranch and dairy near San Bernardino, CA. Also includes letters and pamphlets of their daughter Helen Jane Waterman (1856-?) relating to such subjects as medicine, social hygiene, woman suffrage, prohibition, and white slavery.

871. Webster, Margaret
Papers. 1963. 1 vol.
Open. No guide.
University of California, Berkeley, The Bancroft Library, Manuscripts Division.
Prompt book of Webster (1905-72) contains rehearsal schedule, cast list, and staging directions for her production of *Antony and Cleopatra,* which was performed in 1963 in the Greek Theatre at the University of California.

872. Wedding and Birth Announcements
Collection. 1876-1906. 1 portfolio.
Open. No guide.
University of California, Berkeley, The Bancroft Library, Manuscripts Division.
Announcements from San Jose, CA.

873. Wells, Evelyn
Papers. Nd. 1 carton and 1 box.
Open. No guide.
University of California, Berkeley, The Bancroft Library, Manuscripts Division.
Papers of [Miss] Wells, an author, include manuscripts of her novels and other works; copies of books ghostwritten by her; and letters, 1935-37, from Bessie Beatty, Sara Bard Field, Rose Wilder Lane, Ella Winter, and others pertaining to her biography of Fremont Older.

874. West, Marie de Laveaga (Welch)
Papers. Nd. 9 boxes, 5 cartons, and 1 portfolio.
Open. Unpublished guide.
University of California, Berkeley, The Bancroft Library, Manuscripts Division.
Correspondence, journals, notes, and manuscript poems and prose of [Mrs. George Parsons] West (1905-74), a California poet who published under the name Marie Welch.

875. Westbrook Family
Papers. 1882-86. 5 items.
Open. Published guide.
University of California, Berkeley, The Bancroft Library, Manuscripts Division.
Papers of Texas stock raiser and farmer C. A. Westbrook and his wife Virginia (Whitsitte) Westbrook, whom he married in 1860, include letters and a narrative by Virginia Westbrook, a biographical sketch of the Westbrooks, and an article. Also available on microfilm. See Dale L. Morgan and George P. Hammond, eds., *A Guide to the Manuscript Collections of The Bancroft Library,* vol. I (Berkeley, CA: University of California Press, 1963).

876. Wheeler, Benjamin Ide
Papers. Ca. 1870-1927. 11 boxes, 2 cartons, 1 vol., and 2 portfolios.
Open. Key.
University of California, Berkeley, The Bancroft Library, Manuscripts Division.
Correspondence, photos, genealogies of the Wheeler and Ide families, and other papers of Wheeler (1854-1927). Includes letters from Alice Cunningham Fletcher, Phoebe (Apperson) Hearst, his aunt Amanda Sprague Ide, Lillian (Marsh) [Mrs. Charles Stetson] Wheeler, Susan Lincoln (Tolman) Mills, and his mother Mary Eliza (Ide) [Mrs. Benjamin] Wheeler (1822-84).

877. White, Mrs. Charles Henry
Papers. Nd. 4-page item.
Open. No guide.
University of California, Berkeley, The Bancroft Library, Manuscripts Division.
Historical sketch by White concerning the Protestant Episcopal Old Ladies Home in San Francisco.

878. Whiting Family
Papers. 1924-57. 1 box, 3 vols., and 1 microfilm reel.
Open. No guide.
University of California, Berkeley, The Bancroft Library, Manuscripts Division.
Contains correspondence and clippings of Ethel (Robertson) Whiting (1882-?) and her journal for the years 1924 to 1939, in which she writes about a visit to Washington, DC, for the 1933 inauguration of Franklin D. Roosevelt, her social life while her husband Henry Hyer Whiting was northern California campaign manager for W. G. McAdoo in 1932 and 1938, and other activities. Also included are biographical sketches by Ethel Whiting of her father George M. Robertson, her mother Caroline B. (Story) Robertson, her maternal grandfather Charles R. Story, and other members of the Robertson and Story families.

879. Whitlock, Alma
Papers. 1887. 2-page item.
Open. No guide.
University of California, Berkeley, The Bancroft Library, Manuscripts Division.
Dictation by Whitlock (1839-?) in which she describes San Bernardino, CA. Also available on microfilm.

880. Whitman, Marcus
Papers. 1825-47. 9 items.
Open. No guide.
University of California, Berkeley, The Bancroft Library, Manuscripts Division.
Whitman (1802-47), a New York physician, and his wife Narcissa (Prentiss) Whitman (1808-47) undertook a mission to Oregon Territory for the American Board of Commissioners for Foreign Missions and in 1836 established a pioneer station at Waiilatpu in present-day Washington state. Marcus Whitman's papers include diary notes, letters to his stepfather Calvin Loomis and mother Alice (Green) Whitman Loomis, and a ticket of admission to lectures on midwifery in 1825 at the College of Physicians and Surgeons of the Western District, New York. Narcissa Whitman's papers include letters in which she describes her 1836 journey to her brother-in-law Augustus Whitman and his wife, to her sister and brother-in-law Mary Ann (Prentiss) Judson and Oren Judson, and to her mother-in-law; also includes a letter she wrote from Waiilatpu to a Mrs. Gilbert, mother of an emigrant to Oregon. Narcissa Whitman and her fellow missionary Eliza Spalding were the first white women to cross South Pass in the Rocky Mountains. The Whitmans were killed in 1847 by Cayuse Indians.

881. The Whitman Massacre and Early History of Oregon
Papers. 1839-48. 67 pp.
Open. Published guide.
University of California, Berkeley, The Bancroft Library, Manuscripts Division.
Manuscripts on the Whitman massacre and Oregon history include excerpts from a narrative by Lucinda Bewley [Mrs. William] Chapman. Also available on microfilm. See Dale L. Morgan and George P. Hammond, eds., *A Guide to the Manuscript Collections of The Bancroft Library,* vol. I (Berkeley, CA: University of California Press, 1963).

882. Whitney, Margaret Mason
Papers. Ca. 1923-30. 2 cartons.
Open. Key.
University of California, Berkeley, The Bancroft Library, Manuscripts Division.
Correspondence, biographical sketch, notes and notebooks, financial records, maps, photos, programs, cards, invitations, election material, clippings, pamphlets, and other papers of Whitney (?-1953). Includes minutes, financial records, reports, material on instruction courses for counselors, and other records of the Berkeley Council Camp Fire Girls and a constitution, minutes of the board of directors, reports, worksheets, and other records of the East Bay Girls Service Association.

883. Wiel, Elsa (Rosenbaum)
Oral history. 1971. 19-page item.
Open. No guide.
University of California, Berkeley, The Bancroft Library, Manuscripts Division.
Wiel recalls her 50 years of residence in Atherton, CA.

884. Wiley, Martha
Oral history. 1969. 1 item.
Open. No guide.
University of California, Berkeley, The Bancroft Library, Manuscripts Division.
[Miss] Wiley (1874-1969) discusses her experiences as a Congregational missionary from 1900 to 1947 in China, primarily in the Foochow area of Fukien Province. Recollections of Wiley by Mr. and Mrs. Roderick Scott are appended.

885. Wilkins, Kittie
Papers. Ca. 1887-88. 2 items.
Open. Published guide.
University of California, Berkeley, The Bancroft Library, Manuscripts Division.
Biographical sketch and clipping from an 1887 *San Francisco Examiner* about Wilkins (1861-?), who was the owner of a large herd of horses in Idaho Territory and was known as the "Idaho Horse Queen." Also available on microfilm. See Dale L. Morgan and George P. Hammond, eds., *A Guide to the Manuscript Collections of The Bancroft Library,* vol. I (Berkeley, CA: University of California Press, 1963).

886. Williams, Emma
Papers. 1925-53. 3 items.
Open. No guide.
University of California, Berkeley, The Bancroft Library, Manuscripts Division.
Notes by Williams on residents and old buildings of Dutch Flat, CA; a program for the 1925 Fourth of July celebration there; and a brief history of Dutch Flat by Adeline Gilchrist.

887. Williams, Mary Floyd
Papers. Nd. 618-page item.
Open. No guide.
University of California, Berkeley, The Bancroft Library, Manuscripts Division.
Manuscript of *Fortune, Smile Once More* by Williams (1866-1959), an author.

888. Willis, Mary Eliza (Hyde)
Papers. 1876-1941. 1 portfolio.
Open. No guide.
University of California, Berkeley, The Bancroft Library, Manuscripts Division.
Notes, photos, and clippings of Willis (1854-1934), who founded the first private primary school in Berkeley, pertain to the school.

889. Wilson, Ethel Brodt, Family
Papers. Nd. 2 boxes and 5 cartons.
Access restricted. Partial unpublished guide.
University of California, Berkeley, The Bancroft Library, Manuscripts Division.
Includes correspondence and manuscript poems of [Mrs.] Wilson, a California poet and artist, and of her daughter Virginia Perry Wilson.

890. Wilson, John
Papers. 1840-97. 4 boxes.
Open. Key.
University of California, Berkeley, The Bancroft Library, Manuscripts Division.
Papers of Wilson (1790-1877) include an 1877 marriage record and widow's pension papers of Wilson's widow Ann Robertson (Pulliam) Wilson, a letter by his daughter Mary Eliza (Wilson) Wakeman, and a scrapbook of his granddaughter Katherine (Wakeman) Cooper containing clippings about Ann and John Wilson, Mary (Wilson) Wakeman, and Santa Cruz, CA, social affairs.

891. Wilson, Katie (Adair)
Papers. 1887. 2-page item.
Open. No guide.
University of California, Berkeley, The Bancroft Library, Manuscripts Division.
Dictation by Wilson (1846-?) concerns her move to Monrovia in 1875 and her investments. Also available on microfilm.

892. Wilson, Lila Juliet (Andrews)
Oral history. 1968. 11-page item.
Open. No guide.

University of California, Berkeley, The Bancroft Library, Manuscripts Division.
Wilson (1888-), a resident of Mill Valley, CA, worked during WWII as a visiting observer for the YWCA at the Minidoka Desert War Relocation Center Camp in Idaho. In her interview, she describes her life during 1943 with a Japanese family from Seattle.

893. Winans, Pearl (Fosnot)
Oral history. 1970. 1 vol.
Open. No guide.
University of California, Berkeley, The Bancroft Library, Manuscripts Division.
Transcript of interview with Winans (1891-?) in which she discusses her service in western China from 1921 to 1952 under the sponsorship of the Methodist Church, primarily as dean of women at West China Union University, and her expulsion by the Communists in 1952.

894. Wolf, Rosalie (Walter)
Oral history. 1971. 20-page item.
Open. No guide.
University of California, Berkeley, The Bancroft Library, Manuscripts Division.
Wolf (1908-), a resident of Atherton, CA, from her birth until 1928, describes life and amusements in early Atherton.

895. Women in Politics
Oral history. 1972-73. 3 vols.
Open. No guide.
University of California, Berkeley, The Bancroft Library, Manuscripts Division.
Transcripts of interviews with 33 women in elected or appointed offices in the Los Angeles area, including judges, members of city councils and boards of education, and a mayor, conducted by students in an oral history course at Immaculate Heart College in Los Angeles.

896. Wood, Charles Erskine Scott
Papers. Nd. 10 items.
Open. No guide.
University of California, Berkeley, The Bancroft Library, Manuscripts Division.
Includes a 1913 Christmas poem by Sara Bard Field, who married Wood, and a notice of her lecture on Emily Dickinson in 1928 in San Francisco.

897. Wood, Charlotte Elmire
Papers. 1950-51. 1 item.
Open. No guide.
University of California, Berkeley, The Bancroft Library, Manuscripts Division.
Recollections and notes by Wood (1864-?) concerning the family of her father Charles Wood; their Woodside Farm near Danville, CA; and the Sycamore School in Contra Costa County, CA.

898. Woodruff, Phebe Whittemore (Carter)
Papers. 1880. 6-page item.
Open. Published guide.
University of California, Berkeley, The Bancroft Library, Manuscripts Division.
Autobiographical sketch by Woodruff (1807-85), a Utah resident, concerns her life as the first wife of Wilford Woodruff. Also available on microfilm. See Dale L. Morgan and George P. Hammond, eds., *A Guide to the Manuscript Collections of The Bancroft Library,* vol. I (Berkeley, CA: University of California Press, 1963).

899. Woodson, Rebecca Hildreth (Nutting)
Papers. 1909. 1 vol.
Open. No guide.
University of California, Berkeley, The Bancroft Library, Manuscripts Division.
Autobiography of Woodson (1835-?) in which she recalls an overland journey to California in 1850 with her family, frontier life in Nevada City, her moves within the state after her marriage, and settlers of various counties in which she resided, including Sonoma, Marin, and Monterey. Also available on microfilm.

900. Works, John Downey
Papers. Ca. 1910-17. 11 boxes.
Open. Key.
University of California, Berkeley, The Bancroft Library, Manuscripts Division.
Correspondence and other papers of Works (1847-1928) pertaining to his career in the US Senate and to such subjects as woman suffrage, the Clara Barton tablet, and [Mrs.] Anna M. Foster. Correspondents include the California Federation of Women's Clubs and the WCTU.

901. Wright, Kate H.
Papers. 1935-36. 1 portfolio.
Open. No guide.
University of California, Berkeley, The Bancroft Library, Manuscripts Division.
Papers of Wright relate to La Crescenta Women's Club, of which she was a member, and include notes on the formation of its California history and landmarks department, the text for a pageant on California flags, and photos of members.

902. Yates, Katherine Merritte
Papers. 1918. 54-page vol.
Open. Published guide.
University of California, Berkeley, The Bancroft Library, Manuscripts Division.
Narrative by [Mrs.] Yates (1865-?) concerns a 70-day cruise from San Francisco to the Orient on a Panama Mail Steamship Co. vessel, with descriptions of various cities she visited. Also includes a letter from Yates to the steamship company in Colombo. See Dale L. Morgan and George P. Hammond, eds., *A Guide to the Manuscript Collections of The Bancroft Library,* vol. I (Berkeley, CA: University of California Press, 1963).

903. Yates, Oleta (O'Connor)
Papers. 1934-57. 1 box.
Open. No guide.
University of California, Berkeley, The Bancroft Library, Manuscripts Division.
Notes, speeches, lectures, reports, and translations relating to Yates's activities as a member of the Communist party in California.

904. Young, Clara (Decker)
Papers. 1884. 9-page item.
Open. Published guide.
University of California, Berkeley, The Bancroft Library, Manuscripts Division.
Interview with Young (1828-89) concerns her marriage to Brigham Young at age 16, her experiences crossing Iowa in 1846 and as one of three women on the pioneer journey to Utah in 1847, early housing, and her first year in Salt Lake Valley. Also available on microfilm. See Dale L. Morgan and George P. Hammond, eds., *A Guide to the Manuscript Collections of The Bancroft Library,* vol. I (Berkeley, CA: University of California Press, 1963).

905. Young, Ella
Papers. 1949. 1 portfolio.
Open. No guide.
University of California, Berkeley, The Bancroft Library, Manuscripts Division.
Letters by [Miss] Young (1867-1956), an Irish-born California author, presenting copies of her work to [Miss] Ivander MacIver, acquisition librarian at the University of California, Berkeley.

906. Young, Emma Elinor (Hines)
Papers. Nd. 1 portfolio.
Open. No guide.
University of California, Berkeley, The Bancroft Library, Manuscripts Division.
Manuscripts "The loves and wives of E. J. Baldwin" and "Santa Anita" by Young (1869-?) concern the Santa Anita Rancho and Baldwin. Young wrote the manuscripts in Eagle Rock, CA.

907. Youngman Family
Papers. Nd. 1 portfolio.
Open. No guide.
University of California, Berkeley, The Bancroft Library, Manuscripts Division.
Includes an 1879 letter by Lorinda (Wooster) Youngman (1821-93) describing life in California.

908. Associated Women Students, University of California
Records. 1912-68. 4 cartons.
Open. Key.
University of California, Berkeley, The Bancroft Library, University Archives.
Correspondence and other official records of the organization.

909. Association of Collegiate Alumnae, California Branch
Records. 1894-98. 1 carton.
Open. No guide.
University of California, Berkeley, The Bancroft Library, University Archives.
Records of the Association.

910. California Museum of Vertebrate Zoology, University of California
Records. 1908-49. 5 boxes.
Open. Card catalog and catalog inventory list.
University of California, Berkeley, The Bancroft Library, University Archives.
Records of the Museum include correspondence between Museum directors and Annie Montague Alexander, principal donor of the Museum.

911. Committee on Music and Drama, University of California
Records. 1918-45. 16 cartons.
Open. Card catalog and catalog inventory list.
University of California, Berkeley, The Bancroft Library, University Archives.
Includes correspondence of the Committee with women prominent in theater, dance, and music about performances on the University campus.

912. Daily Californian
Records. 1874- . No size given.
Open. Card index.
University of California, Berkeley, The Bancroft Library, University Archives.
Bound volumes of the *Daily Californian,* a school newspaper that was founded in 1874. The newspaper is also available on microfilm.

913. Department of Dramatic Art, University of California
Records. 1911-70. 20 ft.
Open. Card catalog and catalog inventory list.
University of California, Berkeley, The Bancroft Library, University Archives.
Consists primarily of photo albums of productions and scrapbooks.

914. The Dill Pickle
Records. 1916-35. 1 vol.
Open. Card catalog and catalog inventory list.
University of California, Berkeley, The Bancroft Library, University Archives.
Twenty-eight issues of *The Dill Pickle,* a bogus campus newspaper issued annually by Theta Sigma Phi, the women's journalism honor society. It ceased publication in 1935, the year after its competitor the *Raspberry Press,* a paper put out by men, was banned.

915. Free Speech Movement, University of California
Collection. 1964-65. 4 cartons.
Open. Unpublished guide.

University of California, Berkeley, The Bancroft Library, University Archives.
Consists primarily of papers of individuals involved in the movement.

916. Group for Academic Freedom, University of California
Records. 1950-56. 1 box.
Open. Card catalog and catalog inventory list.
University of California, Berkeley, The Bancroft Library, University Archives.
This faculty organization existed from 1950 to 1956. Includes correspondence and other papers of Margaret T. Hodgen, a professor of sociology and Group member, concerning the loyalty oath controversy.

917. Heller Committee for Research in Social Economics, University of California
Records. 1923-62. 1 carton.
Open. Card catalog and catalog inventory list.
University of California, Berkeley, The Bancroft Library, University Archives.
Correspondence and other records of the Committee, which was founded in 1923 and remained in existence until 1962. The Committee consisted of members of the University faculty, including several women in the field of home economics, and was chaired by Emily Harriet Huntington, an economics professor.

918. Morgan, Julia
Papers. 1926-29. 1 box.
Open. Card catalog and catalog inventory list.
University of California, Berkeley, The Bancroft Library, University Archives.
Correspondence and other papers of Morgan (1872-1957), an architect, relating to the construction of a proposed University art museum.

919. Museum of Anthropology, University of California
Records. 1901-56. 64 cartons.
Open. Card catalog and catalog inventory list.
University of California, Berkeley, The Bancroft Library, University Archives.
Includes correspondence of women prominent in anthropology.

920. Museum of Anthropology, University of California
Records. Nd. 32 cartons.
Open. Published guide.
University of California, Berkeley, The Bancroft Library, University Archives.
Ethnological documents of the Museum include field notes and other papers of such anthropologists as Lila M. O'Neale, Cora A. DuBois, Ruth Benedict, Lucy Freeland, Anna Hadwick Gayton, Erna Gunther, Mary Rosamund Haas, Catherine Holt, Isabel T. Kelly, and Margaret Lantis. See Dale Valory, *Guide to Ethnological Documents (1-203) of the Department of Anthropology, University of California, Now in the University Archives* (Berkeley: Archaeological Research Facility, Department of Anthropology, 1971).

921. Partheneia, University of California
Records. 1912-31. 53 vols.
Open. No guide.
University of California, Berkeley, The Bancroft Library, University Archives.
Texts, musical scores, and reports of the production of the Partheneia, the annual spring pageant written and performed by women students at the University.

922. Phi Beta Kappa Society, University of California
Records. 1900-52. 2 cartons.
Open. Catalog inventory list.
University of California, Berkeley, The Bancroft Library, University Archives.
Correspondence and other records of the Society, including items from Gertrude Atherton, Barbara Armstrong, Gertrude Stein, and other women.

923. Pictures
Collection. 1874- . 13,635 items.
Open. Card index.
University of California, Berkeley, The Bancroft Library, University Archives.
Consists of photos, including a number of pictures of women connected with the University.

924. President, University of California
Papers. 1886-1970. 1256 cartons.
Open. Card catalog.
University of California, Berkeley, The Bancroft Library, University Archives.
Includes letters from Willa Cather, Jane Addams, Frances Perkins, and other prominent women.

925. Prytanean Society, University of California
Records. 1937-70. 4 cartons and 25 tapes.
Open. Card catalog and catalog inventory list.
University of California, Berkeley, The Bancroft Library, University Archives.
Records of this women's honorary society include scrapbooks, a guest book, and trophies of the Mary Bennett Ritter Hall, a women's dormitory and living group sponsored by the Society, and tapes and questionnaires from a 1970 oral history project about the Prytaneans.

926. Student Scrapbooks, University of California
Collection. 1878-1927. 2 cartons.
Open. Card catalog and catalog inventory list.
University of California, Berkeley, The Bancroft Library, University Archives.
Includes scrapbooks kept by women on campus.

927. Women's Dormitory Association, University of California
Records. 1934-65. 1 box and 1 package.
Open. Card catalog and catalog inventory list.
University of California, Berkeley, The Bancroft Library, University Archives.
Correspondence and other records of the Association.

928. Women's Faculty Club, University of California
Records. 1960- . 1 box.
Open. No guide.
University of California, Berkeley, The Bancroft Library, University Archives.
Monthly newsletters and other records of the Club.

929. Young Women's Christian Association, University of California
Records. 1903-24. No size given.
Open. No guide.
University of California, Berkeley, The Bancroft Library, University Archives.
Newsletters of the YWCA, including the *Association Record* for the years 1903 to 1920 and *The Lantern* for 1921 to 1924.

930. Morgan, Agnes (Fay)
Papers. Ca. 1905-62. 4 cartons.
Open. Inventory.
University of California, Berkeley, The Library, Manuscripts Division.
Correspondence and other papers of [Mrs. Arthur Ivason] Morgan (1884-), a chemist, nutritionist, and professor at the University of California, Berkeley.

931. Arnstein, Flora Jacobi
Papers. 1884- . 57 items.
Open. Unpublished guide.
Western Jewish History Center.
Correspondence, poetry, a taped and transcribed interview, photos, clippings, and memorabilia of Arnstein (1886?-) pertain to her careers as poet, author, educator, and cofounder of the Presidio Hill School, a progressive private day school. Contains correspondence with, photos of, and information about musicians, including her cousin the composer Frederick Jacobi, Dame Myra Hess, Ernest Bloch, and Oscar Weill. Also contains an inscribed privately printed autobiographical booklet and photo of Rebecca Godchaux, a music teacher and former social leader of French society in San Francisco; a wedding menu of Edith Brandenstein and Jacob Jacobi; and material on author Harriet Lane Levy, artist Annette Rosenshine, and Helen Salz, who founded Presidio Hill School with Flora Arnstein. Salz was also active with the northern California chapter of the American Civil Liberties Union until her death in 1978.

932. Emanu-El Sisterhood for Personal Service
Records. 1894-1969. 12 ft.
Open. Unpublished guide.
Western Jewish History Center.
Constitution and bylaws, annual reports, minutes, correspondence, reports, photos, scrapbooks, building plans, and brochures of the Sisterhood, earlier known as the Emanu-El Residence Club, which was founded in 1894 as a neighborhood house, evolved into a dormitory for Jewish working girls, and later served as a home for needy girls in the larger San Francisco community. Includes correspondence of Ethel Feineman, Club director from 1915 to 1937, and building plans dated 1922 of architect Julia Morgan. Club developments over the years included the organization of an employment agency in 1894, the creation of residences for girls in 1910, and the building of an expanded multipurpose residential structure for Sisterhood activities in 1923. The facility closed in 1969.

933. Hadassah
Records. 1917- . 36 items.
Open. Unpublished guide.
Western Jewish History Center.
Correspondence, donor books, and brochures of the San Francisco chapter of Hadassah, a Jewish women's group founded in 1917 by Rose Rinder to support the Hadassah Medical Center in Jerusalem. Rinder was the wife of Cantor Reuben Rinder of Temple Emanu-El in San Francisco. Correspondents in the collection include Rose Rinder, Henrietta Szold, Congresswoman Florence Prag Kahn, Marvin Lowenthal, Nathan Straus, Louis Lipsky, and Stephen Wise, a rabbi. Part of the correspondence refers to the founding and history of the chapter.

934. Hassid, Lila B.
Papers. 1960-66. 2 ft.
Open. Unpublished guide.
Western Jewish History Center.
Papers of Hassid, an author and translator, contain correspondence with Malka Heifetz Tussman and other poets and authors and with editors and publishers regarding her work. Also includes English translations Hassid made of Yiddish poems and stories.

935. Jaffa, Adele Solomons
Papers. 1895-1968. 8 folders.
Open. Unpublished guide.
Western Jewish History Center.
Family documents, photos, and pamphlets of Jaffa (1868-1953), a physician and child psychiatrist in San Francisco and Berkeley. Also contains information about her sister Selina Seixas Solomons (1862-1942), who was president of the Votes for Women Club in San Francisco.

936. Kahn, Julius, and Kahn, Florence (Prag)
Papers. 1877-1940. 2 ft.
Open. Unpublished guide.
Western Jewish History Center.
Photos, scrapbooks, a guest book, clippings, and certificates of San Francisco resident Julius Kahn,

an actor who became a US congressman representing California from 1898 to 1902 and from 1904 to 1924, and of his wife Florence Kahn (1866-1948), who succeeded him as US congresswoman after his death in 1925 and served until 1937. Also contains a notebook, a manuscript "My Life Among the Mormons," and photos from ca. 1866 to 1907 of Florence Kahn's mother Mary Goldsmith Prag (1846-1935), an educator who came to San Francisco via Panama in 1852 and then lived in Utah for many years. Prag returned to San Francisco to become a teacher and later served as vice-principal at Girls High School in that city. A member of the San Francisco board of education, she also was a supporter of women's rights.

937. Levitan, Sonia
Papers. Ca. 1968- . Ca. 27 items and 1 tape.
Open. Unpublished guide.
Western Jewish History Center.
Correspondence, manuscripts of her writings, and a taped speech of Levitan (1934-), author of *Journey to America* and other works.

938. Levy and Goodman Family
Papers. 1880- . 20 items.
Open. Unpublished guide.
Western Jewish History Center.
Correspondence, diaries, photos, and scrapbooks of this family of business, civic, and professional leaders in El Paso, TX. Amelia Levy Goodman, Estelle Goodman Levy, Amelia Levy Lemmon, and other family members have been involved in such organizations as the local branch of the National Council of Jewish Women, the Women's Club of El Paso, the El Paso Historical Society, and the Cloudcraft Recreation Camp for the underprivileged.

939. Liederman, Daisy (Cohn)
Papers. 1892-1938. 60 items.
Open. Unpublished guide.
Western Jewish History Center.
Correspondence, photos, a scrapbook, clippings, recital programs, and wedding invitations of Liederman (?-1938), a singer who was married to Cantor Benjamin Liederman of Congregation Sherith Israel in San Francisco. Before her marriage she was the featured soloist of Temple Emanu-El in San Francisco; she also sang for such organizations as the San Francisco Art Association, the Children's Hospital, the Elks, and the YMCA, and she made appearances at the Clunie Opera House in Sacramento. After her marriage to Cantor Liederman she helped organize the Congregation's sisterhood and arranged for many concerts there. At one time she also was social editor of the San Francisco periodical *The Emanu-El.*

940. Lipman, Rowena, Family
Papers. 1876-1970. 25 items.
Open. Unpublished guide.
Western Jewish History Center.
Lipman (1907-), a graphic artist, wrote *The Family of Isaac and Rebecca Harris,* a history of her family, which was published in pamphlet form by the Western Jewish History Center. Manuscripts of her family history publication, photos, invitations, marriage contracts, and other items used in her family history research. Includes photos and memorabilia of Harris descendants Julia Harris Lesser and Irene Lesser Lipman.

941. Mooser, Minnie, and Mooser, Hattie
Papers. 1900-67. 5 ft.
Open. Unpublished guide.
Western Jewish History Center.
As proprietors of the Aladdin Studio Tiffin Room, a night club referred to as a "midnight retreat" during prohibition, and as active supporters of children's theater, Minnie Mooser and her sister Hattie Mooser (1878-1970) were noted for their contributions to the theatrical, civic, and cultural life of San Francisco. Albums containing photos, clippings, and memorabilia about the Aladdin Studio Tiffin Room, the variety of artists who played there, and such Mooser friends and acquaintances as the Duncan Sisters, Rudolph Valentino, Harry Houdini, Sophie Tucker, and Fay King; children's theater and the Racketty-Packetty House; the Golden Gate International Exposition at Treasure Island in 1939; and the Mooser family. Album relating to the Golden Gate International Exposition also contains reminiscences.

942. Oral Histories
Oral history. 1965-75. No size given.
Open. Unpublished guide.
Western Jewish History Center.
Interviews include one with Amy Steinhardt Branden about her work in child welfare and community service, especially her role as chief children's agent for the state of California's department of charities and corrections in 1915; with Dorothy Wormer Coblentz, an architect who discusses her life and career from 1917 to the 1970s; with Elizabeth Elkus, a teacher and widow of Albert I. Elkus; and with Therese Jelenko, a pianist and friend of Michael and Sarah Stein, who reminisces about her life since about 1900.

943. Rosenberg, Abraham, and Rosenberg, Alice (Greenbaum)
Papers. 1860s-1943. 2 ft.
Open. Unpublished guide.
Western Jewish History Center.
Included with correspondence, documents, photos, clippings, and albums of Abraham Rosenberg and his brothers Max and Adolph Rosenberg, who together managed a dried fruit and nut business and whose families supported causes relating to art and civil liberties, are papers of Abraham Rosenberg's wife Alice (Greenbaum) Rosenberg (1876-1943), their daughter Louise (Rosenberg) Bransten Berman, and Alice Rosenberg's mother Sarah Ackerman [Mrs. Louis] Greenbaum, all of whom were civic and social leaders. Also contains information on the town of Jenny Lind and other California cities.

944. Sills, Marion
Papers. 1937-74. 1 folder.
Open. Unpublished guide.
Western Jewish History Center.
Papers of Sills (1916-), a San Francisco worker who was a member of the Department Store Employees Union, Local 110.

945. Stern, Rosalie (Meyer)
Papers. 1842- . 15 ft.
Open. Unpublished guide.
Western Jewish History Center.
Correspondence, photos, invitations, and mementos of Stern (1869-1955), a civic and social leader, patron of the arts, and wife of Sigmund Stern of Levi Strauss & Company. Includes her correspondence with her sisters Aline (Meyer) Leibman, Elise (Meyer) Stern de Souze Dantas, Florence (Meyer) Blumenthal, and Ruth (Meyer) Cook; Rosalie's daughter Elise (Stern) Haas; Rosalie's sister-in-law Agnes (Ernst) [Mrs. Eugene, Jr.] Meyer; Rosalie's mother Harriet Newmark Meyer; various Newmark cousins and aunts; Ernestine Zadoc Kahn and other French relatives; Sara Bard Field; and Supreme Court justice Louis Brandeis. Collection also contains extensive correspondence and other papers of Rosalie's daughter Elise Haas, a San Francisco civic and social leader who married Walter A. Haas, chairman of the board of directors of Levi Strauss & Company. Haas's correspondents include family members, Sara Bard Field, Katherine Burke, Iphigene Ochs Sulzberger, Benjamino Bufano, Ignace Paderewski, and Supreme Court justice Felix Frankfurter.

A noted civic leader, Rosalie Stern was appointed associate field director of military relief for the American National Red Cross in 1918. She also was a member of the San Francisco Recreation Committee and the "Committee of 50" of the city's Community Chest. Charities she supported included the Fatherless Children of France, and she donated Sigmund Stern Grove to the city of San Francisco as a memorial to her husband; a series of free musical events is presented there each summer.

946. Temple Sinai Women's Group
Records. 1914- . 1 folder.
Open. Unpublished guide.
Western Jewish History Center.
Minutes, clippings, and programs of this Oakland, CA, Jewish women's organization, earlier known as the Women's Auxiliary of Temple Sinai and which later changed its name to Temple Sinai Sisterhood. Includes a minute book from 1914, a book of the organization's sewing circle dated 1924, a Sisterhood anniversary booklet from 1929, and information about the Fruit and Flower Mission. The Mission, which was an offshoot of the Daughters of Israel Relief Society, included many members from the Temple Sinai organization. Mission workers visited the sick.

947. Yezierska, Anzia
Papers. Ca. 1950-64. 3 folders.
Open. Catalog cards.
Western Jewish History Center.
Correspondence, manuscripts, and published articles of Yezierska (1885-1970), an author who wrote *The Breadgivers, Salome of the Tenements, Hungry Hearts,* and *Red Ribbon on a White Horse.*

948. Archives
Records. 1975- . Ca. 5 ft.
Access restricted. No guide.
Women Library Workers.
Correspondence, administrative files, a newsletter, and photos of this group, which was organized in 1975 to eliminate discrimination against women library workers.

BEVERLY HILLS

949. Screenplays
Collection. 1915- . 2000 items.
Open. Unpublished guide.
The American Film Institute, Center for Advanced Film Studies, Charles K. Feldman Library.
Collection of motion picture shooting scripts from MGM, Universal, 20th Century-Fox, and other studios include works by such screenwriters as Frances Marion, Anita Loos, Dorothy Parker, Marion Orth, and Isobel Lennart.

950. Seminars
Records. 1969- . More than 300 items.
Open. Unpublished guide.
The American Film Institute, Center for Advanced Film Studies, Charles K. Feldman Library.
Transcripts of weekly seminars held at the Center for Advanced Film Studies with professionals from the motion picture and television industry. Most seminars have been conducted in a question-and-answer format and have lasted about two and one-half hours. Seminars have been held with Liv Ullmann, Lucille Ball, Julia Phillips, Verna Fields, Carol Burnett, Sue Mengers, and Dory Previn.

CAMARILLO

951. Doheny, Estelle (Betzold)
Collection. Nd. 2000 items.
Access restricted. No guide.
St. John's Seminary Library.
Doheny (1875-1958) was the wife of Edward

Laurence Doheny, whose family engaged in oil production. Her collection of manuscripts, which is housed with a collection of rare books and art objects, includes 42 letters Father José Señan wrote from the San Buenaventura Mission in Ventura, CA, between 1806 and 1822. Also contains autograph letters of Elizabeth (Barrett) Browning, Louisa May Alcott, Julia Ward Howe, and many others.

CHICO

952. Barney, Anna Louise
Papers. Nd. Ca. 0.25 in.
Open. No guide.
California State University, Chico, Library.
Travel journals, writings, a scrapbook, college catalogs, and other papers of Barney, dean of women and an English instructor at Chico State Teachers College from 1919 to 1952. After receiving master's degrees from the University of California and Columbia University, Barney was head of Madera High School's English department in Hanford, CA, and dean of women at the State Normal School in Livingston, AL.

953. Bidwell, Annie Ellicott (Kennedy)
Papers. 1855-1913. 5 boxes.
Open. No guide.
California State University, Chico, Library.
Correspondence, diaries, and other papers of Bidwell (1839-1918), an ordained Presbyterian minister, prohibition advocate, suffragist, and wife of General John Bidwell, a California pioneer and congressman. Includes correspondence of the Kennedy family and information about Indians.

954. McQuade, Clara M.
Papers. 1913-19. 6 vols.
Open. No guide.
California State University, Chico, Library.
Record books kept by Clara McQuade of the State Normal School, a teachers school in Chico, include notes regarding courses of instruction and attendance and grade information.

955. Northeastern California Collection, Oral History Project
Oral history. Nd. No size given.
Open. Published and unpublished guides.
California State University, Chico, Library.
Tapes and transcripts of interviews, including ones with Nora L. Abbott regarding life in Washington, Oregon, and California; Agnes A. Dix, a registered nurse, about the founding of the professional nursing program at Chico State College; Ida H. Ellis, a teacher, tax clerk, and member of the cemetery board in Cottonwood, CA; Ruby English, the maid of [Mrs.] Annie E. K. Bidwell from 1914 to 1918; [Mrs.] Frieda Peterson Knott concerning the career of her father Fred Peterson as the Bidwell Mansion gardener, her memories of Mrs. Bidwell and the Bidwell Mansion, the Indian Rancheria, Chico schools, and Knott's flower-arranging at Bidwell Mansion State Park; Selena Lamarr, an Atsugewi Indian woman; Mary Dunbar Lemcke regarding the Grey Lady Corps at the Chico Army airfield during WWII; Phoebe Brownell Steuben about the Brownell Ranch, Chinese employees of the Ranch, Glenn County, and the Wintun Indians; Gertrude Witherow regarding life in Utah and in Shasta County, CA, and the eruption of Mount Lassen; and other women. See Norris A. Bleyhl, comp., *Northeastern California: A Preliminary Bibliography of Books and Periodicals in the Learning Activities Resource Center* (Chico: California State University, 1976).

956. Osborn, Mary M.
Papers. 1926-?. 1 vol.
Open. No guide.
California State University, Chico, Library.
Scrapbook kept by Osborn contains clippings concerning California and the Chico area. Includes clippings regarding such women as [Mrs.] Mary Heckle, an early settler in Quincy in Plumas County, CA; [Mrs.] Cassie Hill, an early Roseville settler and telegraph operator; Annie E. K. [Mrs. John] Bidwell, who was active in the suffrage and temperance movements and a teacher of Indian women in the Chico area; Mary Brown, wife of abolitionist John Brown, and their daughter Sarah Brown; [Mrs.] Mary E. Jones, a member of the Donner party that undertook a trek over the Sierra Nevadas in the 1840s; author Mary Austin; and others.

957. Prey, Ada Jordan
Papers. Nd. 5 folders.
Open. No guide.
California State University, Chico, Library.
Prey (ca. 1880-1958) was a teacher, musician, community social worker, and lecturer. Correspondence; diaries; photos; scrapbook containing theater programs, clippings, and other items; biographical notes; certificates; articles regarding her musical activities; and other papers.

958. Robson, Frances
Papers. Nd. 20 vols. and 48 items.
Open. No guide.
California State University, Chico, Library.
Photos, including portraits and landscapes, of Robson (1885-1949), a photographer, member and secretary of the Photographic Society of America, and founder of the Society's international portfolios division, which arranged exchange exhibits with various foreign countries. Also includes letters of condolence after her death. She was married to Colonel Frederick T. Robson.

959. Trinity Dredging Company
Records. Ca. 1900-59. Ca. 20 ft.
Closed. No guide.
California State University, Chico, Library.
Records of a gold dredging operation on the Trinity River. The business, which was founded in about 1900 and disbanded in 1959, was maintained by Mary E. Smith from 1941 to 1959.

DAVIS

960. Dart and Wolfskill
Papers. 1861-1956. 1145 items.
Open. Unpublished guide.
University of California, Davis, Library, Special Collections.
Included in family papers of John Reid Wolfskill (1809-97), who in 1842 became the first American settler in Solano County, CA, are correspondence, photos, and memorabilia of his wife Susan Cooper Wolfskill and their daughters Melinda, Frances, and Jennie Wolfskill.

961. Davenport and Rankin
Papers. 1852-1908. 1346 items.
Open. Unpublished guide.
University of California, Davis, Library, Special Collections.
Family papers, playscripts, photos, clippings, theater programs, and memorabilia of Edward Loomis Davenport (1815-77) and Arthur McKee Rankin (1841-1914), who were actors and theater managers. Includes papers of family members [Miss] Fanny Lily Gypsy Davenport (1850-98), the daughter of Edward Loomis Davenport and Fanny Vining Davenport; Kitty Blanchard [Mrs. Arthur McKee] Rankin (1847-1911); and Phyllis Rankin (1874-1934), the daughter of Arthur and Kitty Rankin.

962. Glasscock, Anne Bonner
Papers. 1960-66. 31 items.
Open. Unpublished guide.
University of California, Davis, Library, Special Collections.
Papers of Glasscock (1924-), an author who has used the pseudonym Michael Bonner, consist of drafts, manuscripts, and page proofs for books she wrote, among them *Kennedy's Gold* (1960), *The Iron Noose* (1961), *The Shadow of a Hawk* (1963), and *The Disturbing Death of Jenkin Delaney* (1966).

963. Lindley, Thomas Morton
Papers. 1848-1921. 356 items.
Open. Unpublished guide.
University of California, Davis, Library, Special Collections.
Correspondence, bills and receipts, legal papers, photos, and memorabilia of Lindley, a merchant, and his family provide information on women's roles and family life in Sacramento, CA, in the mid-19th century.

964. Living Theatre
Records. 1947- . 2700 items and 22 tapes.
Open. Unpublished guide.
University of California, Davis, Library, Special Collections.
Correspondence, notes, directing scripts, original drawings, taped interviews and videotapes, photos, clippings, and publicity items of this New York theater group, which was founded in 1947 and initiated what became the Off-Broadway movement. Includes information about the theatrical career of Judith Malina, a central figure in the group.

965. Quinn, Frank
Papers. 1955-57. 55 tapes.
Open. Unpublished guide.
University of California, Davis, Library, Special Collections.
Sound recordings made by Quinn, a northern California fieldworker for the American Friends Service Committee, consist of those he made in cooperation with members of the Yurok, Pomo, Hoopa, Karok, and Paiute Shoshoni tribes of northern California; the Oglala Sioux of North and South Dakota; and the Ute of Colorado, Utah, and New Mexico. On tape are remembrances of Indian life and lore, especially music, tradition, attitudes, and values, by women members of the tribes; 28 of the 55 tapes deal with women.

DOWNEY

966. Woman's Club of Downey
Records. 1898- . Ca. 2 ft.
Open. Unpublished guide.
Downey Historical Society.
Certificate of incorporation, bylaws, history, yearbooks, a cookbook, a scrapbook, photos, and clippings of this social and philanthropic club, which was founded in 1898 as the Friday Afternoon Club for the promotion of the "social, moral and intellectual interests of the community" and for the establishment of a public library. The Club's library, which was created in 1901, was the forerunner of a county branch library and the Downey City Library. The group changed its name and was known as the Saturday Afternoon Club until it adopted its current name.

FRESNO

967. Berri, Maud Lillian
Papers. Ca. 1907-14. 1 folder.
Open. Unpublished guide.

Fresno City and County Historical Society.
Clippings and photos of Berri (1871-1958), an actress and singer in several light operas, who was associated with C. William Kolb and Max M. Dill, both actors and comedians.

968. Black and Spanish-speaking People of Fresno County
Oral history. 1977- . Ca. 60 tapes and transcripts.
Open. Unpublished guide.
Fresno City and County Historical Society.
Tapes, transcripts, and photos of primarily retired members of Fresno's black and Spanish-speaking communities, who were and are engaged in a wide range of occupations. Interviews with women, which comprise approximately one-half of those projected, focus on their recollections of life as minority members of a predominantly white society.

969. Covel, Iantha T. (Starbird)
Papers. 1876-1926. 1 folder.
Open. Unpublished guide.
Fresno City and County Historical Society.
Papers of Covel (1860-?) a teacher and writer, include reports about her teaching career, wedding announcements, a pamphlet about the defense efforts Madera County women organized during WWI, photos, and a silent film screenplay she wrote.

970. Haarbauer, Dagmar Frisselle
Papers. 1911-45. 1 box.
Open. No guide.
Fresno City and County Historical Society.
Sketches, photos, clippings, and a personal description by Haarbauer (1895-) of the Kearney Mansion, which she lived in for a time. Haarbauer was an artist, sculptor, and local society leader, who was married to the superintendent of a 5000 acre farm. She also appeared in two silent movies under the name Dagmar Desmond.

971. Harvey Family
Papers. 1848-1965. 2 boxes.
Open. Unpublished guide.
Fresno City and County Historical Society.
Papers of this pioneer Fresno family, which was prominent in land development and the Baptist church, consist of correspondence, diaries, photos, and other documents, most of which were written by Ada, Annie, Constance, Frances, and Louise Harvey, who were daughters of William Harvey, Sr.

972. Taylor, Zella
Papers. 1929-54. 3 vols.
Open. No guide.
Fresno City and County Historical Society.
Scrapbooks of [Mrs. C. S.] Taylor, who was active in local and statewide women's clubs, civic activities, and political campaigns, contain correspondence from nationally prominent political figures, minutes, programs, photos, and clippings.

973. Turner, Florence L.
Papers. 1934-65. 1 folder.
Open. Unpublished guide.
Fresno City and County Historical Society.
Clippings and a photo of [Mrs. George W.] Turner (1878-1965), a prominent Fresno clubwoman who served as director of the California State Department of Social Welfare from 1934 to 1939. In 1937 her duties were increased to cover administration of all types of state relief.

974. Winchell, Ernestine
Papers. 1921-31. 10 folders.
Open. Unpublished guide.
Fresno City and County Historical Society.
Clippings of newspaper articles that [Mrs.] Winchell (1865-1952), a newspaper columnist and historian, wrote for the *Fresno Morning Republican* about recollections of early life in the Fresno area; photos are included as well. Although some of Winchell's articles about pioneer women are general, they are believed to have been based on experiences and reminiscences pioneer women told to Winchell.

GRASS VALLEY

975. Royce, Sarah Eleanor
Papers. 1849-84. 122-page vol.
Open. No guide.
Grass Valley Library.
Manuscript account by Royce (1819-91), an early California settler who married Josiah Royce in 1847, concerns the trip she took with her family across the plains in 1849. Also includes reminiscences she added while rereading her diary. Sarah Royce had three children: two daughters, Hattie and Ruth, and a son, Josiah (1855-?), who became a philosopher.

HAYWARD

976. Jensen Family
Papers. Ca. 1830-1920. Ca. 3000 pp.
Closed. No guide.
California State University, Hayward, Special Collections.
Correspondence, journals, genealogical charts, and photos of various members of this California family and relatives on the island of Föhr, Germany. The material, much of which was written in German script, contains information on daily life in the Hayward-Castro Valley area in California. Includes papers of Emilie (Heinsen) Jensen (1852-1926) and Christianne Emilie (Heinsen) Jensen (1846-1923), two sisters who married the brothers Jens Christian Jensen and Erich Rickert Jensen, respectively.

977. Hayward Hill and Valley Club
Records. 1910-44. 8 in.
Open. No guide.
Hayward Area Historical Society Museum.
Minutes of this women's service organization.

978. Photos
Collection. Ca. 1880s- . Ca. 2000 items.
Open. No guide.
Hayward Area Historical Society Museum.
Includes photos and portraits of many local women and families, including [Mrs.] Emma Oakes (1867-?), who was known as the "mother of Hayward"; Mrs. William Hayward; Edith Beam [Mrs. John Allen] Parks; and [Mrs.] Evelyn Crow.

979. PTA
Records. 1931-58. Ca. 8 in.
Open. No guide.
Hayward Area Historical Society Museum.
Minutes of the PTA at the Edwin Markham School in Hayward, 1931-54, and at the Hayward Union High School, 1948-58. Also includes a register book for the Markham School PTA.

980. Scrapbooks
Collection. 1958- . 73 vols.
Open. Card index.
Hayward Area Historical Society Museum.
Clippings scrapbooks of the Society contain items of local interest and information on the activities of local women.

981. Templeton
Papers. Ca. 1914-40s. 2 vols.
Open. No guide.
Hayward Area Historical Society Museum.
Scrapbooks of clippings collected by Irene Templeton Pratt Jamieson, a city clerk in Hayward from the 1920s to 1950, concern her family, other Hayward residents, and city government.

KING CITY

982. Tape Collection
Oral History. 1971- . Ca. 18 tapes.
Open. No guide.
King City Public Library.
Includes interviews in which Mrs. Santos Nunez, who was one-quarter Jolon Indian, describes her background and her employment and that of her husband at the Dutton Hotel in Jolon, CA; Ramona (Duck) Sutfin tells of her experiences in Jolon, where she was a storekeeper and postmaster for many years; [Miss] Lottie Meeter (1886-), who was born in Illinois and moved to King City at the age of 5, gives details about turn-of-the-century King City and its stores, churches, schools, teachers, and her fellow students; and Dorothea (Pinion) [Mrs. Newton] Heinsen talks about her life and school days at Pacheco School, from which she graduated in 1904. Also contains interviews of other women who discuss events in their lives and the local area, including Leila Currell, who speaks of the Oasis district; Sarah Edrington, who describes Hames Valley; Velma (Adams) Dayton, who talks about Bryson; Marie (Arfsten) Heinsen, who tells about Lockwood, CA; and Rachel (Dayton) Gillett, who also reads a poem on the death of Rachel Ann-Ray Liddle, a member of her family.

LAGUNA NIGUEL

983. Bureau of Indian Affairs (RG 75)
Records. 1867-1952. 3300 cu.ft.
Open. Inventories.
Federal Archives and Records Center, Los Angeles Archives Branch.
Includes correspondence, reports, files, and other records of the Bureau; agency, sub-agency, and reservation records; Indian school records; hospital and health center records, including reports by nurses and doctors; registers of Indian families; book of arrests, police dockets, and court records; and Indian census records. Also contains local Mission Indian Agency records, 1912-55.

984. Bureau of Land Management (RG 49)
Records. 1853-1961. Ca. 370 cu.ft.
Open. Inventory.
Federal Archives and Records Center, Los Angeles Archives Branch.
Financial records, correspondence, land registers, land patents, and survey data of the Bureau, which was founded as the General Land Office in 1812. The records, which concern southern California and Arizona, include information about women who appeared as principals in actions relating to land claims and about women employees of the Bureau, among them Edith Thompson, who began as a stenographer in the surveyor-general's office in ca. 1908 and became office cadastral engineer for Arizona in ca. 1941. Includes correspondence with or records of Isabella Greenway, Arizona congresswoman; Antoinette Funk, assistant commissioner of the General Land Office; and Florence M. Warner, administrator of the Arizona state civil works administration.

985. Los Angeles County Baptismal Records
Records. 1771-1873. 1 microfilm reel.
Open. Name index.
Federal Archives and Records Center, Los Angeles Archives Branch.
Consists of baptismal records for the San Gabriel Mission and the Plaza Church in Los Angeles.

986. United States District Court: Arizona District Court (RG 21)
Records. 1912-46. 681 cu.ft.
Open. Inventory.

Federal Archives and Records Center, Los Angeles Archives Branch.
Records of this federal district court, which was established in 1912, include minute books, commissioners' dockets, correspondence, case files, judgment books, probation files, juvenile records, jury lists, equity dockets, and naturalization petitions. Includes correspondence of [Miss] Effie Botts, senior deputy clerk for the Court, 1912-19 (4 cu.ft.). See Works Progress Administration, Division of Women's and Professional Projects, *Inventory of Federal Archives in the States, Series II: The Federal Courts, No. 3: Arizona.*

987. United States District Court: Arizona Territorial Court (RG 21)
Records. 1864-1912. 200 cu.ft.
Open. Inventory and card index.
Federal Archives and Records Center, Los Angeles Archives Branch.
Minute books, dockets, correspondence, case files, notices of appeal, and other records of the Court, which was established in 1864 and dissolved in 1912. Includes a card index for types of crimes committed and tried, among them adultery, fornication, mailing of obscene material, bigamy, polygamy, incest, prostitution, rape, extradition of illegal aliens (primarily Chinese), murder, theft, and other crimes.

988. United States District Court: Central District of California (RG 21)
Records. 1851-1956. 2763 cu.ft.
Open. Inventory.
Federal Archives and Records Center, Los Angeles Archives Branch.
The Court, which began as the southern district court for California in 1851, adjudicates legal matters in which the US government appears as a party. Includes dockets, minutes, case files, exhibits, and other legal documents. The central district serves Los Angeles.

989. United States District Court: San Diego (RG 21)
Records. 1925-52. 385 cu.ft.
Open. Inventory.
Federal Archives and Records Center, Los Angeles Archives Branch.
Dockets, commissioners' records, law case files, equity cases, correspondence relating to civil and criminal proceedings, and other records of the Court, which was established in 1925 to serve the San Diego jurisdiction.

LOMPOC

990. Advisory Committee of the State Park Contingency Fund
Records. 1934- . 1 carton and other items.
Open. No guide.
La Purisima Mission State Historic Park Archives.
Annual reports, minutes, and correspondence of the Committee, which makes recommendations concerning the expenditure of funds for La Purisima Mission's restoration program. Committee members include Edith Webb, [Miss] Pearl Chase, the present chairperson [Mrs.] Julia Forbes, and other Santa Barbara area women.

991. Webb, Edith
Papers. 1931-62. Ca. 1 ft.
Open. Index.
La Purisima Mission State Historic Park Archives.
Correspondence, research notes, manuscripts, and photos of [Mrs.] Webb, a local historian who has been active in La Purisima Mission's restoration program, contain information on the restoration and surrounding grounds, architecture, local Indians, and her recommendations on the restoration. Also includes *The Story of a Mission Garden* and *Mission Indian Villages* by Webb.

LONG BEACH

992. Dumond
Collection. 1760-1861. Ca. 375 items.
Open. Unpublished guide.
California State University, Long Beach, Library.
Sermons, addresses, political broadsides, reports of societies and convention proceedings, and other material pertaining to antislavery and the abolition movement. Includes a paper by Elizabeth (Coltman) Heydrick, written in 1824, about the abolition of slavery in the West Indies; proceedings of the Anti-slavery Convention of American Women, held in New York in 1837; an 1839 pamphlet in which Maria (Weston) Chapman describes dissension within the Massachusetts Anti-Slavery Society; pamphlets written by Lydia Maria (Francis) Child in 1836 in which she discusses the slavery issue; appeals, an 1835 broadside, and letters to Catharine E. Beecher from Angelina Emily Grimké; an epistle on slavery and letters on the equality of the sexes and the condition of woman by Sarah Moore Grimké; an 1855 leaflet charging mothers to oppose slavery by Mrs. B. L. Follen; and other items. Much of the material was printed by various antislavery societies.

993. Healey, Dorothy Ray
Papers. Ca. 1920s-70s. Ca. 10,000 items.
Open. Unpublished guide.
California State University, Long Beach, Library.
Correspondence, speeches, programs of the Communist party in the US, broadsides, periodicals, books, and other papers of [Mrs.] Healey (1914-), who was a member of the national committee of the Communist party in the US for 12 years and chairwoman of the Communist party's southern California district for ca. 25 years. Includes internal discussion guides and position papers of the American Communist party from the 1940s to the 1960s and documents, pamphlets, and other publications regarding the Soviet Union, Chinese communism in the 1930s, the House Un-American Activities Committee, the first California Conference of the National Negro Congress, Students for a Democratic Society, black Americans from the 1930s to the 1970s, and other groups and topics. Healey was born in Denver and grew up in Oakland, CA. She became a member of the Young Communist League at the age of 14; organized farm laborers and cannery, mill, and municipal workers during the 1940s; and broke with the Communist party in the US over its support for the Soviet invasion of Czechoslovakia in 1968. She resigned from the party in 1973. Presently living in Inglewood, CA, Healey writes, teaches, and conducts a weekly broadcast talk show.

994. Horne, Marilyn
Papers. 1950- . No size given.
Open. No guide.
Long Beach Public Library.
Recordings, tapes, photos, clippings, articles, programs, and other material concerning the career of [Miss] Horne (1934-), an opera singer. Horne attended Long Beach schools and was active in area music events.

995. Long Beach Local History
Collection. Nd. 25 file drawers, ca. 800 vols., and 1450 microfilm reels.
Access restricted. Unpublished guide.
Long Beach Public Library.
Booklets, brochures, photos, scrapbooks, clippings, ephemera, microfilm of Long Beach newspapers, and books provide information about women in Long Beach history, some of whom were nationally known writers, athletes, and movie stars.

LOS ALTOS HILLS

996. Archives
Records. 1633- . No size given.
Access restricted. No guide.
Daughters of Charity of St. Vincent de Paul, Seton Provincialate.
Correspondence of mothers superior, superior-generals, and others; biographies of founders, saints, and deceased sisters of the community; and other records. The order was founded in 1633 in France to serve the sick and poor; Mother Elizabeth Seton established the order in the US in 1809.

LOS ANGELES

997. Sports Library
Records. 20th century. No size given.
Open. No guide.
Citizens Savings Athletic Foundation.
Biographical files, photos, magazines, books, and other records of the Athletic Foundation, which was organized as the Helms Athletic Foundation in 1936. In 1948, the Foundation instituted the World Trophy Award to honor outstanding athletic achievements in the years after 1898. Includes information about the following women who received the Award for tennis: Juliette P. Atkinson, 1898; May Sutton, 1905; Hazel Hotchkiss, 1911; Molla Bjurstedt, 1917; Helen Wills, 1929; Alice Marble, 1939; and Pauline Betz, 1946. Also includes information on swimming award winners Helene Madison, 1931; Ann Curtis, 1944; Keena Rothhammer, 1973; and Shirley Babashoff, 1975. In addition, the collection contains information on Glenna Collett, who was given the golf award for 1930; Patricia McCormick, diving, 1955; and Wilma Rudolph, track and field, 1960. Winners of the awards in other years were men.

998. Archives
Records. 1924- . 24 vols.
Closed. No guide.
Cloistered Dominican Nuns of Perpetual Adoration, Monastery of the Angels.
The Monastery was founded in Los Angeles in 1924. Chronicles, correspondence, biographical information on the Monastery's five founding mothers, photos, and material on the founding by members of this community of the first monasteries for contemplative Dominican Nuns of Perpetual Adoration in Pakistan and the Philippines.

999. Immaculate Heart Community Archives
Records. 1848-1976. No size given.
Open. No guide.
Immaculate Heart College Library.
Correspondence, photos, clippings, and other records of this order of nuns, which established Immaculate Heart College and became a noncanonical organization in 1968. Includes writings by and articles and clippings about Corita Kent, a former member of the order.

1,000. Jewish Community Groups in the Los Angeles Area
Collection. 1854- . 60 ft.
Open. Card catalog.
Jewish Community Library.
Constitutions, bylaws, correspondence, tapes, photos, slides, and other records of various Los Angeles Jewish organizations, including correspondence of Henrietta Szold regarding the founding of Hadassah, a Zionist women's group established by Szold in 1912. Also contains records of organizations in which women were active, such as the Bureau of Jewish Education, the Jewish Federation Council, the Jewish Mothers

Alliance, and the Hebrew Benevolent Society, founded in 1854.

1,001. Jewish Oral History
Oral history. Nd. 23 tapes.
Open. No guide.
Jewish Community Library.
Interviews containing reminiscences of members of the Jewish community include interviews with five women who were descended from prominent Jewish families of early Los Angeles.

1,002. Newspaper Microfilm
Collection. 1847-1921. 69 microfilm reels.
Open. No guide.
Jewish Community Library.
Collection of Jewish community newspapers, including *The American Israelite* of Cincinnati, 1854-1901; *The Asmonean* of New York, 1849-58; the *B'nai B'rith Messenger* of Los Angeles, 1898-; *The Occident* of Philadelphia, 1847-53; *Emanu-El* of San Francisco, 1897-1921; and *The Hebrew* of San Francisco, 1864-87.

1,003. Studies of the Jewish Community
Collection. Ca. 1930-74. Ca. 3 ft.
Open. No guide.
Jewish Community Library.
Unpublished studies regarding the Jewish community and Jewish organizations include a doctoral dissertation regarding the Jewish Family Agency of Los Angeles from 1854 to 1970, and reports of a task force about the Jewish poor in 1973 and about the Jewish Center in the greater Los Angeles area.

1,004. Southern California
Collection. 1770-1975. 200 ft.
Open. Card catalog.
Los Angeles County Museum of Natural History.
Correspondence, photos, assessment rolls, and baptism, marriage, and death records pertaining to the southern California region. Includes correspondence, ca. 45 photos, and clippings relating to Susan B. Anthony; Los Angeles County assessment rolls from 1856 to 1880; baptism, marriage, and death records of 17 California missions from 1770 to 1908; portrait file, including daguerreotypes and ambrotypes, about one-third of which are of women from 1847 to 1920; and correspondence of Ruth I. Mahood, curator of the Los Angeles County Museum of Natural History from 1956 to 1969. The Anthony papers contain letters from Mary Anthony to Jessie Anthony regarding Susan Anthony and the expulsion of John Anthony from the Quaker Church and photos of Anthony and suffragists Ida Husted Harper and Elizabeth (Cady) Stanton. The last photo taken of Anthony before her death is also included.

1,005. Newsclippings
Collection. 1960-67. Ca. 3 ft.
Open. No guide.
Mount St. Mary's College.
Clippings from various newspapers regarding student clubs, sororities, and other aspects of college life at Mount St. Mary's College, which was founded in 1925. Although coeducational, the College's student body is composed predominantly of women.

1,006. Photos
Records. 1929- . Ca. 1.5 ft.
Open. No guide.
Mount St. Mary's College.
Black and white photos of graduating classes; of administrators and teachers, many of whom were nuns of the order of St. Joseph of Carondelet; and of sorority and club activities of Mount St. Mary's College, which was founded in 1925.

1,007. Los Angeles Provincial Archives
Records. 1868- . 24 drawers and other items.
Access restricted. Unpublished guide.
Sisters of St. Joseph of Carondelet, St. Mary's Provincialate.
The Province was established in 1876 in Tucson, AZ. Its members are engaged in teaching, nursing, and related ministries. Financial and administrative records; personnel files; correspondence; chronicles of parochial, educational, and charitable foundations of the Province; memoirs by sisters giving historical data; and diaries of Sister Monica Corrigan describing the journey of seven sisters from St. Louis to Tucson in 1870 and of Sister Berchmans Hartrich concerning her journey from St. Louis to Tucson in 1876.

1,008. Archives
Records. 1923- . Ca. 10 cabinets.
Closed. No guide.
Sisters of Social Service of Los Angeles Motherhouse.
This religious order of women was founded in Hungary in 1908 to work for the alleviation and prevention of social problems and the transformation of society according to the social teachings of the Church. The Sisters began by educating upper middle-class women about social needs and involving them in social service. The order was established in the US in Los Angeles in 1926 by Sister Frederica Horvath. Its members are engaged in pastoral ministry, works of charity, and other forms of social work. Minutes of general chapters and other meetings, correspondence of Sister Frederica and others, records of the founding of each of the houses, biographies of Sister Frederica, histories of the order, taped interviews with Sister Frederica and with eight of the founding Sisters, photos, slides, a community newspaper, and other records.

1,009. Archives
Records. 1848- . 16 drawers and 14 vols.
Access restricted. No guide.
Sisters of the Immaculate Heart of Mary, Mother House.
Minutes of the general government, financial records, correspondence, files of individual sisters, a history, photos, scrapbooks, and clippings of the congregation. The order was founded in Spain in 1848 and was first established in the US in 1871 in Gilroy, CA. Includes histories and other material concerning schools operated by the order.

1,010. Burke, Yvonne Braithwaite
Papers. 1970-73. 0.25 in.
Open. No guide.
Southern California Library for Social Studies and Research.
A politician, Burke was a member of the California Assembly from 1966 to 1972 and of the US House of Representatives from 1972 to the present. Includes correspondence with Mr. and Mrs. Max Kagan regarding the Vietnam War, the Watergate scandal, the California public school crisis, no-fault insurance, and other topics; two newspaper interviews in which Burke discusses political leadership, communication with other politicians and her constituents, her upbringing, her strengths and weaknesses as a politician, and her aspirations; her first newsletter as a member of Congress; and a copy of a federal bill, which she cosponsored, that aimed at preventing the reintroduction of US forces into Vietnam without "prior, specific authorization by Congress."

1,011. California Eagle
Records. 1920-65. No size given.
Open. No guide.
Southern California Library for Social Studies and Research.
Copies of the *California Eagle,* a weekly newspaper that concerned itself with the problems, aspirations, and culture of the black community. The newspaper was founded in 1920 by Carlotta Bass, who intermittently served as editor; publication stopped in 1965.

1,012. Civil Rights Congress of Los Angeles
Records. 1948-54. Ca. 20 ft.
Open. No guide.
Southern California Library for Social Studies and Research.
Formed in 1948 as a coalition between the National Negro Congress and the Los Angeles Mobilization for Democracy, the Los Angeles chapter of the Civil Rights Congress sought to defend the rights of labor, minority groups, and political minorities. Minutes, files of cases undertaken, and a booklet describing local injustices, including incidents involving women and their families. The governing board of the Los Angeles CRC was composed of four women and two men; volunteer services were provided by ca. 40 attorneys, some of whom were women. The Los Angeles CRC disbanded in 1954. There were CRC chapters in 15 other states.

1,013. Coalition for Economic Survival
Records. Ca. 1973-76. 2 in.
Open. No guide.
Southern California Library for Social Studies and Research.
Records of the Coalition, a consumer protection organization, include a letter Lucy Fried, president of the Coalition, wrote California Assembly speaker Leo T. McCarthy urging the appointment of men to the Assembly agriculture committee who would be sympathetic to the plight of consumers; testimony of Fried and Betsy Newburn, a welfare mother, to the US Congressional committee hearing on the Full Employment Act in 1975; and Coalition newsletters and flyers.

1,014. Fight Inflation Together
Records. 1973-75. 2.5 in.
Open. No guide.
Southern California Library for Social Studies and Research.
Announcements, newsletters, pamphlets, and clippings of this organization founded in southern California in about 1972, which was predominantly composed of women dedicated to lowering food prices through political action. Contains information regarding FIT's milk and meat boycotts of 1973 and 1974, their 1973 "Don't Buy Anything Day," and the proposed picketing of the Los Angeles headquarters of Exxon Corporation.

1,015. Granddaughter of Carrie Nation
Papers. Nd. No size given.
Closed. No guide.
Southern California Library for Social Studies and Research.
Correspondence with the Southern California Library for Social Studies and Research regarding the family life of Carrie Nation's granddaughter and her impressions of Nation, family photos, and a recording disc of a musical about Nation's life.

1,016. Women Political Activists
Oral history. Nd. Ca. 30 tapes.
Open. No guide.
Southern California Library for Social Studies and Research.
Collection includes interviews with Barbara Nestor, Mary O'Neal, Rebecca August, Molly Wexler, and Sylvie Thygeson, who were active in the radical left labor movement from 1910 to the 1930s; Ernestine Kettler, who was active in the Socialist party in the early 1900s; Yetta Land, who was an attorney for women's and labor groups; and Grace McDonald.

1,017. Women's Groups and Women's Liberation
Oral history. 1967-73. 9 tapes.
Open. Card catalog.
Southern California Library for Social Studies and Research.
Collection contains interviews from 1967 with members of Women Strike for Peace, including Mrs. Degmar Wilson, [Mrs.] Mary Clark, Mrs. Ben

Riegler, and [Mrs.] Betty Martin, the latter two of whom were mothers of servicemen; interviews and speeches for the Women for Legislative Action by Morris Schappes regarding blacks and Jews, by Ralph W. Jeffs regarding Vietnam and Southeast Asia, and by Paul Perlin regarding unions, higher wages, and monopoly; tapes regarding the 1972 Cambridge, England, debate on women's liberation between Germaine Greer and William F. Buckley, Jr.; an examination of women's liberation by Marsha Hunt and Yvonne Braithwaite in 1971; and interviews with Germaine Greer and Betty Friedan regarding women's liberation. Also contains tapes regarding the women's conference at Immaculate Heart College in 1975 and the People's World 33rd anniversary celebration in 1971.

1,018. Women's Organizations
Records. Nd. No size given.
Closed. No guide.
Southern California Library for Social Studies and Research.
Minutes, correspondence, pamphlets, and other records of such national women's groups as Women for Legislative Action, Women Strike for Peace, Women's Trade Union Auxiliaries, and Emma Lazarus Jewish Woman's Clubs. Also includes records of the women's caucus of the California Democratic Council and the Women's International League for Peace and Freedom.

1,019. Photos
Collection. Ca. 1860- . Ca. 85,000 items.
Open. Partial unpublished guide.
Southwest Museum Research Library.
Photos, negatives, and slides primarily relate to Indians west of the Mississippi River. Includes photos of Indian women and children and women engaged in basketmaking, jewelry making, food preparation, ceremonial worship, and other aspects of Indian culture.

1,020. Warren, Viola Lockhart
Papers. 1846-1968. 1 box.
Open. Unpublished guide.
University of California, Los Angeles, Biomedical Library.
Warren (1896-1968) was author of works on California medical history and first wife of physician Stafford L. Warren, founding dean of the UCLA medical school. Manuscripts, photos, memorabilia, and source material for her works on early medicine and medical education in Los Angeles.

1,021. Dillon, Fannie Charles
Papers. Ca. 1900-47. Ca. 200 items.
Open. Partial inventory.
University of California, Los Angeles, Music Library.
Manuscripts of musical compositions, personal papers, programs, and several published works of Frances "Fannie" Charles Dillon (1881-1947), a pianist and composer who was educated and worked most of her life in the Los Angeles and Pomona, CA, area. Most of her compositions in the collection are songs for solo voice and piano, works for solo piano, and works for full orchestra; also included are a few chamber pieces and choral works.

1,022. Moore, Mary Carr
Papers. Ca. 1900-57. Ca. 80 items.
Open. No guide.
University of California, Los Angeles, Music Library.
Manuscripts of musical compositions, a few personal documents, and programs of Moore (1873-1957), a composer of works for choral and chamber groups, solo piano, and orchestra. She is known best for her operas, including *The Oracle, The Flaming Arrow, Rizzio, Los Rubios,* and *Narcissa,* for which she won the David Bispham Memorial Medal. Most of her operas were produced in San Francisco and Los Angeles in the 1920s and 1930s.

1,023. Schaffer, Helen
Papers. Ca. 1900-50. Ca. 50 items.
Open. No guide.
University of California, Los Angeles, Music Library.
Papers of Schaffer, a composer, consist of manuscripts of her musical compositions for solo piano and chamber groups as well as songs for voice and piano.

1,024. ATAS-UCLA Television Archives
Records. 1948- . 10,000 telefilms and videotapes.
Access restricted. Unpublished guide.
University of California, Los Angeles, UCLA Film, Television, and Radio Archives.
The Library was established in 1965 by the University and the National Academy of Television Arts & Sciences to collect, preserve, and disseminate television programs. Includes such television series as the "Ann Sothern Show" and "The Loretta Young Show"; single programs about such women as Joan of Arc and Martha Washington; television specials on such topics as rape; programs depicting attitudes toward women during the 1950s and 1960s, including "Search for Beauty" and "What a Housewife Can Do"; programs starring such entertainers as Martha Raye and Carol Burnett; and programs produced, directed, or written by women.

1,025. UCLA Film Archives
Records. 1903- . 8000 motion pictures.
Access restricted. Unpublished guide.
University of California, Los Angeles, UCLA Film, Television, and Radio Archives.
The Archives was founded in 1969 to preserve and make available American films primarily from the 1920s through the 1950s. Includes many of the films directed by Dorothy Arzner, including *Anybody's Woman, Working Girls,* and *Honor Among Lovers;* films by screenwriters Phoebe Ephron, Ayn Rand, Dorothy Parker, Mae West, and Zoë Akins; and films starring actresses West, Claudette Colbert, Carole Lombard, Olivia de Havilland, Betty Hutton, Miriam Hopkins, Barbara Stanwyck, Joan Fontaine, Marlene Dietrich, Anne Baxter, Loretta Young, Dorothy Lamour, Irene Dunne, Gale Sondergaard, and Gene Tierney.

1,026. UCLA Radio Archives
Records. 1932-62. 8000 transcriptions.
Access restricted. No guide.
University of California, Los Angeles, UCLA Film, Television, and Radio Archives.
The Radio Archives, founded in 1975, has collected and preserved tapes and discs of 8000 radio programs, including programs concerning Florence Nightingale and Marie Curie and series such as "The Life of Mary Southern," "Joyce Jordan, M.D.," and "The Romance of Helen Trent." Also includes programs such as "Queen Victoria," in which Helen Hayes starred; "The F.B.I. in Peace and War," directed by Betty Mandeville; and "Sorry, Wrong Number," a radio play written by Lucille Fletcher.

1,027. Akins, Zoë (1088)
Papers. Ca. 1915-58. 4 Hollinger boxes.
Open. Unpublished guide.
University of California, Los Angeles, University Research Library, Department of Special Collections.
Literary manuscripts including plays, screenplays, and stories by Akins (1886-1958), a writer.

1,028. Allen, Maud
Papers. Ca. 1910-30s. 2 Hollinger boxes and 2 oversize packages.
Open. Unpublished guide.
University of California, Los Angeles, University Research Library, Department of Special Collections.
Correspondence, photo albums, and books of Allan (1879-1956), a dancer.

1,029. Armstrong, Willimina Leonora
Papers. Ca. 1930-60. 3 Hollinger boxes.
Open. Unpublished guide.
University of California, Los Angeles, University Research Library, Department of Special Collections.
Papers of [Miss] Armstrong (1866-1947), a writer, include correspondence, literary manuscripts, manuscripts of Armstrong's mystical teachings as interpreted by her disciple [Miss] Mattaline G. Crabtree, Crabtree's manuscript biography of Armstrong, and ephemera.

1,030. Austin, Mary Hunter (278)
Papers. 1905-32. Ca. 150 items.
Open. Unpublished guide.
University of California, Los Angeles, University Research Library, Department of Special Collections.
Correspondence, manuscripts, articles, clippings, and ephemera by and about Austin (1868-1934), a writer.

1,031. Bullock, Georgia Philipps (Morgan) (155/22)
Papers. 1913-53. 23 vols. and 1 microfilm reel.
Open. Unpublished guide.
University of California, Los Angeles, University Research Library, Department of Special Collections.
A former judge of the Superior Court for Los Angeles County, Bullock (1878-) practiced law in Los Angeles and held a number of other public offices. Chronologically ordered scrapbooks contain correspondence, pictures, clippings, and ephemera relating to Bullock's career.

1,032. Cole Family (217)
Papers. 1833-1943. 57 Hollinger boxes and 4 packages.
Open. Published guide.
University of California, Los Angeles, University Research Library, Department of Special Collections.
Family collection includes papers of Olive [Mrs. Cornelius] Cole, her daughter Lucretia (Cole) [Mrs. Howard S.] Waring, and granddaughter Olive Howard Waring. Olive Cole's papers consist of correspondence, diaries and reminiscences, writings, and clippings about her, 1851-1922 (Boxes 6-14, 16-21, 32, 33, and 34, envelope 3). Lucretia Waring's papers consist of correspondence, diaries, and miscellaneous papers, 1873-1946 (Boxes 22c-f). Olive Waring's papers consist of correspondence, writings, miscellaneous papers, and memorabilia, 1898-1941 (Boxes 41-43). See Elmo R. Richardson, *The Papers of Cornelius Cole and the Cole Family, 1833-1943. A Guide to Collection 217* (Los Angeles: University of California Library, 1956), which is out of print.

1,033. Desti, Mary
Papers. Ca. 1918-30. 6 Hollinger boxes.
Open. Unpublished guide.
University of California, Los Angeles, University Research Library, Department of Special Collections.
Correspondence and manuscripts of Desti (1871-1931), a writer who was the mother of Preston Sturges and a friend of Isadora Duncan, about whom she wrote a biography.

1,034. Edson, Katherine Philips (235)
Papers. 1909-34. 14 Hollinger boxes and 4 packages.
Open. Unpublished guide.
University of California, Los Angeles, University Research Library, Department of Special Collections.
Correspondence, pamphlets, clippings, and memorabilia regarding political and social welfare campaigns in which [Mrs.] Edson (1870-1933) worked. Subjects include women in industry, minimum wage laws, and woman suffrage.

1,035. Eldredge, Helen (Woodsmall)
Papers. 1908-55. 25 Hollinger boxes.
Open. Unpublished guide.

University of California, Los Angeles, University Research Library, Department of Special Collections. Correspondence, diaries, manuscripts, photos, and printed material of Eldredge (1879-1959), a writer and educator who founded a physical education movement in India and traveled extensively in Europe and the Middle East.

1,036. Faculty Women's Club
Records. Ca. 1918-75. 15 Hollinger boxes.
Open. Unpublished guide.
University of California, Los Angeles, University Research Library, Department of Special Collections. Constitution, bylaws, president's notebooks, minutes, reports, reminiscences, and bulletins of this educational and social group founded in 1918.

1,037. Fadem, Joyce Abrams
Papers. Ca. 1959-67. 10 Hollinger boxes and 17 tapes.
Open. Unpublished guide.
University of California, Los Angeles, University Research Library, Department of Special Collections. Correspondence, tapes, minutes, and printed material of [Mrs.] Fadem (1932-) pertain to the period during which she was secretary of the California Democratic Council board of directors.

1,038. Frankel, Bessie Herbert (Barlett)
Papers. Ca. 1905-59. 7 Hollinger boxes and 1 package.
Open. No guide.
University of California, Los Angeles, University Research Library, Department of Special Collections. Correspondence and scrapbooks of Frankel (?-1959), a musician and composer who founded the Los Angeles Philharmonic Orchestra, the Hollywood Community Chorus, and the California Federation of Music Clubs and held offices in the Federation at the state and national levels.

1,039. Glass, Maude Emily
Papers. Ca. 1912-70. 5 boxes.
Open. Unpublished guide.
University of California, Los Angeles, University Research Library, Department of Special Collections. Correspondence, manuscripts, and other papers of Glass (1897-19??), a free-lance writer, relate to her friendships with the Wilshire family, Julian Hawthorne, and Ruth St. Denis.

1,040. Gregory, Elizabeth (Hiatt) (313)
Papers. Ca. 1900-45. 6 Hollinger boxes.
Open. Unpublished guide.
University of California, Los Angeles, University Research Library, Department of Special Collections. Gregory (1872-1955) was a pioneer aviation journalist and lecturer. Correspondence, lecture notes, articles, photos, and clippings regarding American aviation. Includes an alphabetical file about women in aviation.

1,041. Japanese American Research Project
Records. Ca. 1899-1975. 548 Hollinger boxes and 132 packages.
Open. Unpublished guide.
University of California, Los Angeles, University Research Library, Department of Special Collections. Records pertaining to women in this collection, some of which is in Japanese, include oral history interviews, Issei interview survey questionnaires, correspondence, and family papers.

1,042. Los Angeles Normal School
Records. 1893-1913. 2 Hollinger boxes.
Open. No guide.
University of California, Los Angeles, University Research Library, Department of Special Collections. Minutes of the board of trustees of the School, which was founded in 1881.

1,043. Lybeck, Ruth (901)
Papers. 1944-50. 4 Hollinger boxes.
Open. Unpublished guide.
University of California, Los Angeles, University Research Library, Department of Special Collections. Lybeck and her husband served as campaign managers and political advisers to US Representative Helen Gahagan Douglas from 1944 to 1950. Correspondence, ephemera, and other papers include material relating to Douglas's career.

1,044. McKee, Ruth Eleanor (1151)
Papers. Ca. 1905-72. 11 Hollinger boxes and 2 oversize packages.
Open. Unpublished guide.
University of California, Los Angeles, University Research Library, Department of Special Collections. A writer, McKee (1903-1970?) served as consul for the US Foreign Service in Tokyo and as historian for the War Relocation Authority. Correspondence, manuscripts, and research material, including literary items.

1,045. Marsh, Dorothy
Papers. Ca. 1954-65. 5 Hollinger boxes.
Open. Unpublished guide.
University of California, Los Angeles, University Research Library, Department of Special Collections. Correspondence, clippings, and printed material of Marsh, a doctor of osteopathy, regarding the merger of the California Osteopathic Association and the California Medical Association in 1962. Marsh was president of COA in 1969.

1,046. Meals for Millions Foundation (1107)
Records. Ca. 1946-67. 47 Hollinger boxes and 2 oversize packages.
Open. Unpublished guide.
University of California, Los Angeles, University Research Library, Department of Special Collections. Collection consists of the office and personal files of Florence Rose, the Foundation's executive secretary. Correspondence, financial records, and publications.

1,047. Noel, Frances
Papers. Ca. 1900-60. 10 Hollinger boxes.
Open. Unpublished guide.
University of California, Los Angeles, University Research Library, Department of Special Collections. Correspondence, pamphlets, clippings, and other papers of Noel (1873-?), who apparently was a social reformer, regarding the labor and birth control movements in Los Angeles.

1,048. Ouspenskaya, Maria
Papers. Ca. 1922-42. 4 Hollinger boxes and 1 oversize package.
Open. Unpublished guide.
University of California, Los Angeles, University Research Library, Department of Special Collections. Photos, motion picture scripts, reviews, publicity material, and other papers of Ouspenskaya (1876-1949), an actress.

1,049. Regional Oral History Office, University of California, Berkeley (400)
Oral history. 1954- . No size given.
Open. Unpublished guide.
University of California, Los Angeles, University Research Library, Department of Special Collections. Copies of oral history transcripts. Major subjects discussed by women in 39 interviews are public service, social welfare, civil rights, women's rights, education, and local history. A transcript for each person interviewed is bound with an index of the subjects and persons mentioned.

1,050. Rosecrans, William Starke
Papers. Ca. 1810-1920. 110 Hollinger boxes.
Open. Published guide.
University of California, Los Angeles, University Research Library, Department of Special Collections. Papers of Rosecrans (1819-98) include correspondence between Rosecrans and his wife Ann Eliza (Hegeman) Rosecrans; between Ann Rosecrans and her children Adrian L., Carl F., Lilian, Ann D., and Mary Louise; and between the Rosecrans and Hegeman families. Also includes writings and memorabilia of Ann D. and Mary Louise Rosecrans. See James V. Mink, *The Papers of General William Starke Rosecrans & the Rosecrans Family: A Guide to Collection 663,* UCLA Library, Occasional Paper No. 12 (Los Angeles, 1961).

1,051. St. Denis, Ruth (1031)
Papers. Ca. 1886-1968. 157 Hollinger boxes and 11 oversize packages.
Open. Unpublished guide.
University of California, Los Angeles, University Research Library, Department of Special Collections. Correspondence, diaries, journals, manuscripts, ballet music, tape recordings, photos, and ephemera of St. Denis (1880-1968), a dancer.

1,052. Shepherd, Theodosia Burr (Hall)
Papers. Ca. 1900-40. 3 Hollinger boxes.
Open. No guide.
University of California, Los Angeles, University Research Library, Department of Special Collections. Correspondence, typescript biography, photos, and scrapbooks of Shepherd (1854-1906), a pioneer of seed culture in Ventura County, CA, and in the state of California. Includes a biography written by her daughter Myrtle (Shepherd) Francis.

1,053. Sumner, Anna Emily
Papers. Ca. 1920-60. 20 Hollinger boxes and 3 packages.
Open. Unpublished guide.
University of California, Los Angeles, University Research Library, Department of Special Collections. Correspondence, memoranda, photos, clippings, and ephemera of [Miss] Sumner (1904-), an administrator, concern various UCLA organizations with which she was associated.

1,054. UCLA Oral History Program Interviews (300)
Oral history. 1959- . No size given.
Open. Unpublished guide.
University of California, Los Angeles, University Research Library, Department of Special Collections. Many of the 15 women interviewed are educators, while most of the rest are in the performing arts or social welfare. A transcript for each woman interviewed is bound with an index of the subjects and persons mentioned.

1,055. University Elementary School
Records. 1933-44. Ca. 2 ft.
Open. No guide.
University of California, Los Angeles, University Research Library, Department of Special Collections. Eleven volumes describing activities to be carried out by various grades in the School.

1,056. Woman's Christian Temperance Union
Records. 1909-39. 4 vols.
Open. No guide.
University of California, Los Angeles, University Research Library, Department of Special Collections. Minutes and accounts of the Duarte, CA, chapter of the WCTU.

1,057. Young, Ella
Papers. 1900-56. 5 Hollinger boxes.
Open. Unpublished guide.
University of California, Los Angeles, University Research Library, Department of Special Collections. Papers of Young (1867-1956), a poet, include correspondence, manuscripts of poems and short stories, typescript and galley proofs of her autobiography, horoscopes, and ephemera.

1,058. John Randolph Haynes and Dora Haynes Foundation
Records. 1903-35. 6 ft.
Open. No guide.

University of California, Los Angeles, University Research Library, Public Affairs Service.
Correspondence and clippings that Dora (Fellows) Haynes, the wife of Los Angeles physician John Haynes, collected about woman suffrage activities in Los Angeles.

1,059. Ransome, Amy
Papers. 1873-1941. 2 ft.
Open. Unpublished guide.
University of Southern California Library, Special Collections.
Ransome (ca. 1872-1942) was vice-president and California state chairman of the National Woman's party and treasurer of the World Woman's party. Correspondence, including letters of Martha C. Callan, secretary of the Iowa Equal Suffrage Association; Sarah Ware Whitney, publisher of the Iowa Association's official organ *The Woman's Standard;* Carrie Chapman Catt; Elizabeth Cady Stanton; and others. Also includes publications of the National Woman Suffrage Association and the Woman's Progressive League of California, manuscripts, press releases, clippings, memorabilia, and other items.

1,060. Women's International Association of Aeronautics
Records. 1929-59. 13 ft.
Open. No guide.
University of Southern California Library, Special Collections.
Founded in 1929 as a worldwide organization for women interested in aviation, the Association sought to stimulate interest in air traffic and to promote international peace. Includes papers of Elizabeth McQueen, aviator and founder of the Association; records of the annual Women's Air Derby, dubbed the "Powder Puff Derby" by Will Rogers; correspondence; biographical sketches and photos of women pilots; manuscripts of speeches and articles; clippings; and printed material.

1,061. School of Dentistry
Records. 1898-1974. 18 ft.
Open. No guide.
University of Southern California School of Dentistry Library.
Faculty minutes, ledgers, photos, scrapbooks, announcements, bulletins, yearbooks, and diplomas of the University of Southern California School of Dentistry, which was founded in 1898. Includes a scrapbook containing an article about Emeline Roberts Jones, a pioneer woman dentist, describing her desire to be a dentist, difficulties she encountered, and her success; an article on the role of women dentists during WWI; a note and photo regarding Amy L. Whaley, the oldest practicing woman dentist in the US in 1928; and an article from 1922 by [Miss] Gladys Eyrich concerning dental hygiene in the Jackson, MS, public schools. Also contains the minutes of the USC department of dental hygiene, which was established in about 1943.

LOS BANOS

1,062. Miscellany
Collection. Nd. No size given.
Open. No guide.
Milliken Museum.
Collection contains more than 50 Treasury and Liberty Loan posters from WWI; a 1918 poster announcing an Old Maids Convention; a photo and clipping of Sophia (Bird) McClelland, who joined her husband James L. McClelland, a schoolteacher, in medical training to become the first woman doctor in the area. Also contains a diary in Spanish of [Señora] Alta Gracia y Barcelon y Alvarado (1840-1946), an Indian who had been adopted by the Julian Ursua family; Adelaide (Barcelon) Martin, one of her many daughters, became an artist.

MENDOCINO

1,063. MacCallum
Papers. 1877-?. No size given.
Open. No guide.
Mendocino Historical Research, Inc.
An 1877 letter from Daisy (Kelly) MacCallum to a school friend in Benicia, CA; an 1897 letter from her daughter Jean MacCallum to Daisy MacCallum's mother Eliza Lee (Owen) Kelly; and yearbooks of the Mendocino Study Club, which was organized in 1908 and federated in 1910.

1,064. Mendocino Coast Historical Photos
Collection. Ca. 1860s- . Ca. 20,000 items.
Open. No guide.
Mendocino Historical Research, Inc.
Photos of people and places in the Mendocino coastal area. Many of the photos depict women.

MENLO PARK

1,065. Archives
Records. 1921- . 17 files, 10 boxes, and 4 vols.
Closed. No guide.
Dominican Nuns of Perpetual Adoration, Corpus Christi Monastery.
Papers relating to the foundation of the Monastery, business records, chronicles and history, personal and official correspondence, brief biographies of foundresses, diocesan papers, records of clothing and professions, bequests, records of sisters who entered the Monastery, maps, blueprints, a file about deceased members, clippings, a book, and other records of the Monastery, which was founded in California in 1921. The Dominican order was established in the US in 1880.

1,066. Archives of the San Francisco Province of the Society of the Sacred Heart
Records. 1887- . 20 drawers and 4 cupboards.
Access restricted. No guide.
Society of the Sacred Heart, Provincial Archives.
The San Francisco Province of the Society of the Sacred Heart was founded in 1887. The sisters founded Menlo Academy in 1898 and St. Joseph's School in 1906. Financial and academic records of Menlo Academy; accounts of general and provincial chapters; correspondence with the motherhouse, which was located first in Paris, then in Brussels, and currently in Rome, and with other provinces; photos; house plans; newsletters; and other records. Also includes written accounts of local, national, and international events involving the Society, such as the founding of new establishments and local, national, and international meetings of the Associated Alumnae of the Sacred Heart.

MILL VALLEY

1,067. Local History
Collection. Nd. Ca. 1.5 ft.
Open. Card catalog.
Mill Valley Public Library.
Manuscripts concerning the history of Mill Valley include 1946 reminiscences in which Wiwona Douglas describes the growth of the town and mentions the Outdoor Art Club, which was organized by local women; a story about early life in Mill Valley by Cora Gardner Burt; a 1945 description of home and the young girlhood experiences of Edith M. Pooley; and "Acts of Early Mill Valley and Surroundings, 1579-1947," by Carrie Gray Klyce, who mentions the activities of prominent Mill Valley women and of such women's groups as the Outdoor Art Club and the Order of the Eastern Star.

1,068. Mill Valley
Oral history. 1968- . Ca. 1.5 ft. of transcripts.
Open. Card catalog.
Mill Valley Public Library.
Includes interviews containing reminiscences about early life of such Mill Valley residents as Ida Johnson Allen; Ruth (Boericke) White Bowie; Elinor Burt; Clarissa (Young) Byrne; Helen Clinton, a hostess who was called Mrs. Mill Valley; Karin Lundquist Connelly; Margaret Wosser Dowd; Nora Evans, who is characterized as an outdoorswoman; Thelma Fenton, a nurse; Pearl Heckman Gattini; Valborg "Mama" Gravander, a Swedish weaver; Elsie Maier Kellers; Helen Van Cleave Park, an interior decorator and history writer; Virginia Stolte Spalding; and Marjorie Mills White. Also includes clippings and photos of some of these women.

In addition, the collection contains interviews in which Rita Abrams, a teacher, music composer, and author of the song "Mill Valley," reminisces about writing the song; Helen Thompson Dreyfus describes her early life in Mill Valley and anecdotes about her aunt Kathleen Norris; Constance Karla discusses the cultural development of the town and of the Public Library; S. Edna Maguire, a teacher and principal, talks about her early life as well as education in Mill Valley since 1921; Bella Resek, an Austrian voice teacher who moved to Mill Valley in 1949, reminisces about her life; and Elizabeth Terwilliger, an environmentalist and naturalist, discusses her experiences.

NEVADA CITY

1,069. International Council of Women
Records. 1888. 470-page vol.
Open. No guide.
Nevada City Library.
Reports of a meeting of the Council, which was assembled by the National Woman Suffrage Association in Washington, DC.

1,070. Nevada, Emma
Papers. Nd. 5 items.
Open. No guide.
Nevada City Library.
Clippings about Nevada, a singer.

1,071. Champions of the Red Cross of the State of California
Records. 1876-78. 3 vols.
Open. No guide.
Searls Historical Library.
Proceedings of the seventh, eighth, and ninth annual sessions of the "grand encampment" of the Champions contain minutes and programs of meetings of this organization, which included women members. The group published a newsletter *The Temperance Champion.*

1,072. Cooley, Lucy
Papers. 1910-16. 100 items.
Open. Card file.
Searls Historical Library.
Correspondence and court records of Cooley, superintendent of the German Quartz mine, the Hanley mine, and the Ocean Star mine in Washington, CA, concern mining operations and litigation over infringement of mining rights.

1,073. Early Theater and The Thespians
Collection. Nd. 1 folder.
Open. No guide.
Searls Historical Library.
Includes typescripts, photos, and clippings pertaining to such performers as Sybil Sanderson, Lotta Crabtree, Jenny Lind, Nance O'Neill, Adah

Isaacs Menken, child entertainer La Petite Sue Robinson, and Mary Anderson, a native of Sacramento, CA, who was known as "Our Mary." Also includes information about The Thespians.

1,074. Historical Clippings
Collection. 1851-1942. 225 vols.
Open. Card file.
Searls Historical Library.
Clippings concern the history of Nevada County.

1,075. Masonic and Eastern Star Order
Records. Ca. 1955-74. 1 folder.
Open. No guide.
Searls Historical Library.
Scrapbooks contain programs of activities and clippings of the local chapter as well as notes on the history of the local, state, and national organizations.

1,076. Native Daughters of the Golden West, Columbia Parlor No. 70
Records. 1892-1904. 188-page vol.
Open. No guide.
Searls Historical Library.
Minutes of meetings and a list of members of this chapter of the Native Daughters since its beginning in North San Juan during 1892. The group met at a variety of locations.

1,077. Nevada City Theaters
Collection. 1851- . 1 folder.
Open. No guide.
Searls Historical Library.
A typescript history of local theaters by Doris E. Foley, programs, photos, clippings, and memorabilia relating to the theater and to actors and actresses in the Nevada City area, including Lola Montez and Lotta Crabtree.

1,078. Organizations, Clubs, and Lodges
Collection. Nd. 1 folder.
Open. No guide.
Searls Historical Library.
Scrapbooks contain typescripts, photos, and clippings concerning the activities of local chapters of the AAUW, the WCTU, the DAR, the Order of Eastern Star, the Native Daughters of the Golden West, the Catholic Ladies Relief Society and Donation Day Association, The Salvation Army, and the United Daughters of North San Juan, which is a local group.

1,079. Photographs
Collection. Ca. 1880s- . 2 drawers and 9 cartons.
Open. Card catalog.
Searls Historical Library.
Collection contains photos of local women and of organizations and assemblies. Includes a photo of the Butterfly Club, members of which were dressed in butterfly wings and costumes, and a photo of the KRA women's club.

NEW ALMADEN

1,080. Taped Interviews
Oral history. Ca. 1950s- . No size given.
Open. No guide.
New Almaden Museum.
Includes tapes of interviews with [Mrs.] Amy F. Burnhans and Mrs. Hugh Wright about Christiana Terhune [Mrs. James Butterworth] Randol (1845-1919), who was Burnhans's great-aunt and Wright's grandmother. Randol helped establish the miner's fund at New Almaden, into which miners paid fees and from which they received health care benefits. Also includes interviews in which Mrs. Isadore Miller and [Mrs.] Alva Miller Pringle discuss articles of clothing belonging to Pringle's grandmother Johanna Strabough Miller that are now located in the Museum; they also discuss the personal life of Johanna Miller, who came from Austria to Los Gatos, CA, in 1885. In addition, the collection contains random interviews conducted with old-timers at the Santa Clara County Fair in 1952 and a description by [Mrs.] Constance Perham, Museum curator, of her experiences in Mexico during 1976 as the guest of the governor of Juahaca and her work in interviewing residents there.

OAKLAND

1,081. Bender, Albert M.
Papers. 1920-41. Ca. 6 ft.
Open. Description and register.
Mills College Library, Manuscript Collections.
Correspondence of Bender (1866-1941), an insurance broker, patron of the arts, and trustee of Mills College, includes letters from Gertrude Atherton, Mary (Hunter) Austin, Ina Coolbrith, Bertha Clark Pope Damon, Sara Bard Field, Una Jeffers, Charmian London, Consuela Kanaga McCarthy, Idella Purnell, Ruth St. Denis, Marie Welch, Elizabeth Corbet Yeats, Ella (Flagg) Young, and others. Also includes correspondence and manuscripts of Anne M. Bremer, Hildegarde Flanner, and Genevieve Taggard as well as correspondence of Portia Bell Hume, a physician.

1,082. California Authors
Collection. Ca. 1840- . Ca. 8 ft.
Open. Register.
Mills College Library, Manuscript Collections.
Includes literary manuscripts of *Immortal Marriage* by Gertrude Franklin (Horn) Atherton, *Taos Pueblo* by Mary (Hunter) Austin, poems and prose by Ina Donna Coolbrith, *Grandma Called It Carnal* by [Mrs.] Bertha Clark Pope Damon, and poems by Emma Frances Dawson. Also includes a prose tribute to Albert Bender by Sara Bard Field, poems by Hildegarde Flanner, a poem by Elsa Gidlow, manuscripts relating to Jack London by his wife Charmian (Kittredge) London, poems by Ruth St. Denis, a poem by Margaret Erwin Schevill, a poem by Genevieve Taggard, and poems, manuscripts, and galley proofs of Marie de Laveaga Welch.

1,083. Cameron, James, and Cameron, Emma S.
Papers. 1846-76. 475 items.
Open. Description and register.
Mills College Library, Manuscript Collections.
Papers of James Cameron (1816-?), an American portrait and landscape painter who was born in Scotland, include correspondence with his mother Agnes Cameron and his wife Emma Cameron. Also includes Emma Cameron's correspondence with her mother-in-law Agnes Cameron, her 1862 diary, and notes on her travels in Italy between 1846 and 1848. Collection also contains letters she received from Henrietta (Rossi) [Mrs. Thomas B.] Ashton, 1846-50, the last of which was written after Cameron's marriage; from Sarah Brown (Ingersoll) [Mrs. Halsey Fenimore] Cooper, 1872-76; and from Isabella [Mrs. Joseph] Mozier, 1846-50.

1,084. Clark, Emma Cornelia
Papers. 1822-41. 103 items.
Open. Description and register.
Mills College Library, Manuscript Collections.
Correspondence and a photo of [Miss] Clark (ca. 1806-?), who was a student at Emma Willard's Troy Female Seminary; she later married clergyman William D. Strobel. Letters concern her life as a student at the Seminary; a visit to New York and Washington, DC, and her married life in New York. Correspondents include her cousin Caroline, Anna P. Clark, Abby Ann Strobel, Mary E. Strobel, and Lucretia Maria Davidson, whose letter also contains a drawing, a poem, and minutes. Emma Clark also spelled her maiden name Clarke.

1,085. College Archives
Records. Ca. 1850s- . No size given.
Partially restricted. Index file.
Mills College Library, Manuscript Collections.
Archives of Mills College, which was founded as the Mills Seminary for Young Ladies during the 1850s by Cyrus T. Mills and Susan Lincoln (Tolman) [Mrs. Charles Taggart] Mills, contains texts of speeches of founder's day addresses; minutes of the Women's Faculty Club, 1928-69; secretary's books of the Mu Sigma Sigma sorority; constitution, bylaws, and a list of members of the Mary Atkins Association; a guest book of the Home Management House, 1936-56; records of the Employees' Association, 1940-42; and correspondence, class histories, and papers of Mills College students. The Archives also includes correspondence, a description of the Mills campus, and a Mount Holyoke Seminary notebook of Cyrus and Susan Mills; personal papers of Aurelia (Henry) [Mrs. George Frederick] Reinhardt and papers documenting her presidency of Mills College from 1916 to 1943 and her presidency of AAUW; and papers of Rosalind Keep concerning a history of Mills College, *Four Score Years* (1931), the typescript of which was corrected by Aurelia (Henry) Reinhardt. Also includes Keep's correspondence, school notebooks and report cards from the 1890s, and journals of travels in Europe during 1938 and in South America during 1943 with Reinhardt.

The Archives also contains a variety of correspondence, manuscripts, and other material. It includes papers for a biography of Cyrus and Susan Mills by Elias Olan James; a diary of Amelia Holman [Mrs. Josiah] Keep, 1872-97; correspondence, reminiscences, and interviews with early Mills graduates assembled by Ethel Hunley Coldwell, Mills class of 1894; correspondence, an 1871 receipt for tuition and board at Mills Seminary, rules and regulations for 1909 to 1914, president's reports for 1909 to 1914, and a 1910 notebook of the home life committee of Luella Clay Carson; recollections by Carrie E. Wilson of the early history of Mills Seminary; a text of a speech Louise A. Boyd gave to the Mills assembly in 1940 about her expedition to the Arctic, Northwest Greenland, and Jan Mayen Island; and a lecture Julia Cooley Altrocchi gave at Mills in 1940 on "Ivory Towers Old and New."

1,086. Hitchcock and Coit
Papers. Ca. 1730-1929. 12 ft.
Open. Register.
Mills College Library, Manuscript Collections.
Family papers include correspondence and journals concerning the life of Martha Taliaferro (Hunter) [Mrs. Charles M.] Hitchcock in San Francisco since the 1850s and correspondence, journals, and material concerning her daughter Eliza "Lillie" W. (Hitchcock) Coit (1843-1929), an author who was San Francisco's only volunteer firewoman. Also includes correspondence of Sallie [Mrs. Nathaniel Wyche] Hunter and of Mary E. Lucas as well as notes and clippings of Floride Green, who wrote a biography of Coit.

1,087. Miscellany
Collection. Nd. No size given.
Open. Card index.
Mills College Library, Manuscript Collections.
Collection includes correspondence and manuscripts of Helen Maria (Fiske) Hunt Jackson, Josephine Preston Peabody, Harriet Elizabeth (Beecher) Stowe, Margaret Widdemer, and Ella (Flagg) Young. Peabody's 123-page manuscript is entitled *Fortune and Men's Eyes: New Poem with a Play.*

1,088. Prall, David Wight, and Prall, Margaret C.
Papers. 1908-54. 262 items.
Open. Description and register.

Mills College Library, Manuscript Collections.
Papers of David Prall (1886-1940), a professor of philosophy at Harvard, Cornell, and the University of California, include papers of his sisters Margaret Prall (?-1955), chairman of the Mills music department; Elizabeth (Prall) Anderson, wife of Sherwood Anderson; and Dorothea (Prall) [Mrs. Max] Radin. Margaret Prall's papers consist of correspondence, speeches, lectures, articles, and book reviews she wrote, much of which pertains to music. Elizabeth Anderson's papers consist of a book she translated in ca. 1943 and a high school exhibition program. Dorothea Radin's papers consist of two letters from Delbert E. Prall, sketches of family life, a story, poems, songs for children, and clippings.

1,089. California Authors
Collection. 1874-1965. 1 vol. and 34 items.
Open. Unpublished guide.
Oakland Public Library.
Includes correspondence of Gertrude Atherton, 1926-30; correspondence and cards of Mary Austin, 1912-16; correspondence of Charmian [Mrs. Jack] London, 1909-13; correspondence and a diary of Juanita Miller, a writer who was the daughter of author Joaquin Miller, 1921-53; and letters to Joaquin Miller.

1,090. Coolbrith, Ina Donna
Papers. 1862-1928. 3 boxes, 3 vols., and other items.
Open. Index and catalog cards.
Oakland Public Library.
A manuscript, articles, biographies, photos, scrapbooks of clippings, and books of the poetry of Coolbrith (1841-1928), the first poet laureate of California, from 1915 until her death, and the first librarian of the Oakland Free Library, from 1874 to 1892. Coolbrith was known as the matriarch of a group of California authors, which was called the California Literary Society and included among its members Jack London and Joaquin Miller.

1,091. Stow, Marietta Lucy
Papers. 1879-90. 2 vols. and 5 items.
Open. Unpublished guide.
Oakland Public Library.
A clipping, periodicals, and books of [Mrs. J. W.] Stow (ca. 1830-90), an advocate of equal rights for women who in 1884 organized a new Equal Rights party, which nominated her for Vice-President of the US and another woman for President. In 1882 Stow ran for governor of California.

ONTARIO

1,092. Model Colony
Records. 1881- . Ca. 50 ft.
Open. No guide.
Ontario City Library.
Minute books, ledgers, oral history tapes, photos, scrapbooks, clippings, and other records of the city of Ontario, also known as the "Model Colony," which was founded in 1881. Includes constitutions, bylaws, minute books, ledgers, scrapbooks, yearbooks, histories, and other records of such women's clubs as the Halfhill Club, which was founded in 1920 by Mrs. J. M. Halfhill to encourage participation in community events and provide financial and other types of assistance to churches, schools, and other groups; the Club disbanded in 1974. Other women's clubs represented include the Friday Afternoon Club, a literary club founded in 1896 by Mrs. W. J. Horne and Mrs. Thomas Purvis; the Mountain View Women's Club, which was founded in 1916 by Mrs. J. R. Merrill as a social club for rural women in the area and evolved into a community service club; the Ramblers Club, which was established as a travel and study group and became involved in civic affairs; the East Side Thimble Club; the DAR; the Business and Professional Women's Club; and others. Also includes minutes of the Ontario chapter of the American National Red Cross, 1917-62; minutes and scrapbooks of the Ontario chapter of United Service Organizations, 1942-45; a history of Ontario compiled by Isabel Rose Neales, an early resident of the city; and papers of the Chaffey family, which founded Ontario.

ORANGE

1,093. Archives
Records. 1912- . 16 drawers and 5 shelves.
Open. Unpublished guide.
Sisters of St. Joseph of Orange, Motherhouse.
Minutes, corporate and administrative records, financial records, statistical reports, correspondence, papers of several mothers superior, scrapbooks, and material relating to schools and hospitals established and operated by members of the order in California, Texas, Hawaii, Arizona, New Guinea, and Australia. The congregation was founded in 1912 in Eureka, CA.

PACIFIC GROVE

1,094. Muricata Club
Records. 1911-74. 1 box.
Open. No guide.
Pacific Grove Public Library.
Constitution, bylaws, minutes, correspondence, financial and membership records, programs, yearbooks, photos, clippings, and memorabilia of the Club, a women's study and book review group founded in 1911. The Club, which limited its membership to 20 persons, disbanded in 1974 when several of the original members died.

PASADENA

1,095. Biology Division
Records. 1928-57. 27 cu.ft.
Open. Inventory.
California Institute of Technology Archives.
Administrative records and correspondence of the Division, primarily from 1946 to 1957 when George Beadle, who won the Nobel Prize in 1958, was chairman. Contains correspondence of hundreds of biologists and medical researchers, including such women as Barbara McClintock, a geneticist and cytologist who held a PhD.

1,096. Epstein, Paul S.
Papers. 1910-65. 4 cu.ft.
Open. Inventory.
California Institute of Technology Archives.
Professional and personal papers of Epstein (1883-1966), a physicist, include family correspondence relating to the social and political situation facing Epstein family members in Europe during the 1930s and 1940s. Contains correspondence with his wife Alice Epstein and various cousins; most of the letters are in Russian, German, or Yiddish. Also contains a small amount of material regarding his sister Lida Hedwig Epstein and his mother Sara Lurie Epstein.

1,097. Lauritsen, Thomas
Papers. 1945-73. 5 cu.ft.
Open. Inventory.
California Institute of Technology Archives.
Correspondence, lecture notes, notes on travel and college courses, monographs, conference material, clippings, and other papers of Lauritsen (1915-73), a nuclear physicist. Includes extensive correspondence with Fay Ajzenberg-Selove, also a nuclear physicist, regarding her scientific collaboration with Lauritsen and other topics.

1,098. Millikan, Robert Andrews
Papers. 1889-1953. 24 cu.ft.
Open. Published guide.
California Institute of Technology Archives.
Correspondence, diaries, professional and family papers, photos, scrapbooks, and ephemera of Millikan (1868-1953), an experimental physicist, winner of the Nobel Prize in physics, and chairman of the executive council of Caltech Institute from 1921 to 1945. Contains papers of his wife Greta (Blanchard) Millikan (1876-?), including correspondence with her husband, family, and friends; diaries, including one from her trip around the world in 1940; and papers documenting her community activities. The Millikans were married in 1902. See Albert F. Gunns and Judith R. Goodstein, *Guide to the Robert Andrews Millikan Collection at the California Institute of Technology* (New York: American Institute of Physics, 1975) and Judith R. Goodstein, ed., *Guide to a Microfilm Edition of the Robert Andrews Millikan Collection* (Pasadena: Caltech Archives, 1977).

1,099. Carr
Papers. Nd. 4 boxes.
Open. No guide.
Pasadena Historical Society Museum.
Papers of Jeanne [Mrs. Ezra S.] Carr, an author of historical articles who was also interested in botany and horticulture, include correspondence, deeds and papers pertaining to the Carrs' home in Pasadena, and drawings of California flora and fauna.

1,100. Coleman, Cataline Storms
Papers. Early 1830s-ca. 1918. 1 vol.
Open. No guide.
Pasadena Historical Society Museum.
Notebook of Coleman entitled "The Young Ladies Remembrancer."

1,101. Crank, Mary Agnes
Papers. Ca. 1925. 12-page item.
Open. No guide.
Pasadena Historical Society Museum.
Reminiscences of Crank regarding ranch life from 1876 to 1925.

1,102. Diary
Papers. 1904-05. 1 vol.
Open. No guide.
Pasadena Historical Society Museum.
Diary of an unidentified young woman visiting southern California.

1,103. Greene, Mary Anne
Papers. 1924-37. 1 vol.
Open. No guide.
Pasadena Historical Society Museum.
Scrapbook of Greene (1857-?), an attorney and author of law books, contains personal correspondence, correspondence with newspapers, material regarding the Woman's Baptist Mission Society of Southern California, and clippings. Greene received her law degree from Boston University Law School in 1888.

1,104. Orton, Annie B.
Papers. Nd. No size given.
Open. No guide.
Pasadena Historical Society Museum.
Private accounts of [Miss] Orton, who founded Miss Orton's Private School for Girls.

1,105. Scattergoods Association
Records. 1934-50. 1 vol.
Open. No guide.
Pasadena Historical Society Museum.
Scrapbook compiled by [Mrs.] Mae Reese Johnson regarding the Association, a Negro organization. Includes correspondence, clippings, and other material of female members of the group.

1,106. Washington Heights Study Club
Records. 1905-07. No size given.
Open. No guide.
Pasadena Historical Society Museum.
Minutes of the Club, which was founded in 1905.

1,107. Women's Literary Club
Records. 1907-32. 2 vols.
Open. No guide.
Pasadena Historical Society Museum.
Scrapbooks of the Club, which was founded in 1907 and later known as the Pasadena Study Club, include a history of the Club and clippings regarding meetings and the election of officers.

POMONA

1,108. Ebell Club
Records. 1902-64. 3 ft.
Open. No guide.
Pomona Public Library.
Minutes of the board and secretary's books of this literary and educational society, which was founded in 1902 and is still active.

1,109. Pomona Fruit and Floral Society
Records. 1890-1940. 10 in.
Open. No guide.
Pomona Public Library.
Secretary's and treasurer's books of this ladies organization, which was devoted to social improvement.

1,110. Shakespeare Club
Records. 1904-60. 1 ft.
Open. No guide.
Pomona Public Library.
Secretary's books and membership lists of this literary Club, which was founded in 1904 and is still extant.

1,111. White
Papers. 1878-1955. 4 ft.
Open. No guide.
Pomona Public Library.
Diaries of Mary White, 1878-1930, and of her daughters Alice White, 1892, and Mabel E. White, 1892-1955. Mabel White was an osteopathic physician in Pomona.

REDLANDS

1,112. San Bernardino County Pioneer Women
Collection. 1864-76. 2 vols.
Closed. No guide.
San Bernardino County Museum.
Collection consists of a diary of Mrs. J. A. Rousseau, 1864, and a diary of Ellen W. Steele Sturges, 1876.

1,113. MacNair
Papers. Nd. 1 drawer.
Access restricted. No guide.
University of Redlands Library, Special Collections.
Collection includes correspondence of Florence (Wheelock) [Mrs. Francis] Ayscough (1878-1942), a poet and authority on Chinese literature, 1923-40. Many of the letters are addressed to Harley Farnsworth MacNair, whom she married in 1935. She was married to Ayscough until 1933 and continued to use his surname in her work.

REDWOOD CITY

1,114. Archives Collection of the Redwood City Public Library
Collection. 1898-1976. 81 items and 50 tapes.
Closed. No guide.
Redwood City Public Library.
Collection contains a nearly complete set of minutes of the first American National Red Cross chapter in San Mateo County; a Red Cross roster; a history and scrapbook of the Redwood City Public Library; photos of elementary and secondary Sunday school students; yearbooks; 19th-century school composition books; oral history interviews with pioneer women Pauline Barneson, Emma McCrea, Gertrude Beeger, Petra Cooper, and Margaret Hilton; ledgers; maps; diplomas; and memorabilia.

1,115. Local History
Collection. 1850-1975. 12 drawers.
Access restricted. Unpublished guide.
Redwood City Public Library.
Collection provides information on area pioneers, women educators, social groups, theatrical productions, and WWI and WWI women's activities. Includes histories of women's clubs, pamphlets, programs, rosters, and photos of women in the community.

1,116. Newspaper Clipping File
Collection. 1859- . 25,000 items and microfilm.
Open. Subject heading list.
Redwood City Public Library.
Clippings from the *Redwood City Tribune* and the *Times-Gazette* of Redwood City contain biographical sketches of women active in the community, obituaries, and information on clubs, honors, and related topics.

1,117. Richard Schellens's Local History
Collection. 1850-1974. 184 vols.
Partially closed. Unpublished guide.
Redwood City Public Library.
Correspondence, post cards, biographical material, histories, photos, clippings, and programs contain information about area women's organizations, social events, occupations, and changing roles. Part of the collection also appears on microfilm.

1,118. Archives
Records. 1938- . No size given.
Access restricted. No guide.
Sisters of St. Francis of Penance and Christian Charity, Mount Alverno Convent.
Financial reports; correspondence, including letters from superior generals, provincial superiors, and from other provinces; yearly chronicles of the convents in the province; photos; scrapbooks; newsletters; bulletins; and other records of the province, which was formed in 1938. The order was established in the US in 1874 in Buffalo, NY; its members are involved in all areas of teaching, in health services, and in social work with the poor and underprivileged.

RIVERSIDE

1,119. City Marshal
Records. 1883-1953. 2.5 cu.ft. and 16 vols.
Open. No guide.
Riverside City Archives.
Monthly and annual reports and city and business licenses volumes of the City Marshal, who issued licenses and enforced the civil code. Contains the names and ages of persons applying for various licenses.

1,120. City Treasurer
Records. 1883-1953. Ca. 2 cu.ft. and 44 vols.
Open. No guide.
Riverside City Archives.
Monthly, quarterly, and annual reports; assessment rolls from 1884 to 1907; and demands and warrants volumes of the City Treasurer. The assessment rolls list the names of the heads of households and the value of their property. The demands and warrants volumes contain lists of individual claims against the city for services rendered, including women who demanded payment for feeding prisoners and working in the library.

1,121. Health Department
Records. 1883-1953. Ca. 1 cu.ft.
Open. No guide.
Riverside City Archives.
Monthly, quarterly, and annual reports; health officer's ledger listing patients and employees; correspondence; burial reports; and other records of the Health Department in Riverside, a joint city-county agency that provides health care and services for area residents with an emphasis on preventive medicine. Contains birth and death reports from 1910 to 1939 that are broken down by sex, age, race, and marital status and that list the causes of death, including those related to pregnancy and childbirth. Also includes reports documenting the numbers and rates of communicable diseases, including venereal disease; reports on infant welfare clinics, also known as well-baby clinics, during the 1930s; records from the 1930s regarding the Riverside Women's Rest Room Association, which apparently provided job referral services and hot meals for both men and women; and analyses of nursing activities and projects in the city and county.

1,122. Police Records
Records. 1883-1953. 0.75 cu.ft. and 3 vols.
Open. No guide.
Riverside City Archives.
Law enforcement records for the city of Riverside include monthly police reports, correspondence of police chiefs, citizens' complaints, accident reports, arrest records, and police court dockets. Contains information about two women (one of whom was [Mrs.] Mabel B. Hawley) who were hired by the police department as undercover agents during the Prohibition era; there was only one woman on the force at any one time. Includes a letter from the Riverside Woman's Club relating to alleged misconduct on the part of the chief of police toward certain policewomen. Also includes arrest records for such crimes as rape, illegal cohabitation, and prostitution as well as dockets from 1907 to 1914 containing the name, sex, age, race, crime, and sentence of the offender, some of whom were women.

1,123. Craft, Marcella
Papers. 1880-1959. 8 record storage boxes.
Closed. Index.
Riverside Municipal Museum.
[Miss] Craft (1874 or 1880-1959) was an opera prima donna in Europe between 1905 and 1931 and was founder and, from 1932 to 1957, the general director of the Riverside Opera Association. Personal and business correspondence, post cards, reviews, scores for operas and arias, scrapbooks, photos, and printed material concerning her singing career and the Association, which she founded to produce operas in English. Craft also taught opera techniques at Riverside Junior College.

1,124. Hartmann, Sadakichi
Papers. 1880s-1970. 6 ft.
Partially closed. No guide.
University of California, Riverside, Library, Special Collections.
Papers of Hartmann (1867-1944), a writer and artist, include correspondence with his wives, children, and Ezra Pound; a diary from 1907 to 1908 of Lillian Bonham, an aspiring actress who became Hartmann's common-law wife, who wrote for the most part about her relationship with Hartmann; drafts of Hartmann's literary works; some of his artwork; family photos; and other papers. Contains correspondence dating primarily from the 1930s of Margery Winter, a Los Angeles writer and artist, with Nora and Roy Morgan in Andover, NH, regarding Winter's life at an artists'

enclave on Sargent Circle in Los Angeles and her impressions of Hartmann, Ben Berlin, and other writers and artists. Also contains correspondence between Hartmann's daughter Atma Dorthea Gilliland and Harry Lawton concerning donation of the Hartmann papers to the University of California, Riverside, as well as her feelings for her father.

ROHNERT PARK

1,125. Academic Senate Committee on the Role of Women
Records. 1972-74. 8 in.
Open. No guide.
Sonoma State University Library.
Minutes, correspondence, notes and memoranda, reports, clippings, and newsletters of the Committee at California State College, Sonoma, which functioned from 1972 to 1974. Includes correspondence of Yvette Fallandy, dean of academic planning at the College; reports of women faculty members, including Rita B. Garant from the school's office of educational development, and reports of women faculty members at other California state colleges and universities; official reports of the women's studies program on the Sonoma campus; official report on the status of women at California State University, San Diego; discrimination reports; a list of women's studies sources from the Association of American Colleges; and clippings about such topics as women in education.

1,126. "Change, the Women's Newsletter"
Records. 1973. 11-page item.
Open. No guide.
Sonoma State University Library.
One issue of "Change, the Women's Newsletter," which was published on the Sonoma campus.

1,127. Faculty Women and Wives Club
Records. 1972. 1 item.
Open. No guide.
Sonoma State University Library.
Newsletter of the Club on the Sonoma campus.

1,128. Lee, Hector II.
Papers. 1940s- . 54 vols.
Open. Unpublished guide.
Sonoma State University Library.
Typescripts, manuscripts, interview transcripts, student papers and related items on local history, and photos pertaining to California folklore were compiled into volumes by Lee, who taught courses on folklore at Chico State College and California State College, Sonoma. Many of the items, including some of the interview transcripts, were written by and about women.

1,129. "Sonowoman"
Records. 1971-72. 1 folder.
Open. No guide.
Sonoma State University Library.
Issues of "Sonowoman," an irregularly published newsletter on the Sonoma campus that chiefly consisted of classified personal advertisements.

1,130. Women
Collection. Nd. 1 box.
Open. No guide.
Sonoma State University Library.
Typescripts, bibliographies, announcements, clippings, women's studies program brochures, and mimeograph publications pertain to women students and faculty members at California State College, Sonoma, as well as to community events and issues.

1,131. Archives
Records. Ca. 1970s- . Ca. 12 ft.
Open. No guide.
Sonoma State University, Women's Studies Program Office.
Files, programs, pamphlets, brochures, ephemera, and other records of the University's Women's Studies Program, founded in ca. 1970. Also includes assorted material relating to women and birth control, religion, law, music, and other topics.

SACRAMENTO

1,132. California State Employees Association
Records. Nd. No size given.
Open. No guide.
California State Archives.
Included with reports and other records of the Association are rosters and club files, 1958-68, for the State Women's Club, an employee organization.

1,133. California State Library
Records. Ca. 1920-54. No size given.
Open. No guide.
California State Archives.
Correspondence and papers of various programs of the State Library, among them the home teachers of the blind. Includes reports of the home teachers, most of whom were women, to the state librarian as well as correspondence with other institutions.

1,134. California Supreme and Appellate Court
Records. 1850-1960s. Ca. 23,800 ft.
Open. Unpublished indexes.
California State Archives.
Contains legal arguments on file, trial court records, briefs, and other records. Many of the records concern women involved in civil and criminal actions. Indexes to litigants for 1850 to 1935 are available.

1,135. Census Records
Records. 1790s-1880. Ca. 30 ft.
Open. Published and unpublished guides.
California State Archives.
Consists of 1790s mission censuses, the 1852 state census, the 1860 and 1880 US censuses for California, and special censuses of California cities and towns from 1897 to 1938. The mission censuses for San Carlos (1796), San Luis Obispo (1779 and 1798), San Antonio (1798), and Soledad (1798) list names and ages of all inhabitants under the headings of religious, married couples, widows, widowers, unmarried men, unmarried women, boys, girls, and newborn infants. Special censuses for cities and towns usually provide only names and addresses but occasionally include age, sex, color, and occupation. See *Genealogical Research in the California State Archives* (Sacramento, CA: Office of the Secretary of State).

1,136. Department of Consumer Affairs
Records. Ca. 1900- . No size given.
Open. Unpublished indexes.
California State Archives.
Records of the Department, until 1970 the Department of Professional and Vocational Standards, contain records of approximately 30 boards charged with licensing and regulating individuals in various professions and occupations, among them the cosmetology board, the medical examiners board, the social work examiners board, and the vocational nurse examiners board. Cosmetology board files include applications for various categories of practice, ca. 1927-60, which contain biographical data and a photo of the applicant, report forms, examinations, and records of licensing hearings. Medical examiners board records include physicians biographies, correspondence, and applications, ca. 1906-57, as well as minutes of and records pertaining to applications to the pharmacy board. The social work examiners board records contain correspondence, reports, applications for registration as a social worker, board rulings and responses, and clippings, ca. 1940-67. Vocational nurse examiners board records consist of licenses granted, 1954-55. Some indexing of the records has been done by ethnic group.

1,137. Department of Education
Records. 1850s- . No size given.
Open. No guide.
California State Archives.
Includes annual reports (110 ft.) from county superintendents of schools, 1863-1920, giving the names of teachers, principals, and district clerks; grades taught; salaries; and other information about public education at the local level. Also contains public school records, ca. 1870s-1960s, which include minutes of board of education meetings, material on school programs, and other papers.

1,138. Department of Justice: Women Criminals
Records. 1906. No size given.
Open. Unpublished guide.
California State Archives.
Consists of records of an experimental project that attempted to correlate physical characteristics with a tendency toward criminal activities. The records used were taken from prison "mug books."

1,139. Elections
Records. 1849- . No size given.
Open. Unpublished guide.
California State Archives.
Consists of a master record on statewide elections in California since 1849, giving the vote on a precinct level in every county and providing vote totals for women candidates for office.

1,140. Governor's Office: Administrative Files
Records. 1943-53. No size given.
Open. Published inventory.
California State Archives.
Includes files on institutions (13 folders), which contain correspondence regarding inmates of the California Institution for Women at Tehachapi; records of the department of education (2 folders) concerning child care and day nurseries, with correspondence about rates, eligibility, geographical distribution of centers, and continuance of centers; records of the department of veterans affairs (1 folder), with correspondence about the operation of facilities for women veterans under the Women's Relief Corps Homes; records on women's clubs (11 folders), with information about Governor Earl Warren's appointments of women to executive and administrative positions in state government, the equal rights amendment, compulsory health insurance, and proceedings of the California non-partisan round table luncheons, annual gatherings of women appointees in state government; and records of woman's programs (1 folder), established by the department of education's bureau of business education to create opportunities for self-employment for women. See David L. Snyder, *Records of the Governor's Office,* California State Archives Inventory No. 4 (Sacramento, CA: Office of the Secretary of State, 1974).

1,141. Legislative Records
Records. 1849- . No size given.
Open. Published and unpublished guides.
California State Archives.
Consists of all bills introduced into the California state legislature, including bills introduced by women and those affecting women, as well as petitions to the legislature, legislative hearings, legislative appointments, and other records. See *Genealogical Research in the California State Archives* (Sacramento, CA: Office of the Secretary of State).

1,142. Notary Public Files
Records. 1857-1941. More than 37 vols.
Open. Unpublished guide.
California State Archives.
Consists of appointment records of notaries public, many of whom were women.

1,143. Sacramento Courts
Records. 1850-1879. No size given.
Open. Unpublished guide.
California State Archives.
Records of Sacramento district courts, county courts, courts of sessions, and justices of the peace provide information about divorce, child custody, and domestic matters.

1,144. Secretary of State
Records. 1850s- . No size given.
Open. Unpublished guide.
California State Archives.
Contains applications for permission to practice law, 1880-1920, including the application of Clara Foltz, the first woman admitted to Hastings Law School and to the California bar. Also contains articles of incorporation, from the 1850s to date, for state corporations, including charters, bylaws, names of officers or stockholders, location, and information about economic and other activity.

1,145. Spanish Archives
Records. Pre 1850. No size given.
Open. Unpublished indexes.
California State Archives.
Copies of land grant records, confiscated at Monterey, CA, in 1846, with indexes both to the grant and the grantee, some of whom were women.

1,146. State Department of Corrections: California Institutions for Women
Records. Ca. 1880s-1950s. No size given.
Open. Unpublished guide.
California State Archives.
Includes material about institutions at Corona, Tehachapi, and San Quentin, before it became an exclusively male prison.

1,147. State Department of Corrections: California Prisons
Records. 1850- . More than 1200 cu.ft.
Open. Published guide.
California State Archives.
Consists of records of California prisons, which provide biographical information on prisoners, some of whom were women. The records, which are arranged by prison and occasionally by individual, include prison registers, "mug books," and other information about inmates and conditions in the prisons. More recent records contain information about prison employees. See David L. Snyder, *Records of the Governor's Office,* California State Archives, Inventory No. 4 (Sacramento, CA: Office of the Secretary of State, 1974).

1,148. State Department of Public Health
Records. Nd. No size given.
Open. Unpublished guide.
California State Archives.
Included in records of the Department are applications for public health nursing positions, 1920-41, which provide some biographical information on women applicants.

1,149. State Department of Social Welfare
Records. Nd. No size given.
Open. Unpublished guide.
California State Archives.
Contains county records, ca. 1914-1950s, including reports and other records of county agencies, among them jails and hospitals, which provided programs for women.

1,150. State Relief Administration
Records. 1933-37. No size given.
Open. Unpublished guide.
California State Archives.
Records of cases include descriptions of programs, surveys of areas, and reports of conditions and provide information on women in California during the depression.

1,151. State Youth Authority
Records. Nd. No size given.
Open. Unpublished guide.
California State Archives.
Includes monthly reports for Youth Authority institutions, 1948-49, among them the Los Guilucos School for Girls.

1,152. Warren, Earl
Papers. 1927-53. 25 cu.ft.
Open. Published guide.
California State Archives.
Papers of Warren, governor of California and chief justice of the US Supreme Court, include those of his wife Nina P. (Meyers) Warren and their daughter Nina Elizabeth Warren. Nina (Meyers) Warren's papers are primarily from the years her husband served as governor (1943-53) and include invitations to social functions, requests for use of her name, honorary appointments, requests for information on her family and activities, invitations to and arrangements for annual legislative teas, and information about her work with the governors' wives' committee for a central fountain at the United Nations, 1950-52. Papers of Nina Elizabeth "Honeybear" Warren are primarily from the period after November 1950, when she was stricken with polio. During her illness and recovery, more than 20,000 letters expressing sympathy were received. Also contains a file about her selection and reign as queen of the 25th annual Shenandoah apple blossom festival in 1952. See David L. Snyder, *Index to the Warren Personal Papers, 1927-53,* California State Archives Inventory No. 5 (Sacramento, CA: Office of the Secretary of State, 1976).

1,153. Bidwell, Annie Ellicott (Kennedy)
Papers. 1842-1917. 94 boxes.
Open. Summary.
California State Library.
[Mrs. John] Bidwell (1839-1918), who was born in Meadville, PA, moved to California in 1868 and became a civic leader and philanthropist with special interests in Indians, church affairs, temperance movements, and woman suffrage. Personal and business correspondence, diaries she kept from 1888 to 1911, reminiscences, manuscript and other material on prohibition and the Indians, photos and illustrations, scrapbooks, clippings, ephemera, and periodicals.

1,154. Dill, Theresa Mae (Varney)
Papers. 1934-43. 10 vols.
Open. No guide.
California State Library.
Papers of [Mrs. Robie L.] Dill consist of purchase records and accounts she kept during high school and college in California and Oregon.

1,155. Loyal Orange Ladies' Institution, Purple Star Lodge, No. 131
Records. 1943-49. 300-page vol.
Open. No guide.
California State Library.
Minutes of this Oakland, CA, women's group.

1,156. Maurer, Katharine
Papers. 1913-77. 1 box.
Open. Summary.
California State Library.
Reports and other papers of Maurer, a church welfare worker at the US Quarantine and Immigration Station on Angel Island in San Francisco Bay.

1,157. Photos
Collection. Nd. Ca. 30,000 items.
Open. Card catalog.
California State Library.
Collection of photos contains many portraits of California women, filed alphabetically by name, as well as photos in which women appear in a variety of scenes.

1,158. Sargent Club
Records. 1902-05. 1 vol.
Open. No guide.
California State Library.
Minutes of this San Francisco women's suffrage group.

1,159. Women Peace Officers' Association of California
Records. 1927-70. 2 vols.
Open. No guide.
California State Library.
Scrapbooks of the Association.

1,160. Women's Educational and Industrial Union
Records. 1889-1901. No size given.
Open. No guide.
California State Library.
Reports of the Union, which was established in San Francisco in 1889.

1,161. Irwin, Molly
Papers. 1966. 3 folders.
Partially restricted. No guide.
California State University, Sacramento, Archives.
Official correspondence and reports, campus leaflets, and clippings pertain to the tenure suit of Irwin, a faculty member of the English department at the State University.

1,162. Sime, Ruth
Papers. 1973-74. 1 folder.
Open. No guide.
California State University, Sacramento, Archives.
Clippings and other papers relating to the sex bias suit of Sime, a State University faculty member.

1,163. Women's Advocate
Records. 1972-74. 2 folders.
Open. No guide.
California State University, Sacramento, Archives.
Official records, printed notices, and other publications of the Women's Advocate, an office that existed on the State University campus from 1972 to 1974.

1,164. Women's Caucus
Records. 1971-73. 2 folders.
Open. No guide.
California State University, Sacramento, Archives.
Official reports and papers, announcements, handbills, notices, and other printed matter of the Caucus, a group on the State University campus that promoted awareness in women.

1,165. Women's Studies
Records. 1971- . 1 folder.
Open. No guide.
California State University, Sacramento, Archives.
Official reports and records, printed announcements, handbills, and program brochures of the State University's department of women's studies, founded in 1971.

1,166. Sacramento Union Daily Newspaper Index
Finding aid. 1967- . 136 ft.
Open. No guide.
***Sacramento Union* Editorial Library.**
Files of clippings from the *Sacramento Union* provide information about women in the news and about women's organizations and activities.

ST. HELENA

1,167. Stevenson, Robert Louis, Family
Papers. 1800-1970. Ca. 10 ft. and other items.
Open. Card catalog.
Silverado Museum.
Family correspondence and photos of Stevenson (1850-94), a Scottish author, contain correspondence of his mother Margaret Isabella Balfour Stevenson (1829-97); his wife Fanny Matilda (Van de Grift) Stevenson (1840-1914), an author and artist who was born in Indianapolis; and his stepdaughter Isobel Osbourne Strong Field (1858-1953), who also was an American author and artist. Includes Fanny Stevenson's manuscript cookbook and copies of some of her letters that are housed at Yale University and diaries, correspondence, and manuscripts of Isobel Field, who divorced her first husband Joseph Dwight Strong, an artist, and married playwright Edward Salisbury Field.

SAN ANSELMO

1,168. Marsden, Edward
Papers. Nd. 3 boxes.
Open. No guide.
San Francisco Theological Seminary Library.
Includes four letters from schoolchildren at a missionary school in Sitka, AK, to their former teacher, a Miss Hanna.

1,169. Woman's Christian Temperance Union of California
Records. 1889-1939. 3 vols. and 2 items.
Open. No guide.
San Francisco Theological Seminary Library.
Records of the state WCTU, founded in 1879, consist of an 1889 annual report, minutes of the annual convention held in 1930, and a report of the 1939 annual convention, with constitutions, minutes of meetings and conferences, addresses, reports of department superintendents, membership rosters, and other items. Also includes a 1938 letter that Mrs. Rawlins Cadwallader wrote [Mrs.] Maude Woodruff of Sacramento about WCTU activities in the state and a finance report of the San Francisco YWCA, 1938-39.

1,170. Woman's Congress of Missions of the Panama-Pacific International Exposition
Records. 1915. 1 vol.
Open. No guide.
San Francisco Theological Seminary Library.
Report of the Congress, which was held under the auspices of the Council of Women for Home Missions and the Federation of Woman's Boards of Foreign Missions of the United States, consists of the conference program, reports of meetings, appendixes about policy plans, a treasury report, and a list of members of the Congress.

1,171. Women's Occidental Board of Foreign Missions of the Presbyterian Church, San Francisco
Records. 1873-1920. 4 vols.
Open. No guide.
San Francisco Theological Seminary Library.
The Board promoted mission work in California and abroad from 1873 until 1920, when it was merged with the Woman's Boards of Foreign Missions of the Presbyterian Church in the United States of America. A nearly complete set of annual reports contains handwritten corrections and additions, bylaws, correspondence, notes, history, extracts from missionaries' journals, statistical reports, pamphlets, and other records of the Board and its auxiliaries. Includes information on the California branch of the Woman's Foreign Missionary Society of the Presbyterian Church of San Francisco; mission work in India, China, Siam, Africa, South America, Mexico, and with Indians in the territories of the US and the Chinese in California; and establishment of missionary homes in various areas, including the Occidental Mission School and Home in San Francisco, which was superintended by [Miss] Donaldina M. Cameron. Cameron oversaw the rescue of young Chinese women who were thought to be held captive in Chinatown. Collection also contains a 1903 report by Cameron, letters from pupils at the Home, and a report of the house to house visitation committee, which was intended to help overcome the seclusion at home of women in Chinatown.

1,172. Woodbridge, Sylvester
Papers. Nd. 0.5 box.
Open. No guide.
San Francisco Theological Seminary Library.
Includes ca. 10 letters to a Mr. Drury, a professor at the Seminary, from [Mrs.] Helen Dunning about the life of Woodbridge, a minister.

SAN BRUNO

1,173. Bureau of Agricultural Economics (RG 83)
Records. 1936-49. 23 cu.ft.
Open. Unpublished guide.
Federal Archives and Records Center, San Francisco Archives Branch.
The Bureau was concerned with conducting economic research and studies for the Department of Agriculture. Includes central valley (of California) project studies materials, farm management and farm population project records, and state and local land use planning records relating to western states.

1,174. Bureau of Customs (RG 36)
Records. 1849-1947. No size given.
Open. Unpublished guide.
Federal Archives and Records Center, San Francisco Archives Branch.
Correspondence, reports, memoranda, circulars and instructions, testimony, and exhibits concerning enforcement of navigation and passenger laws, customs regulations, and Chinese immigration after the 1882 Exclusion Act. In 1886 Mary Slicer, an inspectress of customs, testified about the smuggling of opium aboard the *Gaelic,* about her duties as inspectress, and about the life and conditions of stewardesses aboard a passenger liner in the 1880s.

1,175. Bureau of Indian Affairs (RG 75)
Records. 1865-1944. 265 cu.ft. and 28 reels.
Open. Unpublished guide.
Federal Archives and Records Center, San Francisco Archives Branch.
Narrative and statistical reports, correspondence, school and tribal censuses, student folders, accounting records, and registers of vital statistics. Provides information on schools and students and on women as teachers and superintendents of Indian agencies in northern California and northern Nevada.

1,176. Farm Security Administration (RG 96)
Records. 1935-46. 32 cu.ft. and 1 microfilm reel.
Open. Unpublished guide.
Federal Archives and Records Center, San Francisco Archives Branch.
Records relating to the migratory labor camps in the central valley of California, 1935-36. Includes some descriptions of women in reports and correspondence and copies of camp newspapers, which include articles written by women about camp life.

1,177. Government of American Samoa (RG 284)
Records. 1900-66. 183 cu.ft. and 52 microfilm reels.
Open. Unpublished guide.
Federal Archives and Records Center, San Francisco Archives Branch.
Correspondence, reports, memoranda, case files, court records, photos, and other records of the high court, the governor's office, and the attorney general's office. High court records, similar to those of the US district courts, contain wills; probate cases; divorce files (18 ft.), 1960-62; census returns; and other records. The records are indexed. Records of the governor's office contain administrative files and files on Matai names and village matters. Records of the attorney general contain administrative files, prison records, and records on immigration and naturalization. Some portions are available on microfilm.

1,178. United States Attorney: San Francisco (RG 118)
Records. 1913-20, 1944-45. 6 cu.ft. and 37 tapes.
Open. Unpublished guide.
Federal Archives and Records Center, San Francisco Archives Branch.
Correspondence, memoranda, court papers and exhibits, clippings, and other records. Includes files relating to various neutrality cases, 1913-20, among them the Hindu Conspiracy Trial, one of the early major cases of Annette Adams, one of the first women attorneys. Also contains tapes reproducing broadcasts of Radio Tokyo's "Zero Hour" program, 1944-45, which were entered into evidence in US district court case 31712 in which [Mrs.] Iva Toguri D'Aquino was accused of being Tokyo Rose.

1,179. United States District Court: District of Nevada, Carson City and Reno (RG 21)
Records. 1853-1956. 503 cu.ft.
Open. Unpublished guide.
Federal Archives and Records Center, San Francisco Archives Branch.
Contains documents for each individual case brought before the Court, including subpoenas, briefs, pleadings, depositions, judgments, and exhibits. Includes records of civil and criminal actions as well as naturalization proceedings filed in state courts at Reno and Fallon, NV, 1853-1956. Case file indexes provide access to cases with women as plaintiffs or defendants or women who applied for naturalization or citizenship.

1,180. United States District Court: Eastern District of California, Sacramento (RG 21)
Records. 1916-70. 1138 cu.ft.
Open. No guide.
Federal Archives and Records Center, San Francisco Archives Branch.
Contains documents relating to cases brought before the Court, such as subpoenas, briefs, pleadings, depositions, judgments, and exhibits, as well as bound volumes, which include dockets, minutes, orders, final records, and other records and which reflect the work of the Court. Includes records of civil and criminal actions as well as naturalization and other proceedings. Case file indexes provide access to cases with female plaintiffs or defendants.

1,181. United States District Court: Northern District of California (RG 21)
Records. 1851-1951. 4500 cu.ft. and 4 microfilm reels.
Open. Unpublished guide.
Federal Archives and Records Center, San Francisco Archives Branch.
Contains documents relating to individual cases brought before the Court, such as subpoenas, briefs, pleadings, depositions, judgments, and exhibits, as well as bound volumes, which include dockets, minutes, orders, final records, and other records

and which reflect the work of the Court. Includes records of civil and criminal actions as well as naturalization and other proceedings. Case files on Chinese immigrants, who frequently appeared before the Court on a writ of habeas corpus, include passports with photos, statement of wealth or occupation, and occasionally testimony about previous residency in the US. Cases pertaining to Chinese women who were accused of being involved in prostitution may include photos, statements about the personal history and character of the defendant, Court testimony, and other legal papers. Case file indexes provide access to cases with female plaintiffs or defendants.

1,182. War Manpower Commission: San Francisco and Honolulu (RG 211)
Records. 1942-45. 81 cu.ft.
Open. Unpublished guide.
Federal Archives and Records Center, San Francisco Archives Branch.
The Commission was created in 1942 to recruit workers for war and essential civilian industries and to train workers for jobs essential to the war effort. Contains analyses of manpower utilization practices and accumulated information on the national labor market as well as Margaret Kay Anderson and Dennis Mohr's *Survey of Women's Employment at Mare Island Navy Yard* (1943), which was based on observations and interviews at the Yard in California.

SAN DIEGO

1,183. Fitzgerald, Florence (McCartney)
Papers. Nd. 2 pp.
Open. No guide.
San Diego County Law Library.
Papers of Fitzgerald, an attorney who was married to attorney Clifford K. Fitzgerald (1896-1971), consist of a letter from her husband and a statement about him by Leland G. Stanford, which contains mention of her. After her marriage, Fitzgerald became her husband's law partner.

1,184. Foltz, Clara (Shortridge)
Papers. Ca. 1850-1900. 8 items.
Open. No guide.
San Diego County Law Library.
Biographies, an 1888 Fourth of July oration printed in the *San Diego Union,* and notes from that newspaper on Foltz (1849-1934), the first woman lawyer to practice in California. Also includes a letter about Foltz to Leland G. Stanford from the Los Angeles Public Library.

1,185. Stanford: Women Jurors
Papers. 1912-65. Ca. 12 items.
Open. No guide.
San Diego County Law Library.
Material that Leland G. Stanford used to write his article "Early Women Jurors in San Diego" includes a 1912 opinion and letter by the California attorney general about whether women were qualified to act as trial jurors; notes concerning and citing statutes and cases about women jurors in California and elsewhere in the US; ca. 1915 photos of two of San Diego's first women jurors, [Mrs.] Sarah T. Hale and [Mrs.] Nancy J. Eastin; and clippings. Also includes Stanford's manuscript article.

1,186. Stanford: Women Lawyers
Papers. 1800s-1960s. Ca. 18 items.
Open. No guide.
San Diego County Law Library.
Includes notes by Leland G. Stanford for his book *LL.B (Legal Lore & the Bar)* (1968) and a letter in which the secretary of the state bar association lists for Stanford such San Diego woman attorneys as Eveleen K. Bryan, who was admitted to the bar in 1905; Estelle W. Kirk, who was admitted in 1911; Wally Kirk, who was admitted in 1917; and Edwina Kirk. Also includes a 1913 portrait of Estelle Kirk beside Emma Goldman; a biography of attorney Marie (Herney) Mueller; notes on women lawyers and judges in California and elsewhere in the US; a list of 24 San Diego women attorneys; a story that Madge Bradley, a municipal court judge, wrote about [Miss] Alta Hulett, first woman to be admitted to the Illinois state bar; and clippings on Bernice Morris, Vera Lustig Einstien, and Marguerite B. Stein. In addition, the collection contains clippings on Artie Henderson, a judge; [Mrs.] Arline Rossi, a bankruptcy referee; and Mabel (Walker) Willebrandt, an assistant US attorney who retired in 1962.

1,187. Davidson, Winifred
Papers. 1929-63. No size given.
Open. Unpublished guides.
San Diego Historical Society, Library and Manuscripts Collection.
Papers of Davidson (1874-1964), an author, poet, journalist, teacher, and historian, include correspondence, manuscripts of unfinished books regarding San Diego history, documents, notebooks of articles Davidson wrote for local newspapers about local history and place names, clippings, and an obituary. Some of the papers relate to Davidson's work as secretary to Madame Katherine Tingley of the Theosophical Society, of which Davidson and her husband John Davidson were members.

1,188. Hulett, Alta
Papers. 1877-1957. 24 items.
Open. Index cards.
San Diego Historical Society, Library and Manuscripts Collection.
Papers of [Miss] Hulett (1854-77), one of the first female attorneys in the US, include correspondence, financial papers relating to a marker placed on her grave in 1957 by women attorneys in San Diego, a biographical paper written by Judge Madge Bradley in 1947, photos, and clippings. Denied a license to practice law because she was a woman, Hulett drafted legislation, which became Illinois law in 1872, permitting women to enter all professions. It is thought that this was the first such law in the US.

1,189. MacPhail, Elizabeth (Reinbold)
Papers. 1930-76. 2 vols. and 4 items.
Open. Index and catalog cards.
San Diego Historical Society, Library and Manuscripts Collection.
Papers of [Mrs. Alfred] MacPhail (1912-), an attorney, actress, author, and historian, include an oral history transcript in which she discusses San Diego's history and people; a scrapbook regarding her work as an attorney, female attorneys in San Diego, Republican party activities, her speeches, and other topics; a scrapbook pertaining to the theater; and clippings. MacPhail is the author of *Kate Sessions, Pioneer Horticulturist,* which was published by the San Diego Historical Society.

1,190. Rains, Miriam E. (Bliss)
Papers. 1898-1942. No size given.
Open. Index cards.
San Diego Historical Society, Library and Manuscripts Collection.
Scrapbook of [Mrs. J. Frank] Rains (1862-1942), a librarian and the first female police judge in the US, contains correspondence; photos; papers regarding her involvement in the WCTU and a program from 1900-01 and resolutions; clippings regarding her activities as city trustee in El Cajon, CA, city recorder, and judge; and obituaries.

1,191. Rice, Lilian
Papers. 1931-38. No size given.
Open. Index cards.
San Diego Historical Society, Library and Manuscripts Collection.
Papers of [Miss] Rice (1888-1938), an architectural draftsman, designer, and instructor of architecture and mechanical and architectural drawing, contain a portfolio of architectural drawings and photos of buildings designed by Rice, including sketches of private homes and the San Dieguito Union High School and photos of residences and buildings for Rancho Santa Fe, the Zlac Rowing Club in San Diego, and homes in La Jolla; interviews with Samuel Hamill and Waldo Dean Waterman, in which Rice is frequently mentioned; awards from the American Institute of Architects; and biographical information.

1,192. Rowan, Loleta (Levete)
Papers. 1880-1952. No size given.
Open. Index cards.
San Diego Historical Society, Library and Manuscripts Collection.
A singer and voice instructor, [Mrs. Thomas E., Jr.] Rowan (1871-1952) was active in San Diego musical organizations, some of which she founded and for some of which she served as president. Includes a scrapbook containing correspondence requesting her to perform, photos, programs, reviews, a booklet announcing the opening in 1905 of the Rowan Vocal Studio in San Diego, and other material; clippings regarding musical activities, her home, and organizations; and an obituary.

1,193. Scripps, Ellen Browning
Papers. 1897-1932. No size given.
Open. Index cards.
San Diego Historical Society, Library and Manuscripts Collection.
[Miss] Scripps (1836-1932), who was born in London, was a teacher, newspaperwoman, and philanthropist in La Jolla, CA. Includes specifications for the La Jolla Woman's Club, which Scripps had built as a gift to La Jolla; a biographical notebook; a thesis; photos; documents; clippings; and other papers.

1,194. Sessions, Kate Olivia
Papers. 1875-1940. No size given.
Open. Index cards.
San Diego Historical Society, Library and Manuscripts Collection.
Correspondence, diaries, notebooks, a manuscript, photos, scrapbooks, a medal and certificate, and clippings of [Miss] Sessions (1857-1940), a horticulturist, including three interviews with people who knew Sessions and travel diaries containing notes and sketches of vegetation.

1,195. Stevenson, Alice (Barnett)
Papers. Nd. 2 Hollinger boxes and 4 vols.
Open. Index cards.
San Diego Historical Society, Library and Manuscripts Collection.
Papers of [Mrs. George Roy] Stevenson, a musician and composer, include correspondence from Europe, manuscripts of music and verse, lecture notebooks, photo album, scrapbooks, programs, diplomas, and publicity.

1,196. Tingley, Katherine Augusta Westcott
Papers. 1901-29. No size given.
Open. Index cards.
San Diego Historical Society, Library and Manuscripts Collection.
Madame Tingley (1847-1929), who was born in Newburyport, MA, was the leader of the Theosophical Society from 1896 until her death in 1929. Includes translated letters that Staffan Kronberg wrote to his family in Sweden about daily life while he was a student at the Theosophical Society from 1913 to 1921, with frequent mention of Tingley; three interviews, including one with Iverson Harris, who at the age of 9 was brought to the Theosophical Society to live and who later became Tingley's private secretary; a legal ledger;

papers regarding law suits in which she was involved; photos; and clippings. Tingley was married to Richard Henry Cook, then to George W. Parent, and then to Philo Buchanan Tingley.

1,197. Walker, Mary Chase
Papers. 1865-1976. 1 folder and 1 box.
Open. Index cards.
San Diego Historical Society, Library and Manuscripts Collection.
Walker (1828-99), who was born in Massachusetts, was a teacher in San Diego's first official schoolhouse. Includes a manuscript written by Walker describing her arrival in San Diego and her later marriage to Ephraim W. Morse, a school trustee; a manuscript paper regarding an incident in which she was fired as a teacher because of her friendship with a black woman she had met en route to San Diego; a teacher's report and certificate; a marriage license; information regarding a school that was named after her; and clippings.

1,198. Waterman, Hazel (Wood)
Papers. 1901-48. No size given.
Open. Index cards.
San Diego Historical Society, Library and Manuscripts Collection.
Papers of [Mrs. Waldo Sprague] Waterman (1866-1948), an architect, include correspondence, notebooks, working drawings of the 1910 restoration of the Casa de Estudillo, four interviews, clippings, and other papers. Waterman worked under Irving J. Gill, a California architect, and designed various San Diego buildings. She was the daughter-in-law of Governor Robert Waterman and the mother of Waldo D. Waterman, an early aviator.

1,199. Woman's Christian Temperance Union
Records. 1897-1974. No size given.
Open. Index cards.
San Diego Historical Society, Library and Manuscripts Collection.
Correspondence, resolutions, a program, the newspaper *Harbor Light* for 1897 and 1901, clippings, and other records of the first San Diego WCTU, which was founded in 1884. Includes a scrapbook of [Mrs.] Miriam E. Rains, a WCTU officer in Colorado and in El Cajon, San Diego County. In 1887 the WCTU established a fund of $1,000 to build a home for women, thus enabling the Woman's Home Association to become incorporated.

1,200. Woman's Home Association, Inc.
Records. 1887-1904. 3 items.
Open. Index cards.
San Diego Historical Society, Library and Manuscripts Collection.
Records of the Association, founded in 1887 to provide a refuge for indigent women and children "afflicted with any infirmity," include a manuscript history of the Association by Jan Lundie, a deed from the city of San Diego, and articles of agreement with the city regarding use, property, and buildings. The organization changed its name to the San Diego Children's Home Association in 1904.

1,201. Woman's Relief Corps
Records. 1899-1912. 1 vol.
Open. Index cards.
San Diego Historical Society, Library and Manuscripts Collection.
Reports, correspondence, lists of officers, and programs of Jennie W. Snyder, the assistant national press correspondent and president of the local chapter of this auxiliary of the Grand Army of the Republic. Includes letters from chapters throughout the US.

1,202. Woman's Suffrage Association
Records. 1870-1972. 2 folders and 1 item.
Open. Index cards.
San Diego Historical Society, Library and Manuscripts Collection.
Records of the Association, founded in 1870 to "elevate the ballot to woman," include a constitution, bylaws, a manuscript written in 1972 regarding the San Diego suffrage campaign of 1911, and clippings.

1,203. Women's Ambulance and Transport Corps
Records. 1940-42. 1 box.
Open. Index card.
San Diego Historical Society, Library and Manuscripts Collection.
Incorporation records, correspondence, rules and regulations, photos, commendations, programs, and clippings of the Corps, which was founded by Julia Gray Dowell, a colonel in the military during WWII, and then incorporated in 1941. The first organization of its kind in the US, the Corps provided training for women in first aid and in the driving of ambulances and motor transports with physicians, nurses, and medical and other supplies during the war. The Corps expanded to include a cavalry and a parachute corps.

1,204. American National Red Cross
Records. 1917-19. 4 vols.
Open. No guide.
San Diego Public Library, California Room.
Records of the San Diego chapter, founded in 1898, include histories of the war activities of various chapter departments, scrapbooks of clippings, and brochures and other printed material issued by the chapter.

1,205. Anderson, Inez
Papers. Ca. 1913-23. 3 vols.
Open. No guide.
San Diego Public Library, California Room.
Scrapbooks containing clippings of advice-to-the-lovelorn columns written by Anderson, the only San Diego journalist who wrote such a column at that time.

1,206. California Council of Defense, San Diego Division, Women's Committee
Records. 1917-19. 6 folders.
Open. No guide.
San Diego Public Library, California Room.
Correspondence and printed material of the Committee, which was founded in 1917 to support the war effort through the mobilization of housewives in San Diego County for such activities as the food pledge campaign. Includes correspondence of Mabel B. [Mrs. Albert L.] Simpson, chairman of the Committee.

1,207. Committee of Six Hundred
Records. 1933-35. 1 vol.
Open. No guide.
San Diego Public Library, California Room.
Reports, correspondence, pamphlets, and clippings of this San Diego secret crime-fighting organization founded in 1933, sponsored by the San Diego Women's Civic Center, and headed by Mrs. Albert L. Simpson. Its founding was inspired by Mary (Roberts) Rinehart's 1933 article "Can Women Stop Crime?"; the group was disbanded in about 1935.

1,208. Diffendorf, Grace (Baker)
Papers. 1959. 5 pp.
Open. No guide.
San Diego Public Library, California Room.
Correspondence of [Mrs. Walter] Diffendorf (1874?-1961), a California author, teacher, and rancher, regarding the plot of her book *The Long Lane* and the persons on whom the characters were based.

1,209. Griffin, Vashti Rogers
Papers. Ca. 1930. 2 portfolios.
Open. Unpublished guide.
San Diego Public Library, California Room.
Papers of [Mrs. Colin O.] Griffin, a composer and poet, include manuscripts of musical compositions, programs, and clippings.

1,210. Herreshoff, Constance "Connie" (Mills)
Papers. 1934-62. 1 cu.ft.
Open. No guide.
San Diego Public Library, California Room.
Scrapbooks of clippings of [Mrs. James Brown, II] Herreshoff (1880-1966), a San Diego music and drama critic who also worked with and encouraged many aspiring musicians.

1,211. La Jolla Garden Club
Records. 1938-60. 5 vols.
Open. No guide.
San Diego Public Library, California Room.
Minutes, scrapbooks, and other records of this Club, which was founded in about 1937.

1,212. Morning Choral Club
Records. 1923-29. 2 vols.
Open. No guide.
San Diego Public Library, California Room.
Scrapbooks containing photos, programs, and clippings of the Club, which studied and presented choral works written for women's voices.

1,213. San Diego Children's Home Association
Records. 1913-24. 24 pp.
Open. No guide.
San Diego Public Library, California Room.
Correspondence of the Association, which was founded in 1887 to furnish care for orphans and the children of parents unable to provide a proper home. Sponsored by socially prominent women of San Diego, the Association was one of the first social service organizations in the area; it is still in existence. The bulk of the correspondence was generated by Mrs. Edmund Thelen, president of the Association.

1,214. San Diego County Chamber of Commerce, Ladies Annex
Records. 1889-90. 1 vol.
Open. Unpublished guide.
San Diego Public Library, California Room.
Minutes, reports, and contributors' lists of the Annex, which was founded in 1889, pertain to the landscaping of a section of Balboa Park by the Annex.

1,215. San Diego County Federation of Women's Clubs
Records. 1922-56. 0.5 cu.ft.
Open. No guide.
San Diego Public Library, California Room.
Records of this San Diego organization, which was founded in 1898 and is still active, include a notebook containing reports and histories and scrapbooks containing photos, convention information, and clippings documenting the activities of local women's clubs. The San Diego group was the first of the federated women's clubs in the state.

1,216. San Diego County War History Committee
Records. 1918-25. 0.5 cu.ft.
Open. No guide.
San Diego Public Library, California Room.
Correspondence, pictures, information on WWI participants, and printed material of the Committee, which was founded in 1918 to document the role of San Diego County residents in WWI. [Miss] Althea Warren was the secretary, and Fanny J. [Mrs. Edmund] Thelen was the treasurer of the organization.

1,217. Scripps, Ellen Browning
Papers. 1914-59. 3 vols.
Open. No guide.
San Diego Public Library, California Room.
Correspondence, a scrapbook containing clippings, and other papers of Scripps (1836-1932), a southern California philanthropist. Includes a typescript written by her nephew.

1,218. Sessions, Kate Olivia
Papers. 1912-45. 6 vols.
Open. No guide.
San Diego Public Library, California Room.
Journals, a manuscript, and scrapbooks containing correspondence and clippings of [Miss] Sessions (1857 -1940), a horticulturist and nursery owner who contributed to the introduction of non-native plants in San Diego.

1,219. Wallis, Gertrude (Steel-Brooke)
Papers. 1917-53. 1 cu.ft.
Open. Unpublished guide.
San Diego Public Library, California Room.
Correspondence, manuscripts, a photo album, a scrapbook, memorabilia, and other papers of [Mrs. Ross] Wallis (?-1974), general secretary of the YWCA in China and the US. Includes correspondence between Wallis and her mother Louise Holmes Steel-Brooke, a physician who worked in India and China; Steel-Brooke began her career in China at the age of 60. Also contains papers relating to Steel-Brooke's career and the YWCA movement in China.

1,220. Women's Organizations
Collection. Ca. 1921. 19 pp.
Open. Unpublished guide.
San Diego Public Library, California Room.
Brief histories of various early women's clubs of San Diego.

1,221. Archives of New Poetry
Collection. 1914- . No size given.
Open. Inventory and card catalog.
University of California, San Diego, Mandeville Department of Special Collections.
Correspondence, literary manuscripts, photos, clippings, and memorabilia of Marianne Moore, members of the Paul Blackburn family, and others. Includes poems by or about Sara Blackburn; correspondence of Paul Blackburn's first and second wives Freddie and Joan; correspondence, a novel, short stories, and poems by his mother Frances Frost, who was married to W. Gordon Blackburn; and letters to him from many women, including publishers' representatives Ellen Bissart, Jennifer Douglas, Anne Freedgood, Margaret Marshall, and Susan Miller, who worked for Scribner's, Penguin Books, Doubleday, Harcourt-Brace, and Modern Photography, respectively.

1,222. Bancroft Family
Papers. 1844-82. 3 vols.
Open. Card catalog.
University of California, San Diego, Mandeville Department of Special Collections.
Family correspondence and other papers include letters Emily (Ketchum) Bancroft wrote to her family, 1844-68; letters from Kate Bancroft to her father Hubert Howe Bancroft, 1873-82; and a journal she kept during a trip to California missions with her father in 1874 and to Sonoma to visit General Mariano Guadalupe Vallejo.

1,223. Mayer, Marie Goeppert
Papers. Ca. 1950s. Ca. 740 items.
Open. Card catalog.
University of California, San Diego, Mandeville Department of Special Collections.
Correspondence, manuscripts, class lecture notes, photos, clippings, and memorabilia of Mayer (1906-?), a German physicist who immigrated to the US. Includes a manuscript book of German poetry and a copy of a paper she presented in Tokyo on the changing status of women as seen by a scientist.

1,224. O'Neill, James A.
Collection. Nd. 4 Hollinger boxes and 5 cartons.
Open. Inventory and card catalog.
University of California, San Diego, Mandeville Department of Special Collections.
This collection contains correspondence of authors and a few literary manuscripts. The California box contains correspondence, 1938-41, and a poem by Edith Cherrington, which appeared in *The American Mercury;* a 1919 letter to the editor of *Atlantic Monthly* from Mary Stone Bruce; a 1923 letter in which Aurelia Harwood acknowledged the 1871 edition of a book she wrote on Yosemite; poems by Jennette Yeatman; and other items.

The American Literary 20th Century box includes a 1909 letter in which May Morris mentioned Jane Addams to Luther A. Brewer of the Torch Press; correspondence, 1897-1912, of Isabella (Macdonald) Alden, a children's author, primarily letters to Amos R. Wells, editor of *Christian Endeavor World;* an 1891 letter from Jennie Wren, which bears the letterhead "The Doll's Dressmaker: A Magazine for Girls"; a manuscript by Hattie Hateful [Mrs. Sumner] Hayden; and other items.

The Manuscripts boxes contain manuscripts by Mrs. E. Burke Collins, Mary Jane Holmes, and Florence Gerald. In addition, these boxes contain letters to Amos Wells from Katharine Lee Bates concerning Wellesley College and from poet Julia Caroline (Ripley) Dorr as well as letters by authors Mary Hallock Foote; Grace Livingston; Lucy Larcom; Mary Artemisia Lathbury; Alice M. Longfellow, who wrote an article on the home life of college women; Harriett (Stone) Lothrop, who used the pseudonym Margaret Sidney; Katherine "Kate" Abbott Sanborn; Margaret Elizabeth (Munson) Sangster; Catherine Maria Sedgwick; Harriet (Prescott) Spofford; and Sophie Swett. Also includes letters of Anna Jarvis, 1911-12, who founded the Mother's Day movement; letters of Mary (Clement) Leavitt, 1898-99, whose letterhead indicates that she was a lecturer on such subjects as missions, temperance, equal suffrage, and travel; correspondence of Mary Ashton Livermore, 1892-95, who was a suffragist, reformer, editor, and author; and letters of Frances Elizabeth Caroline Willard of the WCTU, 1895.

The Miscellaneous Manuscripts box contains a poem by Abbie Farwell Brown; a Christmas letter and picture of Alden and Mary Clark from 1904, before they went to the Marathi Mission in India; a letter from [Miss] Ethel C. Hatch, one of Lewis Carroll's childhood friends; a manuscript by Harriet Josephine Emerson, apparently concerning the Lafayette family's visit to the US; poems, essays, a family genealogy, and an account of the Indian wars by Polley [Mrs. Bellows] Hartwell; papers of Sister Madeleva; a poem by Edna St. Vincent Millay; a copy of the novel *The Glories of Venus* (New York: Harper's, 1931) about modern Mexico by Susan Smith; and clippings and an edition of *Uncle Tom's Cabin* by Harriet (Beecher) Stowe.

SAN FRANCISCO

1,225. Archives of American Art
Collection. Nd. No size given.
Open. Published guide.
Archives of American Art, West Coast Area Center.
Many of the collections described in the guide for the Smithsonian Institution, Archives of American Art, in Washington, DC, are available on microfilm at the West Coast Area Center as well as at the New England, New York, and Midwest Area Centers. See *Archives of American Art, Smithsonian Institution: A Checklist of the Collection,* 2nd ed. rev. (1977), which identifies the collections that are available on microfilm, and Garnett McCoy, *Archives of American Art: A Directory of Resources* (New York: R. R. Bowker Company, 1972).

1,226. Women's Banking Department, San Francisco and Los Angeles
Records. Ca. 1920s-30s. Ca. 0.5 ft.
Access restricted. Card index.
Bank of America Archives.
Correspondence, reports, photos, and printed items of the Department, which was established to create a comfortable environment for women to do their banking. Staffed by women, the Department provided financial counseling for women and created and distributed leaflets designed to help women manage their money. The San Francisco office of the Department was founded in 1921 under the direction of Mrs. Edward Dexter Knight. The Los Angeles office, founded in 1922, was directed by Grace S. Stoermer. Both offices were consolidated into their respective main branches during the 1930s.

1,227. Adams, Maria Abigail Henry
Papers. 1860-61. 27-page item.
Open. Unpublished guide.
California Historical Society.
Diary in which Adams (1836-1928), a boardinghouse keeper, dressmaker, and mother, describes daily events in Dublin, NH, while her husband was in California. Discusses family contacts, friends, social events, cost of purchases, weather, and occasional feelings of loneliness and frustration.

1,228. Alameda, CA, Resident
Papers. 1858-59. 1 vol.
Open. Descriptive guide.
California Historical Society.
Diary recounting the daily routine of a woman living in California. The woman had left her home in New York and traveled to China before settling in an Alameda boarding house where her husband, who worked in San Francisco, visited her often.

1,229. Allen, Sallie (Brown)
Papers. Nd. 1 folder.
Open. No guide.
California Historical Society.
Notebook, pamphlet, clipping, and other papers of "Sallie Fox" Allen (?-1913), the daughter of Mr. and Mrs. Alpha Brown. Includes a notebook in which she describes the experiences of the Brown, Rose, and Jones wagon train expedition in northern Arizona in 1858, with an account of their rescue by the Smith train at Peach Springs, and the experiences of these pioneers in southern Arizona in 1859. Also contains an account written by Allen's daughter Edith (Allen) [Mrs. Charles H.] Milner regarding her mother's covered wagon experiences as told to Milner by Allen and a 1932 clipping of an account, for which Milner did the research, relating the story of the Brown family: their overland journey, attack by Indians, and their rescue. The pamphlet included in the collection describes the history of the Nut Tree near Vacaville, CA, whose walnut grove was begun from walnuts brought from Arizona in Sallie Brown's pocket.

1,230. Anthony, Susan B.
Papers. 1863-1917. 1 folder.
Open. No guide.
California Historical Society.
Correspondence and other papers of Anthony (1820-1906), a woman suffrage leader, including an 1863 letter from the Women's National League to R. W. Lyman in which League officials acknowledge receipt of a petition and 25 cents, discuss the postponement of the petition's presentation to Congress, note increased interest in the "cause," and express the hope that "all friends of the cause will not think their work done till

every slave is free." Also contains a personal letter from Anthony to [Miss] Hannah J. Clapp and a letter from the National American Woman Suffrage Association to Clapp in Reno, NV, regarding a possible visit of Susan B. Anthony and Anna Howard Shaw to Reno on their way to San Francisco. Also includes proclamations written in Anthony's hand granting equal rights to women and to all citizens of California.

1,231. Atherton, Gertrude Franklin (Horn)
Papers. 1907-09. 1 folder.
Open. Summary in descriptive guide.
California Historical Society.
Correspondence of [Mrs. Henry Bowen] Atherton (1857-1948), an author, primarily with [Miss] Ina Coolbrith regarding the loss of Atherton's manuscripts and possessions during the 1906 earthquake and fire in San Francisco; the Spinners Club volume of tribute to Coolbrith; and a benefit performance, an author's reading, for Coolbrith.

1,232. Auger, Lina
Papers. Ca. 1856-87. 2 vols.
Open. No guide.
California Historical Society.
Account books, in French, of [Mrs.] Auger for the Auger family of San Francisco. Includes an inventory of household contents and biographical information about the Auger and Roberts families.

1,233. Augusta Bixler Farms
Records. 1879-1970. 5 boxes.
Open. Register and summary in descriptive guide.
California Historical Society.
Grain, asparagus, truck crops, and alfalfa were grown on these farms, which totaled ca. 4400 acres on Union Island in the San Joaquin River. The farms were operated by David Bixler from 1879 to 1908 and by the Augusta Bixler Estate from 1920 to 1944; the farm had been in the Hyde-Bixler family for four generations. Annual reports from 1920 to 1939 and financial records of the Farms and Hyde-Bixler family papers including correspondence, Hyde family scrapbook, autograph books of Harriet "Hallie" (Hyde) Irwin, and research notes of William Hyde Irwin, son of Will and Hallie Irwin, for his book about the Farms. Contains papers of Elizabeth Augusta (Hyde) Bixler (1838-1921), including correspondence, an account book of an 1898 European trip, notebook of favorite quotes, inventory of her estate, her wills, and obituaries. Also contains correspondence of or information about Elizabeth Bixler's niece Helen Hyde, Mabel "Daisy" Hyde Gillette, Marietta Butler Hyde, Hallie (Hyde) Irwin, Delphine Gillette Jenks, Grace Luce, and Florence Morrison.

1,234. Austin, Mary
Papers. 1913. 1 item.
Open. No guide.
California Historical Society.
Letter from Austin (1868-1934), an author, to William Kibbler regarding her withdrawal from the Western Drama Society. The letter was written at Wickiup, Austin's residence in Carmel, CA.

1,235. Ayer, Mary Catherine (Norton)
Papers. Nd. 1 folder.
Open. No guide.
California Historical Society.
History of Ayer (?-1921), including photos, written by her grandson Fred C. Hutchinson. Ayer traveled to California via the Isthmus of Panama, returned to the East via the Nicaragua route, and traveled back to California by train in the 1870s. She resided in Calistoga, Napa, and Berkeley, CA, with her son and his family until her death. Ayer was a descendant of Nicholas Norton, Jr., who arrived in America in 1634 and reputedly was an original settler of Martha's Vineyard.

1,236. Babies Aid Society of San Francisco
Records. 1918-50. 2 boxes.
Open. No guide.
California Historical Society.
Functioning as a committee of Associated Charities' baby department from 1908 to 1950, the Society was responsible for the care of foundling babies in San Francisco; it boarded babies with supervised families, maintained an adoption service and medical clinic, and operated such homes as the Mei Lun Yuen cottage for Chinese children. Emphasizing medical care, the Society claimed the world's lowest death rate in foundling homes. Minutes, financial records, and correspondence.

1,237. Baby Hygiene Committee, American Association of University Women
Records. 1905-50. 14 boxes and 2 items.
Open. No guide.
California Historical Society.
Operated by the AAUW from 1905 to 1950, the Committee later came under the control of the Community Chest. Minutes, financial records, correspondence, membership lists, photos, programs, and posters of the Committee pertain to its campaign for certified milk for children. An executive director of the Committee was a Mrs. Graupnor.

1,238. Badger, Ella
Papers. 1875-77. Ca. 0.5 in.
Open. No guide.
California Historical Society.
Programs, advertisements, clippings, and ephemera of [Miss] Badger, an actress and singer, regarding her performances. She was variously referred to as "California's Gifted Young Debutante" and "California's Gifted Child."

1,239. Ball, Katherine M.
Papers. Ca. 1946. 1 folder.
Open. No guide.
California Historical Society.
Letter and text of agreement between Ball and the trustees of the American Theosophical Lodge of San Francisco, to whom she bequeathed her collection of books on metaphysics and related subjects. Also includes clippings regarding Ball's Oriental art collection, which was donated to "the people of San Francisco."

1,240. Beasley, Delilah Leontium
Papers. Ca. 1920s. 1 item.
Open. No guide.
California Historical Society.
Letter from Beasley (1871-1934), an author in Los Angeles to a Mrs. Loomis regarding her experiences in southern California and orders for her book on Negroes in California, which was published in 1919.

1,241. Bennett, Ella Costillo
Papers. 1907-66. Ca. 10 in.
Open. Summary in descriptive guide.
California Historical Society.
Manuscripts and family papers of Bennett (1865-1932), an author; her daughter Mary L. Bennett; and her son Ray Bennett, an actor and author. Contains a manuscript of a play by Ella Bennett, her folder on the Tom Mooney trial, scrapbook pages, and some of her poetry. Also contains papers of Mary Bennett, including material relating to her support of Michael Hannon, pictures of her pets, and a scrapbook.

1,242. Bickerdyke, Mary Ann (Ball) "Mother"
Papers. 1897. 1 folder.
Open. No guide.
California Historical Society.
Correspondence of [Mrs. Robert] Bickerdyke (1817-1901), a Civil War nurse, includes a letter she wrote from Bunker Hill, KS, to Ann Elizabeth Seed [Mrs. Samuel Henry] Chapman regarding an enclosed photo taken at Bickerdyke's birthday celebration, which was attended by many of her patients; her friendship with Chapman; and reminiscences about her nursing career. Also includes a pamphlet from the Grand Army of the Republic in Topeka, KS, proclaiming Mother Bickerdyke Day, in commemoration of the services of army nurses.

1,243. Bidwell, Annie Ellicott (Kennedy)
Papers. Nd. 1 folder.
Open. No guide.
California Historical Society.
Bidwell (1839-1918), the wife of General John Bidwell, was a volunteer Civil War nurse and an ordained Presbyterian minister and missionary to the Indians at Rancho Chico in California; she was particularly concerned with the preservation of Indian culture and education for the women and children. She was also active in woman suffrage and the WCTU. Manuscript of Bidwell regarding California Indians describes her arrival with her husband in Chico in 1868 and the customs and living conditions of the "Digger" Indians of northern California. Also includes an interview with a Mechoopda Indian man of Rancho Chico regarding the courtship and marriage customs of his people.

1,244. Biscaccianti, Elisa
Papers. Ca. 1857. 1 folder.
Open. No guide.
California Historical Society.
Reminiscences of Biscaccianti, a singer, regarding a performance before miners and other residents of San Francisco.

1,245. Black, Annie
Papers. Ca. 1850s-1942. 1 box.
Open. No guide.
California Historical Society.
Family correspondence, including that between J. C. McTarnahan and his wife Adaline "Addie" Chamberlin McTarnahan (1845-?) written from 1880 to 1882 when they were first married; letters to J. C. McTarnahan from his sister Margaret "Maggie" in San Jose, CA, and from his niece Rebecca Gladden; and correspondence between [Mrs.] Annie Black and Anne Fisher. Also included are reminiscences of Adaline McTarnahan, who became Adaline Fowler, assembled by Annie Black and [Miss] Olivia Peterson.

1,246. Blake, Amanda (Farrington)
Papers. 1870-72. 3 items.
Open. Summary in descriptive guide.
California Historical Society.
Letters from Charlotte Farrington and Daniel Farrington to their daughter Amanda Blake, who was caring for her three grandchildren while their mother, Blake's daughter, was attending medical school in Philadelphia. Primarily concerns relatives and friends in Holden.

1,247. Braly, Susannah Hyde
Papers. 1867-96. 30 vols. (1 box).
Open. Summary in descriptive guide.
California Historical Society.
Diaries of Braly (1805-97), wife of John Eusebius Braly, a Cumberland Presbyterian preacher in Missouri and California, concerns Susannah Braly's religious thoughts, family life, and trips to Missouri and San Francisco.

1,248. Brown, Charlotte L.
Papers. 1863-66. 1 folder.
Open. Unpublished guide.
California Historical Society.
Collection pertains to the 1865 case of [Mrs.] Brown, a black woman who sued the Omnibus Rail Road Co. for ejecting her from one of their cars because of her color. Legal documents; notes of Brown's attorneys, including W. C. Burnett; list of jurors; testimony of witnesses; notice of appeal; and

a clipping describing a similar suit brought by a black man William Bowen against the North Beach and Mission Rail Road Co. Also contains material on Maria Cohen.

1,249. Brown, Madie
Papers. Ca. 1918-40. 12 vols.
Open. Unpublished guide.
California Historical Society.
Papers of [Mrs.] Brown include the financial records of an unidentified firm. Clippings and photos of San Francisco, some of which describe or depict local women, have been pasted over the pages in about half of the volumes.

1,250. Buckbee, Edna Bryan
Papers. Nd. 3 boxes.
Open. Register and summary.
California Historical Society.
Papers of Buckbee, a California author, include manuscripts of her historical novels and short stories, many of which were published in the 1930s; notes; and clippings. She wrote about such topics as San Francisco, Calaveras County, and Lola Montez.

1,251. Buckel, Chloe Annette
Papers. 1863-65. 1 folder.
Open. No guide.
California Historical Society.
Correspondence of [Miss] Buckel (1833-1912), a physician and Civil War nurse, includes a recommendation and certification of services performed with the Floating Hospital Nashville near Vicksburg, MS, and a letter from General U. S. Grant providing special orders to escort Buckel, who had been appointed by the governor of Indiana to care for the sick and wounded in the Army of the Tennessee, through the lines. Buckel had graduated from a medical college in 1858 and had practiced in Chicago until 1863. She worked at Woman's Hospital in Boston for 12 years, studied in Vienna and Paris for two years, and came to California in 1877. In 1905 she participated with the Home Club Milk Commission in a project to provide certified milk to Oakland, CA.

1,252. Bunnell, Louise
Papers. 1890. 1 item.
Open. No guide.
California Historical Society.
Letter written to Bunnell from her mother Kate M. Bunnell in Yosemite Valley, CA.

1,253. Burnett, Jane Cromwell (Cleveland)
Papers. Nd. 24-page vol. and other items.
Open. No guide.
California Historical Society.
Reminiscences of Burnett (1834-1923) describing her voyage to California from New York in 1855 and life in Sacramento as the wife of a state senator and in San Francisco after 1857. Burnett presented these reminiscences in 1923 to the Sequoia chapter of the DAR, of which she was a member. Also included are legal papers and related correspondence.

1,254. Butler, Benjamin Franklin
Papers. Ca. 1891. 1 folder.
Open. No guide.
California Historical Society.
Autobiography of Harriet Hitchcock Butler, wife of Benjamin Franklin Butler (?-1864), the first lithographer in San Francisco, regarding the years 1851 to 1891. She describes her voyage from New York via the Isthmus of Panama to San Francisco to rejoin her husband, the San Francisco fire of 1851, vigilance committees, witnessing a murder, and management of the family after her husband's death.

1,255. California Suffrage
Collection. 1896-99. 1 folder.
Open. No guide.
California Historical Society.
Copies of correspondence, including letters to Lillie (Devereux) Blake from Elizabeth (Cady) Stanton; from Carrie Chapman Catt regarding suffrage sentiments in California; from Charlotte G. Hubert regarding the Woman's Parliament of Southern California and the formation of an equal suffrage club; from Susan B. Anthony regarding woman suffrage planks for the People's party, the Prohibition national convention, and the Republican and Democratic conventions; and from Sarah M. Severance in San Jose, CA, regarding legislative barriers to woman suffrage in California.

1,256. Cameron and Martin Family
Papers. Nd. 2 folders.
Open. Descriptive summary.
California Historical Society.
Autobiography of Mary Emma Cameron [Mrs. John] Martin (1851-1932), who claimed to have been the first Anglo-Saxon child born in California, including genealogical information; autobiography written in 1889 by Ina C. Martin (1874-?), the daughter of John Ross Martin and Mary Martin; poem written by Hannah H. Cameron in 1856 regarding her daughter Mary Emma Cameron; and a certificate of membership for Mary Martin in the Association of Pioneer Women of California.

1,257. Cameron, Jessie Anderson
Papers. 1852-58. 1 folder.
Open. Description.
California Historical Society.
Letters from Cameron (1822-1906) to her mother and sister in Scotland regarding her journey, with her two brothers and a niece, from Liverpool, England, through New York, Jamaica, and Panama to Sacramento, CA; her settling in Volcano in Calaveras County, CA; her jobs in Sacramento as a cook and dressmaker; the fire of 1852; her marriage and family life; her husband's and brothers' jobs; establishing a farm and ice-making business; and one brother's mining experiences.

1,258. Carroll, Katharine R.
Papers. 1934. 100-page vol.
Open. Descriptive guide.
California Historical Society.
Diary in which Carroll, a socially active woman in San Francisco, describes meetings of such organizations as the California Historical Society, the California Literary Society, and the California Writers Club.

1,259. Carter, Maude
Papers. 1873-92. 1 folder.
Open. Summary.
California Historical Society.
Correspondence of Carter includes a letter from Mary C. Weeks to Carter describing her family and friends and a letter from a woman in Lowell, MA, to Leon Richardson in California regarding family matters and financial problems.

1,260. Central Presbyterian Church
Records. 1875-77. 1 folder.
Open. No guide.
California Historical Society.
Minute book of this San Francisco church's Young Peoples Aid Society, a social and civic organization, reflects the involvement of women in the group.

1,261. Chandler, Sarah Elizabeth
Papers. Nd. 1 folder.
Open. No guide.
California Historical Society.
Correspondence, teaching certificates, résumé, paintings, and other papers of [Miss] Chandler, a teacher and artist. Includes a note from Annie Frances Briggs of the Sketch Club in San Francisco, of which Chandler was also a member; letters of reference written in 1899 by a Miss Vessaria, president of the Sketch Club, and others; papers regarding California property owned by Chandler; and a 1946 will.

1,262. Chapin, Mary Cheever (Pennie)
Papers. Ca. 1940. 1 folder.
Open. No guide.
California Historical Society.
Reminiscences of Chapin (ca. 1847-?) regarding a journey to California by steamer in 1857 and life in various California cities. Also includes a typescript concerning the 1940 census, which contains Chapin's reminiscences regarding the 1860 census and Albany, NY, where she heard Jenny Lind perform in 1851.

1,263. Cheney, Fannie
Papers. 1869-70. 83-page vol.
Open. Descriptive guide.
California Historical Society.
Composition book of Cheney, a San Francisco schoolgirl, contains descriptions of school and family outings to such places as Stockton, the Mechanic's Fair, and the Grand Music Festival.

1,264. Children of the Confederacy
Records. 1923-29. 1 folder.
Open. No guide.
California Historical Society.
Minutes, membership roster, and clippings of the Nannie Crittenden Van Wyck Chapter of this social organization in San Francisco.

1,265. Club Beaux Arts
Records. Ca. 1924-?. 1 vol.
Open. No guide.
California Historical Society.
Combined scrapbook and register of artists, members, and guests of the Club, which was founded in 1924 to promote and exhibit contemporary art in San Francisco. Contains clippings regarding local artists and interested persons, including Beatrice Judd Ryan and Mae Helene Bacon [Mrs. Angus Gordon] Boggs, both of whom were active in civic affairs.

1,266. Collins, Isabel Margaret (Porter)
Papers. Nd. 1 folder and ca. 1 box.
Open. No guide.
California Historical Society.
Collins (1875-1954) was an artist and photographer. Letter from her son, including a brief biography of Collins; an article illustrated by two of her photos; and negatives and original prints of her photos.

1,267. Cooke, Lucy Rutledge
Papers. 1852-53. 1 folder.
Open. No guide.
California Historical Society.
Letters written by [Mrs.] Cooke to her sister while crossing the plains from Iowa to California. The letters were assembled in a book printed privately for Cooke's descendants in 1923.

1,268. Coolbrith, Ina Donna
Papers. 1898-1925. 1 folder.
Open. Summary.
California Historical Society.
Correspondence and manuscripts of Coolbrith (1841-1928), a poet and librarian. Includes letters to [Mrs.] Eleanor Davenport; Mrs. A. P. Black, with a poem "Woman" enclosed; Harry Noyes Pratt; [Mrs.] Lena S. Simons; and Allen's Clipping Bureau.

1,269. Corlies, Emma
Papers. 1877. 5-page item.
Open. Descriptive guide.
California Historical Society.
Diary of Corlies regarding a train journey from Poughkeepsie, NY, to San Francisco to meet her

father. She expresses anxiety over friends and family left behind and describes people she met, scenery, inconveniences, and tourist gimmicks. She apparently was accompanied by her sister and a "colored maid."

1,270. Crabtree, Lotta
Papers. Ca. 1897-1974. 1 folder.
Open. No guide.
California Historical Society.
Correspondence, manuscripts, biography, clippings, and other papers of Crabtree (1847-1924), an actress whose full name was Charlotte Mignon Crabtree. She sang, danced, and played the banjo in gold rush camps and in San Francisco theaters and formed her own traveling company. Includes correspondence regarding the discovery and possible restoration of Crabtree's piano, a typescript regarding Crabtree's plan to establish a trust fund to rehabilitate San Francisco men discharged from San Quentin and Folsom prisons, a biography of her life in Grass Valley, CA, and clippings from 1974 relating to the rededication of the Lotta Crabtree fountain in San Francisco.

1,271. Cranstone, Susan Marsh
Papers. 1851. 1 folder.
Open. Unpublished guide.
California Historical Society.
Diary regarding an overland journey from the Missouri River to the Columbia River in Oregon includes discussion of such topics as Indians and travel and grazing conditions.

1,272. Crocker, Mary Deming
Papers. 1853-81. 1 folder.
Open. No guide.
California Historical Society.
Letters from [Mrs. Charles] Crocker in New York and California to Hannah DeLamater Jessup, an old friend, reminiscing about the years before her marriage.

1,273. Cronin, Mary
Papers. 1892. 1 folder.
Open. No guide.
California Historical Society.
Abstract of title and deed of trust for Mary Cronin and her husband Patrick. Includes a record of Mary Cronin's personal taxes.

1,274. Crow Family
Papers. 1866-87. 1 folder.
Open. No guide.
California Historical Society.
Correspondence, including letters of Susan Crow Smith of Stockton, CA, regarding the illness and death of Perthania Eastin Crow and Smith's early life at Crow's Landing, CA, with her many brothers and sisters. Perthania Crow was the first wife of John Bradford Crow, for whom Crow's Landing was named.

1,275. Dakin, Laura Maria (Jameson)
Papers. 1872-85. 1 folder.
Open. No guide.
California Historical Society.
Family correspondence and other papers of Dakin (1836-93), a teacher and writer of fiction for *Godey's Lady's Book,* including correspondence of her brothers and her sisters Ellen Jameson and Mary (Jameson) [Mrs. David Morrell] Locke, who wrote using the name of Mary Mountain. Dakin was born in Irasburg, VT, the daughter of Alexander and Sarah (Locke) Jameson. The family moved to Knight's Ferry, CA, where in 1859 she married Isaac Dakin, a wheelwright. In 1876 the Dakins moved to Santa Cruz, CA, where Laura Dakin died. They had three children: Wilbur Jameson Dakin (1860-1947), Henry Robert Dakin (1863-?), and Alice Laura Dakin (1864-?).

1,276. Daughters of Founders and Patriots of America
Records. 1916-62. 9 vols.
Open. No guide.
California Historical Society.
Minutes and programs of the California chapter, which was founded in 1916.

1,277. Daughters of the American Revolution
Records. Nd. 2 boxes.
Open. No guide.
California Historical Society.
California DAR honor rolls, WWII and Korean War service records of members of various California branches, and a scrapbook of the San Francisco chapter, 1952-57.

1,278. Davis, Dulce (Bolado)
Papers. Nd. 1 folder.
Open. No guide.
California Historical Society.
Reminiscences of Doña Josefa Abrego as told to Davis, her granddaughter, regarding her family in early California. Also contains a family genealogy.

1,279. De Ford, Miriam Allen
Papers. 1893-1954. 4 folders and 2 boxes.
Open. Unpublished guide.
California Historical Society.
De Ford (1888-1975) was a suffragist, feminist, and writer. Correspondence, including correspondence between De Ford and her second husband Maynard Shipley (1872-1934), a writer and lecturer whom she married in 1921, and Shipley's correspondence; De Ford's 1905 diary and diary entries from 1939 to 1941; her autobiography; manuscripts of her plays, stories, and articles, including "Feminism—Cause or Effect?," written in 1933; birth certificates, marriage licenses, and divorce papers; academic records; portion of De Ford's will; photos; wills of Shipley and William Armistead Collier; membership cards; clippings; 1906 Philadelphia High School for Girls yearbook; and material on Ella May Clemmons and Mrs. Howard Gould. De Ford attended Wellesley in 1908 and was the youngest member of the Single Tax Society. Among De Ford's works were *They Were San Franciscans* and a biography of Shipley.

1,280. De Losada, Betty Baget
Papers. 1939-64. 1 box.
Open. Unpublished guide.
California Historical Society.
De Losada (1921-) was an official of the International Longshoremen's and Warehousemen's Union, Local 6, during the 1940s. Includes a 1939 high school essay of De Losada on organized labor and a psychology term paper written in 1956 about a typical ILWU steward's conception of self; memorandum and questionnaire for the fair employment practices committee of the ILWU; correspondence of her husband Horace "Ace" De Losada, business agent for Local 6, ILWU, including letters from Wesley Robert Wells; clippings; newsletters; ILWU ephemera; and other papers.

1,281. Dickson, Lillian M.
Papers. 1901-28. 12 vols.
Open. Descriptive guide.
California Historical Society.
Dickson (1872-?) was the wife of Jack F. Dickson, an eye doctor who maintained a practice in Portland, OR, and San Francisco. Diaries regarding her marriage; her relationship with her mother; social life; health problems, including the discovery of a tumor on her uterus; the 1906 San Francisco earthquake and fire; learning to drive a Packard; and registering to vote in 1920.

1,282. Dobbins, Natalia
Papers. 1920s-1930s. 2 boxes.
Open. No guide.
California Historical Society.
Correspondence, programs, clippings, and other papers of Dobbins (?-1975), poet, author, and patron of the arts, relate primarily to her support of foreign artists traveling in the US and of groups such as the Western Athenaeum and the League of Western Writers.

1,283. Draper, Anne Pauline (Kracik)
Papers. Ca. 1971-73. Ca. 7 boxes.
Open. No guide.
California Historical Society.
Draper (1917-73) was a labor organizer, socialist, and founder of Citizens for Farm Labor and Union W.A.G.E., or Union Women's Alliance to Gain Equality. Personal papers and correspondence, including correspondence with labor union people and Christmas cards designed by Anne Draper and Hal Draper, whom she married in 1939; manuscripts of speeches given at her memorial services by local labor and political leaders; and newsletters and ephemera regarding legislation concerning women workers and Union W.A.G.E. The daughter of Polish immigrants, Anne Draper graduated from Hunter College of the City of New York. A longtime member of the Independent Socialist League, she opposed the Vietnam war from the 1950s onward and helped found Union W.A.G.E., the first women's liberation group made up of women trade unionists.

1,284. Dundas, Harriet Thompson Palmer
Papers. Ca. 1953. 1 folder.
Open. No guide.
California Historical Society.
Autobiography of [Mrs.] Dundas (1875-), written when she was 78, reflects her experiences as a young girl and woman in the San Joaquin Valley of California.

1,285. Eastman, Barbara
Papers. 1964-66. 1 folder.
Open. No guide.
California Historical Society.
Letters from [Mrs. George W.] Eastman, a researcher into California history, to Leonary Rehm of Sonora, CA, regarding Eastman's work on Sonora County history.

1,286. Egbert, Eliza Ann (McAuley)
Papers. 1852. 57 pp.
Open. Summary.
California Historical Society.
Diary kept by Egbert (1835-?) while traveling by ox team with her family from Iowa to California. Includes descriptions of the weather, road conditions, and Sioux and Pawnee Indians.

1,287. Ellis, Mrs. E.
Papers. 1900-01. 5 items.
Open. No guide.
California Historical Society.
Letters to "Ma" Ellis, a housewife and mother, in San Francisco from family members in Pacific Grove, CA, who were contemplating the purchase of a hotel. Also included are family women's descriptions of their experiences in Pacific Grove.

1,288. Ely, Charles Arthur
Papers. 1851-60. 1 box.
Open. Unpublished guide.
California Historical Society.
Collection contains material of Ely's wife, Louise (Foot) Ely (1831-?), including correspondence with family and friends; a journal of her sea voyage from New York to Hong Kong and from Hong Kong to San Francisco, including letters to her sister Mary and a friend Nellie; and a diary recording daily events in San Francisco, primarily during her husband's absence. The diary includes descriptions of friends, places, books read, current events in the area, and short journeys south and east of the city.

1,289. Emerich, Regina
Papers. Nd. 1 box.
Open. No guide.
California Historical Society.
Notes by Emerich, a researcher, for a biography of Jose Joaquin Gomez.

1,290. Enloe, Rachael
Papers. 1870. 2 items.
Open. Descriptive guide.
California Historical Society.
Diary of Enloe (1853-?) regarding a hunting trip during which she kept camp for her brothers and a friend and occasionally carried a gun. Also includes an account written by Enloe's son regarding her family's overland journey from Missouri to California in 1853.

1,291. Fargo and Rose Family
Papers. 1864- 1933. 1 folder.
Open. Summary.
California Historical Society.
A diary from 1864 of Martha (True) Fargo (1834-73), wife of Jerome Bonaparte Fargo, regarding her voyage from Wisconsin to San Francisco via the Isthmus of Panama and her life in California as a mother of two girls. Also includes a 1933 letter from Gertrude Atherton to Fannie Fargo Rose in which she reminisces about school friends from the Clarke Institute in San Francisco and an 1878 commencement program from the Institute listing Fannie Fargo.

1,292. Farr, Fred
Papers. 1942-45. 1 folder.
Open. No guide.
California Historical Society.
Correspondence of Farr includes seven letters from two Japanese-American women interned at assembly centers and relocation camps in California during WWII. The letters describe their feelings about removal to the centers and conditions there.

1,293. Flagstad, Kirsten
Papers. 1895-1968. 15 boxes.
Open. No guide.
California Historical Society.
Correspondence, telegrams, photos, clippings, and memorabilia of Flagstad (1895-1968?), a Wagnerian soprano. Particular emphasis is given to the period following her American debut in 1935 and subsequent appearance at the War Memorial Opera House in San Francisco. Also included is material on Flagstad's difficulties with American patriotic groups after WWII for her alleged sympathy with Nazi ideology. The collection material was gathered by Mrs. Milton Esberg, a personal friend of Flagstad.

1,294. Fogg, Georgia
Papers. 1878. 1 vol.
Open. Unpublished guide.
California Historical Society.
Autograph album, containing many original poems, kept by Fogg as a young schoolgirl in Oakland, CA.

1,295. Fortnightly Club of San Francisco
Records. 1895-1960. 1 box.
Open. Descriptive guide.
California Historical Society.
Constitution, bylaws, annual reports from the presidents and section chairwomen, minutes from 1946 to 1960, account books, correspondence, lists of officers and members, and other records of this social and charitable organization, which met in San Francisco and Berkeley, CA.

1,296. Foster, June
Papers. 1849-1910. 4.5 boxes.
Open. No guide.
California Historical Society.
Legal documents, correspondence, and receipts regarding court cases.

1,297. Furlong, Mary
Papers. Nd. 1 folder.
Open. No guide.
California Historical Society.
Reminiscences of [Mrs.] Furlong, a member of the Pacific Grove, CA, DAR, regarding her overland journey to Oregon in 1843.

1,298. Gibbons, Eleanor P.
Papers. Nd. 1 folder.
Open. No guide.
California Historical Society.
Scrapbook, dating from ca. 1878 to 1884, of engravings by Gibbons, an engraver on Bush Street in San Francisco who was the successor to Leila Curtis and Co. Also includes drawings and prints and business forms.

1,299. Gilson Family
Papers. Ca. 1850s-60s. 1 folder.
Open. No guide.
California Historical Society.
Scrapbook of Mrs. Gilson, a housewife, containing clippings and notes of household preparations for cleaning and remedies for various illnesses and afflictions. Photos are also included.

1,300. Girls High School
Records. 1864-1940. 5 boxes and 2 vols.
Open. Descriptive guide.
California Historical Society.
Records of this San Francisco school founded in 1864 and closed in 1940 include a 1930 constitution; student records containing name, address, age, birthplace, previous school, name and occupation of father, grades, and comments about the student; and correspondence regarding scholarships.

1,301. Grandmaitre, Blanche
Papers. 1918-70. 9 vols.
Open. No guide.
California Historical Society.
Grandmaitre, a resident of Minneapolis and later of New York, worked as a schoolteacher in Sacramento, CA, and retired to the San Francisco Bay area. Six diaries, one written in France; two notebooks regarding travel and French history; and a record book.

1,302. Green, Mary Caroline Tilton
Papers. 1913. 1 folder.
Open. Unpublished guide.
California Historical Society.
Letter from Green to her niece May E. Gorham regarding her 1852 journey from New Hampshire to California via Nicaragua describes activities and business ventures undertaken while staying with relatives in California.

1,303. Griswold, Harriet (Booth)
Papers. 1859. 83-page vol.
Open. Summary.
California Historical Society.
Diary of Griswold (ca. 1814-1906) regarding her journey from Illinois to Diamond Springs, CA; she discusses the conditions of the journey, fear of Indians, and care of her three children, particularly of her infant.

1,304. Harland, Hester Ann
Papers. Nd. 1 folder.
Open. No guide.
California Historical Society.
Autobiography of Harland (1857-1940), a suffragist born in Napa County, CA, who was particularly active in the California suffrage campaign of 1896. She was a personal friend of Susan B. Anthony and Anna Shaw, an ordained minister and physician. In 1894 Harland was cofounder of the Child Study Association of California, which later merged with the PTA.

1,305. Hoag, Amanda Josephine Johnson
Papers. 1912-13. 1 folder.
Open. No guide.
California Historical Society.
Account by [Mrs. George W.] Hoag (1833-?) of an 1852 journey by oxteam to California with her mother, two sisters, and two brothers. Contains descriptions of camp life, buffalo, and encounters with Indians as well as a description of a ball in Colusa, CA, with Hoag as the town's only "young lady," and reminiscences of later years in Colusa County, CA. Hoag settled in Red Bluff, CA.

1,306. Hyde, Helen
Papers. 1881-1936. 4 boxes.
Open. Register and summary.
California Historical Society.
Papers of Hyde (1868-1919), an artist, include letters to her sister Mrs. Will Irwin and from the Authors' League of America, illustrated letters from Japan, diaries from 1881 and 1882, sketchbooks, listings of her works and accounts of works sold, photos of WWI posters, articles, clippings, and engraving tools.

1,307. Ina Coolbrith Circle
Records. Ca. 1921-62. 3 boxes and 2 vols.
Open. No guide.
California Historical Society.
The Circle was formed in 1919 by poets, musicians, and artists who gathered at the home of Ina Coolbrith (1841-1928), California's poet laureate; the group promoted poetry, the study of California history and literature, discussion of members' works, and preservation of their personal and literary reminiscences. President's papers; minutes; financial ledger; correspondence; scrapbooks containing manuscript poems and notes, programs, and clippings; meeting registers; material regarding membership elections; photos; guest book; content awards; clippings; newsletters; and other items. After Coolbrith's death the Circle was carried on by her niece Mrs. Finlay Cook until her death. It lapsed for a few years and in 1942 was reorganized by [Mrs.] Ina Cook Craig, Coolbrith's grandniece.

1,308. Keith, Mary McHenry
Papers. 1906. 1 folder.
Open. No guide.
California Historical Society.
Correspondence of Keith (1855-1947), a lawyer and suffragist, regarding a portrait of Susan B. Anthony by Keith's husband William Keith, the Oregon vote for women's suffrage, and the San Francisco earthquake and fire. Correspondents include Mary S. Anthony, Kate M. Gordon, Anna Howard Shaw, and Mary S. Sperry.

1,309. Kellogg, Rhoda
Papers. Nd. 1 carton.
Open. No guide.
California Historical Society.
Kellogg, a children's art educator, ran a day-care center in San Francisco during WWII. She was a suffragist who picketed the White House in 1917. Manuscript and printed articles and books from the late 1940s to the present.

1,310. Kent, Adaline Dutton
Papers. Nd. 1 folder.
Open. No guide.
California Historical Society.
Copy of a typescript regarding [Mrs. William] Kent's mother-in-law's gift of 29 acres in Kentfield in Marin County, CA, for use as an educational, recreational, and civic center. The club house was the first meeting place of the Tamalpais Centre Women's Club founded in 1909.

1,311. Kinkead, Beatrice Reynolds
Papers. 1870-1947. 3 boxes.
Open. Unpublished guide.
California Historical Society.
Papers of Kinkead (1874-1947) contain

correspondence, including a letter regarding the 1906 San Francisco earthquake and fire; her autobiography; her stories and articles; her translations of works by Russian authors; school compositions and catalog; photos; biographical material and obituary; and clippings. Also included is material on Grace Reynolds, who in 1899 became the first graduate of the University of California pharmacy school, and on Kinkead's sons Donald and Robin Kinkead.

1,312. Kirby, Georgiana Bruce
Papers. 1852-53. 25-page vol.
Open. Descriptive guide.
California Historical Society.
Diary of Kirby (1818-87), who was born in Bristol, England, regarding life with her husband Richard Kirby on an isolated ranch near Santa Cruz, CA, while she awaited the birth of her first child; she was concerned about the effect her mental and emotional state might have on the child. The diary also reveals that she came to Santa Cruz to join Eliza Farnham, with whom she had worked as an assistant warden of the women's prison at Sing Sing, NY, and includes comments on the people around her, national leaders, literature, religion, and slavery. In 1886 she published her autobiography regarding the years before she came to Santa Cruz.

1,313. Klussman, Frieda
Papers. Ca. 1940s-58. 3 Hollinger boxes, 13 vols., and 8 items.
Open. No guide.
California Historical Society.
[Mrs. Hans] Klussman, a nurse and wife of a doctor, was in 1940 a delegate to the San Francisco Federation of the Arts; the Federation fostered the 1947 movement to save the Powell Street cable cars that resulted in formation of the Citizens Committee to Save the Cable Cars. Articles, form letters, certificates, clippings, and other material relating to cable cars, the Federation, the Citizens Committee, tree planting in the city, the Community Music School, and the Golden Gate Park Monastery fight.

1,314. Knox Family
Papers. 1867-98. 2 folders.
Open. Descriptive guide.
California Historical Society.
Correspondence, primarily letters from Virginia Knox [Mrs. Harry] Maddox in Europe to her mother [Mrs.] Sarah Knox Goodrich in San Jose, CA, regarding people and places in Europe and mentioning Mrs. Henry Crocker, Mrs. Levi Goodrich, Mrs. George Hearst, Mildred Maddox, and others.

1,315. Le Moyne, Sarah Cowell
Papers. 1901. 1 item.
Open. No guide.
California Historical Society.
Letter from Le Moyne, an actress, to Mrs. Dixwell Davenport thanking her for the roses and expressing her regrets that they will not be able to meet on her short stay in San Francisco.

1,316. League of Women Voters of California
Records. 1911-66. 46 boxes and 1 vol.
Open. Descriptive guide and register.
California Historical Society.
Annual reports, minutes, financial records, correspondence, convention reports, printed material, and other records of the state LWV, founded in 1911, regarding local League chapters, attacks on the LWV and rebuttals, water resources, and other topics.

1,317. League of Women Voters of San Francisco
Records. 1911-72. 10 ft.
Open. Descriptive guide and register.
California Historical Society.
Records of the local LWV, founded in 1911, include local, state, and national bylaws; annual reports; board of directors minutes; financial records; correspondence of presidents and secretaries; scrapbooks of clippings and programs; and other records regarding such topics as counseling and guidance for junior and senior high schools, child care centers, housing, international relations, and the women's court project.

1,318. Lee, Bertha Stringer
Papers. 1912-31. 1 vol.
Open. Descriptive guide.
California Historical Society.
Scrapbook of [Mrs.] Lee (1873-1937), a San Francisco artist, contains a guest register, sketches and dedications, and mementos; numerous prominent artists and authors of California are represented. Lee studied art in New York and abroad and with California artist William Keith. She also was a member of the Sketch Club.

1,319. Llano del Rio Cooperative Colony
Records. 1914-69. 2 ft.
Open. Register and summary.
California Historical Society.
Board of directors minutes, administrative records, correspondence, and clippings of the Colony, which was founded in 1914 and disbanded in 1969. Contains correspondence of approximately 50 women, including Rose Matz Benz, Myrtle Chapin, Ida S. Cole, Clarissa A. Kneeland, Minnie E. Pickett, Nellie Kemp Bradshaw, Anna Loutrel, Erma M. Moore, and Mildred Schlaifer.

1,320. Maloon, Mary Eliza (Warner)
Papers. 1864. 55 pp.
Open. Summary.
California Historical Society.
Diary kept by Maloon (1849-1922) while traveling by wagon train with her family from Illinois through Nebraska, Utah, and Nevada to Sardine Valley, CA. She describes the scenery, weather, and people she met along the way.

1,321. Martin, Anne Henrietta
Papers. 1899-1953. 3 folders.
Open. Register and summary.
California Historical Society.
Papers of Martin (1875-1951), a suffragist and pacifist, include manuscript poems written by Charles Erskine Scott Wood and Sara Bard Field, who was married to Wood, and correspondence with Mary Austin, Herbert Hoover, Una Jeffers, Elizabeth [Mrs. William] Kent, Austin Lewis, John Muir, Kate (Richards) O'Hare, Katherine Schmidt, Edith Newlands Toluectin, and others.

1,322. Mighels, Ella Sterling Cummins
Papers. 1870-1940. 14 boxes.
Open. No guide.
California Historical Society.
Mighels (1853-1934) was an author. Correspondence, primarily of family and friends; manuscripts; records of the California Literary Society and Ark-adians; scrapbooks; and other material. Also includes Mighels's diaries from 1900 to 1927, which she called soulbooks.

1,323. Miller, Juanita
Papers. 1937. 1 folder.
Open. No guide.
California Historical Society.
Letter from Miller to Aimee Woldenberg concerning the involvement of Miller's father, poet Joaquin Miller, in the northern California Indian wars of the 1850s and thanking Woldenberg for her assistance in using Shasta County, CA, data to establish this involvement.

1,324. Native Daughters of the Golden West, Manzanita Parlor, No. 27
Records. Ca. 1933-36. 1 vol.
Open. No guide.
California Historical Society.
Scrapbook compiled by Annie F. Conklin, a charter member of this group, which was organized in 1888 in Grass Valley, Nevada County, CA. Contains poems; photos of local and state chapter members; a tribute to mothers; clippings regarding Nevada County, Lola Montez, and Lotta Crabtree; and other items.

1,325. Ober, Josephine (Robb)
Papers. 1863-1950. 2 folders.
Open. No guide.
California Historical Society.
In 1928 Ober (1882-?) was society editor for *The World* in New York. Correspondence, including letters regarding Ober's work; manuscripts of her short stories; and photos of her family. Ober was born in New York.

1,326. Oliver, Catherine D.
Papers. Nd. 1 item.
Open. No guide.
California Historical Society.
Letter written to [Miss] Oliver from an unidentified young woman who sailed with her sister from Boston to California. Discusses her satisfaction with California, the opportunities available to her in San Francisco, and her "limitations" as a woman seeking employment.

1,327. Pacific Hebrew Orphan Asylum and Home Society
Records. Ca. 1906-57. Ca. 5 ft.
Open. Unpublished guide.
California Historical Society.
Financial records, including register of accounts and receipt books; state aid applications, arranged by child's name; ledger for 1200 Broadway, Inc.; Homewood Terrace children's records; and chart of costs and construction figures on six cottage plants commended by the Russell Sage Foundation, including three in California: Jewish Orphans' Home of Southern California in Huntington Park in Los Angeles, Sacramento Orphanage and Children's Home, and St. Francis Orphanage in Watsonville.

1,328. Peck, Janet
Papers. 1854-1965. 18 boxes.
Open. No guide.
California Historical Society.
Peck (1864-1956) was a philanthropist and friend of the William Randolph Hearst family. Personal and family correspondence, records of the Serbian Relief Society of California, and photos of family and friends.

1,329. Perkins, George Clement
Papers. 1878-1920. 6 boxes and 2 vols.
Open. Unpublished guide.
California Historical Society.
Family correspondence of Perkins and his wife Ruth A. Parker Perkins (?-1921); diaries kept by their daughters during voyages to Alaska, the first in 1886 by Fanny Perkins and the second in 1899 by Pansy Perkins; household bills; and scrapbook of poems collected by Ruth Perkins.

1,330. Photos
Collection. Nd. Ca. 150,000 items.
Open. Card catalog.
California Historical Society.
Prints and negatives of photos of California, including cityscapes, landscapes, and portraits, of which about a third pertains to women. Access to collection is by subject, person's name, or by name of the photographer. Among the photographers represented are Laura Adams Armer and Isabel Porter Collins.

1,331. Porter, Lavinia (Honneyman)
Papers. Nd. 1 folder.
Open. No guide.

California Historical Society.
Papers of Porter (1836-1910) and her family include an account of her journey by ox team to California in 1860 with her husband James J. Porter (ca. 1828-82) and their son Robert Porter (ca. 1855-69). James Porter became involved in the nursery business in Oakland, CA; Lavinia Porter gave embroidery lessons and, after her husband's death, took in boarders. The Porters had three other children: Ida Estelle [Mrs. George Moore] Shaw (1860-1940), Annie Florence [Mrs. Varney] Gaskill (1862-1907), and Gustav Porter (1866-69). James Porter's first marriage was to Lavinia's sister Ida; in 1854, after Ida's death, he and Lavinia were married.

1,332. Post, Jessie M.
Papers. 1891. 1 vol.
Open. Unpublished guide.
California Historical Society.
Diary of Post, a young resident of Rochester, NY, regarding a cross-country vacation with two aunts by railroad; the vacation included visits to relatives, monuments, and cities. Contains observations on the Chinese, Mormons, blacks, and rural and southern women.

1,333. Powers, Laura Bride
Papers. 1923-47. 8 boxes and 1 vol.
Open. Register.
California Historical Society.
Correspondence, manuscripts, biographical information, articles, and other papers of Powers (1867-1947), an historian and preservationist, contain letters to her daughter Mrs. George A. Applegarth, letters to Applegarth from Isabel Hartigan, correspondence and other papers of Applegarth's daughter Laura Bride Applegarth, and papers regarding the Monterey History and Art Association, Charles W. Stoddard, and Powers's death.

1,334. Redding, Mary Frances Driggs
Papers. Ca. 1917-45. 2 folders.
Open. No guide.
California Historical Society.
Redding (1864-1950s) was the first woman notary public in San Francisco. Correspondence, including a letter from Redding to Miss Henderson of the California State Welfare Department regarding an old age pension and a letter from Redding to attorney John McNab regarding Redding's husband's illness and trouble obtaining pension money; reminiscences regarding the years 1864 to 1940; a 1917 notice of appointment of Redding as notary public for the city and county of San Francisco; biography of Redding; clippings regarding the Reddings and old age pensions; and deeds for mining claims. Redding was appointed at the Palace Hotel.

1,335. Richardson, Mary (Curtis)
Papers. Ca. 1926-30. 1 folder.
Open. No guide.
California Historical Society.
Papers of Richardson (1847?-?), an artist, include correspondence with Edythe Foster; Christmas cards designed by Richardson and containing reproductions of her paintings; advertising sheet of [Miss] Abbie T. Grace and [Miss] Leila Curtis, engravers in wood; and clippings regarding Richardson.

1,336. Rix, Alfred, and Rix, Chastina (Walbridge)
Papers. 1849-54. 2 vols.
Open. Descriptive guide.
California Historical Society.
Diaries of Chastina Rix (1824-57), one of which she kept jointly with her husband Alfred Rix beginning with their wedding day in 1849 in Vermont. Her entries in that volume include descriptions of a sea voyage she made in 1853 from New York to San Francisco via the Isthmus of Panama. Accompanied by her sister Clara and her young son Julian, Rix apparently was joining her husband who already was in San Francisco. Her entries also contain descriptions of her management of a boardinghouse in San Francisco, caring for her family, and earning additional money by washing, ironing, and sewing clothes. The other diary was kept by Chastina Rix during her 1853 voyage and contains comments on the hardships of the journey, Cuba and Acapulco, and her longing for her husband in California.

1,337. Rix-Walbridge Family
Papers. 1843-96. 1 folder.
Open. No guide.
California Historical Society.
Correspondence, primarily between the women of the family, includes letters of Roxanna (Brown) Walbridge Watts, Martha Walbridge Gregory, Chastina Walbridge Rix, Sally Walbridge, Clarissa "Clara" Walbridge Rogers, Alice Watts, and Augusta Gregory.

1,338. Rowan, Josephine Morris
Papers. 1900-ca. 1903. 1 vol.
Open. No guide.
California Historical Society.
Scrapbook of Rowan, formerly [Mrs.] Josephine Morris de Greayer, containing photos, autographs of friends, clippings, and memorabilia relating to her social life in San Francisco as wife of Colonel Andrew S. Rowan, who was the celebrated messenger to Garcia during the Spanish-American War.

1,339. San Francisco Earthquake and Fire, 1906
Collection. Ca. 1906-?. 1 box.
Open. Unpublished guide.
California Historical Society.
Correspondence, telegrams, clippings, and other material of the survivors of the 1906 San Francisco earthquake and fire, including letters of Pauline Hemenway Altrocchi, Rosa Bareda, Mrs. T. J. Blight, Edith Bonnell, Rose A. Taylor, Sara Tomlinson, Dolly Brown Anderson, Carrie A. Mangels, Dorothea Torrey, Kate C. Woods, Margie E. [Mrs. Fred W.] Folsom, Jean Ramsey Voigts, Dora Landgrebe, Doris Sharp, Elsie H. Cross, Bernadette A. McKittrick, Tessie Dowd, [Miss] Myrtle Robertson, Inga Soiland, the religious order of the 10th Street Sisters, Rose Felix Poirier, and Agnes Safley Gould.

1,340. Shinn, Milicent Washburn
Papers. 1880-1925. 1 folder.
Open. Descriptive guide.
California Historical Society.
Correspondence of Shinn (1858-1940), editor of the *Overland Monthly,* contains letters from California authors and others, including L. Pearl Boggs, Mary Whiton Calkins, Ina D. Coolbrith, Mary (Mapes) Dodge, Alice Cunningham Fletcher, Martha Hallidie, Phoebe A. Hearst, Edward S. Holden, Helen Hunt Jackson, Franklin D. Roosevelt, Josiah Royce, Katherine Royce, Frederick Slate, Martha Van Rensselaer, and Constance F. Gordon Whiting.

1,341. Shoesmith, Muriel Wilkinson
Papers. 1929-?. Ca. 40 boxes.
Open. Unpublished guide.
California Historical Society.
Correspondence and other material of Shoesmith (?-1975), Women's Council president and active participant in women's groups after her marriage to Earl Shoesmith in 1929. In Tracy, CA, she was president of the Tracy women's group and of the San Joaquin County Federation, Alameda District Federation, and California Federation of women's groups. Shoesmith was known as the dean of the presidents of the GFWC and served as state legislation chairman representing women's groups at the state capitol. She was particularly interested in children's education and participated in the White House Conference on Children and Youth in 1950 and 1960 and in UNESCO programs on children. Shoesmith was the sister of author Bonaro Overstreet and a 1923 graduate of the University of California.

1,342. Smith, Martha Ann Grover
Papers. 1854. 1 folder.
Open. Unpublished guide.
California Historical Society.
Travel diary of Smith (1833-1906), resident of Wiscasset, ME, who at the age of 20 sailed with her new husband Edward Hall Smith from Boston to New York and then to San Francisco via the Isthmus of Panama. Contains descriptions of the weather, the ship's daily progress, tropical flora and fauna, the overland crossing of the Isthmus, the yellow fever epidemic on ship, San Francisco, and the journey to Sacramento, CA, and Kenaha Valley, CA, where they settled.

1,343. Smith, Mary S. D.
Papers. 1853-54. Ca. 2 in.
Open. Unpublished guide.
California Historical Society.
Diary of Smith in the form of letters written during a voyage to California on the ship *Water Witch* and during her residence in San Francisco.

1,344. Sorbier, Louise Agathe Josephine (Bacon)
Papers. 1854-1956. 3 ft.
Open. Descriptive guide.
California Historical Society.
Correspondence, clippings, and other papers of Sorbier (1847-1929) regarding prominent San Francisco women and local organizations in which she was active, including the Women's Educational and Industrial Union, the California State Woman Suffrage Educational Association, the Arguello Boulevard Improvement Club, and the Cemetery Beautifying and Anti-Removal Association. Contains the papers of Sorbier's daughter Cecile Marie Sorbier while she was president of the San Francisco Club. Also includes a personal expense book from 1874, which mentions Cecile Sorbier's birth and Louise Sorbier's divorce.

1,345. Stearly, Annie
Papers. 1968. 1 folder.
Open. No guide.
California Historical Society.
Copy of transcript of oral history interview with [Mrs.] Stearly, descendant of early Fresno County, CA, settlers, concerning her family's history.

1,346. Sutter, John
Papers. 1837-58. 1 folder.
Open. Descriptive guide.
California Historical Society.
Papers of Sutter, a cousin of John A. Sutter, contain an 1856 document from Sutter County, CA, of his wife Anna Sutter in which she declares independent status as a trader, enabling her to do business in her own name and on her own account.

1,347. Taltavall, Jane Shepard
Papers. 1921. 1 vol.
Open. No guide.
California Historical Society.
Account by Taltavall describing a 1921 summer vacation trip by automobile from Redlands, CA, to Boston and back with her husband and 2-year-old son. Inscribed to her friend Sally Kerr Street.

1,348. Thelander, Hulda Evelyn
Papers. 1933-75. 4 boxes.
Open. Unpublished guide.
California Historical Society.
Correspondence, memoranda, and reports of Thelander (1896-), one of the first women physicians in California, relate to her work with the pediatrics department of the Children's Hospital in

San Francisco, the University of California Medical School, the American Academy of Pediatrics, the Committee for the Improvement of Child Health, and other committees as well as to topics such as mental retardation, cerebral palsy, polio, and women in veterans hospitals. Also includes correspondence with California state officials regarding educational programming for handicapped children, medical studies and articles written or collected by Thelander, her curriculum vitae, articles and obituaries on several San Francisco Bay area women physicians, printed material on medical subjects of interest to Thelander, and material concerning Marjorie E. Brush, Kay Flippin, Florence Mabel Holsclaw, Gertrude Flint Jones, Mary Elizabeth Mathes, Helen Brenton Pryor, Evelyn Siris, and Florence Dunlop Strickler.

1,349. Twist, Julia S. (Peck)
Papers. 1861. 1 item.
Open. Unpublished guide.
California Historical Society.
Diary of Twist, a photographer and resident of Beloit, WI, regarding a sea voyage from New York to San Francisco via Panama aboard the *Ariel* on a successful search for her husband in California. Contains description of experiences on the ship and on shore, including mountain climbing. Twist was the author of a published work *Past Made Present, A History of Beloit, 1830-1900.*

1,350. Varney, Thomas
Papers. 1849-78. 5 vols.
Open. Descriptive guide.
California Historical Society.
Papers of Varney include a diary kept from 1852 to 1854 by his wife Maria L. Varney (?-1888), a housewife, writer, and clubwoman. In the diary she expresses her feelings about leaving her mother in the East and traveling to San Francisco to rejoin her husband after a three-year separation and describes the death of her young daughter. The diary also contains letters she wrote to newspapers regarding women's rights, slavery, education, the assimilation of the foreign born, and other topics.

1,351. Watson, Elizabeth Lowe
Papers. 1899-1921. 0.5 box.
Open. Unpublished guide.
California Historical Society.
Correspondence and other papers of [Mrs.] Watson (1843-?), a California suffragist and spiritualist. The collection consists primarily of letters to her son-in-law after her daughter's death regarding spiritualism, but it also includes poems by Watson.

1,352. Watson, Margaret Wickham
Papers. 1921-34. 6 vols.
Open. Unpublished guide.
California Historical Society.
Diary of Watson (1891-1934), French teacher, translator, and author, describes her employment in a New York City publishing house; other writers and literary social events; her meeting with Frederick O'Brien, their friendship and their work together until his death in 1932; her move to the San Francisco Bay area in 1922; and her feelings toward marriage, abortion, parents, and friends. Watson committed suicide after a long period of depression.

1,353. Wilson, Carol Green
Papers. Nd. 1 folder.
Open. Unpublished guide.
California Historical Society.
Research notebook; radio script for Pen Women on the establishment of schools in Santa Clara County, CA; and narration of fashion show for Stanford Mothers' Club.

1,354. Winne, Caroline (Frey)
Papers. 1883-87. 1 microfilm reel.
Open. Unpublished guide.
California Historical Society.
Letters from California written by Winne.

1,355. Women Immigrants to California
Collection. Ca. 1930. 5 items.
Open. No guide.
California Historical Society.
Letters to the Romantic Forty-Niner club from persons requesting membership for their mother or grandmother. Includes information about women who traveled to California between 1852 and the 1860s from France, Ohio, Illinois, Wisconsin, and Iowa.

1,356. Women in California
Oral history. Ca. 1900- . No size given.
Open. No guide.
California Historical Society.
Tapes and transcripts of interviews with California women involved in movements for social change, including the organization of labor unions, the securing of women's legislative and economic rights, pacifist groups, the LWV, unemployment councils, civil rights, and civil libertarian groups organized to protect reformers from vigilante action and illegal jailings. Contains interviews with past presidents of the LWV, including Harriet Judd Eliel, Beatrice Ludlow Flick, and Nan Bamburg Frank; women involved in printing and publishing, including Margaret Murdock and Morris Wagner; and women who organized or worked for labor unions or the Communist party, including Clemmie Barry, Betty De Losada, Katherine Rodin, Elaine Black Yoneda, Louise Lambert, Mildred Edmondson, Violet Orr, Helene Powell, and Caroline Decker Gladstein.

1,357. Women in California Oral History Project: Labor and Radical Leaders
Oral history. Nd. No size given.
Open. Card catalog.
California Historical Society.
Included are interviews with Clemmie Barry (1901-), who was an organizer for the Amalgamated Clothing Workers of America in the 1930s and was active in California unions and the Communist party in the late 1930s and early 1940s; with Betty De Losada (1921-), who was an official of the International Longshoremen's and Warehousemen's Union, Local 6, during the 1940s; with Mildred Edmondson (1914-), who was Trade Union Liaison for the War Manpower Commission during WWII; with Caroline Decker Gladstein, an organizer for agricultural workers in the 1930s and a strike leader, who served time in jail under the Criminal Syndicalism Law; with Louise Todd Lambert (1905-), who was a state leader of the Communist party in California; and with Violet Orr (1905-), a San Francisco leader of the Communist party and a laundry worker who also was active in the peace movement and in church work.

The collection also contains interviews with Helene Powell (1919-), who was a member of the Warehouse Union, Local 6, International Longshoremen's and Warehousemen's Union during the 1940s and an organizer for the international office of the ILWU during the 1940s in Los Angeles; with Katherine Rodin (1907-), who was secretary to Communist party officials during the 1930s and an active party member during the 1930s and 1940s in San Francisco, Washington, and Oregon; with Angela Gizzi Ward who was an organizer for the Office Workers' Union in San Francisco during the late 1930s and early 1940s and an organizer for the Mine, Mill and Smelter Workers' Union and the United Electrical Workers' Union during the 1940s; and with Elaine Black Yoneda (1906-), who was an International Labor Defense official in Los Angeles and San Francisco during the 1930s and 1940s.

Tapes and transcripts are available for many of the above interviews.

1,358. Women's Co-operative Printing Union
Records. Ca. 1869-75. 1 folder.
Open. No guide.
California Historical Society.
Articles of incorporation, receipts, and research notes of this San Francisco union, variously called the Woman's Co-op Printing Union and the Woman's Printing Association. Contains notes relating to various women printers and engravers in San Francisco, including [Mrs.] Agnes Peterson; [Mrs.] Lizzie Richmond; [Miss] Abbie T. Grace; [Mrs.] Leila (Curtis) Chamberlain; [Miss] Eleanor P. Gibbons, who later married Louis H. Sharp; and [Mrs.] Mary (Curtis) Richardson, the sister of Leila Chamberlain.

1,359. Women's Suffrage
Collection. 1910-11. 1 folder.
Open. Unpublished guide.
California Historical Society.
Material primarily concerning the successful 1911 campaign for women's suffrage in California. Includes information on the California Equal Suffrage Association, Fannie McLean, Everis A. Hayes, the Men's League for Woman Suffrage of the State of California, the Political Equality League, and B. Grant Taylor and his wife.

1,360. Women's Suffrage, 1880
Collection. 1880. 1 folder.
Open. Unpublished guide.
California Historical Society.
Record of the negative side of a debate about granting women suffrage presented during a session held at Elk Grove in Sacramento County, CA. The debate was decided in favor of the negative.

1,361. Yoneda, Elaine Black
Papers. 1931-39. 0.5 box.
Open. Unpublished guide.
California Historical Society.
Biographical material and résumé of Yoneda (1906-), material from her 1939 candidacy for the San Francisco Board of Supervisors, International Labor Defense documents, and clippings.

1,362. First Unitarian Church
Records. Ca. 1850s- . Ca. 10 ft.
Open. No guide.
First Unitarian Church of San Francisco.
Records of the Church, which was founded in 1850, consist of bylaws; minute books; records of baptisms, marriages, funerals, and memorial services; pew registers; a card file of names and addresses of persons connected with the Church's history; financial records for the William & Alice Hinckley Fund and the Anna M. Hathaway Fund; historical photos; newsletters; and orders of service.

1,363. Society for Christian Work
Records. Ca. 1893- . Ca. 6 ft., 23 vols., and other items.
Open. No guide.
First Unitarian Church of San Francisco.
This group was founded as a benevolent society in 1873 by men and women members of the First Unitarian Church of San Francisco; in 1880 the Society was reorganized, and the men withdrew from membership. In recent years men have again become members of the organization. Bylaws; minutes of the directors, the membership, and the relief committee; financial records; lists of members; a pew register; and yearbooks listing officers and members of the relief, visiting, needlework, membership, book, decorations, program, tea, alliance, and work committees. Also includes a cashbook and a record book containing lists of parishioners of the post office mission committee. In addition, collection contains bylaws, manuals, service and hymn books, and a cookbook of the General Alliance of Unitarian Women, also known as the General Alliance of Unitarian and Other Liberal Christian Women. The Alliance is

currently known as the Unitarian Universalist Women's Federation.

1,364. St. Mark's Lutheran Church
Records. 1860-1957. 34 vols.
Access restricted. Unpublished guide.
St. Mark's Lutheran Church.
Minutes of annual membership meetings and of the board of trustees, financial records, membership lists for the women's society and for other groups, and registers of weddings, baptisms, deaths, confirmations, and communions of this church, which was founded in ca. 1853 as the First German Protestant Church on the Pacific Coast. The Church's name was changed several times, and its congregation split into at least two churches in 1866.

1,365. Bell, Lizzie
Papers. 1865. 1 vol.
Open. No guide.
San Francisco Public Library.
Journal in which Bell, a pioneer, recorded her overland journey from New York to San Francisco.

1,366. Casserly, Teresa
Papers. 1861-63. 16 items.
Open. No guide.
San Francisco Public Library.
Correspondence of Casserly, a San Francisco resident.

1,367. Coit, Lillie (Hitchcock)
Papers. Nd. 1 vol.
Open. No guide.
San Francisco Public Library.
Pre-Civil War diary of Coit (1843-1929), a prominent San Franciscan.

1,368. Pleasant, Mary Ellen "Mammy"
Papers. 1860-70. 427 items.
Open. No guide.
San Francisco Public Library.
Correspondence, a daybook, financial papers, an address book, cookbooks, a grocery book, photos, and clippings of [Mrs. John] Pleasant (1814?-1904), a black housekeeper who lived in San Francisco.

1,369. Archives
Records. 1854- . 15 boxes and 50 vols.
Closed. No guide.
Sisters of the Presentation Convent.
This religious order of women involved in educational, social, and pastoral ministries was founded in San Francisco in 1854. Annals of all foundations and ministries by the Sisters in California, correspondence, photos, slides, clippings, commemorative booklets, memorabilia, and other records of the order.

1,370. Trinity Episcopal Church
Records. Ca. 1849-1962. 13 microfilm reels.
Open. Unpublished guide.
Trinity Episcopal Church.
Church records consist of such vital statistics as the pew list of names of families, pew number, and amount paid, 1852-97; the parish register, which includes a record of daily events in the life of the rector, 1874-1955; and the marriage register with name, age, residence, marital status, parents' names, and signatures of the bride, groom, and witnesses, 1911-48. Collection also includes minutes of proceedings of the rector, wardens, and vestrymen, 1852-96 and 1916-62; receipt and account records, 1852-84; correspondence and journals; ledgers and other records of St. Mary's Altar Guild; reports of the Church Women; supplementary vital records on baptisms and confirmations, 1929-62; scattered annual reports, 1930-62; surveys; corporation statistics; and scrapbooks containing photos and clippings about Church members and announcements of births, engagements, and marriages.

1,371. Barney, Edna Locke
Papers. 1914-18. 1 folder.
Open. Shelflist and catalog card.
University of California, San Francisco, Archives.
Drafts of papers written by Barney relate to cholelithiasis, goiter, and a discussion of the lipoids concerned in growth with clinical observations on the action of tethelin. The last paper was published in 1918.

1,372. Doyle, Helen MacKnight
Papers. 1934-35. 1 folder.
Open. Shelflist and catalog card.
University of California, San Francisco, Archives.
Letters from Doyle (1872-1957) to Chauncey Depew Leake regarding Doyle's book *A Child Went Forth* (1934).

1,373. Eddie, Bernice U.
Papers. 1948. 1 folder.
Open. Catalog card.
University of California, San Francisco, Archives.
Includes letters to Eddie (1903-69) from the Hooper Foundation, the Phelps Dodge Corporation Hospital branch, and the Arizona department of health about the food poisoning of the Orr family, which lived in Morenci, AZ. The case resulted in two deaths. Includes a report of laboratory findings.

1,374. Gardner, Frances Tomlinson
Papers. 1938?-50?. 17 folders.
Open. Shelflist and catalog card.
University of California, San Francisco, Archives.
Correspondence, notes, typescripts, and galley proofs of Gardner (?-1954), a history librarian at the University of California, San Francisco, whose writings usually concerned early California medicine, San Francisco hospitals, physicians, and "historic" individuals at the University.

1,375. Kalkman, Marion E.
Papers. 1950-67. 1 box.
Open. Catalog card.
University of California, San Francisco, Archives.
Manuscripts for the first through third editions of *Psychiatric Nursing* by Kalkman (1904-).

1,376. Montgomery, Mary F.
Papers. 1936. 2 items.
Open. Catalog card.
University of California, San Francisco, Archives.
Correspondence of Montgomery with Chauncey Depew Leake.

1,377. Rosencrantz, Esther
Papers. 1920-50. 1.2 ft. and 2 cartons.
Open. Shelflist and catalog card.
University of California, San Francisco, Archives.
Papers of Rosencrantz (1876-1950), an author, consist of correspondence with a number of people, her file on tuberculosis, correspondence she collected pertaining to the medical exhibit at the Golden Gate International Exposition, correspondence concerning her collection of Osleriana, and papers concerning the San Francisco and Berkeley campuses of the University and her membership in professional societies.

1,378. Smith, Donna Eloise
Papers. 1967. 23-page item.
Open. Catalog card.
University of California, San Francisco, Archives.
Biographical sketch Smith, a first-year medical student, wrote about George H. F. Nuttall as an elective research project under the direction of Chauncey Depew Leake.

1,379. Smith, Kathryn Muriel
Papers. 1964. 166 pp.
Open. Catalog card.
University of California, San Francisco, Archives.
Consists of Smith's dissertation "Discrepancies in the Value Climate of Nursing Students: A Comparison of Head Nurses and Nursing Educators," which she presented for her Doctor of Education degree at Stanford University. Head nurses used in the investigation were staff members at Herbert C. Moffitt Hospital.

1,380. Thelander, Hulda Evelyn
Papers. 1967-71. Ca. 1 folder and 242 pp.
Open. Catalog cards.
University of California, San Francisco, Archives.
Contains a diary Thelander (1896-) kept while attending the University medical school for the second time; the diary contains a section on the department of pediatrics at Children's Hospital. Also contains memoirs of her family, including her parents' parents, who were from Sweden; articles by Thelander and others on a variety of pediatric topics; and articles relating to women in medicine.

1,381. Toland, Mary Bertha Morrison
Papers. 1888?-97? 1 folder.
Open. Shelflist and catalog card.
University of California, San Francisco, Archives.
Contains letters from [Mrs. Hugh] Toland, an author, to [Mrs.] Sarah Augusta Goodwin; a manuscript poem about Los Angeles; a newspaper obituary of Toland; and a photo of two women.

1,382. University of California, San Francisco, Doctors' Wives' Association
Records. 1919-70. Ca. 3 vols. and 50 pp.
Open. Shelflist and catalog cards.
University of California, San Francisco, Archives.
Includes financial reports, membership lists, a volume relating to annual teas and other events, and a 50th anniversary album containing business reports, committee reports, correspondence, a history, notes, invitations, and clippings of the Association, which is comprised of women faculty members and wives of faculty members at the University of California, San Francisco.

1,383. Wartenberg, Isabelle von Sazenhofen
Papers. 1941-42. 6 folders.
Open. Catalog card.
University of California, San Francisco, Archives.
Includes drafts of a translation of Albert Neisser's "On Modern Syphilotherapy with Particular Reference to Salvarsan," along with notes by Frances Tomlinson Gardner.

SAN GABRIEL

1,384. Baptismal, Confirmation, Marriage, and Death Records
Records. 1771-1978. 42 vols.
Open. Partial index.
San Gabriel Mission.
Records of the San Gabriel Mission, which was founded in 1771 and served the area included in the present counties of Los Angeles, San Bernardino, and Riverside, contain records of 35,948 baptisms, confirmation records from 1778 to 1899, marriage records from 1774 to 1978, death records from 1774 to 1910, and other material. Information provided for each individual includes age, sex, name, parents' names, birthplace, and in the cases of baptisms and confirmations the name of the individual's sponsor.

SAN LEANDRO

1,385. Oakland New Century Club
Records. 1907. 1 vol.
Open. No guide.
San Leandro Community Library.
Annual reports, short essays, and a list of members of the Club, incorporated in 1900 to establish and maintain schools of domestic science, boys' clubs, girls' clubs, free libraries and reading rooms,

kindergarten schools, vacation schools, public playgrounds, and parks. The Club joined both the California Federation of Women's Clubs and the GFWC in 1902; in 1904 it joined the local Council of Women.

1,386. San Leandro Authors
Collection. Ca. 1950s. 1 folder.
Open. No guide.
San Leandro Community Library.
Correspondence and autobiographical essays solicited by [Miss] Marie T. Smith, a librarian of the San Leandro Free Public Library for the California Library Week celebration include a letter and photo from Marguerite Elizabeth (Sprado) Schlichtmann, author of *The Big Oak Flat Road* (1955).

1,387. San Leandro Historical-Centennial Committee
Collection. Ca. 1880s-1960s. Ca. 10 ft.
Open. Index.
San Leandro Community Library.
Copies of documents and photos loaned to the Committee by local families for the city's centennial celebration. Includes photos of the San Leandro Ladies Aid Society of the First Presbyterian Church, which was "dedicated to fighting the 'demon rum,'" 1895; the Alta Mira Ladies Club House and members, 1920; the Cherry Festival Parade; classes at St. Mary's Convent and school; the Ladies Drill Team and Drum Corps of the Sociedade Portuguesa Reinha Santa Isabel (S.P.R.S.I.); and the Holy Ghost Festival, a Portuguese holiday.

1,388. San Leandro Memorial Hospital Auxiliary
Records. 1959-70. 2 vols.
Open. No guide.
San Leandro Community Library.
Scrapbooks contain membership rosters, photos, and clippings relating to the activities of the Auxiliary, most of whose members were women.

1,389. San Leandro Symphony League Auxiliary
Records. 1960-71. 2 vols.
Open. No guide.
San Leandro Community Library.
Scrapbooks of symphony programs and clippings relate to activities of the Auxiliary, which sponsored fashion shows, card parties, home tours, and other events to aid the Symphony. Most members of the Auxiliary were women.

SAN MARINO

1,390. Akins, Zoë
Papers. 1807-1951. 9000 items.
Access restricted. Summary report.
The Huntington Library.
Akins (1886-1958), who married Hugo Rumbold in 1932, was a dramatist, novelist, poet, and screenwriter. Personal and literary papers, business records, photos, and manuscripts of many of Akins's screenplays, poems, and articles, are included along with correspondence with leading literary, theatrical, and motion picture figures. Ninety letters from novelist Willa Cather and several letters each from novelist Edith Wharton and lyric poet Sara Teasdale are also included.

1,391. Anthony Family
Papers. 1844-1945. 162 items.
Open. No guide.
The Huntington Library.
A lecturer and campaigner for woman suffrage, Susan Brownell Anthony (1820-1906) was an officer in the National Woman Suffrage Association and in the National American Woman Suffrage Association. Correspondence, manuscripts, a speech, and other papers of Anthony concern woman suffrage activities, family matters, and ideas about populism, racism, and religion. Correspondents include Joseph Anthony, Lucy Elmina Anthony, Mary S. Anthony, and Anna Howard Shaw.

1,392. Appleton and Foster
Papers. 1717-1897. 73 items.
Open. Summary report.
The Huntington Library.
Most of the papers of the Appleton and Foster families, who were characterized as devout, well-to-do New England settlers engaged primarily in business, consists of early 19th-century correspondence between family members dealing with social life, family matters, Unitarianism, and the War of 1812. Many of the letters are between Sarah (Greenleaf) Appleton Haven (?-1838) and her daughter Mary (Appleton) Foster. Sarah Greenleaf was married to Nathaniel Walker Appleton from 1780 to 1795, then to Joseph Haven from ca. 1814. Her daughter Mary married John Welch Foster in 1824.

1,393. Aram, Joseph
Papers. 1835-1912. 90 items.
Open. Summary report.
The Huntington Library.
Aram (?-1898) was an early California settler, delegate to the first California Constitutional Convention, and member of the first California legislature. Family papers, which include a genealogy, contain material on pioneering in California before and during the gold rush and on the Methodist Episcopal church in California. Also included is a scrapbook compiled by Aram's daughter Sarah Mahala (Aram) Cool (?-1912) containing manuscripts and printed material regarding her family, California pioneers, and the Methodist church. She was married to Peter Y. Cool from 1855 to 1882.

1,394. Archer, Kate Rennie (Aiken)
Papers. 1932-60. Ca. 400 items.
Open. Card catalog.
The Huntington Library.
Archer is a poet and poetry teacher in the San Francisco Bay area. Correspondence with persons active in literary circles of the West, literary manuscripts and poetry by Archer, and a scrapbook concerning literary activities, mainly in California, of Archer and others.

1,395. Atherton, Gertrude Franklin (Horn)
Papers. 1900-25. 53 items.
Open. Item cards in manuscript catalog.
The Huntington Library.
Atherton (1857-1948) was a fiction and nonfiction writer, married to Henry Bowen Atherton from 1876 to 1887. Correspondence to Ina D. Coolbrith, California's poet laureate, and to Mary (Hunter) Austin, as well as an incomplete manuscript of "The Conqueror," Atherton's novel based on the life of Alexander Hamilton.

1,396. Austin, Mary (Hunter)
Papers. 1861-1950. Ca. 11,000 items.
Open. Inventory and item cards in manuscript catalog.
The Huntington Library.
Austin (1868-1934) was a novelist, playwright, and Indian folklorist, married between 1891 and ca. 1903 to Stafford Wallace Austin. Consists of research notes and writing regarding the Indians of the Southwest and Spanish settlers; and personal and literary papers and correspondence documenting her interest in the suffrage and birth control movements, socialism, and other topics.

1,397. Baldwin Family
Papers. 1779-1886. 475 items.
Open. Summary report.
The Huntington Library.
Correspondence of the children of Michael Baldwin (1719-87) depicts their social and daily activities. Included are letters by Ruth (Baldwin) Barlow (1756-1818), who was wife of the American poet and statesman Joel Barlow (1754-1812), and letters to the Barlows from Elizabeth Whitman, whose life was the basis of the popular novel *The Coquette, or, the History of Eliza Wharton,* written in 1797 by Hannah Webster Foster.

1,398. Baldwin, Frank Dwight
Papers. 1860-1923. Ca. 5100 items.
Open. Summary report.
The Huntington Library.
Correspondence, diaries, personal papers, business and military records, army reports, telegrams, and notebooks of Baldwin (1842-1923), a general in the US Army. Includes material documenting Baldwin's Civil War service, his participation in Indian campaigns in the Southwest during 1874 and Montana during 1876, and duty in the Philippines from 1900 to 1903. Also contains letters to Baldwin from his wife Alice (Blackwood) Baldwin and their correspondence with their daughter Juanita (Baldwin) Williams Foote.

1,399. Bartlett, Julia S.
Papers. 1889-98. 109 items.
Open. Card catalog.
The Huntington Library.
Bartlett was a teacher, practitioner, and disseminator of Christian Science. Correspondence, primarily between Bartlett family members regarding religious and family affairs, includes descriptive material about the Boston area.

1,400. Barton, Clara
Papers. 1850-90. 44 items.
Open. Item cards in catalog.
The Huntington Library.
Barton (1821-1912), born Clarissa Harlowe Barton, was the founder of the American National Red Cross and its president for 23 years. Correspondence between Barton family members regarding Barton's nursing experience with the Army of the James in 1864, other Civil War matters, political views, and family affairs.

1,401. Bill, Annie Cecilia (Bulmer)
Papers. 1893-1944. Ca. 4000 items.
Open. Card catalog.
The Huntington Library.
Bill (1861-1936) was a Christian Science schismatic. Correspondence and corrected proofs of her 26 booklets relate to Christian Science doctrine, church government and politics, and Bill's philosophy of Christian Science.

1,402. Bissell, Eleanor
Papers. 1738-1958. 160 items.
Open. Card catalog.
The Huntington Library.
Family papers, correspondence, business records, genealogical notes, photos, autograph album, and guest book of the Bissell and Mills families of Windsor, CT. Also included is a journal, 1893-95, of Eleanor Bissell, who was apparently involved in a small business.

1,403. Bouvier, John
Papers. 1783-1895. 233 items.
Open. Summary report.
The Huntington Library.
Correspondence, personal and professional papers, and legal manuscripts of Bouvier (1787-1851), an editor, judge, and legal scholar, as well as a Bouvier family history he wrote. Contains scrapbook of letters to or about Bouvier's daughter Hannah Mary (Bouvier) Peterson (1811-70), who was an astronomer. Also included is Peterson's *Familiar Astronomy; Or An Introduction to the Study of the Heavens* (1855).

1,404. Burdette, Clara (Bradley)
Papers. 1875-1954. Ca. 50,000 items.
Open. Card catalog.
The Huntington Library.
Burdette (1855-1954), a leader of women's societies, founded Alpha Phi sorority at Syracuse University in 1872, founded and was first president in 1900 of the California Federation of Women's Clubs, and was a trustee of Syracuse University and Mills College. Burdette also was active in Republican party politics and in work for the Southwest Museum; during WWI she was director of food preparation for California.
Correspondence, diaries, manuscripts of books and articles, notes, photos, scrapbooks, and clippings. Included is correspondence from Susan B. Anthony; Carrie Jacobs Bond, a suffrage leader; and Herbert Hoover. Burdette was married to N. Milman Wheeler from 1878 to 1886, to Presley C. Baker from 1890 to 1893, and to Robert J. Burdette from 1899 to 1914.

1,405. Burnett, Wellington C.
Papers. 1830-1935. 869 items.
Open. Card catalog.
The Huntington Library.
Family correspondence of Burnett (1828-1907), a California state senator for Yuba and Sutter counties from 1855 to 1857 who became city and county attorney of San Francisco in 1859, and of his wife Jennie (Cleveland) Burnett.

1,406. Business Women's Legislative Council of California
Records. 1927-43. Ca. 150 items.
Open. No guide.
The Huntington Library.
Minutes, correspondence, and other records of the Council, which sought legal enforcement of equal business opportunities for men and women.

1,407. California Poetry
Collection. Nd. No size given.
Open. Card catalog.
The Huntington Library.
Poems, correspondence, and ephemera of or related to contemporary California poets such as Kate Rennie Archer, Jennette Yeatman, and Julia Altrocchi.

1,408. Caplinger, Leonard J.
Papers. 1835-97. 83 items.
Open. Item cards in catalog.
The Huntington Library.
Correspondence, memoranda, bills, and receipts of Caplinger, an Illinois farmer and a private in the Union Army from 1862 to 1863, including letters exchanged by Caplinger and his wife Mary P. Caplinger during his army duty. His letters discuss the siege of Vicksburg, MS, his illnesses and hospitalization, dissatisfaction with the war, and anti-Negro attitudes.

1,409. Carr, Jeanne C. (Smith)
Papers. 1842-ca. 1903. 192 items.
Open. Summary report.
The Huntington Library.
Carr (ca. 1823-1903), a botanist, and her husband Ezra Slocum Carr, a professor of science, settled in Pasadena, CA, in 1880. Correspondence and manuscripts relate to botany, early California, and Ezra Carr's previous work with the Universities of Wisconsin and California. Included are letters from Helena Modjeska and Mary Ashton Livermore.

1,410. Century Magazine
Records. 1885-1914. 760 items.
Open. Summary report.
The Huntington Library.
Founded in 1870 as *Scribner's Magazine* and renamed *Century Magazine* in 1881, this literary periodical served as a forum for America's most popular writers. Memoranda of editor Richard Gilder to his associate editors and letters to the editor, including 28 letters discussing literary and editorial matters from novelist Anne D. Sedgwick, who married Basil Sélincourt in 1908.

1,411. Chevallié Family
Papers. 1786-1867. Ca. 80 items.
Open. Card catalog.
The Huntington Library.
Legal documents and correspondence of Chevallié, agent in America for the Baron de Beaumarchais who filed claims against the state of Virginia after the American Revolution. Includes letters concerning personal and family matters from his first and second wives Sarah Magee Chevallié and Catharine Power Chevallié.

1,412. Chipman and Dwinelle
Papers. 1845-1943. Ca. 435 items.
Open. Summary report.
The Huntington Library.
Personal papers and business and legal records of William W. and Caroline E. Chipman, John W. Dwinelle, and their heirs chiefly deal with the Chipman family's acquisition of the Encinal San Antonio in California in 1851 and subsequent litigation involving the rancho. Also included are legal records concerning settlement of the estate of Mrs. Timothy Guy Phelphs of San Mateo, CA.

1,413. Clark, Lincoln
Papers. 1758-1942. 690 items.
Open. Summary report.
The Huntington Library.
Family correspondence of Clark (1800-86), a member of the US House of Representatives from 1851 to 1853 and a lawyer practicing from 1837 to 1847 and after 1862, and of his wife Julia A. (Smith) Clark. Included are items regarding the service of Julia Clark and the Clarks' daughter for the US Sanitary Commission in the South during 1864 and 1865 and later letters of Julia Clark regarding women as philosophers. Bulk of the correspondence, written in the 1850s, describes family life.

1,414. Colby, Clara Dorothy (Bewick)
Papers. 1882-1914. 237 items.
Open. No guide.
The Huntington Library.
Colby (1846-1916) was a woman suffrage worker and editor of the *Woman's Tribune,* a newspaper which described itself as containing reliable news about efforts of and for women. Correspondence, business records, and personal papers relate to Colby's life and work. Included are 117 letters from Susan B. Anthony regarding the suffrage movement. Colby was married to Leonard Wright Colby from 1871 to ca. 1904.

1,415. Colorado River Relocation Center
Records. 1942-45. 1408 items.
Open. Card catalog.
The Huntington Library.
Correspondence, bulletins, memos, and issues of *Poston Chronicle* and student newspapers chiefly pertain to the WWII Relocation Center at Poston, AZ, for Japanese-Americans who had lived in the Pacific Southwest. Issues of the *Chronicle* and high school and junior high newspapers give accounts of camp life and the ways in which men, women, and children adjusted. Also included is correspondence by Japanese-Americans relating their attempts to re-enter society outside the camp.

1,416. Coolbrith, Ina Donna
Papers. 1889-1932. 864 items.
Open. Summary report.
The Huntington Library.
A California poet laureate who wrote under the pseudonyms "Ina" and "Meg Merrilies," Coolbrith (1841-1928) was born Josephine Donna Smith but took the name Ina Donna Coolbrith about 1861. Correspondence, personal papers, and literary manuscripts, including a large amount of her poetry, as well as letters from Gertrude Atherton, a California novelist. Coolbrith was married to Robert B. Carsley from 1858 to 1861.

1,417. Cornell, Sara (Hughes)
Papers. 1899-1939. 97 items.
Open. Card catalog.
The Huntington Library.
Correspondence, photos, scrapbook, and clippings of Cornell (1862-1938), a California author and physician, including letters from Edwin Emerson, a war correspondent and editor; from his wife Mary Edith Griswold Emerson; and from Ina Donna Coolbrith, a California poet laureate.

1,418. Dane Family
Papers. 1849-1934. 1030 items.
Open. Card catalog.
The Huntington Library.
Correspondence, which forms the bulk of the collection, and family papers of Ezra Dane (1828-1921), who settled in California during the gold rush and married Lois Anna Nutting in 1859. Largest group of letters were written by Lois Dane's sister Ada Nutting Baker from Decatur, MI.

1,419. Davis, William Heath
Papers. 1843-1906. 634 items.
Open. Summary report.
The Huntington Library.
Correspondence, accounts, and manuscript material of Davis (1822-1909), a prominent San Francisco citizen and store owner, including drafts and a manuscript of the personal recollections of Ellen Josephine (Metcalf) McHenry, which concern life in the San Francisco area from 1851 to 1891.

1,420. Deland, Margaret
Papers. 1890-1928. 116 items.
Open. Card catalog.
The Huntington Library.
Family and personal correspondence of Deland (1857-1945), an author born Margaretta Wade Campbell who was married to Lorin Fuller Deland from 1880 to 1912. Consists primarily of letters to her cousin Madeline Romaine Wade Poindexter.

1,421. Dodge, Mary Elizabeth (Mapes)
Papers. 1866-1900. 76 items.
Open. Item card in manuscript catalog.
The Huntington Library.
Correspondence and a manuscript of Dodge (1831-1905), a children's author and editor of *St. Nicholas* magazine, including letters from Dodge to Horace Scudder, an editor and author who wrote popular stories for juveniles. Dodge was married to William Dodge from 1851 to 1858.

1,422. El Dorado County, California
Records. 1842-1906. Ca. 1600 items.
Open. Inventory.
The Huntington Library.
County assessment rolls and court, land, school, treasury, and mining records provide insight into the roles and economic status of women.

1,423. Eldridge, James William
Papers. 1797-1902. Ca. 15,000 items.
Open. Summary report.
The Huntington Library.
Eldridge (1841-1909) was a Union Army lieutenant and, later, an amateur historian. Correspondence and ephemera, including material he gathered about the Woman's Relief Corps, among which are letters from past WRC presidents who report the dates of their terms of office.

1,424. Fall, Albert Bacon
Papers. 1887-1941. Ca. 50,000 items.
Open. Index.
The Huntington Library.
A US senator from New Mexico, Fall (1861-1944) served as Secretary of the Interior in the Harding

administration and is best known for his role in the Teapot Dome Scandal. Personal and political correspondence includes letters from New Mexico suffrage groups on the Susan B. Anthony Amendment and Fall's replies indicating support of national woman suffrage.

1,425. Farrand, Max
Papers. 1755-1930. Ca. 233 items.
Open. Summary report.
The Huntington Library.
Farrand (1869-1945), a history professor and director of the Huntington Library, collected primary source material. Included are copies of working drafts of the US Constitution and travel journals of Pennsylvania, Connecticut, New York, and Maryland written about 1800 by Susan Johnson, William S. Johnson, William Tully, and W. W. Wolsey. Also included are drafts of *Lantern Slides* by Farrand's mother-in-law [Mrs.] Mary Cadwalder Jones and correspondence to Jones from novelist Edith Wharton and others.

1,426. Fields, James Thomas
Papers. Ca. 1836-1915. 5095 items.
Open. Summary report.
The Huntington Library.
Fields was publisher and editor of *The Atlantic Monthly;* Annie (Adams) Fields (1834-1915), an author, literary hostess, and social worker was his wife from 1854 to 1881. Correspondence and literary manuscripts, most of which were collected by James Fields in connection with his work, include ca. 500 items of Annie Fields's letters, manuscripts, notes, and memoranda. In addition to dealing primarily with literary matters relevant to publication in the magazine, correspondence between authors and James Fields reflects the personal relationship between the authors and James and Annie Fields. Also included are autograph manuscripts of prose and poetry.

Well represented in the collection are Ralph Waldo Emerson, Oliver Wendell Holmes, William Dean Howells, James Russell Lowell, Henry Wadsworth Longfellow, and John Greenleaf Whittier. There are varying numbers of letters from the following women: Jane Addams, settlement founder, social reformer, and peace worker; Louisa May Alcott, author of children's books; Frances Anne (Kemble) Butler, author and actress known as Fanny Kemble who was married from 1834 to 1849 to Pierce Butler; Alice Cary, poet and short story writer; Lydia Maria (Francis) Child, reformer and "woman of letters" married from 1828 to 1874 to David Lee Child; Rose (Terry) Cooke, author married from 1873 to 1892 to Rollin H. Cooke; Rebecca Blaine (Harding) Davis, author of naturalistic novels 30 years before the genre was established in the US, married from 1863 to 1904 to Lemuel Clarke Davis; Margaret Wade Deland, author born Margaretta Wade Campbell and married from 1880 to 1912 to Lorin Fuller Deland; Abby (Morton) Diaz, author, social reformer, and participant in the Brook Farm experiment, married from 1845 to ca. 1850 to Manuel A. Diaz; Mary (Hallock) Foote, author and illustrator who depicted life on the western mining frontier, married from 1876 to 1934 to Arthur De Wint Foote; Jessie (Benton) Frémont, writer and political hostess married from 1841 to 1890 to western explorer and politician John Charles Frémont and daughter of US Senator Thomas Hart Benton; Isabella (Stewart) Gardner, art collector and society leader, married from 1860 to 1898 to John Lowell Gardner; Louise Imogen Guiney, poet, essayist, and literary scholar; Julia (Ward) Howe, woman's club and suffrage leader, author of "Battle Hymn of the Republic," married from 1843 to 1876 to Samuel Gridley Howe; Helen Maria (Fiske) Hunt Jackson, author and crusader for Indian rights, married from 1852 to 1863 to Edward Bissell Hunt and then to William Sharpless Jackson from 1875; Helen Adams Keller, blind and deaf author and lecturer; Lucy Larcom, mill girl, seminary teacher, and magazine editor; Anna Harriette (Crawford) Leonowens, British writer best known as the tutor employed by King Mongkut of Siam to instruct his children (the Rodgers and Hammerstein musical *The King and I* is based on Leonowens's accounts of her experiences as tutor), married until 1858 to T. L. Leonowens; Sara Jane (Clarke) Lippincott, journalist and lecturer also known as Grace Greenwood, married from 1853 to 1876 to Leander K. Lippincott; Mary Ashton (Rice) Livermore, Civil War worker, temperance and suffrage leader, and lecturer, married from 1845 to 1899 to Daniel Parker Livermore; Harriet Martineau, English journalist and social critic; Helena (Opid) Modjeska, classical actress, married from 1861 to 1865 to Gustav Sinnmayer Modrejewski and then from 1868 to 1909 to Karol Bozenta Chlapowski; Mary Noailles Murfree, novelist and short story writer whose pen name was Charles Eggbert Craddock; Mary Traill Spence (Lowell) Putnam, author; Agnes Repplier, essayist; Laura Elizabeth (Howe) Richards, poet and short story writer who was daughter of Julia Ward Howe and from 1869 to 1940 married to Henry Richards; Anna Cora (Ogden) Mowatt Ritchie, author and actress noted in American theatre between 1845 and 1854, married from 1834 to 1851 to James Mowatt and then from 1854 to 1861 to William F. Ritchie; Harriet Elizabeth (Beecher) Stowe, author of *Uncle Tom's Cabin,* married from 1836 to 1886 to Calvin Ellis Stowe; Ida Minerva Tarbell, journalist, muckraker, lecturer, and historian; Celia (Laighton) Thaxter, poet, married from 1862 to 1892 to Levi Thaxter; Edith Matilda Thomas, poet; Elizabeth Stuart Ward, author best known for her prose, who after her mother's death in 1852 changed her given name from Mary Gray Phelps to Elizabeth Stuart and was married from 1888 to ca. 1911 to Herbert Dickinson Ward; Adeline Dutton (Train) Whitney, writer of popular didactic fiction and verse, married from 1843 to 1890 to Seth Dunbar Whitney; Kate Douglas (Smith) Wiggin, author of *Rebecca of Sunnybrook Farm* and other fiction for juveniles as well as an innovative kindergarten educator, married from 1881 to 1889 to Samuel Bradley Wiggin and then from 1895 to 1923 to George Christopher Riggs; Sarah Chauncey Woolsey, author with the pen name Susan Coolidge and lifelong friend of Helen Hunt Jackson; and Anne Whitney, Victorian sculptor.

Also included are varying numbers of literary manuscripts by Butler, Cooke, Davis, Guiney, Howe, Larcom, Lippincott, Martineau, Stowe, Thaxter, Thomas, Ward, Adeline Whitney, and Woolsey.

1,427. Foltz, Clara (Shortridge)
Papers. 1890-1931. 13 items.
Open. Item cards in manuscript catalog.
The Huntington Library.
Foltz (1849-1934), California's first woman lawyer, was active in woman's rights, social welfare, and politics. Correspondence consisting of letters from Foltz to women active in reform movements, including Ida Husted Harper and Alice Park. Foltz was married to Jeremiah Richard Foltz from 1864 to 1877.

1,428. Ford, John Anson
Papers. 1832-1971. Ca. 35,000 items.
Open. Summary report.
The Huntington Library.
Ford (1883-) is a Los Angeles politician who served on the Los Angeles County board of supervisors from 1934 to 1958 and as the board's chairman from 1952 to 1954 and in 1957. Correspondence, early family letters and diaries, reports, and printed material relating to Los Angeles politics, agriculture, education, law enforcement, minority groups, music and art, recreation, and welfare. Includes letters written by George and Jeanette T. Ford while they were missionaries in India from 1846 to 1852 and to the Seneca Indians at Lower Cattarauga, NY, from 1869 to 1870, as well as reminiscences of Juliette T. Holmes concerning her childhood in Quebec and her experiences as a pioneer in Wisconsin from 1856 to 1894. Bulk of the material covers the period 1928 to 1971.

1,429. Foy, Mary Emily
Papers. 1879-1957. 490 items.
Open. Inventory and summary report.
The Huntington Library.
[Miss] Foy (1862-1958) was a Los Angeles educator, community leader, and the city's first librarian, holding that position from 1880 to 1884. Consists of correspondence, personal papers, poems, and manuscripts, including papers, letters, and poems of California's poet laureate Ina D. Coolbrith; material relating to Luisa "Indian Luisa" Loma, 1911-31; and records regarding the Los Angeles Woman's Symphony Orchestra, 1907-10, and the Adams Street Ladies' Woman's Investment Company, 1887-98, a real estate venture in which Foy was a participating investor and secretary.

1,430. Frémont, Jessie Ann (Benton)
Papers. Ca. 1845-95. Ca. 24 items.
Open. Item cards in manuscript catalog.
The Huntington Library.
A writer, Frémont (1824-1902) was the daughter of US Senator Thomas Hart Benton and the wife of western explorer John Charles Frémont from 1841 to 1890. Literary manuscripts and correspondence, some of which Jessie Frémont wrote to her family and others while she and her husband were in Prescott, AZ, where he served as governor of Arizona Territory.

1,431. Gardner, William Bunker
Papers. 1847-1965. 76 items.
Open. Card catalog.
The Huntington Library.
Logbook kept by Gardner, a ship's captain, during a voyage from New Bedford, MA, to San Francisco; journals, including one by his wife Charlotte (Coffin) Gardner describing a journey between 1852 and 1855 from Nantucket, MA, to San Francisco, to Washington Territory, and back to Nantucket; and correspondence, the majority of which is between the Gardners' granddaughter Grace Brown Gardner and Eleanor June Graves regarding the journals and early Nantucket residents.

1,432. Green, Julia (Boynton)
Papers. 1891-1950. 1392 items.
Open. Card catalog.
The Huntington Library.
[Mrs. L. Worthington] Green (1861-1957) was a California poet and writer. Correspondence, including letters from Jessie Benton Frémont, as well as poetry, articles, stories, dramas, and three unpublished books by Green.

1,433. Guiney, Louise Imogen
Papers. 1884-1914. 69 items.
Open. Item cards in manuscript catalog.
The Huntington Library.
Literary manuscripts and correspondence to William H. Ward and to other individuals in the field of literature by [Miss] Guiney (1861-1920), a poet, essayist, and literary scholar.

1,434. Hague, James Duncan
Papers. 1855-1918. Ca. 19,500 items.
Open. Summary report.
The Huntington Library.
Correspondence, reminiscences, personal papers, and business records of Hague (1836-1908), a mining engineer, including ca. 600 letters from author and illustrator Mary (Hallock) Foote to Helena deKay Gilder as well as letters to Hague from his wife Mary and from Mary Foote. Foote was married to Arthur Foote from 1876 to 1934.

1,435. Hale, Sarah Josepha (Buell)
Papers. 1829-76. Ca. 43 items.
Open. Item cards in manuscript catalog.
The Huntington Library.
Hale (1788-1879) was editor for many years of *Godey's Lady's Books,* a leading women's magazine of the mid-1800s. Correspondence between Hale and U. S. Grant, Millard Fillmore, Henry Clay, and other national figures. Hale, who was married to David Hale from 1813 to 1822, had antisuffrage sentiments.

1,436. Harbert, Elizabeth Morrison (Boynton)
Papers. 1863-1925. Ca. 4400 items.
Open. Annotated outline.
The Huntington Library.
A writer and lecturer, Harbert (1843-1925) was president of the Illinois Woman Suffrage Association. Correspondence, manuscripts, scrapbooks, clippings, pamphlets, and books pertain to the woman suffrage movement. Included are letters from temperance leader Frances E. Willard and from such suffrage leaders as Susan B. Anthony, Rachel Foster Avery, Amelia Bloomer, Clara B. Colby, Julia Ward Howe, May Wright Sewell, Elizabeth Cady Stanton, and Lucy Stone. Also included are 128 manuscripts by Harbert regarding suffrage, her 1883 diary, her address books of suffrage leaders, and 48 books by suffrage leaders, which were published between 1868 and 1911.

1,437. Harper, Ida A. (Husted)
Papers. 1841-1919. 235 items.
Open. Item cards in manuscript catalog.
The Huntington Library.
Harper (1851-1931), a journalist and suffragist, was a biographer of Susan B. Anthony. Correspondence gathered by Harper regarding the American woman suffrage movement contains letters from such suffrage leaders as Elizabeth Cady Stanton, Carrie Chapman Catt, and Lucretia Mott; in addition, the attitudes of notable men toward woman suffrage are revealed in letters by William Lloyd Garrison, Abraham Lincoln, Frederick Douglass, Charles Sumner, Henry Ward Beecher, Teddy Roosevelt, and others. Also includes a few letters by Harper, who was married to Thomas Winans Harper from 1871 to 1890.

1,438. Hawthorne, Nathaniel
Papers. 1819-1921. 300 items.
Open. Item cards in manuscript catalog.
The Huntington Library.
Correspondence, fragments of literary manuscripts, and miscellaneous papers of Hawthorne (1804-64), an American novelist, including ca. 165 letters exchanged between Hawthorne and Sophia Amelia (Peabody) Hawthorne, whom he married in 1842. Also included are a few letters from Sophia Hawthorne to others and from Hawthorne's sister Elizabeth M. Hawthorne to her niece Una Hawthorne.

1,439. Hazelton, Elizabeth Clara (Reynolds)
Papers. 1914-54. Ca. 520 items.
Open. Inventory.
The Huntington Library.
Bulk of collection consists of preliminary versions of booklets *Alaskan Forget-Me-Nots* and *Poppy of California* compiled by Hazelton, a southern California writer who was married to W. E. Hazelton from 1897 to 1931. Correspondence, research notes, and business papers relating to her writing are also included.

1,440. Hodge, Benjamin
Papers. 1795-1892. Ca. 380 items.
Open. Summary report.
The Huntington Library.
Correspondence and other papers of the family of Hodge, a horticulturalist and nurseryman, depict the social history of a family moving west from Buffalo, NY, with emphasis on religious and educational matters and post-Civil War business conditions in the Midwest. Included are letters from Hodge's wife Eliza (Patten) Davis Hodge, from their daughters Marie Louisa and Frances Eliza, from an in-law Elizabeth Granger, and from Mrs. Hodge's daughter by a previous marriage, Mary Eliza Davis.

1,441. Hoffman, Elwyn Irving
Papers. 1893-1947. 416 items.
Open. Inventory.
The Huntington Library.
Correspondence, personal papers, and photos of Hoffman (ca. 1870-1949), a California poet and journalist, including 39 letters from Charmian [Mrs. Jack] London, a writer, and 50 photos documenting the experiences of Jack and Charmian London during their voyage on *The Snark* and on their ranch at Glen Ellen, CA. Also includes letters from Mary Hunter Austin, a fiction writer and student of Southwestern Indians.

1,442. Howe, Julia (Ward)
Papers. 1840-1906. 21 items.
Open. Item cards in manuscript catalog.
The Huntington Library.
Howe (1819-1910) was a woman's club and suffrage leader as well as author of "Battle Hymn of the Republic." Literary manuscripts and correspondence of Howe, with letters to Susan B. Anthony, Ida Husted Harper, and Caroline Maria Severance. From 1843 to 1876 Howe was married to Samuel Gridley Howe.

1,443. Jackson, Helen Maria (Fiske) Hunt
Papers. 1852-87. 154 items.
Open. Item cards in manuscript catalog.
The Huntington Library.
Jackson (1830-85) was a crusader for Indian rights and an author who used the pen names "Marah," "H. H.," "Rip Van Winkle," and "Sax Holm." Correspondence from Jackson to other literary figures, generally discussing her writing and opinions, and 24 of her literary manuscripts, the majority of which are verse. Jackson was married to Edward Bissell Hunt from 1852 to 1863; she married William Sharpless Jackson in 1875.

1,444. Janin Family
Papers. 1735-1932. 23,699 items.
Open. Inventory.
The Huntington Library.
Correspondence, diaries, and other papers of Albert Covington Janin, his wife Violet (Blair) Janin, and the Blair and Janin families. Living her entire life in Blair House in Washington, DC, Violet Janin was president of the National Society of Colonial Dames, treasurer of the National Society of Children of the American Revolution, and an active member of the National Society Opposed to Women's Suffrage. Nine boxes of her personal papers supplemented by extensive correspondence provide information about social and diplomatic circles in Washington of the 1860s to 1930 from the point of view of a wealthy upper-class woman. Also included are letters from Julia Clark Jesup to her sister Mary and her niece Violet (Blair) Janin, personal papers of Mary Serena Eliza (Jesup) Blair, and letters from Lucy James (Blair) Wheeler to her mother. Wheeler's letters detailing experiences accompanying her husband Major General George Montague Wheeler to posts in Denver and elsewhere in the US and Europe reveal hardships that ruined the health of both.

1,445. Jewett, Sarah Orne
Papers. Ca. 1890-1906. 10 items.
Open. Item cards in manuscript catalog.
The Huntington Library.
Literary manuscripts and correspondence of Jewett (1849-1909), an author, including holograph copies of "The Coon Dog" and "Jack's Merry Christmas" and letters to other writers and editors.

1,446. Jones, Elbert P.
Papers. 1848-1914. Ca. 100 items.
Open. Card catalog.
The Huntington Library.
Correspondence, legal papers, receipts, and diagrams document the claim by Jones's heirs to Yerba Buena Island, CA. Most of the letters were written to or by [Mrs.] Anna M. R. Jones of West Chester, PA, in connection with her attempt to prove her rights in the case.

1,447. Keeler, Charles Augustus
Papers. 1895-1944. 1700 items.
Open. Inventory.
The Huntington Library.
Correspondence, personal and literary papers, and business records of Keeler (1871-1937), a California poet and ornithologist, including letters from California's poet laureate Ina D. Coolbrith, Mary Mapes Dodge, novelist Gertrude Atherton, writer Mary Hunter Austin, and Julia Ward Howe.

1,448. Keene, Florence R.
Papers. 1896-1950. 2800 items.
Open. Inventory.
The Huntington Library.
Keene (1878-?), a California poet, founded *Westward: A Magazine of Verse* and served as its publisher and editor from 1927 to 1934. Correspondence, business records, personal papers, manuscripts, and photos, including numerous letters and manuscripts by contemporary literary figures, among them Kate Rennie Archer, Julia Altrocchi, and Ella Young.

1,449. Kemble, Fanny
Papers. Ca. 1831-90. 11 items.
Open. Item cards in manuscript catalog.
The Huntington Library.
Kemble, stage name for Frances Ann (Kemble) Butler (1809-93), was an English poet and actress who appeared in the US. Verse and correspondence primarily addressed to other stage and literary personalities. Kemble was married to Pierce Butler from 1834 to 1849.

1,450. Lake, Ann (Getz) Hutchinson Leech
Papers. 1820-72. 53 items.
Open. Summary report.
The Huntington Library.
Correspondence of Lake (ca. 1800-?) and her family largely concerns family matters but includes references to the Civil War. Contains letters from Anna C. (Hutchinson) Brown to her husband describing Civil War "excitement" in Cincinnati. Ann Lake had previous marriages to Edward Hutchinson (which ended in 1839) and to Andrew Leech (which began in 1841).

1,451. Levien, Sonya
Papers. 1908-62. Ca. 1280 items.
Open. Summary report.
The Huntington Library.
Levien (1898-) was an Academy Award-winning scenario writer for Twentieth Century Fox and Metro-Goldwyn-Mayer film studios and wife of Carl Hovey from 1917 to 1956. Personal and professional papers, including correspondence, diaries, manuscripts of scenarios and screenplays, material pertaining to woman suffrage, and discussion of whether to move the *Woman's Journal* from Boston to New York City in 1912. Among the correspondents are F. Scott and Zelda Fitzgerald, D. H. and Frieda Lawrence, George and Ira Gershwin, Fannie Hurst, Emma Goldman, Mabel Dodge Luhan, and Frances Perkins.

1,452. Lieber, Francis
Papers. 1815-88. 6000 items.
Open. Summary report.
The Huntington Library.
Lieber (1798-1872) was a German-American educator, publicist, and first editor of the *Encyclopedia Americana.* Correspondence,

manuscripts, lecture notes, and clippings focus on American social and political thought, with clippings, notes, and a fragment of an article by Lieber on women and on woman suffrage. Also contains letters from suffrage leaders, including Dorothea Dix, and from Lieber's wife and family on personal matters.

1,453. Lilly, Othelia
Papers. 1950-69. Ca. 1000 items.
Open. Card catalog.
The Huntington Library.
Literary papers and manuscripts of [Miss] Lilly (1908-), a California poet, consisting primarily of holograph copies of her poetry.

1,454. Lincoln, Mary Ann (Todd)
Papers. 1848-82. 78 items.
Open. Item cards in manuscript catalog.
The Huntington Library.
Correspondence of Lincoln (1818-82), Washington, DC, hostess and wife of Abraham Lincoln from 1842 to 1865, is primarily addressed to Alexander Williamson, White House tutor for her sons Willie and Tad. The letters have been published in Justin G. Turner and Linda L. Turner, *Mary Todd Lincoln: Her Life and Letters* (Knopf, 1972).

1,455. Lockley, Frederick E.
Papers. 1849-1949. 1520 items.
Open. Summary report.
The Huntington Library.
Correspondence, personal papers, and business records of Lockley (1824-1905), a newspaperman, include material of his son Frederick E. Lockley, Jr. (1871-1958), who was manager of the literary magazine *Pacific Monthly*. Correspondence of writers such as Jack and Charmian London is included in the magazine's records.

1,456. Los Angeles County
Records. 1823-50. Ca. 900 items.
Open. Index.
The Huntington Library.
Archives of the Prefecture (County) of Los Angeles contain a wide variety of administrative, organizational, and statistical material generated during the Mexican period in California.

1,457. Lovell, Mansfield
Papers. 1835-86. 1205 items.
Open. Summary report.
The Huntington Library.
War correspondence and miscellany of Lovell (1822-84), a Confederate general in the Civil War, depicts his life as an itinerant general and that of his family. Included are letters from Emily (Plympton) whom he married in 1849, which describe her life during the War.

1,458. McComas, Gene Frances (Baker)
Papers. 1907-52. 151 items.
Open. Item cards in manuscript catalog.
The Huntington Library.
McComas was the second wife of American artist Francis John McComas (1874-1938). Personal papers of the McComas family, poetry, and correspondence, most of which is addressed to Gene McComas from Grace Hegger Lewis and Carlotta O'Neill.

1,459. McPherson, William F.
Collection. 1773-1861. 330 items and 2 microfilm reels.
Open. Item cards in manuscript catalog.
The Huntington Library.
Copies of mission records, letters, and documents gathered by McPherson, a collector of Californiana, are divided into San Gabriel Mission marriage investigation records, largely in Spanish, and letters and documents of early Californians, particularly missionaries.

1,460. Madison, Dolley (Payne) Todd
Papers. 1803-47. 10 items.
Open. Item cards in manuscript catalog.
The Huntington Library.
Madison (1768-1849) was a Washington, DC, hostess who was married from 1790 to 1793 to John Todd, Jr., and then from 1794 to 1836 to James Madison, fourth President of the US. Correspondence shows the attitudes and activities of the wife of a President.

1,461. Marquis, Neeta
Papers. 1870-1949. Ca. 2740 items.
Open. Inventory.
The Huntington Library.
[Miss] Marquis was a California writer of poetry and short stories, a teacher, and a lecturer. Correspondence including items from Carl Sandburg and H. L. Mencken, Marquis's notes and lectures, and other personal papers.

1,462. Megquier
Papers. 1822-56. 89 items.
Open. Card catalog.
The Huntington Library.
Correspondence and family papers include 53 letters in which Mary Jane (Cole) Megquier, the wife of a medical doctor, tells her children and friends in the East about life in San Francisco during the gold rush years.

1,463. Mellish, George H.
Papers. 1862-65. 187 items.
Open. No guide.
The Huntington Library.
Correspondence between Mellish, a corporal in the Union Army's 6th Vermont Regiment of Volunteers, and his mother Mary Mellish. A small amount of ephemera is also included.

1,464. Merrymount Press
Records. 1893-1948. 214,729 items.
Open. Card index for correspondents.
The Huntington Library.
Merrymount Press was a publishing firm noted for typography and design, particularly in decorative printing and bookmaking. Business records of Daniel Berkeley Updike, founder and president of the Press; correspondence with authors and publishers; and bills and estimates for clients. Included is correspondence with the Women's Educational and Industrial Union and with the Women's National Republican Club.

1,465. Moore, Dorthea (Rhodes)
Papers. 1883-84. 84 items.
Open. Card catalog.
The Huntington Library.
Correspondence written by Moore (ca. 1860-1942) while she was in medical school to her first husband Charles Fletcher Lummis, who was founder and director of the Southwest Museum near Los Angeles and prominent in area literary circles. She later married Ernest Carroll Moore.

1,466. Mormon File
Collection. Ca. 1815-1948. Ca. 1500 items and microfilm reels.
Open. Partial inventory.
The Huntington Library.
Correspondence, journals, diaries, reminiscences, biographical sketches, family histories, and miscellaneous papers of 322 individuals, 58 of them women, contain descriptions of women's pioneering experiences and life in the West. Also included are discussions by Mormon men and women regarding polygamy and its effect on their lives.

1,467. Moulton, Louise (Chandler)
Papers. 1854-1907. 62 items.
Open. Item cards in manuscript catalog.
The Huntington Library.
A poet and literary hostess, Moulton (1835-1908) successfully sought recognition in the US for the English "late Romantics"; among her friends in the group were the Rossettis, A. C. Swinburne, W. B. Yeats, Oscar Wilde, and William Morris. Correspondence regarding literary affairs makes up the bulk of the collection, while a few items of her verse, which concern "the spirit of the age," are included. Moulton was married to William Upham Moulton from 1855 to 1898.

1,468. Muir Family
Papers. 1860-1906. 155 items.
Open. Item cards in manuscript catalog.
The Huntington Library.
Family correspondence of John Muir (1838-1914), an explorer and naturalist, consists chiefly of letters addressed to his brother Daniel H. Muir. Also included are 68 letters by his mother Anne (Gilrye) Muir.

1,469. Newcomb and Johnson
Papers. 1769-1863. 111 items.
Open. Summary report.
The Huntington Library.
Correspondence, chiefly addressed to Daniel Newcomb and his daughter Patty who were part of a New England family moving westward, describes daily life in a small town.

1,470. Newman, Emma E.
Papers. 1845-1921. 200 items.
Open. Inventory.
The Huntington Library.
Newman was an evangelist, mental healer, and "Christian metaphysician" who practiced her craft in the Midwest. Diaries written from 1856 to 1897, holograph sermons, commonplace books, lectures, and other personal papers. Newman was married to Nicholas Newman Emerson.

1,471. Nicholson, Grace
Papers. 1822-1951. Ca. 2560 items.
Open. Summary report.
The Huntington Library.
[Miss] Nicholson (1877-1948) was a collector and dealer in Indian artifacts and oriental art. Correspondence, diaries, business records, notebooks, other personal papers, photos, and scrapbooks. Includes items regarding Nicholson's business activities and various Indian tribes (particularly festivals of southwestern tribes), 11 diaries Nicholson kept from 1906 to 1935, and letters from Evaline Nelson recounting California Indian legends.

1,472. North, John Wesley
Papers. 1849-1947. Ca. 1400 items.
Open. Summary report.
The Huntington Library.
Correspondence and family papers of North, a New York lawyer, and his wife Ann Hendrix Loomis North, including correspondence of Ann North and a photo album she compiled before 1863. Material describes life of North and his family in Minnesota from 1849 to 1861, in Nevada from 1861 to 1865, in Tennessee from 1865 to 1869, and in California from 1870 to 1947.

1,473. Park, Alice (Locke)
Papers. 1798-1953. 795 items.
Open. Card catalog.
The Huntington Library.
Park (1861-1961) was a reformer, pacifist, and woman suffrage worker in California. Correspondence, Park's autobiography, a scrapbook, family papers, and other items relate to her work in movements to improve prison conditions, labor laws, education, and in wildlife and natural resource conservation. She was particularly interested in the welfare of children and advancement of women. Includes scrapbook of mounted notes, broadsides, clippings, and other items related to woman suffrage in California; an article entitled "Why Women Do Not Want the

Ballot"; and a volume of pamphlets regarding suffrage.

1,474. Peck, Orrin M.
Papers. 1878-ca. 1948. Ca. 3000 items.
Open. Card catalog.
The Huntington Library.
Correspondence of Peck (?-1921), a portrait painter, contains that of his sister [Miss] Janet Peck. Also included are ca. 100 letters from Phoebe (Apperson) [Mrs. George] Hearst, the mother of William Randolph Hearst, Sr., and philanthropist with a special interest in educational causes. Phoebe Hearst's letters include many references to her son, to family life in California, and to their travels in Europe.

1,475. Photographic Archives
Collection. Ca. 1850- . Ca. 150,000 prints, negatives, and albums.
Open. Item cards in photo catalogs.
The Huntington Library.
Women appear throughout this collection that pertains to nearly every aspect of the West and of California; the collection also provides a comprehensive record of the development of southern California, particularly Los Angeles, Pasadena, Glendora, La Canada, La Crescenta, Glendale, and Pomona. Of particular interest are post-Civil War photos of the Trans-Mississippi West and photos of nearly every major Indian tribe, especially the California Mission Indians, the Five Civilized Tribes (Cherokee, Chickasaw, Choctaw, Creek, and Seminole), and the Indians of the Southwest; pictured are Indian wars, reservations, and villages with architecture, crafts, ceremonies and dances, living habits, and other aspects of the Indians' "vanishing" lifestyle. Also included are photos of suffrage leaders Susan B. Anthony, Elizabeth Cady Stanton, Ida Husted Harper, and other national figures; and 1,200 negatives by Frances B. Johnston of diplomatic and political activities in Washington, DC, between 1890 and 1910.

1,476. Porter, Clyde H.
Papers. 1928-56. Ca. 4000 items.
Open. Summary report.
The Huntington Library.
Correspondence, research records, photos, and clippings of historians Clyde H. and Mae Reed Porter primarily consist of correspondence, notes, and secondary source material regarding fur traders, adventurers, and German immigration into Texas. Also contains papers pertaining to [Mrs.] Ann Matthew Satterlee, a missionary to Indian tribes.

1,477. Preston, Margaret (Junkin)
Papers. 1862-87. 14 items.
Open. Item cards in manuscript catalog.
The Huntington Library.
Preston (1820-97) was a poet whose writings during the Civil War made her popular in the South. Correspondence, verse, literary notes, and book reviews by Preston, who was married to John T. L. Preston from 1857 to 1890.

1,478. Pumpelly, Raphael
Papers. 1839-1916. Ca. 3500 items.
Open. Summary report.
The Huntington Library.
Family correspondence, professional papers and correspondence, and notebooks of Pumpelly (1837-1923), a geologist and explorer. Also includes diaries by Pumpelly's wife Eliza (Shepard) Pumpelly (?-1911) recounting their 1903-04 trans-Caspian expedition and her extensive family and personal correspondence.

1,479. Randolph and Tucker
Papers. 1723-1901. 630 items.
Open. No guide.
The Huntington Library.
Correspondence between members of two prominent Virginia families, closely allied by marriage, on such subjects as family matters and everyday life. Also included are biographical data and other family papers.

1,480. Rhees, William Jones
Papers. 1744-1906. Ca. 4700 items.
Open. Summary report and collection card.
The Huntington Library.
Correspondence, and personal and professional papers of Rhees (1830-1907) relate primarily to his work as chief clerk of the Smithsonian Institution from 1852 to 1891 and as head of the Smithsonian archives and publications until 1907. Included are letters from reformer Dorothea Lynde Dix and correspondence and personal papers of writers Mary (Howard) Schoolcraft and her husband Henry Rowe Schoolcraft.

1,481. Rust, Horatio Nelson
Papers. 1799-1906. 1,229 items.
Open. Item cards in manuscript catalog.
The Huntington Library.
Correspondence, personal papers, and business records of Rust (1828-1906), a California nurseryman, Indian agent, and collector of anthropological and archaeological objects. Includes correspondence with Jessie Benton Frémont and Helen Hunt Jackson.

1,482. Saunders, Charles Francis
Papers. 1901-41. Ca. 400 items.
Open. Card catalog.
The Huntington Library.
Correspondence, personal papers, and business records of Saunders (1859-1941), a horticulturalist and author of books on California and the Southwest, and of his wife Mary B. Saunders include letters from historian Mary (Ritter) Beard, who was chairman of the World Center for Women's Archives, Inc.

1,483. Severance, Caroline Maria (Seymour)
Papers. 1875-1919. 8400 items.
Open. Summary report.
The Huntington Library.
Correspondence, personal papers, manuscripts, and business records of Severance (1820-1914), a reformer, feminist, and founder of Los Angeles women's clubs. Family correspondence contains letters from her daughter-in-law Annie (Crittenden) Severance regarding Caroline Severance's activities. Correspondents include Jessie B. Fremont, Susan B. Anthony, Elizabeth Morrison Harbert, Phoebe Apperson Hearst, Julia Ward Howe, Helena Modjeska, and Marie Elizabeth Zakrzewska. Severance was married to Theodoric C. Severance from 1840 to 1892.

1,484. Sherman, Ellen Boyle (Ewing)
Papers. 1840-63. 144 items.
Open. Card catalog.
The Huntington Library.
Sherman (1824-88) was the wife of Civil War General William Tecumseh Sherman. Genealogical material pertaining to the Boyle and Ewing families and correspondence, primarily between Ellen Sherman and her mother Maria (Boyle) Ewing (1800-64) regarding family matters.

1,485. Sigourney, Lydia Howard (Huntley)
Papers. 1827-64. 24 items.
Open. Item cards in manuscript catalog.
The Huntington Library.
Sigourney (1791-1865) was one of the first American women to make a successful career in writing. Correspondence and verse reveal her thoughts on death and temperance. From 1819 to 1854 she was married to Charles Sigourney.

1,486. Smith, Lura Case
Papers. 1852-65. 80 items.
Open. Summary report.
The Huntington Library.
Correspondence of Smith, a Long Island, NY, native whose husband Jesse worked for various San Francisco Bay area lumber firms. Smith's letters to her sister Helen Huntting and her family describe daily life in San Francisco and a six-month stay at Vallejo and Mare Island, near San Francisco, in 1855. She tells of buying food and clothes, hunting for rooms, building a house, going to church, sending her 3-year-old daughter Carrie to school, and visiting friends, many of whom also came from the Long Island area.

1,487. Smith, Samuel Francis
Papers. 1822-94. 129 items.
Open. Card catalog.
The Huntington Library.
Smith (1808-95) was a New England Baptist clergyman, educator, poet, and the author of lyrics for the song "America." Correspondence of Smith and members of his family, most of which was written from 1834 to 1840, reflects family, social, and religious life of Baptists in New England. Includes ca. 50 love letters exchanged by Smith and his fiancée during 1834.

1,488. Spofford, Harriet Elizabeth (Prescott)
Papers. 1867-ca. 1921. 13 items.
Open. Item cards in manuscript catalog.
The Huntington Library.
An author, Spofford (1835-1921) was best known as a short story writer and literary critic; she reviewed the works of such writers as the Brontës, George Eliot, and George Sand. Untitled verse and letters by Spofford, two of which are addressed to suffragist Ida Husted Harper. Spofford was married to Richard Smith Spofford from 1865 to 1888.

1,489. Sterling, George
Papers. 1895-1927. 611 items.
Open. Summary report.
The Huntington Library.
Correspondence and poetry of Sterling (1869-1926), a California lyric poet, including letters from Ina D. Coolbrith, the state's poet laureate, and correspondence and poetry by May Snowdrop Greenwood and by poet and journalist Ella Wheeler Wilcox.

1,490. Stetson and Hayes
Papers. 1906-25. 41 items.
Open. Item cards in manuscript catalog.
The Huntington Library.
Letters about Christian Science from Augusta Emma (Simmons) Stetson (1842-1928), a leader in the movement, to James Henry Hayes and his wife Florence Belle Donnelly Hayes.

1,491. Stetson, Augusta Emma (Simmons)
Papers. 1889-1928. Ca. 610 items.
Access restricted. Summary report and item cards in manuscript catalog.
The Huntington Library.
Stetson (1842-1928) was a leader in the Christian Science movement. Personal papers and correspondence regarding Stetson's relationship with Mary (Baker) Eddy, the founder of Christian Science, and with the First Church of Christ, Scientist. Included is material concerning Stetson's teaching and writings on Christian Science and letters by Eddy addressed chiefly to Stetson. Stetson, who built a church and following in New York City, was excommunicated by Eddy in 1909. Stetson was married to Frederick J. Stetson from 1864 to 1901.

1,492. Strong, Harriet Williams (Russell)
Papers. 1815-1939. 1072 items.
Open. Summary report.

The Huntington Library.
Following the death in 1883 of her husband, Strong (1844-1926) established a ranch near Whittier, CA, and became an agriculturalist, civic leader, and student of water supply problems. Personal papers and business records contain material on women's rights, including a 1915 article Strong wrote at Susan B. Anthony's request about the rights of property and of persons, as well as Strong's manuscripts on marriage, childbearing, and the nature and heritage of women. For 20 years Strong was married to Charles Lyman Strong, superintendent of the Gould & Curry mine in Virginia City, NV.

1,493. Stuart, Ruth (McEnery)
Papers. 1893-1917. 14 items.
Open. Item cards in manuscript catalog.
The Huntington Library.
Christened Mary Routh McEnery, Stuart (1849-1917) gained popularity as a writer who faithfully recorded the dialects of the South's poor whites, the Negroes, the Italian and French immigrants in New Orleans, and the Latin-Negro Creoles. Three manuscripts, including her first story "Uncle Mingo's Speculations," and letters from Stuart to Albert Paine, a biographer of Mark Twain. Stuart was married to Alfred Ogden Stuart from 1879 to 1883.

1,494. Susan B. Anthony Memorial
Collection. 1850-1945. Ca. 1000 items.
Open. No guide.
The Huntington Library.
More than 600 pamphlets and broadsides, 150 photos, postcards, posters, buttons, and other items relate to the campaign for woman suffrage and rights in the US and abroad and focus on activities of Anthony (1820-1906) and other suffrage leaders. Included are 45 scrapbooks of clippings and articles that provide a running commentary on the suffrage movement.

1,495. Terhune, Mary Virginia (Hawes)
Papers. 1864-1922. 19 items.
Open. Item cards in manuscript catalog.
The Huntington Library.
Terhune (1830-1922) wrote ca. 25 novels, three books of short stories, and numerous articles on domestic themes. Correspondence, including letters from Terhune to Albert B. Paine, a biographer of Mark Twain, about literary matters. Terhune, the wife of Edward Payson Terhune from 1856 to 1907, was characterized as a well-known writer who was a "helpful wife" and "responsible mother."

1,496. Turner, Frederick Jackson
Papers. 1862-1976. Ca. 20,000 items.
Open. Summary report.
The Huntington Library.
Family and professional correspondence, notes and records on the American Historical Association and the "Bancroft Insurrection" of 1915, working notes, and lectures of Turner (1861-1932), an American historian. Includes boxes of correspondence between Turner and Alice Forbes (Perkins) Hooper, the wife of William Hooper and a member of the Harvard Commission on Western History; letters between Hooper and Max Farrand in which they discuss disposition of Turner's letters and she comments on Turner's life and character; and letters to Turner from the Women's Club of Wisconsin. Much of the Turner and Hooper correspondence was published in Ray Allen Billington, *Dear Lady* (San Marino: The Huntington Library, 1970).

1,497. Vogdes, Ada Adelaide (Adams)
Papers. 1866-72. 2 items.
Open. Item cards in manuscript catalog.
The Huntington Library.
Journal and vocabulary of Sioux, Cheyenne, and Arapaho words compiled by Vogdes, the wife of an Army officer. The journal records her life chiefly at Fort Laramie and Fort Fetterman in Wyoming Territory.

1,498. Walker, Elkanah
Papers. 1837-71. 84 items.
Open. Summary report.
The Huntington Library.
Primarily correspondence and diaries of Walker, a missionary, and of his wife Mary Richardson Walker, concerning their trip across the plains from Maine to Oregon, the establishment of a mission, and difficulties dealing with the Indians.

1,499. Walling, Anna Strunsky
Papers. 1877-1958. 952 items.
Open. Item cards in catalog.
The Huntington Library.
[Mrs. William English] Walling (1879-1964) was a socialist lecturer and writer. Correspondence, manuscripts, papers, and notes document Walling's activities and include letters from Charmian (Kittredge) London, who discusses her own political activities as well as those of her husband Jack London, to whom she was married until 1916.

1,500. Ward, Elizabeth Stuart (Phelps)
Papers. 1877-1910. 46 items.
Open. Item cards in manuscript catalog.
The Huntington Library.
Christened Mary Gray Phelps, Ward (1844-1911) was an author best known for *Gates Ajar,* her novel critiquing the "hellfire and brimstone" religious philosophy. Included are manuscripts of verse and of prose and correspondence from Ward, most of which was addressed to Richard Watson Gilder, editor of *Century Magazine.* She married Herbert Dickinson Ward in 1888.

1,501. Warren, Mercy (Otis)
Papers. 1780-1812. 8 items.
Open. Item cards in manuscript catalog.
The Huntington Library.
Warren (1728 O.S.-1814) was a poet, historian, and patriot. Letters from Warren to Eliza Gerry, whose husband Elbridge Gerry effected a reconciliation between Warren and John Adams after Warren had charged in her book on the Revolutionary War that Adams had forgotten "the principles of the American Revolution." Warren was married to James Warren in 1780.

1,502. Washington, George
Papers. 1749-1806. Ca. 450 items.
Open. Summary report.
The Huntington Library.
Correspondence and personal papers, some of which are copies, of Washington (1732-99), first President of the US, including 12 letters from his wife Martha (Dandridge) Washington (1731-1802) to [Mrs.] Frances Washington regarding personal affairs. Martha Dandridge was married to Daniel Parke Custis from 1749 to 1757 and to George Washington from 1759 to 1799.

1,503. Watkins, Louise (Ward)
Papers. 1871-1974. Ca. 7500 items.
Open. Summary report.
The Huntington Library.
Watkins (1890-1974), a candidate for the US Senate in 1938, was a leader in women's rights, California politics, and Los Angeles organizations. Correspondence, diaries, manuscripts, photos, and scrapbooks reflect her activities. She was a member of the California Committee for Parole Reform in 1934 and the California State Planning Commission in 1934 and 1935 and was founder of a southern California Republican women's group. Married to Edward Francis Watkins in 1915, Watkins supported General Douglas MacArthur in 1951 and 1952 and was honored for fostering Japanese-American relations.

1,504. Weinland, William Henry
Papers. 1853-1946. Ca. 2100 items.
Open. Inventory.
The Huntington Library.
Correspondence, which comprises the bulk of collection, and personal and missionary papers of Weinland (1861-?) and Caroline Yost, whom he married in 1885, largely pertain to missionary work of the Weinlands and of the Moravian Church in Alaska and on the Morongo Indian Reservation near Banning, CA. A subcollection, the Rock Family letters, were written from an Alaskan mission, while the Gilman Family papers include correspondence, land records, and historical notes on the Banning area. Also included are Caroline Weinland's correspondence and diaries, 1885-1932, describing her life as a missionary, as well as letters from Amelia (Stone) Quinton, president of the National Indian Association, to William Weinland regarding Moravian missions in southern California.

1,505. Western Diaries and Journals
Collection. 1840s-80s. Ca. 120 items.
Open. Summary report.
The Huntington Library.
Women wrote 23 of these diaries and journals concerning overland and sea voyages west by pioneers and settlers. Overland trips are described by: Angeline (Jackson) Ashley traveling from Fort Laramie to Salt Lake City in 1852; Mary Stuart Bailey from Ohio to California via Salt Lake City, 1852; unidentified young girl from Collin, TX, to California in 1869; Helen McCowen Carpenter from Kansas to Grass Valley, CA, 1857; Juliette G. Fish across the Plains, 1862; Barsina Rogers [later, French], age 12, from Evansville, IN, to Prescott, AZ, 1867; Catherine Margaret Haun across the Plains, 1849; Susan (Thompson) Parish from Muscatine, IA, to California via Santa Fe and the Spanish Trail, 1850; Maria Christina Shrode from Texas to San Diego following the Butterfield mail route, 1870; Harriet S. Ward from Wisconsin to California, 1853; Mrs. Robert Irion from Pueblo, CO, to Florence, AZ, via Raton Pass, Fort Craig, Silver City, and Globe City, 1877; Joseph Lyman, Butler Lyman, and Esther (Brakeman) Lyman from Fort Kearney to Oregon via Fort Boise and the Malheur River, across the Cascades, to the McKenzie as part of the Lost Wagon Train of 1853; Helen Marnie (Stewart) Love from Pennsylvania to Oregon via South Pass to Fort Hall, 1853; Charlotte Emily (Stearns) Pengra from Illinois to Oregon via South Pass, Fort Boise, and Grande Ronde to the Umatilla River, 1853; Fidelia March Bowers from Missouri to Oregon, as well as the organizational journal for the "Emigrant Train" with which she traveled and which was captained by Solomon Tetherow, 1845; Agnes (Stewart) Warner from Pennsylvania to Oregon via South Pass and Fort Boise to the Malheur and Deschutes River area, 1853; Catherine Amanda (Stansbury) Washburn from Iowa to Oregon via Sublette's Cutoff, Fort Boise, Grande Ronde, the Columbia River, and Cascade Mountains on the Barlow Route, 1853; Catherine (Sager) Pringle to Oregon, 1844; and Esther Belle (McMillan) Hanna from Pittsburgh to Oregon City, OR, via South Pass, Fort Hall, the Dalles, and the Cascades, 1852. Also included with the Lymans's journal are letters concerning their journey; with Warner's diary is a letter from Elizabeth Young Warner concerning the Lost Wagon Train and the Middle Fork Route; and with Pringle's description is an account of life at the mission established by Marcus and Narcissa Whitman and of the Whitman Massacre in November 1847. These overland travels west were started as early as March and sometimes continued into November, but typically they lasted from April into September.

Sea voyages are described by Mary J. Colson traveling on board a whaling vessel *The George and Susan,* 1877-80; Jane McDougal on a sailing ship *California* from San Francisco to Indianapolis via the Isthmus, 1849; and Aphia-Ann Russell

(Tyler) Follansbee on the *Greenfield* from New York to San Francisco, Shanghai, and Cork, Ireland, 1852-53. Also included is an account by Ida F. (Jefferis) Fitzgerald of the life of Plummer Edwards Jefferis with descriptions of voyages from New York to California, 1850 and 1854, and of life in Nevada County, CA, mining towns; with Colson's diary is an unidentified 1830 whaling log.

1,506. Winter, Una Richardson
Papers. 1895-1954. 440 items.
Open. Card catalog.
The Huntington Library.
Director of the Susan B. Anthony Memorial Committee of California, [Mrs.] Winter gathered mementos, particularly original letters, of Anthony and her family. Correspondence regarding Winter's work in the Anthony project includes a series of equal rights letters, 1936-46, and letters from congressmen regarding women's rights, 1938-49.

1,507. Wood, Charles Erskine Scott
Papers. 1846-1974. Ca. 50,000 items.
Open. Summary report.
The Huntington Library.
One-quarter of the papers of Wood (1852-1944), an Army officer, attorney, writer, and defender of civil liberties, consist of material relating to the activities of his wife Sara (Field) Bard Wood (1882-1974), who was a poet, special newspaper correspondent, women's rights worker, and confidante of writers. Correspondence, diaries, literary manuscripts, business records, speeches, notebooks, sketches, photos, scrapbooks, and clippings. Also included are thousands of letters between Charles Wood and Sara, previously married to Ehrgott Bard, written over a period of years before their marriage in 1938, as well as letters to the Woods from Una [Mrs. Robinson] Jeffers, Emma Wold, Ella [Mrs. Lincoln] Steffens, writer Genevieve Taggard, Mark and Dorothy Van Doren, Ella Young, and Virginia Bufano, suffrage worker and politicial radical. Other papers pertaining to Sara Wood include photos of her; boxes of manuscript poetry, articles, a partial autobiography, and biographies of Charles Wood and of Alva E. Belmont; and a scrapbook of the 1915-16 auto trip she made from San Francisco to Washington, DC, to see President Wilson about woman suffrage and of articles she wrote as special reporter for a Portland, OR, newspaper about the 1911 bombing of the *Los Angeles Times* building.

1,508. Yeatman, Jennette (Hayward)
Papers. 1928-60. 2981 items.
Open. Card catalog.
The Huntington Library.
Correspondence, manuscripts, and papers of Yeatman, a contemporary California poet, including letters from Kate Rennie Archer and Julia Altrocchi, letters and poems by other California poets, and manuscript copies of Yeatman's "Fire and Ice" and "The Two Satans."

1,509. Young, Ella
Papers. 1940s-50s. Ca. 24 items.
Open. Card catalog.
The Huntington Library.
Correspondence, verse, prose, and miscellaneous notes and drafts of [Miss] Young (1867-1956), an Irish-born author who remained in the US after obtaining a position as lecturer on Celtic literature and mythology at the University of California, Berkeley. Associated with the Irish literary revival in Dublin after 1900, Young came to the US in 1925.

SAN RAFAEL

1,510. Argüello, Sister Dominica, O.P.
Papers. 1800-1968. 3 folders.
Open. Card catalog.
Dominican Convent of San Rafael, Archives.
Correspondence, memoirs, a baptism certificate and other documents, poems, photos, clippings, and typescripts of plays and articles about Sister Dominica (1791-1857), the first woman to enter the novitiate of the Dominican Order of Monterey. The daughter of the Spanish comandante of the presidio of San Francisco, Doña Maria Concepción Argüello fell in love in 1806 with Count Nikolai Petrovich Rezanov, a Russian who died in Siberia before he could obtain the Czar's permission to marry her. Forty-five years later she became a Dominican sister. Gertrude Atherton later wrote a novel about her.

1,511. Ash, Sister M. Ligouri, O.P.
Papers. Nd. 1 folder.
Open. Card catalog.
Dominican Convent of San Rafael, Archives.
Correspondence and other papers of Sister Ash (1861-1926) and Sister Agnes Cahill, O.P. (1856-1928), members of the Dominican order.

1,512. College Archives
Records. 1917- . Ca. 8 ft.
Open. Card catalog.
Dominican Convent of San Rafael, Archives.
Photos, musical and theatrical programs, and literary, alumni, and student publications of the Dominican College of San Rafael.

1,513. Goemaere, Mother Mary, of the Cross, O. P.
Papers. 1851-1976. Ca. 1 ft. and 7 folders.
Open. List of items.
Dominican Convent of San Rafael, Archives.
Founder in 1850 of the Dominican Order of San Rafael in Monterey, CA, Mother Mary (1809-91) was the first Dominican sister from France and the first woman of a religious order to come to California. Correspondence, including letters from Sister Marie in the Paris convent; copybook of correspondence, some in French, and of *Instructions,* a book by Venerable Mère Marie de Jesus, d'Oegreda; documents regarding baptism, vows, sale of property, and the like; accounts and reminiscences about Mother Mary by Sisters Barry, Ligouri Ash, and Agnes Cahill; books of spiritual instruction; photos; and constitutions and rules governing the Dominican sisters in San Rafael.

1,514. Missions in the State of Nevada
Records. 1932-35. 1 vol. (ca. 3 in.).
Open. Card catalog.
Dominican Convent of San Rafael, Archives.
Records of missionary work done by the Dominican sisters in Nevada include photos and clippings.

1,515. O'Connor, Mother Raymond, O.P.
Papers. Nd. 6 folders.
Open. List of items.
Dominican Convent of San Rafael, Archives.
Correspondence, a biographical outline, retreat notes, and photos of Mother Raymond (1882-1943), a Dominican sister and assistant to Mother Louis O'Donnell, with whom she established the convent school and later the Dominican College of San Rafael.

1,516. O'Donnell, Mother Louis
Papers. 1889-1931. 5 folders.
Open. List of items.
Dominican Convent of San Rafael, Archives.
In 1889 Mother Louis (1852-1931), a Dominican sister, relocated the motherhouse, first established in Monterey and then in Benicia, CA, to its present site at San Rafael; with her assistant Mother Raymond O'Connor, Mother Louis established the convent school and later the Dominican College of San Rafael. Correspondence with lay people, including a Mrs. Buckbee, who was writing an article on her, and correspondence with other nuns, one of whom was Sister Rosalia O'Donnell, her sibling; manuscript of notes on Mother Louis's life by Sister Aloysius O'Brien; a description of Murphys, CA, the mining town where Mother Louis, then Kitty O'Donnell, was raised; articles concerning her golden jubilee; telegrams regarding her death; copies of the eulogy preached by Archbishop Hanna of San Francisco at her funeral mass; and photos.

1,517. O'Neill, Mother Aloysia, O.P.
Papers. Nd. 1 folder.
Open. Card catalog.
Dominican Convent of San Rafael, Archives.
Correspondence, notes, photos, and other papers of Mother O'Neill (1824-95), a Dominican sister, include a manuscript of her biography by Sister Ligouri Ash. Before joining the order Mother O'Neill was known as Fanny O'Neill.

1,518. School and Hospital Archives.
Records. 1850- . Ca. 20 ft.
Open. Card catalog.
Dominican Convent of San Rafael, Archives.
Correspondence, literary works of students and graduates, photos, scrapbooks, clippings, memorabilia, and other material contain complete annals of 22 schools and two hospitals directed by the Dominican sisters of San Rafael in California and Nevada.

1,519. Sisters' Collections
Papers. 1851- . Ca. 20 ft. and 900 items.
Open. No guide.
Dominican Convent of San Rafael, Archives.
Correspondence, photos, scrapbooks, clippings, memorabilia, and other items contain material concerning nearly all the Dominican sisters who have been members of the San Rafael congregation.

1,520. Sisters' Lives
Collection. 1850-1940. 3 vols.
Open. Card catalog.
Dominican Convent of San Rafael, Archives.
Sketches of deceased Dominican sisters written by persons who knew them.

SANTA ANA

1,521. Howe-Waffle, Willella Earhart
Papers. 1880s- . Several items.
Access restricted. No guide.
Bowers Museum.
Photos and clippings of Howe-Waffle (?-1924), an early physician in Santa Ana. She moved to Sonoma County, CA, from Virginia in 1865.

1,522. Miller, Evylena Nunn
Papers. 1920s-?. Ca. 30 items.
Access restricted. No guide.
Bowers Museum.
Sketches, photos of works, paintings, and scrapbooks of Miller (1888-1966), a teacher and painter.

1,523. Modjeska, Helena
Papers. 1876-1909. No size given.
Access restricted. No guide.
Bowers Museum.
Unpublished thesis, a scrapbook of clippings, a passport, photos, and other items of Modjeska (1840-1909), a Polish stage actress who emigrated to Anaheim, CA, in 1876. After studying English after she arrived, Modjeska became known as an actress in this country as well.

1,524. Preble-Nau, Stella Mae
Papers. 1890-1920s. 3 vols. and other items.
Access restricted. No guide.
Bowers Museum.
Diaries and photos of Preble-Nau (?-1965), a young woman who was growing up on a citrus ranch in the Santa Ana area.

SANTA BARBARA

1,525. Local Newspaper Clippings File
Collection. Ca. 1930s- . 12 drawers.
Open. No guide.
Santa Barbara Public Library.
Includes clippings about authors Isobel Field, Mildred George Goertzel, Mira Kimball Ingalls, Margaret Millar, and [Mrs.] Edith Webb; children's authors Helen Bauer, Julia Cunningham, and Gloria Forsyth; Martha Bacon, a poet and novelist; Mrs. Lloyd Chandler, a Grand Ole Opry singer who wrote under the pen name Jerri Jade; and Ruth Runkle, author of an advice column. Includes articles about pioneers [Mrs.] Hattie Stone Benefield, [Mrs.] Celestine Pendola, [Miss] Jennie Kimberly, Hattie Shoults, Elsie and Emma Lawrence, and [Miss] Concepcion Dominguez Sepulveda and typescripts of poems by Sara Teasdale, Marion Craig Wentworth of Santa Barbara, and Edna Holroyd Yillard, who was a San Mateo County librarian.

In addition, collection contains clippings about the women's auxiliary of the Filipino Community Association; the Girl Scouts; La Morada Residence for delinquent girls; nurses and nursing; the Sisters of the Immaculate Heart of Mary and the Franciscan Sisters of the Sacred Heart, both of which maintain novitiate houses in Santa Barbara; the Santa Barbara County Commission on the Status of Women; the Women's City Club of Santa Barbara; and other topics relating to women.

1,526. Community Development and Conservation
Collection. Ca. 1880- . No size given.
Open. Unpublished guide.
University of California, Santa Barbara, Library, Special Collections.
This collection was founded by [Miss] Pearl Chase, a leader in California and national conservation, community planning, historic preservation, and Indian rights; she also was interested in state and national parks. Includes her personal correspondence and other papers, six taped and transcribed interviews with her, papers of her brother Harold Chase, records of many local organizations, pamphlets, photos, scrapbooks, and ephemera. Includes records of the AAUW, the Community Arts Association, the Santa Barbara Indian Defense Association, the Santa Barbara Trust for Historic Preservation, the California Garden Club, and the California Conservation Council, which Pearl Chase helped to found. Also includes early records of the Santa Barbara Chamber of Commerce. Pearl Chase received an honorary doctorate.

1,527. Lehmann, Lotte, Archive
Collection. Ca. 1900- . 15 ft., 4 tapes, and 2 motion pictures.
Open. No guide.
University of California, Santa Barbara, Library, Special Collections.
The Archive was established in 1969 to honor [Mme.] Lehmann (1888-1976), an opera and concert singer, teacher, author, and artist. Business and personal correspondence, business papers and contracts, manuscripts of her books, opera pamphlets, photos, clippings, other papers, mementos, paintings, sculptures, drawings, and other artwork by her. Includes correspondence with Bruno Walter and material documenting her life and work in Vienna, Salzburg, and then Santa Barbara.

1,528. Mitchell, Ruth Comfort
Papers. 1900-61. 164 items.
Open. No guide.
University of California, Santa Barbara, Library, Special Collections.
Correspondence; manuscripts of poems, short stories, and plays; clippings; and printed items of Mitchell (1882-1954), who was an author of novels, short stories, and articles and the wife of a California state senator and grower.

1,529. Stopes, Marie Carmichael
Papers. 1880-1958. 14 ft.
Open. No guide.
University of California, Santa Barbara, Library, Special Collections.
Manuscript and printed material of Stopes (1841-1929), an English physician, author, and pioneer in the advocacy of birth control who lectured in the US. Also includes a box of early contraceptives and paraphernalia.

1,530. Wilson and McAdoo
Papers. 1860-1967. 9 ft.
Open. Unpublished guide.
University of California, Santa Barbara, Library, Special Collections.
Correspondence, typescripts of published works, financial records, photos, scrapbooks, clippings, and other papers of the families of President Woodrow Wilson (1856-1924) and his daughter Eleanor Randolph (Wilson) McAdoo (1889-1967), who was an author of books about the Wilson family, short stories, and articles and the wife of William Gibbs McAdoo (1863-1941), a US senator and secretary of the treasury. Includes correspondence of Woodrow Wilson, his first wife Ellen Louise (Axson) Wilson (1860-1914), and their daughters Eleanor (Wilson) McAdoo, Margaret Woodrow Wilson (1886-1944), and Jessie Woodrow (Wilson) Sayre (1887-1933). Also contains correspondence between Eleanor and William McAdoo and their daughters Ellen Wilson (McAdoo) Henshaw (1915-46) and Mary Faith (McAdoo) Haddad (1920-). Eleanor McAdoo was active in the American Association for the United Nations and other world peace organizations.

SANTA CLARA

1,531. Historic Pictures
Collection. Nd. Ca. 5 cartons.
Open. No guide.
Santa Clara City Library.
Collection of photos contains portraits of members of local families, among them one picture of Josefa Peralta de Fernandez, a member of an early Spanish family of California.

1,532. Oral History Archive
Oral history. 1974- . 28 tapes.
Open. Published guide.
Santa Clara City Library.
Includes an interview in which Mary Botello, a Santa Clara native who has worked in the canneries, reminisces about her life, the Portuguese community, children and family life, seasonal work, Prohibition, the depression, and pre-1940s local families; she was interviewed with her sister Vangie Botello. Also includes interviews in which Ave Bowe, the widow of local historian Earl Bowe, discusses her personal life and schooling after moving to the area in 1939; Freelove Eberhard, wife of a member of the Santa Clara family that owned the Eberhard Tannery, talks about the Tannery, local events, and her personal life; Beryl Hoskin, the first professional librarian at the City Library in 1938 and, since 1940, a reference librarian at the University of Santa Clara, describes her professional interests, her personal life, public schools, Prohibition, and needy families, social life, and clubs and lodges during the depression; Virginia Mayne, a teacher in the Washington and Fremont schools, describes her own education, personal and social life, and her membership in the Rebeccas' Lodge; and Viola Payton, a resident of Agnews Village since ca. 1906, talks with her daughter Delilah Quieto and other participants of the Agnews Village group interview about local history and schooling, Prohibition, the depression, and the interviewees' social lives and personal experiences. See Ronald Campbell, *Guide to an Oral History Archive for the City of Santa Clara, California* (Boulder, CO: Western Interstate Commission for Higher Education, 1974).

1,533. Santa Clara County Genealogical Society
Collection. Nd. More than 1300 vols.
Open. No guide.
Santa Clara City Library
Copies of papers of various families and an index to published and unpublished biographies of early Santa Clara County settlers, including Sarah E. Brelsford, Mary Emma Griswald, Emma Harris Hancock, Malvina A. (Hart) [Mrs. William Kirby] Bennett, Martha Kifer, Nancy Leigh, Sylvia Caroline Loving, Sarah Marshall, and Catherine (Lanker) Walters.

1,534. Santa Clara History File
Collection. Nd. Ca. 15 ft.
Open. Index to headings.
Santa Clara City Library.
Collection of announcements, brochures, clippings, and other material on the city and county of Santa Clara contain information on such artists as Virginia (Smith) Berryman, Emilia Hollman, Kay Inouye, Pamela (Drew) Kerr, Janet Kruskamp, Nancy Papa, Myrtle [Mrs. Ed] Hawkins, Dixie Marshall, Agnes Hennessey, Renate Dollinger, and Miyoka Whittlesey; swimmers Karen Moe, Donna deVarona, and Christine Von Saltza; puppeteer Angeline Judyka; Rose "Travelin' Lady" Wills; Mary Hale Woolsey; Elizabeth Finnegan; Lucie Stern; Margaret Higgins; and Jewel (Spangler) Smaus, who was co-author of *America's First Spaceman.* Also includes information on the Camp Fire Girls, Girl Scouts, the Miss Santa Clara beauty contest, the Carmelite Monastery in the city of Santa Clara, the DAR and other women's clubs, day-care centers, the Dominican sisters, St. Lawrence Girls High School, Santa Clara University, women coaches, the O'Connor School of Nursing, the Committee on Services and Shelter Care for Unwed Mothers, the American National Red Cross, the YWCA, and two national champion synchronized swim teams, the Aquamaids and the California Coralettes. In addition, the collection contains histories of the German and Portuguese colonies in the city, with names of families listed, and miscellaneous records of the Friends of the Library, with minutes of a meeting held in 1964, notes and clippings about activities, information about the membership, and other items.

1,535. Santa Clara Newspaper Index
Finding aid. 1901- . No size given.
Open. No guide.
Santa Clara City Library.
Card catalog index to such Santa Clara newspapers as the *Santa Clara News,* 1901-31; the *Santa Clara Journal,* 1928-70; the *Santa Clara American,* 1974-; and the *Santa Clara Sun,* 1973- . Includes headings for access to items relating to individual women and to the activities of women.

SANTA CRUZ

1,536. Cannon, Annie Jump
Papers. 1905-31. 16 items.
Open. Unpublished guide.
University of California, Santa Cruz, Lick Observatory Archives.
Correspondence of Cannon (1863-1941), an astronomer.

1,537. Furness, Caroline E.
Papers. 1905-34. 22 items.
Open. Unpublished guide.

University of California, Santa Cruz, Lick Observatory Archives.
Correspondence of Furness (1869-1936), an astronomer.

1,538. Harwood, Margaret Spencer Wilson
Papers. 1914-38. 15 items.
Open. Unpublished guide.
University of California, Santa Cruz, Lick Observatory Archives.
Correspondence of Harwood (1885-), an astronomer.

1,539. Hearst, Phoebe (Apperson)
Papers. 1892-1917. 38 items.
Open. Unpublished guide.
University of California, Santa Cruz, Lick Observatory Archives.
Correspondence of Hearst (1842-1919), a philanthropist.

1,540. Shinn, Milicent Washburn
Papers. 1890-1939. 20 items.
Open. Unpublished guide.
University of California, Santa Cruz, Lick Observatory Archives.
Correspondence of Shinn (1858-1940), a writer.

1,541. Sitterly, Charlotte Moore
Papers. 1928-43. 64 items.
Open. Unpublished guide.
University of California, Santa Cruz, Lick Observatory Archives.
Correspondence of Sitterly (1898-), a physicist and astronomer.

1,542. Vinter Hansen, J. M.
Papers. 1940-57. 1 ft.
Open. Unpublished guide.
University of California, Santa Cruz, Lick Observatory Archives.
Correspondence of [Miss] Vinter Hansen, a Danish astronomer who worked in California during WWII.

SANTA ROSA

1,543. College Archives
Records. 1930-76. Ca. 4 ft.
Open. Card catalog.
Santa Rosa Junior College Archives.
The Junior College Archives contains records of the Women's Athletic Association, founded in 1930 by a Miss Clark, who was faculty advisor, and by [Miss] Grace Comstock, athletic manager of the Associated Women Students; these records consist of a constitution; minutes, 1930-36; correspondence with women's athletic associations at other schools; and a manuscript. Also includes commencement addresses, 1960-75, 14 of which were by women; an Associated Women Students handbook, 1968-69; items concerning the Women's Center, 1973-76, with newsletters and programs from a women's day celebration, a women's week, and Emerging Women, an annual women's symposium sponsored by the Center and by the women's concerns committee; and photos of the College and its students.

SHASTA

1,544. Boggs, Mae Helene Bacon
Papers. 1850-1955. 12 boxes.
Access restricted. Unpublished guide.
Shasta State Historic Park, Courthouse Museum.
Personal, family, and business correspondence; scrapbooks; photos; clippings; memorabilia; artworks; and other items of [Mrs.] Boggs (1863-1963), a philanthropist who was interested in women's suffrage, the establishment of parks, western art and artists, and the history of California. The niece of Williamson Lyncoya Smith, division agent of the California Stage Company, Boggs was particularly interested in early northern California stage coaches and transportation and was author of *My Playhouse Was a Concord Coach,* an anthology that was printed privately in 1942.

STANFORD

1,545. Bailey, Margery
Papers. 1912-62. 4 ft.
Open. Unpublished guide.
Stanford University Archives.
Bailey (1891-1963), who held a PhD, was a professor at Stanford University, founder of the Institute of Renaissance Studies, an actress, director, theatrical producer, and an author of children's books as well as of scholarly works. Correspondence with prominent actors, dramatists, and authors and manuscripts and other papers relating to the Institute, theater productions at Stanford, and the Dramatists' Alliance. The Alliance, an organization with which Bailey worked closely, encouraged young playwrights through monetary awards and production of their plays. Bailey also helped develop the Shakespeare Festival at Ashland, OR, and similar community drama festivals.

1,546. Buckingham, Elizabeth Lee
Papers. 1900-70. 6.5 ft.
Open. Unpublished guide.
Stanford University Archives.
Correspondence, student notes dating from 1900 to 1918, course material, and general files of Buckingham, a professor of English and of speech and drama at Stanford from 1910 to 1944 and professor emeritus after 1944.

1,547. Daughters of the American Revolution Blacklist Controversy
Records. 1928. 0.5 ft.
Open. Unpublished guide.
Stanford University Archives.
Correspondence, pamphlets, articles, and clippings pertaining to an alleged DAR blacklist of men and women accused of being communists, socialists, liberals, or pacifists; persons said to have been on the list were not welcome as speakers before DAR members. The inclusion of Stanford University president David Starr Jordan among those cited precipitated the withdrawal of the Palo Alto Chapter from the national DAR.

1,548. Hardy, Irene
Papers. 1900-21. 0.5 ft.
Open. Unpublished guide.
Stanford University Archives.
Manuscript and published poems of Hardy, a professor of English at Stanford University from 1894 to 1901. Also includes her manuscript autobiography.

1,549. Hopkins, Jeanette Hitchcock
Papers. 1932-74. 1 ft.
Open. Unpublished guide.
Stanford University Archives.
A 1914 graduate of Stanford University, Hopkins joined the staff of Stanford Library in 1923, served as keeper of rare books for University Libraries from 1936 to 1947, and was chief of the division of special collections from 1947 to 1955. Principally correspondence, articles, speeches, and unpublished papers concerning both library and non-library topics. Among her correspondents are Arundell Esdaile, Sir Frank Francis, and Patricia Eccles.

1,550. Mirrielees, Edith Ronald
Papers. 1870-1962. 0.5 ft.
Open. Unpublished guide.
Stanford University Archives.
Mirrielees was a professor of English at Stanford University from 1909 to 1944 and professor emeritus from 1944 to 1962. Primarily consists of correspondence with former students and friends regarding their writing and her life at Stanford. Correspondents include Bernard De Voto, Wallace Stegner, and Harry Bush.

1,551. Mosher, Clelia Duel
Papers. 1886-1938. 7 ft.
Open. Unpublished guide.
Stanford University Archives.
Correspondence, diaries, articles, and books by Mosher (1863-1940), a physician, medical advisor to women at Stanford University, and a professor of personal hygiene who was a member of the Stanford faculty from 1893 to 1896 and from 1910 to 1929. Mosher's particular interest was women's health, and she published articles and a multivolume book *The Hygiene and Physiology of Women* on the subject. The collection also contains biographical articles she wrote about prominent women and her studies and notes on the women's movement.

1,552. Stanford, Jane Eliza (Lathrop)
Papers. 1876-1904. 16 Hollinger ms. boxes.
Open. Unpublished guide.
Stanford University Archives.
Correspondence; telegrams; business, legal, and financial papers; speeches; poems; clippings; and printed matter of Stanford (1828-1905) who, with her husband Leland Stanford, governor of California and later a senator from the state, founded Stanford University as a memorial to their only child, a son who died in 1884. After her husband's death in 1893, Jane Stanford helped to keep the University functioning during years of financial crisis during litigation of his estate. A strong supporter of education and suffrage for women, Stanford influenced the social climate of the University as well as its architecture. Her correspondents include Susan B. Anthony.

1,553. Student Letters and Memoirs
Collection. 1891- . 1 ft.
Open. Unpublished guide.
Stanford University Archives.
Letters from Stanford University students to family members and friends and students' reminiscences provide information about the students' experiences at Stanford and events at the school. Correspondents include Harriet Sophia (Hallie) Hyde, a member of the class of 1898; Katherine Taggert, the class of 1914; Rose Payne, the class of 1898, and her sister Theodora Payne, the class of 1900; and Lucy Allabach, the class of 1895.

1,554. Women's Athletic Association and Women's Recreation Association
Records. 1902-75. 8 ft.
Open. Unpublished guide.
Stanford University Archives.
Minutes, correspondence, programs, photos, scrapbooks, and memorabilia of the Athletic Association, which was founded in 1893 to organize and maintain women's athletic teams and other recreational activities for women. The Association, which also organized folk and modern dance groups, changed its name to the Women's Recreation Association in 1955.

1,555. Women's Physical Education Department
Records. 1928-75. 14 ft.
Open. Unpublished guide.
Stanford University Archives.
Minutes of staff meetings, general administrative files, and newsletters of this department, which provided hygiene and physical education training for women students at Stanford. The Department existed as an independent entity until 1975 when it was merged with the Men's Physical Education

Department. Subjects include physical education for women, the Women's Student Health Service, and medical research projects of members of Stanford's faculty.

1,556. Bisbee, Eleanor
Papers. 1918-56. 16 ms. boxes.
Open. No guide.
Stanford University, Hoover Institution on War, Revolution and Peace.
Correspondence, drafts of books and articles, notes, speeches, photos, clippings, and other papers of Bisbee, an American professor at American University in Istanbul, Turkey, regarding the history and government of Turkey in the 20th century. Includes an interview from 1922 with Mustapha Kemal and manuscripts by Bisbee, Resat Guntekin, Milli Partisi, and others.

1,557. International Congress of Women
Records. 1919. 13-page item.
Open. No guide.
Stanford University, Hoover Institution on War, Revolution and Peace.
Resolution of the third Congress, a pacifist women's organization, proposing famine relief in Europe and Asia, lifting the blockade, revision of treaty terms proposed at the Paris Peace Conference, cessation of military attack on Russia and Hungary, amnesty for political prisoners, and the return of prisoners of war.

1,558. Job, Martha
Papers. 1920-41. 0.5 ms. box.
Open. No guide.
Stanford University, Hoover Institution on War, Revolution and Peace.
Journal, pictures, maps, posters, booklets, and clippings of Job, a YWCA secretary in China from 1919 to 1929, regarding the YWCA in China, flood relief, the University of Peking, and internal problems in China from 1920 to 1928.

1,559. Jordan, David Starr
Papers. 1887-1942. 85 boxes, 5 vols., and 8 items.
Open. Unpublished guide.
Stanford University, Hoover Institution on War, Revolution and Peace.
Correspondence, writings, photos, pamphlets, leaflets, and clippings of Jordan (1851-1931), president and chancellor of Stanford University, regarding the Women's International League for Peace and Freedom, civil liberties in the US, immigration, the problems of minorities, personal and family matters, and other topics. Correspondents include Jane Addams, Woodrow Wilson, Herbert Hoover, Elizabeth Tausch, William Howard Taft, Ida Müller, Albert Guérard, Fannie Fern Andrews, Diana Agabey Apcar, Emily Hobhouse, Florence Nasmyth, Theodore Roosevelt, Joseph Swain, Upton Sinclair, Harriet Thomas, and others.

1,560. Mosher, Clelia Duel
Papers. 1898-1937. 7 ms. boxes.
Open. No guide.
Stanford University, Hoover Institution on War, Revolution and Peace.
Correspondence, manuscripts, office files, post cards, and photos of Mosher (1863-1940), who was a physician, medical investigator for the US Children's Bureau, associate medical director for the American National Red Cross's bureau of refugees in Paris from 1917 to 1919, and professor of personal hygiene and medical adviser to women at Stanford University. Relates to Red Cross relief work in France from 1917 to 1919 and the promotion of health education for women in the US. Contains correspondence with Lou Henry Hoover.

1,561. Park, Alice
Papers. 1883-1957. 52 boxes.
Open. Unpublished guide.
Stanford University, Hoover Institution on War, Revolution and Peace.
Correspondence, diaries, pamphlets, leaflets, and clippings of Park (1861-1961), a pacifist, relate to pacifism and the peace movement, the Ford Peace Ship expedition of 1915 to 1916, feminism, socialism, the labor movement, prison reform, child labor legislation, civil liberties, and other reform movements in the US.

1,562. Patrick, Mary Mills
Papers. 1875-1924. 1 ms. box.
Open. No guide.
Stanford University, Hoover Institution on War, Revolution and Peace.
Correspondence and memoirs of Patrick (1850-1940), an American who was president of Constantinople Woman's College in Turkey from 1890 to 1924. Her memoirs, 1919-24, concern conditions in Turkey during the war, Turkish society, and the Turkish educational system.

1,563. Richardson, Grace
Papers. 1919. 1 folder.
Open. No guide.
Stanford University, Hoover Institution on War, Revolution and Peace.
Ephemera, clippings, and memorabilia of Richardson, a volunteer worker for the peace movement, the American National Red Cross, and the Nebraska women's suffrage movement in 1919, include material relating to the League to Enforce Peace, a reception for President Woodrow Wilson in Omaha, NE, and other topics.

1,564. Wales, Nym
Papers. 1931-54. 37 ms. boxes and 30 items.
Access restricted. Unpublished guide.
Stanford University, Hoover Institution on War, Revolution and Peace.
Correspondence, writings, speeches, interviews, photos, organizational records, reports, memoranda, and other papers of Helen Foster Snow (1907-), a journalist and writer whose pseudonym is Nym Wales. She resided in China and the Philippine Islands from 1931 to 1941 and served as a member of the American Committee in Aid of Chinese Industrial Cooperatives board of directors from 1941 to 1951. The collection relates to communism; the industrial cooperative movement; student and labor movements; the 1936 Sian incident, which involved the kidnapping of Chiang Kai-shek; Sino-Japanese conflict; and Chinese art and literature. Correspondents include Rewi Alley, Elsie Fairfax-Cholmeley, Ida Pruitt, Eleanor Roosevelt, Richard J. Walsh, Madame Sun Yat-sen, Dwight Edwards, Geraldine Fitch, Dee C. Chaun, Chiang Kai-shek, Elizabeth Sayre, Dorothy Woodman, and others. Snow was also known as Peggy Snow, Hseuh Hai-lun, and Lo Fu.

1,565. American Authors and Literature
Collection. Nd. 3 ft.
Open. Register.
Stanford University Libraries, Manuscripts Division.
Correspondence, manuscripts, portraits, autographs, pamphlets, and clippings of American authors. Includes correspondence from 1940 and 1941 of Pearl S. Buck, who was married to Richard J. Walsh; correspondence, a poem, and biographical information on Ina Donna Coolbrith; correspondence from 1956 of Jessamyn West McPherson; letters that Carlotta Monterey O'Neill, wife of Eugene O'Neill, wrote to [Mrs.] Kate F. Elkins in 1932 and 1933; letters that Sarah Margaret Fuller, who later married the Marchese d'Ossoli, wrote to [Miss] Georgiana Bruce; an 1884 poem of Lydia Howard [Mrs. Charles] Sigourney; letters that Gertrude Stein wrote to [Mrs. Max] Sloss in 1935; letters from Ida Minerva Tarbell to a Mrs. Norris; and letters that Alice B. Toklas wrote to a Mr. Wilson in 1935. Approximately 33 women are represented in the collection.

1,566. Anderson Family
Papers. 1848-1948. 30 ft.
Open. Register.
Stanford University Libraries, Manuscripts Division.
Bulk of the personal and business correspondence, literary and scientific manuscripts, photos, documents, and clippings of the Anderson family is correspondence between family members. Also includes genealogical notes regarding the Anderson, Best, Gurnee, Playfair, and van Vleck families. Contains correspondence from ca. 1865 to 1945, poems, and business papers of Helen (Best) Anderson, who taught in a girls school established by her mother Isabella Playfair Best in Wolfville, Nova Scotia; correspondence from ca. 1865 to 1923 and diaries from 1875 to 1876 of Charlena (van Vleck) Anderson, who in 1875, while a student at Lawrence College in Wisconsin, married Melville Best Anderson, son of Helen (Best) Anderson and a professor at Stanford University; correspondence from 1883 to 1890 of Mary S. van Vleck, first wife of Balfour H. Anderson; correspondence from 1895 to 1926 of Mary Marvel van Vleck, second wife of Balfour H. Anderson; correspondence from 1901 to 1912 of Mary Elizabeth Gurnee; correspondence from 1926 to 1946 of Elizabeth Gurnee Anderson, who later married a Mr. Lossing; and correspondence of other female family members.

1,567. Angela Davis Defense Committee
Records. Ca. 1971-72. No size given.
Closed. No guide.
Stanford University Libraries, Manuscripts Division.
Correspondence consists primarily of fan mail written from Europe to Davis while she was in jail.

1,568. Artists
Collection. 1800s-1939. Ca. 1 in.
Open. Register.
Stanford University Libraries, Manuscripts Division.
Collection includes a letter that Malvina Hoffman (1887-), a sculptor, wrote to a Mrs. Sloss in 1929.

1,569. Brasch Family
Papers. 1891-1920. 0.5 ft.
Open. Register.
Stanford University Libraries, Manuscripts Division.
Primarily letters written to Frederick E. Brasch, son of Otto and Caroline Brasch, from female family members. Includes letters from his sisters Augusta Brasch, who was married to A. E. Acton; Betty Brasch, who was married to Joseph Picard; and Louise Brasch, who was married to Albert Schmidt. Also contains a 1906 letter from his mother regarding family matters and the San Francisco earthquake and fire, letters from his cousins Mamie and Alice Johannson (variously spelled Johannesen and Johannsen), and letters from his aunt Marie Johanneson (another variation). The bulk of the correspondence was written from San Jose, CA, Santa Clara, CA; San Francisco; and Hawaii.

1,570. Carmichael, Stokely, and Smith, Lorna
Papers. 1963-72. 2.5 ft.
Open. Register.
Stanford University Libraries, Manuscripts Division.
Letters from Carmichael to [Mrs.] Smith regarding her work with the Mississippi Summer Project of 1964 and with the Student Nonviolent Coordinating Committee (SNCC); correspondence between Smith and Sally Belfrage Pomerance, author of *Freedom Summer,* concerning the representation of Carmichael by the press; and an interview with Smith.

1,571. Clarke, Eric, and Clarke, Ruth Johnson
Papers. Ca. 1904-49. 4 ft.
Open. Preliminary accession guide.
Stanford University Libraries, Manuscripts Division.
Correspondence, photos, documents, clippings, printed items, and memorabilia of the Clarkes, who were missionaries in China. Ruth Clarke was born

in China, attended Miss Jewell's School in Shanghai, and graduated from Wilson College in Chambersburg, PA. She returned to China in 1912, taught at Miss Jewell's School, and in 1916 married J. Eric G. Clarke and accepted a position at the Peking American School. Residing in Peking, the Clarkes periodically brought Oriental art collections to the US. During the 1940s they were confined at Lung Hwa Camp near Peking; they now live in the US.

1,572. Colonial and Early American Documents
Collection. 1700s-early 1800s. Ca. 345 items.
Open. Register.
Stanford University Libraries, Manuscripts Division.
Collection contains 18 documents of Mary E. Hastings regarding the alleged romance between Hasting's great-grandmother Alice Adams and Nathan Hale.

1,573. Colt Press
Records. 1920-73. Ca. 3.5 ft.
Open. Register.
Stanford University Libraries, Manuscripts Division.
Ledgers, invoices, legal papers, correspondence, manuscripts, clippings, and other records of Colt Press. Includes letters addressed primarily to Jane Bissell Grabhorn from Beatrice Warde, Janet (Lewis) Winters, and others regarding writing, printing, and typography. Also contains correspondence of Louise Stivers, the Press's bookkeeper; a poem written by Rachel Whimsey; and a seller's permit and manuscripts of Grabhorn.

1,574. Cooke, Philos, and Cooke, Louise Stephens
Papers. 1907-36. 0.5 ft.
Open. Register.
Stanford University Libraries, Manuscripts Division.
Correspondence of Fanny Chapman on Tahiti and a biography of Louise Cooke that Philos Cooke wrote.

1,575. Dall and Oldroyd
Papers. 1890-1927. Ca. 1 in.
Open. Descriptive summary.
Stanford University Libraries, Manuscripts Division.
Correspondence between William H. Dall and [Mrs.] Ida Shepherd Oldroyd regarding shell collecting.

1,576. Daves, Delmer
Papers. 1930-65. No size given.
Open. Register.
Stanford University Libraries, Manuscripts Division.
Correspondence, working papers, play and film scripts, photos, and other papers of Daves pertain to his career in the Hollywood motion picture industry. Contains letters by or about Anne Bancroft; Claudette Colbert; Daves's secretary Muriel Edgarton; Mary Lou Daves; writer Edythe Freeman; Elsa Maxwell; Maureen O'Hara; [Mme.] L. Rouiez, who was secretary to Andre Bernheim; Connie Stevens; and approximately 50 other women. Also includes eight drawers of cartoons, some of which relate to women in war plants and in military uniforms, romance, the maternity ward, "kept women," divorce, and other topics pertaining to women.

1,577. Draper, Anne
Papers. 1959-72. 20 ft.
Open. Register.
Stanford University Libraries, Manuscripts Division.
Correspondence, notes, manuscripts of speeches, reports, photos, posters, articles, clippings, and pamphlets of Draper (1916-73), founder of the Labor Assembly for Peace, a trade union group opposed to the Vietnam War, and cofounder of Union W.A.G.E. (Union Women's Alliance to Gain Equality). A native of New York and a graduate of Hunter College of the City of New York, Draper was an organizer for the Steelworkers Union during the 1930s; she also was active in the Shipyard Workers Union during WWII while she was a welder in Los Angeles. She was West Coast union label director for the Amalgamated Clothing Workers Union, AFL-CIO, and was active in Citizens for Farm Labor. In her later years she worked on behalf of the Farah strikers in El Paso, TX, and the United Farm Workers Union in California, particularly during the grape strike and boycott.

1,578. Elkins, Kate Felton
Papers. Ca. 1882-1927. Ca. 1.5 ft.
Open. Register.
Stanford University Libraries, Manuscripts Division.
Five scrapbooks of [Mrs.] Elkins contain correspondence; autographs; photos; concert, opera, and theater programs; articles; clippings regarding authors and literature; and other papers.

1,579. Field, Isobel Osbourne Strong
Papers. 1949-55. 2 in.
Open. Register.
Stanford University Libraries, Manuscripts Division.
Correspondence of [Mrs.] Field includes letters she wrote her pen pal Hector Bolitho containing comments about her stepfather Robert Louis Stevenson.

1,580. Fiske, Turbese Lummis
Papers. Ca. 1929-48. Ca. 4 in.
Open. Register.
Stanford University Libraries, Manuscripts Division.
Correspondence and manuscripts for plays and stories of Fiske, an author, include correspondence with Nan Blair and rejection letters from publishers.

1,581. Foote, Mary Anna (Hallock)
Papers. 1863-1924. 1 ft.
Open. Register.
Stanford University Libraries, Manuscripts Division.
Correspondence of Foote (1847-1938), an author and illustrator of short stories and novels about the West, includes correspondence with Helena (de Kay) Gilder, with whom Foote was friends for 50 years; with Gilder's husband Richard Gilder, a poet and editor; and with Edith Angus. Foote attended the Poughkeepsie Female Collegiate Seminary in New York from 1860 to 1864 and the school of design for women at Cooper Institute in 1864. She married Arthur De Wint Foote in 1875.

1,582. Gay, Theresa
Papers. Nd. 5 boxes.
Open. Preliminary accession guide.
Stanford University Libraries, Manuscripts Division.
Correspondence, historical research notes, and early California songs and poems of Gay, an author. Also contains a manuscript biography about James Marshall.

1,583. Gerber, Merrill Joan
Papers. Nd. 4 items.
Open. Register.
Stanford University Libraries, Manuscripts Division.
Manuscripts of short stories written by Gerber, an author whose pseudonym is Spiro Merrill.

1,584. Gibbons, A. S., and Gibbons, Sarah Cloud
Papers. 1852-58. 29 items.
Open. Register.
Stanford University Libraries, Manuscripts Division.
Correspondence and other papers of A. S. Gibbons, an itinerant Methodist preacher who taught at Santa Clara College in Santa Clara, CA, for one year, and his wife Sarah Cloud Gibbons. Primarily consists of letters that Sarah Gibbons wrote to her family in Virginia about domestic problems and the temperance movement.

1,585. Hadden, Anne
Papers. 1858-1935. Ca. 100 items.
Open. Register.
Stanford University Libraries, Manuscripts Division.
Letters to Hadden from authors and Stanford University faculty members, including Mary Austin, Margaret W. Beck, Jessie K. Jordan, and Lucie Stern. Also contains correspondence written to or collected by Irene Hardy, with letters of Clara Barton; Ina Coolbrith; Ellen Day Hale; Mary Abigail Dodge, whose pseudonym was Gail Hamilton; and Stanford University faculty member Julia Gilbert. Correspondence and a biographical sketch of [Miss] Maude J. Wilson are also contained in the collection.

1,586. Lewis, James
Papers. 1868-73. 5 vols.
Open. Register.
Stanford University Libraries, Manuscripts Division.
Letters from Lewis to his student Annie Law, whose collection of shells was, in ca. 1891, one of the first collections acquired by Stanford University.

1,587. Lewis, Janet
Papers. 1948-61. Ca. 8 in.
Open. Register.
Stanford University Libraries, Manuscripts Division.
Correspondence, musical and literary manuscripts, photos, reviews, articles, and other papers of Lewis (1899-), an author and wife of Yvor Winters. The bulk of the collection relates to the opera *The Wife of Martin Guerre,* with libretto by Lewis and musical score by William Lawrence Bergsma. Includes correspondence with Bergsma and his wife Nancy-Jane Nickerson Bergsma.

1,588. Lind, Jenny, and Goldschmidt, Otto
Papers. Ca. 1835-76. 2 ft.
Open. Register.
Stanford University Libraries, Manuscripts Division.
Correspondence regarding financial matters and manuscripts of music of Lind, a singer, and Goldschmidt. Also contains correspondence, an account book, photos, a contract with P. T. Barnum, biographical information, and a Royal College of Music exercise book of Lind; music sung by Lind; and papers of Mrs. Raymond Maude regarding Lind.

1,589. Monroe, Will S.
Collection. Nd. 1 ft.
Open. Preliminary accession list.
Stanford University Libraries, Manuscripts Division.
Correspondence and notes regarding Walt Whitman, which Monroe collected from librarians and contemporaries of Whitman. Includes letters from Clara Barrus, Edith Trowbridge, Mary Kennedy Foote, Florance H. Crowell, Dorothea Chambers Blaisdell, Harriet [Mrs. Frank J.] Spraug, Charlotte Endymion Porter, and Florence (Finch) Kelly.

1,590. Nash, Even Rupert
Papers. 1827-1945. Ca. 333 items.
Open. Register.
Stanford University Libraries, Manuscripts Division.
Correspondence of the Nash family concerns their lives in the Oneida Community in New York and the Wallingford Community in Connecticut, their work, activities, and beliefs. Contains correspondence of Sarah B. Nash; Erminia Nash and Almeda Nash, who were sisters; Jennie N. Knowles; Etta Knowles; Florilla "Rillie" Nash; and other women. Also includes genealogical information about the Nash and Poole families.

1,591. Needham, James Carson
Papers. 1893-1936. 5 ft.
Open. Register.
Stanford University Libraries, Manuscripts Division.
Collection includes one box of correspondence, photos, a membership list, and clippings pertaining

to the Covered Wagon Babies Club, founded by Needham to bring together those who were born in covered wagons en route to California.

1,592. Norris, Charles G., and Norris, Kathleen (Thompson)
Papers. Nd. 100 ft.
Open. Register.
Stanford University Libraries, Manuscripts Division.
Collection contains correspondence, 120 folders of manuscripts, and clippings of Kathleen Norris (1880-1966), an author who was the wife of Charles G. Norris. Includes correspondence with R. L. Wilbur and a Mrs. Sloss.

1,593. Noted Women
Collection. Nd. Ca. 2 in.
Open. Register.
Stanford University Libraries, Manuscripts Division.
Collection includes correspondence of Jane Addams, Susan Brownell Anthony, Grace Anna (Goodhue) [Mrs. Calvin] Coolidge, Lou (Henry) Hoover, Helen Adams Keller, Alice Roosevelt [Mrs. Nicholas] Longworth, Anna Eleanor [Mrs. F. D.] Roosevelt, and Helen (Herron) [Mrs. William Howard] Taft. Many of the letters were written to Mrs. M. C. Sloss, R. L. Wilbur, and a Mrs. Snook. Also includes letters that Ellen Karoline Sofia Key wrote to the women's board of the Panama Pacific International Exposition in San Francisco and letters that Sara (Delano) [Mrs. James] Roosevelt wrote to the Motion Picture Research Council.

1,594. Pacific Geographic Society
Records. 1927-40. Ca. 5000 items.
Open. Register.
Stanford University Libraries, Manuscripts Division.
Founded in 1926 as an educational organization to promote western natural history and sciences, the Society, centered in Los Angeles, reorganized in 1929 and was disbanded in ca. 1940. Organizational papers, minutes, correspondence, reports, bills and receipts, notes, memos, photos, legal papers, press releases, programs, clippings, pamphlets, and other records, including correspondence and other items of M. Jeanette Gause, manager and booking agent; Margaret E. Hughs, secretary and manager; Carolyn Ware, manager; and Mrs. Martin Johnson. Contains information regarding aviator Amelia Earhart, conservationist Minerva Hamilton Hoyt, and author Alice (Ames) Winter.

1,595. Pacific Slopes
Collection. 1893-95, nd. Ca. 0.5 ft.
Open. Register.
Stanford University Libraries, Manuscripts Division.
Correspondence, reminiscences, interviews, theses, and term papers written and collected by Mary (Sheldon) Barnes and other faculty members and students at Stanford University relate to the history of the Pacific states. Concerns such topics as the Greek-Russian church of San Francisco, an 1844 overland journey to California, California missions, and the route of Governor Portola's expedition in 1769. Also contains a letter of Jessie [Mrs. John C.] Frémont regarding the conquest of California.

1,596. Park, Alice
Papers. 1920-36. 40 items.
Open. Register.
Stanford University Libraries, Manuscripts Division.
Correspondence and pamphlets of [Mrs.] Park, who was active in the planned parenthood and birth control movements, include correspondence with Mary Ware Dennett, Margaret Sanger, Albert P. Van Dusen, the American Birth Control League, and the Voluntary Parenthood League and pamphlets pertaining to the Northern California Birth Control Committee of One Hundred.

1,597. Parsons, Lucena Pfuffer
Papers. 1850. 1 vol.
Open. Descriptive summary.
Stanford University Libraries, Manuscripts Division.
Journal of Parsons, a pioneer, regarding an overland journey west from Wisconsin.

1,598. Peirce Family
Papers. Ca. 1856-95. Ca. 4.5 ft. and 14 boxes.
Access restricted. Register.
Stanford University Libraries, Manuscripts Division.
Correspondence, a diary, business and legal papers, a ledger, and photos of George H. Peirce and his wife Lydia Ellen (Eaton) Peirce (1839-1903). The collection consists primarily of letters George Peirce wrote while he was a hemp trader in Manila in the Philippines. Also includes notebooks of Lydia Peirce containing verse, expense accounts, and recipes and a register containing Peirce family genealogical information. Includes correspondence from 1856 to 1895 of Lydia Peirce, including a letter regarding Nathaniel Hawthorne's daughter, whom she had met; correspondence from 1856 to 1880 of George Peirce's sister Eliza Peirce; correspondence from 1856 to 1873 of Eliza (Mitchell) Peirce (1784-1887); correspondence from 1856 to 1873 of Emily Mitchell Peirce (1839-1923), who was in Europe; and letters from numerous other family members and friends. Contains information about the Civil War.

1,599. Rose, Alice M.
Papers. 1900-43. 1.5 ft.
Open. Register.
Stanford University Libraries, Manuscripts Division.
Correspondence, journals, autobiographies, and reports of interviews of Rose regarding the Progressive movement and the Lincoln-Roosevelt Republican League. Includes correspondence between Rose and League leaders.

1,600. Smith, Lorna Dysart
Papers. 1928-70. 0.5 ft.
Open. Register.
Stanford University Libraries, Manuscripts Division.
Correspondence, manuscripts, clippings, and other papers of [Mrs. Byron B.] Smith (1897-). Includes correspondence with Molly Castle, wife of William Tucker and mother of Sally Belfrage; Lady Bird Johnson, wife of Lyndon B. Johnson; Alice Scully, wife of Frank Scully; and Jeannette Hopkins. Also contains manuscripts regarding Theodore Dreiser and Frank Scully, notes from the 1965 annual meeting of Women in Community Service (WICS), and a WICS calendar of events at the Cleveland Job Corps center for women.

1,601. Stegner, Wallace
Papers. Nd. 1 box.
Open. Preliminary accession guide.
Stanford University Libraries, Manuscripts Division.
Notes, illustrations, research material, and excerpts from the published works of Stegner, an artist and author, regarding Mary Hallock Foote.

1,602. Urmy, Clarence
Papers. Nd. 1 ft.
Open. Register.
Stanford University Libraries, Manuscripts Division.
Collection includes one folder of letters to Urmy from [Miss] Ina Coolbrith, manuscript poems written by Coolbrith, and manuscripts by Mabel (Urmy) Seares and Laura Bell Everett about Urmy and Coolbrith.

1,603. Wiggin, Kate Douglas (Smith)
Papers. Ca. 1884. 9 items.
Open. Register.
Stanford University Libraries, Manuscripts Division.
[Mrs. Samuel Bradley] Wiggin (1856-1923), an educator, was involved in the development of the kindergarten system. A notebook containing lectures, abstracts, and examples of handicrafts for children compiled by a student in Wiggin's kindergarten training courses and a letter from Wiggin to the student.

1,604. Williams, Mary Wilhelmine
Papers. 1911-43. 1.5 ft.
Open. Register.
Stanford University Libraries, Manuscripts Division.
Correspondence, diaries, manuscripts, photos, and articles of Williams (1878-1944), a history professor at Goucher College in Maryland. Includes correspondence with Heloise Brainerd of the Women's International League for Peace and Freedom, US section, regarding inter-American cooperation; with the US state department concerning a convention for the promotion of inter-American cultural relations; and with Anne (Morrow) Lindbergh in 1931. Also contains letters written from 1926 to 1927 while Williams was in Latin America on an educational survey for the AAUW and other correspondence relating to a meeting of the American Historical Association, to the Kensington Stone Controversy, and to her book about Dom Pedro. Also contains diaries that she kept in Latin America, Mexico, and England; manuscripts of articles she wrote; and printed articles and reviews by and about her. Williams earned her PhD in 1914.

1,605. Younger, J. Arthur
Papers. 1954-64. 12.5 ft.
Partially closed. Register.
Stanford University Libraries, Manuscripts Division.
Manuscripts, bills, and printed material that Younger compiled during his term as a Republican US representative from California. Contains items regarding congresswomen Marguerite Stitt Church from Illinois, Catherine May from Washington, Patsy T. Mink from Hawaii, Edith N. Rogers from Massachusetts, and Katharine St. George from New York; news correspondent Nancy H. Dickerson; newspaper publisher Elizabeth R. Farrington; Republican National Committee member Pearl Carter Pace; author Ruth P. Thompson; and Clare (Boothe) Luce, a playwright, ambassador, and congresswoman from Connecticut. Also includes information on labor, orphanages, the American National Red Cross, housing, civil rights, Indian affairs, and the State Department's report concerning Amelia Earhart.

1,606. Bataan Peninsula, Philippine Islands
Collection. 1941-46. 1 vol.
Open. No guide.
Stanford University Medical Center, Lane Medical Library.
Scrapbook of clippings concerning the experiences of the nurses who were captured on the Bataan Peninsula during WWII.

1,607. Brown, Adelaide
Papers. 1921-30. 1 box.
Open. No guide.
Stanford University Medical Center, Lane Medical Library.
Correspondence, unpublished papers, and pamphlets of Brown (1868-1940), a San Francisco physician, contain information on prenatal care in California, child hygiene, and the health of adolescent girls.

1,608. Lane, Pauline C. (Sampson)
Papers. 1882-1900. 2 vols.
Open. No guide.
Stanford University Medical Center, Lane Medical Library.
Papers of Lane (1837?-1902), wife of Levi Cooper Lane, a San Francisco physician, consist of a poem she wrote, household bills, passenger lists from voyages she made with her husband, and clippings of poems. Levi Cooper Lane was the nephew of Elias C. Cooper, founder of Cooper Medical College, which was established in 1859 in San Francisco and was the forerunner of Stanford University medical school.

STOCKTON

1,609. Booth, Edmund, Family
Papers. Nd. Ca. 2 ft.
Open. No guide.
Pioneer Museum and Haggin Galleries.
Papers collected for a history of this family, which was published as *Edmund Booth, 1810-1905, Forty-Niner: The Life Story of a Deaf Pioneer,* include ca. 25 letters between Booth and his wife Mary Ann Booth, 1849-53.

1,610. Fowler, Grace Georgia
Papers. Ca. 1890-1955. Ca. 5 in.
Open. No guide.
Pioneer Museum and Haggin Galleries.
Papers of [Miss] Fowler (1890-), a Stockton high school teacher and a member of the Mills College class of 1911, consist of diaries she kept between 1904 and 1912; a memory and fellowship book from college, which contains registers of friends at Mills, pamphlets on house rules and activities, greeting cards, photos, and memorabilia; and a ca. 1955 household book in which Fowler recorded her antiques and furniture, her paperweight collection, and various recipes, remedies, and household hints.

1,611. Gordon, Laura (de Force)
Papers. Nd. 1 folder.
Open. No guide.
Pioneer Museum and Haggin Galleries.
Papers of [Mrs. Charles H.] Gordon (1838-1907), an attorney and advocate of women's rights, consist of a diary she wrote at the age of 12, a copy of her appointment to the California bar, a photo, and ephemera.

1,612. Haggin, Eila Butterworth
Papers. Nd. No size given.
Access restricted. Card catalog.
Pioneer Museum and Haggin Galleries.
Personal correspondence, diaries, Haggin and McKee family papers, and photo and post card albums of Haggin (1874-1939), a philanthropist and world traveler who became the Countess Festeties de Tolna and later Mrs. Robert T. McKee. Includes letters from famous persons.

1,613. Lambda Theta Phi Sorority, Zeta Chapter
Records. 1897-1974. 1 vol.
Open. No guide.
Pioneer Museum and Haggin Galleries.
Scrapbooks of the Zeta Chapter of this Stockton high school sorority contain the constitution, bylaws, minutes of meetings, membership rosters, autographs of members, photos, clippings, and memorabilia pertaining to the Chapter's activities.

1,614. Photo Archives
Collection. Ca. 1850-1950. Ca. 4500 items.
Open. Index.
Pioneer Museum and Haggin Galleries.
This collection of photos and post cards contains pictures of women agricultural workers, industry and factory employees, and teachers as well as women engaged in domestic and family activities.

1,615. Stockton High School, Parent-Teacher Association
Records. 1940s-50s. 3 vols.
Open. No guide.
Pioneer Museum and Haggin Galleries.
Scrapbooks of clippings concern the PTA, Stockton women's clubs, the Stockton Presbyterian church, and the Stockton Youth Center, which was sponsored by the PTA Council.

1,616. Stockton Tennis Club
Records. 1897-1908. 1 vol.
Open. No guide.
Pioneer Museum and Haggin Galleries.
Minute book contains information on the establishment and organization of the Club, founded in 1897, as well as bylaws, minutes of meetings, and a roster of members, approximately one-half of whom were women.

1,617. Yardley, Ralph
Papers. Ca. 1880s-1925. 900 items.
Open. Index.
Pioneer Museum and Haggin Galleries.
Original sketches by Yardley (1878-1961), an illustrator for the *Stockton Record,* depict life in Stockton. Includes sketches of women subjects and of families engaged in leisure activities.

1,618. Index to the Stockton Record
Finding aid. Nd. 2 drawers.
Open. No guide.
Stockton-San Joaquin County Public Library.
Card index to this local newspaper, which is still extant, provides access to articles about woman suffrage activities in the area between 1870 and 1897, the woman's congress that met in Stockton in 1897, the AAUW, the LWV, the WACs, the Women's Ambulance and Defense Corps, and the Women's Land Army. Also contains access to information on Stockton women's clubs, apparel shops, and editorials about outstanding achievements of local women.

1,619. Black, James, Family
Papers. 1858-65. 321 pp.
Open. Summary and card index.
University of the Pacific, Pacific Center for Western Studies.
Correspondence of James Black, a Texas pioneer and Confederate officer on coastal defense duty near Galveston, TX, and of his wife Patience Black (1842-69). Also includes a biography written by Patience Black.

1,620. Bolt Family
Papers. 1893-1973. 42 Hollinger boxes.
Open. Unpublished guide.
University of the Pacific, Pacific Center for Western Studies.
Correspondence; diaries; photos, including family portraits and glass slide transparencies; and other papers of the Bolt family. Includes diaries of Beatrice Rebecca (French) Bolt (1880-1974), a genealogist, poet, Methodist, avid reader, and daughter of Henry M. French (1851-1916). She graduated in 1900 from San Jose State Normal School, later known as San Jose State University, in California and in 1905 from Stanford University. In 1908 she married Richard Arthur Bolt (1880-1959), a medical doctor who specialized in child health, and they had four children, Elizabeth, Robert, Marrion Jane, and Richard Henry. In 1969 Beatrice Bolt became a sponsoring member of the Pacific Center for Western Historical Studies at the University of the Pacific.

1,621. Brame, Herbert
Papers. 1934-36. Ca. 6 in.
Open. Inventory and summary.
University of the Pacific, Pacific Center for Western Studies.
Papers of Brame, editor of the *Pony Express Courier,* include correspondence, manuscript articles, and illustrative material from contributors relating to the California gold rush, immigration to California, the Nez Percé Indians, the Donner tragedy, Lake Tahoe, and a history of mining in Nevada. Contains letters from Anne (Bancroft) Graham regarding her grandfather H. H. Bancroft, her upcoming wedding, and her work on a Ben Holladay biography as well as correspondence and a manuscript of [Miss] Effie Johnston, a member of a pioneer family in San Andreas, CA, concerning the life of her father Wade Johnston, sheep ranching, and local pioneers.

1,622. Camp Fire Girls
Records. 1919-22. 4 vols.
Open. Card index.
University of the Pacific, Pacific Center for Western Studies.
Yearbooks from a summer camp of the Camp Fire Girls of Stockton contain notes on daily activities, photos and illustrations, a chronology, texts of songs, and scripts for theatrical productions.

1,623. Cook, Guy
Papers. 1942-46. 5 boxes.
Open. Inventory and summary.
University of the Pacific, Pacific Center for Western Studies.
Papers of Cook relating to Japanese Americans during WWII contain narrative reports of teachers at the Tule Lake Relocation Center near Newell, CA, with accounts of Madelone Carper, Estelle Palonis, Leda R. Lisle, Elsie S. Dunbar, and Dorothy Phillips. Also contains student autobiographies and an account regarding an American woman's experiences in a Japanese camp in the Philippines.

1,624. Dugger, Minnie L.
Papers. 1951-60. 15 vols. and 12 items.
Open. Summary and card index.
University of the Pacific, Pacific Center for Western Studies.
Cashbook, register, and other papers of Dugger, the proprietor of the Hotel Minnie in Stockton.

1,625. Emendian Society
Records. Nd. 1 Hollinger box.
Open. No guide.
University of the Pacific, Pacific Center for Western Studies.
Allegedly the first female literary society west of the Mississippi River, the Society, whose members were students at the University of the Pacific, was organized in 1858. The group became Epsilon Lambda Sigma in 1925 and affiliated with Delta Gamma in 1959. Includes minutes, scrapbooks, and a history.

1,626. Flower, Elsie
Papers. 1900-68. 3.25 ft.
Open. Summary.
University of the Pacific, Pacific Center for Western Studies.
Flower (1886-1968) was a journalist, society editor for the *Stockton Record* from ca. 1925 to 1945, and a news writer for radio station KGMD from 1945 to 1957. Family and business correspondence, notes, writings, typescripts of newscasts, photos, and pamphlets pertaining to Stockton social life, San Joaquin Valley farming, and California history.

1,627. Foulk, Nina
Papers. 1864-1923. Ca. 75 items.
Open. Summary and card index.
University of the Pacific, Pacific Center for Western Studies.
Papers of Foulk, a teacher, consist primarily of family correspondence regarding such topics as the women's rights movement in Mississippi, mining in California, and the San Francisco earthquake and fire of 1906.

1,628. Fountain, Susie Baker
Papers. 1850-ca. 1964. 1 vol.
Open. Card index.
University of the Pacific, Pacific Center for Western Studies.
Scrapbook of Fountain containing a narrative history published serially in the *Blue Lake Advocate* in 1964 and letters that were written in 1903 by Eleanor E. Tracy, a Humboldt County, CA, schoolteacher.

1,629. Goodman, Minerva
Papers. 1904-11. 1 vol. and ca. 75 items.
Open. Summary.
University of the Pacific, Pacific Center for Western Studies.
Goodman was a Stockton physician and secretary of the Political Equality Club, which was affiliated with the California Equal Suffrage Association. Correspondence, a minute book, an annual report for 1908, and broadsides relating to the California woman suffrage movement.

1,630. Hazelton Family
Papers. 1830-1904. 125 items.
Open. Summary.
University of the Pacific, Pacific Center for Western Studies.
Correspondence of a New England family contains descriptions of a post-1849 ocean voyage to California; mining and merchant business; a soldier's life and hospital conditions during the Civil War; social, school, and family matters; and pioneer life in Colorado and Illinois. This collection is published in part in the *Pacific Historian* (1957).

1,631. International Society of Christian Endeavor
Records. 1931. 1 vol.
Open. No guide.
University of the Pacific, Pacific Center for Western Studies.
Scrapbook containing clippings, articles, memorabilia, and ephemera compiled in commemoration of the 50th anniversary of the Society, also known as the Christian Endeavor Society, which was founded in 1881. Includes information about the Society's founder Harriet Elizabeth Abbott, who was married to Francis E. Clark. Abbott was also referred to as Mother Clark.

1,632. Locke and Hammond Family
Papers. 1849-1925. Ca. 20 boxes.
Partially restricted. Inventory and summary.
University of the Pacific, Pacific Center for Western Studies.
Papers of this pioneer family of Lockeford in San Joaquin County, CA, which was named for the Locke family, include diaries and account books of Delia Marcella (Hammond) Locke (1836-1923) and diaries and a Stockton High School secretary's book of Theresa (Locke) Thorpe (1879-?). Also contains records and a history written by Delia Locke of the First Congregational Church of Lockeford; records of the Lockeford Band of Hope, a temperance organization, 1868-70; records of the Mokelumne River Ladies Sewing Circle, 1857-93; records of the Lockeford Soldier's Aid Society, 1864-65; and daily journals of the Locke Family School, ca. 1865-80.

1,633. Miller Family
Papers. 1898-ca. 1905. Ca. 1000 items.
Open. Description.
University of the Pacific, Pacific Center for Western Studies.
Photos of the Miller family depicting Dawson Settlement in the Yukon Territory during the gold rush, Lenora (Huntley) Miller and her daughter [Miss] Gertrude Miller in Dawson, and Gertrude Miller in Stockton, where she was the unified school district librarian.

1,634. Miscellaneous Small Collections
Collection. Nd. No size given.
Open. Card index.
University of the Pacific, Pacific Center for Western Studies.
Included in this collection are ca. 105 items, one volume, and 22 pages pertaining to 14 women and one women's organization from 1852 to 1970. Contains correspondence, a diary, reminiscences, monographs, texts to addresses, business papers, a biographical sketch, an obituary, articles, and other papers regarding travel to and within California; the history of and pioneers in various areas in California, including Yosemite, Napa County, San Joaquin, and Pinole; journeying to Mexico; the Grand Army of the Republic; and other topics. Among the women represented are a poet, a California pioneer teacher and rancher, a museum curator, and the owner of a livery business. Contains family correspondence of Hannah Frances Crabbe, a Portland, OR, resident, regarding home front conditions during WWI and poverty in China; papers of Madie Brown Emparan, a conservationist and historian, including a letter from Linnie Marsh Wolfe, notes regarding John McLaren, and minutes of the John Muir Association for 1941; a notebook of Jeannette Reames, who became the actress Janet Leigh, written while she was a student at the University of the Pacific in 1946; and membership applications of the Pioneers of California ladies auxiliary in Stockton from 1953 to 1957. The applications contain information regarding family history and genealogy.

1,635. Muir, John
Papers. 1858-1914. Ca. 17.5 ft.
Access restricted. Inventory and summary.
University of the Pacific, Pacific Center for Western Studies.
Papers of Muir include letters from his sisters Sarah Galloway and Mary Muir Hand, his daughter Helen Muir, his nieces Anna G. Galloway and Cecilia Galloway, his cousin Susan M. Gilroy, authors Ina Coolbrith and Helen Hunt Jackson, [Mrs.] Annie Kennedy Bidwell, [Mrs.] Jeanne C. Carr, Katherine Merrill Graydon, Mary Francis Kellogg, [Mrs.] Julia Merrill Moores, and other women.

1,636. Oakland, California School Women's Club
Records. 1912-ca. 1942. 6 vols. and ca. 20 items.
Open. Inventory and summary.
University of the Pacific, Pacific Center for Western Studies.
Minutes, a manuscript, a register, bulletins, and clippings of this social and service organization for female schoolteachers, founded in 1912. Its activities included a day nursery, a building bond campaign, and representation in the California Teachers' Association. Also includes research notes for a Club history written by [Miss] Joyce E. Lobner in 1942 for the Club's Loan Fund, which continued operation after the Oakland Teachers' Association took over the Club's functions in 1925.

1,637. Paden, Irene
Papers. 1931-52. Ca. 3 ft.
Open. Summary and card index.
University of the Pacific, Pacific Center for Western Studies.
Manuscripts and research notes and material of Paden, an author and traveler, for her three books on western history. Her notes contain transcriptions of diaries written by travelers on the Oregon Trail. Also includes Paden's journals pertaining to her travels with her husband and friends.

1,638. Pond, Inez (Henderson)
Papers. 1916-65. Ca. 8 ft.
Open. Summary and card index.
University of the Pacific, Pacific Center for Western Studies.
Correspondence, notes, and manuscripts of short stories of Pond, an art collector, columnist, and historian, regarding William Keith, California and Stockton history, and San Francisco Bay area social life and customs.

1,639. Rhodes and Smith
Papers. 1838-1942. Ca. 0.25 ft.
Open. Summary and card index.
University of the Pacific, Pacific Center for Western Studies.
Collection contains letters that Mary W. Kimball Rhodes, wife of Colonel Elisha A. Rhodes, wrote to her son Edward A. Rhodes. Includes an 1843 letter in which she describes General Houston's character and career as president of the Texas republic and an 1861 letter in which she discusses sectional hostilities in California and expresses her pro-South convictions. Also includes poems by Mary Rhodes.

1,640. Sargent, Shirley
Papers. Nd. 1 box.
Open. No guide.
University of the Pacific, Pacific Center for Western Studies.
Papers of Sargent, an author of books about California's Yosemite area, include correspondence with publishers; manuscripts of *Yosemite Tomboy* and of her works on John Muir, Jessie Benton Frémont, and women pioneers in Yosemite; royalty statements; and a book jacket biography of Sargent.

1,641. Stockton Poetry Society
Records. Ca. 1940-50. Ca. 944 items.
Open. Card index.
University of the Pacific, Pacific Center for Western Studies.
Manuscripts of poetry written by Society members, among them Dorothea Amend, Alice C. Beighley, Theodosia Benjamin, Edith Farey, Amanda Field, Grace M. Miller, and Lirrel Starling.

1,642. Stuart, Winifred (Bendel)
Papers. 1950-65. Ca. 10 ft.
Open. Summary and card index.
University of the Pacific, Pacific Center for Western Studies.
Correspondence, business papers, clippings, and other papers of [Mrs.] Stuart, a politician and historian, regarding her service as a councilwoman of Fremont, CA; Fremont politics; and the history of Washington Township, CA, and southern Alameda County, CA.

1,643. Taverner, Margaret B.
Papers. 1951-61. 1 vol. and ca. 350 items.
Open. Summary and card index.
University of the Pacific, Pacific Center for Western Studies.
Notes and a scrapbook of Taverner, a teacher and writer, relating to the lives, travels, and writings of Mark Twain and Bret Harte.

1,644. U.S. Chinese Bureau
Records. Ca. 1904. Ca. 0.5 ft.
Open. No guide.
University of the Pacific, Pacific Center for Western Studies.
San Francisco Chinatown residential inspection records consist of a register listing names, occupations, and addresses of residents and a brief description of living conditions.

1,645. Van Gilder, Florence Scott
Papers. Ca. 1918-33. 1 ft.
Open. Summary and card index.
University of the Pacific, Pacific Center for Western Studies.
Manuscripts and printed material of Van Gilder, a lecturer in Americanization and methods of teaching English to foreigners at the University of the Pacific. Includes lecture notes, texts of public addresses, instructional material, and publications regarding naturalization, assimilation, family, home, and community.

1,646. Withee, Louisa A.
Papers. 1890-1920. 73 items.
Open. Summary and card index.
University of the Pacific, Pacific Center for Western Studies.
Correspondence of Withee with her sister Helen A.

(Manville) [Mrs. Charles A.] Pope, a poet living in South America.

1,647. Woods, Virna
Papers. 1880-1925. 9 Hollinger boxes.
Open. Inventory and summary.
University of the Pacific, Pacific Center for Western Studies.
Correspondence, manuscripts, photos, clippings, an obituary, published items, and other papers of Woods (?-1903), an actress and author of plays, novels, short stories, and poems. Includes correspondence with publishers and producers of her plays and letters from William Ewart Gladstone and Leo Tolstoy's son Latianer Tolstoy expressing their appreciation of her work. Also contains correspondence of Virna Woods's sister Anna Woods, who managed Virna's estate after her death from pneumonia, and papers of the Woods family.

1,648. Young, Eleanor
Papers. Ca. 1901-60. Ca. 60 items.
Open. Summary and card index.
University of the Pacific, Pacific Center for Western Studies.
Papers of [Miss] Young, a Stockton genealogist, include genealogical notes on the Browne, Fagg, Gillum, Martin, Porter, Reynolds, Roberts, and Snowden families and compositions she wrote while attending Stockton High School.

1,649. Zimmermann, Rheta L.
Papers. 1934-53. Ca. 100 items.
Open. Inventory and summary.
University of the Pacific, Pacific Center for Western Studies.
Correspondence, manuscripts, minutes, pictures, clippings, and other papers of [Mrs. W. F. C.] Zimmermann, who was historian for the Yerba Buena Parlor of the Native Daughters of the Golden West and active in the preservation and marking of historical landmarks in the San Francisco Bay area and in Columbia, CA. She also participated in approximately one dozen other area clubs and associations.

SUNNYVALE

1,650. Trubschenck, Ida
Papers. 1870-1952. 152 items.
Open. Unpublished guide.
Sunnyvale Historical Society and Museum Association.
Papers of [Miss] Trubschenck (1886-), city clerk of the city of Sunnydale for 44 years, consist of material from her work, programs of public events in which she performed with her violin, musical scores, insurance records, and memorabilia.

THOUSAND OAKS

1,651. Archives
Records. 1924-77. 10 boxes and 1 vol.
Access restricted. No guide.
Sisters of Notre Dame Convent.
Correspondence of the superior general and others, accounts of the founding of convents, photos, clippings, and other records. Members of the order, which was founded in 1924 in Los Angeles, teach in elementary and high schools.

TOPANGA

1,652. Suffragists and Feminists
Oral history. 1972- . Ca. 25 tapes.
Open. Unpublished guide.
Feminist History Research Project.
Oral histories of eight women who were involved in the suffrage movement in nonleadership capacities between the 1900s and the 1920s contain autobiographical information but focus primarily on these women's suffrage activities. Interviewees discuss the effect of suffrage activities on their later lives and careers, their attitudes toward feminism, and their assessment of the their attitudes toward modern feminism, and their assessment of the strategy and tactics employed during the campaign for suffrage, as compared with those used today.

Consists of interviews with Jessie (Haver) Butler, a Washington, DC, lobbyist for the National Consumers' League and a public speaking teacher, who toured the western states with Carrie Chapman Catt during the 1919-20 ratification drive; Miriam Allen deFord, a writer who became involved with suffrage at the age of 14 in Philadelphia and later in radical politics and labor reporting after her move to California in 1915; May Goldman, a Barnard College student who participated in a suffrage parade in New York in 1915 and later married and became a housewife; Ernestine (Hara) Kettler, who was arrested and served time for picketing the White House in 1917, and who in later years worked with the Industrial Workers of the World and various trade unions; Lorine Pruette, author of *Women and Leisure* and other feminist writings during the 1920s and 1930s; Laura (Ellsworth) Seiler, an advertising executive who formed the first suffrage club at Cornell University in 1913 and who later joined the Women's Political Union, touring the western counties of New York in a suffrage drive; Sylvie Thygeson, a birth control advocate who was involved in the suffrage movement in Minneapolis and St. Paul, MN, during the mid-1910s; and Eva (Marshall) Totah, a Quaker, member of the LWV, and a missionary in Palestine until 1948, who discusses being disappointed about suffrage. In addition, Thygeson talks about the relationship between the birth control and suffrage movements.

1,653. Women and Work
Oral history. 1972. Ca. 25 tapes.
Open. Unpublished guide.
Feminist History Research Project.
Autobiographical interviews in which women employed largely in unskilled jobs during the early part of the 20th century discuss their lives and work. Includes interviews with sharecroppers, tenant farmers, domestics and laundry workers, telephone operators, a cigar maker who became a homesteader in Montana during the 1910s, and saleswomen, including a traveling saleswoman who sold Chautauqua desks during the 1920s.

1,654. Women as Reformers, Radicals, and Revolutionaries
Oral history. 1972- . Ca. 59 tapes.
Open. Unpublished guide.
Feminist History Research Project.
Autobiographical interviews focusing on the political activities of eight women who were active in organizing Socialist party, Communist party, and other left-wing groups, as well as women who were active in early civil rights work in the South and women who ran for political offices representing various Socialist-Communist alliances.

Includes interviews with Genora Johnson Dollinger, founder of a Socialist party local in Flint, MI, during the early 1930s, who later was an organizer and political candidate for the Socialist Workers party until her expulsion from the party in 1953; "Mother" Mary Holloway, a black church and clubwoman who was active in missionary societies and a charter member of the NAACP; Dora Keyser, an anarchist who was involved in cooperative houses in New York and a member of the Ferrer Colony in Stilton, NJ, and Sunrise Farm in upstate New York; Yetta Land, a "people's lawyer" active in International Labor Defense cases and civil rights defense cases, who ran for office on the Farm Labor ticket in Ohio and as a Communist party candidate in Cleveland; Barbara Nestor, a charter member of the Communist party, who was active in the International Labor Defense during the 1920s and the mother of Communist leader Dorothy Healey; and Olive Stone, founder of the Southern Committee for People's Rights during the early 1930s in North Carolina.

1,655. Women in Business, Entertainment, and the Professions
Oral history. 1972- . Ca. 46 tapes.
Open. Unpublished guide.
Feminist History Research Project.
Autobiographical interviews with 19 women who began careers during the first three decades of the century, including schoolteachers, professors, realtors, a funeral parlor operator, a radio announcer, a ventriloquist, and a lawyer, focus on the professional experiences of each as well as discrimination and other kinds of problems each of these women faced in their respective fields.

Includes interviews in which Mildred Baer, a teacher who was fired during the 1920s from a school in San Bernardino, CA, for immoral behavior (wearing her hem above the knee), discusses her life as a single woman; Rosalind Cassidy, the first female full professor (in kinesiology) at UCLA, who was instrumental in introducing modern dance to the West Coast, talks about attitudes toward competition in women's sports and the differences between teaching at a women's college and a coeducational institution; Elizabeth Cuddeback, a public health nurse in Kern County, CA, from 1912 until her retirement at age 82, who served as a midwife and nurse for the Indians; Rosemary Hays, a speech and drama teacher at Stanford and Palo Alto area schools in California and later a realtor, who was raised in a convent until she went to college, and who was married for two years, describes her life as a divorced woman during the 1920s and 1930s; and Mildred Lightfoot, who became a nurse after her father's death forced her to abandon her plans for medical school and whose husband pressured her after WWI to give up her career, discusses her feelings about the conflict between marriage and a career. In the 1940s Lightfoot became an x-ray technician. Also includes interviews with Crystal Marshall, a black entrepreneur who worked as a domestic, a homesteader, and caterer as well as for the black weekly newspaper in Los Angeles, *New Age,* and whose father was a former slave and Mississippi senator during Reconstruction and whose mother was a white New England teacher; and with Barbara Sargent, a teacher, pre-school nursery director, and YWCA executive whose work involved a post in Brazil in 1917.

1,656. Women in the Labor Movement
Oral history. 1972- . Ca. 99 tapes.
Open. Unpublished guide.
Feminist History Research Project.
Tapes of autobiographical interviews with 24 rank and file labor women, whose activities date back to the beginning of the century, focus on organizing, working conditions, and participation in strikes. Most of the women worked in the needle trades, but the collection also contains interviews with cigar makers, an office worker, a UAW founding member, and several middle-class women who were active in labor groups and activities.

Includes interviews of Rebecca August, a clothing trade worker who helped found and organize the Hebrew Trades Council in Chicago from 1904 to 1910 and who also worked with the Industrial Workers of the World in Seattle from 1910 to 1920; Anita Castro, the first Spanish-speaking woman organizer and business agent in the Los Angeles Local of the International Ladies' Garment Workers' Union; Genora Johnson Dollinger, an organizer of the Women's Emergency Brigade during the 1937 sit-ins at General Motors in Flint, MI; Rebecca (Goldberg) Holland, an organizer for the International Ladies' Garment Workers' Union from 1912 to 1925; Yetta Land, a cigar maker and organizer at the age of 14 of a local cigar makers union in Cleveland, who later developed a career as a labor and civil rights attorney; Grace McDonald, founder of the Workers Health Bureau in 1920; and Sarah Rozner, one of the founders and the first woman business agent in the Woman's Local of the Amalgamated Clothing Workers of America in 1920 in Chicago.

1,657. Women's Lives
Oral history. 1972- . Ca. 100 tapes.
Open. Unpublished guide.
Feminist History Research Project.
Autobiographical interviews of ca. 40 women from a variety of backgrounds, who played the traditional female role in the US during the first four decades of the 20th century. Interviewees discuss such topics as clothing, the onset of menses, birth control knowledge and practices, raising children, marriage, and volunteer activities.

WEAVERVILLE

1,658. Shasta College Evening Division
Records. 1970-71. 2 vols.
Open. No guide.
Weaverville Free Library.
Copies of student papers on family history include papers on Mrs. Thayer Bremer and Douglas County, 1880-1908, and Weaverville; [Mrs.] Myrtle Everest and Trinity County, 1918-70; pioneer women from the Hayfork area; and Eliza Todd and Mrs. Michael Perch, pioneer women of the early 1850s. Also includes a diary of [Mrs.] Jessie Wise of Wise Station, Trinity County, 1906-07.

1,659. Trinity County Historical Society
Records. 1955-74. 2 vols.
Open. No guide.
Weaverville Free Library.
Yearbooks of the Society contain sketches of prominent women and families in the area, including Phoebe Allen, Mary Fallon Coyle, Berena Cole Van Matre, Almire Heath Van Matre, Edna Thayer Bremer, Louisa Shufford, and Henrietta Ewing, who was known as the "first lady" of Weaverville.

1,660. Weaverville Name File
Finding aid. Nd. 4 drawers.
Open. No guide.
Weaverville Free Library.
This information and reference file about local residents was compiled from the local newspaper *Trinity Journal* from 1860 to date. It contains several women's names.

YREKA

1,661. Biography Files
Collection. Nd. No size given.
Open. No guide.
Siskiyou County Public Library.
Pamphlet and clippings files contain a three-page radio script about Sophia Bullock "Auntie" Fellows, who was described as the "first lady" of Berryvale, CA. Early settlers of northern California, she and her husband Joseph Fellows started the community of Berryvale; its first industry, a barrel and tub factory; and the Mount Shasta Hotel. Auntie Fellows was also appointed Berryvale's first postmistress.

1,662. Indians of North America, California
Collection. Nd. No size given.
Open. No guide.
Siskiyou County Public Library.
Clippings on local Indians include a 1961 clipping about and photo of Florence Harrie, a Karok Indian basket weaver; a clipping in which Madeline Davis and Alice Dunaway, Karok Indian basket weavers who lived in Happy Camp in Siskiyou County, describe the weaving of baskets and their use for cooking and other household purposes; a 1975 clipping about United Tribes programs for training nurses aides and a photo of graduates; and a photo and clipping of [Mrs.] Anna May Copperfield about her reminiscences of childhood and early Modoc Indian tribal customs. Copperfield was the granddaughter of Winema, who testified in Washington, DC, about the Modoc Indian War.

1,663. Oral History Tape Files
Oral history. Ca. 1970- . Ca. 14 tapes.
Open. No guide.
Siskiyou County Public Library.
Includes an interview in which Gracie Kouts, who moved to Klamathon in Siskiyou County in 1902, describes her journey with her family during the 1890s to Yreka and Klamathon from Washington, KS. She talks about logging, residents, and other aspects of local history; she also describes her early life in Kansas. Also contains interviews in which Ethel C. Ackerman recounts the history of the Ackerman Drug Store in Yreka and provides information on area houses and families; Aura E. Martin, whose mother was a full-blooded Indian, relates the history of the Happy Camp area, where she was born; Lucille Morgan, whose grandfather was Daniel Ream and whose father was a legislator, describes the history of the Mount Shasta and Yreka areas; and Katherine George, a lifelong resident of Missouri Bar in Siskiyou County, relates the history of the area and of other residents as well as reminiscences of her life and childhood as one of seven children. Also includes interviews with [Mrs.] Mabel Glidden, Ethel (Otto) Sargent, and Rose Jane (Bean) Shaffer, whose second cousin was Judge Roy Bean and whose father Pearl Bean helped kill the last large grizzly bear in the area.

1,664. Siskiyou County History
Collection. Nd. No size given.
Open. No guide.
Siskiyou County Public Library.
Manuscript and typescript papers, pamphlets, and clippings about the County's history. Includes a 15-page manuscript in which Mary Shinar of Hornbrook, CA, the daughter of an Indian woman, describes her life and experiences with the Indians of northern California and "My Playhouse Was a Concord Stage Coach," a four-page article by [Mrs.] Mae Helene Bacon Boggs about the difficulties of transportation during the 1880s.

CANAL ZONE

BALBOA HEIGHTS

1,665. Hibbard, Mary Eugenie
Papers. 1938. 10 pp.
Open. Published guide.
Canal Zone Library-Museum.
Memoir of [Miss] Hibbard concerns her experiences as head nurse at Ancon Hospital from 1904 to 1906. She was the first chief nurse in the Canal Zone under the US administration. See *Subject Catalog of the Special Panama Collection of the Canal Zone Library-Museum* (Boston: G. K. Hall, 1964).

1,666. Roosevelt Medal Holders' Reminiscences
Oral history. 1958. 45 pp.
Open. Unpublished guide.
Canal Zone Library-Museum.
Transcriptions of taped reminiscences of 35 persons who were involved in construction of the Panama Canal. The interviews were conducted during a celebration marking the centennial of the birth of Theodore Roosevelt, the President who started construction of the Canal. Women interviewed were Mary Macel (Butler) [Mrs. Alfred W.] Goulet, Gertrude B. Hoffmann, Mary C. (Morrison) [Mrs. George] Lowe, Mrs. John Reese, Mrs. Bruce G. Sanders, Anne Bell [Mrs. Maurice H.] Thatcher, Edith R. [Mrs. Fred DeSales] Willson, and Grace Radcliffe Wright. Six of the women were wives of US citizens who worked on the canal for at least two years during the construction period; the other two worked for the canal administration before their marriages.

COLORADO

BOULDER

1,667. Colorado State Federation of Women's Clubs
Records. 1895-1961. 2 ft.
Open. Unpublished guide.
University of Colorado Libraries, Western Historical Collections.
Yearbooks, history, and a convention program of the Federation, founded in 1895 in Denver to coordinate the activities of women's literary and educational clubs. Also included are pamphlets of affiliated local clubs. In addition to its literary interests, the Federation became involved in penal reform, child protection, and other reforms.

1,668. Colorado Woman's Christian Temperance Union
Records. 1878-1975. 25 ft. and 2 microfilm reels.
Open. Published guide.
University of Colorado Libraries, Western Historical Collections.
Records of the Colorado WCTU, organized in 1880, and of local chapters, particularly the Boulder, Loveland, and Leroy WCTU organizations. Includes annual reports, 1882-1969; minutes of state officers' meetings, 1941-72; correspondence, 1900-54; treasurer's and auditor's reports, 1931-67; a brief history; scrapbooks; photos; and other items that reflect the WCTU's reform activities. Also includes records of the Loyal Temperance Legion and information about Rest Cottage. Records of local unions consist of minutes, 1878-1971; financial records, 1892-1968; yearbooks, 1902-63; and brief histories of the local unions. Items from the national and world WCTU include annual reports, annual convention addresses, handbooks, pamphlets, and extensive runs of *The WCTU Messenger* and *The Union Signal.* See Doris Mitterling, comp., and John A. Brennan, ed., *Guide to the Colorado Woman's Christian Temperance Union Papers,* rev. ed. (Boulder: Western Historical Collections, 1978).

1,669. Costigan, Edward P.
Papers. Ca. 1900-30s. 114 ft.
Open. Unpublished guide.
University of Colorado Libraries, Western Historical Collections.
Papers of Costigan, a founder of the Colorado Progressive (Bull Moose) party, attorney for the United Mine Workers of America, and a US senator from Colorado. Includes correspondence, financial receipts, an article, club records, programs, yearbooks, photos, and other items of his wife Mabel (Cory) Costigan (1873?-1951), a founder of the national LWV, founder and vice-president of the National Consumers League, a supporter of women's suffrage, and the only female member of the committee that directed the presidential campaign of Senator Robert La

Follette. She also founded the Denver chapter of the LWV and the Washington, DC, Consumers League and served in a variety of other civic and political capacities.

1,670. Keating, Edward
Papers. 1900-64. 25 ft.
Partially restricted. Published guide.
University of Colorado Libraries, Western Historical Collections.
Papers of Keating (1875-1965), a journalist and congressman from Colorado who later managed and edited the newspaper *Labor,* include correspondence and articles, 1914-38, written by his wife Margaret Sloan Medill Keating (1875-1939). After working on the *Denver Post,* Margaret Keating was employed as society editor of the *Rocky Mountain News,* where she met her husband; once he was involved in *Labor,* she contributed a humor column to that publication. She also was an early member of the Congressional Club, the Woman's National Press Club, the Woman's National Democratic Club, and the Women's Trade Union League. Collection contains a diary she kept of her experiences and observations in Washington, DC, as the wife of a congressman. See Doris Mitterling, comp., and John A. Brennan, ed., *Guide to the Edward Keating Papers* (Boulder: Western Historical Collections, 1974).

1,671. Kimmerle, Marjorie
Papers. 1942-62. 32 ft. and 1 microfilm reel.
Open. Unpublished guide.
University of Colorado Libraries, Western Historical Collections.
Correspondence, classroom notes, research notes, charts and maps, publications, and material that Kimmerle (1906-63), a PhD who was a member of the University of Colorado's English department faculty, collected on the folklore and language of Colorado and the West. Material documents the changes in language and cultural patterns in the region. Kimmerle also was the Colorado chairman of the American Dialect Society and executive secretary of the Colorado Folklore Society. Includes a microfilm copy of her manuscript "Folk Sayings from Colorado."

1,672. Long, Margaret
Papers. 1850s-1957. 27 ft.
Open. Unpublished guide.
University of Colorado Libraries, Western Historical Collections.
Correspondence, travel journals, daybooks, manuscripts, interviews, post cards, maps of early trails, photos, clippings, and copies of the published books of Long (1873-1957), a physician, pertain to her hobby studying the desert and pioneer trails. Long graduated from Johns Hopkins Medical School in 1903 and came to Denver in 1905, where she founded the Sands Home for tubercular women. She also worked at several other hospitals as well as the Florence Crittenton home for unwed mothers.

1,673. Patterson, Thomas M., Family
Papers. 1850-1925. 10 ft.
Open. Published guide.
University of Colorado Libraries, Western Historical Collections.
Family correspondence, scrapbooks, and photos of Patterson, a US senator from Colorado, and his wife Katherine A. (Grafton) Patterson (1839-1902), an advocate of woman suffrage who also was active in club and charity work. The granddaughter of Alexander Campbell, founder of the Christian Church in America, Kate Patterson planned to become a missionary to India until she married Thomas Patterson, whom she met while teaching at a seminary in Indiana. The couple moved to Denver in 1872, where she became one of the incorporators of the First Christian Church of Denver and one of the founders of the Ladies' Relief Society of Denver, a forerunner of the Charity Organization Society of Denver. Kate Patterson was an active campaigner for the successful effort to ratify women's suffrage in Colorado in 1893, a founder of the Deutsche Damen Club, a charter member of the Denver Woman's Club, and a patron of the Denver Artists' Club. The collection contains her diary for 1898 and extensive correspondence with her daughter Margaret (Patterson) Campbell, the only survivor of her five children, and other family members about family matters, the children's education, and Denver's social and cultural life. See Ellen Arquimbau, comp., and John A. Brennan, ed., *Guide to the Thomas M. Patterson Family Papers* (Boulder: Western Historical Collections, 1977).

1,674. Rippon, Mary
Papers. 1877-1936. 2 ft.
Open. Unpublished guide.
University of Colorado Libraries, Western Historical Collections.
Correspondence, programs and invitations, University announcements, and photos of students and friends of [Miss] Rippon (1850-1935), the first woman faculty member at the University of Colorado; she came to the University in 1878 to teach French and German and was named head of the department of Germanic languages and literature in 1881, a position she held for 28 years. Educated abroad, Rippon was one of the first women in the US to be made a full professor. She also acted as unofficial dean of women at the University until one was appointed in 1901, launched the University's first dramatic productions, and in 1884 founded the Fortnightly Club, which is Boulder's oldest literary group. Collection also contains records of the Mary Rippon Memorial Fund committee and articles about the Mary Rippon Theatre, an amphitheater dedicated to her in 1936. The theater is used for summer productions, particularly those of the Colorado Shakespeare Festival.

1,675. Roche, Josephine Aspinwall
Papers. 1910-70s. 35 ft.
Open. Unpublished guide.
University of Colorado Libraries, Western Historical Collections.
Personal and business correspondence, speeches, notebooks, reports, hearings, photos, clippings, journals, and books reflecting the social, political, and business and union concerns of [Miss] Roche (1886-1976). After developing an interest in social work at Columbia University, Roche became director of the girls' department of Denver's Juvenile Court from 1915 to 1918; she served as a referee in that department from 1925 to 1927. During WWI she did relief work in Belgium and then, as director of the Foreign Language Information Service in New York and Washington, DC, she worked with immigrant women. In 1925 she became director of the editorial department of the Children's Bureau.

When her father died in 1927, Josephine Roche became a director and then president of the Rocky Mountain Fuel Company. Under her leadership, the Company became the first major Colorado coal company to recognize the United Mine Workers, and in 1948 she became a director of the union's new welfare and retirement fund. She also served as assistant secretary of the US Treasury under President Roosevelt from 1934 to 1937, a representative on the President's Cabinet Committee on Economic Security from 1934 to 1940, and chairman of an interdepartmental committee to coordinate the health and welfare activities of the federal government.

1,676. Spring, Agnes Wright
Papers. Nd. 7 ft.
Open. Unpublished guide.
University of Colorado Libraries, Western Historical Collections.
Correspondence, notes, manuscripts, maps, clippings, and publications of Spring (1894-), a western history writer who was Wyoming state librarian and historian from 1913 to 1921, women's editor and feature writer for the *Wyoming Stockman-Journal* from 1916 to 1941, and Colorado state historian from 1955 on; she has also served as activity director and acting curator of the Colorado State Historical Society Museum. Her papers contain material she collected on the cattle industry, Indians, cowboys, outlaws, and other topics, which she used in the writing of her numerous books.

1,677. Wolcott, Rosetta Gordon Lipsia (Bell)
Papers. 1888-1970. 2 ft.
Open. Unpublished guide.
University of Colorado Libraries, Western Historical Collections.
Personal correspondence; diaries, 1904-09 and 1948-70; autograph albums; programs; poetry; calling cards; invitations; photos; and clippings of Wolcott (1879-1974), a professor of French at the University of Colorado from 1920 until her retirement in 1948. Raised in Europe by her Canadian parents, Wolcott moved to Boulder in 1890 when her father James W. Bell was appointed to the University faculty. After his death later that year, her mother Delphine Bell joined the faculty as a French instructor. For years Rosetta Wolcott gave private piano lessons, and she often used songs and folk dances to teach children conversational French and German. She and her husband Charles Wolcott, who owned mining interests in the area, had three children.

1,678. Wolle, Muriel (Sibell)
Papers. 1931-76. 14 ft.
Open. Unpublished guide.
University of Colorado Libraries, Western Historical Collections.
Correspondence, a typed manuscript, photos, selected printed matter concerning the West, memorabilia, and articles, paintings, and sketches by Wolle (1898-1977) a professor of art at the University of Colorado and author and illustrator of books and articles on the history of ghost towns in Colorado and surrounding states. Collection primarily concerns her writing and sketching, her courses at the University, and her special interest in western and southwestern Indian art. Six years after Wolle graduated from Parsons School of Design, she came to the University as an instructor in its newly organized department of fine arts; from 1929 to 1947 she served as head of the department. In 1945 she married Francis Wolle, a professor of English at the University. She was active in civic organizations and the University theater.

1,679. Woman's Club of Boulder
Records. 1901-70s. 10 ft.
Open. Unpublished guide.
University of Colorado Libraries, Western Historical Collections.
Organizational records, minutes of meetings of the directors and the membership, officers' reports, financial records, history, annual announcements, scrapbooks, pamphlets, and publications of this civic and social group, organized in 1901 for public service and development of the individual. At a meeting of representatives from the Fortnightly, Hypatia, and Friday Musical clubs and of ladies auxiliaries of local fraternal organizations, a committee was appointed to draft the Club's articles of incorporation; Mrs. T. A. McHarg served as legal advisor. Later, Mrs. James H. Baker was elected president and Mrs. Horace O. Dodge, first vice-president. The Club established departments of civic science and art and literature; in 1901 it became affiliated with the Colorado

Federation of Women's Clubs and in 1904, with the GFWC.

1,680. Women's International League for Peace and Freedom
Records. 1915-66. 110 ft.
Open. Unpublished guide.
University of Colorado Libraries, Western Historical Collections.
Minutes, correspondence, reports, speeches, appeals and articles, circular letters, bulletins, pamphlets, journals, books, and other records of the WILPF, which was founded in 1915 to study the causes of war and to offer alternatives to it. Much of the collection consists of correspondence between the 75 national sections and the international headquarters in Geneva, Switzerland. Other correspondents include the executive committee and WILPF officers Jane Addams, Emily Greene Balch, Gertrude Baer, Lida Gustava Heymann, and Gertrude Bussey. Also includes files on the League of Nations and the UN, refugees, education, the status of women, and other topics, among them the economic, social, political, and psychological causes of war.

COLORADO SPRINGS

1,681. Colorado College Archives
Records. 1874- . Ca. 100 ft.
Open. Shelflist and card file.
Colorado College Library, Special Collections.
Minutes, financial records, correspondence, literary manuscripts, photos, scrapbooks, and official publications of the College, an independent four-year liberal arts institution founded by Congregational ministers in 1874. Includes correspondence, biographical information, and clippings for each of the deans of women; material about the directors of residence, who usually were women, and about regulations for women students and dormitory activities; records of the Alumni Council and the college's sororities; a file concerning the women's movement since 1974; biographical information about and books and articles by Colorado College faculty members; and college yearbooks, student newspapers, catalogs, and class offerings. Also includes records of the Women's Educational Society, which was founded by the wife of one of the college presidents during the 1920s to promote women's education through the establishment of scholarships.

1,682. Colorado Springs League of Women Voters
Records. 1938- . 85 ft.
Open. Unpublished guide.
Pikes Peak Regional Library District.
Minutes, correspondence, newsletters, pamphlets, publications, and other records of this local LWV branch, founded in 1938. Instrumental in the establishment of the Zebulon Pike Detention Home, the group has also been involved in lobbying for creation and maintenance of city-owned public transportation, preservation and acquisition of park lands, and voter education. The branch also formulated studies of local government.

1,683. Duncan, Fannie May (Bragg)
Oral history. 1972. 1 tape and 1 transcript.
Open. Unpublished guide.
Pikes Peak Regional Library District.
Interview in which [Mrs. Edward R.] Duncan (1920-) describes difficulties she encountered as a black resident of Colorado Springs, the way in which she got her start there, her eventual prosperity and dealings in real estate, and her founding of the Cotton Club, the first black nightclub in Colorado Springs.

1,684. Hamp, Julia
Oral history. 1975. 1 tape and 1 transcript.
Open. Unpublished guide.
Pikes Peak Regional Library District.
Interview in which Hamp (1895-1977), a local civic leader who was a member of the national board of the Girl Scouts from 1955 to 1963, discusses her activities, particularly her involvement with the Girl Scouts and civic affairs. She was a board member of the local YWCA and the Community Chest. She also was the cousin of Sidford Hamp, a participant in the Hayden expedition into the Yellowstone area of Wyoming in 1872.

1,685. Hunt, Inez (Whitaker)
Papers. 1960-64. 2 items.
Open. Unpublished guide.
Pikes Peak Regional Library District.
Manuscripts of books that [Mrs. Nelson V.] Hunt (1892-), an author of works on Colorado, co-authored with Wanetta Draper. Their titles are *Lightning in His Hand: Dr. Nikola Tesla* (1964) and *To Colorado's Restless Ghosts* (1960).

1,686. Morath, Gladys "Glad" (Ramsell)
Oral history. 1975. 1 tape and 1 transcript.
Open. Unpublished guide.
Pikes Peak Regional Library District.
Interview with Morath (1896-), a local piano teacher, editor of the women's page of the Colorado Springs *Gazette-Telegraph,* and mother of ragtime piano player Max Morath. She discusses the events in her life, playing for silent movies in local theaters, raising her two sons alone after her divorce from Fred Morath in 1932, and music in the area.

1,687. Penrose, Julie Villiers (Lewis) McMillan
Papers. 1930-42. 1 ft.
Open. Unpublished guide.
Pikes Peak Regional Library District.
Personal correspondence and household accounts of Penrose (1870-1956), a social leader and wife of mining magnate and philanthropist Spencer Penrose, pertain to her personal life and management of her household at El Pomar, a mansion outside Colorado Springs. Before her marriage to Penrose she was married to James McMillan.

1,688. Stote, Florence (Marshall)
Papers. 1898-1940. 3 ft. and 1 vol.
Open. Unpublished guide.
Pikes Peak Regional Library District.
Correspondence, family records, scrapbooks, clippings, and other papers of [Mrs. William H. R.] Stote (1869-1964), the first white child born on the Kansas Sac Indian reservation, contain information on her interest in local civic affairs, the Republican party, and the DAR. An officer of the state DAR, Stote composed the DAR song "I Pledge Allegiance to My Flag." Manager of her husband's insurance company after his death, Stote also was active in the PTA and the Presbyterian church. During WWI, she was state chairwoman of the Liberty Loan drive.

1,689. Tesker, Wanetta (White) Draper
Papers. 1917- . 1 vol. and 2 items.
Open. Unpublished guide.
Pikes Peak Regional Library District.
Papers of [Mrs. Elmer H.] Tesker (1918-), an author of works on Colorado history who wrote under the name Wanetta Draper, consist of a scrapbook about the effect of WWI on Colorado Springs, especially as a military community, and manuscripts of books she co-authored with Inez Hunt, *Lightning in His Hand: Dr. Nikola Tesla* (1964) and *To Colorado's Restless Ghosts* (1960). Before her marriage to Tesker she was married to Paul Draper.

1,690. Motherhouse Archives
Records. 1863- . No size given.
Open. No guide.
Sisters of St. Francis Motherhouse.
The order was founded in 1863; its members are involved in health care, teaching, orphanages, nursing homes, and social work. Financial records; correspondence; files; bound volumes containing histories of the Motherhouse and of hospitals, schools, orphanages, a home for the aged, and nursing homes administered and staffed by the Sisters; bound volumes containing information about each sister since 1875; photos; scrapbooks; clippings; pamphlets; and books.

DENVER

1,691. Association Archives
Records. 1949- . No size given.
Open. No guide.
Association of Operating Room Nurses Library.
Officially founded in 1954, although it existed from about 1949, the AORN provides education and disseminates information on operating room nursing. Minutes of the board of directors, programs from annual conventions, and publications of the AORN, including the *AORN Journal* and its predecessors.

1,692. Bromwell, Henrietta Elizabeth
Papers. 1885-1917. 77 items.
Open. No guide.
Colorado Historical Society.
Papers of Bromwell, founder of the Artist's Club of Denver, include a diary from 1917, correspondence and other papers relating to Bromwell family genealogy, and a scrapbook of programs and clippings pertaining to artistic endeavors in Denver.

1,693. American Mothers' Committee of the Golden Rule Foundation
Records. 1944-65. 4 vols.
Open. No guide.
Colorado Historical Society.
Reports, scrapbooks of correspondence, speeches, press releases, rules, photos, clippings, and other records of the Denver chapter of the Committee.

1,694. Bailey, Ella
Papers. 1869. 17-page item.
Open. No guide.
Colorado Historical Society.
Diary of Bailey, a resident of Latham in Weld County, Colorado Territory.

1,695. Bane, Elizabeth Evans
Papers. 1890-1936. 300 items.
Open. No guide.
Colorado Historical Society.
Papers of Bane, a Denver resident, include correspondence, personal and business papers, a diary of Isabel Nismith-Evans for 1891 to 1914, scrapbooks of theater bills and programs, clippings, and genealogical material for the Nismith, Evans, and Bane families. Also contains records of the Castle Lake and Resort Company (later known as the Wellington Lake and Reservoir Company), including a minute book for 1890 to 1914, treasurer's records, and stock certificate books.

1,696. Beard, Grace M.
Papers. 1933. 200 items.
Open. No guide.
Colorado Historical Society.
Correspondence and financial records of Beard, a Denver resident.

1,697. Bell, Rose
Papers. 1869. 2 items.
Open. No guide.

Colorado Historical Society.
Original and typescript copy of a diary kept by Bell.

1,698. Bellamy, Frederica (Le Fevre)
Papers. 1908-51. 35 vols.
Open. No guide.
Colorado Historical Society.
Scrapbooks of Bellamy (1884-1963), who in 1912 married Harry E. Bellamy (1874-1956), vice-president of the Kendrick-Bellamy Company in Denver. Contains clippings and memorabilia regarding the Le Fevre and Bellamy families, Denver social events, and horse shows; photos of family members and Denver scenes; and theater bills and programs.

1,699. Bennett, Ella Costillo
Papers. Nd. 90 items.
Open. No guide.
Colorado Historical Society.
Manuscripts of articles and poems, photos, and sheet music of Bennett (1865-1932), a free-lance writer, feature writer for the Portland *Oregonian* and the Denver *Post,* and author of *Letters of Abelard and Heloise.*

1,700. Braun, Evelyn M.
Papers. Nd. 37 vols. and 1905 items.
Open. No guide.
Colorado Historical Society.
Braun was active in the Order of the Eastern Star for 50 years; she also served as administrator of Sands House Sanatorium nursing home for 15 years. Correspondence; a diary; notebooks; administrative records; reports; staff data; an OES constitution, bylaws, chapter rosters, and ritual books; photo and autograph albums; scrapbooks; inspirational books; clippings; and other papers. Includes information about the Sanatorium, various OES chapters, the Grant Avenue United Methodist Church friendship class, the FINS Club, and the American Cancer Society.

1,701. Brown, Mary Butler
Papers. 1906-54. 200 items.
Open. No guide.
Colorado Historical Society.
Correspondence, photos, scrapbooks, clippings, and other papers of Brown (1860-1957), who was secretary of the Society of Colorado Pioneers in addition to her activities in other related organizations. Also includes records of the Society of Colorado Pioneers and material pertaining to the Territorial Daughters of Colorado, the Native Daughters of Colorado, and the Pioneer Ladies' Aid Society.

1,702. Cannon, Frank Jenne
Papers. 1929-39. 2050 items.
Open. Published guide.
Colorado Historical Society.
Papers of Cannon (1859-1933), who was an attorney, newspaper editor, mining entrepreneur, US senator from Utah from 1896 to 1899, and president of the Bimetallic Association in Denver, contain 500 letters of Caroline Evans, secretary of the Bimetallic Association. Cannon devoted the last 10 years of his life to the campaign for the remonetization of silver. See *An Inventory of the Papers of Frank Jenne Cannon (1859-1933), A Holding of the Library of the State Historical Society of Colorado* (Denver: State Historical Society of Colorado, 1969).

1,703. Carr, Benjamin, and Carr, Harriet
Papers. 1854-86. 24 items.
Open. Unpublished guide.
Colorado Historical Society.
Correspondence of Benjamin and Harriet [Mrs. Benjamin] Carr, who settled in Lawrence, Kansas Territory, during the 1850s and moved to Colorado Territory in the 1860s.

1,704. Collier, Alice Light
Papers. 1892-1960. 5 vols.
Open. No guide.
Colorado Historical Society.
Scrapbooks containing correspondence, photos, announcements, programs, and clippings of Robert Collier and the Collier family.

1,705. Colorado Mothers' Committee
Records. 1966-69. 1 vol.
Open. No guide.
Colorado Historical Society.
Scrapbook of clippings pertaining to the selection of the mother of the year.

1,706. Colorado Nurses' Association
Records. 1889-1964. 20 items.
Open. No guide.
Colorado Historical Society.
History of public health nursing in Colorado, a history of the Denver Visiting Nurses' Association, notes on the Denver Tuberculosis Society, pamphlets, photos of uniforms, and other records of the Colorado Nurses' Association.

1,707. Craig, Katherine
Papers. 1905-32. 3 vols.
Open. No guide.
Colorado Historical Society.
Scrapbooks of Craig (1876-1934), state superintendent of public instruction, contain clippings and typescripts about educational programs in Colorado.

1,708. Daughters of the American Revolution
Records. 1895-1950. 38 items.
Open. No guide.
Colorado Historical Society.
Record books from 1895 to 1910 of the Colorado chapter of the DAR and speeches, programs, yearbooks, and other records from various local chapters.

1,709. Davis, Mary O.
Papers. 1898-1940. 10 items.
Open. No guide.
Colorado Historical Society.
Papers of Davis (1881-1964) include photos; articles, booklets, and pamphlets about the Woman's Relief Corps, Grand Army of the Republic; and sight-seeing information on the Pike's Peak region.

1,710. Denver Woman's Press Club
Records. 1953-60. 1 vol.
Open. No guide.
Colorado Historical Society.
Scrapbook of this organization of women journalists contains press releases, programs, and clippings.

1,711. Derbyshire, Mamie C.
Papers. 1868-81. 1 vol.
Open. No guide.
Colorado Historical Society.
Diary of Derbyshire.

1,712. Eisenhower, Mamie (Doud)
Papers. Nd. 200 items.
Open. No guide.
Colorado Historical Society.
Papers of Eisenhower, the wife of Dwight David Eisenhower, US Army general and US President, contain scrapbooks, presidential inaugural programs and invitations from 1953 to 1957, Christmas cards, theater programs, travel brochures, and articles about the Eisenhower family.

1,713. Felt, Margaret
Papers. Nd. 1000 items.
Open. No guide.
Colorado Historical Society.
Papers of Felt, a Denver teacher, include correspondence; post cards; lesson plans, grade books, and other material relating to Byers Junior High School from 1921 to 1929; photos; documents pertaining to Denver public schools and teachers' associations; pamphlets and clippings about the history of Denver and Colorado; and other papers.

1,714. Fisher, Louise A.
Papers. 1887-1929. 50 items.
Open. No guide.
Colorado Historical Society.
Papers of Fisher contain a diary from 1900 to 1929 and such school papers as report cards, her certificates of promotion from one grade to another, and graduation programs.

1,715. Gaynor, Lizzie Mahon
Papers. 1886-1921. 150 items.
Open. No guide.
Colorado Historical Society.
Correspondence, diaries, school recitations, photos, maps, certificates, and diplomas of Gaynor.

1,716. Guerber, Mary Edna Reynolds
Papers. 1899-1956. 250 items.
Open. No guide.
Colorado Historical Society.
Papers of Guerber, a Georgetown, CO, clubwoman and musician, contain a diary for the years 1912 to 1956, which includes notes on Alice Louise Guerber Sheridan, Howard Guerber, and Mary R. Guerber; notes for a biography about Amelia Harriet Nash Reynolds; secretary's and treasurer's records of the Georgetown Shakespeare Club; an album of post cards; programs of recitals by Alice Reynolds' music students; and a scrapbook of clippings about the settlement and development of Georgetown.

1,717. Hill, Alice (Hale)
Papers. 1887-1908. 20 items.
Open. No guide.
Colorado Historical Society.
Travel diaries from 1887 to 1907, journals, photos, and biographical data of [Mrs. Nathaniel Peter] Hill, a Denver resident.

1,718. Hill, Alice (Polk)
Papers. 1896-1947. 100 items.
Open. No guide.
Colorado Historical Society.
Papers of Hill (1854-1921), poet laureate of Colorado, include correspondence, a manuscript of a poem, a membership certificate for Denver's Second Charter Convention, genealogical data, and other items.

1,719. Hill, Crawford, and Hill, Louise Sneed
Papers. 1899-1955. 30,000 items.
Open. Unpublished guide.
Colorado Historical Society.
Personal and business papers of Crawford Hill (1862-1922) and his wife Louise Hill (1861-1955). The son of Colorado smelter and mining entrepreneur Nathaniel P. Hill, Crawford Hill played an active role in such family enterprises as the Republican Publishing Company and the Boston and Colorado Smelting Company. In 1895 he married Louise Sneed, a socially prominent resident of Memphis. Following her husband's death, Louise Hill and her sons managed the family's financial and business interests, which were consolidated into the Hill Land and Investment Company, the Denargo Land Company, and the Hill Securities, Land and Development Company. Also contains business records concerning the Inland Oil and Refining Company and the Dolly Varden Mining Company. Papers of the estates of Crawford Hill, Cora Cowan, and Mary B. Neely are also included.

1,720. Humphreys
Papers. Nd. 225,000 items.
Open. Unpublished guide.
Colorado Historical Society.
Personal and business papers of A. E. Humphreys,

Sr., I. B. Humphreys, and A. E. Humphreys, Jr., and his wife Ruth (Boettcher) Humphreys (1890-1959). Papers of Ruth Humphreys, who was the daughter of Charles Boettcher, span 1900 to 1957 and include correspondence, school compositions, photos, and scrapbooks of articles and clippings about the Boettcher and Humphreys families and their businesses.

1,721. Johnson, Anne Louise
Papers. 1889-1944. 75 items.
Open. No guide.
Colorado Historical Society.
Photos, printed material, clippings, and other papers of Johnson (?-1944), who was instrumental in organizing the playground movement in Denver and the first kindergartens in the Denver public schools. A kindergarten teacher and supervisor of playground departments for the schools and the city, Johnson also was the president of the Wellesley Club and the Woman's Educational Club.

1,722. Kletzsch, Elizabeth Schroeder
Papers. Ca. 1934. 88 items.
Open. No guide.
Colorado Historical Society.
On leave from her position as field and case worker for a Milwaukee relief agency, [Mrs.] Kletzsch went to Denver in 1934 to direct relief work there. Soon after her arrival, relief operations in Denver were federalized and Kletzsch was named director of the Denver Bureau of Public Welfare. Correspondence with her parents and son in Milwaukee and scrapbooks of clippings pertain to her work in Denver and the people with whom she worked. Names cited include Benjamin Glassberg, Helen Hankins, [Mrs.] Carrie Lee Moellendick, Captain C. D. Shawver, Alice Van Diest, and Aubrey Williams.

1,723. Lathrop, Mary Florence
Papers. 1924. 100 items.
Open. No guide.
Colorado Historical Society.
An attorney, Lathrop (1865-1951) was the first woman admitted to the American Bar Association. Includes correspondence, reports, and programs of the American Bar Association and the Canadian Bar Association, photos, and clippings, as well as correspondence and clippings pertaining to the American Bar Association's tour of Europe in 1924.

1,724. Long, Margaret
Papers. 1906-30. 99 items.
Open. No guide.
Colorado Historical Society.
Scrapbooks of clippings regarding woman suffrage and notable women, reading lists, pamphlets, periodicals, and other papers of Long (1873-1957), who received an MD from Johns Hopkins medical school.

1,725. Lonie, Agnes
Papers. 1865-67. 1 vol.
Open. No guide.
Colorado Historical Society.
Diary of Lonie concerns events in Chicago, public reaction to the assassination of President Abraham Lincoln, and her brother Charlie's travels to the West, including Colorado.

1,726. Lord, Charlotte S.
Papers. 1857-69. 1 vol.
Open. No guide.
Colorado Historical Society.
Diary recorded in a Baptist Ladies' Sewing Society cashbook by Lord, a resident of Waverly, IA, contains accounts of travels in the East and Middle West and a genealogy of the Samuel Moss family.

1,727. McCune, Florence
Papers. 1872-85. 5 vols.
Open. No guide.
Colorado Historical Society.
Diaries of McCune, a Denver resident.

1,728. McDonald, Mary M.
Papers. 1929-30. 50 items.
Open. No guide.
Colorado Historical Society.
Photos and scrapbooks of [Mrs. Ralph] McDonald (1881-ca. 1969), a Denver resident, pertain to a veteran's organization, politics, and midwifery.

1,729. McKee, Anna M.
Papers. 1884. 11 items.
Open. No guide.
Colorado Historical Society.
Papers of McKee contain letters written from Taos in New Mexico Territory.

1,730. Maxwell, Martha
Papers. 1805-1958. 1000 items.
Restricted. No guide.
Colorado Historical Society.
Papers of Maxwell (1831-81), a naturalist and artistic taxidermist, include correspondence and the Dartt-Maxwell family Bible, which contains a geneaology. Maxwell married James Alexander Maxwell in 1854, and they moved to the Pike's Peak region in 1860. She established in Boulder the Maxwell's Rocky Mountain Museum, where she displayed her work, and in 1876 she exhibited her work at the Centennial International Exposition in Philadelphia. Correspondents include Maxwell's parents Josiah and Amy (Sanford) Dartt, her half sisters Mary (Dartt) [Mrs. Nathan] Thompson and Elizabeth (Dartt) [Mrs. Hal] Sayre, and her daughter Mabel (Maxwell) [Mrs. Charles] Brace.

1,731. Meredith, Ellis
Papers. 1892-1924. 100 items.
Open. No guide.
Colorado Historical Society.
Correspondence, notebooks, scrapbooks, and clippings of Meredith (1864 or 1865-1955), a Denver suffragist and social worker, concern women's suffrage, child labor in Colorado, and coal miners' strikes.

1,732. Milner, Agnes Finding
Papers. 1862-1947. 3000 items.
Open. No guide.
Colorado Historical Society.
Papers of Milner, a resident of Breckenridge, CO, include diaries, a ledger, photos, material regarding the history of Breckenridge, Denver land records for 1862 and 1863, and clippings. Also contains minutes, correspondence, and yearbooks of the Women's Club; diaries and rosters from 1930 to 1940 of the Pioneer Ladies' Aid Society; a minute book and journals of the Finding Hardware Company; and records of the Fredonia Mine.

1,733. Mitchell, Thomas M., and Mitchell, Elsie
Papers. Nd. 20 items.
Open. No guide.
Colorado Historical Society.
Papers of Thomas Mitchell, an attorney, and his wife Elsie Mitchell, a physician, include Thomas Mitchell's law license, clippings about his legal practice, Elsie Mitchell's medical degrees, certificates, awards, and articles and clippings regarding her medical career.

1,734. Morian, Lelah May
Papers. 1911-63. 250 items.
Open. No guide.
Colorado Historical Society.
Correspondence, manuscripts, radio speeches, scrapbooks, annual reports, yearbooks, brochures, articles, and memorabilia of Morian (1881-1963), a Denver clubwoman, artist, and teacher, relate primarily to the Colorado Federation of Women's Clubs, the GFWC, the Colorado Woman's Service Club, the Civic Garden Club, the Co-operative Club, the Co-Operettes, the Denver Civic Symphony, the Denver Community Players, and the Denver Keramic Club.

1,735. Pioneer Ladies Aid Society
Records. 1896-1911. 500 items.
Open. No guide.
Colorado Historical Society.
Constitution, bylaws, minutes, ledgers, vouchers, canceled checks, receipts, and correspondence of this Denver pioneer women's organization.

1,736. Posten, Anna Garrison
Papers. 1938. 1 vol.
Open. No guide.
Colorado Historical Society.
Scrapbook of Posten contains clippings about pioneer women in Colorado.

1,737. Rickel, Frank H., and Rickel, Dora, Family
Papers. 1886-1962. 333 items.
Open. No guide.
Colorado Historical Society.
Papers of this Denver family include diaries of various family members from 1908 to 1962, a diary and receipt of W. C. Shultz, photos, church material, and other papers.

1,738. Sabin, Florence Rena
Papers. Nd. 22 items.
Open. No guide.
Colorado Historical Society.
A scientist, physician, teacher, and humanitarian, Sabin (1871-1953) was the first woman appointed full professor at the Johns Hopkins school of medicine, where she had received her MD; the first woman president of the American Association of Anatomists; the first woman department head at the Rockefeller Institute for Medical Research; and the first woman member of the National Academy of Sciences. Correspondence, honorary degrees received by Sabin, an AAUW pamphlet dedicated to Sabin, and other papers.

1,739. St. Luke's Hospital, School of Nursing
Records. 1894-1972. 250 items.
Open. No guide.
Colorado Historical Society.
Records of this nursing school, which was in operation from 1881 to 1972, include a constitution, bylaws, correspondence, photos, graduation invitations and programs, a history of the School, and clippings.

1,740. St. Mary's Academy
Records. 1874-1964. 4000 items.
Open. No guide.
Colorado Historical Society.
Records of this Denver parochial school contain correspondence, photos, a history of the Academy, the school's first certificate of credits for Jesse Forshee in 1875, and other material.

1,741. Shellabarger, Mary Elizabeth
Papers. 1898-1916. 250 items.
Open. No guide.
Colorado Historical Society.
Papers of Shellabarger, a Denver resident, include correspondence, photos, announcements of the Woman's Club of Denver, and clippings about Arapahoe County and the San Luis Valley.

1,742. Shinkle, Elizabeth Clark
Papers. 1896-1902. 7 items.
Open. No guide.
Colorado Historical Society.
Papers of Shinkle, a resident of Cripple Creek, CO, contain correspondence, her diary for 1902, and a diary for 1896 regarding Clark family activities.

1,743. Sizer, Ina Cassidy
Papers. 1896-99. 200 items.
Open. No guide.

Colorado Historical Society.
Papers of Sizer contain letters from Frederick G. Perkins to Ellen R. Sizer and photos.

1,744. Spalding, Sarah Griswold
Papers. Nd. 700 items.
Open. No guide.
Colorado Historical Society.
Papers of Spalding (1872-1960), a Denver resident, include correspondence; compositions; notes from her school days at Vassar; prints concerning the Colonial Dames and the Denver Fortnightly Club; scrapbooks of programs and invitations pertaining to the Episcopal church; and engagement books for 1951 to 1959.

1,745. Stapleton, Patience
Papers. Nd. 2 items.
Open. No guide.
Colorado Historical Society.
Papers of Stapleton, a Denver novelist and suffragist, consist of manuscripts of "Dolly Dump" and "The Property Baby," the latter of which was published in *Christmas Dramatic News* (1892).

1,746. Tabor, Horace Austin Warner
Papers. Nd. 10,000 items.
Open. No guide.
Colorado Historical Society.
Correspondence, business records, scrapbooks, and other papers of Tabor (1830-99), who made a fortune in the Leadville, CO, silver boom of 1878-79, was lieutenant governor of Colorado from 1879 to 1883, was a US senator in 1883, lost his wealth in the Panic of 1893, and was appointed postmaster of Denver in 1898. Includes correspondence and other papers of his second wife Elizabeth Bonduel (McCourt) Doe Tabor (1854-1935), better known as "Baby Doe" Tabor, whom he married in 1883; their daughters Elizabeth Bonduel Lily Tabor (1884-) and Rosemary Echo Silver Dollar Tabor (1889-1925); Claudia McCourt; and Peter McCourt. Baby Doe Tabor died at her residence at the Matchless Mine in Leadville.

1,747. Women of Colorado
Collection. Ca. 1957-68. 7 vols.
Open. No guide.
Colorado State Archives.
Scrapbooks contain articles and clippings about Colorado women in the following fields: business and the professions; education; state, local, and national government service; music, art, and literature; and philanthropy. Also includes historical information about women and miscellaneous items.

1,748. Colorado Women's College Archives
Records. 1888- . Ca. 100 ft., 3 files, and a map case.
Open. No guide.
Colorado Women's College Library.
A private four-year liberal arts women's college, Colorado Woman's College was chartered in 1888 with the backing of the state's Baptists. Classes did not begin until 1909, however. Annual reports, minutes of the faculty and of the student council, financial records, memoranda, photos, scrapbooks, brochures, annuals, handbooks, clippings, official college publications, and other records. Historical files contain correspondence, programs, clippings, and other material dating from 1888 to the present. Subject files from the 1950s and 1960s concern such topics as homecoming and freshmen week. The school's association with Colorado Baptists continued until the 1950s. The school's name was changed to Temple Buell College in 1969, and the current name Colorado Women's College was adopted in 1973.

1,749. Arno, May
Papers. 1911-65. 1 box.
Open. Card catalog.
Denver Public Library, Western History Department.
Correspondence, writings, musical compositions, biographical data, articles, clippings, and other papers related to the career of Arno, who for 40 years operated the May Arno School of Music and Drama in Denver. Also included is material relating to the organizations to which she belonged, among them the Dramus Guild, Poetry Society of Colorado, Colorado Pen Women, National League of American Pen Women, Inc., and Colorado Authors' League. Arno was born in Russia and immigrated to the US as a young child, settling in Philadelphia. She was educated in a variety of dramatic and music schools and after a career on the stage moved to Denver with her husband Herman Schwatt.

1,750. Authors
Collections. 1859- . No size given.
Open. Card catalog.
Denver Public Library, Western History Department.
Authors represented include novelists, poets, playwrights, journalists, and historians. Many of the collections contain material relating to western, and especially Colorado, history. A speech given to the Monday Literary Club by author and historian [Mrs.] Elinor Eppich Kingery details the growth and decline of the quarrying industry in Lyons, CO, and includes information on pioneers, mining activities, and toll roads in Boulder County, CO. Manuscript notes for *Faith on the Frontier,* published in 1976 by the Colorado Council of Churches, are contained in the collection of [Mrs.] Louisa (Ward) Arps. Papers of Louise Colbran Harrison, proprietor of Hotel Splendide in Empire, CO, include the manuscripts and notes for *Empire and the Berthoud Pass* (1948) and for her unpublished novel "Mountain Music," while the Helen Rich collection contains a partial manuscript for a novel based on the legend of Silverheels. Other manuscripts include Agnes Wright Spring's *Minute Men of the Rockies,* a book about a Rocky Mountain rescue group, and *Uranium Country* (1955) and *"Aunt" Clara Brown: The Story of a Black Pioneer* (1970) by [Mrs.] Kathleen Bruyn. Also included are story and book manuscripts by Lucretia Payne, wife of western fiction writer Stephen Payne, and 100 light romances and adventure stories written for western pulp magazines by Carolyn St. Clair King, who often wrote under the pseudonyms Sally Lockhart and Carlos St. Clair.

Papers of Colorado Springs author Christine Whiting Parmenter include an autobiographical sketch and letter, while the collection of [Miss] Margaret Hagler contains the manuscript for *Larry and the Freedom Man* (1960), a Civil War novel for teenagers. In a talk entitled "A Little Backstage Gossip," Marian Castle discusses how she wrote the book *Roxana* (1955) and gives suggestions on how to write a novel. Stories, probably unpublished, and an autobiographical sketch are included in the papers of Ida Riner Gleason, while the Mari Sandoz Collection contains correspondence by and about [Miss] Sandoz and a series of clippings based on her memoranda. Also included are a play by Dolores J. Bosley entitled *Mother Seton's Daughters,* which concerns the Sisters of Charity at Trinidad, CO, in the late 19th century; *One Cure for Gold Fever,* a one-act play by Elizabeth Ann Rotolante; and a television script entitled *Silverheels* by Joanna Stevenson Sampson.

Journalists represented include Edith Eudora Kohl, whose scrapbook contains clippings of her series in the Denver *Post* entitled "Denver's Historic Mansions"; Denver *Post* columnist Joanne Ditmer, whose speech to the City Club of Denver discusses how a widely-read columnist can arouse the public into action; and Roleta D. Teal, correspondent for the *Pueblo Chieftain,* whose papers contain a series of clippings describing rural lifestyle and education during the early and mid-20th century in Colorado. Papers of Mrs. Leonel Ross O'Bryan, a Denver journalist who wrote under the name Polly Pry, include correspondence, dramatic scripts, and scrapbooks of her columns on the Mexican Revolution and her trip around the world.

Also included are a volume of poetry by Elizabeth Hyatt Ogden, letters and an autobiographical sketch of poet Catherine Parmenter, and a poem about Silverheels, a dance hall girl at the gold camp of Buckskin Joe, CO, by Grace Pauline Weber. Papers of [Miss] Belle Turnbull include correspondence and business papers, notebooks of her poetry, and stories.

1,751. Autograph Letters
Collections. 1860-1973. Ca. 100 items.
Open. Card catalog.
Denver Public Library, Western History Department.
A number of collections contain autograph letters of women. Among the earliest are letters to her brothers and an autobiography by Fannie Amelia Adriance, wife of pioneer Methodist minister Jacob Adriance; letters by Ellen Roselle Hinsdale describing her life in Pueblo, CO; letters of Catherine Collins from Fort Laramie, CO, where her husband William Oliver Collins had been sent to establish a military fort; and a letter from "Mollie" to "Ann" discussing Portland, OR, and the independence of women there. Correspondence in the collection of Nathan Cook Meeker, president of the Union Colony at Greeley, CO, includes letters by colonists Nellie Davis Patton and Lucy M. Billings and between Meeker and his wife Arvilla Delight Smith Meeker; in one of these Arvilla Meeker writes her children of the White River Massacre where her husband was killed and of her captivity by Ute Indians. Letters of Ida Krus McFarlane, chairman of the University of Denver English department and cofounder of the Central City Play Festival, to author Thomas Sturge Moore are concerned primarily with the theater and her career. Also included are a letter from Mary Elitch Long, cofounder of a public amusement park and of the Elitch summer theater, to a Mrs. Wear; and letters of Susan B. Anthony to [Mrs.] Martha A. Bushnell Conine regarding women's rights and personal matters. A letter by Alice MacHarg Ferril concerns Joanna MacHarg Palmer and other early artists in Colorado. Author Muriel Hazel Wright gives biographical data on her grandfather Allen Wright in a 1925 letter to "Uncle Jim," while letters of artist Alma Wright Feudel concern her painting of William Frederick Cody's portrait. Letters of ex-circus performer Lucia Zora, who was married to Fred Alispaw, are also included. Mrs. James S. Colaw writes about author [Mrs.] Theodora Kracaw Kroeber. A 1971 letter from Mary Ellen Patno to Caroline Bancroft contains anecdotes about Laura Evans, reputed to have been the last of the famed madams of Colorado. Other recent letters include several by author Dawn Langley Simmons, who was known formerly as Gordon Langley Hall, in which she gives biographical information about herself and information on Brownie Adams, and a letter in which Cora H. Foley, a sculptor, reminisces about mining days in Leadville, CO.

1,752. Bancroft, Caroline
Papers. 1965-73. 1 box, 4 envelopes, 6 tapes, and 1 item.
Partially restricted. Partial calendar and card catalog.
Denver Public Library, Western History Department.
Correspondence; notes; manuscripts of articles, a story, research papers, and booklets; film script; and memorabilia of Bancroft (1900-), a Colorado historian and author. In taped interviews [Miss] Bancroft discusses incidents from the life of Margaret (Tobin) Brown that do not appear in her book *The Unsinkable Mrs. Brown.* She also speaks about Baby Doe Tabor, the wife of Horace Tabor, a wealthy mining entrepreneur of Leadville, CO; gives her recollections about Denver's social life, with emphasis on Mrs. Crawford Hill and Evalyn

Walsh McLean; and talks about her own life. Also included is a biographical sketch of Bancroft done as a term paper, which Bancroft has corrected.

1,753. Boyd, Louie Croft
Papers. 1905-24. 1 vol. and 3 mss.
Open. Card catalog.
Denver Public Library, Western History Department. Boyd graduated from the Colorado Training School for Nurses and taught there during the 1910s and 1920s. Short histories by Boyd of the Denver General Hospital, the Colorado Training School for Nurses, and the Arapahoe County Hospital; a scrapbook relating to nursing legislation in Colorado; and material for a proposed biography of Boyd's friend Countess Katrina Murat, reputed to have been the first pioneer woman in Colorado. Included are copies of Murat divorce records.

1,754. Bromwell, Henrietta Elizabeth
Papers. 1905-08. 2 vols.
Open. Card catalog.
Denver Public Library, Western History Department. Collection consists of a diary of trips made by [Miss] Bromwell (1859-1946) to promote her father's Masonic book and a scrapbook containing items relating to art in Denver and to the Artists' Club of Denver, of which Bromwell was cofounder.

1,755. Brown
Papers. 1912-13. 1 vol.
Open. Card catalog.
Denver Public Library, Western History Department. Journal of a young Mormon girl who left Salt Lake City to serve as a missionary in Seattle, WA. She taught Sunday school, "tracted" from house to house to encourage the spread of the Mormon religion, and went to Portland, OR, to proselytize.

1,756. Brown, Margaret (Tobin)
Papers. 1930-60. 22 items.
Open. Card catalog.
Denver Public Library, Western History Department. [Mrs. James J.] Brown (1867-1932) was a Denver society figure and the "Unsinkable Molly Brown" of the *Titanic* disaster. Letters to her housekeeper [Mrs.] Ella Grable, a notebook containing telegrams, and a letter by Joseph P. Brown which informs the Denver Public Librarian that Margaret Brown is interested in undertaking restoration of the Eugene Field house. Included in the Benjamin Poff Draper collection is a typescript entitled "More about 'The Unsinkable Mrs. Brown.'"

1,757. Byers, William Newton
Papers. 1861-1931. 2 boxes.
Open. Calendar and card catalog.
Denver Public Library, Western History Department. Papers of Byers (1831-1903), a Denver pioneer and editor of the *Rocky Mountain News,* include correspondence, receipts, pictures, membership papers, and memorials. Also included is extensive correspondence with his wife Elizabeth Byers and with his daughter Mary (Byers) Robinson.

1,758. Colonial Dames of America
Records. Nd. 1 item.
Open. Card catalog.
Denver Public Library, Western History Department. A summary of the history of Colorado from 1540 to 1861.

1,759. Colorado Constitutional Convention
Records. 1876. 1 item.
Open. Card catalog.
Denver Public Library, Western History Department. Judge Bromwell's minority report on suffrage which was submitted to the Convention.

1,760. Colorado Federation of Colored Women's Clubs
Records. 1903-72. 1 vol.
Open. Card catalog.
Denver Public Library, Western History Department. A scrapbook of items concerning the history, policies, and activities of the Federation includes biographical sketches of members and prominent black women.

1,761. Colorado Press Women, Inc.
Records. 1941-72. 15 items.
Open. Card catalog.
Denver Public Library, Western History Department. Scrapbooks containing annual rosters, monthly bulletins, and clippings of the organization.

1,762. Colorado State Association of Colored Women's Clubs
Records. 1904-60. 1 vol.
Open. Card catalog.
Denver Public Library, Western History Department. Constitution, miscellaneous reports of various chapters, and historical sketch of the Association.

1,763. Conine, Martha A. Bushnell
Papers. Ca. 1896-1910. 1 vol.
Open. Card catalog.
Denver Public Library, Western History Department. Conine was a women's rights and social reform leader who served as a member of the Colorado House of Representatives from 1897 to 1898. Scrapbook containing correspondence, brochures, programs, and clippings regarding her career, woman suffrage, women's club activities, women in politics, and various social reform movements.

1,764. Dailey, John Lewis
Papers. 1833-1952. 1 box and 1 vol.
Open. Card catalog.
Denver Public Library, Western History Department. Dailey (1833-1908) moved to Denver from Nebraska in 1859 and with William N. Byers started the *Rocky Mountain News.* Correspondence, diaries, deeds, patents, tax receipts, and memorabilia. Also included is the scrapbook of Dailey's daughter [Miss] Grace Dailey (1874-1961), which contains a letter in which she describes her early schooling.

1,765. Daughters of the American Revolution, Colorado Chapter
Records. 1895-1910. 2 vols.
Open. Card catalog.
Denver Public Library, Western History Department. Listing of state regents, chapter officers, and other information, and a scrapbook containing patriotic programs sponsored by the Sons and Daughters of the American Revolution.

1,766. Denver Art League, Inc.
Records. 1892-93. 1 vol.
Open. Card catalog.
Denver Public Library, Western History Department. Ledger containing articles of incorporation; bylaws; prospectus; minutes of the preliminary, organizational, regular, and special meetings; and lists of participants in the League, which was established in 1892.

1,767. Denver Fortnightly Club
Records. 1885-1959. 1 vol. and ca. 36 items.
Open. Card catalog.
Denver Public Library, Western History Department. Records of the Club, a study group formed in 1881, include papers written by members, a speech reviewing the history of the Club to 1959, a paper and notes about artist Helen Chain by Mrs. Albert J. Coleman, and a letter by Florence Burton discussing art in the pioneer home and art teacher Mrs. Baxter B. Stiles.

1,768. Denver Woman's Press Club
Records. 1934- . 2 vols.
Open. Card catalog.
Denver Public Library, Western History Department. Collection contains a "Who's Who" of the Club, notebooks giving biographical data and listing published material of each member beginning in 1957, and scrapbooks of clippings and articles concerning Club activities.

1,769. Dewey, Mrs. Elliott Todhunter
Papers. 1941-43. 245-page item.
Open. Card catalog.
Denver Public Library, Western History Department. Manuscript about Dewey's experiences as principal hostess at Lowry Air Force Base in Denver.

1,770. Dodge, Grenville M.
Papers. 1851-1903. 2 boxes.
Open. Card catalog.
Denver Public Library, Western History Department. Personal correspondence, business correspondence and papers, and battle reports of Dodge (1831-1916), major general in the Civil War and chief engineer in the building of the Union Pacific Railroad. Includes a few letters by his wife Anne B. Dodge, which reveal her impressions of camp life during the war. Also contains papers of Dodge's mother Julia Theresa Dodge (1802-88), wife of Sylvanus Dodge; her letters to her son Nathan P. Dodge tell of the life of a pioneer woman on the Nebraska and Iowa frontier and of social life in Council Bluffs, IA.

1,771. Dunagan, Lyda E.
Papers. 1905-16. 3 vols. and 3 items.
Open. Card catalog.
Denver Public Library, Western History Department. [Mrs. Jesse Jackson] Dunagan (?-1932), a Denver pioneer, was president of the Pioneer Ladies Aid Society and matron at the Denver county jail from 1904 to 1915. Scrapbooks contain clippings about pioneers pasted over the minutes of Confidential Council, No. 13; clippings of poetry; and clippings about women criminals pasted over the records of women convicts at the county jail. Also included are testimonials to Dunagan.

1,772. Ensey, Grace E.
Papers. 1933. 459-page item
Open. Card catalog.
Denver Public Library, Western History Department. [Miss] Ensey (?-1935), a Red Cross worker during WW I, was one of the first women to hold a position on the staff of the Veterans Bureau in Denver. Collection consists of a typescript of her autobiography *Dawn, Day and Eventide,* which was published in 1933.

1,773. Ewing, Lizzie Alberta (Merchant)
Papers. 1902. 1 vol.
Open. Card catalog.
Denver Public Library, Western History Department. Ewing's husband was a farmer who brought his family to Washington state. Ewing's diary of the covered wagon trip from Hermosa, SD, to Davenport, WA, also describes events prior to and after the journey.

1,774. Fealy, Maude Hawk
Papers. Ca. 1917-71. 1 vol. and 4 folders.
Open. Card catalog.
Denver Public Library, Western History Department. Papers of Fealy (1881-1971), an actress who began her career at Elitch's Theater in Denver and became a featured player on American and European stages, include a brief history of Denver theater by Fealy; the manuscript of a vaudeville playlet; a notebook with reviews and photos of scenes; programs; advertisements of appearances; and clippings. Fealy spent her later years as a drama coach in Hollywood.

1,775. French, Adelaide A.
Papers. 1882-1974. 3 boxes and 3 vols.
Open. Card catalog.
Denver Public Library, Western History Department. Diaries, research notes and writings, genealogical material, articles, clippings, and other papers of [Miss] French (1878-1974), a resident of Denver

who often lectured on the history of the area. Includes information on Denver and Colorado history and on organizations to which French belonged, including the Morning Study Club, the Colorado Genealogical Society, and the Territorial Daughters of Colorado.

1,776. Gilpin County Pioneer Association
Records. 1882-93. 1 box.
Open. Card catalog.
Denver Public Library, Western History Department.
Officer reports; minutes and resolutions; accounts payable and receivable; correspondence; lists of pioneers, beginning in 1859; and miscellaneous material. Correspondence includes information on a fund drive for Aunt Clara Brown, a Negro born into slavery who came to Colorado after being freed by her mistress in 1858. Brown helped to found the Union Sunday school in Denver and later moved to Central City, where she became identified with the Methodist church and often cared for sick or injured miners in the laundry she operated.

1,777. Gray, Juanita R.
Papers. 1973- . 1 box and 1 tape.
Open. Card catalog.
Denver Public Library, Western History Department.
Collection contains autobiographical and biographical accounts of black Denver leaders and tape recordings of music sung by the choir of Zion Baptist Church and of a panel on black pioneer families of Denver. In connection with her work as community services assistant at the Denver Public Library, [Mrs. George W.] Gray [Jr.] moderated the panel. Panel members Lulu Franklin, Grace McCain, Mrs. R. W. Pinn, Edith Hawkins, and Olietta Moore give biographical information about past and present personalities including Justina Ford and Mrs. Cecil Moore.

1,778. Hale, Irving
Papers. Ca. 1883-1916. 17 boxes and 1 portfolio.
Open. Card catalog.
Denver Public Library, Western History Department.
Hale (1861-1930) was an electrical engineer and general manager of the Rocky Mountain division of the Edison General Electric Company. Collection contains correspondence and memorabilia of Hale's wife Mary Virginia (King) Hale, whom he married in 1887, and correspondence, estate papers, and property records of Martha Elizabeth Hale, wife of Horace Morrison Hale.

1,779. Interviews
Collections. 1950-74. 19 tapes and 3 phonodiscs.
Partially restricted. Card catalog.
Denver Public Library, Western History Department.
Interviews with women or pertaining to women include one with Alice Eastwood, a botanist and author, in which she reminisces about her experiences as a student at Denver's East High School in 1875 and comments about her career. Helene Balch gives her recollections of actress Maude Hawk Fealy, who was her teacher and close associate, while an interview with Linden Stanley Blue concerns his mother Virginia Neal Blue, Denver city councilwoman and real estate broker who was the first woman treasurer of Colorado. [Mrs.] Goldie Griffith Cameron, who appeared as a cowgirl in several Wild West Shows between 1911 and 1922, describes performers, owners, and incidents in Wild West Show life, as well as childhood memories of her father's medicine show. Helen Echovarria discusses [Mrs.] Evelyn "Diamond Tooth Lil" Hildegard, with comments on prostitution interjected by Fred Mazzulla. Interviews with [Mrs.] Carolyn Sporleder Young concern people and events in the Spoon River area near the Spanish Peaks of southern Colorado. Anthropologist and teacher Ruth Murray Underhill reminisces about her early life, her service with the Indian Bureau, and experiences among the Papago, Mohave, Navajo, and Arapahoe Indians. In a joint interview with Skip Scroggins and Emil Bisttram, artist Dorothy Brett talks about Indian dances in various New Mexico Indian pueblos.

An interview with [Mrs.] Rachel B. Noel, a civic leader, teacher, and sociologist who was the first Negro elected to the Denver Board of Education, concerns her family background, education, and career. Elva Jones Dulan gives highlights of her career and personal life; one of the first black nurses hired in Baltimore city hospitals and one of the first black nurses to enter the Army Nurses Corps, Dulan later served as assistant director of Public Health Nursing at the University of Colorado and as a counselor for black students at Loretto Heights College in Denver. Also included is an interview with Florence Rena Sabin, a physician prominent in the fields of tuberculosis and public health. In another interview garment workers Pauline Newman and Judy Ackerman talk about unionism and the International Ladies' Garment Workers' Union. City planner [Miss] Maxine Kurtz discusses the establishment of the Denver City Planning Office, zoning and rezoning in Denver, and various elements of the city's history.

1,780. Kettle, Hazel Olive (Bennet)
Papers. 1853-1914. 11 items.
Open. Card catalog.
Denver Public Library, Western History Department.
Correspondence, including letters by Kettle to her parents when she was a schoolgirl in Denver in the 1900s; reminiscences of her childhood in Conifer, CO, and of Jefferson and Park counties; a paper about Matilda Ann Terril Provost; and a biographical sketch of Colorado pioneer Thomas Hamer. Included in the Daniel C. Oakes collection is a biography of Oakes, a pioneer, businessman, and Ute Indian agent, which his granddaughter Kettle wrote, as well as the marriage record of Oakes and Olive M. Martin.

1,781. Knights of Pythias, Women's Auxiliary
Records. 1902-24. 1 vol.
Open. Card catalog.
Denver Public Library, Western History Department.
Receipt book for membership dues listing names, membership dates, and fees for the Silver Plume, Colorado Free Coinage Temple No. 4 of the Supreme Temple Pythian Sisters.

1,782. Lathrop, Mary Florence
Papers. 1880-95. 1 box and 2 vols.
Open. Card catalog.
Denver Public Library, Western History Department.
Lathrop (1865-1951), member of a Quaker family, was an organizer for the WCTU and an attorney who specialized in probate law; in 1917 she became the first woman member of the American Bar Association. Diaries, 1887 and 1890, record her travels across the country to speak in Protestant churches about temperance and scrapbooks relate primarily to her religious and WCTU work during the 1880s and 1890s. Also includes letters expressing various opinions on Myron Reed's position regarding the Chinese in Denver.

1,783. LeFevre, Eva J.
Papers. 1909-10. 126-page item.
Open. Card catalog.
Denver Public Library, Western History Department.
Diary LeFevre (1851-1948) wrote while she and her family visited England and France. LeFevre was active in charity and civic work and from 1871 was wife of Owen E. LeFevre, a Denver attorney who served as district judge for several years.

1,784. Loretto Heights College
Records. 1864-1958. 1 vol.
Open. Card catalog.
Denver Public Library, Western History Department.
Scrapbook containing historical sketches, pictures, programs of recitals, reviews, clippings, and other material related to this Catholic women's college, which was established in 1918 in Denver by the Sisters of Loretto and which is now coeducational.

1,785. McGrath, Maria (Davies)
Papers. Nd. 3 boxes and 1 vol.
Open. Card catalog.
Denver Public Library, Western History Department.
Papers of [Mrs.] McGrath (1865-1951), founder and president of the Denver Pioneer Museum, include the manuscript of *Real Pioneers of Colorado,* notebooks and records of her interviews; 250 biographies; minute books, record books, and speeches relating to the Pioneer Women of Colorado and the Pioneer Ladies' Aid Society; and scrapbooks of clippings on early pioneers.

1,786. Miscellany
Collections. 1857-1973. No size given.
Open. Card catalog.
Denver Public Library, Western History Department.
Small collections, most of them containing only one or two items, include numerous reminiscences and sketches of life in Colorado. Among them are "Across the Continent in a Brush Runabout, A Pioneer Trip in 1908" by Florence A. Trinkle; "A Christmas Pilgrimage in the Southwest" by Anne Evans; and reminiscences of Chihuahua, Decatur, and Montezuma district by Elizabeth Roller. Sadie J. Boulton provides a sketch of life on Divide Creek and Dry Hollow in the 1900s and 1910s. Mary L. (Costillo) Nichols reminisces about her childhood in Memphis and Denver; and Agnes Hall writes of a trip from Palmer Lake to Pike's Peak and back with a pack horse. "Queen Ann" Bassett Willis, a Colorado rancher and alleged cattle rustler and boss of the Bassett gang, gives her account of the Great Diamond Hoax, while her friend Esther Campbell describes "Queen Ann" as she knew her. Stories by Hannah Shwayder Berry on the Shwayder family, Polish Jews who migrated to Denver and became the largest manufacturers of luggage in the US, include a biographical sketch of midwife Miriam Kobéy, Hannah Berry's grandmother. Minna F. Dickinson provides historical glimpses of the Women's Faculty Club of the University of Denver for the years 1862 to 1949. Material of Carrie A. Hall relates to the art and history of patchwork quilts in the US, while the Minnie F. Wall papers include material on the women who designed and sought the adoption of the Colorado state flag.

The collection of the Shellabargers, who were among the first white ranchers in the San Luis Valley, contains letters of Abigail W. Shellabarger and M. Elizabeth Shellabarger and papers of Blanche Ashley Shellabarger, including an article on ranch life, housekeeping, and agriculture in the San Luis Valley from the 1890s to 1940s; the story of her girlhood in the Colorado towns of Saquache and Moffat; and a history of the Ashley family. A letter by Mrs. Charles Meyrs describes the Convent of the Annunciation, a school founded by the Sisters of Loretto at Mora, NM. Letters by Louise Hawkins Canby to William A. Carter speak of an 1857 trip to Utah and of returning East after the death of her husband General E. R. S. Canby. Other letters include one by Lady Blythe Marvin, the "Original Mechanical Doll," describing her theatrical career and one by Harvey Doe, first husband of Baby Doe Tabor, to his parents explaining why he was in the Lizzie Priston bawdy house when his wife caught him and used that as grounds for divorce. Also included is correspondence of poet Jean Milne Gower.

Scrapbooks include one which belonged to Ethel (Norton) Bancroft and contains items about the Jarvis, Norton, and Bancroft families; one with original art and greeting cards by artist Alice Stewart Hill; and one kept by Mrs. Clyde A. Jack which contains programs from various theaters and from Wolcott School, an exclusive school for girls in Denver founded in 1898 by Anna Wolcott. Mary Brent Parker's scrapbook, kept while she was with Col. Parker at Fort Garland and Fort Union in the 1870s, includes manuscript poems and clippings. Letters, photos, documents, and memorabilia of Nadeen Piatt as well as material relating to William F. Cody are contained in Piatt's scrapbook, while the scrapbook of [Miss] Ina Aulls contains testimonials presented to her on her retirement from the staff of the Denver Public Library. Also included are scrapbooks of society woman Lucretia Pope, author Dora Ladd Keyes, and Elizabeth Keyes, publisher of Gentle Living Publications.

Other items include biographical sketches of Carolyn Lawrence Dier and Sadie M. Likens, part of Likens's will, a journal kept by Harriet Chaffee Ross in 1908 and 1909, a history of the Tuesday Morning Class by Clara C. Blakney, and scripts for Susan O'Brien Hautzinger's radio program. A memorial to Mary Weaver Midkiff describes her life as a minister's wife and missionary in Brazil. Correspondence, brochures, articles, and clippings dealing with the Child Research Council are contained in the papers of Mindell W. Stein, daughter of [Mrs.] Lillian Winter Michelson and assistant to W. Walter Wassor, who were cofounders of the Council. Also included are a biographical sketch of physician Margaret Ethel V. Fraser, who was active in organizations for the improvement of the status of women; a guest register for the dedication of a statue of physician Florence Rena Sabin in Washington, DC; and letters from Sabin to Mabel Mall in the collection of Elinor Bluemel.

1,787. Monday Literary Club
Records. 1881-1956. 3 vols.
Open. Card catalog.
Denver Public Library, Western History Department.
Collection consists of a history of the Club and papers given by members at meetings.

1,788. Music
Collections. 1884-1974. No size given.
Open. Card catalog.
Denver Public Library, Western History Department.
Material on music and musicians includes the Musicians' Society of Denver Collection, which contains short biographies of musicians by Walter C. Nielsen and a history of chamber music in Denver by Miriam S. Campbell. The Colorado Federation of Music Clubs was organized in 1920 to foster music appreciation and encourage musicians and composers by sponsoring festivals, concerts, and contests; its collection contains manuscript and published works, lists of performances, and notebooks of biographical data on Colorado composers. Records of the Denver Area Music Teachers' Association, formed in 1942 to promote music, include a history of the organization, monthly invitations, and publicity brochures for the Denver Metropolitan Piano Festival. Records of the Denver Symphony Society include its constitution, minutes of executive board meetings, financial reports, publicity, and debutante ball committee lists. Two papers, one by Permelia (Curtis) Porter and one by Alice Roeschlaub Williams, concern music in Denver, while a scrapbook by Williams, then Alice Roeschlaub, covers the years 1884 to 1950 and contains musical programs, photos, and biographical sketches of women musicians of Denver. The James Allen Grubb collection contains a scrapbook with biographical sketches, programs, photos, and clippings relating to Denver musicians Margaret Day Grubb, Martha Grubb Bretz, and Margaret Marian Grubb. Other scrapbooks include one with biographical sketches, photos, and clippings of violinist Veda Reynolds; volumes of programs and publicity on the Denver Businessmen's Orchestra, which is conducted by Antonia Brico and is now called The Brico Symphony; and a volume with photos and publicity on the 100-figure miniature of the Denver Symphony Orchestra which was constructed by Cuthbert Powell and his wife Mary Morrison Powell. Another scrapbook contains sketches, photos, and clippings relating to music in Englewood, CO.

1,789. National League of American Pen Women, Inc.
Records. 1941-64. 2 vols.
Open. Card catalog.
Denver Public Library, Western History Department.
Scrapbooks containing yearbooks, correspondence, photos, programs, articles, and clippings of the Denver branch of the League, formed in 1921.

1,790. Pioneer Women
Collections. 1838-1968. No size given.
Open. Card catalog.
Denver Public Library, Western History Department.
Material on pioneer experiences dates from the 1830s to the 1890s and consists of correspondence, diaries, reminiscences, clippings, and scrapbooks. The earliest diary is that of Sarah Gilbert White Smith, written in 1838 and 1839 on a journey from Springfield, MD, to Waiilatpu, Oregon Territory, where she and her husband Asa Smith were to serve as missionaries to the Indians; this journal was published in 1966 as *First White Women Over the Rockies.* An 1854 diary believed to have been written by Mrs. George McGrew describes a trip from Kalamazoo, MI, to Placerville, CA. Diaries of the 1860s include Nellie Slater's record of a journey by horse-drawn wagons from Garden Grove, IA, to Auburn City, OR; "How I Went to Denver," Emily Malone Raymond [Mrs. Isaac Irving] Moore's journal concerning her trip from Omaha by wagon; Sara [Mrs. Andrew Paul] Hively's description of daily life in Denver; and a diary written by Helen E. Clark. The diary of Queen (Mellen) Palmer, wife of railroad entrepreneur William Jackson Palmer, was written in 1870 and 1871 during their honeymoon in Europe. Cara Georgina Whitmore Bell's diary from the years 1872 to 1876 describes her early married life in Colorado Springs, CO, her home Briarhurst, and the important people she met because of the partnership of her physician husband William Abraham Bell with William Palmer. The 1896 diary of Anna Stanley [Mrs. Henry P.] Talhelm contains references to Pike's Peak, the Cog Road, and moving to Rocky Ford where her father was engaged in business.

Other material on pioneer women is primarily from the 1860s and 1870s. Letters by Julia Archibald Holmes, reputed to be the first woman to reach the summit of Pike's Peak, describe her ascent; these letters were used by Agnes Wright Spring in the book *A Bloomer Girl on Pike's Peak, 1858.* Scrapbooks of Annie E. Blake, wife of Denver's first merchant Charles H. Blake, contain articles on the early history of Denver and Pueblo, CO, and on the state of Colorado, obituaries of early Colorado residents, articles about family members, and poems. "The Story of Mary York Cozens" tells of an Irish immigrant who pioneered in Colorado, while a newspaper story concerns a talk in which [Mrs.] Anna Pence describes the hardships of crossing the plains to Idaho. The reminiscences of Flora Ellice (Bishop) Stevens, a poet and journalist who arrived in Denver at the age of five, concern her childhood and reveal contemporary attitudes toward the Sand Creek Massacre. Additional biographical information on Flora Stevens is included in a letter by her son Arthur Ewing Stevens. The Sister Mary Joanna Walsh collection contains her account of a journey to Denver from Santa Fe, NM, and of the opening of St. Mary's Academy there. Biographies of Trinidad, CO, and Las Animas County, CO, pioneers written by Fred Winsor for publication in the Trinidad *Chronicle News,* of which he was editor, are included in the R. E. McClung collection. A paper by [Mrs.] Marian McIntire McDonough is based on the journal Marian Willard Young wrote while traveling from Chicago to Denver; this journal, entitled "Camping Expedition to Colorado," was also the basis for McDonough's novel *Wagon Wheels to Denver.* A series of letters by Isabella Lucy (Bird) Bishop, author of *A Lady's Life in the Rocky Mountains,* concerns her Rocky Mountain experiences; in another letter Cora Belle Wasson Mitchell, a resident of Leadville, CO, in the 1880s, reminisces about her household, daily life, and travels. Also included are the correspondence of Mrs. Thomas Withers and a letter to Henry Moore Teller in which Martha A. [Mrs. James A.] Maxwell, a taxidermist, requests space and financial assistance for her natural history exhibit at the 1878 international Paris Exposition, as well as a talk by Elmer F. Bennett, entitled "Pioneer Women of Colorado—Courage and Sacrifice." The story of the capture of the Box sisters by the Sioux and their eventual rescue is contained in the Lee Herron collection. In letters written from the Wyoming Territory, Robert C. Morris discusses the appointment of his mother Esther Hobart Slack Morris as Justice of the Peace, the first woman in the US to hold that position. The James R. Quinn papers contain a woman's account of a pioneer family in No Man's Land, OK.

1,791. Reviewers' Club
Records. 1892-1972. 7 vols.
Open. Card catalog.
Denver Public Library, Western History Department.
The Club was organized in 1892 for intensive individual study of literary and historic subjects. Minutes of regular meetings and of board meetings dating from 1962, scrapbooks of clippings and other material on Club activities and officers, and material on the Colorado Federation of Women's Clubs, of which the Reviewers' Club was a charter member.

1,792. Round Table Club
Records. 1889- . 3 boxes.
Open. Card catalog.
Denver Public Library, Western History Department.
Constitution, certificate of incorporation, minutes, correspondence, programs, and clippings of the Club, a women's mutual enrichment society in Denver.

1,793. San Juan Women's Club
Records. 1907-23. 2 vols.
Open. Card catalog.
Denver Public Library, Western History Department.
Minutes of the Club, apparently a social club, which met bimonthly at Silverton, CO.

1,794. Spalding, Elizabeth
Papers. Ca. 1909-19. 1 vol., 9 items, and 2 microfilm reels.
Open. Card catalog.
Denver Public Library, Western History Department.
Papers of Spalding, an artist, include correspondence with various artists; a paper on Nantucket Island; and a scrapbook of the Artists' Club of Denver, which in 1917 became the Denver Art Association. Scrapbook contains programs, art notes columns, and clippings on art.

1,795. Spencer, Lillian (White)
Papers. 1920-35. No size given.
Open. Card catalog.
Denver Public Library, Western History Department.
Papers of [Mrs.] Spencer (ca. 1878-1953), a Denver author, poet, and playwright, include correspondence; manuscripts of poems, plays, and lyrics; radio scripts dealing with Indian legends; articles by Spencer from an archaeological magazine; translations of French poetry; biographical information; and critical notices. Correspondents include Lenora Speyer, the *American Poetry Journal,* the Library of Congress, and publishers.

1,796. State Secretary-Treasurers' Association of Colorado, Order of the Eastern Star
Records. Nd. 1 item.
Open. Card catalog.
Denver Public Library, Western History Department.
Constitution, bylaws, and minutes of the first meeting of the Association.

1,797. Territorial Daughters of Colorado
Records. Nd. No size given.
Open. Card catalog.
Denver Public Library, Western History Department.
Papers by members contain biographies, genealogies, and reminiscences about events.

1,798. U.S. Work Projects Administration, Colorado
Records. 1935. 6 boxes, 1 vol., and 24 items.
Open. Card catalog.
Denver Public Library, Western History Department.
Manuscripts of Federal Writers' Projects and the Education-Recreation Division include plays by Lillian Metz Hendrix, Martha Ann Williams, and Charles and Grace Hubbard. The volume gives a summary of activities at the Federal Educational Camp for Unemployed Women held in Palmer Lake, CO, and includes schedules of classes, names of enrollees, entrance requirements, activities, and accomplishments of the Camp.

1,799. Weber, Alice (Lytle)
Papers. 1825-1933. 2 vols. and 2 items.
Open. Card catalog.
Denver Public Library, Western History Department.
Papers of [Mrs. Adam] Weber (1874-1965), a concert contralto and voice instructor, include narratives about Mary Jane McAlister Lytle and about family events, including the discovery of the Black Diamond Gold Mine by Weber's father George Lytle; records of family births, marriages, and deaths; and programs from Weber's musical career.

1,800. Weber, Gretchen
Papers. 1934-49. 1 box.
Open. Card catalog.
Denver Public Library, Western History Department.
Papers of Weber, an artist who worked for the Denver *Post,* include correspondence with David P. Fenwick in which Weber asks for and is granted permission to "crib" an article in her *Post* column and scrapbooks of clippings showing her designs of women's and children's fashions.

1,801. Weber, Lenora (Mattingly)
Papers. Nd. 4 ft. and 6 boxes.
Open. Card catalog.
Denver Public Library, Western History Department.
Correspondence and fan mail, manuscripts of her books, speech notes, articles, short stories, memorabilia, contracts, clippings, and other papers of [Mrs. Albert] Weber (1895-1971), a Colorado author.

1,802. Western States Missionary Baptist Convention
Records. 1909-72. 1 box and 1 vol.
Open. Card catalog.
Denver Public Library, Western History Department.
Minutes, annual reports, lists of officers, church histories, biographical data, photos, and programs of the Convention, which was established in 1908 by members of Zion and Central Baptist churches to insure closer cooperation for church work in Colorado.

1,803. Wolfe Hall
Records. 1886-1948. 2 vols. and 1 item.
Open. Card catalog.
Denver Public Library, Western History Department.
Scrapbook, photo, and miscellaneous papers of Eloise Sargent Lehow, who taught at Wolfe Hall, an Episcopal school for girls which operated in Denver from 1868 to 1913 and served Denver and surrounding states. Included in the Ruth and Jennie Becker collection is a scrapbook of the Wolfe Hall alumnae association containing invitations to and publicity on meetings, programs, recitals, reunions, and class exercises; commencement brochures; articles; and clippings.

1,804. Wolle, Muriel Sibell
Papers. 1926-76. 29 ft.
Open. Card catalog and preliminary inventory.
Denver Public Library, Western History Department.
[Mrs. Francis] Wolle (1898-1977) was a western author, artist, historian, and professor known for her writings on ghost towns and mining camps. Correspondence; journals; field notes; drafts of her book *Stampede to Timberline,* which deals with the mining booms in Colorado; interviews; and 202 scrapbooks of notes, photos, post cards, and clippings on western towns. Wolle, who was born in Brooklyn, NY, received degrees in advertising and costume design from the New York School of Fine and Applied Arts and in art education from New York University. She also received a master's degree in English literature from the University of Colorado, where she taught art for 40 years. Among the books she has written and illustrated are *Ghost Cities of Colorado, Bonanza Trail,* and *Montana Pay Dirt.*

1,805. Women's Christian Union of Silverton
Records. 1914-29. 2 vols.
Open. Card catalog.
Denver Public Library, Western History Department.
Minutes of the Union, a missionary and temperance organization of Silverton, CO.

1,806. Bureau of Indian Affairs (RG 75)
Records. Ca. 1865-1945. 941 cu.ft.
Access restricted. No guide.
Federal Archives and Records Center, Denver Archives Branch.
Correspondence, reports, enrollment books, individual Indian money ledgers, allotment records, medical records, and Indian censuses. Material about women is found primarily in school enrollment lists and census records as well as in records on marriage and divorce, religions, child welfare, social relations, and employment.

1,807. Internal Revenue Service (RG 58)
Records. 1873-1917. 8 cu.ft.
Open. No guide.
Federal Archives and Records Center, Denver Archives Branch.
Tax assessment lists, which give names and addresses of those assessed and the amount assessed. Contains records of Colorado, 1873-1917; New Mexico, 1885-1917; and Wyoming, 1874-79.

1,808. United States Courts of Appeals (RG 276)
Records. 1929-45. 307 cu.ft.
Open. No guide.
Federal Archives and Records Center, Denver Archives Branch.
Case files and correspondence relating to cases heard by the Courts, which were established to hear appeals from cases decided in lower federal courts and to review and enforce orders of federal administrative bodies. Records of cases in the 10th circuit, which includes Colorado, Wyoming, Utah, Kansas, New Mexico, and judicial districts in Oklahoma. Case files are arranged by case file number.

1,809. United States District Courts (RG 21)
Records. Ca. 1860-1945. 2983 cu.ft.
Open. No guide.
Federal Archives and Records Center, Denver Archives Branch.
Docket books, records books, and case files pertaining to cases heard by the Courts in Colorado, New Mexico, and Wyoming. Consists primarily of civil, criminal, and bankruptcy cases but also includes naturalization records for some of the Courts.

1,810. Wage and Salary Stabilization Boards, Economic Stabilization Agency (RG 293)
Records. 1951-53. 16 cu.ft.
Access restricted. No guide.
Federal Archives and Records Center, Denver Archives Branch.
The Board was established in 1950 to administer wage stabilization and labor disputes during the Korean War after Congress imposed wage, price, and other controls. When petitioned, regional boards decided whether salary increases could be granted to employees of specific companies. Includes general subject files, rulings, and opinions case files for Region 11 (Denver), which had program jurisdiction for New Mexico, Colorado, Wyoming, and Utah. Taken from Robert Svenningsen, "Preliminary Guide to the Research Records in the Denver Federal Records Center" (Denver, CO: Denver Federal Records Center, 1969, out of print).

1,811. War Assets Administration (RG 270)
Records. 1940-46. 77 cu.ft.
Access restricted. No guide.
Federal Archives and Records Center, Denver Archives Branch.
Records of the Administration, which was established to dispose of domestic surpluses, contain real property case files from Colorado, Utah, and Wyoming. Some of the cases pertain to women.

1,812. Deaconess Bureau of the Colorado Conference
Records. 1904-41. Ca. 15 vols.
Open. No guide.
Iliff School of Theology, United Methodist Church, Rocky Mountain Conference Archives.
The Bureau supervised operation of the Margaret Evans Deaconess Home. Annual reports of the Colorado Conference Deaconess Board, minutes and treasurer's books of the Deaconess Bureau, and financial records of the Deaconess Home. According to rules of the Methodist Episcopal Church, published in 1904, the deaconesses were unmarried women more than 23 years old who had attended a training school and had given more than two years of probationary service. The governing board of their Conference granted them deaconess licenses upon the recommendation of the head of the training school and other church officials. Their work included care of the sick, poor, and orphans and "other forms of Christian labor." The deaconesses were free to leave the church's service at any time.

1,813. Women's Societies
Collection. 1882-1952. Ca. 20 ft.
Open. No guide.
Iliff School of Theology, United Methodist Church, Rocky Mountain Conference Archives.
Minutes and treasurer's records of the Denver district of the Woman's Home Missionary Society. Also includes annual reports of the Woman's Home Missionary Society, the Woman's Foreign Missionary Society, and the Board of Home Missions and Church Extension, all national organizations.

FORT COLLINS

1,814. Colorado State University Archives
Records. Ca. 1891- . No size given.
Open. No guide.
Colorado State University Library, Special Collections.
Founded as Colorado Agricultural College and renamed Colorado Agricultural and Mechanical

College in 1931, the institution was one of the first schools in Colorado to include a domestic science department. Principally University publications, including yearbooks, faculty manuals, class schedules, student handbooks, a weekly faculty newsletter, student newspapers, and "Here's Help," a home economics newsletter with issues dating from 1966. Also includes a monthly magazine published by an all female staff in 1894 and 1895. First called *The Tourney* and later known as *The Colorado Woman,* the publication was edited by Grace Espy Patton, a member of the English faculty who became state superintendent of public instruction. The magazine was devoted to discussion of sociological subjects and included short stories, essays, editorials, poetry, suffrage articles, and notes on state women's clubs. The College became Colorado State University in 1957.

GREELEY

1,815. Special Collections
Records. 1890- . Ca. 75 ft.
Open. No guide.
University of Northern Colorado Library.
Scattered yearbooks, catalogs, college and faculty bulletins, reprints of articles by faculty members, and other records of this four-year college, which for most of its history was concerned with the education of teachers. The school was founded in 1891 as the State Normal School of Colorado, Greeley; over the years its name was changed to Colorado State Teachers College, Colorado State College of Education, and Colorado State College, until 1970 when the institution adopted its current name. Collection contains papers of Helen Langworthy, who was head of the theater department, and of Katharine Ommanney, a professional actress who was an alumna of the College; oral history interviews in which faculty members discuss their memories of activities and specific events at the University; and master's theses of students at this university, one of the institutions that led in the development of home economics.

LITTLETON

1,816. Babcock, Jessie
Papers. 1881-90. 1 vol.
Open. No guide.
Littleton Historical Museum.
Babcock (1865-?), a resident of Littleton, married John Pollock between 1884 and 1890 and moved to Greenland, CO. Diary with entries from 1881, 1883, 1884, and 1890. During the early portion of the period, Babcock was a young girl living with her parents. In the diary entries, she describes her day-to-day activities, including chores and social activities, and also speaks of farming in eastern Colorado.

1,817. Littleton Business and Professional Women's Club
Records. 1934-56. 12 vols.
Open. Card file.
Littleton Historical Museum.
Scrapbooks of this local group, which was organized in 1934 as a social, educational, and philanthropic club for women in business and the professions. Scrapbooks contain yearly budgets and program books; committee reports; programs from specific events; national, state, and local newsletters; photos; clippings; and other material, including items from the Colorado state convention in 1956 in Glenwood Springs. The scrapbooks reflect the group's activities, which included sponsoring a Camp Fire Girls group, a representative for the Littleton War Memorial Community Center in 1950, and floats for community parades; helping to develop the local Rio Grande Park; and, as part of the state BPW in 1943, supporting a bill for jury service for women. The volumes contain membership lists indicating that members held positions as teachers, secretaries, city employees, bookkeepers, deputy assessor, and owners of beauty shops, grocery stores, and other small businesses.

1,818. Littleton Women's Club
Records. 1906-57. 6 vols. and additional items.
Open. Card file.
Littleton Historical Museum.
The Club was organized in 1897 as a social, philanthropic, and educational group. Secretary's books, treasurer's book, scrapbook with annual reports, and annual program booklets, which include lists of officers and committee chairmen as well as the program for each session. The Club sponsored essay and spelling contests in the local schools and contributed money to scholarship funds and to the municipal Christmas tree fund. The group's program topics included health, fine arts, book reviews, and Colorado history.

PUEBLO

1,819. Archives
Records. 1947- . 3 boxes.
Access restricted. No guide.
Servants of the Blessed Sacrament, American Province.
House journals describing daily events of the order's first foundations in the US, biographies of deceased sisters, photo albums, and scrapbooks of the congregation, which was founded in Waterville, ME, in 1947.

CONNECTICUT

BRIDGEPORT

1,820. Fleck, Ella Conover (Gray)
Papers. 1916-31. 2.5 in.
Open. No guide.
Bridgeport Public Library, Historical Collections.
Correspondence, minutes, reports, and certificates of [Mrs. H. Willard] Fleck (1875 or 1876-1972), a suffrage advocate who lived in Bridgeport. Fleck was active in WWI activities, health and welfare activities, and Republican politics. Includes items on the Bridgeport War Bureau; Fleck was a member of the Bureau's executive committee and chairman of the group's women's committee.

1,821. Hudson, Lillian C.
Papers. 1932-72. 2 in.
Open. No guide.
Bridgeport Public Library, Historical Collections.
Correspondence and other papers of [Mrs. Claude] Hudson (1892-1976) relate to the women's auxiliary of the YMCA of Greater Bridgeport, of which she was president.

1,822. Kirk, Hazel M.
Papers. 19th century-1961. 5 in.
Open. No guide.
Bridgeport Public Library, Historical Collections.
Kirk, an office worker for most of her life, is now retired. Contains personal and family correspondence, including letters from Elizabeth C. Wright, a missionary at the Presbyterian mission in Peking, China, and from Samuel H. and Eileen Moffett, who were missionaries in Korea. Also includes Kirk's diary for 1932 and 19th-century photos of the Tappan and Kirk families, which resided in Union Springs and Muncy, NY, Newark, NJ, Denver, and Bridgeport and Stratford, CT.

1,823. Lind, Jenny
Papers. 1847?-79. 6 items.
Open. Unpublished guide.
Bridgeport Public Library, Historical Collections.
Correspondence of Lind (1820-87), a singer, relates to concert arrangements and acceptances of social engagements. Also includes thank-you notes. P. T. Barnum brought Lind from Sweden to make concert tours in the US.

1,824. Mallett, Anna Smith
Papers. 1861-1907. 3 ft.
Closed. No guide.
Bridgeport Public Library, Historical Collections.
Mallett (1845-1907) was a genealogist. Includes family correspondence; research notes, proofs, and corrections for her book *John Mallet, the Huguenot, and his Descendants, 1694-1894* (Harrisburg, PA, 1895); household accounts for her residences in Bridgeport and Washington, DC; papers relating to land investments in Iowa and Nebraska; and clippings.

1,825. Mosaic Club
Records. 1897-1965. 1 ft.
Open. No guide.
Bridgeport Public Library, Historical Collections.
Minutes and a history of this women's discussion group, which was founded in 1897. Includes notes on talks that members prepared and delivered to the group.

1,826. National League of American Pen Women, Inc.
Records. 1928-75. 2 ft.
Open. No guide.
Bridgeport Public Library, Historical Collections.
President's messages, reports, scrapbooks, and yearbooks of this chapter of the League, a literary organization.

1,827. Seeley, Elizabeth Sterling
Papers. 1920?-74. 10 ft.
Closed. No guide.
Bridgeport Public Library, Historical Collections.
Seeley (1897-1974) was a writer, researcher, and curator of the Barnum Museum in Bridgeport. Includes correspondence, research notes, drafts of articles submitted to popular magazines, and photos, which relate to personal and family matters, local Bridgeport history, the Barnum and Bailey circus, her curatorship, and genealogy.

1,828. Thompson, Caroline Cornelia (Barnum)
Papers. 1848-51. 2 vols.
Open. Unpublished guide.
Bridgeport Public Library, Historical Collections.
Diaries of [Mrs. David W.] Thompson (1833-1911), the daughter of Phineas T. Barnum, concern her trip across New York state to Montreal and Quebec and her return to Bridgeport as well as Jenny Lind's tour through several eastern cities. Lind's tour was under the management of P. T. Barnum.

1,829. Vogel, Anita (Steiber)
Papers. 1949-74. 20 ft.
Open. No guide.
Bridgeport Public Library, Historical Collections.
Papers of [Mrs. Rudolf] Vogel relate to her term as a member of the Bridgeport Board of Education and contain correspondence, reports, studies, minutes, charts, and graphs. Also includes papers pertaining to her unsuccessful race as a Republican candidate for Bridgeport town clerk and her work for the Republican Action League, including research material on issues and strategy, news releases, handbills, brochures, and a leader's manual. Also includes biographical sketches.

1,830. Wednesday Afternoon Musical Club, Inc.
Records. 1898-1976. 2 ft.
Open. No guide.
Bridgeport Public Library, Historical Collections.
Articles of incorporation, minutes, legal records, and yearbooks of the Club, a performing musical group that was made up of women. The Club probably was organized in 1898.

1,831. Women's Auxiliary of the YMCA of Greater Bridgeport
Records. 1931-65. 8 in.
Open. No guide.
Bridgeport Public Library, Historical Collections.
Includes minutes, correspondence, reports, a history, photos, and programs of the Auxiliary, which was founded in ca. 1886 and dissolved in 1965; minutes, reports, and correspondence of the Mother's Club of the YMCA of Greater Bridgeport, which was founded in ca. 1929 and disbanded in 1958; minutes, reports, and programs of the Connecticut Association of Women's Groups of the YMCA; and minutes and reports of the Women's Council of the New England Area YMCA.

1,832. Dental Hygiene
Records. 1913- . 4 boxes and 1 slide-sound show.
Open. Unpublished guide.
University of Bridgeport, Fones School of Dental Hygiene.
Correspondence, journals, minutes, brochures, textbooks, photos, and other items document the work of Alfred Civilion Fones, a dentist who founded the profession of dental hygiene. In 1907 he trained his chairside dental assistant [Mrs.] Irene Newman to perform various intra-oral preventive procedures. The success and effectiveness of her training led to establishment in 1913 of the Fones School, where 33 young women were taught to render educational and clinical services to their patients.

CORNWALL

1,833. Garden Club of Cornwall
Records. 1925-75. Ca. 1 box.
Open. No guide.
Cornwall Historical Society.
Minutes of this gardening group, which was founded in 1925 by Katherine Walker, who was the wife of a local physician. The group, which was disbanded in 1975 because of lack of interest and the advancing age of its members, organized garden and flower shows, plant sales, garden tours, and luncheons.

EAST HARTFORD

1,834. East Hartford Woman's Club, Inc.
Records. 1954-75. 19 vols.
Open. No guide.
East Hartford Public Library.
Scrapbooks and photos of the Club, founded in 1954 to advance and promote "good fellowship in civic, social, charitable and education fields in a non-partisan and non-sectarian manner."

1,835. Laurel Garden Club
Records. 1929-69. 5 vols.
Open. No guide.
East Hartford Public Library.
Constitution, minutes of meetings, and scrapbooks of the Club, founded in 1929 and disbanded in 1971. The group promoted interest in gardening and civic improvements and encouraged the conservation of wild plant life and birds.

FARMINGTON

1,836. Miss Porter's School
Records. 1840- . 60 ft. and 28 boxes.
Access restricted. Unpublished guide.
Miss Porter's School Archives.
Miss Porter's School was founded during the 1840s by [Miss] Sarah Porter, who also was a teacher at and head of the School until her death; the school was operated as a women's academy during the 19th century and as a women's independent secondary school during the 20th century. Correspondence of Sarah Porter with her family and with her students and their parents, diary fragments, class notes, and Bible talks of Porter provide information about her educational and religious ideas. Collection also contains ledgers, 1840-1900, containing names of students and their addresses, textbook lists, and records of students' expenses; school rules for the entire period; student compositions; ca. 20 student diaries, 19th century; ca. 100 student scrapbooks, 1860-1930; and student newspapers, 1850s-60s. In addition, the collection includes material relating to the group of local men who financed the building of the first schoolhouse for Miss Porter's; records of the Sewing Society and the Lodge Society, two alumnae groups that engaged in benevolent work between the 1880s and the 1940s; and material concerning the Farmington Female Seminary.

GREENWICH

1,837. Oral History Project
Oral history. 1973- . 600 tapes and 350 transcripts.
Open. Unpublished guide.
Greenwich Library.
Tapes and transcripts of interviews about the history of Greenwich with local residents, including Mariette [Mrs. Daniel] Badger, who talks about parks and conservation; Sybil [Mrs. George] Bellos, who describes the local public health nursing service; [Miss] Elizabeth Bronk, who discusses the Greenwich Health Association; Elizabeth "Beezie" (Hyde) [Mrs. Kenneth C.] Brownell, who talks about various Greenwich hospitals as well as about Rosemary Hall, a private girls school; Ruth [Mrs. Arthur] Chamberlain, who discusses the North Mianus Community Center; Caroyl [Mrs. Edward G.] Erb, who describes the YWCA; Barbara (Kitchell) [Mrs. Reynolds] Girdler, who talks about the LWV; Marianne [Mrs. Frederick R.] Jeffrey, who tells of the Greenwich Philharmonia; Winifred [Mrs. Stephen L.] Porter, who discusses the American National Red Cross blood program; Nancy (Carnegie) [Mrs. J. Stillman] Rockefeller, who discusses planned parenthood counseling; Hazel [Mrs. John J.] Sargeant, who talks about the school hot lunch program; Mary [Mrs. Donald F.] Updike, who tells of the local housing authority; Helen [Mrs. Joseph] Wilshire [Mrs. William J.] Walsh, who discusses the Republican party; and Gertrude [Mrs. John J.] White, who describes her volunteer work for the YWCA, the Community Chest, and Christ Church. Also includes interviews in which Chancy (D'Elia) [Mrs. J. Lane] Curry discusses her background and ownership of a local retail shop, which bears her maiden name; Olga (Zatorsky) Hirshhorn speaks of her childhood and later life in Greenwich and her marriage to Joseph Hirshhorn, an art collector; Rhoda (Barney) Jenkins and John Barney discuss Nora (Stanton) [Mrs. Morgan] Barney, a Cornell graduate who was the granddaughter of Elizabeth Cady Stanton as well as a civil engineer and architect; and other women, who discuss such topics as nursing, schoolteaching, the Seton Indians, minstrels, and the black, Jewish, Italian, and Polish communities in Greenwich.

HARTFORD

1,838. American Scrapbooks
Collection. 1937-38. 12 vols.
Open. List of subjects.
Archives of the Hartford Seminary Foundation.
Volumes of topically arranged clippings deal with women, marriage, children, and other subjects. The "handwriting" section includes clippings regarding Virginia Drew's method of personality analysis.

1,839. Baxter, Edna May
Papers. 1924-60. Ca. 950 items and 3 ft.
Open. Calendar.
Archives of the Hartford Seminary Foundation.
Baxter (1890-) was professor of religious education at Hartford Seminary Foundation from 1926 to 1960. Correspondence, drafts of essays, notes, catalogs, clippings, and other printed material reflect Baxter's personal interests as well as her work in theology, education, and administration.

1,840. Calverley, Mr. and Mrs. Edwin Elliott
Papers. 1876-1968. Ca. 25,000 items.
Open. Calendar.
Archives of the Hartford Seminary Foundation.
Edwin Calverley (1882-1971) and his wife Eleanor Jane (Taylor) Calverley (1886-1968) were missionary doctors in Arabia; she also was a founder of Alcott Hospital in Kuwait and she lectured on tropical hygiene at Hartford Seminary Foundation from 1930 until 1943. Ca. 1700 pieces of correspondence, most of which were exchanged with her husband; diaries from 1909 to 1950; her autobiography; field reports; account books; lectures; organizational records; bibliographies; class notes; drafts and published versions of articles; photos; and clippings.

1,841. Capen, Mr. and Mrs. Edward Warren
Papers. 1890-1955. Ca. 20,000 items.
Open. Calendar.
Archives of the Hartford Seminary Foundation.
Family papers of Capen (1870-1947) and his wife Elizabeth Lydia (Sanderson) Capen (1872-1955), both of whom were educational administrators; Lydia Capen was a member of the woman's board of the Hartford Seminary Foundation from 1915 to 1954. Correspondence, 15 volumes of Lydia Capen's diaries, a diary she kept with her husband during their 1907-09 trip to the Near East and Asia, her notebooks, and account books, as well as other financial records, sermons, guest books, notes, photos, and clippings.

1,842. Carney, Mabel
Papers. 1928-42. Ca. 340 items.
Open. Calendar.
Archives of the Hartford Seminary Foundation.
A specialist in Negro education, race relations, and rural education in Latin America, Carney taught at the Columbia University Teachers College. Correspondence, course material, notes, lectures, and articles chiefly relate to her visiting lectureship at the Hartford Seminary Foundation Kennedy School of Missions from 1928 to 1942.

1,843. Daniels, Mary Louise (Underwood)
Papers. 1920-36. Ca. 170 items.
Open. Calendar.
Archives of the Hartford Seminary Foundation.
Daniels (?-1933) taught classes on missionary work and the Bible at Hartford Seminary Foundation from 1921 through 1930. Correspondence, clippings, course material, obituaries, and photos chiefly concern her work at the Seminary.

1,844. Donohugh, Agnes Crawford Leaycraft
Papers. 1918-44. Ca. 660 items.
Open. Calendar.
Archives of the Hartford Seminary Foundation.
[Mrs. Thomas A.] Donohugh (1876-1966) taught African ethnology and native life at the Hartford

Seminary Foundation Kennedy School of Missions. Correspondence, drafts of scholarly papers, financial documents, photos, and course material regarding her teaching at the Seminary and her publications.

1,845. Fisher, Annie
Papers. 1916-34. Ca. 165 items.
Open. Calendar.
Archives of the Hartford Seminary Foundation.
Fisher taught both phonetics and methods for teaching English to foreigners at Hartford Seminary Foundation from 1916 until 1936.
Correspondence, lecture notes, class exercises and schedules, lists of students, and articles regarding her work at the Seminary.

1,846. Gates, Katherine (Van Akin)
Papers. 1910-50. Ca. 165 items.
Open. Calendar.
Archives of the Hartford Seminary Foundation.
Gates (?-1949) stressed experiences gained as a missionary in India from 1923 to 1933 in her later scholarly writing and in classes she taught at Hartford Seminary Foundation from 1935 until 1949. Correspondence, school records, copies of publications by and about Gates, photos, and clippings pertaining to her career.

1,847. Gillett, Arthur Lincoln
Papers. 1866-1958. 2 boxes.
Open. Calendar.
Archives of the Hartford Seminary Foundation.
Family papers of Arthur Gillett (1859-1938), a clergyman and educator, and his wife Sarah Colton Phillips Gillett (?-1951), a member of the woman's board of Hartford Seminary Foundation. Diaries, 1917-49; notebooks; correspondence to Sarah Gillett; typescripts of articles; photos; and scrapbooks.

1,848. Hartford Seminary Foundation
Records. 1834- . 4 cases and ca. 230 boxes.
Open. Shelf list.
Archives of the Hartford Seminary Foundation.
Hartford Seminary Foundation was formed in 1913 by the consolidation of Hartford Theological Seminary (founded in 1833) and the Hartford School of Religious Pedagogy (established in Springfield, MA, in 1884 as the School of Christian Workers). Since the parent institutions admitted their first female students in 1889 and 1891, respectively, these records document the education of women for religious work. Collection includes the following records of the Foundation's and parent institutions' woman's boards, which were organized to provide aid to female students: minutes, financial records and accounts, correspondence, historical descriptions, programs, and scrapbooks (including some about Mackenzie Hall, the dormitory opened in 1924 for women students). Foundation records include minutes, financial records, legal documents, correspondence, sermons, lectures, class notes, memoranda books, news releases, reports, catalogs, publications, and photos.

1,849. Hill, Katharine Ledyard
Papers. 1916-27. Ca. 80 items.
Open. Calendar.
Archives of the Hartford Seminary Foundation.
Correspondence documents Hill's work as a teacher of missionary practice at Hartford Seminary Foundation from 1916 through 1922.

1,850. Johnson, Eleanor Hope
Papers. 1908-50. Ca. 6 ft.
Open. Partial calendar and description.
Archives of the Hartford Seminary Foundation.
An educator and social worker, Johnson (1871-1969) taught mental hygiene and psychology at Hartford Seminary Foundation from 1922 until 1937. Correspondence, pamphlets, clippings, and copies of her publications relate to her tenure at the Seminary, her work during WWII, and her studies of race relations.

1,851. Khoobyrarian, Helen
Papers. 1949-66. Ca. 200 items.
Open. Calendar.
Archives of the Hartford Seminary Foundation.
Khoobyrarian taught both religious and Christian education at Hartford Seminary Foundation from 1956 to 1965. Correspondence, course material, transcripts, copies of her publications, photos, and clippings concerning her teaching and scholarly writings.

1,852. Knapp, Lizzie Margaret
Papers. 1877-98. 28 vols. and 2 items.
Open. List.
Archives of the Hartford Seminary Foundation.
Knapp (1863-?) kept diaries from 1877 to 1898 describing life in her home town of Hartford, her travels, and her personal life. Besides 28 diary volumes, the collection consists of genealogical notes and photos.

1,853. Lowell, Marcia Johnson
Papers. 1933-65. Ca. 110 items.
Open. Calendar.
Archives of the Hartford Seminary Foundation.
Lowell (?-1965) was Hartford Seminary Foundation's dean of women from 1933 to 1955. Correspondence, programs, photos, and clippings principally document the conditions of her employment.

1,854. Macdonald, Duncan Black
Papers. 1815-1966. 10 file drawers.
Open. Calendar.
Archives of the Hartford Seminary Foundation.
Family papers of Duncan Macdonald (1863-1943), an author and orientalist, and his wife Mary Leeds Leffingwell (Bartlett) Macdonald (1850-1929), a genealogist and local historian. Collection contains Mary Macdonald's extensive correspondence with her husband and others, her diaries of their 1907-08 trip to Cairo, drafts of her historical writings, photos by and of her, sermons, research material, book reviews, class notes, and articles.

1,855. McLean, Grace B.
Papers. 1923-26. 245 items.
Open. Calendar.
Archives of the Hartford Seminary Foundation.
Correspondence, addresses, notes, obituaries, and clippings concern McLean (?-1935), dean of women at Hartford Seminary Foundation from 1923 to 1933, and the activities of her office.

1,856. Morrill, Belle Chapman
Papers. 1905-58. Ca. 70 items.
Open. Calendar.
Archives of the Hartford Seminary Foundation.
An author, Morrill (1882-1972) was an authority on education of blacks. Correspondence, drafts of her writings, clippings, and files primarily relating to her applications to study and work at Hartford Seminary Foundation.

1,857. Nettleton, Asahel
Papers. 1809-65. Ca. 1310 items.
Open. Calendar.
Archives of the Hartford Seminary Foundation.
Papers of Nettleton (1783-1844), a clergyman, include letters from a large number of women about their spiritual lives and religious feelings. Correspondence, diaries, sermons, accounts, and deeds.

1,858. Platt, Mary (Schauffler)
Papers. 1912-52. Ca. 330 items.
Open. Calendar.
Archives of the Hartford Seminary Foundation.
An educator and author, [Mrs. B. W. Labaree] Platt (1868-1954) taught classes in missionary practice at Hartford Seminary Foundation from 1913 until 1920. Correspondence, drafts of addresses, notes, pamphlets, and clippings relating to her tenure at the Seminary.

1,859. Recordings
Collection. 1955- . 130 tapes.
Open. List naming speaker, title, date, and length.
Archives of the Hartford Seminary Foundation.
Tapes of sermons, public lectures, music, and meetings, some of which relate to women: includes a woman speaking in 1962 on the non-violent philosophy of the Alabama Christian Movement, integration, and the bus boycott; 1960 retirement address by professor Edna May Baxter; and a dialogue between Hartford Seminary Foundation president James N. Gettemy and professor Helen Edick before alumni in 1968.

1,860. Thompson, Augustus Charles
Papers. 1752-1901. 323 vols. and ca. 2500 items.
Open. List of volume contents.
Archives of the Hartford Seminary Foundation.
Family papers of Augustus Thompson (1812-1901), a clergyman and author. Correspondence, reminiscences and autobiography, diaries, memoranda and notes in bound volumes, drafts of articles and lectures, scrapbooks, and leaflets. Among the diaries are those of his daughter-in-law Maria (Dobie) [Mrs. William Augustus] Thompson (1844-1927). Augustus Thompson's subject-classified notebooks include volumes on women, marriage, family, mothers, mothers of missionaries, wives, widows, and women and missions. Two of his scrapbooks, mostly clippings, are also about women.

1,861. Cornelius, Elias
Papers. 1811-1903. Ca. 450 items.
Open. Catalog card.
Connecticut Historical Society.
Correspondence of Cornelius (1794-1832), a missionary to the Indians, includes letters of his sister [Mrs.] Sarah (Cornelius) Perry.

1,862. Dwight and Patrick
Papers. 1772-1866. Ca. 85 items.
Open. Catalog card.
Connecticut Historical Society.
Correspondence of Theodore Dwight (1764-1846), a politician, includes letters to and from his daughter Mary A. (Dwight) [Mrs. Matthew] Patrick.

1,863. Francis, Stillman, Goodrich, and Welles Families
Papers. 1684-1912. Ca. 2300 items.
Open. Catalog cards and a digest.
Connecticut Historical Society.
Correspondence, diaries, account books, receipts, legal papers, sermons, and other papers provide detailed information on the women in these related Connecticut families. Included are school compositions and certificates of Jane Clarissa Francis (1834-ca. 1912), a schoolteacher, letters she wrote, and letters to her from such relatives as Bessie G. Stillman, Clara F. Stillman, Elizabeth Pamela Goodrich [Mrs. Charles] Stillman (1828-1910), Isabel G. Stillman (?-1894), and Maria M. [Mrs. John] Francis (1801-68). Also included are school compositions and letters of Anne Maria Francis (1831-?); correspondence of Mary Ann Welles (1808-73), who was the second Mrs. Joshua Goodrich; and letters from Elizabeth Pamela Goodrich to Maria Francis.

1,864. Hartford Charitable Society
Records. 1792-1871. 1 vol. and ca. 439 items.
Open. Catalog card.
Connecticut Historical Society.
Act of incorporation, constitution, accounts, and lists of subscribers of the Society, organized in 1791 by men and operated by men to provide fuel (wood and later coal), food, and clothing to the town poor, most of whom were women. Names of

the women and men receiving aid appear in the accounts of the firms from which the Society purchased material.

1,865. Hartford Female Seminary
Records. 1827-90. 2 boxes and 1 vol.
Open. Catalog cards.
Connecticut Historical Society.
Fragmentary minutes, financial records, correspondence, newspapers, and other records of this girls school, which was founded by Catharine Esther Beecher.

1,866. Hoadley
Collection. Ca. 1750-1920. 15 boxes.
Open. Catalog cards.
Connecticut Historical Society.
Correspondence, legal and military papers, church records, and other material on New England history collected by Charles Jeremy Hoadley (1828-1900) and his brother George Edward Hoadley (1837-1922) include ca. 400 letters, poems, and other documents to and from Lydia (Huntley) Sigourney, an author. Most of Sigourney's papers concern literary matters.

1,867. Holley, Alexander Lyman
Papers. 1843-82. Ca. 200 items.
Open. Catalog card.
Connecticut Historical Society.
Correspondence, account books, notebooks, and printed matter of Holley (1831-82), a metallurgist and engineer, include letters to and from his mother Marcia (Coffing) Holley, dating primarily from the 1850s.

1,868. Huntington, Benjamin
Papers. 1761-1864. 62 items.
Open. Catalog card.
Connecticut Historical Society.
Correspondence of Huntington (1736-1800), a Connecticut politician, includes that of his wife Anne (Huntington) Huntington (1740-90).

1,869. Hyde, Elizabeth (Waldo)
Papers. 1875-1908. 30 vols.
Open. Catalog card.
Connecticut Historical Society.
Diaries of [Mrs. Alvan Phinney] Hyde, a Hartford resident, contain entries on the weather, family news, travels, and visitors.

1,870. Jocelyn Family
Papers. 1830s-70s. 4 boxes.
Open. Catalog cards.
Connecticut Historical Society.
Diaries of members of this family, which resided in New Haven and Bloomfield, CT, include those of Dorothea Cornelia (Jocelyn) [Mrs. William Hammond] Foster, 1849-64; Elizabeth Hannah (Jocelyn) [Mrs. James Bradford] Cleaveland, 1839-51; Frances M. (Jocelyn) [Mrs. David] Peck, 1839-53; Margaret (Jocelyn) [Mrs. Samuel] Hayes, 1839; Sarah (Jocelyn) [Mrs. Joseph] Wild, 1839-41; and Susan Trowbridge Cleaveland [Mrs. R.L.] Rice, 1874. Entries mention the weather, travels, visitors, family events, and news of the Bloomfield and New Haven communities and of Yale University.

1,871. National Popular Education Board
Records. 1848-52. 2 boxes.
Open. No guide.
Connecticut Historical Society.
The Board was founded in 1847 to recruit teachers, primarily from the New England region, and send them to remote areas of the South, West, and Midwest. Consists primarily of annual reports, lists of teachers, applications for and from teachers, and other records of the Board's committee for the selection of teachers, which chose from among applicants seeking jobs and supervised their training. Most of the records of the committee, which was headquartered in Hartford, are reports from teachers who had already been assigned posts, detailing their experiences to the committee. Although the Board itself only admitted women as honorary members, all committee members and teachers were women.

1,872. New Haven Woman Suffrage Association
Records. 1871-76. 2 vols.
Open. Catalog card.
Connecticut Historical Society.
Constitution, minutes, lists of members and officers, petition, ticket, and clippings of this local suffrage organization, founded in 1871, which admitted both men and women as officers and members. This was the city chapter of the Connecticut Woman Suffrage Association.

1,873. Norwich Ladies Literary Society
Records. 1800-05. 1 vol.
Open. Catalog card.
Connecticut Historical Society.
Articles of agreement, constitution, list of charter members, and minutes of meetings of this local study group.

1,874. Philleo Family
Papers. 1839-79. 4 ft. and ca. 250 items.
Open. Catalog card and checklist.
Connecticut Historical Society.
Correspondence, diaries, account books, legal documents, literary material, memorandum books, and daguerreotypes of Calvin Wheeler Philleo (1822-58), a lawyer, politician, and author, and of his sister Emma (Philleo) Goodwin [Mrs. Charles K.] Whipple, a Boston resident. Included is correspondence of and between Emma Whipple and Calvin Philleo's wife Elizabeth (Norton) Philleo, both of whom comment on national political and military events and on antislavery activities. Emma Whipple's and Calvin Philleo's stepmother Prudence (Crandall) Philleo (1803-89) is mentioned in several letters, including one in which Emma Whipple paraphrases the reminiscences of Sarah (Harris) Fayerweather, the first Negro student at Prudence Crandall's school in Canterbury, CT, in 1833.

1,875. Primus Family
Papers. 1854-95. 300 items.
Open. Catalog card.
Connecticut Historical Society.
Papers of a Negro family whose members lived at least part of their lives in Hartford contain letters and financial documents of Rebecca Primus (1836-1932), an educator who was active in the Hartford Freedmen's Aid Society and who founded and taught at the Primus Institute in Royal Oak, MD, under the Society's auspices. Primus's correspondence contains letters from her friend Addie Brown. Primus later married Charles H. Thomas.

1,876. Sigourney, Lydia Howard (Huntley)
Papers. 1788-1911. 1 vol. and ca. 100 items.
Open. Catalog cards.
Connecticut Historical Society.
Correspondence, poetry, drafts of essays, memoranda, and scrapbook of Sigourney (1791-1865), an author. Consists primarily of letters she and her husband Charles Sigourney (1778-1854) wrote or received on literary and family matters. Many of the letters enclose poems and others contain material on their son Andrew Maximilian Sigourney (1831-50). The longest exchange, 45 letters, is between Lydia Sigourney and Mary Ann Ripley [Mrs. Thomas] Smith. Also included is a scrapbook on the school in Hartford where Lydia Sigourney taught, with catalog of students for 1814 to 1819, a list of her pupils and their children, poetry, obituary verses, and the constitution, minutes, and membership list for the Society of the Former Scholars of Mrs. Sigourney.

1,877. Smith, Julia Evelina
Papers. 1810-76. 4 boxes.
Open. Catalog card.
Connecticut Historical Society.
Papers of Smith (1792-1886), a reformer who married Amos Andrew Parker in 1879, consist of 15 volumes of her diary for 1810 to 1842, written in French, on her travels, readings, and visitors; four volumes of her diary for 1836 to 1857, written in English, with notes on the weather; and a manuscript draft and her corrections for printing her translation of the Bible from Hebrew into English. Smith published the translation at her own expense in 1876.

1,878. Wadsworth Family
Papers. 1749-1883. Ca. 15,700 items.
Open. Calendar.
Connecticut Historical Society.
Correspondence, business papers, account books, military papers, survey plats, maps, and other papers of Jeremiah Wadsworth (1743-1804), a military officer and Connecticut politician, and of his son Daniel Wadsworth (1771-1848), an artist. Included are letters, accounts, and memorandum books of Jeremiah Wadsworth's wife Mehitabel (Russell) Wadsworth (1734-1817) and correspondence of his daughters Catherine Wadsworth (1774-?) and Harriet Wadsworth (1769-93) and of Rose (Terry) [Mrs. Rollin] Cooke. Much of the women's correspondence is between family members. The family correspondence 1792-93, describes Daniel Wadsworth's nursing his sister Harriet, who died of tuberculosis.

1,879. Widows Homes of Hartford
Records. 1860-1928. 2 boxes and 1 item.
Open. Catalog card.
Connecticut Historical Society.
Financial records, correspondence, applications, unfinished history, blueprints, clippings, and other material concerning homes whose rooms were let to poor and older women at modest rates. In 1860 George Beach willed a cottage in which he had housed elderly women to a board of trustees chosen from the rectors and wardens of Episcopal churches in Hartford. The trustees bought a second home in 1885 and built two new ones in 1910.

1,880. Wilcox, Howard
Papers. 1867-97. 2 vols.
Open. Catalog card.
Connecticut Historical Society.
Family correspondence, genealogical chart, map, and photo of Wilcox (1838-83), a resident of Painsville, OH, and West Granby, CT. Includes letters of his first wife Jannette Fancher, his second wife Anna M. Case, and his daughter Henrietta.

1,881. Williams Family
Papers. 1700-1897. 2435 items.
Open. Catalog cards.
Connecticut Historical Society.
Family correspondence and legal and business papers of members of this Connecticut family include more than 100 letters of family women, many of which were exchanged between themselves. Hannah Hopkins Williams (1805-46), Elizabeth Byrne [Mrs. William W.] Williams (1828-1906), and Mary Dyer Williams [Mrs. Charles B.] McLean (1822-1905) are among the major correspondents.

1,882. Women's Organization for War Savings of Hartford
Records. 1942-45. 3 vols. and 1 envelope.
Open. Catalog card.
Connecticut Historical Society.
Scrapbooks of clippings and reports of the Organization for bond sales were kept by its chairman Virginia [Mrs. Houghton] Bulkeley.

1,883. Yale Family
Papers. Ca. 1848-1929. 1 box and 49 vols.
Open. Catalog cards.
Connecticut Historical Society.
Included with the correspondence of Horace Yale (1826-95), a resident of Connecticut and New York City, are letters of his daughter Lilla Charlotte Yale (1855-1929), an artist, which pertain to her education at the Art Students League in NYC. Also included are diaries reflecting Lilla Yale's teaching experiences in Meriden, CT, her artwork, her daily life, and local events.

1,884. Arts and Crafts Club of Hartford (RG 108)
Records. 1909-51. 6 in.
Open. Inventory.
Connecticut State Library, Archives, History, and Genealogy Unit.
Record books of this Club, which existed between 1909 and 1951 to promote the arts, consist of a constitution, officers' reports, minutes, correspondence, membership lists, and programs. Most of the officers and members of the Club, which sponsored workshops, exhibits, demonstrations, lectures, and courses, were women.

1,885. Bates Family (RG 69)
Papers. 1820-78. 7 ft.
Open. Inventory.
Connecticut State Library, Archives, History, and Genealogy Unit.
Personal and business correspondence, diaries, memoranda, notebooks, minutes, and business papers of Carlos Bates (1808-78) and Anson Bates (1799-?), residents principally of East Granby, CT. Includes letters depicting the personal lives of Carlos Bates's sisters Flora (Bates) Metcalf (1806-?), a housekeeper and farm manager in Connecticut and Minnesota; Laura Bates (1813-?), wife of Harry Trumbull and later of Isaac Van Dorn, with whom she resided in Ohio; and Mindwell Dorothy Bates (1819-?), who married twice. Most of Mindwell Bates's letters were written while she was a student at Wesleyan Academy in Wilbraham, MA.

1,886. Buckingham, William Alfred
Papers. 1853-73. Ca. 200 items.
Open. Catalog card.
Connecticut State Library, Archives, History, and Genealogy Unit.
Correspondence and political papers of Buckingham (1804-75), a Connecticut politician. Includes correspondence of his wife Eliza (Ripley) Buckingham (?-1868) and of his daughter Eliza Buckingham, who later married William Aiken.

1,887. Butler, Eva L. (RG 69)
Papers. 1635-1800. 2.5 ft.
Open. Inventory.
Connecticut State Library, Archives, History, and Genealogy Unit.
Transcriptions made by [Mrs.] Butler, a 20th-century anthropologist and local historian, of correspondence, court records, legal documents, town files, and land records out of her scholarly interest in Connecticut history, especially as it pertains to Indians in the 17th and 18th centuries.

1,888. Charitable Society of Vernon
Records. 1814-92. 1 vol.
Open. Catalog card.
Connecticut State Library, Archives, History, and Genealogy Unit.
Constitution, minutes, and a list of members of this local charitable and social organization which was called the Female Society of Vernon from 1814 to 1824.

1,889. Church Records
Collection. Ca. 1670- . Ca. 400 ft.
Open. Detailed list.
Connecticut State Library, Archives, History, and Genealogy Unit.
Records of Connecticut churches include account books, covenants, minutes of church societies, membership lists, pew seating plans, registers of vital statistics, unpublished histories, and sermons preached on the occasion of special events in the church's history. Also included are records of women's societies: the Congregational Church of Bloomfield Ladies Reading Circle, 1915-21; the Congregational Church of East Haven Ladies Benevolent Society, 1846-70; the Congregational Church of East Haven Young Ladies Benevolent Society, 1849; the East Glastonbury Methodist Episcopal Church Ladies Aid Society, 1906-17; the First Baptist Church of Hartford Women's Missionary Society, 1910-22; the First Methodist Church of Hartford Ladies Benevolent Society, 1850-65; the Immanuel Congregational Church of Hartford Widows Home, 1874-1924; the Methodist Church of Hebron Female Benevolent Association, 1837-71; the Center Congregational Church of Manchester Ladies Benevolent Society, 1871; St. Andrew's Episcopal Church of Meriden Ladies Sewing Society, 1852-69; the Methodist Episcopal Church of New Britain Woman's Foreign Missionary Society, 1885-1902; St. Andrew's Church at Northford Ladies Association, 1833-36; the First Congregational Church of Preston Ladies Benevolent Society, 1860-88; the First Congregational Church of Suffield Woman's Missionary Society, 1822-1909; and the West Hartford Baptist Sewing Society, 1858-80.

1,890. Church Records (RG 70)
Records. 1639-1956. 150 ft.
Open. Inventory.
Connecticut State Library, Archives, History, and Genealogy Unit.
Financial records, minutes, membership records, vital statistics, reports, and other records of the missions, clubs, conferences, and committees of various Connecticut churches. Included are records of the Colchester First Congregational Church Auxiliary of the Eastern Connecticut Branch of the Woman's Board of Missions, 1903-08; the Ladies Home Missionary Society of the First Congregational Church of Norwich, 1867-1928; the Ladies Foreign Missionary Society of the Donelson Methodist Church of Kittingly, 1882-1912; the Young Women's Class Sunday School Meetings of the First Baptist Church of Middletown, 1921-26; the Ladies Aid Society for the Hartford North Park Methodist Church, 1931; the Ladies Aid Society of the Hartford South Park Methodist Church, 1896-1927; and the Woman's Home Missionary Society of the Methodist Episcopal Church of Stafford Springs, 1890-1940. Records for societies of the United Church of Chester are detailed, including documentation of the Female Praying and Benevolent Society, 1814-43; the Ladies Benevolent Society, 1853-1909; the Women's Baptist (Foreign) Missionary Society, 1874-1911; and the Women's Baptist Home Missionary Society, 1900-19.

1,891. College Club of Hartford (RG 131)
Records. 1905-44. 3 boxes.
Open. Inventory.
Connecticut State Library, Archives, History, and Genealogy Unit.
Annual reports, minutes, account books, checkbooks, correspondence, and programs of this social, philanthropic, and literary organization which was founded in 1905 at a mass rally of college women in Hartford. The Club was active in founding and managing Spruce Street Settlement House, later known as the Mitchell House; it also sponsored concerts, Americanization programs, and knitting bees during WWI.

1,892. Colonial Dames, Old Houses of Connecticut (RG 143)
Records. 1900-61. Ca. 50 ft.
Open. Inventory.
Connecticut State Library, Archives, History, and Genealogy Unit.
Activities of the Historic Buildings Committee of the Colonial Dames for preserving old structures in Connecticut are reflected in card catalogs, completed forms, registers, bibliographies, drafts of publications, historic and architectural data, drawings, and photos. The Committee, organized in 1900 as the Committee on Old Houses of the Connecticut Society of Colonial Dames of America, initially confined its efforts to homes built during the colonial period but eventually included noteworthy buildings of later periods as well.

1,893. Connecticut Federation of Women's Clubs (RG 142)
Records. 1897-1974. 5 ft.
Open. Inventory.
Connecticut State Library, Archives, History, and Genealogy Unit.
Minutes, financial records, correspondence, officers' records, history, programs, and clippings of this social and charitable organization, founded in 1896, contain detailed documentation on the executive board and the various presidents.

1,894. Connecticut League of Women Voters (RG 106)
Records. 1926-56. 3 ft.
Open. Inventory.
Connecticut State Library, Archives, History, and Genealogy Unit.
Collection of minutes, financial reports, correspondence, memoranda, programs, scrapbooks, publications, and clippings reflect LWV activities in the areas of education of voters on issues and candidates, voter turnout, registration drives, petition campaigns, and work with legislators and government executives. Most of the material is printed or mimeographed.

1,895. Connecticut Military Census (RG 29)
Records. 1917-20. 1093.7 ft.
Open. Inventory.
Connecticut State Library, Archives, History, and Genealogy Unit.
Correspondence, forms, lists, and other material pertaining to a census taken of nurses in the state are included with records of the Census, which was established in 1917 to gather statistics on population and resources.

1,896. Connecticut Woman Suffrage Association (RG 101)
Records. 1858-1921. 3 ft. and 1 microfilm reel.
Open. Inventory,
Connecticut State Library, Archives, History, and Genealogy Unit.
Minutes, correspondence, notes, bills, registers of members and attendance, reports, campaign literature, cartoons, photos, scrapbooks, clippings, publications, and other records of the Association, which was organized in 1869 at a meeting called by Hartford community leaders Isabella B. Hooker, John Hooker, Frances E. Burr, Catharine E. Beecher, and Harriet B. Stowe, and addressed by Henry Ward Beecher, Elizabeth Cady Stanton, Susan B. Anthony, Julia Ward Howe, and William Lloyd Garrison. Working with equal rights, equal franchise, and constitutional union groups, the Association campaigned for women's right to vote in school and local elections and then at state and national levels. Also included are scrapbooks on suffrage kept by Frances Burr.

1,897. Council of Defense (RG 30)
Records. 1917-19. 203 ft.
Open. Inventory.

Connecticut State Library, Archives, History and Genealogy Unit.
Collection includes 40 boxes and one drawer of records of the Woman's Division of the Council, containing minutes, office files, questionnaires completed by volunteers, policy statements, and photos of Division leaders, which document the Division's programs in conservation, fund raising, Americanization, war factory work, child welfare, nursery, and other special projects.

1,898. Crandall, Prudence
Papers. 1833-86. 16 items.
Open. Catalog cards.
Connecticut State Library, Archives, History, and Genealogy Unit.
Papers of Crandall (1803-89), an educator of Negro girls who married Calvin Philleo in 1834, consist of legal documents from the office of the Connecticut secretary of state relating to her school for Negro girls, 1833; an 1833 writ for her arrest; a judgment binding her over for trial; an 1886 petition of the citizens of Canterbury, CT, asking for aid for [Mrs.] Philleo; copies of portraits of her; a photo of the Rhode Island house in which she was born; and a photostat of Crandall's inscribed copy of *Arithmetical Tables for the Use of Schools* (New York) by Samuel Wood.

1,899. Daughters of the American Revolution, Ruth Wyllys Chapter (RG 123)
Records. 1778-1970. 6 ft.
Open. Inventory.
Connecticut State Library, Archives, History, and Genealogy Unit.
Annual reports, minutes, financial records, lists of members, applications, programs, photos, clippings, and other records document the administrative, educational, and social activities of the Hartford DAR chapter, which was organized in 1892. Also contained are records of the Chapter's history study group, including a series of essays, and historical artifacts such as a 1778 muster roll of Captain Witing's Company.

1,900. Davis, Fred C. (RG 69)
Papers. 1723-1951. 10 ft.
Open. Inventory.
Connecticut State Library, Archives, History, and Genealogy Unit.
Correspondence, diaries, account books, pamphlets, memorabilia, children's books, and other material relate to the Davis family of Connecticut and to Fred Davis, who was a 20th-century collector of historical material. Included are correspondence of Eunice Cady (1817-?), who married Alden Davis; of Myrtie Harwood, a schoolteacher who in 1888 married George William Davis; her mother Dorcas Hubbard Harwood; and Laura Stebbins. Records of local groups such as the Ladies Benevolent Society of Somers and records of the Ladies Aid of the Somers Methodist Episcopal Church for 1845 are also contained.

1,901. Diaries
Collection. 1653-1945. Ca. 70 items.
Open. Catalog cards.
Connecticut State Library, Archives, History, and Genealogy Unit.
Collection consists of diaries of Connecticut and New England residents. There are diaries, usually one or two volumes, for the following women: Ellie and Mattie Lynn of Meriden, with entries on their schoolwork in the West school district, 1880; Mrs. S. Smith of Milford, with entries on Lafayette's visit to the town, 1822-25; Mary G. Camp (1799-1841) of Durham, with entries on Miss Pierce's school in Litchfield, a canal trip across New York state in 1828, and social life in Durham, 1818-34; Susan (Howell) Sanford of New Haven, including a copy of a constitution and list of members of a local ladies' society, 1849-58; Mrs. Harry Keeney, with entries on the destruction in the flood of 1869 of the Bunce paper mill, 1865-1949; Amanda Elliott (1789-1839) of Guilford, 1813-21; Abigail Reynolds (1774-1851) of Norwich, who was later married to Giles L'Hommedieu, 1794-1809; Mary (Treadwell) Hooker of Farmington, 1795-1812; and Eliza Ann (Hull) Staples (1804-32), 1815-32. Also includes twelve volumes for both Hannah (Hicock) Smith (1767-1850) of Glastonbury, with entries on her finances, daily events, and the weather, 1819-50, and Ellen Douglas Larned (1825-1912), an historian and genealogist, 1854-1910.

1,902. Female Anti-Slavery Society of Brooklyn
Records. 1834-40. 1 vol.
Open. Catalog card.
Connecticut State Library, Archives, History, and Genealogy Unit.
Minutes, receipts, and correspondence of a local abolition group.

1,903. Female Cent Society of Lebanon
Records. 1814. 1 vol.
Open. Catalog card.
Connecticut State Library, Archives, History, and Genealogy Unit.
Constitution and a list of members and officers of this local social group.

1,904. Female Foreign Missionary Society of South Preston
Records. 1813-24. 1 vol.
Open. Catalog card.
Connecticut State Library, Archives, History, and Genealogy Unit.
Minutes of a local women's group, which was devoted to supporting missionary work abroad.

1,905. Genealogical Materials (RG 74)
Collection. 1895-1973. 75 ft.
Open. Inventory.
Connecticut State Library, Archives, History, and Genealogy Unit.
Genealogical working papers, charts, notes, reference material, drafts, and correspondence contain material on women; on the genealogical activities of women's groups, notably the Colonial Dames of America; and on women genealogists, among them Irene Mix Root, Helen Sharps, and Ellen Douglas Larned. Items such as Dora Bell Leeson's diary are also included.

1,906. Governor's Office (RG 5)
Records. 1630- . 1750 ft.
Open. Inventory.
Connecticut State Library, Archives, History, and Genealogy Unit.
Military, legal, and financial records; correspondence; memoranda; diaries; reports; applications for office; printed proclamations; and certificates of the Office, which was established in 1640 for colonial and state government. Also includes records of earlier agencies. Material relating to women appears throughout and for that generated after 1925 can be found under such headings as Connecticut College for Women, the State Farm for Women, hairdressers, nurses, and child welfare. Also included are 34 boxes of commitment records, 1828-1948, concerning persons admitted to state institutions for the insane, disabled, deaf, blind, and dumb.

1,907. The Grand Army of the Republic, Connecticut Department (RG 113)
Records. 1866-1956. 45 ft.
Open. Inventory.
Connecticut State Library, Archives, History, and Genealogy Unit.
Minutes, financial accounts, correspondence, publications, registers, lists, music, posters, photos, scrapbooks, and printed items of the Department, a veterans' organization which was founded in 1867, and some printed documents of the Army, which was founded in 1866. Although it is primarily concerned with pensions, soldiers' homes, and military cemeteries, the Army also has social functions. Included are letterbooks of the state Women's Relief Corps, 1894-1918, and some records of women's auxiliaries of various posts in the state.

1,908. Hartford Equal Rights Club
Records. 1885-1925. 8 vols. and 1 envelope.
Open. Catalog card.
Connecticut State Library, Archives, History, and Genealogy Unit.
Constitution, treasurers' accounts, minutes, lists of officers and members, programs, pamphlets, photos, and clippings of this local suffrage club.

1,909. Hartford Wellesley Club
Records. 1914-44. 2 vols.
Open. Catalog card.
Connecticut State Library, Archives, History, and Genealogy Unit.
Secretaries' records for a group of local Wellesley College alumnae who met for social and educational purposes.

1,910. Hartford Woman's Club (RG 107)
Records. 1896-1923. 2 ft.
Open. Inventory.
Connecticut State Library, Archives, History, and Genealogy Unit.
A section of the Sociological Society, the Motherhood Club of Hartford was organized in 1896 to study child problems and to socialize; the group engaged in educational, philanthropic, and fund-raising activities, and in 1921 it adopted its current name. The records, which pertain primarily to the Motherhood Club and include material on Club domestic science and home economic sections, consist of minutes, financial records, historical sketches, photos, the Club weekly *Hartford Women,* and other publications.

1,911. Hawkins and Wooster (RG 69)
Papers. Ca. 1856-1934. 3 ft.
Open. Entry on list.
Connecticut State Library, Archives, History, and Genealogy Unit.
Correspondence, diaries, account books, will, deeds, insurance policies, tax receipts, pamphlets, cards, and clippings on the history of Southbury and Oxford, CT, which were collected by Minnie Hawkins and Raymond Wooster. Also includes Hawkins's personal correspondence.

1,912. Hazel Johnson Files on Connecticut Publications (RG 69)
Finding aid. 1755-1800. 5 ft.
Open. Entry on list.
Connecticut State Library, Archives, History, and Genealogy Unit.
File of card lists created by [Miss] Johnson, a bibliographer, as she indexed bills for printing state publications. She intended the lists to be an enlargement of a similar list issued in 1917 by another bibliographer.

1,913. Hearthstone Club of Hartford
Records. 1895-1935. 4 vols.
Open. Catalog card.
Connecticut State Library, Archives, History, and Genealogy Unit.
Minutes of meetings of this woman's organization, founded in 1895 to study "modern social considerations in their bearing upon the home and family life." Members presented and discussed papers on current events and historical topics.

1,914. Jarvis Family (RG 69)
Papers. 1798-1906. 1876 items.
Open. Calendar.
Connecticut State Library, Archives, History, and Genealogy Unit.
Papers of Samuel Farmar Jarvis (1786-1851), a minister, contain correspondence and financial

papers of his wife Sarah M. (Hart) Jarvis detailing family life, travel abroad, and their divorce. In addition, his letters to friends reveal information about the divorce proceedings and their subsequent separate lives.

1,915. Judicial Department (RG 3)
Records. 1636-1972. 4000 ft.
Open. Checklist.
Connecticut State Library, Archives, History, and Genealogy Unit.
Collection of the proceedings of civil and criminal courts (which probably took place first in 1636), exclude those relating to probate but do include dockets, transcripts, drafts of arguments and opinions, rulings, depositions, writs, warrants, registers, affidavits, petitions, pension applications and applications to practice law, licenses, minutes, bills and receipts, correspondence, notes, and reports. Unusually complete files on divorce appear in the Superior Court records for the counties of Fairfield, 1711-98; Hartford, 1740-1849; Litchfield, 1752-1922; Middlesex, 1786-97; New Haven, 1712-1900; New London, 1719-1875; Tolland, 1787-1910; and Windham, 1726-1907. Material on minority women is also available in separate files on Indians which were kept by many of the above Superior Courts and by many of the County Courts.

1,916. Kilbourn, Dwight C. (RG 69)
Papers. 1671-1921. 10 ft.
Open. Inventory.
Connecticut State Library, Archives, History, and Genealogy Unit.
Along with the correspondence, legal papers, historical and genealogical notes, and military documents reflecting the interests of Kilbourn (1837-1914), a lawyer and amateur historian, are correspondence and other papers of his wife Sarah (Hopkins) Kilbourn, whom he married in 1866.

1,917. Labor Department (RG 20)
Records. 1917-41. 70 ft.
Open. List.
Connecticut State Library, Archives, History, and Genealogy Unit.
Correspondence, speech drafts and radio scripts, job notices, applications, reports, press releases, scrapbooks, photos, clippings, printed reference material, and other records of this state agency, which was established in 1873. Included are records of the Employment Service of the Department, 1937-41, and records of the state branch of the US Employment Service of the Department of Labor, 1917-19, with correspondence, press releases, indices, photos, clippings, and other reference material concerning the state Women's Division and employment of women during WWI. Generated by other agencies in the US and abroad, the reference material details the agencies' experience melding women into the work force.

1,918. Larned, Ellen Douglas (RG 69)
Papers. 1850-1908. 5 ft.
Open. Catalog cards.
Connecticut State Library, Archives, History, and Genealogy Unit.
Correspondence, diaries, drafts, genealogical and historical notes, financial accounts, weather records, play, poetry, portraits, scrapbooks, and clippings relate primarily to the research of Larned (1825-1912) on genealogy and history in Connecticut and particularly in Windham County. Letters, notes, and a pamphlet pertaining to Prudence Crandall are also included.

1,919. Lotteries and Divorces (RG 1)
Records. 1718-1820. 613 items.
Open. Index.
Connecticut State Library, Archives, History, and Genealogy Unit.
State and colonial government legal documents pertaining to women include petitions, resolves, depositions, court orders, certificates, and other material relating to marriage, divorce, adultery, and children. Records contain descriptions of unsuccessful marriages and of women's attempts through court action to be freed from them.

1,920. McLean, Charlotte Ellen (RG 69)
Papers. Ca. 1882. 2 ft.
Open. Entry on list.
Connecticut State Library, Archives, History, and Genealogy Unit.
Pencil sketches, watercolors, and oil paintings of wildflowers, scenery, and old Connecticut houses by [Miss] McLean (1835?-?), an artist.

1,921. Monday Afternoon Club (RG 110)
Records. 1887-1938. 6 in.
Open. No guide.
Connecticut State Library, Archives, History, and Genealogy Unit.
Minutes, correspondence, reports, and lists of officers and members of this study group established in 1886. Many of the members of the all-woman Club were professors at Trinity College in Hartford. After voting on an historical topic to study each year, members presented papers on the topic.

1,922. Morris, John Moses (RG 69)
Papers. 1856-89. 4 ft.
Open. Inventory.
Connecticut State Library, Archives, History, and Genealogy Unit.
Included with the correspondence, diary, drafts of essays, photos, and other papers of Morris (1837-73), a chaplain and editor, are 1859-89 letters of his wife Augusta Emily (Griswold) Morris, whom he married in 1863.

1,923. National Society of New England Women, Hartford Colony (RG 104)
Records. 1921-68. 2 ft.
Open. Inventory.
Connecticut State Library, Archives, History, and Genealogy Unit.
Founded in 1921, this group of Hartford women of New England ancestry work together on education, patriotic, and charitable programs. Annual reports, minutes, history, addresses, pamphlets, and scrapbook.

1,924. Noble Collection of Pension Application Files (RG 69)
Papers. 1870-1908. 35 ft.
Open. Entry on list.
Connecticut State Library, Archives, History, and Genealogy Unit.
Files of military pension applications, correspondence, and notes were created by General William H. Noble and his daughter Henrietta Noble of Bridgeport, CT, who acted as agents for Connecticut residents applying for federal pensions arising from their service in the American Revolution, the Civil War, and the Spanish-American War. Also included is personal correspondence of the Nobles.

1,925. Northwest Child Welfare Club, Hartford (RG 115)
Records. 1914-59. 20.5 in.
Open. Inventory.
Connecticut State Library, Archives, History, and Genealogy Unit.
Minutes, financial records, directories, programs, and card file of members of this social welfare organization, which was originally organized as the Mothers Neighborhood Circle; the group adopted its later name in 1936. In addition to lobbying for protective legislation, the Club worked to improve children's lives in homes, schools, church, and the community. In 1959 the Club was disbanded because its members felt their goals had been achieved by means of state laws and welfare programs and that such groups as the PTA were adequately carrying out the Club's programs.

1,926. Norton, Deacon Lewis Mills
Papers. 1834-1917. 7 vols.
Open. Catalog cards.
Connecticut State Library, Archives, History, and Genealogy Unit.
Papers of Norton (1855-?), an historian and resident of Goshen, CT, consist of a volume of records of the Female Bible Class of Goshen, 1834-43, and a four-volume manuscript history of the town. Norton compiled three of the volumes, while his granddaughter [Miss] Mary E. Brooks compiled the fourth and an index.

1,927. People for Question No. 1 (RG 133)
Records. 1974. 4 in.
Open. Inventory.
Connecticut State Library, Archives, History, and Genealogy Unit.
Minutes, correspondence, campaign literature, press releases, and clippings of this organization for the passage of a state constitutional amendment prohibiting discrimination on the basis of sex. The state chairperson was Helen Z. Pearl.

1,928. Platt, Orville H. (RG 69)
Papers. 1880-1950. 17 vols. and 8 folders.
Open. Inventory.
Connecticut State Library, Archives, History, and Genealogy Unit.
Included with the correspondence, biographical sketches, poetry, addresses, and other papers of Platt (1827-1905), a Connecticut politician, are correspondence of his wife (?-1927), his secretary [Miss] Katherine Lawler (?-1938), and [Miss] Alice M. Robertson of Oklahoma.

1,929. Sheffield, Anna D. (RG 69)
Papers. 1834-1948. 18 in.
Open. Entry on list.
Connecticut State Library, Archives, History, and Genealogy Unit.
Correspondence, deeds, drafts of articles, invitations, photos, memorabilia, and clippings gathered by [Miss] Sheffield for historical research on the town of Old Saybrook, CT.

1,930. Sigourney, Lydia Howard (Huntley)
Papers. 1821-65. 19 items.
Open. Catalog cards.
Connecticut State Library, Archives, History, and Genealogy Unit.
Correspondence, poems, and a hymn of Sigourney (1791-1865), an author. Includes letters from her on politics, literature, and personal and family events.

1,931. State Library (RG 12)
Records. 1893-1970. 280 ft.
Open. Inventory.
Connecticut State Library, Archives, History, and Genealogy Unit.
Ledgers, minutes, correspondence, military service records, memoranda, drafts, reports, registers, and other material of the Library, which was established in 1854 to promote scholarship. The war records section contains documents pertaining to Connecticut women who served in various wars or were involved in patriotic activity. These include a card file of nurses, 1940-45, with names and school or hospital affiliation; a list of women who served in WWI; and files of [Mrs.] Mary M. Starr regarding the entertainment during WWII of British seamen at her home in Essex County.

1,932. Thomson and Kinney (RG 69)
Papers. 1673-1905. 12 ft.
Open. Inventory.
Connecticut State Library, Archives, History, and Genealogy Unit.
Correspondence, poems, pamphlets, photos, clippings, and other material collected by Sara

(Thomson) Kinney (1842-1922) and her mother [Mrs.] Susan Belcher Thomson (1809-90), both of whom were Hartford residents. Letters and autographs center on church and political figures. Also included are correspondence and scrapbooks of the Connecticut Indian Association, 1884-1905; the register of visitors to the Connecticut Room of the Women's Building at the International Exposition in Atlanta during 1895; and material on Thomson family history.

1,933. Towns and Boroughs (RG 62)
Records. Ca. 1700-1972. 600 ft.
Open. Inventory.
Connecticut State Library, Archives, History, and Genealogy Unit.
Minutes, receipts, financial accounts, correspondence, licenses, completed forms, reports, registers, and lists document routine fiscal matters of municipal government in Connecticut. Also included are vital statistics, school records on the education of women and employment of women as teachers, and items such as an 1893-97 register of women voters for the town of Preston.

1,934. United States Navy League, Admiral Bunce Section, Comforts Committee (RG 137)
Records. 1917-18. 15 in.
Open. Inventory.
Connecticut State Library, Archives, History, and Genealogy Unit.
Correspondence, ledgers, and clippings of the Hartford chapter of the women's section of the League. A social and patriotic organization of women, this Committee knit woolen garments for men in the US Navy.

1,935. Vital Records (RG 72)
Records. 1635-1972. 500 ft.
Open. Inventories and indices.
Connecticut State Library, Archives, History, and Genealogy Unit.
Birth, marriage, and death information on Connecticut residents is contained in town clerks' files; abstracts from newspapers, church records, and family Bibles; copies of US Census schedules; copies of burial and cemetery records and gravestone inscriptions; reports; and indices.

1,936. War Council (RG 50)
Records. 1940-45. 142 ft.
Open. Inventory.
Connecticut State Library, Archives, History, and Genealogy Unit.
Minutes, directives, correspondence, notes, drafts, surveys, reports, press releases, photos, clippings, publications, and other records of this state agency devoted to coordinating Connecticut's contribution to the Allied cause. Included are general office files, correspondence, memoranda, reports, and reference material of the Women's Division. Also included are records of sections of the Council, such as those of the civilian war services; food conservation; social protection, which dealt with health, recreation, youth, and social matters; the volunteer bureau; the first aid division; and evacuation, which was headed for a period by Eleanor Little.

1,937. Weicker: Watergate (RG 69)
Papers. 1972-74. 17 ft.
Open. Inventory.
Connecticut State Library, Archives, History, and Genealogy Unit.
Copies of correspondence, transcripts, drafts, and reports from the files of Senator Lowell P. Weicker, Jr. (1931-) of Connecticut relate to the work of the Select Committee on Presidential Campaign Activities. Files on Helen Delich Bentley, Sally Harmony, [Mrs.] Beula Hawkins, and Betty Nolan are included, as are items pertaining to Rosemary Woods.

1,938. Welfare Department (RG 19)
Records. 1883-1951. 6 ft.
Open. Accessions list.
Connecticut State Library, Archives, History, and Genealogy Unit.
Minutes, letterbooks, reference material, and other records of this state agency, founded in 1935, and of its predecessor agencies document some of the activities the state undertook to assist the poor, many of whom were women. Included are records of the Temporary Homes of Litchfield and New Haven Counties, 1889-1915, which were devoted to housing neglected children and orphans; minutes and files of the State Board of Charities, 1893-1930, a predecessor of the Department; and reports of several study commissions and emergency planning boards, which led to the creation of the Department in the 1930s.

1,939. Welles, Mary E.
Papers. 1810-56. 110 items.
Open. Catalog cards.
Connecticut State Library, Archives, History, and Genealogy Unit.
Correspondence; financial, business, legal, and military documents; and reports reflect the interest of Welles, a 20th-century local historian of Wethersfield, CT, in the state militia, the state prison system, local seed companies, the Wethersfield poor farm, and the Welles family.

1,940. Welles, Sallie Richard Hamilton (RG 69)
Papers. 1810-1941. 4 boxes.
Open. Inventory.
Connecticut State Library, Archives, History, and Genealogy Unit.
Correspondence, diaries, genealogical charts and research notes, essays, autographs, photos, and scrapbooks reflect the personal life and historical interests of Welles, a family historian and Hartford resident. Included are volumes of her diaries, 1923-41, as well as material concerning the Rodgers, Smith, Perry, and Welles families.

1,941. Wessel, Jennie E. (RG 69)
Collection. 1864-97. 5 ft.
Open. Entry on list.
Connecticut State Library, Archives, History, and Genealogy Unit.
Journals, ledgers, cashbooks, sales books, and design books collected by [Miss] Wessel to document jewelry manufacturing in New Britain during the second half of the 19th century.

1,942. Williams, Comfort (RG 69)
Papers. 1805-22. 5 in.
Open. Entry on list.
Connecticut State Library, Archives, History, and Genealogy Unit.
Papers of Williams (1783-1825), a minister, consist of sermons; letters he exchanged with his cousin Lucy Williams, whom he married in 1811; and three of her diaries.

1,943. Woman's Christian Temperance Union of Guilford
Records. 1878-1904. 2 vols.
Open. Catalog card.
Connecticut State Library, Archives, History, and Genealogy Unit.
Secretary's book of minutes and lists of officers and treasurer's book of accounts of this local WCTU branch.

1,944. Woman's Christian Temperance Union of Hartford
Records. 1881-1931. 7 vols.
Open. Catalog card.
Connecticut State Library, Archives, History, and Genealogy Unit.
Record books and a manuscript history of a local WCTU branch founded in 1881.

1,945. Woman's Parliamentary Club of Hartford
Records. 1893-94. 2 vols.
Open. Catalog card.
Connecticut State Library, Archives, History, and Genealogy Unit.
Minutes of meetings and records of the correspondence secretary of this social club.

1,946. Young Woman's Christian Temperance Union of Rockville
Records. 1882-89. 1 vol.
Open. Catalog card.
Connecticut State Library, Archives, History, and Genealogy Unit.
Secretary's records, consisting of minutes and lists of members and officers, of a local branch of the union.

1,947. Connecticut Branch of the Woman's Auxiliary to the National Convention
Records. 1897-1927. 1 vol., 1 item, and 1 package.
Open. Published guide.
Episcopal Diocese of Connecticut Archives.
Minutes of regular meetings of this church organization, which was founded in 1880, and minutes for the 1927 annual meeting. See Kenneth Walter Cameron, ed., *Historical Resources of the Episcopal Diocese of Connecticut* (Hartford: Transcendental Books, 1963, with additions, 1966).

1,948. Day, Katharine Seymour
Papers. 1800-1964. 178 Hollinger boxes.
Open. Unpublished guide.
Stowe-Day Library.
Bulk of the collection of [Miss] Day (1870-1964), an artist, civic reformer, and philanthropist, is correspondence, but diaries, financial records, bills, inventories, scrapbooks, photos, and ephemera are included as well. After a tour of Europe with her family from 1887 to 1895, Day studied painting in New York City with William Merritt Chase. In 1909 she moved to Paris for a period of years in order to study painting, and from 1916 to 1925 she attended Radcliffe College, the University of California at Berkeley, and Columbia University to study psychology, particularly color perception; in the process, she earned an MA degree. In 1926 she moved into the Hartford home of her great-aunt Harriet (Beecher) Stowe and collected material relating to the abolitionist movement, her ancestors, and Nook Farm. Day also was active in civic affairs and the suffrage movement; a member of the Colonial Dames of America, the DAR, the Berkshire County (MA) Suffrage Commission, the Cosmopolitan Club of New York and the Woman's Municipal League, which later merged with the Citizen's Union of the City of New York; and founder of the Republican League for Party Efficiency. In her correspondence, Day discusses being a third-generation Beecher woman, her status as an "unmarried daughter," and other subjects.

Collection also contains correspondence of Day's sister Alice (Day) Jackson, a student at the Boston School of Cooking and Bryn Mawr College and, later, president of the Consumers League of New York; Day's mother Alice (Hooker) Day (1847-1928), who became a follower of Augusta (Simmons) Stetson and Stetson's sect of Christian Scientists; Katharine Day's cousin Mary Kingsbury Talcott, a genealogist; and other female relatives. Also includes correspondence of Elisabeth (Gillette) Warner with her husband George Warner, both of whom were Nook Farm residents.

1,949. Hartford Art Club
Records. 1901-45. 3 Hollinger boxes.
Open. Unpublished guide.
Stowe-Day Library.
Minutes, financial records, correspondence, manuscripts of papers delivered, and programs of this women's group, organized at the residence of Mrs. Edward B. Hooker of Hartford in 1885 to

study the history of art, art collections, and the lives of artists. Includes information on the Club's criticism of the modern art movement.

1,950. Hooker, Isabella (Beecher)
Papers. 1834-1907. 25 Hollinger boxes.
Open. Unpublished guide.
Stowe-Day Library.
Correspondence, diaries, manuscripts, photos, and broadsides document the career of [Mrs. John] Hooker (1822-1907), a suffragist and youngest daughter of clergyman Lyman Beecher. Includes early correspondence with her husband about women's rights; correspondence with Susan B. Anthony, Henry Blackwell, Olympia Brown, Frances (Hodgson) Burnett, Matilda (Joslyn) Gage, William Lloyd Garrison, Phebe (Coffin) Hanaford, Belva Lockwood, Caroline Severance, Elizabeth (Cady) Stanton, Lucy Stone, Victoria Woodhull, and others; and correspondence about the New England Woman Suffrage Association, the Connecticut Woman Suffrage Association, the National Woman Suffrage Association, and the American Woman Suffrage Association. Also includes correspondence with Lyman Beecher, Catharine E. Beecher, Henry Ward Beecher, Thomas K. Beecher, Harriet (Beecher) Stowe, and other family members.

1,951. Katharine S. Day Collection: Beecher, Catharine Esther
Papers. 1817-78. 2 Hollinger boxes.
Open. Unpublished guide.
Stowe-Day Library.
Bulk of the collection of Beecher (1800-78), an author and educator, is family correspondence, but diaries, bound manuscripts, and photos are also included. Correspondence with Lyman Beecher, Harriet (Beecher) Stowe, Isabella (Beecher) Hooker, Mary (Beecher) [Mrs. Thomas Clap] Perkins, Edward Beecher, and others and correspondence concerning the Hartford Female Seminary, the American Woman's Educational Association, and *A Treatise on Domestic Economy.*

1,952. Katharine S. Day Collection: Gilman, Charlotte (Perkins) Stetson
Papers. 1905-35. 1 Hollinger box.
Open. Unpublished guide.
Stowe-Day Library.
Papers of Gilman (1860-1935), a feminist, author, and lecturer, primarily consist of correspondence with her cousins Katharine Day and Alice (Hooker) Day, who were granddaughter and daughter, respectively, of Isabella (Beecher) Hooker. Also includes typescripts of "A Study in Ethics" and a poem entitled "Hyenas."

1,953. Katharine S. Day Collection: Stowe, Harriet Elizabeth (Beecher)
Papers. 1824-96. 5 Hollinger boxes.
Open. Published guide.
Stowe-Day Library.
Papers of [Mrs. Calvin E.] Stowe (1811-96), an author and Day's great-aunt, include correspondence, diaries, an account book, a guest book, bound manuscripts, photos, and paintings. Includes manuscript pages of *Uncle Tom's Cabin, Oldtown Folks,* and *Palmetto Leaves;* a journal Stowe kept during her visit to Italy in 1859 and 1860, with notes and first draft portions of *Agnes of Sorrento;* religious poems and essays, which were published in such periodicals as *The Independent;* signatures from English and Scottish admirers; and her husband's letters to her and members of the Beecher family. See *The Manuscripts of Harriet Beecher Stowe* (Hartford: The Stowe-Day Foundation, 1976).

1,954. Saturday Morning Club
Records. 1876- . 10 Hollinger boxes.
Open. Unpublished guide.
Stowe-Day Library.
Minutes, financial records, correspondence, manuscripts, scrapbooks, and photos of this young ladies' group, founded in 1876 by Mrs. Charles E. Perkins of Hartford for "culture and social intercourse." Collection contains correspondence by or references to persons who were lecturers to or invited guests of the Club, including George Washington Cable, Samuel L. Clemens, Bret Harte, William Dean Howells, Percival Lowell, Elizabeth Palmer Peabody, Harriet (Beecher) Stowe, and William Butler Yeats. The Club is still in existence.

1,955. Curtis Family
Papers. 1729-1975. Ca. 5000 items.
Open. Description.
Trinity College Archives.
Correspondence, genealogical material, deeds and other legal papers, financial records, and clippings and other printed matter of the Hiester, McLanahan, and Curtis families, including papers of Mary Ann (Scovill) Curtis (1830-1908), who was daughter of a Waterbury, CT, brass manufacturer and wife of William Edmond Curtis (1823-80), a superior court judge in New York. Mary Curtis's correspondence reflects the grief she felt and efforts she made to adjust to the deaths of two of her children in early adulthood.

1,956. Jackson, Abner
Papers. 1830-75. 17 vols. and ca. 50 items.
Open. Card index.
Trinity College Archives.
Family papers of Jackson (1811-74), a minister and president of Trinity College, and of his wife Emily (Ellsworth) Jackson (1816-53). Emily Jackson's papers consist of correspondence from her husband; her copybook of poetry and essays, with clippings; her diary, 1838-52, which details her religious musings; and clippings about her death. Also included are letters to the Jacksons' daughter Emily Elizabeth (Jackson) [Mrs. Philip N.] Nicholas (1845-1935), most of which are from Abner Jackson.

1,957. Jarvis Family
Papers. 1813-1908. Ca. 120 items.
Open. Card index.
Trinity College Archives.
Correspondence, bills and receipts, and legal papers of the family of Samuel Farmar Jarvis (1786-1851) and his son Samuel Fermor Jarvis, II (1825-1910), both of whom were clergymen. Includes personal letters concerning the elder Jarvis's divorce from his wife Sarah McCurdy (Hart) Jarvis.

1,958. Bartlett Family
Papers. 1839-1924. 1 box (ca. 300 items).
Open. No guide.
Trinity College, Watkinson Library.
Correspondence, drafts of local and family histories, genealogical notes, photos, clippings, and other printed material, including papers of Mary Leeds Leffingwell (Bartlett) [Mrs. Duncan Black] Macdonald (1850-1929), a genealogist and local historian. Genealogical correspondence and a copy of the history she wrote in 1915 of the Sunday school of Hartford's Asylum Hill Congregational Church are also included.

1,959. Hartford Residents
Collection. 1807-1947. Ca. 150 items.
Open. No guide.
Trinity College, Watkinson Library.
Among the correspondence, poems, draft essays, photos, invitations, engravings, printed flyers, and other papers of residents of Hartford are 26 letters to Henrietta Gardiner, three of which are from author Laura E. Richards, and signed greeting cards addressed to Gardiner.

1,960. Sibour Family
Papers. 1589-1917. 1100 items.
Open. Inventory.
Trinity College, Watkinson Library.
Correspondence, journal, accounts, wills, contracts, genealogical material, church documents, passports, petitions, and property inventories of a family of French businessmen and statesmen. Included is a copy of Mary Louisa de Sibour's 1903 autobiography detailing her childhood, schooling, marriage, war experiences, family illnesses, travels, and other events. Born in Belfast, ME, in ca. 1837, and educated in Boston, she married Jean Antoine Gabriel de Sibour in 1860. They spent the Civil War years in Charleston, SC, traveled in Europe, and in the 1870s and 1880s lived in Richmond, VA, and Washington, DC.

1,961. Sigourney, Lydia Howard (Huntley)
Papers. 1832-1959. Ca. 75 items.
Open. No guide.
Trinity College, Watkinson Library.
Sigourney (1791-1865) was an author. Correspondence, mostly to the Williams family; manuscript of the school textbook she wrote, which was published as *History of Marcus Aurelius* (Hartford: Belknap and Hamersley, 1836); manuscript and printed poetry; photos and daguerreotypes; clippings; memorabilia; and other material.

1,962. U.S. Civil War
Collection. 1860-89. 2 boxes (ca. 250 items).
Open. Card catalog for items in 1 box.
Trinity College, Watkinson Library.
War documents include a journal of [Mrs.] Mary Trumbull Prime, a Union sympathizer, which consists of clippings linked by text she wrote to provide a history of the battles during 1863; correspondence; telegram book; autograph book; Confederate bonds; blank printed forms; and other printed matter.

1,963. Warner, Charles Dudley
Papers. Ca. 1865-99. Ca. 3050 items.
Open. Card catalog.
Trinity College, Watkinson Library.
Journals, manuscripts of literary works, and correspondence of Warner, including letters to Helen Keller, Varina Anne (Howell) Davis on personal matters, Mary Elizabeth (Mapes) Dodge and Annie (Adams) Fields on personal and literary subjects, Anna Elizabeth Dickinson on her lectures and travels, Constance Fenimore Woolson on travels abroad, and Helen Maria (Fiske) Hunt Jackson on personal, literary, social, and other topics. Also included are a few personal letters from Harriet (Beecher) Stowe to Mrs. Warner.

1,964. Williams Family
Papers. 1721-1908. 2 ft. (ca. 400 items).
Open. Card catalog.
Trinity College, Watkinson Library.
Correspondence, financial documents, legal records, insurance papers, poems, petitions, and invitations of a family of Connecticut residents. Included are three letters from author Lydia Sigourney to Abigail (Ellsworth) Williams and Sigourney's manuscript poem on Abigail Williams's death in 1860; letters of other female family members, such as Mary and Augusta Williams and Ellen (Williams) Vanderbilt; and a scrapbook diary kept in 1835 by Vanderbilt while living in Hartford.

1,965. Women's Fellowship of the Connecticut Conference of the United Church of Christ
Records. 1928- . No size given.
Open. No guide.
United Church of Christ, Connecticut Conference Office.
Annual reports, minutes, treasurers' reports, programs, photos, scrapbooks, clippings, and publications of the state and district boards of the Fellowship. The Women's Fellowship was founded

in 1928 as the Council of Congregational Women of Connecticut with [Miss] Amy Ogden Welcher as its first president.

LITCHFIELD

1,966. Bull, Dorothy
Papers. 1916-30. 2 Hollinger boxes and 150 items.
Open. Unpublished guide.
Litchfield Historical Society.
Bull was an educator and poet. Correspondence and other items pertaining to poet John Masefield and correspondence, photos, and publications relating to the Spring Hill School, an early, progressive, private educational institution.

1,967. Litchfield Female Academy
Records. 1790-1850. Ca. 6 ft. and 4 boxes.
Open. Unpublished guide.
Litchfield Historical Society.
Minutes, financial records, correspondence, diaries, journals, essays, plays, copybooks, albums, scrapbooks, and other records of the Academy, which was in existence between 1792 and 1855, and of its founder Sarah Pierce, an educator. Contains information on Academy board members, teachers, students, and other personalities and about general conditions in Litchfield.

1,968. Phelps, Winthrop H.
Papers. Ca. 1850-1900. 8 boxes and ca. 900 items.
Open. Unpublished guide.
Litchfield Historical Society.
Correspondence, diaries, and battle reports of Phelps (1818-85), chaplain of the Second Connecticut Volunteer Artillery, contain correspondence with his wife Lucy Fassett (Robinson) Benjamin Phelps (1822-1901), most of which pertains to his Civil War service and to her life at home during the war. Also includes a listing Ethel Lowerre Phelps made of Winthrop Phelps's letters and diaries.

1,969. Quincy, Mary Perkins
Papers. 1700-1922. 6 ft. and 18 boxes.
Open. Unpublished guide.
Litchfield Historical Society.
Correspondence, financial records, essays, Perkins and Deming family papers, albums, scrapbooks, and photos of [Miss] Quincy (1866-1921), a Litchfield essayist, world traveler, and collector of historical material who was active in the DAR, the Colonial Dames, and other national patriotic associations. Because of her interest in family history and genealogy, Quincy preserved many documents of her Connecticut ancestors.

1,970. Diaries, Journals, and Albums
Collection. 1796-1841. 3 ft.
Open. Unpublished guide.
Litchfield Historical Society.
Collection contains a journal Electa Marsh kept as a student at Morris Academy in Litchfield, 1799; Jane Lewis's journal for the summer at Miss Pierce's Academy in Litchfield, 1820; a journal Lucy Sheldon kept while she was a student at Miss Pierce's Academy, 1802-03; an album Mary Buel kept while she was a pupil at the Litchfield Seminary, 1831-41; and a friendship album Jane Wadhams kept as a student at the Litchfield Seminary, 1827-31. Also includes volumes by unnamed authors: a diary of life at a school in Litchfield, 1796; a daily journal of a Goshen, CT, student at the Morris Academy, 1810-11; a journal written by a student at boarding school in Litchfield, 1816-18; friendship albums kept by two pupils at Miss Pierce's Academy, 1817 and 1820-21; a friendship album of a resident of Saybrook, CT, 1819; and a friendship album presented to a teacher by her affectionate pupils, 1832.

MIDDLETOWN

1,971. Hall Family
Papers. 1779-1919. Ca. 570 items.
Open. Calendar.
Middlesex County Historical Society.
Correspondence, drafts of speeches and publications, essays, poems, genealogical data, financial documents, business and legal papers, clippings, and printed items of this Middletown family. Contains material of Laura Hall, a schoolteacher in Middletown during the 1870s, including letters she wrote to family members.

1,972. Hulbert and Huntington Family
Papers. 1815-90. Ca. 1500 items.
Open. Calendar.
Middlesex County Historical Society.
Correspondence; diaries; legal, financial, and military documents; broadsides; photos; and clippings and other printed material of this Connecticut family. Includes letters of Mary (Huntington) Hulbert, 1816-75; letters of Marietta Barratt, 1829-39; and letters of other women members of the family.

1,973. Russell Family
Papers. 1796-1929. 20 boxes.
Open. Calendar.
Middlesex County Historical Society.
Correspondence, business papers, and printed material of this Middletown family. Includes letters of Eliza (Hall) Russell, 1809-60, and correspondence and personal financial documents of [Miss] Fanny Russell, 1864-94.

1,974. Atwater, Wilbur O.
Papers. 1840-1943. 13 Paige boxes, 1 Hollinger box, and 1 oversize box.
Open. Preliminary inventories.
Wesleyan University Archives.
Included with the correspondence, diaries, bills and other financial documents, drafts of lectures and publications, notebooks, family papers, and other material of Atwater (1844-1907), a chemist, are correspondence with his wife Marcia (Woodard) Atwater (?-1933); letters to him from his sister Florence, his aunt Harriet [Mrs. L. R.] Atwater, and other female relatives; and papers of his daughter Helen Woodard Atwater (1876-1947), a home economist. Also includes letters that his son Charles Atwater (1885-1946) wrote to his parents, his wife Alice Merriam Atwater, and their daughter Catherine.

1,975. Coeducation at Wesleyan
Records. 1872- . 1 Hollinger box.
Open. No guide.
Wesleyan University Archives.
Founded as a men's college in 1831, Wesleyan was coeducational between 1872 and 1912 and again since 1968. Records for the early period include excerpts from minutes of meetings, reports, a few letters and reminiscences, pamphlets, photos of women students, and clippings. Records for the second period include reports leading up to the decision to make the school coeducational a second time; clippings files on women faculty and students, including one on Sheila Tobias, an historian and administrator who has been active in women's studies programs and equal opportunity efforts; and a file on the math anxiety clinic established in 1975.

1,976. Fisk, Willbur
Papers. 1812-83. 13 Hollinger boxes.
Open. Unpublished guide.
Wesleyan University Archives.
Correspondence, sermons, and other papers of Fisk (1792-1839), a Methodist minister who served from 1831 to 1839 as Wesleyan's first president, include correspondence with his wife Ruth (Peck) Fisk (1795-1884), other family women, and other unrelated women. Also contains papers of Ruth Fisk, including correspondence, financial accounts, manuscript verse on her husband, and information about his death.

1,977. Foss, Cyrus David
Papers. 1850-1910. 9 Hollinger boxes.
Open. Unpublished guide.
Wesleyan University Archives.
Papers of Foss (1834-1910), a Methodist minister who from 1875 to 1880 was president of Wesleyan, consist of correspondence, sermons and other writings, scrapbooks, and information on his travels. Most of his nearly 900 letters are either to his mother Jane (Campbell) Foss or to his wife Amelia (Robertson) Foss. Also included are letters to him from Amelia Foss and letters of his brothers Archibald and William Foss to their mother Jane Foss.

1,978. Kazan, Elia
Papers. 1930s- . 60 cu.ft.
Closed. No guide.
Wesleyan University Archives.
Included with the correspondence, diaries, manuscripts, notes, and scrapbooks of Kazan (1909-), a theatre and film director and novelist, are correspondence, drafts, notes, scripts, scrapbooks, and ephemera of his first wife Molly Day (Thacher) Kazan (1907?-63), a playwright.

1,979. Middletown History
Collection. 1796- . Ca. 50 ft.
Open. Unpublished guide.
Wesleyan University Archives.
Records of organizations, reports, pamphlets, broadsides, clippings, newspapers, photos, books, and other material documenting local history. Includes a copy of the Bible heavily annotated by Julia Evelina Smith in preparation for her translations from the original languages, which was published in 1876. Material on the education of women, for example, includes an 1851 catalog and 1853 issue of the school newspaper of the Middletown Female Seminary, founded in 1849; an 1846 catalog of the Middletown Female Institute, founded in 1843; and the 1870 opening address by Daniel Coit Gilman, an educator, for the Connecticut Industrial School for Girls reformatory.

1,980. Monday Club
Records. 1892-1966. 1 ft.
Open. No guide.
Wesleyan University Archives.
Annual reports, minutes, and programs of this club of Wesleyan faculty wives, which was founded in 1892 for social and intellectual enjoyment and "the furtherance of intimacy among the members of the college community."

1,981. Munson, Gorham
Papers. 1922-64. 37 ft.
Open. Published guide.
Wesleyan University Archives.
Correspondence, memoranda, biographical information, financial and organizational documents, articles, reviews, press releases, pamphlets, bibliographies, legislative material, clippings, scrapbooks, photos, and artifacts of Munson (1896-1969), an author, editor, and reformer, pertain to the American Social Credit Movement and *New Democracy.* Includes correspondence from 1934 to 1943 of Mrs. E. Sohier Welch, leader of the Social Credit

Movement in Boston, and of other women who were active in the Movement. See Clement Vose, *Gorham Munson Papers of the American Social Credit Movement and New Democracy: A Register* (Middletown: Wesleyan University Archives, 1977).

1,982. Olin Family
Papers. 1820-1924. 6 Hollinger boxes.
Open. Unpublished guide.
Wesleyan University Archives.
Correspondence, sermons and lectures, and other papers of Stephen Olin (1797-1851), a Methodist clergyman and educator who served as president of Wesleyan from 1842 to 1851; of his second wife Julia (Lynch) Olin (1814-79); and of their son Stephen Henry Olin (1847-1925), a lawyer who was acting president of Wesleyan from 1922 to 1923. Julia Olin's papers consist of correspondence with her husband, son, aunt, a female cousin, other relatives, and others, as well as a travel diary, commonplace books, notebooks, and 98 compositions.

1,983. Smith, Augustus W., and Family
Papers. 1821-1903. 1 Hollinger box.
Open. No guide.
Wesleyan University Archives.
Correspondence of Smith (1802-66), a professor of mathematics and astronomy who was president of Wesleyan from 1852 to 1857; of his wife Catherine (Childs) Smith (?-1899); and of their son Perry Childs Smith (1827-1903), a lawyer. Consists primarily of Catherine Smith's correspondence with her mother, father, sister, aunt, husband, son, and daughters, as well as letters from her mother to her father.

1,984. Roy Lucas, the James Madison Constitutional Law Institute, and the Population Law Center
Records. 1969-73. 14 ft.
Open. Unpublished guide.
Wesleyan University, Collection on Legal Change.
Roy Lucas, an attorney, has led both the Law Institute, founded in 1969, and the Law Center, founded in 1972, to challenge abortion laws by providing legal protection for physicians and other individuals. Files of abortion cases brought before state and federal courts contain briefs, decisions, trial transcripts, correspondence, and other records. Includes files on abortion-related court cases (in which Lucas participated) in Arizona, California, Colorado, Connecticut, Florida, Georgia, Iowa, Kansas, Kentucky, Louisiana, Massachusetts, Michigan, Mississippi, Missouri, New Jersey, New York, North Carolina, Ohio, Oklahoma, Pennsylvania, South Dakota, Texas, Utah, Vermont, Virginia, and Wisconsin. Also includes records concerning the defense of abortion physician Vuitch in the District of Columbia and Maryland and of a Dr. Hodgson in Minnesota as well as records documenting the participation of Lucas in *Roe v. Wade* (1973), in which the US Supreme Court recognized the constitutional right of women to obtain legal abortions. Philanthropic grants from foundations have helped to fund the Law Institute and Law Center.

MONROE

1,985. Archives
Records. 1896- . 24 Hollinger boxes.
Access restricted. No guide.
Sisters of the Holy Family of Nazareth, Immaculate Heart of Mary Provincialate.
Financial records; correspondence; historical documents; photos; papers of the provincial superiors, foundress, and superiors general; and records of the province, of provincial and general chapters of the order, of Marian Heights Academy, and of parish convents and institutions of the order on the northeast coast of the US. The Immaculate Heart of Mary Province was founded in 1959 and has had its headquarters in Monroe since 1962.

MYSTIC

1,986. Fish Family
Papers. 1810-68. 8 vols. and 2150 items.
Open. Unpublished guide.
Mystic Seaport, Inc., Library.
Papers of the Fish family of Stonington, CT, consist primarily of letters to Asa Fish (1790-1861), who was engaged in maritime commerce, and his wife Prudence (Dean) Fish (1799-?) from their children James D. (1819-?), Sands H. (1821-?), Hannah (1823-?), Silas (1825-?), Asa (1828-?), Prudence (1830-?), Benjamin (1834-?), and Fanny D. Fish (1839-?). The letters, primarily from Brooklyn, NY, and Chicago, also include items from Asa and Prudence Fish's grandchildren. Also contains diaries, accounts, receipts, deeds, and genealogical material.

1,987. Hotchkiss
Papers. 1851-82. 13 vols.
Open. No guide.
Mystic Seaport, Inc., Library.
Collection includes three journals that Emma P. (Hotchkiss) Gray kept on board ships of which her husband Horatio Nelson Gray was master, and a journal she kept on board a ship of which her father Levi J. Hotchkiss was master. These vessels were engaged in trading voyages along the coast, to South America, and to the Orient.

1,988. Mallory Family
Papers. 1808-1958. 82 vols. and 6000 items.
Open. Unpublished guide.
Mystic Seaport, Inc., Library.
Papers of Charles Mallory (1796-1882), Charles Henry Mallory (1818-90), Henry Rogers Mallory (1849-1919), and Clifford Day Mallory (1881-1941), all of whom were engaged in shipbuilding and maritime commerce, contain a few papers of Cora N. (Pynchon) Mallory (1854-1938), a resident of Springfield, MA, whom Henry Rogers Mallory married in 1853. Includes her correspondence with family and friends, 1867-77; school compositions; mementos of a trip she took to Europe with her husband in 1911; Pynchon family genealogies; and clippings relating to the Pynchon family and to Springfield.

1,989. Stover, Calista Meader
Papers. 1859-92. 9 vols. and 46 items.
Open. No guide.
Mystic Seaport, Inc., Library.
Correspondence, diaries, and autograph albums of Stover, the wife of shipmaster Joseph Stover, and her daughter Maria Calista Stover of Bucksport, ME. Calista Stover kept the diaries during voyages to Japan and the Hawaiian Islands aboard the *Daniel Barnes,* of which her husband was master.

1,990. Waterman Family
Papers. 1797-1869. 8 vols. and 895 items.
Open. Unpublished guide.
Mystic Seaport, Inc., Library.
Correspondence, account books, bills, receipts, verse, and photos of Martin Waterman (1793-1860), a shipmaster. Includes correspondence with his wife Joan Cushing Waterman (1795-1845), 1815-45, while she was living in Duxbury, MA, and letters from his mother Silvinia Waterman (1772-1835), 1815-16.

NEW HAVEN

1,991. Association Files
Records. 1939- . No size given.
Open. No guide.
Association of Girl Scout Executive Staff.
Founded in Philadelphia in 1939, the Association promotes contacts among Girl Scout executives and serves as a voice for executive staff members in setting and achieving Girl Scout goals and objectives. Correspondence, administrative files, and biographical data.

1,992. Carmalt, Ethel
Papers. 1878-1940. 0.5 ft.
Open. Inventory.
New Haven Colony Historical Society.
Carmalt (1865-1959) was the daughter of William Henry Carmalt, a professor at Yale University. Her papers primarily relate to the Saturday Morning Club, of which she was a member. The Club, a social and literary club founded in 1881, is composed of women living in the New Haven area. Also includes papers Carmalt wrote on regional planning and her recollections of Ellicottville, NY, as well as photos.

1,993. Daughters of '53
Records. 1853-1972. 1.25 ft.
Open. Inventory.
New Haven Colony Historical Society.
Constitution, a treasurer's book, an annual cash statement, correspondence, a memorandum book, membership lists, a scrapbook, and memorabilia of the Club, an independent Jewish women's club founded as Ahavas Achus in 1853 in New Haven. The club has drawn membership from all over the country and is still active.

1,994. Fortnightly Club
Records. 1886-1971. 1 ft.
Open. Inventory.
New Haven Colony Historical Society.
Bylaws, minutes, papers by members, correspondence, skits, and memorabilia of the Club, a women's organization that was founded in 1886; the Club is still in existence. Members presented papers on selected topics such as social science, political economy, contemporary literature, music, and art.

1,995. Fuller, Hattie (Pierpont)
Papers. 1852-1925. 1.5 ft.
Open. Inventory.
New Haven Colony Historical Society.
Family correspondence of Fuller (1847-1923), a native of New Haven and a daughter of Elias Pierpont and Grace Bradley Pierpont. In 1868 she married Austin B. Fuller, a dentist. They had three children: Pierpont Fuller, a lawyer; Clement A. Fuller (1873-?), also a lawyer; and Grace Pierpont Fuller (1883-1965), a librarian at Yale University Library for many years. Collection primarily consists of letters to Hattie Fuller from her daughter Grace Fuller while she was a student at Smith College, but it also includes correspondence of Hattie Fuller's parents, letters from her husband before and after their marriage, and letters from friends. Also contains a biography of Austin Fuller, which Grace Fuller wrote.

1,996. Little Theater Guild of New Haven
Records. 1922-35. 1.5 ft.
Open. Inventory.
New Haven Colony Historical Society.
Bylaws, minutes, correspondence, blueprints, scrapbooks, sketches for scene design, photos, clippings, and other records of the Guild. Organized in 1922 to provide interested persons with the opportunity to work in all areas of theater, the Guild sold yearly memberships for $5. Later the organization sponsored a children's theater and, during 1934 and 1935, children's symphony

concerts. The organization dissolved in 1935 because of financial difficulties. Includes a motion picture of a production of *Vanity Fair.*

1,997. Lowell House Mothers' Club
Records. 1900-44. 3 ft.
Open. Inventory.
New Haven Colony Historical Society.
Lowell House Settlement was founded in 1900 to begin an "Americanization and humanitarian movement" that would benefit New Haven's foreign population. Minutes, registrar's books, attendance records, program books, membership books, and correspondence, primarily of Susan Bacon Keith, a president of the Club. Records contain information on an American Mothers' Club composed of English-speaking women who met weekly for social purposes and to study such topics as nutrition, child care, and sanitation, and records of other Lowell House-sponsored clubs for children and adults, among them an Italian Mothers' Club.

1,998. Mitchell, Mary Cornwall (Hewitt)
Papers. 1929-50. 7.5 in.
Open. Inventory.
New Haven Colony Historical Society.
Mary Hewitt (1875-1955) taught history at Lake Erie College in Ohio from 1906 to 1909. In 1909 she married Sydney Knox Mitchell, a professor of history and department chairman at Yale University. Consists primarily of drafts and copies of articles and speeches and research notes concerning colonial women of North America, the Irish in New Haven, slavery, and Lydia Sigourney. Also includes some correspondence, photos, and clippings along with biographies of Sarah L. Cady, Carolyn Gorham Dickerman, Charles Loring Brace, and John Pierce Brace. Mitchell was born in New Haven and received her BA from Smith College in 1897 and her PhD in history from Yale in 1901. Her son John H. Mitchell taught at Wellesley College. Mary Mitchell wrote for the *American Biographical Dictionary;* she also gave lectures on topics pertaining to local history. Author of *History of New Haven County, Connecticut* (1930), Mitchell was a member of the Historical Society and other local organizations as well. Additional information on Mitchell is located in the North End Study Club Papers, the West End Institute Papers, and the Papers of the United Church on the Green, which are located at the Historical Society.

1,999. New Haven Study Club
Records. 1892-1974. 7.5 in.
Open. Inventory.
New Haven Colony Historical Society.
Bylaws, minutes of meetings, treasurer's reports, correspondence, reports, bills, histories, lists of topics, photos, clippings, and memorabilia of the Club, which was founded in 1889 by Caroline Atwater Mason, the wife of the pastor of the First Baptist Church. Membership was limited to 20 and restricted to the elite. In 1925 the restrictions on membership were eliminated, permitting any mother to "hold up the Study Club as a possible goal to her most ambitious daughter." A program was set for each year, and every member was assigned a specific topic to study.

2,000. Newcomb, Lydia
Papers. 1897-1903. 2 in.
Open. Inventory.
New Haven Colony Historical Society.
Newcomb, a resident of New Haven, was active in many civic groups and director of The Women's School Association. Papers relate to groups in which she was involved, including the American League for Civic Improvement, the Connecticut State Federation of Women's Clubs, the Pan Republic Congress, the Human Freedom League, the National League for the Protection of American Institutions, and the Public Education Association of New York. Clippings relate to schools, vacation schools, playgrounds, and women leaders.

2,001. North End Club
Records. 1918-67. 2.5 in.
Open. Inventory.
New Haven Colony Historical Society.
Constitution, bylaws, minute books, treasurer's reports, committee reports, correspondence, a history, and programs of the Club, which was founded in 1918 by 14 young mothers to engage in American National Red Cross work and to exchange ideas and information on child rearing and housekeeping. With the end of WWI, the club's emphasis shifted to self-improvement and then to more general community interests.

2,002. Rowell, George Berkeley, Family
Papers. 1829-1902. 1 ft.
Open. Inventory.
New Haven Colony Historical Society.
Primarily correspondence and biographical sketches of George Rowell (1815-84), son of Joseph Rowell and Hannah Chase Rowell, who were residents of Cornish, NH, and of his wife Malvina Jerusha Chapin Rowell (1816-1901), a resident of Newport, NH, and an 1841 graduate of Mount Holyoke Seminary, whom he married in 1842. One month after their marriage the Rowells sailed with the tenth company of missionaries to the Sandwich Islands. Much of the early correspondence concerns the deaths of George Rowell's sister and brother-in-law Martha Laurens (Rowell) Locke (?-1842) and Edwin Locke (?-1842), missionaries in Hawaii who died shortly after the Rowells' arrival, and the future of the Lockes' three children. Lucy Maria Locke (1838-71) and Martha Laurens Locke (1840-89) were adopted by Mr. and Mrs. Asa Bowen Smith, who replaced the Lockes at the Waialua station. The youngest daughter, Mary Sabin, was adopted by her uncle Samuel Newell Rowell of Malta, NY.

The Rowells' children were Malvina Chapin (1843-70), William Edwards (1845-1916), Clara Maria (1847-1916), Marion Eliza (1848-1912), George Addison (1850-1904), Ellen Louisa (1852-1924), and Mary Adelaide Rowell (1853-1932). Four of these children were sent to schools in Hawaii and to the US for their education; letters to them from family and friends in Hawaii form the second major portion of the collection. Also includes letters from Frances Eliza Rowell (1856-1904), the daughter of Samuel Newell Rowell (1821-93) and Eliza Benham Rowell (?-1864), to her sister Ella Maria (Rowell) Higgins (1852-1904) and letters to Mary Adelaide (Rowell) Stoltz while she was at Mount Holyoke from her sister Clara (Rowell) Dole, with family news, genealogical notes, and biographical material on missionaries. Frances Eliza Rowell married her first cousin George Addison Rowell.

2,003. Schools
Collection. 1715-1963. 2.5 ft.
Open. Inventory.
New Haven Colony Historical Society.
Notebooks, memorabilia, and other records of public and private schools in and around New Haven date primarily from 1770 to 1963. Includes records of the Joanna Bontecou School, The Female Seminary, Miss Dutton's School at Grove Hall, and the Women's School Association. Correspondence of Lydia Newcomb, director of the Women's School Association, is contained in that group's records.

2,004. Thursday Club
Records. 1906-62. 17 folders, 4 vols., and 4 items.
Open. Inventory.
New Haven Colony Historical Society.
Includes constitution, minutes, financial records, correspondence, membership lists, photos, clippings, and pamphlets of the Club, which was organized in 1906 by Elizabeth Seymour and Katharine Hastings. The Club's interests were literary and social. Members presented papers on various topics at meetings and were involved in some philanthropic activities. The Club apparently stopped meeting in ca. 1962.

2,005. United Order of True Sisters, New Haven No. 4, Jochebed Lodge
Records. 1863-1972. 3 ft.
Open. Inventory.
New Haven Colony Historical Society.
Minutes, executive committee records, accounts, ledgers, philanthropic league records, membership contributions, and other records of this lodge of the Order, which was organized in 1863. The Order is a national Jewish women's organization known for civic, social, and charitable activities. New Haven No. 4 contributed funds and services to local welfare and health organizations, among them the Jewish Welfare Service, the New Haven Blind Association, the Cancer Research Center, the special service committee for the Veterans Hospital, and the New Haven Committee for Retarded Children. Early records are in Yiddish.

2,006. West End Institute
Records. 1887-1949. 10 in.
Open. Inventory.
New Haven Colony Historical Society.
Correspondence, lists of students, penmanship and exercise books, photos, clippings, school catalogs, books, and memorabilia of the Institute, originally Mrs. Cady's School for Girls, which was founded in 1870 and existed until 1900. Primarily a day school, the institution took in some boarders, who had the added advantage of French conversation in the evenings.

2,007. Woman's Choral Society of New Haven
Records. 1927-59. 2.08 ft.
Open. Inventory.
New Haven Colony Historical Society.
Annual reports of committee chairmen, complete minutes of meetings, lists of executive board members and active and associate members, clippings, and concert programs of the Society, which was founded in 1927 by [Mrs.] Mary Loveridge Robbins, who served as its first president. Composed primarily of nonprofessional singers who gathered to study and present choral works, the group presented concerts of their own as well as concerts in combination with other musical organizations; the Society also assisted at public functions requiring musical talent. The Society was affiliated with the Connecticut State Federation of Music Clubs and with the National Federation of Music Clubs. It disbanded in 1959.

2,008. Woman's Seamen's Friend Society of Connecticut
Records. 1859-1968. 13 in.
Open. Inventory.
New Haven Colony Historical Society.
Nearly complete minutes, reports of the trustees from 1902 to 1911, an account book, and a register of the Society, which was chartered in 1860 to help sailors and improve their conditions.

2,009. Women
Collection. 1704-1930. 2 ft.
Open. Inventory.
New Haven Colony Historical Society.
Includes letters from Charlotte Beers of New Haven to her future husband Henry C. Rossiter of New York, in which she describes life in New Haven during the War of 1812; of Sara M. Denison, a resident of New Haven, in which she discusses with Thomas P. Rossiter in Florence, Italy, her social life in New Haven, friends, and relatives, 1842; and of Lucy Hotchkiss, who tells Amanda Johnson in Meriden about a trip to Grandview, IL, and settling in the town, 1837. Also includes letters to Frances Ives, a resident of North Haven, CT, from her brother Robert Ives,

who was touring with the Doyle-Carte Company in England, 1877-79. Also contains correspondence, reports, a scrapbook, and clippings of Hortense [Mrs. Arthur] Booth, a resident of New Haven, which relate to the New Haven Woman's Club, of which she was a member and an officer. Diaries include those of Eunice Carew [Mrs. Joseph] Huntington, a resident of Norwich, CT, 1792-94; of Mabel Lancraft, a teen-ager who lived in Fair Haven, CT, and attended the Hillhouse High School, 1887-90; of Thalia Maria McMahon [Mrs. Alexis] Painter, a resident of West Haven, CT, who wrote about her family and her religious life; and of Rae Mortimer Seymour Dwight, a Washington, DC, resident visiting Pine Orchard, CT, during the summer of 1893, who describes Grover Cleveland's inauguration, a visit to Clara Barton, and the Lizzie Borden case. Also includes an account book of Mary Griswold Chauncy, a resident of New Haven, ca. 1765; a notebook of Electra S. Landcraft that includes recipes and home medicines; and a friendship album and notebook of Laura Gilbert Daggett, a resident of New Haven, containing poetry and prose she copied and poetry from friends in Wilbraham, MA, ca. 1828 and 1886. Other papers relate to organizations and include a constitution, minutes, a treasurer's account book, receipts and expenditures, lists of garments distributed and recipients, lists of officers, and other records of the Dorcas Society For the Relief of Poor Female Professors of Religion, 1813-70; rules and regulations of the Disciples of Christ, apparently a New Haven women's organization, 1814; and a constitution and letter of the Female Auxiliary Bible Society of New Haven, 1824.

2,010. China Records Project: Brown, Velva V.
Papers. 1920-71. 2 ft.
Open. Unpublished guide.
Yale Divinity School Library.
Printed matter and correspondence concerning the life of Brown, a physician and missionary to China who was superintendent of the Scott Thresher Memorial Hospital in Swatow.

2,011. China Records Project: Carr, Ruth M. (White)
Papers. 1917-26. 1.5 ft.
Open. Unpublished guide.
Yale Divinity School Library.
Diaries and memorabilia of [Mrs. Clarence] Carr (1889-), a missionary to China, are included with extensive letters she wrote home about her activities in China.

2,012. China Records Project: Dawson, Mary E. S.
Papers. 1921-31. 5 in.
Open. Unpublished guide.
Yale Divinity School Library.
Letters from Dawson, a missionary to China, to family members at home concern her activities in China.

2,013. China Records Project: Hartwell, Emily Susan
Papers. 1875-1949. 1.5 ft.
Open. Unpublished guide.
Yale Divinity School Library.
Papers of Hartwell (1858-1951), a missionary to China for 50 years who established schools and orphanages and taught at Foochow College, consist of correspondence, biographical material, printed matter, and papers that take a position against the custom of foot binding.

2,014. China Records Project: Hinman, Kate (Bailey)
Papers. 1908-61. 1.5 ft.
Open. Unpublished guide.
Yale Divinity School Library.
Papers of [Mrs. George W.] Hinman (1871-1970), a missionary to China, consist of correspondence, diaries, and notebook records of her correspondence.

2,015. China Records Project: Perkins, Elizabeth S.
Papers. 1907-27. 1 ft.
Open. Unpublished guide.
Yale Divinity School Library.
A missionary, Perkins (?-1971) was assigned to China in 1907 by the American Board of Commissioners of Foreign Missions; she taught and was principal of a girls school in the Foochow area. Letters home describing her activities, a scrapbook, and clippings.

2,016. China Records Project: Personal Papers
Collection. 1834-1973. 64 ft.
Open. Unpublished guide.
Yale Divinity School Library.
Small amounts (five inches or less) of papers of women missionaries to China, including correspondence, clippings, and printed matter of Alice Alsup, 1919-49; correspondence and printed matter of Margaret Hart (Bailey) Barbour, 1912-48; a report about the internment of Ruth M. Brack by the Japanese, ca. 1942; autobiographical material of Eliza Jane (Gillett) Bridgman; memoirs of Elizabeth Gordon Bruce, 1970; memoirs of Mina (Van Cleave) Buck, 1968 and 1969; correspondence and the script "Women in War-Time China" of Ruth M. Chester, 1927-50; correspondence, clippings, and other material of Nettie R. DeJong, 1915-45; a manuscript of Mary (Porter) Gamewell, ca. 1899-1926; correspondence and a scrapbook of Anne M. Groff, 1921-48; a manuscript "Women in a Changing China: The YWCA" of Jean (McCown) Hawkes, 1971; and correspondence and a diary of Anna (Moffett) Jarvis, 1920-49.

2,017. Foster Family
Papers. 1851-1951. 6 ft.
Open. Unpublished guide.
Yale Divinity School Library.
Clara (Hess) Foster (1859-1945) and her husband John Marshall Foster were Baptist missionaries to China from 1888 to 1894 and 1898 to 1900; from 1900 to 1915 Clara Foster remained in the US with her children and then returned to work in China from 1915 to 1921. Includes correspondence, 1889-1916, and journals, 1915-16, concerning her daily life.

2,018. Hartwell Family
Papers. 1849-1969. 7 ft.
Open. Unpublished guide.
Yale Divinity School Library.
Includes papers of Eliza H. (Jewett) [Mrs. Jesse] Hartwell (1837-70) and her daughter Anna Burton Hartwell (1870-1961), both of whom were Baptist missionaries to China. Eliza Hartwell's correspondence is primarily with her husband during their courtship in America and then after they were married and living in China between 1858 and 1869. Anna Hartwell's notebook diaries containing correspondence, poetry, and clippings reflect her daily life and personality. She went to China in 1892, where she became involved in educational and evangelical work. The correspondence from China contains information on the sentiment against foreigners, mission history, and daily living conditions.

2,019. Smith Family
Papers. 1894-1971. 6 ft.
Open. Unpublished guide.
Yale Divinity School Library.
Includes ca. one foot of correspondence and writings of Helen Huntington Smith (1902-71), appointed a missionary to China in 1929 by the American Board of Commissioners for Foreign Missions; for 20 years she taught at a girls school in Foochow, where she also participated in counseling, cooperatives, and relief work for orphans and destitute students. After missionaries were expelled from China in 1951, Smith held various positions, including director of women's work of the Ohio Conference of the United Church of Christ and research consultant for the Library's China Records Project. Her correspondence, 1910-70, is primarily family related, but later letters also concern her professional activities. Her writings contain addresses, resources for worship, short stories that appear to have been written by her, examinations, material concerning the Council for Lay Life and Work, and other papers.

2,020. Love Family
Papers. 1888-1960. 1400 items.
Open. Unpublished guide.
Yale University, Music Library.
Correspondence, autographed photos, clippings, and printed matter of Lucy Cleveland Prindle [Mrs. Edward Gurley] Love, a New York City resident who was active in the musical life there, and her daughter Helen Douglas (Love) Scranton (?-1969), who was secretary for Franz Kneisel, the founder of the Kneisel Quartet, and then after 1917 secretary of the Society of the Friends of Music and of the Beethoven Association of New York. Although the correspondence touches on some family and personal matters, the bulk of the material concerns musical life in New York and the US between 1885 and 1925. Almost all of the letters relate to musical personalities, composers, conductors, and singers. Includes correspondence of members of the Quartet; of American composers whose works were first played by the Quartet, among them Charles Wakefield Cadman and George Whitefield Chadwick; and of Alfred Cortot, Ernest Bloch, Frank Damrosch, Arthur Foote, Leopold Godowsky, Leopold Stokowski, and others.

2,021. Ornstein, Leo
Papers. 1913- . Ca. 20 archival boxes.
Open. Unpublished guide.
Yale University, Music Library.
Correspondence, manuscripts, programs, photos, and clippings of Ornstein (1892-), a composer. Includes essays on the substance of music and analyses of his music by his wife and assistant Pauline (Mallet-Prevost) Ornstein (ca. 1890-). Because Leo Ornstein dictates his music to his wife, all the manuscripts in the collection are in her hand. She also acts as his secretary and writes his correspondence for him.

2,022. Schneeloch
Papers. 1886-93. 2 boxes.
Open. Unpublished guide.
Yale University, Music Library.
Correspondence, diaries, concert programs, and photos of Emma Waleska Schneeloch (1862-?) and Emelie "Millie" A. Schneeloch (1868-?), sisters and singers who joined the concert band of Patrick Sarsfield Gilmore for a western tour in 1891 and an eastern tour in 1892. Their diaries concern their trip west and contain information on their audiences, including audiences of gold miners in Leadville, CO, and the closing of stores and schools in the Midwest so all the inhabitants of the town could attend their matinee concerts. Millie Schneeloch apparently married Frank Busse later in her life.

2,023. Wright, Helen Madeline
Papers. 1907-54. 1 box.
Open. Unpublished guide.
Yale University, Music Library.
Correspondence, autographed photos, and clippings of Wright, a pupil of Dame Myra Hess and Teresa Carreño, both of whom were pianists and teachers. Includes letters to Wright from Hess and Carreño. Hess, who was born in London, received a scholarship at the age of 13 to study at the Royal Academy of Music. Carreño, a native of

Venezuela, was successful as a pianist, composer, conductor, and singer. She died in New York.

NEW MILFORD

2,024. Ingleside School
Records. 1892-1913. 21 vols. and other items.
Open. No guide.
New Milford Historical Society.
Yearbooks, a scrapbook, notes, cards, photos, and trophies of this secondary school for girls, founded in 1892 by Mrs. William D. Black; the School closed in 1913, soon after her death. The curriculum at the School, which had 30 pupils when it opened and 110 by 1910, included English, foreign languages, art, history, science, sports, and other activities.

OLD LYME

2,025. Ladies Library Association of the Phoebe Griffin Noyes Library, Inc.
Records. 1872- . 4 ft.
Closed. No guide.
Old Lyme—Phoebe Griffin Noyes Library.
Notes on meetings and other records of the Association.

ROCKY HILL

2,026. Ladies Benevolent Society of the Rocky Hill Congregational Church
Records. 1850-1977. 2 ft.
Access restricted. Unpublished guide.
Rocky Hill Historical Society.
Minutes, financial reports, histories, and scrapbooks of the Society, which was organized in 1850 for "Christian benevolence, expressly for the advancement of Christ's cause and kingdom in the world." The Society's early records contain lists of material and accessories purchased to make clothing and knitted items and of the freight charges for shipping boxes of goods. Superseded in its functions by the Elderly Ladies Knitting Society, which was formed in 1841, the Ladies Benevolent Society continues to meet twice monthly.

WEST HARTFORD

2,027. Archives
Records. 1852- . 30 shelves.
Access restricted. No guide.
Sisters of Mercy of Connecticut.
Financial reports, correspondence, papers of several mothers superior, retreat notes, photos, scrapbooks, and other records of the order, which was founded in Hartford, CT, in 1848, relate to institutions operated by the Sisters.

DELAWARE

GREENVILLE

2,028. Crowninshield, Francis B., and Crowninshield, Louise Evelina (du Pont)
Papers. 1829-1957. Ca. 10,000 items.
Open. Published guide.
Eleutherian Mills Historical Library.
Papers of Francis Crowninshield (1869-1950) and his wife Louise Crowninshield (1877-1958), a philanthropist, include tax papers and returns, bills, receipts, invoices, and correspondence concerning her activities with the Kenmore Association of Virginia and the Garden Club of America, cruises she made around the world, and real estate holdings in Delaware and Washington, DC. See John Beverley Riggs, *A Guide to the Manuscripts in the Eleutherian Mills Historical Library* (Greenville, DE: Eleutherian Mills Historical Library, 1970).

2,029. Huston, Charles L.
Papers. 1806-1972. Ca. 5000 items.
Access restricted. Unpublished guide.
Eleutherian Mills Historical Library.
Correspondence, deeds, reports, bulletins, and other papers of Huston (1856-1951), who became vice-president of the family iron business, the Lukens Steel Company. Includes a few items concerning Rebecca (Pennock) Lukens, the mother-in-law of his father Charles Huston (1822-97).

2,030. Longwood Manuscripts: du Pont, Pierre Samuel
Papers. ?-1954. Ca. 1,000,000 items.
Open. Published and unpublished guides.
Eleutherian Mills Historical Library.
Personal and business papers of du Pont (1870-1954), a business executive in E. I. du Pont de Nemours & Co. and in General Motors and a member of the Association Against the Prohibition Amendment, contain ca. 39,000 items of his wife Alice (Belin) du Pont (1872-1944). These include childhood correspondence and scrapbooks, material from her years as an undergraduate at Bryn Mawr College, and information concerning her many philanthropic interests and financial matters. As mistress of Longwood, the du Pont estate, Alice du Pont was able to develop her strong interest in horticulture and gardening. She was a member of the American Orchid Society. See John Beverley Riggs, *A Guide to the Manuscripts in the Eleutherian Mills Historical Library* (Greenville, DE: Eleutherian Mills Historical Library, 1970).

2,031. Lukens Steel Company
Records. Ca. 1798-1917. Ca. 650 ft.
Access restricted. Published and unpublished guides.
Eleutherian Mills Historical Library.
Business records of the Lukens Steel Company, which traces its beginning to 1790 when Isaac Pennock built the Federal Slitting Mill in Chester County, PA, and thus became the first manufacturer of boiler plates in the US. Collection includes records from the period beginning in 1840 when his daughter Rebecca Webb (Pennock) Lukens (1794-1854) operated R. W. Lukens & Co. after the death of her husband Charles Lukens, who had become involved in the business. Seven years later, she served as president and manager of the Company. Rebecca Lukens's son-in-law Abraham Gibbons, Jr., entered the partnership, and the firm changed its name to Lukens Steel Company. See John Beverley Riggs, *A Guide to the Manuscripts in the Eleutherian Mills Historical Library* (Greenville, DE: Eleutherian Mills Historical Library, 1970).

2,032. Webb, Elizabeth
Papers. 1697-99. 38 pp.
Access restricted. Published guide.
Eleutherian Mills Historical Library.
Journal which Webb (1663-1726), a minister of the Society of Friends in England, kept of her mission to the American colonies, beginning with her departure from Bristol, arrival in Virginia, and overland travel with stops in Maryland, Pennsylvania, New Jersey, New York, New Hampshire, and Rhode Island. Webb visited Quaker meetings along the way. The journal, which is also available on microfilm, includes details of travel problems, names of prominent Quakers, and some comments on her religious feelings. See John Beverley Riggs, *A Guide to the Manuscripts in the Eleutherian Mills Historical Library* (Greenville, DE: Eleutherian Mills Historical Library, 1970).

2,033. Winterthur Manuscripts: du Pont, Henry Francis
Papers. 1588-1926. 150,000 items.
Open. Published guide.
Eleutherian Mills Historical Library.
Correspondence, diaries, financial records, transcripts, scrapbooks, photos, and memorabilia of members of the family of E. I. du Pont, a manufacturer of gunpowder. Includes correspondence in French, 1050 items, about family matters of Nicole Charlotte Marie Louise Le Dée de Roccourt de Nemours (1743-84) to her husband Pierre Samuel du Pont de Nemours; some writings and correspondence in French, 1025 items, of Gabrielle Josephine (de la Fite de Pelleport) [Mme. Victor] du Pont (1770-1837) pertaining to family matters, New York state, Franco-American topics, frontier life, and society in New York, Philadelphia, and Charleston, SC; diaries and correspondence on family and religious matters, 5225 items, of Sophie Madeleine (du Pont) Du Pont (1810-88), wife of Admiral Samuel Francis Du Pont; correspondence, 4200 items, depicting social life in New York during the 1870s of Mary Pauline (Foster) du Pont (1849-1902), wife of US senator Henry A. du Pont; and family letters in French, scattered diaries, household accounts, copybooks, and drawings of Sophie Madeleine Dalmas [Mrs. Eleuthère Irénée] du Pont and of her daughters. See John Beverley Riggs, *A Guide to the Manuscripts in the Eleutherian Mills Historical Library* (Greenville, DE: Eleutherian Mills Historical Library, 1970).

WILMINGTON

2,034. Armstrong, Eleanor
Papers. 1834. 1 vol.
Open. Unpublished guide.
Historical Society of Delaware.
School book contains notes from lectures about chemistry, electricity, drawing, and other subjects.

2,035. Bailey, Mrs. Joseph T.
Papers. 1863-64. 1 vol.
Open. Unpublished guide.
Historical Society of Delaware.
Recipe book of Bailey, a housewife, contains recipes common for the period.

2,036. Bayard
Papers. 1800-1930. 6 Hollinger boxes.
Open. Unpublished guide.
Historical Society of Delaware.

2,037. Bissell, Emily Perkins
Papers. Ca. 1930-40. 18 items.
Open. Unpublished guide.
Historical Society of Delaware.
[Miss] Bissell (1868-1948) was a philanthropist, supporter of education, and author who wrote prose and poetry under the pen name Priscilla Leonard; she also was one of Delaware's staunchest opponents of woman suffrage. Manuscript prose and poetry, tributes to Bissell, and a program from the 1946 Christmas Seal campaign. Bissell helped found the Christmas Seal fund-raising drive. Her writings were published in *Youth's Companion, Harper's Bazaar,* and *The Outlook.*

2,038. Bradford, Phoebe (George)
Papers. 1832-39. 22 vols.
Open. Published and unpublished guides.
Historical Society of Delaware.
Diaries of Bradford (1794-1840), wife of Moses Bradford, who was editor of the *Delaware Gazette* and the *Delaware Journal,* reveal her deep interest

in religion. She was a member of the Trinity Episcopal Church in Wilmington, attended other Protestant churches, and entertained their pastors in her home. She also was involved in the Female Colonization Society, the purpose of which was to return manumitted slaves to Africa. Her other interests included music, gardening, and her family. See W. Emerson Wilson, ed., *Diaries of Phoebe George Bradford, 1832-1839* (Wilmington: Historical Society of Delaware, 1976).

2,039. Brian, Sarah
Papers. 1827-33. 3 vols.
Open. No guide.
Historical Society of Delaware.
Volumes contain occasional diary entries but consist primarily of extracts from literature and poems and verse written by friends of Brian.

2,040. Burton, Hannah (Wolfe)
Papers. 1811-24. 1 vol.
Open. No guide.
Historical Society of Delaware.
Diary of Burton, a housewife who was married to clergyman Josiah Burton, concerns everyday life in Sussex County, DE.

2,041. Cannon, Annie Jump
Papers. 1922-59. 14 items.
Open. Unpublished guide.
Historical Society of Delaware.
An astronomer, Cannon (1863-1941) was the first woman elected to the Royal Astronomical Society of Great Britain and the first woman to receive the Henry Draper Gold Medal for outstanding work in the field of astronomy. Correspondence, articles, photos, and clippings.

2,042. Delaware Equal Rights Association
Records. 1891-1943. 6 items.
Open. Unpublished guide.
Historical Society of Delaware.
The Association was founded in ca. 1895 to agitate for woman suffrage and equality and protection under the law. Minutes of a meeting of the Woman's Club of Orange, NJ, and histories of woman suffrage in Delaware. Includes information on such Delaware suffrage leaders as Martha S. Cranston and Mary deVou.

2,043. Equal Rights Magazine
Records. 1923-44. 20 vols.
Open. No guide.
Historical Society of Delaware.
Complete yearly volumes of the *Equal Rights Magazine,* founded in 1923, which advocated complete equality for women in the US. The *Magazine* was the official weekly organ of the National Woman's party.

2,044. Female African School Society
Records. 1833-61. 5 vols.
Open. Unpublished guide.
Historical Society of Delaware.
The Society was founded in ca. 1922 in Wilmington to meet a "concern for the proper instruction of female children of the African race" in reading, writing, arithmetic, sewing, and other subjects. Minute books, account books, and a subscription list of supporters. Martha Hilles, Margaret H. Hilles, Rachel Bassett, and Lydia Seal were participants in the Society. The group was a parallel organization to the Men's African School Society, which educated black Wilmington boys.

2,045. Female Benevolent Society
Records. 1800-1970. 1 Hollinger box and 29 vols.
Open. Unpublished guide.
Historical Society of Delaware.
The oldest charitable organization in Delaware, the Society was founded in 1800 to provide relief to less fortunate Wilmington residents regardless of color or national origin. Constitution, bylaws, minute books, account books, bills and receipts, and a brief history. The Society attempted to find employment for men and piecework for women unable to leave their homes. The 1876 account book of Laura Webb contains details on the status of various families, their problems, and what assistance they were being given. Society founders included Gertrude Gilpin, Ann and Edith Ferris, Deborah Bringhurst, and Margaret, Fanny, and Mary Canby.

2,046. Female Bible Society
Records. 1822-1906. 6 vols.
Open. Unpublished guide.
Historical Society of Delaware.
The Society was founded in 1822 to provide Bibles to those who could not afford them and to give instruction in the Bible to those who had never had such. Account books and an index of members listing several hundred Wilmington women. The chief Bible readers were Margaretta Barr, Annie Irwin, and Miss M. C. Meteer.

2,047. Ferris, Anna M.
Papers. 1854-56. 3 vols.
Open. Unpublished guide.
Historical Society of Delaware.
Diaries of [Miss] Ferris (1815-90), a founder of the Home for Friendless Children, member of the Female Benevolent Society, and a trustee of Swarthmore College, concern her daily life in Wilmington.

2,048. Fromberger, Susan Maria
Papers. 1834. 1 vol.
Open. Unpublished guide.
Historical Society of Delaware.
Recipes of Fromberger (?-ca. 1863), who later married Thomas McKean Rodney, US consul at Havana.

2,049. Gilpin, Elizabeth
Papers. 1830. 41-page vol.
Open. Unpublished guide.
Historical Society of Delaware.
Journal of Gilpin (?-1850) concerns a journey from Wilmington to Johnstown, NY, and back. She records details about people she met and places she stayed.

2,050. Justis, Eleanor C.
Papers. 1890-96. 3 vols.
Open. No guide.
Historical Society of Delaware.
Cash accounts of Justis for 1890 and a daily journal for 1896.

2,051. Parrish, Anne
Papers. 1904-55. 88 items.
Open. Unpublished guide.
Historical Society of Delaware.
An author and sometimes illustrator of 18 novels and stories between 1923 and 1953, [Miss] Parrish (1888-1954?) won the Harper Prize for *The Perennial Bachelor* in 1925. Correspondence, childhood drawings, book reviews, photos, and clippings.

2,052. Porter, Hannah (Armstrong)
Papers. 1917-50. 8 items.
Open. Unpublished guide.
Historical Society of Delaware.
Notes and clippings describe the work of [Mrs. Willard Hall] Porter (1860-1958) in France and Switzerland during WWI and later for the American National Red Cross. She became the leader of the Red Cross's women volunteer workers in Delaware following her return to Wilmington in 1917.

2,053. Richardson Family
Papers. 1803-78. Ca. 8 vols.
Open. No guide.
Historical Society of Delaware.
Manuscript books of sewing instructions, poetry, personal accounts, a daybook, and a journal of an excursion to Warm Springs, VA. Most of the material relates to Thomazine Richardson and her friends, but also included is an account book of Ann S. Richardson.

2,054. Robinson, Hannah
Papers. 1850-76. Ca. 3 vols. and 80 items.
Open. Unpublished guide.
Historical Society of Delaware.
Raised in a family of silversmiths, [Miss] Robinson (1803-78) was a jeweler and the only known woman silversmith in Delaware between 1700 and 1850. Inventory of stock, 1850; building expenses for house and store, 1860; a diary, 1876; and miscellaneous business papers.

2,055. The Suffragist
Records. 1915-21. 6 vols.
Open. No guide.
Historical Society of Delaware.
Bound volumes of *The Suffragist,* founded to promote women's rights and particularly suffrage for women, contain information on developments in the women's movement and the progress of women's suffrage in various states in the US.

2,056. Swift, Gertrude Horton (Dorr)
Papers. 1864-1917. 392-page vol.
Open. No guide.
Historical Society of Delaware.
Diary chronicles events in the life of [Mrs. Joseph] Swift (1844-1917), a housewife.

2,057. Tatnall, Frances Dorr (Swift)
Papers. Nd. 1 vol.
Open. No guide.
Historical Society of Delaware.
Reminiscences of [Mrs. Henry Lea] Tatnall (1874-?) concern her life between 1874 and 1960.

2,058. Warner, Emalea (Pusey)
Papers. 1861-1940. 1 Hollinger box and 20 vols.
Open. Unpublished guide.
Historical Society of Delaware.
Correspondence, diaries, drafts of essays, a passport, certificates, photos, clippings, and other papers [Mrs. Alfred D.] Warner (1853-1948) and Emma Worrell (1834-1931), both of whom were active in Wilmington civic affairs, the movement for women's rights, improvements in education, and health and prison reform. Includes a typescript of Warner's book *Childhood Memories of the Civil War Years, 1861-1865* (Wilmington: 1939). A founder of the New Century Club in Wilmington in 1889, Warner was elected its president in 1890; she also was active in the British-American peace crusade of 1929. The city of Wilmington named its first junior high school after her.

2,059. Wilmington Manuscripts
Collection. 1739- . 2 ft.
Open. Unpublished guide.
Historical Society of Delaware.
Includes a report by Mrs. L. N. D. Mann of the WCTU of Wilmington, which chronicles the temperance movement in Delaware from 1873 to 1875. At the group's first meeting, held in 1874, Mrs. E. W. Smith was elected president and [Miss] Emma Worrell, secretary.

2,060. Wilmington Meeting of Woman Friends
Records. 1832-34. 1 vol.
Open. No guide.
Historical Society of Delaware.
Minute book of the Meeting, kept by Ann S. Richardson, contains information about supervision of the religious lives of female members of the Wilmington community of Friends. Members included Martha Hilles, Hannah Gibbons, and Fanny Ferris.

2,061. Wilson, Elle (Andrews)
Papers. 1860-82. 5 vols.
Open. Unpublished guide.
Historical Society of Delaware.
Scattered diaries of Wilson (?-1900), who in 1866 married James Harrison Wilson, a general in the Union Army, concern her early schooling and, later, daily thoughts and activities. Also contains personal accounts.

2,062. Wilson, Jane
Papers. 1828. 1 vol.
Open. Unpublished guide.
Historical Society of Delaware.
Manuscript book of recipes of Wilson, a housewife, for food as well as home cures for cancer and consumption. Also includes recipes for dyes.

2,063. Women's Suffrage Movement
Collection. 1895-1943. 1 Hollinger box.
Open. No guide.
Historical Society of Delaware.
Clippings from local and national newspapers primarily concern ratification of the woman suffrage amendment, 1915-19. Also includes issues of *The Woman's Journal* and of the GFWC's *Magazine,* an official program of the Woman Suffrage Procession in Washington, DC, in 1913, and articles providing both prosuffrage and antisuffrage views. Much of the material was collected by Florence Bayard Hilles. Includes information on Hilles, Emily P. Bissell, and Martha Cranston.

DISTRICT OF COLUMBIA

WASHINGTON

2,064. American Association of University Women Archives
Records. 1882-1977. 144.5 ft.
Partially restricted. Partial unpublished guide.
American Association of University Women Archives.
Minutes of conventions and other meetings, financial records, correspondence, oral history tapes, diaries, photos, scrapbooks, the AAUW journal, printed items, books, and other records of the AAUW, which was founded in 1882 to promote increased access to higher education for women and greater use for education in all phases of life. Includes information on the organization's legislative activities, international relations, affiliation and liaison with the International Federation of University Women, the Arts Resources Center, fellowships and grants to women for advanced study, and biennial study topics. Also includes material on the Committee on the Economic and Legal Status of Women, on histories of the state division and branches, and on the White House Conference on Children and Youth. Also available on microfilm.

2,065. Arts Program
Records. 1926-63. 8 boxes.
Open. Unpublished guide.
American Association of University Women Archives.
The Arts Program of the AAUW was founded in 1926 to encourage members to study the arts. Includes correspondence, primarily with [Miss] Lura Beam, the consultant for the Arts Resources Center; articles; guides to encourage members in their artistic pursuits; pamphlets; and brochures. The Program ended in 1963. Collections of art produced by the members are housed in the Archives of American Art in New York.

2,066. Association of Collegiate Alumnae
Records. 1881-1921. 10 boxes.
Open. Unpublished guide.
American Association of University Women Archives.
Minutes, registers, scholarly papers, and clippings of the Association, a predecessor of the AAUW. Records deal with the work of the founding members of the Association and provide information on their meetings and establishment of regional branches.

2,067. Board of Directors and General Director
Records. 1921- . 3 drawers.
Open. No guide.
American Association of University Women Archives.
Correspondence and files of the board of directors of the AAUW, which comprises the general director, the president, vice-presidents, and regional and committee members. Papers concern the activities of Mary Woolley, Meta Glass, Margaret Morriss, Helen (Magill) White, Susan Kingsbury, judges Sarah Hughes and Lucy (Somerville) Howorth, Constance Warren, Virginia Gildersleeve, and others.

2,068. Committee on the Economic and Legal Status of Women
Records. 1926-63. 18 boxes.
Open. No guide.
American Association of University Women Archives.
The Committee, which was founded in 1926, was known as the Status of Women Committee after 1944. Correspondence, form letters, brochures, and pamphlets relate to the Committee's studies of women in gainful occupations, vocational training, the employment of married women, and legislation affecting women. Includes Susan Kingsbury's "Economic Status of University Women in the USA" (1939). The Committee was dissolved in 1963.

2,069. Education Program
Records. 1921- . 52 boxes.
Open. Unpublished guide.
American Association of University Women Archives.
Minutes, conference reports, special studies by committee members or staff, correspondence, bibliographies, brochures, and pamphlets of the Program, which was formed in 1921 to study and improve all aspects of education from preschool through higher education. Includes papers of Lois Hayden Meek, who helped organize the Washington Child Research Center, including study guides covering such topics as children's libraries and museums, toys, parent education, better radio programs, career opportunities, vocational opportunities for girls and young women, standards and recognitions for colleges admitting women, women's health and living conditions in colleges, and access to teaching and higher education opportunities for women.

2,070. Hyde, Ida Henrietta
Papers. 1898-1931. 1 drawer.
Open. No guide.
American Association of University Women Archives.
Personal and other correspondence, diaries, a photo collection, and scientific papers of Hyde (1857-1945), a zoologist and researcher. Hyde received her bachelor's degree from Cornell in 1891. The first woman to gain entrance to a German university, she earned her PhD with high honors from the University of Heidelberg in 1896. In 1899, after doing research at the Harvard medical school, she went to the University of Kansas where she taught physiology. She later established a department of physiology there and was the head of it for more than 20 years. Also includes minutes, 1898-1903, of the Association to Promote Scientific Research by Women, prize committee reports, and reports of the American Woman's Table at the Zoological Station at Naples.

2,071. International Federation of University Women
Records. 1920- . 15 boxes.
Open. No guide.
American Association of University Women Archives.
Minutes of triennial conferences and the annual or biennial council meetings, as well as photos of the Federation, which was founded in 1920 and is still in existence. The Federation coordinates all associations of women graduates in all countries of the world. Records contain information on conferences, descriptions of the places where conferences were held, and material on the use of funds for the advancement of scholarly work.

2,072. International Relations
Records. 1924-70. 27 boxes.
Open. No guide.
American Association of University Women Archives.
Minutes and correspondence, including those of the Committee on the Cause and Cure of War; studies; bibliographies; study guides; and brochures of the group, which was formed in 1924 and in 1963 changed its name to World Problems. The organization studied international relations and participated in adult education in foreign policy, peace movements, international education, the Committee on the Cause and Cure of War, the exchange of teachers with other countries, refugee aid and war relief, international economic policy, and the UN.

2,073. League of Nations Association
Records. 1934-43. 3 folders.
Open. No guide.
American Association of University Women Archives.
Correspondence and brochures relate to the AAUW's efforts to continue interest in the League of Nations, even though the US had not joined, and to further world peace. The Association was organized in 1943 but was disassociated from the AAUW in the same year.

2,074. Legislation: Women's Joint Congressional Committee
Records. 1920-51. 6 folders.
Open. No guide.
American Association of University Women Archives.
Correspondence and some printed items of the Committee, which was organized in 1920 to lobby in Congress for passage of bills concerning women.

2,075. Legislative Program
Records. 1921- . 16 boxes.
Open. Unpublished guide.
American Association of University Women Archives.
Statements in support of or in protest against certain legislation, correspondence, indexes to congressional committees, lists of bills to be supported or defeated, pamphlets, and brochures of the Program, which was organized in 1921 to further the aims of the AAUW in such areas as equal pay for women, child care, establishment of an office of education, equal rights, suffrage and the use of it, social security, foreign trade and aid, UN and UNESCO activities, and federal aid to education. The Program still exists.

2,076. National Council of Women
Records. 1932-47. 1 folder.
Open. No guide.
American Association of University Women Archives.
Correspondence of the Council, which became affiliated with the Association of Collegiate Alumnae, later the AAUW, in 1915.

2,077. National Peace Conference
Records. 1933-41. 6 folders.
Open. No guide.
American Association of University Women Archives.
Consists of correspondence of the AAUW with the Conference, which was formed and worked from 1933 to 1941 to achieve world peace.

2,078. Pan Pacific Women's Association
Records. 1932-44. 1 folder.
Open. No guide.
American Association of University Women Archives.
Minutes and correspondence of the Association, which functioned from 1932 to 1944 to lobby and work for the interests of women in Pacific countries and the western US. The group's primary interest was the field of education.

2,079. Southern Association of College Women
Records. 1903-21. 9 folders and 1 box.
Open. Unpublished guide.
American Association of University Women Archives.
Minutes, scholarly papers, lists of members, and clippings of the Association, a group of college women in the southern states. The Association existed from 1903 to 1921 to promote higher education for women. It later became part of what is now the AAUW.

2,080. Southern Women's Educational Alliance
Records. 1931-37. 1 folder.
Open. No guide.
American Association of University Women Archives.
Correspondence of the Alliance, which existed from 1931 to 1937. The group worked to create a guidance service for boys and girls in rural areas and a program to help rural educators.

2,081. Susan B. Anthony Forum Foundation
Records. 1934-37. 1 folder.
Open. No guide.
American Association of University Women Archives.
Correspondence relates to efforts made to have Susan B. Anthony's sculpture included at the Mount Rushmore Memorial. The Foundation existed from 1934 to 1937.

2,082. Western Association of Collegiate Alumnae
Records. 1883-89. 3 folders.
Open. Unpublished guide.
American Association of University Women Archives.
Minutes, scholarly papers, and clippings of the Association, a collegiate women's group in the western states that existed from 1883 to 1889 to promote higher education for women. It was later absorbed into what is now the AAUW.

2,083. White House Conference on Children and Youth
Records. 1930-62. 4 boxes and 19 vols.
Open. No guide.
American Association of University Women Archives.
Minutes, proceedings, correspondence, pamphlets, and books of the Conference, which was formed in 1930 to discuss the problems and concerns of children and youth.

2,084. Woman's Centennial Congress
Records. 1940- . 1 folder.
Open. No guide.
American Association of University Women Archives.
Correspondence and brochures of the Congress, which was formed in 1940 by Carrie Chapman Catt to celebrate the sentiments expressed at the women's suffrage meeting at Seneca Falls, NY, in 1848.

2,085. World Center for Women's Archives
Records. 1935-40. 3 folders.
Open. No guide.
American Association of University Women Archives.
Correspondence, primarily of Mary Ritter Beard, relates to her efforts and the efforts of others to establish the Center, a central point for the collection of records pertaining to all kinds of women's activities. Records also pertain to the closing of the Center because of a lack of funds and support.

2,086. Archives
Records. 1846- . Ca. 720 cu.ft.
Access restricted. No guide.
American Psychiatric Association.
Official records of the Association, secretary's correspondence, correspondence of founders, membership records, and copies of Association publications; oral history tapes and transcripts of interviews with persons involved in the mental health field, including eight women; photos of psychiatrists, mental hospitals, and psychiatric meetings; private papers and collections of persons who were notable in the history of psychiatry; and memorabilia. Includes material concerning the Association's task force on women, which was created in 1972; minutes, reports, agendas, and files of the Association's committee on psychiatric nursing; and records of the nursing consultant, with correspondence, reports, training manuals, course outlines, annual reports from 1954 of accredited schools of nursing, and questionnaires arranged by states and by hospital. The women included in the oral history interviews were physicians [Miss] Hilde Bruch, Charlotte (Malachowski) Buhler, [Miss] Henriette Klein, and Portia (Bell) Hume; [Mrs.] Margaret C. Schweinhaut, a state senator; Marie (Collins) McGuire; [Miss] Mary E. Switzer; and Edith (Mendel) Stern.

2,087. Archives
Records. 1947-72. 1894 ft.
Open. Unpublished guide.
American Red Cross, National Headquarters Library.
Records of the Red Cross, founded in 1881, contain board minutes, correspondence, reports on war and disaster relief and other Red Cross activities, and material concerning international conventions and conferences and Red Cross societies in other countries. Includes information on the Red Cross nursing service, service to military families, service to military hospitals, and supplemental recreation activities overseas, all of which were run almost entirely by women. Collection also contains papers of Jane A. Delano, Clara D. Noyes, Ida F. Butler, Mary Beard, and Ann K. Magnussen, all of whom were nurses and were unmarried. Pre-WWII records of the Red Cross have been deposited with the National Archives and Records Service in Washington.

2,088. Abbott, Maude Elizabeth Seymour
Papers. 1907-21. 1 vol.
Open. No guide.
Armed Forces Medical Museum, Otis Historical Archives.
Correspondence, minutes, membership lists, programs, bulletins, and clippings of Abbott (1869-1940), a physician and pathologist who was known for her work on congenital cardiac defects; she also was director of the medical museum at McGill University. Papers contain records concerning the founding and early days of the International Association of Medical Museums, for which Abbott served as first secretary and treasurer.

2,089. Ludlow, Clara S.
Papers. Ca. 1900-10. 2 vols.
Open. No guide.
Armed Forces Medical Museum, Otis Historical Archives.
Correspondence and reprints of Ludlow, a PhD, relate to her work as an entomologist at the Army Medical Museum and to her research on mosquitoes.

2,090. Sabin, Florence Rena
Papers. 1925-38. 1 item.
Open. No guide.
Armed Forces Medical Museum, Otis Historical Archives.
An unpublished manuscript on studies of the cells of the blood and connective tissues with reference to their reactions in tuberculosis by Sabin (1871-1953), a physician noted for her research on the lymphatic system. The first woman teacher at Johns Hopkins medical school, Sabin was also the first woman appointed to the staff of the Rockefeller Institute of Medical Research in New York and the first woman elected to life membership in the National Academy of Sciences.

2,091. Vogel, Emma E.
Papers. Ca. 1919-67. Ca. 1 ft.
Open. No guide.
Armed Forces Medical Museum, Otis Historical Archives.
Correspondence, manuscripts, certificates, charts and graphs, pamphlets, a Legion of Merit medal, and photos of Vogel, who was a US Army nurse and pioneer physical therapist at Walter Reed General Hospital and first chief of the Women's Medical Specialist Corps.

2,092. Archives
Records. 1892- . 53 containers.
Access restricted. Unpublished guide.
Association for Childhood Education International.
Minutes, committee reports, yearbooks, conference programs, a journal, a newsletter, bulletins, promotional flyers, publications list, photos, books, and other records of the Association for Childhood Education International, its projects, policy and philosophy, branch activities, and cooperation with other organizations. Founded in 1892 as the International Kindergarten Union, the Association for Childhood Education acquired its new name as a result of the merger in 1930 of the Union and the National Council of Primary Education; in 1946 the word International was officially added to the Association's title. The Association works for the education and well-being of children, from infancy to early adolescence, by promoting desirable conditions and practices and by alerting the public to the needs of children.

2,093. Bain, Winifred E.
Papers. 1905-65. 10 containers and 3 tapes.
Access restricted. Register, index, and other unpublished guides.
Association for Childhood Education International.
The bulk of the correspondence, diaries, scrapbooks, photos, tapes, and books of Bain (1889-1965), an educator, lecturer, and author, pertains to her work as president of Wheelock College in Boston from 1941 to 1955 and as president of the Association from 1947 to 1949. Bain also was a member of the faculty of Teachers College, Columbia University, from 1930 to 1939; principal of the Wheelock School in 1940; and chairman of the board of editors of the Association's journal *Childhood Education* from 1940 to 1947. Bain's work at Teachers College included service from 1932 to 1939 on the faculty of New College, an experimental college in teacher education that involved Manhattanville, a community adjacent to Columbia.

2,094. Blow, Susan Elizabeth
Papers. 1877-1916. 1 container.
Access restricted. Register, index, and other unpublished guides.
Association for Childhood Education International.
Correspondence and a picture of [Miss] Blow (1843-1916), a lecturer and educator who taught kindergarten students, trained kindergarten teachers, and helped to introduce kindergartens into the public school system in the US. Includes 113 items of correspondence with [Miss] Fanniebelle Curtis concerning the International Kindergarten Union Committee of Nineteen, which was established in 1903 to formulate contemporary thought on kindergartens. The correspondence reveals ideological divisions within the Union; it also provides insight into Blow's spiritual commitment and her philosophy of life.

2,095. Leeper, Mary E.
Papers. 1898-1965. 6 containers and 3 tapes.
Access restricted. Register, index, and other unpublished guides.
Association for Childhood Education International.
Papers of Leeper (1887-1965), an educator and executive who was vice-president of the International Kindergarten Union in 1930 and executive secretary of the Association from 1930 to 1953, include correspondence, notes on a trip she took to Europe in 1935, speeches, articles, biographical material, memos to the Association's executive board, a volume of expressions from friends and coworkers, honors and awards, photos, and a notebook containing newsletters, notes, and comments on the changes in Association policies and procedures between 1930 and 1960. A primary school teacher from 1910 to 1930 and an instructor and demonstration teacher from 1922 to 1926, Leeper also was a representative of the US Office of Education at the International Conference on Education in Geneva in 1935 and chairman of the Women's Joint Congressional Committee from 1937 to 1939.

2,096. Library
Records. 1920s- . 171 drawers and boxes, 1425 vols., 900 tapes, 400 recording discs, and 1000 ft. of microfilm.
Open. Unpublished guide.
Broadcast Pioneers Library.
Correspondence, scripts, research studies, photos, scrapbooks, pamphlets, clippings, periodicals, books, and oral history tapes and transcripts document the history of radio and television broadcasting and allied fields. Radio broadcasting began during the 1920s.

2,097. Archives
Records. Nd. Ca. 300 tapes.
Open. Unpublished guide.
Business and Professional Women's Foundation.
The Foundation was formed in 1956 to advance the status of women; to administer educational scholarships, loans, and grants for research on women; and to conduct seminars. Includes interviews with Rachel Carson, Margaret Mead, Ayn Rand, Eleanor Roosevelt, Sarah Hughes, Eva Hansl, and Clare (Boothe) Luce; speeches or addresses by Roosevelt, Margaret Chase Smith, Perle Mesta, Martha Griffiths, Patsy Mink, and Margaret Hickey; and taped discussions about job options for women, the role of women during the 1960s, the working mother, day care, legislation concerning women, and other topics.

2,098. Jones, Mary Harris
Papers. 1885-1925. 8 in.
Open. No guide.
Catholic University of America, Archives and Manuscripts.
Correspondence, photos, and clippings of Jones (1830-1930), who was known as Mother Jones, relate to her activities in support of the labor rights of the United Mine Workers of America.

2,099. Merrick, Mary V.
Papers. 1900-54. 5 ft.
Open. No guide.
Catholic University of America, Archives and Manuscripts.
Correspondence, diaries, minutes, and photos of Merrick (1886-1955), founder of the Christ Child Society, relate to the activities and social work of the Society.

2,100. Vertical Files
Records. 1700s- . Ca. 50 drawers.
Closed. No guide.
Corcoran Gallery of Art, Curatorial Library.
Correspondence, exhibition notices, pamphlets, clippings, and other material received in the course of business of the Corcoran Gallery, which houses a collection of sculpture, painting, and graphics. Most of the material is from the period between the 1880s and 1940s, and approximately 25 percent of it pertains to women artists.

2,101. White, Ellen Gould (Harmon)
Papers. 1846-1915. 250 ft.
Access restricted. Indexes.
Ellen G. White Estate, Inc.
Correspondence and manuscripts that [Mrs. James Springer] White (1827-1915), a religious writer and cofounder of the Seventh-day Adventist Church, addressed to various individuals and institutions associated with the Church. Also includes diaries, financial papers, photos, and printed material concerning her life and work.

2,102. Benson, Elizabeth English
Papers. 1926-73. 257 items.
Open. No guide.
Gallaudet College Archives.
[Miss] Benson (1904-72) was dean of women and a faculty member at Gallaudet College for 44 years, a world renowned interpreter for the deaf, and an expert on the language of signs. Correspondence, speeches, biographical material, programs, published articles, photos, clippings, and memorabilia. Associate editor of the *American Annals of the Deaf* for six years, Benson also was a founder and charter member of the Registry of Interpreters for the Deaf, a member of the WACs during WWII and the first woman to receive a direct commission, and the recipient of many awards and citations.

2,103. Billone, Carol Jean
Papers. 1964-76. 15 items.
Open. No guide.
Gallaudet College Archives.
Articles, news releases, photos, and clippings of [Miss] Billone (1943-), a deaf teacher of deaf children, who teaches science and drama and travels with her drama class to perform for various organizations. Many of the performances are done with music and sign language. A task force member of the California Advisory Council of Vocational Education, Billone is also a member of the Professional Educators of Los Angeles and of the National Association of Professional Educators. In addition, she is president of the Faculty Association at Marlton School for the Deaf.

2,104. Bove, Linda Ann Marie
Papers. 1963-76. 83 items.
Open. No guide.
Gallaudet College Archives.
A professional actress who is deaf, Bove (1945-) is married to professional actor Edmund Waterstreet, Jr. Correspondence, articles about her, news releases, and clippings. Bove has been a member of the National Theatre of the Deaf since 1968 and of the Little Theater of the Deaf since 1971; the Little Theater troupe tours schools to perform for children with reading and learning problems. Bove appeared in the children's program "Sesame Street," was a cast member of the television program "Search for Tomorrow" in 1973, and appeared in CBS's "A Child's Christmas in Wales" in December 1973. A participant in a theatrical summer camp for young children, Bove also has made acting tours in eastern and western Europe, the Middle East, the Soviet Union, and Australia. She has received various awards.

2,105. Fabray, Nanette
Papers. 1955-76. 120 items.
Open. No guide.
Gallaudet College Archives.
Correspondence, addresses, releases, photos, and clippings of Fabray, a hearing-impaired motion picture, stage, and television actress who is also a lecturer, an active participant in organizations for the deaf, and a campaigner on behalf of the deaf and handicapped. Fabray had a role in "Caesar's Hour" and had her own television show. She won three Emmy Awards as well as other awards and honorary degrees. She is chairman of the National Advisory Committee on the Education of the Deaf, vice-president of the National Association of Hearing and Speech Agencies, a trustee and member of the board of the Eugene O'Neill Foundation and of the National Theatre of the Deaf, and campaign chairman for the UCLA Hope for the Hearing Foundation. Fabray was married to the late Ranald MacDougall.

2,106. Hanson, Agatha Mary Agnes (Tiegel)
Papers. 1887-1975. 4 Hollinger boxes.
Open. No guide.
Gallaudet College Archives.
Hanson (1873-1959) was a poet; writer for periodicals; editor of the *Seattle Observer;* founder and first president of the O.W.L.S., the first sorority at Gallaudet College, the world's only liberal arts college for the deaf; and wife of clergyman and architect Olof Hanson. Correspondence, a book of poems she wrote, articles about her, photos, and clippings. In 1893, Agatha Hanson, who was deaf, became the second woman to graduate from Gallaudet. She served as president, secretary, and treasurer of the Puget Sound Association of the Deaf.

2,107. Hughes, Regina Mary (Olson)
Papers. 1934-76. 156 items.
Open. No guide.
Gallaudet College Archives.
[Mrs. Frederick] Hughes (1895-) is a deaf poet, author, illustrator for the Smithsonian Institution in Washington, and a scientific illustrator in botany and translator for the US Department of Agriculture, Agricultural Research Service, in Maryland. Correspondence, biographical material, programs, photos of botanical illustrations, and clippings. She is a translator to English of scientific papers in French, Spanish, Portuguese, Italian, and Latin. Her artworks have been exhibited by such institutions as the National Arboretum in Washington, an International Exhibition of Botanical Art & Illustration at the Carnegie-Mellon University of Pittsburgh, and the International Art Center of Roerich Museum in New York City. In addition, Hughes has received various awards and an honorary degree from Gallaudet.

2,108. Keller, Helen Adams
Papers. 1888-1970. 1715 items.
Open. No guide.
Gallaudet College Archives.
[Miss] Keller (1880-1968) was a deaf-blind author, poet, lecturer, and humanitarian. Correspondence, articles by and about her, programs, photos, clippings, medals, and books she wrote. Keller was a counselor to the Bureau of National and International Relations of the American Foundation for the Blind and was instrumental in establishment of the department of services for the deaf-blind in the American Foundation for the Blind. A 1904 graduate of Radcliffe College, she was the first woman to receive an honorary degree from Harvard University. She also was the recipient of many other honorary degrees and awards.

Between 1920 and 1924, Keller went into vaudeville and toured the US; in later years, she toured the world and was received by such notable persons as Sir Winston Churchill of Great Britain and Jawaharlal Nehru of India. She also was received by every US President from Grover Cleveland to John F. Kennedy. Mark Twain said she and Napoleon were "the two most interesting characters in the 19th Century." A regular contributor to such national magazines as *Youth's Companion,* the *Atlantic Monthly,* and *The New York Times Magazine,* Keller also wrote a number of books, including *The Story of My Life,* which contains a supplemental account of her education with Anne Mansfield (Sullivan) Macy. Several films, such as *The Miracle Worker,* were based on Keller's life.

2,109. Low, Juliette Magill Kinzie (Gordon)
Papers. 1928-74. 5 items.
Open. No guide.
Gallaudet College Archives.
Articles and clippings about [Mrs. William Mackay] Low (1860-1927), a deaf woman who founded the Girl Scouts.

2,110. McVan, Alice Jane
Papers. 1928-75. 39 items.
Open. No guide.
Gallaudet College Archives.
A deaf poet, author, and expert on Hispanic material, [Miss] McVan (1906-70) worked for the Hispanic Society of America in New York City, serving from 1929 to 1966 in successive positions from third assistant in publications to curator of membership records. Correspondence, biographical material, articles by and about her, memorial programs, and photos. During WWII, she taught English and citizenship to deaf refugees under the auspices of the New York State division of vocational rehabilitation. Her publications include *Tryst* (1953) and *Antonio Machado* (1959). She also was the first woman editor of Gallaudet's student publication *The Buff and Blue.* She married Karl Bernard Stein.

2,111. Macy, Anne Mansfield (Sullivan)
Papers. 1894-1969. 36 items and 1 motion picture.
Open. No guide.
Gallaudet College Archives.
Articles, programs, releases, clippings, and other papers of [Mrs. John Albert] Macy (1866-1936), an author and lecturer who for 60 years was the teacher of Helen Keller. Macy lost her sight twice, but her vision was restored through operations. Macy received an honorary degree, and awards were created in her honor, among them the Anne Sullivan Macy Service for Deaf-Blind, which was established by the Industrial Home for the Blind. The 100th anniversary of her birth was observed in 1966 in Washington. Various books were written about Macy, one of which was by Keller.

2,112. May, Florence Watermon (Lewis)
Papers. 1914-58. 51 items.
Open. No guide.
Gallaudet College Archives.
[Mrs. William] May (1899-) is a deaf author, poet, translator, and member of the Hispanic Society of America in New York City. She also is a world authority on Spanish lace and textiles. Correspondence, biographical material, programs, advertisements for and copies of her publications, photos, and clippings. Her books include *Silk Weaving in Spain* and *The Deaf Woman.* She also instructed Steve McNally and Helen Craig in the language of signs for their roles in the Broadway play *Johnny Belinda.* In addition, she received an honorary degree from Gallaudet College.

2,113. Norton, Audree Lauraine (Bennett)
Papers. 1952-74. 28 items.
Open. No guide.
Gallaudet College Archives.
Photos and clippings of [Mrs. Ken] Norton (1927-), a deaf professional actress who is a member of the National Theatre of the Deaf and who has appeared in television commercials.

2,114. Peet, Elizabeth
Papers. 1900-61. 7 Hollinger boxes.
Open. No guide.
Gallaudet College Archives.
A deaf educator, [Miss] Peet (1874-1961) was dean of women at Gallaudet College from 1910 to 1950, an instructor and professor of language at Gallaudet, a lecturer and authority on the language of signs, an author, and assistant editor of *American Annals of the Deaf* from 1942 to 1945. She also was the granddaughter of Harvey Prindle Peet and daughter of Isaac Lewis Peet, both pioneer educators of the deaf. Correspondence, articles, biographical material, speeches, scrapbooks, photos, clippings, and memorial programs. Awarded numerous honorary degrees, Peet also was a member of such organizations as the AAUW, the DAR, the American Association of Deans of Women, the League of Republican Women, and the ladies' committee of the board of directors of the New York School for the Deaf. She also was a member and president of the Columbian Women of the George Washington University.

2,115. Switzer, Mary E.
Papers. 1956-73. 142 items and 2 recording discs.
Open. No guide.
Gallaudet College Archives.
Speeches and articles, biographical material, programs, plaques and awards, and clippings of [Miss] Switzer (1900-72), administrator of the social and rehabilitation service of HEW from 1967 to 1970, director of the Office of Vocational Rehabilitation from 1950 to 1967, and assistant to the administrator of the Federal Security Agency from 1939 to 1950. She also was a council member of the Association for Aid to Crippled Children, president of the American Hearing Society, vice-president of the World Rehabilitation Fund, first vice-president of the National Conference on Social Welfare, member of the board of various schools and other organizations, a trustee of Assumption College and Radcliffe College, and the recipient of honorary degrees and awards.

2,116. Kleuser, Louise C.
Papers. 1890-1974. 3 ft.
Open. Register.
General Conference of Seventh-day Adventists Archives.
From 1942 to 1958 [Miss] Kleuser (1890-1976), as an associate secretary in the General Conference Ministerial Association, worked to enlist and train women for Bible work. Notes and outlines for Bible studies, talks, sermons, and courses she taught; correspondence; booklets; certificates and credentials; personal mementos; and books she wrote or compiled. Earlier in her life Kleuser was involved in various church-related activities in the East Pennsylvania Conference, the Southern New England Conference, and the Greater New York Conference. She was born in Barmen, Germany, and died in Takoma Park, MD.

2,117. Archives
Records. 1889- . Ca. 84 ft.
Open. No guide.
General Federation of Women's Clubs.
The GFWC was founded in 1890 to promote communication among women's clubs throughout the world; its work is carried out by its conservation, education, home life, international affairs, public affairs, and arts departments as well as by its community improvement program and legislative and resolutions committees. Speeches and articles; reports and addresses delivered at annual GFWC conventions; a subject file, with records of the GFWC's programs and projects, club histories, legislation, and other material; histories and directories of the State Federations of Women's Clubs; bound volumes of the GFWC's official publication; and other records.

2,118. Georgetown University Archives
Records. 1787-1976. Ca. 1500 ft. and 2500 tapes.
Open. Unpublished guide.
Georgetown University Library, Special Collections.
Minutes, correspondence, ledgers, photos, and tapes of the University, which was founded in 1789 and which gradually became a coeducational institution during the 20th century. Includes accounts concerning female employees of the University and material pertaining to the founding of the nursing school and the University hospital in 1898.

2,119. Richards, Janet Elizabeth
Papers. 1800-1948. 2.1 ft.
Open. Unpublished guide.
Georgetown University Library, Special Collections.
Correspondence, daybooks, minute books, lecture notes, family papers, and photos of [Miss] Richards (1859-1948), a lecturer, teacher, advocate of women's suffrage, and secretary of the board of lady managers of the National Homeopathic Hospital Association. The National Homeopathic Hospital was located in Washington, DC.

2,120. Wagner, Robert F.
Papers. 1911?-49. 882 ft.
Open. Unpublished guide.
Georgetown University Library, Special Collections.
Papers primarily pertain to the period from 1927 to 1949 when Wagner (1877-1953) served as a US senator from New York. Includes correspondence with Frances Perkins, Lillian Wald, Mary (Kingsbury) Simkhovitch, and Mary Van Kleeck and with such agencies concerned with protective legislation for women as the American Association for Labor Legislation, the Survey Associates, and the National Association of Social Workers. Also includes material concerning early proposals for an equal rights amendment, birth control, maternity, child labor laws, and the US Children's Bureau.

2,121. Convent and School Archives
Records. 1799- . 8 boxes and 8 vols.
Access restricted. No guide.
Georgetown Visitation Convent and Preparatory School.
The School was founded in 1799 as a boarding and day school for girls. A junior college was added in 1919 and closed in 1964; the high school is still in operation. Account books, correspondence, alumnae bulletins, photos, written records of events, printed historical material, and published material by sisters and alumnae.

2,122. Archives
Records. 1972- . No size given.
Closed. No guide.
Graphic Arts International Union.
Records of the Graphic Arts International Union, a trade union formed in 1972 through the merger of the Lithographers and Photoengravers Union and the International Brotherhood of Bookbinders, contain material concerning development of the Union's policy on women. Includes records of meetings, memoranda, promotional material, and a contract between the Union and the Department of Labor, which helped fund the Union's Project for Equal Progression program. The program was designed to facilitate the entry of women into the industry's more highly skilled and higher-paying jobs. Also includes correspondence, written descriptions, and motion pictures concerning the Career Equity for Workers program, which the Union is seeking to develop with HEW to assist women, local Union leaders, and employers in assessing women's job opportunities within the printing and publishing industry.

2,123. Anderson, Marian, and the DAR Controversy
Records. 1939-45. 9 ft. and microfilm reels.
Open. Unpublished guide.
Howard University, Moorland-Spingarn Research Center.
Material resulting from denial of permission to [Miss] Anderson (1902-), a contralto, to present a concert in April 1939 in Constitution Hall in Washington. Correspondence, reports, broadsides, programs, press releases, and clippings relating to the Marian Anderson Citizens Committee formed to protest the action and to the Marian Anderson Mural Fund Committee. Correspondents include Charles H. Houston and John Lovell, Jr., respectively chairman and secretary of the Citizens Committee; Mrs. Henry M. Roberts, Jr., DAR president; [Mrs.] Marian Wade Doyle, president of

the District of Columbia Board of Education; and Canon Anson Phelps Stokes. The Citizens Committee was endorsed in letters from Eleanor Roosevelt and Leopold Stokowski. Includes speeches by Oscar L. Chapman, Harold L. Ickes, and Charles Houston.

2,124. Bennett, Elizabeth
Papers. 1819. 1 item.
Open. No guide.
Howard University, Moorland-Spingarn Research Center.
Holograph bill of sale from Martin County, NC, in which Elizabeth Bennett grants three Negroes—Jacob, Cora, and Ben—to Bryant Bennett.

2,125. Branch, Mary Elizabeth
Papers. 1909-48. 5 in.
Open. Unpublished guide.
Howard University, Moorland-Spingarn Research Center.
[Miss] Branch (1882-1944) was an educator and president of Tilloston College in Austin, TX. Collection contains correspondence documenting Sadie Daniel St. Clair's efforts to compile information on Branch's life, biographical data, form letters, and addresses and writings which grew out of Branch's career as a faculty member at Virginia State College in Petersburg, VA, and as president of Tilloston.

2,126. Carr, Mary A.
Papers. 1842. 1 item.
Open. No guide.
Howard University, Moorland-Spingarn Research Center.
Holograph deed of gift signed in Georgetown District, SC, by which Mary Carr gave Sarah E. Carr two female slaves, Annette and Ivina.

2,127. Carter, Jeannette
Papers. 1927-63. 5 in.
Open. Unpublished guide.
Howard University, Moorland-Spingarn Research Center.
Carter was a black political activist, founder and president of the National Political Study Club, an executive officer of the National Negro Press Association, and editor of *Women's Voice,* a magazine published in the interest of the Republican party. Correspondence; reports; press releases; pamphlets; programs; speeches, including one by her nephew; and clippings, some of which refer to her brother William Justin Carter.

2,128. Cary, Mary Ann (Shadd)
Papers. 1844-88. 5 in.
Open. Unpublished guide.
Howard University, Moorland-Spingarn Research Center.
Cary (1823-93) was editor of *The Provincial Freeman,* suffragist, and army recruiter. Correspondence, articles, editorials, reports, and other papers about her work in the US and Canada.

2,129. Clarke, Emma R.
Papers. Ca. 1946. 1 vol.
Open. No guide.
Howard University, Moorland-Spingarn Research Center.
Volume entitled "Why Visit Fort Stevens, DC? A Narrative about President Abraham Lincoln That Every One Should Read" by Clarke, a black teacher emeritus of Washington's Randall Junior High School.

2,130. Cooper, Anna Julia
Papers. 1881-1958. 3 ft. 4 in.
Open. Unpublished guide.
Howard University, Moorland-Spingarn Research Center.
A scholar and educator, Cooper (1858-1964) wrote *A Voice from the South by a Black Woman of the South,* earned a PhD from the University of Paris in 1925, taught at numerous schools, and served as principal of M Street High School in Washington and as teacher and president of Frelinghuysen University from 1930 to 1941. Collection contains correspondence, biographical material, manuscripts, photos, scrapbooks, an album, and clippings. Cooper, who addressed the Pan-African Conference in London, also taught at Wilberforce University in 1884 and 1885, at St. Augustine's Normal and Collegiate Institute in Raleigh, NC, from 1885 to 1887, at Lincoln Institute in Jefferson City, MO, and at Dunbar High School in Washington from 1910 to 1930.

2,131. Daniel, Portia Bird
Papers. 1933. 1 item.
Open. No guide.
Howard University, Moorland-Spingarn Research Center.
"The Value of an Art Exhibit," a holograph address of Daniel, a black, before Cardoza Night School about a Negro art exhibition at the National Museum in Washington.

2,132. Evans, Claiborne
Papers. 1797. 1 item.
Open. No guide.
Howard University, Moorland-Spingarn Research Center.
Holograph deed of emancipation signed in Richmond, VA, by which Evans frees a female slave, Aggy.

2,133. Fauset, Crystal (Bird)
Papers. 1946-50. 4 vols.
Open. Unpublished guide.
Howard University, Moorland-Spingarn Research Center.
Fauset (?-1965) was the first black woman in the Pennsylvania state legislature. Scrapbooks of clippings reflect Fauset's activities with the inter-cultural committee of the United Nations Council of Philadelphia.

2,134. Goins, Georgia (Fraser)
Papers. 1883-1964. 4 ft. 7 in.
Open. Unpublished guide.
Howard University, Moorland-Spingarn Research Center.
A black musician, Goins (1883-1964) studied music at Syracuse University in New York and in Paris and operated a music studio in Washington. Correspondence, diaries, photos, scrapbooks, clippings, and other papers reflect Goins's interest in music, gardening, community affairs, theology, and her homeland the Dominican Republic. Goins's mother Sarah Marinda Loguen Fraser was the second black woman physician in the US and the first woman physician in the Dominican Republic.

2,135. Green, Constance Winsor (McLaughlin)
Papers. Ca. 1962. 1 vol.
Open. No guide.
Howard University, Moorland-Spingarn Research Center.
Green (1897-1975) was an historian. Typescript copy of *Washington, Village and Capital, 1800-1878, and Washington, Capital City, 1879-1950* (Princeton, NJ: Princeton University Press, 1962).

2,136. Grigger, Ann
Papers. 1859. 1 item.
Open. No guide.
Howard University, Moorland-Spingarn Research Center.
Holograph agreement signed in Newby District, SC, by which William H. Garland agrees to purchase from Ann Grigger, "a free woman of color," two acres of land for $400.

2,137. Grimké, Angelina Weld
Papers. 1887-1958. 6 ft. 8 in.
Open. Unpublished guide.
Howard University, Moorland-Spingarn Research Center.
Grimké (1880-1958) was a black teacher, writer, and poet. Correspondence, diaries, manuscripts of plays, short stories, lesson outlines, school reports, clippings, pamphlets, and other papers. Grimké was the great-niece of Angelina Grimké Weld.

2,138. Grimké, Francis James
Papers. 1834-1937. 15 ft.
Open. Unpublished guide.
Howard University, Moorland-Spingarn Research Center.
Diaries of Charlotte L. (Forten) Grimké (1837-1914), a black abolitionist and teacher, are included among the papers of her husband Francis J. Grimké (1850-1937), a minister in Washington. Charlotte Grimké's diaries date from 1854 to 1892. Also included are correspondence, sermons, addresses, scrapbooks, and albums.

2,139. Hubbard, Charlotte (Moton)
Papers. 1934-70. 2 ft.
Open. Unpublished guide.
Howard University, Moorland-Spingarn Research Center.
A black, Hubbard (1920-) has worked in education and public relations, both in the private sector and for the federal government. Correspondence, biographical material, notebooks, programs, invitations, photos, scrapbooks, press releases, and clippings.

2,140. Hunt, William Henry
Papers. 1898-1941. 5 ft. 6 in.
Open. Unpublished guide.
Howard University, Moorland-Spingarn Research Center.
Bulk of collection is correspondence of Ida (Gibbs) Hunt, who was wife of William Hunt (1869-1951), a black diplomat. Also included are manuscripts, pamphlets, photos, clippings, magazines, and memorabilia.

2,141. Langhorne, Ann
Papers. 1795. 1 item.
Open. No guide.
Howard University, Moorland-Spingarn Research Center.
Holograph affidavit from New York in which Lucy, a mulatto, is sworn to be the property of Samuel Bayard.

2,142. Lankford, Charlotte J.
Papers. 1937. 1 item.
Open. No guide.
Howard University, Moorland-Spingarn Research Center.
Description of the invention by Lankford, a black, of an automobile cover.

2,143. Murray, Pauli
Papers. 1943-44. 5 in.
Open. Unpublished guide.
Howard University, Moorland-Spingarn Research Center.
A black, Murray (1910-) was a tactician and advisor to undergraduate activists during the sit-in demonstrations of the civil rights committee at Howard University in 1943 and 1944. Correspondence, biographical material, reports, minutes, press releases, notes relating to committee activities, and clippings.

2,144. Ovington, Mary White
Papers. Nd. 148-page item.
Open. No guide.
Howard University, Moorland-Spingarn Research Center.
Ovington (1865-1951) was an author. Draft of

chapters and notes for an unpublished book "The Walls Came Tumbling Down."

2,145. Pool, Rosey Eve
Papers. 1959-67. 1 ft. 3 in.
Open. Unpublished guide.
Howard University, Moorland-Spingarn Research Center.
Pool (1905-71) was a black patron and critic of black poets as well as author of *Beyond the Blues* (Hand and Flower Press, 1962) and *ik ben Nieuwe Neger (i am the New Negro)* (Den Haag: Bert Bakker, 1965).

2,146. Porter, Dorothy (Burnett)
Papers. 1932. 92-page item.
Open. No guide.
Howard University, Moorland-Spingarn Research Center.
Columbia University master's thesis by Porter (1905-), a black who is a curator of Moorland-Spingarn Research Center and librarian, concerns Afro-American writers published after 1835.

2,147. Sewing Circle of Philadelphia
Records. 1860. 1 item.
Open. No guide.
Howard University, Moorland-Spingarn Research Center.
Unsigned holograph verses honoring the women of the Circle.

2,148. Sheppard, Madeline
Papers. Nd. 307-page item.
Open. No guide.
Howard University, Moorland-Spingarn Research Center.
Holograph copy of the Freedmen's Bureau Act.

2,149. Slowe, Lucy Diggs
Papers. 1919-43. 5 ft.
Open. Unpublished guide.
Howard University, Moorland-Spingarn Research Center.
A black, Slowe (1885-1937) was dean of women at Howard University from 1922 until 1937 and served as president of the National Association of College Women. Correspondence, biographical data, photos, speeches, and articles, including information on her national activities and community affairs.

2,150. Smoot, Maggie Wilson
Papers. 1882-89. 1 vol.
Open. No guide.
Howard University, Moorland-Spingarn Research Center.
Smoot (1870-1954) was a black singer. Holograph logbook of travels with the Fisk Jubilee Singers.

2,151. Spiller, Isabele (Taliaferro)
Papers. 1906-54. 2 ft.
Open. Unpublished guide.
Howard University, Moorland-Spingarn Research Center.
Correspondence, biographical data, publicity programs, broadsides, clippings, and other material pertaining to Spiller (1888-), a black musician, music teacher, and educator. From 1912 until 1926 she was a member of "The Music Spillers," an instrumental group formed by her husband William N. Spiller which performed around the world. Isabele Spiller helped organize the Spiller School of Music in 1929 and became its codirector.

2,152. Staupers, Mabel Eloise Doyle Keaton
Papers. 1937-70. 10 in.
Open. Unpublished guide.
Howard University, Moorland-Spingarn Research Center.
Staupers (1890-) worked for integration of black nurses in professional nursing, organized the Harlem Committee of the New York Tuberculosis and Health Association, and wrote *No Time for Prejudice.* Correspondence, biographical data, reports, programs, and clippings.

2,153. Terrell, Mary (Church)
Papers. 1884-1954. 2 ft. 6 in.
Open. Unpublished guide.
Howard University, Moorland-Spingarn Research Center.
Terrell (1863-1954) was a black writer and social worker who championed human rights. Correspondence, biographical sketches, manuscripts, articles, clippings, and other papers relate to her organizational affiliations. Included are letters from Mrs. Booker T. Washington.

2,154. Truth, Sojourner
Papers. 1864. 1 item.
Open. No guide.
Howard University, Moorland-Spingarn Research Center.
Truth (ca. 1797-1883) was a black abolitionist, preacher, and lecturer. Typescript copy of a letter from Freedman's Village, LA, to Rowland Johnson in Orange, NY.

2,155. Washington Conservatory of Music
Records. 1887-1966. 12 ft.
Open. Unpublished guide.
Howard University, Moorland-Spingarn Research Center.
Founded in 1903 to preserve and develop Negro music, the Washington Conservatory of Music and School of Expression merged in 1937 with and became a department of the National Negro Music Center, which had been founded in New York in 1922. Includes Conservatory correspondence, student records, notebooks, music scores, sheet music, programs, scrapbooks, and clippings. Also included are personal correspondence and papers of Conservatory founder Harriet (Gibbs) Marshall. The first black woman to graduate from the Oberlin Conservatory of Music in Ohio, Marshall served as director of music for the Washington public schools.

2,156. Waties, Charlotte A.
Papers. 1818. 1 item.
Open. No guide.
Howard University, Moorland-Spingarn Research Center.
Bill of exchange by which Waties agrees to trade her Negro man Scipio for her father's Negro man Cutter in order to prevent their separation from their families.

2,157. Ackerman, Carl William
Papers. 1833-1970. 86 ft.
Open. Published guide.
Library of Congress, Manuscript Division.
An author, newspaper correspondent, and public relations consultant, Ackerman (1890-1970) also was dean of the graduate school of journalism at Columbia University. His papers contain material of his wife Mabel L. (VanderHoof) Ackerman (?-1954), including diaries for the period 1932-54; notes; extensive correspondence with her husband, her mother Emma F. VanderHoof, other family members, and Edith M. Smith; and an article Mabel Ackerman wrote about "the baby plague" in Germany. See *Carl William Ackerman: A Register of His Papers* (Washington: Library of Congress, 1973).

2,158. Adams Family
Papers. 1776-1914. Ca. 225 items.
Open. Published guide and inventory.
Library of Congress, Manuscript Division.
Correspondence, writings, and deeds of President John Adams (1735-1826) and other family members. Includes a few letters, 1790-1815, to Abigail (Smith) Adams (1744-1818), who was John Adams's wife, and a few letters and poems, 1832-48, of Louisa Catherine (Johnson) Adams (1775-1852), who was John Quincy Adams's wife. See *The National Union Catalog of Manuscript Collections, 1969* (Washington, DC: The Library of Congress, 1970).

2,159. Adams, Maude
Papers. Nd. 2 boxes.
Open. Published guide.
Library of Congress, Manuscript Division.
Copies of the writings of [Miss] Adams (1872-1953), an actress, include her autobiography, as well as *Thumbs Up for Joy and Adventure, The Spoken Word,* and other works; notes for a proposed radio program with Homer St. Gaudens; a 1939 commencement address she delivered at Stephens College; and Phyllis Robbins's biography of her. Taken from *The National Union Catalog of Manuscript Collections, 1962* (Hamden, CT: The Shoe String Press, Inc., 1964).

2,160. Aldrich, Nelson Wilmarth
Papers. 1777-1930. 58 ft.
Open. Published guide.
Library of Congress, Manuscript Division.
Papers of Aldrich (1841-1915), US senator from Rhode Island between 1881 and 1911, include correspondence, diaries for 1904 and 1912, and engagement books of his wife Abby (Chapman) Aldrich. Also included are boxes of research notes Jeannette Paddock Nichols collected while she was assistant to Nelson Aldrich's biographer Nathaniel W. Stephenson and correspondence of Lucy Aldrich, Katharine Babbitt, Bertha Knobloch, Kathleen Lawler, and Abby (Aldrich) Rockefeller. Also contains a few letters to Nelson Aldrich from each of the following: Abbie M. Hay, Caroline Hazard, Endora S. Kelly, Phoebe J. Lachmeyer, Mary Martin, and Sally A. Rodman. Collection is also available on microfilm. See *Nelson W. Aldrich: A Register and Index of His Papers* (Washington: Library of Congress, 1973).

2,161. Alexander, Frances
Papers. 1820. 1 item.
Open. No guide.
Library of Congress, Manuscript Division.
Letter in which Alexander requested an affidavit from Thomas Swann to be used in her case against Edward A. May for assault and battery.

2,162. Alexander, Julia G., and the Alexander and Graham Family
Papers. 1812-61. Ca. 35 items.
Open. No guide.
Library of Congress, Manuscript Division.
Julia Alexander's collection of Alexander and Graham family papers consists of correspondence and a notebook of Sarah Ann (Graham) Alexander (1807-39?), a teacher in New York and Tennessee, as well as correspondence of William Grenville Graham (1794-1827), who may have been her brother; of her father Joseph Graham (1759-1836); of Hepzibah Graham and her niece Jane Maria Graham (1796-?); of Jane Graham's father James Graham (1773-1829); and of Dicks Alexander and his wife Deborah Alexander.

2,163. Allen, Florence Ellinwood
Papers. 1907-65. Ca. 2700 items.
Open. Published guide and register.
Library of Congress, Manuscript Division.
A lawyer and judge, Allen (1884-1966) was also an author and lecturer. Correspondence, speeches, honors and citations, photos, scrapbooks, clippings, and other material relate to her service as associate justice of the Ohio Supreme Court between 1922 and 1934 and as judge of the Federal Court of Appeals between 1934 and 1966, in addition to her activities on behalf of women's rights and peace through international law. Correspondents include Nancy Witcher Langhorne, who became the Viscountess Astor; Eleanor Roosevelt; Margaret Chase Smith; and members of the International Federation of Women Lawyers. Taken from *The*

National Union Catalog of Manuscript Collections, 1973-74 (Washington, DC: The Library of Congress, 1975).

2,164. Alston Family
Papers. 1735-1957. 1 Hollinger box.
Open. Published guide.
Library of Congress, Manuscript Division.
Papers of this South Carolina family include a genealogical chart; a poem by John Williamson Palmer romanticizing the death of Theodosia (Burr) [Mrs. Joseph] Alston (1783-1813), who was Aaron Burr's daughter; an account of her death by her descendant Jacob Motte Alston; a memoir Jacob Alston wrote in the form of a letter to his daughter Hessie (Alston) [Mrs. Richard Shubrick] Trapier; and a scrapbook of clippings of another of his daughters, Mary Motte Alston. See *The National Union Catalog of Manuscript Collections, 1968* (Washington, DC: The Library of Congress, 1969).

2,165. American Association of University Women Community Arts Survey
Records. 1937-40. 16 Hollinger boxes.
Open. No guide.
Library of Congress, Manuscript Division.
Undertaken by the AAUW beginning in ca. 1937 through its local chapters, the Survey was an effort to identify the extent of and support for literature, music, theater, dance, painting, sculpture, and architecture in 126 variously sized US communities; the data obtained from the Survey provided the basis for the AAUW's decision to add the arts to its educational program.
Correspondence and notes relating to the rationale and design of the Survey, including a discussion of whether the Survey was appropriate for AAUW. Also includes the data collected by local chapters and written reports on community size, population composition, educational level, social services, institutions, community spirit, and details on the status of the arts in each community surveyed.

2,166. The American Scholar
Records. 1932-65. Ca. 28 ft.
Access restricted. Published guide and register.
Library of Congress, Manuscript Division.
The American Scholar, which is published by the United Chapters of Phi Beta Kappa, was established in 1932. Editorial correspondence with authors, some of whose manuscripts were rejected, including Florence E. Allen, Florence Bennett Anderson, Ruth Benedict, Meribeth E. Cameron, Babette Deutsch, Beulah France, Frances Frost, Elizabeth Stanton Hardy, Hannah Kahn, Katharine Kellock Louise Lamprey, Phyllis McGinley, Margaret Mead, L. Ruth Middlebrook, and Eve Triem. Also includes correspondence, reports, and other material concerning publication of the magazine; its policy, organization, editorial board, and relationship with advertising representatives, printers, and Phi Beta Kappa; and items pertaining to Marjory Hope Nicolson, acting and consulting editor, and Irita Van Doren, an editorial board member. See *The National Union Catalog of Manuscript Collections, 1966* (Washington, DC: The Library of Congress, 1967).

2,167. Ames, Harriet Ann (Moore) Page Potter
Papers. Ca. 1893. 30-page item.
Open. No guide.
Library of Congress, Manuscript Division.
In her reminiscences of life as a settler in Texas between 1836 and 1842, [Mrs. Charles] Ames (1810-?) describes living on a prairie where she was deserted by her first husband Solomon C. Page; her marriage to Robert Potter in ca. 1837 and moving to Caddo Lake, TX; the murder of her husband Potter and daughter; and her court battle to convict their murderers. She also describes relations between settlers and Indians.

2,168. Ames, Louise (Bates)
Papers. 1915-75. 10 ft.
Open. Published guide and register.
Library of Congress, Manuscript Division.
A child psychologist and author, Ames (1908-) was cofounder and with Frances Ilg codirector of the Gesell Institute of Child Development in New Haven, CT. Correspondence with family, friends, and professional associates; a sampling of letters from "Parents Ask," a newspaper column she co-authored between 1951 and 1973; and correspondence concerning and manuscripts of several of her books, including *Child Care and Development* (Philadelphia: Lippincott, 1970) and *Don't Push Your Pre-Schooler* (New York: Harper & Row, 1974). From 1952 to 1955 and in 1960 and 1961 Ames also gave a weekly television program on child behavior. See *The National Union Catalog of Manuscript Collections, 1966* (Washington, DC: The·Library of Congress, 1967).

2,169. Amory Family
Papers. 1697-1823. Ca. 600 items.
Open. No guide.
Library of Congress, Manuscript Division.
Business and family correspondence and other business records of this merchant trading and shipping family of Ireland, South Carolina, and Boston. Includes estate papers, 1697-1724, relating to Sarah [Mrs. William] Rhett of Charles Town, SC, as executrix of the estates of Martha Amory and her husband Jonathon Amory; correspondence among members of the immediate family of Rebekah (Holmes) Amory, who was wife of Thomas Amory (1682-1728); and a receipt book of Rebekah Amory. Some of the material has been published in Gertrude E. Meredith, *Descendants of Hugh Amory* (London: Chiswick Press, 1901).

2,170. Andersen, Hendrik Christian, Family
Papers. 1880-1940. 14 ft.
Open. Published guide.
Library of Congress, Manuscript Division.
Papers of Andersen (1872-1940), a sculptor and author who was interested in the world peace movement, include diaries for the period 1920-40, which he wrote in the form of letters to his sister-in-law Olivia Donaldson (Cushing) Andersen (1871-1917), and correspondence with his mother Helen Monsen Andersen (1842-?), as well as with [Mrs.] Fanny Hapgood, [Mrs.] Grace Elly Channing-Stetson, [Mrs.] Fanny Petterson, Anna J. H. [Mrs. Percy V.] Pennybacker, Mary Garrett Hay, [Mrs.] Anna Sturges Duryea, [Mrs.] Belva Lockwood, [Mrs.] Mary Berenson, and the GFWC's organ *General Federation Magazine.*

Included in the collection are papers of Olivia Andersen, who was an author, playwright, and peace advocate. Her material consists of three notebooks of love letters between her and her fiancé Andreas Martin Andersen (1869-1902); correspondence concerning her, her illness and death, and writings on a "world city"; 63 volumes of diaries for the period 1882-1917 in which she details her childhood, marriage and widowhood in 1902, move to Italy in ca. 1906, work writing plays, and plans for the world city; notes; poems, essays, articles, a novel, and a partial biography of Hendrik and Andreas Andersen, all of which she wrote; and drafts and published versions of many of her plays, including *First in Peace, Emperor and Pope,* and her *Creation and Other Biblical Plays* (Geneva: Albert Kundig, 1929). See *The National Union Catalog of Manuscript Collections, 1963-1964* (Washington, DC: The Library of Congress, 1965).

2,171. Anderson, Isabel Weld (Perkins)
Papers. 1857-1949. Ca. 860 items.
Open. Published guide.
Library of Congress, Manuscript Division.
Papers that [Mrs. Larz] Anderson (1876-1948), an author, poet, and playwright, collected on her father George Hamilton Perkins (1835-99), a naval officer, include correspondence of Anderson with her mother Anna (Weld) Perkins and other relatives, correspondence of Anderson concerning her father's death and memorials to him, a letter concerning an honorary award conferred on Anderson in 1918 by George Washington University, and clippings about Anderson, her parents, and her father's sister [Miss] Susan George Perkins (1838-1911). Also includes papers, 1937-49, relating to a 1949 board of arbitration hearing to decide for tax purposes whether Isabel Anderson's legal residence was Massachusetts or New Hampshire. See *The National Union Catalog of Manuscript Collections, 1972* (Washington, DC: The Library of Congress, 1974).

2,172. Anderson, Margarite
Papers. 1905-ca. 1919. 4 items.
Open. No guide.
Library of Congress, Manuscript Division.
Papers of [Mrs.] Anderson, a poet who lived in Chillicothe, OH, consist of poems she wrote and quotations she collected about peace.

2,173. Anderson, Marguerite S.
Papers. 1955-56. 1 vol.
Open. No guide.
Library of Congress, Manuscript Division.
Journal in which [Mrs.] Anderson, an historian, describes a sesquicentennial journey retracing the Lewis and Clark expedition with a Shoshoni Indian guide who was great-great-grandaughter of Sacajawea, Lewis and Clark's Indian interpreter. Includes information on Sacajawea's life as well as clippings.

2,174. Anderson, Robert
Papers. 1819-1919. 5 ft.
Open. Published guide and register.
Library of Congress, Manuscript Division.
Papers of Anderson (1805-71), an artillery officer who was commander of the Union garrison during the bombardment of Fort Sumter, include correspondence of his wife Eliza Bayard (Clinch) Anderson and of his daughter Eba (Anderson) [Mrs. James Marsland] Lawton (1830-1919), who was an historian and his biographer. Included are letters to Eliza Anderson from her sister and father soon after her marriage, letters to her concerning her husband's military career, and correspondence of Lawton, which pertains to her efforts to gain public recognition for her father through a memorial and publication of a book she edited, *History of the "Soldier's Home," Washington, D.C.* (New York: G. P. Putnam's Sons, 1914). See *The National Union Catalog of Manuscript Collections, 1959-1961* (Ann Arbor, MI: J. W. Edwards, 1962).

2,175. Anthony, Susan Brownell
Papers. 1846-1934. 3 ft.
Open. Published guide and register.
Library of Congress, Manuscript Division.
Correspondence, diaries, speeches, scrapbooks of clippings, and printed matter of [Miss] Anthony (1820-1906), a reformer and suffragist, pertain to her activities for the women's suffrage movement. Also included is a speech by Elizabeth Cady Stanton. Collection is available on microfilm. Taken from *The National Union Catalog of Manuscript Collections, 1972* (Washington, DC: The Library of Congress, 1974).

2,176. Antin, Mary
Papers. Ca. 1934. 2 items.
Open. No guide.
Library of Congress, Manuscript Division.
Letters of Antin (1881-1949), an author who married Amadeus William Grabau in 1901, are addressed to a Mrs. Bernnard; one of them mentions the Gould Farm colony in Great Barrington, MA, where Antin was living.

2,177. Arendt, Hannah
Papers. 1935-63. 5 ft.
Partially restricted. Published guide and register.
Library of Congress, Manuscript Division.
[Miss] Arendt (1906-75) was an author and political scientist. Manuscripts of some of her published and unpublished books and articles, drafts of lectures, lecture notes, memoranda, outlines, a notebook, some of her newspaper articles from the Jewish weekly *Aufbau,* and correspondence with Judah Leon Magnes and the Judah L. Magnes Foundation concerning the UN discussion in 1948 of the status of Palestine. Taken from *The National Union Catalog of Manuscript Collections, 1965* (Washington, DC: The Library of Congress, 1966).

2,178. Armstrong, Richard, Family
Papers. 1831-1929. 172 items.
Open. Published guide.
Library of Congress, Manuscript Division.
Correspondence, poems, and clipping of Richard Armstrong (1805-60) and his wife Clarissa (Chapman) Armstrong, who were missionaries to the Hawaiian Islands for the American Board of Commissioners for Foreign Missions. Includes letters in which Clarissa Armstrong details for her brother and sister-in-law the difficulties of being a missionary's wife and raising children as well as the religious training she desired for one of her daughters, who was living with her brother's family between 1842 and 1844. In their correspondence Richard and Clarissa Armstrong's daughters, Mary Jane and Caroline, describe for their brother, William Nevins Armstrong, their activities as adolescents helping with their parents' mission work during the early 1850s. See *The National Union Catalog of Manuscript Collections, 1962* (Hamden, CT: The Shoe String Press, Inc., 1964).

2,179. Arnold, Henry Harley
Papers. 1907-57. 110 ft.
Partially restricted. Published guide and register.
Library of Congress, Manuscript Division.
Papers of Arnold (1886-1950), a US Army officer and pioneer aviator who was instrumental in the development of US air power, include correspondence of his wife Eleanor A. (Poole) Arnold, his daughter Lois E. (Arnold) [Mrs. Ernest E.] Snowden, Katherine V. Harley, and [Mrs.] Elizabeth Poole. Also included are papers of his wartime secretary Edna M. Adkins, which consist of her personal file on Henry Arnold, biographical material on him, and items concerning his death. See *The National Union Catalog of Manuscript Collections, 1963-1964* (Washington, DC: The Library of Congress, 1965).

2,180. Arthur Family
Papers. 1817-1972. 31 ft.
Open. Published guide and register.
Library of Congress, Manuscript Division.
Papers of Chester Alan Arthur II (1864-1937), a sportsman; his first wife Myra Fithian (Andrews) Arthur (?-1935); his sister Ellen Herndon (Arthur) Pinkerton (1875-1915); and his son Chester Alan Arthur III (1901-72), an author. Included are correspondence, detailed but routine diaries for the period 1902-35, Fithian and Andrews family papers, a guest book, address books, and a scrapbook of Myra Arthur and correspondence of Ellen Pinkerton. Also includes correspondence, 1877-99, of Ellen Lewis (Herndon) Arthur (1837-80), the wife of President Chester Alan Arthur; diaries of his sister Malvina Ann (Arthur) Haynesworth, 1853-69; correspondence of Charlotte (Wilson) Arthur, who was married to Chester Arthur III from 1922 to 1932; correspondence and canceled checks of Esther Murphy (Strachey) Arthur, who was married to Chester Arthur III from 1935 to 1961; and correspondence of Edith L. DeSavary. See *National Union Catalog of Manuscript Collections, 1977* (Washington, DC: Library of Congress, 1978).

2,181. Asbill, J. J.
Papers. 1861-62. 8 items.
Open. No guide.
Library of Congress, Manuscript Division.
Correspondence in which Asbill, a Confederate soldier, describes army life to his wife.

2,182. Astor, William Waldorf
Papers. 1904-10. Ca. 50 items.
Open. No guide.
Library of Congress, Manuscript Division.
Collected by [Mrs.] Amy Small Richardson of Washington, DC, the papers of Astor (1848-1919), a financier and journalist, consist primarily of letters he wrote her concerning their mutual interest in his English home Cliveden.

2,183. Atherton, Gertrude Franklin (Horn)
Papers. 1889-1943. 1 ft.
Open. Published guide.
Library of Congress, Manuscript Division.
Correspondence of [Mrs. George Henry Bowen] Atherton (1857-1948), an author, is addressed to Joseph Marshall Stoddard of Philadelphia, who was editor of *Lippincott's Monthly Magazine.* Also included are manuscripts of *The Golden Peacock* and of two other novels she wrote. Taken from *The National Union Catalog of Manuscript Collections, 1963-1964* (Washington, DC: The Library of Congress, 1965).

2,184. Bachmann, Sophie E.
Papers. 1888. 1 item.
Open. No guide.
Library of Congress, Manuscript Division.
Notebook containing a poem about a dog, written and illustrated by [Miss] Bachmann, a poet.

2,185. Bailey, Orra B.
Papers. 1862-64. Ca. 75 items.
Open. No guide.
Library of Congress, Manuscript Division.
Addressed to his wife, letters from Bailey, a Union soldier who served in 1864 as an orderly for the provost marshal, contain candid descriptions of army life during southern campaigns and in Washington.

2,186. Baker, Ray Stannard
Papers. 1836-1946. 61 ft.
Open. Published guide and register.
Library of Congress, Manuscript Division.
A journalist, author, and biographer of Woodrow Wilson, Baker (1870-1946) also participated in the 1919 Paris Peace Conference. His papers include correspondence with Edith (Bolling) [Mrs. Woodrow] Wilson, Ida Tarbell, Jane Addams, Carrie Chapman Catt, Lucy M. Salmon, and Katharine E. Brand, as well as research notes taken by Katharine Brand for Baker on the activities of Woodrow Wilson between 1911 and 1918. See *The National Union Catalog of Manuscript Collections, 1959-1961* (Ann Arbor, MI: J. W. Edwards, 1962).

2,187. Ball, Mary
Collection. 1859-1922. 2 ft.
Open. No guide.
Library of Congress, Manuscript Division.
In an attempt to determine the authenticity of a portrait of Mary Ball (1708-89), who became the second wife of Augustine Washington and mother of George Washington (1732-99), Caroline P. [Mrs. James H.] Campbell of Grand Rapids, MI, collected relevant correspondence, notes, pamphlets, monographs, graphic material, and copies of books such as *The Mother of Washington and Her Times* by Mrs. Roger A. Pryor (New York: Grosset & Dunlap, 1903).

2,188. Bancroft and Bliss Family
Papers. 1788-1928. 5800 items.
Open. Published guide and register.
Library of Congress, Manuscript Division.
Family and general correspondence and other papers of the Bancroft and Bliss families include papers of Elizabeth (Davis) Bancroft (1803-86), who was an author; her husband from 1825 to 1827, Alexander Bliss (1792-1827), who was a lawyer; their son Alexander Bliss II (1827-96), who was an author, soldier, and secretary of the US legation in Berlin; and her second husband, whom she married in 1838, George Bancroft (1800-91), who was an historian, secretary of the US Navy, and US minister to England and Germany. Contains correspondence of Elizabeth Bancroft, dating from her boarding school days through both marriages, with her parents, husbands, sons Alexander Bliss II and William D. Bliss, and others; 1820 issues of a newspaper she produced with her classmates at Miss Cushing's school in Hingham, MA; and manuscripts of her *Letters from England, 1846-1849* (New York: C. Scribner's Sons, 1904). Also included are correspondence of her daughter-in-law Eleanor (Albert) [Mrs. Alexander, II] Bliss (?-1874), writing from Germany between 1866 and 1874, to her mother Emily Albert; a few post-WWI letters from Elizabeth S. Woodruff to [Miss] Elizabeth B. Bliss and others about schools for Italian war orphans; a 1790 poem by Margaret Stevenson to Penelope Russell; and an 1821 sermon by Rev. J. P. K. Henhan on the death of Helen [Mrs. Talbot] Jones of Baltimore. Part of the collection is available on microfilm. See *The National Union Catalog of Manuscript Collections, 1959-1961* (Ann Arbor, MI: J. W. Edwards, 1962).

2,189. Banister, Marion (Glass)
Papers. 1933-51. 2 ft.
Open. Published guide and register.
Library of Congress, Manuscript Division.
A teacher, writer, and leader in women's political affairs, Banister (?-1951) was editor and publisher of the *Washingtonian* magazine from 1929 to 1933 and from 1933 until her death assistant treasurer of the US. Correspondence, publicity material, and memorabilia, some of which relate to the Democratic National Committee. Taken from *The National Union Catalog of Manuscript Collections, 1959-1961* (Ann Arbor, MI: J. W. Edwards, 1962).

2,190. Barnard Family
Papers. 1714-1901. 2 ft.
Open. Published guide.
Library of Congress, Manuscript Division.
Papers dealing with the business activities and social and family life of five generations of the Barnard family in Connecticut and western New York. Includes correspondence of Harriet Barnard (1787-1847), daughter of Revolutionary War commissary officer and judge Timothy Barnard (1756-1847), with her niece Julia Barnard Strong, wife of missionary Eben Strong, who was living on the Missouri frontier during the 1830s. Harriet Barnard's other correspondents include her uncle Ebenezer Barnard, Jr. (1748-1827), a soldier, merchant, and land speculator; her brothers E. Henry Barnard and Daniel D. Barnard (1796-1861), who was a diplomat and US representative; and Ann Perkins. Also contained is correspondence of Sophia Griswold [Mrs. E. Henry] Barnard of Hartford, CT, and Mendon, NY, with her cousins Roxana P. Clark and Sarah Clark, Julia Strong, and several other female friends. See *The National Union Catalog of Manuscript Collections, 1962* (Hamden, CT: The Shoe String Press, Inc., 1964).

2,191. Barnes, Christian
Papers. 1768-84. 54 items.
Open. Published guide.

Library of Congress, Manuscript Division.
Correspondence that [Mrs. Henry] Barnes, a Loyalist and merchant's wife, wrote to her friends Elizabeth Campbell Smith Inman and Dorothy (Murray) Forbes about her activities in Marlborough, MA, before the Revolutionary War and in the Loyalist colony in Bristol, England, during the 1780s. Collection is available on microfilm. See *The National Union Catalog of Manuscript Collections, 1976* (Washington, DC: The Library of Congress, 1977).

2,192. Barrett, John
Papers. 1861-1943. Ca. 100 ft.
Open. Register.
Library of Congress, Manuscript Division.
Papers of Barrett (1866-1938), a journalist and diplomat who served in Siam, the Philippines, and South America, contain papers that Mary X. (Ferguson) Barrett collected in preparation for a biography she wrote of him. Includes correspondence concerning her research, notes, and the manuscript of her unpublished biography. Mary Barrett was the wife of his nephew John Walton Barrett.

2,193. Barrett, Kate Harwood (Waller)
Papers. 1895-1950. 2 ft.
Open. Published guide.
Library of Congress, Manuscript Division.
[Mrs. Robert South] Barrett (1857-1925) was a physician and sociologist. Correspondence, speeches, articles, master's thesis, certificates of appointments to civic organizations, and scrapbooks of clippings reflect her work on behalf of women's rights, particularly her efforts to secure such national legislation as the Mann Act. Material contains information on her associations with the DAR, the National American Legion Women's Auxiliary, the National Council of Women, the National Florence Crittenton Mission, and the Needlework Guild of America. Taken from *The National Union Catalog of Manuscript Collections, 1972* (Washington, DC: The Library of Congress, 1974).

2,194. Bartlett, Paul Wayland
Papers. 1887-1949. 33 ft.
Open. Published guide and register.
Library of Congress, Manuscript Division.
Papers of Bartlett (1865-1925), a sculptor, include correspondence with other sculptors, architects, artists, and craftsmen. Also includes correspondence of his wife Suzanne (Earle) Bartlett, whom he married in 1913 after her marriages to Mahlon Ogden Jones and Samuel Franklin Emmons ended. Her letters, primarily addressed to Paul Bartlett and her daughter Caroline (Jones) [Mrs. Armistead] Peter, reveal her involvement in her husband's career and her life in Paris after his death. See *The National Union Catalog of Manuscript Collections, 1962* (Hamden, CT: The Shoe String Press, Inc., 1964).

2,195. Barton, Bathsheba
Papers. 1819. 1 vol.
Open. No guide.
Library of Congress, Manuscript Division.
Copybook of Barton, a student at the Weston School in Pennsylvania, includes poems and essays she wrote or copied, penmanship exercises, and an account of the death of Lucy A. Pancoast at age 17.

2,196. Barton, Clara
Papers. 1830-1957. 76.8 ft.
Open. Register.
Library of Congress, Manuscript Division.
Barton (1821-1912), whose full name was Clarissa Harlowe Barton, was a welfare worker, philanthropist, and founder and first president of the American National Red Cross. Consists of her diaries and journals for the period 1849-1911; an autobiography, biographies of her by her brother and a grandniece, and genealogical material; poems; lectures; bills, receipts, ledgers, personal accounts, estate items, and other financial documents; and scrapbooks and clippings on her and on the Red Cross. Also includes records of the Red Cross, 1863-1947, and Red Cross secretary Lucy Graves's diary of her work in Cuba in 1898. Bulk of the collection, however, is correspondence concerning Barton's teaching career between 1836 and 1854, work with the US Patent Office between 1857 and 1861, Civil War work, organization and administration of the Red Cross, and personal matters. Correspondents include Dorence Atwater, Harriet Austin, Minna Kupfer, Rachel Stone, Lucy Larcom, M. Louise Thomas, Susan B. Anthony, Sarah A. Spencer, Lucy Stone, E. Florence Barker, Lucy M. Hall, Mary Weeks Burnett, Frances E. Willard, Rachel G. Foster, Antoinette Margot, Leonora B. Halsted, Marietta Holley, Mabel Boardman, Lucy E. Bertram, Saidee F. Riccius, Stephen E. Barton, and clergyman William E. Barton. Part of the collection is available on microfilm.

2,197. Beale Family
Papers. 1794-1957. 8 ft.
Open. Published guide and list.
Library of Congress, Manuscript Division.
Material documenting the careers of several Beale family members includes papers of author Marie (Oge) Beale (1881-1956), who became the second wife of diplomat Truxtun Beale (1856-1936) in 1903. Her papers consist of speeches, radio scripts, and writings on Spanish culture in California and on Central and South America, among them her *Flight into America's Past: Inca Peaks and Maya Jungles* (1932); articles on women as responsible voters; correspondence with the YWCA's Professional Writers' Club and the Naval Historical Foundation concerning the preservation of the Decatur House, which was the Beale family residence in Washington; and letters relating to her fund-raising activities during WWII. See *The National Union Catalog of Manuscript Collections, 1959-1961* (Ann Arbor, MI: J. W. Edwards, 1962).

2,198. Beard, Daniel Carter
Papers. 1798-1941. 105 ft.
Open. Published guide and register.
Library of Congress, Manuscript Division.
Papers of Beard (1850-1941), an author, illustrator, and cofounder of the Boy Scouts of America, contain correspondence with Daisy Barrett, Evangeline Cory Booth, Elizabeth Custer, Anna George deMille, Amelia Earhart, Mrs. Charles Dana Gibson, Helen Keller, Mary A. Nichols, Helen Talbot Porter, Mary Cochrane Rogers, Edith K. Roosevelt, Helen H. Taft, Ida Tarbell, Irita Van Doren, Margaret Woodrow Wilson, the Camp Fire Girls, and the United Daughters of the Confederacy. See *The National Union Catalog of Manuscript Collections, 1959-1961* (Ann Arbor, MI: J. W. Edwards, 1962).

2,199. Beauregard, Pierre Gustave Toutant
Papers. 1844-83. 7 ft.
Open. Published guide and register.
Library of Congress, Manuscript Division.
Papers of Beauregard (1818-93), a Confederate Army officer, engineer, and railroad official, contain letters in which he discusses with Augusta Jane Evans, a novelist who married Lorenzo Madison Wilson in 1868, military strategy for the Civil War and, later, the future of the South and Evans's unfulfilled plan to write a history of the War from the southern point of view. Evans believed strongly in the rightness of the South's cause and corresponded about strategy throughout the War with Beauregard and other Confederate officers. See *The National Union Catalog of Manuscript Collections, 1963-1964* (Washington, DC: The Library of Congress, 1965).

2,200. Becker, George F.
Papers. 1814-1928. 15 ft.
Open. Published guide and inventory.
Library of Congress, Manuscript Division.
Papers of Becker (1847-1919), geologist-in-charge of the US Geological Survey, contain correspondence with his mother Sarah Cary (Tuckerman) [Mrs. Andrew C.] Becker, his second wife Alice "Elsie" Theodora (Watson) Becker (?-1880), and, during the last years of his life, with his third wife Florence S. D. Becker. His mother's papers also include a review of a book she compiled with Federico Mora, *Spanish Idioms and Their English Equivalents* (Boston: Ginn & Co., 1887); her reminiscences of her father Joseph Tuckerman (1778-1840); and correspondence with her father and aunts [Miss] Harriet Cary and [Miss] Ann M. Cary. Alice Becker's papers also include diaries for 1782 to 1789 and a notebook. See *The National Union Catalog of Manuscript Collections, 1959-1961* (Ann Arbor, MI: J. W. Edwards, 1962).

2,201. Beetham, Asa
Papers. 1861-65. 16 items.
Open. No guide.
Library of Congress, Manuscript Division.
Correspondence in which Beetham, a sailor in the US Navy, describes to his sister, [Miss] Emily Beetham of New York, naval duty and life and battles with "rebels." Also includes a broadside.

2,202. Bell, Alexander Graham
Papers. 1834-1972. 397 containers.
Open. Register.
Library of Congress, Manuscript Division.
Professional and personal papers of Bell (1847-1922), an inventor and educator of the deaf, contain papers of his mother Eliza Grace (Symonds) [Mrs. Alexander Melville] Bell (1809-97); of his wife Mabel G. (Hubbard) Bell (1858-1923); of his daughters Marian Hubbard (Bell) [Mrs. David G.] Fairchild (1880-1962), a suffragist and author, and Elsie May (Bell) [Mrs. Gilbert] Grosvenor (1878-1964), a suffragist, explorer, and officer in various women's groups; and of his mother-in-law Gertrude McCurdy [Mrs. Gardiner Greene] Hubbard. Eliza Bell's papers consist of family and general correspondence; journals for 1850 to 1884; a ca. 1889 diary; poems, plays, and articles she wrote; an account book; will and estate papers; notebooks; and scrapbooks. His wife Mabel Bell's papers consist of family and general correspondence, diaries for 1870 to 1907, an autobiography, a biography of her father, an account book, financial papers, notebooks, and certificates. Marian Fairchild's papers consist of correspondence, an article she wrote, invitations, and clippings. Elsie Grosvenor's papers consist of correspondence, speeches and articles she wrote, biographical material, financial papers, and drawings. Gertrude Hubbard's papers consist of correspondence, much of it with her daughter; legal papers; address books; engravings; and printed matter. Papers of more than 40 other women, usually consisting of a few letters to Alexander and Mabel Bell, are contained in the collection. Included is material of various female members of the Bell, Fairchild, Grosvenor, Hubbard, McCurdy, and Symonds families and of Carrie Blatchford, Gertrude Hubbard Grossman, Sophie C. Home, Emily Jordan, Roberta Marsh, Sarah Griswold Marsh, Nancy Bates Marston, and Gertrude G. Pillot. Some items are available on microfilm.

2,203. Bell, Lillian
Papers. Nd. 1 item.
Open. No guide.
Library of Congress, Manuscript Division.
Letter in which Bell (1867-1929), an author who married Arthur Hoyt Bogue, describes to a friend her schedule of public readings, fees, and plans for a reading tour of Europe.

2,204. Benson, Stella, and Lampson, Robin
Papers. Ca. 1923-34. Ca. 108 items.
Open. No guide.
Library of Congress, Manuscript Division.
Benson (1892-1933) was a British author who lived for some time in San Francisco; she was married to J. C. O'Gorman Anderson. Lampson (1900-) is a poet. Benson's papers consist of letters she wrote from China and elsewhere to Albert M. Bender of California; manuscripts of some of her works, including *Goodbye, Stranger* (New York: Macmillan, 1926); drawings by her; and photos. Lampson's papers consist of a few of her poems.

2,205. Bernays, Edward L.
Papers. 1897-1965. 120 ft.
Closed. Published guide and register.
Library of Congress, Manuscript Division.
Papers of Bernays (1891-), a public relations counselor and author, contain the papers of his wife and associate Doris Elsa (Fleischman) Bernays (1891-), a public relations counselor; the papers of both contain information on various of their clients and on the development of mass media, advertising, and public opinion research and analysis.

Doris Bernay's papers consist of correspondence about the Authors Guild, the New York Committee for Young Audiences, the Woman Pays Club, the Women's Conference Group, and a luncheon for a Dr. Treat on behalf of Negro colleges; general correspondence; short stories; speeches; and an appointment book. Also included are correspondence and statistical data concerning *An Outline of Careers for Women: A Practical Guide to Achievement* (Garden City, NY: Doubleday Doran, & Co., 1928), which she compiled and edited, and research notes, interviews, and other papers relating to her unpublished "Going Steady" and "The Last Strike.

Edward Bernays's papers include family correspondence with and about Sigmund Freud and with Anne F. Bernays, Doris Bernays, and Judith Heller; general correspondence with Elizabeth Otis, Marguerite Clark, and others; and correspondence with clients. These clients include the American Nurses Association, Inc.; Countess Mara, Inc.; *Good Housekeeping; Ladies' Home Journal;* the Lucy Stone League; *McCall's;* the ladies auxiliary of the Veterans of Foreign Wars; and such individuals as Agnes E. Benedict, Frances P. Bolton, Anna Duncan, Mary Lewis, Estelle L. Lipton, Joan Lowell, Helen Bullitt Lowry, Clare (Boothe) Luce, Edna Walker Macloskey, Ina Leland Orvis, Jacqueline T. Patenotre, Barbara Hutton Troubetzkoi, and Ethel H. Wise.

See *The National Union Catalog of Manuscript Collections, 1967* (Washington, DC: The Library of Congress, 1968).

2,206. Bickerdyke, Mary Ann (Ball)
Papers. 1856-1905. 1800 items.
Open. Published guide and inventory.
Library of Congress, Manuscript Division.
[Mrs. Robert] Bickerdyke (1817-1901) was a nurse, an agent for the US Sanitary Commission, and a pension attorney who worked to secure pensions for Civil War veterans and nurses. Correspondence, biographical data, financial papers, photos, clippings, and printed matter include material relating to the Commission, her guardianship of James H. Cook, and the Woman's Relief Corps of the Grand Army of the Republic. Also included is correspondence with her sons James Bickerdyke and Hiram Bickerdyke, members of the Ball family, veterans seeking her aid to secure their pensions, and Mary A. Livermore and Lucy Stone. See *The National Union Catalog of Manuscript Collections, 1976* (Washington, DC: The Library of Congress, 1977).

2,207. Biddle, George
Papers. 1899-1969. 7 ft.
Partially restricted. Published guide and register.
Library of Congress, Manuscript Division.
Papers of Biddle (1885-), a painter, sculptor, public official, and war correspondent, include those of his third wife Hélène Sardeau Biddle (1899-), a sculptor. Among her papers are correspondence with her husband, letters concerning her work, her journal of a trip through Mexico in 1945 with archaeologist Franz Blum, a poem, financial papers, a will, photos of her works, and passports. Also included are George Biddle's correspondence with his first wife Anne "Nancy" (Coleman) Biddle, his second wife Jane (Bello) Biddle, and Mary Cassatt, Babette Deutsch, Grace Moore, Frances Perkins, Ione Robinson, Eleanor Roosevelt, Margherita Sarfatti, and Dorothy Thompson. See *The National Union Catalog of Manuscript Collections, 1962* (Hamden, CT: The Shoe String Press, Inc., 1964).

2,208. Binckley, John Milton
Papers. 1816-1943. Ca. 200 items.
Open. Published guide.
Library of Congress, Manuscript Division.
Papers of Binckley, a journalist and public official, include letters his wife Mary (Michel) Binckley wrote him about her financial and physical difficulties during the Civil War while she managed the family farm in Eastville, OH or VA; letters in which his mother-in-law Jane W. Michel, an ardent southern sympathizer, expains her position to Binckley, who was a Union sympathizer; and letters, 1816-17, in which Eliza Patterson discusses beaux with her young friend Charlotte Stoker, who later married a Mr. Binckley. See *The National Union Catalog of Manuscript Collections, 1962* (Hamden, CT: The Shoe String Press, Inc., 1964).

2,209. Blackwell Family
Papers. 1830-1950. 40 ft.
Open. Published guide.
Library of Congress, Manuscript Division.
Papers of Lucy Stone (1818-93), an editor and suffragist; of her husband Henry Brown Blackwell (1825-1909), a reformer and suffragist; of their daughter Alice Stone Blackwell (1857-1950), an editor and author; of Elizabeth Blackwell (1821-1910), a physician; and of her adopted daughter and secretary Kitty Barry Blackwell (1848?-1936). Family and general correspondence; biographical material; poems, speeches, articles, and other writings; financial papers; notes; book reviews; photos; and other miscellany. Also included are items concerning *Lucy Stone, a Chronicle Play* by Maud Wood Park, as well as diaries of Henry Blackwell, 1845-96; of Alice Blackwell, 1872-1937; of Elizabeth Blackwell, 1836-1908; and of Kitty Blackwell, 1917. Collection also contains material of other family members, among them Agnes (Blackwell) Jones, Anna Blackwell, Antoinette Louisa (Brown) [Mrs. Samuel] Blackwell (1825-1921), Emily Blackwell (1826-1910), Emma (Lawrence) Blackwell, Ethel (Blackwell) Robinson, and others. The collection is available on microfilm. See *The Blackwell Family, Carrie Chapman Catt, and the National American Woman Suffrage Association: A Register of Their Papers* (Washington: Library of Congress, 1975).

2,210. Blaine, James Gillespie
Papers. 1777-1945. 20 ft.
Open. Published guide and register.
Library of Congress, Manuscript Division.
Papers of Blaine (1830-93), US representative and senator from Maine and US secretary of state, include papers of his wife Harriet (Stanwood) Blaine (?-1903), of his daughter Margaret (Blaine) [Mrs. Walter Johannes] Damrosch (1865?-1949), and of his confidante and biographer Mary Abigail Dodge, who wrote under the name Gail Hamilton. Harriet Blaine's papers consist of correspondence with her daughter, son Walker Blaine (?-1890), and others and her account of the assassination of President Garfield. Damrosch's papers consist of correspondence concerning her father's career; correspondence with her daughters; diaries she kept in 1887 and 1888 before she was married, particularly of two trips she took to Europe; and a notebook of poems she copied. Also included are letters in which Dodge makes comments and suggestions to James Blaine on his political career as well as correspondence concerning her biography of him. See *The National Union Catalog of Manuscript Collections, 1963-1964* (Washington, DC: The Library of Congress, 1965).

2,211. Blair, Francis Preston, Family
Papers. 1755-1940. 21 ft.
Open. Published guide and register.
Library of Congress, Manuscript Division.
The bulk of the collection consists of professional papers of members of the Blair family, but also included is correspondence of Mary Elizabeth (Woodbury) Blair, predominantly from her husband Montgomery Blair (1813-83), a lawyer and from 1861 to 1864 postmaster general, and from her sons Montgomery Blair, Woodbury Blair, and soldier and lawyer Gist Blair (1860-1940). Also included is a 38-page letter from Mrs. Jefferson Davis to Mr. Blair in 1865. Correspondence of Gist Blair includes letters from his sister Minna (Blair) [Mrs. Stephen Olin] Richey and correspondence, 1900-25, from his wife Laura (Lawson) Ellis Blair, who was divorced from Frank Ellis in 1912. See *The National Union Catalog of Manuscript Collections, 1967* (Washington, DC: The Library of Congress, 1968).

2,212. Blatch, Harriot Eaton (Stanton)
Papers. 1908-15. 12 vols.
Open. No guide.
Library of Congress, Manuscript Division.
A lecturer and suffrage leader, [Mrs. William Henry] Blatch (1856-1940) was president of the New York State Women's Political Union, a group formed to lobby for a suffrage amendment. Scrapbooks containing correspondence, accounts of meetings, transcriptions of debates in the state assembly, propaganda, and photos detail the strategy and activities of the Union's campaign for suffrage.

2,213. Blavatsky, Helena Petrovna (Hahn)
Papers. Ca. 1878. 1 item.
Open. No guide.
Library of Congress, Manuscript Division.
Letter in which [Mrs. Nikifor Vasilievich] Blavatsky (1831-91), a theosophist and occultist, gives a fantastic autobiographical sketch and discusses the Theosophical Society.

2,214. Boardman, Mabel Thorp
Papers. 1853-1945. 5 ft.
Access restricted. Published guide.
Library of Congress, Manuscript Division.
Personal and professional correspondence, diaries for the period 1882-1902, memoranda, genealogical data, notebooks, addresses, sketchbooks, and photos of [Miss] Boardman (1860-1946), an official of the American National Red Cross. Nearly 600 letters from William Howard Taft to Boardman are included along with information on the domestic and foreign issues of every presidential administration from McKinley to Franklin D. Roosevelt. Taken from *The National Union Catalog of Manuscript Collections, 1962* (Hamden, CT: The Shoe String Press, Inc., 1964).

2,215. Bollingen Foundation
Records. 1939-73. 95 ft.
Partially closed. Published guide and register.
Library of Congress, Manuscript Division.
The Foundation was established by Paul and Mary Conover Mellon to fund scholarly research and publication in the humanities. Minutes, legal documents, correspondence, reports, clippings, printed matter, and other items relate to the Foundation's fellowship and contribution programs. Included are files concerning the Bollingen Prize in

Poetry and publication of the collected works of Carl Jung and Paul Valéry in the Bollingen series by Princeton University Press, in addition to material on women who worked for the Foundation, among them advisor Elinore Marvel, secretary and trustee Mary C. Ritter, and Maud Oakes. Also included are files of correspondence, grant applications, Bollingen advisors' comments on each application, and samples of research of more than 50 women, including Marianne Moore, Irma Brandeis, and Maria Santangelo. See *National Union Catalog of Manuscript Collections, 1977* (Washington, DC: Library of Congress, 1978).

2,216. Book-of-the-Month Club
Records. 1939-58. Ca. 23 ft.
Open. Published guide and register.
Library of Congress, Manuscript Division.
Editorial and publishers' correspondence concerning books submitted by publishing houses for consideration by the Club; preliminary readers' reports, mostly for books not selected finally in the form of reviews and candid evaluations of the suitability of books for distribution by the Club; and printed material. Included are preliminary readers' reports by Rosemary Benét, Elizabeth Easton, and Amy Loveman. See *The National Union Catalog of Manuscript Collections, 1963-1964* (Washington, DC: The Library of Congress, 1965).

2,217. Booth, Mrs. Lionel F.
Papers. 1864-67. 2 items.
Open. No guide.
Library of Congress, Manuscript Division.
Booth was the widow of a Negro army officer. A letter Abraham Lincoln wrote to Charles Sumner about his support for the pension rights of widows of Negro soldiers is included with a letter introducing Booth as job applicant for a position with the US Department of the Treasury.

2,218. Borglum, John Gutzon de la Mothe
Papers. 1895-1953. 59 ft.
Open. Published guide and register.
Library of Congress, Manuscript Division.
Papers of Borglum (1871-1941), a painter, author, and sculptor whose projects included the Georgia Confederate Memorial and the faces on Mount Rushmore. Contains papers of his wife Mary (Montgomery) Borglum (?-1955), an Assyriologist, which largely pertain to assistance she gave her husband in his career. Included are diaries from her first years of marriage, which provide a detailed account of her activities in New York and Stamford, CT, as an artist's wife; letters from friends, one of which discusses Borglum's work with the National Woman's Party in Connecticut; and letters to her from Leila Venable [Mrs. Frank Tucker] Mason, a Georgian, which concern the maneuvering Mason undertook among state and national politicians and Confederate memorial groups to facilitate completion of Gutzon Borglum's monument at Stone Mountain, GA. Also included is material on Susan B. Anthony and Mount Rushmore and on Isabella Greenway. See *The National Union Catalog of Manuscript Collections, 1959-1961* (Ann Arbor, MI: J. W. Edwards, 1962).

2,219. Bowen, Catherine (Drinker)
Papers. 1793-1974. 34 ft.
Open. Register.
Library of Congress, Manuscript Division.
Correspondence, contracts, speech material, personal calendars, scrapbooks, photos, clippings, and printed matter of [Mrs. Ezra] Bowen (1897-1973), an author. Also includes manuscripts of *Miracle at Philadelphia: The Story of the Constitutional Convention, May to September, 1787* (Boston: Little, Brown, 1966), *Family Portrait* (Boston: Little, Brown, 1970), and others of her books.

2,220. Bower, May
Papers. 1923-28. 8 items.
Open. No guide.
Library of Congress, Manuscript Division.
Poems by Helena May Bower, a poet, which were published on greeting cards.

2,221. Boyd, Sarah Taylor (Johnson)
Papers. 1913. 2 items.
Open. No guide.
Library of Congress, Manuscript Division.
Reminiscences in which [Mrs. Alfred Davis, Jr.] Boyd describes slaves' duties on her father's plantation in Dallas County, AL, before the Civil War.

2,222. Bradford, Ellen Knight
Papers. 1896. 2 items.
Open. No guide.
Library of Congress, Manuscript Division.
Letter from Bradford, a poet, in which her hymn "Over the Line" is enclosed.

2,223. Brannigan, Felix
Papers. 1861-63. 28 items.
Open. No guide.
Library of Congress, Manuscript Division.
Correspondence in which Brannigan (1843-1907), a union soldier who was later a lieutenant in the US Colored Troops, describes to his sister Daliah (Brannigan) [Mrs. R.] Hall of Pittsburgh his life in the army and battles in Maryland and Virginia.

2,224. Breckinridge, Sophonisba Preston
Papers. 1750-1949. 16 ft.
Open. Preliminary inventory.
Library of Congress, Manuscript Division.
A social worker and educator, [Miss] Breckinridge (1866-1948) worked to develop social work as a profession. Correspondence, lectures by her, minutes of the University of Chicago senate, and family papers reflect her interest in all facets of social work, especially through her association with the Chicago School of Civics and Philanthropy, which became the University of Chicago's graduate school of social service administration. Also included is material for her book *Women in the Twentieth Century: A Study of Their Political, Social and Economic Activities* (New York: McGraw-Hill, 1933). Correspondents include Grace Abbott, Edith Abbott, Jane Addams, Madeleine Leliepre, Florence Kelley, Julia Lathrop, and [Mrs.] Amelia Freeman, as well as the Immigrant Protective League, the American Association of Schools of Social Work, the Association of Social Workers, and the Children's Bureau.

2,225. Brent, Charles Henry
Papers. 1886-1949. 30 ft.
Open. Published guide.
Library of Congress, Manuscript Division.
A clergyman and author, Brent (1862-1929) was a bishop of the Protestant Episcopal church. His papers include correspondence of his sister [Miss] Helen C. Brent concerning a biography of him and the disposition of his papers. See *Bishop Charles Henry Brent: A Register of His Papers* (Washington: Library of Congress, 1959).

2,226. Bristol, Mark Lambert
Papers. 1887-1939. 47 ft.
Open. Published guide and register.
Library of Congress, Manuscript Division.
Papers of Bristol (1868-1939), a naval officer and diplomat who was US high commissioner to Turkey and commander of the Asiatic fleet, include those of his wife Helen (Moore) [Mrs. William Bailey] Thomas Bristol (1867?-1945), whom he married in 1908. Contained are correspondence, greeting and post cards, dance programs, and memorabilia documenting her life as a debutante in Mobile, AL, her marriage, and her activities and duties as the wife of a diplomat and naval officer in Turkey. Also included are engagement calendars and notebooks containing her diary entries, poems, and essays. See *The National Union Catalog of Manuscript Collections, 1959-1961* (Ann Arbor, MI: J. W. Edwards, 1962).

2,227. Brown, Marian Katherine
Papers. 1942. 1 item.
Open. No guide.
Library of Congress, Manuscript Division.
Poem about war by Brown, a poet, was written for Archibald MacLeish.

2,228. Browne, Charlotte
Papers. 1754-57. 1 vol.
Open. No guide.
Library of Congress, Manuscript Division.
Journal of a trip [Mrs.] Browne, an Englishwoman, made to the US contains details of travel and lodging conditions. She visited Bellhaven, VA; Fort Cumberland, MD; Frederick's Town, MD; Philadelphia; and New York.

2,229. Browning Family
Papers. 1824-1917. 2 ft.
Open. Published guide and register.
Library of Congress, Manuscript Division.
Included with papers of Browning family members is family correspondence, the majority of which is between Robert Lewright Browning (1803-50), a naval officer, and his wife Eleanor (Hanlon) Browning (1809-57) from 1834 to 1850 while he was on duty on various ships. In detailed letters she describes her activities in Dayton and Cincinnati, OH, and in Portsmouth, NH, during his long absences. Also included is her correspondence with her sons Robert Lewright Browning, Jr. (1835-60), who was a marine officer, and Charles Henry Browning (1846-1926), who was a genealogist; with her friend Mary Caldwell; and with naval authorities concerning her widow's pension. See *The National Union Catalog of Manuscript Collections, 1971* (Washington, DC: The Library of Congress, 1973).

2,230. Bruce, Blanche Kelso
Papers. 1878-90. 2 items.
Open. No guide.
Library of Congress, Manuscript Division.
Bruce (1841-98) was a US senator from Mississippi. Collection consists of one of his letters and a scrapbook of clippings about his wife Josephine B. (Wilson) Bruce and her reception in Washington society as the wife of a Negro senator. The Bruces were married in 1878.

2,231. Bruce Family
Papers. 1792-1892. 2 ft.
Open. Published guide.
Library of Congress, Manuscript Division.
Financial and other papers of the Bruce family include bills, receipts, and an inventory of the estate of Elvira A. (Cabell) [Mrs. James] Bruce (?-1858), which document expenses she incurred over nearly 20 years while living in Richmond, VA. Before marrying Bruce, she was married to Patrick Henry, Jr. See *The National Union Catalog of Manuscript Collections, 1963-1964* (Washington, DC: The Library of Congress, 1965).

2,232. Bryan, William Jennings
Papers. 1877-1940. 30 ft.
Open. Published guide and register.
Library of Congress, Manuscript Division.
Papers of Bryan (1860-1925), an orator, US secretary of state, and candidate for the presidency, contain correspondence with Evangeline Booth and with evangelist Aimee Semple McPherson. Also includes correspondence of his daughter Grace Dexter (Bryan) Hargreaves, who was compiling a biography of him, and a copy of that biography. See *The National Union Catalog of Manuscript Collections, 1959-1961* (Ann Arbor, MI: J. W. Edwards, 1962).

2,233. Bryson, Lyman Lloyd
Papers. 1908-60. 15 ft.
Open. Published guide and register.
Library of Congress, Manuscript Division.
Papers of Bryson (1888-1959), an educator, contain correspondence with Lucy Wilcox Adams of the California Association for Adult Education, Mary L. Ely of the American Association for Adult Education in New York, Theodora George of the League of Red Cross Societies in Paris, Anne E. M. Jackson of the University of California's extension division, and Mary Wallace Weir of the Near East College Association. See *The National Union Catalog of Manuscript Collections, 1962* (Hamden, CT: The Shoe String Press, Inc., 1964).

2,234. Buchanan, James, Family
Papers. 1825-87. 2 ft.
Open. Published guide, register, and index.
Library of Congress, Manuscript Division.
Correspondence and other papers of Buchanan (1791-1868) pertain primarily to the period prior to his election as US President. Also included is personal correspondence of his niece Harriet (Lane) [Mrs. Henry Elliott] Johnston (1830-1903), most of which dates from 1856 to 1860 when she served as mistress of the White House for her uncle. Her major correspondent was her close friend Sophie W. Plitt, a Philadelphian. Collection is also available on microfilm. See *The National Union Catalog of Manuscript Collections, 1962* (Hamden, CT: The Shoe String Press, Inc., 1964).

2,235. Buckalew, Charles Rollin
Papers. 1839-90. 300 items.
Open. Published guide.
Library of Congress, Manuscript Division.
A lawyer, Buckalew (1821-99) was a state legislator and US senator from Pennsylvania. His papers include a diary his wife Permelia Stevens (Wadsworth) Buckalew kept during her stay in Ecuador while her husband served there as US minister to Ecuador. She records her activities and comments on the country and its people. See *The National Union Catalog of Manuscript Collections, 1972* (Washington, DC: The Library of Congress, 1974).

2,236. Burke, Jane Revere
Papers. Ca. 1936. 1 vol.
Open. No guide.
Library of Congress, Manuscript Division.
An author and psychic, [Mrs. Nicholas P. Trist] Burke claimed to be able, at the bidding of her husband and others, to produce "automatic writing," to write in a language and script unknown to her. Resembling Chinese characters, the results of her writing were undecipherable but were claimed to be from Lemuria, the hypothetical continent in the Indian Ocean that is allegedly represented by Madagascar today. Collection consists of pages of Lemurian she produced by automatic writing, transcripts of meetings with a psychic describing automatic writing, and excerpts from her book *The Bundle of Life* (New York: E. P. Dutton & Co., 1934).

2,237. Burling, Judith
Papers. 1914-34. 1 ft.
Open. No guide.
Library of Congress, Manuscript Division.
Diaries of [Mrs. Arthur Hart] Burling (1900-), an Orientalist, concern travel, a sojourn in the Orient, and Chinese art, poetry, and theater. Also included is a book containing poetry copied by Burling, an address book, and family photos.

2,238. Burlingame Family
Papers. 1810-1937. 1 ft.
Open. Published guide and register.
Library of Congress, Manuscript Division.
Family papers include correspondence of Jane Cornelia (Livermore) Burlingame, who in 1847 married Anson Burlingame (1820-70), a US representative from Massachusetts and from 1862 to 1867 US minister to China. Addressed to her father Isaac Livermore, her sister Mrs. Leland, and her sons Edward Livermore Burlingame (1848-1922) and Walter Burlingame, her lengthy letters begin with her trip with her husband to Peking; she details her official and private activities and comments on the country and on the people, both natives and foreigners. Later letters are from London, Paris, Berlin, and St. Petersburg where Anson Burlingame was negotiating treaties for the Chinese government. Also includes correspondence of Jane Burlingame with her husband and with others about his death, letters by her mother Eunice Hovey Livermore, and correspondence between her parents. See *The National Union Catalog of Manuscript Collections, 1959-1961* (Ann Arbor, MI: J. W. Edwards, 1962).

2,239. Burt, Elizabeth Johnston (Reynolds), Family
Papers. 1797-1917. Ca. 200 items.
Open. No guide.
Library of Congress, Manuscript Division.
A volunteer nurse during the Civil War, Burt (1839-1926) married Andrew Sheridan Burt. Her family papers include the 346-page manuscript "An Army Wife's Forty Years in the Service, 1862-1902," which she wrote describing her life on the western frontier, and letters to her daughter Edith Sanders (Burt) [Mrs. Harry G.] Trout (1867-?). Also includes correspondence of her husband's grandmother Mary Gano and an item of Rachel Reynolds. Portions of Elizabeth Burt's manuscript are quoted at length in Merrill J. Mattes, *Indians, Infants and Infantry: Andrew and Elizabeth Burt on the Frontier* (Denver: Old West Publishing Co., 1960).

2,240. Cadwallader, Sylvanus
Papers. 1849-1904. 250 items.
Open. Published guide.
Library of Congress, Manuscript Division.
Included with the papers of Cadwallader (1825 or 1826-1905?), a journalist, Civil War correspondent, and public official, are papers of his wife Mary I. (Paul) Cadwallader, a suffragist and journalist, which contain clippings of articles she wrote for the *Milwaukee News* under the name Isabella on manners, suffrage and other women's rights, shorthand, and other topics. Also included is correspondence with her husband on the death of their daughter. See *The National Union Catalog of Manuscript Collections, 1966* (Washington, DC: The Library of Congress, 1967).

2,241. Cain, James Mallahan
Papers. 1925-60. 8 ft.
Open. Published guide and register.
Library of Congress, Manuscript Division.
Papers of Cain (1892-1977), an author who wrote *The Postman Always Rings Twice* (1934), *The Magician's Wife* (1965), and other novels, pertain primarily to his work in Hollywood. Includes correspondence with his mother Rose C. [Mrs. James W.] Cain and his sisters Rosalie (Cain) McComas and Genevieve Cain, all of whom were residents of Baltimore, and with Rae [Mrs. William] Blizzard, Ruth (Goodman) Goetz, Barbara Stanwyck, and Rebecca West. See *The National Union Catalog of Manuscript Collections, 1972* (Washington, DC: The Library of Congress, 1974).

2,242. Cairns, Huntington
Papers. 1925-64. 35 ft.
Access restricted. Published guide and register.
Library of Congress, Manuscript Division.
Personal and professional papers of Cairns (1904-), an author, lawyer, and government official who served as federal censor of imported books and movies, include correspondence with Lilian Gish, Edith Hamilton, Mary (Ritter) Beard, Frances P. Bolton, Clare (Boothe) Luce, Anaïs Nin, Katherine Anne Porter, Gloria Swanson, and others. See *The National Union Catalog of Manuscript Collections, 1966* (Washington, DC: The Library of Congress, 1967).

2,243. California Women of the Golden West
Records. 1941-50. 1 vol.
Open. No guide.
Library of Congress, Manuscript Division.
Scrapbook of the Women, a group organized in 1929 to recognize southern California women of civic, cultural, or educational achievement, contains biographical sketches of such members as Queen Walker Boardman, Mrs. William Montague Hunt, Margaret Edgerton Moore, Georgia P. Bullock, Mrs. Claude M. Sneden, and others.

2,244. Call, Annie Payson
Papers. 1914. 1 item.
Open. No guide.
Library of Congress, Manuscript Division.
Essay in which Call (1854-1940), an author, discusses ways to achieve peace with family, friends, and children and in social life, work, and religion.

2,245. Carlton, Caleb Henry
Papers. 1831-1954. 3 ft.
Open. Published guide and register.
Library of Congress, Manuscript Division.
Papers pertaining to the career of Carlton (1836-1923), a US Army officer, include letters he wrote to his wife Sadie (Pollock) Carlton during his Civil War service, even during the five months he was a prisoner of war in Libby Prison in Richmond, VA. Also included are diaries his wife kept while living with him between 1879 and 1894 in forts in Nebraska, Texas, and South Dakota; she lists monthly expenses, letters received and sent, and descriptions of her activities. Also contained is a biographical sketch of him by his daughter Mabel (Carlton) [Mrs. John K.] Horner (?-1961). See *The National Union Catalog of Manuscript Collections, 1966* (Washington, DC: The Library of Congress, 1967).

2,246. Carpenter, Esther Bernon
Papers. 1869-1927. 56 items.
Open. No guide.
Library of Congress, Manuscript Division.
Correspondence of [Miss] Carpenter (1848-?), an author, primarily concerns her writings on Rhode Island history. Many of the letters are from Oliver Wendell Holmes, who comments on articles she had written and sent him.

2,247. Carpenter, Frank G.
Papers. 1875-1960. 4 ft.
Open. Published guide and register.
Library of Congress, Manuscript Division.
Papers of Carpenter (1855-1924), a journalist, contain items pertaining to his daughter Frances Carpenter (1890-), who married William Chapin Huntington, and to the book *Carp's Washington* (New York: McGraw-Hill, 1960), which she edited and arranged. Includes correspondence between her and the *Washington Star* and reviews of her book. See *The National Union Catalog of Manuscript Collections, 1972* (Washington, DC: The Library of Congress, 1974).

2,248. Carrington, Elizabeth Jaquelin (Ambler) Brent
Papers. 1780-1823. Ca. 30 items.
Open. No guide.
Library of Congress, Manuscript Division.
A resident of Richmond and York, VA, [Miss] Ambler (1765-1847) married William Brent and then Edward Carrington. Correspondence to her sister Ann (Ambler) Fisher (1772-?), childhood friend Mildred (Smilks) Dudley, and English friend Frances Caines provides detailed descriptions of their lives. Also included is a manuscript novel entitled "Variety, or; the Vicissitudes of Life," in

which Elizabeth Ambler gives a fictionalized account of her experiences up until the time of her first marriage in 1785.

2,249. Carroll, Daniel
Papers. 1662-1910. 5 ft.
Open. Published guide.
Library of Congress, Manuscript Division.
Business papers of Carroll (1764-1849), a landowner and businessman, include correspondence, legal documents, and receipts concerning administration of his estate by [Miss] Anne C. Carroll, particularly the sale of property in Washington. Also included is an album of Clara Goszler, 1860-73, which contains poems and inscriptions by friends. See *The National Union Catalog of Manuscript Collections, 1963-1964* (Washington, DC: The Library of Congress, 1965).

2,250. Carter, Clarence Edwin
Papers. 1763-1956. 14 ft.
Partially restricted. Published guide and register.
Library of Congress, Manuscript Division.
Included with the papers of Carter (1881-), an editor, author, and historian who edited the *Territorial Papers of the United States,* are letters from his mother Anna Rogers Carter, 1914-25. See *The National Union Catalog of Manuscript Collections, 1959-1961* (Ann Arbor, MI: J. W. Edwards, 1962).

2,251. Carter, Thomas Henry
Papers. 1883-1917. Ca. 9000 items.
Open. Published guide and register.
Library of Congress, Manuscript Division.
A lawyer and US representative and senator from Montana, Carter (1854-1911) was also chairman of the Republican National Committee. His papers contain correspondence with his wife Ellen (Galen) Carter, most of which he wrote her while he was in Washington, and reminiscences of the Carter family by Julia C. Lang, which contain genealogical information and her recollections of growing up in Ohio, Illinois, Iowa, and Montana from the 1860s to 1880s. Collection is available on microfilm. See *The National Union Catalog of Manuscript Collections, 1959-1961* (Ann Arbor, MI: J. W. Edwards, 1962).

2,252. Cartter Family
Papers. 1836-93. Ca. 800 items.
Open. Published guide.
Library of Congress, Manuscript Division.
Most of this collection of family papers consists of papers of Nancy (Hanford) Cartter, a resident of Cleveland and Akron, OH, who was the wife of judge and diplomat David Kellogg Cartter (1812-87). Includes correspondence with her husband; with her sons David Kellogg Cartter, Jr. (?-1862?), a Civil War soldier, and William H. Cartter, a naval officer; with her brothers; her nephew; and with her mother Mrs. W. H. Hanford of Scottsville, NY. Also contained is a diary for 1858 to 1861 that Nancy Cartter began when her son William left home for a naval career; her entries record, almost exclusively, the loss she felt as a result of his absence. See *The National Union Catalog of Manuscript Collections, 1968* (Washington, DC: The Library of Congress, 1969).

2,253. Casson, Esley D. (Hake)
Papers. Ca. 1942. 4 items.
Open. No guide.
Library of Congress, Manuscript Division.
Poems about world peace were written by Casson, a poet and resident of Tacoma, WA.

2,254. Cater, Douglas J., and Cater, Rufus W.
Papers. 1859-65. 60 items.
Open. Published guide.
Library of Congress, Manuscript Division.
Douglas and Rufus Cater were brothers who were Confederate soldiers from Alabama. Their letters written from the field to their cousin [Mrs.] Fannie S. Cater reflect southern soldiers' view of Confederate military losses at the battles of Shiloh, Vicksburg, Atlanta, and Nashville. See *The National Union Catalog of Manuscript Collections, 1963-1964* (Washington, DC: The Library of Congress, 1965).

2,255. Caton, John Dean
Papers. 1826-95. 14 ft.
Open. Published guide and card index.
Library of Congress, Manuscript Division.
Papers of Caton (1812-95), a lawyer who served as chief justice of the Supreme Court of Illinois, contain a small amount of correspondence of his wife Laura A. (Sherrill) Caton (?-1892), whom he married in 1835. See *The National Union Catalog of Manuscript Collections, 1962* (Hamden, CT: The Shoe String Press, Inc., 1964).

2,256. Catt, Carrie Clinton (Lane) Chapman
Papers. 1848-1950. 13 ft.
Open. Published guide.
Library of Congress, Manuscript Division.
A lecturer and author, [Mrs. George William] Catt (1859-1947) was a leader in the women's suffrage movement. Correspondence, travel diaries for 1911 to 1923, a speech and article file, a subject file, and biographical material relate chiefly to women's rights, settlement of international problems, and the establishment of a world peace organization. Included is material concerning the Woman's Centennial Congress of 1940 and the National Committee on the Cause and Cure of War. Correspondents include Alice Stone Blackwell, Ida Husted Harper, Maud Wood Park, Rosika Schwimmer, and Edna Lamprey Stantial. Collection is available on microfilm. Taken from *The Blackwell Family, Carrie Chapman Catt, and the National American Woman Suffrage Association: A Register of Their Papers* (Washington: Library of Congress, 1975).

2,257. Champion, Deborah
Papers. 1775. 1 item.
Open. No guide.
Library of Congress, Manuscript Division.
Letter in which Champion, who was daughter of the Continental Army's commissary-general, describes to a friend her September night ride from Westchester, CT, to Boston to carry military dispatches to General Washington.

2,258. Chase, Lewis Nathaniel
Papers. Ca. 1892-1948. Ca. 89,000 items.
Open. Series description.
Library of Congress, Manuscript Division.
Papers of Chase (1873-1937), an author, editor, and educator, contain correspondence with his mother Augusta (Field) [Mrs. Ethan Allen] Chase, his sister Florence (Chase) Newell, his first wife Pearl Chase, his sister-in-law Mary Chase, and Anne A. Chase. Also included are papers of his first and second wives. He married Pearl Adell (Rowell) Mikesell Chase in 1906, was divorced from her in 1931, and married Emma Service (Lester) Chase in 1932.

Pearl Chase's papers consist of material from a trip through Brittany that she and Lewis Chase took in 1913, with business correspondence and receipts, drafts of her book about the trip *A Vagabond Voyage through Brittany* (1915), and hundreds of photos. Also includes other correspondence and writings, clippings, and printed matter.

Emma Chase was a poet and a Methodist Episcopal church missionary to China, where she served as an English teacher in a Shanghai girls school and college, ca. 1920-29. Her papers consist of correspondence with her sister Julia (Lester) [Mrs. William Bennett] Dillon, who was landscape architect for the city of Sumter, SC; with women friends in China after Chase returned to the US; and business letters concerning her submissions of poems for publication and concerning her association with the missionary board of the church. Also included are scattered diaries that she kept beginning in China and ending after her husband's death, copies of her manuscript and published poems, and clippings. Collection will be available on microfilm.

2,259. Chase, Salmon Portland
Papers. 1755-1874. 25 ft.
Open. Published guide and register.
Library of Congress, Manuscript Division.
Papers of Chase (1808-73), secretary of the treasury and chief justice of the US Supreme Court, contain letters to his third wife Sarah Bella (Ludlow) Chase (?-1852), whom he married in 1846, and to his daughters Janette (Chase) [Mrs. William S.] Hoyt and Catherine "Kate" Jane (Chase) [Mrs. William] Sprague (1840-99). Kate Sprague was her father's political confidante; in some of their correspondence they discuss his career. In other letters Chase advises her, on religious grounds, against seeking a divorce. See *The National Union Catalog of Manuscript Collections, 1962* (Hamden, CT: The Shoe String Press, Inc., 1964).

2,260. Cheney, John Vance
Papers. 1862-1927. 4 ft.
Open. Published guide and register.
Library of Congress, Manuscript Division.
Papers of Cheney (1848-1922), a librarian, poet, and essayist, contain letters he wrote discussing his work and giving instructions to his assistant and secretary Jessie Sherk. Also included is a letter in which Susan B. Anthony urges Cheney to buy *History of Woman Suffrage* for his library. See *The National Union Catalog of Manuscript Collections, 1971* (Washington, DC: The Library of Congress, 1973).

2,261. Chester, Sophy
Papers. 1867-70. 6 items.
Open. No guide.
Library of Congress, Manuscript Division.
Correspondence of [Mrs. Edw.] Chester, a missionary in South India, primarily concerns her brother's ill health but also contains mention of her mission work.

2,262. Child, Lydia Maria (Francis)
Papers. 1856-76. 26 items.
Open. No guide.
Library of Congress, Manuscript Division.
Correspondence of [Mrs. David Lee] Child (1802-80), an author and reformer, is addressed primarily to John Greenleaf Whittier. In her early letters she discusses her publication of the recollections of a slave girl; fugitive slaves; her early reservations about the Republican party, particularly Abraham Lincoln and William H. Seward; her respect for Charles Sumner; and the death of Colonel Robert Shaw, who commanded a troop of Negroes during the Civil War. In later, more personal letters, she writes of Whittier's work, mutual friends, and her husband David L. Child, whom she married in 1828.

2,263. Children's Crusade for Children
Records. 1939-40. 11 ft.
Open. Published guide and register.
Library of Congress, Manuscript Division.
Founded in the winter of 1939-40 by Marion G. [Mrs. Henry Seidel] Canby and Dorothy (Canfield) Fisher for the relief of children who were exiled from their homes by the war in Europe, the Crusade's purpose was to make American children aware of the blessings of living in a democratic country and to give them the opportunity to help less fortunate children by contributing pennies. Official records of the organization, which was run primarily by women; correspondence of Canby and Fisher; speeches and articles by Fisher; posters; photos; scrapbooks; and clippings. See *The National Union Catalog of Manuscript Collections,*

1962 (Hamden, CT: The Shoe String Press, Inc., 1964).

2,264. Choate, Joseph Hodges
Papers. 1745-1927. 16 ft.
Open. Published guide and register.
Library of Congress, Manuscript Division.
Papers of Choate (1832-1917), a lawyer, author, and diplomat, contain correspondence with his mother Margaret Manning (Hodges) [Mrs. George] Choate and with his wife Caroline Dutcher (Sterling) Choate, whom he married in 1861. Extensive correspondence between Caroline and Joseph Choate covers their entire married life and contains her descriptions of her activities in Wallingford, CT, Stockbridge, MA, Newport, RI, and Europe. Also included are her letters to her mother-in-law, condolences to Caroline Choate upon the death of her husband, and letters to their daughter Mabel Choate concerning posthumous publication of her father's memoirs. See *The National Union Catalog of Manuscript Collections, 1959-1961* (Ann Arbor, MI: J. W. Edwards, 1962).

2,265. Churchill, Ann Maria
Papers. Ca. 1830. 3 items.
Open. No guide.
Library of Congress, Manuscript Division.
Penmanship exercise notebooks and an exercise sheet of Churchill (1818?-?), a 12-year-old student who lived in Chatham, CT.

2,266. Churchill, Sarah J.
Papers. 1900. 600-page vol.
Open. No guide.
Library of Congress, Manuscript Division.
Journal that [Mrs.] Churchill (1835-1915) kept on her journey through Japan and China includes comments on the Boxer Rebellion, which broke out during her trip. Also contained are post cards, photos, and clippings.

2,267. Clark, Edward Tracy
Papers. 1923-35. 8 ft.
Open. Published guide and register.
Library of Congress, Manuscript Division.
Correspondence of Clark (1878-1935), a lawyer, businessman, and secretary to President Calvin Coolidge, includes letters from Coolidge, Mrs. Coolidge, and their sons. Taken from *The National Union Catalog of Manuscript Collections, 1962* (Hamden, CT: The Shoe String Press, Inc., 1964).

2,268. Clarkson, Levinus
Papers. 1772-93. 93 items.
Open. No guide.
Library of Congress, Manuscript Division.
Included with the business papers of Clarkson, a merchant and slave trader in Charleston, SC, are papers pertaining to business transactions Ann Van Horne of New York had with Clarkson in her capacity as executor of the estate of Clarkson's father-in-law David Van Horne. Included are correspondence, receipts, and legal documents.

2,269. Clay, Thomas H.
Papers. 1852-61. 15 items.
Open. No guide.
Library of Congress, Manuscript Division.
Primarily correspondence from Clay to his wife Mary Clay while he was in Washington nursing his father Henry Clay. He comments on his father's health, the 1852 Democratic convention, and her activities at their home in Kentucky during his absence.

2,270. Clay, Thomas J.
Papers. 1737-1927. Ca. 15,000 items.
Open. No guide.
Library of Congress, Manuscript Division.
Papers of the Clay family of Kentucky include letters from Henry Clay (1777-1852), US senator and secretary of state, to his wife Lucretia (Hart) Clay (?-1864), whom he married in 1799; papers of Susan M. (Jacob) Clay (1823-1905), who married Henry and Lucretia Clay's son James Brown Clay (1817-64), a lawyer, congressman, and diplomat, in 1843; and papers of Susan and James Clay's daughter Lucretia H. Clay. Susan Clay's papers contain correspondence with her father John I. Jacob, her father-in-law, husband, sisters, brothers, and children. In correspondence with her husband, a Confederate supporter who exiled himself to Canada from 1862 until his death, Susan Clay describes operating the family estate Ashland near Lexington, KY, and her eventual sale of possessions to pay debts; in later letters to her children and grandchildren, she interprets the Bible as a guide to living. Also included is a diary she kept in the form of letters during 1880 and 1881. Lucretia Clay's papers consist of correspondence, a diary in the form of letters to her brother in 1880 and 1881, a manuscript biography she wrote of her grandfather Henry Clay, and other items.

2,271. Coan, Titus
Papers. 1818-1923. 5000 items.
Open. Published guide and register.
Library of Congress, Manuscript Division.
Papers relating to the missionary work of Coan (1801-82), a Presbyterian minister, and of his wife Fidelia (Church) Coan (1810-72), whom he married in 1834, document the work of the Coans in Hilo, Hawaii, between 1834 and 1882. Includes correspondence of the Coans with each other; with their daughter Harriet Fidelia Coan (1839-1906), who was a teacher at Punahou, Hawaii; with Fidelia Coan's sister Mary (Church) Robinson, who was a missionary to Siam between 1834 and 1847; with other sisters and relatives; with other missionaries; with friends at home who supported missionary work; with Sophie Madeleine DuPont; and with Mary and Sarah Oliphant of Auburn, NY. Also included is Fidelia Coan's diary covering her trip to Hawaii and the early years of her marriage and missionary work, 1834-37; her diary for 1837 to 1841; a register of letters she sent; writings and poems by her; and items concerning the estate of her daughter. In addition, the book *Coan: A Memorial* by Titus Coan's second wife Lydia (Bingham) Coan and copies of *The Missionary Herald* are also contained. See *The National Union Catalog of Manuscript Collections, 1976* (Washington, DC: The Library of Congress, 1977).

2,272. Coblentz, Catherine (Cate)
Papers. 1936-47. 16 items.
Open. No guide.
Library of Congress, Manuscript Division.
Papers of Coblentz, an author who married William Weber Coblentz in 1924, relate to her children's book *Martin and Abraham Lincoln.* Includes correspondence with Martin's descendants and a draft of another reminiscence of a meeting with Lincoln.

2,273. Coleman, Juliet Cox
Papers. Ca. 1939. Ca. 100 items.
Open. No guide.
Library of Congress, Manuscript Division.
Research notes of [Mrs.] Coleman, an author and resident of Richmond, VA, pertain to her proposed book on John Laurens, who was a Revolutionary War soldier and envoy to France.

2,274. Columbia Broadcasting System
Records. 1929-60. 85 ft.
Open. Published guide and container list.
Library of Congress, Manuscript Division.
Radio scripts of entertainment programs CBS broadcast during the 1930s and 1940s include scripts from the programs "Sunday Morning at Aunt Susan's," "Maudie's Diary," "Stepmother," "Tillie the Toiler," "Mrs. Miniver," and "Young Love." See *The National Union Catalog of Manuscript Collections, 1971* (Washington, DC: The Library of Congress, 1973).

2,275. Connor, Jeannette Thurber
Papers. Ca. 1913-26. Ca. 900 items.
Open. No guide.
Library of Congress, Manuscript Division.
Papers of Connor (?-1927), an historian and translator who married Washington Everett Connor in 1913, consist of material relating to her research and writing on colonial Florida. Included are correspondence, research notes, manuscripts of her *Colonial Records of Spanish Florida* (1925) and other works, and copies of her translations.

2,276. Cosway, Maria Cecilia Louisa (Hadfield)
Papers. 1820-24. 3 items.
Open. No guide.
Library of Congress, Manuscript Division.
Letters of [Mrs. Richard] Cosway (1759-1838), an Italian painter, musician, and friend of Thomas Jefferson, are addressed to a Mr. Menasi, a Mr. Northcote, and a Mr. Stanley. Translations accompany the two letters written in Italian.

2,277. Cotton, Josiah Dexter
Papers. 1846-68. Ca. 350 items.
Open. Published guide.
Library of Congress, Manuscript Division.
Correspondence of Cotton (1822-?), a physician, primarily with his wife Ann (Steece) Cotton during his service as surgeon of the 92nd Regular Ohio Volunteer Infantry and of Turchin's Brigade. He comments on his care of the sick and wounded and on Sherman's campaign in Georgia. She describes her loneliness during his absence and her activities in Marietta, OH. See *The National Union Catalog of Manuscript Collections, 1963-1964* (Washington, DC: The Library of Congress, 1965).

2,278. Craven, John Joseph
Papers. 1849-1939. 75 items.
Open. Published guide.
Library of Congress, Manuscript Division.
Papers of Craven (1822-93), an inventor, physician, and army officer, contain letters to his wife Catherine S. (Tichenor) Craven, most of which he wrote in 1849 while he was on a voyage, as well as a diary she kept in 1863 when she was with her husband while he was serving as chief medical officer of the department of the South for the Union. She comments on naval movements, including those of the "Iron Clads." The Cravens were married in 1845. See *The National Union Catalog of Manuscript Collections, 1973-74* (Washington, DC: The Library of Congress, 1975).

2,279. Crawford, Laura Jones
Papers. 1859. 182-page vol.
Open. No guide.
Library of Congress, Manuscript Division.
Diary in which [Miss] Crawford (1838?-?), daughter of R. R. Crawford, who was mayor of Georgetown, DC, from 1857 to 1859, notes her daily activities and plans for future work. Some records of William H. Jones are included, for Laura Crawford kept her diary in his old account book.

2,280. Crawford, Rebekah, and Clarke-Smith, Linda
Papers. 1752-1926. Ca. 7 ft.
Open. No guide.
Library of Congress, Manuscript Division.
A music teacher, author, and philanthropist, [Miss] Crawford (1845-1934) raised funds for French victims of WWI and for crippled Italian soldiers. Her niece [Miss] Clarke-Smith, a linguist and an archaeologist, also was a social worker for crippled Italian soldiers. Correspondence, notes, Crawford family genealogical material, manuscript articles and plays, photos, scrapbooks, clippings, artifacts, printed matter, and other items pertain to Crawford's philanthropic work with the American

National Red Cross; the Duryea Committee of War Relief, which was organized by [Mrs.] Nina Larrey Duryea to collect supplies for war victims in France; and other groups. Material also pertains to Clarke-Smith's relief work and contains her records and receipts for administering a program for the soldiers and her letters to her aunt about this work. Also included are books by Crawford and by her sister Alethea (Crawford) Parcells Cox (?-1909) as well as biographical sketches of American authors by Cox.

2,281. Crèvecoeur, Michel-Guillaume St. Jean de
Papers. 1783-88. Ca. 50 items.
Open. Published guide.
Library of Congress, Manuscript Division.
A partial manuscript of an essay on Crèvecoeur, an author, by [Mrs.] Julia Mitchell Kunkle. Also includes his correspondence with such Americans as George Clinton, Robert R. Livingston, and George Washington, the originals of which are in the Public Library in Nantes, France. Taken from *The National Union Catalog of Manuscript Collections, 1970* (Washington, DC: The Library of Congress, 1971).

2,282. Croffut, William Augustus
Papers. 1774-1933. 12 ft.
Open. Published guide and register.
Library of Congress, Manuscript Division.
Papers of Croffut (1835-1915), an author, editor, and poet, contain papers of his wife Bessie B. Croffut, an author, and journals of Dr. Henry A. Robbins concerning medical practice in Europe during the 1870s. Bessie Croffut's papers consist of correspondence relating to her research on Ethan Allen Hitchcock and family, publication of her articles and of her husband's memoirs *Now I Recollect,* and the disposition of his papers; her research notes; poems; articles; and other writings. Also included are several letters to Hitchcock in which Mrs. Nathaniel Hawthorne discusses her thoughts on alchemy, mysticism, and religion. See *The National Union Catalog of Manuscript Collections, 1963-1964* (Washington, DC: The Library of Congress, 1965).

2,283. Crofts, Margaret (Lee)
Papers. 1917-52. 13 items.
Open. No guide.
Library of Congress, Manuscript Division.
Letters to [Mrs. F. S.] Crofts, who may have been an author, from Willa Cather, Kahlil Gibran, and Robert Penn Warren, primarily consist of social notes and some discussion of writings.

2,284. Cronyn, Hume, and Tandy, Jessica
Papers. 1934-60. 23,800 items.
Open. Unpublished guide.
Library of Congress, Manuscript Division.
Papers of actress Jessica Tandy (1909-) and of her husband Hume Cronyn (1911-), an actor, writer, and director, consist of correspondence; financial and legal documents; scripts for films, television, and the stage; engagement books; playbills; clippings; printed matter; and theater miscellany. Includes family letters, fan mail, and correspondence on acting with Virginia Kirkus Glick, Gertrude Wickes, Audrey Wood, Kitty Lilly, Marjorie Winfield Cahn, Estelle Buchele, Ruth Hedgpeth, and Kathleen Ward; material on casting, agents, and bookings; and information on the Actors Equity, the American Federation of Television and Radio Artists, the Theater Guild, and a strike by the Screen Actors Guild. Also included is material on red-baiting of actors on the Committee for Cultural Freedom. Tandy was married to Jack Hawkins in 1932 and to Cronyn in 1942; Jessica Tandy is her stage name.

2,285. Cuban Educational Association of the United States of America
Records. 1898-1954. 2 ft.
Open. Published guide and register.
Library of Congress, Manuscript Division.
Minute book; correspondence; canceled checks; student application forms, rosters, and photos; and a scrapbook of the Association, which was organized in 1898 to help Cuban and Puerto Rican students secure an education in the US. The group ceased to function in 1901 when its secretary-treasurer Gilbert K. Harroun died. Included is correspondence of his assistant [Miss] Laura Darby Conger with former students. See *The National Union Catalog of Manuscript Collections, 1962* (Hamden, CT: The Shoe String Press, Inc., 1964).

2,286. Cullum, George Washington
Papers. 1833-78. 27 items.
Open. No guide.
Library of Congress, Manuscript Division.
A US Army officer, Cullum (1809-92) served with the Army engineer corps at Fort Adams and Washington. Much of his correspondence is addressed to his sister Catharine (Cullum) Huidekoper and her husband Alfred Huidekoper while they were living in Meadville, PA.

2,287. Curtin, Mary Amelia
Papers. 1868. 1 vol.
Open. No guide.
Library of Congress, Manuscript Division.
Curtin (1836-87) was a resident of Washington; she later married Samuel Taylor. Consists of a photo and a scrapbook containing calling cards and invitations to social functions in Washington.

2,288. Cushman, Charlotte Saunders
Papers. 1828-76. 8 ft.
Open. Register.
Library of Congress, Manuscript Division.
Papers of Cushman (1816-76), an actress, consist of correspondence, primarily with family and friends; notebooks of her expenses; poetry; play and dramatic reading scripts; theater programs; and clippings about Cushman.

2,289. Cutter, Carrie Eliza
Papers. Nd. 1 item.
Open. No guide.
Library of Congress, Manuscript Division.
Biographical sketch of Cutter (1842-62), a Civil War nurse who traveled with 21st New Hampshire Regiment to Maryland and North Carolina. She died of fever contracted while she was nursing the troops.

2,290. Cutts Family
Papers. 1755-1905. Ca. 100 items.
Open. Published guide.
Library of Congress, Manuscript Division.
Family papers include correspondence of Anna Holyoke [Mrs. Samuel] Cutts (1735-1812), who was the daughter of the president of Harvard University. Her correspondents include her mother, sister, daughters, and son Charles Cutts (1769-1846), who became a US senator from New Hampshire. Also included is correspondence of Charles Cutts's wife Lucy Henry Southall Cutts (1786-1868) with her husband, brother, cousin, and sister-in-law. See *The National Union Catalog of Manuscript Collections, 1969* (Washington, DC: The Library of Congress, 1970).

2,291. Dana, Caroline
Papers. 1819. 1 vol.
Open. No guide.
Library of Congress, Manuscript Division.
Penmanship book of Dana (?-1822) while she attended Mr. Dunham's School in Windsor, VT, contains exercises dealing primarily with geography. The daughter of Lucy Dana, Caroline Dana married Russell Jarvis (1790-1853).

2,292. Daniels, Josephus
Papers. 1829-1948. 365 ft.
Open. Published guide.
Library of Congress, Manuscript Division.
Papers of Daniels (1862-1948), a journalist, secretary of the US Navy, and ambassador to Mexico, contain correspondence, invitations, and social notes of his wife Adelaide "Addie" (Bagley) Daniels (1869-1943), whom he married in 1888. In her letters to him she occasionally mentions her activities with the United Daughters of the Confederacy and with the YWCA establishing hostess houses during WWI at army and navy training centers, as well as her work as chairman of the Naval Auxiliary of the American National Red Cross and as US delegate to the 1920 World Woman's Suffrage Conference. Also includes her correspondence with her mother Adelaide (Worth) Bagley (1844-?), with her sister Ethel Bagley (?-1939) concerning activities in Washington, and with her sister Belle Worth Bagley (?-1939) concerning Belle Bagley's work as a statistician with the US Geological Survey during the 1890s and then with the US Bureau of Mines until the 1930s. See *Joseph Daniels: A Register of His Papers* (Washington: Library of Congress, 1976).

2,293. Daughters of the American Revolution
Records. 1938-40. 22 items.
Open. No guide.
Library of Congress, Manuscript Division.
Many of these scripts for radio broadcast were written by members of the Daniel Newcomb Chapter of the DAR in Yankton, SD, about pioneering in Dakota Territory during the 19th century. One sketch concerns Alice Bulfinch Cramer, and another, Sarah Wood Ward.

2,294. Daughters of Union Veterans of the Civil War
Records. 1922-27. 1 vol.
Open. No guide.
Library of Congress, Manuscript Division.
The Daughters, whose official title was National Alliance Daughters of Veterans, were organized in 1885 by daughters and granddaughters to commemorate their fathers who were loyal to the Union during the Civil War; the group functioned to aid War veterans and the widows and orphans of veterans. A scrapbook, compiled by the Daughters' national press correspondents Louise Chandler of Chicago and Mary M. North of Herndon, VA, consists of promotional items and clippings concerning the group's activities in each state.

2,295. Davenport, Marcia (Gluck)
Papers. 1932-67. 13 ft.
Open. Published guide and register.
Library of Congress, Manuscript Division.
Davenport (1903-), who was the first wife of Russell W. Davenport, is an author and music critic. Correspondence, notes, drafts, literary manuscripts, and clippings concern her books. Carol Brandt is one of her correspondents. Taken from *The National Union Catalog of Manuscript Collections, 1970* (Washington, DC: The Library of Congress, 1971).

2,296. Davis, Jefferson
Papers. 1835-1913. Ca. 630 items.
Open. Published guide.
Library of Congress, Manuscript Division.
Papers of Davis (1808-89), president of the Confederate States of America, contain correspondence and other items of his wife Varina (Howell) Davis (1826-1906), whom he married in 1845. Her correspondence to Mary Hunter Southworth Kimbrough, her husband Judge A. McC. Kimbrough, and Major William H. Morgan concern her husband's capture, conversion of the Davis residence Beauvoir into a home for Confederate veterans, and her life after her husband's death. Collection is also available on microfilm. See *The National Union Catalog of*

Manuscript Collections, 1963-1964 (Washington, DC: The Library of Congress, 1965).

2,297. Davis, Mary J.
Papers. 1863-65. 1 vol.
Open. No guide.
Library of Congress, Manuscript Division.
Remembrance book of Davis, a resident of Portageville, NY, contains inscriptions from her friends.

2,298. Dawes, Henry Laurens
Papers. 1833-1933. 30 ft.
Open. Published guide and register.
Library of Congress, Manuscript Division.
Papers of Dawes (1816-1903), for 37 years a congressman and senator from Massachusetts, include papers of his wife Electa (Sanderson) Dawes (1822-1901), whom he married in 1844, and of his daughter Anna L. Dawes (1851-1938), who was a journalist, author, Indian reformer, and antisuffragist. Electa Dawes's papers include correspondence by means of which she kept her husband informed about events in his district. Anna Dawes's papers include correspondence as well as diaries and a journal, which concern her education at Abbott Academy, her work as a journalist in Pittsfield, MA, her 1889 trip to California, her tour of Indian territory with her father in 1894 and 1895, her 1902 tour of Indian schools in the Midwest, and her work compiling a biography of her father. Her correspondents include ethnologist and Indian reformer Alice C. Fletcher, who describes working with Harvard University's Museum of American Archaeology and Ethnology, the US Bureau of Education, and the US Indian Service. Other correspondents are the Indian Rights Association; the YWCA; Iowa College (later Grinnell), which described and offered Anna Dawes a position as "lady principal"; the American Missionary Society, which explained its system of employing women as traveling secretaries; and Bliss Perry, who wrote about Anna Dawes's research on her father. See *The National Union Catalog of Manuscript Collections, 1962* (Hamden, CT: The Shoe String Press, Inc., 1964).

2,299. Deen, Mrs. E. W.
Papers. 1865. 1 vol.
Open. No guide.
Library of Congress, Manuscript Division.
Essay by Deen, an author, concerns her work "The Fixed Stars; or, The Goddess of Truth and Justice."

2,300. Deland, Margaret Wade (Campbell)
Papers. 1926-32. Ca. 3 ft.
Open. No guide.
Library of Congress, Manuscript Division.
[Mrs.] Deland (1857-1945) was an author. Manuscripts of her books *Captain Archer's Daughter* (New York: Harper & Bros., 1932); *The Kays* (New York: Harper & Bros., 1926); and *If This Be I, As I Suppose It To Be* (New York: D. Appleton-Century Co., 1935).

2,301. DeMille, Anna Angela (George)
Papers. 1947. 1 Hollinger box.
Open. No guide.
Library of Congress, Manuscript Division.
[Mrs. William Churchill] DeMille (1877-1947) was a lecturer. Manuscript of her biography of her father Henry George (1839-97), an economist and reformer, which is entitled *Henry George, Citizen of the World* (Chapel Hill: University of North Carolina Press, 1950).

2,302. Dewey, George
Papers. 1820-1919. 36 ft.
Open. Published guide and register.
Library of Congress, Manuscript Division.
Papers of Dewey (1837-1917), a naval officer and commander in the Far East during the Spanish-American War, contain the diary of his second wife Mildred (McLean) Hazen Dewey, whom he married in 1899. In her diary Mildred Dewey records her activities from 1900 to 1907 while living with her husband in Washington, her ill health, and the amounts she sent to charities. See *The National Union Catalog of Manuscript Collections, 1962* (Hamden, CT: The Shoe String Press, Inc., 1964).

2,303. Dickinson, Anna Elizabeth
Papers. 1860-1932. 12 ft.
Open. Published guide and register.
Library of Congress, Manuscript Division.
[Miss] Dickinson (1842-1932) was an abolitionist, actress, author, and suffragist. Correspondence, speeches, legal and financial documents, clippings, and other papers concern abolition and the rights of Negroes, woman suffrage, temperance, Republican party election campaigns, and the theater and lecture circuit. Also included are manuscripts for some of her plays, such as *Crown of Thorns* and *An American Girl,* and research notes of Giraud Chester, who wrote her biography *Embattled Maiden* (1951). Her correspondents include Susan B. Anthony, Fanny (Davenport) Price, and Wendell Phillips. Taken from *The National Union Catalog of Manuscript Collections, 1963-1964* (Washington, DC: The Library of Congress, 1965).

2,304. Dickinson, Charles Monroe
Papers. 1897-1923. 1 ft.
Open. Published guide.
Library of Congress, Manuscript Division.
Papers of Dickinson (1842-1924), a lawyer, editor, and diplomat, pertain primarily to his work as diplomatic representative to Turkey and Bulgaria from 1897 to 1908 and contain material relating to [Miss] Ellen M. Stone, an American missionary to Macedonia who was abducted in 1901 and held for nearly six months pending payment of ransom. Dickinson negotiated her release. Includes correspondence with Dickinson's superiors, Stone, and her abductors; reports; and depositions. See *The National Union Catalog of Manuscript Collections, 1962* (Hamden, CT: The Shoe String Press, Inc., 1964).

2,305. District of Columbia School
Records. 1848-52. 1 vol.
Open. No guide.
Library of Congress, Manuscript Division.
Register lists the names, addresses, and ages of girls and boys who attended an unidentified school in Washington. Several of the teachers are listed as "Sister."

2,306. District of Columbia Training School for Nurses
Records. Ca. 1881. 2 vols.
Open. No guide.
Library of Congress, Manuscript Division.
Receipt books of the Washington Training School for Nurses, founded in 1877, contain donors' names and descriptions of art objects Washington residents loaned to the School for a benefit exhibit. The institution's name was later changed to Capital City School of Nursing.

2,307. District of Columbia Woman's Relief Corps
Records. 1905-30. 1 vol.
Open. No guide.
Library of Congress, Manuscript Division.
Scrapbook contains annual reports, correspondence, a photo, and printed matter concerning the activities of the Corps, Department of the Potomac. Included are copies of proceedings of the annual convention in 1921 and of council meetings. Founded in 1883 as an auxiliary to the Grand Army of the Republic, the Corps was incorporated as the National Woman's Relief Corps; its state subdivisions were known as departments.

2,308. Dix, Dorothea Lynde
Papers. 1859-73. 2 items.
Open. No guide.
Library of Congress, Manuscript Division.
Consists of two letters from Dix (1802-87), a reformer, one of which is a note concerning an appointment, the other of which is a lengthy letter to the boys at the Illinois Institution for the Education of Deaf Mutes.

2,309. Dock, Lavinia L.
Papers. 1908-48. Ca. 150 items.
Open. No guide.
Library of Congress, Manuscript Division.
Papers of Dock (1858-1956), a nurse and author, include correspondence concerning the International Council of Nurses, the Henry Street Settlement, and the American National Red Cross. Correspondents include Gladys Stephenson, Cora Simpson, Alice Lewiston, George Dock, Anna Schwarzenberg, Isabel M. Stewart, Elizabeth Pickett Chevalier, Portia B. Kernodle, and Helen McDowell. Also included are clippings and newsletters of various nursing organizations.

2,310. Dock, Mira Lloyd
Papers. 1814-1947. 3 ft.
Open. Published and unpublished guides.
Library of Congress, Manuscript Division.
An educator, clubwoman, horticulturist, conservationist, and landscape artist, Dock (1853-1945) was a member of the State Forest Commission of Pennsylvania and chairman of forestry for the State Federation of Pennsylvania Women. Correspondence, family papers, maps, photos, clippings, and printed matter concern forestry, gardening, park development, city beautification, conservation, and nature study in Pennsylvania and elsewhere in the US, as well as in Germany. Also included is correspondence with Marion A. Crocker, Florence Bascom, and others. Taken from *The National Union Catalog of Manuscript Collections, 1959-1961* (Ann Arbor, MI: J. W. Edwards, 1962).

2,311. Dodge, Mary Abigail
Papers. 1856-77. Ca. 140 items.
Open. No guide.
Library of Congress, Manuscript Division.
An author, [Miss] Dodge (1833-96) wrote under the pseudonym Gail Hamilton. Correspondence, clippings of articles Hamilton wrote for *The Congregationalist,* and a photo.

2,312. Donelson, Andrew Jackson
Papers. 1779-1943. 6 ft.
Open. Published guide and register.
Library of Congress, Manuscript Division.
A soldier, diplomat, lawyer, and planter, Donelson (1799-1871) worked in various capacities for President Andrew Jackson. Donelson's papers include correspondence with his cousin and wife Emily Tennessee (Donelson) Donelson (1807-36). Her correspondence, some of which dates from the period when she served as mistress of the White House for Jackson, is with her parents Mary P. and John Donelson, her sisters, niece, and friends. Also included are papers of Andrew and Emily Donelson's daughter Mary Emily (Donelson) Wilcox (1829-?), which consist of an album in which her friends wrote poems or inscriptions, journal entries from a trip she made to Europe, engravings, and clippings. Correspondence, notes, and photos of the Donelsons' granddaughter Pauline Wilcox [Mrs. Moncure] Burke, which pertain to her research on her grandparents, are included as well. Entire collection is available on microfilm. See *The National Union Catalog of Manuscript Collections, 1962* (Hamden, CT: The Shoe String Press, Inc., 1964).

2,313. Doolittle, Lucy (Salisbury)
Papers. 1864-68. 10 items.
Open. No guide.

Library of Congress, Manuscript Division.
After obtaining funds through the New York National Freedman's Relief Association, [Mrs. Myrick H.] Doolittle (1832-1908) opened and taught in an industrial school for Negro women in Georgetown, DC. Papers consist of correspondence and a notebook in which she recorded class attendance and articles of clothing her students completed.

2,314. Dorman, Deborah
Papers. 1699-1754. 1 vol.
Open. No guide.
Library of Congress, Manuscript Division.
Notebook of Dorman contains fragmentary notes by her, Elizabeth Towne, Joseph Towne, and Topssule Howe.

2,315. Douglass, Frederick
Papers. 1841-1964. 7300 items.
Open. Published guide.
Library of Congress, Manuscript Division.
Papers of Douglass (1817?-95), an abolitionist, orator, journalist, diplomat, and public official, pertain to his work and interest in such issues as emancipation and women's rights and suffrage. Included is correspondence with members of the Webb and Richardson families, who collected money to buy Douglass's freedom. Also included is a biographical sketch of his first wife Anna (Murray) Douglass (?-1882), which was written by their daughter Rosetta (Douglass) Sprague, and papers of his second wife Helen (Pitts) Douglass, a lecturer and women's rights activist whom he married in 1884. Her papers contain correspondence; a diary she kept while traveling during 1886 in Europe and Africa with her husband; her speeches and writings on women's rights, lynching, her husband, and other topics; an account book; check stubs; and memorabilia. Her correspondence has been interfiled with that of her husband; their correspondents include Susan B. Anthony, Gertrude and Sarah Blackall, Julia Boardman, Mary Carpenter, Anna E. Dickinson, Amelia Douglass, Phoebe Hathaway, Catherine Impey, Elizabeth Palmer Peabody, Caroline F. Putnam, Anna W. and Lydia Shackleton, Estelle Sprague, Elizabeth (Cady) Stanton, Lucy Stone, Jane E. Thompson, Ida B. Wells, and Frances Willard. Also includes correspondence and financial notes of Fredericka D. S. Perry. Collection is available on microfilm. See *Frederick Douglass: A Register and Index of His Papers* (Washington: Library of Congress, 1976).

2,316. Duclaux, Mary
Papers. 1932-39. 33 items.
Open. No guide.
Library of Congress, Manuscript Division.
Agnes Mary Frances (Robinson) Duclaux (1857-1944) was a poet and author. Includes a letter and a manuscript with corrections of her unpublished book of poetry "More Ways Than One: A Book of Songs and Spiritual Dances."

2,317. Dumont, Henry, and Dumont, Nina (Webster)
Papers. 1905-38. 5 ft.
Open. Published guide.
Library of Congress, Manuscript Division.
Papers of Henry Dumont (1878-1942), who was a businessman and author, and of his wife Nina (Webster) [Mrs. Leslie D.] Smith Dumont (1887-), a statistician. Her personal and administrative correspondence and financial papers pertain to two studies she conducted in California during 1935 and 1936: one a study of cost of living; the other of occupation, mortality, and morbidity. Nina Dumont conducted statistical surveys for the US Bureau of Labor Statistics, the Public Health Service, the WPA Bureau of Home Economics, and other governmental agencies. See *The National Union Catalog of Manuscript Collections, 1959-1961* (Ann Arbor, MI: J. W. Edwards, 1962).

2,318. Dunlap, Katharine
Papers. 1941-55. Ca. 1 ft.
Open. No guide.
Library of Congress, Manuscript Division.
Manuscripts and proofs of [Mrs. Robert H.] Dunlap, an author. Several are of such of her works as *The Glory and the Dream* (New York: William Morrow & Co., 1951) and *Once There Was a Village* (New York: W. Morrow & Co., 1941).

2,319. DuPuy, Elisabeth
Papers. 1894-1924. Ca. 1 ft.
Open. Register.
Library of Congress, Manuscript Division.
DuPuy (1868-1932), who spelled her first name Elisabeth and Elisabethe, was an author, poet, and playwright. Correspondence; typescripts of plays, stories, and poems; a scrapbook of reviews of her book of poems *The Queen's Quire* (St. Louis: Woodward & Tiernan Printing Co., 1892); and an address book.

2,320. Eaton, Margaret L. (O'Neale)
Papers. 1873. 1 vol.
Open. No guide.
Library of Congress, Manuscript Division.
Manuscript autobiography of Eaton (1799?-1879), which was published as *The Autobiography of Peggy Eaton* (New York: C. Scribner's Sons, 1932). In her autobiography, Eaton spelled her maiden name O'Neil, but her father spelled it O'Neale. In 1816 she married John B. Timberlake (?-1828); in 1829, John Henry Eaton (1790-1856), who was Andrew Jackson's secretary of war and later governor of Florida and minister to Spain; and in the 1860s she married Antonio Buchignani.

2,321. Eddy, Mary (Baker)
Papers. 1866-1905. 5 items.
Open. No guide.
Library of Congress, Manuscript Division.
Eddy (1821-1910) was the founder of the Church of Christ, Scientist. A certificate, notes to a prospective student, and a letter in which she describes to Julius Dresser her slip on the ice in 1866 and then asks Dresser to take the place of her deceased mentor Phineas P. Quimby. In 1843 Mary Baker married George Washington Glover; in 1853, Daniel Patterson, from whom she was divorced in 1873; and in 1878 she married Asa Gilbert Eddy.

2,322. Eustis, William
Papers. 1761-1901. 1 ft.
Open. Published guide.
Library of Congress, Manuscript Division.
A physician, Eustis (1753-1825) was a US representative, secretary of war for Presidents Jefferson and Madison, minister to the Netherlands, and Massachusetts governor. His papers include letters of his wife Caroline (Langdon) Eustis (?-1865?), most of which were written while she was in the Netherlands with her husband, others of which concern her management of her property after his death. Also included are two 1808 letters in which Theodosia (Burr) Alston told William Eustis about her health while at Ballston Springs, NY. See *The National Union Catalog of Manuscript Collections, 1963-1964* (Washington, DC: The Library of Congress, 1965).

2,323. Evans, Mrs. Wealthy Cleveland
Papers. 1860s?. 1 item.
Open. No guide.
Library of Congress, Manuscript Division.
In this essay written as a letter, Evans uses Biblical evidence to support women's rights.

2,324. Everts, Lillian
Papers. 1937-56. 14 Hollinger boxes.
Open. No guide.
Library of Congress, Manuscript Division.
Everts was the pen name of Lillian (Epstein) [Mrs. Murray] Levine (1898?-1960), a poet and author. Correspondence concerning praise and criticism of her poetry, efforts to have it published, requests for copies, and awards it won. Also included are clippings of Everts's published poems and a few stories.

2,325. Ewing, Charles, Family
Papers. 1769-1950. 12 ft.
Open. Published guide and inventory.
Library of Congress, Manuscript Division.
Papers of the Ewing Family, the male members of which were lawyers, diplomats, and US senators and representatives, contain correspondence of attorney Charles Ewing (1835-83) with his wife Virginia Larwill (Miller) Ewing (1846-1937) and with his sisters Eleanor Boyle (Ewing) [Mrs. William T.] Sherman and Maria Theresa (Ewing) [Mrs. Clement F.] Steele. Also includes correspondence of his wife with children and friends, among them Charles Ewing II, Virginia M. Ewing, John K. M. Ewing, Maria Ewing, and Kathleen E. Daly. See *The National Union Catalog of Manuscript Collections, 1965* (Washington, DC: The Library of Congress, 1966).

2,326. Ewing, Jane
Papers. 1789. 1 item.
Open. No guide.
Library of Congress, Manuscript Division.
Letter in which Ewing describes to her brother a trip to Trenton, NJ, where women and girls in patriotic costumes greeted General Washington with a symbolic triumphal arch. A sketch of the arch, which was inscribed "the protector of mothers will also protect their daughters," accompanies her description of the pageant.

2,327. Ewing, Thomas, Family
Papers. 1754-1941. 123 ft.
Open. Published guide and register.
Library of Congress, Manuscript Division.
Papers of the Ewing family, male members of which were lawyers, diplomats, cabinet officers, and government officials, pertain to the Civil War, westward expansion, frontier life, and other matters. Includes correspondence between Ellen (Cox) Ewing (1833-1919), a resident of Lancaster, OH, and her husband Thomas Ewing II (1829-96) while he was serving as a Union officer; her correspondence with her children; and a long 1879 letter in which [Mrs.] Elizabeth L. Palmer describes to William Lloyd Garrison the atrocities of the "Red Shirts" in South Carolina. Also included is a series of letters between Maria (Boyle) Ewing (1801-64), who married Thomas Ewing (1789-1871) in 1820, and her daughter Ellen Boyle (Ewing) Sherman (1824-88), who married General William T. Sherman in 1850. Beginning when Ellen was away at school at the Academy of Visitation in Georgetown, DC, these letters continue through the early years of Ellen's marriage until her mother's death. The letters contain advice and news about Lancaster by Maria Ewing, discussion of their Catholic religion, and Ellen Sherman's descriptions of life in Civil War camps where she joined her husband. See *The National Union Catalog of Manuscript Collections, 1965* (Washington, DC: The Library of Congress, 1966).

2,328. Feamster Family
Papers. 1794-1967. 2 ft.
Open. Published guide and register.
Library of Congress, Manuscript Division.
Correspondence and financial papers of the Feamster and Cary families, including correspondence between William Cary (1798-1857), a lawyer and state legislator in Virginia, and his

wife Ophelia (Mathews) Cary, while she was living at their home in Lewisburg, VA, and 1830s correspondence in which his sisters Eliza (Cary) Green and Eleanor (Cary) [Mrs. Henry Colgate] Brish describe to him their feelings about leaving their homes in Maryland and moving to Ft. Ball, OH. Also includes correspondence of Martha (Alerson) [Mrs. William] Feamster (1797-1885) with her son Thomas L. Feamster (1829-1906), while he was serving as a Confederate soldier; letters from her brother and sister-in-law in Atchison, KS; a notebook she kept of family birth and death dates; and an account book of housekeeping expenses, 1908-17, which Maude Inez (Simmons) [Mrs. Claude N.] Feamster kept in San Antonio, TX. See *The National Union Catalog of Manuscript Collections, 1962* (Hamden, CT: The Shoe String Press, Inc., 1964).

2,329. Fisher, Albert Kenrick
Papers. 1827-1957. 24 ft.
Open. Published guide and register.
Library of Congress, Manuscript Division.
Papers of Fisher (1856-1948), a naturalist and author, contain correspondence with his mother Susan Elizabeth (Townsend) Fisher (1817-1906) about financial arrangements she made after the death of her husband Hiram Fisher. Also included are papers of Albert Fisher's daughter-in-law Anne (Benson) Fisher (1898-), an author and bacteriologist who married naturalist and author Walter Kenrick Fisher (1878-1953); these consist of a journal of her trip to Europe in 1923, reviews of her books, and letters of condolence on the death of her husband. See *The National Union Catalog of Manuscript Collections, 1962* (Hamden, CT: The Shoe String Press, Inc., 1964).

2,330. Fiske, Minnie Maddern (Davey)
Papers. 1884-1932. 56 ft.
Open. Published guide and register.
Library of Congress, Manuscript Division.
[Mrs. Harrison Grey] Fiske (1865-1932) was an actress. Correspondence; financial papers reflecting the expenses of theatrical production; drafts of speeches, articles, and books written by her and her husband; prompt books she annotated; and scrapbooks. Information on the controversy between the Fiskes and theatrical trusts is included. Gertrude Atherton, James M. Barrie, Jack London, and Florenz Ziegfield are among the correspondents. Taken from *The National Union Catalog of Manuscript Collections, 1962* (Hamden, CT: The Shoe String Press, Inc., 1964).

2,331. Flanner, Janet
Papers. 1925-67. 8 ft.
Open. Published and unpublished guides.
Library of Congress, Manuscript Division.
Includes correspondence received by [Miss] Flanner (1892-) and by [Miss] Solita Solano, both of whom were journalists, writers, and literary editors. Also included are articles by Flanner from *The New Yorker;* articles, poems, and lectures by Nancy Cunard, Isak Dinesen, and others; and printed works. Correspondents include Margaret Anderson, Kay Boyle, Elizabeth Jenks Clark, Gilbert Highet, Anita Loos, Gertrude Stein, and Alice B. Toklas. Taken from *The National Union Catalog of Manuscript Collections, 1970* (Washington, DC: The Library of Congress, 1971).

2,332. Fleetwood, Christian Abraham
Papers. 1797-1945. 1 ft.
Open. Published guide and register.
Library of Congress, Manuscript Division.
Papers of Fleetwood (1840-1914), a black Civil War soldier, Congressional Medal of Honor recipient, and civic leader, pertain to civic and social problems of the Negro community, particularly in the District of Columbia. Included are correspondence, a draft of a speech on literary clubs, photos, printed matter, and other papers of his wife Sara (Iredell) Fleetwood (1811-1908), a teacher and nurse whom he married in 1869. She served as superintendent of nurses at the Freedmen's Hospital in Washington and as a member of the District Nurses Board of Examiners. Also includes correspondence with her daughter Edith Fleetwood and an 1865 letter in which Ann Maria Fleetwood describes to Christian Fleetwood the reaction in Baltimore to Lee's surrender. Entire collection is available on microfilm. See *The National Union Catalog of Manuscript Collections, 1959-1961* (Ann Arbor, MI: J. W. Edwards, 1962).

2,333. Flexner, Abraham
Papers. 1870-1955. 9 ft.
Partially closed. Published guide and register.
Library of Congress, Manuscript Division.
Papers of Flexner (1866-1959), an author and educator, pertain to his interest in medical education. Also included are correspondence with his wife Anne (Crawford) Flexner, a playwright whom he married in 1898, and with his daughters Jean (Flexner) [Mrs. Paul] Lewinson, while she was a student at Bryn Mawr College, and Eleanor Flexner, who is an historian. See *The National Union Catalog of Manuscript Collections, 1966* (Washington, DC: The Library of Congress, 1967).

2,334. Foster, Isaac, Family
Papers. 1769-1898. 69 items.
Open. No guide.
Library of Congress, Manuscript Division.
Papers relating to the career of Foster (1740-81), a physician who served as superintendent of a military hospital, include correspondence of his second wife Mary (Russell) Foster with her mother and with him while he was in the army and she, in Boston.

2,335. Frank, Clara C. S.
Papers. 1880s?. 1 item.
Open. No guide.
Library of Congress, Manuscript Division.
Copy of a lecture that [Miss] Frank, a lecturer, gave on the eye and its diseases.

2,336. Frankfurter, Felix
Papers. 1864-1965. 105 ft.
Open. Published guide.
Library of Congress, Manuscript Division.
Papers of Frankfurter (1882-1965), a professor of law, associate justice of the US Supreme Court, and author, contain information on his career and on numerous organizations. Includes a substantial amount of correspondence in which he and his wife Marion (Denman) Frankfurter (?-1975), whom he married in 1919, discuss their personal feelings and philosophy as well as their activities. In her early letters, Marion Frankfurter describes her graduate work in social work and her work for suffrage and with the American National Red Cross war camp activities bureau; in later letters she discusses her research and editing her husband's articles. Her papers also include correspondence in which she wrote her mother about her activities at Smith College between 1910 and 1912 and correspondence in which her sister Helen Denman describes her work as a traveling secretary-organizer for the YWCA in 1923.

Felix Frankfurter's subject files contain information on Mary W. Dewson and the California minimum wage, 1923-25; Elizabeth Brandeis and the Minimum Wage Board, 1919-21; Josephine Goldmark, Florence Kelley, and the National Consumers League, 1915-49; Belle Moskowitz and the presidential elections of 1928 and 1932; and Alice H. Grady and savings bank insurance, 1929-36. His correspondents include Grace Abbott, Catherine (Drinker) Bowen, Ada L. Comstock, Dorothy Canfield Fisher, Ruth Gordon, Alice Hamilton, Freda Kirchwey, Frances Perkins, Cornelia (Bryce) Pinchot, Eleanor Roosevelt, and Dorothy Thomspon. See *Felix Frankfurter: A Register of His Papers* (Washington: Library of Congress, 1971)

2,337. Frémont, Jessie (Benton)
Papers. 1890, nd. 3 items.
Open. No guide.
Library of Congress, Manuscript Division.
Frémont (1824-1902) was an author who married John Charles Frémont in 1841. Consists of a letter about the career of her father Thomas Hart Benton, a letter about her life in retirement, and lecture notes.

2,338. French, Daniel Chester
Papers. 1848-1962. 29 ft.
Partially closed. Published guide and register.
Library of Congress, Manuscript Division.
Family correspondence and other papers relating to the career of French (1850-1931), a sculptor who created the seated figure of Abraham Lincoln for the Lincoln Memorial in Washington, and to that of his daughter Margaret (French) Cresson (1889-), a sculptor and author. Includes correspondence to his sister Harriette V. (French) [Mrs. Abijah] Hollis, his stepmother Pamela M. (Prentiss) [Mrs. Henry Flagg] French, and Evelyn Beatrice Longman. Also includes correspondence of his secretary Margaret F. [Mrs. Charles Davis] Jameson concerning his work, correspondence in which his sister Sarah (French) Bartlette describes to her brother William Marchant Richardson French her activities in Concord, MA, during the early years of marriage and motherhood, and reviews of and correspondence concerning the book *Memories of a Sculptor's Wife* (Boston: Houghton-Mifflin, 1928), written by his cousin Mary (French) French (1859-1939), whom he married in 1888.

Papers of Margaret Cresson largely concern her career. Includes correspondence with her parents; correspondence, 1919-32, between her and William Penn Cresson, whom she married in 1921; correspondence relating to Samuel Chamberlain's book *The Berkshires* (New York: Hastings House, 1956), for which she wrote two chapters; a manuscript and background material for her book *Journey into Fame: The Life of Daniel Chester French* (Cambridge, MA: Harvard University Press, 1947); and articles and speeches concerning sculpture. Daniel French's papers are available on microfilm. See *The National Union Catalog of Manuscript Collections, 1963-1964* (Washington, DC: The Library of Congress, 1965).

2,339. French-Sheldon, Mary
Papers. 1885-1935. Ca. 3 ft.
Open. Published guide.
Library of Congress, Manuscript Division.
French-Sheldon (1847-1936) was an author, lecturer, and explorer of Africa, particularly the Belgian Congo. Although she was born in the US, she spent most of her adult life in England where, in 1892, she was elected a fellow of the Royal Geographical Society. Correspondence; research notes; book, story, and play manuscripts; address book; passports; drawings; awards; photos; clippings; and books largely concern her African interests. Her works include the play *Salammbô; or, The Sacred Veil,* a book on the Belgian Congo, and a translation of Gustave Flaubert's *Salammbô.* Also included is information on her sister Belle French-Patterson. French-Sheldon was born Mary French; after her marriage to Eli Lemon Sheldon she used a hyphenated form of her name. See *The National Union Catalog of Manuscript Collections, 1959-1961* (Ann Arbor, MI: J. W. Edwards, 1962).

2,340. Furman, Bess
Papers. 1919-60. 32 ft.
Access restricted. Published guide and register.
Library of Congress, Manuscript Division.
A journalist and author, Furman (1894-1969) worked on the Kearney, NE, *Hub, The New York*

Times, and other newspapers. Her papers primarily concern politics in Washington but also include notes for and manuscripts of her books *Washington By-line* and *White House Profile.* Correspondents include Eleanor Roosevelt, Ruth (Bryan) Owen Rohde, Bess Truman, Malvina Thompson, and Edith Helm. Taken from *The National Union Catalog of Manuscript Collections, 1962* (Hamden, CT: The Shoe String Press, Inc., 1964).

2,341. Gallaudet, Thomas Hopkins, and Gallaudet, Edward Miner
Papers. 1806-1958. 5ft.
Open. Published guide and container list.
Library of Congress, Manuscript Division.
Papers of Thomas Gallaudet (1787-1851) and of his son Edward Gallaudet (1837-1917), both of whom were pioneers in education of the deaf, contain papers of Edward Gallaudet's biographer Maxine (Tull) [Mrs. Edmund Burke] Boatner (1903-). Includes correspondence concerning and page proofs for her book *Voice of the Deaf: A Biography of Edward Miner Gallaudet* (Washington: Public Affairs Press, 1959), articles she wrote on Gallaudet, and publicity for her book. See *The National Union Catalog of Manuscript Collections, 1959-1961* (Ann Arbor, MI: J. W. Edwards, 1962).

2,342. Galloway, Joseph, Family
Papers. 1743-1823. 260 items.
Open. Published guide.
Library of Congress, Manuscript Division.
Galloway (1731-1803) was a Loyalist and a member of the Continental Congress and of the Pennsylvania assembly. His papers primarily consist of correspondence and poems on women, love, or religion by his wife Grace (Growdon) Galloway (?-1782). In correspondence with her husband and her daughter Elizabeth Galloway, both of whom fled to New York and later London while Grace Galloway stayed at home to protect the family property, she describes attacks on their property, the need to smuggle her letters through enemy lines, and other difficulties experienced by Loyalists in Philadelphia. See *The National Union Catalog of Manuscript Collections, 1973-74* (Washington, DC: The Library of Congress, 1975).

2,343. Galloway, Maxcy, and Markoe Families
Papers. 1654-1888. 25 ft.
Open. Published guide and register.
Library of Congress, Manuscript Division.
Family papers contain correspondence of Mary (Galloway) Maxcy (1787-1849), who was the wife of attorney and politician Virgil Maxcy (1785-1844), and of their daughters Mary (Maxcy) Markoe, who married Francis Markoe (?-1871), and Ann Sarah (Maxcy) [Mrs. George W.] Hughes (1812-?). Written largely while Virgil Maxcy was away from home, these letters provide descriptions of the women's activities running the family estate Tulip Hill in Anne Arundel County, MD. Also includes a few letters between the sisters. See *The National Union Catalog of Manuscript Collections, 1970* (Washington, DC: The Library of Congress, 1971).

2,344. Gamow, George Antony, and Gamow, Barbara
Papers. 1915-75. Ca. 7500 items.
Partially closed. Published guide and register.
Library of Congress, Manuscript Division.
George Gamow (1904-68) was a scientist, author, and educator; Barbara (Perkins) Gamow (1905-76), whom he married in 1958, was an editor and translator who worked in the publishing business. Their professional papers contain information on theoretical physics, genetic coding, parapsychology, the role of women in society, and other topics. Her correspondence is with such writers, illustrators, and editors as Mary Bowen, Kate Pinsdorf DePierri, and Hope Newell. Barbara Gamow was previously married to J. R. de la Torre Bueno, from whom she was divorced in ca. 1943. See *The National Union Catalog of Manuscript Collections, 1968* (Washington, DC: The Library of Congress, 1969).

2,345. Garfield, Harry Augustus
Papers. 1855-1961. 29 ft.
Open. Published guide and register.
Library of Congress, Manuscript Division.
Papers of Garfield (1863-1942), a lawyer, educator, government official, and son of President James A. Garfield, include correspondence in which his mother Lucretia (Rudolph) Garfield (1832-1918) discusses politics and intellectual pursuits. Also includes a notebook of her reflections on marriage, which she wrote for her children in 1912, and correspondence between her and her granddaughter Lucretia (Garfield) Comer (1894-1968), Harry Garfield's daughter who married John P. Comer in 1925. In these letters, Lucretia Comer describes her life at Bryn Mawr College and her thoughts and activities pertaining to WWI, peace, and social reform. Correspondence between Lucretia Comer and her mother Belle (Mason) Garfield (1865?-1944), whom Harry Garfield married in 1888, is included as well. These letters concern Comer's life at boarding school at St. Timothy's in Baltimore, her teaching and speaking tours for the Pine Mountain Settlement School in Pine Mountain, KY, and her biography of her father *Harry Garfield's First Forty Years: Man of Action in a Troubled World* (1965). Collection also contains correspondence of Garfield to his wife and correspondence with his sister Mary (Garfield) Stanley-Brown (1867-1947) and later with her husband Joseph Stanley-Brown, whom she married in 1888. Her letters concern her education in Cleveland and at boarding school at Miss Porter's in Farmington, CT. See *The National Union Catalog of Manuscript Collections, 1967* (Washington, DC: The Library of Congress, 1968).

2,346. Garfield, James Abram
Papers. 1831-81. Ca. 80,000 items.
Open. Published guide.
Library of Congress, Manuscript Division.
Papers of President Garfield (1831-81) contain correspondence with Lucretia (Rudolph) Garfield (1832-1918), whom he married in 1858, from the years of their courtship when she was a teacher in Ravenna, OH, until their later years when she lived in Hiram, OH, and he, in Washington. Also includes his correspondence with his mother Eliza (Ballou) [Mrs. Abram] Garfield (1801-88), who was a resident of Solon, OH; with his daughter Mary (Garfield) [Mrs. Joseph] Stanley-Brown (1867-1947); and with Susan B. Anthony, Almeda A. Booth, Anna T. Boynton, Mary Fuller, Annie E. Hull, Maria Learned, Lucy Stone, and Frances Willard. Collection also contains diaries in which his mother recorded her activities and feelings during the 1860s and '70s, an autobiographical sketch discussing her religion Disciples of Christ and other subjects, and books in which his daughter noted her music lesson assignments and the time she practiced. All the material is available on microfilm. See *Index to the James A. Garfield Papers* (Washington: Library of Congress, 1973).

2,347. Garfield, James Rudolph
Papers. 1879-1950. 98 ft.
Open. Published guide and register.
Library of Congress, Manuscript Division.
A son of President James A. Garfield, James R. Garfield (1865-1950) was a lawyer, politician, and government official. His papers include correspondence with his mother Lucretia (Rudolph) Garfield as well as papers pertaining to the personal life and social reform activities of his wife Helen (Newell) Garfield (1866-1930), whom he married in 1890. Contains correspondence with her husband and her mother-in-law, diaries for 1881 to 1915, visiting notebooks, speeches and articles, photos, clippings, and printed matter. Helen Garfield shared her husband's interest in progressive Republican politics. While living in Washington with her husband between 1902 and 1909, she became active in the Visiting Nurses Association. After returning to live in Mentor, OH, she helped found the Cleveland Association for the Hard of Hearing and chaired local chapters of the Belgian Relief Fund in 1914 and the Fatherless Children of France in ca. 1920. See *The National Union Catalog of Manuscript Collections, 1967* (Washington, DC: The Library of Congress, 1968).

2,348. Garfield, Lucretia (Rudolph)
Papers. 1807-1958. 70 ft.
Access restricted. Published and unpublished guides.
Library of Congress, Manuscript Division.
Garfield (1832-1918) was the wife of US President James A. Garfield. Correspondence, biographical material, memorial poetry, addresses, articles, family papers, photos, scrapbooks, clippings, and other items pertain to the assassination of President Garfield and to Lucretia Garfield's interest in genealogy, literature, and the publication of her husband's works and his biography *The Life and Letters of James Abram Garfield* (1925) by Theodore Clarke Smith. Includes correspondence of James and Lucretia Garfield's children Abram Garfield, Irvin McDowell Garfield, and Mary (Garfield) Stanley-Brown and of other family members. Taken from *The National Union Catalog of Manuscript Collections, 1967* (Washington, DC: The Library of Congress, 1968).

2,349. Garson, Barbara
Papers. Ca. 1966. 1 item.
Open. No guide.
Library of Congress, Manuscript Division.
Manuscript play "MacBird" by Garson, an author who lived in Berkeley, CA, pertains to the career of Lyndon B. Johnson from the Democratic National Convention of 1960 until the first years of his presidency.

2,350. Gates, Ellen M. (Huntington)
Papers. 1880. 1 item.
Open. No guide.
Library of Congress, Manuscript Division.
Letter by Gates (1845-1920), an author of hymns who married J. E. Gates in 1861, contains an autobiographical sketch that includes the dates she composed hymns.

2,351. Gates, Isabel Likins
Papers. 1919. 1 item.
Open. No guide.
Library of Congress, Manuscript Division.
A poem in which Gates, a poet affiliated with the Grand Army of the Republic, commemorates the bravery of the American Legion in WWI.

2,352. George, Emma L.
Papers. 1915-20. 52 items.
Open. No guide.
Library of Congress, Manuscript Division.
Papers of George relate to her WWI relief activities, particularly to her association with the Woman's Land Army of America, which recruited and trained women to work farms during the absence of the men. Includes letters from appreciative farmers, poems and songs about the "farmerettes," schedules of farm work for women in various states, and recruiting and training material. Also includes correspondence from the American Society for the Relief of French War Orphans about George's adoption of an orphan, letters about her work from the Duryea American Relief Clearing House, and information on the National War Garden Commission of Washington, which sponsored victory gardens.

2,353. Gesell, Arnold Lucius
Papers. 1870-1961. 110 ft.
Partially restricted. Published guide and register.
Library of Congress, Manuscript Division.
Director of the Yale Clinic of Child Development, Gesell (1880-1961) was a child specialist who also worked with the Yale School of Medicine, the Connecticut Child Welfare Survey, and the Gesell Institute of Child Development. Papers include correspondence with Catherine Amatruda, Louise (Bates) Ames, Frances L. Ilg, Helen Thompson, and others with whom he worked, in addition to Charlotte Buhler and Glenna Bullis. Also included is correspondence of his wife and collaborator Beatrice (Chandler) Gesell (1875-1965), whom he married in 1909, and that of their daughter Katherine (Gesell) [Mrs. Joseph Whitelsen] Walden. See *The National Union Catalog of Manuscript Collections, 1966* (Washington, DC: The Library of Congress, 1967).

2,354. Gilbert, Cass
Papers. 1802-1961. 13 ft.
Open. Published guide and register.
Library of Congress, Manuscript Division.
Papers of Gilbert (1859-1934), an architect who designed the Woolworth Building in New York City, the US Supreme Court Building in Washington, and three state capitols, contain correspondence of his wife Julia (Finch) Gilbert (1862-1952). Includes correspondence between her and Gilbert before their marriage while she was living in Milwaukee and he, in St. Paul, MN; correspondence between the couple after their marriage in 1887; business correspondence concerning her work with the American Committee for Devastated France, 1919; with the women's division of the Architect's Emergency Committee, 1933; and items concerning her support for the Republican party. See *The National Union Catalog of Manuscript Collections, 1963-1964* (Washington, DC: The Library of Congress, 1965).

2,355. Gill, Daisy Sanial
Papers. 1941-47. 34 items.
Open. No guide.
Library of Congress, Manuscript Division.
[Mrs.] Gill was a poet who lived in Dade City, FL. Consists of manuscript poems, many of which she inscribed and sent to Archibald MacLeish, and clippings of published versions of some of her poems.

2,356. Gilman, Charlotte (Perkins) Stetson
Papers. 1914. 4 items.
Open. No guide.
Library of Congress, Manuscript Division.
Gilman (1860-1935) was a feminist, author, and lecturer. Correspondence with Alice Paul concerns a suffrage bill before the US House of Representatives and Gilman's inability to attend an advisory committee meeting. Gilman married Charles Walter Stetson in 1884, was divorced in 1894, and married George Houghton Gilman in 1900.

2,357. Gish, Lillian
Papers. 1920-70. 8 ft.
Open. Published guide and register.
Library of Congress, Manuscript Division.
An actress, [Miss] Gish (1896-) performed in such plays as *I Never Sang for My Father,* the movie *The Night of the Hunter,* and a television production of *Arsenic and Old Lace.* Scripts of plays, movies, and television scenarios, some of which are annotated; synopses of silent films; correspondence relating to her activities on behalf of the America First Committee; financial papers; interviews; and printed matter. Taken from *The National Union Catalog of Manuscript Collections, 1973-74* (Washington, DC: The Library of Congress, 1975).

2,358. Gist Family
Papers. 1776-1865. Ca. 100 items.
Open. Published guide.
Library of Congress, Manuscript Division.
Papers of members of this Maryland family include correspondence of Mary S. Gist with her nephews Richard J. Gist (?-1864) and Branford P. Gist and with her brother George W. Gist, all of whom apparently were Union soldiers during the Civil War. Their letters concern military campaigns, being wounded, and Mary Gist's work nursing the wounded. Also included are letters from Mordecai Gist (1743-92) to Polly Gist about military matters. See *The National Union Catalog of Manuscript Collections, 1968* (Washington, DC: The Library of Congress, 1969).

2,359. Goldmark, Pauline Dorothea, Family
Papers. 1865-1932. 16 items.
Open. No guide.
Library of Congress, Manuscript Division.
A social investigator, Goldmark (1873?-1962) was secretary of the National Consumers League. Includes correspondence from Joseph Teal about the issue of Catholicism in the 1928 election and from her brother-in-law Louis Brandeis about Thomas Jefferson and railroad passes that were issued to Goldmark for 1918 and 1919 in her capacity as manager of the women's service section of the division of labor. Also includes correspondence of her sister Josephine Goldmark (1877-1950), who also was a social investigator. Her correspondence includes letters from Louis Brandeis while she was at Bryn Mawr College and another he wrote in 1924 about Palestine, one letter each from Florence Kelley and Jane Addams about Josephine Goldmark's book *Fatigue and Efficiency* (1912), and a letter urging her to write a biography of Kelley.

2,360. Gordon, Ruth
Papers. 1924-69. 6000 items.
Open. Published and unpublished guides.
Library of Congress, Manuscript Division.
[Miss] Gordon (1896-) is an actress and playwright. Correspondence relating to her career and her plays, scripts, screenplays, biographical data, box office statements and other business papers, reviews, programs, and publicity material. Correspondents include Edna Ferber, Alec Guinness, Vivien Leigh, and Anita Loos. Taken from *The National Union Catalog of Manuscript Collections, 1973-74* (Washington, DC: The Library of Congress, 1975).

2,361. Gould, Alice Bache
Papers. Ca. 1833-1909. 17 containers.
Open. Container list.
Library of Congress, Manuscript Division.
An American historian, Gould (1869-1953) studied Christopher Columbus's voyages across the Atlantic Ocean. Much of her correspondence, diaries, research and lecture notes, legal papers, sermons, clippings, and printed matter relate to her study and particularly to Puerto Rico. Also includes her personal collection of publications about or published in Puerto Rico, correspondence concerning this collection, and notes on her visits to libraries in the Lesser Antilles.

2,362. Gratz, Rebecca
Papers. 1797-1860. 48 items.
Open. No guide.
Library of Congress, Manuscript Division.
A philanthropist, Gratz (1781-1869) helped found the Philadelphia Orphan Society in 1815, the Hebrew Sunday School Society in 1838, and the Jewish Foster Home; she is also said to have been the basis for the character of Rebecca in Sir Walter Scott's *Ivanhoe.* Includes letters to her niece Sarah and to Maria E. Fenno, who married Ogden Hoffman.

2,363. Greble, Edwin, Family
Papers. 1855-86. 82 items.
Open. Published guide.
Library of Congress, Manuscript Division.
Papers of the Greble family include diaries in which Mary L. Dreer, a young Philadelphia resident, recorded her social activities and courtship. Also included are letters Edwin Greble wrote his sister Sue Volkmar Greble while he was living in New Orleans from 1860 to 1865. Some of the family correspondence is available on microfilm. See *The National Union Catalog of Manuscript Collections, 1966* (Washington, DC: The Library of Congress, 1967).

2,364. Greely, Adolphus Washington
Papers. 1753-1959. 70 ft.
Open. Published guide and register.
Library of Congress, Manuscript Division.
An army officer, Greely (1844-1935) was also an explorer of the polar regions. His papers include correspondence with his wife Henrietta (Nesmith) Greely, whom he married in 1878. See *The National Union Catalog of Manuscript Collections, 1962* (Hamden, CT: The Shoe String Press, Inc., 1964).

2,365. Green, Constance (McLaughlin)
Papers. 1920-69. Ca. 22,000 items.
Open. Published guide and register.
Library of Congress, Manuscript Division.
An historian and author, Constance Green (1897-1975) married Donald Ross Green in 1921. Correspondence, research notes, manuscript speeches and writings, minutes, reports, charts, clippings, and printed material, most of which relate to her publications *Washington, Village and Capital, 1800-1878* and *Washington, Capital City, 1879-1950.* Also includes letters from Charles A. Lindbergh about her book *Vanguard: A History* and letters concerning *Notable American Women, 1607-1950.* See *The National Union Catalog of Manuscript Collections, 1976* (Washington, DC: The Library of Congress, 1977).

2,366. Greenewalt, Mary Elizabeth (Hallock)
Papers. 1918-42. Ca. 1 ft.
Open. Published and unpublished guides.
Library of Congress, Manuscript Division.
Known as Mary Hallock-Greenewalt, [Mrs. Frank Lindsay] Greenewalt (1871-1950) was a concert pianist and inventor of nourathar, which is the art of light-color play, and of the sarabet, which is the instrument on which nourathar is played. Correspondence, autobiographical data, research notes, speeches, manuscript articles, legal and financial papers, photos, clippings, and printed matter pertain to patents Hallock-Greenewalt obtained for her inventions. Also includes manuscripts of her books *Text Book for Fine Art of Light-Color Play,* "Nourathar" (1939), and *The Fine Art of Nourathar (Light-Color Playing).* See *The National Union Catalog of Manuscript Collections, 1976* (Washington, DC: The Library of Congress, 1977).

2,367. Gribble, Mary W.
Papers. 1886. 1 vol.
Open. No guide.
Library of Congress, Manuscript Division.
Journal kept by [Mrs. Harry] Gribble while she was traveling by steamer from San Francisco to Hawaii, Japan, and China.

2,368. Grimké, Sarah Moore
Papers. 1844-61. 5 items.
Open. No guide.
Library of Congress, Manuscript Division.
Correspondence of Grimké (1792-1873), an abolitionist and women's rights pioneer, is addressed to her friend Sarah M. (Douglass) Douglass, a free Negro who married William Douglass in 1855. Grimké's letters primarily consist of advice on the never-ending nature of women's

work, Douglass's future husband, her later marital unhappiness, and the need for Douglass to continue teaching in order to maintain her independence.

2,369. Gruenberg, Benjamin Charles, and Gruenberg, Sidonie (Matsner)
Papers. 1895-1965. Ca. 8000 items.
Open. No guide.
Library of Congress, Manuscript Division.
Benjamin Gruenberg (1875-1965) and his wife Sidonie Gruenberg (1881-1974) were writers and educators who specialized in the problems of children. Their professional papers consist of correspondence, diaries and journals, manuscript writings, notes, lecture and course material, financial papers, photos, scrapbooks, printed matter, and books. Also included are personal and family correspondence.

2,370. Guiney, Louise Imogen
Papers. 1884-1916. 2 ft.
Open. Published guide.
Library of Congress, Manuscript Division.
Correspondence and poems of [Miss] Guiney (1861-1920), a poet, essayist, journalist, and librarian. Correspondents include Frederick Holland Day, Louise (Chandler) Moulton, Alice Brown, Annie Fields, Mrs. Richard W. Gilder, Edmund Gosse, Alice M. Jordon, F. Eva Lewis, and Annie M. Stanton. Collection is available on microfilm. Taken from *The National Union Catalog of Manuscript Collections, 1968* (Washington, DC: The Library of Congress, 1969).

2,371. Hale Family
Papers. 1698-1916. 7500 items.
Open. Published guide and register.
Library of Congress, Manuscript Division.
Included are papers of Edward Everett Hale (1822-1909), an author and clergyman, which primarily consist of personal correspondence with his assistant [Miss] Harriet Elizabeth Freeman of Massachusetts. Detailing daily events, thoughts, and feelings, these letters also contain information on Freeman's trips through Europe, the US, and Canada and her activities in the movements for forest conservation and the rights of Indians. Freeman was financially independent. See *The National Union Catalog of Manuscript Collections, 1959-1961* (Ann Arbor, MI: J. W. Edwards, 1962).

2,372. Hale, Sarah Josepha (Buell)
Papers. 1856. 1 item.
Open. No guide.
Library of Congress, Manuscript Division.
Letter by which [Mrs. David] Hale (1788-1879), an author and editor, introduced a Mrs. Hicks of Virginia, who also was an editor, to a Miss Gilman in Charleston, SC.

2,373. Hall, Margaret (Hunter)
Papers. 1827-28. 267 pp.
Open. No guide.
Library of Congress, Manuscript Division.
Letters that [Mrs. Basil] Hall (1799-1876), a British traveler, wrote to her sister Jane (Hunter) [Mrs. D. C.] Guthrie while touring the US and Canada with her husband and daughter. In the form of a daily journal, the letters contain Hall's observations on American customs and way of life; she also discusses the rigors of traveling with an infant and nurse. The letters were edited by Una Pope-Hennessy and published as *The Aristocratic Journey: Being the Outspoken Letters of Mrs. Basil Hall Written During a Fourteen Months' Sojourn in America* (New York: G. P. Putnam's Sons, 1931).

2,374. Hall, Olivia Bigelow
Papers. 1869-1905. 300 items.
Open. Published guide.
Library of Congress, Manuscript Division.
Hall was a suffragist and resident of Ann Arbor, MI. Correspondence, photos, and printed matter relate to the woman suffrage movement. Correspondence with Susan B. Anthony is included. Taken from *The National Union Catalog of Manuscript Collections, 1962* (Hamden, CT: The Shoe String Press, Inc., 1964).

2,375. Hall, Sarah
Papers. 1813. 1 vol.
Open. No guide.
Library of Congress, Manuscript Division.
Geography and science exercise book that [Miss] Hall (1761-1830) completed while she was a student at Mrs. Seton's School in Cornish, NH.

2,376. Hamilton, Florence, Collection of Markhamiana
Papers. 1900-50. 17 ft.
Partially restricted. Published guide and inventory.
Library of Congress, Manuscript Division.
[Mrs.] Hamilton was a poet and secretary and lecture manager for poet Edwin Markham. Collection consists primarily of his writings and speeches, but it also contains correspondence of Hamilton with Markham and others, a typescript of her unpublished biography of him, photos of her, and books inscribed to her from Markham. Markham's correspondence with Mary Austin, Alice H. Bartlett, Anna Branch, Amelita Galli-Curci, Ida Benfield Judd, Caroline Stebbins, Mabel Wagnalls, and Myrtle Walgreen is included as well. See *The National Union Catalog of Manuscript Collections, 1959-1961* (Ann Arbor, MI: J. W. Edwards, 1962).

2,377. Hamilton, William
Papers. 1838-96. 300 items.
Open. Published guide.
Library of Congress, Manuscript Division.
Hamilton (1824-96) was a lawyer and Union officer. His letters to his mother Rosanna (Boyd) [Mrs. Hugh] Hamilton in Harrisburg, PA, which comprise the bulk of the collection, contain descriptions of battles, skirmishes, and the living conditions of soldiers during the Civil War. Also includes letters his brother John Hamilton wrote to their mother about family matters and the difficulties of living in Texas. Taken from *The National Union Catalog of Manuscript Collections, 1963-1964* (Washington, DC: The Library of Congress, 1965).

2,378. Hamlin, Charles Sumner
Papers. 1869-1955. 85 ft.
Open. Published guide and register.
Library of Congress, Manuscript Division.
Papers of Hamlin (1861-1938), a statesman who served as governor of the Federal Reserve Board, contain papers of his wife Huybertie (Pruyn) Hamlin (1874-1964), whom he married in 1898, and those of their daughter Anna Hamlin (?-1925). Includes correspondence in which Charles Hamlin discusses political events with his wife; their daughter's diaries and scrapbooks about showing horses and her other activities as a debutante in Washington; letters she wrote her mother about her social life; and condolences to the Hamlins on Anna Hamlin's death. Also included are articles that Huybertie Hamlin wrote using excerpts from her diaries about memories of Washington as a child and then of life in Washington from 1913 until 1925, with comments on politics as well as social and civic activities; her recollections of Franklin Delano Roosevelt; and an account of her six-week stay at the White House in 1941. See *The National Union Catalog of Manuscript Collections, 1959-1961* (Ann Arbor, MI: J. W. Edwards, 1962).

2,379. Hanna and McCormick Family
Papers. 1792-1951. Ca. 53 ft.
Open. Published guide and register.
Library of Congress, Manuscript Division.
Papers primarily pertain to the political activities of suffragist Ruth (Hanna) McCormick (1880-1944), particularly her successful congressional campaign in 1928, her unsuccessful Senate campaign, and her activities on behalf of the Republican National Committee. Includes correspondence about her campaigns, constituents' letters, and correspondence with her daughter Ruth McCormick; speeches of Ruth H. McCormick and of her husband Joseph Medill McCormick (1877-1925), who was a congressman and senator from Illinois; biographical data; campaign working papers; items from the Senate investigation of her primary campaign expenditures; proceedings; reports; and scrapbooks. Also includes correspondence of her husband and of her father Marcus "Mark" Alonzo Hanna (1837-1904), a US senator from Ohio. In 1931 Ruth (Hanna) McCormick married Albert G. Simms. See *The National Union Catalog of Manuscript Collections, 1969* (Washington, DC: The Library of Congress, 1970).

2,380. Hanschurst, Sarah
Papers. 1762. 1 vol.
Open. No guide.
Library of Congress, Manuscript Division.
Letter book of Hanschurst, a New York City resident, contains letters she wrote to Sally Forbes and other friends about friendship and beaux.

2,381. Hardee, Elizabeth B.
Papers. 1895. 2 items.
Open. No guide.
Library of Congress, Manuscript Division.
Hardee was a resident of Savannah, GA. Collection consists of poems she collected and copied for a history of the Confederacy and a letter in which she explained why she chose the poems she did.

2,382. Harriman, Florence Jaffray (Hurst)
Papers. 1912-50. 12 ft.
Open. Published guides and register.
Library of Congress, Manuscript Division.
Harriman (1870-1967) was an author and diplomat. Correspondence, memoranda, speeches, reports, articles, pamphlets, photos, clippings, memorabilia, and other papers primarily concern her service as minister to Norway from 1937 and 1941 and her subsequent activities in organizations for world peace. Also includes material relating to her work during WWI as a member of the Federal Industrial Relations Commission and as chairman of the American Federation of Labor committee on women in industry. Correspondents include Albert Einstein, Duke Ellington, Helen Hayes, George C. Marshall, and Eleanor and Franklin Delano Roosevelt. See *Florence Jaffray Harriman: A Register of Her Papers* (Washington: Library of Congress, 1958). See also *The National Union Catalog of Manuscript Collections, 1959-1961* (Ann Arbor, MI: J. W. Edwards, 1962).

2,383. Harris, William Torrey
Papers. 1866-1908. Ca. 13,475 items.
Open. Published guide and register.
Library of Congress, Manuscript Division.
Harris (1835-1909) was an educator, editor, and philosopher. His papers consist of notes and writings on the benefits of education for men and women and on other topics. See *The National Union Catalog of Manuscript Collections, 1959-1961* (Ann Arbor, MI: J. W. Edwards, 1962).

2,384. Harrison, Burton Norvell, and Family
Papers. 1812-1926. 21 ft.
Open. Published guide and register.
Library of Congress, Manuscript Division.
Harrison family papers are largely comprised of the papers of Constance (Cary) Harrison (1843-1920), who in 1867 married Jefferson Davis's private secretary Burton Harrison (1838-1904), a lawyer. Constance Harrison was an author; she wrote

satirically about southern and New York society and manners. Her correspondence and diaries reveal her private thoughts on these matters, whereas her article and book manuscripts show her public views. Includes family correspondence with Burton Harrison during the Civil War and after their marriage and with her mother, sons, and her cousin and daughter-in-law Hetty (Cary) [Mrs. Fairfax] Harrison; among other things, Constance Harrison describes her activities and frequent trips to England and Europe. Also includes her diary of a trip to Europe before marriage; a journal of her weekly visits to Bellevue Hospital wards as a volunteer in 1875 and 1876; and diaries detailing her activities in New York City between 1889 and 1904 and then in Washington from 1904 to 1910. Also contains drafts of articles and of her autobiography *Recollections Grave and Gay,* a genealogical study, a record book of funds she collected for New York charities by sponsoring entertainments, legal and financial papers, clippings, and business correspondence. Correspondents include Matthew Arnold, Andrew Carnegie, Frances F. Cleveland, Varina Howell Davis, Minnie Maddern Fiske, and Walt Whitman. See *The National Union Catalog of Manuscript Collections, 1970* (Washington, DC: The Library of Congress, 1971).

2,385. Harshaw, Ruth (Hetzel)
Papers. 1947-67. 4 ft.
Open. Published and unpublished guides.
Library of Congress, Manuscript Division.
Harshaw (1897-1968) was an author and publicist. Correspondence, scripts, program listings, and other material concern her radio programs "Battle of Books," "Carnival of Books," and "The Hobby Horse." Taken from *The National Union Catalog of Manuscript Collections, 1972* (Washington, DC: The Library of Congress, 1974).

2,386. Hawks, Esther H.
Papers. 1856-67. 515 items.
Open. Published guide.
Library of Congress, Manuscript Division.
Hawks was a nurse and a resident of Manchester, NH. Correspondence and other papers relate to work with her physician husband J. Milton Hawks caring for sick and wounded soldiers in military hospitals during the Civil War and establishing schools and distributing supplies throughout the South for the National Freedman's Relief Association. Most of the letters were written to Esther Hawks by wounded soldiers, but others are from her husband and from Alden M. Lander, who was a superintendent of women nurses. Taken from *The National Union Catalog of Manuscript Collections, 1963-1964* (Washington, DC: The Library of Congress, 1965).

2,387. Hawley, Mrs. Joseph Roswell
Papers. Ca. 1856-86. 1 ft.
Open. No guide.
Library of Congress, Manuscript Division.
A Civil War nurse who worked in the South, Harriet Ward (Foote) Hawley (1831-86) also was a philanthropist who organized and from 1882 until her death was president of the Washington auxiliary of the Women's National Indian Association. Correspondence, calling cards, biographical material, pamphlets, and clippings. Includes letters from her sisters and sisters-in-law during the War, from other family members, and from soldiers she helped.

2,388. Hay, John
Papers. 1785-1914. 35 ft.
Open. Published guide and register.
Library of Congress, Manuscript Division.
Papers of Hay (1838-1905), who had been assistant private secretary to Abraham Lincoln, include correspondence with his wife Clara (Stone) Hay (1849-1914) while he was ambassador to Great Britain from 1897 to 1898 and US secretary of state from 1898 to 1905. Also included are condolences to her on the death of her son in 1901 and on the death of her husband and letters concerning the collection of John Hay's letters for publication. In addition, an autograph collection relating to slavery in the US is included. Many of the items are available on microfilm. See *The National Union Catalog of Manuscript Collections, 1959-1961* (Ann Arbor, MI: J. W. Edwards, 1962).

2,389. Helm, Edith (Benham)
Papers. 1918-53. 7 ft.
Access restricted. Published and unpublished guides.
Library of Congress, Manuscript Division.
Helm (1874-1962) was social secretary at the White House during the Wilson, F. D. Roosevelt, and Truman administrations. Bulk of the collection is scrapbooks, but also included are correspondence, notes, photos, and memorabilia, some of which contain information on the Paris Peace Conference which President Wilson attended. Taken from *The National Union Catalog of Manuscript Collections, 1959-1961* (Ann Arbor, MI: J. W. Edwards, 1962).

2,390. Hickey, Agnes MacCarthy
Papers. 1926-36. 7 items.
Partially restricted. No guide.
Library of Congress, Manuscript Division.
Consists of poems by Hickey, a poet, which are tributes to Nathan Hale, Anne (Sullivan) Macy, and General Pulaski.

2,391. Hillcrest Children's Center
Records. 1815-1966. 25 ft.
Open. Published guide and register.
Library of Congress, Manuscript Division.
The center was founded in 1815 as the Washington Female Orphan Asylum to provide care and protection for homeless girls; it remained an orphan asylum until 1953 when it became an institution for the treatment of emotionally disturbed children. Minutes, correspondence, memoranda, committee and staff reports, and financial records of the board of lady managers, which supervised daily management of the Center and care of the children. Also included are legal documents, admittance and applications records, and financial data. See *The National Union Catalog of Manuscript Collections, 1972* (Washington, DC: The Library of Congress, 1974).

2,392. Hobart, Hannah (Pratt), and Family
Papers. 1783-89. 15 items.
Open. No guide.
Library of Congress, Manuscript Division.
Letters to [Mrs. Enoch] Hobart (?-1804), a Philadelphia resident, and to her son Enoch Hobart from Mary and Enoch Story, their son, and a Mr. and Mrs. Browne. Hannah Hobart was the mother of John Henry Hobart (1775-1830), a Protestant Episcopal bishop.

2,393. Hobby, Oveta (Culp)
Papers. 1941-52. Ca. 6 ft.
Open. No guide.
Library of Congress, Manuscript Division.
Papers documenting the work of [Mrs. William P.] Hobby (1905-) with the US War Department consist of correspondence, engagement calendars, invitations, transcript of an interview, photos, clippings, and printed matter such as yearbooks and army publications. Hobby was a US Army colonel and director of the WACs from 1943 to 1945. She also was publisher of the *Houston Post* and secretary of HEW from 1953 to 1955.

2,394. Hoffman, John Dell
Papers. 1847-69. 17 items.
Open. No guide.
Library of Congress, Manuscript Division.
Letters to Hoffman (?-ca. 1869), a New York resident, are primarily from his sister Sophy (Hoffman) Chester, who was a missionary in South India. She describes her trip to India, her mission work, and the dispensary her husband Edward Chester ran.

2,395. Holmes, Georgianna (Klingle)
Papers. 1887-1935. Ca. 1 ft.
Open. No guide.
Library of Congress, Manuscript Division.
A poet and author who wrote under the name George Klingle, [Mrs. Benjamin Proctor] Holmes (1842?-1940) was also a philanthropist; she founded the Larue Holmes Nature Lovers League as well as the Arthur Home for underprivileged children, which was later renamed the Arthur Home for Blind Babies. Includes detailed letters to Frank L. Stickney, biographical material, scrapbooks, photos, and clippings. Also includes poems and articles by George Klingle.

2,396. Holmes, John Haynes
Papers. 1906-67. Ca. 84,000 items.
Access restricted. Published guide, register, and index.
Library of Congress, Manuscript Division.
A Unitarian clergyman and author, Holmes (1897-1964) was involved with such organizations as the NAACP, the American Friends Service Committee, and the Foster Parents' Plan for War Children. Includes correspondence with Emma Goldman, Edith Lovejoy Pierce, Minnie Loewenthal, Lillian Laub, Henrietta Posner, Blanche G. Watson, and Ethelwyn Doolittle. Also includes personal correspondence with Mr. and Mrs. Hans Baasch, Cynthia and Gus Fraser, Anna Gillingham, Marie Heynemann, Margot Pieksen, Julia Way Wagner, and Mrs. H. Lincoln Way. See *The National Union Catalog of Manuscript Collections, 1971* (Washington, DC: The Library of Congress, 1973).

2,397. Hopkins, Charlotte Everett (Wise)
Papers. 1900-18. Ca. 2 ft.
Open. No guide.
Library of Congress, Manuscript Division.
A social reformer, [Mrs. Archibald] Hopkins (1851-1935) was chairman of the District of Columbia section of the woman's department of the National Civic Federation and chairman of the DC woman's committee of the Council of National Defense. Correspondence concerning reforms in such areas as housing, clean milk, schools as social centers, settlements, labor legislation, working conditions in stores and hospitals, loan sharking, garbage collection, prisons, playgrounds, juvenile delinquency, and war relief. Correspondents include Mary E. Lazenby, executive secretary of the Federation; Maude Wetmore, chairman of the Federation woman's department; Gertrude (Beeks) Easley; and Katherine Peckham. Also included are minutes, reports, press releases, circulars, pamphlets, and clippings concerning the Federation woman's department, the Council woman's committee, and the Associated Charities of Washington.

2,398. Hoskins, Katherine deMontalant (Lackey)
Papers. Ca. 1943-57. 1 Hollinger box.
Open. No guide.
Library of Congress, Manuscript Division.
[Mrs. Albert L.] Hoskins (1909-) is a poet. Manuscripts of *Villa Narcisse: The Garden, the Statues, and the Pool* (New York: Noonday Press, 1956) and other poems; a speech by Hoskins; a pencil sketch; and clippings of book reviews by Hoskins, which appeared in the *Washington Post.*

2,399. Howe, Julia (Ward)
Papers. 1861-1917. 2 ft.
Open. Published guide.
Library of Congress, Manuscript Division.
Howe (1819-1910) was an author and reformer.

Sermons, correspondence, addresses, lectures, poems, articles, and others of her writings on religion, literature, politics, suffrage, the Negro, education, and social work. Taken from *The National Union Catalog of Manuscript Collections, 1962* (Hamden, CT: The Shoe String Press, Inc., 1964).

2,400. Howland, Harriet
Papers. 1811. 1 vol.
Open. No guide.
Library of Congress, Manuscript Division.
Journal that [Miss] Howland kept while traveling in England with her sister and brother-in-law Abby (Howland) Woolsey and G. M. Woolsey. Howland later married James Roosevelt.

2,401. Howland, Marie (Stevens)
Papers. Nd. 6 items.
Open. No guide.
Library of Congress, Manuscript Division.
An author and reformer, Howland (1836?-1921) helped establish the Pacific City colony at Topolobampo Bay in Mexico and helped edit the colony's publication *Credit Foncier.* Manuscripts of "The S.P.C. A Bicycle Romance" and other stories by Howland as well as photos of her. Marie Howland married Lyman Case in the 1850s and Edward Howland (1832-90) in 1865.

2,402. Hoxie, Vinnie (Ream)
Papers. 1853-1937. 4 ft.
Open. Published and unpublished guides.
Library of Congress, Manuscript Division.
Papers of Hoxie (1847-1914), a sculptor, and of her husband Richard Leveridge Hoxie (1844-1930), a US Army officer, contain correspondence, business and legal papers, biographical and genealogical data, poetry by Vinnie Hoxie and Albert Pike, scrapbooks, printed matter, memorabilia pertaining to her work, and other items. Her correspondents include Olivia Briggs, Elizabeth B. Custer, Thaddeus Stevens, and Daniel W. Voorhees. Also included are letters about Richard Hoxie, which were written to his second wife Ruth (Norcross) Hoxie. Taken from *The National Union Catalog of Manuscript Collections, 1965* (Washington, DC: The Library of Congress, 1966).

2,403. Huebsch, Benjamin W.
Papers. 1893-1964. 17 ft.
Open. Published guide and register.
Library of Congress, Manuscript Division.
Papers of Huebsch (1876-1964), a publisher, contain literary manuscripts of Dorothea Angermann. Also includes correspondence with Jane Addams, Gertrude Atherton, Mary (Ritter) Beard, Pearl S. Buck, Babette Deutsch, Molly Dewson, Elizabeth G. Flynn, Charlotte P. Gilman, Ellen Glasgow, Emma Goldman, Sidonie Gruenberg, Lillian Hellman, Fannie Hurst, Fola La Follette, Amy Lowell, Mabel Dodge Luhan, Frances Perkins, Margaret H. Sanger, Sylvia Townsend Warner, Mary van Kleeck, and other authors and reformers. See *The National Union Catalog of Manuscript Collections, 1966* (Washington, DC: The Library of Congress, 1967).

2,404. Hume, Fannie Page
Papers. 1862. 1 vol.
Open. No guide.
Library of Congress, Manuscript Division.
Diary in which Hume (1838-65) recorded her daily domestic and social activities living in her family's home Selma near Orange, VA; in addition, she mentions soldiers passing through or staying in her home. Also includes genealogical material. In 1865 Hume married Carter M. Braxton.

2,405. Hunt, Virginia Livingston
Papers. 1882-1957. 15 items.
Open. No guide.
Library of Congress, Manuscript Division.
[Miss] Hunt was a resident of Washington. Accounts in which Hunt comments on the guests and conversation at functions given by Franklin D. Roosevelt, a book about a ship on which her father was ensign, and correspondence of her mother Mrs. Ridgely Hunt.

2,406. Ingersoll, Henrietta (Crosby)
Papers. 1838-90. 95 items.
Open. Published guide.
Library of Congress, Manuscript Division.
[Mrs. George W.] Ingersoll was an essayist and a resident of Bangor, ME, and Washington. Letters concerning personal and political matters from Ralph Waldo Emerson, Horace Greeley, Lucy Stone, and others. Also includes a letter to her husband from John P. Hale. Taken from *The National Union Catalog of Manuscript Collections, 1965* (Washington, DC: The Library of Congress, 1966).

2,407. International Council of Women
Records. 1931-54. Ca. 200 items.
Open. No guide.
Library of Congress, Manuscript Division.
Organized in 1888, the Council was a member of the peace and disarmament committee of the Women's International Organisations, and the bulk of the collection is minutes, correspondence, reports, and press releases of that committee. Also included is material on international conferences in which the Council participated, such as the League of Nations Conference for the Reduction and Limitation of Armaments, 1932-34; the League's International Institute of Educational Cinematography, 1934; the Conference of Consultative Non-Governmental Organizations, which was associated with the UN, 1949-54; and the Institute of Public Affairs at the University of Virginia, 1942. Also contains copies of the Council's *Bulletin.*

2,408. Izard, Sr., Ralph, Family
Papers. 1778-1826. Ca. 600 items.
Open. No guide.
Library of Congress, Manuscript Division.
Papers of Izard (1742-1804), a US senator, include weekly correspondence of his wife Alice (De Lancey) Izard with her daughter M. (Izard) Manigault, her daughter-in-law Elizabeth (Middleton) [Mrs. Ralph, Jr.] Izard, her granddaughter Ann Middleton Izard, and her son. These three generations of women spent their winters in Charleston, SC, and summers outside Philadelphia. In detailed letters, Manigault and Elizabeth Izard discuss their young families and social life, while Ann Izard writes of her activities during the years she was growing up. Manigault's letters also contain information on local reactions to the War of 1812.

2,409. Jackson, Ada
Papers. 1938. 1 item.
Open. No guide.
Library of Congress, Manuscript Division.
Consists of "Twenty Years After," a poem about war by Jackson, a poet.

2,410. Jackson, Shirley
Papers. 1932-65. 16 ft.
Open. Published and unpublished guides.
Library of Congress, Manuscript Division.
Jackson (1919-65) was an author who was married to Stanley Edgar Hyman. Correspondence, diaries, literary manuscripts, college notebooks, watercolors, pencil and ink drawings, and other papers. Taken from *The National Union Catalog of Manuscript Collections, 1969* (Washington, DC: The Library of Congress, 1970).

2,411. Jameson, John Franklin
Papers. 1822-1956. 40 ft.
Access restricted. Published guide and register.
Library of Congress, Manuscript Division.
Papers of Jameson (1859-1937), an historian, relate to the early history of the American Historical Association, the movement for the National Archives, and the *Dictionary of American Biography.* They also contain the files of Leo F. Stock and Elizabeth Donnan for their book *An Historian's World* (1956). Collection includes correspondence of Jameson with his wife Sara (Elwell) Jameson from the period of their courtship in 1892 and 1893 and his professional correspondence with Edith Abbott, Mabel T. Boardman, Caroline Hazard, Marion D. Learned, Ruth Putnam, Lucy Salmon, Mary E. Woolley, and others. See *The National Union Catalog of Manuscript Collections, 1971* (Washington, DC: The Library of Congress, 1973).

2,412. Jeremy, Lizzie
Papers. 1881-85. 7 items.
Open. No guide.
Library of Congress, Manuscript Division.
[Miss] Jeremy (1860-?) was an actress. Biographical material listing companies with which she played, playbills for productions she appeared in, and photos.

2,413. Johnson, Adelaide
Papers. 1875-1947. 40 ft.
Open. Published guide.
Library of Congress, Manuscript Division.
A sculptor and suffragist, [Miss] Johnson (1859-1955) created the monument to Susan B. Anthony, Lucretia Mott, and Elizabeth (Cady) Stanton, which is now located in the crypt of the US Capitol. Correspondence, diaries, speeches, articles, and notes include information on sittings by Anthony, John Burroughs, Ella (Wheeler) Wilcox, and others of whom Johnson sculpted portrait busts. Correspondents include Anthony, Ida Husted Harper, Emmeline Pankhurst, Alice Paul, May (Wright) Sewall, and Emma Cecilia Thursby. Taken from *The National Union Catalog of Manuscript Collections, 1963-1964* (Washington, DC: The Library of Congress, 1965).

2,414. Johnston, Frances Benjamin
Papers. 1885-1953. 12 ft.
Open. Published and unpublished guides.
Library of Congress, Manuscript Division.
[Miss] Johnston (1864-1952) was a photographer of Southern architecture and gardens. Correspondence, articles, lectures, a draft of her book *Early Architecture of North Carolina* (1941), financial papers, sketches, drawings, maps, and clippings. Also included are papers of her aunt Cornelia Juliaette (Benjamin) Hagan, histories and genealogical data of the William Bryant Johnston and Lewis Craig families, the constitution and an 1885 list of members of the Art Students' League in Washington, DC, and a scrapbook and other records of the Army and Navy Historical Association, Inc., of Washington. Frances Johnston's correspondents include Frances (Folsom) Cleveland, Margaret Mitchell, and Edward Bok. Taken from *The National Union Catalog of Manuscript Collections, 1966* (Washington, DC: The Library of Congress, 1967).

2,415. Johnston, Mercer Green
Papers. 1860-1954. 46 ft.
Open. Published guide and register.
Library of Congress, Manuscript Division.
An educator, social reformer, and author, Johnston (1868-1954) served as an Episcopal clergyman in the US and the Philippines. Includes professional correspondence with Elisabeth Gilman and family correspondence with his wife Katherin (Aubrey) Johnston, his mother, sisters, aunts, and nieces. See *The National Union Catalog of Manuscript Collections, 1959-1961* (Ann Arbor, MI: J. W. Edwards, 1962).

2,416. Jonas, Irene Iris
Papers. Ca. 1940s. 6 items.
Open. No guide.

Library of Congress, Manuscript Division.
Letters and poems by Jonas, a poet, deal with peace and Franklin Delano Roosevelt.

2,417. Keatinge, Harriette C. (Harned)
Papers. 1903-09. 6 items.
Open. No guide.
Library of Congress, Manuscript Division.
Reminiscences of [Mrs. Edward C.] Keatinge (1837-1909), a physician residing in Columbia, SC, in 1865, relate to her experiences during the burning of Columbia by General Sherman's army. After her husband Edward Keatinge, a bank note engraver for the Confederacy, was taken prisoner, she joined Sherman's army to travel to her family; she accompanied the army to Fayetteville, NC, and then traveled by steamer to New York. In ca. 1855 Keatinge had married Henry A. Veazie.

2,418. Keene, Laura
Papers. 1855-76. 107 items.
Open. Published guide.
Library of Congress, Manuscript Division.
[Miss] Keene (1826-73) was an actress and theater manager. Business records, including correspondence, trusts, insurance policies, contracts with players, and material on publishing ventures, as well as printed matter and clippings relating to her presence at Ford's Theater the night President Lincoln was assassinated. Taken from *The National Union Catalog of Manuscript Collections, 1963-1964* (Washington, DC: The Library of Congress, 1965).

2,419. Keller, Helen Adams
Papers. 1907-54. Ca. 1.5 ft.
Open. No guide.
Library of Congress, Manuscript Division.
Papers of [Miss] Keller (1880-1968), an author and lecturer, were compiled by Paul Sperry, minister of the General Convention of the New Jerusalem (Swedenborgian), on the basis of their mutual interests. Includes Sperry's correspondence with Keller and other Swedenborgians about the writing, publication, and translation of Keller's book *My Religion* (Garden City, NY: Doubleday, Page & Co., 1927); manuscripts of the book; and reviews. Also included are articles about Keller, particularly her 1953 trip to Mexico, Peru, Panama, and Brazil; photos of Keller; and manuscripts of works by Evelyn M. Watson, which were edited and prepared for transcription into Braille.

2,420. Kennan, George
Papers. 1840-1937. 44 ft.
Open. Published guide and register.
Library of Congress, Manuscript Division.
Papers of Kennan (1845-1924), an explorer, author, journalist, and lecturer, contain papers of his wife Emeline (Weld) Kennan (1854?-1940), who collaborated with him on his lectures and publications. Includes her general correspondence; correspondence with her husband, mother, and friends; a diary, 1895-96; and a journal she kept while accompanying her husband on a lecture tour in 1890. Also includes correspondence of Emeline Kennan with Mabel [Mrs. Alexander Graham] Bell and with the Bells' daughters Daisy Bell, who married David Fairchild, and Elsie Bell, who married Gilbert Grosvenor. See *The National Union Catalog of Manuscript Collections, 1959-1961* (Ann Arbor, MI: J. W. Edwards, 1962).

2,421. Kerr, Helen Culver
Papers. 1918-20. 2 vols.
Open. No guide.
Library of Congress, Manuscript Division.
A philanthropist, [Mrs. John Clapperton] Kerr was chairman of the musical committee of the National Aeronautic Committee, which was associated with the War Department Commission on Training Camp Activities; she also was chairman of the Bethany Day Nursery Shelter for children orphaned during the influenza epidemic and an American National Red Cross worker. Letters thanking Kerr for hospital supplies and for musical and athletic equipment she procured for soldiers, reports concerning the Shelter, and photos of war relief activities she initiated.

2,422. Kilmer, Joyce, and Kilmer, Aline (Murray)
Papers. 1915-31, nd. 9 items.
Open. No guide.
Library of Congress, Manuscript Division.
Both Joyce Kilmer (1886-1918) and his wife Aline Kilmer (1888-1941), whom he married in 1908, were poets and authors. Includes condolences to her on her husband's death and a notebook of poetry she wrote.

2,423. King, Georgiana Goddard, and Lowber, Edith Hunn
Papers. 1926. 159 pp.
Open. No guide.
Library of Congress, Manuscript Division.
King (1871-1939) was an author and professor at Bryn Mawr College; Lowber was a photographer. Manuscript of their book *Heart of Spain* (Cambridge, MA: Harvard University Press, 1941), for which King wrote the text and Lowber supplied photographs. The book was edited by Agnes Mongan.

2,424. Kingsbury, John Adams
Papers. 1840-1960. Ca. 51,000 items.
Open. Published guide and register.
Library of Congress, Manuscript Division.
Kingsbury (1876-1956) was a social worker who served with various organizations, including the American National Red Cross and the WPA. His papers contain information on public health, unemployment, venereal disease, war relief, welfare, world peace, and other topics. Correspondents include Pearl Buck, Katharine Cornell, Mary E. Dreier, Alice Hamilton, Helen Keller, Fola La Follette, Frances Perkins, Margaret Sanger, and Mary van Kleeck.

Also includes a book of poems his mother Annie (Adams) [Mrs. J. F.] Kingsbury copied while she was a student at Elmira College in Elmira, NY, from 1862 to 1863 and her letters to her sister while living in California from 1864 to 1883. In addition, collection contains correspondence of John Kingsbury with his wife Mabel (Glass) Kingsbury and poems she wrote. Also includes correspondence with their daughters Jean Kingsbury, while she was a student at Swarthmore College in Pennsylvania, and Virginia (Kingsbury) [Mrs. Belden] Hyatt, while she lived in Shady, NY, and correspondence with his sister Letty (Kingsbury) Thomas, who was a Seattle resident. See *The National Union Catalog of Manuscript Collections, 1963-1964* (Washington, DC: The Library of Congress, 1965).

2,425. Kite, Elizabeth Sarah
Papers. 1620-1946. Ca. 1 ft.
Open. No guide.
Library of Congress, Manuscript Division.
[Miss] Kite (1864-1954) was an historian. Research notes, genealogical material, articles, and photos she collected while writing articles on 18th-century America pertain primarily to the Carroll family of Maryland, John Fitzgerald, Pierre Charles L'Enfant, and the initiation of the Franco-American alliance in the 1770s. Also included are manuscripts of books.

2,426. Klees, Mrs. John
Papers. Nd. 1 item.
Open. No guide.
Library of Congress, Manuscript Division.
Play written by playwright Klees during the late 19th century pertains to the reaction of the women in one household to the beginning of the Revolutionary War.

2,427. Knapp, Charlotte C.
Papers. 1837. 1 item.
Open. No guide.
Library of Congress, Manuscript Division.
Letter in which Knapp, a missionary to Hawaii, describes in detail her mission work.

2,428. Knox, Rose Bell
Papers. 1930s. 20 items.
Open. No guide.
Library of Congress, Manuscript Division.
Knox (1879-) was the author of a children's book on the antebellum South. Her papers include the manuscript of her book, photo of a river boat, sketches of a cotton gin, and Confederate money.

2,429. Knox, William Franklin "Frank"
Papers. 1898-1954. 8 ft.
Open. Published guide and register.
Library of Congress, Manuscript Division.
Papers of Knox (1874-1944), a newspaper executive and statesman, contain papers of Annie (Reid) Knox (1876-1958), whom he married in 1898. Includes correspondence with her while he was in the army during WWI and she, in Manchester, NH; letters from him on later trips; and letters from her while she was traveling in Europe during 1927. Also includes Annie Knox's correspondence about the establishment of the Frank Knox Memorial Fellowship at Harvard University, a diary in which she recorded her activities in Washington during WWII while her husband was secretary of the navy, and a notebook listing guests, menus, and comments on luncheons and dinners that were given for the Knoxes. See *The National Union Catalog of Manuscript Collections, 1959-1961* (Ann Arbor, MI: J. W. Edwards, 1962).

2,430. Kraus-Boelté, Maria
Papers. 1904-53. Ca. 1.5 ft.
Open. No guide.
Library of Congress, Manuscript Division.
A kindergarten educator, Kraus-Boelté (1836-1918) helped found in 1873 and operate the New York Seminary of Kindergartners, a school for the education of kindergarten teachers that was based on the theories of Friedrich Froebel. Compiled by her student [Miss] Alice Hirsch, the collection contains Kraus-Boelté's letters to Hirsh, notebooks she kept of class lectures by Kraus-Boelté, art assignment sketchbooks of Hirsh, poems she wrote about her mentor, pamphlets about Kraus Alumni Kindergarten Association meetings, and articles about Kraus-Boelté. Born Maria Boelté, she married John Kraus in 1873 and was known as Mrs. Kraus-Boelté.

2,431. Kroll, Lucy
Papers. Ca. 1937-74. Ca. 80,000 items.
Open. No guide.
Library of Congress, Manuscript Division.
Kroll is a public relations executive. Her business papers relate to her career, the Lucy Kroll Agency, and to her clients, most of whom are theatrical or literary figures.

2,432. La Follette Family
Papers. 1781-1970. 597 ft.
Access restricted. Register.
Library of Congress, Manuscript Division.
Papers of Robert M. La Follette, Sr. (1855-1925); Belle (Case) La Follette (1859-1931), whom he married in 1881; and their children Robert M. La Follette, Jr. (1895-1953), and Fola La Follette (1882-1970), who married George Middleton in 1911. Robert La Follette, Sr., was a US senator from Wisconsin, founder of *La Follette's Magazine,* and a presidential candidate in 1924; his papers contain information on contemporary events, including woman suffrage. His son was also a US senator from Wisconsin.

Belle La Follette was a lawyer and suffragist. Correspondence, memoranda, biographical material, financial papers, research notes, book manuscripts, reports, and printed matter concern political and social movements of the Progressive era and after WWI, including suffrage, the civil rights of Negroes, child labor laws, education, social hygiene, the peace movement and disarmament, the Emily Bishop League for physical culture, the National Council for Prevention of War, the National LWV, the National Popular Government League, and the Women's International League for Peace and Freedom. Papers also document her involvement in the 1912 and 1924 presidential campaigns and her work with *La Follette's Magazine* and with *The Progressive*. Correspondents include Jane Addams, Emily M. Bishop, Alice Goldmark Brandeis, Elizabeth G. Evans, Vinnie Ream Hoxie, Helen Keller, and Emma Wold.

Fola La Follette was an actress and suffragist. Correspondence, research notes, notebooks, financial papers, interview transcripts, book manuscripts, and printed matter primarily pertain to her biography of her father *Robert M. La Follette* (1953), which was started by her mother. Also includes information on her career and suffrage work.

2,433. LaMotte, Ellen Newbold, Collection on the League of Nations Opium Committee
Papers. 1919-40. 36 containers.
Open. Container list.
Library of Congress, Manuscript Division.
[Miss] LaMotte (1873-1961) was an author, nurse, and social reformer. Material she collected because of her interest in curbing drug abuse, particularly opium addiction, consists of minutes and reports of the League of Nations Opium Committee proceedings and clippings from British, European, and Far Eastern newspapers about drug trafficking and addiction.

2,434. Lander, Jean Margaret (Davenport)
Papers. 1836-98. Ca. 1 ft.
Open. No guide.
Library of Congress, Manuscript Division.
An actress, [Mrs. Frederick West] Lander (1829-1903) also was a hospital nurse during the Civil War. Correspondence from admirers of her acting, letters about the death of her husband in 1862 and her claims against the US War Department for his back pay, a poem about her husband, reviews of her performances on stage, playbills and advertisements, and receipts of her father Thomas Donald Davenport.

2,435. Landon, Margaret Dorothea (Mortenson)
Papers. Ca. 1939-43. Ca. 1.5 ft.
Open. No guide.
Library of Congress, Manuscript Division.
[Mrs. Kenneth Perry] Landon (1903-) is an author. Manuscripts and reviews of her book *Anna and the King of Siam* (New York: John Day Co., 1944).

2,436. Lane, Gertrude Battles
Papers. 1915-35. Ca. 200 items.
Open. No guide.
Library of Congress, Manuscript Division.
Correspondence of [Miss] Lane (1874-1941) concerns her work as editor of *Woman's Home Companion.* She also was a publishing executive of the Crowell Publishing Co.

2,437. Laramore, Vivian Yeiser
Papers. Ca. 1942. 1 item.
Open. No guide.
Library of Congress, Manuscript Division.
Poem "Lincoln Walks Again" by Laramore, who was poet laureate of Florida.

2,438. Leadership Conference on Civil Rights
Records. Ca. 1963-74. 95 containers.
Open. Container list.
Library of Congress, Manuscript Division.
Established in 1949, the Conference is a coalition of groups organized to study the civil rights movement. Subject files on various titles of the Civil Rights Act and related legislation, financial records, correspondence, memoranda, reports, press releases, and printed matter. Includes correspondence with Coretta (Scott) King, Shirley Chisholm, Yvonne Braithwaite, Patricia Roberts Harris, Esther Peterson, and Mrs. Malcolm Peabody.

2,439. League of Women Voters of the United States
Records. 1892-1956. 612 ft.
Access restricted. Published and unpublished guides.
Library of Congress, Manuscript Division.
Detailed records include minutes of board meetings, open conferences, committees, and convention debates of the LWV; correspondence between members of the national board, state and local officers, public officials, and other organizations; material about the activities of the League's various departments of work; and political analyses. Correspondents include Carrie Chapman Catt, Edith Abbott, Grace Abbott, Jane Addams, Eleanor Roosevelt, Frances Perkins, Julia Lathrop, Sophonisba Breckinridge, Alice Hamilton, Florence Kelley, and Ruth Hanna McCormick. Taken from *The National Union Catalog of Manuscript Collections, 1962* (Hamden, CT: The Shoe String Press, Inc., 1964).

2,440. Lear, Susan
Papers. 1788. 4 items.
Open. No guide.
Library of Congress, Manuscript Division.
An annotated transcription of a journal kept by Lear (ca. 1770-?), a Philadelphia resident, during her trip to Boston before her marriage in 1788 to James Duncan. She mentions the people with whom she visited and stayed.

2,441. Lee and Palfrey Family
Papers. 1780-1934. Ca. 750 items.
Open. Brief description.
Library of Congress, Manuscript Division.
William Lee (1770-?) was secretary to the US legation in Paris and second auditor of the US. Contains his correspondence with his wife Susan (Palfrey) Lee (?-1834) and their daughters Susan Palfrey Lee and Mary Elizabeth Lee and correspondence of William and Susan Lee with his sister Mary (Lee) Tremain, his mother Mary Lee, his wife's brother John Palfrey, and her friend [Mrs.] Ann White Smith. Also included is a diary that Louise Kalisky, a German woman, kept of her activities while she was visiting the William Lee family in Washington during 1823.

2,442. Lee, Elsie Fullerton
Papers. 1877-1940. 5 items.
Open. No guide.
Library of Congress, Manuscript Division.
A resident of Baltimore, Lee (1878-1937) was a poet. Biographical notes and poems she wrote before her marriage to Paul Irwin Zimmerman. One of the poems concerns the death of her father.

2,443. Lee Family of Virginia
Papers. 1700-1935. Ca. 860 items.
Open. No guide.
Library of Congress, Manuscript Division.
Correspondence of this family, male members of which were soldiers and statesmen, was primarily collected by [Miss] Ethel Armes while preparing *Stratford Hall: The Great House of the Lees* (Richmond, VA: Garrett and Massie, 1935). Correspondents include Elizabeth Collins [Mrs. Richard Bland] Lee, Eleanor Calvert [Mrs. David] Stuart, Cornelia Lee [Mrs. John] Hopkins (1780-1815), Lucy Lee [Mrs. Bernard] Carter, Ann Hill Carter [Mrs. Henry] Lee, Mary (Custis) [Mrs. Robert E.] Lee, and Nancy Shippen. Also includes correspondence of Eleanor Berry, a slave who was owned and freed by Elizabeth Lee.

2,444. Lee, Mary Jane Charlton (Greenhow)
Papers. 1837-65. 380-page vol.
Open. No guide.
Library of Congress, Manuscript Division.
Diary of [Mrs. Hugh Holmes] Lee (1819-?), a Confederate spy who lived in Winchester, VA, primarily concerns her activities during and comments on the Civil War. Lee was the sister-in-law of Confederate spy Rose (O'Neale) Greenhow (ca. 1815-64).

2,445. Lee, Mary Randolph (Custis)
Papers. 1823-73. 20 items.
Open. No guide.
Library of Congress, Manuscript Division.
Papers of Lee (1806-73), who married Robert E. Lee in 1831, consist of letters to "Letty," Benson J. Lossing, and others and a manuscript she copied or wrote about the French revolution and Napoleon Bonaparte.

2,446. Leland, Waldo Gifford
Papers. 1844-1966. 45 ft.
Open. Published guide and register.
Library of Congress, Manuscript Division.
Papers of Leland (1879-1966), an historian and archivist, include correspondence with his mother Ellen M. (Gifford) [Mrs. Luther E.] Leland while she was living in Newton Lower Falls, MA; with Gertrude (Dennis) Leland, whom he married in 1904; and with his sister Minerva Eliza Leland (1859-1926), who describes teaching at Newton High School, work with the Baptist Women's Missionary Society, and studying at the University of Chicago where Sophonisba Breckinridge was one of her professors. Also included are diaries in which his mother details her activities in 1867 and from 1873 to 1878; diaries, 1905-44, of his wife, the most detailed of which concern the Lelands' life in Paris during the 1920s; and poetry and articles by his sister, one of which pertains to her life as a student at Colby College during the 1880s and another of which contains information about the Sigma Kappa sorority at Colby. Part of the collection is available on microfilm. See *The National Union Catalog of Manuscript Collections, 1968* (Washington, DC: The Library of Congress, 1969).

2,447. Leslie Woman Suffrage Commission
Records. 1911-18. 1200 items.
Open. Published guide.
Library of Congress, Manuscript Division.
Correspondence, articles, reports, and press releases that were written by Ida (Husted) Harper in her capacity as chairman of the department of editorial correspondence of the Commission. Taken from *The National Union Catalog of Manuscript Collections, 1963-1964* (Washington, DC: The Library of Congress, 1965).

2,448. Lincoln, Abraham
Papers. 1833-1916. 41 ft.
Open. Published guide.
Library of Congress, Manuscript Division.
Correspondence and other papers pertaining to the presidency of Lincoln (1809-65) include correspondence with Jessie B. Frémont, Eliza P. Gurney, Mrs. S. Harlow, Emily Todd Helm, Mary Todd Lincoln, and Sarah Josepha Hale. Entire collection is available on microfilm. See *Index to the Abraham Lincoln Papers* (Washington: Library of Congress, 1960).

2,449. Lincoln, Mary (Todd)
Papers. 1861-1930. 17 items.
Open. No guide.
Library of Congress, Manuscript Division.
[Mrs. Abraham] Lincoln (1818-82) was First Lady from 1861 to 1865. Her letters contain

information on her endorsement of two men as loyal to the Union, her prediction of the election of 1864, her life after her husband's assassination, and her attempts to obtain a pension from Congress. Also includes a telegram from Abraham Lincoln to his wife about the departure of their son Robert Lincoln on a trip.

2,450. Lindbergh, Anne Spencer (Morrow)
Papers. 1943-44. Ca. 1 ft.
Open. No guide.
Library of Congress, Manuscript Division.
[Mrs. Charles Augustus] Lindbergh (1906-) is an aviator, poet, and author. Notes, drafts, manuscripts, dust jacket designs, and reviews of her book *The Steep Ascent* (New York: Harcourt, Brace and Co., 1944).

2,451. Lindsey, Benjamin Barr
Papers. 1838-1957. 142 ft.
Partially closed. Published guide and register.
Library of Congress, Manuscript Division.
Professional papers of Lindsey (1869-1943) pertain to his service as a judge and social reformer in Colorado and California; he helped develop the juvenile court system in those states. Topics include child welfare, child labor laws, penal reform, women's suffrage, birth control, marriage and divorce, sex education and hygiene, and the Women's Protective League. Correspondents include Jane Addams, Carrie Chapman Catt, Harriet Ford, Eleanor Roosevelt, Margaret Sanger, and Mrs. Frederic Schoff.

Also included are writings by Henrietta (Brevoort) Lindsey, whom he married in 1913. These consist of a manuscript of her play *"New Love"; A True Story of the "New Justice"* and a scenario for a play about white slave traffic. See *The National Union Catalog of Manuscript Collections, 1959-1961* (Ann Arbor, MI: J. W. Edwards, 1962).

2,452. Lippincott, Sara Jane (Clarke)
Papers. 1852-79. 4 items.
Open. No guide.
Library of Congress, Manuscript Division.
A journalist and lecturer, [Mrs. Leander K.] Lippincott (1823-1904) wrote under the pseudonym Grace Greenwood. Poem about her pen name, a document of citizenship, and letters, one of which concerns an article she wrote.

2,453. Litchfield, Grace Denio
Papers. 1870s-1902. 3 vols.
Open. No guide.
Library of Congress, Manuscript Division.
Diaries in which Litchfield (1849-1944), an author and poet, discusses her activities in New York and Europe from the 1860s through the 1880s and then in Washington after 1888. She also describes her writing and publication.

2,454. Logan, John Alexander, Family
Papers. 1847-1923. 61 ft.
Open. Published guide and register.
Library of Congress, Manuscript Division.
Papers of Logan (1826-86), a Union Army officer and US representative and senator, and of Mary S. (Cunningham) Logan (1838-1923), whom he married in 1855, pertain primarily to the Civil War and postwar period. Mary Logan served during the War as a nurse and as her husband's amanuensis; she campaigned for and advised him on his political career, and after his death she began a career of writing, editing, and lecturing. Her papers reflect these activities as well as her founding and participating in the Woman's Relief Corps of the Grand Army of the Republic, her presidency of the Ladies' Association of Garfield Hospital in Washington, her membership on the board of lady managers of the World's Columbian Exposition, her friendship with Clara Barton and association with the American National Red Cross, her work with the DC Belgian Relief Fund, and her support of woman suffrage. Includes professional correspondence; correspondence with her husband and with her daughter Mary (Logan) [Mrs. William F.] Tucker (ca. 1860-?), who was an author; speeches Mary C. Logan gave, many of which were addressed to women's groups or were about women; articles she wrote on subjects ranging from Civil War memorials to philanthropy to marriage; manuscripts of various of her writings, including *The Part Taken by Women in American History* (1912) and *Reminiscences of a Soldier's Wife* (1913); and scrapbooks she kept, most of which deal with the Spanish-American War in which her son John A. Logan, Jr. (1865-99), was killed. Also included are scrapbooks containing correspondence, invitations, programs, clippings, and memorabilia of her daughter Mary Tucker, which pertain to Tucker's childhood and family, activities of the GAR, and the Navy League of the United States. See *The National Union Catalog of Manuscript Collections, 1963-1964* (Washington, DC: The Library of Congress, 1965).

2,455. Lord, Mrs. William Wilberforce
Papers. 1863. 1 item.
Open. No guide.
Library of Congress, Manuscript Division.
Lord, a Confederate supporter, was the wife of a chaplain in the Confederate Army. In her diary she describes the six weeks she spent living in caves with her children and other families after their flight from Vicksburg, MS; the surrender of Vicksburg; her return to the city; and the destruction of her home and its contents by Union troops.

2,456. Louchheim, Kathleen "Katie" (Scofield)
Papers. 1914-74. 29.6 ft.
Access restricted. Published guide and register.
Library of Congress, Manuscript Division.
Papers relating to the work of [Mrs. Walter C., Jr.] Louchheim (1903-), a writer and public official, with the Democratic National Committee and the Department of State. She was director of women's activities and then vice-chairman of the Democratic National Committee between 1953 and 1961, consultant on women's activities for the Department of State in 1961 and 1962 and then deputy assistant secretary of state from 1962 to 1968, assistant to the director of the UN Relief and Rehabilitation Administration from 1942 to 1946, and ambassador and US board member of UNESCO in 1968 and 1969. Correspondence; unpublished plays, poems, and a novel by Louchheim; her published articles and speeches; family papers; working papers; scrapbooks of photos, clippings, mementos, and other items; and her book of poems *With or Without Roses* (Garden City, NY: Doubleday, 1966) and her *By the Political Sea* (Garden City: Doubleday, 1970). Includes Department of State material on welfare projects in foreign countries, programs relating to women, women's organizations, international cultural affairs, the Office of Community Advisory Services, and education. Also includes material about women's activities in the Democratic National Committee, the First Lady's (Lady Bird Johnson's) Committee for a More Beautiful Capitol, UNRRA, UNESCO, and Washington social and political life. See *National Union Catalog of Manuscript Collections, 1977* (Washington, DC: Library of Congress, 1978).

2,457. Low and Mills Family
Papers. 1795-1959. 8 ft.
Open. Register.
Library of Congress, Manuscript Division.
Papers of a New York merchant family engaged in Far Eastern trade primarily consist of correspondence and diaries of Ellen (Low) Mills (1827-98), who married Ethelbert Smith Mills in 1849. Her correspondents include her husband, her sons, and her sisters, including Harriet (Low) [Mrs. John H.] Hilliard (1809-77). Ellen Mills's diaries include a journal of a trip to Europe in 1846 and 1847, a diary of events in New York City during the Civil War and in Washington during Lincoln's inauguration, and 20 diaries recording her daily activities after the death of her husband in 1873. Also included is a journal Harriet Hilliard wrote for her sister about traveling to and living in Macao and China from 1829 to 1834 before her marriage; this detailed record of her daily activities indicates she was visiting a family engaged in trade. Correspondence of her daughter Mary (Hilliard) [Mrs. Stephen] Loines (1844-1944), a teacher, with Union officer George Haven Putnam is also included; he describes his experiences in the South during the Civil War and later in the publishing business. In addition, the collection contains a diary about the activities of Mary Loines's sister Frances "Fanny" Hilliard (1841-62).

2,458. Luce, Clare (Boothe)
Papers. 1923-68. Ca. 335 ft.
Access restricted. Register.
Library of Congress, Manuscript Division.
An author and playwright, Luce (1903-) was a congresswoman from Connecticut from 1943 to 1947 and US ambassador to Italy from 1953 to 1957. Papers deal primarily with her public life and literary, political, and diplomatic interests. Included are correspondence; biographical material; manuscript and printed speeches, articles, stories, plays, and reviews; research material; notes; legal and financial papers; reports, studies, and proceedings; engagement books; invitations; calling and greeting cards; photos; scrapbooks; clippings; and memorabilia. Also included are letters from military men and women to Luce as a member of the House Military Affairs Committee and information on aviation. After marrying George Tuttle Brokaw in 1923, she was divorced from him in 1929. In 1935 she married Henry Robinson Luce.

2,459. Lynd, Robert Staughton
Papers. 1922-67. 3 ft.
Open. Published guide and register.
Library of Congress, Manuscript Division.
Both Lynd (1892-) and his wife Helen (Merrell) Lynd (1896-) are social philosophers and educators. Correspondence, drafts and notes for major publications, lectures, research material on selected topics for the Lynds' Middletown studies, book and article reviews, clippings, and other papers concerning their careers. Taken from *The National Union Catalog of Manuscript Collections, 1969* (Washington, DC: The Library of Congress, 1970).

2,460. Lyon, Mary
Papers. 1839. 1 item.
Open. No guide.
Library of Congress, Manuscript Division.
Letter in which Lyon (1797-1849), an educator who founded Mount Holyoke Female Seminary, describes her recently opened Seminary to a prospective teacher, [Miss] Martha M. Green of Westmoreland, NH.

2,461. McCabe, Flora Morgan, Collection of Morgan, Garrett, and Walker Papers
Papers. 1855-78. Ca. 70 items.
Open. No guide.
Library of Congress, Manuscript Division.
Consists of family correspondence, receipts, and bills of the Daniel J. Morgan and Edward J. Garrett families, most of which pertain to the life of Confederate soldiers. Includes letters from Morgan, a resident of Chillicothe, MO, and his brothers John H. and William C. Morgan to their mother and their sister. McCabe was a descendant of Daniel Morgan.

2,462. McClellan, George Brinton, Sr.
Papers. 1823-98. 44 ft.
Open. Published guide and register.

Library of Congress, Manuscript Division.
Papers relating to the Civil War service of McClellan (1826-85), an army officer who later was governor of New Jersey, include correspondence in which he describes to Ellen (Marcy) McClellan (?-1915), whom he married in 1860, his military activities during the War. Also included are diaries she kept, beginning in 1865, during his three-year trip to Europe and diaries, 1881-84, concerning the social activities of their daughter Mary McClellan (1861-1945), a debutante who spent her time in New York City, Washington, and Orange, NJ, before marrying Paul Desprez. Entire collection is available on microfilm. See *The National Union Catalog of Manuscript Collections, 1968* (Washington, DC: The Library of Congress, 1969).

2,463. MacDowell, Marian Griswold (Nevins)
Papers. 1876-1969. 3.8 ft.
Open. Published guide and register.
Library of Congress, Manuscript Division.
A musician and philanthropist, MacDowell (1857-1956) founded the MacDowell Colony in Peterborough, NH, in 1907 to foster talent in the creative arts. Papers largely relate to her activities with the Colony; also included are papers of Edward A. MacDowell, whom she married in 1884, and records of the Edward MacDowell Assoc., Inc., which finances and administers the Colony. Marian MacDowell's papers consist of her writings; correspondence with Thornton Wilder, Edward Arlington Robinson, and others; a scrapbook on Marian MacDowell Day; clippings; and memorabilia. Collection also contains papers of Nina Maud Richardson, including correspondence with MacDowell, Van Wyck Brooks, O. Louis Guglielmi, Hermann Hagedorn, and Jean (Starr) Untermeyer; greeting cards; financial papers; clippings; and memorabilia. See *The National Union Catalog of Manuscript Collections, 1976* (Washington, DC: The Library of Congress, 1977).

2,464. McGee, Anita (Newcomb)
Papers. 1688-1932. 5 ft.
Open. Published guide and register.
Library of Congress, Manuscript Division.
A resident of Washington, McGee (1864-1940) was an anthropologist and physician. Correspondence, diaries, notebooks, scientific and medical notes, an "idea book," photos, clippings, and memorabilia. Includes correspondence with her father Simon Newcomb, who was a mathematician and astronomer, and with her son Eric McGee Newcomb, who changed his surname, and letters she wrote as acting assistant surgeon of the US Army during the Spanish-American War. Also included are lectures and articles on hygiene and medical matters; articles pertaining to her studies of communal societies in the US, among them the Shakers and the Bethel and Oneida communities; and material relating to the formation of the Women's Anthropological Society of America. Correspondents include Charles B. Davenport, Edward S. Holder, Alcander Longley, and Gifford Pinchot. Papers also contain correspondence of Anita McGee's grandfather Charles A. Hassler, who was a US Navy surgeon, with James Madison and others. Taken from *The National Union Catalog of Manuscript Collections, 1962* (Hamden, CT: The Shoe String Press, Inc., 1964).

2,465. McKee, Mary T.
Papers. Ca. 1863-64. 5 items.
Open. No guide.
Library of Congress, Manuscript Division.
A native of Baltimore, McKee left home with her family in 1863 and moved to New York where her father John McKee was arrested and imprisoned in Fort La Fayette as a southern sympathizer. Collection consists of a notebook in which Mary McKee describes the trip to New York, her father's southern sympathies, his arrest, and her weekly visits to see him at the Fort; she also includes excerpts from "The Right Flanker," which was the Confederate prisoners' newspaper at the Fort. Collection also contains a letter concerning her pass to see her father, a letter from his fellow prisoners requesting food, and drawings of Confederate flags and banners sketched and signed by prisoners.

2,466. Mackey, Ann Jane
Papers. 1822. 1 item.
Open. No guide.
Library of Congress, Manuscript Division.
A poem "The Violet" written and illustrated by Mackey, a poet.

2,467. McLean, Evalyn (Walsh)
Papers. 1886-1948. 40 ft.
Open. Published guide and register.
Library of Congress, Manuscript Division.
Correspondence of McLean (1886-1947) reflects her leadership in the social life of Washington from the 1910s until her death. Also included are business papers relating to Walsh family mining interests and to McLean family publishing interests in the *Cincinnati Enquirer* and the *Washington Post;* legal papers, including divorce proceedings, probates, and libel suits; other papers concerning McLean's interest in the Lindbergh kidnapping case, the Teapot Dome scandal, and her ownership of the Hope diamond; and the manuscript of her book *Father Struck It Rich* (1936). Taken from *The National Union Catalog of Manuscript Collections, 1965* (Washington, DC: The Library of Congress, 1966).

2,468. Madison, Dorothea "Dolley" (Payne) Todd
Papers. 1794-1851. Ca. 2600 items.
Open. No guide.
Library of Congress, Manuscript Division.
Madison (1768-1849) was First Lady from 1809 to 1817. She married John Todd, Jr., in 1790; he died in 1793, and in 1794 she married James Madison. Correspondence with her sister, nieces, nephews, son John Payne Todd (1792-?), Eliza [Mrs. R. B.] Lee and other friends; a poem; legal and financial papers; and a volume of visiting cards.

2,469. Maggio, Graziella
Papers. 1944. 2 items.
Open. No guide.
Library of Congress, Manuscript Division.
"For George Washington Carver," a prize-winning poem in a New York poetry contest, was written by Maggio (1928-), then a high school student. Also includes a clipping about the poem.

2,470. Mamreof, Anna F.
Papers. Ca. 1926-27. 32 items.
Open. No guide.
Library of Congress, Manuscript Division.
Manuscript of a book and correspondence of [Miss] Mamreof, a writer, concerning the attempt of Fred E. Woodward of Washington to publish the book, which is a catalog of original articles on Biblical themes. Mamreof's name was also spelled Mamreov.

2,471. Mann, Mary Tyler (Peabody)
Papers. 1863-76. 75 items.
Open. Published guide.
Library of Congress, Manuscript Division.
Correspondence, newspapers, clippings, and printed matter of [Mrs. Horace] Mann (1806-87), an educator, relate to the educational programs of President Sarmiento for Argentina and to industrial and educational matters in South America. Correspondents include Domingo Faustino Sarmiento, Juana Manso, and Manuel Rafael Garcia, who was Argentine minister to the US; much of the material is in Spanish. Also included are letters from Mann's niece Maria R. Mann while she was stationed at the Freedmen's Camp in Helena, AR; these were addressed to clergyman William L. Ropes and to her family. Taken from *The National Union Catalog of Manuscript Collections, 1966* (Washington, DC: The Library of Congress, 1967).

2,472. Manning, Daniel
Papers. 1885-1921. 2 ft.
Open. Published guide.
Library of Congress, Manuscript Division.
A journalist and financier, Manning (1831-87) was US secretary of the treasury. Correspondence and reports, including letters to his second wife Mary Margaretta (Fryer) Manning (1845-1928) from Frances F. [Mrs. Grover] Cleveland and letters acknowledging receipt of the report of the board of lady managers of the Louisiana Purchase Exposition of 1904. Mary Manning was president of that board. See *The National Union Catalog of Manuscript Collections, 1963-1964* (Washington, DC: The Library of Congress, 1965).

2,473. Manning, Helen Herron (Taft)
Papers. 1917-51. Ca. 300 items.
Open. Published guide.
Library of Congress, Manuscript Division.
Correspondence of [Mrs. Frederick Johnson] Manning (1891?-), an educator who was a professor, dean, and president of Bryn Mawr College. Includes lengthy letters with advice on her career from her father William Howard Taft and letters from her mother and her brother Robert A. Taft. See *National Union Catalog of Manuscript Collections, 1977* (Washington, DC: Library of Congress, 1978).

2,474. Markell, Grace Elizabeth
Papers. Nd. 3 items.
Open. No guide.
Library of Congress, Manuscript Division.
Poems by Markell, a poet, about the Kellogg-Briand peace pact, war, and Charles F. D. Belden.

2,475. Marquand, Eleanor (Cross)
Papers. Nd. 1 item.
Open. No guide.
Library of Congress, Manuscript Division.
Article by [Mrs. Allen] Marquand (1874-1950), an art consultant, concerns art collector John G. Johnson.

2,476. Marshall, Peter, and Marshall, Sarah Catherine (Wood)
Papers. 1933-61. 13 ft.
Open. Published guide and register.
Library of Congress, Manuscript Division.
A Presbyterian clergyman, Peter Marshall (1902-49) was chaplain of the US Senate; his wife Catherine Marshall (1914-) is an author and lecturer. In 1959, Catherine Marshall married Leonard Earl LeSourd; she has continued to use Catherine Marshall as her pen name. Correspondence and fan mail from her readers make up the bulk of the collection. Also included are manuscripts of *Beyond Our Selves* (New York: McGraw-Hill, 1961), *A Man Called Peter* (New York: McGraw-Hill, 1951), and others of her books and articles as well as material concerning the movie version of *A Man Called Peter,* with transcripts of Marshall's conference with the movie company, film scripts and revisions, and extensive correspondence with screenwriter Eleanor Griffin, producer Samuel G. Engel, and film performers Richard Todd, Jean Peters, and Marjorie Rambeau. In addition, the collection contains correspondence and printed matter concerning Peter Marshall and his death as well as reviews and publicity for Catherine Marshall's books and the movie. Also available on microfilm. See *The National Union Catalog of Manuscript Collections, 1967* (Washington, DC: The Library of Congress, 1968).

2,477. Martineau, Harriet
Papers. 1835. 1 item.
Open. No guide.
Library of Congress, Manuscript Division.
Letter in which Martineau (1802-76), a British author, describes to clergyman Charles Brooks her stays in Philadelphia, Baltimore, and Washington, which were later recorded in greater detail in her book *Society in America* (1837).

2,478. Maury, Betty Herndon
Papers. 1861-63. 2 vols.
Open. No guide.
Library of Congress, Manuscript Division.
Diary in which [Mrs. William A.] Maury describes living in Washington at the outbreak of the Civil War, her trip to her family in Fredericksburg, VA, her activities during the War, and the progress of the War.

2,479. Maury, Matthew Fontaine
Papers. 1825-ca. 1951. 15 ft.
Open. Published guide and register.
Library of Congress, Manuscript Division.
Papers of Maury (1806-73), a naval officer and oceanographer who was superintendent of the combined Naval Observatory and the Hydrographic Office; he also attempted to establish a colony of southern families in Mexico after the Civil War. Includes correspondence with his wife Ann (Herndon) Maury (1811-1901), who lived in Virginia during the War; her correspondence with her children; and correspondence of their daughter Mary H. (Maury) [Mrs. James Rhodes] Werth (1844-1928) about his career. Also includes a study by Catherine Cate Coblentz of Matthew Maury's career. See *The National Union Catalog of Manuscript Collections, 1963-1964* (Washington, DC: The Library of Congress, 1965).

2,480. Mew, Charlotte Mary
Papers. 1916. 2 items.
Open. No guide.
Library of Congress, Manuscript Division.
Letter by Mew (1869-1928), a poet, and typescript of her sonnet "There Shall Be No Night There."

2,481. Meyer, Agnes Elizabeth (Ernst)
Papers. 1863-1972. 90 ft.
Open. Register.
Library of Congress, Manuscript Division.
[Mrs. Eugene, Jr.] Meyer (1887-1970) was an author and social reformer. Correspondence; diaries, 1909-70; manuscripts of her speeches, articles, and books; research notes; financial papers; reports; pamphlets; photos; printed matter; memorabilia; and other papers. Includes notes of Meyer while she was a student at Barnard College, family correspondence and correspondence pertaining to her work, and subject files on the many committees, commissions, and activities in which she participated, including the Westchester (NY) County Recreation Commission.

2,482. Michener, James Albert
Papers. 1945-68. 75 ft.
Partially closed. Published guide and register.
Library of Congress, Manuscript Division.
Literary manuscripts, correspondence, and other papers of Michener (1907-), an author and novelist. Includes correspondence with Pearl S. Buck. See *The National Union Catalog of Manuscript Collections, 1959-1961* (Ann Arbor, MI: J. W. Edwards, 1962).

2,483. Millay, Edna St. Vincent
Papers. 1908-60. Ca. 630 items.
Partially restricted. Published guide and register.
Library of Congress, Manuscript Division.
A poet and author, [Miss] Millay (1892-1950) married Eugen Jan Boissevain in 1923. Correspondence; diaries and notebooks containing published and unpublished poems; short prose selections; manuscripts of poetry collections, books, and a play; galley proofs of published works; and a photo of a bust of Millay. Includes letters and essays on government and civil liberties and prose and poetry concerning the Sacco-Vanzetti trial, the rise of totalitarianism during the 1930s, and controversial issues of the 1940s. The diaries and notebooks are also available on microfilm. Taken from *The National Union Catalog of Manuscript Collections, 1970* (Washington, DC: The Library of Congress, 1971).

2,484. Miller, Harriet (Mann)
Papers. 1891-1909. Ca. 35 items.
Open. No guide.
Library of Congress, Manuscript Division.
An ornithologist, lecturer, and author, [Mrs. Watts Todd] Miller (1831-1918) wrote under the name Olive Thorne Miller. Letters to Florence (Merriam) Bailey, notes Miller took while she was observing North American birds in various states and Canada, and daguerreotypes of the Miller family.

2,485. Miller, Olive Kennon (Beaupré)
Papers. 1929-33. 1 Hollinger box.
Open. No guide.
Library of Congress, Manuscript Division.
Typescript essays by Miller, author of *My Book of History,* a series of history books for children, are about such explorers as Sir Walter Raleigh, Ponce de Leon, Vasco da Gama, Cartier, Coronado, and others.

2,486. Miner, Myrtilla
Papers. 1839-64. 2 ft.
Open. Published and unpublished guides.
Library of Congress, Manuscript Division.
Correspondence, notes, pamphlets, photos, clippings, and other papers relate to the efforts of [Miss] Miner (1815-64) to establish and maintain a school for Negro girls in Washington. Bulk of the papers were collected by Lester G. Wells, whose unfinished biography of Miner is also included. Correspondents include Samuel Rhoads, Benjamin Tatham, and members of the Miner family. Taken from *The National Union Catalog of Manuscript Collections, 1959-1961* (Ann Arbor, MI: J. W. Edwards, 1962).

2,487. Miramova, Elena, and Leontovich, Eugenie
Papers. 1943. 1 item.
Open. No guide.
Library of Congress, Manuscript Division.
"Dark Eyes," a play Miramova wrote in collaboration with Leontovich, concerns a young American woman and a Russian prince in New York. Both Miramova and Leontovich were playwrights.

2,488. Mitchell, Margaret
Papers. 1936-42. 4 items.
Open. No guide.
Library of Congress, Manuscript Division.
[Miss] Mitchell (1900-49) was a novelist who married Berrien K. Upshaw in 1922 and was divorced from him in 1924; in 1925 she married John Robert Marsh. Correspondence in which she discusses with Gilbert Govan her book *Gone With The Wind* and the subject of "vanity publishing."

2,489. Mitchill, Catherine (Akerly) Cock
Papers. 1806-1936. Ca. 100 items.
Open. No guide.
Library of Congress, Manuscript Division.
A resident of Washington, Mitchill was the wife of US Congressman and then Senator Samuel Latham Mitchill. Detailed correspondence in which she describes life in the capital to her sister Margaret (Akerly) [Mrs. Silvanus] Miller, pamphlets and clippings pertaining to Samuel Mitchill, and a letter to the donor of the collection.

2,490. Montgomery, Benjamin, Family
Papers. 1872-1971. 12 items.
Open. No guide.
Library of Congress, Manuscript Division.
Montgomery was a businessman and former slave who, in 1867, purchased the Mississippi estate of his former owner Joseph E. Davis and that of Joseph's brother Jefferson Davis. Includes theses about Montgomery and his family as well as printed material about Mound Bayou, MS, which was the all-Negro town established by Montgomery's son Isaiah T. Montgomery (1847-1924); Isaiah Montgomery also was the only Negro delegate to the 1890 Mississippi Constitutional Convention. In addition, the collection contains biographical sketches of Isaiah Montgomery's daughter Mary Cordelia (Montgomery) Booze and her husband Eugene P. Booze, both of whom were active in Mound Bayou, and an 1872 diary in which Isaiah Montgomery's sister Mary Virginia Montgomery (1852-?) sketched her daily activities as bookkeeper and cotton picker for the family cotton business. She also recorded the books and journals she read in preparation for entering Oberlin College and her first weeks at the school.

2,491. Moore, Merrill
Papers. 1904-58. 211 ft.
Partially closed. Published guide.
Library of Congress, Manuscript Division.
Papers of Moore (1903-57), a psychiatrist and poet, include correspondence with Alexandra Adler, Olga Barsis, Babette Deutsch, Charlotte Lowell, and Jean (Starr) Untermeyer. Also includes correspondence of Ann Leslie (Nichol) Moore, whom he married in 1930; of his mother Mary (Daniel) [Mrs. John Trotwood] Moore; and of Helen Moore [Mrs. Whitford] Cole. See *Merrill Moore: A Register of His Papers* (Washington: Library of Congress, 1972).

2,492. Morrill, Florence Barry
Papers. 1915-16. Ca. 40 items.
Open. No guide.
Library of Congress, Manuscript Division.
A suffragist, Morrill was a member of the Congressional Union. Photos and clippings concern the work she and [Mrs.] Ida Mae Waters accomplished for the Union on the Susan B. Anthony Amendment to the Constitution.

2,493. Morris, Gouverneur
Papers. 1771-1834. 5 ft.
Open. Published guide and register.
Library of Congress, Manuscript Division.
Papers of Morris (1752-1816), minister to France and a US senator, include such financial papers of his wife Anne Cary Morris as notes regarding her settlement of his estate, a receipt book in which she detailed her expenditures for goods and services, and her account book with the Bank of New York. Entire collection is available on microfilm. See *The National Union Catalog of Manuscript Collections, 1959-1961* (Ann Arbor, MI: J. W. Edwards, 1962).

2,494. Morris, Martha Elizabeth (Wright)
Papers. 1911-16. 4 items.
Open. No guide.
Library of Congress, Manuscript Division.
Reminiscences in which Morris (1832?-1919), a worker for the US Sanitary Commission during the Civil War, discusses life in Cincinnati and Washington as well as the War. Also included are clippings.

2,495. Mott, Lucretia (Coffin)
Papers. 1843-59. 4 items.
Open. No guide.
Library of Congress, Manuscript Division.
A Quaker minister, Mott (1793-1880) was an abolitionist and pioneer for women's rights. Correspondence about the fugitive slave law, John

Jackson, and the death of a Dr. Channing. Also includes a resolution that was passed by the Philadelphia Female Anti-Slavery Society in 1851 condemning the return of fugitive slaves. Lucretia Coffin married James Mott in 1811.

2,496. Moulton, Ellen Louise (Chandler)
Papers. 1853-1907. 52 vols.
Open. No guide.
Library of Congress, Manuscript Division.
Moulton (1835-1908) was a poet and author who married William U. Moulton (?-1898) in 1855. Correspondence, primarily notes of acknowledgment to Louise Moulton for invitations, poems, or letters; many of the correspondents were poets who often included manuscript poems in their letters. Also contains correspondence of poet Philip Bourke Marston, clippings about him, poems by Moulton, and programs.

2,497. Mowrer, Edgar Ansel
Papers. 1910-66. 56 ft.
Open. Published and unpublished guides.
Library of Congress, Manuscript Division.
Mowrer (1892-1977) and his wife Lilian (Thomson) Mowrer (1889-) were authors and lecturers. Family and general correspondence; manuscripts of speeches, articles, and books; lectures; records of the magazine *Western World;* and other papers, most of which pertain to foreign affairs, particularly the diplomatic policies of Germany, France, Italy, and the US. Correspondents include Dean Acheson, John Dos Passos, and Hubert H. Humphrey. Taken from *The National Union Catalog of Manuscript Collections, 1972* (Washington, DC: The Library of Congress, 1974).

2,498. Munroe, Kirk
Papers. 1850-1940. 10 ft.
Open. Published guide and register.
Library of Congress, Manuscript Division.
Papers of Munroe (1850-1930), an author, include letters he wrote his mother Susan M. (Hall) [Mrs. Charles W.] Munroe (?-1896) while he was surveying land in the West for railroads. Also included are papers of his first wife Mary (Barr) Munroe (1853-1922), an author whom he married in 1883, with diaries in which she recorded her daily activities between 1884 and 1922 while living in Coconut Grove, FL, during the winters and in Massachusetts during the summers; although the diaries contain little information about her writing, they deal with her interest in helping Seminole Indians and a woman's club, perhaps in Miami. Her correspondence also pertains to the Seminoles and includes some letters from her husband. Collection also contains correspondence of his second wife Mabel Kittredge (Stearns) Noble Munroe, a social worker whom he married in 1924, most of which pertains to her proposed biography of Kirk Munroe. Manuscripts of short stories by Mabel Stearns before she married Munroe are included as well. See *The National Union Catalog of Manuscript Collections, 1965* (Washington, DC: The Library of Congress, 1966).

2,499. Murdock, Victor
Papers. 1866-1945. 51 ft.
Open. Published guide and register.
Library of Congress, Manuscript Division.
Papers of Murdock (1871-1945), a newspaper editor, pertain to his tenure in the US House of Representatives. Correspondents include Mabel T. Boardman, Florence Kelley, Edith Kermit Roosevelt, Ida Tarbell, Alice Paul, Edith (Bolling) Wilson, Edna Ferber, and Sallie White. Also includes correspondence of Pearl (Allen) Murdock (1875-1940), whom he married in 1890. See *The National Union Catalog of Manuscript Collections, 1971* (Washington, DC: The Library of Congress, 1973).

2,500. Mytinger, Caroline
Papers. Ca. 1942-46. Ca. 150 items.
Open. No guide.
Library of Congress, Manuscript Division.
Typescripts and drawings for such books by Mytinger, an author and artist, as *Headhunting in the Solomon Islands Around the Coral Sea* (1942) and *New Guinea Headhunt* (1946); the books concern painting in New Guinea during the 1930s.

2,501. National American Woman Suffrage Association
Records. 1839-1961. 40 ft.
Open. Published guide.
Library of Congress, Manuscript Division.
In 1890 the National American Woman Suffrage Association was created from the merger of the National Woman Suffrage Association and the American Woman Suffrage Association, both of which had been organized in 1869 to win the right of suffrage for women. Correspondence, subject files that relate primarily to state and local suffrage organizations and leaders in the movement, published writings, photos, scrapbooks compiled by Ida Porter Boyer, and printed matter. Correspondents include Abby K. Foster, William Lloyd Garrison, Sarah M. Grimké, Ida Husted Harper, Mary Garrett Hay, Julia (Ward) Howe, Florence Kelley, Belle Case La Follette, Mary A. Livermore, Lucretia Mott, Maud (Wood) Park, Jeannette Rankin, Rosika Schwimmer, Anna Howard Shaw, Elizabeth Cady Stanton, and Emma Willard. See *The Blackwell Family, Carrie Chapman Catt, and the National American Woman Suffrage Association: A Register of Their Papers* (Washington: Library of Congress, 1975). See also *The National Union Catalog of Manuscript Collections, 1971* (Washington, DC: The Library of Congress, 1973).

2,502. National Association for the Advancement of Colored People
Records. 1909-69. Ca. 1,000,000 items.
Partially restricted. Published guide.
Library of Congress, Manuscript Division.
Organized in 1909 to work for equal treatment for Negroes, the Association adopted NAACP as its name in 1910. Correspondence, memoranda, speeches, notes, unpublished manuscript books and plays, legal briefs, trial transcripts, reports, resolutions, charts, serials, press releases, articles, clippings, and other printed matter. The records document the growth and development of the NAACP and deal with such subjects as discrimination in business and government; segregation in schools, government, and private establishments; lynching and mob violence; anti-lynching measures; race riots; Negro suffrage in the South; labor disputes; unions; and politics. The collection provides extensive background on Negro life in urban and rural America, particularly during the 1930s. Includes correspondence and other material relating to NAACP branches.

Correspondence of Jane Addams, Mary McLeod Bethune, Lucille Black, Ruby Darrow, Addie W. Hunton, Juanita Jackson, Kathryn M. Johnson, Florence Kelley, Daisy Lampkin, Catharine D. Lealtad, May Childs Nerney, Mary White Ovington, Richetta Randolph, Eleanor Roosevelt, Mary B. Talbert, and Frances Williams is included; personal correspondence of NAACP officers Jackson and Ovington is also included. The correspondence is available on microfilm.

In addition, the collection contains office diaries of Hunton, 1921; Lealtad, 1921; and Ovington, 1920-21. Also included are speakers bureau papers pertaining to Jackson and Ovington and papers relating to the estates of Lola A. Balis, Eva Channing, Delphine Eubanks, a Miss Flagg, Mollie Galloway, Mary McMurtie, Frances Quinn, Marie S. Reavis, and Mattie Roberts, all of whom left money to the NAACP. Material pertaining to women is also located in files on the National Training School for Girls, the National Woman's Party, the women's auxiliary to the NAACP, the YWCA, and woman suffrage. See *The National Association for the Advancement of Colored People: A Register of Its Records,* Volume I, 1909-1939 (Washington: Library of Congress, 1972).

2,503. National Child Labor Committee
Records. 1904-53. 21.7 ft.
Open. Published guide and register.
Library of Congress, Manuscript Division.
The Committee was formed in 1904 to eliminate abuses of child labor. Minutes of Committee meetings, proceedings of annual meetings, reports of investigations into industries that employed children, correspondence of Alexander J. McKelway while he was secretary for the southern states of the Committee, press releases, and clippings about the Committee and child labor. See *The National Union Catalog of Manuscript Collections, 1959-1961* (Ann Arbor, MI: J. W. Edwards, 1962).

2,504. National Consumers League
Records. 1882-1972. 69.6 ft.
Open. Register.
Library of Congress, Manuscript Division.
Organized in 1899 to coordinate the work of local consumers leagues formed during the 1890s, the League and these local groups were founded to curb abuses of workers, particularly women at first, by organizing consumers to boycott goods produced under poor working conditions, by publicizing such conditions, and by supporting protective legislation. League articles of incorporation, constitution, bylaws, annual reports, executive committee minutes, minutes and correspondence of the board of directors, office correspondence, ledgers, state Leagues' records, card indexes, scrapbooks of League form letters and clippings, publications, and miscellaneous material pertaining to Florence Kelley. Also included are records of the now defunct National Council on Agricultural Life and Labor.

Collection also contains projects and programs files on the minimum wage, wages and hours, child labor, the Sheppard-Towner Act, the Children's Bureau, the Women's Bureau, unemployment compensation, the Equal Rights Amendment, radium poisoning, the candy white list, civil liberties, consumers' labeling, education, equal pay, the Fair Labor Standards Act, food and drugs, the US Department of Labor, health, housing, national labor relations, migratory labor, social security, and workmen's compensation. Also included are speeches, articles, and books by Florence Kelley, Josephine Goldmark, Elizabeth S. Magee, Emily Sims Marconnier, Mary W. Dewson, Lucy R. Mason, Mary Dublin Keyserling, Louise Stitt, and Sarah Newman, as well as legal briefs for cases bearing on League work in California, the District of Columbia, Illinois, Massachusetts, New Jersey, New York, Ohio, and Oregon. Most of the League minutes are available on microfilm.

2,505. National Library for the Blind
Records. 1911-54. 1 ft.
Open. Published guide.
Library of Congress, Manuscript Division.
Founded in 1911, the Library merged with the Library of Congress's division of the blind in 1946. The NLB worked to provide literature for the blind by printing and distributing Braille books throughout the US and by attempting to establish a uniform system of Braille. Prior to 1932 the financial records, correspondence, memoranda, reports, clippings, and other records were primarily those of [Miss] Etta Josselyn Giffin, NLB founder and its director from 1911 to 1932. The material relates to library services for the blind, Giffin's role in initiating the services, her becoming director, Braille translations, communication with other institutions serving the blind, appointment of NLB directors, and funding from Congress.

Correspondence after 1931 is primarily that of her successor Paul Sperry, a clergyman. Also included are minutes; financial reports; lists of volunteer workers at the Library, who for the most part were women; and information on the daily activities of the workers. See *The National Union Catalog of Manuscript Collections, 1959-1961* (Ann Arbor, MI: J. W. Edwards, 1962).

2,506. National Society of Arts and Letters
Records. 1944-65. 2 ft.
Open. Published guide.
Library of Congress, Manuscript Division.
Composed of professional women engaged in creative work in art, music, or literature, the Society was formed in 1944 and incorporated in 1949 to encourage and assist young American artists through scholarships, workshops, and sponsoring exhibitions and marketing outlets for the artists' work. Minutes of the Society's national conferences and of executive board meetings; bylaws; scrapbooks of correspondence, invitations, convention programs, poetry, catalogs, brochures, awards, photos, and clippings pertaining to the work of local society chapters, including the Washington chapter; volumes of the Society's newsletter; and volumes of its annual publication, which list activities for the year and names of members. See *The National Union Catalog of Manuscript Collections, 1965* (Washington, DC: The Library of Congress, 1966).

2,507. National Society of the Colonial Dames of America
Records. 1961-66. 2.5 ft.
Open. No guide.
Library of Congress, Manuscript Division.
Organized in 1892, the Society sponsored through its state chapters a survey of historical information about the county courthouses in various states. Scrapbooks of survey results, compiled by Society members, contain historical sketches and photos of county courthouses in Vermont, Maine, Missouri, New Hampshire, New York, Massachusetts, Rhode Island, Tennessee, New Jersey, North Carolina, and Virginia. Also includes the published book of the Alabama courthouse survey, *Early Courthouses of Alabama Prior to 1860* (Mobile, AL: Jordan Printing Co., 1966).

2,508. National Woman's Party
Records. 1911-36. 333 containers.
Open. Container list.
Library of Congress, Manuscript Division.
The Party was formed in 1916 to work for passage of the Susan B. Anthony woman suffrage Amendment to the Constitution; it was successor to the Congressional Union for Woman Suffrage, which had been organized in 1913 to work for suffrage through a federal amendment, as opposed to the state-based activity that was emphasized by the National American Woman Suffrage Association. Collection includes records of the Union and records through 1920 of the Party. Convention minutes; proceedings of committees; committee reports; correspondence; files on picketing and demonstrations, with correspondence, affidavits of jailed suffragists, lists of participants, police permits, clippings, and material from a California antisuffrage group; transcripts of Congressional hearings; Party literature; press releases; poems; photos; lantern slides; cartoons; and clippings. Also includes correspondence of state suffrage organizations and workers, Party chairman Alice Paul, the vice-chairman, the executive secretary, the headquarter's secretary, and of the Party's press, organization, supply, hospitality, membership, and legislative departments. In addition, the collection contains subscription and editorial correspondence of the Party publication *Suffragist,* including correspondence of Lucy Burns, and letters from congressmen about the Amendment.

2,509. National Women's Trade Union League
Records. 1903-50. 11 ft.
Open. Published guide and register.
Library of Congress, Manuscript Division.
Minutes of meetings; proceedings of national conventions; correspondence between local Leagues and the national League; material on the International Congresses of Working Women in 1919, 1921, and 1923; biographical information on League officers; reports; and memorabilia. Much of the correspondence concerns labor and social legislation; it also reflects the League's later interest in education, civil rights, and price control. Correspondents include Samuel Gompers, Jane Addams, Eleanor Roosevelt, Sophonisba P. Breckinridge, Margaret Dreier Robins, Mary Anderson, Alice Henry, Rose Schneiderman, Elizabeth Christman, and Frances Perkins. Also available on microfilm. Taken from *The National Union Catalog of Manuscript Collections, 1959-1961* (Ann Arbor, MI: J. W. Edwards, 1962).

2,510. Nesbitt, Victoria Henrietta (Kugler)
Papers. 1933-49. 4 ft.
Open. Published and unpublished guides.
Library of Congress, Manuscript Division.
Housekeeper for President Franklin D. Roosevelt, Nesbitt (1874-?) also was an author. Correspondence, diaries, manuscripts of her books *The Presidential Cookbook* and *White House Diary,* a nearly complete set of White House menus, memoranda on White House entertainments and other household matters, recipes, lists, and accounts. Includes correspondence with Eleanor Roosevelt and others on White House domestic matters. Taken from *The National Union Catalog of Manuscript Collections, 1959-1961* (Ann Arbor, MI: J. W. Edwards, 1962).

2,511. Newell, Frederick Haynes
Papers. 1885-1931. 10 ft.
Open. Published guide and description.
Library of Congress, Manuscript Division.
Professional and personal papers of Newell (1862-1932), a consulting engineer and public official, include correspondence with Ida M. Tarbell. See *The National Union Catalog of Manuscript Collections, 1959-1961* (Ann Arbor, MI: J. W. Edwards, 1962).

2,512. Nicolay, John George
Papers. 1811-1943. 7.2 ft.
Open. Published guide and register.
Library of Congress, Manuscript Division.
Papers of Nicolay (1832-1901) relate to his tenure as private secretary to Abraham Lincoln; Nicolay also was a biographer of Lincoln. Includes letters to his fiancée Therena Bates, whom he married in 1865, and correspondence of their daughter Helen Nicolay (1866-1954) concerning her father's association with Lincoln and her own writings on Lincoln. Her correspondents include Robert T. Lincoln, George Kennan, James Grant Wilson, John Hay, A. R. Spofford, and Alice C. Fletcher. Also includes research material Helen Nicolay collected for her book *Personal Traits of Abraham Lincoln* (New York: Century, 1912). See *The National Union Catalog of Manuscript Collections, 1968* (Washington, DC: The Library of Congress, 1969).

2,513. Niebuhr, Reinhold
Papers. 1913-66. 12 ft.
Partially restricted. Published guide and register.
Library of Congress, Manuscript Division.
Papers of Niebuhr (1892-1971), a theologian, relate to his interest in religious, social, and political affairs. Correspondents include Helen (Gahagan) Douglas, Freda Kirchwey, Erika Mann, Margaret Mead, Helen Sobell, and Dorothy Thompson. Also included are papers of June (Rossbach) Bingham, a writer, with correspondence, her collection of Niebuhr's letters, and material relating to her book *Courage to Change: An Introduction to the Life and Thought of Reinhold Niebuhr* (New York: Scribner, 1961). See *The National Union Catalog of Manuscript Collections, 1967* (Washington, DC: The Library of Congress, 1968).

2,514. Oliphant, Benjamin F., and Oliphant, Catherine
Papers. 1864-1916. 22 items.
Open. No guide.
Library of Congress, Manuscript Division.
Papers relate to the Civil War service of Benjamin Oliphant, a sergeant with the 3rd Maryland Cavalry, and of his wife Catherine Oliphant, who volunteered to work as a laundress with the same regiment; she seems to have functioned more as a nurse than laundress. Orders and army documents of promotion and discharge, a letter concerning her pension, and a tribute to her War service by a member of her regiment.

2,515. O'Neill, Dorothy Kitchen
Papers. 1918-19. 69 items.
Open. Published guide.
Library of Congress, Manuscript Division.
Letters that [Mrs.] O'Neill wrote her parents while she was stationed at the American National Red Cross headquarters at Savenay Base Hospital Centre, Savenay, France. Also includes a scrapbook of letters, photos, and clippings. Taken from *The National Union Catalog of Manuscript Collections, 1972* (Washington, DC: The Library of Congress, 1974).

2,516. Orr, William
Papers. 1890-1939. 2 ft.
Open. Published guide and register.
Library of Congress, Manuscript Division.
Papers pertain primarily to the period during the 1920s when Orr (1860-1939), educational secretary for the YMCA, studied adult education in Europe. Includes manuscript and printed articles by him and Charlotte (Pettis) Orr (?-1931), whom he married in 1889. Her travelog articles concern travels with her husband through Greece, Albania, Macedonia, Poland, and Sweden and contain some mention of women in these countries. See *The National Union Catalog of Manuscript Collections, 1965* (Washington, DC: The Library of Congress, 1966).

2,517. Painter, Clara Searle
Papers. 1962, nd. 2 items.
Open. No guide.
Library of Congress, Manuscript Division.
Extracts of a letter and reminiscence of [Mrs.] Painter (ca. 1888-) about the period between 1894 and 1900 when she was a student in Lawrence, MA, at the private school run by [Mrs.] Belle Moodie Frost and her son Robert Frost.

2,518. Palmer, Phoebe (Worrall)
Papers. 1855. 1 item.
Open. No guide.
Library of Congress, Manuscript Division.
Letter in which Palmer (1807-74), an evangelist preacher and wife of homeopathic physician Walter Clark Palmer, describes articles she has written and her work as corresponding secretary of the New York Female Assistance Society for the Relief and Religious Instruction of the Sick Poor.

2,519. Pan-American Congress, Women's Auxiliary Conference
Records. 1915-27. Ca. 3000 items.
Open. No guide.
Library of Congress, Manuscript Division.
Organized in 1916 as an adjunct to the second Congress, the Conference provided a forum for women of the Americas to foster understanding among their countries. Minutes of the executive committee, proceedings and reports of the Conferences of 1916 and 1924, and correspondence in Spanish of the Conference's executive secretary

Emma (Bain) [Mrs. Glen Levin] Swiggett of Washington with prominent Latin and South American women. Also includes her correspondence with Conference officials Eleanor (Foster) Lansing, Antoinette (Carter) Hughes, Eva (Perry) Moore, and Julia C. Lathrop.

A major activity of the Conference was sponsorship in 1923 of Columbus Day conferences in 20 national capitals, at which women's contributions to their countries' progress were highlighted. Collection also includes proceedings, correspondence, printed matter, and speeches by Sophonisba Breckinridge, Grace Abbott, and Anna (Garlin) Spencer, which contain information on women's conditions and achievements.

2,520. Pennell, Joseph, and Pennell, Elizabeth (Robins)
Papers. 1597-1935. 104 ft.
Open. Published guide and register.
Library of Congress, Manuscript Division.
Personal and professional papers of Joseph Pennell (1857-1926), an etcher, and of his wife Elizabeth Pennell (1855-1936), an author and art critic, include their collection of the papers of artist James Abbott McNeill Whistler and the papers of Elizabeth Pennell's uncle Charles Godfrey Leland. Includes correspondence between Joseph and Elizabeth Pennell; correspondence with Elizabeth Bertin, Florence McIntyre, Louise Chandler Moulton, Helen Whistler, and Helen Wright; letters to the Pennells about James Whistler; and manuscripts of books, articles, and lectures by both Pennells. Whistler's papers include correspondence and a diary of his mother Anna Matilda McNeill Whistler. Leland's papers include correspondence with his mother Mrs. Charles F. Leland, his sisters Charlotte and Emily, and his niece Elizabeth Pennell. See *The National Union Catalog of Manuscript Collections, 1966* (Washington, DC: The Library of Congress, 1967).

2,521. Perkins, George Hamilton
Papers. 1857-1936. Ca. 500 items.
Open. Published guide.
Library of Congress, Manuscript Division.
Perkins (1835-99) was a naval officer. His papers include letters to his wife Anna Perkins and his daughter Isabel (Perkins) Anderson. Also includes Isabel Anderson's letters to Daniel Chester French about commissions for statues of her father and to Carroll Storrs Alden, Perkins's biographer. Taken from *The National Union Catalog of Manuscript Collections, 1972* (Washington, DC: The Library of Congress, 1974).

2,522. Phillips, Philip, Family
Papers. 1826-1914. 9 ft.
Open. Published guide and register.
Library of Congress, Manuscript Division.
Papers relating to the law practices of Philip Phillips (1807-84) and his son William Hallett Phillips (1853-97), including copies of the reminiscences of Eugenia (Levy) Phillips (1820-1902), whom Philip Phillips married in 1836, about her imprisonment by Benjamin F. Butler as a Confederate spy in New Orleans. Also includes the commonplace book of her mother Fanny (Yates) [Mrs. Jacob Clavius] Levy, which contains lengthy poems written to her by friends, correspondence, and passages copied from published works. Letters to Eugenia Phillips's sister Martha Levy from Varina [Mrs. Jefferson] Davis and letters to Eugenia Phillips from her sister Phebe Levy are also included. See *The National Union Catalog of Manuscript Collections, 1962* (Hamden, CT: The Shoe String Press, Inc., 1964).

2,523. Piccard Family
Papers. 1600s-1968. 45 ft.
Partially closed. Published guide and register.
Library of Congress, Manuscript Division.
Papers largely relate to the careers of Jean Felix Piccard (1884-1963), a chemist, balloonist, and educator, and of his wife Jeannette (Ridlon) Piccard (1895-), a balloonist, educator, and Episcopal priest. Material on Jeannette Piccard covers her education at Bryn Mawr College, from which she received her BA in 1918; at the University of Chicago, from which she received an MA in 1919; and at the University of Minnesota, where she received a PhD in 1942. Also includes information about her ballooning, her work as a consultant on stratospheric matter for General Mills and for the National Aeronautics and Space Administration, her efforts with emotionally disturbed children and youth rehabilitation, and her interest in the Episcopal church and in feminism. Her papers include diaries, 1914-63, and "spiritual meditations," 1932-68; correspondence with her husband and their correspondence with their parents, brothers, sisters, aunts, uncles, children, grandchildren, nieces, nephews, and foster children they raised; other personal and general correspondence; Jeannette Piccard's speeches and writings on ballooning, religion, and women as well as some fictional pieces; financial papers; biographical material; notebooks she kept; scrapbooks; photos; clippings; and memorabilia. See *The National Union Catalog of Manuscript Collections, 1971* (Washington, DC: The Library of Congress, 1973).

2,524. Pilsbury, Moses Cross, and Family
Papers. 1843-1907. 26 items.
Open. No guide.
Library of Congress, Manuscript Division.
Family papers of Pilsbury (1778-?), a prison warden, include correspondence and printed matter pertaining to his daughter Lois C. (Pilsbury) Walker (1820-1900); her husband Galen C. Walker (?-1856), who also was a prison warden; and their daughter Mary E. (Walker) [Mrs. S. T.] Walker (1852-1907). Includes Lois Walker's correspondence with her parents about her visit to a house of correction in Boston in 1843, her marriage, and her husband's work and death at the hands of a prisoner. Also included are newspaper obituaries and a printed tribute to the life of Mary Walker.

2,525. Pinchot, Cornelia Bryce
Papers. 1918-60. 567 containers.
Open. Container list.
Library of Congress, Manuscript Division.
A politician, [Mrs. Gifford] Pinchot (1881-1960) ran unsuccessfully for Congress twice; she was an active supporter of labor legislation and served as a delegate to the UN Scientific Conference on the Conservation and Utilization of Resources in 1949. Correspondence contains material about suffrage, the National Women's Trade Union League, and political campaigns. Also included are speeches and speech material, a book manuscript, account books and other financial papers, journals, address books, date books, brochures, pamphlets, photos, blueprints, and clippings.

2,526. Pinchot, Gifford
Papers. Ca. 1830-1947. 1411 ft. and 1 microfilm reel.
Open. Published guide and register.
Library of Congress, Manuscript Division.
Papers of Pinchot (1865-1946), an agriculturist, conservationist, and governor of Pennsylvania, include diaries of his mother Mary Eno [Mrs. James W.] Pinchot. See *The National Union Catalog of Manuscript Collections, 1959-1961* (Ann Arbor, MI: J. W. Edwards, 1962).

2,527. Pinckney Family
Papers. 1694-1898. Ca. 8000 items.
Open. Container list.
Library of Congress, Manuscript Division.
Papers of Charles Cotesworth Pinckney (1746-1825) and his brother Thomas Pinckney (1750-1828) pertain to the years they fought in the Revolutionary War, Charles Pinckney's service as a diplomat, lawyer, and plantation owner; and Thomas Pinckney's tenure as governor of South Carolina and US minister to Great Britain. Includes letters of the brothers to their mother Elizabeth "Eliza" (Lucas) [Mrs. Charles] Pinckney (ca. 1722-93) and their sister Harriott (Pinckney) [Mrs. Daniel] Horry. Also included are letters Eliza Pinckney wrote her sons and friends; letters she wrote to family and friends in England about her husband's death while visiting South Carolina and her subsequent plans; another of her letter books, the original of which is at the South Carolina Historical Society in Charleston; and a volume of Charles Pinckney's second wife Mary (Stead) Pinckney containing letters she wrote while accompanying her husband on a diplomatic mission to France. Collection also contains a plantation book, 1812-61, kept by Charles Pinckney and his successors, which lists male and female slaves, their birth dates, and the work they performed.

2,528. Pittman, Key
Papers. 1898-1951. 77 ft.
Open. Published guide and register.
Library of Congress, Manuscript Division.
Papers of Pittman (1872-1940), a lawyer and prospector, relate to his career as a Democratic US Senator from Nevada and to his support of suffrage being granted to women by the states. They also reflect his changing position on the Susan B. Anthony Amendment. Correspondents include the National American Woman Suffrage Association, the Congressional Union, the Nevada Equal Franchise Society, and other suffrage groups. Also included are papers of Mimosa (Gates) Pittman (1872-1952), whom he married in 1900, containing correspondence with her husband, friends, and her family in Nevada and California; letters she wrote while staking claims in Alaska; and letters that provide information about her civic and social activities as a senator's wife. Also includes correspondence and financial and legal papers concerning her property. See *The National Union Catalog of Manuscript Collections, 1959-1961* (Ann Arbor, MI: J. W. Edwards, 1962).

2,529. Polk, James Knox
Papers. 1775-1891. Ca. 20,500 items.
Open. Published guide.
Library of Congress, Manuscript Division.
Papers of President Polk (1795-1849) include those of Sarah (Childress) Polk (1803-91), whom he married in 1824. She took an active interest in her husband's political career and, particularly after 1839, acted as his secretary and political counselor. Included are ca. 90 letters between James and Sarah Polk from the time he left Congress through the years of his presidency. Bulk of her papers are checks, receipts, invoices, and other financial material from the years when she was living in Nashville as a widow. Entire collection is available on microfilm. See *Index to the James K. Polk Papers* (Washington: Library of Congress, 1969).

2,530. Pollard, Josephine
Papers. Ca. 1870s. 2 items.
Open. No guide.
Library of Congress, Manuscript Division.
One of the poems by Pollard, a poet, is about the seasons; the other is about prayer.

2,531. Poole, Caroline B.
Papers. 1835-37. 1 vol.
Open. No guide.
Library of Congress, Manuscript Division.
Diary in which [Miss] Poole (1802-44), a Boston resident, recorded her daily life as a teacher in Monroe, LA.

2,532. Porter, Eunice R.
Papers. Nd. Ca. 600 items.
Open. Published guide.
Library of Congress, Manuscript Division.
Porter was a genealogist. Correspondence, copies

of wills, Bible and tombstone records, biographical sketches, memorandum books, notes, and printed matter. Much of the correspondence relates to genealogical research on the Goff, Gray, Hewitt, Johnston, Porter, and related families of Virginia, West Virginia, Maryland, and Pennsylvania. Taken from *The National Union Catalog of Manuscript Collections, 1962* (Hamden, CT: The Shoe String Press, Inc., 1964).

2,533. Post, Emily Price
Papers. 1930-31. 30 items.
Open. No guide.
Library of Congress, Manuscript Division.
Radio speeches given by [Mrs. Edwin M.] Post (1873-1960), an author, about various points of etiquette.

2,534. Potter, Samuel
Papers. 1860-81. 150 items.
Open. Published guide.
Library of Congress, Manuscript Division.
Primarily consists of correspondence of Potter, a soldier, with his wife Sophie Potter while he was serving with the Pennsylvania Volunteer Infantry. He writes about military camp life. Taken from *The National Union Catalog of Manuscript Collections, 1973-74* (Washington, DC: The Library of Congress, 1975).

2,535. Powel, Mary Edith
Collection. 1745-1922. 21 ft.
Open. Published and unpublished guides.
Library of Congress, Manuscript Division.
Powel (1846-1931) was a collector of material about naval history. Correspondence, biographical data on American and foreign naval officers, notes, autographs, commissions, pamphlets, illustrations, photos, and clippings on US Navy ships, disasters at sea, Arctic expeditions, Navy educational institutions, marine natural history, and the merchant marine. Correspondents include Stephen B. Luce, Roderick Terry, and Ada C. Wilson. Taken from *The National Union Catalog of Manuscript Collections, 1969* (Washington, DC: The Library of Congress, 1970).

2,536. Powell, Mary (Keane)
Papers. Ca. 1940. 40-page item.
Open. No guide.
Library of Congress, Manuscript Division.
Reminiscence in which Powell (1859-?), a Wyoming settler who was born in Colorado and then moved to Wyoming in about 1868, describes growing up in Laramie helping her mother run a boarding house, marriage at age 15 to Fred Powell, and her subsequent ranching and homesteading before and after the murder of her husband. Also includes an excerpt from a letter of another Wyoming settler, Nettie Penny Rudkins, which corroborates Mary Powell's account of her husband's death.

2,537. Powers, Catherine
Papers. Ca. 1940s. 1 item.
Open. No guide.
Library of Congress, Manuscript Division.
Consists of "Oh the Man Behind the Man Behind the Gun," a poem by Powers, a poet.

2,538. Pruessner, Anna C.
Papers. 1924. 1 vol.
Open. No guide.
Library of Congress, Manuscript Division.
A writer, [Mrs. J. D.] Pruessner (1861?-?) was an advocate of world peace; because she believed that the Versailles Treaty was unduly harsh toward Germany, she judged it a deterrent to peace. Her views, argued on the basis of Christian ethics and numerology, are developed in her book manuscript "Gods Hand Guides the United States to Free the World from War," which also contains clippings and correspondence. The manuscript is the carbon copy of the one she sent to President Calvin Coolidge in 1924.

2,539. Rand, Rose
Papers. 1963. 1 item.
Open. No guide.
Library of Congress, Manuscript Division.
Manuscript of an article "A Study of the Notions 'Real' and 'Unreal,'" by Rand, who may have been a psychiatrist. The article was based on interviews in 1938 with mental patients in a clinic in Vienna.

2,540. Randall, James Garfield
Papers. 1850-1952. 19 ft.
Open. Published guide and register.
Library of Congress, Manuscript Division.
Papers of Randall (1881-1953), an historian, relate to his works on Abraham Lincoln and the Civil War and to his tenure as professor at the University of Illinois, Urbana. Correspondents include Olive Carruthers, Norma Cuthbert, Josephine Harper, Marie Hochmuth, Ella Lonn, Sister Mary Barbara McCarthy, Jeannette Nichols, and Emma Lou Thornbrough. Also included is the manuscript of a book by Randall's wife Ruth Elaine Painter Randall (1892-), *Mary Lincoln: Biography of a Marriage* (Boston: Little, Brown, 1953). See *The National Union Catalog of Manuscript Collections, 1968* (Washington, DC: The Library of Congress, 1969).

2,541. Randolph, William Beverly
Papers. 1696-1884. 7 ft.
Open. Published guide and register.
Library of Congress, Manuscript Division.
Randolph (1793-187?) was a prosperous plantation owner in Virginia before the Civil War. His papers contain information on the economics of managing an extensive plantation with a large number of slaves. Included is correspondence with his mother Elizabeth [Mrs. Peter Skipwith] Randolph (?-ca. 1810), who married Richard Adams in ca. 1802, about his education in Culpepper, VA; Elizabeth Adams's correspondence with her mother-in-law and sisters; and correspondence of William Randolph with his aunt Ann (Meade) Page about his daughter Elizabeth Randolph, who was recuperating from an illness at the Page's home in Virginia. Page's letters contain details of the treatment of his daughter, which included leeching and bleeding. Also included are letters Elizabeth Randolph wrote her father while she was convalescing. See *The National Union Catalog of Manuscript Collections, 1971* (Washington, DC: The Library of Congress, 1973).

2,542. Reid Family
Papers. 1795-1971. 275 ft.
Open. Published guide and register.
Library of Congress, Manuscript Division.
The Reids were a wealthy family of newspaper executives and philanthropists. Collection contains the papers of Whitelaw Reid (1837-1912); of his wife Elisabeth (Mills) Reid (1858-1931), whom he married in 1881; of their son Ogden Mills Reid (1882-1947); and of their daughter-in-law Helen (Rogers) Reid (1882-1970), who married Ogden Reid in 1911. Correspondents of Whitelaw Reid, who worked his way up from writer to managing editor and owner of the *New York Tribune* before he served as ambassador to Great Britain, include Susan B. Anthony, Catharine E. Beecher, Mabel T. and Florence S. Boardman, Mary L. Booth, Anna C. Brackett, Jennie Cunningham Croly, Charlotte Cushman, Mary A. Dodge, Margaret Eaton, Lucretia R. Garfield, Grace Greenwood, Isabella B. Hooker, Julia Ward Howe, Florence King Howland, Helen Hunt Jackson, Mary P. Jacobi, Laura Keene, Mary A. Livermore, Josephine Shaw Lowell, Louise Chandler Moulton, Elizabeth P. Peabody, Lucy Stone, Ellen Terry, and Frances E. Willard.

Correspondence, financial papers, subject files, and miscellany of Elisabeth Reid concern her active interest in the American National Red Cross in New York and London as well as the Nurses' Training School at the Bellevue Hospital in New York, the D. O. Mills Training School for Nurses at the Trudeau Sanatorium in Sarnac Lake, NY, the Sanatorium itself, and the construction of a hospital in San Mateo, CA. In letters to her son written just after he had assumed editorship of the *Herald Tribune,* she coaches him in editorial policy. Others of her papers detail the management of her townhouse and country estate.

Also included are correspondence; financial papers, family papers, a speech and article file, subject files, and miscellany of Helen Reid, which focus on her work as advertising director, vice-president, and then president of the *Herald Tribune.* Correspondents include newspaper staff members Irita Van Doren, Fanny Fern Fitzwater, Walter Lippman, and Dorothy Thompson and Presidents Coolidge, Hoover, Roosevelt, Truman, and Eisenhower. Includes information on the *Herald Tribune's* Forum on Current Problems, which she developed; the newspaper's Fresh Air Fund; her alma mater Barnard College; the Hall of Fame of New York University; the President's Commission on the Status of Women; and woman suffrage.

Whitelaw Reid's papers are available on microfilm. See *Whitelaw Reid: A Register of His Papers* (Washington: Library of Congress, 1958).

2,543. Reignolds, Kate
Papers. Late 19th century. 2 vols.
Open. No guide.
Library of Congress, Manuscript Division.
Reignolds's working copy of the two-act play *Youthful Days of Richelieu* with stage directions and scenery notes.

2,544. Religion
Collection. 18th century. 23 items.
Open. No guide.
Library of Congress, Manuscript Division.
Collection of miscellaneous and anonymous sermons and notes includes a notebook containing a 31-verse hymn composed by a member of the Moravian Sisters in Bethlehem, PA, in 1782.

2,545. Remey Family
Papers. 1855-1932. 10 ft.
Open. Container list.
Library of Congress, Manuscript Division.
Personal papers of George Collier Remey (1841-1928), a US naval officer; of Mary Josephine (Mason) Remey (1845-1938), whom he married in 1873; of their son Charles Mason Remey (1874-?), who was an architect, author, and genealogist; and of Mary Remey's father Charles Mason (1804-82), justice of the Iowa territorial supreme court and federal commissioner of patents. An advocate of women's rights, Charles Mason was particularly interested in equal pay for equal work. His daily diaries for 1836 to 1882 contain mention of his activities for women's rights. Also included are manuscripts of the *Life and Letters of George Collier Remey* (1939) and the *Life and Letters of Mary Josephine Mason Remey* (1939), which Charles Remey compiled from his parents' diaries and letters, and Mary Remey's reminiscences of childhood. Her *Life and Letters* contain extracts from diaries covering her childhood and youth in Burlington, IA, and Washington and from letters she wrote her son about her daily activities as a naval officer's wife in Portsmouth, NH, and Washington.

2,546. Resnik, Muriel
Papers. 1961-68. Ca. 2 ft.
Open. No guide.
Library of Congress, Manuscript Division.
Most of the correspondence, literary manuscripts, financial papers, contracts, and reviews of Resnik (1921?-), an author and playwright, pertain to her play *Any Wednesday.* Also included are

manuscripts of her *Son of Any Wednesday* (New York: Stein and Day, 1965), *House Happy* (New York: Crowell, 1958), and *Life Without Father* (New York: Vanguard Press, 1956).

2,547. Richards, Janet Elizabeth Hosmer
Papers. 1913-46. 1 ft.
Open. Published guide.
Library of Congress, Manuscript Division.
[Miss] Richards (1859-1948) was a lecturer in public affairs. Invitations to social functions at the White House, printed material, and diaries concerning her activities lecturing in Washington, Baltimore, Philadelphia, New York, and Boston, as well as her interviews with various public officials and routine personal matters. Taken from *The National Union Catalog of Manuscript Collections, 1972* (Washington, DC: The Library of Congress, 1974).

2,548. Ridg, Sarah
Papers. 1809. 1 item.
Open. No guide.
Library of Congress, Manuscript Division.
Excerpts of a diary in which [Miss] Ridg describes social events she attended in Burlington, NJ, Philadelphia, and Washington, including James Madison's inaugural ball. She later married Anthony Dry Schuyler.

2,549. Riis, Jacob August
Papers. 1870-1952. 8 ft.
Open. Published guide and register.
Library of Congress, Manuscript Division.
Papers of Riis (1849-1914), a journalist, author, and philanthropist, primarily relate to his work improving the condition of urban slum-dwellers. Included is correspondence with civic and reform organizations, Theodore Roosevelt, and Josephine (Shaw) Lowell. Most of the items are available on microfilm. See *The National Union Catalog of Manuscript Collections, 1959-1961* (Ann Arbor, MI: J. W. Edwards, 1962).

2,550. Rives, William Cabell
Papers. 1674-1939. 67 ft.
Open. Published guide and register.
Library of Congress, Manuscript Division.
Papers of Rives (1793-1868), a US representative and senator from Virginia, diplomat, and historian, contain correspondence, a 70-page autobiography, family papers, a copybook of original verses, and manuscript novels of Judith Page (Walker) Rives (1802-82), an author whom he married in 1819. Includes correspondence with her husband and her children concerning her activities at the family home Castle Hill in Albemarle County, VA. Also included is a journal in the form of letters to her sister which Judith Rives kept while accompanying her husband to France where he served as US minister. She describes her travels in France, Switzerland, and the Netherlands, as well as the 1830 revolution that took place while she was in Paris and a visit to General Lafayette. Family papers are available on microfilm. See *The National Union Catalog of Manuscript Collections, 1971* (Washington, DC: The Library of Congress, 1973).

2,551. Roberts, Elizabeth Madox
Papers. 1920-40. 4 ft.
Access restricted. Published guide.
Library of Congress, Manuscript Division.
Manuscripts for each of the published works of [Miss] Roberts (1881-1941), an author, are included with notes, unpublished writings, sketches, clippings, and a yearbook. Taken from *The National Union Catalog of Manuscript Collections, 1962* (Hamden, CT: The Shoe String Press, Inc., 1964).

2,552. Roberts, Ellwyn Clare
Papers. 1942. 1 item.
Open. No guide.
Library of Congress, Manuscript Division.
Poem "The War of Survival" by Roberts, a poet.

2,553. Robertson, James Alexander
Papers. 1898-1939. Ca. 21,000 items.
Open. Container list.
Library of Congress, Manuscript Division.
Papers of Robertson (1873-1939), a scholar, editor, and archivist, contain correspondence with Emma Helen Blair about their bibliography *The Philippine Islands* (55 vols., 1903-09) and with Irene Wright about collecting material on colonial Florida in the General Archives of the Indies in Seville, Spain.

2,554. Robinson, Lydia S. M.
Papers. 1914-36. 6 ft.
Partially restricted. Published guide and register.
Library of Congress, Manuscript Division.
Robinson was the secretary of the Navy League of the US, Dept. No. 6, in Philadelphia. Consists of military service records and other material relating to American men who died in WWI but who did not receive recognition because they were members of the Allied Powers' forces, not the American. Also included are letters that soldiers or their families wrote Robinson when they were returning service record forms. See *National Union Catalog of Manuscript Collections, 1977* (Washington, DC: Library of Congress, 1978).

2,555. Robson, May
Papers. 1882-1942. Ca. 9 ft.
Open. No guide.
Library of Congress, Manuscript Division.
May Robson is the stage name that Mary Jeanette Robison (1858-1942), an actress born in Australia, took after her name was thus misspelled on the program of her debut performance. Correspondence, scrapbooks of reviews and photos of Robson in her roles, playbills, and her itinerary for 1908 to 1913. Robson moved to the US after her first marriage in 1877 to Edward H. Gore; in 1889 she married Augustus Homer Brown. A character actress and make-up expert, she appeared on the Broadway stage, in vaudeville, and in the movies. Also included are scrapbooks of correspondence and autographs of Hollywood actors and actresses, which were presented to Robson as a tribute in 1933.

2,556. Rodgers Family
Papers. 1740-1957. Ca. 40 ft.
Open. Published guide and register.
Library of Congress, Manuscript Division.
Papers of the Rodgers family, male members of which were career naval officers, include extensive correspondence between John Rodgers (1773-1838), a commodore in the US Navy; his wife Minerva (Denison) Rodgers (1784-1877); their daughters Ann "Nannie" (Rodgers) [Mrs. John Navarre] Macomb (1824-1916) and Louisa (Rodgers) [Mrs. Montgomery Cunningham] Meigs (1817-79); their son John Rodgers (1812-82); and other close relatives. Includes correspondence of John Rodgers, the elder, with his friend Ann Pinckney, who acted as emissary by keeping him apprised of the feelings of his future wife (Minerva Denison). Also includes correspondence documenting the personal relationship and daily activities of John and Minerva Rodgers while he was at sea and she was managing the family home at Sion Hill near Havre de Grace, MD, and later in Washington; correspondence of Nannie Macomb with her husband while he was chief of the army's topographical engineers; correspondence of Louisa Meigs with her soldier husband while she was in Washington, DC; and correspondence of John Rodgers, the younger, with his wife Ann (Hodge) Rodgers while he was at sea and she in Germantown, PA, and Washington. Also included is correspondence of Ann Rodgers's husband with her mother Sarah (Bayard) [Mrs. William L.] Hodge, as well as Sarah Hodge's correspondence while she was in France and New Orleans. Contained as well is correspondence of Nannie and John Macomb with their daughter Minerva (Macomb) [Mrs. Thomas Willing] Peters, who wrote of life in Wyoming Territory during the 1880s and Europe in the 1890s, and Louisa and Montgomery Meigs's correspondence with their daughter Mary (Meigs) [Mrs. Joseph Hancock] Taylor, who was married to an army officer. Autobiographical sketches of Minerva Rodgers and Nannie Macomb concern their childhoods. See *The Rodgers Family: A Register of Their Papers in the Library of Congress, Naval Historical Foundation Collection* (Washington: Library of Congress, 1972).

2,557. Roedel, Josephine Forney
Papers. 1863-64. 1 vol.
Open. No guide.
Library of Congress, Manuscript Division.
Diary in which [Mrs. William D.] Roedel (1825-1904), writing about her trip from her home in Wytheville, PA, to visit her family and friends in Gettysburg, PA, Baltimore, and Washington, records difficulties she encountered traveling through the lines of both Union and Confederate armies as well as meetings with Thaddeus Stevens and General Benjamin F. Butler to obtain passes. An annotated transcription of the diary was printed in *The Pennsylvania Magazine of History and Biography* (Oct., 1943).

2,558. Roosevelt, Kermit, Family
Papers. 1885-1964. 70 ft.
Open. Published guide and register.
Library of Congress, Manuscript Division.
Papers of Roosevelt (1889-1943), a soldier, author, explorer, and businessman, and of his wife Belle Wyatt (Willard) Roosevelt (1892-1968), an author and businesswoman who organized and directed Your Secretary, Inc. His correspondents include Edith Kermit Roosevelt and other family members, Edith Helm, Fannie Hurst, Ruth Hanna McCormick, Frances Perkins, Margaret Sanger, and Madame Sun Yat-sen. Also included is general and family correspondence of Belle Roosevelt, particularly with her sister Elizabeth (Willard) Herbert and her mother Belle (Wyatt) Willard; Belle Roosevelt's diaries, 1908-23 and 1940-63; subject files on her WWII work and various Roosevelt memorial associations; bills and receipts, a budget book, real estate records, taxes, and other business papers; articles she wrote; and a guest book, passports, poems, scrapbooks, photos, and clippings. See *National Union Catalog of Manuscript Collections, 1977* (Washington, DC: Library of Congress, 1978).

2,559. Roosevelt, Theodore
Papers. 1759-1920. Ca. 276,000 items.
Open. Published guide.
Library of Congress, Manuscript Division.
Papers of Roosevelt (1858-1919), US President, contain correspondence of his second wife Edith (Carow) Roosevelt (1861-1948), whom he married in 1886, much of which was written while she was First Lady. Entire collection is available on microfilm. See *Index to the Theodore Roosevelt Papers* (Washington: Library of Congress, 1969).

2,560. Royall, Anne (Newport)
Papers. 1824-47. 8 items.
Open. No guide.
Library of Congress, Manuscript Division.
An author, traveler, and journalist, [Mrs. William] Royall (1769-1854) is sometimes termed the first newspaperwoman in the US. Correspondence primarily concerns business, the sale of her publications, and her claim for a Revolutionary War widow pension.

2,561. Royce, Sarah Eleanor (Bayliss)
Papers. 1890s? 110-page vol.
Open. No guide.

Library of Congress, Manuscript Division.
Reminiscence by [Mrs. Josiah] Royce (1819-91), a California settler, concerns the trip she took with her family from Iowa across the plains to California during the gold rush of 1849.

2,562. Russell, Charles Edward
Papers. 1864-1941. 16 ft.
Open. Register.
Library of Congress, Manuscript Division.
Papers of Russell (1860-1941), a journalist, author, and socialist, include information on civil rights, prison reform, and women's suffrage. Included are correspondence with actress Julia Marlowe during his writing of *Julia Marlowe: Her Life and Art* (1926); his correspondence with Ruby Darrow, Fannie Hurst, and Mary Mae Swiney; notes for four lectures on Shakespeare which were given in ca. 1900 by his first wife Abby Osborne (Rust) Russell (1866-1901); and manuscript poems by Louise A. McGaffey. Julia Marlowe was the stage name used by Sarah Frances Frost.

2,563. Russian Orthodox Greek Catholic Church of North America, Diocese of Alaska
Records. 1772-1936. Ca. 150,000 items.
Open. Published guide, container list, and index.
Library of Congress, Manuscript Division.
Ecclesiastical documents dealing with the administration of the 17 Church parishes located in Atka, Belkofsky, Ikogmut, Juneau, Kenai, Kalesnoo, Kodiak, Kuskakwim, Nushagak, Nutchek, St. George Island, St. Michael Island, St. Paul Island, Sitka, Taitlek, Unalaska, and Unga, AK, and of the 36 chapels on the other islands. Registers of births, marriages, and deaths; records of confessions and communion; registers of converts; records of income and expenditures of Church funds; reports about churches and lists of clergy; diaries and travel journals; and photos of bishops, priests, church members, churches, and local scenery. Includes vital statistics on Alaskan Indian women who joined the Church and women's petitions to and correspondence with the Church. Vital statistics are available on microfilm. See *The National Union Catalog of Manuscript Collections, 1963-1964* (Washington, DC: The Library of Congress, 1965).

2,564. Salamanca, Lucy
Papers. 1943?. 1 item.
Open. No guide.
Library of Congress, Manuscript Division.
Book manuscript "Fortress of Freedom," an unpublished history of the Library of Congress, by Salamanca, an author who was head of the Library's congressional research section of the Legislative Reference Service.

2,565. Salz, Helen
Papers. 1931-40. 5 items.
Open. No guide.
Library of Congress, Manuscript Division.
Poems by Salz, a poet, include one entitled "Country Poor House."

2,566. Schoolcraft, Henry Rowe
Papers. 1788-1906. 28 ft.
Open. Published guide.
Library of Congress, Manuscript Division.
Papers of Schoolcraft (1793-1864), an author, explorer, geologist, and Indian agent, contain his writings on Indian legends which include stories about Indian women in the Michigan area. Also included are papers of his first wife Jane (Johnston) Schoolcraft (1800-42), a part Ojibwe Indian educated in England whom he married in 1823; of their daughter Jane A. Schoolcraft (1827-?); and of his second wife Mary (Howard) Schoolcraft, an author whom he married in 1847.

His first wife's papers consist of a journal she kept in 1828 of her farming, gardening, and other activities presumably near Sault Ste. Marie, MI, while he was away from home; volumes of poems she wrote before and after marriage and one of devotional poetry, 1788-1828; and manuscript magazines she, her sisters and brothers (writing under Indian pseudonyms), and Henry Schoolcraft compiled in 1826 and 1827 for their own entertainment. *The Muzzeniegun; or Literary Voyager* contained Ojibwe tales, legends, and history as well as an article about an Indian girlhood.

Henry and Jane Schoolcraft's daughter Jane continued the family tradition and with her brother John edited *The Garland*, a literary magazine that contained essays and poems by the editors and works copied from other sources. Collection contains 30 issues from 1844 to 1846.

Papers of Mary Schoolcraft consist of correspondence with her husband Henry, her sisters, brother, and mother; business and financial papers, including three account book records of boarders she took in between 1861 and 1865, which she used primarily as notebooks for her thoughts on women, servants, and other matters; articles she wrote on southern women and slavery; and reviews of her novel *The Black Gauntlet* (Philadelphia: Lippincott, 1860), which concerned the nature of life and manners on a South Carolinian plantation. A member of a wealthy, slave-owning South Carolinian family, Mary Schoolcraft moved to Washington after her marriage to Henry Schoolcraft and remained there until her death. Loyal to the Union, she nevertheless felt compelled to defend southern institutions to the North. The majority of her papers are letters in which she candidly discusses her view of political life in Washington, the Civil War, and Reconstruction; she also wrote on women, particularly their need for economic independence. Her financial and business papers document her management of her husband's and her own finances. Entire collection is available on microfilm. See *Henry Rowe Schoolcraft: A Register of His Papers* (Washington: Library of Congress, 1973).

2,567. Schureman, James Wall
Papers. 1839-44. 20 items.
Open. No guide.
Library of Congress, Manuscript Division.
Letters of Schureman (?-1852), a US Army officer, to his sister [Miss] Mary E. Schureman of Monmouth County, NJ, while he was a student at West Point and later while he was stationed at Fort Wood, LA.

2,568. Schuyler, Louisa Lee
Papers. 1852-1915, nd. 15 items.
Open. No guide.
Library of Congress, Manuscript Division.
A promoter of scientific philanthropy, [Miss] Schuyler (1837-1926) worked for the US Sanitary Commission, the State Charities Aid Association of New York, Bellevue Hospital, and the National Committee for the Prevention of Blindness. Correspondence, a journal recording her re-entry in 1871 into active charity work after a seven-year hiatus, her reminiscences of childhood, pamphlets concerning organizations in which she was interested, and photos of Schuyler.

2,569. Schwimmer, Rosika
Papers. 1930-48. 15 items.
Open. No guide.
Library of Congress, Manuscript Division.
Correspondence of Schwimmer (1877-1948), a pacifist and feminist, is primarily with Oliver Wendell Holmes about his dissenting opinion to the Supreme Court decision denying Schwimmer US citizenship. Also included are a copy of Holmes's opinion, an article based on a 1933 interview Schwimmer had with Holmes, and an obituary of Schwimmer. In 1911 Schwimmer married a Mr. Bédy; in 1913 they were divorced.

2,570. See, Thomas Jefferson Jackson
Papers. 1887-1960. 52 ft.
Open. Published guide and register.
Library of Congress, Manuscript Division.
Papers of See (1866-1962), an astronomer and mathematician, contain correspondence with Carrie Harrison. Also included are correspondence with his fiancée Frances Graves, an office worker in St. Louis whom he married in ca. 1907, and correspondence in which his sister Anna M. (See) Weeks describes her activities in Montgomery City and Mineola, MO. See *The National Union Catalog of Manuscript Collections, 1963-1964* (Washington, DC: The Library of Congress, 1965).

2,571. Shaw Family
Papers. 1636-1892. 1.6 ft.
Open. Published guide and inventory.
Library of Congress, Manuscript Division.
Family correspondence between Elizabeth (Smith) Shaw Peabody (1750-1815), her son William Smith Shaw, her daughter Abigail Adams (Shaw) [Mrs. John Barlow] Felt (1790-1859), and Peabody's sister Abigail (Smith) [Mrs. John] Adams (1744-1818). Also included are copybooks of Felt and miscellaneous writings by Peabody, who was married to John Shaw before she married Stephen Peabody. See *The National Union Catalog of Manuscript Collections, 1963-1964* (Washington, DC: The Library of Congress, 1965).

2,572. Shepherd, Alexander Robey
Papers. 1776-1945. 7.2 ft.
Open. Published guide and register.
Library of Congress, Manuscript Division.
A businessman and governor of the District of Columbia, Shepherd (1835-1902) became involved in silver mining in Mexico from 1879 until his death. His papers include letters he and his wife May (Young) Shepherd (?-1930) wrote their daughters May (Shepherd) [Mrs. E. A.] Quintard and Grace (Shepherd) [Mrs. Francis D.] Merchant (1869-?) about the family's life and daily routine at the mining site. Also included are a diary in which Mary Shepherd describes her first journey to Mexico in 1880, camping along the way with her seven children, and reflections on Mexican women and a diary in which May Quintard, then approximately 16 years old, records her activities during her first years living on the site. See *The National Union Catalog of Manuscript Collections, 1959-1961* (Ann Arbor, MI: J. W. Edwards, 1962).

2,573. Sheridan, Philip Henry
Papers. 1853-88. 53 ft.
Open. Published guide.
Library of Congress, Manuscript Division.
Papers of Sheridan (1831-88), a US Army officer and author, contain accounts of the smuggling by Rebecca Wright, a Quaker and Union supporter living in Winchester, VA, in September 1864, of military intelligence to General Sheridan, the result of which was that he was able to capture the town. Two of the accounts were written by Wright, who later married a Mr. Bonsal; two were by Sheridan. See *Philip H. Sheridan: A Register of His Papers* (Washington: Library of Congress, 1962).

2,574. Shippen Family
Papers. Ca. 1671-1936. 11.5 ft.
Open. Container list.
Library of Congress, Manuscript Division.
Papers of William Shippen, a physician; his daughter Ann Home (Shippen) Livingston; his son Thomas Lee Shippen; Thomas's son William Shippen, a physician; Edward Shippen, a descendant who was a physician; and other family members. Included is correspondence, 1773-1828, of Ann Livingston with her parents, brother, mother-in-law, and friends about her separation from her husband Henry Beekman Livingston, whom she married in 1781, and the custody of their daughter and correspondence over 20 years in

which an unidentified friend discusses with her their friendship and mutual support during many hardships. Also included is correspondence, 1790-1826, of her sister-in-law Elizabeth (Carter) Banister Shippen Izard with her second husband Thomas Lee Shippen during their courtship, with their son William Shippen, and with her mother; she married Shippen in 1791 and later married George Izard. Collection also contains letters to Izard's daughter-in-law Louisa S. Shippen, a Philadelphia resident, from friends; letters, 1882-1916, to Rebecca Lloyd Shippen from her sons and her husband Edward Shippen while they were on trips to Europe and Canada, 1882-1916; and letters to Rebecca (Lloyd) [Mrs. Joseph Hopper] Nicholson of Annapolis, MD, from her mother, children, and grandchildren, 1788-1849. All items available on microfilm.

2,575. Shufeldt, Robert Wilson
Papers. 1836-1910. 15 ft.
Open. Published guide.
Library of Congress, Manuscript Division.
Papers, the bulk of which pertain to the naval and diplomatic career of Shufeldt (1822-95), a naval officer, shipmaster, explorer, and diplomat, include letters his wife Sarah (Abercrombie) Shufeldt (?-1871) wrote him while he was on duty and she in New Canaan, CT. Also included are letters Mary (Miller) Shufeldt wrote her mother, who probably was Robert Shufeldt's sister-in-law Martha A. Miller, while in Japan during the late 1880s and letters she wrote Robert Shufeldt, who seems to have adopted her after her mother's death. See *Robert Wilson Shufeldt: A Register of His Papers* (Washington: Library of Congress, 1969).

2,576. Sifton, Paul, and Sifton, Claire (Ginsburg)
Papers. 1933-38. 2 items.
Open. No guide.
Library of Congress, Manuscript Division.
Typescripts of plays *Blood on the Moon* and *The Doctors* written by playwrights Paul Sifton (1897-1972) and his wife Claire Sifton (1897-).

2,577. Sims, William Sowden
Papers. 1856-1951. 61.8 ft.
Open. Published guides.
Library of Congress, Manuscript Division.
Papers relating to the military activities of Sims (1858-1936), a US Navy officer, include letters to his mother and sisters, letters his wife Anne (Hitchcock) Sims wrote him while he was on duty, and calendars for 1932 to 1935 recording her social engagements after her husband had retired in Boston. See *William Sowden Sims: A Register of His Papers* (Washington: Library of Congress, 1971). See also *The National Union Catalog of Manuscript Collections, 1971* (Washington, DC: The Library of Congress, 1973); *National Union Catalog of Manuscript Collections, 1977* (Washington, DC: Library of Congress, 1978).

2,578. Singleton Family
Papers. 1758-1860. Ca. 800 items.
Open. No guide.
Library of Congress, Manuscript Division.
Letters to Marion (Singleton) Deveaux (1815-?), a resident of Sumter County and Stateburg, SC, from her mother Rebecca T. (Coles) [Mrs. Richard] Singleton (?-1849) and from Rebecca Singleton's sister in Charlottesville, VA. The letters concern the period from 1827 to 1831 when Marion Singleton was a student in Philadelphia and continue through her courtship and marriage in 1835 to Robert Marion Deveaux and her second marriage in ca. 1849 to August L. Converse. Also included are Robert Deveaux's letters to his wife, letters to his father while he was a student at the University of Virginia, and business correspondence. Marion Deveaux apparently left her husband August Converse in ca. 1853 and resumed using her previous married name.

2,579. Smith, Jessica Randolph
Papers. 1868-1932. 2 items.
Open. No guide.
Library of Congress, Manuscript Division.
Clipping of Smith, a Washington resident, concerns the nomination of U. S. Grant. Also included is her reminiscence of her father's invention of a cotton picker and his refusal to swear allegiance to the US government in order to become examiner of patents.

2,580. Smith, Lucy H. King (Cunningham)
Papers. Nd. 1 item.
Open. No guide.
Library of Congress, Manuscript Division.
Poem written and illustrated by [Mrs. Alfred Franklin] Smith (1872-1940), a poet and composer, is a tribute to Samuel Chester Reid and Betsy Ross.

2,581. Smith, Lucy Walker
Papers. 1902. 1 item.
Open. No guide.
Library of Congress, Manuscript Division.
Statement in which Lucy Smith, a resident of Salt Lake City, swears she was a plural wife of the Mormon prophet Joseph Smith. She also briefly describes her decision to marry him in 1843.

2,582. Smith, Margaret (Bayard)
Papers. 1789-1874. Ca. 7 ft.
Open. No guide.
Library of Congress, Manuscript Division.
An author, [Mrs. Samuel Harrison] Smith (1778-1844) was an early chronicler of Washington society. Family correspondence, diaries, and commonplace books record the activities and thoughts of a Washington hostess who entertained both Whigs—her political preference—and her husband's Jeffersonian friends. Her correspondents include her sister Jane (Bayard) [Mrs. Andrew] Kirkpatrick, her sister-in-law [Miss] Mary Ann Smith, her son Jonathan Bayard Harrison Smith (1810-?), her daughters Anna Maria Harrison Smith (1811-?) and Susan Harrison Smith (1804-?), and her friend Maria Templeton. Also includes letters from her husband to his sister Mary Ann Smith. Margaret Smith's diaries and commonplace books, 1799-1840s, contain quotations and poems she copied, essays she wrote prompted by her readings, a reminiscence on Jefferson's presidency, and copies of letters James Madison wrote to "my dearest."

Collection also contains diaries and commonplace books in which her daughter Anna Smith copied poems and quotations, drew sketches, and recorded her activities between 1822 and 1834. Also contained are diaries and commonplace books, 1810-19, of [Miss] Susan Bayard Smith in which she intersperses records of her religious beliefs and activities with copied poems and her own writings.

2,583. Smith, Pamela Seward
Papers. 1815-16. 1 vol.
Open. No guide.
Library of Congress, Manuscript Division.
Journal which Pamela Seward (1797-?), a Vermont resident, kept during an eight-month trip to New Jersey prior to her marriage in 1816 to Luther Smith. She mentions relatives and friends. Also included is a poem she wrote describing her renunciation of worldly finery and her struggle to be "born again" in baptism.

2,584. Southworth, Emma Dorothy Eliza (Nevitte)
Papers. 1895. 2 items.
Open. No guide.
Library of Congress, Manuscript Division.
Letter in which [Mrs. Frederick Hamilton] Southworth (1819-99), a novelist, describes an incident in childhood when she met Benjamin King.

2,585. Sparrow, Louise Winslow (Kidder)
Papers. 1930-58. 1 vol.
Open. No guide.
Library of Congress, Manuscript Division.
[Mrs. Herbert George] Sparrow (1884-) is a sculptor and writer. Papers pertaining to her career as a sculptor, which she began at age 40, consist of a copy of a journal she kept between 1930 and 1934, her reminiscences, catalogs and photos of her work, and a few poems she wrote. She married Sparrow in 1909 and Paul E. H. Gripon in 1940, but professionally she was known as Louise Kidder Sparrow.

2,586. Speyer, Lenora (Von Stosch)
Papers. Ca. 1917-41. 21 items.
Open. No guide.
Library of Congress, Manuscript Division.
[Mrs. Edgar] Speyer (1872-1956) was a poet and author. Longhand poems, most of which have been published; a letter discussing them; and a list of poetry awards she won.

2,587. Spingarn, Arthur Barnett
Papers. 1911-64. 28.8 ft.
Partially restricted. Published guide and register.
Library of Congress, Manuscript Division.
Papers of Spingarn (1878-1971), a lawyer, author, and founder of the NAACP, pertain to his work with the NAACP, the New York State Social Hygiene and Tuberculosis Association, and the Manhattan Council of the New York State Committee Against Discrimination. Includes letters from Mary White Ovington to Roy Wilkins. See *The National Union Catalog of Manuscript Collections, 1966* (Washington, DC: The Library of Congress, 1967).

2,588. Stanton, Elizabeth (Cady)
Papers. 1814-1946. 5 ft.
Open. Published and unpublished guides.
Library of Congress, Manuscript Division.
Consists of scrapbooks containing correspondence, speeches, and miscellaneous material and of speeches, articles, and draft writings by [Mrs. Henry Brewster] Stanton (1815-1902), a reformer and suffragist. Papers document her career as a champion of women's rights, including the right to vote, and touch upon her activities on behalf of such other reform movements as the abolition of slavery. Correspondents include her husband, Susan B. Anthony, Daniel Cady, William Henry Channing, Lydia Maria Child, Frederick Douglass, Lucretia Mott, Lydia Mott, Edith Kermit Roosevelt, Lucy Stone, and John Greenleaf Whittier. Taken from *The National Union Catalog of Manuscript Collections, 1971* (Washington, DC: The Library of Congress, 1973).

2,589. Steefel, Genevieve (Fallon)
Papers. 1944-50. 1 ft.
Open. Published guide and register.
Library of Congress, Manuscript Division.
A Minneapolis political worker, [Mrs. Lawrence D.] Steefel (1899-) was national committeewoman-at-large for the National Progressive party. Correspondence traces her involvement in the party from her work as vice-chairman of the executive committee of the Independent Voters of Minnesota, to cochairman of Women for (Henry A.) Wallace, to committeewoman-at-large. Correspondents include Elinor S. Gimbel of Women for Wallace and Henry Wallace. Bulk of the collection, however, consists of copies of press releases, policy statements, speeches, and committee minutes of the National Progressive party, which she collected in connection with her work. Topics include Progressive Citizens of America, the 1948 Wallace presidential campaign, the party, civil rights, and repeal of the Taft-Hartley law. See *The National Union Catalog of Manuscript Collections, 1967* (Washington, DC: The Library of Congress, 1968).

2,590. Steinhardt, Laurence Adolph
Papers. 1929-50. 42 ft.
Open. Published guide and register.
Library of Congress, Manuscript Division.
Papers of Steinhardt (1892-1950), US ambassador to Peru, the USSR, Turkey, Czechoslovakia, and Canada, include correspondence with Ruth (Bryan) Owens, who was the American minister to Copenhagen. See *The National Union Catalog of Manuscript Collections, 1965* (Washington, DC: The Library of Congress, 1966).

2,591. Stevens, Margaret Talbott
Papers. 1935. 1 item.
Open. No guide.
Library of Congress, Manuscript Division.
Article which Stevens (1892-1955), an author and librarian for the Baltimore and Ohio Railroad, wrote commemorating the 100th anniversary of the Railroad's first train to Washington.

2,592. Stoddert, Rebecca (Lowndes)
Papers. 1769-1800. 33 items.
Open. No guide.
Library of Congress, Manuscript Division.
Financial papers and correspondence in which Stoddert (?-ca. 1800) describes to her niece Eliza Gantt her activities in Georgetown, MD, and Philadelphia as the wife of a merchant and later secretary of the navy, Benjamin Stoddert.

2,593. Stowe, Harriet Elizabeth (Beecher)
Papers. 1865-85. 15 items.
Open. No guide.
Library of Congress, Manuscript Division.
Family and business correspondence of [Mrs. Calvin Ellis] Stowe (1811-96), an author and reformer.

2,594. Stull, Lydia J.
Papers. 1865. 23 items.
Open. No guide.
Library of Congress, Manuscript Division.
A reformer and nurse, [Mrs.] Stull was an agent for the US Sanitary Commission; her duty apparently was to review court martial cases, particularly of prisoners at Fort Whipple, VA, and to help secure prisoners' release. Consists primarily of letters in which prisoners state their cases and ask Stull's help but also includes a few letters in which she details her work and describes the prisoners she aided.

2,595. Suggett, Laura (Steffens)
Papers. 1925-29. Ca. 600 items.
Open. No guide.
Library of Congress, Manuscript Division.
[Mrs. Allen Holman] Suggett (?-1946) was the sister of Lincoln Steffens. In 1924 she was appointed chairman of the GFWC committee of library extension and in this position coordinated a survey of the county library service in the US. Collection contains survey results, with summaries of her activities as chairman, of the committee's recommendations and financial expenses, and of the state-by-state findings.

2,596. Sullivan, Mark
Papers. 1900-35. 15 ft.
Open. Published guide and register.
Library of Congress, Manuscript Division.
Papers of Sullivan (1874-1952), a journalist and author, contain correspondence with Ethel C. Roosevelt Derby; Mary L. D. Ferris; Katharine Gay of the *New York Evening Post;* Florence K. [Mrs. Warren G.] Harding; Amy Loveman, who was assistant editor of the "Literary Review" of the *Post;* Agnes Pendleton, who was secretary to Edwin F. Gay of the *Post;* Edith Kermit [Mrs. Theodore] Roosevelt; Rose Shuman; [Miss] Bess Smith; Helen H. Taft; Ida M. Tarbell; and Ethel M. Thackray of Scribner's. Also included are letters to Sullivan's wife Marie B. Sullivan from William Jennings Bryan, Ethel Roosevelt Derby, Florence Harding, Edith Kermit Roosevelt, and William Howard Taft and to Mabel Shea from Katharine A. Fisher, who was director of the Good Housekeeping Institute. See *The National Union Catalog of Manuscript Collections, 1968* (Washington, DC: The Library of Congress, 1969).

2,597. Susan B. Anthony Foundation
Records. 1896-1943. 3 ft.
Open. Published guide.
Library of Congress, Manuscript Division.
Constitution, bylaws, minutes, correspondence, reports, financial and other records, a membership list, a scrapbook, clippings, and printed matter of the Foundation, which was known as the Anthony League of the District of Columbia from its establishment in 1912 until 1924. Correspondents include the District of Columbia Federation of Women's Clubs, the GFWC, the Juvenile Protective Association of the District of Columbia, and the National LWV. Contains information on [Mrs.] Anna E. Hendley, a founder and in 1960 president of the Foundation; biographical papers of Anthony; and records of the District of Columbia Woman Suffrage Association. Taken from *The National Union Catalog of Manuscript Collections, 1965* (Washington, DC: The Library of Congress, 1966).

2,598. Swart, Rose C.
Papers. 1910-18, nd. 43 items.
Open. No guide.
Library of Congress, Manuscript Division.
Correspondence, research notes, and clippings of Swart, who was associated with the State Normal School in Oshkosh, WI, concern the story "Nurnberg Stove" by "Ouida," who was Marie Louise de la Ramée.

2,599. Taft, William Howard
Papers. 1810-1930. Ca. 780 ft.
Open. Published guides.
Library of Congress, Manuscript Division.
Papers of President Taft (1857-1930) include correspondence with Mabel Boardman. Also available on microfilm. See *Index to the William Howard Taft Papers* (Washington: The Library of Congress, 1972). See also *The National Union Catalog of Manuscript Collections, 1962* (Hamden, CT: The Shoe String Press, Inc., 1964).

2,600. Talbot, Theodore
Papers. 1838-67. Ca. 200 items.
Open. No guide.
Library of Congress, Manuscript Division.
Papers relating to the career of Talbot (?-1862), an explorer and soldier, include letters in which he described to his mother Adelaide Talbot and his sister Mary L. Talbot, both of Washington, his explorations in Oregon and elsewhere in the West and later his garrison duty at army posts, including Fort Sumter in 1861 prior to the bombardment. Also included are letters which author Jessie (Benton) Frémont, whose husband John Charles Frémont headed the Oregon expedition that Theodore Talbot joined, wrote to Adelaide Talbot about the condition and return of the group.

2,601. Terhune, Albert Payson
Papers. 1890-1941. 7 ft. (ca. 580 items).
Open. Published guide and register.
Library of Congress, Manuscript Division.
Papers of Terhune (1872-1942), an author, include articles by his wife Anice (Stockton) Terhune (1873-1964), who was a composer and novelist, and her reminiscences of him. See *The National Union Catalog of Manuscript Collections, 1959-1961* (Ann Arbor, MI: J. W. Edwards, 1962).

2,602. Terrell, Mary (Church)
Papers. 1886-1954. 20 ft.
Open. Published and unpublished guides.
Library of Congress, Manuscript Division.
Terrell (1863-1954) was a Negro leader and author. Correspondence; diaries; manuscripts of her autobiography *A Colored Woman in a White World,* short stories, and poems; speeches; articles; notebooks; datebooks; photos; clippings; printed matter; and memorabilia. Includes information on politics, the rights of women, and desegregation in the District of Columbia. Jane Addams, Mary (McLeod) Bethune, Carrie Chapman Catt, Ruth Hanna McCormick, and Booker T. Washington are among the correspondents. Taken from *The National Union Catalog of Manuscript Collections, 1959-1961* (Ann Arbor, MI: J. W. Edwards, 1962).

2,603. Thaxter, Celia (Laighton)
Papers. Late 1800s. 1 item.
Open. No guide.
Library of Congress, Manuscript Division.
Poem "The Blind Lamb" by [Mrs. Levi] Thaxter (1835-94), a poet.

2,604. Thayer, William Sydney
Papers. 1835-1901. Ca. 600 items.
Open. Published guide and notes.
Library of Congress, Manuscript Division.
Papers of Thayer (1830-64), a newspaper correspondent, editor, and US consul general in Egypt, include a family genealogy and correspondence, 1845-65, and poems of his sister Sarah S. Thayer, who was a teacher and poet in Massachusetts. See *The National Union Catalog of Manuscript Collections, 1959-1961* (Ann Arbor, MI: J. W. Edwards, 1962).

2,605. Thomas, Cora de La Matyr
Papers. 1884-1940. 69 items.
Open. No guide.
Library of Congress, Manuscript Division.
Most of these brief letters to [Miss] Thomas from friends seem to have been saved for their autographs. Correspondents include Susan B. Anthony, Julia Ward Howe, Frances Willard, Margaret Deland, and Pauline Bigelow.

2,606. Thomas, Maria Louise (Palmer)
Papers. 1824-1906. 200 items.
Open. No guide.
Library of Congress, Manuscript Division.
Family correspondence includes documentation of the activities of Thomas (ca. 1830-?) in such women's groups as Sorosis, of which she was president in 1887; the Association for the Advancement of Women; and the National Council of Women of the United States. Also included are autograph letters she collected; letters to her husband Abel Charles Thomas (1807-80), a Universalist clergyman; and legal papers of her father Strange N. Palmer.

2,607. Thompson, Eliza Jane (Trimble)
Papers. 1898. 1 item.
Open. No guide.
Library of Congress, Manuscript Division.
Speech which [Mrs. James Henry] Thompson (1816-1905), a temperance reformer, made before the Friday Club in Hillsboro, OH, on the development of the WCTU as a result of the temperance crusade of 1873 and 1874.

2,608. Thornton, William
Papers. 1741-1865. 27 vols.
Open. Container list.
Library of Congress, Manuscript Division.
Papers of Thornton (1759-1828), a Washington architect, inventor, and public official, include papers of his wife Anna Maria (Brodeau) Thornton (1774?-?), a writer. Her correspondence with Margaret (Bayard) Smith, John Quincy Adams, Louisa Catherine Adams, and others; manuscripts of essays, a play, novels, a story about what a woman ambling about Washington would see, and a biographical sketch she wrote of her husband; a

visiting book listing guests, those who had moved or died, and those who were removed from the list; an expense book her husband began before he died and she completed after his death; an account book listing rents she received and the maintenance of her properties; a bankbook; and commonplace books. Also included are diaries for the years 1792 through 1864, with some omissions, beginning when Anna Thornton lived in Tortola in the British Virgin Islands and then in Philadelphia and Washington. The volumes usually contain brief notes on her activities and daily expenses but those for 1800 through 1818 are particularly detailed concerning social life in Washington. All items are available on microfilm.

2,609. Toner, Joseph Meredith

Papers. 1741-1896. 100 ft.
Open. Published guide and register.
Library of Congress, Manuscript Division.
A physician and author, Toner (1825-96) also was a collector of manuscript medical dissertations and of material relating to the Washington family. His papers include material on Anne Washington, 1764; Martha Washington, 1799-1800; Mary Washington, 1759-78; Sarah Washington, 1815; and Betty Lewis, 1779-96. Also included is a 1769 manuscript on the history of midwifery, with a few pages of practical notes of instruction; a commonplace book of Sarah Ann MacCary; and records of the Ladies Association of the First Presbyterian Church, Washington, 1868-71, with a constitution, minutes, financial records, an attendance record, and a list of charter members. Toner's correspondence with Sarah Madeleine V. Dahlgren is included as well. See *The National Union Catalog of Manuscript Collections, 1967* (Washington, DC: The Library of Congress, 1968).

2,610. Traubel, Horace L., and Traubel, Anne (Montgomerie)

Papers. 1888-1955. 14 ft.
Partially restricted. Published guide and register.
Library of Congress, Manuscript Division.
Papers of Horace Traubel (1858-1919), a poet, critic, and biographer of Walt Whitman, pertain to Traubel's belief in Marxist socialism and his interest in Whitman. Proofs of a periodical *The Conservator,* which Traubel founded to express his social philosophy, are included as is correspondence of his wife Anne Traubel (1864-1954), a student of Whitman's who compiled a book of Whitman's thoughts on nature.

Correspondents of the Traubels include Minnie Maddern Fiske, Ellen Glasgow, Henrietta Hovey, Helen Keller, Margaret Lacey, Horace Traubel's parents Katherine Grunder Traubel and Maurice Henry Traubel, and Anne and Horace Traubel's daughter Gertrude Traubel. Also included is business correspondence of Horace and Anne Traubel. See *The National Union Catalog of Manuscript Collections, 1970* (Washington, DC: The Library of Congress, 1971).

2,611. Trommer, Marie

Papers. 1925-37. 6 items.
Open. No guide.
Library of Congress, Manuscript Division.
Letters to Trommer (1895-), an editor, concern her articles on artists and her magazine *American-Russian Review.*

2,612. Tunstall, Nannie Whitmell

Papers. Late 1800s?. 1 vol.
Open. No guide.
Library of Congress, Manuscript Division.
Partial manuscript by Tunstall, an author who published a book in 1884, is of chapters for the book "Love or Loyalty? A Story of Lynch Law."

2,613. Tutty, Ida

Papers. 1936-41. Ca. 500 items.
Open. No guide.
Library of Congress, Manuscript Division.
A West Salem, OH, evangelist, Tutty believed she was a prophet, although her prophecies went unheeded. Collection consists of material she used to enlighten the public and includes letters to various public figures in which she explained her work, her prophecies, and the powers God had given her; letters and pieces she wrote and collected; and an article "God's Gentiles."

2,614. Underwood, John Curtis

Papers. 1856-98. 140 items.
Open. Published guide.
Library of Congress, Manuscript Division.
Papers of Underwood (1809-73), a lawyer, planter, and US district court judge of Virginia, primarily consist of correspondence concerning political and judicial matters as well as abolition and the Civil War. Includes letters from Lydia Maria Child, from Susan B. Anthony to his wife Maria P. Underwood, and from Harriet Beecher Stowe to Alice Underwood. See *The National Union Catalog of Manuscript Collections, 1968* (Washington, DC: The Library of Congress, 1969).

2,615. United Daughters of the Confederacy

Records. 1915-32. 2 items.
Open. No guide.
Library of Congress, Manuscript Division.
Copy of a report by the UDC committee on design of the stars and bars, the flag of the Confederate states, and notes by Jessica Randolph Smith about the validity of the report. The UDC was organized in ca. 1894.

2,616. Van Buren, Angelica (Singleton)

Papers. 1823-53. 240 items.
Open. No guide.
Library of Congress, Manuscript Division.
Correspondence of [Mrs. Abraham] Van Buren (1816-77), who was hostess for her father-in-law Martin Van Buren in the White House and at the family estate Lindenwald in Kinderhook, NY, with her mother Rebecca T. (Coles) Singleton (?-1849) and her sister Marion (Singleton) Deveaux (1815-?). In early letters to Angelica and Marion Singleton at school in Philadelphia, their mother, who was at home in South Carolina, gives advice on their manners and education. A number of later letters concern the period during which Angelica Van Buren served as White House hostess.

2,617. Van Doren, Irita Bradford (Taylor)

Papers. 1920-66. 12 ft.
Access restricted. Published and unpublished guides.
Library of Congress, Manuscript Division.
Correspondence; subject file; file of original manuscripts of speeches, articles, and poems by various authors; and book reviews of Van Doren (1891-1966), a literary editor. Includes material on Wendell L. Willkie and correspondence with Stephen Vincent Benét, Willa Cather, Theodore Dreiser, E. M. Forster, Ellen Glasgow, Sinclair Lewis, W. Somerset Maugham, and others. Taken from *The National Union Catalog of Manuscript Collections, 1969* (Washington, DC: The Library of Congress, 1970).

2,618. Wade, Isaac R., and Wade, Catherine E.

Papers. 1848-61. 9 items.
Open. No guide.
Library of Congress, Manuscript Division.
Letters to the Wades, who were Claiborne County, MS, residents, from Sarah Jane and Pascal Woodson, the Woodsons' son Grandville Woodson, York Walker, and Peter Ross, all of whom were former slaves who settled in Liberia. The letters describe difficulties living in Liberia, particularly disease, native hostility, and the lack of answers to their letters.

2,619. Warren, Mercy (Otis)

Papers. 1805. Ca. 0.5 ft.
Open. No guide.
Library of Congress, Manuscript Division.
Longhand manuscript by [Mrs. James] Warren (1728-1814), a poet, playwright, and historian, of her book *History of the Rise, Progress and Termination of the American Revolution,* 3 vols. (Boston: printed by Manning and Loring for E. Larkin, 1805). Also included is a copy her son James Warren (1757-?) made in 1805, which includes additions attached to the pages.

2,620. Washington Family

Papers. 1582-1915. Ca. 800 items.
Open. Published guide and register.
Library of Congress, Manuscript Division.
Primarily photocopies of correspondence and legal and financial papers of members of the family of George Washington, which are held in other repositories or privately. Included are legal documents of Hannah (Fairfax) Washington (ca. 1738-1810); correspondence, financial papers, and papers concerning the estate of Martha Dandridge [Mrs. Daniel Parke] Custis [Mrs. George] Washington (1731-1802); and copies of the will and an indenture of Mary (Ball) [Mrs. Augustine] Washington (1708-89). Included as well is an original journal for 1779 to 1796 in which Elizabeth Foote [Mrs. Lund] Washington recorded her thoughts on her marriage, on marriage in general, and on the conduct of a household. She mentions concern over her servants' disrespect for her religion. See *National Union Catalog of Manuscript Collections, 1977* (Washington, DC: Library of Congress, 1978).

2,621. Washington, George

Papers. 1592-1937. 165 ft.
Open. Published guide.
Library of Congress, Manuscript Division.
Papers of Washington (1732-99), army officer and President, include correspondence with Washington family members and with Sarah (Franklin) Bache, Martha Dangerfield Bland, Sarah Fairfax Carlyle, Elizabeth (Graeme) Ferguson, Charlotte de la Saussaye Hazen, Alice De Lancey Izard, Judith (Sargent) Murray, Mercy (Otis) Warren, Lucretia Wilhemine Van Winter, and others. Entire collection is available on microfilm. See *Index to the George Washington Papers* (Washington: Library of Congress, 1964).

2,622. Wason, Betty

Papers. 1941-43. Ca. 25 items.
Open. No guide.
Library of Congress, Manuscript Division.
An author whose real name is Elizabeth Wason, "Betty" Wason (1912-) was a Columbia Broadcasting System war correspondent in Europe from 1938 to 1941, and from July 1940 until July 1941 she was stationed in Greece where she made nightly broadcasts to the US. Collection consists of material relating to her work in Greece and includes a journal with brief entries made during and after the German invasion of Greece about her difficulties in making broadcasts and about her trip, arranged by the Germans, from Athens via Berlin and Lisbon to New York. Also includes photos taken during a tour of the Albanian front in 1941 and her manuscript *Miracle in Hellas: The Greeks Fight On* (New York: Macmillan Co., 1943), which describes the war in Greece.

2,623. Watterston, George

Papers. 1815-66. 480 items.
Open. No guide.
Library of Congress, Manuscript Division.
Papers of Watterston (1783-1854), Librarian of Congress, contain correspondence of his daughter Eliza Watterston, a Washington resident, with her sister Mrs. A. A. Holcombe, her niece Florence Holcombe, and Major J. C. Pattridge of

Watertown, NY, who wrote about the current political scene as he perceived it.

2,624. Webb, Mary L.
Papers. Ca. 1920s. Ca. 350 items.
Open. No guide.
Library of Congress, Manuscript Division.
A Boston resident who was an advocate of world peace, [Miss] Webb (1861-?) believed that peace could be achieved if the money represented by US trusts were put to constructive, not destructive, use. The holder of the last share of the Colorado and Red River (Texas) Land Co., which after extensive research she believed to be the predecessor of the J. P. Morgan and John D. Rockefeller holdings, she proposed to give her certificate, which she thought provided control over these holdings, to the US government provided that the money it represented would be used for peaceful, constructive purposes. Research notes, maps, pamphlets, and clippings relate to her legal research which formed the basis of her claim.

2,625. Webster, Margaret
Papers. 1837-1974. 11 ft.
Open. Published guide and register.
Library of Congress, Manuscript Division.
A British-American actress, director, lecturer, and Shakespearean authority, [Miss] Webster (1905-72) also was the author of a technical book *Shakespeare Without Tears* (1942) and of family biographies *The Same Only Different: Five Generations of a Great Theater Family* (1969) and *Don't Put Your Daughter on the Stage* (1972). Collection contains family correspondence with and between her parents Dame May Whitty and Benjamin Webster, a diary of Whitty, a genealogy, and speeches and writings, notes, programs, press releases, and awards pertaining to the professional careers of her parents. Also included are Margaret Webster's correspondence, memoranda, research notes, manuscripts of writings, lectures, articles about the theater, prompt copies of plays and operas, setting and staging diagrams, musical scores, photos, scrapbooks of clippings, and printed matter on such professional organizations and projects as the American National Theater and Academy, the Actors Equity, and blacklisting. Papers contain information on her career in American theater; her involvement with Eva Le Gallienne and Cheryl Crawford in the American Repertory Theater in New York; her interest in experimental theater with Marweb Productions, which was a Shakespearean company; and her work as a US state department specialist in South Africa. See *National Union Catalog of Manuscript Collections, 1977* (Washington, DC: Library of Congress, 1978).

2,626. Weeks, Estella T.
Papers. 1946. 3 items.
Open. No guide.
Library of Congress, Manuscript Division.
Papers of [Miss] Weeks, an historian, relate to her research on the hymnody of the Shakers. Includes a typescript of an illustrated talk wherein she acted out the life of a Shaker woman through hymns for the Hymn Society of America, a summary of the talk, and a Society newsletter describing her presentation.

2,627. Weinheim, Tess (Ott)
Papers. 1932-33, nd. 14 items.
Open. No guide.
Library of Congress, Manuscript Division.
Clippings of poems by Weinheim, a poet, which deal with the Wyomissing, Reading, and Philadelphia areas of Pennsylvania. Also included is a letter discussing one of her poems.

2,628. Welch, Marie de Laveaga
Papers. 1935. 2 items.
Open. No guide.
Library of Congress, Manuscript Division.
Poem by Welch (1905-74), a poet, on the death of author Stella Benson and a letter to their mutual friend and literary patron Albert M. Bender.

2,629. Weld, Theodore Dwight
Papers. 1783-1888. 32 items.
Open. No guide.
Library of Congress, Manuscript Division.
Papers relating to the abolitionist activities of Weld (1803-95) and Angelina (Grimké) Weld (1805-79), whom he married in 1838. In her letters she discusses at length the value of associations of women, her views on the question of the "second advent," bloomers, her philosophical disagreements with her sister Sarah Grimké, and a justification to an unsympathetic relative of the tract *American Slavery As It Is,* which she compiled with her sister and husband. Also included are a letter in which Anne Warren Weston writes Theodore Weld about the Boston Female Anti-Slavery Society and estate inventories of slave owners.

2,630. Welles, Roger
Papers. 1884-1926. 2.5 ft.
Open. Published guide and register.
Library of Congress, Manuscript Division.
Papers of Welles (1862-1932), a US Navy officer, contain letters he wrote his mother Mercy (Aiken) [Mrs. Roger] Welles while on naval tours of duty between 1885 and 1908 and a diary his wife Harriet D. Welles kept while accompanying her husband in ca. 1910 on tour of duty aboard the USS *New Orleans.* She wrote about Navy life and local people and customs in Shanghai, Yokohama, Chuzenji, Hong Kong, and Manila. See *The National Union Catalog of Manuscript Collections, 1970* (Washington, DC: The Library of Congress, 1971).

2,631. Wickes, Frances (Gillespy)
Papers. 1929-66. 3.5 ft.
Partially restricted. Register.
Library of Congress, Manuscript Division.
An author and lay psychologist and analyst, Wickes (1875-1967) was a pioneer in therapeutic work with disturbed children. Professional correspondence, book manuscripts, source material, and drawings relate primarily to her *The Inner World of Choice* (New York: Harper & Row, 1963), *The Inner World of Childhood: A Study in Analytical Psychology* (New York: D. Appleton and Co., 1927), and *The Inner World of Man* (New York: Farrar & Rinehart, 1938). Also included are notes she took on dreams of her patients and correspondents, articles she wrote for the *Bulletin* of the Analytical Psychology Club of New York, and letters from dancer Martha Graham and stage designer Robert E. Jones. Other correspondents include Thomas Mann, Mrs. Walter Kotschnis, Gerhard Adler, Ethel Dangerfield, Mabel Luhan, and Violet Watt.

2,632. Wilbour, Charlotte Beebe
Papers. 1871. 1 item.
Open. No guide.
Library of Congress, Manuscript Division.
An address on "Honor Among Women" delivered by [Mrs. Charles E.] Wilbour (1833-1914), cofounder of Sorosis, on the third anniversary of the group.

2,633. Wiley, Anna (Kelton)
Papers. 1798-1964. 132 ft.
Open. Published and unpublished guides.
Library of Congress, Manuscript Division.
Papers of Wiley (1877-1964), a Washington feminist and clubwoman, relate to her activities on behalf of women's rights and her work with such clubs and associations as the American Pure Food League, the Columbian Women, the Consumers' League, the DC Federation of Women's Clubs, the Housekeepers' Alliance, the Kalorama Citizens' Association, and the 20th Century Club. General and family correspondence, notes, speeches and articles, financial papers, appointment books, invitations, scrapbooks, photos, clippings, and printed matter. Includes some papers of her husband Harvey W. Wiley (1844-1930) and material relating to her father General John C. Kelton (1828-93) and her grandfather William S. Campbell. Taken from *The National Union Catalog of Manuscript Collections, 1970* (Washington, DC: The Library of Congress, 1971).

2,634. Wilkes, Charles
Papers. 1607-1959. 12 ft.
Open. Published guide and register.
Library of Congress, Manuscript Division.
Papers relating primarily to the naval career of Wilkes (1798-1877), a naval officer and explorer, contain correspondence with his first wife Jane Jeffrey (Renwick) Wilkes (?-1848); their children John, Eliza, and Jane Wilkes; and his second wife Mary H. (Lynch) [Mrs. William C.] Bolton Wilkes. Also includes correspondence of John Wilkes with his cousin Jeanie R. Smedberg. Entire collection is available on microfilm. See *The National Union Catalog of Manuscript Collections, 1962* (Hamden, CT: The Shoe String Press, Inc., 1964).

2,635. Willard Family
Papers. 1800-1955. 106 ft.
Open. Register.
Library of Congress, Manuscript Division.
Papers of Antonia (Ford) Willard (1838-71), a Confederate spy commissioned as an aide-de-camp by General Jeb Stuart, who later married Union major Joseph Clapp Willard; of their son Joseph E. Willard (1865-1924), a soldier, lieutenant governor of Virginia, and US ambassador to Spain; and of his wife Belle Layton (Wyatt) Willard (?-1954), a businesswoman.

Antonia Willard's papers consist of correspondence with her husband, his family, her mother, and her sister; school books she used at the Female Collegiate Institute in Buckingham, VA; an 1871 account book of her husband; and correspondence, research notes, and clippings her daughter-in-law Belle Willard collected about her commission and her part in the Confederate capture of Union general Stoughton.

Belle Willard's papers consist of correspondence with her husband and family; diaries, 1890-1927; correspondence with her financial advisors Thomas B. Love and Joseph W. Wyatt; account books, bills and receipts, bank records, and other material concerning the Fairfax Development Corp., the Willard Hotel (Virginia Hotel Co.), and real estate; genealogical papers; writings on her travels and other topics, including a memoir of her childhood, which was published in *Scribner's* in 1923; and miscellany.

2,636. Willard, Frances Elizabeth Caroline
Papers. 1889-97. 18 items.
Open. No guide.
Library of Congress, Manuscript Division.
Letters from [Miss] Willard (1839-98), a feminist who was president of the WCTU, to Reba Butler and her husband A. L. Butler of Evanston, IL, concern mutual friends and work.

2,637. Williams, Gertrude Gideon
Papers. Nd. 2 items.
Open. No guide.
Library of Congress, Manuscript Division.
Poems about war by Williams, a poet who lived in Springfield, MO.

2,638. Williams, John Sharp
Papers. 1902-24. 61 ft.
Open. Published and unpublished guides.
Library of Congress, Manuscript Division.
Correspondence relating to the career of Williams (1854-1932), a US representative and later senator from Mississippi, concerns various topics, including the woman suffrage amendment. Taken from *The*

National Union Catalog of Manuscript Collections, 1959-1961 (Ann Arbor, MI: J. W. Edwards, 1962).

2,639. Williams, Margaret D.
Papers. 1921. 5 items.
Open. No guide.
Library of Congress, Manuscript Division.
Reminiscence of [Miss] Williams, a Philadelphia resident, concerns the first inauguration of Abraham Lincoln. Williams, her father, and her sister met the Lincolns in Philadelphia and were asked to join their party to Washington. Williams describes this trip and the events preceding the inauguration and ball; she also includes the words to "Alone," a ballad she sang at Lincoln's request.

2,640. Wilson, Edith (Bolling) Galt
Papers. 1833-1961. 27 ft.
Open. Published and unpublished guides.
Library of Congress, Manuscript Division.
Wilson (1872-1961) was wife of President Woodrow Wilson (1856-1924). Family and general correspondence, diary notes, drafts and correspondence concerning her book *My Memoir* (1938), financial and legal papers, genealogical material, printed matter, and memorabilia. Most of the social correspondence is from leaders in American political life. Correspondents include Presidents and wives of Presidents: Calvin Coolidge, Grace Coolidge, Dwight D. Eisenhower, Mamie (Doud) Eisenhower, Florence (Kling) Harding, Herbert Hoover, Lou (Henry) Hoover, Lyndon B. Johnson, John F. Kennedy, Jacqueline Kennedy, Franklin D. Roosevelt, Eleanor Roosevelt, and William Howard Taft. Taken from *The National Union Catalog of Manuscript Collections, 1965* (Washington, DC: The Library of Congress, 1966).

2,641. Wilson, Helen Hopekirk
Papers. 1885-94. 17 items.
Open. No guide.
Library of Congress, Manuscript Division.
A pianist and composer, [Mrs. William A.] Wilson (1856-1945) was known professionally as Mme. Hopekirk. Consists primarily of letters from Oliver Wendell Holmes while she was living and performing in Vienna. Also includes a letter in which Mary Abigail Dodge urges Mme. Hopekirk to visit Holmes and a clipping about an interview between Mmes. Hopekirk and Holmes.

2,642. Wilson, Sophie S.
Papers. 1831. 1 vol.
Open. No guide.
Library of Congress, Manuscript Division.
Diary that Wilson, a resident of Charleston (SC?), kept of a trip she made with her husband and daughter by carriage from Charleston to various baths in Virginia. She describes travel and lodging conditions and comments on people and activities at the watering places they visited: Red Sulphur Springs, White Sulphur Springs, Salt Sulphur Springs, Warm Springs, and Sweet Springs.

2,643. Wister, Owen
Papers. 1829-1936. 40 ft.
Partially restricted. Published guide.
Library of Congress, Manuscript Division.
Papers relating to the literary career of Wister (1860-1938), a novelist, include correspondence with Elizabeth C. Agassiz, Anna (Roosevelt) Cowles, Sarah Orne Jewett, Amy Lowell, Agnes Repplier, M. Carey Thomas, and Edith Wharton. Also included are papers of his grandmother Fanny Kemble (1809-93), an actress who was married to Pierce Butler in 1834 and divorced in 1848; of his mother Sarah (Butler) [Mrs. Owen Jones] Wister (1835-1908), an author; and of his cousin and wife Mary Channing (Wister) Wister (1869-1913), a civic reformer.

Fanny Kemble's papers consist of correspondence with her grandson Owen Wister and with her daughter Frances (Butler) [Mrs. James Wentworth] Leigh (1838-?), who discusses at length the activities of Negroes in Darien, GA, during the 1870s; poems written or copied by Kemble; notes; and reminiscences.

Sarah Wister's papers consist of correspondence with her son Owen Wister, letters from the period she was writing *Worthy Women of Our First Century* (1877), letters from her close friend Henry James, and clippings of some of her articles in *City and State.*

Mary Wister's papers consist of correspondence with her husband Owen Wister about her activities in the Pennsylvania State Federation of Women's Clubs and her founding of the Civic Club of Philadelphia. See *Owen Wister: A Register of His Papers* (Washington: Library of Congress, 1972).

2,644. Withee, Louisa A.
Papers. 1883-1918. 23 vols.
Open. No guide.
Library of Congress, Manuscript Division.
Diaries of [Mrs. Nisan H.] Withee (1841-?), a resident of La Crosse, WI, consist of brief, intermittent entries that concern her financial transactions and business and farming activities managing the family farm and her husband's estate after his death in 1887. The diaries also contain mention of her afternoon calling, entertaining, china painting, and traveling in Europe and include recipes and directions for mixing colors for china painting.

2,645. Wittenmyer, Annie (Turner)
Papers. 1862-66. 5 items.
Open. No guide.
Library of Congress, Manuscript Division.
Correspondence of [Mrs. William] Wittenmyer (1827-1900), a Civil War relief worker and temperance reformer, concerns her work with the Iowa Sanitary Committee during the War. Included are letters of introduction, military passes, and a letter about a soldiers' orphans home in Davenport, IA.

2,646. Woman's Titanic Memorial Association
Records. 1912-31. Ca. 100 items.
Open. No guide.
Library of Congress, Manuscript Division.
The Memorial Association was organized in 1912 to collect money from women to erect a statue to honor the men who died trying to save women and children on the *Titanic;* the group appears to have been disbanded in 1931 after the statue was erected in Washington. Correspondence concerning the collection of funds and erection of the statue; financial statements, bills and receipts, account books, check book, bank book, and contract for construction; and minutes of a 1916 executive committee meeting concerning the commissioning of Gertrude (Vanderbilt) Whitney to prepare the statue.

2,647. Women's Joint Congressional Committee
Records. 1921-62. 5 ft.
Open. Published guide and register.
Library of Congress, Manuscript Division.
Composed of representatives of such groups as the National Consumers' League, the National Educational Association, and the National Council of Jewish Women, the Committee was organized in 1920 to serve as an information center on pending legislation of interest to its members, particularly legislation concerning social welfare, education, and women's rights. Working committees' minutes and reports, financial records, correspondence, membership lists, clippings, and printed matter contain information on legislation the Committee supported and the methods it used to publicize that support. See *The National Union Catalog of Manuscript Collections, 1966* (Washington, DC: The Library of Congress, 1967).

2,648. Women's Loyal National League
Records. 1863. 1 item.
Open. No guide.
Library of Congress, Manuscript Division.
Form letter signed by Susan B. Anthony, secretary of the League, which was organized to collect signatures on petitions calling for Negro emancipation.

2,649. Women's Organization for National Prohibition Reform
Records. 1932-33. Ca. 100 items.
Open. No guide.
Library of Congress, Manuscript Division.
The Organization was a temperance group working for repeal of the 18th Amendment because it believed temperance could better be achieved through other methods, such as establishment of a liquor control system. Correspondence in which Grace C. [Mrs. Edward Wales] Root, director of research for the Organization, asked various consulates for material on their countries' liquor control systems, responses from the consulates, and copies of liquor control laws and reports on their effectiveness in various countries.

2,650. Wood, Leonard
Papers. 1875-1942. 146 ft.
Open. Published guide and register.
Library of Congress, Manuscript Division.
Papers, the bulk of which pertain to the military career of Wood (1860-1927), a US Army officer and governor general of the Philippine Islands, also include papers of Louise A. (Condit-Smith) Wood (1869-1943), whom he married in 1890. Contains correspondence concerning her husband's career and her work with the New York chapter of the American National Red Cross, personal correspondence with her sons and such friends as Edith K. [Mrs. Theodore] Roosevelt and Mabel W. [Mrs. Henry L.] Stimson, speeches she gave for the Red Cross, a 1940 diary with occasional entries about her activities, and a manuscript of a calendar she prepared with literary quotations for each day in 1927. See *The National Union Catalog of Manuscript Collections, 1959-1961* (Ann Arbor, MI: J. W. Edwards, 1962).

2,651. Woodbury, Levi, and Woodbury, Charles Levi
Papers. 1638-1899. 30 ft.
Open. Published guide and register.
Library of Congress, Manuscript Division.
Correspondence of Levi Woodbury (1789-1851), secretary of the navy, secretary of the treasury, governor of New Hampshire, a US senator, and US Supreme Court justice, and of his son Charles Levi Woodbury (1820-98), a lawyer. Includes correspondence of Levi Woodbury with Elizabeth (Clapp) Woodbury during their courtship and early years of marriage, 1818-21; letters he wrote her while he was in Washington and she at home in Portsmouth, NH, and at her parents' home in Portland, ME; and letters she wrote her parents and children while in Washington. Also includes papers of Levi and Elizabeth Woodbury's daughter Virginia (Woodbury) Fox, with a legal contract between her and Gustavus Vasa Fox stating that all her present and future property would remain in her control after their marriage in 1855, correspondence of her husband, and a detailed daily diary she kept from 1860 to 1876 while living in Washington and then in Boston and Lowell, MA. See *The National Union Catalog of Manuscript Collections, 1963-1964* (Washington, DC: The Library of Congress, 1965).

2,652. Woodrow, Mary
Papers. 1813. 1 item.
Open. No guide.
Library of Congress, Manuscript Division.
Letter in which Woodrow, a resident of Alexandria, VA, asks the help of the mayor of Alexandria in compelling the owner of a female slave who had

been burned and abandoned to take care of the woman.

2,653. Woodward, Mary Alethea
Papers. 1926-29. 38 items.
Open. No guide.
Library of Congress, Manuscript Division.
[Miss] Woodward was a poet living in Portland, OR, when this material was collected by her cousin [Miss] Rebekah Crawford. Consists of letters from Woodward to Crawford about Woodward's poetry and Crawford's interest in music as well as manuscript poems, clippings of poems, and photos of Woodward.

2,654. Wotherspoon Family
Papers. 1836-1918. Ca. 150 items.
Open. Published guide.
Library of Congress, Manuscript Division.
Correspondence between Alexander Somerville Wotherspoon (?-1854), a US Army surgeon serving in the Mexican War, and his future wife Louisa Kuhn (?-1877), a Washington resident. Also included are letters he wrote her after they were married and letters from their grandson Alexander Somerville Wotherspoon (1892-), a US Navy officer, to his wife Peggy while he was aboard the *USS New York* during WWI. See *The National Union Catalog of Manuscript Collections, 1972* (Washington, DC: The Library of Congress, 1974).

2,655. Wright, Anna Elizabeth (Steele)
Papers. 1846-1912. 17 vols.
Open. No guide.
Library of Congress, Manuscript Division.
Diaries in which Wright (1825-1913), a resident of Prairie du Sac, WI, made almost daily entries recording her activities over a period of 66 years. Her husband John Wright was an itinerant lecturer, and until 1851 the diary records the family's almost constant travel in the South and Midwest while he lectured; then from 1852 until 1862 the Wrights traveled only during the winters, spending summers at their home in Wisconsin. After her husband's death in an accident in 1862, Elizabeth Wright remained home to raise her family. Inserted in the diaries are correspondence, financial records, photos, clippings, an article by her daughter Jennie (Wright) English on "Those Early Days in Wisconsin," and a transcript with annotations of the diaries kept by Elizabeth Wright's granddaughter Anne Elizabeth [Mrs. Charles Thomas] Watson from 1846 to 1850.

2,656. Wright, Frances
Papers. 1843-96. Ca. 100 items.
Open. No guide.
Library of Congress, Manuscript Division.
Wright (1795-1852) was a writer and reformer who founded Nashoba, a biracial cooperative near Memphis, TN; in 1831 she married Guillaume Sylvan Casimir Phiquepal D'Arusmont and in 1850 divorced him. Papers, largely of her daughter Frances Sylva (D'Arusmont) Guthrie, primarily concern Wright. Included are correspondence of Sylva Guthrie, some of which pertains to her parents; a diary she kept in French, 1851-56; a copy of the divorce proceedings of her parents; a deed giving her title to the land of Nashoba; and a notebook of Phiquepal D'Arusmont concerning property in Cincinnati, Memphis, and Nashoba.

2,657. Wright, Irene Aloha
Papers. 1785-1932. Ca. 1 ft.
Open. No guide.
Library of Congress, Manuscript Division.
An author, journalist, archivist, and US state department official, [Miss] Wright (1879-1972) was working as a free-lance researcher in Seville, Spain, when the Florida State Historical Society hired her to copy papers concerning Florida in the General Archives of the Indies, located in Seville. Collection consists of correspondence in which Wright describes to James A. Robertson and John B. Stetson, respectively recording secretary and benefactor of the project at the Society, her copying work and the material she found. Also included are lists of documents relevant to Florida in the Archives and letters in Spanish, 1785-1812, which Wright copied.

2,658. Wylie, Elinor
Papers. 1918-29. 37 items.
Open. No guide.
Library of Congress, Manuscript Division.
Elinor Morton (Hoyt) Wylie (1885-1928) was a poet and author who wrote under the name Elinor Wylie; in 1905 she married Philip Hichborn, in 1916 Horace Wylie, and in 1923 William Rose Benét. Manuscripts of poems; of her book of poetry *Angels and Earthly Creatures* (New York: A. A. Knopf, 1929); of stories; of her novel *The Venetian Glass Nephew* (New York: George H. Doran Co., 1925); and of an article for the *Saturday Review of Literature,* "The Sage in Meditation." Also includes research notes on St. Louis and Mexico.

2,659. Wyse, Wickliffe, and Phillips Family
Papers. Ca. 1810-1924. Ca. 250 items.
Open. No guide.
Library of Congress, Manuscript Division.
Papers of the three families relate to politics and the military careers of some of the male members. Also included are reminiscences of a shipwreck survived by Mrs. F. O. Wyse, wife of US Army officer Francis O. Wyse. She reports traveling on the steamer *San Francisco* with her husband, who was to be stationed in California; failure of the engines; the steamer's sinking; and rescue by a passing ship. Also included is a journal in which Eugenia (Levy) [Mrs. Philip] Phillips (1820-1902) reminisces about her experiences during the Civil War. An outspoken southern sympathizer living in Washington in 1861, she was imprisoned for several weeks. When she was released, she and her family moved to New Orleans. She describes life in New Orleans under the military government of Benjamin F. Butler, her arrest by Butler as a Confederate spy, and her subsequent imprisonment on Ship Island. Throughout the journal she expresses her contempt for the "Yankees" and praise for the strong women of the South.

2,660. Young, Ella
Papers. 1903-45. Ca. 50 items.
Open. No guide.
Library of Congress, Manuscript Division.
An Irish author and poet, [Miss] Young (1867-1956) was a professor of Celtic mythology and language at the University of California beginning in 1931. Correspondence from William Butler Yeats, Maude Gonne, Eva Gore-Booth, and others; longhand poems sent to her by various Irish poets; pamphlets, drawings; and photos.

2,661. Young, John Russell
Papers. 1829-1923. 10 ft.
Open. Published guide and register.
Library of Congress, Manuscript Division.
Papers of Young (1840-99), a journalist, diplomat, and Librarian of Congress, include papers of his third wife May (Dow) [Mrs. George W.] Davids Young, with social notes and letters from her son and daily diaries she kept between 1891 and 1923. Also included is correspondence of her parents James Gilman Dow and Mary Ann Dow. Her father went to California during the 1849 gold rush, but his wife did not join him until the 1860s. In letters to him she discusses her difficulties raising the family alone in Boston, politics, and her interest in universalism. Journals of a voyage she took to California during 1852 and 1853 with her children to visit her husband are also included as are letters she wrote her daughter May Young during James Dow's last illness.

In addition, the collection contains letters in which John Young's daughter-in-law Dorothy (Mills) [Mrs. Gordon Russell] Young describes in detail to her mother her activities in Europe with the YMCA at the end of WWI. See *The National Union Catalog of Manuscript Collections, 1962* (Hamden, CT: The Shoe String Press, Inc., 1964).

2,662. Zorach, William
Papers. 1822-1967. 18 ft.
Open. Published guide and register.
Library of Congress, Manuscript Division.
Papers relating to the artistic career of Zorach (1887-1966), a sculptor and painter, include correspondence with New York art dealer Edith Halpert, sculptor Ellin A. Ross, and with a former student of his, Maũa Yaromila Levá. Levá's sketches are also included.

In addition, the collection contains papers of Marguerite (Thompson) Zorach (1887-1968), a painter and weaver whom he married in 1912, and of their daughter Dahlov (Zorach) [Mrs. Adolph] Ipcar (1917-), who is also a painter. Includes correspondence of William Zorach with his fiancée Marguerite Thompson while he was in Cleveland and she in India and California, letters she wrote him about their art work, and poems she wrote. Also includes letters in which Dahlov Ipcar writes her parents about painting and farming in Robinhood, ME, photos of her paintings and collages, clippings, and printed matter. See *The National Union Catalog of Manuscript Collections, 1963-1964* (Washington, DC: The Library of Congress, 1965).

2,663. Farrar, Geraldine
Papers. 1897-1965. 22 ft.
Partially closed. Published and unpublished guides.
Library of Congress, Music Division.
[Miss] Farrar (1882-1967) was a singer who also composed and arranged music. Correspondence, manuscript of her biography *Such Sweet Compulsion* (1938), scripts for Metropolitan Opera broadcasts and for pageants, contracts, articles, recordings, and other papers pertain to her career, her involvement in the Republican presidential campaigns of 1936 and 1944, and to such groups as the American National Red Cross, The American Women's Voluntary Services, and the Women's Army Corps. Correspondents include Crown Prince Wilhelm and Crown Princess Cecilie of Germany, Lucrezia Bori, Ruth A. Businger, Emma Eames, Olive Fremstad, Amelita Galli-Curci, Daisy Humphreys, Lilli Lehmann, and Kate Douglas Wiggin. Taken from *The National Union Catalog of Manuscript Collections, 1967* (Washington, DC: The Library of Congress, 1968).

2,664. Hull, Anne A.
Papers. 1912-57. Ca. 200 items.
Open. Published guide and calendar.
Library of Congress, Music Division.
Hull was a pianist and teacher at the Greenwich House Music School in New York City and at the Juilliard School of Music. Includes correspondence, lecture notes, other teaching material, programs, and clippings. Correspondents include Mary Howe, Ernest Hutcheson, John Charles Thomas, and Celius Dougherty. Taken from *The National Union Catalog of Manuscript Collections, 1970* (Washington, DC: The Library of Congress, 1971).

2,665. Menter, Sophie
Papers. 1865-1916. 102 items.
Open. Published and unpublished guides.
Library of Congress, Music Division.
Menter (1846-1918) was a pianist and teacher. Correspondence from musicians and theatrical personalities about music and the role of Prince von Bülow as a special emissary who attempted to keep Italy out of WWI. Correspondents include Mily Alexeyevich Balakirev, Marie von Bülow, Franz Liszt, Hans Richter, and Carl Tausig. Taken from *The National Union Catalog of Manuscript*

Collections, 1967 (Washington, DC: The Library of Congress, 1968).

2,666. Archives
Records. 1974- . 2 drawers.
Closed. No guide.
Mexican American Women's National Association.
Minutes, photos, and scrapbooks of the Association, which was founded in 1974 to promote leadership and communication among Chicanas (Mexican American women), to seek parity for Chicanas in Hispanic organizations, to support the activities of groups responsive to the Association's goals, and to create a national awareness of the presence and concerns of Chicanas. Includes information on the Association's annual national training conferences and on its participation in the national women's conference held in Houston in 1977.

2,667. National Academy of Sciences, Central Files
Records. 1863-1972. 510 cu.ft.
Access restricted. Unpublished guide.
National Academy of Sciences-National Research Council, Archives.
Minutes, correspondence, and reports of the National Academy of Sciences, a nonprofit organization chartered by Congress in 1863 to advise the government on matters of science and technology, and of the National Research Council, the operating arm of the Academy, founded in 1916. Material is organized according to the structure and functions of the Academy and of its components; finding aids provide access to activities of individual women scientist committee members. Academy projects have included studies of nutrition, industrial fatigue, endocrinology, human reproduction, and manpower.

2,668. National Academy of Sciences, Deceased Members
Records. 1863- . 10 cu.ft.
Access restricted. Published and unpublished guides.
National Academy of Sciences-National Research Council, Archives.
Roster files for each Academy member contain biographical and bibliographical data, records on the member's participation in Academy activities, and photos. These files document the work of Academy members and provide source material for the Academy's biographical memoir series. Scientists are elected to the Academy on the basis of their additions to basic scientific knowledge. Thirty-eight women have been elected members, including Florence Rena Sabin, Margaret Floy Washburn, Libbie Henrietta Hyman, Gerty Cori, and Maria Goeppert Mayer. See *National Academy of Sciences Annual Report: Fiscal Year 1975-76* (Washington, 1976) for a listing of deceased members with birth and death dates and year of election to the Academy.

2,669. National Research Council Committee for Research in Problems of Sex
Records. 1921-65. 8.5 cu.ft.
Access restricted. Published and unpublished guides.
National Academy of Sciences-National Research Council, Archives.
By means of research grants, conferences, and a limited fellowship program, the Committee fostered research in sex behavior and biology, including such topics as female reproduction and endocrinology. Bulk of the collection consists of folders on grantees, with applications, status reports, and other administrative material, but minutes, correspondence, and other reports of the Committee are included as well. Women scientists were members and participants of the Committee and its conferences and were recipients of grants and fellowships. Founded in 1921, the Committee disbanded in 1963. See Sophie D. Aberle and George W. Corner, *Twenty-Five Years of Sex Research: History of the National Research Council Committee for Research in Problems of Sex, 1922-1947* (Philadelphia, 1953).

2,670. National Research Fellowships in the Natural Sciences
Records. 1919-54. 2 in. and 30 reels.
Access restricted. No guide.
National Academy of Sciences-National Research Council, Archives.
This program, which existed from 1919 to 1954, provided postdoctoral fellowship awards to Americans and Canadians to enable them to pursue their research at institutions of their choice in the US and abroad. Listings of all fellows by name, institution, research program, and subsequent employment and roster files of fellows' applications, related correspondence, and material on the status of their awards. Of the 1039 fellows selected between 1920 and 1950, 51 were women.

2,671. Adjutant General's Office (RG 94)
Records. Ca. 1783-1917. 38,107 cu.ft.
Open. Published guides.
National Archives and Records Service.
Although the Continental Congress appointed an adjutant general in June 1775, no further provision was made for such an officer until March 1792. A separate head for the adjutant general's department was provided in March 1821 to handle records, orders, and correspondence of the Army. The Office is charged with matters pertaining to the command, discipline, and administration of the military and has had duties of recording, authenticating, and communicating to troops orders, instructions, and regulations issued by the Secretary of War.

Includes general records of the Office, which contain correspondence, orders, muster rolls, and records relating to the regular army, volunteers, wars, and the US Military Academy; records of the divisions of the Adjutant General's Office; records of the record and pension office; records of commissions; and cartographic and audiovisual records.

In the records of the record and pension office are carded medical records, 1812-1912, including carded service records of hospital attendants, matrons, and nurses, 1861-65 (36 ft.), which are arranged alphabetically by surname; carded medical records of civilians, 1894-1912 (18 ft.), showing name, husband's or father's rank and organization, age, race, birthplace, date and cause of admission, hospital to which admitted, and disposition of the case; carded birth records, 1884-1912 (2 ft.), showing mother's maiden name, father's name and rank and organization, name and sex of child, number of children by this marriage, and date and place of birth; carded death records of civilians, 1884-1912 (9 in.), showing husband's name, rank, and organization, and the name, sex, age, date, place and cause of death; carded marriage records, 1884-1912 (3 in.), showing name of man and rank or occupation, name of woman and age and birthplace, and the date and place of marriage for persons married on Army posts.

In records of and pertaining to medical installations, which are in medical records, 1814-1919, are Mexican War hospital records, 1846-48 (2.5 ft.), including registers of nurses and matrons. In the records concerning medical personnel, 1839-1914, are monthly returns of nurses, 1861-65 (10 ft.), showing name and date of contract, and returns of matrons, 1876-87 (6 ft.), showing names of hospital matrons at posts and in military divisions and departments with number of matrons at the post and the date of appointment.

Also includes fragmentary records of the US Christian Commission, 1861-66 (ca. 19 ft.), including the record of contribution of the ladies' auxiliary Christian commissions, 1864-65 (1 in.), showing location, name of church if a church organization, name of the officers, address of the secretary, date of organization, and contributions. See *Preliminary Inventory of the Records of the Adjutant General's Office*, PI 17 (1949). See also *Guide to the National Archives of the United States* (Washington, DC: General Services Administration, 1974).

2,672. Bureau of Employment Security (RG 183)
Records. 1907-49. 859 cu.ft.
Open. Published guide.
National Archives and Records Service.
The Bureau was created in 1907 as the division of information in the Bureau of Immigration and Naturalization of the Department of Commerce and Labor. It administered public employment service and unemployment insurance programs until it was abolished in 1949. Correspondence, surveys, reports, files of Bureau units, subject-classified files of the Bureau of Unemployment Compensation and of the Bureau of Employment Security. Includes labor market area reports, 1940-49 (ca. 160 cu.ft.), which are arranged by state and city. These narrative and statistical reports describe war-related industries and other establishments and provide information on employment of women, occupations available, labor requirements, migration, and the work of women employed by specific companies. See *Guide to the National Archives of the United States* (Washington, DC: General Services Administration, 1974).

2,673. Bureau of Human Nutrition and Home Economics (RG 176)
Records. 1913-41. 253 cu.ft.
Open. Published and unpublished guides.
National Archives and Records Service.
The Bureau, which was established in 1915 and abolished in 1953, conducted research on food, fiber, and other agricultural products; housing and household buying; textiles and clothing; uses of income; and household management and equipment. Includes correspondence, reports, studies, and survey materials.

Correspondence of Louise Stanley, chief of the Bureau of Home Economics from 1923 to 1943, is in the central file, general correspondence, 1917-39 (202 ft.), which includes a special series, subject correspondence of the chief of the Bureau of Home Economics, 1917-30 (7 ft.). The Bureau conducted two studies relating to women, one a study of women living in towns and on farms, 1926-27 (10 ft.), which was directed by Mrs. Chase Going Woodhouse. Study records include card check lists; summaries; questionnaires on farm households, especially those in Colorado, Illinois, and Vermont, with names, addresses, amount and kind of education, number of hired help for individual households, and records of expenses for clothing, rent, and fuel. Similar information is available for women in towns. The second study concerned the use of time by homemakers on farms, 1925-30 (6 ft.); study records include individual file folders for women who kept detailed records of how they spent their time each day for a week.

The record group also includes correspondence of Edith Hawley, 1929 (4 in.), relating to the American Home Economics Association; records pertaining to the White House conferences on child health and protection, 1929-31, including some conference reports and studies; and correspondence of Clarice Scott, 1930-31 (1 in.), head of the division of textiles and clothing. See *Guide to the National Archives of the United States* (Washington, DC: General Services Administration, 1974).

2,674. Bureau of Indian Affairs (RG 75)
Records. 1794-1967. 16,329 cu.ft.
Open. Published guides.
National Archives and Records Service.
The Bureau was established in 1824 within the War

Department, which from the establishment of the federal government had exercised jurisdiction over the civilian aspects of Indian affairs. The Bureau is responsible for most of the federal government's relations with Indians, including their education, economic development, and legal rights. The Bureau's responsibility extends to Indians living on reservations or maintaining their tribal affiliation in some manner. Indians and Eskimos of Alaska came under the Bureau's jurisdiction in 1931.

Contains general correspondence; records of the land, law and probate, irrigation, education, health, extension and industry, finance, inspection, statistics, employees, construction, and rehabilitation divisions; records of the field offices; and cartographic and audiovisual records.

In the records of the statistics division are census rolls and supplements, 1885-1940 (420 ft.), which provide information on individuals, including English and/or Indian name, date of birth, sex, relationship to head of family, and after 1930 degree of Indian blood, marital status, and residence. Records of the education division include annual school census reports, 1912-39 (32 ft.), which provide information on standard forms requesting name, sex, age, tribe, and degree of Indian blood. Enrollment records include, for selected agencies or reservations, a register of Indian families, 1884-1909 (2 ft.), which lists the head of family and provides information on him or her as well as on grandparents, parents, uncles, aunts, brothers, sisters, and children. Records relating to the enrollment of California Indians include applications for compensation, 1928-32 (20 ft.), with information submitted by the applicant concerning age, sex, birthdate, and degree of Indian blood claimed. Records of nonreservation schools, particularly the records of the Carlisle Indian Industrial School, 1879-1918 (ca. 90 ft.), contain information on Indian school children. Student information cards and enrollment cards are divided into boys and girls groupings and then arranged alphabetically.

Central classified files, 1907-39 (8033 ft.), contain information about women under the titles of census matters, for family history; Indian customs, for marriage customs; health and social relations, for training nurses for hospitals, nurses employment and work, and social relations, including marriage, intermarriage, divorce, and polygamy; reports of supervisory nurses; industries and employment, for housekeeping and field matrons' work; and employment, for Indians as nurses.

Other information concerning Indian women may be found in the records concerning tribal and individual money and payments to Indians, annuity payment rolls, 1841-1949 (138 ft.). Information about women employees of the Bureau is found in rosters of agency employees, 1853-1909 (7 ft.), which include name, age, sex, position, salary, race, marital status, and birthplace of employee. Rosters of school employees, 1884-1909 (5 ft.), provide name, position, sex, age, salary, dates of service, marital status, state from which appointed, and former occupation. Records of the health division contain reports of field nurses, 1931-43 (14 ft.), including statistical and narrative reports of activities of field nurses.

The records of the office of the commissioner of Indian affairs contain personal and semi-official files, 1921-32 (2 in.), including correspondence with Stella M. [Mrs. H. A.] Atwood, chairman of the committee on Indian welfare of the GFWC. See *Preliminary Inventory of the Records of the Bureau of Indian Affairs,* PI 163 (2 vols., 1965). See also *Guide to the National Archives of the United States* (Washington, DC: General Services Administration, 1974).

2,675. Bureau of Refugees, Freedmen, and Abandoned Lands (RG 105)
Records. 1865-1879. 711 cu.ft.
Open. Published and unpublished guides.
National Archives and Records Service.
The Bureau, usually known as the Freedmen's Bureau, was established in March 1865 and abolished in June 1872. It was a military organization created to supervise all activities relating to refugees and freedmen and to assume custody of all abandoned or confiscated lands or property. Officers of the Bureau issued rations, clothing, and medicine to destitute refugees and freedmen; operated or leased abandoned or confiscated lands; established hospitals; and cooperated with benevolent societies in establishing schools.

Annual and monthly reports, correspondence, circulars, special orders, appointment registers, and registers of claimants from the Washington headquarters, the freedmen's branch of the Adjutant General's Office, and the district or field offices.

The records group is organized by Washington headquarters and the district offices (usually an individual state) and subordinate offices in each district. Reports providing information about women are included at each level. Material about women involved in the Bureau as teachers is found in the education division of the Washington headquarters records and in the records of the superintendent of education in the district offices. There are, for example, school reports in the Washington headquarters records, 1865-1870 (14 ft.), which give the number, age, and sex of pupils and the kind of education offered at the schools. Teachers' reports give information on the number of pupils, attendance habits, and teaching hours.

District records contain registers of marriage which vary in quantity among the districts; they provide the names of the couple, date of marriage, information on previous marriages, number of children from previous marriages, and the minister who performed the ceremony. Ration reports give the number of rations issued to men, women, and children. Labor contracts between freedmen and employers witnessed by Bureau officers indicate period of service, rate of wages, and type of work. Reports of sick and wounded indicate the number of women and men under treatment at reporting hospitals.

See *Preliminary Inventory of the Records of the Bureau of Refugees, Freedmen, and Abandoned Lands, Washington Headquarters,* PI 174 (1973). See also *Guide to the National Archives of the United States* (Washington, DC: General Services Administration, 1974).

2,676. Bureau of the Census (RG 29)
Records. 1790-1965. 8434 cu.ft. and 27,988 microfilm reels.
Access restricted. Published guides.
National Archives and Records Service.
The Census Office was established in 1902 as a permanent bureau in the Department of the Interior; before then, a census office had been established for each decennial census and closed when work on the particular census was completed. The Bureau is responsible for providing basic statistics about the people and economy of the nation in order to assist the Congress, the government, and the public in planning, carrying out, and evaluating programs. It was formally designated the Bureau of the Census in 1954.

Administrative records of the Census Office and the Bureau of the Census, census schedules and supplementary records, and cartographic and audiovisual records.

Population schedules for censuses before 1850 give only the name of the head of each family and such family information as the number of dependents by age and sex. Most of the schedules for the 1890 census were destroyed by fire, and the 1900 and subsequent census schedules are restricted. Beginning in 1850, however, the schedules show the name, age, sex, and color of every person enumerated; place of birth; if married within the year; literacy; and the number of those deaf, dumb, blind, insane, idiots, and paupers. In 1870 the category for profession, occupation, or trade was expanded to include the occupations of women and children. The 1870 schedule also includes a category for parentage which shows whether parents were foreign born or native born. The 1880 schedule shows the relationship of each person enumerated to the head of the family.

In addition to population schedules the Census Office used separate schedules, known collectively as nonpopulation schedules, on industry, agriculture, social statistics (1850-70), the dependent classes (1880), and mortality. The National Archives has acquired only some of these on microfilm; the originals are in the custody of state and private institutions.

Numerous publications, which are available from the National Archives, describe census schedules and indexes to them.

See *Preliminary Inventory of the Records of the Bureau of the Census,* PI 161 (1964). See also *Guide to the National Archives of the United States* (Washington, DC: General Services Administration, 1974).

2,677. Children's Bureau (RG 102)
Records. 1912-49. 530 cu.ft.
Open. Published guides.
National Archives and Records Service.
The Bureau, which was established in April 1912, investigates and reports on all matters pertaining to childlife, including maternity care, infant mortality, working mothers, the birth rate, orphanages, juvenile delinquency, desertion, dangerous occupations, employment, accidents, childhood diseases, and state and local administration of child welfare.

Contains a central file, which includes correspondence, memoranda, reports with indexes, 1914-40, and an index to files relating to the first and second child labor laws, 1916-19; partial documentation for published survey reports, 1912-40; state plans for child welfare administration, 1936-49; and motion pictures and film strips.

The bulk of the record group consists of the Bureau's central file (450 ft.), arranged in six chronological segments and according to the Bureau's subject-numeric filing system. Principal file classifications include maternal and child health, with material concerning nursing, nursing and midwifery education, maternal mortality statistics, infant mortality statistics, maternity, and hygiene; child labor and industrial conditions affecting children, with material concerning women in industry and working mothers; legislation, with material concerning maternity laws and women's work laws; maternal and child health services under the social security act; and Children's Bureau studies concerning child labor, maternity and infant health, and health problems.

Because the Bureau administers federal aid to state agencies for child welfare, maternal and child health, and crippled children, the record group includes material documenting the functions, policies, procedures, and operations of the Bureau in these areas, 1936-49 (216 ft.), as well as plans submitted by states to show compliance with federal requirements for health and welfare grants.

Material about numerous women employees of the Bureau is found throughout the record group. See *Preliminary Inventory of the Records of the Children's Bureau,* PI 184 (1976). See also *Guide to the National Archives of the United States* (Washington, DC: General Services Administration, 1974).

2,678. Committee on Fair Employment Practice (RG 228)
Records. 1940-46. 200 cu.ft.
Open. Published guides.
National Archives and Records Service.
The Committee, which was established in June 1941 and terminated in June 1946, formulated and

interpreted policies to combat racial and religious discrimination in employment; received, investigated, and adjusted complaints of such discrimination; and assisted employers, labor unions, and government agencies with problems of discrimination. The Committee handled 14,000 complaints of discrimination, of which 80 percent concerned race and primarily involved Negroes; 14 percent concerned national origin and primarily involved Mexican-Americans; and 6 percent concerned religion and primarily involved Jews. Sara E. Southall of Illinois, a supervisor of employment and service for the International Harvester Corporation, served as a member of the Committee.

Office files of headquarters officials, including correspondence, memoranda, and reports; records relating to hearings, with indexes; statistics; issuances; records of the 12 regional offices; and case records with indexes.

Information on women on the staff of the Committee is found in office files of Marjorie M. Lawson, assistant director of the division of review and analysis, 1942-45 (4 ft.); and in the office files of two compliance analysts, Carol Coan, 1943-45 (2 ft.), and Joy P. Davis, 1943-45 (10 in.). In the legal division are office files of Evelyn N. Cooper, trial attorney, 1944-45 (5 in.). The legal division also contains records relating to hearings, 1941-46 (24 ft.), which include records of such cases as *Amertorp Corporation v. Lillian D. Reynolds et al.*, case no. 61, St. Louis, 1944; and *McDonnell Aircraft Corporation v. Sarah J. Bundy et al.*, St. Louis, 1944.

The record group also contains case files involving complaints about discrimination by private employers, labor unions, and federal government agencies. Active case files and closed case files, 1941-46 (17 and 76 ft., respectively), contain correspondence regarding complaints and investigations and reports of investigations. The files include a form which gives the number of women employed by each company; these are arranged by region and party charged. For both sets of cases there is an index that gives the name and address of the party charged; the name, address, and sex of the party aggrieved; and the date of complaint, type of discrimination charged, and disposition of the case. See *Preliminary Inventory of the Records of the Committee on Fair Employment Practice*, PI 147 (1962). See also *Guide to the National Archives of the United States* (Washington, DC: General Services Administration, 1974).

2,679. Council of National Defense (RG 62)
Records. 1916-21. 385 cu.ft.
Open. Published guides.
National Archives and Records Service.
The Council was established in August 1916 to coordinate resources and industries for national security and welfare. It was the first large emergency agency of WWI and the parent agency of most of the other special war agencies. Its activities were suspended in June 1921.

Minutes, correspondence, periodic and special reports, memoranda, bulletins, circulars, tables, press releases, abstract card records, and indexes.

Includes records of one of the major divisions of the Council, the committee on women's defense work (ca. 80 ft.), which was headed by Anna Howard Shaw. Committee records include a central correspondence file (32 ft.), which is arranged by state division, government agency, organization, and person, with an index to the file; a correspondence file of Shaw (1.5 ft.); and other materials (ca. 10 ft.), including circulars, weekly and monthly reports, reports from the women's committee conference of 1918, publications relating to war and social and economic conditions, and lists of officers and department chairmen of state women's committees.

Also contains records of six departments within the women's committee. Records of the news department (ca. 14 ft.), which was headed by Mrs. Joseph R. Lamar, include general correspondence, publications, papers dealing with women and war, the correspondence of Gertrude Mathews Shelley, *Newsletters* and other publications, bulletins, news stories, photos, and abstracts regarding the organization and work of state divisions, economic and social problems abroad with emphasis on women's problems, and women's war work. Records of the women in industry department, which was headed by Agnes Nestor, include publications and summaries relating to the employment of women (4 in.). Records of the education propaganda department, which was headed by Carrie Chapman Catt and Martha E. Martin, contain correspondence, publications, and reports about Americanization activities and patriotic education (4 ft.). Also contains records of the state organization department, which was headed by Mrs. Joseph R. Lamar (3.5 ft.); the child welfare department, which was headed by Jessica Peixotto (3 in.); and the department of registration, which was headed by Hannah J. Patterson. The latter records include summaries of state reports on registration of women by occupation (1 binder).

In addition to records of the committee, the record group contains records of the medicine and sanitation committee, which included a committee on nursing headed by M. Adelaide Nutting. Nursing committee records include reports on assignments of student nurse reserve applicants to hospital training schools (8 in.). Also contained in records of the medicine and sanitation committee are records of the central governing board of the volunteer medical service corps, with card records pertaining to a census of women physicians (ca. 19 ft.), which provide names and addresses of women physicians. The cards are arranged alphabetically by state.

Records of the committee on labor, which was headed by Samuel Gompers, include those of the women in industry subcommittee, which was headed by Mrs. J. Borden Harriman (4.5 ft.). These records include general correspondence, oaths of allegiance from state committees on women in industry, reports, minutes, publications, and tables, lists, and statistics dealing with employment at the Brooklyn Navy Yard in 1918.

Other records pertaining to the work of the committee on women's defense work are filed in the state councils section (16 in.) and in the field division (2 ft.). See *Preliminary Inventory of the Council of National Defense Records*, PI 2 (1942). See also *Guide to the National Archives of the United States* (Washington, DC: General Services Administration, 1974).

2,680. Department of Health, Education and Welfare (RG 235)
Records. 1857-1970. 403 cu.ft.
Open. Published guides.
National Archives and Records Service.
The predecessor of HEW, the Federal Security Agency, was established in 1930 and operated until 1953 when it was abolished and replaced by HEW, which administers federal and federal-state programs in public health, education, and social and economic security. Consists primarily of correspondence but also includes surveys, reports, legal opinions, and files of various officials, among them Oveta Culp Hobby, who was federal security administrator in 1953 and secretary of HEW from 1953 to 1955. Records provide information on such matters as statutes affecting common law marriages in 22 states, 1937-38 (11 in.), which are found in the records of the office of the general counsel: legal opinions and reports—numeric file, report 438. HEW records also contain records of Gallaudet College, 1857-, including correspondence and financial records. See *Preliminary Inventory of the Records of the Department of Health, Education and Welfare*, PI 181 (1975). See also *Guide to the National Archives of the United States* (Washington, DC: General Services Administration, 1974).

2,681. Department of Labor (RG 174)
Records. 1907-68. 1921 cu.ft.
Access restricted. Published and unpublished guides.
National Archives and Records Service.
The Department of Labor, which was created in March 1913 as one of the successor agencies of the Department of Commerce and Labor, has jurisdiction over matters relating to the welfare of American wage earners, including the improvement of their working conditions and the advancement of profitable employment opportunities.

Contains central files of the office of the secretary of labor and records of the secretaries, under secretaries, and assistant secretaries of labor and of their special assistants.

The record group consists primarily of the records of high-level officials of the Department of Labor and of units concerned with matters that affect the Department as a whole. It includes records of secretary of labor Frances Perkins (ca. 67 ft.); correspondence relating to the Women-in-Industry Service, the Children's Bureau, and the Women's Bureau; records of the special assistant to the secretary, Aryness Joy Wickens; and scripts for radio broadcasts by Frances Perkins. The Children's Bureau records include a file of endorsements of Julia Lathrop for the position of chief of the Bureau. See *Guide to the National Archives of the United States* (Washington, DC: General Services Administration, 1974).

2,682. Federal Extension Service (RG 33)
Records. 1888-1952. 911 cu.ft.
Open. Published guides.
National Archives and Records Service.
The Service, which was organized in July 1923, combined various extension activities of the Department of Agriculture. It coordinates extension activities of Department of Agriculture bureaus with those of state agricultural colleges, assists farmers in carrying out new farming and home enterprises through the services of county agricultural and home demonstration agents, makes known results of agricultural research, and presents displays and exhibits at fairs and expositions.

Includes annual narrative and statistical reports, general correspondence with indexes by author and subject, records relating to departmental participation in fairs and expositions, records relating to the farm labor program, and audiovisual records (5565 items).

Material about women involved in extension activities as home demonstration agents and girls club agents is found in annual narrative and statistical reports, 1908-44 (3577 microfilm reels) and 1945 (151 ft.) and in reports and other records concerning boys and girls club activities, 1911-22 (2 ft.). Records concerning the farm labor program, 1943-48 (31 ft.), contain material on the women's land army division, including annual narrative and statistical reports, general correspondence, and a history of the work accomplished by the women's land army division.

In the records of the extension service, general correspondence files, 1943-46 (57 ft.), is material under classifications such as associations, clubs, and societies, for information about farm women and the Associated Country Women of the World; under farm labor, for the women's land army; under personnel, for home demonstration agents; under programs and projects (general only), for home demonstration work; and under public relations, for a list of farm women and farmers. See *Preliminary Inventory of the Records of the Extension Service*, PI 83 (1955). See also *Guide to the National Archives of the United States* (Washington, DC: General Services Administration, 1974).

2,683. Immigration and Naturalization Service (RG 85)

Records. 1787-1954. 959 cu.ft. and 11,476 microfilm reels.
Access restricted. Published and unpublished guides.
National Archives and Records Service.
The Immigration and Naturalization Service administers laws relating to admission, exclusion, deportation, and naturalization of aliens; investigates alleged violations of those laws; patrols US borders; supervises naturalization work; and registers and fingerprints aliens in the US. General supervision over immigration had been exercised by the Secretary of the Treasury from 1882 until 1891, when an office of superintendent of immigration was created within the Department of the Treasury. Responsibility for administering functions was placed in the Department of Commerce and Labor in 1903, in the Department of Labor in 1913, and finally in 1940 in the Department of Justice, where the Service assumed its current name.

Contains records of general immigration, Chinese immigration, passenger arrival, Americanization, naturalization, field offices, and alien internment camps. Also contains audiovisual records.

Passenger arrival records, 1883-1954, are microfilm copies (11,476 reels) of ship and airplane passenger and crew lists, including names of immigrants, visitors, and citizens returning from abroad. Forms prescribed by the federal government, and in use by 1893, include the name of the vessel and master, the names of the ports of arrival and embarkation, and the date of arrival. For each passenger there is given name, age, sex, marital status, occupation, nationality, last residence, port of arrival in the US, and final destination in the US; whether the person had been in the US before and, if so, when and where; and whether the person was going to join a relative and, if so, the name and address of the relative and his or her relationship to the passenger. Passenger list forms were revised in 1903 to include race, in 1906 to include a personal description, and in 1907 to include the name and address of the alien's nearest relative in the country from which he or she came.

Major ports and arrival dates are Baltimore, 1891-1909; Boston and Charlestown, 1891-1943; New Orleans, 1903-45; New York, 1897-1942; and Philadelphia, 1883-1945. See *Guide to the National Archives of the United States* (Washington, DC: General Services Administration, 1974).

2,684. National Recovery Administration (RG 9)

Records. 1927-37. 5168 cu.ft.
Open. Published guides.
National Archives and Records Service.
Created under the authority of the National Industrial Recovery Act in 1933, the NRA worked to rehabilitate industry and trade in the US, expand employment, and improve labor conditions. Before its termination in 1936, it drafted a series of codes of fair competition for the separate regulation of every important branch of trade and industry.

Consolidated files on approved and unapproved codes, including correspondence, reports, memoranda, and questionnaires; transcripts of hearings; records of the various divisions, boards, and committees of NRA; records of regional and territorial offices; and records of code authorities.

Records relating to specific industries in which women were employed, among them the laundry trade, the cotton garment industry, and the light sewing industry, are found in three series: the consolidated files on industries governed by approved codes (2200 ft.), which are arranged alphabetically by names of the 757 industries for which codes were approved; transcripts of hearings (109 ft.), which cover proposed codes, amendments, modifications, exemptions, and code interpretations; and code histories for industries under approved codes (31 ft.), which document the process of formulating codes for approximately 750 industries. The transcripts of hearings files on the laundry trade, for example, include an appendix with statistical information on the marital status, race, and occupations of female laundry workers 15 years old and over in 19 states.

Also contained are records of the public relations division, which include the records (1 ft.) of [Miss] Marshall Coles, director of the division during 1935, and records of the women's section, 1933-35 (ca. 4 ft.), including correspondence, reports, questionnaires, and a history of the section, which was headed by Margie E. Neal. In the classified general files, 1933-35 (160 ft.), is correspondence relating to the employment of married women, domestic workers, and the NRA codes. The records of the division of industrial economics contain five studies by the legal staff concerning the wages of working women.

See *Preliminary Inventory of the Records of the National Recovery Administration,* PI 44 (1952). Women employed by the NRA are listed in appendices 11 and 12 of the *Inventory.* See also *Guide to the National Archives of the United States* (Washington, DC: General Services Administration, 1974).

2,685. National Youth Administration (RG 119)

Records. 1934-44. 993 cu.ft.
Open. Published and unpublished guides.
National Archives and Records Service.
Established in June 1935, the NYA conducted two major programs for needy persons between the ages of 16 and 24: an out-of-school work program, which provided employment and vocational training on public projects, and a student work program, which furnished parttime employment on projects devised by school authorities for students who were unable to continue their education. The NYA was terminated in January 1944.

Correspondence, reports, reference files, and data files of the national advisory committee, the office of the administrator, the various divisions, and regional offices. Also contains audiovisual records.

Information about NYA aid to young women is found in records concerning educational aid, which include records of the national advisory committee on educational camps for unemployed young women, with correspondence of the chairman and the deputy executive director of NYA with state youth and camp directors on camp politics and problems (10 in.). Hilda W. Smith chaired the advisory committee, and Mary McLeod Bethune represented NYA to it. Also includes records of educational camps and educational aid, with correspondence of the director with applicants for enrollment in the camps (5 in.), copies of letters sent by the director concerning administration of the camps (1 in.), a special file of the director concerning educational camps in Pennsylvania (5 in.), and correspondence of the director concerning meetings of the educational committee (2 in.).

Related material is found in the records of the deputy executive director and deputy administrator, correspondence of the deputy executive director concerning NYA girls camps (5 in.). Records about women who held positions in the NYA are in records of the office of Negro affairs, records of the director Mary McLeod Bethune (5 ft.), which include the general subject file of the director, the director's file of reports of state directors of Negro affairs, and the final report of the division. Other material about women in NYA is found in the records of the division of youth personnel, records of the director Mary H. S. Hayes (ca. 33.5 ft.), including correspondence, administrative and reference files, and field inspection reports received by the director; records of the division of reports and records (ca. 2.5 ft.), including statistical data concerning approved applicants for NYA student aid; and records of the director of music Margaret Valinat, consisting of correspondence concerning administration of the music program of NYA (3 ft.).

The NYA publications file (82 ft.) includes information about the women's educational camp program at Camp Seeley, CA; a description of girls resident centers in Colorado; the secretarial field as a career for Negro girls and boys; vocational problems of girls in Maine; and reports on camps and projects. See *Guide to the National Archives of the United States* (Washington, DC: General Services Administration, 1974).

2,686. Office of Civilian Defense (RG 171)

Records. 1939-45. 606 cu.ft.
Open. Published and unpublished guides.
National Archives and Records Service.
The Office, which was established in May 1920 and terminated in June 1945, coordinated federal, state, and local defense relationships regarding the protection of civilians during air raids and other emergencies. It also facilitated civilian participation in war programs.

Consists of records of the national headquarters, including central files; records of the various divisions; records of the regional office in San Francisco (Region IX), the only regional office whose records are extant; cartographic records; and photos.

The record group provides information about the volunteer aspects of women's service during WWII. The central file general correspondence section (130 ft. with indexes), for example, has subjects such as nurseries, child welfare, nurses, nurses' aides, women, women in defense, and physical training for women. The classified file (3 ft.) contains correspondence about women in defense.

The division of federal-state cooperation contains miscellaneous records (10 in.) with memoranda to Eleanor Roosevelt; a file of Mrs. Henry Morgenthau, Jr.; and records relating to day care of children of working mothers. The federal-state division records also contain records relating to activities of volunteers in civilian defense (11 in.), which are arranged by subject, including American women's voluntary services, girl scouts, women's voluntary services, child care, nurses' aides, the Women's Army Auxiliary Corps, women in war work, and the National Organization for Public Health Nursing. Division records also contain records relating to the welfare of children (ca. 2 ft.).

The medical division includes data relating to nursing (ca. 2 ft.), with files on such subjects as nursing education, nursing executives in emergency base hospitals, state nurses' associations bulletins, state registration for nursing legislation, and home nursing. Also contains lists of schools of nursing and a study by Martha M. Eliot, a physician, on civil defense measures for the protection of children in Great Britain. The public counsel division records include a clippings file (12.5 ft.) with subjects such as child care and welfare, civilian mobilization, boy and girl scouts, women, and women's organizations.

The record group contains Office of Civilian Defense publications on volunteer nurses' aides, day care for children of working mothers, nursing participation in emergency medical services, and the use of women volunteers in civilian defense. See *Guide to the National Archives of the United States* (Washington, DC: General Services Administration, 1974).

2,687. Office of Community War Services (RG 215)

Records. 1940-48. 237 cu.ft.
Open. Published guides.
National Archives and Records Service.
The Office was established in April 1943 to succeed the Office of Defense Health and Welfare Services, which had been established in September 1941. The latter superseded the Office of the Coordinator of Health, Welfare and Related Defense Activities, which had been established in November 1940. The Office of War Community Services was terminated in June 1946, with the

exception of the recreation division, which existed through June 1947.

Contains general records, including central files, as well as correspondence, reports and surveys, and minutes.

One of the principal operating units of the Office was the social protection division, which was responsible for organizing and conducting a national program to prevent the spread of venereal disease and to repress prostitution in defense areas. General records of the division, 1941-46 (4 ft.), include material on the activities of various communities and agencies involved in repression of prostitution, on the social treatment of girls described as sexually delinquent, and on the use of policewomen as protective officers. In addition, the division files include reports, 1942-46 (4 ft.), from area representatives to headquarters summarizing the community's social protection programs; statistics and studies, 1941-45 (3 ft.), which include material on prostitution conditions within defense communities and on the number, age, and race of women held on prostitution charges; and a public relations file, 1942-46 (3 ft.), which includes correspondence with women's groups soliciting their endorsement and support.

Additional information about the social protection division is found in the subject-classified central file, 1940-47 (209 ft.), of the headquarters records of the Office of Community War Services, which contains files and minutes of the National Women's Advisory Committee on Social Protection, a nongovernmental agency which aided the division.

Information about women is also found in the records of the day care division, 1942-43 (5 ft.), relating to state plans and budgets for services to children of working mothers; minutes and records of the family security committee, 1941-43 (1 ft.); and records of the health and medical committee that relate to nursing recruitment, 1941-42 (5 in.). Records of the recreation division contain material on juvenile delinquency, youth centers, and youth problems, 1941-46 (3 ft.). See *Preliminary Inventory of the Records of the Office of Community War Services,* PI 132 (1960). See also *Guide to the National Archives of the United States* (Washington, DC: General Services Administration, 1974).

2,688. Office of Price Administration (RG 188)

Records. 1940-49. 8860 cu.ft.
Access restricted. Published guides.
National Archives and Records Service.
The Office of Price Administration was established in May 1940, became an independent agency in January 1942, and consolidated with other agencies in December 1946 to form the Office of Temporary Controls. It was terminated in June 1947.

Contains general records and records of various officials, committees, advisors, boards, departments, and regional offices, including budgets, minutes, correspondence, reports, legal opinions, speeches, publications, transcripts of hearings, and press releases.

In the records of the community service division and its predecessors are records of the consumer division and of the group services branch. Records of Harriet Elliott, commissioner in charge of consumer protection from July 1940 to December 1941, are in the general records, series I (10 ft.), of the consumer division. Also found in the consumer division records, editorial branch (2 in.), are field reports and activity reports prepared by Florence Reynolds, liaison officer to the Department of Agriculture.

The group services branch records contain records of the women's section, 1941-46 (1 ft.), including progress reports of the staff showing the type and degree of assistance given to OPA programs by women's associations, correspondence with national associations, and correspondence with and records relating to Negro associations. A history of the women's section is in the general records of the group services branch, 1942-45 (2 in.).

Also contains transcripts of 16 speeches and radio addresses delivered by Harriet Elliott, among them "Women's Part in Defense Plans," and ten consumer compliance studies and surveys concerning women's knowledge of and attitudes toward price control, price ceilings, and rationing. See *Preliminary Inventory of the Records of the Information Department of the Office of Price Administration,* PI 119 (1959). See also *Guide to the National Archives of the United States* (Washington, DC: General Services Administration, 1974).

2,689. Office of the Quartermaster General (RG 92)

Records. 1792-1957. 22,942 cu.ft.
Open. Published and unpublished guides.
National Archives and Records Service.
Although the first quartermaster general was appointed in 1775, the Quartermaster's Department was not created by Congress until 1818. The quartermaster general ensured efficient systems of supply, movement of the Army, and accountability of officers and agents charged with moneys or supplies. The Office of Quartermaster General was abolished in July 1962.

Correspondence; letter books; reports; personnel records; records relating to supplies, cemeteries, and transportation; field records; and cartographic and audiovisual records.

In the special files of the central records, 1917-54, are records of the gold-star mothers' and widows' pilgrimage to Europe, 1930-33, a pilgrimage made to the graves of sons and husbands killed in WWI in Europe. These consist of general correspondence of the New York office (32 ft.); general correspondence of the Paris office (10 ft.); a ledger of obligations and expenditures relating to the gold-star pilgrimage (1 vol.); a scrapbook of Colonel Richard T. Ellis, who was in charge of the Paris office (1 vol.); and transportation requests of the gold-star pilgrimage. See *Guide to the National Archives of the United States* (Washington, DC: General Services Administration, 1974).

2,690. Office of the Surgeon General (RG 112)

Records. 1775-1949. 4500 cu.ft.
Open. Published and unpublished guides.
National Archives and Records Service.
The Office, which was established in April 1818, is the headquarters of the Army medical department, whose mission is to maintain the health of the Army. Contains records relating to fiscal matters, general correspondence, issuances and reports, and records relating to military personnel; records of subordinate administrative units; records of medical department field installations; and cartographic and audiovisual records.

Includes the records of the Army Nurse Corps, among them records relating to military personnel, 1775-1947, regular Army personnel, nurses, which contain historical files of the Corps, 1900-47 (6 ft.); case files of candidates seeking appointment as Army nurses, 1898-1917 (34 ft.), including successful and unsuccessful candidates; register of military service of members of the Army Nurse Corps, 1901-02 (3 in.); annual efficiency reports on nurses, 1898-1917 (9 ft.); and a list of nurses who served with the Army Nurse Corps during WWI, 1917-21 (1 in.).

Corps records also contain records relating to civilian personnel, 1862-1939, contract nurses, including correspondence relating to Spanish-American War contract nurses, 1898-1910 (2 ft.); registers of service of Spanish-American War contract nurses, 1898-1900 (2 ft.); personal data cards of Spanish-American War contract nurses, 1898-1939 (6 ft.); and correspondence relating to the service of Spanish-American War contract nurses, 1898-1939 (6 ft.). Also contains a list of female nurses, cooks, and laundresses employed in Army hospitals during the Civil War (0.5 in.) and a register showing gains and losses of hospital matrons on duty at Army posts, 1893-1904 (0.5 in.).

Corps records also include records of individual medical department officers, 1820-1936, which contain journals of Anita Newcomb McGee, a physician, 1898-99 (2 ft.). Records of the nursing division contain records of the Army School of Nursing, 1918-33 and 1951 (3 ft.). The records of the women's health and welfare unit, professional administration, contain records relating to the preparation of field manual 35-20, 1942-44 (1 ft.). See *Guide to the National Archives of the United States* (Washington, DC: General Services Administration, 1974).

2,691. Office of War Information (RG 208)

Records. 1941-48. 4630 cu.ft.
Access restricted. Published guides.
National Archives and Records Service.
The Office of War Information was established in June 1942 and terminated in December 1945. It formulated and carried out programs to disseminate information in the US and abroad about the progress of the war and about government policies, activities, and objectives.

Minutes, reports, memoranda, and correspondence of the domestic operations branch and the overseas operations branch. Also contains audiovisual records.

Records of the domestic operations branch contain records of the deputy director for labor and civilian welfare, including records of Natalie Davison, program manager for home front campaigns (4 ft.), including correspondence, reports, and pamphlets relating to child care, maternity and infant care, womanpower in industry, recruitment for the WAVES and WACs; records of the senior deputy director for production and manpower, in which are records of the program manager for the recruitment of women (1 ft.), including records of program manager Mary Keelor dealing with government campaigns to recruit women for the armed services and the Army Nurse Corps; records of the radio bureau's editorial and production division in which are records of the "Women's Radio War Program Guide" (10 in.), including copies of the guide and related correspondence.

Also contained in the records of the domestic operations branch are records of the news bureau's editing division for "Women's Page" (2 ft.), including press releases containing news items from official sources to editors of women's pages; and records of the news bureau's news writing division, which contain reports on phases of the war effort (3 ft.), including reports on topics such as the employment of women, women in the armed services, the effects of war production adjustments on employment of women, child care services for children of working mothers, and the shortage of nurses. See *Preliminary Inventory of the Records of the Office of War Information,* PI 56 (1953). See also *Guide to the National Archives of the United States* (Washington, DC: General Services Administration, 1974).

2,692. President's Organization on Unemployment Relief (RG 73)

Records. 1930-33. 107 cu.ft.
Open. Published guides.
National Archives and Records Service.
The President's Organization was established in October 1930 as the President's Emergency Committee for Employment (which was also known as the [Colonel Arthur] Woods Committee) and reorganized in August 1931 as the President's Organization on Unemployment Relief. It was created to stimulate and coordinate employment and relief activities during the economic depression that began in 1930. The Organization worked with state and local governments, quasi-public and private organizations, and relief and employment

agencies in sponsoring programs, encouraging public works, and serving as a clearinghouse for information and ideas. The Organization was terminated in June 1932.

Consists of central files, including minutes, reports, issuances, correspondence, memoranda, and publications; card index of members and staff; and records of officials and the various sections and divisions of the Committee and the Organization.

Contains the records of the women's division of the President's Emergency Committee, 1930-31 (ca. 5 ft.). General records of the division include correspondence, memoranda, telegrams, reports, and lists of women leaders and organizations concerned with the unemployment problem in the US. These records pertain to the division's campaign for home improvement and repair, prudent spending, and economical and nutritious food; to activities of women's groups assisting the unemployed and providing relief; and to the question of replacing women workers whose husbands held jobs. The reading file contains correspondence and memoranda of the division's director Lillian M. Gilbreth and the assistant director Alice M. Dickson. The state files include reports relating to the gathering of information about women's work in providing relief and employment and the effect of unemployment on women's health and morale. Included are questionnaires related to surveys of employment and economic conditions.

Also contains publications of the Committee and the Organization about community planning for women without resources, activities of the women's division, activities of women's organizations, and other topics. These are scattered throughout the record group. See *Preliminary Inventory of the Records of the President's Organization on Unemployment Relief,* PI 137 (1962). See also *Guide to the National Archives of the United States* (Washington, DC: General Services Administration, 1974).

2,693. Social Security Administration (RG 47)

Records. 1934-63. 374 cu.ft.
Access restricted. Published guides.
National Archives and Records Service.
The Social Security Board was established in August 1935 and abolished in July 1946, the same date that the Social Security Administration was established. Both administered the provisions of the Social Security Act of 1935 relating to federal old-age and survivors insurance and authorizing grants-in-aid to the states for administration of unemployment compensation, old-age assistance, and assistance to the blind and to dependent children.

Minutes, correspondence, reports, charts, and other records are in master files, state files, regional files, and alphabetical files. Also contains audiovisual records.

Members of the Social Security Board included Mary W. Dewson, 1937-38, and Ellen S. Woodward, 1938-46; material relating to them is in the records of the Board, including agenda and minutes, 1935-36 (ca. 10 ft.), and subject, state, and alphabetical files, 1935-40 (ca. 59 ft.). Material relating to domestic employment and the Children's Bureau and scattered material on maternal, wives', and widows' benefits are found in the master file, 1935-47 (102 ft.). Records of the Committee on Economic Security, which preceded the Social Security Board, contain files of Helen Greenblatt, a member of the editorial staff, 1934-35 (2 ft.); correspondence regarding proposals for the economic security program, 1934-35 (2 ft.), including that of Katharine Lenroot, Isador Lubin, and Frances Perkins; and staff correspondence, 1934-35 (2 ft.). The Committee's staff included 24 women.

See *Preliminary Inventory of the Records of the Social Security Administration,* PI 183 (1976). See also *Guide to the National Archives of the United States* (Washington, DC: General Services Administration, 1974).

2,694. United States Food Administration (RG 4)

Records. 1917-20. 2995 cu.ft.
Open. Published guides.
National Archives and Records Service.
The Administration, which was headed by Herbert Hoover, was created in August 1917 to assure the supply, distribution, and conservation of foods during the wartime emergency; to facilitate their movement and prevent monopolies and hoarding; and to maintain government control over foods chiefly by means of voluntary agreements and a licensing system. It was terminated in August 1920.

Contains records of the central office, including minutes, reports, memoranda, agreements, license approvals, procedural material, hearings, legal documents, tables, graphs, data files, press releases, and clippings; records of state food administrations, the milling division, the sugar distributing committee, and the food purchase board; and still pictures, 1917-20 (3550 items).

Women were involved in the Food Administration in two areas, the home conservation division and the educational division. Includes general correspondence, 1917-19 (ca. 46 ft.), of the home conservation division, which was directed by Sarah F. Splint and Martha Van Rensselaer. Division records also contain correspondence (2 in.) of Ida M. Tarbell, who was the Food Administration's representative to the woman's committee of the council of national defense; a file of Sarah L. Arnold, which consists of correspondence concerning conferences at colleges and universities (1 in.); and correspondence of Mrs. Duncan McDuffie, Frances Wardwell, and Mrs. Vernon Kellogg (5 in.).

Education division records include correspondence (18 in.) of Mrs. Alice B. Allen, photographic editor and chief of the illustrations and plate section, with state educational directors and federal food administrators; photos of division personnel and others; a file (29 in.) of Harriet Anderson, who succeeded Gertrude B. Lane as director of the magazine and feature section; a file of Alice B. Norton (2 in.), who was home economics editor; correspondence (22 in.) of Frances Moore, head of the information division; and correspondence of Gertrude Mosshard, chief of the retail stores section. See *Preliminary Inventory of the Records of the United States Food Administration, Part 1, The Headquarters Organization,* PI 3 (1943). See also *Guide to the National Archives of the United States* (Washington, DC: General Services Administration, 1974).

2,695. United States Housing Corporation (RG 3)

Records. 1917-52. 444 cu.ft.
Open. Published guides.
National Archives and Records Service.
The Corporation was formed in 1918 to house workers migrating to congested areas to produce war materials during WWI. Construction activities were completed in 1919 and thereafter, until its termination in 1952, the Corporation was concerned with the operation and sale of properties and the liquidation of other assets.

Financial records, correspondence, investigative reports, memoranda, questionnaires, records of various divisions and committees, field office records, and cartographic records.

Records of the Washington, DC, division of the US homes registration service, 1918-19, include information on matrons employed to ensure the satisfactory operation of commandeered lodging houses in the District; [Mrs.] Elizabeth A. Helmick was in charge of inspectors and matrons. Records of the government hotels, 1919-30 (10.5 ft.), concern housing constructed for clerical workers, who were primarily women, in the District; managers of these hotels were [Miss] Harlean James and her successor [Mrs.] Sarah E. Sumner. See *Preliminary Inventory of the Records of the United States Housing Corporation,* PI 140 (1962). See also *Guide to the National Archives of the United States* (Washington, DC: General Services Administration, 1974).

2,696. United States Railroad Administration (RG 14)

Records. 1917-45. 1353 cu.ft.
Open. Published and unpublished guides.
National Archives and Records Service.
Established in December 1917 during the wartime emergency, the Administration controlled railroad and certain allied activities, specified steamship lines, canals, and the American Express Company. Although the Administration was terminated in March 1920, matters of liquidation and final settlement extended into the 1940s.

Minutes, general files of correspondence, memoranda, records of agreements and contracts with railroads, transcripts of hearings, case files, reports relating to labor disputes, inventories, accounts, statements, and indexes.

Records of the division of labor contain a general subject file of the women's service section, 1918-20 (12 ft.), which was headed by Pauline Goldmark. The files include fiscal and budget material, questionnaires completed by railroad companies concerning the number and occupations of employed women, correspondence relating to complaints by women railroad workers about wages and working conditions, and inspection reports on working conditions at railroad facilities where women worked. See *Guide to the National Archives of the United States* (Washington, DC: General Services Administration, 1974).

2,697. United States Senate and House of Representatives (RG 46 and 233)

Records. 1789-1975. 31,199 cu.ft.
Access restricted. Published guides.
National Archives and Records Service.
The Senate and House of Representatives were established by the constitution as the legislative branch of government. The Senate is empowered to try all impeachments and to judge the elections, returns, and qualifications of its members; it shares in executive responsibility with the president by providing advice and consent in the negotiation of treaties and the appointment of certain federal officials. The House shares legislative power with the Senate, originates all bills for raising revenue, and, by custom, general appropriations bills. The House has the sole power to impeach US civil officers. It judges elections, returns, and qualifications of its members.

Consists of journals and minute books, committee records, petitions and memorials, presidential messages and messages sent by executive departments and agencies, election records, cartographic and audiovisual records, and other legislative records.

Records of the Senate (RG 46) and House (RG 233) are arranged by Congress and thereunder by three major classifications: papers accompanying specific bills and resolutions; committee papers, arranged by committee; and petitions and memorials, resolutions of state legislatures, and related documents which were referred to committees, arranged by committee. The last classification, for example, contains petitions concerning woman suffrage made to at least 18 Congresses between 1855 and 1921; these are found in the records of the House, where they were usually referred to the committee on the judiciary. Similar petitions made to at least 14 Congresses between 1867 and 1919 are found in the records of the Senate.

Many of the records generated by the Congress have been published and serve as finding aids to unpublished materials. Among these are the

Congressional Record and its predecessors, the *Congressional Globe,* the *Register of Debates,* and the *Annals of Congress;* the *Congressional Serial Set,* a compilation of reports by the House and Senate; *Printed Hearings of the House of Representatives* and *Printed Hearings of the Senate;* and the *Journal of the House of Representatives* and the *Journal of the Senate.* See *Preliminary Inventory of Records of the United States Senate,* PI 23 (1950) and *Preliminary Inventory of Records of the United States House of Representatives,* PI 113 (1959). Both inventories are available on microfilm (M 248). See also *Guide to the National Archives of the United States* (Washington, DC: General Services Administration, 1974).

2,698. Veterans Administration (RG 15)
Records. 1773-1964. 76,203 cu.ft.
Access restricted. Published and unpublished guides.
National Archives and Records Service.
The present Veterans Administration, which was created in July 1930, resulted from policies and programs that date back to the American Revolution. The VA administers laws relating to benefits and relief for veterans and is responsible for extending relief to dependents of disabled or deceased veterans.

Administrative and legal records, financial records, war risk insurance records, vocational-rehabilitation records, records relating to pension and bounty land claims, and audiovisual records.

In records relating to pension and bounty land claims (64,250 ft.) are individual case files containing birth, marriage, and death records; copies of military records; medical histories; personal histories of dependents; affidavits and testimonials; correspondence; examiners' reports; and decisions of adjudicating agencies. There are case files of disapproved pension applications of widows and other dependents of veterans of Indian Wars, 1892-1926 (70 ft.), and of approved pension applications for the same wars (272 ft.); case files of disapproved pension applications of widows and other dependents of veterans of the Mexican War, 1887-1926 (55 ft.), and of approved applications for the Mexican War (493 ft.); case files of disapproved pension applications of widows and other dependents of Navy veterans, 1861-1910 (105 ft.), and of approved applications (591 ft.); and case files of disapproved pension applications of widows and other dependents of veterans of the Army and Navy who served primarily in the Civil War and the War with Spain, 1861-1934 (3040 ft.), and of approved applications for the same wars (31,267 ft.).

Although there are no separate series of case files for widows of the Revolutionary War and the War of 1812, information about approved and disapproved claims of veterans, widows, and other dependents is found in case files of pension and bounty-land warrant applications based on Revolutionary War service, 1800-1900 (1098 ft.), and case files of pension and bounty-land warrant applications based on service in the War of 1812, 1812-1910 (1279 ft.).

Financial records, 1805-1933 (2639 ft.), include pension payment rolls, registers of pension applications, registers of pension certificates, and lists of veterans and widows. Major series are pension payment rolls of widows and other dependents of Army veterans, 1863-76 (118 vols.); registers of pension applications of widows and other dependents of veterans based on service in the War of 1812, 1871-1916 (6 vols.); registers of pension applications of widows and other dependents of veterans who served in the Army and Navy after March 4, 1861, 1883-1912 (48 vols.); and registers of pension certificates issued to widows and other dependents of Army and Navy veterans between 1862 and 1914 (73 vols.). See *Preliminary Inventory of the Administrative Records of the Bureau of Pensions and Pension Service,* PI 55 (1953). See also *Guide to the National Archives of the United States* (Washington, DC: General Services Administration, 1974).

2,699. War Department General and Special Staffs and Army Staff (RG 165 and 319)
Records. 1908-64. 25,136 cu.ft.
Open. Published and unpublished guides.
National Archives and Records Service.
The War Department General Staff was authorized in February 1903, and special staff divisions were formed during WWII. In 1947 the War Department became the Department of the Army, and the Army Staff was created in place of these predecessor offices. The duties of these staffs include preparing plans relating to national defense, investigating and reporting Army efficiency and preparedness, and supervising Army operations.

Correspondence and reports of the chief of staff and of various component offices and divisions as well as cartographic and audiovisual records.

Records of the Women's Army Corps are found in both the records of the War Department General and Special Staffs (RG 165) and the Army Staff (RG 319). War Department records contain records of the office of the director of personnel and administration, which include WAC records consisting of security classified general correspondence, 1942-50 (56 ft.); historical and background material relating to the legislation and administration of the Women's Army Auxiliary Corps and its successor, the Women's Army Corps, 1942-49 (14 ft.), including the records of the director of the Corps, Oveta Culp Hobby; and general correspondence of the special civilian assistant to the director, 1942-43 (5 ft.).

Army staff records contain records of the directors of the Corps, 1942-50 (22 ft.), which consist chiefly of correspondence relating to the recruiting, classification, overall utilization, and separation of personnel. In addition to Corps records, material about women can be found in records of the office of the chief of information, 1940-54, which contain records of the women's interest section, 1941-49 (4 ft.). These records consist primarily of correspondence with the advisory council. The presidents of most of the large national women's associations were members of the advisory council. See *Guide to the National Archives of the United States* (Washington, DC: General Services Administration, 1974).

2,700. War Labor Policies Board (RG 1)
Records. 1918-19. 12 cu.ft.
Open. Published guides.
National Archives and Records Service.
Established in May 1918 and terminated in March 1919, the Board formulated uniform policies for war labor administration, promoted better housing conditions for war workers, and after the Armistice considered proposals for canceling government contracts and for demobilization. It also studied domestic and foreign wartime labor conditions and labor policies relating to immediate postwar conditions in the US.

Minutes, correspondence, bulletins, and clippings.

Correspondence of the chairman and the executive secretary (8.5 ft.) includes file folders on subjects such as employment of women; employment service (of the Labor Department), women's division; Labor Department, supply of female workers in the garment trade; night work for women, correspondence with federal and state departments of labor, the general order of the Secretary of War, and resolutions of the Board.

Also includes folders on Grace Abbott; Helen V. Bary, a field agent; C. T. Clayton, on placement of women in war industries; Susan M. Kingsbury, director of the Carola Woerishoffer graduate department at Bryn Mawr; Clara Mortenson, Edith Rockwood, and Ruth True, investigators for the Board; Mary Van Kleeck, director of the women-in-industry service, on working conditions of women employees of arsenals and navy yards; and William B. Wilson, Secretary of Labor, on the committee on employment of women in hazardous occupations, for standards governing employment of women and the unreliability of statistics on the number of women workers.

Minutes of the Board (6 in.) include the statement of policy in regard to women in industry with specific reference to the safeguards that were to be provided. The *Preliminary Inventory of the Records of the War Labor Policies Board,* PI 4 (1943), is out of print. See *Guide to the National Archives of the United States* (Washington, DC: General Services Administration, 1974).

2,701. War Manpower Commission (RG 211)
Records. 1940-47. 1130 cu.ft.
Open. Published guides.
National Archives and Records Service.
The Commission, which was established in April 1942 and terminated in September 1945, recruited labor for war and essential civilian industries, trained labor for jobs essential to the war efforts, analyzed manpower utilization practices to increase labor efficiency, and accumulated national labor market information. It operated through a headquarters office, regional and state offices, area offices, and local US employment offices.

Minutes, correspondence, reports, and memoranda relating to the officials of the Commission and the various committees, services, and bureaus within the Commission at the headquarters, regional, state, and local levels.

Records relating to women are found throughout the record group. Records of the women's advisory committee, 1942-45 (6 ft.), which was established in August 1942 and consisted of 13 women members, include verbatim and summary minutes of meetings with lists of the committee's members and its plans, policies, and programs for the use of women in war industry; issuances of the committee; speeches and broadcasts of Margaret A. Hickey, committee chairman; and correspondence of the chairman and executive secretary of the committee.

Central files of the Commission contain file classifications for the women's land corporation, the health of women, and the women training program. Under labor mobilization and utilization are files for women, the Women's Army Auxiliary Corps, registration of women, and women's auxiliary volunteer emergency service.

The procurement and assignment service records include general files, 1941-46, which contain material on the nursing section, with agenda and minutes, 1941-45, of various nursing committees and the committee on women physicians. Nursing data forms, 1944-45, provide statistical tables and charts on students in nursing schools and the availability of nurses. Katherine Tucker and Laura Grant represented the nursing profession on the governing board of the service.

Commission records provide information on women involved in the Commission. The subject-classified general records of the historical analysis section, 1940-46, include files on the women's advisory committee, the training of women, and job requirements for women. Constance A. Kiehel served as chief historian of the historical project and was also chief of the foreign labor market section from 1943 to 1944. General records of the executive secretary (8 ft.) include information about Marjorie R. Nash, who served as executive secretary of the management-labor policy committee from 1942 to 1945. Records of the office of the assistant executive director for field service contain records of May (Thompson) Evans (7 ft.), who served as a special assistant; these files contain private and government publications relating to women in wartime employment, their recruitment for the armed forces, and their postwar employment prospects.

Information service records include files of Verda W. Barnes (2 ft.), who served as assistant to the director of the service; these files contain material relating to the planning, preparation, and execution of publicity campaigns for recruitment of women. Information service records also include office files of Mary B. White (1 ft.), who served as manager of women's campaigns in the program division and office files of Miriam B. Marshall (4 ft.), who served as chief of the field section. Records of special services (4 ft.) provide information on the position of clearance officer, which was held successively by Verda W. Barnes, Sophie Nack, and Agnes S. Hathaway. Bernice Lotwin served as acting general counsel of the legal service, 1944-45, and her papers are filed in the general records of Bernard C. Gavit and Charles M. Hay, previous general counsels.

The record group also contains scattered material on the employment of women and the utilization of women. In the records of the bureau of placement, for example, are records relating to the steel industry, forges and foundries, and the cotton textile industry. Records of F. W. Hunter, 1940-43 (2 ft.), contain information on plans for the organization of the women's emergency land service and the proposed national voluntary registration of women. In the bureau of manpower utilization are issuances and publications of the division of occupational analysis for the employment of women in war production and other selected occupations. Issuances of the War Manpower Commission include histories of the women's advisory committee and of the nursing section of the procurement and assignment section as well as publications regarding training and utilization of women, wartime responsibilities of women, and related topics. See *Inventory of the Records of the War Manpower Commission, Record Group 211* (1973). See also *Guide to the National Archives of the United States* (Washington, DC: General Services Administration, 1974).

2,702. War Relocation Authority (RG 210)
Records. 1941-47. 2990 cu.ft.
Access restricted. Published guides.
National Archives and Records Service.
The WRA, which was established in March 1942 and terminated in June 1946, provided for the removal, relocation, maintenance, and supervision of approximately 110,000 persons of Japanese ancestry who were excluded from military areas; some German and Italian aliens were also affected.

Consists of headquarters records, including general files, evacuees files, and fiscal, statistical, management, and personnel files; field office records; and records of other agencies.

The bulk of the material pertaining to persons removed from military areas is in the evacuee case files (3058 ft.), which consist of individual folders, arranged alphabetically by name, for each evacuee. The files contain name, birthplace, birthdate, religion, marital status, education, languages spoken, employment history, military records, previous addresses, date of entry into relocation center, parents' and relatives' names and country of origin, and health records. There are also evacuee summary data cards (17 ft.), also arranged alphabetically by name, that give name, place and date of birth, sex, marital status, religion, occupation, parents' birthplaces, and father's occupation. Records of the Tule Lake Segregation Center, which was created for evacuees who had requested repatriation to Japan, renounced their American citizenship, or were suspected of disloyalty, contain lists of evacuees transferred from, remaining at, and transferred to the Center. The lists (11 in.) provide name, age, sex, and place of birth. Other sources of similar information are the population statistics (8 ft.), which include quarterly summaries, 1942-46, of relocation population and give information on age groups and marital status by sex and citizenship; basic family cards for evacuees (158 ft.); final accountability rosters of evacuees (2 ft.); the wartime civil control administration's master index of evacuees (27 microfilm reels); and social data registration forms (29 microfilm reels). The WRA historian was Ruth E. McKee. See *Preliminary Inventory of the Records of the War Relocation Authority,* PI 77 (1952). See also *Guide to the National Archives of the United States* (Washington, DC: General Services Administration, 1974).

2,703. Women's Bureau (RG 86)
Records. 1918-67. 667 cu.ft.
Open. Published and unpublished guides.
National Archives and Records Service.
The Woman-in-Industry Service was established in July 1918 and succeeded by the Women's Bureau in June 1920. A division of the Department of Labor, the Bureau develops standards, policies, and programs pertaining to the welfare, efficiency, and working conditions of working women; publishes reports on trends, opportunities, and characteristics of the female work force; digests existing labor laws and regulations affecting women; and makes recommendations on proposed legislation.

Correspondence, reports, survey materials relating to Bureau studies and bulletins, charts, graphs, posters, special subject maps, photos (2125 items), and motion pictures. Also contains copies of the *Newsletter* and *The Woman Worker,* which were issued by the Bureau from 1921 to 1956.

The record group contains records of the Woman-in-Industry Service, 1918-20 (5 ft.), a wartime emergency service most of whose records were destroyed in a fire in 1930. Includes general correspondence of Mary Van Kleeck, director of the Service, and her correspondence with members of the war labor policies board.

Records of the Women's Bureau provide extensive information on wages, hours, and working conditions for women in various states; on legislation affecting women; and on the occupations available to women. Includes correspondence of the Bureau with women's organizations, unions, the public, and government agencies as well as correspondence concerning the Bureau's published and unpublished reports.

Contains survey material for the Bureau's published bulletins (286 were published by 1963), among them *The Immigrant Woman and Her Job,* Bulletin 74, 1930 (ca. 6 ft.); *Women Unemployed Seeking Relief in 1933,* Bulletin 139, 1936 (7.5 ft.); *The Legal Status of Women in the United States, January 1, 1938,* Bulletin 157, 1941 (ca. 6 ft.); *Conditions in the Millinery Industry in the United States,* Bulletin 169, 1939 (ca. 10 ft.); *Office Work and Office Workers in 1940,* Bulletin 188, 1942 (ca. 21 ft.), which includes individual worker record cards for surveys in Los Angeles, Houston, Kansas City, Philadelphia, and Richmond, VA; and *First Jobs of College Women—Report of Women Graduates, Class of 1957,* Bulletin 268, 1959 (ca. 12 ft.).

Photos and photos of artworks (ca. 11 ft.) concern women at work in defense and peacetime industries, working conditions and the equipment used by women in the home and in industry, women in agriculture, and women in the professions. See *Guide to the National Archives of the United States* (Washington, DC: General Services Administration, 1974).

2,704. Work Projects Administration (RG 69)
Records. 1933-45. 4637 cu.ft.
Open. Published and unpublished guides.
National Archives and Records Service.
The Works Progress Administration was established in May 1935. It succeeded the Federal Emergency Relief Administration and the Civil Works Administration, both of which were established in 1933. The Works Progress Administration became the Work Projects Administration in July 1939 and carried that name until the agency was abolished in June 1943. The WPA, which was responsible for the government's work-relief program, operated at four organizational levels, namely the central administration in Washington, regional offices, state administrations, and district offices.

Contains central correspondence files of CWA, FERA, and WPA, which are organized into state files, with material relating to programs in a single state, and general subject files, which relate to programs in more than one state or to the relief program as a whole; FERA and WPA divisional, office, and project records; and cartographic and audiovisual records.

In CWA, FERA, and WPA central files is the FERA "old" general subject series, 1933-35 (34 ft.), which contains material on women's camps; the 1933 White House conference on emergency needs of women, over which Eleanor Roosevelt presided; and on transients, which includes correspondence with Ellen C. Potter, director of medicine of the New Jersey department of institutions and agencies. The FERA "new" general subject series, 1935-36 (38 ft.), contains a section on women's work, which includes correspondence with federal departments, Congress, the White House, clubs, and organizations. The FERA state series, 1933-36 (137 ft.), contains a section on women's projects, which includes correspondence with the director of women's work and with state administrators.

The WPA central files' general subject series, 1935-44 (309 ft.), has classifications for the women's work program, 1935-39, which includes correspondence with nine regional offices, general and regional reports, projects, and exhibits; for women's projects, 1939, which includes material on sewing, home economics, and museum, public health, and library projects; and for health and welfare projects, 1934-43, which includes material on sewing, clothing, home economics, feeding, nursing, and child care projects. The WPA state series, 1935-44 (870 ft.), has a section on the women's work program, 1935-39, and health and welfare projects, 1935-43.

The FERA work division series, 1934-36 (12 ft.), contains correspondence and reports about the mattress-making project of the women's section and records of the WPA division of women's and professional projects, 1934-37 (4 cu.ft.), including material on sewing, school lunch, household workers' training, and gardening projects.

Information about women is also found in records pertaining to the WPA federal project no. 1, which included the federal art, music, theater, and writers' projects and the historical records survey, 1935-42 (792 ft.). Other records pertaining to federal project no. 1 are in the WPA general subject series under individual programs and in the WPA state series under projects, arranged there by individual program. Filed separately from the WPA state series are final state reports of the WPA division of women's and professional projects, 1936, which include reports from individual counties. In April 1936, approximately 40 percent of the 6686 persons employed in the federal writers' project were women.

See *Preliminary Inventory of the Records of the Federal Writers' Project, Works Progress Administration, 1935-44,* PI 57 (1953). See also *Guide to the National Archives of the United States* (Washington, DC: General Services Administration, 1974).

2,705. Archives
Records. 1919-77. Ca. 60 drawers.
Open. File cards.
National Federation of Business and Professional Women's Clubs, Inc.
The Federation was established in 1919 to elevate standards for women in business and the professions, to promote the interests of and cooperation among these women, and to expand their opportunities by providing industrial, scientific, and vocational education. Records of executive board meetings and of annual membership conventions, lists of members and

chartered clubs, biographies and photos of national presidents and members who were leaders in their fields, histories of the organization, handbooks, and copies of *National Business Woman.* Records also include material concerning operation of the Federation's program, accounting, membership, magazine and public information, production, and sales order departments as well as resource information on the Equal Rights Amendment.

2,706. Historical Files
Records. 1944- . 7 ft.
Open. No guide.
National Women's Association of Allied Beverage Industries, Inc.
Correspondence, administrative files, biographical data, programs, pamphlets, and photos of the Association, founded in 1944 in New York City to perform charitable work in communities and to provide information about the alcoholic beverage industry. Includes descriptions of community work undertaken by various Association chapters throughout the US.

2,707. Administrative Histories of WW II
Records. 1944-47. 300 vols.
Open. Published and unpublished guides.
Naval Historical Center, Operational Archives.
These histories, prepared by major US Naval commands during WWII, include a two-volume history of the Women's Reserve, with details concerning the decisions leading to establishment of the Reserve, procurement of personnel, the establishment of training facilities, and duties undertaken by women. Appendices include histories of some WAVES training schools, instructions, and legislative documents. See William C. Heimdahl and Edward J. Marolda, comps., *Guide to United States Naval Administrative Histories of World War II* (Washington: Naval History Division, 1976).

2,708. Administrative History
Records. 1941-47. 166 ft.
Open. Unpublished guide.
Naval Historical Center, Operational Archives.
Correspondence, reports, histories, and manuals pertaining to administrative histories for the WWII period of major offices and commands in the Navy. Includes a 109-page history of the Naval Reserve Midshipman's School in Northampton, MA, where WAVE officers were trained. This history contains information on the establishment of the program, training provided, and evaluations by commanding officers of WAVE officers who completed the program.

2,709. Office of Chief of Naval Personnel, Assistant Chief of Naval Personnel for Women
Records. 1942-72. 14 ft.
Open. Unpublished guide.
Naval Historical Center, Operational Archives.
Correspondence, studies, statistics, surveys, reports, press releases, scrapbooks, photos, motion pictures, clippings, and tapes pertain to all aspects of the development of the WAVES, which was formerly the women's branch of the US Navy.

2,710. Oral History Collection
Oral history. 1969-74. 15 ft.
Open. Unpublished guide.
Naval Historical Center, Operational Archives.
Transcripts of oral history interviews conducted by the U.S. Naval Institute with US Naval personnel, including Captain Mildred McAfee, Captain Jean Palmer, and Captain Joy B. Hancock, directors of the Women's Reserve; Lieutenant Commander Mary Shelly, who became the first director of the Women's Air Force; and Captain Dorothy Stratton, the first director of SPARS which is the Women's Coast Guard Reserve. The name for the SPARS was coined from the Coast Guard motto: Semper Paratus-Always Ready. Duplicates of these interviews are held at the United States Naval Institute at Annapolis, MD.

2,711. The Advocate
Records. 1896- . 6 ft.
Access restricted. No guide.
Retail Clerks International Union.
Copies of *The Advocate,* the official publication of this labor union, which was founded in 1890, contain articles on women in the labor movement. The March 1975 issue was devoted to the subject of women in the Union.

2,712. Baird, Spencer F.
Papers. 1833-89. 24.3 cu.ft.
Open. Registers and indexes.
Smithsonian Institution Archives.
Correspondence, journals and diaries, scientific notes, drafts of publications and administrative reports, biographical data, financial papers, drawings, forms, and circulars of Baird (1823-87), a scientist. Includes correspondence of his wife Mary Helen (Churchill) Baird (1821-1913) and of his daughter Lucy Hunter Baird (1848-1913), which document their lives in Washington. Also includes correspondence with such scientists as naturalist Grace Anna Lewis.

2,713. Braun, Emma Lucy
Papers. Ca. 1932-40. 1 vol.
Open. Description.
Smithsonian Institution Archives.
Photo album of Braun (1889-1971), a forest ecologist at the University of Cincinnati, contains photos of Kentucky and Tennessee forests, mostly of virgin timber that has since been destroyed by lumbering or mining, and of individuals and groups. Many of the photos appeared in Braun's published works.

2,714. Cochran, Doris Mable
Papers. Ca. 1891-1968. 4 cu.ft.
Open. Inventory.
Smithsonian Institution Archives.
Papers of Cochran (1898-1968), a herpetologist who specialized in the fauna of Central and South America and of Haiti, include correspondence, diaries, school records, scientific notes and data, drafts of publications, records from her work as curator of the Division of Reptiles and Amphibians in the National Museum of Natural History, drawings, photos, memorabilia, and clippings. Cochran began work as an aide in the Museum in 1919 and eventually became curator before retiring in 1968. She earned a PhD from the University of Maryland in 1933; a scientific illustrator, she also wrote popular books on herpetology and presented speeches and radio programs for the general public. Collection also includes material relating to the work of Bertha Lutz, a noted Brazilian herpetologist.

2,715. Croffut, Bessie Nicholls
Papers. Nd. 2 items.
Open. Description.
Smithsonian Institution Archives.
Reminiscences in which Croffut, the second wife of journalist and government employee William Augustus Croffut (1835-1915), describes her life with her husband in Washington, DC, during the 1880s and 1890s.

2,716. Dall, William H.
Papers. Ca. 1839-1927. 22 cu.ft.
Open. Inventory.
Smithsonian Institution Archives.
Correspondence, memoranda, diaries, scientific notebooks, drafts of publications, financial documents, reports, scrapbooks, clippings, and other papers of Dall (1845-1927), a scientist. Includes correspondence, reminiscences, financial papers, and biographical items relating to his mother Caroline Wells (Healey) Dall (1822-1912), an editor and feminist. Also includes his correspondence with anthropologist Alice Cunningham Fletcher and with female relatives of his scientific friends, among them Lucy Hunter Baird, who was daughter of Spencer F. Baird, and with Mary S. Kennicott, who was mother of Robert Kennicott.

2,717. Division of Reptiles and Amphibians
Records. 1873-1968. 11.3 cu.ft.
Open. Inventory.
Smithsonian Institution Archives.
Correspondence, memoranda, reports, and other administrative records of the Division of the Reptiles and Amphibians of the National Museum of Natural History. Includes correspondence and other items reflecting the administrative and scientific work of Doris Mabel Cochran, a herpetologist.

2,718. Hardy, Thora M. Plitt
Papers. 1940-48. 0.34 cu.ft.
Open. Inventory.
Smithsonian Institution Archives.
Correspondence, research notes, and drafts of publications of Hardy, a microanalyst, reflect her research on fur fibers and animal hides for the Fish and Wildlife Service of the Department of the Interior and then for the Bureau of Animal Industry of the Department of Agriculture.

2,719. Heller, Edmund
Papers. Ca. 1898-1918. 3.5 cu.ft.
Open. Inventory.
Smithsonian Institution Archives.
Included with the journals, field notes, drafts of publications, maps, and photos of Heller (1875-1939), a scientist and explorer, is material from the American Museum of Natural History expedition to China during 1916 and 1917, with photos taken by Yvette Borup Andrews for the Museum.

2,720. Henderson Family
Papers. 1868-1893. 2.7 cu.ft. and 1 vol.
Open. Inventory.
Smithsonian Institution Archives.
Correspondence, literary and scientific drafts, photos, clippings, and other papers of this Washington family. Includes correspondence, notebooks, drafts, and financial records of Mary (Foote) Henderson (1841-1931), a patron of the arts, advocate of temperance and woman suffrage, author of children's books and of books on health, and the wife of John Brooks Henderson (1826-1913).

2,721. Henry, Joseph
Papers. 1808-ca. 1903. 20 cu.ft.
Open. Computer index and other indexes.
Smithsonian Institution Archives.
Correspondence, diaries, biographical data, scientific research material, drafts of publications, speeches, and lecture notes of Henry (1797-1878), a scientist. Includes correspondence of his wife Harriet (Alexander) Henry (1808-82), which reflects her life in an upwardly mobile family in Albany, NY, until 1833; in Princeton, NJ, from 1833 to 1846; and then in Washington. Also includes his correspondence with Dorothea L. Dix and other female contemporaries and correspondence, diaries, and research notes of his daughter Mary Ann Henry (1834-1903), an historian, as well as her unpublished biography of him.

2,722. Holmes, William Henry
Papers. 1870-1931. 1.4 cu.ft. and 7 microfilm reels.
Open. Unpublished guide.
Smithsonian Institution Archives.
Correspondence, biographical information, field notes, drafts of publications, drawings, and memorabilia of Holmes (1846-1933), a scientist, artist, and administrator. Also includes volumes of

reminiscences, which contain information on Washington women and on such scientists as Matilda Coxe (Evans) Stevenson, Ellen Leary, May S. Clark, and Alice Cunningham Fletcher.

2,723. Peters, James A.
Papers. 1927-73. 15.5 cu.ft.
Open. Inventory.
Smithsonian Institution Archives.
Correspondence, drafts of publications, invoices, note cards, documents concerning research, computer material, records of organizations and meetings, administrative records, and slides of Peters (1922-72), a herpetologist. Contains material relating to herpetologist Doris Mabel Cochran, including her professional correspondence, requests for reprints of her works, and some records of the Division of Reptiles and Amphibians of the National Museum of Natural History from the years when she was the Division's curator.

2,724. U.S. Department of the Interior, Fish and Wildlife Service
Records. 1860-1961. 44 cu.ft.
Open. Inventory.
Smithsonian Institution Archives.
The Service was formed in 1940 from the merger of the Bureau of Fisheries, which was founded in 1871 in the Commerce Department, and the Bureau of Biological Survey, which was founded in 1885 in the Agriculture Department. Field notes; reports on birds, mammals, and plants; and physiography reports. Includes work by Florence (Merriam) Bailey, Winifred A. Hunter, and Althea Rosina Sherman.

2,725. Vail Telegraph
Collection. 1830-1912. 4.5 cu.ft.
Open. Inventory.
Smithsonian Institution Archives.
Amanda (Eno) Vail helped her husband Alfred Vail (1807-59) document the early history of the telegraph. Included are her correspondence with inventors, lawyers, and businessmen; files and scrapbooks of research material that she organized; notes; account books; copies of contracts; patents; and drafts of publications.

2,726. Walcott, Charles D.
Papers. 1870-1939. 34 cu.ft.
Partially restricted. Calendar and lists.
Smithsonian Institution Archives.
Correspondence, diaries, financial records, biographical material, drafts of speeches and publications, minutes, and reports of Walcott (1850-1927), a geologist. Includes information about his first wife Lura Ann (Rust) Walcott (1843-76); extensive correspondence with his second wife Helena B. Walcott (1858-1911); research notes gathered by his third wife Mary Morris (Vaux) Walcott (1860-1940), a scientific illustrator, and by Adele Jenny; and Jenny's unpublished biography of him.

2,727. Albers, Anni
Papers. 1924-69. 200 items (1 microfilm reel).
Open. Card catalog.
Smithsonian Institution, Archives of American Art.
Born in Berlin, Germany, Albers (1889-) is a weaver, designer, and writer who moved to the US in 1933. Articles by or about her, her Bauhaus training, her Black Mountain College (NC) weaving classes, and the history and function of weaving; exhibition catalogs and reviews; a bibliography; clippings; and photos of her work. Collection is also available at Archives of American Art area centers in Boston, New York, Detroit, and San Francisco.

2,728. American Association of University Women
Records. 1942-52. Ca. 2000 items.
Open. Published guide and card catalog.
Smithsonian Institution, Archives of American Art.
Correspondence, notes, clippings, and other items pertain to a series of traveling art exhibitions sponsored by the AAUW. Collection is also available at Archives of American Art area centers in Boston, New York, Detroit, and San Francisco. See Garnett McCoy, *Archives of American Art: A Directory of Resources* (New York: R. R. Bowker Company, 1972).

2,729. Armer, Ruth
Papers. 1911-71. 291 items.
Open. Card catalog.
Smithsonian Institution, Archives of American Art.
Papers of Armer (1896-) a San Francisco painter, consist of correspondence, writings and notes, business papers, a scrapbook, clippings, and printed material pertaining to her painting techniques and to exhibitions. Collection is also available at Archives of American Art area centers in Boston, New York, Detroit, and San Francisco.

2,730. Ascher, Mary
Papers. 1956-68. 376 items (2 microfilm reels).
Open. Card catalog.
Smithsonian Institution, Archives of American Art.
Business correspondence, biographical material, catalogs, announcements, photos, and clippings of Ascher (1900-), a painter, also include a book of poetry and paintings and two photographic series with commentary by her on "Corridors of Power in Contemporary American Life" and "Women of the Bible." Collection is also available at Archives of American Art area centers in Boston, New York, Detroit, and San Francisco.

2,731. Bacon, Peggy
Papers. 1893-1972. Ca. 3100 items (7 microfilm reels).
Open. Card catalog.
Smithsonian Institution, Archives of American Art.
Correspondence of Bacon (1895-), a painter and writer, including that with and of her parents Charles and Elizabeth Bacon. Also included are school reports and notebooks, publisher's statements, contracts, drawings, and photos of her work. Collection is also available at Archives of American Art area centers in Boston, New York, Detroit, and San Francisco.

2,732. Baker, Mildred
Papers. 1930s-55. Ca. 500 items.
Open. Card catalog.
Smithsonian Institution, Archives of American Art.
Papers of Baker, who was assistant director of the WPA's Federal Art Project, consist of official files on the Index of American Design, community art centers, and exhibitions and general files of correspondence, notes, drafts of reports and speeches, surveys and statistics, technical guides, articles, photos, and clippings. Collection is also available at Archives of American Art area centers in Boston, New York, Detroit, and San Francisco.

2,733. Beaux, Cecilia
Papers. 1863-1968. 2391 items (8 microfilm reels).
Open. Published guide and card catalog.
Smithsonian Institution, Archives of American Art.
A figure and portrait painter, Beaux (1855-1942) lived in Paris and England between 1888 and 1896, Philadelphia and New York between 1900 and 1910, Paris between 1919 and 1921, and New York thereafter. Correspondence, including letters to her family in Philadelphia and to members of the Drinker, Leavitt, and Gilder families; diaries for 1868 to 1928; notes; poetry, essays, and lectures; draft of Beaux's autobiography *Background with Figures;* catalogs; exhibition notes; awards; photos; clippings; and miscellany. Also included are letters to Abram Piatt Andrew. Collection is also available at Archives of American Art area centers in Boston, New York, Detroit, and San Francisco. See Garnett McCoy, *Archives of American Art: A Directory of Resources* (New York: R. R. Bowker Company, 1972).

2,734. Bertha Schaefer Gallery
Records. 1932-71. 4 vols. and 1550 items (3 microfilm reels).
Open. Published guide and card catalog.
Smithsonian Institution, Archives of American Art.
Bertha Schaefer (1895-1971) was a New York City interior and furniture designer and an art dealer who opened her own gallery in 1944. Material pertaining to the business includes correspondence about the sale, exhibition, shipping, and loan of works by artists the gallery handled; inquiries from artists desiring to be represented by her; files of accounts, containing such items as fabric samples, floor plans, and price lists; photos of interiors Schaefer designed; exhibition catalogs; clippings; and printed items. Also included is a scrapbook concerning Alfred H. Maurer as well as information on Schaefer's personal affairs and on mutual friends she shared with various artists. Collection is also available at Archives of American Art area centers in Boston, New York, Detroit, and San Francisco. See Garnett McCoy, *Archives of American Art: A Directory of Resources* (New York: R. R. Bowker Company, 1972).

2,735. Betty Parsons Gallery
Records. 1935-69. 7800 items (15 microfilm reels).
Open. Published guide and card catalog.
Smithsonian Institution, Archives of American Art.
Records of the Gallery, which dealt exclusively in contemporary art, consist of business records; correspondence with artists, museums, buyers, and others; catalogs and reviews; lists; photos; and published material. Also includes correspondence, catalogs, and clippings relating to the sale and promotion of paintings by Betty Parsons and information on the Wakefield Gallery, which she was associated with between 1940 and 1944. Collection is also available at Archives of American Art area centers in Boston, New York, Detroit, and San Francisco. See Garnett McCoy, *Archives of American Art: A Directory of Resources* (New York: R. R. Bowker Company, 1972).

2,736. Bishop, Isabel
Papers. 1935-75. Ca. 680 items (5 microfilm reels).
Open. Published guide and card catalog.
Smithsonian Institution, Archives of American Art.
Bishop (1902-) is a painter and etcher. Correspondence, including letters from such personal friends as Peggy Bacon and Clare Leighton; sketchbooks with notes for Bishop's painting "Subway Scene"; list of works and owners of her works; photos; clippings; and publications relating to her paintings. Collection also available at Archives of American Art area centers in Boston, New York, Detroit, and San Francisco. SeeGarnett McCoy, *Archives of American Art: A Directory of Resources* (New York: R. R. Bowker Company, 1972).

2,737. Bowditch, Nancy Douglas (Brush) Pearmain
Papers. 1898-1973. 2154 items.
Open. Card catalog.
Smithsonian Institution, Archives of American Art.
Correspondence of Bowditch (1890-) includes letters with her first husband William Robert Pearmain, her father George De Forest Brush, family members, and friends. Also includes drawings, personal photos, printed items, and a manuscript of her biography of her father, published in 1970. Collection is also available at Archives of American Art area centers in Boston, New York, Detroit, and San Francisco.

2,738. Bry, Edith
Papers. 1922-70. 1 ft. (2 microfilm reels).
Open. Published guide and card catalog.

Smithsonian Institution, Archives of American Art. A New York painter, Bry (1898-) has been an active member of the Federation of Modern Painters and Sculptors. Correspondence with portrait subjects, colleagues, and art institutions; notes on classes she took in 1948 and 1949 at the New School for Social Research in New York City with Abraham Rattner, notes on experiments with fused glass; financial papers; inventories of works sold or consigned; price lists; scrapbooks; photos; and published material. Collection is also available at Archives of American Art area centers in Boston, New York, Detroit, and San Francisco. See Garnett McCoy, *Archives of American Art: A Directory of Resources* (New York: R. R. Bowker Company, 1972).

2,739. Cassatt, Mary
Papers. 1869-1966. 1 vol. and 470 items (4 microfilm reels).
Open. Published guide and card catalog.
Smithsonian Institution, Archives of American Art. Papers of Cassatt (1844-1926), a painter, primarily consist of correspondence during the 1880s on politics and art in France with such family members as Electra Havemeyer, [Miss] Sarah Hallowell, Mrs. Fredrick MacMonnies, and Mrs. Potter Palmer. Also includes genealogical data, a scrapbook, clippings, and printed items. Collection is also available at Archives of American Art area centers in Boston, New York, Detroit, and San Francisco. See Garnett McCoy, *Archives of American Art: A Directory of Resources* (New York: R. R. Bowker Company, 1972).

2,740. Chittenden, Alice B.
Papers. 1880-1972. 1 vol. and 919 items (1 microfilm reel).
Open. Card catalog.
Smithsonian Institution, Archives of American Art. Correspondence of Chittenden (1859-1944), a San Francisco painter, is included with school notebooks; a financial logbook; drawings and sketches; catalogs; photos of her paintings, family, and friends; and daguerreotypes of her mother and herself as a child. Collection is also available at Archives of American Art area centers in Boston, New York, Detroit, and San Francisco.

2,741. Citron, Minna Wright
Papers. 1930-76. 855 items (2 microfilm reels).
Open. Published guide and card catalog.
Smithsonian Institution, Archives of American Art. Citron (1896-) is a painter and printmaker. Personal and business correspondence; articles and lectures on abstract art, particularly in Cuba and Brazil, and on art education; price lists; sketches; catalogs; announcements; and clippings. Includes material relating to *Venus Through the Ages* by Citron and Jan Gelb. Collection is also available at Archives of American Art area centers in Boston, New York, Detroit, and San Francisco. See Garnett McCoy, *Archives of American Art: A Directory of Resources* (New York: R. R. Bowker Company, 1972).

2,742. Clark, Adele C.
Papers. 1936-43. 800 items (1 microfilm reel).
Open. Published guide and card catalog.
Smithsonian Institution, Archives of American Art. Papers of Clark relate to her work as director of the WPA's Federal Art Project in Virginia. Correspondence; notes; directives; lists; sketches by WPA artists; photos of administrators, students, and works of art; clippings; publications; and exhibition material. Collection is also available at Archives of American Art area centers in Boston, New York, Detroit, and San Francisco. See Garnett McCoy, *Archives of American Art: A Directory of Resources* (New York: R. R. Bowker Company, 1972).

2,743. Collier, Nina Perera
Papers. 1934-36. 1500 items (2 microfilm reels).
Open. Card catalog.
Smithsonian Institution, Archives of American Art. Collier was administrator for the Federal Emergency Relief Administration section for professional and nonmanual projects and publicist for the WPA information service. Correspondence and other material relate to the Index of American Design, the Federal Recreation Project, National Symphony Orchestra summer concerts, the New York World's Fair, the Federal Writers Project, the Federal Music Project, and the Federal Theater Project. Also included is information on federal art projects and on the movement in 1941 for a permanent government art program. Collection is also available at Archives of American Art area centers in Boston, New York, Detroit, and San Francisco.

2,744. Cowdrey, Mary Bartlett
Papers. 1830-1960. 4000 items (11 microfilm reels).
Open. Published guide and card catalog.
Smithsonian Institution, Archives of American Art. [Miss] Cowdrey (1910-74) was an historian, critic, and archivist. Her sizeable files on and collections of books illustrated by 19th-century American painters; correspondence and notes relating to alphabetical indexes and other information she compiled on artists who exhibited at the National Academy of Design between 1861 and 1890, which was intended to be a continuation of her book *National Academy of Design Exhibition Record, 1826-1860* (1943); extensive notes for a book on William S. Mount, which she wrote with Hermann W. Williams; and a bibliography of her writings. Includes articles, catalogs, photos, reproductions, clippings, and other publications. Collection is also available at Archives of American Art area centers in Boston, New York, Detroit, and San Francisco. See Garnett McCoy, *Archives of American Art: A Directory of Resources* (New York: R. R. Bowker Company, 1972).

2,745. Cunningham, Imogen
Papers. 1903-73. Ca. 4300 items.
Open. Card catalog.
Smithsonian Institution, Archives of American Art. Cunningham (1883-1976) was a San Francisco photographer and teacher. Bulk of collection is correspondence with family, friends, photographers, galleries, museums, and publishers. Also included are items pertaining to her family history, business papers, teaching material, curriculum vitae of other artists, transcripts of interviews in which she describes her life and career between 1901 and 1973, her acceptance speech for a doctor of fine arts degree she was awarded in 1968 by the California College of Arts and Crafts, photos of her and her family, and other printed material. Collection is also available at Archives of American Art area centers in Boston, New York, Detroit, and San Francisco.

2,746. Cushing, Lily Emmet
Papers. 1929-72. 1860 items (2 microfilm reels).
Access restricted. Card catalog.
Smithsonian Institution, Archives of American Art. Correspondence of Cushing (1909-69) is included with biographical information, statements and an account book from the Maynard Walker Gallery in New York City, lists of paintings, exhibition catalogs, oil paintings, and photos of Cushing and of her work. Also included are papers relating to the Chinese Women's Anti-Aggression League. Collection is also available at Archives of American Art area centers in Boston, New York, Detroit, and San Francisco.

2,747. Davis, Gladys Rockmore
Papers. 1925-66. Ca. 450 items (2 microfilm reels).
Open. Published guide and card catalog.
Smithsonian Institution, Archives of American Art. Davis (1901-67) was a painter and illustrator. Correspondence with family, dealers, museums, and publishers; biographical information; a travel journal in which she comments on her travels in Europe and the Far East; business papers; a sketchbook; catalogs; photos; and clippings. Collection is also available at Archives of American Art area centers in Boston, New York, Detroit, and San Francisco. See Garnett McCoy, *Archives of American Art: A Directory of Resources* (New York: R. R. Bowker Company, 1972).

2,748. Davis, Helen Stuart
Papers. 1936-49. 200 items (1 microfilm reel).
Open. Published guide and card catalog.
Smithsonian Institution, Archives of American Art. Davis (1869-1966) worked as a sculptor for WPA Federal Art Projects in Miami and in Berkeley, CA. Correspondence includes many letters she wrote her son Stuart Davis describing in detail her work for the Projects and difficulties she encountered therein. Also included are sketchbooks and photos of FAP work in Florida. Collection is also available at Archives of American Art area centers in Boston, New York, Detroit, and San Francisco. See Garnett McCoy, *Archives of American Art: A Directory of Resources* (New York: R. R. Bowker Company, 1972).

2,749. De Mare, Marie
Papers. 1811-1955. Ca. 1000 items (1 microfilm reel).
Open. Published guide and card catalog.
Smithsonian Institution, Archives of American Art. Papers of De Mare, an author, consist of draft writings and research papers for her book on her grandfather George Peter Alexander Healy (1813-94), which was published in 1954; correspondence between De Mare and various family members; diaries of De Mare and of Healy; a list of Healy's paintings; notes; and clippings. Collection is also available at Archives of American Art area centers in Boston, New York, Detroit, and San Francisco. See Garnett McCoy, *Archives of American Art: A Directory of Resources* (New York: R. R. Bowker Company, 1972).

2,750. Dehner, Dorothy
Papers. 1927-74. 2116 items (4 microfilm reels).
Access restricted. Published guide and card catalog.
Smithsonian Institution, Archives of American Art. Personal and business correspondence, reminiscences, and business papers of Dehner (1908-), a sculptor and printmaker, are included with sketchbooks, catalogs, announcements, press releases, and clippings concerning her sculpture. Also included is material relating to her first husband David Smith. Collection is also available at Archives of American Art area centers in Boston, New York, Detroit, and San Francisco. See Garnett McCoy, *Archives of American Art: A Directory of Resources* (New York: R. R. Bowker Company, 1972).

2,751. Delano, Annita
Papers. 1909-75. 1012 items.
Open. Card catalog.
Smithsonian Institution, Archives of American Art. Delano (1894-) is an artist and teacher. Correspondence with museums, galleries, universities, and other artists; a travel journal; biographical information; business receipts; items pertaining to her teaching career; files of analyses of paintings; lecture notes; notes on artists and galleries in Europe; poems by Barbara Morgan; catalogs and announcements; photos of the artist and her work as well as of the works of Sonia and Robert Delaunay; and clippings. Collection is also available at Archives of American Art area centers in Boston, New York, Detroit, and San Francisco.

2,752. Dochterman, Lillian
Papers. 1960-68. Ca. 3000 items.
Open. Published guide and card catalog.
Smithsonian Institution, Archives of American Art.
Correspondence, notes, lectures, articles, photos, and publications of Dochterman, a teacher. Includes working papers for her dissertation on Charles Sheeler, papers written by former students, and miscellany. Collection is also available at Archives of American Art area centers in Boston, New York, Detroit, and San Francisco. See Garnett McCoy, *Archives of American Art: A Directory of Resources* (New York: R. R. Bowker Company, 1972).

2,753. Dreier, Dorothea
Papers. 1887-1916. 1500 items (3 microfilm reels).
Open. Published guide and card catalog.
Smithsonian Institution, Archives of American Art.
Dreier (1870-1923) studied art in Italy, Germany, and Holland. Correspondence, primarily that of Dreier and her three sisters and her brother, pertains to family activities, travels abroad, and such interests as art, politics, and woman suffrage. Also included are sketchbooks, catalogs, photos, clippings, and other publications. Collection is also available at Archives of American Art area centers in Boston, New York, Detroit, and San Francisco. See Garnett McCoy, *Archives of American Art: A Directory of Resources* (New York: R. R. Bowker Company, 1972).

2,754. Eckman, Jeanette
Papers. 1937-41. Ca. 400 items (1 microfilm reel).
Open. Published guide and card catalog.
Smithsonian Institution, Archives of American Art.
Papers of Eckman pertain to her work as director of Delaware WPA projects in art, music, theater, writing, and an historical records survey. Included are official records of her work with employees in the field, including budget and personnel records, her 1939 report, project reports, and news releases, as well as correspondence, directives, and lists. Collection is also available at Archives of American Art area centers in Boston, New York, Detroit, and San Francisco. See Garnett McCoy, *Archives of American Art: A Directory of Resources* (New York: R. R. Bowker Company, 1972).

2,755. Erlanger, Elizabeth N.
Papers. 1950-68. Ca. 750 items.
Open. Card catalog.
Smithsonian Institution, Archives of American Art.
Erlanger (1901-75) was a New York City lithographer and painter. Correspondence relating to her work and to art organizations she participated in, biographical data, catalogs, photos, and clippings. Collection is also available at Archives of American Art area centers in Boston, New York, Detroit, and San Francisco.

2,756. Exhibition of Sculpture by Women
Records. 1910. 115 items (1 microfilm reel).
Open. Card catalog.
Smithsonian Institution, Archives of American Art.
The Exhibition was held in 1910 at the New York School of Applied Design for Women. Business information, correspondence of officers and committee members, a membership list, lists of sculptures, an exhibition catalog, announcements, and clippings. Collection is also available at Archives of American Art area centers in Boston, New York, Detroit, and San Francisco.

2,757. Fasano, Clara
Papers. 1933-72. Ca. 200 items (3 microfilm reels).
Open. Card catalog.
Smithsonian Institution, Archives of American Art.
Correspondence, sketchbooks, drawings, catalogs, awards, and certificates of Fasano (1900-), a sculptor. Also includes her 1955 diary, in which she provides detailed accounts of her daily activities, domestic obligations, and her work, and photos of her and her sculpture. Collection is also available at Archives of American Art area centers in Boston, New York, Detroit, and San Francisco.

2,758. Feigin, Dorothy Lubell
Papers. 1924-69. 245 items (1 microfilm reel).
Open. Published guide and card catalog.
Smithsonian Institution, Archives of American Art.
A teacher in the New York City public school system, [Mrs.] Feigin (1903-69) also served as treasurer for the Federation of Modern Painters and Sculptors in New York. Correspondence, including letters from the National Association of Women Artists, the National Association of Women Painters and Sculptors, and others discussing exhibition plans and sales; letters and notes pertaining to the NYC school system; catalogs; photos; and a scrapbook of clippings, which contain comments on the various women artist associations with which Feigin was involved. Also included are Federation papers, with treasurer's reports and material on dues and membership. Collection is also available at Archives of American Art area centers in Boston, New York, Detroit, and San Francisco. See Garnett McCoy, *Archives of American Art: A Directory of Resources* (New York: R. R. Bowker Company, 1972).

2,759. Flanagan, Hallie
Papers. 1935-42. 4000 items (15 microfilm reels).
Open. Published guide.
Smithsonian Institution, Archives of American Art.
Hallie (Ferguson) Flanagan Davis (1890-1969) was director of the Federal Theater Project of the WPA during the second half of the 1930s. Her correspondence, scripts, photos, clippings, and publications pertain to the operation and administration of the Project. Collection is also available at Archives of American Art area centers in Boston, New York, Detroit, and San Francisco. See Garnett McCoy, *Archives of American Art: A Directory of Resources* (New York: R. R. Bowker Company, 1972).

2,760. Frisbie, Ruth E.
Papers. 1946-63. 1000 items (1 microfilm reel).
Open. Published guide and card catalog.
Smithsonian Institution, Archives of American Art.
Scrapbooks of [Mrs.] Frisbie (1906-), an artist and teacher, reveal her work organizing art and related cultural activities in and around Cleveland and Parma, OH. Also included are photos and a résumé of Frisbie. Collection is also available at Archives of American Art area centers in Boston, New York, Detroit, and San Francisco. See Garnett McCoy, *Archives of American Art: A Directory of Resources* (New York: R. R. Bowker Company, 1972).

2,761. Fulda, Elisabeth (Rungius)
Papers. 1895-1967. 290 items (1 microfilm reel).
Open. Published guide and card catalog.
Smithsonian Institution, Archives of American Art.
A painter and illustrator, Fulda (1879-1968) was best known for her depictions of animals. Correspondence, including letters from the National Association of Women Artists; a transcript of the divorce proceedings in 1916 between Elisabeth and Carl Fulda; and material on her brother Carl Rungius. Also included are manuscript writings, biographical notes, sketchbooks, catalogs, and photos. Collection is also available at Archives of American Art area centers in Boston, New York, Detroit, and San Francisco. See Garnett McCoy, *Archives of American Art: A Directory of Resources* (New York: R. R. Bowker Company, 1972).

2,762. Gardner, Isabella (Stewart)
Papers. 1760-1956. Ca. 6860 items (38 microfilm reels).
Partially restricted. Card catalog.
Smithsonian Institution, Archives of American Art.
Gardner (1840-1924) was an art collector who began buying works of art in 1867 and then built the Fenway Court in Boston to house and display her collection. Unrestricted papers, which form the bulk of the collections, include early Gardner family correspondence, correspondence of Isabella Gardner, and later correspondence of the Gardner Museum. Her personal papers include an 1874 diary she kept in Egypt, including sketches; a diary she kept in Shanghai and India during 1883 and 1884; her funeral directions; and her suggestions for running a museum. Gardner Museum records include dealers' files with invoices, notes, canceled checks, and letters; a book recording the prices paid for paintings in 1917; and photos of the Museum. Restricted material consists of Isabella Gardner's personal and official correspondence with Bernard and Mary Berenson, the originals of which are housed at the Harvard University Center for Renaissance Studies in Florence, Italy. Collection is also available at Archives of American Art area centers in Boston, New York, Detroit, and San Francisco.

2,763. Gelb, Jan
Papers. 1922-72. 1045 items (4 microfilm reels).
Open. Card catalog.
Smithsonian Institution, Archives of American Art.
Correspondence of Gelb (1906-), a painter and printmaker, includes letters from Mary Spencer Nay, Minna Citron, and Lois Barlett Tracy. Also included are business and personal letters from her cousin Constance Blitz in Holland; a diary of a trip Gelb made to Europe in 1929; sketches; poems, notes, and other writings; catalogs; photos of Gelb, her friends, and her work; clippings; and material relating to the Society of American Graphic Artists. Collection is also available at Archives of American Art area centers in Boston, New York, Detroit, and San Francisco.

2,764. Genauer, Emily
Papers. 1930-57. Ca. 300 items (1 microfilm reel).
Open. Published guide and card catalog.
Smithsonian Institution, Archives of American Art.
Papers of [Miss] Genauer (1910-), an influential art critic and writer, consist of photos, publications, and correspondence from artists, dealers, and museums. Collection is also available at Archives of American Art area centers in Boston, New York, Detroit, and San Francisco. See Garnett McCoy, *Archives of American Art: A Directory of Resources* (New York: R. R. Bowker Company, 1972).

2,765. Gold, Fay
Papers. 1927-70. Ca. 360 items (1 microfilm reel).
Open. Published guide and card catalog.
Smithsonian Institution, Archives of American Art.
A 1958 journal describing in detail elements in the personal and artistic life of Gold (1907-), a painter, is included with her correspondence, poems, biographical data, a sketchbook, exhibition catalogs, photos, slides, a scrapbook, and clippings. Also included is a long letter in which Helen West Heller describes her struggles as an artist. Collection is also available at Archives of American Art area centers in Boston, New York, Detroit, and San Francisco. See Garnett McCoy, *Archives of American Art: A Directory of Resources* (New York: R. R. Bowker Company, 1972).

2,766. Goldthwaite, Anne Wilson
Papers. 1910-40. 115 items (1 microfilm reel).
Open. Published guide and card catalog.
Smithsonian Institution, Archives of American Art.
After studying in Paris during the early 20th century, Goldthwaite (1869-1944) worked as a painter and teacher. Personal reminiscences and photos dealing with her childhood in Alabama and Texas, catalogs, and clippings. Collection is also available at Archives of American Art area centers in Boston, New York, Detroit, and San Francisco.

See Garnett McCoy, *Archives of American Art: A Directory of Resources* (New York: R. R. Bowker Company, 1972).

2,767. Goulet, Lorrie
Papers. 1939-72. 1250 items (2 microfilm reels).
Open. Card catalog.
Smithsonian Institution, Archives of American Art.
A sculptor, Goulet (1925-) is also an instructor. General correspondence; letters pertaining to her association with The Contemporaries, a New York City gallery; files on one-man shows at The Contemporaries and elsewhere; material concerning "Around the Corner," a CBS television program for children; and photos of her, her work, family, and friends. Collection is also available at Archives of American Art area centers in Boston, New York, Detroit, and San Francisco.

2,768. Greenman, Frances Cranmer
Papers. 1925-57. 372 items (1 microfilm reel).
Open. Published guide and card catalog.
Smithsonian Institution, Archives of American Art.
A Minneapolis portrait and figure painter, Greenman (1890-) also wrote a column for the Minneapolis *Tribune.* Manuscript of and correspondence relating to her autobiography *Higher Than the Sky;* correspondence with dealers, collectors, and friends, some of which relates to her column; and photos of her paintings. Collection is also available at Archives of American Art area centers in Boston, New York, Detroit, and San Francisco. See Garnett McCoy, *Archives of American Art: A Directory of Resources* (New York: R. R. Bowker Company, 1972).

2,769. Gurr, Lena
Papers. 1908-75. 3950 items (1 microfilm reel).
Open. Card catalog.
Smithsonian Institution, Archives of American Art.
Gurr (1897-) is a painter and graphic artist. Correspondence with various artists and others; notes; a partial listing of exhibitions she participated in; scrapbooks, including one on Mary Cecil Allen; and photos of Gurr and of sculpture she created at the Art Students League school in New York City. Also included are catalogs, sketches, and paintings. Collection is also available at Archives of American Art area centers in Boston, New York, Detroit, and San Francisco.

2,770. Hartwig, Cleo
Papers. 1938-71. 814 items (2 microfilm reels).
Open. Card catalog.
Smithsonian Institution, Archives of American Art.
Hartwig (1911-) is a sculptor who exhibited her work in a show that traveled in Canada during 1949 and 1950. Correspondence concerning her work and the show, contracts and photos relating to the show, biographical material, lists of exhibitions and works, and photos of her sculpture. Collection is also available at Archives of American Art area centers in Boston, New York, Detroit, and San Francisco.

2,771. Hatt, Mabel
Papers. 1944-65. 558 items (2 microfilm reels).
Open. Card catalog.
Smithsonian Institution, Archives of American Art.
Correspondence, catalogs and announcements, scrapbooks, clippings, and photos of the work of Hatt (?-1971), an artist. Collection is also available at Archives of American Art area centers in Boston, New York, Detroit, and San Francisco.

2,772. Jones, Nell Choate
Papers. 1924-68. 545 items (3 microfilm reels).
Open. Card catalog.
Smithsonian Institution, Archives of American Art.
A painter, Jones was also a civic leader and president of the National Association of Women Artists. Correspondence, biographical material, sketchbooks, drawings, catalogs, announcements, a scrapbook, clippings, photos of Jones's work, and lists of exhibitions of the Association. Collection is also available at Archives of American Art area centers in Boston, New York, Detroit, and San Francisco.

2,773. Katz, Ethel
Papers. 1880-1972. 551 items (1 microfilm reel).
Open. Card catalog.
Smithsonian Institution, Archives of American Art.
Personal and business correspondence of Katz (1900-), a painter and instructor, is included with sketchbooks, drawings, catalogs, announcements, clippings, and photos of her, her family, friends, and work. Collection is also available at Archives of American Art area centers in Boston, New York, Detroit, and San Francisco.

2,774. Kent, Adaline
Papers. 1931-61. 1015 items.
Open. Card catalog.
Smithsonian Institution, Archives of American Art.
Kent (1900-57) was a sculptor and painter in San Francisco. Correspondence, diaries, manuscript notes, business papers, photos, and printed material. Collection is also available at Archives of American Art area centers in Boston, New York, Detroit, and San Francisco.

2,775. King, Marian
Papers. 1955-64. 1085 items.
Open. Published guide and card catalog.
Smithsonian Institution, Archives of American Art.
An author, King chiefly wrote books for children. Correspondence, most of which is from museums, galleries, and libraries responding to her requests for information and reproductions for her books; research notes and writings; a book manuscript; and photos and reproductions of paintings. Included are several letters from Mrs. George Bellows. Collection is also available at Archives of American Art area centers in Boston, New York, Detroit, and San Francisco. See Garnett McCoy, *Archives of American Art: A Directory of Resources* (New York: R. R. Bowker Company, 1972).

2,776. Knight, Frances (Beall)
Papers. 1855-56. 2 vols. (1 microfilm reel).
Open. Published guide and card catalog.
Smithsonian Institution, Archives of American Art.
Diaries in which Knight describes her daily activities in Rome with her husband, places she visited in the area, and artists living there. Collection is also available at Archives of American Art area centers in Boston, New York, Detroit, and San Francisco. See Garnett McCoy, *Archives of American Art: A Directory of Resources* (New York: R. R. Bowker Company, 1972).

2,777. Kuh, Katherine
Papers. 1935-74. 1028 items (2 microfilm reels).
Partially restricted. Card catalog.
Smithsonian Institution, Archives of American Art.
Kuh (1904-) is an art critic and art consultant. Included with the correspondence, articles, synopses of articles, and her unpublished textbook "Looking at Modern Art," written for a course given in Chicago in 1935, are writings by Kuh on Central American culture, reviews of her book *The Open Eye,* and clippings reviewing exhibitions at the Katherine Kuh Gallery in Chicago. Collection is also available at Archives of American Art area centers in Boston, New York, Detroit, and San Francisco.

2,778. La Tour, Onya
Papers. 1928-69. Ca. 3500 items (7 microfilm reels).
Open. Card catalog.
Smithsonian Institution, Archives of American Art.
A painter, collector, and dealer, La Tour founded the Indiana Museum of Modern Art in Brown County, IN. Correspondence with family, friends, and artists; diaries for 1930 to 1969, some of which are illustrated; poems and short stories written for her; photos; and a scrapbook of sketches by artist friends. Also includes material relating to the Federal Art Gallery of the WPA and to the Onya La Tour Gallery, both of which were established in New York City, and information on a proposal for an art gallery in Puerto Rico. Collection is also available at Archives of American Art area centers in Boston, New York, Detroit, and San Francisco.

2,779. Le Maire, Eleanor
Papers. 1928-70. 583 items.
Open. Card catalog.
Smithsonian Institution, Archives of American Art.
Papers of Le Maire (1897-1970), a New York City interior designer, include records relating to her interior design firm in the City, with interoffice memoranda; correspondence with clients; scale drawings, blueprints, and photos of designs by Le Maire, most of which were for NYC businesses; publicity scrapbooks; and published items on various of the firm's projects. Also included are speeches and articles by Le Maire on design. Collection is also available at Archives of American Art area centers in Boston, New York, Detroit, and San Francisco.

2,780. Leighton, Clare
Papers. 1931-67. 400 items (3 microfilm reels).
Open. Published guide and card catalog.
Smithsonian Institution, Archives of American Art.
A writer, book illustrator, and wood engraver, [Miss] Leighton (1901-) was born in London but moved to the US in 1939. Personal and business correspondence, the latter of which relates chiefly to her work as an illustrator; extensive notes; sketchbooks; a list of her engravings; photos; and published biographical and critical items. Collection is also available at Archives of American Art area centers in Boston, New York, Detroit, and San Francisco. See Garnett McCoy, *Archives of American Art: A Directory of Resources* (New York: R. R. Bowker Company, 1972).

2,781. Levy, Florence Nightingale
Papers. 1890-1947. 10,000 items (5 microfilm reels).
Open. Published guide and card catalog.
Smithsonian Institution, Archives of American Art.
Levy (1870-1947) was editor of *American Art Annual.* Card files relating to the biographical section of the *Annual;* correspondence, pamphlets, handbooks, and clippings pertaining to collections and to artwork in public buildings and in churches; and manuscript lectures and articles. Collection is also available at Archives of American Art area centers in Boston, New York, Detroit, and San Francisco. See Garnett McCoy, *Archives of American Art: A Directory of Resources* (New York: R. R. Bowker Company, 1972).

2,782. Lippard, Lucy
Papers. 1950-74. 3500 items.
Open. Published guide and card catalog.
Smithsonian Institution, Archives of American Art.
Correspondence, announcements, catalogs, posters, clippings, and other printed material of Lippard (1937-), a writer, pertain to art, particularly Pop Art, in the US, France, Italy, and elsewhere in Europe during the 1950s and 1960s; to such social and political action projects as the Art Workers Coalition, urban development, and anti-Vietnam activities; and to "conceptual art." Also includes correspondence with Kay Sage Tanguy and Philip Evergood and "mail art" sent to Lippard during the 1960s. Collection is also available at Archives of American Art area centers in Boston, New York, Detroit, and San Francisco. See Garnett McCoy, *Archives of American Art: A Directory of Resources* (New York: R. R. Bowker Company, 1972).

2,783. Longacre Family
Papers. 1810-1952. 1090 items (4 microfilm reels).
Open. Card catalog.
Smithsonian Institution, Archives of American Art.
Financial papers and correspondence between James B. Longacre (1794-1869), engraver of the US Mint in Philadelphia, and his wife Eliza Longacre are included with letters which Lydia Longacre (1870-1951) wrote to her parents from Europe at the turn of the century, Lydia Longacre's sketchbooks, and photos of her and of her miniature collection. Collection is also available at Archives of American Art area centers in Boston, New York, Detroit, and San Francisco.

2,784. McCausland, Elizabeth
Papers. 1877-1960. 24,600 items (16 microfilm reels).
Partially restricted. Published guide and card catalog.
Smithsonian Institution, Archives of American Art.
A journalist, art critic, and art history teacher at Sarah Lawrence College, McCausland (1899-1965) also organized art exhibitions and participated in many art organizations. Bulk of the collection, which is unrestricted material, reflects her interest in photography as an art, government's support of the arts, the role of the artist in society, the ability of the artist to earn a living, the role of the artist during WWII, and the difficulty she had trying to support herself as an independent "career woman." Includes correspondence with artists, transcripts of interviews, manuscripts of writings, articles, art columns for the *Springfield Republican,* photos of artworks, and printed items. Restricted papers pertain to a biography McCausland planned to write on Marsden Hartley and include Hartley's notebooks, correspondence, documentation of his travels and work, photos of his works, and bibliographical items. Collection is also available at Archives of American Art area centers in Boston, New York, Detroit, and San Francisco. See Garnett McCoy, *Archives of American Art: A Directory of Resources* (New York: R. R. Bowker Company, 1972).

2,785. MacKendrick, Lilian
Papers. 1923-75. 4 vols. and 4700 items (3 microfilm reels).
Open. Card catalog.
Smithsonian Institution, Archives of American Art.
Papers of MacKendrick (1906-), a painter, include personal correspondence, records of sales and gifts of her works, scrapbooks, photos of her work, and printed material. Collection is also available at Archives of American Art area centers in Boston, New York, Detroit, and San Francisco.

2,786. Marcus, Marcia
Papers. 1943-75. Ca. 1300 items.
Open. Card catalog.
Smithsonian Institution, Archives of American Art.
Correspondence, business papers, catalogs, a high school yearbook, filmstrips, tape recordings, clippings, and photos of the work of Marcus (1928-), a painter. Collection is also available at Archives of American Art area centers in Boston, New York, Detroit, and San Francisco.

2,787. Margaret Brown Gallery
Records. 1921-58. 13,118 items (13 microfilm reels).
Open. Card catalog.
Smithsonian Institution, Archives of American Art.
Correspondence of this Boston art gallery with artists it represented and with other persons, financial records, customer lists, and other business items. Includes the Gallery's file of photos of the works of 61 artists. Collection is also available at Archives of American Art area centers in Boston, New York, Detroit, and San Francisco.

2,788. Mason, Alice Trumbull
Papers. 1922-70. 750 items (3 microfilm reels).
Open. Published guide and card catalog.
Smithsonian Institution, Archives of American Art.
Correspondence, personal budget books, notebooks of writings and poems, sketches and sketchbooks, price lists, announcements, career résumés, clippings, and catalogs of the works of Mason (1904-71), a New York abstract painter. Also included are records of the American Abstract Artists, 1935-63, with treasurer's reports, minutes, membership lists, and correspondence. Collection is also available at Archives of American Art area centers in Boston, New York, Detroit, and San Francisco. See Garnett McCoy, *Archives of American Art: A Directory of Resources* (New York: R. R. Bowker Company, 1972).

2,789. Mayer, Bena Frank
Papers. 1917-73. 275 items.
Open. Card catalog.
Smithsonian Institution, Archives of American Art.
Papers of Mayer (1900-), a painter, consist of personal correspondence and letters with galleries, minutes of a 1960 meeting of the commodity standards division of the Department of Commerce concerning the quality of artists' supplies, early Whitney Museum catalogs, material relating to the New York Society of Women Artists, photos of Mayer and of her work, and clippings. Collection is also available at Archives of American Art area centers in Boston, New York, Detroit, and San Francisco.

2,790. Moholy-Nagy, Sibyl Dorothy
Papers. 1918-71. 7 boxes (6 microfilm reels).
Open. Card catalog.
Smithsonian Institution, Archives of American Art.
Papers of Moholy-Nagy, an actress and then architectural historian, consist of correspondence, a diary of travel in South America during 1959, diaries for 1918 to 1959, manuscripts for articles and lectures, notes for books she wrote, course outlines, Architectural League papers, and family, childhood, and professional photos, including portrait shots from silent movies she made in Berlin between 1924 and 1931. Collection is also available at Archives of American Art area centers in Boston, New York, Detroit, and San Francisco.

2,791. Nevelson, Louise
Papers. 1922-72. 25 boxes and 3000 items (6 microfilm reels).
Open. Published guide and card catalog.
Smithsonian Institution, Archives of American Art.
[Miss] Nevelson (1900-) is a sculptor who was born in Kiev, Russia. Bulk of her papers consists of reviews and comments in art magazines on her work. Also includes correspondence with family, associates, organizations, and museums; lists; catalogs; photos; clippings; and books. Collection is also available at Archives of American Art area centers in Boston, New York, Detroit, and San Francisco. See Garnett McCoy, *Archives of American Art: A Directory of Resources* (New York: R. R. Bowker Company, 1972).

2,792. Oakley, Violet
Papers. 1898-1935. 900 items (1 microfilm reel).
Open. Card catalog.
Smithsonian Institution, Archives of American Art.
Oakley (1874-1961) was a painter, sculptor, illustrator, and writer. Scrapbooks, clippings, and exhibition catalogs, including a catalog of original drawings and studies for mural decorations in the Pennsylvania Capitol and at the Corcoran Gallery of Art in Washington. Collection is also available at Archives of American Art area centers in Boston, New York, Detroit, and San Francisco.

2,793. Paris, Dorothy
Papers. 1940-70. 580 items (2 microfilm reels).
Partially restricted. Card catalog.
Smithsonian Institution, Archives of American Art.
Papers of [Miss] Paris (1902-), a painter, include correspondence with her family, with members of the American Society of Contemporary Artists during her presidency of that group, and with such friends as Faith and Harold Weston, Mary Ascher, and Ann Mittleman. Also included are photos of Paris and of her work, exhibition notices, and clippings. Collection is also available at Archives of American Art area centers in Boston, New York, Detroit, and San Francisco.

2,794. Peggy Guggenheim Galleries
Records. 1938-47. 400 items (1 microfilm reel).
Open. Published guide and card catalog.
Smithsonian Institution, Archives of American Art.
Scrapbooks concerning Peggy Guggenheim's London art gallery, the Guggenheim Jeune, and her New York City gallery, the Art of the Century, contain exhibition catalogs, clippings, and other published material. Collection is also available at Archives of American Art area centers in Boston, New York, Detroit, and San Francisco. See Garnett McCoy, *Archives of American Art: A Directory of Resources* (New York: R. R. Bowker Company, 1972).

2,795. Pereira, I. Rice
Papers. 1932-64. 8000 items (10 microfilm reels).
Open. Published guide and card catalog.
Smithsonian Institution, Archives of American Art.
An abstract painter, Pereira (1907-71) was also a poet and philosopher. Extensive personal and business correspondence; a diary; notes; philosophical treatises; manuscript lectures, essays, and poems; exhibition catalogs; scrapbooks; reviews; clippings; periodicals; and published writings. Includes a series of lectures Pereira delivered to students at the Design Laboratory, which was sponsored by the Federal Art Project during the late 1930s at the Pratt Institute in New York City. Collection is also available at Archives of American Art area centers in Boston, New York, Detroit, and San Francisco. See Garnett McCoy, *Archives of American Art: A Directory of Resources* (New York: R. R. Bowker Company, 1972).

2,796. Pewabic Pottery
Records. 1891-1973. 29 vols. and 3000 items (10 microfilm reels).
Open. Card catalog.
Smithsonian Institution, Archives of American Art.
Order books; daybooks; correspondence; files on commissions, consignments, and exhibitions; photos; and information on the building that houses the Pottery, which was founded by Mary Chase Stratton. Also included are daybooks and records of the Revelation Kiln, owned by Stratton, and some of her personal papers, such as tax returns, property documents, teaching papers, and a scrapbook. Collection is also available at Archives of American Art area centers in Boston, New York, Detroit, and San Francisco.

2,797. Philadelphia School of Design for Women
Records. 1852-1932. 2 microfilm reels.
Open. Card catalog.
Smithsonian Institution, Archives of American Art.
Incorporated in 1852, this Philadelphia art school's name was changed in 1932 to the Moore Institute of Art, Science, and Industry. Document of incorporation; first annual report; and, dating mostly from the 1920s, constitution, bylaws, catalogs and course announcements, and a scrapbook of photos of and clippings about the School and classes. Collection is also available at Archives of American Art area centers in Boston, New York, Detroit, and San Francisco.

2,798. Philbrick, Margaret Elder
Papers. 1931-71. 575 items (1 microfilm reel).
Open. Card catalog.

Smithsonian Institution, Archives of American Art. Correspondence of Philbrick (1914-), a painter and printmaker, is included with a chronological listing and photos of her works; a group of original etchings; exhibition material from the Society of American Graphic Artists, the Library of Congress, the Carnegie Institute, and other organizations; awards; and clippings. Collection is also available at Archives of American Art area centers in Boston, New York, Detroit, and San Francisco.

2,799. Picard, Lil
Papers. 1955-72. Ca. 500 items.
Open. Card catalog.
Smithsonian Institution, Archives of American Art. Picard was an art critic, painter, and sculptor. Notes and comments in German on American and English writers and artists, catalogs, photos, and clippings. Includes material relating to the feminist art movement in the US and to the Art Workers Coalition. Collection is also available at Archives of American Art area centers in Boston, New York, Detroit, and San Francisco.

2,800. Pollack, Naomi Newman
Papers. 1949-64. Ca. 460 items (1 microfilm reel).
Open. Card catalog.
Smithsonian Institution, Archives of American Art. Correspondence of Pollack (1930-), an opera singer, includes letters to her husband Reginald Pollack, an artist, and letters concerning her concerts and singing engagements. Also included are drawings by her and personal photos. Collection is also available at Archives of American Art area centers in Boston, New York, Detroit, and San Francisco.

2,801. Read, Helen Appleton
Papers. 1922-50. 70 items (2 microfilm reels).
Open. Published guide and card catalog.
Smithsonian Institution, Archives of American Art. Papers of [Mrs.] Read (1887-1974), an art historian and critic, consist of scrapbooks of columns she wrote for the *Brooklyn Eagle* from 1922 to 1935, a lecture on new horizons for art in federal buildings, reports on a survey of art in such buildings, notes on the Hudson River School, and articles about art. Collection is also available at Archives of American Art area centers in Boston, New York, Detroit, and San Francisco. See Garnett McCoy, *Archives of American Art: A Directory of Resources* (New York: R. R. Bowker Company, 1972).

2,802. Reynal, Jeanne
Papers. 1942-68. Ca. 300 items (1 microfilm reel).
Open. Published guide and card catalog.
Smithsonian Institution, Archives of American Art. Correspondence, notes, and printed material of Reynal (1903-), a mosaic artist, concern the mural she made for the Nebraska Capital Mural Commission in 1965 and 1966, research on her teacher Arshile Gorky, exhibits of her work, the history and technique of mosaics, and the Tougaloo College, MS, art committee. Collection is also available at Archives of American Art area centers in Boston, New York, Detroit, and San Francisco. See Garnett McCoy, *Archives of American Art: A Directory of Resources* (New York: R. R. Bowker Company, 1972).

2,803. Richardson, Constance
Papers. 1935-57. 350 items (1 microfilm reel).
Open. Card catalog.
Smithsonian Institution, Archives of American Art. Financial papers, catalogs, and clippings of Richardson (1905-), a painter, are included with correspondence, most of which is from Hazel J. Lewis of the MacBeth Gallery in New York concerning the sale and exhibition of Richardson's works. Collection is also available at Archives of American Art area centers in Boston, New York, Detroit, and San Francisco.

2,804. Roberts, Mary Fanton
Papers. 1900-56. 2500 items (4 microfilm reels).
Open. Published guide and card catalog.
Smithsonian Institution, Archives of American Art. Correspondence, lists, articles, photos, and printed matter of Roberts (1871-1956), a writer and editor whose interests included art, theatre, dance, and music. Collection is also available at Archives of American Art area centers in Boston, New York, Detroit, and San Francisco. See Garnett McCoy, *Archives of American Art: A Directory of Resources* (New York: R. R. Bowker Company, 1972).

2,805. Rolick, Esther
Papers. 1941-70. 801 items (2 microfilm reels).
Open. Card catalog.
Smithsonian Institution, Archives of American Art. Papers of Rolick (1922-), an author and illustrator of children's books, consist of correspondence with such friends as May Swenson, Babette Deutsch, and Elizabeth Sparhawk-Jones; catalogs and announcements; exhibition guest books and a scrapbook; photos of Rolick, her friends, and her work; two illustrated children's stories by Rolick; and sketches and drawings by her classmates from the Art Students League in New York City. Collection is also available at Archives of American Art area centers in Boston, New York, Detroit, and San Francisco.

2,806. Rose Fried Gallery
Records. 1944-73. 9 cartons and 300 items (1 microfilm reel).
Open. Published guide and card catalog.
Smithsonian Institution, Archives of American Art. Correspondence, catalogs, photos, clippings, and publicity material relating to purchases, exhibitions, and artists represented by this New York City art gallery, which was founded in the 1930s as the Pinacothea Gallery. Also includes a brief account of the Gallery, which [Miss] Fried wrote. Collection is also available at Archives of American Art area centers in Boston, New York, Detroit, and San Francisco. See Garnett McCoy, *Archives of American Art: A Directory of Resources* (New York: R. R. Bowker Company, 1972).

2,807. Rush, Olive
Papers. 1886-1966. 3150 items (1 microfilm reel).
Open. Published guide and card catalog.
Smithsonian Institution, Archives of American Art. Correspondence, diaries for 1886 to 1892, biographical material, notes and lectures, records of the dispensation of paintings, sketches, woodcuts and lithographs, catalogs, photos, scrapbooks, and clippings of Rush (1873-1966), an artist who painted in Santa Fe, NM, from the 1920s on, primarily concern her career in New Mexico. Collection is also available at Archives of American Art area centers in Boston, New York, Detroit, and San Francisco. See Garnett McCoy, *Archives of American Art: A Directory of Resources* (New York: R. R. Bowker Company, 1972).

2,808. Ruth White Gallery
Records. 1955-70. 3 boxes and 2650 items (7 microfilm reels).
Open. Published guide and card catalog.
Smithsonian Institution, Archives of American Art. Correspondence and scrapbooks of this New York City art gallery, opened in 1956 to specialize in contemporary painting, sculpture, and graphics, include material on such artists associated with the Gallery as Audrey Skaling. Contains correspondence between Ruth White and Skaling arranging for four exhibitions and letters between White and various museum curators and newspaper critics about Skaling's work. Collection is also available at Archives of American Art area centers in Boston, New York, Detroit, and San Francisco. See Garnett McCoy, *Archives of American Art: A Directory of Resources* (New York: R. R. Bowker Company, 1972).

2,809. Ryerson, Margery
Papers. 1920-60. 100 items.
Open. Published guide and card catalog.
Smithsonian Institution, Archives of American Art. A painter and etcher, Ryerson (1886-) also was the compiler of Robert Henri's *The Art Spirit.* Correspondence, a lecture, catalogs, photos, and clippings include material on *The Art Spirit,* letters from Henri, and items concerning her career. Collection is also available at Archives of American Art area centers in Boston, New York, Detroit, and San Francisco. See Garnett McCoy, *Archives of American Art: A Directory of Resources* (New York: R. R. Bowker Company, 1972).

2,810. Saarinen, Aline
Papers. 1891-1971. 6 boxes.
Partially restricted. Card catalog.
Smithsonian Institution, Archives of American Art. Correspondence, a manuscript, scripts, photos, and clippings of Saarinen (1914-72), a writer, art critic, and NBC news correspondent. Restricted material pertains to her unpublished book on Stanford White; unrestricted material pertains to her career. Collection is also available at Archives of American Art area centers in Boston, New York, Detroit, and San Francisco.

2,811. Saarinen, Aline, and Saarinen, Eero
Papers. 1952-69. Ca. 5000 items.
Access restricted. Card catalog.
Smithsonian Institution, Archives of American Art. Papers of Aline Saarinen (1914-72), a writer, art critic, and NBC news correspondent, include correspondence between Aline and Eero Saarinen; letters from her son Donald Loucheim; research notes and drafts for articles, speeches, and lectures; and items for the NBC program "For Women Only." Collection is also available at Archives of American Art area centers in Boston, New York, Detroit, and San Francisco.

2,812. Saarinen, Lily Swann
Papers. 1924-72. Ca. 4000 items.
Open. Card catalog.
Smithsonian Institution, Archives of American Art. Correspondence with artists, writers, publishers, and architects, much of which concerns illustrations Saarinen drew for government and children's publications; detailed diaries; manuscripts for children's books; sketches and drawings; catalogs; photos; and clippings of Saarinen. Collection is also available at Archives of American Art area centers in Boston, New York, Detroit, and San Francisco.

2,813. Sawyer, Esther (Hoyt)
Papers. 1916-65. 500 items (1 microfilm reel).
Open. Published guide and card catalog.
Smithsonian Institution, Archives of American Art. Correspondence of [Mrs. Ansley W.] Sawyer, an art collector, provides a record of personal friendships she established with various artists. Collection is also available at Archives of American Art area centers in Boston, New York, Detroit, and San Francisco. See Garnett McCoy, *Archives of American Art: A Directory of Resources* (New York: R. R. Bowker Company, 1972).

2,814. Scaravaglione, Concetta
Papers. 1924-67. Ca. 800 items.
Open. Card catalog.
Smithsonian Institution, Archives of American Art. A New York City sculptor, Scaravaglione (1900-75) also was a faculty member of Black Mountain College in North Carolina. Personal and biographical notes, business files, catalogs, address books, photos of her and of her sculpture, and clippings. Collection is also available at Archives of American Art area centers in Boston, New York, Detroit, and San Francisco.

2,815. Schmid, Elsa
Papers. 1910-67. Ca. 600 items (1 microfilm reel).
Open. Card catalog.
Smithsonian Institution, Archives of American Art.
Papers of Schmid (1897-), a mosaicist, consist of personal and professional correspondence, including letters from Helen Chase, Georgia O'Keeffe, and Barbara Morgan; notes and lectures about mosaics; drawings; catalogs; articles; clippings; and photos of Schmid's mosaics. Collection is also available at Archives of American Art area centers in Boston, New York, Detroit, and San Francisco.

2,816. Schwabacher, Ethel
Papers. 1940-75. 3 boxes and 300 items (2 microfilm reels).
Open. Published guide and card catalog.
Smithsonian Institution, Archives of American Art.
Schwabacher (1903-) is a painter and art critic. Personal correspondence, correspondence concerning business and social matters and plans for an Arshile Gorky retrospective exhibition at the 1962 Venice Biennale, research notes on Gorky, notes for a projected work on post-WWII abstract artists, material compiled from interviews with artists, catalogs, photos, and clippings. Collection is also available at Archives of American Art area centers in Boston, New York, Detroit, and San Francisco. See Garnett McCoy, *Archives of American Art: A Directory of Resources* (New York: R. R. Bowker Company, 1972).

2,817. Spaeth, Eloise.
Papers. 1941-70. 1525 items (1 microfilm reel).
Open. Published guide and card catalog.
Smithsonian Institution, Archives of American Art.
Correspondence, scrapbooks, and other papers of [Mrs. Otto L.] Spaeth (1904-), an art collector and writer, include letters, reviews, photos, and clippings pertaining to the Dayton Art Institute in Dayton, OH, and to the Religious Art Exhibition held there in 1944; organizational records and correspondence with artists and collectors concerning the Archives of American Art, the American Federation of Artists, and other groups; and letters about the Meta Mold Aluminum Company exhibition in Wisconsin. Collection is also available at Archives of American Art area centers in Boston, New York, Detroit, and San Francisco. See Garnett McCoy, *Archives of American Art: A Directory of Resources* (New York: R. R. Bowker Company, 1972).

2,818. Spencer, Lilly (Martin)
Papers. 1825-1971. 550 items (2 microfilm reels).
Open. Card catalog.
Smithsonian Institution, Archives of American Art.
Correspondence, family histories, photos, and clippings of Spencer (1822-1902), a painter in Ohio and New York City. Includes letters concerning the immigration of her parents Giles and Angelique Martin to the US from England; correspondence to the Martins from Frances Dana (Barker) Gage, Mary Moody Emerson, Caroline M. Severance, and other Ohio and Massachusetts reformers active in women's rights, temperance, antislavery, and labor movements; and letters in which Spencer describes to her parents life and work in Cincinnati, New York, and Newark, NJ. Also included are journals and clippings, recent articles on Spencer's life and work, and lists of her paintings. Collection is also available at Archives of American Art area centers in Boston, New York, Detroit, and San Francisco.

2,819. Sterne, Hedda
Papers. 1944-70. Ca. 500 items.
Open. Published guide and card catalog.
Smithsonian Institution, Archives of American Art.
Papers of [Miss] Sterne (1916-), a painter, consist of correspondence, notes and journals, a biographical sketch, a sketchbook, an interview with Sterne, an exhibition catalog, and photos of paintings by Sterne. Collection is also available at Archives of American Art area centers in Boston, New York, Detroit, and San Francisco. See Garnett McCoy, *Archives of American Art: A Directory of Resources* (New York: R. R. Bowker Company, 1972).

2,820. Story, Ala
Papers. 1941-70. 1445 items (2 microfilm reels).
Open. Published guide and card catalog.
Smithsonian Institution, Archives of American Art.
A collector, Story (1907-72) was executive director of the American British Art Center, Inc., in New York City and staff specialist in art at the University of California, Santa Barbara. Correspondence, notes, lists, business records, catalogs, photos, and published material include items relating to her work for the Center and to five exhibitions she organized for the University between 1948 and 1970. Collection is also available at Archives of American Art area centers in Boston, New York, Detroit, and San Francisco. See Garnett McCoy, *Archives of American Art: A Directory of Resources* (New York: R. R. Bowker Company, 1972).

2,821. Stratton, Mary Chase
Papers. 1846-1961. 1 vol. and 68 items (2 microfilm reels).
Open. Card catalog.
Smithsonian Institution, Archives of American Art.
A ceramicist and educator, [Mrs. William B.] Stratton (1867-1961) founded the Pewabic Pottery in Detroit. Correspondence, primarily with her father William Walbridge Perry; a 144-page unpublished autobiography, which Stratton wrote during the 1930s; and photos of her, her family, her home, and scenes in Europe. Collection is also available at Archives of American Art area centers in Boston, New York, Detroit, and San Francisco.

2,822. Swan, Barbara E.
Papers. 1927-74. 820 items (2 microfilm reels).
Open. Card catalog.
Smithsonian Institution, Archives of American Art.
Correspondence, a diary, catalogs, photos, a scrapbook, clippings, and miscellany of Swan (1922-), a painter. Collection is also available at Archives of American Art area centers in Boston, New York, Detroit, and San Francisco.

2,823. Taylor, Arlene
Papers. 1938-65. 3000 items.
Open. Published guide and card catalog.
Smithsonian Institution, Archives of American Art.
Taylor was a decorator and pioneer in the use of decals. Correspondence, notes, business records, lists, photos, scrapbooks, and published material she accumulated as a result of her association with the Meyercord Decal Company. Collection is also available at Archives of American Art area centers in Boston, New York, Detroit, and San Francisco. See Garnett McCoy, *Archives of American Art: A Directory of Resources* (New York: R. R. Bowker Company, 1972).

2,824. Varian, Dorothy
Papers. 1902-71. Ca. 500 items (2 microfilm reels).
Open. Card catalog.
Smithsonian Institution, Archives of American Art.
Papers of Varian (1895-) consist of correspondence, including letters she wrote from Paris between 1920 and 1922, letters from Alexander and Peggy (Bacon) Brook during the same years, and letters from Lenore Marshall, many of which concern Herminie Klienert. Also included are poems and writings; sketchbooks; catalogs and announcements; photos of Varian, her friends, and her work; and clippings. Collection is also available at Archives of American Art area centers in Boston, New York, Detroit, and San Francisco.

2,825. Waite, Harriet Endicott
Papers. 1923-30. 1650 items (2 microfilm reels).
Open. Published guide and card catalog.
Smithsonian Institution, Archives of American Art.
Papers of Waite relate to her research on Currier and Ives. Includes correspondence with dealers, notes, price lists, catalogs, summaries of her findings, and lists, a card file, photos, and glass negatives of prints. Collection is also available at Archives of American Art area centers in Boston, New York, Detroit, and San Francisco. See Garnett McCoy, *Archives of American Art: A Directory of Resources* (New York: R. R. Bowker Company, 1972).

2,826. Walter, Valerie Harrise
Papers. 1924-61. 600 items (1 microfilm reel).
Open. Published guide and card catalog.
Smithsonian Institution, Archives of American Art.
Correspondence, a sketchbook, exhibition catalogs, photos, scrapbooks, and clippings of Walter, a Baltimore sculptor. Collection is also available at Archives of American Art area centers in Boston, New York, Detroit, and San Francisco. See Garnett McCoy, *Archives of American Art: A Directory of Resources* (New York: R. R. Bowker Company, 1972).

2,827. Weinberg, Helen Joy
Papers. 1927-70. 1113 items.
Open. Card catalog.
Smithsonian Institution, Archives of American Art.
Correspondence of Weinberg (1900-) concerning her work as an artist devoted to Jewish subjects and causes is included with biographical material, sketchbooks, notes and writings, catalogs and announcements, and photos of her and her work. Collection is also available at Archives of American Art area centers in Boston, New York, Detroit, and San Francisco.

2,828. Wildenhain, Marguerite
Papers. 1940-75. Ca. 900 items.
Open. Card catalog.
Smithsonian Institution, Archives of American Art.
Wildenhain was a potter who lived in Guerneville, CA. Correspondence concerning sales, exhibits, symposia, and other professional matters; letters from former students; variant chapters of *Pottery: Its Form and Expression,* which Wildenhain originally delivered as lectures at the 1952 International Conference of Potters and Weavers; lectures on art education, pottery as a craft, and form in pottery; a scrapbook containing letters, photos, and clippings; and a paper by Mildred Newton on Wildenhain's 1971 lectures at the University of Utah. Collection is also available at Archives of American Art area centers in Boston, New York, Detroit, and San Francisco.

2,829. Williams, Esther
Papers. 1899-1964. 729 items (3 microfilm reels).
Open. Card catalog.
Smithsonian Institution, Archives of American Art.
Papers of Williams (1907-), a painter, consist of correspondence with her parents, which is frequently lengthy and descriptive; correspondence with other artists and friends; routine business correspondence with galleries, institutions, and associations; clippings; and printed matter. Also includes letters and other papers of her mother Esther Baldwin [Mrs. O. E.] Williams and a family photo album. Collection is also available at Archives of American Art area centers in Boston, New York, Detroit, and San Francisco.

2,830. Winter, Edward, and Winter, Thelma
Papers. 1908-73. 525 items (1 microfilm reel).
Open. Card catalog.
Smithsonian Institution, Archives of American Art.
Papers of Edward Winter (1908-), an artist, include a portfolio of correspondence, biographical data, awards, a scrapbook, and miscellany, as well as a scrapbook of his wife Thelma Winter, who also

was an artist. In addition, collection contains photos of the Winters, their home, and their work. Collection is also available at Archives of American Art area centers in Boston, New York, Detroit, and San Francisco.

2,831. Withers, Margret Craver
Papers. 1929-74. 1881 items.
Partially restricted. Card catalog.
Smithsonian Institution, Archives of American Art.
Withers was a silversmith in Newburyport, MA. Restricted material, which is the bulk of the collection, includes personal and professional correspondence with craftsmen, customers, and the silversmiths Handy and Harman; biographical data; notes and reference material pertaining to Withers's work; business records; and photos of her work on a post-WWII occupational therapy project and of crafts designed by her, exhibitions, her studio, and her family. Unrestricted material includes radio scripts, press books, exhibition notices, catalogs, photos, and clippings primarily concerning the National Silversmithing Workshop Conference held between 1948 and 1950, Handy and Harman's traveling silver exhibitions, and the activities of the firm's craft service department. Collection is also available at Archives of American Art area centers in Boston, New York, Detroit, and San Francisco.

2,832. Action Anthropology Project Among the Fox Indians
Records. 1932-62. 21 boxes.
Open. Preliminary inventory.
Smithsonian Institution, National Anthropological Archives.
Fiscal records, field journals and notes, correspondence, memoranda, reports, population data, psychological testing material, drafts and reprints of publications, maps, and clippings of this University of Chicago work-study program, which was directed by professor Sol Tax. Information on Indian women and girls of the Fox tribe include kinship profiles, patterns of marriage, child-training practices, and customs surrounding menstruation. Collection also includes information on the training of women as anthropologists during their participation in the Project; field notes, drafts of papers, and copies of reports are available for Marie L. Furey, Marjorie Gearing, and Lisa R. Peattie, who worked with the Project from ca. 1948 to 1957.

2,833. American Anthropological Association
Records. 1917- . 81 boxes.
Partially restricted. Inventory.
Smithsonian Institution, National Anthropological Archives.
Constitution, bylaws, minutes, financial records, office files, ballots, correspondence, reports, and programs of this professional society include material of Association presidents, including Margaret Mead, who was president in 1960, and Frederica de Laguna, who was president in 1967. Also includes information about anthropologists who were active in the Association, among them Ruth Bunzel, Cora DuBois, Betty J. Meggers, and Ruth Benedict.

2,834. American Ethnological Society
Records. 1842- . 11 boxes.
Open. Preliminary inventories.
Smithsonian Institution, National Anthropological Archives.
Annual reports, minutes, financial and membership records, correspondence, programs, and clippings of the Society, a professional organization founded in 1842, include material on such persons as Viola Garfield, who was editor for the group; on Alice James, Ernestine Friedl, and Catherine McClellan, all of whom served as secretary-treasurer; and on Margaret Mead and Ruth Benedict, who were Society members.

2,835. American Society for Ethnohistory
Records. 1953- . 13 boxes.
Open. Register.
Smithsonian Institution, National Anthropological Archives.
Bylaws, minutes, fiscal records, correspondence, subscription lists, and news releases of the Society, a professional organization founded in 1953, include items of Erminie Wheeler-Voegelin, who was the first chair of the Society and until 1964 editor of its journal *Ethnohistory.*

2,836. Anthropological Society of Washington, D.C.
Records. 1879-1965. 17 boxes.
Open. Inventory.
Smithsonian Institution, National Anthropological Archives.
Constitution, bylaws, officers' reports, minutes, correspondence, photos, publications, and other records of the Society, a professional organization founded in 1879, include abstracts of papers presented to the Society by such anthropologists as Margaret Lee, Zelia Nuttall, and Ellen Russell Emerson. Many of these papers were subsequently published.

2,837. Bureau of American Ethnology
Records. 1878-1965. 132 cu.ft. and 47 microfilm reels.
Partially restricted. Inventories.
Smithsonian Institution, National Anthropological Archives.
Financial records, correspondence, memoranda, personnel files, reports, and other administrative records of this government agency, which was founded in 1879 and functioned until 1964 when it was succeeded by the Department of Anthropology, document the work of women who were scientists and administrators with the Bureau. Included is correspondence of Erminnie Smith, Matilda Coxe Stevenson, Alice Fletcher, Frances Densmore, and others.

2,838. Fletcher, Alice Cunningham, and La Flesche, Francis
Papers. Ca. 1860-1932. 34 boxes.
Open. Inventory.
Smithsonian Institution, National Anthropological Archives.
Papers of [Miss] Fletcher (1838-1923) and of [Mr.] La Flesche (?-1932), both of whom were anthropologists, including correspondence; diaries; lecture, reading, and field notes, which include vocabularies, kinship charts, transcriptions of songs, and drawings of artifacts; drafts and reprints of publications; minutes, programs, reports, and other records of organizations; maps; and clippings. Material documents Fletcher's personal and professional life; her particular interest in the Nez Percé, Omaha, and Osage Indian tribes; and her work advocating changes in the federal government's policy toward Indians.

2,839. Hilger, Sister Inez
Papers. 1932-71. 82 in.
Open. Register.
Smithsonian Institution, National Anthropological Archives.
Notes, drafts and reprints of publications, photos, sound recordings, and clippings of Hilger (1891-), a cultural anthropologist, relate primarily to her fieldwork on the Chippewa, Araucarian, and Arapahoe Indian tribes. Also included are notes on other tribes and lecture notes for the series "Anthropology of the Americas," which was broadcast on television in St. Paul, MN, during 1957 and 1958.

2,840. Indian Personality and Administration Research Project
Records. 1939-54. 14 ft.
Access restricted. Register.
Smithsonian Institution, National Anthropological Archives.
The purpose of the Project, which was conducted between 1941 and ca. 1950, was to study the personalities of a sample of children between the ages of 6 and 18 from the Hopi, Navaho, Papago, Sioux, and Pueblo Indian tribes. Case files, test results and analyses, school and medical records, notes on interviews, reports, reprints of articles, and photos primarily document fieldwork conducted for the Project. In addition to containing detailed information about the lives of various Indian girls, the material also contains information on such anthropologists involved in the Project as Laura Thompson, Ruth Benedict, Jane Chesky, Alice Joseph, and Rosamond B. Spicer and on social psychiatrist Dorothea Cross Leighton and psychometrist Grace Arthur.

2,841. Leighton, Dorothea Cross
Papers. 1937-74. 3.5 ft.
Access restricted. Register.
Smithsonian Institution, National Anthropological Archives.
A social psychiatrist and educator, Leighton (1908-) worked as a special physician for the Indian Education Research Project beginning in 1941, during which time she concentrated on Indians of the Navaho and Zuñi tribes. Correspondence, memoranda, drafts of publications, case files, health records, reports, maps, photos, and clippings document this work; they include information on Indian women and girls as well as correspondence with other women anthropologists.

2,842. Photographs
Collection. Ca. 1860-1930. Ca. 90,000 items.
Open. Lists and some microfiche.
Smithsonian Institution, National Anthropological Archives.
Photos, organized by tribe, document Indian life in North America and reveal, for example, the change or continuity in southwestern Indian women's dress after exposure to non-Indian styles. Also included are photos of women anthropologists at work in the field.

2,843. Stevenson, Matilda Coxe (Evans)
Papers. 1801-1915. 2 ft.
Open. Register.
Smithsonian Institution, National Anthropological Archives.
Correspondence, financial records, legal documents, reading and field notes, drafts and copies of publications, photos, memorabilia, maps, and clippings of Stevenson (1849-1915), an ethnologist, document her professional life, particularly her study of the Pueblo Indians of Arizona and New Mexico. Material also relates to her work on anthropology displays at exhibitions between 1892 and 1904 and to her association with the Women's Anthropological Society between 1885 and 1899. Stevenson first became interested in anthropology in ca. 1872 and formally joined the staff of the Bureau of American Ethnology in 1890.

2,844. Central Administrative Files
Records. 1908-74. 43 cu.ft.
Access restricted. Inventory.
Smithsonian Institution, National Collection of Fine Arts.
Fiscal records, correspondence, memoranda, statements of policy and procedures, reports, and exhibit material of the administration office of the National Collection of Fine Arts, which was known as the National Gallery of Art from 1906 to 1937. Included is correspondence of Adelyn Breeskin, an NCFA staff member; of Edith Gregor Halpert, a dealer who worked with the Downtown Gallery; Mrs. J. Lee Johnson, a Smithsonian Art Commission member between 1968 and 1970; and Leila Mechlin, a Commission member from 1921 to 1929. Also included is material from the 1960s on such artists as Lucy Spandorf, Hilda Katz, Ida

Kohlmeyer, and Georgia O'Keeffe and items documenting involvement with the museum during the 1960s and early 1970s of such Washington groups as the American Women in Radio and Television, the Association of American Foreign Service Women, the Junior League of Washington, the DAR, the National League of American Pen Women, the Woman's National Democratic Club, and the Women's National Press Club.

2,845. Department of Twentieth-Century Painting and Sculpture
Records. 1965-1974. 27.4 cu.ft.
Access restricted. Inventory.
Smithsonian Institution, National Collection of Fine Arts.
Correspondence, memoranda, research notes, biographies, bibliographies, reports, forms, lists, and photos, which are organized by exhibit, were created by Adelyn (Dohme) Breeskin, an historian of contemporary art who was special consultant at the NCFA from 1964 to 1967 and then curator of the Department from its creation in 1967 until 1974. Material reflects the work of women members of the curatorial staff, lenders, donors, and artists and includes, for example, items on a 1973-74 exhibit of the art of Marguerite Zorach for the years 1908 to 1920 and a 1971 exhibit of the work of Romaine Brooks.

2,846. Inventory of American Paintings Executed Before 1914
Finding aid. 1971- . 190,000 entries.
Access restricted. Published guide.
Smithsonian Institution, National Collection of Fine Arts.
Consisting of a computer printout and photographic reproductions, the Inventory contains information on privately and publicly owned paintings executed as early as the 1600s; it provides access to paintings by, of, or concerning women. Entries include the artist's name, the title and owner of the painting, and a subject classification, such as Figure-Female, Interior-Kitchen, or Child-Female. In some cases entries contain additional data such as the artist's birth and death dates; the medium, date, and dimensions of the painting; additional subject classifications; citation to a photographic reproduction of the painting; citation to a bibliographic reference to the painting; and an indication of the existence of supplementary information in the Inventory's files. The collection is available on microfiche. See *Bicentennial Inventory of American Paintings Executed Before 1914, Directory* (New York: Arno Press, 1976).

2,847. Office of Exhibition and Design, Miscellaneous
Records. 1964-73. 19.4 cu.ft.
Access restricted. Inventory.
Smithsonian Institution, National Collection of Fine Arts.
Correspondence, memoranda, drafts of proposals, minutes, conference records, schedules for shows, reports, and photos of the NCFA Office, which was established in 1964 and operated as the Office of Exhibits until 1970. Included is material on such art patrons as Nancy Paterson Pigott [Mrs. Estes] Kefauver, who was involved in the Art for Embassies Program between 1964 and 1967; on such lenders as Mrs. Stuart Davis; and on such artists as Mary Cassatt. Also included is information on displays where women were subjects of the artworks, among them the "Mother and Child in American Art" exhibit.

2,848. Office of the Director: Beggs, Thomas M.
Records. 1912-65. 25.9 cu.ft.
Access restricted. Inventory.
Smithsonian Institution, National Collection of Fine Arts.
Records of the Director of the NCFA consist of correspondence with administrators, artists, advisors, scholars, patrons, donors, and lenders, some of whom were women; personnel records, which document the careers of such staff members as Louise A. Rosenbusch and Annemarie H. Pope, who were associated with the Institution from 1920 to 1937 and from 1951 to 1964, respectively; and exhibit material, which contains data on such artists as Christine Deichmann, whose works were displayed in 1949 and 1950, and on the shows of groups of women, among them the National League of American Pen Women. Also included are memoranda and photos.

2,849. Office of the Director: Holmes, William H., and Tolman, Ruel P.
Records. 1906-54. 11.2 cu.ft.
Access restricted. Inventory.
Smithsonian Institution, National Collection of Fine Arts.
Records of the Director of the NCFA consist of correspondence with staff, donors, board members, lenders, patrons, and artists, some of whom were women; memoranda; research notes; drafts and copies of publications; reports; catalogs; lists; and photos. Also included are files on exhibits of the works of such artists as Mary Vaux Walcott, whose art was displayed in 1939; Ethel H. Hagen, 1940-41; Leonora Quarterman, 1942-43; and Alice S. Acheson, 1943-44. Also contains files on "Twenty Women Painters and the Landscape Club," a 1937 exhibit, and on the National League of American Pen Women, whose work was shown between 1946 and 1948.

2,850. Office of the Director, Special Services
Records. 1964-69. 4.8 cu.ft.
Access restricted. Inventory.
Smithsonian Institution, National Collection of Fine Arts.
Correspondence, memoranda, budgets, personnel records, exhibit material, reports, scripts of radio and television broadcasts, articles, clippings, and scrapbooks of the Department, founded in 1966 to provide public and community relations work for the NCFA. Included is information on women docents at the museum; on such staff members as Mary Nell Sherman, who has been assistant for Special Services since 1968; on such benefactors as the Ladies Committee of the Smithsonian; and on artists, among them Mary Cassatt, whose work was exhibited at the museum.

2,851. Publications Editor
Records. 1967-70. 1.4 cu.ft.
Access restricted. Inventory.
Smithsonian Institution, National Collection of Fine Arts.
Budgets, price lists, funding proposals, correspondence, memoranda, copyright data, and reports document the work of Georgia M. Rhoades from 1968 to 1972 and of Carroll [Mrs. George] Clark since 1972 as editor of NCFA catalogs, brochures, popular and scholarly articles, posters, and in-house material on works of art.

2,852. Williams, Mary Elfrieda "Mary Lou" (Scruggs)
Oral history. 1973. 6 tapes and 187-page transcript.
Access restricted. No guide.
Smithsonian Institution, National Endowment for the Arts Jazz Oral History Project.
Interview of [Mrs. John] Williams (1910-), a black pianist and composer, covers her early life and musical education; her musical career in Pittsburgh, the Kansas City area, and then in New York and Europe; her family life and marriage; and her religious faith and spiritual experiences.

2,853. War Production Board: Timepieces
Collection. 1943-45. 2.3 cu.ft.
Open. Unpublished guide.
Smithsonian Institution, National Museum of History and Technology, Division of Mechanisms.
Correspondence and reports reflect the work of Sara Y. Scrogin and H. L. Clary of the Board's Consumer Durable Goods Division regulating the production and allocation of timepieces during WWII.

2,854. Adams Family
Papers. 1775-1856. 0.4 cu.ft.
Open. Item list.
Smithsonian Institution, National Museum of History and Technology, Division of Political History.
Correspondence of the Adams family includes letters of various family women, particularly Abigail Adams, on social life and routine activities.

2,855. Baird, Lucy Hunter
Papers. 1874. 2 vols.
Open. Brief description.
Smithsonian Institution, National Museum of History and Technology, Division of Political History.
Scrapbooks of Baird (1848-1913), a Washington resident, contain clippings about the death of US Senator Charles Sumner. Lucy Baird was the oldest daughter of Spencer F. Baird, who was second secretary of the Smithsonian.

2,856. Johnson, Adelaide
Papers. Ca. 1878-1946. 0.6 cu.ft.
Open. Inventory.
Smithsonian Institution, National Museum of History and Technology, Division of Political History.
Pamphlets, photos, obituaries, clippings, newspapers, and periodicals of Sarah Adeline Johnson, a sculptor noted for her portrait busts of famous persons, particularly of workers for woman's suffrage. Material documents her artistic work and her interest in such reforms as suffrage and, to a lesser degree, temperance, spiritualism, the peace movement, and vegetarianism. In ca. 1878 Johnson began calling herself simply Adelaide Johnson.

2,857. Lockwood, Belva Ann (Bennett) McNall
Papers. 1881-1916. 0.6 cu.ft.
Open. Inventory.
Smithsonian Institution, National Museum of History and Technology, Division of Political History.
Lockwood (1830-1917) was an attorney, candidate for US President, and worker in the peace movement. Correspondence, speeches, pamphlets, broadsides, and clippings reflect her work in politics, her feminist activities, and her concern for the achievement of a durable peace. Lockwood was the first woman admitted to practice before the US Supreme Court.

2,858. National Woman's Party
Records. 1914-64. 0.15 cu.ft.
Open. Description.
Smithsonian Institution, National Museum of History and Technology, Division of Political History.
Records of the NWP, founded in 1913 to obtain woman suffrage, consist of letters to parents and friends in which Elsie Lancaster describes her fieldwork for the NWP in Wyoming, clippings on the Party's efforts to unseat Democrats in Congress who were hostile to suffrage, and a suffrage anthology.

2,859. Temple, Grace Lincoln
Papers. 1892-1944. 0.5 cu.ft.
Open. Inventory.
Smithsonian Institution, National Museum of History and Technology, Division of Political History.
Correspondence, invitations, notes, lectures, sketches, programs, samples of material, scrapbooks, and clippings of Temple, a designer and decorator, document her professional career. Included is information on her interior designs for buildings at the 1895 Atlanta Exposition, the 1940 St. Louis Louisiana Purchase Exposition, and for

private homes, as well as her teaching at the Cleveland School of Art from 1892 to 1894.

2,860. U.S. Political History
Collection. Ca. 1789- . Ca. 25 cu.ft.
Open. Card catalog.
Smithsonian Institution, National Museum of History and Technology, Division of Political History.
Correspondence, invitations, calling cards, tickets, programs, ballots, press releases, sheet music, mimeographed items, engravings, lithographs, photos, memorabilia, souvenir books, and clippings provide extensive documentation of the woman suffrage movement as well as material relating to the wives of US Presidents, women candidates for office, and other women in the families of male candidates.

2,861. Catalog of American Portraits Files
Finding aid. Nd. Ca. 50,000 files.
Partially restricted. Card index.
Smithsonian Institution, National Portrait Gallery, Catalog of American Portraits.
Beginning in 1966 the Catalog collected information on portraits in private and public collections of men and women who contributed significantly to the history and culture of the US; the Catalog also collects information on portraits by noteworthy American artists. These portraits, some of which were executed as early as the 18th century, are usually paintings, sculptures, drawings, and miniatures, but silhouettes and daguerreotypes are also included. Arranged alphabetically by sitters' names and cross-indexed by artist, the files typically contain a photo of the portrait; data on its size, medium, execution date, and condition; provenance; bibliographic references; and biographical material on the artist and the sitter. Martha Washington, for example, is portrayed in a variety of settings and modes of dress.

2,862. Portrait Index, Antiques
Finding aid. 1922-72. 10 microfiche.
Open. No guide.
Smithsonian Institution, National Portrait Gallery, Catalog of American Portraits.
An index by artist and sitter of American portraits described or mentioned in articles and advertisements in *Antiques,* a trade journal first published in 1922, provides access to portraits painted by and of women, some of which date back to the 18th century.

2,863. Library and Archive
Records. 1925- . 20 ft., 706 vols., and 112 cassettes.
Access restricted. Card indexes.
Society of Woman Geographers.
The Society of Woman Geographers was established in 1925 to provide association among women engaged in work in geography and the allied sciences of ethnology, archaeology, anthropology, astronomy, botany, natural science, sociology, folklore, and arts and crafts. An archive of material by and about Society members, the collection contains correspondence, oral histories, biographical and professional activities data, administrative files, *Bulletins,* a history of the Society, photos, theses, pamphlets, and books. Also includes information on the awarding of the Society's highest honor—the Gold Medal—to Amelia Earhart in 1933, Margaret Mead in 1942, Blair Niles in 1944, Irene Wright in 1950, and in 1975 to archaeologist Marion I. Stirling, ichthyologist Eugenie Clark, and paleontologist Mary D. Leakey and on the conferring (in 1978) of the first Outstanding Achievement Award, to Elisabeth Shirley Enochs. Admission in the Society is by invitation to women from any country who have added to knowledge in their field; widely traveled women interested in advancing geographical exploration and research are admitted to associate membership.

2,864. Archives of Trinity College
Records. 1897- . Ca. 500 cu.ft.
Open. Register and card catalog.
Trinity College Archives.
Founded in 1897 by the Sisters of Notre Dame de Namur in Washington, the College is the oldest Catholic liberal arts college for women in the US that was incorporated as a college; the first students began attending the school in 1900. Records consist of complete minutes of the board of trustees and minutes of the ladies auxiliary board, the advisory board, various lay boards, faculty meetings, and of student society meetings; early correspondence and journals of the founders; reports of the presidents and deans; student activity records; incomplete files on former faculty; records relating to contracts, agreements with donors, and accreditation; a complete set of College catalogs; copies of the *Alumnae Journal,* 1927-76; photos of students, faculty, buildings, and activities; scrapbooks of clippings; and a motion picture.

2,865. National Civil Rights Library
Records. 1960s- . 30,000 items.
Open. No guide.
United States Commission on Civil Rights.
The Library, which was established in 1964 when the Commission on Civil Rights was established, contains manuscripts, drafts of published items, periodicals, books, and microfilm copies of material concerning minority and women's rights. Also includes papers of Marija Matich Hughes, a law librarian and author, and working papers for and correspondence related to *The Sexual Barrier: Legal, Medical, Economic and Social Aspects of Sex Discrimination* (1977).

2,866. Women Marines in WW I
Collection. 1918-73. No size given.
Open. No guide.
United States Marine Corps, History and Museums Division.
Correspondence, a history, articles, photos, clippings, and memorabilia pertain to the 305 women who enlisted in the Marine Corps Reserve. In 1918 women were called to join the Corps for clerical duty, primarily at the Marine Corps headquarters, but also at other Corps offices in nine major US cities, thereby releasing male Marines for combat duty. [Mrs.] Opha Mae Johnson was the Marine Corps's first enlisted woman; later Women Marines were rated from privates to sergeants. Collection also includes interviews with 32 veterans about their experiences during the war; these interviews were conducted in 1972 by members of the Women Marines Association.

2,867. Women Marines in WW II
Collection. Nd. No size given.
Open. No guide.
United States Marine Corps, History and Museums Division.
Histories, articles, pamphlets, clippings, and other items pertain to the Marine Corps Women's Reserve, which was established in 1942. More than 20,000 women served in the Reserve during WWII, thereby releasing male Marines for combat duty. Women Marines were trained in a variety of fields; the majority of them held clerical and sales positions, but others worked in professional, mechanical (particularly aviation), and other fields. They were stationed throughout the country and in Hawaii and held ranks ranging from second lieutenant to colonel. Officer training classes for Women Marines were held in conjunction with those for the WAVES at the US Naval Midshipmen's School in Northampton, MA. [Mrs.] Ruth Cheney Streeter was first director of the Reserve.

FLORIDA

BARTOW

2,868. Holland Family
Papers. Ca. 1892-1971. Ca. 12 cu.ft.
Open. No guide.
Polk County Historical Comission.
Correspondence, diaries, sketchbooks, photos, scrapbooks, newspapers, programs, awards, diplomas, announcements, and memorabilia of the family of Spessard Holland (1892-1971), a Florida politician who was governor from 1940 to 1944 and US senator from 1946 to 1970, and his wife Mary Agnes Groover Holland. Contains material on his mother, Fanny Virginia [Mrs. B. F.] Holland, who came to Bartow in 1889 to teach at Summerlin Institute, now Bartow High School. Spessard Holland worked in the US Senate for 13 years before winning approval of a constitutional amendment outlawing the poll tax as a voting requirement in the US. Family albums indicate that Mary Holland was a volunteer worker for the American National Red Cross, took an active part in her husband's campaigns, and participated in Washington society during his senate career. While her husband was governor, Mary Holland was involved with the Junior Salvage Army, a school program to collect scrap materials. In Washington, she was a member of the Home Hospitality Committee. Her papers include a guest log from the early 1940s and memoranda from such women's groups as Ladies of the Senate.

2,869. Polk County Events and People
Collection. 1887-1975. Ca. 2 ft.
Open. No guide.
Polk County Historical Commission.
Volumes of clippings which record political and social events of local importance. Included is material on local schools, civic organizations, pioneers and settlers, social groups, and social events, including weddings. A story and photos from 1939 feature Florida's then-oldest woman, 112-year-old Martha Weeks of Lithia.

2,870. Polk County Photographic Archives
Collection. Ca. 1860-1975. Ca. 8.67 ft.
Open. No guide.
Polk County Historical Commission.
Photos and negatives, dating from the County's initial settlement in ca. 1861, depict many women of prominent area families, pioneer women, and women in early high school classes and social organizations. Includes photos from the Bartow-area family of Florida governor Spessard Holland, particularly of his mother Mrs. B. F. Holland. Photos portray home and family life in the communities of Bartow, Old Chicora, Davenport, De Land, Dundee, Fort Meade, Frostproof, Haines City, Homeland, Lakeland, Midland, Winterhaven, and Auburndale.

DELRAY BEACH

2,871. Archives
Records. 1960- . 1 binder.
Closed. No guide.
Poor Clare Nuns, Christ the King Monastery.
Volume containing a history of this community of Franciscan contemplative nuns, which was founded in Delray Beach in 1960, includes the book of elections and chapters of election, canonical visitations, an account of the founding of the Monastery, names of persons who entered and left the community, and descriptions of community events.

GAINESVILLE

2,872. Hurston, Zora Neale
Papers. 1926-60. 31 in.
Open. Card catalog and index.
University of Florida Libraries, Rare Books and Manuscripts Department.
A Florida native and graduate of Barnard College where she studied anthropology, Hurston (1901-60) was a sociologist, teacher, author, and folklorist whose works included *Men and Mules* (1935), *Jonah's Gourd Vine* (1934), *Tell My Horse* (1938), *Moses: Man of the Mountain* (1939), and her autobiography *Dust Tracks on the Road* (1943). Correspondence, manuscripts, financial records, leaflets, clippings, and other material; includes letters from Margrit Sabloniere, E. O. Grover, Marjorie (Kinnan) Rawlings, and Frank Smathers about Hurston's work, racial problems, personal matters, and other topics. Hurston worked with the Federal Negro Theatre Project, with a college drama department, and as a librarian at Patrick Air Force Base.

2,873. May, Phillip Stockton
Papers. 1942-48. 3.5 ft.
Open. Card catalog and index.
University of Florida Libraries, Rare Books and Manuscripts Department.
A Jacksonville, FL, attorney, May (1891-1969?) defended author Marjorie (Kinnan) Rawlings in a celebrated libel suit filed after publication of her book *Cross Creek*. Correspondence between Rawlings and May; May's correspondence with others involved in the trial; letters supporting Rawlings's position; transcripts from the Florida Supreme Court and the Circuit Court of Alchua County, FL; reviews of her book; clippings about the trial and social functions; and other material. The trial, which involved a definition of the right of privacy, slander, and libel, was based on charges of Zelma Cason, a Cross Creek resident.

2,874. Pickren, Pansy
Papers. 1952-60. 15 in.
Open. Card catalog and index.
University of Florida Libraries, Rare Books and Manuscripts Department.
Correspondence, manuscripts, autobiographical material, rejection notes, poems, and a notebook of Pickren (1904-64?), a schoolteacher in Palatka, FL, who wrote stories dealing with life in Florida. The stories were never published. Pickren wrote about her experiences and portrayed the way of life of lower-class white Floridians.

2,875. Pope, Edith (Taylor)
Papers. 1920-61. 10.5 ft.
Partially restricted. Card catalog and index.
University of Florida Libraries, Rare Books and Manuscripts Department.
Family and personal correspondence, diaries, notebooks, manuscripts, published and unpublished poems, photos, clippings, and memorabilia of Pope (1905-61), an author. Includes manuscripts of her novels *Colcorton* (1944), *Castaways*, and *River in the Wind* (1954). Her early correspondence deals with her school days and study at Bryn Mawr, the political career of her father Senator F. Taylor, dresses, and trips to Europe. After 1940 her correspondence centers on her writings, her activities in the Pen Women Club of St. Augustine, FL, and participation in the political life of her husband Senator Earle Pope. Her later letters reflect her delicate health. Correspondents include Julia Scribner Bingham, James Branch Cabell, Anna Farkes Liddell, Hardwick Moseley, Maxwell Perkins, Kitty Poole, Orville Prescott, Marjorie (Kinnan) Rawlings, Charles Scribner, and Owen Young.

2,876. Rawlings, Marjorie (Kinnan)
Papers. 1916-60. 14 ft. and 14 microfilm reels.
Open. Card catalog and index.
University of Florida Libraries, Rare Books and Manuscripts Department.
A recipient of the Pulitzer Prize for fiction, Rawlings (1896-1953) wrote *The Yearling* and other books depicting the life of poor whites at her home in Cross Creek and other backcountry palmetto regions of Florida; Rawlings moved to Florida from New York in 1928. Correspondence; early drafts of novels, short stories, poems, and speeches; manuscripts; autobiographical writings; notes, letters, and other material Rawlings collected for a projected biography of Ellen Glasgow; personal and family photos; scrapbooks; social and formal programs; clippings; and memorabilia. Includes manuscripts related to *Cross Creek* (1942), *The Secret River, The Sojourner, South Moon Under* (1933), and *The Yearling* (1938). Contains material concerning a legal suit that grew from invasion of privacy charges lodged by Zelma Cason, a Cross Creek resident, following publication of *Cross Creek*. Rawlings's correspondents included her editor Maxwell Evarts Perkins, Zora Neale Hurston, Sigrid Undset, James Branch Cabell, Margaret Mitchell, Charles and Julia Scribner, Marcia Davenport, Marjorie Douglas, Douglas Southall Freeman, Bernice Gilkinson, Ellen Glasgow, and Thorton Wilder. Rawlings, who married Norton Sanford Baskin in 1941, continued to use the surname of her first husband Charles Rawlings in her writing.

2,877. Rawlings, Marjorie (Kinnan): Glasgow, Ellen
Papers. 1906-45. 2 ft.
Open. Unpublished guide.
University of Florida Libraries, Rare Books and Manuscripts Department.
Material collected by Rawlings (1896-1953) for a projected biography of Glasgow, an author, includes correspondence between Ellen and her brother Arthur, Glasgow's writings, criticism of her work, essays about Glasgow, poems, interviews, posthumous tributes to Glasgow, speeches, photos, watercolors of Glasgow's house and old Richmond, and a watercolor of Glasgow by Margaret Dashiell. Also includes correspondence from Dashiell, Carrie Duke, Inez Freeman, and Hunter Stagg.

2,878. Robins, Margaret (Dreier)
Papers. 1855-1949. 51 ft.
Open. Card catalog and index.
University of Florida Libraries, Rare Books and Manuscripts Department.
A labor leader and social reformer, Robins (1868-1945) worked for women's rights and was among the founders of the National Women's Trade Union League and the Women's Municipal League of New York; she also was director of the Training School for Active Workers and co-editor of the magazine *Life and Labor*. Correspondence, diaries, biographical material, speeches, articles, financial records dealing with the Chinsegut Hill Estate, memoranda and convention minutes of the Trade Union League and International Congresses of Working Women, photos, clippings, and memorabilia reflect Robins's interest in the labor movement, social work, suffrage, and the "outlawry of war." Letters from Leonora O'Reilly pertain to the founding of the Trade Union League. Also included are papers of Katherine Dreier (1877-1952), Mary E. Dreier (1875-1963), and Raymond Robins (1873-1955), whom Margaret married in 1905 in New York. In 1908 Margaret Robins was elected to the executive board of the Chicago Federation of Labor; in 1912 she was elected a member of the state Progressive party executive committee and campaigned for Teddy Roosevelt. The Robinses moved to Brooksville, FL, in 1928 and in 1932 gave their Brooksville estate to the US government for a wildlife sanctuary. Her correspondents include Mary Anderson, Jane Addams, Margaret Bonfield, Mrs. J. T. Bowen, P. H. Callahan, Carrie Chapman Catt, and Elizabeth Cristman.

2,879. Smith, Lillian Eugenia
Papers. 1935-65. 11 ft. and 1 tape.
Partially restricted. Card catalog and index.
University of Florida Libraries, Rare Books and Manuscripts Department.
Smith (1897-1966) was a writer, journalist, and reformer who edited *The South Today* (a periodical formerly known as *The North Georgia Review* and *Pseudopodia*); she was deeply interested in southern social issues of the 20th century. Personal and business correspondence; business records and copies of *The South Today;* manuscripts, typescripts, and galley proofs of Smith's books; a tape of a lecture by Smith on autobiography; photos; articles; and clippings document Smith's interest in integration, labor organization, and Christian responsibility for social justice. Included are manuscripts of *The Journey* (1954), *Killers of the Dream* (1949), *Strange Fruit* (1944), and *Our Faces, Our Words* (1954). Smith's correspondents include Louis Adamic, Howard Odum, Mary R. Beard, Mary (McLeod) Bethune, Erskine Caldwell, W. E. B. DuBois, David Lilienthal, Margaret Mitchell, and Walter White, as well as such organizations as Afro-American newspapers, the CIO committee to abolish discrimination, the Congress of Southern Mountain Workers, the Congress for Democracy in South Carolina, the Fellowship of Southern Churchmen, the Highlands Folk School, Morehouse College, the NAACP, and the Workers' Defense League.

2,880. Florida Blacks
Oral history. 1965- . 105 interviews.
Access restricted. No guide.
University of Florida, Oral History Project.
The interviews include 31 with black students at the University of Florida, 13 of them women, and 61 interviews with black elected officials, 10 of whom were women. Female students were asked whether they were accepted by white students; they also discussed life in interracial dormitories, dating, shopping in downtown Gainesville, their relationship with their families, and other topics. Female officials were asked about campaigning for office and serving in an elective post; specific questions concerned the sources of their support and financing, how they were treated by the media, and whether they received preferential or discriminatory treatment because they were women. The women officials were not asked about family or personal matters.

2,881. Florida Local History
Oral history. Nd. 411 interviews.
Access restricted. No guide.
University of Florida, Oral History Project.
Tapes of interviews with Florida community leaders, about 25 to 33 percent of whom were women, include reminiscences of the period from ca. 1900 to the present. The persons interviewed were selected by historical societies and community groups. They represented urban and rural areas and included residents of Alachua, Columbia, Dade, Dixie, Duval, Escambia, Hillsborough, Lake, Lee, Palm Beach, Polk, Putnam, St. Johns, St. Lucie, Seminole, Volusia, and Wakulla counties.

2,882. Florida Personalities
Oral history. Nd. 35 interviews.
Access restricted. No guide.
University of Florida, Oral History Project.
Three women were among the political, religious, education, social, and business leaders interviewed. The women were Arna Boutemps of Columbia University, who discusses Florida author and folklorist Zora Neale Hurston; Josephine Beckley, daughter of a Florida governor; and Alma Warren, who served as hostess for her brother Governor Fuller Warren before he was married.

2,883. Southeastern Indians
Oral history. Nd. Ca. 857 tapes and other items.
Access restricted. No guide.
University of Florida, Oral History Project.
Tapes of 747 interviews, transcripts, photos, Indian newspapers, and other items concern the history and lifestyle of contemporary Indians; about 20 percent of the persons interviewed were women. The collection contains categories for eight tribes: Seminole, Miccosukee, Creek, Florida Choctaw, Mississippi Choctaw, Lumbee, Catawba, and Cherokee. Most of the women's interviews deal with their role in the Indian community, and many focus on tasks such as food processing and pottery making. Catawba women discuss attitudes toward birth control and contraception. Reminiscences of the interviewees reach back to the early 20th century. Forty of those persons interviewed were Lumbees from the Washington, DC-Baltimore area. The newspapers include those published by the Lumbees, Choctaws, and Cherokees.

2,884. University of Florida
Oral history. Nd. 66 interviews.
Access restricted. No guide.
University of Florida, Oral History Project.
Reminiscenses from ca. 1900 to the present of persons connected with the University include those of six women: Marna V. Brady, a professor of logic and former dean of women; Maybell (Williams) [Mrs. John] Benton, wife of a dean and active participant in campus women's organizations; Frances (Sledd) [Mrs. John] Blake, whose father was the first president of the University; Bernice (Ashburn) Mims, assistant director in the general extension division who held a title in the college of education; and Edith (Bristol) [Mrs. John J.] Tigert, who was active in local women's organizations and was a University president's wife. Blake's interview concerns her early life in Gainesville and her memories as a member of the family of University president Andrew Sledd. The 66 interviews include 21 with women.

2,885. Jacksonville Woman's Club Yearbooks
Records. 1897-1952. 11 vols.
Open. Card catalog.
University of Florida, P. K. Yonge Library of Florida History.
Yearbooks of this Florida group, which was organized in 1897 and which combined self-improvement and consideration of contemporary issues with literary, social, and philanthropic objectives. The first yearbooks show emphasis on self-improvement through the reading of papers on such topics as the automobile, household economics, and hygienic cooking. The WWI period led to a greater focus on international and political questions; an international relations and world events class was featured as was a travel class with discussions of Thailand, Mayan civilization, Spanish missions, and the importance of Chautauqua, NY, to Americans. The Edith Gray Canteen Reserve Corps of the American National Red Cross was formed in 1918, and Jacksonville Club members formed a separate unit. Contributions were made to the scholarship fund, the Community Chest, the Tuberculosis Association of Duval County, and the Christmas Seal Fund. The group also was active in conservation work. In the 1920s the Club conducted classes in current events, political science, Spanish conversation, and literature. The 1930s saw new efforts to aid women workers through the Club's department of public welfare. In the 1940s and early 1950s the women supported organized attempts to improve race relations.

2,886. Jennings, May (Mann)
Papers. 1889-1928. 18 Hollinger boxes.
Open. Card catalog.
University of Florida, P. K. Yonge Library of Florida History.
Daughter of state senator Austin Shuey Mann and wife of Florida governor William Sherman Jennings, Jennings (1872-1928) was state director of the GFWC from 1918 to 1920, president of the Florida Federation of Women's Clubs from 1914 to 1917, and a member of the state Audubon Society executive committee from 1919 to 1924. Correspondence, business receipts, speeches, telegrams, official invitations, and correspondence and material of the FFWC. A worker for woman suffrage and conservation, Jennings promoted compulsory education, creation of an institution for the feeble-minded, state parks, bird sanctuaries, state game refuges, and Liberty Loan Campaigns. Included are her reports on the FFWC's department of conservation, the group's endowment fund, and her report as state GFWC director. Her correspondents include newspaper editors and such organizations as the Anti-Saloon League.

2,887. "Women as Lawyers"
Papers. Ca. 1898-1938. 5 items.
Open. Card catalog.
University of Florida, P. K. Yonge Library of Florida History.
Horatio Davis, a local judge, delivered the talk "Women as Lawyers" as a commencement address for a law class that included women. Collection consists of the speech and four letters of response. Davis told the graduates that woman's sphere was extending rapidly and that the first women had been licensed to practice law in Florida just weeks before his address. He contended, however, that a woman's "noblest station is retreat/ Her fairest virtues fly from public sight/ Domestic worth—that shuns too strong a light." The responses include a 1938 letter from James Gwynn, research secretary to the Florida Supreme Court, in which he discusses whether women could have had official authorization to practice law in the state before 1925 and one from Louise R. Pinell who was licensed to practice law in 1898 and was the first woman to take the Florida bar examination.

PENSACOLA

2,888. Abercrombie
Papers. 1930-70s. Ca. 1 Hollinger box and 11 tapes.
Open. Unpublished guide.
Pensacola Historical Museum, Lelia Abercrombie Historical Library.
[Miss] Lelia Abercrombie (1892-) was involved in banking, church activities, and the establishment of the Pensacola Historical Museum. Correspondence, oral history tapes, and other items relating to family and area history.

2,889. Bell Family
Papers. 1817-1920. 2 Hollinger boxes.
Open. Unpublished guide.
Pensacola Historical Museum, Lelia Abercrombie Historical Library.
Correspondence, diaries, journals, and other papers of family members, many of them women teachers. Includes Anna Bell's journal about her voyage to America, the diary Adelaide "Addie" Merritt Bell kept while she was in New Orleans in 1865, and Addie Bell's journal for 1867.

2,890. Cary Family
Papers. 1880s. 10 pp.
Open. Unpublished guide.
Pensacola Historical Museum, Lelia Abercrombie Historical Library.
Papers of the related Cary and Sheppard families include Civil War recollections of Lou Lee Sheppard, who was a young girl during the Civil War.

2,891. Fleming
Papers. Late 1800s-1940s. 2 Hollinger boxes.
Access restricted. Unpublished guide.
Pensacola Historical Museum, Lelia Abercrombie Historical Library.
[Mrs.] Mary Louise Robson Fleming (ca. 1917-), a teacher, has been involved in arts and social activities. Manuscripts, surveys, and historical scrapbooks include a fine arts survey and a history of the arts. Contains information about WPA activities and women's participation in projects during the depression and WWII.

2,892. Mallory
Papers. 1846-96. 2 Hollinger boxes.
Open. Unpublished guide.
Pensacola Historical Museum, Lelia Abercrombie Historical Library.
Correspondence of Stephen R. Mallory (1810-73), Confederate secretary of the Navy, and his wife Angelo Sylvaria Moreno Mallory. Includes her letters to her husband, their sons, and to Mrs. Jefferson Davis.

2,893. Merritt
Papers. 1857-68. 1 Hollinger box.
Access restricted. Unpublished guide.
Pensacola Historical Museum, Lelia Abercrombie Historical Library.
Correspondence of Lucius Merritt (1824-93) and his wife Lizzie includes letters they exchanged while he was a prisoner at Fort Pickens during the Civil War.

2,894. Pensacola Art Club
Records. 1932-34. 20 pp.
Open. Unpublished guide.
Pensacola Historical Museum, Lelia Abercrombie Historical Library.
Minutes, clippings, and other records of this group, which sought to encourage art in Pensacola. Many of the group's members were women.

2,895. Sisters of Charity
Records. 1861. 10 pp.
Open. Unpublished guide.
Pensacola Historical Museum, Lelia Abercrombie Historical Library.
Diary concerning the work of the Sisters, who were nurses at the Warrington hospital during the Civil War. Portions of the diary were published in *Pensacola Historical Society Quarterly,* III, no. 3 (July 1967).

2,896. United Daughters of the Confederacy
Records. 1940-50s. 70 items.
Open. Unpublished guide.
Pensacola Historical Museum, Lelia Abercrombie Historical Library.
Correspondence, programs, and other records.

2,897. Wright, Ella Rupert
Papers. 1950-60s. 1 Hollinger box.
Open. Unpublished guide.
Pensacola Historical Museum, Lelia Abercrombie Historical Library.
Writings by Wright (1896-1963) concern early Pensacola families and their descendants.

2,898. American Association of University Women
Records. 1925-74. 2 ft. and 18 vols.
Open. Unpublished guide.
University of West Florida, John C. Pace Library, Special Collections.
Correspondence, typescripts, a history, programs, photos, clippings, and printed items of the Pensacola Chapter, which was formed in 1925.

2,899. Azalea Garden Club
Records. 1967-74. 7 vols.
Open. Unpublished guide.
University of West Florida, John C. Pace Library, Special Collections.
Scrapbooks containing correspondence, programs, announcements, and clippings reflect the activities of Pensacola's oldest garden club.

2,900. Clubbs, Occie
Papers. 1860-1970. 1588 items.
Open. Unpublished guide.
University of West Florida, John C. Pace Library, Special Collections.
[Miss] Clubs (1888-1971) was a teacher, school principal, and historian. Correspondence chiefly relating to her master's thesis on Stephen Russell Mallory and to her presidency of the Florida Historical Society, scrapbooks, family photos, house plans by her father A. V. Clubbs, and educational periodicals dating from before 1920. Most of the material relates to [Miss] Clubbs's historical interests, her career, and her interest in S. R. Mallory.

2,901. Collier Family
Papers. 1916-60. Ca. 550 items.
Open. Unpublished guide.
University of West Florida, John C. Pace Library, Special Collections.
Correspondence, programs, photos, clippings, and printed items assembled by [Mrs.] Daisy Adams Collier reflect her interest in the DAR, the United Daughters of the Confederacy, the Pensacola Garden Club, and other local organizations.

2,902. Hanshaw, Cella
Papers. 1908-54. 27 items.
Open. Unpublished guide.
University of West Florida, John C. Pace Library, Special Collections.
Hanshaw was a Santa Rosa County schoolteacher. Correspondence, including that with her family and friends; post cards; school papers; educational certificates; and other material.

2,903. Hargis, Modeste
Papers. Nd. 1 item.
Open. Unpublished guide.
University of West Florida, John C. Pace Library, Special Collections.
Typescript of historical notes about Pensacola and Escambia County, FL, by Hargis, a pharmacist, journalist, and musician.

2,904. Hargis, Modeste, and Grant, Isabel R.
Papers. 1939-40. 1 item.
Open. Unpublished guide.
University of West Florida, John C. Pace Library, Special Collections.
Hargis and Grant were journalists. Typescript prepared for the American Guide Series of the Federal Writers Project concerns Pensacola during the Spanish-American War; it consists principally of excerpts from local newspapers and notes about volunteer regiments.

2,905. Ingraham, Isabella
Papers. 1972. 1 folder.
Open. Unpublished guide.
University of West Florida, John C. Pace Library, Special Collections.
Correspondence, photos, clippings, and memorabilia of Ingraham, a founder of the Pensacola Girl Scout Council.

2,906. League of Women Voters, Pensacola Chapter
Records. 1957-75. 817 items.
Open. Unpublished guide.
University of West Florida, John C. Pace Library, Special Collections.
Financial records, correspondence, tapes, photos, and printed items of the Pensacola LWV, organized in 1957, include files on the Chapter's projects on voting, conservation, antipollution work, and services rendered by government offices.

2,907. Mallory, Cora
Papers. 1881-1973. 63 items.
Open. Unpublished guide.
University of West Florida, John C. Pace Library, Special Collections.
Mallory (1881-1973) was the granddaughter of Stephen Russell Mallory, who served as secretary of the Confederate Navy. Correspondence and clippings concern Pensacola history.

2,908. Moreno, Elizabeth
Papers. 1898-1965. 256 items.
Open. Unpublished guide.
University of West Florida, John C. Pace Library, Special Collections.
[Miss] Moreno was a concert pianist and piano teacher. Correspondence; drafts of poems, stories, and other writings; concert and recital programs; and family photos and memorabilia relate to Moreno's school days and career and to the Moreno family of Pensacola.

2,909. Murphy, B. A.
Papers. 1802-1960. Ca. 1375 items.
Open. Unpublished guide.
University of West Florida, John C. Pace Library, Special Collections.
[Miss] B. "Bert" A. Murphy (1872-1967) was a realtor, collector, and civic leader. Correspondence, business records, account books, photos, scrapbooks, maps, and clippings relate primarily to Pensacola and western Florida. Scrapbooks reflect Murphy's interest in state and local political and civic affairs and in WWII events and leaders.

2,910. Oral History
Oral history. 1971. 2 tapes.
Open. Unpublished guide.
University of West Florida, John C. Pace Library, Special Collections.
Reminiscences of two schoolteachers, [Miss] Daisy McAllister (1878-1973) and [Miss] Lelia Abercrombie (1898-). McAllister's interview deals with the role of women in Pensacola from 1919 to 1925, while Abercrombie discusses events at the local Naval Air Station from 1914 to 1919.

2,911. Pensacola: Jones, Corinne
Papers. 1967. 1 item.
Open. Unpublished guide.
University of West Florida, John C. Pace Library, Special Collections.
A history of Negro recreation in Pensacola written by Jones, an educator.

2,912. Santa Rosa County: Deen-Crist
Papers. 1909-51. 13 items.
Open. Unpublished guide.
University of West Florida, John C. Pace Library, Special Collections.
Photos and clippings include reminiscences of a Santa Rosa County, FL, schoolteacher. The schoolteacher, a woman, apparently lived from about 1880 to about 1955.

2,913. Santa Rosa County: Ladies' Aid Society of St. Mary's Episcopal Church, Milton, FL
Records. 1868-79. 1 item.
Open. Unpublished guide.
University of West Florida, John C. Pace Library, Special Collections.
Minutes from 1868 to 1879 of the Ladies' Aid Society, founded in about 1868.

2,914. Santa Rosa County: Shakespeare Club
Records. 1971. 1 item.
Open. Unpublished guide.
University of West Florida, John C. Pace Library, Special Collections.
Organized in 1911 in Milton, FL, this group organized presentations concerning Shakespeare and his works. Consists of a history of the Club from 1911 to 1971 which reflects the literary interests of residents in a small Florida town.

2,915. Simpson, Leah Reemar, and Simpson, Rebecca Calhoun
Papers. 1834-65. Microfilm.
Open. Unpublished guide.
University of West Florida, John C. Pace Library, Special Collections.
Correspondence of Leah Simpson (1798-?) and Rebecca Simpson (1800-?), members of a Bagdad, FL, family that operated a lumber business for many years.

2,916. Smith, Mrs. Daniel
Papers. Ca. 1900-68. 6 folders.
Open. Unpublished guide.
University of West Florida, John C. Pace Library, Special Collections.
Typescripts of Smith's writings on Pensacola history, invitations and programs for various ceremonial occasions, and photos of historic places.

2,917. Stowe, Harriet Elizabeth (Beecher)
Papers. Nd. 2 items.
Open. Unpublished guide.
University of West Florida, John C. Pace Library, Special Collections.
[Mrs. Calvin Ellis] Stowe (1811-96) was a writer. These letters by Stowe, one of which was addressed to her publisher, were included in the first volume of her novel *Uncle Tom's Cabin.*

2,918. Tempest, Ruth
Papers. 1942-64. 92 items.
Open. Unpublished guide.
University of West Florida, John C. Pace Library, Special Collections.
A short story writer, [Mrs.] Tempest is in charge of University publications. Correspondence with literary agents, typescripts, and tearsheets. Tempest had several stories published in women's magazines during the 1940s, 1950s, and 1960s.

ST. AUGUSTINE

2,919. Archives
Records. 1866- . Ca. 67.5 ft.
Open. Unpublished guide.
Sisters of St. Joseph Motherhouse.
The order was established in Florida in 1866. Its members are involved in religious, educational, benevolent, and charitable work in convents, schools, academies, orphanages, asylums, and hospitals. Financial and statistical reports; correspondence, including personal letters to sisters in France about pioneer life; chronicles and annals of the community; tapes of meetings; photos; slides; brochures; clippings; publications; and other records. Includes material relating to the Sisters' work in the 19th century nursing during yellow fever epidemics and the Spanish American War, operating schools for black freedmen in Florida and Georgia and for Indian prisoners, and operating private residential academies, a home for dependent children, and a teacher training institute. During the 20th century, the Sisters have founded special education centers for handicapped children and operated various hospitals and high schools; they also have been involved in catechetical instruction for the deaf and blind.

ST. LEO

2,920. Archives
Records. 1888- . No size given.
Closed. No guide.
Benedictine Sisters of Florida, Holy Name Priory.
Financial records, daily logs, correspondence, photos, scrapbooks, and artifacts of the Sisters, a religious order of women founded in 1888 in San Antonio, FL.

ST. PETERSBURG

2,921. Woman's Town Improvement Association
Records. 1912-31. Ca. 1 Paige box.
Open. Card catalog.
St. Petersburg Historical Society.
Constitution, bylaws, minutes, organizational papers, and handbills of the Association, which sought "to promote and encourage the improvement and beautifying of our city" through creation of public parks, improvement of private grounds, and development of hotels. A successor to the Village Improvement Society formed in ca. 1889, the Association included members of the town's early mercantile and civic groups as well as its social elite. The group was instrumental in initiating St. Petersburg's park system and continued its work through the town's boom period of the 1920s. It occasionally sponsored a flower, fruit, and vegetable show to promote local interest in gardening and beautification.

SARASOTA

2,922. Palmer, Bertha (Honoré)
Papers. 1910-?. 4 folders.
Open. Card catalog.
Sarasota Historical Commission.
Palmer (1849-1918) was a businesswoman, land developer, and civic leader in Chicago and Sarasota. Correspondence, property assessment papers, Palmer farm records from 1917 to 1931, a Department of Natural Resources report on an inspection of the Palmer ranch in 1973, biographical essays on Palmer, her will, and clippings. A leading Chicago socialite after her marriage to Potter Palmer in 1871, Bertha Palmer was elected president of the board of lady managers of the Chicago World's Columbian Exposition in 1893 and visited Europe to interest foreign governments in the event. As a result of her group's efforts, a woman's building was constructed to house examples of women's art and handicrafts from around the world. At her husband's death in 1902, Bertha Palmer inherited about $8,000,000, an amount she increased to more than $20,000,000 before her death. She supported tourism and was active in the development of the Sarasota area after she came to the region in 1910. Palmer successfully promoted the citrus industry and furthered ranching through introduction of Brahma cattle. She controlled more than 80,000 acres in Hillsborough and Sarasota counties before she died.

2,923. Sarasota Historical Commission Photo Albums
Collection. 1839-1962. Ca. 6 in.
Open. No guide.
Sarasota Historical Commission.
Photos dating from the area's earliest settlement portray families, farmsteads, and white settlers on the tropical agricultural frontier. Includes photos of the area's Scottish colonists of the 1880s and 1890s, the Brownings, Gillespies, and the Dunns; of schoolchildren; of women playing golf, strolling on the downtown boardwalks in ca. 1904, or sitting on the porches of their frame houses. Contains photos of woman's club festivities with the names of participants recorded.

TALLAHASSEE

2,924. Florida Association of School Librarians
Records. 1950-72. 4 cu.ft.
Open. Published guide.
Florida State Archives.
The Association, which was originally the school and children's section of the Florida Library Association, merged with the Florida Association for Media in Education in 1972. Minutes, financial records, committee and other reports, correspondence, information on scholarships, and publications. Also includes records of the Florida high school library council, a section of the Association. Taken from the *Catalog of the Florida State Archives* (Tallahassee, FL: Department of State, Division of Archives, History and Records Management, 1975).

2,925. Johnson, Beth McCollough
Papers. 1957-69. 12 cu.ft.
Open. Published guide.
Florida State Archives.
Papers of [Mrs. George W.] Johnson (1909-73), a member of the Florida house of representatives from 1957 to 1962 and the first woman member of the Florida Senate, where she served from 1962 to 1968. Includes speeches, material about her campaigns and elections, and information about her work on reapportionment, mental health, traffic safety, and higher education. Also contains records dealing with her work on the education and welfare committee of the constitution revision committee and some personal papers. Taken from the *Catalog of the Florida State Archives* (Tallahassee, FL: Division of Archives, History and Records Management, 1975).

2,926. State Archives
Records. Nd. No size given.
Open. Published and unpublished guides.
Florida State Archives.
Records of the state, including those created by officials and agencies of state, county, and municipal governments. Material about women is found, for example, in the constitutional revision collection (P69-02), 1957-68 (23 cu.ft.), which includes correspondence with the League of Women Voters; the state board of pensions, records (P69-10), which include application files of Civil War veterans and widows, ca. 1885-1957 (140 cu.ft.); and county court records, which contain extensive marriage, probate, and other records. See the *Catalog of the Florida State Archives* (Tallahassee, FL: Department of State, Division of Archives, History and Records Management, 1975).

2,927. Archives Biography
Collection. 1909- . Ca. 2.5 ft.
Open. Vertical subject file.
Florida State University Library, Special Collections.
Clippings form the bulk of the collection which also includes correspondence, memoranda, manuscripts, social announcement cards, pamphlets, and printed material. Primarily contains biographical information on former members of the faculty and administration personnel at Florida State College for Women and Florida State University. Contains some papers of presidents, including a manuscript by President Edward Conradi concerning FSCW, which he headed from 1909 to 1941, as well as addresses, poems, and reminiscences. Included is biographical material on Louise Richardson, FSCW-FSU librarian from 1919 to 1960; Sara Srygley, librarian; Katherine Warren, dean of women; Margaret V. Campbell and Dorothy Hoffman, modern languages professors; Ruth S. Breen, a botanist; Betty Jane Grimm, a voice professor; and Ann Kirn, an author and artist.

2,928. Authors Manuscripts
Collection. Ca. 1856- . 11.75 ft.
Open. Card catalog.
Florida State University Library, Special Collections.
Manuscripts, letters, background material for manuscripts, and minutes and other records of organizations related to Florida State College for Women and Florida State University. Includes manuscripts of Florida authors Gloria Jahoda, Kathryn Abbey, [Mrs.] Mary B. Alfriend, Louise Blackwell, Doak Sheridan Campbell, Cora Cheney, [Mrs.] Helen Cruickshank, Florence Fritz, Janet Burroway, and Vivian Ahlsweh Williams and memoirs of Helen M. Edwards. Doak Campbell's material includes *A University in Transition: Florida State College for Women and Florida State University, 1941-1957.* Also contains articles by Teresa Holloway, a journalist and popular author; correspondence, background material, outlines, and other items of Jahoda; and books, illustrations, and manuscripts of Ann Kirn, an illustrator and children's author.

2,929. Diamond, Ruby
Papers. 1783-1969. 17 in.
Open. Sketchbook.
Florida State University Library, Special Collections.
[Miss] Diamond, a Tallahassee philanthropist, is the daughter of Julius Diamond, a merchant who lived in Tallahassee from 1870 to 1914 and who served as chairman of the Leon County board of commissioners from 1889 to 1899. Correspondence in German, Hebrew, and English; Civil War letters and documents; family files, bookkeeping journals, and cashbooks of Julius Diamond; legal documents; manuscripts from the American Jewish Archives' Ruby Diamond Collection; biographical sketches; photos, including ones of late 19th-and early 20th-century Tallahassee; university reports; memorials; clippings, including items on Florida history; and other material. Julius Diamond's business records reflect the period's economic conditions and development in the area.

2,930. El Destino and Chemonie Plantations
Records. 1822-59. 1 vol., 16 items, and 65 pp.
Open. Sketchbook.
Florida State University Library, Special Collections.
Records and documents concerning the operation of two plantations near Tallahassee and the estate of William B. Nuttall, who, with his father and brother, established the two plantations. Includes papers of conveyance of land and slaves, lists of names of slaves sold at public auction and prices obtained, lists of Florida inventories, account sales for cotton and other agricultural goods, and reports by executors of Nuttall's estate. The papers were signed by Mary W. Savage; Mary W. (Savage) Nuttall, administratrix; Hector W. Braden as trustee for Mary W. Nuttall, who was the widow of William B. Nuttall; and Mary W. Nuttall's second husband George Noble Jones, who with Mary Jones were joint administrators of William B. Nuttall's estate.

2,931. Florida and Tallahassee Biography
Collection. 1905- . 8.5 ft.
Open. Vertical subject files.
Florida State University Library, Special Collections.
Clippings, articles, announcements, and some correspondence and memoranda contain biographical information on prominent Tallahassee and Florida residents. Includes material on Harriet M. Bedell of Collier County, who was an Episcopal deaconess and missionary; Mary McLeod Bethune, a black educator; Dorothy Dodd, Tallahassee state librarian; Beth Johnson, a state senator; Anna Forbes Liddell, a Florida State University professor emeritus of philosophy; Ellen Call Long, an author and reformer from Tallahassee; circus women Audrey and Edith Ringling; and Shirley Martin, former FSU dean of nursing. The Tallahassee biography file consists of material on area settlers and prominent residents during the 19th and 20th centuries. Includes information on Princess Achille Murat, an active member of the preservation movement in the 19th century and the great-grandniece of George Washington; she worked to restore Mount Vernon.

2,932. Florida Author File
Collection. Ca. 1909- . Ca. 2 ft.
Open. Vertical subject file.

Florida State University Library, Special Collections. Book lists, citations, pamphlets, dust jackets, articles, and clippings accumulated by the Florida State College for Women-Florida State University Library. Primarily consists of clippings containing biographical and publications information on Florida authors, among them Anita Bryant, Marjorie Stoneman Douglas, Rubylea Hall, Helen King Hastings, Teresa Holloway, Mildred Lawrence, Virginia Ormsby, Marjorie (Kinnan) Rawlings, Marjory Bartlett Sanger, Elizabeth Seibert, Ann Kirn, and Dorothy Worley.

2,933. Florida Flambeau

Records. 1915-75. Ca. 83 vols. and other items.
Open. Card catalog.
Florida State University Library, Special Collections. Bound volumes of *Florida Flambeau,* the student newspaper of Florida State College for Women and its coeducational successor Florida State University, record political and social activities at the school as well as student concerns. During the early 1920s, the paper included a YWCA column announcing social events, projects, and a thought-for-the-day poem. Society and gossip columns were also contained. Papers from the WWII era reveal a greater emphasis on general news and a greater institutional complexity. In 1972 the newspaper became an independent venture financed and managed by students.

2,934. Florida State College for Women Alumnae Publications

Records. 1914-47. Ca. 1 ft. and 4 vols.
Open. Card catalog.
Florida State University Library, Special Collections. Founded in 1905, Florida State College for Women became Florida State University, a coeducational institution, in 1947. Bound volumes of the FSCW *Alumnae News;* the FSCW *Bulletin, Alumnae Edition;* the *Bulletin of Alumnae Association of FSCW;* and other material reflecting the alumae organization's growth. Physical expansion, increasing enrollments, and postgraduate opportunities were also discussed. Bulletins include lists of alumnae organization members and minutes of the group's meetings. FSCW had a student body of 1800 when it became coeducational.

2,935. Florida State College for Women and Florida State University Catalogs

Records. 1905-76. Ca. 59 vols.
Open. Card catalog.
Florida State University Library, Special Collections. Catalogs illustrate academic requirements, social rules, disciplinary practices, and educational programs of Florida State College for Women from 1905 to 1947 and of Florida State University from 1947 to the present. Bound volumes of catalogs for all regular and most summer sessions and individual graduate school handbooks. The catalogs provide information about the expansion of a women's liberal arts college into a coeducational institution. Faculty qualifications are listed. In 1906-07 the school included a college of liberal arts, a school of industrial arts (predecessor of the school of home economics), the state school for teachers, and the school of fine arts.

2,936. FSCW-FSU Student Literary Magazines

Records. 1926-72. 2 boxes, 29 vols., and 3 items.
Open. No guide.
Florida State University Library, Special Collections. Copies of Florida State College for Women's *Distaff* and Florida State University's *Talaria, Smoke Signals, Embryo,* and *Legend* contain poems, short stories, and essays by college women, which reveal their attitudes toward themselves, their role as women, and their involvement in political and social issues. *Distaff* articles included "The Sorrows of Eve" in 1927, "Students Look at Russia" in 1946, and in 1947 "On American Women," "In Defense of Women," "The Humanities: A Means to Educational Unity," and "Tell It to Grandma, Mother's Busy."

2,937. In-As-Much Circle of the International Order of the King's Daughters and Sons, Inc.

Records. 1894-1966. 2 ft.
Open. Sketchbook.
Florida State University Library, Special Collections. Charter, bylaws, president's papers, minutes, treasurer's records, bank statements, notebooks, reports, clippings, and other material of the Circle, founded in 1894 as the Florida branch of a national group organized in New York in 1886 to provide care for the sick. The New York founders were women, and women apparently played a large role in the Florida branch. The Circle supported construction and helped endow the Silver Cross Hospital near Tallahassee.

2,938. Lenski, Lois

Papers. Ca. 1893-1973. 2 drawers, 8 shelves, and several portfolios.
Open. Card catalog.
Florida State University Library, Special Collections. Lenski (1893-1974), who often wrote about Florida, was a writer and illustrator of children's books, among them *Strawberry Girl, Indian Captive,* and the *Mr. Small* books. Business and personal correspondence, poems, sketches, manuscripts for published and unpublished works, speeches, photos, scrapbooks, articles, clippings, books, and other material, including taped interviews with Lenski, her "Migrant Plays," articles she wrote, "Lois Lenski's USA" (a map), studies of her work, scrapbooks with background material for *Strawberry Girl* and other works, original illustrations for *Mr. Small* books, regional books, songbooks, eight original lithographs, 13 original block prints, three original woodcuts, bookmarks, and Christmas cards.

2,939. Tally Ho

Records. 1900-73. 61 vols.
Open. Card catalog.
Florida State University Library, Special Collections. Student yearbooks of Florida State College for Women and Florida State University record information on the academic, organizational, and social life of students at a women's college that became a coeducational institution in 1947. Volumes of the yearbook, which was titled *The Argo of the Suwanee* in 1900, *The Argo* in 1903, *Flastacowo* from 1910 until 1947, and *Tally Ho* from 1948 to 1973. Early editions include information on members of the faculty, senior photos, poems, normal school graduating classes, domestic arts classes, sorority rolls, athletic organizations, the "Anti-Fat Club," and the YWCA. Later editions reflect the school's growth and feature photos, histories of the school, and membership lists of such organizations as the F Club (a club for women in physical education), the Garnet Key (an honorary women's group), sororities, and the alumnae association.

2,940. State Photographic Archives

Collection. 1850s-1970s. Ca. 71,000 items.
Open. Card and name indexes.
Florida State University Library, State Photographic Archives.
Photos, negatives, slides, color transparencies, post cards, and stereo views of Florida and Florida-related subjects portray women in roles ranging from pioneers who traveled to Florida in covered wagons in the 1840s to black women representatives in the Florida legislature during the 1970s. The collection was begun in 1952.

2,941. Regional Oral History

Oral history. Nd. Transcripts of 46 interviews and tapes.
Open. No guide.
Florida State University, Project in Oral History. Transcripts and some tapes of interviews with persons, most of whom were more than 50 years old, include reminiscences of politicians, farmers, housewives, children of railroad employees, philanthropists, and persons in other professions. The student-collected interviews include one with Ruby Diamond, a Tallahassee philanthropist and daughter of a local merchant and developer. Diamond, a patron of Florida State University, describes Tallahassee in the early 20th century. Other persons interviewed include Helen Cate, who was associated with the FSU school of home economics for more than 35 years; Pattie Odom Smith, widow of a state senator; Rosalie Gates, a native of Geneva, FL; and Annie May Brown, an agent for a black Tallahassee insurance agency.

TAMPA

2,942. Call, Richard Keith

Papers. 1801-1911. 4 Hollinger boxes and 1 vol.
Open. Index and card catalog.
Florida Historical Society, University of South Florida.
Papers of Call (1792-1862), who twice served as Florida's territorial governor, include those of his wife Mary L. Call and their daughter Ellen (Call) Long (1826-1904?), an author, naturalist, conservationist, and reformer. Ellen Long's papers include her letters to her parents, correspondence from friends, a letter from Harriet (Beecher) Stowe regarding suffrage, Long's manuscripts, family memoirs written by her, organization documents, legal papers, and articles from ca. 1876 concerning suffrage. Best known for her book *Florida Breezes,* Long also wrote about her father's estate, her own family, and her father's career.

2,943. El Destino Plantation

Records. Ca. 1820-1900. 3 Hollinger boxes and 2 vols.
Open. Card catalog and index.
Florida Historical Society, University of South Florida.
Correspondence, business records, and legal documents record the transfer of El Destino and Chemonie plantations from William Nuttall to his widow Mary Nuttall and their management by her lawyer and, later, by her second husband George Noble Jones. The records document the plantations' operation and include information on costs, slave sales and purchases, and financial arrangements.

2,944. Florida Historical Society Miscellaneous Papers

Records. 1492- . 8 Hollinger boxes and other items.
Open. Index.
Florida Historical Society, University of South Florida.
Correspondence, including a 1492 letter of Spanish monarchs Ferdinand and Isabella; manuscripts; army discharges; Civil War ordinances and military orders; plantation orders; WWI prisoner-of-war lists; speeches; and songs. A number of the collection's letters are to or from women and many date from the Civil War years. Included is a manuscript by Florida writer Marjorie Stoneman Douglas concerning historical research in the Everglades area.

2,945. Florida Negroes, Federal Writers' Project

Records. Ca. 1936-40. Ca. 2 ft.
Open. No guide.
Florida Historical Society, University of South Florida.
This section of the Project focused on the culture and lives of Florida Negroes. Manuscripts, some correspondence, transcripts of interviews, and

historical clippings provide information on women in Negro culture. Contains some biographical material on nurse Clara Frye, founder of Tampa's Negro hospital, and Thelma Livingston Roberts, an artist. Collection includes interviews with ex-slaves and free blacks, who often were called "colored" or "creoles." Contains interviews with Ellen M. Allen of Miami and Florida Clayton of Tallahassee, both of whom lived in Florida in the antebellum period, and Georgia Love of Lakeland, a faith healer who discussed religion. The collection illuminates the history, art, education, folklore, religion, occupations, living conditions, and legal status of Florida Negroes.

2,946. Florida Negroes, Florida Slaves
Records. Nd. Ca. 5 ft.
Open. No guide.
Florida Historical Society, University of South Florida.
Directed by black folklorist and writer Zora Neale Hurston, workers in the Negro Writers' Unit of the Federal Writers' Project interviewed aged ex-slaves about life in slavery and after the Civil War in Florida. Many interviews were done by women fieldworkers, including Viola B. Muse, Pearl Randolph, Modeste Hargis, and Rachel A. Austin. Four of the 24 ex-slaves interviewed were women: Patience Campbell of Jackson County, Mary Minus Biddle of Pensacola, Christine Mitchell of St. Augustine, and Margaret Nickerson of Leon County. The interviews contain information about the physical conditions of life in slavery, the making of soap and salt, cooking, gardening, work, and relaxation; life after slavery, large-scale civil marriages performed to legitimize slave unions, life in all-Negro communities such as Amelia Island (near St. Augustine); and descriptions of illnesses and the achievements of slaves and former slaves.

2,947. Florida Negroes, Manuscripts, "Slave Days in Florida"
Records. Ca. 1941. 1 item.
Open. No guide.
Florida Historical Society, University of South Florida.
Drawn from interviews with elderly ex-slaves, the Federal Writers' Project manuscript by Martin Richardson describes the lives of slaves and post-emancipation Negroes in Florida. Eleven of the 32 former slaves interviewed were women. The manuscript discusses the beginning of slavery in Florida in ca. 1687 and the growth after 1819 of large-scale plantation agriculture in the state. Topics discussed include rural and urban slavery; such foods as wild squash, potatoes, tannion leaves, corn bread, coffee made from parched corn meal, okra seeds and potatoes, pilfered eggs, potato bread, and molasses; such women's jobs as candlemaking, home dyeing, cooking, and food preparation; methods of reprisal, escape, pursuit, and hiding; escapes to Seminole settlements and Negro-Indian relationships; "breeders" and marriage; religion and superstitions; cures; amusements and celebrations; and "freedom at last."

2,948. Florida Negroes, Manuscripts, "The Florida Negro"
Records. Ca. 1941. 200-page item.
Open. No guide.
Florida Historical Society, University of South Florida.
Produced by the Federal Writers' Project, the manuscript focused on the history, religion, and community and family life of Florida Negroes. The manuscript, which was gathered from oral history interviews and other sources, includes biographical sketches of sculptor Augusta Savage; author Zora Neale Hurston; and Helen Louise Dillet Johnson, mother of James Weldon Johnson and the first black woman to teach in Florida's public schools. Contains information on bolita; gaming and gambling practices; folk remedies; ghost and childbirth superstitions; hoodoo and voodoo; conjure shops, their products, and the products' effects; notable Florida Negroes; and unusual Negro communities such as Eatonville, an all-Negro town in ca. 1937 that was the scene of Hurston's *Their Eyes Were Watching God.* The manuscript also noted that Pensacola was unusual in the 1930s because "there are no sharp dividing lines at all" between Negro and white housing areas. Writers of the manuscript observed that, "Of Negroes it can be said even more truly than is often said of women: No one knows what they can do, because they are only just beginning to have a chance."

2,949. Love and Allied Families
Papers. 1743-1941. 1 Hollinger box.
Open. General information and card catalog.
Florida Historical Society, University of South Florida.
Correspondence, family history manuscripts, and manuscript index of the Loves, a landholding family in Quincy, FL, that traced its origin to Alexander Love who lived in North Carolina in 1743. Genealogical study, written by [Mrs.] Pearl Trogden Love in 1941, includes references to many women. The Loves were Presbyterians who came to Gadsden County, FL, in 1824 and served in the Confederate Army. The papers provide information about the social and political structure of the plantation town of Quincy.

2,950. Reid, Mary Martha
Papers. 1860-92. 1 Hollinger box.
Open. Index.
Florida Historical Society, University of South Florida.
Correspondence, business records, brochures, newspaper notices, and clippings of Reid, the wife of Florida's fourth territorial governor Robert Raymond Reid. Papers, the bulk of which date from the Civil War years, include correspondence of Mary Reid with her son who was killed in Virginia while serving with a Florida unit of the Confederate Army. Also contains wartime correspondence with friends in Montgomery, AL; Lake City, FL; Madison, FL; Monticello, FL; Richmond, VA; Fayetteville, NC; Savannah, GA; and near Petersburg, VA. Clippings include a memorial tribute to Mary Reid and an essay about her. Collection material reflects life, health, and society during the Civil War.

2,951. Seminole Indians of Florida, Federal Writers' Project
Records. 1936-59. Ca. 2.5 ft.
Open. No guide.
Florida Historical Society, University of South Florida.
Project correspondence, manuscripts, notes, and clippings regarding the life and culture of the Seminoles. Material from interviews and other sources describes the role of Seminole women. Topics discussed include the women's preparation of such food as garfish, flatbread, and conti (an arrowroot bread); women's washday practices; clothing design, production, and ornamentation; marriage and religious ceremonies; childrearing; and folklore. Descriptions of the cultivation of corn, taro, sweet potatoes, Indian pumpkins, bananas, beans, and other vegetables include the observation that on moonlit nights "women walked with hair unbound thru corn rows to encourage growth of ears on corn stalks."

2,952. Walker, Hester (Perrine)
Papers. 1840-85. 2 items.
Open. Card catalog and index.
Florida Historical Society, University of South Florida.
Walker (1824-post 1885) was the daughter of Henry Perrine, a physician and botanist who was killed in 1840 by the Seminoles during a massacre at Indian Key. Walker's journal, written in 1885 for her grandchildren, describes how she and her mother, sister, and younger brother hid in a turtle crawl under the wharf during the massacre. The journal includes a hand-drawn plan of the Perrine house on Indian Key showing the route followed in their escape. Also contains extensive biographical information, descriptions of life in a 19th-century pastor's family, and a cataloging of the virtues of the Perrine women, for example, positivism, practicality, patriotism, and piety.

2,953. Collins, LeRoy
Papers. Ca. 1950-70. 480 boxes and ca. 250 tapes, phonodiscs, and motion picures.
Open. No guide.
University of South Florida Library, Special Collections.
Collins (1909-) was governor of Florida from 1955 to 1961, president of the National Association of Broadcasters, director of the Community Relations Service, and undersecretary of commerce in 1965 and 1966. Correspondence, personal papers, speeches, campaign records, phonodiscs, videotapes, sound tapes, and motion picture reels relate chiefly to Collins's term as governor. Also includes information concerning his 1968 campaign for the US Senate. Much of the material was generated by or relates to women.

2,954. Jackson, James
Papers. Ca. 1880-1910. 3 Hollinger boxes.
Open. Card catalog and index.
University of South Florida Library, Special Collections.
A builder and business manager, Jackson was the father of Tampa civic leader Kate Jackson. Correspondence, notebook diaries, business records, bills and invoices, photos, and other papers. Includes articles on Kate Jackson, material on women's suffrage, and Kate Jackson's books pertaining to the Women's Civic League, the Tampa Business and Professional Women's Club, and other groups.

2,955. Jackson, Kate
Papers. 1909-53. 1 Hollinger box.
Open. Index.
University of South Florida Library, Special Collections.
Correspondence, speeches, and other papers of [Miss] Jackson, a member of one of Tampa's pioneer families who was active in the Tampa Civic Association, the Tampa Business and Professional Women's Club, and the Florida Federation of Women's Clubs and who also helped establish the first city playground. Included is organizational correspondence from the FFWC, the Tampa Business and Professional Women's Club, the Tampa *Tribune,* the DAR, the United Daughters of the Confederacy, the Tampa Civic Association, and the Hillsborough County superintendent of schools. Also includes Tampa *Tribune* clippings about Jackson and her family.

2,956. Simmons Family
Papers. 1772-1942. 5 Hollinger boxes.
Open. Card catalog and index.
University of South Florida Library, Special Collections.
Correspondence, legal and business records, and portions of copybooks of the Simmonses, a family of plantation owners. Material related to women includes correspondence of Mary L. Simmons and other female family members and business records and documents signed and attested by women.

GEORGIA

ATHENS

2,957. Abby, Miss
Papers. 1864. 2 items.
Open. Unpublished guide.
University of Georgia, Special Collections.
Journal written from New Year's Day to July 1864, by [Miss] Abby, an ardent Union sympathizer who lived near Atlanta.

2,958. Akehurst and Lines
Papers. 1850-1914. 483 items.
Open. Unpublished guide.
University of Georgia, Special Collections.
Correspondence, diaries, and photos of the families of Jennie Akehurst and Sylvanus Lines. Includes letters of Daisy Lines, daughter of Jennie and Sylvanus Lines, and a Civil War diary of Jennie Lines.

2,959. American Association of University Women, Athens Branch
Records. 1945-54. 66 items.
Open. Unpublished guide.
University of Georgia, Special Collections.
The Athens branch of the AAUW was formed in 1924. Minutes, committee reports, correspondence, programs, yearbooks, clippings, and other records include bylaws of the AAUW's Georgia division, memorials, maps of Georgia showing the location of women 25 years or older who completed four or more years of college, and Athens branch membership lists.

2,960. American National Red Cross, Athens Chapter, Nutrition Committee Chairman
Records. 1947-48. 11 items.
Open. Unpublished guide.
University of Georgia, Special Collections.
Correspondence, booklets, and other material of the Committee chaired by [Miss] Catherine Newton.

2,961. Athens Ladies Memorial Association, Objects of Association
Records. Ca. 1867-68. 1 item.
Open. Unpublished guide.
University of Georgia, Special Collections.
Manuscript lists the goals of the Association, which was organized shortly after the Civil War to perpetuate the memory of those "who fell in Southern defense" and to raise memorials to the Confederate dead.

2,962. Athens Social and Cultural Events
Collection. 1860-1947. 42 items.
Open. Unpublished guide.
University of Georgia, Special Collections.
Correspondence, invitations, programs, broadsides, and clippings pertain to Athens and the University of Georgia and include a letter from "Jennie" to Mrs. R. J. Wilson regarding weddings in Athens in 1882, a letter from "Miss Mollie" to John Carithers in 1887, and a wedding invitation for Henry W. Grady and Julia King. The letter from "Miss Mollie" was a teacher's letter to a child.

2,963. Atkisson, George Baber
Papers. 1851-1914. 84 items.
Open. Unpublished guide.
University of Georgia, Special Collections.
Correspondence, essays, poems, photos, daguerreotypes, scrapbook material, deeds, drawings, programs, and clippings pertain to the family, life, and interests of Atkisson, a physician. Included are letters to [Miss] Fannie Atkisson, photos of Frances Ann Harden Atkisson and 10 sketches by her, and pictures of other family members, among them Eva and Anne Atkisson.

2,964. Atlanta Typographical Union No. 48, Women's Auxiliary
Records. 1899-1934. 10 items.
Open. Unpublished guide.
University of Georgia, Special Collections.
Minute books, including minutes of the Auxiliary's organizational meetings in 1899; membership rolls; committee reports; and information about reaction to the group's activities, which included cooking schools, labor conferences, and social events.

2,965. Baber and Blackshear
Papers. 1796-1939. 3216 items.
Open. Unpublished guide.
University of Georgia, Special Collections.
Correspondence, journals, ledgers, account books, family papers, invitations, newspapers, clippings, and other papers pertaining to this Macon, GA, family, principally the male descendants of Ambrose Baber (1793-1846), a physician and US ambassador to Sardinia. Includes letters from [Madame] Sophie Sosnowski, [Miss] Callie Sosnowski, and [Miss] Fannie Atkisson.

2,966. Barnsley, Godfrey: B. F. A. Saylor Division
Papers. 1878-1930s. 13,761 items.
Open. Unpublished guide.
University of Georgia, Special Collections.
Business and personal correspondence, letter and account books, ledgers, deeds, promotional literature, and house plans pertain to the descendants and property of Barnsley (1805-72), an English consul in Savannah, GA, and agent for traders in Liverpool, England. Included are letters of his daughter Julia (Barnsley) Baltzelle and her daughter Adelaide (Baltzelle) Saylor.

2,967. Barrow, Colonel David Crenshaw
Papers. 1817-1915. 3886 items.
Open. Unpublished guide.
University of Georgia, Special Collections.
Business and social correspondence, Civil War letters, diaries, overseer's correspondence and records, plantation and church records, account books, bills, receipts, and deeds of the Barrow family. Includes letters of Lucy, Clara, and Ella Barrow.

2,968. Bates, Lucy
Papers. 1911-69. 892 items.
Open. Unpublished guide.
University of Georgia, Special Collections.
Correspondence, diaries, photos, scrapbook, post cards, programs, and articles of Bates. Includes programs of plays, concerts, operas, and recitals in New York and other places from 1906 to 1923 and in 1938. The programs describe performances of such artists as Maude Adams, Julia Marlowe, Ethel Barrymore, Geraldine Farrar, Emma Eames, Emmy Destinn, Margarete Motzenauer, Frances Alda, Amelita Galli-Curci, Maria Jeritza, and Florence Eaton. The collection's dance division includes programs, articles, and photos of such dancers as Fred Astaire and Ginger Rogers, Isadora Duncan, Adeline Genee, Anna Pavlova, Ruth St. Denis, and Mary Wigman.

2,969. Battey, Adrienne
Papers. 1925-29. Ca. 60 items.
Open. Unpublished guide.
University of Georgia, Special Collections.
Correspondence and clippings concern the death of [Miss] Frances Newman (1883-1928), author of *The Hard-Boiled Virgin, Dead Lovers Are Faithful Lovers,* and other works. Correspondents include Hansell Baugh, compiler of Newman's *Letters* (New York, 1929); Winifred Rothermel; Frank Daniel; and Battey, who was Newman's close friend.

2,970. Belt, Elizabeth Talbot
Papers. 1857-?. 4 items.
Open. Unpublished guide.
University of Georgia, Special Collections.
A paper concerning Georgia's readmission to the union by [Mrs.] Belt; an account of the "wreck of the Pulaski" by Rebecca J. (Lamar) McLeod; memorial to Belt, written after 1911; and a 1911 photo of Belt at age 83.

2,971. Bland, Clara Ophelia
Papers. Nd. 1 item.
Open. Unpublished guide.
University of Georgia, Special Collections.
Autograph and verse by Bland of Macon, GA.

2,972. Boardman, Mabel Thorp
Papers. 1916. 1 item.
Open. Unpublished guide.
University of Georgia, Special Collections.
Letter written by [Miss] Boardman (1860-1946) in Quebec, Canada, to John J. Fitzgerald, a member of the US House of Representatives, concerns a proposed tablet for Clara Barton in the Memorial Building to heroic women of the Civil War. Boardman says the American National Red Cross executive committee opposes the plan because it believes Dorothea Dix rendered the greatest service of any woman during the war and because [Miss] Barton allegedly misused Red Cross funds while she was the group's president.

2,973. Bogardus and Allgood Family
Papers. 1800-1944. 189 items.
Open. Unpublished guide.
University of Georgia, Special Collections.
Correspondence, documents, and records of the Bogardus and Allgood families, including correspondence of Margaret Bogardus, her daughter Susan (Bogardus) Farmer (?-1899), Farmer's daughter Susan Allgood (?-1935), and another granddaughter of Margaret Bogardus, Susie M. Wright. Also includes Bogardus's will. Several of the letters written prior to 1870 were by Susan Allgood while she was at a convent school; her later letters, written after her marriage to de Forrest Allgood, were chiefly to her son and mother. Some of the letters were written to Andrew Allgood by young ladies.

2,974. Boston, Mrs. John H.
Papers. Nd. 16 items.
Open. Unpublished guide.
University of Georgia, Special Collections.
Miscellaneous manuscripts, typescripts, and a clipping of Nancy S. (Smith) Boston consist chiefly of her poems, essays, and sketches. The clipping is dated 1934.

2,975. Brown, Alma McLain Coleman
Papers. 1919. 1 vol.
Open. Unpublished guide.
University of Georgia, Special Collections.
Mr. and Mrs. Claud Brown answered an advertisement for a position with [Mrs.] Corra Harris. Diary contains a description of their life with and their opinion of Harris.

2,976. Brown, Joseph Emerson, and Brown, Elizabeth (Grisham)
Papers. 1823-1930. More than 2244 items.
Open. Unpublished guide.
University of Georgia, Special Collections.
Correspondence, notes, speeches, essays, tax receipts, indentures, genealogical material, photos, scrapbooks, clippings, mementos, and other items of Joseph Brown, his wife Elizabeth Brown (1826-96), Joseph M. Brown, Julius L. Brown, Cora Brown, and other family members. Joseph and Elizabeth Brown had two daughters and several granddaughters.

2,977. Brown, Marel
Papers. 1931-68. 7223 items.
Open. Unpublished guide.
University of Georgia, Special Collections.
[Mrs.] Brown is a writer and poet.

Correspondence, manuscripts, poems, photos, scrapbooks, yearbooks, bulletins, articles, clippings, and other papers, including tear sheets of published articles and photos and other items concerning Brown's activities with such groups as the Atlanta Writers' Club, Georgia Writers' Association, Laramore-Rader Poetry Group, Opti-Mrs. Club, the Atlanta branch and nationwide organization of the National League of American Pen Women, Poetry Society of America, Poetry Society of Georgia, Scribblers' Club, and TEL Sunday school. Also contains clippings concerning literary figures.

2,978. Brown, Nathan Atkinson
Papers. 1850s-1936. 58 items.
Open. Unpublished guide.
University of Georgia, Special Collections.
Majority of the collection consists of Civil War correspondence of Confederate captain Nathan Brown with his wife Louisa Nicholia Brown of White Oak Plantation in Camden County, GA.

2,979. Browne, William M.
Papers. 1864-77. 123 items.
Open. Unpublished guide.
University of Georgia, Special Collections.
Browne was a general who lived in Athens. Correspondence, diaries, catalog of books in Browne's library, post card, and clipping. Includes a letter from John A. Cobb to Browne inviting him to a "family breakfast" before the wedding of Ella Barrow, the sister of Cobb's wife Lucy (Barrow) Cobb, and Bourke Spalding; a letter to Browne from Mary McK. Cobb, the wife of Howell Cobb, Jr.; and [Mrs.] Eliza Jane Brown's obituary from a Memphis newspaper.

2,980. Bruce, Robert E., and Bruce, Annie J.
Papers. 1869-72. 13 items.
Open. Unpublished guide.
University of Georgia, Special Collections.
Correspondence of Robert Bruce, a student at University High School and the University of Georgia, with his sister Annie Bruce, who apparently was teaching school in Lowndesville, SC.

2,981. Bryan, Mary Givens
Papers. 1953-66. More than 67 items.
Open. Unpublished guide.
University of Georgia, Special Collections.
A librarian and archivist, Bryan (1910-64) was director of the Georgia department of archives and history. Correspondence, notes, cards, and clippings; the correspondence deals principally with reference questions and business between the state archives department and the University of Georgia Special Collections Department. Also includes a few personal notes.

2,982. Bulloch, Emma Hamilton
Papers. Nd. 1 item.
Open. Unpublished guide.
University of Georgia, Special Collections.
Bulloch was a Georgia lyric poet who published *The Marshes of Georgia and Other Poems* (Washington, DC: W. F. Roberts Company, 1913). Galley proofs containing corrections and notations of an earlier manuscript "Poems."

2,983. Callaway, Morgan, and Callaway, Leila
Papers. 1850-64. 99 items.
Open. Unpublished guide.
University of Georgia, Special Collections.
Correspondence, consisting almost entirely of Civil War letters between Morgan Callaway, a chaplain, and his wife Leila (Hinton) Callaway. In her letters she asks about the purchase of a home and discusses their children and families, her teaching duties and pupils, and the birth of their fourth child in late 1862. Morgan Callaway's letters relate news of the war, sermons he preached, and dress of Richmond, VA, ladies. He also chides his wife for her continued pleas that he return home.

2,984. Camak
Papers. Ca. 1817-1947. Ca. 5000 items.
Open. Unpublished guide.
University of Georgia, Special Collections.
Business and personal correspondence, genealogical material, photos, post cards, invitations, recipes, valentines, and other papers chiefly pertain to descendants of James A. Camak, a founder and first president of the Georgia Railroad. Bulk of the collection is business and personal correspondence of his daughter-in-law [Mrs.] Mary W. Camak and her son Louis. Also includes Mary Camak's correspondence with Thomas E. Watson.

2,985. Campbell, John Archibald
Papers. 1842-85. 3 items.
Open. Unpublished guide.
University of Georgia, Special Collections.
Letters from Judge Campbell to his sister [Mrs.] Rebecca A. Butler of Macon, GA, in which he gives her advice and news of his apparently deteriorating health. The third document, dated 1843, is a record of a deed of a gift of slaves from Campbell to Butler, in which he gives permission to hire out the slaves.

2,986. Carlton, Newton, and Mell
Papers. 1814-1932. 4230 items.
Open. Unpublished guide.
University of Georgia, Special Collections.
Correspondence, diaries, ledgers, account books, bills, receipts, photos, deeds, invitations, programs, Confederate money, and other papers. Includes fragments of a diary of Elizabeth Ann Espey Carlton, account books of Marian Carlton, and material relating to Georgia State Teachers' College from 1927 to 1932.

2,987. Carver, George Washington
Papers. 1924-43. 18 items.
Access restricted. Unpublished guide.
University of Georgia, Special Collections.
Monthly letters written by Carver to Julia Florida (Collier) [Mrs. Julian] Harris of Columbus, GA.

2,988. Cate, Margaret Davis
Papers. 1938-61. 129 items.
Open. Unpublished guide.
University of Georgia, Special Collections.
Correspondence, programs, cards, clippings, and other papers of [Mrs.] Cate. Includes her letters to University of Georgia Library staff members, letters to Cate from Margaret (Mitchell) Marsh and her husband John Marsh, and research notes of Cate.

2,989. Chandler, Artic, Memorial
Collection. Ca. 1800-67. 12 items.
Open. Unpublished guide.
University of Georgia, Special Collections.
Includes a receipted bill for school expenses for 1815-16 for [Miss] Anna Franklin at Salem Boarding School, a broadside announcing a fair planned by the Ladies Memorial Association of Athens, and a valentine mailed from Augusta, GA, to [Miss] M. O. Yerby, care of [Mrs.] S. H. Yerby of Athens.

2,990. Cheney
Papers. 1887-1956. 688 items.
Open. Unpublished guide.
University of Georgia, Special Collections.
Maude and Frances Cheney were sisters involved in two superior court civil cases. Correspondence, a complaint of police brutality, schoolwork, Clarke County deeds, receipts, photos, scrapbooks, post cards, autograph book, Christmas cards, clippings, and other items concerning the sisters' family. Much of the material relates to the suits in which the sisters were involved.

2,991. Christian Commonwealth
Records. 1896-1900. 54 items.
Open. Unpublished guide.
University of Georgia, Special Collections.
Photos of the Commonwealth, a utopian community of about 300 persons that was located in Commonwealth, GA, between 1896 and 1900. The photos, which belonged to Ralph Albertson, a leader of the community, show such scenes as a July 4th picnic, young people and farm children at play, farm industries and buildings, and work scenes at the sawmill. The community was disbanded because of a typhoid epidemic.

2,992. Cobb, Erwin, and Lamar
Papers. 1796-1928. 17,920 items.
Open. Unpublished guide.
University of Georgia, Special Collections.
Business and social correspondence, notebooks, account books, bills, receipts, tax notices, Civil War order books, legal papers, case books, biographical and genealogical material, photos, scrapbook, mementos, and other items related to four generations of these families. Mary Ann Lamar (1818-99), the daughter of Zachariah Lamar and Mary Ann Robinson Lamar, married Howell Cobb (1815-68) in 1835. The couple had several children, one of whom, Mary Ann Lamar Cobb (1850-1930) married Alexander S. Erwin (1843-1907) in 1872. Includes a garden record and account book that Mary Ann (Lamar) Cobb kept while she and her husband lived in Athens from 1850 to 1858.

2,993. Coleman Family
Papers. 1878-1911. 1515 items.
Open. Unpublished guide.
University of Georgia, Special Collections.
William Lewis Coleman, Jr. (1853-1940) owned a general store and farm in Devereaux in Hancock County, GA. Correspondence, bills, receipts, advertisements, broadsides, brochures, cards, clipping, and other items. Many of the items pertain to operation of Coleman's farm and store and include information about the store's sales. Many of the store's customers were women.

2,994. Coleman, Kenneth, and Temple, Sarah Gober: "Georgia Journeys"
Papers. 1732-81. Ca. 8733 items.
Open. Unpublished guide.
University of Georgia, Special Collections.
[Mrs.] Temple did much of the research and some of the writing for *Georgia Journeys* (1961), a history of life in colonial Georgia; after her death, Coleman completed the research and wrote the book as co-author. Manuscript sheets and note cards assembled for the book.

2,995. Daniel, Frank
Papers. 1927-67. 189 items.
Open. Unpublished guide.
University of Georgia, Special Collections.
Correspondence and other papers relate to such southern and Georgia authors as Susan Myrick, Julia Peterkin, Frances Newman, Flannery O'Connor, and Jeannette Rankin.

2,996. Davis, Varina Anne (Howell)
Papers. 1888. 1 item.
Open. Unpublished guide.
University of Georgia, Special Collections.
Letter from [Mrs. Jefferson] Davis (1826-1906) to [Miss] Eleanor Tschudi of Athens concerns a lock of Jefferson Davis's hair requested by Tschudi. Davis's letter also mentions her daughter's visit to Athens and includes messages to Tschudi from the daughter Winnie Davis (1864-98).

2,997. De Baillou, Katherine Cowen
Papers. 1922-74. 1002 items.
Open. Unpublished guide.
University of Georgia, Special Collections.
Correspondence, cards, sheet music of Paul Bowles, photos, 509 post cards, passport, and printed material of de Baillou. Includes letters she wrote to her parents from France, Sweden, Malaga,

North Africa, Germany, Mexico, and New York detailing her experiences and providing information about social life and political climates in countries she visited. Also includes letters from Richard Curle, first editions of Curle's books autographed for de Baillou, and correspondence from Lilia Kidder and Wolfgang Schoenborn.

2,998. Dearing, Katherine G.
Papers. 1914. 1 item.
Open. Unpublished guide.
University of Georgia, Special Collections.
Notebook kept by Dearing, an Athens resident, during a model sewing class at the State Normal School contains notes and outlines on procedures, stitches, styles, and methods. Also includes samples of cloth and stitches.

2,999. Delony, William Gaston
Papers. 1829-1915. 379 items.
Open. Unpublished guide.
University of Georgia, Special Collections.
Correspondence, genealogical material, legal documents, newspapers, and a book of the Delony, Huguenin, and Baker families. Bulk of papers consists of Civil War letters of Colonel William Gaston Delony and his wife Rosa Huguenin Delony.

3,000. Dern, Peggy Gaddis
Papers. Ca. 1944-68. 98 items.
Open. Unpublished guide.
University of Georgia, Special Collections.
[Mrs.] Dern (1895-1966) was an actress, scenario writer, and novelist. Correspondence, completed novels, outlines for novels, novelettes and short stories, contracts for books, biographical information, book lists, and manuscripts of other authors, including Adelaide Humphries and Peter Gorman. Dern published more than 300 book-length romances, about 25 percent of which were nurse stories. Many of the stories had Georgia settings. She wrote under various pseudonyms: Peggy Gaddis, Georgia Craig, Perry Lindsay, Gail Jordan, Roberta Courtland, and Joan Sherman.

3,001. Diamond, James, Family
Papers. 1831-91. 149 items.
Open. Unpublished guide.
University of Georgia, Special Collections.
Correspondence, travel account, and a newspaper of the family of James and Nancy Cornwell Diamond of DeKalb County, GA. Letters of such female family members as Catherine Diamond Crow, Nancy Jane Diamond, Lizzie Towles Diamond, Rebecca Diamond Burton, Sallie and Emma Diamond, Amanda J. Diamond, and Nancy Cornwell Diamond make up the bulk of the collection.

3,002. Elbert County Documents
Records. 1836-80. 9 items.
Open. Unpublished guide.
University of Georgia, Special Collections.
Documents include a letter written in 1877 by Alice Ann Mildred Deadwyler to her husband and children concerning disposal of her property after her death and an indenture, dated 1880, between [Mrs.] Mary Gaines, Wiley S. Gaines, and Deadwyler. The indenture pertains to the sale of land by the Gaineses to Deadwyler.

3,003. Enters, Angna
Papers. 1968. 4 items.
Open. Unpublished guide.
University of Georgia, Special Collections.
Note to [Miss] Lucy Bates regarding a Christmas card she is sending to [Miss] Enters; a card made and autographed by Enters; and biographical sketches about Enters from *The Biographical Encyclopedia* and *Who's Who of the American Theatre.*

3,004. Ethridge, Willie Snow: Summer Thunder
Papers. Ca. 1959. 1 vol.
Open. Unpublished guide.
University of Georgia, Special Collections.
Ethridge was an author. Uncorrected proofs of *Summer Thunder* (New York: Coward-McCann, Inc., 1959).

3,005. Evans, Louise
Papers. 1861. 1 item.
Open. Unpublished guide.
University of Georgia, Special Collections.
A social letter from "Eugenia T." at Buena Vista, GA, to "Dear Sallie." The writer and recipient of the letter donated by [Miss] Evans are unknown.

3,006. Family Visitor Office
Records. 1849-56. 1 item.
Open. Unpublished guide.
University of Georgia, Special Collections.
Manuscript daybook of the office of *Family Visitor,* a Madison, GA, magazine edited by [Miss] C. W. Barber, a Massachusetts native, and then by Charles L. Wheler. Accounts for the magazine run through 1850; the remaining material consists of personal accounts and notes from 1856.

3,007. Farrow, Henry Patillo
Papers. 1855-1937. 4413 items.
Open. Unpublished guide.
University of Georgia, Special Collections.
Correspondence, memoranda, ledgers, account books, bills, receipts, hotel registers, employee books, photos, broadsides, pamphlets, newspapers, clippings, and other items of Farrow, owner of a Porter Springs, GA, hotel and a leading Georgia Republican during Reconstruction. Includes letters from Rebecca Latimer Felton and her husband William H. Felton, a physician and clergyman.

3,008. Felton, Rebecca Ann (Latimer)
Papers. 1851-1930. 4817 items.
Open. Unpublished guide.
University of Georgia, Special Collections.
The first woman to serve in the US Senate, Felton (1835-1930) was a writer, speaker, educator, pioneer in temperance movements, and an advocate of women's suffrage and penal reform. Correspondence, speeches, manuscripts of articles, bills, receipts, tax assessments and returns, canceled checks, photos, scrapbooks, sheet music, greeting cards, and clippings concern Georgia politics, particularly her controversies with John B. Gordon, Benjamin Harvey Hill, Joseph E. Brown, and Alexander H. Stephens. Material also reflects her opposition to the convict lease system, her interest in and writings on education, and her ideas on religion and banking laws. A Cartersville, GA, resident, Felton became a US senator in 1922. She was the wife of William Harrell Felton, a physician, clergyman, and member of the US Congress and Georgia legislature.

3,009. Floyd, Dolores Boisfeuillet
Papers. 1962. 1 item.
Open. Unpublished guide.
University of Georgia, Special Collections.
Copy of "Little Toona-how-i and His Big Gold Watch, A Story of Colonial Days in Georgia," by Floyd, a Savannah, GA, author.

3,010. Forbes, Walter Tillou, I
Papers. 1908-67. 253 items.
Open. Unpublished guide.
University of Georgia, Special Collections.
Correspondence, photos, marriage certificate, and clippings pertain to Forbes's daughter Helen Forbes and to the work of the WCTU. Helen Forbes married E. A. Ross.

3,011. Franklin, Mary
Papers. Nd. 6 items.
Open. Unpublished guide.
University of Georgia, Special Collections.
Notes about Athens residents by [Miss] Franklin; her typescript regarding Tunis, Tunisia; her obituary; photos; and other items.

3,012. Gannon, Nell Upshaw
Papers. 1933-73. 52 items.
Open. Unpublished guide.
University of Georgia, Special Collections.
Gannon earned a PhD from the University of California in 1933. Diaries, family budget books, guest lists, menus, clothing chart, commencement programs, and copies of a campus tour Gannon prepared for the University Newcomer's Club. Her diaries provide a social history of the Athens area from the 1930s through the early 1970s and include descriptions of trips to various parts of the US, the World's Fair in Chicago, and a trip to Cuba. Gannon's husband earned a master's degree in 1934.

3,013. Gardner, Thomas J.
Papers. 1900-09. 3 items.
Open. Unpublished guide
University of Georgia, Special Collections.
Letter to Gardner, evidently a Georgia schoolteacher, from S. R. Ellington of Oxford, GA, in which he offers Gardner a teaching job and states that the "female teacher" already hired would take an assistant's place; Gardner's roll book; and a report card for Pauline Rivers from the John Means Institute.

3,014. Garebold, Elizabeth
Papers. 1888-ca. 1889. 18 items.
Open. Unpublished guide.
University of Georgia, Special Collections.
Garebold was the daughter of John A. Garebold. Her papers include a letter and verse of a poem to a "Mr. H.," asking his opinion of her songs; words and music for the song "Garden of Memories"; poems; and a sketchbook of European scenes of 1888 and 1889.

3,015. Georgia Female College
Papers. 1854. 1 item.
Open. Unpublished guide.
University of Georgia, Special Collections.
Letter on college stationery from "Ann Eliza" in Madison, GA, to a male friend includes school and family news.

3,016. Georgia Miscellaneous
Collection. 1812-89. 8 items.
Open. Unpublished guide.
University of Georgia, Special Collections.
Includes an undated poem "To a Lady by a Female Maniac."

3,017. Greensboro, GA
Collection. 1886. 9 items.
Open. Unpublished guide.
University of Georgia, Special Collections.
Manuscript of items copied from the *Georgia Home Journal* by Margaret (Adams) [Mrs. Leroy] Hart, who originally was from Union Point, GA. Most of the items are social notes, while others are poems and meeting notices.

3,018. Grogan, Elmira: Memoir of Mrs. Edward T. Brown
Papers. Nd. 13 pp.
Open. Unpublished guide.
University of Georgia, Special Collections.
Memoir by [Miss] Grogan about Mary Celestine Mitchell [Mrs. Edward T.] Brown and a pamphlet copy of a speech made by Brown.

3,019. Hall, Gertrude
Papers. 1911-62. 3877 pp.
Open. Unpublished guide.
University of Georgia, Special Collections.
Hall, an author, was the sister of Grace Hall and wife of William Crary Brownell. Correspondence,

notes, notebooks, manuscripts of novels, short stories, plays, poems, articles, essays, photos, a scrapbook, clippings, and other papers, including letters by Hall's husband and Hall's letters to Virginia Hale.

3,020. Hall, Grace
Papers. Ca. 1912-44. 824 pp.
Open. Unpublished guide.
University of Georgia, Special Collections.
Hall, the sister of Gertrude Hall, was an author. Manuscripts of books, plays, short stories, poems, and essays by Grace Hall make up the bulk of the collection, which also includes a short story by female writer George (Madden) Martin, a letter from Hall's husband Edwin Howland Blashfield to [Miss] Lucy Bates, biographical notes, other papers pertaining to Blashfield, and a baptismal certificate.

3,021. Hancock, Joy Bright
Papers. 1918-72. 2529 items.
Open. Unpublished guide.
University of Georgia, Special Collections.
Hancock, a captain in the US Navy, was the ranking officer in the WAVES during and after WWII; she served as a yeoman in WWI. Correspondence, speeches, manuscripts, biographical material, photos, scrapbooks, articles, and citations. Includes articles by and about Hancock and versions, from rough draft to final galleys, of her book *Lady in the Navy*. Correspondents include Bess Truman, US senator Margaret Chase Smith, Secretary of the Navy Frank Knox, Admiral Nimitz, Anna Rosenberg, Margaret Chung, and other persons in government and armed forces.

3,022. Hancock, Joy Bright: Edith Langdale Stallings
Papers. 1943-62. 152 items.
Open. Unpublished guide.
University of Georgia, Special Collections.
Correspondence, pamphlets, and clippings concerning [Mrs.] Stallings's career in the WAVES and the Navy. She attained the rank of commander before retiring to become dean of women at the University of Georgia. Hancock was Stallings's friend and commanding officer.

3,023. Hankinson
Papers. 1824-1902. Ca. 25 items.
Open. Unpublished guide.
University of Georgia, Special Collections.
Legal papers pertaining to the family of Stephen Hankinson and his wife Mary C. Speights Hankinson; a letter, dated 1902, from Mrs. Pope McWhorter to [Miss] Corneille Schiefflin regarding family news; a scrapbook of clippings; herbarium; autograph book; and a miniature book *The Language of Flowers,* which belonged to Marie Essie Hankinson.

3,024. Harden, Jackson, and Carithers
Papers. 1779-1963. 2782 items.
Open. Unpublished guide.
University of Georgia, Special Collections.
Correspondence, including church letters; diaries; ledgers, bills, and receipts; accounts; photos; scrapbooks; deeds; music; clippings; and other papers pertain chiefly to the families of General Edward Harden (1784-1849); his daughter Mary Elisa Greenhill Harden (1811-87), who is described as the "sweetheart of John Howard Payne"; his great-niece Eveline Harden Jackson (1848-1928); and his great-great-niece Elizabeth Carithers (1874-?). Also includes material concerning the Lucy Cobb Institute in Athens. The items reflect the social history of Georgia's Piedmont region.

3,025. Harden, William, and Harden, Nell
Papers. 1826-1936. 970 items.
Open. Unpublished guide.
University of Georgia, Special Collections.
Correspondence, speeches, notes, family records, mementos, clippings, and other items of the Harden, Maxwell, Baker, King, and related families. Includes a letter from Caroline Miller.

3,026. Harman, Hattie
Papers. 1855-57. 23 items.
Open. Unpublished guide.
University of Georgia, Special Collections.
Letters from Hattie L. Harman in Georgia and Alabama to her cousin Annie Carleton, who lived on a plantation near Jeffersonville, GA. Several of Harman's letters were written from Forsyth, GA, before her move to Notasulga and Loachapoka, AL; the letters discuss family matters and describe her lifestyle and her reactions to westward migration. Also contains information about courses and activities at a female seminary, college experiences, and other topics related to education.

3,027. Harmon, Selene Armstrong
Papers. Ca. 1898-1926. 309 items.
Open. Unpublished guide.
University of Georgia, Special Collections.
Harmon was a feature writer for the *Washington Times* and, later, a free-lance writer for magazines and newspapers. Correspondence, articles, manuscripts, biographical information, photos, scrapbook, clippings, and printed material. Included are articles about notable women in Washington, DC, during the Taft and Wilson administrations and a series about the "St. Nicholas Girl" program sponsored by the *Times* in 1910. The program featured Harmon, then [Miss] Armstrong, as the St. Nicholas Girl who collected and distributed Christmas toys for poor children.

3,028. Harris, Corra May (White)
Papers. 1906-44. 39,682 items.
Open. Unpublished guide.
University of Georgia, Special Collections.
A Georgia author, Harris (1869-1935) was the wife of Lundy Howard Harris. Correspondence, manuscripts of books and articles, contracts, canceled checks, photos, clippings, and other items. Includes correspondence from Gertrude Atherton, Caroline Miller, Ruth (Bryan) Owen, Julia Peterkin, and Mary Pickford as well as from Harris's husband, her daughter Faith (Harris) Leech, Faith Leech's husband Harry Leech, and Bettie and Trainie Raines.

3,029. Harris, Mrs. Arthur
Papers. 1951. 1 item.
Open. Unpublished guide.
University of Georgia, Special Collections.
Letter from "Rose" to Harris relates events in the Atlanta area.

3,030. Harris, Safford
Papers. 1859-1938. 822 items.
Open. Unpublished guide.
University of Georgia, Special Collections.
Correspondence; financial records, including canceled checks, bankbooks, and tax receipts; legal documents, including indentures, deeds, and notes; poems; recipes; pamphlets; broadsides; mementos; clippings; and other items of the Wray family of Wrayswood in Greene County, GA, and Athens and the family of C. W. Harris and [Miss] Sarah H. Harris of Winterville, Wrayswood, Madison, and Athens.

3,031. Hatton and Lovejoy
Papers. 1833-87. 1 item.
Open. Unpublished guide.
University of Georgia, Special Collections.
"Memoirs of My Mother and Her Family," memoirs by an unknown author, concern the Hatton and Lovejoy families. The narrative begins with the arrival of the writer's great-grandfather Hatton in Meriwether County, GA, in 1833. The great-grandfather had moved his family and slaves from Newberry District in South Carolina. The narrative follows the family from Greenville, GA, to Atlanta, Oxford, Clarkston, and Lovejoy's Crossing and includes mention of prominent persons and events of the mid-19th century.

3,032. Hazelrigg
Papers. 1862-69. 29 items.
Open. Unpublished guide.
University of Georgia, Special Collections.
Correspondence, stock certificates, Confederate money, and clippings include one letter from [Mrs.] Marie Allen to P. H. Mell asking help in securing a teaching position.

3,033. Head
Papers. 1858-1917. 57 items.
Open. Unpublished guide.
University of Georgia, Special Collections.
Correspondence and receipted bills, including a letter, dated 1861, from Virginia Holliday in Fulton County, GA, to her parents concerning family news. Most of the bills are from Athens merchants to Howell P. Betts or [Mrs.] Lula Betts; also includes tax receipts for Mrs. Lula Betts and Howell P. Betts for 1917 and notes and mortgages for property apparently rented by Howell P. Betts from [Mrs.] Mattie Whitehead.

3,034. Henslee, Mrs. E. P.
Papers. 1865. 1 item.
Open. Unpublished guide.
University of Georgia, Special Collections.
Personal letter from Henslee to her husband includes comments on the revival in Georgia.

3,035. Hillyer
Papers. 1805-74. 3 items.
Open. Unpublished guide.
University of Georgia, Special Collections.
Manuscript books and notes include a memoir by Judge Junius Hillyer (1807-86), which contains a chapter about his parents and one about his grandmother.

3,036. Hillyer, Mrs. John Freeman: Account of Trip to Texas
Papers. 1847-49. 3 pp.
Open. Unpublished guide.
University of Georgia, Special Collections.
An account, apparently taken from a diary kept during the Hillyer family's trip to Texas; the family lived in Galveston for a time before moving on to Goliad. John Hillyer evidently was a preacher.

3,037. Hine, Lewis W.: Photographic Study of Child Labor in Georgia
Collection. 1909-13. 126 items.
Open. Unpublished guide.
University of Georgia, Special Collections.
Photos taken for the National Child Labor Committee portray child labor in Augusta, Columbus, LaFayette, LaGrange, Lindale, Macon, Rome, Rossville, Tifton, and Valdosta, GA. Includes portraits of mill children, spinners, doffers, and meal toters at their work and grouped before the mills. A few photos show the shanty towns surrounding the mills. Also includes copies of Hine's comments on each photo.

3,038. Hiram, Ida Mae Johnson
Papers. 1910-65. 89 pp.
Open. Unpublished guide.
University of Georgia, Special Collections.
Articles by Hiram, the first Negro woman dentist in Georgia, and photos. The articles include items about dentistry and its relation to general health, the African Methodist Episcopal Church, Christianity, and Sunday school topics. Hiram practiced dentistry in Athens from 1910 to 1965.

3,039. Holt, Narcissa Boykin
Papers. 1854-88. 9 items.
Open. Unpublished guide.
University of Georgia, Special Collections.
Contains letters to Holt of Eatonton, GA, and

Shelby County, AL, that include information about the Presbyterian Manual Training Institute, a Gwinnett County, GA, boys school.

3,040. Howell, Jennie Wright
Papers. 1933. 8 items.
Open. Unpublished guide.
University of Georgia, Special Collections.
Letters to [Miss] Johnnie Peterson regarding [Mrs.] Howell's poems and manuscript copies of Howell's poems "To a Mother Bird" and "Black Mammy."

3,041. Hunt, Sarah
Papers. 1862. 1 item.
Open. Unpublished guide.
University of Georgia, Special Collections.
Letter from Hunt at Piedmont, GA, to her son in which she encloses money and offers financial advice. Commenting on the Civil War, she says, "This war is a terrible affair on Mothers."

3,042. Jefferson County Schools
Records. 1870-81. 1015 items.
Open. Unpublished guide.
University of Georgia, Special Collections.
Annual reports, teachers' reports, salary account, vouchers, correspondence, school roll registers, teachers' licenses and contracts, and printed items provide a record of the County's school professionals and their activities. Included are letters from state and county school commissioners.

3,043. Johnston, Marcus
Papers. 1837-61. 12 items.
Open. Unpublished guide.
University of Georgia, Special Collections.
Correspondence, lists, and accounts regarding property of Marcus Johnston, the brother of Georgia author Richard Malcolm Johnston, and his wife, the former [Mrs.] Elizabeth Pendergrass. Includes correspondence regarding the sale of slaves and property, part of Johnston's account book, a notebook concerning the S. Pendergrass estate, and the will of Elizabeth Pendergrass Johnston.

3,044. Jones, Charles Colcock, Jr.
Papers. 1749-1909. 2433 items.
Open. Unpublished guide.
University of Georgia, Special Collections.
Correspondence, documents, and other papers of Charles Colcock Jones, Sr. (1804-63), and his wife Mary Sharpe (Jones) Jones (1808-69) of Liberty County, GA, and of their son Charles Colcock Jones, Jr. (1831-93).

3,045. Jones, Elissa W.
Papers. 1834-75. 10 items.
Open. Unpublished guide.
University of Georgia, Special Collections.
Correspondence consists primarily of letters to female members of the John T. Grant family including Mrs. John T. Grant and Mrs. W. D. Grant, both of whom lived in the Atlanta area, and two letters to Mrs. W. D. Grant from her grandfather W. H. Jackson.

3,046. King, Julia
Papers. 1930-41. 18 items.
Open. Unpublished guide.
University of Georgia, Special Collections.
Letters from [Miss] King of Colonel's Island to Mr. and Mrs. Victor Bassett of Savannah, GA, and to [Mrs.] Margaret D. Cate deals with the King family and its property. Also contains biographical, historical, and genealogical information concerning Georgia families.

3,047. Kinsland, Mary
Papers. 1863. 1 item.
Open. Unpublished guide.
University of Georgia, Special Collections.
Letter from Kinsland to her husband Joshua Kinsland describes home life in Haywood County, NC, during the Civil War.

3,048. Kollock
Papers. 1815-89. 134 items.
Open. Unpublished guide.
University of Georgia, Special Collections.
Correspondence, largely of a family nature, of members of this Savannah, GA, family. One of the letters was published in Susan M. Kollock, "Letters of the Kollock and Allied Families, 1826-1884," *Georgia Historical Quarterly,* vols. 30-35.

3,049. Ladies Benevolent and Missionary Society of the Presbyterian Church
Records. 1883-90s. 1 vol.
Open. Unpublished guide.
University of Georgia, Special Collections.
Volume contains this local Society's constitution, minutes, correspondence, notes, membership roll, clippings, an 1892 wedding invitation, and resolutions passed following the death of Mrs. F. W. Lucas.

3,050. Ladies Garden Club
Records. 1894-1973. 832 items.
Open. Unpublished guide.
University of Georgia, Special Collections.
Correspondence, photos, scrapbooks, booklets, programs, certificates, a map, ribbons, clippings, and other records pertain to the history and activities of this state organization, which was America's first garden club. The group's headquarters are in Atlanta. Material relates to markers, Founders Memorial Garden, the Club's cemetery projects, and a "Floral Menagerie" flower show. Also includes executive board minutes and other records of the Garden Club of Georgia and issues of *Garden Gateways.*

3,051. Langdon
Papers. 1838-64. 5 items.
Open. Unpublished guide.
University of Georgia, Special Collections.
Papers of this Augusta, GA, family include a letter from Thomas W. Cumming to his cousin [Miss] Sarah W. Cumming, written while he was aboard the *USS Relief* at Hampton Roads, VA, in 1838; a Civil War era letter from P. H. Langdon to his fiancée; and an inventory of the estate of Elizabeth Sewall of York, SC.

3,052. Linton
Papers. 1784-1873. 21 items.
Open. Unpublished guide.
University of Georgia, Special Collections.
Correspondence, explanatory notes, indenture, articles, and clippings, including letters from William Henry Waddell to Julia Hull, letter to Lucy Ann Hull Linton from John S. Linton in New York and a letter from John Linton in Boston to "My Dear Annie." The final letter was reprinted in *Cotton History Review* (April 1960).

3,053. Lipscomb Hall, The Honor Dormitory
Records. 1967-68. 3 items.
Open. Unpublished guide.
University of Georgia, Special Collections.
Scrapbook compiled by [Mrs.] Alice Kirkpatrick, the dormitory housemother, contains a constitution, correspondence, notices, rules, photos, programs, clippings, and other material relating to the 1967-68 school year. Also includes the last "Best-Dressed" plaque awarded at the University.

3,054. Long, Crawford W., Family
Papers. 1842-1939. 381 items.
Open. Unpublished guide.
University of Georgia, Special Collections.
Correspondence, bills and receipts, account book, genealogical material, photos, scrapbooks, clippings, and miscellany pertain to Long, a surgeon; his family; his discovery of ether anesthesia; and his death. Included are love letters from Long to his future wife and several letters to Crawford Long's daughter Frances "Fannie" Long from her mother after her husband's death. The genealogical material concerns the McKinne, Aycock, Lane, Swain, Ware, Long, Taylor, and allied families.

3,055. Lucy Cobb Institute
Records. 1800s-1958. No size given.
Open. Unpublished guide.
University of Georgia, Special Collections.
Minute books, correspondence, school papers, programs, photos, brochures, announcements, broadsides, invitation, promotional material, mementos, and clippings of the Institute, a private girls school in Athens from 1858 to 1931. Includes a photo album kept by Ellen Wolff in 1914.

3,056. Lumpkin Family
Papers. Nd. 15 items.
Open. Unpublished guide.
University of Georgia, Special Collections.
Correspondence, bill and receipt for Martha Lumpkin's funeral, copy of Martha Lumpkin's will, deeds, and other items concerning the Lumpkin family.

3,057. Lumpkin, Joseph Henry
Papers. 1748-1919. 715 items.
Open. Unpublished guide.
University of Georgia, Special Collections.
Correspondence, diaries, bills and receipts, legal documents, maps, broadsides, and newspapers relate to Lumpkin and his family. Henrietta Whitney was among the correspondents.

3,058. Lumpkin, Wilson
Papers. 1828-58. 46 items.
Open. Unpublished guide.
University of Georgia, Special Collections.
Correspondence, diary, and a broadside of Lumpkin and his family contain a letter from Martha Wilson Lumpkin Compton to Chancellor D. C. Barrow of the University of Georgia.

3,059. McCullers, Carson: "The Heart Is a Lonely Hunter"
Papers. Nd. 1 vol.
Open. Unpublished guide.
University of Georgia, Special Collections.
Script of the screenplay made from Carson Smith McCullers's *The Heart Is a Lonely Hunter* (New York: Houghton-Mifflin, 1951).

3,060. Mackintosh Family
Papers. 1792-1860. 10 pp.
Open. Unpublished guide.
University of Georgia, Special Collections.
Letters of the Mackintosh family and of Robert Toombs and Young L. G. Harris, all copied and annotated by Annie Cassandra Mackintosh Wall.

3,061. Macon, Jane
Papers. 1925-55. 3 items.
Open. Unpublished guide.
University of Georgia, Special Collections.
Correspondence, including that regarding [Miss] Macon's diploma and her examination in English, her minor field; photos; clippings; and other papers.

3,062. Miles, Emily Winthrop
Papers. Nd. 53 items.
Open. Unpublished guide.
University of Georgia, Special Collections.
Biographical material; photos, including those of [Mrs.] Miles and her property in Sharon, CT, now called the Miles Wild Life Sanctuary of the Audubon Society; photo files of animals, ceramics, designs, landscapes, seashells, and silhouettes; sculpture by Miles; and lists of books.

3,063. Miller, Caroline
Papers. 1933. 1 item.
Open. Unpublished guide.

University of Georgia, Special Collections.
Letter from [Mrs.] Miller in Baxley, GA, to Duncan Burnet of the University of Georgia Library concerning her book *Lamb in His Bosom.*

3,064. Mitchell, Margaret
Papers. 1943. 2 items.
Open. Unpublished guide.
University of Georgia, Special Collections.
Letter from Mitchell to [Miss] Norene Holliday regarding a copy of the French translation of *Gone With The Wind.*

3,065. Mitchell, Margaret
Papers. Ca. 1905- . More than 57,178 items.
Access restricted. Unpublished guide.
University of Georgia, Special Collections.
Author of *Gone With The Wind,* Margaret (Mitchell) Marsh (1900-49) used her maiden name in her work. Correspondence makes up the bulk of the collection, which principally concerns publication of *Gone With The Wind,* the aftermath of the publication, and production of the film version. Included are letters from literary figures of the 1930s and 1940s, including Eudora Welty, Willie Snow Ethridge, and Medora Perkerson and from other prominent southerners. The correspondence includes groupings related to Negro and general correspondence and domestic and foreign fan mail. Also includes family letters and history, condolences, and other items, such as papers of [Miss] Susan Myrick, a longtime friend of Marsh, whose script for the *Gone With The Wind* film is included. Marsh's first husband was Berrien K. Upshaw; she was married to John Robert Marsh at the time of her death.

3,066. Myers, Jennie Belle: Memorial Fund
Records. 1950. 12 items.
Open. Unpublished guide.
University of Georgia, Special Collections.
Correspondence and other material concerning establishment of a scholarship fund created in memory of [Mrs.] Myers (?-1950), a housemother and later head of all women's dormitories at the University of Georgia. She served in housing administration positions at the University from 1924 until her death; her first job was as social director of the school's first women's dormitory.

3,067. Myrick, Susan
Papers. 1937-39. 25 items.
Open. Unpublished guide.
University of Georgia, Special Collections.
Correspondence between [Miss] Myrick and Margaret (Mitchell) Marsh concerning the movie production of *Gone With The Wind.* Most of the letters were addressed to Myrick while she was in Hollywood, CA, working as a technical advisor on the film.

3,068. Noyes School of Rhythm
Records. 1913- . No size given.
Open. Unpublished guide.
University of Georgia, Special Collections.
Correspondence, folders, photos, newsletters, leaflets, posters, articles, clippings, and other material concern winter classes at the School and the institution's summer camp for adults and children. Many of the school's teachers and students were women. The material is included in the papers of Lucy Bates: Dance Division.

3,069. Parr, Charles D.
Papers. 1850. 1 item.
Open. Unpublished guide.
University of Georgia, Special Collections.
Letter from Parr in Atlanta to four ladies who applied for a charter for a Daughters of Temperance chapter provides information about temperance in Georgia.

3,070. Perkerson, Medora Field
Papers. 1914-60. 3015 items.
Open. Unpublished guide.
University of Georgia, Special Collections.
Perkerson (1892-1960) was an author and journalist. Correspondence, writings, speeches, typescripts of books, biographical and genealogical material, photos, autographs, clippings, and other items pertain to the work of Perkerson and her husband Angus Perkerson. Includes letters exchanged by the couple and items concerning her column "Marie Rose"; her books *Blood on Her Shoes, Who Killed Aunt Maggie?,* and *White Columns in Georgia;* Margaret Mitchell; and *Gone With The Wind.*

3,071. Peterson, Johnnie Inez
Papers. 1933-42. 330 items.
Open. Unpublished guide.
University of Georgia, Special Collections.
Manuscripts by and about Georgia authors and others, photos, and clippings. The collection provides biographical material about Martha Berry, Agnes Cochran Bramblett, Annie Johnson Burns, Isa Glenn, Corra Harris, Nelle Womack Hines, Caroline Miller, Minnie Hite Moody, Mrs. Maxfield Parrish, Medora Field Perkerson, Diana Pittman Quarles, Ina Dillard Russell, and Edith Tatus. Women's manuscripts include an autograph and verse of Clara Ophelia Bland and letters and a poem by Jennie Wright Howell.

3,072. Programs
Collection. 1854-1913. 7 items.
Open. Unpublished guide.
University of Georgia, Special Collections.
School programs include three from Georgia Female College in Madison, GA, marking exhibitions and commencement in 1854, and a commencement week program from South Georgia Male and Female College in Dawson, GA, from 1885.

3,073. Radford, Ruby Lorraine
Papers. 1961-69. 21 items.
Open. Unpublished guide.
University of Georgia, Special Collections.
[Miss] Radford, writing under the names Marcia Ford and R. L. Radford, has published 50 books since 1927. Manuscripts of five of her books, including *Juliette Low: Girl Scout Founder* (Champaign, IL: Garrard Publishing Co., 1965), and correspondence concerning them.

3,074. Rankin, Jeannette
Papers. 1917-73. 1 vol. and 16 items.
Open. Unpublished guide.
University of Georgia, Special Collections.
Letters of [Miss] Rankin (1880-1973), many of them to Vernon Edenfield of Millen, GA. Also includes a tape of a 1973 memorial service for Rankin and a scrapbook containing photos, articles, and clippings concerning Rankin, World Peaceways, the National Council for the Prevention of War, and similar organizations.

3,075. Rawlings, Marjorie (Kinnan)
Papers. 1918-63. 243 items.
Open. Unpublished guide.
University of Georgia, Special Collections.
Rawlings (1896-1953) was a novelist. Correspondence; notes; manuscript poems; drafts of *Sojourner* and of "Centennial," apparently an unpublished work by Rawlings; clippings; and published material. Most of the correspondence is between Rawlings and Norman S. Berg of Dunwoody, GA.

3,076. Reed, Eunice Williams
Papers. 1883-1951. 1372 items.
Open. Unpublished guide.
University of Georgia, Special Collections.
Correspondence, speeches, scrapbooks, programs, and other papers primarily concern the tenure of [Mrs. Thomas Walter] Reed as president of the Athens chapter and Georgia division of the United Daughters of the Confederacy and as state chairman of the group's education division. The papers, most of which are from the early 1930s, include material relating to Mildred Rutherford, the Laura Rutherford Chapter of the UDC, the Mrs. L. H. Raines Memorial, and Winnie Davis Hall.

3,077. Reese, Nelle
Papers. 188?-1962. 1270 items.
Open. Unpublished guide.
University of Georgia, Special Collections.
Correspondence; manuscripts of talks and papers given by [Miss] Reese; scrapbooks; mementos; minute books and scrapbooks of University Women's Club at the University of Georgia; and committee reports of Delta Kappa Gamma, an honorary society. Scrapbooks contain material about Corra Harris; old Georgia houses and gardens; the Reese family of Pana, IL; and Walter O. Reese's collection of art work. Manuscripts concern such topics as *Cheaper by the Dozen,* women in Dickens's writings, and the Brownings and George Eliot in Florence, Italy.

3,078. Reeve, Jewell B.
Papers. 1860-1967. 88 items and 2434 pp.
Open. Unpublished guide.
University of Georgia, Special Collections.
The author of two books, [Mrs.] Reeve wrote for the *Calhoun Times* in Calhoun, GA. Speeches; manuscripts of Reeve's *Calhoun Times* stories, which dealt with Gordon County, GA, history and people; copies from manuscript to final print of Reeve's *Climb the Hills of Gordon;* a copy of her other book *A Whimsical Collection;* and clippings.

3,079. Rudulph, Marilou Alston
Papers. 1953-72. 593 items.
Open. Unpublished guide.
University of Georgia, Special Collections.
Papers of [Mrs. Charles Murray] Rudulph, concerning artist George Cooke and her writings about him, include copies of the wills of Cooke and his wife.

3,080. Rutherford, Mildred Lewis
Papers. 1883-1930. 838 items.
Open. Unpublished guide.
University of Georgia, Special Collections.
An Athens educator and writer, [Miss] Rutherford (1851-1928) was principal of the Lucy Cobb Institute, president of the Ladies Memorial Association, historian general of the United Daughters of the Confederacy, and historian for the Georgia UDC. Correspondence, manuscripts, photos, pamphlets, and printed items, including articles and historical writings by Rutherford as well as material relating to the Lucy Cobb Institute, UDC, Children of the Confederacy, and Bible study.

3,081. Screven, Ellen Buchanan
Papers. 1915. 1 item.
Open. Unpublished guide.
University of Georgia, Special Collections.
Autobiography of Screven, written for her daughters, provides an account of life in Annapolis, MD, and Savannah and Athens, GA, and includes some material on the Civil War and Reconstruction.

3,082. Scudder, Nina, Memorial
Papers. 1839-1956. 1738 items.
Open. Unpublished guide.
University of Georgia, Special Collections.
[Miss] Nina Wilkins Scudder (1897-1956) was an Athens artist, art teacher, flower show judge, and garden club lecturer. Correspondence, speeches, biographical records, material concerning flower shows and floral arrangements, drawings, sketches, paintings, articles, and awards. Includes material about the Ladies Garden Club, the first garden club

in America; the Founder's Memorial Garden, a memorial located on the University of Georgia campus that honors the founders of the Ladies Garden Club; the Scudder School of Art; and the Bessie Mell Industrial Home.

3,083. Scudder, Nina, Memorial: Bessie Mell Industrial Home
Records. 1901-30. 31 items.
Open. Unpublished guide.
University of Georgia, Special Collections.
Constitution, bylaws, minute and treasurer's books, bank statements, canceled checks, correspondence, resolutions, contracts, clippings, and other records concern this Athens charitable organization, which sought to provide "aid for the weak and work for the strong." Nina (Wilkins) Scudder, mother of Nina Wilkins Scudder, was an officer of the Home. Founded in 1889, the organization ultimately transferred its building to the YWCA.

3,084. Sears, Zelda, and Wiswell, Louis C.
Papers. 1910-41. 344 items.
Open. Unpublished guide.
University of Georgia, Special Collections.
[Miss] Sears was an actress and playwright while her husband Louis Wiswell was a theatrical manager. Correspondence, notebooks, scripts, photos, scrapbook, and music. Includes scripts written by Sears and letters and telegrams from show business figures, including Billie Burke and Jeanette MacDonald. The scrapbook contains photos, reviews, and clippings, many of them concerning *The Nest Egg,* a successful play in which Sears starred. The notebooks contain anecdotes, jokes, quips, and brief outlines evidently used as background for Sears's plays.

3,085. Sell, Edward S.: History of the State Normal School
Papers. 1923. 141-page item.
Open. Unpublished guide.
University of Georgia, Special Collections.
Typed manuscript with penciled notes of Sell's history of the Athens school.

3,086. Sexton, Margaret Branch
Papers. 1830-1961. 859 items.
Open. Unpublished guide.
University of Georgia, Special Collections.
Correspondence, letter books, rosters of various Georgia companies in the Civil War, photos, scrapbooks, autograph books, broadsides, mementos, newspapers, and other papers concern [Mrs.] Charlotte Sawyer Branch (1814-94), a housewife and volunteer Civil War nurse, and her sons Hamilton McDevitt Branch (1843-99), a Confederate soldier and head of the Central Railroad and Ocean Steamship Company of Savannah, GA; John Lufburrow Branch (1838-61), a Confederate soldier killed at Manassas, VA; and Sanford W. Branch, who also served in the Confederate army. Includes Charlotte Branch's Civil War correspondence with her sons.

3,087. Sibley, Samuel Hale
Papers. Nd. 7-page item.
Open. Unpublished guide.
University of Georgia, Special Collections.
Character sketch and reminiscences by Judge Sibley (1873-1958) concerning his grandmother.

3,088. Slappey, George Hiley, and Slappey, Pansy Aiken
Papers. 1851-1977. Ca. 150 items.
Open. Unpublished guide.
University of Georgia, Special Collections.
George Slappey and his wife Pansy Slappey were Georgia educators and writers. Correspondence, manuscripts, notes, genealogical material, scrapbook, and clippings. Includes published and unpublished manuscripts concerning problems of Georgia education, educational reform, and the public school system; a scrapbook and notes taken by the Slappeys as Georgia delegates to the World Organization of the Teaching Profession conference in Glasgow, Scotland, in 1947; genealogical material on Slappey, Aiken, Shi, Hollis, Singleton, Howard, and allied families; and scrapbooks of Jimmy Carter's presidential campaign, kept by Pansy Slappey.

3,089. Slaves, Bills of Sale
Records. 1848-50. 2 items.
Open. Unpublished guide.
University of Georgia, Special Collections.
One of the bills of sale was made out in the name of John C. Greer for Milly, who was about 13 years old. The girl was sold for $550 to satisfy a mortgage claim of Edward P. Clayton on Philip Clayton.

3,090. Smith, Garland
Papers. 1920s-68. 188 items.
Open. Unpublished guide.
University of Georgia, Special Collections.
Smith (1880-1968), a native of Athens, was an author, artist, poet, and librarian. Published and unpublished articles; poems, nursery rhymes, and stories in French; children's stories; and sketches about people and places.

3,091. Smith, James Rembert
Papers. 1853-58. 29 items.
Open. Unpublished guide.
University of Georgia, Special Collections.
Correspondence, chiefly by Smith, a medical doctor and Methodist preacher of Sandersville, GA, includes a few letters from his daughter Anna Maria Smith. Also includes a covering letter from Mary Bond Smith in which she speaks of "Uncle James' letters" and encloses a composition about a tonsil operation she had recently undergone.

3,092. Smith, Jennie
Papers. 1863-1941. 1023 items.
Open. Unpublished guide.
University of Georgia, Special Collections.
Oneita Virginia "Jennie" Smith (1862-1946) was an artist and head of the Lucy Cobb Institute art department in Athens. Correspondence, notebooks, manuscripts of stories, diary of a Yankee soldier, sketches, engravings, photos, watercolors, a descriptive list of the watercolors, daguerreotypes, broadsides, clippings, obituaries, and other items. Includes material relating to the Cobb Institute.

3,093. Smith, Thomas
Papers. 1767-1912. 68 items.
Open. Unpublished guide.
University of Georgia, Special Collections.
Smith (1745-1809) was a surveyor and colonial officer in Pennsylvania and a member of the Continental Congress in 1781 and 1782. Includes two letters to his mother [Mrs.] Elizabeth Lawrence in Aberdeenshire, the first written from London shortly before Smith left for America, and a letter from his widow Letitia Vanderen Smith to Peter Smith, a physician, concerning Thomas Smith's death. Also includes the will of Letitia Smith and contemporary notes concerning her death.

3,094. Sosnowski, Sophie; Sosnowski, Callie; and the Home School
Papers. 1869-1917?. 30 items.
Open. Unpublished guide.
University of Georgia, Special Collections.
[Madame] Sophie Sosnowski and [Miss] Callie Sosnowski operated the Home School, a private girls school in Athens. Correspondence, typescripts, report cards, photos, programs, menus, clippings, and other School items. Includes letters of Callie Sosnowski and a minute notebook of the Home School Club.

3,095. Southern Female College, Cox College Archives
Records. 1853-1962. 816 items.
Open. Unpublished guide.
University of Georgia, Special Collections.
Cox College, organized as Southern Female College in 1842 or 1843, was directed by Cox family members from 1857 until its closing in 1923. Speeches, committee reports, examinations, poems, photos, scrapbooks, programs, catalogs, and other items, including Cox-Bacon family correspondence. The school was chartered in 1850 as the LaGrange Collegiate Seminary for Young Ladies. The school was known as the Southern and Western Female College and Southern Female College before it was renamed Cox College in honor of I. F. Cox, who served as its president. In 1895-96 the college was moved to College Park near Atlanta. The school was revived from 1932 to 1938.

3,096. Stanton, Lucy May
Papers. 1891-1942. 105 items.
Open. Unpublished guide.
University of Georgia, Special Collections.
Correspondence, sketches, photos, programs, and clippings by and about [Miss] Stanton and her family.

3,097. Stanton, Lucy May
Papers. 1889-1970. Ca. 3288 items.
Open. Unpublished guide.
University of Georgia, Special Collections.
[Miss] Stanton (1875-1931) was a painter of miniatures. Correspondence, diaries, sketchbooks and notebooks, account books, lists of works, photos, a scrapbook, exhibition catalogs, reproductions of Stanton's works, photo album, clippings, and other items. Includes Stanton's manuscript notes with photos and sketches concerning the history of architecture, painting, and sculpture, and diaries and sketchbooks that provide a commentary on Stanton's methods. Correspondents include John Burroughs, Laura Coombs Hills, George and Mabel Sarton, and May Sarton.

3,098. State Normal School, Athens
Records. 1902-63. 115 items.
Open. Unpublished guide.
University of Georgia, Special Collections.
Records concern the curriculum, finances, alumni, history, and other aspects of the School. Also includes correspondence, photos, programs, and clippings pertaining to the school.

3,099. Tate, Edna Ferguson
Papers. Ca. 1758-1958. 5 items.
Open. Unpublished guide.
University of Georgia, Special Collections.
Notebook, manuscripts, and typescripts of [Mrs.] Tate deal with Tate, Ferguson, and Byrd family history in Virginia, North Carolina, and Pickens and Gordon counties in Georgia. One manuscript is a chronology of Tate's education, her children's births, and family activities. The other is her incomplete autobiography.

3,100. Theater
Collection. 1866-1911. 5 vols.
Open. Unpublished guide.
University of Georgia, Special Collections.
Scrapbooks contain playbills, programs, clippings, and photos of performers in theaters in New York, Boston, Paris, and other cities. Bulk of the material dates from 1900 to 1902. Some of the women represented include Mrs. Leslie Carter, Helena Modjeska, Julia Marlowe, Annie Clarke, Mary Anderson, Ellen Terry, Carlotta LeClercq, Maggie Mitchell, Maude Adams, Annie Russell, [Mrs.] Lillie Langtry, Sarah Bernhardt, Eleanor Robson, Lulu Glaser, Mary Mannering, Ethel Barrymore, Isadora Duncan, Anna Pavlova, Julia Sanderson, Nora Bayes, Blanche Bates, Marie Dressler, and Julia Opp.

3,101. Thurmond, Swift, and Tutt
Papers. 1817-1963. 573 items.
Open. Unpublished guide.
University of Georgia, Special Collections.
Correspondence, genealogical material, photos, daguerreotypes, broadsides, mementos, clippings, and other material of the families of Samuel Pinckney Thurmond and Elizabeth (Long) Thurmond, Isaac Swift, and William Duncan Tutt. Includes items relating to Crawford Long, a surgeon who was Elizabeth Thurmond's brother; a letter from Alexander H. Stephens recommending [Mrs.] Catherine C. Trippe as a school teacher in the Martin Institute; and programs and an invitation for an 1852 leap year party.

3,102. Toccoa, GA, School Census
Records. 1893. 34-page item.
Open. Unpublished guide.
University of Georgia, Special Collections.
The census, taken during the spring of 1893 by W. M. Ward, includes lists of the city's white and colored residents.

3,103. Tschudi, Eleanor B.
Papers. 1887-96. 10 items.
Open. Unpublished guide.
University of Georgia, Special Collections.
Papers of [Miss] Tschudi include a letter from Varina (Howell) [Mrs. Jefferson] Davis at Beauvoir House in Mississippi and bills, invitations, programs, advertisements, and other material relating to Athens.

3,104. Tuck, Henry Carlton
Papers. 1878-1954. 85 items.
Open. Unpublished guide.
University of Georgia, Special Collections.
Correspondence, legal documents, and notices of Judge Tuck. Includes the will of [Miss] Evie Jackson and notices and correspondence regarding the Confederate Veterans' Organization.

3,105. Twiggs County Board of Education
Records. 1884-1942. 1267 items.
Open. Unpublished guide.
University of Georgia, Special Collections.
Teacher's monthly, quarterly, and annual reports; superintendent's annual report; list of school houses and supplies; library reports; account books; teacher contracts and lists of teachers; school population figures; book lists; curriculum programs; state school commissioner circulars; printed material; and other items.

3,106. University of Georgia, Library Book Hour
Records. 1936. 24 items.
Open. Unpublished guide.
University of Georgia, Special Collections.
Organized by librarian Duncan Burnet and staff members [Miss] Charlotte Newton and [Miss] Elizabeth LaBoone, the Book Hour was a series of talks on books and readings sponsored by the University of Georgia Library. Notes concerning the meetings, speeches, notices, posters, and attendance lists.

3,107. University of Georgia, Library Freshman Reading Survey
Records. 1936-37. 25 items.
Open. Unpublished guide.
University of Georgia, Special Collections.
Conducted by [Miss] Charlotte Newton and [Miss] Elizabeth LaBoone, the Survey was a study of the reading background of University of Georgia freshmen. Notes, lists of books checked, correlations, and the report given by Newton before a section of the Georgia Library Association.

3,108. Vance, Carolyn
Papers. 1918-33. 53 items.
Open. Unpublished guide.
University of Georgia, Special Collections.
Correspondence, programs, and other items dealing with the speech department of the State Normal School at Athens and later at the University of Georgia.

3,109. Vaughan, John B.
Papers. 1884-1938. 252 items.
Open. Unpublished guide.
University of Georgia, Special Collections.
Vaughan was a composer and publisher. Correspondence, manuscripts, music, and printed items, including verses written by Vaughan's wife Eulalia (Mewbourn) Vaughan.

3,110. Von Meysenbug
Collection. 1896-1964. 1 vol.
Open. Unpublished guide.
University of Georgia, Special Collections.
Correspondence, cards, and autographs include items of Phyllis Bottome, Ann Bridge, Clara and Margaret Bruch, Dorothy Dix, Ellen Terry, and Ella Wheeler Wilcox.

3,111. Ware, Runa Erwin
Papers. 1888-1971. 14 items.
Open. Unpublished guide.
University of Georgia, Special Collections.
[Mrs.] Ware was the author of *All Those in Favor Say Something!*. Annotated manuscript of her book; notices and illustrations for the book and some of the original cartoons by Charles Wickersham, III; clippings about Ware; and a social letter from William H. Barrett, Jr., to [Miss] Lamar Rutherford.

3,112. Way, Sarah Sims
Papers. 1879. 2 items.
Open. Unpublished guide.
University of Georgia, Special Collections.
Papers of [Mrs.] Way consist of two invitations, one honoring [Miss] Sallie Vickers and J. Wilkes Sanders and the other, a wedding invitation of [Miss] S. Annie Maxwell to George Palmer.

3,113. White, Henry Clay
Papers. 1880s-1927. 293 items.
Open. Unpublished guide.
University of Georgia, Special Collections.
Correspondence, telegrams, speeches, poems, biographical material, photos, cards, pamphlets, clippings, a Phi Beta Kappa certificate, and other papers, including material on the Georgia Federation of Women's Clubs.

3,114. White Oak Presbyterian Church
Records. 1837-71. 80 pp.
Open. Unpublished guide.
University of Georgia, Special Collections.
Copies of manuscript minutes of this Coweta County, GA, church, which was part of the Flint River Presbytery. Mary Russell, Mary Atcherson, Elizabeth Thompson, Esther Young, Margaret McLure, Mary Evans, Margaret Wadel, and Isabella Holinghead are listed among the charter members.

3,115. Wilson, William E.
Papers. 1883-93. 203 items.
Open. Unpublished guide.
University of Georgia, Special Collections.
Photos, glass plate negatives, and contact prints depict coastal Georgia as photographed by Wilson. Photos show ex-slaves, Negro children, cotton patches, cotton wharves, scenic views, landmarks, Sunday picnics, and other subjects.

3,116. Women's Student Government Association
Records. 1950-69. 22 items.
Open. Unpublished guide.
University of Georgia, Special Collections.
Scrapbook contains clippings, charts, printed material, and other items pertaining to the Association's activities. Also includes Association handbooks.

3,117. Woodward, Emily Barnelia
Papers. 1916-57. 1769 items.
Open. Unpublished guide.
University of Georgia, Special Collections.
Woodward (1885-1970) was a journalist and newspaper editor. Correspondence, speeches, radio programs, scrapbooks, invitations, programs, greeting cards, and clippings deal primarily with the Georgia Press Association, the women's committee of the national Democratic party, and the Public Forums of the State of Georgia. Correspondents include Emily Post, Corra Harris, Willie Snow Ethridge, Martha Berry, Eleanor Roosevelt, and Margaret Mitchell.

3,118. Works Progress Administration: Ex-Slave Interviews
Records. 1932-37. 260 items.
Open. Unpublished guide.
University of Georgia, Special Collections.
Depositions of interviews with Negroes who were born into slavery. The items are arranged alphabetically by interviewee's name.

3,119. Works Progress Administration, Georgia Records Survey
Records. 1935-40. 2600 items.
Open. Unpublished guide.
University of Georgia, Special Collections.
Typescripts and notes by WPA researchers in Georgia contain material on the federal archives survey, which included federal district courts in Savannah and Augusta, various post offices, customs houses, and government warehouses; workers education reports, instructional guides, survey handbooks, clippings, and correspondence relating to WPA activities in the state; life histories and reminiscences of the WWI era and the depression; Georgia educational institutions records and data sheets; and the Georgia bibliography survey.

3,120. Works Progress Administration in Georgia
Records. 1936. 478 items.
Open. Unpublished guide.
University of Georgia, Special Collections.
Scrapbooks and loose photos depict WPA activities in Georgia's Fulton and DeKalb counties, including such projects as construction of community houses, parks, roads, and sewer systems; theater productions; and immunization clinics.

3,121. Works Progress Administration: Indian Notes
Records. Nd. 588 pp.
Open. Unpublished guide.
University of Georgia, Special Collections.
Notes from various sources concern Indians in Georgia and include information on burial rites and beliefs, customs, home, migration, organized life, and religion.

3,122. Zebulon, GA, Academy, Trustees
Records. 1837-1939. 1 vol.
Open. Unpublished guide.
University of Georgia, Special Collections.
Manuscript book includes cash accounts for 1838-39 and records the courses of study, tuition fees, rules for male and female branches, details of hiring teachers, receipts, and expenditures.

3,123. Creswell, Mary Ethel
Papers. 189?-1960. 145 items.
Open. Unpublished guide.
University of Georgia, University Archives.
Associated with the University of Georgia for all but five years of the period from 1911 to 1949, [Miss] Creswell headed the school's department of home economics for 27 years. Correspondence, speeches, biographical material, pictures, programs,

mementos, clippings, and printed material. From 1913 to 1918, Creswell was a field agent for the US Department of Agriculture.

3,124. Homecon Club
Records. 1936-45. 30 items.
Open. Unpublished guide.
University of Georgia, University Archives.
The Homecon Club, an affiliate of a national organization, was made up of home economic students at the University of Georgia. Correspondence, programs, outlines, and copies of the national organization's magazine *Colhecon.*

3,125. Lyndon, Martha Dorothy
Papers. 1895-1964. No size given.
Open. Unpublished guide.
University of Georgia, University Archives.
[Miss] Lyndon was the first woman to earn a degree at the University of Georgia and the University's first dean of women. Correspondence, photos, programs, clippings, diplomas, master's robe and hood, and other items. Includes diplomas and certificates from Wesleyan Female College in Macon, GA; a teaching license from the State Normal School in Athens; and copies of a memorial service for Lyndon.

3,126. President's Papers: Barrow, David Crenshaw
Records. 1859-1929. 54,641 items.
Open. Unpublished guide.
University of Georgia, University Archives.
A civil engineer, planter, and mathematics professor, Barrow (1852-1929) was chancellor of the University of Georgia from 1906 to 1925, the period during which the first women students were admitted to the school. General and trustees correspondence, annual reports of the University, speeches, accounts, photos, scrapbooks, mementos, and other items. Barrow served as chancellor emeritus from 1925 to 1929.

3,127. University of Georgia, University Woman's Club
Records. 1923- . Ca. 144 items.
Open. Unpublished guide.
University of Georgia, University Archives.
Minute books, treasurer's reports, membership records, notes, photos, scrapbooks, yearbooks, programs, and clippings of the Club. Includes scrapbooks of the Newcomers Club, a division of the University Woman's Club; a tape of 1971 Georgia Day Dinner proceedings; and a history of the group.

ATLANTA

3,128. Acree, Eugene G.
Papers. 1861-1930. 6 items.
Open. Published guide.
Atlanta Historical Society.
Papers of Acree include a 1926 essay on the Atlanta Woman's Club and an 1892 excerpt from minutes of the board of trustees of Appleton Church Home in Columbus, GA. Taken from D. Louise Cook, comp., *Guide to the Manuscript Collections of the Atlanta Historical Society* (Atlanta: Atlanta Historical Society, Inc., 1976).

3,129. Adair, Augustus Dixon
Papers. 1865-1950. 3 items.
Open. Published guide.
Atlanta Historical Society.
Letter by Adair's mother Octavia Hammond Adair depicts Atlanta just before the end of the Civil War; it contains information on residents, servants, prices, and the difficulty of obtaining supplies. Taken from D. Louise Cook, comp., *Guide to the Manuscript Collections of the Atlanta Historical Society* (Atlanta: Atlanta Historical Society, Inc., 1976).

3,130. Adams, A. G.
Papers. 1913-38. 12 items.
Open. Published guide.
Atlanta Historical Society.
Clippings pertaining to the Lucy Cobb Institute, a women's preparatory school in Athens, GA, and correspondence relating to the Capital City Club and Oglethorpe Park. Taken from D. Louise Cook, comp., *Guide to the Manuscript Collections of the Atlanta Historical Society* (Atlanta: Atlanta Historical Society, Inc., 1976).

3,131. Allen, Willette A.
Papers. 1937-40. 8 items.
Open. Published guide.
Atlanta Historical Society.
Correspondence between [Miss] Allen, an Atlanta educator and founder of the Atlanta Kindergarten Normal School, and Ruth Blair about Allen's membership in the Atlanta Historical Society. Also included are biographical essays on Allen's professional work, one of which was written by Ada S. Woolfolk, the other by D'Nena Bridger Beckan. Taken from D. Louise Cook, comp., *Guide to the Manuscript Collections of the Atlanta Historical Society* (Atlanta: Atlanta Historical Society, Inc., 1976).

3,132. Anderson, Constance Spalding
Papers. 1867-1972. 2 cu.ft.
Open. Published guide.
Atlanta Historical Society.
Papers pertaining to the family and friends of [Mrs. Albert] Anderson include photos, invitations, and clippings. Also included are the charter and related records of the Second Ponce de Leon Baptist Church and scrapbooks which contain information on Girls' High School and Saint Simon's Island. Taken from D. Louise Cook, comp., *Guide to the Manuscript Collections of the Atlanta Historical Society* (Atlanta: Atlanta Historical Society, Inc., 1976).

3,133. Anderson, Katherine
Papers. 1810-1954. 134 items.
Open. Published guide.
Atlanta Historical Society.
Correspondence of [Miss] Anderson with Senator Walter F. George, Secretary of War George H. Dern, and others pertains to her attempts to secure the Civil War amnesty records of her grandfather William Patrick Anderson. Also included are prints, etchings, and lithographs depicting female fashions of the 19th century. Taken from D. Louise Cook, comp., *Guide to the Manuscript Collections of the Atlanta Historical Society* (Atlanta: Atlanta Historical Society, Inc., 1976).

3,134. Anti-Tuberculosis Association
Records. 1909. 40-page item.
Open. Published guide.
Atlanta Historical Society.
Casebook of the Association contains case histories of 40 patients in the Atlanta area and photos illustrating environmental conditions such as substandard housing which facilitate the spread of tuberculosis. Taken from D. Louise Cook, comp., *Guide to the Manuscript Collections of the Atlanta Historical Society* (Atlanta: Atlanta Historical Society, Inc., 1976).

3,135. Arkwright, Dorothy Colquitt
Papers. 1917-39. 50-page item.
Open. Published guide.
Atlanta Historical Society.
An Atlanta civic and social leader, Arkwright was the daughter of Georgia Governor Alfred H. Colquitt and wife of Preston S. Arkwright, who was president of the Georgia Power Co. Scrapbook of clippings pertains to the Arkwright family and to the American National Red Cross, the Cornelia Moore Day Nursery, the Sheltering Arms Association, and the Community Chest. Taken from D. Louise Cook, comp., *Guide to the Manuscript Collections of the Atlanta Historical Society* (Atlanta: Atlanta Historical Society, Inc., 1976).

3,136. Atlanta Association for Childhood Education
Records. 1949-51. 0.5 cu.ft.
Open. Published guide.
Atlanta Historical Society.
Scrapbooks containing correspondence, photos, and clippings of the Association, which lobbied for improvements in education and for establishment of a free kindergarten system. Taken from D. Louise Cook, comp., *Guide to the Manuscript Collections of the Atlanta Historical Society* (Atlanta: Atlanta Historical Society, Inc., 1976).

3,137. Atlanta Council of Church Women
Records. 1940-51. 1.5 cu.ft.
Open. Published guide.
Atlanta Historical Society.
Scrapbooks of the Council contain correspondence, photos, and clippings, some of which relate to the Mission Kindergarten sponsored by the Council. Taken from D. Louise Cook, comp., *Guide to the Manuscript Collections of the Atlanta Historical Society* (Atlanta: Atlanta Historical Society, Inc., 1976).

3,138. Atlanta Federation of Women's Clubs
Records. 1898-1951. 7 cu.ft.
Open. Published guide.
Atlanta Historical Society.
Constitution, bylaws, membership application forms, a golden anniversary and other yearbooks, and programs for the 1899 meeting of the Georgia Federation of Women's Clubs and for various meetings of the Atlanta Federation. Also included are scrapbooks containing correspondence, photos, yearbooks, bulletins of member clubs, clippings about activities, and scrapbooks on international relations. Taken from D. Louise Cook, comp., *Guide to the Manuscript Collections of the Atlanta Historical Society* (Atlanta: Atlanta Historical Society, Inc., 1976).

3,139. Atlanta Historical Society
Records. 1922-51. 6 cu.ft.
Open. Published guide.
Atlanta Historical Society.
Scrapbooks of clippings and other items relating to the Society and to the history of Atlanta. One volume deals with Atlanta homes, three contain obituaries, and one deals exclusively with women. Taken from D. Louise Cook, comp., *Guide to the Manuscript Collections of the Atlanta Historical Society* (Atlanta: Atlanta Historical Society, Inc., 1976).

3,140. Atlanta Kindergarten Alumnae Club
Records. 1882-1939. 1 cu.ft.
Open. Published guide.
Atlanta Historical Society.
The Club was formed by graduates of the Atlanta Kindergarten Normal School to stimulate interest in kindergartens and to keep members in touch with educational developments. Correspondence, manuscripts, biographies, clippings, and other material relating to the history of the establishment of kindergartens in Georgia and particularly in Atlanta. Included are correspondence and biographies of [Miss] Willette Allen, who in 1891 opened Atlanta's first free kindergarten in the old Barclay Mission, and of Mary Dickinson, who in 1897 aided Allen in establishing the Normal School. In addition there is material on the Atlanta Free Kindergarten Association, which was established by Nellie (Peters) Black in 1896; the Georgia Education Association; the Georgia Kindergarten Association; and the Sheltering Arms Mission. Correspondence about the enactment of a bill providing for kindergartens in Georgia public schools is also included. Taken from D. Louise Cook, comp., *Guide to the Manuscript Collections*

of the Atlanta Historical Society (Atlanta: Atlanta Historical Society, Inc., 1976).

3,141. Atlanta Pioneer Women's Society
Records. 1909-47. 1.5 cu.ft.
Open. Published guide.
Atlanta Historical Society.
Material regarding the Club's founding in 1909; minutes of meetings; treasurer's notebooks; applications for membership; lists of officers and charter members; and biographies of such members as Mrs. Joseph Thompson, Mrs. Richard Peters, Mrs. William King, Mrs. Frank P. Rice, [Mrs.] Augusta Moore, [Mrs.] Virginia Shelton Wilkinson, Mrs. G. J. Foreacre, Mrs. R. M. Massey, Mrs. Alfred Austell, Mrs. Henry Lumpkin Wilson, and [Mrs.] Lollie Belle Wylie. Also included are a manuscript by Wylie on the early days of Atlanta, which was first known as Terminus and then as Marthasville, as described by pioneer women and manuscripts relating to old-fashioned gardens, social life, Christmas, pioneer men, fashions, and Episcopal churches. Taken from D. Louise Cook, comp., *Guide to the Manuscript Collections of the Atlanta Historical Society* (Atlanta: Atlanta Historical Society, Inc., 1976).

3,142. Atlanta Woman's Club
Records. 1895-1962. 6 cu.ft.
Open. Published guide.
Atlanta Historical Society.
The Club was founded in 1895 to involve women in civic and cultural affairs. Constitution, bylaws, yearbooks, bulletins, and scrapbooks and press books of bulletins, clippings, and ephemera. Taken from D. Louise Cook, comp., *Guide to the Manuscript Collections of the Atlanta Historical Society* (Atlanta: Atlanta Historical Society, Inc., 1976).

3,143. Avary, Myrta (Lockett)
Papers. 1884-1946. 5 cu.ft.
Open. Published guide.
Atlanta Historical Society.
Papers of Avary, an Atlanta author and newspaperwoman, include correspondence concerning her writing; notes; manuscripts of her poetry, short stories, and books; an autobiography by her father Harwood Alexander Lockett; Avary's will and items relating to her estate; scrapbooks; and clippings. Manuscripts included are *A Virginia Girl in the Civil War* (1903), *Diary from Dixie* (1905), and *Letters and Recollections of Alexander H. Stephens* (1910). Among the clippings are human-interest stories by Avary and columns by other women authors as well as clippings relating to [Mrs.] Alice M. Birney, Frank Stanton, and southern women editors. Taken from D. Louise Cook, comp., *Guide to the Manuscript Collections of the Atlanta Historical Society* (Atlanta: Atlanta Historical Society, Inc., 1976).

3,144. Bailey, Rosalie Davis
Papers. 1915-40. 1 cu.ft.
Open. Published guide.
Atlanta Historical Society.
Correspondence, guest lists, menus, and household inventory of Bailey, wife of Brigadier General Benjamin Bailey, and a motion picture film of the Bailey family. Taken from D. Louise Cook, comp., *Guide to the Manuscript Collections of the Atlanta Historical Society* (Atlanta: Atlanta Historical Society, Inc., 1976).

3,145. Barker, Jennie Meta
Papers. 1840-1964. 23 cu.ft.
Open. Published guide.
Atlanta Historical Society.
Correspondence, notes, manuscripts, and clippings used by [Miss] Barker in writing a history of Atlanta relate to such subjects as the Civil War, Reconstruction, city government, business, race relations, labor unions, education, religion, and public health. Other manuscripts by Barker concern Atlanta theater and the development of railroads in Georgia. Taken from D. Louise Cook, comp., *Guide to the Manuscript Collections of the Atlanta Historical Society* (Atlanta: Atlanta Historical Society, Inc., 1976).

3,146. Battey, Robert
Papers. 1872-81. 34 items.
Open. Published guide.
Atlanta Historical Society.
Battey was a physician who supervised Confederate hospitals during the Civil War and maintained a gynecological practice in Rome, GA. Letters from physicians, including J. Marion Sims, who was known as "the father of gynecology," deal principally with gynecological consultation, in particular ovariectomies, the use of antiseptics in surgery, and types of sutures used. Taken from D. Louise Cook, comp., *Guide to the Manuscript Collections of the Atlanta Historical Society* (Atlanta: Atlanta Historical Society, Inc., 1976).

3,147. Bealer, Emily Jane
Papers. 1876-86. 69-page item.
Open. Published guide.
Atlanta Historical Society.
Diary of Bealer describes home life, school, neighbors, illnesses, employment of children, church services of various denominations, Atlanta's Jewish community, and the Southern Baptist Convention of 1879. Taken from D. Louise Cook, comp., *Guide to the Manuscript Collections of the Atlanta Historical Society* (Atlanta: Atlanta Historical Society, Inc., 1976).

3,148. Bell House Boys
Records. 1898-1952. 35 items.
Open. Published guide.
Atlanta Historical Society.
Established by [Mrs.] Emma Bell in 1878, the Bell House served as a home for bachelors, many of whom were prominent Atlanta businessmen. Records of the Bell House Boys, a club organized in 1913 by residents of the House, include correspondence, rosters of members, notes on the history of the House, speeches, a transcript of a television interview, photos, and clippings. Taken from D. Louise Cook, comp., *Guide to the Manuscript Collections of the Atlanta Historical Society* (Atlanta: Atlanta Historical Society, Inc., 1976).

3,149. Benning, Augustus H., and Benning, Margaret R.
Papers. 1867-1942. 5.5 cu.ft.
Open. Published guide.
Atlanta Historical Society.
Papers of Captain Augustus Benning (1840-1904), founder of the Benning Coal Co., include business and personal correspondence and documents relating to his service as a steamer captain in China. Papers of his wife Margaret Rowena (Russell) Benning, who owned extensive rental property in Atlanta, include personal and business correspondence, household account books, receipts, composition books, a lawsuit against the city of Athens, GA, concerning a right-of-way agreement, genealogical notes on the Benning family, photos, material relating to the Baptist church, and scrapbooks. Taken from D. Louise Cook, comp., *Guide to the Manuscript Collections of the Atlanta Historical Society* (Atlanta: Atlanta Historical Society, Inc., 1976).

3,150. Berry, Carrie
Papers. 1864-74. 0.25 cu.ft.
Open. Published guide.
Atlanta Historical Society.
Diaries in which Berry describes the siege, occupation, and burning of Atlanta; family activities; and school life. Also included is a friendship book with biographical information on her friends. Taken from D. Louise Cook, comp., *Guide to the Manuscript Collections of the Atlanta Historical Society* (Atlanta: Atlanta Historical Society, Inc., 1976).

3,151. Black, Nellie (Peters)
Papers. 1895-1941. 6 items.
Open. Published guide.
Atlanta Historical Society.
[Mrs. G. R.] Black, daughter of Richard Peters, was prominent in such Atlanta social service organizations as the Atlanta Free Kindergarten Association and the Georgia Federation of Women's Clubs; she also was a member of the board of the Woman's Building of the Cotton States and International Exposition of 1895, held in Atlanta. Notes by Black on her mother's reminiscences of Civil War hospitals in Atlanta and excerpts from these reminiscences, a biographical booklet on Black by the Georgia Federation of Women's Clubs, and a clipping on the Exposition. Taken from D. Louise Cook, comp., *Guide to the Manuscript Collections of the Atlanta Historical Society* (Atlanta: Atlanta Historical Society, Inc., 1976).

3,152. Blackburn, Mary J.
Papers. 1899. 3 items.
Open. Published guide.
Atlanta Historical Society.
Letter and statement by rental agent John J. Woodside concerning properties owned by [Mrs.] Blackburn and an original watercolor postcard of the slave auction and surrounding buildings drawn by Blackburn. Taken from D. Louise Cook, comp., *Guide to the Manuscript Collections of the Atlanta Historical Society* (Atlanta: Atlanta Historical Society, Inc., 1976).

3,153. Blanchard, Mary H.
Papers. 1876-77. 2 items.
Open. Published guide.
Atlanta Historical Society.
Examination papers of [Miss] Blanchard from Girls' High School and a memorial to Blanchard written by her high school classmates. Taken from D. Louise Cook, comp., *Guide to the Manuscript Collections of the Atlanta Historical Society* (Atlanta: Atlanta Historical Society, Inc., 1976).

3,154. Bomar and Killian Family
Papers. 1816-1926. 2 cu.ft.
Open. Published guide.
Atlanta Historical Society.
Includes correspondence, an account book, and obituaries of Benjamin F. Bomar, second mayor of Atlanta; a scrapbook and sketchbook of his daughter Amaryllis (Bomar) Killian; clippings of the memoirs of his wife Sarah Elizabeth (Lumpkin) Hayes Bomar; and photos of the Bomars and Killians. Taken from D. Louise Cook, comp., *Guide to the Manuscript Collections of the Atlanta Historical Society* (Atlanta: Atlanta Historical Society, Inc., 1976).

3,155. Brooks, Abbie M.
Papers. 1865-70. 0.25 cu.ft.
Open. Published guide.
Atlanta Historical Society.
An 1865 diary of [Miss] Brooks, a schoolteacher living in Edgefield, TN, gives observations on the end of the Civil War, descriptions of Confederate troops returning to the South, her feelings of animosity toward the North, the life confronting the southern civilian, and attitudes toward Negroes. A later diary records her move to Atlanta and then to Madison, GA, Augusta, GA, and Savannah, GA, in an effort to earn a living selling religious publications. Taken from D. Louise Cook, comp., *Guide to the Manuscript Collections of the Atlanta Historical Society* (Atlanta: Atlanta Historical Society, Inc., 1976).

3,156. Brown, Elizabeth (Grisham)
Papers. 1883-96. 46 items.
Open. Published guide.

Atlanta Historical Society.
Papers of [Mrs. Joseph E.] Brown (1826-96) include correspondence, financial documents, an annual report of the Pullman Palace Car Company, and a scrapbook of telegrams, family photos, greeting cards, and articles on travel. Taken from D. Louise Cook, comp., *Guide to the Manuscript Collections of the Atlanta Historical Society* (Atlanta: Atlanta Historical Society, Inc., 1976).

3,157. Brown, Harriett Johnson
Papers. 1880-1937. 1 cu.ft.
Open. Published guide.
Atlanta Historical Society.
[Mrs. Elijah A.] Brown was active in Atlanta civic and social organizations, including the Georgia Committee on Interracial Cooperation. Minutes, pamphlets, flyers, and bulletins of the Committee; a scrapbook of poetry by Lena Johnson and others; items from the Woman's Union Christian College in Foreign Fields; commencement programs for the University of Georgia and LaGrange Female College in LaGrange, GA; invitations; calling cards; club notices; opera programs; clippings; and other material. Taken from D. Louise Cook, comp., *Guide to the Manuscript Collections of the Atlanta Historical Society* (Atlanta: Atlanta Historical Society, Inc., 1976).

3,158. Brown, Joseph Mackey
Papers. 1846-1921. 3 cu.ft.
Open. Published guide.
Atlanta Historical Society.
Brown was an author, attorney, and governor of Georgia from 1909 to 1913. Correspondence, manuscripts of Brown's novel *Astyanax* (1907) and of the "Karl Oter Letters," speeches, campaign literature, and clippings. Correspondence deals with such subjects as Negro voting rights, women's suffrage, elections and voting irregularities, labor unions, prohibition, and the state sanitarium. Correspondents include Helen Dortch Longstreet. Taken from D. Louise Cook, comp., *Guide to the Manuscript Collections of the Atlanta Historical Society* (Atlanta: Atlanta Historical Society, Inc., 1976).

3,159. Brown, Marel
Papers. 1932-68. 111 items.
Open. Published guide.
Atlanta Historical Society.
Papers of [Mrs.] Brown, the author of *Hearth-Fire* (1943), *Fence Corners* (1952), and *The Shape of a Song* (1968), include her history of the Georgia Federation of Women's Clubs; advertisements and reviews of her books; clippings about her speaking engagements, literary friends, prizes, and awards; and a program and yearbook of the Atlanta branch of the National League of American Pen Women. Taken from D. Louise Cook, comp., *Guide to the Manuscript Collections of the Atlanta Historical Society* (Atlanta: Atlanta Historical Society, Inc., 1976).

3,160. Brown, Sallie Eugenia
Papers. 1888-1927. 1 cu.ft.
Open. Published guide.
Atlanta Historical Society.
Papers of Brown (1862-1942), daughter of Joseph E. Brown and Elizabeth (Grisham) Brown, include correspondence, greeting cards, receipts, and Bibles with family photos and clippings pasted inside. Taken from D. Louise Cook, comp., *Guide to the Manuscript Collections of the Atlanta Historical Society* (Atlanta: Atlanta Historical Society, Inc., 1976).

3,161. Browne, M. S.
Papers. 1881-1940. 1 item.
Open. Published guide.
Atlanta Historical Society.
Ledger used by physician M. S. Browne of Cassville, GA, as an account book for his medical practice and later used by his daughter Mrs. J. W. Chambers of Mississippi to record poultry operations, accounts of servants and neighbors, and other records of indebtedness. Taken from D. Louise Cook, comp., *Guide to the Manuscript Collections of the Atlanta Historical Society* (Atlanta: Atlanta Historical Society, Inc., 1976).

3,162. Business and Professional Women's Club of Atlanta
Records. 1939. 1 item.
Open. Published guide.
Atlanta Historical Society.
Manuscript on air pollution and the burning of coal prepared by the smoke abatement committee of the Club. Taken from D. Louise Cook, comp., *Guide to the Manuscript Collections of the Atlanta Historical Society* (Atlanta: Atlanta Historical Society, Inc., 1976).

3,163. Camp Fire Girls
Records. 1914-74. 4 items.
Open. Published guide.
Atlanta Historical Society.
Award letter; a history of the organization; a list of groups; 1914 Camp Fire Girl instruction book; a yearbook of Atlanta Camp Fire Girls for 1926 to 1927, including a list of members on the board of directors of the Greater Council; and a letter describing the early uniform. Taken from D. Louise Cook, comp., *Guide to the Manuscript Collections of the Atlanta Historical Society* (Atlanta: Atlanta Historical Society, Inc., 1976).

3,164. Children of the Confederacy
Records. 1898-1965. 44 items.
Open. Published guide.
Atlanta Historical Society.
Minutes of state conferences of the 1910s and of the 53rd annual convention in 1965, programs of the third state conference and 10th general convention, a brief history of the organization, yearbooks of the Alfred Holt Colquitt Junior Chapter from the 1960s, correspondence, and clippings. Taken from D. Louise Cook, comp., *Guide to the Manuscript Collections of the Atlanta Historical Society* (Atlanta: Atlanta Historical Society, Inc., 1976).

3,165. Cohen, Natalie
Papers. 1895-1948. 3 cu.ft.
Open. Published guide.
Atlanta Historical Society.
Correspondence and photos of [Miss] Cohen's parents and grandparents; photos of Atlanta; scrapbooks containing Girls' High School memorabilia and clippings from her senior year at the University of California in 1934; a souvenir book of the Atlanta Yaarab Temple trip to San Francisco, Mexico, and Canada; her baby book; programs; clippings; and miscellaneous items. Taken from D. Louise Cook, comp., *Guide to the Manuscript Collections of the Atlanta Historical Society* (Atlanta: Atlanta Historical Society, Inc., 1976).

3,166. Cole, Edda A.
Papers. 1898. 1 cu.ft.
Open. Published guide.
Atlanta Historical Society.
Scrapbook of clippings on the Ladies' Memorial Association, [Miss] Winnie Davis, and other subjects. Taken from D. Louise Cook, comp., *Guide to the Manuscript Collections of the Atlanta Historical Society* (Atlanta: Atlanta Historical Society, Inc., 1976).

3,167. Cole, Paul Boneau
Papers. 1929-39. 16 items.
Open. Published guide.
Atlanta Historical Society.
Correspondence relating to author Frances Newman, biographical material on poet Ernest Hartsock, and other material. Taken from D. Louise Cook, comp., *Guide to the Manuscript Collections of the Atlanta Historical Society* (Atlanta: Atlanta Historical Society, Inc., 1976).

3,168. Connally, Mary V.
Papers. 1830-1930. 1.5 cu.ft.
Open. Published guide.
Atlanta Historical Society.
[Mrs. E. L.] Connally, daughter of Joseph E. Brown, was active in civic and social organizations, including the Second Baptist Church and the Atlanta Woman's Club. Correspondence, photos, genealogical material, and clippings on the E. L. Connally family; legal documents; clippings on Atlanta society; and postcards and guidebooks from Europe and South America. Taken from D. Louise Cook, comp., *Guide to the Manuscript Collections of the Atlanta Historical Society* (Atlanta: Atlanta Historical Society, Inc., 1976).

3,169. Cox, Mrs. D. Mitchell
Papers. 1880-1930. 3 cu.ft.
Open. Published guide.
Atlanta Historical Society.
Scrapbooks of clippings covering the history of the DAR, the Daughters of the Confederacy, and the Georgia Federation of Women's Clubs include a series of articles concerning the reaction of the organizations to the women's suffrage movement. Taken from D. Louise Cook, comp., *Guide to the Manuscript Collections of the Atlanta Historical Society* (Atlanta: Atlanta Historical Society, Inc., 1976).

3,170. Crane, Sara Clayton
Papers. 1876-1942. 53 items.
Open. Published guide.
Atlanta Historical Society.
Manuscript of [Mrs.] Crane's memories of life in Atlanta during the Civil War concerns her education at Atlanta Female Academy from 1860 to 1863, her improvised education at the Second Baptist Church, epidemics, care of those wounded in the War, the growing military crisis, and the Battle of Atlanta. Also included are correspondence, essays and poems, postcards, and religious tracts. Taken from D. Louise Cook, comp., *Guide to the Manuscript Collections of the Atlanta Historical Society* (Atlanta: Atlanta Historical Society, Inc., 1976).

3,171. Crew, Jane Louisa Killian
Papers. 1865-1931. 4 items.
Open. Published guide.
Atlanta Historical Society.
Extracts from a diary in which Crew comments in 1865 on Lincoln's assassination, the end of the war, and the murder of her husband James R. Crew. Also included is a 1931 letter to Wilbur G. Kurtz concerning the diary, together with transcriptions of the diary. Taken from D. Louise Cook, comp., *Guide to the Manuscript Collections of the Atlanta Historical Society* (Atlanta: Atlanta Historical Society, Inc., 1976).

3,172. Crisson, Margaret
Papers. 1914-18. 1 cu.ft.
Open. Published guide.
Atlanta Historical Society.
Scrapbooks of Crisson contain photos, memorabilia, and clippings relating to her service in France in the 43rd General Hospital Unit, known as the "Emory Unit." Also included are US Army documents, illustrations of WWI from *Ladies Home Journal,* and clippings. Taken from D. Louise Cook, comp., *Guide to the Manuscript Collections of the Atlanta Historical Society* (Atlanta: Atlanta Historical Society, Inc., 1976).

3,173. Crumley Family
Papers. 1864-1918. 1 cu.ft.
Open. Published guide.
Atlanta Historical Society.
W. M. Crumley was the chaplain of Georgia Hospitals during the Civil War. Diaries and

reminiscences by Crumley and his wife during the Civil War, manuscript by and daily account book of Crumley, WWI correspondence of their son William Crumley, and memory book of their daughter Zulette Crumley. Taken from D. Louise Cook, comp., *Guide to the Manuscript Collections of the Atlanta Historical Society* (Atlanta: Atlanta Historical Society, Inc., 1976).

3,174. Daniel, Frank
Papers. 1924-71. 0.5 cu.ft.
Open. Published guide.
Atlanta Historical Society.
Correspondence, drawings, reviews, clippings, and manuscripts by Georgia authors, including Caroline Miller, author of *Lamb in His Bosom* (1933), and Frances Newman. Among the correspondents are Ella Mae Thornton and June and Susie Ray. Taken from D. Louise Cook, comp., *Guide to the Manuscript Collections of the Atlanta Historical Society* (Atlanta: Atlanta Historical Society, Inc., 1976).

3,175. Daughters of American Colonists
Records. 1929-73. 5 items.
Open. Published guide.
Atlanta Historical Society.
Membership roster of 1973 for the James Edward Oglethorpe Chapter; a report on historic landmarks and memorials; yearbooks containing bylaws, officers' reports, a list of officers and new members and a list of chapters; and a booklet issued by Georgia chapters containing a list of national and Georgia officers, a membership roster, and a history of this and similar organizations. Taken from D. Louise Cook, comp., *Guide to the Manuscript Collections of the Atlanta Historical Society* (Atlanta: Atlanta Historical Society, Inc., 1976).

3,176. Davidson, John Mitchell, and Davidson, Julia (Dunn)
Papers. 1851-1970. 0.5 cu.ft.
Open. Published guide.
Atlanta Historical Society.
Correspondence between John M. Davidson and his wife Julia Davidson (1836-90) concerns their courtship and family experiences during the Civil War. John Davidson, who served in the 29th North Carolina Regiment, writes of troop movements, camp life, and battles, while his wife describes life in Atlanta, the problems of inflation, and the difficulty of obtaining provisions. Correspondence between John L. Davidson and Franklin Garrett from 1968 to 1970 contains biographical and genealogical information on the Davidson family. Taken from D. Louise Cook, comp., *Guide to the Manuscript Collections of the Atlanta Historical Society* (Atlanta: Atlanta Historical Society, Inc., 1976).

3,177. Davis, Olive Bell
Papers. 1953-68. 2.5 cu.ft.
Open. Published guide.
Atlanta Historical Society.
Manuscripts by Bell, an Atlanta author, poet, and playwright, include an unpublished novel, *Exodus: 20* (1959), and short stories, poems, and one-act plays, which were published together in 1965 under the title *Between Two Novels.* Also includes a letter from Flannery O'Connor and other correspondence, notes, articles, and reviews. Taken from D. Louise Cook, comp., *Guide to the Manuscript Collections of the Atlanta Historical Society* (Atlanta: Atlanta Historical Society, Inc., 1976).

3,178. Democratic Party, Fulton County Woman's Division
Records. 1939-41. 0.25 cu.ft.
Open. Published guide.
Atlanta Historical Society.
List of officers and scrapbook of clippings on activities of the Division. Taken from D. Louise Cook, comp., *Guide to the Manuscript Collections of the Atlanta Historical Society* (Atlanta: Atlanta Historical Society, Inc., 1976).

3,179. Dick, Jackson P., and Dick, May (Atkinson)
Papers. 1870-1972. 9 cu.ft.
Open. Published guide.
Atlanta Historical Society.
Photos, memorabilia, and clippings of the family of Jackson P. Dick, Sr., vice-president of the Georgia Power Co.; correspondence and photos from North Africa of Jane LeRoux, who later married Jackson P. Dick, Jr.; and photos of the LeRoux family and of the families of H. M. Atkinson, Richard Peters, and Jackson P. Dick, Jr. Taken from D. Louise Cook, comp., *Guide to the Manuscript Collections of the Atlanta Historical Society* (Atlanta: Atlanta Historical Society, Inc., 1976).

3,180. Dobbs, Mary Butts Griffith
Papers. 1915-40. 1 cu.ft.
Open. Published guide.
Atlanta Historical Society.
Photos, programs, clippings, and periodicals relating to Dobbs and the Griffith School of Music in Atlanta, which she organized in 1915 and subsequently directed. Taken from D. Louise Cook, comp., *Guide to the Manuscript Collections of the Atlanta Historical Society* (Atlanta: Atlanta Historical Society, Inc., 1976).

3,181. Draper, Jesse
Papers. 1917-46. 8 cu.ft.
Open. Published guide.
Atlanta Historical Society.
Draper was an alderman and a commanding officer in the navy during WWII. Correspondence between Draper and his wife Constance (Knowles) Draper during WWI and WWII and photos of the Draper family. Taken from D. Louise Cook, comp., *Guide to the Manuscript Collections of the Atlanta Historical Society* (Atlanta: Atlanta Historical Society, Inc., 1976).

3,182. English Speaking Union
Records. 1940-71. 0.5 cu.ft.
Open. Published guide.
Atlanta Historical Society.
The Atlanta branch of the Union, organized in 1940, was active in raising funds, offering homes to English children, and establishing relief services for Americans in England. Official reports, photos, invitations, bulletins, and pamphlets relate to the activities of the local and national organization primarily during WWII. Taken from D. Louise Cook, comp., *Guide to the Manuscript Collections of the Atlanta Historical Society* (Atlanta: Atlanta Historical Society, Inc., 1976).

3,183. Equal Suffrage Party of Georgia
Records. 1914-15. 15 items.
Open. Published guide.
Atlanta Historical Society.
Records of the Georgia branch of the National American Woman Suffrage Association include charter, financial records, correspondence, and a manuscript by Henry Grady Bell on the legal status of women with statistics on women in professions. Taken from D. Louise Cook, comp., *Guide to the Manuscript Collections of the Atlanta Historical Society* (Atlanta: Atlanta Historical Society, Inc., 1976).

3,184. Everhart Family
Papers. 1850-1960. 0.5 cu.ft.
Open. Published guide.
Atlanta Historical Society.
Naval records for the years 1885 to 1904, a patent, photos, articles of US Naval Commander Lay H. Everhart, and papers of his sister Adelaide Everhart, including original sketches, a scrapbook of bookplates she designed, and clippings about her portraits of historical figures. Taken from D. Louise Cook, comp., *Guide to the Manuscript Collections of the Atlanta Historical Society* (Atlanta: Atlanta Historical Society, Inc., 1976).

3,185. Foreacre, Ella Thomas
Papers. 1888. 2 items.
Open. Published guide.
Atlanta Historical Society.
Wedding souvenir album of Foreacre and Archibald Philip Brantley includes letters, a honeymoon diary, photos, and signatures of witnesses. Taken from D. Louise Cook, comp., *Guide to the Manuscript Collections of the Atlanta Historical Society* (Atlanta: Atlanta Historical Society, Inc., 1976).

3,186. Frank, Leo Max
Papers. 1913-16. 2.5 cu.ft.
Open. Published guide.
Atlanta Historical Society.
Frank (1884-1915), superintendent of the National Pencil Company in Atlanta, was convicted of the murder of Mary Phagan and lynched by a mob in Marietta, GA, in 1915 after his sentence had been commuted. The bulk of the material consists of correspondence about the case and includes letters and telegrams expressing sympathy and support for his wife Lucile Frank, letters from Lucile Frank to Leo Frank in the three weeks following the commutation of his sentence, letters from his attorneys concerning their appeals strategy, and letters from publishers and writers reflecting Frank's attempts to publicize his plight. Also included are petitions, poems about the case, Lucile Frank's household accounts, notes, sympathy cards, clippings and publications on the case, and other material. Taken from D. Louise Cook, comp., *Guide to the Manuscript Collections of the Atlanta Historical Society* (Atlanta: Atlanta Historical Society, Inc., 1976).

3,187. Garden Clubs
Records. 1930-75. 29 cu.ft.
Open. Published guide.
Atlanta Historical Society.
Minutes, correspondence, lists of officers and members, newsletters, scrapbooks, programs, yearbooks, articles, clippings, and booklets of the Clifton Road, Ivy, Peachtree Park, Rose, Clay Hills, Druid Hills, and Neighborhood Garden Clubs; the Garden Club of Georgia; the Georgia Botanical Society; the Georgia Gladiolus Society; the Men's Garden Club of Atlanta; and the Tulip Study Club. Also included are scrapbooks of the Iris Garden Club, 1928-74, and of the Pinetree Garden Club, 1938-74. Taken from D. Louise Cook, comp., *Guide to the Manuscript Collections of the Atlanta Historical Society* (Atlanta: Atlanta Historical Society, Inc., 1976).

3,188. Georgia Botanical Society
Records. 1937-41. 90 items.
Open. Published guide.
Atlanta Historical Society.
Includes a membership roster of the Society, a report concerning the establishment of a botanical garden in Fulton County, GA, with a description of the garden, correspondence in which [Miss] Adrienne Morris details her efforts to establish a botanical garden, and clippings relating to fund raising, gardening, and activities of various garden clubs. Taken from D. Louise Cook, comp., *Guide to the Manuscript Collections of the Atlanta Historical Society* (Atlanta: Atlanta Historical Society, Inc., 1976).

3,189. Georgia Federation of Women's Clubs
Records. 1912-47. 4 cu.ft.
Open. Published guide.
Atlanta Historical Society.
Manuscripts on the history of the Federation to 1921, programs from meetings, yearbooks, and a booklet on Nellie (Peters) Black. Taken from D. Louise Cook, comp., *Guide to the Manuscript*

Collections of the Atlanta Historical Society (Atlanta: Atlanta Historical Society, Inc., 1976).

3,190. Georgia State Nurses' Association
Records. 1939-46. 9 items.
Open. Published guide.
Atlanta Historical Society.
Proceedings of annual conventions, including minutes, lists of officers, addresses, reports, and programs; a program for the 33rd convention; issues of the official publication "Georgia Nursing"; and a booklet listing rules and holdings of the Association's Library and Information Bureau. Taken from D. Louise Cook, comp., *Guide to the Manuscript Collections of the Atlanta Historical Society* (Atlanta: Atlanta Historical Society, Inc., 1976).

3,191. Girls' High School
Records. 1873-1976. 3.5 cu.ft.
Open. Published guide.
Atlanta Historical Society.
Class rosters, photos, commencement programs, diplomas, scrapbooks, yearbooks, and clippings kept by students; a manuscript on the history of the school to 1938; reports of the Mallonian Society; a scrapbook prepared for [Miss] Jessie Muse, principal of Girls' High, on her retirement in 1938; issues of the *Girls' High Times;* and ephemera from class reunions. Taken from D. Louise Cook, comp., *Guide to the Manuscript Collections of the Atlanta Historical Society* (Atlanta: Atlanta Historical Society, Inc., 1976).

3,192. Gone With The Wind
Collection. 1935-76. 6 cu.ft.
Open. Published guide.
Atlanta Historical Society.
Material relating to the book *Gone With The Wind,* to its author Margaret (Mitchell) Marsh (1900-49), and to the movie includes costume designs for the movie; programs, tickets, and memorabilia from the Atlanta premiere of the movie in 1939; scrapbooks of clippings and photos; a folio of watercolors by Wilbur G. Kurtz, Sr., and other items for movie publicity; and an article and clipping file. Taken from D. Louise Cook, comp., *Guide to the Manuscript Collections of the Atlanta Historical Society* (Atlanta: Atlanta Historical Society, Inc., 1976).

3,193. Grady Hospital Aid Association
Records. 1894-1900. 4 items.
Open. Published guide.
Atlanta Historical Society.
Constitution, history, list of committee members, and record book with a list of members and the amount of money contributed. Taken from D. Louise Cook, comp., *Guide to the Manuscript Collections of the Atlanta Historical Society* (Atlanta: Atlanta Historical Society, Inc., 1976).

3,194. Green, Pyatt
Papers. Ca. 1875-95. 0.5 cu.ft.
Open. Published guide.
Atlanta Historical Society.
[Miss] Green was an Atlanta author who wrote under the pseudonym Paul Grant. Includes manuscript stories on the fall of Constantinople, the Romanoffs, and Turkey and scrapbooks of miscellaneous clippings and newspaper stories by Green. Taken from D. Louise Cook, comp., *Guide to the Manuscript Collections of the Atlanta Historical Society* (Atlanta: Atlanta Historical Society, Inc., 1976).

3,195. Grove, Dorothy Haverty
Papers. 1938-55. 1 cu.ft.
Open. Published guide.
Atlanta Historical Society.
Scrapbook on the arts in Atlanta compiled by [Mrs. Lon] Grove, an Atlanta author and arts patron, contains articles on musical topics by Grove, a radio script, information on American National Red Cross activities during WWII, and correspondence, programs, articles, and clippings dealing with the Atlanta Symphony Orchestra, the Atlanta Symphony Guild, the Atlanta Music Club, and the Atlanta Junior League. Taken from D. Louise Cook, comp., *Guide to the Manuscript Collections of the Atlanta Historical Society* (Atlanta: Atlanta Historical Society, Inc., 1976).

3,196. Harling, Ada May
Papers. 1929-34. 0.5 cu.ft.
Open. Published guide.
Atlanta Historical Society.
Scrapbook of photos, articles, and clippings on gardens in Atlanta and elsewhere includes items concerning the Atkins Park Garden Club, the Southeastern Flower Show of 1929, and the Garden Club of Georgia. Taken from D. Louise Cook, comp., *Guide to the Manuscript Collections of the Atlanta Historical Society* (Atlanta: Atlanta Historical Society, Inc., 1976).

3,197. Harris, Corra May (White)
Papers. 1927-41. 16 items.
Open. Published guide.
Atlanta Historical Society.
Letters by [Mrs. Lundy Howard] Harris (1869-1935), author of *A Circuit Rider's Wife* (1909), to Frank Daniel of the *Atlanta Journal* and clippings about Harris, her home, and a memorial chapel built by her nephews. Taken from D. Louise Cook, comp., *Guide to the Manuscript Collections of the Atlanta Historical Society* (Atlanta: Atlanta Historical Society, Inc., 1976).

3,198. Harwood-Arrowood, Bertha
Papers. 1909-12. 0.5 cu.ft.
Open. Published guide.
Atlanta Historical Society.
Harwood-Arrowood was founder and president of the Federation of Women's Clubs in Atlanta. Includes accounts of the founding of the Federation and the Tuberculosis Hospital in Atlanta, an account of the formation of school bands and orchestras, and an essay on blacks and black music. Also included is a scrapbook containing correspondence, programs, and clippings relating to opera, performers who came to Atlanta, and the Atlanta Musical Association, of which she was president. Taken from D. Louise Cook, comp., *Guide to the Manuscript Collections of the Atlanta Historical Society* (Atlanta: Atlanta Historical Society, Inc., 1976).

3,199. Haverty, Mary E.
Papers. 1905-19. 0.5 cu.ft.
Open. Published guide.
Atlanta Historical Society.
Scrapbook containing clippings of poems, editorials, and newspaper stories about society, plays and players, and the Rhodes-Haverty Co., an Atlanta furniture firm. Taken from D. Louise Cook, comp., *Guide to the Manuscript Collections of the Atlanta Historical Society* (Atlanta: Atlanta Historical Society, Inc., 1976).

3,200. Hinton, Fanny D.
Papers. 1939-49. 0.5 cu.ft.
Open. Published guide.
Atlanta Historical Society.
Scrapbook of photos and clippings concerning [Miss] Hinton's term as director of Atlanta's Carnegie Library. Taken from D. Louise Cook, comp., *Guide to the Manuscript Collections of the Atlanta Historical Society* (Atlanta: Atlanta Historical Society, Inc., 1976).

3,201. History Class of 1884
Records. 1884-1974. 0.5 cu.ft.
Open. Published guide.
Atlanta Historical Society.
Records of the History Class, the oldest literary group in Atlanta, include manuscripts about Percy Bysshe Shelley, Walter De La Mare, and St. Francis of Assisi; scrapbooks containing the constitution, correspondence, membership lists, history, clippings, and other records; programs; and reprints. Taken from D. Louise Cook, comp., *Guide to the Manuscript Collections of the Atlanta Historical Society* (Atlanta: Atlanta Historical Society, Inc., 1976).

3,202. Hogan, Mary Grace
Papers. 1923-32. 0.5 cu.ft.
Open. Published guide.
Atlanta Historical Society.
Photos and clippings of Hogan, an Atlanta dancer who performed in Broadway musicals. She and her sister Kathleen used the stage surname Van Noy. Taken from D. Louise Cook, comp., *Guide to the Manuscript Collections of the Atlanta Historical Society* (Atlanta: Atlanta Historical Society, Inc., 1976).

3,203. Howell, Rosalie, Family
Papers. 1858-1965. 3 cu.ft.
Open. Published guide.
Atlanta Historical Society.
[Miss] Howell was a nurse with the American National Red Cross during WWI. Correspondence with former patients, official Red Cross documents, family genealogies, photos, postcards, scrapbooks of photos and clippings on hospital facilities and personnel compiled during her tour of duty in France from 1916 to 1919, clippings about her receipt of the Croix de Guerre from the French government, and memorabilia. Papers of her father Evan Park Howell, who was one of the founders of the *Atlanta Constitution,* mayor of Atlanta, and husband of Julia Adelaide Erwin Howell, include his Civil War correspondence and service documents and a scrapbook of clippings. A diary kept in 1873 and 1874 by Evan Howell's stepmother Mary Davis Hook Howell, who was the third wife of Clark Howell, concerns Atlanta church services, daily affairs, and the weather. Taken from D. Louise Cook, comp., *Guide to the Manuscript Collections of the Atlanta Historical Society* (Atlanta: Atlanta Historical Society, Inc., 1976).

3,204. Hubner and Whitney
Papers. 1879-1970. 50 items.
Open. Published guide.
Atlanta Historical Society.
Poems, a lyrical drama, an opera, and correspondence of Charles W. Hubner, who in 1928 was poet laureate of the South. Papers of Mary Frances Whitney Hubner contain a sketch written for the Atlanta Woman's Pioneer Society and broadsides and clippings of the Atlanta Amateurs, a theatrical group. Also included are items relating to W. Whitney Hubner, who was director of the Pittsburgh Musical Institute, 1900-08, and a clipping on a book being written in 1970 by Mary Hubner Walker about Charles W. Hubner. Taken from D. Louise Cook, comp., *Guide to the Manuscript Collections of the Atlanta Historical Society* (Atlanta: Atlanta Historical Society, Inc., 1976).

3,205. Huff, Sarah
Papers. 1862-1939. 0.5 cu.ft.
Open. Published guide.
Atlanta Historical Society.
Scrapbooks containing poems and articles by [Miss] Huff and photos, pamphlets, and clippings on the Atlanta Woman's Pioneer Society, the Civil War, and other subjects. Also included are a partial manuscript of *My 80 Years in Atlanta* (1937), Huff's report as historian of the Pioneer Society, a notebook with biographies of members of the Society, and her diary for the period 1887-91 which deals with such subjects as government, education, social life, prohibition, yellow fever refugees, and an influenza epidemic. Taken from D. Louise Cook, comp., *Guide to the Manuscript*

Collections of the Atlanta Historical Society (Atlanta: Atlanta Historical Society, Inc., 1976).

3,206. Hughs, Susanna M.
Papers. 1880-1965. 0.5 cu.ft.
Open. Published guide.
Atlanta Historical Society.
Manuscripts include one by Lucile Smith Hughs, which deals with the history of Atlanta and West End, which was chartered in 1868 and incorporated into Atlanta in 1894; one by Mother Mary Monica containing family memories; and one by Albert S. Mead, which chronicles a trip through the northern Georgia mountains. Also included are other items relating to the Hughs family and a biography of John Flynn, a member of the first Atlanta school board. Taken from D. Louise Cook, comp., *Guide to the Manuscript Collections of the Atlanta Historical Society* (Atlanta: Atlanta Historical Society, Inc., 1976).

3,207. Johnson, Ann
Papers. 1889-90. 16-page item.
Open. Published guide.
Atlanta Historical Society.
Copy of *The People's Common Sense Medical Adviser,* which [Mrs.] Johnson used as an account book. Purchases were entered by a storekeeper and paid for by washing done by Johnson. Taken from D. Louise Cook, comp., *Guide to the Manuscript Collections of the Atlanta Historical Society* (Atlanta: Atlanta Historical Society, Inc., 1976).

3,208. Jones, Dunwoody
Papers. 1788-1907. 100 pp.
Open. Published guide.
Atlanta Historical Society.
Lists of purchases from British merchants [Mrs.] Elizabeth Munro made between 1788 and 1792. Also included are biographical notes on Dunwoody Jones's father John Jones (1815-94), a Presbyterian minister, and addresses containing Jones's personal memories of Civil War battles, the prison camp at Andersonville, GA, and life on a coastal plantation. Taken from D. Louise Cook, comp., *Guide to the Manuscript Collections of the Atlanta Historical Society* (Atlanta: Atlanta Historical Society, Inc., 1976).

3,209. Junior League
Records. 1926-75. No size given.
Open. Published guide.
Atlanta Historical Society.
Records of the Atlanta League include annual reports, histories, programs, a pamphlet about cultural activities in Atlanta, and the periodicals *Cotton Blossoms* and *Peachtree Papers.* Taken from D. Louise Cook, comp., *Guide to the Manuscript Collections of the Atlanta Historical Society* (Atlanta: Atlanta Historical Society, Inc., 1976).

3,210. Kurtz, Wilbur G., Jr.
Papers. 1912-73. 4 cu.ft.
Open. Published guide.
Atlanta Historical Society.
Papers of Kurtz, archivist for the Coca-Cola Company of Atlanta, include personal and business correspondence, manuscripts, notices, and clippings about *Gone With The Wind,* actress Olivia de Havilland, author Minnie Hite Moody, the Atlanta Historical Society, and various historical events. Papers of Kurtz's mother Annie Laurie Fuller Kurtz include her reminiscences about the filming of *Gone With The Wind,* her will and an accompanying letter to her children, and photos of her. Also included are correspondence, pamphlets, and clippings pertaining to Wilbur G. Kurtz, Sr., exhibitions of his paintings, a history of the Fuller-Kurtz family, and William A. Fuller's account of Andrews' Raid. Taken from D. Louise Cook, comp., *Guide to the Manuscript Collections of the Atlanta Historical Society* (Atlanta: Atlanta Historical Society, Inc., 1976).

3,211. Ladies' Burns Club
Records. 1938-70. 1 cu.ft.
Open. Published guide.
Atlanta Historical Society.
The Club was organized in 1937 to study the poetry of Robert Burns. Minutes; yearbooks containing constitution, bylaws, and lists of officers and members; and scrapbooks of correspondence, photos, and clippings. Taken from D. Louise Cook, comp., *Guide to the Manuscript Collections of the Atlanta Historical Society* (Atlanta: Atlanta Historical Society, Inc., 1976).

3,212. Ladies Memorial Association
Records. 1864-1974. 8 cu.ft.
Open. Published guide.
Atlanta Historical Society.
The Association, formed in 1866, is dedicated to the honor and memory of Confederate veterans. Minutes; resolutions; fiscal records; correspondence; documents concerning memorials, markers, and monuments; membership lists; reports; history of the Association by Alberta Malone; programs; and genealogies of members. Also included are an eyewitness account of Atlanta on the day after General W. T. Sherman's departure in 1864, correspondence and documents relating to the Stone Mountain Memorial Association, and other items. Taken from D. Louise Cook, comp., *Guide to the Manuscript Collections of the Atlanta Historical Society* (Atlanta: Atlanta Historical Society, Inc., 1976).

3,213. Ladies of the Old Guard of the Gate City Guard
Records. 1954-67. 1 cu.ft.
Open. Published guide.
Atlanta Historical Society.
Membership in the group, which was organized in 1954, is open to wives of members of the Old Guard. Scrapbooks contain correspondence about organization activities, rosters, invitations, programs, photos, and clippings. Taken from D. Louise Cook, comp., *Guide to the Manuscript Collections of the Atlanta Historical Society* (Atlanta: Atlanta Historical Society, Inc., 1976).

3,214. Lamar, Clarinda Huntington (Pendleton)
Papers. 1911-38. 0.25 cu.ft.
Open. Published guide.
Atlanta Historical Society.
Articles and clippings relate to Lamar (1856-1943), who was president of the National Society of the Colonial Dames of America and a member of the Women's Council of National Defense during WWI, and to her husband Joseph R. Lamar, who was a US Supreme Court Justice. Taken from D. Louise Cook, comp., *Guide to the Manuscript Collections of the Atlanta Historical Society* (Atlanta: Atlanta Historical Society, Inc., 1976).

3,215. Lattimer, Emma
Papers. 1833-1931. 0.5 cu.ft.
Open. Published guide.
Atlanta Historical Society.
[Miss] Lattimer was one of the first teachers hired by the Atlanta school board (1872). Scrapbook of clippings relating to the Atlanta Fire Department, programs and class rolls of Girls' High School for the years 1872 to 1880, a history of Atlanta public schools by W. W. Gaines, receipts for the purchase of Negro slaves by the Lattimer family, and other material. Taken from D. Louise Cook, comp., *Guide to the Manuscript Collections of the Atlanta Historical Society* (Atlanta: Atlanta Historical Society, Inc., 1976).

3,216. Lauren, Thomas C., and Lauren, Elizabeth M.
Papers. 1815-1957. 0.5 cu.ft.
Open. Published guide.
Atlanta Historical Society.
Scrapbook of photos, programs, and clippings includes documents concerning Elizabeth Lauren's $500,000 bequest for the children's ward at Grady Hospital, a religious education certificate she was awarded in 1886 as a girl in Ireland, and an American National Red Cross certificate she received in Atlanta in 1917. Taken from D. Louise Cook, comp., *Guide to the Manuscript Collections of the Atlanta Historical Society* (Atlanta: Atlanta Historical Society, Inc., 1976).

3,217. League of Women Voters
Records. 1927-74. 0.5 cu.ft.
Open. Published guide.
Atlanta Historical Society.
Official publications of the Atlanta League, including *The Pilgrim, Facts,* handbooks, and a booklet entitled *Studies in Citizenship for Georgia Women,* published in 1923. Taken from D. Louise Cook, comp., *Guide to the Manuscript Collections of the Atlanta Historical Society* (Atlanta: Atlanta Historical Society, Inc., 1976).

3,218. Logan, Joseph Clayton
Papers. 1903-39. 0.5 cu.ft.
Open. Published guide.
Atlanta Historical Society.
Papers of Logan, an Atlanta attorney who in 1905 helped organize the Associated Charities, include manuscripts on the history of Georgia, Mercer University, the Atlanta Woman's Club, early Georgia churches, and social service agencies in Atlanta. Also included are correspondence of Margaret Leary concerning Logan genealogy, a report and notes of the Associated Charities, and biographies of L. P. Grant and Joseph Logan. Taken from D. Louise Cook, comp., *Guide to the Manuscript Collections of the Atlanta Historical Society* (Atlanta: Atlanta Historical Society, Inc., 1976).

3,219. Longstreet, Helen Dortch
Papers. 1904-55. 2.5 cu.ft.
Open. Published guide.
Atlanta Historical Society.
Longstreet (1863-1962) was widow of General James Longstreet. Correspondence with Mrs. P. S. Rothrock, General Julius F. Howell, and others; manuscripts including *Lee and Longstreet at High Tide* (1904) and "Sure Road to World Peace" (1914); speeches; pamphlets; and clippings. Correspondence deals with such subjects as her efforts to vindicate her husband's actions at the Battle of Gettysburg, the establishment of the Longstreet Memorial Association, WWII, the No Foreign War Committee, the United Daughters of the Confederacy, the white primary system, and voting rights. Taken from D. Louise Cook, comp., *Guide to the Manuscript Collections of the Atlanta Historical Society* (Atlanta: Atlanta Historical Society, Inc., 1976).

3,220. Loyal Star of America, Atlanta Lodge No. 56
Records. 1921-54. 21 items.
Open. Published guide.
Atlanta Historical Society.
The Loyal Star is the ladies' auxiliary to the Brotherhood of Railway Carmen of America. Constitution, minutes of a 1952 meeting, financial reports, correspondence, officers report to the 1950 convention, convention proceedings, Frankfort, IN, membership list, directory of grand and subordinate lodges, installation cards, and clippings. Taken from D. Louise Cook, comp., *Guide to the Manuscript Collections of the Atlanta Historical Society* (Atlanta: Atlanta Historical Society, Inc., 1976).

3,221. Lumpkin, Martha
Papers. 1843-1949. 0.5 cu.ft.
Open. Published guide.

Atlanta Historical Society.
Papers of Lumpkin, later Mrs. T. H. Compton, include correspondence; her will; a notebook of poems, epigrams, and diary entries for the years 1845 to 1848; a history by Idolene Lumpkin-Huddleston of the naming of Atlanta; scrapbooks containing diary entries, greeting cards, clippings and Lumpkin's comments on news reports that she had been poisoned by her husband; and *Miss Beecher's Domestic Receipt-Book* (1858) annotated by Lumpkin. Correspondence includes a letter concerning a pin given to Lumpkin by Dolley Madison and a letter to Lumpkin from her father Wilson Lumpkin. Taken from D. Louise Cook, comp., *Guide to the Manuscript Collections of the Atlanta Historical Society* (Atlanta: Atlanta Historical Society, Inc., 1976).

3,222. McCallie, Samuel Washington
Papers. 1888-1948. 1.5 cu.ft.
Open. Published guide.
Atlanta Historical Society.
McCallie (1856-1933) was Georgia's state geologist from 1908 to 1933. Correspondence, autobiographical essay, minutes of the Association of American State Geologists, scrapbooks of clippings, and other material. Papers of McCallie's wife Elizabeth Hanleiter McCallie, who was a member of the executive committee of the Atlanta Historical Society, include correspondence, notes on Atlanta in the 1850s and on the fire of 1917, a speech on the area around Forrest Avenue in 1913, her notes and essay on being a "business girl" in the 1890s, and a genealogy of the Houston-McCallie family. Taken from D. Louise Cook, comp., *Guide to the Manuscript Collections of the Atlanta Historical Society* (Atlanta: Atlanta Historical Society, Inc., 1976).

3,223. McCrary, John Mathew
Papers. 1862-64. 0.25 cu.ft.
Open. Published guide.
Atlanta Historical Society.
Correspondence between McCrary and his wife Mary Boyd McCrary; a list of his taxable property, pay, clothing, and bounty; a furlough order; and a contract between McCrary and his former slaves. Taken from D. Louise Cook, comp., *Guide to the Manuscript Collections of the Atlanta Historical Society* (Atlanta: Atlanta Historical Society, Inc., 1976).

3,224. McCutcheon, Evelyn W.
Papers. 1920-60. 70 items.
Open. Published guide.
Atlanta Historical Society.
Personal correspondence of [Mrs. Howard C.] McCutcheon, including a letter concerning the site for Girls' High School; her deposition in the contempt-of-court citation in the case of *State of Georgia v. Atlanta Newspapers, Inc.;* family photos; PTA correspondence; the Atlanta Woman's Club audit and yearbook; material pertaining to the Better Films Committee; and the will of Vivan Hamilton Boey. Taken from D. Louise Cook, comp., *Guide to the Manuscript Collections of the Atlanta Historical Society* (Atlanta: Atlanta Historical Society, Inc., 1976).

3,225. Marsh, Margaret (Mitchell)
Papers. 1923-71. 0.5 cu.ft.
Open. Published guide.
Atlanta Historical Society.
Papers of [Mrs.] Marsh (1900-49), a journalist and author of *Gone With The Wind,* include correspondence, guest book, clippings, articles by and about Marsh, program for the unveiling of a bust of Marsh by the Georgia Hall of Fame, and reminiscences by Major Stephen Pierson. Correspondents include Ruth Blair and the Atlanta Historical Society. Taken from D. Louise Cook, comp., *Guide to the Manuscript Collections of the Atlanta Historical Society* (Atlanta: Atlanta Historical Society, Inc., 1976).

3,226. Matthews, Antoinette Johnson
Papers. 1885-1974. 1.5 cu.ft.
Open. Published guide.
Atlanta Historical Society.
[Mrs.] Matthews was headmistress of the Out-of-Doors School. Correspondence, travel diaries for 1954 to 1963, manuscript of *Oakdale Road...* (1972), photos, memorabilia from her reign in 1974 as one of the Top Ten Ladies of the Year, enrollment lists for her school for the years 1947 to 1956, and clippings. Included is material relating to her family, her school, Tullie Smith, the Edgewood Public School class of 1908, and Dame Sybil Hathaway of Sark. Taken from D. Louise Cook, comp., *Guide to the Manuscript Collections of the Atlanta Historical Society* (Atlanta: Atlanta Historical Society, Inc., 1976).

3,227. Mims, Sue Harper
Papers. 1876-87. 0.25 cu.ft.
Open. Published guide.
Atlanta Historical Society.
Scrapbook of [Mrs. Livingston] Mims, organizer of the Christian Science Church in Atlanta and a prominent Atlanta hostess, consists of excerpts from her diary. The excerpts, which include her observations on Reconstruction and Atlanta's social growth and contain references to the visits of such figures as President Hayes, President Cleveland, and Jefferson Davis, were published in the *Atlanta Constitution* in 1914. Taken from D. Louise Cook, comp., *Guide to the Manuscript Collections of the Atlanta Historical Society* (Atlanta: Atlanta Historical Society, Inc., 1976).

3,228. Moore, Charlotte (Palmer)
Papers. Ca. 1875-1906. 0.5 cu.ft.
Open. Published guide.
Atlanta Historical Society.
Photos of [Mrs. R. F.] Moore and her sister Ellen Palmer, which were taken by their father, a professional photographer, provide a study of changing dress styles as the sisters grew from children to young women. Taken from D. Louise Cook, comp., *Guide to the Manuscript Collections of the Atlanta Historical Society* (Atlanta: Atlanta Historical Society, Inc., 1976).

3,229. Moore, Cornelia Jackson
Papers. 1865-1949. 2.5 cu.ft.
Open. Published guide.
Atlanta Historical Society.
Moore was active in the Atlanta Music Club, the Order of Old Fashioned Women, and the Southeastern Fair; she was married to Wilmer L. Moore, president of the Southern States Insurance Company and the Atlanta Chamber of Commerce. Diaries and scrapbooks of the Moore family contain clippings and notes on Atlanta society, the debut of their daughter Jacquelyn Moore (1897-1949), Cornelia Moore's travels in Europe, and aiding the wounded at Fort MacPherson. Taken from D. Louise Cook, comp., *Guide to the Manuscript Collections of the Atlanta Historical Society* (Atlanta: Atlanta Historical Society, Inc., 1976).

3,230. National League of Pen Women
Records. 1948-72. 74 items.
Open. Published guide.
Atlanta Historical Society.
Yearbooks containing bylaws, officer and membership lists, and programs; issues of the League's newsletter *Pen-Graphs;* and a program for the placement of a stone memorializing Lillian Barker. Taken from D. Louise Cook, comp., *Guide to the Manuscript Collections of the Atlanta Historical Society* (Atlanta: Atlanta Historical Society, Inc., 1976).

3,231. Needlework Guild
Records. 1926-52. 1 cu.ft.
Open. Published guide.
Atlanta Historical Society.
Scrapbook of the Atlanta branch of the Guild contains correspondence, brochures, programs, and clippings pertaining to Guild activities. Taken fromD. Louise Cook, comp., *Guide to the Manuscript Collections of the Atlanta Historical Society* (Atlanta: Atlanta Historical Society, Inc., 1976).

3,232. Newman, Frances
Papers. 1924. 1 item.
Open. Published guide.
Atlanta Historical Society.
Letter regarding Newman's novel *Dead Lovers Are Faithful Lovers.* Taken from D. Louise Cook, comp., *Guide to the Manuscript Collections of the Atlanta Historical Society* (Atlanta: Atlanta Historical Society, Inc., 1976).

3,233. Nicholson, Marie
Papers. 1938-75. 3.5 cu.ft.
Open. Published guide.
Atlanta Historical Society.
Photos, awards, programs, scrapbooks, and clippings of [Mrs. J. J.] Nicholson, a nationally known tulip expert, reflect her involvement with various garden clubs, the Atlanta Tulip Study Club, the Atlanta Tulip Show Association, and the National Tulip Society. Taken from D. Louise Cook, comp., *Guide to the Manuscript Collections of the Atlanta Historical Society* (Atlanta: Atlanta Historical Society, Inc., 1976).

3,234. Nicolson, William Perrin, and Crane, Carolyn C.
Papers. 1776-1949. 1.5 cu.ft.
Open. Published guide.
Atlanta Historical Society.
Papers of William Nicolson, the first dean of the Southern Medical College and a pioneer in surgery for appendicitis and craniotomies, include personal correspondence for 1913 to 1946, family photos, biographical sketches of him, scrapbooks of trade and greeting cards, and clippings. Also included are a 1776 letter describing fighting around Norfolk, VA, between soldiers of Lord Dunsmore and colonists, a pamphlet by "Attica" opposing woman suffrage on the grounds that women are not human beings, and a catalog from the International Exposition in Philadelphia. Taken from D. Louise Cook, comp., *Guide to the Manuscript Collections of the Atlanta Historical Society* (Atlanta: Atlanta Historical Society, Inc., 1976).

3,235. 1908 History Class
Records. 1908-72. 1 cu.ft.
Open. Published guide.
Atlanta Historical Society.
The Class was a women's study group organized in 1908 by [Mrs.] Belle Fleet Matheson. Minutes, manuscripts, membership lists, programs, and clippings about Matheson. Taken from D. Louise Cook, comp., *Guide to the Manuscript Collections of the Atlanta Historical Society* (Atlanta: Atlanta Historical Society, Inc., 1976).

3,236. 1900 Study Club
Records. 1900-75. 0.5 cu.ft.
Open. Published guide.
Atlanta Historical Society.
Organized in 1900 to study literary topics, cultural and political affairs, and life in other countries, the Club is one of the oldest members of the Atlanta Federation of Women's Clubs. Manuscript on the history of the Club, which was first known as the Literary Circle and later as the Inman Park Students Club, and programs listing members and study topics. Taken from D. Louise Cook, comp., *Guide to the Manuscript Collections of the Atlanta Historical Society* (Atlanta: Atlanta Historical Society, Inc., 1976).

3,237. Nineteenth Century Class
Records. 1912-52. 0.5 cu.ft.
Open. Published guide.
Atlanta Historical Society.
Minutes, correspondence, membership lists, study topics, programs, and receipts of the Class, a women's group for the study of historical topics. Taken from D. Louise Cook, comp., *Guide to the Manuscript Collections of the Atlanta Historical Society* (Atlanta: Atlanta Historical Society, Inc., 1976).

3,238. Orr, Dorothy
Papers. 1847-1965. 0.5 cu.ft.
Open. Published guide.
Atlanta Historical Society.
Manuscript of Orr's book *Gustavus John Orr, The Man and His Period, 1819-1887* (1965) and a letter to G. J. Orr from his fiancée in 1847 concerning their upcoming wedding plans. Taken from D. Louise Cook, comp., *Guide to the Manuscript Collections of the Atlanta Historical Society* (Atlanta: Atlanta Historical Society, Inc., 1976).

3,239. Our Lady of Perpetual Help Home
Records. 1971-73. 3 items.
Open. Published guide.
Atlanta Historical Society.
Records relating to this Atlanta nursing home for terminal cancer patients include brochures with the history of the Home and a commendatory editorial from the *Atlanta Journal*. Taken from D. Louise Cook, comp., *Guide to the Manuscript Collections of the Atlanta Historical Society* (Atlanta: Atlanta Historical Society, Inc., 1976).

3,240. Paul, Emma V.
Papers. 1912-14. 0.13 cu.ft.
Open. Published guide.
Atlanta Historical Society.
Scrapbook containing a list of objectives, handbills, editorial cartoons, and clippings which chronicle the woman suffrage movement in Atlanta and activities of the local chapter of the Georgia Woman's Suffrage Association. Photos of leaders of the movement and notes by Paul are contained in an issue of *The Georgia Patriot,* which was published weekly by [Mrs.] Margaret McWhorter of Gainesville, GA. Taken from D. Louise Cook, comp., *Guide to the Manuscript Collections of the Atlanta Historical Society* (Atlanta: Atlanta Historical Society, Inc., 1976).

3,241. Powell, Evelyn Knox
Papers. 1922. 0.25 cu.ft.
Open. Published guide.
Atlanta Historical Society.
Scrapbook of photos, autographs, clippings, and memorabilia from [Mrs.] Powell's senior year at Girls' High School. Taken from D. Louise Cook, comp., *Guide to the Manuscript Collections of the Atlanta Historical Society* (Atlanta: Atlanta Historical Society, Inc., 1976).

3,242. Prescott, Emma J. Slade
Papers. 1882. 1 item.
Open. Published guide.
Atlanta Historical Society.
[Mrs. Alfred] Prescott's reminiscences of the Civil War, during which she spent two years in Decatur, GA, and then evacuated to Columbus, GA, with her four children. Taken from D. Louise Cook, comp., *Guide to the Manuscript Collections of the Atlanta Historical Society* (Atlanta: Atlanta Historical Society, Inc., 1976).

3,243. Principals' Club
Records. 1930-45. 0.25 cu.ft.
Open. Published guide.
Atlanta Historical Society.
Scrapbook containing correspondence, committee reports, membership rosters, programs, and puzzles and games for elementary school children. Taken from D. Louise Cook, comp., *Guide to the Manuscript Collections of the Atlanta Historical Society* (Atlanta: Atlanta Historical Society, Inc., 1976).

3,244. Rabun Gap-Nacoochee School
Records. 1928-74. 1 cu.ft.
Open. Published guide.
Atlanta Historical Society.
The Nacoochee Institute and the Rabun Gap School merged in 1926 to form an educational institution for mountain families. Annual reports, minutes, a manuscript history of the School, a history and membership lists of the Rabun Gap-Nacoochee Guild, yearbooks, photos of students and the school site, programs, bulletins, and articles. Taken from D. Louise Cook, comp., *Guide to the Manuscript Collections of the Atlanta Historical Society* (Atlanta: Atlanta Historical Society, Inc., 1976).

3,245. Randall, Helen McCrary
Papers. 1907-65. 1 cu.ft.
Open. Published guide.
Atlanta Historical Society.
Papers relating to Randall and her daughter Helen (Randall) Shreve include family photos, clippings pertaining to society events, ephemera of Helen Randall while at Washington Seminary, and publications of the Atlanta Junior League. Taken from D. Louise Cook, comp., *Guide to the Manuscript Collections of the Atlanta Historical Society* (Atlanta: Atlanta Historical Society, Inc., 1976).

3,246. Raoul Family
Papers. 1829-1953. 1.5 cu.ft.
Open. Published guide.
Atlanta Historical Society.
Correspondence and business records of Captain William G. Raoul and his brother-in-law William M. Wadley, executives of the Central of Georgia Railroad, and of James F. Ball and James M. Ball. Also included are an 1829 letter George Wendrell wrote to be given to his wife upon his death, diaries from the 1890s of Mary and Norman Raoul, a DeKalb County land grant to Thornton Ward's six orphans, notebooks of pencil sketches by Rosine Raoul, and 400 pages of memoirs by Mary Raoul Millis, who married Captain John Millis in 1893, concerning their life in Georgia, various US cities, Paris, and the Orient. Taken from D. Louise Cook, comp., *Guide to the Manuscript Collections of the Atlanta Historical Society* (Atlanta: Atlanta Historical Society, Inc., 1976).

3,247. Rawson, Mary
Papers. 1864. 3 items.
Open. Published guide.
Atlanta Historical Society.
Diary in which Rawson, who was the daughter of Edward E. Rawson of Atlanta and later the wife of Captain John D. Ray of the First Georgia Volunteers, Confederate States Army, describes the capture, occupation, and civilian evacuation of Atlanta in 1864. Taken from D. Louise Cook, comp., *Guide to the Manuscript Collections of the Atlanta Historical Society* (Atlanta: Atlanta Historical Society, Inc., 1976).

3,248. Ray, Hypatia Bowdoin
Papers. 1886-1945. 0.5 cu.ft.
Open. Published guide.
Atlanta Historical Society.
Scrapbooks of [Mrs.] Ray contain theater programs from Atlanta and New York, items concerning Atlanta society and Hollywood movie stars, and clippings. Taken from D. Louise Cook, comp., *Guide to the Manuscript Collections of the Atlanta Historical Society* (Atlanta: Atlanta Historical Society, Inc., 1976).

3,249. Robson, Kate Hester
Papers. 1910-12. 51-page item.
Open. Published guide.
Atlanta Historical Society.
Memoirs of Robson cover the years 1840 to 1912. Robson moved with her husband from Madison, GA, to Atlanta in 1859 and during the Civil War made uniforms for soldiers and worked in a hospital. She describes her experiences during the War and mentions the destruction and demoralization which followed. Taken from D. Louise Cook, comp., *Guide to the Manuscript Collections of the Atlanta Historical Society* (Atlanta: Atlanta Historical Society, Inc., 1976).

3,250. Service Star Legion
Records. 1924-52. 15 items.
Open. Published guide.
Atlanta Historical Society.
Booklet on the Fulton County chapter of the Legion with list of officers, history, membership roster, and list of WWI dead; programs for the eighth and 10th conventions; and issues of the *Service Star.* Also includes a publication by the War Mother's Service Star Legion, a branch of the Legion formed by Fulton County mothers to support their sons who served in WWI and to honor the memory of those who died; the publication gives the history and purposes of the group and lists officers, members, and soldiers who died in combat. Taken from D. Louise Cook, comp., *Guide to the Manuscript Collections of the Atlanta Historical Society* (Atlanta: Atlanta Historical Society, Inc., 1976).

3,251. Seydell, Mildred (Woolley)
Papers. 1915-67. 20 items.
Open. Published guide.
Atlanta Historical Society.
Papers of Seydell, who wrote for many Georgia newspapers, include correspondence and fan mail, an interview with Gary Cooper, an article, clippings of her *Georgian-American* column, and two issues of the *Seydell Quarterly.* Taken from D. Louise Cook, comp., *Guide to the Manuscript Collections of the Atlanta Historical Society* (Atlanta: Atlanta Historical Society, Inc., 1976).

3,252. Shafe, Anne
Papers. 1921-73. 0.75 cu.ft.
Open. Published guide.
Atlanta Historical Society.
Scrapbooks of clippings and items concerning [Miss] Shafe's activities in high school and as a teacher of expression. The bulk of the material focuses on her efforts on behalf of shut-ins and the International Shut-ins Day Association. Taken from D. Louise Cook, comp., *Guide to the Manuscript Collections of the Atlanta Historical Society* (Atlanta: Atlanta Historical Society, Inc., 1976).

3,253. Sheltering Arms Association of Day Nurseries
Records. 1909-74. 0.5 cu.ft.
Open. Published guide.
Atlanta Historical Society.
Constitution, bylaws, annual reports, manuscript histories, and clippings of the Association, which grew out of the Barclay Sewing Circle in 1888 and which was founded by Dorothy Colquitt Arkwright. The Association established several nurseries primarily for the care of children of textile mill workers; the Dorothy Arkwright, Osgood Sanders, Cornelia Jackson Moore, and Hay-Silverman Day Care Centers are still in existence. Taken from D. Louise Cook, comp., *Guide to the Manuscript Collections of the Atlanta Historical Society* (Atlanta: Atlanta Historical Society, Inc., 1976).

3,254. Slaton, Sarah Francis Grant
Papers. 1864-1921. 2 cu.ft.
Open. Published guide.
Atlanta Historical Society.
Business and personal correspondence, constitution and bylaws of the Capital City Club and the

Cotillion Club, business receipts given to [Mrs. John M.] Slaton and Mrs. W. D. Grant, receipts given to W. D. Grant by the Confederacy, family photos, and business cards and advertisements. Taken from D. Louise Cook, comp., *Guide to the Manuscript Collections of the Atlanta Historical Society* (Atlanta: Atlanta Historical Society, Inc., 1976).

3,255. Snipes, Ethel Taylor
Papers. 1922-72. 0.25 cu.ft.
Open. Published guide.
Atlanta Historical Society.
Scrapbook and memorabilia collected by [Mrs.] Snipes while a student at Girls' High School in the class of 1922 and signatures of those who attended the 50th class reunion. Taken from D. Louise Cook, comp., *Guide to the Manuscript Collections of the Atlanta Historical Society* (Atlanta: Atlanta Historical Society, Inc., 1976).

3,256. Spalding, Mary (Connally)
Papers. 1868-1952. 7 cu.ft.
Open. Published guide.
Atlanta Historical Society.
Scrapbooks compiled by Spalding and her mother Mrs. E. L. Connally contain correspondence, notes, clippings, and memorabilia on Atlanta society and family members and include items pertaining to Girls' High School, the Second Baptist Church and its Women's Missionary Society, and Atlanta author Myrta Lockett Avary. Also included are a manuscript by Spalding on her family's activities during the Battle of Atlanta, personal and business account books of A. T. Spalding and Mr. and Mrs. Elijah L. Connally, and genealogical material on the Connally, Spalding, and other families. Taken from D. Louise Cook, comp., *Guide to the Manuscript Collections of the Atlanta Historical Society* (Atlanta: Atlanta Historical Society, Inc., 1976).

3,257. Thompson, C. Mildred
Papers. 1881-1975. 2.5 cu.ft.
Open. Published guide.
Atlanta Historical Society.
An author, historian, and educator, [Miss] Thompson served as dean of Vassar College from 1923 to 1948 and was a member of the American delegation to the Conference of Allied Ministers of Education in 1944 in London. Collection contains correspondence and photos with Franklin D. Roosevelt, Harry Truman, John F. Kennedy, and Adlai Stevenson; correspondence, bulletins, and clippings relating to Vassar College and current political affairs; and articles by Thompson. Thompson is the author of *Reconstruction in Georgia: Economic, Social and Political, 1920.* Taken from D. Louise Cook, comp., *Guide to the Manuscript Collections of the Atlanta Historical Society* (Atlanta: Atlanta Historical Society, Inc., 1976).

3,258. Thompson, Kate
Papers. 1842-1963. 3.5 cu.ft.
Open. Published guide.
Atlanta Historical Society.
Family correspondence, family photos, a Georgia land grant, a report sent by the University of Georgia to parents in 1842 grading students on character traits and studies, and a scrapbook and picture album containing greeting cards and picture postcards of Atlanta scenes. Taken from D. Louise Cook, comp., *Guide to the Manuscript Collections of the Atlanta Historical Society* (Atlanta: Atlanta Historical Society, Inc., 1976).

3,259. Thompson, Mary J. Stafford
Papers. 1846-64. 18 items.
Open. Published guide.
Atlanta Historical Society.
Family letters describing Decatur, GA, and Rome, GA, provide insights into daily life. Taken from D. Louise Cook, comp., *Guide to the Manuscript Collections of the Atlanta Historical Society* (Atlanta: Atlanta Historical Society, Inc., 1976).

3,260. Thornton, Ella Mae
Papers. 1948-68. 0.5 cu.ft.
Open. Published guide.
Atlanta Historical Society.
Letter from Princess Elizabeth in 1948 thanking [Miss] Thornton and other ladies for sending Georgia commemorative china as a wedding present, an account by Thornton of Graham Jackson's reminiscences of the day President F. D. Roosevelt died in Warm Springs, GA, her account concerning the figure atop the dome of the capitol, and a biographical sketch of the life of John Smith Prather. Taken from D. Louise Cook, comp., *Guide to the Manuscript Collections of the Atlanta Historical Society* (Atlanta: Atlanta Historical Society, Inc., 1976).

3,261. Uncle Remus Memorial Association
Records. 1920-27. 2 items.
Open. Published guide.
Atlanta Historical Society.
History of the Association and a program for Uncle Remus Day. Taken from D. Louise Cook, comp., *Guide to the Manuscript Collections of the Atlanta Historical Society* (Atlanta: Atlanta Historical Society, Inc., 1976).

3,262. United Daughters of the Confederacy
Records. 1861-1974. 2.5 cu.ft.
Open. Published guide.
Atlanta Historical Society.
Minutes and programs of annual conventions, a history of the Atlanta chapter, a list of members, and historical essays prepared under the sponsorship of the Atlanta chapter. Scrapbook of the College Park chapter contains letters of a Georgia Confederate soldier from a prisoner-of-war camp in Ohio, a Civil War commission, a list of Georgia volunteers in the service of the Confederacy, a program of a Memorial Day observance, Confederate money and postage stamps, and a 1905 *Atlanta Journal* supplement entitled "Our Women in the War." Scrapbook of the Robert E. Lee chapter contains historical manuscripts by [Miss] Mildred Rutherford, pamphlets, photos, and clippings. Taken from D. Louise Cook, comp., *Guide to the Manuscript Collections of the Atlanta Historical Society* (Atlanta: Atlanta Historical Society, Inc., 1976).

3,263. Warren, Irene
Papers. 1939. 0.5 cu.ft.
Open. Published guide.
Atlanta Historical Society.
Scrapbook containing correspondence, programs, and clippings pertaining to the world premiere of the movie *Gone With The Wind.* Included is a letter from Margaret (Mitchell) Marsh. Taken from D. Louise Cook, comp., *Guide to the Manuscript Collections of the Atlanta Historical Society* (Atlanta: Atlanta Historical Society, Inc., 1976).

3,264. Washington Seminary
Records. 1892-1947. 0.5 cu.ft.
Open. Published guide.
Atlanta Historical Society.
Founded in 1878 by [Miss] Anita Washington and [Miss] Lola Washington, the Washington Seminary was a college preparatory school for women which in 1953 merged with the Westminster Schools. School catalogs; programs for commencements, recitals, and other school events; and issues of the school newspaper *Missemma.* Taken from D. Louise Cook, comp., *Guide to the Manuscript Collections of the Atlanta Historical Society* (Atlanta: Atlanta Historical Society, Inc., 1976).

3,265. Wesley Sisters
Papers. 1909-61. 17.5 cu.ft.
Open. Published guide.
Atlanta Historical Society.
Scrapbooks of Rusha, Bonnie, and Emma Wesley, Atlanta schoolteachers and principals, contain greeting cards, picture postcards, a program from the Quota Club convention, and clippings including items on the Georgia bicentennial. Taken from D. Louise Cook, comp., *Guide to the Manuscript Collections of the Atlanta Historical Society* (Atlanta: Atlanta Historical Society, Inc., 1976).

3,266. Whitner, Sarah Martha Cobb
Papers. 1857-1900. 0.67 cu.ft.
Open. Published guide.
Atlanta Historical Society.
Whitner was the daughter of Georgia governor Howell Cobb (1815-68) and the wife of Major John C. Whitner, president of the Fulton County Bimetallic League. Scrapbooks contain clippings about the careers, weddings, and deaths of family members, including her uncle Thomas R. R. Cobb, who founded the Lucy Cobb Institute for Women. Also included are clippings relating to the General Assembly of the Presbyterian Church in the United States and to the Central Presbyterian Church of Atlanta. Taken from D. Louise Cook, comp., *Guide to the Manuscript Collections of the Atlanta Historical Society* (Atlanta: Atlanta Historical Society, Inc., 1976).

3,267. Whitten, Willie May
Papers. 1909-27. 0.25 cu.ft.
Open. Published guide.
Atlanta Historical Society.
Scrapbook of programs, photos, and clippings about the performances of [Mrs. James H.] Whitten, an Atlanta vocalist who performed at the Howard Theatre and was a soloist at the First Baptist Church and All Saints churches. Taken from D. Louise Cook, comp., *Guide to the Manuscript Collections of the Atlanta Historical Society* (Atlanta: Atlanta Historical Society, Inc., 1976).

3,268. Williams, Mr. and Mrs. Jesse Parker
Papers. 1860-1941. 15 items.
Open. Published guide.
Atlanta Historical Society.
Upon the death of her husband Jesse Williams, Cora Best (Taylor) Williams assumed the presidency of the Georgia, Florida, and Alabama Railroad, the first woman known to have held such a position. Correspondence, Cora Taylor's diary describing her fiancé and impending marriage, her report cards from Wesleyan Female College, biographical information, and an invitation to the dedication of the Jesse Parker Williams Hospital which, built with funds provided by Cora Williams, served women and children whether or not they were able to pay. Taken from D. Louise Cook, comp., *Guide to the Manuscript Collections of the Atlanta Historical Society* (Atlanta: Atlanta Historical Society, Inc., 1976).

3,269. Williams, Mrs. Beaufort Mathews
Papers. Ca. 1880-1900. 1 cu.ft.
Open. Published guide.
Atlanta Historical Society.
Scrapbooks of clippings pertaining to the Civil War, southern Negroes, and romantic prose. Taken from D. Louise Cook, comp., *Guide to the Manuscript Collections of the Atlanta Historical Society* (Atlanta: Atlanta Historical Society, Inc., 1976).

3,270. Wilson, Benjamin J.
Papers. 1850-96. 1 cu.ft.
Open. Published guide.
Atlanta Historical Society.
An Irish immigrant and Atlanta businessman, Wilson (1825-96) was involved in real estate, cotton, and brickmaking. Business and personal correspondence, drafts and receipts from Atlanta merchants, commercial and legal documents including an 1863 receipt for slaves purchased and a letter to Wilson itemizing prices and purchase

information for 14 slaves, architect's specifications for a building erected by Wilson, photos, and other material. Also included is a scrapbook kept by Mrs. Wilson of poems, recipes, and stories about West End. Taken from D. Louise Cook, comp., *Guide to the Manuscript Collections of the Atlanta Historical Society* (Atlanta: Atlanta Historical Society, Inc., 1976).

3,271. Winship and Flournoy Family
Papers. 1822-1951. 1 cu.ft.
Open. Published guide.
Atlanta Historical Society.
Collection contains letters describing life in Atlanta and the area battlefields as they appeared just after the Battle of Atlanta, notes made by Anna Winship during her studies at Wesleyan Female College from 1846 to 1850, a notebook containing sermons and theological ideas of Robert Flournoy, a property settlement agreement between Josiah A. Flournoy and Anna E. Winship prior to their marriage, Georgia land deeds, a receipt for the purchase of slaves, a listing of Macon County family units in 1859, reprints of Macon newspapers from the 19th century, and other material. Taken from D. Louise Cook, comp., *Guide to the Manuscript Collections of the Atlanta Historical Society* (Atlanta: Atlanta Historical Society, Inc., 1976).

3,272. Woman of the Year of Atlanta
Records. 1944-73. 1 cu.ft.
Open. Published guide.
Atlanta Historical Society.
Secretary's subject file containing bylaws, minutes, and programs of the annual award dinner of the organization, which was founded in 1943 to honor achievements of Atlanta's women; the group was sponsored each year by a different business firm. Taken from D. Louise Cook, comp., *Guide to the Manuscript Collections of the Atlanta Historical Society* (Atlanta: Atlanta Historical Society, Inc., 1976).

3,273. Women's Auxiliary of the Medical Association of Atlanta
Records. 1923-70. 11 cu.ft.
Open. Published guide.
Atlanta Historical Society.
Scrapbooks of correspondence, articles, photos, and clippings about the Association, its members, structure, projects, programs, and awards. Projects of the Association covered such areas as career guidance, mental health, public health, safety, and community services. Taken from D. Louise Cook, comp., *Guide to the Manuscript Collections of the Atlanta Historical Society* (Atlanta: Atlanta Historical Society, Inc., 1976).

3,274. Women's Relief Corps
Records. 1912-44. 4 items.
Open. Published guide.
Atlanta Historical Society.
Records of the Corps, whose purpose was to care for graves in the National Cemetery in Marietta, GA, and to do relief work with the American National Red Cross, include the club book containing minutes, correspondence, and membership lists; a history of the organization; and ephemera. Taken from D. Louise Cook, comp., *Guide to the Manuscript Collections of the Atlanta Historical Society* (Atlanta: Atlanta Historical Society, Inc., 1976).

3,275. Wooten, Katherine
Papers. 1884-1917. 1.5 cu.ft.
Open. Published guide.
Atlanta Historical Society.
Scrapbooks of [Miss] Wooten contain programs and clippings relating to theatrical events and personalities in Atlanta. Also included are clippings about Marthasville, GA, and the Cotton States and International Exposition in 1895, programs for the first Metropolitan Opera concert in Atlanta in 1896 and for a carnival benefiting Grady Hospital, and an invitation for commencement exercises at Agnes Scott Institute. Taken from D. Louise Cook, comp., *Guide to the Manuscript Collections of the Atlanta Historical Society* (Atlanta: Atlanta Historical Society, Inc., 1976).

3,276. Wylie, Lollie Belle
Papers. 1909-26. 40 items.
Open. Published guide.
Atlanta Historical Society.
Clippings of [Mrs. Hart] Wylie's series in the *Atlanta Journal* on pioneer women and an account of her part in establishing the author's grove in Piedmont Park, Atlanta. Taken from D. Louise Cook, comp., *Guide to the Manuscript Collections of the Atlanta Historical Society* (Atlanta: Atlanta Historical Society, Inc., 1976).

3,277. Young Matrons Circle for Tallulah Falls School
Records. 1929-67. 6 cu.ft.
Open. Published guide.
Atlanta Historical Society.
Minute books and scrapbooks of the organization. Taken from D. Louise Cook, comp., *Guide to the Manuscript Collections of the Atlanta Historical Society* (Atlanta: Atlanta Historical Society, Inc., 1976).

3,278. Mitchell, Margaret Munnerlyn
Papers. Nd. 1418 items.
Access restricted. Inventory list.
Atlanta Public Library.
Manuscripts, memorabilia, and books of Mitchell (1900-49), the author of *Gone With The Wind.* Mitchell was married to John R. Marsh from 1925 until her death, but she continued to use her maiden name in connection with her writing career.

3,279. Association of Southern Women for the Prevention of Lynching
Records. 1920-43. 1 vol. and 11,575 items.
Open. Unpublished guide.
Atlanta University, Trevor Arnett Library, Negro Collection.
An integral part of the Commission on Interracial Cooperation, the Association grew out of and in 1930 supplanted the Commission's woman's work committee, with [Mrs.] Jessie Daniel Ames as its executive director. Members of the Association, most of them churchwomen, worked to mobilize antilynching sentiment throughout the southern states and to repudiate the fiction that lynching was necessary for the protection of white southern womanhood. Organizational records; correspondence; literature; miscellaneous office file material; lynching data for the years 1931 to 1941, including statistical studies, eye-witness reports, accounts of prevented lynchings, pledge forms signed by members and peace officers, comments on pending antilynching legislation, and clippings; and records of state councils from Alabama, Arkansas, Florida, Georgia, Kentucky, Louisiana, Mississippi, Missouri, North Carolina, Oklahoma, South Carolina, Tennessee, and Texas.

3,280. Atlanta University Archives
Records. 1865-1947. 24,847 items.
Open. Unpublished guide.
Atlanta University, Trevor Arnett Library, Negro Collection.
Material pertaining to Atlanta University, a coeducational institution established in 1865, and to its board of trustees, college faculty, staff, students, and the growth of its physical plant. Included are minutes of trustees meetings, presidents' reports, legal documents, financial statements, memoranda, speeches, administrative correspondence, curricula outlines, building plans, photos, publications, clippings on Negro life after the Reconstruction period, and letters dealing with financial support for Negroes attending the University and with maintenance of the facilities. Among the correspondents are Jane Addams, Mary (McLeod) Bethune, Charlotte Hawkins Brown, Nannie H. Burroughs, Annie Smith-Derricotte, Harriet E. Giles, M. Agnes Jones, Lucy (Craft) Laney, Florence M. Read, Lucy H. Spelman, and Alice Tapley.

3,281. Atlanta University Archives: Horace Bumstead
Papers. 1886-1907. 1830 items.
Open. Unpublished guide.
Atlanta University, Trevor Arnett Library, Negro Collection.
Administrative and business correspondence of Bumstead, second president of Atlanta University, includes letters accompanying contributions from religious and philanthropic societies and letters from former students reflecting how difficult it was for Negro children to obtain an education, especially in the South. Other papers deal with the beginnings of the Atlanta University Conferences under the leadership of W. E. B. DuBois and with various student organizations.

3,282. Chautauqua Circle
Records. 1913-70. 5 vols. and 121 items.
Open. Unpublished guide.
Atlanta University, Trevor Arnett Library, Negro Collection.
One of the oldest Negro women's clubs in Atlanta, the Circle was organized by Henrietta (Curtis) [Mrs. James R.] Porter and in 1913 became a permanent organization. Includes minutes books, financial records, an official account of the group's activities from 1913 to 1963, records of the Circle's assistance to local social welfare agencies, correspondence among members, and a pamphlet entitled *The Home League,* apparently from the early 1900s, which is concerned with women's rights. The Circle was inspired by the National Chautauqua Movement, an influential development in popular education that originated in 1874 in New York state. The Circle's primary activity was a study program involving reports made by members at monthly meetings on political ideologies and issues, civil rights, international relations, economics, art, literature, science, religious philosophies, current social issues, the American Negro, and topics of special interest to women. In addition the Circle sponsored lectures, debates, summer courses, dramatic readings, and social entertainment.

3,283. Commission on Interracial Cooperation
Records. 1919-43. 61,967 items.
Open. Unpublished guide.
Atlanta University, Trevor Arnett Library, Negro Collection.
The Commission was founded in 1919 to reduce mounting racial tensions, to improve the status of the Negro population, and to educate the white and Negro races in mutual tolerance, understanding, and cooperation. In 1943 the Commission merged with the newly formed Southern Regional Council. Minutes of annual meetings of executive councils, boards of directors, and the membership; correspondence; office files; reports and surveys; research projects; studies of the economic status of the Negro; lynching data; theses; miscellaneous material; and records of such CIC state committees as Alabama, Arkansas, Florida, Georgia, Kentucky, Louisiana, Mississippi, North Carolina, Oklahoma, South Carolina, Tennessee, Texas, Virginia, and Ohio. Each of the state committees either had women members or separate women's committees, the records of which are also included. [Mrs.] Jessie Daniel Ames, [Mrs.] Mary (McLeod) Bethune, and [Mrs.] Charlotte Hawkins Brown were among the founding and guiding members of the original organization; much of the correspondence and other records were generated by Ames, who was the director of the woman's work committee.

3,284. Cullen-Jackman Memorial Collection: Bontemps, Arna Wendell
Papers. Nd. No size given.
Open. Unpublished guide.
Atlanta University, Trevor Arnett Library, Negro Collection.
Personal correspondence of Bontemps (1902-) with Harold Jackman and Langston Hughes includes drafts of several poems and an article on Negro poets. In connection with Bontemps's compilation of an anthology of Negro poets, he received letters from Dorothy Vena Johnson, Georgia (Douglas) Johnson, Helene Johnson, Catherine McCarthy, Cora Bell Moten, Effie Lee Newsome, Henrietta Sharon, and others.

3,285. Cullen-Jackman Memorial Collection: Cullen, Countee
Papers. 1928-45. Ca. 30 items.
Open. Unpublished guide.
Atlanta University, Trevor Arnett Library, Negro Collection.
Papers of Cullen (1903-46), a playwright and poet, contain literary correspondence with a number of Harlem Renaissance figures, among them Langston Hughes, Carl Van Vechten, and W. E. B. DuBois; manuscripts of Cullen's plays; photos of Cullen by Carl Van Vechten; reviews; and clippings of Cullen's poems. Correspondence includes a letter concerning the approaching wedding of DuBois's daughter Yolande to Cullen; letters to Harold Jackman and his sisters Ivie and Lola reflecting Cullen's travels in Europe and Jerusalem; a letter to Arna Bontemps giving names and addresses of Negro literati of the New York area; and letters from Cullen's widow Ida written shortly after his death, which refer to the critical reception of his posthumously published *On These I Stand* and to his play *St. Louis Woman.*

3,286. Cullen-Jackman Memorial Collection: Dunbar, Paul Lawrence
Papers. Nd. No size given.
Open. Unpublished guide.
Atlanta University, Trevor Arnett Library, Negro Collection.
Correspondence and other papers of Dunbar (1872-1906), including a poem accompanied by an explanatory letter from Dunbar's wife Alice N. Dunbar.

3,287. Cullen-Jackman Memorial Collection: Hughes, Langston
Papers. 1924-66. No size given.
Open. Unpublished guide.
Atlanta University, Trevor Arnett Library, Negro Collection.
Correspondence, autobiographical material, manuscripts, playbills, programs, advertisements, broadsides, clippings, and other papers of Hughes (1902-67), a poet, author, and playwright. Includes correspondence addressed to a Mrs. Blanchard and to others, which reflects Hughes's place in the Harlem Renaissance, his writing and publishing activities, and his concern for little theatre opportunities for Negroes.

3,288. Cullen-Jackman Memorial Collection: Johnson, Georgia (Douglas)
Papers. 1938-56. No size given.
Open. Unpublished guide.
Atlanta University, Trevor Arnett Library, Negro Collection.
Johnson (1886-1966), a writer, poet, and playwright, was the author of *White Men's Children, Bridge to Brotherhood,* and *Dreams in Me.* Copies of poems from the 1940s, most of them published in *Phylon,* and correspondence written from her home in Washington, DC, addressed almost entirely to Harold Jackman, which reflects Johnson's writing and publishing activities and her interest in such literary friends and acquaintances as William S. Braithwaite, Sterling Brown, Angelina Grimké, Langston Hughes, Bruce Nugent, Ann Petrey, Jean Toomer, and Carl Van Vechten. In her letters, Johnson frequently alludes to plays and biographical sketches in progress and to verse published in national periodicals.

3,289. Cullen-Jackman Memorial Collection: McKay, Claude
Papers. Nd. No size given.
Open. Unpublished guide.
Atlanta University, Trevor Arnett Library, Negro Collection.
Papers of McKay (1890-1948), a poet, include a radio script, correspondence with Arna Bontemps, and literary and personal letters to Harold Jackman and [Miss] Ivie Jackman.

3,290. Cullen-Jackman Memorial Collection: Miscellany
Collection. Nd. No size given.
Open. Unpublished guide.
Atlanta University, Trevor Arnett Library, Negro Collection.
Founded in 1942 to record the contributions of Negroes to literary, graphic, and performing arts in 20th-century America, the Cullen-Jackman Memorial Collection contains assorted papers as well as some manuscripts of scholarly articles and a few belles-lettres by individuals such as Marian Anderson, Gwendolyn Bennett, Stella B. Brookes, Gwendolyn Brooks, Hallie B. Brooks, Pearl Buck, Selma H. Burke, Sarah F. Chenault, Lucia T. Cheney, Nancy Cunard, Ellabelle Davis, Katherine Dunham, Evelyn Ellis, Blanche Ferguson, Margaret L. Fisher, Pearl Fisher, Grace P. Goens, Margaret Taylor Goss, Shirley Graham, Angelina Grimké, Juanita Hall, Caroline G. Harlow, Louise R. Holly, Alicja Iwanska, Ivie A. Jackman, Catarina Jarboro, Dorothy L. Keur, Bette D. Latimer, Rosetta LeNoire, Margaret Linley, Amy Loveman, Gertrude P. McBrown, Hattie McDaniel, Miriam Matthews, Maudelle, Anne Mercer, Abbie Mitchell, Estelle M. Osborne, Ann Petrey, Rosey E. Pool, Dorothy B. Porter, Caryl Posner, Elizabeth Prophet, Florence M. Read, Philippa D. Schuyler, Lillian Smith, Lucy Smith, Paula Snelling, Juanita G. Starke, Era Bell Thompson, Lois Towles, Clara Urquhart, Lillian W. Voorhees, A'lelia Walker, Margaret Walker, Val J. Washington, Dorothy West, and Jane White; the United Negro College Fund and the Negro Actors Guild of America are represented as well. Also included are items by individuals prominent in the latter 19th-century history of the Negro in America, among them Julia W. Howe.

3,291. Cullen-Jackman Memorial Collection: Robeson, Eslanda Goode
Papers. Ca. 1930-36. No size given.
Open. Unpublished guide.
Atlanta University, Trevor Arnett Library, Negro Collection.
Correspondence between Harold Jackman and [Mrs. Paul] Robeson (1896-1965), an anthropologist and author of *African Journey* (1946), which concerns her travels and residence in Europe, Russia, and Africa. Also includes a number of letters showing her interest in drama and in the possibilities of her acting and writing for the theatre.

3,292. Cullen-Jackman Memorial Collection: Van Vechten, Carl
Papers. 1940s-1950. No size given.
Open. Unpublished guide.
Atlanta University, Trevor Arnett Library, Negro Collection.
Papers of Van Vechten (1880-1964), a photographer, contain notes and letters about his interest in the racial integration of a New York City canteen for military personnel. Also includes a copy of an address on the life and accomplishments of Ethel Waters delivered at a dinner given in her honor.

3,293. Hamilton, Grace (Towns)
Papers. 1928-76. 103 ft.
Open. Unpublished guide.
Atlanta University, Trevor Arnett Library, Negro Collection.
Correspondence, organizational records, official reports, announcements, and printed material trace the involvement of Hamilton (1907-) in several social service and race relations agencies and her political career. Hamilton served as secretary of the National Student Council and of the National Commission on Ethnic Minorities of the YWCA; material from this period shows the intensification of efforts to include the Negro in YWCA activities. As executive secretary of the Atlanta Urban League from 1943 to 1961, Hamilton worked toward improvement of public facilities, voter education, and public housing. She also served on the advisory board of the Hughes Spalding Pavilion, which is the Negro wing of Atlanta's municipal Henry Grady Hospital; papers from this period deal with building the Pavilion and its use as a training facility for Negro physicians. Hamilton became a member of the board of trustees of Meharry Medical College of Nashville, and then in 1966 she was the first black woman to be elected to Georgia's house of representatives. Recent material reflects her activities as a member of various Democratic committees, as cochairman of the Georgia Humphrey-Muskie presidential campaign of 1968, and as a member from 1966 to 1972 of the National Citizens Advisory Committee on Recreation and Natural Beauty.

3,294. Hare, Maud (Cuney)
Papers. 1900-36. Ca. 100 items.
Open. Unpublished guide.
Atlanta University, Trevor Arnett Library, Negro Collection.
Papers of Hare (1874-1936), a concert pianist, writer, and lecturer, include manuscript music, photos of Marian Anderson and others, biographies of noted musicians, programs, photos, clippings, and printed sheet music. Among the composers represented are E. Azalia Hackley, Nora Douglas Holt, and Etta Moten.

3,295. Henry P. Slaughter Collection: Douglass, Frederick, Jr.
Papers. 1880s-90s. No size given.
Open. Unpublished guide.
Atlanta University, Trevor Arnett Library, Negro Collection.
Correspondence of Douglass from Anacostia, DC, to Magnus L. Robinson mentions Douglass's grief over his wife's death and other topics. Douglass also comments on the progress made by the black man and the many obstacles still placed in his path.

3,296. Henry P. Slaughter Collection: Douglass, Frederick, Sr.
Papers. 1850s-89. No size given.
Open. Unpublished guide.
Atlanta University, Trevor Arnett Library, Negro Collection.
Correspondence of Douglass (1817?-95) reflects his lecturing and other activities. In addition, a letter to Mrs. Lewis Tappan refers to his feeling that occupations open to freedmen are rooted in servility and that an industrial school for Negroes should therefore be established.

3,297. Henry P. Slaughter Collection: Garrison, William Lloyd
Papers. Nd. No size given.
Open. Unpublished guide.
Atlanta University, Trevor Arnett Library, Negro Collection.
Correspondence of Garrison (1805-79) includes letters alluding to the American Anti-Slavery Society, to the *Liberator,* and to persons associated with the antislavery movement, as well as a letter to [Mrs.] Maria W. Stewart recounting with praise her lifelong work on behalf of her race.

3,298. Henry P. Slaughter Collection: Miscellany
Collection. 1800s-early 1900s. No size given.
Open. Unpublished guide.
Atlanta University, Trevor Arnett Library, Negro Collection.
Emphasizing the early history of the Negro in the US, this collection is composed primarily of slave papers and correspondence of Negro leaders, abolitionists, and outstanding political figures. Among the women represented in subgroups, most of which consist of a few items written by the individual, are Lydia Maria Child, Sarah M. Douglass, Maud Cuney Hare, Georgia (Douglas) Johnson, Lois Mailou Jones, Harriet Martineau, Ann H. Pettigrew, Prudence Crandall Philleo, Sarah Pugh, Vestarine W. Slaughter, and Harriet B. Stowe. The School for Negro Children in Philadelphia is also represented.

3,299. Henry P. Slaughter Collection: Phelps, John W.
Papers. 1862-70s. No size given.
Open. Unpublished guide.
Atlanta University, Trevor Arnett Library, Negro Collection.
Correspondence of Phelps, brigadier general of the 12th Connecticut Volunteers, who was known as the "Abolition General." Letters from fellow officers support Phelps in his efforts to organize and train black regiments for the Union forces; letters from Thomas Webster, a member of the Supervisory Committee for Recruiting Colored Regiments, Philadelphia, provide detailed accounts of the Committee's efforts, including fund raising for schools for Negro children in Louisiana.

3,300. Henry P. Slaughter Collection: Slavery Papers
Collection. Late 1600s-1860s. No size given.
Open. Unpublished guide.
Atlanta University, Trevor Arnett Library, Negro Collection.
Business and legal documents related to slaveholding include bills of sale for slaves; legal conveyances of slaves, which were incorporated into marriage settlements; and material on various types of litigation. Slave-trading activities are exemplified by a three-way correspondence between 1835 and 1837 wherein business partners in Abingdon, VA, Nashville, and Livingston, MS, discuss financing, shipment, and the state of the market. Also included are manumission papers dating from the late 18th century through the 1850s, contracts for the rental of slaves, indenture and apprenticeship papers for freedmen, and broadsides and circulars dealing with the welfare of freedmen in the post-Civil War period. The documents originated in various southern states and Pennsylvania, New York, and Massachusetts. One lengthy document is a legal attack on slavery, probably from the early 1800s, which was prepared by William Lewis for the defense of the slave Flora, who was suing for her freedom under the laws of Pennsylvania.

3,301. McDuffie, Elizabeth (Stanfield?), and McDuffie, Irvin Henry
Papers. 1921-66. 2 vols. and 304 items.
Open. Unpublished guide.
Atlanta University, Trevor Arnett Library, Negro Collection.
Elizabeth McDuffie (1881-1966) and her husband Irvin McDuffie (1882-1946) were maid and valet, respectively, to Franklin Delano Roosevelt prior to and during Roosevelt's presidential terms. Correspondence, reminiscences, photos, clippings, printed material and memorabilia. In her reminiscences, published in *Ebony* under the title "FDR Was My Boss," Elizabeth McDuffie reviews interesting events in Washington, DC, and at the Little White House in Warm Springs, GA; she also gives her views on President and Mrs. Roosevelt's concern for the black man. Elizabeth McDuffie described herself as "the President's self-appointed secretary on colored peoples' affairs." She writes about campaigning for Roosevelt in the elections of 1936, 1940, and 1944, and about her work with the Colored National Democratic League, the Ohio State Democratic League, and the United Government Employees Association, of which she was treasurer in 1938. She also tells about the impact that the Atlanta Riot of 1906 had upon her, other aspects of her childhood, and her audition for the role of Mammy in *Gone With The Wind.* Also includes Irvin McDuffie's journal of his trip to South America with President Roosevelt aboard the USS *Indianapolis* as well as material relating to the activities of Elizabeth McDuffie's godchild Hazel (Dixon) Payne with the American National Red Cross during WWII.

3,302. Neighborhood Union
Records. 1908-61. 7 vols. and 761 items.
Open. Unpublished guide.
Atlanta University, Trevor Arnett Library, Negro Collection.
The Union was a private social welfare agency in Atlanta, which was organized in 1908 by Negroes to provide assistance to Negroes. Organizational records, correspondence, and printed material detail the Union's work in the areas of family assistance, fund raising, liaison with other local agencies, and efforts toward civic improvements for the Negro community. Correspondence of the Union's founder Lugenia (Burns) Hope reveals early race relations successes and failures within organizations with which she was affiliated, among them the YWCA, the Urban League, the National Association of Colored Women, the Commission on Interracial Cooperation, the Negro civic welfare committee of the Council of Social Agencies, the Social Science Research Council, and the International Council of Women of the Darker Races of the World. Others of her letters relate to work by her and her husband John Hope with troops at Camp Upton, NJ, during WWI and to her appointment by Secretary of Commerce Herbert Hoover to advise on conditions of flood victims in Greenville, MS, in 1927. Correspondents in the collection include Jane Addams, Mary (McLeod) Bethune, Margaret James (Murray) [Mrs. Booker T.] Washington, Georgia "Georgia Boy" (Douglas) Johnson, Charlotte Hawkins Brown, Juliette Derricotte, and Janie Porter Barrett.

3,303. Southern Conference for Human Welfare
Records. 1938-67. 15,478 items.
Open. Unpublished guide.
Atlanta University, Trevor Arnett Library, Negro Collection.
Official files of the Conference, later known as the Southern Conference Educational Fund, include minutes, financial records, correspondence, memoranda, drafts of speeches, press releases, and printed matter. The material reflects the Conference's principal activities, in particular its support of Henry A. Wallace's presidential campaign, its attitude toward and relations with labor organizations, and the investigation of the Conference in 1947 by the US House Un-American Activities Committee for evidence of Communist domination. Among the correspondents are Marian Anderson, Mary (McLeod) Bethune, Charlotte Hawkins Brown, Dorothy Parker, Eleanor Roosevelt, and Lillian Smith.

3,304. Tanner, Henry Ossawa
Papers. 1907-71. 1 vol. and 16 items.
Open. Unpublished guide.
Atlanta University, Trevor Arnett Library, Negro Collection.
Correspondence by and about Tanner (1859-1937), an American Negro painter, primarily concerns donation of the Tanner material to Atlanta University by Margaret (Clifford) Bryant of Swarthmore, PA, whose father Wesley N. Clifford taught with Tanner at Clark College in Atlanta. Collection also contains a scrapbook compiled by Bryant of clippings and photos of the Clifford and Tanner families, an oil painting by Tanner, several reproductions of his works, and printed biographical data.

3,305. Towns, George Alexander
Papers. 1851-1956. 2 vols. and 1338 items.
Open. Unpublished guide.
Atlanta University, Trevor Arnett Library, Negro Collection.
Papers of Towns (1870-1961), a professor of English literature and pedagogy at Atlanta University from 1895 to 1930, include correspondence, drafts of poems and prose articles, notes for class lectures, and data relating to Atlanta University. Some of his correspondents are Roberta Bosley, Judia J. Harris, Grace (Nail) Johnson, Rosamond Johnson, and Maude Trotter Steward. The collection also contains letters to Towns, diaries, and autobiographical and genealogical material of Lucy Elizabeth (Merriam) Case, a teacher sent to Atlanta University during its formative years by the American Missionary Association. Her diaries from 1851 to 1855 include entries from the year she was enrolled at Mount Holyoke Seminary. The collection also contains material reflecting the community service activities and interests in art and music of Towns's wife Nellie MacNair Towns (1879-1967), including notebooks, a sketch of her activities, photos of her and of her family, certificates of award for community service, and yearbooks from the Inquirers, a study club to which she belonged. Nellie Towns was the first black woman to serve on the board of the Atlanta YWCA.

3,306. Woman's Christian Temperance Union
Records. 1883-92. 1 vol.
Open. No guide.
Emory University, Pitts Theology Library.
Minutes of the Oxford, GA, branch of the WCTU.

3,307. Woman's Missionary Society, Methodist Episcopal Church, South
Records. 1878-1937. 1 box and 23 vols.
Open. No guide.
Emory University, Pitts Theology Library.
Minutes, financial records, and correspondence of the Woman's Missionary Society of the North Georgia Conference of the Methodist Episcopal Church, South, which was founded in 1878. Includes material of the Atlanta, Oxford, and South Atlanta districts of the Conference and of the Oxford Methodist Episcopal Church, South. The Society promoted Methodist missionary activity at home and abroad.

3,308. Barker, Mary Cornelia
Papers. 1918-64. 14 ms. boxes.
Open. Detailed survey.
Emory University, Robert W. Woodruff Library, Special Collections Department.
An Atlanta public school teacher and labor union activist, [Miss] Barker (1879-1963) was president of the American Federation of Teachers from 1925 to 1931 and a founder, secretary, and member of the board of directors of the Southern Summer School for Women Workers in Industry, organized in 1927. Correspondence, notes, memoranda, clippings, and printed material provide information about Barker's work with the Atlanta Public School Teachers' Association, the AFT, and the Southern School. Also contains material relating to the LWV and other groups with which she was affiliated and to her sister Tommie Dora Barker (1888-), a librarian and library educator.

3,309. Battey, Robert
Papers. 1810-94. 2 ms. boxes.
Open. Detailed survey.

Emory University, Robert W. Woodruff Library, Special Collections Department.
Correspondence between Battey (1828-95), a physician specializing in gynecology and obstetrics in Rome, GA; his wife Martha Baldwin Allen (Smith) Battey; and his aunt Mary (Battey) Halsey. Also contains genealogical material, photos, clippings, and material relating to Adrienne Battey (ca. 1890-), an actress who was the granddaughter of Robert Battey.

3,310. Bone, Robert Donnell
Papers. 1861-63. 60 items (microfilm).
Open. Detailed survey.
Emory University, Robert W. Woodruff Library, Special Collections Department.
Correspondence between Bone (1832-92), a physician in Cherokee and Nacogdoches counties, TX, and his wife Griselda Minerva (Burk) Bone. Griselda Bone's letters give details of life in a rural Texas community, household duties, social affairs, and religion. Robert Bone served in 1861 and 1862 as assistant surgeon in the 12th Texas infantry regiment.

3,311. Bradley, Frances (Sage)
Papers. 1893-1965. 401 items.
Open. Detailed survey.
Emory University, Robert W. Woodruff Library, Special Collections Department.
Bradley (ca. 1862-1949), a physician, worked with the US Children's Bureau from 1914 to 1924, with the American National Red Cross in 1918, and in health care and child welfare in Arkansas and Montana; she also practiced medicine in Atlanta. Correspondence, manuscripts of her short stories and an unfinished autobiography, photos, clippings, and mementos. Included are sketches and miscellaneous material relating to her husband Horace James Bradley, an artist. Most of the correspondence and photos concern Frances Bradley's work with the Children's Bureau and in Arkansas and Montana.

3,312. Bramblett, Agnes Cochran
Papers. 1902-68. 1 ms. box.
Open. Inventory.
Emory University, Robert W. Woodruff Library, Special Collections Department.
Letters, manuscript poems, notebooks, photos, and memorabilia of Bramblett (1886-), a Forsyth, GA, resident who was the state's poet laureate from 1963 to 1972.

3,313. Burge Family
apers. 1832-1952. 5 ms. boxes (705 items).
Open. Detailed survey.
Emory University, Robert W. Woodruff Library, Special Collections Department.
Correspondence, diaries, notebooks, sermons, account books, clippings, and miscellaneous papers of a family of planters and ministers. Includes letters and diaries of Dolly Sumner (Lunt) Burge (1817-91) and her daughter Sadai (Burge) Gray and a diary of her stepdaughter Louisiana Burge. Subjects discussed include plantation life, social customs, religion, education, slavery, the Civil War, and the Reconstruction South. Contains papers relating to the Lewis family of Portland, ME, the Burge family of Newton County, GA, and the Parks family of Franklin and Newton counties, GA. The Burge and Parks families were closely associated with Emory College.

3,314. Burns, Susan
Papers. 1848. 1 microfilm reel.
Open. Detailed survey.
Emory University, Robert W. Woodruff Library, Special Collections Department.
Burns was a schoolteacher in Pennsylvania and North Carolina. Fourteen-page journal of Burns's trip from Philadelphia to Salisbury, NC.

3,315. Chunn, William Augustus
Papers. 1837-79. 168 items.
Open. Detailed survey.
Emory University, Robert W. Woodruff Library, Special Collections Department.
Correspondence between Chunn (1840-1921), a farmer in Cassville, GA, and his wife Lila (Land) Chunn include Civil War letters written while he was serving in Company I, 1st Regiment, 1st Brigade, Georgia State Troops, and in Company I, 40th Regiment, Georgia Infantry. His letters describe his activities, particularly during the siege of Vicksburg, MS. Lila Chunn's letters describe life on the home front.

3,316. Cooper, Augusta (Skeen)
Papers. 1925-70. 2 ms. boxes.
Open. Inventory.
Emory University, Robert W. Woodruff Library, Special Collections Department.
[Mrs. Samuel Inman] Cooper was a chemistry instructor at Emory University from 1943 to 1945 and a civic worker associated with the Fernbank Science Center in Atlanta, the Atlanta World Service Committee, and the YWCA. Correspondence, photos, and memorabilia relating to Emory and her civic activities.

3,317. Davidson, John Mitchell
Papers. 1851-1960. 381 frames of microfilm.
Open. Detailed survey.
Emory University, Robert W. Woodruff Library, Special Collections Department.
Davidson (1829-1917) was a storekeeper and railway station agent in Copper Hill, TN, in North Carolina, and in Georgia; his wife Julia (Dunn) Davidson (?-1890) was a housewife. Correspondence, consisting primarily of Civil War letters; genealogical material; and a scrapbook. Residing in Ducktown, TN, and after October 1862 in Atlanta, Julia Davidson wrote of hardships encountered by civilians, religious and social affairs, news of family and friends, the siege of Atlanta, and her decision in 1864 to refugee to South Carolina. John Davidson served in Company C, 39th Regiment, North Carolina Volunteer Infantry.

3,318. Dewey, Maybelle Jones
Papers. 1908-47. 3 ms. boxes.
Open. Inventory.
Emory University, Robert W. Woodruff Library, Special Collections Department.
A newspaperwoman from Cartersville, GA, Dewey (1888-1963) was the wife of Malcolm H. Dewey, professor of Romance languages at Emory and director of the Emory Glee Club. A scrapbook from 1908 and a copy of Maybelle Dewey's autobiographical account of life at Emory during the 1920s and 1930s. Malcolm Dewey earned a PhD from the University of Chicago in 1918.

3,319. Dobbins, John S., Family
Papers. 1834-1916. 2 microfilm reels.
Open. Detailed survey and calendar.
Emory University, Robert W. Woodruff Library, Special Collections Department.
Correspondence, legal and business records, genealogical material, memorabilia, and other papers of Dobbins (1800-66), a merchant and farmer in Calhoun and Clarksville, GA, including letters of his second wife Sarah (Williams) Dobbins (1816-?); his daughter from his first marriage, Mary Emma Dobbins; and their relatives Mamie Starr and Mrs. E. F. Herrington. Specific topics reflected in the papers include agriculture, slavery, education, transportation, and communications in antebellum, Confederate, and Reconstruction Georgia.

3,320. Edge, Andrew J.
Papers. 1862-64. 20 ft. of microfilm.
Open. Detailed survey.
Emory University, Robert W. Woodruff Library, Special Collections Department.
Correspondence, much of it written by Alpha (Davis) Edge to her husband Andrew Edge (1836-1926), a Baptist minister and farmer from Lumpkin County, GA, who served in Company C, 52nd Georgia Infantry.

3,321. Evans, Letitia (Pate)
Papers. 1947-69. 55 items.
Open. Inventory.
Emory University, Robert W. Woodruff Library, Special Collections Department.
Evans (?-1953), an Atlanta philanthropist, was the first woman to serve on the Emory University board of trustees. Correspondence, genealogical information, photos, brochures, and clippings.

3,322. Every Saturday Club
Records. 1895-1973. 1 ms. box.
Open. List.
Emory University, Robert W. Woodruff Library, Special Collections Department.
A women's discussion group organized in ca. 1895, the Club was affiliated with the Atlanta Federation of Women's Clubs. Programs, which provide names of members and officers and a schedule of members' presentations. The group studied a wide range of subjects with a single topic selected for investigation each year.

3,323. Featherston, Lucius H., Family
Papers. 1836-ca. 1948. 15 ms. boxes.
Open. Detailed survey.
Emory University, Robert W. Woodruff Library, Special Collections Department.
Correspondence, business and legal records, notebooks, clippings, and memorabilia of Featherston (1814-86), a lawyer and judge in Franklin and Newnan, GA; Civil War correspondence and other papers of his daughter Zerlina Catherine "Katie" and her husband George Peddy, a surgeon with the 56th Georgia Infantry; correspondence, diary, notebooks, school records, and mementos of another daughter Mary (Featherston) Wright and her daughter Kathleen Wright. Subjects discussed include social and economic conditions in Georgia, family life, politics, and education, principally during the middle and late 19th century. Contains genealogical material on the Featherston, Peddy, Tompkins, and Cuttino families.

3,324. Greene, Eleonore (Raoul)
Papers. 1850-1950. Ms. boxes.
Open. Inventory.
Emory University, Robert W. Woodruff Library, Special Collections Department.
A suffrage leader and civic worker, Greene (1888-) was an organizer of the Atlanta LWV. Correspondence, estate papers, photos, serials, clippings, printed material, and memorabilia provide information about Greene's suffrage activities, including her work as an organizer in West Virginia; the Atlanta chapter of the LWV; and the Raoul family. Includes numerous letters of the five Raoul sisters, their mother Mary (Wadley) Raoul, and her sister Sarah Wadley.

3,325. Harris, Corra May (White)
Papers. 1900-34. 115 items.
Open. Detailed survey.
Emory University, Robert W. Woodruff Library, Special Collections Department.
[Mrs. Lundy Howard] Harris (1869-1935) was a journalist and novelist who lived in Elbert and Banks counties and in Rydal, GA. Correspondence, photos, clippings, and a few manuscripts of articles and short stories. Her correspondence is primarily with her friend Mrs. Donald McClain. The letters concern family and health problems, her writings, social activities, friends, visitors, and travel.

3,326. Harris, Julian LaRose
Papers. 1890-1968. 33 ms. boxes and 25 vols.
Open. Detailed survey and inventory.
Emory University, Robert W. Woodruff Library, Special Collections Department.
Harris (1874-1963) and his wife Julia Florida (Collier) Harris (1875-1967) were journalists and writers. Correspondence, diaries, notebooks, literary manuscripts, interoffice memoranda, and scrapbooks. Contains correspondence exchanged between the Harrises and their professional correspondence. Julia Harris's correspondents included H. L. Mencken, Geraldine Farrar, Jessie Daniel Ames, Myrta Lockett Avary, Lucy R. Mason, and Helen Woodward. Also contains material relating to the Pulitzer Prize awarded in 1926 to the Harrises' newspaper in Columbus, GA, and to the Association of Southern Women for the Prevention of Lynching.

3,327. Harrison, Emily
Papers. Ca. 1850-1950. Ms. boxes.
Open. Inventory.
Emory University, Robert W. Woodruff Library, Special Collections Department.
[Miss] Harrison was an educator and journalist from Atlanta. Correspondence, writings, photos, and printed material relate to her educational work, including her service with the American National Red Cross in Czechoslovakia in 1920 and 1921, and reflect her interest in rural education, outdoor schools, wildlife preserves, and travel. Also includes family papers and church records.

3,328. Haygood, Atticus Greene
Papers. 1861-1952. 435 items.
Open. Detailed survey.
Emory University, Robert W. Woodruff Library, Special Collections Department.
Correspondence, diary, sermons, addresses, genealogical material, photos, and clippings of Haygood (1839-96), a Methodist bishop and president of Emory College from 1875 to 1884. Included are a diary and letterbook of his sister Laura Askew Haygood (1845-1900), an educator and Methodist missionary to China. Also contains material concerning his daughter Mamie (Haygood) Ardis, the first female student at Emory College.

3,329. Hicks, Mildred
Papers. 1917-45. 6 ms. boxes (2686 items).
Open. Detailed survey.
Emory University, Robert W. Woodruff Library, Special Collections Department.
Mildred Hicks (ca. 1880-?), an active clubwoman, managed the Hicks estate in Bainbridge, GA, while her sister Mary was a schoolteacher; both women joined the Socialist party in 1915. Principally correspondence concerned with the women's work in a campaign to redistribute wealth. They carried on a mail campaign from their Bainbridge home and corresponded with Socialist politicians and leaders. Also includes promotional literature, published articles and letters, clippings, and printed material.

3,330. Hood, Rebecca
Papers. 1862-65. 28 frames of microfilm.
Open. Detailed survey.
Emory University, Robert W. Woodruff Library, Special Collections Department.
Memoir recounting the wartime experiences in Cartersville, GA, of Hood, a mother and second wife of William Henry Hood of York District, SC, and Cartersville.

3,331. Jett, Richard B.
Papers. 1863-87. 38 items.
Open. Detailed survey.
Emory University, Robert W. Woodruff Library, Special Collections Department.
Correspondence, brief diary, and a labor agreement of Jett, a Fulton County, GA, farmer and Confederate soldier, and his wife N. E. "Mae" Jett, who operated the mill and farm in her husband's absence during the war. Mae Jett's letters to her husband give details of home life and describe the effect of the Federal invasion on the community.

3,332. Knight, Mary Lamar
Papers. Ca. 1930-70. 6 ms. boxes.
Open. Box inventory.
Emory University, Robert W. Woodruff Library, Special Collections Department.
A journalist and author from Atlanta, [Miss] Knight (1899-) was one of the first woman correspondents for United Press International. Correspondence, photos, clippings, and memorabilia relating to Knight's career.

3,333. Lovett, Robert Watkins
Papers. 1787-1916. 466 items.
Open. Detailed survey and inventory.
Emory University, Robert W. Woodruff Library, Special Collections Department.
Correspondence, essays, speeches, legal records, genealogical material, and mementos of Lovett (1818-1912), a physician and Methodist minister in Screven County, GA. Included are letters and papers of his grandmother Elizabeth Lovett; letters from Sarah Isabell Price, Robert Lovett's financée and later his wife; letters from Henrietta (Smith) Meriwether to her sister Marietta (Smith) Lovett, Robert Lovett's second wife; and material relating to other women of the Lovett family. Subjects include family news, home and community life, and education.

3,334. McBlair, Virginia (Myers)
Papers. 1818-94. 265 items.
Open. Detailed survey.
Emory University, Robert W. Woodruff Library, Special Collections Department.
McBlair (1821?-91), a resident of Pensacola, FL, and Richmond, VA, was the wife of Confederate naval officer William McBlair. Principally correspondence, including letters from her mother Louisa (Marx) Myers concerning personal, domestic, social, and religious matters; letters dating from 1818 to 1824 from Virginia's father Samuel Myers to Louisa Myers; and Civil War correspondence to Virginia McBlair from her husband and other family members. The Marx and Myers families were Jewish.

3,335. Martin, Harold H.
Papers. 1837-1975. 38 ms. boxes.
Open. Box inventory.
Emory University, Robert W. Woodruff Library, Special Collections Department.
Correspondence, literary manuscripts, photos, and clippings of Martin (1910-), an Atlanta journalist and free-lance writer. Includes papers of Marian Hamilton and Nancy (Hamilton) Ogden, aunts of Martin's wife Boyce Lokey Martin. In 1918 and 1919 Hamilton and Ogden served on the American National Red Cross mission to Palestine. Their papers include scrapbooks, which relate to their work in Palestine, and Ogden's poems, short stories, lectures, and her diary and letters written between 1925 and 1927 in Hong Kong.

3,336. Mitchell, Margaret
Collection. Ca. 1936-70. 6 ms. boxes.
Open. Box inventory.
Emory University, Robert W. Woodruff Library, Special Collections Department.
Correspondence, photos, articles, clippings, and memorabilia of and about Mitchell (1900-49), an Atlanta journalist and novelist who wrote *Gone With The Wind.* Includes reviews of *Gone With The Wind.*

3,337. Monks, Zerah Coston
Papers. 1859-67. 1 microfilm reel.
Open. Detailed survey.
Emory University, Robert W. Woodruff Library, Special Collections Department.
Correspondence, notes, and family papers consist primarily of letters between Monks (1841-1909), a carpenter, schoolteacher, and Union soldier from Vanango County, PA, and [Miss] Hannah Rohrer (1842-1912), a Stewart's Run, PA, resident whom he married in 1865. Hannah Rohrer lived with her grandparents and apparently alternated between attending and teaching school; her letters recount her activities and community news.

3,338. Moody, Minnie (Hite)
Papers. 1914-ca. 1970. 1 ms. box.
Open. Accession lists.
Emory University, Robert W. Woodruff Library, Special Collections Department.
Moody (1900-) is a novelist, short story writer, and journalist who has lived in Atlanta and Granville, OH. Correspondence, unpublished short stories, articles, clippings, and mementos relate to her writing career.

3,339. Murfree, Mary Noailles
Papers. 1877-1928. 314 items.
Open. Detailed survey.
Emory University, Robert W. Woodruff Library, Special Collections Department.
A southern regional writer who lived in Murfreesboro, TN, [Miss] Murfree (1850-1922) published under the name Charles Egbert Craddock. Correspondence, primarily with her publishers, literary manuscripts, photos, and clippings. Literary manuscripts include a book-length story, short stories, and three stories by her father William Law Murfree, Sr.

3,340. Myrick, Susan
Papers. Ca. 1937-72. 3 ms. boxes and 5 vols.
Open. Box inventory.
Emory University, Robert W. Woodruff Library, Special Collections Department.
[Miss] Myrick was a journalist with the *Macon Telegraph* in Macon, GA. Correspondence, photos, clippings, and memorabilia relating primarily to Myrick's work as technical advisor for the movie *Gone With The Wind.* Also includes clippings and photos relating to her newspaper career.

3,341. Old South Miscellany
Collection. Nd. 1 ms. box.
Open. Detailed survey.
Emory University, Robert W. Woodruff Library, Special Collections Department.
Groups of manuscripts and single items relating to the antebellum South include an account by Cornelia E. (Parker) Read of her experiences as a teacher in the South and North between 1853 and 1865. A Connecticut native, Read taught on a Mississippi plantation in 1857 and 1858 and at various locations in Kentucky, Connecticut, and New York.

3,342. Orr Family
Papers. 1825-1970. 14 ms. boxes.
Open. Detailed survey and inventory.
Emory University, Robert W. Woodruff Library, Special Collections Department.
Correspondence, writings, speeches, and family papers of Gustavus John Orr (1819-87), an educator from Atlanta and Oxford, GA, who served as state school commissioner from 1872 to 1887. Also includes correspondence and other papers of his granddaughter, Martha Reynolds "Dorothy" Orr, a teacher, school principal, and author of a history of education in Georgia and a biography of Gustavus John Orr. Also contained are papers of other women family members, Mary E. Orr and Eliza C. Orr.

3,343. Paschall, Eliza K.
Papers. 1958-ca. 1970. 34 Hollinger boxes.
Open. Inventory.

Emory University, Robert W. Woodruff Library, Special Collections Department.
A civic worker active in interracial and women's organizations, Paschall served from 1961 to 1967 as executive director of the Greater Atlanta Council on Human Relations and in 1967 and 1968 as head of its successor, the Community Relations Commission. Correspondence, minutes, reports, interoffice memos, press releases, and clippings principally relate to Paschall's work with the Council and Commission and reflect efforts of this local group to facilitate desegregation and promote racial understanding. Also includes material concerning the LWV, the Agnes Scott College Alumni Association, and the National Organization for Women, as well as a diary Paschall kept while serving with the American National Red Cross in England during WWII.

3,344. Pitts, Thomas Henry
Papers. 1856-75. 246 items (microfilm).
Open. Detailed survey.
Emory University, Robert W. Woodruff Library, Special Collections Department.
Correspondence, chiefly items exchanged between Pitts (1834-71), a planter, Confederate soldier, farmer, and commission merchant from Clinton, SC, and Calhoun, GA, and his fiancée and wife Lizzie (Craig) Pitts. Letters of Lizzie Pitts date chiefly from the post-Civil War period and contain information about social and economic conditions of former planters.

3,345. Plane, Caroline Helen (Jemison)
Papers. 1914-24. 1 ms. box.
Open. Box inventory.
Emory University, Robert W. Woodruff Library, Special Collections Department.
An Atlanta resident, Plane (1829-1925) was founder of the Georgia division of the United Daughters of the Confederacy and president of the Stone Mountain Confederate Memorial Association. Correspondence, minutes, financial records, and clippings relate primarily to the planning of the Stone Mountain Memorial. Bulk of the collection is correspondence between Plane and sculptor Gutzon Borglum.

3,346. Pollard, Marie Antoinette Nathalie
Papers. 1865-96. 46 items.
Open. Detailed survey.
Emory University, Robert W. Woodruff Library, Special Collections Department.
An actress and lecturer who lived in Norfolk and Richmond, VA, Pollard (?-1896?) was the wife of Edward Alfred Pollard. Correspondence, broadsides advertising her performances, and clippings of her reviews.

3,347. Rainey, Glenn Weddington
Papers. 1917-74. 21 ms. boxes (ca. 8000 items).
Partially restricted. Inventory.
Emory University, Robert W. Woodruff Library, Special Collections Department.
Rainey (1907-) is a college professor and civic worker from Atlanta. Principally correspondence, 1933-49, that deals with Rainey's activities in such organizations as the Commission for Interracial Cooperation, the Committee for Georgia of the Southern Conference for Human Welfare, the Citizen's Fact-finding Committee, and the Southern Regional Council. Includes letters from Lillian Smith, Jessie Daniel Ames, Mary C. Barker, Lucy Mason, and Paula Snelling.

3,348. Richardson, Sue
Papers. 1863-65. 4 vols.
Open. Detailed survey.
Emory University, Robert W. Woodruff Library, Special Collections Department.
Diary of Richardson, a resident of Rose Hill Plantation near Front Royal, VA, includes descriptions of family activities, occupation by Federal troops, and the war's effects on her family and friends.

3,349. Rowland, Kate (Whitehead)
Papers. 1863-78. 273 frames of microfilm.
Open. Detailed survey.
Emory University, Robert W. Woodruff Library, Special Collections Department.
Journals of Rowland (1838-?), a wife and mother who lived in Augusta, GA, are dated 1863-64, 1877-78, and 1878 and include accounts of time she spent in camp with her husband as well as home front activities of an upper-class Georgia family during the Civil War. Postwar journals tell of weddings and other social events, religious meetings, family life, and education.

3,350. Seydell, Mildred (Woolley)
Papers. 1842-1973. 64 ms. boxes.
Open. Inventory.
Emory University, Robert W. Woodruff Library, Special Collections Department.
A journalist, author, and lecturer, [Mrs.] Seydell (1899-) was associated with the *Atlanta Georgian* from 1924 to 1939; she was active in the Atlanta branch of the National Woman's Party and belonged to the Atlanta Federation of Women's Clubs and other women's groups. Personal and professional correspondence, photos, scrapbooks, clippings, printed material, and memorabilia; includes letters, clippings, and memorabilia of her aunts Lamar (Rutherford) Lipscomb and Mildred Rutherford. Seydell's correspondence contains items from readers of her books and newspaper column and letters regarding her lectures and travels. Other material relates to her membership in organizations.

3,351. Smith, Lillian Eugenia
Papers. 1940-62. 1 ms. box.
Partially restricted. Inventory.
Emory University, Robert W. Woodruff Library, Special Collections Department.
Correspondence between Smith (1897-1966), a Clayton, GA, author, and George Leonard; an unpublished speech; and articles and clippings by and about Smith.

3,352. Snelling, William Amos, Family
Papers. 1873-1950. 676 items.
Open. Detailed survey.
Emory University, Robert W. Woodruff Library, Special Collections Department.
Principally correspondence between Snelling (1856-1907), a merchant in Washington, Dooly, and Chatham counties, GA; his wife Nannie (Palmer) Snelling (1857-1950); and numerous relatives. The letters describe neighborhood events, church activities, household chores, weddings and other social occasions, and agriculture and business conditions.

3,353. Tilly, Dorothy Eugenia (Rogers)
Papers. 1868-1970. 562 items.
Open. Detailed survey.
Emory University, Robert W. Woodruff Library, Special Collections Department.
An Atlanta church and civil rights worker, [Mrs. Milton Eben] Tilly (1883-1970) was a member of President Truman's Committee on Civil Rights in 1947 and 1948 and an organizer of the Fellowship of the Concerned. Correspondence, records of the Committee on Civil Rights and the Women's Missionary Society of the Methodist Church, biographical information, clippings, and memorabilia.

3,354. Union Microfilm Miscellany
Collection. 1860-65. 1 microfilm reel.
Open. Detailed survey.
Emory University, Robert W. Woodruff Library, Special Collections Department.
Correspondence between Ephraim Girdner, a captain from Greenville, IN, in Company H, 66th Regiment, Indiana Infantry Volunteers, and his fiancée Mary A. Murphy; narrative of the 66th Regiment; genealogy; and family photos.

3,355. Wilson, Alpheus Waters
Papers. 1854-1916. 124 items.
Open. Detailed survey.
Emory University, Robert W. Woodruff Library, Special Collections Department.
Chiefly correspondence of Wilson (1834-1916), bishop of the Methodist Episcopal Church, South, in Baltimore, and his wife Susan B. (Lipscomb) Wilson concerning church affairs, slavery, and family matters.

3,356. Woodward, Comer McDonald
Papers. 1892-1945. Ca. 1700 items.
Open. Box inventory.
Emory University, Robert W. Woodruff Library, Special Collections Department.
An Atlanta sociologist, Woodward (1874-1960) served as dean of men at Emory University from 1924 to 1942. Correspondence and printed material contain items relating to Woodward's activities with such organizations as the Atlanta LWV, the Family Welfare Society, the Georgia Conference on Social Work, the Georgia Department of Public Welfare, and the Georgia Training School for Girls.

3,357. Woodward, Emily Barnelia
Papers. 1918-66. 11 ms. boxes (ca. 3200 items).
Open. Detailed survey and inventory.
Emory University, Robert W. Woodruff Library, Special Collections Department.
A Vienna, GA, journalist and civic leader, [Miss] Woodward (1885-1970) was editor of the *Vienna News* from 1918 to 1930 and president of the Georgia Press Association from 1926 to 1928. Correspondence concerns her organizational work, prison reform, the Georgia Forestry Association, state politics, race relations, and other activities. Also includes articles and addresses relating to Woodward's work with the Georgia Public Forums and the Georgia Press Institute.

3,358. Agerton, Zillah Lee (Bostick) Redd
Papers. 1863-1967. 10 cu.ft.
Open. Inventory.
Georgia Department of Archives and History.
A poet, genealogist, and civic worker, Agerton (1871-1967) was poet laureate of Burke County, GA, and historian of the Waynesboro, GA, Presbyterian church. Personal, organizational, and genealogical correspondence; organizational records, including minutes, yearbooks, magazines, programs, and other material; genealogical records, including information on 100 families; poetry, including Agerton's published and unpublished poetry and poems by her mother Alma Bostick; photos; clippings; books; and other items. Contains records and other material relating to the Millen, GA, Wayside Home Association; the Edmund Burke Chapter of the DAR; the Waynesboro Garden Club; the Waynesboro Woman's Club; the Women's Auxiliary of the Presbyterian church; the WCTU; and the Margaret Jones Chapter of the United Daughters of the Confederacy. A native of New Orleans, Agerton died in Waynesboro.

3,359. Alexander, Iraminta Antoinette
Papers. 1860-96. 1 folder.
Open. Inventory.
Georgia Department of Archives and History.
Correspondence between "Nettie" Alexander and her family and friends while she was attending Monroe Female Academy in 1860; compositions by Alexander and friends; report cards of Alexander's son Benjamin F. Hill and of Stella Baker, who later married Benjamin Hill; a letter from Benjamin Hill to Stella; a funeral notice of the Hills' daughter; poems; and other material.

3,360. American Association of University Women, Georgia Division
Records. 1926-75. 10 cu.ft.
Open. No guide.
Georgia Department of Archives and History.
Officers' reports, branch president reports, minutes for the Division and some branches (particularly Atlanta), branch histories and directories, and yearbooks.

3,361. Atlanta Business and Professional Women's Club
Records. 1920-75. 30 cu.ft.
Open. No guide.
Georgia Department of Archives and History.
Minutes, committee reports, biographical records of members, a Club history, scrapbooks, copies of the national magazine, and other material.

3,362. Atlanta League of Women Voters
Records. 1894-1972. 18 cu.ft. and 1 folder.
Open. Partial inventory.
Georgia Department of Archives and History.
Minutes, financial records, reports, membership rolls, scrapbooks, clippings, and publications of the Atlanta LWV and early Georgia suffrage records. Suffrage material consists of correspondence, telegrams, yearbooks, and a speech by Rebecca (Latimer) Felton, "The Subjection of Women and The Enfranchisement of Women." LWV records include minutes of the board of directors and annual meetings from 1920 to 1954 and of the officers' committee; these deal with such subjects as organization, registration of women voters, the legal status of women, birth control, child welfare, tax reform, immigration, local political investigations, public health, housing, consumerism, juvenile delinquency, war work, local government studies, and racial integration of the LWV. Also included are treasurer's records, budgets, financial statements, donation records, donor lists, and finance committee records for 1922 and 1930 to 1959; membership reports; material relating to publicity, the charter campaign, Atlanta LWV history, investigations of Atlanta graft in 1930 and 1931 and of child labor; and speeches of Eleanor Roosevelt. Voter registration records reflect the LWV's interest in candidates, the poll tax, secret balloting, and in elections in general. Also contains office topic files and LWV publications.

3,363. Atlanta Normal Schools
Records. 1897-1916. 13 vols.
Open. No guide.
Georgia Department of Archives and History.
Minute books of faculty meetings.

3,364. Atlanta Public Schools
Records. 1870-1914. 2 items.
Open. No guide.
Georgia Department of Archives and History.
Survey of the Atlanta Public Schools compiled in 1914 by Celestia Parrish of the state school department and a personnel directory for these schools from 1870 to 1900.

3,365. Atlanta Writers Club
Records. 1938-71. 0.5 cu.ft. and 14 vols.
Open. No guide.
Georgia Department of Archives and History.
Minutes from 1938 to 1946, scrapbooks, and miscellaneous papers.

3,366. Baldwin, Martha Harper
Papers. 1831. 1 vol.
Open. No guide.
Georgia Department of Archives and History.
Copy of a diary of [Mrs. John] Baldwin of Monticello, GA, describing a journey through Tennessee, Kentucky, Ohio, and New York to Connecticut.

3,367. Barili
Papers. 1865-1959. 6 cu.ft.
Open. Description.
Georgia Department of Archives and History.
Papers of Adelina Patti (1843-1919), an opera singer born in Madrid; her nephew Alfredo Barili (1854-1935), a native of Florence, Italy, who emigrated to the US; Emily Vezin Barili (1856-1940), a Philadelphia native who married Alfredo Barili and with him in ca. 1889 established the Barili School of Music in Atlanta; and Louise Vezin Barili (1880-), eldest daughter of Alfredo and Emily Barili. Correspondence, unpublished musical compositions, notebooks, scrapbooks, recital programs, sheet music, magazines, and other material. Bulk of the material pertains to Patti's international career and to activities of the Barili family in Atlanta. Includes letters from Patti and family letters written on visits to her; biographical sketches of Patti and Alfredo Barili written by the family; genealogical information on the Vezin and Barili families; photos of family members and Patti's Welsh castle; Louise Barili's poetry; marriage and death notices; *A Memory of Song,* a book about Patti; and articles about the Barili family and their music school. Adelina Patti was married to the Marquis de Caux, then to Ernest Nicolini, and then to Baron Rolf Cederstrom.

3,368. Barker, Lillian Marion
Papers. 1906-08. 8 cu.ft. and 6 vols.
Open. Inventory.
Georgia Department of Archives and History.
A native of Atlanta, Barker (1888-1968) was a writer, biographer, reporter and feature writer for the New York *Post,* and a foreign correspondent; she obtained an interview with Benito Mussolini during WWII, served as a district publicity director for the USO, and wrote about the Dionne quintuplets. Personal and business correspondence with friends, agents, and publishing firms; manuscripts; clippings, scrapbooks, and other material about the Dionne quintuplets and the Dionne family's litigation against their personal physician; résumés of Barker's work and awards; information regarding property she owned and estates of three of her female relatives; subject files on writing, including bylaws, yearbooks, and rosters of the National League of Pen Women; photos; miscellaneous material; and copies of Barker's 10 published works, which included "Cabaret Love" and "Trilby of the Tenements."

3,369. Baskerville, Jessie B.
Papers. 1910-ca. 1942. 1 item (microfilm).
Open. No guide.
Georgia Department of Archives and History.
A pianist and teacher at the Metropolitan Opera Studio for ca. 30 years, Baskerville was a coach and friend of such opera stars as Lillian Nordica, Ernestine Schumann-Heink, and Enrico Caruso. Scrapbook contains photos, clippings, and other material relating to Baskerville's career, life, and travels.

3,370. Bealer, Emily Jane Winkler
Papers. 1876-86. 1 file.
Open. No guide.
Georgia Department of Archives and History.
Diary of Bealer, a widow who lived in Atlanta with four children, reflects her work running her household, her financial problems, and her difficulties with her children. Includes several poems and a few recipes.

3,371. Black, Mary Ellen "Nellie" (Peters)
Papers. 1870s-1914. 49 items.
Open. No guide.
Georgia Department of Archives and History.
A civic leader and clubwoman, Nellie Black (1851-1919) was the wife of George Robison Black. Correspondence, including personal letters from friends and family, many of which were written just before her marriage in the 1870s; two letters pertaining to a girls' orphanage in Macon, GA; and a 1914 letter from Nellie Black to John Marshall Slaton regarding his appointment of Peyton Wade as a judge. Also includes a biographical pamphlet prepared by the Georgia Federation of Women's clubs.

3,372. Blitch, Iris (Faircloth)
Papers. Nd. 60 cu.ft.
Closed. No guide.
Georgia Department of Archives and History.
Papers recording the political career of [Mrs. Brooks Erwin] Blitch (1912-), a Normantown, GA, native who was a US congresswoman during the 1950s. A graduate of the University of Georgia, Blitch served as Georgia's Democratic national committeewoman in 1949 and from 1952 to 1956 and as a member of the executive committee of the Democratic National Committee from 1952 to 1956. She also was assistant secretary and acting secretary of the state Democratic executive committee in 1946 and from 1950 to 1954, a member of the Georgia House of Representatives from Clinch County in 1949 and 1950, and a representative from the 5th district in the Georgia Senate in 1947, 1948, 1953, and 1954.

3,373. Boulware Family
Papers. 1826-1927. 18 items.
Open. Inventory.
Georgia Department of Archives and History.
Correspondence, deeds, receipts, Confederate currency, and other material of members of the Boulware, Ryland, and Taliaferro families of Virginia. Contains correspondence of the daughters of Lee Boulware and his wife Caroline Miller Boulware: Caroline [Mrs. Andrew] Broaddus (?-1848), Catherine [Mrs. John] Kidd (?-1867), Amanda]Mrs. Richardson] Lumpkin (?-1872), Susan [Mrs. Alexander] Taliaferro, and Josephine [Mrs. Robert] Ryland. Includes letters Josephine wrote to Robert Ryland mentioning scarlet fever and difficult times in the family and letters from Susan Taliaferro to her daughter Carrie, a missionary. Also contains a deed of gift dated 1842 for a 15-year-old Negro named Horace from Catherine Boulware to William Taliaferro.

3,374. Bradbury, Janette Lane
Papers. 1883-1968. 8 cu.ft.
Open. Inventory.
Georgia Department of Archives and History.
Correspondence, a diary for 1936, organizational records, photos, scrapbooks, clippings, and other personal papers of [Mrs. Thomas] Bradbury (1908-68), a civic leader and clubwoman who held bachelor's and master's degrees from the Atlanta Law School. Family and organizational correspondence makes up the bulk of the collection. Also contains financial records; records, including bylaws, minutes, programs, yearbooks, and rosters from more than 40 organizations; material relating to Bradbury's three children Janette Lane Bradbury, Lynda Lane Bradbury, and Thomas Lane Bradbury; memorabilia from travel through the South, the Caribbean, and Europe; and religious clippings and others regarding Bradbury's activities in organizations. Papers reflect Bradbury's work in such groups as the Woman's Auxiliary of the Architects and Engineers' Institute, the Four Seasons and Covenant Garden Clubs, the Atlanta Civic Ballet, the Atlanta Art Association, the Atlanta Music Club, the Atlanta Symphony Guild, the Cherokee chapter of the DAR, the Magna Carta Dames, the YWCA, and the Shakerag Hounds. Born in Meriwether, GA, Bradbury was married in 1936.

3,375. Brady, Sara M.
Papers. 1893-95. 4 items.
Open. No guide.
Georgia Department of Archives and History.
Letters to [Mrs.] Brady written from different parts of Georgia by relatives, including Lizzie Adams, M.

A. Skelton, her granddaughter Lizzie, and son Benton.

3,376. Bryan, Willingham, and Lawton Families

Papers. 1844-68. 10 items.
Open. No guide.
Georgia Department of Archives and History.
Correspondence of S. C. Bryan, M. A. Willingham, S. I. Rhodes, Annie Bryan Lawton, Sarah Jane Willingham Bryan, and Sarah Jane [Mrs. George] Rhodes. The families lived in South Carolina and in Albany and Forsythe, GA.

3,377. Bryson Family

Papers. 1900-30. 6 cu.ft.
Open. No guide.
Georgia Department of Archives and History.
Correspondence of Cassie L. Bryson, M. Turner, Ethel Thompson, and W. C. Thompson as well as business records of L. C. Thompson.

3,378. Buckhead Business and Professional Women's Club

Records. 1965-73. 4 vols.
Open. No guide.
Georgia Department of Archives and History.
Scrapbooks.

3,379. Chunn and Land Families

Papers. 1794-1925. 562 items.
Open. Description.
Georgia Department of Archives and History.
Family and business correspondence, including love letters and Civil War letters, and notes, deeds, receipts, promissory notes, poems, invitations, clippings, and other material of the family of William Augustus Chunn, the son of Samuel Love Chunn (1806-63) and Elizabeth Word Chunn, and his wife Lila (Land) Chunn, one of nine children of Nathan C. Land (1812-80) and Mona Ricks Arrington Land. Includes Civil War correspondence of Elizabeth Chunn with her son, letters to Elizabeth Chunn from various family members, and correspondence of Lila Chunn, Mona Arrington, Sarah E. Howard, and Harriet and Jane Beaver. Also contains family correspondence of the Adaline Smith family of Vicksburg, MS, and the will of Rosanna Mitchell. Nathan Land, elected Cass County ordinary in 1850, donated the property for Cassville Female College.

3,380. Cofer, Mrs. C. J.

Papers. 1941-46. 3 items.
Open. No guide.
Georgia Department of Archives and History.
Scrapbooks containing letters, cards, clippings, and other material about the participation of Cofer's daughter and other Atlanta residents in WWII, particularly in England, Europe, and North Africa.

3,381. Compton, Martha (Lumpkin)

Papers. 1832-1917. 1 cu.ft., 7 vols., and 2 items on microfilm.
Open. Description.
Georgia Department of Archives and History.
Correspondence, receipt books, and scrapbooks of Compton (1827-1917), who was the daughter of Georgia governor Wilson Lumpkin and for whom Atlanta was named "Marthasville" for a time. Includes correspondence and clippings concerning the name change in 1844 from "Terminus" to "Marthasville"; a clipping about a petition Compton made to the city council declaring that cows and boys had ruined her spring and that she had paid taxes for 27 years and had no protection; a clipping regarding the admission of a woman to the University of Georgia, with the comment that the "next woman will want to play football and study law"; articles regarding divorce laws; an obituary for Robert Battey, a Rome, GA, physician who invented the Battey gynecological operation; and a clipping regarding insanity in Negroes. Also includes letters from Elizabeth Hopkins to her granddaughter Mrs. Wilson Lumpkin, which contain news of New York and comments about Universalist religion; a letter dated 1854 in which Martha asks her father to resign as trustee of Franklin College; a letter to Thomas M. Compton; and a burial notice of Martha Compton.

3,382. Coolidge, Mrs. C. W.

Papers. 1890s-1954. 1 folder.
Open. No guide.
Georgia Department of Archives and History.
Copies of articles by Louise Thomson concerning her life as a missionary teacher among the Indians in Oklahoma; a 1954 clipping about Thomson from the Shawnee, OK, *News-Star;* a copy of a photo of Mary Meed Thomson; and copies of a letter and diary.

3,383. Council of National Defense, Georgia Division, Woman's Committee

Records. 1917-19. 10 cu.ft.
Open. No guide.
Georgia Department of Archives and History.
Founded in 1917 to support the Council of National Defense, the Woman's Committee also reflected many of the long-term reform goals of its leaders through organization of standing committees not directly related to the WWI effort. Correspondence, reports, bulletins, and clippings concerning the Committee's business include material on war work of individual County Woman's Committees and of the American National Red Cross, the YWCA, the DAR, the United Daughters of the Confederacy, suffrage and antisuffrage leagues, mission societies, the WCTU, and the Georgia Federation of Women's Clubs. In addition to standing committees for promotion of the draft, sale of war bonds, food conservation and preservation, home and foreign relief, and patriotic education, the Georgia Woman's Committee also formed committees to consider health and recreation, maintenance of existing social agencies, women in industry, and child welfare.

3,384. Cox College

Records. 1895-1950s. 1342 items.
Open. Partial inventory.
Georgia Department of Archives and History.
Founded as LaGrange Female Seminary in 1843, this now defunct college became Southern and West College in 1852, Southern Female College in 1854, and Cox College in 1904; the school moved to College Park, GA, in 1895. Student records from 1913 to 1917, teachers' grade reports from 1916 to 1921, annual reports of Cox College, photos, catalogs, and other material. Includes a souvenir picture album, a history of the school, pamphlets and clippings about College Park, municipal records of College Park, and a manuscript history of the College Park Woman's Club from 1896 to 1954, compiled by Mrs. Oscar Palmour and [Mrs.] Eva Thornton.

3,385. Daughters of the American Revolution Chapters

Records. Nd. 2.5 cu.ft. and 4 items.
Open. No guide.
Georgia Department of Archives and History.
Records of the Cherokee, Fort Peachtree, Oglethorpe, and Hannah Clarke Chapters; three scrapbooks of the Georgia division of the DAR; and a scrapbook that includes material about Georgia history from 1932 to 1938 and the DAR in Georgia.

3,386. Donalson, Agnes Graves

Papers. 1908. 1 item.
Open. No guide.
Georgia Department of Archives and History.
Diploma from the Presbyterian Hospital of the Atlanta Training School for Nurses.

3,387. Dowda, Earline

Papers. 1941-45. 0.67 cu.ft.
Open. No guide.
Georgia Department of Archives and History.
Correspondence, post cards, photos, and greeting cards of Dowda, an employee of Standard Oil of Atlanta who carried on extensive correspondence with men who left the company to become soldiers in WWII; she sent out "Kysomunique," a magazine for her correspondents. Consists primarily of letters to Dowda from the soldiers and letters to the service men's committee of Standard Oil of Atlanta. Also includes material on East Point, GA, and the Old South Bend Cemetery in Atlanta.

3,388. Everitt Family

Papers. 1883-1918. 20 items.
Open. Inventory.
Georgia Department of Archives and History.
Family, farm, and Bible records and miscellaneous papers of Richard Mills Everitt (1823-?) of Newton County, GA, and his daughter Julia Everitt (1852-?), including a diary of domestic affairs from 1892 to 1896 and books of household accounts for 1908 and 1909, all recorded by Julia Everitt. The household book indicates she kept a boardinghouse.

3,389. Few, William

Papers. 1802-69. 1 cu.ft.
Open. Inventory.
Georgia Department of Archives and History.
Papers of Few (1748-1829), a Revolutionary War figure, delegate to the Constitutional Convention, and one of Georgia's first US senators, include letters from Mary Telfair to Few's daughter Mary Few. Telfair, the daughter of Georgia governor Edward Telfair of Savannah, wrote to Mary Few from her home, from the North, and from abroad where her family traveled to avoid the summer heat and disease in Savannah. Telfair, who never married, expressed her views on marriage, political figures and events, and the role of single women in society. Her letters portray the social life and living conditions of a wealthy young woman in antebellum Savannah.

3,390. Fletcher, Louisa Warren Patch

Papers. 1857-98. 0.25 cu.ft.
Open. No guide.
Georgia Department of Archives and History.
Journal and family documents of Fletcher (1808-84), a Massachusetts native who moved to Savannah, GA, in the 1830s and in 1849 to Marietta, GA, where she and her husband Dix Fletcher managed a hotel. In her journal for the period 1857 to 1883, Fletcher reflects on her activities and those of her husband, her three daughters, her sister, and patrons of the hotel. While not a daily record of her life, the journal includes comments about her reading, church attendance, the Civil War and its effect on Marietta, and her feelings about her life. The journal also records a trip the Fletchers took north just after the war to visit friends and family. Also contains two letters concerning restitution for wartime damages to Fletcher property.

3,391. Fletcher, Lydia Bates

Papers. 1632. 3-page item.
Open. No guide.
Georgia Department of Archives and History.
Copy of a letter from Fletcher in Massachusetts colony to her sister Ruth Fletcher in Scrooby, England.

3,392. Georgia State College for Women

Records. 1926. 1 item.
Open. No guide.
Georgia Department of Archives and History.
Copy of a College bulletin, which lists the names of those who graduated from the Milledgeville, GA, school between 1892 and 1926.

3,393. Gordon
Papers. 1834-40?. 2 items.
Open. No guide.
Georgia Department of Archives and History.
Letters from Sarah Anderson Stiles Gordon to her husband William Washington Gordon. The Gordons were grandparents of Juliette (Gordon) Low.

3,394. Gordon, Fannie (Haralson)
Papers. 1864. 1 folder.
Open. No guide.
Georgia Department of Archives and History.
Letters from Gordon (1837-1931) to her husband John Brown Gordon (1832-1904), a Confederate general who became a US senator and governor of Georgia, are personal in nature and express her love for her husband and her fears for his safety. Gordon generally accompanied her husband, staying in towns near where his army was camped. In one letter she wrote from Hanover Junction, VA, she tells how she arrived and found lodging for herself and her son Frank. In another letter she speaks of her "secret," evidently pregnancy, and asks whether anyone other than her husband knows of it.

3,395. Holland, Benjamin F.
Papers. 1835-69. 2 items.
Open. No guide.
Georgia Department of Archives and History.
A memory album of Sophronia Bingley dated 1835 to 1837 and an 1869 letter to [Miss] Jennie Webb discussing folk medicine. The material relates to Virginia and South Carolina.

3,396. Huey, Catherine M.
Papers. 1858. 2 items.
Open. No guide.
Georgia Department of Archives and History.
Two slightly differing descriptive accounts of the execution of the slave Henry Jackson in DeKalb County, GA; both were written by [Mrs.] Huey, apparently for publication by a weekly newspaper.

3,397. Jasper County, GA, Schools
Records. 1887-95. 1 folder.
Open. No guide.
Georgia Department of Archives and History.
Correspondence, bulletins, teachers' contracts, and monthly school reports.

3,398. Johnson, Martha Amelia Allen
Papers. 1888-98. 1 folder.
Open. Partial description.
Open. Partial description.
Georgia Department of Archives and History.
Personal correspondence of the Hill family, primarily letters to [Mrs.] Ellen Ward.

3,399. Kaufman, Rhoda
Papers. 1906-56. 2.5 cu.ft.
Open. Inventory.
Georgia Department of Archives and History.
A social worker and organization executive, [Miss] Kaufman (1888-1956) headed the Georgia Department of Welfare and the Atlanta Family Welfare Society. Personal, business, and organizational correspondence; work diaries; photos; clippings; publications; and other material, including letters and telegrams to clubwomen and professional organizations through which Kaufman organized support for social programs. Also contains copies of her speeches; correspondence and records of the Atlanta chapter of a UN organization that Kaufman supported during the last years of her life; and copies of publications for which she was responsible, including studies of recreational needs, day-care facilities, hospital beds, and medical requirements in metropolitan Atlanta. A Columbus, GA, native whose right leg was amputated when she was 12, Kaufman received her bachelor of science degree from Vanderbilt in 1912. From 1913 to 1915 she was president of the Atlanta AAUW and organized Georgia women in a campaign to build a state training school for girls. While serving as assistant secretary to the Atlanta Associated Charities, she was appointed to the Commission for the Feeble-Minded and was the group's executive secretary in 1918 and 1919. She then served as assistant secretary and later as executive secretary of the newly formed state welfare department. Kaufman resigned from the welfare department in 1926 because of ill-health and became executive secretary of the Atlanta Family Welfare Society, where she worked until 1937. She then became executive secretary of the Atlanta Social Planning Council, the coordinating agency for the city's health and welfare agencies. Kaufman also was chairman of the State Council of Social Agencies executive committee, a member of the executive committee of the American Association of Social Workers and of the Child Welfare League of America, and a member of President Hoover's White House Conference on Children. Kaufman was Jewish.

3,400. Lamar, Charles Augustus Lafayette
Papers. 1858-67. 38 items.
Open. Inventory.
Georgia Department of Archives and History.
Personal correspondence between Lamar and his wife Caro, letters to Caro Lamar from her mother, and other letters she received regarding the death of her husband.

3,401. Lee, Lucinda "Sukie"
Papers. 1796. 2 items.
Open. No guide.
Georgia Department of Archives and History.
Personal letters from Lee at Smithfield to Polly Uphsur at White Hall, VA.

3,402. McCall, Ann Margaret
Papers. 1836. 1 item.
Open. No guide.
Georgia Department of Archives and History.
Copy of a detailed account of Indian depredations written to Captain John H. Moegart in Charleston, SC. The account was written in Muscogee County, GA, and posted from Columbus, GA.

3,403. Madison, GA, Young Matron's Club
Records. 1893-96. 1 item.
Open. No guide.
Georgia Department of Archives and History.
Record book of this social club, including constitution, bylaws, minutes, and records of dues.

3,404. Marye, Florence (Nesbit)
Papers. Ca. 1930s-40s. 7 cu.ft.
Open. Inventory.
Georgia Department of Archives and History.
[Mrs. Phillip Thornton] Marye was a writer. Family and business correspondence, unpublished manuscripts and notes, original verse, photos, sketches of Georgia historic sites, a compilation of historical recipes, pamphlets, brochures, and other material. Includes Florence Marye's correspondence with publishing houses concerning her manuscript for *Georgia Scenes* and WWII correspondence from the Pacific theater of Lieutenant Junior Grade George Alexander Heard, a Marye family relative. Also contains essays; research notes; endorsements for *Georgia Scenes;* "Annals of the Group," an account of a private service organization in Atlanta during the depression; and photos, including a few depicting Marye as a USO hostess during WWII.

3,405. Means, Alexander
Papers. 1853-1909. 1 folder and 11 items.
Open. Unpublished guide.
Georgia Department of Archives and History.
Correspondence of Means (1801-83), a minister, scientist, doctor, and president of the Southern Masonic Female College; of Oreon Mann, who taught at the Covington, GA, women's school from 1853 to 1855, and of Rufus Smith, whom Mann married. Correspondence relates to Mann's employment at the College, activities of two of her sisters in connection with the school, an honorary master's degree for Mann from Wesleyan College, and the possibility of a Spanish translation of some of Means's sermons. A teacher in northern Georgia academies and colleges for 50 years, Mann spent her last 22 years at LaGrange College where her husband was president.

3,406. Means, Sarah Virginia
Papers. 1874-76. 1 vol.
Open. No guide.
Georgia Department of Archives and History.
Diary-composition book in which [Miss] Means, who probably was the daughter of Matthew Harvey Means, relates her experiences while attending Wesleyan Female College in 1874 and 1875. Some entries date from after her graduation. Includes letters to her cousin and copies of mathematics and Latin lessons.

3,407. Michael, Moina
Papers. Nd. 6 cu.ft.
Open. Inventory.
Georgia Department of Archives and History.
Correspondence, transcripts of speeches, manuscripts, ledgers, photos, scrapbooks, clippings, certificates of appreciation, and other papers of [Miss] Michael, who originated the use of the red poppy in commemoration of soldiers killed in WWI. Consists chiefly of correspondence between Michael and WWI soldiers and memorabilia from her extensive letter-writing career.

3,408. Millis, Mary (Raoul)
Papers. 1953. 0.25 cu.ft.
Open. No guide.
Georgia Department of Archives and History.
Unpublished memoir of Millis (1870-1958), an early supporter of woman suffrage who became a socialist. The daughter of a railroad executive, she married John Millis, a captain in the Corps of Engineers, in 1893. The memoir, which deals only with the period from 1870 to 1913, illuminates the life style of a well-to-do young woman of the late 19th century and conveys some of her private feelings. She indicates that she was discontented because she could not become an architect, that she wished to avoid marriage, and that she found the low status of a wife and mother unsatisfactory. Includes extensive information about the Wadley, Raoul, and Millis families.

3,409. Mitchell, Ella L.
Papers. 1888-94. 9 items.
Open. No guide.
Georgia Department of Archives and History.
Mitchell (1855-1924) was a teacher and school principal. A letter of recommendation, a notification dated 1888 of her reelection as principal of the Sandersonville, GA, grammar school, a biographical sketch, and four teaching licenses.

3,410. Mitchell, Nathaniel R.
Papers. 1866-75. 1 cu.ft.
Open. No guide.
Georgia Department of Archives and History.
Mitchell, the father of Anna Green (Mitchell) Tilson, owned a cotton plantation in Thomasville, GA. Family correspondence, ship manifests, plantation records, account books, bills, receipts, promissory notes, McKinnon and McIntosh family records, and a will of Thomas Mitchell. Includes Tilson's letters to her father, her brother George W. Mitchell, and others as well as domestic records concerning the price of household goods, medical assistance, and food. While most of the collection relates to the cotton business before and after the Civil War, family correspondence also includes discussion of finding a wife for Nathaniel Mitchell.

3,411. Moran, Dorothy J.
Papers. 1878. 9-page item.
Open. No guide.
Georgia Department of Archives and History.
Copy of a valedictory speech of Molly Antoinette Sheehan.

3,412. Oliver, Curtis
Papers. 1851-63. 28 items.
Open. No guide.
Georgia Department of Archives and History.
Civil War correspondence of Oliver, a captain in the Georgia Militia from Dahlonega, GA; his wife Nancy; and his sister Mary.

3,413. Osborn, Katherine Elizabeth "Lizzie"
Papers. 1845-1921. 0.5 cu.ft.
Open. Inventory.
Georgia Department of Archives and History.
Lizzie Mangum (1834-?) taught school in the Atlanta area and married James Ozburn in 1854; the Ozburns had five children and maintained a general store in Atlanta until 1861 when he joined the army in Virginia. Family correspondence, including letters exchanged by the Ozburns while James was in Virginia, letters from Lizzie Ozburn to her sister Emily, and letters relating to the Ozburns' oldest daughter Kate Story; business and personal diaries of J. R. and Lizzie Ozburn; and legal documents, including Lizzie Ozburn's teacher's contracts and property deeds of the Mangum and Ozburn families. In 1893, after the deaths of her husband and two of her children, Lizzie Ozburn apparently ran a boardinghouse. The family name was also spelled Osborn.

3,414. Oxford, Edward
Papers. 1793-1837. 639 items.
Open. Inventory.
Georgia Department of Archives and History.
Oxford, justice of the peace for Jones County, GA, served as administrator of the estate of Elizabeth McFarlin, who probably was the wife of Captain Peter McFarlin and Oxford's sister. Correspondence, records of Oxford's office, accounts, receipts for taxes and other payments, records of cotton sales, and legal records. Contains the Elizabeth McFarlin estate papers, including accounts for Negro hire, a letter appointing Oxford estate administrator, an inventory of fees paid from 1824 to 1826, receipts, and other material dating from 1801 to 1830.

3,415. Perkins, Mary Louise Martin
Papers. 1925-62. No size given.
Partially restricted. Inventory.
Georgia Department of Archives and History.
A Fleming, GA, native who graduated from the University of Georgia in 1931, Perkins (1911-62) was a genealogist and painter. Personal, business, and genealogical correspondence; genealogical material about more than 35 families; items relating to the Daughters of the American Colonists and the Midway Church; photos; brochures; miscellaneous religious matter; and other items. Perkins married Percy Harold Perkins, Jr., in 1933.

3,416. Presbyterian Church, Synod of Georgia, Women of the Church
Records. Nd. 0.5 cu.ft.
Open. No guide.
Georgia Department of Archives and History.
Minute books from annual meetings and miscellaneous documents.

3,417. Reese, Mamie (Mathews)
Papers. 1899. 1 item.
Open. No guide.
Georgia Department of Archives and History.
Copy of a prosuffrage speech that Reese, who was 14 at the time, gave during a debate at Briarcreek Institute at Warrenton, GA.

3,418. Reynolds, Lily Elizabeth
Papers. 1854-1931. 0.5 cu.ft.
Open. Description.
Georgia Department of Archives and History.
Reynolds (1866-?) was an historian of Coweta County, GA. Civil War correspondence, journals, poems, Coweta County records, photos, a scrapbook, invitations and memorabilia, clippings, a songbook, and other items. Includes letters exchanged by Reynolds's mother, her brothers, and her husband during the Civil War; clippings regarding prohibition and Reynolds's writings on the subject; an autograph album compiled at Wesleyan Female Institute in Stauton, VA; clippings regarding the Sarah Dickinson Chapter of the DAR in Coweta County; and issues of the *Orphan's Message* from 1899 to 1906.

3,419. Rogers, Loula Winifred Kendall, Family
Papers. 1791-1954. 5 cu.ft.
Open. Inventories and description.
Georgia Department of Archives and History.
[Mrs.] Rogers (1839-1931) was poet laureate of the United Daughters of the Confederacy and a teacher at the Gordon Institute in Barnesville, GA. Correspondence; diaries; journals; published and unpublished poetry; speeches; household accounts; land records; records of the Rogers, Kendall, Franklin, and related families; photos; scrapbooks; pamphlets; clippings; and newspapers. Includes biographical information about Rogers, Louisa Hanson Rogers (Steele) Kendall (1804-81), and Helen Graham Rogers Franklin (1870-1938) and correspondence of Rogers, Kendall, [Mrs.] Julia Kendall Lockett, Fannie Graham Paine, and Sallie Rogers Shaw. Rogers's journals and diaries begin when she was a 15-year-old student at Georgia Episcopal Institute at Montpelier, GA; she describes her life at school, plantation life at Bellwood in Upson County, GA, her married life, her UDC activities, her work at the Gordon Institute, and the Battle of Atlanta. Also contains writings and poetry of Rogers, Franklin, Kendall, Lockett, and Dollie Rogers McCray; records of the Woman's Shakespeare and Literary Club of Barnesville; papers relating to the death of Franklin; organizational records of the national, state, and several local divisions of the UDC, the Confederated Southern Memorial Association, and the United Friends of Temperance, Georgia Council; programs and catalogs of Wesleyan Female College, the Gordon Institute, Jackson Institute, and Tenille High School; and Georgia newspapers, including a 1901 copy of *Woman's World* of Athens.

3,420. Ross, Mary Letitia
Papers. 1885-1973. 125 cu.ft.
Open. Unpublished guide.
Georgia Department of Archives and History.
A student of historian Herbert Eugene Bolton, [Miss] Ross (1885-1971) was an historian and geographer who studied the Spanish occupation of the Southeast, particularly of Georgia and Florida. Personal correspondence; research material, including transcriptions of documents from archives in Spain, Mexico, and Cuba and volumes on history, literature, religion, and travel; maps; and other items. The majority of the collection relates to Ross's research on the Spanish in Georgia. Includes her correspondence with Bolton, which reflects her development as an historian and the problems that Ross faced as a woman in her study of Latin American history.

3,421. Shores, Helen (Hopkins) Keanum
Papers. Nd. 18-page item.
Open. No guide.
Georgia Department of Archives and History.
Typescript of "Miriah's Legacy," a narrative that concerns Miriah Shelnut, a Cherokee woman from North Carolina who married George Washington Cochran and settled in Campbell County, GA, in 1850.

3,422. Shropshire, Mollie H.
Papers. 1874. 6 items.
Open. No guide.
Georgia Department of Archives and History.
Collection consists of material donated by Shropshire's daughter concerning College Temple, a woman's college at Newnan, GA. Includes a note from the donor, a school essay, commencement and concert programs, an 1874 diploma, and other material.

3,423. Smith, Clifton B.
Papers. Nd. 4 items.
Open. No guide.
Georgia Department of Archives and History.
An 1881-82 catalog of LaGrange Female College containing the school's curriculum and names of students, faculty, and graduates as well as a 1900 clipping from the *Atlanta Journal* concerning an upcoming statewide DAR conference.

3,424. Smith Family
Papers. 1817-1905. 8 folders, 78 items, and 163 pp.
Open. Inventory.
Georgia Department of Archives and History.
Correspondence and miscellany of Aaron Smith of Forsyth County, GA, who came to Georgia from North Carolina in 1817; his wife Nancy J. Smith; his children Mariah Louisa, Mary Jane, Atha C., Wilbur F., Eliza A., Telitha A., Horace, and Samuel; and Adaline Smith. Mariah Louisa Smith's correspondence includes letters from boyfriends. Miscellany includes cake recipes.

3,425. Smith, Fannie Pickelshimer Kerby
Papers. 1880-1910. 11 items.
Open. Inventory.
Georgia Department of Archives and History.
Diary, a register book, photos, post cards, and a clipping of Smith, who operated an inn called Aunt Fannie's Cabin in Sinking Mountain, GA, deal primarily with her hotel and excursions during the 1890s and early 1900s to Tallulah Falls, GA. The register provides the name and home city of each guest during the 1890s. The diary, dating from the 1880s, was written by an unidentified man and woman, apparently husband and wife, and includes entries about their travels abroad as well as drawings by the man.

3,426. Smith, Henrietta C.
Papers. 1897-1905. 1 vol.
Open. No guide.
Georgia Department of Archives and History.
Diary of Smith, a resident of Hephzibah, GA.

3,427. Smith, Jane J.
Papers. Nd. 4 items.
Open. No guide.
Georgia Department of Archives and History.
Includes a post card album, dating from ca. 1904, of Cox College.

3,428. Southern Masonic Female College
Records. 1872. 1 item.
Open. No guide.
Georgia Department of Archives and History.
Circular of this Covington, GA, school.

3,429. State of Georgia, Executive Department (Civil War Section)
Records. 1861-65. 30 cu.ft.
Open. Alphabetical list of correspondents.
Georgia Department of Archives and History.
Contains 152 letters written by women to the Georgia governor during the Civil War.

3,430. Toombs, Adah (Knight)
Papers. 1951-67. 1 cu.ft.
Open. Limited description.
Georgia Department of Archives and History.
A Florida native, Toombs (1907-) is a civic leader and prison reformer who attended Agnes Scott

College and William and Mary; she married Henry J. Toombs in 1948. Correspondence, organizational records, clippings, three tapes, and slides reflect Toombs's long interest in prison reform, especially the imprisonment of children in common jails. Most of the material is devoted to her activities, frequently as legislative chairman, in the Georgia Legislative Forum for Women, the Georgia Federation of Women's Clubs, and the United Church Women of Atlanta; other items record her participation in the Fulton County Juvenile Board, the City Executive Council, and the State Board of Family and Children's Services, and as a representative to the Georgia Citizens Committee for Children and Youth. Includes records and personal correspondence concerning Toombs's unsuccessful campaign in 1965 for the Georgia House of Representatives from district 140 and correspondence of Mamie K. Taylor, a civic leader. Also includes tapes of a live interview with a prison guard and a mother of an inmate who died in a Georgia prison and of a radio program about a prisoner broadcast over WGST.

3,431. United Daughters of the Confederacy Chapters

Records. Nd. No size given.
Open. Partial inventory.
Georgia Department of Archives and History.
Civil War material, including minute books, correspondence, diaries, and documents of the Lizzie Rutherford Chapter; correspondence and a transmittal of land grant of the Peachtree Creek Chapter; Atlanta Chapter scrapbooks, 1965-66; and records of the Frankie Lyle Chapter and the LaGrange Chapter, 1901-31.

3,432. Van der Vrede, Jane

Papers. Ca. 1919-40. 3.5 cu.ft.
Open. No guide.
Georgia Department of Archives and History.
A Wisconsin-born nurse who graduated in 1907 from the Milwaukee General Hospital School of Nursing, Van der Vrede (1880-1972) was director of the American National Red Cross's southern division during WWI and Georgia director of Professional and Service Projects for the WPA during the 1930s. Speeches, notebooks, reports, photos, scrapbooks, magazines, and miscellany reflect Van der Vrede's WWI and WPA work and include personnel records for public health nurses in Alabama, Florida, South and North Carolina, Louisiana, and Georgia for the years 1919 to 1921; an analysis of Red Cross and public health nursing in the southern division for the same period; and other Red Cross publications and administrative material. WPA material includes scrapbooks of service projects; radio scripts; records of county "achievement week" functions, including minutes of the Chatham County colored achievement dinner; and other records. Van der Vrede was a Red Cross nurse from 1912 to 1925, a member of the Georgia Board of Examiners from 1914 to 1933, executive secretary of the Georgia State Nursing Association in ca. 1925, a member of the American Nurses' Association board of directors for 14 years, vice-president of the National Organization for Public Health Nursing, and in 1970 the first president of the southern division of the National League for Nursing.

3,433. Van Valkenburgh, Mary Wealthy Bradley

Papers. 1865-66. 7 items.
Open. No guide.
Georgia Department of Archives and History.
Correspondence of Van Valkenburgh (?-1866), a resident of Bibb County, GA, written from Macon, GA.

3,434. Wade, J. D.

Papers. 1887-95. 15 items.
Open. Inventory.
Georgia Department of Archives and History.
School records from Jasper County, GA, consist of letters from book companies to Willis Newton, county school commissioner; teachers' contracts made with the county board of education; school reports compiled by teachers in 1890 and 1891 giving name and age of pupil, name of pupil's parent or guardian, and monthly attendance; and bulletins listing textbooks officially adopted for various Georgia counties.

3,435. Washington Seminary

Records. 1913. 1 vol.
Open. No guide.
Georgia Department of Archives and History.
Copy of *Facts and Fancies,* the yearbook of the Seminary, a now defunct private girls school established in 1878 in Atlanta.

3,436. Whittle and Powers Family

Papers. 1833-94. 124 items.
Open. Inventory.
Georgia Department of Archives and History.
Family, business, and miscellaneous correspondence; legal records; and other papers of the Virginia families of Fortescue Whittle and Mary Ann Davies, whom he married in 1804; Lewis Neale Whittle, the ninth of 15 children of Fortescue and Mary Ann Whittle; and Sarah M. Powers of Georgia, who married Lewis Whittle. Includes letters from Mary Ann Whittle to her son Lewis, who became a lawyer in Georgia after his marriage in the 1830s, and letters of Elizabeth Julia Whittle, her niece Narcissa Whittle, Mrs. Sidney Lanier, and Zillah Emmel. Mary Ann Whittle's letters contain family news, descriptions of Civil War events, and comments about slavery; in an 1859 letter she asks Lewis Whittle to dispose of her servants in Georgia. Also contains correspondence of the Griffin and Powers families; a letter from Nellie (Peters) Black, who complains that the bishop of Georgia is not doing his duty because he will not come to baptize her children; wills of Mary Murray Davies of Mecklenburg County, VA, and Zillah Emmel of Georgia; and receipts for money from the estates of Julia A. Powers, Sarah M. Whittle, and Mary Ann Whittle.

3,437. Winter, Mary Sarah (Carter)

Papers. 1890-1965. 18 cu.ft.
Partially restricted. No guide.
Georgia Department of Archives and History.
A journalist who worked for Georgia newspapers, including the *Augusta Herald,* the *Augusta Chronicle,* and the *Atlanta Constitution,* Winter (1890-1975) participated in a WPA adult education project at Benjamin Franklin High School in Brooklyn, NY, from ca. 1934 to 1938 and worked at the arsenal in Augusta, GA, during WWII. Correspondence, manuscripts, copies of her published articles, notes, photos, pamphlets, clippings, books, and memorabilia. Includes manuscripts of her unpublished books "The Echoing Ages," a genealogy of the Ruffin family, and "Signposts for Freedom," an anti-Catholic tract, as well as a 1911 *Constitution* article "Why Should Women Be Denied Admission to the Bar?" Also contains material about her work during the early 1920s for the Children's Founders Roll of the Stone Mountain Memorial Association in Atlanta and for the New York WPA project. Correspondence from 1908 and 1909 reflects her frustration at being allowed to write only women's stories for the Augusta newspapers. Carter joined the newspapers after graduating from Brenau College in 1906 and teaching school for a year. She moved to Atlanta in ca. 1911 and became the first female courthouse reporter for the *Constitution.* She also was executive editor for the tri-weekly *Atlanta Journal.* A Burke County, GA, native, she married Rogers Winter in 1912. She went to New York to begin research on a book in 1930; in 1932 she helped with publicity for Roosevelt's presidential campaign. By WWII Winter had returned to Georgia where she did publicity work for the American National Red Cross in addition to her duties at the arsenal. After the war she was rehired by the *Augusta Chronicle* and worked as a feature writer and assistant editorial writer until about 1960. In 1948 she headed the women's division of the Georgia States Rights Democratic party. Later she was appointed to the state's Commission on Constitutional Government.

3,438. Women's Auxiliary of All Saints Church, Diocese of Atlanta

Records. 1949-66. 0.5 cu.ft.
Open. No guide.
Georgia Department of Archives and History.
Three yearbooks.

3,439. Women's Organizations

Records. Nd. No size given.
Open. No guide.
Georgia Department of Archives and History.
Records of the Daughters of the American Colonists, Georgia Society, the Garden Club of Georgia, Inc., 1 cu.ft.; the Georgia Association of Women Lawyers, 1 cu.ft.; the Georgia Dietetic Association, 0.5 cu.ft.; the Georgia Federation of Business and Professional Women's Clubs, 20 cu.ft. of records dating to 1975; the Georgia Federation of Women's Clubs, 4 cu.ft., 9 scrapbooks, and 18 folio boxes; the Georgia Home Economics Association, 3.5 cu.ft. and 1 scrapbook, 1920-70; the Georgia Mothers' Committee, microfilm of scrapbooks, 1935-69; the Georgia Nutrition Council, 0.5 cu.ft.; the Georgia Society of Colonial Dames of the 17th century, 3 minute books and 5 scrapbooks; the League of American Pen Women, 0.5 cu.ft.; the Magna Carta Dames, 0.5 cu.ft.; the National Society of the Daughters of Founders and Patriots of America, Georgia Chapter, 3 vols.; the Soroptimist Club, 2.5 cu.ft.; the US Daughters of 1812, 1 scrapbook; and the Women's Pharmaceutical Auxiliary, 6 scrapbooks.

3,440. Word, Lucy

Papers. 1866-1965. 1 cu.ft.
Open. Limited description.
Georgia Department of Archives and History.
An historical preservationist, [Mrs. M. P.] Word (1884-) was chairman of Marking Historic Spots in Georgia, a group within the Georgia division of the United Daughters of the Confederacy. Correspondence, clippings, and miscellany, the bulk of which relates to her UDC work. Includes her correspondence about erecting historical markers and validating proposed markers. Also contains clippings, copies of deeds, copies of marker inscriptions, and programs from events honoring the Confederacy. Much of the correspondence relates to the unfurling of the first Confederate flag in Georgia and to a tribute to [Mrs.] Elizabeth Camp Glover.

3,441. Historic Preservation in Georgia

Records. 1951- . No size given.
Partially restricted. No guide.
Georgia Department of Natural Resources, Historic Preservation Section.
Correspondence, research files, scrapbooks, clippings, and other records of the Georgia Historical Commission and of the Historic Preservation Section. [Mrs.] Mary Gregory Jewett was executive secretary-director of the Georgia Historical Commission from 1967 until her retirement in 1974. Many other women have been involved in historic preservation efforts in the state. Includes material illustrating the work of these women and papers of women who owned or were associated with structures that became historic sites.

3,442. AFL-CIO Region VIII

Records. 1920s-60s. 50 records center boxes.
Open. Unpublished guide.

Georgia State University, Southern Labor Archives. Correspondence of Connie Anderson, Elizabeth Sasuly, and Mary Lou Koger, organizers of the CIO's Food, Tobacco, Agricultural and Allied Workers Union during the 1940s, is included among the financial documents, correspondence, convention proceedings, pamphlets, scrapbooks, printed material, recording discs, and films of AFL-CIO Region VIII. Anderson and Sasuly were directors of the union's political action committee, while Anderson also headed the education committee and Sasuly, the legislative panel.

3,443. Atlanta Labor Council
Records. 1915-69. Ca. 13 ft.
Open. Unpublished guide.
Georgia State University, Southern Labor Archives.
The Council, the political action arm of organized labor in Atlanta, was formed in 1958 through merger of the AFL's Atlanta Federation of Trades and the CIO's Atlanta Industrial Union Council. Minutes, financial documents, membership records, office files, photos, and printed material, the bulk of which was generated after 1956. Includes records of the AFL-CIO and the 5th Congressional District Committee on Political Education, including office files of Sally Ponikarski, director of the Committee's women's activities department, and information regarding the department and its role in voter registration.

3,444. Georgia Nurses Association
Records. 1907-72. Ca. 70 ft.
Open. Unpublished guide.
Georgia State University, Southern Labor Archives.
Chartered in 1907 as a professional membership organization for Georgia's registered nurses, the Association is the state branch of the American Nurses Association. Financial records, correspondence, organizational files, photos, scrapbooks, and audiovisual material provide information about this predominantly female organization. Records from the 1960s reflect the Association's role as an active collective bargaining agent for nurses. Also includes records of the southern division of the American Nurses Association, which was formed in the 1920s but dissolved during the 1950s, and of the Georgia Nurses Association's 17 district organizations.

3,445. International Woodworkers of America, District 4
Records. 1943-59. 50 ft.
Open. Unpublished guide.
Georgia State University, Southern Labor Archives.
Financial documents, weekly work reports, contract notes and proposals, correspondence, photos, and printed material of the union, founded in 1937, include papers of Rosella Chestner, an organizer who worked primarily in Virginia from 1952 to 1959. Her papers include correspondence, weekly reports, and expense vouchers.

3,446. Lucia, Carmen
Papers. 1930s-50s. 1 ft. and 6 tapes.
Open. No guide.
Georgia State University, Southern Labor Archives.
Lucia (1902-), an Italian immigrant and longtime organizer, served as international vice-president of the Hat, Cap and Millinery Workers Union for several years after 1946. Clippings regarding unions Lucia organized across the country; pamphlets concerning union organization, which she wrote, designed, and had printed; and tapes in which she describes her arrival in America at the age of 2, her work as a union organizer, and union history in America.

3,447. McGill, Eula
Papers. 1938-64. 5 in. and 2 tapes.
Open. Unpublished guide.
Georgia State University, Southern Labor Archives.
McGill (1911-) is a union organizer and staff member of the Amalgamated Clothing Workers of America. Scrapbook material, biographical oral history tapes, a transcript, and photos. Newspapers, clippings, and programs in scrapbooks pertain to her organizing activities in Tennessee, particularly to the union's jurisdictional dispute with the United Mine Workers, and to her work with price control and rationing programs during the 1940s. Photos record conventions of the ACWA and of the Tennessee State Industrial Union Council from 1938 to 1944.

3,448. Service Employees International Union, Southern Region
Records. 1962-70. 6 Hollinger boxes.
Open. Unpublished guide.
Georgia State University, Southern Labor Archives.
Minutes, financial and legal documents, correspondence, and printed matter of the Union, founded in the 1920s. Includes correspondence of Huda Aycock, president from 1965 to 1968 of the Service Employees International Union Local 543 of Sheffield, AL.

3,449. True, Martha
Papers. 1964-69. 10 in.
Open. Unpublished guide.
Georgia State University, Southern Labor Archives.
Correspondence, printed material, and reports gathered by True (ca, 1936-), the secretary of the Georgia state AFL-CIO and vice-president and financial secretary of the Atlanta Labor Council. True was vice-president of the state AFL-CIO from 1964 to 1972, vice-president and president of the Communication Workers of America Local 3204 for 19 years, and a member of the CWA constitution and collective bargaining policy committees. Committee material includes information regarding the US economic situation, proposed amendments, membership, and forced overtime.

3,450. United Textile Workers of America
Records. 1930-75. 42 ft.
Open. Unpublished guide.
Georgia State University, Southern Labor Archives.
Minutes, financial records, correspondence, periodicals, photos, and printed material of the union, founded in 1901. Included are papers of Madeleine Parent, and organizer for the Textile Workers in Canada during the 1940s and early 1950s; and Mary Taccone, executive council member and vice-president of the Federation of Woolen and Worsted Workers Union from 1940 to 1947.

AUGUSTA

3,451. Augusta's Citizens
Oral history. 1974- . 14 vols. and ca. 20 transcripts.
Open. Unpublished guide.
Augusta Regional Library, Oral History Project.
Interviews with local residents, about one-third of them women, include oral memoirs of Marguerite (Aycock) Blackstone, an Augusta businesswoman who speaks of Augusta in the early 1900s; Flo (Crouch) [Mrs. Jack] Browning, chief operator for the telephone company during a fire in Augusta in 1916; Alma (Effert) [Mrs. Ralph] Chaney, who founded the Women's Unit of the USO in Augusta and has served as president of the local YWCA board of directors; [Miss] Jean Cochran, who retired in 1975 after 26 years as director of the Augusta-Richmond County Public Library; Gertrude (Donahue) [Mrs. James] Daley, who grew up in an Irish community and worked at Camp Gordon during WWII; [Miss] Laura Garvin, a retired schoolteacher who is the daughter of one of the founders of Morehouse College; [Miss] Margaret L. Laney, a teacher and juvenile court worker who was the niece of a prominent black educator; Margaret (Loyless) [Mrs. Patrick] Mell, the daughter of the editor of the *Augusta Chronicle;* [Miss] Wallace North, who discusses the women's movement in the Augusta area in the early 1900s; Ruby (Mabry) [Mrs. Herman] Pfadenhauer, who worked at the Augusta Arsenal; and Mildred (Abernathy) [Mrs. Montgomery] Ridgely, a former schoolteacher and retired YWCA director. In the interviews, the women speak of their own careers, those of family members, and their lives in the Augusta region. Ridgely reminisces about the educational system in Richmond County during the depression, the actions taken against married women teachers, and the fight to save their jobs. Garvin tells about the work of her father Henry B. Garvin, who worked for the Augusta Post Office for many years and was editor of the Negro section of the *Augusta Chronicle.*

DECATUR

3,452. Agnes Scott College
Records. 1889- . Ca. 50 ft.
Open. No guide.
Agnes Scott College Library.
The College, a private liberal arts school for women, was founded in 1889. Annual reports, including those submitted by President James Ross McCain and Treasurer J. C. Tart, 1923-51; minutes of two literary societies and the debating club; photos of faculty, students, and campus scenes; scrapbooks; college catalogs, 1889- ; complete set of alumnae quarterlies; student handbooks, newspapers, and directories; faculty and alumnae publications; clippings; and other records.

MACON

3,453. Baptist Missionary Society
Records. Nd. Ca. 95 microfilm reels.
Open. No guide.
Mercer University Library, Georgia Baptist Historical Society.
Annual reports, financial records, memorials, obituaries, and other records of various Georgia units of the Society, which has included many women. Many of the reports were printed in connection with the Society's annual meetings. The reports deal with such topics as Sunday schools, foreign and home missions, and temperance and document the activities of various women's missionary unions and women's missionary societies.

3,454. Christian Index
Records. 1822-1968. 2 vols. and more than 5500 cards.
Open. Indexes.
Mercer University Library, Georgia Baptist Historical Society.
Founded in 1822 as the *Columbian Star,* the weekly *Christian Index* was moved from Philadelphia to Washington, GA, in 1833 after it was purchased by Jesse Mercer. Issues of the paper include news about Georgia Baptists and other southern Baptists, war news, advertisements, marriage records, obituaries, and other information. The *Index,* which became the newspaper of Georgia Baptists, absorbed a Southwestern Baptist paper published in Alabama and Tennessee as well as Florida Baptist papers during the 1870s. Also available on microfilm.

3,455. Churches
Records. 1800- . No size given.
Open. No guide.
Mercer University Library, Georgia Baptist Historical Society.
Records of various local churches include the records of the Women's Missionary Society of the

First Baptist Church of Macon. These records, which date from 1906 to 1959, provide information about topics of discussion at monthly meetings, officers, deaths of members, and other topics. Portions of the material have been microfilmed.

3,456. Ebenezer Baptist Association
Records. 1888-1964. 3 vols.
Open. No guide.
Mercer University Library, Georgia Baptist Historical Society.
Scrapbooks contain photos, meeting favors, meeting announcements, and other printed matter of the Women's Missionary Union of the Ebenezer Baptist Association of Georgia. Includes a history of the WMU in the Association and in the Southern Baptist Convention and a map of the area covered by the Association. The scrapbooks illustrate the courses taught by women in the Association.

3,457. Southern Baptist Convention Annuals
Records. 1845- . No size given.
Open. No guide.
Mercer University Library, Georgia Baptist Historical Society.
Annuals of the Convention include information about its woman's auxiliary, the Woman's Missionary Union, which was founded in 1888. Annuals dating from 1845 to 1952 are available on microfilm.

3,458. Women's Missionary Societies
Records. 1880- . More than 90 microfilm reels.
Open. No guide.
Mercer University Library, Georgia Baptist Historical Society.
Records of women's missionary society units in local Georgia churches, which make up the state's 96 Baptist associations. Annual reports of the separate churches include information about the officers, finances, and topics discussed by women's society branches. Societies were formerly known as women's missionary unions.

3,459. Broome, Christine
Papers. ?-1976. 9 vols. and 1 item.
Closed. No guide.
Washington Memorial Library, Genealogical and Historical Room.
[Miss] Broome (1894-1976) taught Spanish, German, French, and Portuguese at Wesleyan College in Macon. Notebooks containing genealogical data and a family chart.

3,460. Everett, Nettie Ward Frierson
Papers. Nd. 34 folders.
Open. Unpublished guide.
Washington Memorial Library, Genealogical and Historical Room.
Genealogical data that [Mrs.] Everett (1886-1971) compiled over a 30- to 40-year period. Includes index and cross index.

3,461. Ayars, Rebecca Caudill
Papers. Nd. 4.5 in.
Open. No guide.
Wesleyan College, Candler Alumnae Center.
Correspondence, clippings, books, and other printed material of [Mrs. James] Ayars, an author who graduated from Wesleyan College in 1920. Believed to be the first Wesleyan College student to pay her way through school, she worked in the bursar's office in return for tuition, room, and board. She taught English and history in Portland, TN, in 1920-21 and then went to Rio de Janeiro where she headed the English department at Collegio Bennett. For six years she was editor of *The Torchbearer,* a Methodist magazine for girls. Ayars is the author of more than 17 books, most of them for children. She lives in Urbana, IL, and Green Valley, AZ.

3,462. Harmon, Mamie
Papers. Nd. Ca. 1 in.
Open. No guide.
Wesleyan College, Candler Alumnae Center.
Correspondence, photos, and printed matter of Harmon, an editor, artist, and free-lance writer. She began her career as a dean of women and English professor at Centenary College in Cleveland, TN. She edited reference works, wrote for Funk and Wagnall, and traveled and studied art in Europe and the Orient. Harmon, who now lives in New York City, earned her AB degree at Wesleyan College in 1926 and an MA from the University of Chicago in 1927.

3,463. Horn, Annabel
Papers. Nd. Ca. 2 in.
Open. No guide.
Wesleyan College, Candler Alumnae Center.
Correspondence, photos, clippings, and textbooks of [Miss] Horn (?-1969), a classics scholar who taught for many years at Atlanta High School for Girls; after her retirement she became dean of the Wesleyan College conservatory and school of fine arts and later assistant to the dean. After earning her AB at Wesleyan College in 1906 and an MA at the University of Chicago, she studied at The Academy in Rome. She was co-author of a series of high school Latin textbooks.

3,464. Johnson, Rosalie Voigt
Papers. Nd. Ca. 0.5 in.
Open. No guide.
Wesleyan College, Candler Alumnae Center.
Correspondence and photos of Johnson, a physician, and her husband Morgan Johnson, a minister, teacher, and artist; both have served as missionaries in Africa since 1961. Rosalie Johnson earned her AB degree at Wesleyan College in 1956 and her MD at Emory University in 1960. She worked at Rhodesian hospitals until she and her husband were deported in 1975 because of their protest against the Rhodesian government's treatment of black Africans. After a year in the US, the Johnsons went to serve as missionaries in Livingstone, Zambia. They have five children.

3,465. Lamar, Eugenia Dorothy Blount
Papers. Nd. Ca. 1 in.
Open. Unpublished guide.
Wesleyan College, Candler Alumnae Center.
Correspondence, photos, and clippings of [Mrs. Walter Douglas] Lamar (?-1955), a student of southern history and literature who was historian general of the United Daughters of the Confederacy from 1934 to 1937 and UDC president general from 1937 to 1939. Lamar received her AB degree from Wesleyan College in 1883 and a doctor of laws degree from Mercer University.

3,466. Matthews, Sara E. Branham
Papers. Nd. Ca. 1.5 in.
Open. No guide.
Wesleyan College, Candler Alumnae Center.
A pioneer woman bacteriologist, [Mrs. P. S.] Matthews (1887 or 1888-1962) was chief of the bacterial toxius section of the US Health Service when she retired in 1958. Correspondence, articles about Matthews, photos, and news releases. Matthews, who received an AB degree from Wesleyan College in 1907 and PhD and MD degrees from the University of Chicago, wrote numerous books on bacteriological research.

3,467. Powell, Kathleen Mackay
Papers. Nd. Ca. 1 in.
Open. No guide.
Wesleyan College, Candler Alumnae Center.
Correspondence, photos, clippings, and printed material of [Mrs. J. Edward] Powell (?-1974), a medical illustrator who founded the Emory University school of medicine's medical illustration department in 1939. Powell graduated from Wesleyan College in 1928 and founded the Emory department after working at the Mayo Clinic from 1929 to 1939. She was a charter member of the International Association of Medical Illustrators, which was organized in 1945.

3,468. Seawell, Eugenia Rawls
Papers. Nd. Ca. 5 in.
Open. No guide.
Wesleyan College, Candler Alumnae Center.
Correspondence, photos, programs, books, and other papers of Seawell, a stage and television actress who uses the name Eugenia Rawls in her work, and of her husband Donald Seawell, a publisher. She made her Broadway debut in Lillian Hellman's *The Children's Hour* and has acted in other plays, including *The Little Foxes, The Great Sebastians, Strange Fruit,* and *Private Lives.* A member of the Wesleyan class of 1932, she lives in New York City and Denver.

3,469. Tilly, Dorothy Rogers
Papers. Nd. Ca. 1.5 in.
Open. No guide.
Wesleyan College, Candler Alumnae Center.
A crusader for civil rights, [Mrs. M. E.] Tilly (1883-1970) served on President Truman's Committee on Civil Rights, helped found the Georgia Negro Training School for Delinquent Girls, and was a member of the Georgia Interracial Committee and the Atlanta Urban League. Correspondence, photos, clippings, and other printed material. Tilly, who received an AB degree from Wesleyan College in 1901, was director of women's work and a field representative for the Southern Regional Council.

MILLEDGEVILLE

3,470. Georgia College Archives
Records. 1889- . 33 ft. and 37 manuscript boxes.
Open. No guide.
Georgia College Library.
Founded in 1889, the College was a women's school until 1967 when it became coeducational. Correspondence, photos, scrapbooks, annuals, college catalogs, and other records of the school, which was known as Georgia Normal and Industrial College from 1889 to 1922, as Georgia State College for Women from 1922 to 1961, The Woman's College of Georgia from 1961 to 1967, and as Georgia College beginning in 1967.

3,471. O'Connor, Flannery
Papers. 1940- . No size given.
Access restricted. Unpublished guides.
Georgia College Library.
[Miss] O'Connor (1925-64) was an author. Correspondence, manuscripts, critical writings, audio recordings, photos, motion pictures, various editions and translations of O'Connor's works, and volumes from her personal library.

3,472. General
Collection. 1600s- . 69 ft. and ca. 24 tapes.
Open. Unpublished guide.
Georgia College, Museum and Archives of Georgia Education.
Manuscript research material and taped recollections concern education in Georgia from the colonial period to the present. The material contains information about public and private institutions from kindergarten to the university level.

3,473. Georgia College
Records. 1889- . 16 ft.
Open. Unpublished guide.
Georgia College, Museum and Archives of Georgia Education.
Founded in 1889 as a women's college with courses for teachers and in home economics and business,

the College is now a coeducational liberal arts institution. Correspondence, memoirs and recollections of alumnae, notebooks, photos, scrapbooks, annuals, programs, textbooks, and other items. Includes information about a laboratory school for children. The College, first called Georgia Normal and Industrial College, became coeducational in 1967.

3,474. Oral History
Oral history. Ca. 1976- . Ca. 24 tapes.
Open. Unpublished guide.
Georgia College, Museum and Archives of Georgia Education.
Tapes and transcripts of interviews with persons who reminisce about their experiences as school administrators, teachers, and students. Also includes interviews with persons who had other connections with Georgia schools.

3,475. School Systems
Collection. 1600s- . 6 ft.
Open. Unpublished guide.
Georgia College, Museum and Archives of Georgia Education.
Annual reports, curriculum guides, report cards, photos, slides, and other items concerning teaching and learning in individual schools and in Georgia county and city school systems. Most of the authors and the subjects of the papers are women.

ROME

3,476. Wilson, Ellen "Ellie" Louise (Axson)
Papers. 1860- . 1 drawer and 28 vols.
Partially restricted. Unpublished guide.
Carnegie Library.
Ellen Axson (1860-1914) met her future husband, Woodrow Wilson, in this Georgia town. Correspondence, photos, brochures, and other papers about Ellen Wilson were given to the Library in connection with the dedication of a portrait of her in 1972. The portrait was given to the Library by the Berry Schools in 1921.

ST. SIMONS ISLAND

3,477. Kemble, Fanny
Papers. Nd. Folders and ca. 14 vols.
Open. No guide.
Coastal Georgia Historical Society.
Kemble (1809-93) was an English-born actress, author, and abolitionist. Clippings, including reviews of plays and dramatic readings in which she performed, and volumes of poetry and other rare books by and about Kemble. Regarded for nearly 40 years as a leading Shakespearean actress, Kemble married Pierce Butler, a rice plantation owner who held nearly 750 slaves. Although Kemble, who had been unaware of the effects of slavery, stayed on Butler's plantation for only four months, she later published a graphic account of the cruelties of slavery. Also included is material on the Butler plantation.

3,478. Slave Photos
Collection. Nd. Ca. 20 items.
Open. No guide.
Coastal Georgia Historical Society.
Pictures of slaves who lived on St. Simons Island, some of whom are identified by name.

3,479. South Georgia Conference Archives
Records. 1879- . No size given.
Open. Published guide.
The Methodist Museum.
Records of organizations and agencies within the South Georgia Conference of the United Methodist Church pertain to the growth of Methodism in America, especially in the South. Includes annual reports, 1888-92, of the Woman's Missionary Society of the Methodist Episcopal Church, South, and reports, 1879-1940, of the Woman's Missionary Society, the Woman's Foreign Missionary Society, and the Woman's Home Missionary Society of the South Georgia Conference of the Methodist Episcopal Church, South. Also includes annual reports of the following divisions of the South Georgia Conference of the Methodist Church and, later, of the United Methodist Church: the Woman's Society of the Christian Service, the Woman's Division of Christian Service, the Board of Missions and Church Extension, and the Board of Missions. Also includes issues of the periodical *Methodist Woman.* See *Georgia Archive* II (Winter 1974).

SAVANNAH

3,480. American Association of University Women
Records. 1928- . No size given.
Open. Inventory.
Georgia Historical Society.
Constitution, bylaws, reports of the president and committee chairmen, minutes of the Savannah branch of the AAUW and of the 1955 state convention, budgets, correspondence, membership material, lists of officers and chairmen, scrapbooks, and other records. Includes historical sketches about the branch, correspondence of the committee that compiled a list of outstanding Savannah women in 1945, local AAUW publications, and material of the state AAUW and branches in other states.

3,481. Arnold, Richard Dennis
Papers. 1838-55. 3 items.
Open. Unpublished guide.
Georgia Historical Society.
Papers of Arnold (ca. 1808-76), a Savannah physician and mayor of the city when it was surrendered to Federal forces in 1864, include the will of Maria Cohen, "a free woman of color" of Chatham County, GA. Cohen left her estate, including real and personal property and slaves, to Arnold as trustee and executor for her children Hannah and Abraham. Her will stated that Arnold was to receive the entire estate if the children predeceased him. Also includes a letter from Sarah A. Paport, who asked Arnold for $30 to pay a medical bill, and a receipt for the sum signed by Paport. Arnold was the first president of the Savannah Board of Education.

3,482. Bassett, Victor Hugo
Papers. 1907-38. 789 items.
Open. No guide.
Georgia Historical Society.
Bassett (1871-1938), a physician, was Savannah city bacteriologist and, later, city and county health officer. His papers include speeches, book reviews, and other writings by Bassett; notes on a training class for midwives; correspondence and notes pertaining to milk and dairies; minutes and correspondence of the board of sanitary commissioners; papers of the Savannah health department and vital statistics about the city; clippings about Bassett's career; clippings and pamphlets concerning diseases and public health; and other items.

3,483. Beck, Sallie Didd
Papers. 1860-81. 1 vol.
Open. Unpublished guide.
Georgia Historical Society.
Commonplace book of Beck contains entries dating principally from 1860 to 1866. During part of that period Beck was a student at the Synodical Female College at Griffin, GA. Her entries contain poetry and letters by fellow students, family members, and soldiers camped near Griffin. Later entries were made by her husband Joseph H. Johnson and their children Joe, Ella H., and Mary B. Johnson. Also includes a notebook with a list of autographs.

3,484. Berry, Martha McChesney
Papers. 1921. 1 item.
Open. Unpublished guide.
Georgia Historical Society.
[Miss] Berry (1866-1942) was the founder of The Berry Schools at Mount Berry near Rome, GA. Letter in which Berry asked Mrs. Sylvanus Johnson for a donation to the Berry Schools.

3,485. Bosomworth, Mary
Papers. 1759. 1 item.
Open. Unpublished guide.
Georgia Historical Society.
The daughter of an English trader and a Creek woman, Bosomworth (ca. 1700-63), whose Indian name was Cousaponakeesa, was married in ca. 1716 to John Musgrove, an Indian trader; to Jacob Mathews, a captain in the rangers, in ca. 1739; and to Thomas Bosomworth in ca. 1742. Copy of a document that constituted the settlement of a land claim by Mary Bosomworth, who was better known as Mary Musgrove. She and Thomas Bosomworth, who came to Georgia as a clerk but became an official of the Church of England, fostered Indian unrest to support her claim that she should be given land as a reward for her service to the English government. The document consists of instructions from Governor Henry Ellis for the survey of St. Catherine's Island for Bosomworth.

3,486. Bouknight, Lula
Papers. 1870. 1 item.
Open. Unpublished guide.
Georgia Historical Society.
A letter, apparently to Bouknight from a cousin, contains a description of a railroad trip from South Carolina through the Georgia towns of Macon, Fort Valley, Americus, and Andersonville. The letter also concerns social life in Newton, GA, friends, and relatives.

3,487. Boyd, Laura Johnson (Broyles)
Papers. 1885-1932. 2 items.
Open. Unpublished guide.
Georgia Historical Society.
Boyd was the wife of Montague Lafitte Boyd, a physician. Diaries dating from 1885 to 1904 and from 1913 to 1932. The first deals with her early married life in Bulloch County, GA, and in Savannah, while the second concerns her grandchildren and family and social life in Savannah.

3,488. Bragg, Lillian (Chaplin)
Papers. 1858-1967. 911 items.
Open. Unpublished guide.
Georgia Historical Society.
A teacher and journalist for the Savannah *Morning News,* Bragg (1895-1967) was the daughter of Nellie Wallis Chaplin and Albert Vernon Chaplin, who was superintendent of the Bethesda Orphan Home from 1876 to 1914. Personal and family correspondence, stories, articles, genealogical information, photos, and other papers. The largest part of the collection concerns the Orphan Home. Bragg wrote many short stories, articles, and books about the history of Savannah and Georgia.

3,489. Burroughs
Papers. Ca. 1820s-30s. 7 items.
Partially restricted. Inventory.
Georgia Historical Society.
Scrapbook of Rosa M. E. (Williams) Burroughs (ca. 1799-1853), the wife of clergyman Benjamin Burroughs, and photos, miniatures, and daguerreotypes of the Burroughs and Williams families. The scrapbook contains genealogies of the Burroughs and Williams families; engravings of

Oglethorpe College, the US Capitol, and the White House; sentimental poems; and other items.

3,490. Butler, C. Ann
Papers. 1865. 1 item.
Open. Unpublished guide.
Georgia Historical Society.
Letter to William Butler, a member of Company H, 2nd US Colored Troops, in Cedar Keys, FL, from his wife C. Ann Butler in the Freedmens Village at Arlington, VA. Writing in January, C. Ann Butler says she is worried because she has not heard from her husband since October; she also gives information about their children.

3,491. Callaway
Papers. 1860-1919. 6 items.
Open. No guide.
Georgia Historical Society.
Scrapbooks and other papers of Mary Ann (Irwin) [Mrs. Merrell Price] Callaway (ca. 1817-82); her son James Callaway, a Georgia newspaperman who worked for the *Macon Telegraph;* and other family members. Mary Callaway's scrapbook principally concerns the Civil War. The Callaway family moved to Wilkes County, GA, from Virginia in 1783.

3,492. Carson, John Avery Gere
Papers. 1881-98. 9 items.
Open. Unpublished guide.
Georgia Historical Society.
Letter books, a personal account book, scrapbooks, and other papers of Carson (1856-1930), a Baltimore native who founded Carson Naval Stores Company in 1898 in Savannah, and of Carrie Gordon (Cubbedge) Carson, whom he married in 1879. John Carson's correspondence includes letters to his wife and other family members as well as business correspondence. Carrie Carson's papers include a scrapbook containing historical articles, poetry, anecdotes, recipes, and clippings pertaining to family weddings, deaths, social entertainments, and civic affairs. Also includes a scrapbook of needlework patterns. John Carson was a city alderman and member of the Chatham County Commission.

3,493. Chatham County PTA
Records. 1917-65. 3 boxes.
Open. Unpublished guide.
Georgia Historical Society.
Bylaws; presidents', treasurer's, and historians' reports; minutes; correspondence; reports of committees for juvenile protection, publications, parent education, music, television, health, endowment, and safety and citizenship; lists of officers; scrapbooks; material of the Georgia PTA; and other records. Includes a personal scrapbook of Mrs. Thomas Purse.

3,494. Christ Church
Records. 1782-1920. 8 boxes.
Open. Unpublished guide.
Georgia Historical Society.
Records of such women's organizations as the Widows and Orphans Fund, the Sacristan Society, and the Altar Society are included with the vestry minutes, account books, marriage records, and other records of this local church. The women's organizations' material dates from 1888 to 1897.

3,495. Civil War Letters
Papers. 1862-63. 2 items.
Open. Unpublished guides.
Georgia Historical Society.
Two letters, one to "Darling Cousin" from "Nell," which concerns social life during the Civil War, and the other to a soldier, which includes a love poem.

3,496. Cohen and Hunter
Papers. 1826-1913. 2 items.
Open. Unpublished guide.
Georgia Historical Society.
Commonplace book of Cecilia Cohen, the daughter of clergyman Moses C. Cohen, and a scrapbook of Hunter, Pearce & Battey, a firm of cotton and naval store factors and wholesale grocers. Cohen's commonplace book dates from 1826 to 1830 and contains original and copied poems.

3,497. Daughters of the American Revolution
Records. 1893-1975. 4 boxes and 10 vols.
Open. Unpublished guide.
Georgia Historical Society.
Bylaws, regents' reports, minutes, correspondence, research notes, scrapbooks, programs, yearbooks, and certificates of the Savannah chapter, which was founded in about 1893. Also includes a pamphlet about the activities of the DAR.

3,498. Daughters of the American Revolution, Lachlan McIntosh Chapter
Records. 1901-73. 1 box and 7 vols.
Open. Unpublished guide.
Georgia Historical Society.
Registers, a membership list, and scrapbooks of the Chapter, which was founded in about 1901. Also includes proceedings of the fourth annual state DAR conference in 1903.

3,499. Dorsett Family
Papers. 1834-93. 15 items.
Open. Unpublished guides.
Georgia Historical Society.
Correspondence, essays, poems, and other papers of this Georgia family. Includes a letter from Sarah Ten Brook in New Brunswick, GA, to her son R. K. Ten Brook, a note by Charles Dorsett to his mother telling of the birth of his daughter Josie, children's letters, essays by Charles Dorsett's sister Fannie A. Dorsett, a commonplace book of Fannie Dorsett, and a poem by K. Humphreys on the death of a 14-year-old girl, Marie Dawsey.

3,500. Duncan, William
Papers. 1860. 22 items.
Open. Unpublished guide.
Georgia Historical Society.
Letters to Duncan from his niece Mary D. Smith discussing family affairs and a contested will; a letter from M. M. Wilman thanking Duncan for his interest in the Savannah Female Asylum, which was founded in 1801; and other correspondence.

3,501. Dwyer, Mary Ann
Papers. 1853-54. 1 item.
Open. Unpublished guide.
Georgia Historical Society.
Dwyer, who married a man named McIntosh, was a native of Ireland who lived in Brunswick, GA. Commonplace book containing poetry.

3,502. Elliott, Stephen
Papers. 1855-66. 2 items.
Open. Unpublished guide.
Georgia Historical Society.
Papers contain a letter dated 1855 in which Amelia Matilda Murray at Menton House in Norfolk, England, states her views on slavery. The letter was published in the *Georgia Historical Quarterly* (Dec. 1949).

3,503. English Academy Booklet
Records. 1786. 1 item.
Open. Unpublished guide.
Georgia Historical Society.
A dissertation issued in connection with the opening in Savannah of an English academy for young ladies. The dissertation, which was written by the academy's preceptor, concerns "virtue in general, and female education & manners in particular. . . ."

3,504. Fielding, Elizabeth
Papers. 1831. 1 item.
Open. Unpublished guide.
Georgia Historical Society.
Letter from Fielding, a schoolgirl, to her grandmother in Salem, GA, includes information about her family and school.

3,505. Forman, Bryan, and Screven
Papers. 1797-1901. 226 items.
Open. Unpublished guide.
Georgia Historical Society.
Family correspondence and memorabilia of the Forman family of Cecilton, MD, and the Bryan and Screven families of Wilmington Island, GA, and Savannah. Includes letters of Augusta Forman, H. Georgia (Bryan) [Mrs. James Proctor] Screven, Virginia S. Bryan, [Mrs.] Delia Byran, Mrs. Joseph Bryan, [Miss] C. B. Screven, and Ada Screven.

3,506. Fraser and Couper
Papers. 1810-84. 106 items.
Open. Unpublished guide.
Georgia Historical Society.
Family correspondence; financial records, including bills of sale for slaves and disbursements; recipes; and home remedies. Includes correspondence of family members Ann L. Fraser, Rebecca L. M. Fraser, Caroline G. Couper, Isabella H. Couper, Louise C. Shaw, Grace Minto, Isabella Wilson, Anne Rebecca Fraser, and Marie W. Menzies; letters from Fanny Kemble; a letter in which Charles Menzies provides Mrs. John Fraser, a widow, with instructions about how to get on the pension list; love letters; and a recipe for a cure for dysentery and diarrhea.

3,507. Froebel Circle
Records. 1897-1972. 3 boxes.
Open. Unpublished guide.
Georgia Historical Society.
The Circle was a women's service organization formed in about 1897. Constitution, bylaws, annual reports, minutes, finance committee reports, account books, correspondence, corresponding secretary papers, an historical sketch, donor lists, photos, yearbooks, clippings, and other records. Also includes annual reports of the superintendent, accounts, and inventories of the Fresh Air Home as well as programs and booklets of other organizations.

3,508. Georgia Infirmary
Papers. 1833-1960. 1 folder and 5 vols.
Open. Unpublished guide.
Georgia Historical Society.
Minutes of the board of trustees of the Infirmary, the first black hospital in Georgia. The Infirmary, which cared for both male and female patients, closed after other hospitals were integrated.

3,509. Georgia Society, Colonial Dames of America
Records. Nd. No size given.
Open. Descriptions.
Georgia Historical Society.
Collection of miscellaneous historical items includes a subscription list for the relief of two ladies and a child who were captured by pirates; a letter that Elizabeth (Marshall) Martin wrote to her brother Thomas Marshall stating that General Braddock and his staff have camped on her place on the way to join General Washington and that she fears for her family's safety; letters of Martha Berry, some of which concern her unsuccessful application for membership in the Colonial Dames; a love letter dated 1783 from John Habersham to his fiancee Sarah Camber in Savannah; and a land grant dated 1768 to Abigail Minis from the Georgia Colony. The subscription list sought contributions for the women and the child, asserting that the pirates had robbed them of their money and clothes and had put them aboard a French brig, which had also been captured and plundered. The document continued that the three arrived in Savannah without means of support and

with no money for passage to their destination. Some of the material has been published.

3,510. Gilbert, Maria Rita Madam
Papers. 1832. 1 item.
Open. Unpublished guide.
Georgia Historical Society.
Letter to [Mrs.] Gilbert from her mother includes news of family and friends. She also describes Darien, GA, and asks Gilbert to tell her husband to prepay postage on letters for appearance's sake.

3,511. Gilmer, Louisa Frederika (Alexander)
Papers. 1864. 2 items.
Open. Unpublished guide.
Georgia Historical Society.
Letters to [Mrs. Jeremy F.] Gilmer from Mary Lavinia [Mrs. John] Stoddard contain news of family and friends and uncomplimentary references to Phoebe Pember.

3,512. Goldsmith, Esther
Papers. 1866-76. 82 items.
Open. Unpublished guide.
Georgia Historical Society.
Estate papers of Goldsmith include receipts, bills, and papers pertaining to the illness and death of her daughter Henrietta in the Georgia State Lunatic Asylum. Richard D. Arnold, a physician, served as executor of Esther Goldsmith's estate.

3,513. Gosling, Charlotte M.
Papers. Nd. 1 item.
Open. Unpublished guide.
Georgia Historical Society.
Letter of application for a position as lady's maid, addressed from 27 Washington Square in New York City.

3,514. Granger, Mary
Papers. Nd. 3 boxes.
Open. Unpublished guide.
Georgia Historical Society.
Educated at Barnard and Columbia, Granger (1897-) was an author and editor. Correspondence; manuscripts, including those for *Light and Shadow, Widow of Ephesus* (1926), and *Wife of Platt;* and reviews of Granger's writings. In 1947 Granger edited *Savannah River Plantations* for the Georgia Historical Society.

3,515. Guerard
Papers. 1789-1882. 32 items.
Open. Unpublished guide.
Georgia Historical Society.
Correspondence and other papers of this Georgia family. Includes an account by William B. Bulloch as executor of Sarah B. Moul's estate in 1836, marriage settlements of Peter Godin Guerard and Emma B. Moul in 1835 and of Mary Emma Guerard and Richard W. Adams in 1840, and tax returns of Mrs. E. B. Guerard for 1856 and papers concerning her husband's estate.

3,516. Gwinnett, Button
Papers. 1771-77. 5 items.
Open. Unpublished guide.
Georgia Historical Society.
Correspondence of Gwinnett (ca. 1732-77), a signer of the Declaration of Independence and governor of Georgia, and of his wife Ann Gwinnett. Includes letters she wrote from Savannah to the president and members of the Continental Congress appealing for redress and describing her husband's death in a duel. Also includes other letters she wrote to John Hancock and the Congress asking for action against the principals in the duel.

3,517. Habersham, Leila Elliott
Papers. 1861-62. 1 item.
Open. Unpublished guide.
Georgia Historical Society.
Scrapbook of Civil War clippings.

3,518. Habersham, William Neyle
Papers. 1832-99. 30 items.
Open. Unpublished guide.
Georgia Historical Society.
Correspondence of Habersham includes a love letter from his wife Josephine (Clay) Habersham and letters concerning the estates of Mary Habersham Elliott, Lydia Hunter, Alberta Telfair (Welter) Gould, Mary E. (Ritchie) Wallbridge, and Maria Elliot White.

3,519. Hale
Papers. 1858. 1 item.
Open. Unpublished guide.
Georgia Historical Society.
Letter by Joshua and Ellen Hale at the Savannah River to Thomas and Josiah Hale contains a postscript in which Ellen Hale tells of hearing a sermon by Andrew Marshall, a Negro preacher, and mentions her sister Caroline and others.

3,520. Hall, Selina Cole
Papers. 1900. 13 items.
Open. Unpublished guide.
Georgia Historical Society.
Seven copies of a chain letter sent by [Mrs.] Hall requesting contributions of 10 cents each for a free public library in Savannah. Also includes six replies.

3,521. Hamilton, Isabelle Caroline
Papers. 1824-76. 103 items.
Open. Unpublished guide.
Georgia Historical Society.
[Mrs.] Hamilton was the daughter of Aimé Marie De la Rocheaulion, a physician, and Sarah Catherine Wigg Floyd De la Rocheaulion of Camden County, GA. Correspondence, including letters from Alice Van Yeveren Alexander, Letitia De Renne, John B. Gordon, William Washington Gordon, and Mary Telfair; oaths of allegiance to the US signed by Isabelle and Sarah and Isabelle's amnesty oath, all dated 1865; French genealogical records; deeds; tax notices; contracts; and other papers. The letters of Alice Alexander and Mary Telfair provide insights into life in Savannah after the Civil War.

3,522. Hardee, Harriett Brailsford
Papers. 1897-98. 4 items.
Open. Unpublished guide.
Georgia Historical Society.
A daily kindergarten workbook, worksheets used in kindergarten training, and other school material.

3,523. Haskell-Pape School
Records. 1906-07. 1 item.
Open. Unpublished guide.
Georgia Historical Society.
Marion Alexander Haskell and Nina Anderson Pape were proprietors of the School, which was founded as a girls school in about 1906. A roll book for the senior department provides students' names, ages, parents, fathers' occupations, attendance records, and deportment reports. The School, now coeducational, is called the Savannah Country Day School.

3,524. Heidt
Papers. 1840?-70?. 78 items.
Open. Unpublished guide.
Georgia Historical Society.
Family correspondence of John Heidt, prosecutor for the eastern district of Georgia in 1863 and pastor of Trinity Methodist Episcopal Church, South, in Atlanta in 1879, includes letters exchanged between Heidt and his wife Leila, letters to Leila from her mother Harriet E. Villard and her sister Kate Villard, and other correspondence of the Heidt and Villard families.

3,525. Heidt, Christian I.
Papers. 1804-05. 1 item.
Open. Unpublished guide.
Georgia Historical Society.
Document filed with the superior court in Effingham County, GA, concerning the divorce of Christian I. and Mary Heidt.

3,526. Hopkins, Jane D.
Papers. Ca. 1880s. 16 items.
Open. Unpublished guide.
Georgia Historical Society.
Commonplace book of Jane W. Davidson, who later became [Mrs.] Jane de Bruyn Kops; a commonplace book of Jane de Bruyn Kops; assorted greeting cards; and two bound poems.

3,527. Hopkins, John Livingstone
Papers. 1826-1913. 15 items.
Open. Unpublished guide.
Georgia Historical Society.
Correspondence of Hopkins includes a letter he wrote telling his brother Benjamin how he had selected and trained his wife and discussing life in Monroe County, TN. Also includes a letter from J. F. Cooke to his daughter Mary, who was away at school; letters from John L. Hopkins II to his wife, the former Mary Cooke; and letters from Nannie Kefauver to her sister Mollie Hopkins.

3,528. Houston and Wylly
Papers. 1827-1922. 9 items.
Open. Unpublished guide.
Georgia Historical Society.
Includes letters dated 1827 and 1828 in which M. W. Houston wrote to her mother Mrs. John Thomas describing the home life of Alexander Campbell Wylly. She also gives details of life in St. Simons, GA.

3,529. Houstoun, Mary Williamson
Papers. 1802-75. 175 items.
Open. Unpublished guide.
Georgia Historical Society.
Estate papers of Houstoun, kept by her executor Richard D. Arnold, include correspondence; personal accounts; land records; dower releases; slave and tax lists; wills of other family members, including Houstoun's mother Mary Ann Thomas; and accounts dating from 1840 to 1865 for the care of Mossman Houstoun in the Pennsylvania Hospital for the Insane.

3,530. Hunter, Anna Colquitt
Papers. 1943-44. 7 folders.
Open. Unpublished guide.
Georgia Historical Society.
Orders, troop newspapers, and other papers relating to Hunter's service with the American National Red Cross in North Africa and Italy.

3,531. Johnston, Edith Duncan
Papers. 1913-62. No size given.
Open. Unpublished guide.
Georgia Historical Society.
Johnston was the first national secretary of the Girl Scouts. Manuscript of her book *The Houstons of Georgia* (University of Georgia Press, 1950) and items related to the Girl Scouts, including correspondence, her reminiscences about her work with the Girl Scouts and with Juliette Low, a photo album, handbooks, and other records.

3,532. Johnston, Richard Malcolm
Papers. 1838-1951. 9 boxes.
Open. Unpublished guide.
Georgia Historical Society.
Johnston was a folklorist. Correspondence, copies of his manuscripts and publications, and clippings. Includes letters to Johnston and his biographer Richard T. Long from such correspondents as Alexander H. Stephens, Sidney Lanier, Joel Chandler Harris, and James W. Riley. Family correspondence contains letters from Julia A. Toombs; Amy, Effie, and Ruth Johnston; and Mary Waldon Johnston Charlton.

3,533. Jones, George Noble
Papers. 1817-88. 152 items.
Open. Unpublished guide.
Georgia Historical Society.
Family, social, and business correspondence and personal and plantation accounts of this Georgia family descended from Revolutionary War figures. Female correspondents include Mary Telfair, Margaret Telfair Hodgson, Delia Tudor (Stewart) Parnell, and Mary G. Hauson.

3,534. Karow
Papers. 1899-1918?. 1 item.
Open. No guide.
Georgia Historical Society.
Scrapbook compiled by Anna Belle Welso [Mrs. Edward] Karow contains items of local interest, such as the reburial of the body of Major General Nathanael Greene in Savannah, and information about deaths, marriages, and other events relating to the Karow family.

3,535. Kate Baldwin Kindergarten and Alumnae Association
Records. 1900-39. 110 items.
Open. Unpublished guide.
Georgia Historical Society.
Organizational records, pamphlets on kindergartens, photos, clippings, and other records of the Baldwin Kindergarten, founded in about 1899. Includes extracts from annual reports; minutes; treasurer's reports; membership, alumnae, and graduate lists; notes pertaining to the history of the kindergarten movement in Savannah; lesson plans; records of [Miss] Sallie McAlpin and [Miss] Harriett B. Hardee; resolutions on the deaths of George J. Baldwin and Hortense May Orcutt; programs; an annual report of the Georgia division of the Association for Childhood Education; and pamphlets of the National Kindergarten Association and the New York Kindergarten Association.

3,536. Lachlison, Sarah
Papers. 1902. 1 item.
Open. Unpublished guide.
Georgia Historical Society.
Account written by Lachlison at The Ridge in Darien, GA, about her experiences following General Sherman's order in 1864 that the wives of Confederate officers be evacuated from Savannah.

3,537. Ladies Memorial Association, Savannah
Records. 1867-97. 4 items.
Open. Unpublished guide.
Georgia Historical Society.
Members of the Association, founded in 1867, cared for the graves of Confederate soldiers in a Laurel Grove cemetery and gathered funds for a Confederate monument. Minute book, an account book, a thank-you letter to the Association from George Wimberly Jones De Renne, and a scroll. The Association merged with the United Daughters of the Confederacy in 1897.

3,538. Lamar, Eliza Anderson
Papers. 1866-67. No size given.
Open. Unpublished guide.
Georgia Historical Society.
A journal in which Lamar wrote about Brandon in Virginia; her travels in France, Switzerland, and England; and her voyage on the steamboat *The China.*

3,539. Lanier, Mary Day
Papers. 1889-1904. 22 items.
Open. Unpublished guide.
Georgia Historical Society.
Letters, notes, and post cards written by [Mrs. Sidney] Lanier from various points in the North and the South following her husband's death.

3,540. Lawton, Sarah Gilbert Alexander
Papers. 1841-76. 4 items.
Open. Unpublished guide.
Georgia Historical Society.
Diary that [Mrs. Alexander Robert] Lawton (1826-?) kept in the pages of *Hostetter's Illustrated US Almanac* for 1876, a letter to Henry R. Jackson, and two commonplace books containing poems and clippings. The Lawtons were married in 1845.

3,541. LeConte and Furman
Papers. 1810-96. 66 items.
Open. Unpublished guide.
Georgia Historical Society.
Personal correspondence, account books, and miscellaneous papers of these families, which were joined by the marriage of Emma LeConte and Farish Carter Furman. Includes letters of Emma LeConte before and after her marriage, her accounts from 1855 to 1896, and Furman estate records.

3,542. Levy, Mrs. R. A.
Papers. Nd. 1 vol.
Open. Unpublished guide.
Georgia Historical Society.
Volume of original poems dedicated to Levy's family and friends.

3,543. Louisa Porter Home for the Friendless
Records. 1875-1955. 2 folders and 4 vols.
Open. Unpublished guide.
Georgia Historical Society.
Originally known as the Industrial Relief Society and Home for the Friendless, the organization's name was changed in 1890 to the Louisa Porter Home for the Friendless and then to the Louisa Porter Foundation. Annual reports, general minutes and minutes of the board, treasurer's accounts, deeds, and other records.

3,544. McAlpin
Papers. 1839-ca. 1882. 6 items.
Open. Unpublished guide.
Georgia Historical Society.
Miscellaneous papers include a notebook containing notes, addresses, lists of linen and silver, and a recipe for household remedies.

3,545. McAlpin, Ellen
Papers. 1913. 1 vol.
Open. Unpublished guide.
Georgia Historical Society.
McAlpin operated a boarding house. Guest book contains names and addresses of McAlpin's guests and her comments about them.

3,546. MacDonell, George G. N.
Papers. 1859-1905. Ca. 30 vols.
Open. Unpublished guide.
Georgia Historical Society.
Diaries of MacDonell, a Methodist minister in Georgia, and his mother [Mrs.] Ann Elizabeth Nowlan MacDonell.

3,547. Mackay, Eliza Ann (McQueen)
Papers. 1807. 1 item.
Open. Unpublished guide.
Georgia Historical Society.
Letter from Isabella Hunter to [Mrs. Robert] Mackay (1778-1862) in London contains news of family, friends, and social life.

3,548. Mackay Family
Papers. 1828-54. 35 items.
Open. Unpublished guide.
Georgia Historical Society.
Correspondence of members of the Robert Mackay family of Savannah and Etowah.

3,549. McNish, Adelaide S. Baynard Guerard
Papers. 1812-94. 14 items.
Open. Unpublished guide.
Georgia Historical Society.
Correspondence, deeds, and other papers of [Mrs.] McNish. Includes letters from Sarah Rosamund Davenport and Sarah C. Guerard; a marriage settlement between William P. Guerard and McNish, who then was Adelaide S. Baynard; and correspondence relating to the historic Davenport House.

3,550. McQueen, John J.
Papers. 1765-91. 16 items.
Open. Unpublished guide.
Georgia Historical Society.
Miscellaneous colonial records and indentures, including a renunciation of dower dated 1773 for Aim [Mrs. James] Fox to John Glen. Fox's property was located in Georgia.

3,551. Mason, Elizabeth Welch (Backus)
Papers. 1861-65?. 1 vol.
Open. Unpublished guide.
Georgia Historical Society.
Scrapbook chiefly containing items relating to the Confederacy includes poems by Latienne, a pen name for Mason; drawings; church programs; post cards; and clippings. Also includes some post-Civil War items.

3,552. Meldrim
Papers. 1920-38. 114 items.
Partially restricted. Unpublished guide.
Georgia Historical Society.
Frances Pamela Bird Casey Meldrim was one of the prime supporters of the effort to restore Arlington Mansion as a memorial to General Robert E. Lee and his wife Mary Custis Lee. Correspondence concerning the restoration, a typescript of an article by Meldrim concerning the Mansion, photos, pamphlets, and clippings.

3,553. Metzger, Sophronia Kennedy
Papers. 1860-61. 1 item.
Open. Unpublished guide.
Georgia Historical Society.
Commonplace book containing poems written for Metzger by her friends.

3,554. Minis Family
Papers. 1768-1912. 12 items.
Open. Unpublished guide.
Georgia Historical Society.
Correspondence and miscellaneous papers include a letter Abigail Minis wrote in 1780 from Charleston, SC, to Mordecai Sheftall, whereby she sought the return of certificates for provisions she supplied to the allied army in 1779 so that she could collect the money due her. Also includes a writ of attachment that Abigail Minis filed against John and Joseph Gibbons for a debt of 1000 pounds.

3,555. Mitchell, Margaret
Papers. 1940-71. 8 items.
Open. Unpublished guide.
Georgia Historical Society.
Correspondence and clippings of Mitchell (1900-49), the author of *Gone With The Wind.* Includes a letter she wrote thanking Joseph W. McAvoy in Atlanta for a Hibernian Society program; she also tells why she selected "Tara" as the name for the plantation in her novel.

3,556. Moore, Susannah (Bolton)
Papers. 1774-1802. 24 items.
Open. Unpublished guide.
Georgia Historical Society.
The widow of William Moore, Susannah Moore was a shopkeeper. Receipt books and loose receipts.

3,557. Morgan, Caroline
Papers. 1840. 1 item.
Open. Unpublished guide.
Georgia Historical Society.
Letter from Julia Morgan at Sand Hills in Augusta,

GA, who describes her new home and furnishings and encloses a sketch of the floor plan.

3,558. Mother's Letter
Papers. 1864. 1 item.
Open. Unpublished guide.
Georgia Historical Society.
A letter that a mother wrote to her son in Fredonia, AL, about family and friends, crops, and the prices of staples.

3,559. Munro, Edward V.
Papers. 1862. 1 item.
Open. Unpublished guide.
Georgia Historical Society.
Letter from Carrie (Munro) Baldy in New Market, GA, to her father Edward V. Munro, who was assistant surgeon for the 51st Regiment of the Georgia Volunteers, includes news of family and friends and mention of scarcity and high prices.

3,560. Nellums, Mrs. William
Papers. 1842. 1 item.
Open. Unpublished guide.
Georgia Historical Society.
Letter in which Hannah Salmon in Montevideo, GA, told Nellums that she would stay with Nellums on "living terms."

3,561. Owens and Thomas
Papers. 1837-1954. 2 boxes.
Open. Unpublished guide.
Georgia Historical Society.
Personal and business papers of this Georgia family include estate papers of Mary W. Owens, George W. Owens, and Mrs. J. G. Thomas; a cashbook of [Miss] Margaret Thomas with items from 1894 to 1913; an account book of Mary W. Owens with entries from 1896 to 1905; letters of Margaret Thomas regarding the Owens-Thomas House, which is now a museum; recipes; and a cookbook. Also includes the constitution, bylaws, and correspondence of the Telfair literary and art union.

3,562. Palmes
Papers. 1837-1912. 3 folders and 3 vols.
Open. Unpublished guide.
Georgia Historical Society.
Papers, most of which relate to the grocery firm of Webster and Palmes, include rewards of merit issued to [Miss] Mary Palmes for diligence and good behavior as well as for proficiency in spelling and history. Also includes an invitation to a New Year's Eve ball in 1840.

3,563. Pape, Nina Anderson
Papers. 1857-1937. No size given.
Open. No guide.
Georgia Historical Society.
Diaries and travel books.

3,564. Parsons, Edwin
Papers. 1759-1862. 40 items.
Open. Unpublished guide.
Georgia Historical Society.
Autographs, including a letter from Fanny Kemble to Mrs. Theodosius Barton declining an invitation, and a letter from Eliza Logan, an actress, to an unidentified man expressing her sorrow about the yellow fever epidemic in Savannah. Also includes a photo of Logan.

3,565. Pigman
Papers. 1840-1943. 29 items.
Open. Unpublished guide.
Georgia Historical Society.
Correspondence, including personal letters Mary (Springman) Pigman wrote to her husband William Penn Pigman while he was imprisoned at Johnson Island, a Union prisoner-of-war camp; a pocket diary she kept during a visit to her husband at the prison; diaries of her husband, including an account of his capture and imprisonment; and diaries of Mary Pigman's mother Margaret Elizabeth Cooper Springman. Also contains compositions and clippings.

3,566. Quachenbush, Sarah
Papers. 1864. 1 item.
Open. Unpublished guide.
Georgia Historical Society.
A letter from Quachenbush to her husband includes news of home and wedding plans.

3,567. Read, Keith
Collection. Nd. No size given.
Open. Unpublished guide.
Georgia Historical Society.
Miscellaneous papers and Savannah customs records. Includes correspondence of Valeria G. Berrien [Mrs. Joseph H.] Burroughs; correspondence of Eliza (McQueen) Mackay, Eliza Anne Mackay Stiles, Mary Anne (Mackay) Stiles, and other Mackay family members; a letter James Jackson in Savannah wrote in 1844 to Mrs. Palmes, saying that he would perform funeral services for her daughter; a bond and an account of payments by Eliza (Lucas) Pinckney as executrix for the estate of her husband Charles Pinckney; and a 1775 letter of Hannah [Mrs. Thomas] Vincent in London concerning her claim to land in Georgia and the trouble between America and Britain.

3,568. Reid, Ruth Erwin Welman
Papers. 1841. 1 item.
Open. Unpublished guide.
Georgia Historical Society.
Recipe book with instructions for cooking and preparation of home remedies of Reid (1799-?), the wife of cotton merchant John Hope Reid.

3,569. Roosevelt, Eleanor
Papers. 1940. 1 item.
Open. Unpublished guide.
Georgia Historical Society.
Letter in which Roosevelt states to William S. Rockwell that her visit to a Civilian Conservation Corps camp in Yosemite was pleasant.

3,570. Saussy, George Nowlan
Papers. 1864-1909. 13 items.
Open. Unpublished guide.
Georgia Historical Society.
Contains family letters and letters to Saussy from Varina (Howell) Davis, wife of Jefferson Davis, from her home in Mississippi and from Atlantic City, NJ. Davis's letters concern the illnesses of herself and her daughter Margaret (Davis) Hayes, who had traveled to Colorado Springs, CO, for her health. One of the letters thanks Saussy for sending his condolences following the death of Jefferson Davis.

3,571. Savannah Federation of Women's Clubs
Records. 1913-20. 5 items.
Open. Unpublished guide.
Georgia Historical Society.
Minute book, treasurer's reports, president's address, and a clipping.

3,572. Savannah Home for Girls
Records. 1810- . No size given.
Partially closed. Unpublished guide.
Georgia Historical Society.
Founded as the Savannah Female Asylum in 1801, the institution later became known as the Savannah Home for Girls; it merged with the Savannah Childrens Center and the Chatham County department of family and children's services in 1972. Annual reports for 1966 to 1969; bylaws from 1911; incomplete minutes of the board extending from 1810 to 1974; treasurer's records; correspondence; matron's reports; admissions and dismissions books; lists of officers, board members, teachers, physicians, directresses, secretaries, and others; an historical sketch by Mrs. B. F. Bullard; photos; a scrapbook; clippings; and other records.

3,573. Savannah Kindergarten Association
Records. 1893?-98. 1 item.
Open. Unpublished guide.
Georgia Historical Society.
Minutes for all meetings include the group's constitution and the names of some officers.

3,574. Savannah Kindergarten Club
Records. 1904-28. 2 vols. and 82 items.
Open. Unpublished guide.
Georgia Historical Society.
Constitution, bylaws, annual reports, president's reports, minutes, treasurer's reports, correspondence, a membership list, programs, pamphlets, clippings, and other records. Includes records relating to the Kate Baldwin Free Kindergarten Association and to the Tallulah Falls Industrial School, which is owned by the Georgia Federation of Women's Clubs.

3,575. Savannah Pharmaceutical Association, Women's Auxiliary
Records. 1934-69. No size given.
Closed. Unpublished guide.
Georgia Historical Society.
Minute books, including one of the first district division of the Auxiliary; scrapbooks; and a photo album.

3,576. Scudder
Papers. 1850-90. 612 items.
Open. Unpublished guide.
Georgia Historical Society.
Business and personal papers include correspondence that reflects quarrels over wills, marriages and deaths, and arrangements to safeguard the family's southern property during the Civil War. Includes correspondence of the Scudder sisters: Mary (Scudder) Maggie, Emily (Scudder) Marsh, Cornelia Matilda (Scudder) Buckner, Cate, and Sarah. The correspondence contains information about the family's transferring its property to the name of Amos Picton Scudder, a brother who lived in the North, in order to avoid confiscation and the working of the family farm by tenant farmers after the War. The correspondence also includes discussion of Mary Scudder's marriage to a man much older than she.

3,577. Sheftall, Josephine
Papers. 1871-73. 1 item.
Open. Unpublished guide.
Georgia Historical Society.
A notebook containing correspondence, themes, poetry, and clippings that Sheftall compiled as a student at Chatham Academy.

3,578. Sinclair, Carrie Bell
Papers. 1864. 3 items.
Open. Unpublished guide.
Georgia Historical Society.
Letter that Sinclair wrote responding to an unknown admirer describing herself and the qualities she expected in the man who would win her love. Also includes a second letter and a poem dedicated to the soldiers of the South.

3,579. Sister's Letter
Papers. 186?. 1 item.
Open. Unpublished guide.
Georgia Historical Society.
Letter from a sister to a brother in the army.

3,580. Smith, Hannah Cooke
Papers. 1833. 1 item.
Open. Unpublished guide.
Georgia Historical Society.
Letter in which Amos D. Smith in Columbus, GA, tells his daughter Hannah that he is glad to be in a community with good schools. He comments that education is very meager in other places because the political situation makes it unsafe to educate slaves.

3,581. Stiles, Maryanne
Papers. 1825. 1 item.
Open. Unpublished guide.
Georgia Historical Society.
Letter from [Mrs. B. E.] Stiles in Savannah to Elizabeth Gilpin concerns social life, Lafayette's anticipated visit to Savannah, and other topics.

3,582. Strickland, Lillian E.
Papers. 1898-1901. 1 item.
Open. Unpublished guide.
Georgia Historical Society.
Account book of Strickland, a piano teacher at the Savannah Conservatory of Music, contains a list of her pupils.

3,583. Strong, Louisa Hall
Papers. 1864-65. 5 items.
Open. Unpublished guide.
Georgia Historical Society.
Strong was the wife of Paschal N. Strong, a founder and the first treasurer of Tulane University in New Orleans. Bill of goods delivered to Louisa Strong by the last blockade runner to Wilmington, NC, from Nassau, a receipt of Kate Beauregard Gugal to Cora Strong for French lessons, a scrapbook, and other papers.

3,584. Sturtevant, Julia E.
Papers. 1881-84. 1 item.
Open. Unpublished guide.
Georgia Historical Society.
Commonplace book includes an entry dated 1883 by Alexander H. Stephens.

3,585. Sutline, John Laffitteau
Papers. 1959-71. 9 items.
Open. Unpublished guide.
Georgia Historical Society.
Papers read by Sutline, who was associated with the *Savannah Evening Press,* to the Madiera Club in Savannah include reports concerning Savannah society from 1916 to 1927 as reflected in a woman's letters, Rebecca (Latimer) Felton and General John B. Gordon, and Savannah society as reported by Harriet Ross Colquitt.

3,586. Sweet, Mary Eliza
Papers. 1824-89?. 1 item.
Open. Unpublished guide.
Georgia Historical Society.
Commonplace book of Sweet, who later became Mrs. Ambrose Baber.

3,587. Telfair Family
Papers. 1750-1875. 31 boxes.
Open. Special catalog.
Georgia Historical Society.
Papers, financial and plantation records, memorabilia, and other items of Edward Telfair, a Revolutionary War patriot and early Georgia governor; his daughter Mary Telfair (1798-1875), a Savannah philanthropist; and other members of the Telfair and Gibbons families. Mary Telfair bequeathed the family mansion and fortune to Telfair Academy of Arts and to Hodgson Hall, the home of the Georgia Historical Society; she also gave money to the Presbyterian church and Telfair Hospital. Her papers include correspondence, journals of her travels to England and Europe during the 1850s and 1860s, journals she kept while in Savannah, account books, school notebooks, commonplace books, tenant receipts and rents, and a codicil of her will, dated 1866.

3,588. Telfair Hospital Board of Managers
Records. 1902-13. 2 items.
Open. Unpublished guide.
Georgia Historical Society.
Letter book of Louisa Porter (Gilmer) [Mrs. J. Florance] Minis, chairman of the Board, contains information about construction of the Hospital and housekeeping personnel matters. Also contains rules and regulations of the Hospital, list of patients with a description of their illnesses, and names of doctors at the Hospital from 1886 to 1906.

3,589. Telfair, Mary
Papers. 1875. 1 item.
Open. Unpublished guide.
Georgia Historical Society.
Letter from Telfair in Savannah to Sophie H. Gibbes Couper [Mrs. Duncan L.] Clinch includes Savannah gossip and comments about books she was reading.

3,590. Threadcraft, Georgia, and Threadcraft, Sallie
Papers. 1876-79. 3 items.
Open. Unpublished guide.
Georgia Historical Society.
A letter by Sallie Threadcraft, a grade report of Georgia Threadcraft, and a clipping regarding the 1742 will of George Treadcraft of South Carolina. The family's surname, Threadcraft, was sometimes spelled Treadcraft.

3,591. Walker, Mattie Jane
Papers. 1855-61. 1 item.
Open. Unpublished guide.
Georgia Historical Society.
Pocket diary with personal accounts, quotations, and clippings.

3,592. War Camp Community Service Club of Savannah
Records. 1918-20. 37 items.
Open. Unpublished guide.
Georgia Historical Society.
Minute books, ledgers, dormitory receipts, committee reports, a history of the Club by Mary C. [Mrs. Horace A.] Crane, an application signed by 10 volunteers for assignment as workers, letters of appreciation for the Club's services, a record of workers, visitors' registers, and other records. Includes a diary of operation kept by Mrs. I. G. Bishop, who served as superintendent and housemother, and private accounts. The Club was dissolved in 1920.

3,593. Waring, Joseph Frederick
Papers. Ca. 1832-65. 4 items.
Open. Unpublished guide.
Georgia Historical Society.
Papers of Waring, a lieutenant colonel in the Jefferson Davis Legion, Georgia Hussars, of the Confederate Army, include a letter dated 1865 in which one woman tells another of family and friends and reports of the death of Mauma Doll, a Savannah Negro; a paper on temperance from ca. 1832; and a description of the illness of a Negro girl named Nelly.

3,594. Wayne, Stites, and Anderson
Papers. 1791-1870s. 4 boxes and 25 vols.
Open. Unpublished guide.
Georgia Historical Society.
Correspondence, a sales book, account books, court dockets, photos, and other papers of these related families include records for the account of Mrs. William Washington Gordon, the mother of Juliette (Gordon) Low, with George Wayne Anderson; records of money spent for clothes and medicine for Negroes; income from rental of Negroes and sale of produce; and a household and personal account book of Mrs. E. C. Anderson from 1876.

3,595. Weed Family
Papers. 1850-1934. 52 items.
Open. Unpublished guide.
Georgia Historical Society.
Correspondence of the family of Henry D. Weed I and Henry D. Weed II include letters from Lydia Maury Skells and Gertrude Weed Billington. Most of the letters were written in Savannah and include news of the family, friends, schools, travels, and social life.

3,596. White, Anna M.
Papers. Nd. 1 item.
Open. Unpublished guide.
Georgia Historical Society.
Book containing compositions, poetry, recipes, household remedies, and penmanship exercises. The book, which is dated 1932, bears two names, that of White and that of Catherine Bulloch.

3,597. Wilkins, Emma Cheves
Papers. 1877-1957. 496 items.
Open. Unpublished guide.
Georgia Historical Society.
Wilkins, an artist, painted portraits and miniatures. Correspondence, a biography, photos, a catalog of her exhibit at the Telfair Academy, clippings, and other items. Includes correspondence with her mother, her brothers Edgar and Langdon, and her sister Mame, much of it written while she was in school; correspondence concerning her paintings and exhibits; membership lists from the Telfair Academy, dating from her term as membership chairman; a photo album of her family and friends; and a membership card in the Georgia Society of Colonial Dames of America.

3,598. Woodbridge, Caroline Lamar
Papers. 1895. 1 item.
Open. Unpublished guide.
Georgia Historical Society.
Cookbook with some recipes from Leila Habersham's cooking class of 1895 and others from friends.

3,599. Wray and Smith
Papers. 1861. 2 items.
Open. Unpublished guide.
Georgia Historical Society.
Civil War letters, including one from Elizabeth B. Smith to [Mrs.] Amelia Dautin and [Mrs.] Susan Seares of Coosa, GA, with mention of scarcities and high prices, activities of women, and news of family and friends.

3,600. Historical Files
Records. 1868-1927. 3 drawers.
Open. No guide.
Juliette Gordon Low Girl Scout National Center.
Juliette "Daisy" Kinzie (Gordon) [Mrs. William Mackay] Low was the founder of Girl Scouts of the USA. Correspondence of Low and the Gordon family; diaries of Low; files generated by the Girl Scouts between the group's founding in 1912 in Savannah and 1915, when the national organization was moved to Washington, DC; files about persons involved in scouting, 1912-15; material concerning the house in which Low was born and efforts to have it preserved as a national landmark; photos; clippings; and other records.

SNELLVILLE

3,601. Archives
Records. 1949- . 10 drawers and 12 boxes.
Open. Unpublished guide.
Monastery of the Visitation.
Correspondence, photos, and clippings of the Monastery, which was the first community of cloistered nuns in Georgia. Includes letters of several mothers superior and correspondence regarding the founding of the Monastery in 1954 in Atlanta by Reverend Mother Francis de Sales Cassidy and nine nuns she brought from the Visitation Monastery in Toledo, OH. Also includes material concerning the founding of the first monastery of the Visitation in Ireland, in which three American sisters (one from Atlanta, one from St. Paul, MN, and one from Brooklyn, NY) participated.

STATESBORO

3,602. Coleman, Leodel
Papers. 1942-45. 40 items.
Open. Description.
Georgia Southern College Library.
Letters by Margaret Mitchell, author of *Gone With The Wind,* to Leodel Coleman, a Statesboro resident who was a combat correspondent with the Marine Corps during WWII, contain descriptions of life in Atlanta and Georgia during the war years. The letters concern Mitchell's work with the American National Red Cross and her involvement in the campaign to raise funds for a new cruiser *Atlanta*. The letters also include news of such mutual friends as Ralph McGill, Edna Cain Daniel, and other persons involved in Georgia journalism. Mitchell wrote for the *Atlanta Journal Sunday Magazine* from 1922 to 1926.

VALDOSTA

3,603. Carter, Catherine McRee
Papers. 1949-76. 2 items.
Open. Unpublished guides.
South Georgia Regional Library.
Tribute written by Carter about a woman known as Aunt Lou (1843-1926) and a manuscript history of events from 1838 to 1949 in Kinderlou, the Lowndes County, GA, community in which Lou lived. Kinderlou, named in honor of Lou, was the site of the Ruskin commune for about two years at the turn of the century.

3,604. Chinkypin
Papers. 1975-76. 436 pp.
Open. Unpublished guide.
South Georgia Regional Library.
Written by Dorothy Price and her Echols County High School composition classes, these two manuscripts pertain to events in the County from 1858 to 1975. The manuscripts were published by the school.

3,605. Daughters of the American Revolution
Records. 1908-48. 4 vols.
Open. Unpublished guide.
South Georgia Regional Library.
Minutes, photos, clippings, and other records of the DAR's Valdosta chapter, which was founded in 1908.

3,606. Echols County, 1858-1958
Records. 1958. 15-page item.
Open. Unpublished guide.
South Georgia Regional Library.
Genealogical records compiled by the Echols County Centennial History Committee, of which Iona C. Buckley was secretary. The volume provides names of persons listed in the 1870 census whose descendants still reside in the County.

3,607. Lake Park, Georgia
Collection. Nd. 1 vol.
Open. Unpublished guide.
South Georgia Regional Library.
Compilation of correspondence, photos, clippings, and other information about the history of Lake Park, a Lowndes County community, from 1859 to 1942.

3,608. Lowndes County Board of Health
Records. 1930. 16-page item.
Open. Unpublished guide.
South Georgia Regional Library.
The Board's 10th annual report was compiled by Gordon T. Crozier, a physician; [Mrs.] Blanche Mixer, a technician; [Miss] Mary Roberts, a visiting nurse; and [Mrs.] A. B. Jordon, secretary. The report reflects health conditions in Valdosta in 1930.

3,609. Lowndes County Census
Records. 1850. 127 pp.
Open. Unpublished guide.
South Georgia Regional Library.
Census material.

3,610. Lowndes County, GA, Historical Society
Records. 1972-77. 1 vol.
Open. Unpublished guide.
South Georgia Regional Library.
Newsletters of the Society contain information about the County's history and include interviews with such persons as Susan Frances Elder Thomas, a teacher; Elsa Horn, a pianist at a local theater during the silent movie era; and Elizabeth Thame Sirmons, a descendant of the area's early settlers.

3,611. McNeil Families
Papers. 1899. 12-page item.
Open. Unpublished guide.
South Georgia Regional Library.
History of the family, typed and slightly edited by Anne McNeil Ward Cork, concerns family relationships, occupations, education, locations, and anecdotes for the period from 1725 to 1899. Laura Virginia Lee (McNeil) [Mrs. George Varnadoe] Baker originally transcribed the sketch, which was dictated by her father Curtis McNeil.

3,612. McPherson, Elizabeth Weir
Papers. Nd. 50-page item.
Open. Unpublished guide.
South Georgia Regional Library.
Manuscript by McPherson concerning the history of the Gaston, Harvey, Reid, Simonton, and Tomlinson families. The Gaston family genealogy dates from 876 A.D.

3,613. Old Cemetery at Troupville
Papers. 1966. 3-page item.
Open. Unpublished guide.
South Georgia Regional Library.
Manuscript pertaining to the cemetery at Troupville, which was the county seat from 1835 to 1859, includes information about families represented by names on the tombstones.

3,614. Sandel, Mary Eleanor Williams, and Sandel, Elias, Jr.
Papers. 1972. 41-page item.
Open. Unpublished guide.
South Georgia Regional Library.
Genealogy of the Touchstone family, members of which lived in Maryland, Virginia, North and South Carolina, Georgia, Mississippi, and Louisiana. Contains information about family events dating from 1679 to 1950.

3,615. Tombstone Records from Sunset Hill Cemetery
Records. Nd. 12-page item.
Open. Unpublished guide.
South Georgia Regional Library.
Manuscript compiled by the General James Jackson Chapter 1010 of the DAR in Valdosta lists tombstones bearing birthdates before 1875. Also contains listings from the Ousley Cemetery located near Valdosta.

3,616. United Daughters of the Confederacy
Records. 1959-68. 5 vols.
Open. Unpublished guide.
South Georgia Regional Library.
Scrapbooks contain minutes, photos, clippings, and other records of the UDC's Valdosta Chapter No. 471, which was founded in 1901.

3,617. Wisenbaker, Mrs. E. D.
Papers. Nd. 58-page item.
Open. Unpublished guide.
South Georgia Regional Library.
Reminiscences of Thannie (Smith) Wisenbaker reflect her first impressions of Valdosta, the community she arrived in as a 10-year-old child in 1863. Includes references to family relationships, occupations, locations of the town's buildings, health in the community, and the first newspaper. Also includes a list of pupils at the Varnadoe school in 1866.

3,618. Zipperer, Nathaniel A., and Seckinger, Ann Eliza
Papers. Nd. 1 item.
Open. Unpublished guide.
South Georgia Regional Library.
Genealogy of Zipperer and Seckinger, dating from 1750 to 1976, was compiled by Jo Ann Hartman and W. J. Coody, a minister.

HAWAII

HONOLULU

3,619. Archives
Records. 1790- . 6000 cu.ft. and 30,000 photos, and 1,000 microfilm reels.
Partially restricted. Unpublished guide.
Hawaii State Archives.
Records of the state of Hawaii document its history as a pre-constitutional government, a constitutional monarchy, a provisional government, an independent republic, a territory, and finally a state. Records pertaining to women can be found in many of the Archives' files, for example, in pre-1900 files on public instruction, which contain material about education and teachers dating back to the 1840s, and vital statistics files, which include marriage records kept by missionaries from 1826. Records from after 1900, the year in which Hawaii became a territory, consist primarily of legislative records and records of the attorney general, the department of public instruction, the department of health, the land office, and the tax office. All of the pre-1900 and most of the post-1900 records are open. The collections described below are part of the State Archives.

3,620. Army and Navy File
Records. 1844-1900. 6 cu.ft.
Open. No guide.
Hawaii State Archives.
Included with correspondence, reports, accounts, and court martial records are records of the military commission, which tried Queen Liliuokalani for misprision of treason in 1895.

3,621. Cooper, Lucy C. (Vrooman)
Papers. 1911-37. 1 cu.ft.
Open. No guide.
Hawaii State Archives.
Diaries in which [Mrs. William Jonathan] Cooper (1878-1947), an innkeeper, describes homesteading on the island of Maui in 1911, an automobile trip across the US in 1919, and the operation of Cooper Ranch Inn at Hauula on the island of Oahu. Cooper was born in Australia, the daughter of missionaries; she received a nursing degree from French Hospital in San Francisco and an MD from Stanford University Medical School before moving to Hawaii in 1907. In 1923 she and her husband purchased land for a ranch, which became the hotel-ranch Cooper Inn; they operated it for more than 20 years.

3,622. Delegates File: Elizabeth (Pruett) Farrington
Records. 1954-56. 10 cu.ft.
Open. No guide.
Hawaii State Archives.
Farrington (1898-), a newspaperwoman, served as delegate to Congress for the Territory of Hawaii from 1954-1956. Consists of her official files as

delegate, including correspondence with US and Territorial departments and with constituents and others, congressional bills with related correspondence and reports, campaign material, and clippings.

3,623. Foster, Mary Elizabeth (Robinson)
Papers. 1844-1961. 14 cu.ft.
Open. Unpublished guide.
Hawaii State Archives.
Primarily business and land records of [Mrs. Thomas R.] Foster (1844-1930), a Honolulu-born landowner, investor, and philanthropist who was a major shareholder in Hui of Kahana. Deeds, accounts, business correspondence, papers relating to estate administration, and records concerning the ownership of land in Kahana Valley on the island of Oahu. Also includes papers of other members of the Robinson family.

3,624. Howland, Deborah Melville (Dowsett)
Papers. 1847-49. 2 vols.
Open. Card catalog.
Hawaii State Archives.
Journals kept by Howland (1827-53), the wife of sea captain Henry Howland, during voyages from Honolulu to New Bedford, MA, in 1847 and from the US to Hawaii in 1848 and 1849. Howland was born in Australia and brought to Hawaii in 1828 by her parents Captain James and Mary Dowsett.

3,625. League of Women Voters of Hawaii
Records. 1922-36. 6 items.
Open. Card catalog.
Hawaii State Archives.
Minute books and treasurer's records of the League, which was organized in 1922 to educate women as voters and to influence legislation and political activities. In 1936 the League, which also was known as the Hawaii League of Women Voters and the League of Women Voters of Honolulu, merged with the Honolulu chapter of AAUW. The League was not a predecessor of the current LWV.

3,626. Liliuokalani Trust
Records. 1852-1937. 3 cu.ft.
Open. Unpublished guide.
Hawaii State Archives.
The Liliuokalani Trust was established in 1909 to administer a trust created by Queen Liliuokalani to benefit children of Hawaiian ancestry. Correspondence and reports of the trustees, records of her death and settlement of her estate, personal financial accounts of the queen, inventories of personal property and land holdings, and information on the welfare and education fund.

3,627. McKay, Helen (Willis)
Papers. 1895-1946. 15 in.
Open. No guide.
Hawaii State Archives.
Memoirs and a journal of McKay (1873-1971), who worked as a private tutor for a few years before becoming a homemaker. The memoirs, which cover the period from 1895-1941, were planned for publication but were never published. The journal was kept from Dec. 7, 1941, to April 7, 1946.

3,628. Montano, Mary Jane Kekulani (Fayerweather) Davison
Papers. 1901-30. 1.5 in.
Open. No guide.
Hawaii State Archives.
Manuscripts, including poems, legends, chants, and incomplete reminiscences of Montano (1842-1930), a poet, composer, and folklorist who was born in Honolulu. Davison married Benoni Richmond Davison in 1864 and Andres Avelino Montano in 1877.

3,629. Nurses Association, Territory of Hawaii
Records. 1918-58. 3 items.
Open. No guide.
Hawaii State Archives.
Scrapbooks of the League, a professional organization for nurses that was established in 1917, contain constitution and bylaws, minutes, photos, and clippings about the Association and nursing in Hawaii. The Association was also known as the Hawaii League of Nursing.

3,630. Nye, Lydia Rider (Drew)
Papers. 1842-47. 60 items.
Open. No guide.
Hawaii State Archives.
Papers of Nye, the wife of sea captain Gorham Nye, include correspondence; diaries of two sea voyages and of daily life in Honolulu, 1842-43; invitations; and two pencil sketches of Honolulu scenes. Nye was born in Massachusetts and came to Hawaii with her husband in 1842.

3,631. Queen Emma
Papers. 1851-85. 1 cu.ft.
Open. Unpublished guide.
Hawaii State Archives.
Primarily correspondence, some of which is in Hawaiian, of Queen Emma (1836-85), the queen consort and dowager queen of the Hawaiian Kingdom. Queen Emma, whose Hawaiian name was Kaleleonalani, married Alexander Liholiho, King Kamehameha IV, in 1856.

3,632. Queen Liliuokalani
Papers. 1831-1917. 4 cu.ft.
Open. Unpublished guide.
Hawaii State Archives.
Queen Liliuokalani (1838-1917) was the ruling monarch of Hawaii from 1891 to 1893 and a composer. Correspondence, including that regarding claims to Crown Lands of Hawaii; diaries for 1887-89, 1893-94, and 1906; business records that primarily concern land holdings; music and lyrics to Hawaiian songs she composed; invitations; and calling cards. Also includes papers of her father-in-law Captain John Dominis, 1831-47; her mother-in-law Mary [Mrs. John] Dominis, 1847-88; and her husband John Owen Dominis, 1844-91. Born in Honolulu, Liliuokalani was educated in the Royal School and a private day school there. She was proclaimed heir apparent to the throne in 1877 and became queen in 1891 after the death of her brother David Kalakaua. Deposed in 1893, she was arrested in 1895 for taking part in a revolution to restore the monarchy. She was eventually pardoned.

3,633. Taylor, Emma Ahuena (Davison)
Papers. 1851-1938. 9 in.
Open. No guide.
Hawaii State Archives.
[Mrs. Albert Pierce] Taylor (1866-1937) was a writer and folklorist. Correspondence, including Fayerweather family correspondence and that relating to her work as a member of the Hawaiian Historical Commission and the Hawaiian Legend and Folklore Commission; manuscript of her book *From Brilliant Feather Cape to Eagle;* reminiscences; papers of the Sons and Daughters of Hawaiian Warriors, of which she served as premier; and scrapbooks of clippings.

3,634. Tennent, Madeline "Madge"
Papers. 1923-68. 2 cu.ft.
Open. No guide.
Hawaii State Archives.
Manuscripts of published books, scrapbooks containing photos of drawings and paintings and letters received, notes for lectures on arts, catalogs, and press clippings of Madeline Grace "Madge" (Cook) [Mrs. Hugh Cowper] Tennent (1889-1972), an artist who was born in London and lived in South Africa, New Zealand, and Samoa before moving to Hawaii in 1923. She studied in a convent school in Paris, at Capetown School of Art in South Africa, and at *Academie Jullian* in Paris. She began her own art school in Capetown.

3,635. Women's War Work Council
Records. 1917-18. 1 vol.
Open. No guide.
Hawaii State Archives.
Minutes of the Council, which operated from September 1917 through June 1918 as a "clearing house for all social activities for enlisted service men."

3,636. Alexander and Baldwin
Papers. 1824-1911. Ca. 10 ft.
Open. Unpublished guide.
Hawaiian Mission Children's Society Library.
Includes papers of William Patterson Alexander (1805-84), his wife Mary Ann (McKinney) Alexander (1810-88), Dwight Baldwin (1798-1886), and his wife Charlotte (Fowler) Baldwin (1805-73), all of whom were Protestant missionaries in Hawaii. Contains correspondence between mothers and their daughters, who were at school on the US mainland; correspondence between husbands and wives; and diaries, journals, and writings of Abigail (Baldwin) Alexander. Many letters contain references to the wives of 19th-century whaling captains, who often stayed with the Baldwins on Maui while their husbands were at sea.

3,637. American Board of Commissioners for Foreign Missions, Hawaiian Evangelical Association
Records. 1820-1920. Ca. 2 ft.
Open. Unpublished guide.
Hawaiian Mission Children's Society Library.
The Board and the Association were Protestant missionary associations, which sought to convert people to Christianity and to establish schools and churches. The Board was founded in 1810 and the Association in 1853, 10 years before the Board formally ended its support of the Hawaii mission. Includes correspondence between missionaries of the Sandwich Islands Mission and the Board in Boston, agreements, requests for appropriations, and other papers. The bulk of the correspondence is between men, but several items relate to the role expected of missionary women. Board instructions to the missionary women are included also.

3,638. Bingham Family
Papers. 1816-1908. Ca. 13 ft.
Open. Unpublished guide.
Hawaiian Mission Children's Society Library.
Includes correspondence of Sybil (Moseley) Bingham (1792-1848), a teacher and missionary who married Hiram Bingham (1789-1869), a minister and leader of the first company of Protestant missionaries to the Hawaiian Islands. Her letters are chiefly to her family, friends, husband, and children. Also includes correspondence of Lydia (Bingham) Coan, the youngest daughter of Hiram and Sybil Bingham, and of Clarissa (Brewster) Bingham, the second wife of Hiram Bingham II, a missionary to the Gilbert Islands.

3,639. Children of the Mission
Collection. 1830-1900. Ca. 6 ft.
Open. Unpublished guide.
Hawaiian Mission Children's Society Library.
Correspondence and other papers of children of American missionaries in Hawaii. At least half of the correspondence is by women.

3,640. Damon
Papers. 1810-76. 8 boxes.
Open. No guide.
Hawaiian Mission Children's Society Library.
Business and personal correspondence of Samuel Chenery Damon (1815-85), a pastor of Seamen's Chapel of Bethel Union Church in Honolulu, who was married to Julia Sherman (Mills) Damon (1817-90), the first president of the Stranger's Friend Society. Also includes Mills family correspondence from 1810, genealogy, sermons, and other papers. Samuel Damon was also editor

and publisher of *The Friend,* an early Hawaiian newspaper.

3,641. Dole
Papers. 1840-1926. Ca. 6 ft.
Open. No guide.
Hawaiian Mission Children's Society Library.
Includes correspondence, clipping books, and scrapbooks of Sanford Ballard Dole (1844-1926), president of the Republic of Hawaii and first governor of the Territory of Hawaii. Some of the correspondence is by women, and Dole frequently discussed his wife and children in his correspondence.

3,642. Hawaiian Evangelical Association, Micronesian Mission
Records. 1852-1900. Ca. 5 ft.
Open. Unpublished guide.
Hawaiian Mission Children's Society Library.
Includes accounts, reports, correspondence, ship logs, essays, drawings, printed forms, and maps generated or collected by the missionaries to Micronesia and to the Caroline, Gilbert, and Marshall Islands. Includes letters to friends, family, and sponsoring officials.

3,643. Journals
Collection. 1819-1900. Ca. 17 ft.
Open. Unpublished guide.
Hawaiian Mission Children's Society Library.
Chiefly diaries and journals of Protestant missionaries to Hawaii, including those of women and children. Also includes diaries of others who were not missionaries.

3,644. Lahaina Restoration Foundation
Records. 1840s. 3 ft.
Partially restricted. Unpublished guide.
Hawaiian Mission Children's Society Library.
Notes taken during research for restoration of the whaling port of Lahaina on the island of Maui. Includes excerpts from letters written by missionary women and the wives of whaling captains.

3,645. Mission Station
Records. 1822-65. Ca. 4 ft.
Open. Unpublished guide.
Hawaiian Mission Children's Society Library.
Annual reports that missionaries sent from 22 stations on the Hawaiian Islands to general meetings held in Honolulu. The reports are written by men but contain many references to the activities of missionary women.

3,646. Missionary Letters
Collection. 1819-1900. Ca. 32 ft.
Open. Unpublished guide.
Hawaiian Mission Children's Society Library.
Personal correspondence of the Protestant missionaries to the Hawaiian Islands includes many letters by and between women.

3,647. Non-missionary Letters
Collections. 1820-1900. Ca. 1 ft.
Open. Unpublished guide.
Hawaiian Mission Children's Society Library.
Correspondence and other papers of early foreign residents of Hawaii, including ship captains, traders, and New Englanders. Includes material on government, business, and native Hawaiians.

3,648. Photos
Collection. 1850s-1950s. Ca. 12,000 items.
Open. Unpublished guide.
Hawaiian Mission Children's Society Library.
Includes photos of missionary men and women and their descendants, women teachers, scenic views of the Hawaiian Islands, and buildings.

3,649. Wilcox, Abner, and Wilcox, Lucy Eliza (Hart)
Papers. 1823-68. Ca. 2.5 ft.
Open. Unpublished guide.
Hawaiian Mission Children's Society Library.
Correspondence, journals, manuscripts, account books, and other papers of Lucy Wilcox (1814-69) and her husband Abner Wilcox (1808-69), who were teachers and missionaries to the Hawaiian Islands.

3,650. Wilder, S. G.
Papers. 1858-81. Ca. 2 ft.
Open. Unpublished guide.
Hawaiian Mission Children's Society Library.
Correspondence, business records, and other papers of the Wilder family include those of Samuel Gardner Wilder (1831-88), who was involved in agriculture and other activities, and his wife Elizabeth Kinau (Judd) Wilder (1831-1918). Also includes papers of the Judd and Dickson families.

3,651. Continuing Education for Women
Records. 1968-75. Ca. 6 ft. and ca. 36 tapes.
Open. No guide.
University of Hawaii at Manoa Archives.
Correspondence, programs, background files, tapes, and clippings on the development and operation of this program, which was established in the University's college of continuing education and community service in 1968 and which seeks to assist adult women in planning for education and reeducation "to meet Hawaii's changing lifestyles." The collection contains information on programs, workshops, and courses offered. Includes videotapes, sound tapes, and computer tapes.

3,652. Women's Campus Club
Records. 1920-72. 7.5 ft.
Open. No guide.
University of Hawaii at Manoa Archives.
Minutes, correspondence, financial records, reports, newsletters, and clippings of this club for wives of faculty members and women instructors at the University, which was founded in 1920. The Club operates a thrift shop, publishes a monthly want ad bulletin, offers two annual scholarships, organizes fund-raising and other social activities, and serves as a welcoming group for new faculty wives and women instructors.

3,653. Hawaii War Records Depository
Collection. 1940-50. Ca. 315 ft. and 56 microfilm reels.
Open. Unpublished guide.
University of Hawaii at Manoa Library, Hawaii War Records Depository.
Material documenting the history of the Hawaiian Islands during WWII includes correspondence, memoranda, cablegrams, personal diaries and narratives, transcripts of interviews and radio broadcasts, articles, pamphlets, photos, maps and charts, clippings, books, and federal, territorial, and municipal documents. Includes correspondence, personnel files, a brief history, and training material of the Women's Army Volunteer Corps and information on the wartime activities of the AAUW, the Business and Professional Women's Club, the DAR, the Daughters of Hawaii, the Girl Scouts and Girl Reserves, the Hawaii Public Health Association, American National Red Cross units, the YWCA, and women's defense service groups. Portions of the material concern day-care and other child-care centers, education, the Equal Rights Commission, evacuation, the Hawaii Library Association, health organizations and hospitals, labor, racial groups, religion, social welfare and social conditions, war relief, and censorship, which was a job often performed by women.

3,654. Franklin, Jane (Griffin)
Papers. 1860-81. Ca. 100 items and 2 microfilm reels.
Open. No guide.
University of Hawaii at Manoa Library, Hawaiiana Collection.
Lady Franklin (1792-1875) was the wife of Arctic explorer John Franklin. Correspondence, journals for 1861 to 1865, and miscellaneous notes and papers by Lady Franklin, Sophia Cracroft, Queen Emma of Hawaii, and others concerning Lady Franklin's visit to Hawaii in 1861.

IDAHO

BOISE

3,655. Boise Catholic Women's League
Records. 1912-73. 3 cu.ft.
Open. No guide.
Boise State University Library, Special Collections.
Annual reports to the membership, financial records, and scrapbooks of the League, which was created in 1912 to promote "religious, civic, and intellectual culture" among local Catholic women. League activities included supporting a Catholic orphanage, sponsoring a Girl Scout group, and planning fund-raising projects for the improvement of schools, hospitals, and public libraries.

3,656. Boise Council of Church Women
Records. 1941-74. 1 cu.ft.
Open. No guide.
Boise State University Library, Special Collections.
Minutes, correspondence, and scrapbooks of the Council, which was founded in 1916 to unify and coordinate volunteer activities of various women's church groups in the Boise area and to sponsor ecumenical Protestant church programs, such as World Day of Prayer, in cooperation with hospitals, schools, and welfare services. All of the Protestant churches in Boise were represented on the Council.

3,657. Knight, Gladys (Bowman)
Papers. 1964-78. 1 cu.ft.
Open. Unpublished guide.
Boise State University Library, Special Collections.
[Mrs. Leonard R.] Knight (1899-) is an author, family historian, and Republican party worker from Council, ID, a rural community. Correspondence and manuscripts of published booklets reflect her interest in local and state social and political issues.

3,658. Ada County Republican Women's Club
Records. 1938-70. 0.2 ft.
Open. Unpublished guide.
Idaho State Historical Society.
Correspondence and articles relating to the 1966 Idaho Republican assembly, scrapbook, clippings regarding Republican elections, from 1964 to 1969, and printed material of the National Federation of Republican Women.

3,659. American Association of University Women
Records. 1939-66. 4 ft.
Open. Unpublished guide.
Idaho State Historical Society.
Reports, correspondence, and publications of the Idaho AAUW. Includes state presidents' files, state and branch reports, and national AAUW publications and reports.

3,660. Amphictyonic Council
Records. 1897-1918. 10 items.
Open. Unpublished guide.
Idaho State Historical Society.
Founded in 1897 as a service organization, social center, and the first women's club of Parma, ID, the Council was instrumental in bringing the first church to the town. Minutes, an 1864 diary of Council member Mrs. E. C. Shipley, yearbooks, and historical notes on the Parma area.

3,661. Bemis, Polly
Papers. 1894-96. 2 items.
Open. Unpublished guide.

Idaho State Historical Society.
Bemis (?-1933), a Chinese dancing girl and laborer in the gold-mining town of Warrens, ID, married Charles A. Bemis after he won her in a poker game; they settled in the Salmon River Canyon in Idaho to farm. Copies of Bemis's certificates of residence and marriage. She was also known as China Polly and Lulu Nathoy.

3,662. Bird, Annie Laurie
Papers. 1919-72. 1 ft.
Open. Unpublished guide.
Idaho State Historical Society.
Bird (1893-1972) was a Nampa, ID, historian and columnist for the *Idaho Free Press;* a schoolteacher for 35 years; a writer; and a publisher. Correspondence, texts, a scrapbook, research material, maps, and clippings, all of which pertain to her column "Nampa Vignette."

3,663. Boulware, Bertha
Papers. 1889-1941. 1 ft.
Open. Unpublished guide.
Idaho State Historical Society.
Boulware was treasurer of the Idaho State Federation of Music Clubs and a resident of Caldwell, ID. Correspondence with family, with local and state club officers, and with Mrs. E. H. Gue of Caldwell; receipts; and memorabilia.

3,664. Brown, Nellie Somers
Papers. 1969. 4 items.
Open. Unpublished guide.
Idaho State Historical Society.
Letters from [Mrs.] Brown to [Mrs.] Nina M. Ogden, librarian in Pierce, ID, concerning the history of the Weippe-Pierce area and a copy of Brown's article on the Clearwater Timber Company and the Clearwater Fire Protective Association.

3,665. Bureau of Indian Affairs, Lapwai Agency
Records. 1871-83. 6 vols.
Open. Unpublished guide.
Idaho State Historical Society.
Correspondence and other material relating to the administration of the Nez Percé Reservation in Idaho and to the Nez Percé Indians for the years surrounding the 1877 Nez Percé war. Includes correspondence of agents Charles E. Montieth, John B. Montieth, and Charles D. Warner and records of decisions that affected the health, education, and welfare of the Indians.

3,666. Chipps, Nettie R.
Papers. 1886-1959. 1 Hollinger box.
Open. Unpublished guide.
Idaho State Historical Society.
Collection centering on the WCTU in Idaho includes annual reports; office records, 1886-1959; correspondence, 1911-54; photos; publications; and copies of the WCTU organs *Gem State Signal, Idaho White Ribboner, South Idaho White Ribboner,* and *Words to Women.*

3,667. Circle C Ranch
Records. 1944-58. 1 Hollinger box.
Open. Unpublished guide.
Idaho State Historical Society.
Marguerite Campbell (1895-1966), wife of Ranch president Rollie Campbell, was a teacher, state board of education member, state senator from Adams County, ID, from 1947 to 1952, and chairman of the University of Idaho board of regents. Includes letters from Idaho governor C. A. Bottolfsen, John Corlett, US senator Henry Dworshak, US senator Joseph R. McCarthy of Wisconsin, Idaho governor C. A. Robins, and Robert E. Smylie and letters pertaining to education, Marguerite Campbell's University of Idaho regent appointment, and the estate of her mother Ambia W. Allen.

3,668. Clark Family
Papers. 1894-1920. 2 items.
Open. Unpublished guide.
Idaho State Historical Society.
Diary of Alice Clark, 1918-20, and minutes, beginning in 1894, of a political discussion club for which she served as secretary. The minutes also contain an account of her household expenditures for 1902.

3,669. Cobb, Calvin
Papers. 1896-1947. Ca. 2 ft.
Open. Unpublished guide.
Idaho State Historical Society.
Correspondence, business records, family mementos, and other items of Cobb, editor and co-owner of the *Idaho Statesman.* Includes family correspondence, 1896-1960; correspondence concerning the Lyon Company, which was established to handle the business interests of Cobb's mother-in-law Mrs. J. S. Lyon of Chicago, 1898-1929; correspondence of US senator William E. Borah, 1908-12; and correspondence and papers of Cobb's daughter Margaret (Cobb) Ailshie (1883-1959), publisher and editor of the *Idaho Statesman,* regarding family matters, the newspaper's status, and Ailshie's work with the American National Red Cross in France in 1919.

3,670. Columbian Club
Records. 1898-1970. 17.5 ft.
Open. Unpublished guide.
Idaho State Historical Society.
Founded in 1892 to furnish the Idaho Building at the World's Columbian Exposition in Chicago, the Club continued as a Boise civic service organization and became affiliated with the General Federation of Women's Clubs. Minutes, president's correspondence, reports, membership and dues records, scrapbooks, and clippings.

3,671. Cosho, Maude L.
Papers. 1973. 142-page item.
Open. Unpublished guide.
Idaho State Historical Society.
Unpublished manuscript, including photos, of the autobiography of Cosho (1896-). In 1907 Cosho came to Canyon County, ID, as a pioneer. She served as an Idaho state legislator during the 1931, 1933, and 1937 sessions and was a physiotherapist in the WACs during WWII. Cosho also lived in Arizona for 14 years where she taught first grade to Papago Indian children.

3,672. D'Amant, Mae
Papers. Nd. 0.5 ft.
Open. Unpublished guide.
Idaho State Historical Society.
A Boise resident, [Mrs.] D'Amant donated rose bushes for the city's parks and assisted in community tree planting. Scrapbooks, 1933-42, regarding the Woman's Relief Corps and the Grand Army of the Republic; clippings concerning D'Amant's activities, organizations, and Boise landmarks; and articles about pioneers.

3,673. DAR, Electra Thomas Clithers
Records. 1915-25. 1 vol.
Open. Unpublished guide.
Idaho State Historical Society.
Scrapbook of clippings regarding Idaho pioneer history prepared for the DAR by Clithers, a member of the Pioneer chapter in Boise.

3,674. DAR, Mrs. James E. Babb
Records. 1925-37. 1 vol.
Open. Unpublished guide.
Idaho State Historical Society.
Scrapbook of clippings prepared for the Idaho DAR by Babb, a Lewiston, ID, resident who was the organization's state historian.

3,675. Davis, Gladys Riley
Papers. 1976. 6 items.
Open. Unpublished guide.
Idaho State Historical Society.
Correspondence and reminiscences of Davis concern her experiences as a settler from 1900 to 1908 in Culdesac, ID.

3,676. Dawson, Nelle
Papers. 1934-1976. 1 folder.
Open. Unpublished guide.
Idaho State Historical Society.
Reminiscences of a 1930s trip from the Midwest to Idaho by Dawson (1895-?), who hitchhiked and walked. Also included is a 1976 copy of the *Champaign County Gazette* from Illinois.

3,677. Dieter, Alice
Papers. 1966- . 5 Hollinger boxes.
Open. Unpublished guide.
Idaho State Historical Society.
Dieter (1928-) was a feature writer for the *Intermountain Observer* and president of the Idaho Farm Workers' Service, Inc., board of directors. Personal correspondence, Dieter's articles and working papers, and board minutes, correspondence, administrative records, and clippings concerning the Farm Workers' Service from 1966 to 1968.

3,678. Dunbar, Etta C.
Papers. 1913. 1 item.
Open. Unpublished guide.
Idaho State Historical Society.
Diary of Dunbar, with photos by Harold C. Finch, chronicles a camping trip from Boise to "the end of the road beyond Lowman." Lowman is in Idaho.

3,679. Duprey, Annie
Papers. 1883-1916. 9 items.
Open. Unpublished guide.
Idaho State Historical Society.
Quitclaim deeds, indentures, tax deeds, and other records of Duprey (?-1916), a Hailey, ID, resident.

3,680. Elsensohn, Sister M. Alfreda
Papers. 1947-70. 0.5 ft.
Open. Unpublished guide.
Idaho State Historical Society.
Elsensohn is a Benedictine nun and schoolteacher at a Catholic school in northern Idaho. Manuscripts of volumes one and two of *Pioneer Days in Idaho County* (Caldwell, ID: Caxton Publications), published in 1947 and 1951 respectively, and of *Idaho Chinese Lore* (Cottonwood, ID: Idaho Corporation of Benedictine Sisters, 1970).

3,681. Equal Suffrage Association of Idaho
Records. 1895-1916. 4 items.
Open. Unpublished guide.
Idaho State Historical Society.
Minutes and correspondence of the Association, which worked for "full citizenship" for women in the state. Correspondents include US senator William E. Borah; Mrs. T. J. Walsh of the Helena, MT, Business Woman's Equal Suffrage Club; and [Miss] Alice Paul, chairman of the National American Woman Suffrage Association congressional committee.

3,682. Flat Top Sheep Company
Records. 1926-53. 2.5 ft.
Open. Unpublished guide.
Idaho State Historical Society.
Bank statements, bills, receipts, tax records, and ledger sheets of the Company, which was based in Rupert and Carey, ID, and which was owned by Mary (Thomas) Brooks, director of the US Mint; her father John Thomas; and her first husband A. J. Peavey, Jr.

3,683. Fletcher, Mary Augusta
Papers. 1901. 1 Hollinger box.
Open. Unpublished guide.
Idaho State Historical Society.
Text and photos documenting a summer botanical and vacation expedition from Pocatello, ID, to St. Anthony, ID, via Yellowstone National Park. The party consisted of Fletcher, Hattie Clearman, Lucy Cavanaugh, and a Mr. Cameron.

3,684. Fouch, Altha
Papers. 1934-37. 5 items.
Open. Unpublished guide.
Idaho State Historical Society.
Letters from US senator William E. Borah to [Mrs.] Fouch (1868-1937), who was appointed secretary and librarian of the Idaho State Historical Society in 1931, primarily concern the preservation of a book he gave to the Society.

3,685. Gates, Gertrude Lewis
Papers. 1924-25. 40 items.
Open. Unpublished guide.
Idaho State Historical Society.
[Mrs.] Gates was a Ketchum, ID, resident and owner of the D. A. Ranch near Cornville, AZ. Correspondence between Gates and Mr. and Mrs. J. L. Lay, managers of the D. A. Ranch, regarding ranch management and Gates's travels.

3,686. Glasson, Mrs. Josiah
Papers. Nd. 1 item.
Open. Unpublished guide.
Idaho State Historical Society.
Reminiscences of a 1905 trip through Yellowstone Park from Wardner, ID, to Spokane, WA, contain descriptions of transportation, sites, and accommodations.

3,687. Green, Emma Edwards
Papers. 1923-38. 0.5 ft.
Open. Unpublished guide.
Idaho State Historical Society.
Correspondence, writings, sketches, and other papers of Green, who designed the state seal of Idaho in 1891. Includes correspondence with Caxton Printers of Caldwell, ID, and Company Flagmakers in New York City regarding the incorporation of the seal on the state flag in 1938 and a 1938 letter of recommendation from Governor Barzilla W. Clark.

3,688. Greenleaf Woman's Christian Temperance Union
Records. 1920. 85-page vol.
Open. Unpublished guide.
Idaho State Historical Society.
Cookbook of the WCTU in Greenleaf, ID, which was a Quaker community.

3,689. Hawkes, Mrs. John
Papers. 1901-59. Ca. 33 ft.
Open. Unpublished guide.
Idaho State Historical Society.
Legal papers and scrapbooks from 1901 to 1908 of John Hawkes of Kalispell, MT, and 159 scrapbooks from 1940 to 1959 of Mrs. Hawkes of Boise concerning music, theater, the classics, geography, hobbies, and other subjects.

3,690. Idaho Council of Churches, Southern Idaho Migrant Ministry
Records. 1958-71. 9 ft.
Open. Unpublished guide.
Idaho State Historical Society.
Organized in 1965 by the Idaho Council of Churches to aid the southwestern Idaho farm laborer, the federally funded Ministry was an early antipoverty program in Idaho. Correspondence, reports, newsletters, and pamphlets relating to the Council and the Ministry. Programs designed to assist women in the home and those who wanted to enter the work force included organized health services, day-care centers, and planned parenthood programs.

3,691. Idaho Farm Workers' Services, Inc.
Records. 1966-69. 60 ft.
Open. Unpublished guide.
Idaho State Historical Society.
Growing out of the Migrant Ministry that assisted Chicanos, this organization was an early antipoverty program of the 1960s in Idaho. Board minutes, financial reports, correspondence, program reports, personnel files, vouchers, and requisitions. Many of those receiving assistance were women who needed medical care, counseling, and other forms of aid.

3,692. Idaho Federation of Music Clubs
Records. 1923-62. Ca. 3 ft.
Open. Unpublished guide.
Idaho State Historical Society.
Minutes of the state board of the Federation, 1940-62; scrapbooks compiled by the Federation historian and relating to the years 1939 through 1961; and a history of the organization, which had a predominantly female membership.

3,693. Idaho Legisladies
Records. 1933-63. 0.5 ft.
Open. Unpublished guide.
Idaho State Historical Society.
Minutes, rosters, club history by Mrs. Charles Winkler, and a scrapbook of this bipartisan luncheon club for the wives of Idaho legislators, which was founded in 1921 by Mrs. Peter Johnson of Blackfoot, ID.

3,694. Idaho Press Women's Archives
Records. 1948-75. 7.5 ft.
Open. Unpublished guide.
Idaho State Historical Society.
An affiliate of the National Federation of Press Women, the Idaho chapter was organized in 1944 by Claire Goldsmith of New Plymouth, ID, and Gladys Swank of Lewiston, ID. Presidents' correspondence, membership files, scrapbooks containing articles written by members and announcements of activities held in conjunction with the National Federation, and the Idaho chapter newsletter.

3,695. Idaho State PTA
Records. 1914-71. 40 ft.
Open. Unpublished guide.
Idaho State Historical Society.
The Idaho branch of the National Congress of Mothers was organized in 1905 by the national president Mrs. Fredric Schoff; it later became the Idaho State PTA. Minutes of meetings of the Idaho Congress of Mothers and the Idaho PTA, 1914-32 and 1957-69; correspondence; scrapbooks; bulletins and public relations material; national PTA convention proceedings; and a history of the Idaho chapter to 1950.

3,696. Idaho Tuberculosis Association
Records. Ca. 1950-59. 4 items.
Open. Unpublished guide.
Idaho State Historical Society.
Scrapbooks and a folder concerning the Idaho chest x-ray program, which was a joint project of the Idaho Tuberculosis Association and the Idaho department of public health, and the Idaho State Tuberculosis Hospital in Gooding, ID. The folder contains statement of purpose and policies of the program. The scrapbooks portray the activities of the program's staff and community volunteers, most of whom were women.

3,697. Idaho Writers' League
Records. 1941-73. 2.5 ft.
Open. Unpublished guide.
Idaho State Historical Society.
An affiliate of the League of Western Writers, this organization was founded in 1938 to promote the interests of Idaho writers, many of whom were women. Correspondence, including letters from Boise chapter president Faith Turner, 1942-57; public relations material from similar organizations; clippings regarding the achievements of League members; and copies of the League's newsletter *Leagazett*.

3,698. Johnesse, Mr. and Mrs. Frank
Papers. 1898-1948. 7 ft.
Open. Unpublished guide.
Idaho State Historical Society.
Correspondence from 1942 to 1947, notebooks, financial records, contracts, and mining material of Frank Johnesse (1869-?), president of the Consolidated Mining Syndicate in Boise. Includes political correspondence and related printed material of his wife Mary Louise Patton Johnesse (1880?-1962?), Democratic state chairman in the 1930s and an unsuccessful congressional candidate in 1938.

3,699. Ladies of the Grand Army of the Republic
Records. 1918. 1 item.
Open. Unpublished guide.
Idaho State Historical Society.
Copy of a letter to General John J. Pershing, commander of American forces in France, from the Ladies of the GAR, Circle 5, in Boise regarding Memorial Day observances.

3,700. Langmaid, Mrs. George W.
Papers. Nd. 1 Hollinger box.
Open. Unpublished guide.
Idaho State Historical Society.
Langmaid was a resident of Middleton, ID. Logbook of a trip made in a Ford in 1916 from Baltimore to Boise, photos, sketches of maps of various states, and a history of Company H, 19th Iowa Volunteer Infantry, published by an Ottumwa, IA, publishing firm in 1890.

3,701. League of Women Voters of Boise
Records. 1965-74. 2.5 ft.
Open. Unpublished guide.
Idaho State Historical Society.
Board minutes, newsletters, public relations material, and national LWV publications.

3,702. League of Women Voters of Idaho
Records. 1950-72. 14 ft.
Open. Unpublished guide.
Idaho State Historical Society.
Minutes of the biennial councils, correspondence, membership files, a scrapbook, and public relations material.

3,703. League of Women Voters of Idaho Falls
Records. 1946-73. 4.5 ft.
Open. Unpublished guide.
Idaho State Historical Society.
Executive board minutes, correspondence, scrapbooks, pamphlets, and other material of the Idaho Falls LWV. Also included are records of the following Idaho chapters: Caldwell, Burley, Twin Falls, Coeur d'Alene, Pocatello, Lewiston, Boise, Nampa, Moscow, and Blackfoot.

3,704. Lingenfelter, Mr. and Mrs. C. H.
Papers. 1902-49. 31 items.
Open. Unpublished guide.
Idaho State Historical Society.
Correspondence, scrapbook, and programs and brochures concerning the National Congress of Mothers' First International Congress, held in 1908 in Washington, DC. Bea (Dally) [Mrs. C. H.] Lingenfelter was Idaho's delegate to the conference.

3,705. Luzadder, Helen Wilson
Papers. 1958-59. 3 items.
Open. Unpublished guide.

Idaho State Historical Society.
Typescripts of biographical articles about Luzadder (1867-1963), a schoolteacher in Nampa, ID, and in McCall and Skagway, AK, and superintendent of schools for Boise County, ID, in the early 1900s.

3,706. McBeth and Crawford
Papers. 1853-1936. 6 ft.
Open. Unpublished guide.
Idaho State Historical Society.
Correspondence, journals and diaries, manuscript of a book, scrapbooks, clippings, and other material pertain to the missionary work of Susan Law McBeth (1830-93), her sister Kate McBeth (1833-1915), and their nieces Mary Crawford (1861-1945) and Elizabeth Crawford (?-1925) among the Nez Percé Indians in Kamiah, ID, and Lapwai, ID. Includes correspondence of the McBeth sisters, 1853-1915; of the Crawfords, 1901-36; and of William Thaw, 1894-1913. Also contains manuscripts of Kate McBeth's book "The Nez Percés Since Lewis and Clark," a Nez Percé English dictionary, diaries and journals of the McBeth sisters, and scrapbooks, clippings, and other material relating to mission business.

3,707. Morton, Maralyn
Papers. Ca. 1953. 7 Hollinger boxes.
Open. Unpublished guide.
Idaho State Historical Society.
Copies of research information for Morton's annotated bibliography on Idaho writers and writings about Idaho by other writers.

3,708. Music Week
Records. 1913-75. 2 ft.
Open. Unpublished guide.
Idaho State Historical Society.
Begun in 1919 by the Boise Civic Chorus and Eugene Farner, this annual May festival has since spread throughout the US. Board minutes, memoranda, scrapbook from 1913 to 1957, programs, and brochures. Women have participated as board members and performers.

3,709. Northman, May L. Scott
Papers. 1902-14. 1 vol.
Open. Unpublished guide.
Idaho State Historical Society.
Scrapbook of [Mrs.] Northman of Boise regarding her term as state superintendent of public instruction from 1902 to 1906 and her unsuccessful bid for the state treasurer's office in 1914.

3,710. Palmer, Carolyn Hunton
Papers. 1918. 1 folder.
Open. Unpublished guide.
Idaho State Historical Society.
Copy of an unpublished autobiographical manuscript of Palmer, a pioneer who settled in Boise, regarding family life, the individual's role in family sustenance, Indians, mining, schools, and weather.

3,711. Parker, Nellie B.
Papers. 1910. 1 vol.
Open. Unpublished guide.
Idaho State Historical Society.
Bound typescript of *The Roughnecks Home Companion,* a privately published monthly magazine written by Nellie Parker and Leslie B. Taylor of Mountain Nest in Valley Camp, a Baker County, OR, mining camp. A family enterprise, the publication contained human interest stories, humorous items, and poetry.

3,712. Parrish, Ella (Knox)
Papers. 1871-1960. 0.5 ft. and 12 items.
Open. Unpublished guide.
Idaho State Historical Society.
Clippings, pamphlets, and publications of Parrish (1868-1964), a resident of Emmett, ID, concern Idaho history, the WCTU, and unidentified flying objects. Also includes letters from Mrs. M. B. Nash, Idaho state historian, regarding her appointment as county historian and letters from senators John Thomas and D. Worth Clark, representatives Compton I. White and Henry Dworshak, and Richard W. Morin of the US Department of State regarding world peace after WWII. The collection also contains a copy of part of a map of Idaho Territory in 1871 and an 1875 declaration of homestead by Parrish's father Douglas Knox.

3,713. Reed, Ella Cartee
Papers. 1881-91. 36 items.
Open. Unpublished guide.
Idaho State Historical Society.
Reed was the second secretary and, from 1921 to 1931, librarian of the Idaho State Historical Society. Notebooks of C. M. Hays containing reminiscences and transcribed extracts from Boise Basin, ID, newspapers; practice booklets for typists containing the stories of J. N. Kimball; bulletins of the Idaho State Historical Society from 1908 and 1910; "The Sheepeater Campaign: Idaho—1879," a booklet by Colonel W. C. Brown with a foreword by Reed; and other items.

3,714. Robinson, Dorothy Clapp
Papers. 1907-19. Ca. 40 items.
Open. Unpublished guide.
Idaho State Historical Society.
Robinson (1892-1968) was an early Idaho schoolteacher and writer. Biography, photos, autograph book, high school memorabilia, and a Blackfoot, ID, high school yearbook.

3,715. Rosquist, August
Papers. 1915-51. 43 Hollinger boxes.
Open. Unpublished guide.
Idaho State Historical Society.
Rosquist, a labor leader, was secretary of the Pocatello Central Labor Union and Building Trades Council, and secretary-treasurer of the Idaho State Federation of Labor from 1924 to 1946. Correspondence, Council minutes, material regarding labor legislation, clippings, and pamphlets contain information on the percentage of women in the labor force and the positions they held from 1924 to 1946.

3,716. Ruby City, Owyhee County
Papers. Ca. 1868. 1 item.
Open. Unpublished guide.
Idaho State Historical Society.
Letter from Lydia R. Walbridge to her cousin Rebecca Williams Hawes regarding her journey from the east coast to Ruby City, ID, via the Isthmus of Panama.

3,717. St. Margaret's School
Records. 1883-1940s. 1 Hollinger box.
Open. Unpublished guide.
Idaho State Historical Society.
The forerunner of Boise State University, St. Margaret's was founded by the Episcopal church in 1892 as a boarding and day school for girls in Boise. Minutes of faculty meetings, 1921-22 and 1930-31; financial ledger, 1919-30; records of student enrollment, grades, and classes, 1912-21; clippings; School pamphlets; papers relating to the women's auxiliary of the Episcopal Church missionary district of Idaho, 1930s-40s; and issues of the *Idaho Churchman,* 1883-86.

3,718. Schuster, Mary
Papers. 1893-1954. 3 Hollinger boxes.
Open. Unpublished guide.
Idaho State Historical Society.
Workbooks and diploma from Western Normal College in Lincoln, NE, and correspondence and personal cards received by Schuster, who lived in Nampa, ID, from 1945 to 1954.

3,719. Seamans, Marie
Papers. 1905. 1 item.
Open. Unpublished guide.
Idaho State Historical Society.
A letter written by Amelia J. Frost of Blackfoot, ID, concerning Seamans's gift of songbooks to the Fort Hall Reservation Church.

3,720. Shawver, Ira
Papers. 1916-19. 1 item.
Open. Unpublished guide.
Idaho State Historical Society.
Notebook containing expenditures for food and cooking utensils, recipes and household hints, and clippings.

3,721. Shearer, George Martin
Papers. 1864-89. 172 items.
Open. Unpublished guide.
Idaho State Historical Society.
Correspondence and business and military records of Shearer (1841-90), a US Army officer and ferry boat operator. Includes correspondence of Shearer with his wife; letters he received while in the Fort Delaware, MD, prisoner of war camp; and reports concerning the 1877 Nez Percé war and the Sheepeater war, which was fought in 1878 and 1879 in Idaho between the US Army and Sheepeater Indians.

3,722. Smith, Jean Conly
Papers. 1895-1960. 1 folder.
Open. Unpublished guide.
Idaho State Historical Society.
Correspondence and articles regarding a 1911 trip through a proposed national park area. Includes letters to Jean Conly [Mrs. G. E.] Smith of Boise, a letter from Smith's daughter Josephine Conly (Smith) Vaughn to US senator Frank Church concerning his Sawtooth National Park bill, photos of the Sawtooth area, and a list of Idaho birds compiled by Jean Smith.

3,723. Spalding, Henry Harmon
Papers. 1836-1945. 0.5 ft.
Open. Unpublished guide.
Idaho State Historical Society.
Spalding (1804-74) founded a Lapwai, ID, mission in 1836 for the Nez Percé Indians. Correspondence, including letters to Levi Hart and his family; diary kept from 1836 to 1840 by Spalding's wife Eliza (Hart) Spalding (1807-51); petition from citizens of Washington and Idaho territories and Oregon seeking Spalding's reappointment; and material regarding the Idaho Spalding Centennial.

3,724. Steuenberg, Edith (Farrer)
Papers. 1975. 1 folder.
Open. Unpublished guide.
Idaho State Historical Society.
Copy of reminscences of Steuenberg regarding her life in Delamar, ID, from the 1890s to 1914. Describes mining, farming, school, family life, and minority groups in the area, particularly the Indians and Chinese.

3,725. Storm, Mrs. Wash, Jr.
Papers. 1923-38. 9 items.
Open. Unpublished guide.
Idaho State Historical Society.
Storm was a childless housewife who looked after orphans. Photos, a letter to [Miss] Mallie Phegley of Houston from US senator William E. Borah's secretary Cora Rubin regarding personal matters, and a letter to Mrs. Augie Jackson of Gause, TX, from Mattie B. Rinhard of Fairfield, IL, concerning family and personal matters.

3,726. Tate, Emma
Papers. 1878-1920. 1 ft.
Open. Unpublished guide.
Idaho State Historical Society.
Tate (1873-1962) was a pioneer and Boise civic

leader who came to Idaho from Kansas in 1879 with her family. Incomplete biography of Tate, receipts, mortgages, and other material. Tate's sons David and John P. Tate founded the Triangle Dairy.

3,727. Towell, Emily Fletcher
Papers. 1881-1959. 1 folder.
Open. Unpublished guide.
Idaho State Historical Society.
Copy of diary kept by Towell on an 1881 journey from Mercer County, MO, to Middle Valley, ID. Also included are poetry by Ethel Pickett Hooper and her 1959 account of the Edson and Pickett families of Middle Valley.

3,728. Tupper, Cornelia Moulton
Papers. Ca. 1930. 1 folder.
Open. Unpublished guide.
Idaho State Historical Society.
Copy of an incomplete autobiography of Tupper (1890-), an Emmett, ID, settler, in which she describes life on a ranch near Emmett in the 1890s and early 1900s.

3,729. Visiting Nurse Association
Records. 1919-23. 2 folders.
Open. Unpublished guide.
Idaho State Historical Society.
The Association was founded in Boise by the American National Red Cross home service department during the Spanish flu epidemic in 1918-19 to provide public nursing and home medical care. Minutes, correspondence, weekly reports, papers concerning the group's work, and advertising circulars.

3,730. Walsh, Mrs. H.
Papers. Nd. 1 folder.
Open. Unpublished guide.
Idaho State Historical Society.
Copy of reminiscences of Walsh (1841-?), an Idaho settler, describes the Nez Percé war of 1877 and fear caused by isolation from other families.

3,731. Walters, Louise Cook
Papers. 1862-65. 7 items.
Open. Unpublished guide.
Idaho State Historical Society.
Copies of letters from Walters, a settler in the Placerville, ID, mining district, to her sister and friends in the East describe life in Idaho and relate her disappointment that the Indians were not the noble savages portrayed by some authors.

3,732. Williams, Ivy Currin
Papers. 1896-1901. 1 folder.
Open. Unpublished guide.
Idaho State Historical Society.
Report cards and examination papers of [Mrs.] Williams, a Payette, ID, resident, from a school in Currinsville, OR, and Payette high school and a 1901 Payette high school commencement program.

COTTONWOOD

3,733. Archives
Records. 1882- . 9 file cabinets, 1 storage cabinet, 5 microfilm reels, and ca. 50 tapes.
Access restricted. Unpublished guide.
Priory of St. Gertrude.
This priory of Benedictine women was founded in 1882. Minutes, financial records, correspondence, diaries, manuscripts, chronicles, photos, papers of prioresses, books, and other records, including material relating to hospitals and a long term care unit operated by the sisters and to the sisters' educational activities in elementary and high schools and colleges.

MOSCOW

3,734. Jewett, George Frederick, Sr.
Papers. 1853-1950. 66 cu.ft. and 21 vols.
Open. Published guide.
University of Idaho Library, Special Collections and Archives.
Correspondence, business papers, financial records, legal documents, and reports of the families of Jewett, his father James Richard Jewett, and his grandfather George Washington Jewett (?-1879), a sea captain; the families were involved in such businesses as lumbering and transportation. Includes correspondence from ca. 1853 to 1900 of Annie M. [Mrs. George Washington] Jewett with her husband, relatives, and friends regarding everyday life and correspondence of Mrs. James Jewett with such socialites as Mrs. F. Weyerhaeuser. Also contains correspondence of Mary C. Jewett and her husband George Frederick Jewett, Sr., with philanthropic organizations. The two were active in the Republican party, the YWCA, Spokane charitable institutions, and the English Speaking Union. See *Descriptive Inventory of the Papers of George Frederick Jewett, Sr.,* University of Idaho Library Publication No. 5 (Moscow: 1969).

3,735. Pfost, Gracie (Bowers)
Papers. 1953-62. 170 cu.ft.
Open. Records transmittal forms.
University of Idaho Library, Special Collections and Archives.
Correspondence, speeches, reports, photos, legal papers, news releases, excerpts from the *Congressional Record,* and other papers of Pfost (1906-63), a congresswoman from Idaho's First District from 1953 to 1962. The bulk of the papers pertains to Congresswoman Pfost's involvement in the controversy over construction of a dam at Hell's Canyon on the Snake River; she assisted the conservationists in opposing it. Pfost worked in real estate and was active in Democratic politics on the local level before she became a congresswoman.

REXBURG

3,736. Daughters of the Snake River Pioneers
Records. 1924-50. 9 in.
Open. No guide.
Ricks College Archives.
This organization was founded in 1924 to perpetuate the names and achievements of men and women who were pioneers in the Upper Snake River Valley in Idaho. Minutes, research notes, and typescripts of reminiscences, family and community histories, individual biographies, and descriptions of pioneer life, which were presented at the group's monthly meetings.

3,737. Daughters of the Utah Pioneers
Records. Ca. 1945-55. 3 vols.
Open. No guide.
Ricks College Archives.
Records of the Fremont County, ID, Association of the DUP, which was dedicated to the perpetuation and honor of pioneers who entered Utah before the transcontinental railroad arrived in Utah in May 1869, contain stories and histories written by Association members and ca. 250 biographies of Fremont County women.

3,738. Hoopes, Ella Clarinda Hinckley Cardon
Papers. Nd. 24-page item.
Open. No guide.
Ricks College Archives.
Reminiscences of Hoopes (1867-?), a Mormon settler in the Snake River Valley of Idaho, who was educated at the Brigham Young Academy at Provo, UT, when Karl G. Maeser, James E. Talmage, Susa Young Gates, and Zina Young Card were teaching there. Hoopes was the third wife of her polygamous husband. The reminiscences cover the years to 1935.

3,739. Upper Snake River Valley
Oral history. 1966-70. 67 tapes.
Open. Register.
Ricks College Archives.
Collection consists of interviews with many of the early settlers of the Valley concerning agriculture, business, and Mormon church activities. Includes interviews in which Zina Larsen Hill, who was born in Denmark, tells of her immigration to the US and later life in the Darby area of the Teton Valley; Kirsten Marie Sorenson Jensen, a Dane who immigrated with her parents to Orderville, UT, recounts her memories of Basalt, ID, where she later moved; and Kate B. Carter, president of the Daughters of the Utah Pioneers, discusses the group's history, organization, purposes, and accomplishments.

3,740. Walz, Christina Magdelena
Papers. Nd. 50-page item.
Open. No guide.
Ricks College Archives.
Biography of Walz (1845-1920), which was compiled by her oldest daughter Eliza (Walz) Tadje, concerns Walz's activities in the Mormon church, work as the community midwife, her life in the Upper Snake River Valley, and her personal experiences.

ILLINOIS

AURORA

3,741. College Archives
Records. 1893- . Ca. 60 ft.
Open. Unpublished guide.
Aurora College Library.
The College, which was founded in 1893, is a coeducational liberal arts college affiliated with the Advent Christian Church. Includes minutes, financial records, correspondence, statistical data, reports, photos, yearbooks, catalogs, bulletins, newspapers, and publications. Items pertaining to women include records of the dean of women, women's studies curricula, and information on women's athletics, the women's debate club, and annual woman's day programs.

3,742. Jenks Memorial
Collection. 1830- . Ca. 216 ft. and 1800 vols.
Open. Unpublished guide.
Aurora College Library.
Collection pertains to the Millerite Movement and the history of the Advent Christian Church. Includes correspondence, diaries, sermons, notes, tracts, photos, periodicals, and books. An American religious leader, William Miller began to preach the second coming of Christ in 1831. Miller's teachings, sermons, revival meetings, and prophesies led to a nation-wide Adventist movement. Dissension between Miller's adherents and established Protestant churches led to the formation in 1845 of a separate Adventist Church. Includes correspondence, of the Woman's Home and Foreign Mission Society, 1897-1914, including items pertaining to Sarah K. Taylor, first president of the Society, and Harriet B. Hastings. Also includes two papers, "Created in God's Image: Religious Issues in the Woman's Rights Movement of the Nineteenth Century," a PhD dissertation presented to Northwestern University in 1975 by Donna A. Behnke, and "Female Preachers in the Advent Christian Denomination," presented to the Andover-Newton Theological Seminary in Newton, MA, in 1978 by Shirlee M. Bromley.

BATAVIA

3,743. Local History
Collection. 1840-1975. 2 Hollinger boxes.
Closed. No guide.
Batavia Historical Society.
Contains reminiscences, business records, photos, clippings, and yearbooks pertaining to Batavia. Includes medical records and artifacts related to Mary Todd Lincoln's confinement in Bellevue Hospital in 1875 as well as items relating to individual women and women's organizations, among them the Batavia Woman's Club, PEO, Young Mother's Club, LWV, and Girl Scouts.

BELLEVILLE

3,744. Archives
Records. 1910- . Ca. 10 vols.
Open. No guide.
Ursuline Sisters Convent.
Chronicles, school reports, photos, and other records of the Convent. The order was first established in the US in 1910.

BLOOMINGTON

3,745. Pantagraph Clippings and Microfilm
Collection. 1881- . 4 cabinets and 800 microfilm reels.
Access restricted. Catalog card index.
Bloomington Public Library.
Correspondence, notes, programs for events, clippings, and ephemera concern such Bloomington area women as Kate Condon, a singer; Hester (Merwin) [Mrs. Edward L.] Ayers, an artist; Florence (Fifer) [Mrs. Jacob A.] Bohrer, the first woman state senator in Illinois and a founder of the McLean County LWV; Rachel Crothers, a Pulitzer Prize-winning playwright; Margaret Illington, who starred in London and New York theaters; Marie Litta, a singer called "the second Jenny Lind"; Sarah E. (Raymond) [Mrs. Francis J.] Fitzwilliam, who in the 1880s became the first female superintendent of schools in the state; Hazle (Buck) [Mrs. Davis] Ewing, a philanthropist whose father was involved in the founding of the Wrigley chewing gum company; and Minnie (Saltzman)-Stevens, a singer.

3,746. University Archives
Records. 1850- . Ca. 75 ft.
Open. Inventory.
Illinois Wesleyan University Archives.
Founded in 1850 by the Methodist Episcopal Church, the University admitted women in 1870 and graduated its first women students in 1872. Includes minutes of the board of trustees, 1850-, and of the faculty, 1861-, including information on the Woman's Educational Association, which purchased a building and operated it as a women's dormitory. Also includes records for the college of music, 1876-; the school of nursing, 1959-; the department of home economics, ca. 1950-70; and the IWU League, an organization for faculty wives, 1960- . Publications include college catalogs and issues of the *Argus*, the student newspaper, 1894-; the *Wesleyana*, the yearbook, 1895-; and the *Orange*, the yearbook of Hedding College, a coeducational institution absorbed by Wesleyan, 1913-23.

3,747. Arts, Crafts, and Recreation
Collection. 1965. 3 items.
Open. Unpublished guide.
McLean County Historical Society.
Essays include "Circus Lore," by Betty Holzhauer; "The Art of Weaving," by [Mrs.] Mary T. Kerr; and "Recent Tendencies in the Drama," by Frances G. Sitherwood.

3,748. Black History
Collection. Nd. 2 items.
Open. Unpublished guide.
McLean County Historical Society.
Includes an historical essay by Frances G. Sitherwood, "Hampton Institute, Virginia," and articles by Vickie Price relating to black history and Joseph Johnson.

3,749. Bohrer, Florence (Fifer)
Papers. 1880-1945. 226-page item.
Open. No guide.
McLean County Historical Society.
Autobiographical memoirs of [Mrs. Jacob A.] Bohrer, who in 1924 became the first woman elected to the Illinois State Senate. The daughter of Illinois governor Joseph Fifer, Bohrer was active in the Illinois LWV and various civic, cultural, and welfare organizations.

3,750. Business and Professional Women's Club
Records. 1925-65. 1 ft.
Open. No guide.
McLean County Historical Society.
Minutes, scrapbooks, directories, and memorabilia of the Club, a social and service organization for working women.

3,751. Businesses
Collection. 1950-77. 6 items.
Open. Unpublished guide.
McLean County Historical Society.
Includes recollections of Inez Dunn concerning the First National Bank of Normal, IL; of Jean Stubblefield concerning the banks in Bloomington; of [Mrs.] Donna M. Eichstaedt concerning the Dillon family which operated a draft horse business; of Elizabeth Masters concerning the arrival of the telephone in McLean County; and of Mrs. A. M. Thayer concerning early milliners and dressmakers of Bloomington. Also includes an article by Wilma Tolley about Adam Guthrie.

3,752. Civil War
Collection. 1861-1911. 4 items.
Open. Unpublished guide.
McLean County Historical Society.
Contains pension records of Albert D. J. Cashier, a woman private in the US Army, including information by Deanne Hillfinger; an address by a Miss Cradlebaugh on flag presentation, 1861; an item by [Mrs.] Mary L. P. Evans on flag presentation to Civil War units; and an item by Adda P. Wertz on the Christian Sanitary Commission, 1911.

3,753. Communities and Sites
Collection. Ca. 1927-74. 15 items.
Open. Unpublished guide.
McLean County Historical Society.
Contains historical essays and reminiscences, including those by Ida Blair concerning Franklin Park, IL; by Beulah Butler about historical spots in McLean County, 1941; by Gertrude Castle Cox about Chenoa and Gridley township; by Eileen Foley concerning theaters in Bloomington and Normal, IL; by Mrs. M. A. Marmon about Dawson township; by Mary McCorvie concerning animal remains at the Grand Village of the Kickipoo, an excavation site; by [Mrs.] Charlotte Scott on Bloomington business; and by Frances Wagers concerning Dawson Lake and Morraine State Park.

3,754. Early Settlers
Collection. Ca. 1837-1956. 35 items.
Open. Unpublished guide.
McLean County Historical Society.
Collection consists of correspondence, autobiographies, reminiscences, biographies, historical sketches, and genealogies. Includes correspondence dealing with early settlers in Bloomington, 1837-75; a compilation of correspondence and genealogy by Virginia Miles dealing with the Castle family and Mrs. J. G. M. G. Mills; memoirs of Amelia Louise Boggs; reminiscences of Judith Bradner relating to early settlers and women's history in Bloomington; a biography of T. L. Buck, an early settler, by Buck's daughter Oral Buck; reminiscences of Maria Dawson-Paist concerning farming, early settlers, and Indians; an item by Etta Havens Carrithers dealing with Havens family genealogy, Indian history, Hudson township, and Havens Grove; a sketch about Omen and Zena Olney, early settlers in Blooming Grove, by J. B. Orendorff; a biography of John Magoun by Mrs. Gordon H. Read, dealing with Magoun and the temperance movement; and an item by Harriet Smock concerning the Illinois wilderness.

3,755. Education
Collection. Ca. 1972-76. 7 items.
Open. Unpublished guide.
McLean County Historical Society.
Includes reminiscences, historical sketches, and articles by Mrs. E. E. Cox concerning Chenoa's first school, by Rudy M. Hundley on the history of Irving Schools, by Florence Mildred Edwards concerning Richard Edwards and early education, by F. A. Walker concerning Sarah E. Beers and a school in Normal township, and by Dortha C. Tompkins about a local school district.

3,756. Farming
Collection. Nd. 4 items.
Open. Unpublished guide.
McLean County Historical Society.
Contains essays and personal reminiscences by Mrs. Herbert Garling dealing with farming, especially winter conditions, in Downs township; by Betty Holzhauer concerning corn farming, 1973; by Mrs. William J. Rhoades relating to farming, farm politics, and the Grange; and by [Mrs.] Hilda Cox Deems concerning making maple syrup in Blooming Grove.

3,757. Hutton Family
Papers. 1884-1944. 4 ft.
Open. Unpublished guide.
McLean County Historical Society.
Correspondence, notebooks, business records, photos, publications, and memorabilia of members of the Hutton family, who were farmers and business proprietors in Saybrook, IL. Includes personal correspondence of L. L. Hutton (?-1927) and his wife Mary Blair Hutton (?-1944), who were married in 1894, including courtship letters, as well as descriptions of farming in Indiana and North Dakota, college life, travel, family, and friends. Also includes records relating to the Hutton music store and an insurance business.

3,758. Jessamine Withers Home
Records. 1955-65. 0.5 ft.
Open. No guide.
McLean County Historical Society.
Minutes, correspondence, and clippings of the Home, a private retirement residence for women that was founded in 1913.

3,759. Kessler, Clara Louise
Papers. 1900-50. 5 vols.
Open. Index.
McLean County Historical Society.
Consists of "Home Town in the Corn Belt," a source history of Bloomington from 1900 to 1950 collected by Kessler. Contains excerpts from correspondence, diaries, reminiscences, and poetry.

3,760. Law and Politics
Collection. Ca. 1914-77. 5 items.
Open. Unpublished guide.
McLean County Historical Society.
Includes historical sketches and essays by [Mrs.]

Edith Packard Kelley concerning local events and people in the 1840 campaign in Bloomington, 1914; by Elizabeth Masters concerning naturalization, 1977; by Laurel Quaid concerning courts, law, and justice in McLean County; by Frances G. Sitherwood concerning the electoral commission in 1876; and by Marie S. White concerning David Davis and the Compromise of 1877, 1972.

3,761. McLean County Home Bureau
Records. 1918-50s. 6 ft.
Open. No guide.
McLean County Historical Society.
Minutes, ledgers, notebooks, receipts, reports, photos, scrapbooks, clippings, and genealogies of the Bureau, a rural and farm women's organization founded in 1918 to promote homemaking skills and crafts. The name has since been changed to McLean County Homemakers Extension Association.

3,762. Religion
Collection. Ca. 1898-1949. 6 items.
Open. Unpublished guide.
McLean County Historical Society.
Historical sketches by [Mrs.] Elizabeth Coale concerning the Quakers in Dawson township, 1898; by Mrs. E. E. Cox concerning the Chenoa Methodist Church, 1949; by Maureen Day concerning the American passion play; by Eileen Dixon concerning the history of the Centennial Christian Church; by Imogene Holder concerning the First Methodist Church of Bloomington; and by Mrs. Gordon H. Read concerning the temperance movement in McLean County.

3,763. Travel
Collection. Nd. 4 items.
Open. Unpublished guide.
McLean County Historical Society.
Includes personal essays and reminiscences by Hillary Conroy concerning travel via stagecoach; by Emeline Dodson concerning a trip to California in 1850; by M. W. Packard concerning John Wells Dawson, Anna Cheney Dawson, and travel to California; and by Frances G. Sitherwood about Tierra del Fuego.

3,764. Women
Collection. 1800s-1900s. 20 items.
Open. Unpublished guide.
McLean County Historical Society.
Chiefly reminiscences and recollections, the collection also includes correspondence, essays, clippings, and programs. Contains items by Charles Capen about Sarah Raymond Fitzwilliam, a Bloomington teacher; by Sarah Raymond Fitzwilliam concerning bird songs of central Illinois, 1894, and the origin of the song "Arkansas Traveler"; by Mrs. F. W. Disbrow concerning Sarah Josepha (Buell) Hale; by Ida Evans about the life of her mother Mary Lucretia Parke Evans; by William Hammit concerning Florence (Fifer) Bohrer, the first woman elected to the Illinois State Senate; by Mrs. L. S. Rupert concerning the medical career of Caroline Flatt; and by Frances G. Sitherwood concerning the life and works of Mary Lyon. Also includes a prospectus for a biographical study of playwright Rachel Crothers by Blake Leach, a brief sketch of the life of Amalia Kraft Graff by Margaret McCain-Snow; an anonymous biography of Hannah Orme Newell; a biography of Melinda Rankin by J. C. Rayburn, dealing with the Presbyterian Church; and biographical data compiled by Ethel Sinclair about Josephine Sanders, who used the stage name Irene Delroy, and her interest in music.

3,765. Woman's Foreign Missionary Society, Central Illinois Conference, Kankakee District
Records. 1885-1933. 2 vols. and 1 envelope.
Open. Unpublished guide.
United Methodist Central Illinois Conference Commission on Archives and History.
The national WFMS was founded in the 1870s to support mission work abroad. Minutes, ledger consisting of reports by local societies to the District secretary, and other reports of the District.

3,766. Woman's Foreign Missionary Society, Illinois Conference, Decatur District
Records. 1885-1940. 3 vols.
Open. Unpublished guide.
United Methodist Central Illinois Conference Commission on Archives and History.
Minutes and secretary's records.

3,767. Woman's Home Missionary Society, Central Illinois Conference
Records. 1889-1939. 5 vols.
Open. Unpublished guide.
United Methodist Central Illinois Conference Commission on Archives and History.
The WHMS was founded in 1882 in Cincinnati to minister to the needs of city women and girls for recreation, worship, and study; the Central Illinois Conference of the WHMS was part of the Methodist Episcopal Church. Minutes; treasurer's books; programs of annual meetings in Bloomington and Jacksonville, IL; and the will of Helen E. Hazen.

3,768. Woman's Home Missionary Society, Illinois Conference, Decatur District
Records. 1910-40. 1 box, 2 ledgers, and 2 envelopes.
Open. Unpublished guide.
United Methodist Central Illinois Conference Commission on Archives and History.
Founded in Cincinnati in 1882, the Society initially supported settlement houses and other projects to minister to women and girls in cities. Minutes, treasurer's report, receipts and payments, and monthly auxiliary reports. By 1940 the Society had a membership of 263,000 women and girls and annual receipts of $1,250,000.

3,769. Woman's Society of Christian Service, Illinois Conference
Records. 1940-67. 5 boxes and 10 vols.
Open. Unpublished guide.
United Methodist Central Illinois Conference Commission on Archives and History.
The WSCS was formed in 1940 through the merger of seven Methodist women's groups. Minutes of the WSCS executive committee of the Illinois Conference, treasurer's book, reports and programs of annual meetings, correspondence, directory, yearbook, and other records. Includes treasurer's records of the WSCS Bloomington District and minutes, financial records, and other records of the WSCS Peoria District.

3,770. Women's Missionary Association
Records. Nd. No size given.
Open. Unpublished guide.
United Methodist Central Illinois Conference Commission on Archives and History.
Records of the Women's Missionary Association in the Branch Society of the Lower Wabash Conference of the Church of the United Brethren in Christ contain secretary record books, 1879-1918; a manuscript history of the first 30 years of the Lower Wabash Branch; and printed material, including constitutions and bylaws, convention records, bulletins, and handbooks. The Lower Wabash Branch of the WMA was part of the national organization, which merged with a similar organization of the former Evangelical Church in 1947 to become the Women's Society of World Service.

CARBONDALE

3,771. Boyle, Kay
Papers. Nd. 25 ft.
Partially closed. Unpublished guide.
Southern Illinois University Archives.
The winner of two O. Henry short story awards and now a professor emeritus at San Francisco State University, Boyle (1902-) was investigated during the McCarthy era for alleged communist sympathies. Correspondence, manuscripts, photos, clippings, and books. Includes Boyle's books *Being Geniuses Together, The Long Walk at San Francisco State,* and *The Underground Woman.* Born in Minneapolis, Boyle traveled extensively. Her first husband was a Frenchman she met in Cincinnati. From 1927 to 1941 she lived in France where she knew Ernest Hemingway, James Joyce, Samuel Beckett, and other authors. After her second marriage, to Laurence Vail, ended in divorce, she married Joseph Franckenstein, an Austrian. Her correspondence with Franckenstein during the McCarthy period will be closed until 10 years after her death.

3,772. Clapp, Elsie Ripley
Papers. 1910-43. 2 cu.ft.
Open. Unpublished guide.
Southern Illinois University Archives.
[Miss] Clapp (1879-1965), a teacher and writer, studied with educator John Dewey from 1907 until 1927. Correspondence; notes and published material about Dewey; employment and biographical data; material on Rosemary, Ballard, and Arthurdale schools; and photos. After Dewey's retirement Clapp taught in high schools and developed plans to experiment with Dewey's concepts of progressive education. With the help of Eleanor Roosevelt, Clapp became head of the school system in Arthurdale, WV, a resettlement project for unemployed miners. In 1936, the Arthurdale school became part of the state school system, and Clapp became editor of the educational magazine *Progressive Education.*

3,773. Dunham, Katherine Mary
Papers. 1919-68. 106 boxes.
Partially restricted. Unpublished guide.
Southern Illinois University Archives.
Dunham (1910-) choreographed and danced in stage productions and motion pictures; opened dance schools in New York City, Stockholm, Paris, and Rome; and founded The Chicago Negro School of Ballet Theatre and the Dunham Company. Correspondence, manuscripts, notes, records of the Dunham Company, photos, drawings, sketches, art material, and other papers. Letters Dunham wrote to her parents while she and her troupe were working in Hollywood in 1942 contain information about racial discrimination in the movie industry. Born in Chicago, Dunham enrolled at the University of Chicago in 1928 to major in anthropology with special emphasis in dance. In 1935-36 she received a fellowship from the Rosenwald and Guggenheim foundations for master's research in Jamaica and Haiti. Her theatrical career began in 1934. Pupils from her Chicago School formed the core of her group, the Dunham Company. Dunham choreographed and danced in *Tropics, Le Jazz Hot, Pardon My Sarong,* and *Carnival of Rhythm.* She is the author of several books, including *Las Danzas de Haiti* and *Island Possessed.* In 1967 she was appointed cultural affairs consultant in public administration and metropolitan affairs at Southern Illinois University at Edwardsville.

3,774. International Ladies' Garment Workers' Union
Records. 1937-64. 12 boxes.
Open. Unpublished guide.
Southern Illinois University Archives.
Minutes and attendance records of the ILGWU's

educational committee and records of the committee's programs, regional summer meetings, and university institutes.

3,775. Kelley, Edith (Summers)
Papers. 1903-58. 0.5 cu.ft.
Open. Unpublished guide.
Southern Illinois University Archives.
Kelley (1884-1956), an author, served as Upton Sinclair's secretary for two years while beginning her own writing career. Correspondence; manuscripts of parts of two novels, short stories, poetry, and a play; clippings; and a review of her novel *Weeds* (1923). Born in the Canadian province of Ontario, Edith Summers graduated from the University of Toronto in 1903 and moved to New York where she worked for Sinclair. For part of the period she lived in Helicon Hall in Englewood, NJ, a commune of young writers, artists, and others. There she met author Sinclair Lewis. She married Lewis's friend and roommate Allan Updegraff in 1908. After a six-year marriage to Updegraff, she married C. F. Kelley, a sculptor. The couple farmed in Kentucky, New Jersey, and California where she wrote *Weeds,* which was based on her experiences living among the poor in Kentucky. She wrote another novel, short stories, and poems, none of which were published during her lifetime. The second novel, *The Devil's Hand,* was published by Southern Illinois University Press in 1974. Also available on microfilm.

3,776. Rittenhouse, Isabella Maud
Papers. 1881-95. 6 vols.
Open. Unpublished guide.
Southern Illinois University Archives.
Diary kept by Rittenhouse, a Cairo, IL, resident, during her youth. The diary was published as Richard Lee Strait, ed., *Maud* (New York: Macmillan, 1939).

3,777. Topping, Helen F.
Papers. 1872-1968. 18.5 cu.ft.
Open. Unpublished guide.
Southern Illinois University Archives.
[Miss] Topping (1889-), the daughter of two American missionaries, became a religious worker, missionary, and teacher. Correspondence, sermons, addresses, articles, book typescripts, name and address files, subscription orders for books, photos, scrapbooks, post cards, clippings, and other papers. Born in Rochester, NY, Topping moved with her family to Japan in 1895. She returned to the US six years later and attended the Francis W. Parker School in Chicago. In 1925 she became a follower of Japanese evangelist Toyohiko Kagawa, serving as his English secretary and organizer in America. She edited and distributed Kagawa's English language magazine *Friends of Jesus* and calendar. Topping also worked in the Philippines and taught at Clark College in Atlanta.

3,778. Woodhull, Victoria
Papers. 1870-1962. 1 cu.ft.
Open. Unpublished guide.
Southern Illinois University Archives.
Victoria California (Claflin) Woodhull (1838-1927) was an author, editor, lecturer, and feminist who, with her sister Tennessee Claflin, opened a New York City bank and stock brokerage office in 1870. Correspondence, articles, horoscope readings, astrology information, and published pamphlets and speeches. Woodhull and Claflin published *Woodhull and Claflin's Weekly,* which advocated equal rights for women, a single standard of morality, free love, and an end to prostitution. Woodhull was the presidential candidate of the Equal Rights party in 1872. In 1871 she spoke on woman suffrage before the US House Judiciary Committee and began to give lectures on that topic. The collection includes notes concerning charges of adultery Woodhull leveled against Henry Ward Beecher, pastor of Plymouth Church in New York City. Also available on microfilm.

CHICAGO

3,779. Archives
Records. 1908- . No size given.
Closed. No guide.
Alpha Kappa Alpha Sorority.
Founded in 1908, the Sorority is committed to rendering service to others. Correspondence, files, photos, pamphlets, and other records.

3,780. Archives
Records. 1967- . No size given.
Closed. No guide.
American Society for Nursing Service Administrators.
Minutes, administrative files, correspondence, biographical data, newsletters, and pamphlets of the Society, which was founded in 1967 to facilitate the exchange of ideas and information among persons involved in nursing service administration. The Society also provides a vehicle through which nursing service administrators may speak on nursing and health care issues.

3,781. Burnham, Daniel Hudson
Papers. 1890-1912. 21 vols.
Open. Unpublished guide.
Art Institute of Chicago, Burnham Library.
Office correspondence and journals of Burnham (1846-1912), an architect and city planner. Includes letters concerned with the Woman's Building at the World's Columbian Exposition in Chicago in 1893, which was designed by Lois Lilley Howe.

3,782. Griffin, Marion Mahony
Papers. Ca. 1942-47. Ca. 5 ft.
Open. Unpublished guide.
Art Institute of Chicago, Burnham Library.
Griffin (1871-1962), an artist and architect, was married to Walter Burley Griffin. Includes her unpublished biography of her husband; notes, drawings, and renderings for her husband's architectural publications; project plans for transforming Chicago into a livable industrial center; and drawings for private residences, planned towns, and a world fellowship center in New Hampshire.

3,783. Exhibition Catalogs
Collection. 1892- . No size given.
Open. Unpublished guide.
Art Institute of Chicago, Ryerson Library.
Catalogs for exhibitions by women artists and sculptors include those for exhibitions of the National Association of Women Artists in New York, 1892; the Women Etchers of America in Boston, 1887; sculpture by Gertrude V. Whitney in Chicago, 1923; the Woman's Club of Evanston, IL, 1941; Women As Artists in the 20th Century in Chicago, 1973; and Illinois women painters, 1928. Also includes scrapbooks of clippings on art and artists in the Chicago area.

3,784. Chicago Board of Education Proceedings
Records. 1867-1977. Ca. 135 vols.
Open. No guide.
Chicago Board of Education Library.
Reports of meetings, legal and financial statements, correspondence, statistics, and resolutions of the Board, which was established in 1840 to supervise public education in Chicago. Records concern all aspects of administration of the finances, buildings and grounds, supplies, personnel, curriculum, and programs of the public schools.

3,785. Chicago Schools
Records. 1854-1978. 8 vols.
Open. No guide.
Chicago Board of Education Library.
Consists of looseleaf notebooks containing an alphabetical listing of all public schools in Chicago, brief descriptions of their building and site, a list of principals, and discussions of special programs. Includes explanations of why the schools were named after prominent people, including Hannah (Greenebaum) Solomon; Kate Douglas Wiggin; Mary Jane McLeod Bethune; Lucy Flower; Ellen Henrietta Richards, an author who organized a domestic science curriculum for Chicago; Beulah Shoesmith, mathematics department chairman at Hyde Park High School from 1909 to 1945; Helen Maley Hefferan, a board of education member from 1923 to 1941 and president of the Illinois PTA; Mary Margaret Bartelme, the first woman judge in Illinois and a juvenile court judge from 1923 to 1933; and Theolene Simpson, who organized the city program for education of pregnant girls.

3,786. Curriculum Guides
Collection. 1866-1978. Ca. 10,000 microfiche.
Open. No guide.
Chicago Board of Education Library.
Consists of officially adopted curriculum guides and study outlines for use in kindergarten through 12th grade. The guides reflect such changes in curriculum as the introduction of domestic science and industrial training for girls and the fluctuation of course offerings in art, music, nature study, and other subjects.

3,787. School Reports
Records. 1854-1968. 59 vols.
Open. No guide.
Chicago Board of Education Library.
Consists of annual reports by the president of the Board of Education, the superintendent of schools, and the heads of major departments of the school system. These reports contain financial records, statistics, data on buildings and supplies, lists of personnel, and histories of the school system. Includes information on women members of the board of education, including [Mrs.] Ellen Mitchell, who in 1888 was the first woman appointee; Jane Addams; Anita (Emmons) McCormick Blaine; Helen Maley [Mrs. William H.] Hefferan; Mrs. Walter Heineman; and [Mrs.] Marge Wild, the current major negotiator with the teachers' union. Other records include information on Ella Flagg Young, the principal of the Chicago Normal School, the superintendent of schools from 1909 to 1915, and the only woman superintendent in Chicago's history; the development of specialized programs for education of handicapped children, immigrants, and school dropouts; the influence of organizations such as the Woman's City Club and the Citizens Schools Committee on reform efforts in the school system; and the relations of the board of education with teachers' organizations and the organization of the Chicago Teachers' Federation and Chicago Teachers' Union.

3,788. Chicago Conservatory College
Records. 1917- . 24 drawers and ca. 15 oversize vols.
Access restricted. No guide.
Chicago Conservatory College.
Founded in 1857, the College offers BA and MA degrees for students who plan careers as music teachers, composers, performers, and conductors. Includes financial ledgers, 1952-, and other financial records; student records; correspondence; invitations; registration material; yearbooks and catalogs, 1917-; commencement announcements; and programs. Women formerly made up 20 to 30 percent of the College's student enrollment, but presently 50 percent of the students are women. Among the well-known women connected with the College are Fannie Bloomfield-Zeisler, Leontyne Price, and Gladys Swarthout.

3,789. Rizzo School of Music
Records. Ca. 1949-60. 7 ft.
Access restricted. No guide.
Chicago Conservatory College.
Student records, including transcripts, correspondence, and other items; musical

compositions; and examinations of the School, which was closed in ca. 1960.

3,790. Student Musical Compositions and Theses
Collection. Ca. 1938-76. Ca. 175 items.
Open. No guide.
Chicago Conservatory College.
Original graduate and undergraduate musical compositions and graduate theses on music history and theory, approximately half of which were composed or written by women students, many of whom were members of religious communities.

3,791. Abraham Lincoln Centre
Records. 1938-67. 220 items.
Open. Card catalog.
Chicago Historical Society.
Minutes of the board of trustees, treasurer's reports, and other records of the Centre, a Chicago social settlement founded in 1905 by Jenkin Lloyd Jones and the All Souls Church. Social worker Thyra Edwards and many other women, including volunteers, have worked at the Centre; numerous settlement residents have been women; and the facility has offered domestic science and other classes and club activities for neighborhood women and girls.

3,792. Action Committee for Decent Childcare
Records. Ca. 1970-72. 2 ft.
Open. Card catalog.
Chicago Historical Society.
Correspondence, notes and research files, pamphlets, and various published items of the Committee, an interest group in Chicago established in ca. 1970 by women who needed day-care facilities for their children or who worked in day-care centers. The Committee worked for legislation to improve day-care service in the city; its activities were coordinated by Heather Booth, an activist who founded Midwest Academy in Chicago, which offers classes in social action organizing. The Committee has been discontinued.

3,793. Aero Club of Illinois
Records. 1909-48. 7.5 ft.
Open. Inventory.
Chicago Historical Society.
Financial records, membership data, correspondence, reports, specifications, and clippings of this affiliate of the Aero Club of America. Chartered in 1910, the Illinois group fostered the development of aeronautical science and advanced aviation through conferences, contests, meets, and other activities. Of special interest were international competitions held at Chicago's Grant Park in 1911 and at Clearing, IL, in 1912 in which women aviators competed. The Aero Club was disbanded in 1951.

3,794. Albums of Remembrance
Collection. 1829-91. 9 vols.
Open. Card catalog.
Chicago Historical Society.
Collection includes albums kept by Vernera Leonard, Sarah C. Runyon, Catherine M. Wolcott, and Bertha A. Patterson with verses, greetings from friends, and illustrations; an autograph album kept by Elizabeth Emerson Atwater with signatures of statesmen and suffragists; and albums kept by Laura Virginia Johnson containing social and family memorabilia from prominent Chicagoans.

3,795. American Association of University Women, Chicago Branch
Records. 1889-1968. 6 document cases and 3 vols.
Open. Card catalog.
Chicago Historical Society.
Minutes, financial and membership records, correspondence, and reports of the Chicago branch of the AAUW, which was founded in 1889. The chapter earlier had been known as the Chicago Association of Collegiate Alumnae.

3,796. Arché Club
Records. 1891-1976. 6 document cases and 3 vols.
Open. Shelflist.
Chicago Historical Society.
Minutes, financial records, correspondence, yearbooks, and scrapbooks of this women's educational and social group, which was organized in 1891. Members have studied art, history, and literary criticism.

3,797. Authors and Editors
Collection. 1830-1934. Ca. 52 items.
Open. Card catalog.
Chicago Historical Society.
Represented among the correspondence and miscellaneous published and unpublished literary writings of authors and editors are Catherine E. Beecher, Myra C. [Mrs. James B.] Bradwell, Lydia Maria [Mrs. David Lee] Child, Mary Mapes Dodge, Zona Gale, Sarah Josepha [Mrs. David] Hale, Julia Ward [Mrs. Samuel Gridley] Howe, Harriet Martineau, Harriet Monroe, and Lydia Huntley Sigourney. Letter of Sigourney, for example, includes comments on women's work, teachers in the West, and the acceptance by *Harper's* magazine of one of her manuscripts for publication.

3,798. Barnes, Clifford Webster
Papers. 1904-44. 4 document cases.
Open. Card catalog.
Chicago Historical Society.
Correspondence, notes, minutes, reports, and printed matter of Barnes (1864-1944), an educator, social worker, and civic leader. Relates chiefly to his membership in the Committee of Fifteen, a citizen's group that precipitated the investigation between 1911 and 1916 of Chicago's prostitution and vice district, and his activities in such organizations as the Legislative Voters League of Illinois. Barnes also was a Hull-House resident in 1893 and 1894.

3,799. Barnett, Claude A.
Papers. 1920-67. 200 ft.
Open. Inventory.
Chicago Historical Society.
Correspondence, speeches, reports, financial records, news releases, and clippings of Barnett (1889-1967), the director of the Associated Negro Press, which was headquartered in Chicago and produced news releases for most of the black newspapers in the US; he was also director from 1960 to 1963 of the World News Service, which provided news releases to over 100 African newspapers, and was active in social and political affairs on local, national, and international levels. Collection pertains to the black press, education, the arts, economic conditions, black businesses, and international affairs and includes information on black clubwomen and professional women and women reporters, editors, and publishers.

Represented in Barnett's extensive correspondence files are Associated Negro Press correspondents Inez Baskin in Montgomery, AL, 1957-59; S. Grace Bradley; Marguerite Cartwright; Alice Dunnigan in Washington, DC, 1946-64; Thyra Edwards and Gladys P. Graham in New York; Lethia Fleming; and Thelma Thurston Gorham. World News Service correspondents include Irene Diggs, and ANP/WNS correspondents represented are Nancy Cunard in Paris and Jocelyn Francois at Port-au-Prince, Haiti. Represented in other correspondence and clippings are such women in entertainment and art as Margaret Sims, Fay Jackson, Katherine Dunham, Marian Anderson, Zelma Watson George, Eva Jessye, Eslanda [Mrs. Paul] Robeson, and Mercedes Walker. Also includes items about Chicago lawyer Edith Sampson.

Collection contains news releases of the ANP and WNS and other files pertaining to such philanthropic and social organizations as the National Association of Negro Women, 1934-38; Alpha Kappa Alpha, 1936-61; Delta Sigma Theta, 1930-57; Phi Delta Kappa, 1938-62; Zeta Phi Beta, 1938-60; the YWCA; the Phillis Wheatley Foundation, 1932-65; and the National Council of Negro Women, 1937-62.

3,800. Barnett, Etta (Moten)
Papers. 1934-66. 10 document cases.
Open. Inventory.
Chicago Historical Society.
Correspondence, contracts, expense accounts, travel schedules, programs, and news releases of Barnett, a concert singer, actress, and lecturer who was known professionally as Etta Moten. She was married to Claude A. Barnett, the director of the Associated Negro Press and the World News Service. Correspondents include her husband, Eva Jessye, officers of Alpha Kappa Alpha, officials of the American-African Institute, and other friends, relatives, and associates.

3,801. Benton House
Records. 1892-1964. 1300 items.
Open. Card catalog.
Chicago Historical Society.
Board minutes and reports, correspondence, photos, clippings, and other records of this social settlement, which was founded in 1907 as the Providence Day Nursery and was operated by the Episcopal Diocese of Chicago. The House later was called the House of Happiness and then Benton House. Women were active in all phases of the settlement's programs. Records provide information on social and economic conditions in the Bridgeport area of Chicago. Includes minutes of the House of Happiness Guild.

3,802. Blair, Sarah Maria Seymour
Papers. 1851-1921. Ca. 20 items.
Open. Card catalog.
Chicago Historical Society.
Papers of [Mrs. William] Blair (1832-1923), a Chicago social leader, contain her personal reminiscences of early city history, including the Chicago fire of 1871; correspondence; her religious writings and Bible lessons; and a notebook of guests and menus at the Blair residence. Also includes a paper she read at the Second Presbyterian Church in Chicago in 1911 regarding the founding of the Woman's Presbyterian Board of Missions of the Northwest.

3,803. Bowen, Louise Hadduck (deKoven)
Papers. 1864-1953. 4 vols. and ca. 10 items.
Open. Card catalog.
Chicago Historical Society.
Correspondence, reminiscences, phonograph records, minutes, reports, legal records, and scrapbooks containing correspondence, photos, clippings, and published material of [Mrs. Joseph T.] Bowen (1859-1953), a Chicago social reformer and civic leader who worked closely with Jane Addams and was treasurer of the Hull-House Association from 1893 to 1953. She participated in most of Chicago's reform activities after 1893, including establishment of the city juvenile court in 1899, the founding of the Woman's City Club in 1910, and programs of the Chicago and Illinois Equal Suffrage Associations, the Juvenile Protective Association, and other groups. Collection contains information about her personal life, her writings, her work at Hull-House, and extensive recollections of Chicago.

3,804. Boyden, Emily Maria Blakeslee
Papers. 1826-93. 43 items.
Open. Card catalog.
Chicago Historical Society.
Correspondence of Boyden (1828-?), a Chicago author of verses, songs, and children's books,

concerns her needlework exhibit at the World's Columbian Exposition in 1893 and some of her verses and songs. Includes one letter she received from Frances Willard.

3,805. Brotherhood of Sleeping Car Porters, Chicago Division
Records. 1925-56. 13 ft.
Open. Inventory.
Chicago Historical Society.
Included in financial and membership records, correspondence, reports, and news releases of this labor union, established nationally in 1925 and in Chicago in 1931, are seven document cases containing records, ca. 1931-56, of the International Ladies Auxiliary to the Brotherhood of Sleeping Car Porters. Contains correspondence of Auxiliary president [Mrs.] Halena Wilson primarily about internal matters of the organization. Also includes her correspondence with political and civil rights leaders about wage and price controls, consumer education, the poll tax, and civil rights.

3,806. Chapin Hall for Children
Records. 1857-1964. 15 ft.
Open. Card catalog.
Chicago Historical Society.
Founded in 1860 and first known as the Chicago Nursery and Half Orphan Asylum, the Hall provided housing and care for children with only one parent, for orphans, and for others requiring day-care services. Record book containing bylaws, lists of officers and members, and children's records of the lady managers of the Chicago Nursery and Half Orphan Asylum, 1868-71, and minutes, legal and financial records, correspondence, reports, client records, studies, and articles, which provide data on the client population of the Hall and of Ridge Farm Preventorium in Lake Forest, IL. The records also provide information on social workers, administrators, and board members, many of whom were women.

3,807. Chern, Fanny I.
Papers. 1949-72. 30 items.
Open. Card catalog.
Chicago Historical Society.
Correspondence, articles, and published material of Chern, a clubwoman, volunteer, and civic leader involved in the charitable and social service work of various Jewish agencies, particularly the Charles H. and Rachel M. Schwab Rehabilitation Hospital in Chicago.

3,808. Chicago Bible Society
Records. 1848-1906. 6 vols.
Open. Card catalog.
Chicago Historical Society.
Founded in 1835 to distribute Bibles to families, hotels, sailing vessels, jails, railroad stations, and poorhouses, the Society reorganized in 1837 to become a branch of the American Bible Society under the name Chicago and Vicinity Bible Society. In 1840 it reassumed its shorter name. During the Civil War the Society particularly focused on work among Union and Confederate soldiers. Record books contain bylaws, articles of agreement, annual reports, and minutes. Also includes minutes, 1894-1901, and an annual report of the Women's Council of the Chicago Bible Society. The Society included both men and women among its members.

3,809. Chicago Commons
Records. 1893-1966. 23 ft. and 3 vols.
Open. Unpublished guide.
Chicago Historical Society.
Founded in 1894 by Graham Taylor, this social settlement located on Chicago's near north side worked to "provide a center for higher civic and social life, to initiate and maintain religious, educational, and philanthropic enterprises . . . and to investigate and improve conditions in the industrial district of Chicago." Minutes, correspondence, reports, neighborhood census data, surveys, research data and materials, employment applications, camp items, and printed matter and publications document neighborhood social and economic conditions and racial and ethnic changes. Also contains material about the settlement work of Lea Demarest Taylor, who succeeded her father Graham Taylor and served as head resident of Chicago Commons from 1921 until 1954, and minutes and other records of the Chicago Commons Woman's Club, 1894-1921.

Among Chicago Commons programs were a kindergarten and day nursery, a milk station, clubs for women and girls, and classes in domestic culture, arts and crafts, and other fields of study. For many years the settlement also operated the Chicago School of Civics and Philanthropy, founded by Graham Taylor in 1903.

3,810. Chicago Council on Community Nursing
Records. 1919-72. 8 document cases.
Open. Card catalog.
Chicago Historical Society.
Founded in 1919 as the Central Council for Nursing Education and renamed the Chicago Council on Community Nursing in 1946, this group of public health, practical, and other community nurses has worked to improve nursing services in the metropolitan Chicago area and to promote the professional development of its membership. Minutes, financial records, correspondence, and photos.

3,811. Chicago Exchange for Woman's Work
Records. Ca. 1880. 1 vol.
Open. Card catalog.
Chicago Historical Society.
Volume listing names and addresses of managers and members of the Exchange, which was founded in 1879 to provide retail sales outlets for handmade articles made by needy women. The Exchange also maintained a sewing school for girls.

3,812. Chicago Fire
Collection. 1871-1928. Ca. 20 items.
Open. Card catalog.
Chicago Historical Society.
Among sources documenting the Chicago fire are reminiscences of Jennie Elizabeth Otis Counselman and Catherine Jefferson; one letter of Aurelia R. King; correspondence of Myron Winslow Reed with Mrs. William O. Carpenter, describing the fire and women's status and position in Indiana; and letters of Frances L. Roberts to her mother Sarah L. Roberts, containing details about relief efforts after the fire.

3,813. Chicago Lung Association
Records. 1906-77. 5 ft.
Open. Shelflist.
Chicago Historical Society.
Minutes, financial records, correspondence, histories, reports, surveys and statistics, research proposals, legislative files, scrapbooks, and clippings of the Lung Association reflect its concern for research and public education regarding lung disease and also provide information about medical services it offered for lung-related illnesses. The Association was founded in 1906 as the Chicago Tuberculosis Institute, which grew from a tuberculosis committee organized by the local Visiting Nurse Association in 1903. It was renamed the Tuberculosis Institute of Chicago and Cook County in 1937 and later became known as the Chicago Lung Association. Women on its founding board included Mrs. Arthur T. Aldis, Mrs. E. L. Gaylord, Mrs. L. A. Hamlin, and [Miss] Harriet Fulmer; after the death of physician Theodore Sachs in 1916, his wife assumed his leadership role on the board. Women also were and continue to be active in the Association's auxiliary. Association programs have included support of open-air and fresh-air schools in Chicago; dispensaries and public health nursing; maintenance of sanitariums, one of which was donated and supported for three years by Eudora Hull Spaulding; and research and education. The Association is now affiliated with the National Tuberculosis Association and operates the local Christmas Seal program.

3,814. Chicago Peace Society
Records. 1909-19. 5 vols. and 900 items.
Open. Card catalog.
Chicago Historical Society.
Constitution, minutes, cashbook detailing expenditures and membership dues, reports, addresses, journals, and clippings of the Society, a branch of the American Peace Society devoted to spreading the doctrine of peace between nations and among individuals. The group was founded in 1910 by members of a predecessor Chicago peace society; local members of the American Peace Society, which was organized in 1902; and local delegates to the National Peace Congress. Women represented in the collection include Jane Addams, who helped found the Society and served as an executive committee member and honorary vice-president, and members Louise deKoven [Mrs. Joseph T.] Bowen, [Mrs.] Ellen M. Henrotin, Mary E. McDowell, Mary Rozet Smith, Mary J. Wilmarth, and Ella Flagg Young.

3,815. Chicago Polonia
Oral history. 1976-77. 6 ft. and ca. 300 tapes.
Open. Published and unpublished guides.
Chicago Historical Society.
Collection of taped interviews, included with interview translations, index data, and notes, in which Polish Americans (most of them women) now residing in Chicago discuss aspects of the immigrant experience, particularly for those who came to the US between the 1880s and the 1930s. A number of those interviewed are members of women's religious orders. Topics discussed include pre-immigration conditions and views of the US, reasons for leaving their homeland, passage and arrival, working and living conditions, religious life, family relationships, social organization, and attitudinal changes. The collection was created under Title IX of the Elementary and Secondary Education Act. See *Master Index for the Oral History Archives of Chicago Polonia* (Chicago, 1977).

3,816. Chicago Society of Decorative Art
Records. 1878-ca. 1884. 1 vol. and ca. 50 items.
Open. Card catalog.
Chicago Historical Society.
Established in 1878 to "seek, encourage, and develop female talent, tastes, and industry in all kinds of decorative art," the Society was patterned after a similar group in New York City and sponsored classes, exhibitions, and a work and sales room. Classes in various arts were offered for the education of teachers who in turn pledged to give their services voluntarily to the mission schools of the city. Constitution and amendments, articles of association, minute book, presidential circulars, the first paper read before the Society by its president, and committee reports. Members included Janet Hopkins [Mrs. Benjamin F.] Ayer, Ellen Martin [Mrs. Charles] Henrotin, Emily Eames [Mrs. Franklin] MacVeagh, Katharine Patrick [Mrs. Joseph] Medill, and Bertha Honoré [Mrs. Potter] Palmer.

3,817. Chicago Teachers' Federation
Records. 1864-1968. 39 ft.
Open. Inventory.
Chicago Historical Society.
Minutes, correspondence, reports, and other records of Chicago's first teachers' union, which was organized in 1897 and disbanded in 1969, relate to the Federation's efforts to assure proper funding for teachers' salaries, to advance the teachers' pension fund, to secure a tenure law, and to advance the position of teachers and improve

the schools. Also contains the papers, including the unpublished autobiography, of Margaret Angela Haley, a vice-president and business representative for the Federation who also was a women's rights and suffrage activist.

3,818. Chicago Teachers Union
Records. 1914-71. 63 ft.
Open. No guide.
Chicago Historical Society.
Minutes, financial records, correspondence, reports, speeches, photos, press releases and clippings, and publications of the Union. Also includes financial and other records of the School Clerks Union of Chicago, 1930-67; minutes and leaflets of the Federation of Women High School Teachers, 1914-37; and a scrapbook of clippings concerning education and unionism between 1914 and 1928 compiled by Margaret Angela Haley, a business representative for the Chicago Teachers' Federation.

3,819. Chicago Temperance Union
Records. 1894. 288 items.
Open. Card catalog.
Chicago Historical Society.
Correspondence and broadsides of the Temperance Union pertain to a temperance demonstration it organized. Correspondence, which chiefly concerns ticket sales, shows that Lucy L. Flower, Bertha Honoré Palmer, and Frances Willard were among subscribers.

3,820. Chicago Woman's Club
Records. 1876-1962. 23 ft.
Open. Card catalog.
Chicago Historical Society.
Records of the Club, a prestigious charitable, civic, cultural, and social group founded in 1876, include minutes, legal and financial records, correspondence, reports, photos, scrapbooks, and clippings. Among Club members were Bertha Honoré [Mrs. Potter] Palmer and Louise deKoven [Mrs. Joseph T.] Bowen. The Club was closely associated with settlement house reforms, education, the juvenile court, the kindergarten movement, reform of penal institutions, relief, and woman's suffrage.

3,821. Chicago Women's Liberation Union
Records. 1968-77. 25 ft.
Open. Shelflist.
Chicago Historical Society.
The Union was founded in 1968 as a radical, anticapitalist feminist organization; it disbanded in 1977. Correspondence; staff reports on such topics as child care, employment, health, and legal issues; office log; clippings and press releases; leaflets; newsletters; and issues of the newspaper *Womankind.*

3,822. Christopher House
Records. 1917-66. 3 document boxes.
Open. Card catalog.
Chicago Historical Society.
Records of Christopher House, a settlement in the Lake View community of Chicago founded in 1907 by the First Presbyterian Church of Evanston as an outgrowth of a mission Sunday school for social and religious work. Contains minutes, fund-raising and other financial records, reports, correspondence, pamphlets, and copies of the Christopher House *News.* Also includes information on the settlement's nursery school and its programs for pre-teens and teens. Among services and activities offered were a kindergarten, a modified milk station, and sewing, cooking, home hygiene, and millinery classes.

3,823. Citizens Committee on the Juvenile Court
Records. 1962-72. 23 document cases.
Open. Shelflist.
Chicago Historical Society.
Minutes, reports, correspondence, clippings, and printed matter of the Committee, created in ca. 1962 by the executive committee of the circuit court of Cook County to investigate operations of the juvenile court. Originally it was named the Citizens Committee on the Family Court. Records include papers of the Committee's executive director Eleanor Macey.

3,824. Citizens Schools Committee
Records. 1911-72. 20 ft.
Open. Card catalog.
Chicago Historical Society.
Minutes, reports, correspondence, clippings, and various published items of the Committee, a watchdog citizen organization formed in 1933 when a tax delinquency threatened closure of legally mandated school programs in Chicago. Originally called the Citizens' Save Our Schools Committee, the group later assumed its shorter name and has continued to work for improvements in the Chicago public school system. Collection also includes papers of Chicago teacher and activist Mary Herrick as well as material, chiefly from the 1920s and 1930s, on the Chicago Teachers Union and other teachers' organizations.

3,825. Clark, Herma Naomi
Papers. 1899-1959. Ca. 6400 items.
Open. Unpublished guide.
Chicago Historical Society.
Personal and business correspondence, book and play manuscripts, speeches, notes, and readers' contributions of Clark (1871-1959), an author and journalist who worked for the William Blair family from 1897 to 1923 as reader, companion, and secretary. Collection chiefly relates to her column "When Chicago was Young," which was published in the *Chicago Tribune* from 1929 to 1959. Her correspondents include Bess (Streeter) Aldrich, Fanny Butcher, Louise (deKoven) Bowen, Edna Ferber, Alice Gerstenberg, and Bessie Louise Pierce.

3,826. Clement, Grace Groves
Papers. 1877-1950. 30 items.
Open. Card catalog.
Chicago Historical Society.
Correspondence, minutes, and other organizational records of Clement pertain to the work of her mother Adelaide B. Groves, a teacher and social worker, at the Cook County, IL, Jail School and in the Woman's Christian Association, a predecessor of the YWCA, in Chicago. Included is a record of two meetings in 1877 of the WCA and the Central Homeopathic Society regarding a fund-raising carnival.

3,827. Connelly, Polly
Papers. 1965-74. 7 boxes.
Partially restricted. Shelflist.
Chicago Historical Society.
Personal correspondence, speeches and articles, appointment books, research material, audio cassettes, videotapes, photos, clippings, and various feminist publications of Connelly (1940-), a feminist who has been active in the women's liberation movement since 1965; she cofounded the publication *Cassandra* with Ti-Grace Atkinson in 1967. Connelly also was the first woman member of the Chicago Flat Janitors Union, American Federation of Labor, Local 1, and has worked as a labor organizer. Her papers include information about her involvement in other groups, such as the Abortion Coalition, the Chicago Women's Liberation Union, the Chicago Peace Action Coalition, the (Chicago) Loop YWCA, the National Organization for Women, and Women Mobilized for Change.

3,828. The Cordon
Records. 1922-57. 1 box and 3 vols.
Open. Card catalog.
Chicago Historical Society.
The Cordon was founded in 1915 by women who had studios in Chicago's Fine Arts Building, which then was the center of the city's arts community; the club was created to foster independence and to "guard and protect self expression beyond domestic bounds." Articles of association; yearbooks containing bylaws and lists of committees, officers, and members; minutes; financial reports; a guest book; and scrapbooks filled with announcements of social and cultural events offered by The Cordon, clippings, club newsletters, and bulletins. Members, chosen on the basis of achievement in the arts and the professions, included Edith Abbott, Jane Addams, Jessie Binford, Louise (deKoven) Bowen, Mary (Hastings) Bradley, Sophonisba P. Breckinridge, Alice Gerstenberg, Alice Hamilton, Mary McDowell, Harriet Monroe, Agnes Hope Pillsbury, and Fannie Bloomfield Feister.

3,829. Correspondence
Collection. 1835-86. Ca. 200 items.
Open. Card catalog.
Chicago Historical Society.
Small collections, individually cataloged, of correspondence of 19th-century women pertaining to settlement of Chicago, travel to Illinois and throughout the Midwest, Indian warfare, conditions during the Civil War, and daily life and business activity in the region. Included are Civil War letters of Lizzie Little Avery, recollections of Fort Dearborn by Susan M. Callis, family correspondence of Harriet Louise Hubbard Hamilton, descriptions of daily life and activities of Margaret A. Hoard, European travel letters of Harriet Kimball, comments on religious conditions in Chicago in 1832 by Caroline Strong, and accounts of a trip to Detroit and living conditions in Illinois in 1852 by Vienna Y. Winslow.

3,830. Counselbaum, Stella Levinkind
Papers. 1950-53. Ca. 350 items.
Open. Card catalog.
Chicago Historical Society.
Correspondence, biographical data, and certificates of awards in race relations of Counselbaum (ca. 1910-), a social worker involved with the National Conference of Christians and Jews. Includes letters of Mary McLeod Bethune.

3,831. Dahlem, Margaret M.
Papers. 1910-1919. 1 box and 1 vol.
Open. Card catalog.
Chicago Historical Society.
Papers reflecting the high school and early womanhood experiences of Peggy Dahlem (ca. 1898-) include letters she received from army private Harry "Ellie" E. Stevens between 1917 and 1919; a scrapbook she kept about her student years at John Marshall High School in Chicago, containing notes from friends, photos, report cards, and school programs, 1912-16; and a memory book album of photos, programs, and personal mementos, 1910-18.

3,832. Davis, William James
Papers. 1879-1914. 5 vols. and 240 items.
Open. Inventory.
Chicago Historical Society.
Correspondence of Davis (1844-1919), a theater manager, includes professional and personal correspondence of his wife Jessie (Bartlett) Davis (1859-1905) and of Jessie Davis's niece Belle Fremont Davis (1879-1901) pertaining to their careers as performers and to family matters.

3,833. Dean, Emily (Washburn)
Papers. 1902-57. Ca. 430 items.
Open. Inventory.
Chicago Historical Society.
Papers of Dean (1870-1958), a social worker, consist of her correspondence, financial records, addresses and speeches, reports, lists, and various published items. Includes material on the Juvenile

Protective Association and its long-time executive Jessie F. Binford as well as information about the Republican Women's Club.

3,834. Diaries
Collection. Ca. 1852-1920. Ca. 88 vols.
Open. Card catalog.
Chicago Historical Society.
Diaries and journals, cataloged individually, include those kept by Sara A. Blakely while touring the Midwest as a member of a concert troupe, 1852-54; personal diaries of Emma Briggs reflecting her teaching experiences in Wisconsin, 1863-72; one volume kept by Jennie E. Hariford as a 13-year-old girl in Aurora, IL; diary of Laura Bartlett Kane describing her life and work on a Lake County, IL, farm, 1879-84; daybook of Nellie Rhue containing business accounts of a store in 1859; one volume kept by Emily Frankstein describing social life and family in Chicago's Hyde Park neighborhood, 1918-20; and 65 volumes of Jane Stowell [Mrs. Samuel R.] Haven containing her notes on family events, travels, Chicago social history, and the Chicago fire, 1865-1905.

3,835. Edwards, Thyra
Papers. 1932-42. 1 ft.
Open. Card catalog.
Chicago Historical Society.
Correspondence, research notes, notes for her unpublished autobiography, photos, scrapbook, and printed matter of Edwards, a black social worker and journalist. Papers document her career at the Abraham Lincoln Centre, a Chicago social settlement founded by Jenkin Lloyd Jones, and her research into housing discrimination, venereal disease control in Chicago, and social conditions in Europe in the 1930s. She participated in efforts to relocate Loyalists in Mexico after the Spanish Civil War.

3,836. Emerson House
Records. 1910-60. 1 document case.
Open. Card catalog.
Chicago Historical Society.
Minutes of the board and of regular, annual, and special meetings; financial records; and other material of Emerson House, a social settlement established in 1910 in the West Town community of Chicago; the facility merged in 1948 with Chicago Commons. Emerson House maintained regular mothers' meetings, a woman's club, and domestic science classes. Many women residents and volunteers were involved in its programs.

3,837. Erie Neighborhood House
Records. 1905-66. 400 items.
Open. Card catalog.
Chicago Historical Society.
Founded in 1915, the House was a Presbyterian social settlement in the West Town community of Chicago. Board minutes, reports, correspondence, contracts regarding a new settlement building, and photos. Includes information on the Erie Chapel Sunday school.

3,838. Fine Art Opera Club
Records. 1938-60. 1 folder.
Open. Card catalog.
Chicago Historical Society.
Constitution, minutes, committee lists, photos of members, and programs of the Club, which was organized in Chicago in 1923 by a group of student singers to present operas, to further the musical knowledge of young singers, and to offer them opportunities not readily available through professional productions or organizations. Women were actively involved in the organization and Zerline Muhlman [Mrs. Fritz] Metzger was a founding member. Apparently the Club was affiliated with and conducted fund-raising efforts for the Fine Art Opera Company. Later the Club became known simply as the Fine Art Opera.

3,839. Fitzpatrick, John
Papers. 1887-1965. 18 ft., ca. 175 items, and 6 microfilm reels.
Open. Inventory.
Chicago Historical Society.
Papers of Fitzpatrick (1872-1946), who was president from 1902 to 1946 of the Chicago Federation of Labor, a group established in 1896, include his correspondence with socialist Nellie Baldwin, 1917-19; with Mary Harris Jones, 1921-28; with Margaret Dreier Robins, 1911-32; and with [Mrs.] Lillie May Burgess of Hyattsville, MD, the proprietor of the Mother Jones Rest Home. Also contains financial records; general minutes, 1903-22, and executive board minutes and reports, 1911-18, of the Chicago Federation of Labor; minutes, 1887-90, and correspondence of the Trade and Labor Assembly of Chicago, which preceded the CFL; and broadsides. Other records in the collection pertaining to women include those of the Chicago Teachers' Federation and the Amalgamated Clothing Workers of America.

3,840. Flavelle, Mary E.
Papers. 1858-1917. 17 vols.
Open. Card catalog.
Chicago Historical Society.
Correspondence, diaries, and legal and financial records pertain to Chicago real estate holdings and world travels of Flavelle (1847-1914), a Chicago socialite.

3,841. Flower, Lucy Louisa (Coues)
Papers. Ca. 1859-1912. 5 vols.
Open. Card catalog.
Chicago Historical Society.
Scrapbooks of Flower (1837-1921), an educator and social reformer, chiefly contain clippings on social service and educational topics. Also includes a ledger listing grades she gave her students while she was teaching in Madison, WI.

3,842. Francis W. Parker School
Records. 1884-1960. 80 ft.
Open. Inventory.
Chicago Historical Society.
Correspondence, speeches, reports, and printed material of this progressive private elementary and secondary school in Chicago, founded in 1901 by Anita McCormick Blaine and named for educator Francis Wayland Parker; the records relate to school administration and to the activities of the Progressive Education Association. Includes papers of Flora J. Cooke, who taught at the School from 1899 to 1901 and then served as its principal until 1934. Also contains extensive material on the School's founder and patron Anita McCormick Blaine.

3,843. Friends of American Writers
Records. 1922-61. 9 ft. and 6 oversize vols.
Open. Shelflist.
Chicago Historical Society.
Minutes, financial records, membership records, correspondence, reports, speeches, photos, clippings, and newsletters of this women's literary organization, which was founded in 1922 to study American literature and encourage excellence in writing.

3,844. Friendship House
Records. 1937-74. 40 ft.
Closed. Card catalog.
Chicago Historical Society.
Staff meeting and annual convention reports, correspondence, photos, and other records of the Chicago national headquarters of Friendship House, a Roman Catholic interracial movement established by Baroness Catherine de Hueck Doherty that seeks to improve race relations, particularly by helping the white community to understand and eliminate racial injustice. The first Friendship House was established in Toronto, Canada, in 1932 by Baroness Doherty; the first American Friendship House was established in New York in 1938; and the Chicago Friendship House was founded in 1942. Collection includes records from Friendship Houses in Shreveport, LA; New York City; Portland, OR; and Washington, DC. The records pertain to operation of the Houses, the position of the Roman Catholic Church in matters of race and social change, and, more specifically, to racial discrimination in Chicago-area schools, hospitals, and housing. Betty Schneider succeeded Baroness Doherty as national director of Friendship House in 1951. Other women associated with the movement have included Mary Dolan and Betty Plank.

3,845. Gads Hill Center
Records. 1898-1963. 11 ft.
Open. Register.
Chicago Historical Society.
Minutes, financial records, reports, correspondence, photos, and published material of this social settlement in Chicago that was operated by the Presbyterian Church. Founded in 1898, Gads Hill has served a community of predominantly Polish ancestry for most of its history. Records include information on Ruth Austin and Meta K. Schweibert, former head residents at Gads Hill.

3,846. Gaines, Irene (McCoy)
Papers. 1917-1968. 4 ft.
Open. Register.
Chicago Historical Society.
Correspondence, speeches, reports, clippings, and published material of Gaines (ca. 1896-1964), a Chicago Negro clubwoman and Republican party candidate, reflect her involvement in the National Association of Colored Women's Clubs, the Chicago Council of Negro Organizations, and the Chicago and Northern District Association of Colored Women.

3,847. Gerstenberg, Alice
Papers. 1962. 696-page item.
Open. Card catalog.
Chicago Historical Society.
Unpublished autobiography of Gerstenberg (1885-1972), a playwright active in drama and the little theater movement, contains her reminiscences about Chicago social and cultural life, particularly theater.

3,848. Gerstenberg, Julia (Wieschendorff)
Papers. 1872-1942. Ca. 130 items.
Open. Card catalog.
Chicago Historical Society.
Correspondence, clippings, and other papers of [Mrs. E.] Gerstenberg (1861-1938), a Chicago social leader and mother of playwright Alice Gerstenberg (1885-1972), pertain to social and cultural leaders and organizations in the city, including the Arts Club of Chicago and the Chicago Opera.

3,849. Glessner, Frances (Macbeth)
Papers. 1872-1921. 53 vols.
Access restricted. Card catalog.
Chicago Historical Society.
Journals of Glessner (1848-1932), a socially prominent Chicago resident with interests in the arts, contain occasional entries by her husband John J. Glessner, an officer of International Harvester Company. Included are their comments on social activities, family life, the operation of the household, illnesses, travels, summers spent in New Hampshire, and the construction of their home in Chicago, which was designed by Henry Hobson Richardson. Collection also includes a diary kept from 1872 to 1880 by Frances Glessner's sister Helen Macbeth.

3,850. Gold Star Mothers
Records. 1919-33. 0.5 ft.
Open. Card catalog.

Chicago Historical Society.
The Mothers, a Chicago memorial organization for women who lost sons in WWI, was a predecessor to the national American Gold Star Mothers group founded in 1928. Correspondence and statistics relate to the Gold Star memorial, the Gold Star Sons of the Chicago Historical Society, and the Gold Star Sons of the University of Chicago. Separately filed are two volumes compiled by Lillian A. White entitled "Chicago Overseas Dead and Chicago Gold Star Mothers."

3,851. Graphics
Collection. 1600s- . Ca. 500,000 items.
Open. Partial card catalog.
Chicago Historical Society.
Included in this collection of prints, broadsides, cartoons, posters, and other illustrations are ca. 450,000 photos pertaining primarily to Chicago history. Arranged by subject, items depicting women may be found throughout the collection, but particularly under the following headings: amusements, beauty contests, biography, celebrations, charities, clubs, ethnic groups, exhibitions (arts and crafts), children, home activities, social service and settlements, suffragettes, theatricals, and women. Separately filed are items pertaining to the Visiting Nurse Association, the Infant Welfare Society, and the Associated Negro Press.

3,852. Hart, Pearl M.
Papers. Ca. 1940s-60s. Ca. 60 ft.
Closed. No guide.
Chicago Historical Society.
Legal files of Hart (1890-1975), a lawyer who was one of the first women probation officers in Chicago. She pioneered juvenile court reforms and actively participated in the Chicago Committee to Defend the Bill of Rights. She was also a founding member, first chairman, and general counsel of The Midwest Committee for Protection of Foreign Born.

A graduate of the Metropolitan Business College and the John Marshall Law School, Hart was admitted to the bar in 1914 with a specialty in criminal law. From 1915 to 1917 she was an adult probation officer and then became the first public defender to be appointed to the Women's Court. She crusaded for women's rights. Hart's concern with child welfare and juvenile delinquency also encouraged her involvement in drafting Illinois children's adoption and other laws. In addition, she became active in deportation and denaturalization cases and issues relating to human rights, especially rights for homosexuals. Hart also served as counsel for many witnesses brought before the House Committee to Investigate Un-American Activities and was involved with the summer school of painting in Saugatuck, MI.

3,853. Hedlund, Marilou
Papers. 1917-75. 23 document cases.
Open. Card catalog.
Chicago Historical Society.
Papers of Hedlund, who served as Democratic alderman from Chicago's 48th ward from 1971 to 1974, consist of her correspondence, reports, memos, constituent and general reference files, and clippings. Included in her office files are items pertaining to neighborhood organizations, political issues and city governance, and constituent services.

3,854. Herstein, Lillian
Papers. 1920-58. 225 items.
Open. Card catalog.
Chicago Historical Society.
Speeches, articles, clippings, and various published items of Herstein (1886-) relate to her teaching career and activities as a union leader with the Women's Trade Union League of Chicago.

3,855. Hubbard, Hannah Root
Papers. 1863-83. 1 vol.
Open. Card catalog.
Chicago Historical Society.
Journal report of Mothers' Meetings, an organization concerned with the religious and moral improvement of children as well as the duties of mothers. Hubbard, who organized mothers' groups in Chicago, apparently kept the record book.

3,856. Huncke, Olga H.
Papers. 1911-74. 4 folders and 8 vols.
Open. Card catalog.
Chicago Historical Society.
Correspondence and scrapbooks containing correspondence, photos, wedding and other invitations, band programs, and clippings of Huncke (1881?-1974), a kindergarten teacher at the Haines School in Chicago's Chinatown district who, after her retirement in 1956, worked at the nursery school of the Chinese Christian Union Church. The scrapbooks reflect her relationships with families of her students and events in the Chinese community; one volume is devoted to Ruth Ann Koesun and follows her life from childhood through her ballet career. At the Haines School, Huncke became especially known for developing a children's rhythm band, which was called upon to perform at various benefits, particularly for China war relief in the 1940s. The rhythm band also performed for Madame Chiang Kai-shek when she visited Chicago in 1943.

3,857. Hyde Park Travel Club
Records. 1891-1971. 11 document cases and 8 vols.
Open. Card catalog.
Chicago Historical Society.
Founded in 1888 as the Hyde Park Travel Class, this Chicago social group attracted members interested in world travel. The Club was also affiliated with the Illinois Federation of Women's Clubs. Minutes, correspondence, scrapbooks, clippings, and miscellaneous published material.

3,858. Illinois Conference on Legislation
Records. 1931-66. 33 items.
Open. Card catalog.
Chicago Historical Society.
Bylaws, minutes, and other items of the Conference, formed in ca. 1949 as a clearinghouse of information for groups lobbying the Illinois General Assembly for statewide public welfare legislation. The Conference was operated chiefly by older clubwomen.

3,859. Illinois Home Economics Association
Records. 1921-1970. 7 ft.
Open. Shelflist.
Chicago Historical Society.
Annual reports, minutes, financial records, correspondence, committee records, and printed matter of this affiliate of the American Home Economics Association established in ca. 1921. Contains information about home economics as a profession, activities of the Association in promotion of vocational education, and consumer education. Also includes records of the Illinois Future Homemakers of America.

3,860. Illinois League of Women Voters
Records. 1921-61. 1 vol. and 3400 items.
Open. Register.
Chicago Historical Society.
Minutes, financial records, correspondence, and various published items of this state body of the LWV established in 1921. Also includes minutes and reports of the Cook County LWV.

3,861. Illinois Training School for Nurses
Records. 1880-85. 50 items.
Open. Card catalog.
Chicago Historical Society.
Records of the Training School, founded in 1880 and affiliated with Cook County Hospital in Chicago, were compiled by its first president Margaret Marsden [Mrs. Charles B.] Lawrence and contain correspondence, reports, invitations, and a subscribers' list. Among prominent Chicago women involved with the Training School were physician Sarah Hackett Stevenson, Lucy L. [Mrs. James Monroe] Flower, and Sarah Peck [Mrs. Edward] Wright.

3,862. Illinois Woman's Press Association
Records. 1923-51. 3 vols.
Open. Card catalog.
Chicago Historical Society.
Organized in 1885, largely through the efforts of Julia Holmes Smith, as a western branch of the National Association of Women Journalists, this group has worked to advance literary interests of women throughout Illinois. Minutes, treasurer's annual reports, financial statements, committee reports, and clippings from the publication *Pen Points*. Founding members of the Association included Mary A. Ahrens, Susan B. Anthony, Julia Ward Howe, Caroline Alden Huling, Sarah Hackett Stevenson, and Frances E. Willard; other members have included newspaper and magazine writers, editors, and artists. The Association is affiliated with the Illinois Federation of Women's Clubs, the International League of Press Clubs, and the National Editorial Association; it operates primarily within the Chicago area.

3,863. Infant Welfare Society of Chicago
Records. 1903-74. 20 document cases and 45 vols.
Open. Shelflist.
Chicago Historical Society.
Minutes, correspondence, reports, case histories, photos, scrapbooks, and published items of this volunteer organization founded in 1903 as the Milk Commission of the Children's Hospital of Chicago. Members worked to improve child health and welfare in the city.

3,864. Isham Family
Papers. 1873-1959. 4 document cases.
Open. Card catalog.
Chicago Historical Society.
Personal and family correspondence, diaries, photos, and genealogical material of Charles Isham (1853-1919), the son-in-law of Abraham Lincoln's son Robert Todd Lincoln. Includes letters to his wife, 1928-38, and correspondence of his daughter-in-law Leahalma [Mrs. Lincoln] Isham, 1921-29. Other family correspondence and papers relate to portraits of Abraham and Mary (Todd) Lincoln.

3,865. Jewish Community Centers of Chicago
Records. 1904-54. 25 document cases.
Open. Inventory.
Chicago Historical Society.
Minutes, financial and membership records, correspondence, surveys, reports, general working files, and scrapbooks of the Centers, an umbrella social service agency for Jewish residents of Chicago and suburbs, include information on the Daughters of Zion, the Women's Auxiliary, the Institute Woman's Council, Rosa Raisa scholarship competitions, and the agency's nursery program, especially during WWII. Founded in 1903 as the Chicago Hebrew Institute to educate Jewish immigrants in the English language, American customs, and citizenship and to meet their religious needs, the organization was renamed the Jewish People's Institute in 1922, and in 1946 it assumed the name Jewish Community Centers of Chicago. Current programs at the agency's 17 branch centers cover a broad range of educational, social, and cultural activities.

3,866. Jewish Home for the Aged (B.M.Z. of Chicago)
Records. 1899-1972. 53 ft. and 99 microfilm reels.
Open. Inventory.
Chicago Historical Society.
Minutes, financial records, admissions and patient records, personnel files, surveys and statistics, scrapbooks, and newsletters of the Home, a residence for elderly Jews (chiefly Orthodox) in Chicago. Founded in 1899, the first Home residence was opened in 1903 and until 1964 was known as Orthodox Jewish Home for the Aged, B.M.Z. (Beth Moshav Z'Keinim). Includes records of women residents, nurses, and other staff members and records of the B.M.Z. Women's Club.

3,867. Kalo Shop
Records. 1920-70. Ca. 1200 items.
Open. Shelflist.
Chicago Historical Society.
Established in 1900 in Park Ridge, IL, by [Mrs.] Clara Barck Welles, the Kalo Shop built a national reputation for designing and making handwrought silver and jewelry; Welles' designs were continued after her retirement in 1940. Collection contains sketches and patterns for silver hollowware and flatware and an award to Welles from the National Conservation Exposition in 1913 for the best collection of handwrought silver in the arts and crafts category.

3,868. Klio Association
Records. 1887-1901. 3 vols.
Open. Card catalog.
Chicago Historical Society.
Minutes, reports, lists of officers, and photos of the Association, a women's group established in 1887 to nurture mutual improvement in literature and music.

3,869. Ladies' Springfield Soldiers' Aid Society
Records. 1862-89. 9 items.
Open. Card catalog.
Chicago Historical Society.
Annual report, treasurer's report, a letter, photos, clippings, and an invitation of the Society, which was organized in 1861 in Springfield, IL, to pursue Civil War relief work. Members collected food, money, and material for sewing.

3,870. Laflin Family
Papers. 1842-1974. 5 ft.
Open. Inventory.
Chicago Historical Society.
Papers of the Laflin family, whose members were residents of Chicago and Lake Forest, IL, chiefly consist of the papers of Josephine Knowland [Mrs. Louis Ellsworth, Sr.] Laflin, a Lake Forest clubwoman and socialite who held a dramatics circle at her home. Includes correspondence about social and family matters and travel in Europe and the Middle East, diaries kept from 1890 to 1907, articles and speeches, and business records concerning Laflin family real estate.

3,871. Legal Documents
Collection. 1676-1917. Ca. 200 items.
Open. Card catalog.
Chicago Historical Society.
Legal documents and other items pertaining to women include birth registers of St. Anne's parish in Fort Chartres, IL, 1721-65, and of St. Joseph's parish in Prairie de Rocher, IL, 1761-98; marriage contracts, certificates, bonds, and licenses, some with supporting biographical and genealogical information, of such famous people as Abraham and Mary (Todd) Lincoln and unknown persons in Chicago, Ohio, Wisconsin, and New France, 1764-1881; slave ship manifests, bills of sale, indentures, manumission papers, and related correspondence, 1732-1861; and property documents, including indentures for land transfers in 1835 and 1888, a release of dower rights dated 1838, miscellaneous real estate papers dated 1858 to 1917, and an inventory of the estate of [Mrs.] Mary Paddy dated 1676.

3,872. Lillie, Frances Crane
Papers. 1886-1977. Ca. 8 document cases.
Open. Inventory.
Chicago Historical Society.
[Mrs. Frank Rattray] Lillie (1869-1958) was a social leader and philanthropist. Personal correspondence; notebooks she kept on her religious interests, particularly her conversion to Roman Catholicism, and Bible study; and reports and financial records relating to the operation of her estate in Wheeling, IL, and the administration of the Crane Fund for Widows and Children, a private trust that operated the farm "Childerly" in Wheeling. Also contains papers of other members of the Crane family, including correspondence, a European travel diary from 1877, and the typescript "Letters to her Daughter" of Mary Prentice Crane, wife of Richard T. Crane; correspondence, a European travel diary from 1877, and a diary kept from 1849 to 1893 by Elize Prentice Crane; and a 486-page manuscript biography of Frances Crane Lillie, written in 1977, by her daughter Mary Prentice (Lillie) Barrows.

3,873. Malek, Leona A.
Papers. 1918-44. 42 items.
Open. Card catalog.
Chicago Historical Society.
Cards, certificates, invitations, and other items of Malek, who wrote a homemaker's column for the *Chicago Herald and Examiner* under the pseudonym Prudence Penny. Consists chiefly of her membership cards for various professional and social organizations.

3,874. Marillac House
Records. 1945-70. 3 ft.
Open. Card catalog.
Chicago Historical Society.
Board minutes, financial and program attendance records, correspondence, studies, and reports of the House, a settlement located on Chicago's west side, which was founded in 1946 and is operated by the Sisters of Charity of St. Vincent de Paul. Collection also provides information about the operation of the settlement's branch in the Rockwell Gardens Homes, which is administered by the Chicago Housing Authority.

3,875. Mary McDowell Settlement
Records. 1894-1968. 25 ft.
Open. Shelflist.
Chicago Historical Society.
Annual and departmental reports, board minutes, correspondence, case records, articles and speeches, and photos of this social settlement, which was founded in 1894 by the Philanthropic Committee of the Christian Union of the University of Chicago and first known as the University of Chicago Settlement. Its name was changed officially in 1956. Also contains the personal papers of Mary Eliza McDowell, the head resident of the Settlement from 1894 to 1936, reflecting her career as a social worker, union organizer, and civic reformer active in race relations and public sanitation. Under McDowell's guidance, the Settlement conducted investigations into various phases of neighborhood life, working for reforms in such areas as housing, streets and refuse, playgrounds, and public schools. Settlement programs included a kindergarten, providing a resident nurse, citizenship school, a summer tent for sick babies, women's clubs and social activities, and classes in cooking, sewing, music, and dancing. Material in the collection also reveals that the Settlement Woman's Club maintained a loan fund for its members and was instrumental in securing public parks and baths.

3,876. Mary Noble Club
Records. 1875-1935. 2 vols.
Open. Card catalog.
Chicago Historical Society.
Minutes, membership lists, histories, and published items of the Club, a women's social and educational group founded in 1875 on Chicago's south side to promote "mutual improvement and social intercourse." Members supported the Municipal Art League in Chicago and the Kenwood Improvement Association, a neighborhood citizen's organization.

3,877. The Matheon
Records. 1896-1916. 5 vols.
Open. Card catalog.
Chicago Historical Society.
Minutes, correspondence, reports, and a guest book of this women's club, which was founded in 1896. Originally devoted to the study of art and music, The Matheon later affiliated with the GFWC and became involved in child welfare reform and the playground movement.

3,878. Metzger, Zerline Muhlman
Papers. Nd. Ca. 5 items.
Open. Card catalog.
Chicago Historical Society.
Biographical data and clippings of [Mrs. Fritz] Metzger (1891-), a voice teacher who sang under the stage name Anna Busch in German light opera productions at Chicago's Bush Temple Theater; she also founded the Fine Art Opera in Chicago in 1921 and served as its opera producer. In addition, she organized and was a producer for the Chicago Park District Children's Opera Guild from 1948 to 1956. She has been music critic for the *Abendpost,* a German language newspaper.

3,879. Moore, Ruth
Papers. 1955-70. 294 items.
Open. Card catalog.
Chicago Historical Society.
Papers of Moore (ca. 1920-), a journalist and author who is married to Raymond W. Garbe, contain reports, articles, studies, clippings, and by-line columns she wrote pertaining to city planning, urban renewal, housing, and historic preservation. Moore uses her maiden name in her work.

3,880. Morgan, Anna
Papers. 1893-1934. 72 items.
Open. Card catalog.
Chicago Historical Society.
Correspondence and scrapbooks of Morgan (1851-1936), a dramatic reader for Redpath Lyceum programs from 1880 to 1883, a drama teacher at the Chicago Conservatory from 1884 until 1888, and the founder in 1889 of Anna Morgan Studio, where she continued to work for 36 years. Included is her social and literary correspondence with Jane Addams, Edith Rockefeller McCormick, and Bertha Honoré Palmer.

3,881. Morton Family
Papers. 1830-1945. 22 ft.
Access restricted. Register.
Chicago Historical Society.
Correspondence, diaries, financial records, photos, scrapbooks, clippings, and other papers of the Morton family chiefly relate to J. Sterling Morton (1832-1902), a former US secretary of agriculture and the founder of Arbor Day, and his sons Joy Morton (1855-1934), the founder of the Morton Salt Company; Paul Morton (1857-1911), a railroad official and former US secretary of the navy; and Carl (1865-1900) and Mark Morton (1858-1951). Material relating to women is scattered throughout the collection and includes family correspondence, genealogies, photo albums, and family scrapbooks such as that of Carrie Lake Morton, the daughter-in-law of Sterling Morton. Her scrapbook

contains verse, articles, photos, and clippings dating from 1867 to 1906.

3,882. Morton, Sterling
Papers. 1891-1961. 22 ft.
Access restricted. Register.
Chicago Historical Society.
Correspondence, travel diaries, speeches, articles, photos, and clippings of Morton (1885-1961), a businessman and philanthropist, also include correspondence with his sister Jean (Morton) [Mrs. Joseph] Cudahy (?-1953) regarding the Morton Arboretum in Lisle, IL, of which she was chairman from 1948 to 1953; family correspondence relating to his wife Sophia Preston Owsley Morton (1891-1969) and their daughters Suzette (1911-), Carolyn (1915-21), and Millicent (1925-29); and family photo albums dating from 1910 to 1920.

3,883. National Association of Social Workers
Records. 1921-25. 10 ft.
Open. Inventory.
Chicago Historical Society.
The Chicago Area Chapter of the NASW was founded in 1924. Minutes, correspondence, reports, clippings, and printed items relate to issues in professional social work, such as education and professional standards, as well as public issues concerning social activism and welfare.

3,884. National Council of Jewish Women
Records. 1898-1968. 6 ft.
Open. Shelflist.
Chicago Historical Society.
The Chicago Section of the Council was founded in 1893 as an outgrowth of the Jewish Women's Congress at the World's Columbian Exposition; it has since functioned as a religious study, charitable, and social action organization. Annual reports, minutes, correspondence, scrapbooks, and published material. Also includes papers relating to Hannah Greenebaum [Mrs. Henry] Solomon, the founder and first president of the National Council of Jewish Women.

3,885. National League of American Pen Women
Records. 1927-42. 3 vols.
Open. Inventory.
Chicago Historical Society.
Minutes of this local branch of the League, a women's artistic and literary organization. The national body was established in 1897.

3,886. National Woman Suffrage Association
Records. 1880. 743-page vol.
Open. Card catalog.
Chicago Historical Society.
Compilation of documents relating to the meeting in Chicago's Farwell Hall in 1880 of the NWSA, a lobby for suffrage by constitutional amendment, includes correspondence from convention participants and invitees such as Matilda Joslyn Gage and Ernestine Louise Siismondi Potowski Rose, petitions to Congress and state legislatures describing individual disabilities suffered because of voting prohibitions, broadsides urging the Republican party to adopt a suffrage plank, tracts, and clippings. The NWSA was founded in 1869.

3,887. Nestor, Agnes
Papers. 1896-1954. 3 ft.
Open. Register.
Chicago Historical Society.
Correspondence, autobiographical manuscript, reports, clippings, and published material of Nestor (1880-1948), a trade union organizer and union official, pertain to her career in the local and International Glove Workers Union, the Chicago Women's Trade Union League, and the National Women's Trade Union League as well as to her political involvements and lobbying for protective legislation for women and children in Illinois.

3,888. Northwestern Soldiers' Fair
Records. 1863. 1 vol.
Open. Card catalog.
Chicago Historical Society.
Volume listing donors, gifts, and donations to the Fair, a Chicago fund-raising event for Civil War relief organized by Jane C. [Mrs. Abraham Holmes] Hoge and Mary A. [Mrs. Daniel Parker] Livermore. In a two-week period, the Fair raised more than $70,000 for the Sanitary Commission and became a model for similar fund-raising efforts throughout the country. Financial records of the Fair were kept by Martha J. [Mrs. Charles A.] Lamb.

3,889. Notable Women
Collection. 1845-1940. Ca. 70 items.
Open. Card catalog.
Chicago Historical Society.
Small collections, cataloged individually, include correspondence about Hull-House and other items of Jane Addams; personal correspondence of Sarah Bernhardt; business correspondence and a photo of Charlotte Saunders Cushman; personal letters of Varina Anne (Howell) Davis; one letter of Mary Baker Eddy; letter, handwritten verses, and personal sketches of Frances "Fanny" Anne Kemble; a letter to Harriet Beecher Stowe regarding the welfare of a black family in Washington, DC; and a photo of singer Jenny Lind.

3,890. Olander, Victor A.
Papers. 1898-1942. 38 ft.
Open. Register.
Chicago Historical Society.
Correspondence, financial records, minutes, and statistics of Olander (1873-1949), a labor union official who served as secretary-treasurer of the Illinois State Federation of Labor, relate to the administration of the State Federation of Labor, to the International Seamen's Union of America, and to the Illinois Emergency Relief Commission, the latter for the period from 1930 to 1935. Olander's correspondents include Margaret Haley, Agnes Nestor, and Mary Harris Jones.

3,891. Old Settlers Society of Chicago
Records. 1879-1928. 5 vols.
Open. Card catalog.
Chicago Historical Society.
Included with photos and a guest book containing signatures of persons who attended reunions of the Society are autobiographical notes and reminiscences of early residents of Chicago; 14 of these autobiographical sketches are about women. Among those represented are Annie Ward [Mrs. Theodore] Hubbard, Avis Dodge Blodgett, Emily Beaubien Le Beau, Sarah D. [Mrs. R. B.] Brown, Sophronia Conant [Mrs. Samuel] Hoard, Mary Kate Preble, and Cynthia Agatha Cooney, the daughter of Indian chief Alexander Robinson.

3,892. Olivet Community Center
Records. 1909-66. 3 ft.
Open. Card catalog.
Chicago Historical Society.
Bylaws; minutes of the board of trustees and staff meetings; budgetary, fund-raising, and other financial records; contributors' lists; reports and studies; and newsletters of the Center, a Presbyterian settlement house established in 1910 on Chicago's near north side. First known as Olivet Institute, the settlement has always offered a program that includes activities and events for neighborhood women and has utilized the services of women volunteers. Collection relates primarily to financial and administrative matters between the Center and the Presbyterian Church.

3,893. Palmer, Potter
Papers. 1902-20. 28 vols. and 1500 items.
Open. Inventory.
Chicago Historical Society.
Correspondence and financial records of Palmer (1826-1902), a Chicago businessman and civic leader, include papers of his wife Bertha Honoré Palmer (1849-1918) concerning her management of the Palmer estate following her husband's death. Contained are estate account books from 1904 to 1920, Bertha Palmer's investment account book from 1918, and indentures, agreements, and other business papers chiefly relating to real estate between 1849 and 1920.

3,894. Parkway Community House
Records. 1937-57. 1 ft.
Open. Card catalog.
Chicago Historical Society.
Board minutes, financial records, and correspondence of this social settlement, which was founded in 1938 and served the Grand Boulevard, Washington Park, and Kenwood communities of Chicago. The House was formerly known as the Good Shepherd Community Center.

3,895. Planned Parenthood Association
Records. 1959-77. 6 ft.
Open. Card catalog.
Chicago Historical Society.
Minutes, financial records, correspondence, and administrative and topical files of the Chicago chapter of Planned Parenthood founded in 1946. Records document its research and public education programs regarding family planning, sex education for marriage and parenthood, and birth control.

3,896. Pullman, Emily Caroline Minton
Papers. 1830-1913. 20 vols. and ca. 500 items.
Access restricted. Card catalog.
Chicago Historical Society.
Family correspondence, diaries, account books, genealogical data, and clippings of Pullman (1808-92), whose son George Mortimer Pullman invented the sleeper and other specialized railroad cars. Emily Pullman's papers reflect the lives of her husband and children and contain information about her personal and household accounts as well as Minton family genealogy. Includes papers relating to her daughter Emma Caroline (Pullman) [Mrs. William F.] Fluhrer.

3,897. Reminiscences
Collection. Ca. 1850-1970. Ca. 38 items.
Open. Card catalog.
Chicago Historical Society.
Reminiscences, primarily relating to early Chicago and Illinois pioneer life and history, include those of Emma Lilian Baird, who was a student of Mary Baker Eddy; Sarah Hollenback Boyd, who describes family experiences during the Indian outbreak of 1832 and the Black Hawk War; [Mrs.] Ann P. Hosmer, who recalls "sanitary work" in Chicago to aid Civil War soldiers, especially those from Illinois, and discusses her visits to hospitals near the front lines, the Ladies War Committee, and the Chicago Soldier's Home; Mary A. Penrose, wife of Lieutenant James W. Penrose, who provides details about US military headquarters at Fort Dearborn and a cholera epidemic; Bertha (Meyer) [Mrs. William] Severin, who writes about her father Henry C. Meyer and the Illinois Women's Athletic Club in 1923; Anna Sheldon Ogden West, who recalls the Chicago fire of 1871; Zdenka Cerny DeLacey, a cellist who grew up in Chicago; Francelia Colby, one of nine children whose parents moved to Illinois from New Hampshire, who comments about the abolition movement, the Civil War, the Lincoln-Douglas debates, and everyday experiences in Chicago; and Rose Howe, who describes the lives of Indians and Shabonee, a Pottawatomi chief.

3,898. Rew Family
Papers. Ca. 1863-1921. 12 document cases and 2 vols.
Open. Card catalog.
Chicago Historical Society.
Papers of the Rew family contain correspondence, diaries, and other material relating to business interests of Henry C. Rew (1839-1912), who developed gas manufacturing in Chicago, and items reflecting his activities as a Yale alumnus. Also contains papers of his son Irwin Rew, the president of the Natural Gas and Water Company, and Irwin Rew's wife Katherine Jones Rew pertaining to family and social acquaintances and European travel.

3,899. Sikes, Madeleine Wallin
Papers. 1880-1950. 3 document boxes.
Open. Card catalog.
Chicago Historical Society.
Correspondence, notes, poems and other original writings, reports, minutes, family photos, clippings, and handbills of Sikes (1868-1955), a Chicago clubwoman, relate to her involvement in such organizations as the League of Cook County Clubs, the National Consumers' League, the Chicago Child Saving League, the LWV, the Women's Club of Austin, the GFWC, the American Collegiate Association, the Chicago Woman's Club, and the Illinois Congress of Mothers. Also contains information about her work in developing educational, child labor, and protective legislation for women. Her correspondents include Jane Addams and Louise deKoven [Mrs. Joseph T.] Bowen.

3,900. South Shore Country Club
Records. 1905-75. 150 ft.
Open. Card catalog.
Chicago Historical Society.
Financial records, membership files, committee minutes, correspondence, and a scrapbook of this private social club on Chicago's lakefront, which was founded in 1905 and was the site of numerous cotillions and debutante parties before it closed in 1974. Membership files contain biographical information on elite Chicagoans.

3,901. Taylor, Lea Demarest
Papers. 1901-67. 25 document cases.
Open. Inventory.
Chicago Historical Society.
Papers of Taylor (1883-1975), a social worker whose father Graham Taylor was founder of Chicago Commons, contain correspondence, speeches, articles and other writings, minutes, reports, and clippings. Collection provides information about her career as head resident of Chicago Commons from 1921 to 1954 and her association with the Chicago Federation of Settlements, the Chicago Recreation Commission, the Citizens Schools Committee, the Welfare Council of Metropolitan Chicago, and the Women's Trade Union League.

3,902. Travel Accounts
Collection. 1837-1925. 5 items.
Open. Card catalog.
Chicago Historical Society.
Travel accounts include travel journals, 1889-1925, and an album of remembrance of Helen W. Boyden, the daughter of Emily Maria Blakeslee Boyden, who taught at Lincoln School in Chicago and published songs, stories, and poems of children; account by Angela Hopkins Hardy of a journey by covered wagon from Keene, OH, to Beardstown, IL, in June and July of 1837; and a diary kept by Rebecca Ketchum in 1853 while she was traveling from New York state to Oregon, detailing privations and hardships and describing other travelers she met along the way.

3,903. United Charities of Chicago
Records. 1867-1971. 30 ft.
Open. Inventory.
Chicago Historical Society.
Constitutions and bylaws, annual and special reports, minutes, correspondence, statistics, maps, clippings, and miscellaneous published material of United Charities, an umbrella organization founded in 1909 to pursue casework in the city; provide relief assistance, legal aid, and counseling; and operate a day nursery and summer camp. Collection also includes records of the UC's women's auxiliary group and records of such UC antecedent organizations as the Chicago Relief and Aid Society, founded in 1867, and the Chicago Bureau of Charities, founded in 1894.

3,904. Visiting Nurse Association of Chicago
Records. 1883-1968. 15 document cases and 1 vol.
Open. Inventory.
Chicago Historical Society.
Established in 1889 as an outgrowth of a home nursing program created by the local YWCA, the Visiting Nurse Association provides nursing and health care services to patients in their homes throughout Chicago, including postpartum and baby care. Correspondence, notes, statistical data, photos, scrapbook, bulletins, and brochures.

3,905. Welfare Council of Metropolitan Chicago
Records. 1914-76. 250 ft.
Open. Shelflist.
Chicago Historical Society.
Minutes, correspondence, reports, research studies, statistics, clippings, brochures, and published items pertain to the administration and work of the Welfare Council in the planning, research, and coordination of social service programs for the metropolitan Chicago area. Founded in 1914 as the Central Council of Social Agencies, this umbrella organization adopted the name Welfare Council of Metropolitan Chicago in 1948; in 1976 the group merged with the Community Fund of Chicago to form the United Way of Metropolitan Chicago. Records cover such topics as the elderly, education, child welfare, public health, neighborhood and community organization, day care, juvenile delinquency, rehabilitation of the handicapped, housing, race relations, recreation, relief, welfare and public assistance, and illegitimate births.

The Council has also functioned in setting standards for and evaluating member agencies as well as in assisting them to carry out their specific programs. Member agencies have included clubs, settlement houses and neighborhood centers, orphanages and homes for the aged, nurseries, hospitals, citizen organizations, rehabilitation centers, and the YMCA and the YWCA.

3,906. Willing Family
Papers. 1874-1932. Ca. 19 ft.
Open. No guide.
Chicago Historical Society.
Correspondence, diaries, account books, and other financial and business records of Henry Willing, Mark Willing, and other Willing relatives chiefly pertain to real estate, agricultural, and business investments. Included are financial and other records concerning the estates of Elizabeth Ann Willing, Evelyn P. Willing, Mary Jane Willing, and Frances S. Willing along with some business and personal papers of these women.

3,907. Wives of U.S. Presidents
Collection. 1840-1948. Ca. 143 items.
Open. Card catalog.
Chicago Historical Society.
Correspondence and other papers of the wives of American presidents include items of Louisa Catherine (Johnson) [Mrs. John Quincy] Adams, Frances (Folsom) [Mrs. Grover] Cleveland, Grace Anna [Mrs. Calvin] Coolidge, Mamie (Doud) [Mrs. Dwight David] Eisenhower, Mary (Todd) [Mrs. Abraham] Lincoln, Jane Means (Appleton) [Mrs. Franklin] Pierce, and Eleanor [Mrs. Franklin Delano] Roosevelt. Papers of Mary (Todd) Lincoln include her correspondence, reminiscences written in 1921 by her half sister Emily Todd Helm, a copy of her marriage license, and a commitment document for Bellevue Hospital.

3,908. Woman Suffrage
Collection. Ca. 1871-1910. Ca. 25 items.
Open. Card catalog.
Chicago Historical Society.
Papers chiefly consist of letters of leading suffragists, but also include antisuffrage material, all of which is cataloged by individual or organization. Represented are suffragists Susan Brownell Anthony, Ellen (Martin) Henrotin, Nina D. Hess, Mary Ashton Rice Livermore, Belva Ann Lockwood, Lucretia Mott, Elizabeth Cady Stanton, and Mary Edwards Walker. Antisuffrage papers include remarks made by Susan Augusta Fenimore Cooper at Cooperstown, NY, and manuscripts of Caroline Elizabeth Corbin, which also contain a position paper of the Illinois Association Opposed to the Extension of Suffrage to Women.

3,909. Woman's Christian Temperance Union
Records. 1879. 1 item.
Open. Card catalog.
Chicago Historical Society.
Petition that the Illinois WCTU presented to the Illinois House of Representatives and Senate requesting legislation to allow referenda on the licensing of those who wished to sell intoxicating beverages. The petition is in the form of a 10-foot scroll signed by men and women.

3,910. Woman's City Club of Chicago
Records. 1916-66. 1400 items.
Open. Card catalog.
Chicago Historical Society.
Minutes, membership records, correspondence, newsletters, and printed material of the Club, a women's civic and charitable organization founded in 1910. Records document the Club's involvement in housing, child welfare, sanitation, recreation, election reform, women's rights, and other public issues. Notable members of the group have included Hannah (Greenebaum) Solomon, Louise (deKoven) Bowen, Jane Addams, Anita McMormick Blaine, Alice Hamilton, Julia Lathrop, Grace Abbott, Lea Demarest Taylor, Edith Abbott, and Harriet Vittum.

3,911. Women and Education.
Collection. 1850-1933. 103 items.
Open. Card catalog.
Chicago Historical Society.
Papers relating to women's educational institutions and to women as students and teachers include teachers' records of the Chicago Board of Education listing the names of teachers who retired from the Chicago public school system, their date of retirement, and the schools in which they worked, 1933; records of the Dearborn Seminary in Chicago, describing scholarship and departments at this female academy, 1856-99; records of Grant Collegiate Institute, formerly Miss Grant's Private School, listing teachers, pupils, attendance, departments, and study programs, 1869-96; and an account book kept by David A. Smith with trustees of the Jacksonville Female Academy in Jacksonville, IL, 1850-53.

Also contains correspondence and related items of such teachers and students as Florence James [Mrs. Milward] Adams, Helen Humphrey, Alice Kirk, Leona E. Koehne, Lavinia S. Townsend, and Katherine E. Tuley; a diary kept by Nellie Law between 1891 and 1892 describing her school days at St. Mary's School in Knoxville, IL; and correspondence and a register listing the pupils of Frances Langdon Willard.

3,912. World's Columbian Exposition, Board of Lady Managers
Records. 1890-1904. 33 vols. and 2800 items.
Open. Card catalog.
Chicago Historical Society.
Minutes, membership books, correspondence, committee papers, reports, and lists of exhibitors of the Board of Lady Managers reflect the efforts of Board president Bertha Honoré Palmer and her colleagues in promoting women's activities and visibility at the Exposition, which was held in Chicago in 1893 to commemorate the 400th anniversary of Columbus's discovery of America. Under Palmer's leadership the Woman's Building became one of the biggest attractions at the Exposition, and cooperation between the Board and auxiliary congresses of women throughout the world brought many international speakers and visitors to Chicago.

3,913. World's Columbian Exposition, Women's Dormitory Association
Records. 1893. 2-page item.
Open. Card catalog.
Chicago Historical Society.
Certificate for one share of stock in the Association, which was organized in ca. 1893 to provide inexpensive housing for women coming to visit or work at the 1893 world's fair in Chicago.

3,914. Portraits in Psychoanalysis
Records. 1932- . 9 tapes.
Open. Published guide.
Chicago Institute for Psychoanalysis.
The Institute, which was founded in 1932, provides postgraduate medical training. Videotaped interviews with the following past and present Institute staff members: Therese Benedek, Helen McLean, Helen Ross, Edwin Eisler, Fritz Moellenhoff, and Louis B. Shapiro. See *Gitelson Film Library Catalog* (Chicago: Chicago Institute for Psychoanalysis, 1977).

3,915. Harsh, Vivian G.
Collection. 1800s- . Ca. 65,000 items.
Open. Published guide.
Chicago Public Library, Carter G. Woodsen Regional Library.
Includes manuscripts, speeches, tapes, phonodiscs, periodicals, pamphlets, posters, books, and art works pertaining to Afro-American history that Harsh, the chief librarian of the Hall branch of the Chicago Public Library, collected. Includes annual reports of the NAACP, 1910-70; Afro-American newspapers and journals, 1827-; items of the US Committee on Fair Employment, 1943-46; papers of the Chicago Urban League; and papers of the American Missionary Association. Part of the collection is available on microfilm. See *The Dictionary Catalogue of the Vivian G. Harsh Collection of Afro-American History and Literature* (Boston: G. K. Hall and Co., 1978).

3,916. Chicago Lawn Historical Society
Records. Ca. 1900-70s. 8 drawers.
Open. No guide.
Chicago Public Library, Chicago Lawn Branch.
Includes files of the Society, ca. 1935-; a film on Chicago Lawn, 1948; photos of women's social events and residences; and a scrapbook of the Chicago Lawn Woman's Club, which relates to a Club project to organize historical collections, 1976-78.

3,917. Ravenswood and Lakeview
Collection. Ca. 1880-1950. 25 drawers.
Open. No guide.
Chicago Public Library, Hild Regional Library.
Reminiscences, biographies, invitations, reports, photos, scrapbooks, clippings, yearbooks, programs, and pamphlets relate to northeastern Chicago. Includes information on women residents, and such women's organizations and clubs as the Ravenswood Women's Club.

3,918. Englewood Historical Society
Records. Ca. 1880-1940s. 1 cabinet and more than 200 items.
Open. No guide.
Chicago Public Library, Kelly Branch.
A constitution, correspondence, membership lists, and programs of the Society, ca. 1930-60; correspondence, histories, photos, circulars, and commencement programs of Chicago Teachers College, formerly Cook County Normal School, 1861-94; church records, including club records, Sunday school items, photos, and directories; school records, including photos, dedications, commencement programs and yearbooks, 1889-1950s; records of Englewood business and clubs, including the Englewood Women's Club; and an Englewood community handbook and history. Also contains local newspapers, including the *Normal Park Press,* 1888; *The Eye,* 1879-83; and the *Englewood News,* 1907.

3,919. Pullman and Roseland
Collection. Ca. 1880-1940. Ca. 1500 items.
Open. No guide.
Chicago Public Library, Pullman Branch.
Correspondence, biographical files, reminiscences, photos, clippings, and pamphlets relate to the history of Pullman and Roseland, two southeast Chicago communities. Contains the archives of the Pullman Library, including minutes of the executive board, 1916-21; membership records, 1883-86; photos; and scrapbooks. Also contains papers of Pullman librarians Mrs. Frederic L. Fake, who served from 1883 to 1889; of Mrs. Charles B. Smith, who served from 1889 to 1897; and of [Miss] Bertha Stewart Ludlam, who served from 1897 to 1926. Collection also contains records of the Calumet Historical Society, ca. 1935-, including records of meetings and programs, membership records, speeches, and reminiscences. Also included is a local history collection that contains biographical files; a history of Roseland by Edna Myers, 1930; photos of women, residences, women's clubs, and ethnic costumes; and church anniversary publications.

3,920. South Shore Local History
Collection. Ca. 1880-1970s. 6 drawers.
Open. No guide.
Chicago Public Library, South Shore Branch.
The collection relates to the history of this south-side Chicago neighborhood. Includes minutes and membership records of the South Shore Historical Society, 1935-; reports and handbooks of the Windsor Park Women's Clubs, 1880-1930s; *South Shore Scene,* a newspaper, 1950s-1970s; and correspondence of Helen Babcock about the 10th anniversary of the South Shore Branch Library.

3,921. Chicago Theatre Arts
Collection. Ca. 1850s-1930. 50 vols. and ca. 30 items.
Open. Unpublished guide.
Chicago Public Library, Special Collections.
Contains scrapbooks, 1880-1930; broadsides; playbills; and programs, including programs for *Guy Mannering,* in which Charlotte Saunders Cushman acted in 1875; for *La Dame aux Camélias,* in which Sarah Bernhardt acted in 1881; for *The Rivals,* in which Louisa Lane [Mrs. John] Drew acted in 1880; and for *Victoria Regina,* in which Helen Hayes acted in 1937.

3,922. Civil War and American History
Collection. 1820-80. No size given.
Open. Unpublished guide.
Chicago Public Library, Special Collections.
Collection contains correspondence, diaries, legal papers, photos, broadsides, pamphlets, books, and artifacts relating to the Civil War and American history. Contains items of the Grand Army of the Republic Memorial Association, including letters from soldiers to their wives and families and from women of the GAR; a minute book of the Soldiers' Aid Society in Selma, OH, 1863-65; memorials to Mrs. George H. Evens, an originator of Decoration Day Services in Iowa, and to Theresa Kilpatrick, a nurse in Company K, 5th Ohio Volunteer Infantry; and photos of Pauline Cushman, Mary Ann (Ball) Bickerdyke, Julia (Dent) Grant and the Grant family, Mary (Todd) Lincoln, and the Ladies of the GAR at their 23rd annual convention in Mattoon, IL, 1914. Other papers include a history of the North-Western Soldiers' Fair held in Chicago in 1863 with a list of donations and names of donors and a signed copy of the "Battle Hymn of the Republic" by Julia (Ward) Howe.

3,923. Ellsworth, James
Papers. 1891-94. 2 ft.
Open. No guide.
Chicago Public Library, Special Collections.
Ellsworth (1849-1925) was a businessman, banker, and major financial supporter and officer of the World's Columbian Exposition held in Chicago in 1893. Contains items pertaining to the board of lady managers, including reports presented to the board in 1891; correspondence related to badges of identification for board members; correspondence of [Mrs.] Bertha Honoré Palmer, chairman of the board of lady managers, regarding plans for a French loan exhibit; and letters from women throughout the US offering items for sale at the Fair. Also includes correspondence of Harriet Monroe with Ellsworth and others relating to her poem *The Columbian Ode* and printed material of the World's Congress of Representative Women and the World's Congress Auxiliary of the World's Columbian Exposition.

3,924. Goodman Theatre Archives
Records. 1926-74. Ca. 100 cu.ft.
Closed. No guide.
Chicago Public Library, Special Collections.
Annotated scripts, prompt books, stage plans, set designs, and programs of the Theatre, a professional theater in Chicago founded in memory of Kenneth Sawyer Goodman. Includes scrapbooks that Marjorie Robbins [Mrs. John] Hopkins compiled, as well as items concerning Charlotte Charpenning. Hopkins was Goodman's widow.

3,925. Library Archives
Records. 1872-1975. Ca. 5000 cu.ft.
Open. No guide.
Chicago Public Library, Special Collections.
Contains minutes of the board of directors, 1872-; financial records; personnel records; correspondence; photos; scrapbooks; and publications of the Library, which was founded in 1872 to operate central and branch libraries for Chicago. Includes papers of Gertrude Gscheidle, chief librarian of the Library from 1950 to 1967; scrapbooks kept by library workers, particularly members of the Chicago Public Library Staff Association; and a petition to the board of directors from citizens and organizations, including women's clubs, for improved library services. The Library was organized following the Chicago fire of 1871.

3,926. Nunn, Robert R.
Collection. 1800s. Ca. 75 items.
Open. Unpublished guide.
Chicago Public Library, Special Collections.
Correspondence, autographs, and other items that Nunn, a physician and collector, compiled. Includes a letter from Sarah Josepha (Buell) Hale to [Mrs.] Caroline (Howard) Gilman, a poet and humorist, requesting information and a miniature of Gilman for Hale's proposed work "Woman's Record." Also includes a letter from Lydia Sigourney to a Mrs. Salter and an engraving of Sigourney by H. Adlord.

3,927. Weiss, Edward H.
Collection. Nd. 210 items.
Open. Inventory.

Chicago Public Library, Special Collections.
Autograph collection of Weiss, a Chicago advertising executive, contains autographs of 19th-century personalities, including many literary figures. Includes an autographed sentiment by and a photo of Louisa May Alcott, 1878; a poem without a signature by Margaret Deland; a letter from Edna Ferber, 1923; an autographed sentiment by Zona Gale, 1928; a letter from Elizabeth (Cady) Stanton to Sara A. Underwood, editor of *The Index,* concerning the investigation of child prostitution in London and the work of author George Eliot, 1885; an autograph and cabinet photo of Julia (Ward) Howe; an autographed poem by Lucy Larcom, 1878; autographed sentiments and a cabinet photo of Harriet (Beecher) Stowe, 1877, 1882; a letter from Ida Minerva Tarbell, 1923; an autographed sentiment from Laura Dewey Bridgman, 1881; an autograph and photo of Katherine Greenaway, 1881; an autographed poem and photo of Louise Imogen Guiney; a letter from Lucretia Peabody Hale regarding publication of extracts from her works, 1883; an autographed poem by Ella (Wheeler) Wilcox, 1882; and an autographed poem by Mary (Mapes) Dodge, 1882.

3,928. Ženské Listy, Jediný Český Týdenník v Americe Věnovaný Zájmům Zen
Records. 1911-30. 4 vols.
Open. No guide.
Chicago Public Library, Special Collections.
Ženské Listy, or *Women's Record: The Only Czech Weekly in America Devoted to the Interests of Women,* was published by the Chicago Association of Czech-American Women and dealt with home, family, and educational reform issues. Founded as the Bohemian Women's Publishing Company in 1894 in Chicago, the Association is still in existence and publishes *Hlas Jednoty,* or *The Voice of Unity,* in Berwyn, IL. [Mrs.] Josepha Humpal Zeman was an editor and early leader of the company.

3,929. Lawndale-Crawford Historical Society
Records. Ca. 1880-1945. Ca. 6 ft.
Open. No guide.
Chicago Public Library, Toman Branch.
Includes correspondence and membership records of the Society, ca. 1935-, and such local history items as "The Ladies Meet, 1878-1945, The History of the Millard Avenue Woman's Club," by Emma Barr Tosh, 1945. Also contains photos of women's societies and schools as well as art works, some of which have women, girls, and children as subjects.

3,930. Morgan Park and Beverly History
Collection. Ca. 1890-1950. 3 drawers.
Open. Unpublished guide.
Chicago Public Library, Walker Branch.
Contains reminiscences, local histories and newspapers, reports, photos, publications, and artwork pertaining to Chicago's southwest side. Includes membership books of the Morgan Park Woman's Club, 1922-39 and 1947-48, and a DAR historical collection. Among the publications included are *The Post,* 1905-17; *Town Talk,* 1916; and the *Beverly Country Club News,* 1906-08.

3,931. Woodlawn Local History
Collection. Ca. 1900-40. 12 drawers.
Open. No guide.
Chicago Public Library, Woodlawn Branch.
Biographies, reminiscences, annual reports, photos, broadsides, and artifacts pertain to Chicago's southeast side. Includes board minutes of the Woodlawn Woman's Club, 1927-31; correspondence, bulletins, and other records of the Associated Clubs of Woodlawn, 1960s; bills, correspondence, and lists of the Woodlawn Neighborhood Committee, a WWI organization; scrapbooks concerning WWII home activities, particularly price control and rationing; publicity scrapbooks concerned with debutante parties, 1917-38; and photos of people and places in Woodlawn.

3,932. Hospital Records
Records. 1891- . Ca. 5 ft.
Access restricted. No guide.
Children's Memorial Hospital.
Minutes, financial records, and reports of Children's Memorial Hospital, which was known as Maurice Porter Memorial Hospital from its founding in 1882 until 1904, document the role women played in the founding, management, and development of the Hospital and in its early concern for social service as a supplement to medical care. Founded and funded initially by Julia Foster Porter as a memorial to her teenage son Maurice, the Hospital offered free care to all indigent children and strongly opposed "everything which tends to diminish the self respect" of people who need free care. A board of women was organized in 1892 "to assist the founder" in the Hospital's management. Known as the board of managers from 1892 to 1904, as the auxiliary board from 1904 to 1955, and as the woman's board from 1955 to the present, the board has included such women as Louise deKoven Bowen, Edith Rockefeller McCormick, Helen Aldis Lathrop, Sarah B. Tyson, and [Miss] Martha Wilson among its membership. In 1904 the Hospital's name was changed to Children's Memorial Hospital, and the expansion in facilities and services began that led to affiliations as a pediatric teaching center. During Martha Wilson's presidency of the auxiliary board from 1911 to 1923, a social service committee was formed to maintain the Hospital's social service program and dispensary and a junior auxiliary was established to provide in-hospital volunteer service and recreational activity for patients. Records of both groups are included with the Hosptial's records.

The Hospital began to treat private patients in 1926 after Martha Wilson provided a bequest to fund a separate building for that purpose. Until 1951 all paid administrators were women: [Miss] Bena M. Henderson, a nurse who served from 1909 to 1923; [Miss] Mary C. Stewart, a nurse who was administrator from 1923 to 1929; and [Miss] Mabel Binner, who was administrator from 1929 to 1951 after serving for five years as director of social service and dispensary. From 1911 until 1966 all paid directors of social service were women: [Miss] Adelaide Walsh, a nurse, 1910-23; [Miss] Babette S. Jennings, 1929-50; and [Miss] Mary Jean Clark, a leader in the development of Illinois's child abuse law who was director from 1961 to 1966.

3,933. Central Archives of the American Provinces
Records. 1892- . 20 drawers, 10 cabinets, and 10 bookshelves.
Open. Unpublished guide.
Congregation of Our Lady of the Retreat in the Cenacle.
The congregation was founded in 1826 in France and was established in the US in 1892 in New York City. Its members are engaged in retreat work, religious education, spiritual counseling, and other forms of spiritual ministry. Correspondence, journals, manuscripts, tapes, films, photos, slides, scrapbooks, relics, books, and other records.

3,934. Dunmore, Hope I.
Papers. 1905-60. 2.5 ft.
Access restricted. No guide.
Du Sable Museum of African American History.
Correspondence, a diary, minutes, membership and financial records, photos, programs, brochures, and published items of Dunmore, a Negro clubwoman who lived in Chicago. Also includes items concerned with Republican women's organizations and church activities at St. Thomas Episcopal Church in Chicago and a 1935 copy of the "Dunmore's Family Magazine," which gives information on the history of the family and Negro history in Chicago. Dunmore was active in many Negro organizations in Chicago, including the Chicago Old Settlers Social Club, which was founded in 1902; the United Brothers of Friendship and Sisters of the Mysterious Tens; Heroines of Jericho; the United Negro Improvement Association; and the Chicago Negro Old Timers or Early Settlers Club.

3,935. Elam, Mellissia Ann
Papers. 1910-25. 1 ft.
Access restricted. No guide.
Du Sable Museum of African American History.
Papers of [Mrs.] Elam, a civic leader and clubwoman who operated Elam House, a residence for Negro girls who came to Chicago seeking employment. Includes correspondence; financial papers; records of operation of Elam House; items of Lauretta Peyton, a niece of Elam; "Housing of Non-Family Women in Chicago, A Survey," an unpublished manuscript by Ann Elizabeth Trotter, 1921; a bulletin of the National Association of Colored Women, 1910; and programs of the Illinois Association of Colored Women, 1931 and 1935.

3,936. Altar Guild of the Diocese of Chicago
Records. 1931-75. 1 folder.
Open. No guide.
Episcopal Diocese of Chicago, Archives and Historical Collections.
Minutes, correspondence, and invitations of a fellowship founded in 1931 for women interested in doing needlework (i.e., making vestments) for the church.

3,937. Central House for Deaconesses
Records. 1951-68. 1 ft.
Open. No guide.
Episcopal Diocese of Chicago, Archives and Historical Collections.
Minutes of the board, correspondence, brochures, and clippings of the institution, founded in 1951, which was a school and residence for deaconesses who were in training or on leave from their assignments.

3,938. Chicago Training School for Deaconesses
Records. 1917-69. 1 ft.
Open. No guide.
Episcopal Diocese of Chicago, Archives and Historical Collections.
Minutes of the board, clippings, announcements, and brochures of a residence and School founded in 1917 to train women in the office and work of deaconess.

3,939. "Clerica," Diocese of Chicago
Records. 1899-1940. 1 folder.
Open. No guide.
Episcopal Diocese of Chicago, Archives and Historical Collections.
The group, founded in 1899, was a fellowship for clergymen's wives who gathered for recreation and devotional programs. Primarily consists of announcements of programs and meetings.

3,940. Daughters of the King, Chicago Chapter
Records. 1897-1960. 1 folder.
Open. No guide.
Episcopal Diocese of Chicago, Archives and Historical Collections.
Minutes and clippings of a group founded in 1897 to provide devotional fellowship for women who serve the local parish and diocese.

3,941. Episcopal Churchwomen, Diocese of Chicago
Records. 1884-1968. 1 ft.
Open. No guide.
Episcopal Diocese of Chicago, Archives and Historical Collections.
Minutes, correspondence, newsletters, yearbooks,

and clippings of a women's fellowship founded in 1884 to raise money for missions and social work and to assist in the Episcopal church's corporate life.

3,942. Girls' Friendly Society, Chicago Chapter
Records. 1886-1960. 1 ft.
Open. No guide.
Episcopal Diocese of Chicago, Archives and Historical Collections.
Founded in 1886, the Society was a devotional fellowship of girls and women, which provided programs of service, worship, and recreation, particularly camping. Minutes, correspondence, photos, clippings, Society publications, and ephemera.

3,943. Covenant Women
Records. 1916-56. 1 drawer.
Open. No guide.
Evangelical Covenant Church of America Archives.
Minutes; financial records; correspondence; notebooks concerning regional organizations; photos; scrapbooks; and books marking the 15th, 20th, 25th, 30th, and 40th anniversaries of Covenant Women, a national organization of women in the Evangelical Covenant Church of America. The group was founded in 1916 and has been active in church affairs.

3,944. Bureau of Indian Affairs (RG 75)
Records. 1870-1960. 1387 cu.ft.
Open. Unpublished guide.
Federal Archives and Records Center, Chicago Archives Branch.
Administrative files, correspondence, bound volumes, and case files from field offices of the Bureau provide information on the administration of reservations, operation of schools, timber and land use, and several censuses. Contains records of Menominee Indian Mills (500 cu.ft.) and its forestry operations, 1908-60; Michigan reservations (12 cu.ft.), 1924-44; the Tama, IA, agency (130 cu.ft.), 1912-46; and Wisconsin reservations (745 cu.ft.), 1870-1952. A guide is available for some portions of the records.

3,945. Bureau of the Census (RG 29)
Records. 1790-1900. 190 cu.ft. and 16,350 reels.
Partially restricted. Published guides.
Federal Archives and Records Center, Chicago Archives Branch.
Includes index cards to the 1880 population census which contain information on families with children under 10 years of age in Illinois, Indiana, and Michigan. Also includes 16,350 microfilm reels of federal population census schedules, 1790-1900. Access to the 1900 census only is restricted. Published indexes to the federal population census schedules are available.

3,946. Campbell, William J. (RG 200)
Papers. 1927-71. 62 cu.ft.
Access restricted. Unpublished guide.
Federal Archives and Records Center, Chicago Archives Branch.
Papers of Campbell, a judge of the US district court (northern district of Illinois, Chicago), include official and personal correspondence, files, minutes, reports, speeches, scrapbooks, photos, publications, clippings, and "bench files" created during his tenure as judge of the district court. Provides information about his work on conferences and committees, judicial conferences, the National Youth Administration, the Catholic Church, the Catholic Youth Organization and Boy Scouts in Chicago, his private practice, and his work as US attorney for the northern district of Illinois. Campbell was director of the NYA in Illinois.

3,947. Internal Revenue Service (RG 58)
Records. 1870-1920. 32 cu.ft.
Open. No guide.
Federal Archives and Records Center, Chicago Archives Branch.
References to women are found in assessment lists relating to the collection of taxes in Illinois, Indiana, Ohio, and Wisconsin, 1870-1917, and in employee rosters for the Detroit office of IRS, 1892-1920.

3,948. United States Attorneys (RG 118)
Records. 1869-1908. 6 cu.ft.
Open. No guide.
Federal Archives and Records Center, Chicago Archives Branch.
Includes correspondence, case files, and some evidential material for the district of Minnesota (4 cu.ft.), 1869-99, and the western district of Wisconsin (2 cu.ft.), 1892-1908.

3,949. United States District Courts (RG 21)
Records. 1808-1963. 28,157 cu.ft.
Partially restricted. No guide.
Federal Archives and Records Center, Chicago Archives Branch.
Consists of records of cases brought before district courts and of naturalization records. Contains records for three Illinois district courts: the eastern district (Danville), 1905-46; the northern district (Chicago), 1871-1952, with naturalization records (2000 vols.), 1873-1964; and the southern district (Peoria), 1819-1963, with naturalization records (130 vols.), 1856-1957. Contains records of two Indiana courts: the northern district (Hammond), 1879-1946, with naturalization records (53 vols.), 1906-21; and the southern district (Indianapolis), 1819-1946, with naturalization records (65 vols.), 1906-54. Also includes records of two Michigan courts: the eastern district (Detroit), 1816-1946, with naturalization records (42 vols.), 1837-1941; and the western district (Grand Rapids), 1863-1946, with naturalization records (16 vols.), 1870-1929. Includes records of two Ohio courts: the northern district (Cleveland), 1855-1946, with naturalization records (266 vols.) for Cleveland and Toledo, 1855-1943; and the southern district (Columbus), 1808-1946, with naturalization records for Cincinnati and Columbus (84 vols.), 1852-1929. Records of two Wisconsin courts: the eastern district (Milwaukee), 1839-1946; and the western district (Madison), 1850-1946, with naturalization records (11 vols.), 1855-1921. Only the records of the northern district court of Illinois (Chicago) are partially restricted.

3,950. War Manpower Commission (RG 211)
Records. 1942-45. 190 cu.ft.
Open. No guide.
Federal Archives and Records Center, Chicago Archives Branch.
Records of activities in Kentucky, Michigan, and Ohio (Region V); Illinois, Indiana, and Wisconsin (Region VI); and Iowa, Minnesota, Nebraska, North Dakota, and South Dakota (Region VIII).

3,951. Anthropology Department Archives
Records. 1900- . Ca. 50 ft.
Open. No guide.
Field Museum of Natural History, Department of Anthropology.
Correspondence, field notes, and photos of the Department, which is concerned with human development and culture in the Old and New Worlds. Includes items pertaining to internal operation, expeditions, and research of the Department as well as correspondence, clippings, and published items concerning sculptor Malvina Hoffman.

3,952. Women's Board
Records. 1966- . Ca. 60 vols.
Open. No guide.
Field Museum of Natural History, Division of Planning and Development.
Minutes, correspondence, invitations, photos, clippings, programs, and published items of the Board, a Museum auxiliary established in 1966 to coordinate special events and raise funds. The Board is an invitational organization composed of the wives of the Museum's board of trustees. The founder and president emeritus was Ellen [Mrs. Hermon Dunlap] Smith.

3,953. Board of Trustees
Records. 1893- . No size given.
Open. No guide.
Field Museum of Natural History, Registrar.
Minutes, legal and financial records, and correspondence of the Museum, which was established in 1893. According to the minutes, there were occasional women members of the Board until 1966 when the president of the Women's Board, an auxiliary group, became a permanent member of the panel. Also includes correspondence, ca. 1930, between Stanley Field and sculptor Malvina Hoffman regarding her commission to sculpt statues of racial and ethnic "types" for display in the Museum's Hall of Man.

3,954. Cook County School of Nursing
Records. 1929-73. 156 ft.
Open. Inventory.
Health and Hospitals Governing Commission of Cook County, Libraries, Archives, and Administrative Records Center.
Minutes, financial records, reports, correspondence, photos, and scrapbooks of the School, which was founded in 1929 to provide nursing education and training to young women and men. Until 1971 the School provided nursing services to Cook County Hospital. Consists primarily of the official records of the School's directors: Laura Logan, Edna S. Newman, Ada R. Crocker, E. Elizabeth Geiger, and Frances L. A. Powell. Records reveal the problems the School faced during the depression as well as the contributions the School made to the US Cadet Nurse Corps during WWII. In 1971 the School became a part of the newly organized Health and Hospitals Governing Commission of Cook County. Collection also includes some correspondence of Florence Nightingale.

3,955. Women's Union of Pullman
Records. 1892-95. 1 vol.
Access restricted. No guide.
Historic Pullman Foundation.
The Union, a charitable organization composed of the wives of Pullman Company executives, dispensed funds and other aid to needy families during the Pullman Strike of 1894 and the depression preceding it. Includes a journal containing minutes, financial reports, lists of visits and the type of aid given to families, statistics on the number of families helped and funds dispensed, and the names of members.

3,956. Katherine Legge Memorial Association
Records. 1924-74. 3 ft.
Open. Unpublished guide.
International Harvester Corporate Archives.
Minutes, financial records, correspondence, photos, scrapbooks, and printed material of the Association, a club for women employees of International Harvester. The Association was formed in 1924 to promote use of the Katherine Legge Memorial, a recreation and rest spot donated by Alexander Legge, then president of International Harvester, in memory of his wife. The Memorial property, which had been the Legges' summer home, was open for use by all women employees of International Harvester. Eventually a clubhouse, a dormitory, convalescent cottages, and other structures were built at the suburban Hinsdale, IL, location. The property was donated to the town of Hinsdale in 1973. The Memorial Association continues to function, however, planning recreational activities and raising funds for charitable organizations.

3,957. Evald, Emmy Carlsson
Papers. 1912-37. 1.5 ft.
Access restricted. Inventory.
Lutheran Church in America Archives.
Correspondence, a biographical sketch, and photos of Evald, founder and president from 1892 to 1935 of the Women's Missionary Society of the Evangelical Lutheran Augustana Synod. Also includes books she collected and wrote.

3,958. Kugler, Anna Sarah
Papers. 1890-1928. 1.5 ft.
Access restricted. Inventory.
Lutheran Church in America Archives.
Correspondence, notes on biblical studies, reports, photos, and pamphlets of Kugler (1856-1930), a physician and missionary from 1883 to 1930 who founded the American Evangelical Lutheran Mission Hospital in Guntur, India. Includes information on the Missionary Medical School for Women in Vellore, India, which was established in 1917, and the American Evangelical Lutheran Mission Hospital, which was renamed Kugler Memorial Hospital following Anna Kugler's death.

3,959. Lutheran Church in America, Lutheran Church Women
Records. 1962-74. 3 ft.
Access restricted. Inventory.
Lutheran Church in America Archives.
Lutheran Church Women, a national Lutheran women's organization, supports educational and social missions, evangelism in North America and overseas, and Christian fellowship among women. The group also is involved in women's causes. Convention minutes, planning documents, programs, and published items, including the monthly magazine *Lutheran Women.*

3,960. Lutheran Church in America, Women of the Illinois Synod
Records. 1962-72. 2.5 ft.
Access restricted. Inventories and card catalog.
Lutheran Church in America Archives.
Minutes, correspondence, reports, photos, clippings, calendars, and bulletins of the meetings and conventions of the Lutheran women of the Illinois Synod.

3,961. United Lutheran Church Women of the Iowa Synod of the United Lutheran Church in America
Records. 1947-62. 0.5 ft.
Access restricted. Inventory.
Lutheran Church in America Archives.
Constitution, minutes, president's papers, and programs of this women's organization.

3,962. Women's Home and Foreign Missionary Society of the Augustana Synod
Records. 1859-1962. 17.5 ft.
Access restricted. Inventory.
Lutheran Church in America Archives.
Minutes; correspondence; convention programs and other items; scrapbooks; a photo album containing missionary pictures from Africa; histories; religious curriculum guides for children; clippings; periodicals, including *Mission Tidings,* 1906-58, and the *Lutheran Women's World,* 1959-62; pamphlets; calendars; and charts of the Society, which did missionary work in China, India, and Africa. Also includes records of the executive board, the Women's Missionary Society, and the Augustana Lutheran Church Women.

3,963. Women's Home and Foreign Missionary Society of the Chicago Synod of the United Lutheran Church in America
Records. 1887-1940. 1 ft.
Access restricted. Inventory.
Lutheran Church in America Archives.
Minutes and financial records of the Society.

3,964. Women's Mission Society of the American Evangelical Lutheran Church—Danish
Records. 1919-62. 2.5 ft.
Access restricted. Inventory.
Lutheran Church in America Archives.
Constitution, minutes, financial records, correspondence, reports, convention material, newsletters, and clippings of the Society. Also includes *Danske Kvinders Missionsfond,* a periodical in Danish, 1919-36.

3,965. Women's Missionary Society of the Northern Illinois Synod of the United Lutheran Church in America
Records. 1877-1916. 1 ft.
Access restricted. Inventory.
Lutheran Church in America Archives.
Minutes and convention proceedings, 1887-1900, 1911; treasurer's records, 1908-13; and secretary's records, 1883-1906, of the Society. Also includes minutes of the Women's Home and Foreign Missionary Society of the Synod of Northern Illinois.

3,966. Women's Missionary Society of the United Lutheran Church in America
Records. 1900-61. 1 ft.
Access restricted. Inventory.
Lutheran Church in America Archives.
Board and executive committee minutes, 1954-56; reports and booklets; *Lutheran Women's Work,* a monthly periodical; and a convention newspaper.

3,967. Archives
Records. 1873-1970. Ca. 8 ft.
Access restricted. No guide.
Mary Thompson Hospital.
The Hospital was established in 1865 as Chicago Hospital for Women and Children to provide medical care, surgical treatment, and a free dispensary for women and children of the "respectable poor." Records include annual reports of the Chicago Hospital for Women and Children, 1873-84; annual reports of the Woman's Hospital Medical College, 1871-85; board of trustee minutes, 1916-70; secretary's minutes, 1886-97; medical staff minutes, 1916-70; departmental minutes, ca. 1954-70; physicians' records, including those of Josephine Wetman, Caroline Alexander, and Elnora Gilson, 1892-94; and a scrapbook of Hospital memorabilia. Also includes information on Mary Harris Thompson, a physician, surgeon, and administrator, and on the medical and nursing training provided for women.

Woman's Hospital Medical College was established by Thompson in 1870 because women were excluded from midwestern medical colleges at that time. During its early years, the College operated under the same board of trustees as the Chicago Hospital for Women and Children. From 1877 to 1892 it operated independently as Women's Medical College, and in 1892 it became part of Northwestern University.

3,968. Archives
Records. 1881- . 30 drawers.
Access restricted. No guide.
Michael Reese Hospital and Medical Center.
Founded in 1881, the Hospital is a nonsectarian health care facility supported largely by the Jewish community. Annual reports, correspondence, records of the United Hebrew Charities and of the medical staff, five drawers of photos, yearbooks, and hospital publications. In 1890 a training school for nurses was established on the Hospital grounds, and, in 1893, a dispensary was opened about a mile away. Women nurses, psychiatric social workers, and doctors, many of them European immigrants, have made substantial contributions to the institution's work and development. Records reflect the work of these women as well as the activities of several women's sewing groups; the Young Ladies' Aid Society, later known as the Chicago Woman's Aid; and the still extant Women's Board. Other files contain information on obstetrics and gynecology, breast-feeding, abortion, the premature nursery, pediatrics, and fund-raising events.

3,969. Biographical Files
Collection. Ca. 1876-1960. Ca. 400 items.
Open. No guide.
Moody Bible Institute Library.
Contains correspondence, reminiscences, lecture notes, financial papers, legal documents, tributes, photos, clippings, questionnaires, programs, announcements, and publications of people associated with Dwight L. Moody, the Chicago Evangelization Society, the Moody Institute, or the evangelical movement of the late 19th and early 20th centuries. Includes files on such women as Frances C. Allison, assistant director of practical Christian work at the Institute; M. A. Blair, secretary of the Institute's board of trustees; Sarah Brown (Hooker) Capron, an early missionary to Madura, India, where she founded a school and hospital for women and girls, and the first superintendent of women at the Institute; Charlotte Amelia Cary, a superintendent of the women's department; Herma Naomi Clark, a newspaper columnist; Sarah Ann (Bass) Cooke, a mission worker with The Salvation Army; Fanny Crosby, a hymn writer and poet; Mary (McLeod) Bethune and Nellie J. (Arnott) [Mrs. P. L.] Darling, students of the Institute; Adella H. Dunlap, an English teacher at the Institute; Emma Dryer, superintendent of the training school of the Woman's Christian Association in Chicago; Pearl Eytinge, an actress who converted and traveled throughout the US giving evangelical lectures; Gertrude Germann, who worked in the business office of the Institute for more than 40 years; [Miss] E. L. Haines, who was associated with the Chicago Evangelization Society and later the Madison Square Church House in New York City; Gertrude Hulbert, a teacher and organizer of the training school at the Northfield Seminary in Northfield, MA, and an organizer of the women's department of the Chicago Evangelization Society; Emily Kinnaird, a lecturer; Annie A. Konsberg, an organizer of the Woman's Christian Association, later the YWCA; Emily Seymour Strong, a superintendent of the women's department at the Bible Institute for Home and Foreign Missions of the Chicago Evangelization Society; Caroline E. Waite, corresponding secretary for the Bible Institute for Home and Foreign Missions of the Chicago Evangelization Society and a missionary to Cape Town, South Africa; and Frances Elizabeth Caroline Willard, a temperance leader and reformer who was president of the national WCTU.

3,970. Institute Archives
Records. Ca. 1887-1976. Ca. 25 ft.
Open. No guide.
Moody Bible Institute Library.
Organized as the Bible Institute for Home and Foreign Missions of the Chicago Evangelization Society, the Institute became known as the Chicago Bible Institute in 1889. A coeducational, nondenominational school, the Institute was involved in the education and training of Christian workers, teachers, ministers, missionaries, and musicians. Includes a constitution, bylaws, minutes, financial records, correspondence, radio broadcasts, reports, sermons, curricula, photos, scrapbooks, tracts, class schedules, graduation certificates, and publications. Records relate to the history, development, founders, students, and faculty of the Institute. Women involved in the institution's early years included Sarah Brown (Hooker) Carpon, Emma Dryer, Caroline E. Waite, Emily Seymour Strong, and Frances E. Willard.

3,971. College History
Records. 1930- . Ca. 9 ft. and 35 oversize vols.
Access restricted. No guide.

Mundelein College Archives.
Founded in 1930 in Chicago, Mundelein College is a Roman Catholic liberal arts women's college operated by the Sisters of Charity of the Blessed Virgin Mary, an American teaching order. Includes scrapbooks containing correspondence, telegrams, invitations, speeches, addresses, clippings, and programs as well as student newspapers, college catalogs, yearbooks, student and faculty directories, student handbooks, the quarterly literary review, the annual poetry anthology, and commencement, theatre, and exhibit programs. The College was established under the leadership of George Cardinal Mundelein, then archbishop of Chicago, and under the direction of Sister Mary Justitia, B.V.M. Primarily an undergraduate institution, Mundelein established its first master's degree program in religious studies in 1969. The Mundelein Weekend College in Residence was established in 1974 to meet the educational needs of women and men who work full-time. Current enrollment totals ca. 1300 students. Records provide information on faculty and College enrollment, administration, academic programs, student life, social activities, and the relationship between Mundelein and other educational institutions as well as the local community. Records of the president, bursar, and registrar are located in their respective offices.

3,972. Nu Theta Epsilon
Records. 1937-56. 0.5 ft.
Access restricted. No guide.
Mundelein College Archives.
Nu Theta Epsilon, a Mundelein College student organization, was established in 1937 for economics majors who wished to promote the field of economics and to perform service functions. Includes minutes, correspondence, lists of members, photos, clippings, and programs concerned with social activities, lectures, and other events, including an annual Christmas project during which dolls were collected and donated to local orphanages.

3,973. Photos
Records. 1930- . Ca. 7000 items.
Access restricted. No guide.
Mundelein College Archives.
Photos, slides, and negatives document the history of Mundelein College from its founding in 1930 to the present and depict alumnae, faculty, the board of trustees, commencement, art, athletics, buildings, clubs, organizations, academic departments, student life and activities, social events, and persons associated with the growth and development of the College.

3,974. Hegner, Bertha Hofer
Papers. Ca. 1896-1938. 1 vol.
Open. No guide.
National College of Education, Hegner Library.
[Mrs. Herman Frederick] Hegner (1862-1937), a teacher and college president, was a kindergarten specialist. Consists of a scrapbook containing correspondence and letters of condolence concerning her death, post cards, Hofer family genealogy, photos, clippings, membership cards, and announcements. An 1890 graduate of the National Kindergarten and Elementary College in Chicago, Hegner did graduate work at the Pestalozzi Froebel Haus in Berlin, the University of Chicago, and Columbia University. A pioneer in kindergarten work in Chicago, she directed the first kindergarten at Chicago Commons settlement and founded the Pestalozzi Froebel Teachers College in Chicago, which she directed from 1896 to 1936. Hegner was a charter member of the Central Council of Childhood Education in Chicago, a member of the Chicago Woman's Club, and founder of the Mothers' Club at the Chicago Commons settlement.

3,975. National Opinion Research Center Studies Data
Records. 1961- . No size given.
Open. Unpublished guide.
National Opinion Research Center, Data Library.
Survey data and publications relate principally to two studies conducted by the Center, the first involving the college graduating class of June 1961 and the second involving a national sample of adults in 1972. The first study included contacts with the same graduates in 1961, 1962, 1963, 1964, and 1968; the 1964 questionnaire, designed by Alice S. Rossi, contained a section in which women were asked about their roles, attitudes, and career plans. The second study, the Center's annual general social survey, included questions about women in politics, women in the home, working women, the question of a woman president, and other aspects of the role of women.

3,976. National Safety Council Archives
Records. 1912- . Ca. 1000 vols. and 237 sets of microfiche.
Open. Unpublished guide.
National Safety Council Library.
Founded in 1913 as the National Council for Industrial Safety, the Council is a membership organization of individuals and associations with affiliated chapters throughout the US; it promotes accident prevention through research, dissemination of information, advocacy of safety programs, education of professionals and volunteers, and sponsorship of conferences. Contains minutes, program items, and publications, including reports of meetings of the women's section and information concerning the board of directors and home, industrial, school, college, and women's conferences. Publications of the Council include the National Safety Congress's *Transactions,* 1912-, which contain writings by Alice Hamilton, Ida M. Tarbell, Frances Perkins, and Mary Anderson; the family safety publication *Home Safety Review,* 1942-61, a magazine purchased by industrial employers for distribution to more than 1.5 million employee homes; and items concerning such topics as industrial nursing, school safety, and women as industrial workers.

3,977. Vertical Files
Records. 1921- . Ca. 600,000 items.
Open. Unpublished guide.
National Safety Council Library.
Includes reports, studies, clippings, pamphlets, press releases, publications, and other records of the Council, which was founded in 1913 to promote accident prevention through education and development of safety programs. Includes biographical items concerning such leaders in the field as Alice Hamilton, a physician; Marion E. Martin, commissioner of the Maine department of labor and industry; and Marie Scotti, division safety coordinator for the Maxwell House division of General Foods Corporation, as well as files on women as workers in industry, women safety professionals, home safety, industrial hygiene, and nursing.

3,978. Women's Conference
Records. 1955-74. 14 microfiche.
Open. Unpublished guide.
National Safety Council Library.
Contains minutes and a membership roster of the Women's Conference and of the executive committee of the National Safety Council as well as minutes and lists of officers of the Women of the Safety Councils section. The Women's Conference of the Council was founded in 1955 to provide educational and program services in accident prevention through liaison with women's organizations. The Conference has developed such program ideas as "Safety on the Streets" for the prevention of traffic accidents and personal assault and "Home Our Mutual Effort," which is concerned with injury prevention and consumer product safety. Six representatives of the Conference sit on the Council's board of directors. The Women of Safety Councils, a section of the Conference, was established in 1972. Composed of women representatives of state and local organizations affiliated with the Council, the WSOC serves as a liaison between the Women's Conference and the state and local safety councils.

3,979. Allen, Gideon Winan, and Cox, Annie Poad
Papers. 1862-65. Ca. 217 items.
Open. Inventory.
Newberry Library.
Love letters between Allen (1835-1912), who was a law student at the University of Michigan at Ann Arbor, and his future wife Cox, a resident of Madison, WI. The letters contain commentary on the political situation during the Civil War.

3,980. Arts Club of Chicago
Records. 1916- . 71 ft.
Open. Inventory.
Newberry Library.
Records of the Club, which fosters high standards of art and mutual acquaintance between artists and the public by maintaining a gallery and providing traveling exhibits. Includes minutes; files on financial matters and club membership, the operation of the building, art exhibits, lecture series, and patronage of dance, drama, and music; and correspondence with Mary Garden concerning Harriet Monroe, Louise Nevelson, and others. Also includes lectures by Katherine Anne Porter, by Laura C. Bolton on African art, by Nadia Boulanger on music, by Vera Brittain on war and its influence on literature, by Mrs. Patrick Campbell on the art of acting, and by Alexandra Danilova, Alicia Markova, and Ninette de Valois on ballet; photos; clippings; scrapbooks; films; catalogs; blueprints; and architectural drawings. The Club was incorporated in 1916.

3,981. Atwater, Adeline (Lobdell)
Papers. Ca. 1890-1940. 36 items.
Open. Unpublished guide.
Newberry Library.
Autobiography, a diary, and manuscripts of [Mrs. Henry] Atwater (ca. 1887-), an author who became the wife of Henry C. Pynchon. Born in Chicago, Atwater lived in Washington, DC, until after WWI, when she divorced her husband and moved to New York City to manage art galleries. She also traveled in Europe with Helena Rubinstein. Her writings detail her involvement in the women's suffrage campaign and the birth control movement.

3,982. Calhoun, William James, and Calhoun, Lucy (Monroe)
Papers. 1909-13. 13 items.
Open. Unpublished guide.
Newberry Library.
Includes letters primarily written by Lucy Calhoun, who was married to William Calhoun (1848-1916), an American envoy to China from 1909 to 1913. In her letters she describes the final days of the Dragon Throne and the formation of the Republic of China.

3,983. Cather and Hitz
Papers. 1938-49. 331 items.
Open. Inventory.
Newberry Library.
Correspondence of Benjamin Hitz, a collector of first editions of the works of Willa Sibert Cather (1873-1947), concerns his research on Cather. Small collection of Cather letters; letters from booksellers, library consultants, and Cather experts, including Flora Bullock, Dorothy Canfield Fisher, and Louise Pound; and studies on biographies, bibliographies, and literary criticism of Cather.

3,984. Cather, Willa Sibert
Papers. 1912-58. 131 items.
Closed. Inventory.
Newberry Library.
Letters that Cather (1873-1947), an author, wrote to Irene (Miner) [Mrs. Charles] Weisz.

3,985. Catherwood, Mary Hartwell
Papers. 1860-1902. 152 items.
Open. Inventory.
Newberry Library.
[Mrs. James Steele] Catherwood (1847-1902) was the author of *The Days of Jeanne d'Arc* (New York: Century Company, 1897) and *Lazarre* (Indianapolis: Bowen-Merrill Company, ca. 1901). Includes family and professional correspondence; diaries; published and unpublished manuscripts of her poems, plays, articles, and novels; photos; and clippings.

3,986. Cowley, Malcolm
Papers. 1918- . 60 boxes.
Open. Inventory.
Newberry Library.
Correspondence, manuscripts, and clippings of Cowley (1898-), a poet, author, and editor. Correspondents include Katherine Anne Porter, Caroline Gordon, Elizabeth Ames, Louise Bogan, Willa Cather, Harriet Monroe, and Agnes Smedley.

3,987. Cummings, Marion
Papers. 1900-15. 462 items.
Closed. Unpublished guide.
Newberry Library.
Correspondence, published and unpublished writings, and photos of Cummings (1876-1941), an author and poet, who was first married to Stanley Cummings, and later to Henry Slonimsky. Includes correspondence of Sara Teasdale, some items of which contain poems.

3,988. Dell, Floyd
Papers. 1908-69. 3673 items.
Open. Inventory.
Newberry Library.
Correspondence, manuscripts, notebooks, photos, and clippings of Dell (1897-1969), an author and editor who wrote about sociology, marriage and the family, socialism, and literary topics; he also was involved in feminism. Contains letters of his first wife Margery Currey Dell and his second wife B. Marie (Gage) Dell. Other correspondents include Jane Burr, Mollie Price [Mrs. George Cram] Cook, Gladys [Mrs. Arthur] Ficke, Susan Glaspell, Marjory Jones, Edna St. Vincent Millay, and Eunice Tietjens.

3,989. Drury, John
Papers. Ca. 1920-70. 43 boxes.
Closed. No guide.
Newberry Library.
Papers of Drury (1898-1972), a journalist, include those of his wife Marion Neville (?-1968), a columnist for the *Chicago Daily News* until her death. Contains notes, research material, and original artwork for her children's books.

3,990. Durkee, Cora Dana
Papers. 185?-1934. 172 items.
Open. Unpublished guide.
Newberry Library.
[Miss] Durkee was a staff member at the Library. Includes a letterpress book of the Durkee family, which resided in Kenosha, WI, 1850s-60s; items relating to Library collections that Durkee assembled, including translations, literary criticism, photos, sketches, drawings, and mementos; poems and articles by Edith Franklin Wyatt; and notes, sketches, and drawings of Mary L. Watson, a Library staff member.

3,991. Everett, Robert, Family
Papers. 1820-1930. 3911 items.
Open. Inventory.
Newberry Library.
Family papers of Everett (1791-1875), a Congregational minister, owner of a Welsh printing press in Remsen, NY, and husband of Elizabeth Everett (179?-1878). Includes correspondence, printed items, and other papers. Their children included Mary Holywell Everett (1830-1916), one of the first female surgeons in the US and an activist in the temperance and women's rights movement, and Cynthia Everett (1839-76), who taught in a Sunday school for black freedmen in Virginia and South Carolina and worked for the US Christian Commission, which aided Union soldiers.

3,992. Fortnightly
Records. Ca. 1920-76. Ca. 30 ft.
Closed. No guide.
Newberry Library.
Minutes, financial records, correspondence, reports, architectural records of the building, photos, scrapbooks, and guest registers of the group, a social, literary, and cultural organization of Chicago women who were involved in civic and philanthropic activities. Kate Newell [Mrs. William] Doggett founded the group. Its members included Harriet S. Monroe, Jane Addams, and Lucy (Monroe) [Mrs. W. J.] Calhoun.

3,993. French, Alice
Papers. 1871-1934. 684 items.
Open. Inventory.
Newberry Library.
Correspondence; diaries; manuscripts of novels, plays, and short stories; speeches; clippings; and souvenirs of French (1850-1934), an author who used the pseudonym Octave Thanet. Her works include *Knitters in the Sun* (1887) and *A Step on the Stair* (1913). Correspondents include Clara Barton, Mary Kinney Brainerd, Celestine Fyervary, Sarah Orne Jewett, Elizabeth Garver Jordan, Edith Kermit Roosevelt, and Ida M. Tarbell.

3,994. Gerstenberg, Alice
Papers. 1913-65. 1225 items.
Open. Inventory.
Newberry Library.
Gerstenberg (1885-1972) was a playwright, director, and a leader of the Little Theatre movement, chiefly in Chicago. Includes correspondence, her works, scrapbooks, photos, and playbills. Correspondents include Maude Adams, Margaret (Ayer) Barnes, Edna Ferber, Lilian Bell, Mary Hastings Bradley, Rachel Crothers, Dorothy (Canfield) Fisher, Zona Gale, Eva Le Gallienne, Harriet Monroe, Caroline Kirkland, Amy Leslie, Caroline McIlvaine, and Herma Clark.

3,995. Harrison, Carter Henry, IV
Papers. 1769-1953. 3937 items.
Open. Inventory.
Newberry Library.
Harrison (1860-1953) was mayor of Chicago from 1897 to 1905 and from 1911 to 1915. Contains correspondence, speeches, bills, photos, and clippings relating to his professional and family life. Correspondence relating to civic reform in Chicago is with Jane Addams, Louise DeKoven [Mrs. Joseph T.] Bowen, Helen Keller, Eleanor Roosevelt, and Ella (Flagg) Young.

3,996. Kerr, May Walden
Papers. 1890-1958. 619 items.
Open. Inventory.
Newberry Library.
Includes correspondence, diaries, manuscripts, account books, photos, and clippings of [Mrs. Charles H.] Kerr (1865-1960), a socialist author and lecturer who was at one time married to Charles Kerr, a socialist publisher in Chicago. Correspondents include C. Amelia Hughes, Jenny Ingham, Carrie Rand Herron, Margaret Sanger, and Eleanor Roosevelt.

3,997. The Little Room
Records. 1898-1929. 258 items.
Open. Inventory.
Newberry Library.
Minutes of committee meetings, financial records, correspondence, manuscripts, and photos of this Chicago literary and social club that was founded in 1898. Correspondents include Alice Gerstenberg, Nellie V. Walker, Harriet Monroe, Edith Franklin Wyatt, Fannie (Bloomfield) Zeisler, and Madeline Yale Wynne.

3,998. McIlvaine, Caroline
Papers. 1927-33. 93 items.
Open. Inventory.
Newberry Library.
Correspondence, notes and research material, photos, and clippings of McIlvaine (1868-1945), a local historian and staff member at the Library and the Chicago Historical Society, relate to a study of old streets and landmarks in Chicago.

3,999. Meine, Franklin Julius
Papers. 1922-65. 350 items.
Open. Inventory.
Newberry Library.
Correspondence, speeches, notes, and clippings of Meine (1896-1968), editor of *American People's Encyclopedia* and a collector of American regional and folk humor and literary items. Collection relates primarily to Meine's activities with the Society of Midland Authors and includes notes on the Society by Edith Franklin Wyatt, 1955; items related to Fannie [Mrs. Carl S.] Junge and the Writers Guild, 1928-42; and notes and correspondence of Mary Hastings Bradley and Alice Gerstenberg concerning a 50th anniversary dinner for Meine.

4,000. O'Hara, John Myers
Papers. 1908-42. 447 items.
Open. Inventory.
Newberry Library.
Correspondence, writings, photos, and clippings of O'Hara, a Chicago poet, include letters, some with poetry or writings enclosed, from poets and writers, including Alice Dunne, Catherine Markham, Helene Mullins, Jessie B. Rittenhouse, Corinne (Roosevelt) Robinson, Leonora Speyer, Sara Teasdale, Blanche Shoemaker Wagstaff, and Calla Wallace.

4,001. Pearce, Christopher Gardner
Papers. 1839-51. 175 items.
Open. Inventory.
Newberry Library.
Correspondence of Pearce (1811-82), a captain on various commercial river vessels, with his wife Jane Ann (Sackett) Pearce, whom he married in 1840 and who was living in Cincinnati.

4,002. Rich, Charles, and Rich, Albina
Papers. 1853-54. 103 items.
Open. Inventory.
Newberry Library.
Weekly correspondence that Charles Rich and his wife Albina Rich exchanged while he was working in Illinois for the Illinois Central Railroad. In the letters Charles Rich writes about his work and Albina's running of the farm in Milo, ME, while she writes about her loneliness, the difficulties of running the farm herself, and their three children.

4,003. Taylor, Graham
Papers. 1862-1938. 62 boxes.
Open. Inventory.
Newberry Library.
Taylor (1851-1938) was a Chicago clergyman, professor, social worker, and civic leader. Includes correspondence, diaries, speeches, journals, biographical material, printed and manuscript articles, reports, photos, scrapbooks, clippings, and programs. Papers relate chiefly to the history and growth of Chicago Commons, a settlement house

that Taylor founded in 1894; the history of the Chicago School of Civics and Philanthropy, which he also founded and directed and which eventually was transferred to the University of Chicago; social welfare and settlement activity locally and nationally; civic reform; housing; labor; education; and unemployment. Also includes items concerning his daughter Lea Taylor (1883-1975), who succeeded him as director of Chicago Commons. Correspondents include Edith Abbott, Grace Abbott, Jane Addams, [Mrs.] Henrietta Octavia Barnett, Sophonisba P. Breckenridge, Julia C. Lathrop, Catharine (Waugh) McCulloch, Mary E. McDowell, and Margaret Dreier Robins.

4,004. Taylor, Harriet
Papers. 1872-1931. 234 items.
Open. Inventory.
Newberry Library.
Correspondence, diaries, a finance book, photos, clippings, and mementos of Taylor (?-1931), a staff member of the Library from 1894 to 1931 who worked primarily in the genealogy section. Papers relate to the history of the Library and to Taylor's professional life.

4,005. Tietjens, Eunice (Hammond)
Papers. Ca. 1910-43. 4263 items.
Open. Inventory.
Newberry Library.
Correspondence, post cards, manuscripts, photos, and clippings of Tietjens (1884-1944), an author, poet, and lecturer who joined the staff of *Poetry* in 1913. She married Cloyd Head, her second husband, in 1920. Correspondents include Mary Hastings Bradley, Ada Booth, Anna Hempstead Branch, Pearl Buck, Fanny Butcher, Elizabeth Cooper, Rheta (Childe) Dorr, Alice D. Lippmann, Amy Lowell, Harriet Monroe, Sara Teasdale, Marguerite Wilkinson, and Elinor Wylie.

4,006. Wingreen, Amy Eleanor
Papers. 1898-99. 129 items.
Open. Inventory.
Newberry Library.
Wingreen (1870-1919) was an army nurse. Includes correspondence, telegrams, photos, a scrapbook, clippings, and maps relating to her service during the Spanish-American War. In her letters she describes her feelings and problems and gives a first-hand account of the War. Wingreen was one of the first trained women nurses to be sent to a foreign country during wartime.

4,007. Wyatt, Edith Franklin
Papers. 1894-1955. 430 items.
Open. Inventory.
Newberry Library.
Correspondence, drafts, contracts, scrapbooks, clippings, and mementos of Wyatt (1873-1958), an author, as well as copies of her works, including newspaper and magazine contributions. Correspondents include Jane Addams, Mary Hastings Bradley, Zona Gale, Alice Gerstenberg, Florence Kelley, Edith Kermit Roosevelt, Mary Rozet Smith, and Ida M. Tarbell. Among Wyatt's works are *Every One His Own Way* (1901) and *The Invisible Gods* (1923).

4,008. University Archives
Records. Ca. 1954- . Ca. 90 ft.
Open. No guide.
Northeastern Illinois University Library.
Founded in 1867 as Cook County Normal School, Northeastern Illinois University assumed its present name in 1971. Includes minutes, budgets, correspondence, research papers, reports, photos, scrapbooks, clippings, yearbooks, catalogs, bulletins, programs, curricula, student handbooks, announcements, and publications from the files of the University president, board of governors, academic departments, and the University committee and council. Contains data on student enrollment and information on educational policy, accreditation, the faculty senate, and faculty organizations. The University is a coeducational public institution with an enrollment of ca. 10,000 that offers graduate and undergraduate programs; it has always enrolled a large number of women students. Also includes minutes, reports, and announcements of the University and College Women of Illinois, Northeastern Illinois University Chapter, 1972-73; invitations, memoranda, and announcements of the Faculty Wives Club, 1967-70; minutes, announcements, and a newsletter of the women's studies program, 1972-76; and a scrapbook containing photos and clippings of the Future Teachers of America, 1954-56.

4,009. Chicago Homeopathic Medical College, J. S. Mitchell School of Nursing
Records. 1897-1905. Ca. 1 cu.ft. and 1 microfilm reel.
Access restricted. No guide.
Northwestern Memorial Hospital Archives.
Student records, diary kept by a student nurse, and class photos of the School, which was founded in 1897 and merged with Hahnemann Hospital School of Nursing in 1905.

4,010. Chicago Lying-In Dispensary and Chicago Maternity Center
Records. 1895-1973. 1100 cu.ft.
Access restricted. Unpublished guide.
Northwestern Memorial Hospital Archives.
Annual reports, audits, patient records, photos, and clippings of the Dispensary, which was founded in 1895 in the Maxwell Street Dispensary located in Chicago's westside immigrant neighborhood. Records of the Center, which continued the work of the Dispensary from 1932 to 1973, relate to out-patient services as well as to home delivery service, which was under the direction of physician Beatrice Tucker. The Center is now a part of Prentice Women's Hospital and Maternity Center of Northwestern Memorial Hospital.

4,011. Chicago Memorial Hospital School of Nursing Alumnae Association
Records. 1914-78. Ca. 1 cu.ft.
Access restricted. No guide.
Northwestern Memorial Hospital Archives.
Memos, newsletters, and annual reunion photos of the Association, a social and fund-raising organization founded in 1914.

4,012. Chicago Memorial Hospital Woman's Board
Records. 1922-54. 2 cu.ft.
Access restricted. No guide.
Northwestern Memorial Hospital Archives.
Annual reports, minute book, and announcements of the Board, which was founded in 1922 and was involved in volunteer and fund-raising activities. The Board was incorporated into the Wesley Woman's Board when Chicago Memorial Hospital merged with Wesley Hospital in 1954 to become Chicago Wesley Memorial Hospital. The chief activity of the group was a summer outing at the South Shore Country Club in Chicago held for medical staff, nurses, and patients. Merissa [Mrs. Paul] Bucy was a leader of the Board.

4,013. Chicago Memorial School of Nursing
Records. 1922-35. Ca. 1 cu.ft. and 1 microfilm reel.
Access restricted. No guide.
Northwestern Memorial Hospital Archives.
Student records, catalogs, and publications of the School, which was founded in 1922 and closed in 1935.

4,014. Chicago Wesley Memorial Hospital School of Neurological Nursing
Records. 1969-72. 9 cu.ft.
Access restricted. No guide.
Northwestern Memorial Hospital Archives.
Student records, curriculum notes, applications, and catalogs of the School, which offers a postgraduate program for nursing specialties.

4,015. Hahnemann Hospital, Attending League
Records. 1855-1921. Ca. 1 cu.ft.
Access restricted. No guide.
Northwestern Memorial Hospital Archives.
Minute book, newsletters, and photos of members of the League, a fund-raising group that existed from 1855 to 1921 when Hahnemann Hospital, a homeopathic hospital, became the Chicago Memorial Hospital. The League was composed of the wives of the Hospital's attending staff. Its records include items relating to a fund-raising bazaar held in 1873.

4,016. Hahnemann Hospital School of Nursing
Records. 1897-1921. Ca. 1 cu.ft.
Access restricted. No guide.
Northwestern Memorial Hospital Archives.
Curriculum material, publications, and other items of the School, which existed from 1897 to 1921 when Hahnemann Hospital became Chicago Memorial Hospital. Hahnemann Hospital's student nurses were praised for their public health activities during a 1918 influenza epidemic.

4,017. Monroe Street Hospital School of Nursing
Records. 1899-1914. Ca. 1 cu.ft.
Access restricted. No guide.
Northwestern Memorial Hospital Archives.
Annual reports, curriculum materials, and other records of the School, which was founded in 1899 and became the Washington Boulevard School of Nursing in 1914. The School was the first all-white Chicago school of nursing to admit a black woman student.

4,018. Passavant Memorial Hospital Woman's Board
Records. 1897-1972. 22 cu.ft.
Access restricted. No guide.
Northwestern Memorial Hospital Archives.
Annual reports, minutes, audits, correspondence, photos, directories, and yearbooks of the Board, which was founded in 1897 as the Woman's Aid Society. In addition to raising funds for the hospital and recruiting hospital volunteers, the group sponsored the Woman's World's Fair in Chicago in 1928 and the annual Passavant Debutante Cotillion held in Chicago beginning in 1948.

4,019. Passavant School of Nursing
Records. 1898-1972. 40 cu.ft. and 9 microfilm reels.
Access restricted. No guide.
Northwestern Memorial Hospital Archives.
Correspondence, student records, curriculum materials, speeches, clippings, student newspaper, catalogs, and yearbooks of the School, a diploma school of nursing founded in 1898. From 1948 to 1972 the School was known as the James Ward Thorne School of Nursing.

4,020. Passavant School of Nursing Alumnae Association
Records. 1912- . Ca. 1 cu.ft.
Access restricted. No guide.
Northwestern Memorial Hospital Archives.
Correspondence, invitations, photos, newsletters, and other items of the Association, a social and fund-raising organization founded in 1912.

4,021. Prentice Women's Hospital and Maternity Center, Northwestern Memorial Hospital
Records. 1968-74. 19 cu.ft.
Access restricted. No guide.
Northwestern Memorial Hospital Archives.
Minutes, grants and proposals, blueprints, architectural drawings, and promotional literature of the Center, which was founded in 1968 to

provide health services to women. The members of the Passavant Memorial Hospital Woman's Board, the members of the Chicago Maternity Center, and patrons of the hospital, including Abra Rockefeller Prentice and Abbie Cantrill Rockefeller Prentice, were influential in the planning of the Center.

4,022. Washington Boulevard Hospital School of Nursing
Records. 1915-41. Ca. 1 cu.ft. and 1 microfilm reel.
Access restricted. No guide.
Northwestern Memorial Hospital Archives.
Student records and curriculum materials of the School, which was founded in 1915 and merged with Wesley Memorial Hospital School of Nursing in 1941.

4,023. Wesley Memorial Hospital School of Medical Records Librarianship
Records. 1943-54. 3 cu.ft.
Access restricted. No guide.
Northwestern Memorial Hospital Archives.
Student records and catalogs of the School, which trained medical records librarians. Includes information on two prominent women in the field of medical records librarianship, Marjorie Quandt and Edna K. Huffman.

4,024. Wesley Memorial Hospital School of Nursing Alumnae Association
Records. 1903-78. 14 cu.ft.
Access restricted. No guide.
Northwestern Memorial Hospital Archives.
Correspondence, invitations, photos, newsletters, brochures, and other records of the Association, a social and fund-raising group of nursing alumnae founded in 1903. The Association is still extant.

4,025. Wesley Memorial Hospital Woman's Board
Records. 1899- . 28 cu.ft.
Access restricted. No guide.
Northwestern Memorial Hospital Archives.
Bylaws, annual reports, minutes, financial records, correspondence, membership records, photos, clippings, and a poster of the Board, which was founded in 1899. The group operates a patient library in the Hospital and performs other volunteer and fund-raising functions. Incorporating 19 organizations, the Board is officially titled the Service League of Northwestern Memorial Hospital.

4,026. Wesley School of Nursing
Records. 1885-1935. 32 cu.ft. and 17 microfilm reels.
Access restricted. No guide.
Northwestern Memorial Hospital Archives.
Annual reports, student records, curriculum notes, photos, and yearbooks of the School, which Lucy (Rider) Meyer founded in 1885 as the Chicago Training School as part of a program for Methodist deaconesses. In 1914 the Wesley School of Nursing became the Wesley Memorial Hospital School of Nursing. From 1943 to 1945 the School was one of 17 training sites for the US Navy Cadet Corps of Nurses program, a group of women who were trained to provide public health and visiting nurse care for military families so other nurses could take overseas duty. In 1972 the School merged with Passavant School of Nursing to form the Wesley-Passavant School of Nursing. The School is scheduled to close in 1981.

4,027. Women's Hospital Medical College
Records. 1892. 1 vol.
Access restricted. No guide.
Northwestern Memorial Hospital Archives.
Scrapbook of the College, which was founded in 1871 to train women as physicians, contains photos of students, doctors, and buildings. Founded and administered by Mary Harris Thompson, a physician and surgeon, the College was affiliated with the Chicago Hospital for Women and Children, which is now known as the Mary Thompson Hospital.

4,028. Archives
Records. 1919- . No size given.
Access restricted. No guide.
Oriental Institute of the University of Chicago.
Founded in 1919, the Institute is concerned with research, field excavation, teaching, and museum activities related to ancient cultures of the Near and Middle East. Includes annual reports, records of the governing board, archaeological field records, correspondence, field notes, journals and drawings from digs, photos, newsletters, and publications. Women have been involved in all phases of the Institute. Professors Nabia Abbott and Helena Kantor were among the research scholars, and [Mrs.] Ursula Wolff Schneider, a German immigrant who was a photo journalist in Europe in the 1930s, worked for many years as technical photographer at the Institute.

4,029. Heisler, Tibor
Papers. 1412-1913. 85 items.
Open. Unpublished guide.
Roosevelt University Archives.
Holograph letters and documents, dating chiefly from the 19th century, include letters of Susan (Franklin) Bandemer and those of contemporary Europeans.

4,030. Roosevelt University Development Office
Records. 1945-63. 3 ft.
Open. Unpublished guide.
Roosevelt University Archives.
Correspondence, speeches, news releases, biographical data, programs, and clippings concern persons, including Eleanor Roosevelt, who spoke during special events at Roosevelt University. Also includes material on Vijaya Lakshmi Pandit, Indian ambassador to the US from 1949 to 1952.

4,031. Roosevelt University Women's Scholarship Association
Records. 1949-63. 1 ft.
Open. Unpublished guide.
Roosevelt University Archives.
The Association was founded in 1949 to raise funds for scholarships; it holds bazaars and runs a small shop. Correspondence, news releases, programs, and clippings concerning the bazaar, special speakers, organization of the scholarship, and other activities of the group.

4,032. Roosevelt University Oral History Project in Labor History
Oral history. 1970-76. 47 transcripts.
Open. Unpublished guide.
Roosevelt University Library.
The Project's interviews include those with 12 women, among them Lillian Herstein, a retired teacher and member for 25 years of the Chicago Federation of Labor executive board; Mollie Levitas, retired secretary of the Chicago Federation of Labor; Sophie Kosciolowski, a Polish immigrant who was a member of the grievance committee of the United Packinghouse Workers of America; Esther Dolgoff, who with her husband Sam was a socialist and organizer for the Industrial Workers of the World; and Myrna Kassel, former executive secretary of community services for the Chicago Industrial Union Council. Herstein's interview includes comments about her youth in Chicago, the Women's Trade Union League, the Bryn Mawr School for Women Workers in Industry, Brookwood Labor College, efforts of the Jewish Labor Committee to aid the labor victims of fascism during WWII, the International Ladies' Garment Workers' Union, teachers unions, and other topics. Kosciolowski discusses her emigration from Poland, work in the stockyards in the 1930s, helping to organize the CIO, the position of women and blacks in the union, the McCarthy era and its effect on the union, and other subjects.

4,033. Sears, Roebuck and Co. Catalogs
Records. 1888- . Ca. 3000 items.
Access restricted. No guide.
Sears, Roebuck and Co. Archives.
Complete catalogs of the Company, a major retail and catalog store founded in 1886.

4,034. Stereoptican Slides
Records. Ca. 1907. 50 slides.
Access restricted. No guide.
Sears, Roebuck and Co. Archives.
Stereoptican views of mail order operations of the Company, a major retail and catalog store founded in 1886. Many slides show women employees writing letters, opening mail, operating the long-distance telephone switchboard, and working in the stenographic department. Also includes slides of the training school, employees' hospital, and girls' cafeteria.

4,035. Province Archives
Records. 1846- . 3 storage rooms.
Partially restricted. No guide.
Sisters of Mercy, Province of Chicago.
Minutes, corporate documents, financial records, correspondence, photos, scrapbooks, and other records of the order, which was founded in Chicago in 1846. Includes papers of mothers superior, records of chapters, and material about community service institutions established and operated by members of the order.

4,036. Archives
Records. 1840- . Ca. 55 vols.
Access restricted. No guide.
Society of the Sacred Heart, Chicago Province.
Correspondence of superiors general and others, biographies of members, histories of the order, studies of its constitution and rules, photos, and accounts of events and ceremonies in its houses. The order was first founded in the US in 1818 in St. Charles, MO, and is involved in the education of girls.

4,037. Jewish Federation of Metropolitan Chicago, Women's Division
Records. 1933-64. Ca. 5 Hollinger boxes.
Closed. Inventory.
Spertus College of Judaica, Chicago Jewish Archives.
Minutes, reports, correspondence, and forms of the Division, which was established in 1933 to provide information to the Jewish community, to raise funds, and to coordinate volunteer programs.

4,038. Johannah Lodge No. 9, United Order of True Sisters
Records. 1898-1960. Ca. 10 Hollinger boxes.
Closed. No guide.
Spertus College of Judaica, Chicago Jewish Archives.
Minute books, ledgers, membership lists, and scrapbooks of the Lodge, which was founded in 1874 and did philanthropic work, including establishing a free kindergarten, a penny lunchroom, soup kitchens, public baths, and loan and scholarship funds for promoting education and self-sufficiency among immigrants.

4,039. Spiegel Family
Papers. 1845-1956. 2 Hollinger boxes.
Open. No guide.
Spertus College of Judaica, Chicago Jewish Archives.
Correspondence, memoirs, family trees, photos, and daguerreotypes of the Spiegel family, the owners of a furniture store that developed into a mail-order business. Female family members were not involved in the business but developed philanthropic and civic interests. Includes personal memoirs dating to 1943 of Marcus Spiegel's daughter Lizzie Barbe (1856-?), who became the first president of the Industrial School, later the Jewish Manual Training School of Chicago, and

who was an active member and leader in other Jewish women's organizations.

4,040. Baer, Jean Hitchcock
Papers. 1946-75. 4.5 ft.
Open. Accession record.
University of Illinois at Chicago Circle Archives.
Baer (1918-74) was a researcher and authority in the fields of student counseling and career guidance and a professor of education. Includes correspondence, a diary, speeches, unpublished papers, research and class lecture notes, reports, and questionnaires pertaining to Baer's counseling and teaching career at Stephens College in Columbia, MO; at the University of Iowa, where she counseled women, especially those studying nursing; and at the University of Illinois, where she counseled older women students. Papers include information on vocational counseling for the Social Security Disability Program, counseling services in junior colleges throughout the US, mental health, and educational psychology.

4,041. College of Health, Physical Education, and Recreation: Physical Education for Women
Records. 1948-68. 5.5 ft.
Open. Accession record.
University of Illinois at Chicago Circle Archives.
Correspondence, notes, memoranda, reports, course outlines, schedules, and booklets of this women's physical education program, which was begun in 1946. Includes information on conditioning activities, a number of sports, a modern dance group, and the Women's Athletic Association.

4,042. Office of Student Affairs, Dean of Women
Records. 1946-48. 11 ft.
Open. Accession record.
University of Illinois at Chicago Circle Archives.
Constitutions, reports, correspondence, memoranda, photos, clippings, cards, invitations, lists, newsletters, calendars, and programs of the Office, which was organized in 1946 to interpret the needs of women students to the University administration. Records pertain to the dean of women's role in counseling women students on financial aid, personal problems, employment, and extracurricular activities as well as to the dean's duties in advising Alpha Lambda Delta, the national scholastic honor society for freshman women; the Activities Honorary Society; and the University Dance Committee. The dean also was involved in scheduling campus-wide social events.

4,043. Office of the Chancellor, Committee on the Status of Women
Records. 1971-72. 0.1 ft.
Access restricted. Accession record.
University of Illinois at Chicago Circle Archives.
Minutes and agenda of meetings, memoranda, federal statutes and reports, and articles of the Committee, which existed from 1971 to 1972 to investigate hiring and promotion practices for women at the University. Records pertain to the Committee's advice to the Campus Equal Employment Opportunity Office in implementing an affirmative action plan and its assistance to University departments and administrative units in the development of guidelines and procedures to meet state and federal affirmative action requirements.

4,044. University of Illinois Women's Club at Chicago Circle
Records. 1962-77. 1.7 ft.
Open. Finding aid.
University of Illinois at Chicago Circle Archives.
Slides, scrapbooks, newsletters, and yearbooks of the Club, a women's social service organization founded in 1962 to promote fellowship among faculty wives and women members of the faculty and professional staff. Records reflect the Club's social activities and include information about fund-raising projects for a student scholarship and loan fund and the members' participation in the choice of scholarship and aid recipients.

4,045. Aaron, Helen
Papers. 1947-72. 16 ft.
Open. Unpublished guide.
University of Illinois at Chicago Circle Library, Manuscript Collection.
[Mrs. Ely M.] Aaron (ca. 1905-) is a Chicago civic leader. Correspondence, minutes, memoranda, reports, photos, scrapbooks, clippings, newsletters, and press releases reflect her involvement with the local and national LWV; the Woman's College Board; the Chicago Commission on Human Relations; the Community Fund of Chicago, Inc.; the Near North Community Council; the Chicago Hearing Society; and the American Jewish Committee.

4,046. Abortion Rights Association of Illinois
Records. 1966-75. 6.5 ft.
Open. Unpublished guide.
University of Illinois at Chicago Circle Library, Manuscript Collection.
Founded in 1966 as the Illinois Citizens for the Medical Control of Abortion, the Association, incorporated in 1975, lobbies to make abortions legal and safe in Illinois and disseminates public information. Includes minutes, financial and membership records, correspondence, research and reference files on women's reproductive rights, reports, petitions, newsletters, pamphlets, and publications. The Association, an umbrella organization of individuals and chapters, has sponsored such special projects as Citizens for the Extension of Birth Control Services. Members include Lonny Myers and Helen Smith. Collection also includes information on the National Abortion Rights Action League.

4,047. Addams, Jane
Collection. 1866-1978. Ca. 10,000 items.
Open. Unpublished guide.
University of Illinois at Chicago Circle Library, Manuscript Collection.
Addams (1860-1935) was cofounder of Hull-House in Chicago and an international leader in social welfare, peace, and women's rights movements. Contains personal papers, including correspondence, 1866-1935; travel diaries, 1883-85, 1923, 1925; a weight record book, 1922-35; speeches and writings, including annotated manuscripts; school essays and papers from Rockford College; legal and financial documents relating to property, inheritances, and guardianship; family papers; awards; portraits; and artifacts. In addition the collection contains correspondence and published items by and about Addams, Hull-House activities and programs, Hull-House residents and associates, the Jane Addams' Centennial in 1960, and the development of Hull-House as well as material concerning social welfare organizations in Chicago, national and international social welfare, peace, and women's organizations.

Also includes papers related to Edith Abbott, Grace Abbott, Ruth Austin, Jessie Binford, Louise deKoven Bowen, Neva Boyd, Sophonisba Preston Breckinridge, Charlotte Carr, Ethel Dewey, Alice Hamilton, Norah Hamilton, Florence Kelley, Julia Lathrop, Adena (Miller) Rich, Eleanor Smith, Mary Rozet Smith, Ellen Gates Starr, Alzina Parsons Stevens, and Rachelle Yarros as well as to Chicago Commons, the Chicago School of Civics and Philanthropy, Gads Hill Center, the Mary Crane Nursery, the Woman's Peace party, and the Women's International League for Peace and Freedom. Collection also contains numerous photos, including those of Addams, Hull-House residents and associates, the neighborhood, and Hull-House departments, activities, and programs. There is also a book collection consisting of Addams's library, Hull-House publications, and materials about settlement houses, child welfare, immigration, unions, protective legislation, and women's rights.

4,048. Adult Education Council of Greater Chicago
Records. 1926-75. 6 ft. and 4 vols.
Open. Unpublished guide.
University of Illinois at Chicago Circle Library, Manuscript Collection.
The Council, organized in 1924 as the Chicago Forum Council, provided a platform for public discussion of such topics as race relations and Jewish-Christian relations. A private nonprofit membership organization, the Council later became involved in promoting educational opportunites for adults and coordinating programs for educational agencies. Includes the constitution, bylaws, minutes, financial records, correspondence, directories, press releases, photos, programs, and publications. The Council's activities included sponsorship of a speakers' bureau, educational radio and television programming, publication of a guide to colleges and universitites, and publication of adult literacy bibliographies. Jane Addams was a founding member of the Council; Esther [Mrs. Benjamin] Fain served as executive director from 1962 to 1975.

4,049. Alschuler, Rose Greenbaum (Haas)
Papers. 1916-73. 3 ft.
Open. Unpublished guide.
University of Illinois at Chicago Circle Library, Manuscript Collection.
Includes correspondence, minutes, legal and financial papers, photos, clippings, newsletters, bulletins, catalogs, and personal mementos of [Mrs. Alfred S.] Alschuler (1887-), a philanthropist and expert in the field of public school nurseries and curricula. Alschuler attended the University of Chicago and Vassar College. In 1926 she organized and was staff director of the first public school nursery in Chicago. She also organized and directed a nursery school for children of the Garden Apartments housing project in Chicago from 1928 to 1933, training Negro parents as staff assistants. From 1941 to 1943 she was chairman of the National Committee for Young Children in Washington, DC, and she served for many years on the executive board of the National Association for Nursery Education. Alschuler lectured all over the world and wrote several books, including *Play, the Child's Response to Life* (1937).

4,050. American Friends Service Committee, Chicago Regional Office
Records. 1918-68. 86 ft.
Access restricted. Accession record.
University of Illinois at Chicago Circle Library, Manuscript Collection.
The Committee, a nonsectarian pacifist and service organization, was founded in Philadelphia in 1917. Includes a charter, bylaws, annual reports, minutes, financial records, correspondence, tapes, reports, proposals, schedules, clippings, programs, and leaflets of the Chicago regional office as well as publications of the national and regional committees. Founded in response to WWI, the Committee provided channels through which Quakers and others could work for peace. Although the Committee is nonsectarian, it follows the Quaker approach to social issues, dedicating itself to creating conditions under which peace can exist and working to relieve human suffering throughout the world. Records of the Chicago regional office concern its work with youth and its efforts to promote racial harmony. Records also reveal the working relationships between the Chicago regional office and the Women for Peace; Save Our Sons; Women Against War; the Women's International League for Peace and Freedom; the St. Francis Xavier College for Women in Chicago; LWV; Women Strike for Peace; the Christian

Association of Mothers for Peace, Inc.; and the National Committee of Jewish Women.

4,051. Association for Family Living
Records. 1926-70. 8 ft. and 8 oversize vols.
Open. Unpublished guide.
University of Illinois at Chicago Circle Library, Manuscript Collection.
The Association, an educational social service agency, was established in 1925 and incorporated in 1930. Includes annual reports, minutes, correspondence, research studies, unpublished manuscripts, addresses, photos, scrapbooks, clippings, and publications. Growing out of a child study conference held in Chicago in 1925, the Association began by sponsoring annual conferences. Later a permanent staff was added as well as a variety of educational programs, including speakers, counseling, group work with families, preparation and distribution of literature on family living, and consultation and services to agencies such as the Henry Booth House. Traditionally the Association has been staffed and supported by women.

4,052. Ballard, Russell Ward
Papers. 1875-1977. 14 ft.
Access restricted. Register and accession record.
University of Illinois at Chicago Circle Library, Manuscript Collection.
Ballard (1893-), a social worker and educator, was director of Hull-House. Includes correspondence, memoirs, annual and other reports, minutes, speeches, financial records, memoranda, case histories, personal school and college records and course material, photos, scrapbooks, autograph albums, announcements, pamphlets, clippings, and published items. Although Ballard's papers relate primarily to his career, some personal papers are also included. From 1943 to 1962 Ballard served as director of Hull-House, the only man to hold that position. Collection contains information on Hull-House activities and programs during his tenure as well as his association with Hull-House women, including Edith Abbott, Alice Hamilton, Jesse Florence Binford, Sophonisba Preston Breckinridge, Louise (deKoven) Bowen, and Charlotte Carr. Also includes information on Jane Addams and Ellen Gates Starr.

4,053. Berkow, Ira
Papers. Ca. 1975-77. 4 ft.
Access restricted. Unpublished guide.
University of Illinois at Chicago Circle Library, Manuscript Collection.
Oral histories, transcriptions, notes, and research files of Berkow, an author and journalist, pertain to his book *Maxwell Street: Survival in a Bazaar* (New York: Doubleday, 1977). Maxwell Street, considered part of the Hull-House neighborhood, was the trading and merchandising center for the west side immigrant ghetto. Includes interviews with Bertha Epstein and Mrs. Louis Leavitt, Jewish residents and business proprietors; Beatrice Tucker, a physician and head of the Chicago Maternity Center; Goldie Greenberg; Goldie Paley; and Guadalupe Rodriguez.

4,054. Bethlehem Community Center
Records. 1891-1960. 21 ft.
Open. Unpublished guide.
University of Illinois at Chicago Circle Library, Manuscript Collection.
Founded in 1888 as a Protestant mission congregation to the Bohemian community on Chicago's west side, the Center, which merged with Howell Neighborhood House in 1961, offered religious programs of worship and such service and settlement activities as relief, work, clubs, classes, and a summer camp. Includes minutes, legal and financial records, correspondence, reports, motion pictures, church vital statistics, rosters, photos, and blueprints. The collection, part of which is in the Czech language, includes information on founders E. A. Adams, a minister, and his wife; [Miss] Bozena Salava, a church leader and youth worker at the center from 1890 to 1925; the Christian Endeavor, a temperance club; the women's auxiliary; and the day nursery.

4,055. Bickham, Martin H.
Papers. 1905-76. 130 ft.
Open. Unpublished guide.
University of Illinois at Chicago Circle Library, Manuscript Collection.
Bickham (1880-1976) was a sociologist, civil rights worker, community organization leader, and a Methodist church social issues activist. Contains family papers with correspondence and memorabilia of his wife Edith Baker Reid Bickham (1877-ca. 1960) and their daughters Catherine Ann (Bickham) [Mrs. James] Bean (1909-), Margaret Reid (Bickham) [Mrs. Dorrance] Nygaard (1913-), Emma Hayes (Bickham) [Mrs. William] Pitcher (1915-), and Frances Louise (Bickham) [Mrs. John] Boyle (1922-). Also contains diaries, minutes, manuscripts of published and unpublished works, speeches, research notes, reports, photos, and scrapbooks as well as information pertaining to Bickham's organizational affiliations, including the Illinois Temperance Council and Temperance Education, Inc.; the United Charities of Chicago; the WPA in Illinois, for which Bickham served as director of the Cook County work relief program and a member of the work relief advisory committee; and the Service Bureau for Unemployed Women. Collection also includes photos of and a scrapbook containing scenes of immigrant families.

4,056. Birmingham, Alma
Papers. 1907-70. 4 ft. and oversize items.
Open. Unpublished guide.
University of Illinois at Chicago Circle Library, Manuscript Collection.
Correspondence, articles, photos, scrapbooks, clippings, yearbooks, proceedings, bulletins, programs, and artwork of Birmingham, a pianist and music teacher who taught at the Hull-House Music School from 1922 to 1938, served as associate director of the Music School from 1938 to ca. 1942, and was acting head resident of Hull-House during the summer of 1934. Papers contain information on artists, musicians, and social workers as well as musical concerts in Chicago. Includes correspondence and other items by or pertaining to Jane Addams, Ellen Gates Starr, Eleanor Smith, Mary Rozet Smith, Adena (Miller) Rich, Louise deKoven Bowen, Agnes Hope Pillsbury, Enella Benedict, the Hull-House Music School, the Lake View Musical Society in Chicago, the Woman's Symphony Orchestra of Chicago and its director Ebba Sundstrom, and the Woman's City Club concerts.

4,057. Bohemian Women's Publishing Company
Records. Ca. 1895-1900. 1 vol.
Open. Register.
University of Illinois at Chicago Circle Library, Manuscript Collection.
Scrapbook of the Company, a commercial printing firm formed and run entirely by 50 Bohemian women in the Pilsen area of Chicago between ca. 1894 and 1900. Contains photos of stockholders, clippings, and samples of printing. The Company also published *Ženské Listy,* the first Bohemian women's weekly in Chicago. Josefa Humpal-Zeman, who briefly resided at Hull-House, edited the journal.

4,058. Bowe, Mary Gwinn
Papers. 1926-74. 4.2 ft.
Open. Accession record.
University of Illinois at Chicago Circle Library, Manuscript Collection.
[Mrs. William John] Bowe (1901-) is a clubwoman, founding member of the Woman's College Board of Chicago, and a member of the women's board of the Lyric Opera of Chicago. Includes correspondence; organizational records, including bylaws, minutes, financial reports and records; a genealogy of the Gwinn, Roche, Bowe, and Caravan families; family papers; clippings; press releases; and programs. Papers relate primarily to Bowe's activities with the Woman's College Board (an outgrowth of women's college alumnae activities at the 1933-34 Chicago World's Fair), which served as a clearing house for information on women's colleges, a center for recruiting prospective students, and a social group for the alumnae. The Board ceased operations in 1974. Bowe also was a trustee of Trinity College and of Chicago's educational television station WTTW.

4,059. Boyd, Neva Leona
Papers. 1911-71. 7.2 ft.
Open. Register.
University of Illinois at Chicago Circle Library, Manuscript Collection.
Boyd (1876-1963) was an educator, educational theorist, social group worker, and author. Includes correspondence, a diary for 1945 to 1947, notes, an unpublished manuscript, case studies, outlines, lists, charts, photos, clippings, programs, published material, and a copy of Paul Simon, ed., *Play and Game Theory in Group Work: A Collection of Papers by Neva Leona Boyd* (Chicago: University of Illinois at Chicago Circle, 1971). A pioneer sociologist, Boyd attended the Chicago Kindergarten Institute and in 1911 founded the Recreation Training School of Chicago, which she directed until it closed in 1914. She served as an assistant professor of sociology at Northwestern University from 1927 to 1941, and from 1941 until her death she was a consultant to the active therapy department of the Illinois department of public welfare. From 1947 to 1960 Boyd was a resident of Hull-House. Her principal interest was the development and practice of a theory of group work and play that she applied to institutionalized children and adults.

4,060. Boyden, William Cowper
Papers. 1888-1976. 15 ft.
Open. Unpublished guide.
University of Illinois at Chicago Circle Library, Manuscript Collection.
Boyden (1894-1965) was a lawyer. Includes correspondence, speeches, scrapbooks, clippings, and Boyden family papers. Contains papers of Boyden's wife Sarah Brown Boyden, a Chicago journalist and social leader, including correspondence, post cards, unpublished writings, speeches, class notes, invitations to social and literary societies, syllabi, examinations from Northwestern University for 1921 and 1922, photos, and clippings. Also includes notes of Ellen M. Brown on Amelia Sears's lectures at the University of Chicago, 1912, and a journal by an unknown author containing accounts for a woman's club, household accounts, verse, clippings, and recipes, 1894-1900.

4,061. Bradley, Mary Hastings
Papers. 1882-1976. Ca. 104 ft.
Open. Unpublished guide.
University of Illinois at Chicago Circle Library, Manuscript Collection.
[Mrs. Herbert E.] Bradley (ca. 1882-1976) was an author, lecturer, world traveler, and social leader in Chicago. Includes correspondence; diaries; notes and research files; drafts and manuscripts of published articles, short stories, and novels; legal and financial papers; speeches; lecture notes; genealogies; itineraries; photos; scrapbooks; maps; clippings; publicity material; and publications. Among Bradley's novels are *The Wine of Astonishment* and *I Passed for White.* She also drew upon her expeditions to Africa and the Far East to write a series of travel books, including *On the Gorilla Trail* and *Alice in Jungleland.* She

lectured extensively during the 1930s about her travels. During WWII she was a war correspondent for *Collier's* and toured Italy and Germany. Her reports on the Nazi concentration camps were published in *Cosmopolitan, Ladies' Home Journal,* and *Saturday Evening Post.* Bradley was a trustee and member of the woman's board of the Illinois Children's Home and Aid Society, a member of the Illinois Woman's Press Association, a board member and president of the Society of Midland Authors, and a governing life member of the Art Institute of Chicago. Collection also includes information on Bradley's daughter Alice Bradley [Mrs. Huntingdon] Sheldon, an art critic and author, and Bradley's mother Lena Rickords Corwin.

4,062. Bundy, John C.
Papers. 1878-90. 15 vols.
Open. Unpublished guide.
University of Illinois at Chicago Circle Library, Manuscript Collection.
Bundy (1841-?) was an editor and publisher of the spiritualist weekly *Religio-Philosophical Journal.* Consists of letterpress books of Bundy's business correspondence. Correspondents include his wife Mary Bundy, Frances E. Willard, and Phoebe Hull, a niece of Charles Hull. Contains information on women mediums and spiritualists of the era.

4,063. Camp Fire Girls, Salt Creek Council, Illinois
Records. 1911-76. 11.5 ft.
Open. Unpublished guide.
University of Illinois at Chicago Circle Library, Manuscript Collection.
Includes annual reports, correspondence, membership lists, photos, scrapbooks, clippings, newsletters, program material, publications, and artifacts of this branch of the Camp Fire Girls, which was founded in 1912 by Lucy Babcock, a teacher. The interests of the Council, which is an umbrella organization of Camp Fire groups in western and southwestern Chicago suburbs, include conservation, Indian lore, and camping as a means for personal growth and development. Among its leaders were Betty Collins, Reva Ebert, and Dixie [Mrs. A. L.] Elder. Nancy Cech is the current executive director.

4,064. Cartwright, Jessie Whitney
Papers. 1897-1977. Ca. 1 ft.
Open. Unpublished guide.
University of Illinois at Chicago Circle Library, Manuscript Collection.
Correspondence, speeches, unpublished poetry and short stories, tapes, photos, and clippings of Cartwright (ca. 1891-1977), who worked from the age of 50 until the age of 75 at the Norge Corporation where she developed a number of patentable improvements on home appliances. She also served as a national home services director at the Corporation.

4,065. Central Baptist Children's Home
Records. 1896-1967. 12 ft.
Access restricted. Unpublished guide.
University of Illinois at Chicago Circle Library, Manuscript Collection.
The Home, which was organized in 1895 as the Central Baptist Orphanage, maintains a residence for children aged 4 to 12 years in Lake Villa, IL, and provides group and foster homes, day-care services, and family counseling. Includes minutes, financial records, correspondence, case records, applications for adoption and foster homes, reports, conference items, and scrapbooks. Collection contains items concerning girls associated with the Home, women staff members, women members of the board of directors, and the Woman's Auxiliary Board.

4,066. A Century of Progress International Exposition
Records. 1928-40. 555 ft.
Open. Unpublished guide.
University of Illinois at Chicago Circle Library, Manuscript Collection.
The Exposition was a world's fair held in Chicago during the summers of 1933 and 1934 in commemoration of the centennial of Chicago's incorporation. Includes minutes, legal and financial records, correspondence, notes, reports, statistics, publicity files, charts and graphs, blueprints, photos, clippings, and publications. The collection relates primarily to the planning, construction, operation, demolition, and writing of the official history of the fair. Women were involved as staff members, artists, trustees, and exhibitors, and women's organizations, including long-lived groups that grew out of fair activities, took an active role. Includes items of such women as Louise Lentz Woodruff, the sculptor of the Fountain of Science; Helen Bennett, the manager of the social sciences division; Helen Tieken Geraghty, producer of the Pageant of Transportation; Bertha [Mrs. Jacob] Baur, a member of the board of trustees; Mrs. Rufus Dawes, chairman of social functions; Mrs. Kellogg Fairbank, a member of the board of trustees and the executive committee; Jane Addams; Eleanor Roosevelt; Ruth (Hanna) McCormick; and Jessie F. Binford. Women's organizations that were involved in the fair include the Woman's Benefit Association, the WCTU, the Woman's City Club of Chicago, the Woman's Interior Decorators Association, the Woman's Symphony Orchestra, the Women's Aeronautical Association of the USA, the Illinois Federation of Women's Clubs, the Women's Trade Union League, and the Women's Worlds Fair, Inc. Collection also includes publicity items for special events, including Woman's Day, a women's billiard championship match, the World's Congress of Representative Women, ethnic and nationality days, shorthand and typing competitions, and beauty contests.

4,067. Chicago Council on Foreign Relations
Records. 1922-75. 70 ft.
Open. Register.
University of Illinois at Chicago Circle Library, Manuscript Collection.
The Council, which was founded in 1922, is an educational organization that gathers to discuss US foreign policy and international relations. Includes articles of incorporation, bylaws, minutes, correspondence, speeches, reports, photos, clippings, and publications. Women have been involved in the Council since its founding, and among the first board members were Mrs. William Gold Hibbard and Mrs. Arthur Ryerson. Louise L. Wright served as executive director from 1942 to 1952 and, with Emily (Taft) [Mrs. Paul] Douglas, cofounded the Pamphlet Shop, a publishing operation that prepared and distributed foreign affairs material. Includes speeches given at meetings by Pearl S. Buck, Eleanor Roosevelt, Agnes Smedley, Barbara Ward, and Gwendolyn Carter.

4,068. Chicago Exchange for Woman's Work
Records. 1880-85. 3 items.
Open. No guide.
University of Illinois at Chicago Circle Library, Manuscript Collection.
The Exchange was organized in 1879 by women of independent means to help needy women become self-sufficient by using their talents and skills and to provide a place for women to sell their handiwork or valuable items in times of need. Includes annual reports containing a constitution, bylaws, treasurer's report, committee reports, resolutions, summaries of goods deposited and sold, and lists of officers, members of the board of managers, and subscribers.

4,069. Chicago Home for the Friendless
Records. 1867-79. 5 items.
Open. Unpublished guide.
University of Illinois at Chicago Circle Library, Manuscript Collection.
Annual reports of the Home, which was founded in 1858 to provide aid to indigent women and children through the maintenance of a temporary residence and placement in homes. Includes committee reports, mortality and morbidity statistics, and lists of donations. The Home was incorporated in 1869 by 14 women, including Jane Currie (Blaikie) Hoge; in cooperation with numerous Chicago churches, the Home cared for foundling children, wards of the court, the elderly, and women needing temporary shelter. The Home maintained an industrial school for girls aged 8 to 12 years as well as the Bever Mission and Industrial School, which was under the direction of Mrs. S. J. Moody.

4,070. Chicago Nutrition Association
Records. 1942-72. 2.5 ft.
Open. Accession record.
University of Illinois at Chicago Circle Library, Manuscript Collection.
The Association, which was founded in 1942, is an interest group of dieticians, physicians, and home economists working for the improvement of the nutritional status of the people of Chicago. Includes constitution, bylaws, articles of incorporation, annual reports, minutes, financial records, correspondence, an audio tape, a motion picture film, membership lists, newsletters, and brochures. Ruth Cowan Clouse was chairman of the planning committee of the Association, which grew out of the Chicago Nutritional Committee, a wartime agency. Initially members of the Association were delegates representing organizations and agencies related to nutrition, but in 1943 membership was opened to all. The first president of the Association was Margaret Hessler Brooks, who served from 1945 to 1947. The Association has been involved in supplying educational material to libraries, assisting in the operation of school lunch programs, lobbying for mandatory enrichment of bread and flour, and sponsoring educational membership meetings and public awareness programs. Most members of the Association have been women.

4,071. Chicago Public School Art Society
Records. 1894-1968. 2.2 ft.
Open. Accession record.
University of Illinois at Chicago Circle Library, Manuscript Collection.
Minutes, financial records, appointment books, reports, form letters, photos, lantern slides, publicity material, catalogs, brochures, and programs of the Society, which was founded as an all-female organization in 1894 to sponsor and promote art education and aesthetic development in Chicago's public schools. An outgrowth of women's art activities that took place during the World's Columbian Exposition in Chicago in 1893, the Society had Ellen Gates Starr, a cofounder of Hull-House, as its first president. The membership, which consisted entirely of women for many years, included delegates from women's organizations and clubs. The Society's first activities, centered in the Goodrich School in the Hull-House neighborhood, included the placement of works of classic beauty in the School. The Society continues its work by awarding scholarships to the Art Institute of Chicago, developing art curricula, and selling art reproductions at cost in inner-city schools.

4,072. Chicago Relief and Aid Society
Records. 1874-95. 16 items.
Open. Unpublished guide.
University of Illinois at Chicago Circle Library, Manuscript Collection.
Annual reports of the Society, which was established in 1857 to coordinate distribution of

private charity for those needing temporary assistance. Early programs included distribution of commodities to individuals and institutions such as hospitals. The Society was selected to administer relief funds sent from around the world following the Chicago fire, and its programs subsequently involved monetary assistance distributed to applicants based on findings of an investigative committee. The Society's officers were men, but the annual reports contain extensive information concerning female charity cases.

4,073. Chicago Urban League
Records. 1932-71. Ca. 200 ft. and 30 microfilm reels.
Open. Unpublished guide.
University of Illinois at Chicago Circle Library, Manuscript Collection.
Founded in 1916, the League works to promote economic and social welfare in Chicago's Negro community and to foster interracial cooperation. Includes a constitution, annual reports, minutes, legal and financial records, correspondence, speeches, research and reference files, photos, press releases, and publications. Also includes files of women staff and board members. The League is concerned with training, employment, fair housing, relief, community organization, liaison with other human relations and civil rights organizations, and civil rights, especially voter registration. Includes items pertaining to the West Side Women's Division, the Junior Women's Auxiliary, the Urbanaides, the Miss Chicago Urban League contest, and the Women's Joint Committee on Adequate Housing.

4,074. Chicago Woman's Aid
Records. 1882-1972. 14 ft.
Open. Unpublished guide.
University of Illinois at Chicago Circle Library, Manuscript Collection.
Annual and special reports, minutes, correspondence, directories, scripts for anniversary shows, photos, programs, and publications of the CWA, a social, educational, and service club, which was organized in 1882 as the Young Ladies Aid Society and chartered in 1895 as the Chicago Woman's Aid. Early activities included providing flowers and books for patients at Michael Reese Hospital. Later the club's interests included aid for the blind and visually handicapped, improvement of public schools, the provision of birth control facilities at Jewish social agencies, and sponsorship of children's facilities at the Hospital and programs for senior citizens. Although CWA's membership has always been predominantly Jewish, the group's activities are not restricted to the Jewish community.

4,075. Chicago Women in Broadcasting
Records. 1974-76. 24 items.
Open. Accession record.
University of Illinois at Chicago Circle Library, Manuscript Collection.
Includes newsletters, programs, and the publication *Chicago Women in Broadcasting* of this professional organization, which was founded in 1972 by eight women who wished to improve the status of women working in radio and television. Membership is limited to women presently or formerly employed by a Chicago-area radio or television station, free-lance workers at these stations, and students of radio and television at local universities. Activities of the group include surveying television and radio for affirmative action compliance, sponsoring public speaking and leadership training, supporting the Equal Rights Amendment, presenting awards, and printing a "job mart" in their newsletter.

4,076. Cirese, Helen Mathilde
Papers. 1933-63. 4.5 ft.
Open. Register.
University of Illinois at Chicago Circle Library, Manuscript Collection.
Cirese (1899-) is a lawyer, judge, and leader in professional organizations. Includes correspondence, memos, campaign literature, photos, scrapbooks, clippings, form letters, flyers, National Association of Women Lawyers directories, and issues of *Women Lawyer's Journal.* Cirese graduated from De Paul University in 1920; she was admitted to the bar in 1921 and served as justice of the peace in Oak Park, IL, from 1945 to 1961. She also was president of the National Association of Women Lawyers from 1930 to 1931, of the West Suburban Bar Association from 1949 to 1950, and of the Central Business and Professional Women's Club from 1942 to 1944.

4,077. Clarence Darrow Community Center
Records. 1954-66. 7 ft.
Open. Unpublished guide.
University of Illinois at Chicago Circle Library, Manuscript Collection.
Founded in 1953 as the Ryder Community Center, this neighborhood center is located in a public housing project on Chicago's south side. Includes constitution, bylaws, annual and service reports, minutes, financial records, correspondence, photos, scrapbooks, clippings, and publications. Sponsored by the Universalist Service Committee, the Center was originally developed to offer recreation to residents of the housing project, but later it provided group work and community service, primarily to young adults. Irene M. Smith is the executive director.

4,078. Clarke, Philip Ream
Papers. 1917-66. 15 ft.
Open. Unpublished guide.
University of Illinois at Chicago Circle Library, Manuscript Collection.
Correspondence, minutes, speeches, legal and financial records, photos, clippings, and published items of Clarke (1889-1966), an investment banker and a chairman of civic fund-raising drives. Includes records of the Cook County Taxpayers' Warrant Trust, which raised $74,000,000 to pay public employees' salaries, 1930; of the Community Fund-Red Cross Joint Appeal, a major public funding agency for social services in Chicago, 1959; and of the King-Bruwaert House in Hinsdale, IL, a residence for elderly women, 1946-52. Also includes correspondence with Doris Nash Wortman, who constructed Double-Crostic word puzzles for the *Saturday Review,* 1953-66.

4,079. Community Fund of Chicago, Inc.
Records. 1930-75. 241 ft.
Access restricted. Accession record.
University of Illinois at Chicago Circle Library, Manuscript Collection.
The Fund, an umbrella fund-raising organization for social agencies in the Chicago metropolitan area, was founded in 1931. Includes constitution, bylaws, minutes, financial records, correspondence, historical files, committee files, reports, membership lists, clippings, and press releases as well as annual reports, correspondence, and publications of agencies that received money from the Fund. Agnes Nestor, an officer in the National Women's Trade Union League, was the only woman member of the first board of directors. In 1943 [Mrs.] Linn Brandenburg became an assistant director, and in 1946 she became associate executive director, a post she held for more than 10 years. The women's division of the Fund was operated as an auxiliary and raised funds on a neighborhood basis from other women through door-to-door solicitation and visiting women's clubs and organizations. In 1976 the Fund merged with the Welfare Council of Metropolitan Chicago to form the United Way of Metropolitan Chicago. Collection includes information on the Camp Fire Girls, Chicago Area Council; the Association for Family Living; the Hull-House Association; the Chicago Child Care Society; the Florence Crittenton Anchorage; the Chicago Maternity Center; the Chicago Nursery and Half Orphan Asylum; the Infant Welfare Society of Chicago; the Mary Bartelme Home for Girls; the YWCA of Metropolitan Chicago; the Mary Crane League; the Visiting Nurse Association; the Juvenile Protective Association; the Travelers Aid Society; the Immigrants' Service League; and the Mary McDowell Settlement.

4,080. Cook County Socialist Party
Records. 1913-35. 1 ft.
Open. Unpublished guide.
University of Illinois at Chicago Circle Library, Manuscript Collection.
The Party is a political organization founded in ca. 1901 to protect the rights of workers and to support Socialist candidates for state and local office. Minutes of the executive and delegate committees as well as broadsides, which include lists of officers, members, and applicants for membership; descriptions of political efforts in state and local elections between 1913 and 1919; and discussions of financial problems. Includes information on Ellen Gates Starr, cofounder of Hull-House, who in 1915 was a member of the executive committee and served on the propaganda committee and the special committee on the unemployed. These committees met with the mayor and city council to discuss the issue of unemployment, took action in the 1915 Chicago street car workers strike, organized lectures, and secured halls for speakers. In 1916, Starr ran unsuccessfully for alderman on the Socialist party ticket. Other women mentioned in the collection include Aleksandra Mikhailovna Kollontai and Emma Goldman.

4,081. Cotton, Sylvia
Papers. 1945-72. 7 ft.
Open. Accession record.
University of Illinois at Chicago Circle Library, Manuscript Collection.
Cotton (1913-) is an educational activist and founder and president of the Day Care Crisis Council of Chicago. Includes budget statements, subject files, memos, reports, items concerning segregation cases, election information regarding Cotton's candidacy for the Chicago board of education, a Jeannette Rankin clipping file and other clippings, newsletters, and open letters. Cotton worked to establish the first integrated nursery school in Hyde Park, IL.

4,082. Council on Population and Environment
Records. 1969-75. 5 ft.
Open. Unpublished guide.
University of Illinois at Chicago Circle Library, Manuscript Collection.
Founded in 1969, the Council, a national organization with headquarters in Chicago, produces research proposals and sponsors conferences. Includes legal and financial records, correspondence, speeches, reports, lists, questionnaires, resolutions, proposals, and photos. Records relate primarily to the First National Congress on Optimum Population and Environment held in Chicago in 1970 and subsequent conferences on improving the quality of urban life in Chicago and elsewhere. Janet H. Malone serves as executive director.

4,083. Dieckmann, Annetta Maria
Papers. 1934-74. 3.75 ft.
Open. Accession record.
University of Illinois at Chicago Circle Library, Manuscript Collection.
Dieckmann (1892-1974) was an industrial division organizer for the National YWCA. Includes correspondence, legal papers, reports, notes, clippings, awards, and published items, which pertain to her career. Dieckmann served as the first industrial secretary for the national board of the YWCA from 1918 to 1924, traveling across the

US to establish programs for working women. In 1924 she came to Chicago to serve as industrial secretary of the Chicago YWCA. After her retirement from the YWCA in 1951, she organized a workers' education program for the Retail Clerks Union in St. Louis, and in 1956 she became a full-time volunteer board secretary for the Illinois American Civil Liberties Union in Chicago, developing statewide educational programs on the civil liberties of women. The Illinois ACLU has established an annual Annetta Dieckmann award for the volunteer who does the most to advance civil liberties in Illinois.

4,084. Elizabeth McCormick Memorial Fund
Records. 1909-1963. 8 ft.
Open. Register.
University of Illinois at Chicago Circle Library, Manuscript Collection.
The Fund is a private philanthropic trust organized to improve child welfare and health in Chicago and the US. Includes legal and financial records; items pertaining to the establishment, administration, general programming and dissolution of the Fund; correspondence; project reports; files of funded fellowships awarded for research; clippings; and photos and memorabilia of Elizabeth McCormick (1892-1905) and her family. Cyrus H. and Harriet McCormick created the trust fund to commemorate their only daughter. The Fund, which was incorporated in 1913, began its work combating disease and high mortality rates among inner-city children in 1909. It established "fresh-air" and "open air" schools to prevent tuberculosis, provided mothers with hygiene and nutritional guidance, and established and encouraged innovative child health practices. After 1949 monies were concentrated almost solely on individual research projects to advance knowledge in meeting the needs of children, and from 1957 to 1961 fellowships were awarded to researchers in these areas. In 1951 the Fund transferred its assets to the Chicago Community Trust. Several women have served as the Fund's executive director, among them Mrs. Ira Couch Wood, who served from 1918 to 1923; Mary E. Murphy, who served from 1925 to 1948; and Martha Branscombe, who served from 1949 to 1954.

4,085. Ethical Humanist Society of Chicago
Records. 1882-1956. 8 ft.
Open. Unpublished guide.
University of Illinois at Chicago Circle Library, Manuscript Collection.
Constitution, bylaws, minutes, financial records, correspondence, speeches, reports, clippings, announcements, bulletins, and programs of the Society, organized in 1882 as a quasi-religious liberal organization devoted to the study and application of ethical and humanist principles. The Society sponsored social welfare activities in Chicago, including Relief Works, a group of public health nurses; Henry Booth House, a social settlement founded in 1898 on Chicago's near west side, residents of which included Emma Pischel, Helen Whitehead, Margaret Young, Edna Hanson, and Lillie Lynem; and the Legal Aid Bureau, which provides legal assistance for needy individuals. Women have been active participants on the board as well as in the Women's Union and the Young People's Association. Jane Addams and other women frequently lectured at the Society in its early years.

4,086. The Feminist Voice
Records. 1971-72. 9 items.
Open. Unpublished guide.
University of Illinois at Chicago Circle Library, Manuscript Collection.
An irregularly issued, collectively produced, feminist newspaper, *The Feminist Voice* carried a variety of feature articles on such issues as abortion, rape, sexuality, and women and work as well as on women's literature.

4,087. Firman House
Records. 1953-67. 9 ft.
Open. Unpublished guide.
University of Illinois at Chicago Circle Library, Manuscript Collection.
Founded in ca. 1872 as a Congregational church mission and Sunday school, this settlement house was incorporated in 1912 as Firman House. Includes constitution, minutes, financial records, correspondence, reports, program items, photos, scrapbooks, and newsletters. The House is located in the Robert Taylor Homes Housing Project, which is comprised of black residents. Records relate to the woman's auxiliary as well as to women staff members, volunteers, and board members. Includes information on the floor captain system employed in the Robert Taylor Homes, a system in which women act as liaisons between residents and the agency.

4,088. Florence Crittenton Anchorage
Records. 1880-1974. 14 ft. and oversize items.
Access restricted. Accession record.
University of Illinois at Chicago Circle Library, Manuscript Collection.
The Anchorage, which was organized in 1887, offered residence facilities and assistance to unmarried pregnant women. Includes bylaws, annual reports, minutes, financial records, correspondence, insurance records, director and caseworker reports, records of mothers, a history, applications for employment, residents' rules, adoption forms, manuals, photos, clippings, newsletters, programs, publicity material, catalogs, and other items. After Frances Willard gave a speech in Chicago in 1886 about saving unfortunate women, the WCTU organized the Anchorage to aid destitute and alcoholic women as well as unwed mothers. In 1893 Charles Nelson Crittenton came to Chicago to organize rescue work, but finding the Anchorage well-established, he arranged with officers of the National WCTU, through Frances Willard, to donate $1000 provided the name was changed to the Florence Crittenton Anchorage. The Anchorage was terminated in 1974 because few women were using the home and because of financial problems.

4,089. Foster, Hazel E.
Papers. 1915-70. 1.25 ft.
Open. Unpublished guide.
University of Illinois at Chicago Circle Library, Manuscript Collection.
Foster (1885-) is an educator, social worker, and Presbyterian minister. Includes correspondence, minutes, resolutions, a memorial tribute to Jane Addams, newsletters, leaflets, brochures, programs, and published items. Foster was active in many women's groups and religious organizations, including the Women's International League for Peace and Freedom, the Fellowship of Reconciliation, the American Association of Women Preachers, and the LWV. Papers relate primarily to her organizational activities with WILPF and include information on planning the League's celebration of the Jane Addams Centennial. Correspondents include Edith Abbott, Grace Abbott, Jane Addams, Mabel Wing Castle, Alice Hamilton.

4,090. Gary Urban League
Records. 1941-65. 14 ft.
Open. Unpublished guide.
University of Illinois at Chicago Circle Library, Manuscript Collection.
The League was founded in 1945 to promote economic and social welfare among the Negro population in Gary, IN, and to improve race relations. Includes a constitution, bylaws, legal and financial records, correspondence, personnel records, program files, reports, studies and research findings, photos, clippings, and publications. The League's particular interests included increasing education and job opportunities for the Negro community in Gary and working to remove restrictive racial barriers in community life. It maintains an organization of block clubs and councils. Women have participated in the League as staff members, volunteers, and block club leaders. Collection also includes information on cooperation with other organizations such as the Visiting Nurse Association of Gary.

4,091. Geraghty, Helen Tieken
Papers. 1931-69. 4.5 ft.
Open. Unpublished guide.
University of Illinois at Chicago Circle Library, Manuscript Collection.
[Mrs. Maurice P.] Geraghty (1902-) is a theatrical producer and director in Chicago. Includes director's notes, budgets, attendance records, scripts, set designs, costume drawings, photos, and programs relating to Geraghty's work as a producer and director of historical pageants, including those at A Century of Progress International Exposition in 1933 and 1934 and the Chicago Railroad Fair in 1948 and 1949. Also includes material concerning Geraghty's production of trade shows, exhibitions, and charity benefits and her employment as a drama instructor at the Francis Parker School and Hull-House.

4,092. German Aid Society of Chicago
Records. 1878-1949. 12 ft.
Access restricted. Register.
University of Illinois at Chicago Circle Library, Manuscript Collection.
A charitable organization, the Society was formed in 1854 to assist German immigrants. Includes bylaws, annual reports, minutes, financial records, correspondence, case histories, lists of contributors, photos, and leaflets as well as correspondence and publications of other German social and benevolent societies across the US. Financed largely by annual membership fees and contributions, the Society dispensed funds for particular needs such as lodging, food, clothing, or coal; provided medical referrals and legal advice; located employment; procured reduced train fares and, in special cases, transportation back to Germany; received letters for immigrants having no permanent homes; and restored lost baggage. Few women were members of the Society, but a number of women were the recipients of its aid. Also includes correspondence from the Women's Trade Union League of Illinois describing the League's immigration department and programs to assist young girls coming from abroad to Chicago through New York to find their friends and employment.

4,093. Greater Lawndale Conservation Commission
Records. 1953-68. 4.5 ft.
Open. Unpublished guide.
University of Illinois at Chicago Circle Library, Manuscript Collection.
Founded in 1954, this community organization works for improved housing, educational opportunities, and health care in a predominantly black neighborhood. Includes bylaws, minutes, financial records, correspondence, reports, clippings, programs, and published items. The Commission, which serves a central west side Chicago community, has an active women's auxiliary involved in fund raising; women are leaders of block club councils and youth committees.

4,094. Groves, Alma Zola
Papers. 1937-74. 11.25 ft.
Open. Accession record.
University of Illinois at Chicago Circle Library, Manuscript Collection.
Groves (1898-) served as assistant attorney general in Illinois; she also is active in women's professional and service organizations. Includes correspondence, minutes, speeches, notes, bylaws, financial records, agendas, memos, reports,

histories, membership lists, conference material, clippings, publicity items, newsletters, professional journals, and other items. Groves graduated from Gem City Business College in 1920, studied law, and was admitted to the bar in 1948. In 1949 she began working for Illinois attorneys general, primarily in the appellate division where she argued cases before the Illinois Supreme Court and the Illinois Appellate Court. She was active in such professional and service organizations as the Zonta Club, the Federation of Business and Professional Women, the Women's Bar Association of Illinois, the National Association of Women Lawyers, and the Friends of Literature. She also organized the Monmouth, IL, chapter of the Business and Professional Women's Club, served as its first president from 1941 to 1943, and served as state president of the group from 1958 to 1960.

4,095. Haldeman-Julius Family

Papers. 1833-1961. 14 ft.
Open. Register.
University of Illinois at Chicago Circle Library, Manuscript Collection.
Includes correspondence, diaries, notes, manuscripts, legal and financial records, genealogies, photos, clippings, and published items of the Addams, Haldeman, and Haldeman-Julius families. Papers relate to John Huy Addams (1822-81), the father of Jane Addams and a resident of Cedarville, IL, who after the death of his wife Sarah (Weber) Addams (1817-63) married Anna (Hostetter) Haldeman (1828-1919), the widow of William Haldeman (1823-66) and a resident of Freeport, IL. John Addams became stepfather to her sons George Bowman Haldeman (1861-1909) and Henry Winfield Haldeman (1848-1905). Henry Haldeman married Jane Addams's sister Sarah Alice (Addams) Haldeman (1853-1915), and they had one child, Anna Marcet Haldeman (1887-1941), who married Emanuel Julius (1889-1951), at which time their names were combined as Haldeman-Julius. Correspondence of Jane Addams relates to her early life and family relationships from 1888 to 1929.

Collection also contains extensive papers of Anna Addams, including correspondence and legal and financial papers, 1844-1919. Papers of S. Alice Haldeman include diaries, 1872 and 1888-89; personal correspondence, 1871-1915; and business papers, 1905-15. In addition, collection contains personal and business correspondence, 1903-41; diaries, 1897-1900 and 1929-30; legal and financial papers, 1915-41; and published and unpublished articles, short stories, and novels of Anna Marcet Haldeman-Julius. Her papers pertain to her career as an actress; administrator of the State Bank of Girard, KS; author and journalist; and, with her husband, owner of the Haldeman-Julius Publishing Company in Girard and publisher of *The Debunker, The Haldeman-Julius Monthly,* and the Little Blue Books series

4,096. Henry Booth House

Records. 1935-69. 3 ft. and 100 oversize items.
Open. Unpublished guide.
University of Illinois at Chicago Circle Library, Manuscript Collection.
This settlement house, founded in 1898 by what is now known as the Ethical Humanist Society, is located in the Dearborn Homes of the Chicago Housing Authority. Includes constitution, bylaws, correspondence, service reports, photos, a scrapbook, brochures, and pamphlets. Records document the activities of Edna Hanson and Lillie Lynem, both head residents of the House. Includes records of the women's board, a volunteer and fund-raising auxiliary.

4,097. Hjorth, Eric

Papers. 1880-1940. 0.5 ft.
Open. Unpublished guide.
University of Illinois at Chicago Circle Library, Manuscript Collection.
Hjorth was an actor with the Hull-House Players and other little theater groups in Chicago and the surrounding area. Papers include clippings, articles, a publicity booklet for 1879 and 1880, and playbills of Laura Dainty [Mrs. Fred] Pelham, an actress and Hull-House resident who founded the Hull-House Players in 1899 and the Chicago City Garden Association, an organization that provided garden tracts for the poor to cultivate. Pelham also was active in the Hull-House Women's Club for many years and served as its president.

4,098. Home Economists in Business

Records. 1948-73. 2 ft. and 6 oversize vols.
Open. Accession record.
University of Illinois at Chicago Circle Library, Manuscript Collection.
Bylaws, annual reports, minutes, financial records, correspondence, project files, a history, convention items, questionnaires, newsletters, and handbooks of the Chicago branch of Home Economists in Business, a section of the American Home Economics Association. A professional organization, the Home Economists is involved in career counseling and professional development. The Chicago organization was formed in 1924, and Dorothy Knight served as its first president from 1924 to 1926. Members must belong to the American Home Economics Association, hold a degree in home economics, and be employed in a business or similar organization. Activities include publication of a newsletter and educational pamphlets, sponsorship of programs, and attendance at the national American Home Economics Association meetings. The group has largely been organized and maintained by women.

4,099. Howell Neighborhood House

Records. 1914-66. 2 ft.
Open. Unpublished guide.
University of Illinois at Chicago Circle Library, Manuscript Collection.
Minutes, correspondence, reports, bulletins, photos, and publications of the House, founded in 1905 as the Bohemian Settlement House by the Women's Presbyterial Society for Home Mission in the presbytery of Chicago. The House operates church and settlement programs in a west side Chicago neighborhood, which originally was a Czech settlement though later residents included Croatians, Mexicans, and Negroes. The House offered clubs, recreation, classes, relief, and aid; it also operated a kindergarten program that was staffed partially by student teachers from the National College of Education in Evanston, IL. Includes items relating to Helen Duncan, the first resident and a kindergarten teacher; Alice Rowell, head resident from ca. 1909 to 1915; Gertrude Ray, head resident from ca. 1917 to 1945; and Margaret Howell, a member of the Women's Presbyterial Society, a volunteer at Howell, and a donor of funds for construction of an addition to the settlement. Collection also contains records pertaining to Howell Memorial Church, which was established in 1916 at the settlement.

4,100. Hull and Culver

Papers. 1848-1955. 1 ft.
Open. Unpublished guide.
University of Illinois at Chicago Circle Library, Manuscript Collection.
Papers pertain to Charles Jerold Hull (1820-89), the original owner of Hull-House, and his family, particularly to his cousin Helen Culver (1832-1925) who turned his mansion over to the settlement that bore his name. Includes correspondence, telegrams, invitations, poems, quarterly reports, financial papers, receipts, descriptions of land plots, flyers, lists, and announcements. Contains information on Hull's business affairs, Hull-House, the 1940 Woman's Centennial Congress, and the Immigrants' Legal Aid Society as well as correspondence of Jane Addams, Helen McCormick Blair, Louise deKoven Bowen, Charlotte Carr, Helen Culver, Adena (Miller) Rich, Margaret (Dreier) Robins, and Mary Rozet Smith.

4,101. Hull-House Association

Records. 1889-1970. 30 ft. and 160 vols.
Open. Unpublished guide.
University of Illinois at Chicago Circle Library, Manuscript Collection.
Founded in 1889 by Jane Addams and Ellen Gates Starr, Hull-House was the first social settlement in Chicago. Consists of the corporate records of the board of trustees, records of the residents of the settlement, items on Jane Addams and the Jane Addams Centennial in 1960, and a comprehensive file on the Near West Side Planning Board, a citizen-participation project in redevelopment of the neighborhood, 1948-62. Contains minutes, financial and legal records, correspondence, photos, scrapbooks, programs, and publications. The settlement developed programs and services for the immigrant community in which it was located and supported many of the major reforms of the progressive era, including factory inspection and legislation, child welfare, the juvenile court system, and trade union organization. Forced to vacate its original site in 1963 for the Chicago Circle campus of the University, Hull-House decentralized and began operating settlement and neighborhood programs in a variety of Chicago locations and one suburban location. The collection also includes information concerning Louise (deKoven) Bowen, longtime treasurer of the Hull-House board; Adena (Miller) Rich, successor to Jane Addams as head resident; Charlotte Carr, successor to Rich; and such Hull-House residents as physician Alice Hamilton, Sophonisba P. Breckinridge, Julia Lathrop, and Florence Kelly.

4,102. Hyde Park Neighborhood Club

Records. Ca. 1910-73. 49.5 ft. and 10 oversize vols.
Open. Unpublished guide.
University of Illinois at Chicago Circle Library, Manuscript Collection.
Organized in 1909 as the Hyde Park Center of the Hyde Park Juvenile Protective League, the Club is involved in interracial community organization in the Hyde Park and Kenwood area of Chicago. Includes bylaws, annual reports, minutes, financial records, correspondence, contracts, personnel records, client files, program items, directories, photos, scrapbooks, and publications. The Club has provided recreation, services, and counseling to children and youth of its area; women have been active on its board and staff and as volunteers. Program innovations begun by women include street work with teen-agers and a study center for assisting schoolchildren. The collection also includes items concerning the day-care program and such fund-raising auxiliaries as the Business and Professional Women's Auxiliary and the Women's Auxiliary.

4,103. Illinois Children's Home and Aid Society

Records. 1883-1970. 41 ft. and 3 oversize vols.
Open. Unpublished guide.
University of Illinois at Chicago Circle Library, Manuscript Collection.
Founded in 1883 in Aurora, IL, as the American Educational Aid Association by Martin Van Buren Van Arsdale and his wife Isabella Van Arsdale, the Society is a private agency involved in adoptive and foster home placement., providing casework and counseling services, and operating specialized residential centers. Includes a constitution, bylaws, annual reports, minutes, financial records, correspondence, studies and statistics, memos, histories, photos, clippings, and publications. Women have been active in all aspects of the Society, and Lois Wildy served as executive director for many years. Correspondents include

Sophonisba P. Breckinridge, Louise (deKoven) Bowen, Jane Addams, Edith Abbott, and Grace Abbott. Collection includes extensive information about dependent children and juveniles as well as the programs and services that are offered to them throughout Illinois.

4,104. Illinois Commission on the Employment of Youth
Records. 1934-67. 11 ft.
Open. Unpublished guide.
University of Illinois at Chicago Circle Library, Manuscript Collection.
Founded in 1919 as the Illinois Child Labor Committee, the Commission was a protective organization for working children and minors. Includes bylaws, articles of incorporation, annual reports, minutes, financial records, correspondence, speeches, legislation, statistics and research reports, clippings, directories, and publications. The Commission, a volunteer organization throughout much of its history, sought to improve working conditions, legal protection, and educational opportunities for minors. Commission workers included Jessie Binford, Esther (Loeb) Kohn, Agnes Nestor, Edith Abbott, and Sophonisba P. Breckinridge. In 1957, under the leadership of Mrs. Francis E. McMahon, the Commission was reorganized with a paid staff.

4,105. Illinois Humane Society
Records. 1879-1961. 273 ft.
Access restricted. Unpublished guide.
University of Illinois at Chicago Circle Library, Manuscript Collection.
Founded in 1869 as the Illinois Society for the Prevention of Cruelty to Animals, this group formerly provided protective services to women and children as well as to abused animals. Includes minutes, correspondence, reports, case records, proceedings, photos, clippings, programs, and publications. Since affiliation in 1969 with Chicago Commons, a federation of settlement agencies, the Society has functioned chiefly as a fund-raising organization.

4,106. Illinois IWY Coordinating Committee
Records. 1977-78. 8 ft.
Open. Unpublished guide.
University of Illinois at Chicago Circle Library, Manuscript Collection.
Established by national legislation, the Illinois International Women's Year Committee held statewide meetings of women to elect delegates and sponsor resolutions for discussion at the 1977 National Women's Conference. Records comprise the office files of the Coordinating Committee and related files from the offices of Illinois state representative Susan Catania, chairperson of the Committee; Margaret Cowden, executive director of the Illinois Commission on the Status of Women; and other Committee members. Includes minutes, transcriptions, correspondence, conference packets, program planning items, reports, registration forms, publications, and artifacts. Also includes items concerning the statewide organization and preparation for events of the Illinois IWY meeting in Bloomington, IL, in 1977; files concerning the Illinois delegation's participation in the National Women's Conference in Houston in 1977; and items concerning the concluding of the Illinois IWY Committee business.

4,107. Illinois Soldiers' Orphans' Home
Records. 1871-82. 5 items.
Open. Unpublished guide.
University of Illinois at Chicago Circle Library, Manuscript Collection.
Consists of annual reports of the Home, which was established in 1865 in Normal, IL, to provide a residence and education for indigent children under 14 years of age whose fathers were disabled or deceased Union soldiers. Contains lists of women employees, including the superintendent, teachers, household workers, and others; names of children admitted to the Home along with their parents' names and residences; and reports on programs offered to the children.

4,108. Illinois Training School for Nurses
Records. 1881-1930. 18.5 ft. and 9 oversize vols.
Access restricted. Accession record.
University of Illinois at Chicago Circle Library, Manuscript Collection.
The School, which existed from 1880 to 1929, was the first training school for nurses in Chicago. Includes financial records, students' transcripts and files, Cook County School of Nursing records, class lists, probation lists, test reports, applications, and matriculation cards as well as *A History of the Illinois Training School for Nurses* (Chicago: Board of Directors of the Illinois Training School for Nurses, 1930) by Grace Fay Schryver. Controlled and administered by women, the School was closely associated with Cook County Hospital, and from its earliest days, student nurses worked in the Hospital wards. The School experienced steady growth, especially under the leadership of Isabel Adams Hampton, superintendent from 1886 to 1889. It established a social service department at the Hospital, and its nurses served in the Spanish-American War and WWI. In 1929 the School terminated and the students were transferred to the Cook County Hospital School of Nursing.

4,109. Illinois Women's Political Caucus
Records. 1974-76. 0.5 ft.
Open. Accession record.
University of Illinois at Chicago Circle Library, Manuscript Collection.
The Caucus was formed in 1973 to promote women candidates and to inform and educate women as party members and voters. Includes bylaws, minutes, agendas, membership lists, resolutions, proposals, biographical sketches, questionnaires, convention packets, clippings, newsletters, and flyers. The Caucus grew out of a meeting in Houston in 1973 at which the National Women's Political Caucus was founded. Organized by Rose Economou, Susan Bellow, and Shirley Starr, the Illinois Caucus began as a small study group made up of women from Hyde Park, Chicago, and Evanston, IL. In 1975, after other chapters had formed, a founding meeting for the statewide Caucus was held in Macomb, IL, with Illinois state representative Susan Catania as chairman. After this meeting the original group changed its name to Chicago Women's Political Caucus to reflect its geographic focus. Membership is open to those who agree with the organization's principles and pay its dues. Activities include fund raising, legislative and elective action, public relations, forums, publication of newsletters, and educational meetings.

4,110. Immigrants' Protective League
Records. 1909-70. 19 ft.
Access restricted. Register.
University of Illinois at Chicago Circle Library, Manuscript Collection.
The League was organized in Chicago in 1908 to assist, encourage, protect, and educate newly arrived immigrants to the US. Includes annual reports, minutes, financial records, correspondence, investigative reports, case histories, lectures, statistical data, photos, programs, press releases, and publications. The League was formed in response to the problems and hardships of immigrants as witnessed in the Hull-House neighborhood. During the early years its headquarters were at Hull-House, and Grace Abbott served as the first director. In 1919 the state of Illinois took over the League and extended its work to cover all of Illinois, conducting studies and publishing documents related to the problems of immigrants. State support was cut off in 1921. League activities have included investigation and publication of documents concerning the legal, economic, and housing conditions of immigrants in Chicago; uniting separated families; assisting immigrants with legal forms and documents as well as medical and employment referrals; lobbying for legislative reform to liberalize immigration law and policy; and offering citizenship and English classes. The League also lobbied successfully for change in federal laws that stripped American citizenship from native-born women who married immigrants. Women associated with the League have included Jane Addams, a trustee and vice-president; Sophonisba P. Breckinridge, a secretary; Edith Abbott, second vice-president; Esther (Loeb) Kohn and Julia Lathrop, both executive committee members; Lea Demarest Taylor, a member of the board of directors; Adena (Miller) Rich, director; and Ione Duval, director. In the mid-1960s the League was incorporated by the Travelers Aid Society, but it retains a separate identity within the Society.

4,111. Institute for Sex Education
Records. 1916-71. 15.5 ft. and 5 oversize vols.
Open. Unpublished guide.
University of Illinois at Chicago Circle Library, Manuscript Collection.
Annual reports, minutes, financial records, correspondence, photos, clippings, publicity material, newsletters, and other publications of the Institute, founded as the Red League in 1916 to combat venereal disease and educate the public in social hygiene. From 1918 until the late 1960s, the group was known as the Illinois Social Hygiene League. Rachelle (Slobodinsky) Yarros, a physician and founding member of the American Social Hygiene Association, was instrumental in organizing the Hygiene League and served as director of the League and of its educational department. Members of the advisory council included Edith Abbott, dean of the school of civics and philanthropy at the University of Chicago; Jane Addams, a founder of Hull-House; and Alice Hamilton, a physician and professor of industrial medicine. The Institute, under its current executive director Shirley Bryan, continues its program of public education.

4,112. Institute of Design
Records. 1927-70. 5 ft.
Access restricted. Unpublished guide.
University of Illinois at Chicago Circle Library, Manuscript Collection.
The Institute was a school of art and design that attempted to achieve a synthesis between art and technology. Includes annual reports, minutes, financial records, correspondence, memoranda, lectures, biographical data concerning faculty and students, applications, class schedules, course descriptions, faculty and student lists, photos, exhibit catalogs, bulletins, news releases, and published items. After Nazi authorities closed the German Bauhaus, the New Bauhaus, directed by Laszic Moholy-Nagy, was organized in Chicago in 1937. The institution's title later was changed to Institute of Design. Women students or faculty members included Sibyl Moholy-Nagy, Marli Ehrman, Else Regensteiner, Marianne Willisch, Sarah Leavitt, and Jane Downey.

4,113. Japanese-American Service Committee
Records. 1945-65. 1 ft.
Open. Unpublished guide.
University of Illinois at Chicago Circle Library, Manuscript Collection.
Annual reports, minutes, financial records, correspondence, programs, directories, and published items of the Committee, which was organized in 1945 as the Chicago Resettlers' Committee to assist with the heavy influx of Japanese-Americans coming to Chicago from relocation centers. The Committee provided counseling and other services. Women have been

active members, officers, and supporters of the Committee.

4,114. Juvenile Protective Association
Records. 1904-55. 12 ft. and 13 oversize vols.
Access restricted. Unpublished guide.
University of Illinois at Chicago Circle Library, Manuscript Collection.
Incorporated in 1907, the Association is a private, non-profit protective and investigative agency that aids dependent and delinquent children. Includes charter, bylaws, minutes, financial records, correspondence, case records, speeches, surveys, reports, petitions, affidavits, reference files, photos, clippings, statutes and criminal code, and published items. The Association was an outgrowth of the Juvenile Court Committee, which was organized to support the work of the juvenile court and to employ probation officers and raise funds for their salaries. When the work of the Committee began to broaden, the Association coordinated the work of local juvenile protective leagues throughout Chicago; studied and attempted to suppress conditions that produced juvenile delinquency; prosecuted persons contributing to the dependency, truancy, or delinquency of children; cooperated with the juvenile court, state factory inspector, and other child welfare agencies; fostered public sentiment for establishment of parks, playgrounds, free baths, vacation schools, and community social centers; and investigated individual cases of dependency and delinquency. The Association was instrumental in the movement to have probation and detention home officers placed under county civil service and paid with public funds rather than from fund-raising and private contributions. After investigating baby farms, illicit street trades, prostitution, gambling and liquor violations, public dance halls, and employment of children in such places as bowling alleys, traveling stage companies, factories, and home manufacture, the Association successfully lobbied for child labor and other protective legislation. Collection contains extensive material by and about Jessie Florence Binford who served as executive director from 1916 to 1952. Many Hull-House figures were actively involved in organizing the Association.

4,115. Kawin, Irene, and Kawin, Ethel
Papers. 1922-69. 0.75 ft.
Open. Accession record.
University of Illinois at Chicago Circle Library, Manuscript Collection.
Includes correspondence, published and unpublished articles, and reports of Irene Kawin (1887-), a social worker and probation officer, and of her sister Ethel Kawin (1890-1969), an educator and researcher in child development and psychology. Irene Kawin first taught in elementary schools. In 1912 she became a social worker; from 1918 to 1927 she was head of the mothers' pension division of the juvenile court of Cook County, IL; and in 1927 she became deputy chief probation officer. Ethel Kawin received her MA from the University of Chicago in 1925. In 1934 she became a guidance counselor for the Glencoe, IL, public school system. She began teaching at the University of Chicago in 1938 and joined a group of educators in Pasadena, CA, to formulate plans for adult education. Her program Parenthood in a Free Nation was adopted by the group and used throughout the US.

4,116. Kenagy, Nina M.
Papers. 1897-1961. 0.5 ft.
Open. Accession record.
University of Illinois at Chicago Circle Library, Manuscript Collection.
Kenagy (1878-1971) was a preschool educator. Includes correspondence, notes, text, and photos for a proposed book on nursery schools; Mary Crane Nursery School brochures; teaching certificates and diplomas; and published articles and papers relating to preschool education. Kenagy worked as the first director of the Mary Crane Nursery School at Hull-House in Chicago from 1925 to 1946. Serving an immigrant community of working mothers, the School offered classes on personal hygiene to parents, student teachers, and child-care volunteers; neighborhood improvement was another of the School's concerns. Kenagy developed an experimental curriculum for preschoolers, which was used at the School. Additional information on Kenagy is available in the Mary Crane League Papers at the Library.

4,117. Kohn, Esther (Loeb)
Papers. 1896-1965. 15.5 ft.
Open. Register.
University of Illinois at Chicago Circle Library, Manuscript Collection.
A resident for 30 years of Hull-House in Chicago, [Mrs. Alfred D.] Kohn (1875-1965) was interested in medical social work, child welfare, and immigrants. Includes correspondence, speeches, articles, photos, clippings, and records of her many organizational affiliations, with annual reports, minutes, agendas, narrative and statistical reports, resolutions, manuals, and membership and contribution lists. Kohn was an active board member and officer of more than 15 organizations and agencies, including the Immigrants' Protective League, the Cook County department of welfare, the Cook County Hospital School of Nursing, and the Jewish Social Service Bureau of the Jewish Charities. As a member of the Illinois Child Labor Committee and the Illinois Committee on Child Welfare Legislation, she was an active lobbyist for progressive child labor laws in Illinois. She also organized support for the national child labor amendment to the Constitution, a minimum wage law, and the Child Health Act. The collection includes correspondence of and items concerning Jane Addams, Edith Abbott, Grace Abbott, Julia Lathrop, and Sophonisba Preston Breckinridge.

4,118. Ladies' Education Society
Records. 1834-67. 31 items.
Open. Unpublished guide.
University of Illinois at Chicago Circle Library, Manuscript Collection.
The Society was founded in 1833 in Jacksonville, IL, with the goals of improving education for women, assisting young women to become teachers, and increasing the number of teachers in the western states. Includes annual reports containing a constitution, minutes, secretary's and treasurer's reports, committee reports, correspondence, addresses delivered at annual meetings, and lists of officers and directresses. The Society was run by a board of women officers and directresses. Involved in raising funds to provide tuition and books for women who could not afford to educate themselves, the Society placed strong emphasis on assisting those women of high moral character who showed promise of leading useful and productive lives. While most of the work was done in Illinois, the Society had directresses from several surrounding states as well as from the East; contributions came from these areas as well.

4,119. Lake Michigan Federation
Records. 1968-75. 2.25 ft.
Open. Unpublished guide.
University of Illinois at Chicago Circle Library, Manuscript Collection.
Founded in 1970, the Federation is composed of citizens' action and conservation groups interested in the ecology of Lake Michigan and related land resources. Includes proceedings, correspondence, memoranda, reports, photos, clippings, newsletters, and published items. The Federation grew out of a 1969 conference of conservationists from Wisconsin, Illinois, Indiana, and Michigan concerning the preservation of Lake Michigan. Conference coordinator [Mrs.] Lee Botts became the Federation's first executive secretary and worked to establish the Federation as an independent educational and scientific organization. Records concern Botts's leadership of the Federation.

4,120. Larson, Marian Louise (Anderson)
Papers. 1953-74. 3 ft.
Open. Accession record.
University of Illinois at Chicago Circle Library, Manuscript Collection.
[Mrs. Robert M.] Larson (1918-) is a journalist and public relations specialist. Includes correspondence, minutes, photos, press releases, publicity, and newsletters relating to her professional life. In 1964 Larson founded the Chicago chapter of Partners of the Alliance for Progress, a foreign aid organization. She also founded the Pan American Assembly and served as its first president from 1963 to 1966. She is a member of the American Women in Radio and Television, the National Federation of Press Women, and the Illinois Woman's Press Association.

4,121. League of Women Voters of Chicago
Records. 1909-66. 12 ft.
Open. Unpublished guide.
University of Illinois at Chicago Circle Library, Manuscript Collection.
Includes bylaws, minutes, agendas, correspondence, reports, charts, studies and questionnaires, photos, clippings, press releases, and publications of the Chicago LWV, which was organized in 1950 as a superstructure for 10 Chicago-area chapters of the LWV of Cook County, IL. Involved in voter education and political education for members, the Chicago LWV has been active in providing voter services. Includes records of predecessor organizations, such as the Chicago Political Equality League; of branches of the League; and of the LWV of Illinois and the LWV of the US.

4,122. League of Women Voters of Oak Park-River Forest
Records. 1909-45. 1.2 ft. and 1 oversize vol.
Open. Unpublished guide.
University of Illinois at Chicago Circle Library, Manuscript Collection.
Annual reports, minutes, financial records, clippings, programs, and published items of the Oak Park, IL, and River Forest, IL, branch of the LWV, which was founded in 1924 to provide voter education and political education for members. This branch was also interested in industrial conditions for women and in international relations. Also includes records of predecessor organizations, among them the Suburban Civics and Equal Suffrage Association, 1909-21, and the Oak Park Civic League, 1921-24.

4,123. Lohr, Lenox Riley
Papers. 1911-68. 66 ft.
Open. Unpublished guide.
University of Illinois at Chicago Circle Library, Manuscript Collection.
Correspondence, minutes, notes, speeches, manuscripts, legal and financial papers, and other material of Lohr (1891-1968), a business executive, museum director, and general manager of A Century of Progress International Exposition held in Chicago during 1933 and 1934. Includes files on Mary Thompson Hospital in Chicago, 1945-67, and the University of Illinois, Jane Addams Memorial Fund, 1963-67; items of Martha S. McGrew, Lohr's executive assistant for A Century of Progress, 1930-37; and papers of Martha S. McGrew and Janet Irwin, Lohr's assistants at the Museum of Science and Industry, 1942-68. Collection also contains personal and family correspondence of Lohr and his wife Josephine Wimsatt Lohr (1888-1975) and their children.

4,124. Lulkin, Sheli A.
Papers. 1960-77. 12 ft.
Access restricted. Accession record.

University of Illinois at Chicago Circle Library, Manuscript Collection.
Lulkin, a high school teacher, is a women's rights and union activist. Includes correspondence, minutes, hearings and testimony, notes, contracts, reports, organizational mailings, clippings, brochures, leaflets, programs, conference material, press releases, and newsletters. Collection contains information on the Chicago Teachers Union, the American Federation of Teachers, the Coalition of Labor Union Women, the Illinois Women's Political Caucus, the Illinois Commission on the Status of Women, the Women's Action Alliance, and ERA Illinois. Also contains extensive subject files on such topics as abortion, sex discrimination, rape, day care, affirmative action, employment, women in education, and women's athletics.

4,125. Lunde, Laura Hughes

Papers. 1931-67. 0.5 ft.
Open. Unpublished guide.
University of Illinois at Chicago Circle Library, Manuscript Collection.
[Mrs. Erling H.] Lunde (1886-1966) was a volunteer, civic leader, reformer, and lobbyist concerned with education, election reform, and public health. Contains correspondence, primarily letters of condolence to Erling Lunde upon the death of his wife; minutes pertaining to Laura Lunde's legislative, civic reform, and charitable activities; memoranda; reports; statements; photos; bulletins; awards; and citations. Lunde was a member of the LWV, the Illinois Hospital Board, the Woman's City Club of Chicago, and the Chicago Citizens Schools Committee. Collection also reflects her involvement with the Citizens of Greater Chicago, the Joint Civic Committee on Elections, the Committee for Modern Courts in Illinois, and the Illinois Conference on Legislation. In 1962 the National Municipal League presented Lunde with the Distinguished Citizens Award.

4,126. McCallister, Frank

Papers. 1923-71. 20 ft.
Open. Unpublished guide.
University of Illinois at Chicago Circle Library, Manuscript Collection.
McCallister (1908-70) was a labor organizer and political activist on behalf of civil and human rights. Includes correspondence, minutes, published and unpublished writings, memoranda, speeches, financial statements, reports, photos, clippings, newsletters, programs, appointment calendars, proceedings, press releases, memorial tributes, awards, and published items. McCallister served as director of the labor education division at Roosevelt University in Chicago from 1949 to 1970; the director of the Georgia Workers Education Service from 1946 to 1949; a labor member of the National War Labor Board, Atlanta Region, from 1943 to 1946; and executive director of the Southern Workers Defense League. Throughout his career he worked on behalf of and with women workers and leaders. Correspondents include the International Ladies' Garment Workers' Union, Coretta (Scott) King, Lillian Eugenia Smith, and Eleanor Roosevelt.

4,127. Marcy-Newberry Center

Records. 1891-1969. 88.5 ft. and 4 oversize vols.
Open. Unpublished guide.
University of Illinois at Chicago Circle Library, Manuscript Collection.
Bylaws, annual reports, minutes, legal and financial records, correspondence, program material, photos, scrapbooks, and publications detail the founding in 1883 and operation of Marcy Center, a settlement affiliated with the Methodist Woman's Home Missionary Society, Rock River Conference. Elizabeth E. (Smith) Marcy began the program at Marcy Center to serve the Bohemian and Polish population. Anna Heistad later directed the Center in its programs of social work as its population became largely Jewish. When the Marcy Center moved to new quarters, the women of the First Methodist Church of Evanston, IL, continued to work in the old location, which in 1934 became Newberry Center. The two centers were merged in 1969 and now serve predominantly Negro communities. Since 1883 women have administered and financed the centers.

4,128. Mary Crane League

Records. 1927-71. 3 ft.
Open. Unpublished guide.
University of Illinois at Chicago Circle Library, Manuscript Collection.
Founded in 1932, the League was a fund-raising and volunteer auxiliary to the Mary Crane Nursery in Chicago. Includes minutes, legal and financial records, correspondence, photos, scrapbooks, publicity and press releases, and publications. The Mary Crane Nursery School was started in 1907 as a day nursery at Hull-House in a building donated by Richard T. Crane in memory of his wife Mary. The program was reorganized in 1925 under the direction of Edna Dean Baker, dean of the National College of Education in Evanston, IL, as a demonstration project in progressive preschool education. Serving an immigrant community in the Hull-House neighborhood, the Mary Crane Nursery offered programs for children beginning at age 3 and provided lengthened day services for working parents. The League was organized in 1932 when the Nursery faced serious financial difficulties. League members were chiefly responsible for fund-raising projects for the Nursery. The school moved to a public housing project on Chicago's northwest side in 1963, where its program serves an interracial constituency. Collection includes information on the Nursery and its director Nina M. Kenagy.

4,129. Metropolitan Housing and Planning Council

Records. 1922-76. 55 ft., 3 cabinets, and oversize items.
Open. Unpublished guide.
University of Illinois at Chicago Circle Library, Manuscript Collection.
Founded in 1934, the Council is a non-profit organization composed of urban planners, realtors, and concerned citizens that attempts to improve housing and the quality of life in the Chicago metropolitan area through education, research, planning, lobbying, and coordinating activity with other organizations. Includes constitution, bylaws, annual reports, minutes, financial records, correspondence, speeches, testimony, official statements, subject files, statistics, officers' lists, photos, slides, scrapbooks, clippings, housing codes, press releases, newsletters, maps, bulletins, programs, questionnaires, surveys, and publications. Activities of the Council were centered around a comprehensive city planning effort, redevelopment of blighted areas, slum prevention, new housing construction for all income groups, and enforcement of building, housing, and zoning codes.

Collection includes records of the Women's Joint Committee on Adequate Housing, which was founded in 1940 and represented more than 30 women's organizations. The Committee educated members and the public about housing issues and worked to solve urban housing problems. The Committee's activities included surveys, exhibits, speakers, investigating conditions in and sponsoring tours of slum areas, furnishing observers at Housing Court, and attending city council meetings and hearings. In 1954 the Committee became the Woman's Council for City Renewal, narrowed its focus to educational work, and eventually merged with the Metropolitan Housing and Planning Council. Collection also concerns the organizational activities of Dorothy Rubel, a member of the Committee, who in 1942 was a delegate to the Metropolitan Housing and Planning Council. She became executive director of the Council in 1946, a post she held for 27 years.

4,130. Morton, Annie Malvin

Papers. 1934-78. 13 ft. and oversize items.
Open. Unpublished guide.
University of Illinois at Chicago Circle Library, Manuscript Collection.
Morton (1906-) is an editor, author, and social welfare agency administrator. Includes correspondence, minutes, poems, published and unpublished works that Morton wrote or edited, radio scripts, speeches, annual reports, contracts, photos, a scrapbook, clippings, proceedings, newsletters, and programs. Morton was public relations director for the United Charities in Chicago from 1947 to 1952, executive director of the Chicago Federation of Settlements and Neighborhood Centers from 1952 to 1961, and editor of the *Public Welfare Journal* from 1961 to 1971; she became public relations consultant of the Florence Crittenton Association of Chicago in 1972. The collection reflects Morton's work with the National Conference on Social Welfare, both the National and Chicago Federations of Settlements and Neighborhood Centers, the American Public Welfare Association, the Clarence Darrow Community Center, the Peoria Neighborhood House, and the Welfare Public Relations Forum. Includes correspondence of Lea Demarest Taylor.

4,131. Myers, Caroline "Lonny" Rulon

Papers. 1955-75. 4 ft.
Open. Unpublished guide.
University of Illinois at Chicago Circle Library, Manuscript Collection.
Lonny Myers (1922-) is a physician and author who is married to Mr. Shu-Yu Wang. Contains correspondence, including letters to the editors of newspapers and professional journals; published and unpublished writings, including articles she contributed to popular journals; tapes of her debate with syndicated columnist Ann Landers; research notes and files; speeches; photos; and clippings. Myers, who was trained and practiced as an anesthesiologist, became interested in the social issues surrounding sexuality in the late 1950s. She was a founding member of the Illinois Citizens for the Extension of Birth Control Services, which lobbied successfully for providing birth control in public health programs. In 1966 she was instrumental in founding the Illinois Citizens for the Medical Control of Abortion, a lobbying organization that assisted in the formation of the National Association for Repeal of Abortion Laws. After her retirement from private practice, Myers founded the Midwest Population Center in Chicago, where she serves as a clinician performing vasectomies. She also is director of medical education and a frequent workshop leader for the Midwest Association for the Study of Human Sexuality.

4,132. National Black Feminist Organization, Chicago Chapter

Records. 1974-75. 0.5 ft.
Open. Accession record.
University of Illinois at Chicago Circle Library, Manuscript Collection.
Bylaws, minutes, correspondence, memos, clippings, and newsletters of this chapter of the Organization, which was formed in 1974 to promote the social, political, and economic welfare of black women. The national Organization was established in 1973 in New York City, and membership was open to women of African descent. Activities included consciousness raising, rape crisis work, educational meetings, cultural events, and education. The Chicago branch was founded by Brenda Eichelberger, LaVerne Bennett, and Michele Gautreaux. In 1975 the Organization became defunct, and in 1976 these same three women formed the National Alliance of Black Feminists, which has its headquarters in Chicago.

4,133. National Congress of Parents and Teachers
Records. 1897-1965. 12 ft.
Open. Unpublished guide.
University of Illinois at Chicago Circle Library, Manuscript Collection.
Minutes, reports of conventions, and magazines of the Congress, which was organized in 1897 as the National Congress of Mothers to promote child welfare and educational cooperation between home and school. Founded by Alice Josephine Birney and Phoebe Apperson Hearst, the Congress became the advocate of protective measures for children and improvements in the educational system.

4,134. Near West Side Community Committee
Records. 1938-75. 46 ft.
Access restricted. Register.
University of Illinois at Chicago Circle Library, Manuscript Collection.
Founded in 1932, the Committee is a community organization that serves the near west side of Chicago. Includes constitution, bylaws, minutes, agenda, financial records, contracts, correspondence, invitations, case studies, applications, reports, photos, scrapbook, newsletters, bulletins, posters, leaflets, press releases, clippings, and other records. The Committee fosters and supports social, recreational, civic, and educational programs for neighborhood children and adults. Local residents form the leadership of the Committee; active women supporters have included Florence Scala, who was involved in the fight to save Hull-House from demolition when the University's location was announced; Frances Moreno; and Mary Placente. The Women's Auxiliary, which was formed in 1941, involves women in program planning, block clubs, social events, and fund raising. The Committee provides summer camps for children and has long fought juvenile delinquency through counseling and other programs.

4,135. Northwestern Sanitary Fair
Records. 1865. 1 vol.
Open. Unpublished guide.
University of Illinois at Chicago Circle Library, Manuscript Collection.
Consists of copies of *Voice of the Fair,* a newspaper published by the Fair, which was organized in 1864 to raise funds for the Soldiers' Home in Chicago and the US Sanitary Commission. The chief organizers of the Fair were Mary Ashton Livermore and Jane Currie (Blaikie) Hoge.

4,136. Off-the-Street Club
Records. 1902-75. 5.5 ft.
Open. Unpublished guide.
University of Illinois at Chicago Circle Library, Manuscript Collection.
Constitution, annual reports, correspondence, schedules, program material, photos, clippings, and publications of the Club, which was founded in 1898 to provide settlement activities for children on Chicago's west side. The Club, which began as a private charity to offer recreation to neighborhood children, was incorporated in 1916. Open to boys and girls, it sponsored a wide range of activities, classes, recreation, and camping. The collection includes information about women's participation as teachers, leaders, and fund raisers.

4,137. Old Ladies' Home of Chicago
Records. 1867-71. 5 items.
Open. No guide.
University of Illinois at Chicago Circle Library, Manuscript Collection.
Founded in 1865, the Home provided a residence for ladies who were at least 60 years old. Includes annual reports containing a charter, bylaws, lists of expenditures and donors of cash and other contributions, and lists of officers, managers, and committees. The Home was directed by the officers and a board of managers composed of representatives from various Protestant denominations. Many women held positions in these groups; the committee on admission and the committee on visitation were composed entirely of women. The matron, [Miss] Isabella Harvey, exercised virtually absolute control over the residents, of which there were 11 to 13 per year for the period represented by the reports. There was great concern for their spiritual lives and a committee on religious instruction provided prayer meetings every Sabbath, while another committee visited each inmate weekly to inquire about her spiritual and temporal welfare.

4,138. Old People's Home
Records. 1875-91. 9 items.
Open. Unpublished guide.
University of Illinois at Chicago Circle Library, Manuscript Collection.
The successor to the Old Ladies' Home, the Old People's Home was founded in 1874 and was supported by the Chicago Relief and Aid Society. Annual reports contain financial reports, the matron's report, and statistics on admittances, residents, and deaths. The board of trustees was composed of male members, but all officers, managers, and committee members were women.

4,139. Onward Neighborhood House
Records. 1926-69. 1.5 ft.
Access restricted. Unpublished guide.
University of Illinois at Chicago Circle Library, Manuscript Collection.
Articles of incorporation, annual reports, minutes, financial records, correspondence, case studies, photos, blueprints, and clippings of the House, which was founded in 1926 as a community center on Chicago's northwest side, a primarily Italian neighborhood. The early activities of the organization centered around church-related programs and clubs. After erection of a new building in 1928, the program became more oriented toward casework and community services. Women have been active in the organization throughout its history.

4,140. Orkney and Shetland Literary, Social, and Benevolent Society
Records. 1885-1970. 1.5 ft.
Open. Register.
University of Illinois at Chicago Circle Library, Manuscript Collection.
Founded in 1885, the Society was a Chicago social and philanthropic organization formed to dispense aid to needy persons and to advance the cultural and intellectual lives of its members. Membership and assistance were limited to persons connected with the Orkney and Shetland islands through birth, parentage, residence, or marriage. Includes a constitution, bylaws, financial records, correspondence, membership lists, photos, and decorative medals. Among the Society's social services were assisting with funeral costs, death benefits, and financial aid to widows and the infirm. Beginning in 1892, women could become honorary members of the Society by paying the initiation fee and annual dues, but they had no voting rights.

4,141. Paulson, Evelina Belden
Papers. 1904-68. 21 ft.
Open. Register.
University of Illinois at Chicago Circle Library, Manuscript Collection.
[Mrs. Henry T.] Paulson (1885-1966) was a social worker who served as the first social service director of the Chicago Boy's Court. Includes correspondence, notes, published and unpublished writings, financial accounts, casework files, surveys, reports, school records, questionnaires, and schedules. A graduate of Oberlin College, Paulson became resident social worker at Hiram House in Cleveland, where she directed the Boys' Game Club, activities for girls on the settlement playground, and other recreational activities. While attending the Chicago School of Civics and Philanthropy she lived and worked at Northwestern University Settlement. In 1913 and 1914 she served as a special officer to the Cook County jail's juvenile division. After her appointment as director of Boy's Court, she became an investigator of infant mortality and social agencies in New Bedford, MA, and illegitimate births in Boston. From 1921 to 1922 she was a member of the American Red Cross Commission to Poland. She retired because of illness in 1942. Includes correspondence or other items of Neva Boyd, Adena (Miller) Rich, Julia Lathrop, Lea Taylor, Edith Abbott, Harriet E. Vittum, and Jessie Binford.

4,142. Phyllis Wheatley Association
Records. 1908-66. 15 items.
Open. Accession record.
University of Illinois at Chicago Circle Library, Manuscript Collection.
Constitution, an auditor's report, membership lists, leaflets, brochures, and a program of the Association, whose predecessor the Phyllis Wheatley Woman's Club was founded in 1896 by [Mrs.] Elizabeth Lindsay Davis and other Negro women. In 1908 the Club established the Phyllis Wheatley Home for Girls, a residence for Negro women seeking employment in Chicago, and organized the Association to support the Home. Funded chiefly by donations from Negro women and an annual Tag Day and Tea, the Home aided Negro women by providing low-cost housing, job placements, and cultural opportunities.

4,143. Polacheck, Hilda (Satt)
Papers. 1910-58. 0.5 ft.
Open. Unpublished guide.
University of Illinois at Chicago Circle Library, Manuscript Collection.
[Mrs. William] Polacheck (1887?-1967) was a resident of the Hull-House neighborhood, a laborer, and an author. Includes correspondence, her unpublished autobiography "I Came A Stranger," a typescript of a play "The Walking Delegate," a character sketch of "Hilda," photos, and articles she wrote for *The Butterfly,* a literary magazine of the Butterfly Association, "an association for the betterment of humanity." Born near Warsaw, Poland, Polacheck came to Chicago with her family in 1892. She began factory work when she was 13; at the age of 16 she joined a literary club and edited a paper at Hull-House. Her dramatization of the novel *The Walking Delegate* was performed by the Hull-House Players in 1912. Her autobiography contains information on Hull-House, Jane Addams, the Women's International League for Peace and Freedom, and woman suffrage. Correspondents include Jane Addams, Florence Kelley, and Alice Hamilton.

4,144. Protective Agency for Women and Children
Records. 1888. 1 item.
Open. No guide.
University of Illinois at Chicago Circle Library, Manuscript Collection.
A protective agency established in 1886 under the auspices of the Chicago Women's Club, the Agency provided legal protection to women and children who could not otherwise afford it. Consists of the second annual report, which contains a constitution and bylaws, officers' reports, reports of complaints entered, and lists of officers, members of the governing board, and subscribers. Governed by a board composed of representatives of local women's organizations, the Agency investigated and provided support for complaints dealing with such topics as false imprisonment, abduction, sewing machine frauds, chattel mortgage foreclosures, criminal assaults, complaints of wives against husbands, and money claims. The Agency

also provided or secured legal advice and settled monetary claims.

4,145. Reitman, Ben Lewis
Papers. 1905-63. 17.75 ft. and ca. 20 oversize items.
Access restricted. Register.
University of Illinois at Chicago Circle Library, Manuscript Collection.
Reitman (1879-1942), a physician who specialized in the control and treatment of venereal disease, was the business manager of Emma Goldman. Contains correspondence, including love letters from Goldman, which also relate to politics, and correspondence with Lucy (Gathings) [Mrs. Albert] Parsons; speeches; notes; manuscripts of published and unpublished writings, including his autobiography *Following the Monkey* and *Sister of The Road: The Autobiography of Box-Car Bertha;* legal and financial papers; reports on birth control, venereal disease, prostitution, and women itinerants, which Reitman prepared during his years as head of the venereal disease clinic at the Cook County jail, as director of the Chicago Society for the Prevention of Venereal Disease, and as a staff member of the Chicago Syphilis Control Program; statistics; and photos. Also includes telegrams, post cards, programs, clippings, and published items relating to Goldman's speaking tours and her management of *Mother Earth,* an anarchist journal.

4,146. Rich, Adena (Miller)
Papers. 1890-1966. 7 ft.
Open. Register.
University of Illinois at Chicago Circle Library, Manuscript Collection.
[Mrs. Kenneth] Rich (1888-1967) was a social worker. Includes correspondence, notes, unpublished manuscripts, minutes, speeches, reports, photos, clippings, pamphlets, and published items as well as records of Hull-House and the Immigrants' Protective League. Rich graduated from Oberlin College and in 1912 became supervisor of visitors for the Immigrants' Protective League, later the Immigrants' Service League, and supervisor of fieldwork for the Chicago School of Civics and Philanthropy from 1914 to 1916. Rich served as executive director of the Immigrants' Protective League from 1926 to 1954. Selected to succeed Jane Addams as head resident of Hull-House in 1935, she resigned that position in 1937. Correspondents include Julia Lathrop, Neva Leona Boyd, Nina M. Kenagy, Louise (deKoven) Bowen, Alice Hamilton, Edith and Grace Abbott, and Robert Morss Lovett.

4,147. Ross, Edith T.
Papers. 1914-69. 0.5 ft.
Open. Unpublished guide.
University of Illinois at Chicago Circle Library, Manuscript Collection.
Photo, clippings, programs, and broadsides of Ross, a black English teacher at DuSable High School in Chicago. Papers concern Ross's education and teaching career; her activities and affiliation with the Sixth Grace United Presbyterian Church of Chicago and its clubs and organizations. Includes the first issue (1914) of "The Alpha Suffrage Record," a broadside of the first Negro suffrage club in Chicago, which was founded by Ida B. Wells-Barnett, as well as a 1940 broadside and newspaper concerning the naming of a Chicago Housing Authority public housing project in honor of Wells-Barnett.

4,148. St. Mary's High School and Center for Learning
Records. 1899-1975. 11 ft.
Access restricted. Register.
University of Illinois at Chicago Circle Library, Manuscript Collection.
The High School was a Catholic girls school operated from 1899 to 1976 on Chicago's near west side by the Sisters of Charity of the Blessed Virgin Mary. Includes annual reports; minutes; financial records; student transcripts; subject folders regarding the Fathers' Club, the Mothers' Club, pregnancy and abortion, racism, and Puerto Rican high schools; state reports; papers on educational theory; tapes; motion pictures; library accession books; photos and slides; programs; bulletins; and school publications. The School served the multi-ethnic and working-class community on the west side of Chicago. In 1968 the School reorganized into the Center for Learning, where innovative techniques and procedures, including an extensive day-care facility, were used. After the archdiocese of Chicago withdrew its financial support in 1973, the Center was unable to continue. The adult program relocated to Malcolm X College in Chicago, and the day-care program continued autonomously.

4,149. Saperstein, Esther
Papers. 1949-75. 63 ft.
Open. Register.
University of Illinois at Chicago Circle Library, Manuscript Collection.
Saperstein (1903-) is a Chicago alderman. Includes correspondence; state committee, commission, and task force records, including minutes, agendas, and reports; motion pictures; state legislative bills; studies; calendars; veto lists; clippings; form letters; and published items. Saperstein was elected to the Illinois House of Representatives in 1956, where she served until 1966 when she was elected to the Illinois Senate, an office she held until 1975. In that year she became alderman of Chicago's 49th ward. Before running for political office, she was a founding member of City of Hope, president of the Chicago region Illinois Congress of Parents and Teachers, secretary of the Juvenile Protective Association, and a public affairs chairman of Hadassah. As state representative and senator, her primary interests were equal rights for women, education, and mental and public health. She was instrumental in securing passage of several bills in these areas and initiated the legislation that led to creation of the Illinois Commission on the Status of Women, which she chaired.

4,150. Scholarship and Guidance Association
Records. 1913-71. 12.5 ft.
Access restricted. Register.
University of Illinois at Chicago Circle Library, Manuscript Collection.
Founded in 1911, the Association provides financial assistance and counseling to secondary school students and sponsors research on educational guidance. Includes minutes, reports, speeches, correspondence, tapes, photos, clippings, and printed items regarding the activities of the Association and its auxiliary agency the Children's Scholarship Association. Originally established as the Joint Committee on Vocational Training of Girls, the Scholarship and Guidance Association worked to secure employment for female high school dropouts. Anne Davis, a social worker, directed the Committee and was assisted by Edith Abbott, Sophonisba P. Breckinridge, and Ella [Mrs. Addison W.] Moore, the first president. In 1912 services were extended to boys, and school loans were given to children. In 1913 the Chicago Board of Education assumed responsibility for the vocational bureau, although scholarships and salaries were still privately funded. By 1916 the group was raising money, lobbying to increase the compulsory school attendance age to 16, providing scholarships, and offering vocational planning and job placement for handicapped children. Services were then expanded to include the study of parent-child relationships, training of and assistance to Chicago schools guidance personnel, and sponsorship of research studies on school dropouts and other educational topics.

4,151. School of Living
Records. 1935-68. 7 ft.
Open. Unpublished guide.
University of Illinois at Chicago Circle Library, Manuscript Collection.
Articles of incorporation, bylaws, financial records, correspondence, questionnaires, lists of members, announcements, bulletins, charts, and publications of the School, which was established in 1934 as an experimental living arrangement emphasizing small group organization and living close to the land. Founded in Suffern, NY, by Ralph Borsodi, the School operated until 1940. Reestablished in Melbourne, FL, in 1950, the School chartered the University of Melbourne, and Borsodi served as chancellor. A branch of the School was organized in Brookville, OH, by Mildred Loomis and her husband John. Mildred Loomis was editor of *The Interpreter,* a publication of the School; she also was in charge of the annual school of living conferences and dean of the National School of Living. Her correspondents include Madalyn Murray and Dorothy Thompson.

4,152. Senior Centers of Metropolitan Chicago
Records. 1955-68. 3 ft.
Open. Unpublished guide.
University of Illinois at Chicago Circle Library, Manuscript Collection.
Founded in 1956, the Centers provide social and recreational services to older persons. Includes minutes, financial records, correspondence, committee reports, agency and service reports, proposals, studies, and clippings. Sponsored by service clubs, including the Chicago Woman's Aid and the Welfare Council of Metropolitan Chicago, the Centers incorporated the predecessor Senior Citizens' Hobby Center. The first location was opened in 1957 at the Mary Pomeroy Green Center under the direction of Mary A. Young. With additional funding from the US Office of Economic Opportunity, more centers were added, and eventually 12 were operating in different sections of the city. The Centers became affiliated with Hull-House Association in 1970.

4,153. Smith, Eleanor
Papers. 1887-1959. 2 ft.
Open. Unpublished guide.
University of Illinois at Chicago Circle Library, Manuscript Collection.
Smith (1858-1942), a director of Hull-House Music School, composed children's music and developed courses of music instruction. Includes correspondence, manuscript music, speeches, a memorial tribute, photos, clippings, recital and concert programs, music and song books by Smith, and Hull-House publications. Papers contain information on the Hull-House Music School, as well as correspondence and speeches concerning Jane Addams.

4,154. Smith, Louise Hulbert
Papers. Ca. 1840-1905. 1 ft.
Open. Unpublished guide.
University of Illinois at Chicago Circle Library, Manuscript Collection.
Correspondence, post cards, photos, clippings, programs, pamphlets, brochures, catalogs, and published items of Smith, a grandniece of Jane Addams (1860-1935). Collection contains Addams family papers, including letters to Jane Addams from her stepbrother George Bowman Haldeman (1861-1909) and sisters Sarah Alice (Addams) Haldeman (1853-1915) and Mary Catherine (Addams) Linn as well as correspondence of Anna (Hostetter) Haldeman Addams (ca. 1828-1919) and information on the Ladies Reading Club of Girard, KS, 1904-05.

4,155. Society of Midland Authors
Records. 1915-71. 4.25 ft.
Open. Unpublished guide.

University of Illinois at Chicago Circle Library, Manuscript Collection.
Minutes, reports, correspondence, membership records, photos, clippings, awards, and publications of the Society, a social organization of midwestern authors founded in Chicago in 1915 to promote greater public awareness of the talents of midwestern authors and to foster their closer association. Members included Jane Addams, Edna Ferber, Zona Gale, Harriet Monroe, Mary Evans Andrews, and Mary (Hastings) Bradley.

4,156. Stewart, Lucy Tilden
Papers. 1869-1930. Ca. 200 items.
Open. Unpublished guide.
University of Illinois at Chicago Circle Library, Manuscript Collection.
Unpublished writings, clippings, newspapers, government documents, programs, pamphlets, and other papers of Stewart (1873-1940), a clubwoman and social worker. Born in Flint, MI, Stewart trained in social work at Hull-House and worked there as a kindergarten teacher. Later she returned to Flint, opened an art shop, and continued her social work activities. Collection documents the interest of Stewart and her mother Mrs. Damon Stewart in women's suffrage and prohibition. Includes a manuscript by Lucy Stewart, "The Earnings of Women," 1890; copies of *The Revolution,* 1869-70; an annual report of the New York State Woman Suffrage Association, 1895; a statement of the executive council of the National Council of Women, 1892; a program from the 40th anniversary celebration of the International Council of Women—National Woman Suffrage Association, 1882; and published items, including the *Woman's Tribune* and *The Woman's Journal.*

4,157. Swiss Benevolent Society of Chicago
Records. 1915-70. 2.5 ft.
Open. Unpublished guide.
University of Illinois at Chicago Circle Library, Manuscript Collection.
Bylaws, annual reports, financial records, correspondence, and printed items of the Society, which was founded in 1871 with funds remaining from Swiss contributions for relief of Swiss victims of the Chicago fire of 1871. The bulk of the collection dates from 1918 and relates to aid and assistance given to individuals and families. Early Society activities often included attempts to find employment for persons applying for aid. In recent years the Society has been involved chiefly in assistance to aged and institutionalized Swiss. Women have been involved in the organization as members and beneficiaries. The collection also includes information on Schweizer Damen Verein, the group's women's auxiliary.

4,158. Taylor, Lea Demarest
Papers. 1888-1968. 8.5 ft.
Open. Register.
University of Illinois at Chicago Circle Library, Manuscript Collection.
Taylor (1883-1975) was a social worker. Includes minutes, published and unpublished writings, annual reports, budgets, reports, memoranda, photos, and pamphlets. Taylor grew up in the Chicago Commons settlement house, which was founded by her father Graham Taylor in 1894. She served as head resident of Chicago Commons from 1921 to 1954. She also was president of the Chicago Federation of Settlements and the National Federation of Settlements and vice-president of the American Association of Social Workers. The first woman to sit on the Metropolitan Housing and Planning Council of Chicago, she founded the Highland Park, IL, Committee on Human Relations and helped promote racial peace at Gage Park High School in Chicago.

4,159. Temperance
Collection. 1871-1939. Ca. 200 items.
Open. Unpublished guide.
University of Illinois at Chicago Circle Library, Manuscript Collection.
Includes correspondence, petitions, invitations, photos, leaflets, flyers, programs, articles, and books relating to Frances Willard, the WCTU, and temperance. Also includes personal correspondence of Willard, 1871-95.

4,160. Travelers Aid Society of Metropolitan Chicago
Records. 1914-75. 51 ft. and 3 oversize items.
Open. Register.
University of Illinois at Chicago Circle Library, Manuscript Collection.
Articles of incorporation, bylaws, minutes, financial records, correspondence, invitations, reports, photos, clippings, newsletters, programs, and booklets of the Society, an adjunct of the YWCA that was organized in 1888 to station volunteers in railroad terminals to help newly arrived women make suitable housing arrangements. Later the group's focus expanded to include immigrants, servicemen, runaway children, and old or sick travelers. In 1914 the Society became independent and established branches throughout the state. In 1939 a woman's board was created to interest women in the programs of the Society. In 1967 the Immigrants' Service League was incorporated as part of the Society.

4,161. Tucker, Irwin St. John
Papers. 1903-75. 11 ft. and 2 oversize vols.
Open. Unpublished guide.
University of Illinois at Chicago Circle Library, Manuscript Collection.
Tucker (1886-) is a journalist, priest, author, and Socialist reformer. Contains correspondence, a diary, manuscripts, legal papers, photos, and clippings. Includes correspondence of his wife Ellen Dorothy O'Reilly Tucker (1883-1953), who was an illustrator for *The Daily Socialist,* an author, and an artist's model, along with information on the Hunger March in 1915, at which he became associated with anarchist Lucy Parsons and a number of Hull-House residents, including Jane Addams, Ellen Gates Starr, and Sophonisba P. Breckinridge.

4,162. United Hebrew Charities
Records. 1876-95. 9 items.
Open. Unpublished guide.
University of Illinois at Chicago Circle Library, Manuscript Collection.
Annual reports of the United Hebrew Charities, which was founded in 1859 to perform relief work, maintain an employment bureau, support the Michael Reese Hospital in Chicago, and maintain a burial society. In addition to organizational reports containing names of donors, these publications include reports concerning charity cases and patients at Michael Reese Hospital. Collection also includes annual reports of the women's affiliates, Jochannah Lodge, the Sewing Societies, and the Young Ladies' Aid Society, which is now the Chicago Woman's Aid, as well as information on the training school for nurses at Michael Reese Hospital.

4,163. Vittum, Harriet Elizabeth
Papers. 1890-1954. 2 ft.
Open. Register.
University of Illinois at Chicago Circle Library, Manuscript Collection.
Vittum (1872-1953) was a social worker. Includes correspondence, diaries, financial papers, articles and other writings, engagement calendars, memorial and retirement tributes, photos, clippings, and publications of the Northwestern University Settlement. Vittum came to Chicago in 1893 to work at the World's Columbian Exposition and afterwards worked with the Illinois Children's Home and Aid Society. In 1904 she became a volunteer at Northwestern University Settlement, and in 1906 she became head resident, a post she held until 1947. An unsuccessful candidate for Chicago alderman and county commissioner, she lobbied for protective labor laws for women and children, women's rights, and suffrage. She helped found the first Infant Welfare Station in Chicago at the Northwestern University Settlement, which initiated a program to make pasteurized milk available to mothers of infants. She also was a founding member and president of the Woman's City Club of Chicago.

4,164. Washingtonian Home
Records. 1865-1917. 0.5 ft.
Open. Unpublished guide.
University of Illinois at Chicago Circle Library, Manuscript Collection.
Organized in 1863, the Home maintained a residence and provided treatment for alcoholics. Includes annual reports, correspondence, histories, receipts, and lists. The Home received early financial support from the Grand Lodge of Good Templars and a ladies' committee. Eliza Edwards was an early and active supporter of the organization. In 1869 a female department was organized, and in 1882 a separate residence, the Martha Washington Home, was opened. Women served on two special committees, the visiting committee and the committee on admissions and discharge, which was concerned with the Martha Washington Home's management. The Home's facilities and programs were later subsumed within the Martha Washington Hospital in Chicago.

4,165. West Side Historical Society
Records. Ca. 1830-1965. 100 ft., 69 oversize vols., and 17 microfilm reels.
Open. Accession record.
University of Illinois at Chicago Circle Library, Manuscript Collection.
The Historical Society was established and housed at the Legler branch of the Chicago Public Library in 1930 where it operated for more than 25 years. During this period a large quantity of papers and records of the people and institutions of the area was gathered and deposited in the Society's files. Includes information on such women as Jane Addams, Ruth Austin, Judge Mary M. Bartelme, [Mrs.] Louise (deKoven) Bowen, Mother Frances Xavier Cabrini, Charlotte Carr, Ellen Gates Starr, Harriet Vittum, and Mary Zimmerman. Also includes records of such women's clubs and organizations as the Austin Home Culture Club, the Belmont Woman's Club, the Daughters of Isabella, the Girl Scouts, the LWV of the West Side, and the West Area Business and Professional Women as well as such girls schools as Notre Dame Academy, Providence High School, and Lucy Flower Technical High School. Collection also includes copies of several west side newspapers dating from the 1930s to the 1960s.

4,166. Woman's City Club of Chicago
Records. 1910-55. 2.4 ft.
Open. Unpublished guide.
University of Illinois at Chicago Circle Library, Manuscript Collection.
The Club, a civic improvement organization, was founded in 1910. Includes a yearbook, the club *Bulletin,* photos, lantern slides, announcements, and programs. The Club worked to secure improvements in housing, child welfare, sanitation, women's rights, education, recreation facilities, electoral politics, and the courts. Prominent members included Jane Addams, Louise (deKoven) Bowen, Harriet E. Vittum, Lea Demarest Taylor, Julia Lathrop, Alice Hamilton, Edith Abbott, and Grace Abbott.

4,167. Woman's College Board of Chicago
Records. 1933-74. 7.25 ft. and 2 oversize vols.
Open. Accession record.

University of Illinois at Chicago Circle Library, Manuscript Collection.
The Board functioned from 1933 to 1974 to recruit prospective college students. Includes bylaws, minutes, financial records, correspondence, reports, a tape, photos, clippings, and publications. Formed at the Chicago World's Fair where the Board maintained a lounge, the Board became a permanent organization in 1935. The group provided information about women's colleges to the general public and to prospective students and stimulated alumnae activities. Member colleges included Barnard, Bryn Mawr, Goucher, Mills, Mount Holyoke, Smith, and Vassar.

4,168. Women for Peace
Records. 1963-71. 0.5 ft.
Open. Unpublished guide.
University of Illinois at Chicago Circle Library, Manuscript Collection.
Announcements, newsletters, bulletins, pamphlets, and form letters of this pacifist women's organization, which was founded in 1961 to protest nuclear testing by the US and the Soviet Union. The founders included Shirley [Mrs. Sidney] Lens, Ethel Taylor, and Bella Abzug. The group has lobbied for nonproliferation of nuclear weapons and the nuclear test-ban treaty; it also protested the Vietnam War. Members take part in letter-writing campaigns, public vigils, and disseminating information through publications.

4,169. Women In Communications, Inc.
Records. 1919-75. 11 ft.
Open. Register.
University of Illinois at Chicago Circle Library, Manuscript Collection.
Constitution, bylaws, articles of incorporation, annual reports, minutes, financial records, correspondence, committee reports, a history, photos, scrapbooks, clippings, articles, membership directories, and newsletters of this group, a Chicago branch of a professional organization of women involved primarily in journalism. Formerly Theta Sigma Phi, the group was founded in 1919 and elected Astrid Dodge Johnson as its first president. The objectives of the organization are to promote professional development for women, recognition of women journalists, recruitment of students for careers in journalism, and a free and responsible press. Current activities include job placement and sponsorship of professional conferences and awards.

4,170. Women Mobilized for Change
Records. 1966-71. 2.5 ft.
Open. Unpublished guide.
University of Illinois at Chicago Circle Library, Manuscript Collection.
Correspondence, reports, memoranda, notes, news releases, clippings, and publications of the Women Mobilized for Change, which was founded in Chicago in 1966 as a response to the urban rioting of the poor and minorities in Los Angeles and Chicago. Growing out of a meeting with Coretta (Scott) King, the group was associated with the YWCA of Metropolitan Chicago. In keeping with their goals to end racial injustice and achieve a humane society, the group began such programs as civil rights marching, sit-ins, Vietnam War protests, and lobbying with the city and state governments. The organization also sent representatives to Cairo, IL, in 1972 to survey the causes and effects of the Cairo race riot. The organization ceased regular functioning in 1972 and was disbanded in 1975.

4,171. Women's Advertising Club of Chicago
Records. 1917-72. 16.5 ft. and 13 oversize vols.
Open. Register.
University of Illinois at Chicago Circle Library, Manuscript Collection.
Bylaws, minutes, presidents' books, financial records, correspondence, a motion picture, photos, scrapbooks, yearbooks, newsletters, and brochures of the Club, which was established in 1917 to encourage women in advertising careers and to utilize women's advertising skills for community service programs. Other activities have focused on professional development and education. The Club publishes the newsletter "Chicago's Advertising Woman."

4,172. Women's Suffrage
Collection. 1873-1902. Ca. 25 items.
Open. Unpublished guide.
University of Illinois at Chicago Circle Library, Manuscript Collection.
Correspondence, including that of Susan B. Anthony; letters from Helen H. Mitchell to George Bowen concerning politics in Illinois, her regard for John P. Altgeld, her political interests, and plans for a publication; and letters from Lucinda B. Chandler in which she writes of her experience with spiritualism, her feelings about child labor, her writing, and other topics. Also includes leaflets and pamphlets, among them Francis Parkman's "Some of the Reasons Against Woman Suffrage."

4,173. Women's Trade Union League of Chicago
Records. 1908-22. 1 ft.
Open. Unpublished guide.
University of Illinois at Chicago Circle Library, Manuscript Collection.
In existence from 1903 to 1950, the League, which was composed of middle- and working-class women, organized women into trade unions and obtained protective legislation and better working conditions for women. Includes correspondence, clippings, and leaflets concerning the activities of the League and of the National Women's Trade Union League. Collection also includes information on a telephone company strike; garment workers' strikes; strikes of women agents of the elevated railway in Chicago in 1911; protective laws for women and children; the Wage Earner's Suffrage League; English classes for immigrant working women; training of union organizers; minimum wage; fire drills and inspection of factories; the struggle for the 10-hour and eight-hour day; the Household Workers Association headed by [Miss] Lilly Bruemerhoff (the only such organization in the country in 1913); promotion of union labels on clothing; organization of sales clerks; organization of Illinois hospital nurses and attendants; and opposition in 1922 to the Equal Rights Amendment as endangering protective legislation. Membership was open to all who would assist in forming trade unions; the majority of executive board members had to consist of women who were, or had been, trade unionists in good standing. Women active in the Chicago branch included Margaret (Dreier) Robins, Agnes Nestor, Mary Eliza McDowell, Jane Addams, and Ellen Gates Starr.

4,174. Workingwoman's Industrial Home of Chicago
Records. 1880. 2 items.
Open. No guide.
University of Illinois at Chicago Circle Library, Manuscript Collection.
The Home, a transient home for working mothers with children, was organized in 1879 and incorporated by [Mrs.] Anna Schock in 1880. Consists of the first annual report and a revised edition of it, which contain a certificate of organization, lists of donations and cash contributions, correspondence, rules of the home, reports from the press, the manager's narrative report and history of the home, and a report concerning the number of women taken in, illnesses, births, and the number of children inmates. Established at a time when county institutions and poorhouses separated children from their mothers, the Home provided shelter, food, supervised school and play for children, and gave instruction in domestic and other labor. Women were requested to pay board if they could; attempts were made to make the Home self-supporting through the manufacture of women's underclothing.

4,175. Young Women's Christian Association of Metropolitan Chicago
Records. 1876-1960. 36 ft.
Open. Unpublished guide.
University of Illinois at Chicago Circle Library, Manuscript Collection.
Bylaws, minutes, financial records, agendas, correspondence, reports, photos, scrapbooks, and publications of this branch of the YWCA, which was founded in 1876 as the Women's Christian Association and aided single women coming to Chicago to seek employment. Founding members included Mrs. Denison Groves, Mary [Mrs. E. G.] Clark, Ida [Mrs. William] Tilden, Harriet [Mrs. Cyrus H.] McCormick, and Effie J. [Mrs. Frederic L.] Fake. Early YWCA activities included an employment bureau, assistance to incoming travelers, a dispensary, and residences for women. The Chicago YWCA lobbied to end child labor and improve working conditions for women; it also promoted racial equality.

4,176. Zonta Club of Chicago Loop
Records. 1924-75. 8.5 ft. and 3 oversize vols.
Open. Register.
University of Illinois at Chicago Circle Library, Manuscript Collection.
Articles of incorporation, bylaws, minutes, auditor's reports, financial records, correspondence, membership forms and rosters, photos, clippings, newsletters, and publications of this chapter of Zonta International, a business and professional women's service club, which was founded in 1925. Membership is by invitation and is limited to one representative per club from each type of business or profession. Activities include establishment of a scholarship, support for the Ramallah School for Palestinian refugee women, and sponsorship of the girls division of the Chicago Boys' Club. The Zonta Club raises funds through cookbook sales, raffles, fun nights, fashion shows, white elephant sales, and auctions. Prominent members include Alma Zola Groves and B. Fain Tucker.

4,177. Women's Council of Realtors® Governing Board
Records. 1939- . 10 vols.
Closed. No guide.
Women's Council of Realtors® of the National Association of Realtors.®
Minutes and monthly publications of the governing board of the Council, which was founded in 1939 to promote association among its members, to promote participation in the activities of the National Association of Realtors®, and to encourage recognition of women and their contributions to the real estate business.

DEKALB

4,178. Schubach, Bernice W.
Papers. 1876-1922. 63 vols.
Open. Unpublished guide.
Northern Illinois Regional History Center.
Diaries and household expense ledgers of Frances (Coleman) Forsythe (1835-1920?), the wife of a Sandwich, IL, businessman, and her daughter Nellie (Forsythe) Woodbury (1869-post 1922), who married the local superintendent of schools. The diaries record activities of an upper-middle-class mother and daughter and their roles as social leaders in a small northern Illinois community.

DES PLAINES

4,179. Des Plaines Woman's Club
Records. 1898-1945. 8 vols.
Open. No guide.
Des Plaines Historical Society.
Journals of the Club, a civic and social organization founded in 1894, contain minutes and lists of officers and members.

4,180. Local History
Collection. Ca. 1880- . No size given.
Open. No guide.
Des Plaines Historical Society.
Includes reminiscences, histories, photos, scrapbooks, clippings, and yearbooks relating to such topics as education, early settlers, women's organizations, and women's church activities.

DOWNERS GROVE

4,181. Anderson, Charlotte Drees
Papers. 1900-50. 1 folder.
Open. Unpublished guide.
Downers Grove Historical Society.
Correspondence, photos, clippings, programs, and other papers of [Mrs.] Anderson (?-1969), a teacher, dean of girls, and assistant principal at Downers Grove North High School. Anderson began her career at Tenney School, a county school near Downers Grove; the collection includes attendance records and other data about this rural school. Anderson retired in 1965 after 42 years of service in the Downers Grove school system.

4,182. Dutcher, Phoebe
Papers. 1930- . 1 folder.
Open. Unpublished guide.
Downers Grove Historical Society.
Correspondence, photos, clippings, and other papers of [Mrs. William] Dutcher (1905-), the first woman recorder of deeds for Du Page County, IL. Dutcher was responsible for initiating the program to microfilm deed ledgers generated over a 122-year period. Dutcher, who now is retired, lives in northern Wisconsin.

4,183. O'Neill, Lottie Holman
Papers. 1922-68. Ca. 30 items.
Open. Unpublished guide.
Downers Grove Historical Society.
[Mrs. William J.] O'Neill (1878-1967), the first woman elected to the Illinois General Assembly, served 13 terms in the legislature. Correspondence, legal documents, photos, clippings, programs, awards, citations, and political memorabilia concern her career as a Republican from the 41st District.

4,184. Selig, Clara, and Selig, Laura
Papers. 1900-70. 1 folder.
Open. No guide.
Downers Grove Historical Society.
Beginning as milliners, Clara Selig (1880-1970) and her sister Laura Selig (1890-1951) built a millinery and dry goods store in Downers Grove, which they operated for more than 50 years. Includes correspondence concerning the business, photos of the Seligs, and clippings about the women.

4,185. Women Authors
Collection. Nd. Ca. 25 items.
Open. Unpublished guide.
Downers Grove Historical Society.
Includes research studies, clippings, and published items of Alice Tisdale (Nourse) Hobart, a resident of China from 1908 to 1921 and the author of *Oil for the Lamps of China;* manuscripts and clippings of Ella Porter, a teacher and a children's author; and clippings of Mrs. Montrew Dunham, a teacher and author of biographies of famous Americans for children at the fourth through sixth grade levels.

DUNDEE

4,186. Columbia Literary Club
Records. 1899-1932. 1 drawer.
Access restricted. Unpublished guide.
Dundee Township Historical Society, Inc.
This literary study group, which was in existence from 1899 until 1932, furnished equipment for the domestic science room at the grade school. Minutes and yearbooks document the group's programs, which dealt with American literature and Italy, France, England, and other European countries.

4,187. Daughters of the World
Records. Ca. 1890-98. No size given.
Access restricted. No guide.
Dundee Township Historical Society, Inc.
Minutes, treasurers' reports, and annual programs of the Daughters, a fraternal organization founded in 1890.

4,188. Dundee Home Welfare Club
Records. 1915-26. 5 vols. and 3 items.
Access restricted. Unpublished guide.
Dundee Township Historical Society, Inc.
Constitution, bylaws, membership and attendance record, and yearbooks of the Club, which was organized in 1915 to protect the health of local residents, particularly the children. The group was discontinued in 1926.

4,189. Dundee Woman's Club
Records. 1932-72. 4 drawers.
Partially restricted. Unpublished guide.
Dundee Township Historical Society, Inc.
Minutes of monthly meetings, treasurer's reports, scrapbooks, yearbooks listing programs and names of members, clippings concerning fund-raising events, and other records of the Club, which was organized in 1932 to undertake projects for civic improvement, to protect the health of the community, to encourage youth through scholarships, and to keep informed about the best in science, literature, and the arts. Includes a history of the Club.

ELMHURST

4,190. Elmhurst Evening Woman's Club
Records. 1939-72. 34 vols.
Open. No guide.
Elmhurst Historical Museum.
Annual scrapbooks containing correspondence, program reports, yearbooks, photos, clippings, and other items of the Elmhurst Junior Women's Club, an educational and social organization that became the Elmhurst Evening Woman's Club in 1951.

4,191. Elmhurst Garden Club
Records. 1950-70. 5 vols.
Open. No guide.
Elmhurst Historical Museum.
Scrapbooks containing photos, clippings, and other records.

4,192. Elmhurst Junior Woman's Club
Records. 1942-51. 4 vols.
Open. No guide.
Elmhurst Historical Museum.
Correspondence, annual scrapbooks, membership information, clippings, and programs of the Club, a civic and social organization.

4,193. Elmhurst Methodist Church, Women's Society of Christian Service
Records. Ca. 1941-45. 1 vol.
Open. No guide.
Elmhurst Historical Museum.
Histories, biographical information, clippings, and lists of the Society, which provided support activities for men and women serving in WWII who were considered part of the Elmhurst Methodist Church family. Includes information on nurses and members of the WACs.

4,194. Elmhurst Panhellenic
Records. 1931-56. 3 vols.
Open. No guide.
Elmhurst Historical Museum.
Includes correspondence, membership lists, photos, scrapbooks, clippings, and programs of the group, an umbrella organization of the alumnae of Greek-letter social sororities.

4,195. Elmhurst Woman's Club
Records. 1935-73. 41 vols.
Open. No guide.
Elmhurst Historical Museum.
Annual scrapbooks contain correspondence, membership data, photos, clippings, programs, and other records of the Club, a civic and social organization founded in 1933. Also includes items concerning the Elmhurst Choral Women's Club.

4,196. Photos
Collection. Ca. 1880- . 2.5 ft.
Open. No guide.
Elmhurst Historical Museum.
Includes photos of homes, schools, churches, special events, leading citizens, and early residents as well as women telephone operators, business proprietors, and doctors. Also includes wedding certificates.

4,197. Vertical Files
Collection. 1845- . Ca. 10 ft.
Open. No guide.
Elmhurst Historical Museum.
Includes correspondence; reminiscences of Ruth Patrick concerning the Pearce family farm in Addison, IL; biographies of Lovella Hagans, Julia Bryan Lathrop, Margaret Chant Papendreau, and Martha Swan Scott; and files on organizations, including the AAUW, American Legion Auxiliary, Artists Guild, Dance Club, Hospital Guild, LWV, and the Elmhurst Lioness Club. Also contains vital statistics, including births, 1880-1934; deaths, ca. 1900-22; Du Page County marriage records, 1889-97; tombstone records for Bloomingdale township and a Du Page County cemetery list, both compiled in 1951.

ELSAH

4,198. Ames, Lucy Virginia (Semple)
Papers. Ca. 1865-1924. More than 450 items.
Open. No guide.
Principia College Library.
Daughter of the founder of Elsah, Ames (1837-1925) became a businesswoman. She provided financial assistance for her brother Eugene Semple, who was governor of Washington Territory. Correspondence, including letters written by Ames and her brother; two tapes by persons who knew her; photos; and other papers. The correspondence between Ames and her brother includes discussion of their business affairs. Ames's two sons became businessmen.

4,199. Morgan, Mary (Kimball)
Papers. 1897- . No size given.
Closed. No guide.
Principia Corporation Archives.
A leader of midwestern Christian Scientists, [Mrs. William Edgar] Morgan founded The Principia, was

chairman of its board of trustees, and was an authorized teacher of Christian Science for many years. Correspondence, speeches, photos, records of Principia, and other papers. Morgan founded Principia, a coeducational school, in 1897. The institution now has an enrollment of more than 1500 students on two campuses, one a preschool, elementary, and high school and the other an undergraduate college. A recent compilation of her writings has been published as *Education at The Principia.*

EVANSTON

4,200. Whitefield, Fannie B.
Papers. Ca. 1900. 3 Hollinger boxes.
Open. No guide.
Evanston Historical Society.
Correspondence, poetry, and scrapbooks of [Mrs.] Whitefield, a poet and resident of Evanston.

4,201. Chicago Training School
Records. Ca. 1910-28. 10 ft.
Open. Unpublished guide.
Garrett-Evangelical Theological Seminary Library.
Founded by [Mrs.] Lucy Jane Rider Meyer (1849-1922) in ca. 1910, the School provided certification for Methodist Episcopal Church deaconesses, education for directors of Christian education for the Church's local and conference units, and training for women in urban social work and in home and foreign missions. Standardized letters, flyers, catalogs, photos, and other material, some of which is mounted in scrapbooks, document Meyer's fund-raising activities and the School's recruitment efforts. In ca. 1928, following Meyer's death, the School merged into the Garrett Biblical Institute.

4,202. Colbert, William
Papers. 1739-1834. 65 items (3 ft.).
Open. Unpublished guide.
Garrett-Evangelical Theological Seminary Library.
Correspondence, journals, and other papers of Colbert (1765-1833), a Methodist minister. Includes correspondence with his wife Elizabeth Stroud Colbert, Francis Asbury, Charles and John Wesley, and George Whitefield. The journals are available on microfilm.

4,203. Dempster, John
Papers. 1827-96. 54 items.
Open. Unpublished guide.
Garrett-Evangelical Theological Seminary Library.
Dempster (1794-1863) was a Methodist minister and educator, a missionary to Argentina, and founder of Garrett Biblical Institute (now Garrett-Evangelical Theological Seminary). Correspondence, sermon notes, and miscellaneous papers, including correspondence of Dempster's daughter Sara (Dempster) McKee and his son William Dempster as well as items regarding family matters and the founding of the Institute.

4,204. Harkness, Georgia
Papers. 1920-73. 5 ft.
Open. Unpublished guide.
Garrett-Evangelical Theological Seminary Library.
A prominent Methodist theologian and apologist following WWII, Harkness (1891-1973) was also a preacher, writer, and educator. Correspondence, lectures, lecture notes, and sermons.

4,205. Hemenway, Francis Dana
Papers. 1853-1904. 589 items.
Open. Unpublished guide.
Garrett-Evangelical Theological Seminary Library.
Family and personal correspondence, sermons, lectures, speeches, notebooks, and photos of Hemenway (1830-84), a Methodist minister and educator. Includes letters to his wife Sara Bixby Hemenway and papers regarding the revision of the Methodist Episcopal Church hymnal in 1878.

4,206. Lesemann, Louis Frederick William
Papers. 1894-1920. 153 items.
Open. Unpublished guide.
Garrett-Evangelical Theological Seminary Library.
Lesemann (1869-1941), a Methodist minister and educator, was superintendent of the Chicago Northern District of the Methodist Episcopal Church between 1912 and 1917. Sermons; reports he made as district superintendent; lectures on the Bible, religious education and training, and other topics; articles; and other papers, some of which relate to the Chicago Training School.

4,207. Ridgaway, Henry Bascom
Papers. 1844-1916. 776 items (4 ft.).
Open. Unpublished guide.
Garrett-Evangelical Theological Seminary Library.
A Methodist minister, Ridgaway (1830-95) was president of Garrett Biblical Institute (now Garrett-Evangelical Theological Seminary). Correspondence, journals of his travels abroad from 1870 to 1892, notebooks, sermons, speeches, lectures, miscellaneous papers concerning theology and other subjects, and photos. Includes 13 letters from Frances Elizabeth Willard and material regarding Richard Cobden and Beverly Waugh.

4,208. Stuart, Charles Macaulay
Papers. 1878-1932. 4904 items.
Open. Unpublished guide.
Garrett-Evangelical Theological Seminary Library.
A Methodist minister and editor, Stuart (1853-1932) was president of Garrett Biblical Institute (now Garrett-Evangelical Theological Seminary). Correspondence, 1908-12 editorials from the *Northwestern Christian Advocate,* sermons, speeches, lectures, notebooks, poems, photos, and other papers re rhetoric, French history, the Bible, hymnody, religious education, and the Sunday School Board and the Board of Education of the Methodist Episcopal Church. Correspondence, most of which relates to Stuart's presidency of the Institute, includes letters of his wife Emma R. Littlefield Stuart; of H. A. Wheeler, an Institute trustee; and of Emory R. Buckner regarding the J. D. M. Buckley controversy on modernism in the Church. Other letters concern Bishop Naphtali Luccock.

4,209. Young, Kimball
Papers. 1830-1962. 18 ft. and 12 microfilm reels.
Open. Unpublished guide.
Garrett-Evangelical Theological Seminary Library.
Young (1893-) was an educator and sociologist who did research on Mormons and polygamy. Correspondence, bibliography, typescripts of Young's *Isn't One Wife Enough?,* research material for the book, personal histories of Mormon plural marriages, journals of early Mormons, and other papers concerning the United Order, James J. Strang, the Strangite schism, and Mormonism in Iowa, Michigan, Missouri, and Nauvoo, IL. Includes copies of newspaper accounts from 1831 to 1849 on Mormons and Mormonism, transcripts of interviews on the sociological and social-psychological aspects of polygamous family life, and student term papers on the same topic.

4,210. Baker, Edna Dean
Papers. Ca. 1900-56. Ca. 2 ft.
Open. No guide.
National College of Education, Harris Library.
Baker (1883-1956) was an educator, college president, and author. Contains correspondence, including some family letters; published and unpublished writings, including articles, books, and poems; a biographical sketch; a memorial tribute; photos; clippings; press releases; and publications of the National Kindergarten and Elementary College and the National College of Education. After receiving a bachelor's degree in education from the National Kindergarten College in 1908, Baker earned a BA and an MA in education from Northwestern University. In 1915 Baker became an assistant to Elizabeth Harrison, president of the National Kindergarten College; in 1920 she became president of the National Kindergarten and Elementary College, later the National College of Education, a position she held until 1949. Under her direction the school moved from Chicago to Evanston, educational programs expanded, the Mary Crane Nursery at Hull-House became a training center for the College's students, and the Children's School, the laboratory school of the College, was established. Among her books is *An Adventure in Higher Education: The Story of the National College of Education* (1956). Collection also contains writings, biographical items, a memorial tribute, and photos of Baker's sister Clara Belle Baker (1885-1961), who founded the Children's School at the College in 1918 and directed it for 34 years.

4,211. Harrison, Elizabeth Letcher
Papers. Ca. 1891-1927. Ca. 8 ft.
Open. No guide.
National College of Education, Harris Library.
[Miss] Harrison (1849-1927) was an educator, a leading figure in the development of progressive education, a pioneer in the kindergarten training movement and parental education, an author, and a college president. Includes correspondence; published and unpublished writings, including manuscripts of her autobiography *Sketches Along Life's Road;* speeches and addresses; manuscript journals of games, crafts, and stories; notes and other items on Friedrich Froebel's life and works; a scrapbook, 1918; memorial tributes and resolutions; photos; clippings; announcements and publications of the Chicago Kindergarten Training School and College; and published items concerning child welfare, kindergarten training, and music and art education. Harrison studied kindergarten training with a Mrs. Putnam in Chicago; she later studied the Froebel method of education as well as the Maria Montessori system. Harrison began a training class for teachers in 1886. In 1887 she founded the Chicago Kindergarten Training School with her friend Mrs. John N. Crouse. The Training School evolved into the National College of Education. The goal of the school's program was to give students broad training for kindergarten and primary school teaching; the arts, handicrafts, and literature, as well as attention to the individual child, were emphasized. Harrison was active in the International Kindergarten Union, the National Education Association, the National Congress of Mothers, the Chicago Woman's Club, and the Art Institute of Chicago. The author of many training manuals and books on child education, she also collected and adapted stories for children, some of which were published. Her books include *A Study of Child Nature* and *The Unseen Side of Child Life.* Correspondents include Jane Addams and Jean Carpenter Arnold, a teacher at the College.

4,212. National College of Education
Records. Ca. 1890- . Ca. 14 ft.
Open. No guide.
National College of Education, Harris Library.
Founded in 1887 by Elizabeth Harrison as the Chicago Kindergarten Training School, the College trains teachers for nursery schools, kindergartens, and elementary schools. Financial records, correspondence, addresses, speeches, historical files, reports, curricula, photos, school newspapers, clippings, annual catalogs, faculty bulletins, yearbooks, and publications of the College contain information on the Chicago Kindergarten Training School; the Chicago Kindergarten College for Teachers, Mothers, and Nurses; and the Chicago Kindergarten Club. Also includes information about presidents Elizabeth Harrison and Edna Dean Baker and students, faculty, and alumnae, all of whom were women during the College's early

years. Records contain letters from Kate Douglas Wiggin.

4,213. Associated Women Students: Mortar Board, Women's League, Women's Athletic Association, and Student Governing Board
Records. 1906- . 1.5 boxes.
Open. No guide.
Northwestern University Archives.
Mortar Board, an honorary society for college women in their senior year, was organized at Northwestern in 1923. The Women's League, which was succeeded by the Student Governing Board, legislated for self-government and unity among women's organizations. The Women's Athletic Association, formed in 1912, promotes intercollegiate sports and such annual events as a musical comedy revue. Charter, constitutions, lists of members and officers, organizational histories, photos, bulletins, and other records of the four organizations. The Women's League records date from 1906 to 1920.

4,214. Lunt, Cornelia Gray
Papers. 1866-1934. 1 letter-size Hollinger box.
Open. Unpublished guide.
Northwestern University Archives.
[Miss] Lunt (1843-1934), a philanthropist, arts patron, and writer, was trustee of Northwestern University from 1896 to 1920. Correspondence, journals, a date book, bookplates, articles, clippings, and other papers. Lunt was the oldest of four children and the only daughter of one of the founders of Northwestern University. She founded and was president of the University Guild.

4,215. Northwestern Female College, Evanston College for Ladies, and Northwestern University Women's College
Records. 1855-1901. 3 boxes and 1 vol.
Open. No guide.
Northwestern University Archives.
Founded by professor W. P. Jones in 1855 as the Northwestern Female College, this women's institution became Evanston College for Ladies in 1871 and Women's College in 1873 when it became a component of Northwestern University. Constitution, bylaws, minutes, correspondence, expense accounts, class lists, photos, a scrapbook, catalogs, articles, mementos, and other records. Northwestern Female College records include a history of the school by [Mrs.] Jennie Wheeler Pearce and copies of *The Casket and Budget,* which was the first newspaper published in Evanston. The Women's College records include correspondence of Frances E. Willard and Ellen Soule, both of whom served as deans of the College; an historical sketch about the school; and photos and autobiographical sketches of Willard, Soule, Jane Bancroft, and other women associated with the school.

4,216. Northwestern University Archives Reference Subject Files
Records. 1874- . 11 folders.
Open. No guide.
Northwestern University Archives.
Correspondence, reports, bulletins, pamphlets, articles, clippings, and other material in the reference subject files contain information about Northwestern University's women graduates and students, the school's deans of women, women in the Reserve Officer Training Corps, Women's Day, the Women's Building, the Women's Education Aid Association, the Women's Interhouse Council, and about Northwestern's first Women's Invitational Gymnastic Meet in 1975. The first woman graduated from Northwestern in 1875. The Women's Building material dates from 1911 to 1938; the Women's Aid Association records, from 1871 to 1949; and the women's ROTC records, from 1973 to the present. Women's Day is an annual campus event begun in 1973.

4,217. Northwestern University: Women's Medical School
Records. 1893-1902. 2 folders.
Open. No guide.
Northwestern University Archives.
The Women's Medical School was founded in 1870 and incorporated into Northwestern University in 1892. Correspondence, photos, commencement programs, schedules, articles, clippings, a published history of the Women's Medical School, and other records. Includes clippings and articles about the School and its graduates; a document concerning establishment of the Elizabeth Skelton Danforth Memorial Scholarship in 1898; and a book about Mary Harris Thompson, a graduate of the School and founder, head physician, and surgeon of the Mary Thompson Hospital of Chicago for Women and Children. Most of the School's records were lost or destroyed after it was dissolved in 1902.

4,218. School of Domestic Arts and Sciences
Records. 1901-52. 5 letter-size Hollinger boxes and 4 vols.
Open. Unpublished guide.
Northwestern University Archives.
The School, incorporated in 1901, was purchased and discontinued by Northwestern University in 1943. Bylaws, annual reports, minutes of the board and executive committee, treasurer's reports and other financial records, correspondence, course outlines and grades, membership lists, a history of the School, news releases, bulletins, clippings, and other records, including files of Anna R. Cross, a trustee of the School.

4,219. Student Guidance and Counseling, Office of
Records. 1925-74. 73 boxes.
Open. Unpublished guide.
Northwestern University Archives.
Correspondence, records of individual student groups, news releases, clippings, and other material include records of or information about cheerleaders, honorary and social sororities, the Married Women's Club, women off campus, the Women's Athletic Association, the YWCA, Women's Defense Efforts, the Associated Women Students, the Big Little Sister program, the Women's Interhouse Council, the Panhellenic Association, sororities, and the Intercollegiate Association of Women Students. The Married Women's Club records are dated 1945.

4,220. Student Organizations and Activities: WAA-MU Show, May Week, May Day, Fraternities and Sororities
Records. 1896- . 4 boxes.
Open. No guide.
Northwestern University Archives.
The WAA-MU Show began in 1929 with the merger of the annual productions of the Women's Athletic Association and the Men's Union; the Show is an annual original musical comedy revue performed by students. Programs, souvenir books, librettos, photos, articles, clippings and some correspondence.

The May Week-May Day observance, which began informally in the 1890s, became an official spring event in 1910. Photos, programs, publicity articles, and clippings reporting on events and students honored

Sororities appeared on the Northwestern campus in 1885. Correspondence, informational brochures, pamphlets, articles, clippings, and other material, including individual folders on the Panhellenic Council, Omega Psi, and Zeta Phi Eta sororities

4,221. Technological Institute: Women in Engineering
Records. 1971-76. 2 folders.
Open. No guide.
Northwestern University Archives.
Press releases, a newsletter and membership lists of the Society of Women Engineers, pamphlets, articles, and other material concerning women in engineering, particularly women in Northwestern's engineering program.

4,222. Ward, Winifred
Papers. 1917- . 10 letter-size Hollinger boxes and 2 packages.
Open. Unpublished guide.
Northwestern University Archives.
[Miss] Ward (1884-1975) founded the Children's Theatre of Evanston in 1925. Correspondence, diaries, speeches and lectures, creative dramatics material, biographical and genealogical information, Children's Theatre records, scrapbooks, annotated play scripts, and other papers. The Archives also holds photos of Ward, books by and about Ward, and disc recordings concerning Ward's career.

4,223. Willard, Frances "Frank" Elizabeth
Papers. 1817-1976. 3 folders.
Open. No guide.
Northwestern University Archives.
Originally a teacher, [Miss] Willard (1839-98), who served as dean of women at Northwestern University, founded the World WCTU in 1883. Correspondence, journal excerpts, material concerning the centenary of her birth, pamphlets, articles, clippings, books by and about Willard, and other items. The Archives' photographic files contain a folder of photos of Willard.

4,224. Women's Activities at the Columbian Exposition
Collection. 1893. 2 vols.
Open. No guide.
Northwestern University Archives.
Scrapbooks contain promotional and informational material, articles, clippings, and other items about the participation of women and women's groups in the Exposition. Includes information about such diverse women as architects, belly dancers, Chicago church women, and "exotic blue-faced women" from the Middle East.

4,225. Women's Medical School: Alumni Biographical Files
Records. 1872-1902. 1 box.
Open. Unpublished guide.
Northwestern University Archives.
Biographical files contain information about graduates of the Women's Medical College, which was founded in 1870 and merged with Northwestern University in 1892. Files contain such items as correspondence, matriculation cards, general alumnae register cards, addresses, death notices, name change cards, clippings and publicity about individuals, and short personal histories.

4,226. Authors and Literary Figures
Collection. Ca. 1855-1936. Ca. 20 items.
Open. Card Catalog.
Northwestern University Library, Special Collections.
Includes correspondence of Alice (Morse) Earle, the author of *Sun-Dials and Roses of Yesterday* (New York: MacMillan, 1902), 1901-04; of Amy Lowell, 1916 and 1922; of Harriet (Beecher) Stowe; and of Gene Stratton-Porter regarding her experience in writing her book *Birds of the Bible,* 1909. Also includes letters from Harriet Monroe to Marguerite Ogden Bigelow Wilkinson, 1914; from Sarah Orne Jewett to Harriet (Prescott) Spofford, 1905; from Elizabeth (Robins) Pennell, an author, to Theodore Koch, 1936; from Agnes Repplier, an essayist to J. Thomson Willing, 1920; from Gertrude Stein to Allen Tannier, ca. 1925; and from Alice B. Toklas to a professor Sanchez, 1935. Also contains manuscripts of "Gladness," a poem by Genevieve Taggard, a poet, and "I Didn't Think," a poem by Ella (Wheeler) Wilcox.

4,227. Breit, Harvey
Papers. 1940-65. Ca. 134 items.
Open. Card catalog.

Northwestern University Library, Special Collections. Correspondence and post cards of Breit, a book reviewer for *The New York Times,* including letters from such literary figures as Faith Baldwin, Elizabeth Bishop, Louise Bogan, Marianne Moore, Katherine Anne Porter, Dorothy Rodgers, Nancy Wilson Ross, and Lillian Roth.

4,228. Brett, Dorothy
Papers. 1923-69. 1 box.
Open. No guide.
Northwestern University Library, Special Collections. Correspondence, typescripts, manuscripts, diaries, and ephemeral material of Brett (1891-), a British author who lived in the US for more than 40 years. Includes her letters to Leland H. Roloff and her drafts of "America" and "Katherine & Myself," which concerns Brett and Katherine Mansfield.

4,229. Goldman, Emma
Papers. 1905-39. Ca. 40 items.
Open. Card catalog.
Northwestern University Library, Special Collections. Goldman (1869-1940) was an anarchist, author, and editor of *Mother Earth,* a journal for anarchists. Includes correspondence, pamphlets by Goldman, articles about her, announcements of her lectures, and a complete set of *Mother Earth.* Correspondence relates primarily to fund raising for *Mother Earth* and scheduling meetings and lectures. Includes letters to James B. Pond, the manager of Goldman's 1934 speaking tour of the US, and to Ruth S. Olsen regarding lecture dates in St. Paul, MN.

4,230. Marx, Erica
Papers. Nd. No size given.
Open. No guide.
Northwestern University Library, Special Collections. Marx (1909-69) ran the Hand & Flower Press. Notes for a speech, papers about her, tributes and obituaries, broadsides, and other items.

4,231. Massachusetts Woman Suffrage Association
Records. 1886. 1 item.
Open. Card catalog.
Northwestern University Library, Special Collections. A notice concerning a bazaar to be held in Massachusetts to further the cause of woman suffrage.

4,232. Nin, Anaïs
Papers. 1929-64. 10 boxes.
Open. Unpublished guide.
Northwestern University Library, Special Collections. Manuscripts of Nin (1903-77), an author, include those for many of her major novels, short stories, and some unpublished works, among them *Under a Glass Bell and Other Stories, House of Incest, Children of the Albatross, Winter of Artifice,* and *D. H. Lawrence, An Unprofessional Study.* Also includes some annotations by Henry V. Miller.

4,233. Notable Women
Collection. Ca. 1886-1962. Ca. 88 items.
Open. Card catalog.
Northwestern University Library, Special Collections. Includes letters by Jane Addams to a Miss Hinterminster accepting her offer to help with Italian immigrants, 1890; by Mary Ashton (Rice) Livermore to [Miss] Frances Willard regarding a copy of *The Story of My Life,* which she was sending to Willard, 1897; by Miriam [Mrs. Kenneth] Patchen to Mr. and Mrs. John Webb; and by Anne Whitney, a sculptor, to Frances Willard and Lady Henry Somerset inviting them to lunch. Also includes correspondence of Frances Willard regarding the ballot for women and subsequent end to liquor advertisements, 1887, as well as correspondence of Clare (Boothe) Luce, Florence Nightingale, and Eleanor Roosevelt.

4,234. Nutting, Helen
Papers. 1913-32. 1 box.
Open. No guide.
Northwestern University Library, Special Collections. Includes diaries, notebooks, and manuscripts of Nutting, a writer and associate of James Joyce, containing descriptions of and comments about her travels in Europe. Also includes her poetry, drawings, stories, and notes on literature, dreams, authors, art, and women. Contains drawings by Elena Nutting.

4,235. O'Brien, Kate
Papers. 1921-70. 3 boxes.
Open. Unpublished guide.
Northwestern University Library, Special Collections. Papers of O'Brien (1897-) contain typescripts and manuscripts of such novels as *The Last of Summer* and *The Flower of May;* plays, including *Without My Cloak, Ante Room, The Last of Summer, Esa Senora,* and *The Flower of May;* short stories; unpublished works; and talks. Also includes autobiographical items, radio scripts, and correspondence with Denys Blakelock and others.

4,236. Pankhurst, Sylvia
Papers. 1928. 5 pp.
Open. No guide.
Northwestern University Library, Special Collections. Letter by Pankhurst describes a book she was planning to write about the history of women's suffrage.

4,237. Riding, Laura
Papers. 1928-72. 1 box.
Open. No guide.
Northwestern University Library, Special Collections. Correspondence with her publisher David McKain, Martin Seymour-Smith, Joyce Wexler, and Sam Hynes; galleys; manuscripts and typescripts; and publisher's proof notices of Riding (1901-), a poet and novelist who lives in Florida.

4,238. Shiras, Myrna
Papers. 1966- . 17 folders.
Open. Unpublished guide.
Northwestern University Library, Special Collections. Correspondence, transcript of a 1976 interview, photos, clippings with reviews, announcements, and programs of Shiras (1936-), a feminist artist and sculptor who lives in California. Includes correspondence with galleries and correspondence in which Shiras discusses her techniques, artistic credo, and feminism.

4,239. Slavery
Collection. 1803-63. 6 items.
Open. Card catalog.
Northwestern University Library, Special Collections. Includes sale documents for Lucy and her child Flora in South Carolina, 1803; for Margaret and an infant, 1857; and for Mary in Richmond, VA, 1863. Also includes a receipt of payment for 419 days of work in a chain gang by Nancy, a slave, 1843; a reward poster for Eliza Cousey, a Negro girl, 1857; and a leaflet concerning the 24th National Anti-Slavery Bazaar.

4,240. Women's Franchise League
Records. 1890-95. Ca. 150 pp.
Open. No guide.
Northwestern University Library, Special Collections. First minute book of the League, founded in 1889, includes the signatures of Emmeline Pankhurst, Harriet (Stanton) Blatch, and others.

4,241. Women's Liberation
Collection. Late 1960s- . 34 ft. and 75 cu.ft.
Open. Unpublished guides.
Northwestern University Library, Special Collections. Position statements, newsletters, newspapers, and ephemera concerning the women's liberation movement, women's centers, abortion, child care, feminism, and related issues. Includes records of the national and regional levels of the National Organization for Women, the Chicago Women's Liberation Union, Seattle Radical Women, the Feminist Coordinating Council, the Los Angeles Feminist Theater, and the Spokeswoman Archives.

4,242. Moldenhauer Archives
Collection. 1500s- . Ca. 10,000 items.
Open. Unpublished guide.
Northwestern University, Music Library. Collection includes correspondence, music manuscripts and scores, photos, and scrapbooks. Contains correspondence, manuscript sketches for "Northwestern Sketches," and the manuscript of "Prelude" by Dorothy Cadzow-Hokanson.

4,243. Union Signal
Records. 1883- . Ca. 9 ft.
Open. Published and unpublished guides.
Woman's Christian Temperance Union National Headquarters, Frances Willard Memorial Library. The official weekly newspaper of the WCTU, the *Union Signal* was established in 1883 by the merger of *Our Union,* a WCTU periodical founded in 1875, and *The Signal,* a periodical of the Illinois WCTU. Issues of the publication reflect the WCTU's interest in social, economic, and political aspects of temperance and prohibition. Frances E. Willard, Anna A. Gordon, Mary H. Hunt, Lillian M. N. Stevens, Cora Frances Stoddard, Ella Boole, and other temperance leaders have written articles for the periodical. Editorial responsibility was held by Mary Bannister Willard, 1883-85; Mary Allen West, 1885-92; Frances Willard, 1892-98; Lillian M. N. Stevens, 1898-1914; Anna A. Gordon, 1914-26; Ella Boole, 1926-33; and Ida B. Wise Smith after 1933. Special columns were included for children and young people. News was reported from state, local, national, and international branches of the WCTU. Other topics, such as the woman's movement, welfare and prison reform, work with child laborers and immigrants, and peace and disarmament movements, were also discussed. Issues from 1883 to 1933 are available on microfilm from the Ohio Historical Society. See Randall C. Jimerson *et al.,* eds., *Guide to the Microfilm Edition of Temperance and Prohibition Papers* (Ann Arbor, MI: University of Michigan, 1977).

4,244. Woman's Christian Temperance Union
Records. 1852- . More than 20 ft.
Open. Published and unpublished guides.
Woman's Christian Temperance Union National Headquarters, Frances Willard Memorial Library. Records of the national headquarters of the WCTU, which was founded in 1874, focus on the careers of Frances E. Willard and Anna A. Gordon. Included are annual reports, minutes of annual conventions and of local Michigan chapter meetings, correspondence, speeches, biographical material, photos, scrapbooks, pamphlets, and other items. Correspondence of the national headquarters includes information about the founding of WCTU chapters in all states, petition drives, the Prohibition party, woman suffrage campaigns, temperance and prohibition efforts in the US and Great Britain, and other subjects. Also contains scrapbooks compiled by Frances Willard and her mother Mary T. Willard that document the work of the WCTU, speaking tours, conventions and politics, and the activities of Frances Willard. Correspondents include Frances Willard, Anna Gordon, Annie Wittenmyer, Esther Pugh, Clara Hoffman, Susan B. Anthony, Rachel Foster Avery, Carrie Chapman Catt, Frances (Folsom) Cleveland, [Mrs.] Varina Davis, Anna Dickinson, Lucretia Garfield, Phebe Hanaford, Elizabeth Phelps Ward, Lucy Stone, and Mary Virginia Terhune. National headquarters' records dating from 1852 to 1932 are available on microfilm through the Ohio Historical Society. See Randall C. Jimerson *et al.,* eds., *Guide to the Microfilm Edition of Temperance and*

Prohibition Papers (Ann Arbor, MI: University of Michigan, 1977).

GALENA

4,245. Local History
Collection. 1816- . 100 microfilm reels and other items.
Partially restricted. Card catalog.
Galena Public Library, Historical Collection.
Diaries, memoirs, census and cemetery records, genealogies, Civil War material, city directories, maps, and microfilm of newspapers and early records provide information about the history of Galena, Jo Daviess County, and the lead mine region of Iowa, Wisconsin, and Illinois. Includes material concerning local women.

GALESBURG

4,246. Armes, Ethel
Papers. 1897-1917. 52 items.
Open. Unpublished guide.
Knox College Archives.
Correspondence and photos of Armes, a writer and journalist. Includes letters from American writers in which they reply to requests for interviews and letters containing comments about writing techniques in general and those of Armes in particular.

4,247. Baldwin, Faith
Papers. 1929-42. 50 items.
Open. Unpublished guide.
Knox College Archives.
Faith (Baldwin) Cuthrell (1893-), a writer, uses her maiden name in her work. Correspondence concerns her private life, travels, habits, finances, activities, publications and writing, residences, and a Miss Gonyaw, whom Baldwin termed a "house comrade."

4,248. Bickerdyke, "Mother" Mary Ann (Ball)
Papers. 1897-1901. 13 items.
Open. Unpublished guide.
Knox College Archives.
Bickerdyke (1817-1901) was a Civil War nurse. Correspondence of Bickerdyke, her brother, and others concerns Bickerdyke's health, the location of the family's plot in Lynwood Cemetery in Galesburg, and arrangements for her burial there. Also includes mention of men in the Civil War.

4,249. Burkhalter, Savina Karl
Papers. 1693-1959. 6 in.
Open. Unpublished guide.
Knox College Archives.
Burkhalter (1888-1959) was a nurse in Illinois hospitals. Correspondence, documents, photos, and clippings primarily provide genealogical information about Burkhalter and her family.

4,250. Burnham, Clara Louise Root
Papers. 1921-24. 19 items.
Open. Unpublished guide.
Knox College Archives.
Correspondence and notes of Burnham (1854-1927), a writer, concern her personal plans, writing, reading, home addresses, health, and social activities.

4,251. Burton, Sarah Fenn
Papers. 1835. 3 items.
Open. Unpublished guide.
Knox College Archives.
Burton's diary contains her description of a steamboat trip from Connecticut to Illinois in the spring of 1835. She describes life on the boat, plants she saw along the way, and a temperance meeting.

4,252. Carey, Amelia L.
Papers. 1866-67. 14 items.
Open. Unpublished guide.
Knox College Archives.
Accounts by Carey (?-1871), who graduated from Knox Seminary in 1869, concerning her life as a student.

4,253. Carroll, Louisa Thomas
Papers. 1939-45. 25 items.
Open. Unpublished guide.
Knox College Archives.
Correspondence and manuscripts of Carroll, a writer, provide information about her writing, health, and family.

4,254. Deming, Abigail Barnum
Papers. 1835-49. 4 items.
Open. Unpublished guide.
Knox College Archives.
Copies of correspondence of Deming concern the life of a widow in Galesburg.

4,255. Dickinson, Lora (Townsend)
Papers. 1846-1902. 15 items.
Open. Unpublished guide.
Knox College Archives.
Papers of Lora [Mrs. Frederick] Dickinson (1878-) and Christina Cornelia Woods Townsend (1854-?) contain descriptions of life in Scotland in the early 1800s; of London in 1873, including the Crystal Palace; and of pioneering in the Avon area of Illinois from 1845 to 1870. Also contains recollections of Galesburg High School, of Lombard College in Galesburg from 1896 to 1899, and of Carl Sandburg.

4,256. Farnham, Jerusha Brewster (Loomis)
Papers. 1837-38. 5 items.
Open. Unpublished guide.
Knox College Archives.
Diary, photos, and *Log City Days,* a published edition of the diary of [Mrs. Eli] Farnham (1806-72). Included is a description of a trip to Log City and life there.

4,257. Finch, Alida Elizabeth
Papers. Nd. 3 items.
Open. Unpublished guide.
Knox College Archives.
Finch (1871-1954) was an insurance underwriter for Pennsylvania Mutual Life Insurance Company in Philadelphia. Letters written to Earnest Elmo Calkins in 1934 in which she describes people and places in Galesburg from about 1837 to about 1891.

4,258. Finley, Georgia E.
Papers. 1916-19. 1 ft.
Open. Unpublished guide.
Knox College Archives.
Correspondence, diary, and mementos of Finley (1872-1943) contain a description of her WWI experiences as an American National Red Cross dietitian with the army at Base Hospital No. 32 in Contrexeville, France.

4,259. Gayman, Esther Palm
Papers. 1910-74. 5 ft.
Open. Unpublished guide.
Knox College Archives.
A life-long resident of Galesburg, Gayman (1891-1974) was a homemaker. Diaries, notes, scrapbooks, and photo albums contain her recollections of Galesburg's early factories, the Weston School, telephone service, the Grand Army of the Republic, building, radio, streets, and people.

4,260. Hitchcock, Margaret (Gale)
Papers. 1835-43. 2 items.
Open. Unpublished guide.
Knox College Archives.
Description by [Mrs. Henry Ethan] Hitchcock (1831-1914) of her trip west with her family.

4,261. Hurd, Ethel (Edgerton)
Papers. 1861-63. 1 item.
Open. Unpublished guide.
Knox College Archives.
[Mrs. Tyrus I.] Hurd (1845-1929), who graduated from Knox in 1865, was a physician, surgeon, and prominent suffragist. Article written for *Knox Alumnus* in which Hurd reminisces about life at Knox Academy from 1861 to 1863 and about professors at the school.

4,262. London, Charmian (Kittredge)
Papers. 1925-44. 39 items.
Open. Unpublished guide.
Knox College Archives.
Correspondence and notes of [Mrs. Jack] London (1883-1955), a writer, concern problems with her writing and publications and some of her personal plans.

4,263. Losey, Lucretia (Hitchcock)
Papers. 1810-1921. 3 items.
Open. Unpublished guide.
Knox College Archives.
Losey (1810-91) was the wife of Nehemiah Homand Losey, founder and professor of Knox College. Notebook, copy of obituary, and clipping. Includes Lucretia Losey's autobiography, written in 1884, describing her childhood, early life in New York, the trip west by canal boat, and life in Log City and Galesburg.

4,264. Milner, Vivian Irene
Papers. 1940-45. 16 items.
Open. Unpublished guide.
Knox College Archives.
Correspondence of Milner, an American writer, includes a discussion of her health. Also contains a photo.

4,265. Morse, Lucy Smith
Papers. 1881-92. 156 items.
Open. Unpublished guide.
Knox College Archives.
Week-by-week letters of [Miss] Morse (1864-1941), a student, describe events, people, organizations, and other aspects of life at Knox Academy and Knox College from 1881 to 1886. They also provide a description of the Boston area in 1889. Also contains post cards, explanatory notes, biographical data, and pictures. Morse later married Edward Caldwell.

4,266. Parminter, Nellie Mabel
Papers. 1893-98. 5 in.
Open. Unpublished guide.
Knox College Archives.
[Miss] Parminter (1873-1969), formerly of Downers' Grove, IL, became the wife of Edward M. Wetmore. Private papers, class notes, written papers, and programs of college events attended reflect Parminter's life as a student at Knox College.

4,267. Phelps, Caroline
Papers. 1830-40. 2 items.
Open. Unpublished guide.
Knox College Archives.
Transcripts by [Mrs. William] Phelps provide a description of life with the Indians on the Mississippi River and of trips to St. Louis and to Oquawka and Lewiston, IL.

4,268. Sengenberger, Ella
Papers. 1914-58. 1 box.
Open. Unpublished guide.
Knox College Archives.
Correspondence, talks, articles, honors, and awards of [Miss] Sengenberger (1890-1964), a 1914 graduate of Lombard College in Galesburg, concern her career as a teacher at Avon High School in Avon, IL, and as advisor of publications at Arsenal Technical High School. She was a teacher from 1914 to 1958.

4,269. Seymour Family
Papers. 1917-47. 12.5 ft.
Open. Unpublished guide.
Knox College Archives.
Family papers contain those of Flora Warren [Mrs. George Steele] Seymour (1888-1948), who graduated from the Washington College of Law in 1915, attended the Chicago-Kent College of Law in 1916, and became a member of the Board of Indian Commissioners in 1922. Correspondence, diaries, scrapbooks, published and unpublished works, and business records. Includes Seymour's exchange with Thomas Kearny regarding Philip Kearny and Stephen Watts Kearny and many letters about the work of the Board of Indian Commissioners. Seymour served as editor of *Quest* from 1908 to 1912, as associate editor of the *Woman Lawyers' Journal,* and on the State Council of Defense in 1917 and 1918.

4,270. Walker, Kenneth James, and Walker, Ursula (Genung)
Papers. 1913-65. 6 ft.
Open. Unpublished guide.
Knox College Archives.
Kenneth Walker (1913-65) and his wife Ursula Walker (1913-), editors and copublishers of a Louisiana newspaper, attempted to improve racial relations in the South. Personal and business correspondence, diaries, financial records, photos, clippings, plaques, and other items.

4,271. Ward, Grace R.
Papers. 1870-1900. 6 in.
Open. Unpublished guide.
Knox College Archives.
Ward (1844-1922), an 1865 Knox graduate, was a teacher and missionary to India. Photos showing locations in Europe and the Middle East.

4,272. Whiting and Tyron
Papers. 1850-1940. 4 ft.
Open. Unpublished guide.
Knox College Archives.
[Mrs.] Maria Whiting (1827-94) was principal of Knox Female Institute while Louise J. Tryon (1863-1942) was an English teacher at Knox College. Correspondence, speeches, and photos relate to Whiting's business and personal life, particularly during her work at Knox Institute from 1879 to 1894, and to family matters.

GENEVA

4,273. Women's Organizations
Collection. 1890- . No size given.
Open. Unpublished guide.
Geneva Historical Society.
Minutes of meetings, correspondence, reports, clippings, programs, and published items of women's social, civic, and charitable clubs in Geneva. Includes records of the Geneva Improvement Association, 1890-1913; the Geneva Woman's Club, 1913-; the Woman's Relief Corps, Grand Army of the Republic, 1913-67; the Geneva Community Club, 1922-76; the Nursery Auxiliary, 1915-, which was formed from the American Fund for French Wounded Children; the Geneva Garden Club, 1928-; the Young Mothers' Club, 1940-, which originally provided dental care to indigent children; and the Woman's Auxiliary, 1945-, a hospital fund-raising group.

HICKORY HILLS

4,274. Monastery Archives
Records. 1893- . No size given.
Closed. No guide.
Chicago Poor Clares Monastery.
Correspondence, photos, and other records of the Monastery, which was founded in 1893. Contains correspondence pertaining to the founding of the order in Chicago, letters from the order's founders to prospective candidates, and information about the births, professions, and deaths of Chicago Poor Clares. The first Poor Clare Colettine House was founded in the US in 1877.

HIGHLAND PARK

4,275. Local History
Collection. Ca. 1890- . No size given.
Open. No guide.
Highland Park Historical Museum.
Reminiscences, family histories, photos, clippings, programs, and published items provide information on women's clubs, early settlers, and organizers and patrons of the Ravinia Festival, a summer arts and music festival.

HINSDALE

4,276. Fresh Air Association
Records. 1898-1929. 3 vols. and ca. 25 items.
Open. No guide.
Hinsdale Public Library.
Constitution, annual reports, minutes, legal and financial records, and clippings of the Association, which was established in 1892 with funds from the estate of Athalia A. Walker. The group operated a residence in suburban Hinsdale as a summer retreat for women and children from slum districts in Chicago. Records chiefly relate to the financial details of operating the residence but include some information on programs the Association offered and people they served.

4,277. Fuller Family
Papers. 1835-1925. Ca. 50 items.
Open. No guide.
Hinsdale Public Library.
Reminiscences, legal papers, and clippings of Mr. and Mrs. Jacob Fuller and their six daughters, including Mary and Nella, who were early settlers in Fullersburg, IL, which is now a part of Hinsdale. Also contains papers of another daughter Loie Fuller (1862-1928), a modern dancer whose choreographic works were praised at the 1906 Paris Exhibition. Includes her autobiography *Fifteen Years of a Dancer's Life* (1913).

4,278. Hinsdale Clubs and Organizations
Records. 1920-48. Ca. 10 items.
Open. No guide.
Hinsdale Public Library.
Includes correspondence, histories, reminiscences, lists, and programs of such clubs and organizations as the Hinsdale Woman's Club, Hinsdale Music Club, Hinsdale Community Service Club, Captain Hubbard Burrows Chapter of the DAR, American Legion Auxiliary, Chapter CK of the PEO Sisterhood, Hinsdale AAUW, and Hinsdale Junior Infant Welfare.

4,279. Photos
Collection. Ca. 1890-1915. 10 vols. and ca. 50 items.
Open. Unpublished guide.
Hinsdale Public Library.
Consists of photos and slide transparencies with identifying notes and captions, including portraits of Mrs. Jacob Fuller, Loie Fuller, Lilian Walker Wentworth Hopkins, and Mary (Fuller) Van Velser, the first schoolteacher in DuPage County. Also includes photos of schoolteachers, women's club members, girls' athletic events, members of the Fresh Air Association, and women participants in May festivals and Independence Day parades.

4,280. Ross Family
Papers. 1885-1911. 1 vol.
Open. No guide.
Hinsdale Public Library.
Scrapbook compiled by Mrs. J. C. Ross, a housewife and social leader in Hinsdale, contains correspondence, photos, clippings, and programs, which primarily relate to births, weddings, travel, social events, and deaths of members of her family and friends.

JACKSONVILLE

4,281. College Archives
Records. 1846- . Ca. 365 ft.
Access restricted. No guide.
MacMurray College Archives.
Established in 1846 as a Methodist church-related women's school, MacMurray College became coeducational in 1955. Includes reports and papers of the presidents, reports of the business office, registrar's records, records of faculty members and student organizations, student directories and publications, library records, papers of alumnae and other persons associated with the College, photos, clippings scrapbooks, centennial items, catalogs, programs, and promotional items.

JOLIET

4,282. Religious Congregation of Women Archives
Records. 1865- . Ca. 400 cu.ft.
Access restricted. No guide.
Sisters of St. Francis of Mary Immaculate.
The first Franciscan congregation of religious women in Illinois, the Congregation was founded in Joliet in 1865 and is dedicated to education and to spreading the Catholic faith. Minutes of the corporation, proceedings of the chapters, financial records, annals, correspondence, diaries, personal papers of members, photos, scrapbooks, and other records of the Congregation and of institutions owned and managed by its members. Includes annals from missions throughout the US and Brazil.

KANKAKEE

4,283. Archives
Records. 1860- . 13 boxes.
Open. No guide.
Servants of the Holy Heart of Mary, Provincial House.
This religious order of women was founded in 1860 in Paris, France, and established in Beaverville, IL, in 1889. Provincial and corporation minutes, financial records, correspondence, retreat notes, photos, and records relating to the founding and closing of various missions. Includes correspondence of the founders, superiors general, and superiors provincial and archival notes of all the houses established by the order.

LA GRANGE PARK

4,284. Archives
Records. 1899- . Ca. 7 document cases.
Partially restricted. No guide.
Sisters of St. Joseph of La Grange.
Minutes, financial records, correspondence, oral history tapes, diaries, chronicles, theses, photos, scrapbooks, and other records of this religious congregation of women, which was founded in 1899 in La Grange, IL. Includes papers of several major superiors and material relating to Nazareth Academy, St. Joseph Academy, Our Lady of

Bethlehem Academy, and the Alexine Learning Center, all of which were established and operated by members of the congregation.

LEBANON

4,285. McKendree College Archives
Records. 1828- . No size given.
Access restricted. No guide.
McKendree College Library.
McKendree, a liberal arts college, was founded as a coeducational institution in 1828. Students were separated by sex, however, in about 1834, and women apparently were no longer students after about 1837. Trustees' minutes, correspondence, financial records, records of literary societies, photos, catalogs, programs, and other records. Tuition records from 1836 indicate that drawing, painting, and needlework were taught in the "Female Department." [Miss] Polly Thorp was chosen principal of the Department in that year. Women were again admitted as college students in ca. 1870. The Clionian Literary Society, which included women, was founded in 1869.

LEMONT

4,286. Archives
Records. 1894- . Ca. 50 ft.
Closed. No guide.
Franciscan Sisters of Chicago.
Chapter minutes, financial records, legal papers, correspondence, autobiographies, photo albums, and retreat papers of the order, which was founded by Mother Mary Theresa Dudzik in 1894. The order was known as the Franciscan Sisters of Blessed Kunegunda until 1968 and was the first sisterhood founded in Chicago. Includes correspondence of the superior generals, names of 500 orphans cared for at St. Vincent's Orphanage in Chicago from 1900 through 1911, and legal papers and correspondence of all institutions operated by the order, among them the Orphanage, the St. Joseph Home for the Aged and Crippled in Chicago, St. Elizabeth Day Nursery, and various schools and hospitals. The motherhouse of the order is located in Lemont. Mother Mary Theresa, who was born Josephine Dudzik, came to Chicago from Poland in 1881.

LIBERTYVILLE

4,287. Local History
Collection. 1835- . Ca. 50 tapes and other items.
Access restricted. Card file.
Libertyville-Mundelein Historical Society, Inc.
Histories, essays, minutes, biographical material, oral history tapes, photos, scrapbooks, and other items pertain to the Society, which was founded in 1955, and to other local organizations, businesses, churches, and schools. Also includes a genealogical library and records of early area events. The collection is housed in the Ansel B. Cook Home, headquarters of the Society.

LISLE

4,288. Prints
Collection. Ca. 1750-1935. Ca. 100 items.
Access restricted. No guide.
Morton Arboretum Library.
Consists of prints of plants, including watercolors of mushrooms and exhibit notes by Helene Warder Beggs, 1930, and sketchbooks and plant specimen books of women, including Bertha Jaques of Chicago.

4,289. Watts, May Theilgaard
Papers. 1916-75. Ca. 6 ft., 50 vols., and 200 oversize items.
Access restricted. No guide.
Morton Arboretum Library.
[Mrs. Raymond] Watts (1893-1975) was a naturalist and author of nature guides and such books as *Reading the Landscape,* rev. ed. (New York: Macmillan, 1975). Includes correspondence; diaries and sketchbooks of her travels; drawings and manuscripts for her published books; lecture notes and research files; unpublished essays, poetry, and short stories; field notebooks; recordings of her lectures and conferences; invitations; photos; clippings; programs; caricatures of people; part of her personal library with annotations; and awards. Born in Chicago and educated at the University of Chicago, Watts was a student of Henry C. Cowles. She was a naturalist at the Morton Arboretum from 1941 until her retirement in 1961. She was responsible for establishing the Illinois Prairie Path, a part of the US National Trail System; she also wrote a column on ecology for the *Chicago Tribune.*

LOMBARD

4,290. Martin, Ellen Annette
Papers. 1847-1916. 1 folder.
Open. No guide.
Lombard Historical Society.
Correspondence, clippings, and other papers of Martin (1847-?), the first woman law student in Chautauqua County, NY, document her effort to have Lombard's women residents vote in the local election of 1891. She believed that women had the right to vote because of a unique provision in the town's charter. Martin was admitted to the Illinois state bar but not to the Chicago Bar Association.

MACOMB

4,291. Macomb Business and Professional Women's Club
Records. 1930-78. 20 vols.
Open. No guide.
Western Illinois University Libraries, Archives and Special Collections.
Scrapbooks containing photos, clippings, and programs of the Club, a professional women's social and service organization.

4,292. St. Agness Guild, St. George's Episcopal Church
Records. 1885-92. 1 vol.
Open. No guide.
Western Illinois University Libraries, Archives and Special Collections.
Consists of a record book containing a constitution, bylaws, minutes, accounts of programs, and attendance records of the Guild, a charitable women's service organization organized in 1883 as the Children's Guild of St. George's Mission.

4,293. Soldiers' Aid Society of Rushville, IL
Records. 1861-64. 1 vol.
Open. No guide.
Western Illinois University Libraries, Archives and Special Collections.
Record book of the Society, a ladies' relief and aid organization active during the Civil War, includes records of donations and expenses and rosters of members. Also includes information on the Society's contributions to the Illinois State Sanitary Commission in Springfield, IL.

4,294. Treadway, Martha N.
Papers. 1908-41. 5 vols.
Open. No guide.
Western Illinois University Libraries, Archives and Special Collections.
Diary in which Treadway (1864-1941?), a farm wife in McDonough County, IL, describes chores, the weather, prices obtained for poultry, and family life. The volumes also contain financial accounts, photos, and clippings.

4,295. Western Illinois University, Grote Hall
Records. 1971-73. 2 vols.
Open. No guide.
Western Illinois University Libraries, Archives and Special Collections.
Scrapbooks of the Hall contain student writings and photos compiled during the final two years in which Grote Hall was used as a women's dormitory.

MOKENA

4,296. Archives
Records. 1866- . No size given.
Closed. No guide.
Franciscan Sisters of the Sacred Heart, Motherhouse.
Minutes of the general chapter, general council, and board of directors; financial reports; property deeds; correspondence of superiors general; a history of the congregation and its works, which is written in German; photos; and other records of this religious order of women dedicated to nursing and teaching apostolates and the care of priests. The order was founded in the US in 1876 at Avilla, IN. Mother M. Anastasia Bischler was the foundress of the Mokena congregation.

MOLINE

4,297. Black Hawk College Classified Committee
Records. 1968-71. 2.5 in.
Open. No guide.
Black Hawk College Library.
Organized in 1968 as the Non-Academic Woman's Club of Black Hawk College, the Committee sought to further its members' intellectual and social interests and to advance the welfare of this junior college's nonacademic women employees. Constitution, minutes, correspondence, membership lists, lists of officers, pamphlets, and information sheets about secretarial skills. The group adopted the final form of its name in 1968 and began to emphasize issues involved with salaries and benefits.

MOUNT CARMEL

4,298. Mount Carmel Woman's Club
Records. 1938- . No size given.
Open. No guide.
Mount Carmel Public Library.
The Club, organized in 1938 with 235 charter members, was involved in civic and social activities. Includes scrapbooks of clippings, programs, and other items. The Club organized and supported the first youth center in Mount Carmel, raised funds for the public library, and made memorial book contributions to the library.

4,299. Reviewer's Matinee
Records. 1894- . 10 vols.
Open. No guide.
Mount Carmel Public Library.
Minutes of the Reviewer's Matinee, a literary organization that [Mrs.] Marie Petitdidier founded in 1894. The group holds monthly meetings and is involved in cultural activities in the community. Instrumental in founding and supporting the Mount Carmel Carnegie Library, the organization was

responsible for the establishment of the first high school PTA and the first American National Red Cross unit in Mount Carmel.

MOUNT CARROLL

4,300. College Archives
Records. 1852- . Ca. 20 ft.
Open. No guide.
Shimer College.
Legal and financial records, correspondence, complete student records, yearbooks, catalogs, and publications of Shimer College, which was founded in 1853 as Mount Carroll Seminary by Frances Shimer and Cinderella Gregory. The school began as a coeducational institution but became a women's school during the Civil War. The College, which is known for its experimental curriculum, has long been associated with the University of Chicago. Includes correspondence of Frances Shimer with William Rainey Harper.

NAPERVILLE

4,301. Alspaugh, Hannah Ditzler
Papers. 1864-1910. 1.5 ft.
Open. No guide.
Caroline Martin-Mitchell Museum.
Alspaugh (1848-1938) was a teacher and amateur historian. Her diaries contain a record of her teaching experiences, notes about local history, clippings, samples of fabric from dresses of local women, Civil War commentary, and other items.

NAUVOO

4,302. Local History
Collection. 1839- . No size given.
Open. No guide.
Nauvoo Public Library.
Collection contains research files of Lillian M. Snyder, including notes and clippings on Icarian history in Nauvoo, with an emphasis on women; a cemetery list for Hancock County, IL; photos, including those of historic buildings and sites. Includes *Colonie Icarienne,* 1856-75; *Times and Seasons,* 1839-46; *The Wasp; Nauvoo Neighbor; Hancock Eagle; New Citizen; Expositor; Hancock Patriot;* and the *Nauvoo Independent,* 1890- . Most of the newspapers are available on microfilm.

4,303. Archives
Records. 1874- . No size given.
Closed. No guide.
Sisters of St. Benedict, St. Mary Priory.
Financial records, papers of superiors, correspondence, records relating to members and to schools taught by members, photos, and clippings of this community of religious women founded in 1874.

NORMAL

4,304. Colby, June Rose
Papers. Ca. 1857-1932. 5 boxes.
Open. Unpublished guide.
Illinois State University Archives.
Correspondence, diaries, manuscripts, student and professional writings, scrapbook, and other papers of [Miss] Colby, a graduate of the University of Michigan and a professor of literature at Illinois State University. Also contains correspondence, diaries, financial records, and other papers, dating from the early 1880s to the 1930s, of the Colby family. Colby's doctoral dissertation, lecture notes, an essay entitled "A Nineteenth Century Problem—Woman," and her *Book of Poems and Impressions* are included as are letters to Colby's mother Celestia R. Colby and a scrapbook of Celestia Colby's publications. June Colby's correspondents included Jane Addams, Carrie Chapman Catt, Alice Paul, Mary Livermore, Julia Ward Howe, and Lucy Stone.

4,305. Felmley, David
Papers. 1857-1932. Ca. 2 ft.
Open. No guide.
Illinois State University Archives.
Papers of Felmley (1857-1930), president of Illinois State University, relate to the University and include board minutes; expense and budget reports; records of the department of health, physical education, and physical sciences; papers regarding teacher certification; and excerpts from literary society publications. Also includes correspondence with Ella Flagg Young, an educator and school administrator, while she was an education professor at the University of Chicago, managing editor of *The Elementary School Teacher,* and Chicago superintendent of schools.

4,306. Lenski, Lois
Papers. 1927-60. 18 ft.
Open. No guide.
Illinois State University Archives.
An author of children's books, Lenski (1893-1974) won the Newbery Medal of the American Library Association in 1946 for her book *Strawberry Girl.* Correspondence, articles, speeches, plays, illustrations by Lenski, a tape recording of an interview with Lenski, publisher's catalogs, review clippings, and books. Includes the manuscripts of Lenski's *Corn Farm Boy, Houseboat Girl, Coal Camp Girl, San Francisco Boy, Bayou Suzette,* and *Judy's Journey.* Lenski spent much of her childhood in Springfield, OH, where her father was a minister. In 1915 she graduated from Ohio State University and then studied art in New York City for four years. She later worked in Italy and England writing and illustrating books. Lenski was the wife of Arthur S. Covey.

4,307. Saltzmann-Stevens, Minnie A.
Papers. 1883-1950. 568 items.
Open. Unpublished guide.
Illinois State University Archives.
[Mrs.] Saltzmann-Stevens (1874-1950), an opera singer in the US and Europe, was an interpreter of Wagnerian roles. Correspondence, autobiography, biographical sketch, photos, scrapbook, contracts, programs, and clippings. Includes letters from Florence Fifer Bohrer, an Illinois state senator, and Jean D. Reszke, who was Saltzmann-Stevens's voice instructor.

OAK FOREST

4,308. Archives
Records. 1951- . 7 vols.
Open. No guide.
Benedictine Sisters of Our Lady of Sorrows.
Established in Chicago in 1951, the Sisters operate a Slovak Cultural Center in connection with the Slovak Catholic Charitable Organization of Chicago. Correspondence, a history of the community, photos, scrapbooks, newspapers, souvenir books, and other records, including records of members of the order who attended workshops, conventions, meetings of former teachers, and other gatherings. At the Cultural Center the Sisters teach the Slovak language and attempt to keep Slovak customs and traditions alive. They maintain a Slovak museum and library and contribute to at least six Slovak language newspapers in the US and Canada.

OAK PARK

4,309. Nineteenth Century Women's Club of Oak Park
Records. 1938-64. Ca. 1 ft.
Open. Register.
Historical Society of Oak Park and River Forest.
Founded in 1898, the Club is a social organization that provides cultural and educational programs for its members. Includes annual reports, financial reports, speakers' contracts, correspondence, clippings, yearbooks, bulletins, and programs. Among the founding members was May Estelle Cook, an Oak Park author. In later years the Club also began to provide scholarships for local girls.

4,310. Woman's Club of Oak Park
Records. 1912-72. Ca. 1 ft. and oversize items.
Open. Register.
Historical Society of Oak Park and River Forest.
Founded in 1912, the Club was a women's organization sponsoring social and educational programs as well as service projects. Includes a certificate of incorporation, correspondence, a list of charter members, photos, clippings, programs, and the club banner. The group disbanded in 1972. Marguerite C. Walleck, a founding member, was active in the organization throughout its history.

PEORIA

4,311. Fortnightly Club
Records. 1893-1941. 1 folder.
Open. No guide.
Peoria Historical Society.
Minutes, reminiscences, report of the nominations committee, correspondence, and calendars of the Club, a local women's literary society founded in 1893.

QUINCY

4,312. Brown, Katherine Holland
Papers. Nd. 1.5 ft.
Closed. No guide.
Historical Society of Quincy and Adams County.
Correspondence, manuscripts, clippings, and memorabilia of Brown, a novelist and short story writer.

4,313. Local History
Collection. Ca. 1860- . No size given.
Closed. Unpublished guide.
Historical Society of Quincy and Adams County.
Contains correspondence, manuscripts, reminiscences, reports, photos, and scrapbooks relating to Quincy and Adams County history. Includes autobiographical reminiscences by Mary Busbey, 1862; "Outstanding Women of Quincy" by Mary Stone; "A Pioneer Woman's Story of Illinois" by Christiana Holmes Tillson; and annual reports of the Needle Pickets, a women's organization that provided supplies to the Union forces, 1861-65.

RED BUD

4,314. Ruma Provincial House
Records. 1870- . 3 file cases and additional boxes.
Closed. No guide.
Adorers of the Blood of Christ, Province of Ruma.
This religious order of women transferred to Piopolis, IL, from Gurtweil, Germany, between 1870 and 1873, settling in the town of Ruma; the sisters bought the building of the former Sacred Heart College in 1876. Correspondence, including letters of the American foundress; historical data; photos; clippings; obituaries of pioneer sisters; and

other records, including material about schools opened by the sisters. The Ruma area is now served by the Red Bud post office.

RIDGWAY

4,315. Gallatin County Historical Society
Records. 1966-77. No size given.
Open. Unpublished guide.
Gallatin County Historical Society.
Scrapbooks and photos of the Society, which was formed in 1966 to preserve the County's history. Also includes books by Lucille [Mrs. J. T.] Lawler and a slide show titled "Story of Shawneetown."

RIVER FOREST

4,316. College Newspaper
Records. 1935- . 21 portfolios.
Open. No guide.
Rosary College Archives.
Consists of issues of the Rosary College student newspaper with material concerning college events and personalities. A liberal arts college, the school originated in 1901 in Sinsinawa, WI, as St. Clara College. In 1922 it was moved to River Forest and was renamed Rosary College, becoming the first Catholic women's college in the Chicago area. The College became coeducational in 1970.

4,317. Literary Magazine
Records. 1922- . 2.67 ft.
Open. Unpublished guide.
Rosary College Archives.
Literary magazines of the College contain fiction, nonfiction, poetry, book reviews, photos, and student art.

RIVERSIDE

4,318. Riverside Woman's Club
Records. 1913- . 50 items.
Open. Unpublished guide.
Riverside Public Library.
Clippings, 1913-35, and yearbooks, 1948-, of the Club, a civic and social club founded in 1913.

ROCK ISLAND

4,319. Andreen, Gustav Albert, Family
Papers. 1864-1940. 16 ft. and 36 vols.
Open. Unpublished guide.
Augustana College Library.
Included with the correspondence, diaries, financial records, writings, lecture notes, photos, and scrapbooks of Andreen (1864-1940), president of Augustana College from 1901 to 1935, are papers of his wife Mary (Strand) Andreen (1870-1948), their children, and of Mary Andreen's family the Jacob Hendrik Strands. Contains letters to Mary Andreen from Edla Lund, a Swedish singer, composer, and professor of music who taught at Bethany College in Lindsborg, KS, and Augustana College, and from Emmy (Carlsson) Evald, leader of the Augustana Lutheran Church Women's Missionary Society and wife of Carl A. Evald, who was pastor at Augustana Lutheran Church. Writings, short stories, and other correspondence constitute the balance of the papers of Mary Andreen, who was a member of the Augustana Women's Missionary Society. Lund's letters are in Swedish.

4,320. Augustana Endowment Society
Records. 1894- . 10 in. and 5 vols.
Open. Unpublished guide.
Augustana College Library.
Formed by Augustana College faculty women in 1894, the Society, which admits both faculty and local women, raises funds for the school and other educational endeavors. Application for charter, minutes from 1902 to 1915 and from 1959 to 1974, and yearbooks.

4,321. Augustana Swedish Institute
Records. 1940-73. 2 cartons.
Open. Unpublished guide.
Augustana College Library.
Minutes, correspondence, brochures, and other records of the Institute, formed in 1940 to promote US-Swedish cultural relations. Includes letters from Sigrid Undset, a Norwegian novelist, to Augustana College and from Hanna Astrup Larsen, an author of Norwegian ancestry, a translator, and editor of the *American-Scandinavian Review*.

4,322. Bremer, Fredrika
Papers. 1861. 5-page item.
Open. Unpublished guide.
Augustana College Library.
Letter of Bremer (1801-65), a Swedish novelist and feminist, to friends in America includes a self-portrait and information about the position of women in Sweden and the US. Bremer visited Minnesota territorial governor Alexander Ramsey and his wife from 1850 to 1851.

4,323. Glaspell, Susan Keating
Papers. Nd. 1 item.
Open. Unpublished guide.
Augustana College Library.
Letter written in Boston by Glaspell (1876?-1948), a novelist and short story writer, welcomes Virginia Hersch, a friend from overseas, for a visit in the Glaspell home at Provincetown.

4,324. Lagerlöf, Selma Ottiliana Lovisa
Papers. 1901. No size given.
Open. Unpublished guide.
Augustana College Library.
Letter to Samuel H. Hill written in Swedish with an English translation; an autographed photo; and clippings of Lagerlöf (1858-1940), a Swedish novelist who won the Nobel Prize for Literature in 1909.

4,325. Lind-Goldschmidt, Jenny Maria
Papers. 1850-61. 3 items.
Open. Unpublished guide.
Augustana College Library.
Lind-Goldschmidt (1820-87), a 19th-century Swedish singer known as Jenny Lind, gave concerts in the US and contributed thousands of dollars to charities and institutions, including Augustana Church. A letter, a brochure for an 1850 Boston concert, and an 1850 Swedish poem with an English translation.

4,326. Olsson, Olof, Family
Papers. 1869-1946. 3 cartons and 4 vols.
Open. Unpublished guide.
Augustana College Library.
Family correspondence, diaries, manuscripts, records, scrapbooks, and memorabilia of Olsson (1841-1900), the third president of Augustana College and pastor of Augustana Lutheran Church. Includes letters, a diary, manuscripts for published books, and a confirmation record of his daughter Anna Olsson (1866-1946), an author.

4,327. Shipley, Marie Adelaide (Brown)
Papers. 1888. 1 item.
Open. Unpublished guide.
Augustana College Library.
Shipley (1842-1900) was an American author and translator who used the pen name Marie A. Brown. Subscription letter sent from Washington, DC, concerns Shipley's interest in establishing that Norsemen discovered and colonized America.

4,328. Archives
Records. 1853- . No size given.
Closed. No guide.
Sisters of the Visitation Monastery.
Minutes of the corporation, records of each sister professed, biographies of early sisters, correspondence, photos, scrapbooks, programs and advertisements of the school, artifacts, and other records of this Monastery of Visitation Nuns. The community established a boarding and day school for young women.

ROCKFORD

4,329. Archives
Records. 1916- . 2 folders and 2 vols.
Access restricted. No guide.
Corpus Christi Monastery of Poor Clares.
Members of this cloistered contemplative community, which was founded in 1916 in Rockford, engage in baking, cutting, and packing of altar breads; making first communion veils, spiritual bouquet cards, other artwork, and rosaries; and gardening. Annual reports, financial records, property deeds, contracts for buildings and repairs, diary, correspondence, photos, slides of the building and grounds, and volumes containing histories of the community, accounts of council meetings, and the names of persons who entered the community.

4,330. Rockford College Archives
Records. 1845- . Ca. 430 ft.
Open. Unpublished guide.
Rockford College Library.
Founded as Rockford Female Seminary in 1847, the College became coeducational in 1960. Trustees' minutes, presidential correspondence, financial records, faculty publications, videotapes of speakers, oral history tapes, photos, building blueprints, yearbooks, catalogs, and other records of the school. Includes papers of Jane Addams, an alumna of the College, and papers of Julia Lathrop, Addams's assistant at Hull-House and founder of the US Children's Bureau.

4,331. Rockfordiana
Collection. Nd. No size given.
Open. No guide.
Rockford Public Library, Local History and Genealogy Division.
Clippings and other papers concern local events and persons who have lived in the community. Includes 58 pages of clippings, 1930-68, pertaining to Jane Addams, social worker and founder of Hull-House.

SHELBYVILLE

4,332. Gordon, Beulah
Papers. Early 1930s-60. 1 box.
Open. No guide.
Shelby County Historical and Genealogical Society.
A reporter, editor, and photographer, Gordon (1909-63) did reporting and feature writing for the *Illinois State Journal* and *Illinois State Register* in Springfield, IL, before becoming director of publicity for the Lincoln Library in Springfield. Notes, historical pageant, articles and poems by Gordon, scrapbook of articles, and copy of her unpublished historical novel, which was set in the local area. Gordon wrote a historical pageant for Springfield's Capitennial in 1957. Several of the articles and poems were published in *Here and There in Shelby County* (Shelbyville: Shelby County Historical and Genealogical Society, 1973).

4,333. Saylor, Ann
Papers. 1865. 11 items.
Open. No guide.

Shelby County Historical and Genealogical Society. Letters by Saylor (1829-68), a housewife, to her husband Philip Saylor, a captain in the Union Army, contain family news and expressions of her concern for his safety. The letters indicate the responsibilities placed on women because of the wartime absence of their husbands. Also contains two daguerreotypes and one photo.

4,334. Shelbyville Woman's Club
Records. 1900-59. No size given.
Open. No guide.
Shelby County Historical and Genealogical Society.
Organized in 1900 by a Methodist minister's wife, the Club provided cultural opportunities for women of the community. Minutes of monthly meetings; histories of the Club's departments, which included those devoted to child welfare, home economics, music and drama, and the Chautauqua reading circle; scrapbook of clippings; and a complete set of yearbooks containing meeting programs. The Club disbanded in 1959 for lack of leadership.

SPRINGFIELD

4,335. Convent Archives
Records. 1873- . 50 drawers and 17 boxes.
Closed. No guide.
Dominican Sisters of Springfield, Sacred Heart Convent.
Financial records, correspondence, diaries, personal files of sisters, annals of the community, customs, manuscripts of books written by sisters, histories of schools and hospitals operated by the Sisters, blueprints, specifications and contracts for buildings, registers of mothers general, photos, scrapbooks, slides, tapes, motion pictures, memorabilia, ceremonial books, prayer books, and other records of the community, which was founded in 1873 in Jacksonville, IL.

4,336. Department of Registration and Education (RG 208)
Records. 1877-1973. 390 vols.
Open. Published guide.
Illinois State Archives.
The Department was established in 1917 to regulate the practice of various professions in Illinois; it received the records of several earlier agencies responsible for licensing professions. Consists of registers of professional licenses issued, which contain names, addresses, birth dates, certificate or license numbers, names of professional schools attended and dates of attendance and graduation; and of grade sheets for professional examinations conducted by the state, which give the date of examination and the results. Includes records of the following professions: architects, 1897-1951; beauty culturists, 1926-52; dental hygienists, 1946-50; dentists, 1881-1951; midwives, 1877-1930; nurses, 1898-1952; public health nurses, 1938-51; special obstetrical licenses, 1924-36; pharmacists, 1881-1952; physicians and surgeons, 1877-1952; real estate brokers, 1927-53; real estate salesmen, 1922-53; and veterinarians, 1913-51. See Illinois State Archives, *Descriptive Inventory of the Archives of the State of Illinois* (Springfield, IL: Office of the Secretary of State, 1978).

4,337. Illinois Board of World's Fair Commissioners (RG 506)
Records. 1891-95. 1 vol.
Open. Published guide.
Illinois State Archives.
The Board was created in 1891 to manage the exhibits at the World's Columbian Exposition; at the same time a woman's board was established to expend 10 percent of the Board's total appropriation in representing the industries of Illinois women at the Exposition. Consists of a woman's board expense book which records all disbursements for officers' salaries, hospital costs, and personal, labor, and kitchen expenses. Both boards went out of existence in 1895. See Illinois State Archives, *Descriptive Inventory of the Archives of the State of Illinois* (Springfield, IL: Office of the Secretary of State, 1978).

4,338. Illinois Soldiers' Widows' Home (RG 260)
Records. 1895-1963. 11 cu.ft.
Access restricted. Published guide.
Illinois State Archives.
The Home, located at Wilmington, IL, was created in 1895 to house indigent mothers, wives, widows, and daughters of honorably discharged veterans. Financial records, admission files, resident card files, and photos of the Home's eight matrons. Includes information about the applicants' date and place of birth, race, trade or occupation, literacy, and number and age of living children. Also includes amount of pension received, value of property, physical condition, relationship to veteran and veteran's military service record, and date of death and occasionally place of burial. When the Home closed in 1963, its residents were transferred to the Illinois Soldiers' and Sailors' Home at Quincy. See Illinois State Archives, *Descriptive Inventory of the Archives of the State of Illinois* (Springfield, IL: Office of the Secretary of State, 1978).

4,339. Illinois Veterans' Home (RG 259)
Records. 1877-1967. 89 cu.ft.
Access restricted. Published guide.
Illinois State Archives.
The Home was established in 1885 as the Illinois Soldiers' and Sailors' Home to provide subsistence and a home for honorably discharged and disabled veterans of the Mexican and Civil Wars. In succeeding years Illinois veterans of all wars became eligible for admission. In 1903 wives of veterans at the Home were admitted if they met certain age and marriage requirements, though some who did not were also admitted as were some mothers and daughters of veterans. Women residing at the Soldiers' Widows' Home when it closed in 1963 were transferred to the Veterans' Home; admission regulations now allow women to be admitted directly to the Home. The Home assumed its present name in 1973.

Consists of financial records, men's and women's admission records and case files, hospital admissions, and furlough registers. Women's admission records and case files, 1908-67 (8 cu.ft.), provide date and place of birth; town and county of residence; physical features, nature of any disability; medical examination reports; dated notes concerning admission, readmission, furloughs, discharge, or death; name, rank, company, and regiment of the veteran whose relation to the woman allowed her admission; and correspondence concerning admission to and activities while at the Home. See Illinois State Archives, *Descriptive Inventory of the Archives of the State of Illinois* (Springfield, IL: Office of the Secretary of State, 1978).

4,340. State Council of Defense
Records. 1917-20. 70 cu.ft.
Open. Published guide.
Illinois State Archives.
The Council, which was created in 1917 and dissolved in 1919, coordinated efforts of various groups in Illinois to ensure effective utilization of state resources during WWI. Annual and other reports, minutes, financial records, correspondence, membership lists of cooperating organizations, Liberty Loan subscription file, publicity material, and bulletins of state and federal agencies. The woman's committee, the largest unit of the Council, was responsible for organized drives to solve problems of food, health, morals, education and recreation, citizenship, and social and industrial democracy for women and children. It coordinated all women's organizations in the state and supervised a registration department for employment. Records of the woman's committee (ca. 8 cu.ft.) consist of minutes, financial records, correspondence, pamphlets, press releases, bulletins, and published reports. The Committee continued its work into 1920. See Illinois Historical Records Survey, *State Council of Defense of Illinois: 1917-1919,* series three in *Inventory of the State Archives of Illinois* (Chicago, IL, 1942).

4,341. Superintendent of Public Instruction (RG 106)
Records. 1861-1961. 175 cu.ft.
Open. Published guide.
Illinois State Archives.
The office of Superintendent was created in 1854 to collect annual reports from county superintendents of schools, to assist them in complying with laws, to grant teaching certificates, to inspect state schools, and to report annually to the governor on the state's school system. The office was abolished in 1973 and replaced by an appointive superintendent of education. County superintendents' annual reports, 1861-1961; correspondence, 1863-1925; records of state teaching certificates granted, 1861-1925; blueprints of Illinois schoolhouses; photos of students, classrooms, and exteriors of school buildings; radio address about education; and newsletters and magazines.

The county superintendents' annual reports contain financial, personnel, and property statistics, including wages of administrators; number of teachers categorized by sex; number of houses owned or rented for teachers; number of schools in each county and number of rooms within each; monthly average wages of teachers by sex, with highest and lowest salaries given; number of public school pupils broken down by age, sex, and race; names of teachers who attended a normal school and whether they graduated; number of special teachers for such subjects as drawing, manual training, or domestic arts; number of physicians, nurses, dentists, and truant officers employed; and number of handicapped children and schools operating specifically for their benefit. Correspondence primarily concerns interpretations of school laws, especially about employee qualifications, courses taught, buildings, insurance, school elections, textbooks, and school funds. Also concerns employment applications from teachers, student discipline, and problems of women as teachers in the state educational system. See Illinois State Archives, *Descriptive Inventory of the Archives of the State of Illinois* (Springfield, IL: Office of the Secretary of State, 1978).

4,342. Academy of Visitation, Illinois
Records. Ca. 1835-50. 2 microfilm reels.
Access restricted. Unpublished guide.
Illinois State Historical Library.
The Academy was a Kaskaskia, IL, girls school established in 1833 and run by the Sisters of Visitation. Ledger; cash, receipt, and expense books; journal; correspondence; baptismal records; school certificates; photos; a broadside; and other papers. Includes a history of the school by Sister Josephine Barber from its establishment in Kaskaskia until it was moved to St. Louis, a thesis digest by Sister Francis Marie O'Connor concerning the Academy from 1833 to 1849, and correspondence with the Georgetown chancery in 1832 and 1833 concerning the school's move west.

4,343. Addams, Jane
Papers. 1870-1942. 23 microfilm reels.
Open. Unpublished guide.
Illinois State Historical Library.
Chronologically arranged correspondence of [Miss] Addams (1860-1935), a social worker and peace advocate. Also includes an index to the main body of the correspondence. The originals of this

correspondence are part of the Swarthmore College Peace Collection.

4,344. Aiken, Sarah
Papers. 1833-36. 6 items.
Open. Card.
Illinois State Historical Library.
Correspondence of Aiken, an 18-year-old resident of a prairie farm in Peoria County, describes her journey from Keeseville, NY, to Illinois and comments on education, Indians, plants, language, household chores, and other subjects. Excerpts from the letters were published in the *Peoria Journal Star* on Dec. 29, 1968.

4,345. Armstrong, Elsie Strawn
Papers. Ca. 1860. 1 vol.
Open. Unpublished guide.
Illinois State Historical Library.
Armstrong (1789-1871) settled with her sons in LaSalle County, IL, about 1830. Autobiographical poem in irregular ballad form primarily concerns her life in Illinois. The poem was used by her grandson James Elder Armstrong in his biography of his grandmother, *Life of a Woman Pioneer* (Chicago, 1931). Extensively edited stanzas from the poem were published in the biography.

4,346. Bacmeister, Theodore
Papers. 1846-1911. 4200 items.
Open. Unpublished guide.
Illinois State Historical Library.
Bacmeister (1830-1911) was a doctor who emigrated from Wurtemberg, Germany; graduated in 1856 from the Homeopathic Medical College of Pennsylvania; and established a medical practice in Toulon, IL. Correspondence of Bacmeister's wife Laura (Ogle) Bacmeister and their children: Emily, William O., Charles A., Theodore, Louise, Otto, and Laura Pauline. Most of the children's letters, particularly those of Emily and her brothers, are concerned with education, travel, employment, and family matters.

4,347. Bailhache and Brayman
Papers. 1815-1905. 1550 items.
Open. Inventory.
Illinois State Historical Library.
Correspondence and miscellaneous papers of John Bailhache (1787-1857), editor of the *Alton Telegraph* and a state legislator in 1835; his son William H. Bailhache (1826-1905), co-editor of the *Illinois State Journal* and participant in the early Illinois Republican party; Sarah Adaline "Ada" (Brayman) Bailhache, wife of William H. Bailhache; and Adaline Bailhache, the daughter of William and Ada Bailhache. Ada Bailhache was the daughter of Mary (Williams) Brayman (1816-86) and Mason Brayman, a lawyer who was editor of the Quincy *Whig*, coproprietor of the *Illinois State Journal*, and governor of Idaho. Ada Bailhache wrote to her parents and husband from Springfield, New York, Albuquerque, and Santa Fe, NM; she described sewing bees, cholera in Springfield, Civil War news, a trip to New York, and a move to the West. Also includes letters of Mary (Williams) Brayman, among them Civil War correspondence from Cairo, IL; Bolivar, TN; Camp Dennison, OH; New Orleans; and Natchez, MS. Letters from Sarah Brayman, sister of Mason Brayman, and Nellie Brayman, sister of Ada Bailhache, are also contained in the collection.

4,348. Black, Elizabeth (Gundaker)
Papers. 1852. 1 vol.
Open. Card catalog.
Illinois State Historical Library.
[Mrs. William M.] Black (1823-1902), a Springfield resident, was a neighbor and frequent visitor in the Abraham Lincoln home. Her diary mentions social and religious activities in Springfield. The diary was published in the *Journal of the Illinois State Historical Society* (Spring 1955).

4,349. Bohrer, Florence (Fifer)
Papers. 1861-1956. 5 ms. boxes.
Open. Unpublished guide.
Illinois State Historical Library.
Bohrer (1877-1960), the daughter of Governor Joseph Fifer, was the first woman elected to the Illinois Senate. Correspondence, including letters from Bohrer's daughter Gertrude Bohrer; unpublished memoir; invitations; articles; and miscellaneous papers. Florence Bohrer, a Bloomington, IL, resident, served in the state senate from 1925 to 1932.

4,350. Booth, Mary Josephine
Papers. 1917-19. 107 items.
Open. Unpublished guide.
Illinois State Historical Library.
Librarian at Eastern Illinois University in Charleston, IL, from 1904 to 1945, Booth (1876-1965) volunteered for service with the American National Red Cross and the American Library Association during WWI and set up libraries in France and Coblenz, Germany. Letters to Booth's aunt Mrs. Josephine Smiley in Beloit, WI, contain details of Booth's preparations for her passage to Europe and of her work there, first with the American Canteen at the Third Aviation Instruction Center and later at the Central Library in Paris, at General Pershing's headquarters at Chaumont, and in Germany. During her first assignment, Booth set up a library and wrote to the ALA concerning employment with the Library War Service. She helped establish the Central Library and reorganized the Red Cross medical library at Chaumont. From January to May of 1919, she directed the library at the Coblenz "leave area." She was hospitalized through much of May, then completed her assignment and returned to the US in July, 1919. Also includes copies of *Plane News*, a paper published at the Third Aviation Instruction Center.

4,351. Bradwell, Myra (Colby)
Papers. 1864-70. 9 items.
Open. Unpublished guide.
Illinois State Historical Library.
Bradwell (1831-94), Illinois's first woman attorney, established the *Chicago Legal News* in 1882 and served as the publication's editor; she was admitted to practice before the US Supreme Court in 1892. Correspondence of Bradwell and her husband James Bolesworth Bradwell includes a letter she wrote to Governor John M. Palmer in 1870 outlining her efforts to advance the legal status of married women. Bradwell won legislative approval of laws to allow all persons freedom in selecting their profession.

4,352. Buckmaster and Curran Family
Papers. 1801-1918. Ca. 1350 items.
Open. Unpublished guide.
Illinois State Historical Library.
Correspondence, diaries, business records, and miscellaneous documents of Anna (Durkee) Young (1753-1839); her granddaughter Harriet Ann Bartling (1811-40), who married Nathaniel Buckmaster in 1832; and her great-granddaughter Catherine M. Buckmaster (1837-1918), who married Isaac Bush Curran, private secretary and chief of staff of Governor Joel A. Matteson. A Norwich, CT, resident and daughter of Revolutionary War colonel John Durkee, Anna Durkee was married twice, first to Dominic Tauzin and then to a Philadelphia physician named Young. She assumed custody of Henry Tauzin Bartling and Harriet Ann Bartling, the children of her daughter Mary (Tauzin) Bartling and Daniel Bartling, and moved with them to Illinois in 1817. Her papers include letters from Daniel Bartling, a lieutenant in the War of 1812, concerning his problems after the War and documents concerning disposal of her property before her move west. Harriet Buckmaster's material contains letters to her husband during the Black Hawk War and to the Buckmaster family in Virginia as well as five of her poems. Catherine Curran's papers include letters to her husband, letters from her sons and from her sister during a world tour in 1890 and 1891, diaries for 1899 and 1900, a biographical paper she wrote about Anna (Durkee) Young in 1914, and genealogical material.

4,353. Casteen, Lucinda
Papers. 1832-39. 18 items.
Open. Unpublished guide.
Illinois State Historical Library.
Casteen (1797-1839) was a pioneer in Schuyler City, IL. Correspondence, primarily letters to her parents Mr. and Mrs. James Peters of Versailles, KY, includes descriptions of farming, schools, society, and family affairs in Illinois.

4,354. Chester, Cordelia Adelaid (Perrine) Harvey
Papers. 1863-65. 3 items.
Open. Unpublished guide.
Illinois State Historical Library.
Cordelia Harvey was the sanitary agent in St. Louis from 1862 to 1865 and the wife of Wisconsin governor Lewis Harvey. Manuscript of a lecture she gave after the Civil War and two photos. The lecture contains her recollections of wartime hospital conditions and detailed accounts of four conversations she had with President Abraham Lincoln seeking improved hospital conditions in the North. Her lecture was published in *Wisconsin Magazine of History*, vol. 1, no. 3 (March 1918).

4,355. Corneau, Octavia Roberts
Papers. Ca. 1907-59. 4 ms. boxes.
Open. Unpublished guide.
Illinois State Historical Library.
An author, Corneau (?-1972) was a Springfield native who married Barton Corneau, an attorney, and lived in Boston. Manuscript of her unpublished book "The Governor's Mansion, 1853-1953, A Social History of the Illinois Executive Mansion" as well as 29 folders of research notes gathered for the book, notebooks, story typescripts, essays, commonplace book dated from 1927 to 1929, story ideas, book outlines, guest book, and clippings. Includes typescript pages from "The Road of Remembrance."

4,356. Davis, David
Papers. 1816-1943. Ca. 19,000 items.
Open. Unpublished guide.
Illinois State Historical Library.
Correspondence of Davis (1815-86), associate justice of the US Supreme Court from 1862 to 1877 and US senator from Illinois from 1877 to 1883; of his first wife Sarah (Walker) Davis (1814-79); of his second wife Adeline (Burr) Davis; of his daughter Sarah (Davis) Swayne [Mrs. John T.] Lilliard; and of his daughter-in-law Ella Hanna Davis with her husband George Perrin Davis. Included are letters from Mary (Todd) Lincoln, which were written between 1861 and 1878 and nearly all of which discuss the Lincoln estate, Mary Lincoln's personal finances, and expenditures for the support of Thomas Lincoln. Also includes letters from Sarah (Walker) Davis's parents William Perrin Walker and Lucy Walker of Lenox, MA, and from her three sisters: Lucy [Mrs. Julius] Rockwell of Pittsfield, MA; Fanny [Mrs. Daniel R.] William of Stockbridge, MA; and Cornelia [Mrs. Joseph] Scranton of Scranton, PA.

4,357. Douglas, Adele (Cutts)
Papers. 1857-65. 8 items.
Open. Unpublished guide.
Illinois State Historical Library.
Correspondence of Douglas (1835-99), the wife of US Senator Stephen A. Douglas of Illinois, includes a letter she wrote in Chicago to her mother discussing personal matters; letters to a friend William A. Seaver concerning social matters and her financial affairs following her husband's death;

and a letter she wrote in April, 1865, to Governor Richard Yates offering her condolences to Mary (Todd) Lincoln.

4,358. Duncan, Joseph
Papers. 1804-1920. 1500 items.
Open. Unpublished guide.
Illinois State Historical Library.
Copies of correspondence and diaries of Duncan (1794-1844), a congressman from Illinois from 1827 to 1834 and governor of Illinois from 1834 to 1838, and his wife Elizabeth Duncan. Elizabeth Duncan's papers include correspondence, diaries dating from 1824 to 1846, a "History of Early Societies in Jacksonville," and biographical sketches of John Hardin, John Wilkinson, and Joseph Duncan. Also contains a biographical sketch of Elizabeth Duncan by her daughter Julia Duncan. Originals of the material are at the Davenport Public Museum in Davenport, IA.

4,359. Eberhart, Lovicy Ann (May)
Papers. 1894-1901. 2 items.
Open. Unpublished guide.
Illinois State Historical Library.
[Mrs.] Eberhart (1832-?) was sent to teach freedmen in Vicksburg, MS, by the American Missionary Association of New York. Typescripts of her reminiscences contain descriptions of her first visit to a military camp in March 1863, of the end of the Civil War, and of her experiences as a teacher. Eberhart's husband Uriah Eberhart was a chaplain in the 20th Iowa Volunteer Infantry.

4,360. Edwards, Elizabeth Parker (Todd)
Papers. 1862-81. 8 items.
Open. Unpublished guide.
Illinois State Historical Library.
Correspondence of [Mrs. Ninian Wirt] Edwards (1813-88), a Springfield resident and sister of Mary (Todd) Lincoln, includes seven letters she wrote to her daughter Julia (Edwards) Baker and her son-in-law Edward Baker from Washington, DC, following the death of her sister's son Willie Lincoln, in 1862. Also includes a letter to Mary (Todd) Lincoln describing the activities of Ninian Edwards and another man on behalf of her pension.

4,361. French, Augustus C., Family
Papers. 1830-1900s. 1500 items.
Open. Brief description.
Illinois State Historical Library.
Correspondence, diary, business receipts, and miscellaneous documents of French (1808-64), a lawyer, receiver of public money, Illinois state legislator, college professor, and governor of Illinois from 1846 to 1853. Includes letters from his wife Lucy French (1818-?) and letters of his daughter Augusta (French) Wicker (1849-89) to her husband Cassius Wicker. Also includes letters from Harriet C. Haskell, third principal of Monticello Seminary, to her cousin Cassius Wicker. Most of Haskell's letters were written at the Seminary, a woman's college in Godfrey, IL. The Frenches had five children.

4,362. Gregg, Sarah
Papers. 1861-66. 29 items.
Open. Unpublished guide.
Illinois State Historical Library.
Gregg was a volunteer nurse during the Civil War. Letters from Gregg's husband David R. Gregg concerning his service with the 1st Illinois Artillery in Missouri, Tennessee, Alabama, Mississippi, and Georgia; Sarah Gregg's diary, which dates from 1863 to 1865 and includes entries concerning sick and wounded soldiers at Camp Stebbins, Camp Butler in Illinois, and at Vicksburg in Mississippi; and letters and documents from nurses, doctors, and soldiers concerning nursing services at Camp Butler.

4,363. Grimsley, Elizabeth (Todd)
Papers. 1861. 7 items.
Open. Unpublished guide.
Illinois State Historical Library.
[Mrs.] Grimsley (1825-95) was a cousin of Mary (Todd) Lincoln who accompanied the Lincoln family to Washington, DC, in 1861 and remained there for six months to help with White House social functions. Letters Grimsley wrote from Washington to her cousins Mr. and Mrs. John Todd Stuart describing White House events and Grimsley's manuscript concerning her White House visit. The material was published in the *Journal of the Illinois State Historical Society* (Oct. 1926).

4,364. Hubbard, Mary Hedges
Papers. 1854-59. 8 items.
Open. Unpublished guide.
Illinois State Historical Library.
[Miss] Hubbard (1837-1934) was an East Coast resident who visited her uncle Illinois governor Joel Matteson from 1854 to 1859. Letters Hubbard wrote from Springfield to the Ward Hubbard family in Champion, NY, in which she discusses personal and social affairs and describes Springfield; an 1859 letter to her sister Ellen tells of playing euchre with Abraham Lincoln. Also includes a letter from Lydia Matteson to her mother.

4,365. Hudson, Anna (Ridgely)
Papers. 1860-72. 10 vols.
Open. Unpublished guide.
Illinois State Historical Library.
[Mrs. James L.] Hudson (1841-1926) was a Springfield resident. Her diaries constitute a weekly record of a young woman's social and religious life and include references to the Abraham Lincoln family, to John Hay, and to the Civil War. Portions of the diaries appeared in the *Journal of the Illinois State Historical Society* (Oct. 1929).

4,366. Illinois Federation of Women's Clubs
Records. 1895-1965. 3 archival boxes and 141 vols.
Open. Unpublished guide.
Illinois State Historical Library.
The Federation was formed in Chicago in 1894 in the Woman's Hospital club rooms following the participation of women in the World's Columbian Exposition of 1893. Alice Bradford Wiles became the organization's president during the group's second annual meeting in 1895 in Springfield. Minutes of the board of directors and executive committee; treasurers' account, and dues books, dating chiefly from the first 30 years of the group's existence; proceedings of the annual conventions from 1905 to 1965; reports submitted to the state board; subscription book; departmental files and reports; and other records. Among the first legislative measures supported by the Federation were compulsory education laws, state aid for traveling libraries, and a dormitory for women at the University of Illinois.

4,367. Illinois Nurses Association
Records. Ca. 1902-69. Ca. 125 ft.
Open. No guide.
Illinois State Historical Library.
Minutes; business papers; economic security papers; subject files, including one on legislation; correspondence of standing committees; and correspondence with state sections and with the American Nurses Association.

4,368. Illinois Women
Papers. 1893. 1 vol.
Open. Unpublished guide.
Illinois State Historical Library.
Compiled by the Illinois Woman's Exposition Board for the World's Columbian Exposition, the volume contains narratives of 17 women who told of their schooling, religious and social life, setting up households on the prairie, Indians, and the hardships of motherhood in early Illinois.

4,369. Illinois Women
Papers. 1893. 8 items.
Open. Unpublished guide.
Illinois State Historical Library.
Letters written for display at the World's Columbian Exposition describe the experiences of the following women who were pioneers in early Illinois: Elizabeth Crawley, Elizabeth McDowell Hill, Mrs. P. B. Purkett, Mrs. Jacob Moore, Mrs. Andrew McCormick, Caroline M. Beers Lane, Mrs. E. W. (Bowling) Logan, and Melissa Stockdale of Crawford, Pike, and Sangamon counties.

4,370. Ives, Elizabeth (Stevenson)
Papers. 1858-1963. 18 ft. and 4 tapes.
Access restricted. Description.
Illinois State Historical Library.
The granddaughter of Vice-President Adlai Stevenson and the sister of Illinois Governor Adlai E. Stevenson, [Mrs. Ernest] Ives (1898-) is an Illinois author. Correspondence, diaries, book drafts and manuscripts, articles, clippings, recordings, tapes, scrapbooks, and items related to her brother's campaigns. Includes papers of Letitia (Green) Stevenson, wife of Vice-President Adlai Stevenson, and of Helen (Davis) [Mrs. Lewis] Stevenson as well as Ives's childhood and school letters, family letters from early trips abroad, and letters Ives wrote from Europe and Africa during her husband's assignments in the diplomatic corps. Also contains drafts of other papers regarding publication of Ives's *My Brother Adlai* and a file she kept in ca. 1952 while serving as hostess for her brother at the Illinois governor's mansion.

4,371. Lincoln, Mary Ann (Todd)
Papers. 1848-82. 192 items.
Open. Unpublished guide.
Illinois State Historical Library.
Correspondence, telegrams, notes, invitations, and other papers of Lincoln (1818-82), the wife of President Abraham Lincoln and for many years a Springfield resident. The bulk of the material was published in Justin and Linda Turner, *Mary Todd Lincoln, Her Life and Letters* (New York: Knopf, 1972).

4,372. Marianna Club
Records. 1954-75. Ca. 1500 items.
Open. Unpublished guide.
Illinois State Historical Library.
Founded in 1954 and dissolved in 1974, the Club was a nonprofit, charitable corporation in Springfield that sponsored a nonsectarian home for teen-age girls. President's papers, minutes, treasurer's reports, business records, scrapbooks, published material, and miscellaneous items.

4,373. Matheny, James H.
Papers. 1780-1940. 7 archival boxes.
Open. Unpublished guide.
Illinois State Historical Library.
Correspondence, cards, and memorabilia of Matheny (1818-90) relate primarily to the family of Fanny (French) Matheny, the wife of James Matheny's son James H. Matheny, Jr. (1856-1918), a Springfield attorney. Papers of Fanny Matheny, daughter of Amos Willard French, a Springfield dentist, include her letters to her parents and children. James Matheny, Sr., a Sangamon County Court judge, was the son of Illinois pioneer Charles R. Matheny (1786-1839).

4,374. Monticello College
Records. 1835-1971. 37,500 items.
Open. Inventory.
Illinois State Historical Library.
Founded as Monticello Female Seminary in 1835 in Godfrey, IL, by Benjamin Godfrey, the College opened in 1838 with Theron Baldwin as principal. General and administrative office files, business ledgers, correspondence, essays, church records, photos and photo albums, scrapbooks, autograph albums, memorabilia, and other records, including

minutes of alumnae societies, most of which postdate a fire at the college in 1888. The records contain correspondence of faculty members, including Harriet Haskell, who served as principal from 1866 to 1907, and teachers Emily G. Alden and Julia Kellogg. Also includes administrative records of George E. Rohrbough, president of the school; John D. Schweitzer, academic dean; Marguerite Shewman, dean of students; and of the public relations office. Papers of early students at the school, among them Eliza Brown, Julia Godfrey, and Catherine E. Snediker and Mary "Mollie" F. Chapman of Jerseyville, IL, are also found in the collection. The school was renamed Monticello Ladies Seminary in 1868, Monticello Seminary in ca. 1907, and Monticello College in ca. 1935. This women's school closed in 1971.

4,375. Stevenson Family
Papers. 1830-1967. 500 items.
Open. Inventory.
Illinois State Historical Library.
Correspondence, diaries, published and unpublished papers, genealogies, photos and photo albums, scrapbook, and speeches, buttons, badges, and other campaign material of Adlai E. Stevenson (1835-1914), who served as a US congressman from Illinois for four years and as vice-president of the US from 1893 to 1895; his wife Letitia (Green) Stevenson (1843-1913); and his daughter Julia (Stevenson) Hardin (1879-1958), an author. Letitia Stevenson's papers include letters from Mrs. Grover Cleveland concerning White House social functions. Hardin's papers include letters written in 1890 by her parents while she was in school in Chicago; two diaries, one of them kept in 1897 while her father was an envoy in Europe and one kept in 1925 and 1926 during a world cruise aboard the *SS Belgenland;* research notes for her writings; and a memoir written in 1945. Hardin, then Julia Stevenson, accompanied her father during his service as an envoy in France, Germany, and Great Britain.

4,376. Turchin, Nadine
Papers. 1863-64. 1 vol.
Open. Unpublished guide.
Illinois State Historical Library.
Born Princess Nadezhda Lvova, Nadine Turchin (1826-1904) was the wife of Brigadier General John Basil Turchin. Turchin and her husband came to the US, settling in Mattoon, IL, soon after the Crimean War. Her diary, which she wrote in French, includes reports and reflections on current events. A translation of the diary is included. Educated at home, Turchin spoke four languages. Turchin's husband was commissioned a colonel of the 19th Illinois Infantry at the outbreak of the Civil War; she accompanied him when his regiment went into training at Quincy, IL, and traveled with him throughout the war.

4,377. Willard, Samuel
Papers. 1783-1883. Ca. 200 items.
Open. Unpublished guide.
Illinois State Historical Library.
Correspondence of the family of Willard (1821-1913), an Illinois physician, includes letters of his aunt Frances Langdon Willard, proprietor and principal of young ladies' schools in New York and Illinois. Her letters to Julius Willard, Samuel Willard's father, describe her activities at schools she operated in Adams, NY, in 1832 and 1833; in Chicago from 1836 to 1838; in Carrollton, IL, in 1850 and 1851; and elsewhere. She also considered opening schools in Alton, IL, and St. Louis, and her letters include references to these cities and to family gossip and religion. The Willard family came to Illinois in 1831 after living in Maine and Massachusetts.

URBANA

4,378. Bane, Lita
Papers. 1919-54. 1.3 cu.ft.
Open. Control card.
University of Illinois Archives.
Bane (1887-1957) was a professor of home economics at the University of Illinois from 1936 to 1949. Correspondence, notes, drafts and copies of publications, corn sugar project reports, home economics department cost surveys, MA thesis topics, files, and a booklet. Includes correspondence relating to a 1944 portrait of Isabel Bevier, a professor of household science at the University of Illinois from 1900 to 1921; files relating to Bane's biography of Bevier, which contain correspondence, notes, statements by Bevier, and two drafts of Bane's manuscript; and notes for Bane's talks and articles.

4,379. Bauer, Frances (Myers)
Papers. 1923-64. 4.7 cu.ft.
Open. Published guide and control card.
University of Illinois Archives.
[Mrs. Edward E.] Bauer (ca. 1906-64) was university editor of the Champaign Urbana *News-Gazette* from 1928 to 1964. Correspondence, manuscripts, typescript articles, speeches, scrapbooks, programs, and clippings. Includes correspondence regarding the University of Illinois; clippings of her column "The Broadwalk Tattler" from 1928 to 1964, financial columns for 1929 and 1930, and by-line and feature stories; drafts of columns; source material for her feature articles; biographical clippings and articles; and programs for social events and theatrical productions. See Maynard J. Brichford, Robert M. Sutton, and Dennis F. Walle, *Manuscripts Guide to Collections at the University of Illinois at Urbana-Champaign* (Chicago: University of Illinois Press, 1976).

4,380. Bevier, Isabel
Papers. 1879-1955. 4.7 cu.ft.
Open. Published guide and control card.
University of Illinois Archives.
[Miss] Bevier (1860-1942) was a household science professor at the University of Illinois from 1900 to 1921. Correspondence, diaries, manuscripts, notes about home economics and other subjects, biographical and autobiographical accounts, anecdotes, photos, obituaries, memorials, clippings, publications, and other papers. Includes publications by Bevier and the household science department, scattered diaries dating from 1917 to 1940, and notes, clippings, and photos regarding the education of women, departmental administration and enrollments, the Woman's Building and laboratories, farm houses, food and nutrition, the family, budgeting, sanitation, Farmer's Institutes, extension work, and European travel in 1927 and 1931. The collection includes *The House, Its Plan, Decoration and Care* (1907, 1914) and *The Home Economics Movement* (1906) by Bevier, *The Story of Isabel Bevier* (1955) by Lita Bane, books by Ellen (Swallow) Richards, and a biography of Richards. Correspondents include Eugene Davenport, Edmund James, and American Home Economics Association officers. See Maynard J. Brichford, Robert M. Sutton, and Dennis F. Walle, *Manuscripts Guide to Collections at the University of Illinois at Urbana-Champaign* (Chicago: University of Illinois Press, 1976).

4,381. Cheever, Alice
Papers. 1871-75. 0.3 cu.ft.
Open. Published guide and control card.
University of Illinois Archives.
Alice Cheever [Mrs. A. H.] Bryan (1854-1917) graduated from the University of Illinois in 1874. Student notebooks include notes on regent John M. Gregory's lectures on education, ancient and constitutional history, moral philosophy, the history of civilization, political economy, duty, religion, young writers, and young ladies. Also contains German themes, physiology lectures by professor Don C. Taft, and notes on music teaching at Seymour in Illinois. See Maynard J. Brichford, Robert M. Sutton, and Dennis F. Walle, *Manuscripts Guide to Collections at the University of Illinois at Urbana-Champaign* (Chicago: University of Illinois Press, 1976).

4,382. Dean of Student Personnel and Dean of Women
Records. 1909-73. 23 cu.ft.
Access restricted. Control card.
University of Illinois Archives.
Correspondence, memoranda, reports, constitutions, bylaws, histories, personnel files, chaperone applications, questionnaires, notebooks, pamphlets, and other material concern such subjects as Panhellenic activities, the Student Affairs Committee, enrollment statistics from 1922 to 1943, Negro women students from 1923 to 1940, the Women's Group System and Woman's League, the residence government system, Feathers service group, the National Independent Student Association, disciplinary actions, discrimination and affirmative action, *Illini Guides,* poverty and the Job Corps, and graduate work.

4,383. Dunbar, Louise B.
Papers. 1896-1975. 2 cu.ft.
Open. Control card.
University of Illinois Archives.
Dunbar (1894-1975), who received her MA in 1917 and her PhD in 1920, was a history professor at the University of Illinois from 1927 to 1962. Personal and professional correspondence, including that with her mother [Mrs.] Belle Hanchett Dunbar; diaries from 1940 to 1943; and programs, photos, publications, and clippings relating to social life in White River Junction, VT, and in Urbana. Also includes material about academic life at the University of Illinois, research in American colonial and Revolutionary War history, Kemper Hall, the Episcopal church, the British coronation in 1937, Alpha Delta Theta, and radio lectures and extension courses in history.

4,384. Erlanger, Margaret
Papers. 1908-74. 11.8 cu.ft.
Open. Published guide and control card.
University of Illinois Archives.
[Miss] Erlanger (1908-75) was a professor of dance and of physical education for women at the University of Illinois. Correspondence, autobiographical material, minutes, a thesis on dance drama, photos, scrapbooks, films, recordings, posters, articles, and other papers. Includes letters of appreciation, dance division annual reports, and constitution, minutes, financial records, reports, scrapbooks, and other records of Orchesis. Correspondents include Merce Cunningham, Agnes De Mille, Ann Halprin, Katherine Litz, Ruth St. Denis, Halim El-Dabh, Al Huang, Claude Kipnis, Masami Kumi, and Paul Taylor. Material provides information about dancers-in-residence, Contemporary Arts Festivals from 1956 to 1967, dance curricula, and sabbaticals in New Zealand and Japan. See Maynard J. Brichford, Robert M. Sutton, and Dennis F. Walle, *Manuscripts Guide to Collections at the University of Illinois at Urbana-Champaign* (Chicago: University of Illinois Press, 1976).

4,385. Filbey Family
Papers. 1900-69. 1 cu.ft.
Open. Published guide and control card.
University of Illinois Archives.
Edward J. Filbey (1879-1959) was a professor of accounting at the University of Illinois from 1919 to 1947. Correspondence; commencement, dance, and social announcements; programs; tickets; and accounts. Includes a university scrapbook of Dorothy M. Filbey Ross, a member of the class of

1929, and a 1969 paper by [Mrs.] Mary L. Filbey about deans of women from 1897 to 1923. See Maynard J. Brichford, Robert M. Sutton, and Dennis F. Walle, *Manuscripts Guide to Collections at the University of Illinois at Urbana-Champaign* (Chicago: University of Illinois Press, 1976).

4,386. Glover, Anna C.
Papers. 1909-52. 0.7 cu.ft.
Open. Published guide and control card.
University of Illinois Archives.
Glover was secretary at the University of Illinois experiment station and, from 1915 to 1954, manager and editor of publications. Correspondence, biographical material, photos, and publications. Included is correspondence with Eugene Davenport concerning honors, vacations and travel, family matters, publications, and agricultural education; biographical material about Davenport; minutes, a report, and correspondence of the Eugene Davenport portrait committee; correspondence and publications relating to the experiment station's 50th anniversary in 1937-38; a file on *Timberland Times;* and articles, obituaries, and memorials concerning Herbert W. Mumford and Henry P. Rusk. See Maynard J. Brichford, Robert M. Sutton, and Dennis F. Walle, *Manuscripts Guide to Collections at the University of Illinois at Urbana-Champaign* (Chicago: University of Illinois Press, 1976).

4,387. Goldthwaite, Nellie E.
Papers. 1909-12. 0.1 cu.ft.
Open. Published guide and control card.
University of Illinois Archives.
Goldthwaite (1868-1946) was a professor of household science at the University of Illinois from 1911 to 1915. Programs, clippings, and other papers include a report on the 75th anniversary in 1912 of Mount Holyoke College and a related series of clippings. See Maynard J. Brichford, Robert M. Sutton, and Dennis F. Walle, *Manuscripts Guide to Collections at the University of Illinois at Urbana-Champaign* (Chicago: University of Illinois Press, 1976).

4,388. Gregory, Louisa (Allen)
Papers. 1873-79. 0.6 cu.ft.
Open. Published guide anc control card.
University of Illinois Archives.
Gregory (1856-?) was the first woman teacher at the University of Illinois and the wife of regent John M. Gregory. Manuscripts of addresses, lecture notes, and other papers. Includes notes on such domestic science subjects as ventilation and food etiquette as well as addresses on domestic science at Illinois Industrial University, "What Every Girl Should Know," "What Should We Teach Our Girls," and other topics. See Maynard J. Brichford, Robert M. Sutton, and Dennis F. Walle, *Manuscripts Guide to Collections at the University of Illinois at Urbana-Champaign* (Chicago: University of Illinois Press, 1976).

4,389. King, Ameda R.
Papers. 1908-71. 4.6 cu.ft.
Open. Published guide and control card.
University of Illinois Archives.
A history professor at the University of Illinois from 1950 to 1962, King (1893-1972) earned her MA in 1925 and her PhD in 1931. Correspondence with her brother, colleagues, students, and others; notes, papers, and a thesis she wrote as a student; lecture notes, grade books, and teaching and research records for courses in American and Latin American history and biography; and items relating to travel, historical society meetings, Monticello College, concerts, plays, and art exhibits. See Maynard J. Brichford, Robert M. Sutton, and Dennis F. Walle, *Manuscripts Guide to Collections at the University of Illinois at Urbana-Champaign* (Chicago: University of Illinois Press, 1976).

4,390. Leonard, Maria
Papers. 1927-66. 0.1 cu.ft.
Open. Published guide and control card.
University of Illinois Archives.
Leonard (1880-) was dean of women at the University of Illinois from 1923 to 1945. Correspondence, lectures and speeches, papers relating to women's war work, photos, certificates, clippings, and publications. Includes material relating to the functions of Leonard's office, the goals and conduct of college women, Alpha Lambda Delta, sororities, and women's war work, including war bond sales, a Women's Army Training Corps unit, and recruiting for the WACs, WAVES, and the Women's Coast Guard Reserves. Also contains publications on fraternity budgets and "The Chaperon and Housemother, Builders of Youth" (1939). See Maynard J. Brichford, Robert M. Sutton, and Dennis F. Walle, *Manuscripts Guide to Collections at the University of Illinois at Urbana-Champaign* (Chicago: University of Illinois Press, 1976).

4,391. Lohrer, Alice
Papers. 1937-73. 20 cu.ft.
Open. Control card.
University of Illinois Archives.
Lohrer was a library science professor at the University of Illinois from 1945 to 1974. Correspondence, reports, minutes, surveys, photos, clippings, and publications relate to the library school curriculum and include faculty meeting minutes, extension course material, local consensus studies, and surveys of school libraries in Oak Park and 28 other Illinois communities. Material contains information on such subjects as foreign students, school libraries, children's conferences, teacher-librarian training, the American Library Association, the Association of American Library Schools, the American Association of School Librarians, the Illinois Library Association, the Illinois Association of School Librarians, and North Central Association accreditation evaluations.

4,392. Pearman Family
Papers. 1877-1951. 0.3 cu.ft.
Open. Published guide and control card.
University of Illinois Archives.
Class history, photos, tintypes, and class album programs of Ida (Pearman) Stevens, Minnie Pearman, and Myrtle (Pearman) Keene, sisters who attended the University of Illinois. Includes a history Ida Pearman wrote about her graduating class (1880), with discussion of attrition, admission standards, professor Joseph C. Pickard's classes, class officers and meetings, social affairs, and dating; an 1880 class photo album; and an 1889 issue of *Sophograph.* See Maynard J. Brichford, Robert M. Sutton, and Dennis F. Walle, *Manuscripts Guide to Collections at the University of Illinois at Urbana-Champaign* (Chicago: University of Illinois Press, 1976).

4,393. Robinson, Florence B.
Papers. Ca. 1949. 0.3 cu.ft.
Open. Published guide and control card.
University of Illinois Archives.
Robinson was a professor of landscape architecture at the University of Illinois from 1929 to 1951. Notes, typescripts, class material, photos, sketches, and other papers. Includes a typescript, photos, sketches, and proof copy for her "Palette of Plants and Its Use" (1949) and a typescript concerning the imperial palaces of Peking, translated from French. See Maynard J. Brichford, Robert M. Sutton, and Dennis F. Walle, *Manuscripts Guide to Collections at the University of Illinois at Urbana-Champaign* (Chicago: University of Illinois Press, 1976).

4,394. Rolfe Family
Papers. 1885-1972. 5 cu.ft.
Open. Published guide and control card.
University of Illinois Archives.
Correspondence, manuscripts, record books, a tape recording, photos, clippings, and publications of the family of Charles W. Rolfe (1850-1934), a geology professor at the University of Illinois. Contains a tape-recorded recollection by Mary Rolfe (1881-1974), a 1902 graduate of the University who apparently was Rolfe's daughter, concerning faculty and student life, student housing, trees on campus, her father, alumni reunions, her commencement exercises at the University, Thomas J. Burrill, and Thomas A. Clark. Also contains correspondence, photos, and publications concerning Mary Rolfe's YWCA and American National Red Cross work in France during WWI. See Maynard J. Brichford, Robert M. Sutton, and Dennis F. Walle, *Manuscripts Guide to Collections at the University of Illinois at Urbana-Champaign* (Chicago: University of Illinois Press, 1976).

4,395. Ross, Betsy
Papers. 1967. 0.1 cu.ft.
Open. Published guide and control card.
University of Illinois Archives.
Ross was the niece of Arthur C. Willard, president of the University of Illinois. Papers and tapes include Ross's recorded comments about social receptions at her uncle's home, deans and faculty members, Anthony Janata, Charles C. Havens, the duties of the president, dormitory construction, Illini Union, University Hall, WWII, trustees, the Medical Center, Amelia Earhart, and Robert Hutchins. See Maynard J. Brichford, Robert M. Sutton, and Dennis F. Walle, *Manuscripts Guide to Collections at the University of Illinois at Urbana-Champaign* (Chicago: University of Illinois Press, 1976).

4,396. Sharp, Katherine Lucinda
Papers. 1881-1963. 1.7 cu.ft.
Open. Published guide and control card.
University of Illinois Archives.
[Miss] Sharp (1865-1914) was a librarian and director of the University of Illinois library school from 1897 to 1907. Correspondence notes, memorial letters, research notes, a University of Illinois library history, photos, announcements, informational circulars and course descriptions, material on library legislation, and other papers. Includes bachelor's and master's diplomas, dated 1892 and 1907, from the New York State Library School; correspondence from the period 1893-97 when she was director of the Armour Institute library school; correspondence with Melvil Dewey and other librarians concerning curricula and Andrew Carnegie; notes on a catechism for librarians, library associations, and public library work; items relating to the Illinois State Library Association; and research notes, correspondence, manuscripts, and photos accumulated by [Miss] Rose Phelps and [Miss] Laurel Grotzinger in separate research about Sharp. See Maynard J. Brichford, Robert M. Sutton, and Dennis F. Walle, *Manuscripts Guide to Collections at the University of Illinois at Urbana-Champaign* (Chicago: University of Illinois Press, 1976).

4,397. Smith, Janice M.
Papers. 1956-67. 2.3 cu.ft.
Open. Control card.
University of Illinois Archives.
Smith (1906-) became a home economics professor at the University of Illinois in 1944 and served as head of the department from 1949 to 1971. Correspondence, notes, hearing material, bulletins, newsletters, reports, schedules, itineraries, and other papers relate to Smith's membership on the National Advisory Commission on Food and Fiber from 1965 to 1967, to home economics in Indiana, and to home economics publications of Indiana universities.

4,398. Sparks, Marion E.
Papers. 1917-28. 0.3 cu.ft.
Open. Published guide and control card.

University of Illinois Archives.
Sparks (1872-1929) was chemistry librarian at the University of Illinois from 1915 to 1929. Notes on chemistry lectures, photo albums, and other materials, including photos of University buildings, chemistry faculty, and students. See Maynard J. Brichford, Robert M. Sutton, and Dennis F. Walle, *Manuscripts Guide to Collections at the University of Illinois at Urbana-Champaign* (Chicago: University of Illinois Press, 1976).

4,399. Spencer, Gwladys
Papers. 1918-34. 0.3 cu.ft.
Open. Published guide and control card.
University of Illinois Archives.
Spencer (1895-1947) was a library science professor at the University of Illinois from 1942 to 1947. Includes correspondence relating to travel and the purchase of artworks for college libraries, notes on music and hygiene courses at Denison University in Granville, OH, and papers written for courses in English, astronomy, and comparative literature at Ohio Wesleyan University. See Maynard J. Brichford, Robert M. Sutton, and Dennis F. Walle, *Manuscripts Guide to Collections at the University of Illinois at Urbana-Champaign* (Chicago: University of Illinois Press, 1976).

4,400. University Woman's Club
Records. 1918-56. 0.3 cu.ft.
Open. Published guide and control card.
University of Illinois Archives.
Constitutions, bylaws, minutes, auditor's and committee reports, correspondence, membership lists, club proceedings, pictures, manuals, clippings, and other material, including house rules, president's calendars, papers and correspondence concerning tax exemption in 1918, and treasurer's accounts and records. See Maynard J. Brichford, Robert M. Sutton, and Dennis F. Walle, *Manuscripts Guide to Collections at the University of Illinois at Urbana-Champaign* (Chicago: University of Illinois Press, 1976).

4,401. University Women's Tuesday Tea Club
Records. 1906-62. 1 cu.ft.
Open. Published guide and control card.
University of Illinois Archives.
The Club, founded in 1906, is a social organization for University of Illinois faculty wives and female faculty members. Constitutions, minutes, correspondence, membership lists, a list of officers from 1942 to 1961, a history of the Club's founding, photos, a scrapbook, clippings, and other material. Includes records and a scrapbook of the Newcomers Club, which was founded as an auxiliary of the Tuesday Tea Club, and minutes and correspondence of the Twenty-Eight Club, the first group of Newcomers. The Newcomers Club records include constitutions, secretary's and board minutes, a history of the group's founding, brief accounts of each year's activities, membership lists, photos, clippings, and information on the duties and activities of interest groups. See Maynard J. Brichford, Robert M. Sutton, and Dennis F. Walle, *Manuscripts Guide to Collections at the University of Illinois at Urbana-Champaign* (Chicago: University of Illinois Press, 1976).

4,402. Welch, Helen M.
Papers. 1948-68. 2 cu.ft.
Open. Published guide and control card.
University of Illinois Archives.
Helen M. (Welch) Tuttle (1914-) served as a bibliographer from 1942 to 1947, as an assistant acquisitions librarian from 1952 to 1968, and from 1962 to 1968 as professor of library administration at the University of Illinois. She also was president of the resources and technical services division of the American Library Association in 1961 and 1962. Correspondence, minutes, and related material concern her career and activities in such groups as the History of Science Society, the American Library Association, the Council of National Library Associations, seminars on the acquisition of Latin American library materials, the Association of Research Libraries, Phi Beta Kappa, and Phi Kappa Phi. Also includes information about her work for the publications *Library Resources* and *Technical Services and Library Trends.* See Maynard J. Brichford, Robert M. Sutton, and Dennis F. Walle, *Manuscripts Guide to Collections at the University of Illinois at Urbana-Champaign* (Chicago: University of Illinois Press, 1976).

4,403. Weston, Janet
Papers. 1912-63. 0.3 cu.ft.
Open. Published guide and control card.
University of Illinois Archives.
Weston became a University of Illinois economics professor in 1945. Report cards from 1912 to 1923, memorabilia, clippings, and other papers. Includes clippings relating to Gold Feather, Alpha Phi, Torch, Alethenai Literary Society, Alpha Lambda Delta, Theta Sigma Phi, and Pi Mu Epsilon and memorabilia relating to these organizations and to Phi Beta Kappa and the Jamesonian Literary Society. Also includes items from a memory book. See Maynard J. Brichford, Robert M. Sutton, and Dennis F. Walle, *Manuscripts Guide to Collections at the University of Illinois at Urbana-Champaign* (Chicago: University of Illinois Press, 1976).

4,404. Wolfe, Cornelia Kelley
Papers. 1875-1964. 2.3 cu.ft.
Open. Published guide and control card.
University of Illinois Archives.
Wolfe (1897-1972), who earned her PhD in 1930, was an English professor at the University of Illinois from 1950 to 1967. Correspondence, diaries, manuscripts, speeches, course material, family photos, student signature books, post cards, clippings, and other items. Includes lecture notes, course outlines, examinations, and student essays regarding English grammar and literature, American literature, and the career and writings of Henry James. The student signature books date from Wolfe's undergraduate days in 1918 at Colby College in Maine; the diaries and picture post cards record her European travels. Also includes *The Early Development of Henry James* (1930) by Wolfe, who then was Cornelia Kelley, and copies of *The Victorian Newsletter.* Correspondents include Leon Edel and members of the Kelley, Pulsifer, Moore, and Thayer families. See Maynard J. Brichford, Robert M. Sutton, and Dennis F. Walle, *Manuscripts Guide to Collections at the University of Illinois at Urbana-Champaign* (Chicago: University of Illinois Press, 1976).

4,405. Todd, David, and Farnsworth, Charlotte
Papers. 1846-74. 74 items.
Open. Inventory.
University of Illinois at Urbana-Champaign, Illinois Historical Society.
Correspondence of Todd (1821-74), a minister who graduated from Oberlin College in 1843, and Farnsworth (1825-47), who also attended the Ohio school. Farnsworth's letters to Todd concern academic and social activities at Oberlin and her affection for him. In his letters he describes the Illinois countryside, his desire to establish a church, and family affairs. Their correspondence ended with her death.

4,406. Alvord, Clarence Walworth
Papers. 1906-20. 41 folders and 24 items.
Open. Inventory.
University of Illinois at Urbana-Champaign, Illinois Historical Survey.
Papers of Alvord (1868-1928), a member of the history department at the University of Illinois and then at the University of Minnesota, include material concerning Elizabeth Murray Shepherd's projected "Woman's History of the World." These papers include a poem by Shepherd, a description and prospectus of the project, and correspondence between Alvord and Shepherd. Also contains articles, court cases, notes, drafts, and other papers of Alvord.

4,407. American Association of University Women
Records. 1902-76. Ca. 7.3 cu.ft.
Open. No guide.
University of Illinois at Urbana-Champaign, Illinois Historical Survey.
Constitution, bylaws, minutes, treasurer's reports, correspondence, journals, reports, photos, scrapbooks, newsletters, magazines, yearbooks, clippings, and other records of the Champaign-Urbana branch of the AAUW. Includes notes from president's conferences and the group's state convention.

4,408. Bancroft, Mrs. George, and Bliss, Alexander
Papers. 1861-65. 18 items.
Open. Unpublished guide.
University of Illinois at Urbana-Champaign, Illinois Historical Survey.
Correspondence of Elizabeth (Davis) Bliss Bancroft (?-1886), the second wife of historian George Bancroft, and her son Alexander Bliss (1827-96), a junior law partner of Daniel Webster. Letters of Bliss, a colonel in the Quartermaster Corps, include comments on assistance rendered by women during the Civil War.

4,409. Brisbane, Albert
Papers. 1830-1936. 250 folders and 17 vols.
Open. Calendar and inventory.
University of Illinois at Urbana-Champaign, Illinois Historical Survey.
Correspondence, diaries, drafts of books and articles, legal records, and papers of Brisbane (1809-90), a spokesman for Fourierist socialism in the US and a columnist for *The New York Times,* and of his second wife Redelia Bates Brisbane. Includes records and papers, 1883-85, about the divorce of Albert and Lodoiska M. Brisbane and unpublished writings and notes of Redelia Brisbane. Her writings concern love, marriage, the family, divorce, prostitution, ethics, the role and history of women, birth control, eugenics, primitive monogamy, religion, and other topics. Also available on microfilm.

4,410. Burr, Amos Shelton
Papers. 1880-1961. 1356 items.
Partially restricted. Published and unpublished guides.
University of Illinois at Urbana-Champaign, Illinois Historical Survey.
Correspondence, documents, and other papers of the family of Burr (1848-1911), who had extensive landholdings in central Illinois and in Rapides Parish, LA; his wife Sydney Amelie (Compton) Burr; and two of their four daughters, Mary (Burr) [Mrs. Lloyd Warfield] Brown and Ellen (Burr) [Mrs. Randolph S.] Simpson. Amos Burr was an early user of fertilizer and drainage systems on his Illinois farm. His daughter Mary Brown became executor of his estate; she and her husband owned a farm near Jacksonville, IL, and leased other land as well. They had two sons, Peter and William. Ellen Burr married Randolph Simpson (?-1918) in 1914. After her husband's death she returned to live with her mother. Her papers contain letters dealing with a gift of $500 to establish a memorial library to her husband at Princeton. See Maynard J. Brichford, Robert M. Sutton, and Dennis F. Walle, *Manuscripts Guide to Collections at the University of Illinois at Urbana-Champaign* (Chicago: University of Illinois Press, 1976).

4,411. Carriel, Mary (Turner)
Papers. 1864-1927. 4 vols. and 120 items.
Open. Inventory.

University of Illinois at Urbana-Champaign, Illinois Historical Survey.
Carriel (1845-1928) was the first woman to serve on the University of Illinois board of trustees. Travel diaries relating to her trips to Europe in 1910 and through South America in 1912 and 1913, essays based on her travel experiences and observations, plot synopses of works she read, notes for lectures on art history and literary figures, items relating to the participation in 1892 of Morgan County women in the Woman's Columbian Exposition Club, and other papers, including correspondence concerning the preparation and marketing of her biography of her father Jonathan Baldwin Turner. Carriel served on the University of Illinois board of trustees from 1897 to 1903. Her husband H. F. Carriel was superintendent of the Jacksonville State Hospital.

4,412. Champaign Business and Professional Women's Club
Records. 1923-53. 1 vol. and 17 items.
Open. No guide.
University of Illinois at Urbana-Champaign, Illinois Historical Survey.
History of the organization, compiled in 1938 with annual additions to 1953. The volume chronicles the group's activities from its founding as the Business Women's Club through its membership in the state and national federations of Business and Professional Women's Clubs. Membership lists are included.

4,413. Cordiner, Jessie C. (Turner)
Papers. Nd. 1 microfilm reel.
Open. No guide.
University of Illinois at Urbana-Champaign, Illinois Historical Survey.
A history of the John Turner family of Roxbury and Medfield, MA, was compiled by Cordiner and others.

4,414. Daughters of the American Revolution, Alliance Chapter No. 642
Records. 1923-56. 4.3 cu.ft.
Open. Inventory.
University of Illinois at Urbana-Champaign, Illinois Historical Survey.
Scrapbooks contain historians' reports and family records of members of this DAR unit, which was located in Champaign-Urbana.

4,415. Daughters of the American Revolution, Illinois Chapter
Records. 1926-36. 15 folders.
Open. No guide.
University of Illinois at Urbana-Champaign, Illinois Historical Survey.
Reports and other records relate to the DAR's effort to publish a guide to historic sites in Illinois. The material is organized by county and town and includes information concerning the location of the graves of Revolutionary War soldiers.

4,416. Deming, Minor Rudd, and Deming, Abigail
Papers. 1826-49. 35 items.
Open. Calendar.
University of Illinois at Urbana-Champaign, Illinois Historical Survey.
Letters from Minor Deming (1810-45), a brigadier general in the Illinois militia, and his wife Abigail to family and friends in Litchfield, CT. The last letters are from Abigail Deming, who moved to Galesburg, IL, to educate her sons at the newly established Knox College. Earlier letters reflect the role of Minor Deming in the dispersal of the Mormons from the Nauvoo, IL, area. Deming was placed in charge of troops in Carthage, IL, after the arrest of Joseph and Hyrum Smith. The Smiths were killed during Deming's absence.

4,417. Duncan Family
Papers. 1849-82. 24 items.
Open. Published guide and card file.
University of Illinois at Urbana-Champaign, Illinois Historical Survey.
Correspondence of Joseph Duncan, who was governor of Illinois from 1834 to 1838; his wife Elizabeth (Caldwell) Duncan (1808-76); and other members of the Duncan family. Provides information about family events, the status of slaves, abolition, the Civil War, and the funerals of Abraham and Mary (Todd) Lincoln. See Maynard J. Brichford, Robert M. Sutton, and Dennis F. Walle, *Manuscripts Guide to Collections at the University of Illinois at Urbana-Champaign* (Chicago: University of Illinois Press, 1976).

4,418. Galloway, Grace (Growden)
Papers. 1778-1934. 5 items.
Open. Unpublished guide.
University of Illinois at Urbana-Champaign, Illinois Historical Survey.
Correspondence, a diary, a family tree, and other papers of Galloway (?-1782), the wife of Loyalist Joseph Galloway. Grace Galloway stayed in Pennsylvania to protect her husband's property after he went to England, but she was turned out of house in 1779. In her diary she describes her "ouster" and her life after that event. Also includes a burial certificate for Joseph Galloway and a letter dated 1934, which provides more information about Grace Galloway's life. Edited portions of the diary were published in Raymond G. Werner, "Diary of Grace Growden Galloway," *Pennsylvania Magazine of History,* vol. 55, no. 1 (1931).

4,419. Gibson, Eva Katherine (Clapp)
Papers. 1885-1905. 106 items.
Open. Inventory.
University of Illinois at Urbana-Champaign, Illinois Historical Survey.
Gibson (1875-1916) was an author and poet who used her maiden name in her work. Manuscript stories, poems, songs, and other papers, including two letters and a deed. Clapp lived in Bradford, IL, until she married C. B. Gibson, a physician, and moved with him to Chicago.

4,420. Gilbert Family
Papers. 1839-40. 4 items.
Open. No guide.
University of Illinois at Urbana-Champaign, Illinois Historical Survey.
Travel journals and biographical notes of [Mrs.] Mary Morse Gilbert. The first journal contains an account of Gilbert's trip from Danville, IL, to Ohio in 1839. The volume, which was recopied by her son James H. Gilbert, contains discussions of relatives, sickness, church meetings, and the weather.

4,421. Grimké, Sarah Moore
Papers. 1856-61. 1 microfilm reel.
Open. Unpublished guide.
University of Illinois at Urbana-Champaign, Illinois Historical Survey.
Grimké (1792-1873) was an antislavery reformer. Correspondence relating principally to the Eagleswood School in Perth Amboy, NJ. The School, the successor of a Fourierist community, carried on many of the principles of communitarianism. Grimké's letters, many of which were written to her friends Sarah G. and August Wattles, concern education, the School and its problems, slavery, the proposed admission of Kansas to the Union, and other subjects.

4,422. Gutmann and Steven Family
Papers. 1807-1918. 8 folders and 1 microfilm reel.
Open. Calendar.
University of Illinois at Urbana-Champaign, Illinois Historical Survey.
Correspondence and birth, baptism, marriage, and citizenship certificates of Laura Ernestine (Gutmann) Steven (1847-1907) and her husband James Steven, Jr. Laura Gutmann moved with her family from Hartford, CT, to Sadorus, IL, in 1857. The majority of her letters are from her school friend Mary Leonora Green, who became Mrs. Horatio Harrison Pollard. Most of the Gutmann family certificates are in German.

4,423. Hutchison, Phebe Jane (Morrison)
Papers. 1930. 1 vol.
Open. Published guide.
University of Illinois at Urbana-Champaign, Illinois Historical Survey.
Born at Cherry Fork, OH, [Mrs. John Rogers] Hutchison (1854-1931) was an Illinois housewife and pioneer. Memoir contains descriptions of school and church events, family and community gatherings, and household and farming experiences; it also contains notes on her reactions to Civil War enlistments, victories, deaths, and the assassination of Abraham Lincoln. The Morrison family moved to Illinois in 1856 and settled near the present-day town of Carlock. See Maynard J. Brichford, Robert M. Sutton, and Dennis F. Walle, *Manuscripts Guide to Collections at the University of Illinois at Urbana-Champaign* (Chicago: University of Illinois Press, 1976).

4,424. King, Margaret A.
Papers. 1864. 17 items.
Open. No guide.
University of Illinois at Urbana-Champaign, Illinois Historical Survey.
Principally letters from King to her husband Philander B. King, who went west to avoid the Civil War draft. She writes of the difficulties that she and the children encountered running their farm and about the prices for goods and produce.

4,425. Knight Family
Papers. 1853-88. 71 items.
Open. Calendar.
University of Illinois at Urbana-Champaign, Illinois Historical Survey.
Correspondence reflects the life histories of Martha and Isabella Gill, two sisters who were orphaned as children in Ireland. The two lived with their grandmother and relatives in Wheeling, VA, until 1853 when Isabella married Harvey J. Knight and went to live on his farm in Leesville, OH. Martha then moved with her aunt and uncle and their family to the Newton, IA, area. In 1856 she married her cousin John T. Mack and moved to a farm near Towanda, IL. The Macks' first child died, but by 1866 they had four living children. Isabella and Harvey Knight had two daughters, Martha "Mattie" and Anna. The Macks convinced the Knights to move to Illinois. They bought a farm near Normal, IL, and Mattie and Anna, who later became schoolteachers, began their schooling there. The correspondence includes information about livestock, land, and crop prices.

4,426. League of Women Voters
Records. 1963-73. 2 boxes.
Open. Published guide and inventory.
University of Illinois at Urbana-Champaign, Illinois Historical Survey.
Minutes and agenda of the LWV of Charleston, IL; reports on annual meetings; issues of the Charleston LWV's annual newsletter *League Link;* and other publications. See Maynard J. Brichford, Robert M. Sutton, and Dennis F. Walle, *Manuscripts Guide to Collections at the University of Illinois at Urbana-Champaign* (Chicago: University of Illinois Press, 1976).

4,427. League of Women Voters
Records. 1923-71. 9 folders, 39 vols., and ca. 1035 items.
Open. Published guide and inventory.
University of Illinois at Urbana-Champaign, Illinois Historical Survey.
Minutes of general meetings and of the board of

directors, financial ledgers and records, scrapbooks, and clippings of the LWV of Champaign County, IL, which was founded in 1923. The clippings were kept by the League's committees and reflect the particular governmental and social problems in which the committees were interested. See Maynard J. Brichford, Robert M. Sutton, and Dennis F. Walle, *Manuscripts Guide to Collections at the University of Illinois at Urbana-Champaign* (Chicago: University of Illinois Press, 1976).

4,428. Lindsey, Martha M.
Papers. Ca. 1850-90. 1 vol.
Open. Unpublished guide.
University of Illinois at Urbana-Champaign, Illinois Historical Survey.
Journal of poetry, autobiographical material, and autograph signatures kept by Lindsey, the wife of Eureka College instructor John Lindsey.

4,429. Maclure, William, and Fretageot, Marie
Papers. 1820-33. 2 microfilm reels.
Open. Unpublished guide.
University of Illinois at Urbana-Champaign, Illinois Historical Survey.
Correspondence between Maclure (1763-1840), a geologist, patron of science and education, and founder of the New Harmony Working Men's Institute, and Fretageot (?-1833), his deputy, provides a record of the New Harmony community.

4,430. Meharry Family
Papers. 1867-1941. 13.5 cu.ft.
Open. Inventory.
University of Illinois at Urbana-Champaign, Illinois Historical Survey.
Personal and business correspondence, farm records, a family history, photos, pamphlets, and maps of the family of Abraham Patton Meharry (1842-1908) and his twin brother Isaac Meharry. [Miss] Martha "Mattie" Jane McMillin married Abraham Meharry in 1879. Their son Charles Leo Meharry (1885-) married [Miss] Clara Esther Burghardt in 1908. The Meharrys were farmers with extensive landholdings in Illinois. Correspondence relates to the farms and to the personal lives of Abraham and Martha Meharry and of Charles and Clara Meharry. The letters of Clara Meharry, who attended Purdue University, provide insight into midwestern college life.

4,431. Morgan, Thomas J.
Papers. 1880-1910. 64 folders and 19 vols.
Open. Inventory.
University of Illinois at Urbana-Champaign, Illinois Historical Survey.
Morgan (1847-1912) was a Chicago lawyer, socialist, and labor leader. His wife Elizabeth (Chambers) Morgan investigated sweatshop conditions among Chicago's women workers in 1891. Correspondence, speeches, minutes of various organizations, reports of trials, a file of Thomas Morgan's weekly publication *The Provoker,* pamphlets, clippings, posters, and other papers. Includes information about women's suffrage, antitrust laws, unemployment, the right to work, the formation of unions and of a labor party, and education. Includes letters from "Mother" Mary (Harris) Jones. Also available on microfilm.

4,432. Mowder, Louisa
Papers. 1857-1903. 1 vol.
Open. No guide.
University of Illinois at Urbana-Champaign, Illinois Historical Survey.
Album of poems and personal sentiments written by friends and relatives of Mowder, a White Hall, IL, resident. Among those who signed the album were Peter Cartwright, a Methodist preacher, and Mowder's granddaughter Ameda Ruth King, who was a member of the University of Illinois history department.

4,433. New Harmony
Collection. 1814-30. 1 microfilm reel.
Open. Unpublished guide.
University of Illinois at Urbana-Champaign, Illinois Historical Survey.
Correspondence of persons involved with the New Harmony community, a village established by Robert Owen in 1825 on the Wabash River in southern Indiana. The community practiced the theories of socialism and human betterment evolved by Owen, including the absolute equality of property, labor, and opportunity as well as freedom of speech and action. Owen admitted the failure of his experiment in 1827 after the absence of authority in the town's government resulted in anarchy. Correspondents include Marie D. Fretageot, Mary Carroll, Martha Chase, and Frances Wright.

4,434. Orvis, Marianne (Dwight)
Papers. 1843-47. 1 microfilm reel.
Open. Published guide.
University of Illinois at Urbana-Champaign, Illinois Historical Survey.
Correspondence of Orvis (1816-1901), a resident member of the Brook Farm community at West Roxbury, MA, in 1846, the year of her marriage to John Orvis. Her letters to Anna Q. T. Parsons contain descriptions of life at Brook Farm, personal events, and the financial affairs of the community. Her first name sometimes was spelled Mary Ann. See Maynard J. Brichford, Robert M. Sutton, and Dennis F. Walle, *Manuscripts Guide to Collections at the University of Illinois at Urbana-Champaign* (Chicago: University of Illinois Press, 1976).

4,435. Owen, Robert Dale
Papers. 1815-58. 111 items and 12 microfilm reels.
Open. Unpublished guide.
University of Illinois at Urbana-Champaign, Illinois Historical Survey.
Owen (1801-77), an industrialist, founded the New Harmony community in Indiana. Correspondence, deeds, and other papers concerning New Harmony and other Owenite experimental communities. Includes letters from Marie Fretageot, Frances Wright, and women involved in New Harmony.

4,436. Pease and Lyman Family
Papers. 1819-1936. 632 items.
Open. Calendar.
University of Illinois at Urbana-Champaign, Illinois Historical Survey.
Correspondence, sermons, poetry, genealogical information, and other family papers of Orange Lyman (?-1851), a Congregational pastor from Madison, OH, who emigrated to Downers Grove Township in Illinois in 1838; his wife Marcia (Dewey) Lyman; their three sons Thomas, Stephen, and Henry Martyn Lyman; Lovancia (Pease) Lyman (1821-1912); her sister Sarah (Pease) Wilson; and other members of the two families. Lovancia Pease attended Oberlin College and taught school for about 10 years before marrying her former schoolmate Henry Martyn Lyman in 1850. The couple settled in Downers Grove, IL, and had two children. Contains correspondence written during their courtship as well as letters that Marcia Lyman wrote to her sons after her husband's death and letters from Sarah (Pease) Wilson in Faribault, MN. Wilson's letters include Pease family genealogy and mention of such technical innovations of the 1890s as cancer operations, the telephone, and electric lights.

4,437. Shakers
Collection. 1806-96. 13 microfilm reels.
Open. Published guide.
University of Illinois at Urbana-Champaign, Illinois Historical Survey.
Minutes, account books, correspondence, diaries, church records and documents, songbooks, and other papers of Shaker colonies in New Lebanon, NY, Canterbury, NH, Union Village, OH, and Pleasant Hill, South Union, Mill Point, and Jasper Springs, KY. The diaries and journals, which were kept by individual members of these utopian communities, concern daily life and religious affairs. Includes the constitution of the New Lebanon community and account books of blacksmiths and storekeepers. The formal name of the sect was the United Society of Believers in Christ's Second Appearing. See Maynard J. Brichford, Robert M. Sutton, and Dennis F. Walle, *Manuscripts Guide to Collections at the University of Illinois at Urbana-Champaign* (Chicago: University of Illinois Press, 1976).

4,438. Stewart and Wilson Family
Papers. 1822-1960. 5 folders, 3 vols., and 193 items.
Open. Unpublished guide.
University of Illinois at Urbana-Champaign, Illinois Historical Survey.
Papers of Fannie Aylworth Stewart (1857-?) and her son-in-law Wilbur Wilson (1881-1958) consist primarily of Wilson's papers concerning atomic bomb tests he witnessed near Bikini atoll in 1946. His papers include government correspondence, a diary, drafts of an article, photos, clippings, three medals, and other items. Fannie Stewart's papers contain reminiscences and copies of birth, death, and marriage records from family Bibles. Stewart was born near New Hampshire, OH, and moved with her family to a farm near Iowa City, IA, in 1865. In 1877 she married Alexander Stewart. Their daughter Teresa married Wilson, who joined the University of Illinois civil engineering staff in 1913.

4,439. Tanner, Sara Jane
Papers. 1874. 1 vol. and 2 items.
Open. No guide.
University of Illinois at Urbana-Champaign, Illinois Historical Survey.
Journal kept by Tanner (1832-?) concerns her trip by train and wagon from Hinckley, IL, to northern and western Iowa and back. She was accompanied by her husband and a family friend. Photos are also included.

4,440. Tawney, Marietta (Busey)
Papers. 1927-49. 393 items.
Open. Published guide.
University of Illinois at Urbana-Champaign, Illinois Historical Survey.
A member of an Urbana pioneer family and an 1899 graduate of Vassar College, Tawney (1879-1949) was a state and local LWV official. Correspondence, notes, drafts, speeches, reports, laws, and other items related to her LWV work. Tawney returned to Urbana in 1930 when her husband Guy Tawney became a professor at the University of Illinois. Her primary interest in the LWV was efficiency in government. She served as downstate LWV chairman and promoted legislation to permit Illinois cities to adopt a city-manager form of government. She also was cochairman of the Illinois Public Health Committee from 1942 to 1947, president of the Community Chest, and a member of the County Emergency Relief Committee. See Maynard J. Brichford, Robert M. Sutton, and Dennis F. Walle, *Manuscripts Guide to Collections at the University of Illinois at Urbana-Champaign* (Chicago: University of Illinois Press, 1976).

4,441. Unity Society
Records. 1881-96. 3 vols. and 27 items.
Open. No guide.
University of Illinois at Urbana-Champaign, Illinois Historical Survey.
The Unity Society, or Unity Church, was formed, apparently in 1882, by members of the Unitarian and Universalist churches in Monmouth, IL. Constitution of the Ladies Social Circle, the Circle's secretary's books with a list of Sunday school receipts and expenses, a treasurer's book of

the Ladies' Society of Unity Church, an account book, correspondence concerning religious matters, and other records.

4,442. Van Sellar, Henry
Papers. 1860-92. 159 items.
Open. Inventory.
University of Illinois at Urbana-Champaign, Illinois Historical Survey.
Correspondence, photos, mementos, invitations, and other papers of Van Sellar (1839-?), a Civil War officer, lawyer, Illinois state senator, and circuit judge, and his wife Sallie (Pattison) Van Sellar. Includes their correspondence from before their marriage in 1864 through the end of the war and correspondence of Sallie Van Sellar with her family and friends. The Civil War letters include accounts of fighting, references to the Lincoln assassination, and some descriptions of the South.

UTICA

4,443. Powell, Maud
Papers. Nd. No size given.
Open. No guide.
La Salle County Historical Society Museum.
Powell (1868-1920) was a violinist who was born in Peru, IL, and died in Uniontown, PA. Photos, record albums, a medal from a Vienna music hall, and other memorabilia.

VANDALIA

4,444. Burtschi, Josephine "Jo" Frances
Papers. 1954- . Ca. 2 ft.
Open. No guide.
Vandalia Historical Society.
Burtschi (1909-), book illustrator and creator of notepaper and post card sketches, is the founder of the Vandalia Historical Society and an historic researcher and preservationist. Includes published and unpublished manuscripts, notes, research files, and photos relating to her interests in historic preservation in Vandalia, the former state capital of Illinois, and Fayette County, IL; correspondence, articles, and files of the Historical Society and the Little Brick House Museum in Vandalia; and Burtschi's collection of manuscripts of James Hall, an author, newspaper editor, and state treasurer of Illinois in 1828, whose papers reflect pioneer life. Burtschi's parents were Joseph Charles Burtschi and Olivia Burtschi (1876-1959); her sister is Mary Burtschi (1911-).

4,445. Burtschi, Mary
Papers. 1949- . Ca. 2 ft.
Access restricted. Unpublished guide.
Vandalia Historical Society.
Burtschi (1911-) is an author, historian, and former high school English teacher. Contains correspondence, including items concerning her writings from such women writers as Louise Callan, Marjorie Erskine, Margaret Flint, Regina Kelly, Lucille Lawler, Betty Madden, Covelle Newcomb, Marguerite Jenison Pease, Ruth Painter Randall, Mary Jo Whittaker, Ellen Whitney, and Adade Wheeler; manuscripts of her published works *Vandalia: Wilderness Capital of Lincoln's Land* (1963), *James Hall of Lincoln's Frontier World* (1977), and *Seven Stories by James Hall* (1975), which she edited; articles she wrote for state and national magazines; travel accounts; lectures; photos; scrapbooks; clippings; and programs. Also includes records of the Literati, 1949-64, a high school literary society sponsored by Burtschi at Effingham High School in Effingham, IL. Burtschi, whose sister is Josephine Burtschi (1909-), is the daughter of Joseph Charles Burtschi and Olivia Burtschi (1876-1959).

4,446. Burtschi, Olivia
Papers. 1905-22. 1 vol.
Open. No guide.
Vandalia Historical Society.
Personal and family photo album of [Mrs. Joseph Charles] Burtschi (1876-1959), a homemaker, whose daughters are Josephine Burtschi (1909-) and Mary Burtschi (1911-).

4,447. Sir Thomas More Society, Mother of Dolores Church
Records. 1971-72. 2 items.
Open. No guide.
Vandalia Historical Society.
Minutes and programs of the Society, a women's study group concerned with the life of Thomas More and the lives of the Roman Catholic saints. The society was organized in 1971 and disbanded in 1972.

WATSEKA

4,448. Woman's Club Cemetery Association of Watseka
Records. 1903-39. 2 vols.
Open. No guide.
Iroquois County Genealogical Society, Old Courthouse Museum.
The Association was established in 1906 to direct the operation of cemeteries under its jurisdiction. Minutes, treasurer's reports, and records of bodies received.

WAUCONDA

4,449. Lake County Home Bureau
Records. 1947-67. No size given.
Open. No guide.
Lake County Museum, Lakewood Forest Preserve.
Correspondence, reference files, studies, reports, announcements, and publications of the Bureau, an extension agency that provides such family services as instruction in household management and safety and child care.

4,450. Local History
Collection. Ca. 1880- . Ca. 70 ft.
Open. No guide.
Lake County Museum, Lakewood Forest Preserve.
The collection concerns the 42 communities in Lake County, IL, and includes files on individuals and organizations, reminiscences, family histories, post cards, photos, publications, and dressmaking patterns.

4,451. Waukegan Women's Clubs
Records. 1911-35. Ca. 25 items.
Open. No guide.
Lake County Museum, Lakewood Forest Preserve.
Consists of a minute book of the Federated Women's Clubs of Waukegan, 1911, and membership books of the Woman's Club of Waukegan, 1911-35. Both clubs focused on civic and social concerns.

WAUKEGAN

4,452. Local History
Collection. Ca. 1900- . Ca. 25 items.
Open. No guide.
Waukegan Historical Society.
Contains correspondence, reminiscences, family histories, photos, scrapbooks, yearbooks and other items. Collection includes yearbooks and scrapbooks of the Waukegan branch of the AAUW, 1928-78, and items concerning Louise (deKoven) Bowen and the Bowen Country Club, a Hull-House summer camp, which serves as the site of the Historical Society.

WHEATON

4,453. Archives
Records. 1872- . Ca. 15 ft.
Partially restricted. No guide.
Franciscan Sisters, Our Lady of the Angels Convent.
This congregation was formed in 1872 when the Sisters came to the US from Germany because of the German goverment's struggle with Catholicism. Correspondence; biographical and historical notes, some of which are in German; reports; photos; and memorabilia relates to the Sisters' early work in parochial schools, their change of emphasis to care of the sick and orphans, their extreme poverty in the early days, hospitals, and the Provincial House. The congregation is engaged in educational, social, and ministerial activities.

WILMETTE

4,454. Garden Clubs
Collection. 1922- . 0.5 ft.
Open. Unpublished guide.
Wilmette Historical Museum.
Includes minutes, correspondence, histories, membership lists, and scrapbooks of local garden clubs, including the Evening Garden Club, founded in 1928, and the Little Garden Club, founded in 1956. Most of the clubs were founded in the 1920s and were devoted to spreading knowledge about and love of gardening and to civic improvement. Includes a 1966 civic improvement contest scrapbook from the Little Garden Club, which relates to their prize-winning project, the beautification of the Chicago Transit Authority station in Wilmette.

4,455. Photos
Collection. 1850- . Ca. 1000 items.
Open. Unpublished guide.
Wilmette Historical Museum.
Includes photos of individuals, families, weddings, school classes, civic activities, recreation, and farm activities.

4,456. Westerfield, Fidelia Burroughs
Papers. 1867-78. 2 items.
Open. Unpublished guide.
Wilmette Historical Museum.
Diaries of Westerfield (1846-1915), a schoolteacher and housewife, in which she writes about daily life in Wilmette.

4,457. Wheelock, Alice
Papers. Ca. 1950. 1 item.
Open. Unpublished guide.
Wilmette Historical Museum.
Autobiographical reminiscence of Wheelock (1885-1960s) concerns children's education, games, and chores in the 1890s.

4,458. Woman's Clubs
Collection. Ca. 1930- . 0.5 ft.
Open. Unpublished guide.
Wilmette Historical Museum.
Includes yearbooks and bulletins of the Woman's Club of Wilmette, which was founded in 1897, and similar items of other social, civic, and recreational women's clubs, including the LWV.

4,459. Ye Olde Towne Folk
Records. 1892-1951. 0.5 ft.
Open. No guide.
Wilmette Historical Museum.
Minutes, membership records, and reminiscences of this social organization, which was founded in 1892 and made up of people who had lived in Wilmette

at least 25 years. The first president was a woman and many women were active members.

ZION

4,460. Orfali, Steffi
Papers. Nd. 1 item.
Open. No guide.
Zion Historical Society.
Unpublished manuscript in which Orfali describes the history of her grandparents, who were Jewish immigrants from Munich. They came to the US in ca. 1830, and the family ultimately moved to Zion.

4,461. Utopian Christian Community
Records. 1894- . No size given.
Open. Unpublished guide.
Zion Historical Society.
The Community, a religious industrial settlement, was founded in 1900 in Zion by John Alexander Dowie, who also was the founder of the Christian Catholic Church. Includes letters of early Zion residents, among them one from Laura Love to her parents, 1907, describing the split in the Church following Dowie's death. Also includes publications that provide information about the local, national, and international activities of the Church, including *Leaves of Healing,* 1894-; *Zion Banner,* 1898-1912; and *The Theocrat,* 1906-20. Also contains published items pertaining to Dowie and his followers, which include information on the practice of commissioning husband-wife missionary teams. Dowie emphasized physical healing and a controlled industrial economy. In 1902 his wife Jane Dowie became overseer of such women's work as lace-making.

4,462. Zion Woman's Club
Records. 1934-75. No size given.
Open. Unpublished guide.
Zion Historical Society.
Scrapbooks containing invitations, clippings, and programs of the Club, a civic and social women's organization.

INDIANA

ANDERSON

4,463. Church of God
Records. 1903- . No size given.
Partially restricted. Card catalog.
Anderson College, School of Theology Library.
Photos, oral history tapes, and books of the Church of God, which was founded in 1880. Many of the Church's ministers were women.

4,464. Church of God, National Woman's Missionary Society
Records. 1932-72. 30 vols. and other items.
Access restricted. Card catalog.
Anderson College, School of Theology Library.
Minutes, financial records, a biography of Nora (Siens) Hunter, photos, and other records. Hunter was the founder of the National Woman's Missionary Society.

4,465. College and Seminary
Records. 1917- . 2 shelves.
Access restricted. Card catalog.
Anderson College, School of Theology Library.
Correspondence, photos, bulletins, and annuals of Anderson College and of the Anderson College School of Theology.

BEECH GROVE

4,466. Convent Archives
Records. 1956- . 3 drawers.
Open. No guide.
Sisters of St. Benedict, Our Lady of Grace Convent.
Financial records, photos, scrapbooks, publications distributed by the community, and other records of this religious order of women, which was founded in 1956 at Beech Grove. Includes material relating to Our Lady of Grace Convent and Academy and to St. Paul Hermitage.

BLOOMINGTON

4,467. Boone
Papers. 1791-1868. 16 items.
Open. Card catalog.
Indiana University, Lilly Library.
Estimate book and correspondence from 1856 to 1868 of Benjamin Pennebaker Douglass (1820-1904), director and president in 1854 and 1855 of the lower division of the New Albany, Lanesville and Corydon, IN, plank road, and of his second wife Queen Victoria (Boone) Douglass (1837-85). In letters to her husband Queen Victoria Douglass speaks of family matters and life in southern Indiana. Benjamin Douglass's papers include letters to his wife as well as his monthly estimate book for the plank road, which also contains his description of the Ladies' Washington Monument Society. The Society, organized in Chicago in 1809 by women's delegations from several states, sought to raise funds for completion of the Washington National Monument.

4,468. Bowers, III
Papers. 1902-72. Ca. 1200 items.
Open. Card catalog.
Indiana University, Lilly Library.
An ambassador and newspaperman, Claude Gernade Bowers (1878-1958) was an author of historical and biographical books, ambassador to Spain from 1933 to 1939, and ambassador to Chile from 1939 to 1953. His papers include letters he exchanged with Sybil (McCaslin) Bowers (1884-1964) before their marriage. Personal in nature, the letters reflect Indiana social customs. Also included are letters by Bowers to his daughter Patricia Bowers (1915-75) relating events in Spain during the Civil War, letters from Sybil Bowers to Patricia, and Sybil Bowers's diaries.

4,469. Champ
Papers. 1836-1931. 134 items.
Open. Card catalog.
Indiana University, Lilly Library.
George W. Champ (1830-1905) was an Indiana physician, businessman, and postmaster; Champ, his wife Elizabeth Ann (Nation) Champ (1833-?), and one of his daughters, Flora A. Champ, were active workers in the Indiana temperance movement. Correspondence of George Champ; programs of the Dublin, IN, branch of the Woman's Missionary Association of the Radical United Brethren Church, for which Flora Champ served as secretary; and minutes of the Dublin WCTU from 1883 to 1894. Dublin was the home of many of the leaders of the state's woman's rights movement.

4,470. Daniels, Edward
Papers. 1869-1920. 3532 items.
Open. Card catalog.
Indiana University, Lilly Library.
Daniels (1854-1918) was a prominent Indianapolis lawyer and trustee of Wabash College in Crawfordsville, IN. Correspondence and papers include letters, beginning in 1896, that concern the admission of women to Wabash College. The letters describe petitions from alumni groups asking that the college become coeducational.

4,471. Davis, Emily
Papers. 1814-1902. 85 items.
Open. Card catalog.
Indiana University, Lilly Library.
Davis was a school teacher in Newhope, Union County, IN. Correspondence, an 1854 employment agreement between Davis and the Newhope school, and Davis's Union County teachers license. The correspondence includes letters from relatives and from Davis's former schoolmates at Liberty Seminary in Liberty, IN, many of whom also were teachers in Indiana schools. In their letters they speak of the pleasures and problems women faced as teachers in mid-19th century Indiana.

4,472. Derwood, Gene
Papers. 1937-56. 100 items.
Open. Card catalog.
Indiana University, Lilly Library.
[Miss] Derwood (1909-54) was a poet and artist. Correspondence; text of *The Poems of Gene Derwood* (Clarke and Way, 1955); folder of miscellaneous papers and criticism; drawings, including two sketch books and three abstract paintings; pictures of works sculpted by Derwood; and photos of her. Correspondence with poetry editors and about her concern for the schooling of her son Strephon. Derwood was the wife of author Oscar Williams.

4,473. Deshon, Florence
Papers. 1917-22. 409 items.
Closed. Card catalog.
Indiana University, Lilly Library.
Correspondence and memorabilia of the career of Deshon (1896-1922), a stage and motion picture actress, including letters exchanged with author Max Eastman in 1919 while she was on tour in the East with a road company of *Among the Girls.* Deshon went to Culver City, CA, that year under contract to Goldwyn but the contract was broken in 1920. She returned to the West Coast in 1921 for more work in movies and on the stage. Deshon committed suicide after returning to New York in 1922. Her letters reflect the experiences of an aspiring actress in the days of silent films.

4,474. Flanagan, Emma Cecelia (Rector)
Papers. 1861-1962. 48 items.
Open. Card catalog.
Indiana University, Lilly Library.
Correspondence, photos, and clippings of [Mrs. Edward E.] Flanagan (1870-1964), a homemaker who was a close friend of the Dreiser family of Terre Haute, IN. In her letters she speaks of her regard for Theodore Dreiser's family and of 19th-century social customs and events in Terre Haute.

4,475. Griffith
Papers. 1831-81. 28 items.
Open. Card catalog.
Indiana University, Lilly Library.
Thomas J. Griffith (1837-?) and his wife Martha E. (Hutchings) Griffith (1842-?) were physicians. Correspondence, diary, and other papers include Martha Griffith's journal containing diaries for 1863 through 1881, obstetrical case histories, medical office accounts for 1871, and medical lecture notes from 1865 and 1866. Also included are her letters from Solon Tilford, a physician; her notebook containing notes from lectures on skin diseases delivered in 1867 by physician Benjamin Jay Jeffries; clinical notes she kept at the Pennsylvania hospital medical clinic; and an account she wrote about early Indiana.

4,476. Hahn
Papers. 1917- . Ca. 12 ft. (5872 items).
Open. Unpublished guide.

Indiana University, Lilly Library.
Emily Hahn (1905-) is a contributor to *The New Yorker* and the author of articles and books, most of which are nonfiction. The wife of Charles R. Boxer, she began her career as a mining engineer in the southwest. Correspondence, research material, and manuscripts for some of her writings; clippings of reviews and tear sheets from her *New Yorker* articles; college notes; photos; nine original Thurber ink drawings; family memorabilia; and other items. Includes letters Hahn wrote to her family describing her experiences in China, Africa, England, India, and other areas. Her correspondence from China concerns the Japanese occupation prior to WWII and her internment by the Japanese from 1941 to 1943. Other writings and research material deal with such subjects as primates, D. H. Lawrence, and Mable Dodge Luhan. Correspondents include her husband, her one-time fiancé William Rose Benét, John Gunther, Rebecca West, editors and writers for *The New Yorker,* Joseph Alsop, Carol Brandt, Hortense Calisher, Milton Caniff, Mme. Chiang Kai-shek, Anna Kavan, and Harold W. Ross.

4,477. Haldeman, Sarah Alice (Addams)
Papers. 1839-1953. 5466 items.
Open. Card catalog.
Indiana University, Lilly Library.
Sister of Jane Addams, Haldeman (1854-1915) was a banker and civic leader in Girard, KS; her papers include those of her daughter Anna Marcet (Haldeman)-Julius (1887-1941), an actress, banker, and author. Family correspondence, including letters from Addams and Anna Haldeman as a student; literary manuscripts; papers concerning Sarah Haldeman's church work and the Kansas Federation of Women's Clubs; genealogical material; legal and financial records; family photos; clippings; and theater programs. Sarah Haldeman became president of Girard's Board of Education and first president of the city's public library association. She succeeded her husband Henry Winfield Haldeman, the son of her stepmother Anna (Hostetter) Haldeman Addams, as president of the State Bank of Girard in 1905, and she was elected district vice-president of the Kansas bankers association in 1914. Anna Haldeman studied at Rockford Female Seminary in Rockford, IL, the Dearborn Seminary in Chicago, Bryn Mawr College, and at the American Academy of Dramatic Arts in New York City between 1908 and 1910. Appearing under the name Jean Marcet, she acted from 1910 to 1913 in stock companies in the US and Canada. In 1915 she returned to Girard where she became vice-president of the State Bank and an officer in the bankers association. She married Emanuel Julius in 1916 and they combined their names legally. The couple were authors and publishers of rationalist and socialist literature; several of Anna Haldeman-Julius's books were published between 1916 and 1931. She also continued as vice-president of the Girard bank until 1925.

4,478. McClure
Papers. 1857-1949. 21,845 items.
Open. Card catalog.
Indiana University, Lilly Library.
Papers of editor Samuel Sidney McClure (1857-1949) consist of family correspondence, diaries, business records, memorandum books, biographical material, and photos of his wife Harriet Sophia (Hurd) McClure (1855-1929). Her papers include eight of her diaries and correspondence, primarily to her sister Mary Charlotte Hurd (1859-1949) and her father Albert Hurd (1823-1906), both of whom were faculty members at Knox College. Also included are diaries, memorandum books, and letters of Mary Charlotte Hurd.

4,479. McCulloch
Papers. 1766-1914. 15,749 items.
Open. Card catalog.
Indiana University, Lilly Library.
Correspondence and family papers of Hugh McCulloch (1808-95), a banker who was US comptroller of the currency, secretary of the treasury, and a partner in the London banking house of Jay Cooke, McCulloch, and Company. Includes personal correspondence, household account books, and scrapbooks of his wife Susan Maria (Man) McCulloch (1818-98) and of their daughter Marie Louise McCulloch, who became Mrs. John Brooks Yale. Dating from the 1870s and 1880s, the women's letters pertain to family and social matters.

4,480. McVitty
Papers. 1952-60. 344 items.
Open. Card catalog.
Indiana University, Lilly Library.
Correspondence, personal papers, and reports of Marion (Etcheverry) McVitty pertain to her work as an officer of the United World Federalist movement. The wife of Edward W. McVitty, she was an accredited observer at the UN for the movement and served as chairman of the movement's United Nations Charter Revision Committee and of the United Nations Liaison Committee of the World Association. An executive committee member of the Conference Group of United States Organizations for the United Nations, Marion McVitty kept 80 to 90 persons informed about events pertaining to UN charter revision. She distributed reports to her correspondents on topics such as UN charter revision, the Suez Canal crisis of 1956, the UN Emergency Force of 1956 to 1960, and disarmament.

4,481. McWhirter, Luella Frances (Smith)
Papers. 1859-1974. 2315 items.
Open. Card catalog.
Indiana University, Lilly Library.
Correspondence; diaries from 1894 to 1941; personal papers; scrapbooks; files of *The Message,* official paper of the Indiana WCTU; and WCTU membership certificates of [Mrs. Felix Tony] McWhirter (1859-?), an officer of the WCTU and of the Woman's Franchise League of Indiana. Born in Perrysville, IN, she attended East Tennessee Wesleyan College at Athens, TN, and DePauw University. She married in 1878 and, in 1888, moved to Indianapolis where she was elected treasurer of the state WCTU in 1893 and president of the group in 1896. She also served as editor of *The Message* from 1897 to 1913 and from 1919 to 1945. She was honorary president of the state WCTU from 1940 to 1952. A founder of the Woman's Franchise League, McWhirter was elected the group's vice-president in 1911. Her papers document efforts of Indiana women to secure temperance reform and the ballot. The papers dating from 1952 to 1974 were gathered by McWhirter's daughter.

4,482. Miner
Papers. 1915- . 4 ft. (ca. 780 items).
Open. Card catalog.
Indiana University, Lilly Library.
A poet who taught for many years at the Pembroke-Country Day School at Kansas City, Virginia Scott [Mrs. Dewey H.] Miner (1901-) reviewed books for a Kansas City newspaper before she retired and moved to Warsaw, IN. Correspondence, notebooks and workbooks of her poems, music and drawings by others for her poems, scrapbooks and other items reflect Miner's career and her influence on her pupils, several of whom became published poets. Correspondents include Margaret Abbott Bartlett, Dorothy Bayley, Stephen Vincent Benét, William Rose Benét, Witter Bynner, Bennett Cerf, Margaret Cousins, Virginia Louise Falkner, Paul Gallico, Mary Carr Hanna, Amy Loveman, Christopher Morley, Gene Stratton Porter, Dorothy Thompson, Grace Tully, Louis Untermeyer, and Hugh Walpole.

4,483. Nolan
Papers. 1914-74. 6536 items.
Open. Card catalog.
Indiana University, Lilly Library.
An Indiana native who lived in Evansville, Bloomington, and Indianapolis, Jeannette (Covert) Nolan (1897-1974) was an author of children's stories, adult novels, and nonfiction works; her husband Val Francis Nolan (1892-1940) was a lawyer and trustee of Indiana University. Correspondence with her literary agents, publishers, Indiana authors, and politicians; speeches; writings; contracts for her works; notebooks; royalties; and artists' drawings for her books. Beginning by writing children's stories based on tales she told her own children, Nolan concentrated on writing as her chief source of income after her husband's death. She also was a staff member for a number of writers' conferences in Indiana and Colorado. Her correspondents included Birch Evans Bayh, Witter Bynner, Bernard Augustine DeVoto, Marilyn Wall Durham, William Herbert Hudnut III, Mabel Leigh Hunt, Clara Ingram Judson, Charles Marion La Follette, Carrie Emma Scott, Adlai Ewing Stevenson, and Marguerite Young.

4,484. Phillips
Papers. 1886-1960. 583 items.
Open. Card catalog.
Indiana University, Lilly Library.
Correspondence of John Sanburn Phillips (1861-1949), an editor and publisher, and of Ida Minerva Tarbell, an author and editor, concerns *McClure's magazine,* of which she was associate editor and staff writer from 1894 to 1906; *American magazine,* of which she was associate editor from 1906 to 1915; and her articles and books on historical and biographical subjects.

4,485. Plath
Papers. 1932-77. 3405 items.
Open. Unpublished guides.
Indiana University, Lilly Library.
Correspondence, writings, and memorabilia of Sylvia Plath (1932-63), a poet and writer; her husband Ted Hughes; and her family. Includes correspondence with various teachers, writers, friends, editors, and family members. After Plath's suicide in 1963, the letters are primarily from Hughes and his family to Plath's mother Aurelia Schober Plath. Correspondents include Elizabeth Bowen, Peter Davison, Paul Hamilton Engle, Lynne Lawner, Russell Lynes, Olive Higgins Prouty, Henry Rago, Richard Sassoon, Byrna Ivens Untermeyer, Edward Augustus Weeks, and William Carlos Williams. Contains a typescript carbon of *Letters Home* (1975), which was edited by Aurelia Plath, as well as scrapbooks of photos and items concerning dances, dates, holidays, and the schooling of Sylvia Plath, who began writing poetry as a child.

4,486. Ralston, Mrs. S. M.
Papers. 1894-1950. 182 items.
Open. Card catalog.
Indiana University, Lilly Library.
Indiana's Democratic national committeewoman from 1934 to 1953, Jennie (Craven) Ralston (1862-1954) was the wife of Samuel Moffett Ralston, Indiana governor and US senator. Correspondence, prose and speeches by Jennie Ralston, pamphlets, and clippings; includes letters from prominent political figures, friends, and members of her family, as well as material pertaining to her work with the national committee.

4,487. Rumely, Fanny (Scott)
Papers. 1883-1973. 2672 items.
Open. No guide.

Indiana University, Lilly Library.
Personal correspondence, diaries, pictures, and printed material of Rumely (1883-). The daughter of Emmet Hoyt Scott and Mary Relief (Niles) Scott, Rumely graduated from La Porte High School in 1895 and Smith College in 1900. She married Edward Aloysius Rumely (1877-?), an educator, in 1910.

4,488. Sinclair, Mary Craig (Kimbrough)
Papers. 1884-1963. 5232 items.
Open. Chronological arrangement of letters.
Indiana University, Lilly Library.
Correspondence and literary writings of Sinclair (1883-1961), a novelist and wife of Upton Beall Sinclair, including items written about Mary Sinclair after her death.

4,489. Thomson, Elizabeth Anna (Williams)
Papers. 1813-81. 20 items.
Open. Card catalog.
Indiana University, Lilly Library.
Thomson (1824-54) was a housewife and poet. Diaries for most of the period between 1834 and 1845, commonplace book containing philosophy notes she made as a student at Wethersfield (CT) Academy in 1841 and 1842, poems she wrote between 1841 and 1845, and an unsigned poem addressed to her entitled "Strike the Cymbal." Born in Middletown, CT, the daughter of minister Joshua Lewis Williams, Elizabeth Williams moved to Terre Haute, IN, in 1838 and attended schools in Terre Haute and Crawfordsville, IN, in 1839 and 1840. She returned to Indiana in 1842 after her study in Connecticut and married Samuel Steele Thomson, a Latin professor at Wabash College in Crawfordsville.

4,490. Tuttle, Elizabeth A.
Papers. 1838-1912. 119 items.
Open. Card catalog.
Indiana University, Lilly Library.
Correspondence of Tuttle (1823?-96), a Civil War nurse and teacher from Colebrook, OH. Tuttle volunteered as an army nurse in 1862 and served until she was honorably discharged in Sept. 1865. She taught at Mound City, IL, in 1869 and 1870 and in Cairo, IL, in 1871. Her correspondence contains items from friends and relatives, including 1863-65 letters to her niece Hattie Tuttle. Others of Elizabeth Tuttle's letters describe her experiences as an army nurse, specifically her work after the battle of Antietam; the establishment of a hospital at Harper's Ferry, VA; the evacuation of Harper's Ferry by canal boats to Washington, DC; and institution of the Army of the Potomac's general hospital at Gettysburg, PA. Also included are letters of gratitude Tuttle received from relatives of men she nursed during the war.

4,491. Wharton
Papers. 1908-52. 4.5 ft. (ca. 2000 items).
Open. Unpublished guide.
Indiana University, Lilly Library.
Edith Newbold (Jones) [Mrs. Edward Robbins] Wharton (1862-1937) was a novelist and short story writer. Correspondence; diaries; unpublished poems; manuscripts of *A Backward Glance, The Gods Arrive,* and *The Age of Innocence;* and photos. Includes correspondence of Bernard Berenson, Walter Berry, E. M. Forster, William Gerhardie, Kenneth Clark, Percy Lubbock, and members of the Tyler family. Includes correspondence of Elisina Royall Tyler, her husband, and their son William Royall Tyler and material that Elisina Tyler collected for a biography of Wharton. R. W. B. Lewis used some of the items in the collection for his *Edith Wharton: A Biography.*

4,492. Committee on Environmental Information
Oral history. 1972-73. 5 tapes and ca. 125 pp. of transcripts.
Open. Unpublished guide.
Indiana University Oral History Research Project.
Interview with Virginia Brodine, one of the Committee's founders. Formerly a labor journalist working for the International Ladies' Garment Workers' Union, Brodine became interested in testing milk for strontium 90 because of her concern about nuclear fallout. She was editor of *Environment* magazine and its two predecessor publications from 1962 to 1969. Since 1969 she has been consulting editor of the magazine.

4,493. Douglas, Melvyn
Oral history. 1972-75. 107 tapes and ca. 3252 pp. of transcripts.
Closed. Unpublished guide.
Indiana University Oral History Research Project.
Biography of Douglas and his acting and political careers through interviews with Douglas, his professional associates, and his friends. Includes interviews with Douglas's wife Helen (Gahagan) Douglas, who is a politician, actress, and singer; Susie Clifton, who has been active in California politics since Upton Sinclair's campaign in 1934; and Selma Hirsh, an administrative assistant in the Office of Civilian Defense during WWII. Hirsh is now associate director of the American Jewish Committee. The women discuss their own careers and their association with Melvyn Douglas.

4,494. History of Indiana University
Oral history. 1968-71. 110 tapes and ca. 2200 pp. of transcripts.
Open. Unpublished guide.
Indiana University Oral History Research Project.
Includes interviews with six women associated with Indiana University during the administrations of University presidents William Lowe Bryan and Herman Wells. The women interviewed were Ivy Leone Chamness, an editor for Indiana University publications; Dorothy Collins, a research and editorial associate for the Institute for Sex Research; Ruth J. McNutt, former secretary to William Lowe Bryan; Mary Rieman Maurer, member of the University's board of trustees from 1945 to 1963; Kate Mueller, dean of women at the University; and Alice Nelson, a former director of the University's residence halls.

4,495. Media-Related Perceptions of Contemporary Problems
Oral history. 1975. 20 tapes and ca. 500 pp. of transcripts.
Closed. Unpublished guide.
Indiana University Oral History Research Project.
Includes interviews with five retired professional women: Theodora Allen and Sada Murayama, who were social workers; Elizabeth Cleland, a chemist and homemaker; Agnes Newton, a teacher and homemaker; and Eunice Roberts, an administrator who was involved in women's education and women's rights at Indiana University. The women discuss current events and their relationship to them. They also discuss their careers and their activities since their retirement.

CRAWFORDSVILLE

4,496. Holloway, Mary M.
Papers. 1855-56. 2 items.
Open. No guide.
Wabash College Library.
Holloway (1831-92) worked her way through Penn Medical College in Philadelphia and returned to Crawfordsville to become one of the first women to practice medicine in Indiana. Her two letters to her father describe her dedication, her financial struggle, and her strong conviction that she should graduate to show people of the West that a woman could be a physician. Holloway later married E. A. Wilhite.

EVANSVILLE

4,497. East Central Province Archives
Records. 1633- . Ca. 102 boxes, 3 vols., and 6 tapes.
Open. No guide.
Daughters of Charity of St. Vincent de Paul, Mater Dei Provincial House.
Correspondence, conference material, biographies of deceased sisters, photos, a record of events, and other records of missions of the Province and of the Provincialate of this order of religious women.

4,498. American Association of University Women
Records. 1923- . 12 vols.
Open. Accession sheet.
Indiana State University, Evansville Campus Library, Special Collections and University Archives.
Minutes, official records, and scrapbooks of the Evansville branch of the AAUW, which was founded in 1923.

4,499. Raintree Girl Scout Council
Records. 1931-74. 9 Hollinger boxes.
Open. Accession sheet.
Indiana State University, Evansville Campus Library, Special Collections and University Archives.
The Raintree Council, established in 1931, consists of Girl Scout groups in southern Indiana. Annual reports, minutes, ledgers, journals, reports, public relations pamphlets, and other records of Scout projects and programs.

4,500. Visiting Nurse Association of Southwestern Indiana
Records. 1926-71. 4 boxes.
Open. List.
Indiana State University, Evansville Campus Library, Special Collections and University Archives.
The Association, formed in 1926, provides nursing service outside the hospital for residents of a three-county area and home nursing care and rehabilitation for persons with acute or chronic illnesses. Scrapbooks and clippings reflect the Association's activities during the depression, following natural disasters such as the Ohio River flood in 1937, and during WWII.

4,501. Westwood Garden Club
Records. 1959- . 2 Hollinger boxes.
Open. List.
Indiana State University, Evansville Campus Library, Special Collections and University Archives.
The Club was founded in 1957 to promote gardening, to protect and conserve natural resources, and to improve the community's natural beauty. Scrapbooks and yearbooks provide information about such Club projects as highway beautification, a national award-winning nature trails project, and restoration of historic log buildings. These projects were undertaken on or near the Indiana State University, Evansville campus.

4,502. Women Community Leaders
Collection. Nd. Ca. 100 items.
Open. List and card file.
Indiana State University, Evansville Campus Library, Special Collections and University Archives.
Consists of questionnaires containing information about women selected as community leaders by members of their own organizations. The project began as a bicentennial project under the sponsorship of the Southern Indiana Status of Women Association; it is being continued.

4,503. Archives
Records. 1875- . 38 boxes and 6 vols.
Closed. No guide.
Monastery of St. Clare.
Financial records, annals, correspondence, a biography of the foundress, a necrology, and other records of the Monastery. Residents of the Monastery are members of the Order of St. Clare, a contemplative order of women founded in 1897 in Evansville.

4,504. Clifford, Emily (Orr)
Papers. 1940-73. 1 Hollinger box.
Open. Unpublished guide.
University of Evansville Archives.
A housewife and civic leader in education history and the arts, [Mrs. George S.] Clifford (1866-1952) was the first woman trustee of Evansville College, now the University of Evansville. Correspondence, her unpublished manuscript concerning philanthrophy in early Evansville, an article she wrote for *Wellesley Magazine* (December 1946) concerning Wellesley in the 1800s, an unpublished autobiography, photos, memorial items, a citation received on presentation of an honorary degree, and other items.

4,505. Faculty Dames of Evansville College
Records. 1919-74. 1 Hollinger box.
Open. Unpublished guide.
University of Evansville Archives.
Constitution, minutes, correspondence, membership lists, programs, and clippings of this group of women who were faculty members or the wives or widows of faculty members at Evansville College, now the University of Evansville. The organization was formed in 1919. The group became Faculty Dames of the University of Evansville in 1967, reflecting the changed name of the University.

4,506. Keena, Ruth (Watkins)
Papers. 1914-77. 20 pp.
Open. Unpublished guide.
University of Evansville Archives.
A doctor of osteopathy for 50 years in Greeley, CO, [Mrs. E. E.] Keena (1892-) was a founder of the Memorial Osteopathic Hospital; she currently is a trustee of the Hospital. Correspondence, her unpublished reminiscence of her life at Moores Hill College, in Moores Hill, IN, and an unpublished manuscript concerning George Washington and Abraham Lincoln. Keena also helped establish a children's cerebral palsy center.

4,507. Smith, Susie (King)
Papers. 1916-76. 1 folder.
Open. Unpublished guide.
University of Evansville Archives.
[Mrs. O. A.] Smith (1904-) is a housewife, world traveler, and writer. Correspondence, photos, clippings, and her unpublished reminiscences about her life as a student at Moores Hill College in Moores Hill, IN. Her father served as the school's president from 1912 to 1916.

4,508. Johnston and Bacon
Papers. 1879-1931. 3 Hollinger boxes.
Open. Inventory.
Willard Library of Evansville.
Annie (Fellows) Johnston (1863-1931), author of the Little Colonel and the Mary Ware books, and Albion (Fellows) Bacon (1865-1933), an urban reformer, were sisters who were born near Evansville. Correspondence between the sisters and members of their families, business correspondence, diary, speeches, poems, articles, minutes and a report of the Indiana Housing Association, photos, pageants, music, paper dolls, clothes, and other items.

Annie Fellows's first poem was published when she was 16. She married her cousin William L. Johnston (?-1892), a widower with three children. After her husband's death, she concentrated on writing. Her Little Colonel books grew from her experiences in Peewee Valley, KY, where she met an old Confederate colonel and his granddaughter who imitated him. The granddaughter was the model for the heroine of the Little Colonel books

Albion Fellows married Hilary Edwin Bacon, an Evansville banker, and volunteered to serve on a local sanitation committee after her four children contracted scarlet fever. She later became interested in various urban reform activities, which led to her leadership in securing laws to regulate multi-family dwellings in the state of Indiana

FERDINAND

4,509. Archives
Records. 1867- . Ca. 12 boxes, 50 vols., and 200 tapes.
Closed. No guide.
Sisters of St. Benedict, Convent Immaculate Conception.
The Sisters are engaged primarily in education, but they are also involved in social work, hospital work, and foreign missions. The Convent was founded in 1867. Financial records, manuscripts, correspondence, oral history tapes, papers of the incumbent prioress and of individual members, biographical information and personal data sheets on women who have become members of the order, photos, and scrapbooks. Also includes material about St. Benedict College of Ferdinand; Academy Immaculate Conception, which is now called Marian Heights Academy; and other schools staffed by the Sisters.

FORT WAYNE

4,510. Jewish Women in Indiana
Collection. Nd. No size given.
Open. No guide.
Indiana Jewish Historical Society.
Records of Congregational Sisterhoods, Indiana branches of the National Council of Jewish Women, ladies aid societies, and other groups. Also contains papers of individual women, including [Miss] Minnette Baum, a pioneer social worker in Fort Wayne and a Zionist leader who worked in Israel and America.

4,511. Lincoln Family
Collection. Nd. Ca. 250 items.
Open. Unpublished guide.
Lincoln Library and Museum.
Correspondence, photos, articles, books, and other items center around Mary (Todd) [Mrs. Abraham] Lincoln (1818-82) and her son Robert Todd Lincoln (1843-1926). Also includes correspondence and documents signed by other Lincoln family members.

FRANKLIN

4,512. Baptist Women's Missionary Society
Records. Ca. 1870- . Ca. 1 ft.
Open. No guide.
Franklin College Library.
Women of Regular, or Missionary, Baptist churches organized themselves into societies to provide support for the church's missionary outreach programs. Yearbooks of Indiana Baptist Women's Missionary Society groups after 1914, programs and related material from Indiana Baptist Women's Summer Conferences after 1940, association and state reports, and state newspapers containing reports about women's missionary work.

GOSHEN

4,513. Kauffman, Christmas Carol
Papers. Nd. 15 in.
Open. Catalog card.
Archives of the Mennonite Church.
Kauffman (1901-69) was a writer of novels and short stories as well as of articles for the *Youth's Christian Companion* and other Mennonite church periodicals. Correspondence, reviews, and notes for talks relating to her various books. Also includes a number of her articles for the *Companion*. Her husband Nelson E. Kauffman (1904-), a minister and bishop at Hannibal, MO, served for many years as president of the Mennonite Board of Education.

4,514. Mennonite Board of Missions
Records. 1881- . Ca. 400 ft.
Open. Inventory.
Archives of the Mennonite Church.
Constitution, minutes, executive committee records, treasurer's records, correspondence, and other records of the Board, which was formed in 1906 as the Mennonite Board of Missions and Charities, and of its predecessor organizations. Includes records of the Board's committees, which dealt with such subject areas as health and welfare, evangelism, and home and overseas missions; correspondence of various women missionaries; and records of the Women's Missionary and Service Commission, which was founded in 1915 by Clara (Eby) Steiner as the Mennonite Woman's Missionary Society. The name of the women's organization was changed to Women's Missionary Committee in 1929, the Women's Missionary Sewing Circle Organization in 1947, and the Women's Missionary and Service Auxiliary in 1955; the current name was adopted in 1971. Mennonite women began meeting in ca. 1894 to sew for mission stations and the poor in their communities. The original purpose of the Mennonite Woman's Missionary Society was to sew for home and foreign missions, to raise money for missionary purposes, to study and discuss missionary books, and to send out and support women foreign missionaries.

4,515. Ressler
Papers. Ca. 1895-1945. Ca. 35 ft.
Open. Inventory and catalog card.
Archives of the Mennonite Church.
Correspondence and other papers of Jacob Andrew Ressler (1867-1936), a missionary to India, and Lina (Zook) Ressler (1869-1948), a missionary and editor whom he married in 1903. The Resslers served together as missionaries in India from 1903 to 1908. Lina Ressler's correspondence dates primarily from before her marriage, much of it from the period when she was a missionary at the Chicago Home Mission, a city mission run by the Mennonite Church. Her papers also include items relating to her work as editor at the Mennonite Publishing House in Scottdale, PA; known as "Aunt Lina," she worked principally on children's periodicals. In 1930 she became president of the Women's Missionary and Service Auxiliary.

4,516. Slagel, Vesta (Zook)
Papers. 1921-23. 3 in.
Open. Catalog card.
Archives of the Mennonite Church.
Correspondence, speech notes, reports, articles, and photos relate to the service of Slagel (1891-), who then was Vesta Zook, as a Mennonite church relief worker in Constantinople, where she directed a children's home. Also contains the diary she kept while crossing the ocean. Before serving as a relief worker, Zook was a professor and dean of women at Goshen College in Goshen. She later married Arthur Slagel, a fellow relief worker.

4,517. Steiner, Clara (Eby)
Papers. 1894-1928. 12 in.
Open. Inventory and catalog card.
Archives of the Mennonite Church.
Correspondence and diaries of [Mrs. Menno] Steiner (1873-1929), organizer and first president of the Mennonite Woman's Missionary Society. Consists principally of correspondence with the Society's executive committee and district secretaries but also includes responses from women's organizations of other religious denominations to her requests for information about their activities. Steiner felt that Mennonite women's organizations could raise money to support missionary activities as well as sewing garments for home and foreign missionaries. She hoped that the women of the local churches, cooperating through the Mennonite Mission Board, could send out and support women foreign missionaries. Steiner's husband established the first Mennonite home mission in Chicago in 1893; Clara Steiner worked at the mission for a year after their marriage in 1894.

GREENCASTLE

4,518. Adams, Marie
Papers. Nd. 1 document case.
Open. List.
Archives of DePauw University and Indiana United Methodism.
Correspondence, autobiographical sketch, manuscripts, photos, clippings, and books of Adams (1890-), a missionary to China. Includes material about cave temples and Peking and her "Leaves from a war prisoner's devotional diary."

4,519. Alvord, Katherine Sprague
Papers. 1915-59. 1 document case.
Open. Typed page.
Archives of DePauw University and Indiana United Methodism.
Correspondence, addresses, articles, alumni newsletter, clippings, and obituaries of Alvord (1871-1959), dean of women at DePauw.

4,520. Beard, Mary (Ritter)
Papers. Nd. 6 folders.
Open. List.
Archives of DePauw University and Indiana United Methodism.
Correspondence, research notes, cards, list of honorary degree recipients at DePauw in 1933, clippings, and articles written by Beard (1876-1958), a writer and historian.

4,521. Caldwell, Sallie (Bowman)
Papers. 1881-1948. 2 file folders.
Open. No guide.
Archives of DePauw University and Indiana United Methodism.
Letters and clippings of Caldwell (1863-1948), daughter of former DePauw president Bishop Thomas Bowman.

4,522. Cammack, Eleanore
Papers. 1922-72. 4 document cases.
Open. Register.
Archives of DePauw University and Indiana United Methodism.
Correspondence, diaries, college notebooks, genealogical material, report cards, photos, clippings, and other papers of [Miss] Cammack (1906-), order librarian at Purdue University and later archivist at DePauw.

4,523. Cooper, Vera Southwick
Papers. 1903-56. 2 document cases.
Open. Register.
Archives of DePauw University and Indiana United Methodism.
Correspondence, provisions from various wills, minutes, budgets, pensions, library accounts and bills, preliminary plans for new library, applications, surveys, US Navy report, and bookplates of Cooper (1890-), head librarian at DePauw.

4,524. Delta Zeta Sorority
Records. 1934-56. 1 document case.
Open. Register.
Archives of DePauw University and Indiana United Methodism.
History, newsletters and reports, Alumnae Club minute book, alumnae programs, manual, clippings, and other records of the sorority's local chapter founded in 1910.

4,525. Dimmitt, Marjorie Alma
Papers. 1920-65. 2 document cases.
Open. Register.
Archives of DePauw University and Indiana United Methodism.
Dimmitt (1895-1965) was a Methodist missionary to India. Correspondence she wrote to her parents and siblings while she was traveling to and from India and while she was on the subcontinent, articles she wrote for the Isabella Thoburn College, and her master's thesis.

4,526. Gaston, Marjorie
Papers. 1916-62. 2 document cases.
Open. Register.
Archives of DePauw University and Indiana United Methodism.
Letters, diaries, musical scores, programs of recitals, and clippings of Gaston (1906-74), a music teacher and writer.

4,527. Gilmore, Eugene Allen
Papers. 1968. 2 items.
Open. Register.
Archives of DePauw University and Indiana United Methodism.
Correspondence of Blanche Basye Gilmore, an 1896 graduate of DePauw, who was married to Eugene Gilmore (1873-1970), a teacher.

4,528. Gilmore, Margaret B.
Papers. 1856-1949. 1 document case.
Open. Register.
Archives of DePauw University and Indiana United Methodism.
[Miss] Gilmore (1869-1946) was a teacher and librarian. Family correspondence, genealogy, rental agreement, Columbia University certificate, marriage license, notes from the Central National Bank, clippings, obituaries, and memorial service program.

4,529. Greene, Lily Dexter
Papers. 1921-42. 1 document case.
Open. Register.
Archives of DePauw University and Indiana United Methodism.
Letters, diary, and biography of Greene (1868-1942), a Methodist missionary in Lahore, India.

4,530. Howard, Liliane Stevens
Papers. 1895-1967. 1 document case.
Open. Register.
Archives of DePauw University and Indiana United Methodism.
[Miss] Howard (1872-1967) was a writer who used the pseudonym Sarah Curtis Mott.
Correspondence, autobiographical sketch, printed articles by Howard, and other papers.
Correspondents include [Miss] Eleanore Cammack, former archivist at DePauw, and John Clark Ridpath.

4,531. Knowlton, Audrey
Papers. 1930-70. 1 document case.
Open. Register.
Archives of DePauw University and Indiana United Methodism.
Bibliographies, conference and workshop material, and folders concerning reference questions received by Knowlton (1904-), a reference librarian.

4,532. Longden, Hazel Day
Papers. 1916-60. 1 document case.
Open. Register.
Archives of DePauw University and Indiana United Methodism.
[Mrs. Grafton J.] Longden is a homemaker. Correspondence, including letters from Marie Adams, a missionary in China and Japan; Ruth McCullough Mack, a 1929 DePauw graduate who lived in China and married a Chinese native; Ellen Studley, a 1921 DePauw graduate and missionary to China; and Marjorie Dimmitt, a 1917 DePauw graduate and missionary to India. Also contains papers written by Longden; articles by Mary Weik, a 1918 DePauw graduate; clippings regarding missionaries and the deaths of DePauw graduates; and program books for Delta Kappa Gamma, the DePauw Women's Club, Over the Tea Cups, and the Progress History Club.

4,533. Mansfield, Belle Aurelia Babb
Papers. Nd. 1 folder.
Open. No guide.
Archives of DePauw University and Indiana United Methodism.
Articles about [Mrs. John Melvin] Mansfield (1846-1911), an educator who in 1871 became the first woman admitted to the bar in the US.

4,534. Ridpath, Martha Jane
Papers. 1879-1926. 1 document case.
Open. Register.
Archives of DePauw University and Indiana United Methodism.
Correspondence, addresses and club speeches, programs, and clippings of [Miss] Ridpath (1855-1926), an educator.

4,535. Royse, Mintie Allen
Papers. 1832-1940. 1 document case.
Open. Manuscript.
Archives of DePauw University and Indiana United Methodism.
Correspondence, diary, genealogy, programs, clippings, and other material of Royse (1872-1963), an educator.

4,536. Schlemmer, Hildegarde
Papers. 1893-1933. 1 document case.
Open. Register.
Archives of DePauw University and Indiana United Methodism.
Correspondence, pamphlets, and clippings of Schlemmer (1893-), a missionary in India. Includes letters from Marie Church in Korea.

4,537. Tarbell, Martha
Papers. 1897-1928. 1 document case.
Open. Register.
Archives of DePauw University and Indiana United Methodism.
Doctoral thesis, typed manuscript, booklets, and clippings of Tarbell (1862-1948), an author.

4,538. Walker, Mary Florence (Morrison)
Papers. 1877-1921. No size given.
Access restricted. Register.
Archives of DePauw University and Indiana United Methodism.
Walker (1850-1921) was a missionary with her husband Wilbur Fisk Walker. Her autobiographical sketch, journal with entries to 1881, an 1877 letter from Mary Walker to the Greencastle *Banner,* and a memorial for her.

4,539. Welch, Winona Hazel
Papers. 1914-76. 12 document cases.
Open. Register.

Archives of DePauw University and Indiana United Methodism.
Welch (1896-) is a botanist, professor, and author. Correspondence, speeches, books and scholarly articles, biographical sketches, scrapbooks, clippings, and material pertaining to her work in the DAR and in various professional organizations.

4,540. Wesleyan Service Guild
Records. Nd. No size given.
Open. Unpublished guide.
Archives of DePauw University and Indiana United Methodism.
Minutes, financial records, correspondence, yearbooks, and programs of a working women's group of the Methodist Church in Indiana.

4,541. Woman's Foreign Missionary Society
Records. Nd. No size given.
Open. Register.
Archives of DePauw University and Indiana United Methodism.
Minutes, financial records, correspondence, yearbooks, and programs of this Indiana Methodist Episcopal Church woman's group.

4,542. Woman's Home Missionary Society
Records. Nd. No size given.
Open. Register.
Archives of DePauw University and Indiana United Methodism.
Minutes, financial records, correspondence, yearbooks, and programs of this state-level Methodist Episcopal Church woman's group.

4,543. Woman's Society of Christian Service of the Methodist Church
Records. Nd. No size given.
Open. Register.
Archives of DePauw University and Indiana United Methodism.
Minutes, financial records, correspondence, yearbooks, and programs of the state-level unit of this Methodist Church woman's group.

4,544. Woman's Society of World Service, Evangelical United Brethren Church
Records. ?-1968. No size given.
Open. Registers.
Archives of DePauw University and Indiana United Methodism.
Minutes, financial records, correspondence, yearbooks, and programs of this state-level Evangelical United Brethren Church woman's group.

4,545. Women's Missionary Association
Records. ?-1968. No size given.
Open. Unpublished guide.
Archives of DePauw University and Indiana United Methodism.
Minutes, financial records, correspondence, yearbooks, and programs of the state-level unit of this United Brethren Church in Christ woman's group.

4,546. Aftermath Club
Records. 1897-1900. 1 folder.
Open. No guide.
Putnam County Historical Society.
Program books of a local women's literary club.

4,547. American Association of University Women
Records. 1936-74. 2 document cases.
Open. No guide.
Putnam County Historical Society.
Minutes, correspondence, reports, and programs of this AAUW chapter, which was formed in 1917. The chapter has been discontinued.

4,548. Beechwood Pleasant Circle
Records. 1903-71. 1 folder.
Open. No guide.
Putnam County Historical Society.
Program books dating from 1903 to 1963 and a 1971 clipping of this women's organization, the primary activities of which were handwork projects, such as knitting, tatting, and embroidery. During the club's early years, members discussed literary topics.

4,549. Boston Club
Records. 1899-1976. 1 folder.
Open. No guide.
Putnam County Historical Society.
Program books and a history of this local group, which was formed by eight Greencastle women in 1899 while they were on vacation in Boston. The group's purpose was cultural and educational development.

4,550. Business and Professional Women
Records. 1925- . 2 document cases.
Closed. No guide.
Putnam County Historical Society.
Minutes, financial records, program books, and scrapbooks of the County chapter, founded in 1925, of the national organization.

4,551. Chaminade Music Club
Records. 1910-12. 1 folder.
Open. No guide.
Putnam County Historical Society.
Program books.

4,552. Colonial Dames, Sir John Ogle Chapter of Colonial Dames of the 17th Century
Records. 1970. 1 item.
Open. No guide.
Putnam County Historical Society.
Clipping concerning the Putnam County Chapter, which was formed in 1970.

4,553. Coterie
Records. 1907-50. 1 folder.
Open. No guide.
Putnam County Historical Society.
Two programs dated 1907-08 and 1919-20 and one clipping of this local literary club, which was founded in 1895 by ladies of the Presbyterian church.

4,554. Council of Clubs
Records. 1929-59. 2 vols.
Open. No guide.
Putnam County Historical Society.
Volumes of minutes of this county-wide organization.

4,555. Country Reading Club
Records. 1895-1971. 1 box and 1 folder.
Open. No guide.
Putnam County Historical Society.
Minute and treasurers' books, a Club history, programs, clippings, and other records of the Club, which was founded by 10 ladies in 1895.

4,556. Crescent Club
Records. 1947-76. 1 folder.
Open. No guide.
Putnam County Historical Society.
The Club was a literary society formed in 1897 in Greencastle. A 1976 program book and clippings.

4,557. Daughters of the American Revolution
Records. Nd. 2 document cases and 7 vols.
Closed. No guide.
Putnam County Historical Society.
Speeches, photos, scrapbooks, books, and other records of the Washburn DAR chapter, which was formed in Greencastle in 1903.

4,558. Daughters of 1812
Records. Nd. 1 document case.
Closed. No guide.
Putnam County Historical Society.
The local chapter of the Daughters was founded in 1956. Charter and members' ancestral papers of the local chapter and a directory of the national group.

4,559. Delta Kappa Gamma, Epsilon Chapter
Records. 1960-66. 5 vols.
Open. No guide.
Putnam County Historical Society.
Yearbooks of the local chapter of this international teachers' sorority.

4,560. Domestic Science Club
Records. 1914-76. 1 folder.
Open. No guide.
Putnam County Historical Society.
Program books of this local group, which was founded in 1908.

4,561. Emera Club
Records. 1916- . 1 folder.
Open. No guide.
Putnam County Historical Society.
Programs of the Club, which is made up of women who are past matrons of Greencastle Chapter No. 255, Order of Eastern Star.

4,562. Federation of Clubs
Records. 1922-73. 1 folder.
Open. No guide.
Putnam County Historical Society.
Program books of this organization, which united clubs throughout Putnam County.

4,563. Fortnightly Club
Records. 1899-1970. 1 folder and 5 vols.
Open. No guide.
Putnam County Historical Society.
The Club, a literary society, was founded in 1895. Minute and program books, a history of the group, and clippings.

4,564. Girl Scouts Council
Records. 1935-73. 2 document cases and 1 vol.
Open. No guide.
Putnam County Historical Society.
Minutes, financial records, a scrapbook, and handbooks.

4,565. Home and Garden Club of Russellville
Records. 1935. 1 folder.
Open. No guide.
Putnam County Historical Society.
Program books of this Russellville, IN, group.

4,566. Home Demonstration Clubs
Records. Nd. 1 folder.
Open. No guide.
Putnam County Historical Society.
Program books of various home demonstration clubs in Putnam County.

4,567. Home Economics Clubs of Clinton and Madison Townships
Records. 1916-66. 1 folder.
Open. No guide.
Putnam County Historical Society.
Program books of the groups, which were organized in 1915.

4,568. League of Greencastle Literary Clubs
Records. 1897-1902. 1 vol.
Open. No guide.
Putnam County Historical Society.
Minutes.

4,569. League of Women Voters
Records. Nd. 1 folder.
Open. No guide.
Putnam County Historical Society.
Correspondence, brochures, and clippings of this LWV branch, which was formed in 1919.

4,570. Martha Washington Club
Records. 1919. 1 folder.
Open. No guide.
Putnam County Historical Society.
Clippings.

4,571. Modern Priscilla Club
Records. 1903-58. 9 vols.
Open. No guide.
Putnam County Historical Society.
Minutes of the Club, which was founded in 1903 in Greencastle.

4,572. Monday Club
Records. 1933-61. 1 folder.
Open. No guide.
Putnam County Historical Society.
Program books and clippings of this local women's group, which was formed before or during 1918. Programs included book reviews, historical discussions, and comments on homemaking topics.

4,573. Morning Musicale
Records. 1925-72. 1 folder.
Open. No guide.
Putnam County Historical Society.
Clippings concerning the Musicale, established in 1925 in Greencastle by women who wanted to broaden their own musical appreciation and that of their community.

4,574. Needlecraft Club
Records. 1920-62. 7 vols.
Open. No guide.
Putnam County Historical Society.
Minutes of this local group, which was formed in 1911 by women who wanted to share ideas about sewing, crocheting, and cooking.

4,575. Over The Tea Cups
Records. 1899-1968. 1 folder.
Open. No guide.
Putnam County Historical Society.
Program books of this club, which was organized in 1895 to promote discussion of current literature and sociability.

4,576. Penelope Club
Records. 1923-76. 1 folder.
Open. No guide.
Putnam County Historical Society.
Program books of the Club, which was organized in 1894 in Greencastle.

4,577. P.E.O. Sisterhood
Records. 1949-68. 1 folder.
Open. No guide.
Putnam County Historical Society.
Program books and clippings of the Greencastle P.E.O. chapter, which was formed in 1923. The national P.E.O. was founded in 1869 at Iowa Wesleyan College in Mount Pleasant, IA.

4,578. Philomath Club of Roachdale
Records. 1961. 1 folder.
Open. No guide.
Putnam County Historical Society.
Clipping concerning this Roachdale, IN, organization, which was founded before 1924.

4,579. Priscilla Club
Records. 1958-62. 1 vol. and ca. 3 items.
Open. No guide.
Putnam County Historical Society.
Volume of minutes and program books of this local group, which was established in 1902.

4,580. Progress History Club
Records. 1916-68. 1 folder.
Open. No guide.
Putnam County Historical Society.
The Club was founded in Greencastle in 1898. Program books, a notebook concerning the group's 70th anniversary, and clippings.

4,581. Putnam County Hospital Guild
Records. 1958-75. 1 folder.
Open. No guide.
Putnam County Historical Society.
Reports and newsletters of this county-wide organization, the members of which did volunteer work at the Hospital.

4,582. Thursday Reading Club
Records. 1940-76. 1 folder.
Open. No guide.
Putnam County Historical Society.
The Club was a social organization formed in 1920. Minutes, treasurers' books, and programs. The group's programs dealt with current events and book reviews.

4,583. Tuesday Reading Club
Records. 1898-1962. 1 folder and 4 vols.
Open. No guide.
Putnam County Historical Society.
Minutes, a history, programs, and clippings of this ongoing organization, which was formed in 1898 by the wives of prominent local business and professional men.

4,584. Twentieth Century Club
Records. 1900-21. 1 folder.
Open. No guide.
Putnam County Historical Society.
Programs of this local group, which was formed by 10 women in 1898, concern literary, musical, governmental, and international topics. The Club was active in civic affairs.

4,585. Veronica Club
Records. 1972. 1 folder.
Open. No guide.
Putnam County Historical Society.
Clipping concerning the history of this literary and sewing society, founded in 1901. The Club was the first group to do sewing for the Putnam County Hospital.

4,586. Woman's Club
Records. 1874-1974. 1 drawer.
Open. No guide.
Putnam County Historical Society.
The Club was a literary study group founded in Greencastle in 1874. Minutes, papers or programs given by members, a history of the organization, program books, and clippings.

4,587. Woman's Study Club
Records. 1926-61. 1 folder.
Open. No guide.
Putnam County Historical Society.
Programs of the Club, which was established in 1916 in Greencastle so that members could discuss book reviews and current events.

HOBART

4,588. American Association of University Women
Records. 1953- . 1 drawer.
Access restricted. No guide.
Hobart Historical Society, Pleak Library.
Minutes and scrapbooks of the Hobart branch of the AAUW. The local unit was formed in 1953.

4,589. Community History
Collection. 1830s- . 16 drawers and other items.
Open. Card catalog.
Hobart Historical Society, Pleak Library.
Memoirs, biographies, and other material concerning the history of Hobart. Contains information about women who contributed to the town's social, cultural, and educational development.

4,590. Hobart Garden Club
Records. 1931- . 2 drawers.
Access restricted. No guide.
Hobart Historical Society, Pleak Library.
Minutes and scrapbooks of this women's club, which was founded in 1931.

4,591. Hobart Woman's Club
Records. 1893- . 2 drawers.
Access restricted. No guide.
Hobart Historical Society, Pleak Library.
Minutes, financial records, and scrapbooks of the Club, which was founded in 1893 as the Hobart Woman's Reading Club.

4,592. Kappa Kappa Kappa
Records. 1950- . 2 drawers.
Access restricted. No guide.
Hobart Historical Society, Pleak Library.
Minutes, scrapbooks, yearbooks, and memorabilia of the Epsilon Zeta chapter of Kappa Kappa Kappa, a social and charitable woman's group. The Chapter was formed in 1950.

4,593. League of Women Voters
Records. 1938-69. 1 drawer.
Open. No guide.
Hobart Historical Society, Pleak Library.
Minutes, financial records, documents concerning studies made by the group, and scrapbooks of the local LWV, which was formed in 1938 and went out of existence in 1969.

HUNTINGTON

4,594. Huntington College Auxiliary
Records. 1904-72. 19 vols. and other items.
Open. Card catalog.
Huntington College Library.
Founded as the Central College Ladies Aid Society in 1903, the Auxiliary raises money to assist Huntington College. Minutes, financial records, and lists of officers and members. Cora [Mrs. F. A.] Loew was a leader of the organization. Central College became Huntington College in 1917.

4,595. Women's Organizations
Records. 1897-1935. 12 vols.
Open. Card catalog.
Huntington College Library.
Constitution, minutes, history, and photos of the Zetalethean Literary Society, which was formed in 1897 and continued through 1953 or 1954, and the YWCA, which was organized in about 1923 and continued through about 1963. The Zetalethean Society held weekly meetings that included training in parliamentary procedure, sponsored college activities, and gave programs for the public. The group's records date from 1897 to 1932. The YWCA, records for which date from 1932 to 1935, also held weekly meetings and sponsored activities; the group also conducted a retreat and gave a tea for mothers. Information about the two groups is included in the college paper, the *Huntingtonian,* and in the annual, the *Mnemosyne.*

4,596. Archives
Records. 1922- . 20 drawers and 31 shelves.
Access restricted. Unpublished guide.
Our Lady of Victory Missionary Sisters.
Members of this religious community of women, which was founded in 1922, are engaged in religious education, nursing, social work, and home and foreign missions. Manuscripts of constitutions, original instructions, correspondence of the founder and first members, diaries, work reports, manuscripts of books written by members, photos, and artifacts.

4,597. Women's Missionary Association of the Church of the United Brethren in Christ, Inc.
Records. 1891-1978. More than 12 vols. and ca. 32 items.
Open. Card catalog.
United Brethren Church Archives.
Annual reports and minutes of the general board and some local branches of the Society, which was founded in 1875 to support missionaries and missionary work. Also includes letters from women missionaries and photos. Society members edited about half of each issue of the *Missionary Monthly* from 1897 to 1954 and have continued to edit portions of the church paper. Cora [Mrs. F. A.] Loew, [Miss] M. M. Titus, and Mrs. Harry Harwood were among the groups's chief leaders.

INDIANAPOLIS

4,598. Butler Family
Papers. 1817-89. 4 in.
Open. Unpublished guide.
Christian Theological Seminary.
Correspondence; financial, church, and legal records; essays; speeches; notebook; plays; drawings; a broadside; and other papers of three generations of the family of Ovid Butler (1801-81), a prominent Indianapolis lawyer for whom Butler University was named. Includes a folder of plays, novels, and notes written by Butler's daughter Anne Butler. Ovid Butler was president of Butler University, formerly North West Christian University, for 20 years.

4,599. Madden
Papers. 1891-1946. 13.83 ft.
Open. Unpublished guide.
Christian Theological Seminary.
Maude (Whitmore) Madden (1867-1948) and her husband Milton B. Madden (1869-?) were missionaries in Japan. Correspondence, notes, manuscripts, photo albums, music, art work, time tables, tickets, clippings, newspapers, museum items, and other material written or collected by the Maddens while they were attending Bethany College in Bethany, WV; while they were missionaries in Japan; and while they were living in the western US. Also contains papers of the Maddens' daughter Grace (Madden) Braley. During her early years in the mission field, Maude Madden was a "living link" missionary of the Morganfield, KY, Christian Church. She served with her husband in Tokyo from 1895 to 1897, in Fukushima from 1897 to 1898, and in Sendai from 1898 to 1914. Their work was under the auspices of the United Christian Missionary Society. During WWI the Maddens lived in the US, but they returned to Japan as independent workers in 1919. They came back to the US just before WWII and settled in Washington state where they worked for Christian churches. Maude Madden died in Seattle.

4,600. Price, Mrs. E. J.
Papers. 1878-89. 1 in.
Open. Card catalog.
Christian Theological Seminary.
Price (ca. 1828-?) taught in the primary school of North West Christian University; in 1870 she was principal of the University's academy. Consists of a diary in which she records her trips to Europe in 1878 and 1889, to Scotland in 1881, and in the US and Canada in 1883, 1887, and 1888.

4,601. Tibbets, Mary Ann
Papers. 1857-96. 2 in.
Open. Unpublished guide.
Christian Theological Seminary.
An author and teacher, [Mrs.] Tibbets (1819-96) participated in the work of the underground railroad during the Civil War. Scrapbook contains religious articles and poems by Tibbets, two obituaries of Tibbets, and an inscription she wrote for her children. Raised a Methodist, Tibbets later became a Baptist. She died in Volga, IN.

4,602. Fletcher, Emily (Beeler)
Papers. 1863-1901. 3 microfilm reels.
Open. List.
Indiana Historical Society Library.
Diaries of Fletcher (1838-1910), the wife of Calvin Fletcher, Jr., and of her daughters Emily Fletcher (185?-1927) and Sarah Hill Fletcher (1854-?). Diaries of Emily (Beeler) Fletcher and [Miss] Emily Fletcher were written in Indianapolis and in Spencer, IN; also includes original poems written by [Miss] Fletcher. The diaries of Sarah Hill Fletcher date from 1863 to 1877.

4,603. Fletcher, Sarah (Hill)
Papers. 1821-38. 1 vol. and other items.
Open. Unpublished guide.
Indiana Historical Society Library.
Fletcher (1801-54) moved to Indianapolis from Urbana, OH, in 1821 with her husband Calvin Fletcher (?-1866), a lawyer, banker, philanthropist, farmer, and ardent antislavery worker who was away from home for long periods. Her diary covers the period during which eight of her 11 children were born and includes information about her reading and self-improvement, home duties, and social life. Also includes some correspondence. Sarah Fletcher's diary has been published in Gayle Thornbrough, ed., *The Diary of Calvin Fletcher, Including Letters of Calvin Fletcher and Diaries and Letters of His Wife, Sarah Hill Fletcher,* vol. I (Indianapolis: Indiana Historical Society, 1972).

4,604. Henderson, Sarah E.
Papers. 1843-45. 34-page vol.
Open. List.
Indiana Historical Society Library.
Diary in which [Miss] Henderson recorded her daily activities as a teacher at St. Mary's Seminary, an Episcopal school in Indianapolis. She also wrote about a trip from her home in Granville, OH, to Indianapolis and back again.

4,605. Holloway, Emma G.
Papers. 1921-49. 64 items.
Partially restricted. List.
Indiana Historical Society Library.
Holloway was a physician at the School for Feeble-Minded Youth in Fort Wayne, IN, from about 1930 to 1935. Papers reflect her professional activities and her participation in the WCTU.

4,606. Hopkins, Martha (Ellis)
Papers. 1914-52. 1 box and 2 packages.
Open. List and manuscript catalog.
Indiana Historical Society Library.
[Mrs. Arthur Herbert] Hopkins (1870-1959) was an active Republican party worker in Jasper County, IN. Correspondence, poll books, broadsides, clippings, printed items, and campaign buttons relating to her political work.

4,607. Humphrey, Margaret
Papers. 1869-72. 1 vol.
Open. Catalog card and partial transcript.
Indiana Historical Society Library.
Diary of [Miss] Humphrey, a young woman who lived with her parents on a southern Indiana farm, reflects her unhappiness with her situation. She found farm life in Switzerland County dull, and the entries indicate that she apparently saw no escape from her unhappiness. She later married Rosman White.

4,608. Judah-Brandon
Papers. 1820-1950. 6 ft.
Open. Unpublished guide.
Indiana Historical Society Library.
Family correspondence and papers include correspondence of Mary (Jameson) [Mrs. John M.] Judah (1851-1930), who lived in Memphis from 1887 to 1900, and her mother Marie Butler [Mrs. Patrick] Jameson (1831-?), who lived in Indianapolis. The letters contain descriptions of social life in the two cities.

4,609. Meredith, Virginia (Claypool)
Papers. 1890-93. 12 items.
Open. List.
Indiana Historical Society Library.
Papers of [Mrs. Henry Clay] Meredith record her activities as chairman of the committee of awards of the board of lady managers of the world's Columbian Commission.

4,610. Morris, Gulielma (Trueblood)
Papers. 1869-75. 2 vols.
Open. Resum|e01.
Indiana Historical Society Library.
[Mrs. Thomas] Morris (1810-89) was a homemaker on a Washington County, IN, farm. Her diaries reflect her feelings about farm life and provide information about such activities as spinning, weaving, quilting, and the gathering and treating of flax.

4,611. Robertson, Carrie Francis (Weed)
Papers. 1890-1929. 26 vols.
Open. List.
Indiana Historical Society Library.
Journals of [Mrs. Alexander M.] Robertson (1852-1941) contain impressions of life abroad, which she recorded during her worldwide travels.

4,612. Scritchfield, Bessie Belle
Papers. 1920-23. 135 items.
Open. Unpublished guide.
Indiana Historical Society Library.
Letters from Scritchfield to her parents Mr. and Mrs. C. H. Scritchfield of Lowell, IN, serve as a diary of her life as a student at Indiana University.

4,613. Stow, Catharine, and Stow, Viola A.
Papers. 1854-62. 2 vols.
Open. Card catalog and partial transcripts.
Indiana Historical Society Library.
Diaries of Catharine [Mrs. Uzziel H.] Stow, a farmer's wife, and her daughter Viola Stow, a schoolteacher, record their activities in Switzerland County in southern Indiana. Catharine Stow's diary was dated 1854, while Viola Stow kept her diary in 1862. Viola Stow later married Francis R. Dufour.

4,614. Thomas, Anne (Butler)
Papers. 1880-1925. 9 vols.
Open. Catalog card and list.
Indiana Historical Society Library.
[Mrs. David Owen] Thomas was the daughter of Ovid Butler, an Indianapolis businessman for whom Butler University was named. Two letter books, six diaries, and a manuscript, which deals with her trip to Japan, India, and Ceylon in 1924 and 1925. The letter books were written in Indianapolis, while the diaries were written at Indianapolis, Vassar College, and Martha's Vineyard, MA.

4,615. Wallace, Lew
Papers. 1799-1923. 9 ft.
Open. Unpublished guide.
Indiana Historical Society Library.
Correspondence and other papers of Wallace (1827-1905), an author, soldier, territorial governor, and US minister to Turkey, and his wife Susan Arnold (Elston) Wallace (1830-1907), an author of novels and articles, who acted as an editor and critic for her husband's writings. The Wallaces were married in 1852. Lew Wallace served in the armed forces during the Mexican War and the Civil War and was governor of New Mexico Territory from 1878 to 1881; from 1881 to 1885 he was minister to Turkey. Susan Wallace traveled with her husband to New Mexico and Turkey; during the rest of the period she lived in her native

city Crawfordsville, IN. Her correspondence includes Civil War letters. Lew Wallace was the author of *Ben Hur.*

4,616. Woman's Christian Temperance Union
Records. 1892-1926. 36 pp. and 1 microfilm reel.
Open. Card catalog.
Indiana Historical Society Library.
Minutes of the Moorefield, IN, branch of the WCTU, 1892-94, and of the South Side WCTU of Wabash, IN, 1912-26.

4,617. Woman's Relief Corps, Winchester, No. 46
Records. 1895-1920. 1 folder.
Open. Catalog card.
Indiana Historical Society Library.
Quarterly reports and printed forms of this Winchester, IN, branch of the Corps.

4,618. Woman's Suffrage Association of Indiana
Records. 1851-81. 1 vol.
Open. Catalog card.
Indiana Historical Society Library.
Constitution and preamble of the Woman's Rights Association of Indiana, which became the Woman's Suffrage Association of Indiana in 1869; minutes from 1851 to 1859 and from 1869 to 1881; and a treasurer's report, 1870.

4,619. Women's Organization for National Prohibition Reform
Records. 1931-33. 33 pp.
Open. Catalog card.
Indiana Historical Society Library.
Minutes and one report of the Marion County, IN, branch of the Organization. The report was written by Roberta W. Nicholson, the branch's executive secretary.

4,620. Baker, Ida Strawn
Papers. 1912-40. 1 Hollinger box.
Open. Card catalog.
Indiana State Library, Indiana Division.
[Mrs. Walter D.] Baker (1876-?) was an artist. Diaries for 1925, 1938, 1939, and 1940; sketchbooks dating from 1912 to 1922; and "Black Billy," a poem by Fay Strawn Campbell. Baker's 1925 diary was written during a trip to Europe; the other diaries concern business and social activities in Indianapolis.

4,621. Balz, Arcada (Stark)
Papers. 1928-68. 2 Hollinger boxes.
Open. Card catalog.
Indiana State Library, Indiana Division.
[Mrs. Fred G.] Balz was the first woman elected to the Indiana state senate. Correspondence, notebooks, information about Balz's family history, speeches, diplomas from the Indianapolis normal school and manual training high school, material on the Indiana Federation of Clubs, information on equal rights for women, and an article on the first women's clubs.

4,622. Bruner, Margaret (Baggerly)
Papers. 1919-71. 4 cu.ft.
Open. Inventory.
Indiana State Library, Indiana Division.
Born in Crawford County, IN, [Mrs. Vate] Bruner (1886-1971) was a poet and columnist. Personal correspondence; diaries; copies of poems, essays, short stories, and newspaper items; business papers; photos; poetry awards; a teachers license; a birth certificate; club membership cards; poetry magazines; and other papers. Bruner spent most of her life in New Castle, IN, where she wrote a weekly column for the New Castle *News Republican* from 1946 to 1970. She published 12 books of poetry, including *The Hill Road* (1932), *In Thoughtful Mood* (1937), *The Constant Heart* (1952), *Above Earth's Sorrow* (1955), and *Eternal Quest* (1968).

4,623. Clarke, Grace Giddings (Julian)
Papers. 1857-1936. 14 in.
Open. Card catalog.
Indiana State Library, Indiana Division.
[Mrs. Charles B.] Clarke (1865-1938) was president of the Indiana Federation of Women's Clubs from 1909 to 1911 and a director of the Woman's Franchise League, which led the suffrage movement in Indiana. Includes correspondence of Carrie Chapman Catt, president of the National American Woman Suffrage Association, regarding suffrage planks for the Democratic and Republican party platforms in 1916; correspondence of Susan B. Anthony concerning Indianapolis civic leader and suffragist May (Wright) Sewall and difficulties in the Indiana suffrage movement; and letters and programs concerning the Indiana Federation of Clubs, the GFWC, the Woman's Franchise League, and various peace organizations. Also includes letters concerning the national election in 1920, scrapbooks, and records of the Equal Suffrage Society of Indianapolis dating from 1878 to 1880. Clarke received her BA from Butler University in 1884. In 1910 she helped found the woman's school commissioner organization that helped win election of the first woman to the Indianapolis school board.

4,624. Coffin, Rhoda M. (Johnson)
Papers. 1902. 9 pp.
Open. Card catalog.
Indiana State Library, Indiana Division.
A prison reformer interested in prisoner rehabilitation, [Mrs. Charles F.] Coffin (1826-1909) was president of the governing board of Indiana's combined women's and girl's prison in Indianapolis and, with her husband, was a delegate to the International Congress for the Protection of Childhood. Manuscript describes the origin and operation of the new women's prison; it also contains information about Coffin's visits to Jeffersonville and Michigan City, IN, prisons in 1868, the new prison's opening in 1870, and the selection of Sarah J. Smith as the first superintendent.

4,625. Grow, Lottie (Lyons)
Papers. 1937-73. 1 Hollinger box and 2 vols.
Open. Card catalog.
Indiana State Library, Indiana Division.
An artist and high school teacher, [Mrs. Walter S.] Grow (1884-) sponsored a program to send art materials to South Pacific hospitals during WWII. Correspondence, miscellaneous papers, scrapbooks on Grow's career, and articles on Indiana artists, the Hoosier salon, the Woman's Department Club in Indianapolis, and the Indiana Federation of Clubs. Born in Sullivan, IN, Grow graduated from Central Normal College in 1904 and studied at the Art Institute of St. Louis, the Herron School of Art, and Marian College. Married in 1910, she and her husband were the parents of one daughter Bernadine. Lottie Grow taught high school in Hymera, IN, for five years. She wrote a column in *Art Digest* from 1938 to 1946 and for the magazine of the Indiana Federation of Women's Clubs from 1937 to 1944. She also exhibited her art work widely and won numerous awards.

4,626. Indiana League of Women Voters
Records. 1910- . Ca. 27 cu.ft. and 103 Hollinger boxes.
Open. No guide.
Indiana State Library, Indiana Division.
Minutes, a secretary's report, correspondence, research notes, a membership list, reports, publicity, broadsides, and pamphlets of the Indiana LWV and its predecessor the Woman's Franchise League. Initially called the Woman's School League of Indiana, the Franchise League was founded in Indianapolis in 1909 to secure the election of [Miss] Mary Nicholson to the city's school board. At first members sought suffrage for women in school elections. In 1911 they broadened their demand to include women's suffrage in all municipal elections and changed the organization's name to the Woman's Franchise League. By the end of the year, League members were committed to full women's suffrage. The group, which had 64 branches by 1914, planned and directed the suffrage campaign in Indiana. The bulk of the collection consists of LWV pamphlets and printed material.

4,627. Jenckes, Virginia Ellis
Papers. 1910-35. 4 Hollinger boxes.
Open. Inventory.
Indiana State Library, Indiana Division.
The first congresswoman from Indiana, Jenckes (1877-1963) became active in politics after her husband's death in 1921 left her sole manager of his elevator business and 1000 acres of Indiana farmland. Correspondence, speeches, photos, and campaign material. Jenckes was instrumental in creation of the Wabash-Maumee River Improvement Association, traveling to Washington, DC, to persuade officials to conduct a flood survey in the area. The Improvement Association gained passage of bond issues to build nine miles of flood control dikes. In 1932 Jenckes won election to the US House of Representatives as a Democrat from Indiana's 6th district, which included Terre Haute. She served until her defeat in 1938.

4,628. Johnston, Margaret Afflis
Papers. 1933-67. 4 cu.ft.
Open. Inventory.
Indiana State Library, Indiana Division.
Indiana state director of probation, Johnston (1907-67) was a member of the Indiana Women's Prison board for 15 years and a Democratic national committeewoman. Correspondence, case histories of women prisoners, psychological test reports of women prisoners, minutes and notes about meetings of the Indiana Women's Prison board of parole, appointment calendars, photos, copies of legislation, post cards, and other papers. Johnston was a Democratic candidate for Congress from Indiana's 2nd district in the 1940s. She served as state director of probation during the administration of Governor Henry F. Schricker.

4,629. Morton, Blanche Liffick
Papers. 1917-66. 2 Hollinger boxes.
Open. Inventory and card catalog.
Indiana State Library, Indiana Division.
Morton was one of seven nurses, all graduates of the Union Hospital School of Nursing in Terre Haute, IN, who served with Unit I, a group of Indiana doctors and nurses who worked overseas during WWI. Correspondence; records of the Overseas Service League, which was an American National Red Cross organization made up of WWI nurses; a card file listing nurses and civilian employees of the Lilly Base Unit during WWI; pictures; a book entitled *Indiana Women in the World War;* magazines; and other items.

4,630. Pierce and Krull
Papers. 1834-1963. 8 cu.ft.
Open. Inventory and card catalog.
Indiana State Library, Indiana Division.
Theresa Vinton (Pierce) Krull (1877-1963) was an active Indianapolis clubwoman and lecturer. Correspondence, speeches, unpublished manuscripts, original music manuscripts, published music, programs, pamphlets, articles, and other papers. Included are clippings of Krull and her husband Frederic Krull, of her parents Mr. and Mrs. Henry Pierce, and of her grandfather Winslow S. Pierce. Also includes copies of her speeches and organizational material from the Woman's Press Club of Indiana, the Woman's Rotary Club, the Vassar College Associated Alumnae of Indiana, the Indiana Vassar Club, the AAUW, the GFWC, and the Indianapolis Woman's Club.

4,631. Sewall, May Eliza (Wright) Thompson
Papers. 1890-1920. 187 items.
Closed. No guide.
Indianapolis-Marion County Public Library.
Founder of the Girls' Classical School, [Mrs. Theodore Lovett] Sewall (1844-1920) was a leader in the woman's movement and was active in the International Council of Women, the National Council of Women, the National American Woman Suffrage Association, and other organizations. Among her correspondents were Anna Howard Shaw, Ruth (McEnery) Stuart, Maud Durbin Skinner, Margaret L. Selenka, Carrie (Lane) Chapman Catt, Rosika Schwimmer, Fanny Zampini Salazar, and Baroness Berthe von Suttner. Sewall was among the founders of the Indianapolis Woman's Club and the Contemporary Club.

4,632. Archives
Records. 1936- . No size given.
Access restricted. No guide.
Marian College Archives.
Marian College, a four-year liberal arts college in Indianapolis conducted by the Sisters of St. Francis, grew out of a normal school and junior college operated by the Sisters in Oldenburg. When it opened in 1937, the College admitted only women; it became coeducational in 1954. Minutes of the board of trustees, 1937-; minutes of the College council, standing committees, and the humanities division; official correspondence of presidents; yearly financial reports; speeches, news releases, and biographical material of presidents; dean's list; photos; yearly College catalogs and brochures; commencement programs; issues of the College newspaper *The Phoenix*, of the College yearbook *The Marian*, and of *The Marian College Magnet*; weekly calendars; dramatic, musical, and recital programs; clippings; student and faculty handbooks and directories; and information relating to accreditation, the faculty, campus ministry, the honors program, various departments, yearly enrollment, medical technology, and honorary degrees conferred.

The College provides programs in elementary and high school teacher training, special education, nursing, early childhood development, the Federal Aviation Administration, an English language school for foreigners, adult education, and associate degrees for military and civilian personnel at Fort Benjamin Harrison; information on these programs is contained in the Archives. Also included are records of the Alumni Association and the constitution, minutes, and other records of the Student Association.

4,633. Harrison, Caroline "Carrie" Lavinia (Scott)
Papers. 1825- . 2 boxes.
Closed. No guide.
President Benjamin Harrison Memorial Home.
Correspondence, notebook, photos, and artwork of Harrison (1832-92), the wife of President Benjamin Harrison, and of her mother, sisters, and daughter.

4,634. Archives
Records. 1922- . 15 ft., 2 drawers, and 2 tapes.
Access restricted. No guide.
Sisters of Our Lady of Mount Carmel, Carmelite Monastery.
Financial records, correspondence, papers by sisters, retreat notes, a history of the order, a custom book, photos, scrapbooks, books of chronicles, and other records of the community, which was founded in 1922 in New Albany, IN, and moved to Indianapolis in 1932. Includes correspondence and other records concerning the hospitality given Icelandic Carmelites during WWII.

LAFAYETTE

4,635. Gougar, Helen Mar (Jackson)
Papers. 1870-1907. 2 Hollinger boxes.
Open. No guide.
Tippecanoe County Historical Association.
[Mrs. John D.] Gougar (1843-1907) was a suffragist and a temperance orator. Correspondence, scrapbook containing clippings about Gougar's speeches, photos, a book, and a research paper about Gougar written by Mary Anthrop.

MUNCIE

4,636. Wakoski, Diane, and Waldman, Anne
Papers. 1968-69, nd. 5 items.
Open. Catalog cards.
Ball State University Library, Special Collections.
Two letters from Wakoski (1937-), a poet, to David Gitin and three undated versions of "Memorial Day" by poet Anne Waldman (1945-).

NEW HARMONY

4,637. Branigin and Owen
Papers. 1832-65. 1 vol. and 42 items.
Access restricted. Unpublished guide.
Workingmen's Institute Library.
Correspondence and journal of Mary Jane Robinson Owen (1813-71), the wife of Robert Dale Owen. She accompanied her husband to Europe during his ministry to Naples and spent time in Stuttgart, Germany, with her sister-in-law Jane Owen Fauntleroy.

4,638. Maclure and Fretageot
Papers. 1820-33. 409 items.
Open. No guide.
Workingmen's Institute Library.
Marie (Duclos) Fretageot (1783-1833), a Pestalozzian schoolmistress, was manager and agent for William Maclure's School of Industry in New Harmony. Correspondence between Fretageot and Maclure contains observations concerning the correspondents' lives in Paris; Alicante, Spain; Philadelphia; the British Isles; New Harmony; and Mexico.

NORTH MANCHESTER

4,639. Myers, Michaele "Mike"
Papers. 1924-74. Ca. 900 items.
Open. Unpublished guide.
Manchester College Library.
Myers (1924-74) acted with stock companies and in Broadway plays. Correspondence, biographical sketch and chronology, photos, scrapbook she kept as a teenager, rehearsal playscripts, programs, reviews, notices, playbills, and memorabilia document Myers's career, particularly the years from 1946 to 1973. Includes a letter from Dore Schary written about the time Myers played Eleanor Roosevelt in Schary's play *Sunrise at Campobello*. Myers never married.

NOTRE DAME

4,640. Wolff, Sister Madeleva
Papers. 1918-64. More than 200 items.
Open. Unpublished guide.
Saint Mary's College Archives.
A religious administrator and educator, writer, lecturer, and member of the Congregation of the Sisters of the Holy Cross, Wolff (1887-1964) was president of Saint Mary's College from 1934 until 1961. Correspondence; annual reports she wrote as president of the College; manuscripts, including one of her autobiography; addresses; citations for honorary degrees and other awards; pamphlets; book reviews; copies of Wolff's published poetry and prose; and other papers. Correspondence, principally literary in nature, includes criticism of other writers' work, advice to persons writing dissertations, and letters to other writers. Includes manuscripts by Thomas Merton, Barbara Ward, Clare (Boothe) Luce, Irene Dunne, and others. Wolff was the founder of the Graduate School of Sacred Theology, which was the first school in the US to offer the degree of PhD in religion to religious and laywomen. She was the fifth president of the Catholic Poetry Society of America. She also addressed the Pittsburgh Diocesan Council of Catholic Women, the Cincinnati chapter of Kappa Gamma Pi, the Catholic Library Association, and several conferences on Christian humanism at Asheville, NC.

4,641. Christian Family Movement
Records. Early 1940s- . 380 ft. and 650 tapes.
Open. Description and shelflist.
University of Notre Dame Archives.
Founded in 1943, the group includes Catholic married couples who, through a program of discussion and action, attempt to help families fulfill their responsibilities in the Catholic lay apostolate. Correspondence, committee reports, tape recordings, scrapbooks, newsletters, programs, and other records of CFM and affiliated organizations. Patricia (Caron) Crowley and her husband Patrick Crowley served as the group's executive secretaries for many years.

4,642. Dolan, Thomas F.
Papers. 1928-29. 2.5 in.
Open. No guide.
University of Notre Dame Archives.
Correspondence, a court transcript, pamphlets, and clippings pertain to the activities of [Mrs.] Neva (Millier) Moss, who was brought to trial in Clarendon, VA, in 1928 and then in Jeffersonville, IN, in 1929 for delivering public lectures that purported to expose abuses in Catholic convents.

4,643. Ewing Family
Papers. 1815-1905. 35.5 ft.
Open. Published guide.
University of Notre Dame Archives.
Correspondence, diaries, sermons, financial records, and legal papers of the family of Thomas Ewing, Sr. (1789-1871), an Ohio lawyer, US secretary of the interior, and US senator. Includes papers of Ewing's wife Maria (Boyle) Ewing (1801-64); his daughter Ellen (Ewing) [Mrs. William Tecumseh] Sherman (1824-88); his son's wife Maria Rebecca (Gillespie) Ewing (1828-?); and Maria Ewing's family, including her sister Eliza Maria Gillespie (1824-87), who became Mother Angela of the Congregation of Holy Cross, and her mother Madelin (Miers) Phelan. The papers of Thomas Ewing, Sr., are also available on microfilm. See *Guide to the Microfilm Edition of the Thomas Ewing, Sr., Papers* (Notre Dame: University of Notre Dame Archives, 1967).

4,644. Guiney, Louise Imogen
Papers. 1883-99. 2.5 in.
Open. Item list.
University of Notre Dame Archives.
Correspondence of Guiney (1861-1920), a poet and essayist, includes letters concerning her work for the *Boston Transcript*.

4,645. Seton, Robert, Family
Papers. 1782-1927. 10 ft.
Open. Partial unpublished guide.
University of Notre Dame Archives.
Correspondence, photos, pamphlets, clippings, and

other papers of Seton (1839-1927), including a limited amount of material of Seton's grandmother Mother Elizabeth (Bayley) Seton (1774-1821), who founded the American Sisters of Charity in 1809. Also includes papers of other female family members.

4,646. Sherman, William Tecumseh, Family
Papers. 1808-1959. 26ft
Open. Published guide.
University of Notre Dame Archives.
Correspondence, diaries, financial papers, photos, scrapbooks, and clippings of Sherman (1820-91), a US Army officer; his wife Ellen (Ewing) Sherman (1824-88); and other female family members. Includes extensive correspondence between William and Ellen Sherman. A portion of the papers are available on microfilm. See *Guide to the Microfilm Edition of the William Tecumseh Sherman Family Papers (1808-1891)* (Notre Dame: University of Notre Dame Archives, 1967).

4,647. Starr, Eliza Allen
Papers. 1856-1902. 2.5 in.
Open. Item list.
University of Notre Dame Archives.
Starr (1824-1901) was an author and lecturer. Correspondence, a manuscript of Starr's history of Isabella of Castile, and clippings about Starr. Some of the correspondence was published in James J. McGovern, ed., *The Life and Letters of Eliza Allen Starr* (Chicago: Lakeside Press, 1904).

4,648. University History
Records. 1842-. 850 ft.
Access restricted. No guide.
University of Notre Dame Archives.
Established in 1842 as a men's school, Notre Dame became a coeducational institution in 1972; however, women had been involved in the institution's history since 1843 when the first group of religious women arrived to staff the school. Correspondence, official records, oral history tapes and transcripts, photos, and scrapbooks. Includes papers of religious women and oral history tapes concerning the period after implementation of the coeducation plan.

OLDENBURG

4,649. Archives
Records. 1851- . No size given.
Access restricted. No guide.
Sisters of St. Francis Convent.
The congregation of the Sisters of St. Francis was established in Oldenburg in 1851. Handwritten books containing the constitution and first rule, with revisions up to ca. 1890; minutes of council meetings, advisory board meetings, and other standing committees; land deeds; financial records; correspondence of the mother superior with archbishops, bishops, pastors, and school superintendents and principals; proceedings of the Chapter of Affairs held in 1968, 1971, 1974, and 1978; records of elections of the reverend mother, the assistant mother, and counsellors, 1851-; circular letters sent by mothers superior to mission homes, 1900-; chronicles, 1851-; records relating to the work of the Sisters as teachers and administrators in schools and in Marian College, which is operated by the Sisters; published and unpublished historical material; photos and blueprints of Convent buildings and the campus and buildings of Marian College; yearbooks of Marian College and academies and high schools staffed by the Sisters; published rule books, 1890-; and material relating to summer programs, such as academic classes, workshops, retreats, assemblies, and catechetical work. The Archives also contains copies of records of Marian College, the originals of which are in the College's archives in Indianapolis.

PLAINFIELD

4,650. Hendricks County Women's Organizations
Records. 1915-49. 7 vols.
Open. No guide.
Plainfield Public Library.
Minutes of the Home Economics Class, which later became the Union Home Economics Club, and of the Ladies' Aid of the Plainfield Monthly Meeting of the Society of Friends. Also includes records of the Union Home Economics Club and the Plainfield WCTU chapter.

4,651. Mills, William Clarkson
Papers. 1839-77. 1 folder.
Open. No guide.
Plainfield Public Library.
Diaries and marriage license of Mills, a Quaker farmer, and his wife Rebecca (Hadley) Mills (1820-?), a homemaker. Her two diaries include commentary on social events, local occurrences, and family problems.

RICHMOND

4,652. Coffin, Charles Fisher, and Coffin, Rhoda M. (Johnson)
Papers. Nd. 8 ft.
Open. No guide.
Earlham College Archives.
Papers of Charles Coffin and his wife Rhoda Coffin (1826-1909). The Coffins were Quaker leaders and prison reformers.

4,653. Simms, Ruthanna
Papers. Ca. 1926-56. Ca. 9 boxes.
Access restricted. No guide.
Earlham College Archives.
Simms (1880-1974) was executive secretary of the Associated Executive Committee of Friends on Indian Affairs. Correspondence, addresses, and reports concerning Quaker work with Indians.

4,654. White, Esther Griffin
Papers. Ca. 1890-1940. 3 ft.
Open. Card catalog.
Earlham College Archives.
[Miss] White (1869-1954) was a local journalist, author, suffragist, and political leader. Correspondence, poems, articles, genealogical material, photos, scrapbooks of clippings, autograph albums, and other papers reflect her work as a writer for the *Richmond Palladium* and other newspapers, her Republican party work, and her activities relating to her Quaker faith and to her position as secretary of the Robert Dale Owen Commission. Also includes information about the Western Association of Writers, of which White was secretary. Publisher of *The Little Paper* from 1915 to the early 1920s and *The People's Paper* in 1921, she was the author of *Indiana Bookplates* (Richmond: Nicholson Press, 1910). She was the first woman delegate to the state Republican convention and a candidate for Congress in 1926 and for mayor of Richmond in 1938.

4,655. The Lily
Records. 1849-56. 1 microfilm reel.
Access restricted. No guide.
Earlham College Library.
Issues of *The Lily,* a woman's journal devoted to temperance and literature that was edited by Amelia Bloomer.

ROCHESTER

4,656. Carter, Myrtle
Papers. 1938. 200 pp.
Open. Unpublished guides.
Fulton County Historical Society.
Diary of [Mrs.] Carter.

4,657. Montgomery, Ethel L.: "The Building of the Michigan Road"
Papers. 1902. 16-page item.
Open. Unpublished guides.
Fulton County Historical Society.
Thesis presented by Montgomery to Purdue University.

4,658. Rochester Normal University
Records. 1895-1912. 16 items.
Open. Unpublished guides.
Fulton County Historical Society.
Annual programs of this institution, which was in operation from 1895 to 1912, and a scrapbook concerning college activities compiled by Flo Delp.

4,659. School Yearbooks
Collection. 1907-78. 104 vols.
Open. Unpublished guides.
Fulton County Historical Society.
Annual copies of *Manitou Ripples,* a Rochester school yearbook; an issue of *Sefhos* of Fulton High School, 1949; an issue of *Aubbeenaubbee,* 1956; issues of *Kewannian,* 1924-69 and 1976-78; and Akron yearbooks, 1962-77.

4,660. Smith, Genevieve Copeland
Papers. 1910-14. 177-page item.
Open. Unpublished guides.
Fulton County Historical Society.
"School Girl Days," a memory scrapbook compiled by Smith, contains items about classmates and faculty at Rochester High School, a class history, photos, and clippings.

4,661. Women's Clubs
Records. Nd. No size given.
Open. Unpublished guides.
Fulton County Historical Society.
Secretary's report, 1908-11, of the Woman's Missionary Society of Rochester's First Baptist Church, founded in 1909; notebooks, 1935-45, containing the constitution, bylaws, and minutes of the Harmony Club of Rochester, a homemakers' group; a yearbook of the Ladies Literary Club, founded in 1874; "Feast of Good Things," a cookbook prepared by the Ladies of the Baptist Church; and magazines, 1930-35, of the local DAR, founded in 1908. Also contains a program book of the Mothers' Study Club, organized in 1913 "for the advancement of intellectual and efficient motherhood through systematic study"; program booklets, 1933-37 and 1940, of the Mount Zion Community Club, founded in 1933; program books, 1901-06, of the Rochester Woman's Club, founded in 1901; and scrapbooks, 1958-63, of Burton Homemakers, which was founded in 1913.

SOUTH BEND

4,662. Allen, Janet
Papers. 1940-70. 2 Hollinger boxes.
Open. Unpublished guide.
Northern Indiana Historical Society.
Personal and political correspondence and campaign material of Allen, a politician.

4,663. As You Like It Club
Records. 1893-1945. 1 Hollinger box.
Open. Unpublished guide.
Northern Indiana Historical Society.
Minutes, membership lists, and programs of this women's literary club.

4,664. Clio Circle
Records. 1898-1951. 2 Hollinger boxes.
Open. Unpublished guide.
Northern Indiana Historical Society.
The Circle was a self-improvement study group. Minutes, treasurer's reports, correspondence, and a group photo from 1910.

4,665. Mother's Club
Records. 1895-1918. 1 Hollinger box.
Open. Unpublished guide.
Northern Indiana Historical Society.
Programs and a photo taken in about 1912.

4,666. Pleiades Club
Records. 1871. Ca. 20 items.
Open. Unpublished guide.
Northern Indiana Historical Society.
Programs and invitations of this literary society.

4,667. Sewing Club
Records. 1871. 1 item.
Open. Unpublished guide.
Northern Indiana Historical Society.
Photo.

4,668. South Bend Women's Civic Club
Records. 1969-71. 4 items.
Open. Unpublished guide.
Northern Indiana Historical Society.
Yearly programs of this women's civic group.

4,669. Sumption Prairie Women's Club
Records. 1963-65. 6 items.
Open. Unpublished guide.
Northern Indiana Historical Society.
Membership and officer lists, programs, and yearbooks of this women's group.

4,670. Woman's Relief Corps of the GAR, Auten Corps No. 14
Records. 1890-1915. Ca. 30 items.
Open. Unpublished guide.
Northern Indiana Historical Society.
Quarterly reports and photos of the 1890 encampment of the Grand Army of the Republic, for which the Woman's Relief Corps served as an auxiliary.

4,671. Women's Council for Human Relations
Records. 1972-73. 3 items.
Open. Unpublished guide.
Northern Indiana Historical Society.
Programs.

4,672. Women's Literary Club
Records. 1874-1961. 1 Hollinger box.
Open. Unpublished guide.
Northern Indiana Historical Society.
Minutes, correspondence, a history, a 1950 photo, and yearbooks.

4,673. Worth Literary Club
Records. 1892-1913. 1 Hollinger box.
Open. Unpublished guide.
Northern Indiana Historical Society.
Programs and membership lists.

4,674. Young Women's Christian Association
Records. 1907-13. Ca. 20 items.
Open. Unpublished guide.
Northern Indiana Historical Society.
Programs and membership lists.

TERRE HAUTE

4,675. Debs, Katherine Metzel
Papers. 1885-1936. 3 vols, and more than 13 items.
Open. No guide.
Eugene V. Debs House.
Kate Debs (1857-1936) was the wife of Eugene V. Debs (1855-1926). A Christmas card and love letter she sent to her husband in 1919 while he was in the Atlanta federal prison; two letters she wrote to her husband's secretary Mrs. George Brewer; letters of condolence from Clarence Darrow, Edgar Lee Masters, and Elizabeth [Mrs. Luther] Burbank; photos of Kate Debs as a bride, in middle age, and as an elderly woman; scrapbooks containing love notes from her husband, clippings about Eugene Debs's career and about her family, and other items; a 1908 interview with Kate Debs from the *Terre Haute Post;* a special issue of the socialist tabloid *The Rip Saw* concerning the Debses' life and work; and an article about Kate Debs from *The Kansas Magazine.* Also included are issues of the magazine of the Brotherhood of Locomotive Firemen, for which Eugene Debs served as editor and Ida Husted Harper as woman's editor.

4,676. Housewives Effort for Local Progress
Records. 1962-72. Several boxes.
Access restricted. No guide.
Vigo County Public Library, Special Collections.
Records of this local organization, which was commonly known by its acronym—HELP. Formed to combat what its members felt was Terre Haute's negative image, HELP encouraged the media and others to scrutinize more carefully actions by local government officials. HELP voted to disband after 10 years because its members felt its work was accomplished.

4,677. Women's Associations
Records. Nd. No size given.
Access restricted. Unpublished guide.
Vigo County Public Library, Special Collections.
Records of organizations, newsletters, scrapbooks, and clippings contain information about such subjects and groups as woman suffrage, women's war work, the Women's Auxiliary Motor Corps, the Women's League Against Waste, the Women's Union Label League, the Franchise League, and the Indiana LWV. Also includes files of the Women's Department Club and Birthright.

VINCENNES

4,678. Rose Ladies Aid Society
Records. 1871-1907. 6 folders and 1 document case.
Open. Unpublished guide.
Vincennes University, Byron R. Lewis Historical Collections Library.
The Society, a Terre Haute, IN, organization, was formed in 1871 to help needy families, particularly older women who had no means of support. Annual reports, financial records listing aid to individuals and costs, receipts for purchases of an "Old Ladies Home," correspondence, and other records.

4,679. Schultheis, Rose
Papers. 1930-65. 1 document case.
Open. Unpublished guide.
Vincennes University, Byron R. Lewis Historical Collections Library.
[Mrs. Leo] Schultheis (1890-1967) was a local historian who lived in Vincennes. Correspondence, notes, articles, and other papers. Includes letters from midwestern historians and letters that reflect local history.

4,680. Warner, Minnie
Papers. 1897. 1 folder.
Open. Unpublished guide.
Vincennes University, Byron R. Lewis Historical Collections Library.
Correspondence of Warner, a homemaker, includes letters she wrote to her husband while she was staying at West Baden Springs Hotel, an Indiana health resort. She writes about the resort, her improving health, and about other persons at the Hotel.

WEST LAFAYETTE

4,681. Earhart, Amelia Mary
Papers. Ca. 1904-37. 10 boxes.
Open. Inventory.
Purdue University Archives.
Earhart (1897-1937), the first woman to make a solo flight across the Atlantic, served in 1935 as a consultant on women's careers at Purdue. Correspondence, essay and other writings by Earhart, notes on her last flight, scrapbooks of clippings about her aviation achievements and personal life, award certificates, maps, and other papers and memorabilia. Includes a typescript of Earhart's book *Last Flight,* an essay and a poem by Earhart, and notes she wrote about Purdue while lecturing and experimenting on aircraft at the school. The Purdue Research Foundation bought an airplane for Earhart to use as a flying laboratory.

4,682. Gilbreth, Lillian Evelyn (Moller)
Papers. 1910-72. 15 manuscript boxes.
Partially restricted. Inventory.
Purdue University Archives.
[Mrs. Frank B.] Gilbreth (1878-1972) was a consulting engineer and professor of management at Purdue University. Correspondence of Gilbreth and her 12 children, diaries, articles by Gilbreth, typescript of her unpublished autobiography, speeches, business records, research findings, audiotapes, photos, scrapbooks, periodicals, clippings, and other papers and memorabilia. Gilbreth received her BA and MA from the University of California, Berkeley, and her PhD in industrial psychology from Brown University in 1915. She worked with her husband Frank Gilbreth (1868-1924) in designing research techniques for motion analysis in industry. Thcy also analyzed fatigue and work simplification for industrial workers. Frank Gilbreth was a lecturer on management at Purdue. Lillian Gilbreth became a lecturer at the school after her husband's death. She was named professor of management in 1935 and served until her retirement in 1948.

IOWA

AMANA

4,683. Amana Colonies
Records. Nd. No size given.
Open. No guide.
Amana Church Society.
Records of the Amana colonies contain religious testimonies. This denomination was first established in 1714.

AMES

4,684. Adams, Austin, Family
Papers. 1842-1901. 2 ft.
Open. Unpublished guide.
Iowa State University Library, Department of Special Collections.
Included in the papers of the Adams family are correspondence, diaries, notes, lectures, and essays of Mary Newbury Adams (1837-1901), wife of Austin Adams, an equal rights advocate, writer and speaker for the woman suffrage movement, member of the Association for Advancement of Women and the American Historical Association, and

vice-chairman of the women's branch of the World's Congress Auxiliary of the Columbian Exposition. She also belonged to numerous literary societies and promoted "culture" in Dubuque, IA, by arranging the visits of Amos Bronson Alcott and Ralph Waldo Emerson to the area. Her correspondents include Ednah Dow Cheney, Bertha M. H. Palmer, Caroline M. Severance, and Emma Ward. Papers also contain items about the Concord (MA) School of Philosophy, which she attended, and an 1872 journal with details about her visit with Alcott and Emerson in Concord.

4,685. Armstrong, Ruth Gallup
Papers. 1958-62. 1.5 ft.
Open. Unpublished guide.
Iowa State University Library, Department of Special Collections.
Manuscripts, galley proofs, photos, and other writings, including short stories of Armstrong (1891-1972), a "cultivated lady author of means" who wrote the book *Sisters Under the Sari.* Based on Armstrong's experiences and friendship with an Iowa State University graduate student from India who lived at her house during the latter's course of study, the book relates how two women from different cultures discovered that they were "sisters under the sari."

4,686. Black, Margaret J.
Papers. 1938-71. 3 ft.
Open. Unpublished guide.
Iowa State University Library, Department of Special Collections.
Correspondence, professional papers, honors, and awards of [Miss] Black (1898-), a natural science professor in the school of education at Drake University, Des Moines, and a member of the Iowa Conservation Education Council, the Iowa chapter of the Nature Conservancy, and the US Soil Conservation Service. Papers pertain to conservation projects and methods for teaching conservation to schoolchildren.

4,687. Iowa Master Farm Homemaker's Guild
Records. 1928-74. 1.5 ft.
Open. Unpublished guide.
Iowa State University Library, Department of Special Collections.
Scrapbooks containing reports and minutes of annual meetings, lists of members, photos, and clippings of the Guild, which since 1928 has promoted the interests of farm homemakers in Iowa.

4,688. Rayness, Gerard M., and Rayness, Velma
Papers. 1929-ca. 1970. Ca. 6 ft.
Open. No guide.
Iowa State University Library, Department of Special Collections.
Correspondence, diaries, notebooks, sketches, and paintings of Gerard Rayness (1898-1946) and his wife Velma Rayness (1896-1977), both painters and art instructors. Diaries reflect the professional and economic difficulties faced by artists during the depression as well as Velma Rayness's struggle to maintain both her home and her artistic career.

4,689. Schmidt, Louis Bernard
Papers. 1884-1957. 3 ft.
Open. Unpublished guide.
Iowa State University Library, Department of Special Collections.
G. Pearle (Wilson) Schmidt (1881-1957), wife of Louis Schmidt, was a homemaker who devoted much time to writing poetry, composing music, and studying genealogy. Correspondence, more than 100 poems, numerous stories and articles, plays, musical compositions, reports, deeds, receipts, photos, clippings, and publications contain information on the DAR, the Society of Mayflower Descendants, the International Society of the Daughters of the Barons of Runnymede, the Iowa Federation of Music Clubs, Antonin Dvorak, the Edward McDowell Colony, and family histories. Schmidt wrote the musical compositions *I Love My Love* (1904) and *The Spirit of Iowa,* which was completed for a state historical pageant in 1920. Her play *Save the Trees* was done for the conservation department of the Iowa DAR. In 1925 she was instrumental in establishing a memorial to Antonin Dvorak. She also ran for the office of state representative in 1920.

4,690. Shattuck, Frederica
Papers. 1918-38. 1.5 ft.
Open. Unpublished guide.
Iowa State University Library, Department of Special Collections.
Correspondence, memoranda, and financial records showing drama expenses of Shattuck (1883-1969), a speech professor at Iowa State University from 1907 to 1956, who organized the campus drama group Iowa State Players and produced and directed plays for 20 years. Shattuck's papers provide information on the speech department, campus life, and the 1918 influenza epidemic that occurred when she was acting dean of women.

4,691. Welch, Mary B.
Papers. 1876- . 0.3 cu.ft.
Open. Unpublished guide.
Iowa State University Library, Department of Special Collections.
Correspondence, handwritten lectures, papers and publications including *Mrs. Welch's Cookbook* (1884), biographical information, clippings, and other items of [Mrs.] Welch (1841-1923), the wife of the first president of Iowa State Agricultural College, a woman suffrage advocate, and the first woman to teach home economics at a land grant college. Soon after Iowa State Agricultural College opened, Welch, who was employed as a lecturer, was asked to give practical and technical housekeeping training to the young women on campus. During her 15 years of service she enlarged the scope of study to include lectures and laboratory work in home care and management, care of the sick, and child training; her work is said to have diminished popular prejudice against the inclusion of domestic economy in university curricula. In addition, Welch first suggested the possibility of extension work in home economics and then initiated a lecture series in Des Moines in 1883. Subsequent lectures followed throughout the state.

4,692. Women in Communications, Incorporated
Records. 1958-75. 1 ft.
Open. Unpublished guide.
Iowa State University Library, Department of Special Collections.
Bylaws, correspondence, reports, membership lists, scrapbooks, manuals, newsletters, and clippings of this organization founded in 1961 for professional women who are active in television, radio, publishing, and other areas of the mass communications field. The group is still in existence.

BOONE

4,693. Kantor, Effie M.
Papers. 1927-30. 1 vol.
Access restricted. Index.
Boone County Historical Society.
Volume consists of the publication *Community Magazine,* later titled the *Community Visitor,* which was edited and distributed by [Mrs.] Kantor (?-1931), a divorced woman who lived in Boone for five years; Kantor's son Mackinlay Kantor, an author, also lived in Boone for several months at that time. Ca. 6000 copies of her publications were mailed on a monthly basis, free of charge, to patrons of the Boone post office, but they were supported by paid advertisements. The *Community Magazine* and its successor the *Community Visitor* were devoted largely to local history topics, and Kantor often printed the reminiscences of elderly Boone residents who had been pioneers in the region. In 1930 the *Community Visitor* ceased publication. Kantor died one year later at her son's home in Des Moines, IA.

4,694. Shelley, Kate
Papers. Nd. No size given.
Access restricted. Partial index.
Boone County Historical Society.
Speech, school and tax records, photo negatives, clippings, and maps concerning Shelley (ca. 1866-?), a Moingona, Boone County, resident who in 1881 assisted in the rescue of trainmen stranded when a torrential rainstorm flooded local Honey Creek and washed out a trestle bridge while an inspection engine was crossing over it. Born in Ireland, Shelley was still an infant when her family emigrated to the US and settled near Moingona. Her father worked as a railroad section foreman until his death in 1878.

BURLINGTON

4,695. Autographs
Collection. Ca. 1850s-1900. Ca. 120 ft.
Open. Card file.
Burlington Public Library.
Autograph signatures and letters and items of correspondence collected for their autograph value pertain to prominent 19th-century figures and include the following women: Frances Folsom [Mrs. Grover] Cleveland (1864-1947); Charlotte "Lotta" Crabtree (1847-1924) and Charlotte Saunders Cushman (1816-76), actresses; Fanny Lily Gypsy Davenport (1850-98), an actress in Augustin Daly's Company; Varina Anne (Howell) [Mrs. Jefferson] Davis (1826-1906); Anna (Price) Dillon (1835-93), wife of lawyer, judge, and author John Forest Dillon and daughter of Iowa congressman Hiram Price; Louisa L. Drew (1820-97), actress and wife of John D. Drew; Eva (Emery) Dye (1855-1947), Iowa author; Annie Florence; Sarah Josepha Buell Hale (1788-1879), writer and the editor of *Godey's Lady's Book* from 1836 to 1877; Phoebe (Apperson) Hearst (1842-1919), educational philanthropist; Grace Elizabeth King (1853?-1932), author known for her works on Louisiana; Mary Ashton Rice Livermore (1820-1905), suffragist and reformer; Belva Ann (Bennett) McNall Lockwood (1830-1917), women's rights leader, lawyer, and nominee in 1888 for US President by the Equal Rights party; Molly Elliot Seawell (1860-1916), novelist; and Harriet Beecher Stowe (1811-96), author and abolitionist.

CEDAR RAPIDS

4,696. Autographs: General
Collection. Ca. 1849- . Ca. 8 ft.
Open. Card file.
Iowa Masonic Library.
Collection established by Theodore Sutton Parvin, who was librarian and grand secretary of the Grand Lodge of Iowa from 1844 to 1851 and from 1853 to 1901, consists of autograph letters and signatures, fragments of literary manuscripts, and items of correspondence that were kept for autograph value but often contain other information. Represented are individuals prominent in politics, literature, the arts, science, and civic and social reform, including Susan B. Anthony; Louise (Whitfield) [Mrs. Andrew] Carnegie; Julia Fletcher Carney, poet; Agnes M. Clerke, astronomer; Frances Folsom [Mrs. Grover] Cleveland (1864-1947); Agnes Crane, scientist and

author; Susan Ann [Mrs. Lawrence] Dean, who in 1832 became the first white woman at Dubuque, IA; Clara A. [Mrs. Augustus C.] Dodge, whose husband was a diplomat and Iowa senator; Lottie E. Granger, president of the Iowa State Teacher's Association in 1889; Alice Le Plongeon, a lecturer, traveler, and explorer; Abbie Gardner Sharp, the sole survivor of the Spirit Lake massacre in northern Iowa; and Annie (Turner) [Mrs. William] Wittenmyer (1827-1900), Civil War nurse and organizer of the Iowa Sanitary Commission who also was first national president of the WCTU from 1874 to 1879. Also includes correspondence from the Sisters of Charity in Dubuque.

4,697. Autographs: Masonic
Collection. Ca. 1850- . Ca. 8 ft.
Open. Card catalog.
Iowa Masonic Library.
Autograph letters and signatures, correspondence, and documents of people prominent in Masonic activities and affairs. Represented among those whose items pertain to the Order of the Eastern Star and its members are Mary C. Agnew, who was worthy grand matron of Keokuk, IA, Grand Chapter of Iowa, from 1884 to 1886; Ella Waite Cobb; Lorraine J. Pitkin, grand secretary of the General Grand Chapter in 1889; Mrs. Theodore F. Ferrell; and the Female Free Masons.

4,698. Erskine, Arthur W.
Papers. 1885-1952. 8 drawers.
Open. Card file.
Iowa Masonic Library.
Papers of Erskine (1885-1952), a physician who pioneered the use of radiology to treat cancer, contain extensive correspondence, speeches, articles, manuscript of his book *Practical X-Ray Treatment,* research data, expense book, photos, records of medical societies to which he belonged, scrapbooks of clippings, medical journals and bulletins, home movies, and a set of printing plates. Included are his speeches and research papers on breast, vaginal, and uterine cancer; research papers on the development of pap tests and speculums for use in treating vaginal cancer; lectures about cancer that were presented to women's groups in ca. 1936; clippings on and correspondence with Chicago physician Maud Slye; and correspondence and other papers pertaining to the Women's Field Army of the American Cancer Society, including both the national and Iowa organizations. Other correspondence pertains to such topics as socialized medicine, health insurance, indigent health care, medical ethics, and Iowa cancer programs and surveys and to numerous medical organizations, including the American Cancer Society, American College of Radiology, the American Medical Association, and the Radiological Society of North America. Erskine was president of the Linn County Medical Society in 1920, president of the Radiological Society of North America in 1925, president of the Iowa State Medical Society in 1938 and 1939, cofounder and secretary of the Iowa X-Ray Club from 1920 to 1952, and a member of the executive board of the American Cancer Society's Women's Field Army in the 1930s.

4,699. Ladies Auxiliary, Order of Railway Conductors of America
Records. Ca. 1889-1941. Ca. 2 ft.
Open. No guide.
Iowa Masonic Library.
Constitution, statutes, rules, minutes, a history to 1940, pamphlets, and the official seal and banner of the Auxiliary, which was founded in 1881 as the Ladies of the Royal Club in Fort Wayne, IN. Also includes photos and printed material about Iowa railway heroine Kate Shelley, who saved a passenger train in 1881 by crawling across a railroad bridge on the Des Moines River near Boone to warn a stationmaster about a bridge washout farther west. The Auxiliary consisted of five divisions, two in Indiana and one each in Iowa, Ohio, and Pennsylvania; together they constituted the Grand Division, which after 1889 assembled annually for social and business meetings. Mrs. J. H. Moore was president of the Auxiliary from 1892 to 1928 and [Mrs.] Agnes M. Whalen was president from 1928 to 1940. The Auxiliary dissolved in 1968 when the Order of Railway Conductors of America merged with another union.

4,700. Sanford S. Kerr Autograph Collection
Collection. Ca. 1930-55. 1.25 ft.
Open. Card file.
Iowa Masonic Library.
Autographs, photos, and memorabilia of persons prominent in sports, politics, theater, and other phases of public life were collected by Kerr, a retired railroad worker of Cedar Rapids who became known as the city's "unofficial roaming ambassador" because of his extensive travels. Women represented in the collection include Patty Berg, professional golfer; Florence Chadwick, who swam the English Channel; Lorraine Corazza, secretary to governor of Colorado William Lee Knows; Mrs. John Luther Jones, wife of Casey Jones; Louise Suggs, professional golfer; and Babe D. Zaharias, golfer and track athlete. Also represented is Minerva Jane Ashlock of Center Point, IA, who celebrated her 95th birthday in 1955.

CHEROKEE

4,701. Brown and Fisher Families
Papers. 1856-69. 7 vols.
Access restricted. No guide.
Sanford Museum and Planetarium.
Diary kept from 1856 to 1858 by Cherokee area pioneer settler and shoemaker James A. Brown (1820-1902), who moved from Rhode Island to Milford, MA, in 1850 and six years later moved to Iowa with the Milford Emigration Society to help establish the Milford Colony, a communal society that dissolved after the Civil War. He also was instrumental in forming the Baptist Church in Cherokee. He began the diary, but it was completed in 1864 by his daughter Clara E. Brown (1850-1919). Also includes six diaries of George Fisher, who married Clara Brown in 1868.

4,702. Sanford
Collection. 1850s-1940. 4 cartons.
Access restricted. No guide.
Sanford Museum and Planetarium.
Papers of the Sanford family and an accumulation of family effects gathered by Maude Emily (Tiel) Sanford (1866-1941), an organizer of the American National Red Cross in Cherokee. The collection furnished the nucleus of the Museum, which was founded in the name of her deceased son Tiel Sanford. Maude Sanford was the wife of William Ackley Sanford.

4,703. Bannister, Nettie
Papers. Nd. 1 item.
Open. No guide.
Whiting Historical Studies, Stiles Archives.
Memoirs of Bannister (ca. 1868-?), whose father came to Cherokee in 1856, chiefly pertain to her family history.

4,704. Brown and Fisher Family
Papers. Ca. 1864-1951. No size given.
Access restricted. No guide.
Whiting Historical Studies, Stiles Archives.
Papers of Cherokee area pioneer settler and shoemaker James A. Brown (1820-1902), who moved from Rhode Island to Milford, MA, in 1850 and then six years later to Iowa with the Milford Western Emigration Society to help establish the Milford Colony, a communal society that dissolved after the Civil War, and papers of Brown's daughter Clara E. (Brown) Fisher (1850-1919), her husband George Fisher, and their daughters Florence Fisher (1873-?) and Annie E. (Fisher) Swanson (1871-?), who was a schoolteacher and farm wife.

Diaries include one volume begun by Brown, but which Clara finished in 1864 at age 14; seven volumes that Clara Fisher kept, 1900-17; two volumes of Florence Fisher, 1892-93, which contain an account of her trip in 1893 to Chicago for the Columbian Exposition; and 12 partial volumes kept by Annie Swanson, which include information about activities at and inmates of the County Poor Farm, where she and her husband once worked.

Collection also contains letters that Clara Fisher received from her daughters in 1893 when she was hospitalized in Chicago, a memoir Annie Swanson wrote at age 80, family photos, and invitations, cards, and other memorabilia. Clara Fisher and George Fisher were married in 1868. Divorced and twice remarried, Annie Fisher's last husband was Aron Johnson.

4,705. Kenyon, Agnes Robertson
Papers. 1929. 1 item.
Open. No guide.
Whiting Historical Studies, Stiles Archives.
A paper for presentation to members of the Cherokee Columbian Club by Kenyon, a Cherokee County school superintendent, relates to pioneer days in Cherokee; she and her family settled in that town in the 1870s.

4,706. Potter, Mary Ann Bailey
Papers. Nd. 6 items.
Open. No guide.
Whiting Historical Studies, Stiles Archives.
Potter (1841-1928), whose family came to the area in 1869, was an early settler in Cherokee County. Photos and several copies of a paper written by Marguerite Whiting, Potter's grand-niece, contain biographical information about Potter.

4,707. Stiles, Nestor L.
Collection. Ca. 1856-1960. Ca. 30 in.
Open. Card file index.
Whiting Historical Studies, Stiles Archives.
Stiles (1884-1960) was a Cherokee banker, amateur historian, and collector of autograph signatures and artifacts. Scrapbooks containing correspondence, photos, clippings, club programs, autographs, and other items that pertain to the history of Cherokee County and the city of Cherokee; the scrapbooks are indexed by an extensive card file. A history major when he attended the University of Wisconsin, Stiles returned to his hometown of Cherokee to enter the banking profession. He maintained an avid interest in local history throughout his lifetime, however. The source material he gathered includes detailed information about the activities of Cherokee women.

COUNCIL BLUFFS

4,708. Bloomer, Amelia (Jenks), and Bloomer, Dexter Chamberlain
Papers. Nd. No size given.
Open. Unpublished guide.
Council Bluffs Free Public Library.
Correspondence, addresses, scrapbooks, and clippings of Amelia Bloomer (1818-94), a temperance reformer, editor, and suffragist, and of her husband Dexter Bloomer, an attorney and antislavery reformer. Includes a poem to Amelia Bloomer, her 1882 certificate of honorary membership in the Woman's National Social Science League, clippings of speeches by Lucy Stone and Antoinette Brown, and material concerning women's rights and temperance. Her correspondents include Stone, Julia (Ward) Howe, and Annie Savery.

DAVENPORT

4,709. Marycrest College Archives
Records. 1939- . 60 ft., 16 drawers, and 12 boxes.
Open. Unpublished guide.
Marycrest College Library.
Established in 1939 as a private liberal arts college for women, Marycrest also has offered professional training leading to degrees in education, science, social work, and nursing as well as a master of arts in education. The College became coeducational in 1970. Contains papers of Mother Mary Geraldine Upham, who as one of the Sisters of Humility founded the College and served as its first president; papers of Sister Sabina Mary Henderson, Sister Mary Helen Rappenecker, and Sister Cathleen Real, succeeding presidents; College accreditation material; minutes of the faculty and all committees; faculty studies on curriculum and grading; data on an institutional study; photos of faculty members and student activities; scrapbooks; and news releases, yearbooks, catalogs, and issues of the College newspaper.

4,710. Palmer, Mabel (Heath)
Papers. 1923- . 3 vols.
Open. No guide.
Palmer College Library.
The wife of B. J. Palmer, the second president of Palmer College, Mabel Palmer (1885-1949) taught anatomy at the College for 30 years. She organized Sigma Phi Chi, the first Greek letter sorority in chiropractic, in 1914. Scrapbook, begun as a memorial to her, with clippings and lists of those who evidently contributed to the Palmer Foundation in her memory and two books she wrote: *Anatomy* (1920), a textbook, and *Stepping Stones* (1942), a travel book. Palmer studied anatomy for one year at Rush Medical College in Chicago before writing *Anatomy.* She established the first Quota Club chapter in Davenport in 1921 and served as the organization's international president in 1928.

4,711. Women's Auxiliary, International Chiropractors Association
Records. 1953. 1 item.
Access restricted. No guide.
Palmer College Library.
Study course about chiropractic with a booklet of the Auxiliary, "Our Creed."

DECORAH

4,712. American Association of University Women
Records. 1946- . 1 ft.
Open. No guide.
Luther College Library.
Minutes, correspondence, and other records of the Decorah branch of the AAUW, established in 1946 to promote the cultural life of members and the community, to discuss books and current issues, and to offer community service.

4,713. Broadway Hospital Unit
Records. 1923-70s. 185 items.
Open. Unpublished guide.
Luther College Library.
Annual reports, secretary's minutes, and clippings of the Unit, a Decorah women's group organized in 1923 to raise money and sew for the local hospital. The Unit functioned until ca. 1970 when all local hospital auxiliaries merged. According to newspaper accounts, Decorah women and local clergy were also instrumental in winning community acceptance for and use of medical care offered at the hospital.

4,714. Dahl, Borghild Margarethe
Papers. 1968. 30 pp.
Open. Unpublished guide.
Luther College Library.
Original manuscript of Dahl (1890-), a writer, for her work *Rikk of the Rendahl Clan* (1968).

4,715. Decorah College for Women
Records. 1929-37. 1 ft.
Open. Published guide.
Luther College Library.
Correspondence, legal documents, and bulletins of the College, founded in 1932 to offer advanced education for local women. The College closed in 1936 when it merged with Luther College, a previously all-male institution.

4,716. Finholt, Mark, and Finholt, Elea
Papers. 1878-1928. 30 items.
Open. Unpublished guide.
Luther College Library.
Correspondence, journals, account books, and cosmetic samples of [Mrs.] Phoebe Lincoln, who managed Phoebe Lincoln Chemical Co., a Decorah cosmetics and drug company. Lincoln sold her cosmetics and drugs to private parties in Decorah and throughout Iowa and to druggists and department stores in other states. Collection chiefly consists of a sales record with a list of her customers.

4,717. Koren, Else Elisabeth (Hysing)
Papers. 1841-1903. 447 items.
Open. Unpublished guide.
Luther College Library.
Diary, several letters, and poems of Koren (1832-1918), who emigrated to the US in 1853 and was the wife of a pioneer pastor. Her diary was published as David T. Nelson, trans., *Elisabeth Koren's Diary* (Norwegian-American Historical Association, 1955).

4,718. Lambda Chi Society
Records. 1957- . 1 ft.
Open. No guide.
Luther College Library.
Secretary's minutes and scrapbooks of this college sorority established in 1957.

4,719. Luther College Women's Club
Records. 1932- . 1 ft.
Open. No guide.
Luther College Library.
Minutes and other records of the Club, which was founded in 1932 to raise money for Luther College projects and furnishings. Open to any woman interested in the College, the group holds monthly meetings with speakers.

4,720. Monday Club
Records. 1896- . 1 ft.
Open. Unpublished guide.
Luther College Library.
Record books, correspondence, and program booklets of a Decorah women's literary group established in 1896. New members are admitted by invitation only.

4,721. Preus, Caroline Dorothea Margrethe (Keyser)
Papers. 1840-69. 176 items.
Open. Unpublished guide.
Luther College Library.
Family correspondence, sketch books, and pencil drawings of Preus (1829-80), who emigrated to the US from Norway in 1851 and became a pioneer pastor's wife. The family correspondence is in Norwegian.

4,722. Preus, Johan Carl Keyser
Papers. 1850-1970. 4618 items.
Open. Unpublished guide.
Luther College Library.
Papers of Preus include 384 letters to and from his sisters Karen [Mrs. Laurence] Larsen (?-1871), Karine [Mrs. J. W. Magelssen] Neuberg, and Henrietta. His sisters' husbands were well-known local Lutheran residents. The letters were written in Norwegian and cover the period from 1865 to 1871.

4,723. Travel Club
Records. 1917-70. 1 ft.
Open. No guide.
Luther College Library.
Records, program folders, and books of this Decorah women's group established in 1917 to pursue study of various countries of the world. The Club is still in existence.

4,724. Women's Missionary Federation
Records. Nd. 16 ft.
Open. No guide.
Luther College Library.
Records and program items of the south central and eastern districts of the Federation, which was founded in ca. 1917 as the women's auxiliary of the Norwegian Evangelical Lutheran Church. The organization's south central district included Iowa, Kansas, Oklahoma, and Texas, while the eastern district took in all states east of the Mississippi River. The Norwegian Evangelical Lutheran Church later became the Evangelical Lutheran Church.

DES MOINES

4,725. Aloha Club
Records. 1897- 1964. 5 vols.
Open. Calendar and card catalog.
Iowa State Historical Department, Division of Historical Museum and Archives, Historical Library.
Organized in 1898 as the Thrice Seven Club, this Des Moines women's group, the purpose of which was cultivation of intellectual, literary, and social culture, changed its name to Aloha Club in 1899. Constitution; secretary's books, 1901-59; cashbooks, 1898-1941; correspondence; annual histories, 1912-57; a complete set of Club yearbooks; clippings; and other items.

4,726. American Association of University Women, Indianola Branch
Records. 1938-40. 1 vol.
Open. No guide.
Iowa State Historical Department, Division of Historical Museum and Archives, Historical Library.
Scrapbook of this local unit of the AAUW in Iowa.

4,727. American Library Association, Library War Service, WWI
Records. 1917-19. 3 vols.
Open. No guide.
Iowa State Historical Department, Division of Historical Museum and Archives, Historical Library.
Financial records, correspondence, pamphlets, brochures, plays, and government agency ephemera of the Library War Service, formed in 1917 by the ALA to provide reading material for soldiers during WWI. The group worked closely with the woman's committee of the Council of National Defense, Iowa Division. Most of the correspondence in the collection reflects the activities of Julia A. Robinson, the chairman of the Iowa registration of women section operated by the woman's Committee to recruit women for service; Robinson also was director and secretary of library extension for the Iowa State Library Commission. As such she played a role in Iowa's participation in the ALA's Cantonment Library movement, organized at the request of War Department secretary Baker in 1917. Collection also contains subscription sheets for War Service funds; index cards of contributions by county from Iowa women's clubs and other groups; a 47-page pamphlet *The ALA in Siberia, Letters Written by Harry Clemons,*

Representative of the ALA War Service with the A.E.F. in Siberia; a play *Every Bite: A Patriotic Burlesque* (ca. 1918) by Ruth Mary Weeks in collaboration with Bertha Goes; a children's play by Claudia Fitzgerald, *The Patriotic Potato;* and a 1919 published report of the war service committee of the ALA.

4,728. Anderson, Mary Audentia S.
Papers. Nd. 1 item.
Open. Card catalog.
Iowa State Historical Department, Division of Historical Museum and Archives, Historical Library.
Folder contains the original manuscript of "Life of Joseph Smith" by [Mrs. B. M.] Anderson.

4,729. Ankeny Family
Papers. Ca. 1850-1930s. No size given.
Open. Card catalog.
Iowa State Historical Department, Division of Historical Museum and Archives, Historical Library.
Family papers of General Rollin Valentine Ankeny, whose parents were pioneers in Polk County, IA, include letters to Mary Ankeny Hunter, an active member of the Iowa Suffrage Memorial Commission during the 1920s and early 1930s, and a scrapbook about the career of her husband Fred H. Hunter, mayor of Des Moines; a notebook containing handwritten essays by Sarah "Sallie" Irvine; an autograph book of Alice Wilson; a school notebook that was converted into a scrapbook of music and theater events from ca. 1895 in Des Moines; a wedding invitation list; photos, including one of the Conversational Club of Des Moines; a scrapbook about the WPA historical survey of Iowa; and clippings about the Des Moines Women's Club and Mrs. Fred Weitz's participation in that group.

4,730. Ankeny, Harriett Louise
Papers. Nd. 1 item.
Open. Card catalog.
Iowa State Historical Department, Division of Historical Museum and Archives, Historical Library.
Consists of a paper soliciting contributions for the maintenance of a cemetery in Somerset, PA, the property for which was given by Captain Peter Ankeny "more than a century ago." Harriett Ankeny was the granddaughter of Captain Ankeny.

4,731. Anthony, Susan Brownell
Papers. 1871-1931. 10 items.
Open. Card catalog.
Iowa State Historical Department, Division of Historical Museum and Archives, Historical Library.
Letters from [Miss] Anthony (1820-1906), a woman suffrage leader and temperance reformer, to Martha Callanan, Quaker minister Joseph Dugdale, and Johnson Brigham regarding suffrage; an article Brigham wrote in 1931 when he was state librarian describing how he met Anthony while he was working as editor of a weekly Brockport, NY, newspaper; and a postage stamp commemorating her.

4,732. Autograph Collection
Collection. 1800s- . Ca. 1500 drawers.
Open. Card catalog.
Iowa State Historical Department, Division of Historical Museum and Archives, Historical Library.
Extensive collection of the autographs of individuals prominent in public affairs, government, the arts, literature, the military, and reform movements; includes autograph letters, cards, and signatures as well as autographed pages from literary manuscripts, photos, biographical sketches, and correspondence collected for autograph purposes but sometimes of substantive value. Of the women represented in the collection, most were prominent 19th-century actresses, artists, authors, novelists, journalists, poets, Civil War nurses, physicians, philanthropists and reformers, pioneers, suffragists, lyceum lecturers, scientists, and women of religious orders; others were wives, mothers, daughters, or nieces of US Presidents and other famous men. Included are items of Mary (Newbury) [Mrs. Austin] Adams (1837-1901), who helped organize the Northern Iowa Woman Suffrage Society in 1869 and pioneered work in the Iowa Federation of Women's Clubs; Elizabeth Cabot (Cary) [Mrs. Louis] Agassiz (1822-1907), president of Harvard Annex, which later became Radcliffe College; Matilda Olivia Aldrich (1836-92), who with her husband Charles Aldrich established the Autograph Collection; Susan Brownell Anthony (1820-1906), a suffragist and temperance leader; [Miss] Anne Ayres (1816-96), a pioneer in American Episcopal sisterhoods, who was consecrated as Sister Anne; Helena Petrovna (Hahn) Blavatsky (1831-91), an occultist and principal founder of the Theosophical Society; [Miss] Laura Dewey Bridgman (1829-89), the first blind deaf-mute to be educated; Margaret W. [Mrs. John] Campbell, who was active in Iowa suffrage work from 1879 to 1901 and president of the Iowa Woman Suffrage Association in 1890; [Miss] Alice Cary (1820-71), a poet and abolitionist who also was the first president of Sorosis, an early New York woman's club; Nettie Sanford Chapin, president of the Marshall County, IA, Woman Suffrage Association in 1870, who also published a semimonthly paper *The Ladies Bureau* from 1875 to 1877 and wrote *American Court Gossip or Life at the National Capitol;* [Miss] Anna Elizabeth Dickinson (1842-1932), an author and reformer who supported Negro suffrage and equal rights for women; Ella Adaline Hamilton [Mrs. Preston B.] Durley (1852-1922), an Iowa author and journalist who was president of the Des Moines Women's Club in 1891 and 1892 and president of the Women's Press Club from 1898 to 1899; Judith Ellen (Horton) Avery [Mrs. Elijah Caleb O.] Foster (1840-1910), who was a temperance leader, lawyer, lecturer, and Republican organizer; Ann E. Harlan, a Civil War nurse whose husband James Harlan, a US senator from Iowa, served as secretary of the interior from 1865 to 1866; Emma Lazarus (1849-87), a poet; Mary Ashton (Rice) Livermore (1820-1905), a lecturer, temperance reformer, and suffragist who worked with the Northwest Sanitary Commission during the Civil War; Jennie McCowen, an MD and the first woman elected president of the Iowa State Medical Society and who also served as president of the Davenport, IA, Academy of Science; Maria Purdy [Mrs. Washington Freeman] Peck (1840-1914), a DAR member who organized the Women's Club of Davenport, IA, formed the Clionian Club in 1874, and was vice-president-at-large of the International Council of Women; Prudence (Crandall) [Mrs. Calvin] Philleo (1803-89), a teacher and abolitionist who unsuccessfully tried to start a school for Negro girls in Canterbury, CT, between 1833 and 1834; Belle E. Smith, an Iowa poet and contributor to the literary magazine *Midland Monthly;* Annie (Turner) [Mrs. William] Wittenmyer (1827-1900), a Civil War army nurse who played a large role in Iowa's participation in the Sanitary Commission, was the first national president of the WCTU, and also was active in the Woman's Relief Corps and the Methodist Episcopal church; and Mary A. Work, an Iowa leader in the Woman's party.

4,733. Barker, Catherine
Papers. 1869-83. 7 vols.
Open. No guide.
Iowa State Historical Department, Division of Historical Museum and Archives, Historical Library.
Reminiscences of Barker (1806-?), an Ohio resident who moved to Iowa in 1844, pertain to her pioneer and domestic experiences. Included are selections from correspondence of Barker with her friends and family, excerpts from her diary, and a biographical sketch. Her sister Frances Dana (Barker) [Mrs. James L.] Gage (1808-84) was an advocate of woman suffrage; excerpts from some of Gage's letters to Barker are also provided.

4,734. Barkluff, Hattie V.
Papers. 1953-54. 2 items.
Open. Card catalog.
Iowa State Historical Department, Division of Historical Museum and Archives, Historical Library.
Newspaper articles by [Miss] Barkluff, a writer from Jewell, IA, were printed in the Iowa newspaper *Ellsworth Press* and pertain to the history of Lakins Grove and Callanan in Hamilton County, IA.

4,735. Beard, Ezra J. H.
Papers. Ca. 1860s-1920s. 2 vols.
Open. Card catalog.
Iowa State Historical Department, Division of Historical Museum and Archives, Historical Library.
An educator and longtime superintendent of Newton, IA, schools, Beard (1842-1924) was married to Lura Alexander Beard and had two daughters, Vesta and Gertrude; Vesta Beard taught in the Newton school system, and Gertrude Beard was a music teacher. Family correspondence, including letters from the Civil War period, some of which have been microfilmed; a telegram; a notebook; Ezra Beard's collection of Spanish-American War material; and a 1912 political scrapbook. Also contains a scrapbook Vesta Beard kept and clippings of articles she wrote for the Newton *Journal* describing her travels in Switzerland, Gibraltar, and Algiers.

4,736. Beaumont, Abbey Louisa
Papers. Nd. 4-page item.
Open. No guide.
Iowa State Historical Department, Division of Historical Museum and Archives, Historical Library.
In her autobiography [Mrs.] Beaumont (1803-ca. 1905) describes childhood experiences at Log Harbor, NY, and also mentions British warships and the Free Masons.

4,737. Blanchard Family
Papers. Ca. 1819-60s. 2 in.
Open. Card catalog.
Iowa State Historical Department, Division of Historical Museum and Archives, Historical Library.
Papers of the Henry E. Blanchard family include correspondence between Henry Blanchard and his mother, sisters, and father; letters his wife Louise Blanchard received from her sister; correspondence of schoolgirls Helen and Maria Blanchard; and invoices of Oliver Blanchard from 1819. Also contains military documents of Henry Blanchard, including his commission to the status of corporal in Troop L, Fourth Cavalry.

4,738. Bloomer, Dexter Chamberlain
Papers. 1839-1900. 5 vols.
Open. Card catalog.
Iowa State Historical Department, Division of Historical Museum and Archives, Historical Library.
Commonplace book, extensive diaries, and other papers of Bloomer (1816-1900), a lawyer and journalist who moved to Council Bluffs, IA, in 1855 and who later was elected mayor of the city; he was married to Amelia (Jenks) Bloomer (1818-94), woman suffrage and temperance leader, and in 1895 he wrote and published the *Life and Times of Amelia Bloomer.* His commonplace book, begun in 1839, was later used as a diary and manuscript book. Other diaries, some combined with his account books, span the period from 1859 to 1900 and contain some mention of his wife's suffrage activity. Also includes fragments of papers, several of which pertain to a religious controversy.

4,739. Briggs, Minerva
Papers. Ca. 1839-96. 4 items.
Open. Card catalog.
Iowa State Historical Department, Division of Historical Museum and Archives, Historical Library.
Included with a brief historical sketch of Briggs (1825-96), a schoolteacher and postmistress, are

several invitations to balls. After teaching school in Athens, MO, Briggs taught at pioneer schools in the Troy, Lebanon, and Croton, IA, area until 1870. She then became postmistress in Croton for 26 years.

4,740. Brown, Mrs. Robert A.
Papers. Ca. 1880-early 1900s. 1.5 in.
Open. Card catalog.
Iowa State Historical Department, Division of Historical Museum and Archives, Historical Library.
Collection donated by Greta Weitz [Mrs. Robert A.] Brown chiefly consists of a photo album and photos of Ankeny family members and their friends, including Mary Ellen Clark, Aurelia [Mrs. Webb] Souers, Harriett Louise Ankeny, Harriet S. Giese Ankeny, and Joseph Ankeny. Also includes a program from a class of 1880 high school graduation reception and miscellaneous cards.

4,741. Carroll, Jennie Dodson
Papers. 1925. 1 item.
Open. Card catalog.
Iowa State Historical Department, Division of Historical Museum and Archives, Historical Library.
Carroll was the wife of Beryl F. Carroll, Iowa governor from 1909 to 1913; they were married in 1886. Program contains a photo of [Mrs.] Carroll that was taken at the unveiling of her portrait in the portrait gallery of the Iowa Historical Building. The portrait was painted by Alice McKee.

4,742. Catt, Carrie Clinton (Lane) Chapman
Papers. Ca. 1871. 1.5 in.
Open. Card catalog.
Iowa State Historical Department, Division of Historical Museum and Archives, Historical Library.
Teacher's record book kept by [Mrs. George William] Catt (1859-1947), a woman suffrage leader and peace advocate, when she taught at a West Point, IA, school. Also includes photos. Catt's first husband was Lee Chapman.

4,743. Cogswell, Celia
Papers. Ca. 1920-32. 4 vols.
Open. Calendar.
Iowa State Historical Department, Division of Historical Museum and Archives, Historical Library.
Photos of theater personalities, scrapbooks of theater clippings, concert programs, and theater magazines and bulletins of Cogswell, an amateur actress. Includes many issues of *The Princess Theatre Bulletin; The Princess Theatre Bulletin, The Ralph Bellamy Players; The Playhouse Magazine, The Kendall Playhouse;* and other magazines. Among the women represented in ca. 97 theater photos are Anne Brouaugh, Rosemary Carlton, Mary Holton, Ruth Allan, Blanche Moulton, Frances McHenry, Janet Allyn, Margaret Lee, Fay Bainter, and Caine Thatcher.

4,744. Covert, Emzie Amelia
Papers. Ca. 1884-?. 3 items.
Open. Card catalog.
Iowa State Historical Department, Division of Historical Museum and Archives, Historical Library.
Covert (1858-1947), the daughter of George Washington Covert and Mary Jane Judd Covert, was a schoolteacher and Nebraska settler. Biographical sketch; a letter of recommendation from Dan Miller, a Jasper County, IA, school superintendent; and school papers of a student group awarded first prize in an 1884 county fair school exhibit. Educated in part at Grinnell College, Covert taught school in Kellogg, IA, and in the Newton area. During the 1880s she filed a homestead claim in Nebraska with her father. She married Alexander "Andy" Armstrong in 1886 and later resided in Nebraska and in Newton, IA, where she was active in the First Methodist Church, taught Sunday school, and served for several years as president of the Women's Home Missionary Society.

4,745. Daughters of Union Veterans of the Civil War
Records. Ca. 1918-57. Ca. 1.5 in.
Open. Card catalog.
Iowa State Historical Department, Division of Historical Museum and Archives, Historical Library.
The national Daughters organization was established in 1885. Rosters of the National Alliance of the Daughters, 1918-21 and 1926-27; a financial statement from the national treasurer, 1957; general orders and circular letters from national headquarters and from the Iowa headquarters of the Daughters; history of the national organization; programs from national conventions and luncheons and from Iowa meetings; a poem "Roll Call"; clippings about and two letters to Lola [Mrs. E. A.] Elliott, president of the Iowa Daughters organization in 1919 and 1920 and president of the national Daughters in 1922 and 1923; and a small souvenir gavel.

4,746. Davis, Varina Anne (Howell)
Papers. Ca. 1890. 3.5 in.
Open. Card catalog.
Iowa State Historical Department, Division of Historical Museum and Archives, Historical Library.
Davis (1826-1906) was an author and the wife of Jefferson Davis, president of the Confederacy. Manuscripts and some proof sheets, notes, and typed correspondence she used in writing *Jefferson Davis, Ex-President of the Confederate States of America, A Memoir by His Wife* (New York: Belford Co., 1890). Two folders from the collection have been microfilmed.

4,747. Deering, Mrs. N. C.
Papers. 1898-1903. 2 items.
Open. No guide.
Iowa State Historical Department, Division of Historical Museum and Archives, Historical Library.
Correspondence of Deering, whose husband may have been Nathaniel Cobb Deering (1827-87), a national bank examiner for the state of Iowa between 1872 and 1877, a member of the US House of Representatives from Iowa from 1877 to 1883, and former regent of the Smithsonian Institute. Consists of one letter to her from James Harlan, a US senator from Iowa, and one letter she wrote to Charles Aldrich, an Iowa newspaper publisher and politician who became curator of the Iowa State Historical Department in 1892.

4,748. Des Moines Federation of Women's Clubs
Records. 1898-1970. Ca. 9.33 ft.
Open. No guide.
Iowa State Historical Department, Division of Historical Museum and Archives, Historical Library.
Organized in 1898, the Federation became affiliated with the Iowa Federation of Women's Clubs in 1901. Minutes, 1924-59; executive committee reports; treasurer's and budget committee reports; check stubs; scholarship loan fund accounts; music committee reports and all-city caroling records; history and other items of the Past Presidents Club, formed in 1918; Philanthropy Club records; the Federation's entries in the Community Achievement Contest, 1898-1958; scattered yearbooks; scrapbooks; program resources and techniques bulletins; and issues of the Iowa *Federation News.*

4,749. Dodge, Grenville M.
Papers. Ca. 1851-1916. 105 vols.
Open. Calendar.
Iowa State Historical Department, Division of Historical Museum and Archives, Historical Library.
Correspondence and business and legal papers of Dodge (1831-1916), a civil engineer, Civil War general, and US congressman from the fifth district who was elected in 1866 and served one term. He also was active as president, member of the board of directors, and engineer for a number of railroad enterprises including the Union Pacific and the Denver and Gulf Railway Company. His personal correspondence includes letters from his mother Julia T. (Phillips) Dodge (1802-?); his wife Anne Dodge; his daughters Lettie, Ella, and Anne; and his sister. Collection also contains recollections of his mother Julia Dodge; papers of his daughter Lettie (Dodge) Montgomery, including personal correspondence with family and friends, business correspondence with the Montgomery family, papers and reports from the Grenville Dodge Trust, and other legal documents; and correspondence and other papers of Lettie Montgomery's son Langford Montgomery.

4,750. Dodge, Nathan P.
Papers. Ca. 1850s-77. 1.5 in.
Access restricted. Card catalog.
Iowa State Historical Department, Division of Historical Museum and Archives, Historical Library.
Biographical and historical papers of Dodge include his 30-page description of Council Bluffs, IA, during the Civil War, recollections of his mother Julia T. (Phillips) Dodge (1802-?) as told to Nathan Dodge in 1876 and 1877, and a 195-page biographical sketch of Dodge family ancestors, which includes typed excerpts from family correspondence dating from the 1850s. Nathan Dodge was the brother of Grenville M. Dodge, a civil engineer, politician, and railroad businessman; he also was the brother of Julia (Dodge) Beard.

4,751. Dubuque Conversational Club
Records. 1869-1916. 3.25 in.
Open. Card catalog.
Iowa State Historical Department, Division of Historical Museum and Archives, Historical Library.
Record books of this Iowa cultural and literary women's group, which was organized in 1868.

4,752. Dubuque Female College
Records. 1854-?. 2 items.
Open. Card catalog.
Iowa State Historical Department, Division of Historical Museum and Archives, Historical Library.
Prospectus dated 1854 of this Iowa women's school and a six-page article by Thornton J. Farnam entitled "Catherine Beecher and the Dubuque Female College."

4,753. Dubuque, IA, Clubs
Papers. 1859-93. 0.5 in.
Open. Card catalog.
Iowa State Historical Department, Division of Historical Museum and Archives, Historical Library.
Records of early Dubuque women's clubs were compiled for a Woman's Building exhibit at the World's Columbian Exposition by Mary (Newbury) Adams, a pioneer worker in the Iowa Federation of Women's Clubs and a leader in founding the Northern Iowa Suffrage Society in 1869. Includes information about and typed extracts of secretaries' reports of the Reading Club, organized in 1859; the Conversational Club, formed in 1868; and the Tuesday Evening Club, founded in 1869.

4,754. Dugdale, Joseph A.
Papers. 1866-73. 26 items.
Open. Calendar.
Iowa State Historical Department, Division of Historical Museum and Archives, Historical Library.
Correspondence of Dugdale (1810-?), a Quaker minister, peace advocate, and reformer who promoted the causes of the insane, the Indian, the Negro, and women; he also helped organize the 1870 Iowa Woman Suffrage Convention in Mount Pleasant. Most of his letters pertain to the Convention in Mount Pleasant as well as to the Iowa Peace Society meeting held in town one day after the suffrage meetings. His correspondents include Amelia Bloomer, Lydia Maria Child, and Joel Bean. Dugdale was born in Pennsylvania and resided there and in Ohio until 1862, when he moved to Mount Pleasant. Long interested in reform, he was a member of the central committee

appointed by the first National Woman Suffrage Convention at Worcester, MA, in 1850. Three years later he helped organize the Longwood Meeting of Progressive Friends, a Quaker group in Chester, PA, which for many years sponsored various reforms. In 1866 Dugdale was elected vice-president of the National Peace Convention. His wife Ruth Dugdale was also a Quaker and shared his reform interests.

4,755. Dunklin, William A., and Dunklin, Jennie
Papers. 1859-68. 1.5 in.
Open. Index and card catalog.
Iowa State Historical Department, Division of Historical Museum and Archives, Historical Library.
A captain in the 44th Georgia Infantry, William A. Dunklin was killed during the Civil War. Papers chiefly consist of correspondence of Dunklin with his wife Jennie Dunklin before their marriage and during the War. Also contains three letters Jennie wrote to a new suitor before her marriage to William; correspondence from family members, including items about Dunklin's death; and his military records.

4,756. Earhart, Amelia Mary
Papers. 1963. 1 item.
Open. Card catalog.
Iowa State Historical Department, Division of Historical Museum and Archives, Historical Library.
Official First Day cover featuring Earhart (1897-1937), an aviator, on an eight-cent US airmail postage stamp. First Day covers were sent to the governor of each state.

4,757. Fifty-First Iowa Mother's Prayer Circle
Records. 1898-1905. 2 vols.
Open. Card catalog.
Iowa State Historical Department, Division of Historical Museum and Archives, Historical Library.
Secretary's books contain the constitution and minutes of the Circle, organized for mothers, wives, and sisters of soldiers in the 51st Iowa Regiment.

4,758. Flannery, Agnes Veronica
Papers. Ca. 1940s-50s. 2 vols.
Open. Card catalog.
Iowa State Historical Department, Division of Historical Museum and Archives, Historical Library.
Correspondence, poetry, programs, and clippings of Flannery (1879-), an author, pertain to the activities of the Iowa Federation of Music Clubs and the Iowa Poets Day Association. Also includes her book *Iowa Centennial 1846-1946 Poetry Anthology,* a pamphlet "What of the Iowa Poets?" by Jessie Welborn Smith, and a program of The Composers and Authors Association of America from 1950.

4,759. Gallagher, Sister Mary Annette
Papers. 1970. Ca. 509 pp.
Open. Card catalog.
Iowa State Historical Department, Division of Historical Museum and Archives, Historical Library.
PhD dissertation completed at the University of Arizona by Sister Gallagher pertains to John F. Lacey, a US congressman who served in the 51st and 53rd through 58th US Congresses.

4,760. Godwin: Flora, Emma, and Eva
Papers. Ca. 1886. 1 vol. and 1 item.
Open. Card catalog.
Iowa State Historical Department, Division of Historical Museum and Archives, Historical Library.
Letter addressed to Flora, Emma, and Eva Godwin, who were Davenport, IA, schoolgirls, from their friend Sadie Robson and the sixth-grade penmanship book of Flora Godwin.

4,761. Gordon: Letter Respecting Women's Rights
Papers. Nd. 2.5-page item.
Open. No guide.
Iowa State Historical Department, Division of Historical Museum and Archives, Historical Library.
Anonymous manuscript entitled "Woman a Peer" was given to the repository by a Mrs. Gordon.

4,762. Gould, Lolita
Papers. 1911. 1 vol.
Open. Card catalog.
Iowa State Historical Department, Division of Historical Museum and Archives, Historical Library.
Diary of a young girl from Sidney, IA, who was studying at the Columbia College of Expression in Chicago.

4,763. Gue, Benjamin F.
Papers. 1850-83. Ca. 0.25 in.
Open. Card catalog.
Iowa State Historical Department, Division of Historical Museum and Archives, Historical Library.
Gue (1828-1904) was lieutenant governor of Iowa from 1866 to 1868, an historian of Iowa history, and a newspaper editor. Consists primarily of personal correspondence with his wife Elizabeth Parker Gue and with his daughters. Elizabeth Gue was an advocate of woman suffrage, and Benjamin Gue also supported this cause.

4,764. Hodges, Joy
Papers. Ca. 1926-68. Ca. 0.5 in.
Open. Index and card catalog.
Iowa State Historical Department, Division of Historical Museum and Archives, Historical Library.
Papers of Hodges, an actress, contain a biographical sketch; photos from theater and stage shows in which she was featured; telegrams for the Blue Bird Twins, who performed on Des Moines radio in 1926, and from Moss Hart and Noel Coward when *I'd Rather Be Right* was performed in 1937 with George M. Cohan; clippings about Hodges; and various programs from theater productions in which she appeared, including *Take Her, She's Mine* with Durwood Kirby in 1964 and *Never Too Late* with Milton Berle in 1965. Also includes photos showing Hodges with Lucille Ball, Margaret Callahan, Anne Shirley, Phyllis Brooks, and Molly Lamont in 1936.

4,765. Howe, Orlando C.
Papers. Ca. 1848-1910. 8 in.
Open. Card catalog.
Iowa State Historical Department, Division of Historical Museum and Archives, Historical Library.
Howe (1824-99) was a lawyer and Barber County, KS, district judge who became a law professor at the State University of Iowa (now known as the University of Iowa) in Iowa City from 1875 to 1880. Earlier Judge Howe had participated in the "relief expedition" sent out after the Spirit Lake Massacre in northern Iowa in 1857, where a small colony of 32 whites were killed by a band of Wahpeton Sioux under the leadership of Inkpaduta. Correspondence, most of which pertains to the early settlement of Newton, IA, to Howe's Civil War experiences, and to his life in Kansas and later as law professor in Iowa, also includes family correspondence of his wife, 1880s-1910, and of other women in his family, 1840s-60s. Also contains his lectures and essays with material on the Spirit Lake Massacre, an 11-page account of the Massacre by Evelyn (Howe) Porter, and Howe's record books with verses and notations.

4,766. Huntington, Ida M.
Papers. Nd. 0.25 in.
Open. Card catalog.
Iowa State Historical Department, Division of Historical Museum and Archives, Historical Library.
Copies of typed articles and a poem by Huntington, a writer. Includes her list of items at a 1916 Swedish art exhibit, a poem "The Country Constituent's Visit to the Legislature," and several pieces on Iowa history.

4,767. Icarian Community
Records. 1853-1947. 5 vols.
Open. Calendar.
Iowa State Historical Department, Division of Historical Museum and Archives, Historical Library.
After an unsuccessful attempt in Texas in 1848, this communal society was established in 1851 in Nauvoo, IL, under the leadership of Etienne Cabet and planned according to his philosophy as expressed in *Le Voyage en Icarie* (1840). Political dissension that forced Cabet to leave the Community in 1856 and economic failures after the Panic of 1857 led the Icarians to move their colony to 3,000 acres of land in Adams County, IA, near Corning in 1860. The bulk of the collection relates to the activities of Icarians in Iowa. Articles of incorporation; laws and regulations; handwritten records of Icarie, 1857-1910; financial receipts and statements; correspondence; journals; photos of men and women; biographical sketches of Community members; drawings of buildings and property, 1857-77; a 10-page typescript account by Corning resident Maude M. Friman about the Young Icarian faction whose dissension in the Community during the 1870s eventually caused older members to form a separate colony on Community property; maps; music; clippings and newspapers; Bibles; books such as *Child of Icaria* (1938) by Marie (Marchand) Ross; and other items. The Young Icarians existed as a group until 1886, and the other "La Nouvelle Communauté Icarienne" colony voted to dissolve in 1895 because of old age and sickness; legal dissolution and land distribution among members was completed in 1898. See Ruth A. Gallaher, "Icaria and Icarians," *Palimpsest,* II (April 1921).

4,768. Iowa Association of Colored Women's Clubs
Records. Ca. 1902-72. 8 in.
Open. Card catalog.
Iowa State Historical Department, Division of Historical Museum and Archives, Historical Library.
Founded in 1902 as the Iowa State Federation of Afro-American Women and by 1905 renamed the State Federation of Colored Women's Clubs, the Association assumed its current name in the early 1970s. Constitution; bylaws and duties of officers; one volume containing programs and minutes of meetings and conventions from 1903 to 1923; convention programs from 1923 to 1967; the 1964 report of Federation president Roberta Frazier; photos, including one of the 1903 convention; scrapbooks containing programs from club affiliates; two issues of *National Notes Magazine;* and other items. Also includes a biography of Hallie Quinn Brown, a black teacher, elocutionist, and clubwoman.

4,769. Junior Federation of Women's Clubs, Des Moines
Records. 1917-73. 8 in.
Open. Card catalog.
Iowa State Historical Department, Division of Historical Museum and Archives, Historical Library.
Records of the Junior Federation, which was organized in 1920 and existed until 1973, contain scattered GFWC reports of the department of junior women's clubs from the 1930s; receipt and attendance books; a Junior Federation history; yearbooks and programs from Clubs in Des Moines and other Iowa towns; constitution, correspondence, yearbooks from ca. 1933 to 1960, and programs of the past presidents group within the Junior Federation; a photo of Florence Kinney; clippings; a 22nd Bicentennial booklet of the Iowa Federation of Women's Clubs, 1937; a Girl Volunteer Aid yearbook, 1917-18; and other items.

4,770. Ladies Club Work in Iowa
Papers. Ca. 1884. 1 in.
Open. Card catalog.

Iowa State Historical Department, Division of Historical Museum and Archives, Historical Library. Report on women's club activity was prepared by Iowa clubwoman and suffrage worker Mary (Newbury) Adams. Also contains her correspondence and club reports and yearbooks she compiled of the Dubuque Ladies Literary Association, the Cedar Rapids Ladies Literary Club, the Nineteenth Century Club of Iowa City, and the Raphael Art Club, also of Iowa City.

4,771. Letts, Albina Brockway
Papers. Nd. 1 item.
Open. Card catalog.
Iowa State Historical Department, Division of Historical Museum and Archives, Historical Library. Literary piece by [Mrs.] Letts of Clarendon, TX, is entitled "Christmas at Uncle Richard's in 1845."

4,772. Lunt, Belle Waldrip
Papers. Nd. 11-page item.
Open. Card catalog.
Iowa State Historical Department, Division of Historical Museum and Archives, Historical Library. Manuscript in which [Mrs. C. L.] Lunt recounts events in the life of Isaac Waldrip, a circuit rider during the 1840s and longtime resident of Lineville, IA. Waldrip's circuit included communities in Iowa, Missouri, and Nebraska.

4,773. Marshall County Pioneers
Collection. 1858-1910. 1.25 in.
Open. Card catalog.
Iowa State Historical Department, Division of Historical Museum and Archives, Historical Library. Pioneer recollections read before the Marshall County Historical Society between 1908 and 1910 were written between 1858 and 1910. Most of the reminiscences contain information about pioneer experiences during the late 1850s. Includes "Early Iowa Trails" by Mrs. H. Howell, "The Topic of the Day" written in 1858 by Marey E. [Mrs. Sylvester] Lacey, and other recollections by [Mrs.] Martha Beeson, Sarah J. Statler, and [Mrs.] Louisa Childs-Coate.

4,774. Methodist Episcopal Church
Records. Ca. 1832-1939. 45 vols.
Open. Card catalog.
Iowa State Historical Department, Division of Historical Museum and Archives, Historical Library. Scattered general conference reports of the Church, 1892-1932; Methodist Disciplines, or ceremony and liturgy records, for the entire period; notebooks on leaders of Methodism; pamphlets containing annual reports for state conferences in Michigan, Minnesota, New Jersey, South Dakota, Indiana, Kansas, and Nebraska, scattered through the period 1871-1939; 141 alphabetized envelopes of data on bishops and ministers of the Church; sermons; photos; and hymn books. Also includes a history of the Des Moines conference, which contains memoirs of preachers' wives from 1880 to 1926, and pamphlets about the Woman's Home Missionary Society, 1882-83, and the Woman's Foreign Missionary Society, ca. 1878-98.

4,775. Monday Club
Records. Ca. 1879-1936. 12 in.
Open. Card catalog.
Iowa State Historical Department, Division of Historical Museum and Archives, Historical Library. Constitution, annual reports, secretary's minutes to 1925, a history, a pamphlet, excerpts from the 50th anniversary program, and other items of the Club, a women's afternoon reading group in Des Moines, which was formed in 1879 and affiliated with the GFWC in 1919.

4,776. Murdock, Marion
Papers. Ca. 1888-1943. 0.25 in.
Open. No guide.
Iowa State Historical Department, Division of Historical Museum and Archives, Historical Library. Sermons, poems, a pamphlet, and a memorial service program of Murdock (1848-1943), an ordained Unitarian minister and poet who was born in Garnavillo, IA. In 1888 she was pastor of the Unity Church in Humboldt, IA; in 1897 she became pastor of a Cleveland, IA, church where she served for six years. Murdock was elected president of the League of Women in the Ministry in 1914. In later life she worked as a missionary minister in the United States and as a teacher of art and literature.

4,777. Northeastern Iowa Teachers' Association
Records. 1916-29. 1 vol.
Open. No guide.
Iowa State Historical Department, Division of Historical Museum and Archives, Historical Library. Bound volume of the proceedings of the Association contains minutes, programs, clippings, and other items.

4,778. Order of Eastern Star
Records. 1886. 1 item.
Open. Card catalog.
Iowa State Historical Department, Division of Historical Museum and Archives, Historical Library. Rituals for this Masonic organization in which women participated.

4,779. Pell, Maria P.
Papers. 1885. 1 item.
Open. Card catalog.
Iowa State Historical Department, Division of Historical Museum and Archives, Historical Library. Letter that Pell, the wife of a Sibley, IA, Congregational minister, wrote to [Miss] May I. Cooper and the Ladies Benevolent Society of the First Congregational Church in Amherst, MA, describing her family's clothing needs and specifying the sizes required.

4,780. Polk County Republican Women's Association
Records. 1938-59. 8 in.
Open. Card catalog.
Iowa State Historical Department, Division of Historical Museum and Archives, Historical Library. Minutes, correspondence, and membership records of the Association.

4,781. Shonemann, A. C. E.
Collection. Ca. 1880s-1920s. 4.25 in.
Open. Calendar and index.
Iowa State Historical Department, Division of Historical Museum and Archives, Historical Library. Autograph collection containing assorted letters, photos, cards, and programs represent individuals involved in music and theater as well as other prominent persons. Among the women identified in the collection are Jane Addams, early 20th-century actress Viola Allen, Susan B. Anthony, actresses Lulu Glaser and Anna Held, novelist Mary J. Holmes, Elizabeth Riis, authors Harriet (Prescott) Spofford and Alice French, and poet Ella (Wheeler) Wilcox. Women represented in the photos are [Miss] Hazel Hirsh, Margaret Illington, [Miss] Jane Salisbury, Vivian Martin, and actresses Maude Adams, May Robson, Sophye Barnard, and Trixie Friganza.

4,782. Smith, Hattie Amelia
Papers. 1863. 1 vol.
Open. Card catalog.
Iowa State Historical Department, Division of Historical Museum and Archives, Historical Library. Daybook that Harriet "Hattie" Amelia Smith (ca. 1841-1923) kept at the age of 22 accompanying her uncle Porter T. Hinman and his family on a journey by ox wagon from Saylorville in Polk County, IA, to Boulder County, CO. She describes their experiences traveling across western Iowa and the unsettled plains of Nebraska and Colorado. Soon thereafter, Smith returned to Iowa, where she lived with her widowed mother and taught school until her marriage to Wesley Nickle in 1881. The daybook has been published in the *Annals of Iowa,* XXXV, No. 2 (Fall 1959) as "To Pike's Peak by Ox-Wagon, the Harriet A. Smith Day-Book," edited by Fleming Fraker, Jr.

4,783. Snyder, Anna
Papers. 1894- 97. 4 items.
Open. Card catalog.
Iowa State Historical Department, Division of Historical Museum and Archives, Historical Library. Teacher's certificates of a schoolteacher were issued in Chariton, Lucas County, IA.

4,784. Thompson, William G.
Papers. 1861-64. Ca. 4.5 in.
Open. Card catalog.
Iowa State Historical Department, Division of Historical Museum and Archives, Historical Library. A lawyer who came to Iowa in 1853, settled in Marion, and was active in Republican party politics, Thompson (1830-1911) held the rank of major in the 20th Iowa volunteer infantry during the Civil War. Correspondence with his wife Harriet Jane Thompson chiefly consists of her love letters to him and letters detailing domestic and family concerns. Also contains photos, clippings, assorted military documents, and a button from a Union Army uniform. In 1879 William Thompson was appointed chief justice of the Idaho Territory and elected to Congress from Iowa's fifth district.

4,785. Walker, Margaret Coulson
Papers. Nd. 2 items.
Open. Card catalog.
Iowa State Historical Department, Division of Historical Museum and Archives, Historical Library. Literary manuscripts by Walker, a writer, which were published as *The Study of Birds* and *Birds and Bird Babies.* Includes illustrations.

4,786. Woman's Christian Temperance Union
Records. 1880-82. 1 vol.
Open. Card catalog.
Iowa State Historical Department, Division of Historical Museum and Archives, Historical Library. Secretary's minutes of the Dexter, IA, branch of the WCTU.

4,787. Woman's Relief Corps
Records. 1883-1913. 8.5 in.
Open. Card catalog.
Iowa State Historical Department, Division of Historical Museum and Archives, Historical Library. Record books, rolls, and quarterly reports of the Iowa Woman's Relief Corps, the state auxiliary body of the Grand Army of the Republic; record books of Iowa county chapters; a list of disbanded posts; and charters of local WRC posts in Fayette, Leon, Magnolia, Orient, Rolfe, West Union, Angency, Stanley, Stanwood, Belmond, Sumner, Sheffield, Maxwell, Moville, Douds-Leando, Adel, Fonda, Valley Junction, and Fairbanks, IA.

4,788. Woman's State Forensic League
Records. 1926. 0.25 in.
Open. No guide.
Iowa State Historical Department, Division of Historical Museum and Archives, Historical Library. Consists of speeches given by League members in a Pella, IA, contest.

4,789. Abraham, Lot
Papers. Ca. 1862-65. 20 in.
Open. Calendar and card catalog.
Iowa State Historical Library.
Correspondence, muster rolls, special orders, morning reports, and other papers of Abraham (1838-1920), a Civil War soldier who reached the rank of captain. Includes personal letters he received in 1864 and 1865 from [Miss] Sarah C.

Alden (1841-88) of Salem, IA, who became his wife in 1865. After the War, Lot Abraham entered politics, and in 1881 he was elected to the Iowa State Senate. He also was active in the Grand Army of the Republic, serving in 1911 as commander of the GAR's Iowa department. Most of this collection has been microfilmed.

4,790. Allen, Amasa Orlando
Papers. 1861-63. Ca. 1.5 in.
Open. Card catalog.
Iowa State Historical Library.
Correspondence between Allen, who was a Civil War soldier, and his wife Agnes Allen. The letters are also available on microfilm.

4,791. Barton, Clara
Papers. 1865-67. Ca. 0.5 in.
Open. Card catalog.
Iowa State Historical Library.
Papers of Barton (1821-1912), a Civil War nurse who founded the American National Red Cross and served as its president for 23 years, consist of printed sheets listing names of and requesting information about missing soldiers.

4,792. Beaty, John, and Beaty, Delilah
Papers. Ca. 1850-60. 14 items.
Open. Card catalog.
Iowa State Historical Library.
Copies of letters to John Beaty and his wife Delilah Beaty from John A. and Mary Beery, S. N. Beery, Noah Beery, and Peter Beery. Most of the letters are addressed from Platte County, MO, and from Jaspar County, IA.

4,793. Callanan, Martha (Cooney)
Papers. 1885. 1 item.
Open. Card catalog.
Iowa State Historical Library.
Letter to [Mrs. James] Callanan (1826-1901), president of the Iowa Woman Suffrage Association from 1876 to 1880, from Iowa state auditor J. W. Cattell. Callanan started the *Woman's Standard,* an Iowa suffrage newspaper, in 1886 and published it for 13 years. She was active in the WCTU and helped organize a Des Moines chapter in 1874.

4,794. Callen, Martin, and Callen, Jane
Papers. Ca. 1845-76. 1.25 in.
Open. Card catalog.
Iowa State Historical Library.
Correspondence between Martin Callen and his wife Jane Callen, chiefly from the 1850s; a handwritten mechanic's dictionary; and a copy of the *Times Illustrated Hand-Book for 1876.*

4,795. Carle, Nancy Charlotte Emmaline Matchett
Papers. Nd. 1 item.
Open. Card catalog.
Iowa State Historical Library.
Reminiscences of Carle are entitled "Battle of Wilson's Creek, Memories of as a Little Girl." Also available on microfilm.

4,796. Clio Club
Records. 1902-75. 7.5 in.
Open. No guide.
Iowa State Historical Library.
Organized in 1900 by women from Drake University as The Leisure Hour Club, an informal sewing circle and social gathering, this Des Moines group assumed the name Clio Club in 1903 when it began to focus on discussions of British and American writers. Secretary's books, 1947-74; treasurer's records, 1910-60 and 1963-73; scrapbooks containing correspondence, scattered yearbooks, a Club history by Irene Smith, membership lists, photos of members, and clippings; and obituaries of members. The Club joined the Iowa Federation of Women's Clubs in 1913. It disbanded in 1975 because the last active members were elderly and unable to attend meetings.

4,797. Davis, Sarah
Papers. 1798-99. 1 vol.
Open. Card catalog.
Iowa State Historical Library.
Journal in which Davis describes her travels in eastern and southern states.

4,798. Dutton, Claude Webb
Papers. Ca. 1903-24. 3 vols.
Open. Card catalog.
Iowa State Historical Library.
Correspondence; legal documents pertaining to the *Gabriel et. al.* v. *Gallatin* case, 1909-17; photos; and souvenirs of Dutton. Includes correspondence of his mother Celinda Parker Dutton.

4,799. Dutton, Jerome
Papers. Ca. 1826-1901. 10 vols. and ca. 20 items.
Open. Card catalog.
Iowa State Historical Library.
Business and personal correspondence, diaries from 1850 to 1869, memorandum books, mortgages, deeds and abstracts, receipts, land patents, commissions, certificates, memorabilia, and other items of Dutton (1826-93), an Iowa businessman, farmer, and local official. Also includes correspondence of his wife Celinda Parker Dutton, a booklet containing her reminiscences and those of other family members as well as genealogical information, an autograph album she kept, and her certificates of membership in the DAR and the Francis Scott Key Memorial Association.

4,800. Eckberg, Minnie
Papers. Ca. 1913-55. 2.25 in.
Open. No guide.
Iowa State Historical Library.
Papers of Eckberg, a Des Moines clubwoman, contain correspondence and a booklet of programs pertaining to the Junior Federation of Women's Clubs, 1925-40; her school report cards; scrapbooks with clippings and programs of banquets and other activities of the Des Moines Junior Federation of Women's Clubs and of the Federation's Past President's Club; clippings about the Des Moines Women's Club; dance programs; invitations; a 1944 issue of *The Iowa Clubwoman* magazine; and other items. Also contains correspondence and other material of and about George Washington Carver.

4,801. Hall, Lynn
Papers. Ca. 1972. Ca. 0.5 in.
Open. Card catalog.
Iowa State Historical Library.
Hall (1937-) has written numerous books for young people. Galley proof from her book *Too Near the Sun* (Dell Publishing Co., 1972) and a biographical sketch of her.

4,802. Hays, Mary Blanche Nichols
Papers. Ca. 1873-1964. 3 items.
Open. Card catalog.
Iowa State Historical Library.
Papers of Hays (1876-1964) consist of a Sunday school teacher's class book, a clipping from the Kansas City *Star,* and a teacher's certificate dated 1873 from Winterset in Madison County, IA.

4,803. Hess, Whitney L.
Papers. Ca. 1834-43. 14 items.
Open. Card catalog.
Iowa State Historical Library.
Correspondence of Hess's grandmother Thankful B. [Mrs. John] Lesan contains descriptions of her experiences while moving to and settling in Iowa.

4,804. Holman, Lois Grant
Papers. 1856. 1 item.
Open. Card catalog.
Iowa State Historical Library.
Typed copy of a letter written by [Mrs. Palmer] Holman, an early Iowa settler, to her family in Rockville, CT, after her arrival in Iowa. Postscripts to the letter were written by her sons Albert and Jerome Holman.

4,805. Iowa Congress of Parents and Teachers
Records. 1934. 3-page item.
Open. Card catalog.
Iowa State Historical Library.
Typescripts of addresses presented for the dedication and unveiling of an oil portrait of Cora Bussey Hillis, the founder of the Iowa Congress.

4,806. Iowa State Teacher's Association
Records. 1872-1905. 1 vol.
Open. Card catalog.
Iowa State Historical Library.
Account book of the treasurer of this teachers' organization.

4,807. Kellogg, Harriett S.
Papers. Nd. 12-page item.
Open. Card catalog.
Iowa State Historical Library.
Article by Kellogg pertains to fiber plants of Iowa.

4,808. King, Grace Elizabeth
Papers. Ca. 1901. 2 items.
Open. Card catalog.
Iowa State Historical Library.
Letter from King (1853?-1932), an author, to Iowa State Historical Department curator Charles Aldrich and eight pages from her manuscript history of Louisiana.

4,809. Kneeland, Dolly
Papers. 1845. 1 item.
Open. Card catalog.
Iowa State Historical Library.
Consists of court papers for the *Dolly Kneeland et al. v. Waitsill Goodrich et al.* case pertaining to a conflict over land. Dolly L. Rice Kneeland was the fourth wife of Abner Kneeland (1774-1844), a New England Universalist minister from 1803 to 1829 who became a free thought advocate and leader of the First Society of Free Inquirers in Boston. In 1831 he founded the *Investigator,* an organ of free thought, and was associated with Robert Dale Owen and Frances Wright; he also established the free thought colony Salubria in 1839 near Farmington, IA. Dolly Kneeland was a widow with four children when she married him in 1834. See Mary R. Whitcomb, "Abner Kneeland: His Relations to Early Iowa History," *Annals of Iowa* 6, no. 5 (April 1904).

4,810. Lady Drummer of 1886
Papers. 1886. 2 items.
Open. No guide.
Iowa State Historical Library.
Handwritten account by an anonymous reporter about a lady drummer, or saleswoman, who sold goods to a Brookings, SD, druggist; the lady drummer apparently was viewed as a local novelty. Also includes a typed copy of the account.

4,811. Lang, Ivan
Papers. Ca. 1860-1934. 1 vol.
Open. Calendar.
Iowa State Historical Library.
Correspondence, tax receipts, insurance and mortgage documents, account books, deeds, books, and other family papers contain information about the Lympus, Springer, and Wheeler families. Includes letters written by women who were family members and friends, among them those that Libbie Wheeler wrote to her parents in 1889 describing the Mitchellville Girl's School, a reform school for girls in Mitchellville, IA.

4,812. Longley, Alice L.
Papers. Ca. 1851-1900. 0.5 in.
Open. Card catalog.
Iowa State Historical Library.
Papers include a diary in which Longley describes a trip to California in 1883; a diary of A. S.

Longley from 1855; a letter M. A. Roe wrote to his family from Bannock City, MT, in 1864; a clothing expense account of Eliza Ann Longley; extracts from reminiscences at the seventh annual meeting of the Old Settlers' Association in Grinnell, IA, in 1900, including those by Maria Parks Kellogg and Joanna Harris Haines; a letter written by Benoni Howard to be read at the 1894 meeting of the Old Settlers' Association; a list of students taking part in an 1858 school program in Grinnell; calling cards; and a piece of centennial calico.

4,813. McGinnis, Gertrude
Papers. Nd. 9-page item.
Open. Card catalog.
Iowa State Historical Library.
Manuscript written by McGinnis pertains to Iowa schools.

4,814. Morrissey, Elizabeth
Papers. 1918-74. Ca. 2 in.
Open. Calendar and card catalog.
Iowa State Historical Library.
Correspondence of Morrissey, a teacher at Mason City (IA) High School during the 1920s who later taught at the College of Notre Dame of Maryland, consists primarily of letters she received between 1918 and 1919 from members of the YMCA Expeditionary Force and the American National Red Cross. Morrissey earned a PhD in labor economics at Johns Hopkins University.

4,815. Needham, Grace (Darland)
Papers. Ca. 1888-1952. 2 vols.
Open. Description and card catalog.
Iowa State Historical Library.
Papers of Needham, a schoolteacher before her marriage to Iowa newspaper editor Sherman W. Needham (1881-1959) and an active clubwoman, consist of her correspondence; a teacher's record book she kept at Williamsburg (IA) High School from 1906 to 1907; scrapbooks, one of which contains a letter from her uncle William Vermillion, autographs, clippings, and programs, and another of which pertains to her husband's career; and assorted yearbooks and programs from numerous Iowa women's clubs and church groups in which she participated. Includes items from the Des Moines, Ames, and Eldora chapters of the DAR and the DAR national organization; material of the national, state, and 10 local chapters of the P. E. O. Sisterhood, which was founded in 1869 at Iowa Wesleyan College; and items from 25 other women's organizations, including the Ames Woman's Club, founded in 1915; the AAUW branch in Ames, formed in 1918; the Ladies Aid Society of the Collegiate Methodist Church in Ames; the Treble Clef Club, established in ca. 1909 in Eldora; the Monday Club, organized in 1896 in Eldora; the Eldora Federation of Club Women, formed in 1913; the LWV; and the Iowa Women's Republican Club, Story County unit.

4,816. Needham, Sherman W.
Papers. Nd. No size given.
Open. Card catalog.
Iowa State Historical Library.
Included in the papers of Needham (1881-1959), a newspaper editor for the Hardin County *Ledger* in Eldora, IA, and the Iowa state superintendent of printing from 1942 to 1959, are teaching certificates and academic diplomas and degrees of his wife Grace (Darland) Needham and of [Mrs.] Mary Vermillion Darland. Grace Needham completed grammar school in Oskaloosa, IA, in 1896, finished high school in Des Moines in 1901, and received a BS and teacher's certificate from the State University of Iowa in 1906. Mary Darland completed a four-year Chautauqua Circle reading course and received a bachelor of pedagogy degree from Oskaloosa College in 1893, earned a doctor of chiropractic degree from the Northwestern School of Chiropractic of Legrand, OR, in 1913, and completed a bachelor of philosophy program at Oskaloosa College in 1914.

4,817. Orwig, Thomas Gilbert, and Orwig, Mary Sipp
Papers. Ca. 1860s. 1 vol.
Open. Card catalog.
Iowa State Historical Library.
Civil War correspondence and photos, a prospectus from the Walkill Academy in Middletown, NY, and clippings of Thomas Orwig and Mary Orwig (?-1907), who were married in 1864. Thomas Orwig fought in Battery E of the 1st Pennsylvania Artillery during the War and also supported prohibition. Before her marriage Mary Orwig was educated in New York schools and at Mount Holyoke, MA; she worked as a schoolteacher, first as an assistant at Walkill Academy for the 1862-63 school year and later at the Culpepper Institute in Virginia. A member of the WCTU and national president of the Women's Foreign Missionary Society, Mary Orwig helped establish the Des Moines Home for the Aged after moving to Des Moines in 1868. She was blind for the last 20 years of her life.

4,818. Partridge, Lucy, and Partridge, Charles P.
Papers. 1832-62. 3 items.
Open. Card catalog.
Iowa State Historical Library.
Papers include a De Kalb County, IL, teacher's license of Lucy Partridge, a schoolteacher, and a document appointing Charles Partridge corporal in the militia of New York state.

4,819. Peterson, Josephine, and Peterson, Anna
Papers. 1878-92. 1 vol.
Open. Card catalog.
Iowa State Historical Library.
Orations, photo album containing photos of the 1880 graduating class at Clarinda (IA) High School, a teaching certificate, a diploma, and commencement programs of Josephine Peterson, a schoolteacher; a photo album of Clarinda resident Anna Peterson, also a teacher, containing photos she received when she taught at a rural school in 1878; an 1883 almanac; and a photo of Mary Helene Peterson. Anna Peterson later married Thomas E. Powers.

4,820. Quigley, Iola B.
Papers. Ca. 1920s-30s. 0.25 in.
Open. Card catalog.
Iowa State Historical Library.
Correspondence and historical articles of Quigley, a teacher at Lincoln High School in Des Moines during the 1920s who also wrote about Iowa history. Several of her articles pertain to the history of railroads in the state.

4,821. Rann, Mary A.
Papers. Nd. 1 item.
Open. Card catalog.
Iowa State Historical Library.
Booklet entitled "Outdoor Sketches" by [Mrs.] Rann, an author from Manchester, IA.

4,822. Remey, Mary Josephine (Mason)
Papers. Ca. 1861-1920. 16 vols.
Open. Card catalog.
Iowa State Historical Library.
Correspondence, diaries from 1861 to 1866, an autobiographical sketch dated 1920, and a notebook on rhetorical abstracts of Remey (1845-1938), who was the daughter of Charles Mason, chief justice of the Iowa supreme court, and the wife of George C. Remey, a rear admiral in the US Navy. Her parents were Burlington, IA, pioneers.

4,823. Roadside Settlement House Association
Records. 1913-14. 1 item.
Open. Card catalog.
Iowa State Historical Library.
Annual report of the Association, incorporated in 1899, includes photos of activities at the Settlement House and a financial statement. The first building owned by this Des Moines social welfare group was opened in 1906 under the direction of Flora Dunlap, a friend of Jane Addams who came to Des Moines to work for the Association in 1904. She was the first successful woman candidate for the Des Moines school board, president of the Iowa Equal Suffrage Association from 1913 to 1915, and first president (1919-21) of the Iowa LWV.

4,824. Rourke, Ellen Mary
Papers. 1916-32. 4 vols.
Open. Card catalog.
Iowa State Historical Library.
In 1913 Rourke (1885-1943?) became the first woman factory inspector in Iowa. Leatherbound notebooks contain items about her career, which lasted for 20 years. Her appointment as factory inspector was hailed as Iowa's first step toward improving the conditions under which women and children worked in Iowa industries.

4,825. Rousseau, Mrs. James
Papers. 1864-?. 3 items.
Open. No guide.
Iowa State Historical Library.
Typed copy of a diary kept by Rousseau containing details about a trip from Knoxville and Pella, IA, to California and a letter and post card in which the diary is discussed.

4,826. Russell, Lillian
Papers. Nd. 1 folder.
Open. Card catalog.
Iowa State Historical Library.
Lillian Russell was the stage name for Helen Louise Leonard (1861-1922), an actress and star of musical comedy who was born in Clinton, IA. Recommendations for beauty treatments, a formula for a cucumber cream and a face bleach, instructions on a treatment with green soap, and a letter she sent with beauty suggestions that was hand stamped with the name Lillian Russell.

4,827. Sackett, Emma
Papers. Ca. 1860s. 1 item.
Open. Card catalog.
Iowa State Historical Library.
Army nurse's certificate of [Mrs.] Sackett was issued in recognition of her services during the Civil War.

4,828. Salisbury, Helen
Papers. Ca. 1890-1927. 1.25 in.
Open. Card catalog.
Iowa State Historical Library.
Letter, documents, photos, programs, a booklet, school diplomas, and magazines collected by Salisbury include photos and programs of the Hospital for the Insane in Independence, IA, some of which depict women; a letter written by Independence resident A. L. Rosenberger regarding pay for Nora Manling; programs from several Hampton High School commencements and from the State University of Iowa school of journalism; and the booklet *Lectures on Cooking* assembled for an 1895-96 class.

4,829. Salter, William
Papers. 1824-1903. 7 vols.
Open. Card catalog.
Iowa State Historical Library.
Correspondence of Salter (1821-1910), a Congregational minister in Burlington, IA, and prominent state historian, includes his correspondence from 1845 and 1846 with Mary Ann Mackintire (1824-93), whom he later married. Salter met Mackintire while he was a student at Andover Theological Seminary and she a student at Bradford Academy. Their letters reflect his early experiences in the Iowa Territory as a traveling

missionary preacher and then in 1846 as pastor of the First Congregational Church of Burlington. Salter had been one of 11 young ministers who formed the Iowa Band in 1843 for the purpose of establishing Congregational churches on the Iowa frontier. He and other Band members also were instrumental in organizing the Free Soil party in Iowa. Portions of the Salter-Mackintire correspondence have been edited by Philip Jordan and published in *Annals of Iowa* 19 (April-July-Oct. 1934).

4,830. Samuelson, Agnes
Papers. Ca. 1932-54. 4 in.
Open. Card catalog.
Iowa State Historical Library.
Samuelson (1887-1963) was Iowa state superintendent of public instruction from 1927 to 1936, president of the National Education Association in 1935 and 1936, and executive secretary of the Iowa State Teachers Association between 1939 and 1945. Speeches she gave, scrapbooks she kept between 1932 and 1954, and a booklet with photos of a trip she made to the site of the first schoolhouse in Iowa in 1932.

4,831. Savery, Annie N.
Papers. 1875. 2 items.
Open. Card catalog.
Iowa State Historical Library.
Bachelor of law diploma and a certificate of admission to Iowa's supreme court for [Mrs. James] Savery (1831-91), one of the first three women to graduate from the law department of the State University of Iowa, now the University of Iowa, in 1875. Savery also was active in organizing the Polk County Woman Suffrage Society and the Iowa Woman Suffrage Association.

4,832. Schermerhorn, Winfield Scott
Papers. Ca. 1849-72. 4 in.
Open. Card catalog.
Iowa State Historical Library.
Schermerhorn was a regimental surgeon with the 16th Wisconsin Volunteers during the Civil War; he also served in the Wisconsin legislature. Family correspondence; diaries, including diary notes of his wife Jane Schermerhorn from 1852; and clippings.

4,833. Schermerhorn, Zella
Papers. Nd. 1 item.
Open. Card catalog.
Iowa State Historical Library.
Manuscript of Schermerhorn on the history of WWI provides information about army divisions and governmental agencies participating in the war effort.

4,834. Schmidt, Mrs. Louis B.
Papers. Ca. 1858-1943. 3 items.
Open. Card catalog.
Iowa State Historical Library.
Short story and poem by G. Perle [Mrs. Louis B.] Schmidt and a clipping about Waterloo, IA, pioneer Mrs. Alpheus Lawrence.

4,835. Scott, Mrs. John
Papers. 1876. 1 item.
Open. Card catalog.
Iowa State Historical Library.
Certificate of award presented to Scott by the women's department at the Centennial International Exposition in Philadelphia for the collection of Iowa women's work that was displayed.

4,836. Sharp, John, and Sharp, Helen Maria
Papers. 1861-65. 1 in.
Open. Card catalog.
Iowa State Historical Library.
Correspondence between John Sharp, a private in the Union Army, and his wife Helen Maria Sharp during the Civil War. Private Sharp served in Company D, Second Iowa Volunteer Infantry, in 1861 and in the 10th Iowa Volunteer Infantry in 1865.

4,837. Smith, Ida B. Wise
Papers. Nd. 1 item.
Open. Card catalog.
Iowa State Historical Library.
Consists of "In God We Trust—Christian Foundations of Our Government," a speech by Smith, who was honorary president of the national WCTU and a member of the Iowa Equal Suffrage Association.

4,838. Social Literary Circle of East Des Moines
Records. 1883-95. 1.5 in.
Open. Card catalog.
Iowa State Historical Library.
Minutes of this social and literary group, which included both male and female members. Mary E. Waldron was the Circle's first secretary, and Isaac Brandt served as first president. A dry goods merchant who moved from Ohio to Des Moines in 1856, Brandt supported abolition and was a friend of John Brown. He was prominent in the Iowa Republican party and held several offices in that state between 1867 and 1894.

4,839. Stern, Millicent B.
Papers. Nd. 1 item.
Open. Card catalog.
Iowa State Historical Library.
A woman suffrage and temperance advocate, Stern (1820-1904) was also active in the Woman's Relief Corps. In 1866 she organized the first Farmer's Club in Iowa, the Harris Grove Farmer's Club, with the help of her husband Jacob B. Stern. Her petition to Congress asking that slavery be abolished contains only one signature and was signed prior to 1857.

4,840. Stevens, Nancy Jane
Papers. 1871. 4-page item.
Open. Description and card catalog.
Iowa State Historical Library.
Account in which Stevens (1846-?), a Jefferson, IA, resident, describes a trip she made in 1864 from Sidney, IA, to Denver.

4,841. Summer, Henry, and Summer, Matilda
Papers. 1887-1950. 19 vols.
Open. Card catalog.
Iowa State Historical Library.
Farm journals of the Summers, who resided in Charles City, IA.

4,842. Taber, Ellen Strang
Papers. Ca. 1859-1923. 1 ft.
Open. Card catalog.
Iowa State Historical Library.
A schoolteacher before her marriage, [Mrs.] Taber (1846-ca. 1931) became a housewife in Albion and Grinnell, IA; at various times she also sold sewing machines from a horse and buggy, sold books, and operated a boarding house for college students. Diaries she kept from 1859 to 1923; a letter she wrote to the Albion Quaker monthly meeting; correspondence of the Strang and Smith families; a report by her sister Sarah Ann Kellogg of an Indian attack at Correctionville, IA, in 1861; school dialogues, an 1859 attendance record, academic exercises, and poems; genealogical material; a recipe for tonic; clippings; and programs. Also contains correspondence of Taber's granddaughter Lida Lisle Greene from ca. 1961 when Greene worked at the Newton, IA, library; currently she is a librarian at the Iowa State Historical Department.

4,843. Talboy, Helen H.
Papers. Ca. 1941-45. 1 folder.
Open. Card catalog.
Iowa State Historical Library.
Mrs. Talboy (1908-69) was a nurse with the American National Red Cross Hospital in Anzio, Italy, during WWII. She won the Purple Heart and was acclaimed a heroine when, after the Hospital was bombed and the head nurse killed, Talboy assumed responsibility and continued caring for patients during the crisis. Letters she wrote home from Italy, documents concerning her career, an autobiographical sketch, and clippings about her.

4,844. Taylor, Jane Wilson
Papers. Ca. 1863. 4 items.
Open. Card catalog.
Iowa State Historical Library.
Letter to [Miss] Taylor from her cousin Augustus Baxter Breed at General Hospital No. 8 in New Albany, IN; a brief biographical sketch of Breed and of Taylor; a photo of her; and an essay "The Costliness of Human Progress," which was read at the graduation exercises at Denmark Academy in Iowa.

4,845. Tedrow, Jane
Papers. Ca. 1849-86. 1 folder.
Open. Card catalog.
Iowa State Historical Library.
Letter that Phoebe Miller wrote to her mother Jane Tedrow in 1849, a letter from James S. Vanscoy to his parents in 1861, miscellaneous notes, and teacher's certificates of Sillah Tedrow for 1884 to 1886.

4,846. Tourist Club
Records. 1892-1963. Ca. 12 in.
Open. Calendar.
Iowa State Historical Library.
Organized in 1892, this Des Moines women's group affiliated with the Iowa Federation of Women's Clubs in 1893 and with the GFWC two years later. Secretary's books to 1958, correspondence, Club yearbooks, a list of charter members, certificates of Club memberships in the Iowa Federation and the GFWC, material pertaining to the 50th anniversary of the Club and its history, obituaries and memorials for members, clippings, a pamphlet on proposed revisions of the Iowa Federation bylaws, and memorabilia.

4,847. Tyler, Pauline
Papers. Ca. 1892-1957. 2 items.
Open. Card catalog.
Iowa State Historical Library.
Correspondence of [Miss] Tyler (?-1957), a schoolteacher, consists of a letter she received in 1892 from W. O. Clure and a second letter containing a brief biographical note about her and about persons mentioned in the 1892 letter. Tyler was a member of the same class as George Washington Carver at Simpson College in Indianola, IA. She also studied with Grant Wood in Stone City, IA, and became a teacher at Melrose Art School.

4,848. Tyrrell, Mrs. J. W.
Papers. Ca. 1925-26. 8 items.
Open. Card catalog.
Iowa State Historical Library.
Consists of correspondence of Sister Mary Claude and some of her pupils in the mission school at Nulato, AK.

4,849. United Brethern in Christ Church
Records. Ca. 1850-1919. 24 in.
Open. Card catalog.
Iowa State Historical Library.
Minutes, including quarterly and annual conference reports; correspondence; autobiographical and historical writings; journals; and other records of the Church pertain to its development in Iowa. Included are items of the Women's Missionary Association, 1910-29; an account book of the Home Frontier and Foreign Missionary Society, organized in 1854 for the Iowa annual conference that year; Sunday school records of the UBC church in Lisbon, IA, 1892-94; records of the Young People's Christian Union in Lisbon,

1904-20; a secretary's book for the Des Moines Conference of Missions, 1898-1909; and minutes of the North Grove Church, 1871-96. Portions of the collection have been microfilmed.

4,850. United States Food Administration
Records. Ca. 1917-19. 2 vols.
Open. Card catalog.
Iowa State Historical Library.
Correspondence; lists of Iowa county food administrators and of county chairmen of the women's committee of the Council of National Defense during WWI; notes on talks to librarians and a certificate of war service to Julia A. Robinson, who was secretary and director of Iowa library extension as well as an administrator within the Iowa division of the woman's committee; dioramas, pamphlets, brochures, cartoons, and posters about wartime food conservation; and issues of the Food Administration's *Weekly Bulletin.*

4,851. Voodry, Alva L.
Papers. 1949. 1 item.
Open. Card catalog.
Iowa State Historical Library.
Reminiscences that Voodry presented before the Des Moines Pioneer Club.

4,852. Wall, Christina McMillen
Papers. 1864. 1 item.
Open. Card catalog.
Iowa State Historical Library.
Handwritten teacher's certificate of Wall (1818-94), who taught in pioneer schools in Hardin, Franklin, and Wright counties, IA, was signed by S. C. Arnold, the Hardin County school superintendent.

4,853. Ward, Viola
Papers. Ca. 1890-1908. Ca. 1.5 in.
Open. Card catalog.
Iowa State Historical Library.
Family correspondence of Ward, a schoolteacher; school board recommendations for her work; photos of her and an unidentified male; Montour (IA) High School programs, including one for commencement in 1906, and alumni invitations; literary society programs and a commencement item dated 1892 from Western College in Toledo, OH; teachers' first class or professional certificates, one of which was signed by Iowa educator Henry Sabin; and wedding invitations.

4,854. Weaver, James Baird
Papers. Ca. 1858-1912. 2 vols.
Open. Card catalog.
Iowa State Historical Library.
Weaver (1833-1912) was an Iowa lawyer, Civil War general, and politician who became a candidate for US President when nominated in 1880 by the Greenback-Labor party and in 1892 by the People's party. Includes love letters which he exchanged with Clara Vinson in 1858 before she became his wife and their correspondence during the War.

4,855. Wilson, Frances Pope (Stokely)
Papers. Ca. 1831-72. Ca. 0.25 in.
Open. Card catalog.
Iowa State Historical Library.
Family correspondence, a photo, a clipping, and other items of [Mrs. Peter] Wilson (?-1868) of Dubuque, IA, the mother of five sons and three daughters; she was also the sister of General Mountford Samuel Stokely. Her sons Thomas Stokely Wilson and David S. Wilson became prominent Iowa judges, her son George Wilson served as a lieutenant under Colonel Zachary Taylor and helped resolve a Dubuque miners dispute, her son Peter Wilson was an agent of the US Treasury department in Washington, DC, and her son Samuel M. Wilson was a lawyer in San Francisco.

4,856. Wilson, Thomas Stokely
Papers. 1834-ca. 1894. Ca. 33 vols.
Open. Card catalog.
Iowa State Historical Library.
While Wilson (1813-94), a lawyer and judge, served as associate judge of the Supreme Court of the Territory of Iowa from 1838 to the 1850s, he rendered the first decision freeing a slave brought by his master to Iowa. Includes correspondence with his wife Mary Stokely Wilson and with his sister Elizabeth Herod and her husband Joseph Herod, correspondence of Mary Wilson with the Herods, the prenuptial agreement Thomas and Mary Wilson made in 1865, extensive scrapbooks containing journals and miscellaneous illustrations he kept during his travels abroad, deeds and land sales, certificates, and appointment documents.

4,857. Wing, Amelia Murdock
Papers. Nd. 44-page item.
Open. Card catalog.
Iowa State Historical Library.
Reminiscences of Wing pertain to early days in Clayton County, IA.

4,858. Wittenmyer, Annie Turner
Papers. 1861-65. 8 vols.
Open. Card catalog.
Iowa State Historical Library.
Correspondence of [Mrs. William] Wittenmyer (1827-1900), an army nurse and Iowa state sanitary agent during the Civil War. In 1874 she also served as the first president of the national WCTU, a position she held until 1879.

4,859. Woman Suffrage
Records. Ca. 1854-1951. Ca. 10 ft.
Open. Calendar and card catalog.
Iowa State Historical Library.
Collection consists of the records of the Iowa Suffrage Memorial Commission, which operated between 1920 and 1951, and extensive material the Commission gathered pertaining to the history of the woman suffrage movement in Iowa. Records of the Commission include articles of incorporation, secretary's and other minutes, treasurer's reports, correspondence, and resolutions. Also contains correspondence, photos, and biographical questionnaires documenting the participation of the Iowa LWV in the work of the Commission and suffrage and antisuffrage papers of Carrie Chapman Catt, including selected correspondence from 1916 to 1947, speeches, suffrage campaign records, and material from South Dakota, Iowa, West Virginia, Maine, and New York.

Material gathered by the Commission concerning the history of the Iowa suffrage movement chiefly consists of records of the Iowa Equal Suffrage Association, which was formed in 1870 as the Iowa Woman Suffrage Association at a Mount Pleasant convention. After passage of the suffrage amendment, the Association merged with the Iowa LWV. Constitution, articles of incorporation, minutes and programs of annual conventions, executive board records, secretary's books, financial records, correspondence, reports, speeches, and suffrage newsletters. Also includes treasurer's books dated 1884-1928 of the Polk County Suffrage Society, formed in 1870; scattered records of the Des Moines Political Equality League, 1870-1920; records of the Men's League for Woman Suffrage in Des Moines, organized in 1910; records of the Des Moines Equal Suffrage Council, ca. 1900-16; and a treasurer's book of the Des Moines Business Women's Equal Suffrage League, 1912.

Other Iowa suffrage records in the collection include secretary's books of the Chariton Suffrage Club, 1892-1908; secretary's books of the Political Equality Club in Independence, 1889-97; general correspondence between Iowa suffrage workers, national suffrage leaders, and state and national politicians, 1869-1920; scrapbooks; suffrage and antisuffrage clippings, flyers, cartoons, and pamphlets; articles and clippings about Susan B. Anthony; national press releases, including issues of the *Weekly Bulletin of Suffrage News* of the National American Woman Suffrage Association, 1917-19; records, subscription letters, and volumes of the Iowa suffrage newspaper *The Woman's Standard,* 1886-1911; volumes of *The Revolution;* published writings about the national suffrage movement; and memorabilia.

In addition, the collection contains records of the Woman's Centennial Congress held in New York City in 1940, including a statement of purpose, reports, correspondence of the Congress's Iowa chairman Mary Ankeny Hunter of Des Moines, clippings, pamphlets and manuals about the role of women, and newsletters.

4,860. Wright, Susie Webb
Papers. 1934. 1 item.
Open. Card catalog.
Iowa State Historical Library.
Paper given by [Mrs. Floyd] Wright before the Mercy Otis Chapter of the DAR concerns historical markers in Iowa.

4,861. Conference on Roles of Women, Iowa State University
Records. 1964. 1 vol.
Open. No guide.
State Library Commission of Iowa.
Proceedings of the Conference, sponsored by the continuing education committee and the college of home economics at Iowa State University and the Governor's Commission on the Status of Women, consist of lectures and addresses on the roles of Iowa women.

4,862. Department of Iowa Woman's Relief Corps
Records. 1884-1934. 1 vol.
Open. No guide.
State Library Commission of Iowa.
Volume containing photos and a listing of the officers and programs of this Iowa auxiliary of the Grand Army of the Republic provides a history of WRC activity in that state.

4,863. Iowa Business Women
Collection. 1950s- . 3 folders.
Open. No guide.
State Library Commission of Iowa.
Clippings include information about individual women in business as well as women's occupations in Iowa.

4,864. Iowa Federation of Women's Clubs
Records. 1893-1970. 32 vols.
Open. No guide.
State Library Commission of Iowa.
Biennium records with reports and lists of officers, 1893-1968, and yearbooks outlining the work and listing committee members of the Federation, 1935-70.

4,865. Iowa Woman Suffrage Society
Records. 1879. 1 vol.
Open. No guide.
State Library Commission of Iowa.
Proceedings of the Society at its eighth annual session in Des Moines contain minutes and the texts of several addresses given at the meetings.

4,866. Iowa Woman's Associations and Clubs
Collection. 1940- . 3 folders.
Open. No guide.
State Library Commission of Iowa.
Clippings and pamphlets include items on the Iowa Press Women from 1949, the Young Business Women from 1969, and the Des Moines Junior League from 1951.

4,867. Iowa Women: Collective Biography
Collection. 1950s- . 1 folder.
Open. No guide.

State Library Commission of Iowa.
Clippings pertain to such topics as Iowa's feminist movement, Iowa women in the stock market, and statewide woman suffrage activity.

4,868. Iowa Women in Art
Collection. 1950s- . 1 folder.
Open. No guide.
State Library Commission of Iowa.
Contained in clippings and pamphlets in the collection is material about [Mrs.] Mary Jean Alexander, Isabel Bloom, [Mrs.] Elizabeth Burnham, [Mrs.] Alice McKee Cumming, [Mrs.] Pearl Lakaski, Nama Lathe, Barbara Lekberg, Marjorie Nuhn, Persis W. Robertson, [Mrs.] Dorothea Tomlinson Marquis, Esther Williams, and Jane Wilson.

4,869. Iowa Women in Politics
Collection. 1950- . 1 folder.
Open. No guide.
State Library Commission of Iowa.
Clippings about Iowa women in politics contain material about Eugenie Anderson, Emma K. Blaise, Sonja Egenes, Willie Glanton, Mary Huncke, Sarah Richardson, Evelyn Schauland, Pat Schroeder, and Roxanne Conlin.

DUBUQUE

4,870. American Lutheran Church Women
Records. 1914- . 16 ft. and 58 microfiche.
Open. Unpublished guide.
The American Lutheran Church Archives.
Minutes, financial records, correspondence, photos, scrapbooks, periodicals, and other records pertain to women's organizations within the ALC and its German and Danish antecedent church bodies. Includes material on the Women's Auxiliary, which under several different names has been an active part of church life since the first Auxiliary was formed in 1914; record books, photos, and mother house periodicals of several orders of Christian Deaconesses; and information on world mission programs.

4,871. Archives
Records. 1964- . No size given.
Closed. No guide.
Our Lady of the Mississippi Abbey.
This community of contemplative nuns, which supports itself through the sale of farm crops and caramels, was founded in 1964. Correspondence, photos, certificates, questionnaires concerning the early years of the community filled out by founding sisters, clippings, and other records.

4,872. Motherhouse Archives
Records. 1833- . Ca. 8 drawers.
Access restricted. No guide.
Sisters of Charity of the Blessed Virgin Mary, Motherhouse.
Financial records, correspondence, journals, papers of mothers general, photos, and material about various schools opened by this religious community of women, which was established in Dubuque in 1843. The order was founded in Philadelphia in 1833.

4,873. Archives
Records. 1864- . 46.5 ft.
Access restricted. Unpublished guide.
Sisters of St. Francis of the Holy Family.
This religious community of women is involved in education of youth in elementary and high schools and colleges as well as in parish ministry, hospital work, and care for the aged. The order was founded by Mother Mary Xavier Termehr in 1864 in Herford, Germany. Financial records, including the account books used by Mother Xavier; correspondence; annals; tapes; photos; slides; films; artifacts; and other records. The Sisters transferred to Iowa City, IA, in 1875 and responded to an invitation from Bishop Hennessey to move to Dubuque in 1878.

4,874. Archives
Records. 1874- . 16 drawers, 3 cabinets, and ca. 50 tapes.
Open. Unpublished guide.
Sisters of the Presentation.
This religious order of women, which is engaged principally in teaching, was founded in 1874 in Dubuque. Minutes, financial records, correspondence, retreat notes, manuscripts, annals, lists of members, biographies, notebooks, photos, scrapbooks, prayer books, programs, obituaries, and other records relating to the community and to the schools established by the Sisters in Iowa, South Dakota, and Illinois.

4,875. Archives
Records. 1871- . 6 drawers and 4 boxes.
Partially closed. No guide.
Visitation Convent.
Correspondence, documents, notebooks chronicling the history of the order, lives of the early sisters, annals, photos, slides, scrapbooks, school transcripts and yearbooks, newspapers, clippings, and books of the Convent, which was established in Dubuque in 1871 and changed to a Diocesan Congregation in 1952. The sisters operated a girls' academy from 1871 to 1970 and are involved in teaching and parish work.

ELDRIDGE

4,876. Archives
Records. Ca. 1908- . No size given.
Access restricted. No guide.
Carmelite Monastery.
The Monastery was founded in 1911 in Davenport, IA, by Mother Clare Nagle and Mother Aloysius Heiker. Financial statements, bills, correspondence, records of membership, photos, scrapbooks, and clippings relate to the history of the Monastery and the Davenport diocese and to the development of this religious community over the years.

FAIRFIELD

4,877. Fairfield Musical Club
Records. 1921-27. 0.5 in.
Open. No guide.
Fairfield Public Library.
Yearbooks, programs, and clippings of this woman's club, which was organized in 1920.

4,878. Fairfield Woman's Club
Records. Ca. 1927-75. 6 in.
Open. No guide.
Fairfield Public Library.
Yearbooks and a scrapbook on the history of the Club, which was founded in 1927, and of the McElhinney House, the Club's meeting house.

4,879. Jefferson County Hospital Auxiliary
Records. 1970. 1 item.
Open. No guide.
Fairfield Public Library.
Anniversary booklet that summarizes the Auxiliary's programs, officers, and members for the period 1960-70.

4,880. Jefferson County Hospital School for Nurses
Records. 1915-70. 3 items.
Open. No guide.
Fairfield Public Library.
The School was organized in 1912 and closed in 1932. List of graduates and their addresses, 1915-32; a paper by Harriett V. Conklin on the history of nursing, with information about the School; and a copy of an address given by James Frederic Clarke during the graduation exercises for the School's first class in 1915.

FORT DODGE

4,881. Art Club
Records. 1900-44. 100 pp.
Open. No guide.
Fort Dodge Historical Museum.
Yearbooks and a scrapbook of this Fort Dodge group established in 1900 to promote fine arts. The Club is still in existence.

4,882. Stevens, Mary
Papers. 1864. 365-page vol.
Open. No guide.
Fort Dodge Historical Museum.
Diary of [Miss] Stevens contains descriptions of her life as a young girl on a small Iowa farm during the Civil War with notes on her chores, the weather, her family and neighbors, and the early settlers in the Fort Dodge area.

4,883. Up-to-Date Club
Records. 1903-69. 300 pp.
Open. No guide.
Fort Dodge Historical Museum.
Minutes, yearbooks, essays and compositions, and scrapbooks of this women's group in Fort Dodge, which was founded in 1903 and remains extant. Members study local and worldwide current events. The Club has been affiliated with the Women's Clubs of Iowa since its earliest years.

4,884. Visiting Nurse Association
Records. 1907-42. 300 pp.
Open. No guide.
Fort Dodge Historical Museum.
Minutes, records of expenditures and of patients, and scrapbooks of the Association, which was established in 1907 and sponsored by Fort Dodge women's clubs to provide nursing care, education, food, and clothing for local underprivileged residents.

GRINNELL

4,885. Bartlet, Eliza Ann
Papers. 1854-64. 42-page item.
Open. No guide.
Grinnell College Archives.
Typescript diary of a pioneer settler in Grinnell.

4,886. College Women's Literary Societies
Records. 1872-1924. Ca. 1 ft.
Open. Card catalog.
Grinnell College Archives.
Constitutions, secretary's minutes, programs, and clippings of four women's literary organizations on campus.

4,887. Noun, Louise Rosenfield
Papers. Nd. 5 drawers.
Open. No guide.
Grinnell College Archives.
Handwritten research notes of [Mrs.] Noun relate to her book *Strong Minded Women* (1969), a history of the woman suffrage movement in Iowa from 1866 to 1920.

INDIANOLA

4,888. Indianola Council of Civic Agencies
Records. 1938-60. 2 in.
Open. No guide.

Indianola Public Library.
Minutes of the Council, which was organized in 1938 to assess the needs of the city of Indianola and its various institutions and to coordinate civic improvements made by local agencies. Represented on the Council were all major civic organizations in Indianola, including the Indianola Woman's Club and the local AAUW chapter; public health nursing; and Simpson College in Indianola.

IOWA CITY

4,889. Adams, Ephraim, and Adams, Elisabeth
Papers. 1835-1907. 7 ft.
Open. Inventory.
State Historical Society.
Correspondence, sermons, and notes of Ephraim Adams (1818-1907), a Congregational minister who helped found Iowa College in Grinnell, and correspondence of his wife Elisabeth Adams (1821-1905). Ephraim Adams came to Iowa in 1843 with the Iowa Band to establish churches; Elisabeth Adams, originally from Hanover, NH, moved to Iowa after their marriage in 1845. Their grandson James Douglass Adams has published a multi-volume collection of the Adamses' letters, which also include excerpts from their diaries.

4,890. American Association of University Women, Iowa Division
Records. 1923- . 15 ft.
Open. Published guide and inventory.
State Historical Society.
Constitution and bylaws of the Division, founded in 1923; board minutes; secretary's minutes, agendas, reports, and correspondence; treasurer's records; convention, legislative, art, educational, and scholarship and loan reports; detailed divisional study project files, 1939-40; organizational histories, historian's reports, and biographies of some AAUW members; notes on the 1965 statewide branch presidents' conference; photos; scrapbooks with programs and related items from state conventions; and other material. Collection also contains reports, officers' lists, correspondence, and histories for numerous Iowa AAUW branches, with additional material on the Iowa City branch, including its constitution, bylaws, minutes, and scrapbooks; records of the national AAUW, including various reports, fellowship histories, convention programs, and ephemera; and records of the International Association of University Women, consisting of its charter, bylaws, conference and council reports, and other material. See Katherine Harris, comp., *Guide to Manuscripts* (Iowa City, IA: State Historical Society of Iowa, 1973).

4,891. AMVETS Auxiliary of Iowa
Records. 1942-62. 10 ft.
Open. Published guide and inventory.
State Historical Society.
Secretary's and treasurer's records, membership lists, correspondence, and scrapbooks with clippings of state, district, and 103 local units of the Iowa Auxiliary of the American Veterans of WWII, which was founded in 1941 as the United Service Women of America, Inc., for Iowa mothers, sisters, spouses, and daughters of men and women in the armed forces. Members organized shipments to service personnel and worked in hospitals and clubs. By 1945 the group had more than 17,000 members in 390 local units, but plans to form a national organization at that time were not carried out; in 1946 the group assumed its present name and affiliation with AMVETS. See Katherine Harris, comp., *Guide to Manuscripts* (Iowa City, IA: State Historical Society of Iowa, 1973).

4,892. Armstrong, Fred C.
Papers. 1898-1963. 0.5 ft.
Open. Published guide.
State Historical Society.
Correspondence, business papers, and photos of Armstrong, an Orient, IA, general store owner. Includes letters, ca. 1926, of his mother Hannah Hennrietta Thacher [Mrs. William Frederick] Armstrong, a schoolteacher, from friends and the Society of Mayflower Descendants and notes for talks she gave to clubs and societies. See Katherine Harris, comp., *Guide to Manuscripts* (Iowa City, IA: State Historical Society of Iowa, 1973).

4,893. Arrowsmith Family
Papers. 1823-1918. 0.5 ft.
Open. Published guide.
State Historical Society.
Papers of this Mount Pleasant, IA, family include correspondence of Eunice, Nettie, Almeda, Lizzie, and Lucy Arrowsmith, ca. 1869-99; unidentified diaries with descriptions of trips from Mount Pleasant to Urbana, OH, and temperance meetings; an account book; a notebook with names of delegates and information about a Mount Pleasant temperance convention in 1881; and a scrapbook. See Katherine Harris, comp., *Guide to Manuscripts* (Iowa City, IA: State Historical Society of Iowa, 1973).

4,894. Atkinson, Wallace, and Atkinson, Buena
Papers. 1889-1935. 1 ft.
Open. Published guide and inventory.
State Historical Society.
Buena Atkinson (1884-1966), a pianist, singer, and vaudeville performer, was married to Wallace Atkinson (1878-?), an optician who played trombone in a traveling orchestra; both were from Storm Lake, IA. Correspondence; diaries, including those Buena Atkinson kept between 1901 and 1915 of her courtship and of performances in Chicago; account books; photos; and scrapbooks with clippings. See Katherine Harris, comp., *Guide to Manuscripts* (Iowa City, IA: State Historical Society of Iowa, 1973).

4,895. Bristol, Myrl Lewark
Papers. 1925-76. 1 Hollinqer box.
Open. Unpublished guide.
State Historical Society.
Early plays and short stories of Bristol, a writer who married a University of Iowa faculty member. Also includes a 1940 radio script, literary criticism for a women's club program on Shakespeare, and "After the Manner of Bassanio," an article she wrote and offered to the Francis Bacon Society of London in 1976.

4,896. Carson, Caroline McKinley
Papers. 1896-1939. Ca. 0.5 ft.
Open. Unpublished guide.
State Historical Society.
Diaries and biographical reminiscences of Carson, who taught school from the 1870s until her marriage in 1889 to a school superintendent, contain descriptions of her childhood experiences on a Cass County, IA, farm; detailed information about her students and their families; and notes about her activities as a school superintendent's wife. Carson moved to Iowa in 1869 with her parents and later taught in rural schools and in Anita, IA; she also attended Callanan University in Des Moines, IA. After her marriage, she and her husband lived in Marengo, IA.

4,897. Catt, Carrie Clinton (Lane) Chapman
Papers. 1898-1940. 0.5 ft. and 1 microfilm reel.
Open. Published guide and inventory.
State Historical Society.
Papers of [Mrs. George William] Catt (1859-1947), a suffragist and peace leader, consist of speeches; photos from a trip around the world and of Catt at her house in Charles City, IA; clippings; some of her writings; printed material from the Woman's Centennial Congress and the Conference on the Cause and Cure of War; and pamphlets concerning the suffrage movement. Microfilm of Catt's personal scrapbook held in the New York Public Library Catt Collection includes clippings from Iowa newspapers, an obituary for Catt's father, and a brochure from the Star Lyceum Bureau advertising her speeches. See Katherine Harris, comp., *Guide to Manuscripts* (Iowa City, IA: State Historical Society of Iowa, 1973).

4,898. Christie, Jeanne
Papers. 1943. 15 pp.
Open. No guide.
State Historical Society.
College student's term paper pertains to Iowa author Margaret Wilson.

4,899. Citizens Historical Association
Records. 1937-40. 1.5 ft.
Open. Published guide and inventory.
State Historical Society.
The purpose of the CHA, a nonprofit organization located in Indianapolis, was to preserve local biography. Of the 1226 biographical sketches the CHA compiled on Iowa residents, eight are about women. Contains sketches of [Mrs.] Eva M. Brebner (1875-?), Blackhawk County recorder; Anna M. Decker (1884-), Blackhawk County treasurer; Marie Catherine (Buhlmann) Jahn (1897-), Plymouth County recorder; Vivian W. Johnson (1896-), a Cedar Falls bank president; Bertha (Graves) Morey (1881-), the president of Morey Clay Products Company in Ottumwa; Christine L. Petersen (1894-), county school superintendent in Le Mars; Carrie E. Wackerbarth, the manager of Independence Canning Company in Independence; and [Mrs.] Mary C. Woolley (1867-?) a Le Mars abstractor. Each sketch contains biographical data on family, career, and activities. See Katherine Harris, comp., *Guide to Manuscripts* (Iowa City, IA: State Historical Society of Iowa, 1973).

4,900. Conway, William B.
Papers. 1838-39. Ca. 0.5 ft.
Open. Published guide and inventory.
State Historical Society.
Among the correspondence and poetry of Conway (1802-), Iowa's first territorial secretary and a resident of Burlington, are letters in which Conway asked his wife Charity Anne Conway in Davenport how she was managing the household without him. See Katherine Harris, comp., *Guide to Manuscripts* (Iowa City, IA: State Historical Society of Iowa, 1973).

4,901. Cox, Henry Givin
Papers. 1897-1964. 0.5 ft.
Open. Published guide and inventory.
State Historical Society.
Cox (1879-ca. 1965) was a music instructor and violinist from Pella, IA. Correspondence, writings, a biography, photos, and music as well as a biography and memorial of his wife Queene Hortense Snow Cox (1881-) and several letters she wrote to him in 1897 and 1899. See Katherine Harris, comp., *Guide to Manuscripts* (Iowa City, IA: State Historical Society of Iowa, 1973).

4,902. Daughters of the American Revolution, Iowa
Records. 1909- . 10 ft.
Open. Published guide and inventory.
State Historical Society.
State and local records of the Iowa DAR include constitution and bylaws, secretary's books, auditor's reports and treasurers' records, historians' books, memorial and necrology material, chaplain's books, chapter officer lists, chapter reports, scrapbooks, and programs. Also contains the 1940 constitution and bylaws of the national DAR, with later amendments; Centennial Congress resolutions of 1958; information about the registrar general, the flag code, and programs sponsored by the DAR; and names of National Board of Management

members. See Katherine Harris, comp., *Guide to Manuscripts* (Iowa City, IA: State Historical Society of Iowa, 1973).

4,903. Daughters of Union Veterans of the Civil War
Records. 1885-1962. 1 ft.
Open. Published and unpublished guides.
State Historical Society.
Records of the Daughters include the organization's national constitution with revisions, a journal for 1942 to 1945 and minutes of conventions, rosters, and a history by Ruth Mueller; state bylaws, reports, programs, and proceedings of annual Iowa meetings in 1937, 1941, and 1945; and local Auntie Marie Hammer Tent No. 26 records, which consist of secretary's books for 1923-62, correspondence, committee reports, officers and membership lists, appointments, member credentials, programs, photos, and a scrapbook. See Katherine Harris, comp., *Guide to Manuscripts* (Iowa City, IA: State Historical Society of Iowa, 1973).

4,904. Diaries
Collection. 1830s-1950s. 24 ft.
Open. Unpublished guide.
State Historical Society.
Collection contains diaries by or pertaining to women, including travel journals of: Betsy (Niles) Breed of Canton, IL, who describes a trip from Stonington, CT, to Canton in 1833; Mr. and Mrs. H. L. Edmunds from Ottumwa, IA, pertaining to travels abroad, 1903; [Mrs.] Jane Augusta Gould, who lived at Holbrook Farm, Mitchell County, IA, regarding her trip from Iowa to Stanton, CA, in 1862; Mrs. E. A. Hadley, who discusses her travels through Iowa on her way to Oregon, 1851; Harriet Martineau, who, while recording events on a trip from Detroit to Chicago via Michigan City, MI, also describes the homes of Pottawattamie Indians, 1836; Margaret Spragg Miller, a Hazelton, IA, farm family member, including references to her trip to the 1893 World's Fair, 1880-95; Esther Pillsbury, an Okoboji, IA, pioneer settler whose travel notes about that area were printed in newspaper installments, 1863; and Jennie Rice of Council Bluffs, IA, regarding general travels, 1919-27. Diaries pertaining to Iowa farm life include those of Maranda J. Cline, a Hills resident, 1907, and [Mrs.] Carrie Blake, a Washington farm wife who later moved to town, 1930-46. Other diaries include those kept by a daughter of James Hall, who came to Clinton, IA, to develop a railroad, though he returned to Portland, ME, 1856-61; Virginia Moore of Keokuk, IA, who describes her experiences at Keokuk High School and a class prophecy she wrote, 1906; Caroline Phelps, a Des Moines River, IA, resident whose husband William Phelps was an Indian trader, which contains her accounts of life with the Indians, 1830-40; and Frances I. [Mrs. Samuel L.] Pillsbury, a member of a prominent Spirit Lake, IA, family, 1930-36.

4,905. Dodge, Augustus Caesar
Papers. 1836-1907. 1.5 ft.
Open. Published guide.
State Historical Society.
Papers of Dodge (1812-83), who served as a US senator from Burlington, IA, from 1848 to 1855, include letters his wife Clara Dodge wrote from Iowa to him while he was in Washington, DC, and an account book, ca. 1856. See Katherine Harris, comp., *Guide to Manuscripts* (Iowa City, IA: State Historical Society of Iowa, 1973).

4,906. Dolliver, Jonathan Prentiss
Papers. 1861-1937. 50 ft.
Open. Inventory.
State Historical Society.
From 1889 to 1910 Dolliver (1858-1910), a lawyer, served as a Republican congressman and senator from Iowa. Included with his correspondence, speeches, scrapbooks, and material about Chautauqua engagements are the papers of his wife Louise (Pearsons) Dolliver (1866-1937), the daughter of George R. Pearsons, a wealthy Fort Dodge, IA, businessman; her papers consist of correspondence, an 1898 diary, scrapbooks, programs, items relating to Wellesley College, and class letters. Louise Dolliver was an 1889 Wellesley College graduate who taught school until her marriage to Dolliver in 1895, spending her last two years of teaching at Northwestern Academy in Evanston, IL. The collection also contains correspondence, speeches, and scrapbooks of Jonathan Dolliver's sisters Mary (Dolliver) Graham (1860-1919), an active member of the Women's Foreign Missionary Society of the Methodist Church and that group's national vice-president in 1917, and Margaret Gay (1864-1938), a teacher who served as dean of women at Morningside College in Sioux City, IA, from 1906 to 1917.

4,907. Enlow Family
Papers. 1850-1941. 1.5 ft.
Open. Published guide and inventory.
State Historical Society.
Correspondence, deeds, and other material of Hulda Enlow, Loretta Enlow Hollingsworth, and [Mrs.] Mattie Enlow Steer, all of whom were WCTU members from West Branch, IA. See Katherine Harris, comp., *Guide to Manuscripts* (Iowa City, IA: State Historical Society of Iowa, 1973).

4,908. Essay Contest
Records. 1923. 12 ft.
Open. Unpublished guide.
State Historical Society.
Essay contest sponsored by the State Historical Society and the Iowa Federation of Women's Clubs in 1923 generated more than 1500 essay entries from local high school students. The essays, three to eight pages in length, were written on the following topics: "The Story of My Grandmother," "The Story of My Grandfather," "An Old Settler's Story," "A Story in the History of My Community," and "What Iowa Means to Me." More than half of the essays were written by women students, and more than 200 essays are about women who were pioneers or rural Iowa residents prior to 1900.

4,909. Etter, Flora (Cotton)
Papers. 1894-1936. 6 folders.
Open. Published guide.
State Historical Society.
Correspondence of [Mrs. W. L.] Etter, a Democratic National Committee member from Sigourney, IA, includes letters from President Franklin D. Roosevelt and his wife Eleanor Roosevelt extending invitations to Etter for White House and other official functions. See Katherine Harris, comp., *Guide to Manuscripts* (Iowa City, IA: State Historical Society of Iowa, 1973).

4,910. Falvey, Lawrence, and Falvey, Katherine
Papers. 1952-63. 4 ft.
Open. Inventory.
State Historical Society.
Scrapbooks containing correspondence, photos, and clippings reflect the Iowa legislative careers of Lawrence Falvey and his wife Katherine (Mull) Falvey (1904-), who succeeded her husband in the Iowa general assembly after his death and served from 1958 to 1963, the only woman member of the body at that time. An Albia, IA, lumberyard owner, Katherine Falvey also was active in the Iowa Library Association trustees section and the Legislative Ladies League. In 1963 she married Ralph Zastrow and was required to resign from her legislative seat because she moved to Charles City, IA.

4,911. Fisher and Hart Family
Papers. 1849-1958. 7.5 ft.
Open. Published guide and inventory.
State Historical Society.
Papers of the Fisher and Hart families, Allison and Cedar Falls, IA, farmers, include will and estate documents of Sally Fisher, 1864 and 1868, and business records, poetry, and a 60-volume diary, 1879-1940, of Mary [Mrs. Irving M.] Fisher. Also contains correspondence of Elizabeth (Biggar) [Mrs. Alexis Crane] Hart (1846-83), including letters she wrote as a Grinnell College student and correspondence with her husband, his sister Mary [Mrs. Irving M.] Fisher, and Hart's son Irving H. Hart; diaries Elizabeth Hart kept in 1871 at Grinnell and in 1883 just before her death; correspondence of Clara Emerson Hart, the second wife of Alexis Crane Hart, with letters she received in 1926 following her husband's death; and a 1914 biography of Alexis Hart. Correspondence, 1912, of Loretta Hart [Mrs. A. B.] Irwin, whose husband was a minister, is included as well. Collection also contains photos. See Katherine Harris, comp., *Guide to Manuscripts* (Iowa City, IA: State Historical Society of Iowa, 1973).

4,912. Hagins, Fanny
Papers. 1866. 2 pp.
Open. Published guide.
State Historical Society.
Notarized divorce records of Hagins cite cruelty, including whipping and beating, as grounds for the proceedings in Iowa City. See Katherine Harris, comp., *Guide to Manuscripts* (Iowa City, IA: State Historical Society of Iowa, 1973).

4,913. Ham, Cornelia Freeman
Papers. 1858-69. 25 items.
Open. Calendar.
State Historical Society.
Consists of letters Ham wrote to her husband James Madison Ham, friends, and family. In 1858 James Ham moved to Clinton, IA, from Baldwinsville, NY; Cornelia Ham came to Iowa after their marriage two years later.

4,914. Haugen, Gilbert N.
Papers. 1882-1940. 81 ft.
Open. Inventory and calendar.
State Historical Society.
Included in papers of Haugen (1859-1933), a Northwood, IA, politician who served as US congressman from Iowa's 4th district from 1899 to 1933, are correspondence and household receipts of his daughter Norma (Haugen) [Mrs. J. O. E.] Johnson (1888-1959), who was active in her father's political campaigns and an officeholder in Republican party organizations for many years. Letters Johnson wrote between 1899 and 1903 to her father in Washington, DC, include descriptions of the family's difficulties adjusting to the congressman's absence; community, school, and church activities; smallpox scares; and other subjects. Letters she wrote to her father from 1903 to 1904 while she attended National Cathedral School in Washington, DC, pertain to classes, social events, and punishments. Also included are tuition bills, school circulars, and letters the School principal and teachers sent to Congressman Haugen concerning his daughter's grades, behavior, and discipline. Johnson's correspondence from 1905 to 1912 is less detailed but documents her education at the Lutheran Ladies Seminary in Red Wing, MN; Downer College in Milwaukee; and the University of Wisconsin at Madison. Her letters and household receipts, 1912-22, from the period after her marriage to J. O. E. Johnson are also included.

4,915. Hillis, Cora Bussey
Papers. 1865-1954. 1 ft.
Open. Published guide, inventory, and calendar.
State Historical Society.
Scrapbook containing correspondence, photos, clippings, and memorabilia of Hillis (1858-1924), a Des Moines child welfare leader, was compiled by her daughter-in-law Hazel M. Hillis. Also includes

an account book with personal and grocery bills. Hillis organized the Iowa Congress of Mothers, the City Union of Mothers Clubs, the Save the Babies Fresh Air Camps, and the Iowa Child Welfare Association. See Katherine Harris, comp., *Guide to Manuscripts* (Iowa City, IA: State Historical Society of Iowa, 1973).

4,916. Hoffman, Sarah Paine
Papers. 1905-36. 2 folders.
Open. Published guide.
State Historical Society.
Hoffman served as an Iowa state DAR officer, regent of the Pilgrim Chapter in Iowa City, and state historian. Correspondence between Hoffman and DAR state regent Alice Brenton, Hoffman's 1936 radio program as state historian, a family history, and a 1905 wedding booklet. See Katherine Harris, comp., *Guide to Manuscripts* (Iowa City, IA: State Historical Society of Iowa, 1973).

4,917. Horack, Frank
Papers. 1891-1955. 0.5 ft.
Open. Published guide.
State Historical Society.
Account books, diaries, and certificates of Horack (1873-1956), a political science professor at the University of Iowa in Iowa City, include a record book, 1907-13, of his wife Elizabeth Collins Horack pertaining to visitors, menus, prices, and social events. See Katherine Harris, comp., *Guide to Manuscripts* (Iowa City, IA: State Historical Society of Iowa, 1973).

4,918. Houghton, Dorothy Deemer
Papers. 1935-64. 7 ft.
Open. Published guide and inventory.
State Historical Society.
Correspondence, speeches, writings, photos, scrapbooks, and certificates of [Mrs. Hiram] Houghton (1890-1972), a Red Oak, IA, clubwoman, reflect her varied activities and interests. Included are letters, speeches, and reports of the Arden House Conference on Family Living from 1962 and biographical data. Scrapbooks she kept document her chairmanships of the GFWC education department, 1940 to 1944, and the 1947 Pan Pacific Conference; her award as Mother of the Year of Iowa in 1948; a term as president of the Iowa Federation of Women's Clubs from 1950 to 1952; her service as refugee and migration vice-director of the Federation for the following three years; leadership in the Chautauqua Woman's Club in 1963; and her work that same year on a project for the International Christian University in Japan. Collection also contains numerous certificates and awards Houghton received, including ones from the State University of Iowa board of education, the National Association of Homebuilders, the Minnesota Chippewa Tribe, the Iowa Council of Republican Women, the DAR, the Foreign Operation Administration, the Order of Van Orange-Nassau, and the Greek Royal Order of Beneficence; honorary degrees from Coe College and the University of Tampa, FL; and recognitions from several states and cities. See Katherine Harris, comp., *Guide to Manuscripts* (Iowa City, IA: State Historical Society of Iowa, 1973).

4,919. Hoxie and Banbury
Papers. 1836-1902. 0.5 ft.
Open. Inventory.
State Historical Society.
Correspondence, land records and business material, Civil War papers, a scrapbook, and clippings of the Hoxie and Banbury families of Iowa City. Includes correspondence of Jane (Hoxie) Robinson (1815-98), an early Iowa City settler who married Thomas Banbury; her scrapbook of clippings; and music and drawings books. Also contains poems of sculptor Vinnie (Ream) [Mrs. Richard Leveridge] Hoxie, whose husband was the nephew of Jane (Hoxie) Robinson Banbury, and an invitation she received to George Yewell's studio.

4,920. Huftalen, Sarah (Gillespie)
Papers. 1836-1952. 5 ft.
Open. Published guide and inventory.
State Historical Society.
A rural Iowa schoolteacher who pioneered efforts to improve and beautify schoolroom and schoolground environments, Huftalen (1865-1952?) later became a school superintendent and an educator in several teachers' training programs. Extensive diaries, including those of her mother Emily Elizabeth (Hawley) Gillespie, 1858-88, and a diary of May Hawley, 1893; Huftalen's writings; an 1836 deed from Michigan Territory and other land records; genealogies; a scrapbook pertaining to women's rights and Huftalen's active support of the Manchester, IA, suffrage organization; and scrapbooks containing photos of her schools and pupils, correspondence with students, and programs. After attending Manchester Academy and Normal School from 1879 to 1882, Huftalen taught in rural Delaware County schools where she encouraged the study of agriculture by organizing crop-growing contests; she also worked in local Farmers' Institutes. From 1910 to 1912 she supervised Page County boys' and girls' summer camps. One year later Huftalen succeeded Jessie Field, also a rural education innovator, as Page County superintendent of schools, a position she held until 1915. From 1917 to 1923 she was an instructor in the rural department of Iowa State Teachers College in Cedar Falls, and for the following 11 years she headed the Muscatine High School normal training department. See Katherine Harris, comp., *Guide to Manuscripts* (Iowa City, IA: State Historical Society of Iowa, 1973).

4,921. Immer, Esther
Papers. 1936-69. 3 ft.
Open. Unpublished guide.
State Historical Society.
A social worker and supervisor in the Iowa state social welfare department, Immer also served from ca. 1948 to 1967 as executive secretary for the Iowa Commission on Children and Youth, a body that was appointed by the governor in response to a request from the National Commission on Children and Youth. Personal and professional correspondence; minutes of the Iowa Commission, which in 1950 sponsored an Iowa White House conference and provided Iowa state representation to the national White House Conference on Children and Youth; minutes and programs from state and national conferences on child welfare; minutes and reports of the Muscatine, IA, migrant council; notes from social work courses Immer completed during 1936 and 1937; and material about the Citizens' Council for Legislation, Iowa chapters of the National Association of Social Workers, and White House conferences on children and youth pertaining to child welfare, migrants, and juvenile delinquency.

4,922. Iowa Federation of Business and Professional Women
Records. 1919- . 17 ft.
Open. Published guide and inventory.
State Historical Society.
Records of the Federation consist of minutes, treasurer's reports, and other material generated prior to the group's incorporation in 1924; articles of incorporation with amendments; board minutes; secretary's books; auditor's reports and other financial records; proceedings of the annual convention; yearly histories of the Federation from 1947 to 1957; programs for state and national meetings; material on Helen Irwin of Des Moines, IA, who was national Federation president in 1953 and 1954; photos; awards, citations, and a song; study manuals; and copies of *The Iowa Business Woman.* Also contains a secretary's book for the Federation's 4th district and scattered annual reports, minutes, scrapbooks, membership certificates, programs, yearbooks, histories and newsletters of local clubs, including the ones in Davenport, Fort Dodge, and Shenandoah. See Katherine Harris, comp., *Guide to Manuscripts* (Iowa City, IA: State Historical Society of Iowa, 1973).

4,923. Iowa Federation of Women's Clubs
Records. 1917-72. 17 ft.
Open. Published and unpublished guides.
State Historical Society.
Federation records consist of a report on club work during WWI, a history of the organization from 1893 to 1927 by Anna B. Howe and a 50-year history completed in 1943 by Mrs. Ernest Frilk and Mrs. John Fitzmaurice, community heritage scrapbooks compiled by 77 local clubs, an appreciation of Mrs. B. B. Clark of Red Oak as a leader in the national and state Federations, and a state anthology of Iowa legends, compiled by Mrs. Marvin Bricker of Williamsburg with Federation assistance. Also contains records of the Iowa City Woman's Club, a local Federation affiliate, including secretary's books of the Club and its literature, public welfare, and social sciences departments; treasurers' records; programs; press books; a project book; scrapbooks, among them those on community improvement, youth, and the nomination of the Club as an honor club and of Myrtle S. Hubbard as Clubwoman of the Year; material about a flower show; and a distinguished service plaque presented by Goodwill Industries of Southeast Iowa. See Katherine Harris, comp., *Guide to Manuscripts* (Iowa City, IA: State Historical Society of Iowa, 1973).

4,924. Irish and Preston
Papers. 1832-1972. 9 ft.
Open. Published guide and inventory.
State Historical Society.
Included with papers of Frederick Irish and his son Gilbert Irish, who was an Iowa City farmer and justice of the peace, are personal diaries, scrapbooks, and an autograph book of Gilbert Irish's wife Josie M. (Strawbridge) Irish, 1860-1921; correspondence, bills and receipts, glass slides, photos, scrapbooks, and penmanship books of their daughter Jane L. Irish, 1890-1959; and letters and a 1905 scrapbook of Gilbert Irish's only sister Ruth Irish. Also contains papers of Gilbert Irish's niece Elizabeth Irish, daughter of Charles Wood Irish and Susannah Abigail (Yarbrough) Irish, consisting of personal correspondence pertaining to business school, her father, and other relatives, 1877-1929; diaries and letters of her mother Susannah (Yarbrough) Irish; diaries and correspondence of Ruth Irish, a second daughter of Charles and Susannah Irish who married Charles Preston; and correspondence of Charles Preston's mother. See Katherine Harris, comp., *Guide to Manuscripts* (Iowa City, IA: State Historical Society of Iowa, 1973).

4,925. Jones, Adalain Kimball
Papers. 1859-1922. 2 ft.
Open. Published guide.
State Historical Society.
Extensive personal diaries of [Mrs. Herbert] Jones, an Iowa City homemaker who was active in the Unitarian church, span her life before and after marriage and include references to the Civil War, the church, and WWI. See Katherine Harris, comp., *Guide to Manuscripts* (Iowa City, IA: State Historical Society of Iowa, 1973).

4,926. Kirkwood, Samuel J.
Papers. 1843-90. 2 ft.
Open. Published guide and inventory.
State Historical Society.
Correspondence, a diary, account books, and certificates of Kirkwood (1813-94), an Iowa governor from Iowa City, include correspondence of his wife Jane (Clark) Kirkwood, 1906-15; her

household accounts, 1845-63; an 1859 diary; and scrapbooks. See Katherine Harris, comp., *Guide to Manuscripts* (Iowa City, IA: State Historical Society of Iowa, 1973).

4,927. Krueger Family
Papers. 1910-66. 6.5 ft.
Open. Published guide and inventory.
State Historical Society.
Krueger family papers contain correspondence, diaries, writings, photos, clippings, and certificates of Amy Krueger, Cora Krueger, Mrs. Fred Krueger, Lydia Krueger Curtis, and Viola Krueger, all of whom were Charles City, IA, teachers. Includes correspondence, diaries for 1910 to 1964, stories, essays, plays, metalsmithing and teaching certificates, and other papers of Amy Krueger, who also served as secretary for the YWCA in Illinois, Minnesota, Mississippi, New York, Ohio, South Dakota, and West Virginia; correspondence, a diary, a Krueger family history, and other items of Cora Krueger, who taught school in Iowa, Nevada, and Michigan; correspondence of Mrs. Fred Krueger; correspondence and other papers of Lydia Krueger Curtis, who married James H. Curtis; and correspondence, business papers, writings, a term paper on developing dictation skills, and other items of Viola Krueger, who taught in Charles City and Parkersburg, IA, and in Michigan. Viola Krueger attended the Iowa State Teacher's College and received an MA from Northwestern University in 1949. See Katherine Harris, comp., *Guide to Manuscripts* (Iowa City, IA: State Historical Society of Iowa, 1973).

4,928. Larrabee, William
Papers. 1848-1943. 6.5 ft.
Open. Published guide and inventory.
State Historical Society.
Correspondence, account books, scrapbooks, and certificates of Larrabee (1832-1912), Iowa's twelfth governor and a Clermont, IA, resident. Also contains papers of his wife Anna Matilda Larrabee, including letters from and photos of French children she sponsored during WWI and items from programs in which she appeared, 1906-21; correspondence and a personal account book of Augusta (Larrabee) [Mrs. Victor] Dolliver; a 1903 wedding invitation of Helen (Larrabee) [Mrs. Charles B.] Robbins and a 1943 memorial service pamphlet relating to her husband; and correspondence of Julia (Larrabee) [Mrs. Don] Love as well as material pertaining to the dedication of the Julia Larrabee Love memorial residence hall in 1939 at the University of Nebraska. See Katherine Harris, comp., *Guide to Manuscripts* (Iowa City, IA: State Historical Society of Iowa, 1973).

4,929. Latimer Family
Papers. 1886-1952. 0.5 ft.
Open. Published guide.
State Historical Society.
Papers of Latimer, a member of the Iowa legislature in 1925 and a Shenandoah, IA, farmer, include correspondence, teaching contracts, and an autograph album of his wife Alma Fellows Latimer. See Katherine Harris, comp., *Guide to Manuscripts* (Iowa City, IA: State Historical Society of Iowa, 1973).

4,930. Lawther, William, and Lawther, Anna
Papers. 1874-1931. 3 ft.
Open. Published guide and inventory.
State Historical Society.
Anna Lawther (1872-1957) and her father William Lawther were members of a family of civic leaders in Dubuque, IA; a suffragist and civic leader, Anna Lawther served as president of the Iowa Equal Suffrage Association from 1916 to ca. 1919, worked on the women's committee of the Iowa Food Administration, and was a member of the Democratic National Committee in 1920. Suffrage material consists of correspondence, including letters from Carrie Chapman Catt; scrapbooks with clippings, some of which are antisuffrage items; pamphlets, broadsides, and other state and national printed material; and various antisuffrage publications from Pennsylvania, Massachusetts, and other states. Collection also contains correspondence and items about the fourth Liberty Loan drive of 1918; form letters Anna Lawther sent to Iowa women in 1920 as a Democratic National Committee member; a speech; correspondence and reports pertaining to the Iowa state board of education from the period when Anna Lawther was both a member and its president, 1922-31; correspondence with WCTU members; biographical material; photos; and programs. See Katherine Harris, comp., *Guide to Manuscripts* (Iowa City, IA: State Historical Society of Iowa, 1973).

4,931. League of Women Voters
Records. 1923- . 1 ft.
Open. Published and unpublished guide.
State Historical Society.
Proposed bylaws and amendments, minutes, financial data, correspondence, reports, requests, publicity, and programs of the national LWV. Iowa state LWV records consist of minutes, radio programs, and studies on education, including higher education, and on tax for schools. Iowa City branch records contain bylaws; annual reports, 1968-70; minutes; statements of purpose; correspondence; officers, committees, and membership lists; studies made, including a 1926 law enforcement report; material about Iowa City water resources in the Upper Mississippi Valley and about the city's public health program; members' guides; calendars; and a scrapbook. See Katherine Harris, comp., *Guide to Manuscripts* (Iowa City, IA: State Historical Society of Iowa, 1973).

4,932. Lewis, Thelma
Papers. 1954-63. 0.5 ft.
Open. Published guide.
State Historical Society.
From 1949 to 1963, [Mrs. Don] Lewis was mayor of Iowa City; she also chaired the education committee of the Iowa state chapter of the LWV. Agendas and minutes of the Iowa City council; studies, reports, and purchase data about water facilities for the city; material relating to the council and the Iowa-Illinois Gas and Light Company case, including Lewis's testimony, 1960-63; minutes, agendas, and recommendations of the citizens committee from its 1950 study of the council-manager plan for city government; and an Iowa LWV education committee report Lewis made on education, organization, and financing of tax supported schools in Iowa. Also includes papers, reports, photos, and other items prepared or written by Lewis in 1947 when she was assistant secretary of the Council of Foreign Ministers to Russia. See Katherine Harris, comp., *Guide to Manuscripts* (Iowa City, IA: State Historical Society of Iowa, 1973).

4,933. Lord, Jeannette (Mather)
Papers. 1890-1945. 1 vol. and 26 items.
Open. Published guide.
State Historical Society.
Scrapbook of [Mrs. Frederick P.] Lord, with colored picture cards and calling cards, a one-page description of making scrapbooks with her sisters as a child, and letters Lord received, primarily during the 1940s when she lived in New Hampshire, from the Shinn family and Hannah Wood of the West Branch, IA, area, near Lord's hometown of West Liberty. See Katherine Harris, comp., *Guide to Manuscripts* (Iowa City, IA: State Historical Society of Iowa, 1973).

4,934. McClain, Emlin
Papers. 1844-1915. 10 ft.
Open. Published guide and inventory.
State Historical Society.
Correspondence of McClain (1851-1915), a lawyer and law professor at the University of Iowa who also served as an Iowa supreme court justice, includes letters his wife Ellen (Griffiths) McClain received after his death, general family correspondence, account books, diaries, speeches and writings, biographical material, photos, and memorabilia. Also contains personal, financial, and business records of McClain's parents Rebecca and William McClain, 1844. William McClain was a schoolteacher in Ohio and Iowa City. See Katherine Harris, comp., *Guide to Manuscripts* (Iowa City, IA: State Historical Society of Iowa, 1973).

4,935. Macy, Jesse
Papers. 1862-1941. 6.5 ft.
Open. Published guide, inventory, and calendar.
State Historical Society.
Among the correspondence, diaries, and writings of Macy (1842-1919), who was a Grinnell College political science professor and author from Grinnell, IA, are letters that his wife Maude Macy wrote on European trips from 1887 to 1913; letters she wrote after Jesse Macy's death; correspondence of his daughter Katharine (Macy) Noyes relating to her father's biography, which she published; and letters between Katharine and her parents while she attended college and after her marriage. See Katherine Harris, comp., *Guide to Manuscripts* (Iowa City, IA: State Historical Society of Iowa, 1973).

4,936. Mather, Samuel
Papers. 1869-1951. 1 ft.
Open. Inventory.
State Historical Society.
Photo albums and clippings of a West Liberty, IA, Quaker family that worked in dry goods and farming. Includes photos depicting the college days, home, relatives, and marriage of Samuel Mather's daughter Rachel Mather, 1890-1919.

4,937. Metcalf, Herbert J.
Papers. 1910-19. 2.5 ft.
Open. Published guide, inventory, and calendar.
State Historical Society.
Correspondence and printed material of Metcalf, who headed the US Public Service Reserve and Iowa council of national defense during WWII. Includes correspondence with Hattie Harl, director of the US Food Administration in Iowa, and items relating to women's activities. See Katherine Harris, comp., *Guide to Manuscripts* (Iowa City, IA: State Historical Society of Iowa, 1973).

4,938. Moffit, John T.
Papers. 1852-1954. 1.5 ft.
Open. Published guide and inventory.
State Historical Society.
Correspondence, photos, a scrapbook, and certificates of Moffit (1862-?), an Iowa district court judge from Tipton, IA; correspondence, clippings, and diplomas of his daughter Margaret (Moffit) [Mrs. Henry] Platner (1897-), who was chief of social service in institutions in Illinois for 20 years; and correspondence and clippings of his wife Winifred (Hecht) Moffit and her mother Mrs. Fred Hecht. See Katherine Harris, comp., *Guide to Manuscripts* (Iowa City, IA: State Historical Society of Iowa, 1973).

4,939. Morgan, Jennie Ham
Papers. 1948-53. 6 vols.
Open. Published guide.
State Historical Society.
Account books for [Mrs.] Morgan's catering service in Iowa City. See Katherine Harris, comp., *Guide to Manuscripts* (Iowa City, IA: State Historical Society of Iowa, 1973).

4,940. Parker, Leonard Fletcher
Papers. 1840-1925. 2 ft.
Open. Published guide and inventory.
State Historical Society.
Correspondence, diaries, speeches, and an autobiography of Parker (1825-1911), an abolitionist and history professor at Grinnell College and the University of Iowa. Includes correspondence of his wife Sarah (Pearse) Parker, also an abolitionist, and his daughter Harriet (Parker) [Mrs. John] Campbell. See Katherine Harris, comp., *Guide to Manuscripts* (Iowa City, IA: State Historical Society of Iowa, 1973).

4,941. Pratt, Walter I.
Papers. 1879-1926. 1 ft.
Open. Inventory.
State Historical Society.
Papers of Pratt (1864-1940), an Iowa City businessman, include a diary and scrapbook of his wife Louise (Shedd) Pratt, 1922-26, and a travel diary and autograph book of his cousin Jennie Rice, 1912-27.

4,942. Remington, Helen
Papers. 1950-70. 3 ft.
Open. Published and unpublished guides.
State Historical Society.
Family histories and genealogical material of [Mrs. Loren] Remington, a Cedar Rapids, IA, genealogist, include her correspondence pertaining to the Bennett, Doane, Francisco, McCabe, Lee, and Lewis families; Beckman Bible records; census records of Michigan and New York; records of the Society of Mayflower Descendants; summarized census reports containing selected surnames of and other records concerning the Budd, Doane, Fousche, Francisco, Havens, Herrington, Houseman, Howe, Hoyt, Johnson, Kessler, Lee, Lewis, Lumm, McKeeby, Markham, Meacham, Parker, Randolph, Remington, Rowley, Tenney, Thomas, Weygand, and Wilson families. See Katherine Harris, comp., *Guide to Manuscripts* (Iowa City, IA: State Historical Society of Iowa, 1973).

4,943. Republican Women's Clubs
Records. 1937-73. 2 ft.
Open. Published guide with updated additions.
State Historical Society.
Scrapbooks and a history of the Iowa Federation, or Iowa Council, of Republican Women, a political organization, and scrapbooks of its first district and the Johnson County Republican Women's Club. See Katherine Harris, comp., *Guide to Manuscripts* (Iowa City, IA: State Historical Society of Iowa, 1973).

4,944. Robeson, Helen (Katz)
Papers. 1903-60. 5 folders.
Open. Published guide.
State Historical Society.
Correspondence, a diary, and writings of Robeson, a music instructor at Yankton, SD, and at the University of Iowa until her marriage in 1919. The diary is one she kept in 1916 while traveling with the Midland Chautauqua Company as a violinist. Also contains diplomas and certificates of her husband George Robeson, a University of Iowa professor from Iowa City. See Katherine Harris, comp., *Guide to Manuscripts* (Iowa City, IA: State Historical Society of Iowa, 1973).

4,945. Rohlf, William A.
Papers. 1885-1955. 2 ft.
Open. Published guide and inventory.
State Historical Society.
Included with diaries, writings and speeches, photos, and a scrapbook of this Waverly, IA, physician are scattered diaries of his wife Lottie (Beed) Rohlf, 1935-55, which largely pertain to her travels in the US and abroad; a speech she gave on doctors' wives of the past; and a memorial given by their daughter Ida C. Rohlf. See Katherine Harris, comp., *Guide to Manuscripts* (Iowa City, IA: State Historical Society of Iowa, 1973).

4,946. Samuelson, Agnes
Papers. 1905-62. 5 ft.
Open. Published guide and inventory.
State Historical Society.
An Iowa educator, [Miss] Samuelson (1887-1963) was state superintendent of public instruction from 1927 to 1939 and president of the National Education Association from 1935 to 1936. Personal and professional correspondence, including recommendations and commendations; a diary; speeches, addresses, and other writings; notes and material pertaining to the 1957 Religious and Educational Conference in Indianola, IA; campaign material relating to her position as state superintendent; a biography and genealogy; photos, programs, and exhibits she used while serving as Iowa State Teachers' Association executive secretary from 1938 to 1945; items prepared for American Education Week; a booklet compiled by Nettie Price and presented to Samuelson when she completed her term as NEA president; and NEA and teaching certificates. In addition to her presidency, Samuelson also served as assistant editor of the NEA *Journal* from 1945 to 1952. SeeKatherine Harris, comp., *Guide to Manuscripts* (Iowa City, IA: State Historical Society of Iowa, 1973).

4,947. Sayre, Ruth B.
Papers. 1920-70. 6 ft.
Open. Published guide and inventory.
State Historical Society.
An Ackworth, IA, farmwoman, [Mrs. Raymond] Sayre (1896-) was actively involved in local and national farm organizations and commissions, among them the Iowa Farm Bureau, the American Farm Bureau Women, and the Associated Country Women of the World. Personal and business correspondence; diary for 1938 to 1954; a biographical outline of her career to 1960; talks she gave pertaining to women and their work, freedom, youth, home economics, safety, and the farm home family; articles she wrote for journals and magazines, including items about her foreign travels to Iran, Egypt, and the Holy Land; material reflecting her work with the AFBW, the ACWW, Farm and Home Weeks in Iowa, 4-H Club and Iowa educational activities, the Iowa Farm Bureau Women, Iowa safety and the President's committee for traffic safety, the White House conference on highway safety, and the Woman's Conference on National Safety; photos, including those depicting her work associates, committees, boards on which she served, visits to foreign countries, Sayre receiving an honorary degree, and her home; scrapbooks; programs; and awards and certificates. See Katherine Harris, comp., *Guide to Manuscripts* (Iowa City, IA: State Historical Society of Iowa, 1973).

4,948. Schenck, Walter Leslie
Papers. 1870-1974. 2.5 ft.
Open. Inventory.
State Historical Society.
Included in papers of Schenck (1882-1964), an Iowa City dentist, are numerous photos of his daughters Bertha Stecker, a physician, and Mary Ethel as well as letters of Stecker and of other women in the family.

4,949. Scrapbooks
Collection. Ca. 1840-1976. 40 ft.
Open. Unpublished guide.
State Historical Society.
Scrapbooks kept by women include those of Marjorie Eames Coast (?-ca. 1920) of Iowa City, with photos, personal records, and clippings about the Carnegie Hero Medal she received at age 11, her marriage to attorney Donald McClain, and her death one year later; Mary Ann Evans of Mount Pleasant and Malvern, IA, with clippings on missions and women's work in the Presbyterian church, religious articles, and poetry; Ruth Hydon [Mrs. Henry W.] Lampe of Iowa City, who was the Iowa Mother of the Year in 1956, with a biographical sketch; Esther McDowell Swisher of Iowa City, relating to her career as a pianist and music teacher, with correspondence, photos, programs for recitals at the University of Iowa music department and clippings, ca. 1903-39; and a scrapbook compiled for the Museum of Textiles and Clothing in the New York state college of home economics, Cornell University, by the husband of Gertrude Heim [Mrs. Charles Mason] Remey, which pertains to her wardrobe, life, and activities, 1888-1939. Other scrapbooks in the collection pertain to subjects such as local news, business, and residents of Iowa towns; marriage and household hints; college life and teaching; Iowa WPA projects; and political campaigns.

4,950. Seagrave, Sadie
Papers. 1890-1961. 3 ft.
Open. Inventory.
State Historical Society.
Seagrave (1882-1972), an author, was secretary at the Oakdale Tuberculosis Sanitarium in Iowa City and a former TB patient at other sanitariums. Correspondence concerning literary criticism, the Torch Press and the Prairie Press; biographies; travelogues; radio programs; manuscripts and printed copies of plays, short stories, poetry, and a novel; scrapbooks with clippings on writers and other friends; and personal memorabilia.

4,951. Smyth, Robert
Papers. 1854-1901. 4 ft.
Open. Published guide and inventory.
State Historical Society.
A real estate businessman and banker, Smyth (1814-98) served as paymaster for the US Army from 1862 to ca. 1866; he was also a member of the Iowa legislature. Business and personal correspondence, including numerous letters between Smyth and his wife Margaret Smyth, his daughters Lizzie and Annie, nieces, and sisters both during and after his Civil War service, and war records and reports regarding the payment of soldiers. See Katherine Harris, comp., *Guide to Manuscripts* (Iowa City, IA: State Historical Society of Iowa, 1973).

4,952. Strawbridge Family
Papers. 1870-1928. 4 folders.
Open. Published guide.
State Historical Society.
Family papers of Jesse K. Strawbridge, a Morse, IA, farmer; his son Frank Strawbridge, a physician in Sigourney, IA; and Jesse Strawbridge's daughter Susan Adda Strawbridge, who homesteaded in Wyoming. Contains early financial records of Jesse Strawbridge and correspondence and financial records of Susan Strawbridge, 1913-28.

4,953. Tatum, Lawrie
Papers. 1847-1906. 0.5 ft.
Open. Inventory.
State Historical Society.
Correspondence, diaries, writings, deeds, an account book, and clippings of Tatum (1822-1900), a Springdale, IA, Quaker farmer who worked as an Indian agent at Fort Sill, OK, during the Grant administration. Also includes correspondence of his wife Mary Ann Tatum with friends and family, ca. 1847-84; a diary she kept at Fort Sill, 1870; and correspondence of Tatum's daughter Ella Tatum.

4,954. U.S. Food Administration
Records. 1917-20. 2 ft.
Open. Inventory.
State Historical Society.
Correspondence and printed material of the USFA in Iowa reflect women's active involvement in food conservation for the WWI war effort, often through home economy lecture tours and the organization

of volunteers. Includes correspondence of USFA Iowa field representative Mrs. Max Mayer; state secretary of volunteer college workers Mrs. Herbert B. Boies; Catherine J. Mackay, who was US Department of Agriculture home economics director; and Cora [Mrs. Francis] Whitley, a chairman of the Council of National Defense women's committee.

4,955. Von Stein, John Peter
Papers. 1838-1928. 0.5 ft.
Open. Published guide and inventory.
State Historical Society.
Included in the papers of von Stein (1819-1903), an Iowa City farmer and shoe repair shop owner, is a personal account book of his daughter Sarah von Stein, 1915-28, which identifies her work and interests, and family and local history writings. See Katherine Harris, comp., *Guide to Manuscripts* (Iowa City, IA: State Historical Society of Iowa, 1973).

4,956. Waite, John Leman
Papers. 1815-1924. 1 ft.
Open. Published guide and inventory.
State Historical Society.
Papers of Waite (1840-1924), an editor and Burlington, IA, postmaster, include correspondence of his wife Letitia (Williams) Waite pertaining to her book *By the Thorn Road,* a diary she kept between 1872 and 1873 of a trip to Cincinnati and her experiences there, and a scrapbook of their daughter Lola Waite concerning a European trip she took in 1900 and 1901. See Katherine Harris, comp., *Guide to Manuscripts* (Iowa City, IA: State Historical Society of Iowa, 1973).

4,957. Weitz, Alice
Papers. 1910-53. 1.5 ft.
Open. Published guide and inventory.
State Historical Society.
[Mrs. Frederick] Weitz was a Des Moines journalist and clubwoman who participated in the GFWC, UNESCO, the Iowa Press and Authors Club, and the Iowa Salvage Committee, a WWII organization. Correspondence with several Iowa writers and a publisher concerning *Prairie Gold,* an anthology of works by Iowa authors and artists, which Weitz edited; speeches and writings; photos; and scrapbooks with clippings. See Katherine Harris, comp., *Guide to Manuscripts* (Iowa City, IA: State Historical Society of Iowa, 1973).

4,958. Women's Biographies and Reminiscences
Collection. Ca. 1840- . Ca. 0.5 ft.
Open. Unpublished guide.
State Historical Society.
Included in a variety of personal reminiscences, biographical sketches, and other items of Iowa women are those of Neva Leona Boyd (1876-1963), who established the first experimental school for adult preparation in recreational activities; Mollie (Brown) Carran, a West Branch resident and former teacher of Herbert Hoover, who describes her first teaching experience at Fairview School; Dubuque, IA, residents Agnes Helbig, a teacher in Iowa and California, and Esther Helbig, who served as president of the Iowa State Teachers Association; Phoebe Sudlow of Davenport, the first female professor at the State University of Iowa; Eleanor Elizabeth Gordon, the minister of the Unitarian church of Iowa City, whose sketch is written by her niece Pearl Avis (Gordon) [Mrs. C. L.] Vastal; Mary Augusta Safford (1851-1927), a suffrage leader and clergywoman of the Iowa City Unitarian Church, with pastorates in other cities; Elizabeth (Wright) Heller (1860-1950), the stepsister of Frank Lloyd Wright and a Marengo resident who in 1881 married John Heller; Mary Josephine (Mason) Remey (1845-1938) of Washington, DC, the daughter of Chief Justice Charles Mason and wife of Rear Admiral George C. Remey, whose sketch was written by her husband; Virginia [Mrs. Harry D.] Couzens of Iowa City, the granddaughter of Governor Robert Lucas and an artist who painted a portrait of Mrs. Samuel Kirkwood; Ethel Probert, who describes the blizzard of 1888; Susannah Willeford of Henry County, who discusses the migration of pioneers from ca. 1820 to 1870; and Martha (Turner) [Mrs. P. C.] Searle, a Denmark resident, describing her Civil War experiences, with edited notes added in 1971 by her granddaughter Helen Holmes [Mrs. Robert D.] Cresap. Neva Boyd's papers also include a letter Jane Addams wrote for the dedication of Boyd Hall.

4,959. Women's Church Societies
Records. 1870-1965. Ca. 1 ft.
Open. Unpublished guide.
State Historical Society.
Scattered minutes, financial records, histories, and scrapbooks for the following Iowa groups: the Woman's Mission Society of the Downey Baptist Church; the Christian Women's Fellowship group of the Iowa City First Christian Church; the Sioux City Diocesan Council of Catholic Women; the Woman's Missionary Union of the Iowa Yearly Meeting of Friends; the Ladies Aid Society and Society of Woman's Home and Foreign Missions of the First English Lutheran Church in Cedar Rapids; the Women's Missionary Society and Young Women's Missionary Society of the First Lutheran Church in Cedar Rapids; the Mount Pleasant Methodist Episcopal Women's Foreign Missions Society; the Ladies Aid Society of the Valley Methodist Episcopal Church in Keokuk; the Westminster Study Club, a Presbyterian group in Cedar Rapids; the Ladies Social Circle, a Unitarian organization; the Unitarian Ladies Working Society; the Woman's Alliance of the First Unitarian Church; and the Council of the United Church Women of Iowa City.

4,960. Women's Clubs
Records. 1862-1976. Ca. 15 ft.
Open. Unpublished guide.
State Historical Society.
Scattered minutes, financial records, correspondence, scrapbooks, programs, and histories, or some portion of the above, exist for such patriotic or veterans' groups in Iowa as the state department of the American Legion Auxiliary, the Daughters of American Colonists of Iowa, the Ladies Soldiers' Aid Society of Iowa City, the Woman's Relief Corps in Kalona and Washington, and the World War Auxiliary Club of Johnson County. Study or social organizations represented include the Poetry Society of Iowa City, the Iowa City Book Club, the Burlington Study Club, the Union Township Woman's Club of Johnson County, the Reading Club and Columbia Circle in Clarence, the Clio Club in Carroll, the Highland Social Club in Washington County, the Solon Study Club, the Solon Teacher's Reading Circle, and the TTT, a national organization founded in Iowa. Suffrage clubs represented include the Charles City Equality Club, the Eagle Grove Equality Club, the Equal Suffrage Association in Iowa City, and the State University of Iowa Equal Suffrage Association. Service organizations include Johnson County 4-H Clubs, the Girls League of Milton High School, the Mount Pleasant Women's Club, and Order of the Eastern Star chapters in Decorah, Fayette, and Iowa City. University or college alumnae and student groups represented include the Elder Daughters, whose members had been students at the State University of Iowa in Iowa City before 1871; the University Club and the University Dames in Iowa City; and the V. V. Club, members of which were alumnae of Des Moines College, Highland Park College, and Des Moines University. Other organizations represented in the collection include state and local chapters of the WCTU, the Des Moines Woman's Press Club, the Iowa League of American Pen Women in Waterloo, and the Wednesday Lookout Club in Clarence.

4,961. Women's Letters
Collection. 1840s-1960s. Ca. 0.5 ft.
Open. Unpublished guide.
State Historical Society.
Correspondence of or pertaining to women that does not appear in larger collections of personal papers includes a letter written in 1862 by Union County, NC, resident Edesa Alden to her husband Joseph Alden, a Confederate soldier, which was found in his knapsack when he was buried at Antietam; letters that Elsie [Mrs. H. O.] Eisslinger of Sheffield, IA, received from persons in military camps in the US and France, 1917-19; letters from Anna T. Harrison, the daughter of President William Henry Harrison, to her cousin Anna (Harrison) Ruder during their school days, 1831; correspondence of Mrs. W. H. Hatch of Fayette and Oelwein, IA, pertaining to her work from 1928 to 1932 in the Farm Bureau and 4-H clubs; letters in which Lois (Grant) Holman of Sergeant Bluffs, IA, describes to her family in Connecticut her life in Iowa with her husband and children, 1856; and letters and pension papers of Calista Sanders [Mrs. Julius] Smith, a Missouri resident and widow of a soldier who served in Company B of the 1st Missouri Cavalry, 1880-1909.

4,962. Wright, Luella Margaret
Papers. 1927-56. 0.5 ft.
Open. Published guide.
State Historical Society.
Personal correspondence of Wright (1881-1963), a poet and English professor at the University of Iowa in Iowa City; correspondence and notes concerning a book of her poetry she desired to publish; biographies of such Iowa writers as Caroline Lee Hentz, Emerson Hough, and Peter Melendy; collected poetry from early Iowa newspapers; and scrapbooks, including one pertaining to her book *The Literary Life of the Early Friends* (1933). See Katherine Harris, comp., *Guide to Manuscripts* (Iowa City, IA: State Historical Society of Iowa, 1973).

4,963. Young, Miller, and Young, William Wray
Papers. 1858-1952. 2.5 ft.
Open. Published guide and inventory.
State Historical Society.
Correspondence, writings, and autograph books of Miller Young, a physician, and William Young, a farmer, both of whom lived in North Liberty, IA. Also includes correspondence of Cora (Moreland) Young, a teacher and wife of William Wray Young, and correspondence and diplomas of their daughters Lillian Rosemary Young and Dorothy Young. See Katherine Harris, comp., *Guide to Manuscripts* (Iowa City, IA: State Historical Society of Iowa, 1973).

4,964. Abraham, Lot
Papers. 1843-1921. 94 items.
Open. Unpublished guide.
University of Iowa Libraries.
Abraham (1838-?), a Mount Pleasant, IA, resident, was a Civil War soldier with the 4th Iowa Cavalry and a state senator. Included with his correspondence, diaries, and military records is a diary of his first wife Sarah Alden Abraham (1841-88), which covers the period from 1864 to 1881.

4,965. Aldrich, Bess (Streeter)
Papers. 1921-54. 22 items.
Open. No guide.
University of Iowa Libraries.
Correspondence of Aldrich (1881-1954), an author, as well as manuscripts and a galley proof of her book *Song of Years* (New York, 1939).

4,966. Anderson, Betty Baxter
Papers. Ca. 1952. 2 boxes.
Open. No guide.
University of Iowa Libraries.
Anderson (1908-66) was an author. Correspondence, drafts, proofs, and other papers relate to her book *Secret of the Old Books* (New York, 1952).

4,967. Associated Women Students, University of Iowa
Records. 1916-70. 2 ft.
Open. No guide.
University of Iowa Libraries.
Founded in 1916, this organization opened membership to all women undergraduates enrolled at the University. Constitutions, minutes, ledger and financial records, correspondence, reports, histories, lists, and publications.

4,968. Athena Literary Society
Records. 1916-24. 2 vols.
Open. No guide.
University of Iowa Libraries.
Ledger and a scrapbook of the Society, a women's group at the University that was founded in 1916 and operated until 1932.

4,969. Aydelotte, Myrtle Elizabeth (Kitchell)
Papers. 1949. 1 Hollinger box.
Open. No guide.
University of Iowa Libraries.
Correspondence of [Mrs.] Aydelotte (1917-) pertains to the reorganization of the University's college of nursing, which had been the University school of nursing, and its choice of Aydelotte, then Miss Kitchell of the University of Minnesota school of nursing, to be the college's first dean.

4,970. Baldwin, Calvin Benham
Papers. 1933-75. 30 ft.
Open. Unpublished guide.
University of Iowa Libraries.
Correspondence, speeches, tape recordings, minutes, proceedings, news releases, photos, scrapbooks, clippings, and broadsides of Baldwin (1902-75), who was a special assistant to Henry A. Wallace from 1933 to 1935 in the US Department of Agriculture and who later held other government appointments, became active in the CIO Political Action Committee and the National Citizens Political Action Committee, and pursued Progressive party politics after 1947. Baldwin was campaign manager for Henry A. Wallace, who was the party's presidential candidate in 1948 and from 1948 until 1955 the Progressive party's national secretary. His papers include material on the CIO Political Action Committee women's division and Women for Wallace as well as items relating to Eleanor Roosevelt, Charlotta Bass, Eslanda Robeson, Anita McCormick Blaine, Virginia Durr, Elinor Gimble, Lena Horne, Vivian Hallinan, Katharine Hepburn, Katherine Van Orden, and Dorothy Parker.

4,971. Bartholomew Family
Papers. 1850-1910. 213 items.
Open. Unpublished guide.
University of Iowa Libraries.
Correspondence chiefly of the family of Bryan Bartholomew and his wife Harriet Ward Bartholomew contains descriptions of settling in Iowa and starting in business in Des Moines and Chariton. Also includes correspondence of the Ward family, Mel L. Webster, Salina Saltsgiver, and F. H. Wyrick.

4,972. Batchelder Family
Papers. 1844-1946. 1 Hollinger box.
Open. Unpublished guide.
University of Iowa Libraries.
Joseph Mayo Batchelder, a minister, and his wife Harriet Kipp Gearhart Batchelder were early settlers in Iowa and Kansas. Family correspondence; account books; diaries, including one volume kept by Harriet Gearhart between 1847 and 1848; sermons; and other items.

4,973. Bissell, Bess G.
Papers. 1884-1974. 2 boxes.
Open. No guide.
University of Iowa Libraries.
Papers of Bissell (1876?-1974), an author from Dubuque, IA, include correspondence, journals, a diary of a 1902 trip to Europe, poems and short stories, and items pertaining to the Dubuque Benevolent Humane Society.

4,974. Booth, Maud Ballington (Charlesworth)
Papers. Ca. 1896-1945. Ca. 256 items.
Open. No guide.
University of Iowa Libraries.
Correspondence, memoirs, notebooks, and photos of Booth (1865-1948), a reformer, include many letters she wrote between 1919 and 1928 to the Redpath Lyceum Bureau in Chicago. Some of the material also relates to her work in prison reform and the Volunteers of America.

4,975. Bradley, Duane
Papers. 1959-67. 2 boxes.
Open. No guide.
University of Iowa Libraries.
Correspondence, outlines, notes, typescripts, proofs, brochures, and a scrapbook of Bradley (1914-), an author, chiefly pertain to her books *Count Rumford* (1967), *Electing a President* (1963), *Our World of Science* (1959), and *Sew IT and Wear IT* (1966).

4,976. Brown, Hazel E.
Papers. Ca. 1972. 3 boxes.
Open. No guide.
University of Iowa Libraries.
Manuscripts of Brown, an author, and source material for her book *Grant Wood and Marvin Cone: Artists of an Era* (Ames, IA, 1972).

4,977. Brown, Paula Watts
Papers. 1930-74. 13 ft.
Open. Unpublished guide.
University of Iowa Libraries.
Brown (1909-74) was a Des Moines, IA, civic leader. Correspondence, diaries, speeches, articles, minutes, reports, agendas, photos, clippings, pamphlets, and other items pertain to such subjects as education in Des Moines schools, billboards, historic preservation, and the Des Moines Art Center.

4,978. Calhoun, Mary
Papers. 1966-70. 1 box.
Open. No guide.
University of Iowa Libraries.
Calhoun (1926-) is an author. Drafts of her book *Magic in the Alley* (New York, 1970).

4,979. Church Women United in Iowa
Records. 1933-72. 7 ft.
Open. Unpublished guide.
University of Iowa Libraries.
Annual reports, minutes, board of managers' files, financial ledgers, audits, local officer files, reports, correspondence, agendas, and scrapbooks of this organization, formerly known as United Church Women or the General Department of United Church Women of the National Council of Churches. Members worked on a number of state projects and were involved in such activities as World Day of Prayer.

4,980. College of Nursing, University of Iowa
Records. 1915-71. 1 ft.
Open. No guide.
University of Iowa Libraries.
Faculty and student organization minutes, correspondence, and publications of the College, established in 1898.

4,981. Committee on International Women's Year, University of Iowa
Records. 1975-76. 1 Hollinger box.
Open. No guide.
University of Iowa Libraries.
Minutes, financial records, and correspondence of the Committee, established in 1975, include items about the IWY "Woman: A Celebration" festival held on campus in early 1976. Festival participants included Susan Brownmiller, Pauline Frederick, and Lily Tomlin.

4,982. Conlin, Roxanne Barton
Papers. 1969-75. Ca. 4 ft.
Open. Unpublished guide.
University of Iowa Libraries.
Papers of Conlin (1944-), an Iowa assistant attorney general and the first chairperson of the Iowa Women's Political Caucus, include correspondence, speeches, subject files, briefs, material on the Iowa Commission on the Status of Women, and photos.

4,983. Crary, Margaret
Papers. 1969-73. 1 box.
Open. No guide.
University of Iowa Libraries.
Crary (1906-) is an author. Drafts, notes, outlines, proofs, clippings, and other items pertain to her books *Mexican Whirlwind* (1969) and *Susette La Flesche: Voice of the Omaha Indians* (1973).

4,984. Department of Home Economics, University of Iowa
Records. 1913-22. 5 vols.
Open. No guide.
University of Iowa Libraries.
Financial records of the Department, organized in 1913.

4,985. Erodelphian Literary Society
Records. 1862-1933. 11 vols.
Open. No guide.
University of Iowa Libraries.
Ledgers and scrapbooks of this University women's group, which was established in 1862 and disbanded in 1933.

4,986. Evans, Mary Ellen
Papers. Nd. 8 boxes.
Open. Unpublished guide.
University of Iowa Libraries.
Correspondence, biographical and editorial material, and book manuscripts of Evans (1912-), an author and editor. She wrote *The Seed and the Glory: The Career of Samuel Charles Mazzuchelli, O. P., on the Mid-American Frontier* (1950) and *The Spirit Is Mercy: The Story of the Sisters of Mercy in the Archdiocese of Cincinnati, 1858-1958* (1959).

4,987. Eyerly, Jeannette Hyde
Papers. Nd. 5 boxes.
Open. No guide.
University of Iowa Libraries.
Correspondence, drafts, proofs, and other items of Eyerly (1908-), an author, largely pertain to her books, including *The Girl Inside* (1968), *Gretchen's Hill* (1965), and *The World of Ellen March* (1964).

4,988. Graham, Alberta Powell
Papers. 1949-56. 11 boxes.
Open. Unpublished guide.
University of Iowa Libraries.
Correspondence, drafts, notes, poems, songs, short stories, photos, and clippings of Graham (1875-1955), an author, pertain to many of her books, among them *Christopher Columbus, Discoverer* (1950); *Clara Barton, Red Cross Pioneer* (1956); *Great Bands of America* (1951); and *Thirty-three Roads to the White House* (1953).

4,989. Graham, Manta S.
Papers. Nd. 7 boxes.
Open. No guide.
University of Iowa Libraries.
Drafts of plays and other writings of Graham, a playwright from Ottumwa, IA.

4,990. Greater Des Moines Chamber of Commerce
Records. 1907-66. 31 ft.
Open. Unpublished guide.
University of Iowa Libraries.
Annual reports, minutes, correspondence, and bulletins of the Chamber of Commerce also include records of the local women's bureau, 1920-61.

4,991. Hall, Lynn
Papers. Nd. 1 box.
Open. No guide.
University of Iowa Libraries.
Notes and typescripts of Hall, an author of children's books, pertain to her works *The Siege of Silent Henry* (1972) and *Too Near the Sun* (1970).

4,992. Herbst, Josephine
Papers. 1928-47. 8 items.
Open. No guide.
University of Iowa Libraries.
Correspondence of Herbst (1897-1969), an author, and printer's copy with revisions of her book *Somewhere the Tempest Fell* (1947).

4,993. Hesperian Literary Society
Records. 1868-1924. 13 vols.
Open. No guide.
University of Iowa Libraries.
Ledgers and scrapbooks of this University women's group which was formed in ca. 1862 and dissolved in ca. 1932.

4,994. Hill, Catherine Snedeker
Papers. 1854-71. 141 items.
Open. Unpublished guide.
University of Iowa Libraries.
Correspondence of [Mrs.] Hill (ca. 1843-90) includes many letters she wrote as a student in Monticello, IL, some with references to Abraham Lincoln, Illinois politics, and the Civil War. She later moved to Mount Pleasant, IA.

4,995. Hinkley, Laura
Papers. Nd. 3 boxes.
Open. No guide.
University of Iowa Libraries.
Hinkley (1875-1949) was an author. Correspondence, notes, drafts, and proofs pertain to her books *Ladies of Literature* (1946) and *The Stevensons: Louis and Fanny* (1950).

4,996. Institute of Child Behavior and Development, University of Iowa
Records. 1913-67. 38 ft.
Open. No guide.
University of Iowa Libraries.
In 1917 the Institute was established at the University by Cora Bussey Hillis to conduct and disseminate research on the normal child and to train students in research techniques. Correspondence, including letters of and about Hillis; forms; sound recordings; and publications. Hillis also was president of the Iowa Child Welfare Association.

4,997. Iowa City Business and Professional Women's Club
Records. 1932-75. 3 ft.
Open. Unpublished guide.
University of Iowa Libraries.
Minutes, financial records, reports, correspondence, subject files, a scrapbook, and newsletters of the Club.

4,998. Iowa Federation of Business and Professional Women's Clubs, Inc.
Records. 1968-76. 2 ft.
Open. Unpublished guide.
University of Iowa Libraries.
Correspondence, form letters, and other records of the Federation.

4,999. Iowa Library Association
Records. 1890-1976. 21 ft.
Open. Unpublished guide.
University of Iowa Libraries.
Annual reports, conference programs, and files; executive minutes; committee reports; correspondence; district meeting files; photos; and publications of the Association, which involved many women.

5,000. Iowa Nurses' Association
Records. 1904-72. 46 ft.
Open. Unpublished guide.
University of Iowa Libraries.
Board minutes, ledgers and financial records, correspondence, membership lists, committee files, annual convention programs and files, district meeting files, collective bargaining material, photos, and newsletters of the Association. Also includes items pertaining to the American Nurses' Association, the Iowa League for Nursing, the National League for Nursing, and the Student Nurses' Association of Iowa.

5,001. Iowa Press Women, Inc.
Records. 1933-73. 2 ft.
Open. Unpublished guide.
University of Iowa Libraries.
Correspondence, reports, subject files, membership records, clippings, and printed material of the Press Women.

5,002. Iowa Suffrage Memorial Commission
Records. 1910-44. 137 items.
Open. Unpublished guide.
University of Iowa Libraries.
Articles of incorporation and contracts of the Commission; correspondence between Mrs. Fred Hunter, president of the Commission, and Carrie Chapman Catt, 1930-41; correspondence with Nellie V. Walker, who wrote memorial reports for Commission members; speeches; bulletins; and pamphlets about women's suffrage.

5,003. Iowa Women's Political Caucus
Records. 1972-75. 2 ft.
Open. Unpublished guide.
University of Iowa Libraries.
Minutes, reports, correspondence, subject files, and other records of the Caucus.

5,004. Johnson, Dorothy M.
Papers. Nd. 4 boxes.
Open. Unpublished guide.
University of Iowa Libraries.
[Miss] Johnson is an author. Correspondence, notes, typescripts, manuscripts relating to her book *The Hanging Tree* (1957), and papers concerning her parents.

5,005. League of Women Voters of Iowa
Records. 1920-68. 27 ft.
Open. Unpublished guide.
University of Iowa Libraries.
Annual reports, convention and board minutes, correspondence, state convention workbooks, memos, press releases, publications, and other records of the LWV of Iowa.

5,006. Levin, Myrtilla Fones
Papers. 1972-75. Ca. 500 items.
Open. Unpublished guide.
University of Iowa Libraries.
Correspondence, clippings, and other items of Levin (1938-), the chairman of the Jasper County, IA, Republican party and mayor of Newton from 1973 to 1975. She also has been an Iowa Confidential Records Council member since 1973 and an alternate delegate to the 1972 Republican National Convention in Miami Beach, FL.

5,007. Lewis, Thelma B.
Papers. 1947-67. 212 items.
Open. Unpublished guide.
University of Iowa Libraries.
Correspondence, notes, manuscripts, and a scrapbook of Lewis, a member of the city council of Iowa City from 1958 to 1963, who also served as mayor in 1961. Lewis had been assistant technical secretary of the US Delegation to the Council of Foreign Ministers in 1947.

5,008. McDonald, Julie
Papers. 1960-73. 1 box.
Open. No guide.
University of Iowa Libraries.
Papers of McDonald, an author, include correspondence, notes, typescripts, proofs, reviews of her books *Amalie's Story* (1970) and *Baby Black* (1960), and items relating to the Iowa Arts Council.

5,009. McDonald, Margaret
Papers. 1966-73. 144 items.
Open. Unpublished guide.
University of Iowa Libraries.
Correspondence, speeches, photos, clippings, press releases, and other papers of McDonald (1925-), an Iowa Republican party member who was vice-chairman of the Cherokee County Republican central committee from 1965 to 1970, a member of the state central committee from the sixth district between 1970 and 1973, and vice-chairman of that state body after 1973.

5,010. McIlvaine Family
Papers. 1862-1931. 325 items.
Open. Unpublished guide.
University of Iowa Libraries.
Correspondence of this Faribault, MN, family chiefly consists of letters to Mrs. Henry B. McIlvaine concerning business, personal matters, and current events. Correspondents include her nephew Herbert Parsons, a US representative from New York.

5,011. Marshall, Lenore (Guinzburg)
Papers. 1943-62. 14 items.
Open. No guide.
University of Iowa Libraries.
Correspondence, poems, and a typescript of *The Hill Is Level* (1959) by [Mrs. James] Marshall (1897-), an author.

5,012. Medary, Marjorie
Papers. 1931-51. 3 boxes.
Open. No guide.
University of Iowa Libraries.
Correspondence, drafts, and proofs of Medary (1890-), an author, relate to her books, including *College in Crinoline* (1950), *Orange Winter, a Story of Florida in 1880* (1931), *Prairie Printer* (1949), and *Topgallant, a Herring Gull* (1935).

5,013. Meigs, Cornelia L.
Papers. Ca. 1946. 1 box.
Open. No guide.
University of Iowa Libraries.
Drafts, proofs, and other items of Meigs (1884-), an author, pertain to her book *The New Moon: The story of Dick Martin's Courage, His Silver Sixpence and His Friends in the New World* (1946).

5,014. Mortar Board, Staff and Circle Chapter, University of Iowa
Records. 1948-71. 1 Hollinger box.
Open. No guide.

University of Iowa Libraries.
Reports and clippings of this women's honorary society, established in 1911.

5,015. Murray, Janette Stevenson
Papers. Ca. 1950. 1 box.
Open. No guide.
University of Iowa Libraries.
Murray (1874-1967) was an author. Drafts and other material relate to her book *The Story of Cedar Rapids* (1950).

5,016. National Angel Flight, Billy Mitchell Squadron, University of Iowa
Records. 1962-72. 1 vol.
Open. No guide.
University of Iowa Libraries.
Scrapbook of the women's auxiliary to the University of Iowa Air Force Reserve Officers Training Corps, founded in 1962, contains correspondence, photos, and clippings.

5,017. Octave Thanet Literary Society
Records. 1901-24. 3 vols.
Open. No guide.
University of Iowa Libraries.
Ledger and a scrapbook of this University women's group which existed between 1900 and 1933.

5,018. Photographs
Collection. 1865-1972. 80 ft.
Open. No guide.
University of Iowa Libraries.
Photos of University activities, people, and buildings include those depicting women involved in home economics, physical education, and other student activities; women faculty members, nurses, staff members, and students; and the interiors and exteriors of home economics rooms and the women's gymnasium.

5,019. Pownall, Dorothy (Ashby)
Papers. 1918-70. 99 items.
Open. Unpublished guide.
University of Iowa Libraries.
Correspondence, a scrapbook, and clippings of Pownall (1895-), an Iowa journalist and author.

5,020. Progressive Party
Records. 1946-54. 30 ft.
Open. Unpublished guide.
University of Iowa Libraries.
Included in business records, reports, directives, correspondence and form letters, speeches, campaign material, fact sheets, articles, press releases, telegrams, and other items of the party, founded in 1948, are folders on women's involvement in party activities.

5,021. Redpath Chautauqua
Records. Ca. 1900-45. 900 ft.
Open. Unpublished guide.
University of Iowa Libraries.
Office files of the Redpath-Vawter Bureau of Cedar Rapids, IA, and of the Redpath-Chicago and Redpath-Kansas City Bureaus, booking agency representatives for Chautauqua circuits. Also includes a major record series containing files on the people who performed in Chautauqua and lyceum programs, many of whom were women.

5,022. Roberts, Katharine Eggleston
Papers. Ca. 1942-46. 5 boxes.
Open. No guide.
University of Iowa Libraries.
Roberts (1895-) is an author. Drafts, proofs, and other papers pertain to her books *And the Bravest of These* (1946), *Center of the Web* (1942), and *Private Report* (1943). Also contains the manuscript of her unpublished novel "Wind from the River."

5,023. Saltzman, Katherine Eleanor
Papers. Ca. 1936-45. 2 boxes.
Open. No guide.
University of Iowa Libraries.
Correspondence, notes, and drafts of Saltzman (1904-46), an author, relate to her books *Ever Tomorrow* (1936) and *Stuart's Hill* (1945).

5,024. Schramm Family
Papers. 1932-71. 18 ft.
Open. Unpublished guide.
University of Iowa Libraries.
Among the correspondence, speeches, subject files, photos, and clippings of this Burlington, IA, family are the papers of Dorothy (Daniell) Schramm (1908-), which contain information about the LWV; the UN Association of the USA, Inc., Iowa Division; and activities in Burlington.

5,025. Seagrave, Sadie Fuller
Papers. Ca. 1918-57. 2 boxes.
Open. No guide.
University of Iowa Libraries.
Papers of Seagrave (1882-1972), an author, include typescripts, a scrapbook, and material relating to her book *The Millwheel Turns* (1948).

5,026. Seals Club
Records. 1921-30. 1 vol.
Open. No guide.
University of Iowa Libraries.
Ledger of this University women's swimming club, established in 1920.

5,027. Shelton Family
Papers. 1864-1908. 4 vols. and 19 items.
Open. Unpublished guide.
University of Iowa Libraries.
Diary kept by Mary E. Shelton between 1864 and 1865 and one kept by Amanda Rhoda Shelton from 1864 to 1866 contain descriptions of nursing experiences they shared with Annie (Turner) Wittenmyer during the Civil War and at the Hospital for the Insane, later renamed the Iowa State Hospital, in Mount Pleasant, IA. Also includes a speech that Amanda Shelton Stewart gave in 1908 about her Civil War nursing experiences.

5,028. Sherman, Edith Bishop
Papers. Ca. 1950. 1 box.
Open. No guide.
University of Iowa Libraries.
Draft, proofs, and other papers of Sherman (1889-), an author, concern her book *Bright College Year* (1950).

5,029. Sizer, Nelson
Papers. 1883. 6 items.
Open. Unpublished guide.
University of Iowa Libraries.
Sizer (1812-97) was a phrenologist. Correspondence, a statement, a catalog, a pamphlet, and a leaflet pertain to his description of the phrenological character of Sarah Lorindia Gillespie Huftalen, which he presented to the Fowler & Wells Phrenological Cabinet in New York City.

5,030. Suckow, Ruth
Papers. 1911-60. 10 boxes.
Open. Published guide.
University of Iowa Libraries.
Suckow (1892-1960) was an author. Correspondence, drafts, notes, notebooks, photos, and manuscripts of many of her books, among them *The Bonney Family* (1928); *Children and Older People* (1931); *Some Others and Myself: Seven Stories and a Memoir* (1952); and *The John Wood Case, a Novel* (1959). See Frank Paluka, "Ruth Suckow: A Calendar of Letters," *Books at Iowa*, No. 1 (October 1964) and No. 2 (April 1965).

5,031. Thane, Elswyth
Papers. Ca. 1943-63. 5 boxes.
Open. No guide.
University of Iowa Libraries.
Correspondence, notebooks, drafts, and tape recordings of Thane (1900-), an author, pertain to her books, including *Dawn's Early Light* (1943), *Kissing Kin* (1948), *This Was Tomorrow* (1951), and *Yankee Stranger* (1944).

5,032. Thaxter, Celia Laighton
Papers. 1872-94. 27 items.
Open. No guide.
University of Iowa Libraries.
Correspondence, a poem, and photos of Thaxter (1835-94), a poet.

5,033. University of Iowa Faculty, Staff, and Student Organizations
Records. Ca. 1900- . 8 ft.
Open. No guide.
University of Iowa Libraries.
Correspondence, clippings, and publications in a vertical file include material concerning women's organizations on campus.

5,034. University of Iowa Library
Records. 1857-1972. 69 ft.
Open. No guide.
University of Iowa Libraries.
Financial records, correspondence, reports, an accession catalog, and publications of the Library, founded in 1855. Women librarians represented in the collection include Grace Wormer, who served as acting director of the Library for many years.

5,035. University of Iowa Personnel
Records. Ca. 1855- . 22 ft.
Open. No guide.
University of Iowa Libraries.
Personnel forms, correspondence, literary manuscripts, speeches, memorabilia, and clippings of University administrators and faculty and staff members include items about [Mrs.] Adelaide Lasheck Burge, dean of women; [Miss] Clara May Daley, assistant professor of history; Kate Daum, professor of dietetics; Margaret Naumann Keyes, home economics professor and director of an historical restoration project; [Miss] Ann Elise Pierce, associate professor of music education; Myrtle Gladys Scott, professor and head of physical education for women; [Miss] Carrie Ellen Stanley, associate professor of English; Beth Lucy Wellman, psychology professor; Sybil Woodruff, professor and head of home economics; [Miss] Grace Wormer, acting library director; Luella Margaret Wright, associate professor of English; Norma Dorothy Young, associate professor of physical education for men; and [Mrs.] May Pardee Youtz, Associate professor of child welfare.

5,036. Van Etten, Winifred Florence (Mayne)
Papers. Ca. 1936. 1 box.
Open. No guide.
University of Iowa Libraries.
Letters to Van Etten (1902-), an author, from the Atlantic Monthly Press concern acceptance and publication of her book *I Am the Fox* (1936). Also includes an autographed draft of chapter eight from that work.

5,037. Veglahn, Nancy
Papers. 1964-72. 4 boxes.
Open. No guide.
University of Iowa Libraries.
Correspondence, typescripts, notes, and proofs of Veglahn (1937-), an author, relate to her books, including *The Buffalo King* (1971); *Peter Cartwright, Pioneer Circuit Rider* (1968); and *The Tiger's Tail: A Story of America's Great Political Cartoonist Thomas Nast* (1964).

5,038. Virden, Helen M.
Papers. 1953-71. 13 boxes.
Open. No guide.
University of Iowa Libraries.
Virden is an author and government official from Mount Pleasant, IA. Correspondence; manuscripts of poetry, prose, and dramatic works; scrapbooks; and material relating to the Civil War centennial and politics in Iowa.

5,039. Walker, Pamela
Papers. 1972-73. 2 boxes.
Open. No guide.
University of Iowa Libraries.
Correspondence, notes, synopses, scenarios, and drafts of Walker, an author, concern her book *Twyla: A Novel* (1973).

5,040. Weaver, James Baird
Papers. 1837-93. 76 items.
Open. Unpublished guide.
University of Iowa Libraries.
Included in the papers of Weaver (1833-1912), a Civil War general and Populist party leader, is personal correspondence of his wife Clara (Vinson) Weaver.

5,041. Weir, Ruth Cromer
Papers. Ca. 1947-60. 5 boxes.
Open. No guide.
University of Iowa Libraries.
Correspondence, drafts, outlines, notes, and clippings of Weir (1912-), an author, pertain to many of her books, including *Benjamin Franklin, Printer and Patriot* (1955); *Leif Ericson, Explorer* (1951); *Rags, an Orphan of the Storm* (1947); *Science, Science, Everywhere!* (1960); and *The Wonderful Plane Ride* (1949).

5,042. Welty, Susan Elizabeth (Fulton)
Papers. 1937-68. 20 boxes.
Open. No guide.
University of Iowa Libraries.
Correspondence, notes, typescripts, proofs, and clippings of Welty (1905-), an author, pertain to her books, including *Knights' Ransom* (1951); *The Light Shines, a Christmas Play* (1940); and *Look Up and Hope! The Motto of the Volunteer Prison League, the Life of Maud Ballington Booth* (1961).

5,043. Wherry, Elizabeth (Cripliver)
Papers. 1931-56. 6 ft.
Open. Unpublished guide.
University of Iowa Libraries.
Wherry (1893-1956) was a farm magazine columnist, author, and radio commentator in Cedar and Jones counties, IA. Research material, articles, family papers, scrapbooks, pamphlets, and other items.

5,044. Whitby Literary Society
Records. 1913-24. 4 vols.
Open. No guide.
University of Iowa Libraries.
Ledger, scrapbook, and yearbooks of this University women's group, which existed between 1913 and 1928.

5,045. Women's Forensic Council, University of Iowa
Records. 1913-33. 3 vols.
Open. No guide.
University of Iowa Libraries.
Ledgers of a speech group, which was composed of all the women's literary societies on campus and which existed between 1913 and 1933.

5,046. Women's Panhellenic Association, University of Iowa
Records. 1907-71. 1 ft.
Open. No guide.
University of Iowa Libraries.
The Association consisted of all the social sororities on campus. Minutes; reports, including annual reports of several sororities; and publications.

5,047. Yambura, Barbara (Schneider)
Papers. Ca. 1960. 3 boxes.
Open. No guide.
University of Iowa Libraries.
Notes, typescripts, and proofs of Yambura (1917-), an author, relate to her book *A Change and a Parting: My Story of Amana* (1960).

JEFFERSON

5,048. Notable County Women
Collection. 1914- . No size given.
Open. No guide.
Greene County Historical Society.
Correspondence, financial records, minutes, photos, scrapbooks, and 30 books collected by the County Historical Society include information about Leta (Dillavou) Jaquis, a teacher in rural, junior high, and senior high schools in Iowa. A graduate of the State University of Iowa in 1917, Jacquis later became president of the English Teachers of the Central District of the Iowa State Education Association and a member of various community groups.

Also includes material about Verna Grisier McCully, who received a degree from the Academy of Fine Arts in Chicago and worked as an illustrator of poems for the *New York Sun* and of interior decorating schemes for *McCall's, The Designer, Woman's Home Companion,* and *Ladies' Home Journal.* She also wrote newspaper articles for the *Chicago News* and, later, stories for children's magazines about life in France, England, and Italy

The collection provides material about Gladys Gallup-Wilson, who earned master's and doctoral degrees in adult education from George Washington University and worked in home economics for the extension service in Washington state; she joined the US Department of Agriculture extension service, for which she was eventually made director of the division of extension research and training. During the late 1950s she served as a consultant on extension methods in Vietnam and India

Also contains information about Doreen V. (Hansen) Wilber (1930-), a resident of Jefferson and a champion archer who won a gold medal in the 1972 Olympic Games as well as other awards

KALONA

5,049. Bender, Mary Swartzendruber Beachy
Papers. 1885-1971. 8.5 in.
Open. No guide.
Iowa Mennonite Museum and Archives.
A homemaker and member of a conservative Mennonite group in Kalona, Mary Swartzendruber first married Walter E. Beachy; after his death, she married Leroy Bender. Scattered diaries from 1926 to 1971; travel journals she kept in 1956 and 1957, which relate to North Dakota, Arkansas, and Harrisonburg, VA; Bible study class and prayer meeting notes; a notebook containing information about sermons and funerals at Upper Deer Creek Mennonite Church; an autograph album of her mother Helena Hershberger; and assorted devotional books containing poetry and stories, many of which are in German. Some of the travel notes concern visits with friends and relatives in other Mennonite communities.

5,050. Gingerich, Mary A.
Papers. Ca. 1972. 2 in.
Open. No guide.
Iowa Mennonite Museum and Archives.
Gingerich (1908-) is an assistant archivist at the Iowa Mennonite Archives of the Mennonite Historical Society of Iowa in Kalona. Original research notes for and copies of her book *Cemetery Directory of Amish and Mennonites in Iowa, Johnson, and Washington Counties of Iowa* (Kalona, 1972).

5,051. West Union Mission Sewing Circle of the West Union Mennonite Church
Records. 1914-23. Ca. 1 in.
Open. No guide.
Iowa Mennonite Museum and Archives.
Minutes and membership and attendance records of this Iowa County, IA, women's church group whose purpose was to sew for mission and relief work.

5,052. Women's Missionary Sewing Circle, Lower Deer Creek Mennonite Church
Records. 1918-60. 3.75 in.
Open. No guide.
Iowa Mennonite Museum and Archives.
Established in 1918 as the Women's Sewing Circle, this Johnson County, IA, organization became known as the Women's Missionary and Service Auxiliary in ca. 1955; it later assumed its present name. Minutes and membership lists for the entire period and financial records to 1924.

MOUNT PLEASANT

5,053. Harlan, James, and Harlan, Ann Eliza (Peck)
Papers. Nd. No size given.
Open. No guide.
Harlan-Lincoln Home.
Unpublished and published papers and memorabilia found in the restored home of Mount Pleasant residents James Harlan (?-1899) and his wife Ann Harlan (1824-84). Their daughter Mary Eunice Harlan married Robert Todd Lincoln, Abraham Lincoln's son. Includes papers from the period when James Harlan was a Whig US senator and material documenting Ann Harlan's service as a Civil War nurse. Also contains a published story about two girls from the Iowa Wesleyan College campus in Mount Pleasant who broke rules by attending a dance given by the Robert Todd Lincoln family at the Harlans' home.

5,054. Arrowsmith, Lizzie
Papers. Ca. 1860s. No size given.
Access restricted. No guide.
Henry County Historical Society.
Correspondence and a biographical account of Arrowsmith provide information about her contributions to the Union effort during the Civil War.

5,055. McCauley
Papers. 1846. No size given.
Access restricted. No guide.
Henry County Historical Society.
Family correspondence and a diary kept by 16-year-old Eliza McCauley while she and her older sister traveled with a cattle drive from Iowa to California and Oregon to meet their father, who already had moved to the West.

5,056. Tiffany, Palmer
Papers. Nd. No size given.
Access restricted. No guide.
Henry County Historical Society.
Reminiscences of Tiffany, which were serialized in Mount Pleasant newspapers, contain details about life on the Iowa frontier, his wife's reaction to settling on the prairie, and her experiences as manager of a Mount Pleasant hotel while Tiffany was in California during the gold rush.

5,057. Willeford, Susannah
Papers. Nd. 5-page item.
Access restricted. No guide.
Henry County Historical Society.
Account by Willeford in which she describes the hardships experienced when she and her family came to Iowa to homestead land. Her husband became ill, leaving her and the children on the prairie without provisions or shelter.

5,058. Foltz, Clara (Shortridge)
Papers. 1969. 1 item.
Open. No guide.
Iowa Wesleyan College Archives.
Clipping pertaining to [Mrs. Jeremiah Richard] Foltz (1849-1934), the first woman lawyer in California. She was educated at Howe's Academy in Mount Pleasant and in 1878 was admitted to the bar.

5,059. Fortnightly Club
Records. 1932-58. 2 vols.
Open. No guide.
Iowa Wesleyan College Archives.
Yearbooks from 1932 to 1933 and from 1957 to 1958 of this Mount Pleasant women's group whose members focused on discussions of history and travel.

5,060. Harlan and Lincoln Family
Papers. Ca. 1862- . Ca. 32 in.
Open. No guide.
Iowa Wesleyan College Archives.
Correspondence, legal papers, photos, articles, clippings, and other items of Mount Pleasant residents James Harlan (?-1899) and his wife Ann Eliza (Peck) Harlan (1824-84) and of the family and descendants of Harlan's daughter Mary Eunice Harlan (?-1937), who married President Abraham Lincoln's son Robert Todd Lincoln in 1868. James Harlan was the fourth president of Iowa Wesleyan College, then Iowa Wesleyan University, serving from 1853 to 1855 and from 1869 to 1870; he was also a Republican US senator and from 1865 to 1866, secretary of the interior. His wife Ann Harlan was active as a Civil War nurse and in the work of the US Sanitary Commission in Iowa; the collection includes a photo and a pass issued by Edwin Stanton in 1862 to permit her to go through military lines for nursing. Also included are a biographical article, photos, an obituary, and legal papers concerning the estate of Mary (Harlan) [Mrs. Robert Todd] Lincoln, who attended Iowa Wesleyan University. Her will provided that part of her estate should go to that institution if the family bloodline died out.

Also contains photos and an obituary of Mary Lincoln Isham and a photo, an obituary, and an article about Jessie Lincoln (1875-1948), who was the daughter of Mary (Harlan) Lincoln and Robert Todd Lincoln. Jessie Lincoln eloped in 1897 with Warren Beckwith. She divorced him in 1907; married Frank Edward Johnson, who later died; and then married Robert J. Randolph. Also contains photos and clippings of Mary Lincoln Beckwith (ca. 1898-?), Jessie Lincoln Randolph's daughter, who was a sportswoman and airplane pilot; photos of Hazel Holland Wilson, who married Jessie Lincoln Randolph's son Robert T. Lincoln Beckwith; and correspondence and other material relating to the restoration of the Harlan-Lincoln family home in Mount Pleasant.

5,061. Iowa Wesleyan College, Classes and Alumni
Records. Ca. 1864- . 27 in.
Open. No guide.
Iowa Wesleyan College Archives.
Records pertaining to Iowa Wesleyan graduates contain correspondence, numerous student photos and class portraits in which women are depicted, historical sketches, literary manuscripts, school catalogs, school report books, clippings and news releases, pamphlets and booklets, a playbill, and other items. Includes historical sketches, catalogs, and other material of the Mount Pleasant Female Seminary, which was established in 1864; the Seminary was not officially connected with the College, but the latter made Seminary graduates honorary alumnae. Also contains items about the Mary Harlan Lincoln Club, an alumnae group named after Mrs. Robert Todd Lincoln, an early Iowa Wesleyan alumna, and a pamphlet describing the history of women students and faculty at the College from 1843 to 1957. The school awarded its first degree to a woman, namely Lucy Webster Kilpatrick, in 1859. Other graduates represented include Mary J. [Mrs. Stafford] Allen, who was one of the original founders of the P. E. O. Sisterhood formed on campus in 1869; Emma Kate Corkhill, a professor at Iowa Wesleyan and at Simpson College and Lawrence College, who received a BA from Iowa Wesleyan in 1889 and a PhD from Boston University; Marsha Fee [Mrs. J. W.] Vorhies, who graduated in 1896 but at one point was expelled from the College for going to a dance given by Mary Harlan Lincoln; and Eva Freeman, who graduated in 1897. The literary manuscripts in the collection consist of Freeman's essays, poetry, and a dramatic sketch.

5,062. Iowa Wesleyan College Departments and Programs
Records. Ca. 1855- . 22 in.
Open. No guide.
Iowa Wesleyan College Archives.
Included with historical sketches, official documents, photos, programs, and clippings about College departments and programs are photos of the Women's Cadet Corps, which was organized in ca. 1887 as a military drill counterpart to the men's corps and was disbanded in 1892; the men's corps disbanded six years later. Also contains a constitution of the Women's Athletic Association and material on women's basketball at the College including photos from 1902 and 1903 of the school's first women's basketball team, later known as the "Tigerettes"; a team photo from 1905; an historical outline of the women's basketball program from 1943 to 1965; programs; and clippings.

5,063. Iowa Wesleyan College Faculty
Records. Ca. 1867- . 22 in.
Open. No guide.
Iowa Wesleyan College Archives.
Files kept on College faculty members contain scattered correspondence, faculty writings, reference sheets with printed information that the College Archives staff compiled about the faculty, biographical sketches and pamphlets, photos, clippings and obituaries, memorial service and other programs, and magazine and journal articles. Women faculty members represented include Belle A. Mansfield, a law student who became the first woman admitted to the bar in the US; Mary L. Powelson [Mrs. C. C.] Warhurst, a Chautauqua orator and drama director; Penelope [Mrs. Campbell] Amber, who taught at the College between 1864 and 1874; Mary Anders, a piano instructor; Paulène Aspel, a poet and professor of French; Ella Mary Belden, a vocal music teacher; Lucy A. Booth, a history and Greek teacher; Linda Boshart, who taught elementary education from 1968 to 1969; Martha Benbow Boyes, a typing teacher; Helen Culver, a vocal music instructor; Grace M. (Coles) Currie, a music instructor; Elizabeth Dean, an English literature teacher and preceptress; Carrie L. Denise, the dean of women from 1910 to 1911; Mathine M. Dietricksen, a vocal music instructor; Phebe Leech Elliott, an English literature professor and preceptress from 1864 to 1865, who was the daughter of College president Charles Elliott and a member of the board of trustees between 1875 and 1879; Margaret Gilchrist, an oratory instructor and preceptress; Sadie Grumbling, a violin teacher; Phebe J. Jenkins, a preceptress; Maria J. Hager Kelly, who taught from 1854 to 1861; Anna-Katherine Barry Koch, a French and German instructor; Emma Layman, a psychology professor; Fanette O'Kell Lines, an art instructor; Julia Baldwin McKibbin, who taught from 1907 to 1909; Carrie Mauch, a music instructor; Jean Smith [Mrs. Roger S.] Morrow, a biology professor; Frances Moser, who was dean of women between 1940 and 1964, a head of the Pioneer College of Business at Iowa Wesleyan from 1943 to 1956, and a business administration professor from 1948 to 1964; Ruth Ann Mosick, an English and mathematics instructor; Ella S. Nicholson, an English literature and history instructor; Mrs. Edwin O. Price, a history instructor; Emma Schliep, a fine arts instructor; Ellen Bryant Voight, a poet and English instructor; Elizabeth Waffle, a biology instructor; and Esther A. Webb, an English literature instructor.

5,064. Iowa Wesleyan College Student Organizations
Records. Ca. 1855- . Ca. 22 in.
Open. No guide.
Iowa Wesleyan College Archives.
Constitutions and bylaws, historical sketches, photos, programs, invitations, clippings, and pamphlets of various student groups, including the P. E. O. Sisterhood, which was formed in 1869 by seven Iowa Wesleyan University (now College) students and which later grew into a national organization; presently all of its chapters but this one represent towns instead of college campuses. Also contains records of the Ruthean Literary Society, which was organized in 1856 by Iowa Wesleyan students; the Society later opened membership to students from Mount Pleasant German College, which was located on the University campus between 1873 and 1909 to provide for German Methodists' needs. Also includes records of the Hypatia Literary Society, which was founded in 1890; the Alpha Kappa Alpha, a black sorority that was formed in 1969 by students from the College and the University of Iowa; the Alpha Alpha, which was organized in 1918 and became a chapter of the national Zeta Tau Alpha society, which was founded in 1819; and the Iowa Alpha chapter of the national Pi Beta Phi society, which became active on campus in 1868 as the I. C. Sorosis club but assumed its present name in 1888. Also includes records of the Alpha Xi Delta sorority, including a program of and clippings about the Beta Province Convention held in Mount Pleasant in 1969, and a photo of Ruthean Literary Society member Louisa Mason, the third Negro woman to graduate from the University in 1891.

5,065. Iowa Wesleyan College Trustees
Records. Ca. 1855- . 6 in.
Open. No guide.
Iowa Wesleyan College Archives.
Correspondence, biographical sketches, photos, clippings, and pamphlets about individuals who have served on the College board of trustees include material on Emily McClure; Martha McClure, a social and civic worker; May Pierce [Mrs. W. C.] Scamman, a 1909 Iowa Wesleyan graduate who was a trustee from 1941 to 1959; Elberta T. Smith, past president of the Woman's Society of Christian Service of the Methodist Church; Olive Cole Smith; and Marjorie [Mrs. Wallace P.] Weirick, an active member of the California P. E. O. Items concerning Olive Smith include Armistice Day essays and a pamphlet she wrote in 1942 about the history of Mount Pleasant.

5,066. Ladies Library Association
Records. Ca. 1915-37. 1 vol. and 1 item.
Open. No guide.
Iowa Wesleyan College Archives.
A photo of members dated ca. 1915 and a 1936-37 yearbook of this Mount Pleasant organization,

formed in 1872 through the merger of the Ladies Reading Club and the Ladies Lecture Association.

5,067. Logan, Isabel "Belly" V. Gardner
Papers. Nd. 1 vol. and 1 item.
Open. No guide.
Iowa Wesleyan College Archives.
"My Mount Pleasant Story, 1864-1881," a volume of reminiscences by Logan (1864-?), contains photos and hand drawn illustrations. Also includes a letter from Miriam Logan to Iowa Wesleyan College concerning the reminiscences.

5,068. Mansfield, Belle A.
Papers. Ca. 1870s-1969. 4.75 in.
Open. No guide.
Iowa Wesleyan College Archives.
Born Arabella Aurelia Babb, [Mrs. John Melvin] Mansfield (1846-1911) was an English literature professor and preceptress at the College, a high school principal, a woman suffrage and temperance advocate, and a peace reformer; in 1869 she also was the first woman to be admitted to the bar in the United States. Correspondence, photos of her, clippings, and a number of biographical sketches, articles, research papers, and other items about Mansfield's life. Also includes research material and an article about her by College president Louis A. Haselmayer, his correspondence with the Babb family and with the National Association of Women Lawyers, and a publicity file about the 1968-69 Mansfield centennial celebration at the College. Mansfield was a student at Iowa Wesleyan University (now College) in the 1860s and a member of the Ruthean Literary Society. In 1872 she received a bachelor of laws degree from the University, and one year later she became preceptress and an English professor at that institution, positions she held full-time until 1879 and half-time until 1884. Then she served as principal at Mount Pleasant High School for two years; in 1886 she became preceptress in the Ladies Hall at DePauw University in Greencastle, IN, where in later years she also served as registrar, history professor, and professor of aesthetics and the history of music. While living in Mount Pleasant, she was president of the Henry County Woman Suffrage Association and a member of the Iowa Peace Society. Although she was admitted to the bar and was a member of the National League of Women Lawyers, a group organized in 1893 that was a predecessor of the National Association of Women Lawyers, Mansfield never actually practiced as a lawyer.

5,069. T. T. T. Society
Records. 1936-50. 2 items.
Open. No guide.
Iowa Wesleyan College Archives.
Articles of incorporation, bylaws and standing rules, and a 25th anniversary program of Chapter Iowa A of the Society, a women's charitable organization, in Mount Pleasant. The Chapter was formed in 1911.

5,070. Warhurst, Mary L. Powelson
Papers. Ca. 1902-43. 0.5 in.
Open. No guide.
Iowa Wesleyan College Archives.
The director of speech arts at the College from 1915 to 1921, [Mrs. C. C.] Warhurst (?-1968) was also a reader, storyteller, and impersonator with lyceum and Chautauqua companies. Papers in the College faculty file include one letter, a 1925-26 employment contract for Des Moines University, recommendations she received from the Columbia School of Oratory and from the College, photos of her, programs and clippings about plays she directed at Des Moines University, a Chautauqua promotional folder and advertisement about her, a pamphlet, and other items. Warhurst was the sister of Ethel Hueston, the author of the "Prudence" books for children.

5,071. YWCA of Henry County
Records. Ca. 1920-26. 1.5 in.
Open. No guide.
Iowa Wesleyan College Archives.
The YWCA of Henry County was organized in 1920, although other YWCA groups existed at a local high school and at Iowa Wesleyan College. Excerpts from the constitution, annual reports to the YWCA national board, monthly reports and minutes of the Henry County Association of the YWCA, a 1923-24 annual report of the YWCA at New London High School, and a post card picture of the Seeley Memorial YWCA in Mount Pleasant.

5,072. Methodist Photos
Collection. Ca. 1867-1947. Ca. 134 items.
Open. No guide.
United Methodist Church Archives.
Approximately one-half of the photos in the collection depict Methodist conferences, meetings, and Methodist college students. Includes a 1931 photo of the Woman's Missionary Association convention, United Brethren in Christ Church, and a 1940 photo of the WMA convention held in Mount Vernon, VA. The remaining photos in the collection are of bishops, ministers, ministers' wives and family members, and prominent church members, including Joseph and Teresa Sartori, who were Methodist philanthropists of Cedar Falls, IA.

5,073. Methodist Women's Organizations
Collection. 1896-1959. 18 in.
Open. No guide.
United Methodist Church Archives.
Consists of pamphlets and booklets containing the constitution and bylaws, annual reports, minutes, yearbooks, and programs of various Methodist women's groups. Represented are the national, state, and Northwest Iowa Conference units of the Woman's Home Missionary Society of the Methodist Episcopal Church; the Des Moines, IA, branch and the national office of the Woman's Foreign Missionary Society of the Methodist Episcopal Church; the Sioux City, IA, and Fort Dodge, IA, districts and the Northwest and North Iowa conferences of the Woman's Society of Christian Service of the Methodist Church; the Boylan Industrial Home in Jacksonville, FL; the Shesler Deaconess Home, Northwest Iowa Conference, which was established in 1901 in Sioux City; the Foochow Woman's Conference and the Yenping Woman's Conference, both of the Methodist Episcopal Church; and the Wall Street Mission, Industrial School and Social Center located in Sioux City.

5,074. Newsom, John Edward, and Newsom, Emma Ellen (Day)
Papers. Ca. 1873-1958. 211 in.
Open. No guide.
United Methodist Church Archives.
Correspondence, essays, invitations, programs, teachers' certificates, and other items of clergyman John Edward Newsom (1856-1930) and his wife Emma Day Newsom (1862-1952), a P. E. O. Sisterhood member and schoolteacher. Also includes a typed pamphlet by [Mrs.] Mary Abbott Delahunt containing personal recollections and genealogical information. John Newsom was a schoolteacher who had studied for one term at Oskaloosa College in 1875 before he decided to become a minister. In 1883 he entered Iowa Wesleyan University to complete the necessary education for admission to the seminary, and while there he met Emma Day. John Newson went on to receive a bachelor of divinity degree from the Theological Seminary of Northwestern. He served as a minister in India, Iowa, New Jersey, and Vermont.

5,075. Women's Organizations of the Evangelical Association and United Evangelical Church
Records. 1903-51. 9.75 in.
Open. Card file.
United Methodist Church Archives.
The Des Moines and Iowa branches of the Evangelical Association, both of which were organized in 1903, merged at a joint convention in 1912; this larger Evangelical Association in turn merged 15 years later with the Des Moines branch of the United Evangelical Church, which had been founded in 1899, and with other units to form the new United Evangelical Church. Records of the Evangelical Association and UEC women's organizations include financial records of the Women's Missionary Society, the Des Moines Conference, 1903-12; items of the WMS of the Iowa Conference, with executive board journals, 1903-26, and other journals, 1903-51, as well as corresponding secretary, young women's work, and general financial records; a record book of the WMS of the Zion Evangelical Church in Laurel, IA; and financial records, 1947-51, of the Women's Society of World Service, Iowa Conference Branch, which was the successor of the WMS organization of the Evangelical United Brethren Church. The EUBC was formed in 1946 when several denominations of the United Brethren in Christ and the UEC merged. Women's organizations of those churches merged in 1951.

5,076. Women's Organizations of the Methodist Episcopal Church
Records. 1883-1940. 7.5 in.
Open. Card file.
United Methodist Church Archives.
Records of the Woman's Home Missionary Society, including journals of the Sioux City district, 1890-1908, and of the Fort Dodge district, 1923-40, both of the Northwest Iowa Conference; journals of the aggregate Northwest Iowa Conference unit, 1883-1901 and 1933-40; and journals of the Ottumwa district, Iowa Conference, 1908-10. Also contains records of the Woman's Foreign Missionary Society, with journals, financial and statistical records, and district corresponding secretary's records of the Algona district, Northwest Iowa Conference, 1898-1940; journals of the Sioux City district, 1914-40; district corresponding secretary's records of the Des Moines branch, 1936-40; and a financial and auxiliary treasurer's book, 1929-40, of the WFMS at Rudd Methodist Episcopal Church in Waterloo district, Upper Iowa Conference.

5,077. Women's Organizations of the United Brethren in Christ Church
Records. 1878-1951. 8.75 in.
Open. Card file.
United Methodist Church Archives.
Financial records of the Woman's Missionary Association, Des Moines Conference, 1892-1925; and minutes for 1948 to 1951, scattered journals for 1878 to 1948, financial records, a history, and a volume entitled "Secretary of Literature, Miscellaneous, 1908-1910" of the WMA, Iowa Conference. The WMA of the United Brethren in Christ and the Woman's Missionary Society of the United Evangelical Church merged in 1951 to form the Women's Society of World Service. Five years earlier the UBC and the UEC church bodies merged to form the Evangelical United Brethren Church; that body and the Methodist Episcopal Church were forerunners of the United Methodist Church.

5,078. Women's Society of World Service, Evangelical United Brethren Church, Iowa Conference
Records. 1951-68. 39.25 in.
Open. Partial card file.
United Methodist Church Archives.
The WSWS was organized in 1951 when the

Woman's Missionary Association of the United Brethren in Christ Church and the Woman's Missionary Society of the United Evangelical Church merged. Annual reports and plans of work, minutes, financial records, correspondence, historical sketches and records, scrapbooks, pamphlets and information sheets, programs, promotional material, and handbooks. Includes correspondence between Iowa branch officers and the national WSWS headquarters in Dayton, OH, 1965-68; minutes, reports, and plans of work of the Missionary Education for Children program, 1959-65; and printed material about United Church Women of Iowa, 1960-65.

MOUNT VERNON

5,079. Cooke, Harriette Jay
Papers. 1873-1964. 2 folders.
Open. No guide.
Cornell College Archives.
[Miss] Cooke (1830-1914), a professor and preceptress at Cornell College, became a social settlement worker in Boston. Composition book containing lecture notes; photos of Cooke; articles about her from the *Cornellian,* the *Sibylline,* and *The Collegian,* ca. 1873-1908; and a paper about Cooke's career in Boston written by Alice Rigby Moore in 1953. Also contains copies of the constitution of the Cornell Association for the Higher Education of Women, of which Cooke was president. In 1853 Cooke graduated from the New Hampshire Conference Seminary. She taught school in Massachusetts until 1857 when she became a teacher of English, drawing, and painting at Cornell College. Two years later she earned an MA from the institution and taught German as well as drawing and painting; she became preceptress in 1866. From 1870 to 1890 she was preceptress and professor of German, history, and government.

After retiring from Cornell, Cooke went to London to study at Mildmay, a social work center. After two years with the Mildmay Association for Female Workers and one year as assistant in a related deaconess training school, she returned to Boston to head the woman's department of the Boston University Settlement, where she helped establish a medical mission. She retired in 1907.

5,080. Holmes, Marjorie
Papers. 1943-75. 1 folder.
Open. No guide.
Cornell College Archives.
Clippings, articles from Cornell College publications, and a printed pamphlet about [Mrs. Lynn Mighell] Holmes (1910-), a novelist and journalist who was a columnist on the Washington *Evening Star* for 18 years and author of a monthly column for *Woman's Day* magazine. She is the author of *Two From Galilee; I've Got to Talk with Somebody, God,* which sold more than a million copies; and other inspirational books. Holmes graduated from Cornell College in 1931.

5,081. Isaacson, Alice Edith
Papers. 1914-56. 1 folder.
Open. No guide.
Cornell College Archives.
Isaacson (1874-1955), a registered nurse, served with the Canadian Medical Corps for more than four years during WWI; she was a nurse at Cornell College from 1923 to 1944. One letter, diary notes, reminiscences, and pamphlets pertaining to her wartime experiences in Britain and France, the "Chicago Unit" of nurses who served in the Canadian Medical Corps in Europe, and the WWI armistice; photos, clippings, and articles from Cornell publications about her career at the College; awards and nursing diploma; memorabilia; and other items. Isaacson received her nurse's training at St. Luke's Hospital in Cedar Rapids, IA, and completed graduate work at the Chicago Lying-In-Hospital. She was honored by the English and French governments for her WWI service.

5,082. Keyes, Margaret
Papers. Ca. 1954- . 1 folder.
Open. No guide.
Cornell College Archives.
Keyes (1918-) has been a home economics professor at the University of Iowa since 1951; her areas of specialization are interior design and architecture. Photos of her, clippings from newspapers and from the *Cornell College Alumnus,* and a 1971 issue of *The Iowan* magazine containing an article she wrote about her grandfather Marsden Keyes, an architect and contractor who lived in the Mount Vernon area. Margaret Keyes graduated from Cornell College in 1939. She supervised the restoration of Iowa's old capitol building in Iowa City, a project that was completed in 1976, and has published a book about 19th-century residential architecture in that area.

5,083. Newbury, Dorothy J.
Papers. 1953- . 1 folder.
Open. No guide.
Cornell College Archives.
Correspondence, journal articles, photos, pamphlet, and clippings from newspapers and Cornell College publications about Newbury, an author who has been assistant, associate, and since 1975 a full professor of education at Cornell College. With the exception of the 1965-66 academic year, which she spent as a Fulbright lecturer at Cuttington College in Liberia, she has taught at Cornell College since 1953. Included are nine letters she sent to the College in 1965 in which she describes her teaching experience in Africa, a letter she wrote from the Canary Islands, and a pamphlet *Broader Learnings Through Poetry,* which she wrote with Marlene Hawke. Newbury also wrote a textbook on the teaching of reading and *For True,* a chronicle of life in West Africa.

5,084. Norton, Mary Florence (Burr)
Papers. Ca. 1877-1950. 1 folder.
Open. No guide.
Cornell College Archives.
Photos, clippings from the *Cornell College Bulletin,* and an obituary notice of Norton (1852-1950), a Cornell College graduate who taught at the institution from 1877 until her retirement in 1919. The 10th child of Isaac Post Burr and Emma Lucretia (Quigly) Burr of Connecticut and western New York, Norton moved with her family to Mount Vernon in 1870. She studied at Cornell, earning a BS in 1877 and an MS and MA in 1880. She taught in the French and mathematics departments from 1877 until 1886 when she began to concentrate her teaching efforts in the mathematics department. In 1895 she did graduate work in mathematics at the University of Chicago. She was married to Cornell geology professor William Harmon Norton.

5,085. Van Etten, Winifred (Mayne)
Papers. 1927-76. 1 folder.
Open. No guide.
Cornell College Archives.
[Mrs. Ben] Van Etten (1902-), a Cornell College English professor from 1928 to 1968, is a novelist whose book *I Am the Fox* won the $10,000 *Atlantic Monthly* novel contest in 1936. Photos, clippings, editions of the Cornell magazine *The Husk* containing selections she wrote, copies of the *Cornell College Bulletin, Alumni Number* with information about her, invitations, and other items. Included in *The Husk* magazine are her stories "The Hat" (1939) and "Still Waters" (1928).

MUSCATINE

5,086. College Archives
Records. 1929- . No size given.
Open. No guide.
Muscatine Community College Library.
Faculty committee minutes, scrapbook, clippings, and campus newspapers of Muscatine Community College, founded in 1929. Includes papers relating to [Miss] Willetta Strahan, the founder and first dean of the College, and [Miss] Louise Gaekle, a faculty member from the 1930s until about 1966. Strahan was born in Omaha, received BA and MA degrees at the University of Iowa, and did additional graduate work at that institution as well as at Oxford and Cambridge universities. From 1916 to 1918 she was a junior high school English teacher in Mason City, IA; from 1919 to 1926 she was a junior high school principal in Denison, IA; and just before the beginning of her career at Muscatine Community College in 1929, she served as principal of the Denison senior high school.

5,087. Women's Organizations in Muscatine
Records. 1913- . No size given.
Open. No guide.
Musser Public Library.
Consists of yearbooks from the Federated Women's Club, the Business and Professional Women's Club, the Ethics Club, and the Atheneum Club in Muscatine.

ORANGE CITY

5,088. Noordhoff, Jeanne
Papers. 1882-1970. 1 box.
Open. Unpublished guide.
Northwestern College Library, Dutch Heritage Collection.
Correspondence, diary, travel descriptions, and photos of Noordhoff (1882-1970), a Reformed Church in America missionary in Japan between 1911 and 1941. She taught at Sturgis School for girls in Shimonoseki for eight years, at Ferris Girls' School in Yokohama for 12 years, and at Keisen Girls' School in Tokyo for three years. She also did general Christian work in Nagasaki for 10 years and in nearby Shimabara for one year. After WWII Noordhoff served in the Japanese Presbyterian Church in Watsonville, CA, and in other churches in the US.

5,089. Women's Auxiliary of Northwestern College
Records. 1928-76. 1 box.
Open. Unpublished guide.
Northwestern College Library, Dutch Heritage Collection.
Charter, minutes, financial records, a history, programs, and clippings of the Auxiliary, established in 1928 to encourage financial support of the College and to promote the institution's general welfare. The Auxiliary is still in existence.

OTTUMWA

5,090. Archives
Records. 1854- . 4 drawers and 4 vols.
Open. No guide.
Humility of Mary Convent.
Records of the Convent, which was established at Ottumwa in 1877, consist of correspondence, photos, scrapbooks, prayer books, artifacts, and material relating to the founding of various missions that were staffed in part by the order, the establishment of a college, and the reuniting of two parts of the congregation. Includes letters of the mothers general and correspondence of sisters with relatives in France.

5,091. Aldrich, Bess (Streeter)
Papers. Nd. 2 vols.
Open. No guide.
Ottumwa Public Library.
Scrapbooks of Aldrich (1881-1954), an author, contain articles she wrote, book reviews, and clippings.

5,092. Ferber, Edna
Papers. Nd. 1 vol.
Open. No guide.
Ottumwa Public Library.
Scrapbook of Ferber (1887-1968), an author who spent her girlhood in Ottumwa between 1890 and 1897, contains clippings and magazine reviews and notices about her career and books.

5,093. Graham, Alberta Powell
Papers. Ca. 1940s-50s. 2 vols.
Open. No guide.
Ottumwa Public Library.
Scrapbooks containing correspondence, photos, clippings, and miscellaneous items of Graham (1875-1955), an author of books for teenagers, songwriter for children, and Ottumwa music teacher who also collected dolls. Her doll collection is housed at the Ottumwa Public Library.

5,094. Morrow, Honore Willsie
Papers. Nd. 3 vols.
Open. No guide.
Ottumwa Public Library.
Scrapbooks of Morrow (1880-1940), an Ottumwa native who became an author of historical novels, including several on Abraham Lincoln. The scrapbooks contain clippings about her career and writings.

5,095. Women of Ottumwa
Collection. 1924-54. 6 vols.
Open. No guide.
Ottumwa Public Library.
Scrapbooks contain clippings about women who were civic and social leaders in Ottumwa.

5,096. Ottumwa Shakespeare Club
Records. 1899-1932. 0.5 in.
Open. No guide.
Wapello County Historical Society.
Records of the Club, a women's literary group organized in 1882, consist of yearbooks, 1899-1910; a 50th anniversary yearbook, 1931-32; program sheet; membership nomination letter; and typewritten comments of members about a Club history written by a Mrs. Keyhoe.

5,097. P.E.O. Sisterhood, Chapter G, Ottumwa
Records. 1896-97. 1 vol.
Open. No guide.
Wapello County Historical Society.
Yearbook of this local chapter of the Sisterhood, organized in 1884. The P.E.O. is a service organization that promotes education for women.

5,098. Young Women's Christian Association
Records. 1902-07. 0.5 in.
Open. No guide.
Wapello County Historical Society.
Records of the local YWCA branch include a yearbook for 1905, an announcement for Bible classes, member's reception booklet, a brochure, and programs from the 20th annual state convention of Iowa YWCAs held in Ottumwa in 1903.

ROCKWELL CITY

5,099. Delphian Chapter
Records. 1890-1970. 4 vols.
Open. No guide.
Calhoun County Historical Society.
Minutes and treasurer's books of this study club, which existed between 1890 and 1970.

5,100. Woman's Christian Temperance Union
Records. 1930-35. 1 vol.
Open. No guide.
Calhoun County Historical Society.
Minute book of a local chapter of the WCTU.

SIOUX CITY

5,101. Dimmitt, Lillian E.
Papers. Nd. No size given.
Open. No guide.
Morningside College Library.
Correspondence, two tapes, and clippings of Dimmitt (1867-1965), an ancient languages professor and dean of women at Morningside College from 1918 to 1940. Dimmitt, who was born in Danville, IL, began her career at the College in 1894 as a Greek and Latin instructor. Three years later she became professor of Latin, a position she held until 1918 when she assumed her wider responsibilities. In later years a women's dormitory on the Morningside campus was named after her.

5,102. Ferguson, Agnes Beveridge
Papers. Nd. 4 folders.
Open. No guide.
Morningside College Library.
Correspondence and clippings of Ferguson (1868-1924), a New York native who became a German professor at Morningside College. During WWI she was employed by the US government to translate German correspondence and documents.

5,103. Woodford, Faith Foster
Papers. Nd. 1 folder.
Open. No guide.
Morningside College Library.
Correspondence and clippings of Woodford (1883-1963), a native of Sergeant Bluff, IA, who was associate professor of pianoforte and music history at Morningside College from 1902 to 1953.

5,104. Call, George R.
Papers. 1850-1974. 1 box.
Open. Unpublished guide.
Sioux City Public Museum.
Correspondence, manuscripts, reports, business papers, photos, scrapbook, clippings, pamphlets, maps, and ham radio memorabilia of Call (1898-1974), a lawyer, real estate agent, and promoter of commercial traffic on the Missouri River. Includes "Early Day Mansion on Rose Hill," a 35-page manuscript by Call's wife Alice (Hawthorne) Call in which she describes the home of Call's parents and writes about the Call family. Drawn mainly from her husband's recollections and completed in 1972, her manuscript provides information about the daily life and social activities of a well-to-do family in the early 1900s.

5,105. Floyd School PTA
Records. 1928-1975. 1 folder, 39 vols., and 1 item.
Open. Unpublished guide.
Sioux City Public Museum.
Records of the PTA at Floyd School in Sioux City chiefly consist of annual scrapbooks that contain minutes; correspondence pertaining to the PTA's involvement in other local, state, and national organizations; lists of officers and members; photos of classes, teachers, and school projects; programs; clippings about school and PTA activities; and documents such as PTA membership and outstanding achievement certificates. Collection also includes a plaque. The PTA disbanded when Floyd School was closed at the end of the 1974-75 school year.

5,106. Harding, William Lloyd, and Harding, Carrie (Lamoreux)
Papers. Early 1800s-1965. 6 folders, 88 vols., and 1 recording disc.
Open. Unpublished guide.
Sioux City Public Museum.
Papers of W. L. Harding (1877-1934), a Sioux City lawyer and governor of Iowa from 1916 to 1920, and his wife Carrie Harding (1879-1965), who pursued various welfare, social, and intellectual interests. Contains correspondence, letter files, diaries, manuscripts, documents, financial records, a recording disc, photos, albums, scrapbooks, clippings, political literature and other campaign material, and memorabilia of family, social life, hobbies, and interests. Also included are family photos and papers of the Harding and Lamoreux families dating to the 1800s.

5,107. Henderson, Gertrude
Papers. 1922-41. 2 boxes.
Open. No guide.
Sioux City Public Museum.
[Mrs. Ralph A.] Henderson (?-1954) was a newspaper writer specializing in historical research of Sioux City and Woodbury County, IA; she also served as curator of the Public Museum while the WPA conducted the Historical Records Survey. Correspondence, research notes, rough drafts, and transcripts of manuscripts pertaining to local and county history, many of which were printed in Sioux City newspapers; and correspondence, photos, clippings, band programs, fund-raising material, and memorabilia of the American Legion Monahan Post Band in Sioux City. The Post, managed by Henderson's husband, won first place in a band competition at the national American Legion convention in 1927. The correspondence reveals her role in arranging for band trips and in representing the band in negotiations for recording and broadcasting engagements and in union matters.

5,108. Historical Records Survey, Works Progress Administration, Division of Women's and Professional Projects
Records. 1868-1941. 113 items.
Open. Unpublished guide.
Sioux City Public Museum.
Of the manuscripts prepared by Records Survey workers from memoirs, diaries, speeches, and independent studies of Sioux City area pioneer settlers, 27 were written by or about women. Includes descriptions of the murder of two Sioux City pioneers by Indians as recorded by the daughter of one of the slain men, the arrival of Sioux City's first white woman and her children, Woodbury County's first schoolhouse, and excerpts from the diary of a woman who came to Sioux City by steamboat in 1858. Many of the manuscripts were written by [Mrs.] Gertrude Henderson, a journalist and local historian.

SPIRIT LAKE

5,109. Spirit Lake Business and Professional Women's Club
Records. 1972-73. 1 vol.
Open. No guide.
Dickinson County Museum.
Scrapbook of this local women's group, founded in 1934, contains state reports, photos, clippings, and an eight-page biographical sketch of Virginia Bedell, a Spirit Lake native who served as the Club's first president and also was president of the state business and professional women's organization. Bedell was admitted to the bar in 1920 and in 1936 became one of the first women in the US to be elected county attorney, a position she held until 1940. Then she was chosen to serve on the state parole board and held that position until 1959. She was also a longtime member of the

DAR and in 1967 was selected mother of the year of Iowa.

STORM LAKE

5,110. Honor Iowans Convocation
Records. 1966. 3.75 in.
Open. No guide.
Buena Vista College Library.
The 75th anniversary convocation at the College presented "Honor Iowans Awards" to ca. 75 native Iowans, individuals nationally prominent in the arts, literature, business, and politics as well as those more closely connected to the school and its immediate geographic area, such as alumni or local residents. Collection consists of correspondence between people honored at the convocation and school officials Wendell Halverson and Charles B. Hoeven. Among the women honored at the convocation and represented in the correspondence are Harriet Nelson, actress and entertainer; Abigail Van Buren, newspaper columnist; Mamie (Doud) Eisenhower; Ruth [Mrs. Norman Vincent] Peale; Marion M. Schrum, dean of the college of nursing at Villanova University; Mary V. Braginton of Rockford College in Illinois; Dorothy D. Houghton; and Marjorie [Mrs. Lynn Mighell] Holmes, author and journalist. Holmes's correspondence contains her reminiscences about her student years at Buena Vista College and life in Storm Lake before she transferred to Cornell College in Mount Vernon, IA.

TOLEDO

5,111. Brownell, Sarah
Papers. 1853-75. 1 vol.
Open. No guide.
Tama County Historical Society Museum.
Autograph album contains illustrations and scattered entries as well as some locks of hair and other mementos.

5,112. Junior Federated Club
Records. Ca. 1940-50. 1 vol.
Open. No guide.
Tama County Historical Society Museum.
Scrapbook containing yearbooks, clippings, and miscellaneous notes of this women's group in Tama. Founded in 1940, the Club joined the Iowa Federation of Women's Clubs and the GFWC that same year.

5,113. Octagon Club
Records. 1917-43. 1 vol.
Open. No guide.
Tama County Historical Society Museum.
Scrapbook of this Tama women's group, which was founded in 1917 as a literary society but which later pursued diverse interests, contains yearbooks, programs, and clippings. The Club affiliated with the Iowa Federation of Women's Clubs the same year it was founded.

5,114. Tama County Unit, Women's Committee, Council of National Defense
Records. 1919. 21-page item.
Open. No guide.
Tama County Historical Society Museum.
Printed report of County participation in the Women's Committee during WWI was written by Mrs. Elmer E. Taylor, the County Unit chairman, and printed in Traer, IA.

5,115. Young Ladies Debating Society of Tama High School
Records. 1876. 1 vol.
Open. No guide.
Tama County Historical Society Museum.
Minutes of the Society.

5,116. Young People's Temperance Society
Records. 1869-72. 1 vol.
Open. No guide.
Tama County Historical Society Museum.
Secretary's book of the Society, whose male and female members assembled for meetings in the "Old School House" in Tama.

WEBSTER CITY

5,117. Business and Professional Women's Club
Records. 1930- . 16 vols.
Open. No guide.
Kendall Young Library.
Scrapbooks containing photos, clippings, and other records of the Club, a Webster City service organization established in about 1930.

5,118. Eberle, Abastenia St. Leger
Papers. 1914-30. 2 vols., 22 slides, and 22 items.
Access restricted. Unpublished guide.
Kendall Young Library.
Scrapbooks filled with personal correspondence, family photos, and clippings of Eberle (1878-1942), a sculptor who was also known as Agnes St. Leger Eberle. Also includes slides of and the original plaster of paris statuettes she created depicting life on Madison Street in New York City's East Side during the years 1914 to 1920. Bronze pieces cast from her plaster models have been displayed at the Chicago Art Institute, the Metropolitan Museum of Art, and the Whitney Museum of American Art in New York and by the Italian Art Society in Venice, Italy.

WEST BRANCH

5,119. Hoover, Herbert: Pre-Commerce Period
Papers. 1894-1921. 75 ft.
Open. Unpublished guide.
Herbert Hoover Presidential Library.
Correspondence, telegrams, memoranda, clippings, printed items, and cross-reference sheets reflect Hoover's activities and interests from the time he graduated from Stanford University until he became secretary of commerce. Papers are arranged into subgroups consisting of general correspondence, subject files, and US Food Administration files. Women with individual files in Hoover's general correspondence include Mary (Hunter) Austin, Mary Gibson, Florence V. Hoyt, Charlotte Kellogg, Alice King, Julia Clifford Lathrop, Edith [Mrs. Everit] Macy, Florence C. Thorne, Martha Van Rensselaer, and Mrs. Henry Villard.

Papers pertaining to women can be found in Hoover's subject files subseries entitled "Presidential Campaign of 1920" and "War Relief and Reconstruction, 1919-23" and in the file on Edith Cavell.

The US Food Administration files consist of printed material, much of which pertains to the role of women in that office's phase of war work.

5,120. Hoover, Herbert: Commerce Period
Papers. 1921-28. 353 ft.
Open. Unpublished guide.
Herbert Hoover Presidential Library.
Personal correspondence, memoranda, reports, clippings, and various printed items document Hoover's career as secretary of commerce and pertain to building and housing, farm relief, foreign debts and loans, regulation of radio broadcasting and aeronautics, flood victim relief in the Mississippi and Vermont river basins in 1927, and the problems of business cycles and unemployment. Hoover also corresponded with many women concerning child health and welfare, suppression of the narcotics trade, home building and ownership, prohibition, and politics. His principal correspondents include Grace Abbott, Jane Addams, Anne [Mrs. William] Hard, Alice [Mrs. Henry] Howard, Julia Clifford Lathrop, Katharine F. Lenroot, Matilda [Mrs. J. H.] Minthorn, Aurelia I. Reinhardt, Arabella [Mrs. Willoughby] Rodman, Ida Tarbell, Mabel (Walker) Willebrandt, and Maud (Wood) Park.

5,121. Hoover, Herbert: Pre-Presidential Period
Papers. 1928-29. 101 ft.
Open. Unpublished guide.
Herbert Hoover Presidential Library.
Papers of Hoover covering the interim between the Republican national convention and Hoover's inauguration as President are divided into the two series of general correspondence and special subjects. General correspondence reflecting the issues of Hoover's campaign consists of correspondence, telegrams, memoranda, clippings, and printed matter and includes files on Jane Addams; Mary Booze, a Negro Republican National Committee member; Clara B. Burdette; Willie W. Caldwell; Ida R. Koverman; Gertrude Lane, editor of *Woman's Home Companion;* Ruth (Hanna) McCormick; Marie M. Meloney of the New York *Herald Tribune;* Lucy W. Peabody of the Woman's National Committee on Law Enforcement; Anna Steese Richardson; Margaret (Dreier) Robins; Caroline Slade; Jennie S. Lathrop Watson; Mabel (Walker) Willebrandt; and Lenna Lowe Yost.

Papers in the special subjects series pertaining to women include a 75-page diary of Ruth (Fessler) Lippman, who was secretary to Lou (Henry) Hoover, (1874-1944), in the Latin American trip file; Lippman evidently accompanied Lou Hoover on this goodwill trip in 1928 and 1929 after the Presidential election. Also contains a file on cabinet appointments, with biographical sketches of prospective appointees and letters endorsing or opposing appointments. Women mentioned in this material include Sally Aley Hert, Maud (Wood) Park, Christine Bradley South, Mabel (Walker) Willebrandt, and Alice (Ames) Winter.

5,122. Hoover, Herbert: Presidential Period
Papers. 1929-33. 656 ft.
Open. Unpublished guide.
Herbert Hoover Presidential Library.
Correspondence, memoranda, reports, executive orders, messages and speeches, press releases, transcripts of trans-Atlantic telephone calls, invitations received, statistical material, editorial analyses, maps and charts, and printed items of Hoover during his Presidency. Includes the following files pertinent to women: Better Homes in America, Inc.; the White House Conference on Home Building and Home Ownership; children, child labor, and the White House Conference on Child Health and Protection; prohibition, the WCTU, and the Wickersham Commission; the controversy generated by Mrs. Hoover's entertaining Mrs. Oscar DePriest, wife of a black congressman, in the White House; women's rights and other matters of general concern to women; the women's division of the Republican National Committee; the Rapidan Community School, established by the President for youngsters in the vicinity of Camp Rapidan; and Gold Star Mothers' pilgrimages to cemeteries in France and elswhere. Hoover's correspondents include Grace Abbott, Jane Addams, Lulah T. Andrews, Mary (McLeod) Bethune, Ada Comstock, Madame Marie S. Curie, Dolly [Mrs. Edward E.] Gann, Lillian Gilbreth, [Miss] Katherine Glover, [Mrs.] Clara C. Grace, Anne [Mrs. William] Hard, Caroline [Mrs. William L.] Honnold, Hannah Clothier [Mrs. William I.] Hull, Helen Keller, [Miss] Gertrude B. Lane, Julia C. Lathrop, Marie [Mrs. William B.] Meloney, Matilda [Mrs. J. H.] Minthorn, Helen Miles [Mrs. Ogden] Reid, Aurelia H. Reinhardt, Arabella [Mrs.

Willoughby] Rodman, Florence Wardwell, Mary Emma Wooley, and Mrs. Ellis S. Yost.

5,123. Hoover, Herbert: Post-Presidential Period
Papers. 1933-64. 500 ft.
Open. Unpublished guide.
Herbert Hoover Presidential Library.
Correspondence, telegrams, reports, notes, memoranda, printed material, routing slips, and cross-reference sheets of Hoover for the period after his Presidency are grouped into general, subject, and individual subseries. The general subseries contains Hoover's correspondence with the general public about a variety of issues and includes correspondence with Prudence Stickney, a Shaker eldress at Sabbathday Lake, ME, about life in a religious communal society.

The subject subseries reflects Hoover's interest in a broad range of organizations during this period. Files pertaining to women and containing correspondence with women are those under the titles American Child Health, the blind, child welfare, the DAR, Food for the Small Democracies, the Girl Scouts, the Girls' Clubs of America, activities of Lou (Henry) Hoover, and women and women's clubs of Republican party affiliation.

The individual subseries contains correspondence with such women in politics as Elva H. Carpenter, Gertrude Hanna, Anna Louise Hicks, Florence P. Kahn, Ida Koverman, Ruth (Hanna) McCormick Simms, Mrs. F. Louis Slade, Margaret Chase Smith, Edith Van de Water, and Mrs. Ellis Yost. Literary figures represented in the papers include Eve Garrette, Laura Winans McDaniel, and Mary (Roberts) Rinehart. Women active in both literary and political affairs include Ruth Alexander, Alice M. Dickson, Gertrude Lane, Rose Wilder Lane, Claire (Boothe) Luce, and Kathleen Norris.

Files reflecting long and close relationships with the Hoover family are those of Aida de Acosta Breckinridge, Clara B. Burdette, and Mildred Hall Campbell. Other files pertaining to social and personal relations include those of Madame Chiang Kai-shek, Charlotte Kellogg, Jacqueline Kennedy, Mrs. Theodore Roosevelt, Jr., and Mrs. Giles Whiting.

Women represented elsewhere in this collection include Lillian Gilbreth; Helen W. Homan; Helen Keller; Hulda Hoover McLean, genealogist of the Hoover family and niece of the President; Bernice Miller, longtime secretary to Hoover; Helen Sioussat, director of the Columbia Brodcasting System; and Countess Alexandra Tolstoy.

5,124. Pegler, James Westbrook
Papers. 1908-69. 63 ft.
Open. Unpublished guide.
Herbert Hoover Presidential Library.
Correspondence, reports and memoranda, press releases, clippings, miscellaneous printed items, and the 2,900-volume personal library of Pegler (1894-1969), a nationally syndicated newspaper columnist. Files he accumulated in connection with writing his column pertain to all facets of US domestic and foreign policy between 1933 and 1963. Included are files on physician Sara Murray Jordan, 1935-59; Lucille Miller, 1947-69; his first wife Julia Harpman Pegler, 1922-66; his third wife Maud Towart Pegler, 1948-55; Eleanor Roosevelt, 1932-63; and Anna Eleanor Roosevelt, 1942-53. Among his correspondents are Doris Stevens and Mabel (Walker) Willebrandt.

KANSAS

ABILENE

5,125. Woman's Relief Corps
Records. 1885-1948. 25 vols.
Open. No guide.
Dickinson County Historical Society.
Minutes, ledgers, journals, and cash books of the Corps, which was founded in 1885 by homemakers and others to help the community's needy residents.

5,126. Adkins, Bertha S.
Papers. 1907-71. 16 ft.
Access restricted. Register.
Dwight D. Eisenhower Library.
Adkins (1906-) was undersecretary of HEW from 1958 to 1961, a Republican National Committee official from 1948 to 1958, and a school administrator. Correspondence, memoranda, speeches, reports, photos, scrapbooks, clippings, recording discs, tape recordings, motion picture film, memorabilia, and other material. Collection reflects the role of women in public life, politics, political campaigns, HEW, and the Lincoln Sesquicentennial Commission. Many of Adkins's duties at HEW pertained to women's participation in government. Prior to her HEW appointment, she headed the women's division of the Republican National Committee. Adkins also represented the US at a 1959 international seminar on women's participation in public life in Bogota, Colombia, and served as vice-chairman of the American National Red Cross's women's division.

5,127. Bacon, Edward A
Papers. 1896-1968. 17 ft.
Access restricted. Unpublished guide.
Dwight D. Eisenhower Library.
Bacon (1897-1968) was a Department of the Army official, a businessman, and a writer. His personal and official correspondence, financial records, poetry, and essays contain items concerning women and other subjects. Includes his unpublished book about his sister, "Dibbie Dear," and 50 pages of poems published in *Light Verse and Worse* (1957).

5,128. Benedict, Stephen
Papers. 1952. 2 ft.
Access restricted. Unpublished guide.
Dwight D. Eisenhower Library.
Benedict (1927-) was a speech writer and research director of Citizens for Eisenhower during the 1952 presidential campaign. Correspondence; campaign speeches, including speech drafts regarding women; and agenda. Also includes letters to women leaders from Katherine Howard, a member of the Eisenhower campaign strategy committee.

5,129. Briggs, Ruth M.
Papers. 1942-45. 326 items and 126 pp.
Open. Unpublished guide.
Dwight D. Eisenhower Library.
Directories, booklets, and 326 photos relate to Briggs's service during WWII as a member of the Women's Army Auxiliary Corps and the Supreme Headquarters Allied Expeditionary Forces staff and as secretary to General Walter Bedell Smith.

5,130. Burgess, W. Randolf
Papers. 1951-62. 600 pp.
Access restricted. Unpublished guide.
Dwight D. Eisenhower Library.
Burgess (1889-) was a Treasury Department official and permanent US representative to the North Atlantic Treaty Organization. Correspondence, press releases, speeches, and statements, the bulk of which concerns Burgess's work during the Eisenhower administration. Includes speeches delivered to two Republican women's clubs and to the National Federation of Business and Professional Women's Clubs.

5,131. Chase, Margaret
Papers. 1942-60. 845 pp.
Access restricted. Unpublished guide.
Dwight D. Eisenhower Library.
Correspondence, diaries, photos, and memorabilia. Bulk of collection concerns Chase's service from 1942 to 1945 as an International Red Cross volunteer in London, North Africa, Italy, and France. Includes correspondence of Chase, her parents, and Dwight D. Eisenhower.

5,132. Cochran, Jacqueline
Papers. 1932-74. 150 ft.
Closed. Accession-registration sheet.
Dwight D. Eisenhower Library.
Cochran, who set numerous speed records for women pilots, was director of the US Army's Women's Air Force Service Pilots during WWII and an officer in several aeronautics associations; she also owned a cosmetics enterprise, helped her husband Floyd Odlum manage a California ranch, and participated in politics on the national and local levels. Correspondence, memoranda, speeches, financial records, galley proofs, scrapbooks, maps, charts, articles, clippings, still and slide photos, photoengraving plates, recording discs, tape recordings, memorabilia, and other material. Principal topics documented are Cochran's career as an aviator and women in aviation. She helped gain a place for women pilots in the US Army during WWII and later maintained close contact with the US Air Force and the National Aeronautics and Space Administration on matters concerning women pilots. Collection contains notes, drafts, and galley proofs for her autobiography *Stars at Noon* (1954) and material reflecting her campaign for the US Congress in 1956 and her ownership of Jacqueline Cochran Cosmetics.

5,133. Doud, Elivera M.
Papers. 1936-57. 11 ft.
Closed. Unpublished guide.
Dwight D. Eisenhower Library.
Doud (1878-1960), the mother of Mamie (Doud) [Mrs. Dwight D.] Eisenhower, collected newspapers, clippings, 18 photos, and a limited amount of correspondence largely regarding her son-in-law's activities, particularly during the 1952 and 1956 presidential campaigns.

5,134. Dulles, Eleanor Lansing
Papers. 1880-1973. 16 ft.
Access restricted. Description and container list.
Dwight D. Eisenhower Library.
Dulles (1895-) was a government official and diplomat as well as an educator, author, and lecturer. Correspondence, diaries, memoranda, speeches, book manuscripts, lecture notes, desk calendars, galley proofs, photos, scrapbooks, articles, clippings, recording discs, tape recordings, memorabilia, and other material. Sister of Allen and John Foster Dulles, Eleanor Dulles was director of financial studies for the Social Security Board from 1936 to 1942, US financial attaché in Vienna, Austria, from 1945 to 1949, special assistant to the State Department's office of German affairs from 1952 to 1962, and a professor at Georgetown University from 1963 to 1971. During the 1960s she wrote books about John Foster Dulles, Germany, the Dominican Republic, and American foreign policy. Personal correspondence includes items regarding the activities and deaths of her brothers.

5,135. Dwight D. Eisenhower Library, Oral History Project: Oral History Transcripts
Oral history. 1964- . Ca. 30,000 pp.
Access restricted. Descriptive summaries.
Dwight D. Eisenhower Library.
About 20 of the collection's ca. 330 interviews, all

of which relate to Eisenhower (1890-1969), are with women. Main subjects of the interviews are the 1952 presidential campaign, the Republican party, and women in government and public life. Others relate to Eisenhower's early life in Abilene, KS, and the Little Rock, AR, school integration crisis of 1957 through 1959. Among women who discuss their careers are Bertha S. Adkins, Jacqueline Cochran, Eleanor Lansing Dulles, Katherine (Graham) Howard, Clare (Boothe) Luce, and Anne W. Wheaton. Majority of the transcripts were produced by the Columbia University Oral History Office's project on the Eisenhower administration, while the others were done by a continuing program of the Eisenhower library.

5,136. Eisenhower, Dwight D., as President
Records. 1953-61. 3242 ft.
Access restricted. Unpublished guide.
Dwight D. Eisenhower Library.
Correspondence, telegrams, memoranda, notes, reports, routing slips, cross reference sheets, printed material, and other items are included in the White House Central Files generated by Eisenhower and his White House staff. Contains material concerning the National Women's Advisory Commission of the Federal Civil Defense Administration, the Department of Labor Women's Bureau, and equal rights for women; endorsements for women for appointive positions in the Eisenhower Administration; and correspondence with such women's groups as the DAR, Girl Scouts of America, and the GFWC as well as with individual women who were friends of the Eisenhower family. Part of the collection is available on microfilm.

5,137. Eisenhower, Dwight D., as President
Papers. 1953-61. 122 ft.
Access restricted. Unpublished guide.
Dwight D. Eisenhower Library.
Correspondence, diaries, notes, minutes, appointment records, memoranda, and printed material of Eisenhower (1890-1969). Material related to women is located primarily within seven series of the Ann Whitman file (named for Eisenhower's personal secretary). The Administration series contains 430 pages of material pertaining to women, the bulk of which concerns Oveta (Culp) Hobby and her activities as secretary of HEW. Other women prominently represented are Clare (Boothe) Luce, Lorraine Knox, and Bela Kornitzer. Among the diary entries, memos of telephone conversations, official White House staff memoranda, summaries of congressional correspondence, presidential appointment schedules, and other material in the Eisenhower diaries series are correspondence and memos regarding telephone conversations with women leaders of the Republican party and the administration, among them Hobby, Luce, and Bertha Adkins. The Name series largely pertains to social and family matters and contains correspondence to and from women, including Barbara Gunderson, Jacqueline Cochran Odlum, and Margaret Chase Smith. The Cabinet series includes material regarding Hobby and her presentations to Cabinet members about social security and other programs. The Speech series contains addresses Eisenhower gave before such women's organizations as the LWV and the National Federation of Republican Women. The Press Conference series contains a reference in 1956 to equal rights for women and others concerning Mrs. Franklin D. Roosevelt's visit to China in 1957. The Ann Whitman diary series, created by Whitman as a file for her daily entries, consists of some 9000 pages of diary entries, correspondence, notes, minutes, appointment records, and printed material. The diaries often include her observations on highlights of the President's day and her views on various issues and people involved with the administration. Some of the material is available on microfilm.

5,138. Eisenhower, Mamie (Doud)
Papers. 1894- . 225 ft.
Closed. Unpublished guide.
Dwight D. Eisenhower Library.
Collection of Eisenhower (1896-), wife of Dwight D. Eisenhower, primarily consists of birthday, get-well, Christmas, and condolence cards; it also contains personal and family correspondence, condolence books regarding the death of General Eisenhower, household files from 1948 to 1950, and photos. Bulk of material covers the period after 1960.

5,139. Fox, Frederic E.
Records. 1953-61. 18 ft.
Access restricted. Unpublished guide.
Dwight D. Eisenhower Library.
The primary duty of Fox (1917-), White House special assistant and staff assistant to the President, was to draft letters for Eisenhower's signature. Correspondence and letter drafts include letters, usually congratulatory or commendatory in form, that Fox drafted to women's organizations throughout the country.

5,140. Hagerty, James C.
Papers. 1953-61. 47 ft.
Access restricted. Unpublished guide.
Dwight D. Eisenhower Library.
Correspondence, diaries, reports, press releases, and transcripts of press conferences held by Hagerty (1909-), President Eisenhower's press secretary. Contains an index to the conferences, which includes references to women and women-related topics. Also includes material on plans for Queen Elizabeth's visit to the US in 1957.

5,141. Hall, Leonard W.
Papers. 1953-57. 111 ft.
Access restricted. Unpublished guide.
Dwight D. Eisenhower Library.
Hall (1900-) was chairman of the Republican National Committee. Correspondence, publications, and reports contain correspondence with Republican women leaders and correspondence and published material regarding individual women and women's organizations.

5,142. Hess, Stephen H.
Papers. 1959-61. 1 ft.
Access restricted. Unpublished guide.
Dwight D. Eisenhower Library.
The principal function of Hess (1933-) as a White House special assistant was the drafting of speeches for Eisenhower and other administration spokesmen. Among the collection's correspondence, speeches, reports, and articles is material relating to speeches that Eisenhower gave before Republican women's clubs and the National Federation of Republican Women.

5,143. Hobby, Oveta (Culp)
Papers. 1940-60. 73 ft.
Access restricted. Container list and summary description.
Dwight D. Eisenhower Library.
Hobby (1905-), a Houston newspaper executive, was an active supporter of Eisenhower's 1952 presidential campaign and the first secretary of HEW, serving from 1953 to 1955. Correspondence, memoranda, notes, speeches, charts, printed documents, press releases, scrapbooks, clippings, and miscellaneous items, the majority of which relate to Hobby's appointment and work at HEW. Among specific topics discussed are the White House Conference on Education, the Salk vaccine controversy, and Hobby's resignation. Collection also includes material regarding her role in Democrats for Eisenhower and Citizens for Eisenhower in 1952, Republican women's clubs, the National Federation of Republican Women, and women in government.

5,144. Jackson, C. D.
Papers. 1931-67. 36 ft.
Access restricted. Unpublished guide.
Dwight D. Eisenhower Library.
Jackson (1902-64) was an executive of Time Inc., a speechwriter and special assistant for President Eisenhower, and deputy chief of the psychological warfare division at Supreme Headquarters Allied Expeditionary Forces in 1944 and 1945. Correspondence, speeches, reports, leaflets, publications, and directives. Material regarding his association with Time Inc. includes résumés and correspondence to and from women employees, women seeking employment, and women submitting articles for publication. Also included are correspondence and memoranda from Ann Whitman, Eisenhower's personal secretary, primarily pertaining to Jackson's requests for information.

5,145. Lambie, James M., Jr.
Records. 1953-61. 25 ft.
Access restricted. Unpublished guide.
Dwight D. Eisenhower Library.
Lambie (1914-) was special assistant to the President in charge of the White House advertising liaison office; he also served unofficially as deputy chairman of the Interagency Commission for Agricultural Surplus Disposal. Correspondence, speeches, minutes, publications, and reports, including correspondence and reports regarding the Advertising Council's campaign on Women in the Services, and correspondence with Ann Whitman, Mary Jane McCaffree, and the National Federation of Republican Women.

5,146. Larson, Arthur, and Moos, Malcolm C.
Records. 1957-59. 2 ft.
Access restricted. Unpublished guide.
Dwight D. Eisenhower Library.
Larson (1910-) and Moos (1916-) were special presidential assistants who helped prepare speeches for Eisenhower. Publications, press releases, and speeches include speech drafts for Eisenhower's appearance before the Republican Women's Meeting in March 1958.

5,147. Lord, Mary Pillsbury
Papers. 1941-72. 1.2 ft.
Access restricted. Register.
Dwight D. Eisenhower Library.
Lord (1904-) was US delegate to the UN General Assembly in 1958 and 1960, alternate US representative to the UN General Assembly from 1953 to 1959, US representative to the UN's Human Rights Commission and to the UN Economic and Social Council from 1953 to 1961, and national chairman of the civilian advisory committee for Women's Air Corps in 1944. Correspondence, articles, clippings, and miscellaneous items regarding her career.

5,148. Lucier, Ruby Norman
Papers. 1913-67. 40 pp.
Access restricted. Unpublished guide.
Dwight D. Eisenhower Library.
Correspondence, photos, memorabilia, and Christmas cards from Eisenhower to Lucier, a childhood friend.

5,149. Mitchell, James P.
Papers. 1953-64. 105 ft.
Access restricted. Unpublished guide.
Dwight D. Eisenhower Library.
Mitchell (1900-64) served as assistant secretary of the army for manpower and reserve forces and as secretary of labor. Correspondence, memoranda, reports, invitations, and printed material, including invitations and personal correspondence of Mitchell's wife. Also includes correspondence and reports concerning personnel in the Labor

Department Women's Bureau and the Department's drafts of a bill concerning sex discrimination in wages.

5,150. National Federation of Republican Women
Records. 1937-60. 62 ft.
Access restricted. Container list.
Dwight D. Eisenhower Library.
Founded in 1938 as the National Federation of Women's Republican Clubs, the organization, an official associate of the Republican National Committee, seeks to build the party through the education and training of women in politics. Minutes, agenda, memoranda, speeches, correspondence, reports, bills, ledgers, receipts, questionnaires, press releases, newsletters, clippings, and miscellaneous items relate to state and local clubs and to national conferences, meetings, and conventions. Contains information on the group's education programs, its training programs (especially the School of Politics), and political campaigns from 1938 to 1960. Also contains information regarding the Republican National Committee, the Committee's women's division, and the Federation's national officers, including Mrs. Glenn Sathers, Mrs. Charles Weis, Mrs. Joseph Farrington, Mrs. Carroll D. Kearns, and Mrs. Peter Gibson.

5,151. Osborn, Genevieve L.
Papers. 1942-57. 15 pp.
Closed. Unpublished guide.
Dwight D. Eisenhower Library.
Correspondence, memorabilia, and printed material of [Miss] Osborn. Includes cards and letters from President Eisenhower, Mamie (Doud) Eisenhower, and A. B. Eisenhower and two letters received by Ida Stover Eisenhower, mother of Dwight D. Eisenhower.

5,152. Phillips, Elizabeth
Papers. 1918-55. 6 ft.
Access restricted. Unpublished guide.
Dwight D. Eisenhower Library.
Correspondence, record books, and newsletters chiefly pertain to [Miss] Phillips's efforts during WWII to organize shipment of relief parcels to British prisoners of war in Europe.

5,153. Picking, Lelia G
Papers. 1945-69. 1210 pp.
Closed. No guide.
Dwight D. Eisenhower Library.
Picking was a high school classmate of Eisenhower. Contains clippings and articles regarding Eisenhower and 10 pages of correspondence regarding the 1959 reunion of the Abilene High School class of 1909.

5,154. Priest, Ivy (Baker)
Papers. 1953-60. 1000 pp.
Closed. Unpublished guide.
Dwight D. Eisenhower Library.
Priest (1905-75) was treasurer of the US. Correspondence concerning personal, political, and governmental matters includes some material on her speaking engagements in 1954. Also contains photos.

5,155. Pyle, Howard
Records. 1955-59. 20 ft.
Access restricted. Unpublished guide.
Dwight D. Eisenhower Library.
A spokesman for the Eisenhower administration, Pyle (1906-) was presidential assistant for intergovernmental relations and a member of the President's Committee on Traffic Safety. Correspondence and speeches include material pertaining to various Republican women's clubs.

5,156. Republican National Committee
Records. 1932-65. 320 ft.
Access restricted. Unpublished guide.
Dwight D. Eisenhower Library.
Clippings, publications, reports, and correspondence maintained as a reference source originally by the Republican National Committee's research and editorial division. Clippings, which make up the bulk of the collection, include items regarding women's organizations, women in the Democratic party, Clare (Boothe) Luce, and other topics related to women. Also included are publications and reports written by the Republican National Committee's research staff concerning women's groups and individual women involved in political activities.

5,157. Richardson, Fannie Belle Taylor
Papers. 1900-60. 11 ft.
Access restricted. Unpublished guide.
Dwight D. Eisenhower Library.
[Mrs.] Richardson, a fifth cousin of Eisenhower, acted as a genealogist for the Eisenhower family. Personal and genealogical correspondence, clippings, photos, and personal business records. Collection primarily consists of correspondence between Richardson and persons who were or claimed to be related to the Eisenhower family. She began compiling the records while she was a clerical employee at the National Archives from 1941 to 1945 and continued her research until the late 1950s. Some of the material is available on microfilm.

5,158. Rogers, William P.
Papers. 1938-62. 23 ft.
Access restricted. Unpublished guide.
Dwight D. Eisenhower Library.
Correspondence, memoranda, and reports of Rogers (1913-), deputy attorney general and US attorney general during the Eisenhower administration. Working papers include ca. 100 pages of correspondence written by Rogers's secretary Maggie Runkle, which chiefly include responses to information requests.

5,159. Wheaton, Anne Williams
Papers. 1957-69. 250 pp. and 1 microfilm reel.
Access restricted. Register.
Dwight D. Eisenhower Library.
Wheaton (1892-) was Eisenhower's associate press secretary from 1957 to 1961 and assistant to the director of publicity for women's activities at the Republican National Committee from 1939 to 1957. Congratulatory correspondence regarding her appointment as associate press secretary, clippings about her appointment and first days in office, and other scrapbook items.

5,160. White House Office, Office of the Special Assistant for Executive Appointments
Records. 1952-61. 33 ft.
Access restricted. Unpublished guide.
Dwight D. Eisenhower Library.
The Office coordinated the filling of presidential appointive positions and other federal jobs not governed by the US Civil Service system. Correspondence, notebooks, résumés, reports, and other records, including biographical sketches of women in the Eisenhower Administration and prospective candidates for appointive positions. Also includes copies of speeches given by Mary Reedick, secretary to Robert Gray and Edward Tait.

5,161. White House Office, Social Office
Records. 1952-61. 342 ft.
Partially closed. Unpublished guide.
Dwight D. Eisenhower Library.
Records of the Office consist of an index to appointments and social functions; files of A. B. Tolley, head of the Office; and papers of Mamie Eisenhower. The Mamie Eisenhower files consist of scrapbooks of social functions, her appointment book, Social Office correspondence, and her personal files, which primarily contain correspondence with family members, friends, and associates within the Eisenhower Administration. The Tolley files, the only segment of the records currently open for research, include references to social functions arranged for and attended by women's groups.

ATCHISON

5,162. Putnam, Amelia (Earhart)
Papers. 1903-76. 20 ft.
Open. No guide.
Atchison County Historical Society.
Amelia Earhart (1897-1937), a pioneer aviator born in Atchison, was inducted into the Women's Hall of Fame at Seneca Falls, NY, about two months after her death in the southern Pacific. Correspondence, photos, articles, childhood items, and clothing document her family's history and her interest in aviation. Includes photos of Earhart from grade school through her graduation from Hyde Park High School in Chicago; of her grandparents, Judge Alfred Otis, a pioneer Atchison attorney, and Amelia Harris Otis; of her parents, Edwin and Amy (Otis) Earhart; of her sister Muriel (Earhart) Morrissey of Boston; of Earhart's cousins; and of others. Also includes correspondence, scrapbook, citations, and other papers concerning the dedication of Amelia Earhart Memorial Airport in Atchison in 1953 and the dedication on Earhart's birthday in 1976 of the local Friendship Forest by the Ninety Nines, a women flyers organization. Earhart married George Putnam in 1931.

5,163. Von Herberg, Eugene (Dennis)
Papers. 1908-48. 1 ft.
Open. No guide.
Atchison County Historical Society.
Von Herberg (1901-48), who was known as Gene Dennis in her work, made a fortune by using her psychic powers to predict the future. Scrapbook and book of clippings and theater programs. Born in Illinois, Eugene Dennis moved to Atchison with her parents in 1917 and graduated from a local high school. Known as the Kansas Wonder Girl, she began her 14-year show business career in Kansas City in 1921. In 1927, she married J. C. Von Herberg, owner of a Washington state theater chain. She retired in 1935 after appearing in theaters in Europe and America. The Von Herbergs made their home in Seattle.

5,164. Congregation of St. Scholastica
Records. 1918-62. 5 ft.
Access restricted. Unpublished guide.
Mount St. Scholastica Convent.
Minutes, reports, and correspondence of Congregation presidents Mother Aloysia Northman, who served from 1918 to 1924; Mother Lucy Dooley, who served from 1926 to 1950; and Mother M. Alfred Schroll, who served from 1950 to 1962. The records concern the founding and development of the Congregation. The Congregation, which was founded in 1918, is the union of a number of Benedictine priories under one president and is governed by a uniform constitution.

5,165. Kremmeter, Mother Evangelista
Papers. 1863-84. 8 folders.
Access restricted. Unpublished guide.
Mount St. Scholastica Convent.
Administrative and personal correspondence, spiritual notes, an account book, a scrapbook, and memorabilia of Mother Evangelista Kremmeter, the first prioress of the Convent, which she founded in 1863.

5,166. Moser, Mother Theresa
Papers. 1884-97. 7 folders.
Access restricted. Unpublished guide.

Mount St. Scholastica Convent.
Administrative and personal correspondence of Mother Theresa Moser, the second prioress of the Convent, which was founded in 1863.

5,167. Northman, Mother Aloysia
Papers. 1897-1924. 1 ft.
Access restricted. Unpublished guide.
Mount St. Scholastica Convent.
Administrative and personal correspondence and memorabilia of Mother Aloysia Northman, the third prioress of the Convent.

BALDWIN CITY

5,168. Baker University Archives
Records. 1859- . No size given.
Open. No guide.
Baker University Library, United Methodist Historical Collection and Library.
Established in 1859 as a Methodist-related college, Baker University also provided preparatory courses because they were not available elsewhere in the area. Records of faculty members, alumni, and organizations; histories of the University; and publications, including yearbooks and *Baker Orange,* the University newspaper.

5,169. Local Churches
Records. Ca. 1860s- . No size given.
Open. No guide.
Baker University Library, United Methodist Historical Collection and Library.
Records of local Methodist churches and church organizations, histories of the churches, photos, dedication leaflets, programs, and other records, including occasional correspondence and diaries. Contains secretary and treasurer records of the Baldwin City auxiliaries of the Woman's Home Missionary Society and the Woman's Foreign Missionary Society, 1889-1940; secretary and treasurer books of the Ladies Sewing Circle of the Baldwin Methodist Episcopal Church, 1863-92; and the 1866 diary of Lizzie Kiefer, a student at Baker University whose parents lived in Baldwin City. Kiefer's diary describes her school experiences and the Sewing Circle's efforts to raise money for construction of a church at Baldwin City.

5,170. Markham, O. G.
Papers. 1891-1909. Ca. 200 items.
Open. Card file.
Baker University Library, United Methodist Historical Collection and Library.
Correspondence of Markham, a professor at Baker University, includes that with former students and faculty members in which he attempts to judge the quality of education at Baker and other letters concerning the University's history during its first 50 years. Many of the letters were from women.

5,171. Methodist Missionaries
Papers. Nd. No size given.
Open. No guide.
Baker University Library, United Methodist Historical Collection and Library.
Correspondence, manuscripts, lectures and devotional speeches, photos, programs, books, and artifacts of several foreign missionaries who were supported by the Methodist Church. Contains papers of women missionaries, including those of Irma Highbaugh (?-1973), a 1915 Baker graduate who served in China before WWII and in Korea under the auspices of the World Council of Churches; Winona Wilson Jett, a missionary in India who graduated from Baker in 1916; Anna Porter Giambarresi, a Baker graduate who taught at a girl's school in Rome, Italy, until the outbreak of WWII when she returned to the US and became involved in social service work in Boston and Providence, RI; and Frances Wilson, a missionary to China.

5,172. Scott, Lilian
Papers. 1897-1909. Ca. 150 items.
Open. Card file.
Baker University Library, United Methodist Historical Collection and Library.
Scott was superintendent of Baldwin City grade school and a professor at Baker University. Correspondence deals primarily with the history of Baker University. Many of the letters were written by women who reminisce about their lives as students or faculty members at Baker. A few letters deal with a short period when Baldwin City had an all-female city council and a woman mayor.

5,173. Women's Societies
Records. 1800s-1900s. No size given.
Open. No guide.
Baker University Library, United Methodist Historical Collection and Library.
Annual reports and conference record books containing minutes, treasurer's records, handbooks, pamphlets, and religious publications of the Woman's Home Missionary Society, the Woman's Foreign Missionary Society, and the Ladies' Aid Society. Most of the material dates from the early 1900s to 1940. Includes issues of the *Ladies Repository,* 1841-77, a monthly periodical of the Methodist General Conference designed specifically for women and devoted to literature and religion; issues of *Heathen Women's Friend,* 1870-89; annual reports of the WHMS, 1881-1925; issues of *Women's Missionary Friend,* 1893-1921; and annual reports of the Kansas Conference WHMS. The WHMS, the WFMS, and the Ladies' Aid Society merged to form the Women's Society of Christian Service.

BONNER SPRINGS

5,174. Conley Family
Papers. Nd. 5 vols.
Open. No guide.
Wyandotte County Historical Society.
Lyda Burton Conley (?-1946), perhaps the first woman of partial Indian ancestry to be admitted to practice law in Kansas; Helena "Lena" Conley (?-1958), an instructor at a Wyandotte Indian reservation in Oklahoma; and Ida Conley were sisters who became involved in a controversy about a Wyandotte burial ground located in what is now downtown Kansas City, KS. Post cards, photos, clippings, and other family papers concern the dispute, which continued from 1906 to 1913, and their legal and personal activities to save the burial ground. They built shacks in the area and defied local authorities who attempted to destroy the burial grounds. Other papers concern the death of the sisters' mother.

5,175. Farrow, Tiera
Papers. Ca. 1900-53. Ca. 2 cu.ft.
Open. Accession inventory.
Wyandotte County Historical Society.
[Miss] Farrow (ca. 1880-), who received bachelor's and master's degrees from the Kansas City School of Law in 1903 and 1930, actively supported the Women's School of Law of Kansas City, which opened in 1925. Manuscript of her autobiography *Lawyer in Petticoats,* a history of the Women's Bar Association of Missouri that she wrote in 1954 with Lois McMullin, legal papers, photos, scrapbooks, articles, clippings, souvenirs, and other papers. The scrapbooks date from 1905 to 1931 and include clippings tracing Farrow's legal career. She was admitted to practice before the Missouri Supreme Court in 1905 and before the US Supreme Court in 1950. She defended Clara T. Schweiger, who was accused of murder.

5,176. Women's Organizations
Records. Ca. 1903- . No size given.
Open. No guide.
Wyandotte County Historical Society.
Minutes, yearbooks, program books, scrapbooks, clippings, and other records of Wyandotte County, KS, women's groups, including the Bonner Springs Chapter of the AAUW, which was organized in 1950, and the Edwardsville Social and Literary Club, which was founded in 1903. Also includes yearbooks of the James Ross Chapter of the DAR, 1923-73, and scrapbooks of the Mary Tenney Gray Travelers Club, a member of the Kansas Federation of Women's Clubs, 1948-49; of the Council of Clubs; of the Federation of Women's Clubs; and of the Grand Army of the Republic, Daughters of Union Veterans, 1938-39. The Edwardsville Social and Literary Club was organized "for the study of the Evolution of Women from the Home into the Mainstream of American Life." The group first considered cultural subjects but soon moved into discussions of woman suffrage, the causes of war, women as a moral power in politics, aviation, and worldwide prohibition. The Club's records date from 1904 to 1953.

CHANUTE

5,177. Johnson, Martin, and Johnson, Osa Helen (Leighty)
Papers. 1884- . Ca. 65 ft., 31 motion pictures, tapes, and other items.
Access restricted. Unpublished guide.
Martin and Osa Johnson Safari Museum.
Martin Johnson (1884-1937) and his wife Osa Johnson (1894-1953) shared careers as explorers, photographers, film makers, authors, and lecturers. Correspondence, fragmentary diaries, oral history tapes by Osa Johnson's mother [Mrs.] Belle Leighty and the Johnsons' pilot Vern Carstens, photos, scrapbooks, films, clippings, books, and other items. The Johnsons were married in 1910 and performed on the Orpheum vaudeville circuit in 1911. Four years later they sailed to the South Seas where Osa Johnson became the first white woman to explore the interior of the New Hebrides and the Solomon Islands and to film the cannibals and headhunters who lived there. Between 1920 and 1933 the Johnsons made five trips to Africa where Osa Johnson shot game for her husband, their native bearers, and herself and drove camera cars while her husband filmed wild animals. In 1932 she obtained her pilot's license. In 1935 the Johnsons returned to the South Seas where they explored the island of Borneo. Martin Johnson was killed in a commercial airplane crash in 1937. Osa Johnson wrote three books, made films to accompany her lectures, produced and starred in two movies, and went to Africa as the technical director for the film *Stanley and Livingstone.* She was planning a color film safari of Africa at the time of her death.

CONCORDIA

5,178. Motherhouse Archives
Records. 1883- . 117 ft. and 27 tapes.
Access restricted. Unpublished guide.
Sisters of St. Joseph, Nazareth Motherhouse and Novitiate.
Correspondence, oral history tapes, photos, memorabilia, and other records of the congregation, which was established in Newton, KS, in 1883 and moved to Concordia in 1884. The records trace the historical and spiritual development of the congregation and the personal lives of its members, who are involved in education, health care, pastoral care, and social service.

GARDEN CITY

5,179. Women's Clubs
Records. 1929- . Ca. 5 ft.
Open. No guide.
Finney County Historical Museum.
Scrapbooks, yearbooks, and program books of women's groups, among them the Business and Professional Women's Club; the Wesleyan Service Guild of the First Methodist Church; the Salmagundi Club; the Opti-Mrs. Club; the Garden City Music Study Club; the Order of the Eastern Star, chapter 359; the American Legion Auxiliary; the DAR, William Wilson Chapter; the Garden City Garden Club; and the Twentieth Century Book Club. Most of the clubs are represented only by yearbooks or program books. The most extensive span of material consists of yearbooks of the Business and Professional Women's Club. The Salmagundi Club, yearbooks of which date from 1971 to 1976, was organized for the mutual improvement of its members in literature and vital questions of the day.

5,180. County Agricultural Agents Annual Reports
Records. 1929-61. 20 items.
Open. No guide.
Finney County Historical Society Research Library.
Annual reports of the agents, state employees who advise farmers on new agricultural techniques and crops, provide information about the activities of girls in 4-H Clubs and about women's home extension groups.

5,181. Garden City Chamber of Commerce
Records. 1935-55. Ca. 9 vols.
Open. No guide.
Finney County Historical Society Research Library.
Scrapbooks of clippings from newspapers in Garden City and surrounding towns concern local events and people.

5,182. Hatch, Daisy
Papers. Nd. 19-page item.
Open. No guide.
Finney County Historical Society Research Library.
Hatch lived in western Kansas after about 1836. Typescript concerns Garfield County, which is now part of Finney County, from the 1870s to the 1890s. Includes comments about people, wildlife, Indians, the founding of towns, and other area events.

5,183. School Districts
Records. Ca. 1887-1940. No size given.
Open. No guide.
Finney County Historical Society Research Library.
Treasurers's books, transcripts, grade and attendance books, and other records of Finney County school districts. Includes treasurers' books, which list the amount paid to teachers; a grade and attendance book of Ella Slade, who taught in District 3 from 1932 to 1935; transcripts dating from the 1920s and 1930s; and a report concenring the curriculum of the Finney County common schools in 1891.

GREAT BEND

5,184. Convent Archives
Records. 1902- . Ca. 50 boxes and ca. 42 tapes.
Access restricted. Unpublished guide.
Sisters of St. Dominic, Immaculate Conception Convent.
Council minutes, tapes of chapter proceedings, financial records, blueprints, correspondence, papers of mothers superior, diaries, files on each sister, chronicles of mission houses, photos, scrapbooks, souvenir booklets, and other records of the order, which was founded in 1902 in Great Bend. Includes material on the four hospitals operated by the Sisters and on mission activities in Nigeria.

HAYS

5,185. College Archives
Records. Ca. 1910- . Ca. 8 cabinets.
Open. No guide.
Fort Hays Kansas State College Archives.
A four-year coeducational institution, the College was founded in 1902 as the Western Branch of the State Normal School. In 1914 it became Fort Hays Kansas Normal School, and in 1923 the name was changed to Fort Hays Kansas State Teachers College. Minute books, correspondence, bulletins, handbooks, College newspapers, and other records. Includes minutes of the faculty senate, student council, and student union; records of the Graduate Club, the Faculty Wives Club, the Faculty Women's Club, Mortar Board, Quill Club, and campus sororities; and records of the home economics, music, and nurses education departments. Also contains regulations for women students dating from 1957 to 1960 and information about Kansas history and Ellis County. The word "Teachers" was deleted from the school's name in the late 1960s.

LEAVENWORTH

5,186. Mother House Archives
Records. 1858- . 45 vols., 3 microfilm reels, 28 tapes, 14 motion picture reels, 3 cabinets, 36 file tiers, 230 document cases, and 8 shelves.
Access restricted. Unpublished guide.
Sisters of Charity of Leavenworth, Mother House.
This religious community of women was founded in Leavenworth in 1858. Its members teach in schools ranging from elementary to the college level and work in hospitals, health centers, homes for children, a center for emotionally disturbed children, a retirement home, missions, and home health care. Patient records, correspondence, diaries, autobiographics, ledgers, press reports, videotapes, cassettes, slides, photos, genealogies, directories, scrapbooks, memorabilia, publications, and books. Includes correspondence of early sisters, a file for each member of the community, correspondence of mothers superior, and histories of the community.

MCPHERSON

5,187. Brethren
Collection. Ca. 1890- . 1.5 cabinets
Open. Card file.
McPherson College Library, Brethren Room.
Minutes, financial records, correspondence, commission reports, church histories, photos, pamphlets, programs, and other material concern activities of the Church of the Brethren in the Midwest. About half the material consists of administrative records of the Church's four Kansas districts. Individual church records include minutes of Antioch Church in Pleasant View, KS, of which Anna Downing was secretary in 1894, and of Cherokee Hills Church in Overland Park, KS, where women served on administrative boards during the period 1959-66. Also includes pamphlets with biographical sketches of female Brethren missionaries who served in China, Nigeria, Vietnam, and India.

5,188. McPherson College Archives
Records. 1890- . 1.5 cabinets.
Open. Card file.
McPherson College Library, Brethren Room.
Founded in 1887 by the Church of the Brethren, McPherson College continues its affiliation with the denomination. Faculty minutes, organization and department records, correspondence, articles by faculty and alumni, photos, college catalogs, student publications, and other records. Includes minutes from the 1890s of the Ciceronian Literary Society, a group that included women; minutes and correspondence of the Moral and Social Reform Committee of McPherson College; and issues of the monthly student magazine and the student newspaper.

MANHATTAN

5,189. Historical Index
Finding aid. 1863-1965. 40,000 items.
Open. Unpublished guide.
Kansas State University Library, Special Collections.
Card index to minutes and books of this land grant institution, which was founded in 1863, provides information about women at the University.

5,190. American Association of University Women
Records. 1921- . 2 cabinets.
Open. No guide.
Riley County Historical Society and Museum.
Minutes, correspondence, scrapbooks, and other records of the Manhattan branch of the AAUW, which was formed in 1921.

5,191. Domestic Science Club
Records. 1876- . 1 cabinet.
Open. No guide.
Riley County Historical Society and Museum.
The Club was organized formally in 1876 by volunteer teachers in the woman's department at Kansas State University. Minutes, financial records, correspondence, scrapbooks, program papers, photos, yearbooks, and clippings. The teachers were homemakers who taught domestic science to college women. They banded together informally in about 1871 to learn from each other and to continue to help the young women. The Club remains in existence.

5,192. League of Women Voters
Records. 1930s- . 1 cabinet.
Access restricted. No guide.
Riley County Historical Society and Museum.
Correspondence, projects records, scrapbooks, and other material of the local LWV.

5,193. Pilot Club
Records. 1950s- . 1 drawer.
Access restricted. No guide.
Riley County Historical Society and Museum.
Charter, minutes, correspondence, project records, gavel, and statuette of the Club, which was formed in 1950 in Manhattan by business and professional women. Associated with Pilot International, the local group has sponsored fund-raising projects for the Federation of Handicapped Citizens, supported two girls baseball teams through the local recreation commission, and carried out a program to help the aged through individual visitation, providing transportation to special events, and holding an annual dinner for senior citizens. Members of the group also prepared infant burial garments and layettes for babies at Irwin Army Hospital.

5,194. Soroptimist Club
Records. 1940- . 1 drawer.
Open. No guide.
Riley County Historical Society and Museum.
Soroptimist is a women's civic club founded in 1940. Scrapbooks, yearbooks, and other records.

5,195. Women's Club
Records. Early 1900s- . 1 drawer.
Open. No guide.
Riley County Historical Society and Museum.
Scrapbooks and other records of the Club, which was organized in 1900 to promote study, social activity, and civic projects.

NORTH NEWTON

5,196. Entz, Frieda (Voth) Regier
Papers. 1895-1949. 13 letter-size Hollinger boxes.
Open. Unpublished guide.
Bethel College, Mennonite Library and Archives.
Entz (1855-1949) was treasurer of the Women's Missionary Association from 1920 to 1949. Correspondence, including letters from missionaries and other women involved in church work; minutes of the Association; financial records; and material related to Entz's father H. R. Voth, a missionary to the Arapaho and Hopi Indians.

5,197. Fast, Aganetha
Papers. 1913-75. 18 boxes.
Open. Unpublished guide.
Bethel College, Mennonite Library and Archives.
Fast (1888-) served from 1917 to 1949 as a missionary to China for the General Conference Mennonite Church. Correspondence, diaries, memoirs, clippings, and other papers, including writings, photos, and memorabilia of Marie K. Fast, who was a relief worker with the UN Relief and Rehabilitation Administration.

5,198. Frantz, Marie J. (Regier)
Papers. Nd. No size given.
Open. Unpublished guide.
Bethel College, Mennonite Library and Archives.
Frantz was a missionary to China from 1926 to 1948, to Paraguay from 1951 to 1954, and to Taiwan from 1955 to 1962.

5,199. Petter, Rodolphe
Papers. Nd. No size given.
Open. Unpublished guide.
Bethel College, Mennonite Library and Archives.
Papers of Petter include items of [Mrs.] Bertha Kinsinger Petter (1872-1967), the first woman of the General Conference Mennonite Church to receive a BA. She received her degree from Wittenberg College in Springfield, OH. She was a missionary to the Cheyenne Indians from 1891 to 1949.

5,200. Women in Christian Church Vocation
Records. 1957-62. 3 boxes.
Open. Unpublished guide.
Bethel College, Mennonite Library and Archives.
Women in Christian Church Vocation, a subcommittee of the Board of Christian Service, was made up of women whose careers involved service to the church or church institutions. Minutes and correspondence of the group, which was active from 1956 to 1962.

5,201. Women's Missionary Association
Records. 1921-72. 7 boxes.
Open. Unpublished guide.
Bethel College, Mennonite Library and Archives.
Organized in 1917 as an auxiliary of the General Conference Mennonite Church, the Association supports home and foreign missions, secures cooperation between the church societies and the missions, and encourages the production and dissemination of literature. Minutes, correspondence, periodical notes, and other records. Mrs. R. A. Goerz was president of this all-women's group for many years. [Mrs.] Frieda Regier was treasurer from 1920 to 1949.

OTTAWA

5,202. Baptist History
Collection. Nd. 4 ft., 1 vol., 1 shelf file, and other items.
Open. No guide.
Ottawa University Library.
Correspondence, reports, programs, pamphlets, clippings, and other items pertain to local and statewide Baptist activities, to the work of overseas missionaries, to the organization of new churches, and to other topics. The items reflect the role of women in the denomination's history.

5,203. Kansas Baptist Women
Records. 1828- . 6 ft.
Open. No guide.
Ottawa University Library.
Photos, scrapbooks, publications, and other records of American Baptist Women, which was founded in 1877, and Kansas Baptist Women, which was established as a statewide group in 1920. The two organizations support gospel missionary activity.

PAOLA

5,204. Archives
Records. 1895- . No size given.
Closed. No guide.
Ursuline Sisters Convent.
Financial journals, correspondence, personal histories, photos, scrapbooks, obituaries, and clippings of the Convent, the members of which engage in teaching and other educational activities. The Convent was founded in 1895 by Mother Jerome Schaub.

PITTSBURG

5,205. Bays, Bertie Cole
Papers. Nd. No size given.
Open. Card catalog.
Kansas State College of Pittsburg Library.
A writer of short stories and a poet, [Mrs. Joshua Willingham] Bays was the wife of a Southern Baptist minister. Correspondence relating to her writing, typescripts of her work with corrections and notations, a notebook she kept while attending a poetry writing workshop, and an autobiography of Bertie and Joshua Bays.

5,206. Brooks, Anne (Tedlock)
Papers. Ca. 1900-50. No size given.
Open. Card catalog.
Kansas State College of Pittsburg Library.
Brooks (1905-), who lived in Jefferson City, MO, and Newport, OR, was the author of two novels, *One Enchanted Summer* and *Paddlewheels Churning,* and numerous children's stories. Correspondence relating to her career, publications containing her stories, and clippings concerning awards she received for her writing. The correspondence concerns her efforts to get her stories published, contracts, criticism of various manuscripts, and general discussions of her writing.

5,207. College Archives
Records. 1903- . No size given.
Open. Card index.
Kansas State College of Pittsburg Library.
Founded in 1903 as a normal school, the institution became Kansas State Teachers College at Pittsburg and then Kansas State College at Pittsburg. Minutes, correspondence, photos, publications, and other records. Includes minutes of the Faculty Association, the Faculty Senate, the Faculty Wives' Club, the library staff, and the Student Assembly; material concerning the school's contribution to the war effort during WWII; records of the Miss Pittsburg State Contest; college bulletins; alumni directories and magazines; faculty and student handbooks; English department publications of student writing; and student yearbooks and newspapers. For many years the school emphasized teacher training; "laboratory schools" were established in which college students acted as student teachers.

5,208. Draper, Edythe Squier
Papers. Nd. No size given.
Open. Card catalog.
Kansas State College of Pittsburg Library.
Correspondence, articles and manuscripts, and clippings document the activities of Draper (1882-1964), an author. She published articles in the *Young People's Paper* and the *Chicago Daily News.* Part of the correspondence deals with publication of her articles, while other items are letters to her family and friends.

5,209. Haldeman-Julius
Papers. Ca. 1910-50. No size given.
Open. Card catalog.
Kansas State College of Pittsburg Library.
Correspondence, photos, clippings, and other items of Emanuel Haldeman-Julius (1889-1951) and his wife Anna Marcet (Haldeman)-Julius (1888-1941). The Haldeman-Juliuses were publishers in Girard, KS, who supported socialist causes. Among other works, they published the *Haldeman-Julius Monthly.* Includes Marcet (Haldeman)-Julius's correspondence with her daughter Alice concerning family matters, Alice's activities at the University of Kansas, her school finances, Marcet's differences with her husband, her opinion of men, her travel, and the people she met. Other correspondence relates to speeches she gave in black churches in Kansas City, her contact with Sinclair Lewis, her concern for Negro students in Kansas, and a mass mailing to members of the Kansas State Bankers Association in 1917 about insurance problems. Correspondents include Jane Addams. The collection includes works by Marcet (Haldeman)-Julius concerning Clarence Darrow's work as a trial attorney, Jane Addams, Edward VIII and Wallis (Warfield) Simpson, and changing morals and the status of women. The originals of some of the Marcet (Haldeman)-Julius correspondence are held at Indiana University, Lilly Library.

5,210. Lowe, Caroline Ann
Papers. Nd. No size available.
Open. Card catalog.
Kansas State College of Pittsburg Library.
Lowe (1885-1933) was a lawyer in Pittsburg who had connections with the labor movement and with socialism. Correspondence from persons reminiscing about Lowe, legal papers concerning the will of Margaret Ella Lowe Abbot who died in 1929, and clippings about Lowe's activities. Margaret Abbot was either the mother or the sister of Caroline Lowe.

5,211. Patterson, Rebecca Elizabeth Coy
Papers. Nd. 16 items.
Open. Card catalog.
Kansas State College of Pittsburg Library.
A member of the Kansas State College of Pittsburg English department, Patterson (1911-75) specialized in the study of the works of Emily Dickinson. Correspondence about Patterson's articles, her scholarly interests, and material she received to critique; a course outline for her modern poetry class; and photos.

SALINA

5,212. Kansas Wesleyan Archives
Records. Ca. 1905- . Ca. 12 ft.
Open. No guide.

Kansas Wesleyan University Library.
A four-year liberal arts institution, Kansas Wesleyan was founded in 1886 by the Kansas West Conference of the Methodist Church. Consists principally of student directories, handbooks, college catalogs, alumni directories, yearbooks, and other publications of the school. The student handbooks list dormitory restrictions for women students while the catalogs list offerings of the home economics department and other divisions. Also includes annual reports dating from the 1950s and 1960s, business manager reports, and a history of the school's first 50 years.

TOPEKA

5,213. Christ Hospital School of Nursing and Christ Hospital
Records. 1882-1949. Ca. 1 box.
Open. No guide.
Episcopal Diocese of Kansas Archives.
Minutes of trustees' meetings, bishop's journals, and photos of the Hospital and School, both of which existed from 1882 to 1949.

5,214. Woman's Auxiliary, Diocese of Kansas
Records. 1884- . 4 Hollinger boxes.
Open. Unpublished guide.
Episcopal Diocese of Kansas Archives.
Minutes of monthly, quarterly, and annual meetings and correspondence of Episcopal Churchwomen, an auxiliary of the Diocese. Founded in 1884, the group assists parishes, missions, and the Diocese in all phases of the church's work. Includes descriptions of fund-raising events.

5,215. Bright, Abbie
Papers. 1870-71. 1 ms. box.
Open. No guide.
Kansas State Historical Society.
Diaries of Bright (1848-1926), who taught grammar school in Indiana during the 1870-71 school year and then moved to Sedgwick County, KS, where she took up 160 acres of Osage Trust Lands. She left Kansas in November after enduring hardships on the frontier. Bright seems to have written the diaries later from notes taken at the time. She married William M. Achenbach in 1873. The diaries were published as Joseph W. Snell, ed., "Roughing It on Her Kansas Claim: The Diary of Abbie Bright, 1870-1871," *Kansas Historical Quarterly*, vol. 37 (Autumn and Winter 1971).

5,216. Cheney Women's Club
Records. 1922-74. 3 ms. boxes and 2 vols.
Open. No guide.
Kansas State Historical Society.
Founded in 1922 as the Civics Club and renamed the Cheney Women's Club in 1925, the organization sponsored a public library, improved parks and school grounds, provided public rest rooms, and supported other projects to improve life in Cheney, KS. Constitution, secretary's and treasurer's records, a history, and a scrapbook. The group's stated interest was "civic, social, and educational culture." The Club disbanded in 1974.

5,217. Dimond, Susan B.
Papers. 1863-1914. 15 vols.
Open. No guide.
Kansas State Historical Society.
Scattered pocket diaries of Dimond, a housewife in Oakdale and Cawker City, KS, detail her daily chores, recreation, and other aspects of her life.

5,218. Farnsworth, Martha O. (Van Orsdol)
Papers. 1882-1922. 2 Hollinger boxes.
Open. No guide.
Kansas State Historical Society.
Diaries of [Mrs. Fred C.] Farnsworth, a housewife. The first entries were written while she was a young unmarried woman; the volumes record her social activities, her first romance, her marriage to a man characterized as a drunkard, his death, and her remarriage to a mail carrier. The diaries provide information about the life of a lower-middle-class family in Topeka. Farnsworth's first husband's name was John Shaw.

5,219. Johnston, Lucy (Browne)
Papers. 1887-1937. 7 Hollinger boxes.
Open. No guide.
Kansas State Historical Society.
A leader in the Kansas women's rights movement, Johnston (1846-1937) was the wife of William Agnew Johnston, chief justice of the Kansas Supreme Court. Correspondence and other papers relate to woman suffrage, prohibition, traveling libraries, and personal matters.

5,220. Lovejoy, Julia Louisa (Hardy)
Papers. 1828-64. 1 ms. box.
Open. No guide.
Kansas State Historical Society.
Diary in which [Mrs. Charles] Lovejoy (1812-82), a minister's wife, describes family events, the family's move to Kansas in 1855, and the hardships they endured. Also includes information about political conditions in Kansas Territory.

5,221. Nichols, Clarina Irene (Howard)
Papers. 1842-1904. 1 ms. box and partial microfilm reel.
Open. No guide.
Kansas State Historical Society.
Correspondence of [Mrs. George W.] Nichols (1810-85), an early woman suffrage leader in Kansas, includes letters of many suffrage leaders.

5,222. Robinson, Charles, and Robinson, Sara Tappan Doolittle (Lawrence)
Papers. 1834-1911. 32 ms. boxes.
Open. Published guide.
Kansas State Historical Society.
Charles Robinson (?-1894) was a leader of the Free State party and served as the first governor of Kansas; his wife Sara Robinson (1827-1911) was the author of *Kansas, Its Interior and Exterior Life.* Correspondence; cash record books, statements of accounts, receipts, records of personal expenses, and other financial papers; business memoranda; compositions by the Robinsons and others; genealogical material; and clippings. Correspondence includes information about Charles Robinson's fight for a free Kansas and Sara Robinson's letters from family and friends. Material after 1894 concerns her philanthropies and her husband's estate. Also available on microfilm. See Joseph W. Snell, ed., *Guide to the Microfilm Edition of the Private Papers of Charles and Sara T. D. Robinson, 1834-1911* (Topeka: Kansas State Historical Society, 1967).

5,223. Woman's Christian Temperance Union
Records. 1898-1920. 13 ms. boxes and 6 vols.
Open. No guide.
Kansas State Historical Society.
Business records, correspondence, and other records concern the organization, finances, and administration of the Kansas Anti-Saloon League, the Kansas State Temperance Union, and the WCTU.

5,224. Lutheran Women's Missionary League, Kansas District
Records. 1943-76. No size given.
Access restricted. No guide.
Lutheran Church—Missouri Synod, Kansas District.
Minutes, newsletters, photos, and scrapbooks of the League, formed in 1943 to aid in international and district mission work. The League provides mites to support mission work in Kansas and around the world and contributes to scholarships for students interested in church work.

5,225. Clippings
Collection. 1953- . Ca. 5 cabinets.
Open. No guide.
Menninger Foundation Archives.
Clippings from state and national newspapers concern all phases of psychiatry and include information about persons involved in the field.

5,226. Dix, Dorothea
Papers. Ca. 1826-86. 2 archival boxes.
Open. No guide.
Menninger Foundation Archives.
Correspondence and speeches of Dix (1802-89), who sought improvements in nursing care, prisons, and hospitals for the insane.

5,227. Law, Mildred
Papers. Ca. 1921-64. 4 archival boxes.
Open. Index.
Menninger Foundation Archives.
[Miss] Law (?-1975), who began work as a lab technician for the Menninger brothers in 1921, retired as a vice-president of the Menninger Foundation in 1964. Office files containing correspondence, memos, reports, and other items relate to her activities at the Foundation.

5,228. Menninger, Catharine "Cay" Wright
Papers. Ca. 1915- . Several drawers and 6 archival boxes.
Open. Card file.
Menninger Foundation Archives.
A 1923 graduate of Columbia University Teachers College, Menninger (1902-) helped her husband William C. Menninger in fund-raising programs for the Menninger Foundation. Correspondence, diary-scrapbooks from her college days, speech notes, records of fund-raising activities, logs of travel with her husband for the Foundation, records from various community activities, and other papers. Cay Menninger kept extensive records of her personal contacts and other activities related to fund raising for the Foundation. Trained in primary education, she helped establish the Westminster School, Topeka's first nursery school, in 1928. Her papers include the School's budgets, minutes, and other records as well as records from the Civilian Defense Volunteer office, which she headed during WWII. Papers also reflect her involvement in groups, including the American National Red Cross; People to People, International; the Community Resources Council; and the Providence Society, which became a division of the Menninger Foundation.

5,229. Menninger, Flo V.
Papers. Ca. 1880-1945. 6 drawers and 3 archival boxes.
Open. Description and partial card index.
Menninger Foundation Archives.
A schoolteacher and leader of Topeka society, Flora Vesta "Flo V." Knisely Menninger (1863-1945) was the mother of physicians William C. and Karl Menninger and the wife of Charles Fredrick Menninger. Diaries, notes for books she wrote, notes for a four-year Bible course she developed, and notes for an art course she taught. Her diaries concern her move from Pennsylvania to Clay Center, KS, and her experiences as a schoolteacher. These experiences are described in her *Days of My Life* (1940). She developed the Bible course after she was asked to teach a class at a Topeka Baptist church and found existing material unsatisfactory. She offered her art course for $2; she also held musicales at her home.

5,230. Menninger, Jeanetta Lyle
Papers. Ca. 1936-70. 4 archival boxes and other items.
Open. Partial index.
Menninger Foundation Archives.
[Mrs. Karl] Menninger (1901-) was the first editor of the *Bulletin of the Menninger Clinic.* Correspondence, including items relating to the

American Medical Writers Association, her involvement with Park College in Kansas City, and to Menninger Foundation activities. Also includes manuscripts of her writings and material about her work for The Villages, Inc., a program that seeks lifelong homes for abandoned children. The concept, introduced by Menninger's husband, is designed to eliminate the use of foster homes.

5,231. Murphy, Lois Barclay
Papers. Nd. Ca. 150 cabinets.
Closed. No guide.
Menninger Foundation Archives.
Correspondence and research data of [Mrs. Gardner] Murphy (1902-), who taught at Sarah Lawrence College in New York from 1928 to 1952. She and her husband then joined the Menninger Foundation staff. Lois Murphy holds a PhD in psychology. Her books concern such subjects as child coping devices.

5,232. Ridenour, Nina
Papers. Nd. 7 archival boxes.
Open. Unpublished guide.
Menninger Foundation Archives.
Ridenour (1904-), who holds a PhD in psychology, was director of the education division of the National Association for Mental Health and secretary of the Ittleson Family Foundation. Correspondence and manuscripts relate chiefly to Ridenour's work in New York City and include some of her ca. 45 publications. Contains plays depicting mental health problems staged by the American Community Theatre Wing. Ridenour was married to N. Arnold Boll but used the name Ridenour in her work.

5,233. Sargent, Helen Durham
Papers. 1910s- . No size given.
Open. No guide.
Menninger Foundation Archives.
[Mrs.] Sargent (1904-), who earned a PhD in psychology from Northwestern University, worked at the Topeka Veterans Administration Hospital before joining the Menninger Foundation staff. Diaries from 1917 to about 1937, speeches, research data, and child development notes. Sargent's research dealt with rehabilitation of the blind, child development, and other subjects.

5,234. Kansas-Oklahoma Conference, United Church of Christ, Congregational Collection
Records. Ca. 1808- . 8 sections of shelving.
Open. Card index.
Washburn University, Mabee Library, Archives.
Correspondence and other Conference records; minutes, histories, membership lists, and marriage and baptism records of local churches; sermons; antislavery material; and published records, including Congregational American Home Missionary Society annual reports, 1827-1903, and the Congregational yearbook, 1854-1952. Also includes such religious publications as *The Panoplist,* 1808-20; *Christian Spectator,* 1823-36; *Missionary Herald,* 1821-1900; and the *Home Missionary,* 1828-80. Specific sections of the collection relate to missions, women, youth, and other topics.

5,235. Washburn University Archives
Records. 1865- . 7 cabinets.
Open. No guide.
Washburn University, Mabee Library, Archives.
Founded in 1865 by the Congregational Church as Lincoln College, the school became Washburn College and, in 1941, Washburn Municipal University. The institution assumed its current title in 1952. Publications, including class schedules, college bulletins, yearbooks, student handbooks, and school newspapers, make up the bulk of the Archives. Also includes some alumni correspondence and lists, photos, and clipping scrapbooks, 1904-33. The material indicates the involvement of women in music, in "rhetorical exercises," and in various organizations.

WICHITA

5,236. Provincial House Archives
Records. 1902- . No size given.
Access restricted. No guide.
Adorers of the Blood of Christ, Provincial House.
The Provincial House oversees the activities of members of this religious women's order in a geographic region. The sisters' work in Wichita dates from 1902. Correspondence, including official letters from religious superiors to members of the province and letters from Wichita sisters who established a foundation in Brazil; financial and educational records; annals of foundations opened by the sisters and later discontinued; theses, dissertations, and books written by sisters; brief individual biographies; taped interviews with older members of the community; photos; scrapbooks; community newspapers, 1945- ; and other records.

5,237. Woodman, H. Rea
Papers. 1879-ca. 1940. Ca. 6 cu.ft.
Open. Unpublished guide.
Wichita Historical Museum.
An author and clubwoman, Woodman (1870-1951) taught school in Wichita and worked to promote culture in her community. Diaries, 1880s-ca. 1900; manuscripts of poems, plays, and other works; ledgers; and type style plates from books. The diaries chronicle her work as a teacher, her opinions on her reading, and descriptions of local events and the role of her socially prominent family. Includes material she used in writing a poem, published in 1913, that concerned the sinking of the Titanic and a manuscript of her history of Wichita.

5,238. Clippings
Collection. Ca. 1900- . No size given.
Open. Card index.
Wichita Public Library.
Clippings from Wichita and Kansas newspapers with separate headings for Wichita women, Kansas women, individual women, and women's groups.

5,239. Families and Individuals
Collection. Nd. No size given.
Open. Partial inventory.
Wichita Public Library.
Occasional correspondence, biographical material, articles, clippings, and photos concerning persons prominent in Wichita's history. Among the women represented in the collection are Ellen Kassim Meagher, who helped found Wichita's Catholic church; Victoria Murdock, a state legislator and wife of the founder of the Wichita *Eagle;* Louise Caldwell Murdock, wife of the *Eagle's* business manager, an art collector, and a member of the group that helped secure a Carnegie library for Wichita; Mary Elizabeth Lease, a leader in the Populist movement; and Olive Ann Beech, who is an executive in the Beech Corporation.

5,240. Hite, Kathleen
Papers. 1955-68. 2.4 ft.
Open. Description.
Wichita State University Library, Special Collections.
Television scripts by Hite, who wrote for such television shows as "Gunsmoke," "Wagon Train," "Laramie," "Empire," "The Guns of Will Sonnett," "General Electric Theatre," "Decision," the "Jane Wyman Show," and Alfred Hitchcock's series.

5,241. University Archives
Records. 1886- . Ca. 45 boxes.
Open. Description and box inventories.
Wichita State University Library, Special Collections.
Established as a liberal arts school called Fairmont College, the institution later became part of the Kansas state university system. Minute books, financial records, correspondence, membership rolls, clippings, and other items, including records of the Philomathean Society, a women's literary society organized in 1896 and discontinued in 1915. Minutes and roll books of the Campus YWCA, 1897-1904, and records of the home economics department, Associated Women Students, Ladies Advisory Board of the Young Woman's Department, sororities, and the Council of University Women are included as well. Contains correspondence of M. Alice Isely, reference librarian of the University Library from about 1905 to 1956.

5,242. Ward, May (Williams)
Papers. 1901-69. 14 ft.
Open. Description and box inventory.
Wichita State University Library, Special Collections.
A poet and writer, [Mrs. Merle] Ward (1882-1975) sold her first poem to *Life* in 1921. Diaries, ledgers, poetry and play manuscripts, short stories, essays, photos, and address books. Ward was president of the Kansas Authors Club and the Poetry Society of Kansas. Five volumes of her poetry were published.

5,243. Wilcox, Mary "Molly" (Warren)
Papers. 1890s-early 1900s. Ca. 600 items.
Open. Description.
Wichita State University Library, Special Collections.
A member of the third graduating class of Fairmont College, [Mrs. Edwin F.] Wilcox (1880-1974) was one of the first woman editors of a Kansas newspaper, the Wichita *Democrat.* Autobiography, short stories, clippings, and other papers, some of which reflect difficulties Wilcox encountered while working in a traditionally male field.

WINFIELD

5,244. Central Kansas Conference, Woman's Society of Christian Service
Records. 1906-68. 1 vol. and 1 folder.
Open. No guide.
Kansas West Conference of the United Methodist Church, Commission on History and Archives.
Constitution, bylaws, minutes, correspondence, photos, programs, and clippings of the WSCS, a woman's Methodist Church organization, document Conference-level activities in directing district and local units. Contains a 1906 minute book of the Conference board of deaconesses.

5,245. Meredith, Mrs. J. W.
Papers. Nd. 48 pp.
Open. No guide.
Kansas West Conference of the United Methodist Church, Commission on History and Archives.
Typescript written sometime after 1945 concerns the life of Margaret Maranda (Baker) Beebe Meredith (1853-1942), a schoolteacher born in Ohio. Written by her son Frank as though it were Meredith's first-person narrative, the typescript tells of her early life; her journey to Kansas; the death of her first husband Thomas Prentiss Beebe, whom she married in 1873; her religious conversion and increasing church activities; and her marriage in 1878 to John William Meredith, a Methodist circuit rider.

5,246. Wilson, Emma Webber
Papers. Ca. 1950-70. 1 folder and 1 box.
Open. No guide.
Kansas West Conference of the United Methodist Church, Commission on History and Archives.
[Miss] Wilson (1897-1970) was a Methodist missionary in Fuchow and Tientsin, China, before WWII and in Korea beginning in 1953. Appointment calendars used as diaries from 1957 to 1965, meditational speeches, tributes from

classes, school yearbooks, and clippings. Wilson began her work in China in 1925. She returned to the US after being held prisoner by the Japanese during the 1930s. She studied at Drew Theological Seminary during WWII and returned to the field in 1953.

5,247. Woman's Home Missionary Society, Dodge City District
Records. 1926-40. 1 vol.
Open. No guide.
Kansas West Conference of the United Methodist Church, Commission on History and Archives.
Annual reports and minutes of Dodge City, KS, District meetings of the Society, which supported missionary work among the Indians. The Society joined with the Woman's Foreign Missionary Society and the Ladies Aid Society in 1940 to form the Woman's Society of Christian Service.

5,248. Women's Society of Christian Service, Hutchinson District
Records. 1940-73. 7 vols.
Open. No guide.
Kansas West Conference of the United Methodist Church, Commission on History and Archives.
Constitution, bylaws, minutes of executive and annual meetings, clippings, and other records of the Hutchinson, KS, District of the WSCS, the primary women's organization of the Methodist Church. The WSCS supported fund-raising projects, missionary and youth work, communication between the conference and local churches, and other programs. The WSCS was formed as the Woman's Society of Christian Service in 1940 through the merger of the Woman's Home Missionary Society, the Woman's Foreign Missionary Society, and the Ladies Aid Society. The name was changed to the Women's Society of Christian Service in 1968. The organization became United Methodist Women in 1974.

KENTUCKY

BEREA

5,249. Campbell, Olive Arnold (Dame)
Papers. 1922-54. 22 items.
Open. No guide.
Berea College Library.
[Mrs. John Charles] Campbell (1882-1954) was director of the John C. Campbell Folk School in Brasstown, NC. Correspondence, pamphlets, and articles relate to her work at the School, which was named for her husband, and to her activities as a ballad collector in the southern highlands.

5,250. Child, Henrietta
Papers. 1910-74. 90 items.
Open. No guide.
Berea College Library.
[Miss] Child (1867-1968) walked to schools in Madison County, KY, to tell stories to schoolchildren. Correspondence, photos, and clippings reflect Child's role in the Berea community. Also includes props she used in her storytelling. She was the daughter of Francis Child, a Harvard University collector of English and Scottish ballads.

5,251. Dingman, Helen
Papers. 1922-67. 20 items.
Open. No guide.
Berea College Library.
Dingman (1885-1978), a Berea College sociology teacher, served as executive secretary of the Council of the Southern Mountains and editor of *Mountain Life and Work.* Correspondence, articles, and clippings pertain to Dingman's role in southern mountain work, to her activities as a community worker for the Presbyterian Board of Home Missions, and to other topics.

5,252. Frontier Nursing Service
Records. 1926-76. 114 items.
Open. Unpublished guide.
Berea College Library.
The Service was founded in 1925 to provide midwifery and nursing services for residents of Kentucky's mountain region. Correspondence, reports, photos, articles, and clippings contain information on midwifery. Correspondence of the Service's founder Mary Breckinridge is included.

5,253. Goodell, Lavinia
Papers. 1846-80. 390 items.
Open. No guide.
Berea College Library.
Correspondence and diaries of Goodell (1839-80), the first woman lawyer in Wisconsin.

5,254. Hindman Settlement School
Records. 1901-77. 174 items.
Open. Unpublished guide.
Berea College Library.
Founded in 1902, this settlement school is located in the Kentucky mountain town of Hindman. Correspondence, photos, pamphlets, articles, and clippings contain information about the role of Katherine Pettit, May Stone, and other women in the School's work.

5,255. Pettit, Katherine
Papers. 1899-1936. 86 items.
Open. Unpublished guide.
Berea College Library.
Correspondence, articles, and clippings of [Miss] Pettit (1868-1936) pertain to the founding and activities of the Hindman and Pine Mountain Settlement schools in Kentucky and to Pettit's 40 years as a settlement worker in the Kentucky mountains.

5,256. Pine Mountain Settlement School
Records. 1913-75. 360 items.
Open. Unpublished guide.
Berea College Library.
The School was founded in 1913. Correspondence, reports, brochures, articles, and clippings concern the School's activities and the role of Katherine Pettit, Ethel de Long, and other women in rural settlement work.

5,257. Ulmann, Doris
Papers. 1930-76. 375 items.
Open. Unpublished guide.
Berea College Library.
Ulmann (1884-1935) was a photographer who photographed southern mountain people during the 1920s and 1930s. Correspondence, minutes of the Doris Ulmann Foundation, her will, articles, and clippings.

BOWLING GREEN

5,258. Bryan
Papers. 1863-1955. 3 Hollinger boxes.
Open. No guide.
Western Kentucky University, Kentucky Library.
[Miss] Fannie Morton Bryan (1870-1964) was a teacher. Correspondence, diaries dating from 1889 to 1895, record and account books, photos, legal papers, pamphlets, and clippings. Includes a manuscript record book of the board of trustees of Russellville Female College in Russellville, KY.

5,259. Calvert, Obenchain, and Younglove
Papers. 1775-1956. 11.5 Hollinger boxes.
Partially restricted. Descriptive inventory and card catalog.
Western Kentucky University, Kentucky Library.
Correspondence, diaries, sermons, writings, business papers, genealogical data, weather records, and clippings of the family of Samuel Wilson Calvert (1796-1837), a Presbyterian minister; his son Thomas Calvert (1826-98); Thomas Calvert's wife Margaret (Younglove) Calvert (1829-1920); Thomas and Margaret Calvert's daughters Margaret (1860-1947), Josephine (1864-1956), and Lida (Calvert) Obenchain (1856-1935); and other relatives. Included within the Samuel Calvert series is correspondence of the Calvert daughters Margaret, a schoolteacher, and Josephine, who worked with a local dressmaker, and Josephine's diary from 1878 to 1881, which reflects the life of a schoolgirl growing up in Bowling Green. Lida Obenchain was a teacher, author, poet, and women's rights advocate. She wrote novels under the name "Eliza Calvert Hall," but she signed her women's rights articles with her initials, "L.C.O." Her husband William Alexander Obenchain (1814-1916) was a mathematics professor and president of Ogden College in Bowling Green; they had four children. Lida Obenchain's papers include family correspondence, notes, abstract of a master's thesis about her, galley and page proofs of books, articles, and clippings. Also contains material of the Younglove family and about Mary (Kendall) Jones (1806?-84), an educator who conducted a school for girls in Bowling Green and later one in St. Louis. The Younglove material includes a diary kept by Jane Younglove (1831-61), sister of Margaret (Younglove) Calvert, during a visit to Bowling Green in 1857.

5,260. Carter, Lillie Mae (Bland)
Papers. 1939-76. 4 Hollinger boxes.
Open. No guide.
Western Kentucky University, Kentucky Library.
Carter (1919-) is a black teacher, author, poet, and homemaker. Correspondence, poems, manuscripts and cards, galley and page proofs, pamphlets, clippings, and printed items relate chiefly to Carter's writing career, but some items pertain to her school activities and to her family. Includes material concerning her books *Black Thoughts* (1971) and *Doing It Our Way* (1975). A Bowling Green native, Carter has lived in Ohio for a number of years.

5,261. Davis, Anne (Pence)
Papers. 1916-73. 3.5 Hollinger boxes.
Open. No guide.
Western Kentucky University, Kentucky Library.
Davis, an author and poet, was born in Kentucky but has lived in Texas since 1926. Correspondence, radio talks, book reviews, page and galley proofs, photos, clippings, professional journals, and printed items concern Davis and her literary career. Includes material about several of Davis's books, among them *Mimi at Camp* (1935), *Wishes Are Horses* (1938), *The Customer Is Always Right* (1940), and *The Top Hand of Lone Tree Ranch* (1960). In addition to her children's books, Davis has published other works of prose and poetry.

5,262. Dunn Family
Papers. 1824-1916. 0.5 Hollinger box.
Open. Descriptive inventory and card catalog.
Western Kentucky University, Kentucky Library.
Family correspondence and tax receipts of James R. Dunn (1802?-81), a farmer in Grayson County, KY; his mother Mary (Rogers) Dunn (?-1857); and his son Zachariah James Dunn (1842-1918). Includes letters from Prudence (Dunn) Rogers Creath (1798-188?), sister of James R. Dunn and second wife of Jacob Creath, Jr. (1799-1886), a Disciples of Christ minister. Prudence Creath's letters include descriptions of her husband's evangelistic travels, farming in Missouri, the Civil War, her trip by steamboat from Kentucky to Missouri in 1868, and family affairs.

5,263. Giles, Janice (Holt) Moore
Papers. 1960-70. 22 items.
Open. Card catalog.
Western Kentucky University, Kentucky Library.
Letters from [Mrs. Henry] Giles (1909-), an author, to her friend Joe Covington in Bowling Green in which she makes references to researching, writing, and publishing her books and to personal matters.

5,264. Giles, Janice (Holt) Moore
Papers. 1948-73. 12 Hollinger boxes.
Open. Descriptive inventory and card catalog.
Western Kentucky University, Kentucky Library.
[Mrs. Henry] Giles (1909-) is a Kentucky author. Manuscript with author's revisions, galley proofs, short stories, articles, speeches, and material Giles used in writing books, including *Hannah Fowler* (1956), *Land Beyond the Mountains* (1958), *Run Me a River* (1964), *G. I. Journal of Sergeant Giles* (1965), *Shady Grove* (1968), *Six Horse Hitch* (1969), *The Damned Engineers* (1970), and *The Kinta Years* (1973). Includes material regarding early Kentuckians, the Shakers at South Union, KY, and other topics.

5,265. Green Family, Falls of Rough, KY
Papers. 1814-71. 43 Hollinger boxes and 8236 items.
Open. Descriptive inventory and card catalog.
Western Kentucky University, Kentucky Library.
Correspondence, business papers and 66 account books, biographical and genealogical data, cards, invitations, programs, and clippings of the Green Family of Falls of Rough, KY. Lafayette Green (1835-1907) and his sons Willis Green (1870-1944), Preston Scott Green (1877-1945), and Robert Scott Green (1882-1943) developed the land at their Grayson County home. The Green family enterprises eventually included farming, lumbering, selling tobacco, raising Shetland ponies, a gristmill, sawmill, post office, bank, and general store. After the death of the three sons in the 1940s, their sister Jennie Scott Green (1879-1965) carried on the family business for another two decades. Included are letters to Willis Green (1794?-1862), a US congressman who was the uncle of Lafayette Green, particularly in connection with Henry Clay's presidential candidacy in 1844; correspondence and other material of Lafayette Green and his wife Rebecca Eleanor "Ella" (Scott) Green (1841-96); and papers of Jennie Scott Green. Ella Green's papers include material of her father Robert Wilmot Scott (1808-84), her letters to her husband, letters from her children, and Scott genealogical material. Papers of Jennie Scott Green contain more than 5000 letters from her family and friends from her school days in Louisville and Princeton, KY; from former residents of Falls of Rough, acquaintances, and charitable organizations. Also included are letters from friends she met during her travels in Naples, FL; Wequetonsing, MI; Chautauqua, NY; Germany; and on cruises. The collection also includes correspondence of many other female members of the Green and Scott families.

5,266. Hamilton, Weston A.
Papers. 1818-1926. 5 items.
Open. Card catalog.
Western Kentucky University, Kentucky Library.
A letter donated by Hamilton in which Cale Young Rice responds to a letter of inquiry regarding an article written about him. Rice's wife Alice Caldwell (Hegan) Rice (1870-1942), a writer, adds a note to the inquirer.

5,267. Knott
Papers. 1776-1953. 5.5 Hollinger boxes.
Open. Descriptive inventory and card catalog.
Western Kentucky University, Kentucky Library.
Correspondence, speeches and writings, sketches and drawings, photos, autograph albums, and clippings of James Proctor Knott (1830-1911), a lawyer who was the attorney general of Missouri from 1858 to 1861, a US representative from Kentucky from 1867 to 1871 and from 1875 to 1883, and governor of Kentucky from 1883 to 1887. Includes his letters to his wife Sarah "Sallie" Rosanna (McElroy) Knott (1833-1915); Sarah Knott's correspondence with family and friends, some of which concerns life in Missouri during 1861 and 1862; and letters and diaries of Maria Irvine (McElroy) Knott (1805-?) of Missouri, mother of James Knott and aunt of Sarah Knott. Maria Knott visited Kentucky in 1861 and 1862.

5,268. Lewis and Starling
Papers. 1784-1970. 11.5 Hollinger boxes and 4 microfilm reels.
Open. Descriptive inventory and card catalog.
Western Kentucky University, Kentucky Library.
Correspondence, Civil War military and personal papers, business records and account books, genealogical data, photos, scrapbooks, and clippings consist principally of correspondence of the Lewis, Bibb, and Starling families, which migrated from Virginia to Kentucky in the early 1800s. Family members represented in the collection include Gabriel Jones Lewis (1775-1864), a surveyor and farmer; his wife Mary (Bibb) Lewis (1782-1819); their daughter Elizabeth Ann Gabriella Lewis (1813-62); her husband Samuel McDowell Starling (1807-90), a farmer and merchant of Logan County and Hopkinsville, KY; Mary (Starling) Payne (1832-96), the eldest of seven children of Samuel and Elizabeth Starling; John Booker Bibb (1789-1884), brother of Mary (Bibb) Lewis; and Thomas Marshall Green (1837-1904), cousin of Mary (Starling) Payne. Mary Starling married William Richardson Payne in 1861, but he died shortly thereafter and she remained with her family, managing the home, especially after her mother's death. She helped rear her brother's children, and, with her sister Anna Irvin Starling (1842-77), helped feed and care for soldiers during the Civil War. Her father served as a Union officer during the war, and the family papers include his letters to Mary and Anna. Mary (Starling) Payne was interested in family records and organized her family's papers. Included in her papers are letters from John Bibb, who practiced law briefly, served in state government, and was an ardent horticulturist, giving his name to a type of lettuce he developed, and from Thomas Green, a newspaper editor whose letters deal chiefly with Kentucky politics from 1880 to 1895.

5,269. Meriwether Family
Papers. 1791-1949. 0.5 Hollinger box.
Open. Descriptive inventory and card catalog.
Western Kentucky University, Kentucky Library.
Correspondence and legal papers of Charles Meriwether (1766-1843), a doctor who moved to Christian County, KY, in 1809; Elizabeth (Meriwether) Gilmer (1861-1951), a newspaper columnist known professionally as "Dorothy Dix," and Caroline Ferguson (Gordon) Tate (1895-), an author and professor. Included are letters from Gilmer to a cousin in Kentucky and from Tate to various relatives relating family news, WWII experiences, and professional activities.

5,270. Murton, Jessie Wilmore (Jones)
Papers. 1927-74. 13 ft.
Open. No guide.
Western Kentucky University, Kentucky Library.
Murton (1886-1973) was a writer best known for her poetry and children's stories. Correspondence, poems, prose, greeting card verses, Burma Shave jingles, lyrics, business records pertaining to her works, memorabilia, clippings, periodicals, and a book printed in Braille. A Kentucky native, Murton lived in Battle Creek, MI, after 1911. She was chosen first poet laureate of the Michigan Federation of Women's Clubs in 1935 and was a member of the National League of American Pen Women.

5,271. Northcott
Papers. 1851-1918. 3 Hollinger boxes.
Open. Descriptive inventory and card catalog.
Western Kentucky University, Kentucky Library.
Correspondence, diaries, journal, and writings of Henry Clay Northcott (1822-1918), a Methodist preacher; his daughter Martha Catherine "Kate" Northcott (1850-89), a music teacher; and her husband Bruce F. Thomas (1853?-82), a Vanceburg, KY, lawyer. Kate Northcott's journal from 1866 and 1867 tells of a stagecoach journey from Shelbyville, KY, to Louisville in 1866 and of the treatment the Northcotts received from Southern sympathizers when they returned to Shelbyville after the Civil War. Correspondence of Kate and Bruce Thomas contains information on his study at Harvard law school in 1873-74, and at a Cincinnati law school in 1874, Kate's work as a music teacher, social life and customs, the struggles of a young lawyer in Vanceburg in the 1870s and 1880s, and steamboat travel and postal service on the Ohio River. Also includes comments and comparisons of operas, music, and theater in Boston and Cincinnati in the 1870s.

5,272. Pace, Pearl (Carter)
Papers. 1902-75. 23.5 Hollinger boxes.
Open. No guide.
Western Kentucky University, Kentucky Library.
A sheriff, homemaker, and businesswoman, Pace (1896-1970) was appointed by President Eisenhower as a member of the War Claims Commission and of the Foreign Claims Settlement Commission. Correspondence, speeches, sheriff's fee book, commission records, photos, clippings, printed material, and campaign mementos. Consists chiefly of papers from the period when she served on the two presidential commissions. Also includes papers of her children, particularly letters from or about her son Stanley while he was a prisoner of war in Europe. Pace served for many years as the Republican national committeewoman from Kentucky.

5,273. Rice
Papers. 1898-1965. 15 Hollinger boxes.
Open. Descriptive inventory and card catalog.
Western Kentucky University, Kentucky Library.
Correspondence, manuscripts, business papers, account book, book reviews, photos, scrapbook, biographical clippings, printed items, and other material of Louisville writers Alice Caldwell (Hegan) Rice (1870-1942) and her husband Cale Young Rice (1872-1943). Among Alice Rice's papers are letters from writers, publishers, and literary agents Brandt and Brandt; business papers, including ones regarding a settlement made with the woman who was portrayed as *Mrs. Wiggs of the Cabbage Patch* (1904); letters concerning movie rights to the book, which was Rice's first and best known novel; contracts and agreements for publication of many books made chiefly with The Century Company; notes and research material; account book containing royalty records; manuscripts of *Our Ernie* (1939) and *Happiness Road* (1942); cartoons drawn by Rice; and other material. Correspondents include authors Anna Hempstead Branch, Harriet Monroe, Jessie Belle Rittenhouse, Elizabeth Madox Roberts, and Ida Minerva Tarbell.

5,274. Rice, Alice Caldwell (Hegan)
Papers. 1904-1917. 2 items.
Open. No guide.
Western Kentucky University, Kentucky Library.
An essay, written in 1904 in letter form, in which Rice (1870-1942), a writer, responds to a request from the editor of *Outlook* for information about books she read as a child, and a 1917 letter in which Rice tells her neighbor of the attractiveness of a book plate owned by the neighbor.

5,275. Rice, L. L.
Papers. Nd. 10 Hollinger boxes.
Open. No guide.
Western Kentucky University, Kentucky Library.
Correspondence, photos, printed items, and other papers of Laban Lacy Rice (1870-1973), an educator. Includes correspondence from his sister-in-law Alice (Hegan) Rice (1870-1942), a writer.

5,276. Rowan
Papers. 1784-1923. 0.5 Hollinger box.
Open. Descriptive inventory and card catalog.
Western Kentucky University, Kentucky Library.
Family and business correspondence of John Rowan (1773-1843), a lawyer, judge, and US representative and senator; his son John Rowan, Jr. (1804-55); and the younger Rowan's wife Rebecca (Carnes) Rowan (1813-97). Included are letters of John Rowan, Jr., to his wife, one of them written before their marriage and others written while he was in Washington, DC, seeking political appointments and she was at home in Bardstown, KY, caring for their children. Also includes a letter of sympathy written to Rebecca Rowan following her husband's death.

5,277. Rowan, Rebecca (Carnes)
Papers. 1855-1976. 0.5 Hollinger box.
Open. Descriptive inventory and card catalog.
Western Kentucky University, Kentucky Library.
Rowan (1813-97), a homemaker, struggled to maintain the farm of her late husband John Rowan, Jr., of Federal Hill at Bardstown, KY, which is known as "My Old Kentucky Home." Correspondence and photos include letters to William Pendleton Boone, a Louisville lawyer, which reveal Rowan's dependence on Boone for legal counsel after her husband's death in 1855. Boone was the husband of Eliza Rowan (Harney) Boone, a granddaughter of Rowan's parents-in-law. Also includes letters to Rowan from her oldest son William Atkinson Hill Rowan (1838?-1900) while he was serving in the Confederate army, photos of her daughter May Rowan (1851?-?) and of Rebecca Rowan, and a 1976 news release and photos of the donor of the collection. Rowan's papers reflect problems encountered by a woman attempting to maintain a household dependent on money gained from farming and business holdings. Her letters indicate she was made to feel she was intruding in "a man's world."

5,278. Sachs, Emanie (Nahm)
Papers. 1933-49. 33 items.
Open. Card catalog.
Western Kentucky University, Kentucky Library.
An author, Emanie (Nahm) Sachs (1893-) took the surname Arling after her divorce in 1939. Consists of correspondence, chiefly letters to Mary (Taylor) Leiper Moore at the Kentucky Library concerning a projected history of Kentucky. Sachs, a Bowling Green native, comments on the writing and revision of the history as well as personal matters. Comments of readers are included.

5,279. Strange
Papers. 1812-1925. 2 Hollinger boxes.
Open. Descriptive inventory and card catalog.
Western Kentucky University, Kentucky Library.
Agatha Jane (Rochester) Strange (1832-96), a homemaker, was a lifelong resident of Bowling Green who was interested in family and local history. Correspondence, journal, manuscript, and scrapbooks. Includes a journal dating from 1852 to 1883 which documents life in Bowling Green and a tour in 1852 of the eastern US, and Strange's manuscript concerning the McDowell families in Kentucky.

5,280. Taliaferro
Papers. 1815-1956. 0.5 Hollinger box.
Open. Descriptive inventory and card catalog.
Western Kentucky University, Kentucky Library.
Elizabeth "Betsy" (Williamson) Taliaferro (1800-50) traveled from her home in Harrisonburg in Catahoula Parish, LA, to her former home at Versailles, KY, in the spring of 1839. Travel diary, correspondence about the diary, manuscript prepared from the diary, and notes about people, places, and events mentioned in the volume. Taliaferro and her husband James Govan Taliaferro (1798-1876); her sons Robert, age 8, and David, age 4; and Kitty, a Negro nurse, first traveled by steamboat to New Orleans for a short visit. Then they retraced their route up the Mississippi River to Natchez, MS, where James Taliaferro disembarked to return to Harrisonburg. Betsy Taliaferro and her party continued by steamboat to Louisville, where they boarded a stagecoagh bound for Versailles. Taliaferro's diary includes descriptions of such aspects of the journey as life in New Orleans, transportation on the Mississippi and Ohio rivers, and steamboat races.

5,281. Underwood
Papers. 1791-1912. 4.5 Hollinger boxes.
Open. Descriptive inventory and card catalog.
Western Kentucky University, Kentucky Library.
Family correspondence, journals, writings, genealogical charts, and research notes of Joseph Rogers Underwood (1791-1876), a lawyer, US senator, Kentucky legislator, judge, and farmer; his brother Warner Lewis Underwood (1808-72); and his son John Cox Underwood (1840-1913). Includes letters of Joseph Underwood and his second wife Elizabeth Threlkeld (Cox) Underwood (1818-84) from 1849 to 1853, the last four years of his term as US senator. During that period Elizabeth remained at home in Bowling Green, KY, and cared for the family business. The correspondence covers such subjects as education, travel, social life and customs, hiring of servants, running the farm, handling business transactions, and planning a new home and reflects the variety of work expected of and accepted by antebellum wives in Kentucky.

FRANKFORT

5,282. Commission on Women
Records. 1964-71. 9 cu.ft.
Open. Unpublished guide.
Kentucky Division of Archives and Records Management, Department of Library and Archives.
The Commission was created in 1964 to research and report on the status of women in Kentucky. Minutes, general files, reports, pamphlets, clippings, and publications.

5,283. Department of Justice, Bureau of Corrections, Kentucky Correctional Institution for Women
Records. 1932-68. 19 boxes.
Access restricted. Unpublished guide.
Kentucky Division of Archives and Records Management, Department of Library and Archives.
Inmates' education folders and inactive case histories of inmates.

5,284. Kentucky Board of Nursing
Records. 1914-77. Ca. 150 cu.ft.
Partially restricted. Unpublished guide.
Kentucky Division of Archives and Records Management, Department of Library and Archives.
Created in 1914, the Board is involved in nursing education and regulation. Personnel records, nursing school records, individual files on registered and licensed practical nurses, and nursing school files from Kentucky hospitals. Prior to mid-1978, the Board was known as the Kentucky Board of Nursing Education and Nurse Registration.

5,285. Adams, Elizabeth
Papers. 1830-78. 1 vol. and 52 items.
Open. Published guide.
Kentucky Historical Society.
Letters to her brother Philip S. Fall, who was a minister, and to Nancy and Mrs. Anne A. Fall. Also available on microfilm. See G. Glenn Clift, *Guide to the Manuscripts of the Kentucky Historical Society* (Frankfort, KY: Kentucky Historical Society, 1955).

5,286. Downing, Lydia
Papers. 1861. 3 pp.
Open. Published guide.
Kentucky Historical Society.
Letter to her teacher, clergyman P. S. Fall, includes news of the death of her son Albert, news of prisoners of war, and information on other subjects. Also available on microfilm. See G. Glenn Clift, *Guide to the Manuscripts of the Kentucky Historical Society* (Frankfort, KY: Kentucky Historical Society, 1955).

5,287. Fall, Mrs. Philip S.
Papers. 1832-76. 1 folder.
Open. Published guide.
Kentucky Historical Society.
In 1821 Anne (Bacon) Fall was married to Philip Fall, a minister who taught at the Nashville Female Academy and established the Female Eclectic Institute in Frankfort. Letters to her husband and children concerning family matters and an 1832 letter from her sister in St. Louis, which contains information about schools there. Philip Fall organized the Christian church in Frankfort in 1832. Also available on microfilm. See G. Glenn Clift, *Guide to the Manuscripts of the Kentucky Historical Society* (Frankfort, KY: Kentucky Historical Society, 1955).

5,288. Fanning, Charlotte Fall
Papers. 1848-93. 142 pp.
Open. Published guide.
Kentucky Historical Society.
Letters to her brother P. S. Fall, principally written from Hope Institute between 1848 and 1880, and personal letters to her niece Betty and to her sister-in-law Mrs. P. S. Fall. Also available on microfilm. See G. Glenn Clift, *Guide to the Manuscripts of the Kentucky Historical Society* (Frankfort, KY: Kentucky Historical Society, 1955).

5,289. Forsythe, Lucy Jane
Papers. 1844. 1 item.
Open. Published guide.
Kentucky Historical Society.
Copybook of Forsythe, a 10-year-old student at Covington Female Seminary. William Orr, a minister, was principal of the school. Also available on microfilm. See G. Glenn Clift, *Guide to the Manuscripts of the Kentucky Historical Society* (Frankfort, KY: Kentucky Historical Society, 1955).

5,290. Foster, Martha
Papers. 1853. 47 pp.
Open. Published and unpublished guides.
Kentucky Historical Society.
Foster was a student at Nazareth College in Bardstown, KY. Letters, school essays, a list of pupils, and school rules. Also available on microfilm. See G. Glenn Clift, *Guide to the Manuscripts of the Kentucky Historical Society* (Frankfort, KY: Kentucky Historical Society, 1955).

5,291. Helm, Emilie (Todd)
Papers. 1836-1930. 8 cases.
Open. Published guide.
Kentucky Historical Society.
Helm, a family genealogist, was the half-sister of Mary (Todd) Lincoln. Manuscript of her Todd family genealogy and letters from Governor J.

Proctor Knott's wife, Mrs. Ninian Edwards, Mrs. Luke Pryor Blackburn, Delia Claiborn [Mrs. S. B.] Buckner, and Mrs. William Stanly. In 1905 Helm sold her Todd family history to a Chambersburg, PA, publishing house. The history was serialized in the first four issues of *The Kittochtinny Magazine*. The magazine ceased publication with the fourth issue, and Helm donated her manuscript to the Kentucky Historical Society. Also available on microfilm. See G. Glenn Clift, *Guide to the Manuscripts of the Kentucky Historical Society* (Frankfort, KY: Kentucky Historical Society, 1955).

5,292. Keets, Louisa Caroline Warburton Fitzherbert
Papers. 1810-14. 25 pp.
Open. Published guide.
Kentucky Historical Society.
Keets established the Ladies Domestic Academy in 1807 in Washington, DC; in 1813 she moved to Washington County, KY, where she started a new domestic academy. Letters to her pupils and others concern troubles with her schools; her teaching career, which began in 1790; her home in Kentucky; rumors and criticisms of her conduct; and her husband, a clergyman who was related to the English poet John Keats. Also available on microfilm. See G. Glenn Clift, *Guide to the Manuscripts of the Kentucky Historical Society* (Frankfort, KY: Kentucky Historical Society, 1955).

5,293. Kentucky Seminary
Records. 1812-30. 35 pp.
Open. Published guide.
Kentucky Historical Society.
Minutes of meetings of this local school's trustees are also available on microfilm. See G. Glenn Clift, *Guide to the Manuscripts of the Kentucky Historical Society* (Frankfort, KY: Kentucky Historical Society, 1955).

5,294. Madison, Dolley (Payne)
Papers. 1810. 6 pp.
Open. Published guide.
Kentucky Historical Society.
Two letters by Madison (1768-1849) to General James Taylor in Newport, KY, tell of her husband and the French situation, news of Virginians, personal news, and other topics. Also available on microfilm. See G. Glenn Clift, *Guide to the Manuscripts of the Kentucky Historical Society* (Frankfort, KY: Kentucky Historical Society, 1955).

5,295. Potts, Eugenia Dunlap
Papers. Nd. 1 vol.
Open. Published and unpublished guides.
Kentucky Historical Society.
Diary of a Kentucky girl "in Dixie" is also available on microfilm. See G. Glenn Clift, *Guide to the Manuscripts of the Kentucky Historical Society* (Frankfort, KY: Kentucky Historical Society, 1955).

5,296. Smith, Laura Ford
Papers. Nd. 3 items.
Open. Published guide.
Kentucky Historical Society.
Smith was a novelist and poet. Manuscripts for her novel *The Hidden Tree* and her stories "Strange Silence of a Woman" and "A Powerful Claw." Also available on microfilm. See G. Glenn Clift, *Guide to the Manuscripts of the Kentucky Historical Society* (Frankfort, KY: Kentucky Historical Society, 1955).

5,297. Temple, Mary (Fall)
Papers. 1850-54. 13 items.
Open. Published guide.
Kentucky Historical Society.
Personal letters to her mother Mrs. P. S. Fall in Frankfort and to other family members. Also available on microfilm. See G. Glenn Clift, *Guide to the Manuscripts of the Kentucky Historical Society* (Frankfort, KY: Kentucky Historical Society, 1955).

HARRODSBURG

5,298. Shaker Journals
Collection. 1842-1911. 10 vols.
Open. Catalog card.
Harrodsburg Historical Society Library.
Business, spiritual, and personal journals kept by members of the Shaker community at Pleasant Hill, KY, which was founded in 1805. The journals reflect events within the Shaker colony and in the world at large. Included is the journal of Polly Harris for 1851 to 1858. The Pleasant Hill community was an outgrowth of the original Shaker settlements In New York and New England. Sister Mary Settle, the last Pleasant Hill Shaker, died in 1923. The Shakers, whose formal title was United Society of Believers in Christ's Second Appearing, believed that Christ would reappear in female form. Celibacy and open confession of sins were basic tenets of the faith.

LEXINGTON

5,299. Christian Churches (Disciples of Christ)
Records. 1866- . No size given.
Open. No guide.
Lexington Theological Seminary, Bosworth Memorial Library.
Includes information on women active in the Disciples of Christ nationally and in the South.

5,300. Kentucky Christian Woman's Board of Missions
Records. 1887-1933. Ca. 1 ft.
Open. No guide.
Lexington Theological Seminary, Bosworth Memorial Library.
Minutes and printed reports of the Board, founded in 1887. The Board, which is the most active missionary group of the Christian Churches (Disciples of Christ), later changed its name to Christian Women's Fellowship.

5,301. Bach, Pearl (Day)
Papers. 1890-1966. 3 boxes, 1 vol., and microfilm.
Open. Inventory.
University of Kentucky Archives.
Bach (1887-1968), the wife of William Everett Bach, was a genealogist and clubwoman born in Hazel Green, KY. Correspondence; historical and biographical sketches concerning Hazel Green, Hazel Green Academy, and the school's Former Students Association and alumni; scrapbook and yearbook of the Kentucky Mountain Club; Former Students Association records, including financial statements, committee reports, meeting records, and member lists; and photos. Bach graduated from Hazel Green Academy in 1905 and later moved to Lexington. She was elected historian of the Former Students Association in 1940 and served as president in 1951-52. She also was a charter member of the Kentucky Mountain Club and headed its sick and hospital committee from 1945 to 1958.

5,302. Breckinridge, Madeline (McDowell)
Papers. 1872-1920. 1003 items.
Open. Inventory.
University of Kentucky Archives.
An active participant in woman suffrage and civic groups, Breckinridge (1872-1920) was president of the Kentucky Equal Rights Association from 1912 to 1915 and in 1919. Chiefly pamphlets, broadsides, and other printed material reflecting Breckinridge's interest in such issues as woman suffrage, child labor, tuberculosis, home rule, labor laws and strikes, civic improvements, and the Lincoln School. Breckinridge attended the State College of Lexington and finished her education at Miss Porter's School at Farmington, CT. She served on the board of trustees of the Fayette County Tuberculosis Sanitarium and of the Fayette County Associated Charities, served on the executive committee of the Lexington Civic League, and was vice-president of the Kentucky Child Labor Commission. She married Desha Breckinridge in 1898.

5,303. Breckinridge, Mary Burch
Papers. 1864-68. 9 items.
Open. Card.
University of Kentucky Archives.
Letters from Breckenridge, the wife of John Cabell Breckinridge (1821-75), to her cousin Mrs. George W. Johnson in Georgetown, KY. Mary Breckinridge wrote the letters as she followed her husband during the last years of the Civil War and during the early postwar period. John Breckinridge was vice president in the James Buchanan administration.

5,304. Caudill, Rebecca
Papers. Ca. 1943-66. 9 boxes.
Open. Card.
University of Kentucky Archives.
Caudill (1899-) is a writer of fiction for children. Notes, background material, drafts, revised pages, and printer's copies of works, including "Barrie and Daughter" (1943); "Happy Little Family" (1947); "Tree of Freedom" (1949); "Saturday Cousins" (1953); "A Place Called Morning"; "Did You Carry the Flag Today, Charley?"; and "My Appalachia."

5,305. Clay, Laura
Papers. 1882-1941. Ca. 7000 items.
Open. Register.
University of Kentucky Archives.
Daughter of abolitionist and ambassador Cassius M. Clay, Laura Clay (1849-1941) was a suffragist. Correspondence, including letters from Anna Howard Shaw, president of the National American Woman Suffrage Association, and Ohio suffrage leader Harriet (Taylor) Upton; diaries; photo albums; scrapbooks; and other papers, including minutes, addresses, and programs of the Kentucky Equal Rights Association; yearbooks of the Woman's Club of Central Kentucky; ca. 1700 cards listing the membership of various suffrage groups; and pamphlets on woman suffrage, child welfare, civil service reform, peace, and temperance. Clay, a native of Madison County, KY, traveled to Oregon, Oklahoma, Arizona, Ohio, and New England in support of the suffrage movement. She was also active in the temperance movement and took part in the Woman's Club of Central Kentucky, the Episcopal church, the peace movement from 1915 to 1917, and the Democratic party. She sought the inclusion of women on the University of Kentucky faculty and on the staffs of state hospitals.

5,306. Collins Family
Papers. 1808-95. 2098 items.
Open. Register.
University of Kentucky Archives.
Correspondence of the family of Richard Collins (1824-89), an author, lawyer, and editor of the *Maysville Eagle*, include letters from women family members concerning births, deaths, visits, clothes, and church and school affairs. More than 200 letters were written by college women, including Lizzie Cox who attended school at Hubersville, KY, from 1845 to 1849, Annie Maria Collins while at Oxford Female College from 1863 to 1865, and Annie Collins's sister Mary Ellen who also attended Oxford Female College. The letters mention class texts, school conditions, and other items.

5,307. Darnell, Mrs. James Samuel
Papers. 1828-1954. 1 vol. and 730 items.
Open. Card and register.
University of Kentucky Archives.
Appointed the first director of Kentucky state parks in 1928, Darnell (1880-1957) served as the first president of the Frankfort, KY, LWV and of the Mothers' Club at the University of Kentucky. Correspondence; a diary of a trip by Darnell and her family through Ohio to New York and Washington, DC, in 1921; volume containing minutes, orders, dedication speeches, letters of invitation, expense accounts, budget analyses, and other items relating to the Kentucky State Park Commission; invitations to inaugurations of Presidents Roosevelt and Eisenhower; and clippings concerning Abraham Lincoln, Lincoln traditions in Kentucky, speeches, ceremonies, pictures, and persons involved with the state parks. She married Frankfort mayor James Samuel Darnell in 1901. She later directed the drive that secured $100,000 in federal funds for the George Rogers Clark Memorial in Pioneer Memorial State Park at Harrodsburg, KY. Active in Republican politics, Darnell also was a member of the Kentucky Federation of Women's Clubs, taught the women's Bible class at the First Methodist Church in Frankfort for more than 20 years, and was on the national board of the DAR.

5,308. Desha, Mary
Papers. 1868-1906. 920 items.
Open. Card.
University of Kentucky Archives.
[Miss] Desha was national secretary of the DAR. Correspondence, principally that with local DAR chapters regarding the group's rules and regulations, prospective members, and organizational problems.

5,309. Dicken, Troutman, and Balke Family
Papers. 1816-1945. 51 vols. and 2972 items.
Open. Register.
University of Kentucky Archives.
Correspondence, notebooks, account books, financial journals, bank books, plantation records, and other papers of Francis Troutman (1820-81), a lawyer and landowner in Lexington; his wife Anna (Dicken) Troutman (1839-1909); and her father General George D. Dicken (1809-74). Includes correspondence of Anna Troutman and letters of [Miss] Margaret Quickert, the fiancée of Frank Simmes Troutman, son of Francis and Anna Troutman.

5,310. Drake, Leah Bodine
Papers. 1918-64. 31 vols. and 110 items.
Open. Register.
University of Kentucky Archives.
A newspaperwoman and poet, [Miss] Drake (1904-64) contributed poetry to such magazines as *The Atlantic Monthly, Poetry, Commonweal, The New Yorker,* and *Saturday Review.* Scrapbooks containing copies of Drake's poems, reviews, correspondence, and other items make up the bulk of the collection, which also includes other correspondence, photos, and sections from *Who's Who in America* (1959) and *International Who's Who in Poetry* (1958). Born in Chanute, KS, Drake attended Miss Kendrick's School for Girls in Cincinnati from 1920 to 1922 and Hamilton College for Women in Lexington from 1923 to 1924. From 1941 to 1951 she was drama editor for the Evansville, IN, *Courier.* During 1957 and 1958 she was poetry books reviewer for *The Atlantic Monthly.* She also became society editor of the Parkersburg, WV, *News* in 1957. Drake's poetry has appeared in various anthologies; in 1950 she published her first book of poems *A Hornbook for Witches* and in 1956, a second volume, *This Tilting Dust.* She was co-editor and a contributor for *The Various Light,* an anthology of young English and American poets.

5,311. Engle, Mary Edith B.
Papers. 1940-45. 2 vols. and 75 items.
Open. Unpublished guide.
University of Kentucky Archives.
[Mrs.] Engle (1916-) was a member of the Women Air Force Service Pilots stationed at Love Field in Dallas. Operations and flight records of Engle, issues of the WASP newsletter, a WASP *Songbook,* the *Final Report on the Woman Pilot Program* by Jacqueline Cochran, and *Wings Over America,* a book containing information about the 5th Ferrying Group based at Love Field. WASPs were civilian volunteers who flew noncombat aircraft to relieve the wartime manpower shortage. One of the women's principal duties was ferrying aircraft between points in the US and Canada. The WASP program was deactivated in December 1944.

5,312. Evans, Catherine (Peter)
Papers. 1724-1968. 18 boxes and 3 packages.
Open. Register.
University of Kentucky Archives.
Includes an extensive Civil War diary of Frances Dallam Peter, daughter of physician, scientist, and educator Robert Peter, and a diary of Miriam Gratz, 1859-62. Catherine Evans transcribed about one-third of Frances Peter's diary, which was written in Kentucky.

5,313. Flanery, Mary (Elliott)
Papers. 1883-1972. 4 boxes and 2 packages.
Open. Description.
University of Kentucky Archives.
A newspaper correspondent, Flanery (1867-1933) was elected to the Kentucky House of Representatives in 1921, becoming the first woman to serve in a southern state legislature. Correspondence, family papers, family scrapbook compiled by Flanery's daughter Dawn (Flanery) Parker, poems by Dawn Parker, pamphlets, programs, political memorabilia, clippings, and other items. Flanery attended Barbourville College in West Virginia and the University of Kentucky. She began to teach in 1892 and married William Harvey Flanery in 1893. He established a law practice in Pikeville, KY, in 1895. Mary Flanery became associated with the Ashland *Daily Independent* in 1904 and later served as correspondent for many newspapers in Kentucky and neighboring states. As a member of the legislature, she introduced the bill that created the Teachers College at Morehead, KY, and sought improved educational conditions in Kentucky. Collection includes papers of the following Flanery children: Merle [Mrs. Davis Monroe] Howerton, Dawn [Mrs. H. Leslie] Parker, Dew [Mrs. Whayne W.] Haffler, and John Elliott Flanery. Merle Howerton was an active member of the Democratic Woman's Club of Kentucky.

5,314. Fouse Family
Papers. 1914-51. 448 items.
Open. Card.
University of Kentucky Archives.
L. B. Fouse was a Negro educator in Lexington while his wife worked with state and local groups seeking advancement of Negroes. Correspondence and personal papers reflect the Fouses' interest in educational and civic affairs and include information on Dunbar High School. Mrs. Fouse's papers, which make up about half of the collection, consist principally of material related to her activities in organizations.

5,315. Fox, Frances Barton
Papers. Nd. 6 boxes.
Open. Card.
University of Kentucky Archives.
[Miss] Fox (1887-1967) was the author of *The Heart of Arethusa* (Small, Maynard, 1918) and *Ridgeways* (Frederick A. Stokes Company, 1934). Typescripts of Fox's novels, short stories, and poems. A Bullitt County, KY, native, Fox was the sister of cartoonist Fontaine T. Fox.

5,316. Jeffrey Family
Papers. 1818-93. 3 manuscript boxes and ca. 700 items.
Open. Register.
University of Kentucky Archives.
The Jeffrey family came to the US from Scotland and built and operated gas plants in several cities. Rosa Griffith Vertner Jeffrey (1828-94), the wife of Alexander Jeffrey, was the author of two novels and three volumes of poetry and was a frequent contributor to magazines and newspapers. Family and business correspondence, including items regarding Rosa Jeffrey's publications; reports on the family's gas works and stock transactions; ledgers of the Lexington Gas Company for 1852 and 1853; and other material. Rosa Jeffrey was born in Natchez, MS, but moved to Lexington during her childhood; she was adopted and reared by her maternal aunt Mrs. Daniel Vertner after the death of her mother Mrs. John T. Griffith. At 17 she married Claude M. Johnson, a wealthy planter who divided his time between homes in Louisiana and Lexington. After his death in 1861 she married Jeffrey. The Jeffreys lived in Rochester, NY, during the Civil War but later returned to Lexington where Rosa Jeffrey died.

5,317. Lindley Family
Papers. 1810-1941. 78 vols. and 1215 items.
Open. Register.
University of Kentucky Archives.
Correspondence, daily journals and diaries, account books, scrapbooks, and manuscript textbooks of this Quaker family. Includes diaries of Martha H. Lindley from 1859 to 1905 and diaries of Kate Lindley from 1885 to 1919. Because of their antislavery attitudes, the Lindleys emigrated in about 1811 from near Salem, NC, to the Blue River settlement in Washington County, IN. The family became community leaders and aided in the establishment of the Blue River academy.

5,318. Neville, Linda
Papers. 1879-1959. Ca. 35,500 items.
Open. Inventory.
University of Kentucky Archives.
[Miss] Neville (1873-1961) founded the Kentucky Society for the Prevention of Blindness and worked particularly to help needy mountain people who suffered from eye disorders. General and personal correspondence, including items regarding individual cases; biographical and autobiographical material about Neville; a genealogy; photos; pamphlets; articles; clippings; awards; and other material, including papers of Neville's mother Mary Payne Neville, her sister Mary Neville, and others. Born and educated in Lexington, Neville received her BA in political economy from Bryn Mawr College in 1895. She returned to Lexington where she and her sister Mary helped local girls prepare for entrance examinations at eastern colleges. In 1908 Neville visited a social settlement and industrial school at the eastern Kentucky village of Hindman and discovered that there was a high incidence of trachoma in the region. She founded the Kentucky Society for the Prevention of Blindness in 1910. In 1914 she lobbied for the law requiring all new-born babies with diseased eyes to be reported to local boards of health and containing a provision for instruction of midwives. Neville's efforts and those of the Kentucky Medical Association led to the establishment in 1913 of three federal trachoma hospitals in rural areas. From 1908 to 1934 she carried on her work for needy persons with eye disorders without state appropriations. Soliciting reduced hospital rates, free medical treatment, and free transportation for indigent patients, she opened her home to persons seeking treatment at Lexington medical facilities. In 1934 the state legislature began annual appropriations to the state health department's section on trachoma and blindness to continue Neville's work.

5,319. Penney Family
Papers. 1835-39. 22 items.
Open. Unpublished guide.
University of Kentucky Archives.
Letters to the Penney family in London from relatives in the US, principally from two sisters, Marian and Margaret Penney. The two left England in 1834 to join their brother Thomas, who worked with a railroad line in Florida. Marian married Edward Winthrop while Margaret married Willard Presby. Both men became Episcopalian clergymen after attending Lexington Theological Seminary. The sisters' letters contain opinions about social, educational, and religious conditions as well as family news.

5,320. Perry Family
Papers. 1837-1952. 7 boxes.
Open. Register.
University of Kentucky Archives.
Roderick Perry was a lawyer, miller, bank president, steamboat owner, court clerk, church treasurer, and local political leader. Correspondence, canceled checks, business vouchers, photos, legal documents, and other papers. Includes letters from Anne Taliaferro to her fiancé William P. Perry, Jr., who was from Warsaw, KY. The letters, which make up the bulk of the collection, reflect a young woman's life at college from 1948 to 1952 and the couple's separations caused by school, family obligations, work commitments, and the Korean War. Also includes school notebooks of Martha Gayle.

5,321. Preston and Johnston
Papers. 1755-1962. Ca. 32,983 items.
Open. Inventory.
University of Kentucky Archives.
Correspondence, diaries, speeches, business papers, account books, scrapbooks, class notes, women's club programs, articles, and other papers of members of the family of William Preston (1816-87), a lawyer, congressman, minister-plenipotentiary to Spain, and Confederate general, and his wife Margaret Preston. Includes correspondence of Margaret Preston; ca. 8000 items of Sarah Brant McDowell (1850-1923), who in 1883 married Wickliffe Preston, the son of William and Margaret Preston; and correspondence, diaries, and an autobiography of Margaret Wickliffe Preston (1885-1964), daughter of Wickliffe and Sarah Preston who married Philip Preston Johnston II in 1917. Sarah McDowell Preston, a leader in Lexington society, twice served as president of the Woman's Club of Central Kentucky. Her papers include personal and family correspondence and women's club programs. Margaret (Preston) Johnston's correspondence includes letters she wrote to her mother from 1904 to 1906 while she was a student at Bryn Mawr College.

5,322. Republican Women's Club of Kentucky
Records. 1888-1965. 2 vols. and 23 items.
Open. Card.
University of Kentucky Archives.
The Club was founded in 1928 in Lexington. Scrapbooks, one containing minutes of the group's annual meetings through 1936 and the other consisting of Buehler family material. The second volume includes articles about the political activities and interests of [Mrs.] Betty Hicks Buehler, the Club's first president.

5,323. Semple, Ellen Churchill
Papers. 1900-32. 74 packages, 4 vols., and 84 items.
Open. Register.
University of Kentucky Archives.
A professor of anthrogeography, [Miss] Semple (1863-1932) graduated from Vassar at the age of 19, studied at the University of Leipzig in 1891 and 1892, and was a member of the Clark University faculty from 1921 to 1928. Personal correspondence, notes on subjects connected with her writing, photos, scrapbook, reprints, clippings, academic hood and gown, and two medals. The papers are devoted to anthrogeography, which is the study of the effect of geographic conditions on human history; her notes deal principally with her work on the Mediterranean region.

5,324. Shackleford, Elise
Papers. 1845-1952. 2 vols. and 413 items.
Open. Unpublished guide.
University of Kentucky Archives.
Shackleford (?-1957) was involved in the racing and breeding of horses. Correspondence, pedigree records for horses that Shackleford worked with from 1916 to 1930, and 257 photos.

5,325. Stewart, Cora (Wilson)
Papers. 1900-40. Ca. 40,000 items.
Open. Unpublished guide.
University of Kentucky Archives.
An educator and author who was particularly interested in adult illiteracy, Stewart (1876-?) headed state, national, and international commissions on illiteracy from 1914 to 1933. Correspondence, unpublished manuscripts, copies of her *Moonlight Schools* and her special readers for adults, statistics about adult illiteracy, records of Cora Stewart and Rowan County schools and of the Moonlight Schools, religious writings by Stewart, material for speeches, financial records, photos, scrapbooks, pamphlets, articles, clippings, and other material. Born in Rowan County, Stewart was educated at Morehead Normal School, National Normal University, and the University of Kentucky. She was superintendent of Rowan schools from 1910 to 1914 and founded the Moonlight Schools in Morehead in 1911. She presided over the illiteracy section of the World Conference on Education in 1923, 1925, 1927, 1929, and 1931; was chairman of the executive committee of President Hoover's Commission on Illiteracy from 1929 to 1933; and served on the executive committee of the National Education Association. Stewart also wrote a group of Country Life Readers and was a frequent contributor to magazines.

5,326. Thompson, May Ringo
Papers. 1780-1940. 110 items.
Open. Register.
University of Kentucky Archives.
Superintendent of Good Samaritan Hospital in Lexington, [Mrs.] Thompson (1868-1940) was an officer of the state and national DAR. Thompson's personal papers, collected during her work with the DAR, include speeches and certificates. Also contains Ringo family papers, including land grants, wills, and letters from a family member serving in the Kentucky legislature in Frankfort. Born in Fleming County, KY, Thompson attended the University of Kentucky and received training at Bellevue Hospital before beginning her work at Good Samaritan Hospital. She was treasurer of the Bryan Station Chapter of the DAR and held DAR posts of state recording secretary, state regent, and national vice-president general.

5,327. Todd Family
Papers. 1841-84. 12 items.
Open. Unpublished guide.
University of Kentucky Archives.
Consists chiefly of letters exchanged between girls attending school at Science Hill Academy in Shelbyville, KY, and members of their family at their home Chestnut Grove.

5,328. Wilson
Papers. 1743-1959. 70,000 items.
Open. Inventory.
University of Kentucky Archives.
Samuel M. Wilson (1871-1940) was a Lexington attorney, WWI soldier, church and civic leader, writer, and collector of books and manuscripts; his wife Mary Shelby Wilson was state woman's chairman for the James M. Cox campaign in 1920 and was among the first women named to the executive committee of Kentucky's Democratic party. Family and general correspondence, genealogical material, legal papers, notes on Samuel Wilson's various projects, and other material, including items regarding Mary Wilson's political activities.

5,329. Wilson: Democratic Woman's Club
Papers. 1910-45. Ca. 1000 items.
Open. Inventory.
University of Kentucky Archives.
Chiefly consists of papers of Mary Shelby Wilson, including items relating to the Kentucky Democratic Woman's Club, the Kentucky Equal Rights Association, and the state LWV. Wilson, the wife of Samuel M. Wilson, was a leader in the early days of women's political participation in Kentucky.

5,330. Women's Liberation Movement
Collection. 1967-74. 6 boxes and 1 package.
Open. Inventory.
University of Kentucky Archives.
Correspondence and clippings from local and national publications deal principally with efforts to gain support for the women's movement on the University of Kentucky campus. Areas of particular interest were equal employment opportunity, abortion, and politics. Includes material regarding University of Kentucky personnel, the Kentucky Women's Political Caucus, the University of Kentucky Women's Studies Committee, and the Reproductive Freedom League of Lexington as well as a report concerning the status of women at the University.

LOUISVILLE

5,331. Barkley, Marianne
Papers. 1828. 1 item.
Open. Card catalog.
The Filson Club.
Letter from Barkley in Nazareth, KY, to her sister J. H. Barkley of Fayette County, KY, in which she describes her life at college and a religious ceremony that took place there. She writes that Naneen Tarascon led a procession of 50 girls; Barkley also mentions a visit to John Rowan's home.

5,332. Breckinridge and Marshall
Papers. 1867-68. 9 items.
Open. Card catalog.
The Filson Club.
Correspondence from Mary Cyrene (Burch) Breckinridge (1822-1906) to her cousin Ann (Viley) [Mrs. George W.] Johnson of Scott County, KY. The letters were written while her husband John Cabell Breckinridge was in Canada and Europe during his exile following the Civil War. Also includes undated letters from Dalton, GA, and Big Lick Station, VA.

5,333. Brown Family
Papers. 1799-1846. 56 items.
Open. Card catalog.
The Filson Club.
Family correspondence of John Brown, a US senator from Frankfort, KY, consists chiefly of letters written by his wife Margaretta (Mason) Brown (1772-1838) concerning family matters, including the health and education of their sons Mason and Orlando. Also includes scattered references to political and diplomatic affairs.

5,334. Clay, Cassius Marcellus
Papers. 1844-1907. 2 boxes.
Open. Card catalog.

The Filson Club.
Papers of Clay (1810-1903), a statesman, include correspondence of his daughter Mary Barr Clay (1839-?), a leader of the women's movement. Her correspondence contains letters from Susan B. Anthony and Lucy Stone concerning woman suffrage as well as letters from Alice Stone Blackwell, Phoebe W. Couzins, Isabella B. Hooker, Emily B. Ketcham, Thomas Witherell Palmer, and May Wright Sewall. Also contains scrapbook of clippings about the Civil War, poetry, recipes, and items of interest to farmers and gardeners; poems addressed to Mary Clay; and two letters from Russians to her mother. Mary Clay was married to Major J. Frank Herrick for a time, but she resumed the use of her maiden name after the marriage ended in divorce.

5,335. Clay, Henry
Papers. Ca. 1844-46. 3 items.
Open. Card catalog.
The Filson Club.
Correspondence of Clay includes three letters from Clay to Octavia Walton Le Vert, an Alabama writer, in which he expresses his hope that [Mrs.] Le Vert will escape a yellow fever epidemic, comments on the corrupt bargaining charges leveled against him by Andrew Jackson, and discusses the war with Mexico, his upcoming representation of a man charged with murder, and family matters.

5,336. Clay, Mary Barr
Papers. 1888. 1 item.
Open. Card catalog.
The Filson Club.
Writing from Whitehall in Madison County, KY, Clay (1839-?) thanks E. F. Strickland, a minister, for including her in his list of renowned women and says she plans to continue working for women's rights.

5,337. Colonial Dames of America
Records. 1907. 1 vol.
Open. Card catalog.
The Filson Club.
A book of remembrances of the Dames' Kentucky Society that was presented to Mrs. Simon Bolivar Buckner by the Louisville Library Committee. The volume is autographed by Committee members.

5,338. Daughters of America, Baxter Council 34
Records. 1917-25. 2 vols.
Open. Card catalog.
The Filson Club.
Minute books of this Louisville group.

5,339. De Navarro, Mary (Anderson)
Papers. Nd. 9 items.
Open. Card catalog.
The Filson Club.
Correspondence by or about [Madame Antonio] Navarro (1859-1940), an actress from Louisville; article about her published in 1939 in the Louisville *Courier-Journal;* biographical notes; and an 1886 diary of Howard Miller in which he describes a dinner with de Navarro at his home. Includes a letter from de Navarro to Levi Bloom in Louisville in which she says she lives in England because the moist climate suits her health and that she will send photos of herself and her son, who lectured on prehistoric archaeology at the University of Cambridge and organized archaeological expeditions. De Navarro was the author of *A Few Memories* (New York: Harper and Brothers, 1896).

5,340. Female High School
Records. 1867-1913. 35 vols.
Open. Unpublished guide.
The Filson Club.
Attendance, deportment, and grade records; admission examination results with pupil names, ages, states of birth, ward schools, and examination grades for the years 1876 through 1881; and an historical sketch of the local school.

5,341. Friends of Kentucky Libraries
Records. 1937-57. Ca. 470 items.
Open. Card catalog.
The Filson Club.
Successor to the Kentucky Citizens Library Committee, founded in 1937, and the Kentucky Citizens Library League, organized in 1939, this group adopted its present name in 1944. Constitutions and bylaws, minutes of the Friends and the Library League, treasurers' reports and financial statements, expense accounts, account book for 1947 and 1948 of the Presbyterian bookmobile, correspondence, record book and lists of officers and members, scrapbook of material about the Kentucky bookmobile project, publicity material, clippings, and other items.

5,342. Giles, Janice (Holt)
Papers. 1951. 1 p.
Open. Card catalog.
The Filson Club.
Letter from Giles (1909-), an author in Knifley, KY, to The Filson Club librarian requesting information on William Whitley and Benjamin Logan.

5,343. Grigsby Family
Papers. 1818-84. Ca. 5241 items.
Open. Card catalog.
The Filson Club.
Papers of Susan Preston (Shelby) Grigsby (1830-91) of Traveller's Rest near Danville, KY; her father Alfred Shelby (1804-32), youngest son of Governor Isaac Shelby of Kentucky; her mother Virginia (Hart) Shelby Breckinridge (1809-59); her stepfather Robert Jefferson Breckinridge (1800-71), a Presbyterian minister and president of Jefferson College in Cannonsburgh, PA; her husband John Warren Grigsby (?-1877), a general in the Confederate Army; a few papers of their children; and papers of the allied Gibson family of Louisiana and the Hart and Wallace families of Kentucky. Susan Grigsby's papers include letters concerning her education at Picot's School for Young Ladies at Philadelphia, her marriage and family life, travel in Europe in 1851 and 1852, her mother's domestic troubles, slavery, the Civil War in Kentucky, confiscation of her property and impressment of slave labor, her husband's military service, financial difficulties she encountered following his death, and her loss of Traveller's Rest in 1883. Also includes her statements of personal and household expenses from 1848 to 1884, canceled checks, receipts for horses and mules confiscated in 1862, land and legal records, and items relating to her litigation with her stepfather, with Rebecca Tevis Hart, and with others. Her correspondents include her mother, stepfather, husband, and other family members. Papers of Virginia Shelby Breckinridge, second wife of Robert J. Breckinridge, consist of letters from her daughter and son-in-law, her second husband, and others; statements of account and receipts; canceled checks; memoranda; and miscellaneous material about social life and the economy in central Kentucky, education, slavery, the history of the Presbyterian Church, and European travel in 1851 and 1852. Papers of Louisiana Grigsby, daughter of John Warren Grigsby and Susan Grigsby, include correspondence, English compositions, and two statements of accounts.

5,344. Guardian Angel Society
Records. 1874. 1 vol.
Open. Card catalog.
The Filson Club.
The Society was a New Castle, KY, temperance organization formed by young ladies to safeguard society from drunkenness among young men. Minute book containing a list of men who supported the Society, memoranda, and recipes.

5,345. Hackett
Papers. 1879-88. 1 box.
Open. Card catalog.
The Filson Club.
Letter from Joseph Hackett, a Louisville manufacturer of metal caskets; two letters from his daughter Mabel Hackett; reports by Mabel from Hampton College in Louisville; English compositions written by Mabel and her sister Belle R. Hackett while studying at Hampton College; sketch book of Belle Hackett; and other material.

5,346. Hill, Patty Smith
Papers. 1878-1942. 1245 items.
Open. Unpublished guide.
The Filson Club.
[Miss] Hill (1868-1946) directed the kindergarten program at Columbia University Teachers College and wrote books and articles about kindergarten and elementary education. Correspondence; transcripts of speeches, articles, and lectures; papers on kindergarten, nursery schools, teacher education, and other topics; an autobiographical sketch; material about her professional trip to Russia in 1929, her honorary degree from Columbia University in 1929, the Patty Smith Hill Fund, the Utopia Children's House, Hilltop, the Patty Smith Hill Farm, and other plans to aid needy children during the depression; lists of books Hill co-authored and material she wrote about the work of Friedrich Froebel, Anna E. Bryan, Susan E. Blow, and Maria Montessori; scrapbooks; photos; clippings; and other material. In her correspondence she discusses her move from Louisville to New York, speaking engagements, activities at Columbia, and establishment and direction of nursery schools. Also contains biographical material about other members of the Hill family and a paper by Pearl Allen Williams about the kindergarten movement in Louisville from 1881 to 1930.

5,347. Jeffrey, Rosa Griffith (Vertner) Johnson
Papers. Nd. 1 vol. and 148 items.
Open. Card catalog.
The Filson Club.
[Mrs. Alexander] Jeffrey (1828-94) was a poet and author. Correspondence; poems by Rosa Jeffrey and others dedicated to her; copyright certificate from 1857 for her poems; accounts of the sale of her writings between 1857 and 1881; a release of a claim against Jeffrey for sale of a Negro woman who proved to be unsound; powers of attorney; statement of cotton captured in 1864 at her plantation near Vicksburg, MS; a claim against the US for damages to the residence of Jeffrey's mother [Mrs.] Elizabeth Vertner during the Civil War; insurance policies; tax receipts from 1864 to 1892; and a scrapbook containing clippings of Jeffrey's poems. Correspondence, chiefly literary, contains some family letters, including those of her husband describing Lexington, KY, during the Civil War. Correspondents include David Bates, Stockton Bates, Charles Augustus Davis, James Cephas Derby, the firm of Derby and Jackson, Julia Deane Freeman, Emily V. Mason, and others.

5,348. Jennie Casseday Rest Cottage
Records. 1893-1901. 78-page vol.
Open. Card catalog.
The Filson Club.
The Cottage, located from 1889 to 1899 in Jefferson and Oldham counties in Kentucky, was founded by Jennie Casseday for the benefit of Louisville working girls during the summer months. Record book kept by Casseday's sister Fannie (Casseday) Duncan, president of the Cottage's board of managers; record of the Cottage's location; lists of officers, members, contributors, donations, and committees; the board of managers' ratification in 1896 of Duncan's action in agreeing

to buy Beech Moor, located near Pewee Valley, for $5,000; leaflets; and clippings.

5,349. Johnston, Annie (Fellows)
Papers. 1895-1911. 5 items.
Open. Card catalog.
The Filson Club.
An author, [Mrs. William "Will" L.] Johnston (1863-1931) was best known for her Little Colonel books. Three pieces of correspondence, a calling card, and a copy of Johnston's *In the Desert of Waiting* (Boston: L. C. Page and Co., 1905). Includes a letter to Mrs. Paul A. McQuaid congratulating her on the birth of her daughter and a letter to Roberts Brothers in Boston in which she says she would be very glad to have "Joel" published in London for a five percent royalty.

5,350. Johnston Family
Papers. 1798-1943. 871 items.
Open. Calendar.
The Filson Club.
Papers of Confederate general Albert Sidney Johnston (1803-62) and his son William Preston Johnston (1831-99) contain papers of the family of Albert Johnston's first wife Henrietta (Preston) Johnston and papers of other female family members. Much of the correspondence concerns military affairs during the Civil War, including administrative communications received by Albert Johnston and letters received by his son, an aide-de-camp to Jefferson Davis. Contains correspondence between William Johnston and his wife Rosa Duncan Johnston (1831-85), discussing wartime conditions and letters from the time of William Johnston's imprisonment and exile. Later correspondence concerns his career from 1866 to 1877 as a faculty member at Washington and Lee College and as president of Louisiana State and Tulane universities. Included are letters of his daughters. Women correspondents include Varina (Howell) [Mrs. Jefferson] Davis; Margaret (Junkin) Preston; Cecilia Viets Dakin Hamilton; Rosa Griffith (Vertner) Johnson Jeffrey; Mary Anna Randolph (Custis) [Mrs. Robert Edward] Lee; Caroline Hancock Preston, wife of William Preston, Jr.; Maria Preston Pope, wife of John Pope, Jr.; and Rosa Duncan Johnston [Mrs. George Anderson] Robinson.

5,351. Kentucky Federation of Music Clubs
Records. 1921-63. 12 vols.
Open. Card catalog.
The Filson Club.
Minute book, correspondence, notes, scrapbooks, and other items. The scrapbooks deal with varying subjects, including the MacDowell Music Study Club, the Federation's history from 1921 to 1954, and Kentucky music as presented by the Federation's Senior Clubs.

5,352. Kentucky Federation of Women's Clubs, Louisville Literature Club
Records. 1909-14. 158 pp.
Open. Card catalog.
The Filson Club.
Minutes include the number of members present at meetings, works read, topics of papers presented, reports about cash on hand and dues, and an account of the presentation of a bust of Madison Cawein to the Louisville Free Public Library.

5,353. Lincoln, Mary (Todd)
Papers. 1856. 1 item.
Open. Card catalog.
The Filson Club.
Letter from Springfield, IL, of [Mrs. Abraham] Lincoln (1818-82) to Emilie Todd [Mrs. Ben Hardin] Helm in which she comments on the recent presidential election and observes that, "Altho' Mr. L. is, or was a Fremont man, you must not include him with so many of those, who belong to that party, an Abolitionist. In principles he is far from it—All he desires is, that slavery shall not be extended, let it remain where it is. My weak woman's heart was too Southern in feeling to sympathise with any but Fillmore." She criticizes immigrants and discusses acquaintances and their activities. Published in Justin G. Turner, *Mary Todd Lincoln: Her Life and Letters* (New York, 1972) and in part in William H. Townsend, *Lincoln and the Bluegrass* (Lexington, KY, 1955).

5,354. Louisville Equal Rights Association
Records. 1889-95. 1 vol.
Open. Card catalog.
The Filson Club.
Minute book containing constitution and bylaws, minutes, and a membership list.

5,355. Louisville Girls High School, Alumnae Club
Records. 1924-41. 81 items.
Open. Card catalog.
The Filson Club.
Primarily a social welfare group, the Club loaned money to alumnae and participated in community, social, and cultural events. Financial statements, reports, correspondence, programs, clippings, the school song, and miscellaneous material.

5,356. Mayors of Louisville
Records. 1870-1909. 24 boxes.
Open. Unpublished guide.
The Filson Club.
Records principally consist of employment applications and recommendations, complaints about municipal services, requests for information or charity, and letters from other city officials, local businessmen, commercial organizations, and Kentucky political figures. Also includes material relating to city contracts and ordinances, petitions, construction proposals and bids, requisitions, payroll lists, receipts, and General Council resolutions. Two of the folders contain material relating to woman's suffrage.

5,357. National League for Woman's Service, Social and Welfare Division
Records. 1917-29. 1 folder and 6 vols.
Open. Card catalog.
The Filson Club.
Minutes, bankbook, correspondence, and records of this Kentucky group. Much of the material deals with the Khaki Club, which was established in Louisville in 1917 by members of the local League and operated until 1919.

5,358. Order of the Eastern Star, Naomi Chapter 14
Records. 1902-45. 14 vols.
Open. Card catalog.
The Filson Club.
Minutes, accounts, and registers of this Louisville Chapter.

5,359. Preston Family
Papers. 1780-1963. 587 items.
Open. Calendar.
The Filson Club.
Papers of this prominent Virginia and Kentucky family, most of which cover the period from 1788 to 1866 and were created by or written to Major William Preston (1770-1821), an early Louisville settler; his wife Caroline (Hancock) Preston (1785-1847); and their children. Correspondence, land and legal records, military papers, certificates and grants, and genealogical material on the Preston, Hancock, Joyes, Lee, Woodson, and Venable families. Much of the correspondence was written by women and concerns the management of farms, household duties such as overseeing weaving and canning, and social activities, including parties and weddings. Principal female correspondents are Caroline Preston and her five daughters: Maria (Preston) Pope, wife of John Pope, Jr.; Henrietta (Preston) [Mrs. Albert Sidney] Johnston; Josephine (Preston) [Mrs. Jason] Rogers; Caroline (Preston) [Mrs. Abram R.] Woolley; and Susan (Preston) Christy Hepburn.

5,360. Rice, Alice Caldwell (Hegan)
Papers. 1903-35. 8 items.
Open. Card catalog.
The Filson Club.
Rice (1870-1942) was a writer best known for her book *Mrs. Wiggs of the Cabbage Patch.* Correspondence, including a letter describing the wedding in 1902 of Alice Hegan and Cale Young Rice; a 1930 letter in which Alice Rice speaks of film rights for "The Buffer," lists her works that had been filmed to date, and says she is eager to have a sound movie made of one of her works; a 1903 letter in which she says she plans to go south soon to gather material for a New York magazine story to protest child labor in mills and factories; and a letter in which she declines an honorary degree from Rollins College.

5,361. Roberts, Elizabeth Madox
Papers. 1921. 1 item.
Open. Card catalog.
The Filson Club.
Manuscript of a collection of poems "Under the Tree" that Roberts (1881-1941), a writer, prepared for [Mrs.] Mary Blythe McElroy.

5,362. Rowley, Gifford, and Clegg
Papers. Nd. 1 box.
Open. Card catalog.
The Filson Club.
Family papers of Helen (Gifford) Clegg of Louisville and William Clegg, whom she married in 1893, include an 1841 proposal of marriage written by Erastus Rowley (1814-97), a clergyman and educator, to Martha Morris; letters from William Clegg of Lafayette, LA, to his future wife Mary Collins during his Civil War service in Virginia as ordnance sergeant in the 2nd Louisiana Regiment; letters from Thomas E. Darden of the Army of Northern Virginia to "Miss Mary" describing the Battle of Chancellorsville; military records of family members, including the Revolutionary War record of Helen Clegg's ancestor Aaron Rowley of Berkshire County, MA; biographical notes and clippings about Erastus Rowley; genealogies of William Clegg and Harley Nelson Gifford; Confederate scrapbook of clippings kept by Martha [Mrs. Erastus] Rowley during the Civil War; clippings announcing the marriage of Helen Gifford and William Clegg; copies of Rowley Bible records; and other papers. Erastus Rowley, who earned a bachelor's degree from Union College in 1834, served as president of Ohio Wesleyan Female College; of Female College at Athens, TN; of DePauw Female College in New Albany, IN, from 1869 to 1881; and of Kentucky College for Young Ladies in Pewee Valley, KY, from 1882 to 1896.

5,363. Savage, Frank A., and Savage, Mary
Papers. 1854-65. 28 items.
Open. Card catalog.
The Filson Club.
Correspondence between Frank Savage and his wife Mary of Germantown, KY, during periods in which he was in Newark, OH, managing his oil refining business. The letters discuss personal concerns, business transactions, land in the Lake Superior region, the Civil War's effect on the Savages and their neighbors, and Civil War battles. Also contains comments about Negroes and hiring-out practices for slaves.

5,364. Shaker Colony at Pleasant Hill, KY
Records. 1815-1917. 40 vols.
Open. Card catalog.
The Filson Club.
Records of this colony of the United Society of Believers in Christ's Second Appearing, called Shakers, include lists of members, business accounts, and daily entries of activities. Includes a family journal kept from 1843 to 1871 by the order

of the Deaconesses of the East House and a journal kept from 1860 to 1884 by the Sisters of the United Society. The latter volume records the Sisters' work in cleaning, cooking, sewing, weaving, and other tasks and notes colony events. Also contains hymn books with hymns written by women of the colony.

5,365. Tachau, Jean (Brandeis)
Papers. 1970. 1 item.
Open. Card catalog.
The Filson Club.
Memoir in which [Mrs. Charles G.] Tachau (1894-1978), niece of US Supreme Court justice Louis Brandeis, describes her experiences from 1917 to 1970 as a social welfare volunteer in Kentucky; her efforts were related primarily to child welfare and planned parenthood. She mentions many social workers and political leaders in her narrative.

5,366. Tafel, Pauline (Autenrieth)
Papers. 1907. 1 item.
Open. Card catalog.
The Filson Club.
Autobiographical sketch of Tafel (1833-?) in which she tells of the emigration of the Autenrieth family from Stuttgart, Germany, to Cincinnati in 1849; her marriage to Karl Tafel; farming in Ohio and Indiana; their removal to Kentucky in 1863; and later family history. The sketch, written in Newport, KY, was translated from German in 1939 by Mary Konersman Tafel.

5,367. Verhoeff, Mary
Papers. 1907-60. 16 boxes.
Open. Card catalog.
The Filson Club.
Correspondence, articles, essays, notes, and speeches by [Miss] Verhoeff (1871?-1962). Subjects include the early history of the Louisville area; exploration, navigation, and shipping on the Ohio and Mississippi rivers; coal and coal mining; and other topics. The speeches include one given in honor of [Miss] Ludie Kinkead upon her retirement in 1953 from The Filson Club. Also contains material regarding Verhoeff's membership in clubs and committees.

5,368. WAC Mothers' Association
Records. 1943-48. 1 box.
Open. Card catalog.
The Filson Club.
Constitution and bylaws, president's messages, reports of annual national conferences, lists of officers, quarterly and semi-annual reports, copies of the official prayer, form letters, and miscellaneous material of the national Association, which had headquarters in Chicago. Constitution, notes, correspondence, and lists of members and activities of the Louisville chapter.

5,369. Woman's Auxiliary, Battery A, 138th Field Artillery
Records. 1917-31. 23-page vol.
Open. Card catalog.
The Filson Club.
Ledger containing minutes, accounts, and description of projects undertaken and events sponsored in Louisville by the Auxiliary, formed by Colonel W. H. Colston to assist the First Kentucky Regiment.

5,370. Women's Synodical Society in the State of Kentucky
Records. 1875-1954. 1 box.
Open. No guide.
Louisville Presbyterian Theological Seminary.
An organization of Presbyterian women, the Women's Missionary Society of the Synod of Kentucky was split in 1876 into the Women's Home Missionary Society and the Women's Foreign Missionary Society; in 1942 the groups were merged again. Minutes of annual meetings, treasurers' records, information on apportionments, reports, bulletins, programs, clippings, and photos. Includes a reprint of an 1889 article by clergyman George P. Hays, "May Women Speak?"; a report on causes of unrest among church women by the special committee to the general council of the national Presbyterian church; and an article by the special committee on women's organizations' financial cooperation with the church.

5,371. Baptist Woman's Missionary Union Training School and the Carver School of Missions and Social Work
Records. 1907-62. Ca. 36 cu.ft.
Open. No guide.
Southern Baptist Theological Seminary Library.
The institution, which operated from 1907 to 1962, prepared women for missionary and church work by providing training in religious education, theology, missions, and social work. Records of the governing board, administrative papers of the presidents, student records, photos, newsletter, published history and catalogs, and other items. The school was known for many years as Woman's Missionary Union Training School; in 1953 the name was changed to Carver School of Missions and Social Work, the title it retained until it merged with the Southern Baptist Theological Seminary in 1962.

5,372. Heines, Sister Virginia, S.C.N.
Records. 1936-76. 3 ft.
Open. Unpublished guide.
Spalding College Archives.
Now a professor emeritus, Sister Virginia Heines (1896-) was a professor of chemistry from 1934 to 1970 and a National Science Foundation professor in 1965. Correspondence, worksheets, slides, reprints, and other papers. She has done research concerning carbohydrates, plant biochemistry, and cancer. She earned a PhD.

5,373. Spalding College
Records. 1920-76. Ca. 250 cu.ft.
Open. Unpublished guide.
Spalding College Archives.
Founded in 1920 by the sisters of Charity of Nazareth as Nazareth College, Spalding College was the first Catholic senior college for women in Kentucky. Annals; personal papers of faculty, students, and alumnae; correspondence; notebooks; photos; scrapbooks; bulletins and catalogs; alumnae newsletters; commencement programs; faculty publications; and other records. Includes files of Sister Mary Charlotte Fowler, S.C.N., who was president of the school from 1961 to 1969, and of Sister Eileen Egan, S.C.N., president of Spalding College after 1969; scientific research material, 1936-76, of Sister Virginia Heines, S.C.N.; and histories of the nursing department and of the Nazareth College Guidance Center and Psychological Clinic. The school, which became coeducational in 1969, integrates liberal education and studies for professional service, especially in nursing, social welfare, education, and library science. The school operated Kentucky's first collegiate nursing program.

5,374. Di Prima, Diane
Papers. 1953-66. 75 items.
Open. No guide.
University of Louisville Library, Rare Book Room.
Di Prima (1934-) is a poet and playwright. Business and personal correspondence, diary, literary manuscripts, notebooks, and notes.

5,375. Thomas, Jeannette Bell
Papers. 1931-68. 227 items.
Open. No guide.
University of Louisville Library, School of Music Library.
Thomas (1881-), who is known as "The Traipsin' Woman," collected and performed Appalachian folklore. Correspondence, literary manuscripts, audiotapes, videotapes, photos, scrapbooks, books, and memorabilia provide information about Appalachian culture. Also contains accounts about Thomas's reception by mountain people. The University's Photographic Archives holds ca. 890 photos pertaining to Thomas.

5,376. Bendl, Gerta
Oral history. 1976. 1 tape.
Open. Unpublished guide.
University of Louisville, Oral History Center.
A Kentucky legislator, [Mrs.] Bendl is a former Louisville city alderman. Interview in which she discusses her early life, education, and her new career in Kentucky politics. She also speaks about her opinions of women in public life and the difficulties they face. Events discussed in the interview date from 1935 to 1976.

5,377. Braden, Anne
Oral history. 1975. 1 tape.
Open. Unpublished guide.
University of Louisville, Oral History Center.
Braden, who remains active in Kentucky's integration movement, has been a civil rights activist for many years; she and her husband Carl Braden were arrested on sedition charges several times during the 1950s. In her interview, Anne Braden discusses her civil rights activities, family history, her education, and her impressions of how the US has changed since the 1950s and 1960s. Her reminiscences deal with events dating from 1925 to 1975.

5,378. Butler, Hilda H.
Oral history. 1977. 1 tape.
Open. Unpublished guide.
University of Louisville, Oral History Center.
Butler is vice-president and secretary of the Mammoth Life Insurance Company in Louisville. Interview in which she discusses her father's founding of Mammoth Life, one of the first large black-owned companies in Kentucky. She also comments on difficulties that black-owned businesses and black women, in particular, encounter in the business world. Reminiscing about events dating back to 1912, she speaks of her early life, education, and her family's history.

5,379. Crowell, Vivian G.
Oral history. 1977. 1 tape.
Open. Unpublished guide.
University of Louisville, Oral History Center.
For 50 years [Mrs.] Crowell was the librarian at the West Branch Library, the first library to extend its services to Louisville's black community. In her interview, Crowell describes the conditions under which she and other black women worked for many years and the events that preceded the opening of the segregated libraries. She also speaks about her family, her education, and her career. Her reminiscences deal with events dating from 1900 to 1977.

5,380. Freibert, Sister Lucy
Oral history. 1976. 1 tape.
Open. Unpublished guide.
University of Louisville, Oral History Center.
A University of Louisville professor who holds a PhD in English, Freibert is a member of the Sisters of Charity of Nazareth, a Catholic teaching and nursing order. In the interview, Freibert discusses her early life and education, her varied career, and her involvement in the women's movement in Kentucky. She also comments on the need for more religious women to become involved in social change and comments about how her involvement affected her life.

5,381. Haddad, Carol
Oral history. 1976. 1 tape.
Open. Unpublished guide.
University of Louisville, Oral History Center.
In her interview, [Mrs.] Haddad, a member of the

Jefferson County Board of Education, talks about her early life, education, and her new career in city politics. She discusses her term on the Board of Education, desegregation of the Louisville school system, and the first year of court-ordered school busing.

5,382. Harry, Ruth, and Crowell, Vivian
Oral history. 1977. 2 tapes.
Open. Unpublished guide.
University of Louisville, Oral History Center.
[Mrs.] Harry and [Mrs.] Crowell were librarians at the West Branch Library of the Louisville Free Public Library, the first library in Louisville and one of the first in the South to open its doors to blacks. Reminiscing about events from 1920 onward, the two discuss their lives as black women and events that preceded the opening of libraries to the black community.

5,383. Jackson, Abbie Clement
Oral history. 1977. 3 tapes.
Open. Unpublished guide.
University of Louisville, Oral History Center.
Interview in which [Mrs.] Jackson tells of her activities in Louisville's black community, particularly in the African Methodist Episcopal Zion Church. She also speaks of her family history and her education.

5,384. Minor, Susan St. Clair
Oral history. 1977. 1 tape.
Open. Unpublished guide.
University of Louisville, Oral History Center.
A 1919 graduate of Central High School and a 1921 graduate of the Louisville Normal School, [Mrs.] Minor taught for many years in the Louisville school system, first in black schools and then in integrated schools. Seventy-eight at the time of her interview, Minor discussed her family history, her education, her career, and the history of Louisville's black community. Central High School, from which she graduated, was the only high school open to Louisville blacks for many years.

5,385. Montgomery, Margie
Oral history. 1977. 1 tape.
Open. Unpublished guide.
University of Louisville, Oral History Center.
[Mrs.] Montgomery is president of the right-to-life group in Louisville; she is also a state organizer for the right-to-life movement. Interview in which she describes her group's activities, her own involvement, and the work of other women in the organization.

5,386. Mulvihill, Mary Margaret
Oral history. 1976. 1 tape.
Open. Unpublished guide.
University of Louisville, Oral History Center.
Interview with Mulvihill, who was Louisville's fourth ward alderman from 1975 to 1977. She discusses her early life, education, and her election to the Board of Aldermen. She also talks about her political contributions and the need for women to be involved in public life. She mentions difficulties that women face in public politics.

5,387. Sales, Estella
Oral history. 1976. 1 tape.
Open. Unpublished guide.
University of Louisville, Oral History Center.
Sales is a young black poet who lives in Louisville. She was interviewed about her early life and education; she also commented on the women's movement and how it affects black women.

5,388. Stovall, Thelma
Oral history. 1976. 1 tape.
Open. Unpublished guide.
University of Louisville, Oral History Center.
Interview in which [Mrs.] Stovall, the first woman lieutenant governor of Kentucky, discusses her personal history, her education, and her 25 years of service in public offices in Kentucky. She also comments on her involvement in the women's movement and emphasizes the long struggle for passage of the Equal Rights Amendment in the state.

5,389. Archives of the Ursuline Sisters of the Immaculate Conception
Records. 1858- . 150 Hollinger boxes, ca. 200 vols., 9 microfilm reels, and ca. 500 tapes.
Open. Unpublished guide.
Ursuline Sisters of the Immaculate Conception.
Constitutions, written and taped minutes of general chapters, correspondence, history, manuscripts, dissertations, administrative records of the congregation, records from Ursuline College and other schools, oral history tapes, tapes of lectures, slides, photos, scrapbooks, high school yearbooks, prayer manuals, index cards concerning church and state relations in Kentucky in the late 1950s, pamphlets, books, and other records. The chief activity of the congregation, which was founded in Louisville in 1858, is education and teaching Christian living.

MAPLE MOUNT

5,390. Archives
Records. 1874- . 24 drawers, 40 vols., and 5 tapes.
Access restricted. No guide.
Mount Saint Joseph Ursuline Motherhouse.
Cashbooks; correspondence, including letters from bishops and priests regarding the work of members and letters of mothers superior; diaries; writings by members; photos; scrapbooks; and other records of this community of religious women, which was founded in 1874 in St. Joseph, KY. The sisters are involved in training prospective members and teaching college, high school, elementary school, and kindergarten.

MELBOURNE

5,391. Convent Archives
Records. 1889- . No size given.
Closed. No guide.
Sisters of Divine Providence, St. Anne Convent.
Council meeting minutes, correspondence, annals, photos, memorabilia, and other records of the congregation, which was established in the US in 1889 in Newport, KY, and is principally concerned with teaching, nursing, and, more recently, social work. Includes correspondence between superiors general and American bishops regarding the congregation's first foundation in the US and annals of schools, homes, hospitals, and other missions.

MIDWAY

5,392. Alumni Files
Records. 1849-1976. Several drawers.
Open. No guide.
Midway College.
Files concerning individual graduates of Midway College include names, dates of graduation, addresses, and other information. The College was founded in 1847 as Kentucky Female Orphan School.

5,393. Midway College
Records. 1847- . Ca. 25 file drawers.
Open. Unpublished guide.
Midway College.
Chartered as the Kentucky Female Orphan School in 1847, Midway College has evolved into a two-year women's college. Students at the College are required to work on campus to help pay for their education. Correspondence and photos of faculty members, most of whom were women, and of students; record books; catalogs; bulletins; a history of the school, published in 1930; and other records. The Kentucky Female Orphan School was founded by officials of the local Christian Church (Disciples of Christ) to help orphans and other girls to become self-supporting. For many years the school's graduates went directly to teaching positions. In 1942 Midway Junior College was opened, and the secondary school became Pinkerton High School. The two institutions operated on the same campus until 1972 when the high school was closed. The College has continued its affiliation with the Christian Church and has carried on the requirement that all students, regardless of their financial status, work to pay part of their educational costs.

MUNFORDVILLE

5,394. Women of Hart County
Collection. 1900- . No size given.
Open. No guide.
Hart County Historical Society.
Brief biographies, articles, programs, clippings, and photos of [Miss] Charlotte Brownlee (1876-1970), a Methodist missionary to Seoul, Korea, where she served from 1913 to 1942 as a kindergarten teacher and a 1910 graduate of the Cincinnati Training School for Deaconesses; of Wanda Catherine [Mrs. Edward H.] Cummings (1914-), a real estate broker, insurance agent, and auctioneer who is a member of several professional underwriting and auctioneers organizations; of Mary Elizabeth Carden (1903-), who operates a business for consulting on interior design and decorating; of Daisie Chaney [Mrs. Hobart] Carter (1897-), a school teacher who, after attending 16 years of summer sessions, obtained her degree from Western Kentucky State College in 1945 and then worked as Hart County superintendent of schools from 1946 to 1954; of Laura Ellen Miller [Mrs. Stephen A.] Derry (1905-), an author and attorney who was reputedly the first woman to try a case before a US Army court-martial in addition to being president of the National Association of Women Lawyers; of Elvena Miller [Mrs. J.H.] Gibson (1905-63), a librarian and English teacher who served as Hart County superintendent of schools from 1943 to 1946; of Edna Sanders [Mrs. Melvin] Hodge (1909-), an educator, poet, and composer of hymns; of Elizabeth Eleanora Thompson Hubbard (1908-), a social worker, Selective Service clerk, and wife of John Buford Hubbard, Jr.; of Jennie Barlow Parr [Mrs. Earl] Holloway (1927-), a pianist; of [Miss] Cattie Lou Miller (1923-), a state official who served as secretary and then assistant to Kentucky governors from 1947 until she took her current job as executive director of the Kentucky Crime Victims Compensation Board; of Gertrude [Mrs. Vernon] Moore (1919-), who with her husband comanages a department store and who is an officer in the Kentucky Order of the Eastern Star; of Clara Hodges Jones (1883-1972), owner and manager of a department store for 62 years; of Margaret Jo Mitchell [Mrs. Clifton Thomas] Snider (1917-), a worker in the mental health and retardation fields who was women's editor for the *Hart County News;* of Nellie Angel Smith (1881-1976), a professor of languages and dean of women at Memphis State University; of Thelma Dewy [Mrs. Lonnie Raymond] Stovall (1919-), the lieutenant governor of Kentucky since 1975, from 1950 to 1955 a state representative, and in terms between 1956 and 1975 Kentucky secretary of state and state treasurer; and of Sarah Felt Richardson (1870-1941), a physician who for years served as local surgeon for the railroad.

MURRAY

5,395. American Association of University Women
Records. 1933-69. 1 Hollinger box and 4 vols.
Open. No guide.
Murray State University, Pogue Library.
Annual reports of the Murray State branch of the AAUW and scrapbooks containing correspondence; programs of state, regional, national, and international conferences; photos; and clippings.

5,396. Murray Woman's Club
Records. 1942-76. 20 vols.
Open. No guide.
Murray State University, Pogue Library.
Scrapbooks of this civic organization, founded in 1900, include photos, clippings, and other items concerning the group's activities.

5,397. Norell, Alney (Allbritten)
Papers. 1896- . 5 Hollinger boxes and 3 vols.
Open. No guide.
Murray State University, Pogue Library.
[Mrs. Henry] Norell (1903-) has worked as a Broadway, Hollywood, and television actress. Correspondence, photos, and scrapbooks relating to Norell's career. Also includes photos and other items relating to the Allbritten family. Norell was given the full name of her father, Robert Alney Allbritten, at birth, but she used Alney as her first name throughout her life.

NAZARETH

5,398. Mother House Archives
Records. 1812-1976. 30 vols.
Open. Unpublished guide.
Sisters of Charity of Nazareth, Mother House Archival Center.
Annals and reports from academies, orphanages, and hospitals served by the Sisters, who work in the areas of health care, social service, and education. In the 19th century the Sisters served in pesthouses during smallpox epidemics, nursed wounded Confederate and Union soldiers during the Civil War, made home visits during cholera epidemics in Kentucky and Tennessee, nursed yellow fever patients in Mississippi, and taught in elementary schools for white children and for Negro children as soon as it was allowed. More recently, members of the congregation have been involved in community health services, working among migrant workers and homeless women and in the inner city, and in pastoral ministry in hospitals, on the *SS Hope,* and elsewhere.

OWENSBORO

5,399. Christian Femininity or The Eternal Woman
Records. 1963- . 3 boxes.
Open. No guide.
Brescia College Archives.
Created by Sister Francesca Hazel in 1963, this course was designed to prepare young women for their role in the contemporary home and society. In 1976, the course was renamed Contemporary Woman. Correspondence, budget records, syllabus, reports, and clippings relate to the course. Also includes annual reports and scrapbooks of the Lafiat Guild, a program for adults that grew from the course. The course was promoted by Philip Law, a retired psychiatrist, surgeon, and general practitioner in Chicago, who believed that many of the current problems of men and women stem from the loss of the arts of femininity.

5,400. Louisville Annual Conference, United Methodist Women
Records. Ca. 1880- . 3 boxes.
Open. No guide.
Kentucky Wesleyan College, Kentucky United Methodist Heritage Center.
Annual reports, minutes, correspondence, histories of local societies, and publications of the Annual Conference. Predecessor organizations of United Methodist Women were formed in about 1879 to promote women's Christian missionary work at home and abroad. The material contains records of various women's auxiliaries, the Woman's Foreign Missionary Society, the Woman's Home Missionary Society, Woman's Missionary Council, the Woman's Society of Christian Service, and the Wesleyan Service Guild.

5,401. Congregation Archives
Records. 1958- . 2 drawers and 20 tapes.
Open. No guide.
Sisters of the Lamb of God, Our Lady of Hope Convent.
Financial records, tapes of conference and retreat notes by the founder, photo albums, and scrapbooks provide a history of the establishment of the congregation's first US house in 1958 in Owensboro and the opening of the Holy Family Kindergarten and Robert Connor Day Care Center. The congregation includes handicapped women in its membership.

PIPPA PASSES

5,402. Appalachian Oral History Project
Oral history. 1970- . Ca. 1700 tapes.
Partially restricted. Published and unpublished guides.
Alice Lloyd College, Appalachian Oral History Project.
The College's portion of the Project comprises interviews with Appalachian area residents who speak about their own experiences and the history of their region. Tapes, transcripts, and photos. Lees Junior College in Jackson, KY; Emory and Henry College in Emory, VA; and Appalachian State University in Boone, NC, also are participating in the Project. Most of the interviewees are elderly persons, with women making up about half of the total. See *Appalachian Oral History Project Union Catalog* (Pippa Passes: Appalachian Oral History Project, 1977).

RICHMOND

5,403. American Association of University Women
Records. 1926- . 6 items.
Open. No guide.
Eastern Kentucky University Library, Townsend Room.
Scrapbooks contain photos and clippings of local AAUW members and events.

5,404. Boonesborough Chapter DAR
Records. 1919. 40 items.
Open. No guide.
Eastern Kentucky University Library, Townsend Room.
Yearbooks and yearbook supplements, both of which contain membership lists.

5,405. Cecilian Club
Records. 1899- . 100 items.
Open. No guide.
Eastern Kentucky University Library, Townsend Room.
Minutes and program yearbooks of this local group, which was founded in 1899 to stimulate musical development.

5,406. Saturday Matinee Musicale
Records. 1926-59. 50 items.
Open. No guide.
Eastern Kentucky University Library, Townsend Room.
Minutes and yearbooks containing membership lists of this Richmond organization, which sought to foster the appreciation and interpretation of music in the community.

5,407. Women's Club of Richmond
Records. 1914-59. 30 items.
Open. No guide.
Eastern Kentucky University Library, Townsend Room.
Yearbooks include membership lists and the creed of the Club, which was formed in 1904 to help its members work for the best interests of their community.

SAINT CATHARINE

5,408. Archives
Records. 1822- . 104 ft., 15 microfilm reels, and 7 tapes.
Access restricted. No guide.
Dominican Sisters of St. Catharine of Siena, Motherhouse.
The order was founded in 1822 in Washington County, KY, and is dedicated to education, health care, and pastoral care. Minutes of the general chapters and the governing board, financial records, correspondence, papers of the major superiors, reports of special apostolic ministries of individual members, historical records, photos, scrapbooks, and data on colleges, academies, schools, and hospitals operated or staffed by members of the congregation.

LOUISIANA

BATON ROUGE

5,409. State Archives
Records. Ca. 1730s- . No size given.
Open. Unpublished finding aids.
Louisiana Archives and Records Division.
Records of state, county (parish), and municipal units of government provide information about women in Louisiana. Includes, for example, microfilm records of the New Orleans censuses of 1791 and 1804, which list the names of white and free people of both sexes; records of the state board of pension commissioners, 1926-31; and marriage records, especially from the offices of parish clerks of courts. Contains St. Helena Parish clerk of court records of marriage, 1809-1944, with marriage licenses issued, affidavits of consent of parents, and records of bonds posted assuring that there were no legal objections to the marriage; Natchitoches Parish clerk of court marriage records, 1855-1900; and St. Charles Parish clerk of court colonial records, 1740-1872, including marriage contracts, inventories of property, family correspondence and other papers, powers of attorney, and wills. Most of the records are available on microfilm; some original records are held by the office that created them.

5,410. WPA Papers
Collection. Ca. 1800-1940. 22 drawers.
Open. Complete inventory.
Louisiana State Library, Louisiana Section.
Manuscripts gathered by the WPA concern Louisiana life and history. Includes black folklore, interviews with ex-slaves, local histories, local and regional recipes, literary papers and documents,

Louisiana French and Creole folk songs, travel accounts, and other items pertaining to such women as "Voodoo Queen" Marie Laveau, Myra (Clark) Gaines, Grace King, Mrs. Josephine Louise (Le Mennier) Newcomb, Eliza Moore Ripley, and Sophie Bell Wright. Subjects discussed include the Acadians of south central Louisiana, witchcraft and black magic, local and regional dialects, hunting and fishing, Indians, local and regional literature, religion, society and culture, education, and Louisiana plantations and their operations. Other papers deal with Louisiana theater of the 19th century, wedding customs, housewifery, fashions, "female characters," celebrations, and New Orleans churches, social agencies, hospitals and clinics, and schools.

5,411. Baton Rouge Business and Professional Women's Club
Records. 1925- . 3 ft. and 38 vols.
Open. Card catalog and inventory.
Louisiana State University, Archives and Manuscripts.
Minutes, correspondence, photos, programs, scrapbooks, and clippings. The scrapbooks, which were compiled by Club historians, contain a history of the Club from 1925 to 1960.

5,412. Edwards, Marianne
Papers. 1855-66. 72 items.
Open. Card catalog and inventory.
Louisiana State University, Archives and Manuscripts.
Letters that Edwards, wife of Guy M. Edwards, a sea captain from Massachusetts, wrote to Edwards family members about her experiences aboard ship and in American and foreign ports. Letters from New Orleans during the Federal occupation contain comments on the social and military conditions in the city and along the lower Mississippi River. Later letters are concerned with family affairs, farming, and the community of Hampton, VA. The letters reveal Marianne Edward's attitudes toward the education of women and child rearing; they also contain descriptions of family life at sea.

5,413. Ferguson, Kate Lee
Papers. 1857-1911. 7 vols. and 38 items.
Open. Card catalog and inventory.
Louisiana State University, Archives and Manuscripts.
A Mississippi novelist, poet, and composer, Ferguson (1841-post 1911) was the wife of Confederate general Samuel Wragg Ferguson. Manuscript writings, a few personal letters, published and unpublished music, and a printed volume of Ferguson's story *Little Mose,* which was dedicated to Jefferson Davis, president of the Confederacy. Also contains poems; short stories, including "Cliquot" and "Sequel to Cliquot"; the operetta *A Tempest in a Teapot;* and a list of household furniture.

5,414. King, Grace
Papers. 1851-1941. 7 vols. and 3800 items.
Open. Card catalog and inventory.
Louisiana State University, Archives and Manuscripts.
A New Orleans writer and historian, King (1853?-1932) was the daughter of William Woodson King. Correspondence, notebooks of literary writings, bound volumes of printed material and financial records, photos, and scrapbooks contain material concerning her travels, literary career, historical interests, and personal matters. Letters from Henry P. Dart, a New Orleans attorney, pertain to activities of the Louisiana Historical Society and its publication *Louisiana Historical Quarterly.* Bound volumes include a bankbook, cashbooks, an index book, notebooks, scrapbooks, and other items. Among her correspondents were such authors and publishers as Charles Dudley Warner, Samuel Clemens, Richard W. Gilder, Francis Parkman, Walter Page, and Charles L. Norton.

5,415. King, Grace
Papers. 1864-1933. 942 items.
Open. Card catalog and inventory.
Louisiana State University, Archives and Manuscripts.
Personal and business correspondence, a few items relating to the Confederacy, and manuscript notes of King (1853?-1932), a New Orleans writer and historian. Material, some of which is in French, includes correspondence pertaining to her literary career, dealings with publishers, and recognition as a writer; European travels; social and family life; and relationships with prominent American, Canadian, and European contemporaries. Also contains some family correspondence, principally of her sister Annie R. King, and letters from Paris by Marie Rosine de St. Roman, daughter of John Slidell. Confederate items include an April 1864 order by Richard Taylor concerning the Battle of Mansfield in DeSoto Parish, LA; manuscript notes on the Federal occupation of New Orleans; and a program for a 1903 New Orleans memorial service for Jefferson Davis.

5,416. Louisiana Association of Student Nurses
Records. 1950-70. 7 ft. and 1 vol.
Open. Card catalog and inventory.
Louisiana State University, Archives and Manuscripts.
Bylaws, financial records, correspondence, memoranda, photos, convention programs, and other material of this state student nurses' group and of the National Association of Student Nurses. Includes records of the executive board, advisors, and state officers of the LASN, bylaws of state and local chapters, committee reports, and other items. Also contains correspondence, convention material, and membership applications of the NASN and papers relating to the Louisiana State Nurses' Association and the National League of Nurses.

5,417. Louisiana State Nurses' Association
Records. 1904-70. 13 ft., 557 vols., and 4984 items.
Open. Card catalog and inventory.
Louisiana State University, Archives and Manuscripts.
Records relate to the professionalization of nursing and to the field's increasing specialization. Agenda for the Association's advisory council and board of directors meetings, presidents' addresses, correspondence, alumnae information, material on the American Association of Industrial Nurses and the Louisiana State Nurses' Association, biographies of prominent nurses, information on institutions in Louisiana and elsewhere, items concerning nursing education, surveys, committee reports, and other records.

5,418. Queyrouze, Leona
Papers. 1800-1950. 54 vols. and 2614 items.
Open. Card catalog and inventory.
Louisiana State University, Archives and Manuscripts.
Leona Queyrouze was the pseudonym of Constant Beauvais (1866-1938), a French language writer, poet, essayist, and musician of New Orleans and New York City. Collection contains correspondence and literary works of Queyrouze, who was the wife of Pierre M. E. Barel, and business and personal papers of her father and other family members, the bulk of which dates from 1860 to 1937. The Queyrouze family was associated with prominent New Orleans Creoles including P. G. T. Beauregard and with writers and members of l'Athénée Louisianais, a group that encouraged the use and study of French language and literature in Louisiana. A number of Leona Queyrouze's essays and poems are published in the *Comtes Rendus de l'Athénée Louisianais.* In New York she translated and adapted French plays for the American stage, and some of her poems were read at the Academy of Sciences at Bordeaux. Her musical composition "Fantasie Indienne" was performed by the Mexican Army Band at the World's Exposition in 1884. Her correspondents include writers Anatole Cousin, Maria Giovanni Callegari, and Mollie (Moore) Davis, a New Orleans novelist who translated many poems by Queyrouze and others.

5,419. Wilkerson, Helen C.
Papers. 1920-58. 3 vols. and 703 items.
Open. Card catalog and inventory.
Louisiana State University, Archives and Manuscripts.
Correspondence, speeches, programs, and other papers of Wilkerson (1905-59), assistant dean of women at Louisiana State University, relate to her career and social life. Contains items concerning her work at LSU and her activities in such Baton Rouge organizations as the Clanjamfry, the Bal Masque, and the Four-Square Bridge Club as well as a 1920 program from the 75th annual commencement of the Natchez Institute in Natchez, MS; Louisiana State University commencement programs; and a 1948 funeral book for Wilkerson's mother Minnie Deardorff.

5,420. Wilkinson, Micajah: Merrit M. Shilg Memorial Collection
Papers. 1853-1935. 149 items.
Open. Card catalog and inventory.
Louisiana State University, Archives and Manuscripts.
Correspondence and pamphlets of Micajah Wilkinson, who farmed near Liberty in Amite County, MS, and his wife Mary Short Wilkinson contain letters from Nancy [Mrs. Dustin] Willard and her granddaughter Thetis Bush of Collingsburg in Bossier Parish, LA. Also includes letters that Micajah Wilkinson wrote to his wife while serving as a Confederate private at Camp Milldale in Warren County, MS, and at Corinth, MS. The Willard and Bush letters, which date from 1855 to 1885, provide information on the people, religious practices, Negro problems, crop conditions, and events of the Collingsburg community as well as descriptions of women's dress, manners, and customs. Pamphlets include information on religious institutions, particularly the Baptist Association of Mississippi and the Mount Zion Church in 1846.

5,421. Women's Social Industrial Association
Records. 1881-99. 6 vols. and 5 items.
Open. Card catalog.
Louisiana State University, Archives and Manuscripts.
Constitution, bylaws, minute books, items removed from minute books, a journal of expenses for the charity committee, and a pamphlet of this New Orleans group organized "for the mutual benefit and improvement of its members and to promote the industries of women."

5,422. Works Progress Administration, Community Service Division
Records. 1940-42. 1 vol.
Open. Card catalog.
Louisiana State University, Archives and Manuscripts.
Addressed to directors and supervisors of WPA projects in Louisiana, these field memos discuss local aspects of the Administration's projects, including personnel, employment regulations, preparation of annual reports, conversion of WPA projects to wartime purposes, and operation of community service division programs. Among projects discussed are those concerning writers, shoe repair, music, arts and crafts, and nursery schools. The memos reflect the role of women in these projects.

5,423. Works Progress Administration, Ex-Slave Narrative Project
Records. 1937-41. 39 items.
Open. Card catalog.
Louisiana State University, Archives and Manuscripts.
Based on interviews with ex-slaves in the Alexandria and New Orleans districts, these narratives describe slave life, the life of blacks after emancipation, and black folklore, music, and religion.

5,424. Works Progress Administration, Historical Records Survey
Records. 1936-40. 21 microfilm reels.
Open. Card catalog and inventory.
Louisiana State University, Archives and Manuscripts.
Microfilm of inventory forms completed by Historical Records Survey workers describing documents in archival collections at various state agencies.

5,425. Works Progress Administration, Historical Records Survey and Survey of Federal Archives
Records. 1935-43. 2 ft.
Open. Card catalog and inventory.
Louisiana State University, Archives and Manuscripts.
Office files, consisting of correspondence, memoranda, reports, and other material, of the Historical Records Survey from 1936 to 1943 and the Survey of Federal Archives conducted in 1936. Included are worksheets and drafts of inventories for the colonial records of Louisiana, Feliciana archives, church archives, manuscripts, police jury minutes, and vital statistics; manuals; instructions and guidelines; and completed inventories.

5,426. Wright, Sophie Bell
Papers. 1889-1906. 3 vols. and 69 items.
Open. Card catalog and inventory.
Louisiana State University, Archives and Manuscripts.
Scrapbooks of [Miss] Wright (1866-1912), a New Orleans educator and reformer, relate to her career as principal of the Home Institute, organizer of the Free Night School for Working Men and Boys, and a philanthropic worker for many New Orleans social service agencies. Contains items regarding the Home Institute, which was a day and boarding school for young ladies; clippings concerning Wright's work with the Free Night School, The Waif's Home, and the Louisiana Chautauqua; letters of acknowledgement from visiting lecturers and artists and from benefactors of Wright's charities; and material concerning her work with the GFWC and her service as state secretary of the King's Daughters and Sons of Louisiana.

COVINGTON

5,427. Archives
Records. 1870- . No size given.
Closed. No guide.
Benedictine Sisters, St. Scholastica Priory.
This branch of the Benedictine Sisters was established in 1870 in New Orleans and is engaged in teaching. Financial records, papers of mothers superior, correspondence, photos, scrapbooks, and other records, including material relating to schools which were staffed and operated by members of the order.

LACOMBE

5,428. Carmel Archives
Records. 1824- . 84.13 ft. and 10 tapes.
Access restricted. No guide.
Mount Carmel Generalate.
Papers of superiors general, school records, congregation records, correspondence, chronicles, photos, juridical works, yearbooks, anniversary commemoration booklets, clippings, and other records of the Generalate, which was founded in 1824. Members of the order are engaged in teaching, hospital work, special education, and church and social services.

LAFAYETTE

5,429. American Association of University Women
Records. 1927-74. 18 ft.
Open. Unpublished guide.
University of Southwestern Louisiana, Southwestern Archives and Manuscripts Collection.
The Lafayette branch of the AAUW was organized in 1927. Minutes, correspondence, journals, and study material for the group's projects. The branch's programs have included work for the Equal Rights Amendment and study of governmental, cultural, and social issues affecting women.

5,430. Campbell, Marie
Papers. Nd. 75 items.
Open. Published and unpublished guides.
University of Southwestern Louisiana, Southwestern Archives and Manuscripts Collection.
Historical notes and essays by [Mrs.] Campbell, a resident of St. James Parish, concern early Louisiana history and genealogy. See *Guide to Southwestern Archives and Manuscripts Collection* (Lafayette, LA: University of Southwestern Louisiana, 1977).

5,431. Denbo, Anna Marshall
Records. Late 1800s-early 1900s. 1 Hollinger box.
Open. Unpublished guide.
University of Southwestern Louisiana, Southwestern Archives and Manuscripts Collection.
Denbo (ca. 1860s-1940s), a longtime resident of Lafayette, and her husband Amzi Denbo, a businessman, were active community and church leaders. Autobiography and an account she wrote based on tales her father told her about Abraham Lincoln's childhood. Denbo's grandfather had lived next door to the Lincoln family.

5,432. Dupré, Edith Garland
Papers. Late 1800s-early 1900s. 2 Hollinger boxes.
Open. Published and unpublished guides.
University of Southwestern Louisiana, Southwestern Archives and Manuscripts Collection.
[Miss] Dupré (1881-1970), a member of a prominent area family, was a member of the first faculty of the University of Southwestern Louisiana. Personal and family correspondence, autobiographical material, photos, clippings, and other items. She was on the Southwestern Louisiana faculty from 1901 until her retirement in 1944. See *Guide to Southwestern Archives and Manuscripts Collection* (Lafayette, LA: University of Southwestern Louisiana, 1977).

5,433. First Lutheran Church of Crowley, LA, and St. John Lutheran Church of Iota, LA
Records. Nd. 1.5 ft.
Open. Published guide.
University of Southwestern Louisiana, Southwestern Archives and Manuscripts Collection.
Constitution in German of the Crowley Church, pastoral letters, financial records, business correspondence, parish reports and bulletins, and other records. Includes minutes of the Ladies Aide Society. See *Guide to Southwestern Archives and Manuscripts Collection* (Lafayette, LA: University of Southwestern Louisiana, 1977).

5,434. Griffin, Lucile Meredith (Mouton)
Papers. 1872-1967. Ca. 5.5 ft.
Open. Published guide.
University of Southwestern Louisiana, Southwestern Archives and Manuscripts Collection.
Papers of Griffin include material about Lafayette's history and society and items about the Mouton family genealogy. Her father Alexander Mouton (1853-1938), a sugar planter and railroad and steamboat engineer, was director of the Mexico City mint from 1880 to 1882 and of the US mint in New Orleans from 1884 to 1888. See *Guide to Southwestern Archives and Manuscripts Collection* (Lafayette, LA: University of Southwestern Louisiana, 1977).

5,435. Labranche, Jean
Papers. Nd. No size given.
Open. Published guide.
University of Southwestern Louisiana, Southwestern Archives and Manuscripts Collection.
Papers of Labranche include an 1845 dowry declaration of Elizabeth Athenais Brown and Brisce Similien Labranche and a copy of the partition, dated 1851, between heirs of Euphemie Labranche [Mrs. William] Brown. See *Guide to Southwestern Archives and Manuscripts Collection* (Lafayette, LA: University of Southwestern Louisiana, 1977).

5,436. Louisiana Colonial Records
Records. 1605-1803. Ca. 250 microfilm reels.
Open. Published guide.
University of Southwestern Louisiana, Southwestern Archives and Manuscripts Collection.
Records relating to the French colonial era in Louisiana, Canada, and to a lesser degree Santo Domingo, Martinique, Guadaloupe, and the Windward Islands include correspondence, reports, orders, memoranda, commissions, and other documents. Includes correspondence of the colonial administrators of Louisiana. See *Guide to Southwestern Archives and Manuscripts Collection* (Lafayette, LA: University of Southwestern Louisiana, 1977).

5,437. University Archives
Records. 1898-1966. Ca. 450 ft.
Partially restricted. Published guide.
University of Southwestern Louisiana, Southwestern Archives and Manuscripts Collection.
Official University records include records of the office of the school's president, 1900-66; faculty senate minutes, 1957- ; records pertaining to admissions, housing, and student life, 1900-38; alumni affairs material; photos; scrapbooks; bulletins; student newspapers; and other records. Contains records of the Intercollegiate Athletics and Oratorical Association and a sampling of material of the testing and guidance bureau from 1940 to 1964. See *Guide to Southwestern Archives and Manuscripts Collection* (Lafayette, LA: University of Southwestern Louisiana, 1977).

NATCHITOCHES

5,438. American Association of University Women
Records. Ca. 1925-65. 6 cu.ft.
Open. Unpublished guide.
Northwestern State University of Louisiana, Archives Division.
Minutes, correspondence, directives, booklets, yearbooks, and other records of the national, regional, state, and local AAUW.

5,439. Carver, Ada Jack
Papers. 1923-36. 2 cu.ft.
Open. Unpublished guide.
Northwestern State University of Louisiana, Archives Division.
Carver (ca. 1895-?) was a short story writer and author of *The Cajun, The Clock,* and other plays. Correspondence, manuscripts, photos, playbills, clippings, and published works. The correspondence begins shortly before Carver won the first prize in a 1925 short story contest with her story "Redbone." Her letters tell of happiness and problems in her personal life and her successes and difficulties in writing.

5,440. Cloutier
Papers. 1725-1941. 12 cu.ft.
Open. Unpublished guide.

Northwestern State University of Louisiana, Archives Division.
Correspondence, bills, receipts, promissory notes, cotton accounts, and slave sale records of this cotton-growing family provide information about women family members and female slaves.

5,441. Cross
Papers. 1924-76. 1494 items.
Open. Unpublished guide.
Northwestern State University of Louisiana, Archives Division.
Ruth Cross (ca. 1895-) is a writer, novelist, and playwright. Correspondence, manuscripts of books and articles, research notes, photos, clippings, and printed works. Cross, who sometimes uses a pseudonym, has written volumes dealing with gardening subjects and scripts for radio programs and a motion picture.

5,442. Dormon
Papers. Ca. 1910-71. 52 cu.ft.
Open. No guide.
Northwestern State University of Louisiana, Archives Division.
Caroline Dorman (1889-1971) was a naturalist, botanist, anthropologist, landscape designer, artist, and writer. Correspondence; interview notebooks; manuscripts for published and unpublished stories, articles, and books; photos; drawings; blueprints; maps; paintings; and artifacts.

5,443. Dormon Collection: Storm, Willie G.
Papers. 1919-63. 0.5 cu.ft.
Open. Unpublished guide.
Northwestern State University of Louisiana, Archives Division.
Correspondence of Willie G. [Mrs. A. F.] Storm (ca. 1870-1965), a clubwoman who was president of the Louisiana Federation of Women's Clubs and of the South Carolina Garden Clubs, is part of the Dormon Collection. While holding the two offices, Storm supported conservation laws, highway beautification, the Kistachie National Forest, and the appointment of a woman to the Louisiana Highway Commission. Her letters from South Carolina also deal with her gardening interests and her own garden in Monck's Corner.

5,444. Egan
Papers. 1787-1955. 8 cu.ft. and 31 microfilm reels.
Open. No guide.
Northwestern State University of Louisiana, Archives Division.
Correspondence, accounts, receipts, and clippings of this family provide information about the lives and activities of women family members. Includes correspondence dealing with women's suffrage and writings of Lavina Egan, which date from the late 1800s.

5,445. Federation
Records. 1925-46. 1 cu.ft.
Open. Unpublished guide.
Northwestern State University of Louisiana, Archives Division.
Speeches, resolutions, study guides, and other convention material; yearbooks; and handbooks of the Federated Women's Club and the Natchitoches Women's Club. The records illustrate the group's interest in national, sociological, artistic, and human rights subjects. Directories list local clubs, officers, and committee members.

5,446. Harris
Papers. 1784-1960. 13 cu.ft.
Open. Unpublished guide.
Northwestern State University of Louisiana, Archives Division.
Family correspondence, household accounts, records relating to the cotton business, and other family papers. Includes correspondence of women family members and bills and notices of the Keachie Female College, 1859-63.

5,447. Lesche Club
Records. 1898-1945. 2 cu.ft.
Open. Unpublished guide.
Northwestern State University of Louisiana, Archives Division.
A literary group, the Lesche Club is the second oldest women's organization in Louisiana. Minute books, correspondence, reports, yearbooks, and entries submitted for an annual one-act play contest. The group fosters community improvement and cultural preservation and sponsors literary contests and awards.

5,448. Melrose
Papers. 1731-1946. Ca. 300 cu.ft.
Open. Unpublished guide.
Northwestern State University of Louisiana, Archives Division.
Assembled by Mrs. Cammie G. Henry, the collection pertains to Louisiana history and includes correspondence, diaries, manuscripts of published and unpublished works, legal documents, scrapbooks, drawings, and other papers of women writers, artists, and suffragists, among them Rachel Lyman Field, Caroline Dormon, Lavinia Egan, Doris Ulmann, Alberta Kinsey, Mary Belle McKellar, Hilda Perini, Ada Jack Carver, and Gustine Courson Weaver.

5,449. Melrose and Dormon Collections: Moore, Dosia
Papers. Ca. 1931-38. Ca. 150 pp.
Open. Unpublished guide.
Northwestern State University of Louisiana, Archives Division.
Correspondence and recollections of Moore (ca. 1850-1940) provide information about the life of an elderly woman who suffered ill health. She wrote short sketches about her life before and after the Civil War and about wartime events at her family's plantation, and she worked with Caroline Dormon, probably a kinswoman, in writing an unfinished account of her family's life in Alabama and Louisiana. Her vignettes about travelers, Indians, neighbors, and other persons provide information about local history. Her papers are included in both the University's Melrose and Dormon collections.

5,450. Melrose Collection: Field, Rachel Lyman
Papers. Ca. 1928-42. Ca. 1 cu.ft.
Open. Unpublished guide.
Northwestern State University of Louisiana, Archives Division.
Correspondence, photos, clippings, and other items of Field (1894-1942), a writer, are part of the Melrose Collection. The letters, some of which were written to Cammie (Garrett) [Mrs. J. H.] Henry, provide information about Field's personal life, thoughts about writing, and advice about publishing. Also includes letters from Field's friends on her death, reviews, published works, and a studio portrait.

5,451. Melrose Collection: McKellar, Mary Belle
Papers. 1922-41. Ca. 1 cu.ft.
Open. Unpublished guide.
Northwestern State University of Louisiana, Archives Division.
Papers of [Miss] McKellar (?-1941), a newspaperwoman and writer who was an American National Red Cross worker in France during WWI, are part of the Melrose Collection.
Correspondence and clippings of her feature stories. McKellar wrote commentaries about people and events in Shreveport, LA, as well as memoirs about her Red Cross work.

5,452. Natchitoches Art Colony
Records. 1920-30. 1 cu.ft.
Open. Unpublished guide.
Northwestern State University of Louisiana, Archives Division.
Correspondence, memoirs, brochures, and other records of the Colony, a summer art school which was the first of its kind in the South. Reports about the Colony appeared in the *Saturday Evening Post,* eastern newspapers, and other publications.

5,453. Roach Collection: Coleman, Patricia
Papers. Ca. 1936-53. 1 cu.ft.
Open. Unpublished guide.
Northwestern State University of Louisiana, Archives Division.
Papers of [Miss] Patricia Coleman (1916-?), a playwright from Mansfield, LA, are part of the Roach collection. Correspondence, play manuscripts and typescripts, drafts, author's comments, and other literary working papers. Contains notes about early 20th-century Mansfield.

5,454. University Archives
Records. 1884- . 200 cu.ft.
Open. Partial unpublished guides.
Northwestern State University of Louisiana, Archives Division.
The University was founded in 1884 as a normal school; it later began to offer a college program. Annual reports, correspondence, legal papers, Public Works Administration forms, and other records. From about 1919 to about 1939 the records reflect the raising of standards for teacher certification and female deportment.

NEW ORLEANS

5,455. Adams, Inez
Papers. 1914-68. 5000 items.
Open. Description.
Amistad Research Center.
A PhD, Adams (1904-67) was a teacher and anthropologist who was particularly interested in Africa and islands of the Caribbean; she also studied race relations and was involved in civil rights activities in the US. Correspondence; accounts and business papers; course materials for classes at Fisk University and Brooklyn College; writings, including anthropological articles, prose, and poems; and field notes dealing with Trinidad and Calypso songs, East Indians in the Caribbean, Africa, school desegregation, and civil rights demonstrations.

5,456. American Home Missionary Society
Records. 1816-1936. 1,000,000 items.
Open. Published guide.
Amistad Research Center.
Founded in 1826 as an interdenominational organization, the Society carried on the home missionary activities of the Congregationalists and Presbyterians under the Plan of Union. Archives chiefly consist of correspondence, including letters and reports from missionaries in the field and letters from Society supporters. The material reflects conditions on the frontier and includes information on slavery, the Civil War and northern churches, and economic, social, and political problems. Also includes biographical material. The Society's work was carried on primarily west of the Appalachians, but correspondence includes items from throughout the US. See David G. Horvath, ed., *A Guide to the Microfilm Edition of the Papers of the American Home Missionary Society 1816 (1826-1894) 1936* (Glen Rock, NJ: Microfilming Corporation of America, 1975).

5,457. American Missionary Association
Records. 1839-1960. Ca. 450,000 items and microfilm.
Partially restricted. Published guide, description, and card catalog.
Amistad Research Center.
Established in 1846 as an outgrowth of the Amistad Defense Committee, the Association is an interdenominational, evangelical, and abolitionist organization. Archives consisting principally of correspondence from missionaries and others, many of them women. Prior to the Civil War, the Association supported missionary work in Sierra Leone, Egypt, Jamaica, Siam, and Hawaii as well as on the American frontier, in border slave states, and among fugitive slaves in Canada. The organization also worked with minority groups in eastern cities, the Chinese in California, Welsh miners, and Indians in Minnesota. Beginning with the Civil War, the Association turned its attention to education of the freedman and has continued to support education for Negroes; it also has provided educational opportunities for Appalachian whites, Chinese Americans, Indian families, and Mexican Americans and has supported health facilities in Puerto Rico. The archives contain material on the Amistad case, evangelical abolitionism, Congregationalism, the Free Presbyterian Church, and the Wesleyan Methodist Connection. The group supported many women schoolteachers who went south after the Civil War. See *Author and Added Entry Catalog of the American Missionary Association Archives* (Nashville: Amistad Research Center, 1969).

5,458. Bethune, Mary Jane (McLeod)
Papers. 1923-36. Ca. 700 items.
Open. Description, card catalog, and register.
Amistad Research Center.
An educator, racial leader, and feminist, Bethune (1875-1955) was a founder in 1904 and president of Bethune-Cookman College in Daytona Beach, FL, and longtime president of the National Association of Colored Women. Correspondence, diaries, writings, speeches, lists of contributions, articles, clippings, biographical news stories, and other material. Includes correspondence with John Hope, Frank S. Horne, Mary W. Ovington, William Pickens, Adam Clayton Powell, Sr., Mrs. John D. Rockefeller, John J. Tigert, Walter White, Roy Wilkins, and Plummer Barnard Young. Bethune kept one of the diaries during a 1927 trip to Europe sponsored by the National Medical Association. A second diary was recorded by her friend Josie Roberts as she toured California in 1926 with Bethune on behalf of the NACW. Includes addresses on behalf of NACW and Bethune-Cookman, of which Bethune was president from 1932 to 1942 and in 1946 and 1947.

5,459. Brice, Carol
Papers. 1905- . 4 vols. and ca. 4000 items.
Open. Unpublished guide.
Amistad Research Center.
Correspondence, scrapbooks, programs, clippings, and memorabilia of Brice, a teacher and vocalist who has sung in Europe and North and South America, reflect her career, the musical development of her brothers Jonathan and Eugene Brice, and her family's contributions to Negro education. A native of Indianapolis, she grew up and received her early education at Palmer Memorial Institute at North Carolina, which was founded and directed by her aunt Charlotte (Hawkins) Brown. Her father served as the Institute's chaplain and her mother taught history. Brice majored in music at Talladega College and after graduation won a fellowship to the Juilliard graduate school. She received the Naumberg Award in 1944, which led to her debut at Town Hall. She then made concert tours in the US, Canada, and South America, often accompanied by her brother Jonathan. She sang at the White House for Franklin D. Roosevelt's third inauguration at the invitation of Eleanor Roosevelt and at the 1948 Democratic National Convention. Brice lives in Norman, OK, with her husband Thomas Carey, a member of the University of Oklahoma music faculty. She has served as guest professor of voice at the University.

5,460. Cartwright, Marguerite (Dorsey)
Papers. 1927- . Ca. 30,000 items.
Open. No guide.
Amistad Research Center.
A stage and movie actress in her youth, Cartwright received a PhD and has taught at Hunter College, Brooklyn College, and the New School for Social Research. She was a correspondent in the UN press corps and was a member of the Provisional council and the board of trustees of the University of Nigeria. Correspondence, newspaper columns written by Cartwright, notes, photos, scrapbooks, invitations, clippings, memorabilia, and material related to her work with the University of Nigeria. Includes her scrapbooks on Negroes in the UN and on the Second Annual Institute of Race Relations held at Fisk University in 1945. A significant part of the collection is records of the University of Nigeria, which document the founding of the school and its early history. Cartwright has made 25 study tours of Africa during which she developed friendships with such African leaders as Kwame Nkrumah, Komla Gbedemah, and Nnamdi Azikiwe.

5,461. Chamberlain, Mary E.
Papers. 1886-1906. 32 items.
Open. Unpublished guide.
Amistad Research Center.
Correspondence, photos, and a scrapbook of [Miss] Chamberlain, a teacher of violin and music, who taught from 1886 to 1906 at Fisk University under appointment from the American Missionary Association.

5,462. Committee on Civil Rights in Metropolitan New York
Records. 1949-66. Ca. 50,000 items.
Open. Description.
Amistad Research Center.
Archives of this interracial, independent organization, which from 1949 until 1966 worked for the elimination of racial discrimination in Manhattan. Led by Edna Mercer and supported completely by volunteers, many of them women, the Committee first worked to end racial discrimination in East Manhattan restaurants. Later the group expanded to include all of metropolitan New York and concentrated its efforts on housing desegregation.

5,463. Congregational Church Extension Boards
Records. 1928-36. 15,000 items.
Open. Description.
Amistad Research Center.
Correspondence of the Boards, which were established in 1928 through merger of the Congregational Home Missionary Society, the Congregational Church Building Society, and the Congregational Sunday School Extension Society.

5,464. Congregational Home Missionary Society
Records. 1894-1928. 150,000 items.
Open. Description.
Amistad Research Center.
Correspondence of the Society, which was called the American Home Missionary Society until 1893. It became part of the Congregational Church Extension Boards in 1928.

5,465. Cullen, Countee
Papers. 1921-69. 8 ft. and 7 microfilm rolls.
Open. Published guide, description, and card catalog.
Amistad Research Center.
A lyric poet, playwright, and novelist who was a leading figure of the Harlem Renaissance, Cullen (1903-46) taught French, English, and creative writing for 11 years at Frederick Douglass Junior High School in New York City; his wife Ida Mae (Roberson) Cullen, co-owner for about five years of the Afro-Arts Bazaar, tried to carry on her husband's interests in publication of *On These I Stand* (1947). Correspondence, a fragmentary diary, writings, financial records, legal papers and certificates, teaching plan books and other teaching records, scrapbooks, clippings, and memorabilia. Includes correspondence with Zora Neale Hurston, Sadie Alexander, Anna Alexander, Florence Adams Allen, Grace I. Alston, M. Margaret Anderson, Harriette Ashbrook, Elsie Johnson Ayer, Janet Barber, Willie Louise Barbour, Gertrude Ryder Bennett, Gwendolyn Bennett, Mary McLeod Bethune, Helen Keller, Helene Johnson, Jessie Fauset, Dorothy Peterson, Leah Salisbury, and Dorothy West. Papers of Ida Cullen primarily deal with literary rights to her husband's works and other business matters, including the Afro-Arts Bazaar, which sold imported jewelry and artifacts. See *Guide to the Microfilm Edition of the Countee Cullen Papers, 1921-1969* (New Orleans: Amistad Research Center, 1975).

5,466. Dobbs, John Wesley, Family
Papers. 1873-1975. Ca. 1000 items.
Open. Description.
Amistad Research Center.
Correspondence, speeches, photos, clippings, and articles of Dobbs (1881-1961), president of the Georgia Voters League in 1935 and national vice-president of the NAACP, and his six daughters: Irene Jackson, chairman of the North Carolina Central University modern language department; Willie Blackburn, chairman of the Jackson State University language division in Jackson, MS; Millicent Jordan, professor of English and Afro-American literature at Spelman College; Josephine Clement, a member of the city-county library board and the city board of education in Durham, NC, and a director of Durham's Better Health Foundation; Mattiwilda Janzon, opera and concert coloratura; and June Butts, who teaches at the University of Massachusetts. Jackson and Butts earned PhD degrees.

5,467. Douglass, Harlan Paul
Papers. 1889-1953. Ca. 400 items.
Open. Unpublished guide.
Amistad Research Center.
An official of social and religious organizations, Douglass was general secretary for the American Missionary Association from 1910 until WWI. Correspondence, journals, speeches, writings, photos, scrapbooks, clippings, and other papers, including family histories that Douglass's parents wrote in 1913 to mark their 55th wedding anniversary. In the histories Truman O. Douglass and Maria Greene Douglass reminisced about their respective families, with references to western migration, the abolitionist crusade, the Civil War, and the development of Congregationalism in the West.

5,468. Jamison, Anna Marie (Hansen)
Papers. Ca. 1917-72. Ca. 170 items.
Open. Description.
Amistad Research Center.
[Mrs.] Jamison taught from 1917 until 1937 in southern schools for Negroes under the auspices of the American Missionary Association. Correspondence with students and colleagues, files of yearbooks and student newspapers, class records, clippings, and interviews recorded with Jamison in 1972. Jamison taught at Chandler Normal School in Lexington, KY; Ballard Normal School in Macon, GA; Tillotson College in Austin, TX; Tougaloo College in Tougaloo, MS; and Straight College and Dillard University in New Orleans.

5,469. Julius Rosenwald Fund
Records. 1917-48. 140,789 microfilm exposures and 50 microfilm reels.
Open. Description and register.
Amistad Research Center.
Founded by Julius Rosenwald (1862-1932), this Fund was chartered in 1917 with an endowment of $20 million; it sought to equalize opportunities among Americans by supporting Negro education and health programs, fellowships for Negroes and white southerners, and other activities. Records relating to the Fund's fellowships and scholarships, trustees, administration, and to the Rosenwald family; financial records; correspondence; publications; and studies. The Fund concluded its activities in 1947. Correspondents include Eleanor Roosevelt, Marion (Rosenwald) Ascoli, Adele (Rosenwald) Levy, Edith (Rosenwald) Stern, Pearl S. Buck, Lillian Smith, and Sara Southall; there is material regarding rural education and schoolhouses, teacher training and universities, social and research studies, and race relations projects. The fellowships section contains correspondence, application papers, progress reports, and biographical material on such individuals as Marian Anderson, Fannie S. Belcher, Anne M. Cook, Lula S. Green II, Hilda Lawson, Mary Adelaide Norton, Mrs. Edward M. Palmer, Ruth M. Smith, Frances S. Thompson, and Jessie Covington Dent as well as social scientists Virginia M. Argrett, Mary Louise Broom, Eloise W. Clark, Edwina Lowe, Estelle H. Scott, Josie Belle Sellers, Thelma K. Shelley, Juanita Williams, and Edmonia White Grant. Also includes material on Marie Beverly Johnson, Elsie Mae Lewis, Dorothy Burnett Porter, Pearl Eileene Primus, Paula Snelling, Bonita Harrison Valien, Preston Valien, and Margaret Walker.

5,470. Keller, Rosa (Freeman)
Papers. 1961-63. 35 items.
Open. Unpublished guide.
Amistad Research Center.
A New Orleans resident, Keller is a member of the Dillard University board of trustees, chairman of the Flint-Goodridge Hospital board of trustees, and a graduate of Hollins College. Correspondence, financial records, legal documents, and clippings pertaining primarily to Keller's support for the legal suit which led to desegregation of Tulane University. Keller was principal supporter of the suit filed on behalf of Pearlie H. Elloie and Barbara M. Guillory, graduates of Dillard University.

5,471. Lewis, Hylan Garnet
Papers. Nd. Ca. 100,000 items.
Open. Description.
Amistad Research Center.
Lewis is a sociologist who has written extensively on the black family. Correspondence, research notes, manuscripts of his writings, and manuscripts by other scholars in history, anthropology, and sociology contain material concerning women and the family.

5,472. Lincoln Academy
Records. 1915-57. 50 items.
Open. Description.
Amistad Research Center.
Founded in 1888 in Kings Mountain, NC, by [Miss] Emily C. Prudden, a New England woman, the Academy was for decades the only institution in several counties to offer secondary education to Negroes. Consists of correspondence, manuscripts, bulletins, and pamphlets and includes correspondence deposited by Mrs. Walter Edward Ricks, whose husband became the Academy's first Negro principal in 1922. The Rickses' correspondence dates from the couple's first meeting in 1915. Also contains a manuscript "Reminiscences" by [Mrs.] Eule Wellmon Dunlap, a graduate of the Academy who came to Kings Mountain with her family at age 3; the family moved to the town so the children could attend the Academy. Prudden founded 15 southern educational institutions between 1884 and 1910. Lincoln Academy was the only one of the 15 devoted to the education of Negroes.

5,473. Nelson, John P.
Papers. 1957-74. Ca. 2500 items.
Open. Unpublished guide.
Amistad Research Center.
Correspondence, speeches, financial records, minutes, court briefs, exhibits for plaintiffs and defendants, and other papers of Nelson, including items that pertain to the suit he brought in behalf of Barbara Marie Guillory, Pearlie Hardin Elloie, and others seeking admission of black students to Tulane University. Among the correspondents are Katherine Skelly Wright, who served as Nelson's associate on the Tulane suit, and Rosa Keller. Also includes a letter from Dorothy Taylor, the first black woman elected to the Louisiana legislature.

5,474. Opportunity Foundation Corporation
Records. 1962-76. Ca. 1500 items.
Open. Unpublished guide.
Amistad Research Center.
Founded by Margaret Callender McCulloch, the Corporation worked to help residents of Memphis and Shelby County, TN, to further their education and to alleviate past discrimination by health, education, and welfare agencies through contributions to new agencies and improvements in existing ones. Bylaws, minutes, accounts and financial statements, correspondence, scholastic and testing records, photos, clippings, and other records of the Corporation's board of directors and trustees. Includes material on educational grants, child welfare, and day-care centers. Correspondents include Frances Coe, Santa (Reul) Schoof, LeMoyne-Owen College in Tennessee, Memphis Academy of Arts, and Memphis city schools.

5,475. Robinson, James H.
Papers. 1938-72. Ca. 35,000 items.
Open. Description, card catalog, and register.
Amistad Research Center.
Robinson (1907-72) was a Presbyterian minister and, in 1958, founder of Operation Crossroads Africa, a program through which more than 4000 American college students and teachers, many of them women, participated in projects in Africa. Correspondence, manuscripts of writings, published and unpublished articles, speeches, sermons, books, clippings, and other material dealing with Operation Crossroads, which served as a model for the Peace Corps. The project's workers helped build more than 100 schools as well as medical clinics, orphanages, village water systems, and other facilities in Africa. Since 1960 more than 300 African youth leaders have visited the US as part of the Crossroads program. Robinson was awarded an honorary doctor of divinity degree by Dartmouth College.

5,476. Tureaud, Alexander P.
Papers. 1799-1974. Ca. 31 ft.
Open. Unpublished guide.
Amistad Research Center.
Correspondence, reports, financial records, biographical sketches, news releases, photos, clippings, and other papers of Tureaud, a New Orleans civil rights lawyer. Includes more than 100 letters from Constance Baker Motley, a US district judge in New York state; the correspondence spans the years 1948 to 1966 and pertains primarily to civil rights cases on which Motely and Tureaud collaborated.

5,477. Voorhees, Lillian Welch
Papers. 1892-1973. Ca. 14,500 items.
Open. Unpublished guide.
Amistad Research Center.
A college professor and civil rights activist, Voorhees (1894-1972) taught English, speech, and dramatics from 1917 to 1963 at Tougaloo College in Mississippi, Talladega College in Alabama, and Fisk University in Tennessee. Correspondence, diaries, autobiography, plays, thesis and dissertation for Columbia Teachers College, bills, receipts, material related to organizations, photos, clippings, memorabilia, and other material; a number of the plays were performed under Voorhees's direction and relate to black history. Voorhees was treasurer of Fisk Union Church, a United Church of Christ church, from 1944 to 1969 and was a member of the board of directors and treasurer of the Eighteenth Avenue Youth Center in Nashville from 1958 until her death. She was a charter member of the National Association of Dramatic and Speech Arts, serving as its executive secretary from 1937 to 1942 and from 1947 to 1952, and a life member of the American Education Theatre Association and the Speech Association of America. She earned a doctorate in education at Columbia University.

5,478. Washington, Fredi
Papers. 1925-75. Ca. 750 items.
Open. Description.
Amistad Research Center.
Correspondence, photos, a scrapbook, programs, invitations, and clippings of Washington, a dancer, actress, and newspaper columnist. A Savannah, GA, native who was educated in Pennsylvania and New York, Washington made her stage debut in *Shuffle Along,* in which she appeared from 1922 to 1924. For the next three years she was the featured dancer at New York's Club Alabama and appeared with Paul Robeson in the drama *Black Boy.* In 1927 and 1928 she toured in Europe and appeared in New York supper clubs with Al Moore as a ballroom dance team, Moiret and Fredi. During the next 15 years she performed on the stage and in movies. In 1937, she was a cofounder of the Negro Actors Guild and served as the group's executive secretary for its first two years and again in 1948 and 1949. Her column "Fredi Says" appeared in *People's Voice* from 1943 to 1947. She is the widow of H. Anthony Bell, a Stamford, CT, dentist.

5,479. Williams, Camilla
Papers. 1944-73. 1010 items.
Open. Unpublished guide.
Amistad Research Center.
Williams was one of the first black women to sing a leading role with a major opera company. During the 1940s she was a leading soprano with the New York City Opera. Correspondence, receipts, photos, programs, and memorabilia.

5,480. Benjamin Franklin Butler Proclamation
Papers. 1862. 1 item.
Open. Catalog.
Historic New Orleans Collection.
Butler (1818-93), a major general, commanded the US Army Department of the Gulf and Federal occupation forces in New Orleans during the Civil War. A reprint of General Order No. 28, in which he declared that all women who behaved discourteously toward Union occupation troops were to be considered "no more than women of the streets" and were to be treated as such.

5,481. Butler Family
Papers. 1778-1975. 2034 items.
Open. Calendar.
Historic New Orleans Collection.
Papers of Edward George Washington Butler (1800-88), a planter and professional military man who served in the Mexican War, and his wife Frances Parke Lewis, a great-granddaughter of Martha Washington. Correspondence, military orders, pamphlets, books, and other papers. Butler, a member of a Revolutionary War family, became the ward of Andrew Jackson after his parents died when he was a child. He and his wife established their home on the western side of the Mississippi River between New Orleans and Baton Rouge in

1831. Collection includes letters that Nelly Parke (Custis) Lewis wrote to her daughter Frances Butler after the Butlers moved from Virginia to Louisiana and other letters of women of the Butler family, which contain comments on the times and mention of public figures in Virginia and Washington, DC.

5,482. Davis, Varina Anne (Howell)
Papers. 1902-06. 3 items.
Open. Descriptions.
Historic New Orleans Collection.
Letters written from New Orleans in 1902 and New York in 1906 by Davis (1826-1906), widow of Confederate President Jefferson Davis, reflect hardships she encountered during her later years.

5,483. Gottschalk, Louis Moreau
Papers. 1842-1911. 284 items.
Open. Calendar.
Historic New Orleans Collection.
Papers, consisting chiefly of correspondence, of Gottschalk, a composer regarded as controversial during his lifetime, and his sister Clara (Gottschalk) Peterson. The letters contain discussions of Louis Gottschalk, whose music was described by many as dissonant. Also contains photos of Clara Peterson and others.

5,484. Greenwood, Moses
Papers. 1844-1952. 810 items.
Open. Calendar.
Historic New Orleans Collection.
A New Orleans businessman, Greenwood headed the Louisiana Relief Committee, which helped persons forced to emigrate by Union occupation troops because they refused to pledge allegiance to the Federal government during the Civil War. Based in Mobile, AL, the Committee attempted to place the refugees or to provide food, clothing, shelter, and other essentials. Collection principally consists of correspondence. Eleven letters from women during the Civil War period provide a view of southern women; some involve the sale or attempted sale of valuables by women who found themselves in financial difficulty. Six letters from the Reconstruction period are from women, most of whom appeal for loans.

5,485. Grima Family
Papers. 1856-1921. 444 items.
Open. Calendar and general description.
Historic New Orleans Collection.
The Grima family has long been prominent in Louisiana, especially during the flowering of Creole culture during the 19th century. Adelaide Grima, the wife of notary Felix Grima, was the family's matriarch. Collection consists chiefly of correspondence between family members during and after the Civil War. Included are letters of Adelaide Grima describing the effect of the War on her family, which was forced to leave Louisiana in 1864. She describes the lack of work, shortage of money, illnesses, rationing of coal and wood, the change of planters' crops from sugar to cotton, the loss of household goods during the family's emigration to Augusta, GA, and the high cost of living in the Georgia town. Also includes letters from a daughter Marie Grima and a cousin Eugenie Lavie. A letter from Amelie Martin, a friend residing in Marseilles, France, concerns events of the Franco-Prussian War in 1871.

5,486. Hobbs, Morris Henry, and Hobbs, Alice "Judy" Seddon
Papers. 1959-68. 8 items.
Open. Catalog.
Historic New Orleans Collection.
Christmas newsletters of Morris Hobbs (1892-1967), an artist, and his wife Judy Hobbs (?-). The Hobbses were botanists and wildlife enthusiasts who lived in New Orleans for many years while he made prints of the city and related subjects. Their annual, personally illustrated newsletters contain details about their travels; some family news; such interests as the wildlife, natural settings, and life styles of Costa Rica, Guatemala, and southern Florida; and gardening and ornithology. A 1968 letter contains a poem by their son Bill Hobbs.

5,487. Merrick Family
Papers. 1865-1913. 35 items.
Open. Collection statement and calendar.
Historic New Orleans Collection.
Papers of Edwin Thomas Merrick (1809-?), a Wilbraham, MA, native who twice was elected chief justice of the Louisiana Supreme Court; his wife Caroline Elizabeth (Thomas) Merrick (1825-1908), a women's rights advocate and author of *Old Times in Dixie,* a volume about the Merrick family before and after the Civil War; and their son David Thomas Merrick, who served in the Confederate Army. Collection, the bulk of which dates from 1866 to 1889, consists of correspondence, official papers, and receipts and includes letters from Frances E. Willard and Susan B. Anthony to Caroline Merrick, a Louisianan who was president of the New Orleans WCTU. Also included are two oaths of allegiance and a federal pardon, all dated 1865, and voter registration from 1868 of Edwin Merrick, who served as a district judge before moving to Jefferson City (now part of New Orleans) to assume his state Supreme Court position in 1855. Letters from Willard and Anthony to Caroline Merrick chiefly relate to organization of women's rights groups and requests that she seek legislation to protect women and girls from attacks by men, that she attend a northern convention, and that she appear before a congressional committee to destroy the illusion that the women's rights cause was merely "a Northern women's craze." Merrick also received a letter from a Point Coupee Parish school board official, who discusses his attempts to hire women teachers and vows his support and that of an area judge for women's rights.

5,488. New Orleans Arts and Crafts Club
Records. 1920s-40s. Ca. 2 ft.
Open. No guide.
Historic New Orleans Collection.
This group assisted the fine arts and artists in the New Orleans area by sponsoring classes in various media, by holding exhibits, and occasionally by providing a sales outlet for members and students. Correspondence, scrapbooks, brochures, and clippings include items regarding the group's inception, artists, exhibits, classes, awards, and artists' sponsors. Among the artists included are Caroline Durieux, Enrique Alferez, Conrad Albrizio, and John McCrady.

5,489. Phelps, Edwin Ledyard
Papers. 1783-1969. Ca. 200 items.
Open. Calendar.
Historic New Orleans Collection.
Phelps, an itinerant portraitist, was a native of the Northeast who was educated in Kentucky; he traveled as far south as New Orleans before settling in Ohio. Chiefly correspondence, travel diaries, a sketch of his father, and genealogical research completed in ca. 1969 regarding the Phelps family. Contains family correspondence, including letters of Phelps's sisters, and information concerning Phelps's father's Revolutionary War record, his wife Cornelia, and their son. Material provides a picture of family life in the late 18th and the 19th centuries.

5,490. St. Geme, Henri de
Papers. 1799-1904. 849 items.
Open. Calendar and general description.
Historic New Orleans Collection.
Correspondence from managers of the Louisiana plantation of St. Geme, who moved to Louisiana from Santo Domingo in ca. 1809 and remained there until 1818 when he returned to France. The letters of plantation managers and others provide detailed information about the life, customs, and social history of early 19th-century Louisiana women, particularly in New Orleans. Also contains accounts, business records, official documents, and clippings. St. Geme's plantation was located at Gentilly, now a part of New Orleans.

5,491. Slavery in Louisiana
Collection. 1785-1869. 2 Hollinger boxes.
Open. Calendar and general description.
Historic New Orleans Collection.
Legal documents and records related to slavery in Louisiana, which in 1860 ranked seventh among southern states in total number of slaves held but first in the number of owners who held 100 or more slaves. Includes acts of sale, 1821-60; promissory statements by New Orleans mayors for contracted slave labor; receipts for taxes paid on slaves, 1820-60; and mortgages on slaves in St. James, Jefferson, and Orleans parishes. Also included are items regarding slave trade with Africa and runaway slaves, reports on New Orleans municipal work performed by hired and slave-contracted Negroes, and a record book containing scattered listings of slaves (men, women, and children), their births and deaths, the dates of sale of runaways, entries regarding the owner's family, and some postwar accounts.

5,492. Waters, Henry Harcourt
Papers. 1875-1954. 4 Hollinger boxes.
Open. Calendar and general description.
Historic New Orleans Collection.
Waters (1844-1902), a Canadian native and curate of St. James Cathedral in Toronto, came to New Orleans in 1875 to become rector of St. Paul's Episcopal Church, where he served until his death. Letters, records, books, and travel diaries, the bulk of which dates from 1877 to 1902. Includes Waters's diary for 1901; verse notebooks, a travel diary for 1877, and a flower press of May Carroll, whom he married; religious books of the Waters family; six items regarding property and tax transactions of St. Paul's Church; and clippings regarding Waters's career and death. Waters won the allegiance of the city in 1878 when he returned from a vacation to care for those afflicted during an epidemic.

5,493. Hotel Dieu Hospital
Records. 1917- . 9 shelves.
Access restricted. No guide.
Hotel Dieu Hospital Library.
Founded in 1859 by the Daughters of Charity of St. Vincent de Paul, the Hospital has been administered by members of the order, beginning with Sister Theresa Frances Sheridan. Hospital and medical staff publications, photos, brochures, clippings, a history of the hospital by Roger Baudier entitled *A Century of Service* (1943), artifacts, and other items. Founded in France in 1633, the Daughters of Charity is described as the world's largest religious order for women. Their mission is nursing, teaching, and social welfare. An American counterpart of the order was founded in 1809 by Saint Elizabeth Ann (Bayley) Seton in Emmitsburg, MD. Mother Seton's Sisters of Charity became affiliated with the Daughters of Charity in 1850.

5,494. Hotel Dieu School of Nursing
Records. 1904-74. 1 file drawer and 1 vol.
Access restricted. No guide.
Hotel Dieu Hospital Library.
Opened by Sister Raphael Jones in 1899, the School had trained nearly 2000 women and 22 men under the direction of the Daughters of Charity of St. Vincent de Paul by 1974 when it became a part of the Louisiana State University system. Nursing school and hospital publications, a history, school yearbooks, photos and albums, clippings, and

reports on National League for Nursing accreditation visits.

5,495. French Superior Council of Louisiana
Records. 1718-69. Ca. 144 ft.
Open. Unpublished guide.
Louisiana State Museum.
The Council, a court of justice created in 1712, was abolished in 1769 by Governor Alexandro O'Reilly after cession of Louisiana from France to Spain. Records of judicial proceedings; successions; manumissions; personal and business contracts; wills; birth, death, and marriage certificates; personal estate and ship inventories; and other items reflecting the political, cultural, and legal history of French colonial Louisiana.

5,496. Spanish Cabildo of Louisiana
Records. 1769-1803. Ca. 144 ft.
Open. Unpublished guide.
Louisiana State Museum.
The Cabildo was a court and administrative council created in 1769 and abolished in 1803. Records of judicial proceedings; successions; manumissions; personal and business contracts; wills; birth, death, and marriage certificates; personal estate inventories; and other items provide information about Spanish colonial Louisiana.

5,497. Louisiana Division
Collection. Nd. No size given.
Open. Unpublished guides.
New Orleans Public Library.
Includes material pertaining to the New Orleans Mardi Gras, more than 30,000 photos concerning Louisiana-related topics, and the City Archives collection, which includes manuscript and printed material produced by New Orleans city agencies since 1769. Also includes microfilm editions of Louisiana census schedules, the civil court records of 42 parishes, theses and dissertations, and early New Orleans notarial records. The Division's material contains information about New Orleans women from the city's early days.

5,498. Davis, Mollie (Moore)
Papers. 1897-1927. 80 items.
Open. No guide.
New Orleans Public Library, Louisiana Division.
Davis (1852-1909), whose full name was Mary Evelyn "Mollie" (Moore) Davis, was a novelist and poet whose works include *Jaconetta: Her Loves* (1901), *The Little Chevalier* (1903), *The Price of Silence* (1907), and *Selected Poems* (1927), which was published as a memorial volume. Personal correspondence; letters relating to publication of *Selected Poems,* a copy of Grace King's introduction for the volume, and galley proofs; typescripts of Davis's poems; and other papers.

5,499. ERA Club
Records. 1914-19. 300-page vol.
Open. No guide.
New Orleans Public Library, Louisiana Division.
While primarily a woman's suffrage organization, the ERA Club also concerned itself with local sanitation, public schools, and mayoral elections and international issues including the Paris peace conference in 1919. Minutes, correspondence, list of members and officers, political broadsides, and clippings. The Club, the full title of which was the Equal Rights Association Club, was reorganized in 1914 after a period of inactivity. The predecessor organization dated from at least 1903. Kate Gordon, a philanthropist who helped form the Louisiana State Tuberculosis Commission, and Florence Loeber, a New Orleans attorney, were involved in the Club's work. The collection is also available on microfilm.

5,500. Local Council of Women of New Orleans
Records. 1898-1903. 100 items.
Open. No guide.
New Orleans Public Library, Louisiana Division.
Founded in 1898 as part of the National Council of Women, the Local Council was made up of representatives of all New Orleans women's groups. Charter; bylaws; minutes of the Local Council and its committee on sanitation; correspondence; lists of members, officers, and member organizations; and clippings. Sophie B. Wright, an educator and philanthropist, was president of the Local Council, which was committed to progressive movements, including sanitation, city beautification, and improved public education.

5,501. Tallant, Robert
Papers. Ca. 1930-57. Ca. 1000 items.
Open. Unpublished guide.
New Orleans Public Library, Louisiana Division.
Notes and research material, typescripts of oral interviews, and book manuscripts of Tallant (1909-57), an author. Includes typescripts of interviews with contemporaries of Marie Laveau, who was called the voodoo queen of New Orleans, and interviews dealing with Mrs. Lorenzo Blanc, Mother Mary, Madame Brent, Mother Kate Francis, Mother Anderson, Mother Catherine, and other women involved in voodoo, clairvoyance, and spiritualism. The interviews provide extensive information about spiritualism in late 19th-and early 20th-century New Orleans.

5,502. Woman's Anti-Lottery League
Records. 1891-92. 70 items.
Open. No guide.
New Orleans Public Library, Louisiana Division.
Created in 1881 in New Orleans as an adjunct to the all-male Anti-Lottery League of Louisiana, the Woman's League sought revocation of the Louisiana Lottery Company's charter. Minutes of the Woman's League and its executive committee, correspondence, membership lists, political broadsides and pamphlets, and clippings. The Lottery Company was founded in 1868.

5,503. Archives
Records. 1856- . No size given.
Closed. No guide.
Our Lady of Holy Cross, Marianite Provincial House.
This religious order of women devoted to teaching, nursing, and social work was founded in France in 1841 and established in Louisiana in 1849. Council minutes, proceedings of provincial chapter sessions, financial records, circular letters, chronicles of the houses, records of visitations, and other records. Much of the material is in French.

5,504. Boggs, Corrine M. "Lindy" Claiborne
Papers. Ca. 1935- . 1 folder.
Open. No guide.
Tulane University Archives.
Articles and clippings of Boggs, who has represented a New Orleans district in the US House of Representatives since her husband T. Hale Boggs disappeared during an Alaskan plane trip in 1972. Born in Pointe Coupee Parish, LA, Lindy Boggs taught history in Romeville in St. James Parish, LA, after graduating from Sophie Newcomb College.

5,505. Dix, Dorothy
Papers. 1861-1951. 1 folder.
Open. No guide.
Tulane University Archives.
Clippings of Dix (1861-1951), a New Orleans newspaperwoman who became known internationally through her advice to the lovelorn column. Dix also covered sensational stories for William Randolph Hearst's *New York Journal,* among them the trials of Harry K. Thaw, Nan Patterson, and Ruth Wheeler and the Hall-Mills case.

5,506. Many, Anna Estelle
Papers. 1907- . Ca. 1 in.
Open. No guide.
Tulane University Archives.
Correspondence, a copy of a vita, biographical information, pamphlets, and booklets of Many (ca. 1890-), who served as dean of H. Sophie Newcomb Memorial College for Women for periods between 1943 and 1953. Many had a long career at Newcomb, which is a distinct yet integral part of Tulane University. She received her bachelor's degree from the school in 1907 and a master's from Tulane in 1913. In 1918 she served in France with the Newcomb Relief Unit, the only relief unit sent by a southern women's college; the unit was organized originally under the American National Red Cross. In 1921 she was appointed counselor to women at Newcomb with the title of assistant professor of mathematics. She has been a member of the National Education Association, the AAUW, the AAUP, the National Association of Women Deans and Counselors, Phi Beta Kappa, the American Mathematical Society, and the Mathematical Association of America.

5,507. Newcomb, Josephine Louise (Le Monnier)
Papers. 1880- . Ca. 2 in.
Open. No guide.
Tulane University Archives.
Correspondence, pamphlets, brochures, and clippings of [Mrs.] Newcomb (1816-1901), who provided a donation that funded the establishment of H. Sophie Newcomb Memorial College for Women in 1886. The College, a distinct yet integral part of Tulane University, was named in honor of Josephine Newcomb's deceased daughter Harriett Sophie Newcomb.

5,508. Tulane University Women's Association
Records. 1910- . Ca. 6 in.
Open. No guide.
Tulane University Archives.
Founded in 1910 as the Tulane University tea committee, this social organization originally included faculty wives; it has been known as the Tulane University Women's Club and later as the Tulane University Women's Association. Announcements of social engagements, organizational announcements, and clippings relating to the club's actitivies. Projects have included a book exchange, bridge groups, French and Spanish language groups, a mother's club, gourmet cooking, needlework, tennis, sketching, and ikebana, or, Japanese floral art.

5,509. Beer, William
Papers. 1892-1924. 3608 items.
Open. Card catalog.
Tulane University Library, Special Collections.
Beer (1849-1929) was librarian of Tulane's Howard Memorial Library (now Howard-Tilton Memorial Library) from ca. 1888 to 1894. Correspondence and notes on Louisiana history and bibliography. Includes exchanges with noted scholars, writers, and librarians, among them Eleanor McMain, head resident of Kingsley House, and short story writer Ruth McEnery Stuart.

5,510. Christian Woman's Exchange
Records. 1881-1967. 1304 items.
Open. Unpublished guide.
Tulane University Library, Special Collections.
The oldest women's organization in New Orleans, the Exchange was founded in 1881 to sell homemade items and family belongings of needy women; the group's facilities later expanded to include a library, lunchroom, homemaking classes, and a rooming house. Minutes, financial records, and correspondence of the Exchange, which has its headquarters and shop in the Hermann-Grima House, a French Quarter home it helped to restore.

5,511. Collins, Dorothy (Spencer)
Papers. 1908-74. 1487 items.
Open. Unpublished guide.

Tulane University Library, Special Collections. Collins is the daughter of Walter B. Spencer, a print and map collector. Personal and social correspondence, social diaries, photos, clippings, and memorabilia. Includes correspondence from Paul Tillich, Adlai E. Stevenson, Alf Landon, Lyle Saxon, Frances Parkinson Keyes, Stanley Reed, Thomas F. Green, James A. Pike, British Air Minister Arthur Henderson, and Francis B. Sayre. Portions of the correspondence relate to the Episcopal church in the Baltimore area and to Episcopalian missions in Asia. Social diaries dating from 1908 to 1974 contain entries about parties attended, luncheons, and travel in New Orleans, Washington, DC, Maryland, Europe, and the Orient.

5,512. De Milt, Clara
Papers. 1891-1953. 1196 items.
Open. Unpublished guide.
Tulane University Library, Special Collections. Appointed assistant professor in the Newcomb College chemistry department in 1925 and department head in 1926, de Milt (1880-1958) later joined the Tulane graduate school faculty where she served as chairman of the chemistry department until 1949. Correspondence, notes, lectures, manuscripts and reprints of her works, her doctoral dissertation, course material, photos, and other papers. Includes letters of Walcott Gibb and Ann Hero; notes, lectures, manuscripts, and reprints relating to de Milt's work on organic chemistry and the history of chemistry and science; two manuscripts of a translation done by Hero and de Milt; papers written about de Milt after her death; and a funeral announcement for George Urbain.

5,513. Hodgson, Daisy
Papers. 1870-1935. 165 items.
Open. Unpublished guide.
Tulane University Library, Special Collections. [Miss] Hodgson was a leader in the Ladies' Confederate Memorial Association. Correspondence, programs, circulars, and clippings. Includes letters from [Mrs.] Mary D. Robinson of Robinson Springs, MS, about her mineral water business; letters addressed to Mrs. W. J. Behan, president of the Confederated Southern Memorial Association; letters, programs, circulars, and clippings about the Robert E. Lee memorial services and statue; and reunion orders dating from 1902 to 1917 of the United Confederate Veterans.

5,514. Hutson, Ethel
Papers. 1921-47. 3714 items.
Open. Unpublished guide.
Tulane University Library, Special Collections. [Miss] Hutson was a New Orleans newspaperwoman. Correspondence, manuscripts, clippings, and printed material pertaining to her public activities and interests and to woman suffrage, particularly in Louisiana. Hutson's civic interests included education, public utilities, child welfare, preservation of the St. Louis Hotel, public finance, and transportation.

5,515. Kingsley House
Records. 1899-1970. 47,740 items.
Partially restricted. Inventory and card catalog.
Tulane University Library, Special Collections. Established by Trinity Church in 1896, Kingsley House was incorporated in 1902 as a New Orleans settlement house without religious affiliation. Administrative papers including board reports and papers of the head residents, financial records, material related to House services and programs, papers concerning historical studies of the institution, photos, scrapbooks, drawings, and printed matter. Most of the material is related to the administrations of head residents Eleanor McMain, who held the post from 1902 to 1934, and Emeric Kurtagh, who headed the institution from 1941 to 1949. McMain urged the House's incorporation as an institution without religious affiliation and worked to expand the House's services and to establish Camp Onward, a summer camp for neighborhood children. Kurtagh, a professional social worker, introduced a program emphasizing group work and data recording. The House became a fieldwork post for students of the Tulane school of social work. Kurtagh also enhanced relations between the House and the city's other social service agencies. Contains material regarding head resident Katherine Hardy, labor education, Eleanor McMain Girls' High School, Margery Sandfield, Margery Schreiver, the Textile Workers' Union of America, and welfare conditions in New Orleans.

5,516. Louisiana Women's War Relief Association
Records. 1898-99. 742 items.
Open. Index and card catalog.
Tulane University Library, Special Collections. Established in New Orleans during the Spanish-American War, the Association sent food and clothing to US soldiers and assisted destitute families of men in active service. Included in the Louisiana Historical Association Collection, the Women's Association's records consist of minute books, financial records, and correspondence concerning the group's activities in raising money and supplies for camps and hospitals in Miami, Tampa, Key West, FL, and Santiago de Cuba. Included are letters from Louisiana and Mississippi women volunteering to aid the Association and from camp commanders and enlisted men thanking the group for its assistance. The financial records include correspondence, bills, receipts, canceled checks, vouchers, and lists of expenditures and of Association officers and members.

5,517. McConnell Family
Papers. 1723-1962. 4565 items.
Partially restricted. Inventory and card catalog.
Tulane University Library, Special Collections. Included with the correspondence, legal records, photos, clippings, and other papers of the McConnell family are those of Elizabeth Logan McConnell (?-1941), a New Orleans suffrage worker, and of Delphine Margaret McConnell as well as items relating to H. Sophie Newcomb College for Women. Elizabeth McConnell was particularly active in the efforts of the New Orleans ERA Club between ca. 1908 and 1912 to have women placed on the Louisiana State Board of Education. Delphine McConnell's papers include documents and correspondence dated from 1914 to 1934 concerning curatorship of the estate she inherited from her father James McConnell, Sr. The Newcomb College papers, which date from 1887 to 1912, include correspondence between [Mrs.] Josephine Louise Newcomb and her attorney James McConnell concerning the founding and progress of the College and legal arrangements she made to leave the bulk of her estate to the school.

5,518. Mitchell, Lise
Papers. 1838-1932. 336 items.
Open. Calendar and card catalog.
Tulane University Library, Special Collections. Personal correspondence and a diary from 1862 to 1867 of Mitchell (1838-1932), a Louisiana woman who was the goddaughter of Jefferson Davis, president of the Confederacy. Mitchell was adopted as a young child by her grandparents Joseph E. Davis and Eliza Van Benthuysen Davis following the death of her mother Mary (Davis) Mitchell. Includes letters to Lise Mitchell from her father Charles Jewett Mitchell, from Jefferson Davis to her and her brother Joseph, and from her husband William D. Hamer, her stepmother Lucy Bradford Mitchell, her stepsister Amanda M. Ganier, and other family members. The Jefferson Davis letters chiefly concern family matters after the Civil War. At the suggestion of her grandfather, Mitchell began her diary with a description of an 1862 trip she made with her grandparents and others to visit the Jefferson Davises in Richmond, VA. She concludes her diary by expressing concern for the fate of her homeless family and despair for her grandfather and father.

5,519. New Orleans Girls' High School Alumnae Association
Records. 1894-1925. 1 vol.
Open. Card catalog.
Tulane University Library, Special Collections. Minutes, including those of annual meetings; reports on special activities; brief biographical sketches of members; and an essay on the early history of New Orleans high schools by [Miss] Harriett A. Sater.

5,520. Poydras Home
Records. 1778-1960. 90 vols. and 31,260 items.
Open. Inventory and card catalog.
Tulane University Library, Special Collections. Founded as the Female Orphan Society in 1817, Poydras Home was maintained by wealthy New Orleans women as a charitable institution for widows, children, and girls; the facility is now a home for the aged. Charter, constitution, and bylaws of the Society as well as annual reports; administrative, financial, and medical reports; asylum rules; correspondence; and building plans of the Home. Includes salaries, memoranda, and lists (some from 1820) of names and short histories of widows and children at the Home. Correspondence principally relates to management of the Home and the children housed there. Financial records pertain to rental, improvements, and taxes on properties owned; also included are leases, mortgages, vouchers, bills, bank statements, and realtors' statements concerning income on property.

5,521. Robinson, Martha: Silver Thimble Fund
Papers. 1925-50. 591 items.
Open. Card catalog.
Tulane University Library, Special Collections. Correspondence of [Mrs.] Robinson (ca. 1890-), a New Orleans reformer and preservationist, chiefly consists of correspondence with [Miss] H. E. Hope-Clarke of Wimbledon, England, concerning Robinson's efforts to establish a Silver Thimble Fund group in the US during WWII, the success of her efforts, other war relief activities, and the two women's comments on the war. Also includes wartime clippings from England and America and printed material concerning the Fund.

5,522. Saxon, Elizabeth Lyle
Papers. 1784-1946. 10 vols. and 3448 items.
Open. Card catalog.
Tulane University Library, Special Collections. Papers of Saxon, a poet and newspaper writer in New Orleans during the 1880s and 1890s, are included in those of Lyle Saxon (1879-1936), a Lousiana writer who may have been Elizabeth Saxon's son. Her papers consist of correspondence, manuscripts and writings, a photo, scrapbooks, and clippings of her poems and newspaper items she wrote on such subjects as Union sentiment in the South during the Civil War, personal reminiscences, Helena P. Blavatsky, the gold question, women's rights and suffrage, and prison reform.

5,523. Southern States Art League
Records. 1921-47. 907 items.
Open. Unpublished guide.
Tulane University Library, Special Collections. Correspondence, membership lists, bulletins, press lists, clippings, and records of prizes of annual exhibitions and of donors to the Woodward Award Fund.

5,524. Stanton, Adele Townsend
Papers. 1874-1928. 133 items.
Open. Unpublished guide.
Tulane University Library, Special Collections.
Correspondence and manuscripts of essays, stories, and poems by Stanton, a New Orleans author. Includes personal letters from Mollie (Moore) Davis and from admirers of Stanton's literary work.

5,525. Stein, Gertrude
Papers. 1933-35. 18 items.
Open. Card catalog.
Tulane University Library, Special Collections.
[Miss] Stein (1874-1946) was an American author best known for her stylistic experiments with language and formal construction.
Correspondence, including letters from Stein, Alice B. Toklas, Bernard Fay, and Marvin Chauncey Ross to Rosseau Voorhies; post cards; a list of lecture topics; a photo; and a clipping announcing a lecture in Chicago by Voorhies. In one of her letters, Stein discusses her writing technique and refers to her consideration of verb tenses; other items deal with her lectures in Chicago in 1934.

5,526. Stuart, Ruth (McEnery)
Papers. 1879-1912. 90 items.
Open. Card catalog.
Tulane University Library, Special Collections.
Correspondence, notes and memoranda, manuscripts, and a scrapbook of Stuart (1849-1917), a Louisiana short story writer. Contains letters to C. Augusta and Emily F. Pope of Boston, a typescript of "The Final Triumph of Jeremiah Prophet Elizah," and a manuscript of "The Luck of Batture Baptiste."

5,527. Thompson, Eleanor P.
Papers. 1869-1939. 366 items.
Open. Unpublished guide.
Tulane University Library, Special Collections.
Miscellaneous material dealing with social and business life in New Orleans from 1870 to 1940. Includes items concerning fairs, expositions, balls, receptions, concerts, theater performances, social and religious organizations, dedications, and women's fashions. Also contains souvenir booklets, city maps, and business advertisements.

5,528. Townsend, Mary Ashley
Papers. 1850-1911. 916 items.
Open. Unpublished guide.
Tulane University Library, Special Collections.
[Mrs.] Townsend was a New Orleans writer. Collection contains personal and business correspondence, including letters from Oliver Wendell Holmes, William Preston Johnson, J. B. Lippincott, and George Moorman; manuscripts of Townsend's stories, essays, and poems; and diaries, clippings, and other material pertaining to her book *Here and There in Mexico.*

5,529. Armstrong, Lillian Hardin
Papers. 1923- . 2 folders, 200 recording discs, and 2 tapes.
Open. Card catalog.
Tulane University Library, William Ransom Hogan Jazz Archive.
Lil Armstrong (ca. 1898-1973) was a jazz pianist and composer and from 1924 to 1938 the second wife of musician Louis Armstrong. Correspondence relating to her early music lessons and life in Chicago, to her experiences as a musician in the New Orleans Creole Jazz Band, and to her marriage to Louis Armstrong; includes as well a taped interview and transcripts, biographical material and clippings, records on which Lil Armstrong's band is featured, records on which other musicians and bands perform her arrangements and compositions, and a number of records of King Oliver and Louis with her band, which was variously named New Orleans Bootblacks and New Orleans Wanderers. She studied arranging and composing for two years at Fisk University in Nashville. During the early 1930s she led her own all-woman band. Her compositions included "My Heart," "You're Next," "King of the Zulus," and "Hotter Than That."

5,530. Holiday, Billie
Papers. 1933- . 1 folder and ca. 25 recording discs.
Open. Card catalog.
Tulane University Library, William Ransom Hogan Jazz Archive.
Born Eleanora Fagan in Baltimore, Holiday (1915-59) became an internationally known jazz singer and songwriter whose compositions included "Strange Fruit," "God Bless the Child," and "Billie's Blues." Biographical material, clippings, and recordings of "Fine and Mellow," "Strange Fruit," "Sentimental and Melancholy," "The Mood I'm In," "Easy Living," "Foolin' Myself," and many other songs. The illegitimate daughter of guitarist Clarence Holiday, she moved to New York City in the late 1920s and worked for a time as a "$20 call girl." Nicknamed Lady Day, Billie Holiday had her first major engagement at the Log Cabin Club in New York. She made a recording in 1933 with Benny Goodman and sang with Teddy Wilson combos from 1935 to 1939. She began recording under her own name in 1936. Holiday had a severe narcotics habit that led her to seek treatment several times; she served a jail sentence on a narcotics charge. Other information on Holiday may be found in Jazz Archives material on Bessie Smith and Hazel Scott.

5,531. Morton, Jelly Roll
Papers. 1885- . 2 folders and ca. 200 recording discs.
Open. Card catalog and subject file.
Tulane University Library, William Ransom Hogan Jazz Archive.
The self-proclaimed inventor of jazz, Ferdinand Joseph "Jelly Roll" Morton (1885-1941) was a jazz composer, pianist, combo leader, and arranger. Phonograph records and biographical material, including correspondence, announcements, clippings, and interview transcript. The composer of "Tiger Rag," "Jelly Roll Blues," "Pearls," "Kansas City Stomp," "The Crave," "Shoe Shiner's Drag," and many other pieces, Morton was a major early jazz figure whose piano compositions blended the New Orleans style with ragtime. Morton began his career in the early 1900s in the bawdy houses of the New Orleans Storyville district. He composed and performed risqué songs about women, and he talked of women in many of his performance numbers.

5,532. Pierce, Billie
Papers. 1951- . 3 folders, ca. 25 recording discs, and ca. 18 tapes.
Open. Card catalog and subject file.
Tulane University Library, William Ransom Hogan Jazz Archive.
Wilhelmina "Billie" Pierce (1907-74), a classic blues singer, was a lifelong exponent of the improvisational New Orleans jazz style, which is characterized as having more flexibility and spontaneity than Dixieland. Typescripts of interviews, records, tapes, articles, a few items of correspondence, pamphlets, and publicity material. Born in Marianna, FL, Pierce grew up in Pensacola, FL, where in 1922 she played piano for vocalist Bessie Smith. Pierce worked with Ma Rainey's troupe and also backed Ida Cox. She moved to New Orleans in 1929 and married cornetist De De Pierce in 1939. The couple worked in New Orleans clubs and halls for nearly 20 years. In the early 1960s, after a series of illnesses, the Pierces began to make appearances at Preservation Hall and eventually became part of the Hall's band. Collection includes interviews with the Pierces which contain information on their individual careers and their work together as jazz musicians.

5,533. Smith, Bessie
Papers. 1923- . 1 folder, ca. 75 recording discs, and 2 tapes.
Open. Card catalog and subject file.
Tulane University Library, William Ransom Hogan Jazz Archive.
Termed the greatest of the blues singers, Smith (1894-1937) made more than 160 recordings and spent nearly her entire career singing before black audiences. Phonograph records, tape reels, articles of music criticism, press releases, and printed material reflect her career. She began singing in her hometown of Chattanooga, TN, then in southern carnivals and tent shows, then with blues artist Ma Rainey, and finally began recording for Columbia Phonograph Company. Her recordings included "Downhearted Blues," "Gimme a Pigfoot," "Nobody Knows You," and "Money Blues."

5,534. Williams, Mary Lou
Papers. 1920s- . 1 folder and ca. 30 recording discs.
Open. Card catalog and subject file.
Tulane University Library, William Ransom Hogan Jazz Archive.
Born Mary Elfrieda Winn in Pittsburgh, Williams (1910-) became prominent as a jazz pianist and arranger-composer. Printed material and phonograph records. Best known for her compositions and piano arrangements, Williams toured as a teenager under the name Mary Lou Burleigh. In 1925 and 1926 she played the vaudeville circuit in a band led by alto saxist John Williams, whom she married. During the 1930s she wrote many arrangements for the Andy Kirk band and was billed as "The Lady Who Swings the Band." She later worked as an arranger for Duke Ellington and wrote the famous arrangement of "Trumpet No End (Blue Skies)." She also arranged for Benny Goodman, Louis Armstrong, Cab Calloway, Tommy Dorsey, Glen Gray, Gus Arnheim, and Earl Hines. After the mid 1940s she worked in clubs in New York, France, and England. Among her compositions are "Froggy Bottom," "Mary's Idea," "Mess-a-Stomp," "Dirge Blues," "The Devil," "Black Priest of the Andes," "Night Life," and "Mary Lou's Mass." The collection includes recordings by Andy Kirk and His Clouds of Joy featuring Williams's "Twinklin," "Walkin' and Swingin'"; recordings by Goodman and his orchestra of Williams's "Roll 'Em"; and her own piano solos of "Drag 'Em" and "Night Life."

5,535. Christian, Marcus Bruce
Papers. Ca. 1850-1976. Ca. 60 ft.
Access restricted. No guide.
University of New Orleans, Earl K. Long Library, Archives and Manuscripts Department.
Correspondence, manuscripts, notes, and historical papers of Christian (1900-76), a black New Orleans poet, journalist, printer, author, and historian who specialized in the history of Louisiana blacks. Includes transcripts of four interviews with women who were ex-slaves and other items relating to women.

5,536. Dart and Dart
Records. 1848-1962. 1.25 ft.
Open. Unpublished guide.
University of New Orleans, Earl K. Long Library, Archives and Manuscripts Department.
Among the legal files of the law firm Dart and Dart, which contain correspondence, wills, memoranda, and miscellaneous documents, is one extensive file concerning services the firm rendered for author Grace King, her estate, and her family. King wrote books and articles including *New Orleans, The Place and the People* (1895); *Creole Families of New Orleans* (1921); and *Memories of a Southern Woman of Letters* (1932).

5,537. Deutsch, Hermann B.
Papers. Ca. 1920-45. 422 items.
Open. Unpublished guide.

University of New Orleans, Earl K. Long Library, Archives and Manuscripts Department.
Deutsch (1889-1970) was a newspaper reporter, columnist, and author. Included with correspondence, news articles, notes, pamphlets, newspapers, periodicals, sheet music, government documents, clippings, and other papers are items concerning Hattie (Wyatt) Caraway, who served from 1932 to 1945 as US senator from Arkansas. Deutsch reported on the 1932 campaign by US Senator Huey P. Long of Louisiana for Caraway's election. A poem signed by Caraway is also included.

5,538. Lamar, Marta B.
Papers. 1951-76. 6.5 ft.
Open. Unpublished guide.
University of New Orleans, Earl K. Long Library, Archives and Manuscripts Department.
[Mrs.] Lamar (1902-), a New Orleans horticulturist and historical preservationist, has been a leader in local controversies over neighborhood preservation, highway and bridge construction, and damage to the ecology. Correspondence, petitions, transcripts of New Orleans City Council hearings and resolutions, unpublished studies and reports on transportation and bridge sites, scrapbooks, political campaign literature, clippings, publications, posters, cartoons, and other material. Bulk of collection concerns proposed sites for a new Mississippi River bridge in New Orleans.

5,539. Louisiana Folklore Society
Collection. Ca. 1948. 50 items.
Open. Unpublished guide.
University of New Orleans, Earl K. Long Library, Archives and Manuscripts Department.
Recording discs of Louisiana French folk songs and stories, which were recorded by Corinne Lelia Saucier, a folklorist, author, and teacher of Spanish and French at Louisiana State Normal College, now Northwestern State University, at Natchitoches, LA. Her book *Folk Tales from French Louisiana* (1962) was based largely on the phonodiscs.

5,540. Luke, Leontine G.
Papers. 1966-74. 15 items.
Open. Unpublished guide.
University of New Orleans, Earl K. Long Library, Archives and Manuscripts Department.
An interviewer for the Orleans Parish juvenile court, [Mrs.] Luke (1909-) is active in civic affairs in her home area, New Orleans's predominantly black Ninth Ward. Photos, clippings, and publications collected by Luke, a black woman, since her election in 1956 as president of the Ninth Ward Civic and Improvement League, a group dedicated to improving conditions in an area marked by high unemployment and poor housing.

5,541. Orleans Gallery
Records. 1956-73. 11 ft. and 18 items.
Open. Unpublished guide.
University of New Orleans, Earl K. Long Library, Archives and Manuscripts Department.
Founded in 1956 and closed in 1972 or 1973, this nonprofit, community-oriented art gallery sought to foster contemporary art in New Orleans and included numerous women among its directors, board members, and exhibiting artists. Bylaws, minutes, account books, bank and tax records, receipt books, invoices, inventories, shipping orders, correspondence, membership lists, artists' résumés, newsletters, photos, and other papers, including items collected by Jerah Johnson while he was active with the Gallery.

5,542. Ormond, Suzanne (Levy)
Papers. Ca. 1951-72. 1.5 ft.
Open. Unpublished guide.
University of New Orleans, Earl K. Long Library, Archives and Manuscripts Department.
[Mrs. John W.] Ormond (1926-) is a New Orleans ceramist, board member of the Louisiana State Museum, and a leader in local controversies over neighborhood preservation and new highway and bridge locations. Correspondence, notes, speeches, minutes, questionnaires, position papers, studies, zoning regulations, clippings, maps, and other papers. Bulk of material concerns a proposed Riverfront Expressway and a new Mississippi River bridge in New Orleans. Ormond has been president and chairman since 1971 of the board of the Crescent Council of Civic Associations.

5,543. Toledano, Ben C.
Collection. 1848-1963. 332 items.
Open. Unpublished guide.
University of New Orleans, Earl K. Long Library, Archives and Manuscripts Department.
Correspondence, notes, lecture programs, clippings, and other items compiled by Nell Henson, a New Orleans book reviewer and wife of C. C. Henson, a local educator who held a PhD. Includes letters from [Mrs.] Elizabeth Meriwether Gilmer, who wrote a newspaper column and several books under the pseudonym Dorothy Dix. Also included are correspondence, recital programs, invitations, pamphlets, post cards, photos, and clippings relating to the Southern College of Music, which was established in New Orleans in 1895 and continued into the mid-1930s. Many faculty members were women and the founder's wife, Mrs. Arthur J. Shoenfeld, directed the school after his death.

SHREVEPORT

5,544. Business Girls' Inn
Records. 1929-74. 15 in. and 3 oversize vols.
Open. Unpublished guide.
Centenary College of Louisiana, Magale Library.
Founded in 1928 by the Woman's Missionary Society city mission board of the Methodist Episcopal Church, South, and closed in 1972, the Inn provided a Shreveport residence for working girls. Minutes of the city mission board, which administered the Inn; business and financial records of the Inn, also called the Jubilee Inn; correspondence; photos; and scrapbooks.

5,545. Centenary Women's Club
Records. 1928-70. 5 in. and 1 vol.
Open. Unpublished guide.
Centenary College of Louisiana, Magale Library.
Founded in 1928 for mothers of Centenary students, the group provided financial support for the school; during the 1930s it opened its membership to all women interested in helping the College. Minutes, account books, membership rolls, correspondence, programs, clippings, college memorabilia, and photos. The Club raised money for scholarship programs and for purchase of library equipment.

5,546. Demoiselle Ball
Records. 1948-74. 19 vols.
Access restricted. Unpublished guide.
Centenary College of Louisiana, Magale Library.
The Demoiselle Club sponsors spring debutante balls in Shreveport. Scrapbooks consist of photos, clippings, and other material about the planning and execution of coming out parties, the customs of debutantes, and Shreveport society.

5,547. Dodd College
Records. 1930s. 7.5 in.
Open. Unpublished guide.
Centenary College of Louisiana, Magale Library.
Founded in ca. 1927, the College was a private women's Christian junior college in Shreveport. Student papers, a cashbook, documents on accreditation of the school, college bulletins, yearbooks, newspapers and a literary magazine, photos, and memorabilia. The College was closed in 1943; its permanent student records are held by the Centenary College registrar.

5,548. League of Women Voters of Shreveport
Records. Ca. 1947-74. 6.5 ft.
Open. Unpublished guide.
Centenary College of Louisiana, Magale Library.
Minutes, financial records, correspondence, and subject files of the Shreveport LWV, founded in 1947 or 1948, document the group's activities and interest in municipal, parish, state, and federal governments.

5,549. Marshall and Furman Family
Papers. 1773-1941. 12 ft. and 1 vol.
Partially restricted. Unpublished guide.
Centenary College of Louisiana, Magale Library.
Correspondence, writings, business and financial records, photos, pamphlets, newspapers, and other family papers of Henry Marshall (1805-64), a DeSoto Parish, LA, planter and slaveholder who was a member of the Confederate Congress, contain extensive material of women family members, including Mary Taylor Furman (?-1913), a granddaughter of Marshall who taught school in Shreveport and served as an officer in local civic groups; Sarah Chandler Furman (?-1910), sister-in-law of Mary Furman; Sadie Marshall, a daughter of Henry Marshall; and Emma Marshall. Mary Furman's papers include correspondence; notes and pictures for an art history class; announcements, invitations, and calling cards; printed material regarding the Chautauqua movement, the DAR, the Louisiana Federation of Women's Clubs, the Era Civic Association, and Hypatia; and memorabilia from trips to the East Coast and Europe. Also contains an 1872 diary and a purse book of Emma Marshall and memorabilia of Sadie Marshall.

5,550. Marshall, Helen Ruffin
Papers. 1946-61. 5 in. and 1 vol.
Open. Unpublished guide.
Centenary College of Louisiana, Magale Library.
Clippings, programs, and photos reflect [Mrs.] Marshall's work as a professor of music at Centenary College and organizer of the Shreveport Civic Opera Association and the Centenary Opera Workshop.

5,551. Methodist Church, Louisiana Conference
Records. 1847- . No size given.
Open. Inventories.
Centenary College of Louisiana, Magale Library.
Collection includes archives of the Conference and records of the Woman's Missionary Society, the Woman's Society for Christian Service, and Mansfield College. Conference archives contain minutes, correspondence from various Conference boards, and some individual church records such as registers and reports. The women's groups' records primarily consist of minutes and programs. Mansfield College, now defunct, was a four-year women's college located in Mansfield, LA, and supported by the Louisiana Conference; its records are administered by the Centenary College registrar, but its yearbooks and catalogs are stored in this collection.

5,552. Oursler, Loree
Papers. 1961-75. 7 in.
Open. Unpublished guide.
Centenary College of Louisiana, Magale Library.
A Shreveport bank employee, [Mrs.] Oursler (?-ca. 1975) was also a free-lance journalist who wrote about local history. Correspondence, notes, drafts, manuscripts, research material, clippings, and photos, most of which pertain to her research and writing on Huddie Ledbetter "Leadbelly," a black folk singer who is buried near Shreveport; General

Kirby Smith; women in banking; and Melrose, a plantation located near Natchitoches, LA, which was owned until about 1948 by Leudivine Carmelite Garrett Henry.

5,553. Rives, Mary Elizabeth (Carter)
Papers. 1851-1940. 7.5 in. and 1 microfilm reel.
Open. No guide.
Centenary College of Louisiana, Magale Library.
Widowed in 1859, Rives (1829-1900) apparently managed her DeSoto Parish plantation while raising her family; in later years she moved to Shreveport to live with her children. Diaries, dating from 1865 to 1870 and from 1887 to 1900, reflect the life of a woman living on a plantation after the Confederacy's defeat. Also contains a few pictures and clippings, particularly family obituaries. In the diary entries Rives details chores, such as "today made vinegar" or "hemmed six towels," and describes trips to New Orleans and Shreveport. Later entries are concerned mainly with the health of her grandchildren and friends and with the weather. Rives's diaries were compiled into a typescript in 1938 by her granddaughter Mai Rives Phillips.

5,554. Wesleyan Service Guild
Records. 1940-68. 2.5 in.
Open. Unpublished guide.
Centenary College of Louisiana, Magale Library.
Minutes and clippings of the Guild, which was organized in 1940 at the First Methodist Church of Mansfield, LA, as a group through which employed women could take part in the Methodist Church's Woman's Society of Christian Service. The group supports missionary work and local church activities.

5,555. North Louisiana Historical Association
Collection. 1824- . 9 record center cartons and 8 microfilm reels.
Open. Catalog.
North Louisiana Historical Association Collection.
Correspondence, diary, journals, and financial records collected by the Association. Includes papers of Henry Marshall and members of his family and the related Furman family and a diary of Mary Elizabeth Carter Rives. Also includes a diary, 1853-57, of Joseph C. Hunter, a physician who used the diary to record his medical cases, and an 1870 diary of Henry Gerary Hall, a lawyer who includes mention of his wife, sister, and daughters. The collection is housed in the Centenary College of Louisiana Library.

5,556. Archives
Records. 1638- . 28 ft. and 2 microfilm reels.
Access restricted. Card index.
St. Vincent Sisters, Daughters of the Cross Convent.
The mission was founded in Cocoville, LA, in 1855 and in 1870 was moved to Shreveport.
Constitution and rules of the order in French and English, customs of the Louisiana congregation, financial records, register of members beginning in 1855, correspondence, retreat notes, history, photos, scrapbooks, albums, prayer manuals, ceremonials for rites of profession of vows, brochures, articles, and clippings. Includes letters by the Louisiana foundress and photos of the faculties, students, alumni, and facilities of schools run by the Sisters and of mothers general of the Louisiana mission.

MAINE

AUBURN

5,557. Auburn Art and Literature Club
Records. 1890-1906. 3 vols.
Open. No guide.
Auburn Public Library, Maine Room.
Minutes, lists of members and officers, and programs of this study group, which was founded in 1890 with the consent of the Auburn Art Club by women who were on the Art Club's waiting list. Members devoted themselves to the same cause of intellectual improvement through readings, lectures, and discussions of history, current events, art, and great works of literature.

5,558. Auburn Art Club
Records. 1880- . Ca. 4 ft.
Open. No guide.
Auburn Public Library, Maine Room.
Minute books, treasurer's account books, correspondence, histories, programs, and scrapbooks of clippings of this study group, founded in 1880. Initially the Club concentrated on studying classical Greek and Roman art, but soon they branched out to later periods, other regions, and different disciplines such as history, literature, and biography. Members discussed topics, often following one member's reading a paper on the particular subject. The Club also sponsored public lectures and civic improvements; it is credited with supporting the town's public library, a kindergarten, and other educational reforms.

5,559. Gardeners' Union of Lewiston and Auburn
Records. 1914-20. 1 vol.
Open. No guide.
Auburn Public Library, Maine Room.
Constitution, bylaws, treasurer's reports, minutes, lists of prizes awarded, and a history of the founding of the Union, a women's horticultural group that existed between 1914 and 1920. The Union held an annual flower show, joined in town improvement and beautification projects, and worked on educating the public about horticulture.

5,560. Philharmonic Club
Records. 1900-56. 13 vols.
Open. No guide.
Auburn Public Library, Maine Room.
In 1899 three local music clubs—the Spinet, Clef, and Clavier clubs—joined to form a Musical Union that sponsored public concerts and similar events of interest to members of all three clubs and to the public. The Union's name was changed to the Philharmonic Society in 1913; in 1917 the separate clubs dissolved in order to regroup as the Philharmonic Club. Included is a volume of treasurer's accounts for the Spinet Club; volumes of minutes, lists of members and officers, and clippings of the Clef Club; volumes of constitution, bylaws, minutes, lists of members and officers, and clippings of the Musical Union; and volumes of minutes, treasurer's accounts, lists of members and officers, programs, clippings, and other records of the Philharmonic Club.

AUGUSTA

5,561. Adjutant General's Department, Civil War
Records. 1861-69. Ca. 240 vols.
Open. Indexes.
Maine State Archives.
Correspondence received by this state agency, established in 1820 when Maine became a state, is extensive for the War period. Includes letters of application from women desiring appointment as nurses, many of whom provided biographical information and a statement of their motivations for the work. Also included are letters relating to families of servicemen seeking state financial aid for subsistence during the War; because town selectmen normally authorized family aid funds, these letters often contain descriptions of economic plight as well as the difficulties women had with officials.

5,562. Augusta Mental Health Institute
Records. 1836-1941. 363 vols.
Access restricted. Inventory.
Maine State Archives.
Records of this state hospital for mentally ill persons, established in 1834, include payrolls and time books with data on women and men who worked with patients; commitment records; an 1892 register of patients; records showing the allowances given patients, 1933-41; and town clerks' memoranda on the death of Institute patients who had formerly resided in the clerks' towns, 1908-14. Minutes of the board of trustees, 1843-98, include information on hospital policy and rules and the physical surroundings and the condition of patients. Collection also includes financial ledgers and records of the dry goods, grocery, and farm and industrial departments.

5,563. Delayed Returns of Vital Statistics
Records. Ca. 1650-1892. 315 boxes.
Open. List.
Maine State Archives.
Index cards, copied from files in Maine town clerk offices, contain population data for 72 towns and are arranged chronologically by surname. They may include name and race of person; place of birth, death, or marriage; age at death or marriage; parents' names and occupations; and other information. These records precede the creation of the state Registrar of Vital Statistics in 1891.

5,564. Industrial Safety Division of the Department of Labor and Industry
Records. 1873-1971. Ca. 240 boxes.
Open. Preliminary inventory.
Maine State Archives.
Financial statements, correspondence, memoranda, reports, surveys, work sheets, certificates, and clippings of this state agency, founded in 1911, and of its predecessor agencies, contain material on the employment of women in industry, particularly between 1950 and 1970. Includes information on violations of minimum wage and maximum hours rules and on job related injuries and occupational hazards.

5,565. Legislature of Maine
Records. 1820-1970. No size given.
Open. Inventory.
Maine State Archives.
Records of the Maine legislature, including minutes, resolutions, petitions, drafts of bills, correspondence, and referenda relating to Maine laws that were enacted as well as measures that were proposed or advocated but not passed. Material documents repeated attempts at laws and resolutions regarding temperance, the abolition of slavery, and woman suffrage; it may also provide information on women activists and women's groups that supported legislation.

5,566. Maine Census
Records. 1850-70. 128 vols.
Open. Contents lists.
Maine State Archives.
Population census schedules for counties and towns in Maine, conducted by the federal government, list data on name, address, age, sex, race, health, property, place of birth, schooling, literacy, and civil status (whether a pauper or convict) for all individuals, though occupation was listed only for adult males. In the 1860 census occupation for

females was added, and in 1870 the census also noted citizenship and whether the parents were foreign born.

5,567. Maine Town Records
Records. 1614-1969. 526 microfilm reels.
Open. List.
Maine State Archives.
Made by the Latter Day Saints for genealogical research, these films of vital statistics registers, card indexes, and other records in Maine town offices also include a few genealogically significant family records and other items.

5,568. Municipal and County Courts
Records. 1760-1935. 9190.25 ft.
Open. Inventory.
Maine State Archives.
Maine civil and criminal court records from the state judicial system consist of docket books, case abstracts, court transcripts, lists of jurors, correspondence, and other records documenting women as plaintiffs, defendants, lawyers, jurors, and judges. Constituting an index, the dockets give names of complainants and defendants, type of case, date, and docket number, which lead to information on women involved in legal proceedings as alleged prostitutes, adulterers and fornicators, murderers, and other kinds of criminals. Also included is information on divorce proceedings.

5,569. Secretary of State
Records. 1820- . Ca. 3000 ft.
Open. Inventories, indexes, and lists.
Maine State Archives.
The Secretary of State tabulates election returns in Maine. Election records include poll lists and tabulations of votes on such referenda as the 1917 woman suffrage amendment and for such candidates as Margaret Chase Smith.

5,570. U.S. Agricultural, Industrial, and Social Censuses
Records. 1850-80. 33 vols.
Open. Contents lists.
Maine State Archives.
These censuses provide social data on all Maine residents and agricultural and industrial data on residents of some Maine counties. The agricultural series includes statistics on the value of homemade manufactures and amounts of such produce as butter and cheese; if a woman owned a farm, her name appears on the schedule. The 1850 and 1860 industrial censuses record the average number of female employees in firms within the county as well as average wages paid to these workers; the 1870 and 1880 censuses only note the number of female employees. The 1850, '60, and '70 social statistics volumes contain information about educational institutions, whether male or female, the size of staff, number of students, and sources of funding; pauperism; crime; and wages, including data on weekly wages paid in addition to board to female domestics. The 1880 social volume contains names, residence, economic condition, health, and information about the institutionalization of deaf-mutes, blind people, homeless children, and mentally retarded and insane persons; also included are profiles of inhabitants of prisons, with names, residence, place of imprisonment, and notes on whether the person was indicted, convicted, serving out time or a fine, or facing execution.

5,571. U.S. Census of Population of Maine
Records. 1790-1890. 172 microfilm reels.
Open. Lists.
Maine State Archives.
Copies of census schedules for towns and counties.

5,572. Vital Records from Various Maine Towns
Records. 1831-95. 18 boxes.
Open. List.
Maine State Archives.
Registers of births, deaths, and marriages, submitted by the clerks of Maine towns to the secretary of state, are included with some copies of intentions of marriage and certificates of birth, death, and marriage.

5,573. Vocational Rehabilitation
Records. 1921-72. 1 box and 4 tapes.
Open. Inventory.
Maine State Archives.
Records of this state social welfare agency, founded in 1917, consist of a list of rehabilitation programs in Maine and tapes of recollections back to 1921 by welfare workers on such topics as services for crippled children and maternal health.

5,574. Ballard, Martha Moore
Papers. 1785-1812. 2 vols.
Open. Published guide.
Maine State Library.
Diary in which [Mrs.] Ballard (1735-1812), an Augusta midwife, recorded her medical work, personal experiences, and detailed local news. Excerpts from the diary have been published in Charles Elverton Nash, *The History of Augusta: First Settlement and Early Days as a Town* (Augusta: Nash, 1904, 1961). See Elizabeth Ring, *A Reference List of Manuscripts Relating to the History of Maine* (Orono: University of Maine, 1938).

5,575. Caswell, Mina Holway
Papers. Ca. 1941. 12 folders.
Open. Catalog card.
Maine State Library.
Manuscript by Caswell, an historian, on the history of welfare work in Maine to 1932, the research for which she started as a WPA project.

5,576. Emerson, Susanna Hovey Perkins
Papers. 1796. 1 vol.
Open. Catalog card.
Maine State Library.
In this diary, Emerson (1737-?), a resident of York, ME, records the weather, her health, and her religious thoughts.

5,577. Finch, Adelaide Victoria
Papers. 1892-1934. 8 vols.
Open. Catalog card.
Maine State Library.
Scrapbooks of poetry, printed and draft articles, photos, clippings, and other papers of Finch (1864-?) relate to the Dingley Normal Training School of Lewiston, ME, during the years she was a teacher and then from 1907 to 1934 while she was the principal there. Finch also was a textbook writer.

5,578. Lowell, Mary Chandler
Papers. Ca. 1940. 6 vols. and 1 envelope.
Open. Catalog card.
Maine State Library.
Research notes of Lowell (1863-1949), an historian, for a history of various towns and families of Piscataquis County, ME.

5,579. Maine Federation of Women's Clubs
Records. 1893-1967. No size given.
Open. Catalog cards.
Maine State Library.
Scrapbooks of this social organization contain programs and lists of members for each club in the Federation for 1893 and later correspondence, programs, and clippings relating to the Federation and its Clubs.

5,580. Maine State Authors
Collection. 1922- . 7 ft.
Open. No guide.
Maine State Library.
Correspondence between the state librarian and authors whose books were purchased for this collection is included with some biographical data, photos, and clippings. Correspondents include authors Mary Ellen Chase, Louise Bogan, Gladys (Hasty) Carroll, Fannie (Hardy) Eckstrom, Mary Childs Jane, Edith Lowell, Ida S. Proper, and Elinor Stevens Walker.

5,581. Maine Woman Suffrage Association
Records. Ca. 1917-19. 1 box.
Open. Catalog card.
Maine State Library.
Records of this political organization consist primarily of petitions signed by persons from Lincoln, Penobscot, Somerset, Washington, and Aroostock counties who favored the suffrage referendum, which was placed on the state special election ballot for 1917. Also included are correspondence, lists of officers and members, and publications such as programs, pamphlets, brochures, and clippings.

5,582. Music by Maine Composers
Collection. 1887- . Ca. 1000 items.
Open. List.
Maine State Library.
Scores and lyrics of popular and classical music composed by Maine residents were first assembled by the Maine Federation of Music Clubs. Included are manuscript compositions by Harriet Russell Collver, Anita Gray Little, Helen Cooper Lord, Edith Lowell, Gladys Pitcher, and Ethel Watson Usher.

5,583. Nurses Registered in Maine
Records. 1916-65. 1 vol.
Open. Catalog card.
Maine State Library.
List of registered nurses, nursing attendants, and practical nurses.

5,584. Pilsbury, Caroline
Papers. 1824-26. 1 vol.
Open. Catalog card.
Maine State Library.
Diary of Pilsbury (1793-?), a native of Newburyport, MA, includes an account of her teaching experiences in Maine.

5,585. Yeaton, Mary
Papers. 1801. 1 vol.
Open. Catalog card.
Maine State Library.
Diary of Yeaton, a resident of Eastport, ME, and daughter of Captain Hopley Yeaton, concerns social and personal events and contains religious reflections.

5,586. Crosby, Cornelia "Flyrod" Thurza
Papers. Ca. 1890s. 1 vol.
Open. No guide.
Maine State Museum.
Scrapbook of biographical clippings and ca. 165 photos that "Flyrod" (1854-1946), Maine's first licensed guide, took of fishing and hunting parties she guided to her favorite locations in the Rangeley area. Includes a few photos of her dressed in a skirt and felt hat decorated with flies and holding a string of trout she had just caught. The photos indicate that occasionally women accompanied the men on expeditions with Flyrod.

5,587. League of Women Voters of Maine
Records. Ca. 1917-69. 2 Paige boxes.
Open. No guide.
Maine State Museum.
Correspondence, pamphlets, broadsides, issues of *The Woman Citizen,* clippings, and other items concerning suffrage and the Maine LWV, founded in 1920. Includes correspondence of [Miss] Mabel Connor, a suffragist who was president of the Maine Women's Suffrage party from 1917 to 1920, with Carrie Chapman Catt and others concerning pressure Maine women exerted upon their congressmen for a federal suffrage amendment and

upon the Maine legislature for a bill to enfranchise women so they could vote in presidential elections. Also includes information on LWV efforts on behalf of the Sheppard-Towner federal maternity act, which became law in 1921, but funding for which was consistently vetoed by the governor of Maine. There are suggestions in Catt's letters that the Maine suffragists had not "turned on the steam sufficiently."

BANGOR

5,588. Burpee, Louise Coburn
Papers. 1893-94. 1 vol.
Open. No guide.
Bangor Public Library.
Photos and a diary in which [Miss] Burpee (?-1941), a Maine resident, describes her educational and social experiences during a year she spent as a student at Miss Morgan's school in Portsmouth, NH. She later married William Otis Sawtelle (1874-1939).

5,589. Crosby, Eliza Leland (Adams)
Papers. 1825-45. 1 vol.
Open. No guide.
Bangor Public Library.
Poems, short stories, and religious and oratorical essays composed by [Mrs. John Leland] Crosby (1806-98), a Bangor resident, some of which she read to a local Bible class and to the Young People's Literary Society.

5,590. Curran, Mary Harris (Ellison)
Papers. 1898-1916. 18 items.
Open. Published guide and catalog card.
Bangor Public Library.
Research notes, drafts of articles, and photos of [Mrs. Nicholas F.] Curran (1839-1917), an author. Contains transcriptions of manuscript documents, which she assembled in preparation for her publications on religious history, local history, and other historical topics. See Elizabeth Ring, *A Reference List of Manuscripts Relating to the History of Maine* (Orono: University of Maine, 1938).

5,591. Harkness, Mrs. E. W.
Papers. 1875-77. 1 vol.
Open. No guide.
Bangor Public Library.
Diary of Harkness, a Maine resident, concerns her voyage around the world on the *J. H. Bowers* with her husband as captain. She describes in detail ports they visited, among them Liverpool, Montevideo, and Honolulu, as well as socializing with other captains' wives at sea.

BAR HARBOR

5,592. Eckstorm, Fannie (Hardy)
Papers. 1930-46. 1 vol.
Open. No guide.
Robert Abbe Museum of Stone Antiquities.
Letters from [Mrs.] Eckstorm (1866-1946), an historian, to [Miss] Mary C. Wheelwright.

BETHEL

5,593. Harris, Hattie
Papers. 1911-59. 1 ft.
Open. Unpublished guide.
Bethel Historical Society.
Harris (1873-1959) was a milliner and executive secretary in Chelsea, MA. Diaries reflecting her activities and attitudes as a retired woman in Bethel, correspondence about business transactions and gifts, and financial records.

BIDDEFORD

5,594. Biddeford Scrapbooks
Collection. Ca. 1910-70. 8 vols.
Open. Indexes.
McArthur Public Library.
Scrapbooks of clippings from local newspapers, indexed by person and subject, provide information on Biddeford residents, institutions, and events. Includes, for example, material on such women's groups as the Thursday Club, a literature study group founded in 1894.

5,595. Historic Notes and Biddeford Biography Index
Finding aid. Ca. 1910- . Ca. 3 ft.
Open. No guide.
McArthur Public Library.
Index cards created by Dane Yorke and his successors at the Library consist of items from local newspapers, the Library's Scrapbook Collection, and other sources from as early as the 17th century. Index provides historical data and bibliographic information on such local women's groups as the American National Red Cross and on such local women as Rebecca (Hitchcock) Emery, who was known for her charitable deeds.

5,596. Photo Prints
Collection. Ca. 1880- . Ca. 1300 items.
Open. Card index of subjects.
McArthur Public Library.
Prints of photos of persons, places, and events in Biddeford provide documentation of the lives of local women through such pictures as a 1913 portrait of the Camp Fire Girls, a 1902 photo of employees of the Pepperell Mills, and a picture of the St. Andre Convent. Sheets on which the prints are pasted give information on the names of persons, events, and settings.

BLUE HILL

5,597. Auxiliary of the Horace Duffy Post of the American Legion
Records. 1940-48. 2 in.
Open. No guide.
Blue Hill Public Library.
Minutes of the women's Auxiliary of the Blue Hill Post of the Legion, a patriotic organization.

5,598. Blue Hill Public Library
Records. 1796- . Ca. 4 ft. and 29 vols.
Open. No guide.
Blue Hill Public Library.
Annual reports, treasurer's accounts, and other records, 1796-1849, of the Blue Hill Social Library, a circulating library founded in 1796. Also contains records of the Blue Hill Ladies Social Library from 1868 to the 1970s; these consist of minutes, annual reports on circulation and finances, treasurer's accounts, correspondence, records of gifts of money, lists of books borrowed by users of the Library, and other material. In 1962 the organization adopted its current name.

5,599. Chase, Mary Ellen
Papers. 1940s? 29 vols.
Open. No guide.
Blue Hill Public Library.
Papers of Chase (1887-1973), an author, consist of notes for her biography *Jonathan Fisher, Maine Parson 1768-1847* (New York: Macmillan, 1948). Included are Chase's transcriptions of Fisher's sermons, letters, and diaries written in a code that she broke.

5,600. Women's Relief Corps of the James A. Garfield Post of the Grand Army of the Republic
Records. 1886-1971. 19 vols.
Open. No guide.
Blue Hill Public Library.
Minutes, lists of officers, ledgers, and cashbooks of the Blue Hill auxiliary of the GAR, a patriotic organization.

BRUNSWICK

5,601. Furbish, Kate
Papers. 1870-1908. 16 folio vols.
Open. Unpublished guide.
Bowdoin College Library.
Watercolor drawings of Maine wild flowers and sketches of Maine mushrooms by [Miss] Furbish (1834-1931), an artist and botanist.

5,602. Richards, Laura Elizabeth (Howe)
Papers. 1914-38. 45 items.
Open. Unpublished guide.
Bowdoin College Library.
Letters from [Mrs. Henry] Richards (1850-1943), an author, to Edwin F. Edgett, who was literary editor of the Boston *Transcript.*

5,603. Wiggin, Kate Douglas (Smith)
Papers. Nd. Ca. 500 vols.
Open. No guide.
Bowdoin College Library.
Journals, manuscripts, press notices, scrapbooks of clippings and notes, ephemera, and books of [Mrs. Samuel Bradley] Wiggin (1856-1923), an author. Included with published copies of her own writings are copies of books presented to her by Helen Keller, Sinclair Lewis, and others.

CUMBERLAND

5,604. Cumberland Womans Missionary Society
Records. 1870-71. 1 vol.
Open. No guide.
Cumberland Historical Society, Prince Memorial Library.
Constitution, minutes, and lists of members and officers of this religious organization, founded in 1870 to improve the spiritual lives of its members and to raise money to support missionary efforts in the US and abroad.

5,605. Female Benevolent Society of Cumberland and the Cumberland Female Seamans Friends Society
Records. 1829-44. 1 vol.
Open. No guide.
Cumberland Historical Society, Prince Memorial Library.
Constitutions, minutes, treasurers' accounts, and lists of members of the Benevolent Society for 1829 to 1833 and of the Seamans Society for 1842 to 1844. Founded in 1829, the Benevolent Society made and sold clothing and used the funds for charitable causes. Founded in 1842, the Seamans Society raised money to support missionary efforts among mariners.

GORHAM

5,606. Baxter, James Phinney
Papers. 1807-1920. Ca. 12 ft.
Open. No guide.
Baxter Memorial Library.
Correspondence, a diary, drafts of speeches and articles, photos, a family Bible, portraits and oil paintings, published material, and printed copies of

the works of Baxter (1831-1921), an historian. Correspondence reflects the events and daily lives, education, social activities, and travel of his mother Sarah (Cone) Baxter (1787-1873); his first wife Sarah Kimball (Lewis) Baxter (1830-72); his second wife Mehetable Cummings (Proctor) Baxter (1837-1914), an artist who specialized in oil painting; and his daughters Emily Poole Baxter (1874-1921) and Madeleine Cummings (Baxter) Tomlinson (1879-1938). His diary also contains information about the activities of these women.

HOULTON

5,607. Houlton Woman's Club
Records. 1904- . Ca. 200 items.
Open. Catalog card.
Cary Library.
Minutes, financial records, and yearly programs of the Club, which was founded in 1904. The group sponsored a public health nursing program during the late 1930s, which is still extant and operated by the town; the Club also became involved in zoning, a free milk program, and the establishment of a dental clinic for underprivileged children in 1929.

KENNEBUNK

5,608. Soldiers' Relief Society
Records. 1861-?. 1 vol.
Open. No guide.
Kennebunk Free Library.
Constitution, correspondence, lists of members, lists of donors and of articles they gave, and an historical sketch of the Society, a charitable women's organization founded in 1861. This Kennebunk Society raised funds, made clothing, and gathered hospital supplies for Union soldiers. After the Civil War, its members devoted themselves to other relief projects such as collecting money to aid Chicago residents who suffered in the fire of 1871. They also helped erect a Civil War memorial tablet.

LEWISTON

5,609. Lewiston Normal Training School
Records. 1895-1935. 1 vol.
Open. Published guide.
Lewiston Public Library.
Scrapbook of the School, an institution that trained schoolteachers between 1869 and 1934 and virtually all of whose staff and students were women, contains annual reports and other printed material, clippings, and photos relating to the institution, its staff, and students. Material is interspersed with a narrative history of the School written by [Miss] Adelaide Finch, principal from 1894 to 1934. Volume also contains Finch's list of School graduates, with dates of attendance and in some cases a summary of the student's subsequent career as a teacher. See Elizabeth Ring, *A Reference List of Manuscripts Relating to the History of Maine* (Orono: University of Maine, 1938).

MACHIAS

5,610. Hannah Weston Chapter of the DAR
Records. 1901- . 15 vols.
Open. No guide.
Burnham Tavern Museum.
Complete secretary's minutes and information on the activities of this local DAR chapter, which was founded in 1901. Also includes a few photos and clippings.

OGUNQUIT

5,611. Ogunquit Woman's Club
Records. 1918- . Ca. 2 ft.
Open. No guide.
Ogunquit Free Library.
Minutes, treasurer's account books, correspondence, a history, annual programs, awards, and certificates of this study and social group. Founded in 1918 as the Ogunquit Literary Club, the Club was dedicated to intellectual improvement through discussion of essays on various subjects presented by members. In 1921 it adopted its current name, and the constitution was amended to include civic improvement projects among its activities. The Club planted trees in the town, donated books to the library and special equipment to the school, and raised funds for scholarships. During WWII, it was particularly active in bond sales and patriotic support work.

OLD ORCHARD BEACH

5,612. Bell, Clara Lizette (Pierce)
Papers. 1891-1933. 2 vols.
Open. No guide.
Old Orchard Beach Historical Society.
Scrapbooks of [Mrs. James H.] Bell (1859-?), a poet and short story writer who resided in Quincy, MA, and Old Orchard Beach, contain manuscript and printed copies of her works, photos, and clippings documenting her literary career.

5,613. Old Orchard Beach Women's Civic Group
Records. 1953-69. 4 vols.
Open. No guide.
Old Orchard Beach Historical Society.
Constitution, minutes, treasurer's accounts, correspondence, photos, and clippings for the term of existence of the Group, which was a town beautification society. The Group planted trees and flowers, placed benches along the beach, sponsored art shows, and worked on rubbish removal problems. In connection with these projects and with zoning ordinances, members worked closely with town officials.

5,614. Woman's Improvement Society at Old Orchard
Records. 1919-47. 1 vol.
Open. No guide.
Old Orchard Beach Historical Society.
Treasurer's reports, minutes, correspondence, and an historical sketch of the Society, which was founded in 1907 as the woman's auxiliary to the Orchard Beach Camp Meeting Association; in 1919 it changed its name. The Society was devoted to raising funds for the preservation and maintenance of the campground in town that was used for religious revivals by various Protestant groups until ca. 1958 when The Salvation Army purchased the site and took over its care. The Club was then disbanded.

ORONO

5,615. Barrows, Alice Prentice
Papers. 1820-1956. 200 items.
Open. Unpublished guide.
University of Maine at Orono, Raymond H. Fogler Library, Special Collections.
Correspondence, autobiographical manuscript, family papers, publications, and clippings of Barrows (1878-1954), an educator.

5,616. Baumann, Eunice Nelson
Papers. 1949-70. 3 cu.ft.
Open. Unpublished guide.
University of Maine at Orono, Raymond H. Fogler Library, Special Collections.
Personal papers, notes, and manuscripts relating to the work of [Mrs.] Baumann, an anthropologist, sociologist, and educator, in human relations and anthropology.

5,617. Bean, Paul W.
Collection. Ca. 1860-75. 5 boxes.
Open. No guide.
University of Maine at Orono, Raymond H. Fogler Library, Special Collections.
Correspondence, diaries, record books, scrapbooks, photos and prints, and memorabilia collected by Bean relate to the Civil War and Reconstruction period. Included are diaries in which Serena M. Chaplin of Massachusetts records events in her daily life and the weather and diaries in which Mary F. (Chaplin) Hodson of Maine describes the course of the War and deaths of relatives.

5,618. Chadbourne, Ava Harriet
Papers. 1915-64. 3 cu.ft.
Open. Unpublished guide.
University of Maine at Orono, Raymond H. Fogler Library, Special Collections.
Notes of and material collected by Chadbourne (1875-1964), a Maine educator, for research on the history of Maine academies.

5,619. Chase, Mary Ellen
Papers. 1900-69. 1 cu.ft.
Open. Unpublished guide.
University of Maine at Orono, Raymond H. Fogler Library, Special Collections.
Correspondence, book manuscripts, and portrait of Chase (1887-1973), author of more than 30 books.

5,620. Coatsworth, Elizabeth Jane
Papers. 1928-73. 1 box.
Open. Catalog card.
University of Maine at Orono, Raymond H. Fogler Library, Special Collections.
Correspondence, diaries, drafts of poems and books, notebooks, and a checklist of books pertain primarily to the publications of Coatsworth (1893-), a writer. Her notebooks contain research for the books on Maine which she wrote for adult readers, while most of the drafts are of books she wrote for younger readers. Travels she made in 1928 and 1936 are described in her diaries.

5,621. Dana, Olive E.
Papers. 1880-1969. 2 boxes.
Open. Catalog card.
University of Maine at Orono, Raymond H. Fogler Library, Special Collections.
Dana (1859-?) was a novelist, poet, and story writer. Correspondence, drafts of stories and poems, receipts and financial accounts, clippings, and printed articles, essays, reviews, and copies of her books all pertain to her career.

5,622. D'Arcy, Belle
Papers. 1894-1940. 2 cu.ft.
Open. Unpublished guide.
University of Maine at Orono, Raymond H. Fogler Library, Special Collections.
Diaries, programs, playbills, autograph album, photos, and clippings of [Miss] D'Arcy, an actress.

5,623. Delano, Mrs. Washington Warren
Papers. 1886-88. 2 vols. and 1 item.
Open. No guide.
University of Maine at Orono, Raymond H. Fogler Library, Special Collections.
Diaries in which Elizabeth (Hartwell) Delano (1847-1922), a Maine resident, records the weather, progress in her household work, and family news.

5,624. Eckstorm, Fannie Pearson (Hardy)
Papers. Nd. 12 cu.ft.
Open. Unpublished guide.

University of Maine at Orono, Raymond H. Fogler Library, Special Collections.
Correspondence, research notes, journal reprints, and photos of [Mrs.] Eckstorm (1865-1946), an authority on the language and customs of Maine Indians, on lumbering in the state, and on Maine and US ballads.

5,625. Elliott, Maxine
Papers. Nd. 3 cu.ft.
Open. Unpublished guide.
University of Maine at Orono, Raymond H. Fogler Library, Special Collections.
Correspondence, diaries, notes, and theater memorabilia of Elliott (1868-1940), an actress.

5,626. Greenwood, Isabel Whittier
Papers. 1900-20. 3 boxes (ca. 6 ft.).
Open. No guide.
University of Maine at Orono, Raymond H. Fogler Library, Special Collections.
Material collected by [Mrs. Chester] Greenwood of Farmington, ME, on women's suffrage organizations in Maine consists primarily of printed items such as pamphlets, broadsides, reprints, magazines, and newspapers issued by the Maine Woman Suffrage Association. Also included are 10 letters to Greenwood from other Maine suffrage leaders; drafts of essays she wrote in support of suffrage; a record book with bylaws, minutes of meetings, and lists of officers and members of the Franklin County Equal Suffrage Association; publications relating to child labor laws, prohibition, and other causes she espoused; and a few personal items and high school yearbooks of Greenwood's.

5,627. Hamlin Family
Papers. 1823- . 15 drawers.
Open. Item index.
University of Maine at Orono, Raymond H. Fogler Library, Special Collections.
Collection consists almost entirely of correspondence of this family of Maine residents but also includes diaries; notes on family history; political, legal, and financial documents, and other papers. Hannibal Hamlin (1809-91), a prominent politician in Maine, is represented in the correspondence, as are his wife Ellen Vesta (Emery) Hamlin (1832-1920), Sarah Purinton Thompson Hamlin (?-1905), and Myra Sampson Hamlin. Ellen Hamlin's papers contain letters received and sent to her and her husband's relatives. Some items are avialable on microfilm.

5,628. Jane, Mary C.
Papers. 1950-72. 2 ft.
Open. Catalog card.
University of Maine at Orono, Raymond H. Fogler Library, Special Collections.
Correspondence and drafts, proofs, and first editions of books written by Jane (1909-), an author of mystery stories for children.

5,629. Johnson, Ethel McLean
Papers. 1913-69. 7 items.
Open. Unpublished guide.
University of Maine at Orono, Raymond H. Fogler Library, Special Collections.
Articles written by Johnson, who was active in the suffrage movement in Massachusetts before she became a writer for the *Woman's Journal.*

5,630. League of Women Voters of Maine
Records. 1950-71. 9 cu.ft.
Open. Unpublished guide.
University of Maine at Orono, Raymond H. Fogler Library, Special Collections.
Correspondence, pamphlets, publications, and other records of the state LWV.

5,631. Maine Federation of Women's Clubs
Records. 1893-1970. 2 cu.ft.
Open. Unpublished guide.
University of Maine at Orono, Raymond H. Fogler Library, Special Collections.
Minutes, newsletter, clubs, publications, and other records of the Federation, which was established in 1892 to promote education and the literary arts.

5,632. Mengers, Marie Christiansen
Papers. 1930-60. 3 ft.
Open. Catalog card.
University of Maine at Orono, Raymond H. Fogler Library, Special Collections.
Correspondence; drafts of lectures, articles, and books; research notes; and student examinations document the teaching and scholarly work on French literature by Mengers, a professor of French. Mengers's special interest was the poetry of Henri de Régnier.

5,633. Patch, Edith Marion
Papers. 1910-54. 1 cu.ft.
Open. Unpublished guide.
University of Maine at Orono, Raymond H. Fogler Library, Special Collections.
Correspondence and manuscripts for articles, speeches, and stories of Patch (1876-1954), a naturalist who also was an author of children's books.

5,634. Remick, Oliver P.
Papers. 1686-1945. 15 ft.
Open. Catalog card.
University of Maine at Orono, Raymond H. Fogler Library, Special Collections.
Correspondence, diaries, drafts of literary works, financial papers, school and research notes, and military organizations' records of Remick (1853-1913), an Army officer and historian. Included is material on various Remick family women: letters, 1901-05 diaries, and drafts of the poems and novels of Martha Remick (?-1906), an author; diary of Edith Remick, written in 1875 while she was still a child; diary of Julia (Hanscom) Sargent Grant, writing primarily on religious topics; and 16 volumes of the diaries of Fannie Remick for 1914 through 1931, in which she noted visitors, travels, the weather, and local events. The class notes of Fannie Remick cover her studies for two years at the State Normal School at Gorham, ME, from which she graduated in 1886.

5,635. Smith, Sallie F.
Papers. 1923-28. 3 vols.
Open. No guide.
University of Maine at Orono, Raymond H. Fogler Library, Special Collections.
Diaries of Smith, a Maine resident, contain entries about the YWCA and meetings Smith attended, plays she saw, and daily events in her life.

5,636. Thayer, Clarissa, and Thayer, Hollis
Papers. Ca. 1830-50. 2 ft.
Open. Catalog card.
University of Maine at Orono, Raymond H. Fogler Library, Special Collections.
Correspondence, notes, and business receipts, ledgers, and other documents of the Thayers' general store in Winterport, ME, in which Clarissa Thayer seems to have played an active role.

5,637. Wilson, Dorothy Clarke
Papers. 1880-1973. 5 boxes and 1 tape.
Open. Catalog card.
University of Maine at Orono, Raymond H. Fogler Library, Special Collections.
Papers relate to the career of Wilson (1904-), a writer of fiction, plays, works on religion, and biographies of women. Correspondence, diaries of her trip to India in 1948 and 1949, research notes, drafts and published copies of her plays and books, articles, and clippings.

5,638. Abbott, Berenice (966)
Oral history. 1975. 2 tapes and 6 pp.
Open. Unpublished guide.
University of Maine, Northeast Archives of Folklore and Oral History.
Interview with Abbott concerns her life as a professional photographer.

5,639. Anderson, Anna (662)
Oral history. 1972. 4 tapes and 140-page transcript.
Open. Published guide.
University of Maine, Northeast Archives of Folklore and Oral History.
Interview with Anderson, the Swedish grandmother of John Kelly, Jr., relates to her life. Taken from Florence Ireland, *The Northeast Archives of Folklore and Oral History* (Orono, ME: The University Press, 1973).

5,640. Charlotte, Sister (592)
Papers. 1950. 21-page item.
Open. Published guide.
University of Maine, Northeast Archives of Folklore and Oral History.
An account that Sister Charlotte, a former nun, wrote about her "horrible" experiences in the convent before she "escaped." Taken from Florence Ireland, *The Northeast Archives of Folklore and Oral History* (Orono, ME: The University Press, 1973).

5,641. Christie, Augusta (Kalloch) (878)
Oral history. 1975. 2 tapes and 44-page transcript.
Open. Unpublished guide.
University of Maine, Northeast Archives of Folklore and Oral History.
Interview with [Mrs. Walter A.] Christie (1887-), a member of the Maine state legislature, relates to her experiences with the WCTU, the DAR, and the legislature.

5,642. Country and Western Music (848)
Oral history. 1975. 2 tapes and a 7-page item.
Open. Unpublished guide.
University of Maine, Northeast Archives of Folklore and Oral History.
Includes interviews with musicians Ray and Ann Little in which they describe their experiences in Maine, Massachusetts, and Canada and country and western music in those places.

5,643. Country Dances (1060)
Oral history. 1976. 5-page item.
Open. Unpublished guide.
University of Maine, Northeast Archives of Folklore and Oral History.
Interview with Gladis [Mrs. Russel] Mace, a wife and mother, who describes kitchen dances of the early 1900s and tells stories about poachers.

5,644. Course Themes
Collection. 1975-76. 14 tapes.
Open. Unpublished guide.
University of Maine, Northeast Archives of Folklore and Oral History.
Includes interviews about Maine towns and people, among them interviews with Verna (Comins) [Mrs. Rosco] Higgins (accession number 1035) and [Miss] Gracie Strang (a.n. 1036) about the town of Eddington, ME, around the turn of the century; with Mary Turner (a.n. 1052) about farm life and her memories; with Florence Baker (a.n. 1054) about farming, maple syrup, and her early life and work; with H. [Mrs. Parker] Vincent (a.n. 950) about the gift shop she runs in Boothbay Harbor; with Suzy Thompson (a.n. 953) about her life on the Maine coast; with Eva Peters (a.n. 951) about the Broiler Festival and her life and work in Belfast, ME; with [Mrs.] Ester Burton (a.n. 984) about the Columbia Street Baptist Church and its history from 1890 to 1910; with [Mrs.] Vivian Gallupe (a.n. 983) about spool mill operation, logging associated with the spool mill, her family and social life, and a boarding house for mill workers; with Gerardine Hale (a.n. 1068) about

Cowan's Tavern, a fire, the 1936 flood, a snow roller, and the history of the town of Lisbon Falls, ME; and with [Miss] Addie Weed (a.n. 969 and 997), who discusses the history of the University and gives autobiographical information. Interviews conducted by the Department of Conservation for the Penobscot Bay Island Project include those with [Mrs.] Clara Orcutt (a.n. 990) about Hog Island, Pond Island, and Western Island; with Abby Weed (a.n. 995) about Butter Island, Bear Island, and Eagle Island; and with Vida Sylvester (a.n. 994) and Laura Brown (a.n. 996) about Eagle Island.

5,645. Davis, Katherine (540)
Oral history. 1969. 1 tape and 53-page transcript.
Open. Published guide.
University of Maine, Northeast Archives of Folklore and Oral History.
Interview in which Davis (1894 or 1895-), a wife and homemaker of Irish ancestry who was married to a dairy farmer, gives detailed information about rug braiding and the tools and material used in the work. Includes photos. Taken from Florence Ireland, *The Northeast Archives of Folklore and Oral History* (Orono, ME: The University Press, 1973).

5,646. Dinsmore, Florence (589)
Oral history. 1971. 1 tape and 18-page transcript.
Open. Published guide.
University of Maine, Northeast Archives of Folklore and Oral History.
Interview with [Mrs.] Dinsmore, a University secretary, relates to her experiences in her work. The interview was conducted as a part of a project on the history of the University. Taken from Florence Ireland, *The Northeast Archives of Folklore and Oral History* (Orono, ME: The University Press, 1973).

5,647. Dr. Clearwater Medicine Company (755)
Oral history. 1973. 1 tape and 18-page transcript.
Open. Unpublished guide.
University of Maine, Northeast Archives of Folklore and Oral History.
Transcript of taped interviews with Eulalie McKeaggan, a secretary at the Company, who gives information about the Company and her work.

5,648. Dowsing (730)
Oral history. 1972. 1 tape and 34-page transcript.
Open. Published guide.
University of Maine, Northeast Archives of Folklore and Oral History.
Interview with Theresa Couture, a wife, mother, and swimming instructor, relates to her experience when she found she could dowse, or water witch, successfully. It also provides information on dowsing and includes photos and interviews with other dowsers. Taken from Florence Ireland, *The Northeast Archives of Folklore and Oral History* (Orono, ME: The University Press, 1973).

5,649. Early Country Music in the Bangor, ME, Area (847)
Oral history. 1975. 2 tapes and 10 pp.
Open. Unpublished guide.
University of Maine, Northeast Archives of Folklore and Oral History.
Interview with Eva Littlefield, a wife and mother, concerns the musical career of her husband Seth Littlefield.

5,650. Goodwin, Elizabeth (535)
Oral history. 1969. 2 tapes and 33-page transcript.
Open. Published and unpublished guides.
University of Maine, Northeast Archives of Folklore and Oral History.
Interview that Hilda Fife conducted with Goodwin concerns Sarah Orne Jewett, an author whose works include *The Country of the Pointed Firs.* Taken from Florence Ireland, *The Northeast Archives of Folklore and Oral History* (Orono, ME: The University Press, 1973).

5,651. Little Musquash Lake (1075)
Oral history. 1976-77. 1 tape and 8 pp.
Open. Unpublished guide.
University of Maine, Northeast Archives of Folklore and Oral History.
Interview with Goldie Averill in which she describes her experiences working with her husband Blaine Averill, who was a woods cook at Little Musquash Lake in 1945 and 1946. The Averills continued as cooks for the same woods operator until 1954.

5,652. McGraw, Natalie (259)
Papers. 1962. 82 pp.
Open. Published and unpublished guides.
University of Maine, Northeast Archives of Folklore and Oral History.
Folk tales told to McGraw, which she later transcribed, concern the Maine towns of Dyer Brook, Smyrna Mills, Merrill, and Oakfield. Includes "Madge Crandall, Girl Heroine of Oakfield," a story about Crandall, who was a mail carrier. Taken from Florence Ireland, *The Northeast Archives of Folklore and Oral History* (Orono, ME: The University Press, 1973).

5,653. McKeaggan, Eulalie (536)
Oral history. 1969. 1 tape and 32-page transcript.
Open. Published and unpublished guides.
University of Maine, Northeast Archives of Folklore and Oral History.
Interviews with McKeaggan, a singer, relate to her singing. Also includes journal entries by Florence Ireland concerning the interviews, which she conducted. Taken from Florence Ireland, *The Northeast Archives of Folklore and Oral History* (Orono, ME: The University Press, 1973).

5,654. Maddan, Jessie Flora (Ash) (690)
Oral history. 1972. 3 tapes and 119-page transcript.
Open. Published guide.
University of Maine, Northeast Archives of Folklore and Oral History.
Interview with Maddan (1886-), a mother and operator of sporting camps in Cardville, ME. She discusses her family life, school, social activities, married life, the illnesses and deaths of her father and husbands, sporting camps, trapping and hunting, herbs used for medicines, maple sugaring, and soap making. Maddan was first married to Remington Maddan and then to Chester James Maddan. Taken from Florence Ireland, *The Northeast Archives of Folklore and Oral History* (Orono, ME: The University Press, 1973).

5,655. Maine Folklore (5)
Papers. 1963. 31 pp.
Open. Published and unpublished guides.
University of Maine, Northeast Archives of Folklore and Oral History.
Folk tales transcribed by Robert Allen. One concerns Mary Wood, a gypsy who wandered about the Wesley, Northfield, and Machias, ME, area. Taken from Florence Ireland, *The Northeast Archives of Folklore and Oral History* (Orono, ME: The University Press, 1973).

5,656. Megquier, Marie (599)
Oral History. 1971. 1 tape and 10-page transcript.
Open. Published guide.
University of Maine, Northeast Archives of Folklore and Oral History.
Transcript and tape of [Mrs.] Megquier, who discusses how to water witch or dowse, and those who are able to do it. Includes photos. Taken from Florence Ireland, *The Northeast Archives of Folklore and Oral History* (Orono, ME: The University Press, 1973).

5,657. Music in Maine (864 and 866)
Oral history. 1975. 7 tapes and 23 pp.
Open. Unpublished guide.
University of Maine, Northeast Archives of Folklore and Oral History.
Interviews with pianists Cherry Noble Feuchette and Mary Lou (Francis) Paul, who was a Penobscot Indian.

5,658. Penobscot Indian Songs (1055)
Oral history. 1976. 1 tape and 9 pp.
Access restricted. Unpublished guide.
University of Maine, Northeast Archives of Folklore and Oral History.
Tape and transcript of Penobscot Indian songs sung by Teresa Sappier, a Penobscot Indian. The original tape is deposited at the Ethnomusicology Archives of the University of Illinois, Champaign-Urbana.

5,659. Porter, Mabel, and Goodwin, Ethel (539)
Oral history. 1973. 1 tape and 22 pp.
Open. Published and unpublished guides.
University of Maine, Northeast Archives of Folklore and Oral History.
Interview with [Mrs.] Porter and her daughter Ethel Goodwin, homemakers in Searsport, ME, concerns food preservation and preparation techniques from more than 50 years ago. Taken from Florence Ireland, *The Northeast Archives of Folklore and Oral History* (Orono, ME: The University Press, 1973).

5,660. Quilting in the State of Maine (778)
Oral history. 1973. 100-page transcript.
Open. Unpublished guide.
University of Maine, Northeast Archives of Folklore and Oral History.
Transcript of taped interviews with five women about quilting. Includes pictures.

5,661. Savage, Elizabeth (874)
Oral history. 1974. 1 tape and 38-page transcript.
Open. Unpublished guide.
University of Maine, Northeast Archives of Folklore and Oral History.
Interview concerning [Mrs. Paul] Savage's role in the women's movement. She was 86 at the time of the interview.

5,662. Schrumpf, Ellen (Brown) "Brownie" [Mrs. William] (586)
Oral history. 1971. 3 tapes and 45-page transcript.
Open. Published guide.
University of Maine, Northeast Archives of Folklore and Oral History.
Interview with Schrumpf, who was a staff writer for the *Bangor Daily News* in Maine, a home economics instructor, assistant to the alumni director at the University, and an assistant 4-H leader at the University, concerns her work experiences. The interview was conducted as part of a project on the history of the University. Taken from Florence Ireland, *The Northeast Archives of Folklore and Oral History* (Orono, ME: The University Press, 1973).

5,663. Scribner, Myrtle (McPheters) (590)
Oral history. 1971. 1 tape and 17-page transcript.
Open. Published guide.
University of Maine, Northeast Archives of Folklore and Oral History.
Interview with [Mrs. John] Scribner, a secretary at the University, who describes her job experiences. The interview was conducted as part of a project on the history of the University. Taken from Florence Ireland, *The Northeast Archives of Folklore and Oral History* (Orono, ME: The University Press, 1973).

5,664. Shea, Mrs. James M. (552)
Oral history. 1970. 1 tape and 15-page transcript.
Open. Published guide.
University of Maine, Northeast Archives of Folklore and Oral History.
Interview with Shea (1901-), who describes the location of woods camps, gathering spruce gum, camp food, lumbering songs, wangan, and superstitions in the Aroostook County, ME, lumbering area. Taken from Florence Ireland, *The Northeast Archives of Folklore and Oral History* (Orono, ME: The University Press, 1973).

5,665. Skinner Settlement Project (840)
Oral History. 1974. 7 tapes and 77-page transcript.
Open. Unpublished guide.
University of Maine, Northeast Archives of Folklore and Oral History.
Interview with Grace (Johnson) [Mrs. Deane L.] Clark (1887-), a wife and mother, concerns family life on a farm in East Corinth, ME, at the turn of the century.

5,666. Viles, George (408)
Papers. 1964. 23 pp.
Open. Published and unpublished guides.
University of Maine, Northeast Archives of Folklore and Oral History.
Folk tales that Thelma Lyon told Viles in Paris Hill, ME. Includes three stories about Molly Ockett, a Saint Francis Indian. Taken from Florence Ireland, *The Northeast Archives of Folklore and Oral History* (Orono, ME: The University Press, 1973).

5,667. Women in Maine
Oral history. 1975-77. 24 tapes.
Open. Unpublished guide.
University of Maine, Northeast Archives of Folklore and Oral History.
Interviews with wives and mothers, who provide their life histories and opinions of the influences that shaped their lives. The interviews were done to study speech patterns. See interviews 876, 880, 882, 884, 886, 888, 904, 938, 997, 998, 999, 1005, 1006, 1010, 1013, 1015, 1019, 1084, 1087, 1091, 1092, 1095, 1096, and 1097, which are housed at the Archives.

5,668. Women in Maine (872)
Oral history. 1975. 1 tape and 27-page transcript.
Open. Unpublished guide.
University of Maine, Northeast Archives of Folklore and Oral History.
Interview with [Mrs.] Catherine Smith, who wrote for a movie magazine from 1914 to 1920, concerns her career as a writer and as secretary to General Chamberlain.

PORTLAND

5,669. Akers, Elizabeth Anne (Chase)
Papers. 1852-1914. 1 box.
Open. Published guide and card catalog.
Maine Historical Society.
A poet and journalist, Akers (1832-1911) later married a Mr. Allen. Correspondence; literary manuscripts, including drafts of her poems "The Pearl Diver" and "The Proud Lady of Stavoren"; biographical sketches; photos; and clippings. Also includes letters wherein Akers discusses her Portland newspaper work, literary efforts, and personal life. See Elizabeth Ring, *A Reference List of Manuscripts Relating to the History of Maine* (Orono: University of Maine, 1938).

5,670. American Guild of Organists
Records. 1919-56. 5 vols.
Open. No guide.
Maine Historical Society.
Minutes; financial accounts; lists of members and officers, many of whom were women; programs; and clippings of this organization founded in 1919, which conducted concerts, listened to lectures, taught classes, held dinners, and sponsored contests. In these records the group is sometimes referred to as the Maine branch of the Guild, at other times as the Portland chapter.

5,671. Black, Persis (Sibley) Andrews
Papers. 1841-53. 5 vols.
Open. Card catalog.
Maine Historical Society.
Diaries of [Mrs. Alvah] Black (1813-91), a resident of Freedom, Dixfield, and Paris, ME, contain descriptions of local customs and society. In 1842 Persis Sibley married Charles Andrews (1814-52), who was a US congressman at the time of his death.

5,672. Brown Family
Papers. 1791-1924. 5 boxes.
Open. No guide.
Maine Historical Society.
Correspondence and financial records of this family of Maine farmers, of which Ephraim Brown (1765-1840) was patriarch. Includes letters to and from women members such as Abigail Brown (1792-?), Hannah Brown (1800-26), another Hannah Brown (1830-1923), Emma Brown (1839-1920), and Mary Burnham Brown.

5,673. Cargill, Knight, and Norcross Families
Papers. 1807-70. 2 boxes.
Open. Correspondence list.
Maine Historical Society.
Correspondence, diaries, deeds, receipts, expense memoranda, essays, penmanship exercises, and school registers of three Maine families. Includes an 1852-61 diary and letters of Chancel Norcross to her parents and brother about school and family events.

5,674. Chapman, Leonard Bond
Papers. 1726-1915. 15 boxes.
Open. List of folders' contents.
Maine Historical Society.
Correspondence, genealogical notes, daybook, and muster rolls of Chapman (1834-1915), a genealogist. Contains letters by Elizabeth Akers reflecting on the death of her husband Paul Akers, her family history, and Portland social life.

5,675. Davison, Eliza Ann (Gannett)
Papers. 1842-93. 3 in.
Open. No guide.
Maine Historical Society.
Davison (1811-?), a resident of Augusta, ME, was the wife of sea captain John Davison. Correspondence, John Davison's diary, poetry, legal documents, and invitations. Includes letters to Eliza Davison from her husband, her parents, her sister Olive Gannett, her brother George Gannett, her daughter-in-law Birta M. Davison, her grandson John A. Davison, and other relatives.

5,676. Goodenow, Robert
Papers. 1759-1863. Ca. 300 items.
Open. List of folders' contents.
Maine Historical Society.
Correspondence, diary, deeds, and other legal papers of Goodenow (1800-74), a lawyer and US congressman from Maine. Tyler family correspondence is included, with letters by Sarah (Collins) Tyler and Valeria (Goodenow) Stone (1802-84) and correspondence between Goodenow and his wife Mary Reed (Cutler) Goodenow (1806-73) wherein she describes personal news and he mentions the Kossuth Revolution and persons such as Daniel Webster, whom he met in Washington, DC.

5,677. Haskell, Winifred
Papers. 1881-1954. 34 vols.
Open. No guide.
Maine Historical Society.
Papers of [Miss] Haskell (1895-1954), a resident of South Windham, ME, consist of an autograph book and 1881 diary of Jessie Haskell, and diaries Winifred Haskell kept from childhood, detailing her experiences at school, her jobs, travel, and household and family events.

5,678. Hawes, Beulah (Nickerson)
Papers. Nd. 68-page item.
Open. Card catalog.
Maine Historical Society.
Autobiographical account of Hawes (1896-) concerns life in Stockton Springs, ME, at the turn of the century.

5,679. King, William
Papers. 1760-1834. 24 boxes and 4 packages.
Open. No guide.
Maine Historical Society.
King (1768-1852) was a businessman, politician, Army officer, and governor of Maine whose papers consist of correspondence, bills, receipts, deeds, indentures, insurance papers, and military records. Included are letters to King from his wife Ann; letters from Lucy Flucker Knox concerning completion of her education, which the King family paid for; and letters about the Coney Female Academy of Augusta, ME. Lucy Knox was probably the daughter of General Henry Knox and, later, wife of Ebenezer Thatcher.

5,680. Maine Association Opposed to Suffrage for Women
Records. 1914-17. 2 boxes.
Open. No guide.
Maine Historical Society.
Bylaws, minutes, financial records, correspondence, index cards and postcards, and printed material of this group, founded in 1914 and predominantly composed of women as officers and members. Correspondence is between the Association and state and national legislators, the National Association Opposed to Woman Suffrage, influential citizens, and other antisuffrage groups. Collection also contains information about Maine Association members and supporters, with lists by town of members' names and occupations for men, marital status for women; postcards with names and addresses of members; and index cards on those who pledged to oppose suffrage whenever it appeared on the ballot, giving supporters' names, addresses, occupations, and names of the persons who solicited their support.

5,681. May, Abigail
Papers. 1789. 1 vol.
Open. Card catalog.
Maine Historical Society.
Diary in which May (1775-1800), a resident of Portland, details her trip from Boston to Portland by ship. May describes social life on board, the course of the journey, and some passengers, including a man searching for a runaway slave.

5,682. Muzzey, Franklin
Papers. 1835-73. 236 items.
Open. No guide.
Maine Historical Society.
Correspondence of Muzzey (1806-73), a blacksmith, consists of exchanges about family news with his wife Caroline (McComber) Muzzey while she was in Bucksport, ME, and he was in Bangor, ME.

5,683. Pidgin, Mrs. William A.
Papers. 1874-1902. 2 vols.
Open. Published guide.
Maine Historical Society.
Household accounts of Pidgin (?-1918), a Lewiston, ME, housewife, for 1874 through 1878 and 1899 through 1902. See Elizabeth Ring, *A Reference List of Manuscripts Relating to the History of Maine* (Orono: University of Maine, 1938).

5,684. Portland Anti-Slavery Society
Records. 1844-66. 1 box.
Open. Correspondence list.
Maine Historical Society.
Constitution, minute book, correspondence, sermon, and manuscript essay of the Society, established in 1844 to promote abolition of slavery. Some of the Society's founders were women; the correspondence secretary was Elizabeth Mountford, and most of the records reflect Mountford's work. Includes her letterbook of correspondence to antislavery leaders such as Wendell Phillips and replies to her from Frederick Douglass, William Lloyd Garrison, and others. Also contained are personal letters Mountfort received from William Willis and a manuscript by Elizabeth Turner on rules for teaching formulae and other mathematical exercises.

5,685. Portland Girls' High School
Records. 1851-63. 4 vols.
Open. No guide.
Maine Historical Society.
Manuscript copies of the School literary magazines *The Aspirant* and *The Constellation,* which consist of essays, short stories, and poetry.

5,686. Portland Provident Association
Records. 1854-1964. 14 vols.
Open. Card catalog.
Maine Historical Society.
Records of the Association, established in 1854 as a charitable organization, include those of the women's auxiliary, the Portland Female Provident Association; in 1965 the two groups merged. Constitutions and bylaws, minutes, accounts, correspondence, lists of officers and members, and a history. The women's auxiliary was managed by women, supported by bequests from the estates of wealthy women, and devoted to donating food and clothing to needy widows.

5,687. Portland Widows' Wood Society
Records. 1850-1945. 7 vols.
Open. Card catalog.
Maine Historical Society.
Act of incorporation, bylaws, minutes, and financial accounts of the Society, a charitable organization founded in 1850, which was run by men although "any citizen" was allowed to join. The Society supplied fuel to destitute widows, orphans, and poor women; in 1903, for example, it purchased and gave away $75 worth of wood. Several wealthy women left bequests to the Society.

5,688. Smith, Ann Bryant
Papers. 1806-07. 1 vol.
Open. No guide.
Maine Historical Society.
Diary of Smith (1753-1835), a storekeeper of Westbrook and Lisbon, ME, graphically reflects her life helping her husband in the store, raising a family, and being involved in the local church and other community organizations.

5,689. Usher, Rebecca
Papers. 1841-99. Ca. 250 items.
Open. Correspondence list.
Maine Historical Society.
Correspondence, diary, essay, photos, and printed reports of Usher (1821-1919), a Civil War nurse from Maine. The diary, essay on political rights for women, and some letters concern Usher's training during 1841 in French at an Urseline convent in Three Rivers, Canada. Other material relates to her Civil War experiences, with information about conditions at the Belle Isle prisoner-of-war camp and details of a feud over the US Army Hospital at Chester, PA, which involved Hospital surgeons and the local ladies' aid society. Usher's sisters Martha (Usher) Osgood (1823-93) and Ellen (Usher) Bacon (1817-?) are among her correspondents.

5,690. Waldo, Samuel
Papers. 1631-1824. 2 boxes.
Open. Published guide.
Maine Historical Society.
Correspondence, deeds, indentures, depositions, receipts, bills, accounts, and shipping papers of Waldo (1695-1759), a politician and army officer. Included are legal and fiscal documents relating to his wife Sarah Tyng (Winslow) Waldo (1765-1826), with papers concerning her administration of the Waldo estate between 1773 and 1802; an account of a sale of land to her; and deeds to her, one of which was from the trustees of the Portland Academy. Sarah Waldo later married Salmon Chase. See Elizabeth Ring, *A Reference List of Manuscripts Relating to the History of Maine* (Orono: University of Maine, 1938.)

5,691. Wildes, Elizabeth (Perkins)
Papers. 1789-93. 1 vol.
Open. No guide.
Maine Historical Society.
Diary in which Wildes (1765-1844), a Maine resident who was daughter of Thomas and Susannah (Hovey) Perkins and wife of Israel Wildes, discusses her household, travels, local news, visitors, and the weather.

5,692. Woodman Family
Papers. Ca. 1824-1973. 85 ft.
Open. No guide.
Maine Historical Society.
Correspondence, diaries, and business and legal records of this Maine family which owned lumbering and railroad businesses; Cyrus Woodman (1814-89) is the individual central to the collection. Papers of female family members include letters of Caroline (Bowers) [Mrs. Edward] Woodman, 1874-86; Mary Woodman, 1847-1928; and Hannah Woodman, 1892-1973. Also includes documents pertaining to the estate of Norah Durand Woodman and to other family estates.

5,693. Archives
Records. 1940- . 4 ft.
Open. No guide.
Victorian Society of Maine Women, Morse-Libby-Holmes Mansion.
Constitution and charter, minutes, correspondence, lists of members, programs, and photos of the Society, an historic preservation group founded in 1943. In 1940 [Miss] Clara Holmes and her brother William Henry Holmes bought the Mansion and began work with several prominent Portland women creating an organization to restore the building and to open it to the public as a museum; the Victorian Society of Maine Women grew out of their efforts. The Society has also been devoted to commemorating achievements of Maine women in the arts and in civic affairs by lectures and other educational programs, dedicating rooms in the Mansion, and conferring special membership in the Society on notable Maine women.

5,694. Maine Women Writers
Collection. 1804- . Ca. 3500 items.
Open. No guide.
Westbrook College.
Correspondence, diaries, manuscripts, photos, memorabilia, and books of more than 325 women authors, including [Miss] Sarah Orne Jewett, author of *The Country of the Pointed Firs;* [Miss] Harriet Plimpton, a poet, teacher, and sculptor, whose published works include *Out of the North* (Oxford University Press, 1960); Florence (Burrill) [Mrs. George] Jacobs, a poet and essayist whose publications include *Stones* and *Neighbors;* Virginia (Chase) [Mrs. Wallace] Perkins, a short story writer, essayist, and author of such novels as *The End of the Week;* her sister [Miss] Mary Ellen Chase, a novelist and author of books on the Bible; Celia (Laighton) Thaxter, an essayist, artist, and poet whose works include "The Sandpiper" and "Courage"; her granddaughter [Miss] Rosamond Thaxter, who wrote a biography of her; novelist Gladys (Hasty) Carroll, who wrote *The Road Grows Strange;* poet Jessie Wheeler Freeman, whose works include *Town Down East;* [Miss] Rachel Field, a playwright, Newbery prize-winning author of children's stories, and novelist, whose works include *All This and Heaven Too;* and Audrey White [Mrs. Walter] Beyer, a teacher at Westbrook and author of such stories for juveniles as *Capture at Sea* and *The Sapphire Pendant.*

Also includes correspondence, photo scrapbooks, and other items of Josephine (Diebitsch) Peary, wife of Admiral Robert E. Peary, who discovered the North Pole, and of her daughter Marie Stafford (Peary) [Mrs. William] Kuhne. After accompanying her husband to Greenland in 1891, Josephine Peary wrote *My Arctic Journal* and other books. Included as well are papers of Elizabeth (Chase) [Mrs. Benjamin Paul] Akers [Mrs. E. M.] Allen, assistant editor of the *Portland Transcript* in 1855, literary editor of the *Portland Daily Advertizer* in 1874, and author of "Rock Me to Sleep" and other poems; Anna Stephens, an editor and publisher of periodicals and a novelist who sometimes used the pseudonym Jonathan Slick; and Blanche Willis Howard, a teacher, novelist, and foreign correspondent for the *Boston Transcript* who became Countess von Teuffel.

In addition, the collection contains papers of Elizabeth Coatsworth, a poet, essayist, author of literature for children, and resident of Nobleboro, ME, who was married to the late Henry Beston; gothic novelist Sarah Sayward (Barrell) Keating Wood (1759-1855); [Miss] Toby Shafter, a biographer of Edna St. Vincent Millay; Elizabeth (Payson) Prentiss, author of children's stories, including *Stepping Heavenward;* Kate Douglas Wiggin, author of *Rebecca of Sunnybrook Farm;* [Miss] Ola Elizabeth Winslow, professor and historian who won a Pulitzer Prize for her biography of Jonathan Edwards; dime novelist Elizabeth Oakes (Prince) [Mrs. Seba] Smith, who wrote and lectured on women's suffrage; Sara Payson (Willis) Parton, a novelist who used the pen name Fanny Fern and who wrote *Ruth Hall,* a satirical portrait of her brother Nathaniel Parker Willis, a poet, journalist, and dramatist; May Sarton, a poet and novelist who lives in York, ME; Abba (Goold) Woolson, a poet, critic, and lecturer; and Harriet Prescott Spofford, Margaret Wade (Campbell) Deland, and Harriet (Beecher) Stowe.

SACO

5,695. Cutts Family
Papers. Nd. No size given.
Open. Card catalog.
Dyer-York Library.
Letters of [Miss] Eunice Cutts, one of which is from Thomas Geyers; a letter Sarah Chauncey Cutts wrote to her mother while attending a boarding school in Dorchester, MA; a poem and watercolor painting of Betsey Cutts; and a letter Foxwell Cutts wrote to his wife and children.

5,696. Diaz Union
Records. Ca. 1882. No size given.
Open. Card catalog.
Dyer-York Library.
Constitution and bylaws of the Union, a Saco group which was organized to "consider and present practical methods for securing women higher intellectual, moral, and physical conditions, with a view to the improvement of all domestic and social relations."

5,697. Fairfield Family
Papers. Nd. No size given.
Open. Card catalog.
Dyer-York Library.
Deposition concerning Anne Payne Fairfield.

5,698. Female Temperance Society of Saco and Biddleford
Records. 1838. No size given.
Open. Card catalog.
Dyer-York Library.
Address delivered to the Society by George Packard, a Saco physician.

5,699. Haley Family
Papers. Nd. No size given.
Open. Card catalog.
Dyer-York Library.
A memorial address for Lizzie H. Haley, a minister, delivered in 1889 by Ellen Gustin, a minister; a note concerning the death of [Miss] Nuldah Haley; and a letter to Adelaide Haley from the Mifflin Co. concerning her father's Civil War diary.

5,700. Miscellaneous Manuscripts
Collection. Nd. No size given.
Open. Card catalog.
Dyer-York Library.
Includes a manuscript describing the frivolous ways of young ladies seeking beaux, a diary of Georgianna Allen for 1860 to 1862, a 1763 indenture between Elizabeth Ayer of Salem, NH, and Timothy Ayer, an 1830 description of the provisions Benjamin and Mercy Simpson made for their foster child Mercy Emerson, and a note from Mercy Emerson.

5,701. Scamman Family
Papers. Nd. No size given.
Open. Card catalog.
Dyer-York Library.
Letter, cards, invitations, and a clipping concerning the appointment of Edith Scamman as field secretary of the Woman's Home Missionary Federation of Congregational Churches. Also includes a clipping about the death of Sarah O. Scamman and another about the funeral of Georgianna Allen, who was the niece of Edith Scamman.

5,702. Suicide
Collection. 1815. 1 item.
Open. Card catalog.
Dyer-York Library.
An account of suicides of four York County women, which apparently were committed out of religious enthusiasm.

5,703. Tucker Family
Papers. 1809-23. 1 vol. and 1 item.
Open. Card catalog.
Dyer-York Library.
Writing book of Lydia E. Tucker and a letter which Elisabeth Tucker wrote to her father while she was attending boarding school.

5,704. York Manufacturing Co.
Records. 1841. 1 item.
Open. Card catalog.
Dyer-York Library.
Clipping from the York County *Herald* concerns the strike by female employees of this company's mills.

5,705. Provincial Archives
Records. 1882-1977. No size given.
Open. No guide.
Servants of the Immaculate Heart of Mary.
Minutes, financial records, correspondence, annals, photos, and other records of the province, including papers of the mothers general. The congregation was established in the US in 1882 in Biddeford, ME. The sisters, who also are known as the Good Shepherd Sisters of Quebec, are engaged in teaching, social works for the rehabilitation of women and the protection of youth, health services, special ministries, and foreign missions.

SEARSPORT

5,706. Diaries
Collection. 1862-71. 4 vols.
Open. No guide.
William H. Pendleton (Personal Collection).
Includes a diary in which Emma W. Pendleton (ca. 1847-70) recorded her life in a small coastal town during 1863 and her thoughts about her future and the Civil War. Pendleton later married Captain James Blanchard, Jr., and was lost with him and her child when the bark *Trovatore* sank en route from Trieste to Palermo, Sicily. Also includes diaries her cousin [Miss] Mary Abigail Bailey (1838-ca. 1910) kept during 1862, 1864, and 1871.

5,707. Shipboard Women
Collection. Late 19th century. No size given.
Open. No guide.
William H. Pendleton (Personal Collection).
Correspondence and journals that women wrote while on voyages with their fathers or husbands, who were ship captains, include a journal Emily (Perry) Pendleton, second wife of Captain Phineas Pendleton, III, kept on her 147-day honeymoon trip in 1882 and 1883 aboard the *Elizabeth* from Baltimore to Japan via the Cape of Good Hope; she describes life at sea as well as people and places she visited. Also includes a journal that Lucy and Lettie Pendleton wrote, in the form of weekly letters home to their sister Rose (Pendleton) Havener, while on a 130-day voyage from New York City to San Francisco aboard the *Henry Hyde,* which was commanded by their father Phineas Pendleton, III. The sisters describe shipboard life and their stay in San Francisco, including a large parade sponsored by Republicans promoting the election of William McKinley.

SPRINGVALE

5,708. Nasson Women
Records. 1912- . Ca. 18 drawers, 200 vols., and 30 files.
Access restricted. Unpublished guide.
Nasson College Library.
Minutes, financial records, correspondence, honors theses, catalogs, yearbooks, scrapbooks, photos, clippings, and memorabilia of Nasson College, a two-year college for women founded in 1912 to provide career training in home economics, business, nursery education, secretarial skills, and other fields. Later the school expanded into a coeducational liberal arts college. Includes biographies of College deans and teachers; chronologies of events and women's activities, including athletics; and information on the life of College women.

SUNSET

5,709. Martha Washington Benevolent Society
Records. Ca. 1870-1935. 1 vol. and 3 items.
Open. No guide.
Deer Isle-Stonington Historical Society.
A minute book, two captioned photos of the membership, and a history written by Frances Hosmer in 1935 of the Society, a charitable organization founded by women of Sunset in 1835 as the Martha Washington Temperance Society. Devoted to good works from its inception, the Society adopted its later name to reflect those activities and then dissolved in the late 1930s when its functions were taken over by a local church. During its existence, the Society was a source of food, fuel, and clothing for poor families in the area. The group raised money by selling knitted goods and quilts made by members. The Society was also involved in village improvement, for it paid to add a community room to the new schoolhouse in 1854, was instrumental in creating a new town cemetery during the 1860s, and was active in starting a community library during the 1890s.

WATERVILLE

5,710. Case, Isaac
Papers. 1785-1880. 12 folders.
Open. No guide.
Colby College Library, Special Collections.
Papers of Case (ca. 1761-1852), a Baptist missionary to the Indians in Maine, include letters he wrote his wife Joanna Case while he was traveling during his missionary work between 1785 and 1836. Collection also contains his diary, 1789-1825, and correspondence and diary sheets of his daughter Hannah (Case) Harley, which primarily consist of religious reflections and news of daily events. Her correspondents are her daughter Amanda (Harley) Stevens, her other children, and her grandchildren.

5,711. Chase, Mary Ellen
Papers. 1910-68. 6 folders, 31 vols., and 45 items.
Open. Unpublished guide.
Colby College Library, Special Collections.
Papers of Chase (1887-1973), an author and teacher, consist of personal correspondence, the bulk of which is letters to Carl J. Weber about their mutual interest in Thomas Hardy, Colby College affairs, and social matters; diaries, 1910, 1932-35 and 1940-55; and essays, short stories, and book-length manuscripts.

5,712. Flint, Margaret
Papers. 1936-59. 2 ft., 24 vols., and 120 items.
Open. Unpublished guide.
Colby College Library, Special Collections.
Papers of Flint (1891-1960), an author who was married to Lester W. Jacobs, consist of correspondence, primarily letters from her publishers Dodd, Mead & Co.; congratulatory messages concerning her novel *The Old Ashburn Place;* diaries chronicling her life in rural Maine, 1936-59; manuscripts of unpublished novels, short stories, poems, and speeches; and other documents. Flint wrote her fiction under her maiden name, but used the name Margaret Flint Jacobs in writing Christian Science publications.

5,713. James, William, Family
Papers. 1825-1900. Ca. 13 vols. and 1200 items.
Open. Unpublished guide.
Colby College Library, Special Collections.
Papers of James (1797-1868), a Presbyterian minister, include correspondence of his wife Marcia Lucretia (Ames) James (1797-1896), daughter of portrait painter Ezra Ames, about family matters; letters to the family and a diary, 1842-47, of their daughter Anna McBride (James) Edwards (1826-1907), who married Isaac Edwards, a lawyer and dean of the Albany law school; letters to Elizabeth Tillman (James) Seelye (1833-81), a daughter of William and Marcia James who married Julius Seelye, president of Amherst College, from the period of her schooling and early marriage; and correspondence about the charitable activities of another daughter of William and Marcia James, Katherine Barber (James) Prince (1834-90), who married psychiatrist William H. Prince. Katherine Prince's correspondents include a teacher and students at a Unitarian mission in Calcutta, Julia B. Wilson of the Mission to Colored Refugees and Children's Home in Baxter Springs, KS, and a teacher and students at a church school in Tougaloo, MS. Also includes letters to Prince from her niece Katherine James Edwards, daughter of Anna and Isaac Edwards, who wrote during her adolescence and young womanhood, and a ca. 1884 diary containing short entries about daily life,

which Katherine Edwards appears to have kept and sent periodically to Katherine Prince.

5,714. Jewett, Sarah Orne
Papers. 1879-1908. 8 folders and 290 items.
Open. Unpublished guide.
Colby College Library, Special Collections.
Correspondence; manuscripts of single poems and the short story "In Dark New England Days"; secondary source material; and published works of Jewett (1849-1909), an author and poet. Correspondents include Horace E. Scudder and other editors as well as authors Julia Dorr, Louise Imogen Guiney, Harriet Spofford, Laura Richards, Violet Paget, Alice Brown, and Mary Wilkins Freeman.

5,715. Costley, Clara
Papers. 1926-58. 24 vols.
Open. No guide.
Waterville Historical Society.
Diaries in which Costley, a Waterville resident, made references to her work in an office, local events, family news, and occasionally major national events such as the beginning or end of wars.

5,716. Parmenter, Harriet May
Papers. 1892-1952. 52 vols.
Open. No guide.
Waterville Historical Society.
Diaries of Parmenter (1867-1955), a Waterville resident, contain quotations from newspapers, lectures, and friends' letters; descriptions of events in her life and those of other townspeople; notes on her visitors and travels; and clippings concerning local and national news.

5,717. Silence Howard Hayden Chapter of the Daughters of the American Revolution
Records. 1952-60. 2 vols.
Open. No guide.
Waterville Historical Society.
Scrapbooks contain histories, programs, photos, clippings, and artifacts of the Chapter, a patriotic group organized in 1898.

MARYLAND

ANNAPOLIS

5,718. United States Naval Academy Museum
Papers. 1661-1952. 615 items.
Open. Unpublished guide.
United States Naval Academy Museum.
In collections of personal and family papers held by the Museum is material relating to the US Navy, including correspondence between wives, sisters, mothers, and Naval officers on such subjects as battles, camp life, and the duties of midshipmen. Invitations to social functions and letters containing family news are also included. Items relating to women include a letter by William Crowninshield Endicott regarding the disposition of $4000 upon the death of Polly Fay, an 1819 letter by which Stephen Decatur emancipated his slave Philis Ash, and a 1797 letter from Martha Washington to her sister [Mrs.] Elizabeth Henley concerning the health of Washington family members and the return of Washington's niece Fanny Bassett Washington Lear to her parents. Letters, diaries, and other papers of the Charles E. Thorburn family are contained as well.

5,719. Oral History Collection
Oral history. 1942- . 20 tapes.
Open. Unpublished guide.
United States Naval Institute.
Tapes and transcripts of interviews with 14 women concerning their activities in the WAVES. Includes interviews with Captain Mildred McAfee, who in 1942 was the first director of the WAVES; Captain Robin Quigley, who in 1975 retired as head of the WAVES; and Captain Dorothy Stratton, who began as a member of the WAVES but then organized the SPARS for the US Coast Guard. Also includes an interview with Margaret Chase Smith, a US senator from Maine who helped establish the WAVES. Duplicates of these interviews are also held at the Naval Historical Center, Operational Archives, in Washington, DC.

BALTIMORE

5,720. Szold, Henrietta
Papers. 1866-1944. 18 microfilm reels.
Open. No guide.
Baltimore Hebrew College Library.
[Miss] Szold (1860-1945) was a Zionist, philanthropist, and founder and first president of Hadassah, the Women's Zionist Organization of America. Correspondence about Szold's world travels, impressions of people, and opinions about the settlement of Palestine and various Jewish communities.

5,721. Cone
Papers. 1904- . No size given.
Access restricted. Unpublished guide.
The Baltimore Museum of Art.
Correspondence, diaries, financial records, scrapbooks, and photos of Claribel Cone (1864-1929), a physician, and her sister [Miss] Etta Cone (1870-1949), both of whom were art collectors. Contains information on their collection and purchase of works by Pablo Picasso, Henri Matisse, and other artists. Includes correspondence with Picasso, Matisse, and other artists the Cones knew who were working in Paris during the early 20th century.

5,722. Archives
Records. 1642- . Ca. 10 boxes.
Closed. No guide.
Carmelite Monastery.
The Monastery, founded in 1790 at Port Tobacco, MD, was the first community of religious women in the original thirteen colonies. Although this order of contemplative women is devoted chiefly to prayer, the community also operated an academy for young girls from 1831 to 1851. Financial and legal records, a Rule, correspondence, annals, profession and death records, wills, retreat material, sermons, custom books, songs, poems, biographical material, a scrapbook of clippings, and other records. Includes correspondence with the first Catholic bishops in this country, with Jesuits, with founders and foundresses of religious communities, and with religious men and women in Europe as well as a diary kept by one of the sister foundresses, an English woman, on a boat trip from Antwerp to southern Maryland after the Revolutionary War. Material that predates the founding in Port Tobacco includes a handwritten Rule, correspondence, lists of sisters and families, spiritual notebooks, death notices, poems, books brought from the Low Countries, and a 1674 deed to the first property owned by the nuns in southern Maryland. Also contains material gathered for a lawsuit in the 1820s over property that belonged to the community in Port Tobacco.

5,723. Lucas, Bertha
Papers. Ca. 1900s-30s. Ca. 5 boxes.
Open. No guide.
Enoch Pratt Free Library, George Peabody Department.
Diaries, scrapbooks, and clippings of Lucas. The clippings relate to nursing and nursing schools in Maryland.

5,724. Medical Archives
Records. Nd. No size given.
Access restricted. No guide.
Johns Hopkins University Medical Archives.
Records concerning the history of medicine include two letters of application to medical schools by Elizabeth Blackwell, 1840s, and two boxes of correspondence of physician Florence Sabin, 1903-41.

5,725. Admission of Women to Hopkins
Records. Ca. 1877-93. Ca. 100 items.
Open. Unpublished guide.
Johns Hopkins University, Milton S. Eisenhower Library, Special Collections.
Correspondence, memoranda, and other material, including 75 letters from women applicants to Johns Hopkins and memos on the admission of women from Hopkins faculty members.

5,726. Boehm, Margaret Donaldson
Papers. 1908-56. 159 items.
Open. Unpublished guide.
Johns Hopkins University, Milton S. Eisenhower Library, Special Collections.
Correspondence and diaries of Boehm (1894-1956), a resident of Baltimore. The minutiae of daily life are described in her 47 diaries; the letters are from Henry W. Nevinson, a writer.

5,727. Collitz, Klara Hechtenberg
Papers. 1904-36. 575 items.
Open. Unpublished guide.
Johns Hopkins University, Milton S. Eisenhower Library, Special Collections.
Correspondence of Collitz (1863-1944), a philologist who was married to Hermann Collitz, a professor of German at Johns Hopkins.

5,728. Franklin, Christine (Ladd)
Papers. 1893-1900. 14 items.
Open. Unpublished guide.
Johns Hopkins University, Milton S. Eisenhower Library, Special Collections.
[Mrs. Fabian] Franklin (1847-1930) was a mathematician and one of the first graduate students at Johns Hopkins. Principally addressed to Daniel C. Gilman, the first president of Hopkins, her correspondence includes some items relating to the admission of women to the University.

5,729. Garrett, Mary E.
Papers. 1887-95. 30 items.
Open. Unpublished guide.
Johns Hopkins University, Milton S. Eisenhower Library, Special Collections.
Correspondence of Garrett, a philanthropist, addressed to president Daniel C. Gilman of Johns Hopkins reveals her interest in education for women. She made her donation to the Hopkins medical school contingent upon women being admitted to the school on the same terms as men.

5,730. Lanier, Mary Day
Papers. 1864-1918. Ca. 1000 items.
Open. Unpublished guide.
Johns Hopkins University, Milton S. Eisenhower Library, Special Collections.
Correspondence of Lanier, wife of poet Sidney Lanier, with her husband and members of his family.

5,731. Thomas, Martha Carey
Papers. Ca. 1880-1920. 50 items.
Open. Unpublished guide.
Johns Hopkins University, Milton S. Eisenhower Library, Special Collections.
Correspondence of Thomas (1857-1935), an educator who was president of Bryn Mawr College, includes letters to presidents Gilman, Goodnow, and Remsen and to professors Adams, Collitz, and Gildersleeve, all of Johns Hopkins.

5,732. Turnbull, Eleanor
Papers. 1934-57. 150 items.
Open. Unpublished guide.
Johns Hopkins University, Milton S. Eisenhower Library, Special Collections.
Correspondence of Turnbull (1875-1964), a translator of Spanish poetry and other works, includes letters from Pedro Salinas.

5,733. Turnbull, Francese Hubbard (Litchfield)
Papers. 1888-1925. 40 items.
Open. Unpublished guide.
Johns Hopkins University, Milton S. Eisenhower Library, Special Collections.
Correspondence of [Mrs. Lawrence] Turnbull (1844-1927), an historical novelist, is addressed chiefly to President Gilman of Johns Hopkins and to other members of the University community.

5,734. Wharton, Edith Newbold (Jones)
Papers. Ca. 1914-34. 47 items.
Open. Unpublished guide.
Johns Hopkins University, Milton S. Eisenhower Library, Special Collections.
Personal correspondence of Wharton (1862-1937), an author, is addressed primarily to Mr. and Mrs. John W. Garrett of Baltimore.

5,735. Nightingale
Collection. Ca. 1889-1945. Ca. 100 boxes.
Access restricted. No guide.
Johns Hopkins University, Welch Medical Library.
Collection of material pertaining to nursing and nursing education contains correspondence, diaries, notebooks, reports, scrapbooks, photos, and clippings of Katharine Amberson, Vashti Bartlett, Elizabeth Burgess, Emma O. Cleaver, Charity Babcock Fisk, Alice Fitzgerald, Caroline Hampton, Elizabeth Hobson, Elsie Lawler, Adelaide Nutting, Isabel Hampton Robb, Isabel Stewart, Effie Taylor, Carolyn Van Blarcom, Anna Wolf, and Ellen M. Wood. Also includes records of the Johns Hopkins Hospital School of Nursing, the National Council for War Service, the Committee on Grading of Nursing Schools, the Office of Civilian Defense subcommittee on nursing, the National Nursing Planning Committee, and other organizations and agencies.

5,736. Aiken, John Adams
Papers. 1865-88. Ca. 1500 items.
Open. No guide.
Maryland Historical Society.
Correspondence of Aiken (1850-1927), a lawyer, judge, and member of the Massachusetts state legislature, was written primarily while he was a student at Phillips Academy in Andover, MA, and at Dartmouth College in Hanover, NH. Includes letters in which his mother M. E. [Mrs. David] Aiken gives her son advice and describes her activities in Greenfield and Amherst, MA; letters in which Katherine "Kate" Abbott Sanborn mentions to him her work as an author, lecturer, and teacher in New York, Hanover, and Northampton, MA; and letters in which Mary Willard describes to him her activities in New York and her readings.

5,737. Aircraft Warning Service
Records. 1941-45. 1 vol.
Open. No guide.
Maryland Historical Society.
Scrapbook of Ingreet Bowen [Mrs. Joseph Elmer] Weisheit contains poems, comic strips, advertisements, photos, and clippings concerning the Service, Filter Centers, and the Women's Auxiliary Army Corps, particularly in Maryland, Virginia, and New York. Also includes Weisheit's army pass, her certificate of honorable service, and a 1943 copy of the Filter Center volunteers' magazine *Flash*.

5,738. Arundell Club (36, 988, and 1181)
Records. 1890-1952. 20 vols. and ca. 500 items.
Open. No guide.
Maryland Historical Society.
Minutes, financial papers, correspondence, a roll book, membership lists, programs, and printed matter of the Arundell Club, a women's civic, philanthropic, and social club founded in 1894 and dissolved in 1952; of its subsidiary the Arundell Good Government Club, a reform branch founded in 1896 and dissolved in 1905; and their predecessor the Woman's Literary Club of Baltimore, founded in 1890 to encourage literary work among Baltimore women. In 1894 a group of women split from the Literary Club to form the Arundell Club, which limited its membership; to allow more women to participate in civic and reform activities, the Good Government Club was organized. Collection consists of Arundell Club annual reports, minutes, financial records, and correspondence, most of which concerns finances; Arundell Good Government Club minutes; and Woman's Literary Club minutes containing detailed summaries of original papers Club members presented at each monthly meeting and programs of papers presented.

5,739. Baltimore Birth Control Clinic
Records. 1935. 22 items.
Open. No guide.
Maryland Historical Society.
Correspondence, guest lists, and programs concerning Margaret Sanger's speech in Baltimore on federal birth control legislation. Also includes material on the decision of the Baltimore Birth Control League not to join the American Birth Control League and lists of Baltimore social work agencies, Maryland family welfare agencies, and member clubs of the Maryland Federation of Women's Clubs.

5,740. Blake, Helen D.
Papers. 1922-26. 4 vols.
Open. No guide.
Maryland Historical Society.
Diaries of Blake, a Baltimore resident, cover her high school days and social activities. Much of her social life revolved around the Epworth League, a Methodist young people's group; she describes the League's conventions, week-long training programs for Sunday school teachers that she attended, and other experiences.

5,741. Bonaparte, Charles Joseph
Papers. 1911-18. Ca. 40 items.
Open. No guide.
Maryland Historical Society.
Correspondence between Bonaparte (1851-1921), a lawyer and municipal and civil service reformer, and Anne G. (Hall) Carey concerns their work as Baltimore civic reformers and officers of the Consumers' League of Maryland. They discuss protective labor legislation for women and children.

5,742. Bonaparte, Elisabeth (Patterson)
Papers. 1800-1956. Ca. 1500 items.
Open. Calendar.
Maryland Historical Society.
Bulk of the papers of Bonaparte (1785-1879), a resident of Baltimore and Europe, concerns her marriage in 1803 to Napoleon Bonaparte's brother Jerome, the annulment of their marriage, and her subsequent years in Europe, during which she attempted to have her son recognized as a legitimate Bonaparte heir and to obtain a pension and title for herself. Correspondence with family members about her finances, with friends about life in Baltimore during the Civil War, with French officials concerning her pension and custody of her son, and with European society members about their social activities; legal papers pertaining to her inheritance from her father, the legal difficulties with Napoleon III, and her real estate; business account books, accounts of her real estate holdings, and inventories of her property; poetry; essays; notes; address books; scrapbooks and clippings about her; and printed matter.

5,743. Boone
Papers. 1865-97. 15 vols.
Open. No guide.
Maryland Historical Society.
Diaries and journals of William Marshall Boone (1836-79), a Baltimore businessman; of Sarah P. (Kennedy) Boone (1842-83), a Baltimore resident whom he married in 1866; and their daughter Agnes Boone. In her diary Sarah Boone records her daily activities, many of which centered around the Catholic church, during the year before her marriage. Agnes Boone's journals are of trips she took to Europe, the Middle East, Scotland, and the western US between 1888 and 1897.

5,744. Bowie, Lucy Leigh
Papers. 1790-1958. Ca. 500 items.
Open. No guide.
Maryland Historical Society.
Bowie (1872-1966) was a Baltimore resident and local historian. Letters from friends, some of which concern her articles on Maryland history; research notes for her articles; a diary; genealogical material; and papers relating to the Bowie, Davis, and Gardiner families of Maryland. Also includes correspondence, 1840s-90s, of [Mrs.] Eliza C. Gardiner and her daughters or nieces Mary S. Gardiner, Lottie Leigh Gardiner, and Lucy Leigh Gardiner, all of whom seem to have been connected with running St. Mary's Seminary, a girls school in St. Mary's County, MD.

5,745. Bradford, Phoebe (George) (1077 and 1778)
Papers. 1832-39. Ca. 2500 pp.
Open. No guide.
Maryland Historical Society.
Diaries of [Mrs. Moses] Bradford (1794-1840), a Wilmington, DE, resident, pertain to her participation in the Female Bible Society, the Female Hospitable Society, and the Female Colonial Society of Wilmington. Also contains information on her interest in religion and references to slavery and to the situation between Mexico and the US during the 1830s.

5,746. Briggs and Stabler (139, 146, and 147)
Papers. 1770-1920. Ca. 12 ft.
Open. Description.
Maryland Historical Society.
Business papers and family correspondence of Isaac Briggs (1763-1825), a civil engineer and surveyor, and of James P. Stabler (?-1840), a postmaster in Sandy Spring, MD, and employee of the B & O Railroad, contain information on Quakers in Virginia and Maryland, medicine, farming, and other topics. Includes correspondence from the 1790s to the 1860s between Briggs, his wife Hannah (Brooke) Briggs (?-ca. 1851), and their daughters Deborah Briggs, Mary Briggs, Elizabeth Briggs, Sarah Briggs, and Anna (Briggs) [Mrs. Caleb?] Bentley (1796-?) about the family's life in Sandy Spring. Also includes ca. 50 letters in which Anna Bentley describes her family's migration to New Lisbon, OH. Deborah Briggs may later have married Joseph Bond and Sarah Briggs, James P. Stabler.

5,747. Bronson, Loosie
Papers. 1881. 1 vol.
Open. No guide.
Maryland Historical Society.
Diary in which Bronson (ca. 1867-?), a Baltimore schoolgirl, recorded her daily activities, which included housework, lessons, sewing school, prayer meetings, and Sunday school.

5,748. Buchanan, Robert Christie
Papers. 1811-90. Ca. 600 items.
Open. No guide.

Maryland Historical Society.
Papers of Buchanan (1811-78), a US Army officer, contain letters from his mother Carolina Virginia Marylandia (Johnson) [Mrs. Andrew] Buchanan [Mrs. Nathaniel, Jr.] Frye and from Louisa Catherine (Johnson) [Mrs. John Quincy] Adams (1775-1852), both of whom lived in Washington, DC.

5,749. Cannon, Lucy A.
Papers. Ca. 1823-65. 3 vols.
Open. No guide.
Maryland Historical Society.
Diary in which Cannon describes her activities as a schoolgirl in Natchez, MS, during the Civil War; an 1820s letter book of a W. Shipp, which she used as a sketchbook; and an autograph album, 1845-47, with inscriptions and poems to an unidentified Mary by her girl friends in Baltimore.

5,750. Carroll, Anna Ella
Papers. 1854-90. Ca. 550 items.
Open. Index.
Maryland Historical Society.
[Miss] Carroll (1815-94) was an author and a military strategist who was influential in keeping Maryland in the Union. Professional papers concerning her claim that she planned the Tennessee campaign for the Union, a report to the assistant secretary of war about a trip to the West, recollections of Abraham Lincoln, and manuscripts pertaining to John Minor Botts, John C. Calhoun and secession, and Andrew Johnson. Correspondents include Lincoln, Botts, Governor Thomas Hicks, Robert J. Breckinridge, Millard Fillmore, J. F. Polk, Thurlow Weed, and Fernando Wood.

5,751. Coale Family
Papers. 1792-1900. 21 vols.
Open. No guide.
Maryland Historical Society.
Material kept or collected by women members of the Coale and Buchanan families of Baltimore includes scrapbooks of clippings, etchings, engravings, and verse; 19th-century cookbooks; and commonplace books of copied verses.

5,752. Coleman, Anne Caroline
Papers. 1830-33. 233 items.
Open. No guide.
Maryland Historical Society.
Detailed letters that Coleman (1818-96), a student at Miss Mercer's Academy in West River, MD, received during the school year from friends writing about their activities in her hometown of Lebanon, PA, and during the summer from school friends writing of their activities in Maryland. Correspondents included Sarah F. Cocke, Harriet Fenwick, Ann C. Hall, Christiana Lippincott, Agnes Riddell, and Lucretia Van Bibber.

5,753. Cradock and Walker Families
Papers. 1734-1900. Ca. 1000 items.
Open. No guide.
Maryland Historical Society.
Papers of these Maryland families include manuscript articles by author and military strategist [Miss] Anna Ella Carroll (1815-94) on women's suffrage, Thomas A. Scott, the Civil War, Republicanism, and other matters.

5,754. Davis, Allen Bowie (285 and 1511)
Papers. Ca. 1825-1932. Ca. 200 items.
Open. No guide.
Maryland Historical Society.
Davis (1809-89) was a farmer, businessman, and member of the Maryland House of Delegates. Papers primarily relate to his second wife Hester A. (Wilkins) Davis (1809-88), whom he married in 1839, and to their children W. Wilkins Davis, Rebecca Dorsey Davis (ca. 1844-1921), Mary Dorsey Davis (?-1939), and Ester Davis. Detailing the lives of these women on the family estate, Greenwood, near Brookville in Montgomery County, MD, are Hester Davis's letters to her children, diaries for 1850 to 1864, and an 1830s notebook of her poems and letters; Rebecca Davis's letters from her sister and friends, some of which relate to her work with the Episcopal church, and an 1868 diary of her activities at home; Mary Davis's diary for 1888 to 1891 in which she describes nursing her mother at Greenwood; and Ester Davis's commonplace book of poems and personal inscriptions.

5,755. De Roth, Lydia Howard (de Ford)
Papers. 1836-1970. Ca. 800 items.
Open. No guide.
Maryland Historical Society.
Papers of [Mrs. Herbert Charles] de Roth, a sculptor, primarily concern her civil defense work during WWII. Includes her diary of experiences as an air raid warden during the London blitz, a copy of a handbook she wrote for training other wardens, and correspondence pertaining to her work for the Massachusetts Committee on Public Safety from 1941 to 1944 and as a recruiter for the nation's civil defense program. Also includes some material on her education at Bryn Mawr College and at the Maryland Institute of Art and her efforts for the US War Department in 1919, poetry she and other family members wrote, and clippings about her family in Baltimore.

5,756. Dickinson Family
Papers. 1680s-1943. Ca. 500 items.
Open. No guide.
Maryland Historical Society.
Included with legal papers relating to the Samuel Dickinson land holdings in Talbot County, MD, are personal papers of his descendant Laura D. Dickinson (1856-1934), with papers concerning her property, bills and receipts, and correspondence, primarily letters to her while she was at school in Baltimore from her friend Alice Kemp, who describes activities at home in Trappe, MD. Also includes letters in which Laura Dickinson's mother Catherine (Willard) [Mrs. Samuel Philemon] Dickinson describes her family and life in Trappe to her sister in Massachusetts.

5,757. Done
Papers. 1858-87. 2 vols.
Open. No guide.
Maryland Historical Society.
Notebooks of Rachel Anne (Kerr) Done (1814-92), who married John Haynie Done in 1842, and their son Josiah Bayly Done (1845-?). Her notebook contains history lessons she used to teach her children in 1864 and an autobiographical sketch she wrote in 1887. The sketch contains information about her childhood near Easton, MD; schooling in 1829 and 1830 at Miss Mercer's Academy in West River, MD; an operation for breast cancer in 1835; and her married life in Snow Hill and Princess Anne, Somerset County, MD, until her husband's death in 1856. Josiah Done's notebook contains a genealogical sketch of his mother's family.

5,758. Electric Sewing Machine Society
Records. 1891-98. 1 vol.
Open. No guide.
Maryland Historical Society.
Minute book of the directors of the Society, which was established in Baltimore in 1891 to train women in the use of electric sewing machines so they could become self-supporting. Minutes include discussion of the number of women trained, their success in making a living with this skill, their wages, and the nursery that the Society provided.

5,759. Fayhey, Nellie
Papers. 1906. 1 vol.
Open. No guide.
Maryland Historical Society.
Notebook kept by Fayhey while she was a student at the Academy of Mercy, a Catholic school in Merion, PA, contains poems and essays she wrote on such topics as the dignity of woman, life, Italian art, and Henry Wadsworth Longfellow.

5,760. Female Bible Society of Annapolis
Records. 1829-32. 2 vols.
Open. No guide.
Maryland Historical Society.
Constitution, bylaws, minutes, and financial records of the Society, an auxiliary of the American Bible Society, which was organized in ca. 1821 in Annapolis, MD, to distribute Bibles and testaments.

5,761. Female Christian Home
Records. Ca. 1874. 1 item.
Open. No guide.
Maryland Historical Society.
Annual report of the Home, a boardinghouse established in 1865 to provide a supervised home for young women working in Baltimore.

5,762. Female City Mission of Baltimore
Records. Late 19th century. 1 item.
Open. No guide.
Maryland Historical Society.
Report of the Mission, organized in 1865 by evangelical churches in Baltimore to send women missionaries among outcast women, particularly "the fallen." The report lists the Mission's accomplishments and expenses for one year, including the number of visits made, prayer meetings held, Bibles distributed, families fed, children clothed, "houses of ill-fame" broken up, and saloons closed.

5,763. Ferguson, Blanche (Smith)
Papers. 1953-64, nd. 11 items.
Open. No guide.
Maryland Historical Society.
Notebooks of [Mrs. James H., Jr.] Ferguson, an author and poet, contain notes on her works "When You See William," "Strolling Along," and "Golden Wedding." Also includes a few letters and a notebook of James H. Ferguson, Jr., a dentist whom she married in 1917.

5,764. Fitzgerald, Alice Louise Florence
Papers. 1916-56. Ca. 100 items.
Open. No guide.
Maryland Historical Society.
Papers of Fitzgerald (1874-1962), a registered nurse and educator, pertain to her nursing career, particularly during WWI, after the war when she was director of Red Cross Nurses of America, and later when she surveyed nursing and public health practices in the Philippines and the Far East. Collection contains a diary she kept during WWI, an unpublished 500-page autobiography, a few letters, manuscript and printed copies of her articles on nursing training and public health nursing, and photos.

5,765. Forman, Thomas Marsh (403 and 1277)
Papers. 1732-1937. 14 vols. and 165 items.
Open. No guide.
Maryland Historical Society.
Papers of Forman (1758-1845), a Revolutionary War officer and Cecil County, MD, planter, primarily consist of papers of his second wife Martha Brown [Mrs. James Rorke] Callender Forman (?-1864). Includes letters from her husband and her sister and diaries for the period 1814-54 in which she details her daily activities as the mistress of the large Cecil County plantation known as Rose Hill. Also includes correspondence, legal papers, and exercise and account books of other family members.

5,766. Free Summer Excursion Society
Records. 1873-1960. Ca. 4 ft.
Open. No guide.
Maryland Historical Society.
The Society was incorporated in 1875 to provide

day excursions with food and medical care for poor children and overworked mothers of Baltimore; in 1960 the group was dissolved. Annual reports, minutes of meetings of the directors, financial records, and scrapbooks. Although the selection of women and children for the trips was made by volunteer women, the collection contains their names only and not the records of their work. The directors of the organization were male.

5,767. Fulton, Jean Boyd
Papers. 1876-80. 4 vols.
Open. No guide.
Maryland Historical Society.
Diaries in which Fulton (1860-?), a teacher and resident of Salisbury in Wicomico County, MD, recorded her daily and social activities, most of which centered around her father's Protestant church. Also includes mention of her schoolteaching in the area.

5,768. Gilman, Elisabeth
Papers. 1941. 1 vol.
Open. No guide.
Maryland Historical Society.
Gilman (1867-1950) was a Baltimore reformer, socialist, and author. Scrapbook contains letters and telegrams of congratulations, programs, and photos relating to a testimonial dinner held in her honor.

5,769. Gittings, Victoria
Papers. Ca. 1944. Ca. 20 items.
Open. No guide.
Maryland Historical Society.
A manuscript book and stories about supernatural apparitions by Gittings (1879-1965), an author, and letters to her concerning psychic phenomena.

5,770. Gordon and Blackford (398, 398.1, 399, 399.1, 404, and 1584)
Papers. 1828-1951. Ca. 6000 items.
Open. No guide.
Maryland Historical Society.
Personal and business papers of John Montgomery Gordon (1810-84), a lawyer and banker, and of his son-in-law Eugene Blackford (1840-1908), a Confederate officer. Bulk of the collection is correspondence of John Gordon with his wife Emily (Chapman) Gordon (?-ca. 1852) while she was living in Baltimore and papers of their daughters [Miss] Susan Fitzhugh Gordon (1838-58) and Rebecca (Gordon) [Mrs. Eugene] Blackford (1841-?). The daughters' papers include diary-letter books from their childhood and correspondence with friends and relatives, containing information about their lives in Baltimore from the 1850s to the 1880s. Also contains correspondence of L. M. Blackford, principal of the Episcopal High School of Virginia.

5,771. Graves Family
Papers. 1793-1899. 21 vols. and 100 items.
Open. No guide.
Maryland Historical Society.
Collection primarily consists of papers from the period before the marriage in 1831 of Ann Jane (Baker) Graves, a poet and Baltimore resident, to John James Graves (1800-90), a physician. Letters to girl friends; her essays on religion, missionaries, intemperance, and other topics; notebooks of poems, many of which she wrote between 1819 and 1860 on friendship and on women; commonplace books of copied poetry; a diary from 1824 to 1840 in which she recorded her thoughts and impressions, particularly concerning religion; and Bible study notes. Also includes items relating to the medical career of her husband and correspondence with her sons William B. and Henry M. Graves, who were Confederate officers, and her daughters Lilly and Annie M. Graves.

5,772. Guest, Rebecca (Hall)
Papers. 1800-1917. 1 vol.
Open. No guide.
Maryland Historical Society.
Daily entries in which [Mrs. John] Guest (ca. 1775-?), a Quaker and resident of Philadelphia and London, recorded her domestic activities while she was living in England between 1800 and 1810. Also includes genealogical notes added in 1912 and 1917.

5,773. Hammond, Maria Johns
Papers. 1880-1930. 4 vols.
Open. No guide.
Maryland Historical Society.
Notebook with copies of letters to Hammond (1862-1949), a Baltimore poet, from authors, editors, politicians, and artists discussing her poems and other matters.

5,774. Harper, Robert Goodloe, Family (430, 431, 1304, and 1305)
Papers. 1701-1912. Ca. 2000 items.
Open. Published guide.
Maryland Historical Society.
Personal and business papers of Harper (1765-1825), a lawyer and US senator from South Carolina and from Maryland. Includes letters that his sisters Frances, Letitia, Mary, and Cathy Harper wrote to him while they were living at home in Granville, NC, during the period 1784-90s; letters from Catharine (Carroll) Harper (1775-1861), whom he married in 1801, for the period 1803-40s; letters from their daughters Mary Diana Harper (1804-18), who wrote concerning her education by Mother Elizabeth Ann Seton in Emmitsburg, MD, and in France and Emily Louisa Harper (1812-92), who wrote about her education in Emmitsburg during the 1820s and her life in Baltimore and Newport, RI, during the 1840s; and letters that Mother Seton, who founded the Sisters of Charity, wrote about the education of the Harper children. Most of the collection is available on microfilm. See Bayly Ellen Marks, *Guide to the Microfilm Edition of the Robert Goodloe Harper Family Papers* (Baltimore: Maryland Historical Society, 1970).

5,775. Harris, Mrs. Benjamin G.
Papers. 1850-91. 20 vols.
Open. No guide.
Maryland Historical Society.
In almost daily entries throughout 41 years, Martha Elizabeth (Harris) Harris records her life in Baltimore as the wife of US representative Benjamin Harris.

5,776. Hinkley, Edward Otis
Papers. 1790-1894. Ca. 4 ft.
Open. Container list.
Maryland Historical Society.
Business papers of Hinkley (1824-96), a Baltimore lawyer, contain personal correspondence of various family members. Includes letters Anne (Keemlé) Hinkley, whom he married in 1861, wrote to her husband and cousins while she was away from Baltimore; correspondence in which her mother Anna Maria (Mather) Keemlé, who married Samuel Keemlé in 1815, describes life in Philadelphia; and letters she received from Philadelphia while she was elsewhere.

5,777. Hollingsworth
Papers. 1802-37. Ca. 124 items.
Open. No guide.
Maryland Historical Society.
Letters from Ann Maria Hollingsworth and Lydia Hollingsworth, both Baltimore residents, to their relatives about their activities.

5,778. Holy Cross Alumnae Association of St. Catherine's Normal Institute
Records. 1900-72. 3 vols.
Open. No guide.
Maryland Historical Society.
Organized in 1900, the Association was related to St. Catherine's Institute, a Catholic girls school in Baltimore operated by the Sisters of the Holy Cross. Association minutes, 1921-23, and scrapbooks of clippings, programs, and memorabilia kept by Association members contain information on the Association, the Institute, the Sisters of the Holy Cross, and the Maryland chapter of the American Federation of Catholic Alumnae.

5,779. Hunter, Elizabeth A.
Papers. 1911-59. 7 vols.
Open. No guide.
Maryland Historical Society.
Diaries of Hunter, a resident of Roland Park, Baltimore, who married army officer Thomas Meredith Hunter in 1922, contain details on her daily life, except during the 1930s and the early 1950s. Also includes journals of trips she made to Europe in 1911 and 1913. Before marrying Hunter, she was married to a Mr. Cole.

5,780. Isaacs, Bertha Patience
Papers. 1821-1943. Ca. 500 items.
Open. No guide.
Maryland Historical Society.
Isaacs (1865-?) was a legal secretary, genealogist, and resident of Elkridge in Howard County, MD. Her papers largely relate to her family in England. Includes letters from her English cousins, diaries of trips she took to England and Europe during the 1920s and in 1931, and genealogical material on the Bowmer, Bull, Shirley, and Sutton families.

5,781. Jackson, Leonora
Papers. 1852-1931. Ca. 4 ft.
Open. No guide.
Maryland Historical Society.
Correspondence, concert programs, photos, and other papers of Jackson (1879-1969), a concert violinist, include diary-scrapbooks detailing her concert career from the 1890s to 1906 in the US and Europe; these volumes contain public notices and her lengthy private comments. Also includes an album kept by her mother from 1852 to 1859 and articles by William Duncan McKim, whom she married in 1915.

5,782. Johnson, Mary Ann
Papers. Ca. 1830. 1 vol.
Open. No guide.
Maryland Historical Society.
Notebook of Johnson contains manuscript music, some of which was contemporary.

5,783. Kahn, Florence (Ring)
Papers. 1930-53. 2 vols. and 50 items.
Open. No guide.
Maryland Historical Society.
Papers of [Mrs. Howard] Kahn (1883-1964), a poet and playwright, concern her poems, plays, and work with the National League of American Pen Women. Correspondence, scrapbooks, clippings, and printed matter. Includes her play *The Cry of Laughter* (1947) and a pageant she wrote about the B & O Railroad Transportation Museum.

5,784. Keech, Lillian Sue (Anspach) (1100)
Papers. 1921-28. 1 vol.
Open. No guide.
Maryland Historical Society.
Scrapbook with printed and manuscript poems by [Mrs. Edward P.] Keech (?-1942), a poet.

5,785. King, Jane R.
Papers. 1840-41. 1 vol.
Open. No guide.
Maryland Historical Society.
Receipt book for tuitions and supplies paid to King for a school in Baltimore, of which she was mistress.

5,786. Kingsworth, Eliza
Papers. 1824-28. 13 vols.
Open. No guide.
Maryland Historical Society.
School exercise books kept by Kingsworth while she was a schoolgirl (perhaps in England), most of which deal with English history and grammar, one with geography. She later was governess to the Ridgely family of Baltimore.

5,787. League of Nations Non-Partisan Association
Records. Ca. 1928-51. Ca. 4 ft.
Open. No guide.
Maryland Historical Society.
Records of the Maryland branch of the Association, which was organized to promote peace, consist of material arising from the work of Jessie Snow as executive secretary of the branch from 1928 to 1945. Includes minutes of executive committee meetings, correspondence, reports, clippings, printed matter, and items concerning Snow's lectures on peace. Also includes material Snow collected concerning her work with the Association's allied organization, the Committee to Defend America by Aiding the Allies, and efforts to organize the UN.

5,788. Litchfield, Grace Denio
Papers. 1872-79. 3 vols.
Open. No guide.
Maryland Historical Society.
Papers of Litchfield (1849-1944), an author and poet, consist of a pictorial letter compiled by her friends to celebrate the publication of her first book; a scrapbook containing a romantic tale about her future, "The Adventures of Grace Litchenfels"; and an alphabetic catalog of her experiences, "An ABC Book."

5,789. Lloyd Family
Papers. 1660-1890. Ca. 30,000 items.
Open. Published guide.
Maryland Historical Society.
Personal and business papers spanning seven generations of this Maryland family, the bulk of which pertain to Edward Lloyd IV (1744-96), a patriot and politician; Edward Lloyd V (1779-1834), governor of Maryland; and Edward Lloyd VI (1798-1861), a farmer. Includes 19th-century correspondence of Ann "Nannie" Lloyd Buchanan, Mary Ellen Lloyd Goldsborough, Elizabeth Lloyd Harwood, Mary Tayloe Lloyd Key, Elizabeth C. McBlair Lloyd, Sally Scott Lloyd Lowndes, Anne Murray Mason, Sarah Elizabeth Murray, Rebecca Lloyd Nicholson, Elizabeth Tayloe Lloyd Winder, and other family women. Entire collection is available on microfilm. See Gary Arnold, *A Guide to the Microfilm Edition of the Lloyd Papers* (Baltimore: Maryland Historical Society, 1973).

5,790. Mason, Louisa G.
Papers. 1864-65. 1 vol.
Open. No guide.
Maryland Historical Society.
Diary in which Mason, a Baltimore resident, describes her social activities in Baltimore, Washington, DC, and Philadelphia.

5,791. Mayer, Brantz
Papers. 1791-1896. Ca. 350 items.
Open. No guide.
Maryland Historical Society.
Correspondence and other papers of several generations of this Baltimore family, one member of which was Brantz Mayer (1809-79), a lawyer and diplomat. Includes letters to Katrina (Baum) Mayer (?-1843) from her husband Christian Mayer while she was in Baltimore, correspondence of Eliza C. (Blackwell) [Mrs. Charles F.] Mayer with her father while she was living in Baltimore, and letters from Eliza Mayer's daughter-in-law Kitty D. (Goldsborough) Mayer (?-1868) to Kitty's future husband Alfred M. Mayer while she was in New York in 1864. Also includes an 1861 diary Kitty Mayer kept of her daily activities while she was living in Frederick, MD.

5,792. Misses Hall's School Alumnae Association (417 and 1958)
Records. 1914-40s. Ca. 500 items.
Open. No guide.
Maryland Historical Society.
Organized in 1912 and dissolved in 1947, the Association was an offshoot of Misses Hall's School, a private girls school in Baltimore that functioned between ca. 1863 and 1900. Minutes, legal and financial records, correspondence, and printed matter relate to the incorporation, operation, and dissolution of the Association. Includes routine lists of alumnae, dues, receipts, replies to invitations to alumnae luncheons, a scrapbook history of the Association, a brief history of the School, and material on the Association's major project, which was the maintenance of a dormitory for women art students.

5,793. Moale (1371 and 1372)
Papers. 1811-1906. Ca. 125 items.
Open. No guide.
Maryland Historical Society.
Correspondence and genealogical notes of William Armistead Moale (1800-80), a merchant, and of Mary (Winchester) Moale (1812-89), a Baltimore resident whom he married in 1841. Collection largely consists of letters she received from her parents George and Ann Winchester while she was a student in Baltimore from 1825 to 1827, letters from her husband W. A. Moale, and letters from Mary Winchester, who may have been her aunt.

5,794. Morris, Thomas John
Papers. 1815-1955. Ca. 4000 items.
Open. No guide.
Maryland Historical Society.
Primarily personal correspondence of Morris (1837-1912), a lawyer and judge in Baltimore; of Sarah P. (Cushing) Morris, whom he married in 1867; and of their daughter Josephine Cushing Morris. Sarah Morris's papers consist of letters written by friends in Baltimore while she was away at school during the 1860s, letters from her daughter Josephine who was traveling in Europe on various trips between 1898 and 1912, and diaries Sarah Morris kept of her activities as a schoolgirl and then as wife of a judge. Josephine Morris's papers primarily consist of letters from friends. Also includes letters in which Thomas Morris's sister Sarah Morris (1842-94) describes her nursing training in New York City and miscellaneous papers concerning both the Morris and Cushing families.

5,795. National League of American Pen Women
Records. 1921-71. 15 vols.
Open. No guide.
Maryland Historical Society.
Organized in 1921, the Baltimore Branch of the League promoted creative and educational activities of women in art, letters, and music. Scrapbooks containing clippings and printed matter detailing the chapter's annual activities; minutes, 1925-30; financial statements, 1970-71; and chapter publications.

5,796. Norbury, Tacy Burges
Papers. 1813-19. 2 vols.
Open. No guide.
Maryland Historical Society.
Daily class behavior record book for Norbury, a student at Mr. Beardsley's Select School for Girls, perhaps in Baltimore, from 1813 to 1815 and her arithmetic exercise book, 1819. [Miss] Norbury married Thomas MacKenzie in 1823.

5,797. Oden
Papers. 1755-1836. Ca. 260 items.
Open. No guide.
Maryland Historical Society.
Business and financial papers of Maryland tobacco merchants Stephen West, Jr. (1727-90) of Prince Georges County and his son-in-law Benjamin Oden (1762-1836) of Patuxent. Includes letters from Oden's daughter Maria West (Oden) [Mrs. James] Mullikin [Mrs. Thomas] Jackson (ca. 1791-?) to her father about her activities in Leesburg and Richmond, VA, between 1821 and 1836. Part of collection is available on microfilm.

5,798. Patapsco Female Institute
Records. 1832-91. Ca. 600 items.
Open. No guide.
Maryland Historical Society.
Records relating to the organization and financial management of the Institute, a private girls school in Ellicott Mills, MD, which was opened in ca. 1833 and closed in ca. 1890. Consists of complete minutes of the meetings of the board of trustees, account books, and correspondence about funding, leasing the school to school principals, and buildings.

5,799. Preston, Margaret (Smith)
Papers. 1862-64. 3 vols.
Open. No guide.
Maryland Historical Society.
Diaries of the daily activities of [Mrs. William P.] Preston (1811-80) at the family estate, Pleasant Plains, near Baynesville and Towson, MD. She mentions the progress of the Civil War and, particularly, skirmishes with the rebels close to her home.

5,800. Preston, William P.
Papers. 1778-1916. Ca. 7000 items.
Open. No guide.
Maryland Historical Society.
Papers of Preston (1811-80), a criminal lawyer in Baltimore, contain proceedings, warrants, wills, and indentures; proceedings of the Moot Court of the Friday Evening Club, 1833-35; and information on slavery. Also includes correspondence, 1830-80, of his wife Margaret (Smith) Preston (1811-80) concerning her early life in Gettysburg, PA, as well as her marriage and her subsequent life at the Preston estate, Pleasant Plains, near Towson, MD. In addition, the collection contains correspondence of their daughter May (Preston) [Mrs. Joshua Vansant] McNeal (1849-1913), primarily that with her mother while she was a student at St. Joseph's, a Catholic boarding school, during the 1860s; a young wife in Baltimore; and then a resident of Indianapolis from 1881 to 1887.

5,801. Quigg, Jane (Townsend)
Papers. 1857-76. Ca. 35 items.
Open. No guide.
Maryland Historical Society.
Letters in which [Mrs. John B.] Quigg, a resident of New Market and Chestertown, MD, and South Easton, PA, describes her life as the wife of a Methodist circuit rider and her bitter feelings about marriage and motherhood.

5,802. Randall, Giddings, and Clunas
Papers. 1850-58. 23 items.
Open. No guide.
Maryland Historical Society.
Primarily letters to Catherine (Randall) [Mrs. Luther?] Giddings (ca. 1829-?) from her sister Elizabeth (Randall) [Mrs. J. A.?] Clunas (ca. 1830-?), a resident of New Orleans and New Brighton, LA, who writes about life in New Orleans during the 1850s and about her views on marriage. Includes an exchange of letters in which the sisters discuss the mastectomy, slow recuperation, and subsequent death of their aunt Catherine (Wirt) [Mrs. Alexander] Randall (ca. 1807-53).

5,803. Redwood
Papers. 1694-1940. Ca. 3500 items.
Open. No guide.
Maryland Historical Society.
Family correspondence of Anne (Hopkinson) Coale (1745-1817), a Baltimore resident who married Samuel Stringer Coale in 1775, and of Mary B. (Coale) Redwood (1861-1940), a Baltimore resident who married Francis T. Redwood in 1887. Anne Coale's correspondence includes that with her daughters Eliza (Coale) [Mrs. John Greene] Proud (1786-1838) and Mary Abigail Willing (Coale) [Mrs. William T.] Proud (?-1831); with her son-in-law John Greene Proud (1776-1865), who was a farmer and insurance man; with her granddaughter Anna Maria Proud; and with other family members. Mary Redwood's papers include letters regarding WWI and notebooks pertaining to her son's service in the war. Also includes papers of Hopkinson family of Philadelphia, 1755-1800, with correspondence, business papers, speeches, and other material of both male and female family members.

5,804. Reizenstein, Jennie
Papers. 1908-41. 13 vols.
Open. No guide.
Maryland Historical Society.
Journals Reizenstein kept on trips to Europe throughout the period and on one to California in 1940.

5,805. Ridgely, Helen West (Stewart) (715, 716, and 954)
Papers. 1789-1921. Ca. 5000 items.
Open. No guide.
Maryland Historical Society.
Ridgely (1854-1929), who married John Ridgely (1851-1938), was an author and socialite who lived in Towson, MD. The collection consists primarily of letters from her husband and eight children, but it also includes letters in which her mother L. Josephine (Moulton) [Mrs. John] Stewart (1834-?) and grandmother Leonice M. (Sampson) [Mrs. Joseph W.] Moulton give her advice on the ways of marriage, childrearing, and education in a socially prominent family. Also contains letters in which Baltimore author Sarah E. Bennett discusses her works and those of Helen Ridgely; letters from Annie (Leakin) [Mrs. Albert] Sioussat, an historian of women; and letters concerning Ridgely's work for the Jamestown Exposition in 1907 and the Colonial Dames, particularly the book she compiled for the Colonial Dames about graveyards in Maryland. Other papers include her diaries for 1886 to 1909, reminiscences of her childhood in Baltimore, and scrapbooks of clippings. In addition, the collection contains a diary kept in 1834 and 1835 by Eliza Kingsworth, who was governess for the Ridgelys; an 1842 diary in which Eliza "Didy" Ridgely recorded her activities as a schoolgirl in Baltimore; and an anonymous story, probably written in the 1840s, about two women visiting the springs in Virginia.

5,806. Rost, Ida Sophie
Papers. 1928-57. Ca. 60 items.
Open. No guide.
Maryland Historical Society.
Papers of Rost (1880-1966), a nurse, primarily relate to her career as a poet in Baltimore. Correspondence concerning publication of her poems, copies of poems, grades from high school classes she took at night, and her scrapbook about her doctor J. M. T. Finney.

5,807. Rowland and Harrison
Papers. 1761-1950. Ca. 500 items.
Open. No guide.
Maryland Historical Society.
Primarily consists of calling cards, invitations, and correspondence of Henrietta (Harrison) [Mrs. Henry A.] Rowland (1865-1950), a Baltimore resident, including letters from her mother while she was a student at St. Timothy's School for girls in Catonsville, MD, from 1882 to 1885 and letters in which her nephew and a friend, Mrs. Mab. McLachlan, describe life in London during WWII. Also includes some papers concerning Henrietta Rowland's father George L. Harrison, her brother George L. Harrison, Jr., and her son Henry A. Rowland, Jr. (1893-1921).

5,808. Scarborough
Papers. Ca. 1930-60. Ca. 1000 items.
Open. No guide.
Maryland Historical Society.
Research notes and drafts of articles on Maryland and Virginia history by Katherine Scarborough (1900-60), an historian, are included with clippings of many of her articles printed in the Baltimore *Sun* newspaper.

5,809. Social Service Club of Maryland
Records. 1906-11. 2 vols.
Open. No guide.
Maryland Historical Society.
Minutes and membership lists of the Club, which was founded in 1906 to promote unified philanthropic work in Baltimore. The group used guest speakers and lobbied for legislation in the areas of clean milk, protective legislation, charity organization societies, and settlements. Women active in the group included Aimee Guggenheimer, Ellen N. LaMotte, Lucy F. Friday, Mary Sherwood, and Lilian Welsh.

5,810. Stafford, Mary J.
Papers. 1841-44. 2 vols.
Open. No guide.
Maryland Historical Society.
A penmanship exercise book and a commonplace book with essays and poems copied or written by Stafford, a schoolgirl.

5,811. Stump and Forwood
Papers. 1821-46. 11 vols.
Open. No guide.
Maryland Historical Society.
School exercise books and an account book of Rachel (Stump) [Mrs. S.] Forwood (1806-30); her son William Stump Forwood (1830-92), who was a physician; and her sister Kezia (Stump) [Mrs. Richard I.] Jackson. The exercise books for 1821 to 1828, which appear to have been completed in Philadelphia, contain arithmetic and penmanship exercises as well as poetry and a long poem which Rachel Forwood's husband wrote on her death. Also includes some of her letters and an account book of her expenses in 1822.

5,812. Taylor, Nannie
Papers. 1861-67. 30 items.
Open. No guide.
Maryland Historical Society.
Correspondence of Taylor, a nurse at the Camp Winder Hospital in Richmond, VA, during the Civil War, includes letters about her work, letters from her uncle and brother describing their experiences as Confederate soldiers, and detailed letters between Taylor and the mother of a patient who died at the Hospital. One of these letters contains excerpts from a journal Nannie Taylor kept while she worked at the Hospital. Also includes an 1865 military order whereby all ladies of Richmond were commanded to sit by their east windows so they could be admired; noncompliance would result in court-martial. Taylor married David Griffith in 1867.

5,813. Thomas, Elizabeth (Todhunter)
Papers. 1836-37. 2 vols.
Open. No guide.
Maryland Historical Society.
Journals in which Thomas, a Baltimore resident who married Evan Philip Thomas in 1835, provides a detailed account of people and customs she observed during a trip to England, France, and Italy.

5,814. Towson, Sophia (Bingham)
Papers. 1822-43. 36 items.
Open. No guide.
Maryland Historical Society.
A resident of Washington, DC, Towson married army officer Nathan Towson in 1816. Letters, primarily to her sister-in-law in Baltimore, concern the health of family members and social activities in Washington.

5,815. Turnbull
Papers. 1840-1947. Ca. 3 ft.
Open. No guide.
Maryland Historical Society.
Collection primarily consists of papers relating to the literary activities of Francese Hubbard (Litchfield) Turnbull (1844-1927), a novelist, poet, and cofounder of the Woman's Literary Club of Baltimore. Includes correspondence and printed material concerning a poetry lecture series she and her husband Lawrence Turnbull sponsored at Johns Hopkins University, with letters from such poets and literary figures as Sidney Lanier, Robert Browning, William Dean Howells, Henry Wadsworth Longfellow, Oliver Wendell Holmes, Gabriela Mistral, and Louise (Chandler) Moulton; manuscripts of novels *Catholic Man* (1890) and *Val Maria* (1893) by Francese Turnbull; and school compositions she wrote at B. H. Academy. Also includes letters about and poems by her sister Grace Denio Litchfield, a poet, and papers of Francese's daughter Eleanor Turnbull (1875-1964), a poet and translator.

5,816. Turnbull, Grace Hill
Papers. 1891-1973. Ca. 300 items.
Open. No guide.
Maryland Historical Society.
Papers concerning the artistic career of Turnbull (1880-1976), a sculptor, consist of correspondence from other artists, a list of her sculptures, and a scrapbook of reviews of her work. Also includes a typescript of her novel *The Uncovered Well.*

5,817. Tyler, Adeline (Blanchard)
Papers. 1861-64. 20 items.
Open. No guide.
Maryland Historical Society.
[Mrs. John] Tyler (1805-75) was an Episcopal deaconess and a nurse during the Civil War. Correspondence concerning her job superintending nurses in military hospitals in Chester, PA, and Annapolis, MD, and manuscript accounts by friends of her work.

5,818. United Daughters of the Confederacy
Records. Ca. 1860-1940. 18 vols.
Open. No guide.
Maryland Historical Society.
Scrapbooks of the Maryland division of the UDC, which was founded to commemorate relatives who were connected with the Confederate States of America. Includes correspondence, poems, and essays dating from the Civil War, but the bulk of the collection is clippings collected after 1900 about the War and the UDC.

5,819. Waller, Mary Virginia E.
Papers. 1864. 1 vol.
Open. No guide.
Maryland Historical Society.
In her diary Waller, a resident of Green Hill and Quantico, Wicomico County, MD, describes her work teaching in Green Hill. Attendance records for her students are also included.

5,820. Warden, David Bailie
Papers. 1797-1851. Ca. 5 ft.
Open. Published guide.
Maryland Historical Society.
Correspondence and scientific and literary notes of

Warden (1772-1845), a diplomat and scientific writer. Includes letters to him from Eliza Parke Custis, who was well known in political circles; Elisabeth (Patterson) Bonaparte, who wrote about her travels; and novelist Helena Maria William. Also includes an 1808 autobiography by Custis. Entire collection is available on microfilm. See Bayly Ellen Marks, *Guide to the Microfilm Edition of the David Bailie Warden Papers* (Baltimore: Maryland Historical Society, 1970).

5,821. Warfield, Susanna
Papers. 1845-85. 5 vols.
Open. No guide.
Maryland Historical Society.
Scattered daily diaries in which Warfield (1797-1890), a resident of Sykesville, MD, discusses her activities at her home, Groveland, and with the Episcopal church in Sykesville. She also comments on the Mexican War, the Civil War, slavery, natural history, Indians, the railroad, politics, and Roman Catholics.

5,822. White, John Campbell
Papers. 1764-1928. Ca. 300 items.
Open. No guide.
Maryland Historical Society.
Papers relating to the business and property interests of White, a lawyer and clerk of the Baltimore branch of the Second Bank of the US; of his son Henry White; of Henry's daughter-in-law Eliza (Ridgely) White; and of an Ann White. Includes Eliza White's journal of a trip she took to England, France, Germany, and Italy from 1845 to 1846 before her marriage in 1849 to John Campbell White; account books for her property holdings in Maryland and the administration of her estate, 1853-65; notebooks of poems copied or written by Ann White of Baltimore, 1803-09; and an anonymous 300-page epic poem entitled "Louise."

5,823. Wilson (833 and 833.1)
Papers. 1790-1955. Ca. 1000 items.
Open. No guide.
Maryland Historical Society.
Papers of Franklin Wilson (1822-96), a Baptist minister in Baltimore; Virginia (Appleton) Wilson (1824-1902), whom he married in 1848; their daughter [Miss] Adelaide S. Wilson; their son John Appleton Wilson (1851-1927), an architect in Baltimore; and his daughter [Miss] Virginia Appleton Wilson (1881-1957), a philanthropist. Franklin Wilson's papers pertain to his ministry, editorship of *True Union,* Columbian College, and the Maryland Industrial School for Girls. His wife's papers consist of diaries in which she recorded her activities as a minister's wife from 1849 to 1851 and a notebook containing her recipes. Adelaide Wilson's papers consist of a diary for 1880 to 1896 in which she provides a detailed description of her life caring for her elderly parents and her church-related activities, a journal of a trip to Rome in 1906, and copybooks of poems, one of which she compiled for her young niece. Virginia Wilson's papers consist of an 1892 diary in which she records her activities as a schoolgirl and an 1899 notebook of school notes and poetry.

5,824. Wirt, William (1011 and 1014)
Papers. 1784-1864. Ca. 8000 items.
Open. Published guide.
Maryland Historical Society.
Primarily correspondence of Wirt (1772-1834), a lawyer, US attorney general, author, and historian of Bladensburg, MD, with his second wife Elizabeth (Gamble) Wirt (1784-1857), an author whom he married in 1802, and with their daughters Laura (Wirt) [Mrs. Thomas] Randall (1803-33), Elizabeth (Wirt) [Mrs. Louis M.] Goldsborough (ca. 1807-?), Catherine (Wirt) [Mrs. Alexander] Randall (ca. 1807-53), Ellen (Wirt) [Mrs. Edmund Brooke] Vass [Mrs. Charles] McCormick (ca. 1812-?), and [Miss] Agnes C. Wirt (1815-31). Also includes correspondence of Elizabeth (Gamble) Wirt and of Catharine Randall with her sisters. This extensive family correspondence details family relations, childrearing, and education in an antebellum family in Virginia and Florida; in addition, the correspondence provides insight into Elizabeth Washington (Gamble) Wirt's work as an author of popular books, among them a giftbook *Flora's Dictionary.* Entire collection is available on microfilm. See John B. Boles, *A Guide to the Microfilm Edition of the William Wirt Papers* (Baltimore: Maryland Historical Society, 1971).

5,825. Woman's Eastern Shore Society of Maryland
Records. 1926-56. 5 vols.
Open. No guide.
Maryland Historical Society.
Founded in 1926 by women natives of the area who were interested in its history, the Society organized social activities and raised funds for student loans to Eastern Shore girls. Scrapbooks containing programs, clippings, and articles on the history of the Eastern Shore, particularly Kent and Dorchester counties.

5,826. Wyman
Papers. Ca. 1867-1907. Ca. 100 items.
Open. No guide.
Maryland Historical Society.
Family and business papers of William Wyman (1825-1903), a Baltimore businessman, and of his daughter Helen de St. Prie (Wyman) [Mrs. Daniel] Rollins (1857-1949). Her papers consist of diaries of her activities as a schoolgirl in Baltimore from 1867 to 1870, an account book in which she recorded the amounts she donated to various charities, and a minute book, 1879-86, of the Altar Society of St. John's Church, Waverly (in Baltimore), of which she was secretary.

5,827. Maryland Diocesan Archives
Records. 1676- . 53,856 items and 2 microfilm reels.
Open. Partial published guide and card catalog.
Maryland Historical Society, Maryland Diocesan Archives.
Official records and other items associated with the Episcopal church in Maryland and the District of Columbia from its organization in 1780, with some manuscripts concerning the colonial Church of England and extensive records regarding the Episcopal church throughout the US and abroad. The bulk of the collection dates from the 19th century.

Contains minutes, reports, and correspondence concerning such organizations as the Church Home and Infirmary in Baltimore, the Ladies' Church Home Society, the Baltimore Female Union Society for the Promotion of Sunday Schools, the Baltimore Female Tract Society, the Girls' Friendly Society, the Ladies' Prayer Book and Tract Society, the Protestant Episcopal Female Beneficial Society, the Corporation for the Relief of Widows and Children of Deceased Clergymen, the US Sanitary Commission, and girls schools in the 19th century. The records are illustrative of the role of women in the Episcopal church, particularly in education; in social services; in charitable and missionary enterprises; in sisterhoods, especially the Clewer Sisterhood, the Sisters of All Saints, the Sisters of Charity, the Sisters of the Good Shepherd, and the Sisterhood of St. John; in fund raising for church buildings; and in work as deaconesses.

Records pertaining to girls schools include substantial holdings on the Hannah More Academy in Reistertown, MD, 1832-1974, and the Patapsco Female Institute in Ellicott City, MD, 1840-80.

Contains correspondence of Episcopal bishops, clergymen, and their families as well as of such laypersons as Sarah Josepha Hale, editor of *Godey's Lady's Book,* and Almira Hart Lincoln Phelps, a pioneer educator and author. Includes 149 letters of Mary Ann (Rollinson) [Mrs. Richard] Whittingham, a religious writer and linguist who was the mother of William Rollinson Whittingham, the fourth bishop of Maryland.

The Maryland Diocesan Archives are on deposit at the Maryland Historical Society but remain the property of the Diocese of Maryland and are under the care of the Diocesan historiographer.

See *Inventory of the Church Archives of Maryland, Protestant Episcopal: Diocese of Maryland* (Baltimore: Works Project Administration, Maryland Historical Records Survey Project, 1940).

5,828. McKeldin, Theodore R., and Jackson, Lillie May
Oral history. 1976-77. 98 tapes and 40 transcripts.
Open. Unpublished guide.
Maryland Historical Society, Oral History Office.
McKeldin was governor of Maryland twice and mayor of Baltimore twice during the period from 1935 to 1970. Jackson (1889-1975), who received an honorary PhD from Morgan State University in Baltimore, was president of the Baltimore chapter of the NAACP and president of the Maryland conference of the NAACP from 1942 to 1962. Jackson played a leading role in efforts to open stores, schools, jobs, neighborhoods, recreational facilities, and voting rolls to blacks by means of fund raising, lawsuits, and door-to-door organizing.

The oral history project consisted of interviews with persons associated with McKeldin or Jackson, among them Jackson's daughters Virginia (Jackson) Kiah and Juanita (Jackson) Mitchell. Kiah and Mitchell speak about their mother's early years, family, marriage, and the growth of her religious beliefs. They also discuss other black organizations, nonviolence, Jackson's opposition to violence as a tactic, CORE, freedom rides, the riots in Baltimore, and her relationship with Mitchell and with McKeldin. Kiah, who was an artist and membership secretary for the Baltimore branch of the NAACP during the 1930s, discusses her mother's becoming qualified to work as a minister, her disapproval of Kiah's marriage, the role of the "upper crust" in the civil rights movement, and Kiah's own acquaintance with Mary McLeod Bethune and Eleanor Roosevelt. In seven hours of interviews, Mitchell, who also has been active in civil rights efforts, gives an account of her feelings about her mother, her mother's religion, her values as an "old-fashioned Methodist," her mother as a businesswoman, her mother's legal education, her own work with the NAACP, civil rights victories, and her close and continuing relationship with her mother in civil rights activities. Mitchell's husband Clarence Mitchell has been director of the Washington, DC, bureau of the NAACP since 1950.

The collection also contains interviews with Lane Berk, who was a member of the State Human Relations Commission, CORE, the NAACP, and the Urban League and a consultant for the US Civil Rights Commission; she speaks about her personal involvement in the civil rights movement, the relationship of the civil rights movement and the women's movement, and the relationship of various factions within the civil rights movement. Mrs. John B. Ramsay, a civic leader who served on the State Human Relations Commission from 1951 to 1973 and was president of the Baltimore LWV from 1947 to 1951, discusses desegregation of the Ford and Lyric theatres, discrimination in restaurants, and the Urban League. Verda D. Welcome, a Maryland state senator, talks about the general direction of civil rights in Maryland under Jackson, various black factions, the relationship between blacks and Jews in Baltimore, and the contrast between Governor McKeldin and Governor Spiro Agnew. Susie Murphy, a civil rights worker for the NAACP, provides anecdotes and recollections of Jackson, the office operations of the NAACP, and the involvement of black churches in the civil rights movement.

5,829. Maryland Oral History
Oral history. 1971- . Ca. 400 tapes.
Open. Unpublished guide.
Maryland Historical Society, Oral History Office.
Interviews with 65 Maryland women, including Anna Catherine Drozd Yarmalow, a member of the Fells Point Polish community, who discusses working in a cannery, the depression, and prohibition; Lubov Keefer, a music and Russian language instructor at Johns Hopkins University and author, who discusses her early life in Russia, teaching at Catonsville High School and the Peabody Institute, her philosophy of teaching, and Baltimore as a music center; Pauline Prevas, the daughter of Greek immigrants, who talks about her educational experiences through college, living in an ethnic community, Greek customs and music, and resistance to assimilation; and Sirkka Tuomi Lee, a daughter of immigrant Finns, who discusses her activities in politics, socialism, the depression, the House Un-American Activities Committee, cooperatives, and the Finnish community in Baltimore.

Also includes interviews in which Reba Silver, who came to Baltimore with her family in 1905, speaks of her childhood in a Jewish community, her work as secretary for the Baltimore City Water Department from 1940 to 1965, the depression, WWII, and Hadassah; Cheryl Pearce discusses Mormonism in the Baltimore-Washington, DC, area; Mildred A. Stelfax talks about her work as a public health nurse at Sparrows Point during the 1930s; Josephine [Mrs. Eric] Jacobsen discusses her duties as Library of Congress consultant in poetry from 1971 to 1973, the reasons people write poetry, and women as poets; Frances Morton [Mrs. Hans, Jr.] Froelicher, founder and executive director of the Citizens Planning and Housing Association from 1945 to 1969, speaks of the Baltimore Housing Authority, planning, and the use of volunteers; Adelyn Dohme Breeskin, director of the Baltimore Museum of Art from 1947 to 1962, speaks about the Museum's print collection, Mary Cassatt, museum development, and other art museums and galleries; Mildred Otenasek, an instructor at Trinity College in Washington, DC, from 1940 to 1954 and at the College of Notre Dame of Maryland in Baltimore since 1956 and member of the Democratic National Committee from 1956 to 1973, mentions Eleanor Roosevelt, President John F. Kennedy and his family, women in politics, and the vote for 18-year-olds; and Phoebe Stanton, a professor of art at Johns Hopkins University and member of state and local committees concerned with community development and historic preservation, discusses the history and future of Baltimore, the rationale for city planning, and public art in the 20th century.

5,830. Archives
Records. 1890- . 420 boxes and 42 vols.
Open. Unpublished guide.
Mission Helpers of the Sacred Heart.
Financial records, chapter records, correspondence, journals, photos, scrapbooks, and other records of the order, which was founded in Baltimore in 1890 and is involved in religious education. Includes papers of several mothers general and records from missions throughout the US, Puerto Rico, and South America where sisters have been or are working.

5,831. Oblate Archives
Records. 1829- . 30 boxes.
Open. No guide.
Oblate Sisters of Providence, Our Lady of Mount Providence Convent.
Financial records, correspondence, papers of mothers superior, retreat notes, photos, scrapbooks, and other records of the Convent, which was founded in 1829 in Baltimore. Includes material about St. Frances Academy, which was established and operated by members of the order.

5,832. Archives
Records. 1847- . 18 drawers, 95 boxes, and 6 tapes.
Open. Unpublished guide.
School Sisters of Notre Dame Provincial House.
Members of the congregation, which was established in the US in 1847, are involved in teaching, nursing, religious education, pastoral ministry, and social and missionary work with the underprivileged. Constitutions, minutes of general and provincial chapter meetings, financial records, legal papers such as wills and deeds, correspondence concerning the founding of convents and the establishment of schools to serve German immigrants, chronicles, registers of sisters who entered the convent and of those who left, a necrology, circulars, biographical sketches, photo albums, slides, directories, issues of the Province magazine *The Notre Dame Sister,* blueprints, material relating to Province education and to the early founders and foundresses, magazines, and books, including biographies of Mother Caroline Friess, who established many of the Province's first schools and set up a system of education.

5,833. Richmond, Sarah Elizabeth
Papers. 1858-1922. 4 Hollinger boxes and other items.
Open. Unpublished guide.
Towson State University Archives.
Official correspondence, a diary, photos, clippings, and memorabilia of [Miss] Richmond (1843-1921), a member of the first Maryland State Normal School class, who became a faculty member in 1866, vice-principal in 1872, principal in 1909, and dean of the School from 1917 until her death. As a result of her work with the School, she exerted a great influence on public education in Maryland. She also was a member of the Maryland Woman's Suffrage Association.

5,834. Tall, Lida Lee
Papers. 1920-42. 3 Hollinger boxes and other items.
Open. Unpublished guide.
Towson State University Archives.
Tall (1873-1943) was an author, associate editor of the *Atlantic Educational Journal,* and an academic administrator at Towson State College. Correspondence, photos, clippings, memorabilia, and published works. Tall, who received an honorary doctorate from the University of Maryland in 1926, was principal of State Normal School at Towson from 1920 until 1935 when the institution became State Teachers College. She served as president of the College until 1938.

5,835. Towson State University
Records. 1886- . Ca. 612 Hollinger boxes, vols., and 225 tapes.
Partially restricted. Unpublished guide.
Towson State University Archives.
Minutes of the faculty, departments, and committees; financial records; correspondence; records of students and faculty organizations; student academic records, notebooks, and class histories; scrapbooks; and photos of the University, founded in 1866 as the Maryland State Normal School. In 1935 the school changed its name to State Teachers College at Towson; in 1963 the name was changed to Towson State College, and the institution became a general purpose educational institution. In 1976 the school became Towson State University. Women students and faculty predominated at the coeducational college, which until 1963 trained teachers for Maryland public schools. Collection contains information on curricula provided to students over the years as well as some official and private papers and memorabilia of Sarah E. Richmond, who headed the school from 1909 to 1917; of Lida Lee Tall, who headed it from 1920 to 1938; and of M. Theresa Wiedefeld, who headed the college from 1938 to 1947.

5,836. Wiedefeld, Mary Theresa
Papers. 1899-1971. 8 Hollinger boxes.
Open. Unpublished guide.
Towson State University Archives.
Wiedefeld (1886-) was a teacher and public school administrator before she became president of State Teachers College at Towson in 1938. Correspondence, speeches, unpublished manuscripts, publications, photos, and clippings, including manuscripts for social studies teachers that reflect Wiedefeld's view of social roles. Wiedefeld, who earned a doctorate in education from Johns Hopkins University in 1937, was known professionally as M. Theresa Wiedefeld.

5,837. Citizens' Planning and Housing Association of Baltimore
Records. 1937-71. 80 ft.
Open. Unpublished guide.
University of Baltimore, Baltimore Region Institutional Studies Center.
Minutes; correspondence; reports; general, research, and reference files; speeches; and a doctoral dissertation on the history of the Association, which was founded during the 1940s because of Frances Morton's efforts to promote cooperation among Baltimore residents in city planning, improved land use, and other measures to achieve a more livable community. The Association used research, education, public discussion, legislation, law enforcement, and other methods to attain their goals. With extensive use of volunteers from and ties to such groups as the LWV, the Women's Civic League, and the Negro and Professional Women's Clubs, the Association's women members helped to create a housing court and worked for code enforcement, slum clearance, urban renewal, and zoning.

5,838. Independent Order of Odd-Fellows, Rebekah Assembly
Records. 1819-1971. Ca. 15 cu.ft.
Open. Unpublished guide.
University of Baltimore, Baltimore Region Institutional Studies Center.
The Rebekah Assembly is the women's auxiliary of the Odd-Fellows, a fraternal, secret organization that provides benevolent services and social activities for members. Bylaws, minute books, financial records, correspondence, proceedings, membership rosters, ceremonial papers and memorabilia, slides, photos, and publications. The Rebekahs raise funds and plan such activities as the annual pilgrimage to the Odd-Fellows' Home in Frederick, MD.

5,839. League of Women Voters of Baltimore
Records. 1927-72. 19 ft.
Open. Unpublished guide.
University of Baltimore, Baltimore Region Institutional Studies Center.
Minutes, financial records, correspondence, reports and recommendations, research studies, membership lists, biographies, and publications of the LWV document the work of women volunteers who provided impartial studies on such topics as the examination of government functions, the city budget, charter revision, reapportionment, health and welfare, housing, poverty, water resources, transportation, and disarmament.

5,840. Maryland Conference of Social Concern
Records. 1909-76. 25 ft.
Open. Unpublished guide.
University of Baltimore, Baltimore Region Institutional Studies Center.
The mission of the Conference, an organization of social workers and informed laymen, is to study and discuss social work in Maryland and to coordinate statewide efforts for improved

legislation; the group's previous names were Maryland Conference of Social Welfare, the Maryland Conference of Social Work, the Social Service Club of Maryland, and the Maryland Conference of Charities and Corrections. Minutes, financial records, correspondence, memoranda, reports, directories, press releases, case histories, publications, reference material, and oral history tapes of several past presidents. The Conference's interests included social work as a profession and such matters of social concern as adoption, child welfare and abuse, equal opportunity, foster care, family income and expenditure, recreation, rehabilitation, malnutrition, mental health, food programs, and aid for families with dependent children.

5,841. Maryland Council of Churches
Records. 1904-70. 340 cu.ft.
Open. Unpublished guide.
University of Baltimore, Baltimore Region Institutional Studies Center.
The Council was founded in 1937 as a cooperative effort among Protestant and orthodox denominations in Maryland to address matters of religious concern and social problems; it was formed by the merger of the Baltimore Federation of Churches, the Baltimore Council of Religious Education, and the Maryland-Delaware Council of Religious Education. Minutes, financial records, correspondence, administrative files, research reports, photos, published material, and the reference library of the Council, which was disbanded in 1970. The Council's origins can be traced to the Baltimore Sunday School Union in 1842. The Council not only established the first child-care center for migrant workers in Hurlock, MD, but also concerned itself with improving the status of women throughout the world. It was involved in ecumenicism, Christian social relations and education, urban and rural ministry, migrant ministry, and church planning. [Mrs.] Mildred Atkinson was director of the division of social relations. The United Church Women, which was a branch of the Council, coordinated the services and activities of all denominational women's groups.

5,842. Planned Parenthood of Maryland
Records. 1929-72. 29 ft.
Open. Unpublished guide.
University of Baltimore, Baltimore Region Institutional Studies Center.
Planned Parenthood provided clinical counseling and educational activities to regulate childbirth; it also provided sterility treatment and marriage counseling. Minutes of the board of directors, the medical advisory committee, and the clergy advisory committee; financial records; correspondence; family planning policy papers; socioeconomic statistics on clients; clinic statistics; status reports; effectiveness evaluations; scrapbooks; reference material; and records concerning fund raising. The collection documents substantial change in public attitudes toward birth control, abortion, sex education, illegitimacy, and the role of women in society. Physician Bessie Moses, Ann Huppmann, and Annette Lieberman were active in the Planned Parenthood movement.

BETHESDA

5,843. Flower, Mrs. J.
Papers. 1887?. 12-page item.
Open. Catalog card.
National Library of Medicine.
Consists of a history of the Illinois Training School for Nurses in Chicago in the form of a letter to the editor by Flower.

5,844. Gatewood, James Duncan
Papers. 1893. 2 vols.
Open. Catalog card.
National Library of Medicine.
Notes of Gatewood (1857-1924) on a training school for nurses are included with notes on medical schools and naval hospitals and a sketch of the history of hospitals.

5,845. National League for Nursing
Records. 1894-1952. 6 ms. boxes.
Open. Catalog card.
National Library of Medicine.
Minutes of meetings, proceedings of annual conventions, correspondence, photos, and other records of the League. Also includes biographical data on early League leaders.

COLLEGE PARK

5,846. Maryland League of Women Voters
Records. 1911-63. 45 ms. boxes.
Open. Unpublished guide.
University of Maryland Library, Archives and Manuscripts.
Minutes, financial statements, budgets, correspondence, reports, speeches, pamphlets, newsletters, and other records of the Maryland LWV, which was known as the Suffrage League of Maryland until 1921. The group's interests ranged from social legislation and public welfare in its early years to voter education in its later years. Includes information on suffrage, almshouses, child labor, child welfare, maternity, and infant hygiene. Mrs. Charles Elliott was the state LWV's first president, and, in 1921, Lavinia Engle was its research director.

EMMITSBURG

5,847. Archives
Records. 1786- . 78 ft.
Open. Partial card catalog.
Daughters of Charity of St. Vincent de Paul, St. Joseph's Provincial House.
This religious order of women, whose members work in schools, hospitals, and social centers, was founded at Emmitsburg in 1809 by Mother Elizabeth Ann Seton. Correspondence, journals, histories of religious foundations made by the Daughters of Charity, photos, and scrapbooks. Includes correspondence and other papers of Mother Seton, correspondence of the American hierarchy with the order, and reports of sisters serving in field ambulances during the Civil War and the Spanish-American War.

ILCHESTER

5,848. Archives
Records. 1804-1977. 22 drawers, 28 boxes, and ca. 100 tapes.
Access restricted. Unpublished guide.
Sisters of Notre Dame de Namur, Maryland Provincial House.
Minutes, financial records, correspondence, diaries, photos, tapes, scrapbooks, and other records of the order, which was founded to teach the poor. The Sisters came to the US in 1840.

REISTERSTOWN

5,849. Caples, Louise Skinner Leigh
Papers. 1938-39. Ca. 3 folders.
Open. No guide.
Reisterstown Public Library.
Correspondence and scrapbooks of [Mrs. D. Delmas] Caples (1915-), a registered nurse and community leader born in Hertford, NC, contain information on nursing, medicine, the church, schools, clubs, and patriotic and historical topics.

5,850. Goodwin, Louise Bland
Papers. 1930-77. Ca. 3 folders.
Open. No guide.
Reisterstown Public Library.
A retired Baltimore County teacher and librarian of the Baltimore County Historical Society, [Mrs.] Goodwin has published historical articles, taught seminars on the history of Reisterstown at a community college, and was responsible for the establishment of the Public Library's Reisterstown Room, which is a depository for historical material. Correspondence, typed accounts, booklets, photos, scrapbooks, and clippings provide a history of the town. Past president of a local business and professional women's group, Goodwin has also held office in the local chapter of the DAR and the Colonial Dames XVII Century.

RIDGELY

5,851. Archives
Records. 1852- . No size given.
Access restricted. No guide.
Benedictine Sisters, St. Gertrude Priory.
History, photos, and clippings of the Priory, which was founded in 1857. Members of the Priory are engaged in teaching.

TOWSON

5,852. Goucher College Archives
Records. 1885- . Ca. 130 ft.
Open. Card catalog.
Goucher College Library.
Founded in 1885 by the Baltimore Conference of the Methodist Church and opened in 1888 as the Woman's College of Baltimore, this liberal arts college for women was renamed Goucher College in 1910; it later severed its affiliation with the Methodist Church. Miscellaneous administrative committee minutes, correspondence, and student records for 1888 to 1900; financial records; representative course syllabi starting in 1934; complete College catalogs; pamphlets; promotional literature; a yearly scrapbook of clippings about the College; photos; and tape recordings. Also includes minutes of the faculty club, 1943-51; correspondence with prospective faculty members, 1890-95; copies or reprints of scholarly works by faculty; and faculty handbooks. In addition, the collection contains complete runs of the student newspaper, various literary magazines, the student yearbook, and the alumnae magazine; minutes of the executive board of the student government organization, 1901-60; student handbooks and songbooks; and a few scrapbooks kept by various students.

5,853. Mencken, Sara Powell Haardt
Papers. 1918-36. 16 vols.
Open. Card catalog.
Goucher College Library.
[Mrs. H. L.] Mencken (1898-1935) was a writer. Correspondence, telegrams, memorandum books, diaries, notes, manuscripts, short stories, movie scenarios, address books, clippings, and books. Includes correspondence of H. L. Mencken about publishing her stories as *Southern Album* (Garden City, NY: Doubleday, Doran & Co. Inc., 1936) with a preface by him and copies of *Southern Album* and of *The Making of a Lady* (Garden City: Doubleday, Doran & Co. Inc., 1931) by Sara Haardt.

WESTMINSTER

5,854. Shellman, Mary Bostwick
Papers. 1849-1938. 17 folders.
Open. Unpublished guide.
Historical Society of Carroll County.
Correspondence, an autobiography, a biography, transcripts, and clippings of Shellman (1849-1938), author of accounts of early Westminster history, poetry, and songs, including William McKinley's campaign rally song. She also was a newspaper correspondent, chairman of the Carroll County League of Republican Women, a member of the Civic League and the American National Red Cross, and an advocate of woman suffrage. Shellman worked to improve conditions at the local almshouse.

5,855. College Archives
Records. 1867- . 350 ft. and 8 microfilm reels.
Access restricted. Unpublished guide.
Western Maryland College Archives.
Annual reports, minutes of faculty and College committees, budget records, correspondence, diaries, studies, reports, College and faculty publications, clippings, and memorabilia of Western Maryland College, a coeducational liberal arts college founded in 1867 under the sponsorship of the Methodist church. The first coeducational college below the Mason-Dixon line, the College has always had more female than male students. The collection reflects the interests and activities of College women, their social life, academic studies, curriculum, and two women's literary debating societies. The College is no longer affiliated with the Methodist church.

MASSACHUSETTS

ACTON

5,856. Adams and Bixby Family
Papers. 1808-20s. 8 items.
Closed. No guide.
Iron Work Farm in Acton, Inc.
Family memorabilia include a biographical sketch that Moses Adams (1749-1819), a Congregational minister in Acton, wrote about his daughter Abigail "Nabby" (Adams) [Mrs. Luke] Bixby (1780-1808) for the benefit and instruction of her daughter Martha Abigail Adams (Bixby) [Mrs. Winthrop Emerson] Faulkner (1806-97).

5,857. Campbell, Sir Francis, and Campbell, Lady
Papers. Ca. 1885-1933. Ca. 380 items.
Closed. No guide.
Iron Work Farm in Acton, Inc.
Correspondence, manuscripts, photos, and clippings pertain to the work of Sir Francis Campbell and Sophia Elizabeth (Faulkner) Campbell (1849-1933) at the Royal Normal College for the Blind in London, England, which Sir Francis Campbell founded. Recognized as an outstanding teacher of the blind, Lady Campbell was associated with the Normal College from 1875 to 1914 and with the Perkins School in Boston and the Columbus School for the Blind in Ohio.

5,858. Faulkner Family
Papers. 1796-1909. 15 vols. and 433 items.
Closed. No guide.
Iron Work Farm in Acton, Inc.
Papers of this prominent Acton family include letters to Rebecca (Keyes) [Mrs. Francis] Faulkner (1736-1812) from her daughters, who describe their domestic activities, family news, and related topics; similar letters to her daughter Elizabeth "Betsey" Faulkner (1765-1813); correspondence concerning family matters addressed to Mary (Wright) [Mrs. Winthrop] Faulkner (1777-1855); two letters from Asa Dodge Smith, a student at and later president of Dartmouth College, concerning Mary Faulkner's search for teachers for the academy at Acton; cooking recipes used by several generations of the Faulkner family, ca. 1820-1900; household accounts kept by Martha A. A. (Bixby) Faulkner, 1880s; and correspondence and genealogical and historical research material of Charlotte "Lottie" Cornelia (Faulkner) [Mrs. George F.] Flagg (1838-1909), an Acton schoolteacher.

5,859. First Universalist Church
Records. 1858-1969. 11 vols. and 90 items.
Closed. No guide.
Iron Work Farm in Acton, Inc.
Collection contains minutes, 1871-1926; notes; membership lists; and descriptions of projects undertaken for the benefit of this South Acton, MA, church and the community by the Church's Social Circle, which was open to all members of the Church but which consisted primarily of women.

AMHERST

5,860. Bogan, Louise
Papers. 1930-70. 21 Hollinger boxes.
Open. Unpublished guide.
Amherst College Library.
Bogan (1897-1970) was a poet, translator, educator, and poetry critic. Personal and business correspondence; diaries; manuscript poetry, short stories, translations, criticism, articles, introductions, and lectures; journals; notebooks; photos; and clippings. Contains Bogan's reflections on her career as a poet in the male-dominated literary society of the 1920s and 1930s and on her struggles in her personal life.

5,861. Brownell, William Crary
Papers. 1871-1928. 5.5 ft.
Open. Unpublished guide.
Amherst College Library.
Correspondence and clippings of Brownell (1851-1928), editor of the *New York World, The Nation,* and the *Philadelphia Press,* are included in the notebooks he kept for his editorial work. Includes letters from Edith Wharton, Viola Roseboro, Martha Gilbert Dickinson Bianchi, Helen Reese Aldrich, Linnie Blaskfield, Olive (Tilford) Dargan, Annie Flint, Pauline Forney, Lucia (Fairchild) Fuller, Antoinette R. Peterson, and Emily James Putnam.

5,862. Dickinson, Emily
Papers. 1844-86. 27 ft. and 2 microfilm reels.
Open. Published guide and card index.
Amherst College Library.
Papers of [Miss] Dickinson (1830-86), a poet, include her correspondence and poems, correspondence between Mabel (Loomis) Todd and those involved in publication of the first editions of Dickinson's *Poems and Letters,* and printer's copies of *Bolts of Melody* (1945) and other collections of Dickinson's poetry. See Thomas H. Johnson, *Poems and Letters of Emily Dickinson.*

5,863. Dwight, Harrison Griswold
Papers. 1902-59. 9.5 ft.
Open. Unpublished guide.
Amherst College Library.
Correspondence, diaries, manuscript articles, notebooks, and photos of Dwight (1875-1959), an author and critic. Includes correspondence with Willa Cather, Alice B. Toklas, Edith Wharton, Eleanor Roosevelt, Maud Clapp, Georgia O'Keeffe, Martha Saxton, Grace Guest, Elisa Willard, and Mary Willard.

5,864. Emerson, Benjamin Kendall
Papers. 1844-1933. 6 ft.
Open. Unpublished guide.
Amherst College Library.
Emerson (1843-1932) was a geologist of the Massachusetts and New England areas. Late 19th-century surveys of these areas, diaries, account books, deeds, notebooks, maps, pamphlets, and other papers, including correspondence of Emerson's wife, mother, and daughter.

5,865. Garman, Charles Edward
Papers. 1849-1907. 26.5 ft.
Open. Unpublished guide.
Amherst College Library.
Papers of Garman (1850-1907), a professor of mathematics, philosophy, and metaphysics at Amherst College. Includes diaries and notebooks kept by Eliza Garman and correspondence of Charles Garman's mother, sister, wife, sister-in-law, and other women.

5,866. Hitchcock, Edward
Papers. 1815-1934. 8.75 ft.
Open. Unpublished guide.
Amherst College Library.
Papers of Hitchcock (1793-1864), a geologist and president of Amherst College from 1845 to 1854. Includes diaries of Orra White Hitchcock, a painter; music books of Mary Hitchcock; articles by Jane Elizabeth Hitchcock; and correspondence of Edward Hitchcock's wife, mother, daughter, and other women.

5,867. James, William
Papers. 1825-64. 2 ft.
Open. Unpublished guide.
Amherst College Library.
Correspondence, sermons, and photogravures of James (1797-1868), a Presbyterian minister. Includes letters from James to Marcia Ames James and Catherine Barber James Prince and from Prince to Elizabeth Tillman (James) Seelye concerning causes and contemporary cures for mental illness. Prince was institutionalized several times in the Northampton-Springfield area.

5,868. Seelye, Julius Hawley
Papers. 1825-1915. 6.5 ft.
Open. Unpublished guide.
Amherst College Library.
Papers of Seelye (1824-95), a professor from 1858 to 1875, a US congressman from 1875 to 1877, president of Amherst College from 1877 to 1890, a lecturer, and a minister. Includes correspondence of 19 female members of the Seelye family, who wrote from India, Washington, and other locations, about family matters, politics, small town affairs, travels to Japan, Amherst College business, health, and social obligations.

5,869. Williams, Talcott
Papers. 1875-1928. 54 ft.
Open. Unpublished guide.
Amherst College Library.
Correspondence, manuscript articles, pamphlets, and clippings of Williams (1849-1928), a journalist who worked for the *New York World,* the *New York Sun,* the *Springfield Republican,* and the *Philadelphia Press;* Williams also was director of the school of journalism at Columbia University. Collection contains extensive correspondence with [Mrs.] Sophia Williams, much of which is literary in nature and which provides commentary on the period.

5,870. Du Bois, W. E. B.
Papers. 1885-1964. Ca. 140 ft.
Closed. No guide.
University of Massachusetts Library.
Primarily correspondence of Du Bois (1868-1963), an author, sociologist, historian, and a founder of the NAACP and editor of its journal *The Crisis* from 1910 to 1934; late in life he also was involved

in the peace movement. Correspondents include Jane Addams, Dorothy Canfield Fisher, Amy Garvey, Shirley (Graham) Du Bois, Georgia Douglas Johnson, Maud Cuney Hare, Alice Hamilton, Margaret Sanger, Mary White Ovington, Eleanor Roosevelt, Amy Spingarn, Mary McLeod Bethune, and E. Sylvia Pankhurst. Collection also contains organizational minutes, financial records, and photos.

5,871. Massachusetts Cooperative Extension Service
Records. 1918-63. 105 ft.
Open. No guide.
University of Massachusetts Library.
Annual reports, yearly plans, correspondence, narratives, pictures, and clippings of the Extension Service, founded in 1908 to provide out-of-school education for adults and children on the subjects of improved farming practices and the domestic conditions of farm families; programs with and for women constituted approximately one-third of the Service's efforts. Women involved in Service programs included Harriet J. Haynes, state home economist, 1914-49; Mildred C. Thomas, a Worcester County home economist; May E. Foley, nutrition state specialist; Esther Cooley Page, clothing state specialist; and Ruth McIntire, recreation state specialist.

5,872. Massachusetts, University of: Advisory Council of Women
Records. 1921-64. 1 box.
Open. No guide.
University of Massachusetts Library.
Minutes, correspondence, plans for legislative action, studies of needs for women's courses and scholarships, biographical material, membership lists, photos, clippings, and one film.

5,873. Massachusetts, University of: Faculty Senate Committee on the Status of Women
Records. 1970- . 1 box.
Open. No guide.
University of Massachusetts Library.
This standing committee of the Faculty Senate was founded in 1970 to discuss and recommend action on all matters affecting women at the University. Minutes, membership lists, and reports of subcommittee investigations concerning benefits, search committees, affirmative action, administration, part-time students, the women's studies program, day care, and motions brought to the floor of the Faculty Senate.

5,874. Obrebsky, Joseph, and Obrebsky, Tamara
Papers. 1928-73. 34.5 ft.
Open. Unpublished guide.
University of Massachusetts Library.
Field notes, draft essays, autobiographies of peasants, photos, and tapes, most of which are in English, pertain to the ethnography and anthropology of Macedonia, 1931-32; Polesie, eastern Poland, 1934-36; and Jamaica, 1947-48. Also includes material on the sociology and anthropology of developing nations in the post-WWII period.

5,875. Samizdat
Collection. 1955- . 4 ft.
Open. Unpublished guide.
University of Massachusetts Library.
Unpublished poetry, prose, and social and literary criticism by dissident authors inside the USSR and by Soviet émigrés to other countries. The poetry is primarily of a personal nature, and the collection as a whole provides insight into the lives and characters of Russian women, some of whom emigrated to the US.

ANDOVER

5,876. Abbott, Charlotte Helen
Papers. Ca. 1910s. 55 vols.
Open. Unpublished guide.
Memorial Hall Library.
Notebooks of genealogical data, which Abbott (1844-1921) gathered about prominent Andover families from the colonial period to the early 20th century.

5,877. Abbot Academy
Records. 1829-1973. 33 ft.
Open. Unpublished guide.
Phillips Academy Library.
Records of this secondary girls school include minutes of the trustees, deeds and legal documents, financial records, correspondence of several school departments, general files from the dean's office, folders on faculty and other Academy employees, principal's reports, information on students' term charges, library reports, notes on the history of Abbot, student government records, albums of clippings and programs, publicity brochures, catalogs, bulletins, yearbooks, and school songs.

ATHOL

5,878. Athol Associated Charities
Records. 1920-47. 1 vol.
Open. Index.
Athol Historical Society, Inc.
Record book of accounts and other material on the activities of this local charitable society, which functioned between 1904 and 1947 with Alice V. Goodnow as its treasurer.

5,879. Athol High School Class of 1900
Records. 1896-1900. 1 vol.
Open. Index.
Athol Historical Society, Inc.
Bylaws and minutes of this Class.

5,880. Fuller, Evelyn
Papers. 1908-46. 10 vols.
Open. Index.
Athol Historical Society, Inc.
Scrapbooks of [Miss] Fuller (1878-ca. 1946) contain clippings of local interest.

5,881. General William T. Sherman Camp, Sons of Union Veterans Auxiliary
Records. 1924-42. 5 vols. and 1 item.
Open. Index.
Athol Historical Society, Inc.
Charter and minutes of the ladies auxiliary of the Camp's Sons of the Union Veterans, which existed from 1916 to 1942.

5,882. George H. Hoyt Post No. 3, Matrons of the Republic
Records. 1878-84. 2 vols.
Open. Index.
Athol Historical Society, Inc.
Bylaws and minutes of the ladies auxiliary to the Grand Army of the Republic, Parker Post No. 123, which was in existence between 1878 and 1953.

5,883. Hale, Florence M.
Papers. 1931. 5 items.
Open. Index.
Athol Historical Society, Inc.
Letters and clippings of [Miss] Hale (1880-?), a teacher who was president of the National Education Association.

5,884. Hazzard, Marion (Lord)
Papers. Nd. 1 vol.
Open. Index.
Athol Historical Society, Inc.
Scrapbook of [Mrs.] Hazzard (1891-), a government employee.

5,885. Holbrook, Lillian
Papers. 1897-ca. 1940. 1 vol.
Open. Index.
Athol Historical Society, Inc.
Scrapbook of Holbrook (1879-ca. 1965) concerns her classmates from the Athol High School class of 1897.

5,886. Lake Park Village Improvement Society
Records. 1908-32. 1 vol.
Open. Index.
Athol Historical Society, Inc.
Minutes of this civic and social organization.

5,887. Lewis, Sarah A.
Papers. 1859-65. 3 vols.
Open. Index.
Athol Historical Society, Inc.
Diaries in which [Miss] Lewis (1847-1937) discusses current events.

5,888. Newton, Marion (Bromley)
Papers. Ca. 1890-1940. 1 vol.
Open. Index.
Athol Historical Society, Inc.
Scrapbook of Newton (1880-ca. 1960), a musician, contains autobiographical items.

5,889. Parent-Teacher Association, Hapgood School
Records. 1928-38. 2 vols.
Open. Index.
Athol Historical Society, Inc.
Minutes and a scrapbook of clippings about school events of this Athol school's PTA.

5,890. School Districts
Records. 1795-1875. 4 vols.
Open. Index.
Athol Historical Society, Inc.
Minutes of the school committees for district no. 7, West Royalston, 1795-1858; district no. 20, New Salem, 1805-37; district no. 11, Athol, 1837-64; and district no. 5, Athol, 1836-68. Also includes minutes, 1857-75, of the town of Athol's school committee, which was founded in 1829.

5,891. Stone, Sarah
Papers. Ca. 1900. 1 vol.
Open. Index.
Athol Historical Society, Inc.
Scrapbook of [Mrs.] Stone contains clippings and samples of hand sewing and fancywork.

5,892. Waterman, L. May
Papers. 1962. 6 pp.
Open. Index.
Athol Historical Society, Inc.
Copy of a radio speech [Mrs. R. Burton] Waterman (1894-), president of the Athol Historical Society, gave about the Society.

AUBURN

5,893. Auburn Woman's Club
Records. 1924-75. 5 vols. and 6-page item.
Open. No guide.
Auburn Public Library.
Yearbooks and a history written by a member of the Club, which was founded in 1924 to bring women together to serve their community.

BARRE

5,894. Barre Churches
Records. 1763-1940s. 10 ft.
Open. No guide.
Barre Historical Society, Inc.
Minutes and other records of the Barre Methodist-Episcopal Church, the First Parish Unitarian Church, which originally was a Congregational church called the Church of God; the First Baptist Society of Barre; the Barre Plains Chapel Association; and the Orthodox-Congregational Society. Includes secretaries' records, ledgers, programs, and other material of various women's groups associated with these churches and societies.

5,895. Barre District Schools
Records. 1827-1900s. 3 ft.
Open. No guide.
Barre Historical Society, Inc.
School records, registers, and lists of teachers, attendance, and terms, 1827-68, and printed reports of the Barre School Committee, 1846-1900, contain information on teachers' names and salaries; minutes of committee meetings of the district schools; receipts; information on subjects taught, purchases, and the selection of committees; and pictures of early teachers, pupils, and schools. Also includes a teachers certificate of Elizabeth Rawson, 1846, and a statement of the workers' salaries at Dr. Brown's Institution for Feeble Minded Youth, which was one of the first schools of its kind in the US.

5,896. J. Slater and Co. Cotton Manufactory
Records. 1826-30. 1 vol.
Open. No guide.
Barre Historical Society, Inc.
Ledger of the company, which manufactured cotton goods, lists male and female workers and the amounts they were paid for piecework. The firm later became Boston and Barre Manufacturing Co.

5,897. Jenkins and Gorham
Papers. 1840s-80s. 2 ft.
Open. No guide.
Barre Historical Society, Inc.
Family correspondence and legal papers of J. Martin Gorham (1830-80), an attorney who practiced in Barre, include correspondence of his mother Elizabeth (Jenkins) Gorham (1810-95), who was the third wife of Jason Gorham (1787-1881) and one of the 11 children of James Wright Jenkins and Elizabeth (Whipple) Jenkins. Most of her correspondence is with female members of the Gorham and Jenkins families.

BEVERLY

5,898. Beverly Female Charitable Society
Records. Ca. 1818-1970s. 1 box.
Open. No guide.
Beverly Historical Society.
A history, a pamphlet concerning the 100th anniversary, bankbooks, treasurers' and secretaries' reports, membership lists, and other records pertaining to meetings of this group, organized in 1810 to benefit the poor and to provide for the improvement of members through the reading of instructive books at meetings.

5,899. Larcom, Lucy
Papers. Ca. 1830-1970s. 1 folder and 1 display case.
Open. No guide.
Beverly Historical Society.
A mill girl, Larcom (1824-93) was also an author, seminary teacher, and magazine editor. Correspondence, poems, issues of the *Lowell Offering* and *The Operatives' Magazine and Lowell Album,* Larcom family genealogical information and other items, articles, clippings, a memorial service program, correspondence of the Historical Society about Larcom, and a portrait of Larcom by Beverly artist Mary Woodbury.

5,900. Trask, Sarah E.
Papers. 1849. 1 vol.
Open. No guide.
Beverly Historical Society.
Diary in which Trask (1828-?), a Beverly resident, describes the weather and her activities, which included working at home stitching shoes. Also contains poems.

BOSTON

5,901. Archives of American Art
Collection. Nd. No size given.
Open. Published guide.
Archives of American Art, New England Area Center.
Many of the collections described in the guide for the Smithsonian Institution, Archives of American Art in Washington, DC, are available on microfilm at the New England Area Center as well as at the New York, Midwest, and West Coast Area Centers. See *Archives of American Art, Smithsonian Institution: A Checklist of the Collection,* 2nd ed. rev. (1977), which identifies the collections that are available on microfilm, and Garnett McCoy, *Archives of American Art: A Directory of Resources* (New York: R. R. Bowker Company, 1972).

5,902. American Academy of Arts and Sciences
Records. 1781-1934. 6 vols.
Open. Unpublished guide.
Boston Athenaeum.
Minutes of council meetings and reports of committees of the Academy, a national honorary society founded in 1780 to sponsor interdisciplinary studies on topics of public interest. Includes references and reports, 1921-43, on the advisability of electing women to the Academy.

5,903. Morison Collection of Autograph Letters: Julia (Ward) Howe
Collection. 1866-1905. 20 items.
Open. No guide.
Boston Athenaeum.
Brief personal letters and social invitations of Howe (1819-1910), a woman's club and suffrage leader, were addressed for the most part to Emily Marshall (Otis) Eliot and members of the Samuel Eliot family and were later collected by Emily and Samuel Eliot's daughter Emmy (Eliot) [Mrs. John Holmes] Morison. Also includes a letter in which Howe comments on the difficulties of organizing an association of women ministers.

5,904. Adams, Abigail (Smith)
Papers. 1770-1813. 38 items.
Open. Item catalog.
Boston Public Library.
Correspondence of Adams (1744-1818) includes letters she wrote to John Thaxter on subjects ranging from the Revolutionary War to her husband John Adams (1735-1826), second President of the US.

5,905. Alcott, Louisa May
Papers. 1860-1909. 27 items.
Open. Item catalog.
Boston Public Library.
Correspondence, receipts, and autographs of Alcott (1832-88), an author, including letters to [Miss] Maggie Lukens and to the Lukens sisters about their magazine *Little Things.*

5,906. Alexander, Francesca
Papers. 1882-1908. Ca. 317 items.
Open. Typed list; some items cataloged.
Boston Public Library.
An American who lived in Italy for most of her life, [Miss] Alexander (1837-1917) was an artist, author, and dispenser of charity. Correspondence includes letters between Alexander and John Ruskin, from Ruskin to Alexander's mother Lucia Gray Swett Alexander (1814-1916), and from Alexander to Lilly Nelson [Mrs. Charles] Fairchild.

5,907. Antislavery Manuscripts
Collection. Ca. 1798-1902. Ca. 15,000 items.
Open. Cataloged.
Boston Public Library.
More than 5000 manuscripts pertain to women involved in the antislavery movement. In addition to various documents concerning many of these women, the collection contains correspondence of Elizabeth Buffum Chace, antislavery and woman suffrage leader; Lydia Maria Frances Child, author and reformer; Sarah Mapps Douglass Douglass, black teacher and abolitionist; Angelina Emily Grimké and Sarah Moore Grimké, abolitionists and woman's rights pioneers; Jane Elizabeth Hitchcock Jones, antislavery and woman's rights lecturer; and Sarah Parker Remond, black antislavery lecturer and physician. Much of the correspondence of Abigail Kelley Foster, abolitionist, was addressed to Maria Weston Chapman and William Lloyd Garrison; of Mary Grew, abolitionist and suffragist, addressed to William Lloyd Garrison and Helen Eliza Benson Garrison; of Sallie Holley, abolitionist and educator of southern freedmen, addressed to Samuel May; of Prudence Crandall Philleo, teacher and abolitionist, addressed to William Lloyd Garrison; and most of the correspondence of Anne Terry Greene Phillips was written with her husband Wendell Phillips. Besides correspondence and other documents, the papers of Maria Weston Chapman, abolitionist, include poems, notes, drafts, memoranda, reports of meetings, and manuscripts relating to her memorial of Harriet Martineau; papers of Lucretia Coffin Mott, Quaker minister, abolitionist, and woman's rights pioneer, include correspondence to Hannah Webb and Richard Davis Webb as well as an article Mott wrote in 1843 for *Liberty Bell,* which was published under the title "Diversities"; papers of Sarah Pugh, teacher, abolitionist, and suffragist, include a manuscript as well as correspondence to Hannah Webb, Richard Davis Webb, Maria Weston Chapman, and Elizabeth Pease Nichol.

Also included in the collection is a small number of items of Elizabeth Margaret Chandler, Betsey Mix Cowles, Ellen Craft, Frances Dana Barker Gage, Abigail Hopper Gibbons, Josephine Sophia White Griffing, Caroline F. Putnam, Emily Howland, Abigail Jemima Hutchinson, Paulina Kellogg Wright Davis, Sojourner Truth, Harriet Tubman, and Frances Wright. In addition, records of such organizations as the Boston Female Anti-Slavery Society are included.

5,908. Bassett, Sara Ware
Papers. Nd. 153 items and 1 box.
Open. Typed list; some items cataloged.
Boston Public Library.
Correspondence, memorabilia, and other papers of Bassett (1872-1968), an author, including manuscripts written by her, notes she took at lectures, and letters and poems from Clara Endicott Sears.

5,909. Batchelder, Mary Wellington
Papers. 1866-88. 21 vols.
Open. Card catalog.
Boston Public Library.
Diaries of a woman living in Lynn, MA.

5,910. Beach, Amy Marcy (Cheney)
Papers. 1899-1921. 5 items.
Open. Card catalog.
Boston Public Library.
Beach (1867-1944) was a composer and pianist. Manuscript of "The Year's at the Spring," a song

written by Beach with accompaniment for piano and words by Robert Browning (published in Boston, 1899); correspondence with R. G. Appel discussing revisions in Beach's *Te Deum;* and letters to Elizabeth Porter Gould.

5,911. Bishop, Anna (Rivière)
Papers. 1856-73. 1 vol.
Open. Cataloged.
Boston Public Library.
Scrapbook of Bishop (1810-84), a singer, contains programs and clippings. Also included are financial accounts of her appearance at the Prince of Wales Theatre in Sydney, Australia, and other material from Bishop's concerts in Australia, Canada, Bermuda, and the US.

5,912. Boston Gleaning Circle
Records. 1805-14. 10 vols.
Open. Cataloged.
Boston Public Library.
The Circle was a women's literary and social club. Includes recitations and financial and other records.

5,913. Brown, Alice
Papers. Ca. 1891-1921. 40 items.
Open. Some items cataloged.
Boston Public Library.
Brief letters from Brown (1856-1948), an author, and a collection of poetic tributes to Brown on the occasion of her 65th birthday from members of the Boston Authors Club, most of whose members were women. Tributes from Club members are filed with the Club's records.

5,914. Cary, Alice
Papers. 1847-69. 21 items.
Open. Item catalog.
Boston Public Library.
Correspondence and manuscript poems by Cary (1820-71), an author, including letters to Rufus Wilmot Griswold on publishing matters as well as one in which she describes her own personality and appearance.

5,915. Cary, Phoebe
Papers. 1847-69. 11 items.
Open. Item catalog.
Boston Public Library.
Correspondence and poems by Cary (1824-71), an author, including letters to Rufus Wilmot Griswold on publishing matters and one in which she describes her own personality and appearance.

5,916. Castilian Club, Boston
Records. 1888-91. 7 vols.
Open. Cataloged.
Boston Public Library.
This women's club was devoted to the study of Spain. Includes papers written and read by members.

5,917. Cheney, Ednah Dow (Littlehale)
Papers. Ca. 1862-1901. 148 items.
Open. Some items cataloged.
Boston Public Library.
Cheney (1824-1904) was a writer, reformer, and philanthropist who lived in Boston. Manuscript of Cheney's remarks at a Saturday morning meeting in Boston and correspondence, including letters from Elizabeth Hyde Botume and from Booker T. Washington's second and third wives, respectively, Olivia A. Davidson Washington and Margaret James Murray Washington.

5,918. Cobb, Eunice Hale Waite
Papers. 1821-80. 5 vols.
Open. Card catalog.
Boston Public Library.
Diaries kept by Cobb, a Bostonian who was wife of Universalist clergyman Sylvanus Cobb (1798-1866), are interleaved with mementos and clippings. Diaries cover 1821 to 1826 and 1864 to 1880.

5,919. Cushman, Charlotte Sanders
Papers. Ca. 1840-73. Ca. 40 items.
Open. Some items cataloged.
Boston Public Library.
Correspondence of Cushman (1816-76), an actress, includes letters to Kate Field.

5,920. Daniels, Mabel Wheeler
Papers. 1917-40. Ca. 5 boxes.
Open. Cataloged.
Boston Public Library.
Daniels (1878-) is a musician and composer. Includes original scores and some correspondence.

5,921. Deland, Margaret Wade Campbell
Papers. 1893-1938. 38 items.
Open. Item catalog.
Boston Public Library.
Correspondence and social invitations of Deland (1857-1945), an author. Many of the letters are to Lilian Whiting.

5,922. Dickinson, Emily
Papers. 1862-93. 140 items.
Open. Item catalog.
Boston Public Library.
Correspondence and 48 manuscript poems by Dickinson (1830-86), a poet. Letters to Thomas Wentworth Higginson are included as well as other letters relating to Dickinson.

5,923. Dix, Dorothea Lynde
Papers. 1836-75. 42 items.
Open. Calendar.
Boston Public Library.
Dix (1802-87) was an humanitarian crusader for the mentally ill and for prison reform. Manuscript poems and hymns by Dix and correspondence, including letters to George Barrell Emerson about personal matters and her work.

5,924. Field, Kate
Papers. 1860-96. 15 vols. and 4 boxes.
Open. Card catalog.
Boston Public Library.
Known as Kate Field, [Miss] Mary Katherine Keemle Field (1838-96) was a journalist, lyceum lecturer, actress, playwright, and literary critic. Manuscripts and typescripts of some of her lectures, plays, and interviews; correspondence, including letters from such well-known persons as English novelist Anthony Trollope; scrapbook of correspondence concerning the removal in 1895 of John Brown Fort from Chicago to Harper's Ferry and scrapbooks about the restoration in 1878 of Memorial Church in Stratford-on-Avon, England; and photos of Field.

5,925. Fields, Annie (Adams)
Papers. Ca. 1860-1909. Ca. 285 items.
Open. Card catalog.
Boston Public Library.
[Mrs. James Thomas] Fields (1834-1915) was an author, literary hostess, and social welfare worker. Correspondence, much of which was from Sophia Amelia (Peabody) Hawthorne and Celia (Laighton) Thaxter; a manuscript of reminiscences of Sophia Hawthorne by Fields, which incorporates portions of Hawthorne's original letters to Annie and James Fields and which was published in *Boston Public Library Quarterly,* July 1957; and photo of Fields.

5,926. Follen, Eliza Lee (Cabot)
Papers. 1830-62. 92 items.
Open. Item catalog.
Boston Public Library.
Correspondence of Follen (1787-1860), an abolitionist and author of children's stories, includes letters to Maria (Weston) Chapman and others active in the antislavery movement. In addition, reference to Follen is made in letters of Mary Ann Estlin and of the sisters Anne Warren Weston, Deborah Weston, and Caroline Weston.

5,927. Friends, Society of Philadelphia Yearly Meeting of Women Friends
Records. 1767-84. 8 items.
Open. Cataloged and item list.
Boston Public Library.
Extracts of minutes sent to the Yearly Meeting of Women Friends in Maryland.

5,928. Gill, Sarah Prince
Papers. 1743-64. 1 vol.
Open. Card catalog.
Boston Public Library.
In her diary Gill (1728-71), a Boston resident, describes her religious state as well as a few actual incidents.

5,929. Gould, Elizabeth Porter
Papers. Ca. 1876-1906. Ca. 252 items.
Open. Card catalog.
Boston Public Library.
Papers of Gould (1848-1906), an author, consist of a commonplace book which includes poems Gould wrote; descriptions and financial records of her travels; copy of a lecture; index of books owned; and correspondence with Mellen Chamberlain and various literary figures.

5,930. Griswold, Rufus Wilmot
Papers. 1834-56. Ca. 1200 items.
Open. Cataloged and item list.
Boston Public Library.
Griswold (1815-57) was editor of *Female Poets of America* (1848). Includes correspondence and manuscripts from many 19th-century literary women.

5,931. Guiney, Louise Imogen
Papers. Ca. 1881-1920. Ca. 46 items.
Open. No guide.
Boston Public Library.
Correspondence and manuscript of Guiney (1861-1920), a poet, essayist, and literary scholar.

5,932. Harrington, Elizabeth Davis Locke
Papers. 1880-84. Ca. 25 items.
Open. Cataloged.
Boston Public Library.
Much of the correspondence of Harrington was written with her husband Henry Francis Harrington (1814-87) while they were living in New Bedford, MA, and was addressed to their grandchildren Elsie Tetlow and Helen Tetlow.

5,933. Hawthorne, Sophia Amelia (Peabody)
Papers. 1861-71. 220 items.
Open. Item catalog.
Boston Public Library.
Hawthorne (1809-71) was an artist, writer, and wife of Nathaniel Hawthorne (1804-64). Most of the correspondence was written to Annie Adams Fields about personal and family news or to Annie's husband James Thomas Fields about publishing and business matters.

5,934. Howe, Julia Ward
Papers. 1860-1908. 51 items.
Open. Some items cataloged.
Boston Public Library.
A woman's club and suffrage leader, Howe (1819-1910) founded the Boston Authors Club. Poems and one book review by Howe; correspondence, including letters to Kate Field, Elizabeth Porter Gould, and Lilian Whiting; tributes to Howe; photos; and material in the records of the Club.

5,935. Jewett, Sarah Orne
Papers. 1859-1909. 60 items.
Open. Item catalog.
Boston Public Library.
Correspondence, manuscript poems, and writing practice book of Jewett (1849-1909), an author, including letters with Mellen Chamberlain, Lilly

Nelson [Mrs. Charles] Fairchild, and Louise Imogen Guiney.

5,936. Lang, Frances Morse (Burrage)
Papers. 1876-1920. 24 vols.
Open. No guide.
Boston Public Library.
Lang (1839-1934) was a singer and wife of composer Benjamin Johnson Lang. Includes material on meetings with contemporary composers and musicians.

5,937. Lang, Margaret Ruthven
Papers. 1887-1967. 1 box and 3 vols.
Open. No guide.
Boston Public Library.
Lang (1867-1972) was a musician and composer. Includes scrapbooks and scores.

5,938. Larcom, Lucy
Papers. 1858-89. 75 items.
Open. Typed list.
Boston Public Library.
Larcom (1824-93) was a mill girl, author, seminary teacher, and magazine editor. Correspondence, the bulk of which is addressed to Ada Elise Locke.

5,939. Livermore, Mary Ashton (Rice)
Papers. 1863-1903. 45 items.
Open. Item catalog.
Boston Public Library.
Livermore (1820-1905) was a Civil War worker, lecturer, and temperance and suffrage leader. Correspondence consists primarily of letters to Lilian Whiting containing information about Livermore's interest in spiritualism; also included are letters to William Lloyd Garrison as well as a 16-page letter from Harriet (Beecher) Stowe to Livermore discussing Elizabeth (Cady) Stanton's attitude toward French author George Sand.

5,940. Lothrop, Harriett Mulford (Stone)
Papers. Ca. 1875-1959. Ca. 140 items.
Open. Typed list.
Boston Public Library.
Correspondence, poem, legal documents and other papers of Lothrop (1844-1924), an author who was better known as Margaret Sidney. Included are notes for an illustrated collection of her stories; papers relating to mortgages on various properties; and letters to Lothrop, her husband Daniel Lothrop (1831-92), her daughter Margaret Mulford Lothrop (1884-), or the publishing firm D. Lothrop & Company from authors and personal friends. Also included are letters from Daniel Lothrop to Harriet expressing his love for her.

5,941. Lukens Family
Papers. 1870s-1930s. Ca. 80 items.
Open. Typed list.
Boston Public Library.
Correspondence, poems, magazines, and photos of a family of women who between ca. 1871 and 1874 in Brinton, PA, published a magazine entitled variously *Little Things* and *Young Folks Journal.* Collection contains subscription requests, letters from authors, photos of the Lukens sisters and their father, and issues of their publication. Also included are poems, notes, and letters by Carrie E. (Lukens) Smith, Maggie W. (Lukens) Pratt, and Margaret (Lukens) Smith Adamson; and material relating to Louisa May Alcott, with letters from Alcott to the Lukens sisters and letters from Belle Moses to Carrie Smith about Alcott's relationship with the sisters.

5,942. Mifflin, Mary Crowninshield
Papers. 1841-93. 52 vols.
Open. Card catalog.
Boston Public Library.
A Boston resident, [Mrs. Charles] Mifflin was mother of George Harrison Mifflin (1845-1921), who was president of Houghton, Mifflin Co. publishing firm. Her diaries were written in interleaved issues of *The (Old) Farmers' Almanac* by Robert B. Thomas.

5,943. Morrissey, Elizabeth M.
Papers. 1876. 385-page vol.
Open. Card catalog.
Boston Public Library.
Diary Morrissey kept as a student at Girls' High School in Boston.

5,944. Moulton, Ellen Louise (Chandler)
Papers. Ca. 1852-1905. Ca. 60 items.
Open. Item catalog.
Boston Public Library.
Correspondence and manuscript poems of Moulton (1835-1908), author and literary hostess, includes personal letters to Thomas Wentworth Higginson and business letters about selling her books to Phillips, Sampson and Company.

5,945. National Federation of Afro-American Women
Records. 1895. 1 folder and 1 item.
Open. Card catalog.
Boston Public Library.
Organized in Boston in ca. 1895, the Federation was a women's reform club. Report, written by Richard Theodore Greener, of what appears to have been the organizational meeting of the Federation; a folder of notes on the proceedings of that meeting, probably kept by [Mrs.] Florida R. Ridley of Brookline, MA; and clippings and a printed announcement for the 1st Federation convention, held in Washington, DC.

5,946. National Society of United States Daughters of 1812
Records. 1901. 1 vol.
Open. Cataloged.
Boston Public Library.
Letters and clippings of this Massachusetts organization relate to the Old Ironsides Fair held in Boston to raise funds for the rehabilitation of the US frigate *Constitution.*

5,947. Oliver, Susan Lawrence Mason
Papers. 1878. 1 vol.
Open. Card catalog.
Boston Public Library.
Diary of a resident of Boston who was married to Fitch Edward Oliver (1819-92), a physician.

5,948. Osgood, Frances Sargent (Locke)
Papers. Ca. 1842-1970. Ca. 40 items.
Open. Some items cataloged.
Boston Public Library.
Correspondence and manuscript poems of Osgood (1811-50), an author, include a letter from Elizabeth Fries (Lummis) Ellet retracting her charges about Osgood's relationship with Edgar Allan Poe. Also included is material on Osgood, which was collected by Helen Ingersoll Tetlow.

5,949. Ossoli, Sarah Margaret (Fuller), Marchesa d'
Papers. Ca. 1836-1904. Ca. 250 items.
Open. Some items cataloged.
Boston Public Library.
Ossoli (1810-50), usually referred to as Margaret Fuller, was an author, critic, teacher, feminist, transcendentalist, and revolutionary. Poems and other brief manuscripts by Fuller; letters from Fuller to friends, particularly William Henry Channing and Ralph Waldo Emerson, discussing the *Dial,* teaching plans, personal experiences, family, and travel, especially in Italy; letters and notes from Fuller to James Nathan Gotendorf expressing affection for him and relating personal news; extracts concerning Fuller from the diaries of Amos Bronson Alcott; and correspondence pertaining to the biography of Fuller written in 1884 by Thomas Wentworth Higginson.

5,950. Peabody, Elizabeth Palmer
Papers. 1839-94. 32 items.
Open. Card catalog.
Boston Public Library.
Peabody (1804-94) was a transcendentalist, teacher, author, and educational reformer. Correspondence, with letters to Charles Folsom, John Sullivan Dwight, and James Thomas Fields; and reminiscences of Peabody, written by Sarah Freeman Clarke and others.

5,951. Phillips, Mary Elizabeth
Papers. Ca. 1880-1945. Ca. 1000 items.
Open. Typed list.
Boston Public Library.
Phillips (1857-1945) was an author who wrote biographies of Edgar Allan Poe and James Fenimore Cooper. Correspondence includes letters from members of Cooper's family concerning her biography of him; letters pertaining to her biography of Poe; and letters from publishing firms, research libraries, and Adelaide E. Dewey in Paris, Roger Gregory Lewis, Victor Hugo Paltsits, Henry Wharton Shoemaker, and Rudolf Drescher. Also included are boxes of pamphlets, clippings, and ephemera on Cooper, Poe, and other subjects.

5,952. Prang, Louis
Papers. 1858-80. 1 vol.
Open. Card catalog.
Boston Public Library.
Diary of Prang (1824-1909), a lithographer in Boston, which was written in German by Prang and his wife Rosa Gerber Prang (?-1898) for their daughter Henriette, contains entries about Henriette's physical and mental development.

5,953. Quincy, Abby A.
Papers. 1887. 1 vol.
Open. Card catalog.
Boston Public Library.
Journal of a trip to Japan and Europe, with particular emphasis on Italy. A photo, clippings, and other material are inserted.

5,954. Ristori, Adelaide
Papers. 1867-86. 30 items.
Open. Item catalog.
Boston Public Library.
Papers of Ristori (1822-1906), an actress, including a poem written in tribute of one of her performances; theater programs; Kate Field's season theater tickets; and letters written to Field by Ristori about her work and travel in Cuba, Argentina, Chile, Switzerland, Paris, Rome, and cities in the US.

5,955. Root, Sarah C.
Papers. 1859-64. 50-page vol.
Open. Card catalog.
Boston Public Library.
Diary and household accounts of a woman living in Belchertown, MA.

5,956. Sanborn, Katherine Abbott
Papers. Ca. 1870s-1900s. 20 items.
Open. Item catalog.
Boston Public Library.
Correspondence of Sanborn (1839-1917), an author, teacher, and lecturer, includes letters to Harriet Mulford (Stone) Lothrop about Sanborn's book on the wit of American women and another letter in which Sanborn comments on Edith Newbold (Jones) Wharton.

5,957. Sigourney, Lydia Howard (Huntley)
Papers. 1810-52. 30 items.
Open. Item catalog.
Boston Public Library.
Papers of Sigourney (1791-1865), an author, consist of manuscript poems, correspondence concerning publishing matters, and letters to Edgar Allan Poe.

5,958. Society to Encourage Studies at Home, Boston
Records. 1873-99. 2 boxes and 21 vols.
Open. Cataloged.
Boston Public Library.
The Society was a correspondence school for women, founded and run by Anna Eliot Ticknor. Includes correspondence, outlines of courses, papers by students, and a catalog of the school's lending library.

5,959. Spofford, Harriet Elizabeth (Prescott)
Papers. 1862-1915. 41 items.
Open. Item catalog.
Boston Public Library.
Correspondence of Spofford (1835-1921), an author, includes letters written from Deer Island, Newburyport, MA, to Lilian Whiting with references to Ellen Louise (Chandler) Moulton. Also included are personal letters to Harriet Mulford (Stone) Lothrop.

5,960. Stanard, Mary Mann Page Newton
Papers. 1920-26. 23 items.
Open. No guide.
Boston Public Library.
Correspondence of Stanard (1865-1929), an historian, includes letters written from Richmond, VA, to Mary Elizabeth Phillips.

5,961. Stanton, Elizabeth (Cady)
Papers. Ca. 1831-82. 21 items.
Open. Item catalog.
Boston Public Library.
Papers of Stanton (1815-1902), women's rights leader, include an autograph and commonplace book which belonged to her before marriage and which she took on her wedding trip to Europe in 1840; correspondence, with letters to Lucretia (Coffin) Mott and William Lloyd Garrison; and a printed notice of the 11th National Woman's Rights Convention in 1866.

5,962. Stoddard, Elizabeth Drew (Barstow)
Papers. Ca. 1856-91. 40 items.
Open. Item catalog.
Boston Public Library.
Correspondence of Stoddard (1823-1902), a novelist and poet, includes letters to Lilian Whiting about family news and literary matters.

5,963. Stone, Lucy
Papers. 1848-93. 52 items.
Open. Item catalog.
Boston Public Library.
Correspondence of Stone (1818-93), a feminist, abolitionist, and suffragist, includes letters to Samuel May and William Lloyd Garrison as well as letters about Stone written by persons active in the antislavery and suffrage movements.

5,964. Stowe, Harriet Elizabeth (Beecher)
Papers. 1851-72. Ca. 86 items.
Open. Item catalog.
Boston Public Library.
Papers of Stowe (1811-96), an author, include a manuscript; promissory notes to antislavery fairs; letters to William Lloyd Garrison; and letters mentioning Stowe, written between persons active in the antislavery movement.

5,965. Sutherland, Evelyn Greenleaf Baker
Papers. Ca. 1890-1905. 146 items.
Open. Index of correspondents' names.
Boston Public Library.
Papers of Sutherland (1855-1908), a writer for newspapers and magazines and a playwright, include correspondence and a manuscript poem Sutherland wrote to Julia Ward Howe.

5,966. Thaxter, Celia (Laighton)
Papers. 1860s-92. 145 items.
Open. Typed list.
Boston Public Library.
Correspondence and poems of Thaxter (1835-94), a poet, including letters written from such places as Newtonville, MA, Portsmouth, NH, and the Isles of Shoals, NH/ME, to Annie (Adams) Fields, James Thomas Fields, Sarah Orne Jewett, Kate Field, and Isabella Mack Hinckley.

5,967. Thomas, Edith Matilda
Papers. 1885-88. 23 items.
Open. Typed list.
Boston Public Library.
Manuscript poem of Thomas (1854-1925), a poet, and correspondence to Lilian Whiting.

5,968. Wallace, Susan (Arnold) Elston
Papers. 1896-1905. 40 items.
Open. No guide.
Boston Public Library.
Correspondence of Wallace (1830-1907), an author married to Lewis Wallace (1827-1905), was written from Crawfordsville, IN, and addressed to Mary Elizabeth Phillips.

5,969. Waltham Woman Suffrage Society
Records. 1879-91. 112-page vol.
Open. Card catalog.
Boston Public Library.
Constitution and minutes of meetings of the Waltham, MA, Society.

5,970. Ward, Elizabeth Stuart (Phelps)
Papers. 1868-99. 36 items.
Open. Item catalog.
Boston Public Library.
Papers of Ward (1844-1911), an author, include manuscripts for her short stories "Fourteen to One" and "Jack" as well as correspondence, with several personal letters from Henry Wadsworth Longfellow.

5,971. Wednesday Morning Club
Records. 1900-06. 1 vol.
Open. Card catalog.
Boston Public Library.
Programs of this Boston women's club and letters written by members to Elizabeth Porter Gould.

5,972. Weston Family
Papers. Ca. 1834-1900. 29 vols.
Open. Card catalog.
Boston Public Library.
All of six Weston sisters from Weymouth, MA, were involved in the antislavery movement. Correspondence and diary entries of Caroline Weston (1808-82), a teacher, and of Deborah Weston, a teacher; and correspondence of Anne Warren Weston (1812-90), Lucia Weston (?-1861), and Emma Forbes Weston (1825-?), with Anne Weston's letters constituting the bulk of the collection. Papers of the eldest sister Maria (Weston) Chapman are located in the Antislavery Manuscripts collection. Most of the letters were written among the sisters, but some were written to others active in the antislavery movement. Also included is material of male members of the Weston family and of other female members.

5,973. Whiting, Lilian
Papers. Ca. 1870-1940. Substantial holdings.
Open. Some items cataloged.
Boston Public Library.
Whiting (1847-1942) was a journalist and author. Manuscripts of poems and a 237-page unpublished study of Italy under Mussolini, entitled "Italy Transformed"; publishers' announcements and order blanks for various of her books; clippings of articles by Whiting; and correspondence with Margaret Wade Campbell Deland, Julia Ward Howe, Mary Ashton Rice Livermore, Harriet Elizabeth (Prescott) Spofford, Elizabeth Drew (Barstow) Stoddard, and Edith Matilda Thomas.

5,974. Woman's Education Association, Boston
Records. 1894-1902. 60 items.
Open. Card catalog.
Boston Public Library.
The Association was founded to promote educational opportunities for women; one of its projects was creating the West End Branch of the Boston Public Library. Correspondence and memoranda relating to establishment of the Branch; volumes of recommendations for purchase by the Association of material for the Branch, which include an 1896 finding list of Branch books; and a scrapbook of other material about the Branch.

5,975. Women's Centennial Executive Committee of Massachusetts
Records. 1875-77. 12 vols. and 1 package.
Open. Card catalog.
Boston Public Library.
The Committee was founded to plan for the centennial celebration of the US. Included are treasurers' records, meeting and financial records, clippings, and correspondence, with letters to Annie (Adams) Fields, who served on the Committee, from women in various Massachusetts towns planning centennial celebrations. Also included are some records of the Old South Church Preservation Committee, to which funds unexpended by the Centennial Committee were donated.

5,976. Woolson, Abba Louisa (Goold)
Papers. 1873-99. 21 items.
Open. Some items cataloged.
Boston Public Library.
Correspondence of Woolson (1838-1921), a teacher, author, and dress reformer, includes letters to Mellen Chamberlain.

5,977. Kallen, Miriam
Papers. 1736-1975. 71 cartons.
Open. Box list.
Boston State College Library.
A graduate of Boston State College and an educator, Kallen (ca. 1900-) taught there from 1929 to 1964. She was an advocate of John Dewey's concept of progressive education, particularly through her best-selling book *A Primary Teacher Steps Out* (1936). Includes school textbooks, spellers, arithmetics, children's stories, and other material she collected for use in her teaching and research; poetry; tests; report cards; games; classroom material; master's theses and doctoral dissertations; bibliographies; catalogs; pamphlets; reprints; and clippings. Also includes correspondence, notebooks, texts of speeches and drafts of publications, menus, recipes, and photos. Some items document her concern with progressivism. Also contained is material of her brother Horace M. Kallen (1882-1974), a philosopher and Judaist.

5,978. Abbott, Jane Ludlow Drake
Papers. 1925-62. 0.5 box.
Open. Inventory.
Boston University, Mugar Memorial Library, Special Collections.
Papers of Abbott (1882-1962), an author, consist of manuscripts of short stories, clippings about her, and a reminiscence of Abbott written by her daughter Elizabeth (Abbott) Kerr, with photos appended.

5,979. Alman, David, and Alman, Emily
Papers. 1922-70. 28 boxes plus supplement.
Open. Inventory.
Boston University, Mugar Memorial Library, Special Collections.
David Alman (1919-) and his wife Emily Alman are both film producers and authors who sometimes write individually, sometimes jointly. Personal correspondence between the couple, family correspondence, and some professional correspondence; manuscripts of their published and

unpublished works, including poems and short stories; TV script for "The 91st Day" and material pertaining to airing the program; material concerning the "Martinsville Seven," the execution in 1951 of seven Negro men in Martinsville, VA; reviews; scrapbooks; photos; and personal memorabilia. Collection also contains extensive material about Ethel and Julius Rosenberg and Morton Sobell, with letters to the Rosenbergs' sons; material pertaining to the American Peace Crusade in 1951; and transcripts of hearings before the US House Committee on Un-American Activities during 1955.

5,980. Astor, Mary
Papers. 1958- . 11 boxes.
Open. Inventory.
Boston University, Mugar Memorial Library, Special Collections.
Papers of Astor (1906-), an actress and author, contain correspondence concerning her conversion to Catholicism and the problem of alcoholism as presented in her book *My Story*. Also included are manuscripts of her published and unpublished works and of her TV scripts, correspondence with publishers and newspaper editors, fan mail, reviews, publicity material, and photos.

5,981. Babb, Sanora
Papers. 1962- . 1 box.
Open. Inventory.
Boston University, Mugar Memorial Library, Special Collections.
Manuscript of and items pertaining to *An Owl on Every Post* by author Babb (1907-), as well as a copy of an article.

5,982. Babson, Naomi Lane
Papers. 1920- . 14 boxes.
Open. Inventory.
Boston University, Mugar Memorial Library, Special Collections.
Manuscripts of published and unpublished writings of Babson (1895-), an author of short stories, articles, and novels. Also included are correspondence, reviews, clippings, photos, memorabilia, and scrapbooks, one of which was kept by Babcock's mother to document Babcock's high school days.

5,983. Baldwin, Faith
Papers. Ca. 1930- . 18 boxes.
Open. Inventory.
Boston University, Mugar Memorial Library, Special Collections.
Bulk of the correspondence, notes, typescripts, galleys, photos, interviews, and other papers of Baldwin (1893-), an author who is also referred to as Faith (Baldwin) Cuthrell, pertains to works she has had published since 1967. Included are photos of Baldwin and various notable people, a film of a TV interview of Baldwin by Edward Murrow, and a phonorecord of another interview by Bennett Cerf, as well as reviews, publicity material, memorabilia, and papers relating to war work Baldwin performed between 1942 and 1945.

5,984. Banister, Margaret Sandford
Papers. 1905-77. 8 boxes.
Open. Inventory.
Boston University, Mugar Memorial Library, Special Collections.
An author, Banister also worked at the Pentagon from 1942 through 1956, first in the public information bureau of the War Department and then in the information office of the Secretary of Defense. Correspondence, memos, ratings, and papers from her Pentagon work are included with manuscripts of her novels *Burn Then, Little Lamp* and *Tears Are for the Living* and short stories and essays she wrote for Sweet Briar College. Collection also includes correspondence with the publishing firm Houghton Mifflin, fan mail, letters from Banister's friends, copies of speeches, memos, photos, clippings, and memorabilia.

5,985. Banning, Margaret (Culkin)
Papers. 1917-60s. 109 boxes.
Open. Inventory.
Boston University, Mugar Memorial Library, Special Collections.
Banning (1891-) is an author of novellas, novels, short stories, magazine articles, nonfiction, and radio programs. Correspondence with publishers and magazine editors, with Brandt & Brandt and Harper and Brothers; notes, manuscripts, and copies of some of her works; lecture material; fan mail; press clippings and reviews; publicity material; and photos.

5,986. Barbour, Harriot Buxton
Papers. 1918-72. 5 boxes.
Open. Inventory.
Boston University, Mugar Memorial Library, Special Collections.
An author of music education texts in collaboration with Warren Samuel Freeman, Barbour (1901-) also wrote pamphlets, articles, short stories, poems, and other books. Included are correspondence; manuscripts; research notes; galleys and page proofs of *Old English Tales Retold,* of *Sandwich: The Town That Glass Built,* and of *Music for Family Fun;* printed copies of others of her works; scrapbooks; and memorabilia.

5,987. Barry, Jane Powell
Papers. 1959-68. 3 boxes.
Open. Inventory.
Boston University, Mugar Memorial Library, Special Collections.
Correspondence, notes, manuscripts, and reviews, all of which relate to works of Barry (1925-), a newspaper woman and author. Barry wrote *A Shadow of Eagles, The Carolinians, A Time in the Sun,* and other novels.

5,988. Benton, Patricia
Papers. 1900s- . 41 boxes plus supplement.
Open. Inventory.
Boston University, Mugar Memorial Library, Special Collections.
Papers of Benton (1907-), a poet and lecturer, contain material relating to the National Society of Arts and Letters and to National Poetry Day observances in Arizona and New York in the 1950s and early 60s; poems by children; correspondence, most of which relates to Benton's work; manuscripts of her poems and plays; musical scores with lyrics by Benton; phonorecords whose texts she wrote; photos and watercolors of Pueblo Indians; reviews, publicity; and other items.

5,989. Betts, Doris June Waugh
Papers. 1953- . 10 boxes plus supplement.
Open. Inventory.
Boston University, Mugar Memorial Library, Special Collections.
Betts (1932-) is a newspaper woman and author of short stories. Collection contains manuscripts of various of her works, including *The Scarlet Thread, Tall Houses in Winter,* and *The River to Pickle Beach;* copies of lectures and speeches she gave; correspondence with publishers and contemporary authors; publicity material; and clippings.

5,990. Bonime, Florence Cummings
Papers. 1967-68. 1 box.
Open. Inventory.
Boston University, Mugar Memorial Library, Special Collections.
Letter and manuscripts of *A Thousand Imitations* by Bonime (1907-), an author.

5,991. Borden, Mary
Papers. 1919-60s. 20 boxes.
Open. Inventory.
Boston University, Mugar Memorial Library, Special Collections.
Borden (1886-1968) was an author who originally wrote under the pseudonym Bridget Maclagan; she also was director of field hospitals for the French during WWI and WWII. Manuscripts of her works, correspondence with publishers, an account of her interview with Albert Einstein, her 1938 diary, and personal letters from French generals with whom she worked during the wars and from prominent Englishmen.

5,992. Borowik, Ann
Papers. 1960s. 1 box.
Open. Inventory.
Boston University, Mugar Memorial Library, Special Collections.
Papers of Borowik (1930-), an author of poems, short stories, and novels, consist of manuscripts of some of her works, including her novels *How Many Miles to Babylon* and *Lions Three: Christians Nothing;* several leaves of a diary or journal; a few letters; and a clipping.

5,993. Bothwell, Jean
Papers. 1924- . 46 boxes.
Open. Inventory.
Boston University, Mugar Memorial Library, Special Collections.
An author who wrote under the pseudonyms Elizabeth Midland Rodgers and Priscilla Jane Millward, Bothwell (1892?-1977) also served as a Methodist Episcopal Church business manager-missionary to India. Correspondence with publishers and fan letters from children; manuscripts of her published and unpublished works; personal financial accounts; photos; clippings; and memorabilia from her years in India, her college years from 1912 to 1916 at Nebraska Wesleyan University, and from 1945 to 1970 at the MacDowell Colony in New Hampshire.

5,994. Carrighar, Sally
Papers. 1943-70. 11 boxes.
Open. Inventory.
Boston University, Mugar Memorial Library, Special Collections.
Papers of Carrighar, an author, consist of correspondence with publishers and with Walt Disney Productions, financial papers, manuscripts, some original drawings for illustrations of her books, articles by her, photos, clippings, and memorabilia.

5,995. Carroll, Gladys (Hasty)
Papers. 1910- . 41 boxes.
Open. Inventory.
Boston University, Mugar Memorial Library, Special Collections.
A trustee of Bates College in Lewiston, ME, Carroll (1904-) is an author of short stories, articles, and novels. Manuscripts of her works and clippings and publicity pertaining to them are included with motion picture and folk play versions of *As the Earth Turns.* Collection also includes correspondence relating to Bates College, letters from national political figures about Carroll's interest in the Republican party, and letters to Robertine Howe Rice and William H. Remy.

5,996. Carter, Mary (Arkley)
Papers. 1952- . 8 boxes.
Open. Inventory.
Boston University, Mugar Memorial Library, Special Collections.
Manuscripts of some of the novels, short stories, essays, and lectures of Carter (1923-), an author. Also included are notes and correspondence with publishers and with agent Brandt & Brandt.

5,997. Chase, Ilka
Papers. Ca. 1940s- . 13 boxes.
Open. Inventory.

Boston University, Mugar Memorial Library, Special Collections.
Manuscripts of some of the literary works of Chase (1905-), an author and actress.

5,998. Chase, Mary Ellen
Papers. Ca. 1965. 1 box.
Open. Inventory.
Boston University, Mugar Memorial Library, Special Collections.
Letters and manuscripts of *The Story of Lighhouses* and *A Journey to Boston* by Chase (1887-1973), an author and professor of English.

5,999. Clarke, Mary Stetson
Papers. 1935- . 4 boxes.
Open. Inventory.
Boston University, Mugar Memorial Library, Special Collections.
Papers of Clarke (1911-), an author and journalist, consist of literary manuscripts and articles she wrote for *The Christian Science Monitor,* research notes, publicity material, and correspondence with Elizabeth George Speare, Ellen Nelson, Barbara Cooney, Ruth Henshaw, and others.

6,000. Cockrell, Marian Brown
Papers. 1935-65. 1 box.
Open. Inventory.
Boston University, Mugar Memorial Library, Special Collections.
Manuscripts of a novel *The Revolt of Sarah Perkins* and a screenplay *What Every Young Bride Should Know* by Cockrell (1909-), an author. Also includes her diary of 1935 through 1940.

6,001. Cooper, Jamie Lee
Papers. Nd. 2 boxes.
Open. Inventory.
Boston University, Mugar Memorial Library, Special Collections.
Papers of Cooper, an author and illustrator, consist of an ink drawing, typescripts, and notes for *Shadow of a Star* and manuscripts of *The Horn and the Forest.*

6,002. Corbett, Elizabeth Frances
Papers. 1954- . 10 boxes.
Open. Inventory.
Boston University, Mugar Memorial Library, Special Collections.
Outlines and manuscripts of many of the works, particularly poems, of Corbett (1887-), an author. Also included are correspondence, publicity material, photos, and mementos.

6,003. Crawford, Joanna
Papers. 1964- . 4 boxes.
Open. Inventory.
Boston University, Mugar Memorial Library, Special Collections.
Manuscripts of the novel *Birch Interval* by Crawford (1941-), an author and actress; a copy of the screenplay version of the novel; notes; and manuscripts of other screenplays and novels.

6,004. Cullman, Marguerite Wagner
Papers. 1948-63. 3 boxes.
Open. Inventory.
Boston University, Mugar Memorial Library, Special Collections.
An author and lecturer, Cullman (1908-) also backs Broadway plays with her husband. Manuscripts of *Ninety Dozen Glasses* and *Occupation: Angel,* copies of magazine articles by Cullman, and publicity material.

6,005. Davis, Bette
Papers. 1910s- . 18 boxes and 59 vols.
Open. Inventory.
Boston University, Mugar Memorial Library, Special Collections.
Scrapbooks and photo albums of Davis (1908-), an actress, consist of correspondence, drawings, reviews, telegrams, photos of Davis and other actors and actresses, programs, publicity items, and clippings. Collection also contains appointment diaries and luncheon menus, scripts of plays and films in which she performed, musical scores and lyrics to songs from her movies, tape recordings and phonorecords of Davis, copies of speeches by Davis, and drawings and portraits of her.

6,006. Deal, Babs Hodges
Papers. 1956-68. 12 boxes.
Open. Inventory.
Boston University, Mugar Memorial Library, Special Collections.
Manuscripts of *Fancy's Knell, High Lonesome World,* and *The Walls Came Tumbling Down* by Deal (1929-), an author; correspondence with her agents and publishers; and personal correspondence with Margaret Cousins and Jimmy Joiner.

6,007. Dee, Sylvia
Papers. 1940s-60s. 11 boxes and 27 packages.
Open. Inventory.
Boston University, Mugar Memorial Library, Special Collections.
Dee (1914-67) was an author and song lyricist whose married name was Josephine Moore Proffitt. Manuscripts of Dee's novels, short stories, children's books, poetry, lyrics, and narrations for phonorecord albums; recordings of songs by Dee; scrapbooks containing some correspondence; and memorabilia.

6,008. Deutsch, Helen
Papers. 1890s-1960s. 56 boxes and 5 packages.
Open. Inventory.
Boston University, Mugar Memorial Library, Special Collections.
Papers of Deutsch, a theatrical press agent, film writer, and author, including a diary of her father, written in Hebrew, and a poem and letter from him to her mother during their courtship; records of the New York Drama Critics Circle from the period during which Deutsch was its secretary; and memorabilia of the Provincetown Players of Provincetown, MA, from the 1920s. Also contained are items Deutsch wrote as a high school and college student; correspondence between Deutsch and Theresa Helburn of the Theatre Guild and from other colleagues, actors, and actresses; business correspondence and fan mail; manuscripts of TV and film scripts she wrote; copies of her short stories; publicity material and other papers relating to her career; scrapbooks; photos; and memorabilia.

6,009. Distinguished Graduates of Boston University
Collection. Nd. No size given.
Open. No guide.
Boston University, Mugar Memorial Library, Special Collections.
A few papers of women graduates of BU include clippings about Eva Channing, class of 1877, who was granddaughter of William Ellery Channing; letters and poems by Marie Molineux, class of 1879, a lecturer and biologist with the Massachusetts Board of Health; material pertaining to the college education of women and to the AAUW and a few manuscripts by Marion Talbot, class of 1880, an educator and author who was one of the AAUW founders; printed material and manuscripts by Alice Stone Blackwell, class of 1881, an author and feminist who was daughter of Lucy Stone; and manuscript poems by Ada A. Cole, class of 1899, a poet.

6,010. Dolim, Mary Nuzum
Papers. 1942-67. 5 boxes.
Open. Inventory.
Boston University, Mugar Memorial Library, Special Collections.
Dolim (1925-) is an author of novels, books for juveniles, articles, and short stories. Manuscripts of her writings, correspondence pertaining to her writing, and copies of pieces she wrote for her high school newspaper.

6,011. Eaton, Evelyn Sybil Mary
Papers. Ca. 1930s- . 26 boxes.
Access restricted. Inventory.
Boston University, Mugar Memorial Library, Special Collections.
A war correspondent in the Far East during WWII, Eaton (1902-) is an author and lecturer. Manuscripts of her published and unpublished writings; copies of articles she wrote; material such as articles, reports, press releases, photos, and mementos pertaining to her work as war correspondent; notes for lectures and courses she taught; reviews of her writings; musical scores by various composers, based on some of her poems; tape recordings of readings by her and interviews with her; scrapbooks; and personal and business correspondence. Also included are items pertaining to Sweet Briar College and the MacDowell Colony, NH.

6,012. Fisher, Frederick, and Fisher, Welthy
Papers. 1902- . 66 boxes.
Open. Inventory.
Boston University, Mugar Memorial Library, Special Collections.
Papers of Frederick Bohn Fisher (1882-1938), a bishop of the Methodist Episcopal Church and missionary to India, and of his wife Welthy Blakesley (Honsinger) Fisher (1879-), an author and teacher and missionary in China and India, consist of correspondence, her diaries, autobiographical material from her years in the Far East and marriage to Fisher, sermons and lectures, biographical and genealogical material, manuscripts of writings, tapes, photos, scrapbooks, clippings, and memorabilia. Collection also includes material on literacy projects and organizations, on women's organizations in India, and on the Methodist Episcopal Church, as well as letters from Mohandas Karamchand Gandhi, Rabindranath Tagore, other East Indians, and Americans living in India.

6,013. Fitzgerald, Ella
Papers. Nd. 8 boxes.
Open. Inventory.
Boston University, Mugar Memorial Library, Special Collections.
Photos of and musical scores for Fitzgerald (1918-), a singer and composer, which have been variously arranged by Buddy Bregman, Nelson Riddle, and Billy May.

6,014. Flagg, Mildred (Buchanan)
Papers. 1896-1960s. 14 boxes.
Open. Inventory.
Boston University, Mugar Memorial Library, Special Collections.
Notebooks of Flagg (1886-), a writer and lecturer, contain notes pertaining to her speaking engagements, with clippings and letters interleaved. Collection also includes scrapbooks with correspondence, letters on the death of her husband, photos, articles, correspondence with authors whom she invited to speak to the Boston Authors Club, and manuscripts of her writings.

6,015. Fletcher, Grace (Nies)
Papers. 1924- . 10 boxes.
Open. Inventory.
Boston University, Mugar Memorial Library, Special Collections.
Papers of Fletcher (1895-), an author, include business, personal, and family correspondence and fan mail; notes; manuscripts of her writings; reviews and publicity material; photos; and memorabilia.

6,016. Forbes, Kathryn
Papers. 1941-60. 2 boxes.
Open. Inventory.

Boston University, Mugar Memorial Library, Special Collections.
Papers of Forbes (1909-66), an author, consist of galleys of *Mama's Bank Account;* material pertaining to the adaptation of the book as a play, including script, watercolors of costumes and a set, and photos from the original production; and articles by and about Forbes.

6,017. Fountain, Leatrice
Papers. 1967- . 1 box.
Open. Inventory.
Boston University, Mugar Memorial Library, Special Collections.
Manuscripts of published and unpublished works by Fountain (1924-), author of articles and *Love to the Irish* and *Get Out of the Garden, Nellie, the Flowers Are Gone!*

6,018. Freedman, Benedict, and Freedman, Nancy
Papers. 1942- . 25 boxes plus supplement.
Open. Inventory.
Boston University, Mugar Memorial Library, Special Collections.
Papers of Benedict Freedman (1919-), a radio and film writer, and of his wife Nancy (Mars) Freedman (1920-), an actress and author, primarily consist of outlines, research notes, and manuscripts generated by each of them or by them jointly. Also included are correspondence, drawings and watercolor illustrations by Nancy Freedman for some of their books, notebooks and writings by their children, tape recordings of TV interviews, musical scores, photos, publicity material, and memorabilia.

6,019. Freeman, Lucy Greenbaum
Papers. 1952-69. 5 boxes.
Open. Inventory.
Boston University, Mugar Memorial Library, Special Collections.
Manuscripts of *The Story of Psychoanalysis, The Cry for Love,* and *Farewell to Fear* by Freeman (1916-), an author who also worked as a newspaper reporter.

6,020. Fromm, Bella
Papers. 1917-70. 61 boxes and 2 packages.
Open. Inventory.
Boston University, Mugar Memorial Library, Special Collections.
An author, Fromm (1890-1972) left her native land of Germany and in 1938 came to live in the US. Correspondence contains material about the help during WWII Fromm and her husband gave the US government uncovering Nazi agents, as well as information about the Nazis' confiscation of her property and about her move to the US. Correspondence with friends and colleagues, diaries for the entire period, manuscripts, scrapbooks, photos, and printed items, including articles and lectures by Fromm, publicity and reviews of her book *Blood and Banquets,* research notes, and other material.

6,021. Gardner, Nancy (Bruff)
Papers. 1924- . 4 boxes.
Open. Inventory.
Boston University, Mugar Memorial Library, Special Collections.
Writing under the name Nancy Bruff, Gardner (1915-) is an author of articles, novels, poetry, and books for juveniles. Correspondence, manuscripts of her writings, research notes and drafts, reviews, publicity items, photos, clippings, and memorabilia.

6,022. Gartner, Chloe Maria
Papers. 1937- . 2 boxes.
Open. Inventory.
Boston University, Mugar Memorial Library, Special Collections.
Papers of Gartner (1916-), an author, consist of manuscripts of her "Gypsy Earrings" and *Drums of Khartoum,* copies of her play *Perchance to Dream* and articles, correspondence, photos, clippings, and mementos.

6,023. Gellhorn, Martha Ellis
Papers. 1920s- . 17 boxes.
Access restricted. Inventory.
Boston University, Mugar Memorial Library, Special Collections.
An author, Gellhorn (1908-) was also a war correspondent, a foreign correspondent, and third wife of Ernest Hemingway. Correspondence, diary entries, manuscripts, notes, photos, and other material generated by Gellhorn in connection with her literary or newspaper activities include information about Hemingway, France during WWII, the Spanish Civil War, the Vietnam War, Mexico, Arab-Israeli conflicts, Africa, and American political events. Major correspondents include Leonard Bernstein, Hortense Flexner, Sybille Bedford, Bernard Berenson, Eleanor Roosevelt, and various American politicians. Collection also contains an incomplete draft of Gellhorn's memoir, business papers, copies of many of her magazine and newspaper articles, and memorabilia.

6,024. Geva, Tamara
Papers. 1970s. 1 box.
Open. Inventory.
Boston University, Mugar Memorial Library, Special Collections.
Born in Russia, Geva is a dancer, actress, and choreographer who now lives in the US. Correspondence, typescripts of her book *Split Seconds,* and reviews and publicity items pertaining to the book.

6,025. Geyer, Georgie Anne
Papers. 1970s. 2 boxes.
Open. Inventory.
Boston University, Mugar Memorial Library, Special Collections.
Typescripts of *The New Latins* and *The New 100 Years War,* which were written by Geyer (1935-), a journalist and author.

6,026. Giovanni, Nikki
Papers. 1960s- . 12 boxes and 7 packages.
Open. Inventory.
Boston University, Mugar Memorial Library, Special Collections.
Papers of Giovanni (1943-), a black poet, include correspondence, manuscripts, photos, and published copies of her poems and other writings such as articles and reviews, book reviews of her *Gemini,* articles about her, book jackets, publicity items, and memorabilia.

6,027. Glennon, Maurade
Papers. 1968- . 1 box.
Open. Inventory.
Boston University, Mugar Memorial Library, Special Collections.
Proofs of *No More Septembers* and *The Waiting Time* by Glennon (1926-), an author born in Ireland who now resides in the US.

6,028. Goldman, Emma
Papers. 1907-39. 4 boxes.
Open. Inventory.
Boston University, Mugar Memorial Library, Special Collections.
Correspondence of Goldman (1869-1940), an anarchist and author, with Alexander Berkman, physician Ben Lewis Reitman, and Almeda Sperry. Also included are notes for a speech or article on rebellion and anarchism, memorabilia with flyers advertising Goldman's appearances, and clippings. Originals of letters from Goldman to Reitman are located at the University of Illinois at Chicago Circle Library, Special Collections.

6,029. Greenberg, Joanne (Goldenberg)
Papers. 1950s- . 21 boxes.
Access restricted. Inventory.
Boston University, Mugar Memorial Library, Special Collections.
Papers of Greenberg (1932-), an author, contain personal correspondence, fan mail, and business correspondence, much of which is with her literary agent. Also includes manuscripts of her writings, some of them done while she was a college student; research notes; publicity material; photos; and memorabilia.

6,030. Guthrie, Anne
Papers. 1962. 1 box.
Open. Inventory.
Boston University, Mugar Memorial Library, Special Collections.
Manuscripts of *Madame Ambassador* by Guthrie (1890-), an author who contributed to newspapers and periodicals.

6,031. Halsell, Grace Eleanor
Papers. 1959- . 27 boxes.
Open. Inventory.
Boston University, Mugar Memorial Library, Special Collections.
Halsell (1923-) was formerly a newspaper columnist and correspondent as well as a White House staff writer during the Johnson administration. Correspondence, diary Halsell kept in Peru and articles she wrote from Latin America during 1959 and 1960, and research material, taped interviews and transcripts, copies of drafts, business letters, publisher's proofs, and photos, all relating to her books *Soul Sister, Peru, Black/White Sex,* and *Evers, A Frank Autobiography of Charles Evers,* which she co-authored, and "The Ladies and King Sorrel," which has not been published.

6,032. Haycraft, Molly Costain
Papers. 1950s-60s. 2 boxes.
Open. Inventory.
Boston University, Mugar Memorial Library, Special Collections.
Correspondence, manuscripts, pencil sketches of costumes, and research material of Haycraft (1911-), an author.

6,033. Holman, Libby
Papers. 1860s-1970. 23 boxes and 2 packages.
Open. Inventory.
Boston University, Mugar Memorial Library, Special Collections.
Papers of the singer and actress born Elizabeth Holman (1905-71) consist of family correspondence and personal letters from Holman's friends, genealogical records and family scrapbooks containing photos, phonorecords and recordings of Holman singing, tape recordings of interviews with her, publicity material, and memorabilia.

6,034. Hunter, Beatrice Trum
Papers. Ca. 1927- . 35 boxes plus supplement.
Open. Inventory.
Boston University, Mugar Memorial Library, Special Collections.
Hunter (1918-) is a lecturer, free-lance writer, and advocate of natural foods, organic gardening, and consumer's rights. Manuscripts of her writings; business and personal correspondence and fan mail, including correspondence with Rachel Louise Carson and Adelle Davis; tape recordings of lectures by Hunter; poems written as a child and high school student; information and fan mail concerning her series on natural food for WGBH-TV, Boston's public broadcasting station; research material; publicity; photos; and memorabilia.

6,035. Hunting, Constance
Papers. 1920s- . 6 boxes plus supplement.
Open. Inventory.

Boston University, Mugar Memorial Library, Special Collections.
An author of short stories, poems, and novels, Hunting (1925-) is also the founder, publisher, and editor of Puckerbrush Press in Orono, ME. Collection includes copies of her writings, some of which were written during childhood; correspondence, with letters from Mary Gray Hughes; galleys of works by others, which Hunting edited for Puckerbrush Press; reviews and publicity material; photos; and memorabilia.

6,036. Hutchins, Maude Phelps (McVeigh)
Papers. 1920s- . 38 boxes.
Open. Inventory.
Boston University, Mugar Memorial Library, Special Collections.
Papers of Hutchins, a sculptor and author, consist of manuscripts of her writings; research notes; family correspondence and correspondence with artists, critics, writers, and publishers; business papers; material on her sculpture exhibitions; publicity material; photos; and memorabilia.

6,037. Jordon, Mildred
Papers. 1958-68. 1 box.
Open. Inventory.
Boston University, Mugar Memorial Library, Special Collections.
Typescripts of *Echo of the Flute* and *Proud To Be Amish* by Jordan (1901-), an author.

6,038. Kampen, Irene Trepel
Papers. 1960s- . 5 boxes.
Open. Inventory.
Boston University, Mugar Memorial Library, Special Collections.
Correspondence of Kampen (1922-), an author, with her agent and publishers, fan mail, manuscripts of various of her writings, research notes, and publicity material.

6,039. Karmel, Ilona
Papers. Ca. 1969. 3 boxes.
Open. Inventory.
Boston University, Mugar Memorial Library, Special Collections.
Typescripts of *An Estate of Memory,* published in 1969, which was written by Karmel (1925-), an author.

6,040. Kellner, Esther
Papers. Ca. 1966. 2 boxes.
Open. Inventory.
Boston University, Mugar Memorial Library, Special Collections.
Manuscripts of *Cry to the Hills,* written by Hunter Lewis and Kellner, an author who was also editor of a children's magazine.

6,041. Kenney, Lona B.
Papers. 1953- . 3 boxes.
Access restricted. Inventory.
Boston University, Mugar Memorial Library, Special Collections.
Papers of Kenney, a singer and author, consist of a notebook of observations she made between 1953 and 1955 at a Veterans' Administration hospital in New York City, which served as the basis for her book *A Caste of Heroes,* as well as manuscripts of that book and of *Mboka.*

6,042. Kumin, Maxine (Winokur)
Papers. 1940s- . 8 boxes plus supplement.
Open. Inventory.
Boston University, Mugar Memorial Library, Special Collections.
Kumin (1925-) is an author who is best known for her poetry. Correspondence, primarily concerning publishing matters; papers written during the 1940s while Kumin was a student at Radcliffe College; research notes; card file of published poems; fan mail; reviews of her work; and manuscripts and galleys of poems, short stories, and books, including *The Passions of Uxport, Through Dooms of Love,* and *The Wonderful Babies of 1809 and Other Years.*

6,043. Lawrence, Josephine
Papers. 1913- . 7 boxes.
Open. Inventory.
Boston University, Mugar Memorial Library, Special Collections.
Manuscripts of the writings of Lawrence (1897?-), a newspaper columnist and author, are included with copies of articles she wrote and of the column she produced during the 1940s for the *Newark Sunday Call* of Newark, NJ, articles and clippings about Lawrence, business correspondence, and publicity material.

6,044. Lewis, Flora
Papers. 1937- . 101 boxes.
Access restricted. Inventory.
Boston University, Mugar Memorial Library, Special Collections.
Papers of Lewis (1921?-), a journalist and foreign correspondent, consist primarily of research material, notes, variant drafts, publisher's proofs, and correspondence pertaining to her newspaper and magazine articles, syndicated columns, and books. Also included are letters from Lewis to her parents and to her children as well as other personal correspondence, letters from readers, business papers, clippings about Lewis, photos, and memorabilia.

6,045. McCall, Monica
Papers. 1936-65. 72 boxes.
Open. Inventory.
Boston University, Mugar Memorial Library, Special Collections.
Office files of [Miss] McCall, a literary agent, contain correspondence from clients, publishers, and agents. Correspondents include Sylvia Ashton-Warner, Vera Caspary, Pamela Frankau, Irene Trepel Kampen, Muriel Rukeyser, Elswyth Thane, and Margaret Webster.

6,046. McHugh, Arona
Papers. Ca. 1958-73. 10 boxes.
Open. Inventory.
Boston University, Mugar Memorial Library, Special Collections.
Manuscripts of *The Calling of the Mercenaries, The Luck of the Van Meers, A Banner with a Strange Device,* and *The Seacoast of Bohemia* by McHugh (1924-), an author and librarian.

6,047. MacIver, Joyce
Papers. 1960s. 4 boxes.
Open. Inventory.
Boston University, Mugar Memorial Library, Special Collections.
Papers of an author, whose pseudonym is Joyce MacIver, consist of notes and manuscripts of *The Exquisite Things;* manuscripts relating to her play *The Frog Pond* with notes by Michael Myerberg, who produced it; reviews; and programs.

6,048. Maddux, Rachel
Papers. 1943-60s. 2 boxes.
Open. Inventory.
Boston University, Mugar Memorial Library, Special Collections.
Holographs of *The Green Kingdom* and *Abel's Daughter* by Maddux (1912-), an author.

6,049. Mannes, Marya
Papers. 1910- . 25 boxes plus supplement.
Open. Inventory.
Boston University, Mugar Memorial Library, Special Collections.
Author of novels, plays, short stories, poetry, lyrics and songs, nonfiction, and TV and radio scripts, Mannes (1904-) is also a magazine editor, columnist, and lecturer. Family and business correspondence, manuscripts of many of her published and unpublished works, brief diaries, manuscript speeches, reviews, fan mail, photos, publicity items, and other material. Also included are financial records and correspondence of Short Wave Research, Inc., a group Mannes was president of, which tried to provide personnel for foreign language broadcasts and publications during WWII.

6,050. Marshall, Lenore (Guinzburg)
Papers. 1935-71. 1 box.
Open. Inventories.
Boston University, Mugar Memorial Library, Special Collections.
Marshall (1897-1971) was a poet and novelist. Notes and manuscripts of her novels *Only the Fear* and *Hall of Mirrors;* manuscripts of poems in her collection *Latest Will;* printed poems, and a memorial booklet on Marshall, containing her poems and tributes from others, which was published by her family.

6,051. Massachusetts Society for the University Education of Women
Records. 1875-1973. 9 boxes.
Open. No guide.
Boston University, Mugar Memorial Library, Special Collections.
Organized in 1876 as the Boston University Women's Education Society to provide financial assistance to young women desiring to attend Boston University or other institutions of higher learning, the Society later expanded its goals in an attempt to assure equal access to higher education for all women. The Society was a major force in the creation in 1878 of the Girls' Latin School in Boston. Minutes, financial records, correspondence, reports, lists of members, programs of social events, invitations, and other records of this on-going group.

6,052. Mehdevi, Anne Marie Sinclair
Papers. Ca. 1963-64. 1 box.
Open. Inventory.
Boston University, Mugar Memorial Library, Special Collections.
Manuscripts of *Persia Revisited* by Mehdevi (1921?-), an author.

6,053. Meyer, Edith Patterson
Papers. 1967-74. 4 boxes.
Open. Inventory.
Boston University, Mugar Memorial Library, Special Collections.
Meyer (1895-) is a librarian and author and editor of children's books. Manuscripts of her works *That Remarkable Man, Justice Oliver Wendell Holmes, First Lady of the Renaissance, For Goodness' Sake!,* and *Not Charity, But Justice.*

6,054. Moats, Alice Leone
Papers. 1908- . 47 boxes and 2 packages.
Open. Inventory.
Boston University, Mugar Memorial Library, Special Collections.
Papers of Moats (1908-), an author and foreign correspondent, consist of correspondence, primarily from her to her family; manuscripts of some of her writings; and scrapbooks with articles and memorabilia.

6,055. Molinaro, Ursule
Papers. Ca. 1945- . 20 boxes.
Open. Inventory.
Boston University, Mugar Memorial Library, Special Collections.
Molinaro was a translator and author of short stories, magazine articles, poetry, plays, novels, and song lyrics, some of which she wrote in French. Correspondence pertaining to and manuscripts of many of her writings; correspondence with publishers, agents, and friends; business and financial papers; tape recordings; publicity material; photos; and memorabilia.

6,056. Moore, Ruth
Papers. 1934-60s. 20 boxes.
Open. Inventory.
Boston University, Mugar Memorial Library, Special Collections.
Moore was a newspaper woman and author of scientific magazine articles and of books. Manuscripts of her works in variant drafts; clippings of articles Moore wrote for the *Chicago Sun-Times* on the Office of Price Administration, personal letters and correspondence with scientists, research notes, reviews, clippings, photos and drawings used in her books, and publicity items.

6,057. Morgan, Berry
Papers. 1960s- . 1 box.
Open. Inventory.
Boston University, Mugar Memorial Library, Special Collections.
Manuscripts of some of the short stories of Morgan (1919-), an author, which were published in *The New Yorker,* manuscripts of others of her writings, and publicity material.

6,058. Morris, Edita deToll
Papers. 1940s-60s. 1 box.
Open. Inventory.
Boston University, Mugar Memorial Library, Special Collections.
Typescripts of *Three Who Loved, The Seeds of Hiroshima,* and *Love to Vietnam* by Morris (1902-), an author born in Sweden who resides in the US.

6,059. Mossiker, Frances Sanger
Papers. 1960s. 5 boxes.
Open. Inventory.
Boston University, Mugar Memorial Library, Special Collections.
Papers of Mossiker (1906-), an author and writer of radio scripts, consist of notes and drafts of *Napoleon and Josephine: The Biography of a Marriage,* original illustrations for the book, reviews by Mossiker, correspondence, and publicity material.

6,060. Mystery and Suspense Novel Writers
Collection. 20th century. No size given.
Open. Inventories.
Boston University, Mugar Memorial Library, Special Collections.
Collection contains more than 380 boxes of typescript drafts, galleys, and page proofs of manuscripts written by women novelists. Those with a substantial amount of material include Martha Albrand, who also uses the pseudonyms Christine Lambert and Katrin Holland and whose real name is Heidi Huberta Freybe Loewengard Lamon; Charlotte Armstrong, who also uses the name Jo Valentine; Evelyn Domenica Berckman, who also uses Joanna Wade and Constance Cleve; Doris Miles Disney; Mignon (Good) Eberhart; DeLoris Florine Stanton Forbes, who also uses the pseudonyms Stanton Forbes, Tobias Wells, DeForbes, Michaela Boston, and jointly with Helen Rydell, the pseudonym Forbes Rydell; Mildred Nixon Gordon, who writes in collaboration with her husband Gordon Gordon; Elizabeth Linington, who also uses Anne Blaisdell, Lesley Egan, Dell Shannon, G. L. Chapin, Egan O'Neill, Barbara Egan, and Dale Egan; Helen McCloy; Melissa Mather; Barbara Gross Mertz, who also uses Barbara Michaels; Audrey Kelley Roos, who writes with her husband and jointly with him uses the pseudonym Audrey Roos; and Phyllis Ayame Whitney.
Those with fewer boxes of material include Cecily Crowe; Ursula Reilly Curtiss; Mildred Davis; Rosemary Gatenby; Dorothy Gilman, who also uses the name Dorothy Gilman Butters; Dolores (Birk) Olsen Hitchens, who also uses the pseudonyms Dolan Birkley, Noel Burke, and D. B. Olsen; Helen Bernice Nielsen, who also uses Kris Giles; Lillian Udvardy O'Donnell; Merriam Modell, who also uses Evelyn Piper; Phoebe Atwood Taylor, who also uses Alice Tilton; Elizabeth Fenwick Way, who also uses Elizabeth Fenwick and Betty Phillips; and Dorothy Uhnak.

6,061. Niedecker, Lorine
Papers. 1960s. 1 box.
Open. Inventory.
Boston University, Mugar Memorial Library, Special Collections.
Correspondence and manuscripts of poetry anthologies of Niedecker (1903-70), a poet. The anthologies, which seem to have been published privately, are entitled *The Earth and Its Atmosphere, The Very Veery,* and *Harpsichord and Salt Fish.*

6,062. Osterman, Marjorie K.
Papers. 1952-60s. 4 boxes.
Open. Inventory.
Boston University, Mugar Memorial Library, Special Collections.
Papers of Osterman, an author, consist primarily of correspondence, notes, research material, tape recordings, reviews, drafts, and other material pertaining to her *Damned If You Do—Damned If You Don't.* Also included are manuscripts of others of her published and unpublished writings, correspondence, and a short autobiographical sketch.

6,063. Owens, Rochelle
Papers. 1954- . 6 boxes.
Open. Inventory.
Boston University, Mugar Memorial Library, Special Collections.
Papers of Owens (1936-), a poet and playwright, include manuscripts of her plays, poems, a novel, and a short story; book reviews; correspondence; articles about her; advertisements; programs; photos; and clippings.

6,064. Peden, Rachel
Papers. 1932-60s. 4 boxes.
Open. Inventory.
Boston University, Mugar Memorial Library, Special Collections.
Peden was a newspaper columnist and author of short stories and plays. Manuscripts of her writings, including *Rural Free* and *The Land, The People,* and clippings of her column "The Hoosier Farm Wife Says," which was published in *The Indianapolis Star* between 1946 and 1966.

6,065. Peterson, Virgilia
Papers. 1931-60s. 5 boxes.
Open. Inventory.
Boston University, Mugar Memorial Library, Special Collections.
Peterson (1904-66) was a book reviewer, lecturer, translator, moderator between 1952 and 1955 of the TV program "The Author Meets the Critics," and author, whose works were published under her first married name Virgilia Peterson Ross and under her second married names Princess Paul Sapieha or Virgilia Sapieha. Correspondence; typescript of *A Matter of Life and Death* and related reviews, tearsheets, advertisements, and clippings; copies of speeches, book reviews, and articles by her; tape recording of a TV appearance; and memorabilia, including a stone on wood bust of Peterson sculpted by Marya Mannes during the 1940s.

6,066. Petry, Ann (Lane)
Papers. 1940- . 19 boxes.
Open. Inventory.
Boston University, Mugar Memorial Library, Special Collections.
Notes, drafts, and manuscripts of various of the writings of Petry (1911-), a black author, are included in the collection along with business and personal correspondence and fan mail, copies of articles by Petry, reviews, tape cassettes, publicity material, photos, and memorabilia.

6,067. Polite, Carlene Hatcher
Papers. 1960s. 1 box.
Open. Inventory.
Boston University, Mugar Memorial Library, Special Collections.
Manuscripts of the novel *The Flagellants* by Polite (1932-), an author, former professional dancer, and "organizer of political action-education activities."

6,068. Pomeroy, Miggs
Papers. 1960s. 1 box.
Open. Inventory.
Boston University, Mugar Memorial Library, Special Collections.
Pomeroy is an author. Correspondence and manuscripts of *The Janus Lovers* and of a book she co-authored with Catherine Collins, *The Great Sahara Mouse Hunt.*

6,069. Potter, Nancy A. J.
Papers. 1960s. 1 box.
Open. Inventory.
Boston University, Mugar Memorial Library, Special Collections.
Correspondence with the editors at Alfred A. Knopf, drafts of short stories, and manuscripts of the collected short stories of Potter, an author, published as *We Have Seen the Best of Our Times.*

6,070. Price, Eugenia
Papers. 1930s- . 34 boxes plus supplement.
Access restricted. Inventory.
Boston University, Mugar Memorial Library, Special Collections.
Price (1916-) is an author, former serial writer for radio, and owner of a radio programs production company named Eugenia Price Productions. Collection consists primarily of manuscripts of her writings; radio scripts; a synopsis of her radio series "In Care of Aggie Horn"; business and personal correspondence and fan mail; reviews, clippings, and articles by Price; promotion and publicity material; appointment books; photos; memorabilia; and a manuscript by Joyce Knight Blackburn.

6,071. Rama Rau, Santha
Papers. 1943- . 14 boxes.
Access restricted. Inventory.
Boston University, Mugar Memorial Library, Special Collections.
Rama Rau (1923-) is an East Indian author who was educated in an American college. Correspondence, articles, reviews, and photos relating to *Passage to India;* manuscripts of some of her writings and speeches; personal and business correspondence and fan mail, including letters to Elizabeth Lawrence; business papers; newspaper and magazine articles by and about her; research material; reviews; tape recording; photos; and mementos.

6,072. Randall, Florence Engel
Papers. 1960- . 8 boxes plus supplement.
Open. Inventory.
Boston University, Mugar Memorial Library, Special Collections.
Manuscripts of novels *Hedgerow, The Place of Sapphires,* and *The Almost Year* and of short stories by Randall (1917-), an author.

6,073. Roget, Elizabeth
Papers. 1960s-70. 1 box.
Open. Inventory.
Boston University, Mugar Memorial Library, Special Collections.
Manuscript of the book *Shagbark Hill* by Roget (1900-), an author, and a manuscript of *Journal of Jules Renard,* which was translated by Roget and Louise Bogan.

6,074. Rothchild, Sylvia
Papers. 1945- . 14 boxes.
Open. Inventory.
Boston University, Mugar Memorial Library, Special Collections.
Rothchild (1923-) is an author who uses the pseudonym Sylvia Rossman. Notes and manuscripts of some of her published and unpublished writings; reviews and articles by Rothchild; personal and business correspondence with editors, publishers, and agents; business papers; tape recordings; and research material.

6,075. Samuels, Gertrude
Papers. 1949- . 58 boxes.
Open. Inventory.
Boston University, Mugar Memorial Library, Special Collections.
Samuels was a journalist, foreign correspondent, author, and photographer. Files of magazine articles by Samuels, most of which appeared in *The New York Times Magazine,* contain correspondence, notes, drafts of articles, newsletters, clippings, maps, and other material. Also included are boxes of black and white photos by Samuels, several of which were exhibited as "Portrait of Israel: A Coming of Age"; copies of articles, a book review, and plays by Samuels; and other material.

6,076. Sand, Froma
Papers. 1910- . 13 boxes.
Access restricted. Inventory.
Boston University, Mugar Memorial Library, Special Collections.
Born Bertha Froma Slosberg and raised in South Africa, Sand came to the US in 1941; although she had used her maiden name in her writing, the author changed it to Sand after she underwent analysis in Los Angeles. Outlines and manuscripts of novels, plays, screenplays, television programs, essays, articles, short stories, and poems Sand wrote; outlines for unsold television program and movie ideas; correspondence with publishers, agents, and movie producers; and other material. Also included are personal letters, diaries, an autobiography, a tape recording "Words to a Future Biographer," mementos from Sand's schooling in South Africa, and family photos and mementos.

6,077. Sandburg, Helga
Papers. 1929- . 49 boxes and 1 package.
Open. Inventory.
Boston University, Mugar Memorial Library, Special Collections.
Helga Sandburg (1918-), an author, is the daughter of Carl Sandburg. Research material, notes, variant drafts, correspondence, illustrations, advertisements, and proofs of her novels, young adult novels, nonfiction books, books of poetry, children's books, short stories, and poems. Also included are personal and business correspondence; printed copies of some of her works; page proofs of *Steichen the Photographer,* a biography of Edward Steichen by Carl Sandburg; and publicity material.

6,078. Saylor, Carol
Papers. 1960s. 2 boxes.
Open. Inventory.
Boston University, Mugar Memorial Library, Special Collections.
Manuscripts of *The Equinox* and *God in the Dust* by Saylor, an author.

6,079. Schneir, Walter, and Schneir, Miriam
Papers. 1950s- . 8 boxes plus supplement.
Open. Inventory.
Boston University, Mugar Memorial Library, Special Collections.
Papers of Walter and Miriam Schneir, a husband and wife who were authors and who sometimes wrote jointly, contain manuscripts of their investigation of the case against Julius and Ethel Rosenberg, entitled *Invitation to an Inquest;* reviews and publicity material pertaining to the book; and clippings concerning the Rosenbergs. Also included are copies of Miriam Schneir's *Feminism: The Essential Historical Writings,* copies of articles by both Schneirs and of *Ms.* articles by Miriam Schneir, material relating to the Chicago Democratic convention riot of 1968, clippings, and other papers.

6,080. Schoonover, Shirley
Papers. 1960s-70. 3 boxes.
Access restricted. Inventory.
Boston University, Mugar Memorial Library, Special Collections.
A few diary entries and personal notes of Schoonover, an author, are included with manuscripts of her short stories, poetry, and other writings; correspondence; and photos.

6,081. Scott, Natalie Anderson
Papers. 1930s-60s. 2 boxes.
Open. Inventory.
Boston University, Mugar Memorial Library, Special Collections.
Earlier writings of Scott (1906-), who was born in Russia, were published under the name Natalie B. Sokoloff; now a US citizen, the author uses the name Scott. Manuscripts of some of her novels and unpublished short stories, correspondence about publication of her works, tearsheets of her stories published in *Adventure,* reviews and advertisements for her works, and fan mail.

6,082. Seid, Ruth
Papers. 1922-60s. 37 boxes plus supplement.
Open. Inventory.
Boston University, Mugar Memorial Library, Special Collections.
An author who uses the pseudonym Jo Sinclair, Seid (1913-) has written novels, short stories, articles, and radio, stage, and television plays. Notes and manuscripts of her works, including the novels *Anna Teller, The Changelings, Sing at My Wake,* and unpublished novels "Approach to Meaning" and "They Gave Us a Job"; a series of radio broadcasts Seid wrote in 1947 for the Jewish Community Council of Cleveland; correspondence with publishers, agents, and friends; fan mail; clippings of reviews of some of her books and plays; rejection slips; and high school memorabilia.

6,083. Seifert, Elizabeth
Papers. 1938- . 24 boxes plus supplement.
Open. Inventory.
Boston University, Mugar Memorial Library, Special Collections.
Correspondence of Seifert (1897-), an author, with her publisher Dodd, Mead & Company and outlines, notes, manuscripts, and research material relating to some of her novels.

6,084. Seifert, Shirley Louise
Papers. 1962. 1 box.
Open. Inventory.
Boston University, Mugar Memorial Library, Special Collections.
Typescript of *By the King's Command* by Seifert (1888-1971), an author.

6,085. Selznick, Irene Mayer
Papers. 1940s-60s. 63 boxes.
Access restricted. Inventory and name index.
Boston University, Mugar Memorial Library, Special Collections.
Selznick (1910-) is a theatrical producer with her own production company, named the Irene Mayer Selznick Company. Boxes of material pertain to her productions, with correspondence, financial papers and legal documents, rehearsal and script notes, reviews, programs, photos, clippings, and publicity and other items. Also included are scripts, both solicited and unsolicited, with original, revised, and final versions of those plays which were produced; volumes of reprints of reviews by New York City theatre critics; and correspondence with persons such as Tennessee Williams, Hugh Beaumont, novelist and playwright Enid Bagnold, literary agent Monica McCall, and stage designer Jo Mielziner.

6,086. Seton, Anya
Papers. 1878-1967. 1 box (ca. 100 items).
Open. Inventory.
Boston University, Mugar Memorial Library, Special Collections.
Primarily correspondence of Seton (1916-), an author. Also included are papers and letters of her mother Grace (Gallatin) Seton (1872-1959) and of her father Ernest Thompson Seton (1860-1946), publicity material, and mementos.

6,087. Sewell, Elizabeth
Papers. 1919- . 14 boxes plus supplement.
Open. Inventory.
Boston University, Mugar Memorial Library, Special Collections.
Also referred to as Margaret Elizabeth Sewell, Sewell (1919-) is an author and professor of humanities. Personal, professional, and business correspondence; manuscripts of her short stories, poems, unpublished novel entitled "An Idea," and essays; copies of poetry, essays, articles, and reviews by her and of her work; diary she kept at Jackson State College in Jackson, MS, during the summer of 1966; notes made during the early 1960s while she was elsewhere in Mississippi; notes and documents pertaining to Bensalem College, an experimental college connected with Fordham University, of which Sewell was chairman between 1967 and 1969; typescript lectures and notes; 19th-century photos of her family and of herself as a baby in India; and memorabilia.

6,088. Sexton, Anne (Harvey)
Papers. Ca. 1945- . 36 boxes.
Closed. Partial inventory.
Boston University, Mugar Memorial Library, Special Collections.
Papers of Sexton (1928-74), a poet, include correspondence, primarily business; manuscripts of her poetry, prose, and a play; printed matter such as reviews and publicity items, articles about her, and copies of her poetry; tape-recorded talks by and interviews with Sexton; films of her reading her poetry; photos of Sexton with family, friends, and colleagues; and memorabilia.

6,089. Shedd, Margaret Cochran
Papers. 1930s- . 14 boxes.
Open. Inventory.
Boston University, Mugar Memorial Library, Special Collections.
An author, Shedd (1900-) is also director of the Centro Mexicano de Escritores. Correspondence, notes, outlines, manuscripts, and research material pertaining to her writings are included with printed material and clippings about the Centro.

6,090. Silberman, Rhoda Truax
Papers. 1943-60s. 5 boxes.
Open. Inventory.
Boston University, Mugar Memorial Library, Special Collections.
Papers of an author, who writes under the pseudonyms Rhoda Truax and Rhoda Wyngard, consist of manuscripts of some of her novels and short articles, correspondence with agents and publishers, business papers, and a copy of a speech by Silberman.

6,091. Soman, Florence Jane
Papers. 1958- . 5 boxes.
Open. Inventory.
Boston University, Mugar Memorial Library, Special Collections.
Manuscripts of the novels *Gloria Barney, Picture of Success,* and *A Break in the Weather* and manuscripts and printed copies of short stories and

novellas published in *Good Housekeeping*, all of which were written by Soman.

6,092. Sorensen, Virginia (Eggertsen)
Papers. 1920s- . 41 boxes.
Open. Inventory.
Boston University, Mugar Memorial Library, Special Collections.
A member of the Church of Jesus Christ of Latter-Day Saints, Sorensen (1912-) uses the Mormon Church for background in many of the novels, short stories, articles, and children's books she writes. Personal and business correspondence; fan mail, including letters from children; letters Sorenson wrote from American Fork, UT, to her close friend Carol Reid Holt; manuscripts of Sorensen's writings, speeches, and lectures; manuscripts of other writers; notes and research material on the Mormon Church, Mormon settlers of Utah, and Scandinavian countries; tapes and transcripts of interviews Sorensen conducted with Wesley Dennis, a writer and illustrator of children's books; Sorensen's 1955 diary; business papers; book reviews by Sorensen and reviews of her books; publicity material; scrapbooks; photos; and memorabilia.

6,093. Speare, Elizabeth George
Papers. 1957-67. 3 boxes.
Open. Inventory.
Boston University, Mugar Memorial Library, Special Collections.
Speare (1908-) is an author of historical novels and children's books. Correspondence with Houghton Mifflin and manuscripts of *The Witch of Blackbird Pond, Calico Captive, Life in Colonial America,* and others of her books.

6,094. Stanger, Margaret A.
Papers. Ca. 1966. 1 box.
Open. Inventory.
Boston University, Mugar Memorial Library, Special Collections.
Manuscripts of *That Quail, Robert* by Stanger, an author and psychologist.

6,095. Starkey, Marion Lena
Papers. 1918- . 10 boxes plus supplement.
Open. Inventory.
Boston University, Mugar Memorial Library, Special Collections.
A professor of English at Hampton Institute in Hampton, VA, between 1930 and 1943, Starkey (1901-) is also author of such books as *The Cherokee Nation, The Devil in Massachusetts, Striving To Make It My Home: The Story of Americans from Africa, The Congregational Way,* and *Lace Cuffs and Leather Aprons.* Correspondence, variant drafts, notes, typescripts, galleys and page proofs, and illustrations pertain primarily to these and others of her published works. Also included is material pertaining to Starkey's request to interview Stella Benson, to courses Starkey took at Boston University in 1918 and 1934, and to her teaching at Hampton. Also contains the papers of Malcolm Shaw MacLean, president of Hampton during the early 1940s, which consist of correspondence, diaries, manuscripts, office files, scrapbooks, and printed items.

6,096. Stephan, Leslie Bates
Papers. 1960s. 1 box.
Open. Inventory.
Boston University, Mugar Memorial Library, Special Collections.
Papers of Stephan (1933-), an author, consist of correspondence, primarily with Viking Press; drafts of and material pertaining to her novel *A Dam for Nothing;* and copies of her short stories.

6,097. Stevens, Risë
Papers. 1930s-60s. 29 boxes and 35 packages.
Open. Inventory.
Boston University, Mugar Memorial Library, Special Collections.
An operatic singer, Stevens (1913-) has since 1964 been a cogeneral manager of the Metropolitan Opera National Company. Correspondence relating to her management of the Company, appearances while on tour with the Company, and arrangements for speaking tours and social events; Company budget sheets; musical scores for opera and popular music, many of which were signed by the composers and lyricists who created them; speeches by Stevens; articles about her; and scrapbooks with photos, reviews, and other memorabilia.

6,098. Stewart, Ramona
Papers. 1922- . 14 boxes.
Open. Inventory.
Boston University, Mugar Memorial Library, Special Collections.
Correspondence, notes, drafts, reviews, and research and other material pertaining to novels and short stories written by Stewart (1922-). Also included are journals and notebooks, correspondence and fan mail, legal papers, a screenplay version of her novel *The Possession of Joel Delaney,* tape recording of an interview with her on TV's "Today Show," photos, and other material.

6,099. Stone, Grace (Zaring)
Papers. 1927-71. 2 boxes.
Access restricted. Inventory.
Boston University, Mugar Memorial Library, Special Collections.
Diaries of Stone (1896-), an author who uses the pseudonym Ethel Vance, contain personal entries as well as anecdotes, reminiscences, and sketches of literary figures and well-known people. Correspondence, photos, clippings, and memorabilia are interleaved in the notebooks. Stone's diaries contain information on her residence in or visits to China and Japan, 1927; Mexico, 1936-39; Russia, 1959; and Rome, 1966.

6,100. Suttles, Shirley Smith
Papers. 1949-67. 1 box.
Open. Inventory.
Boston University, Mugar Memorial Library, Special Collections.
Using the pseudonym Lesley Conger, Suttles (1922-) is an author of short stories, television dramas, children's books, radio scripts, and articles. Manuscripts of some of her writings, copies of others, and correspondence between Suttles and her literary agent Howard Moorepark.

6,101. Taber, Gladys (Bagg)
Papers. 1916- . 23 boxes.
Open. Inventory.
Boston University, Mugar Memorial Library, Special Collections.
Occasionally writing under the pseudonym Virginia Hatch, Taber (1899-) is an author of short stories, magazine articles, novels, and nonfiction books, as well as a columnist. Business and personal correspondence and fan mail; manuscripts of many of her writings; copies of short stories, articles, and her columns "Diary of Domesticity" for *Ladies Home Journal* and "Butternut Wisdom" for *Family Circle;* research material she used; reviews of her work; clippings and articles about Taber; photos of her, her home, and her dogs; and memorabilia.

6,102. Tait, Dorothy Fairbairn
Papers. 1950-72. 19 boxes.
Open. Inventory.
Boston University, Mugar Memorial Library, Special Collections.
Tait (?-1972) was an author who wrote under the pseudonym Ann Fairbairn. Notes, manuscripts of some of her published and unpublished writings, reviews and publicity material, and correspondence with her agent and publishers, as well as letters pertaining to a trip Tait took to England from 1964 to 1969 with George Lewis.

6,103. Thane, Elswyth
Papers. Ca. 1876- . 144 boxes plus supplement.
Access restricted. Inventory.
Boston University, Mugar Memorial Library, Special Collections.
Wife of scientist and author William Beebe (1877-1962), Thane (1900-) is a newspaper woman, writer for motion picture studios, and author of historical novels, nonfiction books, articles, and plays. Collection contains correspondence of Beebe family members, including William and his father; personal letters and fan mail of Thane; her 1931-44 diaries; manuscripts of many of her writings; extensive material Thane collected for research on England, Williamsburg, VA, and the Mt. Vernon Ladies' Association, including notes, pictures of costumes, clippings, a bibliography of background source books, guidebooks and maps, and other material; illustrations for some of her books; reviews of her works; publicity and other material; and photos and memorabilia pertaining to her and her husband.

6,104. Trevino, Elizabeth Borton de
Papers. 1928- . 7 boxes plus supplement.
Open. Inventory.
Boston University, Mugar Memorial Library, Special Collections.
An author and journalist, Trevino (1904-) was born in the US but lives in Mexico, which provides the setting for many of her books. Manuscripts of some of her novels, children's books, and short stories (some in Spanish); clippings of music and theatre reviews and interviews she wrote for the *Boston Herald* between 1928 and 1932; business letters and fan mail, mostly from children; copy of a PhD dissertation on her works; research material; and publicity items.

6,105. Turnbull, Agnes (Sligh)
Papers. 1922-60s. 16 boxes.
Open. Inventory.
Boston University, Mugar Memorial Library, Special Collections.
Papers of Turnbull (1888-), an author of short stories, articles, and books, include notes and manuscripts of her writings, some business correspondence, transcript of a radio review of one of her books, publicity items, photos, and other memorabilia.

6,106. Wallach, Erica
Papers. 1949-60s. 2 boxes.
Open. Inventory.
Boston University, Mugar Memorial Library, Special Collections.
Born in Germany but now a US resident, Wallach (1922-) is a teacher and author who worked as a German magazine editor during 1946 and 1947. After she had crossed into East Germany to search for her foster parents Noel and Herta Field in 1950, Wallach was charged with spying for the US; she spent five years in East German prisons and Russian labor camps until Stalin died, after which she was found innocent and released. Letters, notes, and poem, many of which are in German; typescript of the story of her imprisonment behind the Iron Curtain, entitled *Light at Midnight;* reviews of her book; articles concerning the disappearance and reappearance of her foster parents and her internment; pencil sketches; and memorabilia.

6,107. Walter, Dorothy Blake
Papers. Ca. 1950s-60s. 7 boxes.
Open. Inventory.
Boston University, Mugar Memorial Library, Special Collections.
A free-lance writer who uses the pseudonyms Katherine Blake, Kay Blake, and Katherine Ross, Walter (1908-) is also a teacher, nurse, secretary,

and textbook writer and editor. Correspondence, manuscripts, and copies of Walter's articles, poems, and serializations for magazines, most of which were written for children and appeared in Sunday school publications.

6,108. Ward, Mary Jane
Papers. 1943-70. 5 boxes.
Open. Inventory.
Boston University, Mugar Memorial Library, Special Collections.
Correspondence of Ward (1905-), an author, as well as typescripts of *The Snake Pit, It's Different for a Woman, The Other Caroline,* and others of her books. Also included are the movie and TV scripts for two of her books.

6,109. Warner, Esther Sietmann
Papers. 1948- . 4 boxes.
Open. Inventory.
Boston University, Mugar Memorial Library, Special Collections.
Papers of Warner (1910-), an artist and author, include typescript, reviews, clippings, and publicity for her *Seven Days to Lomaland;* manuscripts of and correspondence pertaining to Prince Modupe's *I Was a Savage,* for which Warner was ghost rewriter; personal and business correspondence and fan mail; and memorabilia from Africa, where she lived from 1941 to 1943.

6,110. Welch, Galbraith
Papers. Ca. 1965. 3 boxes.
Open. Inventory.
Boston University, Mugar Memorial Library, Special Collections.
Manuscripts of *Africa Before They Came* by Welch, an author who founded Brandt & Brandt literary agency and a former London correspondent for *The New York Times Book Review.*

6,111. Wertenbaker, Lael Tucker
Papers. 1962- . 6 boxes.
Open. Inventory.
Boston University, Mugar Memorial Library, Special Collections.
Correspondence, expense accounts, manuscripts, and research and printed material of Wertenbaker (1909-), a foreign correspondent and author who sometimes wrote under the name Lael Tucker, relate to her books *The Afternoon Women, The World of Picasso, The Hotchkiss School* which she wrote with Maude Basserman, and her TV script "Pierre Laval."

6,112. West, Dorothy
Papers. 1927-49. 1 box.
Open. Inventory.
Boston University, Mugar Memorial Library, Special Collections.
Manuscript, photos, and correspondence of West (1909-), a black woman who edited a 1930s periodical entitled *New Challenge.* Copy of poem "Sonnet in Absence" by Countee Cullen; letters from Cullen, Langston Hughes, Claude McKay, Carl Van Vechten, and black anthropologist and author Zora Neale Hurston; and photos of Hurston and of Hughes with William Christopher Handy.

6,113. Westcott, Jan Vlachos
Papers. 1945- . 9 boxes.
Open. Inventory.
Boston University, Mugar Memorial Library, Special Collections.
Correspondence between Westcott (1912-), an author, and editors, publishers, and agents, as well as notes for and manuscripts of her novels *Condottiere, The White Rose,* and *Set Her on a Throne.*

6,114. White, Hilda Crystal
Papers. 1927- . 3 boxes plus supplement.
Open. Inventory.
Boston University, Mugar Memorial Library, Special Collections.
Papers of White (1917-), an author, include manuscripts of *Song Without End, The Love Story of Clara and Robert Schumann,* and of *Truth Is My Country,* poems she wrote as a child, copies of pieces she wrote in high school and college, a 1933 diary, business correspondence, and photos and childhood memorabilia with information about the Jewish Children's Home in New Orleans where White lived until she was 10 years old.

6,115. Wilchek, Stella
Papers. 1939-60s. 14 boxes.
Open. Inventory.
Boston University, Mugar Memorial Library, Special Collections.
Born in Austria but now a US resident, Wilchek (1922-) is an author of novels and short stories. Notes and manuscripts (some in German) of unpublished stories and a novel "A Question of Guilt," as well as of published novels *Ararat, Judith,* and *Tale of a Hero.* Also included are photos of Vienna and other background material for *Tale of a Hero.*

6,116. Winwar, Frances
Papers. 1920s-60s. 4 boxes.
Open. Inventory.
Boston University, Mugar Memorial Library, Special Collections.
Born Francesca Vinciguerra in Sicily but now a US citizen, Winwar (1900-) is a book reviewer, author, and translator. Manuscripts of some of her writings, copies of translations she wrote of two opera librettos, articles by and about her, a brief biography, reviews of her works, and lecture notes on English literature.

6,117. Wolff, Ruth
Papers. 1960s. 4 boxes.
Open. Inventory.
Boston University, Mugar Memorial Library, Special Collections.
Manuscripts of *A Crack in the Sidewalk, I, Keturah, A Trace of Footprints,* and *The Space Between,* all of which were written by Wolff (1909?-72), an author.

6,118. Wright, Constance Choate
Papers. 1917- . 3 boxes.
Open. Inventory.
Boston University, Mugar Memorial Library, Special Collections.
Manuscripts and copies of pieces written during college by Wright (1897-), an author, as well as notes and manuscripts of her *Beautiful Enemy, A Royal Affinity, Silver Collar Boy,* and *Fanny Kemble and the Lovely Land.*

6,119. Yates, Elizabeth
Papers. 1927- . 24 boxes plus supplement.
Open. Inventory.
Boston University, Mugar Memorial Library, Special Collections.
Yates (1905-) is a lecturer and author of short stories, articles, plays, and children's books. Correspondence, including fan mail and business letters; drafts and other copies of many of Yates's works and lectures; reviews, clippings, and publicity material; tape recordings of Yates talking about her work for the "Meet the Authors" series for children; a "Bio-Bibliography" of Yates by Sister Margaret Lillian Trudell; photos of Yates and her New Hampshire home; and memorabilia. Collection also contains material pertaining to Yates's study of clergyman Howard Thurman, as well as drawings by artist Nora S. Unwin and recorded dramatizations of and other material concerning Yates's children's book *Amos Fortune, Free Man.*

6,120. Yezierska, Anzia
Papers. 1922-70. 2 boxes.
Open. Inventory.
Boston University, Mugar Memorial Library, Special Collections.
Yezierska (1885-1970) was an author who was born in Russia but became a US citizen. Correspondence; manuscripts of short stories, articles, a lecture entitled "What Makes a Writer," and chapters of *Red Ribbon on a White Horse;* copies of stories and articles; *The New York Times* tearsheets of book reviews by her; reviews of her books; articles about her; and publicity items.

6,121. Yorck, Ruth Landshoff
Papers. 1930s-60s. 49 boxes.
Open. Inventory.
Boston University, Mugar Memorial Library, Special Collections.
Papers of Yorck (1909-66), a German-born author, include a 302-page autobiography and manuscripts of some of her novels, novella, poetry, articles, short stories, songs, lectures, plays, and essays, some of which were written in German, some in French. Collection also contains correspondence, primarily from agents and publishers; manuscripts by Anne Hessel; photos from the 1930s; drawings; private press editions of Yorck's works; and periodicals.

6,122. American Journal of Nursing Company, Inc.
Records. Ca. 1900-60s. 47 boxes and 18 vols.
Open. Inventories.
Boston University, Mugar Memorial Library, Special Collections, Nursing Archive.
Established in 1900 to publish the *American Journal of Nursing,* the Company owned by the American Nurses' Association later expanded to publish *Nursing Research* and another journal and to administer various services for the nursing profession. Minutes of the editorial board of *Nursing Research* which was founded in 1952 to publish scientific articles on nursing and to encourage nurses to write such articles, manuscripts submitted to the journal, correspondence, and other business records; material pertaining to the International Nursing Index; scrapbooks of correspondence, clippings, and publications pertaining to the Nursing Information Bureau and to the profession during WWII; and papers of Mary May Roberts and Nell V. Beeby, who were nurses and editors of *American Journal of Nursing.* Roberts's and Beeby's papers include personal and business correspondence; manuscripts of addresses, articles, and books; photos; clippings; memorabilia; and autobiographical and biographical material of Roberts. Also included are 325 biographical histories of and manuscripts by such prominent nurses as Sarah Lillian Clayton, Mary Adelaide Nutting, Linda Anne Judson Richards, Lillian Wald, Lavinia Lloyd Dock, Annie Warburton Goodrich, Jane A. Delano, Katharine DeWitt, Stella Goostray, Mary Hamer Greenwood, Lystra E. Gretter, Julia Catherine Stimson, and Anne A. Williamson.

6,123. American Nurses' Association
Records. 1897-1970s. 487 boxes.
Partially closed. Inventory.
Boston University, Mugar Memorial Library, Special Collections, Nursing Archive.
Originally formed in 1896 as the Nurses' Associated Alumnae of the United States and Canada, the present name of this national professional organization of registered nurses was adopted in 1911. Bylaws and constitutions; reports of and often verbatim minutes and comments of the board of directors and the advisory council; correspondence; memorabilia; ephemera, including conference reports and printed pamphlets on topics of interest to the nursing profession; and ANA publications. Collection also contains the following major series of records:

Biennial ANA conventions and committees. Correspondence, verbatim records of discussions at conferences, copies of addresses and papers presented, announcements and agenda, press releases, and other material. Committees represented include those devoted to economic and general welfare, standards, credentials, civil service, civil defense, and geriatric nursing.

House of delegates special section and conference groups. Verbatim copies of comments made during meetings, which were held at biennial ANA conventions for voting on resolutions and bylaws and conducting the business of the Association. The house of delegates consists of nurse representatives from each state; the number from each is based on ANA membership in the particular state.

State nurses' associations. Correspondence, committee reports, histories, state nurse practice acts, surveys of nursing needs in various states, and state board of nurse examiners records. Although they are constituents of the ANA, these associations act independently on matters for which there is no ANA area of conformity required.

Professional registries. Correspondence, memoranda, surveys, report forms, and other material reflect registry developments for nurse practitioners.

National Health Council. Correspondence, programs and reports, items concerning the proceedings of the Third National Health Careers Conference and the Commission on Health Careers, names of ANA representatives, ANA dues information, copies of *Health Forum* (1954-62), and news releases.

International Council of Nurses. Founded in 1899, the ICN consists of two representatives from the official nursing organization of each member country. Conference minutes, list of officers, reports of ICN congresses, material on UN representatives for ICN, a history of the organization, and various publications.

Material about Florence Nightingale and items pertaining to the National Association of Colored Nurses, Inc., are also found in the collection.

6,124. American Nurses' Foundation
Records. 1953-70s. 44 boxes.
Partially restricted. Inventory.
Boston University, Mugar Memorial Library, Special Collections, Nursing Archive.
The Foundation was established in 1955 by the American Nurses' Association to conduct and promote scientific nursing research in patient care. Minutes, agenda, financial records, memoranda, correspondence, and reports of the board of directors, the technical committee, the technical and research advisory committee, the International Council of Nurses, and ANF members. Also contained are files of ANF research grant inquiries and proposals; questionnaires and other material generated by ANF research projects, conferences, and conventions; and published research reports.

6,125. Arnold, Virginia
Papers. 1945-74. Ca. 2 boxes.
Open. Inventory.
Boston University, Mugar Memorial Library, Special Collections, Nursing Archive.
Arnold (1907-) is a public health nurse who was a supervisor with the UN Relief and Rehabilitation Administration in Egypt and Greece, and assistant executive secretary to the International Council of Nurses in London during 1945 and 1946; in 1956 and 1957 she worked with the Rockefeller Foundation. Correspondence, diaries, transcript of an interview with Arnold, biographical material, copies of speeches and articles, photos, and published items.

6,126. Arnstein, Margaret Gene
Papers. 1929-72. 27 boxes.
Open. Inventory.
Boston University, Mugar Memorial Library, Special Collections, Nursing Archive.
Arnstein (1904-72) was a professor of public health nursing and served as dean of the Yale University School of Nursing from 1967 to 1972. Personal and professional correspondence; notes, outlines, and other material for courses she taught between 1930 and 1972; notes and other material pertaining to her participation in Rockefeller Foundation study teams abroad during 1958, 1964, and 1965; speeches and articles; photos; and memorabilia.

6,127. Blanchfield, Florence A.
Papers. 1916-67. 4 boxes.
Open. Inventory.
Boston University, Mugar Memorial Library, Special Collections, Nursing Archive.
Personal correspondence, biographical papers, speeches, photos, and other material of Blanchfield (1884-1971), an army nurse who served as superintendent of the US Army Nurses Corps during WWII. Includes executive minutes of the American Nurses' Association and official correspondence of and manuscripts concerning the Corps.

6,128. Boston City Hospital School of Nursing
Records. Ca. 1886-1960s. 8 boxes.
Open. Inventory.
Boston University, Mugar Memorial Library, Special Collections, Nursing Archive.
Collection of photos, clippings, memorabilia, ephemera, and official publications of the School, established in 1878 as the Boston City Hospital Training School for Nurses, also includes correspondence, addresses, and reports of Marion Geneth Parsons, a teacher at the School; correspondence of Lucy Lincoln Drown, the first superintendent of nurses at Boston City Hospital; and publications of the Boston City Hospital Nurses' Alumnae Association.

6,129. Brooks, Ethel Grant
Papers. 1904-50s. 5 boxes.
Open. Inventory.
Boston University, Mugar Memorial Library, Special Collections, Nursing Archive.
Brooks (1887-1976) was an army nurse during WWI who became the first administrator of Massachusetts public health nurses. Papers relating to her WWI service at US Army Base Hospital No. 5 in France contain correspondence with and among members of her family in Massachusetts, military papers and passes, photos, clippings, and memorabilia. Also included are correspondence pertaining to public health nursing during the 1930s; photos, memorabilia, and clippings relating to her work with the Wheeling, WV, chapter of the American National Red Cross in the 1920s and 1930s; and family photos.

6,130. Brown, Esther Lucile
Papers. 1929-70s. 3 boxes.
Open. Inventory.
Boston University, Mugar Memorial Library, Special Collections, Nursing Archive.
Correspondence; manuscripts of talks, speeches, articles, book forewords, and book reviews; a tape; photos; memorabilia and awards; and published items by Brown, a social anthropologist with the Russell Sage Foundation who studied, lectured, and authored books and articles about the nursing profession and improvement of patient care.

6,131. Brown, Mary Magoun
Papers. 1897-1962. 6 boxes.
Open. Inventory.
Boston University, Mugar Memorial Library, Special Collections, Nursing Archive.
Brown (1869-1962) was a nurse who served with the American National Red Cross in the US and the Near East. Correspondence; 41 notebooks and diaries with daily notes about Brown's work, with references to the Henry Street Settlement visiting nurse service in New York City and the American National Red Cross; reports of her work for the Red Cross nursing service; reports written while Brown was in college; alumnae reunion material from 1933 to 1952 for the Presbyterian Hospital School of Nursing in New York City; diplomas, certificates, and citations; photos; and memorabilia. Biographical material Brown compiled about other nurses is also included: correspondence, notes, articles by Brown, letters by some of the nurses, and clippings pertain to Anna Caroline Maxwell, Sarah Lillian Clayton, Lillian Wald, Annie Warburton Goodrich, and Florence Merriam Johnson.

6,132. Capital City School of Nursing, Washington, DC
Records. Ca. 1879-1970s. 34 boxes and 11 packages.
Open. Inventory.
Boston University, Mugar Memorial Library, Special Collections, Nursing Archive.
Founded in ca. 1879 as the Washington Training School for Nurses, this institution was later known as the Gallinger General Hospital School of Nursing and eventually the Capital City School, affiliated with the DC General Hospital, until it ceased operation in 1972. Minutes and reports of committees; material pertaining to accreditation; correspondence, including that of Catherine E. Moran, superintendent of nurses; records of students in training; course outlines; tape recordings of commencement and convocation ceremonies; photos of graduating classes; scrapbooks; clippings; memorabilia; and early bulletins and commencement programs. Also included are historical accounts and reminiscences of persons connected with Gallinger General Hospital.

6,133. Carnegie, Mary Elizabeth Lancaster
Papers. 1943-75. 1 box.
Open. Inventory.
Boston University, Mugar Memorial Library, Special Collections, Nursing Archive.
Manuscripts of speeches, a tape, and printed articles of Carnegie (1916-), a black nurse who is editor of *Nursing Outlook*. Earlier she had been associate editor of that publication and assistant editor of the *American Journal of Nursing;* she also has served as dean and professor of the Florida Agricultural and Mechanical College School of Nursing and assistant director of the Hampton, VA, Institute School of Nursing.

6,134. Clarke, Alice R.
Papers. Ca. 1935-50s. 18 boxes.
Partially closed. Inventory.
Boston University, Mugar Memorial Library, Special Collections, Nursing Archive.
Manuscripts, printed material, and correspondence of Clarke, editor of *Nursing Forum*. Included are American Nurses' Association committee reports, convention material, and press releases; records pertaining to the ANA's Professional Counseling and Placement Service and the ANA's State Board of Nursing and Registration; material about the mobilization of nurses during WWII; and information on federal legislation affecting the nursing profession. Also included are correspondence, articles, and other material by Janet Marie Louise Sophie Geister, a nurse.

6,135. Deutsch, Naomi
Papers. 1916-73. 1 box.
Open. Inventory.
Boston University, Mugar Memorial Library, Special Collections, Nursing Archive.
Deutsch (1890-) is a nurse who served as director of the US Department of Labor Children's Bureau from 1935 to the 1940s. Biographical information; correspondence, including letters and documents related to her Children's Bureau appointment;

speeches and articles by Deutsch, primarily about public health nursing; a tape; photos; and clippings.

6,136. Dunbar, Virginia M.
Papers. 1919-70. 4 boxes.
Open. Inventory.
Boston University, Mugar Memorial Library, Special Collections, Nursing Archive.
Collection of Dunbar (1897-), a nursing educator, includes material and illustrations on nursing history, papers concerning her stay in 1935 and 1936 in London as a Florence Nightingale International Foundation scholarship student, correspondence, addresses and articles by her, photos, memorabilia, and ephemera. Also contains a notebook from anatomy classes during 1920 and 1921 at Johns Hopkins School of Nursing.

6,137. Flores, Florence
Papers. 1909-68. 2 boxes and 3 items.
Open. Inventory.
Boston University, Mugar Memorial Library, Special Collections, Nursing Archive.
Flores (1903?-) has been a nurse and nursing educator. Correspondence, professional papers including reports and surveys she conducted concerning the nursing profession, papers by Flores's students, photos, and memorabilia. Also contains letters and memorabilia of famous nurses.

6,138. Freeman, Ruth Benson
Papers. 1959-74. 1 box.
Open. Inventory.
Boston University, Mugar Memorial Library, Special Collections, Nursing Archive.
Papers of Ruth (Freeman) Fisher (1906-), a leader in the public health nursing movement who was professor and chairman of the public health nursing administration at the Johns Hopkins School of Public Health, include correspondence with and articles by Janet Marie Louise Sophie Geister, a nurse; speeches by Lucile Petry Leone, also a nurse; and tapes.

6,139. Geister, Janet Marie Louise Sophie
Papers. 1900-64. 27 boxes.
Open. Inventory and partial name index.
Boston University, Mugar Memorial Library, Special Collections, Nursing Archive.
Papers relating to the writings of Geister (1885-1964), a nurse and author of articles on nursing and hospitals, include manuscripts, notes, correspondence, and copies of articles, some of which appeared in *The Trained Nurse and Hospital Review.* Also included are notes for speeches, material pertaining to her nursing career and the American Nurses' Association, copies of non-professional and autobiographical stories and articles, photos, scrapbooks, citations, memorabilia, and printed material.

6,140. Germain, Lucy D.
Papers. 1927-70. 2 boxes.
Open. Inventory.
Boston University, Mugar Memorial Library, Special Collections, Nursing Archive.
Professional correspondence, articles and speeches on nursing care and the nursing profession, photos, clippings, memorabilia, and publicity items of Germain, a nurse, nursing educator, and Pennsylvania Hospital administrator.

6,141. Goostray, Stella
Papers. 1899-1969. 23 boxes and 1 package.
Open. Inventory.
Boston University, Mugar Memorial Library, Special Collections, Nursing Archive.
Goostray (1886-1969) was a nurse who also served her profession as an educator, administrator, and author of articles and books on nursing; in 1977 she was elected to the American Nurses' Association Hall of Fame. Professional correspondence, addresses and articles, tapes, photos, citations, memorabilia, an untitled manuscript for a biochemistry textbook, and correspondence and other material pertaining to Goostray's *Memoirs: Half a Century in Nursing.* Also included are tributes and biographies she wrote and material she collected concerning such nurses as Florence Nightingale, Mary Adelaide Nutting, Sophia French Palmer, Linda Anne Judson Richards, Mary May Roberts, Isabel Maitland Stewart, Julia Catherine Stimson, and Effie Jane Taylor.

6,142. Gregg, Elinor Delight
Papers. Ca. 1908-53. 8 boxes.
Open. Inventory.
Boston University, Mugar Memorial Library, Special Collections, Nursing Archive.
Gregg (1889-1970) served as the first professional nurse supervisor of public health nursing in the medical division of the Bureau of Indian Affairs from 1922 to 1936; previously she had worked for two years in a similar capacity for the American National Red Cross on loan to the Indian Service. Correspondence and reports to the Commissioner of Indian Affairs and the Indian Service, notebook of places she visited for the Service, rules and regulations for nurses and inspectors, manuscripts about nursing Indians, photos of various Indian tribes, memorabilia, and printed articles by Gregg. Also contains BIA releases, memos, and published items as well as copies of a news sheet *Indians at Work,* 1937-44.

6,143. Henderson, Virginia A.
Papers. Ca. 1930-71. 15 boxes.
Open. Inventory.
Boston University, Mugar Memorial Library, Special Collections, Nursing Archive.
A nurse practitioner and nursing professor, Henderson also edited the *Nursing Studies Index, Textbook of the Principles and Practice of Nursing,* and *The Nature of Nursing,* which was published in many languages. Correspondence, course outlines and notes for classes she and others taught during the 1930s and 1940s, reports, speeches, manuscripts of articles and books, photos, and published material. Also contains correspondence of Annie Warburton Goodrich, the dean of the Yale University School of Nursing.

6,144. Leahy, Kathleen M.
Papers. 1932-71. 1 box.
Open. Inventory.
Boston University, Mugar Memorial Library, Special Collections, Nursing Archive.
Correspondence of Leahy, a nurse and author; copies of her autobiographical accounts, reviews, nonfiction, and professional writings; photos; printed articles she wrote; and a bibliography of her publications.

6,145. Leone, Lucile Petry
Papers. 1940-60s. 18 boxes.
Open. Inventory and partial name index.
Boston University, Mugar Memorial Library, Special Collections, Nursing Archive.
Leone (1902-) was the first nurse Assistant Surgeon General and directed the Cadet Nurse Corps during WWII; she is also a nursing educator and author. Professional correspondence, copies of her articles and speeches, tapes, photos, clippings, memorabilia, and reports, surveys, newsletters, brochures, conference material, and periodicals pertaining to her career and to the nursing profession.

6,146. McIver, Pearl
Papers. 1917-70s. 10 boxes.
Open. Inventory.
Boston University, Mugar Memorial Library, Special Collections, Nursing Archive.
A public health nurse, administrator, and author, McIver (1893-1976) was the founder and director of the division of public health nursing, US Public Health Service. Personal and business correspondence, notebooks containing copies of her speeches and articles, tapes, photos, citations, memorabilia, clippings and other publicity about her career, ephemera, and nursing periodicals.

6,147. Massachusetts Nurses' Association
Records. 1903-60s. 17 boxes and 29 packages.
Open. Inventory.
Boston University, Mugar Memorial Library, Special Collections, Nursing Archive.
Established in 1903 as the Massachusetts State Nurses' Association, this group is the state division of the American Nurses' Association. Constitution and bylaws; minutes and reports of sections, committees, annual meetings, and conventions; correspondence; lists of members; and photos of prominent nurses. Collection also contains histories of the MNA, the ANA, and other related organizations; surveys conducted by the Professional Counseling and Placement Service; ANA surveys and reports; reports on the education and economic security of nurses; and material about legislation of interest to the nursing profession, including minutes, reports, and correspondence of the legislation committee.

6,148. Muller, Theresa Grace
Papers. 1915-60s. 8 boxes.
Open. Inventory.
Boston University, Mugar Memorial Library, Special Collections, Nursing Archive.
A nursing educator and author, Muller (1895-1962?) was known for her pioneering work in the field of psychiatric nursing. Professional and personal correspondence, manuscripts of her writings, biographical and bibliographical material on Muller, papers by her students, photos, memorabilia, and printed research material on psychiatric nursing.

6,149. Nahm, Helen
Papers. 1929-70. 3 boxes.
Open. Inventory.
Boston University, Mugar Memorial Library, Special Collections, Nursing Archive.
A nurse and nursing educator who served as director of Nurse Testing Services, Nahm (1901-) was dean of the University of San Francisco School of Nursing. Includes professional correspondence; manuscripts of her speeches, reports, studies, MS and PhD theses, and other papers; teaching material; and printed biographical items.

6,150. New England Hospital for Women and Children
Records. 1859-1960s. 7 boxes.
Open. Inventory.
Boston University, Mugar Memorial Library, Special Collections, Nursing Archive.
The Hospital was founded in Boston in 1862 to provide women with medical aid by female physicians. Business and financial records of the Hospital, some of which reflect economic preparations for the Hospital's founding, and material about the Hospital's history. Also includes records of the Hospital's School of Nursing, founded in 1872, with reports of the principal; correspondence; graduation programs; photos of the Hospital, nurses, and student nurses; and nursing periodicals.

6,151. Nurses' Educational Funds, Inc.
Records. 1912-73. 2 boxes.
Open. Inventory.
Boston University, Mugar Memorial Library, Special Collections, Nursing Archive.
Established in 1916 as the Isabel Hampton Robb Memorial Fund in honor of Robb, a professional nurse, this organization, which provides financial assistance to nurses seeking to continue their education, assumed its current name in 1954. Bylaws, minutes and reports of committees, financial statements, lists of contributions, and correspondence.

6,152. Parsons, Marion Geneth
Papers. 1911-50s. 16 boxes.
Open. Inventory.
Boston University, Mugar Memorial Library, Special Collections, Nursing Archive.
Parsons (1871-1968) was the first nurse matron of the Harvard Unit in France during WWI in conjunction with the British Expeditionary Forces; between 1919 and 1923 she set up a nursing school in Czechoslovakia. She also served as an educator at the Boston City Hospital School of Nursing. Material pertaining to her career consists of personal and professional correspondence; financial records, reports, lectures, and curricula from the Czechoslovakian school; photos; clippings; memorabilia; and printed matter.

6,153. Phillips, Elisabeth Cogswell
Papers. Ca. 1920s-65. 3 boxes.
Open. Inventory.
Boston University, Mugar Memorial Library, Special Collections, Nursing Archive.
Phillips was an author and a public health nurse who served in Europe during WWII. Personal and professional correspondence, including letters she wrote to friends and family while stationed at the American National Red Cross Hospital, Harvard Field Hospital Unit, at Salisbury, Wilts, England; diary entries from 1941 interleaved with photos and memorabilia; minutes and reports of nursing committees on which she served; manuscript and printed copies of her articles; photos; memorabilia; and printed material pertaining to the nursing profession.

6,154. Public Health Nursing Service of Dayton and Montgomery County, Ohio
Records. 1898-1970. 4 boxes.
Open. Inventory.
Boston University, Mugar Memorial Library, Special Collections, Nursing Archive.
Founded in 1898 as the Fruit and Flower Mission, this organization was renamed The Visiting Nurse Association of Dayton in 1913 and then in 1962 its present name was adopted. Records include complete minutes of its board; annual reports; correspondence; a history; a manuscript entitled "Standing Orders and Field Guide"; copies of annual health reports for the city of Dayton, scattered from 1947 to 1963; and printed bulletins of the Dayton Division of Health.

6,155. Rhode Island Hospital School of Nursing
Records. 1884-1970s. 26 boxes.
Open. Inventory.
Boston University, Mugar Memorial Library, Special Collections, Nursing Archive.
Established in ca. 1883 as the Rhode Island Hospital Training School for Nurses, the School ceased operation in ca. 1973. Recent minutes of the School's standing committees; office files, including correspondence, nursing records of graduates, photos, clippings, and School publications; and early log books of students and graduates.

6,156. Richards, Linda Anne Judson
Papers. Nd. 7 boxes.
Open. Inventory.
Boston University, Mugar Memorial Library, Special Collections, Nursing Archive.
The first American to earn a diploma in nursing, Richards (1841-1930) was a pioneer nursing educator. Correspondence, including letters Richards wrote between 1886 and 1890 while she was in Japan; speeches; articles; photos; clippings; portraits, certificates, diplomas, and other memorabilia; published copies of her reminiscences; and other books.

6,157. Roberts, Mary May
Papers. Ca. 1919-74. 2 boxes.
Open. Inventory.
Boston University, Mugar Memorial Library, Special Collections, Nursing Archive.
Papers of Roberts (1877-1959), a nurse who was editor of the *American Journal of Nursing,* consist of copies of class notes she took between 1919 and 1921 at Teachers College, Columbia University; material pertaining to her book on the history of American nursing; and printed items she collected for research.

6,158. Shetland, Margaret L.
Papers. 1939-73. 7 boxes.
Open. Inventory.
Boston University, Mugar Memorial Library, Special Collections, Nursing Archive.
Professional correspondence of Shetland (1906-), a nurse and nursing educator who was dean of the Wayne State University College of Nursing, manuscripts and printed copies of articles and papers she delivered at meetings, and material about nursing workshops, conferences, and the nursing profession.

6,159. Slanger, Frances Y.
Papers. 1932-48. 5 boxes.
Open. Inventory.
Boston University, Mugar Memorial Library, Special Collections, Nursing Archive.
A member of the US Army Nurse Corps, Slanger (1914-1944) was the first American nurse killed in Europe during WWII. Correspondence, primarily letters of condolence to her family; obituary notices; copies of her poems and articles; scrapbooks of correspondence, poems, photos, and other items; clippings; and memorabilia.

6,160. Van de Vrede, Jane
Papers. 1914-56. 5 boxes.
Open. Inventory.
Boston University, Mugar Memorial Library, Special Collections, Nursing Archive.
A nurse in the American National Red Cross between 1912 and 1943, Van de Vrede was active in public health nursing, relief work, and professional nursing organizations. Correspondence, reports, lectures, speeches, articles, essays, a manuscript history of nursing and nurses in Georgia, photos, and clippings pertaining to nursing in the 1920s.

6,161. Vassar College, Training Camp for Nurses
Records. 1918-60s. 6 boxes.
Open. Inventory.
Boston University, Mugar Memorial Library, Special Collections, Nursing Archive.
The Camp was established and operated during WWI at Vassar College to train college-educated women in nursing care. Collection consists of material about the Camp which was assembled by Gladys Bonner Clappison in preparation for her book *Vassar's Rainbow Division—1918* (The Graphic Publishing Company, 1964), with correspondence to Clappison from women who attended the Camp, manuscript of the book, photos, and printed material.

6,162. Visiting Nurse Association of Boston
Records. 1884-ca. 1947. 6 boxes.
Open. Inventory.
Boston University, Mugar Memorial Library, Special Collections, Nursing Archive.
This ongoing organization was founded in 1885 as the Instructive District Nursing Association. Reports of superintendents, boards of managers, the president, and nurses; minutes of committees; a secretary's notebook; financial records; records of cases and visits by nurses; correspondence, including letters of Elizabeth P. Cordner, an early president of the Association, and by candidates for the position of director of the Association in 1911, among them Ella Phillips Crandall; correspondence about the Spanish-American War; glass slides; scrapbooks of photos and clippings; and printed material pertaining to the Association, nursing care, and the profession. Also included are 1912-15 reports, financial records, and correspondence of the National Organization for Public Health Nursing.

6,163. Wadsworth, Eliza F.
Papers. 1889-93. 1 box.
Open. Inventory.
Boston University, Mugar Memorial Library, Special Collections, Nursing Archive.
Collection of Wadsworth, a nurse, contains class lecture notes she took in 1889 and 1890 as a student at Boston City Hospital Training School for Nurses; correspondence; and a textbook, manual, and other printed material.

6,164. Waltham Training School for Nurses
Records. 1895-1963. 2 boxes and 2 packages.
Open. Inventory.
Boston University, Mugar Memorial Library, Special Collections, Nursing Archive.
Established in Waltham, MA, in 1885 by physician Alfred Worcester as the first nurses training school without hospital affiliation, the School ceased awarding diplomas in 1935; from 1935 to 1945 it simply offered classes for attendent nurses; and from 1945 to the present the School has granted nursing scholarships. Correspondence, including copies of letters to Florence Nightingale from Charlotte Macleod; a manuscript history of the School by Annette Fiske, a graduate; a few annual reports, 1916-63; photos and memorabilia; and other publications related to the School and its graduates. Also included are articles by and about Alfred Worcester and a brief tribute to Charlotte Macleod. A graduate of the School who in 1906 started the Training School of Visiting Nursing for the Boston Instructive District Nursing Association, Macleod became the chief superintendent of the Victorian Order of Nurses in Canada.

6,165. White, Louisa
Papers. Ca. 1923-59. 7 boxes.
Open. Inventory.
Boston University, Mugar Memorial Library, Special Collections, Nursing Archive.
Professional correspondence of White, a nurse and nursing educator who served as dean of the University of Rhode Island School of Nursing, a paper she wrote in nursing school, research material White used for her history of nursing course at the University of Rhode Island School of Nursing, a scrapbook with autographs of famous nurses, and memorabilia.

6,166. Wolfson, Theresa
Papers. 1953-70. 21 boxes.
Open. Inventory.
Boston University, Mugar Memorial Library, Special Collections, Nursing Archive.
A professor and an economist, Wolfson (1897-) worked for the American Nurses' Association as a consultant in the economic security section. Personal and professional correspondence; papers she generated with the economic security section, including official memoranda, progress reports, and copies of her articles and speeches; and other material pertaining to her work as a professional economist and her special interest in the status of women.

6,167. Biographical Files
Records. 1920s- . Ca. 400 ft.
Open. No guide.
***Christian Science Monitor* Library.**
Biographical information files on persons mentioned in the *Christian Science Monitor* primarily consist of clippings from the newspaper, which was started in 1908.

6,168. Subject Files
Records. 1920s- . Ca. 800 ft.
Open. No guide.

***Christian Science Monitor* Library.**
Information files on ca. 60,000 topics discussed in the *Christian Science Monitor* as well as in *The New York Times* and the Washington *Post.* Includes files on women's rights, roles, education, organizations, and conferences; files on women for each state; and files on women in other countries.

6,169. Jericho Centre, VT, First Congregational Church, Women's Organizations
Records. 1806-1919. 12 vols.
Open. Unpublished guide.
Congregational Library.
Consists of articles of the Feminine Religious Society, 1806; minutes, an historical account, and names of subscribers and members of the Ladies Cent Society, 1817-75; minutes of the women's Missionary Society, 1877-97; constitution and membership records of the Woman's Home Missionary Society, 1892-1917; and records of the founding, a constitution, and minutes of the Woman's Foreign Missionary Society, 1897-1919.

6,170. Kenyon, Helen
Papers. 1934-72. 3 ft.
Open. Unpublished guide.
Congregational Library.
[Miss] Kenyon (1884-) was the official moderator—and first woman to hold this position—of the Congregational Christian Churches. Correspondence, reports, a Kenyon family genealogy, photos, and clippings contain information on the merger of the Congregational Christian Churches and the Evangelical and Reformed Church to form the United Church of Christ.

6,171. Union Maternal Association of Boston
Records. 1869-1930. 5 vols.
Open. No guide.
Congregational Library.
Annual reports of the Association, founded in 1869 to provide prayer meetings and religious instruction, particularly for children.

6,172. Wollaston Congregational Church, Women's Union
Records. 1875-1935. 7 vols.
Open. Unpublished guide.
Congregational Library.
Record books of this women's church service group, founded in 1875.

6,173. Woman's Board of Missions, Rhode Island Branch
Records. 1869-1927. 5 vols.
Open. No guide.
Congregational Library.
Treasurer's records of the Rhode Island branch of the Board, founded in 1869 to direct and coordinate mission activities.

6,174. Women's Board of Missions, Essex South County Branch
Records. 1875-1946. 15 vols.
Open. Unpublished guide.
Congregational Library.
Minutes, treasurer's books, reports, history, and other records of the Essex branch of the Board, which directed mission activity.

6,175. Association for the Work of Mercy
Records. 1890-1973. 5 boxes and 11 vols.
Access restricted. Unpublished guide.
Episcopal Diocese of Massachusetts, Diocesan Library and Archives.
The Association existed from 1895 to 1973. Annual reports; minutes; treasurer's reports and records of specific funds; bank statements, investments, and other financial records; case records and statistics; and a record of births. The Association operated the House of Mercy, a home where young unwed mothers lived during and after their confinement. The purpose of the home was to develop and rebuild the character of each woman.

6,176. Babcock, Mary Kent Davey
Papers. 1935-47. No size given.
Open. Unpublished guide.
Episcopal Diocese of Massachusetts, Diocesan Library and Archives.
Babcock (1864-1947), who was the wife of Samuel G. Babcock, the first suffragan bishop of the Diocese of Massachusetts, was a church historian. Ca. 50 letters to Charles Knowles Bolton, librarian of the Boston Athenaeum; a letter from William King Covell; a manuscript copy of her book on Boston's Christ Church, which is known as Old North Church; her articles in the Diocesan newspaper the *Church Militant;* and her pamphlets and printed books.

6,177. Dakota League
Records. 1872- . 1 file folder.
Open. No guide.
Episcopal Diocese of Massachusetts, Diocesan Library and Archives.
Annual reports for 1873 to 1877 and a cashbook of the League, the purpose of which was to work with the Woman's Association Auxiliary to the Board of Missions to aid Indian tribes.

6,178. Girls' Friendly Society
Records. 1877- . 1 file.
Open. No guide.
Episcopal Diocese of Massachusetts, Diocesan Library and Archives.
Photos and pamphlets of the oldest national girls' organization in the US, which was founded by [Miss] Elizabeth Mason Edson. Sponsored by the Episcopal Church, the Society ran lodges for working girls, supported protective legislation for women workers, and organized discussion groups on college campuses. Today it offers a program of study, worship, play, and service.

6,179. House of the Good Samaritan
Records. 1860-1958. 1 box and 1 folder.
Open. No guide.
Episcopal Diocese of Massachusetts, Diocesan Library and Archives.
The House was founded in 1860 by Anne Smith Robbins "for the sick and feeble—for those disabled by long and lingering disease, who cannot be received into, nor kept in, the Massachusetts General Hospital." The House was incorporated into the Children's Hospital Medical Center in 1958. Annual reports for 1862 to 1886 and legal documents and correspondence relating to the installation of a chapel in the House.

6,180. Margaret Coffin Prayer Book Society
Records. 1855-1963. 3 vols.
Open. Unpublished guide.
Episcopal Diocese of Massachusetts, Diocesan Library and Archives.
The Society was founded in 1856 to procure, circulate, and distribute the *Book of Common Prayer.* Minutes, cashbook, memorandum of Margaret Coffin asking two friends to establish a prayer book society, and other records.

6,181. Order of the Fleur de Lis
Records. Ca. 1925- . 1 folder.
Open. No guide.
Episcopal Diocese of Massachusetts, Diocesan Library and Archives.
Manuals of this organization for girls and women of the Episcopal Church, who pledged "Purity within Ourselves, Loyalty to our Church, Service to Others."

6,182. Society for the Relief of Widows and Orphans of Deceased Clergymen of the Protestant Episcopal Church
Records. 1840-1945. 3 vols.
Open. Unpublished guide.
Episcopal Diocese of Massachusetts, Diocesan Library and Archives.
Bylaws, minutes, and financial records of the Society, which was incorporated in 1846 to provide annuities to widows and orphans of clergymen of the Church.

6,183. Woman's Auxiliary, Massachusetts Branch
Records. 1878-1947. 59 vols.
Open. Unpublished guide.
Episcopal Diocese of Massachusetts, Diocesan Library and Archives.
Annual reports, minutes, treasurer's book, and correspondence of the Auxiliary, which was founded in 1878 to do "women's work for missions."

6,184. Eddy, Mary (Baker)
Papers. 1835-1910. 200 ft.
Access restricted. Unpublished guide.
The First Church of Christ, Scientist, Archives.
Correspondence, diaries, financial records, minutes, photos, and scrapbooks of [Mrs. Asa Gilbert] Eddy (1821-1910), founder of the Church. Includes material concerning her Bible study, her discovery of Christian Science as a healing ministry, and her founding of the Church.

6,185. Gardner, Isabella (Stewart)
Papers. 1600s-1900s. 8 cartons, 75 vols., ca. 6625 items, and 38 microfilm reels.
Access restricted. Unpublished guide.
Gardner Museum.
The work of Gardner (1840-1924) as a collector of art and patron of artists and musicians culminated in 1900 in her founding and directing the Gardner Museum, which was established as a place where visitors can enjoy art, music, and flowers. Correspondence, diaries, travel journals, literary manuscripts, autographed musical scores, concert programs, memorabilia, clippings, photos, and other personal papers are contained with business records of the Museum, including correspondence, account books, dealers' invoices and photos, contracts with musical performers, and collection inventories. Included are letters and photos from such artists as John Singer Sargent, James Abbott McNeil Whistler, John La Farge, Cecilia Beaux, and Paul Manship; such writers as Henry James, Henry Adams, F. Marion Crawford, and Sarah Orne Jewett; such musicians as Charles Martin Loeffler, Nellie Melba, and Edward MacDowell; such actors and actresses as Sarah Bernhardt, Ellen Terry, and Sir Henry Irving; such politicians as Theodore Roosevelt and Mayor Curley of Boston; and Charles Eliot Norton and Bernard Berenson. Also included are letters Gardner collected by Ludwig van Beethoven, Johannes Brahms, Charles Dickens, John Keats, Henri Matisse, Felix Mendelssohn, and Alfred, Lord Tennyson.

Museum records include business correspondence of Morris Carter, Gardner's secretary who assumed directorship of the Museum after her death, and his notes for his published biography of her. Also includes business correspondence of subsequent directors George Stout and Rollin van N. Hadley.

6,186. Alden, Lydia Augusta, and Alden, Hannah Maria
Papers. 1822-44. 1 vol.
Open. No guide.
Harvard University, Baker Library.
A ledger of accounts kept by the guardian of the young Alden sisters of Boston contains records of their tuition, entertainment, wearing apparel, and other expenses, as well as of the sisters' sources of income.

6,187. Boston Manufacturing Company
Records. 1813-1930. 122 ft., 11 boxes, 182 vols., and 15 envelopes.
Open. Unpublished guide.
Harvard University, Baker Library.
Business records of this cotton textile manufacturing company, founded in ca. 1813 in Waltham, MA, include directors' records; stockholders' records; semi-annual reports summarizing into a general financial statement the costs of production, amounts produced, and product values; tax reports; and correspondence. Also included are volumes of payrolls which provide data on women and men working for the firm between 1817 and 1881.

6,188. Cabot, Ella (Lyman)
Papers. 1913-36. 7 vols.
Open. No guide.
Harvard University, Baker Library.
Correspondence and other papers of Cabot (1866-1934), an author and educator, relate to her royalties and investments. After attending private schools in Boston, she took special courses at Radcliffe College, particularly in philosophy and logic. She lectured at the Salem Normal School and at the 1933 summer school of the University of California. In addition, she taught at the Barland and Wellesley Schools of Home Making. Cabot is author of such works as *Seven Ages of Childhood* and *Outline of a Course in Good-Will for the Public Schools.*

6,189. Coes, Mary
Papers. 1883-92. 1 box.
Open. No guide.
Harvard University, Baker Library.
Personal papers of Coes, a dean of Radcliffe College, consist of correspondence, bills, legal documents, and accounts, some of which pertain to property she owned in Worcester, MA, Minnesota, and Colorado.

6,190. Curtis, Sarah
Papers. 1862-66. 2 vols.
Open. No guide.
Harvard University, Baker Library.
A book of invoices and a daybook for the dry goods and millinery store Curtis kept in Hampden, ME.

6,191. D. Mackintosh & Sons Company
Records. 1872-1963. 45 vols.
Open. Unpublished guide.
Harvard University, Baker Library.
Included with the business records of this textile manufacturing firm in Holyoke, MA, is the private ledger account of the investments of Henrietta P. Mackintosh, 1903-17.

6,192. Duren Family
Papers. 1814-69. 1 box and 1 vol.
Open. No guide.
Harvard University, Baker Library.
Samuel Duren was a boot and shoemaker in Woburn and Lexington, MA. Business records contain household accounts and accounts of the wages paid to women working for him. Also included are accounts for Woburn which indicate that the town employed women to keep school.

6,193. Forbes Family
Papers. 1753-1920. 5 boxes, 71 vols., and 5 cases.
Open. Unpublished guide.
Harvard University, Baker Library.
Correspondence, account books, and ships' logs and accounts of several generations of a family engaged in the China trade. Letters of Forbes wives, mothers, sisters, aunts, and others living in Boston and Milton, MA, corresponding between themselves and with their male relatives in Canton, China, provide detailed information about the women's daily lives. Includes correspondence of James Murray and of Dolly (Murray) Forbes from 1753 to 1810 and 19th-century correspondence of Josephine Forbes, Mrs. Ralph Bennet Forbes, and Sarah Perkins. Also included are a large series of letters of Valeria Wright Forbes, 1831-86, who kept a journal in the form of letters while her husband Paul Siemen Forbes was in China; correspondence between her, her husband, and their children Nellie, DeCourcey, and Paul Forbes; 1832 letters to Emma P. Forbes from her brother Robert Bennet Forbes; and an 1845 letter from Anna H. Forbes to her grandmother.

6,194. Gardner Family
Papers. 1853-1934. 4 ft. and 33 vols.
Open. Unpublished guide.
Harvard University, Baker Library.
Trust accounts relating to interests of this Boston family include an account of the estate of Catherine Endicott (Peabody) Gardner (1808-83) of Brookline, MA. Also included is a diary kept by an unidentified woman traveling in Europe in 1849.

6,195. Hamilton Manufacturing Company
Records. 1825-1917. 93 ft., 15 boxes, 794 vols., and 6 cases.
Open. Unpublished guide.
Harvard University, Baker Library.
Business records of this textile manufacturing company, founded in ca. 1825 in Lowell, MA, include minute books, general account books, production records, sales records, and letterbooks. Also included are volumes of payrolls for 1826 to 1902.

6,196. Heard Family
Papers. 1754-1898. 261 ft., 272 boxes, and 800 vols.
Open. Unpublished guide.
Harvard University, Baker Library.
Personal papers of several generations of an Ipswich, MA, family engaged in the China trade, and business records of Augustine Heard & Co. contain correspondence of women family members. Included is correspondence of Ellen W. [Mrs. Joseph] Coolidge, writing from Boston, Macao, Geneva, London, Dresden, Naples, and Paris between 1835 and 1847; letters contain information on Boston social life, her husband's relations with his other partners in Russell & Co., and schools for her children. Also included is a diary she kept during a voyage she made alone to China in 1839 and papers relating to the divorce of Mary Livingston Heard from Albert Heard during the 1870s.

6,197. Kinsman, Rebecca Chase
Papers. 1843. 1 vol.
Open. No guide.
Harvard University, Baker Library.
Personal journal in the form of letters home, which Kinsman kept during her five-month journey to China on the ship *Probus.*

6,198. Lawrence Manufacturing Company
Records. 1831-1926. 121 ft., 103 boxes, and 924 vols.
Open. Unpublished guide.
Harvard University, Baker Library.
A nearly complete set of business records of this cotton textile manufacturing company, founded in ca. 1831 in Lowell, MA, include general account books, production records, sales records, payrolls for 1833 to 1882, and correspondence.

6,199. Loring, Cornelia
Papers. 1835-59. 3 vols.
Open. No guide.
Harvard University, Baker Library.
Personal accounts of Loring, a Boston resident, detail her expenses for books, wardrobe, charitable contributions, and sundries. Her parents were her only recorded source of income.

6,200. Oliver, Matilda
Papers. 1833-85. 4 vols.
Open. Card listing.
Harvard University, Baker Library.
Personal accounts of Oliver reveal that she was a frugal Bostonian who earned from $150 to $200 per year teaching primary school and taking in knitting and sewing. Large portions of her income went to charity and to support of her parents. Oliver also was a Sabbath School teacher.

6,201. Parton, James
Papers. Ca. 1930-76. 10 cabinets.
Open. Unpublished guide.
Harvard University, Baker Library.
Correspondence, speeches, financial records, and other papers of Parton (1912-), an editor and publisher, primarily concern *American Heritage,* which he founded. Also included are correspondence and other items concerning Mills College in Oakland, CA, of which Parton was a trustee for 11 years, and folders on the Frontier Nursing Service, for which Parton acted as governor for several years. Founded in 1925, the Service pioneered efforts to bring nurse and midwife services to people in remote regions of the country; it was a model for inner-city paramedical services. Parton first worked for the Service in 1928 as a courier, meeting new nurses at the railroad station and escorting them to the Service's headquarters in Wendover, KY.

6,202. Pepperell Manufacturing Company
Records. 1741-1928. 192 ft., 22 boxes, and 1020 vols.
Open. Unpublished guide.
Harvard University, Baker Library.
Financial records of this cotton textile manufacturing company in Biddleford, ME, contain wage and payroll data for the men and women who have worked for the firm since 1850.

6,203. R. H. Macy Co.
Records. 1858-1965. 10 boxes and 3 cases.
Open. Brief description.
Harvard University, Baker Library.
Source material for a study in 1943 of Macy's department store, collected by Ralph M. Hower of Harvard Business School's Business Historical Society, includes a documentary history of the Company which Mildred L. Hartsough prepared in 1928 and 1929 and interviews she conducted. A business historian and member of the Society, Hartsough was author of *From Canoe to Steel Barge on the Upper Mississippi* (Minneapolis: University of Minnesota Press, 1934) and translator of *Jacob Fugger the Rich* by Jacob Strieder (New York: The Adelphi Company, 1931).

6,204. Ship: Reindeer
Records. 1852-60. 1 vol.
Open. No guide.
Harvard University, Baker Library.
Accounts for oil of the Ship's master Edward R. Ashley are included with a diary his wife kept during a voyage in 1859 and 1860 from a Pacific island to New Bedford, MA.

6,205. Ship: William Wirt
Records. 1853-57. 1 vol.
Open. No guide.
Harvard University, Baker Library.
Slop book of the Ship's master Edward R. Ashley includes a diary his wife kept during an 1856-57 voyage.

6,206. Spear, Charles
Papers. 1856-72. 4 vols.
Open. No guide.
Harvard University, Baker Library.
Business records of Spear, a farmer, contain farming and teamsters' accounts and a volume of the register for the Dorchester Workhouse, where

Spear was keeper, listing indigent women and men for 1864 to 1870.

6,207. Walter Baker Chocolate Co.
Records. 1812-1945. 14 ft. and 147 vols.
Open. Unpublished guide.
Harvard University, Baker Library.
Business records of this chocolate manufacturing company, founded in ca. 1765 in Dorchester, MA, include payrolls for 1868 to 1884 and 1918 to 1928, which list wages for men and women. In the 1918-28 payrolls, men's and women's wages are detailed in separate volumes.

6,208. William Appleton & Company
Records. 1840-89. 93 boxes and 87 vols.
Open. Unpublished guide.
Harvard University, Baker Library.
Included with the business records of this Boston family of shipping merchants, who were involved in trade with California, Latin America, the Pacific Islands, and the Far East, are letterbooks of correspondence to and from Mary Ann [Mrs. William] Appleton between 1815 and 1836 and correspondence to Sarah Appleton [Mrs. Amos A.] Lawrence between 1836 and 1861. Also included are diaries of S. Abbott Lawrence, a young woman traveling in 1851 from Rome to Baden Baden to Paris.

6,209. Baumgartner, Leona
Papers. 1837- . Ca. 100 ft.
Access restricted. No guide.
Harvard University, Countway Library of Medicine.
Correspondence, memoranda, diaries, research notes, drafts of speeches, administrative reports, clippings, and copies of publications of Baumgartner (1902-), a physician and health administrator who was married to Nathaniel M. Elias. The collection documents Baumgartner's career from her medical education and training in public health at Yale University, through her association from 1937 with the health department of New York City where she served as commissioner of health from 1954 to 1961, to her work as an advisor to the Agency for International Development. Her files also contain family correspondence and information about child welfare, pediatrics, social work, women's groups, medical research institutes, and economic development.

6,210. Blow, Susan Elizabeth
Papers. 1894-1916. 52 items.
Open. Description.
Harvard University, Countway Library of Medicine.
Correspondence of Blow (1843-1916), an educator, author, and philosopher who lived in Cazenovia, NY, consists of letters to James Jackson Putnam, a physician, in which she discusses her own books as well as others she recommends. Philosophy, particularly pragmatism; psychotherapy; education; politics, including women's suffrage; and religion are other subjects discussed.

6,211. Boston Insane Hospital, Austin Farm
Records. 1883-1903. 4 vols.
Access restricted. Card catalog.
Harvard University, Countway Library of Medicine.
The Farm housed men and women for psychiatric care until 1898 when the men were transferred to Pierce Farm. Records consist of a daily register of patients; early admission and discharge registers giving name, age, and place of birth; and later admission records with name, age, birthplace, parents' place of birth, occupation, religion, marital status, diagnosis, and cause of illness.

6,212. Boston Insane Hospital, Pierce Farm
Records. 1857-99. 2 vols.
Access restricted. Card catalog.
Harvard University, Countway Library of Medicine.
Records of the Farm, which housed women and men until 1898 when the women were transferred to Austin Farm, consist of a daily register of patients with name, occupation, marital status, religion, and medical history covering time at the Farm (admission, diagnosis, transfer, discharge, return, and/or death). Also included for the last few years is a weekly summary of statistics by sex on patients admitted, discharged, visiting, and resident.

6,213. Boston Lying-In Hospital
Records. 1881-1901. 174 vols.
Open. No guide.
Harvard University, Countway Library of Medicine.
The Hospital was founded in 1832 to serve maternity cases and in 1966 merged with the Free Hospital for Women. Inpatient and outpatient records for most of the period include case histories and a summary of any treatment prescribed.

6,214. Boston State Hospital
Records. 1839-1954. 63 vols.
Access restricted. Description.
Harvard University, Countway Library of Medicine.
Founded in 1837 as the Boston Lunatic Asylum, the name of this institution for psychiatric care of mentally ill men and women was changed in 1896 to Boston Insane Hospital and then in 1908 to Boston State Hospital. Volumes include case records, 1861-98, some of which were kept by Theodore Willis Fisher; 1880 histories of cases of general paralysis; records of restraints, seclusions, and packs; of visits, escapes, and returns; and of deaths. Also included are admissions records with name, age, sex, marital status, nationality, occupation, and diagnosis; daily censuses of men and of women, detailing admissions, discharges, and visits; weekly summaries; a sick call register of patients receiving rites from the Catholic chaplain, patient accounts; and other data.

6,215. Boston State Hospital, Training School for Nurses
Records. Ca. 1899-1946. 1 vol. and 3 items.
Open. Catalog card.
Harvard University, Countway Library of Medicine.
Records of Training School graduates consist of a register describing students and alumnae, a list of signatures of probationers at the School, a letter from Mary Alice McMahon to Ermy Corser Nokle reporting reasons for declining enrollment at the School, and a letter from W. M. L. Coplin to William Noyes on the admission of School nurses to the Philadelphia Hospital for Nurses.

6,216. Canavan, Myrtelle May Moore
Papers. 1850-1925. 1 box, 1 vol., 3 folders, and 2 packages.
Open. Catalog card.
Harvard University, Countway Library of Medicine.
Canavan (1879-1953) was a physician and brain pathologist. Correspondence and research material, including letters concerning her receipt of the Southard Brain Study in 1925, notes on the causes of death in Duke County and Nantucket, MA, between 1850 and 1890, medical records and photos for cases she studied, and a catalog of pathological specimens.

6,217. Chadwick, James Read
Papers. 1873-84. 6 boxes and 2 vols.
Open. Card catalog.
Harvard university, Countway Library of Medicine.
For his research on the role of women in health and medicine, Chadwick (1844-1905), a physician, collected information on women as medical students, as physicians, and as members of medical societies. Correspondence, including replies to Chadwick's request that medical societies and schools describe their policies on admission of women, and dated clippings from journals and newspapers.

6,218. Clinical Department of the New-England Female Medical College
Records. 1859-62. 2 vols.
Open. Catalog card.
Harvard University, Countway Library of Medicine.
Records kept by "visitors of the month" include brief case histories and statistical summaries. Delegated to report on the work of the Department, the visitors were members of the executive committee of the board of lady managers of the College, which was founded in 1848.

6,219. Dickinson, Robert Latou
Papers. Ca. 1920-50. 17 drawers.
Open. No guide.
Harvard University, Countway Library of Medicine.
Correspondence, case records, research and clinical notes, teaching material, organizations' records, drafts of publications, and photos and slides of Dickinson (1861-1950), a physician and medical reformer. Contains information about gynecology, contraception, sexual counseling, and several major birth control groups.

6,220. Free Hospital for Women
Records. 1875-1924. 96 vols.
Open. No guide.
Harvard University, Countway Library of Medicine.
The Hospital was founded in 1875 to serve gynecological needs and in 1966 merged with the Boston Lying-In Hospital. Inpatient and outpatient records for most of the period, as well as electrotherapy records from 1890 through 1895, detail the patient's symptoms, diagnosis, and treatment, with notes on the treatment's success.

6,221. Gamble, Clarence James
Papers. 1923-66. Ca. 150,000 items.
Open. Inventory.
Harvard University, Countway Library of Medicine.
Gamble (1894-1966) was a physician and philanthropist with interests in sterilization and in providing access to birth control for migrant women, Indians, Puerto Ricans, and the rural poor, especially those in Appalachia. Correspondence; clinical, statistical, and laboratory notes; field reports; drafts of publications; and printed material, including reprints of medical articles, administrative reports of organizations, brochures, and items used in mailings. Sterilization program files, organized by state, include correspondence, research reports, and clinical studies from planned parenthood leagues, maternal health groups, human betterment leagues, and women's hospitals, as well as material from individual women physicians, fieldworkers, reformers, and administrators. Also included are files on such organizations as the National Committee on Maternal Health, the Margaret Sanger Research Bureau, the American Birth Control League, the Birth Control Clinical Research Bureau, the Birth Control Federation of America, the Planned Parenthood Federation of America, the International Planned Parenthood Federation, and other international groups. Among correspondents are women active in the birth control movement, such as Betty U. Kibbee, Emily Mudd, Phyllis Page, Margaret Sanger, Elsie Wulkop, Ellen Watumull, and Doris Davidson.

6,222. Guttmacher, Alan Frank
Papers. Ca. 1930- . Ca. 40 cartons.
Open. No guide.
Harvard University, Countway Library of Medicine.
Correspondence, drafts of publications and speeches, research files, administrative reports, memoranda, and programs of Guttmacher (1898-), a physician who worked in obstetrics and gynecology, first at Johns Hopkins from 1925 to 1952 and then at Mt. Sinai Hospital in New York City until 1962, as well as with the Planned Parenthood Federation of America. Material relates to his work to disseminate accurate information on all aspects of human reproduction,

particularly contraception and childbirth, through clinics, publications, and educational programs.

6,223. Himes, Norman E.
Papers. 1918-56. 132 boxes.
Open. Inventory.
Harvard University, Countway Library of Medicine.
Himes (1899-1949) was a sociologist with special interests in birth control, population problems, and marriage and family counseling. Correspondence; drafts of publications, speeches, and lectures; research files; reports; book reviews; programs of meetings; and organizations' records. Collection relates to Himes's teaching at Simmons College from 1928 to 1930 and at Cornell University between 1937 and 1940; to his publications on marriage, birth control, and population; to his work with reform organizations; and to his colleagues. Included are records of the American Birth Control League, the American Eugenics Society, the Birth Control Federation of America, and the Population Association of America. The records of the American Social Hygiene Association contain correspondence with Janet Fowler Nelson; those of the Birth Control Clinical Research Bureau contain correspondence with Mrs. P. B. P. Huse and Charlotte Kohlberg; and those of the National Committee on Maternal Health contain extensive files as well as correspondence with Louise S. Bryant and Gertrude Sturges, a physician. Also included is material on state and local maternal health and birth control groups and material about the *Birth Control Review*, with correspondence with Mary Sumner Boyd, Stella Hanau, and Mary Travis Wood. Colleagues whose correspondence is contained in the collection include Dorothy Dunbar Bromley, Mary Ware Dennett, Stella Hanau, physician Antoinette F. Konikow, Caroline [Mrs. L. N.] Robinson, and Hazel Zborowski, all writing on birth control; Ruth W. [Mrs. Gilbert] Beebe on marriage studies; Lucia Freeman on a birth control clinic and the American National Red Cross; Gladys Gaylord on the Cleveland Maternal Health Association; Hilda Holland on her book; Helen M. Jordan on a survey of families; Marie E. Kopp on birth control research; Alice B. Lorenz on teaching birth control methods; physician Bessie Moses on a birth control clinic in Baltimore; Emily Mudd on marriage counseling and the Philadelphia Maternal Health League; Marie Munk on family law; physician Hilda Noyes on the Oneida Community; physician Clementine J. Paolone on a marriage guidance book; Ida Lee Rainey on her professional studies; Margaret Sanger on birth control and other reforms; Marian Saunders on translations she made of Himes's books in her capacity as his literary agent; physician Hannah Stone on birth control and marriage counseling; and Amy [Mrs. Frank D.] Watson on marriage and family guidance.

6,224. Katz, Fanny (Bowditch)
Papers. 1901-64. 1 box.
Open. Description.
Harvard University, Countway Library of Medicine.
Correspondence, diary, psychological reminiscences, drafts of poetry, lecture and seminar notes, drawings, pamphlets, photos, and clippings of Katz (1874-1967), a student of psychiatry. Katz's experiences with psychiatry, principally in Zurich between 1910 and 1935, are documented with items to, from, and about her physician husband Johann Rudolf Katz (1880-1938), her analyst Dr. Maria Moltzer, her physican James Jackson Putnam, and teachers and physicians Carl Jung and Alfred Adler.

6,225. Massachusetts Commission on Lunacy
Records. Ca. 1854. 991-page vol.
Open. Catalog card.
Harvard University, Countway Library of Medicine.
Reports, completed forms, correspondence, and drafts of the Commission, which studied the insane and mentally retarded persons living in the state as of 1854, both those cared for privately and those institutionalized in public facilities. Forms for each town list the name, sex, age, race, birthplace, marital status, mental illness, and other data on these persons. Commissioners Levi Lincoln, Edward Jarvis, and Increase Sumner gathered information for the report from physicians, hospitals, state almshouses, and jails.

6,226. Massachusetts Medical Society
Records. 1781-1929. 43 boxes and ca. 30 vols.
Open. Card catalog and partial inventory.
Harvard University, Countway Library of Medicine.
Financial accounts, record books, correspondence, biographical sketches and obituaries, lists, reports, and published material of this group of physicians founded in 1781. Includes documentation of the controversy during the 1870s and 1880s over admitting women to the Society: letters concerning Susan Dimock's nomination for membership; a list of candidates for Society offices running on a platform of admitting women; full committee, minority, and majority reports on the issue; letters by Samuel Augustus Fiske objecting to the admission of women; reports of affiliated societies on their policies; a letter from Henry Ingersoll to Francis Webster Boss about the status of women in the Society; a poll on their admission; and report of the diplomas committee concerning recognition of Mary A. Hall's credentials from the New-England Female Medical College.

6,227. National Committee on Maternal Health
Records. 1923-61. 2 drawers.
Open. No guide.
Harvard University, Countway Library of Medicine.
Minutes, financial reports, correspondence, memoranda, drafts of research results, reports, conference proceedings, publications, and membership lists. Activities of the Committee, established in 1923, included support for medical research on birth control, service as an agency to publish information on contraception, and sponsorship of professional forums on human fertility.

6,228. New England Hospital for Women and Children
Records. 1862-1908. 135 vols.
Open. Card catalog.
Harvard University, Countway Library of Medicine.
Bulk of the records of the Hospital, founded in 1862, consists of maternity, medical, and surgical case records spanning the period from 1862 to 1908. Briefer case histories and notes are found in a 1905 general fee book; in 1908 records of surgical specimens; and in material kept during the Hospital's first years by "visitors of the month" who, representing the board of directors, periodically summarized statistical data on patients. Also included are early rules of the Hospital and an 1892-94 receipt book for patients' room fees.

6,229. Obstetrical Society of Boston
Records. 1861-1940. 6 vols.
Open. No guide.
Harvard University, Countway Library of Medicine.
Constitutions and bylaws, minutes, lists of members, and programs of this medical society founded in 1861. The Society sponsored lunches and dinners at which members discussed cases and reported on research.

6,230. Registry of Nurses
Records. 1880-1914. 21 vols.
Open. No guide.
Harvard University, Countway Library of Medicine.
In 1880 the Massachusetts Medical Society created this Registry to serve as a statewide referral service for recommending home nurses to patients and physicians. Information on a given nurse included name, age, address, marital status, training, experience, specialties, fees charged, whether or not she would eat in the kitchen, and remarks on her ability and character by patients and doctors who had hired her. Some correspondence, photos, and clippings are also included.

6,231. Rock, John
Papers. Ca. 1925- . Ca. 35 cartons.
Open. No guide.
Harvard University, Countway Library of Medicine.
Correspondence, medical records, administrative documents, and publications of Rock (1890-), a physician, including material on his work as director of the Fertility and Endocrine Clinic at the Free Hospital for Women between 1926 and 1956, on his teaching obstetrics and gynecology at Harvard Medical School between 1947 and 1956, and on his work with such organizations as the Planned Parenthood Federation of America.

6,232. Stone, Abraham, and Stone, Hannah (Mayer)
Papers. 1921-59. 14 drawers.
Open. No guide.
Harvard University, Countway Library of Medicine.
Papers of physicians Abraham Stone (1890-1959) and Hannah Stone (1894-1941) include correspondence, drafts of publications, research and clinical notes, financial records, reports of birth control groups and gynecological clinics, conference proceedings, photos, and clippings. Contains information on the Margaret Sanger Research Bureau and the history of the Stones' *Marriage Manual* (published in 1935 but frequently revised and reprinted).

6,233. Museum of Fine Arts Ladies Committee
Records. 1956- . 30 drawers.
Closed. Unpublished guide.
Museum of Fine Arts Library.
Minutes, correspondence, memos, and records concerning members, student members, and events sponsored by the Committee, which was founded by Frances Lawrence to promote Museum membership and to encourage members to participate in activities of this private museum. Over the years, the Committee worked to make the Museum more conscious of its responsibilities to the community at large.

6,234. Families
Collection. 1600s- . 3125 ft. and 200,000 vols.
Open. No guide.
New England Historic Genealogical Society.
Extensive correspondence, diaries, notes, family charts, census and Bible records, papers of genealogists, and other items concern local and family histories and genealogies of families in Vermont, Rhode Island, Connecticut, Massachusetts, Maine, and New Hampshire. The collection provides birth, death, and marriage dates for thousands of New Englanders as well as more personal accounts. Access is by family name or by town through card catalogs and several analytical indexes. Included are ca. three feet of correspondence and diaries of Hannah Adams (1755-1831), an historian and autobiographer.

6,235. Office of Registrar
Records. 1913-67. 2 ft.
Access restricted. Unpublished guide.
Simmons College Archives.
Records of the Simmons College registrar consist of student rosters, which include academic and family background, academic specializations, withdrawals from Simmons, and reasons for such withdrawals. These records reflect the shift in emphasis at Simmons from vocational to liberal arts education.

6,236. Prince School of Retailing
Records. 1906-46. 6 ft.
Partially restricted. Unpublished guide.
Simmons College Archives.
Originally called the Union School of Salesmanship, the Prince School was founded and

directed by Lucinda Wyman (Smith) Prince in 1905 as a program of the Women's Educational and Industrial Union. The original purpose, to educate Boston shop girls in the practical aspects of sales and business methods, was expanded in 1911 to include training women to teach courses in salesmanship. Consists chiefly of Prince's office files, including correspondence with the National Retail Dry Goods Association, of which she was educational director in 1915; with the Federal Board of Vocational Education; and with other national groups. Also contains records of the Prince School, including minutes of faculty meetings, budgets, correspondence, and student records. The School first became associated with Simmons College in 1911, but it remained autonomous until Prince's death in 1935. A strong advocate of vocational education, Prince also served as director of practice in courses of salesmanship for the Boston Public Schools in 1913 and as executive secretary of the US Food Administration in charge of instruction for conservation in stores in 1917.

6,237. Simmons College Corporation
Records. 1905-13. 2 in.
Open. No guide.
Simmons College Archives.
Minutes and reports of Simmons College Corporation, a college incorporated in 1899 to fulfill the wishes of John Simmons, a Boston merchant who left his fortune to found a college that would enable women to earn an independent livelihood. Minutes of the trustees, some of whom were prominent Boston women, contain discussions about the ways in which women should be educated, about vocational education programs available elsewhere in the US and abroad, and about the types of programs Simmons should offer. The trustees also debated whether women should, in fact, be educated. These minutes are supplemented by minutes of committees and special reports and other material tracing the growth of the College and development of its curriculum. Among these is a report by Sarah Louise Arnold, first dean of the College, on "Reconcilement of Cross Purposes in the Education of Women," an address she delivered before the general session of the National Education Association in 1908.

6,238. Simmons College Department of Nursing
Records. 1902-64. 5 ft.
Open. Unpublished guide.
Simmons College Archives.
The first nurses training was offered at Simmons in 1903 by the school of home economics. The school of public health nursing, which was established in 1918 under the directorship of Anne Harvey Strong, a leader in the field of public health nursing, became the School of Nursing in 1934. Correspondence of Strong and other early faculty members, transcripts of lectures, syllabi and curriculum notes, reports of the School, information about faculty appointments, and records of the National Organization for Public Health Nursing. Strong, who graduated from Bryn Mawr College in 1898 and the Albany Hospital Training School for Nurses in 1906, taught in the Columbia University division of nursing education prior to her work at Simmons. She was assistant secretary to the Rockefeller Foundation committee for the study of nursing education and was a member of other committees and nursing organizations.

6,239. White, Eva (Whiting)
Papers. 1907-74. 5 ft.
Open. Unpublished guide.
Simmons College Archives.
Correspondence, notes, lectures, addresses, articles, subject files, programs, pamphlets, photos, and clippings of White (1885-1974), a social worker, professor, and member of many social welfare organizations, women's groups, and Unitarian organizations. After receiving a BS in social work from Simmons in 1907, White undertook graduate studies in social work at the University of Wisconsin and Columbia University before she returned to Boston, where she served as head worker of the Elizabeth Peabody House from 1909 to 1944, director of training for the War Camp Community Service in 1917, director of the Simmons College school of social work and a professor of social economy from 1922 to 1929, director of the Massachusetts board of education's division of Americanization and immigration from 1927 to 1950, and president of the Women's Educational and Industrial Union in Boston from 1929 to 1952. In addition, she was a nonresident lecturer at Bryn Mawr College from 1917 to 1929 and a member of the visiting committee of the department of sociology at Harvard University from 1931 to 1947. Most of the collection concerns her work at the Elizabeth Peabody House and at Simmons College. The bulk of her correspondence is housed at the Schlesinger Library in Cambridge.

BOXBOROUGH

6,240. Hager, Lucie Caroline Gilson
Papers. Nd. 1 vol. and 2 items.
Open. No guide.
Boxborough Library.
Poems that were printed in various periodicals and a book about the history of Boxborough by [Mrs.] Hager (1853-1911). Also includes a ca. 40-page paper about Hager by Jeanne Kangas.

BREWSTER

6,241. Brewster Ladies Library Association
Records. 1852- . 3 ft. and 2 microfilm reels.
Open. No guide.
Brewster Ladies Library.
Complete sets of annual reports, treasurer's account books, and minutes; charter; bylaws; deeds and other legal documents; correspondence; a history; and photos of the Association, which began in 1852 when a group of Brewster schoolgirls decided to increase the availability of books in town by founding a lending library. Originally housed in rooms donated by its supporters, in 1868 the Library was moved into a separate building constructed to house the books, where it has since remained. In addition to maintaining the Library, the Association sponsored public lectures and educational entertainment. Men were gradually given a role in the Association, first as honorary members in 1867, but the Association and its Library have kept the word "Ladies" to acknowledge their beginnings.

6,242. Dugan, Caro
Papers. Ca. 1870-1940. 1 ft.
Open. No guide.
Brewster Ladies Library.
A resident of Brewster, Dugan (?-1941) wrote fictionalized biography, poetry, and essays for a popular audience. Correspondence, diaries, drafts of publications, photos, and scrapbooks of clippings document her work and life in the town.

BRIGHTON

6,243. Congregation Archives
Records. 1873- . 15 files and 7 cabinets.
Access restricted. Unpublished guide.
Sisters of St. Joseph of Boston.
Financial and other administrative records; correspondence; proceedings; personal files; histories; annals of local convents, schools, and institutions; oral history tapes; photos; scrapbooks; clippings; and memorabilia of the congregation, which was founded in 1873. The primary apostolate of the congregation is education.

BROOKLINE

6,244. McDowell, Anne Elizabeth
Papers. 1807-95. 31 items.
Closed. Unpublished guide.
Brookline Public Library.
Correspondence, photos, and clippings of McDowell (1826-1901), an editor and journalist who founded the *Woman's Advocate,* reportedly the first newspaper owned, published, and edited by a woman; particularly concerned with improving working conditions for women, McDowell also was active in the women's movement. Correspondents include Susan B. Anthony; Amelia Bloomer; Lucretia Mott; Mary Grew, an antislavery agitator and preacher; John Wanamaker, a merchant and advocate for better working conditions for women; and Louis A. Godey, who was publisher of *Godey's Lady's Book,* a periodical written primarily by and for women.

CAMBRIDGE

6,245. Champney, James Wells
Papers. 1838-1904. 5 vols. and 435 items.
Open. No guide.
Forbes Library.
Correspondence, poems, bills and receipts, and printed and other material of Champney (1843-1903), an artist. Includes his 1865-66 diaries, which record activities at the Young Ladies Seminary in Lexington, MA, at which he taught drawing; ca. 150 letters addressed mostly to Champney from his mother Sarah E. (Wells) Champney, his wife Elizabeth (Williams) Champney, his daughter Marie M. (Champney) Humphreys, his cousin Etta Champney, his aunt [Mrs.] Ellen Stanwood, and several other aunts; the 1889 diary of his daughter; and letters to his wife, in some of which correspondents discuss publication of her articles and short stories.

6,246. Blavatsky, Helene Petrovna (Hahn)
Papers. 1885-90. 18 items.
Closed. No guide.
Harvard Divinity School, Andover-Harvard Theological Library.
Correspondence from Blavatsky (1831-91), a theosophist, to a Mr. Judge and a Mr. Bridge.

6,247. Bowen, Georgene Esther
Papers. 1925-74. 2 boxes.
Open. Unpublished guide.
Harvard Divinity School, Andover-Harvard Theological Library.
Correspondence, essay, and articles of Bowen (1898-), a Universalist missionary to Japan, relate to her work in Japan. Also included are her memoirs.

6,248. Dolbee, Cora
Papers. Nd. 57-page item.
Open. No guide.
Harvard Divinity School, Andover-Harvard Theological Library.
Typescript of Dolbee (?-1956), based on old correspondence, concerns the Brook Farm experiment and those who participated in it.

6,249. Dolbee, Cora
Papers. 1855-1930. 1 box.
Open. Unpublished guide.
Harvard Divinity School, Andover-Harvard Theological Library.
Papers of Dolbee (?-1956) consist of

correspondence concerning research and publication, notes, and a manuscript, all of which pertain to the Unitarian Church of Lawrence, KS.

6,250. Fahs, Sophia Blanche (Lyon)
Papers. 1903-68. 3 ft.
Open. Unpublished guide.
Harvard Divinity School, Andover-Harvard Theological Library.
Fahs (1876-) was an editor of children's material for the American Unitarian Association in Boston. Correspondence and subject files relate primarily to her work developing the New Beacon Series in Religious Education.

6,251. Foote, Henry Wilder
Papers. Ca. 1776-1964. 61 boxes.
Open. No guide.
Harvard Divinity School, Andover-Harvard Theological Library.
Correspondence of Foote (1875-1964), a Unitarian minister and professor at the Divinity School, includes letters written by Mary Wilder Foote White between 1839 and 1889 and 1840-86 letters by Margaret Harding White.

6,252. Harvard Street Church Women's Alliance
Records. 1907-24. 1 vol.
Open. Unpublished guide.
Harvard Divinity School, Andover-Harvard Theological Library.
Record book of meetings of a women's group of the Harvard Street Unitarian Church in Cambridge.

6,253. Helvie, Clara Cook
Papers. 1902-25. 1 box.
Open. Unpublished guide.
Harvard Divinity School, Andover-Harvard Theological Library.
Correspondence, notes, and articles of Helvie (1876?-1958), a Unitarian minister.

6,254. Lee Street Church Ladies Charitable Society
Records. 1846-85. 1 box.
Open. Unpublished guide.
Harvard Divinity School, Andover-Harvard Theological Library.
Record books of meetings of a women's group of the Lee Street Unitarian Church in Cambridge.

6,255. Newton Centre Unitarian Church Women's Auxiliary
Records. 1887-89. 1 vol.
Open. No guide.
Harvard Divinity School, Andover-Harvard Theological Library.
Record book of meetings of the women's group of the Church in Newton Centre, MA.

6,256. Smith, Julia Evelina
Papers. 1882. 2 items.
Open. No guide.
Harvard Divinity School, Andover-Harvard Theological Library.
Letters of Smith (1792-1886), a Connecticut suffragist, to William Ladd Ropes.

6,257. Tuckerman School
Records. 1910-33. 9 items.
Open. Unpublished guide.
Harvard Divinity School, Andover-Harvard Theological Library.
The Unitarian School was established in Boston to train women to be religious educators. Checkbooks, account book of the students' house, guest book, record book of the School Association of faculty and students, and photos and a scrapbook containing printed material all relate to activities and programs at the School.

6,258. Unitarian Sunday School Society
Records. 1826-1962. 3 ft.
Open. Unpublished guide.
Harvard Divinity School, Andover-Harvard Theological Library.
Record books, correspondence, scrapbooks, and clippings of the Society, founded in 1827, pertain to religious education. Both men and women were members of the Society.

6,259. Crabtree, Charlotte "Lotta" Mignon
Papers. 1877-1935. 9 ft. (ca. 2000 items).
Open. Unpublished guide.
Harvard Law School Library.
Papers arising from probate of the will of Crabtree (1847-1924), an actress and comedienne who became a multimillionaire from investing her money in urban land and properties. Collection primarily consists of biographical material and legal documents which the defense assembled to prove, successfully, that despite some eccentricities, Crabtree was a shrewd, level-headed businesswoman to the end of her life. Carlotta (Crabtree) Cockburn, who claimed to be Crabtree's niece and daughter of Crabtree's brother Jack Crabtree and Annie Leopold, and Ida May Blankenburg, who claimed to be Crabtree's illegitimate daughter, both contested the will on the grounds that Crabtree had been incompetent when she made it. Correspondence between Crabtree and members of her family; interviews with her friends; playbills and reviews of her performances; biographical data; material relating to bank accounts, investments, real estate holdings and transactions, and litigations; drafts of her will and its codicils; research notes; transcripts of legal testimony; briefs; scrapbooks; clippings; and other documents. Files on Cockburn contain information on the position of women in Tombstone, AZ, during the early 1880s; legal material on marriage, legitimacy, and adoption; and evidence for the court of Cockburn's moves from Arizona to California, Missouri, and west again. Files on Blankenburg show that she was found to be an imposter and served four months in jail for perjury.

6,260. Glueck, Sheldon, and Glueck, Eleanor (Touroff)
Papers. 1911-72. 50 ft.
Open. Unpublished guide.
Harvard Law School Library.
Papers of Sheldon Glueck (1896-), a Law School professor, and of his wife Eleanor Glueck (1898-1972), a research criminologist, relate to their joint research and co-authorship of works on juvenile delinquency. Correspondence; diaries; drafts of published and unpublished books, articles, and speeches; notes; bibliographies; tables; reports; minutes of meetings; press releases; clippings; and other items. From 1925 until 1974 Sheldon Glueck was director of a Law School project on the causes, treatment, and prevention of juvenile delinquency. Serving as his research assistant from 1930 to 1953, Eleanor Glueck became research associate and then in 1966 codirector of the project. Collection also pertains to professional associations and meetings the Gluecks participated in concerning mental illness and mental health, social welfare, child psychiatry, delinquency, crime, and penal law. Also contains Eleanor Glueck's diary of a trip she and her husband took to Japan in 1960 and papers of their daughter Anitra Joyce (Glueck) Rosberg (1925-56), a poet, including manuscripts of all of Rosberg's published poems and some unpublished poems, correspondence, and biographical material.

6,261. Holmes, Jr., Oliver Wendell
Papers. 1715-1967. 70 ft.
Access restricted. Unpublished guide.
Harvard Law School Library.
Correspondence, diaries, biographical and family material, and other papers of Holmes (1841-1935), a teacher, attorney, and judge. Includes research material gathered by professor Mark De Wolfe Howe for his writings on Holmes and his editions of selected Holmes correspondence, including Holmes's Civil War letters and diary. Also included is a travel diary of Holmes's wife Fanny Bowditch (Dixwell) Holmes for the summer of 1874, which she and her husband spent in England and on the Continent on a delayed honeymoon; she records in detail observations on the social, literary, and art scene in London. A number of ink sketches she made are interspersed in the text, and menus, lists of invitations, and embroidery patterns she copied are appended. Collection also contains some of her correspondence, photos of her and her sisters, and April Fool's drawings she made for her husband each year.

6,262. James, Eldon Revare
Papers. 1899-1935. Ca. 500 items.
Open. Unpublished guide.
Harvard Law School Library.
Correspondence, diaries, manuscripts of writings, and other papers of James (1875-1949), an attorney, professor of law, law school administrator, and international law expert who became judge of the Supreme Court of Siam, relate to his work as foreign affairs advisor to the Siamese government between 1918 and 1923. His wife Phila S. James lived with him in Siam during these years and accompanied him on diplomatic missions he undertook for the Siamese government to Paris in 1919 and to London in 1921. In her journal letters to her mother and other close relatives in the US, she describes in detail daily life in Bangkok, social engagements and official events, the diplomatic community, and the native scene. Also includes a diary for 1921 to 1925 in which Phila James recorded the weather, family matters, social engagements, and information about recitals she gave and musical productions she organized in Siam.

6,263. Van Waters, Miriam
Papers. 1924-31. 11 ft.
Open. Unpublished guide.
Harvard Law School Library.
Correspondence, memoranda, notes, transcripts of interviews, case histories, statistical summaries, reports, and printed matter of Van Waters (1887-1974), a psychologist, penologist, penal administrator, and author. The papers concern her participation in the Harvard Survey of Crime and Criminal Justice in Greater Boston and her work as a consultant to the National Commission on Law Observance and Enforcement. Van Waters directed the Survey's inquiry into the process of handling juvenile delinquents under 17 years of age in courts, schools, and social agencies, as well as preventive measures and community aspects of juvenile delinquency, including public opinion. As a consultant to the Commission, she directed a study, made under the auspices of the Commission and the White House Conference on Child Health and Protection, of child offenders in the federal system of justice and of the problems they pose for the states; these files contain information on investigations made in individual institutions, social agencies, and court systems that handle juvenile delinquents.

6,264. Advisor for Harvard Wives
Records. 1943-67. 53 vols.
Access restricted. No guide.
Harvard University Archives.
Correspondence, notebooks, reports, petty cashbook, registration cards, and other records of the Advisor, who was originally designated the Advisor for Veterans' Wives.

6,265. Associations of Women at Harvard
Records. 1894- . 22 vols.
Access restricted. No guide.
Harvard University Archives.
Lyman House, the Harvard Teas Association, and

the Harvard Neighbors were groups primarily composed of wives of Harvard faculty members. Minutes of meetings, financial reports and records, correspondence, lists of members, and other records.

6,266. Birkhoff, George David
Papers. 1902-46. 41 vols.
Access restricted. Listing.
Harvard University Archives.
Papers of Birkhoff (1884-1944), a professor of mathematics, include some correspondence of his wife Margaret (Grafius) Birkhoff (1885-1973).

6,267. Bond, William Cranch, and Bond, George P.
Papers. 1845-72. 8 vols.
Open. Listing.
Harvard University Archives.
William Bond (1789-1859) was the father of George Bond (1825-65); both men were astronomers. Included are a biography of the two by George Bond's daughter Elizabeth Bond, family letters, and other items.

6,268. Cabot, Richard Clarke
Papers. 1888-1934. 199 vols.
Access restricted. Unpublished guide.
Harvard University Archives.
Correspondence and other papers of Ella (Lyman) Cabot (1866-1934), a person prominent in the field of education and wife of Richard Clarke Cabot (1868-1939), a Harvard professor and physician.

6,269. Cannon, Annie Jump
Papers. Nd. 1 item.
Open. No guide.
Harvard University Archives.
Biographical material of Cannon (1863-1941), an astronomer.

6,270. Committee on Admission of Women to the Divinity School
Records. 1893. 1 item.
Open. No guide.
Harvard University Archives.
Report to the Overseers of Harvard on the activities of the Committee.

6,271. Committee on Admitting Women to the Medical School
Records. 1867-78. 2 vols.
Open. No guide.
Harvard University Archives.
Report on the activities of the Committee, one of which is addressed to the Corporation of Harvard University, the other to the Overseers.

6,272. Committee on Examinations for Women
Records. 1874-81. 2 vols.
Open. No guide.
Harvard University Archives.
Report to the Faculty of Arts and Sciences on activities of the Committee and sample applications for taking the exam.

6,273. Committee on Instruction and Degrees at Radcliffe College
Records. 1900?. 1 item.
Open. No guide.
Harvard University Archives.
Report of the Committee to the Faculty of Arts and Sciences.

6,274. Committee on Relations with Radcliffe College
Records. 1898-99. 2 items.
Open. No guide.
Harvard University Archives.
Recommendations of the majority of the Committee and a Committee report to the Overseers of Harvard.

6,275. Committee on the Harvard-Radcliffe Relationship
Records. 1970. 1 item.
Open. No guide.
Harvard University Archives.
Report of the Committee to the Corporation of Harvard University.

6,276. Committee on the Status of Women in the Faculty of Arts and Sciences
Records. 1970-71. 2 ft.
Closed. Listing.
Harvard University Archives.
Records of the Committee, established in 1970, include a report to the faculty and material of Committee chairperson Barbara Solomon.

6,277. Day, Mary Anna
Papers. Nd. 1 item.
Open. No guide.
Harvard University Archives.
A sketch of the life of Day (1852-1924), a librarian at the Gray Herbarium of Harvard University for 31 years, was written by B. L. Robinson.

6,278. Eliot, Charles William
Papers. 1869-1926. 370 vols.
Open. Unpublished guide.
Harvard University Archives.
Official correspondence, addresses, articles, and clippings of Eliot (1834-1926), president of Harvard University from 1869 to 1909. Includes letters about the education of women, the founding of Radcliffe College, and the relation of women to Harvard.

6,279. Eliot, Samuel Atkins
Papers. 1817-61. 12 vols.
Open. Listing.
Harvard University Archives.
Papers of Eliot (1798-1862), treasurer of Harvard College and mayor of Boston from 1837 to 1839, include a memory sketch of him and his wife Mary Eliot by their oldest daughter Mary (Eliot) [Mrs. Charles E.] Guild.

6,280. Fleming, Williamina "Mina" Paton (Stevens)
Papers. 1905-09. 3 vols.
Open. Listing.
Harvard University Archives.
An astronomer, [Mrs. James Orr] Fleming (1857-1911) was curator of astronomical photos in the Harvard College Astronomical Observatory. Correspondence, scrapbook of clippings, publications, and reference material.

6,281. Forbes, Edward Waldo
Papers. 1878-1963. 26 boxes.
Access restricted. Unpublished guide.
Harvard University Archives.
Correspondence, poetry, writings, speeches, and other papers of Forbes (1873-1969), who was director of the Fogg Art Museum at Harvard. Includes correspondence of various Forbes and Emerson family women.

6,282. Glueck, Sheldon, and Glueck, Eleanor (Touroff)
Papers. Nd. 4 vols.
Access restricted. Listing.
Harvard University Archives.
Best known for their work in juvenile delinquency, the Gluecks were joint researchers in criminology; Sheldon Glueck was a professor of law at the Harvard Law School and Eleanor Glueck (1898-1972) was a research associate. Publications and reference material.

6,283. Gray, Asa
Papers. 1840-92. 3 vols.
Open. Listing.
Harvard University Archives.
Included with the papers of Gray (1810-88), professor of natural history at Harvard and curator of the Harvard Botanic Garden, are family letters, 1840-52, of his wife Jane Lathrop (Loring) Gray (?-1909).

6,284. Greenough, Chester Noyes
Papers. 1900-38. 18 vols.
Open. Listing.
Harvard University Archives.
Papers of Greenough (1874-1938), a professor of English at Harvard University and dean of Harvard College from 1921 to 1927, include correspondence of his wife Ruth Hornblower Greenough pertaining to her biography of him and a copy of the biography, which was published in 1940.

6,285. Harvard College Observatory
Records. Ca. 1845-1956. 300 vols.
Open. Listing.
Harvard University Archives.
Fairly complete records of the Observatory, founded to conduct astronomical research, include correspondence and other material documenting the work of Annie Jump Cannon (1863-1941), Cecilia (Payne) Gaposchkin, Williamina "Mina" Paton (Stevens) Fleming (1857-1911), Henrietta Swan Leavitt (1868-1921), and others at the Observatory.

6,286. Harvard-Radcliffe Student Organizations and Clubs
Records. Ca. 1880- . No size given.
Access restricted. Listing.
Harvard University Archives.
Minutes, correspondence, publications, and other records of Harvard organizations and clubs, many of which included women after Radcliffe College was founded.

6,287. Harvard University Nursery School
Records. 1944-51. 6 vols.
Open. No guide.
Harvard University Archives.
Account books, correspondence, forms, and other records of the School, which was in operation from 1944 to 1951.

6,288. Harvardevens
Records. 1938-51. 14 vols.
Access restricted. Listing.
Harvard University Archives.
Harvardevens Village was housing at Fort Devens in Ayer, MA, for married Harvard students who were veterans. Correspondence of the resident manager, journal, clinic records, sales records, and material pertaining to the swap shop, kindergarten, and nursery school.

6,289. Housing Office Files and Hunneman and Company
Records. 1942-51. Ca. 50 boxes.
Access restricted. No guide.
Harvard University Archives.
Succeeding the Housing Office, the Company became agent for the University in 1947 in matters relating to the housing of married students. Correspondence, applications for temporary housing, material on apartments available, lists of tenants and waiting lists for Harvardevens Village, forms, and other items.

6,290. Jordan, Wilbur Kitchener
Papers. 1943-59. 18 vols.
Access restricted. Listing.
Harvard University Archives.
Jordan (1902-), a professor of history and political science, was president of Radcliffe College. Correspondence and other material pertaining to his appointment to and resignation from the presidency are included with items concerning women students and Radcliffe.

6,291. Lowell, Abbott Lawrence
Papers. 1909-33. 405 boxes.
Access restricted. Unpublished guide.
Harvard University Archives.
Personal and presidential correspondence, notebooks, speeches, lectures, and other papers of Lowell (1856-1943), president of Harvard University between 1909 and 1933, contain information on the relation of women to Harvard.

6,292. Magruder, Rosalie S.
Papers. 1920-49. 1 vol.
Open. No guide.
Harvard University Archives.
Reminiscences of Magruder, executive secretary of the Harvard Student Record Office from 1920 to 1949, concern her work at Harvard.

6,293. Massachusetts Commission to Study the Question of the Support of Dependent Minor Children of Widowed Mothers
Records. 1912. 1 box.
Open. No guide.
Harvard University Archives.
Minutes and correspondence of the Commission collected by Robert Franz Foerester, a Harvard professor of social ethics.

6,294. Memorial Church Women's Association
Records. 1955-62. 1 item.
Access restricted. Listing.
Harvard University Archives.
Miscellany of the Association.

6,295. Mises, Hilda (Geiringer) von
Papers. 1914-73. 24 boxes.
Open. Listing.
Harvard University Archives.
Hilda Geiringer (1893-1973), a professor of mathematics at Wheaton College, was also the wife of Richard von Mises (1883-1953), a professor of applied mathematics at Harvard. Correspondence, manuscripts of writings, notebooks, lecture notes, speeches, and reprints.

6,296. Pease, Arthur Stanley
Papers. 1914-44. 5 vols.
Access restricted. Listing.
Harvard University Archives.
Papers of Pease (1881-1964), a professor of classics and past president of Amherst College, include a 1944 diary of his wife Henrietta (Faxon) Pease (?-1951) and a 1914 list of visitors to their home.

6,297. Peirce, Jr., Benjamin Osgood
Papers. 1834-1971. 26 vols.
Open. Listing.
Harvard University Archives.
Papers of Peirce (1854-1914), a professor of mathematics and physics, include volumes of early family papers, correspondence of his wife Isabella Turnbull (Landreth) Peirce (?-1937) and of his daughters, and family photos.

6,298. Porter, Arthur Kingsley
Papers. 1863-1957. 50 vols.
Open. Listing.
Harvard University Archives.
Correspondence of Porter (1883-1933), a professor of fine arts; diaries of his wife Lucy Bryant (Wallace) Porter (1876-1962), a photographer; and other family correspondence and photos.

6,299. Presidents of Harvard University
Papers. 1933-71. Ca. 750 boxes.
Closed. Partial index.
Harvard University Archives.
Papers of James Bryant Conant and Nathan Marsh Pusey, who were presidents of Harvard from 1933 to 1953 and from 1953 to 1971, respectively, contain correspondence and other records, some of which concern the education of women.

6,300. Radcliffe College
Records. Nd. 18 vols.
Partially closed. Listing.
Harvard University Archives.
Histories, forms, notices, leaflets, catalogs, clippings, and other reference material on Radcliffe, which was founded in 1879. Because administrative offices of Harvard and Radcliffe have been combined in recent years, archival material on Radcliffe women is increasingly available in various collections of records at the Harvard University Archives. The main body of records is located at the Radcliffe College Archives.

6,301. Schlesinger, Arthur Meier, Sr.
Papers. Ca. 1918-66. 66 boxes.
Access restricted. Listing.
Harvard University Archives.
Personal and professional correspondence, lecture notes, and other papers of Schlesinger (1888-1965), an historian, include information on his early interest in women's history. Also included are letters of condolence to his wife Elizabeth (Bancroft) Schlesinger (1887-1977).

6,302. Sibley, John Langdon
Papers. 1831-85. 109 vols.
Open. Listing.
Harvard University Archives.
Papers of Sibley (1804-85), librarian of Harvard College, include a few publications and reference items pertaining to his wife Charlotte Augusta Langdon (Cook) Sibley (?-1902?).

6,303. Special Committee on the Petitions Regarding Female Education
Records. 1894. 1 item.
Open. No guide.
Harvard University Archives.
Report to the Overseers of Harvard on the activities of the Committee.

6,304. "The Goodies"
Records. Ca. 1770-1800. 1 vol.
Open. Listing.
Harvard University Archives.
Photos and miscellaneous information on the maids at Harvard University, who were known as "The Goodies."

6,305. Winthrop, John
Papers. 1728-89. 17 vols.
Open. Listing.
Harvard University Archives.
Includes diaries, 1779-89, of Hannah (Fayerweather) Tolman Winthrop (?-1790), who was the second wife of astronomer John Winthrop (1714-79), a Harvard professor of mathematics and of natural and experimental philosophy.

6,306. Women at Harvard
Collection. Nd. 1 folder.
Open. No guide.
Harvard University Archives.
Clippings and other material relating to women at Harvard.

6,307. Allen, Lizzie C.
Papers. Ca. 1915. 8 boxes and 274 items.
Open. Catalog card.
Harvard University, Farlow Library.
Papers of Allen, a botanical illustrator, consist of her watercolor drawings of mushrooms and fungi; lists and notes including keys, which give the characteristics used to identify these plants in the field and in the laboratory; correspondence; photos; and reprints by Gertrude S. Burlingham.

6,308. Blackford, Eliza Beulah
Papers. 1898-1934. 12 boxes and 2 vols.
Open. No guide.
Harvard University, Farlow Library.
A Boston artist, scientist, and botanical illustrator, Blackford specialized in drawing mushrooms and other fungi. Her research papers consist of correspondence, drafts of technical papers, watercolor drawings and photos of fungi, and spore prints of mushrooms. Also included are notes and notebooks which record her readings in botanical literature and her study of specimens in the field and in the laboratory.

6,309. Farlow, William Gilson
Papers. 1863-1919. 135 vols.
Open. Partial index.
Harvard University, Farlow Library.
Correspondence on botanical topics of Farlow (1844-1919), a botanist, includes letters with such botanists and women interested in botany as Floretta A. Curtiss, Emily L. Gregory, Sarah Eliza Sigourney (Cushing) Tuckerman, and Elizabeth (Knight) Britton.

6,310. Gray Herbarium Historic Letters
Collection. 1800-1952. 14,820 items.
Open. Authors list.
Harvard University, Gray Herbarium, Library.
Correspondence to Asa Gray (1810-88), a botanist, and to his successors in botany at Harvard are often highly technical in their treatment of botanical topics, especially taxonomy. Correspondents represented by more than nine letters include Kate Barnes, Mary Katherine Curran Brandegee, Elizabeth Bridge, Elizabeth (Knight) Britton, Sarah Paxen Cooper, Kate Furbish, Isabella (Batchelder) James, Emily O. Pelton, Mary O. Rust, Anna Stout, and Mary Treat.

6,311. Gray, Jane Lathrop (Loring)
Collection. 1799-1898. 5 vols.
Open. Item listing.
Harvard University, Gray Herbarium, Library.
Gray (1821-1909) is best known as the biographer of her husband Asa Gray and as editor of his letters. Scrapbooks she compiled contain source material for a history of botany, with correspondence or samples of writings, biographical notes, and portraits of each botanist represented, many of whom were American.

6,312. Women in Astronomy
Collection. Ca. 1880s-1930s. No size given.
Access restricted. No guide.
Harvard University, Harvard College Observatory.
Original research data notebooks and photos of women, posed individually and in groups, who played a large part in astronomical research at the Observatory, which was founded in ca. 1845. Other material pertaining to the work of these women is held at the Harvard University Archives.

6,313. American Board of Commissioners for Foreign Missions
Records. 1812-1960. Ca. 700,000 vols.
Partially restricted. Unpublished guide.
Harvard University, Houghton Library.
Records of the Board include reports from missionaries to the Boston headquarters of the ABCFM, correspondence between missionaries and headquarters, and biographical information. Also includes records of the ABCFM's women's board.

6,314. King, Carol (Weiss)
Papers. 1932-39. Ca. 18 in.
Open. No guide.
Harvard University, Littauer Library, Industrial Relations and Manpower Collection.
Papers of King (1895-1952), a New York City lawyer, relate to her work as secretary of the International Juridical Association. Topically arranged briefs, notes, correspondence, reports, and telegrams contain extensive information about civil rights, police violence, and the right to picket; about such labor matters as yellow dog contracts, sitdown strikes, and injunctions against strikers; and about specific cases, such as the case brought by the Cinderella Theatre Company against Sign

Workers' Local No. 591 in Detroit in 1934 and the coal miners' strike in Bell and Harlan counties in Kentucky during 1932.

6,315. National Women's Trade Union League
Records. Ca. 1920-50. Ca. 8 ft.
Open. No guide.
Harvard University, Littauer Library, Industrial Relations and Manpower Collection.
Some correspondence of the League, a labor organization that existed between 1903 and 1955, is included with press releases, mimeographed material, conference proceedings, pamphlets, government reports, clippings, and union and trade journals, which seem to have comprised part of the League's reference and research files. Arranged topically, the material is particularly extensive on life, group, health, and unemployment insurance; on legislation regarding wages, hours, and the Industrial Recovery Act of 1935; on the farm, steel, automobile, and shoe industries; and on strikes of miners, airline pilots, and garment workers. Included are detailed files concerning textile workers' strikes in Passaic, NJ, in 1926, in New Bedford, MA, in 1928, in Kenosha, WI, during 1928 and 1929, and in Danville, VA, during 1930 and 1931.

6,316. Agassiz
Papers. 1836-1910. 14 ft.
Open. Unpublished guide.
Harvard University, Museum of Comparative Zoology.
Correspondence, diaries, scientific notes, drawings, photos, and clippings of Louis Agassiz (1807-73), a Swiss geologist and naturalist; of his son Alexander Agassiz (1835-1910); and of their associates. Includes items of female members of the family. Also included are records of the Museum, which was founded in 1859 by Louis Agassiz and after his death in 1873 directed by Alexander Agassiz; these contain material on the Penikese Summer School, which was attended by women school and college teachers in 1873 and 1874, and correspondence of Alexander Agassiz's secretary Elizabeth Hannah Clark.

6,317. Brewster, William
Papers. 1865-1919. 26 ft.
Open. Unpublished guide.
Harvard University, Museum of Comparative Zoology.
An ornithologist, Brewster (1851-1919) was a member of the bird department at the Museum from 1883 to 1919. Correspondence, diaries, journals, scientific notes, drawings, photos, and clippings contain information on the developing role of women in ornithology and in ornithological publications and organizations.

6,318. Bryant, Elizabeth Bangs
Papers. Nd. 14 items.
Open. No guide.
Harvard University, Museum of Comparative Zoology.
Correspondence, notebooks, manuscripts of papers, and drawings of Bryant, an arachnologist.

6,319. Deichmann, Elizabeth
Papers. Nd. 17.5 ft.
Open. No guide.
Harvard University, Museum of Comparative Zoology.
Correspondence and photos of Deichman (1896-1975), assistant curator of invertebrates at the Museum from 1930 to 1942 and then curator of invertebrates until 1961.

6,320. Edinger, Tilly
Papers. Nd. 5.5 cu.ft.
Open. No guide.
Harvard University, Museum of Comparative Zoology.
A paleontologist, Edinger (1897-1967) specialized in the development of the vertebrate brain. Correspondence, scientific notes, and photos.

6,321. Museum Manuscripts
Collection. 1860-1940. 44 ft.
Open. Unpublished guide.
Harvard University, Museum of Comparative Zoology.
Correspondence, diaries, journals, scientific notes, field notes, departmental records, drawings, photos, and clippings of individuals associated with the Museum include items of Annie Trumbull Slosson, an author and naturalist; Mary Jane Rathbun, a zoologist who worked at the US National Museum; Elvira Wood, an echinodermologist; Eleanor Omerod, a British entomologist; Emily A. Smith, an entomologist; and Helene Mary Robinson, secretary to Museum of Comparative Zoology director Thomas Barbour.

6,322. Robinson, Helene Mary
Papers. Nd. 1 ft.
Open. No guide.
Harvard University, Museum of Comparative Zoology.
Correspondence, reminiscences, and photos of Robinson (?-1976), secretary to Thomas Barbour, who was Museum director from 1927 to 1946.

6,323. Accessions Cards
Collection. 1866- . Ca. 7 ft.
Open. No guide.
Harvard University, Peabody Museum of Archaeology and Ethnology.
Card files on artifacts accessioned by the Museum since its founding are arranged alphabetically by name of collector. Cards for Adela C. Breton, for example, pertain to artifacts she sent the Museum between 1896 and 1915 in connection with her work in Mexico; on Alice Cunningham Fletcher, material from her studies of ethnology of the Sioux Indians between 1882 and 1898; on Zelia Nuttall, items reflecting her fieldwork in Mexico between 1888 and 1926; on Doris Zemurray [Mrs. Roger T.] Stone, pottery she sent from Central America between 1937 and 1952; and on Cordelia Adelaide Studley, human osteology specimens she collected between 1881 and 1886.

6,324. Bowditch, Charles Pickering
Papers. 1893-1920. 4 cartons and 3 boxes.
Open. Contents lists.
Harvard University, Peabody Museum of Archaeology and Ethnology.
Correspondence, field notes, and drafts of papers of Bowditch (1842-1921), an anthropologist, including letters from Adela C. Breton and correspondence with Alice Cunningham Fletcher on the direction the Archaeological Institute of America ought to take in its interest in American sites. The Institute was primarily devoted to classicist archaeology.

6,325. Carnegie Institution of Washington
Records. Ca. 1909-50s. 4 cabinets.
Open. Card index.
Harvard University, Peabody Museum of Archaeology and Ethnology.
Scientific material generated during the collaboration of the Institution, founded in 1902, with the Peabody Museum on archaeological sites in Yucatan and other areas of Mexico. A few administrative records, correspondence, field notes, drawings of sites and artifacts, and drafts of reports. Includes notes and drawings by anthropologists involved in the project, among them Anna Chowning, Fanny Denison, Jane Jennings, Tatiana Proskowiakoff, Anna O. Shepard, and Laura Wiggins.

6,326. Nuttall, Zelia
Papers. 1886-1914. Ca. 4 in.
Open. No guide.
Harvard University, Peabody Museum of Archaeology and Ethnology.
Papers of Nuttall (1857-1933), an anthropologist, consist of letters to Frederic Ward Putnam and drafts and proofs of her lectures and publications on the ancient Mexican calendar.

6,327. Studley, Cordelia Adelaide
Papers. 1870s. 1 vol.
Open. No guide.
Harvard University, Peabody Museum of Archaeology and Ethnology.
Notebook of Studley (1855-87), a physical anthropologist whose specialty was human osteology, contains her reading notes on studies of shell heaps. After studying medicine in Boston and Michigan, Studley became a special student at the Peabody Museum in 1881 and worked there as an assistant until 1886.

6,328. Tozzer, Alfred Marston
Papers. 1902-45. Ca. 15 in.
Open. No guide.
Harvard University, Peabody Museum of Archaeology and Ethnology.
Correspondence of Tozzer (1877-1954), an anthropologist, including letters of English anthropologist Adela C. Breton, detailing her fieldwork, publications, and work in the International Congress of Americanists.

6,329. Longfellow, Alice Mary
Papers. 1862-1928. 15 ft.
Open. Unpublished guide.
Longfellow National Historic Site.
Correspondence, account books, financial papers, notes, essays, and family photos of [Miss] Longfellow (1850-1928), daughter of Frances E. A. Longfellow and poet Henry Wadsworth Longfellow, a philanthropist, and a founder and trustee of Radcliffe College. Alice Longfellow's particular interests were private and public education, American history, and foreign travel. She and her father entertained many American and European writers, musicians, and artists at the Longfellow home in Cambridge. Their visitors included Ralph Waldo Emerson, Nathaniel Hawthorne, Harriet Beecher Stowe, Edwin Booth, Sarah Orne Jewett, Mark Twain, Charles Dickens, Jenny Lind, the Russian anarchist Mikhail Bakunin, William Makepeace Thackeray, Henry Ford, and Thomas Edison.

6,330. Longfellow Family
Papers. 1700-1945. 16 ft.
Open. No guide.
Longfellow National Historic Site.
Family correspondence, diaries, household account books, scrapbooks, and photos include material of Zilpah (Wadsworth) Longfellow (1788-1851), mother of poet Henry Wadsworth Longfellow and wife of lawyer and congressman Stephen Longfellow; Mary (Longfellow) Greenleaf (1816-1902) and Anne (Longfellow) Pierce (1810-1901), sisters of the poet; and Anne (Longfellow) Thorpe (1855-1934) and Edith (Longfellow) Dana (1853-1915), daughters of the poet. Their papers reflect their thoughts on travel, home economy, and social life.

6,331. Longfellow, Frances "Fanny" Elizabeth (Appleton)
Papers. 1825-61. 5 ft.
Open. No guide.
Longfellow National Historic Site.
A Boston socialite, Longfellow (1817-61) was the daughter of textile manufacturer Nathan Appleton, wife of poet Henry Wadsworth Longfellow, and mother of six children; she also was a literary and art critic. Correspondence, diaries, journals, sketchbooks, and scrapbooks. Her correspondents included Boston and European literati. In 1847 she became the first woman in America to be given ether during childbirth.

6,332. Women at MIT
Collection. 1871- . 10 cu.ft.
Open. No guide.
Massachusetts Institute of Technology Historical Collections.
Incorporated in 1861 as a school for the study of

science and engineering, MIT held its first classes in 1865, admitted its first woman student in 1871, and graduated its first woman student in 1873. Correspondence, financial records, minutes, statistics, surveys, news releases, pamphlets, newsletters, photos, clippings, and other records document the role of women at MIT as students in dormitories, laboratories, and classrooms; as members of sororities, honorary societies, study groups, and clubs; as alumnae; and as subjects of study by committees and historians. Includes extensive files and biographical information on individual students, among them Ellen Henrietta (Swallow) Richards, who was MIT's first woman graduate; Katharine D. McCormick; and Florence Luscomb.

6,333. McCormick, Katharine (Dexter)
Papers. 1820-1964. 3 ft.
Open. No guide.
Massachusetts Institute of Technology, Institute Archives and Special Collections.
A member of the MIT class of 1904, [Mrs. Stanley] McCormick (1875-1967) was a feminist and philanthropist. Correspondence with family and friends, some of whom were feminists; lecture notebooks she kept during her student days; notes on Dexter family genealogy; legal papers and drafts of her will; portfolios of family photos; and clippings.

6,334. Office of the President: Richards, Ellen Henrietta (Swallow)
Records. 1907-24. 28 items.
Open. No guide.
Massachusetts Institute of Technology, Institute Archives and Special Collections.
[Mrs. Robert Hallowell] Richards (1842-1911) was a chemist, professor, and first president of the American Home Economics Association. Letters she wrote while she was a faculty member at MIT are addressed to MIT administrators and concern ventilation and pure water, women students at MIT, and the Association. Also includes correspondence about her death, a resolution passed by the faculty concerning her service to the Institute, and a transcript of an interview Richards conducted with Margaret E. Dayton [Mrs. Jackson L.] Stinson, who was hired as a chemistry assistant at MIT in 1865 becoming the first woman employee at the institution. Stinson held the chemistry assistant's position until 1911. In the interview the two women talk about their experiences as women and as associates of the MIT chemistry department.

6,335. Oral History Project on Women Scientists and Engineers
Oral history. 1976- . 80 tapes and 9 items.
Partially restricted. Table of contents.
Massachusetts Institute of Technology, Institute Archives and Special Collections.
Project interviews examine the life histories of nine women scientists and engineers. During 60 hours of interviews, the women's early home environments, school and research experiences, roles as wives and mothers, and views on the special problems confronting women in science and engineering are explored. In addition to the interview transcripts, the collection includes selected copies of the women's publications, tapes of meetings and forums on women scientists and engineers, and other documents. The interviewees were Mildred S. Dresselhaus, Ellen Henderson, Christina Jansen, Christine Jones, Vera Kistiakowsky, Nancy Kopell, Lisa Steiner, Giuliana Tesoro, and Sheila Widnall.

6,336. Recombinant DNA Controversy
Collection. 1972- . 6.5 ft., 200 tapes, and 45 transcripts.
Open. Unpublished guide.
Massachusetts Institute of Technology, Institute Archives and Special Collections.
This collection was organized under the direction of MIT professor Charles Weiner to document the controversy surrounding recombinant DNA, a form of genetic engineering. The collection covers the development of policies for this technique at the local, state, federal, and international levels. Includes interviews with various women who played a significant role in the controversy, including Maxine Singer, a biochemist at the National Institutes of Health; Elizabeth Kutter, a phage biologist at Evergreen State College in Olympia, WA; Janet Mertz, a molecular biologist at the University of Wisconsin; Jane Setlow, a molecular biologist at Brookhaven National Laboratory; and Susan Wright, an historian of science at the University of Michigan. Also contains interviews with members of the Cambridge Laboratory Experimentation Review Board, organized in 1976 to examine the possibility of regulating recombinant DNA work in the city, including Sister Mary Lucille Banach, who is a nurse; Constance Hughes, a social worker; Mary Nicoloro, an employee of a commercial firm; and Cornelia Wheeler, a former city councilor. In addition, the collection contains interviews with Barbara Franks, a medical technologist and advisor to the Board; Cambridge city councilors Barbara Ackermann and Saundra Graham; and Artemis Simopoulos, a press officer of the National Academy of Sciences. Correspondence of Singer, Wright, and others, including Lorna Salzman, a spokesperson for Friends of the Earth, an environmental organization, and Lois Miller, a molecular biologist at the University of Idaho, is contained as well. Also includes memoranda, minutes, conference proceedings, hearings transcripts, petitions, briefs, committee rosters, draft reports, a press file, videotapes, and other material.

6,337. Stetson, Harlan True
Papers. Ca. 1920-60. 30 boxes.
Open. File list.
Massachusetts Institute of Technology, Institute Archives and Special Collections.
Papers of Stetson (1885-1964), an astrophysicist, contain correspondence with Ruth Aley about publications and personal news, with Roxanna Wells and Margaret E. Richardson about lectures, with Melinda Alexander about lectures and personal news, with Ann Chapman about radio talk shows, with Mildred Hasbrouk about sunspots, with Mrs. E. D. Roe about a telescope, with Mary Ann Jaeger about business matters, and with Mrs. Carroll Hodge about personal affairs. Also includes some material on Florence May (Brigham) Stetson (?-1956), whom he married in 1912.

6,338. Women at MIT
Finding aid. 1873- . 5 in.
Open. Unpublished guide.
Massachusetts Institute of Technology, Institute Archives and Special Collections.
This card index contains entries for each woman who attended MIT, a school for the study of science and engineering. Incorporated in 1861, the school held its first classes in 1865, admitted its first woman student in 1871, and graduated its first woman student in 1873. For each student enrolled in an undergraduate or graduate degree program, the file gives name, class with which she was affiliated, vital dates, and a reference to the source of information. The sources cited are printed material about MIT, such as graduation lists and the class notes and necrology section of *Tech Review*, an alumni magazine. The Archives houses other material on women students, including theses, technical reports, and other publications.

6,339. Radcliffe College
Records. 1879- . Ca. 1249 ft.
Partially restricted. List.
Radcliffe College Archives.
Archives of this women's college, which was founded in 1879, consist of records of the governing boards; president; administrative vice-president; graduate dean; deans of instruction, college relations, and residence; the Student Government Association; the Alumnae Association; the business, publicity, admissions, registrar, and career planning offices; the Health Center; the library; the Women's Archives, which was later named the Schlesinger Library; the Radcliffe Institute for Independent Study; the Harvard-Radcliffe Program in Business Administration; the College marshall; and Education for Action. Also included are the College's photo and sound archives, special collections, student files, a records survey, Radcliffe president Wilbur K. Jordan's speeches, alumnae special collections and publications, and senior honors theses, as well as material on the Institute on Historical and Archival Management, the fund office, publishing procedures, financial aid, deceased alumnae, and other matters. Collection contains information on Elizabeth Cary Agassiz, Mary Coes, Bernice Cronkhite, Edith Stedman, Helen Keller, and other people who were associated with the College as students or administrators.

6,340. Abbott, Mary Adams
Papers. 1920-58. 1 Hollinger box.
Open. Published and unpublished guides.
Schlesinger Library.
Correspondence, diaries, and journals describe an around-the-world journey taken in the 1920s by [Mrs. Grafton S.] Abbott and her daughter Mary. See Arthur and Elizabeth Schlesinger Library on the History of Women in America, *The Manuscript Inventories and the Catalogs of the Manuscripts, Books and Pictures*, vol. III (Boston: G. K. Hall & Co., 1973).

6,341. Adams, Abigail Smith
Papers. 1808. 3-page item.
Open. Published and unpublished guides.
Schlesinger Library.
Letter from Adams (1744-1818), wife of President John Adams, to her daughter Abigail (Adams) Smith (1765-1813) regarding family life and politics. See Arthur and Elizabeth Schlesinger Library on the History of Women in America, *The Manuscript Inventories and the Catalogs of the Manuscripts, Books and Pictures*, vol. III (Boston: G. K. Hall & Co., 1973).

6,342. Adams, Hannah
Papers. 1795-1820. 2 items.
Open. Published and unpublished guides.
Schlesinger Library.
Letters by Adams (1755-1831), a New England historian and author, provide information about herself and Boston life. See Arthur and Elizabeth Schlesinger Library on the History of Women in America, *The Manuscript Inventories and the Catalogs of the Manuscripts, Books and Pictures*, vol. III (Boston: G. K. Hall & Co., 1973).

6,343. Adkinson, Florence Burlingame
Papers. 1867-1927. 1 Hollinger box.
Open. Published and unpublished guides.
Schlesinger Library.
[Mrs.] Adkinson (1847-1925?) was a journalist and secretary of the Indiana State Board of Agriculture women's department. Correspondence pertaining to the Adkinsons' courtship, marriage, and divorce, as well as to her work on the temperance paper *Sentinel*, on the Chicago *Inter Ocean*, 1881-84, and on the *Woman's Journal*, 1891-1910. Correspondents include Bertha E. Clauson and Alice Stone Blackwell, a close friend. See Arthur and Elizabeth Schlesinger Library on the History of Women in America, *The Manuscript Inventories and the Catalogs of the Manuscripts, Books and Pictures*, vol. III (Boston: G. K. Hall & Co., 1973).

6,344. Adlow, Dorothy
Papers. 1923-64. 1 Hollinger box and 37 vols.
Open. Published and unpublished guides.
Schlesinger Library.
An art critic for 40 years, Adlow (1902-64) worked as critic and journalist for the *Christian Science Monitor* and was the wife of Nicholas Slonimsky. Scrapbooks contain Adlow's articles on American and foreign art and other subjects as well as correspondence, including 23 letters by Marianne Moore. See Arthur and Elizabeth Schlesinger Library on the History of Women in America, *The Manuscript Inventories and the Catalogs of the Manuscripts, Books and Pictures,* vol. III (Boston: G. K. Hall & Co., 1973).

6,345. Advertising Women of New York, Inc.
Records. 1912-70. 1 Hollinger box.
Open. Published and unpublished guides.
Schlesinger Library.
Correspondence, articles, and photos of this club, founded in 1912, that seeks advancement and education of women in advertising. Includes material on consumer work, consumer relations, and activities of the club. See Arthur and Elizabeth Schlesinger Library on the History of Women in America, *The Manuscript Inventories and the Catalogs of the Manuscripts, Books and Pictures,* vol. III (Boston: G. K. Hall & Co., 1973).

6,346. Agassiz, Elizabeth Cabot (Cary)
Papers. 1838-1920. 3 Hollinger boxes and 3 folders.
Open. Published and unpublished guides.
Schlesinger Library.
Agassiz (1822-1907) was first president of Radcliffe College and wife of Louis Agassiz. Correspondence, diaries, other personal papers, and photos reflect her interest in science, education, European travel, and the Cary family. Included is information about the Anderson School of Natural History at Penikese Island, Buzzards Bay, MA; a natural history exhibit she was commended for at the World's Columbian Exposition in Chicago; Radcliffe College; and the Perkins Institute-Kindergarten for the Blind. See Arthur and Elizabeth Schlesinger Library on the History of Women in America, *The Manuscript Inventories and the Catalogs of the Manuscripts, Books and Pictures,* vol. III (Boston: G. K. Hall & Co., 1973).

6,347. Age Center of New England
Records. 1956- . 2 Hollinger boxes.
Open. Published and unpublished guides.
Schlesinger Library.
The Center, which was established in 1955, interviews retired persons and maintains records on reminiscences about their youth. The majority of the collection's 40 interviews and questionnaires are from women and reflect American life and customs since the 1890s. See Arthur and Elizabeth Schlesinger Library on the History of Women in America, *The Manuscript Inventories and the Catalogs of the Manuscripts, Books and Pictures,* vol. III (Boston: G. K. Hall & Co., 1973).

6,348. Aitchison, Beatrice
Papers. 1943-56. 2 folders.
Open. Published and unpublished guides.
Schlesinger Library.
Aitchison (1908-) was director of the US Post Office transportation research department in Washington, DC. Articles regarding technical work done by the department, mimeographed speeches, and printed matter. See Arthur and Elizabeth Schlesinger Library on the History of Women in America, *The Manuscript Inventories and the Catalogs of the Manuscripts, Books and Pictures,* vol. III (Boston: G. K. Hall & Co., 1973).

6,349. Aldrich, Mildred
Papers. 1926. 4 vols. and 1 folder.
Open. Published and unpublished guides.
Schlesinger Library.
[Miss] Aldrich (1853-1928) was an author. Manuscript of "Confessions of a Breadwinner," her autobiography describing American and French social life and customs from the late 1800s to 1926. Manuscript of "The Burial of a Fallen Poet" is also included. See Arthur and Elizabeth Schlesinger Library on the History of Women in America, *The Manuscript Inventories and the Catalogs of the Manuscripts, Books and Pictures,* vol. III (Boston: G. K. Hall & Co., 1973).

6,350. Aldrich, Roseltha
Papers. 1853-56. 5 items.
Open. Published and unpublished guides.
Schlesinger Library.
Certificates of Aldrich (1837-?), a teacher in western Massachusetts, declare her qualified to teach in various districts. See Arthur and Elizabeth Schlesinger Library on the History of Women in America, *The Manuscript Inventories and the Catalogs of the Manuscripts, Books and Pictures,* vol. III (Boston: G. K. Hall & Co., 1973).

6,351. Alexander, Francesca
Papers. 1893. 1 item.
Open. Published and unpublished guides.
Schlesinger Library.
Letter from Alexander (1837-1917), a Boston native who lived most of her life in Italy as a philanthropist and artist. See Arthur and Elizabeth Schlesinger Library on the History of Women in America, *The Manuscript Inventories and the Catalogs of the Manuscripts, Books and Pictures,* vol. III (Boston: G. K. Hall & Co., 1973).

6,352. Alger Family
Papers. 1809-1968. 4 Hollinger boxes.
Access restricted. Published and unpublished guides.
Schlesinger Library.
Correspondence, diaries, financial records, photos, and clippings of seven prominent New England and Pennsylvania families all related by marriage: the Alger, Rodgers, Meigs, Taylor, Jackson, Price, and Hubbell families. Topics include WWI and WWII; politics; US history, particularly the Civil War and Reconstruction; and women as physicians. See Arthur and Elizabeth Schlesinger Library on the History of Women in America, *The Manuscript Inventories and the Catalogs of the Manuscripts, Books and Pictures,* vol. III (Boston: G. K. Hall & Co., 1973).

6,353. Alger, Louisa Jackson
Papers. Ca. 1918-70. 4 Hollinger boxes, 1 carton, and 10 folders.
Partially closed. No guide.
Schlesinger Library.
Correspondence, diaries, memos, manuscripts, reports, minutes, financial records, photos, pamphlets, memorabilia, cookbook, and books of a New England family. Includes correspondence from a stay of Alger (ca. 1900-) in Switzerland, her college themes, and remarks at her 25th Radcliffe reunion. Also contains minutes of the Massachusetts Commission Against Discrimination, material on Sarah Sprague, George Eaton correspondence with his children Hanna and Charles, and correspondence from Rosella Ja Ja, Bea Reiner, Sister Eleanor Lucy, Abby Langdon Alger, Elizabeth Frances Cummings Qualey, E. E. Cummings, Marion Cummings, Esther Forbes, and Robert "Alcy" Frelick.

6,354. Allen, Annie Ware (Winsor)
Papers. 1813-1960s. 18 cartons and 1 oversize package.
Access restricted. No guide.
Schlesinger Library.
Allen (1865-1955) was an educator, founder of the Roger Ascham School in White Plains, NY, active member before her marriage of the Social Reform Club in New York City, and wife of Joseph Allen, a City College of New York mathematics professor. Correspondence, diaries, school records, albums, photos, architectural drawings, and other papers include her writings on education, psychology, and child rearing; correspondence from Leonora O'Reilly, clergyman Henry A. Ware, Jr., and other family members; and Roger Ascham School records containing minutes, correspondence, memos, reports, student records, and curriculum and lesson plans. Three of Allen's siblings also founded schools: Mary P. Winsor (the Mary Winsor School, Boston), Frederick Winsor (the Middlesex School, Concord, MA), and Elizabeth (Winsor) Pearson (cofounder of the Eliot-Pearson School of Child Study, Tufts University, Medford, MA).

6,355. Allen, Corinne Marie (Tuckerman)
Papers. 1896-1927. 1 Hollinger box.
Open. Published and unpublished guides.
Schlesinger Library.
[Mrs. Clarence Emir] Allen (1856-1931) was a leader in social welfare, humanitarian pursuits, and educational reforms in Utah. Correspondence, minutes, and manuscripts regarding Mormonism and polygamy, the National Congress of Mothers, the DAR, birth control, the Utah Federation of Women's Clubs, the GFWC, and the Women's International League for Peace and Freedom. See Arthur and Elizabeth Schlesinger Library on the History of Women in America, *The Manuscript Inventories and the Catalogs of the Manuscripts, Books and Pictures,* vol. III (Boston: G. K. Hall & Co., 1973).

6,356. Allen, Florence Ellinwood
Papers. 1921. 1 item.
Open. Published and unpublished guides.
Schlesinger Library.
Letter from Allen (1884-1966), a judge in Cuyahoga County, Cleveland, concerning the suitability of women as jurors. See Arthur and Elizabeth Schlesinger Library on the History of Women in America, *The Manuscript Inventories and the Catalogs of the Manuscripts, Books and Pictures,* vol. III (Boston: G. K. Hall & Co., 1973).

6,357. Allen, Florence Ellinwood
Papers. 1921-58. 1 Hollinger box, 3 scrolls, and 2 vols.
Open. Published and unpublished guides.
Schlesinger Library.
Allen (1884-1966) was a US Circuit Court of Appeals judge in Ohio. Manuscripts, judicial opinions, photos, and articles contain biographical material and show Allen's views on government. See Arthur and Elizabeth Schlesinger Library on the History of Women in America, *The Manuscript Inventories and the Catalogs of the Manuscripts, Books and Pictures,* vol. III (Boston: G. K. Hall & Co., 1973).

6,358. Almy Family
Papers. 1649-1967. 4 Hollinger boxes and 10 folders.
Open. Published and unpublished guides.
Schlesinger Library.
Family collection centers on Helen Jackson (Cabot) Almy (1856-1938), a prominent Boston area woman who was daughter of a physician and wife of a judge; on her parents Samuel Cabot (1815-85) and Hannah Lowell (Jackson) Cabot (1820-79); and on her six children, including daughters Mary (1883-1967), Helen Jackson (1884-1976), Anna Cabot (1886-), and Elizabeth (1892-). Correspondence, diaries, financial records, genealogical charts, composition book, speeches, poems, examinations, reports, photos, articles, pamphlets, clippings, and other material. Bulk of collection is correspondence between members of the Almy, Jackson, and Cabot families. Along with the diaries, the correspondence also describes daily activities of individual women and the social network among upper-class Boston families. Correspondents include Elizabeth Cary Agassiz,

Charles W. Eliot, Ellen Tucker Emerson, and Ralph Waldo Emerson. Also included are records of the Mothers' Club of Cambridge, which pertain to the establishment between 1899 and 1910 of playgrounds and vacation schools in Cambridge, as well as papers of daughter Helen Jackson, a medical social worker, with material on the Massachusetts Conference on Social Work, civil service in Massachusetts, the Boston Symphony Orchestra, the Mothers' Discussion Club, the Monday Lunch Club, and other organizations. SeeArthur and Elizabeth Schlesinger Library on the History of Women in America, *The Manuscript Inventories and the Catalogs of the Manuscripts, Books and Pictures,* vol. III (Boston: G. K. Hall & Co., 1973).

6,359. American Association of University Women, Boston Branch
Records. 1886-1967. 11 Hollinger boxes, 2 cartons, and 2 folders.
Open. Published and unpublished guides.
Schlesinger Library.
Boston AAUW treasurer's and secretary's records, minutes of board meetings, committee reports, office and membership records, notebook, and scrapbooks include information about committees working on domestic service, education, forestry, peace, war, French orphans, and fellowships. The 1965-67 papers of Anne Thomas are also included. See Arthur and Elizabeth Schlesinger Library on the History of Women in America, *The Manuscript Inventories and the Catalogs of the Manuscripts, Books and Pictures,* vol. III (Boston: G. K. Hall & Co., 1973).

6,360. American Association of University Women, International
Records. 1920-61. 1 Hollinger box.
Open. Published and unpublished guides.
Schlesinger Library.
Annual reports and newsletters reflect the growth and purpose of the AAUW's international organization, founded in ca. 1921. See Arthur and Elizabeth Schlesinger Library on the History of Women in America, *The Manuscript Inventories and the Catalogs of the Manuscripts, Books and Pictures,* vol. III (Boston: G. K. Hall & Co., 1973).

6,361. American Association of University Women, Massachusetts State Division
Records. 1936- . 11 Hollinger boxes, 1 carton, 4 folders, and 5 envelopes.
Open. Published and unpublished guides.
Schlesinger Library.
Reports of the state AAUW board and of committees, annual reports, minutes, notices, correspondence, scrapbook, newsletters, and handbook include fellowship committee records and histories of AAUW branches within Massachusetts. See Arthur and Elizabeth Schlesinger Library on the History of Women in America, *The Manuscript Inventories and the Catalogs of the Manuscripts, Books and Pictures,* vol. III (Boston: G. K. Hall & Co., 1973).

6,362. American Association of University Women, National
Records. 1881-1959. 6 Hollinger boxes.
Open. Published and unpublished guides.
Schlesinger Library.
Records of the national AAUW and of its predecessor, the Association of Collegiate Alumnae, founded in 1882, include committee reports, membership lists, publications, and other material. Much of the collection is Committee on the Status of Women publications describing women's gains in the professions and the struggle toward equality. See Arthur and Elizabeth Schlesinger Library on the History of Women in America, *The Manuscript Inventories and the Catalogs of the Manuscripts, Books and Pictures,* vol. III (Boston: G. K. Hall & Co., 1973).

6,363. American Medical Women's Association
Records. 1961. 1 reel.
Open. Published and unpublished guides.
Schlesinger Library.
Recording of annual meeting in Cleveland of this organization of women physicians founded in 1915. See Arthur and Elizabeth Schlesinger Library on the History of Women in America, *The Manuscript Inventories and the Catalogs of the Manuscripts, Books and Pictures,* vol. III (Boston: G. K. Hall & Co., 1973).

6,364. Ames, Blanche (Ames)
Papers. 1860-1961. 7.5 Hollinger boxes, 3 oversize items, 1 oversize vol., and 1 microfilm reel.
Open. Unpublished guide.
Schlesinger Library.
Ames (1878-1969) was an artist, a suffragist active in the Massachusetts Woman Suffrage Association and the LWV, cofounder and president of the Massachusetts Birth Control League, founder of the Family Welfare Foundation, and a president and member of the board of directors of the New England Hospital in Boston. Correspondence, minutes, annual reports, financial records, photos, and printed pamphlets and articles. Largest portion of the collection concerns the New England Hospital (formerly the New England Hospital for Women and Children) controversy in the 1950s over its continuing existence as a women's Hospital and hiring of male physicians; Ames and other board members attempted to obtain funds to continue the Hospital with female physicians only and to re-open the nurses training school. Also included is material on early 20th-century suffrage in Massachusetts and on birth control in Massachusetts during the 1940s.

6,365. Anderson, Mary
Papers. 1918-64. 4.5 Hollinger boxes and 4 phonotapes.
Open. Published and unpublished guides.
Schlesinger Library.
Anderson (1872-1964) was active in labor unions and director of the US Department of Labor Women's Bureau from 1919 to 1944. Bulk of collection consists of correspondence with labor leaders and others on such topics as equal rights, protective legislation, organization of women workers, and Women's Bureau activities. Includes correspondence and printed material regarding right-wing accusations of communist infiltration of women's organizations and the blacklisting of Anderson and others by the DAR. Tapes contain a memorial service for Anderson with Esther Peterson, Pauline Newman, Ernestine Friedman, Senator Wayne Morse, Frances Perkins, Bill Snitzler, and Bill Wirtz, secretary of labor, as speakers; an interview by Esther Peterson concerning the time from Anderson's immigration to the US through the founding of the Women's Bureau; and 1942 radio speeches in which Anderson discussed women's contributions and value in the war effort, their prewar difficulties obtaining jobs in industry, the types of positions held by women, and equal wages for men and women. See Arthur and Elizabeth Schlesinger Library on the History of Women in America, *The Manuscript Inventories and the Catalogs of the Manuscripts, Books and Pictures,* vol. III (Boston: G. K. Hall & Co., 1973).

6,366. Anderson, Stella (Benson)
Papers. 1923-33. 1 folder.
Open. Published and unpublished guides.
Schlesinger Library.
Correspondence, note, and photo of Anderson (1892-1933), an English author and wife of James O'Gorman Anderson of the Chinese Customs Service, reflect social customs in China. See Arthur and Elizabeth Schlesinger Library on the History of Women in America, *The Manuscript Inventories and the Catalogs of the Manuscripts, Books and Pictures,* vol. III (Boston: G. K. Hall & Co., 1973).

6,367. Andrews, Esther Myers
Papers. 1886-1939. 5 folders.
Open. Published and unpublished guides.
Schlesinger Library.
Andrews (1861-1938) was the first woman member of the Massachusetts Governor's Council. Correspondence, a manuscript report of a 24-hour visit to the Charles Street Jail in Boston, certificates of state appointments, death certificate, and clippings. See Arthur and Elizabeth Schlesinger Library on the History of Women in America, *The Manuscript Inventories and the Catalogs of the Manuscripts, Books and Pictures,* vol. III (Boston: G. K. Hall & Co., 1973).

6,368. Andrews, Fannie Fern (Phillips)
Papers. 1896-1941. 163 Hollinger boxes and 91 vols.
Open. Published and unpublished guides.
Schlesinger Library.
Correspondence, diaries, reports, and articles of Andrews (1867-1950), an authority on international law and the international aspects of education. Andrews founded the American School Peace League in 1908, served as US representative at numerous international conferences, and was instrumental in establishment of the International Bureau of Education. Other topics covered include international peace, Radcliffe College, woman suffrage, the AAUW, and the International Council of Women. See Arthur and Elizabeth Schlesinger Library on the History of Women in America, *The Manuscript Inventories and the Catalogs of the Manuscripts, Books and Pictures,* vol. III (Boston: G. K. Hall & Co., 1973).

6,369. Anonymous: Account Book
Papers. 1832-46. 1 vol.
Open. Published and unpublished guides.
Schlesinger Library.
Household expense book of a family living in the Boston area, containing such items as hair cut, 12 cents, and pew rent, $1.04. See Arthur and Elizabeth Schlesinger Library on the History of Women in America, *The Manuscript Inventories and the Catalogs of the Manuscripts, Books and Pictures,* vol. III (Boston: G. K. Hall & Co., 1973).

6,370. Anonymous: Civil War Soldier's Letter
Papers. 1864. 1 item.
Open. Published and unpublished guides.
Schlesinger Library.
A partial letter to "Dear Wife and Children" contains a Civil War soldier's philosophy and advice to his family. See Arthur and Elizabeth Schlesinger Library on the History of Women in America, *The Manuscript Inventories and the Catalogs of the Manuscripts, Books and Pictures,* vol. III (Boston: G. K. Hall & Co., 1973).

6,371. Anonymous: Notebook
Papers. Nd. 1 vol.
Open. Published and unpublished guides.
Schlesinger Library.
A late 18th-or early 19th-century notebook, probably of English origin and brought to the US, containing recipes and prescriptions for the cure of illnesses. See Arthur and Elizabeth Schlesinger Library on the History of Women in America, *The Manuscript Inventories and the Catalogs of the Manuscripts, Books and Pictures,* vol. III (Boston: G. K. Hall & Co., 1973).

6,372. Anonymous: "The Real and Ideal in Politics"
Papers. Ca. 1884. 1 item.
Open. Published and unpublished guides.
Schlesinger Library.
Incomplete manuscript of "The Real and Ideal in Politics," a play in three acts regarding woman suffrage. See Arthur and Elizabeth Schlesinger

Library on the History of Women in America, *The Manuscript Inventories and the Catalogs of the Manuscripts, Books and Pictures,* vol. III (Boston: G. K. Hall & Co., 1973).

6,373. Anonymous: "Three Old Crows"
Papers. 1870. 3-page item.
Open. Published and unpublished guides.
Schlesinger Library.
Satirical poem "Three Old Crows" pertains to Lucy Stone, Mary Livermore, Julia Ward Howe, and other prominent suffragists. It was written for the Woman Suffrage Convention in Burlington, VT. See Arthur and Elizabeth Schlesinger Library on the History of Women in America, *The Manuscript Inventories and the Catalogs of the Manuscripts, Books and Pictures,* vol. III (Boston: G. K. Hall & Co., 1973).

6,374. Anthony, Susan Brownell
Papers. 1815-1954. 2 Hollinger boxes and 5 folders.
Open. Published and unpublished guides.
Schlesinger Library.
Correspondence, diaries, financial records, family papers, manuscript speeches, photos, pamphlets, and clippings of [Miss] Anthony (1820-1906), women's rights leader and reformer. Includes biographical material and information on her activities for temperance, woman suffrage, abolition, and feminism. Also contains letters from Katharine Anthony regarding her biography of Susan B. Anthony. See Arthur and Elizabeth Schlesinger Library on the History of Women in America, *The Manuscript Inventories and the Catalogs of the Manuscripts, Books and Pictures,* vol. III (Boston: G. K. Hall & Co., 1973).

6,375. Arnold, Mary Ellicott
Papers. 1908-58. 2 Hollinger boxes.
Open. Published and unpublished guides.
Schlesinger Library.
Correspondence, reports, photos, and published articles of Arnold (1876-?) who with Mabel Reed built cooperative housing units for Nova Scotia miners and Newfoundland fishermen and established consumer services for lobster fishermen along the Maine coast. Arnold also farmed in Maine, aided the Indians, and managed cafeterias. See Arthur and Elizabeth Schlesinger Library on the History of Women in America, *The Manuscript Inventories and the Catalogs of the Manuscripts, Books and Pictures,* vol. III (Boston: G. K. Hall & Co., 1973).

6,376. Art Workshop of the Rivington Neighborhood Association
Records. 1894-1959. 6 folders.
Open. Published and unpublished guides.
Schlesinger Library.
The Workshop was established in 1929 as an outgrowth of the College Settlements Association (founded in 1889) but changed its emphasis to creative arts after the College Settlements Association's discontinuance. Minutes of the College Settlement executive board, the steering committee, and the finance committee, and report of the Workshop's first year, which includes a brief history of the College Settlement. See Arthur and Elizabeth Schlesinger Library on the History of Women in America, *The Manuscript Inventories and the Catalogs of the Manuscripts, Books and Pictures,* vol. III (Boston: G. K. Hall & Co., 1973).

6,377. Atwell, Grace Parthenia
Papers. 1886-1944. 5 vols.
Open. Published and unpublished guides.
Schlesinger Library.
Scrapbooks of [Miss] Atwell, a stage actress whose career began in Boston, mainly contain theater programs and clippings about plays in which she performed. See Arthur and Elizabeth Schlesinger Library on the History of Women in America, *The Manuscript Inventories and the Catalogs of the Manuscripts, Books and Pictures,* vol. III (Boston: G. K. Hall & Co., 1973).

6,378. Auerbach Service Bureau for Connecticut Organizations
Records. 1945- . 2 Hollinger boxes.
Open. Published and unpublished guides.
Schlesinger Library.
Annual reports of the Bureau, originally called the Service Bureau for Women's Organizations, which was formed to provide background information and technical training for leaders of various women's organizations. It has expanded to include other than women's groups. See Arthur and Elizabeth Schlesinger Library on the History of Women in America, *The Manuscript Inventories and the Catalogs of the Manuscripts, Books and Pictures,* vol. III (Boston: G. K. Hall & Co., 1973).

6,379. Babcock, Caroline (Lexow), and Hurlburt, Olive E.
Papers. 1906-61. 9 Hollinger boxes.
Open. Published and unpublished guides.
Schlesinger Library.
Correspondence, memo book, articles, and publications of Babcock (1882-) and Hurlburt, who were active in the woman's suffrage movement and the National Woman's Party. Babcock was NWP executive secretary from 1938 to 1945 while Hurlburt worked with the NWP's Michigan branch from 1936 to 1947. Large part of collection deals with the controversy within the NWP between 1938 and 1946, which culminated in a lawsuit in 1947 and a split. Babcock's papers also include material about her work for the Women's Peace Union of the Western Hemisphere, woman's suffrage in New York from 1906 to 1915, movements to abolish conscription and capital punishment, and the campaign for world government. Also included is correspondence with and material about Harriot (Stanton) Blatch and Elinor Byrns. See Arthur and Elizabeth Schlesinger Library on the History of Women in America, *The Manuscript Inventories and the Catalogs of the Manuscripts, Books and Pictures,* vol. III (Boston: G. K. Hall & Co., 1973).

6,380. Backus, Louise Burton (Laidlaw)
Papers. Nd. 12 cartons.
Open. No guide.
Schlesinger Library.
[Mrs. Dana] Backus (1906-) was a leader in the Pan Pacific and Southeast Asia Women's Association and was active in suffrage work. Records of the Pan Pacific and Southeast Asia Women's Association, the UN Association, and the Committee of Correspondence.

6,381. Baker, Maxine Eldridge
Papers. 1963-73. 2 folders.
Open. Unpublished guide.
Schlesinger Library.
A member of the Florida House of Representatives for 10 years, [Mrs.] Baker (1898-) specialized in mental health legislation. Brief summary of Baker's years as a legislator, biographical information, campaign material, and clippings about her work and awards. Included is part of The Florida Mental Health Act, also known as The Baker Act.

6,382. Baldwin, Amelia Muir
Papers. 1809-1960. 9 Hollinger boxes and 3 cartons.
Open. Published and unpublished guides.
Schlesinger Library.
A Boston interior decorator, Baldwin (1876-1960) earned a nationwide reputation for tapestry needlework design. Correspondence, financial ledgers and files, client folders, advertising, design material, samples of materials and order book, photos, and memorabilia primarily concern Baldwin's work as an interior decorator. Also included are papers relating to activities with Friends of the Framingham Reformatory and the W. S. Housing Corp., personal correspondence, and family papers. From 1913 to 1919 Baldwin designed and decorated booths for Boston suffrage bazaars. See Arthur and Elizabeth Schlesinger Library on the History of Women in America, *The Manuscript Inventories and the Catalogs of the Manuscripts, Books and Pictures,* vol. III (Boston: G. K. Hall & Co., 1973).

6,383. Barbour, Louise
Papers. 1917-37. 0.5 Hollinger box.
Open. Unpublished guide.
Schlesinger Library.
Barbour's career was in the telephone industry; during WWI she served as a telephone operator with the Signal Corps in France. Correspondence to the American Telephone and Telegraph Company and to friends, memorandum, telephone directories, mementos of the Signal Corps, and Barbour's article for AT&T's *Bell Quarterly* on women in the telephone industry and in the Signal Corps.

6,384. Barker, Burt Brown
Papers. 1932-45. 1 folder.
Open. Published and unpublished guides.
Schlesinger Library.
Collection of correspondence and photo is formed around a statue commemorating Barker's pioneer mother and pertains to the motivation behind the creation of the "Pioneer Mother" statue, its inscription, and its erection on the campus of the University of Oregon, Eugene. See Arthur and Elizabeth Schlesinger Library on the History of Women in America, *The Manuscript Inventories and the Catalogs of the Manuscripts, Books and Pictures,* vol. III (Boston: G. K. Hall & Co., 1973).

6,385. Barron, Jennie (Loitman)
Papers. 1950-63. 1 folder.
Open. Published and unpublished guides.
Schlesinger Library.
Articles and speeches by Barron (1891-1969), a judge in Massachusetts Superior Court, as well as copies of awards and citations presented to her. See Arthur and Elizabeth Schlesinger Library on the History of Women in America, *The Manuscript Inventories and the Catalogs of the Manuscripts, Books and Pictures,* vol. III (Boston: G. K. Hall & Co., 1973).

6,386. Barton, Clara
Papers. 1870-1906. 4 folders.
Open. Published and unpublished guides.
Schlesinger Library.
Barton (1821-1912) was founder and president of the American National Red Cross. Correspondence from Barton and from her relatives, part of a poem "Have Ye Room?", and portions of a speech. See Arthur and Elizabeth Schlesinger Library on the History of Women in America, *The Manuscript Inventories and the Catalogs of the Manuscripts, Books and Pictures,* vol. III (Boston: G. K. Hall & Co., 1973).

6,387. Batten, Pluma B.
Papers. 1930-56. 22 Hollinger boxes and 3 oversize vols.
Open. Published and unpublished guides.
Schlesinger Library.
[Mrs.] Batten (1894-) was in New Jersey public education. Correspondence, manuscripts, notes, official and committee reports, financial records, minutes, handbooks, scrapbooks, and publications document Batten's career. From 1930 to 1943 she was a New Jersey State Helping Teachers Rural Supervisor and from 1943 to 1956 a member of the Pilesgrove, NJ, Board of Education as well as a supervising principal and superintendent of schools in Woodstown Pilesgrove district. Batten also served as president of the American Federation of Soroptimist Clubs, a professional women's organization for the political and economic advancement of women. Included are manuscripts

and notes for *Jobs for the Over Sixty* and for an AAUW cookbook, the resulting published cookbook, and scrapbooks on the status of women compiled by Batten. See Arthur and Elizabeth Schlesinger Library on the History of Women in America, *The Manuscript Inventories and the Catalogs of the Manuscripts, Books and Pictures,* vol. III (Boston: G. K. Hall & Co., 1973).

6,388. Beam, Lura
Papers. 1900-69. 2.5 Hollinger boxes, 1 carton, 1 oversize vol., and certificates.
Open. No guide.
Schlesinger Library.
Correspondence, 1925-69 diary, manuscripts, articles, scrapbook, diplomas, photos, and clippings concerning Beam (1887-), an author. Collection includes correspondence, drafts, and reviews regarding Beam's books; a 1900 Marshfield, ME, tax list with manuscript entries; printed articles and other material on AAUW art exhibitions and classes from the 1940s and 1950s; volumes of material for a seminar on human relations, entitled "Marriage and Sex Adjustment"; and material on the American Missionary Association, the Association of American Colleges, and the Council of Church Boards of Education, with 1922-23 reports of research.

6,389. Beard, Mary Ritter
Papers. 1935-58. 2 Hollinger boxes and 4 folders.
Open. Published and unpublished guides.
Schlesinger Library.
Beard (1876-1958) was an author and historian. Correspondence and articles, including personal letters from Beard to Luella Gettys Key and letters to Gwladys Jones and others about the World Center for Women's Archives. Articles and other correspondence contain material about the Archives' founding, projects, research suggestions, material sought and received, and final disbanding. See Arthur and Elizabeth Schlesinger Library on the History of Women in America, *The Manuscript Inventories and the Catalogs of the Manuscripts, Books and Pictures,* vol. III (Boston: G. K. Hall & Co., 1973).

6,390. Becker, May Lamberton
Papers. 1927. 1 folder.
Open. Published and unpublished guides.
Schlesinger Library.
Letter and an explanatory note by Becker (1873-1958), an author, editor, and lecturer. See Arthur and Elizabeth Schlesinger Library on the History of Women in America, *The Manuscript Inventories and the Catalogs of the Manuscripts, Books and Pictures,* vol. III (Boston: G. K. Hall & Co., 1973).

6,391. Bedinger, Caroline Bowne (Lawrence)
Papers. 1853-55. 1 vol.
Open. Published and unpublished guides.
Schlesinger Library.
[Mrs. Henry] Bedinger (1827-?), granddaughter of Elizabeth Southgate Bowne, was wife of the US Minister to Denmark. Volume of letters to Bedinger's mother and other relatives describe Danish life in the 1850s. See Arthur and Elizabeth Schlesinger Library on the History of Women in America, *The Manuscript Inventories and the Catalogs of the Manuscripts, Books and Pictures,* vol. III (Boston: G. K. Hall & Co., 1973).

6,392. Beecher and Stowe
Papers. 1798-1956. 17 Hollinger boxes and 5 oversize items.
Open. Published and unpublished guides.
Schlesinger Library.
Papers of a prominent New England family noted for its contributions in the fields of education, religion, humanitarianism, and literature. Correspondence, miscellaneous writings, clippings, and memorabilia. Correspondence from Catharine Esther Beecher (1800-78), Esther Beecher, Eunice White (Bullard) Beecher (1812-97), Harriet (Porter) Beecher (?-1835), Lydia (Beals) Jackson Beecher (1789-1869), Eliza Tyler Stowe (1836-?), Harriet Elizabeth (Beecher) Stowe (1811-96), Harriet Beecher Stowe II (1836-?), and Susan (Munroe) Stowe, much of which contains family news, stories, and comments about the times. Also included is material pertaining to Charlotte (Perkins) Gilman, Isabella (Beecher) Hooker (1822-1907), and other family members, as well as Lyman Beecher Stowe's correspondence and research on Charlotte (Perkins) Gilman and actress Charlotte Cushman. Bulk of the collection pertains to Harriet (Beecher) Stowe, her husband Calvin, and their children; their personal and professional correspondence includes letters from publishers and prominent people Harriet Stowe met in England. Most of the papers are available on microfilm. SeeArthur and Elizabeth Schlesinger Library on the History of Women in America, *The Manuscript Inventories and the Catalogs of the Manuscripts, Books and Pictures,* vol. III (Boston: G. K. Hall & Co., 1973).

6,393. Beecher, Catharine Esther
Papers. 1847. 1 item.
Open. Published and unpublished guides.
Schlesinger Library.
Letter wherein Beecher (1800-78), an author and educator writing from Springfield, MA, discusses sending female teachers West. See Arthur and Elizabeth Schlesinger Library on the History of Women in America, *The Manuscript Inventories and the Catalogs of the Manuscripts, Books and Pictures,* vol. III (Boston: G. K. Hall & Co., 1973).

6,394. Beecher, James C.
Papers. 1850-1946. 3 Hollinger boxes.
Open. Published and unpublished guides.
Schlesinger Library.
Family papers of James Beecher (1828-86), son of Lyman Beecher and commander of the First North Carolina Colored Volunteers in the Civil War, contain correspondence, diaries, and photos. Included are James Beecher's correspondence about the Civil War, Reconstruction, and the Freedmen's Bureau, and papers of James's wife Frances (Johnson) Beecher Perkins, of their adopted twin daughters Mary Frances (Beecher) Beecher and Margaret (Beecher) Ward, and of other Beechers and Johnsons. See Arthur and Elizabeth Schlesinger Library on the History of Women in America, *The Manuscript Inventories and the Catalogs of the Manuscripts, Books and Pictures,* vol. III (Boston: G. K. Hall & Co., 1973).

6,395. Bell, George A.
Papers. 1873-97. 1 folder.
Open. Published and unpublished guides.
Schlesinger Library.
Collection formed around the Beecher-Tilton scandal and the position of Bell (?-1897) regarding it. Letters, clippings of a letter by Theodore Tilton, and a memorial to Bell. See Arthur and Elizabeth Schlesinger I ibrary on the History of Women in America, *Th. Manuscript Inventories and the Catalogs of the Manuscripts, Books and Pictures,* vol. III (Boston: G. K. Hall & Co., 1973).

6,396. Bennett, Martha T.
Papers. 1956. 1 item.
Open. Published and unpublished guides.
Schlesinger Library.
Letter from Bennett (1867-?), sister of authors John Bennett and H. H. Bennett, to Jacob Blanck of Harvard University's Houghton Library. See Arthur and Elizabeth Schlesinger Library on the History of Women in America, *The Manuscript Inventories and the Catalogs of the Manuscripts, Books and Pictures,* vol. III (Boston: G. K. Hall & Co., 1973).

6,397. Berkeley Street School
Records. 1862-81. 2 items.
Open. Published and unpublished guides.
Schlesinger Library.
The School, which operated from 1862 to 1912 in Cambridge, offered eight years of instruction for young ladies. Enrollment book listing students and parents and a pamphlet describing the School. See Arthur and Elizabeth Schlesinger Library on the History of Women in America, *The Manuscript Inventories and the Catalogs of the Manuscripts, Books and Pictures,* vol. III (Boston: G. K. Hall & Co., 1973).

6,398. Berkeley Street School Association
Records. 1862-1967. 2 Hollinger boxes.
Open. Unpublished guide.
Schlesinger Library.
Records of the alumnae association of a private girls school that operated in Cambridge from 1862 to 1912 include constitution and bylaws, minutes, financial reports, lists of officers and members, announcements, reminiscences, and material regarding the Margaret Rae Ingols scholarship at Radcliffe College. Records of the School include histories, correspondence, pupil lists, course announcements, programs, and memorabilia. Also contains photos and tintypes of the School's principals Lyman Richards Williston, Justin Edwards Gale, Margaret Rae Ingols, and Constance Bigelow Williston, and of students, a school building, class outings and plays, and a 1914 Association meeting.

6,399. Bernays, Doris Elsa (Fleischman)
Papers. 1919-70. 6 cartons and 2 Hollinger boxes.
Closed. No guide.
Schlesinger Library.
[Mrs. Edward] Bernays (1891-) is a pioneer in the field of public relations. Correspondence, manuscripts, printed articles, and clippings reflect Bernays's interest in feminism. Papers concern The Lucy Stone League, the Woman Pays Club, and household employment; also included are correspondence with Mary Beard, a 1946 *McCall's Magazine* article on the servant problem, and clippings regarding Bernays's book *A Wife Is Many Women.*

6,400. Bernhardt, Sarah
Papers. Nd. 1 item.
Open. Published and unpublished guides.
Schlesinger Library.
Note to "Wolfe" by Bernhardt (1845-1923), a tragedian and wife of Jacques Damala. See Arthur and Elizabeth Schlesinger Library on the History of Women in America, *The Manuscript Inventories and the Catalogs of the Manuscripts, Books and Pictures,* vol. III (Boston: G. K. Hall & Co., 1973).

6,401. Berrien, Laura M.
Papers. Ca. 1945-57. 1 box.
Open. No guide.
Schlesinger Library.
Minutes of the National Woman's Party, an organization in which Berrien, a lawyer, was active, and material on a lawsuit within the NWP.

6,402. Beyer, Clara E. Mortenson
Papers. 1911-ca. 1974. 22 Hollinger boxes and 5 cartons.
Open. Published and unpublished guides.
Schlesinger Library.
[Mrs.] Beyer (1892-) was employed by the US Department of Labor as a labor law specialist. Correspondence, diary, articles, reports, business records, pamphlets, clippings, and photos relate to her professional and personal life. Printed material concerns her service as consultant on labor and on women in US foreign aid, as well as her work for the Agency for International Development and for the 1974 Percy amendment to the Foreign Assistance Act. Beyer was executive assistant on the War Labor Policies Board in 1918, then

executive secretary for the DC Minimum Wage Board from 1919 to 1921; within the Department of Labor she served as economist for the Children's Bureau from 1928 to 1931, as director of the industrial division from 1931 to 1934, as associate director from 1934 to 1957, and then as acting director from 1957 to 1958 of the Bureau of Labor Standards. See Arthur and Elizabeth Schlesinger Library on the History of Women in America, *The Manuscript Inventories and the Catalogs of the Manuscripts, Books and Pictures,* vol. III (Boston: G. K. Hall & Co., 1973).

6,403. Billings, Addie Melvina Stephenson
Papers. 1875-1948. 0.5 Hollinger box.
Open. Unpublished guide.
Schlesinger Library.
Billings (1858-1948) was a teacher in Nebraska in the 1880s; became a lawyer in 1887, earning certification in Nebraska, Iowa, and California; and was an antiprohibition activist and grape grower in California. Correspondence, speeches, school papers, photos, autograph album, and certificates, including correspondence with two adopted daughters, speeches supporting William McKinley for President, and material on Eastern Star membership.

6,404. Birth Control League of Massachusetts
Records. 1916-34. 1 Hollinger box.
Open. Published and unpublished guides.
Schlesinger Library.
The League was established in 1916 to disseminate legally birth control information in Massachusetts. Correspondence, articles, and state statutes concern the early legal difficulties of the League. Correspondents include Blanche (Ames) Ames and Margaret Sanger. See Arthur and Elizabeth Schlesinger Library on the History of Women in America, *The Manuscript Inventories and the Catalogs of the Manuscripts, Books and Pictures,* vol. III (Boston: G. K. Hall & Co., 1973).

6,405. Bisbee, Dorothy Winsor
Papers. 1970-72. 2 Hollinger boxes.
Open. No guide.
Schlesinger Library.
Papers of [Mrs.] Bisbee, an executive in the LWV, chronicle her efforts to improve Boston public schools and her unsuccessful campaign for election to the Boston School Committee.

6,406. Biscoe, Helen Maria
Papers. 1881-1945. 2 Hollinger boxes.
Open. Published and unpublished guides.
Schlesinger Library.
Correspondence, diaries, and notebooks of Biscoe (1860-1946), an author, poet, and traveler. Also included are letters and articles by Beulah Marie (Dix) Flebbe, Ethel B. Osgood, Maud (Wood) Park, and former pupils and friends, which contain extensive biographical material about Biscoe and reveal her personal kindliness and religious nature. See Arthur and Elizabeth Schlesinger Library on the History of Women in America, *The Manuscript Inventories and the Catalogs of the Manuscripts, Books and Pictures,* vol. III (Boston: G. K. Hall & Co., 1973).

6,407. Blackall, Dorothy Brewer
Papers. 1912-58. 3 Hollinger boxes and 19 oversize items.
Open. Unpublished guide.
Schlesinger Library.
Blackall (ca. 1890-1949) was publicity director from 1932 to 1949 for the New England Hospital for Women and Children in Boston. Correspondence, photos, clippings, brochures, pamphlets, and programs for fund-raising events provide information particularly on the Hospital's publicity but also on the Hospital generally and on women in medicine.

6,408. Blackwell, Alice Stone
Papers. 1888-1945. 5 folders.
Open. Published and unpublished guides.
Schlesinger Library.
Blackwell (1857-1950) was a feminist, editor, and humanitarian radical. The collection includes 1904-08 letters to Isaac A. Hourwich, papers about Blackwell's work with the Friends of Russian Freedom, post cards, and a photo. See Arthur and Elizabeth Schlesinger Library on the History of Women in America, *The Manuscript Inventories and the Catalogs of the Manuscripts, Books and Pictures,* vol. III (Boston: G. K. Hall & Co., 1973).

6,409. Blackwell, Anna
Papers. 1893. 1 item.
Open. Published and unpublished guides.
Schlesinger Library.
Letter by Anna Blackwell, member of the Blackwell family of New England, to Antoinette Brown Blackwell. See Arthur and Elizabeth Schlesinger Library on the History of Women in America, *The Manuscript Inventories and the Catalogs of the Manuscripts, Books and Pictures,* vol. III (Boston: G. K. Hall & Co., 1973).

6,410. Blackwell, Antoinette Brown
Papers. 1871-1913. 6 items.
Open. Published and unpublished guides.
Schlesinger Library.
Blackwell (1825-1921) was the first woman ordained minister in the US. Correspondence, most of which is to Emily Howland, regarding Blackwell's travels, writings, and the 1913 suffrage parade. See Arthur and Elizabeth Schlesinger Library on the History of Women in America, *The Manuscript Inventories and the Catalogs of the Manuscripts, Books and Pictures,* vol. III (Boston: G. K. Hall & Co., 1973).

6,411. Blackwell, Elizabeth
Papers. Ca. 1854-1900. 3 items.
Open. Published and unpublished guides.
Schlesinger Library.
Blackwell (1821-1910) was a physician. Copies of letters and a printed prospectus of lectures by Elizabeth and Emily Blackwell. See Arthur and Elizabeth Schlesinger Library on the History of Women in America, *The Manuscript Inventories and the Catalogs of the Manuscripts, Books and Pictures,* vol. III (Boston: G. K. Hall & Co., 1973).

6,412. Blackwell Family
Papers. 1784-1944. 15 Hollinger boxes, 1 oversize package, and 1 oversize folder.
Open. Published and unpublished guides.
Schlesinger Library.
Correspondence, journals, diaries, memoirs, manuscripts, photos, biographical and autobiographical material, memorabilia, and other papers of the Blackwell family, which was notable in the fields of abolition, medicine, religion, prohibition, and woman's suffrage. Family members represented include Samuel Blackwell; his children: doctors Elizabeth (1821-1910) and Emily Blackwell (1826-1910), Henry Blackwell and his wife Lucy Stone (1818-93), Samuel Blackwell and his wife Antoinette Brown (1825-1921); and Alice Stone Blackwell (1857-1950) and five other granddaughters. Papers of Elizabeth Blackwell and Antoinette Brown Blackwell, the first woman ordained as a minister in the US, make up a large part of the collection. Antoinette Blackwell's autobiography is included, as is correspondence from several Blackwell cousins and other relatives. Correspondents include Susan B. Anthony, Elizabeth Cady Stanton, and Gerrit Smith. See Arthur and Elizabeth Schlesinger Library on the History of Women in America, *The Manuscript Inventories and the Catalogs of the Manuscripts, Books and Pictures,* vol. III (Boston: G. K. Hall & Co., 1973).

6,413. Blackwell, Henry B.
Papers. 1869-92. 2 items.
Open. Published and unpublished guides.
Schlesinger Library.
Letters from Blackwell (1825-1909), publisher of the *Woman's Journal,* son of Samuel Blackwell, and husband of Lucy Stone. See Arthur and Elizabeth Schlesinger Library on the History of Women in America, *The Manuscript Inventories and the Catalogs of the Manuscripts, Books and Pictures,* vol. III (Boston: G. K. Hall & Co., 1973).

6,414. Blake, Alde L. T.
Papers. 1897-1919. 1 Hollinger box and 1 oversize folder.
Open. Unpublished guide.
Schlesinger Library.
Correspondence, annual reports, programs, and publications of [Mrs. William F.] Blake, a suffragist and campaign secretary in 1912 of the Michigan Equal Suffrage Association. Includes papers of the MESA and the National American Woman Suffrage Association and extensive correspondence of Alfred W. Wishart, a clergyman who was campaign advisor to the MESA, regarding the recount that followed the 1912 election in which Michigan women narrowly missed winning the vote.

6,415. Blanc, Marie Thérèse (de Solms)
Papers. 1893. 2-page item.
Open. Published and unpublished guides.
Schlesinger Library.
Letter of Blanc (1840-1907), an author who used the pseudonym Theodore Bentzon, to [Miss] Clara A. May at Harvard Annex. See Arthur and Elizabeth Schlesinger Library on the History of Women in America, *The Manuscript Inventories and the Catalogs of the Manuscripts, Books and Pictures,* vol. III (Boston: G. K. Hall & Co., 1973).

6,416. Blanding, Sarah Gibson
Papers. 1940-75. 3 Hollinger boxes, 1 large envelope, and 1 large carton.
Partially closed. No guide.
Schlesinger Library.
Blanding (1898-) was president of Vassar College from 1946 to 1964. Correspondence, oral history interview transcript, speeches, photos regarding family history, scrapbook, book reviews for *The New Yorker,* articles, and clippings concerning Blanding's career as an educator at the University of Kentucky, Cornell, and Vassar, and her retirement. Correspondents include E. B. and Katharine White, Florence C. Wislocki, and Rebecca Lawrence Lowrie.

6,417. Boehner, Ruth P.
Papers. 1943-58. 6-page item.
Open. Published and unpublished guides.
Schlesinger Library.
Letter in which Boehner, a career member of the WACs, describes life in the Corps' early days. See Arthur and Elizabeth Schlesinger Library on the History of Women in America, *The Manuscript Inventories and the Catalogs of the Manuscripts, Books and Pictures,* vol. III (Boston: G. K. Hall & Co., 1973).

6,418. Bolton, Charles Knowles
Papers. 1881-1937. 2 Hollinger boxes.
Open. Published and unpublished guides.
Schlesinger Library.
Diaries and autobiography of Sarah Knowles Bolton (1841-1916), author, humanitarian, and mother of Charles Bolton (1867-1950). Also includes pages from her autobiography and journal that were selected and edited by her son. Diary topics include travel, education of women, the Society for the Prevention of Cruelty to Animals, and the WCTU. See Arthur and Elizabeth Schlesinger Library on the History of Women in America, *The Manuscript Inventories and the Catalogs of the*

Manuscripts, Books and Pictures, vol. III (Boston: G. K. Hall & Co., 1973).

6,419. Bosanquet, Theodora
Papers. 1924-36. 5 items.
Open. Published and unpublished guides.
Schlesinger Library.
Diaries of [Miss] Bosanquet describing her travels in the US and Europe as secretary of the International Federation of University Women. She also was secretary to Henry James. See Arthur and Elizabeth Schlesinger Library on the History of Women in America, *The Manuscript Inventories and the Catalogs of the Manuscripts, Books and Pictures,* vol. III (Boston: G. K. Hall & Co., 1973).

6,420. Boston Parents' Council
Records. 1930-38. 3 Hollinger boxes.
Open. Unpublished guide.
Schlesinger Library.
The Council was founded in 1930 by a small group of professional and volunteer social agency administrators to bridge the gap between scientists of child development and parents who wanted information on normal child growth. Minutes, committee records, correspondence, and mimeographed and printed material include information on the 1930 White House Conference on Child Health and Protection, the Federal Emergency Relief Administration and emergency education programs, the Massachusetts Department of Education, and Council-sponsored events concerning children. In 1938 the Council was disbanded.

6,421. Bowditch, Sylvia Church Scudder
Papers. 1890-97. 1 folder and 1 oversize vol.
Open. Published and unpublished guides.
Schlesinger Library.
Scrapbooks reflect Bowditch's social life and activities as a young woman from a prominent Cambridge family in the 1890s. Contained are memorabilia and invitations, many from prominent individuals and families of Boston and Cambridge. See Arthur and Elizabeth Schlesinger Library on the History of Women in America, *The Manuscript Inventories and the Catalogs of the Manuscripts, Books and Pictures,* vol. III (Boston: G. K. Hall & Co., 1973).

6,422. Bowditch, William L., and Bowditch, Sarah R.
Papers. 1879. 1 item.
Open. Published and unpublished guides.
Schlesinger Library.
Pamphlet explaining to women in Brookline, MA, how to register to vote for the school committee. See Arthur and Elizabeth Schlesinger Library on the History of Women in America, *The Manuscript Inventories and the Catalogs of the Manuscripts, Books and Pictures,* vol. III (Boston: G. K. Hall & Co., 1973).

6,423. Boyd, Rosamonde R.
Papers. 1949. 1 item.
Open. Published and unpublished guides.
Schlesinger Library.
Manuscript of a speech on equal rights for women by Boyd, dean of women at Converse College in Spartanburg, SC, before the 1948 Deans of Women Conference. See Arthur and Elizabeth Schlesinger Library on the History of Women in America, *The Manuscript Inventories and the Catalogs of the Manuscripts, Books and Pictures,* vol. III (Boston: G. K. Hall & Co., 1973).

6,424. Boynton, Grace Morrison
Papers. 1925-51. 3 Hollinger boxes.
Open. Published and unpublished guides.
Schlesinger Library.
Correspondence, diaries, and diary transcripts of [Miss] Boynton (1890-), a missionary educator in China, provide information about her work and Yenching University. See Arthur and Elizabeth Schlesinger Library on the History of Women in America, *The Manuscript Inventories and the Catalogs of the Manuscripts, Books and Pictures,* vol. III (Boston: G. K. Hall & Co., 1973).

6,425. Bradley and Hyde
Papers. 1800-61. 1 Hollinger box.
Open. Published and unpublished guides.
Schlesinger Library.
Correspondence of four generations of the Bradley and Hyde family, which was prominent in Connecticut and Massachusetts. Collection reflects the social life, customs, and education of women in the first half of the 19th century. Abigail Bradley married Lavius Hyde in 1818. See Arthur and Elizabeth Schlesinger Library on the History of Women in America, *The Manuscript Inventories and the Catalogs of the Manuscripts, Books and Pictures,* vol. III (Boston: G. K. Hall & Co., 1973).

6,426. Bridgman, Laura Dewey
Papers. 1877-87. 7 items.
Open. Published and unpublished guides.
Schlesinger Library.
Letters from Bridgman (1829-89) who was deaf, dumb, and blind, reveal her activities and outlook. Also includes an article about her life and condition. See Arthur and Elizabeth Schlesinger Library on the History of Women in America, *The Manuscript Inventories and the Catalogs of the Manuscripts, Books and Pictures,* vol. III (Boston: G. K. Hall & Co., 1973).

6,427. Brooks, John Graham
Papers. 1864-1938. 4 Hollinger boxes and 1 oversize vol.
Open. Unpublished guide.
Schlesinger Library.
Correspondence, scrapbooks, reviews, pamphlets, leaflets, and clippings of Brooks (1846-1938), a Unitarian minister and founder of the National Consumers' League. He lectured for the League for Political Education, investigated strikes for the US Department of Labor, and studied in Germany. Correspondents include Jane Addams, Alice Stone Blackwell, Ednah Dow Cheney, Ada Louise Comstock, Florence Kelley, Grace Norton, and Lillian Wald.

6,428. Brooks, Mrs. Morgan
Papers. 1871-1908. 1 folder.
Open. Published and unpublished guides.
Schlesinger Library.
Correspondence of Brooks, a prominent Bostonian, regarding the Simmons Fund and the Woman's Education Association. Correspondents include Catharine Beecher, Thomas Wentworth Higginson, and Ednah Dow Cheney. See Arthur and Elizabeth Schlesinger Library on the History of Women in America, *The Manuscript Inventories and the Catalogs of the Manuscripts, Books and Pictures,* vol. III (Boston: G. K. Hall & Co., 1973).

6,429. Brown, Abbie Farwell
Papers. 1859-1927. 4 Hollinger boxes and 1 oversize vol.
Open. Published and unpublished guides.
Schlesinger Library.
Brown (1871-1927) wrote children's books and lectured about them. Correspondence, diaries describing European trips of 1899 and 1906, manuscripts of poems and books, a drawing book, financial records, photos, clippings, and published stories. See Arthur and Elizabeth Schlesinger Library on the History of Women in America, *The Manuscript Inventories and the Catalogs of the Manuscripts, Books and Pictures,* vol. III (Boston: G. K. Hall & Co., 1973).

6,430. Brown, Charlotte (Hawkins)
Papers. 1899-1959. 5 Hollinger boxes.
Open. Published and unpublished guides.
Schlesinger Library.
[Mrs. Edward S.] Brown (1882-1961) was a Negro educator, protégé of Alice Freeman Palmer, and founder of the Palmer Memorial Institute in Sedalia, NC. Correspondence, speeches, and memorabilia pertain to Brown's accomplishments in the field of education for Negroes. Institute material includes charter, constitution, student publications, and photos. See Arthur and Elizabeth Schlesinger Library on the History of Women in America, *The Manuscript Inventories and the Catalogs of the Manuscripts, Books and Pictures,* vol. III (Boston: G. K. Hall & Co., 1973).

6,431. Brown, Dorothy Kirchwey
Papers. 1920-56. 4 Hollinger boxes.
Open. Published and unpublished guides.
Schlesinger Library.
Correspondence, working papers, and articles of [Mrs. LaRue] Brown (1888-) reflect her work with the LWV and the Massachusetts Committee for the Ratification of the Child Labor Amendment to promote maternal care and child welfare through the Sheppard-Towner Act. See Arthur and Elizabeth Schlesinger Library on the History of Women in America, *The Manuscript Inventories and the Catalogs of the Manuscripts, Books and Pictures,* vol. III (Boston: G. K. Hall & Co., 1973).

6,432. Brown, Dorothy Kirchwey
Papers. 1920s-72. 22 Hollinger boxes, 3 folders, 3 cartons, 1 vol., and 1 oversize item.
Open. No guide.
Schlesinger Library.
[Mrs. LaRue] Brown (1888-), a Democratic party member, has worked for the social improvement of women and children. Family and general correspondence, manuscripts, photos, scrapbooks, certificates, clippings, newsletter, articles, pamphlets, and programs include material re the Al Smith campaign, the national LWV, woman suffrage, the Youth Services Board, the Planned Parenthood League of Massachusetts, and the Birth Control League of Massachusetts. Also included are pamphlets of Ethel S. Dummer and material on Katharine Driscoll, Mildred Mahoney, and LaRue Brown's mother. Correspondents include Minnie Fisher Cunningham, Texas attorney and executive secretary of the national LWV during its first years; Eleanor and Franklin Roosevelt; and O. W. Holmes.

6,433. Brown, Gertrude Foster
Papers. Ca. 1936-51. 0.5 Hollinger box.
Open. No guide.
Schlesinger Library.
Files of Brown (1867-1956) concerning Carrie Chapman Catt include correspondence of Catt and correspondence, financial papers, clippings, and printed material pertaining to the Carrie Chapman Catt Memorial, Inc., the Suffrage Archives, and the 1936 Argentina Good Neighbor Conference.

6,434. Brown, Katherine Kennedy
Papers. Ca. 1946-60. 1 folder.
Open. Published and unpublished guides.
Schlesinger Library.
Speeches and published items pertain to [Mrs.] Brown's Republican party activities in Ohio and on the national level. She is also active in civic and philanthropic projects nationally and in Dayton, OH. See Arthur and Elizabeth Schlesinger Library on the History of Women in America, *The Manuscript Inventories and the Catalogs of the Manuscripts, Books and Pictures,* vol. III (Boston: G. K. Hall & Co., 1973).

6,435. Brown, Olympia
Papers. 1849-1956. 5 Hollinger boxes and 1 roll of diplomas.
Open. Published and unpublished guides.
Schlesinger Library.
Brown (1835-1926), whose married name was Willis, was an ordained minister who worked for

woman suffrage principally in Wisconsin and on the national level. Correspondence, sermons, speeches, articles, photos, and suffrage material, including programs, leaflets, clippings, and the *Congressional Record.* Includes material on the Federal Suffrage Association of the US, the National Woman Suffrage Association, the National American Woman Suffrage Association, Antioch College, and Victoria C. Woodhull. See Arthur and Elizabeth Schlesinger Library on the History of Women in America, *The Manuscript Inventories and the Catalogs of the Manuscripts, Books and Pictures,* vol. III (Boston: G. K. Hall & Co., 1973).

6,436. Browne, Sarah Ellen
Papers. 1856-59. 0.5 Hollinger box.
Open. Unpublished guide.
Schlesinger Library.
Browne was a student at the girls school conducted by Elizabeth and Louis Agassiz in Cambridge. Notes, transcripts, and correspondence, mainly between Browne and her mother, reveal the social life, study, dress, and other concerns of a young lady at school and describe such current events as the Utah Expedition of 1857 and 1858.

6,437. Browning, Elizabeth Barrett
Papers. Nd. 2 items.
Open. Published and unpublished guides.
Schlesinger Library.
An engraving of and note from Browning (1806-61), a poet. See Arthur and Elizabeth Schlesinger Library on the History of Women in America, *The Manuscript Inventories and the Catalogs of the Manuscripts, Books and Pictures,* vol. III (Boston: G. K. Hall & Co., 1973).

6,438. Bucknall, Joanna Rooker, and Bucknall, Martha Elizabeth
Papers. 1818-1936. 4 Hollinger boxes and 5 oversize items.
Open. Unpublished guide.
Schlesinger Library.
Joanna Bucknall (1816?-95) and Martha Bucknall (?-1880) were sisters who founded and managed a girls' school in Newark, NJ, from 1840 to 1855; in New York City from 1855 to 1866; and in New Brunswick, NJ, from 1866 to ca. 1880. Family correspondence; financial records, both personal and of the schools; and school records, including correspondence with students and their parents, student essays, lectures, and lessons. Collection documents girls school curriculum and women's roles as students and school principals in the mid-19th century.

6,439. Bunker Hill Monument Ladies Appeal
Records. 1830. 1 item.
Open. Published and unpublished guides.
Schlesinger Library.
Manuscript of the Appeal, founded in ca. 1830 in Charlestown, MA, to obtain funds to complete the monument. See Arthur and Elizabeth Schlesinger Library on the History of Women in America, *The Manuscript Inventories and the Catalogs of the Manuscripts, Books and Pictures,* vol. III (Boston: G. K. Hall & Co., 1973).

6,440. Bureau of Vocational Information
Records. 1915-32. 37 Hollinger boxes.
Open. Published and unpublished guides.
Schlesinger Library.
The Bureau was organized in 1919 for research on women's occupations and to counsel individual women and colleges. Correspondence, questionnaires, and clippings concern occupations for women in art, business, law, nursing, social work, statistics, and secretarial work as well as the requirements, training, and advantages of these fields. After the Bureau was disbanded in 1926, [Miss] Beatrice Doerschuk continued research for the manuscript "The Woman Secretary." See Arthur and Elizabeth Schlesinger Library on the History of Women in America, *The Manuscript Inventories and the Catalogs of the Manuscripts, Books and Pictures,* vol. III (Boston: G. K. Hall & Co., 1973).

6,441. Burgess, Martha Palmer
Papers. Ca. 1920-32. 1 folder.
Open. Published and unpublished guides.
Schlesinger Library.
Typed manuscript of poems by Burgess (1905-). See Arthur and Elizabeth Schlesinger Library on the History of Women in America, *The Manuscript Inventories and the Catalogs of the Manuscripts, Books and Pictures,* vol. III (Boston: G. K. Hall & Co., 1973).

6,442. Butler, Mabel (Churchill)
Papers. 1882-1931. 2 folders.
Open. Published and unpublished guides.
Schlesinger Library.
Butler was daughter of Mable (Hall) Churchill and granddaughter of Lucretia Allen Hall, both of whom were active in the suffrage movement, Churchill in New Hampshire and Hall in Missouri. Collection consists primarily of clippings concerning the lives of Churchill and Hall; correspondence is also included. See Arthur and Elizabeth Schlesinger Library on the History of Women in America, *The Manuscript Inventories and the Catalogs of the Manuscripts, Books and Pictures,* vol. III (Boston: G. K. Hall & Co., 1973).

6,443. Cable, George W.
Papers. 1885. 1 folder.
Open. Published and unpublished guides.
Schlesinger Library.
A letter to Colonel Higginson, which states that if women "are not fit to vote, they ought to stop bearing sons." See Arthur and Elizabeth Schlesinger Library on the History of Women in America, *The Manuscript Inventories and the Catalogs of the Manuscripts, Books and Pictures,* vol. III (Boston: G. K. Hall & Co., 1973).

6,444. Cabot, Ella (Lyman)
Papers. 1855-1934. 12 Hollinger boxes.
Open. Published and unpublished guides.
Schlesinger Library.
Cabot (1866-1934) was an author, educator, and member of a prominent Boston family. Correspondence, journal, manuscript, drafts and notes for lectures, articles, photos, and books. Material on Cabot's family life and public activities and for her lectures and books on philosophy, ethics, education, psychology, and religion includes notes from her studies under Josiah Royce and a manuscript in Royce's hand. Also included is correspondence of her father Arthur Theodore Lyman written while he was traveling in Europe. See Arthur and Elizabeth Schlesinger Library on the History of Women in America, *The Manuscript Inventories and the Catalogs of the Manuscripts, Books and Pictures,* vol. III (Boston: G. K. Hall & Co., 1973).

6,445. Cabot, Hugh
Papers. 1786-1945. 9 Hollinger boxes and 2 document boxes.
Open. Published and unpublished guides.
Schlesinger Library.
Collection of papers of a prominent Boston area family consists of correspondence, diaries, travel journals, and 1786-1840 records concerning the slave, tea, and spice trades. Reminiscences in which Lizzie Perkins [Mrs. Samuel] Cabot (1791-1885) describes 19th-century Boston; diaries, travel journals, and correspondence in which Elizabeth (Dwight) [Mrs. James Elliot] Cabot (1840-1902) comments at length on Boston life and the Civil War; diaries in which Mary Anderson Boit [Mrs. Hugh] Cabot describes her school life, 1890-91, and her children's infancy, 1905-08; and the 1930-31 diary in which Louise Cabot, first wife of Hugh Cabot, Jr., details her children's infancy. See Arthur and Elizabeth Schlesinger Library on the History of Women in America, *The Manuscript Inventories and the Catalogs of the Manuscripts, Books and Pictures,* vol. III (Boston: G. K. Hall & Co., 1973).

6,446. Calderone, Mary (Steichen)
Papers. Ca. 1920-75. 25 Hollinger boxes, 4 cartons, 7 folders, and 2 tapes.
Open. Published and unpublished guides.
Schlesinger Library.
Calderone (1904-), a physician, became a leader in public health, birth control, and sex education. Correspondence, speeches, journal articles and reprints, proceedings of panel discussions, clippings, photos, memorabilia, and books. Calderone worked as physician for the public schools in Great Neck, NY; as medical director for the Planned Parenthood Federation from 1953 to 1964; and from 1965 in association with the Sex Information and Education Council of the US. Collection contains extensive material relating to the PPF and SIECUS, including a complete set of SIECUS Newsletters and a report and information regarding abortion, birth control, conception-prevention, the Catholic Church, sex education and instruction, and the 1969-70 sex education controversy. See Arthur and Elizabeth Schlesinger Library on the History of Women in America, *The Manuscript Inventories and the Catalogs of the Manuscripts, Books and Pictures,* vol. III (Boston: G. K. Hall & Co., 1973).

6,447. Callender, Eunice
Papers. 1808-24. 3 vols.
Open. Published and unpublished guides.
Schlesinger Library.
Callender (1785-?) lived in Boston with her parents. Her manuscript diaries, comprising ca. 330 pages, portray everyday life for a busy young woman. See Arthur and Elizabeth Schlesinger Library on the History of Women in America, *The Manuscript Inventories and the Catalogs of the Manuscripts, Books and Pictures,* vol. III (Boston: G. K. Hall & Co., 1973).

6,448. Cam, Helen Maud
Papers. Ca. 1931-69. 0.5 Hollinger box.
Open. Unpublished guide.
Schlesinger Library.
Cam (1885-1968) was an historian, the first woman professor on the Faculty of Arts and Sciences at Harvard University, and a professor at Cambridge University in England. Correspondence, biographical material, articles, pamphlets, and photos reflect Cam's work in education. Also included are personal letters and writings on women in local government in England.

6,449. Cambridge Sewing Club
Records. 1910-60. 1 folder.
Open. Published and unpublished guides.
Schlesinger Library.
This Cambridge social organization, founded in 1910, sews for charity. Correspondence, notebook, and membership list cover the Club's activities from 1910 to 1937 and its 50th anniversary. See Arthur and Elizabeth Schlesinger Library on the History of Women in America, *The Manuscript Inventories and the Catalogs of the Manuscripts, Books and Pictures,* vol. III (Boston: G. K. Hall & Co., 1973).

6,450. Campbell, Dorcas
Papers. 1946-58. 6 folders.
Open. Published and unpublished guides.
Schlesinger Library.
Campbell (?-1959) was a banker and author of books on banking. Personal correspondence between Campbell and Mary R. Beard and other correspondence between Campbell and the Women's Archives. See Arthur and Elizabeth Schlesinger Library on the History of Women in America, *The Manuscript Inventories and the*

Catalogs of the Manuscripts, Books and Pictures, vol. III (Boston: G. K. Hall & Co., 1973).

6,451. Carter and White Family
Papers. Ca. 1860-1940s. 1 Hollinger box.
Open. No guide.
Schlesinger Library.
Family papers of the Carter and White families include letters from Helena (deKay) Gilder to Susan Carter, who helped found the Cooper Union, as well as wills, clippings, drawings, and other material.

6,452. Carter, Morris
Papers. 1920-63. 0.5 Hollinger box.
Open. Unpublished guide.
Schlesinger Library.
Carter (1877-1965) was assistant director of the Isabella Stewart Gardner Museum in Boston from 1919 to 1924, then director from 1924 to 1954. Correspondence to Carter while at the Museum is either personal or concerns Museum social events. Correspondents include Ada Louise Comstock, Laura Coombs Hills, Lotte Lehmann, Eleonora Sears, Booth Tarkington, and Anna Boynton Thompson.

6,453. Cary, Alice
Papers. Ca. 1866. 3 items.
Open. Published and unpublished guides.
Schlesinger Library.
Photo and correspondence of Cary (1820-71), a poet. See Arthur and Elizabeth Schlesinger Library on the History of Women in America, *The Manuscript Inventories and the Catalogs of the Manuscripts, Books and Pictures,* vol. III (Boston: G. K. Hall & Co., 1973).

6,454. Cary, Phoebe
Papers. Ca. 1852-66. 3 items.
Open. Published and unpublished guides.
Schlesinger Library.
Photo and correspondence of Cary (1824-71), a poet. See Arthur and Elizabeth Schlesinger Library on the History of Women in America, *The Manuscript Inventories and the Catalogs of the Manuscripts, Books and Pictures,* vol. III (Boston: G. K. Hall & Co., 1973).

6,455. Catt, Carrie Clinton (Lane) Chapman
Papers. 1898-1947. 3 folders.
Open. Published and unpublished guides.
Schlesinger Library.
Catt (1859-1947) was a national suffrage leader and president of the National American Woman Suffrage Association. Correspondence, financial records, and 1898 reports regarding suffrage in Oklahoma. See Arthur and Elizabeth Schlesinger Library on the History of Women in America, *The Manuscript Inventories and the Catalogs of the Manuscripts, Books and Pictures,* vol. III (Boston: G. K. Hall & Co., 1973).

6,456. Central Committee on Friendship Dinners
Records. 1927-50. 3 Hollinger boxes.
Open. Published and unpublished guides.
Schlesinger Library.
The Committee sponsors dinners for the American Woman's Association awards. Treasurer's reports, secretary's reports, membership lists, a history, and other records contain information about the dinners, guests, and recipients of AWA awards and scholarships. See Arthur and Elizabeth Schlesinger Library on the History of Women in America, *The Manuscript Inventories and the Catalogs of the Manuscripts, Books and Pictures,* vol. III (Boston: G. K. Hall & Co., 1973).

6,457. Chamberlain, Lucy (Parker)
Papers. 1857-1907. 4 Hollinger boxes.
Open. Published and unpublished guides.
Schlesinger Library.
Correspondence, receipts, and reports of [Mrs. Frank H.] Chamberlain (1829-?) who was part of a prominent New England family and a mother. Collection is largely correspondence by Chamberlain to family members, including accounts of European travel from 1869 to 1873, with subjects such as education of children, family, the 1870-71 Franco-Prussian War, and the Civil War. See Arthur and Elizabeth Schlesinger Library on the History of Women in America, *The Manuscript Inventories and the Catalogs of the Manuscripts, Books and Pictures,* vol. III (Boston: G. K. Hall & Co., 1973).

6,458. Chapman, Maria (Weston)
Papers. 1839-77. 2 folders.
Open. Published and unpublished guides.
Schlesinger Library.
Chapman (1806-85) was an author and abolitionist. Correspondence to Catherine Sargent, Henrietta Sargent, and a Mr. Garrison. See Arthur and Elizabeth Schlesinger Library on the History of Women in America, *The Manuscript Inventories and the Catalogs of the Manuscripts, Books and Pictures,* vol. III (Boston: G. K. Hall & Co., 1973).

6,459. Chase, Mary Ellen
Papers. 1941. 1 item.
Open. Published and unpublished guides.
Schlesinger Library.
A letter to professor William G. Howard from Chase (1887-1973), an author. See Arthur and Elizabeth Schlesinger Library on the History of Women in America, *The Manuscript Inventories and the Catalogs of the Manuscripts, Books and Pictures,* vol. III (Boston: G. K. Hall & Co., 1973).

6,460. Cheek, Jeannette Bailey
Collection. Nd. 1 folder.
Open. Published and unpublished guides.
Schlesinger Library.
Named in honor of this former director of the Schlesinger Library, the collection consists of correspondence of Susan B. Anthony, Ednah Dow Cheney, Elizabeth (Smith) Miller, and Amelia Jenks Bloomer. See Arthur and Elizabeth Schlesinger Library on the History of Women in America, *The Manuscript Inventories and the Catalogs of the Manuscripts, Books and Pictures,* vol. III (Boston: G. K. Hall & Co., 1973).

6,461. Cheney, Ednah Dow Littlehale
Papers. 1899. 2 items.
Open. Published and unpublished guides.
Schlesinger Library.
A letter and a 42-page memoir of her husband Seth W. Cheney by Ednah Cheney (1824-1904), an author and reformer. See Arthur and Elizabeth Schlesinger Library on the History of Women in America, *The Manuscript Inventories and the Catalogs of the Manuscripts, Books and Pictures,* vol. III (Boston: G. K. Hall & Co., 1973).

6,462. Chesterfield Female Benevolent Society
Records. 1844-47. 1 folder.
Open. Published and unpublished guides.
Schlesinger Library.
Constitution and report of meetings of the Society, founded in 1844 in Hopkinton, NH, to help the less fortunate. See Arthur and Elizabeth Schlesinger Library on the History of Women in America, *The Manuscript Inventories and the Catalogs of the Manuscripts, Books and Pictures,* vol. III (Boston: G. K. Hall & Co., 1973).

6,463. Child Care Center Parents Association of New York
Records. 1947-54. 2 Hollinger boxes.
Open. Published and unpublished guides.
Schlesinger Library.
The Association, founded ca. 1943, campaigned in the state of New York for funds to maintain and expand child care centers for children of working mothers. Minutes, correspondence, statements, programs, newsletters, bulletins, and clippings concern the Association's campaign. See Arthur and Elizabeth Schlesinger Library on the History of Women in America, *The Manuscript Inventories and the Catalogs of the Manuscripts, Books and Pictures,* vol. III (Boston: G. K. Hall & Co., 1973).

6,464. Child, David Lee
Papers. 1854-57. 1 folder.
Open. Published and unpublished guides.
Schlesinger Library.
Letters to Ellis Gray Loring of David Child (1794-1874), a journalist and husband of Lydia Maria (Francis) Child, concern slavery in Texas and the border states and renting land in Massachusetts. See Arthur and Elizabeth Schlesinger Library on the History of Women in America, *The Manuscript Inventories and the Catalogs of the Manuscripts, Books and Pictures,* vol. III (Boston: G. K. Hall & Co., 1973).

6,465. Child, Julia (McWilliams)
Papers. 1962-73. 12 cartons, 3 Hollinger boxes, 8 vols., 1 oversize vol., 1 tape, and 1 recording disc.
Access restricted. No guide.
Schlesinger Library.
Papers of Child (1912-), author of French cookbooks and star of the "French Chef" television series, contain "French Chef" scripts and photos; audience lists; recipes; manuscripts of her books and correspondence concerning them; material on lectures and courses; articles; clippings; correspondence with Simone Beck, James Beard, and M. F. K. Fisher; and other items.

6,466. Child, Lydia Maria (Francis)
Papers. 1841-79. 10 folders.
Open. Published and unpublished guides.
Schlesinger Library.
Child (1802-80) was an abolitionist, reformer, and author. Correspondence, the bulk of which is to Louisa Loring, her husband Ellis Gray Loring, and Anna Loring, and receipts. See Arthur and Elizabeth Schlesinger Library on the History of Women in America, *The Manuscript Inventories and the Catalogs of the Manuscripts, Books and Pictures,* vol. III (Boston: G. K. Hall & Co., 1973).

6,467. Chivvis, Ada Mary (Chaphe)
Papers. Ca. 1906-37. 2 folders.
Open. No guide.
Schlesinger Library.
Chivvis (1864-1937) was a St. Louis attorney, civic leader, reformer, and member of the Missouri Bar Association. Correspondence, clippings, photos, and printed material re Chivvis's career and activities, including genealogical and biographical information. Chivvis was head of the Girls' Protective Association, court representative for the Board of Religious Organizations, president of the Missouri Federation of Women's Clubs in 1913 and president of the Women's Bar Association of St. Louis in 1936.

6,468. Church, Roberta
Papers. 1953-70. 2 folders.
Open. Published and unpublished guides.
Schlesinger Library.
Church (ca. 1923-) was the minority group consultant for the US Department of Labor Bureau of Employment Security. Correspondence, biographical material, photos, clippings, and speeches and articles on employment opportunities for minorities and related subjects. See Arthur and Elizabeth Schlesinger Library on the History of Women in America, *The Manuscript Inventories and the Catalogs of the Manuscripts, Books and Pictures,* vol. III (Boston: G. K. Hall & Co., 1973).

6,469. Claflin, Adelaide Avery
Papers. 1883-1921. 2 folders.
Open. Published and unpublished guides.
Schlesinger Library.
Claflin (1846-?) was active from the 1880s until 1920 in the suffrage movement in Massachusetts.

Correspondence from Alice Stone Blackwell, Lucy Stone, and Wenona Osborne Pinkham; printed suffrage material; Claflin's high school reports; clippings; and papers concerning the Boston Castilian Club. See Arthur and Elizabeth Schlesinger Library on the History of Women in America, *The Manuscript Inventories and the Catalogs of the Manuscripts, Books and Pictures,* vol. III (Boston: G. K. Hall & Co., 1973).

6,470. Clark, Rosamond
Papers. Ca. 1916. 1 folder.
Open. Published and unpublished guides.
Schlesinger Library.
Correspondence and an article containing two accounts of American girls leaving Germany at the start of WWI. See Arthur and Elizabeth Schlesinger Library on the History of Women in America, *The Manuscript Inventories and the Catalogs of the Manuscripts, Books and Pictures,* vol. III (Boston: G. K. Hall & Co., 1973).

6,471. Clark, Ruth E.
Papers. 1934. 1 item.
Open. Published and unpublished guides.
Schlesinger Library.
Letter from Arthur Tilley, Fellow of Kings College in Cambridge, England, to [Miss] Clark in which he makes reference to [Miss] Alice Longfellow and the founding of Radcliffe College. See Arthur and Elizabeth Schlesinger Library on the History of Women in America, *The Manuscript Inventories and the Catalogs of the Manuscripts, Books and Pictures,* vol. III (Boston: G. K. Hall & Co., 1973).

6,472. Clarke, Elizabeth Lawrence
Papers. 1921-47. 1 folder.
Open. Published and unpublished guides.
Schlesinger Library.
Correspondence, biographical material, articles, and clippings of Clarke, a plant pathologist. The articles concern raising seed potatoes on Dimock Farm in Corinth, VT. See Arthur and Elizabeth Schlesinger Library on the History of Women in America, *The Manuscript Inventories and the Catalogs of the Manuscripts, Books and Pictures,* vol. III (Boston: G. K. Hall & Co., 1973).

6,473. Cleghorn, Sarah Norcliffe
Papers. 1936-45. 6 folders.
Open. Published and unpublished guides.
Schlesinger Library.
Cleghorn (1876-1959) was an author and poet. Correspondence with Elizabeth Kent, galley proof and typescripts, manuscripts of 22 sonnets, and several articles. See Arthur and Elizabeth Schlesinger Library on the History of Women in America, *The Manuscript Inventories and the Catalogs of the Manuscripts, Books and Pictures,* vol. III (Boston: G. K. Hall & Co., 1973).

6,474. Clemmer, Mary
Papers. Nd. 4-page item.
Open. Published and unpublished guides.
Schlesinger Library.
Manuscript entitled "The Lobbyist" by Clemmer (1831-84), a Washington, DC, newspaper columnist. See Arthur and Elizabeth Schlesinger Library on the History of Women in America, *The Manuscript Inventories and the Catalogs of the Manuscripts, Books and Pictures,* vol. III (Boston: G. K. Hall & Co., 1973).

6,475. Clothier, Florence
Papers. Nd. 2 Hollinger boxes and 1 carton.
Partially restricted. No guide.
Schlesinger Library.
A psychiatrist and author, Clothier (1903-), who married George Wislocki, was director of the Planned Parenthood League of Massachusetts from 1945 to 1957 and League president from 1953 to 1956 before becoming assistant to the president of Vassar College in 1957. Correspondence with Rebecca Lowrie and Sarah G. Blanding; journal of a trip to Alaska in 1928; personal, school, and professional material; and information on euthanasia, abortion, and birth control.

6,476. Code, Marion Osborne Graves
Papers. 1953-55. 1 box.
Open. Published and unpublished guides.
Schlesinger Library.
Correspondence and journal of [Mrs.] Code (189?-1955) describe her journey from New York to India via England. Includes a travelog, observations on social life and customs, and descriptions of traveling companions and her participation in social projects. The papers document Code's initial enthusiasm and eventual disillusionment with Indian philosophy and customs. See Arthur and Elizabeth Schlesinger Library on the History of Women in America, *The Manuscript Inventories and the Catalogs of the Manuscripts, Books and Pictures,* vol. III (Boston: G. K. Hall & Co., 1973).

6,477. Coe, Evelyn Peverley
Papers. 1881-1964. 1 folder and 3 oversize items.
Open. Published and unpublished guides.
Schlesinger Library.
Correspondence, certificates, photos, and clippings regarding the work of Coe (1881-1967?) in such Massachusetts woman's suffrage organizations as the Boston Equal Suffrage Association for Good Government and the Women Suffrage Coffee House in Groton and her WWI service at the Soldiers' and Sailors' Club in Boston. See Arthur and Elizabeth Schlesinger Library on the History of Women in America, *The Manuscript Inventories and the Catalogs of the Manuscripts, Books and Pictures,* vol. III (Boston: G. K. Hall & Co., 1973).

6,478. Coes, Mary
Papers. 1909-13. 1 Hollinger box.
Open. No guide.
Schlesinger Library.
Addresses to students, alumnae, and others by Coes (1861-1913), dean of Radcliffe College from 1909 to 1913.

6,479. Coggeshall, Mary Jane Whitely
Papers. 1882-1909. 1 Hollinger box.
Open. Published and unpublished guides.
Schlesinger Library.
[Mrs.] Coggeshall (1836-1911) was a leader of the Iowa woman suffrage movement, an officer of the National American Woman Suffrage Association, and an editor of the *Woman's Journal.* Correspondence, speeches, articles, and clippings reflect Coggeshall's suffrage activities and contain material on such suffrage conventions as the Iowa Equal Suffrage Conventions of 1902 through 1906 and the National Woman Suffrage Conventions from 1904 to 1909. See Arthur and Elizabeth Schlesinger Library on the History of Women in America, *The Manuscript Inventories and the Catalogs of the Manuscripts, Books and Pictures,* vol. III (Boston: G. K. Hall & Co., 1973).

6,480. College Club
Records. 1890-1969. 30 vols. and 1 folder.
Open. Unpublished guide.
Schlesinger Library.
The Club was established in 1890 to provide a place for social meetings of college women in Boston. Minutes; records of the board of directors, board of managers, house committee, and executive committee; annual meeting reports; newsletters; bulletins; and directories.

6,481. Commission on the Education of Women, American Council on Education
Records. 1953-61. 9 Hollinger boxes.
Open. Published and unpublished guides.
Schlesinger Library.
In operation from 1953 to 1961, the Commission conducted research on the role of education in women's lives. Minutes, financial records, correspondence, pamphlets, and clippings describe the Commission's creation and activities. See Arthur and Elizabeth Schlesinger Library on the History of Women in America, *The Manuscript Inventories and the Catalogs of the Manuscripts, Books and Pictures,* vol. III (Boston: G. K. Hall & Co., 1973).

6,482. Committee on the Status of Women at Harvard
Records. 1969-71. 6 Hollinger boxes and 5 reels.
Partially closed. Published and unpublished guides.
Schlesinger Library.
Formed in 1970 to study the status of Harvard's women students and faculty members, the Committee was chaired by Caroline W. Bynum and Michael L. Walzer. Correspondence, memos, notes, questionnaires, page proofs, final draft, transcripts, tapes, articles, and clippings. Contains papers of Bynum pertaining to her work on the Committee, the Women's Faculty Group, and the Committee on the Harvard-Radcliffe Relationship. Tapes contain testimony by Harvard University faculty, employees, and students on Harvard faculty women, day care and health services, part-time teaching and part-time study, graduate student housing, job placement, and discrimination against women. See Arthur and Elizabeth Schlesinger Library on the History of Women in America, *The Manuscript Inventories and the Catalogs of the Manuscripts, Books and Pictures,* vol. III (Boston: G. K. Hall & Co., 1973).

6,483. Comstock, Ada Louise
Papers. 1923-43. 3 Hollinger boxes.
Open. Published and unpublished guides.
Schlesinger Library.
Speeches to groups at Radcliffe College or alumnae and clippings of Comstock (1876-1973), president of Radcliffe from 1923 to 1943, pertain to the American Woman's Association, the Law Enforcement Commission, AAUW, the Institute of Pacific Relations, and other groups in which she was active. See Arthur and Elizabeth Schlesinger Library on the History of Women in America, *The Manuscript Inventories and the Catalogs of the Manuscripts, Books and Pictures,* vol. III (Boston: G. K. Hall & Co., 1973).

6,484. Comstock, Ada Louise
Papers. 1929-71. 0.5 Hollinger box, 5 folders, and 1 certificate.
Partially restricted. No guide.
Schlesinger Library.
Personal and family papers of Comstock (1876-1973), Radcliffe College president from 1923 to 1943. Correspondence regarding the death of Margaret Clark Williams, the Wickersham Commission, and the Radcliffe presidency; notebooks; a binder containing "A Memoir of Ada Comstock With Love"; questionnaires; photos; a framed certificate; and other material. Correspondents include Harvard University president Abbott Lawrence Lowell, Ella (Lyman) Cabot, Helen Keller, L. B. R. Briggs, Frances Reed Jordan, and Comstock's father. Comstock was married to Wallace Notestein.

6,485. Consumers' League of Connecticut
Records. 1902-46. 4 Hollinger boxes.
Open. Published and unpublished guides.
Schlesinger Library.
The League, established in 1902, sought to mobilize public opinion in support of improved conditions for workers. Minutes, reports, leaflets, clippings, and publications contain material on investigations into working conditions, labor legislation, child labor, homework, minimum wage, and related topics. Also included are reports of the Hartford Consumers' League, 1902-19, and of the New Haven Consumers' League, 1909-14. See Arthur and Elizabeth Schlesinger Library on the History of Women in America, *The Manuscript Inventories*

and the Catalogs of the Manuscripts, Books and Pictures, vol. III (Boston: G. K. Hall & Co., 1973).

6,486. Consumers' League of Massachusetts
Records. 1891-1955. 31 Hollinger boxes.
Open. Published and unpublished guides.
Schlesinger Library.
The League, established in 1898, sought to mobilize public opinion in support of improved conditions for workers. Minutes, financial statements, reports, correspondence, membership lists, articles, and publications contain material on child labor, the National Child Labor Committee, the Child Labor Amendment, and efforts to raise the compulsory school attendance age. Also includes items regarding industrial working conditions (particularly of women workers) such as wages and hours, sweatshops, homework, industrial poisoning, strikes, unions, social security, and workmen's compensation. Some records of the National Consumers' League and other state Leagues are also included. See Arthur and Elizabeth Schlesinger Library on the History of Women in America, *The Manuscript Inventories and the Catalogs of the Manuscripts, Books and Pictures,* vol. III (Boston: G. K. Hall & Co., 1973).

6,487. Cooke, Helen Temple
Papers. 1858-1951. 1 Hollinger box.
Open. Published and unpublished guides.
Schlesinger Library.
[Miss] Cooke (1865-1955) was an educator and principal of Dana Hall in Wellesley, MA. Bulk of her papers are college records and English themes, but correspondence for 1933 to 1951 and poems from Laura Spencer Porter Pope are included as well. Collection also contains diaries, 1858-66, in which Cook's grandmother Mrs. Bardwell describes daily life in Walpole, NH, and comments on her travels to Decorah, IA, in 1862 and 1866 to visit her daughter Sarah; the work of the Soldiers' Aid Society, and the Civil War. See Arthur and Elizabeth Schlesinger Library on the History of Women in America, *The Manuscript Inventories and the Catalogs of the Manuscripts, Books and Pictures,* vol. III (Boston: G. K. Hall & Co., 1973).

6,488. Cookery
Collection. 17th-19th centuries. 13 items.
Open. Published and unpublished guides.
Schlesinger Library.
Manuscript sheets of English and American recipes. See Arthur and Elizabeth Schlesinger Library on the History of Women in America, *The Manuscript Inventories and the Catalogs of the Manuscripts, Books and Pictures,* vol. III (Boston: G. K. Hall & Co., 1973).

6,489. Cooper, Lorraine (Rowan)
Papers. 1958-74. 1 Hollinger box, 2 folders, and 13 vols.
Open. No guide.
Schlesinger Library.
A newspaper columnist and civic affairs volunteer worker, Cooper (1906-) is the wife of John Sherman Cooper, who was a US senator from Kentucky and ambassador to the German Democratic Republic. Correspondence, including items from Evangeline [Mrs. David] Bruce; mimeographed newsletters; and scrapbooks containing correspondence, clippings, and photos. From 1960 to 1962 Lorraine Cooper was president of the Republican Congressional Wives Club.

6,490. Court, Cora May (Trawick)
Papers. 1893-1963. 4 Hollinger boxes, 1 oversize vol., and 1 oversize folder.
Open. Unpublished guide.
Schlesinger Library.
Court (1875-?) taught parent education classes in Nashville in the 1930s and at Lesley College in Cambridge in the late 1940s. Material about parent education, with book reviews and articles written by Court, class assignments for her courses at the University of Chicago Extension School and Columbia University Teachers College, and syllabi for courses she taught at Lesley. Also included is a scrapbook containing clippings, which primarily concern race relations. In addition to her parent education courses, papers relate to marriage and the family, the Age Center of New England, and child psychology.

6,491. Cox, Anna P.
Papers. 1879. 1 item.
Open. Published and unpublished guides.
Schlesinger Library.
Letter thanking William Lloyd Garrison's children for a book about him. See Arthur and Elizabeth Schlesinger Library on the History of Women in America, *The Manuscript Inventories and the Catalogs of the Manuscripts, Books and Pictures,* vol. III (Boston: G. K. Hall & Co., 1973).

6,492. Croly, Jane (Cunningham)
Papers. 1876-98. 9 items.
Open. Published and unpublished guides.
Schlesinger Library.
Correspondence of Croly (1829-1901), a journalist. See Arthur and Elizabeth Schlesinger Library on the History of Women in America, *The Manuscript Inventories and the Catalogs of the Manuscripts, Books and Pictures,* vol. III (Boston: G. K. Hall & Co., 1973).

6,493. Cronkhite, Bernice Veazey (Brown)
Papers. 1915-70. 3 Hollinger boxes.
Open. Published and unpublished guides.
Schlesinger Library.
Graduate dean of Radcliffe from 1934 to 1959 and a vice-president of the school from 1923 to 1960, [Mrs. Leonard Wolsey] Cronkhite (1893-) was active nationally and internationally in the field of education. Correspondence, speeches, clippings, and photos pertain to her early career, her work at Radcliffe, and organizations in which she participated such as the US Board of Foreign Scholarships, the Training School for Public Service, the Hall of Fame for Great Americans, and Mundelein College advisory committee. See Arthur and Elizabeth Schlesinger Library on the History of Women in America, *The Manuscript Inventories and the Catalogs of the Manuscripts, Books and Pictures,* vol. III (Boston: G. K. Hall & Co., 1973).

6,494. Crowell, Rhoda
Papers. 1967-72. 1 carton.
Open. No guide.
Schlesinger Library.
Crowell was president of the Somerville chapter and then chairman of the Education Department of the Massachusetts Federation of Women's Clubs. Federation agendas, calls to meetings, correspondence, questionnaires regarding education, programs, chairman's handbooks, manuals, and bulletins.

6,495. Cumming, Adelaide (Fish) Hawley
Papers. 1922-67. 2.5 Hollinger boxes and 1 oversize vol.
Open. Unpublished guide.
Schlesinger Library.
Cumming (1905-) worked as a radio commentator from 1935 to 1948; then from 1950 to 1964 she played the role of Betty Crocker, an advertising agent for General Mills, on radio and television. Correspondence, speeches, program scripts, publicity photos, and articles primarily concern her career. Among topics included are the place of women in American history, women harness racers, Fanny Kemble, the World Center for Women's Archives, and the importance of Women voters. Papers concerning her Betty Crocker role consist mainly of promotional literature and speeches.

6,496. Curie, Marie (Sklodowska)
Papers. 1921. 1 item.
Open. Published and unpublished guides.
Schlesinger Library.
A framed autograph of Curie (1867-1934), who won the Nobel Prize for chemistry after she and her husband discovered radium and polonium. See Arthur and Elizabeth Schlesinger Library on the History of Women in America, *The Manuscript Inventories and the Catalogs of the Manuscripts, Books and Pictures,* vol. III (Boston: G. K. Hall & Co., 1973).

6,497. Curtis, Frances Greeley
Papers. 1957. 4 folders.
Open. Published and unpublished guides.
Schlesinger Library.
Collection includes letters of condolence, tributes, and obituaries on the death of Curtis (1867-1957), a member of the Boston School Committee from 1913 to 1925. See Arthur and Elizabeth Schlesinger Library on the History of Women in America, *The Manuscript Inventories and the Catalogs of the Manuscripts, Books and Pictures,* vol. III (Boston: G. K. Hall & Co., 1973).

6,498. Curtis, Vera
Papers. 1907-62. 1 Hollinger box and 1 vol.
Open. Published and unpublished guides.
Schlesinger Library.
Correspondence, writings, lecture notes, program notes, clippings, portraits, and publicity pictures pertain to the musical career of Curtis (1879-1962), who in 1912 became the first singer trained in America to perform with the Metropolitan Opera Company. See Arthur and Elizabeth Schlesinger Library on the History of Women in America, *The Manuscript Inventories and the Catalogs of the Manuscripts, Books and Pictures,* vol. III (Boston: G. K. Hall & Co., 1973).

6,499. Cushman, Nancy (Cox) McCormack
Papers. 1931-60. 1 folder.
Open. Published and unpublished guides.
Schlesinger Library.
Cushman (1885-1967) was a sculptor and art teacher. Manuscripts and articles include radio talks and interviews for the "Woman's Radio Review" series broadcast over NBC's WEAF in 1931 and 1936, which concern artcraft schools, Jane Addams, and modeling a bust of Gandhi in 1931. See Arthur and Elizabeth Schlesinger Library on the History of Women in America, *The Manuscript Inventories and the Catalogs of the Manuscripts, Books and Pictures,* vol. III (Boston: G. K. Hall & Co., 1973).

6,500. Dall, Caroline Wells (Healey)
Papers. 1841-1909. 2 Hollinger boxes.
Open. Published and unpublished guides.
Schlesinger Library.
Correspondence from John Patton of Toronto, and notebooks, scrapbooks of obituaries, and a poem and printed articles by Dall (1822-1912), a Boston author. One notebook, published in 1895, contains Caroline Healey's abstracts of the 1841 "conversations" of Margaret Fuller on Greek mythology at the house of Boston editor and reformer George Ripley; another contains Caroline Dall's notes on 1864-65 "conversations" of Mrs. R. P. Clarke, the mother of James Freeman Clarke, which were entitled "Studies towards the Life of 'A Business Woman'"; and the last contains hymns by clergyman Charles Henry Appleton Dall, which his wife Caroline Dall copied in 1855 at his request. See Arthur and Elizabeth Schlesinger Library on the History of Women in America, *The Manuscript Inventories and the Catalogs of the Manuscripts, Books and Pictures,* vol. III (Boston: G. K. Hall & Co., 1973).

6,501. Dame, Harriet Patience
Papers. 1891. 1 item.
Open. Published and unpublished guides.

Schlesinger Library.
Letter wherein Dame (1815-1900), a Civil War nurse and later a US Treasury Department clerk, accepts an honorary membership in the Trinity Historical Society. See Arthur and Elizabeth Schlesinger Library on the History of Women in America, *The Manuscript Inventories and the Catalogs of the Manuscripts, Books and Pictures,* vol. III (Boston: G. K. Hall & Co., 1973).

6,502. Dana
Papers. 1829-1956. 14 Hollinger boxes and 4 cartons.
Open. Published and unpublished guides.
Schlesinger Library.
Correspondence, diaries, notebooks, account books, and legal documents, mainly of the women members of the Dana family. Correspondence includes that of Sarah Watson Dana (1814-1907), wife of Richard Henry Dana, Jr. (1815-82), a maritime lawyer and Cambridge-Boston author who wrote *Two Years Before the Mast;* of their children Sarah W., Ruth Charlotte, Elizabeth Ellery (1846-1939), A. Henrietta Channing, Mary Rosamond, and Richard H. Dana III; and many letters written to Mrs. Dana before her marriage in 1841 by her mother, sisters, cousins, and aunts. Diaries and other papers of Mrs. Dana, of daughters Elizabeth Dana and Rosamond (Dana) Wild, and of Dana's sister Ruth Charlotte Dana (1814-1901) reflect their school years and later life. Legal documents such as wills, deeds, and trust accounts of the Dana family and others include material on the legal problems of several women R. H. Dana, Jr., and R. H. Dana, III, represented. See Arthur and Elizabeth Schlesinger Library on the History of Women in America, *The Manuscript Inventories and the Catalogs of the Manuscripts, Books and Pictures,* vol. III (Boston: G. K. Hall & Co., 1973).

6,503. Daniels, Mabel
Papers. Ca. 1903-60. 8 Hollinger boxes, 2 folders, and 1 tape.
Open. No guide.
Schlesinger Library.
Correspondence, musical scores, notebook, diary, photos and album, scrapbooks, articles, clippings, memorabilia, and other papers of Daniels, a composer. Includes correspondence with Mrs. Edward McDowell, Mrs. Stanley McCormick, Walter Piston, and Ada L. Comstock; a card file of music by Daniels; recording of "Three Observations for Three Woodwinds"; material on the Arlington Street Church in Boston and Unitarians; diary of Daniels's father George F. Daniels concerning his eighth trip to Europe; and articles on Edwin A. Robinson.

6,504. Danielson, Sarah
Papers. 1806. 2 items.
Open. Published and unpublished guides.
Schlesinger Library.
Letters regarding education and family matters from General William Eaton to Danielson, his stepdaughter, during her stay at Mrs. Rivardi's School in Philadelphia. See Arthur and Elizabeth Schlesinger Library on the History of Women in America, *The Manuscript Inventories and the Catalogs of the Manuscripts, Books and Pictures,* vol. III (Boston: G. K. Hall & Co., 1973).

6,505. D'Autremont
Papers. 1764-1840. 3 folders.
Open. Unpublished guide.
Schlesinger Library.
Translated correspondence, genealogical material, and portraits of a French widow and her three sons living on the western New York frontier.

6,506. Davies, Daisy Bell (Hitch)
Papers. 1932-35. 1 vol.
Open. Published and unpublished guides.
Schlesinger Library.
Davies (1877-1938) was a school teacher, member of various women's organizations and patriotic organizations, and mother. Correspondence, clippings, and her manuscript describing the effect on her family of the Depression, particularly during 1932 and 1933. See Arthur and Elizabeth Schlesinger Library on the History of Women in America, *The Manuscript Inventories and the Catalogs of the Manuscripts, Books and Pictures,* vol. III (Boston: G. K. Hall & Co., 1973).

6,507. Davis, Helen Clarkson (Miller)
Papers. 1902-54. 2 Hollinger boxes.
Open. Published and unpublished guides.
Schlesinger Library.
[Mrs. Harvey N.] Davis (1879-1968), an author, was headmistress of the Spence School in New York City from 1928 to 1932. Correspondence, autobiographical sketch, speeches, and articles chiefly concern Davis's work with the YMCA, the YWCA, Spence School, peace, world friendship, the League of Nations, and research. She wrote "Aspects of Religious Liberty in the Near East" and "Constitutions, Electoral Laws and Treaties of States in the Near and Middle East." See Arthur and Elizabeth Schlesinger Library on the History of Women in America, *The Manuscript Inventories and the Catalogs of the Manuscripts, Books and Pictures,* vol. III (Boston: G. K. Hall & Co., 1973).

6,508. Davis, Paulina (Kellogg) Wright
Papers. 1873. 1 item.
Open. Published and unpublished guides.
Schlesinger Library.
Letter by Davis (1813-76), a feminist, reformer, and suffragist, to her husband. See Arthur and Elizabeth Schlesinger Library on the History of Women in America, *The Manuscript Inventories and the Catalogs of the Manuscripts, Books and Pictures,* vol. III (Boston: G. K. Hall & Co., 1973).

6,509. Davis, Varina Anne (Howell)
Papers. 1905. 1 item.
Open. Published and unpublished guides.
Schlesinger Library.
Letter of Davis (1826-1906), widow of Jefferson Davis, who was president of the Confederacy, expresses condolences to a Dr. Stockton on the death of his daughter. See Arthur and Elizabeth Schlesinger Library on the History of Women in America, *The Manuscript Inventories and the Catalogs of the Manuscripts, Books and Pictures,* vol. III (Boston: G. K. Hall & Co., 1973).

6,510. Davison, Ann Maria
Papers. Ca. 1814-61. 1 Hollinger box.
Open. Unpublished guide.
Schlesinger Library.
Davison (1783-?) lived in New Orleans most of her life but traveled along the East Coast. Diaries covering 1847 to 1860 and an incomplete manuscript pertain to her religious thoughts, her application of religion to life, antislavery, and the life of blacks on the East Coast. Also included are notes, a notebook, and a penmanship booklet.

6,511. De Vries, Lini Moerkerk
Papers. ?-1975. 3.5 Hollinger boxes, 3 folders, and 1 vol.
Open. No guide.
Schlesinger Library.
An author, public health nurse, and teacher, de Vries worked as chief of American Hospital Number 3 on the Madrid-Valencia Road during the Spanish Civil War, as a public health nurse in New Mexico and in the Mexican mountains, and as a teacher of Mexican history and leader of a discussion group for Mexican and American women in Cuernavaca, Mexico. Correspondence, manuscripts and typescripts, photos, articles, and documents, including correspondence concerning a US re-entry visa, autobiographical pieces and articles about Mexico, manuscript and Japanese translation of *Please God, Take Care of the Mule,* and material about de Vries's work in Mexico and about the Cemanahuac educational community.

6,512. Dean, Vera Micheles
Papers. 1929-65. 6 Hollinger boxes, 3 cartons, and 1 folder.
Open. Published and unpublished guides.
Schlesinger Library.
[Mrs.] Dean (1903-72) was an editor, author, and lecturer associated with the Foreign Policy Association. Correspondence, article manuscripts, speeches, travel notes, biographical data, course syllabi, articles, and other papers of Dean, as well as FPA records. Collection also contains manuscripts or partial manuscripts of her books *Europe in Retreat, The Struggle for World Order, South America Looks at the Future, The United States and Russia, Foreign Policy Without Fear, The United Nations Today,* and of others of her books. See Arthur and Elizabeth Schlesinger Library on the History of Women in America, *The Manuscript Inventories and the Catalogs of the Manuscripts, Books and Pictures,* vol. III (Boston: G. K. Hall & Co., 1973).

6,513. Deland, Margaret Wade (Campbell)
Papers. 1884-1937. 8 items.
Open. Published and unpublished guides.
Schlesinger Library.
Correspondence of Deland (1857-1945), an author, consists of letters dated 1884 concerning her work with unwed mothers and later letters concerning her literary career. See Arthur and Elizabeth Schlesinger Library on the History of Women in America, *The Manuscript Inventories and the Catalogs of the Manuscripts, Books and Pictures,* vol. III (Boston: G. K. Hall & Co., 1973).

6,514. Delta Kappa Gamma Society
Records. 1954-68. 1.5 Hollinger boxes.
Open. Published and unpublished guides.
Schlesinger Library.
The Michigan branch of Delta Kappa Gamma, a society for women in education, was founded in 1938. Issues of the journals *Michigan Heritage, The Delta Kappa Gamma Bulletin,* and *Michigan History;* biographies of women teachers by Society members; and the publications *Brief History of the Delta Kappa Gamma Society, Michigan, 1938-1961,* and *Charlotte, 1863-1963.* The journals also contain biographies of Michigan pioneer women. See Arthur and Elizabeth Schlesinger Library on the History of Women in America, *The Manuscript Inventories and the Catalogs of the Manuscripts, Books and Pictures,* vol. III (Boston: G. K. Hall & Co., 1973).

6,515. Demarest, Victoria Booth
Papers. Nd. 16 cartons.
Partially closed. No guide.
Schlesinger Library.
Correspondence, publicity releases, scrapbooks, ordination scrapbook, and clippings reflect the career of Demarest (ca. 1890s-), an itinerant evangelist, minister, singer, and dramatist, who is the granddaughter of General William Booth, founder of The Salvation Army.

6,516. Denison House
Records. 1891-1961. 6 Hollinger boxes and 15 oversize vols.
Open. Published and unpublished guides.
Schlesinger Library.
Founded in 1892 in Boston's South End by a small group of college-educated women, Denison House was a settlement house which offered camps, clubs, clinics, union organization, and other services for the neighborhood's mixed nationalities; in 1943 the House was moved to the Dorchester-Roxbury area. Minutes, annual reports, day books, photos, scrapbooks, clippings, pamphlets, posters, and invitations. Organizers included Emily Balch, Helen Cheever, Vida Scudder, and [Miss] Helena

Dudley, who was head worker between 1893 and 1912. See Arthur and Elizabeth Schlesinger Library on the History of Women in America, *The Manuscript Inventories and the Catalogs of the Manuscripts, Books and Pictures,* vol. III (Boston: G. K. Hall & Co., 1973).

6,517. Densen-Gerber, Judianne
Papers. Nd. 1 folder.
Open. No guide.
Schlesinger Library.
Trained as a lawyer and a psychiatrist, Densen-Gerber (1934-) founded the Odyssey House, which is a drug rehabilitation center. Consists of material on Odyssey House and Densen-Gerber.

6,518. DeVoto, Avis
Papers. 1952-68. 3 Hollinger boxes.
Closed. Unpublished guide.
Schlesinger Library.
An editor for Alfred A. Knopf Inc. who was associated with academic institutions in Cambridge, DeVoto (1904-) spent much of her life handling correspondence of her husband Bernard DeVoto, an author, editor, historian, and literary critic. Correspondence, manuscripts, recipes, photos, and clippings.

6,519. Dewey, Frances E. (Hutt)
Papers. 1949. 1 item.
Open. Published and unpublished guides.
Schlesinger Library.
Letter of Dewey (1903-70), the wife of Thomas E. Dewey, to Niles R. Becker thanking him for a birthday wire. See Arthur and Elizabeth Schlesinger Library on the History of Women in America, *The Manuscript Inventories and the Catalogs of the Manuscripts, Books and Pictures,* vol. III (Boston: G. K. Hall & Co., 1973).

6,520. Dewson, Mary Williams
Papers. 1896-1959. 3 Hollinger boxes and 1 oversize vol.
Open. Published and unpublished guides.
Schlesinger Library.
[Miss] Dewson (1874-1962), assistant director of the US Department of Labor's Children's Bureau, was active in various organizations, many of which were concerned with improving the status of women. Correspondence, speech manuscripts, fliers, clippings, and published works pertain to Dewson's work in 1917 and 1918 with the American National Red Cross in France, with the National Consumers' League on minimum wage problems, with the Democratic National Committee's women's division on politics, and with the Women's Education and Industrial Union located in Boston and the Massachusetts Industrial School for Girls located in Lancaster. Manuscript biography of her mother Elizabeth Weld (Williams) Dewson (1836-1912) is also included. See Arthur and Elizabeth Schlesinger Library on the History of Women in America, *The Manuscript Inventories and the Catalogs of the Manuscripts, Books and Pictures,* vol. III (Boston: G. K. Hall & Co., 1973).

6,521. Diary of M. I. M.
Papers. 1854. 1 folder.
Open. Published and unpublished guides.
Schlesinger Library.
Diary of M. I. M. (1830-?) gives details of life as a school teacher in Lynn, MA, and reflects social life and customs of the town. See Arthur and Elizabeth Schlesinger Library on the History of Women in America, *The Manuscript Inventories and the Catalogs of the Manuscripts, Books and Pictures,* vol. III (Boston: G. K. Hall & Co., 1973).

6,522. Dickinson, Anna Elizabeth
Papers. 1864-82. 6 items.
Open. Published and unpublished guides.
Schlesinger Library.
Letters by Dickinson (1842-1932), a Civil War orator and lyceum lecturer. See Arthur and Elizabeth Schlesinger Library on the History of Women in America, *The Manuscript Inventories and the Catalogs of the Manuscripts, Books and Pictures,* vol. III (Boston: G. K. Hall & Co., 1973).

6,523. Dignam, Dorothy
Papers. 1876-1960. 5 Hollinger boxes and 3 folders.
Open. Published and unpublished guides.
Schlesinger Library.
An active member and historian of Advertising Women of New York, Dignam (1896-) worked in advertising, particularly of fashion, beauty, and homemaking products. Correspondence, diaries, travel journal, school notebooks, histories, and articles. She spent the 1920s in Europe promoting consumer relations and home appliances, then worked in Philadelphia during the 1930s and in New York City during WWII. Her letters, which contain correspondence with Christine Frederick, and her diaries reflect changing economic and social conditions; her war diaries describe WWII action on the home front. Material on AWNY and women in advertising is included. See Arthur and Elizabeth Schlesinger Library on the History of Women in America, *The Manuscript Inventories and the Catalogs of the Manuscripts, Books and Pictures,* vol. III (Boston: G. K. Hall & Co., 1973).

6,524. Dillon Collection, Series I: Suffrage Miscellany
Collection. 1879-1920. 0.5 Hollinger box.
Open. Published and unpublished guides.
Schlesinger Library.
Woman suffrage cartoons, autographs, calendars, posters, banners, scrapbooks, pictures, and memorabilia. See Arthur and Elizabeth Schlesinger Library on the History of Women in America, *The Manuscript Inventories and the Catalogs of the Manuscripts, Books and Pictures,* vol. III (Boston: G. K. Hall & Co., 1973).

6,525. Dillon Collection, Series II: Catt, Carrie Clinton (Lane) Chapman
Papers. 1904-41. Ca. 1 Hollinger box.
Open. Published and unpublished guides.
Schlesinger Library.
Catt (1859-1947) was a national woman suffrage leader. Biographical material, clippings, memorabilia, and copies of Catt's speeches and articles regarding suffrage and other aspects of women's rights. See Arthur and Elizabeth Schlesinger Library on the History of Women in America, *The Manuscript Inventories and the Catalogs of the Manuscripts, Books and Pictures,* vol. III (Boston: G. K. Hall & Co., 1973).

6,526. Dillon Collection, Series III: Harbert, Elizabeth Morrison Boynton
Papers. 1870-1921. Ca. 0.5 Hollinger box.
Open. Published and unpublished guides.
Schlesinger Library.
[Mrs.] Harbert (1845-1925) was an officer of the Illinois Equal Suffrage Association. Correspondence from Elizabeth Cady Stanton, Isabella Beecher Hooker, and Susan B. Anthony; articles; photos; and scrapbooks of clippings from "Woman's Kingdom," a woman's section of the Chicago newspaper *Inter Ocean.* See Arthur and Elizabeth Schlesinger Library on the History of Women in America, *The Manuscript Inventories and the Catalogs of the Manuscripts, Books and Pictures,* vol. III (Boston: G. K. Hall & Co., 1973).

6,527. Dillon Collection, Series IV: Harte, Grace H.
Papers. 1887-1943. Ca. 0.5 Hollinger box.
Open. Published and unpublished guides.
Schlesinger Library.
Correspondence of Harte, a Chicago lawyer, and articles pertaining to women lawyers, particularly those who graduated from Rockford College. See Arthur and Elizabeth Schlesinger Library on the History of Women in America, *The Manuscript Inventories and the Catalogs of the Manuscripts, Books and Pictures,* vol. III (Boston: G. K. Hall & Co., 1973).

6,528. Dillon Collection, Series V: Women Educators of Illinois
Collection. 1941. Ca. 0.5 Hollinger box.
Open. Published and unpublished guides.
Schlesinger Library.
Biographies of 15 Illinois educators. See Arthur and Elizabeth Schlesinger Library on the History of Women in America, *The Manuscript Inventories and the Catalogs of the Manuscripts, Books and Pictures,* vol. III (Boston: G. K. Hall & Co., 1973).

6,529. Dillon Collection, Series VI: Johnson, Carrie Ashton
Papers. 1891-1941. Ca. 0.5 Hollinger box.
Open. Published and unpublished guides.
Schlesinger Library.
Correspondence, including many letters from Mary E. Holmes, and a scrapbook. See Arthur and Elizabeth Schlesinger Library on the History of Women in America, *The Manuscript Inventories and the Catalogs of the Manuscripts, Books and Pictures,* vol. III (Boston: G. K. Hall & Co., 1973).

6,530. Dillon Collection, Series VII: McCulloch, Catherine Gougar (Waugh)
Papers. 1868-1943. Ca. 13 Hollinger boxes.
Open. Published and unpublished guides.
Schlesinger Library.
An Illinois lawyer in partnership with her husband Frank, McCulloch (1862-1945) also worked for woman suffrage and uniform laws. Biographical material, suffrage correspondence, LWV correspondence, articles, speeches, scrapbook, pamphlets, clippings, and other publications pertaining to the legal status of women in each state from 1910 to 1912 and from 1920 to 1923. In addition to practicing law and raising four children, McCulloch was particularly active with suffrage associations, women's clubs, and the LWV in attempts to remove all disabilities imposed on married women by common law. See Arthur and Elizabeth Schlesinger Library on the History of Women in America, *The Manuscript Inventories and the Catalogs of the Manuscripts, Books and Pictures,* vol. III (Boston: G. K. Hall & Co., 1973).

6,531. Dillon Collection, Series VIII: Reid, Harriet
Papers. 1920-43. Ca. 0.33 Hollinger box.
Open. Published and unpublished guides.
Schlesinger Library.
Correspondence regarding civil service and the appointment of Reid, an Illinois lawyer, as arbitrator with the Illinois Industrial Commission, 1920-27. See Arthur and Elizabeth Schlesinger Library on the History of Women in America, *The Manuscript Inventories and the Catalogs of the Manuscripts, Books and Pictures,* vol. III (Boston: G. K. Hall & Co., 1973).

6,532. Dillon Collection, Series IX: Reilly, Caroline I.
Papers. 1907-41. Ca. 0.33 Hollinger box.
Open. Published and unpublished guides.
Schlesinger Library.
Correspondence with Carrie Chapman Catt, Anna Howard Shaw, and others, as well as articles by Reilly, a suffragist. See Arthur and Elizabeth Schlesinger Library on the History of Women in America, *The Manuscript Inventories and the Catalogs of the Manuscripts, Books and Pictures,* vol. III (Boston: G. K. Hall & Co., 1973).

6,533. Dillon Collection, Series X: Robinson, Lelia J.
Papers. 1887-90. Ca. 0.33 Hollinger box.
Open. Published and unpublished guides.
Schlesinger Library.
An attorney, Robinson was a member of the Equity

Club, a club for women lawyers. Correspondence from lawyers describing their background and legal experience and Club annual containing similar letters. See Arthur and Elizabeth Schlesinger Library on the History of Women in America, *The Manuscript Inventories and the Catalogs of the Manuscripts, Books and Pictures,* vol. III (Boston: G. K. Hall & Co., 1973).

6,534. Dillon Collection, Series XI: Shaw, Anna Howard, and Anthony, Lucy
Papers. 1877-1944. Ca. 6.5 Hollinger boxes.
Open. Published and unpublished guides.
Schlesinger Library.
Shaw (1847-1919) was a minister; a speaker for temperance, woman suffrage, and the peace movement; and president of the National American Woman Suffrage Association from 1904 to 1915. Anthony was her friend and secretary. Correspondence, diaries, appointment books, speeches, tributes, biographical and other articles, photos, and clippings relate to Shaw's varied career activities. Correspondents include Carrie Chapman Catt, Lucy Stone, and Susan B. Anthony. Also included is some of Lucy Anthony's correspondence. See Arthur and Elizabeth Schlesinger Library on the History of Women in America, *The Manuscript Inventories and the Catalogs of the Manuscripts, Books and Pictures,* vol. III (Boston: G. K. Hall & Co., 1973).

6,535. Dillon Collection, Series XII: Stantial, Edna Lamprey
Papers. 1908-44. Ca. 1 Hollinger box.
Open. Published and unpublished guides.
Schlesinger Library.
Correspondence, speeches, articles, reports, leaflets, and clippings of highlights of the women's rights movement, including material about or from such women as Alice Stone Blackwell and Carrie Chapman Catt. See Arthur and Elizabeth Schlesinger Library on the History of Women in America, *The Manuscript Inventories and the Catalogs of the Manuscripts, Books and Pictures,* vol. III (Boston: G. K. Hall & Co., 1973).

6,536. Dillon Collection, Series XIII: Stewart, Ella (Seass)
Papers. 1903-32. Ca. 0.5 Hollinger box.
Open. Published and unpublished guides.
Schlesinger Library.
Stewart (1871-?) held office in the Illinois Equal Suffrage Association and the National American Woman Suffrage Association. Correspondence with such women as Alice Stone Blackwell, Lucy Anthony, Anna Howard Shaw, and Carrie Chapman Catt; articles; and scrapbooks. See Arthur and Elizabeth Schlesinger Library on the History of Women in America, *The Manuscript Inventories and the Catalogs of the Manuscripts, Books and Pictures,* vol. III (Boston: G. K. Hall & Co., 1973).

6,537. Dillon Collection, Series XIV: Leaflets and Pamphlets
Collection. Ca. 1890-1915. Ca. 0.5 Hollinger box.
Open. Published and unpublished guides.
Schlesinger Library.
Pro-woman suffrage leaflets and pamphlets written by a variety of people. See Arthur and Elizabeth Schlesinger Library on the History of Women in America, *The Manuscript Inventories and the Catalogs of the Manuscripts, Books and Pictures,* vol. III (Boston: G. K. Hall & Co., 1973).

6,538. Dingman, Mary Agnes
Papers. 1915-57. 1 Hollinger box and 1 oversize folder.
Open. Published and unpublished guides.
Schlesinger Library.
Dingman (1875-1961) was chairman of the Women's International Organization peace and disarmament committee, 1931-39, and traveled abroad lecturing for the World's YWCA, 1920-35. Correspondence, speeches, articles, clippings, biographical material, minutes, and committee reports, including records of the committee. See Arthur and Elizabeth Schlesinger Library on the History of Women in America, *The Manuscript Inventories and the Catalogs of the Manuscripts, Books and Pictures,* vol. III (Boston: G. K. Hall & Co., 1973).

6,539. Dix, Dorothea Lynde
Papers. 1830. 1 item.
Open. Published and unpublished guides.
Schlesinger Library.
A letter to President Andrew Jackson from Dix (1802-87), an humanitarian who crusaded for the mentally ill and a superintendent of army nurses during the Civil War. See Arthur and Elizabeth Schlesinger Library on the History of Women in America, *The Manuscript Inventories and the Catalogs of the Manuscripts, Books and Pictures,* vol. III (Boston: G. K. Hall & Co., 1973).

6,540. Dodge, Jane Gay
Papers. 1861-1951. 1 Hollinger box and 2 vols.
Open. Published and unpublished guides.
Schlesinger Library.
Dodge's aunt [Miss] E. Jane Gay traveled with [Miss] Alice Cunningham Fletcher, who apportioned land to the Indians. Correspondence, manuscripts, and photos pertain to activities of several women associated with the Nez Percé Indians between 1889 and 1892. Correspondence includes letters from Francis LaFlesche, an Indian whom Fletcher adopted. Also contained are papers, 1861-77, of Dorothea L. Dix, primarily letters from famous contemporaries. See Arthur and Elizabeth Schlesinger Library on the History of Women in America, *The Manuscript Inventories and the Catalogs of the Manuscripts, Books and Pictures,* vol. III (Boston: G. K. Hall & Co., 1973).

6,541. Dodge, Mary Abigail
Papers. Ca. 1895. 2 items.
Open. Published and unpublished guides.
Schlesinger Library.
Letters of Dodge (1833-96), an author who used the pseudonym Gail Hamilton. See Arthur and Elizabeth Schlesinger Library on the History of Women in America, *The Manuscript Inventories and the Catalogs of the Manuscripts, Books and Pictures,* vol. III (Boston: G. K. Hall & Co., 1973).

6,542. Drinker, Sophie Lewis (Hutchinson)
Papers. Nd. 2 cartons, 2 boxes, and 2 recording discs.
Open. No guide.
Schlesinger Library.
Correspondence, notebooks, and card files of [Mrs. Henry Sandwith] Drinker contain material about goddesses, female singers, and music. Included are letters from Mary (Ritter) Beard, Mary Milbank Brown, and Marjorie White.

6,543. Drysdale, Euphemia
Papers. 1922-31. 6 items.
Open. Published and unpublished guides.
Schlesinger Library.
Drysdale was a minister. Letters, articles about Drysdale, and an article by her. See Arthur and Elizabeth Schlesinger Library on the History of Women in America, *The Manuscript Inventories and the Catalogs of the Manuscripts, Books and Pictures,* vol. III (Boston: G. K. Hall & Co., 1973).

6,544. Dummer, Ethel (Sturges)
Papers. 1766-1954. 43.5 Hollinger boxes and 1 folder.
Access restricted. Published and unpublished guides.
Schlesinger Library.
Family papers include those of Dummer (1866-1954), a philanthropist and social welfare leader, and her daughter Katharine (Dummer) Fisher (1892-1961). Correspondence, speeches, photos, reports, minutes, and articles. Material documents Dummer's efforts on behalf of juvenile delinquents, prostitutes, and illegitimate children, as well as her interest in progressive education and Chicago public schools and her work with leaders of the mental hygiene movement. Included is correspondence with her daughter Ethel Mintzer and such sociologists, psychiatrists, social workers, and educators as Jane Addams, Havelock Ellis, Sigmund Freud, Jessie Hodder, Karen Horney, Julia Lathrop, Norman Thomas, Miriam Van Waters, and others.

Katharine Fisher was active in Chicago civic affairs such as education and in the LWV on the local and national levels. Her papers include her correspondence with her husband and others, a note from Supreme Court Justice Felix Frankfurter, records of the LWV of Winnetka, IL, and poetry. Collection also includes 18th-and 19th-century letters and documents of the Sturges and Dummer families, both of which were prominent in Illinois. See Arthur and Elizabeth Schlesinger Library on the History of Women in America, *The Manuscript Inventories and the Catalogs of the Manuscripts, Books and Pictures,* vol. III (Boston: G. K. Hall & Co., 1973).

6,545. Dunaway, Margaret Fowler
Papers. 1922-64. 4 Hollinger boxes.
Open. Published and unpublished guides.
Schlesinger Library.
[Mrs. Maurice Don Carlos] Dunaway was a poet who lived in Missouri and Cambridge. Correspondence from her son Don Carlos and daughter Dorothy who traveled abroad; her poems; articles; and journals which discuss her home and social life, children and grandchildren, the education of children, travels in the US and abroad, and national and international affairs. See Arthur and Elizabeth Schlesinger Library on the History of Women in America, *The Manuscript Inventories and the Catalogs of the Manuscripts, Books and Pictures,* vol. III (Boston: G. K. Hall & Co., 1973).

6,546. Dunham, Catherine Devenney
Papers. Ca. 1884-1920. 0.5 Hollinger box.
Open. Published and unpublished guides.
Schlesinger Library.
[Mrs. William] Dunham was a prominent club woman in Michigan who was active in causes affecting women. Manuscripts of speeches read before women's clubs in Jackson and Concord, MI, concerning the WCTU, temperance, woman suffrage, and the rights of women, particularly the rights of mothers as guardians of their children. See Arthur and Elizabeth Schlesinger Library on the History of Women in America, *The Manuscript Inventories and the Catalogs of the Manuscripts, Books and Pictures,* vol. III (Boston: G. K. Hall & Co., 1973).

6,547. Durr, Virginia Foster
Papers. 1950-74. 1 Hollinger box and 8 folders.
Partially closed. No guide.
Schlesinger Library.
The wife of attorney Clifford Durr, Virginia Durr (ca. 1900-) supported Rosa Parks, a seamstress in the Durr household, in her defiance of laws requiring segregated seating in buses in Montgomery, AL. Correspondence involving Virginia Durr, Clifford Durr (1899-1975), James Dombrowski, Patricia Lee Murphy, Corliss Lamont and his wife Helen Lamb Lamont, and Clark and Mairi Foreman; articles from the *New South* written by Virginia Durr; and a pamphlet describing the memorial service for Clifford Durr. Subjects discussed include McCarthyism, civil rights in the South, and US politics.

6,548. Dutcher, Caroline M.
Papers. 1820-32. 1 item.
Open. Published and unpublished guides.
Schlesinger Library.
Dutcher was a student at the Litchfield Female

Academy in Litchfield, CT, in the 1820s. A remembrance book with a handwritten verse and friend's autograph on each page. See Arthur and Elizabeth Schlesinger Library on the History of Women in America, *The Manuscript Inventories and the Catalogs of the Manuscripts, Books and Pictures,* vol. III (Boston: G. K. Hall & Co., 1973).

6,549. Eames, Emma Hayden
Papers. 1886-91. 1 Hollinger box.
Open. Published and unpublished guides.
Schlesinger Library.
Eames (1865-1952) was an operatic soprano who made her debut in 1891. Consists of letters to Francis Wilson Lee of Boston, treasurer of a fund raised by friends to finance Eames's musical studies abroad. Eames was married to Julian Story from 1891 to 1907 and to Emilio de Gogorza from 1911 to 1932. See Arthur and Elizabeth Schlesinger Library on the History of Women in America, *The Manuscript Inventories and the Catalogs of the Manuscripts, Books and Pictures,* vol. III (Boston: G. K. Hall & Co., 1973).

6,550. Earhart, Amelia Mary
Papers. 1835-1965. 2 Hollinger boxes.
Open. Published and unpublished guides.
Schlesinger Library.
Earhart (1897-1937), who disappeared during a flight around the world, was the first woman to fly and to solo across the Atlantic Ocean, in 1928 and 1932 respectively. Correspondence, genealogies, photos, scrapbooks, clippings, baby books, and commemorative stamps. Includes extensive correspondence of Earhart's sister Muriel (Earhart) Morrissey concerning investigations of Earhart's disappearance; numerous photos of Earhart, her family, and her husband George Palmer Putnam; and genealogies of the families of her parents Edwin S. and Amy (Otis) Earhart. See Arthur and Elizabeth Schlesinger Library on the History of Women in America, *The Manuscript Inventories and the Catalogs of the Manuscripts, Books and Pictures,* vol. III (Boston: G. K. Hall & Co., 1973).

6,551. Eastman, Linda Anne
Papers. 1925-52. 1 Hollinger box.
Open. Published and unpublished guides.
Schlesinger Library.
As librarian of the Cleveland Public Library from 1918 to 1938, Eastman (1867-1963) was responsible for innovations in library service. Correspondence, biographical material, writings including the manuscript of *Portrait of a Librarian: William Howard Brett,* and other papers. See Arthur and Elizabeth Schlesinger Library on the History of Women in America, *The Manuscript Inventories and the Catalogs of the Manuscripts, Books and Pictures,* vol. III (Boston: G. K. Hall & Co., 1973).

6,552. Eastman, Mary F.
Papers. 1875. 1 item.
Open. Published and unpublished guides.
Schlesinger Library.
Letter in which Eastman offers to be of service to Mary (Putnam) Jacobi, a physician. See Arthur and Elizabeth Schlesinger Library on the History of Women in America, *The Manuscript Inventories and the Catalogs of the Manuscripts, Books and Pictures,* vol. III (Boston: G. K. Hall & Co., 1973).

6,553. Eastman, Mary (Reed)
Papers. 1832-77. 2 items.
Open. Published and unpublished guides.
Schlesinger Library.
Diaries in which Mary Reed (1806-78) of Marblehead, MA, who married Ornan Eastman in New York City in 1832, describes her wedding journey by ship and overland from New York City to Charleston, SC, New Orleans, St. Louis, and Cincinnati where she visited Lyman Beecher. Also included are descriptions of church and missionary meetings. See Arthur and Elizabeth Schlesinger Library on the History of Women in America, *The Manuscript Inventories and the Catalogs of the Manuscripts, Books and Pictures,* vol. III (Boston: G. K. Hall & Co., 1973).

6,554. Edmunds, Susan M.
Papers. Nd. 1 item.
Open. Published and unpublished guides.
Schlesinger Library.
December 26 letter to a Mrs. Childs thanking her for a gift. See Arthur and Elizabeth Schlesinger Library on the History of Women in America, *The Manuscript Inventories and the Catalogs of the Manuscripts, Books and Pictures,* vol. III (Boston: G. K. Hall & Co., 1973).

6,555. Ehrmann, Sara Emelie (Rosenfeld)
Papers. 1910-69. 1 Hollinger box.
Open. Unpublished guide.
Schlesinger Library.
Papers of [Mrs. Herbert] Ehrmann (1895-), including bylaws, correspondence, pamphlets, and clippings of the Brookline, MA, branch of the LWV; material of the Massachusetts and national LWV; a few personal items; and correspondence with the Lane Bryant Volunteer Award Committee.

6,556. Eliot, Abigail Adams
Papers. Ca. 1860-1974. 4.5 Hollinger boxes, 2 folders, and other items.
Open. No guide.
Schlesinger Library.
Eliot (1892-), cofounder of the Eliot-Pearson School of Child Study at Tufts University, is interested in education, particularly kindergarten, and in humanitarianism. Correspondence, diaries from trips, lecture notes, photos, articles, clippings, and memorabilia. Includes correspondence with clergyman William G. Eliot, from D. Dix to T. L. Eliot, and Abigail Eliot's letters home during her study in Oxford, England; material on Eliot's sister Martha M. Eliot; honorary degrees; and records of organizations in which Abigail Eliot was involved. Included are items about World Organizations on Early Childhood Education, the New England Association for Nursery Education, and the continuing education committee of the Radcliffe Alumnae Association.

6,557. Eliot, Emily M., and Morison, Emily Marshall (Eliot)
Papers. 1859-1922. 1 box.
Open. No guide.
Schlesinger Library.
Diaries of Emily M. Eliot and Emily M. (Eliot) Morison (1857-?), respectively grandmother and mother of Admiral Samuel Eliot Morison, reflect 19th-and early 20th-century social life and customs.

6,558. Eliot, Martha May
Papers. 1898-1975. 76 Hollinger boxes, 1 oversize folder, and 1 oversize vol.
Partially closed. Unpublished guide.
Schlesinger Library.
A pediatrician and expert on children's health, Eliot (1891-) was a founder of the World Health Organization and the fourth head of the Children's Bureau. Correspondence, speeches, articles, photos, clippings, posters, and other papers document Eliot's career and work in international, national, state, and local organizations which promoted maternal and child health. Includes ca. 550 of Eliot's articles and speeches. Among organizations represented are the Children's Bureau, the World Health Organization, the Harvard School of Public Health, the Massachusetts Committee on Children and Youth, and UNICEF.

6,559. Ellet, Elizabeth Fries (Lummis)
Papers. 1856. 1 item.
Open. Published and unpublished guides.
Schlesinger Library.
Note from Ellet (ca. 1812-77), an author and historian, to O. H. Peck. See Arthur and Elizabeth Schlesinger Library on the History of Women in America, *The Manuscript Inventories and the Catalogs of the Manuscripts, Books and Pictures,* vol. III (Boston: G. K. Hall & Co., 1973).

6,560. Elliman, Claiborne (Catlin)
Papers. 1914. 1 Hollinger box.
Open. Published and unpublished guides.
Schlesinger Library.
Manuscript of "Stirrup Cups," photos, and scrapbook all concern [Mrs. Kenneth] Elliman's four-month tour of Massachusetts, especially Cape Cod, for the National American Woman Suffrage Association. See Arthur and Elizabeth Schlesinger Library on the History of Women in America, *The Manuscript Inventories and the Catalogs of the Manuscripts, Books and Pictures,* vol. III (Boston: G. K. Hall & Co., 1973).

6,561. Emerson and Nichols
Papers. 1806-1953. 6.5 Hollinger boxes.
Open. Unpublished guide.
Schlesinger Library.
Chiefly papers of Marian Clarke Nichols (1873-1953) and her aunt Eugenie Homer Emerson (1854-1940), both of whom were from well-to-do Boston families. Correspondence, diaries, notebooks, clippings, photos, daguerreotypes, lantern slides, and organizational records of civil service reform groups in which Nichols was active. Nichols's papers contain diaries she kept during European trips, 1891 and 1893-94. She was active in the Massachusetts Civil Service Reform Association women's auxiliary, the National Civil Service Reform League, and the Massachusetts State Federation of Women's Clubs' committee on civil service reform. Homer's letters tell of her extensive European travels and life in Roxbury, MA. After her marriage in 1896 to Oliver P. Emerson (1845-1938), a minister, she devotes much attention in her correspondence to health and illness. Additional papers of the Homer and Nichols families can be found in the Nichols and Shurtleff family collection.

6,562. Emerson, Ellen Tucker
Papers. Nd. 1 item.
Open. Published and unpublished guides.
Schlesinger Library.
Emerson (1839-1909) was the daughter of Ralph Waldo Emerson. Letter to M. L. N. Myers comments on medical treatment her father used. See Arthur and Elizabeth Schlesinger Library on the History of Women in America, *The Manuscript Inventories and the Catalogs of the Manuscripts, Books and Pictures,* vol. III (Boston: G. K. Hall & Co., 1973).

6,563. Erin-Go-Bragh
Records. 1894-1953. 1 Hollinger box.
Open. Published and unpublished guides.
Schlesinger Library.
The Erin-Go-Bragh (Ireland forever) Club was founded in 1889 by girls who studied at Miss Ireland's school in Boston. Minutes from 1915 on, photos, and letters exchanged about the Catherine Innes Ireland Travelling Scholarship, which the group established at Radcliffe. Prominent club members included Emily Greene Balch and Alice Bache Gould. See Arthur and Elizabeth Schlesinger Library on the History of Women in America, *The Manuscript Inventories and the Catalogs of the Manuscripts, Books and Pictures,* vol. III (Boston: G. K. Hall & Co., 1973).

6,564. Ernst, Morris Leopold
Papers. 1933-37. 1 vol.
Open. Unpublished guide.
Schlesinger Library.
Ernst (1888-1976) was an attorney who represented physician Hannah Stone in a successful legal action against the US government, which had seized contraceptives shipped to Stone from Japan.

Correspondence, trial and appeal material, other legal papers, articles, clippings, and editorials constitute Ernst's record of the case.

6,565. Evans, Elizabeth Gardiner
Papers. 1882-1937. 9 Hollinger boxes.
Open. Published and unpublished guides.
Schlesinger Library.
[Mrs. Glendower] Evans (1856-1937) was a writer, social worker, and public servant who also worked for woman suffrage and establishment of a minimum wage. Correspondence, diaries, manuscripts, and articles relate to her work and colleagues. Evans was active in the Lawrence, MA, strike of 1919 and on behalf of Sacco and Vanzetti. Correspondents include Alice Brandeis, Louis Brandeis, the Glasier family of England, Jessie Donaldson Hodder, Henry James, William James, Fola LaFollette, Josephine Shaw Lowell, Elizabeth Cabot Putnam, and Miriam Van Waters. See Arthur and Elizabeth Schlesinger Library on the History of Women in America, *The Manuscript Inventories and the Catalogs of the Manuscripts, Books and Pictures,* vol. III (Boston: G. K. Hall & Co., 1973).

6,566. Fahnestock, Elizabeth Shenk Dickey
Papers. Late 19th century. 34-page vol.
Open. Published and unpublished guides.
Schlesinger Library.
Notebook of recipes collected by Fahnestock (1840-1924), a resident of Pennsylvania. See Arthur and Elizabeth Schlesinger Library on the History of Women in America, *The Manuscript Inventories and the Catalogs of the Manuscripts, Books and Pictures,* vol. III (Boston: G. K. Hall & Co., 1973).

6,567. Farragut, Virginia (Loyall)
Papers. Nd. 1 item.
Open. Published and unpublished guides.
Schlesinger Library.
Letter in which Farragut, second wife of Admiral David Farragut (1801-70), accepted a dinner invitation for the admiral and herself. See Arthur and Elizabeth Schlesinger Library on the History of Women in America, *The Manuscript Inventories and the Catalogs of the Manuscripts, Books and Pictures,* vol. III (Boston: G. K. Hall & Co., 1973).

6,568. Ferguson, Lucia
Papers. 1954. 5-page item.
Open. Published and unpublished guides.
Schlesinger Library.
Biography of Elva Shartel Ferguson, an Oklahoma Territory pioneer and newspaperwoman who was the wife of Territorial Governor Tom Ferguson, was written by her daughter-in-law and describes Elva Ferguson's early family life, her settling in Oklahoma, and her husband's appointment as governor. See Arthur and Elizabeth Schlesinger Library on the History of Women in America, *The Manuscript Inventories and the Catalogs of the Manuscripts, Books and Pictures,* vol. III (Boston: G. K. Hall & Co., 1973).

6,569. Field, Rachel Lyman
Papers. Ca. 1924-30. 1 folder.
Open. Published and unpublished guides.
Schlesinger Library.
Letters and cards to Sarah White Davis Emerson from Field (1894-1942), a poet, novelist, and children's writer. See Arthur and Elizabeth Schlesinger Library on the History of Women in America, *The Manuscript Inventories and the Catalogs of the Manuscripts, Books and Pictures,* vol. III (Boston: G. K. Hall & Co., 1973).

6,570. Fields, Annie (Adams)
Papers. 1882-1911. 11 items.
Open. Published and unpublished guides.
Schlesinger Library.
Letters and a poem of Fields (1834-1915), a Boston native descended from early Bay Colony settlers. She was acquainted with various literary figures and wrote prose and verse herself. See Arthur and Elizabeth Schlesinger Library on the History of Women in America, *The Manuscript Inventories and the Catalogs of the Manuscripts, Books and Pictures,* vol. III (Boston: G. K. Hall & Co., 1973).

6,571. Fields, Daisy B.
Papers. Nd. 1 folder.
Open. No guide.
Schlesinger Library.
Printed articles of Fields, an author whose particular concerns are career development for women and affirmative action programs for government and private industry.

6,572. Fisher, M. F. K.
Papers. Ca. 1929-74. 7 cartons and 1 folder.
Closed. No guide.
Schlesinger Library.
Correspondence, manuscripts, typescripts, menus, articles, and clippings of Fisher (1908-), a writer of cookbooks.

6,573. Flagg, Mildred (Buchanan)
Papers. 1900-55. 4 Hollinger boxes.
Open. Published and unpublished guides.
Schlesinger Library.
An active clubwoman in the Boston area, [Mrs.] Flagg (1886-) worked as a writer, lecturer, and organizer of Celebrity Breakfasts. Correspondence, including letters from authors, aviators, members of the clergy, college presidents, explorers, government officials, politicians, royalty, senators, sportsmen, and sportswomen. Also included are ca. 100 autographs of authors popular in the 1930s. See Arthur and Elizabeth Schlesinger Library on the History of Women in America, *The Manuscript Inventories and the Catalogs of the Manuscripts, Books and Pictures,* vol. III (Boston: G. K. Hall & Co., 1973).

6,574. Floyd, Olive B.
Papers. 1910-60. 2 boxes and 4 vols.
Partially closed. No guide.
Schlesinger Library.
Floyd is an author. Correspondence, diary for the year 1910, travel diaries, reading lists, two Westover School yearbooks, autograph book, scrapbooks, photo albums, photos, clippings, book, and memorabilia from trips abroad.

6,575. Follen, Eliza Lee (Cabot)
Papers. 1843-46. 2 items.
Open. Published and unpublished guides.
Schlesinger Library.
Letters by Follen (1787-1860), an antislavery worker and author of children's stories and of a biography of her German-born husband Charles Follen. See Arthur and Elizabeth Schlesinger Library on the History of Women in America, *The Manuscript Inventories and the Catalogs of the Manuscripts, Books and Pictures,* vol. III (Boston: G. K. Hall & Co., 1973).

6,576. Fosdick, Lucy H.
Papers. 1911. 22-page item.
Open. Published and unpublished guides.
Schlesinger Library.
Manuscript describes Fosdick's family's journey across the plains to Colorado between 1861 and 1864. See Arthur and Elizabeth Schlesinger Library on the History of Women in America, *The Manuscript Inventories and the Catalogs of the Manuscripts, Books and Pictures,* vol. III (Boston: G. K. Hall & Co., 1973).

6,577. Foster, Abigail (Kelley)
Papers. 1844-86. 2 items.
Open. Published and unpublished guides.
Schlesinger Library.
Letters of Foster (1810-87), an abolitionist and woman's rights advocate: the first, addressed to Messrs. and Miss Abigail Jemima Hutchinson, discusses the antislavery movement in New Hampshire, while the second declines an invitation, citing reasons of ill health. See Arthur and Elizabeth Schlesinger Library on the History of Women in America, *The Manuscript Inventories and the Catalogs of the Manuscripts, Books and Pictures,* vol. III (Boston: G. K. Hall & Co., 1973).

6,578. Francis, Abigail B. (Allyn)
Papers. 1881. 1 item.
Open. No guide.
Schlesinger Library.
Letter from Francis, the wife of Lydia Child's clergyman brother Convers Francis, to [Mrs.] Caroline Dall describes Child's death and funeral.

6,579. Frank, Adelaide (Schulkind)
Papers. 1925-72. 1 Hollinger box and 2 vols.
Open. Unpublished guide.
Schlesinger Library.
[Mrs.] Frank was for more than 30 years executive secretary of the League for Mutual Aid. Correspondence, mainly letters to Frank concerning League assistance, and bulletins. The League, founded in 1920, has helped individuals in liberal and labor movements with loans and guidance, defraying the cost through annual memberships and other contributions. Correspondents include Ralph J. Bunche, Mary Ware Dennett, Katherine Anne Porter, and Rosika Schwimmer.

6,580. Frederick, Christine (McGaffey)
Papers. Ca. 1910-40. 1 carton, 2 packages, and 1 Hollinger box.
Open. No guide.
Schlesinger Library.
Correspondence, clipping scrapbooks, and photos pertain to the career of Frederick (1883-1970), who promoted household efficiency by lecturing, writing, and consulting.

6,581. Freeman, Frances Tuckerman
Papers. 1956-57. 7 items.
Open. Published and unpublished guides.
Schlesinger Library.
Speeches made by [Mrs.] Freeman, an associate of the AAUW's status of women committee from 1956 to 1957. See Arthur and Elizabeth Schlesinger Library on the History of Women in America, *The Manuscript Inventories and the Catalogs of the Manuscripts, Books and Pictures,* vol. III (Boston: G. K. Hall & Co., 1973).

6,582. Friedan, Betty
Papers. Ca. 1940-76. 50 cartons, 56 file boxes, and 21 tapes.
Access restricted. No guide.
Schlesinger Library.
Friedan (1921-), a writer, publicist, political activist, and speaker on the subject of women, helped found the National Organization for Women. Correspondence, manuscripts, financial reports, leaflets, clippings, printed matter, video cassettes, and recording tapes. Includes material about her career; her book *The Feminine Mystique;* the manuscript for *It Changed My Life;* articles for *McCall's Magazine;* labor articles; poems and short stories written as a student at Smith College; notes and financial records for Friedan's 1972 campaign for delegate to the Democratic Convention; NOW correspondence and leaflets; printed material from NOW's Legal Defense and Education Fund, the National Women's Political Caucus, the National Abortion Rights Action League, and other organizations; and items concerning the International Women's Year and Mexico City conferences (1975), the Community Resources Pool, the World Population Conference in Bucharest, the International Feminist Conference, and the Women's Bank.

6,583. Friends of the Framingham Reformatory
Records. 1948-57. 16 Hollinger boxes.
Open. Published and unpublished guides.
Schlesinger Library.
The group, formed in Boston in 1948, sought to defend the Reformatory's superintendent Miriam Van Waters and to work for enlightened methods of dealing with women offenders. Committee reports, correspondence, 41 scrapbooks, articles, state government documents, and clipping document defense of Van Waters against an attempt to remove her because of alleged irregularities at the Reformatory. She was cleared of all charges. See Arthur and Elizabeth Schlesinger Library on the History of Women in America, *The Manuscript Inventories and the Catalogs of the Manuscripts, Books and Pictures,* vol. III (Boston: G. K. Hall & Co., 1973).

6,584. Friends of the Schlesinger Library
Records. 1970-75. 7 tapes.
Open. Unpublished guide.
Schlesinger Library.
The group, founded in 1970, provides support and aid to the Library. Collection consists of recordings of talks given before the group's annual meetings, with addresses by Elizabeth Koontz, Catharine (Drinker) Bowen and Helen Howe, Kathleen Loucheim, Pauline Kael, Charlotte Curtis, and by Arvonne Fraser, Barbara Mikulski, Jill Ruckelshaus, and C. Delores Tucker on women in politics.

6,585. Frysinger, Grace Elizabeth
Papers. 1919-56. 1 Hollinger box.
Open. Published and unpublished guides.
Schlesinger Library.
[Miss] Frysinger (1885-ca. 1973) was senior home economist for the extension service of the US Department of Agriculture. Correspondence, programs, articles, and photos pertaining to education of rural women in the US and abroad, with items about the 1934 Rural Home Conference in Washington, DC, and the Triennial Conferences of the Associated Country Women of the World, 1936, 1939, and 1953. See Arthur and Elizabeth Schlesinger Library on the History of Women in America, *The Manuscript Inventories and the Catalogs of the Manuscripts, Books and Pictures,* vol. III (Boston: G. K. Hall & Co., 1973).

6,586. Fuller, Jean Wood
Papers. 1954-57. 2 folders.
Open. Published and unpublished guides.
Schlesinger Library.
[Mrs.] Fuller (1913-) was director of women's activities for the Federal Civil Defense Administration. Biographical material, clippings, and speeches on the role of women in civil defense. See Arthur and Elizabeth Schlesinger Library on the History of Women in America, *The Manuscript Inventories and the Catalogs of the Manuscripts, Books and Pictures,* vol. III (Boston: G. K. Hall & Co., 1973).

6,587. Fuller, Sarah Margaret
Papers. Ca. 1840-1901. 1 folder.
Open. Published and unpublished guides.
Schlesinger Library.
Fuller (1810-50), an author and feminist, married the Marchese d'Ossoli. Correspondence, notes she made as a teacher in Providence, photo, and copy of her 1901 memorial service at Fire Island with comments by Julia Ward Howe and T. W. Higginson. See Arthur and Elizabeth Schlesinger Library on the History of Women in America, *The Manuscript Inventories and the Catalogs of the Manuscripts, Books and Pictures,* vol. III (Boston: G. K. Hall & Co., 1973).

6,588. Gage, Frances Dana Barker
Papers. Nd. 1 item.
Open. Published and unpublished guides.
Schlesinger Library.
Letter of Gage (1808-84), an active suffrage worker, to Susan B. Anthony. See Arthur and Elizabeth Schlesinger Library on the History of Women in America, *The Manuscript Inventories and the Catalogs of the Manuscripts, Books and Pictures,* vol. III (Boston: G. K. Hall & Co., 1973).

6,589. Gage, Matilda (Joslyn)
Papers. 1850-1900. 5 folders and 1 microfilm reel.
Open. Published and unpublished guides.
Schlesinger Library.
Correspondence, biographical material, speeches, and articles of Gage (1826-98), who was active in movements for women's rights and to upgrade the status of women. Correspondents include Susan B. Anthony, Lucy Stone, Lucretia Mott, and Matthew Vassar. See Arthur and Elizabeth Schlesinger Library on the History of Women in America, *The Manuscript Inventories and the Catalogs of the Manuscripts, Books and Pictures,* vol. III (Boston: G. K. Hall & Co., 1973).

6,590. Gallison, Marie (Reuter)
Papers. 1949. 1 vol.
Open. Published and unpublished guides.
Schlesinger Library.
[Mrs. Henry] Gallison (1861-?) was a German-born singer who taught at Radcliffe. Typescript of her autobiography "My Life in Two Continents," which describes her early life in Germany, her careers and family in the US, and her return in the late 1920s to Kaiserwerth, Germany. See Arthur and Elizabeth Schlesinger Library on the History of Women in America, *The Manuscript Inventories and the Catalogs of the Manuscripts, Books and Pictures,* vol. III (Boston: G. K. Hall & Co., 1973).

6,591. Gammell, Harriet Ives
Papers. 1898-1900. 1 folder.
Open. Published and unpublished guides.
Schlesinger Library.
Gammell was a wealthy Newport, RI, socialite. Collection includes two letters in French and a clipping about the wedding of Gammell and Thomas Safe of England. See Arthur and Elizabeth Schlesinger Library on the History of Women in America, *The Manuscript Inventories and the Catalogs of the Manuscripts, Books and Pictures,* vol. III (Boston: G. K. Hall & Co., 1973).

6,592. Gardener, Helen Hamilton
Papers. 1890-1942. 4 folders.
Open. Published and unpublished guides.
Schlesinger Library.
Gardener was the pen name used by this author and feminist who was the first woman to serve on the US Civil Service Commission; in her private life she was Alice (Chenoweth) Day (1853-1925), wife of Col. Selden Allen Day. Correspondence, 1907 diary, lists, and clipping provide information about Gardener's will and estate, particularly the bequest of her brain to Cornell University to disprove the theory that women's brains are smaller than men's. See Arthur and Elizabeth Schlesinger Library on the History of Women in America, *The Manuscript Inventories and the Catalogs of the Manuscripts, Books and Pictures,* vol. III (Boston: G. K. Hall & Co., 1973).

6,593. Gardiner Family
Papers. 1826-80. 4 Hollinger boxes.
Open. Published and unpublished guides.
Schlesinger Library.
Correspondence, journals, personal account book, notes, photos, and scrapbooks concern activities, social customs, and relationships among the Gardiners, a large, prominent Boston family. Letters from the related Perkins, Cary, Agassiz, and Cushing families are included, as well as a large number of letters written between 1853 and 1863 by Mary (Gardiner) [Mrs. William Nye] Davis to her parents William H. and Caroline Perkins Gardiner, Davis's travel journals, scrapbooks, and unpublished writings, one of which is a story about New England life in the 19th century. Also included are 12 letters by Elizabeth Cabot (Cary) Agassiz and one by Louis Agassiz. Letters written between 1850 and 1870 contain family and travel news. See Arthur and Elizabeth Schlesinger Library on the History of Women in America, *The Manuscript Inventories and the Catalogs of the Manuscripts, Books and Pictures,* vol. III (Boston: G. K. Hall & Co., 1973).

6,594. Gardner, Mary Sewall
Papers. 1902-54. 4 Hollinger boxes.
Open. Published and unpublished guides.
Schlesinger Library.
Gardner (1871-1961) directed the Providence, RI, District Nursing Association from 1905 to 1931, helped form the National Organization for Public Health Nursing and was its president from 1913 to 1915, traveled in Europe for the American National Red Cross during WWI, and helped organize public health nursing internationally after the war. Correspondence, notebooks, manuscripts, photos, and clippings, which reflect Gardner's life and career interests. Includes material for a study during the 1930s of public health nursing throughout the world. See Arthur and Elizabeth Schlesinger Library on the History of Women in America, *The Manuscript Inventories and the Catalogs of the Manuscripts, Books and Pictures,* vol. III (Boston: G. K. Hall & Co., 1973).

6,595. Garrison, William Lloyd
Papers. 1835-68. 5 items.
Open. Published and unpublished guides.
Schlesinger Library.
Letters by Garrison (1805-79), an abolitionist, to members of the Loring family. See Arthur and Elizabeth Schlesinger Library on the History of Women in America, *The Manuscript Inventories and the Catalogs of the Manuscripts, Books and Pictures,* vol. III (Boston: G. K. Hall & Co., 1973).

6,596. Gellhorn, Edna (Fischel)
Papers. 1919-60. 0.5 Hollinger box.
Open. Published and unpublished guides.
Schlesinger Library.
Correspondence and clippings of [Mrs. George] Gellhorn (1878-1970), a St. Louis civic worker who was director of the National American Woman Suffrage Association, president of the St. Louis and Missouri LWVs, and vice-president of the national LWV. The papers, which pertain to Gellhorn's positions in these organizations, contain extensive correspondence with Carrie Chapman Catt. See Arthur and Elizabeth Schlesinger Library on the History of Women in America, *The Manuscript Inventories and the Catalogs of the Manuscripts, Books and Pictures,* vol. III (Boston: G. K. Hall & Co., 1973).

6,597. Gerstenberg, Alice
Papers. 1921-51. 1 folder and 2 mss.
Open. Published and unpublished guides.
Schlesinger Library.
Gerstenberg (1885-1972) was active in the Chicago theater world from 1893 to 1921 and later wrote and produced plays in Boston, Chicago, New York, and other cities. Articles, theater programs, announcements, and correspondence of Gerstenberg reminiscing about her life and career in Chicago. Also includes correspondence by Nancy (Cox) McCormack Cushman describing her life between 1910 and 1921 as an art student and artist in the city. See Arthur and Elizabeth Schlesinger Library on the History of Women in America, *The Manuscript Inventories and the Catalogs of the Manuscripts, Books and Pictures,* vol. III (Boston: G. K. Hall & Co., 1973).

6,598. Gibbons, Abigail Hopper
Papers. 1890. 1 item.
Open. Published and unpublished guides.

Schlesinger Library.
Letter regarding autographs of the husband and father of Gibbons (1801-93), an abolitionist, philanthropist, and founder of the Infant Asylum and the Diet Kitchen. See Arthur and Elizabeth Schlesinger Library on the History of Women in America, *The Manuscript Inventories and the Catalogs of the Manuscripts, Books and Pictures,* vol. III (Boston: G. K. Hall & Co., 1973).

6,599. Gibson, Irene (Langhorne)
Papers. 1924. 1 item.
Open. Published and unpublished guides.
Schlesinger Library.
Letter from Gibson, the wife of Charles Dana Gibson, to Louis Shipman. See Arthur and Elizabeth Schlesinger Library on the History of Women in America, *The Manuscript Inventories and the Catalogs of the Manuscripts, Books and Pictures,* vol. III (Boston: G. K. Hall & Co., 1973).

6,600. Gilboy, Elizabeth Waterman
Papers. 1938-49. 4 folders.
Open. Published and unpublished guides.
Schlesinger Library.
Correspondence and reprint of a 1938 article "The Propensity to Consume" by [Mrs.] Gilboy (1903-73), an economist who was associate director of the Harvard Economics Research Project and a consultant to the US Bureau of Labor Statistics. She also wrote several books. See Arthur and Elizabeth Schlesinger Library on the History of Women in America, *The Manuscript Inventories and the Catalogs of the Manuscripts, Books and Pictures,* vol. III (Boston: G. K. Hall & Co., 1973).

6,601. Gilder, Jeannette Leonard
Papers. 1865-1917. 1 Hollinger box and 1 folder.
Open. Published and unpublished guides.
Schlesinger Library.
[Miss] Gilder (1849-1916) was a journalist, critic, and author who with her brother Joseph founded the *Critic* in New York City in 1881; she edited the publication until 1906. Personal and professional correspondence, manuscripts, school compositions, and a scrapbook. Included are letters she received from her mother and her brother Richard Watson Gilder while she was a student at Bridgeton Female Seminary in New Jersey and business correspondence with newspaper editors, literary figures, and publishers. See Arthur and Elizabeth Schlesinger Library on the History of Women in America, *The Manuscript Inventories and the Catalogs of the Manuscripts, Books and Pictures,* vol. III (Boston: G. K. Hall & Co., 1973).

6,602. Gilman, Charlotte (Perkins) [Stetson]
Papers. 1846-1961. 29 Hollinger boxes, 6 oversize vols., and 6 folders.
Open. Published and unpublished guides.
Schlesinger Library.
A socialist and deist, Gilman (1860-1935) was an independent thinker, author, and speaker who was an intellectual leader of the women's movement from the late 1890s through the mid-1920s. An advocate of economic independence for women, Gilman considered the ballot of secondary importance. Her interests ranged from sensible dress for women and physical fitness to birth control, Freud, and immigrants. Correspondence, diaries, journals, manuscripts, articles, clippings, photos, and drawings provide information about Gilman's personal and public life. Largest group of letters is to her future husband George Houghton Gilman.

Other correspondence includes a sizable group to her daughter Katharine between 1895 and 1934; letters from William Dean Howells, Jane Addams, and Florence Kelley; and items pertaining to her books and articles. Literary material includes manuscripts and typescripts of chapters for *Sex in Civilization* (1929) and *Woman's Coming of Age* (1930); the plays *A Pretty Idiot* (1889), *Changing Hands* (ca. 1890), and *Three Women;* the books *Social Ethics, A Study in Ethics* (1933), and "A Winter in California"; manuscripts by others; miscellaneous stories; poems; sermons; lectures; and reviews of her works. Entire collection available on microfiche. See Arthur and Elizabeth Schlesinger Library on the History of Women in America, *The Manuscript Inventories and the Catalogs of the Manuscripts, Books and Pictures,* vol. III (Boston: G. K. Hall & Co., 1973).

6,603. Goldman, Sarah Adler
Papers. 1928. 1 folder.
Open. Published and unpublished guides.
Schlesinger Library.
Manuscript of reminiscences of early life of Goldman (1858-1934) in a New York rabbi's family. She became the wife of attorney Julius Goldman and mother of four children. See Arthur and Elizabeth Schlesinger Library on the History of Women in America, *The Manuscript Inventories and the Catalogs of the Manuscripts, Books and Pictures,* vol. III (Boston: G. K. Hall & Co., 1973).

6,604. Goldmark Family
Papers. 1886-1960. 0.5 Hollinger box.
Open. Published and unpublished guides.
Schlesinger Library.
Josephine Clara Goldmark (1877-1950) and Pauline Goldmark (1896-1962) were associated with the National Consumers' League; active in social work, social research, and factory investigation; and supported labor legislation. Correspondence and articles reflect Goldmark family interests. Jane Addams, William James, and Florence Kelley were among the correspondents. See Arthur and Elizabeth Schlesinger Library on the History of Women in America, *The Manuscript Inventories and the Catalogs of the Manuscripts, Books and Pictures,* vol. III (Boston: G. K. Hall & Co., 1973).

6,605. Goodrich, Juliet T.
Papers. 1917-21. 1 Hollinger box.
Open. Unpublished guide.
Schlesinger Library.
Goodrich (1881-1963) sailed to France to work in an American National Red Cross canteen in 1917 and returned home shortly after the armistice in 1918. Correspondence includes Goodrich's letters to her aunt describing life in France, a few letters she wrote after her return, and a number of letters from her aunt Mrs. Magriore.

6,606. Goostray, Stella
Papers. 1917-40. 1 folder.
Open. Published and unpublished guides.
Schlesinger Library.
Goostray (1886-), a nursing educator, was president of the National League of Nursing Education from 1940 to 1944. Correspondence, photos, and mimeographed material pertain to work of the Woman's Committee and the Committee on Nursing of the Council of National Defense, 1917, and national defense planning and policies of the nursing profession, 1940. Included is a 1930 photo of M. Adelaide Nutting. See Arthur and Elizabeth Schlesinger Library on the History of Women in America, *The Manuscript Inventories and the Catalogs of the Manuscripts, Books and Pictures,* vol. III (Boston: G. K. Hall & Co., 1973).

6,607. Gordon, Linda
Oral history. 1976. 0.5 box.
Open. No guide.
Schlesinger Library.
Summaries of interviews conducted for classes of Gordon, an historian and history professor at the University of Massachusetts, Boston, with students' relatives and other women describing their early life, education, work, marriage, children, health, and attitudes toward unions, suffrage, and the women's liberation movement.

6,608. Gould, Elizabeth Porter
Papers. 1890-1904. 1 vol.
Open. Published and unpublished guides.
Schlesinger Library.
A bound volume of 1901-02 issues of *The Patriot Review,* a magazine "devoted to the interests of the Patriotic and Historical Organizations of the United States," and correspondence, notices, programs, sheet music, and photos, all of which Gould gathered to complement the magazine articles. See Arthur and Elizabeth Schlesinger Library on the History of Women in America, *The Manuscript Inventories and the Catalogs of the Manuscripts, Books and Pictures,* vol. III (Boston: G. K. Hall & Co., 1973).

6,609. Grant, Anne
Papers. 1835. 1 item.
Open. Published and unpublished guides.
Schlesinger Library.
Letter which [Mrs.] Grant (1755-1838) of Laggan, probably Scotland, a writer who traveled widely in America, wrote to a Mrs. Brewen in Edinburrogh (Edinburgh?), regarding her work and interest in missions and American Indians, especially the treatment of Black Hawk. See Arthur and Elizabeth Schlesinger Library on the History of Women in America, *The Manuscript Inventories and the Catalogs of the Manuscripts, Books and Pictures,* vol. III (Boston: G. K. Hall & Co., 1973).

6,610. Grant, Ida Honoré
Papers. 1891. 1 item.
Open. Published and unpublished guides.
Schlesinger Library.
Invitation to tea for a Mr. Hatfield from [Mrs. Frederick] Grant, daugter-in-law of U. S. Grant, writing from the US Legation. See Arthur and Elizabeth Schlesinger Library on the History of Women in America, *The Manuscript Inventories and the Catalogs of the Manuscripts, Books and Pictures,* vol. III (Boston: G. K. Hall & Co., 1973).

6,611. Gray, Peter
Papers. Nd. 1 folder.
Open. Published and unpublished guides.
Schlesinger Library.
Typescript of Gray's biography "Foundling's Heritage" of Hannah (Jensen) Kempfer, a Norwegian immigrant who became a teacher and a member of the Minnesota legislature. Kempfer, an orphan who arrived in the US with her foster parents at the age of six, became a state legislator in 1923 and remained in politics for nearly 20 years. See Arthur and Elizabeth Schlesinger Library on the History of Women in America, *The Manuscript Inventories and the Catalogs of the Manuscripts, Books and Pictures,* vol. III (Boston: G. K. Hall & Co., 1973).

6,612. Greeley, Gabrielle
Papers. 1887. 1 folder.
Open. Published and unpublished guides.
Schlesinger Library.
Letter written from Chappaqua, NY, by Greeley, daughter of Horace Greeley, to a Mr. Pringle. See Arthur and Elizabeth Schlesinger Library on the History of Women in America, *The Manuscript Inventories and the Catalogs of the Manuscripts, Books and Pictures,* vol. III (Boston: G. K. Hall & Co., 1973).

6,613. Greene Family
Papers. Ca. 1910-75. 5 cartons, 2 Hollinger boxes, and 1 oversize folder.
Open. No guide.
Schlesinger Library.
The Cambridge family of Henry Copley Greene (1871-1951) and Rosalind Huidekoper Greene (1885-1975) was interested in amateur theater, musicology, French culture, and a variety of social causes. Correspondence, travel notes, poems, manuscripts, wills, and a plaster bust. Family papers of Rosalind Greene and her mother, Henry

Greene, and four Greene daughters include poems by Rosalind Greene; letters from Katrine R. C. Greene (1912-66) to the family and to Richard C. Cabot, Ella (Lyman) Cabot, and others; material concerning Henry Greene's relief work in France during WWI and WWII; and correspondence with the Whiteheads, William James, and Ernest Hocking. Also included is a bust Katrine Greene cast of Henry Greene.

6,614. Gruenberg, Bertha Sanford
Papers. 1906-ca.1953. 3 cartons and 10 Hollinger boxes.
Open. No guide.
Schlesinger Library.
A free-lance writer, Gruenberg (1888-) was society editor of the *Minneapolis Tribune* and director of a summer camp. Collection of reports, books, and other items include articles written between 1906 and 1910 as Bertha B. Sanford, woman's department reporter and society editor of the *Tribune*. Other material pertains to her life in Philadelphia after marriage where by free-lance writing and public speaking she helped popularize such new ideas as housekeeping on a budget, progressive education, and part-time employment for educated women. For many years Gruenberg directed a summer camp which sought to implement John Dewey's philosophy. Collection contains 1923-53 records of Camp Waziyatah in Harrison, ME, including reports on both campers and counselors.

6,615. Gruening, Dorothy Smith
Oral history. Nd. 1 tape.
Open. Unpublished guide.
Schlesinger Library.
Recollections of Gruening (1888-), an active participant in civic organizations and the wife of former US Senator Ernest Gruening, about a 1908 woman's rights meeting which Inez Milholland convened in a Poughkeepsie, NY, cemetery because Vassar College refused to allow it to be held on campus.

6,616. Guion, Connie Myers
Papers. 1840s-early 1970s. 7 cartons, 1 Hollinger box, and 1 oversize folder.
Open. No guide.
Schlesinger Library.
Guion (1882-1971) was a physician and educator. Correspondence with Wellesley and Sweet Briar Colleges, as well as personal and professional correspondence, diaries, speeches, documents, and photos. Subjects are medicine, New York Hospital (Cornell Medical School), Wellesley, and Sweet Briar.

6,617. Hale, Sarah Josepha (Buell)
Papers. 1841-74. 10 items.
Open. Published and unpublished guides.
Schlesinger Library.
[Mrs.] Hale (1788-1879) was editor of magazines such as *Godey's Lady's Book* and editor or author of more than 50 books. Correspondence includes one letter to Hale from Andrew Dickson White, the president of Cornell University. See Arthur and Elizabeth Schlesinger Library on the History of Women in America, *The Manuscript Inventories and the Catalogs of the Manuscripts, Books and Pictures,* vol. III (Boston: G. K. Hall & Co., 1973).

6,618. Hall, Carrie May
Papers. 1917-40. 3 folders.
Open. Published and unpublished guides.
Schlesinger Library.
Hall, superintendent both of nurses and of the Nurses Training School at Boston's Peter Brent Brigham Hospital, was president of the National League of Nursing Education in 1927. Correspondence, biographical material, speeches, articles including items by Hall on nursing, clippings, and photo. Contains WWI letters from France and England to her family, some of which describe the work of nurses during the war. See Arthur and Elizabeth Schlesinger Library on the History of Women in America, *The Manuscript Inventories and the Catalogs of the Manuscripts, Books and Pictures,* vol. III (Boston: G. K. Hall & Co., 1973).

6,619. Hall, Constance H.
Papers. 1915-21. 2 folders and 4 vols.
Open. Published and unpublished guides.
Schlesinger Library.
Correspondence, photos, and scrapbooks of [Miss] Hall (1886-1973), chairman of the New England Clothing Committee working with the *Comité Franco-Américain pour la protection des enfants de la frontière*. Scrapbooks contain records of work by Hall's committee, bills, sample patterns, reports, pictures of children, and other items; folders contain letters from Caroline H. Hill to Hall. Collection provides information on women's work and WWI. See Arthur and Elizabeth Schlesinger Library on the History of Women in America, *The Manuscript Inventories and the Catalogs of the Manuscripts, Books and Pictures,* vol. III (Boston: G. K. Hall & Co., 1973).

6,620. Hall, Margaret Gettys
Papers. 1934-59. 1 folder.
Open. Published and unpublished guides.
Schlesinger Library.
Correspondence and manuscript of [Mrs.] Hall, a California lawyer. Bulk of correspondence, much of it with Mary R. Beard, pertains to women lawyers. Also includes material about the Biblical character Deborah, who was described as the "first judge of them all." See Arthur and Elizabeth Schlesinger Library on the History of Women in America, *The Manuscript Inventories and the Catalogs of the Manuscripts, Books and Pictures,* vol. III (Boston: G. K. Hall & Co., 1973).

6,621. Hamer Family
Papers. 1805-81. 1 folder.
Open. Published and unpublished guides.
Schlesinger Library.
Letters describe the lives and hardships of Cape Cod's sea-faring families of the 1850s (including the Howes, relatives of the Hamers), as well as the experiences of a sea captain's wife on a trip to Galveston and Pensacola in 1851. See Arthur and Elizabeth Schlesinger Library on the History of Women in America, *The Manuscript Inventories and the Catalogs of the Manuscripts, Books and Pictures,* vol. III (Boston: G. K. Hall & Co., 1973).

6,622. Hamilton, Alice
Papers. Ca. 1817-1961. Ca. 31 Hollinger boxes and 10 cartons.
Open. Published and unpublished guides.
Schlesinger Library.
A physician who was the first woman professor at Harvard University, Hamilton (1869-1970) also worked as a resident researcher at Hull House, a researcher of industrial poisons for the US Department of Labor, and a member of the League of Nations Health Organization and of President Hoover's Committee on Social Trends. Included with Hamilton's correspondence, notes, pamphlets, published articles, awards, photos, and clippings reflecting her professional life and interests are letters to Katharine Putnam Bowditch Codman, letters from abroad, and others on civil liberties and equal rights. Also included are papers of the Hamilton family of Ft. Wayne, IN, which consist of correspondence of her sisters Norah, Margaret, and Edith Hamilton, a classicist and teacher; of her mother Gertrude (Pond) and father Montgomery Hamilton; of her uncle Andrew Holman Hamilton, his wife Phoebe (Taber) Hamilton, and cousins Agnes and Jessie Hamilton; of her grandfather Allen and grandmother Emerine Hamilton; and of other aunts and uncles. Also contained are letters from Allen Hamilton's parents in Ireland and diaries of Agnes Hamilton. See Arthur and Elizabeth Schlesinger Library on the History of Women in America, *The Manuscript Inventories and the Catalogs of the Manuscripts, Books and Pictures,* vol. III (Boston: G. K. Hall & Co., 1973).

6,623. Hamilton, Olivia E.
Papers. 1915-19. 1 folder.
Open. Published and unpublished guides.
Schlesinger Library.
Hamilton was a nurse at American Ambulance Hospital in Paris, 1916-17, and later a district nurse behind American lines in the war zone with the medical headquarters in Neuf Chateau de Vosges. Letters to Marian S. DeVictor describe people, hospital conditions, travels through Spain and France, and Hamilton's antiwar beliefs. See Arthur and Elizabeth Schlesinger Library on the History of Women in America, *The Manuscript Inventories and the Catalogs of the Manuscripts, Books and Pictures,* vol. III (Boston: G. K. Hall & Co., 1973).

6,624. Hamlin, Margaret Pomeroy
Papers. 1919-58. 1 folder.
Open. Published and unpublished guides.
Schlesinger Library.
An autobiography and seven articles about women in agriculture by Hamlin, the agricultural counselor for women at the Massachusetts Agricultural College at Amherst. See Arthur and Elizabeth Schlesinger Library on the History of Women in America, *The Manuscript Inventories and the Catalogs of the Manuscripts, Books and Pictures,* vol. III (Boston: G. K. Hall & Co., 1973).

6,625. Hansl, Eva Elise (vom Baur)
Papers. 1939-54. 2 Hollinger boxes.
Open. Published and unpublished guides.
Schlesinger Library.
Hansl (1889-) was program supervisor for the 1939-40 radio series "Women in the Making of America," which was broadcast in cooperation with the WPA's Federal Theatre Radio Division, and "Gallant American Women," broadcast in cooperation with the US Office of Education. Radio scripts for these series and for "Gallery of Women," produced by the University of Michigan in 1954, are included with program outlines, poster, and clippings. See Arthur and Elizabeth Schlesinger Library on the History of Women in America, *The Manuscript Inventories and the Catalogs of the Manuscripts, Books and Pictures,* vol. III (Boston: G. K. Hall & Co., 1973).

6,626. Harbert, Elizabeth Boynton
Papers. 1887. 1 item.
Open. Published and unpublished guides.
Schlesinger Library.
Letter by [Mrs.] Harbert (1845-1925), an officer in the Illinois Equal Suffrage Association, to Alice B. Stockhum. See Arthur and Elizabeth Schlesinger Library on the History of Women in America, *The Manuscript Inventories and the Catalogs of the Manuscripts, Books and Pictures,* vol. III (Boston: G. K. Hall & Co., 1973).

6,627. Hardy, Elisa B.
Papers. 1836-37. 1 vol.
Open. Published and unpublished guides.
Schlesinger Library.
School notebook kept by Hardy at Pittsfield Academy in Pittsfield, MA. See Arthur and Elizabeth Schlesinger Library on the History of Women in America, *The Manuscript Inventories and the Catalogs of the Manuscripts, Books and Pictures,* vol. III (Boston: G. K. Hall & Co., 1973).

6,628. Harreld, Claudia White
Papers. 1952. 1 folder and 2 phonotape reels.
Open. Published and unpublished guides.
Schlesinger Library.
A 30-page memoir by Harreld about her mother Josephine Elizabeth Thomas (1834-?), who was born a slave in Georgia, describes Negro life in the South in the 1800s. See Arthur and Elizabeth

Schlesinger Library on the History of Women in America, *The Manuscript Inventories and the Catalogs of the Manuscripts, Books and Pictures,* vol. III (Boston: G. K. Hall & Co., 1973).

6,629. Harrison, Ella
Papers. 1892-98. 5 folders.
Open. Published and unpublished guides.
Schlesinger Library.
Harrison (1859-1933) worked for woman suffrage in Missouri and for suffrage campaigns in Mississippi and Louisiana in 1897 and in Iowa in 1898. Bulk of collection is correspondence describing her experiences on the campaigns. Susan B. Anthony, Carrie Chapman Catt, and Helen M. Reynolds were correspondents. Also included are clippings and articles. See Arthur and Elizabeth Schlesinger Library on the History of Women in America, *The Manuscript Inventories and the Catalogs of the Manuscripts, Books and Pictures,* vol. III (Boston: G. K. Hall & Co., 1973).

6,630. Harrison, Florence L.
Papers. 1885-1973. 1 folder.
Open. Published and unpublished guides.
Schlesinger Library.
Harrison (1883-1973) was an educator who was active in women's organizations such as the LWV, LWV's Overseas Educational Fund, and the Service Bureau for Women's Organizations. Correspondence, booklet and pamphlets, photos, and clippings. Contains brief biography, photos from a trip, material about her death, and items re Harrison's mother Theresa Virginia Beard, Marguerite M. Wells, Eleanor Holgate Lattimore, and Eleanor Roosevelt. See Arthur and Elizabeth Schlesinger Library on the History of Women in America, *The Manuscript Inventories and the Catalogs of the Manuscripts, Books and Pictures,* vol. III (Boston: G. K. Hall & Co., 1973).

6,631. Hartford Female Seminary
Records. 1852-53. 1 item.
Open. Published and unpublished guides.
Schlesinger Library.
Catalog of the Seminary, founded in 1828 to educate young ladies, lists students and describes courses offered. The enclosed list of students was annotated by Caroline E. Day, the catalog's owner. See Arthur and Elizabeth Schlesinger Library on the History of Women in America, *The Manuscript Inventories and the Catalogs of the Manuscripts, Books and Pictures,* vol. III (Boston: G. K. Hall & Co., 1973).

6,632. Hartshorne, Clementina R.
Papers. 1910-15. 5 folders.
Open. Published and unpublished guides.
Schlesinger Library.
Bulk of collection is correspondence; also included are pamphlets, leaflets, and clippings regarding the Pennsylvania woman suffrage campaign in which [Mrs. Edward Y.] Hartshorne worked. See Arthur and Elizabeth Schlesinger Library on the History of Women in America, *The Manuscript Inventories and the Catalogs of the Manuscripts, Books and Pictures,* vol. III (Boston: G. K. Hall & Co., 1973).

6,633. Harvard Law School Forum
Records. 1966. 4 tapes.
Open. Unpublished guide.
Schlesinger Library.
Recording of Forum meeting, entitled "Dare We Not Discriminate?" Moderator was professor Albert Sacks and panelists were Betty Friedan, Mary I. Bunting, and Pauli Murray.

6,634. Hastings, Ann Eliza (Phipps)
Papers. 1914. 1 folder.
Open. Published and unpublished guides.
Schlesinger Library.
A note from Hastings (1813-ca. 1915) extending birthday greetings to a friend on her 90th birthday. See Arthur and Elizabeth Schlesinger Library on the History of Women in America, *The Manuscript Inventories and the Catalogs of the Manuscripts, Books and Pictures,* vol. III (Boston: G. K. Hall & Co., 1973).

6,635. Hathaway, Katharine Butler
Papers. 1912-47. 1 folder.
Open. Published and unpublished guides.
Schlesinger Library.
Hathaway (1890-1942) was an author. Collection contains manuscript poems by Hathaway, articles about her house in Castine, ME, and poems and letters of her brother Warren Butler. Photos are also included. See Arthur and Elizabeth Schlesinger Library on the History of Women in America, *The Manuscript Inventories and the Catalogs of the Manuscripts, Books and Pictures,* vol. III (Boston: G. K. Hall & Co., 1973).

6,636. Hawthorne, Sophia Amelia (Peabody)
Papers. 1867. 1 item.
Open. Published and unpublished guides.
Schlesinger Library.
Letter of Hawthorne (1809-71), an artist, writer, and the wife of Nathaniel Hawthorne, to Colonel T. W. Higginson. See Arthur and Elizabeth Schlesinger Library on the History of Women in America, *The Manuscript Inventories and the Catalogs of the Manuscripts, Books and Pictures,* vol. III (Boston: G. K. Hall & Co., 1973).

6,637. Hazzard, Florence (Woolsey)
Papers. 1870-1941. 1 folder.
Open. Published and unpublished guides.
Schlesinger Library.
Hazzard (1903-) is an author. Bulk of collection is correspondence, 1940-41, between Hazzard and Lucy E. Anthony regarding a biographical sketch of Susan B. Anthony. Also included is a manuscript poem honoring Anthony. See Arthur and Elizabeth Schlesinger Library on the History of Women in America, *The Manuscript Inventories and the Catalogs of the Manuscripts, Books and Pictures,* vol. III (Boston: G. K. Hall & Co., 1973).

6,638. Henrotin, Ellen (Martin)
Papers. 1865-1921. 4 Hollinger boxes.
Open. Published and unpublished guides.
Schlesinger Library.
[Mrs. Charles] Henrotin (1847-1922), the second president of the GFWC and wife of a Chicago banker, was active in reform movements; she also helped bring the newly organized women's clubs into a national and international movement. Correspondence, speeches, notebooks, pamphlets, albums, clippings, articles, and photos re Henrotin's activities. Her speeches and articles pertain to social welfare, labor, suffrage, and women's roles in education, prostitution, the family, economics, and finance. See Arthur and Elizabeth Schlesinger Library on the History of Women in America, *The Manuscript Inventories and the Catalogs of the Manuscripts, Books and Pictures,* vol. III (Boston: G. K. Hall & Co., 1973).

6,639. Henry, Diana Mara
Papers. 1970s. 4 boxes and 1 envelope.
Open. Unpublished guide.
Schlesinger Library.
Henry (ca. 1947-) is a photographer. Ca. 500 prints of contemporary women of various ages and walks of life and one envelope of descriptive cards.

6,640. Herrick, Elinore (Morehouse)
Papers. 1931-64. 13 Hollinger boxes, oversize photos, albums, and scrapbooks.
Open. Published and unpublished guides.
Schlesinger Library.
[Mrs.] Herrick (1895-1964) became personnel director and an editorial staff member for the *New York Herald Tribune* in 1945 after serving as personnel and labor relations director for Todd Shipyards Corporation, from 1942 to 1945 and director of the New York-New Jersey-Connecticut region for the National Labor Relations Board from 1934 to 1942. Correspondence, manuscripts, notes for speeches, editorials written by Herrick, official documents, reports, pamphlets, publications, clippings, and photos largely concern her career. Labor, women as writers, and the NLRB are subjects reflected in Herrick's papers. Collection also contains material on cases tried by the NLRB, the Board's labor-regulating acts, and investigations; reports on Todd Shipyards personnel, some of whom were women; and information about *Herald Tribune* labor disputes in which Herrick was involved. See Arthur and Elizabeth Schlesinger Library on the History of Women in America, *The Manuscript Inventories and the Catalogs of the Manuscripts, Books and Pictures,* vol. III (Boston: G. K. Hall & Co., 1973).

6,641. Hewes, Patricia Esther Jackson
Papers. 20th century. 1 vol.
Open. Unpublished guide.
Schlesinger Library.
Autobiography in which Hewes (1900-76) recounts her early life in Mexico as daughter of a Mexican mother and an American father who was in charge of a mine. She describes life at a convent school, the family's leaving Mexico during the 1910 revolution, and their settling in San Francisco where Hewes, as oldest daughter, worked as a hat-maker to support her mother and younger siblings after her father died in ca. 1916. The account ends in ca. 1917. Hewes went on to become involved in the city's art community where she knew Dorothea Lange.

6,642. Hodder, Jessie (Donaldson)
Papers. 1873-1931. 2 Hollinger boxes.
Open. Published and unpublished guides.
Schlesinger Library.
Papers of [Mrs.] Hodder (1867-1931), an internationally known penologist who from 1911 through 1931 served as superintendent of the Massachusetts Reformatory for Women at Framingham, consist of personal correspondence with her son Alan and with Elizabeth Gardiner [Mrs. Glendower] Evans; a diary for 1915, 1919, and 1920; a 1921 report on European prisons; articles; and photos. See Arthur and Elizabeth Schlesinger Library on the History of Women in America, *The Manuscript Inventories and the Catalogs of the Manuscripts, Books and Pictures,* vol. III (Boston: G. K. Hall & Co., 1973).

6,643. Holden, Geraldine Weston Dudley
Papers. Ca. 1858-1927. 1 Hollinger box and 4 diplomas.
Open. Unpublished guide.
Schlesinger Library.
Lydia Ann Joslin Smith (1836-1912) and Edna Ione Smith Tyler (1861-1930) were authors. They both began careers as "typewriters" and stenographers in 1885 and then Tyler, in founding Tyler's Business College, became a pioneer in commercial employment and business education of women. Manuscripts including those of Smith and Tyler, biographical material regarding the Smith family, typescripts, pamphlets, diplomas, photos, clippings, memorabilia, and tintypes, as well as material pertaining to stenography and Tyler's Business College.

6,644. Holden, Ruth
Papers. 1907-61. 0.5 Hollinger box.
Open. Unpublished guide.
Schlesinger Library.
A paleobotanist, Holden (1890-1917) worked with the British Red Cross in Russia during WWI, traveling in Europe to help establish refugee hospitals. Correspondence, the bulk of which Holden wrote to her parents or to a Radcliffe classmate Louise Hodge Lahee, pertains to women's work in WWI, Russia, and paleobotanists. Holden traveled extensively in Russia and wrote of hardships involved in distributing hospital supplies.

She contracted typhoid and died of meningitis while helping establish hospitals and doing paleobotany in Kazan. One folder relates to the establishment of a scholarship in her name.

6,645. Holden, Sarah Gilbert
Papers. Ca. 1860-1903. 1 folder and 1 oversize item.
Open. Unpublished guide.
Schlesinger Library.
Notes from school lectures on logic and philosophy, certificates from the State Normal School in Salem, MA, and marriage certificate and other papers of [Mrs. George M.] Holden, a teacher who was grandmother of Franz J. Ingelfinger, a physician who married Sarah Shurtleff.

6,646. Hollingsworth and Kirk
Papers. 1911-64. 3 Hollinger boxes.
Open. Published and unpublished guides.
Schlesinger Library.
Collection chiefly consists of E. Buckner (Kirk) Hollingsworth's professional correspondence concerning the writing and publishing of her two books *Flower Chronicles* (1958) and *Her Garden Was Her Delight* (1962). It also includes correspondence about the research and writing of numerous articles on horticulture and about Hollingsworth's service overseas in 1918 and 1919 with the American National Red Cross, correspondence between her sister Mary Kirk and their mother, material on Wallis (Warfield) Simpson, and financial records, articles, pamphlets, clippings, and photos. See Arthur and Elizabeth Schlesinger Library on the History of Women in America, *The Manuscript Inventories and the Catalogs of the Manuscripts, Books and Pictures,* vol. III (Boston: G. K. Hall & Co., 1973).

6,647. Holman, Anna E.
Papers. Nd. Ca. 1 Hollinger box and 3 envelopes.
Open. No guide.
Schlesinger Library.
Correspondence, post cards, pamphlets, books, and guides to French cities of Holman (ca. 1892-), head of the Radcliffe Unit, which in association with the French Red Cross did relief and settlement work in seven regions of France during 1919 and 1920.

6,648. Holman, Lydia
Papers. 1914-52. 4 folders.
Open. Published and unpublished guides.
Schlesinger Library.
Holman (1868-1960) was a pioneer public health nurse in rural North Carolina. Annual reports from the "Friendly Nurse" printed by her Boston Committee sponsors and correspondence with the Committee document Holman's career. See Arthur and Elizabeth Schlesinger Library on the History of Women in America, *The Manuscript Inventories and the Catalogs of the Manuscripts, Books and Pictures,* vol. III (Boston: G. K. Hall & Co., 1973).

6,649. Holmes, Oliver Wendell
Papers. 1885. 2 items.
Open. Published and unpublished guides.
Schlesinger Library.
Letter states the views of Holmes (1809-94), author and physician, regarding woman suffrage. A typed transcript is included. See Arthur and Elizabeth Schlesinger Library on the History of Women in America, *The Manuscript Inventories and the Catalogs of the Manuscripts, Books and Pictures,* vol. III (Boston: G. K. Hall & Co., 1973).

6,650. Holt and Messer Family
Papers. 1809-1962. 5 Hollinger boxes.
Open. Published and unpublished guides.
Schlesinger Library.
Family papers of Joseph Burt Holt (1828-99) and of Julia Evelyn Rollins Holt (1829-95), who founded the town of Champlin, MN; assisted freedmen in Jackson, MS, between 1868 and 1869; taught school in Atlanta in 1875; and worked on Indian reservations in Lac Court d'Oreilles, WI, and Los Pinos, CO, during the early and late 1870s. Correspondence, diaries, notes, manuscripts, clippings, government documents, maps, photos, and portraits. Contains material on the Civil War and resettlement of the frontier, the Old Northwest, and the Southwest. Included are correspondence and diaries of Emily Burt Holt (1854-1934), Emma North Messer (1852-1938), and Mary Burt Messer (1881-1960), as well as Emma Messer's article "Memories of a Frontier Childhood," published in *Overland Monthly* in 1924. Also contains genealogical information on the Holt, Burt, Berry, and Baker families. See Arthur and Elizabeth Schlesinger Library on the History of Women in America, *The Manuscript Inventories and the Catalogs of the Manuscripts, Books and Pictures,* vol. III (Boston: G. K. Hall & Co., 1973).

6,651. Holway, Amy Richardson
Papers. 1917-49. 0.5 Hollinger box.
Open. Unpublished guide.
Schlesinger Library.
Holway (1894-1949) was a missionary and school principal in China during the 1920s; later she returned to the US where she taught at the Rhode Island State College and earned a doctorate in education at Harvard University. Correspondence, diaries, notes, and clippings pertain primarily to Holway's life in China where she was associated with the Mary Bridgman Normal School.

6,652. Holway, Frances Hope (Kerr)
Collection. 1871-1957. 2 Hollinger boxes and 1 oversize vol.
Open. Published and unpublished guides.
Schlesinger Library.
Correspondence and pamphlets concerning early women teachers and missionaries in the South and West. Includes a manuscript bibliography on women teachers working between 1820 and 1865 and information about the Choctaw Indians in Oklahoma from 1871. See Arthur and Elizabeth Schlesinger Library on the History of Women in America, *The Manuscript Inventories and the Catalogs of the Manuscripts, Books and Pictures,* vol. III (Boston: G. K. Hall & Co., 1973).

6,653. Hooker
Collection. 1788-1890. 2 Hollinger boxes (ca. 300 items).
Open. Published and unpublished guides.
Schlesinger Library.
Correspondence by housewives and women schoolteachers on such subjects as education, politics, marriage, local and family news, and social life and customs. Included are letters between Lucy Gray and her husband, a Cape Cod sea captain; letters from friends and relatives to Weltha Brown, a Hartford, CT, schoolteacher, many of which deal with religious subjects; letters wherein Hannah Buchanan of Maryland describes to her absent husband the problems of running a plantation; letters by authors Sarah Edgarton and Luella J. B. Case; and a letter by Dolley Madison. See Arthur and Elizabeth Schlesinger Library on the History of Women in America, *The Manuscript Inventories and the Catalogs of the Manuscripts, Books and Pictures,* vol. III (Boston: G. K. Hall & Co., 1973).

6,654. Hooker, Isabella (Beecher)
Papers. Nd. 1 item.
Open. Published and unpublished guides.
Schlesinger Library.
Letter to a Mrs. Chittenden wherein Hooker (1822-1907), a suffragist and advocate of women's rights, discusses her activities for women's rights. See Arthur and Elizabeth Schlesinger Library on the History of Women in America, *The Manuscript Inventories and the Catalogs of the Manuscripts, Books and Pictures,* vol. III (Boston: G. K. Hall & Co., 1973).

6,655. Hooper, Ellen (Sturgis)
Papers. Ca. 1840. 1 vol.
Open. Published and unpublished guides.
Schlesinger Library.
Manuscript notebook of Hooper (1812-48), a transcendentalist poet, contains shorter poems by her and a longer poem entitled "The Community—Brook Farm" by Hooper and Susan Sturgis Bigelow. See Arthur and Elizabeth Schlesinger Library on the History of Women in America, *The Manuscript Inventories and the Catalogs of the Manuscripts, Books and Pictures,* vol. III (Boston: G. K. Hall & Co., 1973).

6,656. Hopkins, Charlotte Everett (Wise)
Papers. 1924-42. 8 folders.
Open. Published and unpublished guides.
Schlesinger Library.
[Mrs. Archibald] Hopkins (1851-1935) was a civic leader, social service worker, and "grande dame" who waged a 20-year fight for the abolition of alley homes in Washington, DC, the result of which was the establishment in 1934 of the Alley Dwelling Authority. Correspondence, biographical material, articles, reports, and clippings. Includes her reminiscences and papers on the Authority. See Arthur and Elizabeth Schlesinger Library on the History of Women in America, *The Manuscript Inventories and the Catalogs of the Manuscripts, Books and Pictures,* vol. III (Boston: G. K. Hall & Co., 1973).

6,657. Hopkinson, Corinna Prentiss
Papers. 1856. 1 item.
Open. Published and unpublished guides.
Schlesinger Library.
Letter Hopkinson, a Cambridge resident, wrote from Europe to her husband Thomas about their family life and Elizabeth and Louis Agassiz's school. See Arthur and Elizabeth Schlesinger Library on the History of Women in America, *The Manuscript Inventories and the Catalogs of the Manuscripts, Books and Pictures,* vol. III (Boston: G. K. Hall & Co., 1973).

6,658. Horner, Matina (Souretis)
Oral history. 1971. 1 tape.
Open. Unpublished guide.
Schlesinger Library.
Recording of an interview with Horner (1940-), a professor of psychology and since 1972 president of Radcliffe, which was aired on "The Women's Show" for WGBH-FM radio in Boston.

6,659. Hosmer, Harriet Goodhue
Papers. 1834-1922. 6 Hollinger boxes and 3 oversize items.
Open. Published and unpublished guides.
Schlesinger Library.
After studying with an English sculptor in Rome, Hosmer (1830-1908), a sculptor from Watertown, MA, spent much of her professional and social life in Rome as a member of the English colony there. Correspondence, diary, poetry, manuscripts, dramas, notes on art, photos, articles, and clippings of Hosmer, including papers of Cornelia Carr concerning her writing of *Harriet Hosmer, Letters and Memoirs.* Much of the collection is correspondence; correspondents include Carr, Hosmer's benefactor and lifelong patron Wayman Crow, Elizabeth Cary Agassiz, Susan B. Anthony, Robert and Elizabeth Browning, Annie Fields, Isabella Beecher Hooker, Louise Chandler Moulton, Lydia Maria Child, Elizabeth Palmer Peabody, Kate Sanborn, Mary Somerville, Lucy Stone, Adeline D. T. Whitney, and Abba Goold Woolson. Also included is a letter to "Aunt Dobby" wherein Hosmer discusses friends, relatives, and her own values. See Arthur and Elizabeth Schlesinger Library on the History of Women in America, *The Manuscript Inventories*

and the Catalogs of the Manuscripts, Books and Pictures, vol. III (Boston: G. K. Hall & Co., 1973).

6,660. Houghton, Dorothy Deemer
Papers. 1953-57. 2 folders.
Open. Published and unpublished guides.
Schlesinger Library.
Papers of [Mrs.] Houghton (1890-), Foreign Operations Administration assistant director for refugees and migration, consist of biographical material, articles and speeches by her, photos, and clippings. See Arthur and Elizabeth Schlesinger Library on the History of Women in America, *The Manuscript Inventories and the Catalogs of the Manuscripts, Books and Pictures,* vol. III (Boston: G. K. Hall & Co., 1973).

6,661. Houghton, Nancy Manning
Papers. Ca. 1882-90. 1 folder and 1 vol.
Open. Published and unpublished guides.
Schlesinger Library.
Clippings on women's education, suffrage, and rights; religion; temperance; the treatment of Indians; and other topics. See Arthur and Elizabeth Schlesinger Library on the History of Women in America, *The Manuscript Inventories and the Catalogs of the Manuscripts, Books and Pictures,* vol. III (Boston: G. K. Hall & Co., 1973).

6,662. Howard, Katherine (Graham)
Papers. 1894-1961. 16 Hollinger boxes.
Open. Published and unpublished guides.
Schlesinger Library.
Howard (1898-) has been active within the Republican party as secretary of the National Committee from 1948 to 1952, as a staff member for Dwight Eisenhower during his 1952 campaign, and as a volunteer worker for the Nixon-Lodge ticket in Massachusetts during 1960; she also worked in civil defense between 1954 and 1957 and as US Deputy Commissioner of the Brussels World's Fair during 1957 and 1958. Correspondence, manuscript, notes, speeches, convention records, citation, scrapbooks, and clippings pertain to her career. Also included are a copy of a speech she delivered at Salem College, the citation accompanying the Smith College award she received, and a manuscript of her mother-in-law Emily Pagelsen Howard, a physician, about the state almshouse. See Arthur and Elizabeth Schlesinger Library on the History of Women in America, *The Manuscript Inventories and the Catalogs of the Manuscripts, Books and Pictures,* vol. III (Boston: G. K. Hall & Co., 1973).

6,663. Howe Family
Papers. Nd. 2 cartons, 1 box, and other items.
Open. No guide.
Schlesinger Library.
Papers of Julia (Ward) Howe (1819-1910), author and social reformer; of her daughter Florence Marion (Howe) Hall (1845-1922); of Florence Hall's husband David Prescott Hall, and of the Howe, Ward, Cutler, and Hall families, including correspondence, manuscripts, articles, school notebooks and themes, pamphlets, primers, catechism books, and miscellany. Included are a partial memoir of Julia Howe, articles and speeches she wrote, a remembrance of J. G. Whittier, and letters to her and Samuel Howe from Florence Nightingale; manuscripts of "A Visit to Florence Nightingale," of a book on Laura Bridgman, and of plays, articles, stories, and articles by Florence Hall; and correspondence, poetry, writings, and speeches of David Hall.

6,664. Howe, Julia (Ward)
Papers. 1867-1941. 1 Hollinger box, 10 vols., and 3 folders.
Open. Published and unpublished guides.
Schlesinger Library.
Howe (1819-1910) was an author and social reformer with interests in such causes as antislavery and woman suffrage. Correspondence, manuscripts, articles, scrapbooks of clippings of many of her writings and poems, and other material document her reform activities, her work with women's clubs, and the Association for the Advancement of Women. Also included are letters to Ednah Dow Cheney and correspondence, a speech, and a report on the Women's Department at the New Orleans Exposition of 1884/85. See Arthur and Elizabeth Schlesinger Library on the History of Women in America, *The Manuscript Inventories and the Catalogs of the Manuscripts, Books and Pictures,* vol. III (Boston: G. K. Hall & Co., 1973).

6,665. Howlett, Angelina
Papers. Nd. 1 Hollinger box.
Open. No guide.
Schlesinger Library.
Correspondence, diaries, clippings, and material from the writing and lecturing of Howlett, a social worker and author, include information on the Boys' Club of Boston.

6,666. Hughes, Sarah (Tilghman)
Papers. Nd. 2 Hollinger boxes.
Open. No guide.
Schlesinger Library.
[Mrs. George E.] Hughes (1896-) has practiced law in Texas since 1922; since 1961 she has served as a judge of the US District Court of the Northern District of Texas. Biographical data, writings, photo, clippings, and articles by Hughes on the legal aspects of juvenile delinquency.

6,667. Hull, Josephine (Sherwood)
Papers. 1871-1956. 11 Hollinger boxes and 3 oversize packages.
Open. Published and unpublished guides.
Schlesinger Library.
Correspondence, diaries, notebooks, programs and scripts, photos, and musical scores of [Mrs.] Hull (1877?-1957), a producer of and actress in plays and operas, document her career, early family life, and education at Radcliffe, from which she graduated in 1899. See Arthur and Elizabeth Schlesinger Library on the History of Women in America, *The Manuscript Inventories and the Catalogs of the Manuscripts, Books and Pictures,* vol. III (Boston: G. K. Hall & Co., 1973).

6,668. Humphrey, Helen Florence
Papers. 1942-63. 2.5 Hollinger boxes.
Open. Unpublished guide.
Schlesinger Library.
Papers pertain to the career of Humphrey (1909-63), a lawyer in Washington, DC, and other parts of the US, who specialized in labor-management relations; she was a member of the National Labor Relations Board from 1939 to 1951.

6,669. Huntington, Catharine Sargent
Papers. 1915-74. 10 folders and 1 tape.
Open. Published and unpublished guides.
Schlesinger Library.
A professional actress, Huntington (1889-) became a producer of plays and manager of the Provincetown Playhouse in Massachusetts. Correspondence, photos, clippings, and printed material include information on the Rodgers and Hammerstein Award as well as statements about the Sacco and Vanzetti case and on her arrest for activity in their behalf. Recording is of Huntington reading some of her own poetry entitled "Beloved House" and poetry of Alfred Lord Tennyson and Warren Butler. See Arthur and Elizabeth Schlesinger Library on the History of Women in America, *The Manuscript Inventories and the Catalogs of the Manuscripts, Books and Pictures,* vol. III (Boston: G. K. Hall & Co., 1973).

6,670. Huntington, Margaret Jane Evans
Papers. 1895-1963. 2 folders.
Open. Published and unpublished guides.
Schlesinger Library.
Correspondence, biographical sketches, articles, speech manuscript, and photos of Huntington (1842-1926), dean of women at Carleton College in Northfield, MN, from 1874 to 1908 and from 1895 to 1899 first president of the Minnesota Federation of Women's Clubs. See Arthur and Elizabeth Schlesinger Library on the History of Women in America, *The Manuscript Inventories and the Catalogs of the Manuscripts, Books and Pictures,* vol. III (Boston: G. K. Hall & Co., 1973).

6,671. Hurst, Fannie
Papers. 1933. 1 item.
Open. Published and unpublished guides.
Schlesinger Library.
Letter from Hurst (1889-1968), an author of novels, short stories, and plays, concerning a dinner for the Hon. Ruth B. Owen. See Arthur and Elizabeth Schlesinger Library on the History of Women in America, *The Manuscript Inventories and the Catalogs of the Manuscripts, Books and Pictures,* vol. III (Boston: G. K. Hall & Co., 1973).

6,672. Husted, Marjorie Child
Papers. 1946-54. 2 folders.
Open. Published and unpublished guides.
Schlesinger Library.
Papers of [Mrs.] Husted, a business woman and home economist who was director of the Home Service Department of General Mills, Inc., consist of photos and manuscripts of speeches on the role and position of women, particularly in the business world. See Arthur and Elizabeth Schlesinger Library on the History of Women in America, *The Manuscript Inventories and the Catalogs of the Manuscripts, Books and Pictures,* vol. III (Boston: G. K. Hall & Co., 1973).

6,673. Institute of Women's Professional Relations
Records. 1928-41. 4 Hollinger boxes.
Open. Published and unpublished guides.
Schlesinger Library.
Minutes and published and other matter of the Institute, established in 1928 in New London, CT, to raise the level and number of women in professional working positions. Includes studies and interviews on chemistry, banking, dietetics, and other fields, and studies and reports, carried out in cooperation with Works Progress Administration project 2132 and the LWV, on Connecticut and Rhode Island state governments. See Arthur and Elizabeth Schlesinger Library on the History of Women in America, *The Manuscript Inventories and the Catalogs of the Manuscripts, Books and Pictures,* vol. III (Boston: G. K. Hall & Co., 1973).

6,674. International Assembly of Women
Records. 1946. 1 Hollinger box.
Open. Published and unpublished guides.
Schlesinger Library.
Complete records of the Assembly, which met in South Kortright, NY, and which promoted the consciousness of women and their cooperation with the UN. Includes financial records, correspondence, lists, and the Assembly's final printed report "The World We Live In—The World We Want." See Arthur and Elizabeth Schlesinger Library on the History of Women in America, *The Manuscript Inventories and the Catalogs of the Manuscripts, Books and Pictures,* vol. III (Boston: G. K. Hall & Co., 1973).

6,675. International Federation of Working Women
Records. 1919-23. 1 Hollinger box.
Open. Published and unpublished guides.
Schlesinger Library.
First called by the National Women's Trade Union League, congresses concerning the employment of women were held in Washington, DC, in 1919, in Geneva in 1921, and in Vienna in 1923. Stenographic reports of the congresses, calls,

programs, speeches, articles, and clippings. See Arthur and Elizabeth Schlesinger Library on the History of Women in America, *The Manuscript Inventories and the Catalogs of the Manuscripts, Books and Pictures,* vol. III (Boston: G. K. Hall & Co., 1973).

6,676. Interstate Association of Commissions on the Status of Women
Records. 1969-74. 1 record carton.
Open. No guide.
Schlesinger Library.
Now called the National Association of Commissions for Women, the Interstate Association was founded in 1970 to promote communication among Commissions for Women, conferences, research, and information about equality of the sexes. Includes minutes, drafts, reports, and printed matter.

6,677. Irwin, Agnes
Papers. Ca. 1875. 2 items.
Open. Published and unpublished guides.
Schlesinger Library.
Correspondence about invitations of Irwin (1841-1914), first dean of Radcliffe. See Arthur and Elizabeth Schlesinger Library on the History of Women in America, *The Manuscript Inventories and the Catalogs of the Manuscripts, Books and Pictures,* vol. III (Boston: G. K. Hall & Co., 1973).

6,678. Irwin, Inez (Haynes)
Papers. 1872-1945. 5 Hollinger boxes and 1 oversize vol.
Open. Published and unpublished guides.
Schlesinger Library.
A writer, [Mrs. Will] Irwin (1873-1970) was active in the woman suffrage movement. Includes her autobiography, diaries, and literary notebooks filled with comments on suffrage work, Maud Younger, and other labor leaders in California, her travels in Europe, and literary personalities in the US and abroad. Also included are a diary of a trip she took abroad during WWI; the 1920 volume *Heterodoxy to Marie,* which was addressed to Marie Jenney Howe and consists of pictures and signatures of literary women; photos; and Christmas cards. See Arthur and Elizabeth Schlesinger Library on the History of Women in America, *The Manuscript Inventories and the Catalogs of the Manuscripts, Books and Pictures,* vol. III (Boston: G. K. Hall & Co., 1973).

6,679. Jackson, Edith Banfield
Papers. Nd. 1 Hollinger box and 1 small carton.
Open. No guide.
Schlesinger Library.
Professional papers and correspondence of Jackson (1895-1977), a physician who taught pediatrics and psychiatry at the Yale school of medicine from 1924 to 1959 and at the University of Colorado from 1960.

6,680. Jackson, Ellen
Papers. Ca. 1968. 1 folder and 2 tapes.
Open. Published and unpublished guides.
Schlesinger Library.
Article and transcript of an interview of [Mrs.] Jackson, a black educator and founder of Operation Exodus in Roxbury, MA, provide biographical background and information about Operation Exodus and Metco. See Arthur and Elizabeth Schlesinger Library on the History of Women in America, *The Manuscript Inventories and the Catalogs of the Manuscripts, Books and Pictures,* vol. III (Boston: G. K. Hall & Co., 1973).

6,681. Jacobi, Mary Corinna (Putnam)
Papers. 1851-1923. 1 Hollinger box.
Open. Published and unpublished guides.
Schlesinger Library.
Autobiographical notes, correspondence, stories, addresses, and other personal papers of Jacobi (1842-1906), a physician who was active in woman suffrage, including correspondence with Jacobi's grandmother Catherine Putnam, Alexander Agassiz, Carl Schurz, Oliver Wendell Holmes, and William James. Subjects include religion, medicine in England and Paris, and women at Harvard medical school. Also included is a biography of Jacobi, which was written by Ruth Putnam. See Arthur and Elizabeth Schlesinger Library on the History of Women in America, *The Manuscript Inventories and the Catalogs of the Manuscripts, Books and Pictures,* vol. III (Boston: G. K. Hall & Co., 1973).

6,682. Jacobs, Sophia (Yarnall)
Papers. Ca. 1949-70. 2 cartons and 1 Hollinger box.
Open. No guide.
Schlesinger Library.
Correspondence, articles, speeches, and photos of [Mrs. Reginald Robert] Jacobs (1902-), a Philadelphia civic worker and author, pertain to her presidency of the Urban League and of the National Council of Women, for which she traveled to India and West Africa, and to her involvement with the UN Council of Philadelphia and her 1949 campaign for school committee. Her articles cover such subjects as fashion, decorating, and children's etiquette; her speeches concern civil rights.

6,683. Jacobson, Myrtle Saxe
Papers. 1953. 1 folder.
Open. No guide.
Schlesinger Library.
Papers of Jacobson (1919-74), dean and director of the School of General Studies at Brooklyn College, City University of New York, consist of her thesis entitled "Federal Old-Age and Survivor's Insurance for Employees of the College of New York," memoranda, and other items.

6,684. James, Janet Wilson
Phonotape. Nd. 1 reel.
Open. Published and unpublished guides.
Schlesinger Library.
Recorded speech by [Mrs.] James (1918-), an historian, professor of history, and co-editor of *Notable American Women, 1607-1950,* for a series on changing ideas about women in America. Her speech is entitled "Religious Revival and the New Conservatism: Marriage and the Home, 1800-1825." See Arthur and Elizabeth Schlesinger Library on the History of Women in America, *The Manuscript Inventories and the Catalogs of the Manuscripts, Books and Pictures,* vol. III (Boston: G. K. Hall & Co., 1973).

6,685. Jeffrey, Jennetta A. (Street)
Papers. 1912-15. 1 vol.
Open. Published and unpublished guides.
Schlesinger Library.
Scrapbook of [Mrs. Edward C.] Jeffrey, who was active in the Massachusetts Woman Suffrage Association, contains clippings on suffrage and page proofs of articles for the suffrage pages of the *Boston American.* See Arthur and Elizabeth Schlesinger Library on the History of Women in America, *The Manuscript Inventories and the Catalogs of the Manuscripts, Books and Pictures,* vol. III (Boston: G. K. Hall & Co., 1973).

6,686. Johnson, Ethel M.
Papers. 1919-45. 3 Hollinger boxes.
Open. Published and unpublished guides.
Schlesinger Library.
Papers of Johnson, assistant commissioner of the Massachusetts Department of Labor and Industries between 1919 and 1932, consist of correspondence; speeches and articles pertaining to the Bureau of Women in Industry, minimum wage, child labor, and labor legislation in Massachusetts; and minutes of the Massachusetts Council on Women and Children in Industry. See Arthur and Elizabeth Schlesinger Library on the History of Women in America, *The Manuscript Inventories and the Catalogs of the Manuscripts, Books and Pictures,* vol. III (Boston: G. K. Hall & Co., 1973).

6,687. Jones, Gwladys Webster
Papers. 1929-39. 1 folder.
Open. Unpublished guide.
Schlesinger Library.
Correspondence, play, and speeches of Jones (1891-), who worked with the AAUW, attempted to establish a local branch in Washington, DC, of the World Center for Women's Archives, and who was associated with the Employment Service of the US Department of Labor. Material also pertains to Caroline O'Day, Frances Perkins, Eleanor Roosevelt, Florence E. Allen, and a "Voteless" LWV.

6,688. Jordan, Sara Murray
Papers. 1904-59. 1 Hollinger box.
Open. Published and unpublished guides.
Schlesinger Library.
Correspondence, biographical information, diplomas, awards, citations, clippings, and articles by and about Jordan (1884-1959), a physician who was head of gastroenterology at the Lahey Clinic in Boston from 1923 until 1959. Jordan was born in Newton, MA, graduated from Radcliffe, received a PhD from the University of Munich, Germany, and an MD from Tufts medical school in Boston; she also published widely in medical journals. See Arthur and Elizabeth Schlesinger Library on the History of Women in America, *The Manuscript Inventories and the Catalogs of the Manuscripts, Books and Pictures,* vol. III (Boston: G. K. Hall & Co., 1973).

6,689. Junior League of the City of New York
Records. Ca. 1909-60. 20 cartons.
Open. No guide.
Schlesinger Library.
Established in 1900 as a volunteer organization of women to engage in civic affairs and welfare work, the New York Junior League served as a model for other Junior Leagues which soon thereafter organized in other cities. Minutes of the board of managers and of the executive committee, photos, publications, and files of the project chairmen for program planning, membership activities, children's activities and welfare, schools, hospitals, occupational therapy, League shelters, and the ball and museum committees.

6,690. Keller, Elizabeth (Reed)
Papers. 1944-46. 3 items.
Open. Unpublished guide.
Schlesinger Library.
Diary of [Mrs. Phillips Brooks] Keller, written during her WWII service in Italy as an American National Red Cross staff assistant, a typescript by her husband about army ranks on board ship, and a clipping.

6,691. Keller, Helen Adams
Papers. 1900-68. 1 Hollinger box and 6 folders.
Open. Published and unpublished guides.
Schlesinger Library.
[Miss] Keller (1880-1968) was a blind deaf-mute humanitarian who lectured internationally on behalf of the blind and who served as an advisor to the American Foundation for the Blind, among other organizations. Correspondence, a Keller genealogy, photos, clippings, and printed material. Includes letters by Keller; letters by Ella J. Spooner and others about Keller's Radcliffe experience, which describe some of the difficulties she encountered obtaining her BA degree; a letter by her nephew Phillips Brooke Keller, Jr., about her; letters about her new house; and correspondence between P. B. Keller and M. C. Migel. See Arthur and Elizabeth Schlesinger Library on the History of Women in America, *The Manuscript Inventories and the Catalogs of the Manuscripts, Books and Pictures,* vol. III (Boston: G. K. Hall & Co., 1973).

6,692. Key, Luella (Gettys)
Papers. 1922-48. 0.5 Hollinger box.
Open. Unpublished guide.
Schlesinger Library.
Correspondence of [Mrs. V. O. Jr.] Key, a political scientist, including letters from Mary (Ritter) Beard; correspondence, a contract, and reviews concerning Key's book *The Law of Citizenship* (1948); pamphlets by Key on citizenship and state and county government reorganization; and her dissertation, completed at the University of Illinois in 1925 and entitled "The Effect of Changes of Sovereignty on Nationality."

6,693. Kinderman, Kathy
Papers. Nd. 0.5 Hollinger box and 7 tapes.
Open. No guide.
Schlesinger Library.
Scripts, tapes, and reference material for "In Her Own Right," a program Kinderman produced for Boston's public television channel 2.

6,694. Kirchwey, Freda
Papers. Ca. 1910-58. 9 cartons, 2.5 Hollinger boxes, and 1 oversize folder.
Open. No guide.
Schlesinger Library.
Kirchwey (ca. 1893-1976) began her career as a cub reporter for *The New York Morning Telegraph* in 1915 but soon joined the staff of *The Nation* where she moved through the ranks to become editor and publisher of this magazine in 1937.
Personal and business correspondence, diary, appointment books, personal files, *The Nation* files from the 1930s to the 1950s, a photo album with pictures of speakers at a 1945 anti-Franco demonstration, photos, and clippings. Some of the correspondence and clippings pertain to Kirchwey's son Michael Clark.

6,695. Kitchelt, Florence Ledyard (Cross)
Papers. 1885-1961. 11 Hollinger boxes and 1 oversize vol.
Open. Published and unpublished guides.
Schlesinger Library.
Kitchelt (1874-1961) was executive director of the Connecticut League of Nations Association from 1924 to 1944 and chairman of the Connecticut Committee for the Equal Rights Amendment from 1943 to 1956. Correspondence, manuscripts, scrapbook, pamphlets and leaflets, and clippings reflect her various activities, including social work with immigrants in New York City and Rochester, NY. Also included are her diary of suffrage work in Connecticut during 1918, sections from her journals, and many letters from her family and her husband Richard Kitchelt. See Arthur and Elizabeth Schlesinger Library on the History of Women in America, *The Manuscript Inventories and the Catalogs of the Manuscripts, Books and Pictures,* vol. III (Boston: G. K. Hall & Co., 1973).

6,696. Kittredge, Mabel Hyde
Papers. Nd. 1 folder.
Open. Published and unpublished guides.
Schlesinger Library.
Papers of Kittredge (1867-1955), a sociologist, author, and resident of Cape Cod, MA, consist of biographical material, family photos, and a memorial address by Charles W. Gilkey. See Arthur and Elizabeth Schlesinger Library on the History of Women in America, *The Manuscript Inventories and the Catalogs of the Manuscripts, Books and Pictures,* vol. III (Boston: G. K. Hall & Co., 1973).

6,697. Kittridge, Elizabeth
Papers. 1915-60. Ca. 1 Hollinger box.
Open. No guide.
Schlesinger Library.
Correspondence, minutes, pamphlets, clippings, and other papers of Kittridge, a physician, containing medical articles, articles on women doctors, information about birth control clinics, and biographical material on Ruth A. Parmelee, Ida J. Heiberber, and Lana Edwards, the latter two of whom were physicians. Also included are minutes of the organizational meeting in 1915 of the Medical Women's National Association and a booklet of lectures delivered at the 10th general assembly of the Medical Women's International Association in Norway in 1960.

6,698. Kleinert, Margaret Noyes
Papers. Ca. 1849-1966. 4 Hollinger boxes, 9 folders, 1 oversize folder, and 10 reels.
Open. Published and unpublished guides.
Schlesinger Library.
Correspondence; biographical material; annual, committee, and other reports; newsletters; clippings; and other papers of Kleinert (1879-1971), a Boston area physician. Includes articles by Kleinert, *Liberator* articles concerning the Boston Female Medical School and the New England Hospital for Women and Children, and material on the Woman's Medical College of Pennsylvania. Also included are tapes and transcripts of interviews Kleinert conducted with other women doctors discussing their careers in medicine, specifically with Hanna G. Myrick, Alice Phillips, Marion Ropes, Harriet Hardy, Martha Brunner-Orne, Harriet Frisbee, Anna Churchill, Alice Bigelow, and Madaline Brown. See Arthur and Elizabeth Schlesinger Library on the History of Women in America, *The Manuscript Inventories and the Catalogs of the Manuscripts, Books and Pictures,* vol. III (Boston: G. K. Hall & Co., 1973).

6,699. Kline, Alma
Papers. 1941-71. 0.5 Hollinger box.
Open. Unpublished guide.
Schlesinger Library.
Kline (ca. 1907-) is a sculptor who exhibited her work in two one-woman exhibits in New York City and at group shows. Photos of her sculptures, and articles, announcements, and catalogs pertaining to exhibits in which she participated.

6,700. KneuBuhl, Emily
Papers. 1907-59. 1 Hollinger box and 1 package.
Open. Published and unpublished guides.
Schlesinger Library.
Collection of correspondence, diary, notebook, yearbook, photos, and other papers of [Miss] KneuBuhl (1883-), an educator and official in the federal government. Includes correspondence with friends in Europe; a 1927 thesis on American women's activities for peace; a manuscript written during the late 1930s with Emma Woytinsky, entitled "How Do You Like America?"; charts prepared for the LWV; and material on women's clubs in Minneapolis. See Arthur and Elizabeth Schlesinger Library on the History of Women in America, *The Manuscript Inventories and the Catalogs of the Manuscripts, Books and Pictures,* vol. III (Boston: G. K. Hall & Co., 1973).

6,701. Knox, Maryal
Papers. 1880-1956. 1 Hollinger box.
Open. Published and unpublished guides.
Schlesinger Library.
Correspondence, minutes, pamphlets, and photos of Knox (1879-1955), a social worker who worked at the 110th St. Neighborhood Club in New York City for more than 30 years, contain information on her education and career as well as the genealogy of her great-grandparents John J. and Sarah Curtiss Knox. See Arthur and Elizabeth Schlesinger Library on the History of Women in America, *The Manuscript Inventories and the Catalogs of the Manuscripts, Books and Pictures,* vol. III (Boston: G. K. Hall & Co., 1973).

6,702. Koshland, Lucile Heming
Papers. 1947-74. 2 large cartons.
Open. No guide.
Schlesinger Library.
From 1947 to 1964 Koshland (1892-) was the head of the Carrie Chapman Catt Memorial Fund, which in 1961 became the Overseas Education Fund of the LWV. Her correspondence, financial reports, and other papers contain Fund publications and reports, an evaluation and tributes, a history of the Fund, and information about fund raising and Fund projects in Africa, Asia, Europe, and Latin America.

6,703. Ladies' Physiological Institute of Boston and Vicinity
Records. 1848-1966. 1.5 Hollinger boxes.
Open. Unpublished guide.
Schlesinger Library.
Founded in 1848 for the purpose of "promoting among women a knowledge of the human system, the laws of life, and the means of relieving sickness and suffering," the Institute sponsored a series of lectures. Minutes of early meetings of the Institute and of its executive board, financial records for most of the period, annual reports, correspondence, handbooks, newsletters, photos, clippings, and memorabilia.

6,704. Ladies Sewing Society of the German Orphan Asylum
Records. 1913-35. 0.5 Hollinger box.
Open. Unpublished guide.
Schlesinger Library.
One of two women's auxiliaries of the Asylum located in Anacostia, DC, the Society was established in 1879 to oversee the clothing needs of Asylum children, hold fund-raising benefits, and advise the staff and director on management of the institution. Bilingual constitution, financial reports, minutes, correspondence, photos, and clippings.

6,705. LaFollette, Isabel (Bacon)
Papers. 1945-63. 2.5 Hollinger boxes.
Open. Unpublished guide.
Schlesinger Library.
Under the auspices of the Wisconsin Department of Vocational and Adult Education, during 1952 [Mrs. Philip Fox] LaFollette organized a pilot project for bringing together middle-aged women with employers in Madison. Known as the Woman's Service Exchange, the organization was absorbed by the state Employment Office in 1964. Correspondence, radio talks and speeches, articles and publications, and clippings include material on the Exchange, women and employment, and aging.

6,706. Laidlaw, Harriet Wright (Burton)
Papers. 1851-1948. 10 Hollinger boxes, 1 folder, and 2 microfilm reels.
Open. Published and unpublished guides.
Schlesinger Library.
A teacher who was a leader in the campaign for woman suffrage, Laidlaw (1873-1949) also had social, musical, and philanthropic interests. Correspondence, diary, articles and speeches, pamphlets and leaflets, photos, scrapbooks, and clippings reflect the early life of Laidlaw and, after her marriage, the interests of both her and her husband James Lees Laidlaw. Included is information on her youth, education, work as a teacher, marriage, and family affairs, as well as material on white slave traffic, with correspondence of Rose Livingston and letters from John D. Rockefeller, Jr., and Irene Earll, a minister, on prostitution. Also included is material on the suffrage movement in New York state, with correspondence of the state Woman Suffrage Association and the National American Woman Suffrage Association, and records of the Men's League for Woman Suffrage, the Woman's Pro-League Council, and the LWV. See Arthur and Elizabeth Schlesinger Library on the History of Women in America, *The Manuscript Inventories and the Catalogs of the Manuscripts, Books and Pictures,* vol. III (Boston: G. K. Hall & Co., 1973).

6,707. Lamb, Rosamond
Collection. Ca. 1840-1907. 3 folders.
Open. Published and unpublished guides.
Schlesinger Library.
Material collected by Lamb (1898-), president of the Consumers' League of Massachusetts, consists of correspondence, 19th-century recipe books, and a copy of a speech given by Georgina Schuyler at a meeting memorializing Elizabeth Cary Agassiz. See Arthur and Elizabeth Schlesinger Library on the History of Women in America, *The Manuscript Inventories and the Catalogs of the Manuscripts, Books and Pictures,* vol. III (Boston: G. K. Hall & Co., 1973).

6,708. Lamont, Corliss
Papers. 1929-31. 2 Hollinger boxes.
Open. Unpublished guide.
Schlesinger Library.
A former director of the American Civil Liberties Union, Lamont (1902-) is also an author and philosopher. Correspondence and clippings pertain to his efforts in 1929 to raise money among Harvard University alumni to pay back wages to the scrubwomen in the University library who were fired when President Lowell refused to pay them the minimum wage. The Consumers' League of Massachusetts, which took an active interest in this matter, is one of the correspondents.

6,709. Lamont, Helen Lamb
Papers. 1937-75. 10 Hollinger boxes and 1 oversize folder.
Open. Unpublished guide.
Schlesinger Library.
An economist, [Mrs. Corliss] Lamont (1906-75) was a research analyst for the US government and for the Center for International Studies at MIT; later in life she was active in civil liberties work and a leader of the anti-Vietnam War protest. Correspondence, drafts, notes, speeches, pamphlets, printed articles and leaflets, photos, and memorabilia. Includes personal papers, correspondence with friends and relatives, folders of advertisements and reviews of books that interested Lamont, and material on her work on East Indian economics and about such political issues as China, Cuba, and women's rights. Bulk of the collection pertains to Lamont's work and published writing on Vietnam, including correspondence with individuals and organizations in the US and abroad, interviews with Vietnamese exiles in Paris for a 1963 article in *The Nation,* and material on her book *Vietnam's Will To Live: Resistance to Foreign Aggression from Early Times Through the Nineteenth Century* (1972) and on her 1964 pamphlet "The Tragedy of Vietnam."

6,710. Lamson, Peggy
Oral history. Ca. 1964-67. 0.5 Hollinger box and tapes.
Open. Published and unpublished guides.
Schlesinger Library.
Phonotapes and transcripts of interviews of congresswomen and women in government service, which [Mrs. Roy] Lamson conducted for her book *Few Are Chosen* (1968). Included are interviews with Congresswomen Frances Bolton, Ella Grasso, Martha Griffiths, Margaret Heckler, Patsy Mink, and Senator Margaret Chase Smith, and with government service workers Eugenie Anderson, Esther Peterson, and Antonia Uccello, and with Judge Constance Baker Motley. See Arthur and Elizabeth Schlesinger Library on the History of Women in America, *The Manuscript Inventories and the Catalogs of the Manuscripts, Books and Pictures,* vol. III (Boston: G. K. Hall & Co., 1973).

6,711. Lancaster Industrial School for Girls
Records. Ca. 1856-1942. 38 vols.
Access restricted. No guide.
Schlesinger Library.
One of the oldest girls reform schools in the US, the School was founded in 1856 in Lancaster, MA, as a home to "restore girls to decency, morality, and respectable society." Financial, individual, and visitors' records; annual reports; and daily logs containing observations on the background, behavior, prognosis, and progress of individual girls.

6,712. Landauer, Bella Clara
Collection. Ca. 1821-1943. 1 Hollinger box and 1 oversize folder.
Open. Published and unpublished guides.
Schlesinger Library.
Correspondence, calling cards, bookplates, photos, and other papers of various American women, including title pages of sheet music dedicated to Amelia Bloomer, among others. Also included is material of Abigail Adams, Jacqueline Cochran, Mary Pickford, Harriet Beecher Stowe, Susan B. Anthony, Jane Addams, Clara Barton, Anna E. Dickinson, Zona Gale, Belva Lockwood, Louise Chandler Moulton, and Kate Douglas Wiggin. See Arthur and Elizabeth Schlesinger Library on the History of Women in America, *The Manuscript Inventories and the Catalogs of the Manuscripts, Books and Pictures,* vol. III (Boston: G. K. Hall & Co., 1973).

6,713. Lane, Laura
Papers. 1936-55. 3 Hollinger boxes.
Open. Published and unpublished guides.
Schlesinger Library.
A director of the Country Women's League organization of rural women, Lane (1913-) edited League leaflets and the "Country Gentlewomen" section of the *Country Gentleman.* Both Lane and Sara Bulette were at different times chairman of the US Liaison Committee of the Associated Country Women of the World; their correspondence with the Associated Country Women is included, as are manuscripts of articles submitted in League contests, and records, reports, and convention material pertaining to the Associated Country Women, the Committee, and the US branch of the Associated Country Women. See Arthur and Elizabeth Schlesinger Library on the History of Women in America, *The Manuscript Inventories and the Catalogs of the Manuscripts, Books and Pictures,* vol. III (Boston: G. K. Hall & Co., 1973).

6,714. Larcom, Lucy
Papers. 1877-82. 2 items.
Open. Published and unpublished guides.
Schlesinger Library.
Correspondence of Larcom (1824-93), a mill girl, author, seminary teacher, magazine editor, and poet, consists of a letter to Annie Adams Fields and one to Elizabeth S. Phelps Ward about Ward's book *Dr. Zay.* See Arthur and Elizabeth Schlesinger Library on the History of Women in America, *The Manuscript Inventories and the Catalogs of the Manuscripts, Books and Pictures,* vol. III (Boston: G. K. Hall & Co., 1973).

6,715. Lathrop, Julia Clifford
Papers. 1926. 1 item.
Open. Published and unpublished guides.
Schlesinger Library.
Letter by Lathrop (1858-1932), a social worker and reformer who was the first director of the Children's Bureau, to Florence Kelley on passage of a bill before Congress. See Arthur and Elizabeth Schlesinger Library on the History of Women in America, *The Manuscript Inventories and the Catalogs of the Manuscripts, Books and Pictures,* vol. III (Boston: G. K. Hall & Co., 1973).

6,716. League of Women for Community Service
Records. 1918-38. 1 folder and 3 vols.
Open. Published and unpublished guides.
Schlesinger Library.
Minutes of the League, a social service and civic organization of black Boston women which was founded in ca. 1916 as a WWI soldier's comfort unit. See Arthur and Elizabeth Schlesinger Library on the History of Women in America, *The Manuscript Inventories and the Catalogs of the Manuscripts, Books and Pictures,* vol. III (Boston: G. K. Hall & Co., 1973).

6,717. League of Women Voters of Cambridge
Records. 1916-59. 2.5 Hollinger boxes, 9 cartons, and 1 box.
Open. Published and unpublished guides.
Schlesinger Library.
Records of a branch of the LWV, which until 1920 had been named the Cambridge Political Equality Association, include minutes and reports of the executive board and of annual and regular meetings, correspondence, office files, directories, *League Items* newsletters and other publications, scrapbooks, and material on the Plan E city council-city manager form of government. See Arthur and Elizabeth Schlesinger Library on the History of Women in America, *The Manuscript Inventories and the Catalogs of the Manuscripts, Books and Pictures,* vol. III (Boston: G. K. Hall & Co., 1973).

6,718. League of Women Voters of Massachusetts
Records. 1920-76. 21 Hollinger boxes.
Open. Published and unpublished guides.
Schlesinger Library.
Records on the organization, work, and interests of the state LWV, founded in 1920, include minutes of board of directors meetings, financial records pertaining to the state and national LWVs, correspondence, general files, memos, bulletins, pamphlets, newsletters, photos, clippings, and publications dealing with League projects in government, legislation, education, and welfare and correction. See Arthur and Elizabeth Schlesinger Library on the History of Women in America, *The Manuscript Inventories and the Catalogs of the Manuscripts, Books and Pictures,* vol. III (Boston: G. K. Hall & Co., 1973).

6,719. League of Women Voters of the US
Records. 1920-68. 15 Hollinger boxes.
Open. Published and unpublished guides.
Schlesinger Library.
Records of the League, founded in 1920 as the National League of Women Voters, contain a constitution, minutes, annual reports, and publications of the National League and of 20 LWV chapters, including those in Boston and Watertown, MA, and Milwaukee County, WI. See Arthur and Elizabeth Schlesinger Library on the History of Women in America, *The Manuscript Inventories and the Catalogs of the Manuscripts, Books and Pictures,* vol. III (Boston: G. K. Hall & Co., 1973).

6,720. Lee, Dorothy (McCullough)
Papers. 1905-63. 9.5 Hollinger boxes and 1 oversize folder.
Open. Unpublished guide.
Schlesinger Library.
Correspondence, including a letter from President Eisenhower; speeches; photos from childhood and later life; and clippings on the career of [Mrs. W. Scott] Lee (1901-), a lawyer in California and Oregon who was an Oregon state representative from 1929 to 1931 and state senator from 1932 to 1943. Serving from 1943 to 1948 as commissioner of public utilities for the city of Portland, OR, in 1949 Lee became Portland's mayor, a position she held until 1952. In January 1953 she was made a consultant on women's affairs in Germany for the US Department of State and in August a member of the US Parole Board. From 1956 to 1962 she was a member of the US Subversive Activities Control Board, which she chaired from 1957.

6,721. Lee, Eleanor
Papers. 1919-66. 1.5 Hollinger boxes.
Open. Unpublished guide.

Schlesinger Library.
Correspondence, published and unpublished articles, photos, and memorabilia reflect the life and career of [Miss] Lee (1896-1967), a nurse who was director of nursing and associate nursing dean with the Columbia University Faculty of Medicine. Educated at Radcliffe and trained in nursing at Vassar College and the Presbyterian Hospital Nursing School in New York City, Lee assumed an administrative position at the Presbyterian School. Interested in the history of nursing, Lee was a member of the Committee on Historical Source Material in Nursing of the National League for Nursing, curator of the Florence Nightingale collection, and author of two volumes on the history of nursing at Columbia-Presbyterian Medical Center.

6,722. Lee, Mary
Papers. 1917-35. 4 Hollinger boxes and 2 bundles.
Open. Published and unpublished guides.
Schlesinger Library.
Lee (1891-) is an author and journalist who wrote a controversial book about WWI, which was originally titled "The Farce" but renamed *It's a Great War* when it was finally published in 1929. Correspondence; reminiscences of Radcliffe; manuscripts of articles and of "The Farce"; original version of the book; a German translation of *It's A Great War,* which was never published; articles; and clippings. Collection contains letters Lee wrote to her parents about her work abroad during WWI; she had sailed overseas in 1917 with the Massachusetts General Hospital Unit, then transferred to the US Air Service in Paris. See Arthur and Elizabeth Schlesinger Library on the History of Women in America, *The Manuscript Inventories and the Catalogs of the Manuscripts, Books and Pictures,* vol. III (Boston: G. K. Hall & Co., 1973).

6,723. Lee, Percy Maxim
Papers. Ca. 1940s-60s. 1 carton.
Open. No guide.
Schlesinger Library.
Lee (1906-) was president of the Connecticut LWV and of the League of Women Voters of the US and a member of the President's Consumer Advisory Council. Consists of correspondence concerning the LWV Overseas Education Fund and speeches she made in her presidential positions.

6,724. Leland, Minerva E.
Papers. 1862-1926. 4 Hollinger boxes.
Open. Published and unpublished guides.
Schlesinger Library.
From 1900 a teacher of mathematics in the Newton High School, Newton, MA, Leland (1859-1926) also taught at Scituate, MA, and Springfield, VT, and was an 1882 graduate of Colby College. Correspondence, articles, photos, and clippings, including letters from her family and school and college friends describing life at Colby, Wellesley, and Smith colleges; experiences in teaching for men and women; and the influence a teacher may have on her students. See Arthur and Elizabeth Schlesinger Library on the History of Women in America, *The Manuscript Inventories and the Catalogs of the Manuscripts, Books and Pictures,* vol. III (Boston: G. K. Hall & Co., 1973).

6,725. Leopold, Alice (Koller)
Papers. 1953-55. 2 Hollinger boxes.
Open. Published and unpublished guides.
Schlesinger Library.
[Mrs.] Leopold (1909-) was appointed director of the Women's Bureau in 1953 and assistant to the Secretary of Labor for Women in 1954. Correspondence, biographical material, speeches by Leopold, news releases, clippings about her and her work, and photos. Includes studies of Women's Bureau projects and information on a conference about the effective use of womanpower. See Arthur and Elizabeth Schlesinger Library on the History of Women in America, *The Manuscript Inventories and the Catalogs of the Manuscripts, Books and Pictures,* vol. III (Boston: G. K. Hall & Co., 1973).

6,726. Lerner, Gerda
Papers. Nd. 1 carton.
Closed. No guide.
Schlesinger Library.
Manuscripts and script of Lerner, an author and professor of history.

6,727. Levis, Rosa Marie (Finnochietti)
Papers. 1890-1959. 5 Hollinger boxes, 1 oversize folder and 3 oversize items.
Open. Unpublished guide.
Schlesinger Library.
A volunteer civic service worker in Boston, Levis (1878-1959) was involved in social, political, and religious women's organizations; Boston's Italian community; the Republican party; and woman suffrage. Correspondence, manuscripts, handbook, photos, clippings, and printed material provide information on her personal and family life, organizations in which she was involved, benefits, memorial funds, fund raising, and her WWI- and WWII-related work. Included are letters of gratitude from victorious Republican office-seekers, thanking her for her energetic campaigning, and some from prominent suffragists.

6,728. Lincoln, Alexander
Papers. 1919-40. 6.5 Hollinger boxes and 7 oversize vols.
Access restricted. Published and unpublished guides.
Schlesinger Library.
Lincoln (1873-?) was a Boston lawyer who from 1927 to 1936 was president of the Sentinels of the Republic, a nationwide organization that opposes federal encroachment on the rights of states and of individuals. Correspondence, speeches, minutes, bulletins, scrapbooks, clippings, and publications pertain to the work of the Sentinels in opposition to federal child labor amendments, as well as their work in the fields of maternity care, education, old-age assistance, and social security. See Arthur and Elizabeth Schlesinger Library on the History of Women in America, *The Manuscript Inventories and the Catalogs of the Manuscripts, Books and Pictures,* vol. III (Boston: G. K. Hall & Co., 1973).

6,729. Linderholm, Natalie Walker
Papers. Ca. 1940-70. 1 Hollinger box, 2 vols., and 2 envelopes.
Open. No guide.
Schlesinger Library.
Correspondence, scrapbooks, photos, and manuscripts for speeches, articles, and pamphlets by Linderholm, a Boston and New York social worker. Material pertains to her work for the Greater New York Fund, the Belmont School Committee, the Family Welfare Society of Boston, and the Nursery Training School of Boston. Also included are discussion outlines for the Family Welfare Association of America's Southern Institute, held in Georgia during 1940 and 1941.

6,730. Littledale, Clara (Savage)
Papers. 1913-55. 3 Hollinger boxes.
Open. Published and unpublished guides.
Schlesinger Library.
Articles, radio talks, and speeches on childrearing problems, which were written by [Mrs.] Littledale (1891-1956) during the years she served as first editor of *Parents' Magazine.* Also included are personal correspondence, notes, manuscripts, clippings, and photos, as well as material concerning the Women's Conference Group and the National Council for American-Soviet Friendship. See Arthur and Elizabeth Schlesinger Library on the History of Women in America, *The Manuscript Inventories and the Catalogs of the Manuscripts, Books and Pictures,* vol. III (Boston: G. K. Hall & Co., 1973).

6,731. Livermore, Mary Ashton (Rice)
Papers. 1870-1903. 3 folders.
Open. Published and unpublished guides.
Schlesinger Library.
Correspondence of Livermore (1820-1905), a Civil War worker, lecturer, and temperance and suffrage leader. See Arthur and Elizabeth Schlesinger Library on the History of Women in America, *The Manuscript Inventories and the Catalogs of the Manuscripts, Books and Pictures,* vol. III (Boston: G. K. Hall & Co., 1973).

6,732. Lockwood, Belva Ann (Bennett) McNall
Papers. 1885. 1 item.
Open. Published and unpublished guides.
Schlesinger Library.
The first woman to argue a case before the US Supreme Court, Lockwood (1830-1917) was a lawyer, advocate of women's rights, peace worker, and in 1884 and 1888 a presidential candidate. Letter in which Lockwood discusses her lecture engagements. See Arthur and Elizabeth Schlesinger Library on the History of Women in America, *The Manuscript Inventories and the Catalogs of the Manuscripts, Books and Pictures,* vol. III (Boston: G. K. Hall & Co., 1973).

6,733. Long, Priscilla
Oral history. 1972-73. 1 Hollinger box and 21 tapes.
Open. Published and unpublished guides.
Schlesinger Library.
Manuscripts, tapes, and a syllabus from a course on women in American history which was taught by Long, an instructor at the University of Rhode Island Extension in Providence. Students, some of whose work is included, undertook either social histories of their families or interviews with an older relative or friend. See Arthur and Elizabeth Schlesinger Library on the History of Women in America, *The Manuscript Inventories and the Catalogs of the Manuscripts, Books and Pictures,* vol. III (Boston: G. K. Hall & Co., 1973).

6,734. Longfellow, Annie
Papers. Nd. 1 item.
Open. Published and unpublished guides.
Schlesinger Library.
Letter from Longfellow to [Miss] Clara Howe. See Arthur and Elizabeth Schlesinger Library on the History of Women in America, *The Manuscript Inventories and the Catalogs of the Manuscripts, Books and Pictures,* vol. III (Boston: G. K. Hall & Co., 1973).

6,735. Longfellow, Henry Wadsworth
Papers. 1879-81. 2 items.
Open. Published and unpublished guides.
Schlesinger Library.
Manuscript poem by Longfellow (1807-82), a poet, and a letter to Mrs. F. Crooks. See Arthur and Elizabeth Schlesinger Library on the History of Women in America, *The Manuscript Inventories and the Catalogs of the Manuscripts, Books and Pictures,* vol. III (Boston: G. K. Hall & Co., 1973).

6,736. Lord-Heinstein, Lucile
Papers. 1937-50s. 1 Hollinger box and 1 oversize vol.
Open. No guide.
Schlesinger Library.
Correspondence, court brief, clippings, printed matter, and information on the lectures of Lord-Heinstein, a physician who was a birth control activist. Included is material on the 1937 raid of a Salem, MA, birth control clinic and the subsequent trial, and minutes from the North Shore Mothers' Health Centre.

6,737. Lord, Mary Pillsbury
Papers. Ca. 1950-71. 3 Hollinger boxes and 5 folders.
Open. Published and unpublished guides.
Schlesinger Library.
Papers pertaining to the UN work of [Mrs. Oswald Bates] Lord (1904-), a US representative to the General Assembly of the UN and US representative to the Commission on Human Rights, including correspondence, speeches and articles, photo, clippings, and printed material. Also contained is biographical data, excerpts of an interview with Lord on education at Smith College, and information on Indochina trips and the New York Commission on the Education and Employment of Women. See Arthur and Elizabeth Schlesinger Library on the History of Women in America, *The Manuscript Inventories and the Catalogs of the Manuscripts, Books and Pictures,* vol. III (Boston: G. K. Hall & Co., 1973).

6,738. Loring, Ellis Gray
Papers. 1809-1942. 10 Hollinger boxes, 6 oversize items, and 1 folder.
Open. Published and unpublished guides.
Schlesinger Library.
Correspondence, diaries, business papers, financial records, estate papers, scrapbooks, and photos of Loring (1803-58), a Boston lawyer and abolitionist who used his legal training to aid runaway slaves. Diary in which Loring describes conversations he had with Ralph Waldo Emerson on philosophic and religious issues; material concerning a trust which was established by friends of William Lloyd Garrison to help Garrison and his family financially while retaining some control over the way in which the money was spent; letters in which Elizabeth Preston Peabody discusses the possible establishment during the 1850s and 1860s of a Boston academy; and correspondence, diaries, and scrapbooks of the Loring and Dresel families. Correspondence of three generations of the Loring family includes letters between Ellis Loring, his wife Louisa (Gilman) Loring (1797-1868), their daughter Anna (Loring) Dresel (1830-96), their son-in-law Otto Dresel (1826-90), and their grandchildren Louisa Loring Dresel (1864-195?) and Ellis Loring Dresel (1865-1925). Much of the Dresel family correspondence was written in German. Also included is correspondence of John Glen King and his children, of Lydia Maria Child with the Lorings, and of Loring friends in the antislavery movement, Boston society, literary figures, and European musical personages. See Arthur and Elizabeth Schlesinger Library on the History of Women in America, *The Manuscript Inventories and the Catalogs of the Manuscripts, Books and Pictures,* vol. III (Boston: G. K. Hall & Co., 1973).

6,739. Lowrie, Rebecca (Lawrence)
Papers. 1940s-70s. 2 boxes and 3 folders.
Closed. No guide.
Schlesinger Library.
Correspondence of Lowrie (1891-1976), a civic worker, author, and editor, consists of letters to and from Florence (Clothier) Wislocki, executive vice-president of Vassar College, and letters from Sarah Gibson Blanding, president of Vassar.

6,740. Luckie, Mary O. (Barton)
Papers. 1875-1964. 1 Hollinger box and oversize items.
Open. Published and unpublished guides.
Schlesinger Library.
A founder of the GFWC, [Mrs. S. Blair] Luckie (1862-1964) was a club woman who was active in civic affairs. Clippings, articles, certificates, and programs of Luckie, photos of her and of GFWC members, and other material concerning the Federation. See Arthur and Elizabeth Schlesinger Library on the History of Women in America, *The Manuscript Inventories and the Catalogs of the Manuscripts, Books and Pictures,* vol. III (Boston: G. K. Hall & Co., 1973).

6,741. Lutz, Alma
Collection. 1783-1938. 1.5 Hollinger boxes.
Open. Published and unpublished guides.
Schlesinger Library.
Correspondence of leading abolitionists on antislavery and women's rights, including letters from Hannah Adams, Maria Weston Chapman, Prudence Crandall, Abigail Kelley Foster, Sarah Moore Grimké, Florence Kitchelt, and Rose Arnold Powell. Also included is Mary Grew's diary of the World Anti-Slavery Convention held in London in 1840. Collection also contains correspondence of other notable women such as Alice Stone Blackwell, Antoinette Brown Blackwell, Elizabeth Blackwell, Lydia Maria Child, Mary A. Livermore, Margaret Sanger, Lucy Larcom, Lucy Stone, Carrie Chapman Catt, Julia Ward Howe, Caroline M. Severance, Lydia Huntley Sigourney, and Mercy Otis Warren. See Arthur and Elizabeth Schlesinger Library on the History of Women in America, *The Manuscript Inventories and the Catalogs of the Manuscripts, Books and Pictures,* vol. III (Boston: G. K. Hall & Co., 1973).

6,742. Lutz, Alma
Papers. 1921-70. 9.5 Hollinger boxes and 1 folder.
Open. Published and unpublished guides.
Schlesinger Library.
Collection of correspondence, manuscript, speeches, articles, pamphlets, photos, clippings, and other papers of [Miss] Lutz (1890-1973), a member of the national council of the National Woman's Party, literature chairman, and contributing editor of *Equal Rights,* the NWP's official organ, also contains Party records. All of the material reflects the work of Lutz, the NWP, and other organizations for the equal rights amendment, as well as the Party's concerns with the Women's Charter, protective legislation, equality for working women, women as jurors, and the international status of women. Included are Council minutes and financial reports, *Equal Rights* records, correspondence of its editor Helen Hunt West with Lutz, press releases, reports on Party conventions and conferences, material concerning the 50th anniversary celebration of woman suffrage, and information on the activities of the Massachusetts branch of the NWP. Also included is correspondence of Lutz with such Party members as Caroline Lexow Babcock, Florence Bayard Hilles, Edith Houghton Hooker, Florence Kitchelt, Jeannette Marks, Alice Paul, Jane (Norman) Smith, Doris Stevens, and Anna (Kelton) Wiley. See Arthur and Elizabeth Schlesinger Library on the History of Women in America, *The Manuscript Inventories and the Catalogs of the Manuscripts, Books and Pictures,* vol. III (Boston: G. K. Hall & Co., 1973).

6,743. Lydia Estes Pinkham Medicine Company
Records. 1776-1968. 194 Hollinger boxes, 3 poster rolls, and 92 oversize items.
Partially closed. Published and unpublished guides.
Schlesinger Library.
The Company was founded in 1873 to sell the vegetable compound which Lydia (Estes) Pinkham (1819-83) developed, from a formula probably given to her by a neighbor, as a cure for female maladies; in 1968 the Company was sold to Cooper Laboratories of Connecticut. Fairly complete financial records to date from 1859 when the Pinkham Compound was sold privately, including cashbooks, inventories, and taxes; advertising registers and other records; correspondence; notebooks; research studies; trademark registrations; manufacturing records; photos; pamphlets; and books concerning the Company. Also included are a complete series in various languages of Pinkham pamphlets, which incorporate women's testimonials and Mrs. Pinkham's advice; and detailed studies from the 1950s of herbs and female maladies. A few family papers reveal Pinkham's attitude toward her family, scientific knowledge, and suffering, particularly that of women.

6,744. Lyman, Helen D.
Papers. 1882-1919. 1 Hollinger box.
Open. Published and unpublished guides.
Schlesinger Library.
Correspondence, scrapbooks, and photo album of Lyman, a minister in Benson, VT, contains information on women in the ministry, items on women's ministerial conferences in 1882 and 1895, and a photo album of portraits of American women ministers, which was kept by Julia (Ward) Howe. See Arthur and Elizabeth Schlesinger Library on the History of Women in America, *The Manuscript Inventories and the Catalogs of the Manuscripts, Books and Pictures,* vol. III (Boston: G. K. Hall & Co., 1973).

6,745. McCleery, Mary J.
Papers. 1870. 1 item.
Open. Published and unpublished guides.
Schlesinger Library.
Letter concerning the movement for improving the condition of Negroes. See Arthur and Elizabeth Schlesinger Library on the History of Women in America, *The Manuscript Inventories and the Catalogs of the Manuscripts, Books and Pictures,* vol. III (Boston: G. K. Hall & Co., 1973).

6,746. McCormick, Katharine (Dexter)
Papers. 1912-58. 1 folder.
Open. Published and unpublished guides.
Schlesinger Library.
Correspondence, pamphlets, and clippings of [Mrs. Stanley] McCormick (1875-1967), vice-president of the National American Woman Suffrage Association and corresponding secretary of the International Woman Suffrage Alliance, contain material pertaining to woman suffrage. Pamphlets include a 1913 antisuffrage monologue by Marie Jenny Howe, a 1915 pamphlet by Elsie Clews Parsons entitled "An Aversion to Anomalies," and another by Pelletier entitled "Les Femmes Peuvent-elles avoir du Genie?" See Arthur and Elizabeth Schlesinger Library on the History of Women in America, *The Manuscript Inventories and the Catalogs of the Manuscripts, Books and Pictures,* vol. III (Boston: G. K. Hall & Co., 1973).

6,747. McDowell, Mary Stone
Papers. 1935-55. 1 vol.
Open. Published and unpublished guides.
Schlesinger Library.
Papers of [Miss] McDowell (1876-1955), a peace worker, contain correspondence on her work as a Quaker and on her writings and articles she wrote for religious publications. See Arthur and Elizabeth Schlesinger Library on the History of Women in America, *The Manuscript Inventories and the Catalogs of the Manuscripts, Books and Pictures,* vol. III (Boston: G. K. Hall & Co., 1973).

6,748. MacKay-Scott, Ruth (Jarvis)
Papers. 1928-41. 1.5 Hollinger boxes, 2 oversize vols., and 1 oversize folder.
Open. Unpublished guide.
Schlesinger Library.
Correspondence, photos, clippings, and printed material of [Mrs. Andrew] MacKay-Scott, the wife of a wealthy stockbroker and an officer of the Woman's Club of Evanston, IL. Bulk of the collection relates to her service with the Club, while personal correspondence indicates that she entertained in her home musicians, lecturers, physicians, and other personages who participated in programs she organized or sponsored. MacKay-Scott's civic interests were social service and mental health programs such as the Infant Welfare Society, juvenile justice, venereal disease

education, and the Evanston King's Daughters, which was an organization for dependent girls and women. In 1930 she served as secretary of the Southern California Society for Mental Hygiene and as such was a member of the committee on organization of the First International Congress on Mental Hygiene. MacKay-Scott was also a board member of the Los Angeles Women's Health Center.

6,749. MacKaye, Percy
Papers. Nd. 1 item.
Open. Published and unpublished guides.
Schlesinger Library.
Statement of MacKaye (1875-1956), a dramatist, on woman suffrage. See Arthur and Elizabeth Schlesinger Library on the History of Women in America, *The Manuscript Inventories and the Catalogs of the Manuscripts, Books and Pictures,* vol. III (Boston: G. K. Hall & Co., 1973).

6,750. McLaughlin, Agnes Winifred
Papers. Ca. 1901-27. 1 folder.
Open. Published and unpublished guides.
Schlesinger Library.
The first woman to pass the bar in New Hampshire, McLaughlin (1882-1964) was an attorney who practiced in New Hampshire and New York. Correspondence, autobiography, articles, speeches, essay and manuscript, photos, and clippings document her career. See Arthur and Elizabeth Schlesinger Library on the History of Women in America, *The Manuscript Inventories and the Catalogs of the Manuscripts, Books and Pictures,* vol. III (Boston: G. K. Hall & Co., 1973).

6,751. Mahoney, Mildred (Hodgman)
Papers. 1944-69. 3.5 Hollinger boxes.
Open. Unpublished guide.
Schlesinger Library.
[Mrs. John J.] Mahoney (1896-) was executive secretary of the Massachusetts Governor's Commission for Racial and Religious Understanding from 1943 until 1946, when she was appointed chairman of the Massachusetts Commission Against Discrimination, a position she held until 1964. Correspondence, articles, speeches, notes, and printed material contain information on discrimination in Massachusetts. Also contained are MCAD minutes and annual reports, annual reports of the state Fair Employment Practices Commission, and manuscripts of speeches made before the 1944 Institute on Intercultural Education held at Boston University.

6,752. Maimie
Papers. 1910-22. 3 Hollinger boxes.
Access restricted. Published and unpublished guides.
Schlesinger Library.
Correspondence, reports, and photos of Maimie (1885-?), a Philadelphia prostitute. Bulk of collection is correspondence between Maimie and Fanny (Quincy) [Mrs. M. A. DeWolfe] Howe about Maimie's past, her marriages, her training and work as a stenographer, and her efforts to establish and maintain a halfway house for young prostitutes, which was known as the Montreal Mission for Friendless Girls. Maimie also describes the individual girls, how they came to the Home, their problems and feelings, and their adjustment to life at the Home. Maimie and Howe were introduced by a Philadelphia social worker. See Arthur and Elizabeth Schlesinger Library on the History of Women in America, *The Manuscript Inventories and the Catalogs of the Manuscripts, Books and Pictures,* vol. III (Boston: G. K. Hall & Co., 1973).

6,753. Mannheim, Eunice
Papers. Nd. 3 cartons and 1 Hollinger box.
Open. No guide.
Schlesinger Library.
Correspondence and printed material of Mannheim pertain to her campaigns for public office, the LWV, and the Board of Selectmen of the town of Amherst, MA.

6,754. Marks, Jeannette A.
Papers. 1905-39. 3 cartons and 1 folder.
Open. Published and unpublished guides.
Schlesinger Library.
Papers of Marks (1875-1964), an author who was also a professor of English literature at Mount Holyoke College between 1901 and 1910, concern the National Woman's Party. Also included is correspondence from Marks to Curtis Hidden Page on literary subjects. See Arthur and Elizabeth Schlesinger Library on the History of Women in America, *The Manuscript Inventories and the Catalogs of the Manuscripts, Books and Pictures,* vol. III (Boston: G. K. Hall & Co., 1973).

6,755. Marsh, Mary B.
Papers. 1861. 1 item.
Open. Published and unpublished guides.
Schlesinger Library.
Letter in which Marsh describes, to her cousin Sarah, New York City in the spring. See Arthur and Elizabeth Schlesinger Library on the History of Women in America, *The Manuscript Inventories and the Catalogs of the Manuscripts, Books and Pictures,* vol. III (Boston: G. K. Hall & Co., 1973).

6,756. Martineau, Harriet
Papers. 1837. 1 item.
Open. Published and unpublished guides.
Schlesinger Library.
Letter of Martineau (1802-76), an English abolitionist who visited the US, to Arthur Hill. See Arthur and Elizabeth Schlesinger Library on the History of Women in America, *The Manuscript Inventories and the Catalogs of the Manuscripts, Books and Pictures,* vol. III (Boston: G. K. Hall & Co., 1973).

6,757. Maryland Suffrage
Collection. 1910-20. 1 folder and 1 oversize item.
Open. Published and unpublished guides.
Schlesinger Library.
Yearbook of the Equal Suffrage League of Baltimore, yearbook of the State Equal Franchise League of Maryland, and reports of affiliated suffrage Leagues. See Arthur and Elizabeth Schlesinger Library on the History of Women in America, *The Manuscript Inventories and the Catalogs of the Manuscripts, Books and Pictures,* vol. III (Boston: G. K. Hall & Co., 1973).

6,758. Mason Family
Papers. Nd. 4 Hollinger boxes.
Open. No guide.
Schlesinger Library.
Correspondence, manuscripts, booklets, and clippings pertain to Caroline Mason (1823-90), a poet, to her poetry, and to her sisters. Some of the correspondence relates to woman suffrage and to Lucy Stone.

6,759. Massachusetts Girl Scouts
Records. 1915-67. 2 cartons.
Open. No guide.
Schlesinger Library.
Minutes of annual meetings and of executive board meetings, reports, and other records for the metropolitan, eastern, and western divisions of the Girl Scouts; camping department records; minutes, reports, and financial records of the Massachusetts state camp committee; and minutes of the Local Directors' Association. Also included are correspondence, speeches, reports, and biographical information by and about Massachusetts Scouts leaders Sarah Louise Arnold, Augusta Batchelder Hartt, Lou (Henry) Hoover, and Helen Osborne Storrow.

6,760. Massachusetts Society for Social Health
Records. 1915-65. 9 Hollinger boxes.
Open. Unpublished guide.
Schlesinger Library.
Charter of incorporation, financial records, post-1927 minutes of the executive committee and reports of the executive secretary, manuscripts of speeches and articles, memoranda, photos, clippings, and publications of the Society, which was founded in 1911 "to help people understand and manage sex in its relation to health, good citizenship, marriage, parenthood, and family life." Material describes the educational activities of the Society in Boston as well as those of the branch which operated in western Massachusetts. Subjects include homosexuality, marriage counseling, pornography, prostitution, and venereal diseases. Some of the women active in the Society or employed by it were Maida (Herman) Solomon, Dorothy W. Miller, Miriam Van Waters, and Eva (Whiting) White. Also included are some records of the American Social Hygiene Association.

6,761. Matthews, Annabel
Papers. 1880-1960. 1.5 Hollinger boxes and 1 oversize folder.
Open. Unpublished guide.
Schlesinger Library.
A tax attorney, Matthews (1883-1960) was appointed to the US Board of Tax Appeals in 1930. Correspondence and clippings mostly pertain to her appointment and her not being re-appointed in 1936. Also included are clippings on women officials in the federal government as well as letters from Mabel (Walker) Willebrandt and Vera Mankinen.

6,762. May and Goddard Families
Papers. 1766-1904. 2 Hollinger boxes, 2 oversize vols. and 1 folder.
Open. Published and unpublished guides.
Schlesinger Library.
Correspondence, diaries, financial papers, photos, and other documents of two families who were prominent in New England and descendants of the parents of Abigail Williams May (1829-88). A reformer and cofounder of the New England Women's Club, May was one of the first women to serve as a member of the Boston School Committee, a position she held between 1873 and 1875. Included are Abigail May's papers, with letters from prominent abolitionists, suffragists, and authors; women's diaries and account books; and papers of Samuel and Mehetable Goddard, with letters they wrote home during their residence in England from 1818 to 1827. Other persons represented are Samuel J. May (1797-1871); Samuel May of Leicester, MA; Frederick Warren Goddard May (1821-1904); Louisa May Alcott; Ednah Dow Cheney; Lucy Stone; Julia Ward Howe; and Elizabeth Stuart Phelps. Collection also contains information on social life and customs in Boston and New England. See Arthur and Elizabeth Schlesinger Library on the History of Women in America, *The Manuscript Inventories and the Catalogs of the Manuscripts, Books and Pictures,* vol. III (Boston: G. K. Hall & Co., 1973).

6,763. Mead, Kate Campbell (Hurd)
Papers. Ca. 1939-43. 2 Hollinger boxes.
Open. Published and unpublished guides.
Schlesinger Library.
Papers of Mead (1867-1941), a physician and historian of women in medicine, consist of photos and the manuscript for *The History of Women in Medicine, Vol. 2: Medical Women in the Eastern Hemisphere.* See Arthur and Elizabeth Schlesinger Library on the History of Women in America, *The Manuscript Inventories and the Catalogs of the Manuscripts, Books and Pictures,* vol. III (Boston: G. K. Hall & Co., 1973).

6,764. Metcalf, Eleanor M. Thomas
Papers. 1895-1906. 2 folders.
Open. Published and unpublished guides.
Schlesinger Library.
Correspondence of Metcalf, a granddaughter of author Herman Melville, contains letters between Elizabeth S. Melville and Adeline Dutton (Train) Whitney and letters from Whitney to Metcalf. See Arthur and Elizabeth Schlesinger Library on the History of Women in America, *The Manuscript Inventories and the Catalogs of the Manuscripts, Books and Pictures,* vol. III (Boston: G. K. Hall & Co., 1973).

6,765. Miller, Emma (Guffey)
Papers. 1920-67. 15 Hollinger boxes, 1 carton, and 1 oversize folder.
Open. Published and unpublished guides.
Schlesinger Library.
Collection reflects the political life of [Mrs. Carroll] Miller (1874-1970) who was a Democratic National Committeewoman from Pennsylvania from 1932 to 1970 and a member of the convention platform committee from the mid-1940s; she also was a suffragist, member of the Consumers' League from 1910 to 1914, and from 1961 to 1965 chairman of the National Woman's Party. Correspondence, speeches, reports and mementos, scrapbook, pamphlets, photos, clippings, publications, and other material, which reflect Miller's interests in prohibition repeal, education, equal rights, social welfare, and the National Youth Administration. Correspondents include Harry Truman, Mary Dewson, Hubert and Muriel Humphrey, Lyndon B. Johnson, John F. Kennedy, Robert F. Kennedy, Frances Perkins, Gifford Pinchot, and Adlai Stevenson. Also included is an essay on Miller by Miriam Lois Backer. See Arthur and Elizabeth Schlesinger Library on the History of Women in America, *The Manuscript Inventories and the Catalogs of the Manuscripts, Books and Pictures,* vol. III (Boston: G. K. Hall & Co., 1973).

6,766. Miller, Frieda Segelke
Papers. Ca. 1923-67. 30 Hollinger boxes, 3 cartons, and 5 folders.
Access restricted. Published and unpublished guides.
Schlesinger Library.
Correspondence, manuscripts for speeches, notes, articles, reports, pamphlets, photos, publications, and other papers of Miller (1889-1973) reflect her political career. From 1944 to 1953 she was director of the Women's Bureau; from 1943 to 1944 she was special assistant to the US ambassador in London; and from 1939 to 1942 she was industrial commissioner of the New York State Department of Labor. Also included is information on International Labor Organization conferences, the 1946 conference in London where she served as advisor to the US delegation to the General Assembly of the UN and as the government representative to the ILO's constitutional committee meetings, and later meetings about bringing the ILO into the UN. Material on UNICEF, the National Committee on Household Employment, the International Union for Child Welfare Survey, and Friends of Alliance is included as well as Miller's diary of a trip to Delhi, India. Frances P. Bolton, Herbert Lehman, Clara (Mortenson) Beyer, Pauline Newman, Frances Perkins, and Louise Stitt are correspondents. See Arthur and Elizabeth Schlesinger Library on the History of Women in America, *The Manuscript Inventories and the Catalogs of the Manuscripts, Books and Pictures,* vol. III (Boston: G. K. Hall & Co., 1973).

6,767. Miller, Helen Hill
Papers. Nd. 14 Hollinger boxes, 4 cartons, 1 vol., and 1 folder.
Open. No guide.
Schlesinger Library.
Correspondence, manuscripts, PhD thesis, scrapbook, printed material, and memorabilia of [Mrs. Francis Pickens] Miller (1899-), a journalist and author in Washington, DC, and London. Included are articles Miller wrote, notes for her college courses, correspondence and reviews about her books, correspondence concerning the International Visitors Center in Knoxville, TN, and material about the Women's National Press Club.

6,768. Millette, Minnie Roop
Papers. 1903-?. 1 carton and 2 folders.
Open. No guide.
Schlesinger Library.
Correspondence, manuscripts, photos, clippings, and other papers of Millette, a Dayton, OH, schoolteacher, show the intellectual interests of an educated woman. Included are notes on Austria and on Mexican myths and legends.

6,769. Mooar, Eva Alberta
Papers. 1908-37. 1 folder.
Open. Published and unpublished guides.
Schlesinger Library.
A 1908 graduate of Radcliffe, Mooar was a teacher, for eight years director of the Radcliffe College Appointment Bureau, and from 1927 to 1954 dean of admissions at Pembroke College. Correspondence, notebooks, programs, documents, and memorabilia pertain to Mooar's education and to two trips she took around the world. See Arthur and Elizabeth Schlesinger Library on the History of Women in America, *The Manuscript Inventories and the Catalogs of the Manuscripts, Books and Pictures,* vol. III (Boston: G. K. Hall & Co., 1973).

6,770. Moore, Dorothea May
Papers. 1858-?. 1 Hollinger box.
Open. No guide.
Schlesinger Library.
Moore was a physician. An 1858-71 diary by Louisa Walter Bishop Hughes of New Haven, CT, photos and correspondence from Dorothy (Canfield) Fisher to Moore's mother, and material on the Medical Women's International Association, the Children's Medical Center of the Philippines, and the Center's founder Fe del Mundo, who was a physician.

6,771. Morgan and Howes Families
Papers. 1892-1962. 7 Hollinger boxes.
Open. Published and unpublished guides.
Schlesinger Library.
Primarily the collection of Laura (Puffer) Morgan (1874-1962), a lecturer, writer, teacher, world traveler, suffragist, press correspondent, and worker for disarmament and world organization; papers of her sister Ethel (Puffer) Howes (1872-1950), a psychologist and first director of the Institute for the Co-ordination of Women's Interests at Smith College, are also included. Correspondence, articles, reports, minutes, and press releases document Morgan's career and include information on the 1921-22 Washington Disarmament Conference; the 1930 and 1935-36 London Naval Conferences; the 1932 League of Nations World Disarmament Conference; the 1932-35, 1935-37, and 1938 Geneva Disarmament Conferences; the Institute on World Organization; and the Washington, DC, board of education between 1922 and 1924. Howes's papers contain personal and professional correspondence, with letters to her mother and family, letters to Morgan on Howes's death, biographical material, writings, and clippings. See Arthur and Elizabeth Schlesinger Library on the History of Women in America, *The Manuscript Inventories and the Catalogs of the Manuscripts, Books and Pictures,* vol. III (Boston: G. K. Hall & Co., 1973).

6,772. Morris, Anna Mary (Curtis)
Papers. 1861-89. 1 vol.
Open. Published and unpublished guides.
Schlesinger Library.
Scrapbook of Morris (ca. 1830-?), sister of [Madame] Ellen Louise (Curtis) Demorest, contains poems, clippings, and memorabilia of Morris as well as material relating to the Demorest family and to the Woman's Tea Company of New York. See Arthur and Elizabeth Schlesinger Library on the History of Women in America, *The Manuscript Inventories and the Catalogs of the Manuscripts, Books and Pictures,* vol. III (Boston: G. K. Hall & Co., 1973).

6,773. Morris, Clara
Papers. 1867-1924. 56 vols.
Open. Published and unpublished guides.
Schlesinger Library.
Diaries of Morris (1847-1925), an actress and author of short stories and such books as *Little Jim Crow* (1894), *The Silent Singer* (1898), and *Life on the Stage* (1901). In her diaries she discusses her career on the stage, her writings, and her personal life which was often difficult because of ill health, temporary partial blindness, and lack of money. Married to Frederick C. Harriott from 1874 until his death in 1914, Morris largely supported him, her mother, and others. See Arthur and Elizabeth Schlesinger Library on the History of Women in America, *The Manuscript Inventories and the Catalogs of the Manuscripts, Books and Pictures,* vol. III (Boston: G. K. Hall & Co., 1973).

6,774. Morse, Frances Rollins
Papers. Nd. 2 cartons.
Open. No guide.
Schlesinger Library.
Correspondence and calendars of Morse (1850-1928), a social work volunteer.

6,775. Morton, Emma Little
Papers. Ca. 1925. 1 item.
Open. Published and unpublished guides.
Schlesinger Library.
Autobiography of Morton (1846-192?), who was active in Congregational church work and music and associated with Dwight L. Moody and Henry Ward Beecher. See Arthur and Elizabeth Schlesinger Library on the History of Women in America, *The Manuscript Inventories and the Catalogs of the Manuscripts, Books and Pictures,* vol. III (Boston: G. K. Hall & Co., 1973).

6,776. Morton, Gertrude Eliza (Tyler)
Papers. 1892. 123-page vol.
Open. Published and unpublished guides.
Schlesinger Library.
Account illustrated with photos of two weeks spent on the Bras D'Or lakes of Nova Scotia by Morton, an 1887 graduate of Radcliffe. See Arthur and Elizabeth Schlesinger Library on the History of Women in America, *The Manuscript Inventories and the Catalogs of the Manuscripts, Books and Pictures,* vol. III (Boston: G. K. Hall & Co., 1973).

6,777. Morton, Helen
Papers. 1871-76. 13 items.
Open. Published and unpublished guides.
Schlesinger Library.
Correspondence of Morton, a physician, to [Mrs.] Mary Elizabeth (Watson) Hopkinson illuminates the friendship between the two and Morton's loneliness; in one letter Morton refers to Marie Zakrzewska. See Arthur and Elizabeth Schlesinger Library on the History of Women in America, *The Manuscript Inventories and the Catalogs of the Manuscripts, Books and Pictures,* vol. III (Boston: G. K. Hall & Co., 1973).

6,778. Mosher, Alfreida
Papers. Nd. 3 Hollinger boxes, 3 folders, and 1 vol.
Open. No guide.
Schlesinger Library.
Correspondence, diaries, pamphlets, diplomas, and pictures of Mosher (1873-1966). Includes copies of

the *International Beacon* and letters to Pauline Gardescu, Paul Agnew, and M. Heitzer.

6,779. Mothers' Club of Cambridge
Records. 1881-1942. 2 Hollinger boxes.
Open. Published and unpublished guides.
Schlesinger Library.
Financial records, minutes, reports, manuscripts of speeches, lists, and clippings of the Club, which was founded in ca. 1878 for discussion of problems relating to the members' children. The Club's scope was later expanded to include programs on the conditions of less privileged children, domestic service, and other subjects. See Arthur and Elizabeth Schlesinger Library on the History of Women in America, *The Manuscript Inventories and the Catalogs of the Manuscripts, Books and Pictures,* vol. III (Boston: G. K. Hall & Co., 1973).

6,780. Mothers' Discussion Club
Records. 1899-1958. 1 Hollinger box.
Open. Published and unpublished guides.
Schlesinger Library.
Constitution, financial records, minutes, membership lists, and essays on WWI work by members of this Cambridge Club, founded in 1899 for discussion of problems relating to the members' children, such as physical training, clothing, teaching manners and music, and public schools. Later, the Club broadened its discussion to cover community affairs, clubs, and international affairs. See Arthur and Elizabeth Schlesinger Library on the History of Women in America, *The Manuscript Inventories and the Catalogs of the Manuscripts, Books and Pictures,* vol. III (Boston: G. K. Hall & Co., 1973).

6,781. Mothers' Study Club
Records. 1914-67. 2 Hollinger boxes and 1 oversize item.
Open. Published and unpublished guides.
Schlesinger Library.
Constitution, minutes, and programs of the Club, founded in Cambridge in 1914 to promote discussion and socializing among the membership, reveal aspects of Cambridge social life and customs. Also included are manuscripts of speeches by Club members on such topics as employment for women and feminism. See Arthur and Elizabeth Schlesinger Library on the History of Women in America, *The Manuscript Inventories and the Catalogs of the Manuscripts, Books and Pictures,* vol. III (Boston: G. K. Hall & Co., 1973).

6,782. Mothers' Thursday Club
Records. 1919-72. 1.5 Hollinger boxes.
Open. Unpublished guide.
Schlesinger Library.
Founded in Cambridge in 1920 as the Mothers' Query Club to promote discussion and socializing among the membership, the group changed to its current name in 1921. Constitution, minutes, and membership lists include proceedings of the membership, nominating, and meetings committees. Many of the lectures at Club meetings were given by members of the Harvard University faculty.

6,783. Mott, Lucretia (Coffin)
Papers. 1866. 1 item.
Open. Published and unpublished guides.
Schlesinger Library.
Letter to Susan B. Anthony from Mott (1793-1880), a Quaker minister, abolitionist, and pioneer in the movement for women's rights. See Arthur and Elizabeth Schlesinger Library on the History of Women in America, *The Manuscript Inventories and the Catalogs of the Manuscripts, Books and Pictures,* vol. III (Boston: G. K. Hall & Co., 1973).

6,784. Motter, Ellen Sitgreaves (Vail)
Papers. Nd. 2 cartons and 1 folder.
Open. No guide.
Schlesinger Library.
Manuscript poems and diaries of Motter, photos, and letters from her father Thomas Hubbard Vail, Episcopal bishop of Kansas from 1864 to 1889, who with his wife Ellen Ledlie Bowman Vail founded the College of the Sisters of Bethany. The College later became part of Washburn University in Topeka, KS.

6,785. Moulton, Louise (Chandler)
Papers. Nd. 1 item.
Open. Published and unpublished guides.
Schlesinger Library.
Letter of Moulton (1835-1908), an author and literary hostess, to the publisher Messrs. John Wilson and Son. See Arthur and Elizabeth Schlesinger Library on the History of Women in America, *The Manuscript Inventories and the Catalogs of the Manuscripts, Books and Pictures,* vol. III (Boston: G. K. Hall & Co., 1973).

6,786. Mount Holyoke Female Seminary Memorandum Society
Records. 1862. 1 item.
Open. Published and unpublished guides.
Schlesinger Library.
Catalog of the Society, established in 1837 and evidently a forerunner of the alumnae association, consists of the constitution and a list of members from 1837 to 1862. See Arthur and Elizabeth Schlesinger Library on the History of Women in America, *The Manuscript Inventories and the Catalogs of the Manuscripts, Books and Pictures,* vol. III (Boston: G. K. Hall & Co., 1973).

6,787. Mowatt, Anna Cora (Ogden)
Papers. 183?-1939. 10 folders.
Open. Published and unpublished guides.
Schlesinger Library.
Collection of Mowatt (1819-70), an actress and author of the play *Fashion,* consists primarily of correspondence to Catharine Sargent. Also included are memorabilia from Mowatt's career, articles, photos, and clippings. See Arthur and Elizabeth Schlesinger Library on the History of Women in America, *The Manuscript Inventories and the Catalogs of the Manuscripts, Books and Pictures,* vol. III (Boston: G. K. Hall & Co., 1973).

6,788. Mudd, Emily
Papers. 1932-73. 3 Hollinger boxes and 5 folders.
Access restricted. No guide.
Schlesinger Library.
Mudd (1898-) is a counselor and educator who specializes in marriage and family counseling. Correspondence, reprints of her articles, reports, and photos, including material on the Pathfinder Fund, training for seminary teachers of pastoral care, and the Pennsylvania Abortion Law Commission.

6,789. Munk, Marie
Papers. 1918-50. Ca. 7 Hollinger boxes and 1 oversize vol.
Open. Published and unpublished guides.
Schlesinger Library.
A noted German lawyer and judge, Munk emigrated to this country in 1934; she was admitted to the Ohio bar in 1944. Correspondence, manuscripts, speeches, articles, photos, and other material contain information on Munk's interest in marriage and divorce law and in juvenile justice, and on the International Federation of Women Lawyers and the New York Training School for Girls. Also included are scrapbooks of clippings from German newspapers and manuscripts of *Reminiscences of a Pioneer Woman Judge in Pre-Hitler Germany,* which was written in the 1940s and contains information on the rise and fall of German feminism, and of *The Elements of Love and Marriage* (revised edition, 1950). See Arthur and Elizabeth Schlesinger Library on the History of Women in America, *The Manuscript Inventories and the Catalogs of the Manuscripts, Books and Pictures,* vol. III (Boston: G. K. Hall & Co., 1973).

6,790. Murray, Pauli
Papers. Ca. 1940-72. 11 cartons.
Open. No guide.
Schlesinger Library.
Correspondence, notebooks, financial papers, appointment books, clippings, and printed material and reports of Murray, a black lawyer, author and editor, college teacher, and ordained Episcopal priest, document her education, career, and commitment to work against sex and race discrimination and for improvement in the legal status of black and white women. Files of the National Organization for Women and from the President's Commission on the Status of Women are included with reports of research and legal cases concerning sex discrimination and material on the equal rights amendment and the American Civil Liberties Union.

6,791. Nathan, Maud (Nathan)
Papers. 1890-1938. 12 vols.
Open. Published and unpublished guides.
Schlesinger Library.
These scrapbooks of clippings, available on microfilm, concern the activities of Nathan (1862-1946), a New York society woman and social reformer who was president of the New York Consumers' League from 1897 to 1917; vice-president of the National Consumers' League; a suffrage worker; and delegate to international congresses for peace, suffrage, working girls, and social betterment. Also included are reports of speeches as well as reviews and correspondence concerning her book *The Story of an Epoch-Making Movement.* See Arthur and Elizabeth Schlesinger Library on the History of Women in America, *The Manuscript Inventories and the Catalogs of the Manuscripts, Books and Pictures,* vol. III (Boston: G. K. Hall & Co., 1973).

6,792. National American Woman Suffrage Association
Records. 1899-1915. 1 vol.
Open. Published and unpublished guides.
Schlesinger Library.
Notebook of minutes of the 1899 convention and a program from the 1915 convention of the Association, which was established in 1890 to help attain woman suffrage. The Association was formed by the merger of the American Woman Suffrage Association and the National Woman Suffrage Association. See Arthur and Elizabeth Schlesinger Library on the History of Women in America, *The Manuscript Inventories and the Catalogs of the Manuscripts, Books and Pictures,* vol. III (Boston: G. K. Hall & Co., 1973).

6,793. National Consumers' League
Records. 1912-49. 1 Hollinger box.
Open. Published and unpublished guides.
Schlesinger Library.
Records of the League, founded in 1898 to improve working conditions for employees, include a constitution, correspondence, clippings, copies of addresses before annual meetings, and minutes of the executive committee and of the committee on cooperation. See Arthur and Elizabeth Schlesinger Library on the History of Women in America, *The Manuscript Inventories and the Catalogs of the Manuscripts, Books and Pictures,* vol. III (Boston: G. K. Hall & Co., 1973).

6,794. National Organization for Women
Records. 1966- . 33 cartons, 13 Hollinger boxes, 2 films, and tapes.
Open. No guide.
Schlesinger Library.
Records of national and Massachusetts chapters of NOW, organized in 1966 to work toward the realization of legal, economic, and social equality for women, also include papers of individual

officers such as Wilma Scott Heide, president in 1974. Bylaws, financial records, minutes, correspondence, articles, newsletters, video and sound tapes, and other material, including records of the Joint Committee of Organizations Concerned About the Status of Women in the Catholic Church, the Ecumenical Task Force on Women and Religion, the Catholic Caucus, and the NOW Legal Defense and Education Fund Public Service Advertising Campaign.

6,795. National Women's Trade Union League of America
Records. 1904-50. 7 Hollinger boxes, 1 oversize vol., and 2 oversize items.
Open. Published and unpublished guides.
Schlesinger Library.
The Trade Union League was established in 1903 to organize women workers into unions, thereby helping them to "secure conditions necessary for healthful and efficient work and to obtain a just reward for such work." Correspondence, reports, bulletins, publications of local Leagues, photos, and printed material illustrate the League's work training labor leaders, performing research on working conditions, and supporting strikes, as well as organizing local Leagues. Included is material on working conditions in the garment and textile industry, protective legislation, equal rights for women, the 1910-11 Chicago garment workers' strike, the 1930-31 Danville, VA, textile workers' strike, and the Women's Trade Union Leagues of Chicago, Philadelphia, and New York. In 1950 the League ceased operations. Portions are available on microfilm. See Arthur and Elizabeth Schlesinger Library on the History of Women in America, *The Manuscript Inventories and the Catalogs of the Manuscripts, Books and Pictures,* vol. III (Boston: G. K. Hall & Co., 1973).

6,796. Nealy, Mary E.
Papers. 1868. 1 item.
Open. Published and unpublished guides.
Schlesinger Library.
Letter to a Mr. Tillinghast from Nealy, a poet and author. See Arthur and Elizabeth Schlesinger Library on the History of Women in America, *The Manuscript Inventories and the Catalogs of the Manuscripts, Books and Pictures,* vol. III (Boston: G. K. Hall & Co., 1973).

6,797. New England Hospital
Records. 1914-54. 1 Hollinger box.
Open. Unpublished guide.
Schlesinger Library.
Founded by women in 1862 as the New England Hospital for Women and Children, until the 1950s the Hospital was also staffed exclusively by women. Minutes of the board of directors, correspondence, notes, completed questionnaires, annual reports, lists of staff committees, clippings, and other material on administration of the Hospital, particularly financial difficulties and the controversy during the 1950s over admitting male doctors to practice there. In 1969 the Hospital's name was changed to Dimock Community Health Center.

6,798. New England Women's Club
Records. 1868-1970. 13 Hollinger boxes, 1 oversize folder, and 5 oversize vols.
Open. Published and unpublished guides.
Schlesinger Library.
One of the oldest women's clubs in the US, the Club was founded in 1868 to provide a meeting place for women outside their homes where they could obtain knowledge and inspiration for work inside and outside the home in social causes. A detailed picture of board, annual, and social meetings emerges from officers' reports, financial records, minutes, correspondence, lists of officers and members, committee reports, scrapbook, photos, clippings, and other material. Also included are manuscripts of speeches and articles, biographical data on some Club members, and material on difficulties encountered by the dress reform committee, the financial crisis of 1899, and on the relationship of the Club to the Massachusetts Federation of Women's Clubs and to the GFWC from 1890, when the national group was founded. See Arthur and Elizabeth Schlesinger Library on the History of Women in America, *The Manuscript Inventories and the Catalogs of the Manuscripts, Books and Pictures,* vol. III (Boston: G. K. Hall & Co., 1973).

6,799. New York House and School of Industry
Records. Ca. 1951-57. 4 Hollinger boxes.
Open. No guide.
Schlesinger Library.
Correspondence, questionnaires, registration cards, Women's Bureau publications, and project proposals of the vocational training project of the School. The project was founded in ca. 1951 to retrain older stenographers and typists so that they could return to work. Files also include information on the backgrounds of the women who participated in the program.

6,800. New York State Association Opposed to Woman Suffrage
Records. 1894-1916. 3 folders.
Open. Published and unpublished guides.
Schlesinger Library.
Newsletters, pamphlets, leaflets, and form letters to the press, circulated by the Association whose purpose was distributing information against woman suffrage, were written by such persons as Elihu Root, Francis M. Scott, Harry Stimson, and Alice George. See Arthur and Elizabeth Schlesinger Library on the History of Women in America, *The Manuscript Inventories and the Catalogs of the Manuscripts, Books and Pictures,* vol. III (Boston: G. K. Hall & Co., 1973).

6,801. New Zealand Women's Archives
Records. Nd. 3 Hollinger boxes and 1 oversize folder.
Open. Published and unpublished guides.
Schlesinger Library.
Manuscripts, clippings, and publications collected by several women for the Archives in the Schlesinger Library contain information about the status and accomplishments of women in New Zealand as well as about women's social, political, and civic organizations. Also included are biographies of women, who were important in such fields as journalism, business, education, nursing, medicine, religion, politics, and civic affairs. See Arthur and Elizabeth Schlesinger Library on the History of Women in America, *The Manuscript Inventories and the Catalogs of the Manuscripts, Books and Pictures,* vol. III (Boston: G. K. Hall & Co., 1973).

6,802. Newman, Pauline
Papers. 1974. 5 cartons and 2 tapes.
Open. Unpublished guide.
Schlesinger Library.
Newman was active in the women's labor movement. Interview with her concerns the 1909-10 shirtwaist makers strike in New York City and work in the garment industry. Also included is material from her work with the International Ladies Garment Workers Union's Union Health Center and with the state and national Women's Trade Union League.

6,803. Nichols and Shurtleff Family
Papers. 1780-1953. 17.5 Hollinger boxes.
Open. Unpublished guide.
Schlesinger Library.
Correspondence, diaries, journals, notebooks, financial documents, manuscript articles, photos, and books of women members of this wealthy Boston area family; extensive European travelers, the women were also active in social and civic affairs, woman suffrage, and artistic endeavors. Papers of Elizabeth F. Nichols (1844-1929) pertain to her adult life, with information about her activities as a wife and mother. Papers of Marian Clarke Nichols (1873-1953) and Rose Standish Nichols (1872-1960), daughters of Elizabeth and Arthur H. Nichols (1840-1923), document Marian Nichols's participation in Boston volunteer organizations, suffrage, local government, and civic improvement as well as Rose Nichols's work studying and practicing garden architecture; their correspondence often contains their reactions to their travels abroad. Papers of Margaret H. (Nichols) Shurtleff (1879-1959), third daughter of Elizabeth and Arthur Nichols, reflect her role as a mother and active philanthropist. Also included are papers of the Shurtleff family, with travel diaries written by Margaret Shurtleff's mother-in-law Sarah Ann Keegan Shurtleff who describes her thoughts about people and places she encountered abroad; Keegan family correspondence; and handbound volumes written by Sarah Shurtleff's daughter Gertrude Hope Shurtleff (1872-?), who was an amateur poet, artist, and writer. Photos of family members and of places visited are also included.

6,804. Nichols, Clarina Irene (Howard)
Papers. 1880-82. 2 items.
Open. Published and unpublished guides.
Schlesinger Library.
Letters to Harriet (Hanson) Robinson and Susan B. Anthony from Nichols (1810-85), a newspaper editor and women's rights leader who was born in Vermont but spent her later years in Kansas, Washington, DC, and California. See Arthur and Elizabeth Schlesinger Library on the History of Women in America, *The Manuscript Inventories and the Catalogs of the Manuscripts, Books and Pictures,* vol. III (Boston: G. K. Hall & Co., 1973).

6,805. Nichols, Minerva (Parker)
Papers. Ca. 1880s-90s. 1 Hollinger box and 2 manuscript rolls.
Open. No guide.
Schlesinger Library.
Architectural drawings and plans of Nichols (1861-1949), a Philadelphia architect, for the New Century Club in Philadelphia, the New Century Club in Wilmington, DE, the Browne and Nichols School in Cambridge, and a woman's pavilion at the 1893 Chicago World's Fair.

6,806. Niles, Marion
Papers. 1911-46. 1 Hollinger box.
Open. Published and unpublished guides.
Schlesinger Library.
Photos, clippings, reports, and publications reflect the activities of [Miss] Niles who, out of concern for the working girl, was active in the Massachusetts and National League of Women Workers, the Massachusetts and National League of Girls Clubs, the Community Club of Wellesley Lower Falls, and the Rockport Lodge. See Arthur and Elizabeth Schlesinger Library on the History of Women in America, *The Manuscript Inventories and the Catalogs of the Manuscripts, Books and Pictures,* vol. III (Boston: G. K. Hall & Co., 1973).

6,807. Norris, Katharine Augusta
Papers. 1943-48. 1 Hollinger box.
Open. Published and unpublished guides.
Schlesinger Library.
Minutes, correspondence, and reports of Norris (?-1949) pertain to the Women's Joint Legislative Committee for Equal Rights, of which she was convener. Also included is material concerning the National Woman's Party litigation, Alice Paul, and Anita Pollitzer. See Arthur and Elizabeth Schlesinger Library on the History of Women in America, *The Manuscript Inventories and the Catalogs of the Manuscripts, Books and Pictures,* vol. III (Boston: G. K. Hall & Co., 1973).

6,808. North Bennet Street Industrial School
Records. 1879-1965. Ca. 100 cartons, 15 ft., and 8300 items.
Open. No guide.
Schlesinger Library.
Pauline (Agassiz) Shaw was the guiding spirit and considered the founder of this trade school and settlement house which was founded in the North End of Boston in 1879 to provide a means for self-help to the poor. The North End Industrial Home first established a sewing room managed and staffed mainly by women for women; in 1885 the school was incorporated under its present name to serve the surrounding immigrant community, which after 1900 was mainly Italian, although today the trade School attracts students from all over the US. Administrative and financial records, including minutes of meetings of the Board of Managers, annual reports, and ledgers; correspondence with Board members, social and government agencies, donors, businesses, students, and teachers; internal memoranda; catalogs; 8000 vocational placement index cards; news releases; bulletins; scrapbooks; 300 photos; clippings; and other material.

In addition to the sewing room, the School offered other vocational courses for children and adults, a day nursery, a library, and an industrial training program. For many years, the School also provided vocational training to Boston Public Schools students. Vocational guidance and placement were initiated before WWI but were emphasized particularly during the Depression when the School also helped run a work relief program for the unemployed. After WWII the School participated in government programs to train veterans and handicapped persons.

The settlement aimed to help immigrants become citizens and improve their economic conditions. Its services for them included day care, clubs for young people, a credit union, a lounge for teenagers, summer camps, and The Habit Training School, which was set up to train bright children with behavior problems to be cooperative, useful members of society.

6,809. Norton, Grace
Papers. Nd. 1 Hollinger box.
Open. Published and unpublished guides.
Schlesinger Library.
Manuscripts of lectures and articles on 17th- and 18th-century French literary personages by Norton (1834-1926), an author. One series is on French women. See Arthur and Elizabeth Schlesinger Library on the History of Women in America, *The Manuscript Inventories and the Catalogs of the Manuscripts, Books and Pictures,* vol. III (Boston: G. K. Hall & Co., 1973).

6,810. Odencrantz, Louise C.
Papers. 1909-68. 0.5 Hollinger box.
Open. Unpublished guide.
Schlesinger Library.
Correspondence, manuscripts, programs, reports, photos, and speeches and articles by Odencrantz (1884-1969), who from 1908 to 1946 worked in labor relations, industrial relations, and personnel. Subjects of Odencrantz's speeches and articles include hiring the handicapped, employment of women and children, and training of women. Material from the International Industrial Relations Association is also included.

6,811. O'Hare, Kate Richards
Papers. 1919-20. 1 vol.
Open. Unpublished guide.
Schlesinger Library.
O'Hare (1877-1948) was a socialist who opposed US participation in WWI and who was indicted and found guilty under the espionage act and sentenced to five years in the Missouri State Penitentiary; later she worked for prison reform, particularly in California. In this volume of mimeographed letters to her family during her incarceration, O'Hare discusses conditions of life and work in the prison, her family and friends, politics, books, the psychology of women and developments in psychoanalysis, and her religious and political beliefs. Also included is a photo of O'Hare with her children.

6,812. O'Reilly, Leonora
Papers. 1886-1927. 17 Hollinger boxes and 2 microfilm reels.
Open. Published and unpublished guides.
Schlesinger Library.
Correspondence, diaries, notebooks, speeches, articles, pamphlets, leaflets, and clippings reflect the career of O'Reilly (1870-1927), a factory worker, labor organizer, and social reformer who became vice-president of the New York Women's Trade Union League. O'Reilly wrote speeches and articles on equal rights, suffrage, and the employment of women; these include "Eight Hour Day," "Francis Ferrer Is No More!" and "Women's Opportunities in the Civil Service." Some subjects of the material are the Manhattan Trade School for Girls in New York, the National Women's Trade Union League, the labor movement, strikes, peace, and the 1915 International Congress of Women. Correspondents include Mary (Ritter) Beard, Harriot (Stanton) Blatch, Mary Ware Dennett, Mary and Katherine Dreier, Laura Greshheimer, Harriet H. King, Margaret (Dreier) Robins, Olivia B. Strohm, and Mary Wolfe. See Arthur and Elizabeth Schlesinger Library on the History of Women in America, *The Manuscript Inventories and the Catalogs of the Manuscripts, Books and Pictures,* vol. III (Boston: G. K. Hall & Co., 1973).

6,813. Osborne, Lucy Eugenia
Papers. 1923-55. 7 folders and 1 vol.
Open. Published and unpublished guides.
Schlesinger Library.
A noted librarian, bibliographer, and authority on rare books, Osborne (1879-1955) was custodian between 1922 and 1947 of the Chapin Library at Williams College. Correspondence, biographical material, and articles and manuscripts by Osborne contain information on the Chapin Library and a manuscript history of "the printed book." See Arthur and Elizabeth Schlesinger Library on the History of Women in America, *The Manuscript Inventories and the Catalogs of the Manuscripts, Books and Pictures,* vol. III (Boston: G. K. Hall & Co., 1973).

6,814. Ovington, Mary White
Papers. 1946-51. 1 folder.
Open. Published and unpublished guides.
Schlesinger Library.
Correspondence, cards, and clippings pertain to the death and memorial service of Ovington (1865-1951), a social worker who, in her efforts to improve the civil rights of Negroes, helped found the NAACP. See Arthur and Elizabeth Schlesinger Library on the History of Women in America, *The Manuscript Inventories and the Catalogs of the Manuscripts, Books and Pictures,* vol. III (Boston: G. K. Hall & Co., 1973).

6,815. Owens, Helen (Brewster)
Papers. 1899-1962. 8 Hollinger boxes, 2 vols., and 3 oversize envelopes and maps.
Open. Published and unpublished guides.
Schlesinger Library.
Correspondence, manuscripts for speeches, minutes, reports, and clippings of [Mrs. Fred] Owens (1881-), a New York suffragist and mathematician, contain material on the New York state and Kansas campaigns for woman suffrage and on the achievements of women in mathematics and science as well as copies of doctoral theses and articles by women with PhDs in mathematics and science. Also included are the 1909-12 correspondence files of the Empire State Suffrage Association, with Jenny Cannon, Lillian Huffcut, Helen K. Lee, Harriet May Mills, and Clara M. Schlingheyde as correspondents, and a yearbook of the Ohio Woman Suffrage Association. See Arthur and Elizabeth Schlesinger Library on the History of Women in America, *The Manuscript Inventories and the Catalogs of the Manuscripts, Books and Pictures,* vol. III (Boston: G. K. Hall & Co., 1973).

6,816. Owings, Chloe
Papers. Nd. 3 cartons and 0.5 Hollinger box.
Open. No guide.
Schlesinger Library.
Correspondence, published and unpublished writings, and clippings of Owings (1883-), a sociologist and author. Includes her autobiography, which is entitled *Living Through Covered Wagon to Space Ship Age.*

6,817. Paine, Elsie Miriam
Papers. 1900-48. 4 Hollinger boxes.
Open. Published and unpublished guides.
Schlesinger Library.
Correspondence, manuscript, and 26 volumes of diaries of [Miss] Paine (ca. 1882-) detail her student years at Radcliffe as a member of the class of 1904 and her subsequent employment as a secretary in Fay House. Also included are round-robin letters to Radcliffe classmates and a history and recollections by Paine of the First Congregational Church school in Cambridge. See Arthur and Elizabeth Schlesinger Library on the History of Women in America, *The Manuscript Inventories and the Catalogs of the Manuscripts, Books and Pictures,* vol. III (Boston: G. K. Hall & Co., 1973).

6,818. Painter, Clara (Searle)
Papers. Nd. 1 item.
Open. Published and unpublished guides.
Schlesinger Library.
Reminiscences by [Mrs. H. K.] Painter of Mrs. Frost's School in Lawrence, MA, during the 1890s. [Mrs. William Prescott] Frost was the mother of Robert Frost. See Arthur and Elizabeth Schlesinger Library on the History of Women in America, *The Manuscript Inventories and the Catalogs of the Manuscripts, Books and Pictures,* vol. III (Boston: G. K. Hall & Co., 1973).

6,819. Parisi, Angela R.
Papers. 1951-61. 10 Hollinger boxes and 1 oversize item.
Open. No guide.
Schlesinger Library.
Correspondence, news releases, photos, and clippings of Parisi (1914-61), a lawyer who was Mrs. Leo Louison, contain material on Democratic politics in New York. Parisi was assistant corporation counsel of the city of New York from 1946 to 1954, vice-chairman of the New York State Democratic Committee from 1949 to 1955, chairman of the state's Workmen's Compensation Board from 1955, and president of the Brooklyn Women's Bar Association from 1956 to 1957.

6,820. Parker, Lydia D.
Papers. 1862. 1 item.
Open. Published and unpublished guides.
Schlesinger Library.
Letter to a friend by Parker, wife of Theodore Parker (1810-60). See Arthur and Elizabeth Schlesinger Library on the History of Women in America, *The Manuscript Inventories and the Catalogs of the Manuscripts, Books and Pictures,* vol. III (Boston: G. K. Hall & Co., 1973).

6,821. Parrington, Ruth
Papers. 1873. 1 item.
Open. Published and unpublished guides.
Schlesinger Library.
Letter to George A. Bolles. See Arthur and Elizabeth Schlesinger Library on the History of Women in America, *The Manuscript Inventories and the Catalogs of the Manuscripts, Books and Pictures,* vol. III (Boston: G. K. Hall & Co., 1973).

6,822. Payson, Elizabeth Phillips
Papers. Ca. 1825. 1 vol.
Open. Published and unpublished guides.
Schlesinger Library.
Notebook of material concerning the activities of the Charlestown, MA, female reading society between 1812 and 1817, with a list of members, lists and descriptions of books read, writings on the Bible, and copies of poems and quotations. Includes Payson's extracts from and remarks on some of the books she read from 1806 to 1825. See Arthur and Elizabeth Schlesinger Library on the History of Women in America, *The Manuscript Inventories and the Catalogs of the Manuscripts, Books and Pictures,* vol. III (Boston: G. K. Hall & Co., 1973).

6,823. Peabody, Elizabeth Palmer
Papers. Ca. 1880-86. 1 folder.
Open. Published and unpublished guides.
Schlesinger Library.
Correspondence of Peabody (1804-94), an educator, author, and lecturer who was an associate of Bronson Alcott, concerns events in her life and her work with education of children in kindergartens. See Arthur and Elizabeth Schlesinger Library on the History of Women in America, *The Manuscript Inventories and the Catalogs of the Manuscripts, Books and Pictures,* vol. III (Boston: G. K. Hall & Co., 1973).

6,824. Peabody, Josephine Preston
Papers. 1902-53. 5 folders.
Open. Unpublished guide.
Schlesinger Library.
Correspondence, manuscript children's and other poems, photo, and clippings of [Mrs. Lionel Marks] Peabody (1874-1922), a poet and playwright.

6,825. Peck, Wilda Claire (Strong)
Papers. 1914-34. 2 folders and 1 oversize folder.
Open. Published and unpublished guides.
Schlesinger Library.
Primarily concerning suffrage work in Lynn, MA, the correspondence, notebook, manuscript, flyer, clippings and other material of Peck (1890-1971), an officer in the Lynn Equal Suffrage Association, include Association minutes and a story on suffrage by Peck. See Arthur and Elizabeth Schlesinger Library on the History of Women in America, *The Manuscript Inventories and the Catalogs of the Manuscripts, Books and Pictures,* vol. III (Boston: G. K. Hall & Co., 1973).

6,826. Pedersen, Thyra E.
Papers. 1923-74. 1.5 Hollinger boxes.
Open. Published and unpublished guides.
Schlesinger Library.
A teacher at Union Girls School in Hangchow, China, and at the Sgaw Karen High School in Bassein, Burma, between 1923 and 1925, Pedersen (ca. 1889-) went on to become assistant director of the nursing service of the US Veterans Administration from ca. 1925 until 1943; later she was rehabilitation officer for the American Legion and chief nurse at two VA facilities. Correspondence, manuscripts of speeches, annotated articles and programs, photos, and clippings contain material about her trip around the world between 1923 and 1925, when she spent most of her time in East Asia, and information relating to nursing and veterans. See Arthur and Elizabeth Schlesinger Library on the History of Women in America, *The Manuscript Inventories and the Catalogs of the Manuscripts, Books and Pictures,* vol. III (Boston: G. K. Hall & Co., 1973).

6,827. Perkins, Frances
Papers. 1945-61. 3 items.
Open. Published and unpublished guides.
Schlesinger Library.
Letters from Perkins (1882-1965), secretary of labor from 1933 to 1945, are to J. T. Patterson, James G. Johnson, and Josephine Goldmark. See Arthur and Elizabeth Schlesinger Library on the History of Women in America, *The Manuscript Inventories and the Catalogs of the Manuscripts, Books and Pictures,* vol. III (Boston: G. K. Hall & Co., 1973).

6,828. Perry, Jane (Slidell)
Papers. Ca. 1848. 4 items.
Open. Published and unpublished guides.
Schlesinger Library.
Correspondence of [Mrs. Matthew Calbraith] Perry, a member of a prominent New England family, with her daughter Bell. See Arthur and Elizabeth Schlesinger Library on the History of Women in America, *The Manuscript Inventories and the Catalogs of the Manuscripts, Books and Pictures,* vol. III (Boston: G. K. Hall & Co., 1973).

6,829. Phillips, Lena Madesin
Papers. 1881-1955. 9 cartons and 1 Hollinger box.
Open. No guide.
Schlesinger Library.
Personal and professional correspondence, articles, pamphlets, photos, and clippings of Phillips (ca. 1881-1955), a Kentucky lawyer who in 1930 founded the International Federation of Business and Professional Women in New York. Phillips was also an organizer of the Business and Professional Club of New York and of the National Federation of Business and Professional Women's Clubs.

6,830. Phillips, Wendell
Papers. Ca. 1855. 3 items.
Open. Published and unpublished guides.
Schlesinger Library.
Letters to Elizabeth Cady Stanton and Susan B. Anthony by Phillips (1811-84), a Boston-born reformer who was active in antislavery, prohibition, woman suffrage, and penal reform. See Arthur and Elizabeth Schlesinger Library on the History of Women in America, *The Manuscript Inventories and the Catalogs of the Manuscripts, Books and Pictures,* vol. III (Boston: G. K. Hall & Co., 1973).

6,831. Piper, Helen Jackson
Papers. 1901-59. 1 vol. and 1 microfilm reel.
Open. Published and unpublished guides.
Schlesinger Library.
Papers of Piper (1882-1958), an educator, include a microfilmed journal of her voyage on the *Benjamin Sewall* from Vancouver, Canada, to Fremantle, Australia during 1901 and 1902; letters to family; and "The Girl in the Lifeboat" by Piper, an account of her voyage which was edited in 1959 by William and Esther Prosser. See Arthur and Elizabeth Schlesinger Library on the History of Women in America, *The Manuscript Inventories and the Catalogs of the Manuscripts, Books and Pictures,* vol. III (Boston: G. K. Hall & Co., 1973).

6,832. Poole Family
Papers. Ca. 1905- . 6 folders.
Open. Published and unpublished guides.
Schlesinger Library.
Manuscripts written by Marion Howe Poole McFadden reminiscing about her youth in Chicago document social life and customs of an elite midwestern family with details of Chicago and Poole family life, beginning in the 1870s; another manuscript, written by Marion McFadden's mother Mary Howe Poole, contains a description of the Chicago fire of 1871. See Arthur and Elizabeth Schlesinger Library on the History of Women in America, *The Manuscript Inventories and the Catalogs of the Manuscripts, Books and Pictures,* vol. III (Boston: G. K. Hall & Co., 1973).

6,833. Poor Family
Papers. 1791-1921. 30 Hollinger boxes.
Open. Published and unpublished guides.
Schlesinger Library.
Correspondence, diaries, financial documents, notebooks, sermons, photos, and clippings of five generations of the Poor family, members of which were active in the clergy, business, and social movements in New England. Subjects include social life and customs in New York and New England, Unitarianism, women missionaries, and the rights of women. Collection centers on Henry Varnum Poor (1812-1905), a railroad journalist and economist, and on his wife Mary (Pierce) Poor (1820-1912), a participant in social reform movements and daughter of John Pierce (1773-1849) who for 50 years was minister of the First Church of Brookline, MA. Also included are Pierce family papers, with letters of John Pierce and his wife Lucy (Tappan) Pierce, daughter of Benjamin Tappan who was a progenitor of the abolitionist family; letters of Lucy (Pierce) Hedge and her husband Frederic Henry Hedge (1805-90), a transcendentalist minister; papers of Henry Varnum Poor's children, including Henry William Poor (1844-1915), a New York banker; and papers of Henry Varnum Poor's grandchildren. See Arthur and Elizabeth Schlesinger Library on the History of Women in America, *The Manuscript Inventories and the Catalogs of the Manuscripts, Books and Pictures,* vol. III (Boston: G. K. Hall & Co., 1973).

6,834. Popper, Hermine (Isaacs)
Papers. 1941-68. 3.5 Hollinger boxes.
Open. Unpublished guide.
Schlesinger Library.
An editor, critic, and short story writer, Popper (1915-68) was managing editor and then associate editor and film critic for *Theatre Arts Magazine* between 1936 and 1948. In 1953 she became an assistant editor at Harper and Brothers, but left in 1956 to work at free-lance book editing; among the authors whose works she edited are Victoria Sackville-West, Constantin Stanislavski, Martin Luther King, Jr., and Frank Riessman. Fiction and nonfiction writings by Popper; writings by others, which she edited; correspondence; notes; and research material. Bulk of collection concerns the manuscripts of Martin Luther King, Jr., and the manuscript of *Up from Poverty* by Riessman and Popper. Popper also wrote original articles on film and theater as well as pamphlets.

6,835. Potter, Frances (Squire)
Papers. Nd. 1 Hollinger box.
Open. No guide.
Schlesinger Library.
A professor of English at the University of Minnesota, Potter (1867-1914) was also active in suffrage and the labor movement. Pamphlets, photos, copies of *Life and Labor,* and other material from the Women's Trade Union League.

6,836. Powell, Rose (Arnold)
Papers. 1922-61. 5 Hollinger boxes.
Open. Published and unpublished guides.
Schlesinger Library.
Correspondence, journals, articles, scrapbook, photos, and clippings document the efforts of [Mrs.] Powell (1876-1961) to memorialize Susan B. Anthony. Powell attempted to have Anthony represented at Mount Rushmore; she also used published articles, tributes in libraries, special buildings, stamps, sculptures, schools named in Anthony's honor, The Susan B. Anthony Forum, and the Susan B. Anthony Foundation to memorialize Anthony. See Arthur and Elizabeth Schlesinger Library on the History of Women in America, *The Manuscript Inventories and the Catalogs of the Manuscripts, Books and Pictures,* vol. III (Boston: G. K. Hall & Co., 1973).

6,837. Pratt, Marietta (Harkness)
Papers. 1921-25. 2 vols.
Open. Published and unpublished guides.
Schlesinger Library.
Scrapbooks concern the activities of [Mrs. Walter M.] Pratt, a member of the Massachusetts LWV; some clippings pertain to the Atlantic City Board

Walk, a 1922 charity bazaar in which her state LWV participated. See Arthur and Elizabeth Schlesinger Library on the History of Women in America, *The Manuscript Inventories and the Catalogs of the Manuscripts, Books and Pictures,* vol. III (Boston: G. K. Hall & Co., 1973).

6,838. President's Commission on the Status of Women
Records. 1961-63. 10 Hollinger boxes.
Open. Published and unpublished guides.
Schlesinger Library.
Minutes, transcripts, reports, correspondence, and press releases of the Commission, established in 1961 to examine the needs and rights of women and to make recommendations for "the diminution of barriers that result in waste, injustice, and frustration." Also included are background, interim, and final reports and minutes of meetings of the Commission's subcommittees for home and community, protective labor legislation, education, social insurance and taxes, civil and political rights, federal employment policies and practices, and private employment. See Arthur and Elizabeth Schlesinger Library on the History of Women in America, *The Manuscript Inventories and the Catalogs of the Manuscripts, Books and Pictures,* vol. III (Boston: G. K. Hall & Co., 1973).

6,839. Priest, Alice L.
Papers. 1892-98. 4 items.
Open. Published and unpublished guides.
Schlesinger Library.
Leaflets regarding woman suffrage and political equality. See Arthur and Elizabeth Schlesinger Library on the History of Women in America, *The Manuscript Inventories and the Catalogs of the Manuscripts, Books and Pictures,* vol. III (Boston: G. K. Hall & Co., 1973).

6,840. Priest, Ivy (Baker)
Papers. 1945-55. 2 folders.
Open. Published and unpublished guides.
Schlesinger Library.
Biographical material, photos, speeches by, and articles about [Mrs.] Priest (1905-75), treasurer of the US under President Eisenhower. See Arthur and Elizabeth Schlesinger Library on the History of Women in America, *The Manuscript Inventories and the Catalogs of the Manuscripts, Books and Pictures,* vol. III (Boston: G. K. Hall & Co., 1973).

6,841. Pruette, Lorine Livingston
Papers. ?-1974. 2 cartons and 1 folder.
Open. No guide.
Schlesinger Library.
Pruette (1896-) is an author and sociologist who combines feminist writing for *The Nation* and other publications with writing about psychology, literary reviewing for *The New York Times,* teaching, and the practice of psychotherapy. Autobiography; correspondence; manuscripts of poems, articles, and other writings; financial papers; photos; clippings; and printed material. Includes the typescript "There's Always Surgery."

6,842. Pugh, Sarah
Papers. 1868. 1 item.
Open. Published and unpublished guides.
Schlesinger Library.
Pugh (1800-84) was a teacher, abolitionist, and suffragist. Poem addressed to Pugh and Abby Kimber was written from St. Mary's Hospital in Detroit about the 1840 World's Anti-Slavery Convention in London. See Arthur and Elizabeth Schlesinger Library on the History of Women in America, *The Manuscript Inventories and the Catalogs of the Manuscripts, Books and Pictures,* vol. III (Boston: G. K. Hall & Co., 1973).

6,843. Putnam, James Jackson
Papers. 1907?. 1 item.
Open. Published and unpublished guides.
Schlesinger Library.
Letter on pragmatism by Putnam (1846-1918), a neurologist who was born in Boston and educated at Harvard University, is addressed to [Mrs.] Elizabeth Glendower Evans and concerns the views of Josiah Royce and William James. See Arthur and Elizabeth Schlesinger Library on the History of Women in America, *The Manuscript Inventories and the Catalogs of the Manuscripts, Books and Pictures,* vol. III (Boston: G. K. Hall & Co., 1973).

6,844. Putnam, Mabel Raef
Papers. 1924-38. 0.5 Hollinger box.
Open. Published and unpublished guides.
Schlesinger Library.
Scrapbook of clippings by Putnam and manuscripts by Edwin E. Witte and Howard F. Ohm, all of which concern the Wisconsin equal rights law. See Arthur and Elizabeth Schlesinger Library on the History of Women in America, *The Manuscript Inventories and the Catalogs of the Manuscripts, Books and Pictures,* vol. III (Boston: G. K. Hall & Co., 1973).

6,845. Quick, Frances (Merritt)
Papers. 1850-64. 1 Hollinger box.
Open. Published and unpublished guides.
Schlesinger Library.
Correspondence, scrapbook, and other papers of Quick (1833-1924), including five diaries she kept as a student and later teacher at Framingham, MA, State Normal School, a diary in which she describes her life as wife of clergyman A. J. Quick, and a scrapbook containing a manuscript entitled "Female Education" by Caroline Prescott. See Arthur and Elizabeth Schlesinger Library on the History of Women in America, *The Manuscript Inventories and the Catalogs of the Manuscripts, Books and Pictures,* vol. III (Boston: G. K. Hall & Co., 1973).

6,846. Rankin, Jeannette
Papers. 1879-1976. 12.5 Hollinger boxes, 5 tapes, and 1 motion picture.
Open. Unpublished guide.
Schlesinger Library.
A pacifist and feminist, Rankin (1880-1973) was the first congresswoman, representing Montana for the 1916-18 and 1940-42 terms; she also was the only member of Congress to vote against US participation in both world wars. Correspondence, card files, financial papers, pamphlets and leaflets, scrapbooks, clippings, photos, tapes, and a film focus on her vote against WWII and the consequent public reaction. Other correspondence reflects her involvement in the suffrage movement, Vietnam War protest, election reform, and the women's movement, with information on the Women's International League for Peace and Freedom and the Jeannette Rankin Brigade, which was also called the Jeannette Rankin Rank and File. Also included is family correspondence containing letters from her sisters Mary (Rankin) Bragg, Grace (Rankin) Kinney, and birth control advocate Edna (Rankin) McKinnon.

6,847. Ransom, Eliza Taylor
Papers. 1888-1955. 1 Hollinger box and oversize items.
Open. Published and unpublished guides.
Schlesinger Library.
Correspondence, articles, scrapbooks, clippings, and photos of Ransom (1867-1955), a Boston physician who founded the first Twilight Sleep Hospital in America. From 1900 she was associated with Boston University, between 1917 and 1918 with the French Baby Fund, and from 1936 with the Boston Evening Clinic. See Arthur and Elizabeth Schlesinger Library on the History of Women in America, *The Manuscript Inventories and the Catalogs of the Manuscripts, Books and Pictures,* vol. III (Boston: G. K. Hall & Co., 1973).

6,848. Raushenbush, Elizabeth (Brandeis)
Papers. Ca. 1920-60s. 2 cartons.
Open. No guide.
Schlesinger Library.
Correspondence, drafts, and printed and other material of [Mrs. Paul] Raushenbush (1896-), an economist who was a member of the faculty of the University of Wisconsin, Madison, 1928-66. Included is correspondence with Clara (Mortenson) Beyer, with whom Raushenbush served on the District of Columbia Minimum Wage Board in the early 1920s; a copy of her 1924 master's thesis "A Comparative Study of Private Industrial Law"; and material on the Wisconsin Governor's Commission on Human Rights, labor legislation, the war on poverty, and the Wisconsin LWV.

6,849. Rawalt, Marguerite
Papers. 1966-74. 1 carton and 7 Hollinger boxes.
Access restricted. No guide.
Schlesinger Library.
Papers of Rawalt, a lawyer who serves as legal counsel for the National Organization for Women and the Women's Equity Action League, consist of NOW bylaws, minutes, financial documents, and files; NOW legal committee and legal defense and education fund records; WEAL files; reports from the President's Commission on the Status of Women and various state Commissions; and documents concerning the Mengelkoch, Colgate-Palmolive, and Weeks cases.

6,850. Reynard, Elizabeth
Papers. 1934-62. 14 Hollinger boxes, 3 oversize vols., and other items.
Open. Published and unpublished guides.
Schlesinger Library.
Assistant director of the WAVES during WWII, [Miss] Reynard (1897-1962) was also an author. Correspondence, articles, reports, manuals, photos, phonograph records, and other material reflect Reynard's career in the Navy, including her assignments with the WAVES at WAVES training school, the Naval Training School, and on the U.S.S. *Hunter,* as well as information about WAVES personnel and organization regulations and about other units of military women in the US, Canada, and Great Britain. Also included are manuscripts of poetry and writings on Cape Cod and New England; manuscripts of her *The Narrow Land* (1934) and *Ports of Youth: Fragment of an Autobiography* (1946-47); and a scrapbook of reviews of *The Mutinous Wind* (1951). See Arthur and Elizabeth Schlesinger Library on the History of Women in America, *The Manuscript Inventories and the Catalogs of the Manuscripts, Books and Pictures,* vol. III (Boston: G. K. Hall & Co., 1973).

6,851. Reynolds, Bertha C.
Papers. 1838-1956. 1 folder.
Open. Published and unpublished guides.
Schlesinger Library.
Reynolds added explanatory notes to journals for the years 1838 through 1884 which were written by Betsey Estey Talbot Capen, a spinster, about religious meditations and daily events. Also included is a biography of educator Bessie Tilson Capen, written by her nieces Mary L. B. Reynolds and Bessie Faunce Gill. See Arthur and Elizabeth Schlesinger Library on the History of Women in America, *The Manuscript Inventories and the Catalogs of the Manuscripts, Books and Pictures,* vol. III (Boston: G. K. Hall & Co., 1973).

6,852. Rice, Elizabeth Prince
Papers. Nd. 3 cartons and 1 Hollinger box.
Open. No guide.
Schlesinger Library.
Correspondence, speeches and addresses, and articles written by [Miss] Rice (1900-), an associate professor of public health social work at the Harvard School of Public Health, concern her career in mental health and social welfare.

Included is material on the School and on the American Mental Health Association.

6,853. Richards, Elizabeth Ney
Papers. 1890s-1914. 2 folders.
Open. Published and unpublished guides.
Schlesinger Library.
Correspondence, membership lists, and announcements of [Mrs.] Richards, a suffragist, consist primarily of correspondence with her son Joseph Richards on suffrage activities in Boston and New Hampshire. See Arthur and Elizabeth Schlesinger Library on the History of Women in America, *The Manuscript Inventories and the Catalogs of the Manuscripts, Books and Pictures,* vol. III (Boston: G. K. Hall & Co., 1973).

6,854. Richards, Janet Elizabeth Hosmer
Papers. 1890-1948. 2 folders.
Open. Unpublished guide.
Schlesinger Library.
Papers of Richards (ca. 1859-1948), a lecturer, consist of correspondence with friends, admirers, and the League for Political Education, for whom she lectured; correspondence and an article she wrote on the early days of the National Congress of Parents and Teachers, which was published in 1942; lecture programs; an article about Richards; and photos of her.

6,855. Richards, Laura Elizabeth (Howe)
Papers. 1940. 1 item.
Open. Published and unpublished guides.
Schlesinger Library.
Letter of [Mrs.] Richards (1850-1943), an author of children's books and daughter of Julia Ward Howe, to Olive Floyd. See Arthur and Elizabeth Schlesinger Library on the History of Women in America, *The Manuscript Inventories and the Catalogs of the Manuscripts, Books and Pictures,* vol. III (Boston: G. K. Hall & Co., 1973).

6,856. Richards, Mrs. George
Papers. 1871-72?. 1 item.
Open. Published and unpublished guides.
Schlesinger Library.
Manuscript about education for young women. See Arthur and Elizabeth Schlesinger Library on the History of Women in America, *The Manuscript Inventories and the Catalogs of the Manuscripts, Books and Pictures,* vol. III (Boston: G. K. Hall & Co., 1973).

6,857. Ripley, Sarah Alden (Bradford)
Papers. 1806-67. 1 Hollinger box.
Open. Published and unpublished guides.
Schlesinger Library.
Correspondence of Ripley (1793-1867), the wife of Samuel Ripley (1783-1847) who became minister of the First Church in Waltham, MA; in 1846 she and her husband moved to the Old Manse in Concord, MA, where she lived until her death. Letters to childhood friends Abba Allyn and Mary Moody Emerson reveal her intellectual interests and philosophical outlook. Letters from the 1840s to her son-in-law George F. Simmons contain news of family, friends, and the Waltham parish; reports on her reading and scientific pursuits; and comments on public affairs. Later letters to her daughter Sophy discuss family news and friends, the ravages of the Civil War, and her own failing health and faculties. Ralph Waldo Emerson, Henry David Thoreau, Nathaniel Hawthorne, and other notable writers, ministers, and reformers are mentioned in the letters as neighbors or acquaintances with whom she exchanged ideas. See Arthur and Elizabeth Schlesinger Library on the History of Women in America, *The Manuscript Inventories and the Catalogs of the Manuscripts, Books and Pictures,* vol. III (Boston: G. K. Hall & Co., 1973).

6,858. Roberts, Margaret Stevenson
Papers. 1900-42. 0.5 Hollinger box.
Open. Published and unpublished guides.
Schlesinger Library.
Active in the suffrage movement, [Miss] Roberts (?-1952) worked with the Republican State Committee in Idaho and from 1905 to 1932 as a librarian for the Traveling Library. Correspondence, including letters from people connected with the Republican party and with suffrage, such as Senator Borah of Idaho, Harriot Stanton Blatch, Carrie Chapman Catt, and Alice Paul; speeches; pamphlets; and clippings. Also included is correspondence concerning the founding of the LWV. See Arthur and Elizabeth Schlesinger Library on the History of Women in America, *The Manuscript Inventories and the Catalogs of the Manuscripts, Books and Pictures,* vol. III (Boston: G. K. Hall & Co., 1973).

6,859. Robinson, Harriet Jane (Hanson), and Shattuck, Harriette Lucy (Robinson)
Papers. 1833-1937. 3 Hollinger boxes and 115 vols.
Open. Published and unpublished guides.
Schlesinger Library.
Correspondence, volumes of diaries and scrapbooks, and clippings of [Mrs. William Stevens] Robinson (1825-1911) and of her daughter [Mrs. Sidney Doane] Shattuck (1850-1937). One of the leaders of the woman suffrage movement in New England, Robinson began at an early age to write about the need for reform in the working conditions of women, antislavery, and suffrage; Shattuck also worked for woman suffrage and was active in the founding of women's clubs. Robinson's papers include correspondence with her husband, children, and other family members, as well as Lucy Larcom, several Lowell mill girls, and suffrage leaders Susan B. Anthony, Matilda (Joslyn) Gage, Elizabeth Cady Stanton, and Lucy Stone. Much of the suffrage correspondence concerns setting up the American Woman Suffrage Association and the National Woman Suffrage Association in 1869 and the merger of the two in 1890. Also included are Robinson's annual diaries for 1852 to 1908 and scrapbooks of early published and unpublished writings and material on Lowell mill girls and suffrage. Shattuck's papers consist of diaries for 1867 to 1937, scrapbooks, and an 86-page autobiography. See Arthur and Elizabeth Schlesinger Library on the History of Women in America, *The Manuscript Inventories and the Catalogs of the Manuscripts, Books and Pictures,* vol. III (Boston: G. K. Hall & Co., 1973).

6,860. Rockwood, Edith
Papers. 1932-54. 1 Hollinger box.
Open. Published and unpublished guides.
Schlesinger Library.
A staff member of the Children's Bureau from 1932 to 1952, [Miss] Rockwood (1888-1952) was also active in the LWV. Correspondence, biographical material, reports, photos, clippings, and other papers include manuscripts of speeches and articles she wrote for the Bureau and the LWV and letters to Rockwood upon her retirement from the Bureau. Contains material on the growth, development, welfare, and health of the child; on the National Commission on Children and Youth; the Midcentury White House Conference on Children and Youth; and the Interdepartmental Committee on Children and Youth. See Arthur and Elizabeth Schlesinger Library on the History of Women in America, *The Manuscript Inventories and the Catalogs of the Manuscripts, Books and Pictures,* vol. III (Boston: G. K. Hall & Co., 1973).

6,861. Rogers, Edith (Nourse)
Papers. 1854-1961. 25 Hollinger boxes, 47 oversize vols., 2 oversize folders, and 10 oversize items.
Open. Unpublished guide.
Schlesinger Library.
From 1925 to 1960, [Mrs. John Jacob] Rogers (1881-1960) was a Republican congresswoman from Massachusetts; in the House of Representatives she was chairman of the Veterans' Affairs Committee and a member of the Foreign Affairs Committee. Correspondence Rogers received as Committee chairman and with constituents; speeches she made in the House, over radio, before veterans' groups, and for various events; analyses of her voting record; campaign material, citations, and awards; photos; clippings; and sympathy letters concerning her death. Rogers was elected to the House to fill the vacancy caused by the death of her husband. Re-elected to every successive Congress, she died in office. Legislation attributed to Rogers includes improvement of the Foreign Service, establishment of the WAC, enactment of the G. I. Bill of Rights, enactment of the Korean veterans' benefits bill, establishment of a permanent Nurse Corps for veterans, and other laws providing aid and assistance to permanently disabled American war veterans.

6,862. Rohfleisch, Marjorie (Cherry)
Papers. 1916-60. 6 Hollinger boxes.
Open. Published and unpublished guides.
Schlesinger Library.
Correspondence, mementos, and clippings document the life of [Mrs. Kramer] Rohfleisch (1910-) as a student at Pomona College in Claremont, CA, and as a missionary in Mexico during 1932 and 1933. In 1934 she married Kramer Rohfleisch. She lived in Germany in 1936 and 1937 and later as a housewife in California, Washington, DC, and Chicago. Majority of the correspondence is to her mother Marguerite Cherry and her father E. E. Cherry, Sr., although letters to her mother from Kramer Rohfleisch and Peter Rohfleisch are also included. Correspondence provides information on domestic relations, home economics, social life and customs in Germany, and her interests in music, gardening, and teaching. See Arthur and Elizabeth Schlesinger Library on the History of Women in America, *The Manuscript Inventories and the Catalogs of the Manuscripts, Books and Pictures,* vol. III (Boston: G. K. Hall & Co., 1973).

6,863. Rorer, Sarah Tyson (Heston)
Papers. 1929-38. 1 folder.
Open. Published and unpublished guides.
Schlesinger Library.
Papers of [Mrs.] Rorer (1849-1937), who for 53 years lectured and wrote and edited works about foods, consist of photos of her, letters to her son James on illness and death, the minister's address at her funeral, obituaries, and other items. See Arthur and Elizabeth Schlesinger Library on the History of Women in America, *The Manuscript Inventories and the Catalogs of the Manuscripts, Books and Pictures,* vol. III (Boston: G. K. Hall & Co., 1973).

6,864. Ross, Ishbel
Papers. 1948-59. 1 folder.
Open. Published and unpublished guides.
Schlesinger Library.
Letters to Ross concerning physician Elizabeth Blackwell and Julia D. [Mrs. Ulysses S.] Grant from Alice Stone Blackwell, Howard Lane Blackwell, Nell (Grant) [Mrs. William Pigott] Gronan, Florence Ledyard (Cross) Kitchelt, and others. See Arthur and Elizabeth Schlesinger Library on the History of Women in America, *The Manuscript Inventories and the Catalogs of the Manuscripts, Books and Pictures,* vol. III (Boston: G. K. Hall & Co., 1973).

6,865. Rotch, Helen Gilman Ludington
Papers. 1943-57. 0.5 Hollinger box.
Open. Published and unpublished guides.
Schlesinger Library.
Included with the correspondence, clippings, and other papers of [Mrs. Arthur Grinnell] Rotch (?-ca. 1958) are speeches and statements she prepared in connection with her work for the Americans for Democratic Action, the Joint Council for

International Cooperation, and other political and civic groups in the Boston area. See Arthur and Elizabeth Schlesinger Library on the History of Women in America, *The Manuscript Inventories and the Catalogs of the Manuscripts, Books and Pictures,* vol. III (Boston: G. K. Hall & Co., 1973).

6,866. Rutland Corner House
Records. 1877-1966. 16 Hollinger boxes.
Access restricted. Published and unpublished guides.
Schlesinger Library.
Records of the board of managers, treasurer, superintendent, and recording secretary include annual reports, minutes, financial records, correspondence, visitors books, and card files on residents of the House, which was originally organized as the Home for Working Women where "women desirous of making an honest living, but penniless and friendless, may find shelter and employment until able to secure a permanent position." After temporary addresses, the House was established in 1886 on the corner of Rutland Street in Boston; in 1925 its current name was adopted. Inmates, who had to be poor, respectable, and able to work, were usually referred to the House through social agencies, although some were accepted directly from the streets. During the 1920s the House population was increasingly made up of "undesirable" women. This change continued into the '50s when inmates included unmarried mothers, psychopathic cases, persons discharged from hospitals, young runaways, and court cases, until 1953 when the board of managers voted to turn the House into a transitional residence for women psychiatric patients. See Arthur and Elizabeth Schlesinger Library on the History of Women in America, *The Manuscript Inventories and the Catalogs of the Manuscripts, Books and Pictures,* vol. III (Boston: G. K. Hall & Co., 1973).

6,867. Ryan, Agnes
Papers. 1904-55. 7 Hollinger boxes.
Open. Published and unpublished guides.
Schlesinger Library.
A Boston author, Ryan (1878-1954) was managing editor of the *Woman's Journal* between 1910 and 1917, at which time she moved to Durham, NH, to do freelance writing. Correspondence, diaries for the period 1904 to 1908, manuscripts of unpublished novels and other writings, scrapbook, and published works. Included is correspondence with Alice Stone Blackwell, Emily Blackwell, and Henry Blackwell about the *Journal;* with Marian MacDowell and others concerning the MacDowell Association; with the Freshels, who established the Millenium Guild, on Ryan's interest in vegetarianism; and with her husband Henry Bailey Stevens, Sarah N. Cleghorn, and Bashka Paeff. Subjects include the American Penwomen, Ryan's work for peace, and the School of Non-Violence. See Arthur and Elizabeth Schlesinger Library on the History of Women in America, *The Manuscript Inventories and the Catalogs of the Manuscripts, Books and Pictures,* vol. III (Boston: G. K. Hall & Co., 1973).

6,868. Salisbury, Marguerite Scott
Papers. 1910-13. 16 items.
Open. Published and unpublished guides.
Schlesinger Library.
Letters to [Miss] Salisbury from Rev. and Mrs. George William Brown, who were missionaries to India, concern conditions in India and the difficulties in being missionaries. See Arthur and Elizabeth Schlesinger Library on the History of Women in America, *The Manuscript Inventories and the Catalogs of the Manuscripts, Books and Pictures,* vol. III (Boston: G. K. Hall & Co., 1973).

6,869. Samson, Chloe
Papers. 1819-64. 1 vol.
Open. Unpublished guide.
Schlesinger Library.
Account book of Samson, a seamstress from Pembroke, MA, who later sold foodstuffs and took in laundry, reveals 19th-century economic conditions of women.

6,870. Saturday Morning Club of Boston
Records. 1871- . 10.5 Hollinger boxes and 3 oversize vols.
Open. Unpublished guide.
Schlesinger Library.
Constitutions, minutes, financial records, correspondence, papers by members, lecture notes, Club histories, lists of officers and members, photos, and other records, including those of the executive committee and other committees, secretaries, and treasurers, as well as autobiographical and biographical items of Club members. The Club was founded in 1871 by Julia Ward Howe to promote "culture and social intercourse" for her daughter Maud and other young women. The Club met for lectures by such persons as Lucy Stone, Ralph Waldo Emerson, Abba Woolson, Annie and James Fields, and professors from Harvard University. Beginning in 1874 the Club produced plays and sponsored parties; presentation of original papers by Club members became its major function.

6,871. Saunders, Mary Ball
Papers. 1912. 1 item.
Open. Published and unpublished guides.
Schlesinger Library.
Manuscript speech which Saunders (1822-1918) dictated to her daughter on personal recollections of Concord, MA, for the Friendly Club of Cambridge. See Arthur and Elizabeth Schlesinger Library on the History of Women in America, *The Manuscript Inventories and the Catalogs of the Manuscripts, Books and Pictures,* vol. III (Boston: G. K. Hall & Co., 1973).

6,872. Schlesinger, Elizabeth Bancroft
Papers. 1930-63. 3 Hollinger boxes, 3 folders, and 1 vol.
Open. Published and unpublished guides.
Schlesinger Library.
An author and historian, Schlesinger (1887-1977) was also active in the LWV, the Schlesinger Library, and the Cambridge School Committee. Personal correspondence, lectures and articles by Schlesinger, printed material on Cambridge and other Massachusetts political and educational matters, and a scrapbook. Includes letters from Mary Ritter Beard, which concern writing about the position of women, and other letters regarding Schlesinger's "Jennie June" article on Jane (Cunningham) Croly. See Arthur and Elizabeth Schlesinger Library on the History of Women in America, *The Manuscript Inventories and the Catalogs of the Manuscripts, Books and Pictures,* vol. III (Boston: G. K. Hall & Co., 1973).

6,873. Schoedler, Lillian
Papers. ?-1962. 3 Hollinger boxes, 6 vols., and 1 trunk.
Open. No guide.
Schlesinger Library.
Correspondence, diaries, and clippings reflect the role of Schoedler as executive secretary and travel companion to Boston businessman Edward A. Filene. Included are letters from Schoedler's early life and college years as well as letters written between 1957 and 1962 from Australia, which were used for the manuscript (also included) "Tell Them I Came."

6,874. Schumpeter, Elizabeth Boody
Papers. 1939-53. 6 Hollinger boxes.
Open. No guide.
Schlesinger Library.
Correspondence, speeches, and reprints of articles of Schumpeter, an economist and author associated with the Institute of Pacific Relations, whose specialty was the economy of Japan.

6,875. Scudder, Ida Sophia
Papers. 1843-1967. 3.5 Hollinger boxes, 1 carton, and 1 oversize folder.
Open. Unpublished guide.
Schlesinger Library.
Correspondence, speeches and pamphlets, bulletins, clippings, other printed material, and family photos of Scudder (1870-1960), a medical missionary in India, primarily concern the hospital she built and the Vellore Christian Medical College she founded, which was the first Christian medical school in South India to train women doctors. Also included are letters from Scudder's roommates at the Northfield School for Girls and family correspondence, with letters from Ida Scudder to Dorothy Scudder and material on Ida S. Scudder's niece Ida Belle Scudder, also a physician, who joined her aunt in India in 1931, eventually to become head of radiology at the College.

6,876. Seton, Grace Thompson
Papers. 1911-52. 2 Hollinger boxes.
Open. Published and unpublished guides.
Schlesinger Library.
Correspondence, a manuscript, financial reports, and photos of Seton (1872-1959), an author and suffragist, concern the Connecticut Woman Suffrage Association, the International Woman Writers Conclave held in Chicago in 1933, the Biblioteca Femina, the International Women's Art Exhibit held in New York during 1939 and 1940, and National Poetry Day. See Arthur and Elizabeth Schlesinger Library on the History of Women in America, *The Manuscript Inventories and the Catalogs of the Manuscripts, Books and Pictures,* vol. III (Boston: G. K. Hall & Co., 1973).

6,877. Seven Associated Colleges Alumnae Clubs
Records. 1937-55. 1 Hollinger box.
Open. Unpublished guide.
Schlesinger Library.
Minutes, financial reports, publicity releases, and clippings of the Clubs, organized in 1926 to hold annual meetings in Boston, pertain to those meetings. Also included are speeches of President Margaret Antoinette Clapp of Wellesley College and of President Pusey of Harvard University, speaking at the annual meetings in 1951 and 1954, respectively.

6,878. Severance, H. A.
Papers. 1862-66. 1 vol.
Open. Published and unpublished guides.
Schlesinger Library.
Diary in which Severance (1838-?) writes of her homelife, health, the weather, working conditions in a hoopskirt factory in Northampton, MA, during 1862, and the Civil War. See Arthur and Elizabeth Schlesinger Library on the History of Women in America, *The Manuscript Inventories and the Catalogs of the Manuscripts, Books and Pictures,* vol. III (Boston: G. K. Hall & Co., 1973).

6,879. Shaver, Dorothy
Papers. 1947-56. 1 Hollinger box.
Open. Published and unpublished guides.
Schlesinger Library.
Papers of [Miss] Shaver (1899-), president of Lord and Taylor, Inc., consist of correspondence, clippings, and speeches and articles reflecting her interest in fashion, design, and world affairs. Included are speeches she delivered at American Design Awards luncheons. See Arthur and Elizabeth Schlesinger Library on the History of Women in America, *The Manuscript Inventories and the Catalogs of the Manuscripts, Books and Pictures,* vol. III (Boston: G. K. Hall & Co., 1973).

6,880. Shaw, Pauline (Agassiz)
Papers. Ca. 1887-93. 4 items.
Open. Published and unpublished guides.
Schlesinger Library.
Letters which Shaw (1841-1917), an educational philanthropist, wrote to a Mr. Lee about funds for the North Bennet Street Industrial School and one to a Mrs. Ames about money for an unspecified project. See Arthur and Elizabeth Schlesinger Library on the History of Women in America, *The Manuscript Inventories and the Catalogs of the Manuscripts, Books and Pictures,* vol. III (Boston: G. K. Hall & Co., 1973).

6,881. Sherwin, Belle
Papers. 1880-1950. 1 Hollinger box and 11 vols.
Open. Published and unpublished guides.
Schlesinger Library.
Scrapbooks and photo album of Sherwin (1868-1955), president of the National LWV from 1924 to 1934, a Cleveland civic leader, and a trustee of Wellesley College, from which she graduated in 1890. Also includes information on her interests in politics, education, and social welfare. See Arthur and Elizabeth Schlesinger Library on the History of Women in America, *The Manuscript Inventories and the Catalogs of the Manuscripts, Books and Pictures,* vol. III (Boston: G. K. Hall & Co., 1973).

6,882. Shields, Elizabeth (Smallwood)
Papers. 1883-1960. 1 Hollinger box and 1 vol.
Open. Published and unpublished guides.
Schlesinger Library.
Articles, scrapbook, photos, clippings, and other papers of [Mrs. Bernard C.] Shields (1862-1932) reflect her career as an actress, whose stage name was Bessie Bernard, and as a press agent for the St. Charles Orpheum Theatre in New Orleans; she was the first southern woman to hold the position of press agent. Also includes biographical material and photos concerning her children and grandchildren as well as other family members such as her sister Martha (Smallwood) Field, a New Orleans news reporter who used the pseudonym Catherine Cole. See Arthur and Elizabeth Schlesinger Library on the History of Women in America, *The Manuscript Inventories and the Catalogs of the Manuscripts, Books and Pictures,* vol. III (Boston: G. K. Hall & Co., 1973).

6,883. Shiras, Myrna
Papers. 1970-75. 1 Hollinger box and 1 oversize folder.
Open. No guide.
Schlesinger Library.
Correspondence, photos of paintings, posters, and a drawing entitled "Always a Silent Witness" by Shiras, a feminist artist.

6,884. Sigourney, Lydia Huntley
Papers. Ca. 1834-65. 19 items.
Open. Published and unpublished guides.
Schlesinger Library.
Letters of Sigourney (1791-1865), an author, to such persons as Mary G. Wells and Anna Marie (Fielding) Hall. See Arthur and Elizabeth Schlesinger Library on the History of Women in America, *The Manuscript Inventories and the Catalogs of the Manuscripts, Books and Pictures,* vol. III (Boston: G. K. Hall & Co., 1973).

6,885. Simkhovitch, Mary Melinda (Kingsbury)
Papers. Ca. 1850-1951. 4 Hollinger boxes and 4 cartons.
Open. Published and unpublished guides.
Schlesinger Library.
Papers of Simkhovitch (1867-1951), a New York City social worker, contain family and business correspondence, correspondence with Emily Balch and other friends, a diary, biographical material, a genealogy, speeches and articles, photos, and information on Greenwich House, the Greenwich Village Association, and the New York City Housing Authority. See Arthur and Elizabeth Schlesinger Library on the History of Women in America, *The Manuscript Inventories and the Catalogs of the Manuscripts, Books and Pictures,* vol. III (Boston: G. K. Hall & Co., 1973).

6,886. Simon, Caroline K.
Papers. ?-1976. 24 cartons and 3.5 Hollinger boxes.
Open. No guide.
Schlesinger Library.
Personal and professional correspondence, memos, speeches, articles, reports, bulletins, photos, clippings, other printed material, and memorabilia of Simon, a New York City lawyer who since 1963 has served as judge of the Court of Claims. Contains information on her public service and legal career, including her years on the New York State Commission Against Discrimination in Employment, and her term as New York secretary of state. Also includes material about the Women Lawyers' Centennial Celebration, the National Council of Women and the Law Center, the Women's Social Service for Israel, Inc., the National Council of Women womenpower committee, the National Alliance for Safer Cities, and the USO.

6,887. Simons, Frieda (Hennock)
Papers. 1922-60. 20 Hollinger boxes.
Open. Published and unpublished guides.
Schlesinger Library.
Papers of Simons (1904-60), a New York lawyer who was the first woman member of the Federal Communications Commission, to which she was appointed in 1948, contain personal and professional correspondence, notes, drafts, speeches and opinions, clippings, photos, and official publications, the bulk of which relate to her FCC work. Letters of congratulations on important events in later life reveal her acquaintance with notable persons in business, education, and politics. See Arthur and Elizabeth Schlesinger Library on the History of Women in America, *The Manuscript Inventories and the Catalogs of the Manuscripts, Books and Pictures,* vol. III (Boston: G. K. Hall & Co., 1973).

6,888. Sisters of the Holy Family Motherhouse and Novitiate
Records. 1897. 2 items.
Open. Unpublished guide.
Schlesinger Library.
A letter in which Susan B. Anthony, responding to an appeal by this religious order for money for poor Negroes in New Orleans, also discusses such matters as the 50th anniversary of Seneca Falls. In the second letter she requests funds for the National American Woman Suffrage Association press bureau.

6,889. Smith, E. H.
Collection. 1888-1934. 5 folders.
Open. Published and unpublished guides.
Schlesinger Library.
Letters and autographs of outstanding British women and men suffragists, musicians, educators, physicians, and public figures, many of which were collected by [Miss] Smith of Manchester, England, for the Manchester and District Suffrage Bazaar in 1912. Includes a card from Elizabeth Robins, an American living in England. See Arthur and Elizabeth Schlesinger Library on the History of Women in America, *The Manuscript Inventories and the Catalogs of the Manuscripts, Books and Pictures,* vol. III (Boston: G. K. Hall & Co., 1973).

6,890. Smith, Elizabeth Oakes
Papers. 1852. 2 items.
Open. Published and unpublished guides.
Schlesinger Library.
Letter and engraving of Smith (1806-93), an author, lecturer, and reformer. See Arthur and Elizabeth Schlesinger Library on the History of Women in America, *The Manuscript Inventories and the Catalogs of the Manuscripts, Books and Pictures,* vol. III (Boston: G. K. Hall & Co., 1973).

6,891. Smith, Gerrit
Papers. 1852. 1 item.
Open. Published and unpublished guides.
Schlesinger Library.
Letter by Smith (1797-1874), an abolitionist, to Susan B. Anthony concerns women addressing the legislature, proposed meetings, and other matters. See Arthur and Elizabeth Schlesinger Library on the History of Women in America, *The Manuscript Inventories and the Catalogs of the Manuscripts, Books and Pictures,* vol. III (Boston: G. K. Hall & Co., 1973).

6,892. Smith, Hattie (Hyland)
Papers. 1937-59. 4 Hollinger boxes.
Open. Published and unpublished guides.
Schlesinger Library.
From 1940 through 1950 and from 1953 through 1959, Smith was assistant commissioner of the Massachusetts Department of Labor and Industry; from 1954 through 1959 she also was administrator of the division on employment of the aging. Correspondence, articles, reports, and other material on minimum wages, emergency housing, equal pay, equal rights, household employment, industrial homework, youth conservation, employment of the aging, and the Equal Rights Amendment. See Arthur and Elizabeth Schlesinger Library on the History of Women in America, *The Manuscript Inventories and the Catalogs of the Manuscripts, Books and Pictures,* vol. III (Boston: G. K. Hall & Co., 1973).

6,893. Smith, Hilda Worthington
Papers. 1835-1975. 41 Hollinger boxes, 14 folders, and 13 vols.
Open. Published and unpublished guides.
Schlesinger Library.
A pioneer in workers' education, [Miss] Smith (1888-) was associated with the Bryn Mawr Summer School for Women Workers from 1921 to 1933, the Affiliated Schools for Workers, Inc., from 1927, and various labor organizations including the Workers Service Program of the Federal Emergency Relief Administration, the Communications Workers of America, the WPA, and during the late 1940s the National Committee for the Extension of Labor Education. Correspondence, an unpublished autobiography and other biographical material, family papers, poems, manuscripts, speeches and articles, financial documents, minutes, reports, printed matter, and photos. Includes correspondence concerning the structure of American society with industrial women workers who were active in the labor movement from the 1920s through the 1940s. Also contains material on groups with which Smith was associated, including the Hudson Shore Labor School and the Highlander Folk School. See Arthur and Elizabeth Schlesinger Library on the History of Women in America, *The Manuscript Inventories and the Catalogs of the Manuscripts, Books and Pictures,* vol. III (Boston: G. K. Hall & Co., 1973).

6,894. Smith, Jane (Norman)
Papers. 1913-53. 13 Hollinger boxes and 3 oversize vols.
Open. Published and unpublished guides.
Schlesinger Library.
Papers of [Mrs. Clarence M.] Smith (1874-1953), chairman of the National Woman's Party from 1927 to 1929, consist of correspondence, minutes, financial documents, NWP publications, clippings on suffrage and equal rights, and photos, most of which center on the NWP, its campaign for women's equality, and Smith's special interest in the investment of NWP funds and the industrial equality of women in New York. Also included is information on 1947 lawsuits within the NWP,

other women's organizations, international women's activities, and suffrage in New York. See Arthur and Elizabeth Schlesinger Library on the History of Women in America, *The Manuscript Inventories and the Catalogs of the Manuscripts, Books and Pictures,* vol. III (Boston: G. K. Hall & Co., 1973).

6,895. Smith, Margaret E.
Papers. 1943-50. 4 Hollinger boxes.
Open. Published and unpublished guides.
Schlesinger Library.
Minutes, reports, and files of the Special Services Committee of Ann Arbor, MI, a small and informal organization of friends whose interest was worker education. Contains reports of projects such as a 1944 army orientation program, a study of university programs in labor education made by Caroline F. Ware in 1946 in cooperation with the American Labor Education Service, and work with the Committee for the Extension of Labor Education from 1945 to 1950. See Arthur and Elizabeth Schlesinger Library on the History of Women in America, *The Manuscript Inventories and the Catalogs of the Manuscripts, Books and Pictures,* vol. III (Boston: G. K. Hall & Co., 1973).

6,896. Smith, Mildred E. Buller
Papers. 1919-46. 9 vols. and 1 folder.
Open. Published and unpublished guides.
Schlesinger Library.
Journals of Smith, a Vermont agriculturist, are mainly descriptive of work on the Dimock Farm in East Corinth, VT, a winter in Florida, and a 1929 trip abroad. Also includes correspondence, memoranda, and economic briefs concerning her job as milk price specialist for the Office of Price Administration. See Arthur and Elizabeth Schlesinger Library on the History of Women in America, *The Manuscript Inventories and the Catalogs of the Manuscripts, Books and Pictures,* vol. III (Boston: G. K. Hall & Co., 1973).

6,897. Society for Humane Abortion
Records. Ca. 1960-71. 9.5 Hollinger boxes, 3 cartons, and 6 tapes.
Access restricted. No guide.
Schlesinger Library.
Financial records, correspondence, articles, newsletters, scrapbooks, photos, clippings, and other records of the Society, which referred women from the West Coast to reputable abortionists in Mexico before abortion was legal in the US. Also contains leaflets of the Association to Repeal Abortion Laws.

6,898. Sociologists for Women in Society
Records. Ca. 1972-76. 8.5 Hollinger boxes.
Open. No guide.
Schlesinger Library.
Correspondence, memoranda, reports, lists, and newsletters of this organization, which was organized in 1971 to promote professional opportunities for women in sociology, provide job market services, explore the contributions of sociology to the humanization of sex roles, and serve as guardian for women in the American Sociological Association. Also included are records of its committee on constitutional revision and organization and SWS newsletter editorial files.

6,899. Solomon, Barbara (Miller)
Oral history. 1964. 1 tape.
Open. Unpublished guide.
Schlesinger Library.
Recollections by [Mrs. Peter H.] Solomon, associate dean at Harvard University and director of the Women's Archives, on Mrs. Lyndon Baines Johnson's second White House "Luncheon for Lady Doers."

6,900. Solomon, Maida (Herman)
Papers. 1925-74. 7 cartons and 4 Hollinger boxes.
Access restricted. No guide.
Schlesinger Library.
A psychiatric social worker, [Mrs. Harry Caesar] Solomon (1891-) was head of the Simmons College department of psychiatric social work and vice-president from 1928 to 1956 of the Massachusetts Society for Social Hygiene. Correspondence, minutes, reports, photos, and other material concern Solomon's work with the American Association of Psychiatric Social Workers, the American National Red Cross, the American Association of Schools of Social Work, Boston State Hospital, and Union Park Forum, as well as her fieldwork for the AAPSW, syphilis social work at the Boston Psychopathic Hospital, and service as a psychiatric social work consultant to hospital administration and staff psychiatric workers assigned to VISTA programs. Also included is information on Hecht House.

6,901. Somerville and Howorth Family
Papers. 1852- . 15 Hollinger boxes, 13 oversize items, 2 rolls, and unprocessed addenda.
Open. Published and unpublished guides.
Schlesinger Library.
Correspondence, diaries, scrapbook, autograph album, photo, memorabilia, and other papers of a Mississippi family, women members of which were active in the Methodist church, woman suffrage, and government. Included are correspondence, speeches and articles, a genealogy, and biographical information of Nellie (Nugent) Somerville (1863-1952), a pioneer in Mississippi work for women's rights and the first woman to be elected to the state House of Representatives; she was active in the Mississippi WCTU, the DAR, the First Methodist Church of Greenville, the Monteagle Assembly, the Mississippi Woman Suffrage Association, and women's clubs. Also included are correspondence from notable persons in government and organizational work, speeches, and other papers of her daughter Lucy (Somerville) Howorth (1895-), which reveal Howorth's education, experiences and contacts in the legal profession and in her government work, and her association with such organizations as the Business and Professional Women's Clubs of Jackson, MS, and Washington, DC, and the National and International Federations of Business and Professional Women, the AAUW, Women in World Affairs, and the Assembly of Women's Organizations for National Security. Howorth's papers also contain information on women lawyers and the position of women in government and in appointive positions. Collection contains papers of other family members as well, with an autobiography, diary of religious meditations for 1852 to 1868, and church records of Somerville's grandmother S. Myra (Cox) Smith (1822-87), who was recording secretary of the women's auxiliary of the First Methodist Church of Greenville from 1879 until 1887 when Somerville succeeded her; recollections of Amelia (Lewis) Thomson (1799-?); letters Somerville's father William Lewis Nugent wrote between 1860 and 1865 to his wife Eleanor Fulkerson (Smith) Nugent; a Keith family tree; and material on the Nugent residence and other relatives. See Arthur and Elizabeth Schlesinger Library on the History of Women in America, *The Manuscript Inventories and the Catalogs of the Manuscripts, Books and Pictures,* vol. III (Boston: G. K. Hall & Co., 1973).

6,902. Somerville, Mary
Papers. 1834. 1 item.
Open. Published and unpublished guides.
Schlesinger Library.
Letter wherein Somerville (1780-1872), an astronomer, introduces Harriet Martineau to a Professor Farrars at Harvard. See Arthur and Elizabeth Schlesinger Library on the History of Women in America, *The Manuscript Inventories and the Catalogs of the Manuscripts, Books and Pictures,* vol. III (Boston: G. K. Hall & Co., 1973).

6,903. Sparrow, Louise Kidder
Papers. 1839-1975. 4 Hollinger boxes, 1 drawer, 1 box, 14 folders, and 4 vols.
Open. Published and unpublished guides.
Schlesinger Library.
Papers of [Mrs. Herbert George] Sparrow (1884-), a sculptor and poet, include correspondence, diaries, manuscripts, notebook, family papers, genealogical information, scrapbooks and albums, portraits, photos, and memorabilia. Also contained are pamphlets Sparrow wrote, a manuscript of her first novel *Whispering Tongues: A Fanciful Romance of Rio,* translations she made of foreign poetry, volumes of her poetry, and material concerning her escape from France prior to the German occupation during WWII. See Arthur and Elizabeth Schlesinger Library on the History of Women in America, *The Manuscript Inventories and the Catalogs of the Manuscripts, Books and Pictures,* vol. III (Boston: G. K. Hall & Co., 1973).

6,904. Speare, Florence Lewis
Papers. 1911-68. 1 Hollinger box.
Open. Unpublished guide.
Schlesinger Library.
Collection of [Mrs. M. Edmund] Speare (1886-1965), a Radcliffe graduate who was an author, playwright, and teacher at various New England colleges, consists primarily of published copies of such of her works as the play *Jones versus Jones* (1913), *The Star Gleams: A Community Christmas Choral* (1919), and *The Bride and the Burglar* (1922). Also included are correspondence, a manuscript, photos, and clippings.

6,905. Stanton, Elizabeth (Cady)
Papers. Ca. 1894. 6 items.
Open. Published and unpublished guides.
Schlesinger Library.
Correspondence by Stanton (1815-1902), a women's rights leader, and a poem to Susan B. Anthony on her 90th birthday. See Arthur and Elizabeth Schlesinger Library on the History of Women in America, *The Manuscript Inventories and the Catalogs of the Manuscripts, Books and Pictures,* vol. III (Boston: G. K. Hall & Co., 1973).

6,906. Stearns, Sarah (Ripley)
Papers. 1801-37. 1 Hollinger box.
Open. Published and unpublished guides.
Schlesinger Library.
Papers of Stearns (1785-?), a resident of Greenfield and Shelburne, MA, who was sister of George Ripley, consist of her journals for 1801 to 1818, journals of her daughter Rachel Willard Stearns (1813-?) for 1834 to 1837, and 139 letters to Sarah Stearns from Eunice Callender of Boston. The papers contain news of local events and family affairs as well as extensive discussion of religious concerns. See Arthur and Elizabeth Schlesinger Library on the History of Women in America, *The Manuscript Inventories and the Catalogs of the Manuscripts, Books and Pictures,* vol. III (Boston: G. K. Hall & Co., 1973).

6,907. Stedman, Edith G.
Papers. 1833-1971. 8.5 Hollinger boxes and 12 folders.
Open. Published and unpublished guides.
Schlesinger Library.
Stedman (ca. 1888-) was director of the Radcliffe College Appointment Bureau. Correspondence, including letters from Margaret Deland and Eleanor Roosevelt; manuscript autobiography; diaries of European travel and of her life in England between 1959 and 1961; manuscript entitled "A Yankee in an English Village" by Stedman; material on her restoration of Dorchester Abbey in England and her creation of the "Monastery Cookbook"; and source material for a booklet on Stedman, entitled *Twelve Years on a Shoestring,* by Nancy Creshkoff. Also included are early family papers, with Samuel Munson's journal

of a voyage to Batavia in 1833, Augustus F. Holt's account of transporting fugitive slaves in 1844, guest registers, photo, clippings, and printed material. See Arthur and Elizabeth Schlesinger Library on the History of Women in America, *The Manuscript Inventories and the Catalogs of the Manuscripts, Books and Pictures,* vol. III (Boston: G. K. Hall & Co., 1973).

6,908. Stevens, Doris
Papers. Ca. 1915-60s. 56 cartons, 11 Hollinger boxes, 3 boxes, and oversize items.
Open. Published and unpublished guides.
Schlesinger Library.
Active in organizations for advancement of the rights of women, particularly the Inter-American Commission of Women, for which she served as US delegate and chairman, Stevens (1892-1963) also was a composer, author, collector of information about women, and wife of Jonathan Mitchell. Correspondence; diaries; manuscripts of her books, articles, and speeches, including "Jailed for Freedom" in Spanish and Portuguese translations; IACW financial records, scrapbooks of press releases, and workbooks for the 7th International Conference of American States on the Political and Civil Rights of Women; sheet music and recordings of her compositions; articles about her; tributes to her from women in South America; photos; and memorabilia. Also included is correspondence with James B. Scott and others concerning preparation of a book of the paintings and drawings of Jeannette Scott, which Stevens arranged and for which she wrote a biographical sketch of Scott. See Arthur and Elizabeth Schlesinger Library on the History of Women in America, *The Manuscript Inventories and the Catalogs of the Manuscripts, Books and Pictures,* vol. III (Boston: G. K. Hall & Co., 1973).

6,909. Stillman, Mildred Whitney
Papers. 1932-51. 1 folder.
Open. Unpublished guide.
Schlesinger Library.
Papers of [Mrs. Ernest G.] Stillman (1890-1950), an author, consist of correspondence from, to, and about her; Christmas cards containing poems by her; and a photo.

6,910. Stokes, Caroline, and Stokes, Olivia Phelps
Papers. 1866-1927. 1.5 Hollinger boxes.
Open. Unpublished guide.
Schlesinger Library.
Correspondence, journals, photos, and clippings of Caroline Phelps Stokes (1854-1909) and Olivia Egleston Phelps Stokes (1847-1927), who were daughters of wealthy and religious parents in New York City and who devoted their lives to Christian philanthropy. Includes letters of appreciation from individuals and institutions which benefitted from the sisters' generosity; letters and other documents relating to the Ansonia Library in Connecticut, which the sisters built in memory of their father James Stokes and their maternal grandfather Anson Greene Phelps; and letters from Olivia to Caroline. Also contained are writings of Caroline Stokes, including her travel journals which were the basis for *Travels of a Lady's Maid,* anonymously published in 1908, and a ledger and manuscripts pertaining to the will of Olivia Stokes.

6,911. Stone, Lucy
Papers. 1850-93. 3 folders.
Open. Published and unpublished guides.
Schlesinger Library.
Correspondence of Stone (1818-93), a feminist, suffragist, and abolitionist, to her brother William B. Stone, a minister; Samuel Joseph May; Fanny and Charles Ames; a Miss Holland; and others. See Arthur and Elizabeth Schlesinger Library on the History of Women in America, *The Manuscript Inventories and the Catalogs of the Manuscripts, Books and Pictures,* vol. III (Boston: G. K. Hall & Co., 1973).

6,912. Stoughton, Louise
Papers. 1877-79. 1 Hollinger box.
Open. Published and unpublished guides.
Schlesinger Library.
Correspondence and manuscripts of Stoughton (1851-86), who accompanied her aunt and uncle Edward Wallace Stoughton when he was Minister Plenipotentiary to Russia between 1877 and 1879. In her letters home she describes her travels and experiences abroad in Rome, Venice, Warsaw, and Russia; the Czarevna's palace; the Hermitage palace; dinners in St. Petersburg; and balls and receptions. See Arthur and Elizabeth Schlesinger Library on the History of Women in America, *The Manuscript Inventories and the Catalogs of the Manuscripts, Books and Pictures,* vol. III (Boston: G. K. Hall & Co., 1973).

6,913. Stowe, Harriet Elizabeth (Beecher)
Papers. 1835-94. 15 items.
Open. Published and unpublished guides.
Schlesinger Library.
Letters by Stowe (1811-96), an author, to various correspondents. See Arthur and Elizabeth Schlesinger Library on the History of Women in America, *The Manuscript Inventories and the Catalogs of the Manuscripts, Books and Pictures,* vol. III (Boston: G. K. Hall & Co., 1973).

6,914. Strauss, Anna Lord
Papers. Ca. 1920-75. 13 cartons, 1 box, and 3 bundles.
Open. No guide.
Schlesinger Library.
President of the LWV of the US from 1944 to 1950, Strauss (1899-) has also been active in the New York City and state Leagues as well as in the Overseas Education Fund, the Food and Agriculture Organization of the UN, the UN Association, the Town Meeting of the Air, and various government positions. Correspondence, speeches, reports, pamphlets, diplomas, certificates, photos, and clippings contain material from Strauss's South American trip in 1929 and 1930, the LWV, the President's Commission on Internal Security and Individual Rights, the UN General Assembly, the Woodrow Wilson Foundation, UNICEF, the Committee for Economic Development, the World Foundation, the National Committee for an Effective Congress, the National Center for Education in Politics, Women in World Affairs, the Citizens Committees for Reorganizing Executive Government and for the Courts, and Connecticut and Hampshire colleges.

6,915. Strickland, Edward F.
Collection. 1780-1918. 1 Hollinger box.
Open. Published and unpublished guides.
Schlesinger Library.
Autograph collection consisting of autographs, correspondence, and photos of women prominent in suffrage work and of women authors, artists, and lawyers. See Arthur and Elizabeth Schlesinger Library on the History of Women in America, *The Manuscript Inventories and the Catalogs of the Manuscripts, Books and Pictures,* vol. III (Boston: G. K. Hall & Co., 1973).

6,916. Sturgis, Lucy S.
Papers. 1854-55. 1 vol.
Open. Published and unpublished guides.
Schlesinger Library.
Notebook of abstracts of lectures which were given by Louis Agassiz on geology, biology, and paleontology to a class consisting of his daughter Ida Agassiz and her friends. See Arthur and Elizabeth Schlesinger Library on the History of Women in America, *The Manuscript Inventories and the Catalogs of the Manuscripts, Books and Pictures,* vol. III (Boston: G. K. Hall & Co., 1973).

6,917. Swingle, Maude K.
Papers. 1965-66. 1 folder.
Open. Unpublished guide.
Schlesinger Library.
Letters to Swingle in which Camille Falkett, a Peace Corps volunteer, discusses Bolivian social conditions, climate and geography, political unrest, duties as a Corps volunteer, and transfer because of illness.

6,918. Swisshelm, Jane Grey (Cannon)
Papers. 1878. 1 item.
Open. Published and unpublished guides.
Schlesinger Library.
Letter of Swisshelm (1815-84), a reformer, journalist, and advocate of women's rights, to a Mrs. Stockheim. See Arthur and Elizabeth Schlesinger Library on the History of Women in America, *The Manuscript Inventories and the Catalogs of the Manuscripts, Books and Pictures,* vol. III (Boston: G. K. Hall & Co., 1973).

6,919. Switzer, Mary Elizabeth
Papers. Ca. 1941-70. 61 cartons, 5 Hollinger boxes, 4 folders, 5 vols., and items.
Open. No guide.
Schlesinger Library.
Employed by the US Public Health Service in 1922, Switzer (1900-72) became director in 1950 of the Federal Office of Vocational Rehabilitation and then administrator of HEW's Bureau of Social Services and Rehabilitation. Correspondence, memoranda, speeches, articles, minutes, pamphlets, photos, recording discs, tapes, and clippings primarily concern Switzer's career in HEW. Also included are files from the National Health Assembly, the Health Resources Advisory Commission, the American Hearing Society, the Association for the Aid of Crippled Children, and Alexandria Hospital, as well as material on the deaf, polio, the Patent Board, and nursing and medical care for the indigent.

6,920. Szold, Henrietta Schaar
Papers. 1875-1918. 1 carton and 9 folders.
Open. Published and unpublished guides.
Schlesinger Library.
Personal and professional correspondence of Szold (1860-1945), a founder and from 1912 to 1926 president of Hadassah, relate to her activities on behalf of Hadassah, the Jewish Publication Society of America, and the Young Women's Hebrew Association in New York. Included are letters, 1898-1907, from two German Jewish scholars resident in the US concerning publications undertaken or considered by the Society; 1914 letters on laying the cornerstone in the new YWHA building; and letters on fund raising for Hadassah and its medical work in Palestine during WWI. Also included are articles, photos, and copies of letters and of a diary, which were used by Irving Fineman to write *Woman of Valor,* a biography of Szold. See Arthur and Elizabeth Schlesinger Library on the History of Women in America, *The Manuscript Inventories and the Catalogs of the Manuscripts, Books and Pictures,* vol. III (Boston: G. K. Hall & Co., 1973).

6,921. Tarbell, Ida Minerva
Papers. 1878-98. 1 Hollinger box.
Open. Published and unpublished guides.
Schlesinger Library.
Original manuscript by Tarbell (1857-1944), an historian, journalist, and muckraker, entitled "The Nationalizing of Business," which was edited by Arthur M. Schlesinger and Dixon R. Fox and published as volume nine of *The History of American Life.* Also included are copies of some memos. See Arthur and Elizabeth Schlesinger Library on the History of Women in America, *The Manuscript Inventories and the Catalogs of the Manuscripts, Books and Pictures,* vol. III (Boston: G. K. Hall & Co., 1973).

6,922. Thomas, Edith Matilda
Papers. Nd. 2 items.
Open. Published and unpublished guides.
Schlesinger Library.
Fragments of poems by Thomas (1854-1925), a poet. See Arthur and Elizabeth Schlesinger Library on the History of Women in America, *The Manuscript Inventories and the Catalogs of the Manuscripts, Books and Pictures,* vol. III (Boston: G. K. Hall & Co., 1973).

6,923. Thompson, Anna Boynton
Papers. 1890-1923. 1 Hollinger box, 1 folder, and 1 microfilm reel.
Open. Published and unpublished guides.
Schlesinger Library.
An educator, Thompson (1848-1923) taught at Thayer Academy in Braintree, MA, for 44 years, many of them as chairman of the history department; while employed, she also continued her education at Radcliffe and Tufts colleges where she studied with George Santayana, Josiah Royce, and other professors, some of whom she corresponded with for the rest of her life. Correspondence with Santayana, Royce, Alice Freeman Palmer, Alice M. Longfellow, and Thompson's former student Laurence J. Hawes; journals; photos; clippings; and articles about Thompson by Thayer students and colleagues. In the letters to Hawes, Thompson explains her theories of education. See Arthur and Elizabeth Schlesinger Library on the History of Women in America, *The Manuscript Inventories and the Catalogs of the Manuscripts, Books and Pictures,* vol. III (Boston: G. K. Hall & Co., 1973).

6,924. Thompson, Frances Euphemia
Papers. 1936-75. 0.5 Hollinger box and addenda.
Open. Unpublished guide.
Schlesinger Library.
An artist, Thompson (ca. 1900-) was chairman of the art department at Tennessee Agricultural and Industrial State College. Correspondence, papers Thompson wrote on art and artists, a newsletter, a certificate, photos, clippings, and memorabilia include information about teaching at TAISC and tributes from students and academic organizations.

6,925. Tillinghast, Anna Churchill (Moulton)
Papers. 1911-45. 1 Hollinger box.
Open. Published and unpublished guides.
Schlesinger Library.
Papers of Tillinghast (1874-1951) concern her career as an ordained minister, a speaker for prohibition, Commissioner of Immigration for New England from 1927 to 1933, a suffrage amendment advocate, and a state and local Republican party worker. Correspondence, announcements, dinner programs, photos, and clippings. Correspondents include Calvin and Grace Coolidge, Warren G. and Florence (Kling) Harding, Henry Cabot Lodge, and Edith Kermit Roosevelt. See Arthur and Elizabeth Schlesinger Library on the History of Women in America, *The Manuscript Inventories and the Catalogs of the Manuscripts, Books and Pictures,* vol. III (Boston: G. K. Hall & Co., 1973).

6,926. Tilton, Elizabeth (Hewes)
Papers. 1918-45. 28 Hollinger boxes and 3 oversize vols.
Open. Published and unpublished guides.
Schlesinger Library.
Correspondence, volumes of diaries, an autobiography, speeches, articles, and other manuscripts of [Mrs. William] Tilton (1869-1950) concern her work for social and economic reform with charitable organizations such as the National Congress of Mothers, the PTA, the Unitarian Temperance Society, and other temperance groups. See Arthur and Elizabeth Schlesinger Library on the History of Women in America, *The Manuscript Inventories and the Catalogs of the Manuscripts, Books and Pictures,* vol. III (Boston: G. K. Hall & Co., 1973).

6,927. Toklas, Alice Boyd
Papers. 1934-54. 4 items.
Open. Published and unpublished guides.
Schlesinger Library.
Correspondence from Toklas (1877-1967), a writer who was companion of Gertrude Stein, to Jean Reeder Emmet. See Arthur and Elizabeth Schlesinger Library on the History of Women in America, *The Manuscript Inventories and the Catalogs of the Manuscripts, Books and Pictures,* vol. III (Boston: G. K. Hall & Co., 1973).

6,928. Tousley, Clare M.
Papers. Ca. 1925-70. 1 carton.
Open. No guide.
Schlesinger Library.
Correspondence, speeches, articles, photos, and other material of Tousley, a social work publicist, pertain to her teaching at Barnard College and the University of California at Berkeley, the Community Service Society, and the Family Service Association of America.

6,929. United Nations Commission on the Status of Women
Records. 1946-68. 2 Hollinger boxes.
Open. No guide.
Schlesinger Library.
Mimeographed and printed reports of the Commission.

6,930. U.S. Army Nurse Corps
Records. 1951-58. 17 folders.
Open. Published and unpublished guides.
Schlesinger Library.
A history and description of this auxiliary unit of nurses for the Army, brief biographies and photos of Corps chiefs, articles, and publications. The Corps was established in 1901. See Arthur and Elizabeth Schlesinger Library on the History of Women in America, *The Manuscript Inventories and the Catalogs of the Manuscripts, Books and Pictures,* vol. III (Boston: G. K. Hall & Co., 1973).

6,931. U.S. Defense Advisory Committee on Women in the Services
Records. 1951-70. 3 Hollinger boxes and 2 items.
Open. Published and unpublished guides.
Schlesinger Library.
Minutes, reports, directives, recommendations, publicity material, publications, photos, and biographies of commanders of the Committee, organized in 1951 to assist the Department of Defense on matters relating to Services women. Information on various of the Services is also included. See Arthur and Elizabeth Schlesinger Library on the History of Women in America, *The Manuscript Inventories and the Catalogs of the Manuscripts, Books and Pictures,* vol. III (Boston: G. K. Hall & Co., 1973).

6,932. Upton, Harriet (Taylor)
Papers. 1908. 2 items.
Open. Published and unpublished guides.
Schlesinger Library.
Letter of Upton (1853-1945), a suffragist, to the Knickerbocker Publishing Company and a four-page biography of Susan B. Anthony. See Arthur and Elizabeth Schlesinger Library on the History of Women in America, *The Manuscript Inventories and the Catalogs of the Manuscripts, Books and Pictures,* vol. III (Boston: G. K. Hall & Co., 1973).

6,933. Van Loon, Eliza Ingersoll (Bowditch)
Papers. 1906-07. 0.5 Hollinger box.
Open. Unpublished guide.
Schlesinger Library.
Correspondence and photos of van Loon, first wife of writer-journalist Hendrik Willem van Loon and daughter of Harvard Medical School professor Henry Pickering Bowditch (1840-1911). Includes letters she wrote her family while living in Moscow and Warsaw where her husband was an Associated Press correspondent and letters Hendrik van Loon wrote, all of which depict occurrences in the van Loons' personal lives as well as political and social events abroad.

6,934. Van Waters, Miriam
Papers. 1894-1971. Ca. 52 Hollinger boxes, 10 cartons, 6 recording discs, and 1 microfilm reel.
Access restricted. Published and unpublished guides.
Schlesinger Library.
Correspondence, diaries, notes, lectures, speeches and articles, reports, scrapbooks, photos, clippings, and printed and other material of Van Waters (1887-1974), superintendent of the Reformatory for Women in Framingham, MA, from 1932 to 1957. The family correspondence documents Van Waters's experiences as daughter, sister, mother, and professional; her professional correspondence includes letters from prisoners and from prominent individuals who were concerned with penology and juvenile delinquency. From 1919 to 1920 Van Waters was superintendent of El Retiro, a school for delinquent girls in California; then from 1920 to 1930 she served as referee for the Los Angeles County Juvenile Court, after which she assumed the position at Framingham. In addition, she was director of the juvenile delinquency section of the Harvard Law School Crime Survey from 1926 into the 1930s, a consultant on juvenile delinquency for the National Commission on Law Observance and Enforcement (the Wickersham Commission) from 1928 to 1931, and secretary of the American Youth Commission from 1935 to 1941. See Arthur and Elizabeth Schlesinger Library on the History of Women in America, *The Manuscript Inventories and the Catalogs of the Manuscripts, Books and Pictures,* vol. III (Boston: G. K. Hall & Co., 1973).

6,935. Wambaugh, Sarah
Papers. 1902-49. 1 Hollinger box.
Open. Published and unpublished guides.
Schlesinger Library.
Wambaugh (1882-1955), a 1902 Radcliffe graduate, was an instructor in history and government and an international affairs authority. Correspondence, including letters with comments on her book *The Saar Plebiscite* (1940); notes for speeches; biographical material; and memorabilia such as diplomas, honorary awards, and a medal of the Knight in the Royal Order of the Phoenix, which was awarded in Greece in 1949. See Arthur and Elizabeth Schlesinger Library on the History of Women in America, *The Manuscript Inventories and the Catalogs of the Manuscripts, Books and Pictures,* vol. III (Boston: G. K. Hall & Co., 1973).

6,936. Ward, Elizabeth Stuart (Phelps)
Papers. Nd. 1 item.
Open. Published and unpublished guides.
Schlesinger Library.
Letter of [Mrs. Herbert Dickinson] Ward (1844-1911), an author who was born in Boston, to a Mr. Talbot. See Arthur and Elizabeth Schlesinger Library on the History of Women in America, *The Manuscript Inventories and the Catalogs of the Manuscripts, Books and Pictures,* vol. III (Boston: G. K. Hall & Co., 1973).

6,937. Washburn, Minnie
Papers. Nd. 1 item.
Open. Published and unpublished guides.
Schlesinger Library.
Letter of Washburn (ca. 1835-?) to her father Emery Washburn (1800-77), who was governor of Massachusetts from 1854 to 1855. See Arthur and Elizabeth Schlesinger Library on the History of Women in America, *The Manuscript Inventories and the Catalogs of the Manuscripts, Books and Pictures,* vol. III (Boston: G. K. Hall & Co., 1973).

6,938. Webster, Ellen A.
Papers. 1909-19. 1 Hollinger box.
Open. Unpublished guide.

Schlesinger Library.
Scrapbook and clippings of Webster (1863-1965), a suffragist, concern events in the Wilson administration, some of which concerned women and suffrage.

6,939. Weis, Jessica (McCullough)
Papers. 1925-62. 24 Hollinger boxes, 2 oversize vols., and 2 items.
Open. Published and unpublished guides.
Schlesinger Library.
Active in the Republican party on county, state, and national levels, [Mrs. Charles W., Jr.] Weis (1901-63) was a New York congresswoman from 1958 to 1962. Correspondence, scrapbooks, photos, clippings, and other material relate to her political career from 1937 to 1962, during which years she served as vice-chairman of the Monroe County Republican Committee; a member of the advisory committee of the National Federation of Women's Republican Clubs; vice-chairman of the New York delegation to the Republican National Conventions in 1944, 1948, 1952, and 1956; and as associate campaign manager of the 1948 Dewey-Warren campaign. Included along with her official papers as congresswoman are correspondence and other material relating to her work with the American National Red Cross during WWII, as a member of the national advisory board of the Federal Civil Defense Administration, and as an advisor to the American delegate to the Inter-American Commission of Women in 1953. See Arthur and Elizabeth Schlesinger Library on the History of Women in America, *The Manuscript Inventories and the Catalogs of the Manuscripts, Books and Pictures,* vol. III (Boston: G. K. Hall & Co., 1973).

6,940. Weld, Theodore Dwight
Papers. 1880-90. 2 items.
Open. Published and unpublished guides.
Schlesinger Library.
Correspondence of Weld (1803-95), an abolitionist who married Angelina Grimké, reflects his feelings on his wife's death and his later life. See Arthur and Elizabeth Schlesinger Library on the History of Women in America, *The Manuscript Inventories and the Catalogs of the Manuscripts, Books and Pictures,* vol. III (Boston: G. K. Hall & Co., 1973).

6,941. Wells, Agnes Ermina
Papers. 1924-56. 6 folders.
Open. Published and unpublished guides.
Schlesinger Library.
Correspondence, articles, photos, and clippings of Wells (1876-1959), dean of women at Indiana University, who was active in the AAUW, the National Federation of Business and Professional Women's Clubs, and the National Woman's Party. See Arthur and Elizabeth Schlesinger Library on the History of Women in America, *The Manuscript Inventories and the Catalogs of the Manuscripts, Books and Pictures,* vol. III (Boston: G. K. Hall & Co., 1973).

6,942. Wells, Marguerite Milton
Papers. 1895-1959. 2 Hollinger boxes.
Open. Published and unpublished guides.
Schlesinger Library.
Wells (1872-1959), a suffrage leader, was president of the Minnesota LWV from 1922 to 1932 and president of the National LWV from 1934 to 1944. Consists of scrapbooks of her activities, articles, pamphlets, photos, and some correspondence of the National LWV. See Arthur and Elizabeth Schlesinger Library on the History of Women in America, *The Manuscript Inventories and the Catalogs of the Manuscripts, Books and Pictures,* vol. III (Boston: G. K. Hall & Co., 1973).

6,943. Wesselhoft, Selma
Papers. 1865. 2 items.
Open. Published and unpublished guides.
Schlesinger Library.
An appointment by the New England Freedmen's Aid Society and a commission issued by the American Freedmen's Aid Commission to Wesselhoft, a teacher of southern freedmen. See Arthur and Elizabeth Schlesinger Library on the History of Women in America, *The Manuscript Inventories and the Catalogs of the Manuscripts, Books and Pictures,* vol. III (Boston: G. K. Hall & Co., 1973).

6,944. West, Helen (Hunt)
Papers. 1917-64. 1 Hollinger box and 5 oversize vols.
Open. Published and unpublished guides.
Schlesinger Library.
Correspondence, speeches, photos, and clippings of [Mrs. Byron McG.] West (1892-1963), a Florida lawyer and journalist. Includes information about her activities in the campaign for suffrage, the movement for passage of the Equal Rights Amendment, and the National Woman's Party, for which she served as congressional chairman, national council member, and editor of *Equal Rights.* Also includes some correspondence on a bill calling for equal representation of men and women on party committees, which West sponsored in the Florida state legislature. See Arthur and Elizabeth Schlesinger Library on the History of Women in America, *The Manuscript Inventories and the Catalogs of the Manuscripts, Books and Pictures,* vol. III (Boston: G. K. Hall & Co., 1973).

6,945. Westropp, Lillian Mary, and Westropp, Clara E.
Papers. 1922-68. 1.5 Hollinger boxes, 1 oversize folder, and 8 oversize vols.
Open. Unpublished guide.
Schlesinger Library.
In 1922 Lillian Westropp (1884-1968) and Clara Westropp (1886-1965), who were sisters, founded the Women's Savings and Loan Company of Cleveland. Consists of correspondence, articles, publicity, minutes, photos, and clippings, as well as material relating to Lillian Westropp's work as a municipal judge and Clara Westropp's work raising funds for Catholic missionaries. The Westropps founded the bank to be run by women for women; Lillian Westropp was president and Clara Westropp secretary until 1958 when she became president. The bank is now called the Women's Federal Savings and Loan Association.

6,946. White, Eva (Whiting)
Papers. 1900-57. 6 Hollinger boxes.
Open. Published and unpublished guides.
Schlesinger Library.
A Boston social worker, [Mrs. Wesley Dunn Allen] White (1885-1974) was head of the Simmons College school of social work. Consists of correspondence, articles, reports, scrapbooks, photos, and clippings which reflect her activities, including service as head social worker at the Elizabeth Peabody House from 1909 to 1944 and as president of the Women's Educational and Industrial Union from 1929 to 1952. Correspondents include Jane Addams and Mary Follette; subjects include social settlements, community service, and immigrants. Other items concern the Peabody House's departments and theatre, as well as health, war service, and the Boston Social Union. See Arthur and Elizabeth Schlesinger Library on the History of Women in America, *The Manuscript Inventories and the Catalogs of the Manuscripts, Books and Pictures,* vol. III (Boston: G. K. Hall & Co., 1973).

6,947. White, Marjorie
Papers. Ca. 1930-70. 29 Hollinger boxes and 1 card file.
Open. Unpublished guide.
Schlesinger Library.
Out of an interest in correcting the public view of woman's role in history, White (1894-1972), a resident of Forest Hills, NY, collected published and unpublished articles, photos, and clippings on women throughout history and prehistory, which she inserted along with notes into notebooks. Mary R. Beard gave recognition to the usefulness of White's notebooks in the acknowledgments to her *Woman as Force in History* (1946); and, included in the notebooks, is White's correspondence with Beard. Prehistoric woman as priestess, midwife, and originator of culture is featured in the collection. White's interest in these aspects of woman was stimulated by Mary Milbank Brown, so correspondence with Brown, as well as Brown's notes, outlines, and unpublished writings, are also included; some of this correspondence refers to plans to correct the treatment of women in the *Encyclopaedia Britannica* and *Collier's Encyclopedia* and to prepare an encyclopedia for women, none of which materialized. Other correspondents include Herma Briffault; Dora Edinger; C. Esther Hodge, editor of the English periodical *Women Speaking;* Miriam Y. Holden; Inez (Haynes) Irwin; Blanche Christine Olschak; and Doris Stevens. The notebooks also contain an extensive section on Indian women.

6,948. White, Sallie Elizabeth (Joy)
Papers. 1828-1936. 3 Hollinger boxes, 5 vols., and 1 oversize item.
Open. Published and unpublished guides.
Schlesinger Library.
The first woman journalist in Boston, White (1852?-1909) used the pseudonym Penelope Penfeather. Family correspondence, letters she received from notable persons, volumes of clippings of her newspaper articles and columns, a photo, and papers of her daughter Grace Elinor Joy (White) [Mrs. Chester] Pratt. As special reporter for the Boston *Post* in 1870, White covered woman suffrage conventions and related activities. She continued to report women's rights activities and local news and advised on fashion and household problems for the Boston *Herald* until shortly before her death. See Arthur and Elizabeth Schlesinger Library on the History of Women in America, *The Manuscript Inventories and the Catalogs of the Manuscripts, Books and Pictures,* vol. III (Boston: G. K. Hall & Co., 1973).

6,949. White, Sue Shelton
Papers. 1913-59. 4 Hollinger boxes.
Open. Published and unpublished guides.
Schlesinger Library.
Correspondence, manuscripts, articles, and photos record the career of White (1887-1943) as a suffrage worker in Tennessee and on the national level. She also served as secretary to Senator Kenneth McKellar of Tennessee, assistant to Mary Harriman L. Rumsey, and chairman of the consumers' advisory board of the National Recovery Administration; in addition, she worked in the women's division of the Democratic National Committee. See Arthur and Elizabeth Schlesinger Library on the History of Women in America, *The Manuscript Inventories and the Catalogs of the Manuscripts, Books and Pictures,* vol. III (Boston: G. K. Hall & Co., 1973).

6,950. Whiting, Winifred (Hanus)
Papers. 1893-1944. 7 folders.
Open. Published and unpublished guides.
Schlesinger Library.
Constitution, membership list, correspondence, a pamphlet, a photo, and a clipping of the Mothers' Circle, a Cambridge club founded in 1893 and to which Whiting's mother Mrs. Paul Hanus belonged. Also included are papers Whiting wrote for the Mothers' Study Club and the Mothers' Discussion Club, other Cambridge groups of which she was a member. See Arthur and Elizabeth Schlesinger Library on the History of Women in America, *The Manuscript Inventories and the Catalogs of the*

Manuscripts, Books and Pictures, vol. III (Boston: G. K. Hall & Co., 1973).

6,951. Wiggin, Kate Douglas (Smith)
Papers. Nd. 1 item.
Open. Published and unpublished guides.
Schlesinger Library.
Letter of Wiggin (1856-1923), an author and kindergarten teacher, to Rowena Keit Keyes. See Arthur and Elizabeth Schlesinger Library on the History of Women in America, *The Manuscript Inventories and the Catalogs of the Manuscripts, Books and Pictures,* vol. III (Boston: G. K. Hall & Co., 1973).

6,952. Wilcox, Ella Wheeler
Papers. Nd. 2 items.
Open. Published and unpublished guides.
Schlesinger Library.
Letter and photo of Wilcox (1850-1919), a poet and journalist. See Arthur and Elizabeth Schlesinger Library on the History of Women in America, *The Manuscript Inventories and the Catalogs of the Manuscripts, Books and Pictures,* vol. III (Boston: G. K. Hall & Co., 1973).

6,953. Wiley, Anna (Kelton)
Papers. 1893-1962. 3.5 Hollinger boxes.
Open. Unpublished guide.
Schlesinger Library.
A member of many Washington, DC, clubs, [Mrs. Harvey W.] Wiley (1877-1964) was president of the National Woman's Party from 1930 to 1932 and 1940 to 1942, editor of *Equal Rights* from 1940 to 1945, and a lobbyist on behalf of many of the organizations with which she was involved. Personal and business correspondence; pamphlets and articles on suffrage, equal rights, and social reform; bulletins and programs of various clubs; and clippings. Wiley belonged to more than 10 organizations ranging from the DAR to the Consumers' League.

6,954. Willard, Frances Elizabeth Caroline
Papers. 1877-97. 13 items.
Open. Published and unpublished guides.
Schlesinger Library.
Letters of Willard (1839-98), a temperance leader and feminist, to Mrs. Aaron Macy Powell, John H. Vincent, and others. See Arthur and Elizabeth Schlesinger Library on the History of Women in America, *The Manuscript Inventories and the Catalogs of the Manuscripts, Books and Pictures,* vol. III (Boston: G. K. Hall & Co., 1973).

6,955. Williams, Blanche Colton
Papers. Ca. 1933-43. 1 carton.
Open. No guide.
Schlesinger Library.
A writer and editor, Williams (1879-1944) was also a professor of English at Hunter College. Correspondence, memorabilia, a magazine, photos, and other material include items Williams collected for her biography *Clara Barton,* information on Williams's life, articles she wrote, and a speech by Mrs. B. O. Fields on Williams.

6,956. Wilson, Elizabeth (Millar)
Papers. 1873-1944. 9 folders and 3 vols.
Open. Published and unpublished guides.
Schlesinger Library.
Wilson (1830-1913) was a pioneer who traveled West in 1851 to teach in The Dalles, OR; in 1873 after marriage and then the death of her husband Joseph G. Wilson, a circuit court judge in Oregon, she was appointed by President Grant postmistress of The Dalles. Correspondence, journals, and a manuscript contain accounts of her trip West and life in The Dalles. Also included are recollections by Wilson's daughter Lucy (Wilson) Peters, tributes to Joseph Wilson, and material relating to other Oregon pioneer families. See Arthur and Elizabeth Schlesinger Library on the History of Women in America, *The Manuscript Inventories and the Catalogs of the Manuscripts, Books and Pictures,* vol. III (Boston: G. K. Hall & Co., 1973).

6,957. Wilson, Woodrow
Papers. Nd. 1 item.
Open. Published and unpublished guides.
Schlesinger Library.
Statement by Wilson (1856-1924), US President from 1913 to 1921, on the position and role of women. See Arthur and Elizabeth Schlesinger Library on the History of Women in America, *The Manuscript Inventories and the Catalogs of the Manuscripts, Books and Pictures,* vol. III (Boston: G. K. Hall & Co., 1973).

6,958. Winslow, Mary N.
Papers. 1923-50. 1 Hollinger box and oversize items.
Open. Published and unpublished guides.
Schlesinger Library.
Papers of Winslow (1888-1952), a social worker, consist of correspondence, drafts of *Women at Work,* notes and manuscripts of political speeches and of articles on the employment of married women and the Inter-American Commission of Women, reports of the International Labor Organization Conference of American States held in Havana in 1939, and an autobiography of Mary Anderson as told to Winslow, as well as correspondence concerning publication of the autobiography. Correspondents include Edith Abbott, Mary Dewson, Mary Dingman, Lillian Gilbreth, Agnes O'Connor, Alice T. Post, Margaret Dreier Robins, and Harriet Taylor Upton. See Arthur and Elizabeth Schlesinger Library on the History of Women in America, *The Manuscript Inventories and the Catalogs of the Manuscripts, Books and Pictures,* vol. III (Boston: G. K. Hall & Co., 1973).

6,959. Winsor, Mary
Papers. 1917-40. 13 folders.
Open. Published and unpublished guides.
Schlesinger Library.
Manuscripts, pamphlets, and a newspaper of Winsor (1869-1956), a suffragist, woman's rights leader, and progressive, include biographical material and information about her prison experiences, a "Prison Special" train, sent around the country by the National Woman's Party, suffrage, equal rights, women for Congress, and the Inter-American Commission of Women. See Arthur and Elizabeth Schlesinger Library on the History of Women in America, *The Manuscript Inventories and the Catalogs of the Manuscripts, Books and Pictures,* vol. III (Boston: G. K. Hall & Co., 1973).

6,960. Woman Citizen Corporation
Records. 1916-49. 3 folders.
Open. Published and unpublished guides.
Schlesinger Library.
The Corporation was founded in 1917 to continue publishing the *Woman's Journal* and to advocate woman suffrage. Bylaws, financial reports, minutes of the board of directors for 1917 to 1919, advertising leaflets for the *Journal,* circulars for activities planned by the organization, a program of the Woman's Worlds Fair in 1925, and a lecture leaflet for Gertrude Foster [Mrs. Raymond] Brown. See Arthur and Elizabeth Schlesinger Library on the History of Women in America, *The Manuscript Inventories and the Catalogs of the Manuscripts, Books and Pictures,* vol. III (Boston: G. K. Hall & Co., 1973).

6,961. Woman Suffrage and Equality
Collection. 1860-1961. 8 items.
Open. Published and unpublished guides.
Schlesinger Library.
Manuscripts, post cards, publications, and memorabilia, including an 1877 "special appeal" signed by Lucy Stone, William Lloyd Garrison, and others and a 1961 article by Geoffrey Gorer, which was annotated by Ada (Comstock) Notestein. See Arthur and Elizabeth Schlesinger Library on the History of Women in America, *The Manuscript Inventories and the Catalogs of the Manuscripts, Books and Pictures,* vol. III (Boston: G. K. Hall & Co., 1973).

6,962. Woman's Education Association
Records. 1872-1951. 1 folder.
Open. Published and unpublished guides.
Schlesinger Library.
Annual reports, leaflets, clippings, and other records of the Association, founded in 1873 to promote educational progress for women and disbanded in 1929. Contains information on such Association projects as courses in botany and natural history, foreign scholarships, nursery schools, household aid, and district nursing. Also included is a manuscript of Eleanor W. Allen's "Review of the Instructive District Nursing Association, 1886-1951." See Arthur and Elizabeth Schlesinger Library on the History of Women in America, *The Manuscript Inventories and the Catalogs of the Manuscripts, Books and Pictures,* vol. III (Boston: G. K. Hall & Co., 1973).

6,963. Woman's Land Army of America
Records. 1917-19. 2 folders.
Open. Published and unpublished guides.
Schlesinger Library.
Reports, a diary, a memorandum, and a photo album of the Army, organized in ca. 1917 to train women to replace male laborers on farms during WWI. Records concern various Army training camps; included are annual reports for the Woman's Agricultural Camp in Bedford, NY, and for the Wellesley College Training Camp and Experiment Station. See Arthur and Elizabeth Schlesinger Library on the History of Women in America, *The Manuscript Inventories and the Catalogs of the Manuscripts, Books and Pictures,* vol. III (Boston: G. K. Hall & Co., 1973).

6,964. Woman's National Farm and Garden Association
Records. 1913-76. 42.5 Hollinger boxes, 3 cartons, 29 vols., and 2 drawers.
Open. Published and unpublished guides.
Schlesinger Library.
Constitutions, bylaws, financial reports, minutes, correspondence, membership lists, histories, photos, publications, and other records of the Association, founded in 1914 to promote agricultural and horticultural interests throughout the country. Includes records of the executive, advisory, personnel, education, and international committees; of local divisions; and annual reports of state divisions. Also included are copies of *Home Acres, The Recipe Exchange,* and *Farm and Garden Magazine;* papers of Mrs. David B. Buerger, president of the Association from 1968 to 1970; a history of the Maine division; material on the Lou Henry Hoover Girl Scout Fellowship, the Sarah Bradley Tyson Memorial Fellowship, the Lady Aberdeen Fellowship, and the Grace E. Frysinger Fellowship; and information on Frysinger, the Woman's Land Army, the Associated Country Women of the World, and its US Liaison Committee, which in 1954 was renamed the Country Women's Council USA. See Arthur and Elizabeth Schlesinger Library on the History of Women in America, *The Manuscript Inventories and the Catalogs of the Manuscripts, Books and Pictures,* vol. III (Boston: G. K. Hall & Co., 1973).

6,965. Woman's Relief Corps
Records. 1887-1907. 1 Hollinger box.
Open. Unpublished guide.
Schlesinger Library.
An auxiliary to the Grand Army of the Republic, the Corps was founded in 1883 to foster patriotism through acts of charity; its members were wives and daughters of Union veterans of the Civil War. Pamphlets, directives, speeches, material on

national conventions, notes on local activities and the deaths of prominent members, and other items. Corps activities included giving support to the GAR and erecting memorials to Union war dead and "loyal women."

6,966. Woman's Rights
Collection. 1853-1958. 85 Hollinger boxes, 9 oversize vols., and 39 items.
Open. Published and unpublished guides.
Schlesinger Library.
This collection of manuscripts concerning women and men involved in the woman's rights movement was a gift to Radcliffe from alumna Maud Wood Park; it formed the nucleus of the Women's Archives, which is now the Schlesinger Library. Correspondence, journals, notebooks, speeches, financial documents, reports, minutes, membership lists, agendas, bulletins, pamphlets, manuals, articles, clippings, maps, scrapbooks, photos, posters, memorabilia, plays, books, and other material. Highlighting the work done in Massachusetts, the collection also documents the suffrage movement and the gains for women in government participation, protective legislation, and employment opportunities since 1920. Includes information on little-known women, suffrage leaders, and professional women. Material on such suffrage groups as the Massachusetts Woman Suffrage Association, the National American Woman Suffrage Association, the Boston Equal Suffrage Association for Good Government, the Cambridge Political Equality Association, the National and Massachusetts LWVs, and the National Woman's Party is also included, as is information on the League of Nations Societies and the Women's International League for Peace and Freedom. See Arthur and Elizabeth Schlesinger Library on the History of Women in America, *The Manuscript Inventories and the Catalogs of the Manuscripts, Books and Pictures,* vol. III (Boston: G. K. Hall & Co., 1973).

6,967. Woman's Rights Collection: Allen, Florence Ellinwood
Papers. Ca. 1912-43. 1 folder.
Open. Published and unpublished guides.
Schlesinger Library.
Papers of Allen (1884-1966), an Ohio judge who was the first woman to sit on a state Supreme Court, consist of letters to Maud Wood Park and articles Allen wrote. See Arthur and Elizabeth Schlesinger Library on the History of Women in America, *The Manuscript Inventories and the Catalogs of the Manuscripts, Books and Pictures,* vol. III (Boston: G. K. Hall & Co., 1973).

6,968. Woman's Rights Collection: Ames, Blanche (Ames)
Papers. Ca. 1913-18. 3 folders.
Open. Published and unpublished guides.
Schlesinger Library.
Correspondence and other papers of Ames (1878-1969), an artist, concerning women's rights, suffrage, and the Shafroth Amendment. Ames was treasurer of the Massachusetts LWV from 1915 to 1918, president and cofounder of the Birth Control League of Massachusetts, and president of the New England Hospital from 1952 to 1954. See Arthur and Elizabeth Schlesinger Library on the History of Women in America, *The Manuscript Inventories and the Catalogs of the Manuscripts, Books and Pictures,* vol. III (Boston: G. K. Hall & Co., 1973).

6,969. Woman's Rights Collection: Ames, Fanny B.
Papers. 1907-43. 1 folder.
Open. Published and unpublished guides.
Schlesinger Library.
Correspondence and memorial address of Ames (1840-1931), first president of the Boston Equal Suffrage Association. Includes a letter to Edna Stantial from Alice (Ames) Winter on Winter's mother's mother, Fanny Ames. See Arthur and Elizabeth Schlesinger Library on the History of Women in America, *The Manuscript Inventories and the Catalogs of the Manuscripts, Books and Pictures,* vol. III (Boston: G. K. Hall & Co., 1973).

6,970. Woman's Rights Collection: Bagley, Grace Hodge
Papers. 1905-45. 1 folder.
Open. Published and unpublished guides.
Schlesinger Library.
Papers of Bagley (1860-1944), a social worker at Hull House who also was active in Massachusetts suffrage organizations, contain letters and a speech on suffrage, notes on Mary Meecham, and addresses memorializing Bagley. See Arthur and Elizabeth Schlesinger Library on the History of Women in America, *The Manuscript Inventories and the Catalogs of the Manuscripts, Books and Pictures,* vol. III (Boston: G. K. Hall & Co., 1973).

6,971. Woman's Rights Collection: Blackwell, Alice Stone
Papers. 1893-1946. 5 folders.
Open. Published and unpublished guides.
Schlesinger Library.
Correspondence, biographical information, manuscripts of writings, articles, and memorabilia of Stone (1857-1950), a journalist and suffragist. Stone assisted her parents Lucy Stone and Henry B. Blackwell with *The Woman's Journal* from 1881 until their deaths; in 1893 she became editor-in-chief of the *Journal.* She also was a contributing editor of *The Woman Citizen,* secretary of the National American Woman Suffrage Association for 20 years, and president of the New England and Massachusetts Woman Suffrage Associations. See Arthur and Elizabeth Schlesinger Library on the History of Women in America, *The Manuscript Inventories and the Catalogs of the Manuscripts, Books and Pictures,* vol. III (Boston: G. K. Hall & Co., 1973).

6,972. Woman's Rights Collection: Catt, Carrie Clinton (Lane) Chapman
Papers. 1904-47. Ca. 0.5 Hollinger box.
Open. Published and unpublished guides.
Schlesinger Library.
Correspondence, 1914-17; photos; writings of; and articles, poems, and speeches about Catt (1859-1947), a suffragist. From 1895 she worked with the National American Woman Suffrage Association, of which she was president from 1900 to 1904 and from 1915 on; she was president of the International Woman Suffrage Alliance from 1904 through 1923; and in 1919 she founded the National LWV. See Arthur and Elizabeth Schlesinger Library on the History of Women in America, *The Manuscript Inventories and the Catalogs of the Manuscripts, Books and Pictures,* vol. III (Boston: G. K. Hall & Co., 1973).

6,973. Woman's Rights Collection: Dewson, Mary Williams
Papers. 1917-61. Ca. 0.5 Hollinger box.
Open. Published and unpublished guides.
Schlesinger Library.
Correspondence, reports, scrapbooks, and other papers of Dewson (1874-1962), an industrial economist, including articles by and about her, speeches and material concerning the Reporter plan and the Democratic national campaign of 1936, as well as documents pertaining to Adkins vs. The Children's Hospital, 1922; Gainer vs. Dohrman; and a 1912 Report of the Committee on Minimum Wage Board. Dewson worked for the Democratic National Committee from 1928 to 1937; she was a member of the advisory council of the President's Commission on Economic Security and from 1933 through 1935 of the Consumers' Advisory Board of the National Recovery Administration. She also was a member of the Social Security Board in 1937 and 1938 and director of the International Migration Service. See Arthur and Elizabeth Schlesinger Library on the History of Women in America, *The Manuscript Inventories and the Catalogs of the Manuscripts, Books and Pictures,* vol. III (Boston: G. K. Hall & Co., 1973).

6,974. Woman's Rights Collection: Evans, Elizabeth (Gardiner)
Papers. 1913-43. 1 folder.
Open. Published and unpublished guides.
Schlesinger Library.
Papers of [Mrs. Glendower] Evans (1856-1937), a reformer who was active in labor law reform, suffrage, and the Sacco-Vanzetti case, consist of correspondence on peace and suffrage, Evans's writings on Sacco-Vanzetti, poems by Alice Stone Blackwell and James Russell Lowell, and addresses for a meeting memorializing Evans. See Arthur and Elizabeth Schlesinger Library on the History of Women in America, *The Manuscript Inventories and the Catalogs of the Manuscripts, Books and Pictures,* vol. III (Boston: G. K. Hall & Co., 1973).

6,975. Woman's Rights Collection: Foster, Abigail "Abby" (Kelley)
Papers. Nd. 1 item.
Open. Published and unpublished guides.
Schlesinger Library.
Letter to Lucy Stone concerning Oberlin College by Foster (1810-87), an abolitionist and woman's rights advocate. In 1840 Foster was appointed to the executive committee of the American Anti-Slavery Society; after 1850 she concentrated more on woman's rights and took part in most woman's rights conventions for the next 20 years. See Arthur and Elizabeth Schlesinger Library on the History of Women in America, *The Manuscript Inventories and the Catalogs of the Manuscripts, Books and Pictures,* vol. III (Boston: G. K. Hall & Co., 1973).

6,976. Woman's Rights Collection: Gardener, Helen Hamilton
Papers. 1895-1930. 8 folders and 1 vol.
Open. Published and unpublished guides.
Schlesinger Library.
An advocate of woman suffrage and National American Woman Suffrage Association president, Gardener (1853-1925) was also appointed in 1920 by President Wilson to the Civil Service Commission. Personal and business correspondence, letters about her, writings, photo, clippings, material about suffrage, memorabilia, and obituaries and other material on her funeral and memorial service. A pseudonym, Gardener became her legal name. She was born Alice Chenoweth and married Charles Selden Smart and then Col. Selden Allen Day. See Arthur and Elizabeth Schlesinger Library on the History of Women in America, *The Manuscript Inventories and the Catalogs of the Manuscripts, Books and Pictures,* vol. III (Boston: G. K. Hall & Co., 1973).

6,977. Woman's Rights Collection: Johnson, Ethel McLean
Papers. 1913-45. Ca. 1.5 Hollinger boxes.
Open. Published and unpublished guides.
Schlesinger Library.
An economist, Johnson represented the governors of Massachusetts and New Hampshire at interstate conferences on labor legislation between 1931 and 1935 and then between 1935 and 1943 worked for the International Labor Organization in a number of capacities. Correspondence; speeches; articles she wrote; reports from the New Hampshire Commission on Interstate Compacts, 1934-35, and from the New Hampshire Minimum Wage Office, 1934-36; material on the ILO; publications; clippings; and photos. See Arthur and Elizabeth Schlesinger Library on the History of Women in America, *The Manuscript Inventories and the Catalogs of the Manuscripts, Books and Pictures,* vol. III (Boston: G. K. Hall & Co., 1973).

6,978. Woman's Rights Collection: Johnson, Grace A.
Papers. 1893-1948. Ca. 37 Hollinger boxes.
Open. Published and unpublished guides.
Schlesinger Library.
Johnson (1871-1952) served as state congressional chairman of the Massachusetts Woman Suffrage Association and in 1917 as chairman of its board, as a member of the national council of the National American Woman Suffrage Association, from 1915 to 1917, as a member of the council of the Massachusetts Foreign Policy Association from 1927 on, as chairman of the Educational Committee of the Massachusetts League of Nations Association from 1926 to 1933, and as a lecturer at schools and universities in the Boston area. Correspondence, notes and outlines, financial papers, reports, minutes, membership lists, bulletins, pamphlets, manuals, posters, scrapbooks, photos, memorabilia, and other items. Includes records of 20 Massachusetts and national suffrage organizations, particularly those of the Cambridge Political Equality Association, the Massachusetts Suffrage Association, and the Boston Equal Suffrage Association for Good Government. Also included is material on the national, state, Cambridge, and Boston LWVs. Other material concerns the League of Nations, the World Court, the UN, and societies which disseminated information and advised support of the League, as well as the Foreign Policy Association, the Women's International League for Peace and Freedom, and the National and International Councils of Women. Johnson's writings and documents she collected include information on the status of women; state, national, and international government; and morality. Topics include immigration and naturalization, neutrality law, prohibition, single tax, disarmament, women leaders and world progress, civil service in Massachusetts, India and Gandhi, and birth control and social disease. Authors of some of this material include Maud Wood Park, Ethel M. Johnson, and Jane Addams. See Arthur and Elizabeth Schlesinger Library on the History of Women in America, *The Manuscript Inventories and the Catalogs of the Manuscripts, Books and Pictures,* vol. III (Boston: G. K. Hall & Co., 1973).

6,979. Woman's Rights Collection: Loines, Mary Hilliard
Papers. 1869-1940. Ca. 1 Hollinger box.
Open. Published and unpublished guides.
Schlesinger Library.
Correspondence, writings, reports, pamphlet, photo, and scrapbook of Loines (1844-1944), head of the Brooklyn, NY, Woman's Suffrage Association from 1899 to 1919. Contains material of such organizations as the Brooklyn Association, the New York State Woman Suffrage Association, the National American Woman Suffrage Association, the Interurban Woman Suffrage Council, the Woman Suffrage Party of the City of New York, and the American Equal Rights Association. See Arthur and Elizabeth Schlesinger Library on the History of Women in America, *The Manuscript Inventories and the Catalogs of the Manuscripts, Books and Pictures,* vol. III (Boston: G. K. Hall & Co., 1973).

6,980. Woman's Rights Collection: Luscomb, Florence H.
Papers. 1909-59. Ca. 0.5 Hollinger box.
Open. Published and unpublished guides.
Schlesinger Library.
Formerly a suffragist, Luscomb (1887-) is a civil rights worker; after serving as a leader in the Massachusetts and Boston Equal Suffrage Associations and as executive secretary of the Boston LWV, she became vice-president of the state Civil Liberties Union and state chairman of the Massachusetts Progressive Party. Correspondence, her writings and notes, flyers, photos, clippings, and memorabilia. Includes letters to Alice Stone Blackwell and Edna Stantial as well as material concerning the World Court, the NAACP, the Progressive Peace Party, and civil liberties. See Arthur and Elizabeth Schlesinger Library on the History of Women in America, *The Manuscript Inventories and the Catalogs of the Manuscripts, Books and Pictures,* vol. III (Boston: G. K. Hall & Co., 1973).

6,981. Woman's Rights Collection: Park, Maud (Wood)
Papers. 1870-1951. Ca. 18 Hollinger boxes.
Open. Published and unpublished guides.
Schlesinger Library.
A suffragist and writer, Park (1871-1955) was founder and president of the first branch of the College Equal Suffrage League, secretary of the Boston Equal Suffrage Association for Good Government, and first president of the National LWV. Correspondence, financial reports, minutes, membership lists, bulletins, pamphlets, photos, articles, clippings, scrapbooks, memorabilia, and her manuscripts for the books *Front Door Lobby* and *Lisa* and for short stories, poems, speeches, and plays such as "Abigail Adams," "Lucy Stone," and "Moonstruck." Much of the collection relates to woman's rights, with material on organizations with which Park was involved and on the Massachusetts Woman Suffrage Association and its local chapters, the Woman Suffrage Party, the National American Woman Suffrage Association, the Cambridge Political Equality Association, the state LWV, and the Women's Joint Congressional Committee. Also included is some antisuffrage literature and material concerning the Children's Bureau, the World Woman's Party, the National Woman's Party, and race relations. Also included are Park's notes and reports on her trip around the world in 1909 and 1910, with information on the status of women in 14 countries ranging from Finland and Norway to Turkey, Siam, and Australia. See Arthur and Elizabeth Schlesinger Library on the History of Women in America, *The Manuscript Inventories and the Catalogs of the Manuscripts, Books and Pictures,* vol. III (Boston: G. K. Hall & Co., 1973).

6,982. Woman's Rights Collection: Perkins, Frances
Papers. 1919?-52. Ca. 10.5 Hollinger boxes.
Open. Published and unpublished guides.
Schlesinger Library.
After working as the executive secretary of the New York Consumers' League from 1910 to 1912 and as a factory investigator, Perkins (1882-1965) was industrial commissioner of the state of New York from 1929 to 1933, secretary of the US Department of Labor from 1933 to 1945, and a member of the US Civil Service Commission from 1946 to 1953. Correspondence, manuscripts for speeches and other writings, minutes, annual reports, clippings, and other material, most of which pertains to the Department of Labor, with records of the International Labor Organization and its governing body in Geneva, records of the Committee on Economic Security, and material on other labor-related government agencies. See Arthur and Elizabeth Schlesinger Library on the History of Women in America, *The Manuscript Inventories and the Catalogs of the Manuscripts, Books and Pictures,* vol. III (Boston: G. K. Hall & Co., 1973).

6,983. Woman's Rights Collection: Shaw, Anna Howard
Papers. 1908-43. 5 folders.
Open. Published and unpublished guides.
Schlesinger Library.
A reformer, physician, and minister, Shaw (1847-1919) was vice-president at large of the National American Woman Suffrage Association from 1892 to 1904 and NAWSA's president from 1904 to 1915. Correspondence, pamphlet, clippings, and memorabilia concern her suffrage work. See Arthur and Elizabeth Schlesinger Library on the History of Women in America, *The Manuscript Inventories and the Catalogs of the Manuscripts, Books and Pictures,* vol. III (Boston: G. K. Hall & Co., 1973).

6,984. Woman's Rights Collection: Shaw, Pauline (Agassiz)
Papers. 1900-32. 4 folders.
Open. Published and unpublished guides.
Schlesinger Library.
Correspondence, articles, and other papers of Shaw (1841-1917), a philanthropist who was a pioneer in education and social service. Includes a sonnet to Shaw and information on the Boston Equal Suffrage Association for Good Government. See Arthur and Elizabeth Schlesinger Library on the History of Women in America, *The Manuscript Inventories and the Catalogs of the Manuscripts, Books and Pictures,* vol. III (Boston: G. K. Hall & Co., 1973).

6,985. Woman's Rights Collection: Upton, Harriet (Taylor)
Papers. 1897-1925. 2 folders.
Open. Published and unpublished guides.
Schlesinger Library.
Correspondence, memorabilia, and articles regarding speeches of Upton (1853-1945), a suffragist who was president of the Ohio Woman Suffrage Association from 1899 to 1919 and treasurer of the National American Woman Suffrage Association for 15 years. Includes information on the Ohio Association. See Arthur and Elizabeth Schlesinger Library on the History of Women in America, *The Manuscript Inventories and the Catalogs of the Manuscripts, Books and Pictures,* vol. III (Boston: G. K. Hall & Co., 1973).

6,986. Women in Science
Collection. 1935-40. 10 Hollinger boxes and 1 oversize vol.
Open. Published and unpublished guides.
Schlesinger Library.
Correspondence, financial records, clippings, photos, and publications collected for a Radcliffe College exhibit held in 1936 in connection with Harvard University's tercentenary celebration. Correspondence concerns the exhibit, while the published articles which made up the final exhibit are by women who were conducting research in astronomy, biology, geology, chemistry, physics, and the medical sciences. See Arthur and Elizabeth Schlesinger Library on the History of Women in America, *The Manuscript Inventories and the Catalogs of the Manuscripts, Books and Pictures,* vol. III (Boston: G. K. Hall & Co., 1973).

6,987. Women in the Birth Control Movement and in Maternal and Child Health
Oral history. 1973-75. 11 vols. and 66 tapes.
Open. Unpublished guide.
Schlesinger Library.
This Schlesinger-Rockefeller Series of oral history tapes and transcripts contains the biography, career accomplishments, and views of 11 women working in population control and maternal and child health, as well as their opinions of others working in the field. The women interviewed are registered nurse Elizabeth Arnold, clinic supervisor of the Margaret Sanger Research Bureau from 1957 to 1970, and between 1969 and 1972 with Julia Tsuei, founder of the Maternal and Child Health Demonstration Project in Taipei, Taiwan; physician Mary (Steichen) Calderone, director from 1964 to 1975 and chairman from 1975 of the Sex Information and Education Council of the US; Loraine Leeson Campbell, member of the board from 1941 to 1969 and president from 1957 to 1959 of the Planned Parenthood Federation of America; physician Florence Clothier, director from 1945 to 1957 and president from 1953 to 1956 of the Planned Parenthood League of Massachusetts; physician Martha May Eliot, chief of the Children's Bureau from 1951 to 1957,

professor of maternal and child health at the Harvard School of Public Health from 1957 to 1960, and a founder of the World Health Organization; Frances (Hand) [Mrs. Robert M.] Ferguson, a volunteer worker with the national and International Planned Parenthood Federations; Leonore Guttmacher, wife of physician Alan F. Guttmacher; physician Louise Gilman Hutchins, a public health, maternal and child health, and family planning worker in Kentucky; counselor Emily Hartshorne Mudd, founder in 1933 and director from 1936 to 1937 of the Marriage Council of Philadelphia as well as a founding member and president of the American Association of Marriage and Family Counselors and professor at the medical school of the University of Pennsylvania; Adaline Pendleton Satterthwaite, a physician at the Ryder Memorial Hospital in Humacao, PR, from 1952 to 1963 and a member of the field staff of the technical services division of the Population Council from 1965; and physician Julia Tsuei, a fellow of the Sanger Research Bureau, family planning worker in Taipei, Taiwan, and founder with Elizabeth Arnold of the Demonstration Project in Taipei.

6,988. Women United for the United Nations
Records. Ca. 1966. 2 Hollinger boxes.
Open. No guide.
Schlesinger Library.
Minutes of membership meetings and of the steering committee, correspondence, a general history, scrapbooks, and a magazine of WUUN. Includes slides and scrapbooks on the Woonsocket Project, which was a pilot project consisting of a trip to the UN by members of Woonsocket, RI, organizations and a United Nations Week in Woonsocket, both of which occurred in 1961.

6,989. Women's Educational and Industrial Union
Records. 1878-1955. 11 Hollinger boxes.
Open. Published and unpublished guides.
Schlesinger Library.
Records of the Union, founded in Boston in 1877 to promote the advancement of women, consist of a manuscript history of the Union written by S. Agnes Donham; reports of the research department for 1898 to 1931 on domestic service, immigrant women and their protection, industrial opportunities for women and girls, and old age security; and printed material from 1878 to 1920 on such departments as the domestic reform league, the school of housekeeping, the handiwork shop, school lunches, and the New England kitchen. Other boxes reveal the work of the appointment bureau between 1907 and 1933 and its relation to other "bureaus of occupation." See Arthur and Elizabeth Schlesinger Library on the History of Women in America, *The Manuscript Inventories and the Catalogs of the Manuscripts, Books and Pictures,* vol. III (Boston: G. K. Hall & Co., 1973).

6,990. Women's Equity Action League
Records. 1968-76. 6.5 Hollinger boxes, 4 cartons, and 5 folders.
Partially restricted. No guide.
Schlesinger Library.
Bylaws, correspondence, speeches, newsletters, printed material, and clippings of WEAL, an organization founded in 1968 to promote the equality of women through legal and legislative action. Included is information on the national board and a national convention; the New Jersey, Michigan, and South Carolina divisions; the 1973 annual conference in California; various committees; and Title IX.

6,991. Women's History Research Center and Library
Records. Ca. 1971-75. 9 cartons and 7 boxes.
Partially restricted. No guide.
Schlesinger Library.
The Center was established in Berkeley, CA, in 1968 to collect information on contemporary women and to answer requests for information; financial conditions later caused the Center to curtail its activities. Office and internal files, correspondence of the children's department and of women's periodicals; research letters on law, health, and the press; logbooks of invitations and titles; progress reports; material on interns and volunteers; and memorabilia.

6,992. Women's Travel Club
Records. 1947-73. 1 Hollinger box and 0.5 drawer.
Open. No guide.
Schlesinger Library.
Minutes, correspondence, and other records of the Club, founded in ca. 1940 to foster world exploration by women. Includes material on talks entitled "Breadfruit in the Baggage," "A Seaplane Cruise in the Canadian Arctic," "Pastoral Warriors in Uganda," and "Archaeological Findings in Shantung Province."

6,993. Woodhull, Victoria (Claflin)
Papers. 1873. 1 item.
Open. Published and unpublished guides.
Schlesinger Library.
Letter to "My Dear Friend" written by Woodhull (1838-1927), a reformer and supporter of women's rights, concerns the Tilton case. See Arthur and Elizabeth Schlesinger Library on the History of Women in America, *The Manuscript Inventories and the Catalogs of the Manuscripts, Books and Pictures,* vol. III (Boston: G. K. Hall & Co., 1973).

6,994. Woodward, Ellen (Sullivan)
Papers. 1927-54. 2 Hollinger boxes.
Open. Published and unpublished guides.
Schlesinger Library.
Correspondence, speeches, and articles of Woodward (?-1971), a public official and suffrage advocate, concern the Mississippi State Board of Development, the WPA, the Social Security Board, the UN Relief and Rehabilitation Administration, the Business and Professional Women's Clubs of Washington, DC, Susan B. Anthony, and women in the work force. See Arthur and Elizabeth Schlesinger Library on the History of Women in America, *The Manuscript Inventories and the Catalogs of the Manuscripts, Books and Pictures,* vol. III (Boston: G. K. Hall & Co., 1973).

6,995. World Center for Women's Archives
Records. 1936-38. 2 folders.
Open. Published and unpublished guides.
Schlesinger Library.
Correspondence and publications of the Archives, which was to be a repository for the papers of women, and a manuscript by Maud Nathan. See Arthur and Elizabeth Schlesinger Library on the History of Women in America, *The Manuscript Inventories and the Catalogs of the Manuscripts, Books and Pictures,* vol. III (Boston: G. K. Hall & Co., 1973).

6,996. Yates, John Van Ness
Papers. 1823. 3-page item.
Open. Published and unpublished guides.
Schlesinger Library.
Letter of Yates (1779-1839), an Albany, NY, lawyer, to Benjamin F. Thompson in Suffolk County, NY, about the right of women to vote as "free holders." See Arthur and Elizabeth Schlesinger Library on the History of Women in America, *The Manuscript Inventories and the Catalogs of the Manuscripts, Books and Pictures,* vol. III (Boston: G. K. Hall & Co., 1973).

6,997. Zeiger, Dorothy Child (Cross) Remington
Papers. 1903-62. 1 Hollinger box.
Open. Published and unpublished guides.
Schlesinger Library.
Correspondence, biographical data, photos, memorabilia, and other papers of Zeiger (1890-), the first white teacher at Central State College in Wilberforce, OH, which is a predominantly Negro institution. Includes information on Zeiger's education, activities, and the College; her poems, essays, speeches, and articles on education, human relations, and democracy; and a scrapbook of clippings concerning her presidency of the Roseland PTA. See Arthur and Elizabeth Schlesinger Library on the History of Women in America, *The Manuscript Inventories and the Catalogs of the Manuscripts, Books and Pictures,* vol. III (Boston: G. K. Hall & Co., 1973).

DANVERS

6,998. Autograph and Remembrance Albums
Collection. 1825-62. 8 vols.
Open. Card catalog.
Danvers Archival Center.
Albums containing poetry, sentimental notes, pencil drawings, and watercolors belonged to Lydia P. Tapley, Elizabeth Putnam, Cornelia Benedict, C. A. Preston, Augusta Osborn, Harriet P. Fowler, and Martha C. Black.

6,999. Boardman, Nancy Ellen
Papers. 1854-55. 2 vols.
Open. Card catalog.
Danvers Archival Center.
Diaries in which Boardman (1825-?), a teacher, comments on school, church and social activities in Danvers, the weather, and her marriage to Edward A. Lord in 1855.

7,000. Danvers Women's Association
Records. 1882-1960s. Ca. 104 vols. and 300 items.
Open. Card catalog.
Danvers Archival Center.
Organized in 1882, this social club for women still exists. Records of the treasurer, the secretary, and of meetings; committee reports; reports on special projects; correspondence; programs; a history of the founding and first year of the Association; yearbooks; copies of "The Echo," which contain announcements, news, and poetry; scrapbooks; and other material concerning the Association and Danvers.

7,001. First Church, Congregational
Records. 1800s-1900s. No size given.
Open. Card catalog.
Danvers Archival Center.
Record books, a notebook, and a typescript pertain to women's organizations of the Danvers Church. Included are one volume of records of the Female Domestic Missionary Society, 1832-46; brief records of the Female Society, 1831; and records of meetings, financial accounts, and scrapbooks of the Ladies Benevolent Society, 1832-1959. Also included are a history of the Benevolent Society written in 1932 by Florence Augusta Mudge and an 1815 volume in which Emma Putnam made notes on the sermons of a Rev. Wadsworth.

7,002. Fowler, Harriet P., II
Papers. 1890. 1 vol.
Open. Card catalog.
Danvers Archival Center.
Catalog of pamphlets, photos, curiosities, books, and other items belonging to Harriet P. Fowler II (1806-91).

7,003. Hood Family
Papers. 1803-1926. Ca. 225 items.
Open. Card catalog.
Danvers Archival Center.
Correspondence, diary, receipts, and legal documents of the Danvers family, including essays written by Lizzie Frances Hood (1864-?), papers of Harriet Parker Hood (1834-?), and letters in which

Helen Dodge Hood (1892-) describes her work with the YMCA in France during 1919.

7,004. Maple Street Congregational Church
Records. 1800s-1900s. No size given.
Open. Card catalog.
Danvers Archival Center.
Record books and printed material pertain to women's organizations of the Danvers Church. Included are 1846-1905 volumes containing constitution, meeting records, and membership lists of the Ladies Society, 1846-1905; a volume containing constitution, meeting records, lists of officers, and yearly bulletins of the United Women Workers, 1904-10; volumes of meeting records, annual reports, financial accounts, programs, booklets, and yearbooks of the Women's Society, 1920-68; and volumes containing constitution, meeting reports, and membership lists of the Women's Foreign Missionary Society, 1876-1920.

7,005. Mudge, Sarah Wilson
Papers. 1870-1918. 3 vols.
Open. Card catalog.
Danvers Archival Center.
Diary in which Mudge (1857-1938), a daughter of Edwin Mudge (1818-90), makes notations about family, friends, and activities in Danvers and Boston.

7,006. Philbrick, Julia A.
Papers. 1890. 18-page ms.
Open. Card catalog.
Danvers Archival Center.
Historical monograph of [Mrs. John Dudley] Philbrick (1819-?) concerns the building and occupants of the old school house in Danvers. Also included is information on the Female Benevolent Society in Danvers.

7,007. Proctor, Elizabeth
Papers. 1788-95. 2 vols. and 1 item.
Open. Card catalog.
Danvers Archival Center.
Papers of Proctor (1750-1824), a teacher, consist of accounts concerning the length of time and cost for instructing individual pupils and personal items purchased. Also included are letters and a poem "To the Discontented and Unquiet."

7,008. Putnam, Louisa Jane
Papers. 1840. 1 vol.
Open. Card catalog.
Danvers Archival Center.
Diary in which Putnam, the daughter of Elias Putnam, notes family and neighborhood events in the Putnamville section of Danvers. Also contains information about the Page and Pedrick families, the Whig party, and William Henry Harrison's presidential campaign.

7,009. Putnam, Louisa Lancaster
Papers. 1858-59. 1 vol.
Open. Card catalog.
Danvers Archival Center.
Album containing sentiments written by friends of Putnam, a Holten High School graduate.

7,010. Women's Centennial Society of Danvers
Records. 1876. 1 vol.
Open. Card catalog.
Danvers Archival Center.
Reports of the Society, which was founded to plan for the centennial celebration of the US, concern officers elected, a treasurer's account, and a catalog of an exhibit of historical memorabilia at the Peabody Institute Library in Danvers, MA.

DEERFIELD

7,011. Baker, Charlotte Alice
Papers. Ca. 1850-1909. 7 boxes, 10 vols., and 2 microfilm reels.
Open. No guide.
Pocumtuck Valley Memorial Association Library.
Correspondence, research notes, working papers, manuscripts of writings, scrapbooks, and clippings of Baker (1833-1909), a teacher, principal of private schools in Chicago and Boston, research historian, and preservationist. Baker was responsible for some of the first restoration efforts in Deerfield; she also wrote numerous historical articles and papers.

7,012. Deerfield Industries
Collection. 1896-ca. 1935. 15 boxes.
Open. No guide.
Pocumtuck Valley Memorial Association Library.
Deerfield Industries was the informal title of a local arts and crafts revival movement led by Deerfield women. The movement began in 1896 with the formation of the Society of Blue and White Needlework by [Miss] Ellen Miller and [Miss] Margaret Whiting; in ca. 1899 the Deerfield Society of Arts and Crafts was organized. Correspondence and other records of the Arts and Crafts Society, the basket makers, and other crafts groups; account books; notebooks; programs; exhibit catalogs; extensive holdings of embroidery patterns; photos; scrapbooks; and clippings. Other skills revived included the crafting of handmade rugs, raffia and willow baskets, ceramics, netting, and jewelry as well as blacksmithing and photography. Collection contains information on photographers Frances Stebbins Allen and her sister Mary Electa Allen; Gertrude (Porter) [Mrs. Charles Hart] Ashley, who wrote books on raffia basketry; and authors Madeline (Yale) Wynne, Elizabeth (Williams) [Mrs. James Wells] Champney, Lucy Agnes Pratt, Emma Lewis Coleman, and Edith (Barnard) [Mrs. James] Delano. The revival, influenced by the "new clairvaux" movement in Montague, MA, and through the work of Elbert Hubbard in East Aurora, NY, was best known for its needlework.

7,013. Sheldon, Jennie Maria (Arms)
Papers. Ca. 1890-1938. 5 vols.
Open. No guide.
Pocumtuck Valley Memorial Association Library.
Correspondence, notes, and working papers of [Mrs. George] Sheldon (1852-1938), a scientist, teacher at the Massachusetts Institute of Technology, and local history researcher.

DENNIS

7,014. Fairbank Family
Papers. 1759-1969. 2 drawers.
Open. Card file.
Dennis Historical Society Library, Josiah Dennis Manse.
Family papers, the bulk of which is correspondence of Sarah Elizabeth Gulliver (1801-70) with Josiah Fairbank (1794-1878), before and after their marriage in 1827. Josiah Fairbank was a schoolteacher who opened a private school in Milton, MA, in 1845. Collection also includes correspondence of his mother Deborah (Clark) Fairbank and of her sister Mary (Clark) Fairbank, both of whom were married to his father Josiah Fairbank, Sr. (1761-95). Also includes correspondence and essays by Mary Bumstead, a teacher, and correspondence of other members of the related Gulliver, Clark, Brown, Bumstead, Stone, Vose, and Leonard families. Four years after her husband's death, Deborah (Clark) Fairbank married clergyman Benjamin Stone.

DIGHTON

7,015. Beck, Mabel Lane
Papers. 1917-19. 1 folder.
Open. File cards.
Dighton Historical Society.
Correspondence of Beck (1892-1958), a nurse who served overseas during WWI.

7,016. Ingalls, Marguerite
Papers. 1954-67. 1 carton.
Open. File cards.
Dighton Historical Society.
Dighton news reports written by Ingalls (1888-1971), a housewife and correspondent for the *Taunton Daily Gazette.*

7,017. Lane, Helen H. (Holmes)
Papers. 1690- . Ca. 18 vols. and 5 cartons.
Open. File cards.
Dighton Historical Society.
Lane (1889-) is a retired teacher and local historian who wrote a history of Dighton in 1962. Booklets, photos, clippings, and other historical notes and material she collected include information about the fire and police departments, the military, industries, old homes, prominent persons, and areas in which women were active, particularly the schools, churches, Dighton Rock Grange No. 314, and other town matters.

7,018. Spooner
Papers. 1848-56. 5 vols. and 1 item.
Open. File cards.
Dighton Historical Society.
Journal of Emily Noyes Spooner (1835-59) is included with diaries written by men and a drawing of a toll house.

7,019. White, A. Ruth Staples
Papers. 1917-19. 1 box.
Open. File cards.
Dighton Historical Society.
Correspondence, an entertainment program, and a dinner menu of White (1895?-) who, after serving overseas as a nurse during WWI, became a housewife and mother.

DORCHESTER

7,020. Athena Club
Records. Nd. No size given.
Open. No guide.
Dorchester Historical Society.
Bylaws and minutes of the Club.

7,021. Dorchester Women's Club
Records. Nd. No size given.
Open. No guide.
Dorchester Historical Society.
Includes a history of Dorchester, which was written by the Club's history class.

7,022. Stone, Lucy
Papers. Nd. No size given.
Open. No guide.
Dorchester Historical Society.
Papers of Stone, a suffragist.

EASTHAM

7,023. Archives
Records. Ca. 1644- . No size given.
Access restricted. No guide.
Eastham Historical Society, Inc.
Scrapbooks about life in Eastham and Cape Cod include information about Alice Lowe, author of *Nauset on Cape Cod* and a founder of the Historical Society, and other local women.

Eastham, which originally was known as Nauset, was settled in 1644.

EDGARTOWN

7,024. Bailey, Harriet Frances
Papers. 1930s. 4 envelopes.
Open. Unpublished guide.
Dukes County Historical Society.
A diary, manuscript and printed poems, and clippings of Bailey (1918-38), an author and poet.

7,025. Hamilton, Gail
Papers. 1861-83. 41 items.
Open. Unpublished guide.
Dukes County Historical Society.
Gail Hamilton was the pseudonym of Mary Abigail Dodge (1833-96), an author and reformer. Letters from family members, Ralph Waldo Emerson, Edward N. Kirk, Charles and Lida Nordhoff, and Nathaniel Hawthorne's wife Sophia Hawthorne and his daughters Rose and Una Hawthorne.

7,026. Luce, Nancy
Papers. 1840s-80s. 5 items.
Open. Unpublished guide.
Dukes County Historical Society.
Correspondence, bills, manuscripts, photos, clippings, and a printed booklet of the work of Luce (1820-90), a poet. Living by herself on a farm, Luce kept chickens in her house as pets. Her book of poetry *Poor Little Hearts* is about her chickens. When her favorite chickens died, Luce erected gravestones for them and had poems she had written inscribed on them.

7,027. Smith, Hannah
Papers. 1813-42. 2 vols.
Open. Unpublished guide.
Dukes County Historical Society.
Diaries of Smith (1789-?), a poet, contain poetry.

7,028. Whaling Archives
Collection. Ca. 1780s-1930s. Ca. 10 ft.
Access restricted. Unpublished guide.
Dukes County Historical Society.
Correspondence, logbooks, and other material on whaling contain information on women that was used by Emma Mayhew Whiting and Henry Beetle Hough for their book *Whaling Wives* (Boston, 1953).

FALL RIVER

7,029. Shove, Phila
Papers. 1817-22. 3 vols.
Open. No guide.
Fall River Historical Society.
Diaries of [Miss] Shove (1791-?), a Quaker teacher who married and became a stepmother, concern life in a Quaker family.

FRAMINGHAM

7,030. Fuller, Meta Vaux Warwick
Papers. Nd. No size given.
Open. No guide.
Framingham Public Library.
Articles from periodicals and newspapers of Fuller (1877-1968), a Negro sculptor who studied under Auguste Rodin in Paris. Born in Philadelphia, Meta Fuller married Solomon Fuller, a psychiatrist who practiced in the Framingham area and taught at Boston University; the couple lived in Framingham. Collection also contains one of her sculptures.

7,031. Van Waters, Miriam
Papers. Nd. No size given.
Open. Catalog cards.
Framingham Public Library.
In 1931 Van Waters (1887-1974), a PhD, was appointed superintendent of the State Reformatory for Women at Framingham, which was renamed the Massachusetts Correctional Institution. Pamphlets about the Institution, clippings, a copy of her book *Youth in Conflict* (1925), and a biography of her. An author of articles on social work and capital punishment, Van Waters was named consultant to the Wickersham Commission under President Herbert Hoover because of her expertise in the field of juvenile delinquency. She introduced various innovations at the Correctional Institution, including expansion of the indenture system.

GLOUCESTER

7,032. Annisquam Sewing Circle
Records. 1837-1977. 18 vols.
Access restricted. No guide.
Annisquam Historical Society.
Constitution, bylaws, and complete minutes of the Sewing Circle, which was founded in 1837 as the Annisquam Female Benevolent Society; the group is said to be the oldest continuous society of women in the US. Beginning with 42 women who wanted to help the needy, the Circle has grown to 94 members who perform benevolent acts in Annisquam and the surrounding area and who provide a scholarship fund as well. The Society was founded by [Miss] Eunice C. Fellows; Nancy Leonard, widow of clergyman Ezra Leonard, was the first president. Fellows, with her sister Anstice Fellows, founded the first orphan asylum in Boston; the sisters also were editors of *The Orphans' Advocate* for several years. While living in Pigeon Cove, MA, Eunice Fellows also founded a group similar to the Benevolent Society.

GROTON

7,033. Founder's Corner
Records. 1825- . 30 vols. and other items.
Access restricted. No guide.
Sacred Heart Convent, Provincial House.
Correspondence of Jean Baptiste de Brabant, who founded the order in France in 1825, and of the first members; memoirs and biographies of members; reports on events connected with the work of the congregation; tapes; photos; slides; clippings; and other records. The congregation is involved primarily in teaching. Early correspondence is in French.

HANCOCK

7,034. Amelia, Sister
Papers. 1874-90. 1 vol.
Open. Catalog card.
Hancock Shaker Village, Library.
Diary in which Sister Amelia, a member of the United Society of Believers in Christ's Second Appearing community, recorded her daily activities; also includes unsigned entries by another Shaker sister.

7,035. Blue Dye Department
Records. 1839-65. 1 vol.
Open. No guide.
Hancock Shaker Village, Library.
A detailed journal account of dyemaking by the sisters of the New Lebanon, NY, Shaker community, which was established in 1787, includes a list of materials and explanation of the processing for each batch, revealing that the sisters experimented with dyeing techniques. Abigail Crossman and Betsy Coply kept the journal.

7,036. Cahoon, Hannah
Papers. 1817-99. 1 vol.
Open. No guide.
Hancock Shaker Village, Library.
Notebook made by Cahoon (1799-?), a member of the Hancock Shaker community, contains significant dates in her life as a Shaker worker, remarks on events in the Village, and the names and death dates of members of her family.

7,037. Calver, Amelia J.
Papers. 1875-82. 1 vol.
Open. No guide.
Hancock Shaker Village, Library.
Autograph album of Sister Calver (1844-1929), a schoolteacher in the New Lebanon, NY, Shaker community, contains autographs she requested from her contemporaries in the community and from important members of the sect. Each consists of a religious reflection, a remark on the nature of friendship, or an exhortation to good works, which were signed by the writer and usually dated; in many cases the autographs also included the signer's date of birth.

7,038. Deaconesses
Records. 1843-61. 1 vol.
Open. No guide.
Hancock Shaker Village, Library.
This journal of domestic events and economic transactions contains a description of the daily lives of Shaker sisters and news of their community in New Lebanon, NY. Emphasis is on work the sisters did for sale to the outside world, with lists of products from their laboratory, fruit crop yields and sales, and activities of the kitchen and sewing rooms.

7,039. Scott, Julia Ann
Papers. 1873-1912. 1 vol.
Open. No guide.
Hancock Shaker Village, Library.
Commonplace book of Scott (1839-1919), a member of the Shaker community at New Lebanon, NY, includes songs, financial accounts, and itemized lists of the numbers and types of preserves made between 1873 and 1896. Some entries were recorded by Cornelia French.

7,040. Sisters' Dresses
Records. 1866. 1 folder.
Open. Catalog card.
Hancock Shaker Village, Library.
Correspondence, essays, and patterns contain a meticulous description by Eldresses Ann and Betsy of the New Lebanon, NY, Shaker community of the appropriate dress for sisters, as well as a theological justification for the nature of the garments. Also included is a graduated scale of waist measures and patterns for a woman's apron and a man's jacket.

7,041. Sisters in the Church at Harvard, MA
Records. 1853-66. 1 vol.
Open. No guide.
Hancock Shaker Village, Library.
Journal of the domestic work performed by deaconesses in the kitchen, sewing rooms, and other women's parts of the Village. Personal, theological, economic, and administrative events in the community are also recorded. The Church at Harvard was founded in 1791.

HARVARD

7,042. Alcott, Louisa May
Papers. Ca. 1840s-80s. 36 items.
Open. Card catalog.

Fruitlands Museums.
Correspondence of Alcott (1832-88), a novelist and author of children's books, includes personal letters, some of which she wrote to a Mrs. Stearns with references to the health of her father Amos Bronson Alcott, and a few business letters addressed to Thomas Niles, Jr., and to a Mr. Bacon about her writing.

7,043. Brook Farm
Collection. 1834-1921. 44 items.
Open. Brief inventory.
Fruitlands Museums.
Correspondence of persons active in the Brook Farm experiment in group living in West Roxbury, MA, between 1841 and 1847 was assembled by Henry S. Borneman, a Philadelphia collector. Included are letters to Borneman in 1921 from M. Catherine Allen, daughter of John Allen; letters to Marianne (Dwight) Orvis; and single letters by Anna Q. T. Parsons, Elizabeth Palmer Peabody, and Amelia E. Russell.

7,044. Cooke, George Willis
Papers. 1838-1918. Ca. 125 items.
Open. Brief inventory.
Fruitlands Museums.
A Unitarian clergyman and writer and lecturer on religious, social, and literary topics, Cooke (1848-1923) was considered an authority on New England transcendentalism. Correspondence, much of which was written in response to Cooke's inquiries about certain episodes in the life of Ralph Waldo Emerson, relates to Emerson, the transcendental periodical *The Dial,* Brook Farm, and Bronson Alcott. Included are 11 letters from Julia Ward Howe and a few from each of the following: Mary Ashton Rice Livermore, Lucy Larcom, Lydia Maria (Francis) Child, Ellen Emerson, Ednah Dow (Littlehale) Cheney, and Kate Sanborn. Also contained are single letters from Clara Barton, Caroline Wells (Healey) Dall, Sarah J. Farmer, Charlotte Anna Perkins Stetson Gilman, Annie Adams Fields, Lucy Stone, and Louisa May Alcott's sister Anna (Alcott) Pratt.

7,045. Fuller, Sarah Margaret
Papers. 1843-50. 14 items.
Open. Card catalog.
Fruitlands Museums.
Papers of Fuller (1810-50), an author, critic, teacher, feminist, and transcendentalist who became the Marchesa d'Ossoli, consist of correspondence she wrote to Elizabeth Hoar, who was the daughter of Samuel Hoar of Concord, MA, and to others; a letter from Fuller's mother to a T. Hicks; and fragments of Margaret Fuller's journal, which contain daily observations and drafts of poems, ca. 1844.

7,046. Sears, Clara Endicott
Papers. Ca. 1911-60. 4 drawers.
Access restricted. No guide.
Fruitlands Museums.
Office files and business records of Fruitlands and correspondence of [Miss] Sears (1863-1960), the author who founded Fruitlands. The complex includes an early 18th-century farmhouse where Bronson Alcott and leaders of the transcendental movement attempted to achieve a new social order, an old Shaker house, an Indian museum, and a gallery of portraits by itinerant American painters and landscapes by painters of the Hudson River School.

7,047. Shakers
Collection. Ca. 1790-1911. Ca. 90 vols. and tray cases.
Open. Card catalog.
Fruitlands Museums.
Manuscript correspondence, diaries, poetry, essays, account books, church covenants and records, recipes, scrapbooks, and other material of the communities in Harvard and Shirley, MA, of the United Society of Believers in Christ's Second Appearing. Included are a general journal of extracts from the diaries of several authors, kept by the sisters in the church at Harvard 1824-38; a journal maintained by the deaconesses concerning domestic work performed by the sisters at Harvard, 1867-76; an account of work performed by the sisters, 1872-94; a daybook for the church at Shirley, which was kept by Mary O. Elston, 1870-73; and 25 manuscript hymn and songbooks, several of which show a woman's name on the title page. Also includes a daily journal of Maria Foster, 1893-1911, which was continued after her death by some other person; a journal kept by Susan Wentworth in ca. 1876, which includes poetry; Nancy Orsment's book of 1846, which contains an autobiographical sketch of widow Sarah Putnam Thomas, poems and songs, excerpts from the writings of famous people, and a transcription of a narration by an Indian woman and other accounts; the journal of Alfred Collier containing entries by a woman, which consist of personal reflections and comments on daily events, 1872-80; a volume containing a reminiscence about and reflection on the death in 1850 of Eldress Ruth and a poem, which were probably written by Anna Dodgson of Holy Mount, New Lebanon, NY; an impression of Eldress Ruth, impressions of Hannah Blake, and a communication from Mother Ann, which were probably written by Eunice Bathrick; a book of poetry, ca. 1869, by Mary Rosie Morse; and a book of poetry from the 1870s by a woman named Leoline. In addition, the collection includes a volume containing an 1822 speech by Eldress Ruth, rules concerning wearing apparel for the sisters in the church of New Lebanon from 1840, a recipe for laying down butter for table use, and an explanation of the division of labor in the kitchen.

HAVERHILL

7,048. Bradfordiana
Records. 1803- . Ca. 20,000 items
Partially closed. No guide.
Bradford College Library.
Minutes of the trustees, correspondence, diaries, scrapbooks, photos, books, and other items of Bradford College, which was founded in 1803 as Bradford Academy. Since that time, the school has been a coeducational academy, a women's academy, a women's junior college, and a coeducational college. Includes diaries of Anne Carroll Moore and biographies and pictures of Ann (Hasseltine) Judson and Harriet (Atwood) Newell, Bradford students who were the first American women missionaries for the American Board of Commissioners of Foreign Missions.

HOLYOKE

7,049. Mother House Archives
Records. 1873- . No size given.
Access restricted. No guide.
Sisters of Providence of Holyoke, Mother House.
This religious congregation of women was founded in 1873 in Holyoke by Mother Mary of Providence to provide health care for the sick and the poor. Correspondence, annals of the Mother House and related institutions, a history of Holyoke, material relating to the bishops and Diocese of Springfield, photos, and other records of the congregation. Includes material concerning hospitals; homes for children, the elderly, and unwed mothers; and other institutions with which the Sisters were involved.

HYDE PARK

7,050. Hyde Park Current Events Club
Records. 1908- . No size given.
Open. No guide.
Hyde Park Historical Society.
Secretary's records and yearbooks containing treasurer's reports, programs, and names of officers and members of the Club, founded in 1894 to promote the study and discussion of current events and to advance civic and educational projects. Material concerns the Club's activities and affiliation with the Massachusetts Federation of Women's Clubs.

7,051. Thought Club
Records. 1881-1976. No size given.
Open. No guide.
Hyde Park Historical Society.
Constitution, bylaws, financial records, secretary's reports, yearbooks, scrapbooks, clippings, and some original essays by members of this book review club, established in 1881 "for mutual aid and improvement."

IPSWICH

7,052. Brown, Mary E.
Papers. 1868-69. 1 vol.
Open. No guide.
Ipswich Public Library, Ipswich Historical Society Manuscript Collection.
Diary in which Brown, a young Ipswich resident, describes the weather, her daily activities, farming, and town gossip. Some information in the diary, which also contains drafts of letters, pencil drawings, and clippings, suggests Brown may have been a student at the Ipswich Female Seminary.

7,053. Heard, Elizabeth Ann Farley
Papers. 1842-50. 28 items.
Open. No guide.
Ipswich Public Library, Ipswich Historical Society Manuscript Collection.
Letters written by [Mrs. George Washington] Heard (1802-63), an Ipswich resident, to her son John Heard (1824-94) in Canton, China, and to her son Augustine Heard (1827-1905), who joined John Heard in Canton, contain family and town news.

7,054. Heard, Mary
Papers. 1843-50. 9 items.
Open. No guide.
Ipswich Public Library, Ipswich Historical Society Manuscript Collection.
Letters in which Heard recounts for her nephew John Heard in Canton, China, personal and family news.

7,055. Hosmer
Papers. 1745-1934. 1 folder.
Open. No guide.
Ipswich Public Library, Ipswich Historical Society Manuscript Collection.
Family correspondence, genealogical notes, a deed and survey, photos, and other papers include some material pertaining to Harriet Goodhue Hosmer (1830-1908), a sculptor; Eliza Hosmer, a teacher in Concord, MA; and Jane Hosmer, a teacher. Also includes a note from Henry David Thoreau's sister Sophia E. Thoreau; letters by Elizabeth B. Ripley, Lydia "Lidian" [Mrs. Ralph Waldo] Emerson, and Harriett Mulford (Stone) Lothrop; a copy of a "wail" Louisa May Alcott gave at a tea of the New England Women's Club; and a permit for transportation issued to Jane Hosmer by the Bureau of Refugees, Freedmen, and Abandoned Lands in 1865.

7,056. Ipswich Female Seminary
Records. 1825-74. 4 folders.
Open. No guide.
Ipswich Public Library, Ipswich Historical Society Manuscript Collection.
Incorporated in 1828 as Ipswich Academy, the Seminary's purpose was the education of young ladies. Founding and other legal documents; printed programs, invitations, and catalogs, one of which lists Mary Lyon as assistant principal of the school; a history of the Seminary, written in 1839; book lists and items concerning the acquisition of books for the school library; and copies of songs sung at the Seminary. Also includes an 1829 letter from students in a mission school in Mackinaw; a brief description of a religious experience by Eunice Caldwell; an essay on "home," which was written at Mount Holyoke Seminary in 1850; and Bible lessons kept by Elizabeth Lee Allen in 1835.

7,057. Kinsman, Nancy Green
Papers. 1863-88. 1 vol.
Open. No guide.
Ipswich Public Library, Ipswich Historical Society Manuscript Collection.
Diary, interleaved with clippings, in which Kinsman (1806-86), an Ipswich resident married to William Kinsman (1809-88), records morning and evening temperatures, daily activities, and events in her personal life and in the town. Also contains diary entries, probably made by Kinsman's daughter Berthiah Dodge Kinsman, describing the deaths of Nancy and then William Kinsman.

7,058. Manning, Elizabeth Heard
Papers. 1822-31. Ca. 45 items.
Open. No guide.
Ipswich Public Library, Ipswich Historical Society Manuscript Collection.
Papers of Manning (1808-31), daughter of Thomas Manning and Margaret Manning of Ipswich, consist of letters she wrote her parents while she was a student at a private academy in Dorchester, MA, letters from her father, correspondence between her and her brother John Heard Manning, student notes from 1822, a notebook on her religious views and sermons she heard, poetry, and extracts on Roman and Greek history copied from *Le Sage.*

LANCASTER

7,059. Archives
Records. 1897-1977. 1 box.
Access restricted. No guide.
Lancaster Current Topics Club.
Complete minutes, photos, and scrapbooks of meetings and charitable activities of the Current Topics Club, a women's group organized in 1897 to promote interest in current events and to develop knowledge of the duties and responsibilities of citizenship. The group joined the Massachusetts Federation of Women's Clubs in 1898 and the GFWC in 1952.

7,060. Chandler, Alice Greene
Papers. Ca. 1870-1900. Ca. 2500-3000 items.
Open. Unpublished guide.
Lancaster Historical Commission.
Collection consists of glass plate negatives and photos taken by [Miss] Chandler (1851-1935), librarian and later chairman of the board of trustees of the Lancaster Town Library and a member of the Massachusetts Library Commission. The photos are of a wide range of subjects, including self portraits; pictures of Washington, DC, and of New York, the first Chicago world's fair, construction of the Tremont Street subway in Boston; photos of Lancaster scenes and residents; and experimental sequence shots.

7,061. A Lancaster Girl
Papers. 1842-43. 1 vol.
Open. Unpublished guide.
Lancaster Historical Commission.
Journal of a young Lancaster resident, who appears to have been a seamstress, contains notes on ladies who came to her home for fittings, sewing, the weather, town meetings and elections, deaths of townspeople, christenings, books she read, dances, church services, music lessons, the activities of relatives and friends, and lectures held in town on such subjects as magnetism, phrenological education, mathematics, and temperance. The young woman's mother also was a seamstress.

7,062. Thayer, Pauline Revere
Papers. 1917-19. 1 vol.
Open. No guide.
Lancaster Town Library.
Scrapbook of [Mrs.] Thayer (1861-1934) concerns her work during WWI as chairman of the Massachusetts division of the woman's committee of the Council of National Defense and Home Economics, as director of federal home economics for Massachusetts, and as a member of various other women's organizations. Correspondence from military and government officials, photos, and clippings containing information on the "farmerette" program, stenographers' and nurses' training programs, and educational programs conducted for women during the war on child care, coal conservation, and planning menus to conserve sugar, flour, and other supplies.

LAWRENCE

7,063. Archives
Records. 1892- . Ca. 3 ft. and 4 shelves.
Open. Unpublished guide.
Greater Lawrence YWCA.
Minutes of board and committee meetings, financial records, correspondence, reports, photos, and scrapbooks of this branch of the YWCA, founded in 1892. Includes information on the struggle of local women to convince the YMCA leadership that it was appropriate for them to organize as well as material on early immigrants to the area and on mill strikes.

LENOX

7,064. Woman's Home and Foreign Mission Society of the Advent Christian Denomination
Records. 1888-1967. 5 vols. and 15 items.
Open. No guide.
Berkshire Christian College, Dr. Linden J. Carter Library.
Organized in 1897 and incorporated in 1901, this religious organization worked to convert people in India. Constitution; minutes for 1901 to 1910 and 1921 to 1939; records kept by [Mrs.] Thelma Collins of the Society's intercessory prayer committee, which encouraged Adventists to pray for the success of the Society's missions, as well as Collins's tabulations by name and geographical area of the efforts of local committee representatives; and correspondence and other papers of Sarah K. [Mrs. A. W.] Taylor of Maine, the Society's first president. In 1908 Taylor visited the Society's mission in India and judged that the discipline for children was too severe and that administration was poor. After presenting her case to the Society's board, which failed to back her suggestions for reform, she resigned as president and created a new women's organization, the Bible Faith Mission, which was also devoted to work in India. Collection contains Faith Mission records through 1913 and the constitution, lists of members, and minutes for 1888 to 1895 and 1902 of the Emerald Street Mission in Boston, an earlier missionary group which changed its name in 1902 to the Warren Street Mission. Women were active in the Emerald Street Mission and were well represented among its officers.

7,065. Kemble, Fanny
Papers. 1829-1960. 6 in.
Open. No guide.
Lenox Library Association.
Papers of Frances "Fanny" Anne Kemble (1809-93), an actress and writer who married Pierce Butler in 1834, include letters to Grace Sedgwick, playbills, book reviews, photos, and clippings concerning Kemble's divorce from Butler in 1849. Also includes a biographical article on Kemble, which was written by Grace Wilson in 1920; extracts from the diary of Amelia M. Watson, which chronicle her research on Kemble; and drafts of Watson's poems and essays about Kemble.

LEXINGTON

7,066. St. Joseph Province Archives
Records. 1895- . No size given.
Closed. No guide.
Sisters of Charity (Grey Nuns of Montreal).
Minutes, financial records, correspondence, photos, personnel records, scrapbooks, and other records of the order, which was first founded in the US in 1855. Includes material related to hospitals, nursing homes, orphanages, and homes for the aged operated by the order.

LOWELL

7,067. Lowell Historical Society: Female Operatives
Collection. 1824- . No size given.
Open. Unpublished guide.
University of Lowell, Alumni-Lydon Library.
Items concerning mill girls in Lowell include published and unpublished correspondence; diaries; poetry; statistics; case studies; company and hospital records; magazines and newspapers written, edited, and published by mill girls; rubbings of gravestones of early mill girls; and pamphlets. Material concerning immigrant women who worked in the textile manufacturing companies includes photos and oral histories.

7,068. Lowell Historical Society: Rogers Hall School for Girls
Records. 1892-1974. 27 ft.
Open. Unpublished guide.
University of Lowell, Alumni-Lydon Library.
Correspondence, scrapbooks, photos, and publications of this private girls high school that functioned in Lowell between 1892 and 1974.

7,069. Lowell Historical Society: Women Authors
Collection. 1830-1976. No size given.
Open. Unpublished guide.
University of Lowell, Alumni-Lydon Library.
Unpublished and published works by Lowell women, including Sarah Bagley, Harriot Curtis, Harriet Farley Dunlevy, Sara Swan Griffin, Charlotte Hilbourne, Lucy Larcom, Jane E. Locke, Maria H. Parker, Laura Rice, and Harriet (Hanson) Robinson.

7,070. Proprietors of the Locks and Canals Company on Merrimack River
Records. 1792-1950. 3000 vols. and 4700 items.
Open. Unpublished guides.
University of Lowell, Alumni-Lydon Library.
Founded in 1792, the Locks and Canals Company built a canal system on the Merrimack River for

use by the textile plants in Lowell. Company records, diaries, statistics, scrapbooks, and the Company's technical library contain items concerning women in the textile industry, with 700 architectural drawings and 4000 photos of the textile company and of the boarding houses where women textile workers lived. Also contains regulations of the companies and the boarding houses.

7,071. American Association of University Women, Lowell Area Branch
Records. 1901- . 50 envelopes and other items.
Access restricted. Unpublished guide.
University of Lowell, O'Leary Library.
Minutes, treasurer's books, correspondence, membership records, program material, and scrapbooks of publicity of the AAUW's Lowell branch, which was founded in 1901.

LYNN

7,072. Female Anti-Slavery Society
Records. 1836-38. 1 vol.
Open. No guide.
Lynn Historical Society, Inc.
Constitution, treasurer's and meeting records, accounts of dues, and lists of members of this abolitionist society, founded in 1836. Some of the material documents the participation of Abigail (Kelley) Foster in the Society.

7,073. Female Benevolent Society
Records. 1814-1914. 10 vols.
Open. No guide.
Lynn Historical Society, Inc.
Constitution, bylaws, regulations, treasurers' reports, lists of members and managers, records of annual assessments of members, lists of donations to the needy, and clippings of this charitable organization, founded in 1814 and disbanded in 1914. At some point the Society changed its name to the Ladies Benevolent Society.

7,074. Lynn Female Fragment Society
Records. 1820-81. 8 vols.
Open. No guide.
Lynn Historical Society, Inc.
Constitution, bylaws, treasurer's reports, regulations, lists of members and their annual assessment for $1, and records of articles delivered to the needy by this charitable organization, founded in 1820.

7,075. Lynn Women's Club
Records. 1878-1941. 8 vols.
Open. No guide.
Lynn Historical Society, Inc.
Records of the board of directors and of the secretary, financial and presidents' reports, programs, attendance records, and chronicles by Lucinda M. Lummus of the Club, founded in 1909 to provide a place for local clubs and organizations to meet.

7,076. Manuscripts
Collection. Ca. 1705-1857. Ca. 300 items.
Open. Name index.
Lynn Historical Society, Inc.
Primarily consisting of such legal documents as marriage banns, deeds, and wills, material also includes bills, receipts, and some correspondence. Women are mentioned in or are authors of approximately one-half of the items.

7,077. North Shore Club
Records. Ca. 1891-1916. 1 folder and 3 vols.
Open. No guide.
Lynn Historical Society, Inc.
Treasurer's records, receipts, and material concerning meetings of this Lynn club, founded in 1891 for the "moral, intellectual, and social improvement of women."

7,078. Political Science Club of Lynn
Records. 1912-36. 5 vols.
Open. No guide.
Lynn Historical Society, Inc.
Clippings, membership lists, and other material concerning meetings of the Club, founded in 1912 to promote discussion and study of contemporary political problems. The Club supported the NAACP, suffrage, temperance, the League of Nations, and labor unions.

7,079. Starr Club
Records. Ca. 1892-1928. 6 folders and 10 vols.
Open. No guide.
Lynn Historical Society, Inc.
Constitution, annual reports, committee reports, and printed programs and notices of this Lynn cultural club, founded in 1892 and named after Sarah E. Starr (1820-80).

7,080. Woman's Missionary Union of Lynn
Records. 1908-16. 2 vols.
Open. No guide.
Lynn Historical Society, Inc.
Constitution; reports of the executive board, study committee, and study classes; meeting records; programs; and clippings of the Union, founded in 1908 to support foreign and home missions.

7,081. Women's Auxiliary to the Massachusetts Civil Service Reform Association
Records. 1902-18. 2 vols.
Open. No guide.
Lynn Historical Society, Inc.
Clippings, lists of members, and other material pertaining to meetings of the Lynn branch of the Auxiliary, founded in 1902 to promote reform of the civil service.

MALDEN

7,082. Old and New of Malden
Records. 1878-1977. 1 cabinet.
Closed. No guide.
Malden Public Library.
Minutes, photos, yearbooks, scrapbooks, and original magazines of the Old and New women's club, founded in 1878 by Harriette (Robinson) Shattuck, who served as the club's first president and then secretary; she also was founder and president of the Boston Political Class, an officer of Massachusetts suffrage associations, and author of books on parliamentary law, of a column "The Woman's Hour" that was published in a Ewing, NE, newspaper, and of articles for Boston newspapers and magazines. The club's scrapbooks contain copies of Shattuck's articles on suffrage; clippings from her column; articles she wrote on the Concord School of Philosophy, which were published as *The Story of Dante's Divine Comedy* (1887); poems; and children's stories. Scrapbooks also contain stories, poems, and dramatic pieces by her mother Harriet H. Robinson, who also was an author, speaker, organizer of suffrage associations and women's clubs, and abolitionist. In addition, the collection contains histories of the club, which were written by club historian and treasurer Ruth K. Randall.

MANCHESTER

7,083. Samples, Sally
Papers. Ca. 1776. 6 pp.
Open. No guide.
Manchester Historical Society.
Story by Samples, a pseudonym for Elizabeth Allen (1734-1824), a housewife and proprietor of a notions store, in which she tells about how she walked to Boston, avoiding the British, to get needles for a Manchester woman during the British occupation of Boston.

7,084. Trask, Abigail (Hooper)
Papers. 1822-44. 5 vols.
Open. No guide.
Manchester Historical Society.
Ledgers of Trask (1788-1885), the proprietor of a grocery store and later of a millinery shop.

MARBLEHEAD

7,085. Gregory, Sarah E. Franks
Papers. 1928. 21-page item.
Open. No guide.
Marblehead Historical Society.
Reminiscences of [Mrs. William D.] Gregory (1846?-1931), a Marblehead librarian for more than 50 years, contain information on early Marblehead families and ships, her family, and her life in Marblehead.

7,086. Marblehead Female Humane Society
Records. 1816-1957. 1 envelope.
Open. No guide.
Marblehead Historical Society.
Records of the Society, founded in 1816 and still functioning to provide charity to the indigent, sick, and infirm, consist of an 1816 pamphlet containing rules, regulations, and a membership list; a brief history and annual report for 1916; scattered later annual reports; clippings; and fund-raising items.

7,087. Marblehead Garden Club
Records. 1926-76. No size given.
Open. Unpublished guide.
Marblehead Historical Society.
Three different editions of the Club's constitution, bylaws, and history; a nearly complete set of yearbooks; programs; and other items of the Club, which was founded in 1926 to promote gardening and "a civic conscience." In addition to augmenting the horticultural education of members, the Club conducted various beautification projects in Marblehead.

7,088. Marblehead Visiting Nurse Association
Records. 1896-1976. No size given.
Open. No guide.
Marblehead Historical Society.
The Association was founded in 1896 to provide home nursing and then expanded to maintain "keep well" clinics and administer various restorative therapies. Letters about fund-raising events; annual reports, which contain the constitution and bylaws, secretary's reports, lists of members, rules for the nurse, and nurses' reports; and a clipping.

7,089. Marblehead Women's Club
Records. 1917-75. 1 box.
Open. No guide.
Marblehead Historical Society.
Records of this ongoing charitable and social Club, founded in 1913, consist of yearbooks containing treasurer's reports, lists of members and officers, and programs of monthly meetings; leaflets; and a list of deaths of Club members between 1918 and 1944.

7,090. Poetry and Prose
Collection. 1800s-1900s. 1 vol. and 2 envelopes.
Open. No guide.
Marblehead Historical Society.
Literary manuscripts and printed versions of writings by Marblehead women include *The Tea Party,* a play written by Gertrude Neilson for an anniversary celebration in 1952 of the Commodore Samuel Tucker Chapter of the DAR; "The First Fourth of July," a story written in 1899 by Mary

Lee Etheridge; acrostics devised in the 1860s by Alice B. Chinn, some of which were printed in newspapers; poems written between the 1850s and 1884 by Eliza G. Bonney; poems written between the 1930s and 1950s by Edith DeBlois Laskey Parker; and a poem written in 1886 by one woman to another. Many of the poems by Bonney and Parker were printed in newspapers.

MARLBORO

7,091. Rice Family
Papers. 1700-1851. Ca. 200 items.
Open. Brief description of folder contents.
Marlboro Public Library.
Legal documents, land surveys, and business papers of this Marlboro family include material pertaining to the estate of Sarah Rice (?-1778), with a copy of her will, an inventory of and valuations for each item of her wearing apparel, receipts from persons who benefited from her estate, and receipts for taxes on the estate and on income derived from rental of a piece of her property. In the inventory, Rice's apparel was divided into six equal portions with the name of the woman who was to receive a portion noted next to each.

7,092. Second (West) Parish
Records. 1801-52. Ca. 104 items.
Open. Brief description of folder contents.
Marlboro Public Library.
Church records and correspondence pertaining to parish affairs of this Marlboro church, which was founded in ca. 1800 and is still extant. Includes an attendance book of pupils and teachers of the Sabbath school for 1851 to 1852; lists of teachers, who for the most part were female; attendance records of students of Bible classes; and sermon notes.

MIDDLETON

7,093. King's Daughters Circle
Records. 1922-70. Several vols.
Closed. No guide.
Middleton Historical Society.
Secretarial and financial records of this small, charitable organization of women, founded in 1922 to provide clothing, food, and other necessities to the needy.

NANTUCKET

7,094. Mitchell, Maria
Papers. 1830-89. 3 shelves and 9 microfilm reels.
Open. Unpublished guide.
Maria Mitchell Science Library.
Mitchell (1818-89) was an astronomer, a professor at Vassar College, and the first and only woman member during the 19th century of the American Academy of Arts and Sciences. Correspondence, diaries, meteorological and astronomical observations, lecture notes, and clippings reveal Mitchell's views on life and the education of women.

NEWTON

7,095. Female Benevolent Society
Records. 1836-1930. 5 vols.
Open. Unpublished guide.
Newton Free Library.
Constitution, minutes, and membership records of the Society, a group organized to aid the sick and destitute, which was called variously the Ladies Benevolent Society, the Ladies Temperance Society, and the Ladies Benevolent Total Abstinence Society. Members of the Society sewed for the needy and provided coal and other necessities. Club records indicate that in 1930 the Society "was not called on for any charity work."

7,096. Newton Equal Suffrage League
Records. 1899-1920. 2 vols.
Open. Unpublished guide.
Newton Free Library.
Records of the League, which was also called the Newton Woman's Suffrage League and the Newton Equal Franchise Association. In 1908 the League included men among its 205 members. The group's concerns were equal pay, property and voting rights, political action to elect women, peace, education to change prejudices against women, and support of other voting rights groups, "even if methods differed."

7,097. Rebecca Pomroy Newton Home for Orphan Girls
Records. 1873-88. 1 vol.
Open. Unpublished guide.
Newton Free Library.
Annual reports of directors of the Home, which was originally called the Newton Home for Orphans and Destitute Girls. Includes a treasurer's report, a list of donations received, and information on the condition of the Home and of girls resident at the Home.

NEWTON CENTRE

7,098. Baptist Female Missionary Society of the First Baptist Church
Records. 1831-80. 2 vols.
Open. No guide.
Andover Newton Theological School Library.
Minutes and financial records of the Society, founded in 1831 to support the Watertown, MA, church's proselytizing in the US.

7,099. Benevolent Circle of the First Baptist Church and Society of Boston
Records. 1841-87. 2 vols.
Access restricted. No guide.
Andover Newton Theological School Library.
Minutes of this social and benevolent society, which was organized in 1841 as the Sewing Circle, renamed the Ladies Mission Circle in 1843, and then renamed the Benevolent Circle in 1877.

7,100. Female Foreign Mission Society of the First Baptist Church.
Records. 1845-1910. 3 vols.
Open. No guide.
Andover Newton Theological School Library.
Minutes of the Society, organized in 1845 in Watertown, MA, to support the Church's foreign mission movement.

7,101. Female Mite Society of the First Baptist Church
Records. 1815-51. 34 pp.
Open. No guide.
Andover Newton Theological School Library.
Minutes of the Society, established in 1815 in Framingham, MA, to assist the missionary cause.

7,102. Ladies Aid Society of the Harvard Street Baptist Church
Records. 1883-1909. 1 vol.
Open. No guide.
Andover Newton Theological School Library.
Financial records of this Boston benevolent society, which was named the Harvard Street Sewing Circle until 1896.

7,103. Ladies Home Mission Sewing Circle of the First Baptist Church
Records. 1829-1906. 9 vols.
Open. No guide.
Andover Newton Theological School Library.
Complete set of minutes and partial financial records of this benevolent society, founded in 1829 in Watertown, MA, as the Female Charitable Sewing Society.

7,104. Watertown Branch of the Woman's American Baptist Home Mission Society
Records. 1879-1910. 2 vols.
Open. No guide.
Andover Newton Theological School Library.
Minutes of the Watertown, MA, branch of the Society, established in 1879 to support the work of the national Society and to cultivate a missionary spirit in the local First Baptist Church.

NORTH ADAMS

7,105. Blackinton, Charlotte Palmer
Papers. 1890. 1 vol.
Open. Description.
North Adams State College Library.
Blackinton (1814-99) was a resident of Blackinton, MA. Recollections entitled "To Our Children," which she dictated to her daughter Helen (Blackinton) Archer, contain biographical data on her husband John R. Blackinton.

7,106. City of Adams
Records. 1854-70. 5 vols.
Open. No guide.
North Adams State College Library.
Court records of cases heard before the police court list the date, names of plaintiff and defendant, nature of the complaint, and finding of the court. Women's names appear frequently as complainants and defendants.

7,107. Junior Girls' Club of St. Andrews Mission
Records. 1920. 1 vol.
Open. Description.
North Adams State College Library.
Minutes of meetings of this Catholic girls' social club in Blackinton, MA, as recorded by Constance Haigh, secretary.

7,108. North Adams School Department
Records. 1902-22. 9 vols.
Open. No guide.
North Adams State College Library.
Financial accounts for the schools in North Adams contain information on salaries paid to men and women teachers and educational material purchased.

7,109. Oral History Project
Oral History. 1973- . 64 items and 40 tapes.
Open. No guide.
North Adams State College Library.
Tapes, transcriptions, information sheets, and permission slips from interviews by North Adams State College history students of North Adams residents about their recollections of local history. Women interviewed, most of whom are housewives, include Mary Chenaille Bernard, Florence M. Haigh, Mary G. Dailey, Marie Dean, Amy Marino, Eva Nellie Brown, Josephine Reed, Constance Reed Ashley, a Mrs. Cardillo, Alta O'Neil, Gertrude Moore, Eleanore Miller, Dorothy Briggs, Anna B. Whitney, [Mrs.] Irene Rivers, Mae Breen, a Mrs. Hubbard, Ruth Browne, and Margaret Stewart. Also includes a tape of a Mrs. Simmons reading the diary of Helen (Blackinton) Archer, who came to North Adams in 1905.

7,110. Owens, Annie Evalina
Papers. 1895-1903. 18 vols.
Open. Register.
North Adams State College Library.
Papers of Owens, a student, consist of college catalogs for North Adams Normal School, North Adams State College's predecessor; pamphlets on education topics; and lecture notes, classroom exercises, and homework from classes Owens attended in physiology, language, child study, writing, sketching, music, minerals, geometry, algebra, and literature.

7,111. Paupers' Register, City of Adams
Records. 1868-94. 1 vol.
Open. No guide.
North Adams State College Library.
Completed forms and lists of City residents who were provided with financial support give for each person the name, age, sex, size of family, race, birthplace, health, and other descriptive factors. In some years, only names and amounts received are recorded. Women's names appear frequently.

7,112. Turner, Anne Archer
Papers. Ca. 1930. 1 vol.
Open. Description.
North Adams State College Library.
Recollections of [Mrs. Charles] Turner, a resident of Blackinton, MA, who was also related to the Blackinton family, are entitled "The Garrulity of Age." In her recollections, which she read to the Monday Club, she reminisces about life in early Centerville, the village that was later renamed Blackinton after its most prominent family.

NORTH ANDOVER

7,113. Amos Abbott Company
Records. 1829-1941. 33 ft.
Open. Unpublished guide.
Merrimack Valley Textile Museum.
Business records of this textile manufacturer include payrolls and time books, 1834-1908, which indicate the names of women workers, their positions in the mill, time worked or piece rate, and payments.

7,114. Appleton Company
Records. 1829-1929. 2 ft.
Open. Unpublished guide.
Merrimack Valley Textile Museum.
Letter books and memoranda of this firm, which was engaged in textile manufacturing, include data on wages and employment conditions; strike lists and petitions for shorter hours, which show women's names; and production records.

7,115. Barnes Textile Associates
Records. 1925-54. 60 ft.
Open. Unpublished guide.
Merrimack Valley Textile Museum.
Barnes Associates was a consulting firm for the textile industry; company officers also acted as textile engineers. Reports to individual client companies include reports on labor conditions, job descriptions by department within the mill, and time and motion studies.

7,116. Charlottesville Woolen Mills
Records. 1868-1954. 21 ft.
Open. Unpublished guide.
Merrimack Valley Textile Museum.
Business records of this company, which was engaged in textile manufacturing, include payrolls and time books, 1909-53, indicating names of women workers, their positions in the mill, time worked or piece rate, and payments.

7,117. E. Dole & Company
Records. 1843-1949. 49 ft.
Open. Unpublished guide.
Merrimack Valley Textile Museum.
Business records of this textile manufacturer include payrolls and time books, 1852-1947, indicating names of women workers, their positions in the mill, time worked or piece rate, and payments.

7,118. Louisville Textiles
Records. 1888-1950. 12 ft.
Open. Unpublished guide.
Merrimack Valley Textile Museum.
Records of this textile manufacturer include textile designs by women designers for home furnishing fabrics; scrapbooks of company advertising for such fabrics, which was directed toward women consumers and women's magazines; fabric samples for draperies, upholstery, and other home furnishing textiles; and a scrapbook of employee information, which includes data on some of the women employees of the firm.

7,119. M. T. Stevens & Company Inc.
Records. 1811-1961. 550 ft.
Open. Unpublished guide.
Merrimack Valley Textile Museum.
Includes business records of 10 separate woolen mills throughout New England, which were incorporated into the parent company between 1855 and 1934, with payrolls and time books indicating the names of women workers, their positions in the mill, time worked or piece rate, and payments. Also includes boxes of dossiers, 1900-30, on employees who worked at the original mill in North Andover, with employment applications, Company personnel records, and local vital statistics for supporting data.

7,120. Pemberton Mill Relief Fund
Records. 1860-61. 3 ft.
Open. Unpublished guide.
Merrimack Valley Textile Museum.
Account books of this charitable organization, founded when the Pemberton Mill collapsed and burned in 1860, document cash payments made for medical attention and living expenses of injured employees and funeral expenses and death stipends for those who were killed. The amount of relief was based on the wage scale of employees, 62 percent of whom were women. Accounts include names and condition of employees as well as wage figures.

7,121. R. D. Nesmith & Company
Records. 1845-51. 1 ft.
Open. Unpublished guide.
Merrimack Valley Textile Museum.
Business records of the Company, which was engaged in the manufacture of textiles, include payrolls and time books indicating names of women employees, their positions in the mill, time worked or piece rate, and payments.

7,122. Stevens Linen Works
Records. 1846-98. 2 ft.
Open. Unpublished guide.
Merrimack Valley Textile Museum.
Business records of this textile manufacturing company include payrolls and time books, 1846-48, indicating the names of women workers, their positions in the mills, time worked or piece rate, and payments.

7,123. Sutton's Mills
Records. 1864-1958. 8 ft.
Open. Unpublished guide.
Merrimack Valley Textile Museum.
Business records of this firm, which was engaged in textile manufacturing, include payrolls and time books, 1904-58, indicating names of women workers, their positions in the mill, time worked or piece rate, and payments.

7,124. Talbot Mills
Records. 1830-1957. 90 ft.
Open. Unpublished guide.
Merrimack Valley Textile Museum.
Business records of this textile manufacturer include payrolls and time books, 1857-1937, indicating names of women workers, their positions in the mill, time worked or piece rate, and payments.

7,125. Taylor & Company
Records. 1864-71. 2 ft.
Open. Unpublished guide.
Merrimack Valley Textile Museum.
Business records of the Company, which was engaged in textile manufacture, include payrolls and time books for the period indicating the names of women workers, their positions in the mill, time worked or piece rate, and payments.

7,126. Uxbridge Cotton Mills
Records. 1852-1931. 20 ft.
Open. Unpublished guide.
Merrimack Valley Textile Museum.
Business records of this textile manufacturer include payrolls and time books, 1852-1921, indicating the names of women workers, their positions in the mill, time worked or piece rate, and payments.

7,127. Bradstreet, Anne (Dudley)
Papers. 1612-72. 43 vols.
Access restricted. Unpublished guide.
Stevens Memorial Library.
Collection contains a rare manuscript of Bradstreet (1612-72), the first American poet, as well as copies of all the editions of her works and books about her. The manuscript, "Meditations Divine and morall," includes the contents of another manuscript book her son Simon Bradstreet copied into the volume and a few verses, including "As weary pilgrim, now at rest." Because Bradstreet did not intend her poems for publication and seems simply to have circulated them among her friends in manuscript form, she was surprised to see them printed in an edition published in 1650 in England, where a collection of her poems had been taken without her knowledge.

Born in England, Anne Dudley married Simon Bradstreet at the age of 16 and came to America in 1630 with her husband, her father Thomas Dudley, her mother Dorothy Dudley, and Governor Winthrop's party on the *Arbella.* Her father served several terms as governor of the colony, as did her husband after her death. During the late 1640s, Bradstreet and her husband moved to the original village of Andover, which is now North Andover; she lived there for the rest of her life.

NORTHAMPTON

7,128. Allen Family
Papers. 1773-1866. 102 items.
Open. Catalog cards.
Forbes Library.
Correspondence, poems, notes for sermons, biographical notes, wills, bills, and clippings of this Massachusetts family, including letters to and from Love (Allen) Ripley (1786-1820) on church news, places she visited, her family's health and activities, and the military assignments of her husband Eleazar Wheelock Ripley. Also included are 1827-28 letters by Clarissa (Allen) Breck, an 1805 letter from Catherine Codman, and two poems by Thomas Allen on the death of his daughter Elizabeth (Allen) White.

7,129. Bridgman Family
Papers. 1768-1949. Ca. 130 items.
Open. No guide.
Forbes Library.
Papers of the Bridgman family of missionaries to Africa consist of correspondence, military commissions, lists, photos, clippings, and printed items relating primarily to the family's work in

Natal, South Africa, in a mission which was concerned with education, temperance, and health, as well as religion. Included is material of Amy (Bridgman) Cowles (1866-1948) and of her mother Laura Brainerd Nichols Bridgman (1834-1923), a Mount Holyoke Seminary graduate who worked in Africa with her husband from 1860 until her death. Also included are Laura Bridgman's reminiscences.

7,130. Butler, Hannah M.
Papers. 1825-67. 3 vols.
Open. No guide.
Forbes Library.
Notebook of Butler, a mid-19th-century resident of Northampton, containing quotations from the Bible on various religious themes; a religious journal for the years 1826-27 and 1867-68, in which Butler summarizes sermons and records church news; and a friendship album of poetry, which was copied into the book and signed and dated by friends and relatives of Butler.

7,131. Chadwick, John White
Papers. Ca. 1820-1934. 1 vol.
Open. Catalog cards.
Forbes Library.
Copy of the extra-illustrated volume entitled *Out of the Heart: Poems for Lovers, Young and Old* (Boston: Knight, 1891) by Chadwick, in which have been inserted correspondence and drafts of poems by Anna Hempstead Branch, Emily Dickinson, Julia Caroline Ripley Dorr, Mary Potter Thacher Higginson, Helen Hunt Jackson, Lucy Larcom, Louise (Chandler) Moulton, Sarah Morgan Bryan Pratt, Charlotte Fiske Bates Rogé, Harriet Elizabeth (Prescott) Spofford, and Adeline Dutton Train Whitney. Also included are a few 1890s letters from Harriet Spofford to Annie Cleaveland Bridgman.

7,132. Colonial Club
Records. 1910-52. 3 vols. and 2 items.
Open. Catalog cards.
Forbes Library.
Constitution and bylaws, reports of officers, minutes, resolutions, programs, lists of members, and histories of the Club of Northampton women, which was founded in 1890 to study literature and history. The Club was named the Milton Club from its inception until 1892, changed its name to the Round Robin Club for eight years, and then adopted its most recent name. Members held dinner parties and studied intellectual topics by means of readings and lectures.

7,133. Coolidge, Calvin
Papers. 1875-1957. 23 ft.
Access restricted. No guide.
Forbes Library.
Correspondence, news conference transcriptions, speeches, articles, clippings, photograph albums, and other papers of Coolidge (1872-1933), a Northampton resident who was governor of Massachusetts and US President, and of his wife Grace Anne (Goodhue) Coolidge (1879-1957). Included are copies of articles she wrote for popular magazines, biographical accounts and photos of her, a few fiscal accounts reflecting her management of the White House, clippings on her social and family life, and personal correspondence, notably with Therese (Christiansen) [Mrs. Reuben] Hill of Hampshire County, MA, and Grace (Graham) [Mrs. Carl] Medinus, an Illinois clubwoman.

7,134. Edwards, Anna Cheney
Papers. 1703-1868. Ca. 70 items and 1 box.
Open. Catalog cards.
Forbes Library.
Material used by Edwards (1835-?), a genealogist, in her research on Northampton families, includes correspondence, notes, and legal documents such as tax bills, wills, indentures, deeds, and military commissions.

7,135. Friendship Albums
Collection. 1821-79. 8 vols.
Open. Catalog cards.
Forbes Library.
Blank books which have been inscribed by the owners' friends with signatures, expressions of friendship, and quotations. Includes an 1833-35 volume of Sarah P. Adams of Northampton, an 1857-62 volume of Lizzie S. Smith of Northampton, an 1822 volume of Elizabeth Strong of Northampton, and an 1821-22 volume of Rachel Strong of Hopkins Academy in Hadley, MA.

7,136. Lamb, Martha Joanna Reade (Nash)
Papers. 1880-91. 2 vols. and 51 items.
Open. No guide.
Forbes Library.
Much of the correspondence, diaries, drafts of articles, genealogical and historical notes, and other papers of Lamb (1826-93), an historian and editor, relate to her attendance at meetings of the American Association for the Advancement of Science in Boston in 1880, in Cincinnati in 1881, in Montreal in 1882, and at the meeting of the Royal Society of Canada in Montreal in 1891. Other items stem from her historical research and publications.

7,137. Local WWI Archives
Collection. 1914-24. 2 drawers, 58 vols., and ca. 5000 items.
Open. Unpublished guide.
Forbes Library.
Minutes, correspondence, pamphlets, lists, photos, clippings, and other material documenting the military and patriotic activities of Hampshire County residents during WWI, including financial and administrative reports, minutes, and photos of the county chapter of the American National Red Cross, with brief reports from the Smith College branch added. Also includes minutes and clippings of the Northampton City Conservation Committee, which sponsored patriotic speakers and newspaper ads as well as operating a storefront center to train women in domestic economy; a card index of military records, which includes data on the small number of local women who served either in the armed forces or in support units; completed biographical questionnaires with photos; and clippings on services personnel.

7,138. Local WWII Archives
Collection. 1939-47. Ca. 22 drawers, 110 vols., and 2800 items.
Open. Unpublished guide.
Forbes Library.
Correspondence; drafts of poems, short stories, and books; speeches; photos; and printed and other material documenting the military and patriotic activities of Hampshire County residents during WWII. Women who served in the armed forces are well represented in card files of military records and biographical information for services personnel; also included are completed questionnaires and photos, which provide more biographical detail, and scrapbooks of clippings. Included as well are speeches, pamphlets, postcards, and photos of the Naval Reserve Midshipmen's School, stationed at Smith College and devoted to training women for the WAVES; correspondence addressed to Mrs. Calvin Coolidge on the work of the Northampton War Finance Committee women's division for the sixth war loan campaign; and, from the Books and Authors War Bond Committee of the US Treasury, a draft of *Paradise* (1937) by Esther Forbes and a draft of the short story "Father Never Gets a Valentine" by Elizabeth Reeve (Cutter) Morrow.

7,139. Massachusetts Woman Suffrage Association
Records. 1916-18. Ca. 50 items.
Open. Catalog card.
Forbes Library.
Records of the First Hampshire Representative District Committee of the Association, founded in 1916, consist of constitution; minutes; financial and administrative reports; correspondence with public officials and state and national suffrage organizations; notes on fund raising, voter canvasses, legislative lobbying, and war work; instructions to ward chairmen; lists of members, officers, election workers, and delegates to state and national suffrage conventions; and clippings. Much of the Committee's time was devoted to enlisting voter support for the 1918 suffrage referendum in Massachusetts.

7,140. Northampton Historical Society
Collection. 1777-1932. Ca. 8 ft.
Open. Card index.
Forbes Library.
Correspondence; memoranda; diaries; personal and business account books; poetry; essays; sermons; minutes of organizations; genealogical material; classroom notes; military records; and cookbooks and recipe books documenting the history of Northampton and its residents. Included are personal account books of Electa (Warner) Allen for 1832-57 and of Mrs. F. W. Proctor for 1832-59; and diaries of Hattie Abell for 1932, of [Mrs.] Emma Greene for 1894, of Mrs. Israel Dickinson for 1871, of [Mrs.] Carrie Greene Westover for 1890, of Mrs. Henry L. Williams for 1862, and of Martha Whitmarsh for 1886 and 1891. Also included are a recipe book of Amelia Clark; a manuscript cookbook of Dorcas A. Clark; a copy of a poem "The Happy Warrior," written in 1818 by Sarah Hamilton; an 1800 funeral sermon for Nellie Williams; an 1850 memorandum book of Clara Lathrop; a 1902 essay by Mary Sergeant on Deerfield, MA; and 1859-91 correspondence and other personal papers of Sarah Ann Hopkins.

7,141. Northampton Martha Washington Temperance Society
Records. 1835-47. 1 vol.
Open. No guide.
Forbes Library.
Constitution, minutes, pledge of abstinence, and list of those who made the pledge and were members of the Society, founded in 1843 as the women's auxiliary to the local men's Hampshire Washingtonian Temperance Society. Also included are records of the Northampton Total Abstinence Society, a local women's group which was founded in 1835.

7,142. Northampton Town Records
Collection. 1653-1884. Ca. 15,000 items and 22 microfilm reels.
Open. Preliminary inventory.
Forbes Library.
Official records of the town, which was founded in 1654, and of its departments up to the year in which it was incorporated; a few records of Hampshire County and Commonwealth of Massachusetts records pertaining to Northampton are also included. Minutes, financial and legal documents, correspondence, petitions, completed forms, reports, maps and plans, and other records of the Town, including census records for 1850 and 1857-64, certificates of marriages and lists of marriages, 1730-1858, and an 1853 volume of birth records. Information on women criminals can be found in monthly police reports, 1877-80, and in the 1811-23 Hampshire County jailer's book; on women students and teachers in 1784-1872 school records; and on women paupers in the 1721-1878 records of the Overseers of the Poor, with correspondence, accounts, bills, inventories, lists of almshouses' residents, indentures, and case histories.

7,143. Pomeroy, Seth
Papers. 1668-1912. 2 vols. and ca. 35 items.
Open. Unpublished guide.
Forbes Library.
Correspondence, journals, receipts, deeds and other

legal documents, muster rolls and military commissions, essays, and other papers of Pomeroy (1706-77), a gunsmith and military officer, including the 1732 statement of intention of marriage between Seth Pomeroy and Mary Hunt (1705-77), his journal of a trip with his wife from Northampton to various towns in Connecticut during 1743, and correspondence between him and his wife Mary Hunt Pomeroy. Also included is a diary in which Hannah Wells Pomeroy (1782-1861) describes the difficulties of her journey from Northampton to DeKalb, NY, during 1816 and summarizes the hardships she encountered as an early settler in DeKalb during the 1810s and 1820s.

7,144. Trumbull, James Russell
Papers. 1661-1907. Ca. 21 vols. and 881 items.
Open. Catalog cards.
Forbes Library.
Trumbull (1825-99), an historian, created this collection of correspondence, drafts of articles and chapters, notes, notebooks, sermons, deeds, military documents, town records, maps, plans, and other material during the research and writing of his *History of Northampton, From Its Settlement in 1654* (Northampton: Gazette Printing Co., 1898-1902). Also includes material of his niece Nancy L. Miller, who helped him with the book. After his death, she corresponded with historians and genealogists about Northampton and its families.

7,145. Woodruff
Papers. 1815-1957. Ca. 7 vols., 159 items, and 1 microfilm reel.
Open. No guide.
Forbes Library.
Correspondence; genealogical notes and drafts; deeds, indentures, military commissions, and other legal documents; notebooks; lists; daguerreotypes and photos; and other material collected by Martha Charlicana Woodruff (1863-1961) during her research on Woodruff and related families. Included are an 1841 notebook of Sally Taylor [Mrs. David] Pease, a 1903 catalog of Mrs. Jerusha A. Woodruff's antique collection, and letters to Martha Woodruff from various women.

7,146. Clarke, Anna Laura
Papers. 1823-37. Ca. 4 ft.
Open. No guide.
Northampton Historical Society.
Papers reflecting the career of Clarke (1788-1861), who was a teacher in Northampton and elsewhere before she began touring the US to present lantern slide lectures on national costumes, historical topics, and scientific subjects. Includes her slides; an 1823 pamphlet concerning the use of the magic lantern, for which Clarke wrote a lecture on dress of the Romans; a transcription of the lecture; and hairpieces Clarke apparently wore while lecturing.

7,147. Clef Club
Records. 1906-53. 2 Hollinger boxes and 1 envelope.
Open. No guide.
Northampton Historical Society.
Constitution, bylaws, minutes, lists of members, programs, a clipping, and a history of this Northampton music club, founded in 1905 and disbanded in 1939. Music teachers and professional and amateur musicians were Club members, but men were excluded until 1933 when a few were admitted to lend versatility to the Club's choral programs. The Club sponsored public concerts, promoted the work of local composers, and provided its members with lectures and readings on classical music.

7,148. Hayden Family
Papers. 1863-1973. 1 Hollinger box.
Open. No guide.
Northampton Historical Society.
Bills and other financial papers, military records, school report cards, a page of a soldier's Civil War diary, WWII ration books, post cards, and other material of the family, which resided in Northampton and Haydenville, MA, pertain primarily to Elmer Hayden (1897-1971) and his wife Sarah Elizabeth Shea Hayden (1919-). Includes her notes and drafts of the history and genealogy of the Shea and Hayden families; items pertaining to her education, church affiliation, and activities with the Girl Scouts; and autograph books.

7,149. Lathrop Family
Papers. 1861-1938. 6 in.
Open. No guide.
Northampton Historical Society.
Correspondence, drafts of essays on local and family history, receipts, a passport, photos, clippings, and printed material of this Northampton family pertain primarily to Clarissa Stebbins Lathrop (1823-1908) and her daughters Suzanne Lathrop (1860-1938), Bessie Lathrop (1854-?), and Clara Lathrop (?-1907). Included are photographic portraits of women, photos of the Lathrop sisters' art studio, and an essay on Clarissa Lathrop by Anna C. Bliss.

7,150. Miscellaneous Manuscripts
Collection. 1659-1976. Ca. 600 items.
Open. Index.
Northampton Historical Society.
Correspondence, diaries, financial records, legal documents, commissions and military items, pamphlets, broadsides, and photos document the history of Northampton and its residents, organizations, and historic sites. Includes a diary of Clarissa Stebbins for 1832 to 1843 and a diary of Fannie Wright for 1848 to 1859. Also included are legal documents conveying property to and from various women, among them 1781 articles of indenture for Mary Davis, a 7-year-old, which were signed by the Overseers for the Poor; estate papers of Olive Ames Wright and other women in her family, 1842-89; and late 18th-century financial agreements between Anna Patch and her son Robert Fitts.

7,151. Oral History Project
Oral history. 1963- . 2 ft. and 47 tapes and transcripts.
Partially restricted. Card file.
Northampton Historical Society.
Tapes, transcriptions, research notes, and correspondence relate to interviews in which prominent Northampton residents and older citizens discuss their lives and the town's history. Included are interviews of Alice Bly, Louise (Miller) Hodges, Clara (Cooley) Campbell, Bessie (Campbell) Feiker, Martha (Dickinson) Galbraith, Hilda Hamlin, Mrs. Michael Manning, Isabell (Churchill) Mooney, Mary Walsh O'Keefe, June Parsons Filion, Mrs. Ivan Parsons, Edith Carpenter Shepherd, and Helen O'Shea Woods. Also included are recollections of Grace (Goodhue) Coolidge and other information about women in the interviews of male residents.

7,152. Parsons, Josiah, Family
Papers. 1827-71. 1 vol. and 50 items.
Open. No guide.
Northampton Historical Society.
Papers of this Northampton family consist of letters about teaching, church activities, homesteading in Ohio, travels, family life, and visits with family members and a diary that Anne A. Spaulding of Walpole, NH, kept before her marriage to Elijah Chauncey Parsons in 1874. The diary contains listings of her monthly expenses and a description of a trip she made with her aunt by train to Boston and by ship to Baltimore and back.

7,153. Academic History and Policy
Records. 1904- . 17 boxes.
Open. No guide.
Smith College Archives.
Minutes, correspondence, programs, lists, invitations, and photos primarily pertain to the awarding of honors at Smith College graduation, such campus honorary societies as Sigma Xi and Phi Beta Kappa, and Smith's Junior Year Abroad program. Records for the program in France from 1921 on are particularly detailed; also included are records of the Association of Former Juniors in France.

7,154. Alumnae Association
Records. 1881- . 18 boxes.
Open. No guide.
Smith College Archives.
Detailed minutes of the council, lists of members, correspondence, programs, bulletins, reminiscences, flyers, song sheets, photos, clippings, and artifacts of the Association of Smith Alumnae, founded in 1881, include material on College reunions and on Smith Clubs in various cities.

7,155. Buildings and Grounds
Records. 1875- . 62 boxes, 6 vols., 20 items, and 1 microfilm reel.
Open. No guide.
Smith College Archives.
Correspondence, reports by maintenance personnel, pamphlets, registers and lists, blueprints and drawings, maps, photos, and drafts of histories of sites and of buildings trace the evolution of Smith College environment in dormitories, libraries, classrooms, gymnasiums, laboratories, and landscapes.

7,156. Classes
Records. 1879- . Ca. 650 boxes and 100 vols.
Partially restricted. No guide.
Smith College Archives.
Correspondence, diaries, autobiographical accounts, class letters, dance programs, commencement programs, reunion material, photos, clippings, and artifacts. Includes personal papers of some Smith College students while they were attending Smith and some material from their later lives; folders of biographical information on members of each class, records of each class's group activities, and records of the class secretaries. These data are detailed enough for statistical study.

7,157. Faculty
Records. Ca. 1875- . 33 boxes.
Open. No guide.
Smith College Archives.
Minutes of all Smith College faculty meetings and of the faculty's various committees are preserved with lists of committees, lists of rules, correspondence, memoranda, programs, and other administrative records pertaining to endowed chairs and lectureships; the faculty code of rules by which professors conduct their teaching and administrative business; faculty organizations, including the Faculty Wives Club; and faculty shows, most of which were musicals performed by faculty members for charitable causes.

7,158. Faculty Papers
Collection. 1875- . Ca. 275 boxes.
Open. No guide.
Smith College Archives.
Personal, scholarly, pedagogical, and administrative correspondence; research notes; drafts of scholarly publications; classroom material; and other items of individual Smith College faculty members. Includes some papers and records of Dorothy S. Ainsworth, a teacher in the physical education department; Caroline Brown Bourland, modern languages; Julia H. Caverno, Greek; Mary Ellen Chase, literature and history; Ruth Swan Clark, philosophy; Grace Hazard Conkling, literature; Margaret Brackenbury Crook, religion; Mina (Kirstein) Curtiss, English; Anna Alice Cutler, philosophy; Eleanor Shipley Duckett, Latin and history; Mary Louise Foster, chemistry; Ethel Hale

Freeman, English; Emily Hale, English; Agnes Hunt, history; Mary Augusta Jordan, English; Marie F. Kapp, German; Margaret Kemp, botany; Elizabeth McGrew Kimball, art; Jennette Perry Lee, English; Marine Leland, French; Mary Belle McElwain, classics; Myra Sampson, zoology; Victoria Schrager, English; Frances Grace Smith, botany; Beulah Strong, art; Inez Whipple Wilder, zoology; Katharine S. Woodward, English; and Ruth E. Young, Italian.

Also included are papers of Ada Louise Comstock, Smith College dean and later president of Radcliffe College; Annetta I. Clark, who worked in College administration; Elizabeth Deering Hanscom, who taught editing and literature; Elizabeth A. Drew, a writer and critic; Edith Naomi Hill, an editor; Marjorie Hope Nicolson, an author and administrator; and Laura Lord Scales, an administrator.

7,159. Graduate Work
Records. 1882- . 16 boxes.
Open. No guide.
Smith College Archives.
Minutes, policy statements, course outlines, examinations, bulletins, correspondence, and other administrative and educational records include material of the Cambridge School of Architecture and Landscape Architecture, a Smith affiliate noted for training women at a time when they were not welcome in other professional institutions in architecture; the Alumnae College; the School for Social Work; the Italian and music summer schools; and of Smith's graduate instruction generally, most of which was directed toward master's degrees.

7,160. Official Events and Special Periods and Time
Collection. 1875- . 90 boxes, 37 vols., and ca. 150 tapes.
Open. No guide.
Smith College Archives.
Correspondence, card indexes, articles, programs, newsletters, photos, clippings, and tape recordings concern Smith College history highlights. Includes material on inaugurations of College presidents; anniversaries in 1900, 1925, 1950, and 1975 of the College's founding; special conferences held on campus, such as the Model League of Nations in 1933 and 1946; fires, murders, suicides, and other disasters; College participation in 1898, 1915, and 1933 world fairs; special scholarly symposia held at the school; and distinguished visitors, among them Smith Medal recipients and honorary degree conferees. Also included is material documenting the College's wartime service: the Smith College Relief Unit in WWI and defense courses, bond drives, and work with the WAVES during WWII.

7,161. Presidents
Records. 1873- . 163 boxes.
Open. No guide.
Smith College Archives.
Scholarly, administrative, and to a lesser extent personal papers of presidents of Smith College consist of correspondence, memoranda, drafts of lectures and speeches, reports, minutes, photos, and printed items that document changes in educational policy affecting women students and faculty. Includes some papers of Elizabeth (Cutter) Morrow, an author who served as acting president of Smith from 1939 to 1940.

7,162. Smith Centennial Study
Papers. 1970-76. 15 boxes, 7 drawers, and ca. 175 tapes.
Open. No guide.
Smith College Archives.
Author Jacqueline [Mrs. William] Van Voris conducted a detailed research program employing oral history techniques to document the history of the College at its centennial; her work resulted in the book *College, a Smith Mosaic* (1975). Correspondence, memoranda, research notes, drafts, lists and card indexes, photos, and tape recordings and transcriptions of interviews contain extensive information on College alumnae.

7,163. Smith College History
Collection. 1875- . 30 boxes and 12 vols.
Open. No guide.
Smith College Archives.
Correspondence, diaries, legal documents, biographical data, cartoons, scrapbooks, photos, articles, clippings, and books primarily concern the founding, incorporation, and finances of the College. Also includes some personal papers of Sophia Smith, a philanthropist from Hatfield, MA, and benefactor of the College. Also available are papers and business records of her advisor John Morton Greene, a clergyman whose ideas were influential in Smith's plans for the College.

7,164. Student Activities
Records. 1875- . Ca. 100 boxes and 17 vols.
Open. No guide.
Smith College Archives.
Correspondence, memoranda, fiscal accounts, administrative records, minutes, programs, radio and play scripts, circulars, flyers, posters, and newsletters pertain to Smith College athletics, clubs, dramatics, radio, student government, political demonstrations, and the Smith College Association for Christian Work. Athletics records include material on field days, competitions, and matches; records of athletic clubs; and information on particular sports such as basketball. Club records contain detailed documentation of the Alpha Society and Phi Kappa Psi, debate groups, the Flying Club, and the International Relations Club. Material of the Association, an organization for religious and reform activities, covers the years 1892 to 1945.

7,165. Trustees
Records. 1888- . 11 boxes and 7 vols.
Open. No guide.
Smith College Archives.
Minutes, reports, correspondence, lists, biographical data, photos, clippings, and other administrative records. Includes papers of at least two women trustees at Smith: Charlotte (Cheever) Tucker and Harriet Bliss Ford, a social worker and editor.

7,166. Branch, Anna Hempstead
Papers. 1780-1937. Ca. 10,000 items.
Open. Card index.
Smith College, Neilson Library, Rare Book Room.
Correspondence, drafts of poems and plays, notebooks, biographical material, family papers, and photos of Branch (1875-1937), an author, primarily consist of letters from more than 200 friends, relatives, and authors. Also included are letters to Branch's mother Mary L. (Bolles) Branch as well as information on the Branch and Bolles families, Smith College, the Christadora settlement house, the Poets' Guild and other literary organizations, and publication of Branch's writings.

7,167. Chapelbrook Foundation
Records. 1953-71. 27 boxes.
Access restricted. Card index.
Smith College, Neilson Library, Rare Book Room.
A philanthropic organization for support of the arts and scholarship between 1953 and 1971, the Foundation granted awards particularly in the fields of art, music, literature, psychology, and history. Applications and supporting documents such as résumés, some administrative records, correspondence, notes on action taken, informal reports on the progress of projects that were funded, and other material. Index provides name access to applicants, reviewers of applications, and Foundation administrators. Also includes information on historian Constance McLaughlin Green, modern dancer Ruth St. Denis, author Tillie Olsen, and other artists and scholars.

7,168. Cushman, Maria S.
Papers. 1857-64. 1 vol.
Open. No guide.
Smith College, Neilson Library, Rare Book Room.
Student notebooks of Cushman contain essays written for a composition class at Utica Female Seminary with corrections by a teacher, lists of important dates in history, notes on lectures on the Bible at the Broadway Tabernacle in New York City, recipes, and post cards of St. Augustine, FL.

7,169. Glasgow, Ellen Anderson Gholson
Papers. 1930-45. 51 items.
Open. No guide.
Smith College, Neilson Library, Rare Book Room.
In correspondence to Bessie Judith (Zaban) Jones, Glasgow (1873-1945), a novelist, wrote about the classics, contemporary authors, poetry, her novels, her health, travel plans, the South, and family news; she also commented frequently on publications by Bessie Jones's husband Howard Mumford Jones. Some of these letters have been published in Blair Rouse's edition of Ellen Glasgow, *Letters* (New York: Harcourt, Brace, 1958).

7,170. Lindbergh, Anne (Morrow)
Papers. 1931-35. Ca. 3 ft.
Access restricted. No guide.
Smith College, Neilson Library, Rare Book Room.
Original manuscript and drafts, proofs, drawings, maps, photos, and correspondence of Lindbergh (1906-), an author, relate to her book *North to the Orient* (New York: Harcourt, Brace, 1935) about her airplane flight with her husband Charles A. Lindbergh from Washington, DC, to Japan and China in 1931.

7,171. Miscellaneous Manuscripts
Collection. 1592-1963. 21 in.
Partially closed. Card index.
Smith College, Neilson Library, Rare Book Room.
Correspondence, legal documents, and drafts of books, short stories, essays, and poems include a few letters and/or literary manuscripts by Louisa May Alcott, Susan Brownell Anthony, Josephine Dodge (Daskam) Bacon, Kay Boyle, Willa Sibert Cather, Katherine Garrison Chapin, Mary Ellen Chase, Lydia Maria (Francis) Child, Grace Walcott (Hazard) Conkling, Elizabeth (Bacon) Custer, Emily Dickinson, Julia (Ward) Howe, Helen Adams Keller, Lucy Larcom, Harriet Monroe, Elizabeth Reeve (Cutter) Morrow, Josephine Preston Peabody, Lydia Howard (Huntley) Sigourney, Gertrude Stein, Harriet Elizabeth (Beecher) Stowe, and Kate Douglas (Smith) Wiggin. Also includes 13 letters of Edith Newbold (Jones) Wharton.

7,172. Addams, Jane
Papers. 1904-60. 2 document boxes.
Open. Published guide.
Smith College, Sophia Smith Collection.
[Miss] Addams (1860-1935), a settlement worker and reformer, founded Hull House with Ellen Gates Starr in 1889 in Chicago; Addams also organized the Women's International League for Peace and Freedom in 1915. Letters to friends; typescripts of addresses, 1912-33; photos; biographical notices; obituaries; reprints; WILPF records; and Hull House records, including reports for 1904 to 1933, yearbooks, programs, articles, clippings, and publications. Addresses and articles relate to such subjects as social service, the status of women, the "challenge to Christianity," education, juvenile delinquency, trade unions, child labor, employment, prohibition, prostitution, and women's rights. Taken from Mary-Elizabeth Murdock, *Catalog of The Sophia Smith Collection, Women's History Archive,* 2nd ed. (Northampton, MA: Smith College, 1976).

7,173. Ainsworth, Dorothy Sears
Papers. Ca. 1916-75. 40 document boxes and ca. 7 vols.
Open. Published guide.
Smith College, Sophia Smith Collection.
Papers of Ainsworth (1894-1976), a specialist in women's physical education who was director of physical education at Smith from 1926 to 1960, include personal and professional correspondence; drafts of addresses, articles, and reports; term papers, department reports, and other material relating to physical education at Smith College and to administrative responsibilities; scrapbooks; and items relating to the American Association for Health, Physical Education and Recreation and to other physical education organizations. Taken from Mary-Elizabeth Murdock, *Catalog of The Sophia Smith Collection, Women's History Archive,* 2nd ed. (Northampton, MA: Smith College, 1976).

7,174. Allen, Florence Ellinwood
Papers. 1912-65. 1 document box.
Open. Published guide.
Smith College, Sophia Smith Collection.
Allen (1884-1966) was a lawyer, a judge in the Ohio Sixth Circuit Court of Appeals from 1934 to 1959, and an advocate of peace. Letters to friends, biographical material, photos, papers relating to Ohio suffrage work from 1914 to 1920, and typescripts of her addresses to such organizations as the International Federation of Women Lawyers, the International Bar Association, and the American Bar Association. Also includes papers of her mother Corinne Marie (Tuckerman) Allen (1856-1931) concerning sexual morality, monogamy, family relationships in Utah during the 1910s, and the founding of the National Congress of Mothers, which later became the National Congress of Parents and Teachers. Taken from Mary-Elizabeth Murdock, *Catalog of The Sophia Smith Collection, Women's History Archive,* 2nd ed. (Northampton, MA: Smith College, 1976).

7,175. American Association for Health, Physical Education and Recreation
Records. Nd. 1 document box and 5 items.
Open. Published guide.
Smith College, Sophia Smith Collection.
Annual reports, 1963-65; minutes of the board of directors and the representative assembly, 1963-65; minutes of the executive council division for girls and women's sports, 1958-65; and a volume containing the 1949 yearbook and convention *Proceedings.* Taken from Mary-Elizabeth Murdock, *Catalog of The Sophia Smith Collection, Women's History Archive,* 2nd ed. (Northampton, MA: Smith College, 1976).

7,176. American Association of University Women
Records. Nd. 1 document box and 1 vol.
Open. Published guide.
Smith College, Sophia Smith Collection.
Notices of Boston and Los Angeles branch meetings, convention material, bulletins for 1923 to 1926, reports, pamphlets, clippings, listings of approved colleges and universities whose graduates are eligible for membership in the AAUW, and histories of scholarships and of the AAUW. Taken from Mary-Elizabeth Murdock, *Catalog of The Sophia Smith Collection, Women's History Archive,* 2nd ed. (Northampton, MA: Smith College, 1976).

7,177. American Council of Railroad Women
Records. Nd. 11 document boxes.
Open. Published guide.
Smith College, Sophia Smith Collection.
Constitution, 1948; bylaws, 1945; annual reports, 1951-72; minutes of meetings; treasurer's reports; business correspondence; secretary's files; membership lists; addresses; biographical information on leaders; photos; history of the ACRW; programs of meetings; and bulletins, 1967-72. Taken from Mary-Elizabeth Murdock, *Catalog of The Sophia Smith Collection, Women's History Archive,* 2nd ed. (Northampton, MA: Smith College, 1976).

7,178. Ames Family
Papers. 1856-1967. Ca. 119 document boxes.
Open. Published guide.
Smith College, Sophia Smith Collection.
Correspondence, diaries, notes, financial records, biographical and genealogical material, photos, original works of art, and publications of the family and descendants of Adelbert Ames (1835-1933), a Civil War general and governor of Mississippi during Reconstruction. Includes correspondence of Adelbert Ames and his wife Blanche (Butler) Ames (1845-1939) as well as extensive correspondence and other papers of their daughter Blanche (Ames) Ames (1878-1969), who was married to Harvard botanist Oakes Ames (1874-1950). In addition to Massachusetts Suffrage Association and other suffrage correspondence, there are original suffrage cartoons by Blanche (Ames) Ames and ca. 200 clippings of suffrage cartoons, as well as material relating to women's rights, philanthropy, politics, science and education, religion, art and architecture, the New England Hospital, and business and industry. Also includes the constitution, minutes, correspondence, and history of the Birth Control League of Massachusetts and an account of the church controversy in Massachusetts. Taken from Mary-Elizabeth Murdock, *Catalog of The Sophia Smith Collection, Women's History Archive,* 2nd ed. (Northampton, MA: Smith College, 1976).

7,179. Another Mother for Peace
Records. Nd. 1 document box.
Open. Published guide.
Smith College, Sophia Smith Collection.
Records of the group, established in 1967, include bylaws, correspondence, newsletters for 1967 to 1975, campaign material, samples of peace Christmas cards, flyers, pamphlets, clippings, reprints, and material documenting efforts to establish a federal department of peace in 1968 and 1969. Taken from Mary-Elizabeth Murdock, *Catalog of The Sophia Smith Collection, Women's History Archive,* 2nd ed. (Northampton, MA: Smith College, 1976).

7,180. Anthony, Susan Brownell
Papers. 1873-1970. 2 document boxes.
Open. Published guide.
Smith College, Sophia Smith Collection.
Family and business correspondence, copies of addresses, biographical and genealogical material, photos, clippings, and other papers of suffragist and reformer [Miss] Anthony (1820-1906) documenting the "illegal voting" controversy of 1872 to 1874 and her suffrage work. Also includes correspondence, photos, news releases, clippings, and memorabilia relating to First Day Women Suffrage Stamp Ceremonies in Adams, MA, on August 26, 1970. Taken from Mary-Elizabeth Murdock, *Catalog of The Sophia Smith Collection, Women's History Archive,* 2nd ed. (Northampton, MA: Smith College, 1976).

7,181. Archbald, Mary Ann (Wodrow)
Papers. 1784-1840. 2 document boxes.
Open. Published guide.
Smith College, Sophia Smith Collection.
Papers of Archbald (1762-1841), a Scottish immigrant pioneer, include letter books containing drafts of letters to her family and friends; journals for the years 1785 to 1840 documenting her early life on Little Cumbray Island in Scotland, her marriage, and her emigration in 1807 to a "hard, happy life" in Mohawk Valley, NY; and commonplace books. Taken from Mary-Elizabeth Murdock, *Catalog of The Sophia Smith Collection, Women's History Archive,* 2nd ed. (Northampton, MA: Smith College, 1976).

7,182. Art
Collection. Nd. 3 boxes.
Open. Published guide.
Smith College, Sophia Smith Collection.
Biographical data, scrapbooks, clippings, advertisements, reviews, and books are primarily from the 20th century and relate to women as artists, art critics, and architects. The bulk of the collection consists of six scrapbooks of art critic Helen Appleton Read, who wrote about the New York art scene for the *Brooklyn Daily Eagle* from 1922 to 1936 and for *Vogue* from 1927 to 1932. In addition, there is material on women's participation in the World's Columbian Exposition of 1893, on landscape architecture, and on individual artists, including Katherine S. Dreier, Sarah Jackson Eddy, and Georgia O'Keeffe. Also includes photos, printed biographical information, and other material from the 19th and 20th centuries relating to women sculptors, including Harriet Goodhue Hosmer, Anne Whitney, Adelaide Johnson, and Bashka Paeff. See Mary-Elizabeth Murdock, *Catalog of The Sophia Smith Collection, Women's History Archive,* 2nd ed. (Northampton, MA: Smith College, 1976).

7,183. Association for the Advancement of Women
Records. Nd. 1 folder and several vols.
Open. Published guide.
Smith College, Sophia Smith Collection.
Records of the AAW, which was established in 1873, include reports; essays by Catharine E. Beecher, Julia Ward Howe, Elizabeth Cady Stanton, and many others; an invitation to the First Woman's Congress in 1873; and the 1876 constitution of the AAW. Taken from Mary-Elizabeth Murdock, *Catalog of The Sophia Smith Collection, Women's History Archive,* 2nd ed. (Northampton, MA: Smith College, 1976).

7,184. Association of Collegiate Alumnae
Records. Nd. 4 document boxes.
Open. Published guide.
Smith College, Sophia Smith Collection.
Records of the ACA, which was established in 1882, include the constitution; correspondence; registers; committee, financial, and branch reports; speeches; photos; announcements; a scrapbook; ACA *Journal,* 1918; and essays relating to the medical education of women, college entrance requirements, the history of the ACA, the Domestic Reform League, university extension programs, athletics for women, wages of working women, school lunch programs, and a bibliography on higher education of women. Includes letters to Ellen H. Richards and to internationalist and pacifist Fannie Fern Andrews. Taken from Mary-Elizabeth Murdock, *Catalog of The Sophia Smith Collection, Women's History Archive,* 2nd ed. (Northampton, MA: Smith College, 1976).

7,185. Authors
Collection. Nd. 7 boxes.
Open. Published guide.
Smith College, Sophia Smith Collection.
Biographical data, reviews, clippings, and articles on women as writers are from the 19th and 20th centuries and are primarily biographical accounts of and literary criticism on American and English writers. Among the American writers represented are Louisa May Alcott, Willa Cather, Emily Dickinson, Margaret Fuller, Sarah Orne Jewett, Harriet Martineau, Sylvia Plath, Harriet (Beecher) Stowe, Mabel (Loomis) Todd, and Emma Lazarus. See Mary-Elizabeth Murdock, *Catalog of The Sophia Smith Collection, Women's History Archive,* 2nd ed. (Northampton, MA: Smith College, 1976).

7,186. Bacon, Josephine Dodge (Daskam)
Papers. Nd. 2 document boxes.
Open. Published guide.
Smith College, Sophia Smith Collection.
Manuscripts of works by Bacon (1876-1961), a writer who graduated from Smith College in 1898, include *Memoirs of a Baby* (1904), in which she satirizes pediatrician Luther Emmett Holt's child training; *In the Border Country* (1909), which presents three visions revealing to women their "true" role in society; and *Truth o' Women* (1923), poems in which women of various nationalities speak from the grave about the truth of their lives. Taken from Mary-Elizabeth Murdock, *Catalog of The Sophia Smith Collection, Women's History Archive,* 2nd ed. (Northampton, MA: Smith College, 1976).

7,187. Bailie, Helen (Tufts)
Papers. 1896-1959. 5 document boxes.
Open. Published guide.
Smith College, Sophia Smith Collection.
Correspondence, journals for the years 1896 to 1959, manuscripts of protest writings and fictional works, addresses, press releases, cartoons, articles, and clippings of Bailie (1874-1962), a writer, political activist, and humanist. Includes a complete record of her DAR trial and ouster, which reveals her involvement in the Red Menace scare of the 1920s; statements and reports from her supporters, including Jane Addams and Carrie Chapman Catt; correspondence and other papers documenting the fight to repeal the Teachers' Loyalty Oath in Massachusetts during the mid-1930s; correspondence and articles tracing William B. Shearer's views on the naval disarmament controversy; and publications of such organizations as the Better America Federation, the Massachusetts Public Interests League, and the DAR. Taken from Mary-Elizabeth Murdock, *Catalog of The Sophia Smith Collection, Women's History Archive,* 2nd ed. (Northampton, MA: Smith College, 1976).

7,188. Barton, Clara Harlowe
Papers. 1852-1919. 4 document boxes.
Open. Published guide.
Smith College, Sophia Smith Collection.
[Miss] Barton (1821-1912) was a teacher, Civil War nurse, and organizer of the American National Red Cross. Correspondence with family, friends, and doctors concerning her health, her efforts to become a nurse and to enter relief work, and her Civil War experiences; addresses; biographical material; photos; a scrapbook; a war service album; and articles. Includes material relating to Andersonville Prison, army life, battlefield experiences, her advocacy of women's rights, and her efforts from 1865 to 1900 to establish the International and the American National Red Cross. Taken from Mary-Elizabeth Murdock, *Catalog of The Sophia Smith Collection, Women's History Archive,* 2nd ed. (Northampton, MA: Smith College, 1976).

7,189. Beard, Mary (Ritter)
Papers. 1936-58. 2 document boxes.
Open. Published guide.
Smith College, Sophia Smith Collection.
Correspondence, typescripts of published books, biographical articles, and addresses of [Mrs. Charles] Beard (1876-1958), a scholar, writer, and women's rights advocate, concern her concept of women's rights, the role of women throughout history, her evaluation of the status of women, and the need to establish a world center for women's archives. Letters of Beard to Dorothy Brush relate to the Japanese birth control movement; to the work of Shidzue Ishimoto Kato, an author, stateswoman, feminist, and birth control champion; and to Beard's book *The Force of Women in Japanese History* (1953). Taken from Mary-Elizabeth Murdock, *Catalog of The Sophia Smith Collection, Women's History Archive,* 2nd ed. (Northampton, MA: Smith College, 1976).

7,190. Beggs, Vera (Wadsworth)
Papers. Nd. 2 document boxes.
Open. Published guide.
Smith College, Sophia Smith Collection.
Correspondence from the period 1933 to 1946, minutes, reports, articles, and pamphlets of [Mrs. Frederic] Beggs (?-1968), a suffragist, international relations specialist, and champion of equal citizenship and peace, relate to her work as chairman of the National Committee on the Cause and Cure of War, as chairman of the department of international relations of the GFWC, as cofounder and first chairman of the US section of the Canadian-American Women's Committee and to her involvement with the International Alliance of Women for Suffrage and Equal Citizenship and the Carrie Chapman Catt Memorial Fund. Includes extensive correspondence with Catt concerning work for women's rights and peace. Taken from Mary-Elizabeth Murdock, *Catalog of The Sophia Smith Collection, Women's History Archive,* 2nd ed. (Northampton, MA: Smith College, 1976).

7,191. Billings, Florence
Papers. 1919-41. 2 document boxes.
Open. Published guide.
Smith College, Sophia Smith Collection.
Correspondence, journals for the years 1919 to 1926, writings, photos, reports, articles, and clippings of Billings (1879-1959), who was a relief organizer in France from 1914 to 1918, in the Near East from 1919 to 1923, and from 1926 to 1928 during Armenian-Greek disputes. Includes correspondence with pioneer missionary Annie T. Allen, Turkish writer and feminist Halide Edib Adivar, and from 1925 to 1941 with Reza Shah Pahlevi, the prime minister and later shah of Iran. Taken from Mary-Elizabeth Murdock, *Catalog of The Sophia Smith Collection, Women's History Archive,* 2nd ed. (Northampton, MA: Smith College, 1976).

7,192. Birth Control Clinical Research Bureau
Records. Nd. 10 document boxes.
Open. Published guide.
Smith College, Sophia Smith Collection.
Records of the Bureau, which was established in 1917, include biographical material on birth control pioneers, including Emma Goldman; publications and reports of leagues such as the Neo-Malthusian League, the American Birth Control League, and the Birth Control Federation of America; correspondence, reports, and publications of the National Committee on Federal Legislation for Birth Control and the National Committee on Maternal Health; pamphlets and other material supporting and opposing the international birth control movement, with information on contraceptive methods, birth control laws and legislation, and the religious controversy over birth control; Norman Himes's anatomical slides; and books. The Research Bureau was renamed the Margaret Sanger Bureau in 1943. Taken from Mary-Elizabeth Murdock, *Catalog of The Sophia Smith Collection, Women's History Archive,* 2nd ed. (Northampton, MA: Smith College, 1976).

7,193. Blake Family
Papers. 1871-1943. 1 document box.
Open. Published guide.
Smith College, Sophia Smith Collection.
Papers of Lillie (Devereux) Blake (1833-1913), a writer and suffragist, and her daughter Katherine Devereux Blake (1858-1950), a teacher, suffragist, first woman treasurer of the National Education Association, and champion of the Equal Rights Amendment, progressive education, and peace. Consists of correspondence, addresses, articles, a scrapbook of clippings on the status of women from the period 1871 to 1875, clippings on women's rights, and a copy of Lillie Blake's *The Fables* (1879). Correspondents include Isabel Howland and Matilda Gage. Taken from Mary-Elizabeth Murdock, *Catalog of The Sophia Smith Collection, Women's History Archive,* 2nd ed. (Northampton, MA: Smith College, 1976).

7,194. Brewer, Vivion Mercer (Lenon)
Papers. Nd. 10 document boxes.
Partially restricted. Published guide.
Smith College, Sophia Smith Collection.
[Mrs. Joe Robinson] Brewer (1900-), an integrationist, served on the executive committee and as president of the Women's Emergency Committee to Open Our Schools, Little Rock, AR, during the late 1950s and early 1960s. Correspondence from the years 1956 to 1972 relating to Committee elections, national opinions, and general political support; Brewer's typescript "The Embattled Ladies of Little Rock"; minutes, agendas, memoranda, publicity surveys, clippings, newsletters, and other records of the Committee; material on segregationist activities and on Arkansas elections from 1958 to 1961; and memorabilia. Taken from Mary-Elizabeth Murdock, *Catalog of The Sophia Smith Collection, Women's History Archive,* 2nd ed. (Northampton, MA: Smith College, 1976).

7,195. Brewster Family
Papers. 1884-1930s. 9 document boxes.
Open. Published guide.
Smith College, Sophia Smith Collection.
Papers of Northampton sisters Anna Gertrude Brewster and Caroline Brewster, who were teachers; Mary K. Brewster, who was a writer; and Helen Brewster, who was director of the People's Institute in Northampton. Includes correspondence, diaries for the years 1889 to 1927, children's handwritten newspapers, photos, scrapbooks, theater programs, clippings, and other material relating to Academy of Music events and the Little Theatre Movement in Northampton. Mary Brewster was the author of "The Municipal Theatre in America" and "Theatre in Northampton" as well as newspaper stories, plays, and a book; correspondence relates to her western and Australian tours, to contemporary Northampton news, and to foreign travels of her sisters. Taken from Mary-Elizabeth Murdock, *Catalog of The Sophia Smith Collection, Women's History Archive,* 2nd ed. (Northampton, MA: Smith College, 1976).

7,196. Brown, Helen (Gurley)
Papers. Nd. 16 document boxes, 1 oversize vol., and 2 recording discs.
Open. Published guide.
Smith College, Sophia Smith Collection.
Papers of Brown (1922-), a businesswoman, journalist, and editor of *Cosmopolitan Magazine,* include correspondence, promotional material, articles, and clippings relating to her books *Sex and the Single Girl* and *Sex and the Office* as well as scripts for a radio series, editor's drafts, record albums, and newspaper columns. Taken from Mary-Elizabeth Murdock, *Catalog of The Sophia Smith Collection, Women's History Archive,* 2nd ed. (Northampton, MA: Smith College, 1976).

7,197. Brush, Dorothy
Papers. Nd. 12 document boxes.
Open. Published guide.
Smith College, Sophia Smith Collection.
Brush (1896?-1968) was a writer, crusader for birth control and women's rights, and editor of the International Planned Parenthood Federation "News." Correspondence, articles, and pamphlets relating to her writings and interests, especially birth control and sex education; typescripts of an unpublished play "Margaret"; a photo album of a 1959 trip to the Far East with Margaret Sanger; a complete set of the IPPF "News" periodicals; and research material for books on Sanger, Japanese women, and menopause. Taken from

Mary-Elizabeth Murdock, *Catalog of The Sophia Smith Collection, Women's History Archive,* 2nd ed. (Northampton, MA: Smith College, 1976).

7,198. Bryant, Louise Frances (Stevens)
Papers. 1885-1956. 14 document boxes.
Open. Published guide.
Smith College, Sophia Smith Collection.
Bryant (1885-1956) was a social welfare and public health specialist who held a PhD in medical science. Extensive personal and professional correspondence relates to her involvement with the AAUW, the Girl Scouts, army recruitment and demobilization in WWI, eugenics, and child health, while diaries for the years 1921 to 1955, organizational records, reports, articles, and other papers trace her career as a researcher on school meals and child health for the Russell Sage Foundation, as a statistician on the world food supply and manpower for the US Army, and as a publicist for the United Hospital Fund and National Committee on Maternal Health. Also includes a typescript of Lura Beam's biography of Bryant, *Bequest from a Life.* Taken from Mary-Elizabeth Murdock, *Catalog of The Sophia Smith Collection, Women's History Archive,* 2nd ed. (Northampton, MA: Smith College, 1976).

7,199. Burr, Jane
Papers. 1914-53. 1 document box.
Open. Published guide.
Smith College, Sophia Smith Collection.
Jane Burr (1882-1958) was the pseudonym used by Rosalind Mae (Guggenheim) Winslow, a journalist and a champion of women's rights, birth control, companionate marriage, and reforms relating to divorce laws and dress. Correspondence with Havelock Ellis and others concerning her views on freer sex, birth control, marriage and divorce laws, and the status of women; photos; and articles and clippings by and about Burr. Taken from Mary-Elizabeth Murdock, *Catalog of The Sophia Smith Collection, Women's History Archive,* 2nd ed. (Northampton, MA: Smith College, 1976).

7,200. Bush-Brown Family
Papers. 1835-1969. 14 document boxes and 5 vols.
Open. Published guide.
Smith College, Sophia Smith Collection.
Family correspondence, diaries, biographical material, photos, etchings, drawings, clippings, and article reprints of this family of sculptors, muralists, and painters. Includes two albums of silk murals by Lydia Bush-Brown Head (1887-) and letters concerning her work as an occupational therapist in France in 1918 and 1919, correspondence of Ellen Day Hale, and papers of Margaret Lesley Bush-Brown (1857-1944) and other family members. Taken from Mary-Elizabeth Murdock, *Catalog of The Sophia Smith Collection, Women's History Archive,* 2nd ed. (Northampton, MA: Smith College, 1976).

7,201. Canadian-American Women's Association
Records. 1941-69. 13 document boxes.
Open. Published guide.
Smith College, Sophia Smith Collection.
Records of the American section of the Association, an affiliate of the National Council of Women, include correspondence for 1949 to 1965, financial records, special studies, historical information, and material relating to exchange programs, meetings, special projects, conferences, and reports. The Association existed from 1941 to 1969. Taken from Mary-Elizabeth Murdock, *Catalog of The Sophia Smith Collection, Women's History Archive,* 2nd ed. (Northampton, MA: Smith College, 1976).

7,202. Carey, Ernestine Moller (Gilbreth)
Papers. 1904-65. 6 document boxes.
Closed. Published guide.
Smith College, Sophia Smith Collection.
Correspondence; diaries; notes; typescripts of lectures, short stories, and books; an excerpt from a family log; movie stills; photos; clippings; and memorabilia of Carey (1908-), a writer. Includes typescripts of her books *Jumping Jupiter* (1952), *Rings Around Us* (1956), and *Giddy Moment* (1958); stills of the motion picture made from her book *Cheaper by the Dozen;* and material relating to the Gilbreth and Carey families. Taken from Mary-Elizabeth Murdock, *Catalog of The Sophia Smith Collection, Women's History Archive,* 2nd ed. (Northampton, MA: Smith College, 1976).

7,203. Carpenter, Frank G.
Papers. 1893-1917. 1 document box.
Open. Published guide.
Smith College, Sophia Smith Collection.
Papers of Carpenter (1855-1924), a journalist, include letters from Mabel G. [Mrs. Alexander Graham] Bell, Salvation Army leader Maud B. Booth, and Elizabeth (Cochrane) Seaman, who traveled around the world and whose pseudonym was Nellie Bly; a manuscript poem and letters by Elizabeth Cady Stanton concerning women in Congress and educational qualifications for suffrage, which she devised for the 1894 Ithaca Convention; and questionnaire responses from Susan B. Anthony and Clara Barton relating to the purpose of life, work and marriage, and women in Congress. Taken from Mary-Elizabeth Murdock, *Catalog of The Sophia Smith Collection, Women's History Archive,* 2nd ed. (Northampton, MA: Smith College, 1976).

7,204. Casement, Frances M.
Papers. Ca. 1860-1928. 2 boxes.
Open. Published guide.
Smith College, Sophia Smith Collection.
Pamphlets, periodicals, and other papers gathered by Casement (1840-1928) in her suffrage work in Ohio. See Mary-Elizabeth Murdock, *Catalog of The Sophia Smith Collection, Women's History Archive,* 2nd ed. (Northampton, MA: Smith College, 1976).

7,205. Catt, Carrie Clinton (Lane) Chapman
Papers. 1892-1946. 5 document boxes.
Open. Published guide.
Smith College, Sophia Smith Collection.
Correspondence, typescripts of suffrage addresses, biographical material, photos, suffrage cartoons, pamphlets, brochures, clippings, and other papers of Catt (1859-1947), a suffragist, women's rights advocate, and worker for peace. Includes papers relating to the organization of the International Woman Suffrage Alliance, 1908-23; the National American Woman Suffrage Association, 1902-19; and the LWV. Also includes correspondence from the period 1892 to 1946 with suffrage leaders, congressmen, and government officials, including A. Mitchell Palmer, Caroline Reilly, and Maud (Wood) Park, on such topics as old age, policewomen, the LWV, and WWII. Catt was married to Leo Chapman and then to Charles William Catt. Taken from Mary-Elizabeth Murdock, *Catalog of The Sophia Smith Collection, Women's History Archive,* 2nd ed. (Northampton, MA: Smith College, 1976).

7,206. Clark, Kate (Upson)
Papers. 1862-1935. 2 document boxes.
Open. Published guide.
Smith College, Sophia Smith Collection.
Papers of Clark (1851-1935), a writer, poet, lecturer, and journalist, include correspondence with her sister Mary (Upson) Avery, diaries for the years 1862 to 1868 and 1888 with observations on the Civil War and Reconstruction, a travel journal for 1923 to 1925, manuscript notebooks of her reminiscences, article and lecture notes, and a 1935 memorial tribute from Wheaton College in Norton, MA. Taken from Mary-Elizabeth Murdock, *Catalog of The Sophia Smith Collection, Women's History Archive,* 2nd ed. (Northampton, MA: Smith College, 1976).

7,207. Committee of Correspondence
Records. 1952-69. Ca. 55 document boxes.
Open. Published guide.
Smith College, Sophia Smith Collection.
This New York-based affiliate of Women's International Non-Government Organizations existed from 1952 to 1969 and sponsored leadership training programs and seminars designed to prepare women to assume leadership roles in their emerging nations. Minutes, correspondence, photos, multilingual publications on such subjects as community action and meeting community needs, files relating to the status and problems of the world's women, and other records. Taken fromMary-Elizabeth Murdock, *Catalog of The Sophia Smith Collection, Women's History Archive,* 2nd ed. (Northampton, MA: Smith College, 1976).

7,208. Consumer's League of Kentucky
Records. Nd. 2 document boxes.
Open. Published guide.
Smith College, Sophia Smith Collection.
Constitution; presidents' reports; minutes of meetings, 1901-19; financial records; correspondence, including some from the US Department of Labor; reports, 1919-41; a history of the League through 1941; bulletins of the national and state Consumers Leagues; pamphlets; and publications. The records relate to efforts to secure legislation for minimum wage, control of contagious diseases, women and child labor regulations, pure food, industrial codes, and compulsory education. Taken from Mary-Elizabeth Murdock, *Catalog of The Sophia Smith Collection, Women's History Archive,* 2nd ed. (Northampton, MA: Smith College, 1976).

7,209. Crump, Mary Alletta
Papers. Ca. 1913-70. 2 document boxes.
Open. Published guide.
Smith College, Sophia Smith Collection.
Crump (1887-1970) was co-owner of the Greenwich Village Crumperie Tea Room from 1916 to 1927, an entertainer, and a volunteer worker for the American National Red Cross, the Grenfell Mission, the American Women's Voluntary Services in the 1940s, and for the YMCA. Personal and business correspondence; a taped conversation between Crump and Joyce Grenfell in 1958; photos; menus, sketches, advertisements, clippings, and memorabilia of the Tea Room; and guest books containing Greenwich Village Theatre programs and sketches, poems, and annotations by such Tea Room patrons as Christopher Morley, Charles Coburn, Theodore Dreiser, Fannie Hurst, Laura and William Rose Benét, and Dorothy Dix. Taken from Mary-Elizabeth Murdock, *Catalog of The Sophia Smith Collection, Women's History Archive,* 2nd ed. (Northampton, MA: Smith College, 1976).

7,210. Cushman, Nancy (Cox) McCormack
Papers. 1911-67. 9 document boxes.
Open. Published guide.
Smith College, Sophia Smith Collection.
Personal and business correspondence, diaries for 1930 to 1931, writings, interviews, texts of radio talks, photos, etchings, and papers and memorabilia relating to exhibitions and commissions of Cushman (1885-1967), a sculptor whose subjects included Jane Addams, Mussolini, Gandhi, and Ezra Pound. Correspondents include Mary R. Beard, Laura Benét, Louise (DeKoven) Bowen, Elizabeth Sparhawk Jones, Marian MacDowell, and Ezra and Dorothy Pound. Taken from Mary-Elizabeth Murdock, *Catalog of The Sophia Smith Collection, Women's History Archive,* 2nd ed. (Northampton, MA: Smith College, 1976).

7,211. Davis, Angela
Papers. 1969-72. 2 boxes.
Open. Published guide.
Smith College, Sophia Smith Collection.
Printed material of Davis (1944-), a black activist, including articles and statements, cartoons, clippings, flyers, newsletters, and posters. Also includes material relating to the work of the National Committee to Free Angela Davis and state committees devoted to that cause. See Mary-Elizabeth Murdock, *Catalog of The Sophia Smith Collection, Women's History Archive,* 2nd ed. (Northampton, MA: Smith College, 1976).

7,212. De Forest, Charlotte Burgis
Papers. 1893-1973. 4 document boxes.
Open. Published guide.
Smith College, Sophia Smith Collection.
De Forest (1879-1973) was a writer and president of Kobe College in Japan from 1915 to 1940. Correspondence from the years 1935 to 1951, journal entries, writings, biographical material, an interview, photos, citations, awards, her articles in *International Review of Missions,* and a copy of her *History of Kobe College.* Includes a description of a Japanese relocation center in Manzanar, CA, reflections on Hiroshima and her hopes for postwar Japan, and a taped interview from 1970 concerning Japanese society and culture as well as her career. Taken from Mary-Elizabeth Murdock, *Catalog of The Sophia Smith Collection, Women's History Archive,* 2nd ed. (Northampton, MA: Smith College, 1976).

7,213. De Lussan, Zelie
Papers. 1877-1949. 1 document box.
Open. Published guide.
Smith College, Sophia Smith Collection.
De Lussan (1863-1949) was an opera singer who sang the roles of Carmen, Desdemona, Musetta, and Mignon. Correspondence, including letters from Adelina Patti describing coaching for a performance of *Lakmé;* repertoire notebooks for 1886 to 1896; photos; a scrapbook, clippings, and memorabilia relating to public concerts and command performances before Queen Victoria; and opera and concert programs. De Lussan was married to Angelo Fronani. Taken from Mary-Elizabeth Murdock, *Catalog of The Sophia Smith Collection, Women's History Archive,* 2nd ed. (Northampton, MA: Smith College, 1976).

7,214. De Mille, Agnes
Papers. 1924-73. 11 document boxes.
Access restricted. Published guide.
Smith College, Sophia Smith Collection.
Papers of de Mille (1908-), a dance recitalist, writer, and choreographer, include correspondence with her mother Anna (George) de Mille containing references to Martha Graham, Ruth St. Denis, Edna Millay, Gertrude Lawrence, and Rebecca West; manuscripts of *And Promenade Home* (1954) and *Book of the Dance* (1963); notes and drafts of *Dance to the Piper* (1952); autobiographical and biographical material; notes on the history of dance; and unpublished lectures. Also contains photos, posters, programs, clippings, a US Information Agency publication on dance in America, and a copy of her *Speak to Me, Dance with Me* (1973). Taken from Mary-Elizabeth Murdock, *Catalog of The Sophia Smith Collection, Women's History Archive,* 2nd ed. (Northampton, MA: Smith College, 1976).

7,215. Diaz, Abby (Morton)
Papers. 1879-1900. 1 document box.
Open. Published guide.
Smith College, Sophia Smith Collection.
Papers of [Mrs. Manuel A.] Diaz (1821-1904), an author, suffragist, and advocate of social reform, include articles by and about her, among them her essay "Personal Reminiscences of the Old Anti-Slavery Times" (1879), leaflets on woman suffrage, papers relating to the Women's Educational and Industrial Union, a bibliography of her writings and talks, and a copy of her book *Old Anti-Slavery Days* (1893). Taken from Mary-Elizabeth Murdock, *Catalog of The Sophia Smith Collection, Women's History Archive,* 2nd ed. (Northampton, MA: Smith College, 1976).

7,216. Doty, Madeleine Zabriskie
Papers. 1906-63. 2 document boxes.
Open. Published guide.
Smith College, Sophia Smith Collection.
Doty (1879-1963) was a lawyer, feminist, advocate of prison reform, WWI correspondent, and worker for peace. Correspondence on such subjects as child welfare, suffrage, prison reform, and her trip to Russia in 1917 and 1918; her incomplete and unpublished autobiography; articles by and about her; photos; her doctoral thesis "The Central Organization for a Durable Peace" (University of Geneva, 1945); and a copy of her book *Behind the Battle Line* (1918). Correspondents include her husband Roger Baldwin, Jane Addams, Dorothy Canfield Fisher, John Galsworthy, Charlotte Perkins Gilman, Emmeline and F. W. Pethick-Lawrence, and H. G. Wells. Taken from Mary-Elizabeth Murdock, *Catalog of The Sophia Smith Collection, Women's History Archive,* 2nd ed. (Northampton, MA: Smith College, 1976).

7,217. Dreier, Ethel Eyre (Valentine)
Papers. 1902-57. 7 document boxes.
Open. Published guide.
Smith College, Sophia Smith Collection.
Papers of [Mrs. H. Edward] Dreier (1872-1958), an author, lecturer, suffragist, and crusader for civic reform, include correspondence with her husband, Jane Addams, Carrie Chapman Catt, and others; diaries for 1939 to 1957; drafts of addresses, reports, and agendas; a file on women in politics; photos; records relating to Dreier's presidency of the Women's City Club of New York from 1924 to 1930 and from 1932 to 1936; reports of the New York State Woman Suffrage party, flyers, clippings, memorabilia, and other material relating to suffrage; and a pamphlet on the education of women in a democracy, which was prepared for the Woman's Centennial Congress in 1940. Also includes papers relating to Brooklyn Female Academy, which was established in 1846 and renamed Packer Collegiate Institute in 1854, and to All Sorts and Conditions of Girls (ASACOG), a Brooklyn settlement house. Taken from Mary-Elizabeth Murdock, *Catalog of The Sophia Smith Collection, Women's History Archive,* 2nd ed. (Northampton, MA: Smith College, 1976).

7,218. Drinker, Sophie Lewis (Hutchinson)
Papers. 1859-1968. Ca. 3 folders, 2 document boxes, and 16 vols.
Open. Published guide.
Smith College, Sophia Smith Collection.
[Mrs. Henry S.] Drinker (1888-1967) was a musicologist and specialist on women in music. Correspondence concerning and manuscript volumes of Brahms's *Stimmenhefte,* research material for Drinker's book *Music and Women* (1948), memorabilia, and a copy of her book *Brahms and His Women's Choruses* (1952). Taken from Mary-Elizabeth Murdock, *Catalog of The Sophia Smith Collection, Women's History Archive,* 2nd ed. (Northampton, MA: Smith College, 1976).

7,219. Eastern Association for the Physical Education of College Women
Records. Nd. 20 document boxes.
Open. Published guide.
Smith College, Sophia Smith Collection.
Treasurer's records; written and taped records of conferences and meetings, ca. 1912 to date; executive board and officers' reports; a history; information on the organization of the Association; membership lists; legislation; committee records; newsletters; material relating to special studies and research; and publications of the national and regional Associations. Taken from Mary-Elizabeth Murdock, *Catalog of The Sophia Smith Collection, Women's History Archive,* 2nd ed. (Northampton, MA: Smith College, 1976).

7,220. Eastman, Elaine (Goodale)
Papers. Nd. 7 document boxes and 4 oversize vols.
Open. Published guide.
Smith College, Sophia Smith Collection.
[Mrs. Charles A.] Eastman (1863-1953) was a writer and specialist in American Indian education. Correspondence on the Massachusetts branch of the Women's International League for Peace and Freedom, Indian Bureau policies, and Indian reservations, education, suffrage, and wardship; manuscripts of her unpublished biography of Helen Hunt Jackson, "Spinner in the Sun," of her play *Pontiac,* of her autobiography "Little Sister to the Sioux," and of "The Ghost Dance War and Wounded Knee Massacre of 1890-91"; photos; scrapbooks; clippings; pamphlets; and bulletins, including *The Navajo Language Monthly,* newsletters of the Indian Council Fire, and the *Wi-iyohi.* Also includes short stories; *Mountain Dooryards* (1941) and other poetry; articles on nature; printed material on the Uplands Sanatorium in Tennessee, 1920-46; and other papers of Eastman's sister Dora Reed Goodale (1866-?), a writer and director of the Sanatorium, and plays and verses from the 1890s of their father Henry S. Goodale, a New England farmer and writer. Taken from Mary-Elizabeth Murdock, *Catalog of The Sophia Smith Collection, Women's History Archive,* 2nd ed. (Northampton, MA: Smith College, 1976).

7,221. Ford, Harriet Bliss Chalmers
Papers. 1899-1957. 5 document boxes.
Open. Published guide.
Smith College, Sophia Smith Collection.
Ford (1876-1964) was a civic leader, author, worker for peace, and associate editor of *Century Magazine* from 1899 to 1912. Correspondence with Carrie Chapman Catt, Ada Comstock, Elizabeth (Cutter) Morrow, William Rose Benét, and others concerning her career, her commitment to the League of Nations and international peace, and her involvement in Northampton intellectual and political life; manuscripts of and notes for writings and addresses; plays written for and published by the YWCA; essays; memorabilia; and pamphlets. Taken from Mary-Elizabeth Murdock, *Catalog of The Sophia Smith Collection, Women's History Archive,* 2nd ed. (Northampton, MA: Smith College, 1976).

7,222. Garrison Family
Papers. 1773- . Ca. 16 drawers, 31 document boxes, 20 vols., and 10 binder indexes.
Open. Published guide.
Smith College, Sophia Smith Collection.
Papers of the family of William Lloyd Garrison II (1838-1909), son of abolitionist William Lloyd Garrison, and of the Mott and David Wright families include correspondence, diaries, addresses, daguerreotypes, photos, articles, clippings, memorabilia, and printed material relating to their interest in abolition, freedmen's societies, women's rights, suffrage, free trade, anti-imperialism, immigration problems, antivaccination, antivivisection, socialism, and the single tax. Among the correspondents are Susan B. Anthony, Alice Stone Blackwell, Carrie Chapman Catt, Lucy Conant, Kate Daniel, Matilda Gage, Lucretia C. Mott, Martha Coffin Wright, Emmeline and Sylvia Pankhurst, Caroline Severance, Anna Howard Shaw, Elizabeth Cady Stanton, Lucy Stone, Frances E. Williard, and Marie Zakrzewska. Taken from Mary-Elizabeth Murdock, *Catalog of The Sophia Smith Collection, Women's History Archive,* 2nd ed. (Northampton, MA: Smith College, 1976).

7,223. Goldman, Emma
Papers. 1911-40. 1 document box.
Open. Published guide.
Smith College, Sophia Smith Collection.
Papers of feminist and anarchist Goldman (1869-1940) include correspondence, 1934-36, with Roger Baldwin, clergyman John Haynes Holmes, and others; notes; biographical material; and reprints of articles on anarchism, prison experiences, her philosophy of atheism, the white slave traffic, and deportation. Taken from Mary-Elizabeth Murdock, *Catalog of The Sophia Smith Collection, Women's History Archive,* 2nd ed. (Northampton, MA: Smith College, 1976).

7,224. Grant Family
Papers. 1795-1883. 2 document boxes.
Open. Published guide.
Smith College, Sophia Smith Collection.
Correspondence, journals, legal papers, a catalog of Lake Erie Female Seminary in Painesville, OH, clippings on Sac and Fox Indians and other subjects, and pamphlets. Letters of Zilpah Polly (Grant) Banister (1794-1874) refer to the Ipswich Female Seminary which she established with Mary Lyon, who served as the school's assistant principal, while correspondence of Susan (Boyd) Grant contains references to activities and personnel of Catharine Beecher's girls school in Hartford, CT. Includes material relating to involvement of family members in 1870 in the Silkville Co-operative Farm, a Fourieristic experiment in Kansas. Taken from Mary-Elizabeth Murdock, *Catalog of The Sophia Smith Collection, Women's History Archive,* 2nd ed. (Northampton, MA: Smith College, 1976).

7,225. Green, Ruth (Tuthill)
Papers. 1919-42. 5 document boxes.
Open. Published guide.
Smith College, Sophia Smith Collection.
Green (1895-) taught at Humacao High School, the US government school in Puerto Rico, in 1919 and 1920; she also was the wife of Brigadier General Thomas H. Green, who was executive to the military governor in Hawaii in 1941. Letters of Green to her family and to others concern her work at the Caney Creek Community Center in Kentucky, Puerto Rico; army life; and Hawaiian war experiences. Also includes diaries and photos. Taken from Mary-Elizabeth Murdock, *Catalog of The Sophia Smith Collection, Women's History Archive,* 2nd ed. (Northampton, MA: Smith College, 1976).

7,226. Guion, Connie M.
Papers. Ca. 1941-69. 6 document boxes.
Open. Published guide.
Smith College, Sophia Smith Collection.
Guion (1882-1971), a physician, was appointed professor of clinical medicine at Cornell University medical college in 1946, and in 1952 she became the first woman honorary member of the New York Hospital board of governors. Letters from family, colleagues, patients, and friends; a tape of a 1965 interview; articles by Guion on endocrine diseases; a bibliography of her publications; photos; awards; citations; a poem to her by Dame Edith Sitwell; and clippings. Guion was the first woman in the US to be made a professor of clinical medicine. Taken from Mary-Elizabeth Murdock, *Catalog of The Sophia Smith Collection, Women's History Archive,* 2nd ed. (Northampton, MA: Smith College, 1976).

7,227. Hale Family
Papers. 1780- . 142 document boxes.
Open. Published guide.
Smith College, Sophia Smith Collection.
Correspondence, diaries, writings, photos, lectures, scrapbooks, paintings, clippings, printed matter, and memorabilia of Hale and Everett family members, including Nathan Hale (1784-1863), owner and editor of the *Boston Daily Advertiser;* his wife Sarah Preston (Everett) Hale (1796-1866); their children, including Sarah Hale (1817-51), author and clergyman Edward Everett Hale (1822-1909), artist Susan Hale (1833-1910), and Lucretia Peabody Hale (1820-1900), who was the author of *The Peterkin Papers;* and Edward Everett Hale's daughter Ellen Day Hale (1854-1940). Among the correspondents are Charlotte Perkins Gilman, Isabella (Beecher) Hooker, Ida M. Tarbell, and children's author Eliza Orne White. Taken from Mary-Elizabeth Murdock, *Catalog of The Sophia Smith Collection, Women's History Archive,* 2nd ed. (Northampton, MA: Smith College, 1976).

7,228. Hansl, Eva Elise (vom Baur)
Papers. Nd. 5 document boxes.
Open. Published guide.
Smith College, Sophia Smith Collection.
Correspondence and radio scripts of Hansl (1889-) relate to the radio series "Women in the Making of America," later called "Gallant American Women," of which she was program supervisor. The series dealt with the role and contributions of women in American life from the 18th through the 20th century. Taken from Mary-Elizabeth Murdock, *Catalog of The Sophia Smith Collection, Women's History Archive,* 2nd ed. (Northampton, MA: Smith College, 1976).

7,229. Harris, Julia Florida (Collier)
Papers. 1921-55. 2 document boxes.
Open. Published guide.
Smith College, Sophia Smith Collection.
Papers of Harris (1875-1967), a southern author, journalist, owner of the Columbus, GA, *Enquirer-Sun,* and champion of civic and social reforms, include correspondence with George Washington Carver, Sherwood Anderson, Henry L. Mencken, Dorothy Canfield Fisher, Geraldine Farrar, and others; unpublished and published reform articles; and reviews. Taken from Mary-Elizabeth Murdock, *Catalog of The Sophia Smith Collection, Women's History Archive,* 2nd ed. (Northampton, MA: Smith College, 1976).

7,230. Hazzard, Florence (Woolsey)
Papers. Nd. 1 document box.
Open. Published guide.
Smith College, Sophia Smith Collection.
Papers of Hazzard (1903-), a writer and advocate of women's rights, consist of annotated typescripts documenting the lives of such women as Abigail Adams, Lucretia Mott, Elizabeth Cady Stanton, Margaret Fuller Ossoli, and Emma Willard. Taken from Mary-Elizabeth Murdock, *Catalog of The Sophia Smith Collection, Women's History Archive,* 2nd ed. (Northampton, MA: Smith College, 1976).

7,231. Hemenway, Ruth V.
Papers. 1924-42. 4 document boxes.
Open. Published guide.
Smith College, Sophia Smith Collection.
Twenty volumes of diaries that Hemenway (1894-1974) kept while she was a medical missionary and artist in China from 1924 to 1941 concern her medical-surgical career, the Chinese countryside, and the economic, social, and political temper of China before WWII. Taken from Mary-Elizabeth Murdock, *Catalog of The Sophia Smith Collection, Women's History Archive,* 2nd ed. (Northampton, MA: Smith College, 1976).

7,232. Howland, Isabel
Papers. 1888-1911. 2 document boxes.
Open. Published guide.
Smith College, Sophia Smith Collection.
Papers of Howland (1859-1942), a suffragist and advocate of social reforms who served as corresponding secretary for the Association for the Advancement of Women and the New York State Woman Suffrage Association, include correspondence relating to such subjects as abolition, suffrage, women's rights, and temperance; photos; and memorabilia. Correspondents include Susan B. Anthony, Carrie Chapman Catt, Antoinette (Brown) Blackwell, Julia Ward Howe, Alice Stone Blackwell, and Anna Howard Shaw. Taken from Mary-Elizabeth Murdock, *Catalog of The Sophia Smith Collection, Women's History Archive,* 2nd ed. (Northampton, MA: Smith College, 1976).

7,233. Hudson Family
Papers. 1825-65. 1 document box.
Open. Published guide.
Smith College, Sophia Smith Collection.
Papers of the family of Erasmus Darwin Hudson (1805-80), who was general agent for the American Anti-Slavery Society from 1837 to 1849, include correspondence containing comments on events during the Civil War era and on such personalities as abolitionist and women's rights advocate Abigâil "Abby" Kelley Foster, social reformers Parker Pillsbury and Wendell Phillips, and clergyman Theodore Parker; manuscript addresses "Intemperance" (1828) and "Conquest Through Self Conquest" (1864); and manuscript and typescript copies of *Anti Slavery Campaign, 1842-83.* Taken from Mary-Elizabeth Murdock, *Catalog of The Sophia Smith Collection, Women's History Archive,* 2nd ed. (Northampton, MA: Smith College, 1976).

7,234. Hunt Family
Papers. Ca. 1841-1903. 1 document box.
Open. Published guide.
Smith College, Sophia Smith Collection.
Correspondence and family papers of Elizabeth B. Bisbee Hunt, a suffragist, and her sister Mary Olive A. Hunt, a physician. Includes letters relating to women's medical education during the 19th century and letters from Rose (Hawthorne) Lathrop, daughter of Nathaniel Hawthorne, relating to the suffrage activities of Elizabeth Hunt. Taken from Mary-Elizabeth Murdock, *Catalog of The Sophia Smith Collection, Women's History Archive,* 2nd ed. (Northampton, MA: Smith College, 1976).

7,235. Huntington, Frances Carpenter
Papers. 1927-68. 1 document box and 5 vols.
Open. Published guide.
Smith College, Sophia Smith Collection.
Correspondence, manuscripts of *South American Wonder Tales* and *The Story of East Africa,* scripts of radio talks on such topics as children's books and women of the arts, and scrapbooks containing photos, bibliographies, illustrations, book jackets, reviews, and clippings of Huntington (1890-1972), an author of children's books and a geographer. Taken from Mary-Elizabeth Murdock, *Catalog of The Sophia Smith Collection, Women's History Archive,* 2nd ed. (Northampton, MA: Smith College, 1976).

7,236. Inter-American Commission of Women
Records. Nd. 2 document boxes.
Open. Published guide.
Smith College, Sophia Smith Collection.
Reports, agendas, and other records of meetings and special assemblies, mostly in Spanish; correspondence; biographies; special studies on such topics as equal rights, working women, employment, and education; *Proceedings* (1948); and publications. Taken from Mary-Elizabeth Murdock, *Catalog of The Sophia Smith Collection, Women's History Archive,* 2nd ed. (Northampton, MA: Smith College, 1976).

7,237. International Alliance of Women
Records. Nd. 2 document boxes.
Open. Published guide.
Smith College, Sophia Smith Collection.
The Alliance, established in 1904, was originally known as the International Woman Suffrage Alliance. Constitution, a history, conference and convention records, photos, international triennial meeting reports for 1908 to 1958, and pamphlets

and flyers on equal pay, equal citizenship, and international suffrage. Taken from Mary-Elizabeth Murdock, *Catalog of The Sophia Smith Collection, Women's History Archive,* 2nd ed. (Northampton, MA: Smith College, 1976).

7,238. International Congress of Working Women
Records. Nd. 1 document box.
Open. Published guide.
Smith College, Sophia Smith Collection.
Handbook, songs, flyers, pamphlets, and other records of the first Congress, which was held in 1919, and of the 1921 and 1923 Congresses. Taken from Mary-Elizabeth Murdock, *Catalog of The Sophia Smith Collection, Women's History Archive,* 2nd ed. (Northampton, MA: Smith College, 1976).

7,239. International Council of Women
Records. Nd. 4 document boxes and 3 vols.
Open. Published guide.
Smith College, Sophia Smith Collection.
Constitution; minutes; correspondence; committee reports; membership lists; records of international conference, 1904-70; historical notes; biographical information on such ICW leaders as Lady Ishbel Aberdeen, Rachel (Foster) Avery, May (Wright) Sewall, and Frances Willard; and issues from 1956 to 1958 of the "Monthly News Sheet" of the ICW, which was established in 1888. Includes correspondence of Vera Beggs and Alice M. Stetten and material on such subjects as education, housing, suffrage, and social welfare. Taken from Mary-Elizabeth Murdock, *Catalog of The Sophia Smith Collection, Women's History Archive,* 2nd ed. (Northampton, MA: Smith College, 1976).

7,240. International Federation of University Women
Records. Nd. 4 folders.
Open. Published guide.
Smith College, Sophia Smith Collection.
Committee and council meeting reports; membership lists for 1939; issues of the newsletter for 1956, 1958, and 1959; conference reports, 1924-32; flyers; and clippings of the Federation, which was established in 1920. Taken from Mary-Elizabeth Murdock, *Catalog of The Sophia Smith Collection, Women's History Archive,* 2nd ed. (Northampton, MA: Smith College, 1976).

7,241. Jarrett, Mary C.
Papers. 1913-49. 8 document boxes.
Open. Published guide.
Smith College, Sophia Smith Collection.
Jarrett (1877?-1961) was a specialist in psychiatric social work and gerontology; she also was associate director of the Smith College school for social work, which was established in 1919. Professional and personal correspondence, including letters and notes of Lillian (Moller) Gilbreth, a pioneer specialist in mental hygiene in industry; notes on publications; lectures; reports; articles; and pamphlets. Taken from Mary-Elizabeth Murdock, *Catalog of The Sophia Smith Collection, Women's History Archive,* 2nd ed. (Northampton, MA: Smith College, 1976).

7,242. Kenyon, Dorothy
Papers. 1907-70. 2 document boxes.
Open. Published guide.
Smith College, Sophia Smith Collection.
Kenyon (1888-1972) was a lawyer, a justice in the municipal court of New York City, and a champion of civil liberties and women's rights. Correspondence, biographical material, addresses, reports, photos, legal briefs, articles, and pamphlets relate to such subjects as the status and role of women, prostitution, domestic and foreign policy, abortion, minority legal rights, Senator Joseph McCarthy, the UN, the Equal Rights Amendment, and the Lower West Side Community Program Center. Also includes a copy of Kenyon's statement before the US Senate Committee on Foreign Relations in 1950. Taken from Mary-Elizabeth Murdock, *Catalog of The Sophia Smith Collection, Women's History Archive,* 2nd ed. (Northampton, MA: Smith College, 1976).

7,243. Kitchelt, Florence Ledyard (Cross)
Papers. Nd. 1 document box.
Open. Published guide.
Smith College, Sophia Smith Collection.
Papers of Kitchelt (1874-1961), a settlement worker, writer, and social reformer whose pseudonym was Rachel Hazelwood, include correspondence with her parents and others; journals for 1900 to 1905 relating to her career at New York College Settlement and at Lowell House in New Haven, CT; autobiographical material; poetry; articles and essays on Susan B. Anthony, notable black Americans, and the problems of segregation; programs; and memorabilia. Taken from Mary-Elizabeth Murdock, *Catalog of The Sophia Smith Collection, Women's History Archive,* 2nd ed. (Northampton, MA: Smith College, 1976).

7,244. Kross, Anna (Moskowitz)
Papers. 1947-73. 8 document boxes.
Open. Published guide.
Smith College, Sophia Smith Collection.
Papers of Kross (1891-), a specialist on prisoner rehabilitation, a magistrate, and commissioner of correction for New York City from 1954 to 1966, include biographical material, statements, photos, tapes, clippings, memorabilia, pamphlets, and publications concerning practices in penology through the 1960s. Taken from Mary-Elizabeth Murdock, *Catalog of The Sophia Smith Collection, Women's History Archive,* 2nd ed. (Northampton, MA: Smith College, 1976).

7,245. Ladies' American Home Education Society and Temperance Union
Records. Nd. 9 vols.
Open. Published guide.
Smith College, Sophia Smith Collection.
Annals of this group, which was established in 1836, cover the years 1852 to 1870 and include the constitution, annual reports, treasurer's records, correspondence, board of officers' records, notices of meetings, membership and donor lists, a history of the organization, essays, fiction, and poetry. Taken from Mary-Elizabeth Murdock, *Catalog of The Sophia Smith Collection, Women's History Archive,* 2nd ed. (Northampton, MA: Smith College, 1976).

7,246. Lamb, Martha Joanna Reade (Nash)
Papers. 1838-1915. 9 document boxes and 22 vols.
Open. Published guide.
Smith College, Sophia Smith Collection.
[Mrs. Charles A.] Lamb (1826-93) was an historian, novelist, and editor of the *Magazine of American History* from 1883 to 1892. Personal and professional correspondence, occasional diaries for the period 1857 to 1885, poetry, autobiographical and biographical articles, photos, genealogical material, scrapbooks, obituaries, clippings, and a copy of her *History of the City of New York* (1877). Includes material relating to her club affiliations as well as volumes of the *Magazine of American History* for the period when she was editor. Taken from Mary-Elizabeth Murdock, *Catalog of The Sophia Smith Collection, Women's History Archive,* 2nd ed. (Northampton, MA: Smith College, 1976).

7,247. Lamont, Florence Haskell (Corliss)
Papers. 1880-1968. 16 document boxes.
Open. Published guide.
Smith College, Sophia Smith Collection.
Lamont (1873-1952) was a writer, philosopher, philanthropist, and worker for peace. Correspondence, diaries, childhood writings, manuscripts, poems, photos, tributes, genealogical material, a family history, and obituaries. Includes manuscripts and printed material concerning her philosophical theories, philanthropic commitments, crusades against antiliberalism and the decline of free speech, her advocacy of the League of Nations, the UN, and peace. Among her correspondents are Jan Christian Smuts, Walter de la Mare, and John Masefield. Taken from Mary-Elizabeth Murdock, *Catalog of The Sophia Smith Collection, Women's History Archive,* 2nd ed. (Northampton, MA: Smith College, 1976).

7,248. Lansburgh, Therese Weil
Papers. 1963- . 5 document boxes.
Open. Published guide.
Smith College, Sophia Smith Collection.
Papers of [Mrs. Richard M.] Lansburgh (1919-), a social worker, include correspondence, addresses, notes, minutes, agendas, newsletters, and published reports relating to her leadership role in the Day Care and Child Development Council of America, the Maryland Committee for Day Care of Children, the Maryland Association for Mental Health, the Children's Lobby, and the Richmond Fellowship of America. Also includes selected learning toys. Taken from Mary-Elizabeth Murdock, *Catalog of The Sophia Smith Collection, Women's History Archive,* 2nd ed. (Northampton, MA: Smith College, 1976).

7,249. Laughlin, Clara Elizabeth
Papers. 1903-41. 8 document boxes and 8 vols.
Open. Published guide.
Smith College, Sophia Smith Collection.
Laughlin (1873-1941) was a feminist, writer, dramatist, travel adviser, and businesswoman. Personal and business correspondence; manuscripts of radio talks on travel and of *So You're Going to . . .*; reviews and clippings relating to her plays, short stories, and biography *Foch, the Man* (1918); and books. Taken from Mary-Elizabeth Murdock, *Catalog of The Sophia Smith Collection, Women's History Archive,* 2nd ed. (Northampton, MA: Smith College, 1976).

7,250. Le Gallienne, Eva
Papers. Nd. 1 document box.
Open. Published guide.
Smith College, Sophia Smith Collection.
Papers of Le Gallienne (1899-), an actress, consist of autobiographical notebooks that were published in 1951 as *With a Quiet Heart,* biographical material, and clippings. Taken from Mary-Elizabeth Murdock, *Catalog of The Sophia Smith Collection, Women's History Archive,* 2nd ed. (Northampton, MA: Smith College, 1976).

7,251. League of Women Shoppers, Inc.
Records. Nd. 1 document box.
Open. Published guide.
Smith College, Sophia Smith Collection.
Constitution, bylaws, minutes and agendas of board meetings of the Chicago branch for 1938 to 1944, correspondence, congressional committee hearing reports, general reports, news bulletins, and publications concerning the problems of organized labor, taxes, and Office of Price Administration policies. Taken from Mary-Elizabeth Murdock, *Catalog of The Sophia Smith Collection, Women's History Archive,* 2nd ed. (Northampton, MA: Smith College, 1976).

7,252. League of Women Voters
Records. Nd. 6 document boxes.
Open. Published guide.
Smith College, Sophia Smith Collection.
Records of the National LWV include bylaws, convention material for 1958 to 1968, proceedings of annual conventions, newsletters for 1937 to 1970, 50th anniversary clippings, pamphlets relating to the history of the organization, and publications on the legal status of women. Taken from Mary-Elizabeth Murdock, *Catalog of The Sophia*

Smith Collection, Women's History Archive, 2nd ed. (Northampton, MA: Smith College, 1976).

7,253. League of Women Voters of Northampton
Records. Nd. 6 document boxes.
Open. Published guide.
Smith College, Sophia Smith Collection.
Constitution, bylaws, correspondence, and reports for 1928 to 1958 of the Northampton LWV; Massachusetts LWV bulletins for 1936 to 1970; and news sheets concerning the structure and functions of local government, housing, schools, voter services, and welfare reform. Taken from Mary-Elizabeth Murdock, *Catalog of The Sophia Smith Collection, Women's History Archive,* 2nd ed. (Northampton, MA: Smith College, 1976).

7,254. Leonard, Baird
Papers. Ca. 1910-37. 2 document boxes.
Open. Published guide.
Smith College, Sophia Smith Collection.
Leola Baird (Leonard) Zogbaum (1888?-1941), a writer and critic who used the professional name Baird Leonard, was married to Harry St. Clair Zogbaum. Correspondence, notes, typescripts of essays, lectures, poetry, clippings of her columns "The Book Market" from 1914 and "Mrs. Pep's Diary" from 1928, reviews of her book *Simple Confession* (1930), a Charles Dana Gibson sketch, and articles on Leonard from *Life* magazine. Taken from Mary-Elizabeth Murdock, *Catalog of The Sophia Smith Collection, Women's History Archive,* 2nd ed. (Northampton, MA: Smith College, 1976).

7,255. Long, Margaret
Papers. 1893-1929. 1 document box.
Open. Published guide.
Smith College, Sophia Smith Collection.
Long (1873-1957) was a physician, a specialist in tuberculosis research, and a writer of western history. Correspondence and diaries for the period 1897 to 1907 concern her experiences at Johns Hopkins medical school with Florence Sabin and Dorothy (Reed) Mendenhall and Long's early career. Letters from Mendenhall contain references to Smith College and work at the New York Infirmary for Women and Children in 1902 and the New York City Babies' Hospital from 1903 to 1905. Taken from Mary-Elizabeth Murdock, *Catalog of The Sophia Smith Collection, Women's History Archive,* 2nd ed. (Northampton, MA: Smith College, 1976).

7,256. McCulloch, Rhoda E.
Papers. Nd. 1 document box.
Open. Published guide.
Smith College, Sophia Smith Collection.
Papers of McCulloch (1884-?), an editor, advocate of women's rights, and worker for peace, include notes on educational trends, attitudes of and about married working women, marriage, women's role in the YWCA, and the woman movement as well as a 1933 address "Women Take to Politics" and reprints of articles. Taken from Mary-Elizabeth Murdock, *Catalog of The Sophia Smith Collection, Women's History Archive,* 2nd ed. (Northampton, MA: Smith College, 1976).

7,257. MacKenzie, Jeanne Daisey
Papers. Nd. 2 document boxes.
Open. Published guide.
Smith College, Sophia Smith Collection.
Papers of [Mrs. Norman Ian] MacKenzie (1922-), a writer and crusader for women's rights, include correspondence, research and bibliographical notes for her book *Australian Paradox* (1961), questionnaires and statistical surveys prepared for *Women in Australia* (1963), and files on education, equal pay for equal work, women in war work and public life, feminism, prostitution, and conventions of the UN, UNESCO, and the International Labor Organization. Taken from Mary-Elizabeth Murdock, *Catalog of The Sophia Smith Collection, Women's History Archive,* 2nd ed. (Northampton, MA: Smith College, 1976).

7,258. Marsh Family
Papers. 1915-73. 3 document boxes.
Open. Published guide.
Smith College, Sophia Smith Collection.
Dorothy Marsh (1889-), president of Marsh Tours, Inc., was manager of the American Women's Club in Paris from 1926 to 1927 and of the American National Red Cross Service Clubs from 1943 to 1946; she also was a member of the New York Women's Council. Her sister Marjorie (Marsh) Enfield was her partner in Marsh Tours. Correspondence of and articles by Dorothy Marsh; minutes, conference material, memoranda, itineraries, and pamphlets relating to Marsh Tours; photos; maps; awards; and memorabilia. Taken from Mary-Elizabeth Murdock, *Catalog of The Sophia Smith Collection, Women's History Archive,* 2nd ed. (Northampton, MA: Smith College, 1976).

7,259. Mendenhall, Dorothy Mabel (Reed)
Papers. 1886-1953. 10 document boxes.
Partially restricted. Published guide.
Smith College, Sophia Smith Collection.
Mendenhall (1874-1964), a physician, was a pioneer specialist in public and child health and pathology. Correspondence, diaries, a manuscript autobiography, essays, course outlines, lecture notes, themes, scientific sketches, photos, account books, syllabuses, articles, memorabilia, and pamphlets relate to her years abroad from 1886 to 1889, at Smith College from 1891 to 1895, and at Johns Hopkins from 1896 to 1902 as a medical student, intern, fellow in pathology, and researcher on Hodgkin's disease. Also contains material about her service with the US Children's Bureau from 1917 to 1920, maternity, and child care. Taken from Mary-Elizabeth Murdock, *Catalog of The Sophia Smith Collection, Women's History Archive,* 2nd ed. (Northampton, MA: Smith College, 1976).

7,260. Merchant, Abby S.
Papers. Nd. 1 document box.
Open. Published guide.
Smith College, Sophia Smith Collection.
Papers of playwright Merchant (1883?-) consist of manuscripts of seven plays, including *The New Englander* (1912); *Irish Dew* (1920), which deals with prohibition; and *The Unbent Twig* (1940). Taken from Mary-Elizabeth Murdock, *Catalog of The Sophia Smith Collection, Women's History Archive,* 2nd ed. (Northampton, MA: Smith College, 1976).

7,261. Miller, Olive Kennon (Beaupré)
Papers. Nd. 11 document boxes.
Open. Published guide.
Smith College, Sophia Smith Collection.
Miller (1883-1968) was a writer of children's books. Correspondence, notebooks, research notes, articles by and about Miller, photos, biographical and genealogical material, curriculum guides, paper dolls, and material relating to her unpublished and published works, including *Engines and Brass Bands* (1933) and *My Book House* (1920). Taken from Mary-Elizabeth Murdock, *Catalog of The Sophia Smith Collection, Women's History Archive,* 2nd ed. (Northampton, MA: Smith College, 1976).

7,262. Mink, Patsy (Takemoto)
Papers. Nd. 6 document boxes.
Open. Published guide.
Smith College, Sophia Smith Collection.
Mink (1927-) is a lawyer, Democratic congresswoman from Hawaii, and champion of civil liberties and women's rights. Biographical data, addresses, legislative bills and drafts, news releases, reports, and articles relate to the National Day Care Program, the status of women, atomic energy, affirmative action programs, women in politics, the 1974 Women's Educational Equality Act, China, Micronesia, Vietnam, minority rights, the 1975 Older Americans Act, and election, tax, and governmental reform. Taken from Mary-Elizabeth Murdock, *Catalog of The Sophia Smith Collection, Women's History Archive,* 2nd ed. (Northampton, MA: Smith College, 1976).

7,263. Morris, Clara
Papers. Nd. 1 document box.
Open. Published guide.
Smith College, Sophia Smith Collection.
Papers of Morris (1847-1925) include the manuscript of *Life on the Stage: My Personal Experiences* (1901) with unpublished passages on John Wilkes Booth; photos; theater programs; obituaries; and clippings. Morris was married to Frederick C. Harriott. Taken from Mary-Elizabeth Murdock, *Catalog of The Sophia Smith Collection, Women's History Archive,* 2nd ed. (Northampton, MA: Smith College, 1976).

7,264. Morrow, Elizabeth Reeve (Cutter)
Papers. 1892-1954. Ca. 28 drawers and 161 document boxes.
Closed. Published guide.
Smith College, Sophia Smith Collection.
Morrow (1873-1955) was an educator, writer, and philanthropist; an alumna of Smith College, she served as a trustee, as alumnae association president, as acting president of the College from 1939 to 1940, and as chairwoman of the board of trustees from 1947 to 1950. Correspondence, diaries from her childhood and from the years 1895 to 1953, notes, unpublished and published poems, children's stories, speeches, photos, household records, and articles relate to Smith College, to her husband Dwight Morrow's diplomatic mission to Mexico in 1928 and 1929, and to such subjects as religion, art, charities, literary and peace organizations, community service, wartime appeals, and education. Also contains letters of the Morrows to their children and papers of their children, including manuscripts and photos of Anne Spencer (Morrow) Lindbergh (1906-), a manuscript autobiography of Elisabeth Reeve (Morrow) Morgan (1903-), and correspondence and photos of Dwight Morrow, Jr., and Constance Cutter (Morrow) Morgan (1913-). Taken from Mary-Elizabeth Murdock, *Catalog of The Sophia Smith Collection, Women's History Archive,* 2nd ed. (Northampton, MA: Smith College, 1976).

7,265. Mossiker, Frances S.
Papers. Ca. 1940- . 6 boxes.
Open. Published guide.
Smith College, Sophia Smith Collection.
Correspondence, manuscripts, photos, reviews, and clippings of Mossiker (1906-), an author, relate to her books on history and her biographies. See Mary-Elizabeth Murdock, *Catalog of The Sophia Smith Collection, Women's History Archive,* 2nd ed. (Northampton, MA: Smith College, 1976).

7,266. Motley, Constance Baker
Papers. Nd. Ca. 8 document boxes.
Open. Published guide.
Smith College, Sophia Smith Collection.
Papers of Motley (1921-), a lawyer, judge, New York state senator, and champion of civil rights, include correspondence relating to her appointment in 1966 as a federal judge for the southern district of New York, legal papers, press releases, and addresses on such subjects as urban renewal, antipoverty programs, school integration, the NAACP, day-care centers, and careers for women in law. Taken from Mary-Elizabeth Murdock, *Catalog of The Sophia Smith Collection, Women's History Archive,* 2nd ed. (Northampton, MA: Smith College, 1976).

7,267. Music
Collection. 1880s- . 7 boxes.
Open. Published guide.
Smith College, Sophia Smith Collection.
Biographical material, photos, and sheet music relating to women musicians and composers, including Marian Anderson, Effie Douglas Putnam, Amy Marcy (Cheney) Beach, Sarah Caldwell, Jenny Lind, and Geraldine Farrar, as well as general information on women's participation in popular and classical music. See Mary-Elizabeth Murdock, *Catalog of The Sophia Smith Collection, Women's History Archive,* 2nd ed. (Northampton, MA: Smith College, 1976).

7,268. National American Woman Suffrage Association
Records. Nd. 2 document boxes.
Open. Published guide.
Smith College, Sophia Smith Collection.
Constitution; a history; an account of the final meeting, which was held in 1950; reports; a biographical sketch of Lucy Stone; convention programs; headquarter newsletters, 1915-17; flyers, pamphlets, and brochures by Jane Addams, Anna Howard Shaw, Carrie Chapman Catt, Lucy Stone, Mary Emma Wooley, and others; issues of "Woman Suffrage Leaflet," 1888-1903; issues of convention *Proceedings,* 1884-1916, and *Progress,* 1903-07; and the "Political Equality Series." The Association was established in 1869. Taken from Mary-Elizabeth Murdock, *Catalog of The Sophia Smith Collection, Women's History Archive,* 2nd ed. (Northampton, MA: Smith College, 1976).

7,269. National Committee on the Cause and Cure of War
Records. Nd. 1 document box.
Open. Published guide.
Smith College, Sophia Smith Collection.
Records of the Committee, which grew out of a conference on the cause and cure of war held in 1925, include minutes, agendas and budget records, correspondence, conference programs, delegates' study outlines, workshop material, pamphlets, and conference reports for 1925 to 1933. Includes letters to women's rights advocate Louisa K. Fast from Josephine Schain and others. Taken from Mary-Elizabeth Murdock, *Catalog of The Sophia Smith Collection, Women's History Archive,* 2nd ed. (Northampton, MA: Smith College, 1976).

7,270. National Council of Women of the United States
Records. 1942- . Ca. 65 document boxes.
Open. Published guide.
Smith College, Sophia Smith Collection.
Minutes of executive and other committee meetings, correspondence, biographical material, lectures, photos, taped panel discussions on women's place in crime control, records of cooperation with such organizations as the GFWC and the Women United for United Nations, conference reports, and publications. Includes material on such subjects as gerontology, children, women composers, slavery, and the status of women. Taken from Mary-Elizabeth Murdock, *Catalog of The Sophia Smith Collection, Women's History Archive,* 2nd ed. (Northampton, MA: Smith College, 1976).

7,271. National Woman's Christian Temperance Union
Records. Nd. 1 document box.
Open. Published guide.
Smith College, Sophia Smith Collection.
Records of the Union, which was established in 1874, include convention minutes for 1878 and 1879; reports and programs; writings, addresses, and biographical notes of WCTU president Frances E. Willard; temperance songs; posters; flyers; clippings; pamphlets; and publications. Also includes material relating to the activities of two related organizations—the Non-Partisan National WCTU and the Women's Organization for National Prohibition Reform for 1930 to 1932; minutes and a history of the Western Washington WCTU for 1884 to 1893; correspondence, articles, and clippings of Mary A. Livermore; and biographical information on British temperance leader Lady Henry Somerset. Taken from Mary-Elizabeth Murdock, *Catalog of The Sophia Smith Collection, Women's History Archive,* 2nd ed. (Northampton, MA: Smith College, 1976).

7,272. National Woman's Party
Records. Nd. 3 folders.
Open. Published guide.
Smith College, Sophia Smith Collection.
Records of the Party, established in 1913, include an historical sketch; endorsements of the Equal Rights Amendment by Mary E. Woolley, Alma Lutz, actress Katharine Hepburn, Pearl S. Buck, Helen Hayes, and others; an equal rights amendment proposed in 1943; flyers of national conventions in 1921 and 1949; and pamphlets on discriminatory laws and equal rights for women. Taken from Mary-Elizabeth Murdock, *Catalog of The Sophia Smith Collection, Women's History Archive,* 2nd ed. (Northampton, MA: Smith College, 1976).

7,273. National Women's Trade Union League of America
Records. Nd. 1 document box.
Open. Published guide.
Smith College, Sophia Smith Collection.
Constitution; a history; convention proceedings, handbooks, and official programs; an address on English women in cooperative and labor movements; League pamphlets from 1922 opposing the National Woman's party's Equal Rights Amendment; material on the Labor Extension Service; Mary Van Kleeck's information on how to organize trade unions; and other records of the League, which was established in 1903. Taken from Mary-Elizabeth Murdock, *Catalog of The Sophia Smith Collection, Women's History Archive,* 2nd ed. (Northampton, MA: Smith College, 1976).

7,274. New England Hospital
Records. Ca. 1820-1955. 29 document boxes.
Open. Published guide.
Smith College, Sophia Smith Collection.
New England Hospital, founded in Boston in 1862 by physician Marie Elizabeth Zakrzewska, Lucy Goddard, and Ednah Dow Cheney, was the first hospital in New England to educate women to be physicians, the first training school for nurses in the US, and the first hospital in the US to provide medical care for women by women. Annual reports; minutes of physicians' meetings, 1876-1917; financial records; correspondence; research records in obstetrics, pediatrics, and gynecology; historical material; files on interns and the abortion controversy; and a manuscript report of the London Anti-Slavery Convention in 1840. Includes correspondence and biographical information about physician Susan Dimock, a surgeon at the Hospital; Marie Zakrzewska; Linda Richards, the first graduate nurse in the US; and Mary Eliza Mahoney, the first black graduate nurse in the US. Several hundred letters collected for their autograph value and to be sold at fund-raising fairs during the 19th century are also contained in the collection; among them are letters by Louisa May Alcott, Susan B. Anthony, Alice and Elizabeth Blackwell, Maria (Weston) Chapman, Lydia Maria Child, Margaret Deland, Abby Morton Diaz, Dorothea L. Dix, Harriet Martineau, Ellen H. Richards, Lucy Stone, Harriet E. Beecher Stowe, and M. Carey Thomas. Taken from Mary-Elizabeth Murdock, *Catalog of The Sophia Smith Collection, Women's History Archive,* 2nd ed. (Northampton, MA: Smith College, 1976).

7,275. Pan-Pacific and Southeast Asia Women's Association
Records. Nd. 1 document box.
Open. Published guide.
Smith College, Sophia Smith Collection.
Constitution, bylaws, historical notes, issues of the "Newsletter" for 1963 to 1967 and of *Mid Pacific Magazine* for 1928 to 1933, and conference proceedings of the Association, which was established in 1924 with the US as a founding member. Taken from Mary-Elizabeth Murdock, *Catalog of The Sophia Smith Collection, Women's History Archive,* 2nd ed. (Northampton, MA: Smith College, 1976).

7,276. Parton, Sara Payson (Willis)
Papers. 1829-1966. 4 document boxes.
Open. Published guide.
Smith College, Sophia Smith Collection.
[Mrs. James] Parton (1811-72), whose pseudonym was Fanny Fern, was a writer, advocate of women's rights, and one of the first woman journalists. Correspondence of Parton and her descendents, a memorandum book, legal and business papers, a descriptive bibliography of her articles, family sketches, daguerreotypes, photos, biographical studies, a school album, clippings, and articles she wrote for the *New York Ledger* from 1855 to 1872. Includes letters by Harriet Beecher Stowe. Taken from Mary-Elizabeth Murdock, *Catalog of The Sophia Smith Collection, Women's History Archive,* 2nd ed. (Northampton, MA: Smith College, 1976).

7,277. Peabody Family
Papers. Ca. 1820-53. 1 document box.
Open. Published guide.
Smith College, Sophia Smith Collection.
Elizabeth Palmer Peabody (1804-94), Mary Tyler (Peabody) [Mrs. Horace] Mann (1806-87), and Sophia Amelia (Peabody) [Mrs. Nathaniel] Hawthorne (1809-71) were sisters who lived in Salem and Boston. Correspondence between the sisters and a Salem friend Maria Chase contains literary and philosophical comments, social notes, art news, commentaries on a Cuban trip, and observations on religion and education. Also includes typescripts of letters that Chase's sister Rebecca (Chase) Kinsman, a writer and traveler, wrote to her family concerning a voyage to China in 1842 and 1843 and life in Macao during the 1840s as well as the published journal of her husband Nathaniel Kinsman, which contains an account of his successful involvement in the China trade. Taken from Mary-Elizabeth Murdock, *Catalog of The Sophia Smith Collection, Women's History Archive,* 2nd ed. (Northampton, MA: Smith College, 1976).

7,278. Peace
Collection. Nd. 6 boxes.
Open. Published guide.
Smith College, Sophia Smith Collection.
Reports, flyers, drawings, photos, newsletters, articles, clippings, and pamphlets, primarily from the 20th century, document the involvement of women in peace efforts. Includes information on organizations such as the Order of the Unicorn, Another Mother for Peace, the National Committee on the Cause and Cure of War, Women Strike for Peace, the Women's Committee to Oppose Conscription, and the Peace Department of the WCTU. In addition, there is biographical material on Emily Greene Balch, Lucia True (Ames) Mead, and others and some information on antipacifists. See Mary-Elizabeth Murdock, *Catalog of The Sophia Smith Collection, Women's History Archive,* 2nd ed. (Northampton, MA: Smith College, 1976).

7,279. Pearce Family
Papers. 1880-1962. 2 document boxes.
Open. Published guide.

Smith College, Sophia Smith Collection.
Papers of Charlotte Hays Brown (1862-1951), her sister Rebecca McClure (Brown) Pearce (1860-1911), and Pearce's daughter Katharine Standish Pearce (1895-), who were teachers, librarians, and educational missionaries in Syria and Turkey, include correspondence, diaries, writings, business records, photos, reports, sketches, and memorabilia. Correspondence provides a detailed record of their careers at Sidon Seminary in Syria from the 1880s to the 1930s and at Constantinople Woman's College, which was also called American College for Girls. Taken from Mary-Elizabeth Murdock, *Catalog of The Sophia Smith Collection, Women's History Archive,* 2nd ed. (Northampton, MA: Smith College, 1976).

7,280. Peet, Azalia E.
Papers. 1916-73. 4 document boxes.
Open. Published guide.
Smith College, Sophia Smith Collection.
Peet (1889-1973) was a Christian missionary in Japan, a champion of women's rights, and a worker for peace. Letters to family and friends concerning her work, her philosophy, and Japanese society; diaries for the years 1902 to 1956; a tape and transcript of an interview; a photo album; articles; clippings; and memorabilia. Taken from Mary-Elizabeth Murdock, *Catalog of The Sophia Smith Collection, Women's History Archive,* 2nd ed. (Northampton, MA: Smith College, 1976).

7,281. Picker, Jean S.
Papers. 1969-77. 9 document boxes.
Open. Published guide.
Smith College, Sophia Smith Collection.
Correspondence from 1969 to 1973, addresses, biographical information, press releases, minutes, agendas, and reports of Picker (1921-), a diplomat, relate to her role as a member of the US Mission to the UN, the US Delegation to the Economic and Social Council of the UN, and as US representative to the UN Commission for Social Development. Also includes publications on the status of women, working mothers, family policy and law, social welfare resolutions, the 1971 world conference on adoption and foster home placement, and the UN Association. Taken from Mary-Elizabeth Murdock, *Catalog of The Sophia Smith Collection, Women's History Archive,* 2nd ed. (Northampton, MA: Smith College, 1976).

7,282. Planned Parenthood Federation of America
Records. 1921-53. 98 document boxes.
Open. Published guide.
Smith College, Sophia Smith Collection.
Records of the PPFA and of its predecessors the American Birth Control League, the National Committee on Federal Legislation for Birth Control, and the Birth Control Federation of America. Includes correspondence, birth control campaign material, documents concerning litigation on legislative reform, clinical records, proceedings of family planning conferences, and records of the National Clergymen's Advisory Committee and the National Committee on Mental Health. Also includes records and reports of medical research into new methods of contraception of the Planned Parenthood League of Massachusetts. Among the correspondents are Lydia Allen DeVilbiss, Mary Lasker, and Margaret Sanger. Taken from Mary-Elizabeth Murdock, *Catalog of The Sophia Smith Collection, Women's History Archive,* 2nd ed. (Northampton, MA: Smith College, 1976).

7,283. Planned Parenthood League of Massachusetts
Records. Nd. 159 document boxes.
Open. Published guide.
Smith College, Sophia Smith Collection.
Financial records, correspondence, reports, conference proceedings, subject files, photos, scrapbooks, publicity, and other records of the League, which was organized in 1916 as the Birth Control League of Massachusetts, relate to the struggle to revoke the Massachusetts Comstock Laws, controversy with the Roman Catholic church, and referendum voting in 1942 and 1948 on the right to disseminate information on birth control. Includes personal files of Loraine L. Campbell, president of the Planned Parenthood Federation of America in the 1950s; letters to Margaret Sanger from General Douglas MacArthur in 1950 and 1951, forbidding Sanger to visit Japan; and files on the status of clinical programs, population, eugenics, feminism, maternal and infant health, marriage and sex counseling, and contraceptive research. Taken from Mary-Elizabeth Murdock, *Catalog of The Sophia Smith Collection, Women's History Archive,* 2nd ed. (Northampton, MA: Smith College, 1976).

7,284. Porritt, Annie Gertrude (Webb)
Papers. 1910-34. 4 document boxes.
Open. Published guide.
Smith College, Sophia Smith Collection.
Porritt (1861-1932), a suffragist, was secretary of the American Birth Control League in the 1920s and vice-president of the Hartford LWV. Correspondence, minutes of the American Birth Control League from 1923 to 1932, notes, her unpublished histories of the birth control and suffrage movements, her 1910 essay "Woman as a Metonymy," legislation, flyers, pamphlets, brochures, and reprints. Includes material relating to her interest in the London Society of Friends. Among her correspondents are Margaret Sanger; Stella Hanau, editor of *Birth Control Review;* Alice Stone Blackwell; Mary (Ware) Dennett; and Anna Howard Shaw. Taken from Mary-Elizabeth Murdock, *Catalog of The Sophia Smith Collection, Women's History Archive,* 2nd ed. (Northampton, MA: Smith College, 1976).

7,285. Powers, Beatrice Farnsworth
Papers. 1894-1969. 1 document box and 1 vol.
Open. Published guide.
Smith College, Sophia Smith Collection.
Papers of Powers (1880-1967), a nurse and teacher, include correspondence, notes on European travel, essays, biographical material, photos, an album, annual reports of the Yale-in-China Hospital for 1915 and 1966, and obituaries. Letters, notes, and essays concern her career at Dr. Wilfred Grenfell's mission in Labrador in 1912 and at the Yale-in-China Hospital in Changsha, China, the status of Chinese women, and the impact of missionaries on China. Taken from Mary-Elizabeth Murdock, *Catalog of The Sophia Smith Collection, Women's History Archive,* 2nd ed. (Northampton, MA: Smith College, 1976).

7,286. Richards, Ellen Henrietta (Swallow)
Papers. 1895-1946. 1 document box and 4 vols.
Open. Published guide.
Smith College, Sophia Smith Collection.
[Mrs. Robert Hallowell] Richards (1842-1911), an industrial chemist and specialist in food technology, ecology, and public health, was the first woman graduate of and first woman professor at the Massachusetts Institute of Technology. Correspondence and essays relating to her founding in 1873 of the Society to Encourage Studies at Home for women and girls and to her founding of the Association of Collegiate Alumnae. Also contains photos, tests, diagrams, drawings, and reprints of scientific writings. Taken from Mary-Elizabeth Murdock, *Catalog of The Sophia Smith Collection, Women's History Archive,* 2nd ed. (Northampton, MA: Smith College, 1976).

7,287. Rose, Florence
Papers. 1921-68. 43 document boxes.
Open. Published guide.
Smith College, Sophia Smith Collection.
Rose (1902?-69) was cofounder of Meals for Millions, secretary to Margaret Sanger, and an advocate of equal rights and birth control. Personal and business letters; records of the Committee on Public Progress, 1931-39; contributor's lists; material on legal hearings and legislation; a history of the birth control movement; and reports of the Division of Negro Service, 1940-41. Includes material on Anna M. Kross, the National Woman's party, and the religious controversy sparked by advocates of birth control as well as correspondence with Sanger, Mary R. Beard, Pearl Buck, Shidzue Ishimoto Kato, Lady Dhanvanthi Rama Rau, Lilia Skala, and Ellen Watumull. Taken from Mary-Elizabeth Murdock, *Catalog of The Sophia Smith Collection, Women's History Archive,* 2nd ed. (Northampton, MA: Smith College, 1976).

7,288. Sabin, Florence Rena
Papers. 1881-1953. 32 document boxes.
Open. Published guide.
Smith College, Sophia Smith Collection.
Sabin (1871-1953) was a physician, teacher, public health specialist, and medical researcher in histology and tuberculosis control. Correspondence with family and friends; lecture notes; notebooks; biographical, bibliographical, and genealogical information; photos; citations; reports written for the Rockefeller Foundation and the National Tuberculosis Association; files on such subjects as atomic energy and epidemics; memorabilia; and addresses and scientific studies in histology, the lymphatic system, tuberculosis, public health, and hematology. Correspondents include archaeologist Zelia Nuttall and Dorothy (Reed) Mendenhall. Taken from Mary-Elizabeth Murdock, *Catalog of The Sophia Smith Collection, Women's History Archive,* 2nd ed. (Northampton, MA: Smith College, 1976).

7,289. Sanger, Margaret (Higgins)
Papers. Ca. 1890-1966. 199 document boxes, 166 vols., and 145 microfilm reels.
Partially restricted. Published guide.
Smith College, Sophia Smith Collection.
[Mrs. William] Sanger (1879-1966), an author, feminist, and advocate of marriage counseling and sex reforms, was founder and leader of the international birth control movement. Personal and professional correspondence, diaries for the period 1914 to 1954, addresses, a 1965 motion picture on Sanger narrated by actress Katharine Hepburn, photos, conference proceedings, pamphlets, watercolor paintings, articles, clippings, memorabilia, periodicals, and books relate to facets of the birth control movement such as abortion, the history of contraception, clinical work, litigation and legislation, eugenics, Malthusian theory, population problems, maternal health, religious attitudes, and sex education. Includes material on the American Birth Control League, the Margaret Sanger Clinical Research Bureau, the National Committee on Federal Legislation for Birth Control, the Birth Control Federation of America, the Planned Parenthood Federation of America, and the International Planned Parenthood Federation. Among the correspondents are Dorothy Brush, Lydia Allen DeVilbiss, Helen Keller, Anne Kennedy, Mary Lasker, Katharine (Dexter) McCormick, Juliet Rublee, Hannah and Abraham Stone, H. G. Wells, and Ellen Watumull. Sanger's second husband was Noah Slee. Taken from Mary-Elizabeth Murdock, *Catalog of The Sophia Smith Collection, Women's History Archive,* 2nd ed. (Northampton, MA: Smith College, 1976).

7,290. Schain, Josephine
Papers. 1907-58. 11 document boxes and 4 vols.
Open. Published guide.
Smith College, Sophia Smith Collection.
Schain (1866-1972) was a suffragist, crusader for women's rights, and worker for international cooperation and peace. Correspondence with Carrie Chapman Catt and others, radio scripts, notes, photos, reports, proceedings, scrapbooks,

clippings, and pamphlets relate to food problems, the worldwide status of women, neutrality laws, moral disarmament, the UN, the YWCA, and peace; to her responsibilities as a Democratic National Committee member in the 1940s; and to her leadership role in the Chautauqua Woman's Club, the Girl Scouts, the International Alliance of Women, the Pan Pacific Women's Association, the UN Commission on the Status of Women, the Women's Committee on the World Court, the Women's Centennial Congress, and the National Committee on the Cause and Cure of War. Taken from Mary-Elizabeth Murdock, *Catalog of The Sophia Smith Collection, Women's History Archive,* 2nd ed. (Northampton, MA: Smith College, 1976).

7,291. Schwimmer and Lloyd
Papers. Ca. 1900-48. 4 boxes.
Open. Published guide.
Smith College, Sophia Smith Collection.
Correspondence, photos, biographical material, articles, clippings, and pamphlets documenting the friendships, philosophies, and peace crusades of pacifists Lola Maverick Lloyd (1875-1944), Rosika Schwimmer (1877-1948), and Franciska Schwimmer. See Mary-Elizabeth Murdock, *Catalog of The Sophia Smith Collection, Women's History Archive,* 2nd ed. (Northampton, MA: Smith College, 1976).

7,292. Scudder, Vida Dutton
Papers. 1884-1970. 1 document box.
Open. Published guide.
Smith College, Sophia Smith Collection.
Scudder (1861-1954) was an author, editor, educator, settlement worker, religious enthusiast, and social reformer. Correspondence; journals for the period 1932 to 1946, including the original draft of her autobiography *On Journey;* unpublished essays; biographical notes; photos; a 1908 notebook from the College Settlement in New York; obituaries; articles; clippings; and memorabilia. Taken from Mary-Elizabeth Murdock, *Catalog of The Sophia Smith Collection, Women's History Archive,* 2nd ed. (Northampton, MA: Smith College, 1976).

7,293. Seton, Grace (Gallatin) Thompson
Papers. 1903-40. 4 document boxes.
Open. Published guide.
Smith College, Sophia Smith Collection.
[Mrs. Ernest Thompson] Seton (1872-1959) was an author, explorer, and feminist who worked for the International Writers Conclave in Chicago in 1933. Correspondence relating to her travels, associates, and publications, including *Poison Arrows* (1940); notes; typescripts of articles and addresses; an essay; minutes, agendas, reports, and other records of the National Council of Women, 1931-35, and of the International Council of Women, 1915-26; minutes and correspondence of the Montessori Education Association of New York; information on Mary Stone, a medical missionary in China; and *Biblioteca Femina,* which was assembled by Seton as chairman of letters of the National Council of Women. Taken from Mary-Elizabeth Murdock, *Catalog of The Sophia Smith Collection, Women's History Archive,* 2nd ed. (Northampton, MA: Smith College, 1976).

7,294. Severance, Caroline Maria (Seymour)
Papers. 1860-1914. 1 document box.
Open. Published guide.
Smith College, Sophia Smith Collection.
[Mrs. Theodoric Cordenio] Severance (1820-1914) was an abolitionist and advocate of suffrage, birth control, dress reform, women's rights, and peace. Autograph book of Severance from 1866; a scrapbook of her daughter Julia Long Severance, which contains notes, poems, and pencil and watercolor sketches; and letters from Louisa May Alcott, Alice Stone Blackwell, Sarah Grimké, Lucy Stone, Celia Thaxter, John Greenleaf Whittier, Theodore Dwight Weld, and others; and a published tribute volume *The Mother of Clubs* (1906) which includes correspondence of, addresses by, and biographical information about Severance. Taken from Mary-Elizabeth Murdock, *Catalog of The Sophia Smith Collection, Women's History Archive,* 2nd ed. (Northampton, MA: Smith College, 1976).

7,295. Slavery
Collection. Ca. 1836-70. 2 boxes.
Open. Published guide.
Smith College, Sophia Smith Collection.
Correspondence, biographical material, speeches, photos, drawings, clippings, newspapers, pamphlets, and printed reports on antislavery and Union war activity, including addresses by Elizabeth (Cady) Stanton and Emma Willard, a letter by Maria (Weston) Chapman, some papers of John Brown, drawings of slave life by William A. Stephens, and photos and sketches of emancipated slaves. Also includes biographical sketches and clippings that document the war effort of American women in such organizations as the Ladies' Army Aid Society and the New England Freedmen's Aid Society, which was established in 1862. Includes annual reports, addresses, and pamphlets of several antislavery societies; a copy of *Liberator-Extra* (1837); the American antislavery almanac for 1836, vol. 1, no. 1; "An Appeal to the Christian Women of America" (1836); and a volume entitled *Woman's Work in the Civil War* (1867). See Mary-Elizabeth Murdock, *Catalog of The Sophia Smith Collection, Women's History Archive,* 2nd ed. (Northampton, MA: Smith College, 1976).

7,296. Smith, Grace (Kellogg) Griffith
Papers. Nd. 3 document boxes and 5 vols.
Open. Published guide.
Smith College, Sophia Smith Collection.
Papers of Smith (1885-), a writer and educator, include correspondence relating primarily to her book *The Two Lives of Edith Wharton* (1965), writings, notes, photos, and biographical research material documenting the philosophy, life, and work of Wharton. Taken from Mary-Elizabeth Murdock, *Catalog of The Sophia Smith Collection, Women's History Archive,* 2nd ed. (Northampton, MA: Smith College, 1976).

7,297. Sommer, Jane
Papers. 1964-66. 1 document box.
Open. Published guide.
Smith College, Sophia Smith Collection.
Consists of letters that Sommer, a Peace Corps volunteer in the Philippines, wrote to her family describing her life and work. Taken from Mary-Elizabeth Murdock, *Catalog of The Sophia Smith Collection, Women's History Archive,* 2nd ed. (Northampton, MA: Smith College, 1976).

7,298. Sorosis
Records. Nd. 9 document boxes and 36 vols.
Open. Published guide.
Smith College, Sophia Smith Collection.
Articles of incorporation; a constitution; bylaws; minutes, 1868-1930, including those of the executive committee; committee reports on art, drama, education, music, and legislative programs; membership lists; yearbooks; programs; memorabilia; and other records of this organization, which was established in 1868. Includes biographical information, writings, and photos of the first president Jane "Jennie June" (Cunningham) Croly; material relating to the Women's Congress in New York City in 1873 and 1887 and to the Association for the Advancement of Women, which was established by Sorosis in 1873; and files on temperance, prison reform, peace, and women's status in government, medicine, and law. Taken from Mary-Elizabeth Murdock, *Catalog of The Sophia Smith Collection, Women's History Archive,* 2nd ed. (Northampton, MA: Smith College, 1976).

7,299. Spofford, Grace
Papers. Nd. 6 document boxes.
Open. Published guide.
Smith College, Sophia Smith Collection.
Spofford (1888?-1974) was director of the music school of Henry Street Settlement in New York City from 1935 to 1954 and chairman of the arts, letters, and music committee of the National Council of Women and the International Council of Women. Correspondence relating to the activities and achievements of women musicians, biographical items, minutes, reports, photos, publicity material, programs, bulletins, clippings, and printed matter on women in music and on the Society of Women Musicians, which was established in 1911. Taken from Mary-Elizabeth Murdock, *Catalog of The Sophia Smith Collection, Women's History Archive,* 2nd ed. (Northampton, MA: Smith College, 1976).

7,300. Starr, Ellen Gates
Papers. 1840s-1939. 13 document boxes.
Open. Published guide.
Smith College, Sophia Smith Collection.
Starr (1859-1940), a religious writer, bookbinder, and advocate of labor legislation and other social reforms, was cofounder with Jane Addams of Hull House in Chicago. Correspondence, notebooks, biographical and genealogical notes, poems, photos, lectures, articles, obituaries, and her *Book of Meditations* (1935). Includes correspondence with Addams; Vida Scudder; Alice Hamilton; Thornton Wilder; her bookbinding teacher Thomas J. Cobden-Sanderson; Oberlin College professor Charles Henry Wager, who wrote on literary and religious subjects; and clothing industry labor leaders Jacob Patofsky and Sidney Hillman, who thanked her for her organized labor crusade. Also includes letters, journals, poems, writings of Eliza Allen Starr (1824-1901), and other family papers. Taken from Mary-Elizabeth Murdock, *Catalog of The Sophia Smith Collection, Women's History Archive,* 2nd ed. (Northampton, MA: Smith College, 1976).

7,301. Stern, Geraldine
Papers. Nd. 3 document boxes.
Open. Published guide.
Smith College, Sophia Smith Collection.
Papers of Stern, an artist, author, and lecturer on modern Israeli women, include correspondence, research notes, drafts and a complete manuscript of *Daughters from Afar* (1958), photos, and articles. Papers relate to the fate of European Jews, WWII, kibbutz life, Jewish heritage, Yemenite women, and Arab women in Israel. Taken from Mary-Elizabeth Murdock, *Catalog of The Sophia Smith Collection, Women's History Archive,* 2nd ed. (Northampton, MA: Smith College, 1976).

7,302. Stetten, Alice Mayer
Papers. 1930-72. 4 document boxes.
Open. Published guide.
Smith College, Sophia Smith Collection.
Stetten (1887-1972) was a civic leader and advocate of civil rights and peace. Personal and business correspondence, biographical material, and files containing minutes, agendas, circular letters, reports, programs, and flyers of organizations in which she was involved, among them the American Woman's Association, the Carrie Chapman Catt Memorial Fund, the Common Council for American Unity, the National Council of Women, the Overseas Education Fund, the Women's Action Committee, and the Women's City Club of New York. Taken from Mary-Elizabeth Murdock, *Catalog of The Sophia Smith Collection, Women's History Archive,* 2nd ed. (Northampton, MA: Smith College, 1976).

7,303. Stevens, Risë
Papers. Nd. 4 document boxes.
Open. Published guide.

Smith College, Sophia Smith Collection.
Papers of Stevens, an opera singer, include correspondence for the years 1962 to 1974 with opera colleagues and friends, fan mail, her addresses and articles, a 1966 interview of Stevens by Metropolitan Opera broadcast announcer Milton Cross, legal papers and contracts, a script, concert scores, portraits, clippings about *Carmen,* and memorabilia. Includes material relating to the 1969 Metropolitan Opera labor dispute and the Metropolitan Opera National Company. Taken from Mary-Elizabeth Murdock, *Catalog of The Sophia Smith Collection, Women's History Archive,* 2nd ed. (Northampton, MA: Smith College, 1976).

7,304. Stevenson, Candace Thurber
Papers. 1916-65. 7 document boxes.
Open. Published guide.
Smith College, Sophia Smith Collection.
Papers of Stevenson (1883-1968), an author, include extensive correspondence with colleagues, literary agents, editors, publishers, and friends; manuscripts of her writings; and biographical notes. Taken from Mary-Elizabeth Murdock, *Catalog of The Sophia Smith Collection, Women's History Archive,* 2nd ed. (Northampton, MA: Smith College, 1976).

7,305. Storm, Marian
Papers. 1903-67. Ca. 11 document boxes and 15 vols.
Open. Published guide.
Smith College, Sophia Smith Collection.
Storm (1892?-1975) was a writer, artist, conservationist, and champion of animal welfare. Correspondence with family and friends; typescripts of published and unpublished novels, articles, poems, and short stories; notebooks containing research notes for newspaper stories; scrapbooks containing letters, her New York *Herald Tribune* stories, and other clippings; watercolors; and memorabilia. Includes correspondence with archaeologist Zelia Nuttall and research notes on Mexican towns, music, fiestas, birds, herbs and medicinal plants, the Tarascan language, religion, and ruins. Taken from Mary-Elizabeth Murdock, *Catalog of The Sophia Smith Collection, Women's History Archive,* 2nd ed. (Northampton, MA: Smith College, 1976).

7,306. Suffrage and Antisuffrage
Collection. Ca. 1880- . 22 boxes.
Open. Published guide.
Smith College, Sophia Smith Collection.
Biographical material, congressional speeches, photos, addresses, convention programs, program announcements, poetry, posters, plays, mementos, maps, cartoons, articles, clippings, pamphlets, and periodicals pertaining primarily to the US and English suffrage movements. Includes 15 scrapbooks on woman suffrage compiled by Mary Bartlett Dixon Cullen, covering the years 1909 to 1920; antisuffrage pamphlets and addresses; material on individual states and on such organizations as the International Woman Suffrage Alliance and the National American Woman Suffrage Association; and clippings about the position of women, political prisoners, the vote, White House picketing, and the Catholic position. In addition, there are copies of oral history transcripts of the suffragists project conducted by the University of California, Berkeley. See Mary-Elizabeth Murdock, *Catalog of The Sophia Smith Collection, Women's History Archive,* 2nd ed. (Northampton, MA: Smith College, 1976).

7,307. Tallant, Alice Weld
Papers. 1902-57. 1 document box.
Open. Published guide.
Smith College, Sophia Smith Collection.
Tallant (1875-1958), an obstetrician, was director of the Smith College Relief Unit in France during WWI; she also worked in Joy Settlement and St. Martha's House in Philadelphia. Correspondence with her grandmother Alice Brown, a playwright, and others; poems; radio scripts; photos; clippings; memorabilia; reprints of publications; and material relating to her membership in the Philadelphia County Medical Society and the Johns Hopkins Alumni Association. Taken from Mary-Elizabeth Murdock, *Catalog of The Sophia Smith Collection, Women's History Archive,* 2nd ed. (Northampton, MA: Smith College, 1976).

7,308. Tarbell, Ida Minerva
Papers. 1896-1943. 1 document box.
Open. Published guide.
Smith College, Sophia Smith Collection.
Tarbell (1857-1944) was an author, editor, and advocate of social, economic, and political reforms. Correspondence, articles, and clippings relate to trusts, suffrage, and the status and role of women. Includes numerous letters concerning her research for her articles on Abraham Lincoln, which were published in 1900 in *McClure's magazine.* Taken from Mary-Elizabeth Murdock, *Catalog of The Sophia Smith Collection, Women's History Archive,* 2nd ed. (Northampton, MA: Smith College, 1976).

7,309. Thayer, Eleanor W.
Papers. Nd. 3 document boxes.
Open. Published guide.
Smith College, Sophia Smith Collection.
Thayer (1908?-), a specialist in music education for the blind, taught in the music department at the Perkins School for the Blind in Watertown, MA, from 1929 until 1971. Correspondence, manuscripts of addresses, course outlines, examples of braille music, and workshop and special event material for the Perkins School for the Blind provide information about her role in developing the music curriculum at Perkins. Includes publications of the International Conference of Educators of Blind Youth and the American Association of Instructors of the Blind. Taken from Mary-Elizabeth Murdock, *Catalog of The Sophia Smith Collection, Women's History Archive,* 2nd ed. (Northampton, MA: Smith College, 1976).

7,310. Theatre
Collection. Nd. 11 boxes.
Open. Published guide.
Smith College, Sophia Smith Collection.
Autobiographies; photos; and published and unpublished biographical, critical, and historical works and plays date from the 19th and 20th centuries and pertain to women in the performing arts. Includes material on actresses, burlesque performers, playwrights, and other kinds of theater workers, including Ruth Chatterton, Katharine Cornell, Maude Adams, Sarah Bernhardt, June Havoc, Julie Harris, Rachel Crothers, Rosamond Gilder, Julia Dean Hayne, Charlotte Lennox, Eva LeGalliene, Alla Nazimova, and Cornelia Otis Skinner. See Mary-Elizabeth Murdock, *Catalog of The Sophia Smith Collection, Women's History Archive,* 2nd ed. (Northampton, MA: Smith College, 1976).

7,311. Thomas, Caroline (Bedell)
Papers. Nd. 1 document box.
Open. Published guide.
Smith College, Sophia Smith Collection.
Papers of Thomas (1904-), a physician and specialist in internal and preventive medicine, include biographical and genealogical information on Thomas and on her husband Henry M. Thomas (1891-1966) and father Frederick Bedell (1868-1958), both of whom were physicians; articles relating to the history of women medical students at Johns Hopkins and her work as director of a research project on hypertension and coronary artery disease; photos; and clippings. Taken from Mary-Elizabeth Murdock, *Catalog of The Sophia Smith Collection, Women's History Archive,* 2nd ed. (Northampton, MA: Smith College, 1976).

7,312. Tuttle, Florence (Guertin)
Papers. 1917-48. Ca. 9 document boxes.
Open. Published guide.
Smith College, Sophia Smith Collection.
Tuttle (1869-1951) was a writer, suffragist, and advocate of world federalism, birth control, and peace. Correspondence from 1917 to 1936; social and travel notes; manuscripts of her unpublished autobiography and her unpublished book on women and Reconstruction; poems; photos; press releases; her addresses on feminism, disarmament, the League of Nations, the status and role of women, and suffrage; clippings; and printed sources. Correspondents include birth control advocates Anne Kennedy and Annie G. Porritt, Katherine Devereux Blake, Alice Carpenter, and Portia Willis Berg. Tuttle was the author of *Women and World Federalism* (1918). Taken from Mary-Elizabeth Murdock, *Catalog of The Sophia Smith Collection, Women's History Archive,* 2nd ed. (Northampton, MA: Smith College, 1976).

7,313. United Nations
Records. Nd. 5 document boxes.
Open. Published guide.
Smith College, Sophia Smith Collection.
Material generated by the UN Commission on the Status of Women, including addresses, press releases, resolutions, position papers and reports for 1946 to 1959, articles, clippings, and pamphlets; bibliographies on the status of women and on the activities, publications, and accomplishments of International Women's Year, 1975; and photos of women delegates to the UN. Taken from Mary-Elizabeth Murdock, *Catalog of The Sophia Smith Collection, Women's History Archive,* 2nd ed. (Northampton, MA: Smith College, 1976).

7,314. Upton Family
Papers. 1876-1937. 6 document boxes.
Open. Published guide.
Smith College, Sophia Smith Collection.
Diaries for 1904 to 1937 and letters concerning the travels in South America of Cornelia A. (Babcock) Upton (1854-1941), diaries for 1896 to 1921 and a PhD thesis of her daughter Eleanor Stuart Upton (1886-1974), and diaries for 1909 to 1926 and scientific publications of her other daughter Margaret Frances Upton (1890-1967). Also includes stories, plays, poems, and minutes of meetings from 1897 to 1900 of the Upton children's secret society in Providence, RI, "The Quier Kyds." Taken from Mary-Elizabeth Murdock, *Catalog of The Sophia Smith Collection, Women's History Archive,* 2nd ed. (Northampton, MA: Smith College, 1976).

7,315. Van Kleeck, Mary Abby
Papers. 1906-72. 6 drawers, 113 document boxes, and 98 vols.
Open. Published guide.
Smith College, Sophia Smith Collection.
Van Kleeck (1883-1972), a social researcher, industrial sociologist, and statistician, was a champion of social legislation, scientific management, international peace, and women's rights. She served as director of the department of industrial studies at the Russell Sage Foundation from 1908 to 1948; from 1928 to 1948 she also was active in the International Industrial Relations Institute as associate director. Correspondence, articles and addresses, biographical information, reports and records of IRI conferences and congresses, congressional hearing transcripts, and scrapbooks containing her editorial comments, addresses, news releases, and clippings on such subjects as trade unions, immigration, and the economic status of women. Also includes the Sage Foundation studies of women in industry, which were influential in affecting judicial opinion and protective labor legislation. Correspondents

include Mary L. Fledderus, Alice Hamilton, Rhoda E. McCulloch, M. Carey Thomas, and Lillian D. Wald. Taken from Mary-Elizabeth Murdock, *Catalog of The Sophia Smith Collection, Women's History Archive,* 2nd ed. (Northampton, MA: Smith College, 1976).

7,316. Varèse, Louise (McCutcheon)
Papers. 1915-75. Ca. 25 document boxes.
Open. Published guide.
Smith College, Sophia Smith Collection.
Papers of Varèse (1880-), an author and translator, include correspondence with family, friends, and persons active in the fine arts and performing arts; notes and typescripts of her book on her husband Edgar Varèse (1883-1965), a composer, entitled *Looking Glass Diary* (1972); poems and other writings by Louise Varèse; photos; awards; programs for performances of Edgar Varèse's compositions; material on the MacDowell Colony; genealogical information; sketches; condolences on her husband's death; reviews; memorabilia; two issues of *The Rogue* magazine from 1915; and her published translations of Baudelaire, Proust, Sartre, Stendhal, and Rimbaud. Taken from Mary-Elizabeth Murdock, *Catalog of The Sophia Smith Collection, Women's History Archive,* 2nd ed. (Northampton, MA: Smith College, 1976).

7,317. Walker, Emma Elizabeth
Papers. 1903-48. 1 document box.
Open. Published guide.
Smith College, Sophia Smith Collection.
Papers of Walker (1864?-1954), a physician, writer of children's stories, antisuffragist, and advocate of hygiene, physical culture, sex education, and birth control, include correspondence; typescripts of her published and unpublished articles, writings, and addresses; reviews of her book *The Pretty Girl Papers* (1910); and clippings of her column on beauty and health problems. Taken from Mary-Elizabeth Murdock, *Catalog of The Sophia Smith Collection, Women's History Archive,* 2nd ed. (Northampton, MA: Smith College, 1976).

7,318. Ward, Emma France
Papers. 1922-60. 2 document boxes.
Open. Published guide.
Smith College, Sophia Smith Collection.
Ward (1886-1963) was a pioneer in public health medicine, especially in the areas of industrial hygiene and occupational disease, as well as an advocate of child labor legislation. Personal and professional correspondence, biographical information, reprints of her articles, publications of the US Department of Labor Women's Bureau concerning the status of women in industry during the 1920s, and material relating to her role at the Sixth International Congress on Industrial Accidents and Diseases in Geneva, Switzerland, in 1931.

Also includes papers relating to *Victory Fleet,* digest of news and bulletins from the division of public relations of the US Maritime Commission, to which Ward contributed as shipyard personnel consultant, division of shipyard labor relations of the Commission. Taken from Mary-Elizabeth Murdock, *Catalog of The Sophia Smith Collection, Women's History Archive,* 2nd ed. (Northampton, MA: Smith College, 1976).

7,319. Wead Family
Papers. Nd. 1 document box.
Open. Published guide.
Smith College, Sophia Smith Collection.
Papers of Mary K. [Mrs. Samuel C.] Wead (1812-96?) include letters from the New York headquarters of the US Sanitary Commission relating to the work of women in northern New York state in collecting clothing and supplies for soldiers; correspondence with the New York National Freedman's Relief Association and the New York State Charities Aid Association; and other documents relating to the Civil War and the Reconstruction period. In addition, there are letters to Wead's granddaughter Eunice Wead (1881-1969) from Amy Lowell and others. Taken from Mary-Elizabeth Murdock, *Catalog of The Sophia Smith Collection, Women's History Archive,* 2nd ed. (Northampton, MA: Smith College, 1976).

7,320. Wile, Ira Solomon
Papers. 1915-42. 2 document boxes.
Open. Published guide.
Smith College, Sophia Smith Collection.
Wile (1877-1943) was a physician, author, lecturer, and advocate of birth control. Correspondence with Louise Stevens Bryant, Robert Latou Dickinson, Lydia DeVilbiss, Stella Hanau, Katharine (Houghton) Hepburn, Florence Rose, Margaret Sanger, and others on the social, economic, political, legal, religious, medical, and moral ramifications of the birth control movement. Also includes material relating to birth control conferences, the American Birth Control League, and the Birth Control Federation of America. Originals of these papers are located at the University of Rochester. Taken from Mary-Elizabeth Murdock, *Catalog of The Sophia Smith Collection, Women's History Archive,* 2nd ed. (Northampton, MA: Smith College, 1976).

7,321. Women Strike for Peace
Records. Nd. 1 document box.
Open. Published guide.
Smith College, Sophia Smith Collection.
Records of the group, which was established in 1961, include minutes of the steering committee, 1967 to present; flyers; the group's newsletter, 1963-67; and the periodical *Memo,* 1964-73. Taken from Mary-Elizabeth Murdock, *Catalog of The Sophia Smith Collection, Women's History Archive,* 2nd ed. (Northampton, MA: Smith College, 1976).

7,322. Women's International Democratic Federation
Records. Nd. 3 document boxes and 1 vol.
Open. Published guide.
Smith College, Sophia Smith Collection.
Records of the Federation, which was established in 1945, include agendas, correspondence, statements, reports, appeals, programs, flyers, pamphlets, and publications on many topics, including the status of women throughout the world, the defense of children, working women, and the banning of nuclear weapons; an autobiography of founder and president Eugénie Cotton; documents and proceedings, 1948-69, of congresses concerning the economic and political rights of women; and publications of affiliates in other countries and of the Congress of American Women. Also includes membership lists; "News in Brief," a publication of the Federation, 1953-57 and 1969-72; and records of the World Congress of Women. Taken from Mary-Elizabeth Murdock, *Catalog of The Sophia Smith Collection, Women's History Archive,* 2nd ed. (Northampton, MA: Smith College, 1976).

7,323. Women's International League for Peace and Freedom
Records. Nd. 18 document boxes.
Open. Published guide.
Smith College, Sophia Smith Collection.
Organizational records of international, national, and US branches of the League; annual reports of the national League; international congress proceedings, resolutions, and reports; international circular letters; papers from special topic conferences, including a 1929 conference on chemical warfare; a history of the League beginning in 1919; newsletters and flyers from national committees on civil liberties, conscientious objection, labor, legislation, refugees, the UN, and other subjects; clippings; pamphlets; and publications. Taken from Mary-Elizabeth Murdock, *Catalog of The Sophia Smith Collection, Women's History Archive,* 2nd ed. (Northampton, MA: Smith College, 1976).

7,324. Women's Liberation
Collection. 1950- . 47 boxes.
Open. Published guide.
Smith College, Sophia Smith Collection.
Minutes, biographical material, conference records, reports, calendars, newsletters, cartoons, handbooks, directories, posters, signs, stickers, lapel buttons, flyers, articles, clippings, bibliographies, catalogs, original and reprinted publications and almanacs. The collection documents the work of specific women's groups, including Smith College Women's Liberation; KNOW, Inc., a feminist press in Pittsburgh; the National Organization for Women; Valley Women's Center in Northampton; and the Feminist Press. It contains information on topics such as abortion, child care, health care, lesbianism, men's liberation, sex roles, and sex discrimination. See Mary-Elizabeth Murdock, *Catalog of The Sophia Smith Collection, Women's History Archive,* 2nd ed. (Northampton, MA: Smith College, 1976).

7,325. Women's Rights
Collection. 1848- . 24 boxes, 1 microfilm reel, and microfiche.
Open. Published guide.
Smith College, Sophia Smith Collection.
Minutes, correspondence, reports, biographical material, a scrapbook, articles, newspapers, pamphlets, and periodicals relate to federal employment of women, women's rights conventions and organizations, taxes and insurance paid by women, protective labor laws, political and civil rights for women, and the work of women for and against the Equal Rights Amendment. Includes extensive information on the President's Commission on the Status of Women. See Mary-Elizabeth Murdock, *Catalog of The Sophia Smith Collection, Women's History Archive,* 2nd ed. (Northampton, MA: Smith College, 1976).

7,326. Woodsmall, Ruth Frances
Papers. Nd. Ca. 72 document boxes and 3 vols.
Open. Published guide.
Smith College, Sophia Smith Collection.
Woodsmall (1883-1963) was an executive of the international YWCA from 1932 to 1948 and a champion of women's rights. Correspondence on such subjects as her WWI work, interracial problems, education, and refugees; diaries for 1920 to 1930 and 1940 to 1950; research notes; essays and addresses; manuscripts; educational and business records; biographical sketches; photos; reports; awards; pamphlets; and clippings. Includes manuscripts of her books *Eastern Women Today and Tomorrow* (1933); *The Role of Women, Their Activities and Organizations in Lebanon, Egypt, Iraq, Jordan and Syria* (1955); and *Women and the New East* (1960). Also contains material on Rockefeller Foundation grant research on the changing status of Muslim women and files of her work with the US High Commission for Germany. Taken from Mary-Elizabeth Murdock, *Catalog of The Sophia Smith Collection, Women's History Archive,* 2nd ed. (Northampton, MA: Smith College, 1976).

7,327. Wright, Jane C.
Papers. 1950-75. 2 document boxes.
Open. Published guide.
Smith College, Sophia Smith Collection.
Papers of Wright (1919-), an oncologist and hospital executive, include reprints of articles relating to her work in cancer treatment and research and issues of *Progress Against Cancer* from 1967 and 1969 to 1970. Taken from Mary-Elizabeth Murdock, *Catalog of The Sophia Smith Collection, Women's History Archive,* 2nd ed. (Northampton, MA: Smith College, 1976).

7,328. Wrinch, Dorothy
Papers. 1932-70. Ca. 125 document boxes.
Closed. Published guide.
Smith College, Sophia Smith Collection.
Wrinch (1895-1976), a crystallographer, biochemist, mathematician, and physicist who taught at Smith College, was the originator of the cyclol theory of protein structure. Personal and professional correspondence with Linus Pauling and others, travel diaries, notebooks, Smith College outlines and lectures, a bibliography of her writings, conference reports, symposium records, articles, models, and memorabilia. Also includes letters and writings of her daughter Pamela (Wrinch) Schenkman (1927-75), a political scientist. Taken from Mary-Elizabeth Murdock, *Catalog of The Sophia Smith Collection, Women's History Archive,* 2nd ed. (Northampton, MA: Smith College, 1976).

7,329. YWCA
Records. Nd. 51 document boxes and 3 vols.
Open. Published guide.
Smith College, Sophia Smith Collection.
Records of the national YWCA include conference minutes and reports for 1922 to 1948; records of the business, professional, and industrial departments, including conference material and special studies on such subjects as textile mill villages and the problems of women in industry; historical and biographical information on the secretary of the industrial department Florence Simms and other leaders; a history; bibliographies; bulletins; photos; song sheets; articles; clippings; pamphlets; publications; and material on International Institutes, interracial education, national and international women's movements, women's war effort, and other topics. Taken from Mary-Elizabeth Murdock, *Catalog of The Sophia Smith Collection, Women's History Archive,* 2nd ed. (Northampton, MA: Smith College, 1976).

NORTON

7,330. Women's Education
Collection. 1834- . 192 ft., 500 vols., 14 recording discs, and 75 tapes.
Open. Unpublished guide.
Wheaton College Archives.
Records of Wheaton College, a women's school founded in 1834 as Wheaton Female Seminary, include annual reports of the president, minutes of some faculty meetings, budget records, correspondence, studies, reports, curriculum material, faculty publications, and clippings. Also includes student journals and correspondence from the 19th century, a few class books and autograph albums, a complete file of the literary magazine *Rushlight* since 1855 and *Wheaton News* since 1921, and papers of all the presidents of the College and principals of the Seminary. In addition, the collection contains correspondence, diaries, notebooks, and books of Lucy Larcom, 1859-62; letters to Laban Morey Wheaton and his wife Eliza Baylies (Chapin) Wheaton from Mary Lyon, 1834-35; and tapes of a forum held in 1962 with Eleanor Roosevelt. Laban Morey Wheaton, who with his wife was active in the Seminary's affairs for many years, was the son of Judge Laban Wheaton, who founded the Seminary in memory of his daughter.

PETERSHAM

7,331. Female Benevolent Society
Records. 1823- . 5 ft.
Open. Unpublished guide.
Petersham Historical Society.
Charter, record books, yearbooks, photos, and clippings of the Society, founded in 1823 to sew for those in need and to purchase tracts for distribution. The Society, which is still in existence, was renamed the Petersham Branch Alliance when it became affiliated with the Unitarian Universalist Women's Federation.

7,332. Goodsell, Carolyn
Papers. 1890- . 1 ft.
Open. No guide.
Petersham Historical Society.
Scrapbooks of and paintings by [Mrs. Alson] Goodsell (1890-), a teacher, artist, and American National Red Cross nurse during WWI; she wrote *Evacuation 114* (1919) about her experiences. Her scrapbook concerns the Petersham bicentennial in 1954; her paintings are of Captain John Green Mudge, who organized the local Civil War company, and of a baseball game on Petersham Common. Goodsell taught in a public school, held art classes in her home, and was a Sunday school teacher. She adopted three children who had been orphaned as the result of a fire. Goodsell was head of the Historical Society's committee for a 1966 art exhibit.

7,333. Howe, Sarah
Papers. Nd. No size given.
Open. No guide.
Petersham Historical Society.
Journal in which [Mrs. Joel] Howe (1766-1849), founder of the Female Benevolent Society, describes her education, the Revolutionary War, and Shays' Rebellion. She also remarks on other topics current in her day.

7,334. Williams, Marie E.
Papers. 1883-1960. 5 ft.
Open. Partial unpublished guide.
Petersham Historical Society.
[Miss] Williams (1866-1961) was a teacher, office worker, and researcher who served as president of the Historical Society from 1923 to 1925. Historical notes, reports on Petersham families and organizations, scrapbooks of clippings about local residences, clippings, and other items, including an index that traces changes in ownership of Petersham dwellings.

ROCKPORT

7,335. Gale, Mary Louisa Bigelow
Papers. 1826-61. 9 vols.
Access restricted. No guide.
Sandy Bay Historical Society and Museum.
Diaries of Gale (1807-61), the wife of Congregational minister Wakefield Gale (1797-1881), contain extensive entries beginning two years before her marriage and continuing until shortly before her death. She comments on life with her husband in Eastport, ME, and then in Rockport, concentrating primarily on family news and church events.

7,336. Hatchet Gang
Collection. 1856-1940s. 1 folder.
Access restricted. No guide.
Sandy Bay Historical Society and Museum.
Material concerns the raid a group of women temperance advocates made in 1856 in Rockport. Transcripts of oral interviews with persons who witnessed, remembered, or heard about the raid; a contemporary account from the diary of Joseph H. Bartlett; legal records; photos; memorabilia; and clippings.

SALEM

7,337. Adams, Abigail
Papers. 1784-86. 5 items.
Open. Card catalog.
Essex Institute.
Letters of Adams (1744-1818), who was the wife of US President John Adams.

7,338. Almy, Lydia Hill
Papers. 1797-99. 69 pp.
Open. Card catalog.
Essex Institute.
Diary, which Almy wrote for her husband while he was away working on a whaling ship, contains accounts of visits, family, neighbors, illnesses, church meetings, and her emotions. Almy had at least one child.

7,339. Association for Relief of Aged and Destitute Women in Salem
Records. 1860-1903. 2 envelopes.
Open. No guide.
Essex Institute.
Annual reports, information on investments, correspondence, and records pertaining to the support of needy women in Salem.

7,340. Averill, Martha Jane (Weston)
Papers. 1856-89. 1 Hollinger box and 3 vols.
Open. Card catalog.
Essex Institute.
Averill (1838-?) was a teacher. Diary-account book contains descriptions of classes at the Salem Normal School; at school in Ipswich, MA; and of life in Middleton, MA. Also includes a list of letters she wrote, receipts, genealogical notes, and recipes.

7,341. Baldwin, Mary C.
Papers. 1816-17. 1 vol.
Open. Card catalog.
Essex Institute.
Diary-account book of Baldwin contains listings of debits and credits and of such purchases as foodstuffs and fabrics.

7,342. Barrett, Martha Osborne
Papers. 1848-87. 9 vols.
Open. Card catalog.
Essex Institute.
Diaries in which Barrett (1827-?), a student, teacher, and clerk in a milliner's shop, describes her courses of study, daily activities, meetings, visits, her abolitionist sentiments, and her plans and expectations. Also includes poems and compositions she wrote at the Westfield Normal School in 1849 and an account of a trip to the White Mountains in 1887. Barrett was born in Peabody, MA.

7,343. Bemis, Martha (Wheatland)
Papers. 1831-46. 51 items.
Open. Card catalog.
Essex Institute.
Letters of [Mrs. R. E.] Bemis (1807-?), a Salem native, to her brother Henry Wheatland (1812-93) and from her husband and her daughter Caroline Bemis.

7,344. Benjamin, Anna Northend
Papers. 1901. 4 vols. and 1 envelope.
Open. Card catalog.
Essex Institute.
Diaries and miscellaneous papers relating to a trip Benjamin took to Europe. Includes photos of France and Russia.

7,345. Betton, Elizabeth Ellis (Prescott)
Papers. 1824-48, nd. 1 Hollinger box.
Open. Card catalog.
Essex Institute.
Letters to [Mrs. Charles] Betton, who was born in Derry, NH, and resided in Derry and Salem, NH, from her mother Harriet Prescott and from other members of her family.

7,346. Bowen, Elizabeth
Papers. 1775-1808. 1 envelope.
Open. Card catalog.
Essex Institute.
Diary of Bowen (1734-?), born in Marblehead, MA, consists of a brief autobiography and family genealogy, accounts of smallpox and measles epidemics, and spiritual notes.

7,347. Boyd, Alice Webster
Papers. 1890-92. 3 vols.
Open. Card catalog.
Essex Institute.
Boyd's papers consist of a notebook containing sewing class projects and notebooks from sewing and domestic economy classes she took at St. John's School in Tarrytown-on-Hudson, NY.

7,348. Bradford Female Benevolent Society and Bradford Female Charitable Society.
Records. 1815-68. 1 vol.
Open. No guide.
Essex Institute.
Records of both of these Bradford, MA, societies are contained in the same volume. Consists of records of the Charitable Society, 1815-23, and records of the Benevolent Society, 1861-68.

7,349. Brown, Alice
Papers. 1906-35. 98 items.
Open. Card catalog.
Essex Institute.
Correspondence of [Miss] Brown (1856-1948), an author who lived in Boston and Newburyport, MA.

7,350. Brown, Mary Quincy
Papers. 1847-48, nd. 3 items.
Open. Card catalog.
Essex Institute.
Letters that Brown's father N. Brown wrote to her while she was attending Mount Holyoke Female Seminary.

7,351. Burbank, Timothy: Collins, Hannah (Pickering)
Papers. 1693-1773. 1 vol.
Open. Card catalog.
Essex Institute.
Diary of Burbank contains partial diary of [Mrs. Adoniram] Collins (1708-?). Her entries, dated from 1731 to 1761, contain dates of family births, marriages, and deaths as well as information about school attendance.

7,352. Burnham Family
Papers. 1824-1952. 2 boxes.
Open. Unpublished guide.
Essex Institute.
Papers of this Essex, MA, family include correspondence, school compositions, and legal documents of Ida L. (Angier) Burnham, 1860-1928, and accounts pertaining to the estate of Sally [Mrs. Samuel] Burnham, 1888-95.

7,353. Buxton, Huldah G.
Papers. 1877. 1 vol.
Open. Card catalog.
Essex Institute.
Diary of [Mrs. Joshua, Jr.] Buxton, a housewife, primarily consists of accounts of devotions and of visits by the doctor.

7,354. Buxton, Mary Jane
Papers. 1712-1914. 5 boxes.
Open. Unpublished guide.
Essex Institute.
Correspondence with relatives and friends, diaries, bills and receipts, legal documents, and family papers of Buxton (1821-1915), a resident of Danvers and Peabody, MA. Her 48 volumes of diaries scattered over the period 1861-1911 contain information about the weather and temperatures, partial accounts of social groups and activities for which she appears to have served as treasurer, lists of letters received and sent, addresses, subscription receipts, and notes of funds she loaned to others, stock she owned, and dividends received.

7,355. Carter, Elizabeth Margaret
Papers. 1819-21. 1 envelope.
Open. Card catalog.
Essex Institute.
Account book of goods purchased for Elizabeth Carter (1799-1866) and a list of gifts she received prior to her marriage in 1821 to William B. Reynolds (1797-1866) of Boston; a letter in which Reynolds asked Thomas Smith to be his groomsman; a journal of Anna Quincy (Thaxter) Parsons, which contains a description of Carter's wedding to Reynolds; and a letter from Reynolds to Mrs. Joshua Carter about early married life.

7,356. Chapman, Louisa
Papers. 1848-49. 1 vol.
Open. Card catalog.
Essex Institute.
Diary in which Chapman (1815-?), a seamstress and schoolteacher from Ipswich, MA, reports on her daily activities over a period of 11 months.

7,357. Choate, Abby Parker (Cogswell)
Papers. 1885-1900. 13 vols.
Open. Card catalog.
Essex Institute.
Diaries of Choate (1832-?), a Bradford College alumna who later became a wife and mother, contain notes on the activities of her family, accounts of household expenses, addresses, and entries concerning a trip she made to Europe in 1891.

7,358. Choate, Anna N.
Papers. 1905. 1 vol.
Open. Card catalog.
Essex Institute.
Diary of Choate (1870-?), a housewife, contains information about her household activities, her family, and the weather.

7,359. Cleveland, Elizabeth H.
Papers. 1824-49. 1 vol.
Open. Card catalog.
Essex Institute.
In her diary Cleveland described the final days before the deaths of her mother and then her father and medications used during the last days of her daughter's life. Diary also contains thoughts on her brother's death, characterizations of friends who were deceased, and discussion of the scriptures.

7,360. Cranch, Mary
Papers. 1760-69. 1 vol.
Open. Card catalog.
Essex Institute.
Account book of Cranch, a tavern keeper in Boston.

7,361. Crowninshield Family
Papers. 1789-1906. 32 boxes.
Open. Unpublished guide.
Essex Institute.
Includes letters to and account books of Louise (du Pont) [Mrs. Francis Boardman] Crowninshield (1877-1958); account books of Katherine M. Crowninshield; letters that F. B. C. Bradlee received from his mother Alice Crowninshield [Mrs. Josiah] Bradlee and his sister Sarah Crowninshield Bradlee, which were written from Europe and New Hampshire between 1905 and 1907; and letters that Alice Bradlee received in 1923 from her children in the Caribbean, France, and England. Also includes correspondence and other papers from other female Crowninshield relatives and friends.

7,362. Cummins Family
Papers. 1806-98. 1 box.
Open. Unpublished guide.
Essex Institute.
Papers of this Salem family include correspondence, fan mail, legal papers, writings, and reviews of the works of [Miss] Maria Susannah Cummins (1827-66), an author. Also includes publishing contracts and requests from magazines and newspapers for stories by Cummins.

7,363. Cutts Family
Papers. 1787-93. 1 box.
Open. Card catalog.
Essex Institute.
Correspondence, primarily consisting of letters exchanged by Hannah Tracy (Emery) [Mrs. Benjamin] Abbott of Exeter, NH, and Mary Carter of Newburyport, MA. Carter later married Edward Cutts of Portsmouth, NH.

7,364. Dodge, Mary Abigail
Papers. 1842-96. 1 box.
Open. Card catalog.
Essex Institute.
An author who was born in Hamilton, MA, Dodge (1833-96) used Gail Hamilton as her pseudonym. Correspondence, poetry, prose, notebooks, clippings, and other items.

7,365. Dorcas Society
Records. 1811-75. 4 vols.
Open. Unpublished guide.
Essex Institute.
This religious and charitable society was founded in Salem in 1812 and dissolved in ca. 1892. Record book, an account and dues book, and two volumes of information on the distribution of garments and aid to the needy between 1817 and 1875. The records are filed with those of the Salem Female Charitable Society, to which the Dorcas Society contributed.

7,366. Emerson, Sarah Marsh
Papers. 1859-60. 1 vol.
Open. Card catalog.
Essex Institute.
Diary concerns the first months of a trip to Europe that Emerson (1835-1915) made as companion to Mrs. J. S. Cabot.

7,367. Emery Family
Papers. 1793-1863. 1 envelope.
Open. Card catalog.
Essex Institute.
Includes letters to [Miss] Margaret "Meta" Emery and legal and estate papers of Ella Maria Emery and her husband Moses Emery of Amesbury, MA.

7,368. Emery, Mary Elizabeth "Lizzie"
Papers. 1888-89. 1 vol.
Open. Card catalog.
Essex Institute.
Diary in which Emery, the wife of a farmer, recorded her daily activities and the weather conditions.

7,369. Endicott, Mary
Papers. 1816-71. 1 vol.
Open. Card catalog.
Essex Institute.
Diary in which Endicott (1800-77), a resident of Danvers, MA, recorded her thoughts and daily activities as well as the deaths in Danvers and nearby communities.

7,370. Essex County Teachers Association
Records. 1830-98. 2 vols.
Open. No guide.
Essex Institute.
Record books of the Association.

7,371. Essex North Women's Congregational Fellowship
Records. 1875-1927. 5 vols.
Open. Card catalog.
Essex Institute.
Constitutions, records of meetings, and reports of the Essex North Missionary Association, the Essex North Home Missionary Alliance, and the Essex North branch of the Women's Board of Missions.

7,372. Fairfax Family
Papers. 1753-1815. 1 envelope.
Open. Card catalog.
Essex Institute.
Includes letters from family members to [Mrs.] Deborah Fairfax Anderson and Hannah (Clarke) [Mrs. John] Cabot of Salem and a 1764 inventory of the estate of Hannah Cabot.

7,373. Female Religious and Biographical Reading Society
Records. 1826-33. 1 vol.
Open. No guide.
Essex Institute.
Record book of this Salem organization.

7,374. Female Temperance Society
Records. 1829-34. 1 vol.
Open. No guide.
Essex Institute.
Records of this West Bradford, MA, group.

7,375. French, Mary E.
Papers. 1874-87. 1 envelope.
Open. Card catalog.
Essex Institute.
Correspondence and other writings by French and other missionaries in India and Europe.

7,376. Goodell, Martha Page (Putnam)
Papers. 1914. 1 vol.
Open. Card catalog.
Essex Institute.
Diary in which Page (1834-?) describes her daily activities and the fire of 1914 in Salem. Also contains some notes of bills paid.

7,377. Gould, Elizabeth Porter
Papers. 1884-1906. 1 envelope.
Open. Card catalog.
Essex Institute.
Reviews and letters concerning books by Gould (1848-?), an author who lived in Boston.

7,378. Hale, Ann E.
Papers. 1841. 1 vol.
Open. Card catalog.
Essex Institute.
Diary of Hale, a student at the Young Ladies' Classical Institute in Newburyport, MA, contains descriptions of classes and courses of study over a two-month period.

7,379. Hall, Alma
Papers. 1807-20. 1 envelope.
Open. No guide.
Essex Institute.
School compositions by and letters to Hall.

7,380. Harraden, Lydia Anne
Papers. 1832. 1 vol.
Open. Card catalog.
Essex Institute.
Diary of [Mrs. Benjamin Ives] Harraden (1809-81), which was interleaved in an almanac, contains accounts of the weather, visits, church attendance, deaths in Salem, and celebration of George Washington's birthday.

7,381. Hassam, Eleanor
Papers. 1886-1903. 1 box, 1 vol., and 2 envelopes.
Open. No guide.
Essex Institute.
Correspondence, diaries, a notebook, school compositions, and other papers of Hassam (1879-), including a list of classmates at various schools she attended and accounts of social events in the Boston area.

7,382. Hassam Family
Papers. 1848-1929. 1 box and 7 vols.
Open. No guide.
Essex Institute.
Includes diaries, 1872 and 1877-78; an account book of personal expenses, 1866-81; and an inventory, 1903-07, of furniture, books, silver, and jewelry in the Salem house of Nelly Alden (Batchelder) Hassam.

7,383. Hawthorne and Manning
Papers. 1683-1956. 8 ft.
Open. Unpublished guide.
Essex Institute.
Papers of author Nathaniel Hawthorne (1804-64) and of his and related families include correspondence of Sophia Amelia (Peabody) Hawthorne (1809-71), most of which pertains to financial matters; Una Hawthorne (1844-77), who writes detailing the family's activities in Europe while Nathaniel Hawthorne served as consul to Liverpool, in Dresden where Julian Hawthorne attended school, and in England where she spent her later years; Nathaniel Hawthorne's granddaughter Hildegarde Hawthorne, who describes her work with the YMCA in France during WWI; and Elizabeth Palmer Peabody (1804-94).

Also includes letters Rose (Hawthorne) Lathrop (1851-1926) wrote about such family matters as her marital difficulties and later letters she wrote after she had become a nun, adopted the name Mother Alphonsa, and worked with cancer patients.

Collection also contains correspondence of Rebecca B. Manning (1834-1933), which consists primarily of letters to her nephew Richard C. Manning, Jr., a physician; her correspondence with Manning Hawthorne; family correspondence of Maria Miriam Manning (1786-1814), Mary Manning (1777-1841), Susan (Dingley) Manning, Priscilla Miriam (Manning) Dike (1790-1873), and Elizabeth Manning Hawthorne (1802-83); letters from Maria H. Davis to Maria Manning (1826-1917); and correspondence and legal and financial papers of Rebecca Dodge (Burnham) Manning (1797-1869). In addition, the collection includes a diary for 1805 to 1809 in which an unknown female member of the Tabernacle Church in Salem discusses romances and religious conversion.

7,384. Holyoke, Elizabeth "Betsey"
Papers. 1786-87. 2 vols.
Open. Card catalog.
Essex Institute.
Diaries of Holyoke (1771-89), a native of Salem, contain brief notes on the weather, visits and visitors, and her expenses and clothing purchases.

7,385. Holyoke Family
Papers. 1607-1905. 8 ft. and 85 vols.
Open. Unpublished guide.
Essex Institute.
Primarily consists of the papers of Edward Holyoke (1689-1769), a minister and president of Harvard University from 1737 to 1769, and of his son Edward Augustus Holyoke (1728-1829), a Salem physician. Includes legal papers of Edward Holyoke's third wife Mary (Epes) Holyoke (?-1790); correspondence of Edward Augustus Holyoke with his sister Margaret (Holyoke) Mascarene (1726-92); Margaret Mascarene's diaries, 1783-92; Edward Augustus Holyoke's correspondence with his wife Mary (Vial) Holyoke (1738-1802) about smallpox and military activity during the early days of the Revolutionary War; Mary Holyoke's diaries, 1760-1800, that contain brief daily entries and notations of expenses; Edward Augustus Holyoke's correspondence with his daughter Margaret Holyoke (1763-1825) about her studies, an inoculation, and family matters; and Margaret Holyoke's diaries, 1783-1823, in which she made brief notes about visits, visitors, the weather, and events as well as about some of her expenses.

Collection also contains correspondence about family and financial matters and health by Anna (Holyoke) Cutts (1735-1812), Priscilla Holyoke (1739-82), and Elizabeth (Holyoke) Kneeland (1732-1821) and an 1829 diary in which Mary (Holyoke) Ward (1800-80), a music student, provides accounts of her daily visits and lessons.

7,386. Hook, Elizabeth
Papers. 1785-1844. 1 vol.
Open. Card catalog.
Essex Institute.
Diary-account book in which Hook (1778-?), a Salisbury, MA, milliner who was also a spinner, weaver, and knitter, notes her income, expenses, and major weather events.

7,387. Howard, Cecil Howard Cutts
Papers. 1741-1893. 1 vol.
Open. Card catalog.
Essex Institute.
Includes letters, 1741-96, to Mary Carter and Mary Cutts of Newburyport, MA, from Hannah Smith, Hannah Green, and Eliza Smith of Boston and Philadelphia about family matters, social life, religion, and other topics.

7,388. Hutchinson, Hannah, and Hutchinson, Sarah P.
Papers. 1871-1903. 53 vols.
Open. Card catalog.
Essex Institute.
Diaries of the Hutchinson sisters, residents of Danvers, MA, include accounts of their daily activities, such as homemaking, farming, selling eggs and vegetables, and social visits. Also includes financial papers of Sarah Hutchinson.

7,389. Jewett, Lucy Kinsman
Papers. 1804-11. 1 vol. and 3 pp.
Open. Card catalog.
Essex Institute.
Jewett (1757-1837) was a teacher in Ipswich, MA. Accounts for schooling, 1804-05, and a bill for the education of Lydia Wells, 1804-11.

7,390. Johnson, Samuel
Papers. 1836-81. 5 boxes and 8 envelopes.
Open. Card catalog.
Essex Institute.
Correspondence and writings of Johnson (1822-82), a minister of the Lynn Free Church, including letters from Elizabeth Palmer Peabody, Lucy Stone, Lydia Maria Child, and other women involved in the antislavery and women's rights movements.

7,391. Kenny, Mary Emerson
Papers. 1854-59. 2 vols.
Open. Card catalog.
Essex Institute.
Diaries of [Mrs. Jonathon] Kenny, a housewife, contain notations of daily highlights and shopping lists with prices. Her diaries were interleaved in almanacs.

7,392. King, Kate
Papers. 1868. 1 vol.
Open. Card catalog.
Essex Institute.
Journal of a trip King took to England, Prussia, and Germany with her husband David King.

7,393. Kinsman Family
Papers. 1784-1878. 5 boxes.
Open. No guide.
Essex Institute.
Includes correspondence of Nathaniel Kinsman with his wife Rebecca Kinsman, 1834-47; letters to

her from her family from Macao in 1845, from Manilla in 1845 and 1846, and then from home in 1846 and 1847; and other letters to her from her family and friends, 1852-65.

7,394. Knowlton, Gertrude F.
Papers. 1906-30. 2 vols. and 38 pp.
Open. No guide.
Essex Institute.
Account book pertains to the business of Knowlton, a Hamilton, MA, dealer in wood, hay, and farm products.

7,395. Knowlton, Irene M.
Papers. 1871-88. 4 vols.
Open. Card catalog.
Essex Institute.
Diaries of Knowlton, who took in boarders, contain her notes on the weather, daily tasks, and health.

7,396. Ladies Foreign Missionary Society
Records. 1871-91. 3 vols.
Open. No guide.
Essex Institute.
Record books of the Society of the First Baptist Church in Salem.

7,397. Ladies Reading Society
Records. 1818-46. 1 envelope.
Open. No guide.
Essex Institute.
Record book of this Byfield, MA, group.

7,398. Larcom, Lucy
Papers. 1807-93. 2 ft.
Open. Unpublished guide.
Essex Institute.
Correspondence, poems, and miscellaneous papers of [Miss] Larcom (1824-93), an author. Bulk of the collection is correspondence with [Miss] P. Fobes, who was one of Larcom's teachers; Mary Mapes Dodge, an author of works for children and editor of *St. Nicholas* magazine; Elizabeth Stuart Phelps Ward, an author and advocate of women's rights; and S. I. Spalding.

7,399. Lee, Martha
Papers. 1852. 26 pp.
Open. Card catalog.
Essex Institute.
Journal in which Lee, a resident of Manchester and Bradford, MA, describes her religious experiences.

7,400. Little, Mary Bishop
Papers. 1858-59. 1 vol.
Open. Card catalog.
Essex Institute.
A diary of the daily activities of Little (1836-67).

7,401. Little, Sophronia (Balch)
Papers. 1857. 1 vol.
Open. Card catalog.
Essex Institute.
Diary of [Mrs. Josiah] Little (1793-1872), a Newburyport, MA, housewife, contains accounts of her family's daily activities, her tasks, visits, and expenses.

7,402. Lund, Matilda Barker
Papers. 1831-65. 1 vol.
Open. Card catalog.
Essex Institute.
Diary and financial papers of Lund, a housewife who sold eggs, contain an inventory of accounts, stocks, notes receivable, and bad debts for 1831; a listing of her monthly income for 1864 and 1865; and a description of her daily activities during 1864.

7,403. Lyman, Samuel
Papers. 1795-1841. 1 envelope.
Open. Card catalog.
Essex Institute.
Includes correspondence of Mary Lyman, a resident of Springfield, MA, 1796-1813.

7,404. Marblehead Charitable Society
Records. 1847-91. 1 vol.
Open. No guide.
Essex Institute.
Record book of the Society.

7,405. March, Alice Little (Hale)
Papers. 1852. 1 vol. and 1 item.
Open. Card catalog.
Essex Institute.
A letter to her brother and a diary of [Mrs. John C.] March (1811-?), a housewife. She notes daily highlights, visits, the weather, and her health.

7,406. Mason, Caroline (Atwater)
Papers. 1899-1939. 6 boxes.
Open. Card catalog.
Essex Institute.
Personal letters, letters from supporters and admirers, manuscripts, copies of sketches and stories, notebooks, memoirs, reviews, and a guest book of Mason (1853-1939), an author and poet. Includes letters in support of her prohibitionist and fundamentalist stands.

7,407. Mead, Lucy Irene
Papers. 1910-25. 1 envelope.
Open. Card catalog.
Essex Institute.
Mead was a missionary to China. Letters written from China and a copy of the temporary constitution of the Chinese Christian Church of Peking. Includes accounts of life in China, Taoist worship, the role of Chinese women, education, and military skirmishes in Peking during 1917.

7,408. Miles, Nellie
Papers. 1897-1900. 1 envelope.
Open. Card catalog.
Essex Institute.
Letters of praise, recommendations, a contract for services, programs, and flyers of Miles, a leader of a military band and of a ladies orchestra.

7,409. Millett, Charlotte
Papers. 1809-10. 1 vol.
Open. Card catalog.
Essex Institute.
Daybook of Millett, who kept a general store in Gloucester, MA, contains customers' accounts and information about stock bought for the store.

7,410. Moulton, Susan Whittemore
Papers. 1877-78. 1 envelope.
Open. Card catalog.
Essex Institute.
Love letters to a medical student in New York, original poems, and clippings about the family home Moulton Castle of Susan Moulton (1856-89), a resident of Newburyport, MA.

7,411. Nichols, Charlotte S.
Papers. 1910-33. 5 vols.
Open. Card catalog.
Essex Institute.
Household account books of Nichols, a Salem, MA, resident, show itemized purchases of clothing, cosmetics, and food and list other expenses, among them charitable contributions.

7,412. Nichols, Sarah Pierce
Papers. 1833. 1 vol.
Open. Card catalog.
Essex Institute.
Diary in which Nichols (1804-?) made notes on the weather, 12-mile walks, and sermons she heard.

7,413. Northey Family
Papers. 1721-1896. 13 boxes.
Open. Card catalog.
Essex Institute.
Family papers include letters to Cynthia (Winslow) Northey (1808-65) and her daughter Rebekah Maria (Northey) [Mrs. John Henry] Buffum (1825-?) as well as correspondence of Annie, Helen, and Margaret Anthony (1828-93) and other members of the Anthony family.

7,414. Osborne, Sarah Waters (Whittredge)
Papers. 1879-83. 3 vols.
Open. Card catalog.
Essex Institute.
Diaries in which [Mrs. George] Osborne (1804-?), a housewife and mother, describes the daily activities of her family.

7,415. Parsons, Margaret
Papers. 1831-55. 1 vol.
Open. Card catalog.
Essex Institute.
Diary in which Parsons made notes on Sunday services, recording the name of the minister who preached, the text used, and details about the sermons.

7,416. Peabody, Elizabeth Palmer
Papers. 1835-79. 12 items.
Open. Card catalog.
Essex Institute.
Correspondence and photos of Peabody (1804-94), an educator. Includes letters to Ralph Waldo Emerson and his wife Lydia "Lidian" Emerson, 1838-39, about religion and the insanity of Jones Very and other letters about her reading and religious topics.

7,417. Peabody, Mary S. C.
Papers. 1860-1905. 15 vols.
Open. Card catalog.
Essex Institute.
Scattered diaries in which Peabody (1817-?), an Ipswich, MA, housewife, noted visits, social occasions, letters she wrote, and domestic activities.

7,418. Peatfield, Hannah M.
Papers. 1847. 1 vol.
Open. Card catalog.
Essex Institute.
Accounts of the activities of Peatfield (1837-?), a schoolgirl, in school, church, and at home. She also mentions visits she made.

7,419. Perkins, Mary H.
Papers. 1857-78. 1 vol.
Open. Card catalog.
Essex Institute.
Diary in which Perkins, a schoolgirl, describes her classes, courses of study, and family outings in 1857. Also includes later notes she made on Bible lessons.

7,420. Pickman, Mary Toppan
Papers. 1831-61. 4 vols.
Open. Card catalog.
Essex Institute.
Diaries of Pickman (1816-?), a student and then wife and mother in Salem, concern her daily activities, sermons she heard, authors she read, and people she saw.

7,421. Pierson, Ellen Elizabeth (Perry)
Papers. 1852-85. 4 vols.
Open. Card catalog.
Essex Institute.
Journals concern the travels of Pierson (1828-?) in Spain, Switzerland, Germany, France, and Italy. Journals also contain some dried flowers.

7,422. Pope, Sarah A.
Papers. 1871. 1 vol.
Open. Card catalog.
Essex Institute.
Notes of a trip to England, Holland, France, and Germany that Pope seems to have made alone.

7,423. Porter, Elizabeth
Papers. 1845. 1 vol.
Open. Card catalog.
Essex Institute.
Porter's diary, interleaved in an almanac, contains one-line entries about visits and meetings she attended.

7,424. Putnam, Margaret (Sage)
Papers. 1844-96. 1 vol. and 1 envelope.
Open. Card catalog.
Essex Institute.
Account of a voyage that Putnam (1811-?), a Salem resident, made from Boston to Charleston, SC, and of her stay in the South prior to Lincoln's assassination. Includes information on the observations of former slaves and on visits to Fort Sumter, Fort Moultrie, and Beaufort, SC. Collection also contains correspondence of Putnam with her daughter [Mrs.] Alice L. Boardman concerning daily activities, reading, and news.

7,425. Putnam, Mary H.
Papers. 1855-56. 1 vol.
Open. Card catalog.
Essex Institute.
Journal that Putnam, a resident of Manchester and Londonderry, NH, kept while her husband Horace B. Putnam, a sailor, was away at sea. She speaks of her family and of loneliness.

7,426. Rantoul Family
Papers. 1886. 1 vol.
Open. Card catalog.
Essex Institute.
Diary of a woman, who was living in Paris, contains notes on the weather, visits, and shopping.

7,427. Rantoul, Hannah Lovett
Papers. 1869-70. 1 vol.
Open. Card catalog.
Essex Institute.
Journal of the travels of Rantoul (1821-?), a native of Beverly, MA, to England, Holland, Belgium, Germany, Switzerland, Italy, and France.

7,428. Reynolds, Rebecca Evelina
Papers. 1845-48. 1 envelope.
Open. Card catalog.
Essex Institute.
Correspondence of Reynolds, a resident of Boxford, MA, to her parents.

7,429. Rust, Daniel, and Rust, Elizabeth
Papers. 1799-1817. 1 vol.
Open. Card catalog.
Essex Institute.
Daybook of the Rusts, who were shopkeepers in Salem, contains customers' accounts and shop receipts.

7,430. Salem Female Anti-Slavery Society
Records. 1834-66. 1 ft. and 5 vols.
Open. Unpublished guide.
Essex Institute.
Record books; account books; letters from Susan B. Anthony, Henry W. Beecher, Lucretia Mott, Ralph Waldo Emerson, and others who were involved in the abolition movement; and miscellaneous records of the Society, which was founded in 1834 to promote the abolition of slavery.

7,431. Salem Female Charitable Society
Records. 1801-1963. 4 boxes, 2 vols., and 1 folder.
Partially restricted. Unpublished guide.
Essex Institute.
Organization records, financial accounts, correspondence, lists of members and beneficiaries, and other records of the Society, which was founded in 1801 to aid needy or fatherless girls by placing them in suitable families. The group also helped aged and infirm widows. In 1810 the Society acquired a house and hired a governess for the girls, but as other organizations and the public welfare system began to assume the care of such girls, the Society's function was reduced to providing financial assistance and friendship to needy Salem women. Records are particularly complete for the early period of the Society's history. Includes information on Society anniversaries.

7,432. Salem Female Employment Society
Records. 1861-79. 1 box and 31 vols.
Open. Unpublished guide.
Essex Institute.
Complete records of the Society, founded in 1861 and dissolved in 1879, consist of bylaws and regulations, account books, lists of articles made by employees, work orders, manager's sales records, and subscription lists. Organized to provide sewing for poor women who were unable to procure employment elsewhere and to give them fair wages for their work, the Society hoped "by these means to encourage a spirit of independence, and to diminish daily alms-giving."

7,433. Salem Female School
Records. 1799-1834. 2 envelopes.
Open. No guide.
Essex Institute.
Accounts and receipts, lists of scholars, and a record book of the School, which was also known as Mr. Cole's Female School.

7,434. Salem Women's Club
Records. 1895-1904. 1 envelope.
Open. No guide.
Essex Institute.
Correspondence of guest lecturers and supplementary material of the Club, founded in 1895 to broaden and strengthen "the moral, social, and intellectual life of its members and through them, to make itself a power for good in the community."

7,435. Salem Women's Indian Association
Records. 1885-1909. 10 vols.
Open. No guide.
Essex Institute.
Constitution, treasurer's reports, receipts, an expense book, a dues book, membership lists, an address book, and other records of the Association, founded in 1885 to abolish oppression of Indians within the US and to aid in educational and mission work among Indians.

7,436. Salem Young Women's Association
Records. 1898-1965. 31 vols.
Open. Unpublished guide.
Essex Institute.
Records of meetings, account books, scrapbooks, and other records of the Association, which was formerly known as the Salem Girls Club.

7,437. Sawyer, Alice
Papers. 1881-85. 1 vol.
Open. Card catalog.
Essex Institute.
Cashbook of accounts of Sawyer, who operated a small dry goods shop in her home in Melrose, MA.

7,438. Short, Moses: Short, Abigail
Papers. Nd. 2 vols. and 2 items.
Open. Card catalog.
Essex Institute.
Diaries and correspondence of Abigail Short are contained within the papers of her father Moses Short of Newbury, MA. Abigail Short's diary, 1854-55, concerns her experiences as a schoolteacher in a small southern Wisconsin village; the diary of Moses Short, 1835-41, was completed by his other daughter Ruth Isley Short.

7,439. Silver, William
Papers. 1867. 29 items.
Open. Card catalog.
Essex Institute.
Letters to Silver from his daughter Susan, who was writing from Europe.

7,440. Smith, Rhoda (Parker)
Papers. 1836-54. 1 envelope.
Open. Card catalog.
Essex Institute.
School composition of Smith, a student who lived in West Newbury, MA, and then became a wife and mother. Also includes correspondence about family activities.

7,441. Spinney, Anna G.
Papers. 1885-1912. 5 boxes.
Open. Card catalog.
Essex Institute.
Correspondence of Spinney, who was writing from Peking, Canton, and Shanghai, China, includes descriptions of places and her activities.

7,442. Spofford, Harriet Elizabeth Prescott
Papers. 1860-1916. Ca. 125 items.
Open. Unpublished guide.
Essex Institute.
[Mrs. Richard S.] Spofford (1835-1921) was a Newburyport, MA, author. Poems and letters written to family, friends, and publishers.

7,443. Stearns, Sarah W.
Papers. 1831-32. 1 vol.
Open. Card catalog.
Essex Institute.
Personal receipt and expense account book.

7,444. Stickney, Lucy Waters
Papers. 1899. 1 vol.
Open. Card catalog.
Essex Institute.
Diary in which Stickney (1843-?), a Salem native who went to work as a career woman in an office in Boston, wrote notes on dresses, purchases, visits, and the weather.

7,445. Stickney, Molly
Papers. 1805-63. 1 vol.
Open. Card catalog.
Essex Institute.
Transcriptions by Matthew Adams Stickney of Molly Stickney's letters to him contain genealogical information on the Stickney family.

7,446. Stone, Alice Homan Osborne
Papers. 1892-1947. 2 vols. and 1 envelope.
Open. Card catalog.
Essex Institute.
Family papers, birth and marriage certificates, a biography, bills, music and theater programs, and scrapbooks of clippings of Stone (1865-1952), a librarian, contain information about her life, marriage in 1896, and widowhood beginning at the age of 33.

7,447. Tarr, Susan
Papers. 1822-41. 1 vol.
Open. Card catalog.
Essex Institute.
Account book of Tarr, who worked as a tailor in Ipswich, MA, lists customers, work done, and charges made.

7,448. Thacher, George
Papers. 1787-90. 1 envelope.
Open. Card catalog.
Essex Institute.
Papers of Thacher, a judge who also spelled his name Thatcher, contain letters to his wife, living in Biddeford, ME, from her friends and son.

7,449. Thought and Work Club
Records. 1891-1964. 3 boxes, 24 vols., and 1 bundle.
Open. Unpublished guide.

Essex Institute.
Constitution, bylaws, correspondence, and other records of this Salem group.

7,450. Towne, Abigail W. (Peterson)
Papers. 1891-1908. 2 vols.
Open. Card catalog.
Essex Institute.
Diary and notebook of Towne (?-1945), a teacher, contain descriptions of her activities, organizations, spring flowers she saw, and lectures she attended. Also includes lists of books and articles she read and poems she copied.

7,451. Trask Family
Papers. 1847-79. Ca. 100 items.
Open. Card catalog.
Essex Institute.
Includes correspondence of Abigail Hooper [Mrs. Richard] Trask of Manchester, MA, with her foster child Louisa Lord about daily activities and family news.

7,452. Trefry, Sarah
Papers. 1839-60. 5 vols.
Open. Card catalog.
Essex Institute.
Household accounts of Trefry with merchants in her hometown of Marblehead, MA.

7,453. Tucker, Mary Orne
Papers. 1802. 1 vol.
Open. Card catalog.
Essex Institute.
Diary of [Mrs.] Tucker (1775-1806) contains observations regarding family, friends, and neighbors; notes about discussions with friends; and comments on the role of women, marriage, family relationships, and religious topics.

7,454. Upton Family
Papers. 1873-1906. 1 envelope.
Open. Card catalog.
Essex Institute.
Includes correspondence, 1870-1906, and diaries, 1873-76, of Kate J. Upton, which contain information about her activities and family life.

7,455. Waite, Eliza
Papers. 1786-91. Ca. 100 items.
Open. Card catalog.
Essex Institute.
Letters from Waite, a housewife who lived in Salem and Andover, MA, to Susan Kittredge and others about her social life and family.

7,456. Waldo, Phoebe M.
Papers. 1910-11. 11 items.
Open. Card catalog.
Essex Institute.
Letters to Waldo, a Salem resident, from Louise Nothurst describing her activities and travels in Japan, China, Singapore, and Ceylon.

7,457. Ward, Elizabeth C.
Papers. Ca. 1900. 133-page vol.
Open. Card catalog.
Essex Institute.
Journal of Ward (1839-?), a native of Salem, provides an account of her life in Mexico.

7,458. Ward, Elizabeth Stuart Phelps
Papers. 1867-1900. 1 envelope.
Open. Card catalog.
Essex Institute.
Letters to a Dr. Ward and others and manuscript poems of Elizabeth Ward (1844-1911), a poet and author.

7,459. Ward, Sophia Langdon
Papers. 1869. 13 items.
Open. Card catalog.
Essex Institute.
Letters to Charlotte Nichols from Ward (1855-?), a Salem native.

7,460. Ward, Susannah (Holyoke)
Papers. 1831-56. 26 vols.
Open. Card catalog.
Essex Institute.
Diaries of [Mrs. Joshua] Ward (1779-1860), interleaved in almanacs, contain brief entries noting visits and visitors, meetings, and clothing expenses. Susannah Ward was also known as Susan Ward.

7,461. Waters Family
Papers. Nd. No size given.
Open. No guide.
Essex Institute.
Includes correspondence of Sarah W. Knight, 1792-1864; Esther Waters, 1847-64; Marietta Waters, 1881-89; and Eliza Greenleaf Waters, 1865-83. Also includes miscellaneous papers of Abigail Devereux, 1817-29, and correspondence of Abigail Devereux Waters and William D. Waters, 1827-73.

7,462. Waters, Lucy
Papers. 1865-1919. 2 vols.
Open. Card catalog.
Essex Institute.
Diaries of Waters contain descriptions of travels throughout New England; New York; Washington, DC; North Carolina; Florida; California; and Canada.

7,463. Waters, Susan Louise (Whittredge)
Papers. 1849-52. 7 vols.
Open. Card catalog.
Essex Institute.
Diaries of Waters (1833-?) concern her daily activities at school, visits, social events, and trips to Boston she made as a schoolgirl.

7,464. White, Elizabeth Orne
Papers. 1802-71. 1 envelope.
Open. Card catalog.
Essex Institute.
Correspondence of [Mrs. Daniel A.] White (1784-?), a Salem native, to and about family members. Also includes correspondence of her son William O. White. Elizabeth White was first married to William Wetmore.

7,465. Williams, Frances Ropes
Papers. 1935-59. 1 box.
Open. Card catalog.
Essex Institute.
Correspondence of Williams concerning the Herb Society of America and correspondence with Adeline P. (Dodge) Cole of Wenham, MA.

7,466. Williams, Mary Elizabeth "Lizzie"
Papers. Nd. 1 box.
Open. Card catalog.
Essex Institute.
Correspondence, sketches, clippings, and other papers of Williams (1825-1902), a Salem artist.

7,467. Brooks, Margarette W.
Papers. 1877- . 2 boxes and 1 vol.
Open. No guide.
Peabody Museum of Salem, Phillips Library.
Correspondence, books of notes on natural history, pamphlets, scrapbooks, and clippings of Brooks, a Salem entomologist. Included is a copy of her pamphlet *An Experiment in Silk-Culture,* other material concerning silk culture and The Women's Silk Culture Association, and notes on lectures by Edward S. Morse.

7,468. Crowninshield, Benjamin Williams
Papers. 1700s-1800s. 1 folder.
Open. No guide.
Peabody Museum of Salem, Phillips Library.
Correspondence of Crowninshield (1773-1851), who served as secretary of the navy, includes letters his wife Mary Boardman Crowninshield wrote him describing family activities and events in Salem.

7,469. Crowninshield, Clarissa
Papers. 1818-1908. 5 ms. boxes.
Open. No guide.
Peabody Museum of Salem, Phillips Library.
Papers of Crowninshield (1810-1907), who married Louis Thies, consist of personal correspondence between her when she was a girl and her guardian Benjamin Nichols, a Boston and Salem banker, and his wife; letters Crowninshield wrote from Cambridge, MA, and Europe to her family after she was married; letters she wrote from Dresden, Germany, where she spent most of her adult life; personal correspondence with her banker; and clothes lists, an inventory of the Thies house, papers relating to the German inheritance laws, and other documents pertaining to her estate and to that of her husband.

7,470. Crowninshield, Francis Boardman
Papers. 1816-32. 15 items.
Open. No guide.
Peabody Museum of Salem, Phillips Library.
Correspondence to Crowninshield (1809-77) from his mother Mary Boardman [Mrs. Benjamin Williams] Crowninshield contains family news; some letters were written from Salem, some from Washington, DC. Also included is a letter his wife Sarah Putnam Crowninshield wrote to her parents.

7,471. Crowninshield, Hannah B. Armstrong
Papers. 1809-29. 3 boxes and 1 vol.
Open. No guide.
Peabody Museum of Salem, Phillips Library.
An arithmetic book of Crowninshield, a Salem resident, and sketchbooks of subjects in nature are included with her diary entitled "Private Journal and Poetical or Triffling Effusions, Nonsense, etc., etc."

7,472. Crowninshield, Jacob
Papers. 1770-1808. 5 ms. boxes.
Open. No guide.
Peabody Museum of Salem, Phillips Library.
Correspondence, legal documents, and clippings of Crowninshield (1770-1808), who served as secretary of the navy, including letters from his wife Sally Gardner Crowninshield (?-1807) about his nomination as navy secretary, local news, and personal matters. Also included is material on the deaths of Jacob and Sally Crowninshield, with a funeral oration by William Bentley, a Salem minister.

7,473. Crowninshield, Maria Louise
Papers. 1803-33. 3 items.
Open. No guide.
Peabody Museum of Salem, Phillips Library.
Correspondence of Crowninshield, a Salem resident, is included with her diary of a six-week vacation in Danvers, MA.

7,474. Eckstorm, Fannie Pearson (Hardy)
Papers. 1930s-40s. 1 box.
Open. No guide.
Peabody Museum of Salem, Phillips Library.
Papers of Eckstorm (1865-1946), a writer, ornithologist, and authority on the Indians of Maine, consist of her annotated copy of her book *The Handicrafts of the Modern Indians of Maine* (Abbe Museum Bulletin III, 1932); correspondence concerning the book; correspondence, notes, and photos which pertain to Indian handicrafts; and correspondence concerning her book on Indian place names.

7,475. Endicott, Elizabeth
Papers. 1832-44. 1 box.
Open. No guide.

Peabody Museum of Salem, Phillips Library.
Papers of Endicott (1797-1866), a Salem resident who married Augustus Perry, consist of correspondence with her sister Clarissa (Endicott) [Mrs. George] Peabody (1807-91). In addition to containing family and city news, the letters Elizabeth wrote her sister include comments about her sister's two children, for whom she cared while Clarissa was traveling in Europe. Also included are letters Elizabeth Perry wrote describing her own travels in Europe to her sister, who was then residing in Salem.

7,476. Grew Family
Papers. 1800s-1900s. 4 boxes.
Open. No guide.
Peabody Museum of Salem, Phillips Library.
Includes letters from M. Grew to her children; letters she wrote to her granddaughter Anna Greene Grew [Mrs. James Church] Alvord (1812-92); letters to Alvord from her aunt E. Coltman in England; one box of letters to Alvord from Ann Greene Phillips and Wendell Phillips; Civil War clippings, which probably were compiled by Anne Wigglesworth or Thomas Wigglesworth; and letters to her aunts by a young woman named Jennifer, who was writing from the Far East during the 1860s.

7,477. Hemenway Family
Papers. 1793-1922. 25 boxes, 32 vols., and 1 trunk.
Open. Brief inventory.
Peabody Museum of Salem, Phillips Library.
Correspondence, notebooks, ledgers, checkbooks, business papers, legal documents, photos, and other material of the family. Includes correspondence between Mary Porter (Tileston) Hemenway (1820-94) and her husband Augustus Hemenway (?-1876), Mary Hemenway's biography of her father Thomas Tileston; correspondence between her and Sophia Amelia Peabody Hawthorne and Hawthorne's copy of "Twenty Days with Julian at Lenox" written by her husband Nathaniel Hawthorne in 1851; material pertaining to Mary Hemenway's estate; and letters to her from such prominent women as Julia Ward Howe, Dorothea Dix, Lucy Stone, and Frances Elizabeth Willard. Also included are papers pertaining to the Hillside Home for Boys in Milton, MA.

7,478. Houdlette, Harriet (Lilly)
Papers. 1839-44. 1 ms. box.
Open. No guide.
Peabody Museum of Salem, Phillips Library.
Diary which Houdlette (1816-1911), wife of Captain Franklin Houdlette (1815-87) of Maine, kept while she was visiting in Philadelphia, traveling with her husband on a voyage from New Orleans to Genoa and Madeira and then back to Boston, living in Hallowell, ME, while she awaited her husband's return from sea, and living in Richmond, VA. Also included is an 1844 obituary of her sister Lydia Lilly.

7,479. King, Anna T. Stott
Papers. Ca. 1910. 273-page vol.
Open. No guide.
Peabody Museum of Salem, Phillips Library.
Notebook by King (1843-1931), the daughter of a sea captain, is entitled "The Infant Mariner; Reminiscences of Voyages in the Pacific"; it concerns whaling voyages and life in Honolulu between 1845 and 1862.

7,480. Logbook Collection: Clement (Bark)
Records. 1838. 29-page vol.
Open. Brief description.
Peabody Museum of Salem, Phillips Library.
Journal of a voyage aboard the *Clement* from New Orleans to St. Petersburg, FL, was written by the wife of the ship's master, whose first name was George. Journal also contains a poem, a draft of a letter, and recipes.

7,481. Logbook Collection: Vigilant (Whaling Bark)
Records. 1860-62. 101-page vol.
Open. Brief description.
Peabody Museum of Salem, Phillips Library.
Journal of a voyage aboard the *Vigilant* from New Bedford, MA, to the Pacific coast of South America, was written by Susan A. Cole, wife of the ship's master Fred P. Cole. Journal also contains memoranda and poems.

7,482. McKee, Linda Mitchell
Papers. Nd. 26-page item.
Open. No guide.
Peabody Museum of Salem, Phillips Library.
Account by McKee (1939-) concerns a mutiny on the whaling ship *Globe* while it was en route from Nantucket Island, MA, in 1824.

7,483. Moseley, Elizabeth
Papers. 1780s-1808. 2 boxes.
Open. No guide.
Peabody Museum of Salem, Phillips Library.
Bills and receipts of Moseley, who was the wife of Captain Joseph Moseley of Salem, are from Salem and Boston merchants.

7,484. Nichols Family
Papers. 1770s-1800s. 15 boxes.
Open. No guide.
Peabody Museum of Salem, Phillips Library.
Correspondence, diaries, travel journals, account books, business papers, inventories of house furnishings, school essays, silhouettes, photos, stamps, and a book of this Salem family. Includes a letter in which Amelia Ann (Ainsworth) [Mrs. Charles Sanders] Nichols describes to her son Harry Pierce Nichols a sermon by Henry Ward Beecher as well as other material generated by female members of the family.

7,485. Omori, Annie
Papers. 1900s. 2 boxes.
Open. No guide.
Peabody Museum of Salem, Phillips Library.
Correspondence, postcards, photos, and clippings of Anna B. Shepley Omori, an American artist. Includes letters she wrote from Japan and letters Charles A. Baldwin wrote while traveling to Japan. Omori was married to Hyozo Omori (?-1913), a proponent of physical education in Japan.

7,486. Protheroe, Lorena Reed
Papers. Ca. 1934-39. 1 box.
Access restricted. No guide.
Peabody Museum of Salem, Phillips Library.
Literary manuscript of a story in which Protheroe portrays the life of a young girl in a Maine shipbuilding town during the 1890s and on a ship to Cape Horn and China. Also included is correspondence pertaining to Protheroe's efforts to secure a publisher for the story.

7,487. Snyder, Dorothy Eastman
Papers. Nd. 11 boxes, 2 card files, and 1 item.
Open. Brief inventory.
Peabody Museum of Salem, Phillips Library.
Correspondence, literary manuscripts, notes, a catalog, and other papers of Snyder, who was curator of natural history at the Museum, pertain to her books *Birds of Guyana, The Birds of Massachusetts,* and *The Passenger Pigeon in New England.* Also included is a booklet pertaining to bird and reptile egg collections at the Museum.

7,488. Wallis, Mary Davis Cook
Papers. 1851-53. 1 vol.
Access restricted. No guide.
Peabody Museum of Salem, Phillips Library.
Journal of Wallis, who was wife of Captain Benjamin Wallis, consists of travel descriptions of her voyage aboard the *Maid of Orleans* from Salem to New Zealand, the Fiji Islands, and Manila.

SANDWICH

7,489. Cooke, Alice Rebecca
Papers. 1884-1956. Ca. 50 items.
Open. No guide.
Sandwich Historical Commission.
[Miss] Cooke (1861-1956) was the owner and matron of the Locust Grove Asylum, a mental health facility in East Sandwich, from 1907 to 1938. She had a lifelong interest in wildlife. Includes correspondence from naturalist Thornton W. Burgess, author of *Aunt Sally's Friends in Fur* (Boston: Little Brown, 1954), in which Cooke's observation and feeding of animals are described. A cousin of James Bryant Conant, Cooke was one of the first women licensed to operate an asylum.

7,490. Rose, Annie (Ewer)
Papers. 1890-1972. Folders and other items.
Open. No guide.
Sandwich Historical Commission.
Correspondence, wedding certificates, genealogical records of Quaker families of Sandwich, and photos of [Mrs. William J.] Rose (1867-1972), a Sandwich resident, a Quaker, secretary of the Sandwich Monthly Meeting, and a teacher at the Moses Brown school in Providence, RI. Eighteen local families converted to the Quaker faith of Christopher Holder and John Copeland, two English preachers who arrived in Sandwich in 1657; Rose was a descendant of those families. She copied genealogical material from the Friends' records at Rhode Island.

7,491. Tangney, Lillian (Haynes)
Papers. 1880-1970. 1 carton.
Open. No guide.
Sandwich Historical Commission.
Correspondence, post cards, family papers, photos, and clippings of [Mrs. James H.] Tangney (1873-1971), a Sandwich resident, grade school teacher from 1891 until the 1950s, and a lifelong friend of naturalist Thornton W. Burgess. Tangney was the daughter of Edward Haynes, an English glassmaker who immigrated to Sandwich in 1825 when the Boston & Sandwich Glass Co. was founded. Her papers contain information on glassmaking and local history.

SHARON

7,492. Manuscripts
Collection. 1780-1977. Ca. 2000 vols.
Open. Unpublished guide.
Kendall Whaling Museum.
Includes one foot of diaries and journals of wives of whaling captains, 1800s, and of whale watchers, persons who observe whales in the wild, 1970s. Collection is also available on microfilm.

SOUTH HADLEY

7,493. College History Collection
Records. Ca. 1820- . Ca. 2000 ft.
Open. Card catalog, lists, and two registers.
Mount Holyoke College Library.
The Collection includes the archives of Mount Holyoke College, which was chartered in 1836 and opened in 1837. It contains extensive information about the College's staff and students and about alumnae, many of whom were missionaries or founders or staff members of educational institutions. It also includes a photographic collection dating from the 1850s that documents the architectural development of the campus, student activities, and changes in clothing and decorative styles.

The Collection also contains papers of Mount Holyoke's founder Mary Lyon. During the 1820s she taught with Zilpah Grant Banister in Derry, NH, and Ipswich, MA; in addition, Lyon conducted her own schools in Ashfield and Buckland, MA. Catharine Beecher was one of her correspondents.

7,494. Grant, Zilpah Polly
Papers. 1823-74. Ca. 87 items.
Open. Card catalog.
Mount Holyoke College Library, College History Collection.
Correspondence with former Ipswich pupils of Grant (1794-1874), headmistress of the Ipswich Female Seminary from 1828 to 1839, includes a few letters from Catharine Beecher. Grant married William Banister.

7,495. Memory Books
Records. Ca. 1881-1966. 45 vols.
Open. No guide.
Mount Holyoke College Library, College History Collection.
Scrapbooks of student memorabilia, arranged chronologically by class of the compilers, contain correspondence, greetings exchanged on a variety of occasions, records of extracurricular (including political) activities, and photos of students, their rooms, and recreation.

7,496. Miscellaneous Diaries, Journals, and Account Books
Records. Ca. 1820-1920. Ca. 60 items.
Open. Card catalog.
Mount Holyoke College Library, College History Collection.
Diaries and journals, class notes, autograph albums, and account books, particularly for the early years of Mount Holyoke Seminary. Includes a journal of Zilpah Grant and a journal of a trip an alumna of the 1920s took in 1955.

7,497. Missionaries
Collection. Ca. 1840-1925. 7 ms. boxes.
Open. Card catalog.
Mount Holyoke College Library, College History Collection.
Collected by Anna C. Edwards, an 1859 Mount Holyoke graduate, this material consists of correspondence, lists, notebooks of statistics, photos, and other items. The collection is organized both by country to which Mount Holyoke alumnae traveled as missionaries and chronologically by the classes in which they graduated.

7,498. Mount Holyoke Alumnae
Records. Ca. 1836- . 261 Hollinger boxes.
Open. Card catalog.
Mount Holyoke College Library, College History Collection.
Individual folders for every alumna of the College are arranged chronologically by class and in many cases contain correspondence, diaries, genealogical and biographical information, student papers, questionnaires completed for the College, photos, and clippings. For example, the folder of Cynthia Abram, a nongraduating member of the class of 1862, contains five letters she wrote to her family between 1859 and 1862 with vivid descriptions of the hardships she endured traveling in a wagon train to the Oregon gold rush; the files on Charlotte and Mary Ely, sisters who graduated in the class of 1861, contain correspondence and other material from their years as missionaries in Turkish Armenia until their deaths in 1913 and 1915 and accounts of the Turkish massacres, during which they remained with their missions.

7,499. Mount Holyoke Faculty and Staff
Papers. Ca. 1838- . 105 Hollinger boxes.
Open. No guide.
Mount Holyoke College Library, College History Collection.
Correspondence, biographical material, photos, reprints of articles, and publications of College faculty and staff members. Includes 30 Hollinger boxes of correspondence and other papers of Jeannette Marks, a member of the English Department faculty from 1901 to 1941 and founder of the College's laboratory theater. The collection also includes extensive material (one or more Hollinger boxes) of papers of Margaret Ball, a member of the English department, 1901-39; Cornelia Clapp, a member of the zoology department, 1872-1916; Florabelle Ludington, librarian of Mount Holyoke, 1936-64; and Mary Nutting, who was Mount Holyoke's first librarian, 1870-1901.

7,500. Mount Holyoke Journal Notebooks
Records. 1843-89. 4 ms. boxes and 21 vols.
Open. No guide.
Mount Holyoke College Library, College History Collection.
Journal notebooks about events at Mount Holyoke Seminary, teachers, students, visitors, gifts, and other items of interest to distant alumnae and former teachers were begun by Lucy Lyon, a Seminary teacher, for Fidelia Fiske, who had left her post as a teacher at Mount Holyoke to teach in Persia under the auspices of a mission board. A number of teacher "scribes" followed Lyon, and the mailing list was gradually extended to include all alumnae in mission service in this country and abroad.

7,501. Usher, Melissa, and Usher, Jerusha
Papers. 1852-63. Ca. 60 items.
Open. Card catalog.
Mount Holyoke College Library, College History Collection.
Correspondence and notebooks of Melissa Usher, an 1856 Mount Holyoke graduate, and of her sister Jerusha Usher, an 1857 Mount Holyoke graduate who became a teacher and, later, registrar of Wellesley College. Contains correspondence with each other and with family members.

SOUTHBRIDGE

7,502. Southbridge Newspapers
Collection. 1876-87. 300-page vol.
Open. Index.
Jacob Edwards Memorial Library.
Scrapbook of clippings from local newspapers contains information on social, organizational, political, church, and other events related to women. The volume was presented to the Library by Mrs. C. B. Litchfield.

STOCKBRIDGE

7,503. Cresson, Margaret (French)
Papers. 1900-73. 30 ft. and ca. 75 vols.
Access restricted. No guide.
Chesterwood, Archives.
Correspondence, diaries, drafts of writings, research files, engagement books, blueprints, drawings, and scrapbooks of clippings and other material of Cresson (1889-1973), a sculptor, relate to her sculptures, writings, travels, social life, family, and finances, as well as to her preservation of the studio and home of her father Daniel Chester French.

7,504. French, Mary Adams (French)
Papers. 1925-39. 5 ft.
Access restricted. No guide.
Chesterwood, Archives.
Best known for her *Memoirs of a Sculptor's Wife* (1928), French (1859-1939) was an author, wife of Daniel Chester French, and mother of Margaret (French) Cresson. Drafts of her work and correspondence concerning the estates of her husband and of her son-in-law.

7,505. Ashburner and Sedgwick
Papers. 1780- . Ca. 300 items.
Open. Card catalog of items.
Stockbridge Library Association.
Correspondence, drafts of literary works, legal documents, illustrations, scrapbooks, clippings, and other papers of two Stockbridge families, much of which pertains to women. Correspondence, drafts of writings, clippings about, and photos and an engraving of Catherine Maria Sedgwick (1789-1867), a novelist; correspondence, recollections of Stockbridge life, a diary for 1838 to 1846, a memorandum book, genealogical notes, and photos of Anne Ashburner (1807-94); poems by Grace Ashburner (1813-93) and correspondence, including 26 letters with A. Remenyi, a male acquaintance; and extracts from the journal of and a portfolio of sketches of spring flowers by Sarah Ashburner.

7,506. Field Family
Papers. 1825-1941. 1 carton and ca. 2000 items.
Open. Card index of items.
Stockbridge Library Association.
Correspondence, reminiscences, financial papers, deeds, patent material, transcripts of court hearings, photos, drawings, and clippings of the Stockbridge family. Includes correspondence of and other items pertaining to Henriette Desportes Field (1813-75), author Rachel Lyman Field (1894-1942), and poet Elizabeth Field (1891-).

7,507. Interlaken Thimble Club
Records. 1914-27. 1 vol.
Open. No guide.
Stockbridge Library Association.
Minutes of meetings and memoranda of the Club, also known as the Ladies Aid Society, which was founded in 1914 to sew aprons and other items for sale to raise funds for a church in Interlaken, MA. Alice [Mrs. William J.] Davis was a particularly active member of the Club.

7,508. Laurel Hill Association
Records. 1853- . 4 drawers.
Open. No guide.
Stockbridge Library Association.
Constitution, bylaws, minutes, correspondence, lists of members and officers, programs, photos, clippings, and printed material of the Laurel Hill Association, which was founded in 1853 for the civic improvement of Stockbridge. The Association, many of whose members were women, beautified the town by planting trees, shrubs, and flowers and by maintaining sites such as local cemeteries; erected historical monuments; and was involved in establishing zoning ordinances. Mary Hopkins Goodrich was instrumental in the work of the Association from its founding until her death.

7,509. Literary Manuscripts
Collection. 1921-72. Ca. 200 items.
Open. Card catalog of items.
Stockbridge Library Association.
Memoirs; drafts and proofs of plays, poems, short stories, novels, and books; notes; and clippings. Includes versions of books by Eleanor Hoffman, Irene Hoffman, and Margaret (French) Cresson, with chapters of her *Berkshire Hills, Journey into Fame,* and *Laurel Hill Association.* Also contains drafts of plays and short stories by Rachel Lyman Field, of a book of poetry by Elizabeth Field, and of a book and memoirs of Nina Larrey Duryea.

7,510. Oral History Project
Oral history. 1961- . Ca. 20 items and 58 tapes.
Open. No guide.
Stockbridge Library Association.
Tapes and indexes of the contents of interviews of older Stockbridge residents, including Laura Seelye, Marjorie [Mrs. William] Barrett, Barbara Smith

[Mrs. Robert] Bracknell, Margaret (French) Cresson, Amelia Radell [Mrs. Joseph] Franz, Rosamond Sherwood, Emily Smith, Sarah Cabot [Mrs. William Ellery] Sedgwick, Molly Punderson [Mrs. Norman] Rockwell, Esther Van Deusen [Mrs. Cecil] Babcock, Olivia Stokes [Mrs. J. D.] Hatch, and Alice Schilling. Also included are recollections of many women about the Rising Paper Company of Housatonic, MA, which provide information on women's roles in factories.

7,511. Sergeant, John
Papers. 1742-1885. 1 Hollinger box.
Open. Card catalog of items.
Stockbridge Library Association.
Correspondence, account book, genealogical material, photos, clippings, and printed items of Sergeant (1710-49), a missionary to the Stockbridge Indians. Includes family letters of Abigail Sergeant (1721-91); of Caroline Sergeant, dating from 1843; and of Eunice Sergeant, dating from 1798 and 1800.

7,512. Tuesday Club
Records. 1906- . 1 box and 7 vols.
Open. Card index of items.
Stockbridge Library Association.
Constitution, minutes, histories, lists of members, drafts of plays, programs, and clippings of this Stockbridge women's club, established in 1892 as a literary, dramatic, and historical group for intellectual improvement, education, and entertainment. In addition to studying topics together, Club members sponsored plays, lectures, and tours of historic town sites.

STURBRIDGE

7,513. Bond, Alvan
Papers. 1815-76. 1 box.
Open. Unpublished guide.
Old Sturbridge Village Research Library.
Papers of Bond, a minister who lived in Sturbridge and Sutton, MA, and Norwich, CT, include a diary of his third wife Sibby Ann (Waters) Davis, whom he married in 1849. Kept from 1830 to 1859 while she was living in Concord, MA, and Norwich, the diary is introspective and religious.

7,514. Diaries and Biographies
Collection. 1816-60. 7 vols.
Open. Unpublished guide.
Old Sturbridge Village Research Library.
Collection of New England diaries and biographies includes those of Caroline M. Fitch, a resident of Boston, who describes a trip from Boston to Lyme, NH, 1836; of Warren and Olive Gay, residents of Hampton Falls and Sharon, NH, who comment on social and political matters, 1840-50; of Mary R. (Fitch) [Mrs. I. Henry] Jenks, a resident of Boston, who discusses her social life during the year following her marriage, 1841-42; of Harriet N. Rand, a resident of New Haven, CT, and New York City, who describes boarding school, church services, service as a Sunday school teacher, work in a black Sunday school, and a visit to New York, 1835; of Mary A. [Mrs. Aaron] White, a resident of Boylston, MA, who comments on her family, church, community matters, and the weather, 1836-39, and lists deaths, 1839-60; of Minerva Mayo, a resident of Orange, MA, which she wrote in 1820 when she was 16 years old; and of a resident of Amherst, MA, and western Massachusetts, which is religious in tone, 1816-41.

7,515. Goodale Family
Papers. 1807-82. 3 Hollinger boxes.
Open. Unpublished guide.
Old Sturbridge Village Research Library.
Papers of this Marlborough, MA, family contain items of Meliscent (Warren) [Mrs. David] Goodale (1797-1861), including correspondence with her son Charles while he was at boarding schools. The letters provide details of her domestic life, management of an orchard and dairy farm, and political activity. Also includes her diary for 1848, a draft of a will, and her school exercise books. Other papers include family correspondence, a botany notebook, and school compositions of her daughter Lucy T. Goodale (1820-40).

7,516. Lewis, Hannah
Papers. 1807-16. 1 vol.
Open. Unpublished guide.
Old Sturbridge Village Research Library.
Letter book of Lewis, a resident of Boston and Dorchester, MA, and Augusta, ME. In her letters she comments on religion, Sabbath school work, conducting a school, working as a seamstress, caring for the aged, musical activities, and social and community life.

7,517. New England Women's Organizations
Collection. 1812-1902. 5 vols.
Open. Unpublished guide.
Old Sturbridge Village Research Library.
Constitutions, bylaws, and minutes of the Female Benevolent Society of Brimfield, MA, which made contributions to the American Board of Commissioners for Foreign Missions; of the Female Friendly Society of Coventry, CT, which was a charitable and religious group; of the Female Fragment Society, a charitable organization in Coventry that invited men into the membership in 1837; of the Maternal Association of Marlborough, NH, which was involved in the moral and religious training of children; and of the Maternal Association of Sherburn, which was formed by members of the Evangelical church and was devoted to the rearing of children.

7,518. Saunders, Catharine E. G.
Papers. 1798-1804. 64 items.
Open. Unpublished guide.
Old Sturbridge Village Research Library.
Letters from Saunders, a resident of Salem and Wenham, MA, who was the daughter of a Salem shipowner, to her brother Charles Saunders at Harvard College. Written during the period when she was 16 to 20 years of age, the letters contain descriptions of household matters, her social life, and her family.

7,519. Shrewsbury, MA, Organizations
Records. 1814-98. 13 vols.
Open. Unpublished guide.
Old Sturbridge Village Research Library.
Includes minutes, treasurer's records, a history, and flower show premiums of the Shrewsbury Floral Society, a women's organization; minutes of the Shrewsbury Musical Association; and minutes and other records of the Shrewsbury Social Club.

7,520. Sumner Family
Papers. 1834-45. 15 items.
Open. Unpublished guide.
Old Sturbridge Village Research Library.
Correspondence between the Sumner family and the related Brown, Hartwell, and Usher families, which resided in Brimfield, Spencer, and Waltham, MA; North Coventry, CT; and Providence, RI. The letters relate to family matters, school, teaching experiences, and work at the mill.

7,521. Towne, Salem
Papers. 1772-1841. 2 Hollinger boxes.
Open. Unpublished guide.
Old Sturbridge Village Research Library.
Papers of the Towne family, which lived in Charlton, MA, contain family letters to female family members, including letters to Sally Towne from her husband Salem Towne, Jr., 1820-34.

7,522. Tufts and Appleton Families
Papers. 1815-49. 12 items.
Open. Unpublished guide.
Old Sturbridge Village Research Library.
Correspondence of these families who lived in Boston, Charlestown, Dorchester, and Medford, MA; Dover, NH; and Waterville, ME. Includes letters from Martha (Adams) Tufts (1751-1832) to her daughter Anna Louisa Tufts, a teacher in Dover. In her letters Martha Tufts comments on her sons, clothing costs and fashions, relatives, and family matters. Also includes letters from female relatives, who comment on their children's interests and activities.

7,523. Walker Family
Papers. 1783-1884. 1 small Hollinger box.
Open. Unpublished guide.
Old Sturbridge Village Research Library.
Papers of this Sturbridge family include family correspondence and papers pertaining to the settlements of three estates and household goods for three brides.

WALTHAM

7,524. Abendanone Family
Papers. 1829. 3 items.
Open. Catalog card.
American Jewish Historical Society.
A document in which Grace Abendanone describes family relationships is included with her bequest of a slave to Jacob De La Motta and the oath of American citizenship which was administered to David Abendanone.

7,525. Baron de Hirsch Fund
Records. 1870-1935. 61 boxes.
Open. Catalog card.
American Jewish Historical Society.
Minutes; financial records; mortgages, wills, deeds, and other legal documents; reports; correspondence; and published items of the Fund, founded in 1890 to support charitable, educational, and other organizations. Includes material on such groups as the National Council of Jewish Women, which collaborated with the Fund; such individuals as the Baroness de Hirsch, Henrietta Szold, and Lina Frank Hecht; and such organizations for the improvement of the lives of women as the Clara de Hirsch Home for Working and Immigrant Girls in New York City.

7,526. Cambridge Hebrew Women's Aid Society
Records. 1914-69. 5 vols.
Open. Catalog card.
American Jewish Historical Society.
Minute books of this charitable organization, founded in 1897 in Cambridge, MA, contain discussion of individual needy cases; records of disbursements of funds to persons and organizations, including payments to tuberculosis sanitaria in Colorado and Los Angeles; and accounts of social activities of the Society.

7,527. Columbia Religious and Industrial School for Jewish Girls
Records. 1905-44. 91 items.
Open. Card catalog.
American Jewish Historical Society.
Financial data, correspondence, and reports of this New York City school, founded in 1888, which trained girls for a useful and pious life. Rosalie (Solomons) [Mrs. Naphtali] Phillips served as the School's first vice-president and then as president.

7,528. Ehrenreich Family
Papers. 1841-1971. 1 ft.
Open. Catalog card.
American Jewish Historical Society.
Correspondence, genealogical charts, photos, clippings, artifacts, and published material of the Waterman, Kernsky, and Ehrenreich family. Among these are items relating to Louise

(Waterman) Wise (1874-1947), who was a charity worker, Zionist, and wife of rabbi Stephen S. Wise.

7,529. Franks, Bilhah Abigail (Levy)
Papers. 1733-1968. 2 cartons.
Open. Published guide.
American Jewish Historical Society.
Correspondence of [Mrs. Jacob] Franks (1696-1756), a New York City resident, to her son in England, 1733-48, is included with research notes generated when these letters were edited for publication. See *Lee Max Friedman Collection of American Jewish Colonial Correspondence: Letters of the Franks Family* (New York: American Jewish Historical Society, 1968).

7,530. Friends of Ida Kaminska Theatre Foundation Inc.
Records. 1968-75. Ca. 2500 items.
Open. Catalog card.
American Jewish Historical Society.
Minutes, financial records, correspondence, mailing lists, advertising brochures, and clippings of the Foundation, incorporated in 1970 to assist the New York City Theatre which held plays performed in Yiddish. Includes information on [Mme.] Ida Kaminska, in whose honor the Theatre was established upon her emigration from Poland in 1968. The Foundation was dissolved in 1975.

7,531. Goldstein, Harriet B. L.
Papers. 1918-19. 4 vols.
Open. Catalog card.
American Jewish Historical Society.
Goldstein (1886-1961) was comptroller of the Federation of Jewish Philanthropies of New York and of the American Jewish Joint Distribution Committee; she was also a representative for the American Fund for Jewish War Sufferers. Minutes, financial documents, correspondence, and reports concern her relief activities with the Committee.

7,532. Gomez Family
Papers. 1716-1882. 2 boxes.
Open. Catalog card.
American Jewish Historical Society.
Papers of this New York City family include ca. 1820-80 financial and legal documents of Hetty (Hendricks) Gomez, who married Aaron Lopez Gomez in 1821.

7,533. Gratz, Rebecca
Papers. 1794-1869. 635 items.
Open. Catalog card.
American Jewish Historical Society.
Family and business correspondence and inventory of the estate of Gratz (1781-1869), a Philadelphia philanthropist, including letters from her and her relatives to her brother Benjamin Gratz and his family and letters from her to Maria Fenno Hoffman, wife of a judge who became New York state's attorney general.

7,534. Hays, Sarah Ann
Papers. 1823-33. 21 items.
Open. Catalog card.
American Jewish Historical Society.
Papers of Sarah Ann (Hays) Mordecai (1805-94) consist of manuscript poems, many of which were dedicated to Hays, and scenic illustrations and sketches, some of which were drawn by Charlotte Meade Graham.

7,535. Hebrew Female Orphans Dowry Society of the United States
Records. Nd. 1 vol.
Open. Catalog card.
American Jewish Historical Society.
A charitable organization incorporated in 1874 in New York City, the Society provided dowries for orphaned Jewish girls. A record book lists members and donations.

7,536. Hebrew Orphan Asylum
Records. 1855-1941. 30 ft.
Open. Catalog card.
American Jewish Historical Society.
This New York City organization was devoted to the welfare of Jewish children, particularly orphans and poor or immigrant children. Annual reports, minutes, financial reports, ledgers, registers, correspondence, building specifications, and statistical, medical, legal, and educational reports document the philanthropic and charitable work of Jewish women and the welfare of Jewish girls in the City. Included are minutes, membership lists, and other material of the Ladies Sewing Circle, which was affiliated with the Asylum. Founded in 1822 as the Hebrew Benevolent Society, in 1906 after various name changes the group became known as the Orphan Asylum; in 1940 it merged into the Jewish Child Care Association.

7,537. Jewish Immigration Committee
Records. 1908-17. Ca. 200 items.
Open. Catalog card.
American Jewish Historical Society.
Founded in 1908, the Committee provided relief to immigrants in New York City and its environs. Constitution, bylaws, minutes, and correspondence include information on the Committee's work with the National Council of Jewish Women, the Clara de Hirsch School for Immigrant Girls, and other organizations.

7,538. Jewish Sisters Mutual Aid Society
Records. 1920-58. 3 ft.
Open. Card catalog.
American Jewish Historical Society.
The Society was a social and charitable organization founded in 1920 in New York City. Minutes, membership and financial records, and correspondence document the activities of the group, including its program of providing interest-free loans.

7,539. Johnson, Augusta (Ellis)
Papers. 1869. 5 items.
Open. Catalog card.
American Jewish Historical Society.
Correspondence between Johnson, an American Jew living in Lima, Peru, and the US minister to Peru, General Alvin P. Horey, concerns her request for American intervention for the release of her 14-year-old son Joseph, who had been forcibly abducted and baptized by Spanish friars.

7,540. Kohler, Max James
Papers. 1888-1934. 11 ft.
Open. Catalog card.
American Jewish Historical Society.
Correspondence, biographical items, research notes, reports, scrapbooks, and published material of Kohler (1871-1934), an historian, lawyer, and leader of the Jewish community. Included are papers of his wife Winifred Kohler as well as correspondence, growing out of his reform activities, with the National Council of Jewish Women, the Baroness de Hirsch, and other women's groups and individuals.

7,541. Kohut, George Alexander
Papers. 1891-1933. Ca. 5 ft.
Open. Catalog card.
American Jewish Historical Society.
Correspondence, memoranda, research notes, financial accounts, poems, sermons, and clippings of Kohut (1874-1933), a scholar, educator, and writer. Included are letters of Rebekah Kohut and other family members and items pertaining to the Children's University School in New York City and the American Jewish Joint Distribution Committee.

7,542. Kussy, Sarah
Papers. 1898-1951. 6 items.
Open. Catalog card.
American Jewish Historical Society.
Diary of Kussy (1869-1956), a Jewish community leader of Newark, NJ, from the period of the Spanish American War is included with minutes and other material of the Ladies' Patriotic Relief Society, a Newark group which was organized to help needy families during the War; a history of the Miriam Auxiliary of the Oheb Shalom Congregation in Newark; and a genealogy of the Kussy family.

7,543. Lazarus, Emma
Papers. 1869-87. 165 items.
Open. Catalog card.
American Jewish Historical Society.
Papers of Lazarus (1849-87), a poet and essayist, consist of manuscript poetry and a scrapbook of clippings, most of which were memorial tributes.

7,544. Levy, Jefferson Monroe
Papers. 1901-39. 7 vols. and 16 items.
Open. Catalog card.
American Jewish Historical Society.
Papers of Levy (1852-1924), a lawyer and congressman from New York City, consist of correspondence, military records, photos, and clippings. Also included is correspondence of his sister Amelia (Levy) Mayhoff.

7,545. Litman, Ray (Frank)
Papers. 1878-1957. 150 items.
Open. Catalog card.
American Jewish Historical Society.
Litman (1864 or 1865-1948) was a lecturer, journalist, and adviser to Jewish students at the University of Illinois. Correspondence, including letters of poet Nina Davis Salaman; manuscript and printed poetry, essays, and sermons; a biography by Litman of Salaman; and a scrapbook of clippings, which reflects Litman's interest in women's suffrage and in Judaism.

7,546. Menken, Alice (Davis)
Papers. 1882-1935. Ca. 2200 items and 3 Hollinger cases.
Open. Catalog card.
American Jewish Historical Society.
Correspondence, diaries, biographical material, reports, scrapbooks, and manuscript and published articles of Menken (1870-1936), a social worker, document her involvement in the Society of New York State Women, the National Jewish Welfare Board (originally called the Jewish Welfare Board), the Jewish Board of Guardians, the New York City Woman's Night Court, the Hudson State Training School, the New York State Reformatory for Women, the DAR, the Mayor's Committee of Women on National Defense, the Florence Crittenton League, and the New York Training School for Community Center Workers.

7,547. Mordecai Family
Papers. 1771-1907. 37 items.
Open. Catalog card.
American Jewish Historical Society.
Papers of this family which lived in the eastern US consist of correspondence of Rosa Mordecai, Miriam Mordecai, Laura Mordecai Summerall, and other family members, 1898-1907; a bill of exchange; a military commission; and the draft of a speech.

7,548. National Association of Jewish Social Workers
Records. 1912-16. 1000 items.
Open. Catalog card.
American Jewish Historical Society.
Programs, papers read at meetings, resolutions, and pension plan proposals of the Association, founded in 1908 to improve the lives of immigrant and poor Americans. Included is correspondence of Minnie F. Low, Belle Moskowitz, and other social workers.

7,549. Phillips Family
Papers. 1773-1954. 4 ft.
Open. Catalog card.
American Jewish Historical Society.
Correspondence, research notes, memorabilia, clippings, and published material of this New York City and Philadelphia family, including papers of Rosalie (Solomons) Phillips (1872-1945), which reflect her political activities, work on behalf of various Jewish institutions, interest in the history of the Solomons family and of the Congregation Shearith Israel in NYC, and her acquaintance with Eleanor Roosevelt.

7,550. Picon, Molly
Papers. 1876-1967. 21 ft. (3036 items).
Open. Catalog card.
American Jewish Historical Society.
An actress, Picon (1898-) performed much of her work in collaboration with her husband Jacob Kalich, who was a playwright. Correspondence; manuscript Yiddish plays, musical scores, and television and radio scripts; theater programs and announcements; posters; photos; souvenirs; and clippings. Included are her fan mail and family correspondence of her husband, her mother Clara Picon, and her sister Mrs. William Silverblatt.

7,551. Purim Association
Records. 1865-1906. 3 vols.
Open. Card catalog.
American Jewish Historical Society.
Constitution, bylaws, minutes, correspondence, and list of members of this charitable organization which was founded in New York City in 1862. After raising funds by sponsoring public entertainment, the Association gave the proceeds to a variety of charitable and educational institutions.

7,552. Seixas, Gershom Mendes
Papers. 1783-1815. 26 items.
Open. Catalog card.
American Jewish Historical Society.
Correspondence of Seixas (1746-1816), a New York City rabbi, with his daughters Grace (Seixas) Judah and Sarah (Seixas) Kursheedt, both of Richmond, VA, refers to daily activities, the health and welfare of family and friends, and celebration of Jewish holidays. A sermon is also included.

7,553. Seligman, Henry
Papers. 1870. 1 item.
Open. Catalog card.
American Jewish Historical Society.
Letter in which Seligman writes from Frankfort, Germany, about the need to rescue Mrs. Abraham Lincoln from poverty after Congress rejected the pension bill for presidential widows.

7,554. Solis-Cohen, Emily
Papers. 1923-36. 528 items.
Open. Catalog card.
American Jewish Historical Society.
An author, Solis-Cohen (1886-) also was field secretary for the women's activities of the National Jewish Welfare Board. Minutes, financial records, correspondence, reports, and published material primarily concern the School of the Parents' Education Association in Jerusalem and the American committee working on behalf of the School. Included is correspondence with Deborah Kallen, founder and principal of the School; with Sophie Udin, about the Hebrew University Library; and with Henrietta Szold.

7,555. Solis, Elvira (Nathan)
Papers. 1902-03. 56 items.
Open. Catalog card.
American Jewish Historical Society.
Correspondence, research notes, and lists of Solis (186?-1953), a genealogist, contain material concerning her research on the Etting, Menken, Nathan, and Nones families and on her study of a Jewish soldier who served in the American Revolutionary War.

7,556. Solomons, Adolphus Simeon
Papers. 1882-1903. 104 items and 4 vols.
Open. Catalog card.
American Jewish Historical Society.
Correspondence, biographical material, and scrapbooks of Solomons (1826-1910), a philanthropist. Includes correspondence with Clara Barton and material on the organization and activities of the American National Red Cross.

7,557. University Settlement Society of New York
Records. 1899-1919. 130 items.
Open. Card catalog.
American Jewish Historical Society.
Incorporated in 1892, the Society was concerned with the social, economic, and intellectual improvement of immigrants in New York City. Among its minutes, yearbooks, and other administrative material are records of related organizations involving women, such as the Richman Literary Society, which was named after Julia Richman.

7,558. Waksman, Selman Abraham
Papers. 1886-1975. 4 cartons.
Open. Catalog card.
American Jewish Historical Society.
A Nobel Prize winner, Waksman (1888-1973) was a marine bacteriologist. His papers include correspondence, biographical data, travel notes, photos, and sketches by his wife Deborah Bertha (Mitnik) Waksman.

7,559. Wolf, Gertrude
Papers. 1910-42. 470 items.
Open. Catalog card.
American Jewish Historical Society.
Correspondence, autobiography, sermons, and photos of Wolf (?-1966), who was secretary both to Stephen S. Wise, a rabbi, and to the School of Fine Arts in New York City. Includes material relating to her work for Wise as well as a manuscript play by Rachel Crothers.

WATERTOWN

7,560. Research Library
Records. 1600s- . No size given.
Partially restricted. No guide.
Perkins School for the Blind Library.
This collection of pamphlets, clippings, serials, photos, books, and other items pertaining to blindness and deaf-blindness include biographies of notable blind women as well as correspondence, writings, and photos of Helen Keller and correspondence and a journal relating to the association of Nella Braddy Henney, a writer, biographer of Anne Sullivan Macy, and friend of Helen Keller, with the Keller household from the 1920s to 1969. Collection also includes some items concerning Julia Ward Howe, whose husband was the first director of the Perkins School, which was founded to educate the blind and deaf-blind, and papers of Laura D. Bridgman, a Perkins student who is thought to have been the first deaf-blind person to be educated.

WAYLAND

7,561. Child, Lydia Maria (Francis)
Papers. 1824-83. 1 folder, 14 vols., and 27 items.
Open. No guide.
Wayland Historical Society.
Correspondence, pamphlets, photos, and books of [Mrs. David Lee] Child (1802-80), an author and abolitionist who lived in Wayland. Includes copies of various of her books, including *American Frugal Housewife* (1829), *Philothea* (1861), and *Incidents in the Life of a Slave Girl* (1861); photos of her home and one of her; a pamphlet of her correspondence with Governor Wise of Virginia and Mrs. Mason concerning John Brown; correspondence with Brown; and "A Tract Entitled the Duty of Disobedience to the Slave Act," which she presented to the Massachusetts legislature and which was published by the American Anti-Slavery Society in 1860. Also contains letters of condolence, thank-you notes, and letters in which she expresses her opinions of education, religion, and spiritualism, which she "tended to accept."

WELLESLEY

7,562. Alumnae
Records. 1880- . 14.8 ft. and 4 tapes.
Open. No guide.
Wellesley College Archives.
Minutes, correspondence, reports, tapes, biographical data, scrapbooks, and photos of the Wellesley College Alumnae Association, which was founded in 1880. Records relate to the Association's operation and activities, including its fund-raising efforts.

7,563. Bates, Katharine Lee
Papers. 1866-1929. 3.5 ft.
Open. Unpublished guide.
Wellesley College Archives.
Correspondence, diaries, manuscripts of prose and poetry, scrapbooks, photos, and memorabilia of [Miss] Bates (1859-1929), an educator and poet. Includes papers concerning her poem "America the Beautiful," her teaching at Wellesley, and her prose and poetry.

7,564. College Events
Records. 1875- . 29 ft. and 130 tapes.
Open. Unpublished guide.
Wellesley College Archives.
Tapes and transcripts of addresses, correspondence, and scrapbooks of College events include material on commencement, inaugurations of presidents, celebrations of anniversaries, concert series, lectures and symposia, the Summer Institute for Social Progress, the Wellesley Institute for Foreign Students, conferences on church work and church music, and the New England Institute for International Relations.

7,565. College Government
Records. 1901-72. 4.6 ft.
Partially restricted. Unpublished guide.
Wellesley College Archives.
Minutes, financial records, questionnaires, reports, correspondence, speeches, casebooks, and clippings of the student government, which was founded in 1901. Records concern student government activities, the establishment and enforcement of rules and regulations affecting student conduct, allocation of the student activities fee, and meetings with regional and national student groups.

7,566. Development and Business Management
Records. 1911-74. 25.5 ft.
Open. Partial unpublished guide.
Wellesley College Archives.
Financial records of the operation of the College include correspondence and reports relating to fund-raising efforts.

7,567. Faculty
Papers. 1835-1976. 65 ft.
Partially restricted. Partial unpublished guide.
Wellesley College Archives.
Papers of College faculty members include correspondence, diaries, manuscripts of their publications, lecture notes, and papers on the International Institute for Girls in Spain. Women

represented include Justina Ruiz-de-Conde, Cecile de Banke, Vida Scudder, Mary Whiton Calkins, Margaret Ferguson, Sarah Frances Whiting, Katharine Coman, and Josephine Preston Peabody.

7,568. Founders of the College
Records. 1841-1916. 0.4 ft.
Open. Unpublished guide.
Wellesley College Archives.
Correspondence, photos, clippings, and publications of Pauline Cazenove Durant (1832-1917) and her husband Henry Fowle Durant (1822-81), founders of the College, an institution for the higher education of women. Includes a partial biography of Henry Durant.

7,569. Hazard, Caroline
Papers. 1780-1941. 8 ft.
Open. Unpublished guide.
Wellesley College Archives.
Correspondence, diaries, manuscripts, addresses, financial papers, scrapbooks, photos, clippings, certificates, and memorabilia of Hazard (1856-1945), an educator and author who was a president of the College. Includes her addresses on women and her research on the Hazard family of Peace Dale, RI.

7,570. Information Services
Records. 1924-75. 29 ft.
Open. Unpublished guide.
Wellesley College Archives.
Correspondence, biographical files, press releases, brochures, programs, and other publications of the office of information services, which publicizes and disseminates information about the College. Records concern students, faculty, events, special programs, buildings, gifts, and grants.

7,571. Libraries and Museums
Records. 1875- . 35.8 ft.
Open. No guide.
Wellesley College Archives.
Minutes, financial records, reports, correspondence, and publications of the College libraries and museums concern accessions, buildings, special collections, the Friends of the Library, the Friends of Art, and exhibitions.

7,572. Palmer, Alice Freeman
Papers. 1874-1901. 1 ft.
Open. Unpublished guide.
Wellesley College Archives.
Correspondence, manuscripts, a scrapbook, and photos of [Mrs. George Herbert] Palmer (1855-1902), who taught history in secondary schools and at the College. Papers relate to her presidency of Wellesley from 1881 to 1887, her service as the first dean of women at the University of Chicago from 1892 to 1895, and her membership on the Massachusetts State Board of Education from 1889 to 1902. In addition, she played an active role in the Association of Collegiate Alumnae. Collection also includes information on her relationship with her husband.

7,573. Photo File
Collection. Ca. 1876-1976. 61 ft.
Open. No guide.
Wellesley College Archives.
Photos and slides of College campus scenes, buildings, students, faculty, administrators, staff, events, clubs, and other groups.

7,574. President's Office
Records. 1875-1973. 40.2 ft.
Partially restricted. Unpublished guide.
Wellesley College Archives.
Annual reports of academic departments and administrative offices, minutes, statistics, reports, and correspondence of the presidents of the College. Chartered in 1870 as Wellesley Female Seminary, the school was renamed Wellesley College in 1873 and opened for classes two years later. Represented are Ada Howard, Alice Freeman Palmer, Helen Shafer, Julia Irvine, Caroline Hazard, Ellen F. Pendleton, Mildred (McAfee) Horton, Margaret Clapp, Ruth Adams, and Barbara W. Newell. Records relate to finances, students and student organizations, faculty, curriculum development, growth and maintenance of the physical plant, alumnae relations, the Academic Council, the Seven College Conference, Yenching University in China, exchange agreements, and special programs.

7,575. Student Events
Records. 1877- . 7.4 ft.
Open. Unpublished guide.
Wellesley College Archives.
Financial records, correspondence, reports, photos, clippings, and programs of student-sponsored events, including such traditional events as Tree Day, Float Night, and Hoop Rolling.

7,576. Student Organizations
Records. 1875- . 30.2 ft.
Open. Unpublished guide.
Wellesley College Archives.
Minutes, financial records, reports, correspondence, scrapbooks, photos, publications, and memorabilia of student groups and organizations at the College. Records outline the structure and activities of organizations, among them departmental clubs, chapters of Phi Beta Kappa and Sigma Xi, musical and dramatic groups, literary societies, the athletic association, and service groups.

7,577. Student Services
Records. 1900-75. 7.5 ft.
Open. No guide.
Wellesley College Archives.
Minutes, financial records, correspondence, sermons, and scrapbooks of those administrative offices that deal with such nonacademic services to students as financial aid, on-campus residency, chaplaincy, the student center, and health care.

7,578. Students
Records. 1861- . 116 ft.
Open. Partial unpublished guide.
Wellesley College Archives.
Minutes, financial records, correspondence, reports, scrapbooks, photos, publications, and memorabilia of students. Contains records of class and student activities and interests, as well as biographical information on many students. Contains papers of Sally Carrighar, Madame Chiang Kai-shek, Mary B. Gilson, Margaret L. Law, and Katherine K. Davis.

7,579. Theses
Records. 1882-1976. 79.4 ft.
Open. Unpublished guide.
Wellesley College Archives.
Contains MA and honors theses and student papers.

7,580. Wellesley College Academic Departments
Records. 1875-1975. 64.1 ft.
Partially restricted. Unpublished guide.
Wellesley College Archives.
Financial records, correspondence, reports, questionnaires, curricular material, speeches, working papers, scrapbooks, photos, programs, publications, and memorabilia of the departments concerned with staffing, curriculum development, outside associations and internships, botanic gardens, gifts and grants, and the language laboratory. Includes information on the Anne L. Page Memorial School; the Boston Normal School of Gymnastics, which was absorbed by Wellesley in 1909; and the Wellesley Verse Speaking Choir.

7,581. Wellesley College Admission Office
Records. 1911-71. 72.2 ft.
Access restricted. No guide.
Wellesley College Archives.
Financial records, correspondence, and reports of the Admission Office, as well as admission forms, information sent to prospective students, and statistics on entrants.

7,582. Wellesley College Deans
Records. 1927-75. 24 ft.
Partially restricted. Unpublished guide.
Wellesley College Archives.
Minutes, budgets, correspondence, reports, and notes of academic deans and advisors. Includes items pertaining to exchanges and foreign students.

7,583. Wellesley College Histories
Records. 1869-1975. 4.4 ft.
Open. Unpublished guide.
Wellesley College Archives.
Includes a partial manuscript and notes for Alice Payne Hackett's "Wellesley: Part of the American Story" (1949) and transcripts of oral history interviews and papers used by editor Jean Glasscock during the preparation of "Wellesley College 1875-1975: A Century of Women" (1975). Includes transcripts of interviews with Mildred (McAfee) Horton, Margaret Clapp, Agnes Abbott, Katherine Balderston, M. Margaret Ball, Teresa G. Frisch, Mary Cooper Jewett Gaiser, Edna Heidbreder, E. Elizabeth Jones, Helen T. Jones, Jean V. Crawford, Lucy Killough, Elisabeth Luce Moore, Barbara W. Newell, Louise Overacker, Mary Eleanor Prentiss, Alice T. Schafer, Louise Pettibone Smith, E. Faye Wilson, Blanche DePuy, and Lucy Wilson. Also includes clippings and articles on the College.

7,584. Wellesley College Self-Studies
Records. 1953-71. 2.6 ft. and 1 tape.
Open. Unpublished guide.
Wellesley College Archives.
Minutes, correspondence, reports, questionnaires, and clippings relate to a survey of student and alumnae attitudes toward extracurricular life at the College; the survey was conducted in 1953 under a grant from the Ford Foundation Fund for the Advancement of Education. Records also concern the Commission on the Future of the College, a commission established by the board of trustees in 1969 to make recommendations concerning possible ties to Dartmouth College, visits to other colleges, the question of coeducation, curriculum proposals, admissions, the status of women, Wellesley's role, and other questions. The Commission ceased operation in 1971.

7,585. Whitney, Anne
Papers. 1835-1915. 6.5 ft.
Open. No guide.
Wellesley College Archives.
Correspondence, diaries, a will, and photos of Whitney (1821-1915), a sculptor. Correspondents include Louisa May Alcott, Lydia Maria Child, Louise Imogen Guiney, Sarah Orne Jewett, Frances E. Willard, Adeline Manning, Alice Stone Blackwell, Fredrika Bremer, Maria Weston Chapman, Florence Converse, Harriet Hosmer, Mary Ashton (Rice) Livermore, Vida Dutton Scudder, Alice Freeman Palmer, and Emma Stebbins.

WENHAM

7,586. Richards Family
Papers. Ca. 1827-1900s. 1 envelope.
Open. No guide.
Wenham Historical Association, Timothy Pickering Library.
Papers of this Wenham family consist of genealogical information, poems by Harriet N. Foster, correspondence of John Cushing Richards (1839-1907) in Wenham with his sister Mary Ann

Richards (1834-69) at Thetford Academy, and other items.

WESTWOOD

7,587. Baker Family
Papers. 1700s-1900s. 1 vol.
Open. No guide.
Westwood Public Library.
Papers of this West Dedham, MA, family consist of correspondence, photos, and articles from newspapers and the *Yankee* magazine that pertain to Betsey (Metcalf) Baker (1786-1867). Baker made the first straw bonnet in the US and founded the industry in this country.

7,588. Colburn, Mary E. G.
Papers. 1891. 3 vols.
Open. No guide.
Westwood Public Library.
Journal in which Colburn recorded in detail her 10-week trip to Europe, beginning with her voyage on the *City of Richmond* from New York for Liverpool. The journal contains programs, photos, and other memorabilia.

7,589. Williams, Mary (Nelson)
Papers. 1861-65. 1 box.
Open. No guide.
Westwood Public Library.
Letters that Williams, a housewife living in Greenfield, MA, wrote to her husband Franklin Delano Williams, who was in China on business, provide a picture of life in a small New England town during the Civil War.

WILLIAMSTOWN

7,590. Armstrong, Samuel Chapman
Papers. 1776-1905. 6700 items.
Open. List and catalog cards.
Williams College Library, Williamsiana Collection.
Most of the correspondence and other papers of Armstrong (1839-93), an administrator, relate to his work at the Hampton Institute in Virginia, for which he was noted. Also includes family correspondence of women in the related Armstrong, Williams, and Walker families, which reflects the women's social activities and events in Williamstown, the Institute, Williams College, and the nation. Contains lengthy series of correspondence of Samuel Armstrong's first wife Emma Dean (Walker) Armstrong (1849-78); his second wife Mary Alice Ford Armstrong; his biographer and daughter Edith Hull (Armstrong) Talbot (1872-?); Frances Walker Williams (1817-1903), who was wife of a Williamstown banker; her sister-in-law Clara Williams; and Sarah Walker Davis (1814-79), who was wife of a judge.

7,591. Hopkins, Mark
Papers. 1815-87. 7 vols. and 123 items.
Open. No guide.
Williams College Library, Williamsiana Collection.
Correspondence and other papers of Hopkins (1802-87), an educator, contain correspondence of various women in his family. Includes letters of his grandmother Electra Sergeant Hopkins, his wife Mary Hubbell Hopkins, his daughter Mary Louisa Hopkins, and a long series of his mother Mary Curtis Hopkins.

7,592. Literary Club
Records. 1939-68. 2 vols. and 2 items.
Open. No guide.
Williamstown Public Library, House of Local History.
Initially known as the Shakespeare Club for men and women when it was founded in the 1870s, the group later changed its name and restricted membership to women. Treasurer's reports, minutes, bankbooks, and tables of dues payments and attendance. The Club held dinners and afternoon socials at which members read aloud from literary works.

7,593. Monday Club
Records. 1907-18. 1 vol.
Open. No guide.
Williamstown Public Library, House of Local History.
Minutes, lists of members and officers, and programs of the Club, a women's group founded in 1907 to study classical and popular literature, particularly Shakespeare and the Greeks. Members heard lectures, gave readings, and examined the works of critics.

WINCHENDON

7,594. Alpha Circle of the Chantanqua Literary and Scientific Circle
Records. 1882-90. 3 vols.
Open. Unpublished guide.
Winchendon Historical Society.
Minutes of this women's group, which from 1882 to 1890 held lectures and promoted the writing of essays as well as using "whatever other methods they could to contribute to the prosperity of the Circle in the lines of culture."

7,595. Atlanta Society
Records. 1873-98. 1 vol.
Open. Unpublished guide.
Winchendon Historical Society.
Minutes of this women's group, which existed between 1873 and 1898. The group provided financial assistance for Negro students at Atlanta University.

7,596. Dickens Club of Winchendon
Records. 1884-1909. 1 vol.
Open. Unpublished guide.
Winchendon Historical Society.
Minutes of the Club, a women's group that met twice a month between 1884 and 1909 to read the works of Charles Dickens. In the minutes, members often refer to having a "Dickens" of a time.

WORCESTER

7,597. Abbot, Ephraim
Papers. 1801-1904. 10 octavo vols. and 2 ms. boxes.
Open. Published guide and catalog.
American Antiquarian Society.
Correspondence, diaries for 1812 and 1814, an autobiography, and sermons of Abbot (1779-1870), a minister, missionary, and educator who served as minister and preceptor at the Brackett Academy in Greenland, NH, from 1813 to 1828. Primarily between Abbot and his first wife Mary Holyoke Pearson Abbot (1782-1829), whom he married in 1814, the correspondence illuminates family relationships and activities, his business interests, his ministry in New Hampshire, his work as missionary to the Indians of Eastern Maine, his activity as an agent for the Massachusetts Bible Society, and his interests in temperance and farming. See *Catalog of Manuscripts of the American Antiquarian Society* (Boston: G. K. Hall & Co., 1979).

7,598. Adams, Abigail
Papers. 1784-1816. 1 ms. box.
Open. Published guide and catalog.
American Antiquarian Society.
Correspondence of Adams (1744-1818), wife of US President John Adams, to her sister Mary (Smith) Cranch (1741-1811) and her niece Lucy (Cranch) Greenleaf (1767-1846), begins with the Adamses' crossing to England where John Adams served as minister to the Court of St. James and continues through his Presidency to retirement in Quincy, MA, in 1801. The letters contain comments on political topics, observations on social and economic conditions, and discussion of life in London, New York, Philadelphia, and Washington.

7,599. Bancroft, Elizabeth
Papers. 1793-95. 18-page octavo vol.
Open. Published and unpublished guides.
American Antiquarian Society.
Typescript copy of lost diary of Bancroft (1773-1867) indicating that she taught at a school, evidently in Pepperell, MA; attended a dancing school, religious services, and quilting bees; and visited friends and relatives. See *Catalog of Manuscripts of the American Antiquarian Society* (Boston: G. K. Hall & Co., 1979).

7,600. Barton, Clara
Papers. Ca. 1832-1912. 6 ms. boxes.
Open. Published and unpublished guides.
American Antiquarian Society.
Correspondence, 1881-82 diary entries, notebooks, scrapbook, and other papers of [Miss] Barton (1821-1912), founder and president of the American National Red Cross, including correspondence with Frank Norton and with members of her family, as well as deeds to family property in North Oxford, MA. Originals of most of these papers are at the Library of Congress. See *Catalog of Manuscripts of the American Antiquarian Society* (Boston: G. K. Hall & Co., 1979).

7,601. Bascom, Ruth (Henshaw)
Papers. 1789-1846. 52 octavo vols.
Open. Published and unpublished guides.
American Antiquarian Society.
Consists of diaries spanning 57 years of the life of Bascom (1772-1848), an artist who also was a member of the Henshaw family of Leicester, MA, and wife of Ezekiel Lysander Bascom (1779?-1841), a minister in Phillipston and Ashby, MA. Main subjects are local events, sickness and death, visiting, Bascom's art work, and the weather, although unusual events and natural disasters are noted. Early diaries reveal that Bascom's time as a young girl was occupied by classes and special programs at Leicester Academy, social activities, housework, and family occasions. After her marriage, she helped her husband with his ministerial functions; she carefully noted his sermon topics, funerals, and marriage ceremonies. In addition, she devoted time to visiting, watching the sick, serving local library and temperance societies, and performing household tasks. In 1819 she made the first entry concerning her work with pastel portraits and silhouettes, for which she became known. There are a few notations of receiving money for her sketches, and occasionally she recorded the amounts she spent for art supplies. In 1816 Bascom began keeping track of vital statistics for the town, as well as personal accounts of how long visitors stayed and how many meals they consumed, lists of letters received and sent, and expenses. She also made detailed entries about the many trips she and her husband made to such places as Virginia, Leicester, Boston, and Maine. She recorded the route traveled by stagecoach, number of passengers and their destinations, stops, and road conditions. Also included with Bascom's diaries are two kept by her sister Catherine Henshaw (1784-1806). See *Catalog of Manuscripts of the American Antiquarian Society* (Boston: G. K. Hall & Co., 1979).

7,602. Bigelow, Louise
Papers. Ca. 1930s?. 601-page octavo vol.
Open. Published and unpublished guides.
American Antiquarian Society.
Typescript of *Colonel Timothy Bigelow: A*

Historical Novel (Meador Publishing Company, 1941) by Bigelow, an author who was blind. See *Catalog of Manuscripts of the American Antiquarian Society* (Boston: G. K. Hall & Co., 1979).

7,603. Bliss, Alexander
Papers. 1825. 134-page folio vol.
Open. Published and unpublished guides.
American Antiquarian Society.
Diary in which Bliss (1792-1827), a law partner of Daniel Webster, records the two-month honeymoon trip in 1825 which he took with his bride Elizabeth (Davis) Bliss (1803-86) of Plymouth, MA, to Niagara Falls by way of western Massachusetts, the Mohawk Valley, and the Finger Lakes region. The couple continued on to Montreal and Quebec before returning to Boston by way of Plattsburgh, Saratoga Springs, and Deerfield. Also included are copies of poetry and prose on death, prayer, and the family, which may have been compiled by Elizabeth Bliss. She later married historian George Bancroft. See *Catalog of Manuscripts of the American Antiquarian Society* (Boston: G. K. Hall & Co., 1979).

7,604. Bliss, Sally (Hitchcock)
Papers. 1821-72. 122-page folio vol.
Open. Published and unpublished guides.
American Antiquarian Society.
Diary in which [Mrs. David] Bliss (1791-1872) records numerous church, prayer, and camp meetings of the Methodist Church of Wilbraham, MA. Bliss also describes her spiritual condition, notes the scriptural passages of sermons, and lists death notices. See *Catalog of Manuscripts of the American Antiquarian Society* (Boston: G. K. Hall & Co., 1979).

7,605. Bolton and Stanwood Family
Papers. Ca. 1843-1944. 1 ms. box and 38 octavo vols.
Open. Published guide and catalog.
American Antiquarian Society.
Includes papers of Charles Knowles Bolton (1867-1950), librarian of the Boston Athenaeum; of his wife Ethel (Stanwood) Bolton (1874-1954), an author; of his mother Sarah Knowles Bolton (1841-1916), a poet and biographer; and of his father-in-law Edward Stanwood (1841-1923), editor of *Youth's Companion.* Correspondence, diary entries, record books, and memorabilia include notes by Ethel Bolton, which she probably gathered in preparation for her book on Shirley, MA, which is entitled *Shirley Uplands and Intervales;* correspondence and notes pertaining to her pamphlet *Wax Portraits and Silhouettes;* selections by Charles Bolton of entries, 1894-1915, from the journal of Sarah Bolton, which concern people she met and corresponded with, her literary and temperance interests, and her great concern for animals; and Sarah Bolton's correspondence, which also reflects her literary and humanitarian interests. Correspondents include Mary Abigail Dodge and Frances Elizabeth Caroline Willard. See *Catalog of Manuscripts of the American Antiquarian Society* (Boston: G. K. Hall & Co., 1979).

7,606. Brigham, Cephas
Papers. 1887-90. 7 octavo vols.
Open. Published and unpublished guides.
American Antiquarian Society.
Notebooks of Brigham (1822?-?), a school teacher, broom manufacturer, and lawyer in various Massachusetts towns, contain diary entries and reminiscences in the form of a sketch of his wife Lucy Elmira Graves Brigham (1827-87). Beginning 10 days before her death, Brigham's writings reflect the sense of loss he felt; he attempted to recapture their relationship by reminiscing. The notebooks also include copies of 41 letters between him and his wife. See *Catalog of Manuscripts of the American Antiquarian Society* (Boston: G. K. Hall & Co., 1979).

7,607. Brownell, Abner
Papers. 1779-87. 2 octavo vols.
Open. Published and unpublished guides.
American Antiquarian Society.
Diaries of Brownell (1756-1851), a Quaker from Dartmouth, MA, who became a follower of religious leader Jemima Wilkinson after a conversion experience, record his traveling and preaching throughout southeastern New England, first as part of Wilkinson's retinue and later on his own. Contained is a careful log of meetings conducted in various communities, where meals were taken, and where shelter for the evening was secured. See *Catalog of Manuscripts of the American Antiquarian Society* (Boston: G. K. Hall & Co., 1979).

7,608. Cargill Family
Papers. 1725-1923. 1 ms. box and 6 folio vols.
Open. Published and unpublished guides.
American Antiquarian Society.
Correspondence, genealogical material, business papers, and legal documents of Benjamin Cargill, Sr. (1737-1813), Benjamin Cargill, Jr. (1769-1822), and John Milton Cargill (1806?-90), all of whom were businessmen in Providence, RI, and Pomfret, CT. Also included are late 19th-century and early 20th-century deeds, personal papers, and miscellaneous documents of Mary H. Cargill of East Providence, RI. See *Catalog of Manuscripts of the American Antiquarian Society* (Boston: G. K. Hall & Co., 1979).

7,609. Chace, Mary (Tyler)
Papers. 1737-1879. 1 octavo vol.
Open. Published and unpublished guides.
American Antiquarian Society.
Record book of [Mrs. Charles, Jr.] Chace (1797-?), a resident of Harvard, Lancaster, and Still River, MA, consists primarily of death dates of prominent people and lists of historical events. Also included are records of family expenses and real estate transactions during the 19th century, genealogical data, information on local events, a list of books Chace read between 1872 and 1877, a letter by Chace, a note concerning Chace, a school register kept by her daughter who was a teacher in Lancaster, MA, during the 1860s, and a list written by the daughter of suggestions on commencing school. *Catalog of Manuscripts of the American Antiquarian Society* (Boston: G. K. Hall & Co., 1979).

7,610. Chase Family
Papers. Ca. 1787-1915. 5 ms. boxes and 1 octavo vol.
Open. Published and unpublished guides.
American Antiquarian Society.
Diaries, business and legal documents, school compositions, and correspondence between family members, much of which was generated by Anthony Chase (1791-1879), a Worcester merchant and part owner of the *Massachusetts Spy;* and by two of his children, Lucy Chase (1822-1909), a teacher, and Charles Augustus Chase (1833-1911), treasurer of Worcester County. Papers of Lucy Chase consist of correspondence with her siblings, cousins, and school friends; school compositions; notebooks; and diary excerpts. Beginning in 1863, Lucy and her sister Sarah Earle Chase (1836-1915) taught in contraband camps and freedmen schools in the South; they wrote lengthy and articulate letters home describing their experiences and observations there. In poor health, Sarah Chase stopped teaching in 1866, but Lucy Chase continued to teach in Virginia and Florida until 1869. Between 1870 and 1875 the sisters traveled in Europe, where they wrote letters home and kept journals. In 1902 Lucy Chase visited Cuba; she later wrote several articles based on her observations of Cuban life and social customs. A selection of letters written from contraband camps by Lucy and Sarah Chase to family and friends is included in Henry L. Swint, *Dear Ones at Home* (Nashville: Vanderbilt University Press, 1966). See *Catalog of Manuscripts of the American Antiquarian Society* (Boston: G. K. Hall & Co., 1979).

7,611. Cheever Family
Papers. Ca. 1800-1900. 26 ms. boxes and 9 folio vols.
Open. Published guide and index.
American Antiquarian Society.
Primarily correspondence, diaries, notes, lectures, sermons, legal documents, and clippings of the children of Charlotte Barrell Cheever (1778-1854) and Nathaniel Cheever (1778-1819): George Barrell Cheever (1807-90), a Congregational minister, author, and reformer; and Elizabeth Bancroft (Cheever) Washburn (1812-98), a philanthropist. Much of the correspondence is between George Cheever and his mother, his sister, and his wife Elizabeth Hoppin Wetmore Cheever (?-1886). Most of Elizabeth Washburn's correspondence, which contains informative news about family events, is to family members, including a large network of cousins, aunts, and uncles. Like the rest of her family, she was zealously religious; her letters and ca. 1826-67 diaries reflect unceasing concern for her spiritual health and that of family members. After devoting herself to the care of her mother and service for her brothers, at age 46 Elizabeth Cheever married Ichabod Washburn, a Worcester industrialist. When he died 10 years later, he left a substantial estate generating some legal battles; collection also includes information on these. See *Catalog of Manuscripts of the American Antiquarian Society* (Boston: G. K. Hall & Co., 1979).

7,612. Child, Lydia Maria
Papers. 1845-80. 1 folder.
Open. Published and unpublished guides.
American Antiquarian Society.
Most of the correspondence of Child (1802-80), an author and reformer, is addressed to her friend Marianne Cabot (Devereux) Silsbee, an author. These letters contain information on Child's abolitionist interests and associations, comments on literary figures, political discussion, descriptions of domestic life, and expressions of fondness for Silsbee. Collection is also available on microfilm. See *Catalog of Manuscripts of the American Antiquarian Society* (Boston: G. K. Hall & Co., 1979).

7,613. Civil War
Collection. 1861-65. 4 ms. boxes, 1 octavo vol., and 2 folio vols.
Open. Published and unpublished guides.
American Antiquarian Society.
Included with the military records, account books of commissary supplies, correspondence, reminiscence, and diaries are ca. 350 letters from southern women and a few men seeking employment in the Department of the Confederate States Treasury. Most of the letters are addressed to Treasury Secretary Christopher Gustavus Memminger and a few include endorsements from Mrs. Jefferson Davis; in some of the letters women wrote detailed explanations of their economic status and family situation. Also included is correspondence between Union soldiers and their wives and families. See *Catalog of Manuscripts of the American Antiquarian Society* (Boston: G. K. Hall & Co., 1979).

7,614. Clapp Family
Papers. 1836-56. 1 folder.
Open. Published and unpublished guides.
American Antiquarian Society.
Personal letters to John Drury Clapp (1822-98), a tanner, from his father Levi Clapp (1794-1854), a Worcester merchant, and from his sister Sarah Huntington (Clapp) Holmes (1824-69). See *Catalog of Manuscripts of the American*

Antiquarian Society (Boston: G. K. Hall & Co., 1979).

7,615. Davis, John
Papers. 1812-1902. 1 ms. box, 4 octavo vols., and 1 oversize vol.
Open. Published guide and catalog.
American Antiquarian Society.
Correspondence and official documents pertaining to the public life of Davis (1787-1854), a Worcester lawyer who served as a US congressman from 1825 to 1834, governor of Massachusetts from 1834 to 1835 and from 1841 to 1843, and US senator from 1835 to 1841 and from 1845 to 1853. Included is correspondence between Davis and his wife Eliza (Bancroft) Davis (1791-1872), sister of historian George Bancroft, in which she comments on state and national matters, current legislation, and local Worcester issues; several drafts and copies of his major speeches are in her hand. In his letters to her, most of which were written from Washington, DC, but some of which were written while he was on domestic and European trips, he discusses personal, family, and social matters as well as political activities and events. Her letters, on the same subjects, include discussion of state and national issues particularly as they pertained to current legislation. Also included is correspondence Eliza Davis wrote family and friends during the time she spent in Washington with her husband and letters relating to her life after she was widowed. See *Catalog of Manuscripts of the American Antiquarian Society* (Boston: G. K. Hall & Co., 1979).

7,616. DeWolf and Lawrence
Papers. 1785-1843. 2 folders.
Open. Published and unpublished guides.
American Antiquarian Society.
Family correspondence and legal documents of James DeWolfe (1762-1834); his second wife Nancy (Lawrence) DeWolf (1764-1807), who was daughter of a Congregational minister in Lincoln, MA; and James and Nancy DeWolf's daughter Abby Kane (DeWolf) Bartlett (1794-1842), wife of Boston merchant and horticulturist Enoch Bartlett. Correspondence was written from Massachusetts and from Liverpool, Nova Scotia where the DeWolf family moved after 1755 when New Englanders were encouraged to settle there. Included are letters Nancy DeWolf wrote her mother Love Adams Lawrence and letters from Abby Bartlett to her father, which primarily concern personal and domestic subjects. See *Catalog of Manuscripts of the American Antiquarian Society* (Boston: G. K. Hall & Co., 1979).

7,617. Dixon, Ann Lilley
Papers. 1841-63. 1 folder.
Open. Published and unpublished guides.
American Antiquarian Society.
Personal letters to [Mrs. George] Dixon in Plainfield, CT, and later Webster, MA, are from friends and relatives. Also included are telegrams announcing the death of her husband. See *Catalog of Manuscripts of the American Antiquarian Society* (Boston: G. K. Hall & Co., 1979).

7,618. Draper and Rice Family
Papers. Ca. 1760-1868. 3 ms. boxes and 15 octavo vols.
Open. Published and unpublished guides.
American Antiquarian Society.
For the most part, the correspondence, account books, and judicial documents reflect the career of James Draper (1778-1868), a farmer, teacher, Massachusetts state legislator, and justice of the peace in Spencer, MA. Also included are letters by Draper; his wife Lucy Watson Draper (1788-1848); and their four children Emeline (Draper) Rice (1806-54), Julia Ann (Draper) Lazell Pratt (1808-41), Sophia A. (Draper) White (1811-67), and Lucy (Draper) Rider (1813-?), as well as correspondence between Emeline Rice and her husband William E. Rice (1803-82) and their children James D. Rice, Lucy W. Rice, and William E. Rice (1833-1919). See *Catalog of Manuscripts of the American Antiquarian Society* (Boston: G. K. Hall & Co., 1979).

7,619. Drew, Abigail (Gardner)
Papers. 1799-1817. 49-page octavo vol.
Open. Published and unpublished guides.
American Antiquarian Society.
Daughter of George and Rebecca Coffin Gardner of Nantucket, MA, Drew (1777-1868) married Gershom Drew, Jr. in 1795. In her diary she reminisces about her early life, particularly about her courtship with Gershom and her feelings at that time; later entries reveal that her life changed from one of social pleasures to one of religious commitment. Diary also contains scattered poetry and financial accounts. See *Catalog of Manuscripts of the American Antiquarian Society* (Boston: G. K. Hall & Co., 1979).

7,620. Dunn, Robinson Potter
Papers. 1825-97. 2 octavo vols. and 3 folders.
Open. Published and unpublished guides.
American Antiquarian Society.
Correspondence, sermons, estate documents, clippings, and other papers of Dunn (1825-67), a Presbyterian minister who was also a professor at Brown University. Included are letters written by his parents Theophilus Colhoun Dunn (?-1871) and Elizabeth Robinson Potter Dunn to him and his second wife Mary Stiles Foster Dunn (?-1900) of Worcester and letters of condolence to Mary Dunn on the death of her husband. See *Catalog of Manuscripts of the American Antiquarian Society* (Boston: G. K. Hall & Co., 1979).

7,621. Edes, Sarah Louisa Lincoln
Papers. 1852-53. 2 octavo vols.
Open. Published and unpublished guides.
American Antiquarian Society.
Recording her everyday activities, Edes (1823-?), a young widow living in Cambridge, MA, makes frequent sentimental references to her late husband Henry Augustus Edes (1824-51). See *Catalog of Manuscripts of the American Antiquarian Society* (Boston: G. K. Hall & Co., 1979).

7,622. Fairchild, Thomas B.
Papers. 1834-82. 1 octavo vol. and 1 folder.
Open. Published and unpublished guides.
American Antiquarian Society.
Correspondence and diary of Fairchild, a minister in Hudson, OH, including letters from his mother Nancy Peck Fairchild Tuttle, writing from Cambridge and Lansingburgh, NY, and letters from other relatives and friends. See *Catalog of Manuscripts of the American Antiquarian Society* (Boston: G. K. Hall & Co., 1979).

7,623. Farnum, Mary Barker
Papers. 1806-20. 3 octavo vols.
Open. Published and unpublished guides.
American Antiquarian Society.
Diaries and correspondence of Farnum (1784?-1861), a minister of the Society of Friends who was born on Nantucket Island, MA; she was married first to Walter Allen and later to Moses Farnum, and lived in Smithfield, RI. Diaries of trips she made with companions through several states including Maryland, Virginia, Washington, DC, and Ohio contain careful notations of distances traveled, people encountered, and frequent religious meetings. Diaries also include some mention of expenses and a few personal entries. Enclosed with the diaries are letters apparently written to Mary from Moses Farnum before they were married. See *Catalog of Manuscripts of the American Antiquarian Society* (Boston: G. K. Hall & Co., 1979).

7,624. Fay, Annah C. (Harthan)
Papers. 1904-39?. 2 octavo vols. and 1 folder.
Open. Published and unpublished guides.
American Antiquarian Society.
Papers of [Mrs. Arthur] Fay (1853-1938), owner of the Hitchcock Press and a resident of Princeton, MA, consist of business records of job printing which was performed at the Press prior to and during its ownership by Fay; a book listing subscribers to the publication *Laborers Friend;* biography of Fay, written by her daughter Lois (Fay) Powell (1883-1960); letters of condolence on Fay's death; and obituaries. Dealing primarily with Fay's personal life prior to 1900, the biography contains discussions of her courtship, genealogy, and family and farm life in Princeton; it concludes with several pages of copied poems. See *Catalog of Manuscripts of the American Antiquarian Society* (Boston: G. K. Hall & Co., 1979).

7,625. Flint, Waldo
Papers. 1818-79. 6 ms. boxes.
Open. Published and unpublished guides.
American Antiquarian Society.
Correspondence, diaries, account books, business papers, and other material of Flint (1794-1879), a Boston banker who served as a state representative and senator, and of his wife Catharine (Dean) Flint (1802-69). Includes account books kept by Waldo and Catharine Flint, diaries, 1858-68; and her correspondence with her sister Rebekah Scott (Dean) Salisbury (1812-43) and other relatives and friends. The correspondence and diaries concern personal, family, and social matters. Most of the letters were written from Boston; Charlestown, NH; Leicester, MA; and Worcester. See *Catalog of Manuscripts of the American Antiquarian Society* (Boston: G. K. Hall & Co., 1979).

7,626. Forbes, Esther
Papers. Ca. 1940s-60s. 4 ms. boxes.
Open. Published and unpublished guides.
American Antiquarian Society.
Correspondence, research notes, chapter drafts, and clippings pertaining to the last and unfinished literary project—a history of witchcraft—of [Miss] Forbes (1891-1967), an historical novelist and short story writer. Much of the correspondence is from Forbes's friend "K" [Mrs. Lovell] Thompson of Ipswich, MA, who did research for her. Also included is correspondence from librarians and historians. See *Catalog of Manuscripts of the American Antiquarian Society* (Boston: G. K. Hall & Co., 1979).

7,627. Forbes, Harriette (Merrifield)
Papers. Nd. 4 ms. boxes.
Open. Published and unpublished guides.
American Antiquarian Society.
Papers of [Mrs.] Forbes (1856-1951), an author and local historian, including correspondence from people she surveyed for information for her *New England Diaries 1602-1800: A Descriptive Catalogue of Diaries, Orderly Books and Sea Journals* (1923); letters pertaining to her *Gravestones of Early New England and the Men Who Made Them* (1927); miscellaneous notes; and clippings. See *Catalog of Manuscripts of the American Antiquarian Society* (Boston: G. K. Hall & Co., 1979).

7,628. Forbes, Susan E. P. Brown
Papers. 1841-1908. 2 ms. boxes.
Open. Published and unpublished guides.
American Antiquarian Society.
Born in Epsom, NH, Forbes (1824-1910) married Alexander B. Forbes, a Scotsman who immigrated to the US in 1857 where he founded Forbes and Wallace Department Stores. Alexander and Susan Forbes spent much time and money restoring Fatherland Farm in Byfield, MA, which was the colonial home of Susan Forbes's ancestors and the place where she died. Her diaries concern events in her life before marriage, living with her husband

in Springfield, MA, and their move to Fatherland Farm. Entries, which become longer as the years progress, are primarily domestic in subject matter: they indicate whom she visited, who visited her, household duties she performed, and meetings and lectures she attended. Earlier diary volumes, interleaved in almanacs, include personal accounts and a record of letters sent and received, whereas later volumes include addresses and miscellaneous accounts. See *Catalog of Manuscripts of the American Antiquarian Society* (Boston: G. K. Hall & Co., 1979).

7,629. Foster, Abigail (Kelley)
Papers. 1836-91. 2 ms. boxes.
Open. Published guide catalog.
American Antiquarian Society.
Correspondence of Foster (1810-87) and her husband Stephen Symonds Foster (1809-81), both of whom were abolitionists, advocates of women's rights, and lecturers, provides information on the antislavery movement in New York, New England, and Ohio between 1837 and 1850. Many of the letters are between Abby and Stephen Foster; other correspondents include Maria (Weston) Chapman, Jane Elizabeth (Hitchcock) Jones, Sallie Holley, Caroline F. Putnam, and Lucy Stone. Correspondence also illuminates the role of women in politics and reform movements as well as that of reformers generally. All items available on microfilm. See *Catalog of Manuscripts of the American Antiquarian Society* (Boston: G. K. Hall & Co., 1979).

7,630. Foster Family
Papers. 1750-1884. 34 ms. boxes and 10 octavo vols.
Open. Published and unpublished guides.
American Antiquarian Society.
Included with correspondence, diaries, account books, notebooks, and business and financial papers of five generations of this Massachusetts family is correspondence of mothers, sisters, daughters, cousins, and female friends. Includes extensive correspondence between Rebecca Faulkner [Mrs. Dwight] Foster (1761-1834) and her husband, 1784-1819; letters of Pamela Foster (1784-1807) to her father and brother, 1792-1807; correspondence between Lydia (Stiles) [Mrs. Alfred Dwight] Foster (1806-87) and her father, husband, and children; family correspondence of Sophia Dwight (Foster) [Mrs. Samuel M'Gregore] Burnside (1787-1872?); and letters of Mary Stiles Foster (1830-1900). See *Catalog of Manuscripts of the American Antiquarian Society* (Boston: G. K. Hall & Co., 1979).

7,631. Gale Family
Papers. Ca. 1837-50. 2 octavo vols. and 3 octavo traycases.
Open. Published and unpublished guides.
American Antiquarian Society.
Papers of Frederick William Gale (1816-54), a Worcester lawyer, and of his sister Hannah "Anna" Davis Gale (1818-51) consist of their letters containing descriptions of Worcester social life, Frederick Gale's experiences at Harvard College, and family affairs; journals kept while traveling in Europe; and an 1837-38 journal Anna Gale kept as a student at the Greene Street School in Providence, RI, which includes detailed impressions of her teacher Margaret Fuller. See *Catalog of Manuscripts of the American Antiquarian Society* (Boston: G. K. Hall & Co., 1979).

7,632. Gardner Family
Papers. Ca. 1833-82. 2 folders and 1 octavo vol.
Open. Published and unpublished guides.
American Antiquarian Society.
Correspondence, diary, notebook, account book, genealogical notes, and other documents of the Nantucket Island, MA, family of whalers and farmers. Included are letters Jared M. Gardner (1818-76?) wrote his wife Harriet Gardner during his whaling voyage between 1840 and 1843 in the Pacific Ocean on the brig *Lady Washington,* a letter he wrote her during a later voyage, several letters she wrote him, and incomplete drafts of letters Harriet Gardner wrote her family during a voyage she took with her husband during 1849 and 1850 around Cape Horn to San Francisco. Also included is an 1841 letter to Harriet Gardner from her sisters Rebecca B. Swain and Mary Ann Swain, written from Clinton, MI, in which the sisters complain about the hard life in the West; an 1833 letter from Lucretia Mott to Eunice Gardner; and a recollection by Charlotte Vinette Gardner Fisher of the Centennial Exposition at Philadelphia in 1876. See *Catalog of Manuscripts of the American Antiquarian Society* (Boston: G. K. Hall & Co., 1979).

7,633. Gibbs, Robert
Papers. 1659-1708. 108-page octavo vol. and 33 items.
Open. Published and unpublished guides.
American Antiquarian Society.
Business records of the Boston general store of Gibbs (1634-74), a merchant. The business continued after his death, possibly managed by his wife Elizabeth Sheafe Gibbs (?-1718). See *Catalog of Manuscripts of the American Antiquarian Society* (Boston: G. K. Hall & Co., 1979).

7,634. Gilman, Samuel, and Gilman, Caroline
Papers. 1809-88. 3 folders.
Open. Published and unpublished guides.
American Antiquarian Society.
Papers of Samuel Gilman (1791-1858), a Unitarian minister and author, and of his wife Caroline (Howard) Gilman (1794-1888), a poet, consist primarily of family letters and their poetry. The letters are chiefly to Samuel Gilman's sister Louisa (Gilman) Loring (1797-1868) of Salem, Cambridge, and Boston, MA; to Caroline Gilman's sister Harriet (Howard) Fay of Cambridge; and to Caroline Gilman from Samuel Gilman while he was in Boston or on other East Coast trips. The letters contain discussions of personal, family, and social matters; literature; the literary magazine *Rose Bud* and English writer Harriet Martineau; religious subjects, particularly Samuel Gilman's ministry and Unitarianism; the slavery issue; and antebellum life in Charleston, SC, as observed by the Gilmans, New Englanders who lived there during most of their married life. Sermons by Samuel Gilman and tributes to both Gilmans are also included. See *Catalog of Manuscripts of the American Antiquarian Society* (Boston: G. K. Hall & Co., 1979).

7,635. Grafton, MA
Collection. 1743-1948. 1 ms. box.
Open. Published and unpublished guides.
American Antiquarian Society.
Local land deeds, records of epitaphs, Grafton History Club material, and records of other societies, including a volume of minutes of meetings, annual reports, constitution, and lists of members and officers of the Grafton Female Moral Reform Society, an auxiliary of the Boston Moral Reform Society for "the prevention of licentiousness." See *Catalog of Manuscripts of the American Antiquarian Society* (Boston: G. K. Hall & Co., 1979).

7,636. Green Family of Boston, MA
Papers. 1752-1870. 17 folio vols. and 2 folders.
Open. Published and unpublished guides.
American Antiquarian Society.
Correspondence, account books, business papers, and legal documents of this Boston family of merchants, a judge, a physician, and a librarian, include notebooks and ledgers of Anna Peirce Green (1702-70) relating to her role as executrix of her husband's estate between 1765 and 1770 and correspondence of Edward Henry Green (1821-1902), written while he was abroad between 1848 and 1850. Included are letters from his business associates, personal friends, his mother Anna Amory Tucker Green (1803-75), and other family members. See *Catalog of Manuscripts of the American Antiquarian Society* (Boston: G. K. Hall & Co., 1979).

7,637. Haverhill and Bradford Soldiers Relief Society
Records. 1861. 1 octavo vol. and 1 folder.
Open. Published and unpublished guides.
American Antiquarian Society.
This charitable group of Haverhill and Bradford, MA, women who organized in 1861 to solicit and sew clothing and linen for Union soldiers initially held meetings daily and then several times per month. Minutes, Society accounts with lists of donations of money and goods, inventory lists, and correspondence by Elizabeth Fletcher, Society secretary, including letters to Union officers and physicians informing them that clothing and linen were forthcoming. See *Catalog of Manuscripts of the American Antiquarian Society* (Boston: G. K. Hall & Co., 1979).

7,638. Henshaw Family
Papers. 1759-1892. 5 ms. boxes, 4 folio vols., and 1 oversize folder.
Open. Published guide and catalog.
American Antiquarian Society.
Included with the correspondence, business papers, and military documents of the Leicester, MA, family are ca. 30 letters between William Henshaw (1735-1820) and his second wife Phebe Swan Henshaw (1753-1808), which were written while he served as an assistant to General Gates during the 1775 seige of Boston and during his participation in the 1776 battle of Long Island. See *Catalog of Manuscripts of the American Antiquarian Society* (Boston: G. K. Hall & Co., 1979).

7,639. Holyoke, Priscilla
Papers. 1766. 32-page octavo vol.
Open. Published and unpublished guides.
American Antiquarian Society.
Holyoke (1739-82) was born in Cambridge, MA, where her father Edward Holyoke (1689-1769) was president of Harvard College; in 1780 she married Eliphalet Pearson (1752-1826). Interleaved in an almanac, her diary contains brief information on such everyday occurrences as where she dined, whom she visited, and who preached on Sunday. Also included are a few personal accounts; a copy of a prayer; and references to her father, to her brother who was a physician in Marblehead, MA, and to rejoicing in Boston and Cambridge at the repeal of the Stamp Act. See *Catalog of Manuscripts of the American Antiquarian Society* (Boston: G. K. Hall & Co., 1979).

7,640. Howell, Anna Blackwood
Papers. 1819-39. 12 octavo vols.
Open. Published and unpublished guides.
American Antiquarian Society.
Widow of Joshua Ladd Howell (1762-1818) of Gloucester County, NJ, Anna Howell (1769-1855) inherited fisheries on the Delaware River; she operated these and the family farm after her husband's death. Her diaries, interleaved in agricultural almanacs, include entries concerning farming and fishing, information on preparation of nets and the types of fish in particular catches, and comments revealing her preoccupation with the weather and its possible effect on her livelihood. Also mentioned are visits with her 11 children and such family matters as illness and death. See *Catalog of Manuscripts of the American Antiquarian Society* (Boston: G. K. Hall & Co., 1979).

7,641. Jennison Family
Papers. 1729-1860. 16 ms. boxes, 35 octavo vols., and 1 folder.
Open. Published and unpublished guides.

American Antiquarian Society.
Correspondence, diaries, sermons, poetry, and research notes of this family, who were residents of Worcester and other Massachusetts towns, including an 1848-49 diary in which Ann Elizabeth (Jennison) Barton (1827-69), just before and after her marriage to William Sumner Barton, records her personal, social, familial, and religious life. See *Catalog of Manuscripts of the American Antiquarian Society* (Boston: G. K. Hall & Co., 1979).

7,642. Kent Family
Papers. 1787-1890. 1 folder.
Open. Published and unpublished guides.
American Antiquarian Society.
Correspondence concerns mundane matters in the life of members of the family of William Austin Kent (1765-1840) of Concord, NH. Principal correspondents are Kent, his first wife Charlotte Mellen Kent (1768-1820), his second wife Mary Tucker Kent (1776?-1833), and his daughter Rebecca Prentiss (Kent) Packard (1808-1905). See *Catalog of Manuscripts of the American Antiquarian Society* (Boston: G. K. Hall & Co., 1979).

7,643. Lambert Family
Papers. 1821-87. 1 folder.
Open. Published and unpublished guides.
American Antiquarian Society.
Business papers and correspondence of this family which emigrated to the US from England in the 1820s, settling in Newburyport and East Cambridge, MA. Written by family members and friends to one another and to a relative in England, the letters contain impressions of American life and descriptions of travel to California and to Washington, DC. The women's letters include random comments on well-known contemporary figures in literature and education and on the abolitionist and temperance movements. See *Catalog of Manuscripts of the American Antiquarian Society* (Boston: G. K. Hall & Co., 1979).

7,644. Larned Family
Papers. 1753-1859. 12 ms. boxes, 1 octavo vol., 1 folio vol., and 1 oversize vol.
Open. Published and unpublished guides.
American Antiquarian Society.
Correspondence, business papers, and other papers of Larned family members of Oxford, MA, and of Providence, RI, some of whom spelled the name Learned, including an 1859 diary in which Elizabeth Rand Larned (1820-80) of Oxford notes her daily activities and the weather. See *Catalog of Manuscripts of the American Antiquarian Society* (Boston: G. K. Hall & Co., 1979).

7,645. Lee, Sarah
Papers. 1834-48. 4 octavo vols.
Open. Published and unpublished guides.
American Antiquarian Society.
Diaries of Lee (?-1850), the daughter of John Lee, are interleaved in Robert B. Thomas, *The (Old) Farmer's Almanack, Calculated on a New and Improved Plan* (Boston: 1834, 1843, 1844, and 1848), and were written from the Boston home where Sarah Lee continued to live with her sister Rebecca after their father's death in 1841. The diaries indicate that much of Sarah Lee's time was spent in religious study, for there are numerous Biblical references in addition to notes on the number of visits received from clergymen. Other social events such as attendance at evening lectures and concerts are also recorded. See *Catalog of Manuscripts of the American Antiquarian Society* (Boston: G. K. Hall & Co., 1979).

7,646. Leicester Academy
Records. 1784-1963. 2 ms. boxes, 3 octavo vols., and 3 folio vols.
Open. Published and unpublished guides.
American Antiquarian Society.
Established in 1784 in Leicester, MA, as a private coeducational institution, the Academy was leased in 1921 to the town as public high school and in ca. 1940 it became a junior college. Trustee records for the entire period include minutes, legal documents, financial records and treasurers' reports, correspondence, and other material. Found with the school records are 1798-1824 records of the Social Fraternity of the Academy, a student organization which promoted declamation, and 1908-18 records of the Alumni Association. See *Catalog of Manuscripts of the American Antiquarian Society* (Boston: G. K. Hall & Co., 1979).

7,647. Lincoln Family
Papers. 1667-1937. 12 ms. boxes, 65 octavo vols., 39 folio vols., and 1 oversize vol.
Open. Published and unpublished guides.
American Antiquarian Society.
Correspondence, diaries, genealogical papers, legal and business documents, farm account books, speeches and addresses, poetry, and historical notes of a prominent Maine and Massachusetts family of lawyers, politicians, farmers, druggists, and historians. Included are account books, which were kept by Martha (Waldo) Lincoln (1761-1828), wife of Levi Lincoln, Sr., for a farm in Worcester and a farm account book and general store daybook kept by both Martha Lincoln and her husband. Also included is correspondence of William Sever Lincoln (1811-89), his wife Elizabeth (Trumbull) Lincoln (1816-1900), and their son William Lincoln (1839-69); Trumbull family correspondence; and correspondence of Fanny (Chandler) Lincoln (1852-1939). See *Catalog of Manuscripts of the American Antiquarian Society* (Boston: G. K. Hall & Co., 1979).

7,648. Marble, Annie Russell
Papers. 1888-1929. 1 folder.
Open. Published and unpublished guides.
American Antiquarian Society.
Correspondence of [Mrs.] Marble (1864-1936), an author, teacher, lecturer, and Worcester civic leader, consists of brief notes of greeting, permission to include published verses in forthcoming publications, regrets and acceptances of lecture invitations, and several brief autobiographical notes from literary figures. Correspondents include Willa Cather, Julia (Ward) Howe, Jane (Goodwin) Austin, Ellen Louise (Chandler) Moulton, and Thomas Wentworth Higginson. Marble assembled the letters for their autograph value and for the insight they provide students of chirography, psychology, and personality. See *Catalog of Manuscripts of the American Antiquarian Society* (Boston: G. K. Hall & Co., 1979).

7,649. May, Sophia
Papers. 1800-12. 1 folder.
Open. Published and unpublished guides.
American Antiquarian Society.
Correspondence of May (1784-1870), a Boston resident who was daughter of Colonel John May (1748-1812) and Abigail May (1754-1824), is addressed to May's mother and two of her sisters: Mary Davenport May (1793-1869) and Charlotte Augusta May (1795-1873). Written primarily from Alexandria, VA, or Washington, DC, although a few were from New York, Philadelphia, and Baltimore, the letters provide descriptions of local events, news of numerous visitors, May's impressions of the cities' architecture, and commentary on southern social customs. An 1807 series of more personal letters were written to her sisters in the form of a journal. See *Catalog of Manuscripts of the American Antiquarian Society* (Boston: G. K. Hall & Co., 1979).

7,650. Merrick Family
Papers. 1776-1903. 2 folders.
Open. Published and unpublished guides.
American Antiquarian Society.
Family correspondence and business papers generated by Pliny Merrick (1755-1814) and his wife Ruth Cutler Merrick (1770-1841), who were residents of Brookfield and Worcester, MA, as well as by their children, grandchildren, and friends. Included are instructions on deportment by Pliny Merrick to his daughter Maria (Merrick) [Mrs. Samuel, Jr.] Allen (1790-?), letters in verse by Nancy (Merrick) [Mrs. Henry] Miller (1797-1843), letters by Sarah Reed Merrick (1832-54) about trips to Nantasket, MA, letters to Frances (Fiske) Lincoln, descriptions by Frances Williams Allen of the expansion of Worcester, and letters concerning Worcester social affairs. See *Catalog of Manuscripts of the American Antiquarian Society* (Boston: G. K. Hall & Co., 1979).

7,651. Moulton, Ellen Louise (Chandler)
Papers. Nd. 2 ms. boxes.
Open. Published and unpublished guides.
American Antiquarian Society.
Papers of [Mrs. William Upham] Moulton (1835-1908), an author and literary hostess, consist of correspondence, mostly to her; manuscripts of her poems, a short story, reviews, and an incomplete account of an 1883 trip to Spain; and printed matter such as poems by English authors, clippings, and notes. The manuscripts of Moulton's poems were graded by Herbert Edwin Clarke, the English poet and literary critic, and perhaps by Louise Imogen Guiney. In addition, John Miller Dow Meiklejohn, a Scottish educator, wrote criticisms of some of Moulton's poetry, which are filed with his letters to her. Also included are letters about Moulton to Lilian Whiting, author of the biography *Louise Chandler Moulton, Poet and Friend,* and a brief essay on Moulton by Coulson Kernahan, an English author. See *Catalog of Manuscripts of the American Antiquarian Society* (Boston: G. K. Hall & Co., 1979).

7,652. Nason, Elias
Papers. 1831-84. 1 ms. box and 4 octavo vols.
Open. Published and unpublished guides.
American Antiquarian Society.
Correspondence of Nason (1811-87), a teacher, writer, lecturer, and Congregational clergyman, includes a few letters from his fiancée Mira Anne Bigelow. See *Catalog of Manuscripts of the American Antiquarian Society* (Boston: G. K. Hall & Co., 1979).

7,653. Newton, MA
Collection. 1749-1869. 1 ms. box and 1 octavo vol.
Open. Published and unpublished guides.
American Antiquarian Society.
Real estate valuation lists, legal documents, land surveys, and other local material including school records: a volume kept by Charlotte Ann Bruce (1819-?) which contains rules of the Newton Female Academy and an 1839-44 list of students and their home towns; student lists for Keene Academy in New Hampshire, Hadley Seminary in Massachusetts, and Fulton Female Seminary in New York; and an 1838 letter of appreciation written by Bruce to her teachers. See *Catalog of Manuscripts of the American Antiquarian Society* (Boston: G. K. Hall & Co., 1979).

7,654. Nichols, Charles Lemuel
Papers. 1851-1927. 6 ms. boxes, 2 folio vols., and 7 octavo vols.
Open. Published and unpublished guides.
American Antiquarian Society.
Papers of Nichols (1851-1929), a Worcester physician, bibliographer, and collector of early printed works, include correspondence from his mother Lydia Carter Nichols (?-1888) and his father Lemuel Bliss Nichols (1816-83), entries by

Nichols's sister Anna Lewis Nichols (?-1934) in the *Bryant Birthday Book of Verses* (1882) on family events and anniversaries between 1882 and 1896, research notes, scholarly papers, speeches, and genealogical items. See *Catalog of Manuscripts of the American Antiquarian Society* (Boston: G. K. Hall & Co., 1979).

7,655. Oread Institute School of Domestic Science
Records. 1904. 1050-page folio vol.
Open. Published and unpublished guides.
American Antiquarian Society.
Correspondence of the School, founded in 1898 in Worcester by Henry D. Perky to train young women to become domestic science teachers, consists of letters of [Mrs.] Harriet A. Higbee, the School's principal, concerning her administrative duties, letters of recommendation for students, informative letters to prospective students, and reports to Perky of the School's activities and progress. Also included are personal letters providing news of the School to former students and friends. The School offered a one-year program with such courses as sewing, cooking, laundry, marketing, psychology, pedagogy, elocution, chemistry, and physiology. The School ceased operation in 1904. Its founder, Perky, was the inventor of shredded wheat and president of the National Food Company in Niagara Falls, NY. See *Catalog of Manuscripts of the American Antiquarian Society* (Boston: G. K. Hall & Co., 1979).

7,656. Osborn, Sarah
Papers. 1747-77. 1 folder.
Open. Published and unpublished guides.
American Antiquarian Society.
Correspondence from [Mrs. Henry] Osborn (1714-96), a teacher who founded and until her death was head of a female religious society in Newport, RI, is addressed to Joseph Fish, a North Stonington, CT, minister, and is filled with religious reflection and speculation on the state of her soul. The letters also contain information on Osborn's teaching, her involvement in her female religious society, and her prayer meetings with Negroes and young men of Newport. Her school and prayer meetings were so popular that she supported herself with these endeavors. In addition, collection contains one 1777 letter recounting the British occupation of and then withdrawal from Newport. See *Catalog of Manuscripts of the American Antiquarian Society* (Boston: G. K. Hall & Co., 1979).

7,657. Osgood, Frances Sargent (Locke)
Papers. 1836-1942. 1 folder.
Open. Published and unpublished guides.
American Antiquarian Society.
Papers of [Mrs. Samuel Stillman] Osgood (1811-50), a poet and author, consist of a short story by her, a brief journal in Osgood's hand about her three-week-old daughter Ellen Frances Osgood, correspondence, a clipping about several poems of Edgar Allan Poe, and other items and memorabilia. Also included are letters asking Osgood's grandniece for information about Osgood. See *Catalog of Manuscripts of the American Antiquarian Society* (Boston: G. K. Hall & Co., 1979).

7,658. Page Family
Papers. 1823-64. 4 octavo vols.
Open. Published and unpublished guides.
American Antiquarian Society.
Residents of Danvers, MA, Mary Page (1806-94) and her sister Martha Crosby Page (1808-32) attended Saugus Seminary in Saugus, MA, and Adams Female Seminary in Danvers; in 1831 Mary Page married Alfred Putnam (1804-35) of Danvers. The sisters' commonplace books contain remembrance verses written for graduation and signed by school friends, verses written by relatives and friends in later years, poetry by Martha Crosby Page on such topics as "The Sky" and "The Lover's Serenade," and quotations from Sir Walter Scott and other poets. In addition, Mary Page included color sketches of flowers and birds, while her sister wrote brief stanzas on each monarch of England beginning with William the Conqueror. Collection also includes an 1853 commonplace book kept by a Martha Page, probably a relative, while she was a student at Bradford Female Academy in Bradford, MA. See *Catalog of Manuscripts of the American Antiquarian Society* (Boston: G. K. Hall & Co., 1979).

7,659. Paine Family
Papers. Ca. 1721-1918. 9 ms. boxes, 50 octavo vols., and 20 folio vols.
Open. Published and unpublished guides.
American Antiquarian Society.
Correspondence, diaries, account books, and other business papers, medical documents, court records, genealogical notes, and library catalogs of four generations of the Worcester family, beginning with Timothy Paine (1730-93), a 1748 graduate of Harvard College, an American Loyalist who remained in the US through the Revolution, and an active civic leader in Worcester. Correspondence includes that of members of the Sturgis, Chandler, Perkins, and Rose families who married into the Paine family; some of the letters concern business and trading interests of various family members. Also included is personal correspondence between family members, both male and female, and with friends. See *Catalog of Manuscripts of the American Antiquarian Society* (Boston: G. K. Hall & Co., 1979).

7,660. Park Family
Papers. 1800-90. 234-page octavo vol. and 1 folder.
Open. Published and unpublished guides.
American Antiquarian Society.
Correspondence, diary, poetry, and legal documents of John Park (1775-1852), a physician, of his first wife Louisa (Adams) Park (1773-1813), of his second wife Agnes (Major) Park, and of his children author Louisa Jane (Park) Hall (1802-92), John Cochran Park (1804-?), and Mary Ann (Park) Thomas (1811-?). The family lived in Newburyport, Boston, and Worcester, MA. The 1800-01 diary of Louisa (Adams) Park, which was copied by Dr. Park in 1848 and into which he also copied several letters she wrote him during those years, consists of a stream-of-consciousness description of her daily life and thoughts while Dr. Park was away from home; it includes commentaries on the various medical treatments prescribed to and the eventual death of her infant son, references to the French Revolution and to Thomas Jefferson, descriptions of trips to neighboring towns, details of her dreams, and comments on her life in Windham, NH, and Acton and Salisbury, MA. Collection also includes poetry written by Dr. Park, Agnes Park, and the three children; letters to Dr. Park from his daughter Louisa; letters from Agnes Park to her stepchildren; and letters from Louisa Jane (Park) Hall to her stepsons on social events in Boston, church sermons, her son's precarious health, new household furnishings, rare books, and an 1832 meeting in Boston at which the rights of the Cherokee Indians in Georgia were defended. See *Catalog of Manuscripts of the American Antiquarian Society* (Boston: G. K. Hall & Co., 1979).

7,661. Parkman Family
Papers. 1707-1879. 13 octavo vols., 3 ms. boxes.
Open. Published and unpublished guides.
American Antiquarian Society.
Correspondence, diaries, account books, legal documents, sermons, ecclesiastical papers, and genealogical information of Ebenezer Parkman (1703-82), a minister in Westborough, MA. Includes a 150-page memorial he wrote to Sarah (Breck) Pierpont, the daughter of Nathaniel and Martha Cunnable Breck of Boston, who married James Pierpont, Jr., of New Haven, CT. Parkman's memorial includes 1730s-40s extracts from Pierpont's diary on her spiritual wellbeing. See *Catalog of Manuscripts of the American Antiquarian Society* (Boston: G. K. Hall & Co., 1979).

7,662. Peabody, Stephen
Papers. 1767-1814. 13 octavo vols. and 1 folder.
Open. Published and unpublished guides.
American Antiquarian Society.
Diaries, notes, account book, and clippings of Peabody (1741-1819), a minister of the First Congregational Church of Atkinson, NH, and founder in 1787 of the Atkinson Academy. The diaries contain references to the Academy, which first started with a few scholars living in the parsonage and taking lessons with Peabody. After obtaining incorporation for the Academy, he built a building for the school which he ran with the help of his second wife Elizabeth (Smith) [Mrs. John] Shaw Peabody (1750-1815). When Peabody's daughter insisted on attending the Academy, he admitted her and other females, the result of which was that the Academy was then credited with being the first coeducational school of its type. Diary entries provide extensive details of the administration of the Academy and of the controversies which characterized it. Peabody's account book and diary also reveal the financial arrangements he made with those Academy scholars who boarded with him. Later diaries include descriptions of visits the Peabodys made with former President John Adams and his wife Abigail (Smith) Adams, who was Elizabeth Peabody's sister. See *Catalog of Manuscripts of the American Antiquarian Society* (Boston: G. K. Hall & Co., 1979).

7,663. Perkins, Susanna
Papers. 1786-1804. 56-page octavo vol.
Open. Published and unpublished guides.
American Antiquarian Society.
Volume of 61 songs with lyrics and music compiled by Perkins (1757-?), a resident of Bridgewater, MA, who may have been the daughter of Jonathan Perkins and, later, wife of Robert Howard of Bridgewater. In many cases, the composer is not mentioned for the songs which include "Christmas Hymn," "Appearance," "Andover," and religious hymns. See *Catalog of Manuscripts of the American Antiquarian Society* (Boston: G. K. Hall & Co., 1979).

7,664. Philadelphia, PA
Collection. 1752-1864. 1 ms. box, 1 octavo vol.
Open. Published and unpublished guides.
American Antiquarian Society.
Financial records, bills of lading, legal documents, records of various societies, and petitions, including an 1830 petition signed by 30 women requesting better wages for seamstresses who did piecework in their homes and another petition signed by 24 men supporting the women's petition.

7,665. Poetry
Collection. 1778-1862. 3 octavo vols. and 1 folder.
Open. Published and unpublished guides.
American Antiquarian Society.
Poems on religion, death, politics, childhood, and other subjects are for the most part anonymous, undated, untitled, and unpublished. Included is a collection of poems by Elizabeth (Paine) Trumbull, youngest daughter of Timothy and Sarah (Chandler) Paine of Worcester, which were copied by her grandson George Clap Trumbull in 1834 and which may have been published in the *Massachusetts Spy*. Elizabeth Trumbull's poems reveal that she was well educated; they include references to "Negroes in arms," which appears to be an allusion to Nat Turner; to events in Belgium

and Poland; and to members of the Perkins family of Boston. One of the poems was written to her brother Samuel Paine, an American Loyalist who fled to England. See *Catalog of Manuscripts of the American Antiquarian Society* (Boston: G. K. Hall & Co., 1979).

7,666. Powell, Lois (Fay)

Papers. 1915-58. 2 ms. boxes.
Open. Published and unpublished guides.
American Antiquarian Society.
Daughter of Annah C. Harthan Fay (1853-1938) of Princeton, MA, and a conservationist, Powell (1883-1960) spent 33 years as custodian of the Minns Wildlife Reservation, a sanctuary on Little Wachusett Mountain in Princeton which was given to the state of Massachusetts by Susan Minns of Boston, subject to a life interest by Powell. Supervising the Reservation, Powell developed a deep interest in botany, ornithology, and soil conservation; she frequently wrote articles for newspapers and journals on these subjects. Material gathered by Powell concerning the Reservation includes correspondence with conservation officials, scientists, and Susan Minns; diary entries on Powell's life as caretaker, writings on the early history of Princeton and Mt. Wachusett; maps and photos of the area; and scrapbooks. See *Catalog of Manuscripts of the American Antiquarian Society* (Boston: G. K. Hall & Co., 1979).

7,667. Prang, Louis

Papers. 1856-1921. 1 folder.
Open. Published and unpublished guides.
American Antiquarian Society.
Business correspondence and papers of Prang (1824-1909), a Boston lithographer, and of his second wife Mary Amelia (Dana) Hicks Prang (1836-1937), an art educator. In 1882 Louis Prang established the Prang Educational Company which published drawing books that came to be widely used in schools. Mary Prang worked with him for the Company, and together they established the Prang Normal Art Classes. Included are weekly advertising newsletters sent to Company customers in the US and Canada; correspondence and notices regarding the Centennial Celebration of the Invention of Lithography, held in Philadelphia in 1896, notes about establishing a school for lithography, 1905-08 letters from David Paterson of Scotland to the Prangs with detailed accounts of his work color dyeing with chemicals, and a 1921 application and resume of Mary Prang for a master's degree at Harvard University. See *Catalog of Manuscripts of the American Antiquarian Society* (Boston: G. K. Hall & Co., 1979).

7,668. Randolph Academy

Records. 1835-37. 28-page octavo vol.
Open. Published and unpublished guides.
American Antiquarian Society.
Arranged by seasonal terms and by its male, female, and primary departments, this account book of the Academy lists pupils, their parents' or guardians' names, and tuition charges. In operation from 1833 to 1842 in Randolph, MA, the Academy had a student body of 75 to 100 secondary school pupils. See *Catalog of Manuscripts of the American Antiquarian Society* (Boston: G. K. Hall & Co., 1979).

7,669. Reed, Elizabeth Freeman

Papers. 1929-40. 2 folders.
Open. Published and unpublished guides.
American Antiquarian Society.
A resident of Boothbay Harbor, ME, Reed (1874-?) was president of the Daughters of Colonial Wars and regent of the Pemaquid chapter of the DAR. Notes pertaining to the history of Maine, particularly of Boothbay Harbor and the Pemaquid area, apparently were written or compiled by Reed for the purpose of writing a history of the area. Included is information copied from archives, newspapers, and books on Boothbay Harbor legends; letters written by residents during the American Revolution, the War of 1812, and the Civil War; lists of and official documents pertaining to area soldiers who served during those wars; notes on a 1778 town meeting; and genealogical studies of the Beath, Fullerton, Cowden, and Sawyer families. Also included are copies Reed made of the diary of Jeremiah Person of Essex County, Massachusetts Bay, which was written during his expedition to Quebec in 1749, and of the constitution and 1846 bylaws of the Franklin Forensic Association of Boothbay Harbor. Included as well are articles Reed wrote, probably for publication, including "The Rebel Cruiser *Shenandoah* and the Ships Which She Sank," "Notes on the Anti-Slavery Movement in Maine," and "Rev. Robert Blair, Quaker Preacher and Teacher of Falmouth, Maine." See *Catalog of Manuscripts of the American Antiquarian Society* (Boston: G. K. Hall & Co., 1979).

7,670. Riccius Family

Papers. 1856-1937. 1 folder.
Open. Published and unpublished guides.
American Antiquarian Society.
Material centers on the life in Millbury, Webster, and Worcester, MA, during the 1890s of German immigrant Adolf Gustav Riccius (1841-95?), his wife Ida Adelia (Barton) Riccius (1847-1911) who was a niece of Clara Barton, and the Ricciuses' four children. A 46-page history, written in 1937 by the Ricciuses' oldest child Edith (Riccius) King (1881?-) provides family information through anecdotes as well as descriptions of schools, fashions, housing problems, neighborhoods, Worcester's first telephone and electric cars, interesting town characters, and adjustments to life in Worcester. Also included are Adolf Riccius's notebook account, written in German, of his 1856 voyage to America; an 1856 list of rules and items needed for a voyage; the Ricciuses' 1879 marriage certificate; photos of Adolf and Ida Adelia Riccius; a memorial to Ida Adelia Riccius, written by Clara Barton; and other items. After receiving most of Clara Barton's papers, another daughter Saidee F. Riccius (?-1959) helped organize biographical studies of and memorials to her great-aunt. See *Catalog of Manuscripts of the American Antiquarian Society* (Boston: G. K. Hall & Co., 1979).

7,671. Ripley, Sally

Papers. 1799-1809. 118-page octavo vol.
Open. Published and unpublished guides.
American Antiquarian Society.
Diary of Ripley (1785-?), daughter of merchant and civic and social leader Jerome Ripley of Greenfield, MA, contains entries made before her marriage in 1812 to merchant Charles Stearns (1781-1818) of Shelburne, MA, and the births of their four children. Recording her activities, particularly visits made and visitors received, the diary also includes many of Sally Ripley's school recitations in history, geography, and astronomy; copies of skits performed during her school days; descriptions of the memorial services held in Deerfield, MA, on the death of George Washington as well as of trips to Boston to visit relatives; and poems and extracts on various topics, primarily spiritual, which Ripley took from books and newspapers. Available on microfilm. See *Catalog of Manuscripts of the American Antiquarian Society* (Boston: G. K. Hall & Co., 1979).

7,672. Rockwell, John Arnold

Papers. 1798-1867. 3 ms. boxes.
Open. Published and unpublished guides.
American Antiquarian Society.
Rockwell (1803-61) was a lawyer, Connecticut state politician, and president of the Norwich & Worcester Railroad Company. Correspondence, business papers, legal documents, and personal papers of Rockwell and of other family members, including a diary mentioning the activities of John Rockwell and of his brother and a ca. 1805-30s account book attributed to his aunt Betsey Rockwell (1762-1847), who raised him and his brother in Norwich, CT, after the death of their mother when John Rockwell was an infant. The account book records personal expenses as well as information on a small business selling milk and butter. See *Catalog of Manuscripts of the American Antiquarian Society* (Boston: G. K. Hall & Co., 1979).

7,673. Rogers Family

Papers. 1731-85. 2 octavo vols.
Open. Published and unpublished guides.
American Antiquarian Society.
Diary of the daily activities during 1731 of Daniel Rogers (1707-85), a 1725 Harvard graduate who was born in Ipswich, MA, and a tutor and itinerant preacher before he was established in 1748 as minister of the Second Church in Exeter, NH. The diary of his daughter Martha "Patty" Rogers (1761-1840), an Exeter resident who apparently never married, reveals her daily activities as well as intimate thoughts; in it, she expresses concern for her sickly father and frustration over having to care for him. She also describes her social life with details about her courting relationships with two men. See *Catalog of Manuscripts of the American Antiquarian Society* (Boston: G. K. Hall & Co., 1979).

7,674. Ruff, Deborah (Pratt)

Papers. 1761-76. 61-page octavo vol.
Open. Published and unpublished guides.
American Antiquarian Society.
Poetry by Ruff (1746-96) contains many topical verses in addition to poems dedicated to living and dead friends and expressions of sentiment. Daughter of Henry and Rebecca Claypoole Pratt of Philadelphia and sister of artist Matthew Pratt (1734-1805), Deborah Pratt married Daniel Ruff, a minister in Abington, MD, in ca. 1770. See *Catalog of Manuscripts of the American Antiquarian Society* (Boston: G. K. Hall & Co., 1979).

7,675. Scofield, James Monroe

Papers. 1823-1923. 22 folio vols. and 6 ms. boxes.
Open. Published and unpublished guides.
American Antiquarian Society.
Correspondence, diaries, and account books of Scofield (1824-71), a merchant in Stockton, CA, then newspaper editor and publisher in Connecticut, and then insurance agent in Worcester. Included are diaries of his wife Madilia Ney Houche Scofield (1830-1913) for the years 1856 in Stockton and 1870-72 in Worcester, all of which concern mundane matters until after the death of her husband when she became introspective and wrote at length about her expectation that he would be resurrected; also included are some financial accounts and a journal of her trip in 1877 to Europe with her children. Collection also contains papers of James Scofield's daughter Florence Madilia (Scofield) Thayer (1858-1936); her 1876-77 diary, kept while she was a student at Wellesley College, is included along with correspondence from fellow College students, written after she left Wellesley to travel abroad with her family, and her account of the European trip. See *Catalog of Manuscripts of the American Antiquarian Societv* (Boston: G. K. Hall & Co., 1979).

7,676. Seccomb Family

Papers. 1753-70. 45-page octavo vol.
Open. Published and unpublished guides.
American Antiquarian Society.
John Seccomb (1708-92) served as first minister of Harvard, MA, from 1733 until he was dismissed from the post in 1757; then in 1759 he accompanied the first settlers to Chester, Lunenburg County, Nova Scotia, where he settled

with his family. His wife was Mercy Williams Seccomb, granddaughter of clergyman Solomon Stoddard (1643-1729). Collection consists of copies of John Seccomb's 1759 diary and of the 1753-70 diary of his daughter Mercy Seccomb (1743/44-?), the originals of which are in the Nova Scotia Historical Society. Mercy Seccomb's diary contains sporadic entries on family events such as illnesses, marriages, visitors, laborers, travels, and her father's activities, as well as descriptions of her moods. See *Catalog of Manuscripts of the American Antiquarian Society* (Boston: G. K. Hall & Co., 1979).

7,677. Shaw and Webb Family
Papers. 1756-1936. 10 ms. boxes.
Open. Published and unpublished guides.
American Antiquarian Society.
Correspondence, poems, business papers, recipes, and printed matter of five generations of the family of Anna Leonard (Stetson) Smith Shaw (1766-1847) of Dighton, MA, which eventually settled in Bucksport and Bangor, ME, and Atkinson, NH. Anna Shaw's daughters Nancy Leonard (Smith) Peabody (1785-1856), Harriet (Smith) Goodnow (1787-1869), Maria B. (Smith) Noyes (1790-1875), Emma Augusta (Shaw) Hobbs (1792?-1875), and Hannah King (Shaw) Webb (1800-75) are among the family members who corresponded extensively between themselves, their children, their grandchildren, and friends on such matters as family births, marriages, illnesses, and the intemperance of several relatives.
Correspondence of Anna Shaw includes letters she wrote during the War of 1812 describing the British march up the Penobscot River near her home. Correspondence of Augusta Maria (Noyes) Stover (1817-71) includes detailed letters about her travels around Cape Horn with her sea captain husband and sightseeing in Malaga, Gibraltar, Liverpool, London, and Washington, DC. Copious correspondence of Anna Leonard (Webb) Farris (1821-68) not only concerns her courtship with Thomas C. Farris but also provides information on her suffering from consumption and search for a variety of cures. Ann Mary Hobbs in her letters refers to abolitionist lectures, lectures of William Makepeace Thackeray, and her visit to the 1876 Philadelphia Centennial Exposition.

Correspondents include Mary H. Silsby, writing of her life in Chico, CA, during the 1850s; Henrietta (perhaps Henrietta S. White), who was involved in Universalism in Chicago; Margaret (Tinkham) Peabody, commenting on the Civil War and the need for emancipation; Maine's first US Senator John Holmes, who refers to his controversial courtship of Caroline F. (Knox) Swan, daughter of Revolutionary War General Henry Knox; Maria Antoinette Meservey of Bangor, an 1863 graduate of the New England Female Medical College in Boston, who writes of her struggle to gain acceptance as a doctor in the small southern town of Bridgeville, DE, in 1866-67, referring to the "excesses" of black freedmen and detailing her own medical methods in contrast to the "barbarous" obstetrical practices of southern black women; and Nancy (Colburn) Hartford, who traveled to Pike's Peak, Colorado Territory, to join her husband in his search for wealth. Besides including frequent references to the Civil War, Nancy Hartford's 1860-64 letters to her mother in Maine contain descriptions of her trip through New York City on her way West, of the Colorado scenery, her life in a log cabin, and pioneer life in Russell's Gulch.

7,678. Sibley, Lucretia Cargill Carter
Papers. 1841-76. 2 folders.
Open. Published and unpublished guides.
American Antiquarian Society.
A resident of Uxbridge, MA, and Providence, RI, in 1819 Lucretia Carter married Royal Sibley (1793-1822); their children were George Henry Sibley (1821-?) and Anna Maria (Sibley) Hovey (1822-65), who was wife of Congregational missionary George Lewis Hovey (1810-ca. 1878). Correspondence to Lucretia Sibley and Anna Hovey is primarily from cousins Mary Ann Waterman of Clear Branch, VA; Samary Stedman Sherman (1785-?) of Sterling Bottom, OH; and from their children who settled in various parts of Kansas, Illinois, and Missouri. Letters contain family news and vital statistics, comments on the weather and crops, religious verses, land and housing policies, recipes, and cures for various diseases, including consumption. Also included are descriptions of the Waterman and Sherman children's pioneering in Kansas and Illinois and of Indian troubles and crop failures as well as references to temperance, the coming of the railroads, and the importance of the nativist movement.

Many of these letters from northern and southern cousins contain allusions to the Civil War era with descriptions of slave beatings and rentals, and references to Harper's Ferry, Lincoln's election, the outbreak of war, secession troubles in St. Joseph, MO, and enlistments of family members. In addition, letters contain frequent defenses of slavery by Mary Waterman in response to abolitionist tracts Lucretia Sibley sent her, Waterman's reading of *Uncle Tom's Cabin,* and an explanation of her belief that the South needed better roads and schools. Letters only from the northern cousins are included for the period from 1862 until the end of the War; these include comments on the War's progress and deaths in battle of family members and a copy Samary Sherman made for Lucretia Sibley of the last letter Sherman's grandson Lyman White (?-1864) wrote describing in detail the battle of Ball's Bluff. Postwar letters written by cousins from both the North and South refer to their growing families, the many improvements in Kansas after the 1850s, and a trip to the Philadelphia Centennial Exposition. See *Catalog of Manuscripts of the American Antiquarian Society* (Boston: G. K. Hall & Co., 1979).

7,679. Smith, Elizabeth
Papers. 1820-54. 186-page octavo vol.
Open. Published and unpublished guides.
American Antiquarian Society.
In her diary, Smith (1773-1854), a devout Episcopalian who lived in Worcester, records sermons she heard and lists texts and preachers of morning and afternoon services she attended in Worcester, Boston, Templeton, Weston, and Milton, MA. She also makes personal observations which are primarily religious in substance. See *Catalog of Manuscripts of the American Antiquarian Society* (Boston: G. K. Hall & Co., 1979).

7,680. Smith, Josephine McCurdy Caroline (Lord)
Papers. Ca. 1840-1909. 1 octavo vol. and 1 folder.
Open. Published and unpublished guides.
American Antiquarian Society.
After marrying Charles Worcester Smith (1828-83) in 1856 in her hometown of Canton, IL, Josephine Smith (1834-1910) moved to Worcester where her husband was a millowner, railroad director, and bank president. Autobiographical reminiscences by Smith for her children contain descriptions of the Lord family's overland trip to Illinois from Lyme, CT, in ca. 1840, life in a log cabin, farming, raising livestock, household chores, and her courtship, marriage, and move to Worcester. Also included are a long poem written in tribute to Smith and her ancestors in Lyme by Chauncey Wetmore Wells, a professor at Yale University; a biography of Smith, which was written by her friend Mary E. Wills Kellogg of Canton; and letters of condolence from friends and relatives on the death of Smith's husband. See *Catalog of Manuscripts of the American Antiquarian Society* (Boston: G. K. Hall & Co., 1979).

7,681. Spofford, Harriet Elizabeth (Prescott)
Papers. 1885-1936. 1 folder.
Open. Published and unpublished guides.
American Antiquarian Society.
A prolific writer of fiction and poetry for late 19th-century periodicals, Prescott (1835-1921) married Richard Smith Spofford Jr. (?-1888) in 1865 and lived for a while in Washington, DC, before establishing a home on Deer Island, near Newburyport, MA. Poems by her husband and "Thy Law" by Harriet Spofford; a foreword to a book of her verse that was to have been published posthumously; and correspondence, most of which was written to her friend Herbert Edwin Lombard, a minister in Newbury and Worcester, MA, who was a bibliographer and collector of bookplates; and to his mother Nellie Montimorenci de Callahan Lombard. Letters refer to daily concerns; visits; bookplates Spofford sent Rev. Lombard; descriptions of Deer Island, Newburyport, and Washington, DC; and Spofford's opinions of her own poetry and that of other poets, particularly John Greenleaf Whittier. See *Catalog of Manuscripts of the American Antiquarian Society* (Boston: G. K. Hall & Co., 1979).

7,682. Stoddard, Richard Henry
Papers. 1852-1900. 1 folder.
Open. Published and unpublished guides.
American Antiquarian Society.
Correspondence of Stoddard (1825-1903), an author, includes 1890s letters by his wife Elizabeth Drew (Barstow) Stoddard (1823-1902), a poet and author, concerning her literary works and efforts to have them published. See *Catalog of Manuscripts of the American Antiquarian Society* (Boston: G. K. Hall & Co., 1979).

7,683. Stoughton, Sarah Josephine
Papers. 1869-70. 64-page octavo vol. and 4 items.
Open. Published and unpublished guides.
American Antiquarian Society.
After birth in Jaffrey, NH, Stoughton (1848-71), the daughter of farmer Samuel Stoughton (1815-91), lived with her family in Gill, MA. In her diary, written just prior to her death from tuberculosis, she discusses close friends and family members, daily activities, visits made and received, letters written and received, domestic chores performed, the state of her health, political issues such as woman suffrage, and such events as the 1869 flooding of the area. As her death approached, she increasingly made religious observations. Also included are clippings and genealogical data from the family Bible. See *Catalog of Manuscripts of the American Antiquarian Society* (Boston: G. K. Hall & Co., 1979).

7,684. Sullivan, Anne Mansfield
Papers. 1887-1902. 1 folder.
Open. Published and unpublished guides.
American Antiquarian Society.
[Miss] Sullivan (1866-1936) became the teacher of Helen Keller in 1887 shortly after graduating from the Perkins Institute for the Blind in South Boston. Letters to Michael Anagnos, director of the Institute who recommended Sullivan for the position, provide information on Keller's progress in reading, writing, and speaking during her early life in Tuscumbia, AL, with details on the methods Sullivan used to educate Keller; the gradual development of her disposition, imagination, and literary abilities; the publication of her first short stories; and remarks on her troubled homelife. Some letters refer to Sullivan's use of telegraphy to communicate with the handicapped, her feelings on the contributions which she as a woman made to special education, and her opinions on education of the deaf. Also included is Sullivan's instruction schedule, quotations from passages written by

Keller, details of trips they made together to Washington, DC, and Boston, and references to the financial affairs of the Institute. Sullivan later married John Albert Macy. See *Catalog of Manuscripts of the American Antiquarian Society* (Boston: G. K. Hall & Co., 1979).

7,685. Ticknor, Caroline
Papers. Ca. 1884-1930s. 2 ms. boxes.
Open. Published and unpublished guides.
American Antiquarian Society.
The granddaughter of William Davis Ticknor (1810-64), who founded the publishing house Ticknor & Fields, Caroline Ticknor (1866-1937) was a Boston author of books, plays, short stories, poetry, essays, and biographical sketches. Correspondence consisting of social notes, acknowledgments of receipt of one of her literary works, and a letter by a Mr. Taylor; manuscripts of poems, stories, plays, essays, and sketches; and a manuscript of the introduction which Ticknor wrote to the autobiography of Cornelia Gray Lunt, which was entitled *Sketches of Childhood and Girlhood, Chicago, 1847-1864* (Evanston, IL: 1925). See *Catalog of Manuscripts of the American Antiquarian Society* (Boston: G. K. Hall & Co., 1979).

7,686. Archives
Records. 1887- . 1000 ft.
Open. Unpublished guide.
Clark University Archives.
Minutes, financial records, correspondence, faculty and student records, scrapbooks, photos, and clippings of the University, founded in 1887. Includes information about women who have been graduate students at the University since 1900, members of the faculty since 1921, undergraduate students since 1942, administrators since 1943, and trustees since 1962.

7,687. Clark, Jonas Gilman, and Clark, Susan (Wright)
Papers. 1835-1931. 2.5 ft.
Open. Unpublished guide.
Clark University Archives.
Papers of Jonas Clark (1815-1900), a businessman who founded Clark University, include such papers of his wife Susan Clark (1816-1904) as an autograph album, 1835-37; a notebook, 1845-47; a daguerreotype; papers concerning the purchase of books and works of art; and papers, including clippings, pertaining to her role as executrix of her husband's estate and to her own estate.

7,688. Forbes, Esther
Papers. 1906-67. Ca. 250 items.
Open. No guide.
Clark University Library, Special Collections.
Correspondence, manuscripts, and miscellaneous papers relate to the writings of Forbes (1891-1967), an author.

7,689. Prouty, Olive Higgins
Papers. 1901-61. 12.5 ft.
Open. No guide.
Clark University Library, Special Collections.
Correspondence, a fictional autobiography, literary manuscripts, and related items of Prouty (1882-1974), a writer, include material concerning her book *Stella Dallas.*

7,690. Guiney, Louise Imogen
Papers. 1872-1920. 50 ft.
Open. Unpublished guide.
College of the Holy Cross Library.
[Miss] Guiney (1861-1920), who was born in Boston and lived in Auburndale, MA, and England, was a poet, essayist, editor, and compiler. Correspondence; diaries; manuscripts of poems, prose, and songs; notebooks; contracts with publishers; address books; photos; scrapbooks; and her published books, articles, sheet music, and contributions to anthologies. Includes correspondence with literary figures in the US, England, and Ireland, among them Ralph Adams Cram, Thomas W. Parsons, and Katherine Tynan.

7,691. Wayman, Dorothy (Godfrey)
Papers. 1862-1960. 9 ft.
Access restricted. No guide.
College of the Holy Cross Library.
[Mrs. Charles] Wayman (1893-1975) was a journalist, author, and biographer who worked as a reporter for the *Boston Globe* for many years. She has written articles on women in New England and Japan. Correspondence; a journal of her trip to the Far East in 1939; manuscripts of stories, articles, and books; notebooks; photos; and scrapbooks containing clippings of her articles. Also includes two diaries, one kept in 1891 by a woman traveling from Boston to her new home in California.

7,692. Kelley and Foster
Papers. 1837-93. 118 items.
Open. Published guide.
Worcester Historical Society.
Collection concerns Abby (Kelley) Foster (1810-87) and her conversion to the antislavery movement in 1837; her subsequent activities as an organizer of antislavery societies; her marriage in 1845 to Stephen S. Foster, who also was an abolitionist; and their experiences with the antislavery, woman suffrage, and prohibition movements. Correspondence, cash receipts, a Foster family cashbook for 1874 to 1886, a list of subscriptions to antislavery societies, travel expense accounts, a deed, a marriage certificate, and an address book. Collection also contains Abby Foster's written account of her work as an early abolitionist. See *Guide to the Manuscript Collections in the Worcester Historical Society* (Boston: Historical Records Survey, 1941).

YARMOUTH

7,693. Hallet, Bangs
Papers. 1859-69. 21 items.
Open. List.
Historical Society of Old Yarmouth.
Letters written to Hallet (1807-97), a sea captain, from Yarmouth and Fairhaven, MA, while he was en route to Calcutta; correspondents are his wife Anna Eldridge Hallet (1809-87), his daughter Amelia (Hallet) [Mrs. John] Hawes (1830-1906), and his daughter Anner (Hallet) [Mrs. Job] Tripp (1830-?). Also included are letters to Amelia Hawes. Correspondence reflects the Hallet women's religious activities, social life, and personal and family matters.

MICHIGAN

ADRIAN

7,694. History of the Adrian Dominican Sisters
Records. 1853- . No size given.
Partially restricted. No guide.
Adrian Dominican Sisters, Motherhouse.
Financial records, deeds of houses, correspondence, taped interviews, history, photos, slides, albums, and obituaries of deceased sisters. Includes letters of Mother Camilla Madden and Mother Augustine Walsh, the first mothers general; personal correspondence of Mother Gerald Barry and her letters to sisters during her administration from 1933 to 1961; and correspondence from bishops and priests relating to schools, hospitals, and other ministries of the Sisters. The order was first founded in the US in Williamsburg, NY, in 1853.

7,695. Adrian Woman's Club
Records. 1931-72. 8 vols.
Open. No guide.
Lenawee County Historical Society Museum.
Scrapbooks containing program yearbooks, clippings, and mementos of meetings and luncheons of the Club, a cultural group founded in ca. 1886. The Club is still extant.

7,696. Lenawee County Federation of Women's Clubs
Records. 1905-72. 5.5 ft.
Open. No guide.
Lenawee County Historical Society Museum.
Minutes, financial records, officers' reports, correspondence, registration lists, program yearbooks, and scrapbooks of the Federation in this agricultural, resort, and industrial county in Michigan. The Federation offers cultural programs and promotes various activities in the arts, homemaking, government affairs, and good citizenship.

ANN ARBOR

7,697. Adelia Cheever House
Records. 1924-54. 1 vol. and 10 items.
Open. Card catalog.
University of Michigan, Bentley Historical Library, Michigan Historical Collections.
Minutes of the board of patronesses and board of directors, financial records, and social directors' reports of this University of Michigan residence hall.

7,698. Aldinger, Ella H.
Papers. 1916-33. 35 items.
Open. Card catalog.
University of Michigan, Bentley Historical Library, Michigan Historical Collections.
Aldinger was president of the Michigan LWV and a member of the Legislative Council of Michigan Women. Correspondence, minutes of professional meetings, clippings, and printed material pertain to her activities on behalf of woman suffrage and social reform.

7,699. Allan, Virginia R.
Papers. 1963-75. 10 ft.
Open. Unpublished guide.
University of Michigan, Bentley Historical Library, Michigan Historical Collections.
Allan was a Wyandotte, MI, businesswoman, chairwoman of the President's Task Force on Women's Rights and Responsibilities, and deputy assistant to the secretary of state for public affairs during the Nixon administration. Collection includes material relating to her professional work and reflects her interests in women's rights, Republican party politics, the work of the National Federation of Business and Professional Women's Clubs, the Equal Rights Amendment, and International Women's Year in 1975.

7,700. American Association of University Women
Records. 1902-69. 2 ft.
Open. Card catalog.
University of Michigan, Bentley Historical Library, Michigan Historical Collections.
Minutes, financial records, membership lists, correspondence, and other material of the Ann Arbor and Ypsilanti branch of the AAUW.

7,701. Anderson, Faye Louise
Papers. 1945-47. 12 items.
Open. Card catalog.
University of Michigan, Bentley Historical Library, Michigan Historical Collections.
Correspondence in which Anderson describes to family and friends her experiences with the

American National Red Cross in New Guinea and in European countries during and after WWII.

7,702. Anderson, Katherine
Papers. 1916-21. 1 vol.
Open. Card catalog.
University of Michigan, Bentley Historical Library, Michigan Historical Collections.
Record book of [Mrs. George Potter] Anderson, who was a 1910 graduate of the University of Michigan, includes household and personal accounts of her life in Battle Creek, MI.

7,703. Andrews, Esther
Papers. 1847-50. 20 items.
Open. Card catalog.
University of Michigan, Bentley Historical Library, Michigan Historical Collections.
Correspondence of Andrews, a Defiance, OH, widow of a Mexican War soldier, relates to her pension claims. Also includes letters of the Hatch family of Sylvan and Chelsea, MI.

7,704. Angell, Sarah (Caswell)
Papers. 1746-1903. 9 vols. and ca. 225 items.
Open. Card catalog.
University of Michigan, Bentley Historical Library, Michigan Historical Collections.
Angell (1831-1903) was the wife of University of Michigan president James B. Angell.
Correspondence with her husband and other family members; material pertaining to Caswell family genealogy and the Society of Colonial Dames; and diaries for the period 1880 to 1903 in which she describes events in Ann Arbor and at the University, her travels abroad, and life in China and Turkey during her husband's diplomatic missions there. Climate, cities, customs, and journeys to Greece, Egypt, Palestine, Europe, Turkey, and China are discussed, with special notes on Chinese cities and points of interest near Peking. Angell was particularly interested in social life, church missionary work, the DAR, and art and architecture in foreign countries.

7,705. Ann Arbor Business and Professional Women's Club
Records. 1920-70. 6 ft.
Open. Unpublished guide.
University of Michigan, Bentley Historical Library, Michigan Historical Collections.
Minutes, membership lists, histories, correspondence, photos, scrapbooks, and publications pertain to Club activities, especially state and national conventions from 1921 to 1966, work for better housing in Ann Arbor from 1921 to 1922, and efforts for civil defense from 1950 to 1960.

7,706. Anonymous Diaries
Papers. Ca. 1902. 2 vols.
Open. Card catalog.
University of Michigan, Bentley Historical Library, Michigan Historical Collections.
Diaries of a Benzonia, MI, girl named Velma contain descriptions of daily life; school, perhaps the Benzonia Academy; and social activities.

7,707. Anonymous Paper
Papers. Ca. 1917. 1 item.
Open. Card catalog.
University of Michigan, Bentley Historical Library, Michigan Historical Collections.
Document pertains to the history of University of Michigan sororities and includes rules issued in 1917 for recruiting sorority members and addresses for the sororities.

7,708. Appel, Marie
Papers. 1910-48. Ca. 50 items.
Open. Card catalog.
University of Michigan, Bentley Historical Library, Michigan Historical Collections.
Appel was a Danish immigrant who became a resident of Marlette, MI. Correspondence and post cards in Danish from relatives in Denmark pertain to family matters.

7,709. Armstrong, Louise (Van Voorhis)
Papers. 1936-48. Ca. 750 items.
Open. Card catalog.
University of Michigan, Bentley Historical Library, Michigan Historical Collections.
Papers of Armstrong (1889-1948), who was a county relief administrator and author, include the original manuscript and related notes and correspondence for her book *We Too Are the People.* Also includes reports on relief activities in Manistee County, MI.

7,710. Arnold, Jennie Waterman
Papers. 1967. 1 item.
Open. Card catalog.
University of Michigan, Bentley Historical Library, Michigan Historical Collections.
Reminiscences of Arnold, in which she describes her life as a teacher in northern Michigan, also include her recollections of Woodbridge N. Ferris and the Ferris Institute in about 1914.

7,711. Association for the Promotion of Female Education
Records. 1842. 1 item.
Open. Card catalog.
University of Michigan, Bentley Historical Library, Michigan Historical Collections.
Bequest by the Association of property in Detroit; the bequest was meant to encourage female education and to maintain the female seminary in Detroit.

7,712. Athletic Federation of College Women
Records. 1951. 1 vol.
Open. Card catalog.
University of Michigan, Bentley Historical Library, Michigan Historical Collections.
Report of the 13th national convention of the Federation, which was held in Ann Arbor.

7,713. Bach, Ellen Botsford
Papers. Ca. 1896. 2 vols. and 2 pp.
Open. Card catalog.
University of Michigan, Bentley Historical Library, Michigan Historical Collections.
Papers of Bach (1877-1960) consist of reminiscences about her early life in Ann Arbor; a photo album containing photos of her family, friends, views of Ann Arbor, and interiors of some Ann Arbor homes; and a recipe book. Bach's correspondence and other papers are located in the Bach family papers.

7,714. Baits, Vera (Burridge)
Papers. 1950-59. 6 items.
Open. Card catalog.
University of Michigan, Bentley Historical Library, Michigan Historical Collections.
Addresses given by Baits (1892-1963), who was a University of Michigan regent, and alumni awards.

7,715. Ball, H. Belle
Papers. 1878-1902. 5 vols. and 5 items.
Open. Card catalog.
University of Michigan, Bentley Historical Library, Michigan Historical Collections.
A graduate of the University of Michigan medical school, Ball became a Jackson, MI, physician. Financial records, including account books listing fees charged and a few case histories, and a student notebook with notes on lectures by professor Edward Dunster.

7,716. Ballard, Lusina (Nash)
Papers. 1880-83. 1 vol. and 1 item.
Open. Card catalog.
University of Michigan, Bentley Historical Library, Michigan Historical Collections.
Ballard (1823-?) was the wife of Lyman Ballard, a farmer and storekeeper in Englishville in Kent County, MI. Diary she kept during 1880 includes comments on daily affairs, weather, crops, and community events, especially those of the Church of Christ of Englishville, and an 1883 reminiscence concerning the history of the Ballard family. Religion and housework were Ballard's main interests.

7,717. Ballard, Mary Ethel
Papers. 1911-12. 1 vol.
Open. Card catalog.
University of Michigan, Bentley Historical Library, Michigan Historical Collections.
Travel notes of Ballard pertain to a geology trip to Niagara Falls she made with other University of Michigan students, under the leadership of professor J. H. H. Calhoun of Clemson College, and to her trip to Marquette, MI, for a Michigan Christian Endeavor Union convention. The latter set of notes contains descriptions of meetings and points of interest in Marquette.

7,718. Banér, Skulda Vanadis
Papers. 1926-62. 1 ft.
Open. Unpublished guide and name index.
University of Michigan, Bentley Historical Library, Michigan Historical Collections.
Correspondence and scrapbooks of Banér (ca. 1898-1964), an Ironwood, MI, writer whose works include the novels *First Parting, Latchstring Out,* and *Voice of the Lute* as well as many short stories. Correspondents include Dorothy Canfield Fisher, Ann Harding, Mary Margaret McBride, Agnes Moorhead, and Stella Osborn.

7,719. Banks, Sarah Gertrude
Papers. 1871-1951. 11 items.
Open. Card catalog.
University of Michigan, Bentley Historical Library, Michigan Historical Collections.
Banks (1839-1926) was a Detroit physician. Correspondence, including a letter with biographical information on Banks; receipts; class certificates; and her 1873 University of Michigan medical school thesis, "Insanity: A Sympathetic Accompaniment of Uterine Disease." Correspondents include Anna Howard Shaw.

7,720. Baptist Church
Records. 1833-1932. Ca. 250 items.
Open. Card catalog.
University of Michigan, Bentley Historical Library, Michigan Historical Collections.
Records of this Chelsea, MI, church, which was formerly known as the Sylvan Baptist Church, include records of the Women's Missionary Society, 1904-24.

7,721. Barbour Scholarships for Oriental Women
Records. 1918-69. 1 ft.
Open. Card catalog.
University of Michigan, Bentley Historical Library, Michigan Historical Collections.
Minutes, correspondence, and printed material documenting the work of the University of Michigan Barbour Scholarships committee.

7,722. Barnes, Virginia (Grant)
Papers. 1963. 1 vol.
Open. Card catalog.
University of Michigan, Bentley Historical Library, Michigan Historical Collections.
Interview with Barnes, who was the daughter of Michigan supreme court justice Claudius B. Grant and granddaughter of Governor Alpheus Felch, chiefly concerns Grant and Felch.

7,723. Barrabee, Marcia
Papers. 1961-69. 2 ft.
Open. Unpublished guide.

University of Michigan, Bentley Historical Library, Michigan Historical Collections.
Barrabee was newsletter editor of the Ann Arbor Women for Peace. Correspondence, newsletters, clippings, and printed material pertain to the Women Strike for Peace, the House Un-American Activities Committee, disarmament, the draft, civil defense, and fallout shelters.

7,724. Barton, Lizzie
Papers. Ca. 1878. 1 vol.
Open. Card catalog.
University of Michigan, Bentley Historical Library, Michigan Historical Collections.
Scrapbook of Barton, who lived in Kalamazoo, MI, contains original pencil, pen, and color sketches and clippings of poems and articles.

7,725. Bates, Anna May Lamb
Papers. 1898. 3 items.
Open. Card catalog.
University of Michigan, Bentley Historical Library, Michigan Historical Collections.
Letters from Bates (1877-1953) to her parents discuss her life as a University of Michigan student.

7,726. Bay View Club
Records. 1897-1970. 2 ft.
Open. Unpublished guide.
University of Michigan, Bentley Historical Library, Michigan Historical Collections.
Records of this Fenton, MI, women's social and reading society include minutes, membership lists, papers read before the Club, and programs.

7,727. Bell, Margaret
Papers. 1919-56. 6 ft.
Open. Unpublished guide.
University of Michigan, Bentley Historical Library, Michigan Historical Collections.
Bell was chairperson of the department of physical education for women at the University of Michigan and a physician in the University Health Service. Correspondence, conference and speech material, files relating to women's athletics at the University, clippings, and other items.

7,728. Benjamin, Jeanette Smith
Papers. Ca. 1930. 3 items.
Open. Card catalog.
University of Michigan, Bentley Historical Library, Michigan Historical Collections.
Excerpts from reminiscences of Benjamin, in which she recalls her immigration to the US from England; the excerpts were assembled by her son in 1956.

7,729. Berthelot, Helen W.
Papers. 1948-68. 84 ft.
Open. Unpublished guide.
University of Michigan, Bentley Historical Library, Michigan Historical Collections.
A Democratic party activist, Berthelot was campaign manager for Michigan governor G. Mennen Williams and also legislative representative for the Communications Workers of America. Correspondence, campaign material, clippings, and other items pertain to the Michigan Democratic party since 1948 and Berthelot's work with the CWA. Also included is material on ethnic groups, employment, labor unions, education, communications, and the Women's Power Conference.

7,730. Bingham, Mary (Warden)
Papers. 1862-63. 1 vol.
Open. Card catalog.
University of Michigan, Bentley Historical Library, Michigan Historical Collections.
Diary of [Mrs. Kingsley Scott] Bingham in which she discusses daily activities and reflects on her husband's and son's deaths. Also contains accounts she kept at the back of the volume.

7,731. Blake, Alde L. T.
Papers. 1912-14. 25 items.
Open. Card catalog.
University of Michigan, Bentley Historical Library, Michigan Historical Collections.
Blake was campaign secretary for the Michigan Equal Suffrage Association. Correspondence and printed items pertain to the woman suffrage movement. Correspondents include Jane Addams.

7,732. Bohr Millinery and Dressmaker Shop
Records. 1878-84. 1 vol.
Open. Card catalog.
University of Michigan, Bentley Historical Library, Michigan Historical Collections.
Account book of this Westphalia, MI, business owned by Theresa Bohr.

7,733. Brazer, Marjorie C.
Papers. 1964-75. 1 ft.
Open. Unpublished guide.
University of Michigan, Bentley Historical Library, Michigan Historical Collections.
Brazer was secretary of the Ann Arbor Transportation Authority. Minutes, financial records, and reports of the AATA focus on the problems of mass transportation and development of the "Dial-a-Ride" system. Also included is material about the development of streets and automobile parking facilities.

7,734. Brokaw, Josephine
Papers. 1967-69. 75 items.
Open. Card catalog.
University of Michigan, Bentley Historical Library, Michigan Historical Collections.
Personal correspondence of Brokaw, who was an Ann Arbor teacher, primarily describes her life in India as a teacher with the US Agency for International Development.

7,735. Bronson, Christine Frederica
Papers. 1877-1903. 1 vol.
Open. Card catalog.
University of Michigan, Bentley Historical Library, Michigan Historical Collections.
Scrapbook of a University of Michigan student from the class of 1893 contains programs of University and Ann Arbor musical events.

7,736. Brown, Gloria
Papers. 1964-67. 50 items.
Open. Card catalog.
University of Michigan, Bentley Historical Library, Michigan Historical Collections.
Brown was chairman of the Detroit chapter of the Congress of Racial Equality. Correspondence, news releases, and printed material pertain to the Detroit CORE.

7,737. Brown, Martha A.
Papers. 1856. 1 item.
Open. Card catalog.
University of Michigan, Bentley Historical Library, Michigan Historical Collections.
Account by Brown, a Cass County, MI, resident, describes her husband's death at the hands of a proslavery mob in Kansas in 1856.

7,738. Brucker, Clara (Hantel)
Papers. 1930-73. 3 ft.
Open. Unpublished guide.
University of Michigan, Bentley Historical Library, Michigan Historical Collections.
Brucker was a clubwoman, a Republican party worker, and the wife of Wilber M. Brucker, a former Michigan Republican governor and US secretary of the army. Correspondence, diaries, speeches, and travel briefs relate to her work with the Detroit School of Government and mock Republican conventions. The collection also reflects her interests in the prevention of sex crimes against women and children, GFWC, and various charities. Correspondents include Mme. Chiang Kai-shek.

7,739. Buchanan, Ruth Bacon
Papers. 1928-53. 4 ft.
Open. Card catalog.
University of Michigan, Bentley Historical Library, Michigan Historical Collections.
Collection includes letters Buchanan (1882-1953) received from University of Michigan students and alumni serving in WWII as well as research material on covered bridges in Michigan.

7,740. Buell, Jennie
Papers. 1891-1934. 2 vols. and 20 items.
Open. Card catalog.
University of Michigan, Bentley Historical Library, Michigan Historical Collections.
Papers of Buell (1891-), secretary of the Michigan State Grange, include correspondence, notes, and speeches about agriculture, farm women, and education of farm women.

7,741. Burdge, Emma Spencer
Papers. 1891-1933. Ca. 25 items.
Open. Card catalog.
University of Michigan, Bentley Historical Library, Michigan Historical Collections.
Correspondence, telegrams, and family histories of a Battle Creek, MI, resident.

7,742. Burns, Eunice L.
Papers. 1962-68. 1 ft.
Open. Card catalog.
University of Michigan, Bentley Historical Library, Michigan Historical Collections.
Burns was a Democratic member of the Ann Arbor city council. Correspondence, reports, and clippings pertain to a fair housing campaign and the problems of race relations and police-community relations.

7,743. Burns, Julie C.
Papers. 1975. 1 microfilm reel.
Open. Card catalog.
University of Michigan, Bentley Historical Library, Michigan Historical Collections.
Account by Burns of her experiences as organist at Cristo Rey, a Roman Catholic church in Lansing, MI.

7,744. Burr Family
Papers. 1860. 1 item.
Open. Card catalog.
University of Michigan, Bentley Historical Library, Michigan Historical Collections.
Letter of Mary L. Burr to her brother William Burr of Standish, MI, describes everyday occurrences.

7,745. Burrows, Frances (Peck)
Papers. 1860-67. 2 vols.
Open. Card catalog.
University of Michigan, Bentley Historical Library, Michigan Historical Collections.
Diaries of Burrows (?-1916), who was the wife of US senator Julius Burrows and a resident of Kalamazoo, MI, consist of a daily journal written between January and September of 1860 at Prairie Seminary and an account of a trip to Europe in 1867.

7,746. Business and Professional Women's Club
Records. 1938-66. 1 ft.
Open. Card catalog.
University of Michigan, Bentley Historical Library, Michigan Historical Collections.
Minutes, rosters, bulletins, clippings, and printed items of this Ypsilanti, MI, club.

7,747. Butler, Orma Fitch
Papers. 1843-1936. Ca. 500 items.
Open. Card catalog.

University of Michigan, Bentley Historical Library, Michigan Historical Collections.
Correspondence, manuscripts, genealogical information, deeds, student records, and other papers of Butler (1874-1938), a professor of Latin and curator of archaeology at the University of Michigan.

7,748. Butterfield, Eleanor
Papers. Nd. 1 item.
Open. Card catalog.
University of Michigan, Bentley Historical Library, Michigan Historical Collections.
Questionnaire of Butterfield, a 1923 University of Michigan graduate, includes her personal recollections of college life.

7,749. Campbell, Caroline Bezora (Portman)
Papers. 1910-25. Ca. 100 items.
Open. Card catalog.
University of Michigan, Bentley Historical Library, Michigan Historical Collections.
Correspondence and other papers of Campbell (1859-1926), who was the wife of James H. Campbell and a resident of Grand Rapids, MI, concern the restoration of the Michigan constitution of 1835, replacement of the Michigan plaque in the Washington Monument, and the Michigan state seal.

7,750. Centennial of Admission of Women Committee
Records. 1969-71. Ca. 250 items.
Open. Card catalog.
University of Michigan, Bentley Historical Library, Michigan Historical Collections.
Financial data, correspondence, memos, and printed material relate to the celebration of the 100th anniversary of the admission of women to the University of Michigan.

7,751. Chandler, Elizabeth Margaret
Papers. 1793-1834. Ca. 500 items.
Open. Calendar.
University of Michigan, Bentley Historical Library, Michigan Historical Collections.
Chandler (1807-34) was an abolitionist poet who lived in Adrian, MI. Correspondence, primarily that of Chandler and her brother Thomas Chandler with family members in the East, with Benjamin Lundy, and with others. Also includes family letters of the previous Chandler generation in Pennsylvania and later correspondence about those papers. Collection describes early settlement, agricultural conditions, and local and national antislavery movements.

7,752. Chaplin, Addie F.
Papers. 1880-83. 1 vol.
Open. Card catalog.
University of Michigan, Bentley Historical Library, Michigan Historical Collections.
Diary of a young girl at home in Dowagiac, MI, contains an account of daily life with particular emphasis on flowers and music.

7,753. Chase, Cornelia
Papers. 1863. 1 vol.
Open. Card catalog.
University of Michigan, Bentley Historical Library, Michigan Historical Collections.
[Mrs. John Smith] Chase (1815-1905) was an Elsie, MI, housewife. Diary in which she discusses daily activities and her fears for her two sons in the Civil War. Chase's main interests were her family and the Soldier's Aid Society.

7,754. Child Study Club
Records. 1934-66. Ca. 250 items.
Open. Card catalog.
University of Michigan, Bentley Historical Library, Michigan Historical Collections.
Constitution, minutes, financial records, and correspondence of this Ann Arbor group.

7,755. Child Study Club, Ypsilanti
Records. 1926-46. 3 vols.
Open. Card catalog.
University of Michigan, Bentley Historical Library, Michigan Historical Collections.
Records of this Ypsilanti, MI, organization.

7,756. Clark, Chloe
Papers. 1836. 1 vol.
Open. Card catalog.
University of Michigan, Bentley Historical Library, Michigan Historical Collections.
Diary of an Ann Arbor schoolteacher consists of an account of her journey with her family across New York state and down the Great Lakes to Detroit. Contains detailed notes about the people and countryside.

7,757. Clinton, Anna L.
Papers. 1959. 2 items.
Open. Card catalog.
University of Michigan, Bentley Historical Library, Michigan Historical Collections.
In her reminiscences, Clinton (1871-1960), an Ann Arbor schoolteacher, discusses her early life and career in Ann Arbor. Also included are reminiscences of Katherine Groomes.

7,758. Cloon, Mary (King)
Papers. 1908-65. 1 ft.
Open. Unpublished guide.
University of Michigan, Bentley Historical Library, Michigan Historical Collections.
Cloon is an Ironwood, MI, teacher who participates in local civic affairs. Correspondence, chiefly with her husband city attorney William G. Cloon, and diaries describe her daily activities and interests.

7,759. College Baptist Church
Records. 1864-1940. 1 vol. and 250 items.
Open. Card catalog.
University of Michigan, Bentley Historical Library, Michigan Historical Collections.
Material of the Hillsdale, MI, Church includes records of the Women's Missionary Society, 1864-87.

7,760. Committee on the Defense Training Program for Women
Records. 1941-43. 1 vol.
Open. Card catalog.
University of Michigan, Bentley Historical Library, Michigan Historical Collections.
Notebook of the Committee at the University of Michigan contains correspondence, bulletins of the University War Board, and printed material. The Committee operated under the auspices of the University Committee on National Defense.

7,761. Condict Family
Papers. 1911. 1 item.
Open. Card catalog.
University of Michigan, Bentley Historical Library, Michigan Historical Collections.
Letter from Anna Condict of Adrian, MI, to Alice Condict of Morenci, MI, about family news.

7,762. Connor, Mamie E.
Papers. 1890-1937. 42 vols.
Open. Card catalog.
University of Michigan, Bentley Historical Library, Michigan Historical Collections.
Diaries of Connor, a Plymouth, MI, storekeeper, contain descriptions of social activities, weather, and trips to Detroit and nearby towns.

7,763. Council of Church Women
Records. 1917-31. 1 vol.
Open. Card catalog.
University of Michigan, Bentley Historical Library, Michigan Historical Collections.
Records of this Ypsilanti, MI, organization, formerly known as the Ypsilanti Missionary Federation.

7,764. Creswell, Cordelia
Papers. 1886-1930s. 2 ft.
Open. Unpublished guide.
University of Michigan, Bentley Historical Library, Michigan Historical Collections.
Margaret Creswell and Cordelia Creswell (1868?-1950) were Grand Rapids, MI, special education coordinators. Financial records, including teacher budgets, and annual and individual reports on the students and on the program, delinquency, and education for the retarded.

7,765. Cuddihy, Joan F.
Papers. 1945-72. Ca. 250 items.
Access restricted. Unpublished guide.
University of Michigan, Bentley Historical Library, Michigan Historical Collections.
Collection includes personal correspondence of US supreme court justice Frank Murphy, photos, and clippings.

7,766. Cumings, Grace P.
Papers. 1887-88. 1 vol.
Open. Card catalog.
University of Michigan, Bentley Historical Library, Michigan Historical Collections.
Diary of Cumings (1866-?), who lived in Grand Rapids, MI, and Melbourne Beach, FL, includes a description of a railroad trip to Florida. Cumings made the trip with her father because of his health.

7,767. Curtis, Martha (Leach)
Papers. 1833-54. Ca. 200 items.
Open. Card catalog.
University of Michigan, Bentley Historical Library, Michigan Historical Collections.
Correspondence of Curtis, an Ann Arbor teacher, includes letters exchanged with the Leach family and with her husband William S. Curtis, who was a minister, about social, family, and religious matters.

7,768. Daughters of the American Revolution
Records. 1900-70. 30 ft. and 6 vols.
Open. Card catalog.
University of Michigan, Bentley Historical Library, Michigan Historical Collections.
Minutes of the Michigan DAR state executive board, state officers' reports, Michigan conference proceedings, records of WWI and WWII DAR activities, material pertaining to genealogical work, historical files of individual chapters, scrapbooks, and publications.

7,769. Davidson, Sylvia
Papers. 1848-1918. 12 items.
Open. Card catalog.
University of Michigan, Bentley Historical Library, Michigan Historical Collections.
Reminiscences of pioneer life around Tecumseh, MI, and miscellaneous Civil War material.

7,770. Davis, Mary P.
Papers. 1861-64. 2 items.
Open. Card catalog.
University of Michigan, Bentley Historical Library, Michigan Historical Collections.
Consists of a letter Davis wrote while teaching school in Illinois and a second letter written while she was a matron of the Detroit House of Correction.

7,771. De Jonge, Madge Ann (Brook)
Papers. 1954-63. 3 vols.
Open. Card catalog.
University of Michigan, Bentley Historical Library, Michigan Historical Collections.
Scrapbooks of De Jonge, a resident of Ann Arbor, relate to the activities of the Woman's Auxiliary of the Washtenaw County Medical Society and to local events in Ypsilanti, MI, and Ann Arbor.

7,772. Department of Physical Education for Women
Records. 1924-69. 6 ft.
Open. Card catalog.
University of Michigan, Bentley Historical Library, Michigan Historical Collections.
Annual reports of the Department at the University of Michigan, scrapbooks, a history of physical education for women written in 1937, and curriculum material for the Women's Athletic Association.

7,773. Devin, Alice
Papers. 1870-72. 19 items.
Open. Card catalog.
University of Michigan, Bentley Historical Library, Michigan Historical Collections.
Letters of an Ann Arbor high school student about social life and the University of Michigan.

7,774. Dilts, Adda
Papers. 1955-71. 20 items.
Open. Card catalog.
University of Michigan, Bentley Historical Library, Michigan Historical Collections.
Research material collected by Dilts, who was an historical researcher and teacher, pertains to the history of the Friends church in Michigan and the lives of its members, especially Laura (Smith) Haviland.

7,775. Doner, Mary Frances
Papers. Ca. 1934-74. 5 ft. and 12 vols.
Open. Unpublished guide.
University of Michigan, Bentley Historical Library, Michigan Historical Collections.
Doner was a Ludington, MI, author. Correspondence, manuscripts of writings, contracts with publishers, scrapbooks, clippings, and books.

7,776. Douglass, Esther
Papers. 1864-1914. Ca. 250 items.
Open. Card catalog.
University of Michigan, Bentley Historical Library, Michigan Historical Collections.
Correspondence, reminiscences, and other papers of Douglass, a missionary and teacher in the South after the Civil War, relate to the teaching of free blacks.

7,777. Downs, Lucinda Goodrich
Papers. Nd. 1 item.
Open. Card catalog.
University of Michigan, Bentley Historical Library, Michigan Historical Collections.
Questionnaire that Downs, a public school teacher and 1877 University of Michigan graduate, completed for the University alumnae council contains personal recollections of college days.

7,778. Dunshee, Mariah L. B.
Papers. 1854-64. 1 item.
Open. Card catalog.
University of Michigan, Bentley Historical Library, Michigan Historical Collections.
Diary of a Prairie Ronde, MI, housewife and mother contains notes and reflections on her inner religious life and on death.

7,779. Edwards, Ann
Papers. 1946-57. Ca. 250 items.
Open. Unpublished guide.
University of Michigan, Bentley Historical Library, Michigan Historical Collections.
Papers of Edwards (?-1962), an activist in national activities of the Prohibition party, the Young Prohibitionists Association, and Democracy Unlimited, include correspondence, party records, and other papers she held at the time of her death pertaining chiefly to her activities with the Missouri Prohibition party and the Greater St. Louis Prohibition Clubs. Edwards was an active participant in the groups until 1955.

7,780. Federation of Women's Clubs, Washtenaw County
Records. 1916-59. 4 vols. and 50 items.
Open. Card catalog.
University of Michigan, Bentley Historical Library, Michigan Historical Collections.
Minutes, correspondence, historical sketch, and other items of this Washtenaw County, MI, organization.

7,781. Federation of Women's Clubs, Ypsilanti
Records. 1914-44. 1 vol.
Open. Card catalog.
University of Michigan, Bentley Historical Library, Michigan Historical Collections.
Treasurers' records of this Ypsilanti, MI, organization.

7,782. Felion, Phebe
Papers. 1925-27. 1 vol.
Open. Card catalog.
University of Michigan, Bentley Historical Library, Michigan Historical Collections.
Diary of Felion, a Mount Morris, MI, housewife, records everyday events, visits with friends, and reminiscences.

7,783. Fowler, Minnie (Osborne)
Papers. 1913-28. 11 vols.
Open. Card catalog.
University of Michigan, Bentley Historical Library, Michigan Historical Collections.
Diaries of Fowler (1862-?), a resident of Saline, MI, who moved to Los Angeles in 1913, contain detailed descriptions of everyday life.

7,784. Fox, Emma Augusta (Stowell)
Papers. 1894-1945. 3 vols. and ca. 750 items.
Open. Card catalog.
University of Michigan, Bentley Historical Library, Michigan Historical Collections.
Correspondence of Fox (1847-1945), a parliamentary law teacher and author, chiefly pertains to parliamentary law and women's clubs. Also included are a letter from Jane Addams, galley sheets and notes for parliamentary law books, biographical material, guest books from functions honoring Fox, and clippings.

7,785. Frank, Patricia M.
Papers. 1972. 1 vol.
Open. Card catalog.
University of Michigan, Bentley Historical Library, Michigan Historical Collections.
Master's thesis of Frank consists of an oral history project about Genevieve Gillette, president emeritus of the Michigan Parks Association, and includes a biographical sketch of Gillette and an index to taped interviews with her.

7,786. Freeman, Eeta Bayla
Papers. 1962-65. Ca. 250 items.
Open. Card catalog.
University of Michigan, Bentley Historical Library, Michigan Historical Collections.
[Mrs. Irwin Gershaw] Freeman was a Peace Corps volunteer in Pakistan. Correspondence with her parents in Detroit, a diary fragment, clippings, and other papers relate to social work in the US and Pakistan.

7,787. Friday Club
Records. 1889-1975. Ca. 250 items.
Open. Card catalog.
University of Michigan, Bentley Historical Library, Michigan Historical Collections.
Minutes, reports, membership material, and correspondence of this Jackson, MI, women's literary group.

7,788. Froebel Study Club
Records. 1891-1953. 1 ft.
Open. Card catalog.
University of Michigan, Bentley Historical Library, Michigan Historical Collections.
Minutes, scrapbooks, and other records of this Grand Rapids, MI, women's group, the members of which studied Friedrich Froebel's writings on education.

7,789. Frostic, Gwen
Papers. 1964-72. 1 ft.
Open. Card catalog.
University of Michigan, Bentley Historical Library, Michigan Historical Collections.
Correspondence, poetry, clippings, and publications of Frostic, who is a Benzonia, MI, poet and engraver.

7,790. Fuller, Barbara
Papers. 1976. 1 item.
Open. Card catalog.
University of Michigan, Bentley Historical Library, Michigan Historical Collections.
Fuller (1925-) was a member of a humanitarian delegation sent to Vietnam in April 1976. Account gives her impressions of conditions in the countryside and recounts conversations with North and South Vietnamese government leaders.

7,791. Gardner, Nannette Brown Ellingwood
Papers. 1871-93. 2 vols. and 3 items.
Open. Card catalog.
University of Michigan, Bentley Historical Library, Michigan Historical Collections.
Gardner (1828-1900) was a Michigan leader and lecturer for the woman suffrage movement. Letters to various newspapers; scrapbooks containing photos, clippings, broadsides, and printed articles about the Michigan suffrage movement; and a diary and scrapbook of her daughter Sarah M. Gardner.

7,792. Gelston Family
Papers. 1847-1917. 35 items.
Open. Card catalog.
University of Michigan, Bentley Historical Library, Michigan Historical Collections.
Collection of Gelston family members, who lived in Michigan and New York state, contains letters of Caroline E. Fanning written from Holyoke Seminary and correspondence of Caroline and Anna Gelston, who were University of Michigan students. Correspondents include Jane Addams and Frances Willard.

7,793. Gilbert, Mabelle Agnes
Papers. 1889-1914. 19 vols. and 10 items.
Open. Card catalog.
University of Michigan, Bentley Historical Library, Michigan Historical Collections.
Gilbert was a West Bay City, MI, music teacher. Diaries, account books listing payments for music and dance lessons, school grade reports, and a scrapbook she assembled as a student at the University School of Music, an independent institution that became affiliated with the University of Michigan in 1929.

7,794. Gillette, Emma Genevieve
Papers. 1920-72. 11 ft.
Open. Unpublished guide.
University of Michigan, Bentley Historical Library, Michigan Historical Collections.
Gillette (1898-) is a landscape architect and conservationist who served as president of the Michigan Parks Association and was a member of the Citizen's Advisory Committee on Recreation and Natural Beauty during the Johnson administration. Correspondence, reports, and printed material relate to her work in state and national conservation organizations, but particularly in the Michigan Parks Association and the Michigan Conservation Commission.

7,795. Girl Scouts, Huron Valley Council
Records. 1946-65. 11 ft.
Open. Unpublished guide.

University of Michigan, Bentley Historical Library, Michigan Historical Collections.
Articles of incorporation, board minutes, financial records, agendas, fund-raising and promotional material, and scrapbooks of the Michigan Council. Also included are administrative files of the Ypsilanti, Wayne, and Brighton councils, 1948-58.

7,796. Gomon, Josephine (Fellows)
Papers. 1913-71. 10 ft. and 1 vol.
Open. Unpublished guide and name inventory.
University of Michigan, Bentley Historical Library, Michigan Historical Collections.
Papers of [Mrs.] Gomon (1892-1975), who was a teacher, executive secretary to Detroit mayor Frank Murphy from 1930 to 1933, chairman of the mayor's Unemployment Committee, director of the Detroit Housing Commission, a candidate for public office in that city, and director of women personnel at Ford Motor Company's Willow Run bomber plant during WWII. The collection describes the Murphy mayoralty, Clarence Darrow and the Sweet trial of 1925, and Detroit politics. Includes correspondence, diaries for the period 1913 to 1966, clippings, and material gathered by Gomon for a biography of Murphy.

7,797. Gonzalez, Jane
Papers. 1973. 1 item.
Open. Card catalog.
University of Michigan, Bentley Historical Library, Michigan Historical Collections.
Transcript of an interview with Gonzalez (1918-), who was a Muskegon, MI, court reporter before she became project director of the Muskegon Office of Educational Opportunity, contains a discussion about the Mexican-American community in the Muskegon area during WWII.

7,798. Grand Rapids Kindergarten Training School
Records. 1891-1919. 6 ft.
Open. Unpublished guide.
University of Michigan, Bentley Historical Library, Michigan Historical Collections.
Minutes, financial records, student and alumni registers, notebooks, and scrapbooks of the School.

7,799. Grandmothers' Club
Records. 1920-52. 7 vols.
Open. Card catalog.
University of Michigan, Bentley Historical Library, Michigan Historical Collections.
Minutes and scrapbooks of this Ann Arbor organization.

7,800. Graves, Theresa M.
Papers. 1898-1936. 100-page vol.
Open. Card catalog.
University of Michigan, Bentley Historical Library, Michigan Historical Collections.
Scrapbook of an Ypsilanti, MI, resident consists mainly of clippings about persons, cultural activities, and schools, particularly Cleary College and Michigan State Normal College.

7,801. Greene, Mary Theresa
Papers. 1910-48. Ca. 125 items.
Open. Card catalog.
University of Michigan, Bentley Historical Library, Michigan Historical Collections.
Greene was a member of the University of Michigan medical school graduating class of 1890. Correspondence pertaining to her class, class lists, a biographical sketch of physician Adelle P. Pierce, and scrapbooks with other material on Greene's medical school class and the medical memorial loan fund.

7,802. Griffiths, Martha (Wright)
Papers. 1956-74. 203 ft.
Open. Unpublished guide.
University of Michigan, Bentley Historical Library, Michigan Historical Collections.
[Mrs. Hicks] Griffiths (1912-) is a Detroit attorney who served as a Democratic member of Congress from Michigan's 17th District from 1955 to 1974. Professional correspondence, legislative and case files, speeches, printed items, and other material pertaining to her Congressional career.

7,803. Grimes, Lucia Isabella (Voorhees)
Papers. 1912-49. 4 ft.
Open. Unpublished guide.
University of Michigan, Bentley Historical Library, Michigan Historical Collections.
[Mrs. George] Grimes was a Detroit suffragist and women's rights campaign participant who headed the Michigan branch of the National Woman's party. Correspondence, clippings, pamphlets, periodicals, and other papers relate to her activities in the Congressional Union for Woman Suffrage, the Detroit Equal Suffrage Club, the Michigan Equal Suffrage Association, the Legislative Council of Michigan Women, the National Woman's party, and the Michigan Republican party. Correspondents include the LWV, MESA, the Michigan State Federation of Women's Clubs, the National Civil Service Reform League, the NWP, and Alice Paul.

7,804. Groomes, Katherine S.
Papers. 1957-72. 7 items.
Open. Card catalog.
University of Michigan, Bentley Historical Library, Michigan Historical Collections.
Reminiscences of Groomes, an Ann Arbor historian, in which she describes Ann Arbor at the turn of the century. Also contains notes on area churches and early settlers.

7,805. Haire, Anna M.
Papers. 1873. 1 vol.
Open. Card catalog.
University of Michigan, Bentley Historical Library, Michigan Historical Collections.
Journal of Haire (1822-75), who lived in Georgetown Township of Ottawa County, MI, offers a detailed description of the household and religious duties of a prosperous farmer's wife, her family, and friends.

7,806. Hall, Emma Amelia
Papers. 1866-1935. 7 vols., ca. 250 items, and 1 microfilm reel.
Open. Card catalog.
University of Michigan, Bentley Historical Library, Michigan Historical Collections.
Prominent in prison work in the 1870s and 1880s, Hall (1837-84) was superintendent of the Michigan Reform School for Girls in Adrian. Correspondence; diaries with scattered accounts of and comments about the Reform School; business records, including minutes of the board of control of the State Industrial School, a report to the Detroit House of Corrections inspectors, and superintendent's reports; notebooks containing literary sketches Hall wrote, lists of girls' duties, and personal notes; sermons; and other papers.

7,807. Hall, Gwendolyn (Midlo)
Papers. 1939-74. 2 ft. and 1 vol.
Closed. Unpublished guide.
University of Michigan, Bentley Historical Library, Michigan Historical Collections.
Hall (1929-) is an historian and civil rights activist. Family and professional correspondence, clippings, articles and reviews, and printed material reflect her interests in black history, black activist Robert Williams, and drug reform. Also included are oral interviews Hall conducted focusing on the problem of drug rehabilitation, particularly the methadone treatment.

7,808. Hall, Olivia Bigelow
Papers. 1869-1905. 1 microfilm reel.
Open. Card catalog.
University of Michigan, Bentley Historical Library, Michigan Historical Collections.
Correspondence and other papers of Hall, an Ann Arbor suffragist, relate to the woman suffrage movement. There is extensive correspondence with Susan B. Anthony. The originals of these papers are held by the Library of Congress.

7,809. Hamm, Carolyn L.
Papers. 1966-67. 14 items.
Access restricted. Card catalog.
University of Michigan, Bentley Historical Library, Michigan Historical Collections.
Letters of Hamm (1943-), a worker with the American Friends Service Committee, written to her family while she was stationed in Vietnam.

7,810. Hart, Adelaide Julia
Papers. 1948-70. 20 ft.
Access restricted. Unpublished guide.
University of Michigan, Bentley Historical Library, Michigan Historical Collections.
A Democratic party worker, Hart (1900-) also served as vice-chairperson of the Michigan Democratic party state central committee. Files pertain to party conventions, election issues and campaigns, and the work of the state central committee and reflect the role of women in the party and in the Women for Humphrey organization.

7,811. Hartsuff Family
Papers. 1839-1950. 7 vols. and 100 items.
Open. Card catalog.
University of Michigan, Bentley Historical Library, Michigan Historical Collections.
Correspondence, notebooks, and a history of a Detroit family. Includes a diary of Alice Elliott [Mrs. Albert] Hartsuff for the period 1908 to 1915 containing scattered brief entries describing travels abroad and in the US and daily activities in Detroit. Also includes diaries written by Florence Hartsuff between 1884 and 1890 while she traveled in Europe.

7,812. Haydon, Ione
Papers. 1892-1948. 39 vols.
Open. Card catalog.
University of Michigan, Bentley Historical Library, Michigan Historical Collections.
Diaries of a farm housewife who lived near Decatur, MI, contain descriptions of daily farm and village life and include a brief account of her student experiences at the University of Michigan. Her main concerns are the weather, friends, and domestic matters.

7,813. Hillsdale Woman's Club
Records. 1890-1945. 20 vols. and 16 items.
Open. Card catalog.
University of Michigan, Bentley Historical Library, Michigan Historical Collections.
Minutes from 1890 to 1926, treasurers' reports, student loan fund material, and other records of the Club.

7,814. Hinsdale Family
Papers. 1857-1963. 2 ft.
Open. Unpublished guide.
University of Michigan, Bentley Historical Library, Michigan Historical Collections.
Collection includes papers of the three Hinsdale sisters Ellen Clarinda Hinsdale (1864-1958), Mary Louisa Hinsdale (1866-1946), and Mildred Hinsdale (1871-1971). In 1897 Ellen Clarinda became the fifth woman to receive a PhD from Gottingen University; from 1897 to 1931 she taught Germanic languages and literature at Mount Holyoke College. Correspondence; travel journals from 1888, 1928-29, and 1936; and other papers pertain to her study at Gottingen. Mary Louisa

earned a PhD from the University of Michigan in 1912 and later taught political science and history at Grand Rapids, MI, Junior College. Correspondence, diaries of European trips, a student notebook from Radcliffe College, and an interview with Lucretia R. [Mrs. James A.] Garfield. Mildred graduated in 1895 from the University of Michigan, later taught at Grand Rapids Junior College, and founded the Grand Rapids Alumnae Club. Correspondence, a journal of a trip to Russia in 1928, and transcribed interviews with her about student life at the University of Michigan in the 1890s.

7,815. Hollister, Emily Jane (Areen)
Papers. 1888-1911. 2 items.
Open. Card catalog.
University of Michigan, Bentley Historical Library, Michigan Historical Collections.
Diary of Hollister (1839-1918), who was a practical nurse in Ann Arbor and Whitmore Lake, MI, includes accounts of her nursing experiences, patient care, the nature of illnesses, and doctors with whom she worked. Nursing and family were her main concerns.

7,816. Holmes, Pricilla
Papers. 1867-77. 3 items.
Open. Card catalog.
University of Michigan, Bentley Historical Library, Michigan Historical Collections.
One letter from J. I. Fletcher, Holmes's financé; reminiscence of a boat trip from Detroit to Lake Superior through Sault Ste. Marie; and a memorandum book of a New York trip.

7,817. Hoobler, Icie Macy
Papers. 1921-74. 35 ft.
Open. Unpublished guide.
University of Michigan, Bentley Historical Library, Michigan Historical Collections.
Hoobler (1892-) is an Ann Arbor scientific research consultant. Correspondence, scientific reports and publications, and other papers pertain to her interests in the problems of nutrition and aging; her work with the Merrill-Palmer School in Detroit, the Detroit Institute of Cancer Research, the Children's Fund of Michigan, and the Grand Valley State College in Allendale, MI; and her membership in the White House Conference on Food, Nutrition, and Health and in various White House conferences on children and youth since 1930.

7,818. Huber, G. Carl
Papers. 1874-1943. 9 ft.
Open. Unpublished guide.
University of Michigan, Bentley Historical Library, Michigan Historical Collections.
The collection contains family correspondence of Huber (1865-1934), a University of Michigan professor and dean. Most of the letters are addressed to Huber's wife Lucy (Parker) Huber from her children, including daughter Lucy (Huber) Andrus and daughter-in-law Marion (Kubic) Huber. Also included are social appointment books.

7,819. Hunt, Estelle Louise
Papers. Nd. 1 item.
Open. Card catalog.
University of Michigan, Bentley Historical Library, Michigan Historical Collections.
Questionnaire completed by Hunt, a member of the University of Michigan class of 1905, contains reminiscences of her student experiences.

7,820. Hussey Family
Papers. 1876-1926. 8 ft. and 8 items.
Open. Unpublished guide.
University of Michigan, Bentley Historical Library, Michigan Historical Collections.
Collection includes papers of Ethel (Fountain) Hussey (1865-1915), who was the wife of William J. Hussey, a University of Michigan astronomer. Correspondence; diaries for the period 1905 to 1912, which describe daily events in Ann Arbor and a trip in 1911 to La Plata, Argentina; manuscripts of articles and stories; student essays and papers; and other items relating to Hussey's interest in the Association of Collegiate Alumnae, the University's Women's League, other domestic and social faculty activities, and astronomy.

7,821. Inglis, Elizabeth N.
Papers. 1912-58. 1 vol.
Open. Card catalog.
University of Michigan, Bentley Historical Library, Michigan Historical Collections.
Inglis was the wife of James Inglis and an Ann Arbor resident. Volume of notes about her entertaining at what is now Inglis House includes menus and guest lists.

7,822. International Conference on Alternative Perspectives on Vietnam
Records. 1965-66. 1 ft.
Open. Card catalog.
University of Michigan, Bentley Historical Library, Michigan Historical Collections.
Records of an international conference held at the University of Michigan in 1965. Correspondents include Hannah Arendt, Germaine Bree, and Mary C. Wright.

7,823. International Order of King's Daughters and Sons, Goodwill Circle
Records. 1917-68. 8 vols.
Open. Card catalog.
University of Michigan, Bentley Historical Library, Michigan Historical Collections.
Minutes, account book, and scrapbooks of the Circle in Ann Arbor, which formerly was known as the Homeopathic Hospital Circle.

7,824. International Women's Year Committee
Records. 1975-76. Ca. 250 items.
Open. Card catalog.
University of Michigan, Bentley Historical Library, Michigan Historical Collections.
Minutes of the planning committee, budget and project material, clippings, and other records of this University of Michigan group.

7,825. Jones, Alice (Van Hoosen)
Papers. 1876-1950. Ca. 200 items.
Open. Card catalog.
University of Michigan, Bentley Historical Library, Michigan Historical Collections.
Papers of Jones (1855-1950), who lived in Stony Creek, MI, include personal correspondence with her sister Bertha Van Hoosen and letters of condolence upon the death of her husband Joseph C. Comstock.

7,826. Jones, Sarah Van Hoosen
Papers. 1898-1972. 1 ft.
Open. Unpublished guide.
University of Michigan, Bentley Historical Library, Michigan Historical Collections.
Jones (1892-1972) was a farmer and cattle breeder from Stony Creek and Rochester, MI, who served as president of the Association of Governing Boards of State Universities and Allied Institutions and was a member of the Committee for the White House Conference on Education. Personal and family correspondence from her mother Alice Van Hoosen Jones and her aunt Bertha Van Hoosen pertains to everyday life, primarily for the period 1900 to 1930. Other papers concern her work with the Association of Governing Boards and the White House Committee in 1954 and 1955.

7,827. Judd, Dorothy
Papers. 1935-71. 11 ft.
Open. Unpublished guide.
University of Michigan, Bentley Historical Library, Michigan Historical Collections.
[Mrs. Siegal] Judd was a delegate to the Michigan constitutional convention in 1961 and 1962, chairman of the Michigan state advisory committee to the US Commission on Civil Rights, and a member of the Michigan Civil Service Commission. Correspondence, drafts, reports, studies, convention files, pamphlets, and other papers relate to equal employment in Michigan, development of the merit principle in state employment practices, the Michigan constitutional convention, and local politics in Grand Rapids.

7,828. Kanouse, Bessie Bernice
Papers. 1944-45. 2 items.
Open. Card catalog.
University of Michigan, Bentley Historical Library, Michigan Historical Collections.
Letters to Kanouse (1889-) from Lucille E. Turnquist describe Turnquist's experiences as a sergeant with the armed services in New Guinea.

7,829. King, Julia Anne
Papers. 1872-1908. 1 vol. and ca. 250 items.
Open. Unpublished guide.
University of Michigan, Bentley Historical Library, Michigan Historical Collections.
King (1838-1919) was an educator, preceptress, and head of the history department at Michigan State Normal School at Ypsilanti. Lecture notes, manuscripts, course outlines, and student papers. Also included is a notebook she kept as a teacher at Flint High School, which contains lectures, essays, and personal records.

7,830. Kinney, Mary McKain
Papers. 1904. 1 item.
Open. Card catalog.
University of Michigan, Bentley Historical Library, Michigan Historical Collections.
Letter of Kinney to Effie Mae Adams concerns the death of a relative in a Hart, MI, fire.

7,831. Kleinstuck, Frieda
Papers. 1909-10. 34 items.
Open. Card catalog.
University of Michigan, Bentley Historical Library, Michigan Historical Collections.
Papers of Kleinstuck, a Kalamazoo, MI, resident, pertain to efforts of the Women's League to raise money for Palmer Field and a women's dormitory at the University of Michigan. Many of the letters are from Myrtle White.

7,832. Knights of Pythias
Records. 1926-64. 1 ft.
Open. Card catalog.
University of Michigan, Bentley Historical Library, Michigan Historical Collections.
Material of the Knights, Arbor Temple No. 80, in Ann Arbor also contain records of the Pythian Sisters.

7,833. Knott, Kate Jeffery
Papers. Nd. 1 item.
Open. Card catalog.
University of Michigan, Bentley Historical Library, Michigan Historical Collections.
Alumnae Council questionnaire completed by Knott, who graduated from the University of Michigan in 1902, includes biographical information and reminiscences.

7,834. Kosten, Laurel
Papers. 1963. 1 item.
Open. Card catalog.
University of Michigan, Bentley Historical Library, Michigan Historical Collections.
Interview with Kosten, a state factory inspector, relates to her investigations of working conditions for women in the Grand Rapids, MI, area from 1937 to 1951.

7,835. Ladies Arbeiter Aid Society
Records. 1917-75. 3 vols. and 4 items.
Open. Card catalog.

University of Michigan, Bentley Historical Library, Michigan Historical Collections.
Minute books, membership lists, and a history of a German-American insurance and social society for working women in Ann Arbor. Records generated before 1932 are in German.

7,836. Ladies Library Association
Records. 1866-1916. 6 vols. and 31 items.
Open. Card catalog.
University of Michigan, Bentley Historical Library, Michigan Historical Collections.
Bylaws, minutes, legal documents, correspondence, and clippings of this Ann Arbor organization. Includes a 10th anniversary volume from 1876, which was sealed in that year with instructions that it not be opened until 1976; the volume contains messages for the women of 1976.

7,837. Ladies Literary Club
Records. 1894-1968. 3 ft.
Open. Card catalog.
University of Michigan, Bentley Historical Library, Michigan Historical Collections.
Minutes, financial records, reports, scrapbooks, and other records of this Ypsilanti, MI, organization.

7,838. Ladies Temperance Union
Records. 1874. 1 vol.
Open. Card catalog.
University of Michigan, Bentley Historical Library, Michigan Historical Collections.
Minutes of this Adrian, MI, organization.

7,839. Ladies Universalist Society
Records. 1886. 1 vol.
Open. Card catalog.
University of Michigan, Bentley Historical Library, Michigan Historical Collections.
Constitution of a Port Huron, MI, group, which was created to prepare the way for building a Universalist church. The constitution is part of a book of religious reflections.

7,840. League for Planned Parenthood
Records. 1961-68. Ca. 100 items.
Open. Card catalog.
University of Michigan, Bentley Historical Library, Michigan Historical Collections.
Minutes of the Washtenaw County, MI, League.

7,841. League of Women Voters
Records. 1942-70. 2 ft.
Open. Unpublished guide.
University of Michigan, Bentley Historical Library, Michigan Historical Collections.
Minutes, reports, correspondence, and printed material of the Ann Arbor branch of the LWV pertain to revision of the Ann Arbor city charter, 1948-55; Ann Arbor public schools; Michigan constitutional conventions, 1958-62; city planning; candidates for local public office; and activities of Washtenaw County government.

7,842. League of Women Voters, Monroe
Records. 1959-63. 1 ft.
Open. Unpublished guide.
University of Michigan, Bentley Historical Library, Michigan Historical Collections.
Reports, correspondence, newsletters, and printed material of the Monroe, MI, branch of the LWV concern the formation of the League and local politics and government.

7,843. Lifespan, Inc.
Records. 1969-74. 1 ft.
Open. Card catalog.
University of Michigan, Bentley Historical Library, Michigan Historical Collections.
Promotional material, newsletters, clippings, and other items of an organization formerly known as People Taking Action Against Abortion.

7,844. Lincoln, Martha H.
Papers. 1839. 1 item.
Open. Card catalog.
University of Michigan, Bentley Historical Library, Michigan Historical Collections.
Letter from Lincoln, who lived in Goadwinsville, MI, to her sister-in-law [Mrs.] Olive Lincoln in which she discusses family matters.

7,845. Lloyd, Alice Crocker
Papers. 1931-50. 1 ft.
Open. Card catalog.
University of Michigan, Bentley Historical Library, Michigan Historical Collections.
Lloyd (1893-1950) was dean of women at the University of Michigan. Speeches, biographical material, scrapbooks, and press releases pertain to her administration, the University, and to women students' activities.

7,846. Lowe, Berenice Bryant
Papers. 1937-64. Ca. 175 items.
Open. Card catalog.
University of Michigan, Bentley Historical Library, Michigan Historical Collections.
Papers collected by [Mrs.] Lowe, a local historian of Battle Creek, MI, focus on black abolitionist Sojourner Truth, who settled in Battle Creek in 1857, and on Margaret Nickerson Martin, a writer and poet of Jackson, MI.

7,847. McClure, Grace
Papers. Ca. 1958. Ca. 75 pp.
Open. Card catalog.
University of Michigan, Bentley Historical Library, Michigan Historical Collections.
Reminiscences of McClure (1884-1961), a Saginaw, MI, resident, contain descriptions of her life in Saginaw, prominent families in the area, her activities in Republican politics, and the woman suffrage movement. Also includes several anecdotes about Theodore Roosevelt.

7,848. McGinnis, Esther
Papers. 1948-50. 1 ft.
Open. Card catalog.
University of Michigan, Bentley Historical Library, Michigan Historical Collections.
McGinnis was director of the Merrill-Palmer School. Material relates to the National Conference on Family Life and the White House Conference on Youth in 1950.

7,849. McKenzie, Flora
Papers. 1923. 1 item.
Open. Card catalog.
University of Michigan, Bentley Historical Library, Michigan Historical Collections.
Letter of McKenzie, who lived in St. Cloud, FL, to her mother Della Townsend of Stockbridge, MI, pertains to family matters and mentions Florida Ku Klux Klan activities.

7,850. McLaughlin, Lois Thompson (Angell)
Papers. 1872-1915. Ca. 250 items.
Open. Unpublished guide.
University of Michigan, Bentley Historical Library, Michigan Historical Collections.
McLaughlin was the daughter of James B. Angell and wife of Andrew C. McLaughlin. Contains personal correspondence and letters and diaries that concern her life in China during the Angell diplomatic mission from 1880 to 1882.

7,851. Marston, Mary Olive
Papers. 1870-1924. 125 items.
Open. Card catalog.
University of Michigan, Bentley Historical Library, Michigan Historical Collections.
Marston (1854-1939) was a student at the University of Michigan from 1873 to 1877 and later a professor of Greek at Wellesley College. Includes letters she wrote to her mother while she was attending the University.

7,852. Martha Cook Building
Records. 1915-72. 6 ft.
Open. Unpublished guide.
University of Michigan, Bentley Historical Library, Michigan Historical Collections.
Martha Cook Building is a residence hall for women students at the University of Michigan. Minutes of the board of governors, reports, correspondence, photos, yearbooks, and clippings relate to the activities of the residents and to administration of the Building. Also includes blueprints and other material pertaining to construction and funding of the residence.

7,853. Martin, Ellen Annette
Papers. 1882-85. 7 items.
Open. Card catalog.
University of Michigan, Bentley Historical Library, Michigan Historical Collections.
Letters and other papers about women lawyers, an autobiographical sketch, and diplomas of Martin, who graduated from the University of Michigan law school in 1875.

7,854. Mary Markley House
Records. 1917-50. 5 vols. and ca. 250 items.
Open. Card catalog.
University of Michigan, Bentley Historical Library, Michigan Historical Collections.
Minutes, reports, accounts, correspondence, scrapbooks, and other items of a University of Michigan residence that was called Alumnae House before 1944.

7,855. Mason, Laura Talmadge
Papers. 1838. 10 pp.
Open. Card catalog.
University of Michigan, Bentley Historical Library, Michigan Historical Collections.
Typescript of the journal of Mason (1824-?), who was the daughter of Marshall, MI, minister Steven Mason, contains descriptions of the family's journey to Michigan via the Erie Canal and the Great Lakes and of the beginnings of their new life in Marshall.

7,856. Michigan Abortion Referendum Committee
Records. 1969-72. 5 ft.
Access restricted. Unpublished guide.
University of Michigan, Bentley Historical Library, Michigan Historical Collections.
Organized in 1972 to coordinate support for an abortion reform referendum in that year's election, MARC succeeded the Michigan Coordinating Committee for Abortion Law Reform, which sought the state legislature's approval of a liberalized state abortion law from 1969 to 1971. Includes legislation and petition drive material and campaign files containing MARC publicity and press releases as well as material distributed by the antireferendum Michigan Right to Life Committee.

7,857. Michigan Congregational Church Organizations
Records. 1830-1952. 13 vols. and 7 items.
Open. Card catalog.
University of Michigan, Bentley Historical Library, Michigan Historical Collections.
Records of four Congregational churches or church women's groups, including minutes and other material of the Women's Fellowship in Clinton, 1903-52; Lima church records, 1830-75, containing items of the Women's Society, 1856-63; Pinckney church records, 1853-1924, containing material of the Women's Society, 1870-80 and 1893-99; and records of the Women's Home Missionary Society in Whittaker, 1889-98.

7,858. Michigan Daughters of the American Revolution Chapters
Records. 1838-1974. 6 ft., 1 vol., and ca. 500 items.
Open. Unpublished guide and card catalog.

University of Michigan, Bentley Historical Library, Michigan Historical Collections.
Records of five Michigan DAR chapters include ca. 500 items of the John Biddle Chapter in Trenton, 1957-66; records of the Lewis Cass Chapter in Escanaba, 1909-72, and the Menominee, MI, chapter, 1905-74; scrapbook of the Keziah Cooley Goss Chapter in Ann Arbor, 1949-56; and records of the Sarah Caswell Angell Chapter in Ann Arbor, 1838-1963, containing minute books, reports, membership lists, correspondence, scrapbooks, and programs relating to chapter activities, especially members' work with recent immigrants and their support of national defense efforts during the Spanish-American War and WWI.

7,859. Michigan Female Seminary
Records. 1866-1907. 5 vols.
Open. Card catalog.
University of Michigan, Bentley Historical Library, Michigan Historical Collections.
Minutes, financial records, and subscription lists of the Seminary in Kalamazoo, MI.

7,860. Michigan Grand Army of the Republic Auxiliaries
Records. 1924-54. 8 vols.
Open. Card catalog.
University of Michigan, Bentley Historical Library, Michigan Historical Collections.
Records of three GAR auxiliaries include account book, journal, and scrapbooks of the Estabrook Woman's Relief Corps in Ann Arbor, 1939-54; minutes, account book, and membership list of the Welch Woman's Relief Corps in Ann Arbor, 1938-53; and minutes of the Woman's Relief Corps in East Tawas, 1924-31.

7,861. Michigan League of Women Voters
Records. 1924-63. 7 ft.
Open. Unpublished guide.
University of Michigan, Bentley Historical Library, Michigan Historical Collections.
Records of the state office of the LWV include annual reports, 1945-56; minutes of the state board; financial records; correspondence; convention and conference files; president's letters to the branches; and files on civil service, election law reform, the Fair Employment Practices Commission, the Children's Service, reapportionment, taxation, the Michigan constitutional convention, and the "Know Your State" booklet. Also contained are files, primarily for the 1950s, of LWV branch offices in Allen Park, Bay City, Birmingham, Dearborn, Detroit, Escanaba, Ferndale-Pleasant Ridge, and Flint.

7,862. Michigan Methodist Episcopal Church Organizations
Records. 1847-1960. 4 ft. and 6 vols.
Open. Unpublished guide and card catalog.
University of Michigan, Bentley Historical Library, Michigan Historical Collections.
Minutes and financial statements of the Woman's Home Missionary Society of the Adrian District, 1887-97; minutes of the WHMS in Morenci, 1910-25; constitution and minutes of the WHMS in Pinckney, 1871-91; material about the WHMS in Melford, 1878-1914; and scattered records of the Women's Missionary Federation, Women's Society of Christian Service, Ladies' Aid, WHMS, and Woman's Foreign Missionary Society in Ypsilanti, 1847-1960.

7,863. Michigan Presbyterian Church Organizations
Records. 1823-1940. 57 vols. and ca. 500 items.
Open. Card catalog.
University of Michigan, Bentley Historical Library, Michigan Historical Collections.
Constitution and minutes of the Women's Missionary Society of the First Presbyterian Church of Evart, 1912-17; material of the WMS of the Church in Iron Mountain, also called the Kingsford Presbyterian Church, 1919-40; items of the WMS of the Church in Lapeer; and minutes of a women's society in records of the Church in Pontiac, 1823-1937.

7,864. Michigan Right to Life Committee
Records. 1971-74. 2 ft.
Open. Unpublished guide.
University of Michigan, Bentley Historical Library, Michigan Historical Collections.
Correspondence, newsletters, and campaign and promotional material of the Committee, which was organized to counter 1972 efforts to legalize abortion in Michigan.

7,865. Michigan State Federation of Women's Clubs
Records. 1896-1957. 1 ft.
Open. Unpublished guide.
University of Michigan, Bentley Historical Library, Michigan Historical Collections.
Minutes, reports, and correspondence of the Federation.

7,866. Michigan Woman's Christian Temperance Union
Records. 1873-1970. 4 ft.
Open. Unpublished guide.
University of Michigan, Bentley Historical Library, Michigan Historical Collections.
Collection contains papers of early WCTU workers Alice E. H. Peters and Ella Eaton Kellogg, correspondence with Frances Willard and Anna Adams Gordon, and minutes and treasurers' reports of individual WCTU Michigan districts and chapters, including Eaton, Macomb, and Genesee counties and Dowagiac, Grand Rapids, Vassar, Flint, and Swartz Creek.

7,867. Michigras Committee
Records. 1947-60. 8 vols.
Open. Card catalog.
University of Michigan, Bentley Historical Library, Michigan Historical Collections.
Records of a University of Michigan group sponsored jointly by the Women's Athletic Association and the Michigan Union.

7,868. Morgan, Angela
Papers. 1893-1957. 58 ft.
Open. Unpublished guide and name index.
University of Michigan, Bentley Historical Library, Michigan Historical Collections.
Morgan (1873-1957) was a poet, novelist, and participant in the WWI peace movement. Correspondence, drafts of writings, clippings, and printed material pertain to her writing career and to her interest in the work of the 1915 International Congress of Women, the Henry Ford Peace Ship, the Fellowship of Reconciliation, and the New York City branch of the Woman's Peace party. Correspondents include Jane Addams, Emily Greene Balch, Ruth Standish (Bowles) Baldwin, Zoe Beckley, Evangeline Cory Booth, Anna Hempstead Branch, Isabel (Fiske) Conant, the GFWC, Frances Parkinson Keyes, Margaret Lane, the League of American Pen Women, Eleanor W. McAdoo, the National Woman's party, Corinne (Roosevelt) Robinson, Rebecca Shelley, Ida Minerva Tarbell, Fanny (Garrison) Villard, Lillian D. Wald, Ella (Wheeler) Wilcox, the Women's International League for Peace and Freedom, the Woman's Peace party, the Woman's Pro-League Council, the Women's National Committee for Hands Off the Supreme Court, and the Women's Peace Society.

7,869. Morgan Family
Papers. 1830-1900. 2 ft.
Open. Card catalog.
University of Michigan, Bentley Historical Library, Michigan Historical Collections.
Collection of an Ann Arbor family includes an 1829 autobiography of Polly Morgan and correspondence, drawings, and writings of Lucy Stow Morgan.

7,870. Morgan, Lucy Stow
Papers. 1831. 2 items.
Open. Card catalog.
University of Michigan, Bentley Historical Library, Michigan Historical Collections.
Letter of an Ann Arbor resident to her family in Connecticut contains a detailed account of her domestic duties, household equipment, and housekeeping arrangements as well as detailed notes about Ann Arbor and Jackson, MI.

7,871. Mortar Board Alumnae Club
Records. 1953-73. 50 items.
Open. Card catalog.
University of Michigan, Bentley Historical Library, Michigan Historical Collections.
Minutes, membership lists, and other organizational material of the Ann Arbor chapter of the national senior women's honorary society.

7,872. Mosher, Eliza Maria
Papers. 1846-1934. 3 ft. and 4 vols.
Open. Unpublished guide.
University of Michigan, Bentley Historical Library, Michigan Historical Collections.
Family correspondence of Mosher (1846-1928), who was a physician and dean of women at the University of Michigan; outlines of lectures; manuscripts of articles; notes on trips abroad and scrapbooks with letters and post cards about her travels; and a biographical sketch of her by Florence Hazzard. Mosher's 1875 medical school thesis dealt with the structure and function of the ovaries.

7,873. Mulligan, Joan E.
Papers. 1971-73. 1 ft.
Open. Unpublished guide.
University of Michigan, Bentley Historical Library, Michigan Historical Collections.
Mulligan is a registered nurse and assistant professor of public health at the University of Michigan. Correspondence, notes, conference and committee records, clippings, and other papers pertain to abortion and abortion facilities in Michigan, law reform, anti-abortion groups, and the Michigan Nurses Association.

7,874. Munger, Edith Garnett Cushaway Gotts
Papers. 1907-27. 1 vol. and 300 items.
Open. Card catalog.
University of Michigan, Bentley Historical Library, Michigan Historical Collections.
[Mrs.] Munger (1862-1945) was president of the Michigan Audubon Society. Correspondence, addresses, and other papers deal chiefly with the Society. Also included is a volume of bird-watching records.

7,875. Murphy, Irene (Ellis)
Papers. 1917-75. 1 ft.
Access restricted. Unpublished guide.
University of Michigan, Bentley Historical Library, Michigan Historical Collections.
Correspondence, clippings, and other papers of [Mrs. Harold] Murphy, who was a Birmingham, MI, businesswoman and Democratic regent of the University of Michigan, relate to her life and her interests in the Philippine Islands, especially during her brother-in-law Frank Murphy's administration of the Islands from ca. 1933 to 1936, during WWII, and during the administration of Ferdinand Marcos.

7,876. Murtland, Cleo
Papers. 1917-42. Ca. 130 items.
Open. Card catalog.
University of Michigan, Bentley Historical Library, Michigan Historical Collections.
Murtland (1873-1965) was professor of education at the University of Michigan. Correspondence,

biographical information, and questionnaires completed by her students.

7,877. Nelson, Kaisa
Papers. 1905. 1 item.
Open. Card catalog.
University of Michigan, Bentley Historical Library, Michigan Historical Collections.
Letter of a Crystal Falls, MI, resident to her parents in Finland in which she describes a fire that destroyed her house and killed her two sons. The letter is written in Finnish with an English translation appended.

7,878. Newberry, Marie Anna
Papers. 1915-27. 19 items.
Open. Card catalog.
University of Michigan, Bentley Historical Library, Michigan Historical Collections.
Correspondence of a Dundee, MI, and Toledo, OH, librarian pertains to her interest and work in secondary school libraries, the library section of the Schoolmasters' Club, and organization of a school librarians association.

7,879. Newell, Barbara
Papers. 1966-70. 2 ft.
Open. Card catalog.
University of Michigan, Bentley Historical Library, Michigan Historical Collections.
Newell was acting vice-president for student affairs at the University of Michigan. Files concern student housing and food services at the University.

7,880. Noble, Alice W.
Papers. 1859. 1 item.
Open. Card catalog.
University of Michigan, Bentley Historical Library, Michigan Historical Collections.
Letter by Noble to a Mrs. Cumings of Chelsea, MI, discusses family matters.

7,881. Noggle, Elizabeth (Muncy)
Papers. 1859-77. Ca. 125 items.
Open. Card catalog.
University of Michigan, Bentley Historical Library, Michigan Historical Collections.
Letters of Noggle, who lived in Pierceton, IN, to her brother Levi Muncy.

7,882. Norris, Mark
Papers. 1815-91. 2 ft.
Open. Card catalog.
University of Michigan, Bentley Historical Library, Michigan Historical Collections.
Norris (1796-1862) and his wife Roccina B. Vaill Norris were residents of Ypsilanti, MI. Letters of Roccina Norris relate to education for women. Correspondents include Mary H. Clark, Caroline Kirkland, and Laura Plumb.

7,883. Nye, Kathryn C.
Papers. 1952-75. 4 ft.
Open. Unpublished guide.
University of Michigan, Bentley Historical Library, Michigan Historical Collections.
A resident of East Lansing, MI, Nye was recording secretary of the Michigan Democratic Party State Central Committee from 1962 to 1967. Minutes of the Committee, correspondence, speeches, directories, campaign files, convention material, and publications pertain to state Democratic politics, political campaigns, and Democratic conventions. Includes a few personal items.

7,884. Omega Phi
Records. 1954. 1 item.
Open. Card catalog.
University of Michigan, Bentley Historical Library, Michigan Historical Collections.
Letter from Mrs. Carl S. Wagner to T. Hawley Tapping concerns reasons for the demise of the women's debating society at the University of Michigan.

7,885. Osborn, Stella (Brunt)
Papers. 1916-76. 27 ft.
Open. Unpublished guide and name inventory.
University of Michigan, Bentley Historical Library, Michigan Historical Collections.
A leader in the Atlantic Union movement in the 1950s and 1960s, Osborn (1894-) served as an officer for the Atlantic Union Conference, the International Movement for Atlantic Union, and the Federal Union, Inc. A ward of Chase S. Osborn, she later became his wife.
Correspondence; diaries for 1949 and 1956-63 in which she recorded daily activities, her work on her husband's papers, and her own work on world government; and other papers pertaining to her professional interests, especially her work for world peace through international cooperation. She also was an author.

7,886. Patterson, Barbara Ann
Papers. 1965-70. 1 ft.
Access restricted. Unpublished guide.
University of Michigan, Bentley Historical Library, Michigan Historical Collections.
Patterson (1938-) was personal secretary to G. Mennen Williams, a Democratic governor of Michigan and US ambassador to the Philippine Islands. Personal correspondence and other items relate primarily to her work and activities in the Philippines.

7,887. Patterson, Frances Todd
Papers. 1892-94. 3 vols.
Open. Card catalog.
University of Michigan, Bentley Historical Library, Michigan Historical Collections.
Diaries of Patterson, who was a lady manager from New York at the 1893 World's Columbian Exposition in Chicago, contain descriptions of her domestic and social activities, with emphasis on her participation in preparations for the Exposition; detailed notes about the opening and final weeks of the fair; and references to important persons who planned, managed, or visited the events.

7,888. Perry, Maude Elaine (Caldwell)
Papers. 1891-1948. 1 ft.
Open. Unpublished guide.
University of Michigan, Bentley Historical Library, Michigan Historical Collections.
Perry (1873-1963) was an author and wife of Adrian, MI, journalist Stuart H. Perry.
Correspondence, chiefly family letters; manuscripts of books, plays, short stories, and poetry; book reviews; and a notebook of an 1875 European bicycle tour. She was the author of the novels *Tide House, Yellow Rose Bush,* and *Sea's Edge* and of a play *The Vow.*

7,889. Peterson, Elly (McMillan)
Papers. 1961-77. 25 ft.
Access restricted. Unpublished guide and name inventory.
University of Michigan, Bentley Historical Library, Michigan Historical Collections.
An active Charlotte, MI, Republican party member, Peterson (1914-) was a candidate for the Senate in 1964 and assistant chairwoman of the Republican National Committee in 1969 and 1970.
Correspondence; speeches; her Committee files, which contain letters, speeches, and campaign material as well as the correspondence files of her Committee assistant Juanita Hunter; topical files on women and minorities in the Republican party and on her work for the Equal Rights Amendment; and files relating to her work as deputy chairperson of Gerald R. Ford's presidential campaign in 1976.

7,890. Pfabe, Caroline
Papers. 1897-98. 3 items.
Open. Card catalog.
University of Michigan, Bentley Historical Library, Michigan Historical Collections.
Letters of a German immigrant to Ann Arbor comment on daily life in the 1890s and are addressed to family members. The letters are in German.

7,891. Phelps, Jessie
Papers. 1883-1952. 21 vols.
Open. Card catalog.
University of Michigan, Bentley Historical Library, Michigan Historical Collections.
Phelps (1870-1957) was a teacher at Eastern Michigan College in Ypsilanti. Diaries for part of the period 1885 to 1951 contain her descriptions of student life at Pontiac High School, European trips, and daily activities as a retired teacher; the diaries also reflect her interests in education, reading, nature and gardening, family matters, health in later years, and world affairs. For example, she describes her reaction to events like V-E Day in May 1945, the 1945 San Francisco Conference, and the August 1945 explosion of the atomic bomb. Also included are autograph books.

7,892. Phelps, Mary Merwin
Papers. 1916-56. 2 vols. and ca. 750 items.
Open. Card catalog.
University of Michigan, Bentley Historical Library, Michigan Historical Collections.
Phelps (1865-1944) was an author who lived in Ypsilanti, MI. Correspondence with her publishers and others about her book *Kate Chase* and other manuscripts, her record book listing the dates on which her manuscripts were sent to and were returned from publishers, several unpublished books and articles, and a scrapbook that contains reviews and notices of *Kate Chase.*

7,893. Phillips, Julia Macgruder
Papers. 1891-1904. Ca. 200 pp.
Open. Card catalog.
University of Michigan, Bentley Historical Library, Michigan Historical Collections.
Scrapbook of a 1901 University of Michigan graduate includes programs and clippings pertaining to her life as a University student.

7,894. Political Equality Club
Records. 1894-1900. 2 vols.
Open. Card catalog.
University of Michigan, Bentley Historical Library, Michigan Historical Collections.
Minutes of this Ann Arbor suffrage organization.

7,895. Poole, S. Alicia
Papers. 1925-46. Ca. 250 items.
Open. Card catalog.
University of Michigan, Bentley Historical Library, Michigan Historical Collections.
Research notes and printed material of a Mackinac Island resident relate to all phases of Mackinac Island history. Genealogical material is also included.

7,896. Potter, Louise
Papers. 1912-42. 1 vol. and 6 items.
Open. Card catalog.
University of Michigan, Bentley Historical Library, Michigan Historical Collections.
Correspondence of Potter, a Detroit resident, with Myra B. Jordon and Alfred Lloyd. Also includes a student paper and a scrapbook relating to her student career at the University of Michigan from 1912 to 1916.

7,897. Pratt, Martha Elsie
Papers. 1886-87. 1 vol.
Open. Card catalog.
University of Michigan, Bentley Historical Library, Michigan Historical Collections.
Diary of Pratt (?-1920), who lived in Connersville, IN, has been edited by her daughter Helen H. Ellis and includes notes about games and customs of the day, miscellaneous writings, family photos, and clippings. Ellis details Pratt's interest in drama and representative dramatic pieces.

7,898. Presbyterian Church
Records. 1883-1959. 2 ft.
Open. Unpublished guide.
University of Michigan, Bentley Historical Library, Michigan Historical Collections.
Records of the First Presbyterian Church of Ann Arbor include Women's Foreign Missionary Society secretaries' records for the period 1915 to 1926.

7,899. Presbyterian Church, Big Rapids
Records. 1890-1940. 7 vols.
Open. Card catalog.
University of Michigan, Bentley Historical Library, Michigan Historical Collections.
Constitutions, minutes, and financial reports of women's societies at the Westminister Presbyterian Church of Big Rapids, MI.

7,900. Presbyterian Church, Blissfield
Records. 1845-1969. 6 ft.
Open. Unpublished guide.
University of Michigan, Bentley Historical Library, Michigan Historical Collections.
Collection of the First Presbyterian Church of Blissfield, MI, contains secretaries' records for the Sewing Society, 1852-61, and the Women's Association, 1922-69; secretaries' and treasurers' records of the Women's Home Missionary Society, ca. 1888-1920; and minutes and a cashbook of the Ladies Church Society, 1879-1924. Also includes records of the Young Ladies Guild, 1916-19; Priscilla Circle, 1961-67; and Afternoon Circle, 1951-57.

7,901. Presbyterian Church, Saline
Records. 1831-1960. 19 vols. and 18 items.
Open. Card catalog.
University of Michigan, Bentley Historical Library, Michigan Historical Collections.
Material of a women's society is included in records of the First Presbyterian Church of Saline, MI.

7,902. Presbyterian Church, Stony Creek
Records. 1833-1904. 3 vols. and 1 item.
Open. Card catalog.
University of Michigan, Bentley Historical Library, Michigan Historical Collections.
Stony Creek, MI, church records include the constitution of a local female benevolent society and auxiliary to the home missionary society of Washtenaw County.

7,903. Presbyterian Church, Ypsilanti
Records. 1830-50. 22 vols. and 100 items.
Open. Card catalog.
University of Michigan, Bentley Historical Library, Michigan Historical Collections.
Constitution, annual reports, minutes, financial records, and other material of women's societies in records of the First Presbyterian Church of Ypsilanti, MI.

7,904. Price, Margaret (Bayne)
Papers. 1918-69. 32 ft.
Open. Unpublished guide.
University of Michigan, Bentley Historical Library, Michigan Historical Collections.
Price (1912-68), the wife of Hickman Price, Jr., was a Democratic national committeewoman and women's affairs director of the Democratic party. Minutes of women's affairs meetings, correspondence, speeches, schedules and itineraries, biographies, newsletters, press releases, clippings, and topical files reflect her interests in social, charitable, and youth agencies. Other papers pertain to the Defense Advisory Committee on Women in the Services, women's activities in the Democractic National Committee, and campaign conferences for Democratic women. Correspondents include Helen Berthelot, Martha Wright Griffiths, Adelaide Hart, Maurine (Brown) Neuberger, Eleanor Roosevelt, and Oveta (Culp) Hobby.

7,905. Protestant Episcopal Church
Records. 1885-1928. 15 vols.
Open. Card catalog.
University of Michigan, Bentley Historical Library, Michigan Historical Collections.
Minutes and other material of a church women's association are included in the records of St. Andrews Episcopal Church in Ann Arbor.

7,906. Protestant Episcopal Church, Adrian
Records. 1908-35. 2 vols.
Open. Card catalog.
University of Michigan, Bentley Historical Library, Michigan Historical Collections.
Material of the Daughters of Christ Church and the Women's Auxiliary of Christ Church in Adrian, MI.

7,907. Protestant Episcopal Church, Diocese of Northern Michigan
Records. 1892-1970. 4 ft.
Open. Unpublished guide.
University of Michigan, Bentley Historical Library, Michigan Historical Collections.
Records of the Diocese of Northern Michigan include Women's Auxiliary material dating from 1933 to 1960, a minute book, and a notebook.

7,908. Protestant Episcopal Church, Diocese of Western Michigan
Records. 1866-1968. 31 ft.
Open. Unpublished guide.
University of Michigan, Bentley Historical Library, Michigan Historical Collections.
Records of the Diocese of Western Michigan include files, 1924-37, and a secretary's book, 1906-08, of the women's auxiliary and material from the 1960s pertaining to Episcopal Churchwomen's meetings, projects of the Churchwomen of St. Lukes, and the Conference of Young Women.

7,909. Protestant Episcopal Church, Hudson
Records. 1895-1958. 6 vols. and 10 items.
Open. Card catalog.
University of Michigan, Bentley Historical Library, Michigan Historical Collections.
Minutes of the church guild and women's auxiliary at the Trinity Episcopal Church of Hudson, MI.

7,910. Reed, Minnie
Papers. Nd. 1 vol.
Open. Card catalog.
University of Michigan, Bentley Historical Library, Michigan Historical Collections.
Notes taken for a botany course by a student at the Kalamazoo Female Seminary.

7,911. Reed, Prudence
Papers. 1962-63. 1 item.
Open. Card catalog.
University of Michigan, Bentley Historical Library, Michigan Historical Collections.
Reminiscences of Reed, the daughter of a Methodist minister, in which she reflects upon her family, daily activities, and church affairs.

7,912. Republican Club
Records. 1941-46. 25 items.
Open. Card catalog.
University of Michigan, Bentley Historical Library, Michigan Historical Collections.
Constitution, correspondence, clippings, and other records of the Republican Party Women's Club of Alma, MI.

7,913. Richmond, Rebecca L.
Papers. 1881. 1 item.
Open. Card catalog.
University of Michigan, Bentley Historical Library, Michigan Historical Collections.
Report to the Union Benevolent Association by Richmond pertains to the industrial sewing school opened by the UBA and to the Grand Rapids, MI, school board.

7,914. Romney, Lenore (LaFount)
Papers. 1962-74. 15 ft. and 1 vol.
Open. Unpublished guide.
University of Michigan, Bentley Historical Library, Michigan Historical Collections.
Romney is a civic leader who ran as a Republican candidate for the US Senate in 1970; she is the wife of former Michigan governor George Romney. Correspondence; speeches; political information, topical, and Senate campaign files; audiotapes; and other material relating to the 1970 election and the gubernatorial career of George Romney.

7,915. Root, Minnie Maes
Papers. 1928-42. 11 items.
Open. Card catalog.
University of Michigan, Bentley Historical Library, Michigan Historical Collections.
Correspondence of Root, who was a music publisher in Ann Arbor, and notes concerning the publication of college and patriotic songs.

7,916. Rufus, Maude
Papers. 1916. 1 item.
Open. Card catalog.
University of Michigan, Bentley Historical Library, Michigan Historical Collections.
Letter of Rufus, the wife of professor Carl Rufus of Ann Arbor, describes their educational work in Seoul, Korea.

7,917. Russell, Allie
Papers. Nd. 4 pp.
Open. Card catalog.
University of Michigan, Bentley Historical Library, Michigan Historical Collections.
Reminiscences of Russell (1872-?), an Ann Arbor resident, contain descriptions of her childhood and youth in Ann Arbor.

7,918. Sawtell Family
Papers. Ca. 1850-60. 1 vol.
Open. Card catalog.
University of Michigan, Bentley Historical Library, Michigan Historical Collections.
Notebook kept by a member of the Sawtell family, who was probably a staff member of the Michigan Female College, consists primarily of quotations and notes on the status of women.

7,919. Schaub, Theresa
Papers. Nd. 1 vol.
Open. Card catalog.
University of Michigan, Bentley Historical Library, Michigan Historical Collections.
Contains Schaub's history of the Ladies' Library Association of Ann Arbor from 1866 to 1872.

7,920. Selmon, Bertha Eugenia (Loveland)
Papers. 1932-49. Ca. 2 ft. and 2 vols.
Open. Unpublished guide.
University of Michigan, Bentley Historical Library, Michigan Historical Collections.
Correspondence between Selmon (1877-1949), a Battle Creek, MI, physician, and her medical colleagues about the Medical Women's National Association, early women physicians in Michigan, and birth control. Also includes scrapbooks with pictures and brief biographical sketches of such Michigan women physicians as Minnie Dell Sprague Baker, Dana G. Cook, Margaret Cochrane Cooper, Anna Hall Flatt, Blanche Moore Haines, M. Alice Heney, Margaret McCauley Kellogg, Helen Marie Upjohn Kirkland, Lauretta Kress, Katherine Kindsay, Maria Whittlesey Norris, Eva J. Shedd Outwater, Linda Gage Roth, Frances A. Rutherford, Hattie A. Schwendener, Martha Cochrane Strong, and Millie Kirby Upjohn.

7,921. Session, Vivian Siemon
Papers. 1946. 2 vols.
Open. Card catalog.
University of Michigan, Bentley Historical Library, Michigan Historical Collections.
Student papers of Session include a study of the Political Equality Club of Ann Arbor, which was a suffragist group.

7,922. Sheldon, Mary Downing
Papers. 1872. 5 items.
Open. Card catalog.
University of Michigan, Bentley Historical Library, Michigan Historical Collections.
Letter from [Miss] Sheldon (1850-98) to Alice Williams describes Latin and Greek examinations at the University of Michigan in 1872. Also includes copies of the examinations and explanatory letters.

7,923. Shelley, Rebecca
Papers. 1910-69. 16 ft.
Open. Unpublished guide and name inventory.
University of Michigan, Bentley Historical Library, Michigan Historical Collections.
A pacifist from Battle Creek, MI, Shelley (1887-) was a participant in the WWI peace movement and has been a member of the Fellowship of Reconciliation, Women Strike for Peace, and the Women's International League for Peace and Freedom. Correspondence, reports, clippings, pamphlets, and other material pertain to the 1915 International Congress of Women, the Henry Ford Peace Ship in 1915, the American Neutral Conference Committee, the Emergency Peace Federation, and the People's Council of America. Correspondents include Jane Addams, Emily Greene Balch, Sophonisba Preston Breckinridge, Emma Goldman, Alice Hamilton, Lida Gustava Heymann, Lola Maverick Lloyd, Angela Morgan, Alice Paul, Franciska Schwimmer, Rosika Schwimmer, and Fanny Garrison Villard.

7,924. Skarshaug, Pauline Grant Waite
Papers. 1896-1949. 27 vols. and ca. 1000 items.
Open. Card catalog.
University of Michigan, Bentley Historical Library, Michigan Historical Collections.
Diaries of Skarshaug (1901-50), a University of Michigan librarian who lived in Yakima, WA, and Ann Arbor, cover the period 1911 to 1938 and comment on daily activities in school, at work at the University, and at home.

7,925. Sketching Club
Records. 1893-1900. 1 vol.
Open. Card catalog.
University of Michigan, Bentley Historical Library, Michigan Historical Collections.
Constitution, bylaws, minutes, and clippings of this women's art club in Ann Arbor.

7,926. Slack, E. Elizabeth
Papers. 1936-61. 1 ft.
Open. Card catalog.
University of Michigan, Bentley Historical Library, Michigan Historical Collections.
Clippings and other items of Slack (1881-1973), who lived in Ann Arbor, relate to her work with the Friends of the Ann Arbor Public Library, the Ann Arbor Board of Education, the Northside Improvement Association, and other community organizations.

7,927. Slayton Family
Papers. 1849-1954. 11 ft.
Open. Unpublished guide.
University of Michigan, Bentley Historical Library, Michigan Historical Collections.
Papers of the Slayton and Dunn families of Hillsdale, MI, include correspondence and other papers of Sarah Abbie (Dunn) Slayton (1853-1926) and Helen Elizabeth Slayton and letters of Helen (Dunn) Gates, Sarah Augusta Slayton (1886-), and Abbie Cyrena Slayton (1884-).

7,928. Slayton, Julia A.
Papers. 1881-83. 2 vols.
Open. Card catalog.
University of Michigan, Bentley Historical Library, Michigan Historical Collections.
Diaries of Slayton (1829-?), who was a Grant, MI, resident and wife of William C. Slayton, contain brief entries describing her daily household routine and social events.

7,929. Slayton, Sarah Augusta
Papers. 1899-1918. 9 vols.
Open. Card catalog.
University of Michigan, Bentley Historical Library, Michigan Historical Collections.
Diary of Slayton (1886-), a teacher, includes her reflections on childhood experiences, student life at Hillsdale College, and her teaching experiences in Michigan, Wisconsin, and Georgia.

7,930. Smith, Anna K.
Papers. 1911-39. 5 vols.
Open. Card catalog.
University of Michigan, Bentley Historical Library, Michigan Historical Collections.
Account books of a Monroe County, MI, schoolteacher include earnings and costs of goods and services.

7,931. Smith, Arvilla Almira (Powers)
Papers. 1833-45. 1 vol.
Open. Card catalog.
University of Michigan, Bentley Historical Library, Michigan Historical Collections.
Diary of Smith (1808-95), who was a missionary to the Ottawa and Ojibwe Indians in Michigan and wife of George Nelson Smith, includes comments on her trip from Vermont to Michigan, the births and deaths of her children, other family concerns, and her health. Also contains her reflections on religious matters and personal salvation.

7,932. Smith Family
Papers. 1846-1935. 17 items.
Open. Card catalog.
University of Michigan, Bentley Historical Library, Michigan Historical Collections.
Papers of an Ontonagon, MI, family contain letters of Martha Bracken Smith to her mother describing life as a missionary, an essay on the role of women she wrote as a student at Washington Female Seminary, and memoranda on her life written by her husband James I. Smith, who was a Presbyterian missionary on Michigan's Upper Peninsula.

7,933. Smith, Josie
Papers. 1887-98. 13 vols. and 102 items.
Open. Card catalog.
University of Michigan, Bentley Historical Library, Michigan Historical Collections.
Personal letters, scattered business correspondence, and account books of an Adrian, MI, resident.

7,934. Smith, May K.
Papers. 1909-71. 62 vols. and 50 items.
Open. Card catalog.
University of Michigan, Bentley Historical Library, Michigan Historical Collections.
Smith (1881-) was a schoolteacher, civic leader, and president of the Monroe, MI, Business and Professional Women's Club. Correspondence with former students during WWII, diaries of daily activities, account books, and a history of the Monroe BPWC.

7,935. Spalding Family
Papers. 1808-1910. 3 ft.
Open. Unpublished guide and partial calendar.
University of Michigan, Bentley Historical Library, Michigan Historical Collections.
Correspondence of the Spalding-Sexton family of Connecticut, Alabama, and northern Michigan includes letters of Mary (Spalding) [Mrs. C. P.] Chamberlain discussing family matters and life in New Lisbon, OH, and Canisteo, NY; letters of Miranda (Sexton) [Mrs. William P.] Spalding (1826-1910), which pertain to her early years as a student in Connecticut, teaching in Alabama, life during the Civil War, her administration of a Ruffian, NC, plantation from 1869 to 1874, and family concerns and life in Sault Ste. Marie, MI; correspondence of Mary B. (Sexton) [Mrs. Amos] Lively (1816-91), a teacher in Alabama and Texas, in which she contrasts Alabama with Connecticut and describes Texas before and during the Civil War; letters of Hannah Sexton (?-1848), a teacher in Alabama and Connecticut who commented on her experiences in the 1830s and 1840s; and letters of Adelle Spalding, written after 1900, concerning mining activities in Idaho and Alaska.

7,936. Spaulding, Mary Cecilia (Swegles)
Papers. 1903. 2 items.
Open. Card catalog.
University of Michigan, Bentley Historical Library, Michigan Historical Collections.
Reminiscences of Spaulding, who was the wife of Oliver Lyman Spaulding and daughter of John Swegles, recount the early history of St. Johns, MI, and describe her father. Also contains a letter by her son Oliver Lyman Spaulding with reminiscences of the Ladies Literary Club.

7,937. Spring Weekend Committee
Records. 1955-57. 2 vols.
Open. Card catalog.
University of Michigan, Bentley Historical Library, Michigan Historical Collections.
Records of this University of Michigan organization, which was sponsored jointly by the Women's Athletic Association and the Michigan Union.

7,938. Star Guild
Records. 1913-16. 30 items.
Open. Card catalog.
University of Michigan, Bentley Historical Library, Michigan Historical Collections.
Receipts, correspondence, and an historical sketch of the Hillsdale, MI, Guild.

7,939. Stebbins, Elizabeth R.
Papers. 1871-75. 75 items.
Open. Card catalog.
University of Michigan, Bentley Historical Library, Michigan Historical Collections.
Stebbins was corresponding secretary of the Michigan Orphan Asylum Association in Lenawee County. Constitution and correspondence of the Association and Stebbins's correspondence with Laura Smith Haviland.

7,940. Stockwell, Madelon Louisa
Papers. 1918-21. 24 items.
Open. Card catalog.
University of Michigan, Bentley Historical Library, Michigan Historical Collections.
In 1870 Stockwell (1845-1924) became the first woman student at the University of Michigan. A letter; material about her class, the class of 1872; and recollections about Stockwell assembled in 1954.

7,941. Sunderland, Eliza Jane (Read)
Papers. 1865-1910. 5 ft.
Open. Unpublished guide and name inventory.
University of Michigan, Bentley Historical Library, Michigan Historical Collections.
Correspondence, lectures, sermons, student notebooks, and articles of Sunderland (1839-1910), who was a lecturer, educator, author, and advocate of women's rights. Correspondents include the

Association for the Advancement of Women, Augusta Jane Chapin, the Connecticut Woman Suffrage Association, Caroline Bartlett Crane, Julia (Ward) Howe, Myra (Beach) Jordan, the Michigan Equal Suffrage Association, the Michigan State Federation of Women's Clubs, the National Alliance of Unitarian and Other Liberal Christian Women, Lucinda (Hinsdale) Stone, and the Women's Western Unitarian Conference. Other items among her papers provide information about the Unitarian organizations listed above. Although Sunderland was not an ordained minister, she often took the place of her husband Jabez T. Sunderland in the pulpit; many of her sermons included in the collection pertain to women's topics. From 1886 to 1895 she served on the national board of the Association for the Advancement of Women. She was a prominent speaker at the Women's Congress of the 1893 World's Columbian Exposition in Chicago and in that year became one of the first women to receive a PhD from the University of Michigan. She also was the first woman elected to the Hartford, CT, school board.

7,942. Sutton Family
Papers. 1836-88. Ca. 250 items.
Open. Card catalog.
University of Michigan, Bentley Historical Library, Michigan Historical Collections.
Papers of this Allegan County, MI, family include the correspondence of Susan Sutton Kirtland, written in the 1850s and 1860s, and letters of Harriet Sutton Turner (1820-1902).

7,943. Swadling, Lella (Taylor)
Papers. 1866-1901. 7 items.
Open. Card catalog.
University of Michigan, Bentley Historical Library, Michigan Historical Collections.
Correspondence and papers regarding school activities of Swadling, a Grass Lake, MI, resident.

7,944. Swift, Iva Irene
Papers. 1916-17. 1 vol.
Open. Card catalog.
University of Michigan, Bentley Historical Library, Michigan Historical Collections.
Scrapbook of a graduate student at the University of Michigan contains photos, post cards, clippings, and other memorabilia of student life.

7,945. Tanner, Helen (Hornbeck)
Papers. 1966-69. 1 ft.
Open. Card catalog.
University of Michigan, Bentley Historical Library, Michigan Historical Collections.
Tanner was secretary of the Commission on Indian Affairs of the State of Michigan. Correspondence, reports, clippings, and printed material concern the work of the Commission and the status of the Michigan Indian. Items also focus on such subjects as Indian housing, education, arts and crafts, legislation, and court suits.

7,946. Taylor Family
Papers. 1827-1908. 3 ft. and 18 vols.
Open. Card catalog
University of Michigan, Bentley Historical Library, Michigan Historical Collections.
Papers of the Barton Stout Taylor family include manuscripts of sermons, articles, and speeches on woman suffrage.

7,947. Teed, Florence Ernestine (Schleicher)
Papers. 1919-53. 2 ft.
Open. Unpublished guide.
University of Michigan, Bentley Historical Library, Michigan Historical Collections.
Teed (1901-54) was an ordained Methodist minister. Correspondence, student papers, sermon outlines, clippings, and religious and inspirational writings relate to her preaching, the role and activities of women in the church, and the holiness movement within Methodism. Also includes material about the Women's Society of Christian Service of the Methodist Church and the American Association of Women Ministers.

7,948. Todd, Clara (Patterson)
Papers. 1920-69. Ca. 250 items.
Open. Card catalog.
University of Michigan, Bentley Historical Library, Michigan Historical Collections.
Correspondence, clippings, and printed material of Todd, a temperance leader, pertain to the WCTU. Also included are items about her mother Judge Phoebe Patterson as well as a brief WCTU history written by Phoebe Patterson.

7,949. Treat, Lucretia Willard
Papers. 1892-1904. 1 ft.
Open. Card catalog.
University of Michigan, Bentley Historical Library, Michigan Historical Collections.
Treat (1842-1904) founded the Grand Rapids, MI, Kindergarten Training School. Correspondence, lecture notes, school material, address book, and clippings pertain to kindergarten education. Correspondents include Jane Addams.

7,950. Tuomy, Katherine Genevieve
Papers. 1876-1947. 1 ft.
Open. Card catalog.
University of Michigan, Bentley Historical Library, Michigan Historical Collections.
Family correspondence, clippings, and other items of Tuomy (?-1966), who was an Ann Arbor realtor and president of the Michigan Federation of Business and Professional Women.

7,951. Turner, Sarah E.
Papers. 1849-1939. 3 vols. and 5 items.
Open. Card catalog.
University of Michigan, Bentley Historical Library, Michigan Historical Collections.
Turner (1834-1939) was a temperance worker and member of the WCTU. Correspondence with Benjamin Turner; her 1939 autobiography, which recounts her temperance and other reform activities; and scrapbooks with clippings on temperance and about Adrian, MI.

7,952. Unitarian Church
Records. 1865-1961. 2 ft.
Open. Card catalog.
University of Michigan, Bentley Historical Library, Michigan Historical Collections.
Records of the First Unitarian Church of Ann Arbor include an 1889 report of the King's Daughters and 1888 secretary's report of the Ladies Union.

7,953. United Church Women
Records. 1941-60. 4 vols. and 50 items.
Open. Card catalog.
University of Michigan, Bentley Historical Library, Michigan Historical Collections.
Secretary's books with minutes, reports, and lists; a draft of the Ann Arbor self survey; and other items of the UCW in Ann Arbor.

7,954. U.S. Council of National Defense, Women's Committee
Records. 1918-19. 27 items.
Open. Card catalog.
University of Michigan, Bentley Historical Library, Michigan Historical Collections.
Material of this Washtenaw County, MI, women's organization.

7,955. University of Michigan Alumni Association
Records. 1859-1967. 130 ft.
Open. Card catalog.
University of Michigan, Bentley Historical Library, Michigan Historical Collections.
Records of the Association contain Alumnae Council files, including responses to Council questionnaires; Alumnae Club files; Michigan League Building Fund campaign records; the Henderson House file; and recent material concerning the establishment of the Center for Continuing Education of Women.

7,956. University of Michigan Alumni Association, Alumnae Association
Records. 1916-42. 2 vols.
Open. Card catalog.
University of Michigan, Bentley Historical Library, Michigan Historical Collections.
Minute books of the Association unit in Boston.

7,957. University of Michigan Alumni Association, Alumnae Club
Records. 1931-60. 1 ft.
Open. Card catalog.
University of Michigan, Bentley Historical Library, Michigan Historical Collections.
Minutes, reports, correspondence, and other records of the Sara Browne Smith group in Ann Arbor.

7,958. University of Michigan Alumni Association, Saginaw
Records. Nd. 26 pp.
Open. Card catalog.
University of Michigan, Bentley Historical Library, Michigan Historical Collections.
History of the Saginaw Valley Alumnae Association from 1896 to 1920 was compiled by Kate Jackson Hard and includes addenda to 1957.

7,959. University of Michigan Dean of Women
Records. 1940-66. 3 ft.
Open. Card catalog.
University of Michigan, Bentley Historical Library, Michigan Historical Collections.
Collection includes reports, forms, and items concerning housing for women students and minutes of the League House Directors.

7,960. University of Michigan Faculty Women's Club
Records. 1921-71. 2 ft.
Open. Unpublished guide.
University of Michigan, Bentley Historical Library, Michigan Historical Collections.
The Club is open to University women and faculty wives. General and executive committee minutes, treasurers' reports, proceedings, scrapbooks with publicity clippings, membership cards, newsletters, and other records.

7,961. University of Michigan, Mortar Board
Records. 1906-20. 2 vols.
Open. Card catalog.
University of Michigan, Bentley Historical Library, Michigan Historical Collections.
Photo album and membership rolls of the Pi Sigma Alpha Chapter of Mortar Board, an honorary society for college women in their senior year.

7,962. University of Michigan Women's League
Records. 1891-1963. 32 ft.
Open. Unpublished guide.
University of Michigan, Bentley Historical Library, Michigan Historical Collections.
Presidents' reports, ledgers, scrapbooks, and other records of this social organization, which was interested in housing, self-government, judicial affairs, organizations, and other concerns of women students.

7,963. University of Michigan Women's Research Club
Records. 1902-76. 2 ft.
Open. Unpublished guide.
University of Michigan, Bentley Historical Library, Michigan Historical Collections.
The Club is an organization for University women, faculty members, staff, and graduate students

engaged in independent research. Minutes, financial records, membership lists, correspondence, histories, abstracts of papers presented, and memorials.

7,964. Van Deman, Esther Boise
Papers. 1901-02. Ca. 250 items.
Open. Card catalog.
University of Michigan, Bentley Historical Library, Michigan Historical Collections.
Collection of Van Deman (1862-1937), an archaeologist, contains her manuscript on historical Roman monuments and architecture, lecture notes, diagrams of Greek and Roman buildings, a passport, photos of Roman countryside and art works, and other items.

7,965. Van Duren, Margaret Vining
Papers. 1944-46. Ca. 250 items.
Open. Card catalog.
University of Michigan, Bentley Historical Library, Michigan Historical Collections.
Scrapbook and other papers of Van Duren, an Ann Arbor resident, relate to her volunteer work during WWII with the Office of Civilian Defense, the American National Red Cross, and the Office of Price Administration.

7,966. Van Hoosen, Bertha
Papers. 1880-1952. 2 ft.
Open. Card catalog.
University of Michigan, Bentley Historical Library, Michigan Historical Collections.
Van Hoosen (1863-1952) was a physician in Rochester, MI, and Chicago. Correspondence, diaries, manuscript of her autobiography, appointment books, clippings, and other material relate to student life at the University of Michigan and to her professional activities.

7,967. Van Tyne, Helen Belfield (Bates)
Papers. 1944-71. 3 ft.
Open. Unpublished guide.
University of Michigan, Bentley Historical Library, Michigan Historical Collections.
[Mrs. Josselyn] Van Tyne was an Ann Arbor civic leader and member of the Citizens Advisory Council of the Washtenaw County Juvenile Court. Material reflects her interest in juvenile delinquency problems, the Michigan League of Planned Parenthood, the Michigan Council on Women in Business and Industry, and the James Foster Foundation.

7,968. Vandenberg, Hazel Harper (Whittaker)
Papers. 1928-48. 1 box and 14 vols.
Access restricted. Unpublished guide.
University of Michigan, Bentley Historical Library, Michigan Historical Collections.
Vandenberg (1882-1950) was the wife of Arthur H. Vandenberg, a Republican US senator from Michigan. Diaries in which she describes social activities and daily political life in Washington, DC, also contain photos, programs, clippings, and other items.

7,969. Walter Family
Papers. Ca. 1849-50. 23 pp.
Open. Card catalog.
University of Michigan, Bentley Historical Library, Michigan Historical Collections.
Diary of an unnamed Kalamazoo, MI, woman contains descriptions of her daily activities and religious work in the Methodist church.

7,970. Warber, Esther Maxine
Papers. 1957-65. Ca. 400 items.
Open. Card catalog.
University of Michigan, Bentley Historical Library, Michigan Historical Collections.
Correspondence, clippings, maps, and other papers of a Peace Corps volunteer from Michigan who served in Ecuador.

7,971. Washtenaw County Medical Society, Women's Auxiliary
Records. 1938-68. 1 ft.
Open. Card catalog.
University of Michigan, Bentley Historical Library, Michigan Historical Collections.
Constitution and bylaws, annual reports, minutes, correspondence, a history, and other records of the Auxiliary.

7,972. Whedon, Helen M.
Papers. 1859-98. 4 vols. and 25 items.
Open. Card catalog.
University of Michigan, Bentley Historical Library, Michigan Historical Collections.
Diaries of [Mrs. William W.] Whedon, a Chelsea, MI, housewife, contain brief entries for the period 1859 to 1869, which discuss weather, religious activities, encounters with friends, and current events. Also included are poems and papers delivered before church groups, a history of the Ladies Aid Society of the First Methodist Church of Ann Arbor, and memorial tributes to Eliza Burd, Elizabeth Noyes, and Phoebe Beers Beal.

7,973. Wheeler, Clara Marian
Papers. 1874-1948. 6 ft.
Open. Unpublished guide and partial name inventory.
University of Michigan, Bentley Historical Library, Michigan Historical Collections.
An educator and advocate of kindergarten education, Wheeler (1861-1946) also was principal of the Grand Rapids, MI, Kindergarten Training School. Correspondence, including that with [Miss] Elizabeth Harrison, Lucretia Willard Treat, Kate Douglas Wiggin, and Frances Willard; ledgers and account books; lecture and class notes; programs; scrapbooks with clippings and handwritten material about Grand Rapids educational affairs and poetry and quotations from famous persons; and papers relating to the Froebel Study Club, Kent County Sunday School Association, the national PTA, First Methodist Church of Grand Rapids, and Grand Rapids Kindergarten Training School.

7,974. Wheeler, L. O.
Papers. 1845. 1 item.
Open. Card catalog.
University of Michigan, Bentley Historical Library, Michigan Historical Collections.
Account book of a Saline, MI, seamstress contains a record of daily expenses.

7,975. Willis, Mattie Azalia
Papers. 1928-70. 2 ft.
Open. Unpublished guide.
University of Michigan, Bentley Historical Library, Michigan Historical Collections.
Willis (1912-70) was a Battle Creek, MI, musician, music teacher, and a member of that city's NAACP chapter. Correspondence; diaries scattered from 1928 to 1967 containing notes about daily activities and personal thoughts; essays and papers concerning her professional career and interests; and clippings.

7,976. Wolfe, Joan
Papers. 1962-73. Ca. 250 items.
Open. Card catalog.
University of Michigan, Bentley Historical Library, Michigan Historical Collections.
Papers of Wolfe, an employee of the Michigan department of natural resources, include material pertaining to her work as organizer of Michigan's first environmental teach-in in 1966 and as founder of the West Michigan Environmental Council. The papers reflect her interest in the controversy concerning the use of pesticides.

7,977. Woman's Christian Temperance Union
Records. 1877-1974. 2 ft.
Open. Unpublished guide.
University of Michigan, Bentley Historical Library, Michigan Historical Collections.
Minutes of the Ann Arbor chapter of the WCTU; treasurers' reports; an organizational history; scrapbooks, including one of Lula Bon Rice; and other records.

7,978. Woman's Christian Temperance Union, Battle Creek
Records. 1874-1962. 2 ft.
Open. Unpublished guide.
University of Michigan, Bentley Historical Library, Michigan Historical Collections.
Minutes of the Battle Creek, MI, chapter of the WCTU, its board of trustees, and the Red Ribbon Temperance Union; scrapbook; programs and yearbooks; and clippings.

7,979. Woman's Christian Temperance Union, Evart
Records. 1900-05. 1 vol.
Open. Card catalog.
University of Michigan, Bentley Historical Library, Michigan Historical Collections.
Minutes of the Evart, MI, chapter of the WCTU.

7,980. Woman's Christian Temperance Union, Jackson County
Records. 1912-50. 3 vols.
Open. Card catalog.
University of Michigan, Bentley Historical Library, Michigan Historical Collections.
Minute books and a scrapbook of the Clara Kennedy chapter of the WCTU, which was located in Jackson County, MI.

7,981. Woman's Christian Temperance Union, Osceola County
Records. 1897-1900. 1 vol. and 6 items.
Open. Card catalog.
University of Michigan, Bentley Historical Library, Michigan Historical Collections.
Minutes, roll book, and correspondence of the Osceola County, MI, branch of the WCTU.

7,982. Woman's Christian Temperance Union, Three Oaks
Records. 1879-87. 50 items.
Open. Card catalog.
University of Michigan, Bentley Historical Library, Michigan Historical Collections.
Minutes of the Three Oaks, MI, branch of the WCTU.

7,983. Woman's Christian Temperance Union, Ypsilanti
Records. 1928-68. 3 vols. and 25 items.
Open. Card catalog.
University of Michigan, Bentley Historical Library, Michigan Historical Collections.
Minutes, financial records, membership lists, clippings, and memorabilia of the Ypsilanti, MI, branch of the WCTU.

7,984. Woman's Club
Records. 1905-62. 12 vols.
Open. Card catalog.
University of Michigan, Bentley Historical Library, Michigan Historical Collections.
Records of this Saline, MI, organization.

7,985. Women's Athletic Association
Records. 1905-62. 1 ft. and 20 vols.
Open. Unpublished guide.
University of Michigan, Bentley Historical Library, Michigan Historical Collections.
Constitution, minutes, and reports of this University of Michigan group.

7,986. Women's Club
Records. 1887-1928. 26 items.
Open. Card catalog.

University of Michigan, Bentley Historical Library, Michigan Historical Collections.
Annual reports from 1891 to 1893, financial records, scattered correspondence, and an 1895 manuscript history of this Adrian, MI, group, which originally was known as the Ladies Study Club.

7,987. Women's Education Club
Records. 1925-33. 2 vols.
Open. Card catalog.
University of Michigan, Bentley Historical Library, Michigan Historical Collections.
Minutes, treasurers' records, and clippings of this University of Michigan club.

7,988. Women's International League for Peace and Freedom
Records. 1938-74. 2 ft.
Open. Unpublished guide.
University of Michigan, Bentley Historical Library, Michigan Historical Collections.
Minutes, correspondence, newsletters, and clippings of the Michigan branch of the WILPF and of local units in Ann Arbor, Ypsilanti, Detroit, Rouge Valley, Traverse City, Ingham County, and Oakland County. Also included are items about the national WILPF, branch newsletters, the periodicals *Four Lights* and *Peace and Freedom,* and proceedings of the International Congress.

7,989. Women's Presbyterial Society
Records. 1875-1965. 1 ft. and 15 vols.
Open. Card catalog.
University of Michigan, Bentley Historical Library, Michigan Historical Collections.
Annual reports, minutes, membership registers, district meeting attendance registers, and other records of the WPS in the presbyteries of Lake Superior, Flint, Saginaw, and Lake Huron, MI.

7,990. Women's Presbyterial Society, Lansing
Records. 1878-1957. 1 vol. and ca. 250 items.
Open. Unpublished guide.
University of Michigan, Bentley Historical Library, Michigan Historical Collections.
Annual reports for the periods 1878 to 1916 and 1932 to 1957, minutes, and a history of the activities of the Lansing, MI, Society.

7,991. Wood, Julia Newton
Papers. 1853. 1 vol.
Open. Card catalog.
University of Michigan, Bentley Historical Library, Michigan Historical Collections.
Diary of [Mrs. James] Wood (1827-?) recounts a trip to California and discusses crossing the Missouri River, the Great Plains, and the mountains. Includes reflections on the hardships of travel and her interest in religion.

7,992. Worcester, Nanon Fay (Leas)
Papers. 1909. 1 item.
Open. Card catalog.
University of Michigan, Bentley Historical Library, Michigan Historical Collections.
Worcester was the wife of Dean Conant Worcester, who was the secretary of the interior of the Philippine Islands from 1901 to 1913. Diary contains letters she wrote to her mother describing an inspection trip she took with her husband into the interior of Luzon.

7,993. Young Men's—Young Women's Christian Association
Records. 1895-1955. 27 vols. and 150 items.
Open. Card catalog.
University of Michigan, Bentley Historical Library, Michigan Historical Collections.
Minutes, financial records, scrapbooks, and other records of the Ann Arbor YMCA auxiliary and minutes of the YWCA.

7,994. Young Woman's Christian Temperance Union
Records. 1880-81. 1 vol.
Open. Card catalog.
University of Michigan, Bentley Historical Library, Michigan Historical Collections.
Minutes of this University of Michigan organization.

7,995. Young Women's Christian Association, Battle Creek
Records. 1903-58. 2 ft.
Open. Unpublished guide.
University of Michigan, Bentley Historical Library, Michigan Historical Collections.
Board minutes, secretaries' reports, correspondence, items pertaining to proposed buildings, and a scrapbook of the Battle Creek, MI, branch of the YWCA.

7,996. Young Women's Christian Association, University of Michigan Branch
Records. 1916-23. 2 vols.
Open. Card catalog.
University of Michigan, Bentley Historical Library, Michigan Historical Collections.
Minutes and advisory committee minutes of the YWCA branch at the University of Michigan.

7,997. De Cleyre, Voltairine
Papers. 1885-1950. 146 items.
Open. No guide.
University of Michigan Library, Department of Rare Books and Special Collections.
Papers of De Cleyre (1866-1912), an anarchist lecturer, writer, poet, and teacher, contain correspondence with her mother Harriet Elizabeth (Billings) De Claire (1836-1927), the Livshis family, and Joseph Antoine Labadie (1850-1933) as well as several of Voltairine De Cleyre's articles and poems. Also includes correspondence of her son Harry De Cleyre (1890-1974) and her sister Adelaide (De Claire) Thayer (1864-1945) with Agnes Inglis, the first curator of the University of Michigan's Labadie Collection of social, political protest, and reform literature, who was assembling information for a biography. The spelling of the De Clair surname varied: Voltairine De Cleyre's father's name was Hector Auguste De Clair, and her mother and sister chose to spell the name De Claire. Her son took her surname because she didn't marry his father.

7,998. Goldman, Emma
Papers. 1901-40. 166 items.
Open. Unpublished guide.
University of Michigan Library, Department of Rare Books and Special Collections.
Correspondence, articles, and a scrapbook of Goldman (1869-1940), an anarchist lecturer, writer, and feminist. Contains her correspondence, 1915-32, with Agnes Inglis, the first curator of the Labadie Collection of social, political protest, and reform literature at the University of Michigan. Also includes numerous copies of Goldman's correspondence with noted writers and radicals and her correspondence, 1920-39, with Mark Clevans (formerly Mark Mratchny), the editor of the *Freie Arbeiter Stimme* from 1936 to 1939, and with his wife Johanna (Boetz) Clevans. The latter items are in Russian, German, Yiddish, and English.

7,999. Heinzen, Karl Peter
Papers. 1803-80. 5 Hollinger boxes.
Open. No guide.
University of Michigan Library, Department of Rare Books and Special Collections.
Correspondence, manuscripts, and documents of Heinzen (1809-80), a German immigrant who founded and edited the *Pionier,* a German language journal of opinion, from 1854 to 1878; Heinzen also was a supporter of women's rights. Papers include his correspondence, 1872-78, with [Mrs.] Clara Neymann, a German immigrant who was Wendt's sister-in-law, about her lecture tours on behalf of women's rights as well as Heinzen's criticism of her writings, which she sent to him for critical review. Also includes his correspondence in 1872 with [Mrs.] Mathilde F. Wendt concerning her work on and her loss of *Die Neue Zeit,* which she edited as a women's journal in New York. Wendt's letters concern employment for the *Neue Zeit* staff at the *Pionier* and include mention of the reaction she caused when she demanded to register as a voter in her New York ward.

8,000. Holt, Frederick Holford
Papers. 1915-17. 2 Hollinger boxes and 384 items.
Open. No guide.
University of Michigan Library, Department of Rare Books and Special Collections.
Correspondence, speeches, reports, financial records, photos, and press releases of Holt (1867-1929), a Detroit businessman who was a member of the Ford Peace Expedition in 1915, the personal representative of Henry Ford, and business manager for the 1916 Neutral Conference for Continuous Mediation in Stockholm, Sweden. Includes papers of his wife Lillian (Silk) Holt (1869-1949), a member of the Women's Peace party and the Ford Peace Expedition, and correspondence with Rosika Schwimmer, a Hungarian feminist and member of the Women's Peace Congress in 1915. Lillian Holt's papers contain a speech she gave in 1915 attributing the origins of the Ford Peace Expedition to activities of the Women's Peace party and letters she received from Frederick Holt in 1916 when she returned to Detroit from Stockholm to determine Henry Ford's wishes regarding continuation of the Conference.

8,001. Van Volkenburg and Browne
Papers. Ca. 1883-1971. 142 ft.
Partially restricted. No guide.
University of Michigan Library, Department of Rare Books and Special Collections.
Correspondence; diaries; manuscripts for books, plays, and poems; financial records; photos; scrapbooks; playbills; promptbooks; and family records of Ellen Van Volkenburg (1882-) and Maurice Browne (1881-1955), both actors, producers, and directors who have been credited with founding the little theater movement through their establishment of the Chicago Little Theatre, which operated from 1912 to 1917. Browne was also a poet and Van Volkenburg worked with marionettes. The two were married in 1912 and divorced in 1925. They continued to work together and corresponded until Browne's death; Von Volkenburg has continued to use the name Mrs. Maurice Browne. Included are her diaries for the period 1928 to 1966, her almost daily letters to her parents, her correspondence with Browne, and correspondence with playwright and painter Mary (Reynolds) Aldis, playwright Alice Brown, author Nancy Wilson Ross, author Dorothy Leigh Sayers, and poet Sara Bard Field.

8,002. Child, Lydia Maria (Francis)
Papers. 1836-94. 84 items.
Open. Published guide.
University of Michigan, William L. Clements Library.
Letters from [Mrs. David Lee] Child (1802-80), an abolitionist, to her friends Ellis Gray Loring and his wife and daughter relate to her work as editor of the *National Anti-Slavery Standard,* a weekly newspaper in New York. See Arlene P. Shy, *Guide to the Manuscript Collections of the William L. Clements Library* (Boston: G. K. Hall & Co., 1978).

8,003. Hancock, Cornelia
Papers. 1863-65. 176 items.
Open. Published guide.
University of Michigan, William L. Clements Library.
Correspondence of Hancock (1840-1927), a Civil War nurse, educator, and reformer, with relatives

recording conditions and experiences of the Army of the Potomac. Most items in the collection have been published in H. S. Jaquette, *South After Gettysburg* (Pittsburgh, 1937). See Arlene P. Shy, *Guide to the Manuscript Collections of the William L. Clements Library* (Boston: G. K. Hall & Co., 1978).

8,004. Phoenix Family
Papers. 1801-79. 101 items.
Open. Published guide.
University of Michigan, William L. Clements Library.
Family papers of New York merchant Alexander Phoenix (1778-1863) contain 11 letters of Harriet Beecher Stowe. See Arlene P. Shy, *Guide to the Manuscript Collections of the William L. Clements Library* (Boston: G. K. Hall & Co., 1978).

8,005. Weld and Grimké
Papers. 1822-98. 15 vols.
Open. Published guide.
University of Michigan, William L. Clements Library.
Antislavery and family correspondence of Theodore Dwight Weld, his wife Angelina Emily (Grimké) Weld (1805-79), their son Charles S. Weld, and Angelina Weld's sister Sarah Moore Grimké (1792-1873). Also includes diaries kept by Angelina Weld and Sarah Grimké. See Arlene P. Shy, *Guide to the Manuscript Collections of the William L. Clements Library* (Boston: G. K. Hall & Co., 1978).

8,006. Young Ladies Union Society
Records. 1826-42. 1 vol.
Open. No guide.
University of Michigan, William L. Clements Library.
Annual reports and minutes of the Society, a sewing group that supported religious, educational, and social interests of its members and served as a charitable organization in Danbury, CT.

BATTLE CREEK

8,007. Battle Creek: Cultural Fusion and Urban Development
Oral history. 1977-78. 40 tapes.
Closed. No guide.
Willard Library.
Collection of interviews with 40 businessmen and businesswomen, professionals, students, and skilled and unskilled laborers who are first and second-generation immigrants to Battle Creek from foreign countries and the southern US. Nearly 50 percent of those interviewed were women; they ranged in age from 33 to 89 years. Several of the men discuss their partnerships in business with their wives.

8,008. Lowe, Berenice (Bryant)
Papers. 1896-1977. 1 box.
Partially restricted. No guide.
Willard Library.
Correspondence; research notes; manuscripts of articles, addresses, and an autobiography; and published works of [Mrs.] Lowe (1896-), a local author and historical researcher, reveal details of her methods of work. She has published texts on elementary French grammar, the history of Michigan, and the history of Battle Creek.

8,009. Shelley, Rebecca
Papers. 1887-1977. 1 box and 1 tape.
Open. No guide.
Willard Library.
Clippings and an hour-long videotaped autobiographical interview with Shelley (1887-), a 1910 Phi Beta Kappa graduate of the University of Michigan, a suffragist, and a pacifist. Shelley was the youngest delegate sent to the International Conference on Women held at The Hague in 1915; she also was the founder of Peaceways Nonviolent Community in Battle Creek, an organization devoted to the promotion of pacifism. The interview was taped in 1976.

8,010. Truth, Sojourner
Papers. Ca. 1850-1976. 2 boxes, 1 tape, and 1 microfilm reel.
Open. Unpublished guide.
Willard Library.
Photos of Truth (ca. 1797-1883), a black slave formerly known as Isabella Hardenburgh, who became an abolitionist and women's rights activist; contemporary clippings describing Truth's appearances; notes of researchers about her; copies of various poems and plays commemorating her life; a published autobiography and biographies; microfilm that duplicates the Truth collection at the University of Michigan; and videotape produced in 1976 of a memorial service honoring Truth. The collection relies heavily on contemporary published accounts of Truth's life and places particular emphasis on her last 30 years, which were spent in Battle Creek. Truth used the city as a home base from which she planned and conducted lecture tours throughout the US, decrying black slavery and the oppression of women.

DEARBORN

8,011. Daughters of the American Revolution
Records. 1930-60. 1.5 ft.
Open. Unpublished guide.
Dearborn Historical Museum.
Registrar's reports, yearbooks, and scrapbooks of two local DAR chapters, which were named for Aquila Sturges and Joshua Howard.

8,012. Dearborn Woman's Club
Records. 1927-1976. 8 feet.
Open. Unpublished guide.
Dearborn Historical Museum.
Minutes, treasurer's records, rosters, historical material, scrapbooks, and yearbooks of the Club.

8,013. Garden Club of Dearborn
Records. 1926-34. 2.5 ft.
Open. Unpublished guide.
Dearborn Historical Museum.
Incorporation papers and constitution, attendance records, rosters, a history, and bulletins of the Club, which was founded in 1915. The group's first president was Clara J. (Bryant) [Mrs. Henry] Ford.

8,014. Progressive Club of the Dearborn YWCA
Records. 1939-70. 1 ft.
Open. Unpublished guide.
Dearborn Historical Museum.
Rosters, programs, photos, scrapbooks, clippings, and slides of the Club.

8,015. Winter Study Club of Dearborn
Records. 1902-60. 4 ft.
Open. Unpublished guide.
Dearborn Historical Museum.
Annual reports, minutes, and rosters of the junior and senior branches of the Club.

8,016. Woman's Farm and Garden Society
Records. 1930-73. 1.5 ft.
Open. Unpublished guide.
Dearborn Historical Museum.
Constitution and bylaws, annual reports, minutes, treasurer's records, committee reports, membership lists, rosters, programs, photos, yearbooks, scrapbooks, clippings, and awards of the Dearborn branch of the Society, founded in 1931 to promote better understanding and cooperation between rural and urban members. The Dearborn group was organized by Mrs. Henry Ford and [Miss] Clara Snow at the home of Mrs. E. Roy Bryant. Mrs. Maurice Castell served as the first president.

DETROIT

8,017. Archives of American Art
Collection. Nd. No size given.
Open. Published guide.
Archives of American Art, Midwest Area Center.
Many of the collections described in the guide for the Smithsonian Institution, Archives of American Art in Washington, DC, are available on microfilm at the Midwest Area Center as well as at the New England, New York, and West Coast Area Centers. See *Archives of American Art, Smithsonian Institution: A Checklist of the Collection,* 2nd ed. rev. (1977), which identifies the collections that are available on microfilm, and Garnett McCoy, *Archives of American Art: A Directory of Resources* (New York: R. R. Bowker Company, 1972).

8,018. Adventurer's Club of Detroit
Records. 1927-70. 1 ft. and 3 vols.
Open. No guide.
Detroit Public Library, Burton Historical Collection.
Minutes, scrapbooks, and printed material of the Club, a women's study group which was founded in 1927 and grew out of the Good Cheer Sunday school class of the First Baptist Church of Detroit. Among various Club activities were promotion of a women's cancer detection center and support for the Emma A. Fox Foundation fund.

8,019. Alvord, Edith (Vosburg)
Papers. 1907-56. 1.5 ft.
Open. No guide.
Detroit Public Library, Burton Historical Collection.
Correspondence and other items of Alvord (1876-1961), a Detroit teacher, pertain to her activities with the Federation of Women's Clubs from 1922 to 1956, the International Institute of Detroit from 1926 to 1944, and other women's organizations.

8,020. Banks, Sarah Gertrude
Papers. 1834-1923. 1 ft.
Open. Unpublished guide.
Detroit Public Library, Burton Historical Collection.
Personal and business correspondence, notes, and addresses of Banks (1839-1926), a physician. Also includes correspondence of the Bassett family, neighbors of the Banks family in Oakland County, MI.

8,021. Boltwood Family
Papers. 1754-1906. 21 ft.
Open. Unpublished guide.
Detroit Public Library, Burton Historical Collection.
Letters written between 1867 and 1869 to Clarinda Boardman (Williams) [Mrs. Lucius Manlius] Boltwood from her maid Margaret Maher. Maher also served as a maid for Emily Dickinson during that period.

8,022. Dean, Helen Ryan
Papers. 1858-1971. 7.5 ft.
Open. Unpublished guide.
Detroit Public Library, Burton Historical Collection.
[Mrs.] Dean (1892-1971) was a clubwoman and Republican party fund raiser. Correspondence, scrapbooks, clippings, and printed material reflect Dean's memberships on the Franklin Settlement board and the Republican national finance committee as well as her vice-chairmanship of the Wayne County Republican party.

8,023. Detroit Female Seminary
Records. 1830-66. 2 vols.
Open. No guide.
Detroit Public Library, Burton Historical Collection.
Records of the Seminary, a girls school founded in

1830, which was also referred to as the Association for the Promotion of Female Education.

8,024. Detroit Women Writers' Club
Records. 1900-59. 1 ft. and 1 vol.
Open. No guide.
Detroit Public Library, Burton Historical Collection.
Known from 1900 to 1913 as the Detroit Women's Press Club, the DWWC after 1913 actively promoted the works of local women authors. Correspondence and a scrapbook.

8,025. Fox, Emma Augusta (Stowell)
Papers. 1847-1944. 15 ft.
Open. Unpublished guide.
Detroit Public Library, Burton Historical Collection.
A teacher of parliamentary law, Fox (1847-1945) also participated in women's suffrage and equal rights organizations. Correspondence and material about various women's groups that Fox joined.

8,026. Glenn, Mary E.
Papers. 1894-1973. 11 ft. and 2 vols.
Open. Unpublished guide.
Detroit Public Library, Burton Historical Collection.
Correspondence, photos, scrapbooks, and printed material of Glenn (1902-), who supervised the Detroit Post Office, record her participation in the National Alliance of Postal Employees, the National Association of Postal Employees, the Detroit Model Neighborhood Region Three, and the Second Baptist Church.

8,027. Gragg, Rosa Lee
Papers. 1901-71. 19 ft.
Open. Unpublished guide.
Detroit Public Library, Burton Historical Collection.
Correspondence, scrapbooks, and other papers of [Mrs.] Gragg (1901-), a teacher and public welfare commissioner, reflect her membership in many local Negro organizations and also highlight her activities as president of the National Association of Colored Women's Clubs from 1958 to 1964. She also served on the national volunteers participation committee and the President's Commission on the Status of Women.

8,028. Hampton, Emma Stark
Papers. 1879-1909. 1 ft. and 2 vols.
Open. Unpublished guide.
Detroit Public Library, Burton Historical Collection.
[Mrs.] Hampton (1843-1925) was president of the national Women's Relief Corps and a national counsel. Correspondence, including an 1879 letter about treatment of sick and wounded officers in Libby Prison; letter books; rules and applications for the national WRC home; and a treasurer's ledger for the Detroit Equal Suffrage Club, 1908-09.

8,029. Housewives League of Detroit
Records. 1930-73. 3 ft. and 2 motion pictures.
Open. Unpublished guide.
Detroit Public Library, Burton Historical Collection.
Founded in 1930 to strengthen the economic base of the black community, this group of black housewives worked to encourage black families to purchase goods from businesses owned and operated locally. Includes constitution, bylaws, minutes, financial records, a history, correspondence, membership information, photos, clippings, and printed matter.

8,030. Osborn, Laura Freele
Papers. 1903-56. 6 ft.
Open. Unpublished guide.
Detroit Public Library, Burton Historical Collection.
Correspondence, speeches, resolutions, a biography, items pertaining to club activities, and printed matter of Osborn (1867-1955), a teacher and member of the Detroit Board of Education who was credited with bringing special education into Detroit schools for handicapped and gifted children.

8,031. United Community Services, Women's Committee
Records. 1934-72. 25 ft. and 2 tapes.
Open. Unpublished guide.
Detroit Public Library, Burton Historical Collection.
Established in 1934 to handle Depression-era fund raising for the UCS, the Committee later expanded its program to include educational, community awareness, and social planning projects. Constitution, minutes, reports, correspondence, audiotapes, photos, and pamphlets.

8,032. Woman's Baptist Foreign Mission Society of Michigan
Records. 1891-1914. 5 vols.
Open. No guide.
Detroit Public Library, Burton Historical Collection.
Minute books of the Society.

8,033. Woman's Baptist Foreign Missionary Society of the West
Records. 1891-99. 1 folder and 2 vols.
Open. No guide.
Detroit Public Library, Burton Historical Collection.
Record books and statistical data of the Society.

8,034. Woman's Baptist Home Mission Society of Michigan
Records. 1893-1914. 3 vols.
Open. No guide.
Detroit Public Library, Burton Historical Collection.
Minute books and general records of the Society, which was founded in 1893 to spread the Christian gospel in the US.

8,035. Woman's Baptist Mission Society of Michigan
Records. 1917-52. 10 vols.
Open. No guide.
Detroit Public Library, Burton Historical Collection.
Minute books and general records of the Society.

8,036. Women Lawyer's Association of Michigan
Records. 1947-66. 1.5 ft. and 1 vol.
Open. Unpublished guide.
Detroit Public Library, Burton Historical Collection.
Constitution, history, membership lists, correspondence, scrapbooks, and newsletters of the Association, established in 1919 to advance the interests of and promote a fraternal spirit among women members of the legal profession.

8,037. Women's Aquatic Club
Records. 1923-52. 0.5 ft. and 10 vols.
Open. No guide.
Detroit Public Library, Burton Historical Collection.
Minutes, treasurers' account books and reports, and membership records of the Club, organized in 1914 to promote and encourage all aquatic sports among women in Detroit.

8,038. Women's Historical Club
Records. 1877-1976. 1.5 ft.
Open. No guide.
Detroit Public Library, Burton Historical Collection.
Minutes and scrapbooks of this Detroit group, which was founded in 1877 to study history.

8,039. Women's International Education Council
Records. 1938-49. 1 folder.
Open. No guide.
Detroit Public Library, Burton Historical Collection.
Minutes and general records of the Council.

8,040. Zonta Club of Detroit
Records. 1919-69. 15 ft.
Open. Unpublished guide.
Detroit Public Library, Burton Historical Collection.
Founded in 1919 to assist needy young women, this service organization later expanded its purpose to include help for the aged, scholarship funds, and community assistance. Minutes, reports, correspondence, rosters, and publicity material.

8,041. Alpha Theta Sigma
Records. 1920s-60s. 0.5 ft. and 3 vols.
Open. No guide.
Wayne State University Archives.
Constitution, bylaws, minutes, correspondence, photos, clippings, directories, programs, invitations, and newsletters of this sorority whose purpose was to promote and practice high moral, educational, and social standards in Wayne State University activities and to foster school spirit. Founded in 1923 as the Aa-Tik-Lik Club by a group of women students at Detroit Junior College, an early forerunner of the University, the group became a chapter of the national ATS sorority in 1927. The sorority encouraged education through scholarship awards for University women.

8,042. Bishop, Harriette, and Bishop, Helen
Papers. 1866-1945. 2.5 ft.
Open. Unpublished guide.
Wayne State University Archives.
Correspondence, clippings, and printed items of Harriette Bishop (1846-1944) and her daughter Helen Bishop (1874-1947) pertain to their teaching careers at Detroit and Central high schools and at Wayne State University. Harriette taught high school; Helen taught high school and at the University.

8,043. Chase, Ethel Winifred Bennett
Papers. 1900-48. 2.5 ft.
Open. Unpublished guide.
Wayne State University Archives.
Correspondence, reports, and clippings of Chase (1877-1949) reflect her faculty responsibilities as a Wayne State University botany professor and her administrative role as advisor to women students from 1919 to 1947. Includes information about campus activities and organizations for women students.

8,044. Clark, Nellie M.
Papers. 1894. 1 item.
Open. Unpublished guide.
Wayne State University Archives.
Diary of Clark (1876-?), an 1896 graduate of Detroit Normal School, contains descriptions of her last month at Detroit High School and activities and personalities at the Normal School, including details about her studies, Class Day, and school principal Harriet Scott.

8,045. College of Nursing
Records. 1920-65. 44 ft.
Access restricted. Unpublished guide.
Wayne State University Archives.
Minutes, financial records, reports, correspondence, and clippings of the College, which was established at Wayne State University in 1930 as the department of nursing and assumed its present name in 1945. Includes pre-departmental files; records of the office of the dean, which consist of material of Katharine Faville, 1945-65; medical studies, projects, and programs, including records from 1961 to 1965 of the Polish Project and material pertaining to visiting Polish nurses trained at Wayne State, two trips Katharine Faville made to Poland, and the American Children's Hospital in Cracow; and records of professional organizations and governmental agencies such as the National League for Nursing, the W. K. Kellog Foundation, the Michigan Department of Health, and HEW, as well as Detroit hospitals and clinics, the Detroit Council on Community Nursing from 1924 to 1943, the Basic Nursing Defense Program during WWII, and the Central Bureau of Nursing in Detroit from 1920 to 1929.

8,046. Faculty Wives Club
Records. 1925-76. 4 ft.
Open. Unpublished guide.

Wayne State University Archives.
Annual reports, minutes, correspondence, scrapbooks, and news bulletins of the Club, which was founded in 1925 and continues to encourage service and social activities among faculty families and the Wayne State University community.

8,047. Faculty Women's Club
Records. 1940-61. 0.5 ft.
Open. Unpublished guide.
Wayne State University Archives.
Constitution, bylaws, annual reports, minutes, directories, and newsletters of the Club, organized in 1935 to promote social and professional interests of all University women, especially women faculty members. The Club sponsored luncheon meetings, teas, and lectures; created and supported a scholarship; and worked with the American National Red Cross and a clothing service shop.

8,048. Family Life Project
Records. 1949-54. 1 ft.
Open. Unpublished guide.
Wayne State University Archives.
Minutes, financial data, reports, and correspondence of the Wayne State University Project, conducted in 1950 and 1951 to develop a five-year teaching and research program in family living with the aim of teaching undergraduate students how to achieve physical and mental health, social equilibrium, and spiritual satisfaction within the family and teaching graduate students engaged in professional work about programs in child growth and development and family living. Records also include minutes for 1951 to 1954 of the coordinating committee of the Child Growth and Development Program, the third phase of the Project.

8,049. Graham, Hazel E.
Papers. 1935-70. 1 ft.
Open. Unpublished guide.
Wayne State University Archives.
Correspondence, articles, and brochures of Graham (1906-) pertain to her career as associate professor of education in the department of educational psychology at Wayne State University, particularly her interest and involvement in the introductory clinical psychology course that began in 1935 and terminated in 1970, as well as work with psychological and psychiatric clinics in metropolitan Detroit.

8,050. Knapp, Patricia
Papers. 1943-72. 14 ft.
Closed. No guide.
Wayne State University Archives.
Knapp (1915-72) was a library science professor at Wayne State University. Correspondence, articles, reports, and library science course material, including tape recordings, reflect her roles as educator and librarian and show her involvement with the Monteith Library Project of the early 1960s.

8,051. Pi-Lambda Theta
Records. 1944-47. 1 folder.
Open. Unpublished guide.
Wayne State University Archives.
Minutes and officers' handbook of the Alpha Pi Chapter of this University society.

8,052. Schooten, Sarah
Papers. 1921. 1 item.
Open. Unpublished guide.
Wayne State University Archives.
Laboratory notebook in bacteriology and embryology of Schooten (1895-1974), a physician who graduated from the University school of medicine in 1926.

8,053. Shetland, Margaret L.
Papers. 1939-73. 0.5ft.
Open. Unpublished guide.
Wayne State University Archives.
From 1965 to 1973, Shetland (1906-) was dean of the college of nursing at Wayne State University; she also held various positions in public health nursing as an educator, consultant, and director. Publications and papers she presented, primarily at nursing convocations and conventions.

8,054. Women of Wayne
Records. 1936-75. 6.5 ft.
Access restricted. No guide.
Wayne State University Archives.
Minutes, correspondence, and programs of the University alumnae association, founded in 1933. Women of Wayne has developed community, educational, and cultural programs and University-centered projects such as a women's student fund and a scholarship fund for part-time women students.

8,055. Air Line Pilots Association, Steward and Stewardess Division
Records. 1959-73. 14.5 ft.
Access restricted. Published guide.
Wayne State University, Archives of Labor and Urban Affairs.
Correspondence, seniority lists, agreements, newsletters, and other items of the Division, established in 1960 as an integral part of the ALPA to represent airline flight attendants, cover such topics as organizational elections, schedules, grievances, and mergers. Access to records less than 10 years old is restricted. See Warner W. Pflug, comp. and ed., *A Guide to the Archives of Labor History and Urban Affairs, Wayne State University* (Detroit: Wayne State University Press, 1974).

8,056. Albrier, Frances
Oral history. 1968. 27-page transcript.
Access restricted. Published guide.
Wayne State University, Archives of Labor and Urban Affairs.
Interview with Albrier (1898-), one of the first black female members of the Boilermakers Union, relates to the problems faced by black women welders who tried to enter craft unions in California during WWII. See Warner W. Pflug, comp. and ed., *A Guide to the Archives of Labor History and Urban Affairs, Wayne State University* (Detroit: Wayne State University Press, 1974).

8,057. Alpern, Harriet (Cooper)
Papers. Ca. 1970-76. 3 ft.
Open. No guide.
Wayne State University, Archives of Labor and Urban Affairs.
Correspondence, minutes, reports, newsletters, pamphlets, clippings, and other published items of [Mrs. Bryce] Alpern (1923-), who worked in public relations and was the vice-president of the Detroit chapter of the National Organization for Women. Subjects covered in her papers include NOW; the Equal Rights Amendment; child care; women and employment, education, religion, and poverty; women in the media; women's history; political action; reproductive rights of women; marriage and the family; older women; and women's self-image. Presently Alpern manages her own company, Program Resources, Inc., which creates filmstrips and other audiovisual materials.

8,058. American Federation of Teachers
Records. 1914-72. Ca. 200 ft.
Partially restricted. Published guide and inventory.
Wayne State University, Archives of Labor and Urban Affairs.
Minutes, financial statements, reports, correspondence, proceedings, resolutions, applications for grants and charters, ballots, general files, and clippings of this teachers' union established in 1916. Represented are the records of the AFT executive council, the president's and communications departments, conventions, state federations, defunct locals, and defense cases. Provides information on the history of women in teaching, budgets, elections, factionalism, federal and state aid to education, federal works programs, integration, loyalty investigations, antiwar movements, price controls, vocational education, academic freedom, the National Educational Policies Committee, adult education, college and university teachers, the communist issue, civil rights, tenure, teachers under the WPA, contracts, conventions, charter revocations, finances, grievances, organizing, political action by teachers, teacher ratings, segregated locals, international teachers' organizations, universal military training, strikes, workers' education, collective bargaining, and the problems of the aged. Access to records less than five years old is restricted. See Warner W. Pflug, comp. and ed., *A Guide to the Archives of Labor History and Urban Affairs, Wayne State University* (Detroit: Wayne State University Press, 1974).

8,059. American Federation of Teachers Local 28, St. Paul, MN
Records. 1898-1970. 4 ft.
Open. Published guide.
Wayne State University, Archives of Labor and Urban Affairs.
Minutes, correspondence, bulletins, and other items of the fifth-oldest AFT local still existing in the US and the first teachers' union in Minnesota. The union evolved from the Grade Teachers Federation, which was founded in 1898 and received its AFT charter in 1918 under the name of the St. Paul Federation of Women Teachers; it merged in 1957 with the St. Paul Federation of Men Teachers, which had been chartered in 1919, to form the present group. Records pertain to the formation and merger of Local 28's antecedent unions, the merit pay system, tenure cases, strike efforts, and recruitment of members. See Warner W. Pflug, comp. and ed., *A Guide to the Archives of Labor History and Urban Affairs, Wayne State University* (Detroit: Wayne State University Press, 1974).

8,060. American Federation of Teachers Local 420, St. Louis
Records. 1961-70. 6 ft.
Open. Published guide.
Wayne State University, Archives of Labor and Urban Affairs.
Minutes, correspondence, press releases, clippings, and other items of the AFT local union in St. Louis, established in 1935. Includes the files of AFT vice-president Betty Finneran and information on such topics as tenure, membership drives, and collective bargaining by teachers. See Warner W. Pflug, comp. and ed., *A Guide to the Archives of Labor History and Urban Affairs, Wayne State University* (Detroit: Wayne State University Press, 1974).

8,061. Anderson, Alfred, and Anderson, Rose (Gelb)
Papers. 1920s-30s. 1 ft.
Open. No guide.
Wayne State University, Archives of Labor and Urban Affairs.
Both active members of the Industrial Workers of the World, Alfred Anderson (1899-1973) was secretary of the Metal Workers Industrial Union's Chicago branch, while his wife Rose Anderson (1897-) was an IWW organizer and secretary of the Textile Workers Industrial Union, Chicago branch. Correspondence, articles, minutes, leaflets, pamphlets, and memorabilia relate to the IWW and its activities in the Chicago area.

8,062. Austin, Richard H.
Papers. 1964-71. 23 ft.
Open. Published guide.
Wayne State University, Archives of Labor and Urban Affairs.
Austin (1913-), a certified public accountant, was

a member of the Wayne County board of auditors between 1966 and 1970 and since that time has also been Michigan secretary of state. Correspondence, minutes, reports, studies, notebooks, and clippings include his 1968 files on Westside mothers in Detroit who were receiving Aid to Dependent Children funds, his 1969 files on the Detroit Job Training Center for Women, Inc., and research and speech material on women's liberation. Correspondents include Geraldine Bledsoe Ford and Mildred Jeffrey. See Warner W. Pflug, comp. and ed., *A Guide to the Archives of Labor History and Urban Affairs, Wayne State University* (Detroit: Wayne State University Press, 1974).

8,063. Beasley, Olive
Papers. 1952-65. 0.5 ft.
Open. Published guide.
Wayne State University, Archives of Labor and Urban Affairs.
Correspondence, speeches, agenda, and clippings of Beasley, the director of the Flint, MI, Civil Rights Commission and vice-president of the Michigan State Employees Union, Council 7, American Federation of State, County, and Municipal Employees. Papers pertain to conferences on Michigan fair employment practices. See Warner W. Pflug, comp. and ed., *A Guide to the Archives of Labor History and Urban Affairs, Wayne State University* (Detroit: Wayne State University Press, 1974).

8,064. Beffel, John Nicholas
Papers. 1943-54. 13.5 ft.
Open. Published guide.
Wayne State University, Archives of Labor and Urban Affairs.
Included with correspondence, manuscripts, drafts, notes, and clippings of Beffel (ca. 1895-), a writer, reporter, editor, and publicist, are manuscript writings of Edith Liggett, Helen Parkhurst, Voline, and Rose Pesotta; Pesotta's work contains descriptions of her girlhood in tsarist Russia, immigration to the US, and work in the New York City garment district. Other papers pertain to Voltairine deCleyre and Hetty Green. Correspondents include Margaret DeSilver, Agnes Inglis, Helen Parkhurst, Matilda Robbins, Olga Maximoff Urkevich, and Elizabeth Gurley Flynn. See Warner W. Pflug, comp. and ed., *A Guide to the Archives of Labor History and Urban Affairs, Wayne State University* (Detroit: Wayne State University Press, 1974).

8,065. Billups, Joseph, and Billups, Rose
Oral history. 1967. 16-page transcript.
Access restricted. Published guide.
Wayne State University, Archives of Labor and Urban Affairs.
Joseph Billups (1893-) was one of the first black members of UAW Ford Local 600; his wife Rose Billups was active in organizing UAW women's auxiliaries. In their interview they discuss pre-UAW automobile unionism, black and left-wing union activities, Detroit during the Depression, Unemployed Councils, Nat Turner Clubs, the Ford Hunger March, and the Ford Organizing Drive. See Warner W. Pflug, comp. and ed., *A Guide to the Archives of Labor History and Urban Affairs, Wayne State University* (Detroit: Wayne State University Press, 1974).

8,066. Bishop, Dorothy Hubbard
Papers. 1934-40. 0.5 ft.
Open. Published guide.
Wayne State University, Archives of Labor and Urban Affairs.
Correspondence, reports, educational material, and clippings of [Mrs. Merlin D.] Bishop (ca. 1910-), who supervised the WPA workers education division in Michigan. See Warner W. Pflug, comp. and ed., *A Guide to the Archives of Labor History and Urban Affairs, Wayne State University* (Detroit: Wayne State University Press, 1974).

8,067. Blankenhorn, Ann Washington (Craton)
Papers. 1922-68. 1 ft.
Open. Published guide.
Wayne State University, Archives of Labor and Urban Affairs.
Correspondence, diaries, personal notebooks, and address books of [Mrs. Heber] Blankenhorn (1891-1970), who investigated and publicized the social and economic conditions in the textile, clothing, and coal mining industries during the 1920s and 1930s; her special emphasis was the effect of these conditions on women and children. Papers provide information on the WPA in 1934 and the imprisonment of Elizabeth Gurley Flynn. See Warner W. Pflug, comp. and ed., *A Guide to the Archives of Labor History and Urban Affairs, Wayne State University* (Detroit: Wayne State University Press, 1974).

8,068. Bledsoe, Geraldine
Oral history. 1970. 10-page transcript.
Access restricted. Published guide.
Wayne State University, Archives of Labor and Urban Affairs.
Interview with [Mrs.] Bledsoe, who was the director of the Michigan Employment Security Commission equal employment opportunity program, concerns the CIO and the black community; the Detroit NAACP; Charles Hill, a minister; and civil rights organizations between 1935 and 1945. See Warner W. Pflug, comp. and ed., *A Guide to the Archives of Labor History and Urban Affairs, Wayne State University* (Detroit: Wayne State University Press, 1974).

8,069. Borchardt, Selma Munter
Papers. 1911-67. 100 ft.
Open. Published guide.
Wayne State University, Archives of Labor and Urban Affairs.
Correspondence, speeches, notes, minutes, reports, and press releases of Borchardt (1895-1968), a legislative representative and vice-president of the American Federation of Teachers between 1924 and 1962; she also served as chairwoman of the AFT international regulations committee from 1927 to 1962, secretary of the AFL education committee from 1929 to 1955, and director of the World Federation of Educational Associations between 1927 and 1946. Her papers cover such subjects as child labor, the communist issue within the AFT, equal rights and equal pay for women, exchange teacher programs, federal aid to education, the Institute of World Studies, juvenile delinquency, the National Women's Trade Union League, social security legislation, vocational education, the Washington Trade Union College from 1919 to 1924, and workers' education. See Warner W. Pflug, comp. and ed., *A Guide to the Archives of Labor History and Urban Affairs, Wayne State University* (Detroit: Wayne State University Press, 1974).

8,070. Brewer, George, and Brewer, Grace
Papers. 1905-21. 4 ft.
Open. Published guide.
Wayne State University, Archives of Labor and Urban Affairs.
Correspondence, speeches, lectures, photos, scrapbooks, union membership booklets, pamphlets, newspapers, and clippings of the Brewers. Grace Brewer (1881-) served as secretary to Fred D. Warren, the managing editor of the Socialist party newspaper *Appeal to Reason;* she also edited the "Appeal Army" column and woman's page of that newspaper and later managed the *Appeal* Lecture Bureau as well as the Non-Partisan League Speaking Bureau. From ca. 1907 to 1913 she was secretary to Eugene V. Debs. Her husband George Brewer was chief spokesman for the Socialist party in the southeastern Kansas region, a member of the Kansas legislature from 1914 to 1916, and with his wife publisher of *The Workers Chronicle* in Pittsburg, KS. He also was manager, traveling companion, and secretary to Eugene Debs on his *Appeal* lecture tours. Papers pertain to mining strikes and accidents, WWI pacificism and profiteering, the Navy League, Socialist party activities, antipapism in Detroit and Chicago, the Non-Partisan League, southeastern Kansas politics, speaking engagements of Eugene Debs and the Brewers, and family matters. Correspondents include Debs and his wife Katherine (Metzel) Debs. See Warner W. Pflug, comp. and ed., *A Guide to the Archives of Labor History and Urban Affairs, Wayne State University* (Detroit: Wayne State University Press, 1974).

8,071. Brookwood Labor College
Records. 1921-37. 49 ft.
Open. Unpublished guide.
Wayne State University, Archives of Labor and Urban Affairs.
Founded in 1921, this coeducational, residential workers' institution located in Katonah, NY, attempted to build a militant, intelligent, and powerful labor movement by providing a progressive, nonfactional education for workers; lack of funds forced the College to close in 1937. Minutes, reports, correspondence, memoranda, school records and student files, course outlines, photos, scrapbooks, pamphlets, and clippings were collected by Mark Starr and Helen (Norton) Starr. Correspondents include Mary C. Barker, Selma M. Borchardt, Fannia M. Cohn, Josephine Colby, Cara Cook, Katherine P. Ellickson, Elizabeth Gurley Flynn, Florence Rood, Rose Schneiderman, Helen (Norton) Starr, Florence C. Hansen, and Mary Van Kleeck. Contains material about the National Women's Trade Union League; women's rights; workers' education in the US, Europe, Africa, and Asia; labor politics; labor songs; communism; and the Liberal party in the Borough of Queens and New York City.

8,072. Calvert, Mellie M., and Calvert, Herbert S.
Papers. Ca. 1920-34. 2 in.
Open. No guide.
Wayne State University, Archives of Labor and Urban Affairs.
Mellie Calvert (ca. 1895-) and her husband Herbert Calvert (ca. 1888-) were members of the Industrial Workers of the World; they were also active in and helped plan the Autonomous Industrial Colony Kuzbas in Russia. Correspondence, minutes, agreements, lists of people, and an application form relate to the Colony and the recruitment of workers by its American organization committee.

8,073. Chalmers, W. Ellison
Papers. 1926-38. 13.5 ft.
Open. Published guide.
Wayne State University, Archives of Labor and Urban Affairs.
Correspondence, reports, and press releases of Chalmers (1903-), an economics professor, pertain to women's wages in 1935 in Michigan industries, working women, and workers' education at Bryn Mawr during the 1930s. Correspondents include Frances Perkins. See Warner W. Pflug, comp. and ed., *A Guide to the Archives of Labor History and Urban Affairs, Wayne State University* (Detroit: Wayne State University Press, 1974).

8,074. Christenson, Edith L.
Papers. 1909-74. 3.5 ft. and 1 vol.
Open. Unpublished guide.
Wayne State University, Archives of Labor and Urban Affairs.
Correspondence, diaries, scrapbook, booklets, pamphlets, and clippings of Christenson (1893-), who was active in organized labor, adult education, and social service programs. Includes material on

the organizing of Staunton, VA, women's clothing and textile workers in 1934 and 1935, China during the 1920s, trade unionism, workers' education, and other items about personal matters.

8,075. Coalition of Labor Union Women
Records. Ca. 1970-75. 8 ft.
Open. No guide.
Wayne State University, Archives of Labor and Urban Affairs.
Constitutions and bylaws, minutes, convention proceedings, resolutions, reports, correspondence, tapes, handbills, lists, newsletters, clippings, and other published material of the Coalition, formed in 1974 to address the problems of unorganized working women and to make unions more responsive to the needs of all women, especially minority women. Subjects include child care, the Equal Rights Amendment, equal employment opportunity, occupational health and safety, women's studies, seniority, maternity and unemployment compensation, pensions, and the formation of CLUW and its chapters. The activities of Olga Madar, CLUW's first president, are particularly well documented.

8,076. Coalition of Labor Union Women, Seattle
Records. 1975. 1 in.
Open. No guide.
Wayne State University, Archives of Labor and Urban Affairs.
Founded in 1975 to unify women union members, the Coalition in Seattle works to promote the special concerns of women as union members and workers in the labor force. Letter, proposal, pamphlets, and bulletins of the Coalition for Protective Legislation relate to the 1975 CLUW convention.

8,077. Collier, John, and Collier, Phyllis (Feningston)
Papers. 1881-1967. 11.5 ft.
Open. Published guide.
Wayne State University, Archives of Labor and Urban Affairs.
Correspondence, autobiography, notes, clippings, and other papers of writer and social critic John Collier (1874-1947), also known as William Armistead Collier, Jr., and of his wife Phyllis Collier (1896-). She was the secretary of the American Labor party in New York in 1919 and 1920; she joined the Bookkeepers, Stenographers, and Accountants Union of the AFL in 1919, later becoming its union organizer. From 1932 to 1958 she was a Los Angeles social worker. Included are papers about Garland Farm and the Garland Fund, 1920-26; the Helicon Home Colony, 1906-07; Upton Sinclair's 1934 and 1936 gubernatorial campaigns; single-tax and cooperative colonies; and the Workers' Defense League. Correspondents include Malcolm Cowley, Kate Crawford, Miriam Allen deFord, Theodore Dreiser, Max Eastman, Elizabeth Gurley Flynn, Emma Goldman, Sidney Hook, Mary Craig Kimbrough, Frieda Lawrence, Sinclair Lewis, Mabel Dodge Luhan, Lucille Pittman, Margaret Sanger, Meta Sinclair, Upton Sinclair, Norman Thomas, and Louis Untermeyer. See Warner W. Pflug, comp. and ed., *A Guide to the Archives of Labor History and Urban Affairs, Wayne State University* (Detroit: Wayne State University Press, 1974).

8,078. Craig, Roger
Papers. 1965-70. 24 ft.
Closed. Published guide.
Wayne State University, Archives of Labor and Urban Affairs.
Correspondence and other papers of Craig (1933-), a Michigan state senator from the 10th district from 1964 to 1970, include material about abortion, civil liberties, welfare, and migrant labor. See Warner W. Pflug, comp. and ed., *A Guide to the Archives of Labor History and Urban Affairs, Wayne State University* (Detroit: Wayne State University Press, 1974).

8,079. Daniel, Berthe
Papers. 1937-41. 1 in.
Open. No guide.
Wayne State University, Archives of Labor and Urban Affairs.
Correspondence, reports, poetry, a list of girls, a photo, and clippings of Daniel, an educator and resident director of the National Youth Administration's Resident Work Center for Girls in Shippensburg, PA. The Center, open to young women between the ages of 18 and 25 years, was the federal government's counterpart to the male Civilian Conservation Corps.

8,080. Detroit Household Workers Organization
Records. 1969-76. 1 ft.
Open. Unpublished guide.
Wayne State University, Archives of Labor and Urban Affairs.
Correspondence, speeches, leaflets, and clippings of the DHWO, organized in 1969 by Mary Upshaw McClendon (1922-) to unionize household workers. Material pertains to the group's unionizing efforts, the National Committee on Household Employment, the Household Technicians of America, and a minimum wage for household workers.

8,081. Dollinger, Genora Johnson
Papers. 1937-39. 3 items.
Open. No guide.
Wayne State University, Archives of Labor and Urban Affairs.
Letter and newspapers of Dollinger (1913-), who headed the Women's Emergency Brigade during the 1937 Flint, MI, sit-down strikes, relate to the role played by the Brigade in the strikes and also to the organizing of women workers at the Delco radio plant in Kokomo, IN, in 1939.

8,082. Dunayevskaya, Raya
Papers. 1941-69. 2 microfilm reels.
Open. Published guide.
Wayne State University, Archives of Labor and Urban Affairs.
Correspondence, drafts of articles, clippings, and published items of Dunayevskaya, the author of numerous pamphlets and articles. She also wrote *Marxism and Freedom,* which first suggested the American and humanist roots of Marxism and which contained the first translation of Hegel's *Science and Logic.* Included are her files on the state-capitalist theory, on the Johnson-Forest tendency, and on the committees of *Correspondence* and *News and Letters,* which were Marxist-humanist newspapers. See Warner W. Pflug, comp. and ed., *A Guide to the Archives of Labor History and Urban Affairs, Wayne State University* (Detroit: Wayne State University Press, 1974).

8,083. Edelman, John
Papers. 1926-63. 46.5 ft.
Open. Published guide.
Wayne State University, Archives of Labor and Urban Affairs.
From 1943 to 1963, Edelman (1893-1971) was director of the Textile Workers Union of America's Washington office. Correspondence, speeches, TWUA executive board minutes, memoranda, reports, congressional and legal testimony, press releases, clippings, and publications include material on equal pay and equal rights for women. Mrs. Gifford Pinchot is a correspondent. See Warner W. Pflug, comp. and ed., *A Guide to the Archives of Labor History and Urban Affairs, Wayne State University* (Detroit: Wayne State University Press, 1974).

8,084. El-Messidi, Kathy (Groehn) Cosseboom
Papers. Ca. 1967-73. 1 ft.
Open. No guide.
Wayne State University, Archives of Labor and Urban Affairs.
Correspondence, interviews, questionnaires, notes, manuscripts, clippings, and reviews of El-Messidi (1946-), a history PhD student, pertain to her book *Grosse Pointe: Race Against Race* (East Lansing: Michigan State University Press, 1972).

8,085. Ellickson, Katherine (Pollak)
Papers. 1929-69. 51.5 ft.
Open. Published guide.
Wayne State University, Archives of Labor and Urban Affairs.
Correspondence, lecture outlines, notes, speeches, book drafts, interviews, minutes, reports, statements of testimony, leaflets, bulletins, pamphlets, songs, clippings, and published items of [Mrs. John Chester] Ellickson (1905-), a labor economist who was assistant director of the social security department and associate director of research for the AFL-CIO; she also served on the President's Commission on Equal Opportunity and was executive secretary of the President's Commission on the Status of Women. Papers contain early records of the CIO, records of the Committee on the Status of Women, minutes and her notes concerning Brookwood Labor College in Katonah, NY, and information about West Virginia miners and southern textile workers during the Depression, company unions, and early credit unions. Other subjects covered are workers' education, the guaranteed annual wage, unemployment insurance, social security, Medicare legislation, and women's rights. Correspondents include John Brophy, James B. Carey, Wilbur Cohen, Eleanor Coit, Philip Murray, A. J. Muste, Esther Peterson, David Saposs, Elizabeth Wickenden, and other prominent labor personalities. See Warner W. Pflug, comp. and ed., *A Guide to the Archives of Labor History and Urban Affairs, Wayne State University* (Detroit: Wayne State University Press, 1974).

8,086. Ellmann, Erwin B.
Papers. 1969-71. 4 ft.
Open. Published guide.
Wayne State University, Archives of Labor and Urban Affairs.
Correspondence, minutes, and reports of Ellmann, the attorney and general counsel for the Michigan American Civil Liberties Union, include material on women's rights. See Warner W. Pflug, comp. and ed., *A Guide to the Archives of Labor History and Urban Affairs, Wayne State University* (Detroit: Wayne State University Press, 1974).

8,087. Flynn, Elizabeth Gurley
Papers. 1962. 1 tape.
Open. No guide.
Wayne State University, Archives of Labor and Urban Affairs.
Flynn (1890-1964), a communist, was a founding member of the Industrial Workers of the World. Tape of a talk she gave at Northern Illinois University about her personal recollections of the IWW.

8,088. Gelles, Catherine "Babe"
Oral history. Nd. 20-page transcript.
Access restricted. Published guide.
Wayne State University, Archives of Labor and Urban Affairs.
Interview in which [Mrs. Albert] Gelles, a leader in the UAW women's auxiliary and the CIO national women's auxiliary, describes literature distribution at the Ford Motor Company River Rouge plant, the Battle of the Overpass, the 1936 Bohn Aluminum sit-down strike, the 1938 Federal Screw strike, and the 1941 Ford Motor Company strike. See Warner W. Pflug, comp. and ed., *A Guide to the Archives of Labor History and Urban Affairs,*

Wayne State University (Detroit: Wayne State University Press, 1974).

8,089. Gomon, Josephine
Oral history. 1959. 34-page transcript.
Access restricted. Published guide.
Wayne State University, Archives of Labor and Urban Affairs.
An educator, columnist, and first woman federal court receiver, [Mrs.] Gomon (1892-1975) was also executive secretary to Detroit mayor Frank Murphy. She became the first public housing director in the US when she assumed that position with the Detroit Housing Commission, and as an employee of Ford Motor Company during WWII, she dealt with the problems of women and blacks. In her interview Gomon discusses the 1933 Briggs strike, Mayor Frank Murphy's 1932 unemployment committee, the Ford Hunger March, the Thrift Garden Project, and housing and black employment at Ford Motor Company's Willow Run plant during WWII. See Warner W. Pflug, comp. and ed., *A Guide to the Archives of Labor History and Urban Affairs, Wayne State University* (Detroit: Wayne State University Press, 1974).

8,090. Graves, Anna Melissa
Papers. 1921-48. 5.5 ft.
Open. Unpublished guide.
Wayne State University, Archives of Labor and Urban Affairs.
Graves (1875-1964) was an American citizen who taught English in China, Russia, Latin America, and Africa during the 1920s and 1930s. Correspondence, photos, pamphlets, clippings, and newspapers primarily relate to Victor Raúl Haya de la Torre, a Peruvian political leader of the 1930s who founded the American Popular Revolutionary Alliance and was its unsuccessful presidential candidate in Peru in 1931. Graves worked to free him from prison following his arrest in Peru in 1932. Correspondence she received from Latin Americans, frequently translated into English from Spanish, French, Portuguese, or a Brazilian dialect, includes many letters from South American women providing insight into the political, economic, and cultural conditions on that continent between ca. 1920 and 1940.

8,091. Groves, Phyllis
Papers. 1968-69. 10 items.
Open. Published guide.
Wayne State University, Archives of Labor and Urban Affairs.
Letters to Groves from her mother Bertha Cannon McNeill pertain to coal miners in southern Illinois from ca. 1918 through the Depression. See Warner W. Pflug, comp. and ed., *A Guide to the Archives of Labor History and Urban Affairs, Wayne State University* (Detroit: Wayne State University Press, 1974).

8,092. Henrickson, Merle E.
Papers. 1945-50. 2 ft.
Open. Published guide.
Wayne State University, Archives of Labor and Urban Affairs.
Correspondence, constitutions, financial statements, reports, and newsletters of Henrickson (1913-), the president of the United Public Workers of America, Local 275 of Detroit, in the late 1940s. Includes material about the creation of the UPWA in 1946 through the merger of the State, County, and Municipal Workers and the Federal Workers of America. Also contains items about the LWV. See Warner W. Pflug, comp. and ed., *A Guide to the Archives of Labor History and Urban Affairs, Wayne State University* (Detroit: Wayne State University Press, 1974).

8,093. Herrick, Mary Josephine
Papers. 1932-66. 2 ft.
Open. Published guide.
Wayne State University, Archives of Labor and Urban Affairs.
Long active in the American Federation of Teachers, Herrick (1895-) was its director of research and a vice-president; she also was president of the Women High School Teachers in Chicago from 1933 to 1936. Correspondence, reports, financial statements, resolutions, proceedings, ballots, publicity and other campaign material, and publications contain information about such subjects as the communist controversy in the AFT, federal aid to education, the Workers' Defense League, the constitutional rights of married women teachers, AFT executive council policy and procedures, and national AFT conventions and caucuses. Correspondents include Selma M. Borchardt, Charles Cogen, Paul Douglas, Lillian Herstein, Estes Kefauver, Irvin Kuenzli, and Carl Megel. See Warner W. Pflug, comp. and ed., *A Guide to the Archives of Labor History and Urban Affairs, Wayne State University* (Detroit: Wayne State University Press, 1974).

8,094. Industrial Workers of the World
Records. 1905-72. 80 ft. and 45 microfilm reels.
Open. Published guide.
Wayne State University, Archives of Labor and Urban Affairs.
Proceedings, correspondence, trial records and evidence, pamphlets, and newspapers of the IWW, an industrial union established in 1905, members of which included lumberjacks, miners, farm hands, migrant workers, sailors, and textile mill workers. Correspondents or subjects in the collection include Mary "Mother" Jones, Katie Phar, Matilda Robbins, Hilda Seery, Elizabeth Serviss, Elizabeth Gurley Flynn, and Cora P. Wilson. Also contains records of the Aberdeen, WA, Women's Union, 1917-19, and correspondence, notes, chapter drafts, pamphlets, and other items of Joyce Kornbluh, the author of *Rebel Voices, an IWW Anthology*. See Warner W. Pflug, comp. and ed., *A Guide to the Archives of Labor History and Urban Affairs, Wayne State University* (Detroit: Wayne State University Press, 1974).

8,095. Israel, Joan L.
Papers. Ca. 1970-75. 2 ft.
Open. No guide.
Wayne State University, Archives of Labor and Urban Affairs.
Correspondence, minutes, reports, and published items of [Mrs. Kenneth] Israel (1930-), a feminist psychotherapist and the former president of the Detroit chapter of the National Organization for Women, relate to NOW activities and to the child care committee which reported to the Detroit Common Council on local child care facilities.

8,096. Jeffrey, Mildred Mesurac
Papers. 1951-74. 10 ft.
Open. No guide.
Wayne State University, Archives of Labor and Urban Affairs.
Correspondence, minutes, and reports of Jeffrey (1911-), who was consumer affairs department director of the UAW; she has also participated in civic, community, and political activities and has been a member of the Wayne State University board of governors for many years. Her papers reflect these varied interests and include material on women in politics. Currently Jeffrey serves as chairperson of the National Women's Political Caucus. In 1977 she was appointed by President Jimmy Carter to be program and agenda chair for the International Women's Year national meeting in Houston, TX. She was married to but is now divorced from Newman Jeffrey.

8,097. Jones, Dorothy
Oral history. 1968. 30-page transcript.
Access restricted. Published guide.
Wayne State University, Archives of Labor and Urban Affairs.
Interview with Jones, a Rutgers State University faculty member, relates to the United Federation of Teachers; Kenneth Clark; northern school desegregation; the Ocean-Hill, Brownsville integration episode; the Black Caucus of the American Federation of Teachers; and Albert Shanker. See Warner W. Pflug, comp. and ed., *A Guide to the Archives of Labor History and Urban Affairs, Wayne State University* (Detroit: Wayne State University Press, 1974).

8,098. Lane, Layle
Papers. 1940-69. 8 items.
Open. No guide.
Wayne State University, Archives of Labor and Urban Affairs.
Speeches, legal briefs, clippings, and pamphlets of Lane, a member of the American Federation of Teachers committee on democratic human relations, concern the *Brown vs. Board of Education* case as well as blacks and the AFT.

8,099. McCracken, Elizabeth
Oral history. 1959. 38-page transcript.
Access restricted. Published guide.
Wayne State University, Archives of Labor and Urban Affairs.
Interview with [Miss] McCracken, an employee of the Mechanics Educational Society of America, pertains to the organizing work of MESA and comparisons of that group with other unions, strikes of tool and die workers in 1933, the strike at Motor Products in 1935, the strike at the Michigan Tool Company in 1936, the strike at Kelvinator in 1937, the Auto Labor Board, the Automotive Industrial Workers Association, and the Ku Klux Klan. See Warner W. Pflug, comp. and ed., *A Guide to the Archives of Labor History and Urban Affairs, Wayne State University* (Detroit: Wayne State University Press, 1974).

8,100. McDaniel, John K.
Oral history. 1961-62. 35-page and 43-page transcripts.
Access restricted. Published guide.
Wayne State University, Archives of Labor and Urban Affairs.
McDaniel (1902-) was a skilled trades auto worker, union organizer, and officer of a UAW Packard local. His interview includes information about women workers in the auto industry. See Warner W. Pflug, comp. and ed., *A Guide to the Archives of Labor History and Urban Affairs, Wayne State University* (Detroit: Wayne State University Press, 1974).

8,101. McGhee, Rosa
Papers. 1966-67. 0.5 ft.
Open. Published guide.
Wayne State University, Archives of Labor and Urban Affairs.
Correspondence, reports, and other items of [Miss] McGhee relate to her activities as vice-president of the American Federation of Teachers and to the Southern Regional Caucus. See Warner W. Pflug, comp. and ed., *A Guide to the Archives of Labor History and Urban Affairs, Wayne State University* (Detroit: Wayne State University Press, 1974).

8,102. McGough, Mary
Oral history. 1970. 90-page transcript.
Access restricted. No guide.
Wayne State University, Archives of Labor and Urban Affairs.
Interview with McGough (1885-), an educator who was active in the St. Paul Federation of Teachers and the American Federation of Teachers, includes her comments on the history of both the St. Paul Federation and the AFT as well as reminiscences about her childhood, teaching career, and the lives of family members in Ireland, where she was born.

8,103. Madar, Olga
Papers. 1938-72. 4 ft.
Open. Published guide.
Wayne State University, Archives of Labor and Urban Affairs.
Madar (1915-) was the recreation department director of the UAW; in 1966 she became the first woman to be elected to the UAW international executive board, and in 1970 she became the UAW's first female vice-president. From 1974 to 1977 she was president of the Coalition of Labor Union Women. Correspondence, reports, speeches, articles she wrote, memos and notes, biographical sketches, minutes, petitions, leaflets, photos, and published items pertain to the Citizens Advisory Committee on School Needs in Detroit, 1957-58; the Citizens Advisory Committee on Health, Physical Education, and Physical Fitness in the Detroit Public Schools, 1960-61; the Network for Economic Rights; the Equal Employment Opportunity Enforcement Act of 1971; work and leisure; urban problems; pollution; the problems of aging; conservation of natural resources; UAW regional women's committees; and efforts between 1964 and 1966 to elect the first woman to the UAW international executive board. See Warner W. Pflug, comp. and ed., *A Guide to the Archives of Labor History and Urban Affairs, Wayne State University* (Detroit: Wayne State University Press, 1974).

8,104. Maki, Eleanor
Oral history. 1970. 30-page transcript.
Access restricted. Published guide.
Wayne State University, Archives of Labor and Urban Affairs.
Interview with Maki, a Detroit teacher, pertains to the American Youth Congress; the Civil Rights Federation and Civil Rights Congress, of which she was a member; the Sojourner Truth housing episode; and the American Federation of Teachers in the 1930s and 1940s. See Warner W. Pflug, comp. and ed., *A Guide to the Archives of Labor History and Urban Affairs, Wayne State University* (Detroit: Wayne State University Press, 1974).

8,105. Mason, Hodges
Oral history. 1968. 18-page transcript.
Access restricted. Published guide.
Wayne State University, Archives of Labor and Urban Affairs.
Interview in which Mason (ca. 1907-), one of the first black presidents of a UAW local, namely Bohn Aluminum, describes the placement of the first black women in war production work in 1942 in the Detroit area. See Warner W. Pflug, comp. and ed., *A Guide to the Archives of Labor History and Urban Affairs, Wayne State University* (Detroit: Wayne State University Press, 1974).

8,106. Mezerik, A. G., and Mezerik, Marie (Hempel)
Papers. 1937-38. 1 vol.
Open. Published guide.
Wayne State University, Archives of Labor and Urban Affairs.
Marie Hempel Mezerik and her husband A. G. Mezerik worked for the protection of civil rights; A. G. Mezerik was active in the early days of the UAW and also headed the Aid the Spanish Republic and China Aid committees. Scrapbook containing leaflets, newsletters, bulletins, and clippings relates to the Black Legion Citizens Committee, the Aid the Spanish Republic and China Aid committees, and the 1937-38 Conference for the Protection of Civil Rights. See Warner W. Pflug, comp. and ed., *A Guide to the Archives of Labor History and Urban Affairs, Wayne State University* (Detroit: Wayne State University Press, 1974).

8,107. Michigan AFL-CIO
Records. 1939-58. 303 ft.
Open. Partial unpublished guide.
Wayne State University, Archives of Labor and Urban Affairs.
Minutes, reports, correspondence, memoranda, notes, court decisions, hearings, resolutions, press releases, pamphlets, clippings, posters, and other items of the Michigan CIO and of this federation of craft and industrial unions, which was established in 1955. Includes material on equal rights and pay for women between 1946 and 1958.

8,108. Michigan Welfare League
Records. 1916-65. 30 ft.
Open. Published guide.
Wayne State University, Archives of Labor and Urban Affairs.
Minutes, correspondence, newsletters, and other items of the League, a voluntary and independent group founded in 1912 as the Michigan Conference of Social Work. Records reflect the League's goal of improved public health, welfare, and social services, especially in such areas as family and child welfare, aging, and physical and mental health. See Warner W. Pflug, comp. and ed., *A Guide to the Archives of Labor History and Urban Affairs, Wayne State University* (Detroit: Wayne State University Press, 1974).

8,109. Miles, Isadore
Papers. 1958-61. 15 items.
Open. Published guide.
Wayne State University, Archives of Labor and Urban Affairs.
Correspondence, notes, and bulletins collected by [Mrs.] Miles, who was president of the American Federation of Teachers Local 6 in Washington, DC. See Warner W. Pflug, comp. and ed., *A Guide to the Archives of Labor History and Urban Affairs, Wayne State University* (Detroit: Wayne State University Press, 1974).

8,110. Montgomery, Andrew
Oral history. 1961. 18-page transcript.
Access restricted. Published guide.
Wayne State University, Archives of Labor and Urban Affairs.
A skilled trades auto worker and UAW shop committeeman, Montgomery (ca. 1907-) was also vice-president of the AFL-CIO Council in Pontiac, MI. His interview includes commentary on women employees in auto plants. See Warner W. Pflug, comp. and ed., *A Guide to the Archives of Labor History and Urban Affairs, Wayne State University* (Detroit: Wayne State University Press, 1974).

8,111. Morris, Ken
Oral history. 1963. 52-page transcript.
Access restricted. Published guide.
Wayne State University, Archives of Labor and Urban Affairs.
Interview in which Morris (1915-), a UAW regional director, comments on protection of women's job rights at the close of WWII. See Warner W. Pflug, comp. and ed., *A Guide to the Archives of Labor History and Urban Affairs, Wayne State University* (Detroit: Wayne State University Press, 1974).

8,112. National Sharecroppers Fund
Records. Ca. 1942-69. 37 ft.
Open. Published and unpublished guides.
Wayne State University, Archives of Labor and Urban Affairs.
Established in 1937, this nonprofit, voluntary organization worked for the advancement of all agricultural labor, specifically by directing those in need of help to the appropriate governmental or private aid programs. Minutes, reports, correspondence, statements and testimonies, press releases, newsletters, clippings, and other publications are primarily the papers of Fay Bennett in her capacities as executive secretary of the National Advisory Committee on Farm Labor, executive director of the Fund, and executive secretary of the Migrant Children's Fund. She was also a board member of the National Council on Agricultural Life and Labor and a member of the Citizen's Crusade Against Poverty executive committee. See Warner W. Pflug, comp. and ed., *A Guide to the Archives of Labor History and Urban Affairs, Wayne State University* (Detroit: Wayne State University Press, 1974).

8,113. Nelson, Mercedes
Papers. Ca. 1936-59. 1 ft.
Open. No guide.
Wayne State University, Archives of Labor and Urban Affairs.
Correspondence, reports, minutes, proceedings, and clippings of Nelson (1900-), an educator who was active in the American Federation of Teachers, pertain to the executive board of the AFT and its independent caucus, AFT locals 59 and 238 in Minneapolis, the 1948 Minneapolis public school employees' strike, tenure, WPA locals affiliated with the AFT, Jerome Davis, William Cord, and honors Nelson received.

8,114. Nowak, Stanley, and Nowak, Margaret Collingwood
Papers. 1938-57. 3 ft. and 2 vols.
Open. Unpublished guide.
Wayne State University, Archives of Labor and Urban Affairs.
Stanley Nowak (1903-) was a Michigan state senator between 1938 and 1948, a union organizer, and since 1958 editor of *The People's Voice (Glos Ludowy).* His wife Margaret Nowak (1908-), who worked as his secretary while he was a state senator, ran for the US House of Representatives on the Progressive ticket in 1952. She also was a union organizer, head bookkeeper for a legal firm, and author of articles on feminists.
Correspondence, diaries of Margaret Nowak from 1939 to 1944, speeches, an early draft of Margaret's biography of her husband, biographical material, campaign papers, transcripts of legal testimony and briefs, and scrapbooks.

8,115. Oliver, William
Oral history. 1963. 23-page transcript.
Access restricted. Published guide.
Wayne State University, Archives of Labor and Urban Affairs.
Oliver (1915-) has served as codirector of the UAW Fair Practices and Anti-Discrimination Department. Interview includes information about black women at the Ford Motor Company's Highland Park plant, the "Lady in Red Slacks" case, the Fair Practices Department, and housing. See Warner W. Pflug, comp. and ed., *A Guide to the Archives of Labor History and Urban Affairs, Wayne State University* (Detroit: Wayne State University Press, 1974).

8,116. Overton, Carrie Burton
Papers. 1856-1969. 5.5 ft.
Open. Published guide.
Wayne State University, Archives of Labor and Urban Affairs.
Correspondence, reports, notes, leaflets, and clippings of [Mrs. George W. B.] Overton (1888-1975), who was secretary to civil rights leader Mary White Ovington, stenographer for the NAACP between 1924 and 1928, and executive secretary to Julian D. Rainey, the head of the Colored Division of the National Democratic Committee in 1932, 1936, and 1940. She also held secretarial positions with Howard University, the Vanguard Press, and the Community Church of New York City. Correspondents include Mary Bethune, Gloster Current, James Farley, Harold Ickes, Mary White Ovington, Julian Rainey, Algernon Tassin, Lyman Ward, and Walter White. Her papers contain information about black voters, employment in the federal government for blacks, activities of the NAACP, Democratic Party politics, and Overton's early years in Wyoming. See Warner W. Pflug, comp. and ed., *A Guide to*

the Archives of Labor History and Urban Affairs, Wayne State University (Detroit: Wayne State University Press, 1974).

8,117. Parks, Rosa Lee (McCauley)
Papers. 1950s-70s. 9 ft.
Open. No guide.
Wayne State University, Archives of Labor and Urban Affairs.
A civil rights leader of the 1960s who was instrumental in the Montgomery, AL, bus boycott, Parks (1913-) currently serves on the staff of Michigan Congressman John Conyers. Correspondence, photos, newspapers, and awards largely pertain to her civil rights activities.

8,118. Pollock, Sam
Papers. 1958. 2 ft.
Open. Published guide.
Wayne State University, Archives of Labor and Urban Affairs.
Pollock served as the president of Meat Cutters Local 427 in Cleveland and was an active member of the United Organized Labor of Ohio, a committee established to oppose a right-to-work amendment to the Ohio constitution. Speeches, radio and television scripts, press releases, campaign material, leaflets, newsletters, and newspapers include information on the Women's Security Council of Eastern Ohio. SeeWarner W. Pflug, comp. and ed., *A Guide to the Archives of Labor History and Urban Affairs, Wayne State University* (Detroit: Wayne State University Press, 1974).

8,119. Rahoi, Philip
Papers. 1943-68. 0.5 ft.
Open. Published guide.
Wayne State University, Archives of Labor and Urban Affairs.
Correspondence, speeches, and clippings of Rahoi (1896-), who was elected Michigan state representative from Iron Mountain in 1934 and 1936 and served as state senator from 1954 to 1966. Includes material on aid to dependent children. See Warner W. Pflug, comp. and ed., *A Guide to the Archives of Labor History and Urban Affairs, Wayne State University* (Detroit: Wayne State University Press, 1974).

8,120. Reuther, May (Wolf)
Oral history. 1963. 22-page transcript.
Access restricted. Published guide.
Wayne State University, Archives of Labor and Urban Affairs.
Reuther (1910-70), a teacher, became active in the labor movement in the 1930s, especially with the American Federation of Teachers and the UAW; she was also the wife of labor leader Walter P. Reuther. In her interview she discusses the 1938 Federal Screw strike, the AFT in the early 1930s, UAW Local 174, preparing material for and aiding strikes, and the success of the UAW. See Warner W. Pflug, comp. and ed., *A Guide to the Archives of Labor History and Urban Affairs, Wayne State University* (Detroit: Wayne State University Press, 1974).

8,121. Richard, Zeline (McCullough)
Oral history. 1969. 52-page transcript.
Access restricted. Published guide.
Wayne State University, Archives of Labor and Urban Affairs.
Interview with Richard, an educator who was a leader in the New Caucus of the American Federation of Teachers, includes information about such topics as national AFT conventions, 1964-68; the 1966 "Racism in Education" Conference; the role of Ed Simpkins in the AFT; school decentralization; the emergence of the New Caucus; growth of the Detroit AFT and its response to the needs of black teachers; Albert Shanker and the New York situation; and attitudes of blacks toward unions. See Warner W. Pflug, comp. and ed., *A Guide to the Archives of Labor History and Urban Affairs, Wayne State University* (Detroit: Wayne State University Press, 1974).

8,122. Rinehart, Blanche
Papers. 1949-66. 1 ft.
Open. Published guide.
Wayne State University, Archives of Labor and Urban Affairs.
Correspondence, drafts, and manuscripts of Rinehart (ca. 1883-1976) relate to her biography of Samuel Gompers. Included are her interviews with Mary Anderson, Elizabeth Christman, and Mary Erb. See Warner W. Pflug, comp. and ed., *A Guide to the Archives of Labor History and Urban Affairs, Wayne State University* (Detroit: Wayne State University Press, 1974).

8,123. Robbins, Matilda
Papers. 1900-63. 1 ft.
Open. Published guide.
Wayne State University, Archives of Labor and Urban Affairs.
Robbins (1887-1963), born Tatania Gitel Rabinowitz, was a labor organizer and writer for the Industrial Workers of the World. Correspondence and other personal papers, manuscripts of her articles and stories, photos, and clippings contain information about early labor struggles and the effect of industrialization and urbanization on society, families, and individuals, especially women. Specific subjects covered in the papers include textile organizing; the Lawrence, MA, strike; the Paterson, NJ, strike; "Big Bill" Haywood; and the IWW. See Warner W. Pflug, comp. and ed., *A Guide to the Archives of Labor History and Urban Affairs, Wayne State University* (Detroit: Wayne State University Press, 1974).

8,124. Sherwood, Lillian E.
Papers. 1938-64. 2 ft.
Open. Published guide.
Wayne State University, Archives of Labor and Urban Affairs.
Convention proceedings, photos, and clippings of Sherwood (1913-), a member of the Kent County, MI, Industrial Union Council in 1945; she became secretary-treasurer of the Michigan Congress of Women's Auxiliaries of the CIO and served as president of the CIO's National Congress of Women's Auxiliaries from 1949 to 1957. See Warner W. Pflug, comp. and ed., *A Guide to the Archives of Labor History and Urban Affairs, Wayne State University* (Detroit: Wayne State University Press, 1974).

8,125. Smith, Stanton, and Smith, Nancy
Papers. 1937-42. 1.5 ft.
Open. No guide.
Wayne State University, Archives of Labor and Urban Affairs.
Nancy Smith was an area chairman of the Joint Progressive Caucus of the American Federation of Teachers; her husband Stanton Smith (1905-) was a vice-president of the AFT. Correspondence, minutes, proceedings, ballots, rosters, and transcripts of hearings regarding charter revocation of AFT locals 5, 192, 453, and 537. Includes material about communism in the AFT and the Joint Progressive Caucus.

8,126. Starr, Mark, and Starr, Helen (Norton)
Papers. 1920-56. 33 ft.
Open. Published guide.
Wayne State University, Archives of Labor and Urban Affairs.
Correspondence, minutes, course outlines, photos, pamphlets, and clippings of Helen Starr, an instructor of labor journalism at Brookwood Labor College, and of her husband Mark Starr (1894-), an extension director at the College who also was education director of the International Ladies' Garment Workers' Union and vice-president of the American Federation of Teachers. Collection covers such topics as the National Women's Trade Union League; women's rights; workers' education in the US, Europe, Africa, and Asia; labor politics; labor songs; communism; and the Liberal party in the Borough of Queens and New York City. Correspondents include Fannia Cohn, Josephine Colby, and Katherine P. Ellickson. See Warner W. Pflug, comp. and ed., *A Guide to the Archives of Labor History and Urban Affairs, Wayne State University* (Detroit: Wayne State University Press, 1974).

8,127. Steelink, Nicolaas
Papers. 1912-53. 2 ft.
Open. Published guide.
Wayne State University, Archives of Labor and Urban Affairs.
Correspondence of Steelink (1890-), an Industrial Workers of the World member who was convicted of criminal syndicalism in the California trials of 1920; for many years, under the pseudonym Ennaes Ellae, he was a contributor to the IWW paper *Industrial Worker.* Correspondents include his wife Fannia Steelink, Alice Chase, Lily R. Iverson, and Fanny Bixby Spencer. See Warner W. Pflug, comp. and ed., *A Guide to the Archives of Labor History and Urban Affairs, Wayne State University* (Detroit: Wayne State University Press, 1974).

8,128. Stern, Marjorie
Papers. Ca. 1967-75. 4 ft.
Open. Unpublished guide.
Wayne State University, Archives of Labor and Urban Affairs.
Personal and organizational files of Stern (1918-), an officer of the San Francisco Federation of Teachers, American Federation of Teachers Local 61, and a leader in the AFT's Progressive Caucus and women's rights committee. She also served on the Coalition of Labor Union Women steering committee. Her papers chiefly pertain to women's rights and include material on the National Organization for Women and its task force on union women, the Coalition of Labor Union Women, the Coalition for a Democratic Union, equal employment opportunity, and collective bargaining.

8,129. Topdahl, Manilla P.
Papers. Ca. 1941-65. 2 in.
Open. No guide.
Wayne State University, Archives of Labor and Urban Affairs.
Topdahl, an educator, was president of the St. Paul Federation of Women Teachers, American Federation of Teachers Local 28. Correspondence, constitutions, leaflets, clippings, and background material relate to contract negotiations, Minnesota laws affecting teachers, teacher salaries, the St. Paul teachers' strike of 1946, and St. Paul city ordinances and charter amendments.

8,130. UAW, Community Relations Department
Records. 1953-66. 1.5 ft.
Partially restricted. Published guide.
Wayne State University, Archives of Labor and Urban Affairs.
The Department was organized in 1951 to strengthen the bonds of understanding between the UAW, its members, and the communities in which they live. Correspondence and other office files of Mildred Jeffrey about community meetings and projects, activities of the Committee on Political Education, and such citizens' groups as Citizens for Michigan and Citizens for School. Also includes information on consumer councils and on CIO councils in Michigan and in other states. Access to records less than 20 years old is restricted. See Warner W. Pflug, comp. and ed., *A Guide to the Archives of Labor History and Urban Affairs, Wayne State University* (Detroit: Wayne State University Press, 1974).

8,131. UAW Fair Practices and Anti-Discrimination Department, Women's Bureau
Records. 1946-53. 2.5 ft.
Open. Unpublished guide.
Wayne State University, Archives of Labor and Urban Affairs.
Minutes, reports, correspondence, resolutions, surveys, and printed material of the Bureau, founded in 1946 to promote fair and equitable treatment of women members, chiefly consist of the papers of Lillian Hatcher, a UAW international representative. Reflecting her political activities are items on the National Committee for Fair Play in Bowling, civil rights, equal employment opportunity, the Detroit Urban League, the Michigan Council on Women in Business and Industry, and employment rights of women.

8,132. UAW Local 51
Records. 1939-69. 15.5 ft.
Partially restricted. Published guide.
Wayne State University, Archives of Labor and Urban Affairs.
Minutes, reports, correspondence, clippings, and published items of Local 51, which was organized in 1936 and which represented UAW workers at Plymouth Assembly Plant in Detroit and at Mound Road Engine Plant. Includes correspondence from women workers and material on civil rights and the problems of labor during WWII. Access to records less than 20 years old is restricted. See Warner W. Pflug, comp. and ed., *A Guide to the Archives of Labor History and Urban Affairs, Wayne State University* (Detroit: Wayne State University Press, 1974).

8,133. UAW Local 662
Records. 1934-65. 2 ft. and 1 vol.
Partially restricted. Published guide.
Wayne State University, Archives of Labor and Urban Affairs.
Local 662 represents workers at the Delco-Remy division of General Motors Corporation in Anderson, IN; the union was chartered in 1939 and within a year it supplanted UAW Local 146, which had been organized in 1935. Minutes, correspondence, notebooks, scrapbook, and handbills include material reflecting the activities of the UAW's women's auxiliary 203. Access to records less than 20 years old is restricted. See Warner W. Pflug, comp. and ed., *A Guide to the Archives of Labor History and Urban Affairs, Wayne State University* (Detroit: Wayne State University Press, 1974).

8,134. UAW Recreation Department
Records. 1945-50. 1 ft.
Open. Published guide.
Wayne State University, Archives of Labor and Urban Affairs.
Minutes, correspondence, and reports of the Department, established in 1937 within the UAW's education department and directed by Olga Madar to advise and assist local unions in organizing leisure activities for members and their families. Records relate to the National Committee for Fair Play in Bowling, F.D.R. labor camps, and UAW children's camps. See Warner W. Pflug, comp. and ed., *A Guide to the Archives of Labor History and Urban Affairs, Wayne State University* (Detroit: Wayne State University Press, 1974).

8,135. UAW Research and Engineering Department
Records. 1940-53. 55 ft.
Open. Published guide.
Wayne State University, Archives of Labor and Urban Affairs.
Serving as the general information and fact-finding bureau for the UAW, the Department was created in 1948 following the consolidation of the UAW's research, time study, and wage-contract departments. Reports, correspondence, speeches, contracts, statistical data, questionnaires, surveys, press releases, song sheets, posters, clippings, and printed material cover such subjects as the women's auxiliaries of the UAW and the CIO, WWII and postwar employment of women, women in political action, equal pay for equal work, and child care. See Warner W. Pflug, comp. and ed., *A Guide to the Archives of Labor History and Urban Affairs, Wayne State University* (Detroit: Wayne State University Press, 1974).

8,136. UAW Secretary-Treasurer: Addes, George
Papers. 1936-47. 65.5 ft.
Open. Published guide.
Wayne State University, Archives of Labor and Urban Affairs.
Correspondence, reports, minutes, and other office files of Addes (1910-), who served as the UAW's first international secretary-treasurer from 1936 to 1947. Includes material about the UAW women's auxiliary and the role of women during the UAW sit-down strikes. See Warner W. Pflug, comp. and ed., *A Guide to the Archives of Labor History and Urban Affairs, Wayne State University* (Detroit: Wayne State University Press, 1974).

8,137. UAW Secretary-Treasurer: Mazey, Emil
Papers. Ca. 1941-55. 24 ft.
Open. Published guide.
Wayne State University, Archives of Labor and Urban Affairs.
Mazey (1913-) has been secretary-treasurer of the UAW since 1947. Correspondence, speeches, general files, and grievance files include information about the UAW's women's auxiliary division and women's division from 1941 to 1947, maternity leaves, the seniority of working women after WWII, Michigan labor laws, and women workers. Mazey served as president of UAW-CIO Local 212 from 1937 to 1941 and in 1943, as assistant director of the UAW-CIO's National Ford Department in 1941, and as a regional director of the UAW-CIO in 1946 and 1947. See Warner W. Pflug, comp. and ed., *A Guide to the Archives of Labor History and Urban Affairs, Wayne State University* (Detroit: Wayne State University Press, 1974).

8,138. UAW Unemployment Compensation Department
Records. 1945-55. 6 ft.
Open. Published guide.
Wayne State University, Archives of Labor and Urban Affairs.
Correspondence, hearings and petitions for hearings, determinations, briefs, court transcripts, and related items of the Department, established in 1941 to promote legislation favorable to labor and to assist UAW members in processing contested unemployment compensation and welfare claims. Includes many appeals of women on contested unemployment compensation claims in which the Department acted as an interested party and agent for the claimants. See Warner W. Pflug, comp. and ed., *A Guide to the Archives of Labor History and Urban Affairs, Wayne State University* (Detroit: Wayne State University Press, 1974).

8,139. UAW War Policy Division
Records. 1941-46. 16.5 ft.
Open. Published guide.
Wayne State University, Archives of Labor and Urban Affairs.
Organized in 1941, the Division coordinated the UAW's war efforts and represented the UAW in its dealings with governmental agencies. Minutes; reports; correspondence with Mildred Jeffrey, Dorothy K. Roosevelt, and others; speeches; notes; publicity material; and clippings. Includes information on job transfers, the utilization of labor, job training programs, alien workers, housing, price and rent control, child care, discrimination, fair employment practices, reconversion, postwar planning, and veterans. See Warner W. Pflug, comp. and ed., *A Guide to the Archives of Labor History and Urban Affairs, Wayne State University* (Detroit: Wayne State University Press, 1974).

8,140. UAW War Policy Division, Women's Bureau
Records. 1942-45. 2.5 ft.
Open. Unpublished guide.
Wayne State University, Archives of Labor and Urban Affairs.
Minutes, reports, correspondence, questionnaires, photos, and published items of the Bureau, established in 1941 to develop and recommend policies and programs affecting women union members. Includes material on child care, training and counseling programs, conferences on problems of women in business and industry, equal pay for women, absenteeism and employment turnover, seniority rights, and women war workers. Correspondents include Mildred Jeffrey.

8,141. Van Camp, Lawrence, and Van Camp, Dorothy Chalk
Papers. 1933-57. 0.5 ft.
Open. Published guide.
Wayne State University, Archives of Labor and Urban Affairs.
Correspondence, reports, speeches, minutes, position papers, resolutions, leaflets, songs, clippings, and monographs of the Van Camps pertain to the Socialist party. Correspondents include Roy Reuther, Frank R. Crosswaith, and Fred Henderson. See Warner W. Pflug, comp. and ed., *A Guide to the Archives of Labor History and Urban Affairs, Wayne State University* (Detroit: Wayne State University Press, 1974).

8,142. Van Kleeck, Mary
Papers. 1900-40s. 20 ft.
Open. Published guide.
Wayne State University, Archives of Labor and Urban Affairs.
Correspondence, reports, speeches, articles, minutes, clippings, and published items of Van Kleeck (1883-1972), an industrial sociologist who was the director of the Commission on Women's Work and Industrial Studies, associate director of the International Industrial Relations Institute, and director of industrial studies for the Russell Sage Foundation. Papers concern her work with the Sage Foundation; activities of the United Mine Workers Union; organizing and unionizing of the automobile and steel industries in the 1930s and 1940s; wages, hours, and working conditions of employed women, ca. 1905-44; a fact-finding committee on summer school for women workers in industry at Bryn Mawr; the American Women's Association; The Women's Charter Group; industrial fatigue; the Interprofessional Association for Social Insurance; and the International Industrial Relations Institute. Correspondents include Mary L. Fleddérus and Mary E. Richmond. See Warner W. Pflug, comp. and ed., *A Guide to the Archives of Labor History and Urban Affairs, Wayne State University* (Detroit: Wayne State University Press, 1974).

8,143. Vess, Raymond
Oral history. 1961. 36-page transcript.
Access restricted. Published guide.
Wayne State University, Archives of Labor and Urban Affairs.
Interview with Vess, a skilled trades auto worker and UAW committeeman, includes his comments on women workers in the auto industry. See Warner W. Pflug, comp. and ed., *A Guide to the Archives of Labor History and Urban Affairs, Wayne State University* (Detroit: Wayne State University Press, 1974).

8,144. Vorse, Mary Marvin (Heaton)
Papers. 1841-1966. 77 ft.
Open. Published guide.
Wayne State University, Archives of Labor and Urban Affairs.
A writer, labor journalist, and social critic of the US, Vorse (1874-1966) studied and wrote about strikes, civil and labor disturbances, wars, revolutions, and political upheavals in other parts of the world. Correspondence, daily notes and journals, literary manuscripts, reference and research material, personal and family papers, pamphlets, clippings, and memorabilia. Correspondents include Jane Addams, John Dewey, Katy and John Dos Passos, David Dubinsky, Elizabeth Gurley Flynn, Susan Glaspell, Emma Goldman, John F. Kennedy, John L. Lewis, Sinclair Lewis, Agnes O'Neill, Walter P. Reuther, Theodore Roosevelt, Margaret Sanger, Lincoln Steffens, and many others in labor, literary, and political fields. Papers contain information on the following topics: the 1912 Lawrence, MA, textile strike; the International Women Suffrage Convention of 1913; the Industrial Workers of the World; child labor; the National Consumers' League; the organization of the Provincetown Players in 1915; mining strikes in Michigan and Minnesota in 1916; the rise of Hitler and the invasion of Poland; postwar conditions in Europe after both world wars; the Scottsboro, AL, case; the steel strikes of 1919 and 1936-37; the organizing drive of the Amalgamated Clothing Workers, 1920-21; the Sacco-Vanzetti case; Palmer raids and criminal syndicalist cases, 1921-23; the 1926 textile strikes in Passaic, NJ, and 1929 strikes in Gastonia, NC; the Farmers Holiday Association; migrant workers; automobile sit-down strikes in 1936-37; the UN Relief and Rehabilitation Administration; the Sinarquistas in Mexico in 1949; crime on the New York and New Jersey waterfronts between 1950 and 1954; the Associated Country Women of the World; the Women's International Suffrage Alliance; effects of strikes, family, work, living conditions, leisure, and love on women; infant mortality; the International Congress of Women; Ella Reeve Bloor; and the 1959 textile strike in Henderson, NC. See Warner W. Pflug, comp. and ed., *A Guide to the Archives of Labor History and Urban Affairs, Wayne State University* (Detroit: Wayne State University Press, 1974).

8,145. Weil, Truda
Papers. 1947-59. 0.5 in.
Open. No guide.
Wayne State University, Archives of Labor and Urban Affairs.
Weil (?-1971) was the executive secretary of the original New York Teachers Union and later of the New York Teachers Guild. Correspondence with and speech of John Dewey and photos relate to honoring Henry Richardson Linville, an educator who presided over both the Teachers Union and the Guild.

8,146. Wheeler, Doris B. Preisler
Papers. Ca. 1901-60. 1 ft.
Open. No guide.
Wayne State University, Archives of Labor and Urban Affairs.
Songbooks and songsheets of Wheeler, who was educational director for the International Ladies' Garment Workers' Union, St. Louis locals. Includes labor, folk, and protest songs, some of which pertain to women workers. Wheeler was first married to Paul Preisler; her second husband was Maurice R. Wheeler.

8,147. Wheeler, Mary R.
Papers. 1938-67. 1.5 ft.
Open. Published guide.
Wayne State University, Archives of Labor and Urban Affairs.
Correspondence, reports, minutes, and other papers of Wheeler (1901-), the vice-president of the American Federation of Teachers and an officer in both the West Suburban Teachers Union in the Chicago area and the Illinois Federation of Teachers. Contains material about professional standards for teachers, retirement plans, and negotiations and strikes by teachers. See Warner W. Pflug, comp. and ed., *A Guide to the Archives of Labor History and Urban Affairs, Wayne State University* (Detroit: Wayne State University Press, 1974).

8,148. Whitby, Beulah
Oral history. 1969. 41-page transcript.
Access restricted. Published guide.
Wayne State University, Archives of Labor and Urban Affairs.
[Mrs.] Whitby was a social worker and assistant director of the Detroit Commission on Community Relations. Interview contains her descriptions of employment with the YWCA, her meeting trains carrying migrants from the South, casework with the Detroit Welfare Department, Detroit during the Depression, Muslims, the Sojourner Truth housing project episode in Detroit, race riots in that city in 1943, left-wing activities, the Interracial Commission, the NAACP, the Urban League, and the black community in Detroit. See Warner W. Pflug, comp. and ed., *A Guide to the Archives of Labor History and Urban Affairs, Wayne State University* (Detroit: Wayne State University Press, 1974).

8,149. Women's International League for Peace and Freedom
Records. 1934-75. 6.5 ft. and 7 vols.
Open. Unpublished guide.
Wayne State University, Archives of Labor and Urban Affairs.
Minutes, financial records, correspondence, membership lists, scrapbooks, bulletins, pamphlets, and newsletters of the WILPF, formed in 1915, were collected by Meta Rosenberg Riseman and reflect her activities as president of the organization's Detroit unit, of its Michigan branch, and of the WILPF's US section. She also chaired the group's human rights committee. Subjects include disarmament, peace, universal military training, civil rights, antisemitism, women's rights, and conscientious objectors. Among the correspondents are Mildred Scott Olmsted, Katharine Arnett, Elsie Picon, Alice Bostick, and Annalee Stewart.

EAST LANSING

8,150. Carpenter, Louise
Oral history. 1972. 27 pp. and 1 tape.
Open. No guide.
Michigan State University Archives and Historical Collections.
Interview in which Carpenter, an assistant professor in continuing education at the University, describes the "Adventures in World Understanding" and the "Christmas Adventure" programs that she directed and many of her experiences with foreign students studying in various parts of the US. Carpenter received BS and MS degrees from Michigan State University; from 1948 to 1968 she was employed by the University to work with foreign students.

8,151. Clark Family
Papers. 1848-1939. 11 folders and 11 vols.
Open. Published guide.
Michigan State University Archives and Historical Collections.
Collection consists primarily of letters by Hannah Wall Handy of Augusta, ME, to her sister Mrs. Charles H. Clark of Grand Haven, MI, containing comments on the Civil War, education, politics, religion, business, and fashion. Also included are account and memoranda books of Charles H. Clark, who operated a general store in Grand Haven and later Robinson Township, MI. Taken from Frederick L. Honhart, Suzann M. Pyzik, and Saralee R. Howard, *A Guide to the Michigan State University Archives and Historical Collections* (East Lansing, MI: Michigan State University, 1976).

8,152. College of Human Ecology
Records. Ca. 1900-72. 1 cu.ft. and 388 items.
Open. Published guide and card catalog.
Michigan State University Archives and Historical Collections.
Correspondence, reports, photos, clippings, publications, and other records of the College, formerly known as Home Economics, which in turn developed from the Women's Course organized in 1896. The photos depict students; faculty; alumni; buildings; classes, including early cooking and sewing groups; and research activities. See Frederick L. Honhart, Suzann M. Pyzik, and Saralee R. Howard, *A Guide to the Michigan State University Archives and Historical Collections* (East Lansing, MI: Michigan State University, 1976).

8,153. Crittenden, Mariette C.
Papers. 1959. 1 folder.
Open. Unpublished guide.
Michigan State University Archives and Historical Collections.
Reminiscences of Crittenden (1825-?), originally written in 1907, describe pioneer life in the Saline, MI, area. Crittenden recounts her family's emigration from Vermont to Washtenaw and Livingston counties in 1831, family hardships, housekeeping practices, and her philosophy of life.

8,154. Diaries
Collections. 1830-1956. No size given.
Open. Published guide.
Michigan State University Archives and Historical Collections.
Included are a diary of Hale Estabrook Crosby and his wife Mary Foster (Chamberlain) Crosby, which records their life in Concord, MA, and Ashby, MA, from 1838 to 1842; correspondence and diaries relating to the ministry of Waters Warren and to Caroline C. Parsons, who became Warren's wife; and an 1877 diary of schoolteacher Seneca Freeman Russell. The collection of Mrs. Carl Wolff contains an 1862 diary kept by [Miss] Belle Voorheis describing rural life in Michigan. Diaries of the 1880s and 1890s include those of Mary Emma Lowe, who was the wife of pharmacist Vincent A. Lowe of Benton Harbor, MI, and three by Hattie Foote [Mrs. A. V.] Austin of Milford, MI, concerning her life and travels. The diary of Miriane Ogen describes social life in Manistee County, MI, around the turn of the century, while diaries and account books for the years 1914 to 1932 relate to the farm life of Sue E. Hoyt in McMinnville, TN, and Vassar, MI. See Frederick L. Honhart, Suzann M. Pyzik, and Saralee R. Howard, *A Guide to the Michigan State University Archives and Historical Collections* (East Lansing, MI: Michigan State University, 1976).

8,155. Dye, Marie
Papers. 1910-70s. 1.5 cu.ft.
Open. Unpublished guide.
Michigan State University Archives and Historical Collections.
Correspondence, speeches, reports, notes, and clippings of Dye (1891-1974), a nutrition expert who was dean and professor from 1930 to 1956 in the College of Home Economics, later called Human Ecology, at the University. Her handwritten speech notes pertain to the history of home economics and the education and roles of women during the 1930s, 1940s, and 1950s.

8,156. Edwards, Anna Rebecca
Papers. 1936. 29 pp.
Open. Unpublished guide.

Michigan State University Archives and Historical Collections.
Reminiscences in which Edwards (1863-?), a Benzonia, Benzie County, MI, resident, describes her family's move to Michigan from Ohio in 1859 and the hardships of pioneer life.

8,157. English Family
Papers. 1855-1954. 5.5 cu.ft.
Open. Published guide.
Michigan State University Archives and Historical Collections.
Personal and business correspondence, diaries, financial records, clippings, and other material relating to Albert D. English, his wife Marion Brown (Monteith) English, his daughter Jean (English) Wisner, and his sister Annette English. Albert English was a Manchester, MI, school district assessor, overseer of highways, and farmer who was active in the Democratic party. Collection reflects social, political, and economic interests of the Englishes and the Monteiths, prominent Michigan families, in the latter 19th and early 20th centuries. Diaries, 1886-1930, and monograph histories by Annette English, a local historian, record the histories of individuals, families, societies, buildings, and localities of the Manchester area and contain recollections of longtime residents of the area. Taken from Frederick L. Honhart, Suzann M. Pyzik, and Saralee R. Howard, *A Guide to the Michigan State University Archives and Historical Collections* (East Lansing, MI: Michigan State University, 1976).

8,158. Hale, Mary Taylor
Papers. 1835-80. 8 folders.
Open. Unpublished guide.
Michigan State University Archives and Historical Collections.
The bulk of the correspondence of [Mrs. Richard] Hale, a schoolteacher in Milford, MI, is letters from friends and relatives written between 1864 and 1880. Topics discussed include education and the problems of teaching, the Civil War, the draft, election politics, Abraham Lincoln's death, and farming activities.

8,159. Hallifax, Lillie S.
Papers. 1874-1913. 1 folder and 8 vols.
Open. Unpublished guide.
Michigan State University Archives and Historical Collections.
Diaries of a Henrietta, MI, teacher provide detailed accounts of her daily activities, including classroom instruction and housework.

8,160. Hart, Adelaide
Papers. 1951-69. 3.5 cu.ft.
Open. Unpublished guide.
Michigan State University Archives and Historical Collections.
Correspondence, reports, and pamphlets of Hart, a teacher, relate to her activities as a delegate to the Michigan Constitutional Convention of 1961-62, from the 10th District, Wayne County.

8,161. Jones, Sarah Van Hoosen
Papers. 1856-1960s. 1 cu.ft.
Open. Unpublished guide.
Michigan State University Archives and Historical Collections.
Correspondence, articles, reports, clippings, and material about academic degrees of Van Hoosen (1892-1972), who was a farmer, cattle breeder, and member of the Michigan state board of agriculture and the University governing board. Correspondents include family members, the Michigan Master Farmers Club, and the state board of agriculture. Van Hoosen graduated from the University of Wisconsin in 1921 with a PhD in genetics, the first woman to earn such a degree. After college she managed the family farm near Rochester, MI, and raised purebred Holsteins; from 1943 to 1955 she served on the University governing board and was influential in establishing a University campus at Oakland. Upon her retirement she donated her property to the University.

8,162. Kellog, Lizzy
Papers. 1882. 1 folder.
Open. Unpublished guide.
Michigan State University Archives and Historical Collections.
A partially handwritten transcript of the trial of Kellog, a teacher, in the case versus the First Congregational Church, somewhere in Michigan. Kellog was accused of improper behavior with a man.

8,163. Kellogg, John Harvey
Papers. 1896-1950. 25.67 cu.ft.
Open. Unpublished guide.
Michigan State University Archives and Historical Collections.
Kellogg was a physician and business leader who cofounded the Seventh Day Adventist Church. Business records and correspondence include his letters to Ellen G. White, also a Church cofounder, about their differences of opinion regarding the Church and correspondence between Kellogg and other Church members about White and her activities.

8,164. Letters
Collections. 1823-1958. No size given.
Open. Published guide.
Michigan State University Archives and Historical Collections.
Pioneer life in Michigan is described in an 1845 family letter written primarily by Jane Comstock of Eaton Rapids, MI, to Samuel Hickson of Painesville, OH, and in clippings of letters written in the early 1830s by Elizabeth Chandler of Lenawee County, MI, and printed in the *Adrian Daily Telegram* in 1926. Excerpts of letters from the years 1823 to 1831 by William Montague Ferry and his wife Amanda (White) Ferry, Protestant missionaries on Mackinac Island, MI, contain descriptions of Indians and references to opposition from the Roman Catholic Church, while an 1840 letter from Emeline Churchill to her father Joseph Pope expresses her strong religious feelings. Letters of the 1850s include one to [Mrs.] Sarah K. Vansandt of Beechymire, PA, from her sister expressing loneliness and discussing family affairs; one by Martha C. Bradley to Nancy [Mrs. Jona] Kimball describing the sinking of her husband's whaling ship in the northern seas; one written from Hillsdale College by Abel G. Peck describing experiences of a newly appointed female member of the faculty; and one by Caroline Stoddard to her sister concerning the family's trip from the East to settle in Tuscola County, MI. Letters written by Achsa Waters of Independence, MI, and Union, MI, to her family in New York concern a trip through Memphis to Vicksburg, MS, in 1864 to teach the "colored people" and to deliver barrels of clothing from Ohio and Michigan. Also included are Civil War letters of Benjamin F. Marsh to his mother while he was serving in the 8th Michigan Infantry and correspondence between Marsh and his wife during the 1870s and 1880s concerning family matters. In an 1886 letter Sarah Warner of Evans Mills, NY, discusses family health with her cousin William S. Calkins. Also includes WWI correspondence of Harald Smith Patton and Marguerite Irene Taylor, who later became his wife, as well as correspondence, 1891-1941, of [Mrs.] N. K. Schopp of Eaton and Ingham counties, MI, and of her mother Ada Taylor. Letters which Katie (Kelly) Bullock and her husband Dillman S. Bullock wrote to his parents between 1902 and 1958, while he served as a Methodist missionary and teacher in Chile and as US agricultural trade commissioner in Argentina, contain comments on political, economic, and social affairs of Chile and Argentina; the life of Americans in South America; and wildlife. See Frederick L. Honhart, Suzann M. Pyzik, and Saralee R. Howard, *A Guide to the Michigan State University Archives and Historical Collections* (East Lansing, MI: Michigan State University, 1976).

8,165. MacLeod, Leona
Oral history. 1973. 23 pp. and 1 tape.
Open. No guide.
Michigan State University Archives and Historical Collections.
Interview with MacLeod, who was a home demonstration agent and professor in the University cooperative extension service, contains her descriptions of work as a home economist at the University and also in South Korea under US Agency for International Development sponsorship. She traces the development of the University extension program and the beginnings of consumer programs for women, noting the careers open to women during the 1930s and 1940s.

8,166. Matheson, Elizabeth Cooper
Papers. 1861-73. 5 vols.
Open. Unpublished guide.
Michigan State University Archives and Historical Collections.
Matheson was a Quaker resident of Berrien County, MI. In her diaries she describes her family's move from Pleasantville, PA, to Salem, OH, in 1862 and to Riverside, MI, in 1867. Early entries include many observations about Civil War events; she also provides details regarding Quaker meetings and the Temperance Society she joined in 1866.

8,167. Miscellany
Collections. 1836-1973. No size given.
Open. Published guide.
Michigan State University Archives and Historical Collections.
Small collections include a series of school compositions from 1839 and 1840 by Abby Sheldon (Bagg) Austin; an 1860 certificate of marriage between Perkins Garner and Isabel Irwin of New Hudson, NY; and home remedies, recipes, school themes, and a farm ledger from Saginaw County, MI, in the Mable A. Babion collection. Papers of the Porter and Pierce families include letters from Horace Greeley concerning care of his sick mother as well as printed material dealing with the DAR. Civil War relief fund records from Lenawee County, MI, contain a relief roll recording payments made to families of men in the service and letters of application for such aid. Also included are Civil War letters of Thomas Davis to his wife while he was serving with the Wisconsin Volunteers and with the Army of Tennessee and biographical sketches of Davis and his wife. A minute book of the A. J. Babcock Ladies Auxiliary of the United Spanish War Veterans covers the years 1918 to 1929. Family reminiscences of Virginia Norfleet give a moralistic account of life in the Tidewater area of Virginia, with emphasis on the Civil War and its effects on living conditions. Miscellaneous certificates, pamphlets, and other material relating to American war preparedness, Liberty Bond solicitation, and the temperance and women's suffrage movements are contained in the collection of Mrs. Grant C. Putnam. Also included are tax receipts of Mary E. Fouts for property in Isabella County, MI, in the John C. Beukema collection and account books of Rosadel (Taft) Lansing from her insurance business. In an oral history interview, Bessie Dair, a lifelong resident of Benzie County, MI, describes river drives on the Betsie River, a sawmill her brother operated, and fishing in the area. Also included is an edited manuscript on the history of logging in Benzie County based on an oral history by William and Edith Overlease. See Frederick L. Honhart, Suzann M. Pyzik, and Saralee R. Howard, *A Guide*

to the *Michigan State University Archives and Historical Collections* (East Lansing, MI: Michigan State University, 1976).

8,168. Pendleton Family
Papers. 1774-1887. 7 folders and 3 vols.
Open. Published guide.
Michigan State University Archives and Historical Collections.
Bulk of the collection consists of correspondence of Lottie Pendleton, later Mrs. George W. Bailey, a resident of Cleveland who attended college in Adrian, MI; letters date from the 1850s and 1860s and are from relatives and from school friends attending Albion and Oberlin colleges and the University of Michigan. Also included are manuscripts of poetry illustrated by Caleb Pendleton, manuscript copies of arithmetic books, and an account book of George W. Bailey, which contains expense accounts, poetry, and medicinal recipes. Taken from Frederick L. Honhart, Suzann M. Pyzik, and Saralee R. Howard, *A Guide to the Michigan State University Archives and Historical Collections* (East Lansing, MI: Michigan State University, 1976).

8,169. Porter, Florence Emeline Foote
Papers. 1842-1906. 10 folders and 1 vol.
Open. Published guide.
Michigan State University Archives and Historical Collections.
Class notes and exercises and letters to Hattie Foote, a teacher in Milford, MI, from friends and relatives concerning teaching, education, and college life. Also includes farm and household accounts of the Foote family, financial statements and stockholder reports of Andrew V. Austin of Milford, and other material. Taken from Frederick L. Honhart, Suzann M. Pyzik, and Saralee R. Howard, *A Guide to the Michigan State University Archives and Historical Collections* (East Lansing, MI: Michigan State University, 1976).

8,170. Schools and Teachers
Collections. 1824-1973. Ca. 13 cu.ft., 32 folders, 17 vols., and 7 items.
Open. Published guide.
Michigan State University Archives and Historical Collections.
Michigan school records for Cedar Creek Township and Van Buren, Cass, Grand Traverse, Lenawee, Berrien, and Huron counties include contracts for teachers and other employees; financial records; business correspondence; meeting notes; school histories; records of attendance, examination, and classification of students; school censuses; annual reports; and teachers certificates. Minutes of school board meetings for 1832 to 1866 for Cass County and an 1841 circular from the superintendent of public instruction at Ann Arbor, MI, are also included. Teachers certificates, contracts, school roll books, and other material are contained in the collections of various Michigan teachers, among them Mary E. Bennett, Charlotte and Lucia Rich, Owen Churchill, and [Miss] Grace E. Bradley, who was appointed matron in the Indian Service. Also included are correspondence, teaching materials, essays, and clippings of May McKibbin, principal of Logan School in Lansing, MI. In addition, there are letters to Eliza A. (Clark) Johnson, and her husband Samuel Johnson, both of whom were teachers, from former students and fellow teachers, which reveal teaching conditions from the 1820s to 1860s in Massachusetts, New York, and Pennsylvania. See Frederick L. Honhart, Suzann M. Pyzik, and Saralee R. Howard, *A Guide to the Michigan State University Archives and Historical Collections* (East Lansing, MI: Michigan State University, 1976).

8,171. Stockman, Dora Hall
Papers. 1910-48. 1.75 cu.ft.
Open. Unpublished guide.
Michigan State University Archives and Historical Collections.
[Mrs.] Stockman (1872-?) was a writer; lecturer; member of the Michigan state board of agriculture from 1920 to 1931; member of the governing body of Michigan State University and later the board of trustees; member of the Michigan legislature from the second district of Ingham County from 1938 to 1946; member of an advisory group for the US Children's Bureau; secretary of the National Rural Home Conference and the Michigan state educational advisory committee; and a member of the White House children's conference during the Hoover administration and the Children of Democracy Conference. Correspondence, including items pertaining to her terms of legislative office; an autobiography; portions of her unfinished doctoral dissertation about rural life in America; songs and poetry; articles, pageants, and speeches she wrote; radio broadcast transcripts; a manuscript; tax receipts; photos; a scrapbook; clippings; State Grange rosters, handbooks, and publications, including issues of the *Michigan Patron* that she edited; books; and other material. The State Grange remained her primary interest; Stockman helped establish county Granges throughout the state and held several Grange offices, including that of official State Grange lecturer from 1914 to 1930.

8,172. Thompson, Irma
Papers. 1896-1969. 1.5 cu.ft.
Open. Unpublished guide.
Michigan State University Archives and Historical Collections.
One of four women to graduate from the University in 1900, Thompson (1880-), later Mrs. Mark Ireland, was instrumental in obtaining a lounge for off-campus women students. Correspondence, reminiscences with detailed notes about the campus life of women during the 1890s, programs of social events, photos, and clippings.

8,173. Tobia, Rajee
Papers. 1865-1953. 0.33 cu.ft.
Open. Unpublished guide.
Michigan State University Archives and Historical Collections.
Minutes and clippings pertain to the 41st biennial convention of the PEO Sisterhood, a philanthropic and educational organization, which was held in 1953 in Vancouver, British Columbia.

8,174. University Archives
Collections. 1896-1976. 12 folders and 10 vols.
Open. Published guide.
Michigan State University Archives and Historical Collections.
Collections related to Michigan State University include records of the department of human relations at MSU, which contain information on training programs for women and minority groups; class notes of Emily Kilbourne for 1899 and 1900 on pomology, cooking, and horticulture; and scrapbooks pertaining to MSU compiled by Ruth E. Carrel, Helen Sheldon Lundberg, Ruth I. Rutherford, and Ellen Jean Fry, who graduated from MSU between 1908 and 1915. A scrapbook compiled by Ruth (Ryder) St. John, an American National Red Cross recreation worker in the South Pacific who graduated from MSU in 1936, contains correspondence about an alumni reunion she organized in Manila in 1945, her description of the reunion, a poster, and a newsletter. Also included are correspondence, registration cards, and health certificates of Harriet Irving Robson for the years 1896 to 1907; memos, programs, receipts, and class schedules of Sarah Metzler Boline for 1917 to 1919; and newsletters of the MSU Business Women's Club for 1964 to 1976. See Frederick L. Honhart, Suzann M. Pyzik, and Saralee R. Howard, *A Guide to the Michigan State University Archives and Historical Collections* (East Lansing, MI: Michigan State University, 1976).

8,175. Woman's Christian Temperance Union
Records. 1857-1964. 5 folders.
Open. Unpublished guide.
Michigan State University Archives and Historical Collections.
Constitution; minute books, 1879-87; financial records, 1883-87; and membership lists of the Three Oaks, MI, chapter of the WCTU. Also included are seven annual convention reports and directories of Michigan's state WCTU; a notice of the 1879 state WCTU convention; a 1909 pamphlet, "Ingham County Must Stay Dry," which was published by the women's local option committee; an 1874 copy of the *Woman's State Temperance Records;* and a printed poem by a temperance lecturer.

FARMINGTON HILLS

8,176. Sisters of Mercy: History and Apostolates
Records. 1873- . Ca. 200 cu.ft.
Access restricted. No guide.
Sisters of Mercy, Province of Detroit Archives.
The Sisters of Mercy in Michigan have been involved in health services, education, and social work since 1873; they operate hospitals, sanitaria, schools, and homes for working women, orphans, the aged, and the mentally disturbed. Council and chapter minutes, financial records, correspondence, diaries and journals, chronicles, histories, theses, dissertations, photo and picture albums, slides, reports, and scrapbooks.

FLINT

8,177. Columbian Club of Flint
Records. 1892-1965. 7 boxes.
Open. Unpublished guide.
Alfred P. Sloan, Jr., Museum.
Formed in 1892 to study the 1893 World's Fair program and the proposed exhibits, the Club also worked to "further the cultural status of its members and create new mental stimulus for the changing years" through the study of history, science, literature, art, and ethics. Secretary's reports from 1892 to 1957, treasurer's reports and other financial records, correspondence, reports of members, membership applications, yearbooks, certificates, and pamphlets and publications of the Michigan State Federation of Women's Clubs, of which the Columbian Club was a member. [Miss] Helen V. Walker, a schoolteacher, served as the Club's first president.

8,178. Daughters of the American Revolution, Genesee Chapter
Records. 1849-1929. 7 boxes.
Open. Accessions list.
Alfred P. Sloan, Jr., Museum.
Records of this Flint chapter of the DAR, established in 1897, consist of minutes, financial records, list of charter Chapter members, rosters of officers, and scrapbooks, many of which were kept by early DAR members and contain pictures, photos, cards and invitations, and clippings.

8,179. Flint Parliamentary Law Club
Records. 1938-59. 2 in.
Open. Accessions list and card file.
Alfred P. Sloan, Jr., Museum.
Constitution and bylaws, minutes from 1953 to 1959, treasurer's records and financial statements, correspondence, membership lists, and other items of this women's group devoted to the teaching and study of parliamentary law.

8,180. Hospital Aid Association
Records. 1913-74. 2 boxes.
Open. Accession list and card file.

Alfred P. Sloan, Jr., Museum.
Annual reports, minutes, financial records, correspondence, a history, and other items of the Association, which was founded by local women in 1913 as the Maternity Home and Children's Hospital Association to support new facilities at Hurley Hospital in Flint. The Association assumed its present name in 1950. At that time the group also expanded its activities to include promotion of a health museum, which was established at the Sloan Museum. The collection consists chiefly of Association records from the period after 1950 and includes an annual report of the Hurley Hospital Auxiliary for 1971-72.

8,181. Rankin, Francis Hearn
Papers. Late 1800s-1950s. 13 boxes and other items.
Open. Unpublished guide.
Alfred P. Sloan, Jr., Museum.
Rankin (1854-1925) and his daughter Caroline Arabella Rankin (1888-1964) were owners and operators of the Wolverine Citizen Printing Company, established in Flint in 1850. Francis Rankin was mayor of Flint in 1891, a school board member for many years, and a member of the boards of the Michigan School for the Blind and the School for the Deaf. The collection, one-third of which pertains to Caroline Rankin, consists of personal papers; business papers related to the Wolverine Citizen Company; photos of family, friends, and the community; and publications and other items about the Flint area and about organizations in which the Rankins participated.

8,182. Young Women's Christian Association
Records. 1917-49. 1 box.
Open. Unpublished guide.
Alfred P. Sloan, Jr., Museum.
Ledgers, journals, and other financial records of the YWCA in Flint, which was founded in 1908 and operated a recreational and educational center for women in the community.

HANCOCK

8,183. Finnish-American Temperance Movement
Records. 1887-1972. 75 Hollinger boxes.
Open. No guide.
Suomi College, Finnish American Historical Archives.
Minutes, financial records, and correspondence of national and local branches of the Movement, established in 1885 to encourage temperance among Finnish Americans. Includes minutes of sewing clubs within the organization and records of lending libraries and entertainment committees in which women took part.

8,184. Finnish Relief
Collection. 1939-?. 14 Hollinger boxes.
Open. No guide.
Suomi College, Finnish American Historical Archives.
Minutes, accounts, and correspondence of various Finnish relief organizations, which operated from 1939 through WWII. Includes the records of such women's groups as the Lotta Svard Organization.

8,185. Folklore Oral History Project
Oral history. Nd. No size given.
Open. Index.
Suomi College, Finnish American Historical Archives.
Taped and transcribed interviews with 350 elderly persons, most of them of Finnish-American cultural background; 75 tape recordings of live WMPL Radio Heritage Line broadcasts, including interviews with local residents, writers, and others about local and ethnic history; and additional tapes, writings, and memorabilia pertaining to folklore and social change in the Lake Superior mining region. Finnish-American women are represented throughout the collection, and information is included on prominent women in the Finnish Lutheran Church, women radicals in the Finnish labor movement, and on individuals such as Margareeta Nüranen, who adopted the name Maggie Walz. Walz helped publish a women's magazine in Finnish, sold real estate, and made trips to Finland where she persuaded young women to come to America, usually to work as domestics in non-Finnish homes. The Project was conducted by Suomi College, which also operates the Finnish American Historical Archives.

8,186. Suomi Synod Archives
Records. 1890-1962. 84 Hollinger boxes.
Open. Unpublished guide.
Suomi College, Finnish American Historical Archives.
Minutes, financial records, and correspondence of the Suomi Synod governing body, founded in 1890, and of local churches. The Suomi Synod, which was another name for the Finnish Evangelical Lutheran Church of America, merged with the Lutheran Church in America in 1962. Included are minutes of pastors' wives organizations; speeches, articles, and other items of [Mrs.] Thyra Rautalahti, a well-known minister's wife; and material pertaining to sewing clubs, aid societies, and other women's church groups.

HARTFORD

8,187. Van Buren County Federation of Women's Clubs
Records. 1895-1976. No size given.
Open. No guide.
Van Buren County Historical Society Museum.
Minutes, program yearbooks of various local clubs, and scrapbooks of the Federation reflect the activities of numerous women's groups in this rural Michigan county from ca. 1895 until 1976, when the Federation disbanded. Federation club representatives met annually, and the Federation board kept in touch with officers of the state and national GFWC to coordinate club activities.

HOLLAND

8,188. Holland Woman's Literary Club
Records. 1922-67. 12 microfilm reels.
Open. No guide.
Herrick Public Library.
Annual reports and minutes of the Club, founded in 1922, document its social activities and efforts toward "literary improvement."

8,189. Karsten, Helene P.
Papers. 1929-72. 80 items.
Open. No guide.
Hope College Archives.
[Mrs. Harold J.] Karsten (1898-1972) was a piano instructor at Hope College from 1928 to 1963. Correspondence, a manuscript about emotional problems of high school and college students, course outlines, her reports as president of the west central district of the Michigan Federation of Music Clubs, musical scores for the Cosmopolitan fraternity, programs, and clippings.

8,190. Kollen, Martha (Diekema)
Papers. 1975. 24-page item.
Open. No guide.
Hope College Archives.
Student research paper by Jan Osterhaven pertains to Kollen (1867-1960), a Holland clubwoman and civic leader who served on the local board of education for 30 years and was school superintendent for 10 years, president of the Woman's Literary Club, and a lifelong member of the Century Club. She also taught Sunday school for 40 years.

8,191. Ross, Metta J.
Papers. 1926-74. 3 ft.
Open. No guide.
Hope College Archives.
[Miss] Ross (1890-) was a professor of English and history at Hope College. Correspondence, biographical material, manuscripts of her literary and historical writings, and lecture notes, outlines, examinations, clippings, pamphlets, and bibliographies relating to courses she taught. The course material is arranged under general categories of arts, biography, literature, international affairs, Latin America, Africa, Europe, Asia, and world civilization. Includes her manuscripts of "The Boomerang" and other short stories. Also contains a student research paper written in 1974 by Suzan M. Gould about Ross's career at the College.

8,192. Snow, Esther Mac Farlane
Papers. 1942-74. 140 items.
Open. No guide.
Hope College Archives.
Correspondence, photos, programs, and clippings of Snow (1895-1974), an instructor and professor of organ and piano, the director of the Women's Glee Club, and assistant professor of German at Hope College. Included are letters she wrote to her family while she was serving as chaperone for students attending the Hope College Vienna Summer School in 1957, 1958, 1960, 1961, 1962, and 1965.

8,193. Women's League for Hope College
Records. 1925- . 250 items.
Open. No guide.
Hope College Archives.
Constitution, correspondence between chapters, photos, publicity material, news publications, and other items of the League, established in 1925 to raise money to furnish the girls' dormitories at the College. Since 1957 its chief fund-raising activity has been to conduct the "Village Square" sale of miscellaneous donated items on campus; from 1957 to 1967 this project netted more than $500,000 for the League.

8,194. Holland Musicians' Club
Records. 1928-33. 1 Hollinger box.
Open. Published guide.
Netherlands Museum.
Minutes, treasurer's accounts, correspondence, programs, and other records of this women's group. See "A Guide to the Archives of the Netherlands Museum, 1978."

8,195. Women of Holland
Collection. Nd. No size given.
Open. Published guide.
Netherlands Museum.
Individual accounts and recollections of pioneer women in Holland include items on Elvira (Langdon) Cooper, the first woman teacher in Holland, and on early settlers Anne De Vree, Anna Coatesworth [Mrs. Henry D.] Post, and [Mrs.] Cornelia Hulst Schaddelee. See "A Guide to the Archives of the Netherlands Museum, 1978."

8,196. Divorce, Remarriage, and Planned Parenthood
Records. 1962. 16 pp.
Access restricted. Unpublished guide.
Western Theological Seminary Library.
Reports and recommendations of the Christian action committee of the Reformed Church in America.

8,197. Dykstra, Adelphos A., and Dykstra, Bernice Mollema
Papers. 1932-66. 132 items.
Access restricted. Unpublished guide.
Western Theological Seminary Library.
Personal papers of Adelphos and Bernice Dykstra.

8,198. Holkeboer, Tena
Papers. 1920-63. 37 items.
Access restricted. Unpublished guide.
Western Theological Seminary Library.
Talks, addresses, and articles by Holkeboer (1895-1965), an educational missionary of the Reformed Church in America who worked in China and the Philippines.

8,199. Hostetter, Winifred Hager
Papers. ?-1967. 44 items.
Access restricted. Unpublished guide.
Western Theological Seminary Library.
Hostetter (1926-67) was a Reformed Church in America missionary to the Sudan and Pakistan. Obituary notices, condolences to her husband, and other papers.

8,200. Marriage, Divorce, Remarriage Report
Records. 1957. 24 pp.
Access restricted. Unpublished guide.
Western Theological Seminary Library.
Report of the joint committee from the Reformed Church in America synod of Chicago and Michigan.

8,201. Osterhaven, M. E.
Papers. 1957-58. 100 items.
Access restricted. Unpublished guide.
Western Theological Seminary Library.
Papers of Osterhaven contain letters from Mary B. Allison.

8,202. Otte, Frances Phelps
Papers. 1939. No size given.
Access restricted. Unpublished guide.
Western Theological Seminary Library.
Otte was the first woman graduate of Hope College, a coeducational school in Holland, MI. Included with a history she wrote of the first medical work conducted abroad by the Reformed Church in America are papers of her father and items relating to Hope College.

8,203. Pieters, Jennie A.
Papers. 1904-39. No size given.
Access restricted. Unpublished guide.
Western Theological Seminary Library.
Correspondence, missionary talks, and annual school reports of Pieters, a missionary to Japan.

HOLLY

8,204. Ladies Library of Holly Township
Records. 1877-1947. 3 vols.
Access restricted. No guide.
Northwest Oakland County Historical Society.
Minutes of the Ladies Library organization contain information about purchases and book loan privileges in Holly.

JACKSON

8,205. Sharp, Ella "Nellie" Wing (Merriman)
Papers. Ca. 1835-1912. Ca. 65 boxes and 1 cabinet.
Open. Unpublished guide.
Ella Sharp Museum.
[Mrs. John C.] Sharp (1857-1912), a Jackson clubwoman, was a granddaughter of Abraham Wing of Glen's Falls, NY, who bought Hillside Farm in 1855 for his widowed daughter Mary (Wing) [Mrs. Thomas S.] Farnsworth (1822?-92). Farnsworth later married Dwight Merriman, and they had several children, among them Ella (Merriman) Sharp. Papers and possessions of the Wing, Merriman, and Sharp families include correspondence of women family members on such topics as the status of single women, education and school activities, and the situation of women servants and "bound girls"; diaries; school essays and reports; Ella Sharp's notes for talks she gave at women's clubs and notes she took at forestry conferences; household financial records; deeds, mortgages, and other business records; wills; organizational records, including annual reports of the Home for the Friendless; legislative bills and speeches; photos; scrapbooks; clippings; ca. 25 boxes of newspapers and periodicals; recipes; and other items. Sharp willed Hillside Farm to the city of Jackson for use as a park and museum.

KALAMAZOO

8,206. Ethnographic Field Data: Aleut-Eskimo
Records. 1948- . 6 drawers, ca. 6050 items, and 20 tapes.
Access restricted. Unpublished guide.
American Institute for Exploration.
Field notes of trained ethnographers and linguists supplemented by taped and written interviews, reminiscences, photos, and slides of chiefly small village populations of Aleut-Eskimo natives in Atka, Nikolski, Unalaska, and Akutan of the Aleutian Islands. Collection contains genealogies of Aleut families; narratives of Aleut women about medical lore, midwifery, and superstitions regarding females; biographies of such notable Aleut women as [Mrs.] Anfesia Shapsnikoff of Unalaska, Eva Chercassen and Jenny Krukoff of Nikolski, and Jenny Golley of Atka; linguistic tapes that reveal differences between female language and male language; recipes; and items concerning weaving, painting, cooking, and other female activities.

8,207. Human Sexuality
Collection. Nd. 1 drawer, 220 vols., 200 serials, and other items.
Open. No guide.
American Institute for Exploration.
Collection pertains to human sexuality in American, Eskimo, Danish, and other cultures with particular emphasis on "the new sexual freedom" in the US, the history of American sexual customs and beliefs, and cross-cultural comparisons of the role of women in human sexuality. Letters from sexual freedom groups such as the Berkeley Sexual Freedom League, "swinger" and wife-swapping clubs, and other organizations in the US and Scandinavia; slides of illustrations in classical erotic literature; art prints; and books and magazines of classical and modern erotica, including items regarding the modern exploitation of eroticism and sexuality.

8,208. Women in Exploration
Collection. 1760- . 1 box and ca. 24 vols.
Open. No guide.
American Institute for Exploration.
Books and miscellaneous notes mention, feature, and detail the exploration activities of women in anthropology, biology, and other research fields. Includes accounts of the work of Margaret Mead, the explorations of Osa [Mrs. Martin] Johnson, and the experiences of [Miss] Mary Ann Oatman and [Miss] Olive Ann Oatman as captives of American Indians during the 1850s.

8,209. American Association of University Women
Records. 1914-73. 13 boxes.
Open. Unpublished guide.
Western Michigan University, Regional History Collections.
Bylaws of the Kalamazoo chapter of the AAUW; annual reports, 1929-63; board and branch meeting minutes to 1971; treasurers' reports; membership records; directors' and other correspondence; complete history of the chapter; scrapbooks; material pertaining to senior women honors, women's education, educational center funding in the 1950s, and memorial gifts; and newsletters, directories, and journals.

8,210. Averitt, Kay
Papers. 1972-74. 1 folder.
Open. Unpublished guide.
Western Michigan University, Regional History Collections.
Minutes, correspondence, clippings, and related material of the Kalamazoo Women's Government Caucus were gathered by Averitt, a Caucus member. Formed in 1972, the group consisted of women who were elected officials and members of advisory boards and commissions of various city, county, and state governmental units.

8,211. Barnard, Elizabeth
Papers. 1823-1963. 80 items.
Open. Unpublished guide.
Western Michigan University, Regional History Collections.
Papers of Barnard, who was head of the art department for the Kalamazoo Public Museum and Art Institute, contain program books from the Ladies' Library Association garden group, 1953-58.

8,212. Beisel, Mr. and Mrs. Robert
Papers. 1830-1975. 13 Hollinger boxes.
Open. Unpublished guide.
Western Michigan University, Regional History Collections.
Clippings, group history, and yearbooks of the Philomaths, a ladies' reading circle organized in 1897 in Lima, IN. Alice [Mrs. Robert] Beisel was a charter member of the group.

8,213. Blake, James L.
Papers. 1810-1922. 35 vols. and 1 ft.
Open. Unpublished guide.
Western Michigan University, Regional History Collections.
Included with diaries and other papers of the Blake family, who were Galesburg, MI, residents, is a printed constitution and a 1919 catalog of the local Ladies' Library Association.

8,214. Brown, Mary
Papers. 1873-1906. 40 items.
Open. Unpublished guide.
Western Michigan University, Regional History Collections.
Includes a diary in which Ella Ward of Kalamazoo detailed her daily activities in 1879.

8,215. Buechner, Mrs. J.
Papers. 1970. 1 item.
Open. Unpublished guide.
Western Michigan University, Regional History Collections.
History of the Kalamazoo Business and Professional Women's Club from 1920 to 1970 was compiled by Mrs. Emilia Kennedy.

8,216. Bushell, Bertha
Oral history. Ca. 1963. 1 tape.
Access restricted. No guide.
Western Michigan University, Regional History Collections.
Taped and transcribed interview with [Mrs.] Bushell, a Kalamazoo resident who since 1947 has been affiliated with the labor movement and was secretary of the Kalamazoo Labor Council.

8,217. Case, Eula
Papers. 1861-1974. 2 Hollinger boxes.
Open. Unpublished guide.
Western Michigan University, Regional History Collections.
[Miss] Case was a school teacher who lived in Eaton County, MI. Scattered diaries she kept between 1960 and 1971 reflect her daily experiences while retired and living on the family farm.

8,218. Chrysolite Club
Records. 1914-67. 4 vols.
Open. Unpublished guide.
Western Michigan University, Regional History Collections.
Minutes of this Kalamazoo women's organization, first established in the Hillcrest area to promote self-improvement and literary interests.

8,219. Collins, Ada
Papers. 1855-1967. 60 items.
Open. Unpublished guide.
Western Michigan University, Regional History Collections.
Diary of Caroline E. Honeysett of Springbrook in Kalamazoo County contains scattered entries from 1896 to 1901 pertaining to her daily household activities.

8,220. Comings, Sherman
Papers. 1893-1937. 3 Hollinger boxes and 1 package.
Open. Unpublished guide.
Western Michigan University, Regional History Collections.
Consists of records of the Galesburg, MI, Ladies of the Maccabees, including minutes, 1893-1922; monthly reports; financial records; miscellaneous receipts; correspondence; and rituals manuals.

8,221. Cook, Wallace
Papers. 1870-92. 6 vols. and 1 item.
Open. Unpublished guide.
Western Michigan University, Regional History Collections.
Diaries kept sporadically between 1870 and 1877 by [Miss] Medora Burdick of Muir in Ionia County, MI, relate to her school activities, household duties, and family matters. Also included are 1891-92 diaries of [Mrs.] Polly Burdick, also of Muir, which pertain to household and family matters just before the time of her death and a notebook she kept for a trip to the 1876 Philadelphia Centennial celebration.

8,222. Cornish, Lena
Papers. 1898. 1 item.
Open. Unpublished guide.
Western Michigan University, Regional History Collections.
Journal of Matilda Van Riper Lawrence relates to a trip she and her husband Archie Lawrence took by horse and wagon from Little Prairie Ronde in Cass County, MI, to Akron, CO.

8,223. Crane, Caroline Bartlett
Papers. 1843-1935. 50 Hollinger boxes.
Open. Unpublished guide.
Western Michigan University, Regional History Collections.
Crane (1858-1935), a minister, civic leader, reformer, and writer, was married to Kalamazoo physician Augustus W. Crane. Correspondence between Crane and her husband; correspondence and related material pertaining to her interests in the church, a sanitary survey, meat inspection, civic improvement, suffrage, prison reform, and the Women's Council of National Defense; personal items; reminiscences; notes on family history; clippings; honorary proclamations; and autographs. Council material dates from 1917 to 1920.

8,224. Dibble Family
Papers. 1814-1941. 12 ft.
Open. Unpublished guide.
Western Michigan University, Regional History Collections.
Among business papers, family correspondence, and diaries of the Philo Dibble family of Marshall, MI, whose business interests included banking, railroads, and plank road companies, are ca. 1700 letters between Dibble relatives, many of them women, relating to everyday life.

8,225. Ednie, Mrs. William
Papers. 1878-97. 10 items.
Open. Unpublished guide.
Western Michigan University, Regional History Collections.
Daily household diary of Gusta Evans Smith, who married Frank Smith of Weesaw Township in 1878 and lived near Hill's Corner in Berrien County, MI.

8,226. Ensfield, Mary
Oral history. 1963. 1 tape.
Access restricted. No guide.
Western Michigan University, Regional History Collections.
Interview with [Miss] Ensfield, who in 1919 was elected to serve as a county school commissioner, relates to her career as well as her involvement with and the history of Western Michigan University.

8,227. Every Friday Club
Records. 1908-73. 1 Hollinger box.
Open. Unpublished guide.
Western Michigan University, Regional History Collections.
Minutes, treasurers' reports, membership lists, program schedules, and a history of this Kalamazoo women's group. The Club history was prepared in 1962 by Dorothy Gaultlett.

8,228. Fleming, Greta Wolfe
Papers. 1918. 13 items.
Open. Unpublished guide.
Western Michigan University, Regional History Collections.
Correspondence of [Mrs.] Fleming pertains to her service with an American National Red Cross nurses' group in France during WWI. Her letters begin as she awaits overseas departure and continue after she reaches France.

8,229. Ford, Sina Hutchison
Papers. 1837-1965. 42 vols. and 1 ft.
Open. Unpublished guide.
Western Michigan University, Regional History Collections.
Born in St. Joseph County, MI, [Mrs.] Ford taught school in that area as well as in Kalamazoo County. Extensive diaries she kept between 1899 and 1965 include descriptions of her daily experiences and weather notes.

8,230. Giddings, Allan M.
Papers. 1859-76. 25 items.
Open. Unpublished guide.
Western Michigan University, Regional History Collections.
Papers of several families in the Battle Creek-Augusta, MI, area include 1875-76 diaries of Celia Mowry, who lived in Ross Center, Kalamazoo County, which pertain to school, household, and community activities when she was a young girl and an 1861-63 diary in which Mrs. Philo Pratt describes daily experiences as a housewife.

8,231. Hagle, Jane S.
Papers. 1815-87. 3 vols. and 22 items.
Open. Unpublished guide.
Western Michigan University, Regional History Collections.
Scattered diaries kept between 1861 and 1869 by Margaret Stanford, a resident of Martin in Allegan County, MI, include one volume in which she records her duties as a school teacher in 1862.

8,232. Harrison, Lucia
Oral history. 1958. 8 pp.
Access restricted. No guide.
Western Michigan University, Regional History Collections.
Transcript of an interview with [Miss] Harrison, who from 1909 to 1947 was a member of the Western Michigan University geography department, pertains to her early years at WMU.

8,233. Jackson, Mrs. Clair
Oral history. 1972. 1 tape.
Access restricted. No guide.
Western Michigan University, Regional History Collections.
In a taped and transcribed interview, Josephine Wing Jackson (1877-1972) describes her experiences as secretary for the Western State Normal School from 1904 to 1905 and includes details about many tasks she handled.

8,234. John Gray Memorial Museum, Ladies of the Maccabees
Records. 1864-1950. 1 Hollinger box.
Open. Unpublished guide.
Western Michigan University, Regional History Collections.
Minutes of annual meetings, an 1893 list of charter members, and a reunion book of the Alamo, MI, Ladies of the Maccabees.

8,235. Kalamazoo Chamber of Commerce, Women's Division
Records. 1964-72. 2 vols.
Open. Unpublished guide.
Western Michigan University, Regional History Collections.
Scrapbooks of the Division, now known as the Greater Kalamazoo Federated Women's Club, contain clippings, programs, and other items.

8,236. Kalamazoo Public Library
Collection. 1904-74. 1 vol. and 1 item.
Open. Unpublished guide.
Western Michigan University, Regional History Collections.
Constitution; minutes, 1904-22; and membership lists of the Graduate Nurses' Association of Kalamazoo. In 1920 this organization became a unit of the Michigan State Nurses' Association. Also included is a term paper written in 1974 by Danforth W. Thomas pertaining to Helen Statler's campaign for the 1920 Republican nomination to Congress in the third Michigan district; [Mrs.] Statler was the first woman in Michigan to seek a Congressional nomination.

8,237. Kelly, Eula, and Pellowe, Esther
Papers. 1833-1903. 8 vols.
Open. Unpublished guide.
Western Michigan University, Regional History Collections.
Diaries kept by Esther Copley Lawrence, who lived in the Village of Volina, Cass County, MI, include her descriptions of family life for the period from 1858 to 1903.

8,238. Kleinstueck, Irene
Oral history. 1965. 1 tape.
Access restricted. No guide.
Western Michigan University, Regional History Collections.
Interview in which [Miss] Kleinstueck (1884-1974) discusses her experiences while attending the Michigan Female Seminary in Kalamazoo in 1899.

8,239. Krasean, Thomas
Papers. 1885-92. 1 vol.
Open. Unpublished guide.
Western Michigan University, Regional History Collections.
Diary of [Mrs.] Emily Barden (1813-?) a widow from Bellevue in Eaton County, MI, contains references to local news and weather.

8,240. Ladies' Library Association
Records. 1852-1976. 13 Hollinger boxes.
Open. Unpublished guide.
Western Michigan University, Regional History Collections.
Annual reports and board minutes to 1962 of this

Kalamazoo women's group, founded in 1852; minutes of the secretary; treasurers' books, bills, and receipts; membership lists and program book; press book; catalog of library books; a play written in 1973 by Ada McAllister about her great-great-grandmother Lucinda Hinsdale Stone, who was an Association member; and published historical sketches of Michigan library associations compiled in 1976 by Mrs. A. F. Bixby and Mrs. A. Howell.

8,241. Lamport, Belinda Sophia
Papers. 1838-1921. 12 items.
Open. Unpublished guide.
Western Michigan University, Regional History Collections.
Includes diary kept in 1847 by Lamport (1830-?), a Leonidas, MI, resident.

8,242. League of Women Voters
Records. 1935-72. 35 Hollinger boxes.
Open. Unpublished guide.
Western Michigan University, Regional History Collections.
Minutes, brochures, and printed reports of the Kalamazoo unit of the LWV.

8,243. McKain, Mr. and Mrs. William
Papers. 1838-1954. 2 Hollinger boxes.
Open. Unpublished guide.
Western Michigan University, Regional History Collections.
Papers of this Vicksburg, MI, family include diaries, in which Helen [Mrs. William] McKain describes life in a farming community from 1929 to 1954, as well as a 1931-32 program for the Pavilion Ladies' Aid.

8,244. MacMillian, Margaret Burnham
Oral history. 1958. 10 pp.
Access restricted. No guide.
Western Michigan University, Regional History Collections.
Transcribed interview with MacMillian (1899-), who at age 21 began her teaching career at the Kalamazoo Normal High School, contains her recollections about teaching in the Western Michigan University history department before retiring in 1969. The High School, which operated until ca. 1965, was the teachers training school for Western State Teachers College.

8,245. Michigan Female Seminary
Records. 1872-1905. No size given.
Open. Unpublished guide.
Western Michigan University, Regional History Collections.
Catalogs, programs, yearbooks, and flyers of the Seminary, which was located in Kalamazoo.

8,246. Morton, Mrs. Sidney
Papers. 1941-72. 31 vols.
Open. Unpublished guide.
Western Michigan University, Regional History Collections.
Diaries of Hazel Brown Morton, a Jackson, MI, resident who in later life spent several months each year in Florida and eventually retired there, contain daily accounts of her activities in Michigan and Florida.

8,247. Nobbs, Lucille
Oral history. 1965. 1 tape.
Access restricted. No guide.
Western Michigan University, Regional History Collections.
Nobbs came to Western Michigan University in 1921 to teach English and retired in 1965. In a taped and transcribed interview she discusses her early years at the University.

8,248. Pender, Mrs. H. R.
Papers. 1868-72. 2 vols.
Open. Unpublished guide.
Western Michigan University, Regional History Collections.
Diaries of Theoda [Mrs. Henry] Knappen, an early settler of Richland in Kalamazoo County, and Lizzie Brown, a Richland resident who later married Eugene Knappen, pertain to their daily experiences and activities.

8,249. Playford, Pearl
Papers. 1855-1949. 17 vols. and 1 item.
Open. Unpublished guide.
Western Michigan University, Regional History Collections.
Diaries kept between 1933 and 1949 by Mrs. Ira Leonard of Hartford, MI, include details about her daily activities and the weather.

8,250. Ray, Mrs. Jessie
Papers. 1855-1926. 8 vols. and 115 items.
Open. Unpublished guide.
Western Michigan University, Regional History Collections.
Included with diaries, correspondence, and other items are 1862-69 diaries of Sally (Haner) [Mrs. Sidney] Johnson, who lived in Three Rivers, St. Joseph County, MI, about her daily activities beginning at age 25 and continuing through the first year of her marriage.

8,251. Ritter, Nellie
Papers. 1849-1932. 29 vols.
Open. Unpublished guide.
Western Michigan University, Regional History Collections.
Diaries kept between 1867 and 1910 by Susan Layman Dickson of Berrien Centre, MI, provide descriptions of weather and her daily experiences.

8,252. Rogers, Frederick, and Rogers, Katherine
Papers. 1837-1934. 1 Hollinger box.
Open. Unpublished guide.
Western Michigan University, Regional History Collections.
Included are two incomplete diaries kept by Galesburg, MI, resident Ellen Beattie during her early school years.

8,253. Ross, Nellie Tayloe
Papers. 1901-77. 1 ft.
Open. Unpublished guide.
Western Michigan University, Regional History Collections.
Ross (1876-1977) served as governor of Wyoming from 1925 to 1927 and in 1933 was appointed director of the Bureau of the US Mint. Her extensive correspondence and clippings pertain to family matters. When she was elected to complete the term of her husband Governor William Ross, who died in 1924, she became the first woman governor in America. She retired from the US Mint in 1955 after 22 years of service.

8,254. Rubert, Mrs. John
Papers. 1880-1945. 3 vols.
Open. Unpublished guide.
Western Michigan University, Regional History Collections.
Minutes of the Richland, MI, Ladies' Library Association, 1880-1917, and financial records of the Richland Woman's Christian Temperance Union, 1923-45.

8,255. Sherrod, Mrs. Arthur
Papers. 1894-1926. 5 vols.
Open. Unpublished guide.
Western Michigan University, Regional History Collections.
Secretary's books with minutes of the Ladies' Aid Society of the First Congregational Church in Bangor, MI.

8,256. Smith, Stanley Barney
Papers. 1831-1918. 10 Hollinger boxes.
Open. Unpublished guide.
Western Michigan University, Regional History Collections.
Diaries of Mary Allen Barney of Schoolcraft, MI, span the period from 1862 to 1901 and provide detailed information about her home life and town activities. Also contains a short 1853 journal in which Cynthia Ainsworth, who lived in Yorkville, Kalamazoo County, describes local news.

8,257. Snow, Leta
Oral history. 1962. 1 tape.
Access restricted. No guide.
Western Michigan University, Regional History Collections.
Taped and transcribed interview with [Mrs.] Snow (1880-), who helped to establish the Kalamazoo Michigan Symphony Orchestra, includes her comments about the problems and solutions in that effort.

8,258. Soeters, Wilhelmia Tourman
Oral history. 1974. 1 tape.
Access restricted. No guide.
Western Michigan University, Regional History Collections.
Interview with [Mrs.] Soeters (1888-) pertains to her experiences as she and her family immigrated to America in 1910 and settled in Kalamazoo.

8,259. Spangler, Maude A.
Papers. 1917-19. 128 items.
Open. Unpublished guide.
Western Michigan University, Regional History Collections.
Correspondence of [Miss] Spangler includes letters she received from friends serving overseas during WWI, among them those who worked with the Nurse Corps and hospital groups. Also contains photos of nurses and postcards of military trains in Europe.

8,260. Stoddard, Mrs. Lynn
Papers. 1944-62. 2 Hollinger boxes.
Open. Unpublished guide.
Western Michigan University, Regional History Collections.
Correspondence between members of the Stoddard family consists chiefly of letters from Bernice "Abie" Stoddard to her husband Lynn Stoddard who was stationed at Great Lakes Naval Hospital from 1944 to 1945. The correspondence reflects her struggle to manage their farm in Calhoun County, MI, while her husband served in WWII.

8,261. Streidl, Mr. and Mrs. Jack
Papers. 1967-69. 79 items.
Open. Unpublished guide.
Western Michigan University, Regional History Collections.
Correspondence of Plainwell, MI, resident Diane Streidl, who was the daughter of Mr. and Mrs. Streidl, pertains to her term as a Peace Corps volunteer in Inhamas-Goias, Brazil.

8,262. Travel Club
Records. 1911-70. 1 Hollinger box.
Open. Unpublished guide.
Western Michigan University, Regional History Collections.
A Kalamazoo literary and social group founded in 1911, this women's club met to study various foreign countries. Minutes, 1940-70; program books; a Club history with clippings to 1936; and reminiscences written by Alice Chamberlain Hatfield for the Club's 25th anniversary.

8,263. Tuesday Book Review Club
Records. 1907-74. 2 Hollinger boxes.
Open. Unpublished guide.

Western Michigan University, Regional History Collections.
Bylaws of the Club, which was founded in 1895; minutes to 1968; treasurer's book, 1915-54; lists of officers and members; a Club history, 1895-1938; and lists of books reviewed. Also included is a history of the Twentieth Century Club by Sarah H. [Mrs. George] Foote.

8,264. Wellever, Edith
Papers. 1890-1943. 148 items and 6 vols.
Open. Unpublished guide.
Western Michigan University, Regional History Collections.
Papers include a diary kept from 1899 to 1903 by [Mrs.] Laura Bradley of Battle Creek, MI, recording daily experiences.

8,265. Wiersma, Jennie
Oral history. 1975. 1 tape.
Access restricted. No guide.
Western Michigan University, Regional History Collections.
Taped and transcribed interview with [Mrs.] Wiersma (1891-), who immigrated to America from Holland in 1916, settled in Wisconsin, and later moved to Kalamazoo.

LANSING

8,266. Brotherton, Belle
Papers. ?-1926. 2 boxes.
Open. No guide.
Michigan Department of Education, State Library Services.
Correspondence, files, clippings, pamphlets, and broadsides of [Mrs.] Brotherton relate to the woman suffrage movement in Michigan, particularly to the activities of the Michigan Suffrage Association.

8,267. Michigan State Federation of Women's Clubs
Records. 1895- . 18 ft.
Access restricted. No guide.
Michigan Department of Education, State Library Services.
Minutes and scrapbooks of the Federation.

8,268. Woman's Christian Temperance Union in Michigan
Records. 1876. 1 vol.
Open. No guide.
Michigan Department of Education, State Library Services.
Volume containing histories of local WCTU chapters in Michigan.

8,269. Association of Country Women of the World
Records. 1968. 13 tapes.
Open. Published guide.
Michigan State Archives.
Recordings of Michigan Farm Bureau radio broadcasts about the Association of Country Women of the World include information on projects such as candymaking and gardening. Taken from *Bibliography of Sources Relating to Women* (Lansing, MI: Michigan Department of State, 1975).

8,270. Cook Family
Papers. 1837-96. 3 in.
Open. Published guide.
Michigan State Archives.
Correspondence of members of the Cook family in New York with family members who emigrated to Michigan, especially Charlotte and Sarah Cook. Material on agriculture, transportation, politics, and the Civil War. The family also spelled its name Cooke. Taken from *Bibliography of Sources Relating to Women* (Lansing, MI: Michigan Department of State, 1975).

8,271. Daughters of the American Revolution, Chapter 292
Records. 1896-1972. 7 ft.
Open. Published guide.
Michigan State Archives.
Records of the Lansing chapter of the DAR include minutes of meetings, annual conference proceedings, treasurer's records, brief histories, membership rosters, records of special projects such as essay contests and grave registrations, and scrapbooks. Contains an article about "Deborah Sampson, Maiden Soldier of the Revolution" and an autobiographical sketch of Sarah Huyck, daughter of a Revolutionary War soldier. Taken from *Bibliography of Sources Relating to Women* (Lansing, MI: Michigan Department of State, 1975).

8,272. Daughters of the Grand Army of the Republic, Michigan Department
Records. 1911-61. 3.75 ft.
Open. Published guide.
Michigan State Archives.
Minutes of the board of directors, ledger of accounts, rosters and histories of fortresses, register of department encampments, and records of the General Alpheus S. Williams Fortress. Taken from *Bibliography of Sources Relating to Women* (Lansing, MI: Michigan Department of State, 1975).

8,273. Detroit Federation of Women's Clubs
Records. 1895-1935. 3 in.
Open. Published guide.
Michigan State Archives.
Historical sketch of the Federation, compiled by Sarah A. Grindley, includes constitutions and bylaws, presidents' annual addresses, annual reports of activities, special projects and committee reports, and photos of members. Taken from *Bibliography of Sources Relating to Women* (Lansing, MI: Michigan Department of State, 1975).

8,274. DuMond, Neva
Papers. 1965. 1 in.
Open. Published guide.
Michigan State Archives.
Poems by [Miss] DuMond, a Michigan author and artist from Sanilac County. Also includes photos and clippings about her death. Taken from *Bibliography of Sources Relating to Women* (Lansing, MI: Michigan Department of State, 1975).

8,275. Ferris, Donna
Papers. Nd. 8 in., 6 vols.
Open. Published guide.
Michigan State Archives.
Quilt designs and clippings and reference notes about quilt designs accumulated by [Mrs.] Ferris. Includes letters of appreciation for talks given by Ferris, 1940-50. Taken from *Bibliography of Sources Relating to Women* (Lansing, MI: Michigan Department of State, 1975).

8,276. Governmental Collections
Records. Nd. No size given.
Open. No guide.
Michigan State Archives.
Included in the State Archives are records of the Executive Office, which contain information on the State Industrial Home for Girls, the Girls' Training School, and the Okemos Women's Prison. Other series contain records of or information on the Michigan Reform School for Girls.

Included are legal agreements placing inmates of the State Industrial Home for Girls in private homes for service, letters regarding girls indentured for such service, and letters from the girls in service describing work conditions, pay, problems, and social life. Also includes case histories of the first 120 girls received at the Michigan Reform School for Girls and annual reports and other records of the School. Taken from *Bibliography of Sources Relating to Women* (Lansing, MI: Michigan Department of State, 1975).

8,277. Greenough, Annetta
Papers. 1881-?. 4 in.
Open. Published guide.
Michigan State Archives.
Registered nurse certificates and the war service record of Greenough. Taken from *Bibliography of Sources Relating to Women* (Lansing, MI: Michigan Department of State, 1975).

8,278. Halbert Family
Papers. 1839-1919. 4 in.
Open. Published guide.
Michigan State Archives.
Letters to Emma, Hattie, and Maria Halbert, some of which concern homemaking and early settlement in Ionia and Eaton counties. Taken from *Bibliography of Sources Relating to Women* (Lansing, MI: Michigan Department of State, 1975).

8,279. Hamilton, Isabella
Papers. 1850-1911. No size given.
Open. Published guide.
Michigan State Archives.
Includes diaries kept in 1850 and 1853 by Isabella Hart at Coombe Cottage, Ann Arbor, relating to her studies there; diaries kept by Isabella Hamilton; and *The Ladies Coronal,* 1850, a manuscript periodical edited by Isabella Hart and devoted to moral and intellectual improvement. Taken from *Bibliography of Sources Relating to Women* (Lansing, MI: Michigan Department of State, 1975).

8,280. Hayden Family
Papers. 1840. 1 in.
Open. Published guide.
Michigan State Archives.
Includes a letter from Bessie Stark Chadwick of DeWitt, MI, to Esther M. Martin of Palmyra, NY, commenting on settling of the area. Taken from *Bibliography of Sources Relating to Women* (Lansing, MI: Michigan Department of State, 1975).

8,281. Lansing Woman's Club
Records. 1874-1925. 21 vols.
Open. Published guide.
Michigan State Archives.
Constitutions, annual reports of the presidents, minutes of weekly business meetings, and photos. Taken from *Bibliography of Sources Relating to Women* (Lansing, MI: Michigan Department of State, 1975).

8,282. Lewis Family
Papers. 1952-62. No size given.
Open. Published guide.
Michigan State Archives.
Materials accumulated by Jane Irwin Lewis (1913-66) on the quality of elementary and secondary education in the Ferndale school system. Taken from *Bibliography of Sources Relating to Women* (Lansing, MI: Michigan Department of State, 1975).

8,283. Michigan Nursing Association
Records. 1916-51. 9 ft.
Open. Published guide.
Michigan State Archives.
Registry and other reports, convention bulletins, lantern slides relating to the activities of the Association, and scrapbooks. Taken from *Bibliography of Sources Relating to Women* (Lansing, MI: Michigan Department of State, 1975).

8,284. Michigan State Association of Colored Women's Clubs
Records. 1898-1962. 20 in.
Open. Published guide.
Michigan State Archives.
History and program material of the Association, an account of "Pioneer Women of Afro-American Descent of Detroit," biographical sketches and photos of members, and a scrapbook documenting the history of "The King's Daughters and Sons," an organization for spiritual growth. Taken from *Bibliography of Sources Relating to Women* (Lansing, MI: Michigan Department of State, 1975).

8,285. Patchin, Elizabeth
Papers. 1820-1902. 3 in.
Open. Published guide.
Michigan State Archives.
Journal in which [Mrs.] Patchin comments on life as the wife of a minister, movements to other parishes, and homemaking. Taken from *Bibliography of Sources Relating to Women* (Lansing, MI: Michigan Department of State, 1975).

8,286. Peterson Family
Papers. Nd. 5 in.
Open. No guide.
Michigan State Archives.
Papers of Addie L. Lathrop, a teacher and later a railway telegraph operator, contain correspondence about teaching, business papers and correspondence, teaching certificates, and contracts. Taken from *Bibliography of Sources Relating to Women* (Lansing, MI: Michigan Department of State, 1975).

8,287. Stallworth, Alma G.
Papers. 1971-74. 9 ft.
Open. Published guide.
Michigan State Archives.
Papers of Stallworth, a Michigan state representative, include general legislative files, constituent correspondence, and files of the youth care committee, which Stallworth chaired. Correspondence pertains to such topics as the National Organization of Women Legislators, the League of Women Voters, and the Michigan Black Women's Political Caucus. Taken from *Bibliography of Sources Relating to Women* (Lansing, MI: Michigan Department of State, 1975).

8,288. Stoner Family
Papers. 1843-56. 2 in.
Open. Published guide.
Michigan State Archives.
Letters from Cornelia Stoner in Cortland to her sister in New York comment on homesteading, crops planted and harvested, agriculture, and homemaking. Taken from *Bibliography of Sources Relating to Women* (Lansing, MI: Michigan Department of State, 1975).

8,289. United Spanish-American War Veterans Ladies Auxiliary
Records. 1928-69. 2 ft.
Open. Published guide.
Michigan State Archives.
Reports of officers, financial records, general orders, photos, and scrapbooks relating to the Ladies Auxiliary, especially the Guy V. Henry Post Auxiliary. The collection was donated by Mabel Rogers Witfoth. Taken from *Bibliography of Sources Relating to Women* (Lansing, MI: Michigan Department of State, 1975).

8,290. Women's Relief Corps
Records. 1884-1967. 134 vols.
Open. Published guide.
Michigan State Archives.
Minutes of meetings, proceedings, notes and programs relating to activities of the Corps, clippings, and scrapbooks. Taken from *Bibliography of Sources Relating to Women* (Lansing, MI: Michigan Department of State, 1975).

LIVONIA

8,291. Shaw, Ann
Papers. 1855-81. 1 vol.
Open. No guide.
Livonia Historical Village at Greenmead.
Diary kept by Shaw (1819-91), who came to Livonia from England as a young girl, contains her descriptions of daily activities in what then was a pioneer rural area.

MONROE

8,292. Motherhouse Archives
Records. 1845- . Ca. 250 ft.
Access restricted. No guide.
Sisters, Servants of the Immaculate Heart of Mary Archives.
Records of the congregation and of provinces include minutes of chapters, boards, and committees; financial records; correspondence; personal papers and menologies of deceased Sisters; tapes and cassettes; annual chronicles of convents; photos; slides; memorabilia; and publications. This religious order of women was founded in 1845 in Monroe. In the past its members were engaged primarily in teaching in Catholic schools in Michigan and Illinois. Today the Sisters serve in parish, prayer, and campus ministries and are involved in religious education, pastoral care of the sick and elderly, and other areas of human development and social concern in the US and foreign countries.

MONTAGUE

8,293. Chisholm, Nellie B. (O'Connell)
Papers. 1880-1960. No size given.
Open. No guide.
Montague Museum and Historical Association.
Scrapbooks, tapes, photos, clippings, and various county records of Chisholm (1870-1958), an educator and newspaper writer. After graduating from Montague High School, she taught in rural schools near Montague. She then attended Michigan State Normal College, now known as Eastern Michigan University, at Ypsilanti. With that additional training she began to teach in high schools and then served as principal of two schools. In 1896 she married John A. Chisholm (?-1910), superintendent of the school in Seney, MI, where she was principal.

In 1907 Chisholm was elected county commissioner of schools of Muskegon County, becoming the first woman elected to county office in the county; she held her post for 28 years. In this capacity, she was instrumental in winning the state legislature's approval of a teachers' retirement program. She also gave numerous speeches on education for women and improved instruction for children.

MT. PLEASANT

8,294. Abbot, Elizabeth Bonsfield
Papers. 1890-98. 1 vol.
Open. Unpublished guide.
Central Michigan University, Clarke Historical Library.
Journal of Abbot, a student and socialite in Bay City, MI, reflects her social life and activities in Bay City and her travels in the US and abroad. Includes notes on the literature of American slavery.

8,295. Abbott, Alice (Gilmour) Young
Papers. 1901-32. Ca. 180 items.
Open. Unpublished guide.
Central Michigan University, Clarke Historical Library.
Family correspondence received principally by Abbott, a housewife, relates in part to business profits and prices of household goods. Correspondents include Abbott's second husband Albert J. Abbott, a traveling salesman; her mother Jane Gilmour, while visiting relatives in Canada; her brother John A. Gilmour in Kansas and Texas; and her sister Kate Gilmour in Wyoming.

8,296. Alliton, Silas
Papers. 1860-1916. 3 vols. and 242 items.
Open. Unpublished guide.
Central Michigan University, Clarke Historical Library.
Alliton (1842-?) served in Company G of the Third Michigan Cavalry. Personal correspondence includes letters from his sister Ann about family affairs and from his girl friend Dora Knight concerning education, teaching, and their growing friendship. Also contains diaries.

8,297. American Theater
Collection. 1819-1926. 185 items.
Open. Unpublished guide.
Central Michigan University, Clarke Historical Library.
Personal and business correspondence of American artists and theatrical agents, including Amelia Summerville, Maud Morgan, Dorothy Earle, Mabel Strickland, Fanny Rice, Fanny Davenport, and Cornelia Otis Skinner and receipts of the American Dramatic Fund Association.

8,298. Andrews, Sarah, and Andrews, Winifred
Papers. 1900-14. 7 items.
Open. Unpublished guide.
Central Michigan University, Clarke Historical Library.
Personal correspondence between two Detroit residents and letters from family and friends about family concerns, travels, and social matters.

8,299. Arnold, Amelia Langworthy
Papers. Nd. 1 item.
Open. Unpublished guide.
Central Michigan University, Clarke Historical Library.
In her reminiscences Arnold (1846-1929), a resident of Elk Rapids, MI, describes her trip to Michigan in 1855 and pioneer life in Elk Rapids.

8,300. Ball, John
Papers. 1815-83. 8 vols. and 114 items.
Open. Unpublished guide.
Central Michigan University, Clarke Historical Library.
Business and personal correspondence, diaries, receipts, scrapbooks, and maps of Ball (1794-1884), a Grand Rapids, MI, lawyer. Also included are an 1874 diary of his wife Mary describing her daily activities, social life, and family affairs and two scrapbooks containing family letters between the Ball children and their parents, primarily Mary, on family matters and travel.

8,301. Barrett, Elizabeth B.
Papers. 1923. 1 item.
Open. Unpublished guide.
Central Michigan University, Clarke Historical Library.
Barrett was a member of the Lucy Wolcott Barnum chapter of the DAR and a resident of Adrian, MI. Letter to a Mrs. Wait providing information on the life of Lucy Barnum.

8,302. Beardsley, Clarence B.
Papers. 1890-1951. 2 vols. and 121 items.
Open. Unpublished guide.
Central Michigan University, Clarke Historical Library.
Beardsley was a farmer who served as secretary and treasurer of the Dean Creek Thrashing Company in Sheridan, MI. Family correspondence, including letters in which Lucy Luscombe of Greenville, MI, who later became Beardsley's wife, discusses farming and local social activities; journals, including that of the Thrashing Company, which was kept from 1921 to 1951; indentures; poetry; and broadsides.

8,303. Benedict, Harriet
Papers. 1852-53. 3 items.
Open. Unpublished guide.
Central Michigan University, Clarke Historical Library.
Letters by Benedict, a resident of Tompkins, MI, and C. J. Rhea, to Benedict's sister (who was also Rhea's daughter) Martha Rhea of Wayne County, NY, about family, financial, and social matters.

8,304. Bingham, Abel
Papers. 1778-1909. 26 vols. and ca. 2500 items.
Open. Unpublished guide.
Central Michigan University, Clarke Historical Library.
Papers of Bingham (1786-1865), a Baptist clergyman and missionary to the Indians at Sault Ste. Marie, MI, from 1828 to 1855; of his wife Hannah Bingham; and of their daughters. Correspondence, diaries, journals, account books, and reports relate to Bingham's association with the Baptist Missionary Society of Boston, his ministry at the Tonawanda Indian Mission in New York State and the Baptist Indian Mission at Sault Ste. Marie, and to social activities in Grand Rapids, MI, after 1855. Diaries of Hannah Bingham deal with her daily activities, mission work, social calls, and religion. Diaries of her daughter Sophia Bingham describe school days and life at Sault Ste. Marie; letters to and from daughters Sophia, Ann Hasseltine, Hannah Maria, and Angelina concern daily activities, home life, school, and other subjects.

8,305. Blackwood, Thomas
Papers. 1825-71. 3 vols. and ca. 335 items.
Open. Unpublished guide.
Central Michigan University, Clarke Historical Library.
Correspondence, diaries, and lecture book of Blackwood (ca. 1800-56), a physician and prospector in the California gold rush who had lived in Ann Arbor and Ypsilanti, MI. Correspondence, chiefly between Blackwood and his wife Jane Blackwood, relates to family matters and to business. Includes Jane Blackwood's diary kept during the family's overland journey in 1853 from Council Bluffs, IA, to Sacramento, CA.

8,306. Blanchard, Pearl R.
Papers. 1894-96. 2 items.
Open. Unpublished guide.
Central Michigan University, Clarke Historical Library.
Blanchard was a schoolteacher in Clarenceville and Farmington, MI. Consists of a letter in which businessman Frank M. Lamb of Mt. Pleasant gives advice on teaching and Blanchard's teaching contract with the Farmington school district.

8,307. Bolsoadiris, Leide
Papers. 1897-98. 12 items.
Open. Unpublished guide.
Central Michigan University, Clarke Historical Library.
Correspondence of Bolsoadiris, a resident of Cassopolis, MI, relates to family matters and includes five letters from Charles E. Davis, superintendent of the Eureka Springs Sanitarium, regarding Bolsoadiris's sister who was a patient there.

8,308. Bosworth, Eliza
Papers. 1861-85. 8 items.
Open. Unpublished guide.
Central Michigan University, Clarke Historical Library.
Bosworth was a teacher who lived in Eaton County, MI. Teaching certificates, an announcement of an examination for teachers, and a letter from St. Louis which advertises the sale of a carriage.

8,309. Boughey, Herbert F.
Papers. 1911-34. 118 ft. and 16 vols.
Open. Unpublished guide.
Central Michigan University, Clarke Historical Library.
Financial records, correspondence, and letterpress books of Boughey, a lumber merchant and real estate broker in Traverse City, MI, who was also treasurer of the Carp Lake Lumber Company. Correspondence is primarily family letters from Grace Greenstead Boughey to her children in Illinois and Arkansas about family and social matters.

8,310. Bourgeois, Mary
Papers. 1914-67. 175 items.
Open. Unpublished guide.
Central Michigan University, Clarke Historical Library.
Bourgeois (1884-), a housewife, was a nurse from 1914 to 1918 during the European War. Includes family correspondence reflecting Bourgeois's travels and activities as a nurse at Base Hospital 91 in France in 1918 and 1919, receipts, bills, a Negro lullaby "Go to sleep my husky baby," 89 prayer cards, and the diploma that Julia Bourgeois, Mary's sister, received from Central State Normal School in 1914.

8,311. Brown, Morris
Papers. 1815-1934. 197 items.
Open. Unpublished guide.
Central Michigan University, Clarke Historical Library.
Personal and family correspondence of Brown (?-1878), an employee in Hammondsport and Cooperstown, NY, law offices with his cousin Emoline Whitmore of Hamburg, NY, and with Maria Smith of Cooperstown, whom he later married. Also included are correspondence concerning his daughter's divorce, her 1878-95 legal papers, letters from a friend Eleanor Fitzgerald, and Fitzgerald's family correspondence.

8,312. Carlin, Margot R.
Papers. Nd. No size given.
Closed. No guide.
Central Michigan University, Clarke Historical Library.
Carlin was a member of the Michigan American Revolution Bicentennial Commission from Mt. Pleasant. Material relates to her membership on the Commission and includes minutes of that body, papers of committees, correspondence, and grant proposals.

8,313. Clark, Robert
Papers. 1829-58. 1 vol. and 128 items.
Open. Unpublished guide.
Central Michigan University, Clarke Historical Library.
Correspondence, order book, indentures, and receipts of Clark (?-1837), a soldier and surveyor from St. Joseph County, MI, and of his wife. Clark's correspondence to his wife concerns his work as a government surveyor, while Mrs. Clark's correspondence with her relatives discusses family matters and farm business. Also includes material relating to supplies for the Michigan militia.

8,314. Cloutier, Helen H.
Papers. 1957-60. 9 items.
Open. Unpublished guide.
Central Michigan University, Clarke Historical Library.
Collection of Cloutier (1909-), a radio operator, journalist, and Michigan author, consists of manuscripts of her book *Isle Royale Calling* (1957) and illustrations for her book *The Many Names of Lee Lu* (1960).

8,315. Collet Family
Papers. 1823-1937. 6 vols. and 262 items.
Open. Unpublished guide.
Central Michigan University, Clarke Historical Library.
Diaries and correspondence of members of the Collet and Hall families in Indiana, Iowa, and Michigan, consisting primarily of 1853-79 letters of Emma Collet on family matters, farming prices, and health.

8,316. Compton, Cyrus
Papers. 1876-82. 30 items.
Open. Unpublished guide.
Central Michigan University, Clarke Historical Library.
Family correspondence of Compton, a cattleman in Custer City, Dakota Territory, who had lived in Charlotte, MI, includes letters in which his wife Mary in Charlotte describes to him family matters, social life, and local news.

8,317. Curtis, Marie
Papers. 1932-54. 2 vols.
Open. Unpublished guide.
Central Michigan University, Clarke Historical Library.
Scrapbooks with business correspondence, programs, photos, and clippings pertain to Curtis's work as music director and teacher at East Commerce High School and Southeastern High School in Detroit.

8,318. Custer, Elizabeth (Bacon)
Papers. 1907. 3 items.
Open. Unpublished guide.
Central Michigan University, Clarke Historical Library.
Custer (ca. 1841-1933) was an author and wife of General George Armstrong Custer. Correspondence concerns a proposed statue of her husband to be erected in Michigan and a request that her name be spelled out in a publication.

8,319. Daughters of the American Colonists
Records. 1948-59. 27 items.
Open. Unpublished guide.
Central Michigan University, Clarke Historical Library.
Minutes, reports, correspondence, and bills of the national board of the Daughters and membership rosters and a program for the organization's Michigan state assembly and its Chippewa Trails local chapter.

8,320. Daughters of the American Revolution, Lucy Walcott Barnum Chapter No. 912, Adrian, MI
Records. 1909-21. 1 vol.
Open. Unpublished guide.
Central Michigan University, Clarke Historical Library.
Scrapbook contains minutes, pamphlets, clippings, portraits, and a photo of members of the Chapter, founded in 1909.

8,321. Delta Kappa Gamma Society
Records. 1938-58. 11 items.
Open. Unpublished guide.
Central Michigan University, Clarke Historical Library.
The Society is an international organization to unite women educators. Constitution, a 1938

directory, and programs of annual conferences of the Society's Michigan state chapter; manuscript of a song book compiled by Mabel Bowers; and a "who's who" for the Dearborn, MI, Kappa chapter, which was organized in 1944.

8,322. Diary of a Young Lady
Papers. 1859. 1 vol.
Open. Unpublished guide.
Central Michigan University, Clarke Historical Library.
Diary in which a young lady, apparently from Orangeville, OH, and a student of a professor Walker when she attended school in Columbus, OH, comments on school life and the weather.

8,323. Diary of a Young Lady of a Trip South
Papers. Ca. 1900. 1 vol.
Open. Unpublished guide.
Central Michigan University, Clarke Historical Library.
Diary kept by a young lady, perhaps an Ohio resident, during a trip from Ohio through Indiana and Kentucky to a farm near Tullahoma, TN, contains mention of toll gates, cities along the route, landscapes, and housework. A note on one of the pages reads "Millie's memorandum."

8,324. Edmonds, Sarah Emma (Seelye)
Papers. 1885-97. 7 items.
Open. Unpublished guide.
Central Michigan University, Clarke Historical Library.
Correspondence of Edmonds (1841-98), who served in the Civil War under the name of Frank Thompson, consists of letters to R. H. Halsted about having her photo taken, her membership and participation in the Grand Army of the Republic, and her efforts to obtain an increase in her government pension because of injuries sustained while delivering mail during the War.

8,325. Female Tract Society
Records. Nd. 1 item.
Open. Unpublished guide.
Central Michigan University, Clarke Historical Library.
An agreement by members of this Jonesville, MI, organization to pay an annual amount to the Society lists names of the members and their annual dues.

8,326. Ferguson, A. E.
Papers. 1880. 1 vol.
Open. Unpublished guide.
Central Michigan University, Clarke Historical Library.
Diary in which Ferguson, a resident of Chelsea, MI, describes a trip to Harbor Springs, her visits and impressions of northwestern Michigan, and other activities.

8,327. Ferguson, Sarah J.
Papers. 1914-29. 1 vol.
Open. Unpublished guide.
Central Michigan University, Clarke Historical Library.
Account book of Ferguson, who lived in Birmingham, MI, in which daily expenses for groceries, church collections, and medical bills are recorded.

8,328. Fiske, Jennie (McGraw)
Papers. 1889-91. 1 vol.
Open. Unpublished guide.
Central Michigan University, Clarke Historical Library.
Inventory book of Fiske (1840-81), an Ithaca, NY, resident, contains a listing of articles in her home and their value as well as a pamphlet about the executor's sale in her home in 1891.

8,329. Fox, Frances Margaret
Papers. 1900-52. 34 ms. boxes and 1 vol.
Open. Unpublished guide.
Central Michigan University, Clarke Historical Library.
Born in Framington, MA, Fox (1870-1959) was a resident of Mackinaw City, MI, who wrote books for juveniles. Personal and business correspondence with publishers, relatives, and friends; notebooks and diaries containing research for her books and stories; accounts of people she met on her frequent travels; typescripts and printed articles of her stories; receipts; bills; and photos.

8,330. Freeman, Mary L.
Papers. 1885-91. 2 vols.
Open. Unpublished guide.
Central Michigan University, Clarke Historical Library.
Diaries of [Mrs.] Freeman, a housewife in Peoria, IL, contain entries about family life, meetings of the Women's Foreign Missionary Society, social life, delinquency at home, participation in a Shakespeare reading club, and a trip through Michigan and Mackinac Island to New York in 1885.

8,331. Garrett, Cecilia (Vincent)
Papers. 1853-1927. 60 items.
Open. Unpublished guide.
Central Michigan University, Clarke Historical Library.
Garrett, a housewife, was the wife of Milton W. Garrett of Redford, MI. Correspondence with friends and relatives in Connecticut and New York, scrapbook of poetry, and mortgage for land in Redford. Some of the early letters relate to teaching.

8,332. Goodrich, William Henry
Papers. 1855-88. 2 vols.
Open. Unpublished guide.
Central Michigan University, Clarke Historical Library.
Family correspondence from Goodrich (1825-74), a clergyman and grandson of Noah Webster, and from his wife Mary to his parents and brother Chauncey about family affairs and life in Binghamton, NY, and Cleveland. Also included are letters by Chauncey and his wife Ellen from Dresden, Germany, to their children about travel in Europe.

8,333. Gould, Amos
Papers. 1828-1931. Ca. 153 vols. and 65,000 items.
Open. Unpublished guide.
Central Michigan University, Clarke Historical Library.
Correspondence, diaries, and financial records of Gould (1808-82), who was a lawyer, state senator, and president of the First National Bank of Owosso, MI, relate to banking, land, lumber, railroads, politics, and family matters. Also included are correspondence of his wife Louisa about family and social matters and letters of their daughters Mary, Lena, and Jennie about family affairs, business in Owosso, college life, and a trip in 1873 to the Upper Peninsula.

8,334. Gray, Clarence Arthur
Papers. 1886-1901. 4 vols. and 10 items.
Open. Unpublished guide.
Central Michigan University, Clarke Historical Library.
Included with memory albums of Gray (1874-1934), a store owner and undertaker in Buckley, MI, are memory albums of his wife Nellie Prentice of Scottville, MI, poetry, her teachers certificates, and clippings.

8,335. Grubaugh, Orpha Jane
Papers. 1950-54. 60 items.
Open. Unpublished guide.
Central Michigan University, Clarke Historical Library.
Photos, receipts, school report cards, and various greeting and remembrance cards of Grubaugh, an Alma, MI, high school student. Also includes religious pamphlets issued by the Apostolic Truth Tract Society and other organizations.

8,336. Hammond, Aramintha
Papers. 1864. 3 items.
Open. Unpublished guide.
Central Michigan University, Clarke Historical Library.
Personal correspondence of Hammond, who lived in Constantine, MI, concerns payment of family debts.

8,337. Hampton, Charles George
Papers. 1850-1942. 25 vols. and 1191 items.
Open. Unpublished guide.
Central Michigan University, Clarke Historical Library.
Business and personal correspondence, diaries, journals, record books, and other papers of Hampton (?-1917), a Union Army officer and resident of Detroit, including material of his wife Emma (Stark) Hampton (1843-1925) and items relating to the Hampton and Stark families and to the Civil War. Emma Hampton's papers contain her correspondence, part of which relates to genealogy; diaries concerning her activities in the Woman's Relief Corps in 1882 and the Hamptons' trip to the Bahamas in 1892; a diary and memorandum book she kept in 1917; and a Stark family history she wrote.

8,338. Hannaford, Julia (Barnard)
Papers. 1866-67. 1 vol.
Open. Unpublished guide.
Central Michigan University, Clarke Historical Library.
Typescript of journal in which Hannaford, a housewife and resident of Glen Arbor, MI, describes the tribulations of her family during their first year of settlement and farming in the wilderness near Glen Arbor in Leelanau County. Typescript was prepared by Hannaford's son William H. Hannaford in 1937.

8,339. Hartman, Mrs. Peter G.
Papers. 1902-09. 3 vols.
Open. Unpublished guide.
Central Michigan University, Clarke Historical Library.
Diaries of Hartman, a Brighton, MI, housewife whose husband was a butcher; she records day-by-day accounts of weather, her domestic work, Maccabee meetings, guests, and animals her husband purchased.

8,340. Hinds, Henry Harrison
Papers. 1871-1906. 15 vols. and 15 items.
Open. Unpublished guide.
Central Michigan University, Clarke Historical Library.
Personal and business correspondence of Hinds (1840-?), a Stanton, MI, farmer and cattle breeder; of his wife Mary Sherwood Hinds; and of daughters Alma and Edna Hinds. Business correspondence pertains to the Woman's Relief Corps, the American Short Horn Breeders' Association, the Michigan Live Stock Sanitary Commission, the Patrons of Husbandry, and other interests.

8,341. Hodgdon, Abbie L.
Papers. 1869-71. 1 vol.
Open. Unpublished guide.
Central Michigan University, Clarke Historical Library.
Notebook of Hodgdon contains short essays on various subjects, poetry, and songs.

8,342. Hollands, Hulda Theodate (St. Bernard)
Papers. 1859-1929. 3 vols. and 51 items.
Open. Unpublished guide.
Central Michigan University, Clarke Historical Library.
Hollands (1837-1910) was a teacher and author. Correspondence, diaries of 1907 and 1908 relating to her social life and club activities in Detroit, manuscripts of writings about Michigan history, and an 1859 contract to teach in Port Huron, MI. Includes letters from Peter White, regent of the University of Michigan, concerning Hollands's book *When Michigan Was New* (1906); business letters from the office of Henry Ford; and scrapbooks with clippings about St. Clair, MI, and about Hollands's children's stories.

8,343. Holmes, Adelaide
Papers. 1855-ca. 1868. 1 vol.
Open. Unpublished guide.
Central Michigan University, Clarke Historical Library.
Holmes (1853-?) was a housewife and resident of Peck Village, MI. Journal contains reminiscences of her childhood in Dewitt, NY, from 1853 to 1864 and in Peck Village from 1864 to about 1868. Includes descriptions of farm life and early school days as well as some genealogical data.

8,344. Ina, Lyman
Papers. 1860-1965. 85 vols.
Open. Unpublished guide.
Central Michigan University, Clarke Historical Library.
Diaries and cash account books of Ina (?-1883), a farmer near Brockport, NY, who moved to Galesburg, MI, in 1869; of his daughter Jennie; of her husband James H. Imus, a traveling salesman; and of the Imuses' daughter Genevieve Imus. Diaries contain daily accounts of such family activities on farms in Michigan and Ohio as church attendance, travel, family celebrations, various purchases, gifts, rent, taxes, and other topics. The Imuses' wedding picture is also included. Ina had five daughters: Amelia, Emma, Jennie, Julia, and Netta.

8,345. Ionia Free Fair
Records. 1949-56. 730 items.
Open. Unpublished guide.
Central Michigan University, Clarke Historical Library.
Business correspondence and papers concern the operation of a county fair sponsored by the Ionia, MI, chamber of commerce. Includes rules concerning the election of the fair queen and her court.

8,346. Isabella County Girl Scouts, Inc.
Records. 1951-64. Ca. 2 vols. and 200 items.
Open. Unpublished guide.
Central Michigan University, Clarke Historical Library.
Correspondence, bulletins, directories, and scrapbooks relate to the organization, history, and activities of the Girl Scouts in Mt. Pleasant.

8,347. Jeffers, Ira S.
Papers. 1858-1930. 37 vols.
Open. Unpublished guide.
Central Michigan University, Clarke Historical Library.
Included with diaries and notebooks of Jeffers (1843-?), a furniture dealer in Palo, MI, are an 1858 diary of his mother Sophrona of Binghamton, NY, concerning daily activities, household chores, and her social life; an 1870 diary of his first wife Georgie Jeffers; and diaries kept sporadically from 1874 to 1904 by his second wife Sate Jeffers, with comments on family matters, social life, her health, religion, and life in Lone Tree, NE, and in Palo.

8,348. Johnston, Faith
Papers. 1944. 2 items.
Open. Unpublished guide.
Central Michigan University, Clarke Historical Library.
Personal recollections in which Johnston (1902-), a biology professor at Central Michigan University who lived in Rosebush, MI, describes her school days in Mt. Pleasant and teaching at Central State Normal School. Also included is a letter to Johnston from Douglas Murray, a soldier who was serving in WWII's Pacific theater, concerning textbooks for a class he was taking.

8,349. Keller, Ella Flatt
Papers. 1930-51. 6 items.
Open. Unpublished guide.
Central Michigan University, Clarke Historical Library.
Personal correspondence of Keller (1878-), a resident of Manitou Beach, MI, and North Miami, FL, consists of Christmas cards as well as letters to Gertrude Aldrich of Michigan concerning friends and Florida weather.

8,350. Ladies' Literary Club
Records. 1887-88. 1 vol.
Open. Unpublished guide.
Central Michigan University, Clarke Historical Library.
Scrapbook of this Grand Rapids, MI, club contains minutes, clippings, programs, and other material on Club activities.

8,351. Lander, Jean Margaret Davenport
Papers. 1854-87. 8 items.
Open. Unpublished guide.
Central Michigan University, Clarke Historical Library.
Lander (1829-1903) was an English-born American actress and the wife of General Frederick Lander. Thank-you notes and letters of appreciation for her performances, invitations, and receipts for her expenses paid by the National Theater of Boston.

8,352. Lewis, Milla Witter
Papers. 1892. 1 vol.
Open. Unpublished guide.
Central Michigan University, Clarke Historical Library.
Reminiscences in which Lewis (1809-?) reflects on her childhood on a farm in western New York state and later life in Vermont and Ohio; she describes home life, clothing, religion, customs, and farming.

8,353. Maynard, Mary Wilcoxson
Papers. 1893. 1 vol.
Open. Unpublished guide.
Central Michigan University, Clarke Historical Library.
Diary in which Maynard, who was the wife of John Maynard, a grocer in Ann Arbor, MI, and the mother of Frederick A. Maynard (1852-1950), Michigan's state attorney general from 1895 to 1897, discusses daily activities, the weather, family and social life in Ann Arbor, and church attendance.

8,354. Merrill, Nathan M.
Papers. 1852-90. 952 items.
Open. Unpublished guide.
Central Michigan University, Clarke Historical Library.
Merrill (?-1892) was the superintendent of the Saginaw Valley and St. Louis, MI, Railroad. Business correspondence with railroad employees and officials of other railroad companies, journals, and a letterpress book of Merrill's daughter Lila Merrill of Saginaw, which contains personal correspondence on family matters, her broken engagement, social activities, and business affairs.

8,355. Michigan Child Study Association
Records. 1920-76. 5 boxes and 14 vols.
Open. Unpublished guide.
Central Michigan University, Clarke Historical Library.
The Association was established in 1920 as a voluntary organization devoted to parent education and child nurture. Minutes, convention reports, financial records, correspondence, photos, clippings, and newsletters relate to the history, programs, and activities of the Association. Also included are minutes of related organizations.

8,356. Michigan Music Teachers' Association
Records. 1867-73. Ca. 14 vols. and 1700 items.
Open. Unpublished guide.
Central Michigan University, Clarke Historical Library.
Minutes, papers of past presidents, treasurers' reports, programs, correspondence, photos, scrapbooks, and other records of this professional organization of teachers.

8,357. Oppermann, Gustav F.
Papers. 1892-94. 2 vols.
Open. Unpublished guide.
Central Michigan University, Clarke Historical Library.
Correspondence of Oppermann (1863-1932), the manager of the Oppermann Fur Company in Saginaw, MI, consists primarily of letters between his wife Antoinette "Nettie," writing from New York, and her parents Mr. and Mrs. Charles H. Peters, Sr., in Saginaw, about family affairs and social life and the fur business in New York.

8,358. Otis, Edna M.
Papers. 1973. 2 items.
Open. Unpublished guide.
Central Michigan University, Clarke Historical Library.
Otis is an East Tawas, MI, antique dealer. Typescript and proof of her book *Sawdust Days* (1973).

8,359. Raudman, Dorothy
Papers. 1919-20. 1 vol.
Open. Unpublished guide.
Central Michigan University, Clarke Historical Library.
Diary in which a high school senior in Constantine, MI, describes her school friends, social life, cities visited, and home life. Also contains her photo, poetry, and a list of members of her graduating class.

8,360. Saginaw County League of Women Voters
Records. 1925-41. Ca. 3330 items.
Open. Unpublished guide.
Central Michigan University, Clarke Historical Library.
Annual reports, minutes, correspondence, press releases, programs, circulars, scrapbooks, clippings, and other material of the Saginaw County LWV, founded in 1919. Includes correspondence from Senators James Couzens and Arthur H. Vandenberg; material of the Saginaw Department of Recreation, the Saginaw Garden Club, and the Saginaw Welfare League; and Good Citizenship Bonds.

8,361. Sanford, Mrs. M. L.
Open. 1858-71. 55 items.
Open. Unpublished guide.
Central Michigan University, Clarke Historical Library.
Sanford was a housewife and resident of Sciota in Shiawassee County, MI. Correspondence to her daughter Amanda, a school teacher in the East, depicts social life in Sciota and Antrim, MI, and Sanford's daily chores on a farm and provides detailed descriptions of her house and family affairs. Also contains a few letters from other

family members regarding Universalist preaching, the number of bears around Owosso, and a Dr. Revin who was accused of having performed an abortion.

8,362. Sewall, May Eliza (Wright)
Papers. 1877-1904. 10 vols.
Open. Unpublished guide.
Central Michigan University, Clarke Historical Library.
A feminist, Sewall (1844-1920) was the principal of the Girls' Classical School in Indianapolis. Scrapbooks contain articles in various languages, many of them written or edited by Sewall, on woman's suffrage and her participation in international women's congresses in London in 1899, in Berlin in 1904, and in the World's Columbian Exposition in 1893. Also includes complimentary letters addressed to Sewall, pamphlets, invitations, programs, menu cards, and portraits of famous suffragists.

8,363. Stacy, Consider A.
Papers. 1824-1919. 76 vols. and 701 items.
Open. Unpublished guide.
Central Michigan University, Clarke Historical Library.
Personal and business correspondence of Stacy (1817-88), a lawyer and judge in Tecumseh, MI, and diaries, including those of his wife Maria describing family matters, expenses, and daily activities and diaries of Loana Stacy and Mrs. A. J. Bigelow on family and social life and church activities.

8,364. Starr, Minnie E.
Papers. 1897-1913. 105 items.
Open. Unpublished guide.
Central Michigan University, Clarke Historical Library.
A resident of Royal Oak, MI, Starr taught music in high schools in Villisca, IA, Moline, IL, and Birmingham and Flint, MI. Personal correspondence from family, fellow teachers, and former students.

8,365. Thomas, Jessie
Papers. 1871-72. 1 vol.
Open. Unpublished guide.
Central Michigan University, Clarke Historical Library.
Diary of Thomas, a Michigan resident, includes a list of letters received and sent, music lessons taken, expenses, and a day-by-day account of her trip to Paddock's Grove, IL, where she stayed with relatives while attending school.

8,366. Thompson, Adelaide
Papers. 1860-1927. 2 vols. and 142 items.
Open. Unpublished guide.
Central Michigan University, Clarke Historical Library.
Personal correspondence between Thompson, a nurse in Saginaw, MI, and William R. Longstreet, a Saginaw bookkeeper and religious leader, concerns the nursing of patients, social and religious matters, a trip to New York in 1892, and welfare work of the Jefferson Avenue Epworth League. Also included are a diary of Isabella Longstreet describing her missionary work in China from 1899 to 1901 and a letterpress book of the William Longstreet and Ludwig General Insurance Agency in Saginaw.

8,367. Towler, Lewis
Papers. 1882-86. 33 items.
Open. Unpublished guide.
Central Michigan University, Clarke Historical Library.
Correspondence of Towler, a student at Princeton University, consists chiefly of letters from his mother who was wife of a Presbyterian minister in Spring Lake and later Corunna, MI, concerning the hardships of a minister's life, church affairs, social events, and family matters.

8,368. Turner, Gertrude E.
Papers. 1913-17. 5 items.
Open. Unpublished guide.
Central Michigan University, Clarke Historical Library.
Personal correspondence of Turner, a resident of Tecumseh, MI, consists of letters she received from relatives about family matters, social events, and the weather.

8,369. Van Deusen, Minnie
Papers. 1842-1969. 70 vols. and 173 items.
Open. Unpublished guide.
Central Michigan University, Clarke Historical Library.
Van Deusen (1880-) was the wife of a furniture store owner and undertaker in Elsie, MI. Correspondence; diaries dealing with the weather, her daily activities at home, trips in Michigan, and social events in Elsie; her account books, 1940-45; an account book of her father-in-law R. G. Van Deusen, 1842-49; a cash book containing brief accounts of the year 1894; a volume with minutes of the Knights of the Modern Maccabees, Tent 419, of Elsie; a scrapbook with clippings from the Elsie *Sun* concerning local social events; bills and receipts; and WWII ration books.

8,370. Van Deventer, Dora E.
Papers. 1881-1930s. 3 vols.
Open. Unpublished guide.
Central Michigan University, Clarke Historical Library.
Notebook dated 1881 and 1882 of Van Deventer, the wife of an Ithaca, MI, area farmer, contains questions and answers about world history. Also included are her husband's diary from 1901 to 1903 giving daily accounts of the weather, farm work, church and camp meeting attendance, and visitors and visits, and a scrapbook entitled "China Missionaries" with a map of Honan Province in China, photos, and clippings from Chinese newspapers.

8,371. Van Sickle, Nellie
Papers. 1897-1900. 18 items.
Open. Unpublished guide.
Central Michigan University, Clarke Historical Library.
Correspondence of Van Sickle, who lived in Carson City, MI, includes letters from her father Asher Van Sickle of Concordia, KS, and from other family members and friends about family matters, daily activities, and farming.

8,372. Warden, Selina Clark
Papers. 1856-69. 57 items.
Open. Unpublished guide.
Central Michigan University, Clarke Historical Library.
Correspondence of Clark, wife of a farmer in Milan Township, Washtenaw County, MI, consists principally of letters from her parents concerning family health and hard times on the farm. Includes Civil War letters from her brother Benjamin Clark who served in Company H of the First Michigan Cavalry.

8,373. Webster, Mary L.
Papers. 1846-63. 6 items.
Open. Unpublished guide.
Central Michigan University, Clarke Historical Library.
Correspondence from the Sacramento region of California and Lake of the Mountains, Nevada Territory, in which [Mrs.] Webster, a housewife and former resident of Bellville in Jefferson County, NY, describes to her daughter her voyage by ship to California, gold and copper mining in the West, living conditions, intemperance, and religious infidelity. One letter is from a friend in Rock County, WI, who writes of a trip from New York state to Wisconsin and country life there.

8,374. Wells, Charles William
Papers. 1817-95. No size given.
Open. Unpublished guide.
Central Michigan University, Clarke Historical Library.
A lumberman and businessman, Wells (1841-93) owned a lumberman's supply operation in Saginaw, MI. Included with his correspondence, diaries, and photos relating to the Mexican and Civil Wars, the California gold rush, his business, and activities of the Wells, Cochrane, Smith, Harding, and Craig families are diaries of Eliza J. McLean concerning religious, social, and family matters; correspondence of Janet Craig Cochrane, which contains family news; and correspondence between other female members of the various families.

8,375. Whittier, John Greenleaf
Papers. 1820-92. 574 items.
Open. Unpublished guide.
Central Michigan University, Clarke Historical Library.
Correspondence of Whittier (1807-92), a poet, includes letters from Alice and Phoebe Carey, Mary Abigail Dodge, Annie Fields, Sarah L. Forten, Jessie Fremont, Sarah Orne Jewett, Harriet Martineau, and Celia Thaxter.

8,376. Williams, Maria D. Stowell
Papers. 1850-60. 49 items.
Open. Unpublished guide.
Central Michigan University, Clarke Historical Library.
Williams (?-1868) was a housewife in Dexter in Washtenaw County, MI. Correspondence contains letters from her husband Spencer Williams and son John Williams and other items relating to her articles in the *Waverly Magazine*. Poems and receipts are also included.

8,377. Wing, Josephine
Papers. 1896-99. 11 items.
Open. Unpublished guide.
Central Michigan University, Clarke Historical Library.
Letters recommending [Miss] Wing, a resident of Vicksburg, MI, as a qualified school teacher and three teachers certificates.

8,378. Wolfe, Marjorie Carlisle
Papers. 1967. 3 items.
Open. Unpublished guide.
Central Michigan University, Clarke Historical Library.
Reminiscences of Wolfe, a Philadelphia resident, pertain to her experiences from 1912 to 1916 while attending Central Michigan Normal School in Mount Pleasant. Also includes a typescript of her reminiscences prepared by her daughter Mrs. Reginald Angus and a letter Wolfe wrote concerning the School.

8,379. Woman's Home Missionary Society
Records. 1903-27. 4 vols.
Open. Unpublished guide.
Central Michigan University, Clarke Historical Library.
Record books of the meetings and activities of the Oxford, MI, Society, which was the auxiliary to the Detroit Conference of Home Missions, include membership rolls.

8,380. Woodworth, Ellen L.
Papers. 1863-65. 1 vol.
Open. Unpublished guide.
Central Michigan University, Clarke Historical Library.
Woodworth (1833-1914) was a pioneer resident of Mt. Pleasant and, in 1864, the city's first schoolteacher. Consists of a journal compiled from her correspondence with her husband Samuel

during his Civil War service in Company M, Michigan 1st Engineers and Mechanics. Her letters from Mt. Pleasant and Lincoln, MI, concern family matters, farming, social life, and teaching; his letters from various locations in Tennessee and Bridgeport, AL, deal with camp life and the war in general. Also included are copies of her poems in manuscript and as published in local newspapers.

MUSKEGON

8,381. Muskegon Heights Women's Club
Records. Nd. No size given.
Closed. No guide.
Hackley Public Library.
Yearbooks, scrapbooks, and other records of the Club, which existed from 1926 to 1961 and pursued the literary interests of its members.

8,382. Muskegon Women's Club
Records. 1891- . 12 boxes.
Open. No guide.
Hackley Public Library.
Constitution, bylaws, attendance records, yearbooks, scrapbooks, and programs of the Club, established in 1891 to promote literary and scientific pursuits. The Club, members of which belonged to prominent families in Muskegon, spawned other local organizations, including theatrical and garden groups.

NAZARETH

8,383. Convent Archives
Records. 1880- . More than 3 cabinets, 8 files, and 6 showcases.
Open. No guide.
Sisters of St. Joseph Convent, Nazareth History Room.
The Convent was founded in 1889 in Kalamazoo, MI. The Sisters were originally involved in nursing, teaching, and social work; they are now engaged in pastoral ministries, in inner city and Confraternity of Christian Doctrine (CCD) work, and in other types of work. Financial records, correspondence, diaries, retreat notes, personal papers of the Sisters, tapes, PhD dissertations and MA theses, school and parish histories, slides, photos, scrapbooks, and other records.

NILES

8,384. Ladies Reading Club
Records. 1882- . 30 vols.
Open. No guide.
Niles Community Library.
Minutes of the Club, the second oldest women's organization in the Niles area, reflect interests and activities of the membership at each bimonthly meeting since the group's inception in 1882. Formed to encourage social, cultural, and literary pursuits, the Club later had programs concerning social problems, women's suffrage issues, domestic concerns during the world wars, and women's role in society.

OLIVET

8,385. College Archives
Records. 1844- . 238 ft.
Open. Unpublished guide.
Olivet College Library.
Minutes, financial records, correspondence, biographical data on alumni and faculty members, extensive photo collection, scrapbooks, yearbooks, catalogs, and local and campus newspapers of Olivet College, founded in 1844 as a coeducational institution; the College also offered secondary education in its early years. The College's first graduating class consisted entirely of women.

SAULT STE. MARIE

8,386. Woman's Reading Club of Sault Ste. Marie
Records. 1891-1944. 3 vols. and 3 items.
Open. No guide.
Bayliss Public Library.
Minute books with occasional clippings, an attendance book, and program pamphlets of this social and benevolent group, the membership of which was usually no more than 25 women. The program pamphlets date from 1891-92, 1909-10, and 1939-40. Members and guests performed plays and skits, presented readings and lectures, and gave instrumental or vocal performances. The Club's benevolent activities included making regular donations to various organizations, giving small gifts to the poor, making cookies for soldiers, and cosponsoring fund-raising teas at the local hospital.

WAYNE

8,387. Clubs
Records. 1896-1977. No size given.
Open. No guide.
Wayne Historical Commission.
Records of the Wayne Literary Club, originally the Ladies' Literary Club of Wayne, consist of minutes for the years 1896 to 1945 and yearbooks for 1909 to 1977. Also included are minutes and yearbooks to 1977 of the Arché Club, which was organized in 1903.

8,388. Local Women
Collection. Nd. No size given.
Open. No guide.
Wayne Historical Commission.
Personality sketches, photos, and clippings on women of Wayne. Emma John (1866-1943) was a businesswoman, librarian, and assistant postmaster who served as village treasurer from 1922 to 1943. [Mrs.] Italy Vining (1879-1948), the only woman to serve as justice of the peace in Wayne and the first to serve as such in Wayne County, was elected in 1931 and re-elected until her death; in 1935 she was the first woman appointed to the Wayne County jury commission. Estelle Vining Bunting (1864-1965) was a teacher of elocution and truant officer in the public schools and a clubwoman prominent in local cultural activities. Anna Cady Butler (1878-1973), a Methodist church worker and deacon evangelist in the early 20th century, was probably the first woman licensed as a local preacher in the Detroit Conference.

MINNESOTA

ANOKA

8,389. Anoka County: Historical and Genealogical
Collection. 1855-1965. 68 microfilm reels.
Open. Card file and partial index.
Anoka County Historical Society.
Records from Anoka County townships, schools, and churches were microfilmed for genealogists and local historians; the originals were then returned to the churches and offices where they were found. Public records from township offices include surveyors' records, tax assessment rolls, land ownership and transfer records, including a number of documents issued to women, birth and death records, and naturalization papers. Other public records consist of Anoka school board minutes, 1877-1920, and teachers' reports on school attendance, supplies, and curriculum, 1886-1920. Church records contain several minute books of church business meetings, membership lists, and baptism, confirmation, and marriage records for the following Anoka County churches: St. Stephen's Catholic Church of Anoka; the First Baptist Church of Anoka, established in 1856; the Congregational Church of Anoka, established in 1855; Trinity Episcopal Church of Anoka, established in 1858; the Joyce Chapel (Methodist); the Elim Baptist Church of Anoka; the Glen Cary Lutheran Church of Ham Lake, established in 1870; Our Saviour's Lutheran Church of Ham Lake; and St. John's Lutheran Church of Burns, established in 1876.

8,390. Columbia Heights Garden Club
Records. Ca. 1940-60s. 1 ft.
Open. No guide.
Anoka County Historical Society.
Minute books, membership lists, and programs of the Club, which was organized sometime before 1940 and disbanded in the 1960s.

8,391. Locke, Roberta Pratt
Papers. Ca. 1920-50. 6 in.
Open. No guide.
Anoka County Historical Society.
[Mrs.] Locke was a member of the University of Minnesota graduating class of 1894. She took an active part in organizing class reunions, many of which were held at the Lockes' summer house in Fridley, MN, which now is administered by the Historical Society as an historic site. Papers pertain to her graduating class and its reunions.

BEMIDJI

8,392. Association of Minnesota State University Women
Records. 1975. 1 folder.
Open. No guide.
Bemidji State University Library, Archives Collection.
Minutes.

8,393. Campus Human Rights Commission for Affirmative Action
Records. 1973. 1 folder.
Open. No guide.
Bemidji State University Library, Archives Collection.
Minutes.

8,394. Faculty Wives
Records. 1970- . 1 folder.
Open. No guide.
Bemidji State University Library, Archives Collection.
Correspondence of this social organization on the University campus.

8,395. Geittmann, Ida
Papers. 1957- . 2 folders.
Open. No guide.
Bemidji State University Library, Archives Collection.
Correspondence of Geittmann, associate director of area services who served earlier as assistant to the vice-president for administration at the University.

8,396. Ghostley, Mary (Chapman)
Papers. 1900-56. 1 Hollinger box.
Open. Unpublished guide.
North Central Minnesota Historical Center.
Diaries, personal documents, notes on speeches, and medical records of [Mrs. Fred] Ghostley (1881-1975), a physician.

8,397. Knutson, Coya (Gjesdal)
Papers. 1954-58. 3 bacases.
Open. Unpublished guide.
North Central Minnesota Historical Center.
Legislative papers and election material of Knutson (1912-), a member of the US House of Representatives from Minnesota's ninth district from 1954 to 1958. An Edmore, ND, native, she graduated in 1934 from Concordia College in Moorhead, MN, and taught high school until 1954. In 1940 she married Andrew Knutson.

BLOOMINGTON

8,398. Bloomington Cemetery
Records. 1890-1972. 1 folder.
Open. No guide.
Bloomington Historical Society.
Clippings with a photo pertain to [Mrs.] Marie Pedersen, who served as Cemetery sexton for many years after her husband died.

8,399. Bloomington Families
Collection. Nd. 1 folder.
Open. No guide.
Bloomington Historical Society.
Clippings and newspapers, pamphlets, mimeograph copies of an 1880 township directory and of a guide to Bloomington historical sites, and 1881 and 1895 Bloomington histories contain information about prominent area residents. Included are memorial descriptions of [Mrs.] Sarah Goodrich, [Mrs.] Florence Wells, Agnes Fahley, [Mrs.] Clara Painter, Mrs. Camerson, Bertha [Mrs. Clement] Harrison, and [Mrs.] Marie Scott and an article about [Mrs.] Alta Brown. The 1895 town history was written by Mary Frances (Hopkins) [Mrs. Edward Robert] Pond. The guide to local historical sites tells of a Christianized Dakota girl who was killed by a Chippewa.

8,400. Bloomington Ferry School: Curry, Helen Brown
Papers. Nd. 2-page item.
Open. No guide.
Bloomington Historical Society.
Reminiscence in which Helen Brown Curry describes her childhood experiences as a student at the School in District 14 during the early 1900s.

8,401. Bloomington Grange
Records. 1874-86. 0.5 in. and 1 vol.
Open. No guide.
Bloomington Historical Society.
Minutes from 1874 to 1877 of Grange No. 482 of Patrons of Husbandry, a local political and social group for farmers established in 1874, document women's participation as Grange members. Also contains an 1886 record of the Grange with comments regarding women's experiences and role in the organization.

8,402. Bloomingtonarian
Records. 1919-48. 1 Paige box.
Open. No guide.
Bloomington Historical Society.
Typescript mimeographed magazine published by Bloomington High School contains articles about local school events, clubs, and personal activities of both men and women in the area. Also includes the newsletter "Bloomington Community Service," 1919-25.

8,403. Harrison, Clement, and Harrison, Bertha (Miller)
Papers. 1900-68. 4 items.
Open. No guide.
Bloomington Historical Society.
Obituaries of Clement Harrison (1884-1968), a farmer, and of his wife Bertha Harrison (1879-1960), a schoolteacher, and [Mrs.] Harrison's limited second grade Minnesota county certificate and 1900 contract for teaching.

8,404. Indians
Collection. Nd. 1 folder.
Open. No guide.
Bloomington Historical Society.
Clippings and pamphlets about Indians include the printed item "Little Bird that Was Caught" (1968) by Lillie Gibbs Le Vesconte, which pertains to Jane DeBow Gibbs, a late 19th-century woman who apparently was not an Indian.

8,405. Kelley
Papers. 1911-68. 1 folder.
Open. No guide.
Bloomington Historical Society.
Family correspondence, a notebook, and clippings of Cora Scofield [Mrs. Robert J.] Kelley (1868-1968), an early Bloomington resident who was a teacher. Includes a childhood notebook on the Pilgrims kept by Alice Kelley, Cora Kelley's niece; a letter Alice Kelley wrote as a child to her mother Mrs. J. S. Kelley, Cora Kelley's sister-in-law, in 1925; and two letters by Alice Kelley's sister Regina Kelley.

8,406. Kelley, Cora Scofield
Collection. 1900-69. 1 folder.
Open. No guide.
Bloomington Historical Society.
Clippings assembled in the Historical Society's public reference file on [Mrs. Robert] Kelley (1868-1968), an early Bloomington settler, farmer, schoolteacher, and the first woman member of the Bloomington school board, include articles taken from birthday and other interviews with her. Many items relate to Kelley's unsuccessful attempt to save the family homestead from land developers.

8,407. Letters
Collection. 1885-1902. 1 in.
Open. No guide.
Bloomington Historical Society.
Contains three letters from a schoolteacher named A. J. Davis; three items by women regarding teaching positions; one letter from Edward Robert Pond to W. S. McLeod complaining about an unnamed teacher; two letters about the resignation of a Miss Ames; and one item from an aunt in San Francisco to her niece Carrie.

8,408. McAfee
Papers. Nd. 1 folder.
Open. No guide.
Bloomington Historical Society.
Clippings include one newspaper interview with longtime Bloomington resident Cora Scofield Kelley (1868-1968).

8,409. Olson, Hubert G.
Papers. 1962-64. 1 folder.
Open. No guide.
Bloomington Historical Society.
Clippings of Olson (1902-64), a Bloomington school superintendent, and a one-page reminiscence by his wife Grace Olson, which was published as part of the Historical Society's newsletter.

8,410. Oxborough
Papers. 1964-69. 4 items.
Open. No guide.
Bloomington Historical Society.
Clippings pertain to Mary (Evans) [Mrs. Robert] Oxborough (1884-), an early Bloomington resident.

8,411. Photographs
Collection. Ca. 1880s-1940s, nd. Ca. 440 items.
Open. Index.
Bloomington Historical Society.
Photos of local families, schools, houses, industries, and threshing operations from the late 1800s to the 1940s. Includes photos of Bloomington Auto Club waitresses and cooks dating from 1920 to 1928, with staff names listed.

8,412. Pond
Papers. 1855-1975. 3 folders.
Open. No guide.
Bloomington Historical Society.
Family papers of Gideon H. Pond (1810-78) and his second wife Agnes Carson Johnson Hopkins Pond (1825-?), who were Presbyterian missionaries to the Sioux. Includes an 1864 letter written from Fort Thompson in the Dakota Territory by Mary Frances (Hopkins) Pond, Agnes Pond's daughter by her first marriage, to Mary's brother Frank in Bloomington; reminiscences of Agnes Pond and another of her daughters Scintilla Sexta (Pond) [Mrs. Cyrus] Ritchie; receipts; a typescript of a play; clippings; and pamphlets.

8,413. Vault Miscellany
Collection. 1885. 1 item.
Open. No guide.
Bloomington Historical Society.
Letter from Fanny Pinkerton to [Mrs.] Agnes Hopkins Pond.

8,414. Archives
Records. 1875- . Several drawers.
Closed. No guide.
Monastery of Saint Clare.
Correspondence, diaries, photos, scrapbooks, publications, and other records of the Monastery, which was founded in 1954, and of other US, Canadian, and Korean monasteries. Includes a diary, monastic records from Omaha, and other papers of Mother Mary Magdalen Bentivoglio, the American foundress of the order, and material from the Franciscans of Little Falls, MN, and the Evansville, IL, monastery of Poor Clares. Before becoming a Poor Clare, Mother Mary Magdalen was Countess Annetta Bentivoglio.

BLUE EARTH

8,415. Delphian Society, Alpha Chapter
Records. 1924-53. 4 vols.
Open. Card file.
Faribault County Historical Society.
Secretary's books, attendance records, studies and reports, correspondence, and clippings of this study club, which functioned between 1924 and 1953.

8,416. Faribault County Federation of Women's Clubs
Records. 1945-71. 8 cu.ft.
Open. Card file.
Faribault County Historical Society.
Records of the Federation and its member clubs include annual reports and programs, secretary's and treasurer's books, correspondence, photos, scrapbooks, a directory of federated clubs in Minnesota, and clippings.

8,417. Mitchell Chautauqua Circle
Records. 1882-1966. 5 cu.ft.
Open. Card file.
Faribault County Historical Society.
Minutes, bank statements and other financial records, yearbooks and programs, book lists, reports, and alphabetical file of this ongoing study club, which was established in Blue Earth in 1882. Also included are record books, 1882-1917, of the Society of Hall in the Grove, which was a predecessor of the Circle. The Circle was named for a Mrs. Mitchell.

8,418. Trinity Lutheran Church Women
Records. 1896-1970. 1 vol.
Open. Card file.
Faribault County Historical Society.
Membership, activities, and attendance records of the Church Women.

8,419. Woman's Relief Corps
Records. 1886-1950. 12 cu.ft.
Open. Card file.
Faribault County Historical Society.
Minutes, a history, list of charter members, programs, clippings, framed pictures, an American flag, and a quilt of this local auxiliary to the Grand Army of the Republic. Members of the Corps, which was established in 1886, attended patriotic civic events, welcomed new citizens to the community, and planned charitable events.

8,420. Women's Christian Temperance Union
Records. 1899-1927. 3 vols.
Open. Card file.
Faribault County Historical Society.
Secretary's books and treasurer's county book of a Blue Earth branch of the WCTU which existed between 1899 and 1953.

BUFFALO LAKE

8,421. Johnson, Gloria O.
Papers. 1977. 1 portfolio.
Open. No guide.
Renville County Historical Society.
Portfolio of Johnson (1924-), a homemaker who was chosen Minnesota Mother of the Year in 1977, was submitted to the American Mothers Committee, Inc., in New York in competition for national Mother of the Year honors. Includes her biography and biographical sketches of her husband Arthur B. Johnson and their children, letters of reference, a press release, and other items.

CARLTON

8,422. Business and Professional Women's Club
Records. 1937-44. 2 vols.
Open. No guide.
Carlton County Historical Society.
Secretary's and treasurer's ledgers of this Carlton organization.

8,423. Country Schools
Records. 1922-35. 6 vols.
Open. No guide.
Carlton County Historical Society.
School board meeting records, township clerk's books, teachers' contracts, and ungraded elementary teachers' school records for country schools in the Carlton area.

CHASKA

8,424. Williams, Frances (Ropes)
Papers. 1940-68. 6 ft.
Open. No guide.
University of Minnesota, Andersen Horticultural Library.
Correspondence, notebooks, photos, and slides of hosta plants by [Mrs. Stillman P.] Williams (1883-1969), a 1904 graduate of Massachusetts Institute of Technology in landscape architecture who spent 40 years growing, observing, breeding, and experimenting with hosta plant varieties. Includes letters to horticulturists, nurserymen, and taxonomists in the US, Sweden, and Japan. Also contains the two-volume pictorial reference *The Hosta of Mrs. Frances R. Williams,* which was compiled and edited by Linda Sanford, a University of Minnesota Arboretum staff member.

CROOKSTON

8,425. Province Archives
Records. 1903- . Ca. 250 items, 13 tapes, and 6 cases.
Closed. Inventory.
Sisters of St. Joseph Provincial House.
The Province was founded in 1903 in Argyle, MN; its members are involved in education, health care, pastoral ministry, and social service. Financial and legal records, correspondence, letters, diaries, retreat notes, essays, poetry, memorabilia, and other papers of individual sisters; oral history tapes; circular letter of superiors general and provincial coordinators; slides; photos; scrapbooks; post cards; newsletters; programs; and clippings of the Province. Includes correspondence, school registers, daily attendance record books, faculty meeting books, lesson plans, photo albums, scrapbooks, and school magazines of St. Joseph's Academy in Crookston, which was operated by the Sisters from 1905 until it closed in 1968. Notes and working papers of Mother Agnes Lanctot, who held a PhD, relating to her research on children and their response to literature are also included.

DULUTH

8,426. American Association of University Women
Records. Ca. 1923-70. Ca. 9 ft. and 225 items.
Open. No guide.
Northeast Minnesota Historical Center.
Bylaws of the Duluth chapter of the AAUW, financial records, committee reports, ca. 225 data cards on chapter members, correspondence, bulletins, yearbooks, and AAUW journals. Also included is a history of the Minnesota division of the AAUW.

8,427. American Red Cross
Records. 1917-70s. 11 boxes and 5 in.
Open. No guide.
Northeast Minnesota Historical Center.
Correspondence of the Duluth chapter of the American National Red Cross, a ledger of instructions on surgical dressings and bandages, sample forms, a Red Cross pin collection, and clippings. Also included are boxes of WWI sample items such as manuals, bandages, and dressings.

8,428. Banning, Margaret (Culkin)
Papers. 1913-64. 2 in. and 10 items.
Open. No guide.
Northeast Minnesota Historical Center.
Correspondence, speeches, clippings, and book reviews of Banning (1891-?), an author who graduated from Vassar College and became director of the National Council of Community Chests. She wrote 13 books, including *The Women of the Family, The Iron Will,* and *Letters to Susan;* many of her stories appeared in the *Saturday Evening Post* and other national magazines.

8,429. Bedard, Irene R.
Papers. 1948-59. 2 in.
Open. No guide.
Northeast Minnesota Historical Center.
[Mrs.] Bedard (1901-59) was assistant manager of the Hibbing, MN, *Daily Tribune* and president of the National Federation of Press Women in 1949 and of the Duluth Business and Professional Women's Club. Correspondence, pamphlets, clippings, and reprints of travel articles she wrote.

8,430. Cecilian Chorale Society
Records. 1892-1957. Ca. 1 ft. and 4 vols.
Open. No guide.
Northeast Minnesota Historical Center.
Founded in 1887 to promote music appreciation in the Duluth area, the Society sponsored visiting performers and lecturers and produced local musical performances. Minutes; financial reports; membership lists; correspondence, including letters to the Edward MacDowell Association of New York; scrapbooks; programs; yearbooks; scores; and memorabilia.

8,431. Duluth Women's Club
Records. Ca. 1925-75. 2 in.
Open. No guide.
Northeast Minnesota Historical Center.
Bylaws, correspondence, programs, bulletins, and clippings of the Club, earlier known as the Women's Council of Duluth, which was established to promote civic, educational, literary, and welfare work in Duluth.

8,432. Ely, Catherine Bissell
Papers. 1835-1923. Ca. 0.5 in. and 1 item.
Open. No guide.
Northeast Minnesota Historical Center.
[Mrs. E. F.] Ely (1817-80) was the wife of the first white minister in Duluth. Correspondence, diary dating from 1835 to 1837, a 1923 clipping about Ely, and a photo.

8,433. Hilton, Mrs. Afton B.
Papers. Ca. 1897-1956. 5 in. and 10 items.
Open. No guide.
Northeast Minnesota Historical Center.
A Duluth artist, poet, and novelist, Hilton (1873-1958) actively participated in local cultural and literary societies and helped found the Duluth art institute; from 1890 to 1906 she was customs collector for the port of Duluth. Correspondence, including letters from H. L. Mencken and Harold Stassen; account books; sketches; photos; diplomas and licenses; clippings; and memorabilia. Hilton's most famous works are "The White Plague," a short story about her battle with tuberculosis, and *The Long Roll,* a collection of her father's Civil War diaries.

8,434. Junior League
Records. 1928-71. 2 in.
Open. No guide.
Northeast Minnesota Historical Center.
Programs, clippings, and books of printed photos of the League, which was formed in 1914 in Duluth as the Silver Cross of King's Daughters. The group assumed its present name in 1917 and in 1921 became affiliated with the National Junior League. The League fulfilled its welfare service function in the 1920s by operating a day-care center and by providing other community assistance.

8,435. League of Women Voters of Duluth
Records. 1922-66. 15 ft.
Open. Unpublished guide.
Northeast Minnesota Historical Center.
Annual reports, minutes, research material collected for studies, and scrapbooks with clippings of this local branch of the LWV established ca. 1922. Includes items from the 1930s documenting LWV activities against the equal rights amendment legislation of that period.

8,436. McGiffert, Gertrude Yates
Papers. 1914-31. Ca. 2 in.
Open. No guide.
Northeast Minnesota Historical Center.
[Mrs. G. R.] McGiffert (?-1961) was an American National Red Cross relief worker during WWI and the 1920s in France and Belgium. Correspondence, clippings, and pamphlets pertain to Red Cross relief work. McGiffert was also involved in the public health movement and in the DAR.

8,437. Minnesota-Arrow Chapter, National Secretaries Association
Records. 1946-69. Ca. 1 ft., 7 vols., and 150 items.
Open. No guide.

Northeast Minnesota Historical Center.
Bylaws, minutes, correspondence, rosters, scrapbooks, bulletins, photos, and memorabilia of the Chapter, established in 1946 to elevate the standards of the secretarial profession by uniting women who were or had been secretaries.

8,438. Minnesota Federation of Women
Records. Ca. 1929-71. 1 in.
Open. No guide.
Northeast Minnesota Historical Center.
Clippings and directories of the Federation, which is affiliated with the GFWC and is involved in civic and cultural activities.

8,439. National Federation of Business and Professional Women
Records. Ca. 1921-70. Ca. 1.5 ft., 4 vols., and 11 items.
Open. No guide.
Northeast Minnesota Historical Center.
Bylaws, annual reports, minutes, financial records, committee reports, correspondence, photos, scrapbooks, clippings, and memorabilia of the Duluth chapter of the Federation.

8,440. Nurses
Collection. 1930-72. 1 in.
Open. No guide.
Northeast Minnesota Historical Center.
Includes a 1930 yearbook and 1932 commencement program of the St. Luke's Hospital training program and clippings pertaining to activities of Duluth-area nurses.

8,441. Nute, Grace Lee
Papers. 1650-1960. 12.5 ft.
Open. Unpublished guide.
Northeast Minnesota Historical Center.
Personal correspondence, manuscripts, research notes, primary source material gathered between 1920 and 1970, maps, magazines, and pamphlets of Nute (1895-), an historian who was curator of manuscripts from 1921 to 1946 and then research associate until 1957 for the Minnesota Historical Society; Nute also was a history professor at Hamline University, the University of Minnesota, and Macalester College. The author of many books and articles about exploration and the fur trade in North America as well as about various aspects of Minnesota history, Nute's major publications include *The Voyageur* (1931), *Caesars of the Wilderness* (1943), and *Rainy River Country* (1950). The collection also contains a film on explorer Robert Cavelier, Sieur de La Salle, which she helped produce for the *Encyclopaedia Britannica.*

Nute was born in North Conway, NH; received a BA in 1917 from Smith College; and earned an MA in 1918 and PhD in 1921 at Radcliffe College where she studied with historian Frederick Jackson Turner. During her long career in Minnesota she held offices in various historical organizations and was a Guggenheim Fellow in Europe in 1934 and 1935. She is now retired.

The collection is owned by the University Archives at the University of Minnesota's Duluth campus.

8,442. Richards, Bertha
Papers. 1908-30. 2 in. and ca. 34 items.
Open. No guide.
Northeast Minnesota Historical Center.
[Mrs. George S.] Richards was a board member of the National Federation of Music Clubs and sponsor of the All Star Music Concerts, which brought American and foreign performers to the Duluth area. Correspondence, photos, scrapbooks, advertisements, programs, pamphlets, and clippings.

8,443. Stocker, Clara
Papers. 1927-52. 1 in.
Open. No guide.
Northeast Minnesota Historical Center.
Correspondence, including a letter from Albert Einstein; programs; advertisements; clippings; and memorabilia of Stocker (?-1973), a lecturer, musical performer, and music critic for the Duluth *Tribune* and Duluth *Herald.* Like her mother Stella Prince Stocker, she was also interested in music composition. In addition, she actively supported the UN and the world federalist movement.

8,444. Stocker, Stella Prince
Papers. Ca. 1899-1925. 2 in. and 10 items.
Open. No guide.
Northeast Minnesota Historical Center.
Musical scripts and scores, programs, photos, and clippings of [Mrs.] Stocker (1858-1925), who was a composer, author, lecturer, and founder and director of several Duluth-area musical groups, including the Cecilian Chorale Society. Born in Jacksonville, FL, Stocker studied music in America and Europe, later lecturing at home and abroad on her particular interest, music of the Chippewa and Sioux. She is best known as a composer of choruses, anthems, and opera, and as author of the historical play *Sieur de Lhut.*

8,445. Twentieth Century Club
Records. 1927-71. 2 in.
Open. No guide.
Northeast Minnesota Historical Center.
Programs, directories, and clippings of the Club, which was established in 1898 to centralize the activities of many small Duluth clubs for greater service and efficiency.

8,446. War Records File
Collection. 1914-45. Ca. 10 ft., 2 vols., and 50 items.
Open. No guide.
Northeast Minnesota Historical Center.
Records of the Duluth chapters of the American National Red Cross, the Office of Civilian Defense, and the Victory Aide Association include WWI military service records of Duluth-area women and memoirs describing wartime experiences of several army nurses; data cards of wartime agencies, which provide age, education, marital status, employment history, and skills information for about 10,000 Duluth-area women who were involved in first aid and nursing courses and volunteer activities during WWI or civilian defense and victory garden work during WWII; and WWII scrapbooks, clippings, programs, and newsletters pertaining to the Civilian Defense Homemakers Corps and to the Office of Civilian Defense consumer interest division. Also included is the collection of [Mrs.] Gertrude Yates McGiffert, which contains material about WWI Red Cross activities in Duluth; correspondence regarding relief work in Serbia, France, and Belgium; letters from servicemen in Europe; photos; programs; clippings; posters; and other items.

8,447. War, Women in World Wars
Collection. Ca. 1915-19. Ca. 0.5 in.
Open. No guide.
Northeast Minnesota Historical Center.
Correspondence of the women's division of the United War Work Campaign; a list of women who served in the armed forces in WWI; clippings about the exploits of army nurses, women workers in WWI industrial production, and women involved in relief work; and J. E. L. Moore's "The War Work of the Women of Duluth" (1922).

8,448. Woman's Christian Temperance Union
Records. 1928-50. Ca. 0.5 in.
Open. No guide.
Northeast Minnesota Historical Center.
Clippings of the WCTU in Duluth pertain to local activities and to the group's efforts to promote sobriety and temperance.

8,449. Women's Council of Duluth
Records. 1916-25. 2 in.
Open. No guide.
Northeast Minnesota Historical Center.
Constitution, committee reports, and clippings of a social service organization that was chiefly concerned with education and juvenile delinquency.

8,450. Women's Institute of Duluth
Records. 1940-66. Ca. 3 in.
Open. No guide.
Northeast Minnesota Historical Center.
Clippings and programs of the Institute, which was established in 1940 to promote civic, cultural, and economic progress by sponsoring visits to Duluth by national and international figures in science, literature, and the arts. Visitors sponsored by the Institute included Ruth Bryan Owen, who was US minister to Denmark and daughter of William Jennings Bryan; Cornelia Otis Skinner; Eve Curie, the daughter of Marie Curie; and Mrs. J. Borden Harriman, US minister to Norway.

8,451. Young Women's Christian Association
Records. 1929-75. Ca. 0.5 in.
Open. No guide.
Northeast Minnesota Historical Center.
A 50th anniversary history, yearly programs, directories, and clippings of the Duluth chapter of the YWCA. Also included is material on Camp Wanakiwin, a summer camp for girls.

EDINA

8,452. Edina History
Collection. 1857- . Ca. 200 ft. and 4 drawers.
Open. No guide.
Edina Historical Society.
Manuscripts, including several on pioneer women in Edina and Morningside; minutes of Minnehaha Grange No. 398, 1873-1930; genealogies; pre-1900 elementary school textbooks; and artifacts gathered by the Society that pertain to Edina history. Founded in 1969, the Society's chief function is preservation of local history.

ELYSIAN

8,453. Woman's Relief Corps
Records. Nd. No size given.
Open. No guide.
LeSueur County Historical Society Museum.
Attendance and expense records of the Waterville, MN, auxiliary of the Grand Army of the Republic.

FERGUS FALLS

8,454. Blaisdell, Marie
Papers. 1889-1918. No size given.
Open. Unpublished guide.
Otter Tail County Historical Society.
Widely known as the "Minnesota Blizzard," [Mrs. M. J.] Blaisdell (1846-1918), a pioneer of Pelican Rapids, MN, spent more than 20 years attempting to persuade Congress to increase her husband's Civil War pension, to grant him a back pension, and to give her a pension for her services as an Army nurse. Clippings and a letter written by Mrs. Wilson Harris to Marguerite [Mrs. W. L.] Patterson of the Otter Tail County Historical Society about Blaisdell's activities in Washington, DC. Unsuccessful in her efforts, Blaisdell was considered a "terror" and for a short time was committed to an institution for the insane.

8,455. Johnson, Amelia
Papers. Ca. 1938. 2 items.
Access restricted. No guide.

Otter Tail County Historical Society.
Biographical files include an interview and short sketch published in *New York Mills "Seventy-Five Years of Progress" 1884-1959* about Johnson (1858-?), the first Finnish immigrant to buy land in New York Mills, MN. She also owned the first factory-made wagon in the area and operated a lodging house, which served as a community Finnish-American headquarters.

8,456. Kempfer, Hannah (Jensen)
Papers. 1903-66. No size given.
Open. Unpublished guide.
Otter Tail County Historical Society.
[Mrs. Charles] Kempfer (1880-1943) was a Minnesota state representative for 18 years. Manuscript and articles of Peter Gray's biography of Kempfer entitled "Beyond Herself," which was serialized in the *Fergus Falls Journal* in 1966; photos, including her wedding photo; a campaign article and leaflets; and clippings. Born on the North Sea to an unknown sailor and ship stewardess, Kempfer was adopted and in 1886 brought to America and ultimately to Fergus Falls where, at the age of 11, she worked as a milkmaid. She became a popular teacher and later a legislator. As chairman of the legislature's fish and game committee, Kempfer was influential in passage of a fishing license law and a bill forbidding use of the "cruel" steel game trap. She also helped establish goat husbandry and bee farming in the area, as well as a farm improvement club and the Otter Tail County fair. Collection includes a former pupil's description of her teaching and material regarding her work on behalf of illegitimate children.

8,457. Niggler, Elizabeth
Papers. Nd. No size given.
Access restricted. No guide.
Otter Tail County Historical Society.
Photo, a biographical report, a scrapbook, and a township file pertain to Niggler (?-1876), after whom the town of Elizabeth, MN, was named in 1876. The scrapbook was prepared by the Fergus Falls *Daily Journal* as an Otter Tail County centennial edition in 1968.

8,458. Patterson, Marguerite
Papers. 1927-32. No size given.
Open. Unpublished guide.
Otter Tail County Historical Society.
Correspondence of Patterson, corresponding secretary for the Otter Tail County Historical Society, who attempted to establish corresponding secretaries for each township and village. She was an artist who did much of her work at the Fergus Falls State Hospital where she lived with her husband W. L. Patterson, who was superintendent of the Hospital from 1927 to 1968. In addition, she traveled around the world.

8,459. Tiller, Edith W.
Papers. Nd. No size given.
Access restricted. No guide.
Otter Tail County Historical Society.
Biographical report pertaining to Tiller, who was editor and publisher of the *Battle Lake Review* during the 1920s.

8,460. Tweten, Geneva
Papers. 1963-68. No size given.
Open. Unpublished guide.
Otter Tail County Historical Society.
[Miss] Tweten (1901-68), whose motto was "It's never too late to succeed," was a candidate for the state legislature 12 times and is quoted as saying, "No one will move me until I get elected." Clippings on Tweten's activities in Fergus Falls. She was a designer of trimmings and decorations, manager of the Dotty Dunn Hat Shop, president of the Antique Collector's Club, and a member of the American Legion, Veterans of Foreign Wars auxiliaries, the Eastern Star, the Business and Professional Women's Club, and the Otter Tail County Historical Society. Tweten was also chairman of the Phelps Mill park committee; she succeeded in having the Mill restored and designated as the first Otter Tail County park.

8,461. Whitcomb, Mrs. George F.
Papers. 1935. 1 item.
Access restricted. Card catalog.
Otter Tail County Historical Society.
Obituary and biographical report on Whitcomb (?-1935), the first woman operator of the telegraph office in Fergus Falls.

8,462. Women of Otter Tail County
Oral history. Nd. 10 tapes.
Access restricted. Unpublished guide.
Otter Tail County Historical Society.
Consists of taped interviews with Otter Tail County residents Minne Carlson, Carol Draxton, Edna Fletcher, Florence E. Markle, Helen Quick, Kate Rotzien, Gladys Sandberg, Alma Satersmoen, Marie Stras, and Janette Anthony.

HOPKINS

8,463. Boy Scouts and Girl Scouts
Records. 1931-ca. 1952. 1 folder.
Open. Unpublished guide.
Hopkins Historical Society.
Typescript history, a newspaper, articles on the Boy Scouts, and a galley proof for portions of a book about the Boy Scouts and Girl Scouts. The Girl Scouts were organized in the Hopkins area before 1944.

8,464. Burwell, Louise
Papers. 1928-ca. 1952. 3 items.
Open. Unpublished guide.
Hopkins Historical Society.
Typescript biographical sketches of Burwell and her mother Mary Burwell, both missionaries, and an obituary of Mary Burwell.

8,465. Campbell, Samuel C.
Papers. 1915-53. 1 folder.
Open. Unpublished guide.
Hopkins Historical Society.
Papers of Campbell contain items about Catherine Burnes, a schoolteacher who became the first woman to graduate from the University of Minnesota medical school and was the first physician to practice in Hopkins. Manuscript biography, reminiscences, histories of Hopkins and Hopkins schools, a poem, photos, and clippings. Also includes an obituary for Diana Burnes [Mrs. Samuel C.] Campbell (1856-1938), who was a Hopkins civic leader. The Campbells were married in 1885.

8,466. Carlson
Papers. Ca. 1941-45. 1 item.
Open. Unpublished guide.
Hopkins Historical Society.
Newspaper photo shows June and Katherine Carlson, who are twin sisters, leaving the Minnetonka, MN, area to begin WACs aircraft training sometime during WWII.

8,467. Drahosh, Anna Stodola
Papers. 1937-40. 2 items.
Open. Unpublished guide.
Hopkins Historical Society.
Clippings pertain to the life of Drahosh (1856-1952), who became a raspberry picker after her emigration to Minnesota from her native Bohemia. She married Joseph Stodola (?-1887) in 1876. After Stodola was killed, she married Joseph Drahosh (?-1922). Her second husband's name was also spelled Drahos.

8,468. Empanger, Joseph
Papers. 1901-51. 1 folder.
Open. Unpublished guide.
Hopkins Historical Society.
Family photos, a newspaper, and articles about Empanger and his family. Women family members, some of whom are identified, appear in photos from the early 20th century.

8,469. Fraternal Lodges
Records. 1902-76. 1 file.
Open. Unpublished guide.
Hopkins Historical Society.
Typescript histories, membership certificate, photocopied newspaper, and pamphlet pertain to the Rebekahs, the female affiliate group of the International Order of Odd Fellows, and to the Order of the Eastern Star, a women's organization affiliated with the Masons, which was established locally in 1904 to promote community service, social enjoyment, and civic interest.

8,470. Hopkins, History of
Collection. 1881- . 1 file.
Open. Unpublished guide.
Hopkins Historical Society.
Typescript interviews, clippings, pamphlets, and mimeograph items about the history of Hopkins. Includes a one-page interview with Catherine Schultz, an anecdote of [Mrs.] Mary Shorba, and more than 700 pages of a proposed history of Hopkins by James L. Markham, publisher of the *Hennepin County Review*. The first settlers arrived in the Hopkins area in 1853, and in 1893 the village was incorporated as West Minneapolis. In 1928 the community assumed its present name.

8,471. Larkin, Mrs. Martin
Papers. 1938-57. 3 items.
Open. Unpublished guide.
Hopkins Historical Society.
Typescripts and clippings concern Anna Bridget "Brydie" (Nelson) Larkin's efforts to obtain the back pay of her deceased husband Martin Larkin, a weed inspector for Hennepin County, MN.

8,472. Leathers Family
Papers. Ca. 1950. 1 item.
Open. Unpublished guide.
Hopkins Historical Society.
Typescript description of Mrs. Harry Leathers and Mrs. Daniel Dow, pioneer women who "enjoyed the reputation of being very colorful individuals."

8,473. Maloney, Mrs. Michael
Papers. 1929-ca. 1952. 3 items.
Open. Unpublished guide.
Hopkins Historical Society.
Biographical sketch of and clippings about Albertine Erickson [Mrs. Michael] Maloney (1857-1940), a Hopkins organ teacher.

8,474. Nash, A. H., and Nash, Phoebe
Papers. 1937-57. 2 items.
Open. Unpublished guide.
Hopkins Historical Society.
Obituaries of [Mrs.] Phoebe Nash (1859-1937), who was active in animal protection work.

8,475. Peterson, H. Martin
Papers. Ca. 1880s-1920s. 1 file.
Open. Unpublished guide.
Hopkins Historical Society.
Photos and memorial records of Hopkins area residents include photos of women in the Peterson family.

8,476. Photos
Collection. 1889- . 3 files and 900 items.
Open. Unpublished guide.
Hopkins Historical Society.
Photos depicting Hopkins residents are assembled into several separate groupings and contain items showing women as high school students, teachers,

and school staff members. Also contains photos of a woman at the Clear Springs Creek School in 1905; women employed in general and grocery stores and in millinery and fabric businesses; women in family groups; Hopkins raspberry festival queens; women as Hopkins city employees and staff, including a 1966 photo of a female city recreation department member; women's clubs in 1935; the Sokol Club (gymnastics) in 1910; and families of Little League baseball team members.

8,477. Poetry
Collection. 1879-ca. 1900. Ca. 1 vol. and 1 item.
Open. Unpublished guide.
Hopkins Historical Society.
A scrapbook containing women's poetry as well as clippings and articles about women; "Memories of Hopkins," a poem with references to physician Catherine Burnes; and a poem about the "Pilgrim Fathers" by Felicia Henraus, with designs by [Miss] L. B. Humphrey. The Henraus poem was printed in Boston in 1879.

8,478. Prose
Collection. Ca. 1900-69. 1 folder.
Open. Unpublished guide.
Hopkins Historical Society.
Clippings and a scrapbook entitled "Alice, A Minnesota Girl" with prose reflecting early 20th-century life and expectations of a young woman.

8,479. Raspberry Day
Records. 1935-75. 1 file.
Open. Unpublished guide.
Hopkins Historical Society.
Records of the annual Hopkins Raspberry Day festival, first held in 1934, contain a typescript interview with Helen Kurtz, programs, newspapers, and a pamphlet about Beatrice Bella Shoppe, who in 1948 became Miss Hopkins, Miss Minnesota, and Miss America.

8,480. Redeen, August
Papers. 1942-71. 1 folder.
Open. Unpublished guide.
Hopkins Historical Society.
Photocopied newspaper and article related to oral history reminiscences taped in 1971 of Hilda Redeen (1879-1973), the daughter of August Redeen (1842-1942). August Redeen had been employed at the Minneapolis Threshing Company.

8,481. Women's Clubs
Records. 1908-69. 13 vols.
Open. Unpublished guide.
Hopkins Historical Society.
Records of the Women's Club of Hopkins and of other local women's organizations, among them the LWV, the Agnes Blake Study Club, and the Petal Pushers gardening group, which existed between 1961 and 1969. Included are annual reports, minutes, treasurer's record, correspondence, a history from 1908 to 1921, scrapbooks, and a 50th anniversary scroll of the Women's Club of Hopkins; a volume of Hennepin County Federated Clubs records; and correspondence, histories, clippings, and pamphlets of other women's groups. Formed in 1908 as the Women's Improvement League and later titled the Hopkins Improvement League, the Women's Club of Hopkins encouraged the village council to support clean-up and beautification projects. It also constructed and staffed a women's rest facility at the county fairgrounds and provided food, clothing, and medical care for needy people before the advent of government welfare programs. In addition, the Club provided 51 cemetery lots for indigent people, supported foreign exchange students, and created college scholarships for local girls.

INTERNATIONAL FALLS

8,482. Personal Histories and Women's Clubs
Collection. Late 1800s- . 2 drawers and other items.
Open. No guide.
Koochiching County Historical Society Museum.
Personal histories and photos of numerous early settlers in the Koochiching County area, including material on Annie "Muskeg Annie" (Shelland) [Mrs. Clarence E.] Williams, the first County superintendent of schools; items about Margaret [Mrs. Fred] Corell, who was active in securing libraries for small communities and worked for the affiliation of local women's clubs; and scrapbooks kept since the 1920s of Federated Women's Clubs and other area women's organizations.

LITTLE FALLS

8,483. Motherhouse Archives
Records. 1823- . Ca. 13 files.
Partially restricted. Unpublished guide.
Franciscan Sisters of Little Falls, Motherhouse.
Correspondence, scattered diaries, retreat notes, photocopied documents, sisterhood records, processed interviews, photos, scrapbooks, clippings, and historical artifacts of the Motherhouse of the Franciscan Sisters, a religious order devoted to teaching, works of mercy, and missionary labors. Contains material on the mother foundress and on the mothers general who have governed the autonomous sisterhood of Franciscans, which was established by 16 sisters in 1891 in Little Falls. The Franciscan community in Little Falls grew from a group established by Mother Mary Ignatius Hayes in Bell Prairie, MN, in 1872.

MANKATO

8,484. Alpha Delphian Society of Mankato
Records. 1924-39. 3 vols. and 1 folder.
Open. Catalog.
Blue Earth County Historical Society Museum.
Minutes and a register (roll call) for the study club dedicated to promoting higher education, personal improvement, and social progress. The Society began with a six-year course studying the history of civilization, then proceeded to reviewing novels and current events; it also gave money to scholarship funds. One meeting concerned "the 19th-century idea" of educated women, of women and politics, and of women's suffrage.

8,485. American Association of University Women, Mankato Branch
Records. 1918-60. 8 vols.
Open. Catalog card.
Blue Earth County Historical Society Museum.
Founded in 1918 as the Mankato Branch of the Association of Collegiate Alumnae but known as the Mankato College Women's Group and renamed AAUW in 1923, the group promoted education by sponsoring scholarships, loans, teas for high school girls, community programs on public education issues, and cultural events featuring women. Minutes, treasurer's ledgers, receipt book, and scrapbooks of clippings and programs. Because the AAUW saw its mission as enabling college women to pursue their intellectual growth, furthering the advancement of women, and discharging the special responsibilities that those with higher education have to society, the chapter maintained study groups, including one devoted to creative writing and others for discussion of child rearing; it joined with the LWV to debate legislation affecting women and to sponsor a discussion series on international relations, cooperated with the Minnesota mental health program, and supported the Minnesota Valley Community Day Care Center. In 1939 the chapter led the successful campaign for passage of a local ordinance requiring higher standards for milk.

8,486. Art History Club
Records. 1896-1958. 12 vols.
Open. Catalog card.
Blue Earth County Historical Society Museum.
After studying art history for the first 15 years, members of this Mankato group focused on civic and charitable projects before turning to international concerns in the 1950s when they entertained foreign students, some of whom addressed the group. Club constitution, complete set of minutes, a history of the Club, and programs. Examples of Club projects during the 1910s included efforts to institute and maintain the first city rest room; inspection of restaurants and food suppliers for the Pure Food Campaign, which resulted in higher cleanliness standards; motion picture supervision; and support for social hygiene, birth registration enforcement, public playgrounds, and fire drills in public schools. Members also taught surgical dressing classes and compiled scrapbooks for soldiers during WWI and II.

8,487. Carmel Presbyterian Esther Circle
Records. 1957-69. 1 vol.
Open. Catalog card.
Blue Earth County Historical Society Museum.
Minutes of a Bible study and social group of the Carmel Presbyterian Church, named for former church member Esther (Ellis) Croswell.

8,488. Clio Club, Mankato
Records. 1901-44. 11 vols. and 1 envelope.
Open. Catalog card.
Blue Earth County Historical Society Museum.
For many years after this study group's founding in 1894, the members emphasized history and literature; science was added in the 1930s; and by the 1940s their program consisted of book reviews. Minutes and registers from 1911 and a nearly complete set of programs. Two programs in 1939 and 1940 concerned the relationships of wives and husbands.

8,489. Lovelace, Maud (Hart)
Papers. 1925- . 1 folder.
Open. Unpublished guide.
Blue Earth County Historical Society Museum.
[Mrs. Delos] Lovelace (1892-) is author of the Betsy-Tacy children's books depicting growing up in early 20th-century Mankato. Correspondence, newspaper reviews and clippings, publisher's booklet, biographical accounts of Lovelace, and photos.

8,490. Mankato Council of Camp Fire Girls
Records. 1922-45. 4 items.
Open. Catalog card.
Blue Earth County Historical Society Museum.
A book of "The Guardian" newsletters and Mankato chapter Camp Fire Girls records, consisting of a membership book, a scrapbook of clippings, and a program. One news release contended the organization "was fulfilling a new need for leisure time activities" for girls 10 years and older.

8,491. Tourist Club
Records. 1899-1965. 5 vols.
Open. Catalog card.
Blue Earth County Historical Society Museum.
Record and minute books and scrapbook of a women's study group which, because it had several members who planned to travel to Europe, discussed European history and geography along with English and American poetry in the years following its inception in 1892. Members later expanded their programs to include South America and Asia, literature, and book reviews; in one

program during the 1929-30 season, biographies of important women were presented.

8,492. Wiecking, H. R.
Papers. 1944-73. 17 folders.
Open. No guide.
Blue Earth County Historical Society Museum.
Family papers include those of Anna Wiecking (1887-1973), who served as professor of education for 39 years at Mankato Teachers College (now Mankato State University) and as an historian of the area. Papers concerning activities before and after retirement, including correspondence about her writings, typescripts and photocopies of her histories, manuscripts of her works on education, clippings, and paper dolls. Wiecking was founder and 50-year member of the local AAUW chapter as well as a board member of the Blue Earth County Historical Society and the local American National Red Cross chapter. Also included is correspondence between Wiecking as AAUW representative and author Maud Hart Lovelace concerning a Betsy-Tacy Day in Mankato in 1961. Wiecking, one of the first teachers at the Mankato college to receive a doctorate, earned a BS from the University of Minnesota after studying at Mankato High School and the Mankato Normal School. She received an MS from Columbia University and a PhD from the University of Iowa.

8,493. Zetetic Club
Records. 1905-52. 8 vols.
Open. Catalog.
Blue Earth County Historical Society Museum.
Founded in 1896, the group's activities included musical presentations and readings, the study of literature and history, and various civic projects. Minutes, a register containing annual reports, and a cash book. The Club's civic activities paralleled those of other Mankato women's groups. Because one Club member was advocating women's suffrage, several meetings were devoted to the topic. In 1919 the Club helped found an LWV chapter; it also was associated with Federated Women's Clubs, which was probably the GFWC. Programs on women, children, or the family were held about once a year from 1930 to 1950.

8,494. Heritage Room
Records. 1833- . Ca. 650 items and 11 tapes.
Open. Unpublished guide.
School Sisters of Notre Dame, Our Lady of Good Counsel Convent.
Minutes, correspondence, chronicles, writings of sisters, biographies, sermons, tapes, filmstrip, maps and charts, photos, scrapbooks, obituaries, books, antiques, and artifacts of this religious congregation of women whose primary work is in education. The congregation was founded in Bavaria in 1833.

8,495. Bell, Ione B.
Oral history. 1976. 1 tape and transcript.
Open. Unpublished guide.
Southern Minnesota Historical Center.
Taped and transcribed interview with Bell, a feminist and author in Austin, MN, who discusses her work, inspirations, and the influence of others on her writing.

8,496. Daughters of the American Revolution, Anthony Wayne Chapter
Records. 1899-1976. 6 bacases.
Open. Unpublished guide.
Southern Minnesota Historical Center.
Record books, correspondence, programs, clippings, and printed material of this DAR chapter, which was organized in Mankato in 1899.

8,497. Fletcher, Ella May
Papers. 1912-59. 29 items.
Open. Unpublished guide.
Southern Minnesota Historical Center.
Clippings of newspaper articles by and about Fletcher (1874-1959), the daughter of Susan Dyer Fletcher and L. G. M. Fletcher, who taught in Mankato and Minneapolis schools; she also was the organizer of the first Camp Fire Girls group in Mankato. She was active locally and nationally with Camp Fire Girls for most of her adult life.

8,498. Fletcher, Susan Marshman Dyer
Papers. 1867-1941. 1 folder.
Open. Unpublished guide.
Southern Minnesota Historical Center.
Correspondence, photos, and clippings of Fletcher (1845-1941), a teacher and wife of L. G. M. Fletcher, who was prominent in Mankato business and civic affairs. Includes information about the hiring of Susan Fletcher in 1867 by the newly created Mankato Normal School.

8,499. Ingraham, Eliza M.
Papers. Ca. 1956. 6-page item.
Open. Unpublished guide.
Southern Minnesota Historical Center.
Reminiscences in which Ingraham (1883-1957), a housewife, describes rural life in Leavenworth Township in Brown County, MN.

8,500. Johnson, Mary Pay
Oral history. 1974. 1 tape and 21-page transcript.
Open. Unpublished guide.
Southern Minnesota Historical Center.
In her interview Johnson (1906-), a Mankato resident, reminisces about the various business interests of her grandfather, father, and husband, including ventures in a livery stable, a dray business, a hotel, and a laundry. Johnson assisted her husband in the laundry business.

8,501. Louk, Ione
Oral history. 1976. 1 tape and 22-page transcript.
Open. Unpublished guide.
Southern Minnesota Historical Center.
Taped and transcribed interview with Louk (1912-), a housewife, who discusses her interest in the women's movement and her enrollment as the first student in Mankato State University's women's studies program.

8,502. Mankato Council of Church Women United
Records. 1950-77. 0.5 Hollinger box.
Open. Unpublished guide.
Southern Minnesota Historical Center.
Organized in 1950, the Council functions as an ecumenical fellowship for women interested in church work in Mankato. Minutes, correspondence, reports, yearbooks, programs, and clippings.

8,503. Mankato Rehabilitation Center Auxiliary
Records. 1962-76. 5 folders.
Open. Unpublished guide.
Southern Minnesota Historical Center.
Annual reports, minutes, and financial records of the Auxiliary, founded in 1962 to provide volunteer social and financial support to the Mankato Rehabilitation Center and its clients. Members, all of whom are women, operate a thrift shop and perform various volunteer services.

8,504. Mankato State University, Faculty Wives Association
Records. 1935-77. 1 vol.
Open. Unpublished guide.
Southern Minnesota Historical Center.
Scrapbook containing minutes, lists of members, photos, programs, clippings, and memorabilia of the Association, a social organization formed in 1935 for wives of faculty members at the University.

8,505. Mankato Symphony Guild
Records. 1965-77. 0.5 Hollinger box.
Open. Unpublished guide.
Southern Minnesota Historical Center.
Minutes, correspondence, photos, clippings, and an American Symphony Orchestra League citation of merit won by the Guild, a women's group that was organized in 1965 in cooperation with the Mankato Symphony Orchestra to increase subscription membership and attendance at Orchestra concerts. Members also promote symphony music by operating a music appreciation program for elementary school students in Mankato.

8,506. Mills, Lucius D.
Papers. 1933. 45-page item.
Open. Unpublished guide.
Southern Minnesota Historical Center.
Included in reminiscences of Mills (1848-1936), a farmer, are the reminiscences of Zulu Bartlett [Mrs. James] Baker, a friend of the Mills family, who recalls her arrival and education in Minnesota during the 1860s and 1870s.

8,507. Peterson, Eda Lien
Oral history. 1976. 1 tape and 33-page transcript.
Open. Unpublished guide.
Southern Minnesota Historical Center.
Taped and transcribed interview with Peterson (1892-), a teacher and housewife, who recalls her childhood in rural Delavan, MN.

8,508. Portfolio Club
Records. 1947-61. 1 vol.
Open. Unpublished guide.
Southern Minnesota Historical Center.
Minute book of this women's social and study club, which was organized in Mankato in 1947.

8,509. Saiki, Sue
Oral history. 1975. 1 tape and 14-page transcript.
Open. Unpublished guide.
Southern Minnesota Historical Center.
Taped and transcribed interview with Saiki (1919-), a partner with her husband Taro "Ty" Saiki in a Mankato-based chick sexing business, which operated for the purpose of identifying young chickens as either roosters or egg-laying pullets for poultry buyers. She recalls her childhood in California, her family's move to Mankato in 1942, and some of her family's experiences while living in Minnesota.

8,510. Scherer, Minnie
Papers. 1977. 18-page item.
Open. Unpublished guide.
Southern Minnesota Historical Center.
"Early History of Mankato," a paper by Scherer (1890-), a schoolteacher and housewife, was produced from her reminiscences and research in various local history sources.

8,511. Society of Fine Arts, Inc.
Records. 1963-74. 1 folder and 11 vols.
Open. Unpublished guide.
Southern Minnesota Historical Center.
Minutes, financial records, correspondence, membership lists, and scrapbooks of the Society, incorporated in Mankato in 1963 to promote cultural activities, art, music, dance, and theater in the area; women members were especially active in the formative years of this organization. The Society ceased to function in 1974.

8,512. Wiecking, Emma
Oral history. 1977. 1 tape and transcript.
Open. Unpublished guide.
Southern Minnesota Historical Center.
In her taped and transcribed interview [Miss] Wiecking (1894-) comments on her life and career at Mankato State College, earlier known as the State Normal School at Mankato, where for 37 years she worked as a librarian. Includes information about the College faculty, student life, the library, and education in general.

8,513. Young Women's Christian Association
Records. 1926-76. 27 bacases.
Open. Unpublished guide.

Southern Minnesota Historical Center.
Minutes, financial records, photos, scrapbooks, clippings, and printed matter of the Mankato YWCA, which was organized in 1926.

MARSHALL

8,514. Andrew, Martha Freeman
Papers. 1929-39. 1 Hollinger box.
Open. Unpublished guide.
Southwest Minnesota Historical Center.
Diaries of Martha "Mattie" Andrew (1877-1943), a Tracy, MN, resident and wife of Redwood County farmer Louis Towers Andrew, include one volume she kept during an automobile trip in 1929 from Tracy to California and back with notes on places visited, mileage, prices, and road conditions; a diary from 1932 recounting her activities on the family farm in Springdale Township in Redwood County; and one volume she kept between 1935 and 1939 recording her daily life in Tracy, where her husband was secretary of the Tri-County Co-op Oil Company and where she was active in the local Presbyterian church and in various community groups. The latter diary also contains references to their farm in Springdale Township.

8,515. Carrigan, Minnie Bruce
Papers. Nd. 1 vol.
Open. Unpublished guide.
Southwest Minnesota Historical Center.
Reminiscences of [Mrs.] Carrigan (1856-?), which were published in 1912 by the *News Print* of Buffalo Lake, MN, pertain to her family's settlement at Middle Creek in Renville County, MN, and the 1862 Indian uprising in southwestern Minnesota. According to her account, Carrigan's parents were murdered at Middle Creek by Indians and she was held captive until released by General Henry Sibley.

8,516. Morrison, Alden Leslie, and Buyse, Zedie Jane (Morrison)
Papers. 1877-99. 1 microfilm reel.
Open. Unpublished guide.
Southwest Minnesota Historical Center.
Diaries of Morrison, a farmer and schoolteacher in Little Rock, IA, which was located near the Minnesota-Iowa state line, and of Buyse, the wife of a livestock dealer who lived in southwestern Minnesota and in Sioux Falls, SD. The women were sisters. Morrison's diary contains information about life on the farm and in a rural community.

8,517. Runholt, Vernon, and Runholt, Frances (Harris)
Papers. 1 vol., 21 items, 1 tape, and 42-page transcript.
Open. Unpublished guide.
Southwest Minnesota Historical Center.
Taped and transcribed oral history interview with Lyon County, MN, residents Vernon Runholt and his wife Frances Runholt, who taught school for many years in Lynd, a small community near Marshall. Also includes a scrapbook and 21 slides. Discussed in the interview are her teaching experiences, salary, expenses, and enrollment; her education at St. Cloud State Teachers College, then called Normal School, from the late 1920s to the early 1930s; the fight for quality education in Lynd and the consolidation of schools; early electrical devices in the home and on the farm; Protestant versus Catholic land settlement; the Ku Klux Klan; and various agricultural organizations to which the Runholts belonged, including the Farm Bureau, the Farm Holiday Association, and the Protective Land Use Association.

8,518. Southwest Minnesota History
Oral history. Nd. Ca. 46 tapes and 19 transcripts.
Partially restricted. Unpublished guide.
Southwest Minnesota Historical Center.
Represented in interviews with southwestern Minnesota residents are ca. 50 women, among them homemakers, business professionals, immigrants, and pioneers, who discuss a variety of personal experiences and such topics as family history, home life, technological advances since the 1880s, religion, recreation, club activity, education, politics, business conditions and the depression, the status of women, and social life in small towns and rural communities. Included are interviews with [Miss] Sigrid Frost, a cashier and bookkeeper of Icelandic descent who was born and raised in the Icelandic community of Minneota, MN; Kathryn Kwak [Mrs. John] Ponstein, who came to America from Holland on the ship *Rotterdam* in 1912 (the *Rotterdam* was crossing the Atlantic Ocean just behind the *Titanic* when the latter ship sank) and who discusses that voyage, social life in the 1920s, her household duties, and the WPA and other federal relief programs in Lyon County in the 1930s; Minnie Schwanke Pankonin, who was 100 years old when the interview was conducted and who reminisces about her childhood in Blue Earth County, her German immigrant parents, frontier farming, church life, and early education; Mrs. Ansel Norgrant, a housewife and second-generation Swedish resident of Lakefield, who discusses the Swedish Lutheran Church, women's church organizations and social events, and relations between local Swedes and Norwegians; [Mrs.] Irene Ironheart Howell, a housewife and student, who talks about Indian history in the Granite Falls and Morton area; [Mrs.] Laura S. Wolfe Hanson, a farmer's wife residing near Montevideo, who recounts her and her husband's involvement in Chippewa County cooperative movements, the Farmers' Union, and the Farm Holiday Association; Kathleen B. Smith Jordan, a physician, who describes the work she and her physician husband Lewis Jordan accomplished as superintendent and medical director of the Riverside Sanatorium in Granite Falls, especially in combating tuberculosis between 1930 and 1963; Maude Sylvester, a schoolteacher, who comments on educational techniques and requirements for teachers in the 1930s and 1940s; [Mrs.] Margaret Stevens, a Marshall resident and former librarian, who talks about her active involvement in the women's suffrage movement and about various aspects of women's experience such as childbirth, dating, fashions, and family life; and Achsah Fricke, a housewife, who discusses her early school experiences, dating and entertainment, life during the depression, and her husband's career as a section foreman with the Currie Line, part of the railroad system in southwestern Minnesota.

8,519. Sweet, Lottie
Papers. Nd. 3-page item.
Open. Unpublished guide.
Southwest Minnesota Historical Center.
Letter written by [Mrs.] Sweet in which she describes her arrival as a child in 1873 in Lyon County, MN, and in Marshall.

8,520. Voight, Nell Adams
Papers. 1902. 17-page item.
Open. Unpublished guide.
Southwest Minnesota Historical Center.
Typewritten copy of a diary kept by Voight during a trip from St. Paul, MN, to Seattle on the Northern Pacific Railroad. Includes her impressions of the towns she passed through en route to Seattle.

MINNEAPOLIS

8,521. Sister Kenny Archives
Collection. 1943- . Ca. 450 items.
Access restricted. No guide.
Abbott-Northwestern Hospital Corporation.
Autobiographical account by Sister Kenny, a pioneer and leader in polio rehabilitation medicine, with handwritten annotations; booklets written by staff members of the Sister Kenny Institute, containing information on homemaking, clothing, and sexuality in regard to handicapped women; articles and theses of staff members and others at the Institute; books by and about Sister Kenny, including a biography by Martha Ostenso; and various publications of the American Rehabilitation Foundation, many of which were written by women prominent in the health care delivery field.

8,522. Artists and Sculptors
Collection. Nd. 19 drawers.
Open. No guide.
Minneapolis Public Library and Information Center.
Clipping folders, exhibition catalogs, pamphlets, and articles from periodicals pertain to historical and contemporary male and female artists and sculptors.

8,523. Films
Collection. 1947- . 2733 films.
Open. Published guide.
Minneapolis Public Library and Information Center.
Ca. 22 of the films are specifically about women or the women's movement. Includes one film on Susan B. Anthony. See *16mm Film Catalog of the Minneapolis Public Library and Information Center* (1978).

8,524. Filmstrips
Collection. Nd. No size given.
Open. Card catalog.
Minneapolis Public Library and Information Center.
The collection contains a series of four filmstrips with phonodiscs and a guide, entitled "Woman's Place." In an examination of the status of women in modern society, the series presents information on perceptions of and common stereotypes and myths about women, the progress of the women's movement since 1966, and biological facts.

8,525. Index to Artists and Sculptors
Finding Aid. Nd. 3-drawer card index.
Open. No guide.
Minneapolis Public Library and Information Center.
Index of books, periodicals, and other sources at the Library provides access to research material about historical and contemporary male and female artists and sculptors.

8,526. Nineteenth-Century New England Authors
Collection. 1807-1976. 3630 items.
Open. Unpublished guide.
Minneapolis Public Library and Information Center.
Correspondence, manuscripts, and 3500 pamphlets, periodicals, and books. Includes an 1884 letter by Harriet (Beecher) Stowe and two 1847 letters by educator and reformer Catharine Esther Beecher, the first of which was a recommendation for Evelina Bray, a Marblehead, MA, resident who was one of the first teachers sent by the Board of National Popular Education to work in Ohio, and the second of which was written to encourage an apparently dissatisfied Bray to accept cheerfully her new teaching assignment for the good of "the cause." Also contains a journal that Bray, later Evelina (Bray) Downey, kept while she was teaching in a Memphis school from 1866 to 1867. She and John Greenleaf Whittier were classmates at Haverhill Academy; she reportedly is the lost love described in several of his poems.

8,527. Pictures
Collection. Nd. 25 drawers.
Open. No guide.
Minneapolis Public Library and Information Center.
Files contain loose pictures and photos of men and women, cataloged by each person's name.

8,528. Minnesota Annual Conference, United Methodist Church
Records. 1856- . Ca. 140 ft., 26 drawers, ca. 3000 vols., and 8 cabinets.
Open. Indexes.
Minnesota Conference of the United Methodist Church, Commission on Archives and History.
Records of the United Methodist Church in Minnesota and its antecedent denominations, the Methodist Episcopal Conference, the Evangelical Association, and the Church of the United Brethren in Christ, include minutes and reports, some on microfilm, of statewide denomination organizations, discontinued local churches, and women's groups. Includes yearbooks and journals dating from the organization in 1856 of the state's Methodist Episcopal Conference and of the Evangelical Association. Also contains a complete set of Annual Conference yearbooks; correspondence; photos; periodicals, including issues of *Heathen Woman's Friend*, 1869-89; and books relating to general and United Methodist Church history. The Church of the United Brethren in Christ was organized in the state in 1857. Women have served as ministers of the denominations in Minnesota since about 1889.

8,529. Hospital Archives
Records. 1877- . 35 folders and envelopes, 2 boxes, and 18 vols.
Access restricted. No guide.
St. Mary's Hospital, Staff Library.
The archives of the Hospital, a private acute care facility founded in 1887, contain records of the St. Mary's Hospital school of nursing, female administrators, the Hospital auxiliary, and Hospital personnel. Annual reports, correspondence, photos, scrapbooks, clippings, Hospital publications, and other items.

8,530. Drew, James M., and Drew, Margaret S.
Papers. Ca. 1875-1967. 20 in.
Open. No guide.
University Archives, University of Minnesota Libraries.
Correspondence, diaries, photos, clippings, and memorabilia of James M. Drew (1863-1948), a University school of agriculture faculty member, and his daughter Margaret Salisbury Drew (1894-1966), who received a BS from the University in 1917 and was a dietitian on the home economics staff from 1940 until her retirement in 1963. Her papers consist of correspondence, including letters to Drew about her mother's death in 1945; items concerning her retirement from the home economics department; and letters, cards, clippings, and a tribute written by her sister Helen (Drew) Richardson upon her death. Drew was a member of the National Dietetic Association and was a relief dietitian at the University Hospitals outpatient diabetes clinic until 1966.

8,531. Kerlan Collection
Collections. 1900- . 22 drawers, mss. for 1500 titles, and illustrations for 2350 titles.
Partially closed. Card catalog.
University of Minnesota Libraries, Children's Literature Research Collections.
The Kerlan Collection contains approximately 400 collections of papers of American women authors and illustrators of children's books, most of them 20th century. Collections range in size from one manuscript or original illustration to 14 feet and are composed primarily of manuscripts and illustrations of various sorts and in various stages of preparation. Manuscripts range in form from author's notes, holograph texts, and typescripts to book dummies, galley proofs, and page proofs. Illustration media include pencil and ink sketches, chalk, ink wash, watercolor, collage, paper batik, and woodcuts, as well as color separations and studies for jackets. Also included in the collections are personal, business, and fan mail correspondence; diaries; autobiographical writings; notebooks; acceptance speeches for Caldecott and Newbery awards; photos; memorabilia; original greeting cards and book plates; pamphlets; advertising posters; reviews; bibliographies; articles; clippings; and publishers' catalogs.

Among the authors and illustrators represented in the Kerlan Collection are Wanda Gág (1893-1946), whose papers contain the manuscript and illustrations for *Millions of Cats;* Carol Ryrie Brink (1895-), whose papers include the manuscript for *Caddie Woodlawn,* a book about her pioneer grandmother in Wisconsin; and Eve Merriam (1916-), whose papers contain the manuscript for *Independent Voices,* a book of poetry about seven prominent Americans including Lucretia Mott, Elizabeth Blackwell, and Ida B. Wells. The largest collection is that of Elizabeth Jane Coatsworth (1893-), which includes correspondence, diaries for the years 1915 to 1945, an unpublished autobiography, and notebooks of her poetry, as well as manuscripts for 51 books. The papers of Marie Hall Ets (1895-) contain her acceptance speech for the Caldecott Award for *Nine Days to Christmas,* an autobiographical sketch, illustrations for 18 books, and manuscripts of nine books. Autobiographical notes, a family history, poems, and the manuscript for *Cloud Shoes* are among the papers of Borghild Margarethe Dahl (1890-).

Other authors and illustrators represented in the Kerlan Collection include Adrienne Adams, Ruth Adler, Laura Nelson Baker, Marguerite De Angeli, Margot Benary-Isbert, Emma Lillian Brock, Margaret Wise Brown, Natalie Savage Carlson, Phoebe Erickson, Marguerite Henry, Margaret Hodges, Irene Hunt, Anne Marie Jauss, Clara (Ingram) Judson, Evaline Ness, Emily Cheney Neville, Mary (Leduc) O'Neill, Lucy (Fitch) Perkins, Mary Rodgers, Mary Slattery Stolz, Sydney Taylor, Tasha Tudor, Yoshiko Uchida, Judith Viorst, Margot Zemach, and Charlotte (Shapiro) Zolotow.

8,532. Ad Hoc Committee on the Status of Women
Records. 1971-72. 1 folder.
Access restricted. No guide.
University of Minnesota Libraries, University Archives.
Minutes of the Committee, which was appointed in 1971 at the University's Morris campus to recommend the establishment of a permanent commission for women with a defined scope and goal. The Committee disbanded in 1972 when the commission was established.

8,533. Anderson, Maude (Case)
Papers. 1866. 1 folder.
Open. Unpublished guide.
University of Minnesota Libraries, University Archives.
Personal papers of [Mrs. Frank Maloy] Anderson, an 1895 University graduate, include descriptions of University landmarks of the 1850s and 1860s, among them Cheever House and Cheevertown.

8,534. Baillif, Matilda Victorine
Papers. 1905-09. 1 in.
Open. Unpublished guide.
University of Minnesota Libraries, University Archives.
Scrapbook of Baillif (1883-), a 1909 University graduate, contains student memorabilia.

8,535. Baker, Annie Laurie
Papers. 1921-72, nd. 1 folder.
Open. Unpublished guide.
University of Minnesota Libraries, University Archives.
Correspondence and reports of Baker (1905-), a professor of social work and director of the social service department at the University Hospitals, generally pertain to Minnesota welfare and hospital services and to development of the General Hospitals and Masonic Unit at the University Hospitals. Baker's career began in 1931 at the University where for four years she was a medical social worker. From 1935 to 1942 she was district representative for northwestern Minnesota on the state board of control, now called the state department of public welfare; she also was director of the division of the blind from 1938 to 1942. During WWII she joined the American National Red Cross, working in both domestic and foreign service. Baker returned to University Hospitals in 1948 and remained there until her retirement in 1972.

8,536. Baker, Gertrude Margaret
Papers. 1955. 1 folder.
Open. Unpublished guide.
University of Minnesota Libraries, University Archives.
Manuscript of Baker (1894-1977), a director of University physical education for women, relates to female participation in University physical education programs from 1905 to 1955. A member of the faculty since 1921, Baker became women's physical education director in 1945; she retired in 1962.

8,537. Barnes, Marjorie Dean Mitchell
Papers. 1927-31. 2 in.
Open. Unpublished guide.
University of Minnesota Libraries, University Archives.
Scrapbook of Barnes (1909?-), a 1931 University graduate, contains souvenirs of her student activities. A member in 1952 of the first board of directors of the Minnesota Alumni Club's central Wisconsin chapter, Barnes became the chapter's secretary-treasurer in ca. 1958.

8,538. Biester, Alice
Papers. 1941-55, nd. 1 folder.
Open. Unpublished guide.
University of Minnesota Libraries, University Archives.
Biester (1890-1969) came to the University in 1915 and retired in 1955 as professor and head of the nutrition section of the school of home economics. Includes a list of her professional activities, bibliography of her publications through 1954, and program summary of the nutrition section of a 1941 food and nutrition conference. During her career Biester conducted investigations dealing with the nutritive value of foods, relative sweetness of sugars, blood regeneration in anemia, and nutrition for older women.

8,539. Blakey, Roy Gillespie
Papers. 1865-1964. 47 in.
Open. Preliminary guide.
University of Minnesota Libraries, University Archives.
Correspondence, photos, scrapbook, memorabilia, and publications of Blakey (1880-1967), a University professor, educator, and economist. Includes correspondence and other papers of his wife Gladys McAlphine (Campbell) Blakey, who coauthored with her husband many publications on taxation and tax structure.

8,540. Boynton, Ruth Evelyn
Papers. 1931-61. 42 in.
Open. Preliminary guide.
University of Minnesota Libraries, University Archives.
Papers of Boynton (1896-), an educator and director of the University health service from 1936 to 1961, include correspondence; radiological health subcommittee files of the state board of health, containing minutes and correspondence about oral polio vaccine field studies; and material pertaining to the planning committee of the Fourth National Conference on Health in Colleges. Boynton began her association with the University

health service in 1921. She served as director of the division of child hygiene, Minnesota state department of health, from 1923 to 1927. The health service was renamed Boynton Health Service in 1975.

8,541. Brandsmark, Gertrude Marie
Papers. 1897-1901. 1 folder.
Open. Unpublished guide.
University of Minnesota Libraries, University Archives.
Papers of Brandsmark, a University student from 1897 to 1901, include her original poems and translations from Greek poetry; photos, clippings, programs, and magazines relating to her student activities; and clippings, program, and a copy of the play *The Return of Odysseus,* which was presented in 1900 by the University Lyceum Theater. Brandsmark married George R. Longbrake.

8,542. Brownson, Cora Inez (Brown)
Papers. Ca. 1940-49. 1 folder.
Open. Unpublished guide.
University of Minnesota Libraries, University Archives.
Manuscript of Brownson, an 1880 University graduate, includes information about the University from 1857 to 1880. Brownson wrote the account when she was in her 80s. Also includes an accompanying letter.

8,543. Bruchholz, Elizabeth Roy (Ware)
Papers. 1907-11. 1 in.
Open. Unpublished guide.
University of Minnesota Libraries, University Archives.
Scrapbooks of Bruchholz and her husband Henry Bruchholz, both members of the University class of 1911. Contains correspondence, photos, and clippings about the 1911 May Fete, for which Elizabeth Bruchholz, who then was Elizabeth Ware, served as assistant chairman of the executive committee; letters from [Mrs.] George Vincent, the wife of the University president, regarding Fete activities for faculty and students; and general University memorabilia.

8,544. Butner, Anne Maud
Papers. 1900-12. 2 vols.
Open. Unpublished guide.
University of Minnesota Libraries, University Archives.
From 1900 to 1912 Butner (1870-1932) was director of physical culture at the University. Scrapbooks contain pictures and clippings pertaining to physical education activities; items about the Sargent system of physical training; and clippings and a news comment by Maria Sanford defending basketball as a proper sport for women.

8,545. Christian, Mrs. George Chase
Papers. 1927-28. 1 folder.
Open. Unpublished guide.
University of Minnesota Libraries, University Archives.
Correspondence and memorabilia of [Mrs.] Christian (1875-1964), a Minneapolis social leader and benefactor to the University Hospitals, reflect her activities as president of the Minneapolis chapter of *Sauvegarde de l'Art Francais,* a French society devoted to the preservation of French art.

8,546. Clopath, Henrietta
Papers. 1934-36. 1 folder.
Open. Unpublished guide.
University of Minnesota Libraries, University Archives.
Correspondence of [Miss] Clopath (?-1936), who headed the University art department, concerns a collection of paintings bequeathed to the home economics department and later transferred to the University Gallery. Also included is a copy of Clopath's will. A native of Switzerland who was educated in Europe, Clopath came to Minneapolis in 1895; three years later she was appointed instructor in the University art department.

8,547. College of Education
Records. 1917-50. 120 in.
Open. Preliminary guide.
University of Minnesota Libraries, University Archives.
Minutes, reports, and correspondence of the College, founded in 1905, contain scattered material relating to women and also document the history of several fields that were traditionally filled by women. Correspondence of the department of art education includes letters of Ruth Raymond, who headed the department from its creation in 1919 until her retirement in 1947; home economics education material contains correspondence about federal legislation that provided funds for training home economics teachers; nursing education files include correspondence pertaining to the establishment of nursing schools on a vocational level and a course for training nurses to teach in schools of nursing; and a file concerning reorganization of the department of physical education for women in 1941 contains correspondence, examples of exams given, and reports, including a survey of administrative relationships within women's physical education departments by Gertrude Margaret Baker, acting director of the University department of physical education.

8,548. College of Science, Literature, and the Arts
Records. 1914-45. 61 in.
Access restricted. Unpublished guide.
University of Minnesota Libraries, University Archives.
Minutes, correspondence, and subject files of the College, which was founded in 1868. Includes an AAUW study of experiments in education, with replies from liberal arts colleges that were surveyed.

8,549. Commission for Women
Records. 1970-76. 1 folder.
Access restricted. No guide.
University of Minnesota Libraries, University Archives.
Minutes of the Commission, established in 1972 at the University's Morris campus to study research, programs, and grievances of University women. The Commission set up a "grievance procedure related to sexist behavior affecting classroom learning," which was approved by the Morris campus assembly; it also investigated and made recommendations about women's athletics, minority women, and hiring of women faculty. The Commission dissolved by unanimous agreement in 1976, and a member of the grievance committee assumed the Commission's duties.

8,550. Council for University Women's Progress
Records. Ca. 1970-74. 12 in.
Access restricted. No guide.
University of Minnesota Libraries, University Archives.
The Council was formed in 1969 to represent University women students, staff, and faculty in attempts to provide equal opportunity in hiring, promotions, salaries, job placement, and professional advancement. Annual reports, including those of the University's equal opportunity and affirmative action office; minutes and meeting notices; member and nonmember mailing lists; articles, reports, and miscellaneous information; material about University civil service; and newsletters.

8,551. Countryman, Gratia Alta
Papers. 1888. 1 folder.
Open. Unpublished guide.
University of Minnesota Libraries, University Archives.
Following her graduation from the University in 1889, Countryman (1866-1953) became a librarian at the Minneapolis Public Library where she worked for 47 years. Petition she wrote and submitted to the University president and faculty requesting that women students be allowed to participate in military drill "as an aid to culture." Also includes correspondence pertaining to Company Q, which provided military drills for women.

8,552. Dean of Students
Records. 1916- . 1045 in.
Access restricted. Partial inventory.
University of Minnesota Libraries, University Archives.
Minutes, reports, and correspondence generated in the office of the Dean of Students, which was established in 1917 as the office of the Dean of Student Affairs. Includes correspondence of the office of the dean of women, 1916-40, as well as a 1951 letter pertaining to the controversial formation of a new office of the dean of women; AAUW correspondence concerning the 1961 state convention and AAUW University membership; minutes of the school of nursing's faculty meetings as well as its advisory, student scholastic standing, and student work committees; material about the status and membership requirements of Sigma Kappa sorority, 1956-60; a 1947 study of the geographic distribution of University sorority members; correspondence describing University policies, 1943-52, concerning women in fraternity houses; committee minutes, correspondence, recommendations, and course outlines for a proposed marriage class, 1941-45; marriage conseling material; and correspondence about YWCA activities on campus.

8,553. Densford, Katherine Jane
Papers. 1906-69. 235 in., 9 recording discs, and 8 tapes.
Access restricted. Preliminary guide.
University of Minnesota Libraries, University Archives.
Densford (1890-) was a nurse, educator, and administrator who was director of the University school of nursing from 1930 to 1969. Correspondence, subject files, sound recordings and tapes, travel scrapbook, diplomas, certificates, memorabilia, and textbooks. Material spans Densford's career as a student at Miami University, the University of Chicago, the University of Cincinnati school of nursing, and elsewhere; her marriage to Carl Dreeves; and her teaching and administrative experiences at various hospitals and nursing schools as well as at the University. Items relate to such topics as the *American Journal of Nursing,* the American Nurses Association, the American Nurses Foundation, the Army Nurse Corps, the International Council of Nurses, the National and Minnesota League for Nursing, and the National Nursing Accrediting Service. Other material pertains to the Defense Committee on Womanpower, the Governor's Commission on the Status of Women, minority women, and Florence Nightingale.

8,554. DeReyter, Nellie Molenar
Papers. Ca. 1910-13. 4 in.
Open. Unpublished guide.
University of Minnesota Libraries, University Archives.
Class notes and memorabilia of DeReyter (ca. 1892-), who was a University school of agriculture student from 1910 to 1913.

8,555. Division of Entomology and Economic Zoology
Records. 1890-1959. 270 in.
Access restricted. Unpublished guide.

University of Minnesota Libraries, University Archives.
Division material includes correspondence between Tamarath Knigin Yolles and University professor C. E. Mickel about Yolles's experiences in British Guiana and Trinidad during WWII and correspondence of Nellie Maria de Cottrell Payne, which pertains to *Biological Abstracts,* insect physiology, and job opportunities. Born in Cheyenne Wells, CO, Payne received a BS in 1920 and an MS in 1921 from Kansas State College before earning a PhD in 1925 at the University of Minnesota. From 1918 to 1921 she was an assistant in Kansas State's zoology and entomology department; she taught chemistry and mathematics at Lindenwood College in St. Charles, MO, for two years; and then she served as assistant, librarian, and later lecturer in the University's department of entomology. From 1927 to 1933 Payne was a member of the *Biological Abstracts* science staff; after 1937 she worked for the American Cyanamid Company as an entomologist and zoologist; and after 1957 she worked as a literary chemist, doing abstracting and bibliographic work at Velsicol Chemical Corporation.

8,556. Dooley, Lucile (Collins)
Papers. 1910- . 15 in.
Open. No guide.
University of Minnesota Libraries, University Archives.
Albums with photos, post cards, and memorabilia of [Mrs. Patrick V.] Dooley (ca. 1887-1968), who graduated from the University in 1910, relate to her student experiences. Also includes material about the LWV.

8,557. Drew, Helen L.
Papers. 1910-73. 5 in.
Open. Unpublished guide.
University of Minnesota Libraries, University Archives.
After graduating from the University in 1914, Drew (ca. 1892-) became an English professor and English department head at Rockford College in Rockford, IL. Scrapbook pertaining to her student days; correspondence, including letters from Margaret Sweeney, the University dean of women from 1912 to 1916; and one item about Sweeney's death in 1920. Drew married Robert Kimball Richardson.

8,558. Dunwoody, William Hood
Papers. 1901-08. 1 folder.
Open. Unpublished guide.
University of Minnesota Libraries, University Archives.
Correspondence of Dunwoody (1841-1914), a Twin Cities businessman and benefactor for various University and civic projects, contains letters from University president Cyrus Northrop and Woman's League president Rita Kendall about proposals for a women's building on campus in 1904 and one letter from Ada Comstock concerning a women's dormitory. The Woman's League was succeeded in 1913 by the Women's Self-Government Association.

8,559. Eckert, Ruth Elizabeth
Papers. 1930-73. 20 in.
Open. Unpublished guide.
University of Minnesota Libraries, University Archives.
Eckert (1905-), the first woman regents' professor at the University, developed and served as professor in a higher education program there. Correspondence; studies; reports, including Eckert's report on the status of University women in 1971 and 1972, which she prepared for an AAUP committee; material on University committees, the college of education, the higher education program, professional associations, and statewide planning documents; and publications. Eckert married John H. McComb.

8,560. Enches, Evelyn Leslie
Papers. Ca. 1919-23. 1 folder.
Open. Unpublished guide.
University of Minnesota Libraries, University Archives.
Memorabilia of a 1923 University school of business graduate pertains to her student days.

8,561. Faculty Employment Records
Records. ?-1920. 63 in.
Open. No guide.
University of Minnesota Libraries, University Archives.
Card file of items, most of which are undated, document appointments, promotions, and salary increases of women and men employed at the University prior to 1920.

8,562. Faculty Women's Club
Records. 1911-63. 25 in.
Access restricted. Unpublished guide.
University of Minnesota Libraries, University Archives.
Constitutions, secretaries' minutes, record and treasurers' books, and scrapbooks of the Club, established in 1911 for all faculty women and faculty wives. While the original purpose of the group was social, membership interests soon diversified: in 1914 the Club staged a play to raise money for a women students' loan fund, and by 1961 members pursued various civic, educational, and service activities.

8,563. Faculty Women's Dining Club
Records. 1940-64. 4 in.
Open. Unpublished guide.
University of Minnesota Libraries, University Archives.
Minutes and reports, financial records, membership rosters and attendance records, correspondence, and meeting notices of an organization formed in 1930 to combine professional and social interests of women who were fulltime appointees of the academic and professional staffs of all University colleges and departments. Material reflects changes in the concerns and interests of Club members.

8,564. Firkins, Ina Ten Eyck
Papers. 1917-24, nd. 64.5 in.
Open. Unpublished guide.
University of Minnesota Libraries, University Archives.
Correspondence, lecture notes, notebook, and a scrapbook of Firkins (1866-1937), a University librarian. Includes letters about a new edition of her *Index to Short Stories,* which was a standard reference book in US libraries and abroad; correspondence pertaining to arrangements for completion of her *Index of Plays* (1927); correspondence with Charles Franklin Woods, a librarian at the Riverside, CA, Public Library, arranging for her to be a guest lecturer at the Riverside Library service school; lecture notes and a description of a course she proposed to teach; and notes for a bibliography of University faculty publications. Firkins earned a bachelor of literature degree from the University in 1888, and one year later she became a University library assistant. From 1920 to 1921 she served as acting librarian and then resumed her position as reference librarian with the rank of associate professor. In 1932 Firkins retired to pursue personal interests.

8,565. Folwell Family
Papers. Ca. 1898-1921. 28 in.
Open. Unpublished guide.
University of Minnesota Libraries, University Archives.
Included in the correspondence, diaries, photos, memorabilia, and other papers of the Folwell family are personal letters of Mary H. Folwell (1865?-1946), daughter of first University president William Watts Folwell, in which she describes daily life primarily when she was in Cuba and Trinidad keeping house for her brother William Bainbridge Folwell while he was serving in the army, and her reminiscences of University faculty members. Also includes correspondence and a diary of Sarah (Heywood) Folwell (1838?-1931), the wife of William Watts Folwell.

8,566. Ford, Guy Stanton
Papers. 1885-1959. 205 in.
Open. Unpublished guide.
University of Minnesota Libraries, University Archives.
Correspondence, speeches, reports, subject files, biographical material, and publications of Ford, a University educator, editor, and administrator. Includes his correspondence with Dorothy Agnes Bennett, editor and art director of Golden Books, Simon & Schuster, and from 1937 to 1943 University Press sales manager, pertaining to her career and including recommendations and biographical material; with Helen B. Clapesattle, an editor for and later director of the University Press, concerning her book *The Doctors Mayo;* with Ada Louise (Comstock) Notestein, the University's first dean of women and later a Radcliffe College president, relating to professional matters and Comstock Hall, a campus dormitory; with Margaret (Snodgrass) Harding, director of the University Press from 1927 to 1953, pertaining to professional matters, the American Historical Association and the *American Historical Review,* and her husband's death; and with Patty W. Washington concerning the American Historical Association.

8,567. Ford, Roxana Ruth
Papers. 1939-75, nd. 16.5 in.
Open. Unpublished guide.
University of Minnesota Libraries, University Archives.
Papers of Ford (1910-), a University home economics educator and administrator, include personal papers; speeches; unpublished and published studies, including several done on home economics adult education and continuing education for home economists; files pertaining to national, state, and University committees and organizations, as well as national and Minnesota conferences; and articles and publications. Committees represented in the material include those of the American Home Economics Association, the American Vocational Association, the Committee on Research in Home Economics and its research section, and the Association of Land Grant Colleges and Universities. Organizations represented in the material include the AVA, Delta Kappa Gamma, Gamma Sigma Delta, the National Council on Family Relations, Omicron Nu, Phi Delta Kappa, Phi Upsilon Omicron, Pi Lambda Theta, and the Vocational Rehabilitation Administration. In 1947 Ford joined the University faculty; from 1959 to 1967 she was assistant director of home economics education, and from 1967 until her retirement eight years later, she served as associate director of the program.

8,568. Gale, Isabel
Papers. 1878-84. 2.5 in.
Open. Unpublished guide.
University of Minnesota Libraries, University Archives.
Scrapbook of Gale (ca. 1860-?), containing invitations, announcements, and programs of concerts and plays, provides information about social and cultural life in Minneapolis from 1878 to 1884.

8,569. Girls' Self-Government Association, Brewster Hall, School of Agriculture
Records. 1929-51. 3 in.
Open. Unpublished guide.

University of Minnesota Libraries, University Archives.
Secretaries' records of the Association, which was formed in 1929 by residents of a women's dormitory at the School, reflect changes in attitudes and activities of women students. The School was a subcollegiate program.

8,570. Girls' Swimming Club, School of Agriculture
Records. 1920-21. 1 folder.
Open. Unpublished guide.
University of Minnesota Libraries, University Archives.
Constitution, business minutes, and membership list of the Club, the members of which also belonged to the Girls' Athletic Club of the School of Agriculture, a subcollegiate program.

8,571. Grant, Avis (Winchell)
Papers. 1950. 1 folder.
Open. Unpublished guide.
University of Minnesota Libraries, University Archives.
Letter of Grant (1872-?), the daughter of University geology professor Newton Horace Winchell and wife of geologist and professor Ulysses Sherman Grant (1867-1932), includes reminiscences of her early family life in St. Anthony, MN, and her student years at the University. Avis Winchell met Ulysses Grant, one of her father's graduate students, while she was attending the University. They were married in 1891.

8,572. Grout, Ruth Ellen
Papers. Ca. 1893-1975. 16 in.
Open. Unpublished guide.
University of Minnesota Libraries, University Archives.
Correspondence, reports, photos, unpublished and published writings, and memorabilia of Grout (1901-), a University public health educator who also held health science administrative positions in government and the World Health Organization. Included in her professional papers are reports of the Cattaraugus County, NY, school health project, 1931-38; reports and work material of the Minnesota committee on local health units that spurred legislation for the local units, 1945-47; unpublished WHO documents, working material, and assignment items, 1953-71; records pertaining to US Agency for International Development assignments in Jamaica, West Indies, 1969-71; University school of public health material; Grout's PhD thesis; and a bibliography of her writings through 1973. Her personal papers contain correspondence; curriculum vitae; material about her retirement; photos; clippings; honors, citations, and awards; and family documents, including a copy of a talk given in 1893 at Dorchester Academy in McIntosh, GA, by Laura Miller Grout, Grout's mother, who was principal of the black Academy for one year. Also contains a booklet about Laura Miller Grout and her husband Edgar Homer Grout assembled from highlights of diaries kept by Laura Grout from 1929 to 1950. Ruth Grout graduated from Mount Holyoke College in 1923 and received a master's degree in public health in 1930 and a PhD from Yale University in 1939. After teaching high school biology in Connecticut for eight years, she served as director of the school health education study, a Milbank Memorial Fund project in Cattaraugus County, NY, from 1931 to 1938. From 1930 to 1942 she also was senior supervisor of health education for the Tennessee Valley Authority. Grout then became a consultant for the Office of Education in Washington, DC, serving until 1943. From 1943 to 1967 she was an associate, then full, professor in the University of Minnesota school of public health and college of education. During her years at the University, Grout intermittently served as consultant with WHO regional offices for Europe, Southeast Asia, Africa, and the eastern Mediterranean.

8,573. Hewer, Vivian Humphrey
Papers. Ca. 1949-73. 32 in.
Open. No guide.
University of Minnesota Libraries, University Archives.
Correspondence, professional papers, psychology course material, articles, and publications of Hewer (1908-), a University educator and counselor who did varied research in psychometric procedures, social status, attitudes toward women, and group and vocational counseling. Included are some of her papers about women, "Attitudes of Entering College Freshmen Toward the Occupational Motivations of Married Women" (1963) and "College Freshmen's Attitudes Toward Working Wives" (1964), as well as material about her involvement as a consultant and examiner for the North Central Association of Colleges and Secondary Schools. Hewer was born in Mora, MN, and received her BS in 1929, MS in 1941, and PhD in 1954 from the University. After teaching and counseling in various Minnesota schools, the US Employment Service, and the US Veterans Administration in St. Paul, she was appointed a University senior student counselor and instructor in 1949. She retired in 1973 as a professor of counseling psychology. Also a member of the Student Counseling Bureau, Hewer edited the Bureau's publication *Review* for 25 years.

8,574. Hirsch, Jean E.
Papers. Ca. 1914-60. 9 in.
Open. No guide.
University of Minnesota Libraries, University Archives.
Correspondence, sketches and illustrations, studies, photos, a scrapbook, and advertisement reprints of Hirsch (1893-1974), a medical illustrator and wife of Horace P. Fish. Includes her student biology notebook with the illustrations that prompted University medical school founder Richard Olding Beard to encourage Hirsch toward a career in medical illustration; correspondence between Hirsch and Edith Boyd, who was on the Child Research Council at the University of Colorado school of medicine, concerning Hirsch's illustrations for a book by Boyd and Richard Scammon entitled *Growth;* anatomical sketches; preliminary studies; photos; and reprints of a series of Northwestern National Life Insurance ads that Hirsch illustrated. Hirsch received her early training at the University and at Johns Hopkins University under Max Broedel. An assistant from 1914 to 1919 and then head of the Medical Art Shop until she retired in 1952, Hirsch also helped to found the National Association of Medical Illustrators.

8,575. Hobart, Inez M.
Papers. Ca. 1910-42. 4 folders.
Open. Unpublished guide.
University of Minnesota Libraries, University Archives.
A Minnesota nutrition specialist and associate professor of home economics at the University, Hobart (1885-) also worked with the University agricultural service from ca. 1923 to 1954 and served as an extension nutritionist in the 1930s for the Minnesota State Emergency Relief Administration. She played a major role both in nutrition research projects conducted by the SERA in cooperation with the agricultural extension service and in the organization of relief agencies throughout the state. Material dates largely from the depression years and includes items from scrapbooks used by extension nutritionists in their work on the state level. Also includes material relating to hot school lunches.

8,576. Home Economics Association, School of Agriculture
Records. 1910-20. 2 folders.
Open. Unpublished guide.
University of Minnesota Libraries, University Archives.
Constitution, minutes, secretary's records, and membership records of this social and educational organization, founded in 1910, the members of which were registered in the School's home economics department.

8,577. Hudson, Dorothy Rose
Papers. 1887-1908. 1 vol.
Open. Unpublished guide.
University of Minnesota Libraries, University Archives.
Scrapbook of Hudson (1887-) documents the first 21 years of her life.

8,578. Institute of Agriculture, Director's Office
Records. 1837-1969. 750 in. and 59 vols.
Open. Unpublished guide.
University of Minnesota Libraries, University Archives.
Departmental records, historical and WPA files, speeches, bound volumes, and awards of the Institute, which was established in 1871 as the Department of Agriculture. Scattered items about women's functions in the Institute include a list of names and hometowns of women who lived in the women's dormitory from 1916 until 1948; two folders pertaining to the history of coeducation at the School of Agriculture, a subcollegiate unit within the Institute, including correspondence, reports, and letters to the editors of local newspapers regarding women's admission to the School; records of the department of home economics from 1949 to 1954, containing correspondence about the appointment of a new department director and other matters; and records of the School of Agriculture's YWCA branch, including quarterly reports of the organization's activities and correspondence.

8,579. Iota Sigma Pi, Mercury Chapter
Records. 1922-51. 5 in.
Open. Unpublished guide.
University of Minnesota Libraries, University Archives.
Records of the University chapter of the national honor society for women in chemistry include correspondence, convention programs and reports, directories and membership lists, a history of the national and local groups, Iota Sigma Pi awards, and publications of the national council and society members. The local chapter was founded in 1923.

8,580. Jackson, Elizabeth
Papers. Ca. 1908-60. 160 in.
Open. No guide.
University of Minnesota Libraries, University Archives.
Papers of Jackson (1893-1968), an educator and University English professor, include correspondence; diaries; class and lecture notes, including those she took as a Radcliffe College student; poetry; pictures; and memorabilia. Born in Bridgewater, MA, Jackson received a BA in 1913, an MA in 1914, and a PhD two years later from Radcliffe. She came to the University in 1916 as an English instructor; she retired in 1961 as a full professor. In 1944 her book *The Faith and Fire Within Us* was published.

8,581. Julian, Florence J.
Papers. Ca. 1921-71. 13 in.
Open. No guide.
University of Minnesota Libraries, University Archives.
Reports and publications of Julian (1912-), a nurse, educator, and administrator, include annual reports and a history of the Variety Club Heart

Hospital, histories of other University hospitals, articles Julian wrote, and patient care guides. In 1944 Julian came to the University school of nursing as an instructor for cadets in a government-funded military nurses training program. One year later she became surgical supervisor and instructor at University Hospitals. She was appointed assistant director of nursing services in 1947, and she became director in 1953. From 1971 until she retired in 1974, Julian was associate administrator of the Hospitals.

8,582. Kallio, Anne
Papers. 1943. 1 folder.
Open. Unpublished guide.
University of Minnesota Libraries, University Archives.
Reports of Kallio (1891-1945), a University librarian, pertain to articles in Finnish-American newspapers; the reports were written for the US government.

8,583. Konopka, Gisela
Papers. 1945-75. 204 in. and 1 motion picture reel.
Access restricted. Preliminary guide.
University of Minnesota Libraries, University Archives.
Correspondence, speeches, manuscripts, and committee and conference files of Konopka (1910-), an educator and social worker, focus on her career after 1947 as a University professor of social work and pertain chiefly to her research on group work with children and adolescents, especially adolescent girls. Files include material on Big Sisters in Minneapolis and a committee evaluation of the organization's group work program; Camp Fire Girls in Minneapolis; group work with unmarried mothers; and the committee on the status of women. Born in Berlin, Konopka attended Hamburg University before coming to the US in 1941 as a WWII refugee. She received an MS at the University of Pittsburgh and then a PhD from Columbia University. From 1970 until her retirement in 1978 Konopka served as director of the Center for Youth Development and Research at the University, and she continues to serve as consultant for the National Youthworker Education Project in the Twin Cities.

8,584. Lake, Edith Janet
Papers. 1930-34. 1 in.
Open. Unpublished guide.
University of Minnesota Libraries, University Archives.
Scrapbook of Lake (1912?-), a University school of nursing student from 1931 to 1932, contains clippings about nursing, trends in health, and treatment of diseases as well as nursing student memorabilia. In 1934 Lake received a BS in public health nursing from the college of education.

8,585. Meredith Hall Self Government Association
Records. 1937-39. 1 folder.
Open. Unpublished guide.
University of Minnesota Libraries, University Archives.
Secretary's records of a women's dormitory organization reflect the interests and activities of undergraduate University women. Meredith Hall was originally called the College Girls Dormitory.

8,586. Methven, Mildred Louise
Papers. 1955. 1 folder.
Open. Unpublished guide.
University of Minnesota Libraries, University Archives.
Publication entitled "Bibliomania 1955" by Methven (1899-), a librarian, grew from a library training class she taught at the University of Dacca, East Pakistan, as a Fulbright lecturer in 1954 and 1955. Also includes a clipping concerning the library and library work at the Faribault School for the Blind. Born in Minneapolis, Methven received bachelors degrees from the University of Minnesota and from a New York state institution. She worked at the Faribault, MN, Public Library in 1925. In 1937 she became supervisor of institution libraries for the division of public institutions, state department of social security, in St. Paul, MN.

8,587. Minnesota Women's Center
Records. Ca. 1960-75. 465 in.
Access restricted. No guide.
University of Minnesota Libraries, University Archives.
Established in 1960 as the Planning and Counseling Center for Women, the Center continues to offer educational, personal, and career development counseling; referral and testing services; and information about women's legal rights and responsibilities. Minutes, including those of the Council for University Women's Progress; reports; membership files, including those of the Minnesota Plan: Continuing Education for Women with applications, questionnaires, and correspondence; departmental files; material pertaining to Minnesota Feminists, the women's liberation organization, and the Women Studies Students' Association, a group of women students who sought creation of a women studies program; and publications.

8,588. Moen, Blanche Elvina
Papers. Ca. 1949. 1 folder.
Open. Unpublished guide.
University of Minnesota Libraries, University Archives.
Report by Moen (1895-), a librarian, pertains to Swedish and Norwegian university libraries she visited in 1949. Moen was born in Devils Lake, ND, and after receiving her BA in 1916, she taught in North Dakota and Montana high schools for six years. In 1924 she became an assistant in the University Library reference department; she retired in 1961 as an assistant professor and chief reference librarian. With W. H. Russell and T. P. Flemming, she wrote *The Use of Books in Libraries* (Minneapolis: University of Minnesota, 1933), a syllabus for use in library instruction.

8,589. Moffet, Rebecca Virginia (Baker)
Papers. 1885-89. 1 folder.
Open. Unpublished guide.
University of Minnesota Libraries, University Archives.
Papers of Moffet (1868-?), a University student and member of the class of 1889, relate to student registration and her grades.

8,590. Mohl, Ruth
Papers. Ca. 1909-13. 1 folder.
Open. Unpublished guide.
University of Minnesota Libraries, University Archives.
Student memorabilia of Mohl (ca. 1888-?), a 1913 University graduate who was active in the student government association and was a member of various honorary societies.

8,591. Mudget, Helen Parker
Papers. Ca. 1940s-50s. 255 in.
Open. No guide.
University of Minnesota Libraries, University Archives.
Papers of Mudget (1900-62), an educator and historian, include an unpublished manuscript on the history of the Ojibwe Indians, with early drafts and photos; miscellaneous files pertaining to Indians; radio scripts of her "America Bound" series; and items and files about civil rights. Born in Lisbon, NH, Mudget received a BA from Wellesley College in 1921 and an MA from the University of Minnesota in 1923. She also studied at the University of London and the London School of Economics. In 1928 she was appointed instructor in economic history, European civilization, and current events in the University's general extension division. In the 1940s she edited the *Reading for Wartime* bulletins, which contained selected book reviews and digests of significant publications focusing on various important issues, interpretations of history, current events, and literature. In 1944 Mudget wrote *Democracy for All*, a study guide on racial and cultural groups and human rights. In her "America Bound" radio broadcasts in 1950 and 1951, she continued to pursue those topics. During WWII she helped to found the St. Paul Council of Human Relations and served as a board member. From 1953 to 1955 she was chief coordinator for a series of conferences on Indian affairs conducted by the Center for Continuation Study at the University.

8,592. Museum of Natural History
Records. 1872-1947. 337 in.
Access restricted. Unpublished guide.
University of Minnesota Libraries, University Archives.
Records of the Museum contain office and general correspondence, diaries, notebooks, manuscripts, the Thomas Sadler Roberts papers, and the Minnesota Geological and Natural History Survey. Also included is correspondence of botanist Olga Lakela pertaining to her career from ca. 1922 to 1947. Born in Finland, Lakela was a member of the biology department at the University Duluth campus until she retired in 1958.

8,593. Oerting, Ella K. S.
Papers. 1918-58. 1.5 in.
Open. Unpublished guide.
University of Minnesota Libraries, University Archives.
Master's thesis and other papers of Oerting (1890-1959) document her educational preparation and her University teaching career in rhetoric. Raised in St. Paul, MN, Oerting received a BA in 1921 from the University of Minnesota and taught at Brainerd Senior High School for 11 years before taking positions at rural Minnesota schools. In 1934 she received a master of philosophy degree through the speech department at the University of Wisconsin; her thesis examined "diagnostic and remedial uses of auditorium work for personality training in the junior high school." She joined the University of Minnesota's school of agriculture faculty as an instructor of rhetoric in 1936 and taught there until her retirement in 1958.

8,594. Office of the Dean of Women
Records. 1909-49. 6 in.
Open. Unpublished guide.
University of Minnesota Libraries, University Archives.
Reports and correspondence of the Office, established in 1906 to advise and befriend all University women, pertain primarily to the period from 1923 to 1949 when Anne Dudley Blitz was dean of women. Includes constitutions and correspondence of the All-University Student Council; constitution, bylaws, and correspondence of the National and Minnesota Associations of Deans of Women; AAUW correspondence; material about women and the WWII war effort; and bylaws and policy items of the campus YWCA advisory board. In 1949 the functions of the Office were transferred to that of the dean of students.

8,595. Oldenburg, Margaret Elizabeth
Papers. Ca. 1938-70. 9 in.
Open. No guide.
University of Minnesota Libraries, University Archives.
Correspondence, reports, photos, and memorabilia of Oldenburg (1892-1972), a teacher, botanist, and University librarian who resigned her cataloging job in 1939 to travel extensively, especially in the Canadian Arctic, and collect specimens for the University botany department. Includes accounts of her trips in an unpublished manuscript "Trips to the North, 1939-1952," itineraries, plant collection

numbers, maps, annual letters and reports, and photos from her expeditions. Oldenburg was born in Carlton, MN; she earned a BA in 1915 from Vassar College and received BS degrees in education in 1921 and library science in 1929 from the University. She taught in various Minnesota schools from 1918 to 1928, interrupted only when she held a Northfield, MA, teaching position in 1924 and 1925. She worked at the University library from 1929 to 1939.

8,596. Phelps, Ethel Lowerre
Papers. 1916-55. 1 folder.
Open. Unpublished guide.
University of Minnesota Libraries, University Archives.
Phelps (1888-1968) was a University educator and home economics professor who made contributions to research in the clothing and textiles fields. Publications, including "Outline of Clothing Projects for Girls Clubs" by Phelps and Josephine T. Berry (1916) and "Appraisals of Trends in Home Economics Research" presented at the 1937 Kansas City meeting of the American Home Economics Association research department; a bibliography of Phelps's publications complete through 1954; and professional activities records. Born in Newark, NJ, Phelps received a BS in 1915 from Cornell University and an MS from the University of Minnesota. She was a textiles and clothing instructor in the home economics division as a graduate student and continued to teach at Minnesota after she earned her degree. Phelps completed additional graduate work at Columbia and Yale. She retired in 1955 as a full professor. Her research focused upon the effects of laundering on fabrics, the wearing qualities of chemically manufactured fibers, and the characteristics of yarn and fabrics made of flax produced by the Minnesota method from seed flax straw.

8,597. Phelps, Ruth Shepard
Papers. 1905-28. 5 in.
Open. Unpublished guide.
University of Minnesota Libraries, University Archives.
Material assembled by Phelps (1876-1949), a romance languages professor, focuses on the works of Arthur Upson, a poet and English literature instructor at the University whose death in 1908 led Phelps to donate funds for an Arthur Upson Room in the University Library. Includes Upson's translation of *Die Heilige Elisabeth,* reviews of his works, articles and poems, tributes at the time of his death, statements for books Phelps purchased for the Upson Room from 1921 to 1925, and several of her personal bills. Phelps was born in Aurora, IL, and educated in Minneapolis; she received a bachelor of literature degree from Smith College in 1899 and an MA in 1910 from Columbia University before receiving a PhD in 1924 from the University of Chicago. At the University of Minnesota she was appointed instructor in French in 1910 and instructor in romance languages in 1912; later she became a professor in the romance languages department. In 1929 she resigned to marry University French professor Paul Morand, and she lived in France until her death. Phelps wrote many poems and essays and collaborated with her husband on prose and poetry, which was published in France.

8,598. Practical Nurse's and Home Management Club, School of Agriculture
Records. 1949-58. 2 in.
Open. Unpublished guide.
University of Minnesota Libraries, University Archives.
Constitution, minutes, membership records, and scrapbooks of the Club, established in 1949 and originally called the Practical Nurse's Club. The group prepared young women to become practical nurses and homemakers to supplement professional nursing and home care in the rural community and in rural health programs.

8,599. Reid, Ruth Evangeline LaPlant
Papers. 1911-14. 1 folder.
Open. Unpublished guide.
University of Minnesota Libraries, University Archives.
Photos and personal souvenirs of Reid (ca. 1893-), a University student and member of the class of 1914, include snapshots of the first University geology tour in 1913, the 1911 May Fete, the 1913 University circus, and the first extension tour of the European Club in 1913. Also includes program notes.

8,600. Richards, Carmen (Nelson)
Papers. 1940-61. 2 folders.
Open. Unpublished guide.
University of Minnesota Libraries, University Archives.
An author, editor, and active University alumni club member, Richards (1891?-) helped prepare several successful University publications. Questionnaires, autobiographies, and correspondence from individuals represented in *Minnesota Writers* (1945), a collection of autobiographical stories by Minnesota prose writers, among them Elizabeth Mary Atkins, Mary Ellen Chase, and Ina Ten Eyck Firkins, which was coedited by Richards. Also includes similar material pertaining to Richards's book *Minnesota Writers* (1961), which includes information about Anne Cawley Boardman, Carol Ryrie Brink, Joy Chute, Marchette Chute, Mary Chute Smith, Florence Page Jacques, and Ruth Sawtell Wallis. After she graduated from the University in 1913, Richards spent five years teaching in various Minnesota towns; from 1928 to 1929 she taught in Palmetta, FL, and then returned to Minneapolis where she taught for 30 years. In 1945 she became active in the Minnesota Alumni Club, later receiving its 1967 alumni service award. Richards edited *The Moccasin,* a University poetry magazine, and *Minnesota Skyline* and wrote *Death Stalks the Philippine Wilds* (1951). Several of her poems were published in magazines and anthologies.

8,601. Rietz, Dorothy
Papers. 1943. 1 folder.
Open. Unpublished guide.
University of Minnesota Libraries, University Archives.
A University student's paper for an academic course pertains to student life on campus in the 1890s.

8,602. Robinson, Amy Josephine Cook
Papers. Ca. 1904. 1 folder.
Open. Unpublished guide.
University of Minnesota Libraries, University Archives.
Student sketches drawn by Robinson (ca. 1882-?), a 1904 University graduate, include those of Richard Burton and Burton Hall, which was then the University library; Sid, the rat man; Cyrus Northrop; Oscar Firkins; Charles Savage; Jabez Brooks; Francis Potter, and Matilda Wilkin.

8,603. Rose, Caroline (Baer)
Papers. Ca. 1939-75. 126 in.
Access restricted. No guide.
University of Minnesota Libraries, University Archives.
Personal and professional papers; course notes; University department of sociology records; material by and about women, including clippings, bibliographies, and articles; and publications of Rose (1913-75), an educator, sociologist, and feminist; most of the collection relates to the period just before her death. Born in Wheeling, WV, she earned a BA from West Virginia University in 1935, an MA from the University of Chicago in 1943, and completed most of her work for a PhD at Chicago. Rose joined the University sociology department faculty in 1952. She and her husband Arnold M. Rose, who was also a sociologist and University professor, worked with Swedish sociologist Gunnar Myrdal on *An American Dilemma: The Negro Problem and Modern Democracy* (1944). She also contributed to her husband's work, and wrote numerous papers, articles, and books pertaining to labor, minority problems, and women; her last project was an unfinished book on women. Rose was active in Minnesota Democratic-Farmer-Labor politics for 25 years. She also was a member of the Council for University Women's Progress and served as chairwoman of the University senate judicial committee.

8,604. Rozentāls, Magdalēna
Collection. 1955-62. 3 in.
Open. Unpublished guide.
University of Minnesota Libraries, University Archives.
Latvian journals and articles collected by Rozentāls (1915-), a University librarian, provide information about Latvian female artists Anna Šmits, a University instructor of weaving; Melita Lepko-Kolendro, a St. Paul graphic artist and painter; and Austra Ogulis, of Minneapolis. Other articles pertain to Latvian folksongs and folk poetry. Also included are several editions of the *Bibliography of Latvian Publications Outside Latvia, 1955* (Washington, DC, 1957), which was coedited by Rozentāls. Rozentāls was born in Liepaja, Latvia, and received a BA in 1940 from the University of Latvia at Riga in languages and history. She taught school for one year and then worked at the Jelgava historical museum until 1945. At that time she and her family fled to Germany, where for four years she taught school in a displaced persons camp before coming to the US. In 1954 she received a master of library science degree from Columbia University and came to the University of Minnesota as a junior librarian in the circulation department. From 1959 to 1963 Rozentāls worked in the art library and from 1964 until her retirement in 1977 she was a bibliographer in the acquisitions department.

8,605. Runyon, Florabell
Papers. 1924-28. 1 folder.
Open. Unpublished guide.
University of Minnesota Libraries, University Archives.
High school and college memorabilia of Runyon (ca. 1906-), a 1928 University graduate who also received a BS in library instruction in 1929, are mounted into a Minneapolis telephone directory. Includes letters, clippings, and programs of city and University events and photos of campus buildings.

8,606. Sanford, Maria Louise
Papers. 1869-1922. 2 in.
Open. Unpublished guide.
University of Minnesota Libraries, University Archives.
[Miss] Sanford (1836-1920) was a University professor of rhetoric and elocution. Correspondence, including a letter to the school directors of Chester County, PA, in ca. 1869 defending Sanford's right to be elected and commissioned county school superintendent; a speech; a 1922 tribute given in her honor at a Mankato, MN, DAR meeting; and monographs used by her students in an art lecture course.

8,607. School of Agriculture
Records. 1858-1939. 13 in.
Access restricted. Unpublished guide.
University of Minnesota Libraries, University Archives.
Records of the School, founded in 1888, contain correspondence, petitions and resolutions about the introduction of coeducation at the School, items

pertaining to establishment of a state agricultural college, histories of University agriculture, biographical sketches of men associated with the School, and publications. Also includes the Juniata Shepperd collection, which documents the early development of University home economics. Juniata L. Shepperd established the department of domestic science in ca. 1906. Her papers contain material she compiled, including historical sketches; a manuscript about home economics, both collegiate and subcollegiate, at the University farm from 1894 to 1914; an early history of the agricultural sorority Phi Upsilon Omicron; plans for a home economics building; and letters, photos, and several personal tributes, especially from former students. Born in Chariton, IA, Shepperd earned a BA at Iowa's Oskaloosa College, later called Drake University, in 1881 and an AM degree at the University of Minnesota in 1896 with one year of special work in food chemistry. She was appointed instructor of cooking in 1897 and remained on the regular faculty until 1914, when she became a fieldworker for the agricultural extension division. She retired in 1923.

8,608. School of Agriculture Estelle Literary Society
Records. 1917-22. 1 folder.
Open. Unpublished guide.
University of Minnesota Libraries, University Archives.
Minutes and membership records of the Society, founded in 1917 to train its members in parliamentary procedure, public speaking, and debate. Named for Estelle Cook, a University public speaking instructor, the Society was the only all-female literary group on campus at that time.

8,609. School of Chemistry
Records. 1894-1942. 108.5 in.
Access restricted. Unpublished guide.
University of Minnesota Libraries, University Archives.
Established in 1896 as part of the college of science, literature, and the arts, the School was organized as an independent unit in 1903. Correspondence; enrollment statistics for the School, 1923-35, and for the Institute of Technology, 1935-42; employment statistics; administrative and personnel records for IT; material pertaining to the chemistry show and Engineers Day; and scattered items, including correspondence, by and about University chemistry professor Lillian Cohen. Cohen was born in Minneapolis, graduated in 1900 from the University, and in 1902 began her teaching career as an assistant in chemistry; she received a PhD in 1913. She retired from the faculty in 1946 as an associate professor of chemistry.

8,610. School of Nursing
Records. Ca. 1920-69. 197 in.
Access restricted. Partial guide.
University of Minnesota Libraries, University Archives.
Minutes, reports, correspondence, and scrapbooks of the School, established in 1909 as the School of Nurses. Includes minutes of the faculty, student scholastic standing and student's work committees, and the Association of Collegiate Schools of Nursing; Minnesota board of nursing reports; and reports to and departmental correspondence of the Minnesota Accredited Schools of Nursing. Contains correspondence of School administrators Louise Mathilde Powell, superintendent and then director from 1910 to 1924; Marion Lydia Vannier, director from 1924 to 1930; Katherine (Densford) Dreeves, director from 1930 to 1959; and Edna Lillian Fritz, director from 1959 to 1970. Collection also contains material of such state and national nursing organizations as the Minnesota League of Nursing Service, American Nurses' Association, National Council of Nurses, and National Planning Commission for War Service.

8,611. Scott, Carlyle McRoberts
Papers. 1917-31. 45 in.
Open. Preliminary guide.
University of Minnesota Libraries, University Archives.
Scott was professor and chairman of the University music department for 38 years; in 1919 his wife Verna (Golden) Scott (1876-1964) established the University Artist's Course, an annual series of campus concerts by musicians from around the world. Material pertains almost entirely to the Artist's Course and includes financial records, correspondence of Verna Scott about arrangements for musicians' appearances, programs and announcements, and photos of artists. Verna Scott was born in River Falls, WI, and educated in the Minneapolis public schools. From 1894 to 1898 she studied violin at and then graduated from the Leipzig Conservatorium of Music; there she met Carlyle Scott, whom she married in 1902 after returning to Minneapolis. She managed the Artist's Course until 1944 and served as Minnesota orchestra manager from 1930 to 1938.

8,612. Sigma Alpha Iota, Sigma Sigma Chapter
Records. 1926-53. 10 in.
Open. Unpublished guide.
University of Minnesota Libraries, University Archives.
Records of the University chapter of this women's professional music fraternity, established on campus in 1926, contain a constitution; bylaws; minutes; president's informal notes from business meetings; secretary's and treasurer's reports; calendar of meetings; correspondence, including letters to the association's regional president; material about national conventions and the SAI foundation; manuscripts for *Pan Pipes,* the fraternity's official magazine; directory of members; alumnae news letters; and publications.

8,613. Sikes, George Cushing, and Sikes, Madeleine Wallin
Papers. 1886-1952. 1 in.
Open. Unpublished guide.
University of Minnesota Libraries, University Archives.
Correspondence and photos of Madeleine Sikes (1868-1955), a university graduate, pertain to her life as a student in the 1890s and include her letters to the class of 1892 alumnae organization about 1941 and 1942 class reunions. She married George Cushing Sikes (1868-1928), a fellow University student and graduate, in 1897.

8,614. Smith, Audrey Nina
Papers. 1911. 2 in.
Open. Unpublished guide.
University of Minnesota Libraries, University Archives.
Scrapbook of Smith (ca. 1887-), a University student and member of the class of 1909, contains photos, drawings, clippings, and programs of the 1911 Minnesota May Fete, a social event held for all University faculty and students. Smith was the Fete business secretary.

8,615. Society of Minnesota Dames
Records. 1915-55. 32 in.
Open. No guide.
University of Minnesota Libraries, University Archives.
Established in 1915, the Society promoted social fellowship among wives of all University students. Minutes, treasurers' reports, financial records, scrapbooks, and yearbooks of the National Association of University Dames containing annual reports of each chapter. Also includes a survey from ca. 1933-34 of housing conditions of married students, in which questions were asked of residents in south, southeast, and north Minneapolis and in St. Anthony Park in St. Paul, MN.

8,616. Student Government Association
Records. 1909-30. 4 in.
Open. Unpublished guide.
University of Minnesota Libraries, University Archives.
The Association, which was formed in 1906 for all University women, assumed responsibility for Alice Shevlin Hall, the women's union at that time; it made and enforced the rules for students using the Hall and controlled social functions held in the building. Minutes, with a summary of the 1915 Shevlin Hall standing rules; treasurer's accounts; and a guest book. The Association was succeeded in 1913 by the Women's Self-Government Association.

8,617. Swenson, Lillian Bessie (Marvin)
Papers. 1894-1940. 1 folder.
Open. Unpublished guide.
University of Minnesota Libraries, University Archives.
Papers of Swenson (1876-1961), an 1898 University graduate, include letters of recommendation and items from Maria Sanford and Grace [Mrs. Guy Stanton] Ford; an account book of the Society for the Pro-mulgation of the Education of Aspiring Females; class themes; a necrology of classmate Harriet E. Helliwell, written by Swenson, with samples of Helliwell's poetry; and a notebook concerning student days. Swenson taught history in Minneapolis high schools. Her husband David F. Swenson (?-1940), whom she met while they were University students, became a University philosophy professor. She edited her husband's book *Kierkegaardian Philosophy in the Faith of a Scholar* (Philadelphia: Westminster Press, 1949), and with him translated the Kierkegaardian writings published as *Edifying Discourses, A Selection* (New York: Harper, 1958).

8,618. Templin, Mildred Clara
Papers. Ca. 1947-70. 90 in.
Open. No guide.
University of Minnesota Libraries, University Archives.
Professional correspondence, thesis material, and scientific publications of Templin (1913-), an educator whose career at the University Institute of Child Development from 1943 to 1976 was devoted to teaching and conducting research in speech, language, and thought development in both hearing and deaf children. Contains correspondence pertaining to the Institute and between Templin and contributors to *Monographs of the Society for Research in Child Development,* for which she became editor in 1964, as well as her PhD thesis material, including written explanations of Piaget questions from Deutsche tests by hearing and defective hearing samples, sample summary data, test samples, and analyses. Templin was born in Milwaukee and received her BA in 1936 and MA in 1937 from the University of Wisconsin. In 1947 she earned a PhD at the University of Minnesota.

8,619. Thompson, Faith
Papers. 1955-61, nd. 2 in.
Open. Unpublished guide.
University of Minnesota Libraries, University Archives.
A history professor at the University from 1923 to 1961, Thompson (1893-1961) became recognized as an international authority on English constitutional and legal history, especially the Magna Carta. General correspondence; notes on British antiquaries, statutes, and court cases; clippings on George Bernard Shaw; and a copy of the Magna Carta and other documents. Among her books published by the University Press were *Magna Carta: Its Role in the Making of the English Constitution* (1948) and *Short History of Parliament, 1295-1642* (1953).

8,620. Tilden, Josephine Elizabeth
Papers. 1927. 1 folder.
Open. Unpublished guide.
University of Minnesota Libraries, University Archives.
Correspondence of Tilden (1869-1957), an educator and botanist, pertains to an article in *Popular Science*. Just after receiving an MS in 1896, Tilden became a member of the University botany department; she remained there until her retirement in 1937. She wrote several books on the subject of algae, her special field.

8,621. Training Course in Kenny Technique
Records. 1941-48. 26.5 in.
Access restricted. Unpublished guide.
University of Minnesota Libraries, University Archives.
Sister Elizabeth Kenny was internationally known for her methods of treating poliomyelitis; the records deal with her relationship to the University and courses begun there in 1941 to train health professionals in the Kenny technique. Card index, which provides an incomplete list of names of individuals who attended or graduated from the course; correspondence; course material; and items about the Kenny Institute, the Gillette State Hospital for Crippled Children, the Institute of International Education, the National Foundation for Infantile Paralysis, and epidemics in Little Rock, AR, Los Angeles, and Memphis. The collection reflects both the enthusiasm of those who accepted the Kenny method and the opposition of those who did not.

8,622. University Gallery
Records. 1935-50. 17 in.
Open. Unpublished guide.
University of Minnesota Libraries, University Archives.
The Gallery was established in 1933 to present art exhibitions, develop a permanent University collection, and provide rental service of original art works for students, staff, and faculty; it also now organizes teaching exhibitions for classes in many University departments. Routine departmental files, consisting of minutes, reports, and correspondence, of Gallery curator Ruth Lawrence; WPA files; and Faculty Women's Club material, including minutes, reports, and correspondence, 1938-41, about the new Campus Club and the privileges provided for women in the Club. Ruth Lawrence began her University career in 1932, became gallery curator in 1934, and directed its operations until her retirement in 1957.

8,623. Wilkin, Matilda Jane Campbell
Papers. 1861-1943. 23.5 in.
Open. Unpublished guide.
University of Minnesota Libraries, University Archives.
Papers of Wilkin (1846-1943), a University English and German professor, include correspondence; diaries and personal memoirs; an account book; her school themes while a student; volumes of German and English literature class notes, records, and outlines; students' papers; manuscripts of poems, speeches, and articles; clippings about Wilkin's death; and diplomas. She was born in Maine, graduated from the University of Minnesota with the class of 1877, and that same year was appointed to the University staff as instructor in Latin and German, thus becoming one of the first women teachers at the University. In 1890 she received a master of literature degree and was appointed assistant professor of English and German. Wilkin retired in 1911.

8,624. Women's Liberation
Records. Ca. 1970-73. 7 in.
Open. No guide.
University of Minnesota Libraries, University Archives.
Posters, publicity newsletters, and clippings of a student-feminist organization, which was formed in 1970 and actively studied political and social issues related to women's rights. Includes material about a proposed University women studies department, gay liberation, abortion, the Vietnam War, and child care and announcements and publicity about films, courses, conferences, and lectures by and pertaining to women. The organization disbanded in 1973.

8,625. Women's Self-Government Association
Records. 1924-34. 3 in.
Open. Unpublished guide.
University of Minnesota Libraries, University Archives.
Scrapbook contains photos, clippings, and programs of the Association, a voluntary University group established in 1913 that worked in close cooperation with the dean of women. The Association operated a bookstore to provide scholarship funds for women students; organized social functions for women who did not participate in sororities; and supervised an annual series of vocational conferences for women. Senior advisors from the Association helped welcome incoming women students to campus life.

8,626. Wood, F. John
Papers. 1955-76. 12 in.
Open. Unpublished guide.
University of Minnesota Libraries, University Archives.
Included in material of Wood, a zoological researcher on woodcocks in the US, is his correspondence with zoologist Monica Shorten Viscoso pertaining to her 1974 review of world literature on the European woodcock, woodcock banding in England, her participation in the 1974 Athens, GA, woodcock workshops, establishment of the European Woodcock Research Group in 1975, and personal matters. Viscoso was born in Leadenham, Lincolnshire, England; she received a first class honors degree in zoology from Somerville College at Oxford and has held a number of research positions.

8,627. Young Women's Christian Association
Records. Ca. 1893-1966. 386 in.
Open. No guide.
University of Minnesota Libraries, University Archives.
Annual reports, minute and account books, ledgers, correspondence, and scrapbooks of the University campus YWCA, founded in 1891 to give college women intellectual help, social enjoyment, personal friendship, and spiritual inspiration.

8,628. Young Women's Christian Association, St. Paul Campus
Records. 1938-47. 7 in.
Open. Unpublished guide.
University of Minnesota Libraries, University Archives.
Scrapbooks contain material relating to personnel activities, promotional plans, and educational and recreational programs of the YWCA, the purpose of which was to help students combine cultural and religious values and apply Christian faith and ideals to everyday living. In 1955 the St. Paul campus and Minneapolis campus YWCAs merged.

8,629. Young Women's Christian Association, School of Agriculture
Records. 1913-50. 2 in.
Open. Unpublished guide.
University of Minnesota Libraries, University Archives.
Established in 1897, the YWCA worked to develop the Christian character of students enrolled in the School and to promote religious life in the institution. Minutes and membership records exist for the years up to 1920 and after 1943; Bible study records exist only for the period before 1920.

8,630. Abortion Rights Council
Records. 1967-73. 2 ft.
Open. No guide.
University of Minnesota, Social Welfare History Archives.
Minutes, correspondence, texts of testimony given before legislative committees, publicity releases, newsletters, clippings, and other records of the Council, which was formed in 1966 to seek changes in Minnesota abortion legislation and to further public education on abortion. Also includes material regarding the Dr. Jane Hodgson Legal Defense Fund, which was formed to support a Minnesota physician who was convicted of performing an abortion. Originally called the Minnesota Council for the Legal Termination of Pregnancy, Inc., the organization later was known as Minnesota Organization for the Repeal of Abortion Laws (MORAL).

8,631. American Immigration and Citizenship Conference
Records. 1932-68. 26 ft.
Open. Unpublished guide.
University of Minnesota, Social Welfare History Archives.
Founded in 1960 through the merger of the six-year-old American Immigration Conference and the National Council on Naturalization and Citizenship, which was established in 1930, the AICC is a clearinghouse for information and a coordinator for activities of nonprofit, nonpolitical agencies involved with immigration and naturalization. Minutes of board and committee meetings, correspondence, items used to prepare bibliographies and educational material, conference programs and proceedings, newsletters, and reference information files of the AICC document efforts of the group and its predecessors to monitor and influence government immigration and naturalization policy, particularly the groups' work to alter the national origins quota system and to liberalize other regulations concerning admission of refugees. Also contains records pertaining to the agencies' efforts to assist in the integration of recent immigrants into American society. AICC records reflect the work of such member organizations as the YWCA and the National Council of Jewish Women, New York section. Ruth Z. Murphy was the executive director of the AICC and of its predecessor groups; one inch of her personal papers is included in the collection.

8,632. American Public Welfare Association
Records. 1940-67. 23 ft.
Open. No guide.
University of Minnesota, Social Welfare History Archives.
Founded in 1930, the Chicago-based APWA seeks to monitor, analyze, and influence the formulation and implementation of national and state public welfare policy. Correspondence, speeches, conference proceedings, working papers, and reports, predominantly from the group's Washington, DC, office, include records regarding the Advisory Council on Public Welfare, on which the APWA was represented, and APWA regional conferences from 1953 to 1961 at which many speeches were given by women welfare administrators and workers. The work of Loula Dunn, director of the Association; Elizabeth Wickenden and Marie Lane, APWA representatives in Washington; and Ellen Winston, North Carolina state commissioner of public welfare, is reflected in the records. The collection contains files from two APWA-sponsored studies of the Aid to Dependent Children program, the findings of which were published as *Future Citizens All* (1952) and *An American Dependency Challenge* (1963).

8,633. American Social Health Association
Records. 1900-75. 100 ft.
Partially restricted. Unpublished guide.

University of Minnesota, Social Welfare History Archives.
Founded in 1913 through the merger of the American Vigilance Association and the Federation for Sex Hygiene, the Association seeks the prevention and control of venereal disease and commercialized prostitution; promotes family life education in schools; publishes or has published the *Journal of Social Hygiene, Social Hygiene Papers,* and topical pamphlets; and is involved in drug abuse programs and other projects. Annual reports, board of directors minutes, financial and committee records, correspondence, field and survey reports, educational units, statistical data, publications manuscripts, radio and television scripts, publicity material, photos, scrapbooks, clippings, posters, and other items document the work of the Association and its employees, including Mabel Grier Lesher, educational consultant; Katherine Rahl, liaison with women's branches of the armed services; Eleanor Shenehon, head of the Association's Washington office and, in 1952, acting director of the Association; Esther Emerson Sweeney, director of the community services division; Josephine Tuller, director of the international division; and Jean Pinney, editor of *Journal of Social Hygiene.*

Initially called the American Social Hygiene Association, the Association assumed its current title in 1960. Annual reports and pamphlets provide information about the American Society for Sanitary and Moral Prophylaxis, the American Federation of Sex Hygiene, the American Purity Alliance, the American Vigilance Association, and other early groups that became a part of the Association. Correspondence files include exchanges with military officials concerning prostitution and the incidence of venereal disease around military bases and the distribution of Association publications to enlisted men. Copies of model laws and court decisions provide information about the Association's work for adoption and enforcement of laws on the age of consent, contraceptives, curfews, dance marathons, massage parlors, required premarital and prenatal venereal disease examinations, and other subjects. Public information activity files include records of special projects, chiefly during the 1940s, designed to educate Negroes and industrial workers about the dangers of venereal disease. Records on Association research projects include material about several studies of adolescent behavior during the 1950s. The largest of these studies, directed by Celia Deschin, surveyed teenagers who came to New York City public health clinics for treatment of possible venereal disease infection. Access to reports on studies from 1919 to 1951 concerning the prevalence of venereal disease, medical treatment and control programs, enforcement of vice laws, and the extent of commercialized prostitution in various US cities is restricted. The Association's records include correspondence and other items illustrating its relationship with the GFWC, the National Council of Women, the national YWCA, Planned Parenthood of America, the UN, the International Union against the Venereal Diseases, International Red Cross, the International Bureau for the Suppression of Traffic in Persons, and other groups.

8,634. Association for Voluntary Sterilization
Records. 1929-64. 6 ft.
Partially restricted. Unpublished guide.
University of Minnesota, Social Welfare History Archives.
Founded in 1937 as the Sterilization League of New Jersey, the Association evolved from a group primarily interested in advocacy of compulsory sterilization for persons with mental and physical handicaps to one supporting voluntary sterilization as a legitimate birth control technique. Minutes, financial records, correspondence, statistical reports, and clippings document the group's sponsorship of research into the medical, legal, and socioeconomic aspects of sterilization; its effort to disseminate information to doctors, social workers, and the public; and to help persons seeking sterilizations by providing referrals to cooperating doctors and clinics and financial assistance through a revolving loan fund. The changing emphasis of the group is illustrated by changes in its name; in 1943 it became a nationwide organization called the Sterilization League for Human Betterment. Later the name was changed to Birthright, Inc.; Human Betterment Association of America; Human Betterment Association for Voluntary Sterilization; and, in 1964, the Association for Voluntary Sterilization. The group's records include material concerning annual compilations of statistics, 1932-61, on sterilizations performed under state laws. The information generally is tabulated by state, sex, and reason for sterilization of the subject. Attitudes toward sterilization, particularly the opposition of the Roman Catholic church, are reflected throughout the records. Persons represented most prominently in the collection are Marion Norton Olden, a founder of the Sterilization League of New Jersey and the central figure in the organization until 1948; Robert Latou Dickinson, a gynecologist and educator who was chairman of the Association's medical and scientific committee; and H. Curtis Wood, Jr., an obstetrician and gynecologist who was the Association's president from 1945 to 1961 and its medical consultant from 1961 to 1973. Other individuals and groups represented in the records are Irene Headley Armes, Clarence J. Gamble, Ezra S. Gosney, Alan F. Guttmacher, Mabel Law, Margaret Sanger, the American Institute of Family Relations, the Human Betterment Foundation, and the Planned Parenthood Federation of America.

The Archives also holds a 120-foot supplement covering the period 1944-76. Correspondence, case files, photos, tape recordings, articles, and clippings include information about the group's international program to promote recognition and use of surgical contraception as a birth control method. The case files, access to which is restricted, concern couples who sought referrals or financial assistance for sterilization procedures.

8,635. Association of Junior Leagues of America
Records. 1922-56. 36 ft.
Open. Unpublished guide.
University of Minnesota, Social Welfare History Archives.
Junior Leagues provide volunteer service opportunities for women between the ages of 18 and 45 in cities throughout the United States, Canada, and Mexico. The Association, founded in 1922, helps member leagues to understand their communities and to promote volunteer service in civic activities. The collection comprises files on member leagues in 182 cities and contains correspondence, field visit reports, financial reports, completed questionnaires, training course outlines, material submitted for the Association's magazine, and newspaper clippings. Records describe efforts to place volunteers in existing health, welfare, cultural, and recreational agencies and to initiate and support new projects, such as well-baby clinics, to satisfy unmet community needs. Also documents other areas of leagues' activities, including children's entertainment, civil defense, occupational and physical therapy, and support of settlement houses. Other topics reflected in the collection are birth control, race relations, domestic effects of WWII, the American Women's Volunteer Service Association, the Girl Scouts of America, and the LWV.

A two-foot supplement contains minutes and papers from national board meetings from 1942 to 1969.

8,636. Bartlett, Harriett M.
Papers. 1918-76. 3 ft.
Open. Unpublished guide.
University of Minnesota, Social Welfare History Archives.
A medical social worker and educator, Bartlett (1897-) was associated with the social service department of the Massachusetts General Hospital in Boston from 1921 through 1945 and served as president of the American Association of Medical Social Workers from 1942 to 1944. Correspondence, minutes and reports of committees on which she served, surveys of hospital social service departments, teaching material, and copies of her publications and background papers date primarily from 1935 to 1960 and reflect her work in national social work organizations. Included are minutes, correspondence, and reports of committees of the American Association of Medical Social Workers and its successor, the medical social work section of the National Association of Social Workers. Also included are papers pertaining to visits Bartlett made to 13 medical schools from 1944 to 1947 to observe the teaching of social and environmental factors in medicine and surveys she conducted from 1936 to 1942 in the social service departments of five hospitals. Correspondence and other papers relate to advisory committees of the US Children's Bureau and to courses Bartlett taught at the universities of Denver, Illinois, Minnesota, and Southern California and at Harvard University and Simmons College.

8,637. Benjamin, Paul Lyman
Papers. 1914-71. 2.5 ft.
Open. Unpublished guide.
University of Minnesota, Social Welfare History Archives.
Correspondence, speeches, articles, reports, poems, and clippings of Benjamin (1886-), a social work executive who served as president of the American Association of Social Workers from 1946 to 1947. Benjamin's articles, speeches and reports discuss such issues as the family, day care, foster homes, illegitimacy, sex education, and sexual behavior. Benjamin was an officer of the Indianapolis Family Welfare Society from 1922 to 1924; of the Louisville Family Service Organization from 1925 to 1930; of the Social Hygiene Society in Washington, DC, from 1931 to 1932; of the Buffalo, NY, Council of Social Agencies from 1932 to 1943; of the Public Charities Association of Pennsylvania from 1943 to 1947; and of the Related Activities Council in Schenectady, NY, beginning in 1947.

8,638. Bernhagen, Beatrice
Papers. 1937-67. 1.5 ft.
Open. Unpublished guide.
University of Minnesota, Social Welfare History Archives.
Bernhagen (1910-67), a Minnesota social work practitioner and educator, was director of casework services for the Ramsey County Public Welfare Department from 1950 to 1967. Correspondence, memoranda, speech drafts, reports and supporting papers, clippings, and other items primarily consist of material Bernhagen used in writing speeches on child welfare, adoption, child abuse, neglect and dependence, social work and the law, mental health and retardation, foster care, juvenile delinquency, illegitimacy, and other topics. Includes a daily journal Bernhagen kept during her work in 1937 as a staff member of the Minnesota State Emergency Relief Administration and items she used in writing "The Indian in Minnesota" (1949), a report of the Governor's Interracial Commission of Minnesota. Bernhagen was a child welfare consultant, training consultant, field representative, and supervisor for the Minnesota department of public welfare. From 1945 to 1950 she was a sociology professor at Hamline University in St. Paul, MN.

8,639. Child Study Association of America
Records. 1890-1965. 17.5 ft. and 1 microfilm reel.
Open. Unpublished guide.

University of Minnesota, Social Welfare History Archives.
Established in 1888 as the Society for the Study of Child Nature, the Association disseminated information about child-rearing, both directly and indirectly through such methods as publications, reviews of children's literature, conferences, and radio and television appearances. Annual reports; financial records; correspondence, minutes, and reports from policy-making bodies, standing committees, and study groups; articles and speeches; photos; scrapbooks; guest books; and other records document the Association's attempts to introduce and interpret the findings of psychiatry, psychology, and sociology in a form useful to parents and others who work with children. The group's name was changed in 1908 to the Federation for Child Study, and in 1924 the organization was incorporated as the Child Study Association of America. In 1977 the name was changed to Family Development Association.

Included in the collection are the Association's records, papers of its employees, and records of two organizations that had their origin in the Association. The Association records include such items as minutes of study-group meetings with New York City area parents summarizing discussions about adolescence, discipline, parent roles, breast-feeding, physical care, sex education, moral training, and other subjects; records of the speaker's bureau, which handled lectures, radio programs, symposia, and university courses; and records of the children's book committee, including correspondence regarding awards and preparation of anthologies and lists of recommended books. Among the individuals represented in the collection are Sidonie Matsner Gruenberg, who served as an Association volunteer from 1906 to 1924 and as the group's executive director from 1924 to 1950, and Josette Frank, a staff associate for children's books and mass media. In addition to her work with the Association, Gruenberg's correspondence, articles, and speeches reflect her work to help Jews escape from Nazi Germany. Records of the Inter-Community Study Committee and the National Council of Parent Education, which was formed after a 1925 conference sponsored by the Association, are also included. The Committee was organized in 1929 to deal with the special needs of parent education in Negro communities in such cities as Brooklyn and North Harlem, NY; Montclair and Englewood, NJ; Baltimore; and Washington.

A 45-foot supplement to the collection contains records dating primarily from 1955 to 1970 that document the Association's shift toward training staff members of other agencies who work with parents and children. Particularly prominent are the records of a project to train Head Start workers to involve parents more effectively in their programs.

8,640. Child Welfare League of America
Records. 1917-1951. 4 in.
Open. Unpublished guide.
University of Minnesota, Social Welfare History Archives.
Minutes, reports, correspondence, memoranda, and other records of the Child Welfare League of America, which was organized in 1920, discuss the development of day nurseries to provide care for children of working mothers. Included are items from the Association of Day Nurseries of New York City, organized in 1894, and the National Federation of Day Nurseries, organized in 1898. The two merged in 1938 to form the National Association of Day Nurseries, which in turn became a part of the League in 1943.

A 27-foot supplement covering the period from 1923 to 1976 deals with all aspects of social services for children, particularly foster care, day care, and adoption. Included are records of the League's dealings with the Florence Crittenton Association of America, which became a division of the League in 1976; the American Parents Committee; and the National Council on Illegitimacy and its predecessor the National Association on Services to Unmarried Parents.

8,641. De Schweinitz, Karl, and de Schweinitz, Elizabeth
Papers. 1907-74. 4.25 ft.
Open. Unpublished guide.
University of Minnesota, Social Welfare History Archives.
Karl de Schweinitz (1887-1975) and his wife Elizabeth McCord de Schweinitz (1895-1978) were social welfare administrators and educators who wrote *Interviewing in Social Security* (1961). Correspondence, teaching and research files, and published and unpublished writings contain papers documenting in-service training programs Elizabeth de Schweinitz conducted for agencies, including the District of Columbia board of public health and the California department of social welfare. Initially a caseworker, she became involved in programs pertaining to Social Security and public welfare. She worked with her husband on several writing and consulting projects, including a trip in 1951 to Egypt where the de Schweinitzes served as social security consultants. She also was research assistant for his uncompleted history of social welfare. Research files compiled in connection with the history include correspondence with and about pioneer social worker Mary Richmond.

8,642. Deschin, Celia S.
Papers. 1961-66. 10 ft.
Open. No guide.
University of Minnesota, Social Welfare History Archives.
A professor at the Adelphi University school of social work, Deschin (ca. 1902-), directed a survey that studied the sense of community felt by residents in suburban Nassau County, NY. Interview forms, questionnaire schedules, questionnaires completed by 700 high school juniors and adults in 700 households, keysort cards, clippings, and other items pertaining to the survey. Respondents were asked about their sense of community identity, awareness of local social problems, and attitudes about child rearing. A copy of the report, "The Five Towns: A Community Self-Portrait," is included.

8,643. Dickinson, Ruth Robertson (Allen)
Papers. 1930-63. 2 ft.
Partially restricted. Unpublished guide.
University of Minnesota, Social Welfare History Archives.
Dickinson attended the University of Chicago and was married in 1922. Following her divorce she returned to the University and completed graduate studies in about 1950. From 1950 to 1959 she was a guidance counselor and visiting school social worker in Western Springs public schools near Chicago. In addition to reports, case files, and resource materials related to her employment, the collection contains correspondence, speech notes, minutes, and reports that reflect her involvement in professional and community activities.

8,644. Dunn, Loula
Papers. 1935-65. 1.5 ft.
Open. No guide.
University of Minnesota, Social Welfare History Archives.
[Miss] Dunn (ca. 1900-) was commissioner of public welfare in Alabama from 1937 to 1949 and director of the American Public Welfare Association from 1949 to 1963. Correspondence, reports, and speeches Dunn presented on topics related to public welfare. Includes letters of congratulation she received following her appointment as APWA director, letters recommending her for the directorship of a proposed US department of public welfare in 1949, and working papers of a consultants committee that provided information to the Social Security Administration on the extension of old-age and survivors' insurance benefits. Dunn served on the consultants committee in 1953.

8,645. Family Service of St. Paul
Records. 1894-1974. 9 ft.
Open. Unpublished guide.
University of Minnesota, Social Welfare History Archives.
Articles of incorporation, annual reports, minutes, financial records, statistical reports, agency studies, and other records of Family Service, which was organized in 1892 as the Associated Charities of St. Paul, MN. Reorganized in 1914 as the United Charities of St. Paul and in 1935 as Family Service of St. Paul, the group provides counseling, advice, and other assistance to families in need. Included are minute books, 1897-1914, of the board of lady managers of the St. Paul Free Dispensary, one of the original members of the Associated Charities. The board later became a department of the United Charities.

8,646. Five Towns Community House.
Records. 1907-65. 15 ft.
Partially restricted. Published guide.
University of Minnesota, Social Welfare History Archives.
Founded in Lawrence, NY, in 1907 with funds provided by Margaret [Mrs. Russell] Sage, the House was known initially as the Margaret Sage Industrial School and, from 1911 to 1942, as the Nassau Industrial School. The House assumed its current name in 1942. Bylaws; records of annual meetings; minutes of the board of directors and standing committees; subject files, including material on House programs and activities; records dealing with placement of undergraduate and graduate students in field work positions, group work records and reports of conferences between supervisors and group leaders; studies; photos; clippings; and other records reflect the institution's changing emphasis from a vocational school for boys and girls to an agency providing cultural, recreational, and educational programs for small neighborhood groups in an interracial community. Group work records constitute the bulk of the collection and provide information about group projects, meetings, group leaders, and group work theories. Records include discussion of programs for the aged, housing, juvenile delinquency, National Federation of Settlements and Neighborhood Centers, programs for teens, youth services, and recreation. See *Descriptive Inventories of Collections in the Social Welfare History Archives Center* (Westport, CT: Greenwood Publishing Corporation, 1970).

8,647. Florence Crittenton Association of America
Records. 1951-67. 10 ft.
Open. Unpublished guide.
University of Minnesota, Social Welfare History Archives.
Established in 1950 as the Florence Crittenton Homes Association, the Florence Crittenton Association of America was a federation of autonomous Crittenton agencies that provided social, medical, educational, and legal services to unwed parents and their children; the Association also worked to promote a better public understanding of the needs of unwed parents and their children. Records of the executive director, board of directors, and committees; annual national and area conference records; items concerning personnel standards and practices; public relations material; and other records reflect the Association's concern with such services and issues as prostitution, illegitimacy, birth control, and residential homes for unwed mothers and their children. Correspondence of executive directors Virgil Payne and Mary Louise Allen is included. Also contains correspondence with and other

records concerning the Association's relationship with the Child Welfare League of America with which the Association merged in 1976, the Family Service Association of America, the National Association of Service to Unmarried Parents, the National Association of Social Workers, the National Conference on Social Welfare, the National Social Welfare Assembly, Planned Parenthood Federation of America, and the US Children's Bureau. The Association is now a division within the Child Welfare League of America.

8,648. Fourth District Minnesota Nurses' Association
Records. Ca. 1898-1967. 7 ft.
Open. Unpublished guide.
University of Minnesota, Social Welfare History Archives.
Founded in 1898 as the Ramsey County Graduate Nurses' Association, the Association promotes professional, educational, and economic advancement of nurses as outlined by the Minnesota Nurses' Association and the American Nurses' Association and works to foster high standards of nursing practice and maintain the nursing code of ethics. Constitutions; bylaws; annual reports; board of directors minutes and reports; reports of the executive secretary and Fourth District Association presidents; minute books of committees and sections, including the private duty section, the public health section, and the Red Cross Committee on Nursing Service; financial records; correspondence; biographical material and correspondence of Theresa Ericksen, founder of the Association, most of which relates to her activities as an army nurse in the Philippines during the Spanish-American War; material on the history of the Association and of the history of public health nursing in Minnesota; records relating to the Association's reorganizations; photos; scrapbooks; clippings pertaining to nursing legislation, standards, and developments in the profession; and memorabilia. Also includes records of the Fourth District Minnesota Nursing Students' Association. The Ramsey County Graduate Nurses' Association was renamed Ramsey County Registered Nurses' Association in 1912 and was incorporated as the Fourth District Minnesota State Registered Nurses' Association in 1925. The group assumed its current title in 1950.

8,649. Golden, Mary Katz
Papers. 1927-32. 10 items.
Open. Unpublished guide.
University of Minnesota, Social Welfare History Archives.
Correspondence of Golden, a member of the staff of *Survey* magazine, with Paul Kellogg, editor of *Survey,* concerning the periodical's editorial staff.

8,650. Goodrich, Bessie Bacon
Papers. 1929-40. 6 items.
Open. Unpublished guide.
University of Minnesota, Social Welfare History Archives.
Letters to Goodrich from her cousin Paul Kellogg, who was editor of *Survey* magazine, concern family and personal matters.

8,651. Hall, Helen
Papers. Ca. 1906-75. 14 ft.
Open. Unpublished guide.
University of Minnesota, Social Welfare History Archives.
A settlement leader and reformer, Hall (1892-) served as president of the National Federation of Settlements and was resident director of the Henry Street Settlement on New York City's lower east side from 1933 to 1967. Personal and professional correspondence, manuscripts for articles and books, transcripts of speeches and testimony before legislative bodies, minutes and reports for committees on which she served, and records of the Henry Street Settlement, including board of directors minutes, financial reports, committee studies and reports, and correspondence. Hall's correspondents included Paul U. Kellogg, her husband and editor of *Survey* magazine; Lillie Peck; Helen Harris; Margaret Berry; Jane Addams; Grace and Edith Abbott; Lea Taylor; Mary Van Kleeck; Helen Morton; Mary Keyserling; Lillian Wald; and Albert H. Kennedy. The bulk of the collection deals with Hall's work to combat unemployment during the depression, especially its effect upon home life; consumer education of the urban poor; her advocacy of community health facilities; and health insurance and social security. Also included are files relating to her American National Red Cross work overseas during both world wars; her participation on President Roosevelt's advisory council to the Committee on Economic Security, which drafted the Social Security Act; post-WWII planning and the UN; the Mobilization for Youth and the Lower East Side Neighborhood Association, two New York City groups Hall and others created to combat juvenile delinquency; cooperatives and credit unions; and urban housing for low-income and middle-income dwellers. Hall worked at Philadelphia's University Settlement from 1922 to 1933.

8,652. Hamilton-Madison House
Records. 1898-1965. 2 ft.
Open. Unpublished guide.
University of Minnesota, Social Welfare History Archives.
A settlement house devoted to improving neighborhood conditions on New York City's lower east side, Hamilton-Madison House was formed in 1954 through the merger of Madison House, founded in 1898, and Hamilton House, which was established in 1901. Annual reports, legal and financial records, board and committee records, guest books, and other records, including a scrapbook compiled in 1937 by neighborhood children to mark the 70th birthday of Lillian Wald.

8,653. Hathway, Marion
Papers. 1911-56. 7.5 ft.
Open. Unpublished guide.
University of Minnesota, Social Welfare History Archives.
Hathway (1895-1955) was a professor of social work at the University of Pittsburgh from 1932 to 1951, with the exception of three years during which she served as executive secretary of the American Association of Schools of Social Work; she was a social work professor at Bryn Mawr College from 1951 to 1955. Correspondence, articles, speeches, course material, card files, appointment books, and clippings document her teaching and research career, particularly her concern for the rights of the individual and the role of social welfare in a democratic system. The papers also reflect her activities in professional groups, most notably the American Association of Schools of Social Work, the American Association of Social Workers, and the National Association of Social Workers. They record criticism of her alleged communist leanings, which resulted from her involvement with the Progressive Party and the National Council of American-Soviet Friendship. Her correspondents included Edith Abbott, Sophonisba Breckenridge, Karl de Schweinitz, Harold Ickes, and Mary Van Kleeck.

8,654. Haugen, Ruth Bergliot
Papers. 1933-1975. 1.25 ft.
Open. Unpublished guide.
University of Minnesota, Social Welfare History Archives.
Haugen (1905-) was a social worker and a social work educator at the University of Minnesota and the University of Kentucky. Lecture notes, summaries of reading assignments, case histories, manuals, reports, pamphlets, and clippings. Includes material for courses in casework, interviewing technique, the legal aspects of social work, public welfare administration, and community organization. Also contains material about Haugen's friend Mary Sydney Gold, a social worker in Minnesota and the District of Columbia. The bulk of the material is from the period from 1933 to 1940.

8,655. Henry Street Settlement Urban Life Center
Records. 1896-1971. 150 ft.
Open. Unpublished guide.
University of Minnesota, Social Welfare History Archives.
The Settlement, established in 1893 by Lillian D. Wald and Mary Brewster as Nurses' Settlement, has developed two major action strategies: it provides services for residents of its neighborhood and seeks reform and reconstruction of urban areas through mobilization of political forces and community action. The collection contains minutes, financial records, correspondence, reports, articles, speeches, photos, and clippings; it consists primarily of administrative files generated during Helen Hall's tenure as resident director from 1933 to 1967. Hall succeeded Wald, who directed the Settlement's work from 1893 to 1933. Initially the Settlement provided visiting nurse services throughout New York's lower east side. Incorporated as Henry Street Settlement in 1903, the agency expanded its services to include adult education, art and music instruction, summer camps for children and adults, consumer education, day care, domestic education and planning, drug addiction clinics, employment referrals, mental health clinics, preventive medical care, and recreational and educational opportunities for the emotionally handicapped. The Settlement also worked to provide facilities for a community hospital, offered programs of assistance to the aged, initiated programs to combat juvenile delinquency, supported public housing for the poor, created a credit union and cooperatives, and actively encouraged community support for the UN. Some of the collection's files document the work of Wald, the visiting nurse service, and the administration of Bertram Beck as executive director of the Settlement from 1967 to 1977. The Settlement adopted its current name in 1970.

8,656. Hodges, Barbara (Bailey)
Papers. 1932-70. 2 ft.
Open. Unpublished guide.
University of Minnesota, Social Welfare History Archives.
[Mrs. J. Stanley] Hodges (1909-), a medical social work educator, taught at the National Catholic School of Social Service in Washington, DC, and at Johns Hopkins School of Hygiene and Public Health. From 1951 to 1955 she served as chief of social services in the Office of the Army Surgeon General and from 1955 to 1964 as chief of the bureau of medical assistance and contracts in the District of Columbia department of public health. Notes she used in class lectures; speeches and articles she wrote; minutes of organizations to which she belonged; manuals she drafted; a small amount of correspondence; and reference material concerning social work in the military and medical social work education. Her papers include proposals she developed for establishment of social service departments in various hospitals; a manual she developed for the District of Columbia public health department to use in determining eligibility for medical assistance; and a manual she wrote for the social service department of Morris Cafritz Memorial Hospital. Hodges was head of the Washington, DC, hospital's social service office from 1967 to 1970. Also includes minutes, reports, and other records of the American Association of Medical Social Workers executive and education committees, of the American Association of Social Workers, the American Association of Schools of Social Work, the Council on Social Work

Education, and the American Association of Psychiatric Social Workers.

8,657. International Social Service, American Branch
Records. 1923-67. 6 ft. and 2 microfilm reels. Partially restricted. No guide.
University of Minnesota, Social Welfare History Archives.
Founded in 1924 as the American Branch of International Migration Service, the Branch provides specialized casework services to clients referred by local, national, and international agencies when the problems of individuals and families demand coordinated efforts in two or more countries. Minutes; reports; correspondence, including correspondence files of International Service executives Mary Hurlbutt, Ruth Larned, and Elizabeth W. Clark; and other records. The correspondence documents the involvement of board of directors or national advisory council members Mr. William Burns, Joan Crawford [Mrs. Alfred] Steele, Margaret Curtis, Gertrude Ely, Amelia [Mrs. Raymond] Emerson, Edith B. Jackson, Perle Mesta, Eleanor Neustaedter, Ann Thorpe, Pearl Buck, and Annie Clo Watson. Many of the Service's cases involve families whose members have been separated by national borders and require assistance in such matters as child support, custody, paternity claims, immigration, deportation, and repatriation. Since WWII the emphasis of the Service, which became the International Social Service in 1946, has shifted toward international adoption cases, most of which involve American homes for foreign-born children.

8,658. Kellogg, Paul Underwood
Papers. Ca. 1884-1968. Ca. 21 ft.
Open. Published guide.
University of Minnesota, Social Welfare History Archives.
A journalist, editor, and social reformer, Kellogg (1879-1958) was editor from 1912 to 1952 of *Survey* and *Survey Graphic,* two major journals of social issues. Correspondence, articles, speeches, memoranda, financial and editorial records, minutes, reports, photos, pamphlets, clippings, and other papers relate principally to Kellogg's work as editor of *Survey* and include information on child labor, social work, industrial and international relations, unemployment and workers compensation, pacifism, and other topics. Kellogg's correspondents included Jane Addams, Mary C. Austin, Ann Reed Brenner, Marion Clinch Calkins, Florence Kelley, Frances Perkins, Mary Van Kleeck, Lillian Wald, Miriam Van Waters, and Lea Taylor. Organizations represented by correspondence or other records include the American Union Against Militarism; the Foreign Policy Association, one of whose founders was Kellogg; the American Association for Social Workers; the National Federation of Settlements; and the Woman's Peace Party. Kellogg was married in 1935 to Helen Hall, social worker and head resident of the Henry Street Settlement in New York City. See *Descriptive Inventories of Collections in the Social Welfare History Archives Center* (Westport, CT: Greenwood Publishing Corporation, 1970).

8,659. Kennedy, Albert Joseph
Papers. 1900-69. 5.75 ft.
Open. Unpublished guide.
University of Minnesota, Social Welfare History Archives.
Associated with settlement work and the National Federation of Settlements for nearly 60 years, Kennedy (1879-1968) conducted a nationwide interracial study in ca. 1945 to "gauge the progress of social, educational, and recreational opportunities available to Negroes in homogeneous and in interracial areas and neighborhoods." Correspondence, minutes, reports, memoranda, statistical studies of settlements and cities, notes, clippings, and other papers, most of which pertain to the interracial study, which was sponsored by the National Federation of Settlements. The correspondence, interviews, questionnaires, and other records provide information about city and community planning, the family, housing, immigrant and ethnic groups, recreation, visual arts, and music, feminism, health care, and other topics. Correspondents include Jane Addams, Helen Hall, Lillie M. Peck, Lillian Wald, Mary Simkhovitch, and Lea Taylor.

8,660. Leach, Agnes Brown
Papers. 1927-52. 1 in.
Open. Unpublished guide.
University of Minnesota, Social Welfare History Archives.
Correspondence between [Mrs. Henry Goddard] Leach (1884-1975), a member of the board of directors of Survey Associates and the Foreign Policy Association, and Paul Kellogg, Richard Scandrett, and Joseph Chamberlain concerning fundraising and anniversary celebrations for Survey Associates, publisher of *Survey* magazine.

8,661. Lower Eastside Neighborhood Association
Records. 1955-73. 22 ft.
Open. Unpublished guide.
University of Minnesota, Social Welfare History Archives.
Minutes, financial records, correspondence, personnel files, and other records of the Association, which was founded in New York City in 1955 to counteract the activities of neighborhood youth gangs. The Association's primary function, however, soon became that of a planning and coordinating agency for other neighborhood groups in the areas of health, education, youth problems, recreation, and housing. The Association's records document the assistance given to poor women faced with housing problems and other difficulties. Helen Hall, head resident of the Henry Street Settlement, was one of the Association's founders and served on the group's board of directors. Marta Valle served as the Association's executive director for several years before resigning in 1966 to become deputy administrator for community relations for New York City.

8,662. Lurie, Harry L.
Papers. 1927-58. 2 ft.
Open. Published guide.
University of Minnesota, Social Welfare History Archives.
Lurie (1892-1973), a social work practitioner and educator, was born in Latvia and immigrated to the US in 1898. After working for Jewish social agencies in Buffalo, Chicago, and New York, he served as executive director of the Council of Jewish Federations and Welfare Funds from 1935 to 1954. Professional correspondence makes up the bulk of the collection, which also includes occasional reports, minutes, memoranda, and other papers reflecting Lurie's interests in social reform, social welfare, anti-semitism, birth control, care of the aged, and family welfare. He displayed particular interest in New Deal social and economic programs and their impact on families and communities. Correspondents include Grace and Edith Abbott, Helen Hall, Harry L. Hopkins, Paul Kellogg, and Mary Van Kleeck. See *Descriptive Inventories of Collections in the Social Welfare History Archives Center* (Westport, CT: Greenwood Publishing Corporation, 1970).

8,663. Maxted, Mattie Cal
Papers. 1942-57. 1.25 ft.
Open. Published guide.
University of Minnesota, Social Welfare History Archives.
A social work educator, Maxted (1900-) served as secretary of the National Association of Schools of Social Administration. Correspondence, speeches, minutes, annual proceedings, committee reports, statistical studies, and course material chiefly relate to the need for undergraduate social work education programs to provide trained social workers. The NASSA was formed in 1942 to provide direction to colleges and universities that offered all or part of their social service instruction at the undergraduate level. The already existing American Association of Schools of Social Work recognized only graduate programs. Maxted's correspondents included Ernest B. Harper, Sue Spencer, and H. E. Wetzel. Maxted was a professor of social work at the University of Oklahoma from 1935 to 1940 and at the University of Arkansas from 1940 to 1969. See *Descriptive Inventories of Collections in the Social Welfare History Archives Center* (Westport, CT: Greenwood Publishing Corporation, 1970).

8,664. Mudgett, Mildred Dennett
Papers. 1968-78. 4 in.
Open. No guide.
University of Minnesota, Social Welfare History Archives.
Autobiographical reminiscences of Mudgett (1888-), a social work educator and practitioner, include information about her childhood in New England; her education at Friends School, at Mount Holyoke College from 1905 to 1909, and at New York School of Social Work in 1915 and 1916; and her employment at Philadelphia Girls House of Refuge in 1909, the Philadelphia Society for Organizing Charity from 1910 to 1913, and at the New York Charity Organization Society in 1914 and 1915. The reminiscence, which was written for Mudgett's daughters, also provides information about her work as supervisor of field work at the University of Minnesota from 1919 to 1929, her work with various Minneapolis-St. Paul social agencies from 1930 to 1948, her personal and family activities, and her travel throughout the US and Europe. Among the subjects discussed are her mother's death, her stepmother, rejection of her minister father's orthodox religion, the problems of securing employment as a married woman, combining working and child rearing, and her adjustment to retirement.

8,665. National Association of Social Workers
Records. 1917-63. 52 ft.
Open. Published guide.
University of Minnesota, Social Welfare History Archives.
Formed in 1955, the Association, a membership organization for professional social workers, promotes the quality and effectiveness of social work practice by setting standards, conducting research, and seeking to improve professional education. Board and committee minutes and working papers, financial records, correspondence, memoranda, conference and workshop proceedings, case material prepared for teaching purposes, reports on consultation visits to schools and hospitals, records on local chapters, topical reference files, and other records reflect the growth of the social work profession, a field made up predominantly of women.

Included are records of the seven groups that merged to form the Association, chief among them the American Association of Social Workers, which was founded in 1921. This group's records reflect the work of Edith Shatto King, Neva R. Deardorff, Dorothy C. Kahn, Mary Van Kleeck, Florence Taylor, Elisabeth Mills, and Grace Marcus, most of whom were AASW officers.

The other predecessor groups of the National Association of Social Workers were the American Association of Medical Social Workers, founded in 1918; the National Association of School Social Workers, founded in 1919; the American Association of Psychiatric Social Workers, established in 1922; the American Association of Group Workers, formed in 1936; the Association for the Study of Community Organization, founded in 1947; and the Social Work Research Group, established in 1949. The records of the American Association of Medical Social Workers document the development of hospital social service departments to deal with social factors related to health and medical care. Individuals represented in the group's records include Edith M. Baker, Harriett Bartlett, Ida M. Cannon, M. Antoinette Cannon, Eleanor Cockerill, Dora Goldstine, Mary L. Hemmy, Ruth E. Lewis, and Mary Poole. The American Association of Group Workers began as a visiting teacher movement, which dealt with students' out-of-classroom problems; each of the group's presidents was a woman. Many of the members of the American Association of Group Workers were affiliated with settlements, the YWCA, Girl Scouts, and Camp Fire Girls and were interested in recreational and informal education activities. Among the women represented in the group's records are Ann Elizabeth Neely, Edna d'Issertelle, and Janet W. Korpela.

Collectively, the seven groups' records show their evolution from vocational placement bureaus into professional organizations concerned with raising professional standards and improving education offerings and working conditions. During the 1930s some of the groups studied the impact of depression-era federal social and economic programs. During WWII their attention was focused on the armed forces, including the need for social workers in the WACS. Since 1955, the National Association of Social Workers has continued the work of its predecessors with particular emphasis upon the accreditation of social workers and personnel standards. See *Descriptive Inventories of Collections in the Social Welfare History Archives Center* (Westport, CT: Greenwood Publishing Corporation, 1970).

8,666. National Association of Social Workers, Southern Minnesota Chapter, Medical Social Work Section
Records. 1922-60. 2 ft.
Open. Unpublished guide.
University of Minnesota, Social Welfare History Archives.
Thirty-five Minnesota medical social workers, the majority of them from the Minneapolis-St. Paul area, organized in 1922 to provide a vehicle for communication among hospital social workers and to improve and maintain standards of social work in hospitals, dispensaries, special clinics, and other medical facilities. Minutes, financial records, correspondence, memoranda, committee reports, membership lists, and programs comprise the records of the Chapter under its three titles: the Minnesota District of the American Association of Hospital Social Workers, the Minnesota District of the American Association of Medical Social Workers, and the Southern Minnesota Chapter, Medical Social Work Section, National Association of Social Workers. The group assumed the second form of its name in 1934 and became a branch of the NASW following the formation of the national group in 1955. The records reflect the Chapter's interests in the quality and availability of educational opportunities in medical social work, in social legislation, in medical social work recruitment, in rehabilitation services, and in civil defense preparedness. Includes records of local and national committees that coordinated the merger into the NASW. Minnesota social workers represented in the records include Mary Gold, Elizabeth Gardner, Lydia B. Christ, Florence Parker, Helen Anderson Young, Caroline Manger Iverson, and Marion Tebbets.

8,667. National Council on Family Relations
Records. 1939-75. 13 ft.
Open. No guide.
University of Minnesota, Social Welfare History Archives.
Founded in 1938, the Council promotes consultation and cooperation among such professional family life workers as clergymen, counselors, educators, home economists, nurses, physicians, lawyers, social workers, and psychologists. Financial reports, account ledgers, correspondence, programs, and membership cards. Included is correspondence with state and regional family relations councils and material regarding annual meetings. The records document the activities of Ruth H. Jewson, who has served as the Council's executive director since 1956.

8,668. National Federation of Settlements and Neighborhood Centers
Records. 1891-1965. 35 ft. and 6 microfilm reels.
Open. Published guide.
University of Minnesota, Social Welfare History Archives.
Established in 1911 as the National Federation of Settlements, the organization has sought to promote better neighborhood organization by assistance to individual settlement houses and groups, by conducting research about and studies of community conditions, by securing capable personnel for the settlements, and by supporting state and national legislation suggested by the settlement experience. Minutes of the board of directors and committees, conference proceedings, correspondence, memoranda, reports and studies conducted by the Federation, photos, mimeographed program material distributed to members, and files of records pertaining to nearly 300 settlements in cities throughout the US. Also includes a chronological index to activities of the Federation, which assumed its current name in 1949. The records document the settlement movement in the US, an effort made up primarily of college-aged young people who moved into working class neighborhoods to engage in community improvement activities. Women predominated among the settlement workers. Among the women represented in the Federation's records are Jane Addams; Fern Colburn; Margaret Berry, Federation executive secretary from 1959 to 1971; Ellen W. Coolidge; Helen Hall; Frances Ingram; Florence Kelley; Julia Lathrop; Frances McFarland; Lillie Peck, Federation executive secretary from 1923 to 1948; Jane Robbins; Mary Simkhovitch; Lea Taylor; and Lillian Wald.

Records of the Federation's social education and action committee reflect the group's concerns in housing, public health, industrial medicine, unemployment, municipal political reform, and child welfare, including a concerted effort for creation of the US Children's Bureau in 1912. Other records provide information about the Americanization of immigrants, prohibition, civil rights and civil liberties, settlements in wartime, and settlement recreation and informal educational activities in music, art, drama, and handcraft.

A 44-foot supplement contains records dating from ca. 1921 to 1971 consisting principally of correspondence and reports from member settlements, files on contacts with settlements in other countries, and records of the Federation's training center. The supplement documents the transition of the settlement movement in the 1960s, a decade during which minority representation on national and local staffs and boards was increased. See *Descriptive Inventories of Collections in the Social Welfare History Archives Center* (Westport, CT: Greenwood Publishing Corporation, 1970).

8,669. National Florence Crittenton Mission
Records. 1895-1959. 6.25 ft.
Open. Published guide.
University of Minnesota, Social Welfare History Archives.
Chartered by Congress in 1898, the national Mission organization was an outgrowth of a New York City residence for homeless and pregnant women established by Charles Nelson Crittenton in 1883. Eventually the Mission opened 65 homes around the country, each of them bearing the name of Crittenton's daughter. Annual reports from 1918 to 1928, board of trustees minutes and correspondence, extension committee records, annual conference records, correspondence with individual homes, and employment applications reflect the national Mission's early battles against white slavery and prostitution, the concern for adequate medical care for unwed mothers, the initial Crittenton policy of opposing separation of mother and child by adoption, and frequent local problems created by individual Crittenton homes providing services for Negro unwed mothers.

Charles Crittenton established the national Mission organization to oversee operation of the Crittenton homes. Kate Waller Barrett, a physician, became superintendent of the national Mission in 1896 and succeeded Crittenton as president upon his death in 1909. After her death in 1925 her son Robert South Barrett became president and her daughter Reba (Barrett) Smith became general superintendent. The retirements of Robert Barrett and Reba Smith in 1950 prompted a reorganization that led to more autonomy for member homes. This change is reflected in records, 1948-59, of the Florence Crittenton Homes Association, later called the Florence Crittenton Association of America, which assumed many of the duties of the national Mission. Since 1950 the national Mission has existed primarily to maintain and supervise its invested funds.

Women represented in the collection include the following Crittenton officials: Kate Waller Barrett, Reba (Barrett) Smith, Roxana Jackson, and Mary Louise Allen. See *Descriptive Inventories of Collections in the Social Welfare History Archives Center* (Westport, CT: Greenwood Publishing Corporation, 1970).

8,670. National Social Welfare Assembly
Records. 1911-56. 8 ft.
Open. Published guide.
University of Minnesota, Social Welfare History Archives.
Since its establishment in 1923 as the National Social Work Council, the Assembly has planned and coordinated activities of national voluntary welfare organizations. Minutes and transcripts of meetings, correspondence, and mimeograph and printed material. The collection consists principally of transcripts of monthly meetings of the Council, which was made up of executives of national social work groups, among them the Camp Fire Girls, Girl Scouts, the national board of the YWCA, and the National Travelers Aid Association. The executives met to exchange information and discuss common problems, including financial support for voluntary social welfare activities, social conditions during the depression, the impact of defense mobilization and demobilization, and the role of voluntary organizations in the face of growing public welfare programs. Includes transcripts of presentations made by the following women: Barbara N. Armstrong, Sallie Bright, Josephine C. Brown, Margaret Byington, Joanna C. Colcord, Margaret Creech, Dorothy De la Pole, Sadie Orr Dunbar, Emma Hirth, Charlotte Johnson, Dorothy Kahn, Florence Kelley, Hertha M. Kraus, Bertha McCall, Helen W. Martin, Margaret Murray, Ellen C. Potter, Mrs. Paul Rittenhouse, Myra Smith, Clare Tousley, Mary Van Kleeck, Anna Ward, and Alice Webber. The Council was reorganized in 1945 and renamed the National Social Welfare Assembly. In 1967 it became the National Assembly for Social Policy and Development and in 1973, the National Assembly of National Voluntary Health and Social Welfare Organizations.

Two supplements, totaling 256 feet, contain records of the organization from 1945 to 1967 and include committee records and files on organizations affiliated with the Assembly. Also included are records reflecting the activities of

Bernice Bridges, an Assembly youth specialist who guided the formation of the Young Adult Council (later the United States Youth Council), and Elizabeth Wickenden, the Assembly's social policy and government affairs consultant. See *Descriptive Inventories of Collections in the Social Welfare History Archives Center* (Westport, CT: Greenwood Publishing Corporation, 1970).

8,671. Phillips, Wilbur Carey, and Phillips, Elsie Cole
Papers. 1849-1965. 23 ft.
Open. No guide.
University of Minnesota, Social Welfare History Archives.
Wilbur Phillips (1880-1967?), a social theoretician, devoted most of his life to developing his "social unit plan," a democratic neighborhood structure through which local residents could participate in the control of community affairs. His wife Elsie LaGrange Cole Phillips (1879-1961) was a 1901 graduate of Vassar College who worked as placement secretary at the Manhattan Trade School for Girls and as assistant secretary for the National League of Women Workers before their marriage in 1911. Correspondence, diaries, manuscripts, card files, and scrapbooks document Wilbur Phillips's work with New York, Milwaukee, and Cincinnati projects that sought improved child health through clean milk and education for mothers in the principles of child hygiene. Later records document the Phillipses' efforts to develop and promote the social unit plan. Included is correspondence with [Miss] Ethel Pew, who contributed $50,000 over a 30-year period to their work. Also included is personal correspondence between the Phillipses, other family members, and supporters as well as card files containing names and addresses of individuals, organizations, and foundations identified as actual or potential supporters.

8,672. Planned Parenthood of Minnesota
Records. 1932-1971. 15 ft.
Partially restricted. Unpublished guide.
University of Minnesota, Social Welfare History Archives.
The organization, which had its origins in the Minnesota Birth Control League formed in 1931, seeks to provide family planning information and services to all persons in Minnesota who wish them. Annual reports, minutes, financial and fundraising records, annual meeting summaries, correspondence, clinic statistical reports, scrapbooks, press releases, clippings, and calendars. The collection consists primarily of records, 1945-65, of Planned Parenthood of Minneapolis, which joined with Planned Parenthood of St. Paul in 1971 to form the statewide Planned Parenthood organization. Also included are records (6 in.) of the St. Paul Planned Parenthood group as well as committee and board minutes, annual meeting programs, research reports, news releases, and other items generated by Planned Parenthood-World Population, which formerly was known as Planned Parenthood Federation of America. Most prominently represented in the records is Pamela Getz [Mrs. William] Veerhusen, executive director of Planned Parenthood of Minneapolis from 1956 to 1971; other records document visits to the Twin Cities area by Margaret Sanger, Baroness Ishimoto, Naomi Thomas, and Mary (Steichen) Calderone. In addition to Veerhusen, the collection includes papers of such local leaders as Dorothy B. A. Rood, Mrs. Hill Shepardson, Mrs. John Cowles, and Jane Brown. The records show that until 1968 the organization had a policy of limiting service to married women only. Abortion begins to emerge as an active issue in the later years of the collection.

8,673. Raines, Anna B.
Papers. 1926-55. 16 items and 1 tape.
Open. Unpublished guide.
University of Minnesota, Social Welfare History Archives.
Memoranda and reports prepared by [Miss] Raines in connection with her work as chief of social work service at the Veterans Administration Hospital in Tuskegee, AL, from 1926 to 1956.

8,674. Randall, Ollie A.
Papers. 1915-75. Ca. 30 ft.
Open. No guide.
University of Minnesota, Social Welfare History Archives.
A social worker and gerontologist, Randall (1890-) was one of the founders of the National Council on the Aging (in 1950) and the principal consultant from 1960 to 1970 for the Ford Foundation's program on aging. Correspondence, manuscripts, notes, memoranda, and minutes make up the bulk of the collection. A 1912 graduate of Brown University, Randall worked for the Russell Sage Foundation in 1915. In 1916 she began her work for the elderly with the New York Association for Improving the Condition of the Poor, which was renamed the Community Service Society of New York; she worked for the Society until her retirement in 1955. She served as a board member and vice-president of the National Council on the Aging for many years.

8,675. Sabloff, Janet
Papers. 1927-34. 22 items.
Open. Unpublished guide.
University of Minnesota, Social Welfare History Archives.
Sabloff was personal secretary to Paul U. Kellogg, editor of *Survey* magazine. Personal correspondence between Sabloff and Kellogg, much of it concerning her desire to "do something that counts." The letters also contain Kellogg's advice on how to see Europe.

8,676. Saint Paul Family Centered Project
Records. 1947-68. 14.5 ft.
Open. Unpublished guide.
University of Minnesota, Social Welfare History Archives.
Working under the auspices of the Greater St. Paul Community Chest and Council in St. Paul, MN, from 1954 to 1967, the Project promoted cooperation among agencies to overcome the fragmented nature of social services and sought to identify families that were experiencing difficulties in a number of areas and to provide them with more systematic, effective service. The Project grew out of the Family Unit Report Study, which demonstrated the ineffectiveness of existing practices. Minutes, financial records, correspondence, speeches, studies, sample casework records, publications, clippings, and other records discuss such subjects as Aid to Dependent Children, child-rearing, community organization, dependency, juvenile delinquency, neighborhood centers, sex roles, and social work research. The records document the Project's pioneering efforts to develop diagnostic tools through which data on families known to social agencies could be classified and evaluated as the basis for prescribing treatment. It also attempted to measure changes in the families' ability to function in matters of finances, child-rearing, and marital relationships. Among those associated with the Project were Madeline Berry, Beulah Compton, Mildred Conlan, Alice Overton, Helen Harris Perlman, Virginia Satir, Katherine Tinker, and Alice Voiland.

8,677. Study of Social Work Education
Records. 1946-53. 4.25 ft.
Open. Unpublished guide.
University of Minnesota, Social Welfare History Archives.
Sponsored by the National Council on Social Work Education and directed by Ernest V. Hollis with the assistance of Alice Taylor, the Study examined the objectives and content of social work education as it related to the needs of social work practice, particularly to the lack of trained social workers to work in expanding social programs. Correspondence, minutes, reports, reference material, and questionnaire responses, including questionnaires completed by heads of social work schools and programs as well as material from a 1949 conference called to define the present and future role of social work in a democratic society. The Carnegie Corporation-funded Study culminated in *Social Work Education in the United States: The Report of a Study Made for the National Council on Social Work Education* (Columbia University Press, 1951). Other individuals involved in the Study include Sue Spencer, Jane Hoey, Helen R. Wright, and Harriett M. Bartlett, chairman of the National Council on Social Work Education's study committee.

8,678. Survey Associates, Inc.
Records. 1891-1952. 125 ft.
Open. Published guide.
University of Minnesota, Social Welfare History Archives.
Survey Associates was a membership organization established in 1912 to support publication of *Survey* magazine, which had been published by the New York Charity Organization Society. Minutes, financial records, manuscripts, correspondence, memoranda, photos, and other editorial and production materials. Includes correspondence with Grace Abbott, Jane Addams, Florence E. Allen, Helen Cody Baker, Marion Clinch Calkins, Rossa B. Cooley, Crystal Eastman, Helen Hall, Alice Hamilton, Katharine F. Lenroot, Frances Perkins, Eleanor Roosevelt, Anna Louise Strong, Mary Van Kleeck, Miriam Van Waters, and Lillian Wald. From 1922 until 1949 the Associates supported publication of two periodicals: *Survey Graphic,* which sought to interpret social and economic developments for an audience of concerned laymen, and *Survey Midmonthly,* a digest of the social work field for social workers and agency board members.

The activities of *Survey* associate editors Beulah Amidon, Ann Reed Brenner, Florence Loeb Kellogg, and Gertrude Springer are reflected in the records. Among the subjects discussed frequently are child welfare, civil liberties, economic planning, health and health insurance, housing, immigration, industrial relations and working conditions, international relations, pacifism, relief and unemployment, race relations, settlements, and the social work profession. See *Descriptive Inventories of Collections in the Social Welfare History Archives Center* (Westport, CT: Greenwood Publishing Corporation, 1970).

8,679. Travelers Aid Association of America
Records. 1910-75. 31 ft. and 36 microfilm reels.
Open. Unpublished guide.
University of Minnesota, Social Welfare History Archives.
The Association grew out of late 19th-century efforts of YWCAs and other organizations to help young single women who were migrating to cities to seek employment. The travelers aid organizations later broadened their focus to help all needy traveling persons, including immigrants, black migrant families, and the elderly. Constitutions and bylaws; minutes, reports, agendas, and resolutions of the board of directors and committees; minutes, speech texts, reports, lists of delegates, programs, and delegate packets from national and regional conferences; directories of local travelers aid services; procedural manuals; training material for travelers aid caseworkers; historical summaries; bulletins and newsletters; reports and studies of travelers aid activities; and scrapbooks. Local travelers aid societies banded together in 1917 to form the National Travelers Aid Association, which fostered broader cooperation among the local societies. The national records document Travelers Aid's role in

cooperative efforts between government agencies and voluntary organizations to cope with the large transient population during the depression—particularly through the Committee on Care of Transients and Homeless—and with traveling armed services personnel, their families, and European refugees during WWII. The records reflect the efforts of Bertha McCall, who served as the Association's general director from 1933 to 1949. Most of the Association's records are also available on microfilm.

The name of the National Travelers Aid Association was changed to National Association of Travelers Aid Societies in 1920, to the National Association for Travelers Aid and Transient Service in 1934, to the National Travelers Aid Association in 1938, and the Travelers Aid Association of America in 1966. The Association merged with the International Social Service, American Branch, to form Travelers Aid-International Social Service in 1972, but separated and resumed the title Travelers Aid Association of America in 1977.

8,680. Travelers Aid Society of Minneapolis
Records. 1906-75. 3 ft.
Open. Unpublished guide.
University of Minnesota, Social Welfare History Archives.
The Society was created in ca. 1906 by the Woman's Christian Association and the local YWCA to assist needy travelers. Articles of incorporation, minutes, financial records, correspondence, reports, and clippings. The YWCA and Woman's Christian Association began the work to provide protective services for young women and immigrant groups moving into Minneapolis. They met young women at the train station, provided lodging at a "Women's Hotel," and helped the women find employment. The Society was incorporated as an independent agency in 1929. The Society's later work included casework services to transient men, women, and families during the depression and to military transients and their families during WWII and the Korean War. The Society disbanded in 1975.

8,681. United Neighborhood Houses of New York City
Records. 1898-1961. 48 ft.
Open. Published guide.
University of Minnesota, Social Welfare History Archives.
Formed in 1900 as the New York Association of Neighborhood Workers, the organization enabled its members to compare experiences and to take part in cooperative projects to improve conditions in New York City's tenement districts. Minutes, financial records, correspondence, programs and proceedings of meetings, speeches, testimony given before legislative bodies, reports, photos, scrapbooks, and clippings. Includes records of committees concerned with legislation, housing, consumer affairs, education, and unemployment and reflect the organization's efforts to analyze conditions and influence public policy at the municipal, state, and national levels. Other subjects discussed in the records include day care; clubs for women and girls; settlement art, drama, and music activities; and the Americanization of immigrants. Among the women represented in the collection are Mary K. Simkhovitch, who was a founder of the New York Association of Neighborhood Workers; Helen Hall; and Helen M. Harris, who was the executive director of United Neighborhood Houses from 1947 to 1971. The organization was incorporated under its current name in 1919.

Also included in the collection are two feet of records, 1926-44, of the League of Mothers of United Neighborhood Houses, which was organized in 1912 to bring together New York City mothers' clubs operating under the auspices of settlements, churches, day nurseries, and kindergartens. The League, which became part of United Neighborhood Houses in 1921, sought to help individual women recognize their responsibilities in the home, neighborhood, and community and to transform the mothers' clubs into a significant social and civic force. The League's records describe studies and projects in housing, health, child welfare, consumer affairs, home management, and recreation. See *Descriptive Inventories of Collections in the Social Welfare History Archives Center* (Westport, CT: Greenwood Publishing Corporation, 1970).

8,682. Voluntary Action Center
Records. 1945-74. 8 in.
Open. Unpublished guide.
University of Minnesota, Social Welfare History Archives.
Organized in St. Paul, MN, in 1945 as Volunteer Bureau, Inc., and reorganized in 1975 under its current name, the Center acts as a clearinghouse for placement of volunteers in positions with local health and welfare agencies. Minutes, correspondence, memoranda, reports, a scrapbook, and other records reflect volunteer support for activities, including visits to the elderly; tape recordings for the blind; assistance for unescorted elderly persons, handicapped individuals, and children at the airport; hospital work; transportation for patients and social service agency clients; and distribution of food and toys at Thanksgiving and Christmas. Also contains the motion picture "Volunteers Serve in the City."

8,683. Wartime Committee on Personnel in the Social Services
Records. 1942-46. 3 in.
Open. Unpublished guide.
University of Minnesota, Social Welfare History Archives.
The Committee was formed by professional social work organizations and schools of social work in 1943 to address the shortage of trained social service personnel during WWII. Minutes, correspondence, and reports document the impact the draft and war mobilization had upon the social service field, both in the movement of social workers into the military and in increased needs for social services because of disruptions of peacetime community patterns. Organizations represented on the Committee were the American Association of Social Workers, the American Association of Medical Social Workers, the American Association of Psychiatric Social Workers, the American Association for the Study of Group Work, and the American Association of Schools of Social Work. Harriett M. Bartlett, chairman of the Committee and president of the American Association of Medical Social Workers, and Leona Massoth and Elisabeth Mills, who were president and secretary, respectively, of the American Association of Social Workers, are represented most prominently throughout the collection. Others who were active in the Committee's work included Gordon Hamilton, Grace Coyle, Ann Elizabeth Neely, and Marian Russell. The Committee ceased functioning in 1946.

8,684. Young Women's Christian Association of Mount Vernon, NY
Records. 1917-69. 8.75 ft.
Open. Unpublished guide.
University of Minnesota, Social Welfare History Archives.
Organized in 1917, the Association began its work by operating a residential home and cafeteria for young working women. Later club activities were designed for primary and secondary school students, working women, and homemakers. Board and committee minutes, financial records, reports and evaluations prepared for the national YWCA, project files, scrapbooks, and clippings provide information on the group's programs, which included seminars and classes, a day camp, and a nursery school. The records also reflect the tension that followed the influx of blacks, Italians, and Jews into the community, particularly dissension about providing integrated services for blacks. The Mount Vernon YWCA dissolved in 1969.

8,685. Youngdahl, Benjamin Emanuel
Papers. 1920-66. 10 ft.
Open. Published guide.
University of Minnesota, Social Welfare History Archives.
Correspondence, speeches, articles, poems, and a scrapbook of Youngdahl (1897-1970), who was director of social service for the Minnesota State Emergency Relief Administration from 1933 to 1937, director of public assistance for the Minnesota State Board of Control from 1937 to 1939, and professor at the George Warren Brown School of Social Work at Washington University in St. Louis from 1939 to 1966. Includes Youngdahl's correspondence with Oveta (Culp) Hobby, Jane Hoey, Edna (Fischel) Gellhorn, and Charlotte Towley. Also included are letters of condolence, tributes, and other correspondence upon the death of Washington University faculty members Helen Hayden and Ruth Endicott Lewis as well as Youngdahl's correspondence with Joanna Colcord throughout her lengthy illness. See *Descriptive Inventories of Collections in the Social Welfare History Archives Center* (Westport, CT: Greenwood Publishing Corporation, 1970).

8,686. Zimand, Gertrude (Folks)
Papers. 1915-66. 2 ft.
Open. Published guide.
University of Minnesota, Social Welfare History Archives.
A social worker and reformer, Zimand (1894?-1966) was a founder of the National Committee on Employment of Youth and from 1943 to 1955 general secretary of the National Child Labor Committee. Correspondence, articles and speeches, memoranda, reports, and other papers relate primarily to her work with the National Child Labor Committee and to child labor in general. Also contains some personal papers, including correspondence with her father Homer Folks, a founder of the National Child Labor Committee; Paul Kellogg; Lillian Wald; and Sol Markoff. Zimand was associated with the National Child Labor Committee from 1916 to 1955. She married Savel Zimand (1891-1967), a journalist and health educator, in 1926. See *Descriptive Inventories of Collections in the Social Welfare History Archives Center* (Westport, CT: Greenwood Publishing Corporation, 1970).

MOORHEAD

8,687. Cheston, Mary Godley Starr
Papers. 1902. 12-page item.
Open. Unpublished guide.
Northwest Minnesota Historical Center.
Unpublished reminiscence of Cheston (1902-), a retired teacher living in the Norwegian community of Ullman in Norman County, MN, contains her descriptions of planting time in Ullman at the turn of the century.

8,688. Christianson, Mrs. Marvin E.
Papers. 1969. 1 folder.
Open. Unpublished guide.
Northwest Minnesota Historical Center.
In 1969 Donna Andrae Christianson (1931-) served in the Minnesota House of Representatives from legislative district 66a, replacing her husband who died in office. Correspondence, a House journal, photos, and telegrams.

8,689. Comstock, Soloman Gilman
Papers. 1872-1939. 58 Hollinger boxes and 68 vols.
Open. Unpublished guide.

Northwest Minnesota Historical Center.
Correspondence, diaries, ledgers, and clippings of Comstock. Includes letters dated 1900 to 1939 from his children Jesse Comstock, George Comstock, and Ada (Comstock) Notestein (1876-1973) and clippings concerning Ada Notestein's career in education. A Moorhead native, she attended the University of Minnesota from 1892 to 1894 but received undergraduate and graduate degrees in literature from Smith College. She served as dean of women at the University of Minnesota from 1906 to 1912 and at Smith College from 1912 to 1923. The following year she became the first full-time president of Radcliffe College, a position she held for 20 years. In addition, she was an advisor to the Encyclopaedia Britannica Foundation and a member of the board of the Motion Picture Research Council; she was president of the national AAUW from 1921 to 1923 and continued to be active in that organization until 1938.

8,690. Northwest Minnesota History
Oral history. 1976-77. 19 tapes.
Open. Unpublished guides.
Northwest Minnesota Historical Center.
Taped interviews with 18 women who reside or have resided in northwestern Minnesota chiefly consist of the reminiscences of housewives and teachers but they also include recollections of women from other occupations; ca. one-half of the women interviewed also discuss immigrant or second-generation experiences during the late 19th and early 20th centuries. Represented are Gladys Ray, a Native American teacher and army nurse whose grandparents arrived on the White Earth Indian Reservation in 1912; Beatrice Schaefer, retired registered nurse, who discusses the Norwegian settlement and Norwegian church in Lac qui Parle County, MN, and her career; Hannah Harris, retired insurance saleswoman, who describes her parents' immigration to the US during the 1860s and 1870s as well as her work with the Ancient Order of United Workmen Auxiliary, the forerunner of the Pioneer Mutual Insurance Company; [Mrs.] Gladys Westrum, a housewife, who discusses her Swedish ancestry and the Swedish-American community in Moorhead; [Mrs.] Freda Bjornson, an import store employee whose parents emigrated from Iceland to Canada and then to North Dakota, discussing the Icelandic community in Garder, ND, and her experiences working in the "cook car" for a 24-member threshing crew; [Mrs.] Clara Euren Furcht, daughter of Swedish immigrant Gustaf Euren and an employee of the Great Northern Railroad for nearly 45 years; [Mrs.] Eva Thortvedt, who tells about her experiences at Moorhead Normal School from 1915 to 1918 and her careers as a telephone and Western Union operator, telegrapher, and store clerk in Moorhead from 1930 into the 1940s; and [Mrs.] Faith Evers Sprung, an Ortonville, MN, farmwife who with her husband William Sprung describe life during the depression as well as the prisoners of war during WWII who worked on their farm as part of the Ortonville Camp program.

MORRIS

8,691. Bogie, Mary (Hawn)
Oral history. 1975. 1 tape and transcript.
Open. Unpublished guide.
West Central Minnesota Historical Center.
In a taped and transcribed interview with [Mrs.] Bogie (1879-), she discusses her childhood and youth; her family's migration from an eastern province of Canada, where she was born, to Pope County, MN; and her life on the family farm.

8,692. Burfiend, Helen Margaret (Allanson)
Oral history. 1973. 2 tapes and transcripts.
Open. Unpublished guide.
West Central Minnesota Historical Center.
Taped and transcribed interviews with [Mrs.] Burfiend (1901-), the daughter of George and Bertha Allanson, contain information about her family history, schooling, her participation in high school girls' basketball, job experiences, and social life in Wheaton, MN, where she lived. Burfiend's great-grandfather Major Joseph Brown was the founder of Browns Valley and Henderson, MN.

8,693. Carson, Josephine (Gran)
Oral history. 1967-71. 4 tapes.
Partially restricted. Unpublished guide and transcript.
West Central Minnesota Historical Center.
Born on a farm outside Kensington, MN, [Mrs.] Carson (1886-) is the daughter of John Peter Gran, whose family helped settle Douglas County. Interviews pertain to a wide range of topics, including her family and husband's background; her parents and children; marriage, her home, and activities in the house; immigration and settlement; survival; farming; social life; WWI; medical experiences, including her life as a nurse trainee; Duluth; Sunday activities, churches, and the ladies' society; race relations; wealth distribution and inheritance; holidays and shopping; Indians; peddlers; and meals.

8,694. Cartwright, Mabel (Stone)
Oral history. 1976. 1 tape and transcript.
Open. Unpublished guide.
West Central Minnesota Historical Center.
Interview with [Mrs. Paul] Cartwright (1886-), a Morris resident whose family has been prominent in both business and political activities at local and state levels, pertains chiefly to her personal history and provides some insight into the social history of the community.

8,695. Cunningham, Agnes (O'Leary)
Oral history. 1973. 1 tape and transcript.
Open. Unpublished guide.
West Central Minnesota Historical Center.
For many years [Mrs.] Cunningham (1907-) was a teacher in the Wheaton, MN, area. Interview in which she discusses family and personal history, survival in the early days, schooling in Big Stone County, and diseases and other health problems in the schools. Also included are expressions of her feelings about changing times and practices in the field of education.

8,696. Eames, Camilla (Hendricks)
Oral history. 1975. 1 tape and transcript.
Open. Unpublished guide.
West Central Minnesota Historical Center.
Taped and transcribed interview with [Mrs. Earl] Eames (ca. 1898-), the wife of a prominent businessman and a Morris resident since 1922, contains details about her involvement in and the organization and goals of such Morris area clubs as the American Legion Auxiliary, the First Lutheran Church board, the Ladies Aid Club, the library board, the LWV, and the Literary Club. Also includes her analysis of the past and present position of women in Morris.

8,697. Eddy, Josephine
Oral history. 1975. 1 tape and transcript.
Open. Unpublished guide.
West Central Minnesota Historical Center.
Taped and transcribed interview with Eddy (1889-), a teacher and clubwoman, contains her reminiscences about early work experiences with other women on the WPA as well as comments about her more recent involvement in such women's organizations as the Students Club, the Literary Club, the LWV, the Cancer Society, and the Hospital Auxiliary. Also included are her opinions concerning the status of women over time. Born in Verndale, MN, Eddy attended the University of Minnesota in Minneapolis and taught school for 11 years. Then, after returning to the University for social work courses, she became employed in Stevens and Swift counties. She became an active clubwoman after her retirement.

8,698. Forde, Astrid (Flack)
Oral history. 1976. 1 tape.
Open. No guide.
West Central Minnesota Historical Center.
Interview with [Mrs. G. O.] Forde pertains to the problems faced by Pope County, MN, churches when they switched from Norwegian to the English language in the early 20th century.

8,699. Gramm, Peg
Oral history. 1975. 1 tape and transcript.
Open. Unpublished guide.
West Central Minnesota Historical Center.
In her interview, Gramm (1954-), who was born in Bloomington, IL, and who moved in 1960 with her family to Hancock, MN, discusses the standard practices, customs, philosophies, and activities of the Apostolic Christian church, of which she has been a member since 1971. She places special emphasis on the role of women in the church and on social customs; she also expresses opinions regarding birth control and abortion.

8,700. Grove, Cora
Oral history. 1973. 1 tape and transcript.
Open. Unpublished guide.
West Central Minnesota Historical Center.
In her interview Grove, a former Morris town clerk, recalls that city's social life at the turn of the century, highlighting her experiences at the fair and in community clubs.

8,701. Hanson, Mrs. Oliver
Oral history. Nd. 1 tape and transcript.
Open. Unpublished guide.
West Central Minnesota Historical Center.
Taped and transcribed interview with Ethel (Ellingson) Hanson (1896-), who grew up in Grant and Douglas counties, MN, pertains to her school days and first teachers; church practices, such as burial rites and her confirmation instruction; early transportation; the 1888 diphtheria epidemic; and early Hoffman, MN, businesses.

8,702. Kohn, Kathryn
Oral history. 1975. 1 tape and transcript.
Open. Unpublished guide.
West Central Minnesota Historical Center.
Born in Kiel, Germany, Kohn (1899-) emigrated with her family to the US in 1907, first moving to Luverne, MN, but eventually settling in the Barrett area. Interview includes her reminiscences of early life in Grant County as compared to life in Germany; it also contains her recollection of a speech Theodore Roosevelt gave in Luverne in 1912.

8,703. Larson, Marie (Jacobson)
Oral history. 1974. 1 tape and transcript.
Open. Unpublished guide.
West Central Minnesota Historical Center.
[Mrs.] Larson (1888-), a farmwife, is the last surviving daughter of one of the first families who in 1866 settled in Stevens County, MN. In the interview she provides a short family history, describes the life of an early settler on the prairie, and discusses home remedies. Interview also contains her reflections on childhood experiences, social activities, education, and the depression.

8,704. Mohr, Elsie (Schlueter)
Oral history. 1974. 1 tape and transcript.
Open. Unpublished guide.
West Central Minnesota Historical Center.
Born in Nebraska, [Mrs.] Mohr (1890-) and her family moved in 1901 to Horton Township in Stevens County, MN; she has lived on a farm in that township and in the city of Morris ever since. Interview relates to her early experiences in a rural setting, and she compares life as a

German-American citizen during WWI to life during WWII. Mohr also describes an economic boom and the depression as it affected her community.

8,705. Morris, MN, Indian School
Records. 1887-1909. 6 in.
Open. Unpublished guide.
West Central Minnesota Historical Center.
The School was founded in 1887 by Mother Mary Joseph Lynch and the Sisters of Mercy with the support of the US Bureau of Indian Affairs, and it operated until 1909. Reports pertaining to the School, its faculty, and students; correspondence with the BIA; and letters from parents of pupils at the School. Much of the material consists of items photocopied from National Archives Record Group no. 75.

8,706. Olson, Florence; Norman, Rowland, and Norman, Gertrude; Nygaard, Cora; and Anderson, Emil
Oral history. 1975. 1 tape and transcript.
Open. Unpublished guide.
West Central Minnesota Historical Center.
Interviews include one with Florence J. (Peterson) Olson (1913-), who worked as a nurse's aide for 19 years in and around Granite Falls, MN. She was born on a Chippewa County farm, attended school through the eighth grade, and performed house and farm work until her marriage in 1935. A niece of Olaf Swensson (1843-1923), a self-appointed lay pastor who ran unsuccessfully for Minnesota governor and the state House of Representatives between 1885 and 1895, she spent many summers with her Swensson cousins on their farm. Also included is an interview with Gertrude Branum [Mrs. Rowland] Norman (1908-), a country schoolteacher and farmwife; since 1968 she and her husband have been caretakers of the Swensson House, the brick home, now a museum, built by Olaf Swensson at the turn of the century. In her interview she describes the main floor, various rooms, and artifacts in the House. Born in Wheaton, MN, Norman graduated from country school, completed high school in 1926 in Montevideo, and also took one year of training in that town before becoming a country teacher for four years. After she married, she farmed with her husband. Also contained is an interview with Cora (Anderson) Nygaard (1897-), a neighbor to the Swenssons and friend of the Swensson women, in which she describes her experiences and recollections of the Swensson family. Nygaard was employed in Minnesota in a variety of positions both before and after her marriage in 1923.

8,707. Parson, Lillian
Oral history. 1974. 1 tape and transcript.
Open. Unpublished guide.
West Central Minnesota Historical Center.
In an interview Parson (1896-), who was one of the first woman doctors to practice in Grant County, MN, discusses her personal family background, especially her medical training, experience, and practice.

8,708. Pederson, Mabel (Knutson)
Oral history. 1976. 1 tape.
Open. No guide.
West Central Minnesota Historical Center.
Interview with [Mrs. Elmer R.] Pederson (1901-) pertains to the problems local churches encountered when they switched from Norwegian to the English language.

8,709. Reminiscences of Grant County
Oral history. 1972-75. 7 tapes and transcripts.
Open. Unpublished guide.
West Central Minnesota Historical Center.
Taped and transcribed interviews with Grant County, MN, residents, including Mrs. Tena Fjoslien (1872-), the daughter of Andrew Meyergrins, and a native of Ofstad Township, Otter Tail County; she later had ten children, all of whom were born in a dugout. The interview contains descriptions of her early neighbors, schools she attended and her first teachers, and a diphtheria epidemic. An interview with Emma Brenvold (1883-), whose parents came to Grant County in 1880 and who was born near Pomme de Terre Village, includes her reminiscences about her first teachers, camping wagons on the Abercrombie Trail, local businessmen, the Village farmyard, and Indians on the river. An interview with Mrs. Tosten Hagen (1877-?), who was born in a dugout near the Pomme de Terre Village, contains descriptions of her parents' experiences as a pair of Minnesota's earliest settlers in the 1860s, including her father's fur trapping activity and trade with the Indians; life on the Pomme de Terre River; her first teachers; a Fergus Falls, MN, sewing school; local stagecoach routes; and early area businessmen. An interview with Mrs. Hodgson Nelson (1886-), who was born in Delaware Township, provides details about Bill Moses, his "big farm" with running water, and the local county fair, which he organized; and about her father's education at Hamline University, his discussions about politics with General Barrett, and his participation in the civil war against the Indians in the New Ulm raid. She also recalls her own education at Elbow Lake High School and at the University of Minnesota.

8,710. Schaeffer, Elaine C.
Papers. 1966- . No size given.
Closed. No guide.
West Central Minnesota Historical Center.
Letters to the editor, term papers, and clippings of Schaeffer (1903-), a teacher and academic administrator, pertain to the Frank Schaeffer family and the early history of Pomme de Terre Village, where she was born. After graduating from Elbow Lake High School, Schaeffer attended Macalester College and later earned an MA in history at the University of California, Berkeley. She served as a high school instructor and principal and was the head of the history department at Elgin Academy and Junior College in Elgin, IL. Schaeffer retired in Elbow Lake.

8,711. Schmidgall, Mr. and Mrs. Floyd
Oral history. 1975. 1 tape.
Open. Unpublished guide.
West Central Minnesota Historical Center.
In their interview Floyd Schmidgall (1928-) and his wife Mrs. Schmidgall (1929-) describe the customs, beliefs, and practices of the Apostolic Christian church.

8,712. Schumaker, Mary
Oral history. 1973. 2 tapes and transcript.
Open. Unpublished guide.
West Central Minnesota Historical Center.
Taped and transcribed interview with Schumaker (1888-), an Ortonville, MN, teacher and principal, who describes her family history, teaching, social and intellectual activities, the Grand Army of the Republic, Ortonville and the railroad, WWI and the repression of German citizens, and storms.

8,713. Sherman, Margaret
Oral history. 1975. 1 tape and transcript.
Open. Unpublished guide.
West Central Minnesota Historical Center.
Taped and transcribed interview with Sherman (1912-), a public health nurse, relates to the attitudes of Stevens County, MN, residents toward public health and Sherman's duties as a public health nurse. After graduating from the University of Minnesota school of public health, she began a long nursing career, which has included employment with the Minneapolis Community Health Service and positions in Stevens County; since ca. 1960 she has worked in Wadena County.

8,714. Stahler, Bonnie (Giberson)
Oral history. 1976. 1 tape and transcript.
Open. Unpublished guide.
West Central Minnesota Historical Center.
Interview in which Stahler (1918-) discusses high school sports for women before and during the depression.

8,715. Strandsness, Elisabeth
Oral history. 1975. 1 tape and transcript.
Access restricted. Unpublished guide.
West Central Minnesota Historical Center.
Interview with Strandsness (1896-), a worker for the US Forest Service for 30 years and owner of the Strandsness Prairie tract before The Nature Conservancy, or TNC, acquired it. She has since retired to the farm on which she was born.

8,716. Strandsness, Elisabeth
Papers. 1873-1975. 3 vols.
Open. Unpublished guide.
West Central Minnesota Historical Center.
Papers of Strandsness (1896-) largely pertain to the Strandsness Prairie, a tract of land she owned. Includes correspondence with The Nature Conservancy about the transfer of the Prairie from Strandsness to the TNC, items regarding ownership and management of the land, and a Prairie history she wrote. Also contains clippings about the Strandsness family and her great-grandfather's reminiscences of his coming to a homestead claim from Norway.

8,717. Swanke, Anna (Kaufman)
Oral history. 1973. 2 tapes.
Open. Unpublished guide.
West Central Minnesota Historical Center.
Interview with Swanke (1894-), a Browns Valley teacher whose husband moved to that area in 1886 as an infant, contains her descriptions of early family history, education and college, home and social life as a youth, her early teaching experiences and the teaching methods she used, WWI, the bakery, and church.

8,718. Swanke, Anna (Kaufman)
Papers. 1885-1968. 0.5 ft.
Open. Unpublished guide.
West Central Minnesota Historical Center.
Swanke (1894-), the second wife of Ernst Gustav Swanke, was a Browns Valley, MN, schoolteacher. Unpublished biography she wrote about her husband, which was based on stories and his recollections after moving with his family in 1886 from Wisconsin to Browns Valley; clippings pertaining to the Browns Valley area as well as clippings and place mats about Samuel Brown's famous ride in 1866 from Sisseton, SD, to Browns Valley to warn settlers of an Indian attack; and short writings by some of Swanke's elementary school pupils, which contain reminiscences of pioneer residents in the area as told to the children.

8,719. Wells, Harry H., and Family
Papers. 1880-1961. 17 bacases and 103 vols.
Access restricted. Unpublished guide.
West Central Minnesota Historical Center.
Business records and family correspondence of Wells (1851-1936), a prominent Morris banker, merchant, and legislator; also includes correspondence of Mary March Benedict, the daughter of Wells's business partner and son-in-law Charles H. March. The material provides information about the active involvement of Wells family women in business ventures.

8,720. Wheeler, Clara (Torgerson)
Oral history. 1976. 1 tape and transcript.
Open. Unpublished guide.
West Central Minnesota Historical Center.
Taped and transcribed interview with Wheeler

(1891-), who was a schoolteacher before her marriage, relates to life on a farm in the Glenwood, MN, area and the Sioux Indian uprising. She was one of 14 children born on her parents' Glenwood cattle farm. She attended school in district 40 and was a student at Glenwood Academy.

NORTHFIELD

8,721. First Ladies of Northfield
Collection. Nd. 9 items.
Open. Newspaper index.
Northfield Public Library.
Represented in clippings about notable and early professional and business women in Northfield are Ann Hendrix (Loomis) [Mrs. John W.] North, first woman in the town in 1857; Effie (Stranahan) [Mrs. Gustav] Santino, in 1926 the first woman city official; Laura Baker, in 1898 the first woman in the US to establish a private school for mentally retarded children; Nellie [Mrs. Issac] Lenout, in 1881 the first local feminist; Genevieve Tucker, in 1883 the first woman physician in Northfield; Margaret Jane (Evans) [Mrs. George] Huntington, the first dean of women at Carleton College in Northfield and in 1899 the first woman member of the Northfield school board; and Marie Piesinger, in 1925 the first woman pharmacist and also the first woman to serve on a state board of pharmacy in the US.

8,722. Bacon, Astrid Ihme
Papers. 1976. 1 item.
Open. Unpublished guide.
Norwegian-American Historical Association.
Born in Twedestrand, Norway, Bacon (1903-) emigrated to the US in 1914. A history she wrote of a Norwegian community in San Pedro, CA, chronicles the experiences of its residents.

8,723. Bergh, Bolette Stub
Papers. 1944. 3 items.
Open. Unpublished guide.
Norwegian-American Historical Association.
Clippings contain the memoirs of [Mrs. Johannes E.] Bergh (1852-1940), a Lutheran pastor's wife who lived in Sacred Heart, MN, from 1872 until 1905.

8,724. Boe, A. Sophie
Papers. 1814-1936. 1 vol. and 61 items.
Open. Unpublished guide.
Norwegian-American Historical Association.
[Miss] Boe (1879-1937), whose father N. E. Bøe was a minister, became a teacher and writer. Correspondence, including letters from her grandfather Lars Davidson Reque; a history of Liberty Prairie Church in Deerfield, WI, where many of her relatives were members; material relating to Augsburg Seminary and Svein Nilsson, who was the editor of *Billed-Magazin;* genealogical information; and a biography of her father.

8,725. Brye, Martha M.
Papers. 1880. 1 vol.
Open. Unpublished guide.
Norwegian-American Historical Association.
Scrapbook of Brye (1864-1946), a teacher and nurse from Coon Valley and La Crosse, WI, contains clippings of a poem by Kristofer Janson, an address given by professor O. J. Breda at the Kristofer Janson festival in Decorah, IA, and Laur. Larsen's address at the President Garfield memorial program in Decorah.

8,726. Dahl, Borghild
Papers. 1944-64. 9 items.
Open. Unpublished guide.
Norwegian-American Historical Association.
Correspondence, articles, and brochures of Dahl (1890-), who was a writer, lecturer, and teacher.

8,727. Dahl, Dorthea
Papers. Nd. No size given.
Open. Unpublished guide.
Norwegian-American Historical Association.
Dahl (1883-1958), a Norwegian-born author who came to America at the age of two, wrote several books and many short stories that were published in the Norwegian-American press. Material about and reviews of books by Dahl.

8,728. De Witt, Ruth
Papers. 1976. 1 item.
Open. Unpublished guide.
Norwegian-American Historical Association.
Brochure consists of a descriptive record of the landmarks and history of Dunn Township, Dane County, WI, and was prepared for the US Bicentennial celebration.

8,729. Deen, Tilla R. Dahl
Papers. 1949. 16-page item.
Open. Unpublished guide.
Norwegian-American Historical Association.
Article in which Deen (1868-?) describes pioneer life from 1870 to ca. 1890 in Blue Earth County and in the Cottonwood, MN, area.

8,730. Enochson, Marie Johnson
Papers. Nd. 1 item.
Open. Unpublished guide.
Norwegian-American Historical Association.
Autobiographical sketch by Enochson (1864-1953) contains her reminiscences of Norway, her journey to America, and life in the Wild Rice community, ND, located in the Red River Valley.

8,731. Ernstsen, Oline
Papers. 1939-56. 2 items.
Open. Unpublished guide.
Norwegian-American Historical Association.
Recollections of [Mrs. Daniel] Ernstsen (1882-?), a Norwegian-born pioneer housewife of Bear River, MN, include her descriptions of passage to America and early settlement experiences, religious life, and transportation and communication. Also contains an historical sketch of the founding of the ladies' aid organization in the Bear River Lutheran congregation in 1906.

8,732. Fedde, Elizabeth
Papers. Nd. 2 items.
Open. Unpublished guide.
Norwegian-American Historical Association.
Autobiographical account, translated from Norwegian, and original notes of Fedde (1850-1921), a deaconess and hospital administrator. She began her career in 1873 at the Deaconess Home in Kristiania, now Oslo, Norway, and 10 years later she came to New York where she organized a deaconess program affiliated with the Seaman's Mission Church in Brooklyn. Eventually Sister Elizabeth, as she was known, established deaconess hospitals in Brooklyn and in Minneapolis. Her autobiographical account covers her career in Norway and the first two years she spent in the US.

8,733. Folkedahl, Beulah
Papers. 1958-71. 53 items.
Open. Unpublished guide.
Norwegian-American Historical Association.
[Miss] Folkedahl (1896-1971) was an historian and teacher. Correspondence, working papers for the Norwegian-American *Studies* volumes, and articles. After her retirement in 1960, Folkedahl organized the documents collection of the Norwegian-American Historical Association.

8,734. Fredricksen, Mabel
Papers. Nd. 2 vols.
Open. Unpublished guide.
Norwegian-American Historical Association.
Photo album and book entitled *Den gamle Richards Kunst at blive rig og lykkelig* were family keepsakes of [Mrs.] Fredricksen.

8,735. Garborg, Arne
Papers. 1919. No size given.
Open. Unpublished guide.
Norwegian-American Historical Association.
Correspondence of Garborg, a Norwegian poet, with Mabel Johnson Leland of Kenyon, MN, pertains to publication matters. Leland translated Garborg's *Den burtkomne faderen,* which was published in 1920 as *The Lost Father.*

8,736. Garborg, Hulda
Papers. 1914-15. 10 items.
Open. Unpublished guide.
Norwegian-American Historical Association.
Article written by Garborg, the wife of Norwegian poet Arne Garborg, relates to the American Indian; it was run serially in *Morgen-Posten* after her visit to the US in 1913.

8,737. Gjerset, Knut
Papers. Nd. 2145 items.
Open. Unpublished guide.
Norwegian-American Historical Association.
Material assembled for a biographical encyclopedia of Norwegian-Americans contains information about women who were involved in Norwegian-American activities before 1930, including Anna Margaret Brunsdale, Jorgine Slettede Boomer, Diderikke Ottesen Brandt, Rebekka Oline Giertsen Dahl, Gudrun Løchen Drewsen, Mrs. Manley L. Fossen, Marie Folrvard, Alma A. Guttersen, Aase Haugen, Sofie Jebe, Mabel Johnson Leland, Ingrid Egge Markhus, Berthe Peterson, and Elise Waerenskjold.

8,738. Glesne, Elise Torgrimson Fjelde
Papers. 1915-31. 176 items.
Open. Unpublished guide.
Norwegian-American Historical Association.
Glesne (1869-1946) was the wife of Iowa Lutheran clergyman Ole Glesne. Poems, both original and translated, and a story that appeared in *Familiens Magasin.*

8,739. Grevstad, Mathilde Berg
Papers. Nd. 2 items.
Open. Unpublished guide.
Norwegian-American Historical Association.
Translations of descriptive accounts by [Mrs.] Grevstad (1862-1952?) pertain to the experiences of her parents Ole-Iver Berg and Johanne Berg, who emigrated from Norway to Wisconsin in 1861, later moved to Fillmore County, MN, and finally settled in the Red River Valley.

8,740. Hagen, Petra
Papers. Nd. 1 vol.
Open. Unpublished guide.
Norwegian-American Historical Association.
Diary of Hagen (1876-1959), a St. Olaf College student, contains her comments about the election of 1896, a Foundation Day observance, Alpha Beta Chi programs, dormitory life, college discipline, faculty, students, and courses. Also includes photos.

8,741. Hansen, Anne M., and Hansen, H. J.
Papers. 1853. 1 item.
Open. Unpublished guide.
Norwegian-American Historical Association.
Letter written by a Janesville, Rock County, WI, resident to a relative contains descriptions of

American wages, climate, crops, machinery and tools, food, and work opportunities.

8,742. Hasler, Alice
Papers. 1961. 1 item.
Open. Unpublished guide.
Norwegian-American Historical Association.
An historical sketch of pioneer events in Scandinavia, Waupaca County, WI.

8,743. Hatgren, Thora
Papers. 1874. 1 item.
Open. Unpublished guide.
Norwegian-American Historical Association.
Letter written by an immigrant who settled in Hoboken, NJ, includes her descriptions of health, prices, and unemployment in America.

8,744. Haugen, Kristine
Papers. 1918-58. 93 vols.
Open. Unpublished guide.
Norwegian-American Historical Association.
[Mrs. John] Haugen (1878-1965) was a correspondent for the Norwegian-American press, and from 1928 to 1935 she served as editor of the *Oppdalslagets Yearbook;* her son Einar Haugen became a Harvard University professor. Scrapbooks of clippings from the press on a variety of topics, including the Norwegian-American Historical Association, and letters from Ole E. Rølvaag.

8,745. Hill, Mabel Peterson
Papers. Nd. 1 item.
Open. Unpublished guide.
Norwegian-American Historical Association.
Article written by Hill relates to Methodist missionaries in Utah.

8,746. Hilleboe, Gertrude M.
Papers. 1920-68. 13 boxes and 5 items.
Open. Unpublished guide.
Norwegian-American Historical Association.
[Miss] Hilleboe (1888-1976) was a teacher who in 1915 became the dean of women at St. Olaf College in Northfield; she held that position until 1958. Correspondence, including letters she wrote to the AAUW urging approved status for the College; speeches; records and reports; school notebooks; articles; poems; photos; scrapbooks; programs; citations; and other items. Much of the collection pertains to counseling, campus life, student housing and recruitment, funds solicitation, and WWI and WWII programs at the College. Also included are the records of Roche a Cree Lutheran Church in Arkdale, WI, papers of her grandfather Sjur H. Hilleboe, and correspondence with the family of her other grandfather E. T. Ytterboe.

Gertrude Hilleboe received a BA in 1912 from St. Olaf College and an MA in 1922 from Columbia University. She was a preceptress and teacher at Waldorf College one year before she began her 43-year career as dean of women at St. Olaf College. From 1917 to 1966 she was a member of the National Association of Deans of Women and held several offices in that organization; she also was president of the Minnesota Association of Deans of Women in 1932. Her book *Manitou Analecta* was published in 1968.

8,747. Hogstel, Mildred
Papers. 1976. 1 item.
Open. Unpublished guide.
Norwegian-American Historical Association.
An account of a brief journey made by a Texas resident to the homes of her ancestors in southern Norway also includes a genealogical compilation for the families of Johan and Anna Bronstad and Berger and Anna Rogstad.

8,748. Hougstad, Martha Hove
Papers. 1940. 1 item.
Open. Unpublished guide.
Norwegian-American Historical Association.
Reminiscences in which Hougstad (1867-1945) describes her life as the daughter of a Worth County, IA, farmer; her experiences as a college student; and her career as a piano and organ teacher in Northwood and Decorah, IA, and in Minneapolis. Her husband, a Lutheran clergyman, served parishes in Wisconsin.

8,749. Houkom, Nellie S. Johnson
Papers. Ca. 1948. No size given.
Open. Unpublished guide.
Norwegian-American Historical Association.
Historical sketches of pioneer farm life in Muskego and Trempealeau Valley, WI, were written by [Mrs. A.] Houkom and include descriptions of health, travel, neighbors, and church activity. She and her husband, a Lutheran clergyman, were married in 1894.

8,750. Hoyem, Nell M.
Papers. 1970?. 1 microfilm reel.
Open. Unpublished guide.
Norwegian-American Historical Association.
Microfilmed PhD thesis of Hoyem, submitted to Mankato State Teachers College, pertains to the life and work of John Dahle.

8,751. Jacobson, Clara
Papers. 1943. 2 items.
Open. Unpublished guide.
Norwegian-American Historical Association.
Reminiscences of Jacobson (1864-1949), a teacher, author, and daughter of Lutheran parish pastor Abraham Jacobson, consist of detailed descriptions of her childhood experiences to 1878 at Perry parsonage in western Dane County, WI. Includes comments on church school, books, music, dress, entertainment, trips, playmates, guests, the parsonage, household and farm employees, Monona Academy, and the tornado of 1878. Also contains a scrapbook of clippings from *Decorah-Posten* and *Reform.*

8,752. Jensen, Hanna Bugge
Papers. 1856-ca. 1909. 3 items.
Open. Unpublished guide.
Norwegian-American Historical Association.
[Mrs. Nils E.] Jensen (ca. 1841-1921) was the Norwegian-born wife of a Lutheran pastor at Highland Prairie, MN. Reminiscences, including descriptions of her journey to America, the parsonage, living conditions, her fear of Indians, and parish activities; a copy of the Highland Prairie congregation's formal request to the Norwegian synod for a pastor; and a copy of her husband's first sermon in the parish.

8,753. Johnson, Laura Edseth
Papers. 1953. 1 item.
Open. Unpublished guide.
Norwegian-American Historical Association.
Reminiscences of [Mrs. Severin] Johnson (1876-1962), a housewife who spent her childhood in Halstad, MN.

8,754. Kindem, Anna Sekse
Papers. 1938-68. 79 items.
Open. Unpublished guide.
Norwegian-American Historical Association.
[Mrs. Ingvald] Kindem (1896-1976) emigrated from Norway to the US in 1923 and became a Northfield resident. Clippings from Norwegian newspapers include letters and articles she and others wrote commenting on American prices, employment, politics, crops, the Fourth of July, the 1939 visit of Norwegian royalty to the US, WWII, reminiscences of Norway, St. Olaf College, lefse, Norwegian-American festivities, summer camps, and travel in the US and Norway.

8,755. Kittilsby, Agnes M.
Papers. 1894-ca. 1940. 199 items.
Open. Unpublished guide.
Norwegian-American Historical Association.
Correspondence, biographical notes, and scrapbooks of [Miss] Kittilsby (1880-1925), an Iowa-born college teacher, pertain to her teaching experiences at St. Ansgar Seminary, Waldorf College, Augustana College, St. Olaf College, and the Unity School in Honan, China.

8,756. Kvamme, Vera Joyce Fox
Papers. Nd. 11 vols.
Open. Unpublished guide.
Norwegian-American Historical Association.
Genealogical records of [Mrs. J. P.] Kvamme trace the Norwegian forefathers of the John Peder Kvamme, Sr., family and include a list of the descendants of Olav II, Saint, King of Norway.

8,757. Larsen, Gunhild Andrine Jacobsdatter
Papers. 1923-25. 1 item.
Open. Unpublished guide.
Norwegian-American Historical Association.
Articles in which [Mrs. Tobias] Larsen (1836-1934), a Norwegian-born pastor's wife, recalls her passage across the Atlantic to America, life in Muskego, WI, during the 1840s and 1850s, and her marriage in 1856. Also includes her comments on *Nordlyset* and the 1856 presidential election.

8,758. Larsen, Karen
Papers. 1881-1961. 54 items.
Open. Unpublished guide.
Norwegian-American Historical Association.
Papers of Larsen (1879-1961) contain photos, clippings, pamphlets, and diplomas and decorations that she and her sister Hanna Astrub Larsen and their father Laur. Larsen received.

8,759. Larson, Agnes M.
Papers. 1952-61. 18 items.
Open. Unpublished guide.
Norwegian-American Historical Association.
Correspondence of [Miss] Larson (1892-1967), a history professor at St. Olaf College, consists of letters she received from former students serving at armed forces bases in Germany, Korea, and the US.

8,760. Lutheran Deaconess Home and Hospital, Chicago
Records. 1896-1962. 62 items.
Open. Unpublished guide.
Norwegian-American Historical Association.
Constitution, correspondence, reports, history, and journals of this institution, which was founded in 1897. Collection also includes a biography of Marie Rorem, a deaconess and administrator at the Home and Hospital.

8,761. Lutheran Deaconess Home and Hospital, Minneapolis
Records. 1889-1939. 1 folder, 16 vols., and 32 items.
Open. Unpublished guide.
Norwegian-American Historical Association.
Reports, correspondence, histories, and catalogs of the Hospital, founded in 1888 under the leadership of Sister Elizabeth Fedde of Brooklyn, NY.

8,762. Lutheran Ladies' Seminary
Papers. 1898-1920. 34 items.
Open. Unpublished guide.
Norwegian-American Historical Association.
Reports, photos, catalogs, and journals of a Red Wing, MN, school that was established in 1894 and operated until 1920.

8,763. McMahon, Ruth (Lima)
Papers. 1886-1976. 12 folders.
Open. Unpublished guide.
Norwegian-American Historical Association.
Papers of [Mrs.] McMahon, a housewife, which primarily consist of correspondence of her parents Ole Lima (1860-1931) and Martha Lima

(1862-1900), pertain to the settlement of and pioneer life in Griggs County, Dakota Territory, after 1881. A 1922 St. Olaf College graduate, McMahon studied under and worked with Ole E. Rølvaag.

8,764. Magelssen, Thora
Papers. 1923-32. 1 vol.
Open. Unpublished guide.
Norwegian-American Historical Association.
Scrapbook of Magelssen (?-1968), a Rushford, MN, teacher and homemaker, contains correspondence from Knut Gjerset, Kristian Prestgard, and Ole E. Rølvaag and clippings about the Magelssen family, Ola M. Levang, and Henrik Shipstead, among others.

8,765. Monson, Clara
Papers. 1871-1964. 43 items.
Open. Unpublished guide.
Norwegian-American Historical Association.
Memoirs of [Mrs. Martin O.] Monson (1888-), a housewife from Lafayette County, WI; correspondence written from Wiota and Luther Valley settlements about farming, housing, dress, epidemics, school, church, and social activities in pioneer days; histories of the Synstelian, Tollefsrude, and Brenum families; and a photo.

8,766. Nordic Arts Clubs
Records. 1936- . 86 items.
Open. Unpublished guide.
Norwegian-American Historical Association.
Records of two Northfield women's organizations, most of whose members belonged to the St. Olaf College faculty or were faculty wives. One of the groups existed only from 1939 to 1950.

8,767. Norse American Centennial Daughters of St. Paul
Records. 1922-46. 342 items.
Open. Unpublished guide.
Norwegian-American Historical Association.
Correspondence, reports, clippings, articles, and brochures of a Norwegian-American women's society that was organized in 1925 following the Norse American centennial celebration in Minneapolis that year. The group has participated in such activities as the Minnesota Leif Erikson Monument Association program and Norwegian royal visitors entertainment; it also has been involved in city library, music, museum, and welfare projects.

8,768. Norwegian-American Historical Association
Records. 1925-77. 40 boxes.
Open. Unpublished guide.
Norwegian-American Historical Association.
Founded in 1925, the Historical Association strives to preserve the record of Norwegian-American experience by maintaining archives and publishing books on Norwegian-American history, literature, art, and culture. Among correspondence, source material, and manuscripts of books the NAHA edited and published are a diary of Elizabeth Fedde, correspondence and reports of Lise Linbaek, letters of Agnes Larson concerning her biography of John A. Johnson, a manuscript of Karen Larsen's biography of her father Laur. Larsen, a manuscript of the Verdandi Study Club's translation of *Frontier Parsonage,* and copies of *Frontier Mother* by Gro Svendsen and *Lady With a Pen* by Elise Waerenskjold.

8,769. Norwegian-American Women's Club of Detroit
Records. 1940-50. 178 items.
Open. Unpublished guide.
Norwegian-American Historical Association.
Correspondence, clippings, and other records of the Club, established to raise WWII relief funds for Norway. Prominent leaders of this group included Mrs. Guttorm Miller, Mrs. Henry Glicman, and Mrs. N. H. F. Olsen.

8,770. Norwegian Lutheran Deaconesses' Home and Hospital, Brooklyn, NY
Records. 1895-1960. 114 items.
Open. Unpublished guide.
Norwegian-American Historical Association.
Reports, histories, catalogs, and brochures of the Hospital, founded in 1883 by Sister Elizabeth Fedde. In 1956 this institution merged with the Lutheran Hospital of Manhattan to form the Lutheran Medical Center.

8,771. Odland, Lisa
Papers. Nd. 1 vol.
Open. Unpublished guide.
Norwegian-American Historical Association.
Typescript of Odland's collection of poems entitled "The Mystic Star."

8,772. Oftedahl, Maria
Papers. Ca. 1930. 5 items.
Open. Unpublished guide.
Norwegian-American Historical Association.
Articles and clippings of [Mrs. Einar L.] Oftedahl (1861-1948), a Cottonwood, MN, housewife, pertain to childhood memories, the "snow winter" of 1880-81 in Lyon County, and local church history.

8,773. Øglaend, Kirsten
Papers. 1949. 1 item.
Open. Unpublished guide.
Norwegian-American Historical Association.
Manuscript of an address Øglaend gave at St. Olaf College.

8,774. Olsen, Emily Veblen
Papers. 1885-1941. 9 items.
Open. Unpublished guide.
Norwegian-American Historical Association.
Olsen (ca. 1865-1953) was the wife of Lutheran clergyman Sigurd Olsen and sister of Thorstein Veblen and Andrew A. Veblen. Memoirs, biographies she wrote of her husband and of her father-in-law Johan Olsen, a sermon by Johan Olsen, a history of the St. Ansgar congregation, a tribute to Claus L. Clausen by Sigurd Olsen, a letter by Ole Nilsen, and a photo album.

8,775. Olson, Eleanora
Papers. Nd. 1 item.
Open. Unpublished guide.
Norwegian-American Historical Association.
Dialect monologue entitled "Sogne-Kjerring" by Olson (1870-1946), a Chicago and Minneapolis declaimer and singer. The piece appeared in *Yust for Fun* (1925), a compilation of dialect stories she and Ethel Olson presented on concert tours throughout the Northwest.

8,776. Pederson, Maren Pol
Papers. 1956? 1 item.
Open. Unpublished guide.
Norwegian-American Historical Association.
Biography of Pederson (1849-1935), a Norwegian-born boarding house operator and wife of Andreas Pederson, was written by her two daughters. They describe her experiences in Norway before emigration, hardships at sea on a trip to Hawaii and California via Cape Horn, and details about Hawaiian sugar plantations she visited.

8,777. Peterson, Berthe C.
Papers. Nd. No size given.
Open. Unpublished guide.
Norwegian-American Historical Association.
Photos and clippings of Peterson (1872-1941), a Norwegian-born Chicago clubwoman. In addition to being president of the Federation of Norwegian Women's Societies, she was active in the Norwegian National League and the Norse-American Centennial Committee; she also promoted the idea of Leif Erikson Day. In 1940 she received the St. Olav Medal from Haakon VII of Norway.

8,778. Pierson, Harriet
Papers. 1846. 2 items.
Open. Unpublished guide.
Norwegian-American Historical Association.
Letters Pierson wrote in English from Hartland, MI, to Sarah and Nancy Austin of Orleans County, NY, pertain to family matters.

8,779. Raaen, Aagot
Papers. 1929-50. 25 items.
Open. Unpublished guide.
Norwegian-American Historical Association.
Articles and clippings of [Miss] Raaen (1878-1957), a public school teacher and author in North Dakota, contain descriptions of pioneer life in that state. Raaen wrote *Grass of the Earth* (1950), published by the Norwegian-American Historical Association; *Measure of My Days* (1953); and a Hamarsbøn-Raaen family genealogy, compiled in 1954.

8,780. Rasmussen, Mathilde
Papers. 1945. 1 item.
Open. Unpublished guide.
Norwegian-American Historical Association.
A history of the P. A. Rasmussen family as told by daughter Mathilde Rasmussen (1865-1952) includes information on their Norwegian heritage; activities of her father's scattered parishes in Illinois, Wisconsin, Iowa, Minnesota, and Missouri; life in the Lisbon, IL, parsonage; synodical affairs; and family anniversaries and memorials.

8,781. Reierson, Helena
Papers. 1860. 1 item.
Open. Unpublished guide.
Norwegian-American Historical Association.
Letter written by Reierson, who was the wife of Georg Reierson, a commission merchant in Shreveport, LA, pertains to slaves, railroad building, and her husband's business; it also includes references to the Bache family and to Elise Waerenskjold.

8,782. Ritter, Mattie W.
Papers. 1867-69. 2 items.
Open. Unpublished guide.
Norwegian-American Historical Association.
Diary of Ritter and a teaching certificate issued by the county superintendent in Coles County, IL.

8,783. Rollag, Grace
Papers. 1929. 1 item.
Open. Unpublished guide.
Norwegian-American Historical Association.
Manuscript in which [Mrs. Ole] Rollag (1851-1943) recounts her pioneer experiences primarily at Beaver Creek, MN, since 1873, the year of her marriage. Also includes a Rollag genealogy.

8,784. Rølvaag, Ole Edvart
Papers. 1899-1956. 49 boxes.
Open. Unpublished guide.
Norwegian-American Historical Association.
Papers of Rølvaag (1876-1931), an educator and author, include correspondence of his wife Jennie Marie (Berdahl) Rølvaag and that of his colleague and biographer Nora Olava Solum, reminiscences of his daughter Ella Valborg (Rølvaag) Tweet, and Evelyn Berdahl's reflections about her work with Rølvaag. Following his death, [Mrs.] Rølvaag corresponded with many individuals about topics relating to her husband's work; she also compiled scrapbooks, indexed some of his papers, and made notes on his biography.

8,785. Sebo, Mildred M.
Papers. 1954. 3 items.
Open. Unpublished guide.
Norwegian-American Historical Association.
Articles by a La Molle, MN, resident consist of a history of the Sebo-Myhre family of Cedar Valley, the story of their centennial celebration, and an account of their first Christmas in America.

8,786. Semmingson, Ingrid
Papers. Nd. 1 item.
Open. Unpublished guide.
Norwegian-American Historical Association.
Article by [Mrs.] Semmingson (1910-), an American history professor at the University of Oslo in Norway, consists of a critique of [Mrs.] Gudrum Hovde Gvale's biography of Ole E. R Rølvaag. Semmingson is the author of *Utvandringen og det utflyttede Norge* (1952) and *Veien mot Vest* (1942).

8,787. Solberg, Elizabeth Ronning
Papers. 1967. 1 item.
Open. Unpublished guide.
Norwegian-American Historical Association.
Autobiography in which Solberg (1911-) describes farm and village life in North Dakota, her working career in Evanston, IL, and her years as an invalid in California.

8,788. Solum, Nora Olava
Papers. 1904-69. 375 items.
Open. Unpublished guide.
Norwegian-American Historical Association.
Papers of Solum (1889-1971), an English professor at St. Olaf College from 1919 to 1960. She co-authored *Ole Edvart Rølvaag: A Biography* (1939) with Theodore Jorgenson and translated a number of Norwegian works, including *Laengselens Boat* (1921), *Peder Seier* (1928), *The Boat of Longing* (1933) by Rølvaag, and *Norway's New Saga of the Sea* (1969) by Lise Lindbaek.

8,789. Stolen, Lena Kjellesvig
Papers. 1857-ca. 1932. 4 items.
Open. Unpublished guide.
Norwegian-American Historical Association.
Papers of [Mrs. Knut] Stolen (1869-1937) consist of her father's emigration health certificate, her mother's emigration church certificate, a letter from Norway, and a genealogy of the Anon Kjellesvig family.

8,790. Syse, Sophia Stuegaarden
Papers. 1853-ca. 1930. 10 items.
Open. Unpublished guide.
Norwegian-American Historical Association.
Emigration documents and correspondence of [Mrs.] Syse (1866-1947) pertain to the Anders Stuegaarden family.

8,791. Thompson, Julia
Papers. 1881-92. 1 vol.
Open. Unpublished guide.
Norwegian-American Historical Association.
Autograph album of Thompson, a Scandinavia, WI, resident.

8,792. Thompson, M. Burnette
Papers. 1939. 1 item.
Open. Unpublished guide.
Norwegian-American Historical Association.
Paper by [Miss] Thompson, who graduated from St. Olaf College in Northfield in 1930, pertains to the St. Olaf Lutheran Choir and its significance in American choral music. Includes information on the history of the Choir, a biography of F. Melius Christiansen, an analysis of the ideals and influence of the Choir, and a list of Christiansen's compositions. Thompson wrote the paper to fulfill the thesis requirement for an MA degree in the musicology department at the Eastman School of Music, University of Rochester, in Rochester, NY.

8,793. Thykesen, Anna
Papers. 1903-34. 6 items.
Open. Unpublished guide.
Norwegian-American Historical Association.
Thykesen (1879-) taught Norwegian at St. Olaf College. Letter written by Bjørnstjerne Bjørnson, a scrapbook of clippings and a pamphlet relating to Bjørnson and the 100th anniversary of his birth, scrapbooks of clippings pertaining to Ole E. Rølvaag and other writers and to the reorganization problem in the Norwegian Lutheran Church of America during the early 1930s, and a pamphlet by Einar Bjørnson.

8,794. Torbenson, Mary Syverson
Papers. 1965. 1 item.
Open. Unpublished guide.
Norwegian-American Historical Association.
Historical sketch of pioneer life in Moore Township, Ransom County, ND, by [Mrs. Oscar] Torbenson (1880-), a native of the area.

8,795. Tracts
Collection. 1866-1945. 447 items.
Open. Unpublished guide.
Norwegian-American Historical Association.
Tracts on religious subjects, which were published in English and Norwegian by such groups as the Norwegian Evangelical Lutheran Church in America, include an item written by Mrs. O. E. Rølvaag pertaining to the founding in 1840 of the first kvindeforening, or ladies' aid, in Norway by Gustava Kjelland.

8,796. Turli, Irene
Papers. Nd. 1 item.
Open. Unpublished guide.
Norwegian-American Historical Association.
Unpublished manuscript of the first portion of a novel by Turli (1926-), "The Three Red Hills," which is set on the western prairie during the decade following 1912; hunger for land is its central theme.

8,797. Tuve Family
Papers. Nd. 1 folder.
Open. Unpublished guide.
Norwegian-American Historical Association.
Clippings pertain to the descendants of a Norwegian immigrant family. Anton Tuve, the son of Gulbrand Tuve and Torbjør Tuve, was president of Augustana College in Sioux Falls, SD, from 1892 to 1918. His children George, Merle, Rosemond, and Richard Tuve all earned PhDs at American universities, and all were awarded honorary degrees in 1964 at Carleton College commencement exercises in recognition of their career accomplishments.

8,798. Ueland, Brenda
Papers. 1967. 1 vol.
Open. Unpublished guide.
Norwegian-American Historical Association.
Biography of Clara (Hampson) [Mrs. Andreas] Ueland (1860-1927), a Minnesota suffragist and civic reformer, was written by her daughter Brenda Ueland. Contains descriptions of family attitudes, in part drawn from correspondence between family members, about war, women's suffrage, child discipline, the LWV, politics, religion, education, and manners. Brenda Ueland also wrote about her grandfather Ole Gabriel Ueland, who was the founder of the Bonde party in Norway.

8,799. Vallon, Julia (Sando)
Papers. 1937. 1 item.
Open. Unpublished guide.
Norwegian-American Historical Association.
Article in which Vallon describes the way in which her father Halvor Lars Sando scouted for land in the Red River Valley, ND.

8,800. Vangen, Christina
Papers. 1892. 1 vol.
Open. Unpublished guide.
Norwegian-American Historical Association.
Diary of a St. Olaf College student from Cannon Falls, MN, contains her comments on housing, social life, study, and classes.

8,801. Waerenskjold, Elise Tvede
Papers. 1851-66. 2 items.
Open. Unpublished guide.
Norwegian-American Historical Association.
Letters written by [Mrs.] Waerenskjold (1815-95), one of which was published in *Morgenblad* in 1852 as a response to T. Andreas Gjestvang's request for information about Texas to counteract the negative view presented by Captain A. Tolmer in his published series of letters. She wrote the other letter, which was published in 1867 in *Adressebladet,* from Prairieville, TX; it provides her detailed account of the murder of her husband Wilhelm Waerenskjold by N. T. Dickson.

8,802. Widen, Gudrun
Papers. Nd. 2 items.
Open. Unpublished guide.
Norwegian-American Historical Association.
Manuscripts of romantic novels by Widen, including *Varden,* a story from Norway centered around the cairn, or varden, and written in Norwegian, and *Why Don't They Go Home?,* the story of a girl who immigrated to Brooklyn, NY.

8,803. Wolsted, Mabel Ewen
Papers. 1966. 1 item.
Open. Unpublished guide.
Norwegian-American Historical Association.
Article written by Wolsted pertains to the culture of the Norwegian immigrant and the hardships of the emigration journey to America.

8,804. Women's Missionary Federation
Records. 1911-57. 33 items.
Open. Unpublished guide.
Norwegian-American Historical Association.
Constitutions, reports, handbooks, articles, and pamphlets provide historical information about the Federation, which was part of the Norwegian Lutheran Church.

8,805. Buckley, Joan Naglestad
Papers. 1976. 1 item.
Open. Unpublished guide.
St. Olaf College Archives.
[Mrs.] Buckley is an English teacher at Concordia College in Moorhead, MN. Her PhD thesis, completed at the University of Iowa, consists of a critical study of the novels of Martha Ostenso, a second-generation Norwegian-American writer who won professional acclaim and a literary prize for her first novel *Wild Geese.* Most of Ostenso's writings deal with rural life in the midwestern US and Canada, where she spent most of her life.

8,806. Dieson, Georgina, and Hegland, Martin
Papers. 1880-1972. 1 ft. and 2 tapes.
Open. Unpublished guide.
St. Olaf College Archives.
Georgina Dieson (1882-), who married Martin Hegland (1880-1967), was a teacher and preceptress at the College; she also served as a community and church volunteer in Northfield. Correspondence about local news and travels abroad; memoirs and taped reminiscences in which she reflects on her experiences as a St. Olaf student between 1900 and 1904, on married life, and on her professional and community activities from the 1920s to the 1940s; manuscripts; articles; addresses; programs; pamphlets; clippings; and her book *As It Was in the Beginning,* a history of the early days of the College that focuses particularly on the activities of women students.

8,807. Felland, O. G.
Papers. 1886-1928. 3200 items.
Open. Unpublished guide.
St. Olaf College Archives.
Photos and glass plate negatives of Felland (1853-1938), a religion professor at the College, principally depict campus life between 1886 and 1928. Approximately 100 of the photos show the activities and living conditions of women students before 1910.

8,808. Frayseth, Inez
Papers. 1927-75. 6 ft.
Open. Unpublished guide.
St. Olaf College Archives.
Records created by [Miss] Frayseth (1912-) while she served as assistant registrar, recorder, and registrar at the College from 1935 to 1973 consist of correspondence, reports, minutes, lists, schedules, pamphlets, programs, and clippings. Correspondents include the president and dean of the College, faculty members, colleagues at St. Olaf and at other institutions, and parents.

8,809. Hilleboe, Gertrude M.
Papers. 1911-62. 1 Hollinger box and 1 tape.
Open. Unpublished guide.
St. Olaf College Archives.
From 1915 to 1958, Hilleboe (1888-1976) was dean of women and a teacher of Latin at the College. Correspondence, including letters she wrote to St. Olaf servicemen describing campus activities during WWII; a tape of "Living Stones," which was a talk about the College and its ideals; constitutions and minutes of the Women's Self-Government Association on campus, which she helped establish and operate; photos; programs; scrapbooks; clippings; and her published reminiscences *Manitou Analecta,* in which she describes her career at the College and reflects on events and personalities.

8,810. Lewis, Mildred (Schelde)
Papers. 1917-21. 1 vol.
Open. No guide.
St. Olaf College Archives.
Album of Lewis (1900-73) contains photos and memorabilia she assembled reflecting her experiences as a St. Olaf College student between 1917 and 1921.

8,811. Mohn, Anna E. (Ringstad)
Papers. Ca. 1910. 6 pp.
Open. No guide.
St. Olaf College Archives.
Reminiscences that Mohn (1852-1923), the wife of the first president of St. Olaf, wrote in Norwegian contain information about the founding of the College.

8,812. Peterson, Julie
Papers. 1975. Ca. 68 pp.
Open. No guide.
St. Olaf College Archives.
Unpublished MA thesis "Pluck and Perseverance: The History of Women at St. Olaf College, 1874-1914" by Peterson (1950-), a Sarah Lawrence College graduate student, contains information about the lives, activities, schedules, and attitudes of women students between 1874 and 1914. Also included are data sheets from questionnaires she sent to alumnae as part of her research.

8,813. Phi Kappa Phi Literary Society
Records. 1908-41. 1 Hollinger box.
Open. Unpublished guide.
St. Olaf College Archives.
Constitution, minutes, lists, a history, and a published cookbook of this College student women's group that existed between 1913 and 1967. The cookbook was published in 1908 to raise funds for a new women's dormitory.

8,814. Roe, Ella (Hjertaas)
Papers. 1904-71. 1 ft.
Open. Unpublished guide.
St. Olaf College Archives.
Correspondence, committee minutes, photos, programs, scrapbooks, and clippings of [Mrs. Herman] Roe (1889-1972), a music and voice teacher at the College from 1919 to 1960. Photos document many of the US and European concert tours of the St. Olaf Choir.

8,815. Solum, Nora Olava
Papers. 1920-66. 2 ft.
Open. Unpublished guide.
St. Olaf College Archives.
[Miss] Solum (1889-1971) taught English at the College from 1919 to 1960. Correspondence, lecture notes and manuscripts of scholarly lectures, radio talks, student papers, and a draft of an MA thesis. Correspondents include Gertrude Hilleboe, St. Olaf's first dean of women; George Weida Spohn, chairman of the English department; and L. W. Boe, College president, whose letter concerns the death of author Ole E. Rølvaag.

RED WING

8,816. Hobart Women's Christian Temperance Union
Records. 1891-1945. 11 vols.
Open. No guide.
Goodhue County Historical Society.
Minute books, treasurer's reports and records, membership lists, items from the annual Minnesota 26th district convention, photos, scrapbooks, programs, song books, and issues of the *White Ribbon,* the newspaper of the Minnesota WCTU. Founded in 1877 as the Red Wing WCTU, the organization changed its name to Hobart WCTU in the early 20th century in recognition of Harriet A. Hobart, who was president of the state WCTU. Items about the 26th district WCTU and its conventions provide information on temperance work in Goodhue, Dakota, and Rice counties. Also includes a history written in 1919 of the Minnesota WCTU soldiers and sailors department, also known as the home and allied relief department, and a scrapbook of the Sterling WCTU, founded in 1921 in Burnside, MN. The chapter was named after Isabella Sterling, a charter member of the Hobart group.

8,817. Lutheran Ladies' Seminary
Records. 1892-1962. 2 Paige boxes.
Open. No guide.
Goodhue County Historical Society.
Photos, yearbooks, pamphlets, catalogs, and student newspapers of the Seminary, first proposed by clergyman H. A. Preus in 1874 and incorporated in 1889 as a liberal arts religious college for women by the Red Wing Lutheran Ladies' Seminary Association. Classes, including instruction in science, literature, art, and music, were offered for the first time in 1894. Although the Seminary was destroyed by fire in 1920 and classes were never resumed, an active alumnae group continued to meet until 1962. Minutes of the group's meetings and numerous histories by members are included in the collection.

8,818. Red Wing School of Nursing
Records. 1912-27. 5 vols.
Open. No guide.
Goodhue County Historical Society.
Founded in 1912 and affiliated with the Red Wing Hospital, the School of Nursing ceased operation in 1927 as a result of increasingly strict standards developed for such institutions by the Minnesota Board of Nursing. Correspondence, class records, and student nurses' reports provide information about the nursing curriculum and the School's relationship to the Hospital. Records also document progress and performance criteria used by supervisors to evaluate student nurses.

ROCHESTER

8,819. American Association of University Women
Records. 1933-61. Ca. 1 in.
Open. No guide.
Olmsted County Historical Society.
Collection consists of material pertaining to Rochester house tours conducted by the AAUW from 1959 to 1961; a history of the AAUW Minnesota division from 1923 to 1953, written by Vera Hanawalt Frohlicher; a program of the eighth national AAUW convention, which was held in 1933 in Minneapolis; a 1958 yearbook; and several publications of the national AAUW educational office.

8,820. Daughters of the American Revolution
Records. Ca. 1919-56. 1 in.
Open. No guide.
Olmsted County Historical Society.
Bylaws, programs, scrapbook with clippings, a sample DAR ancestral chart, handbooks, and yearbooks of this organization.

8,821. Graff, Ella A.
Papers. 1888-1963. Ca. 2 in.
Open. No guide.
Olmsted County Historical Society.
Correspondence, photos, and biographical information about Graff (1872-1963), a secretary for Rochester attorney Burt W. Eaton who helped found the Olmsted County Historical Society. Graff was active in the YWCA and the Business and Professional Women's Club.

8,822. Linton, Laura
Papers. 1903-54. 6 items.
Open. No guide.
Olmsted County Historical Society.
Biographical sketch, photos, and clippings of Linton (1853-1915), a physician who, after attending MIT and graduating from the University of Minnesota medical school, supervised the women's ward at Rochester State Hospital and became an instructor at the state training school for nurses. She was also a member of the American Association for the Advancement of Science and the Association for the Advancement of Women.

8,823. Mayo, Edith Graham
Papers. Ca. 1940-53. Ca. 1 in.
Open. No guide.
Olmsted County Historical Society.
[Mrs. Charles H.] Mayo (1871-1943) instructed the first nurses trained for the Mayo Clinic and was one of the first anesthesiologists in Minnesota. Collection consists of material about her 1940 American Mother of the Year award and the construction of her memorial in 1953.

8,824. Olmsted County American Red Cross
Records. 1919-25. 0.5 in.
Open. No guide.
Olmsted County Historical Society.
Correspondence of Olmsted County American National Red Cross director J. H. Kahler includes correspondence with division headquarters and the national organization. Also contains clippings and a list of local Olmsted County chapters and their officers.

8,825. Olmsted County Federated Women's Club
Records. 1922-40. 3 in.
Open. No guide.
Olmsted County Historical Society.
Constitution and bylaws, minutes, membership lists, a history, and scrapbooks of the Club, which was established in 1922 to unite the county's women to improve their communities and homes and to promote work endorsed by the Minnesota FWC.

8,826. Planned Parenthood
Records. 1938-48. 1 in.
Open. No guide.
Olmsted County Historical Society.
Articles of incorporation of this Planned Parenthood office, bylaws, annual reports, clinic reports, a list of the first board of directors, and inventory lists. Annual clinic reports for 1943 to 1946 contain information concerning the religion and occupation of women served by Planned Parenthood.

8,827. Ringe Mothers and Daughters Club
Records. 1913-67. 2 in.
Open. No guide.
Olmsted County Historical Society.
Constitution and bylaws, minutes, membership lists, and yearbooks of an organization founded in 1913 to help mothers to "cultivate social qualities," study their work as wives and mothers, help each other in the community, and study the environment's influence on children.

8,828. Rochester Barettes
Records. 1925-73. 1 in.
Open. No guide.
Olmsted County Historical Society.
Made up of wives and mothers of Olmsted County attorneys, the Barettes was organized in 1925 as an auxiliary of the Olmsted County Bar Association to help that group host the Minnesota Bar Association convention. Minutes, membership lists, correspondence, and clippings.

8,829. Rochester Business and Professional Women's Club
Records. Ca. 1931-63. 2 in.
Open. No guide.
Olmsted County Historical Society.
Bylaws, treasurers reports, receipt books, membership lists, a history of the group written in 1963, programs, yearbooks, clippings, and memorabilia of the Club, founded in 1922 to promote the interests and elevate the standards of women, especially employed women. Grace Nye Willson and [Mrs.] Alice Dodge were among the Club's members.

8,830. Rochester Flower and Garden Club
Records. 1930-64. 7 in.
Open. No guide.
Olmsted County Historical Society.
Minutes and scrapbooks of the Club.

8,831. Sloan, Marion
Papers. Ca. 1855-1942. Ca. 1 in.
Open. No guide.
Olmsted County Historical Society.
Marion Sloan (1846-1942) was vice-president of the Minnesota state women's suffrage association and chairwoman of the Republican Women of Olmsted County. Correspondence, including letters from Clara Barton about the status of Sloan's brother who was missing in action during the Civil War and letters from Agnes Hathaway, a Universalist missionary to Japan; diaries from 1872 to 1874 and diary excerpts from 1856 and 1864; certificates; a notebook of calling cards of visitors to the Sloan home; and memorabilia.

8,832. Study Club
Records. 1885-1960. Ca. 1 in. and 2 vols.
Open. No guide.
Olmsted County Historical Society.
List of officers, programs, clippings, and a history of the Rochester Study Club, a local unit of the Chautauqua movement. The movement sought to bring adult education and "mental refreshment to isolated communities" through year-round meetings, summer institutes, and readings in science, art, history, literature, and philosophy. Also includes information about the Rochester Women's Monday Club, the Senior History Club, and the Monday Study Club and Chautauquan publications, including prescribed courses of study for 1885.

8,833. Willson, Grace Nye
Papers. 1936-60. Ca. 2 in.
Open. No guide.
Olmsted County Historical Society.
Correspondence, speeches and articles, programs, photos, and clippings of Willson, who served the Olmsted County Historical Society as secretary from 1936 to 1941, as president from 1941 to 1947, and as curator from 1947 to 1958. She also was active in the YWCA and the Business and Professional Women's Club at local and national levels.

8,834. Woman's Christian Temperance Union
Records. 1908-65. 14 in.
Open. No guide.
Olmsted County Historical Society.
Financial records and minute books contain annual and committee reports, membership lists, and clippings of five Minnesota WCTU groups including chapters in Pleasant Grove, Rochester, and Stewartville. Also contains a scrapbook of the 1963 WCTU state convention which was held in Pipestone, MN.

8,835. Woman's Relief Corps
Records. 1887-1953. Ca. 1 ft.
Open. No guide.
Olmsted County Historical Society.
Minutes, ledger, and cash and account books of the Corps, an auxiliary to the Grand Army of the Republic, Custer Corps No. 28, department of Minnesota.

8,836. Women's Civic League of Rochester
Records. 1910-58. Ca. 10 in.
Open. No guide.
Olmsted County Historical Society.
Secretary's minutes of the League reflect human service needs in the Rochester area. Out of this organization grew additional public health and public welfare services as well as various private organizations. Currently the League operates the Civic League Day Nursery for ca. 100 children.

8,837. Women's Foreign Missionary Society
Records. 1878-1940. Ca. 4 in.
Open. No guide.
Olmsted County Historical Society.
Minutes and financial records of this Dover, MN, organization, which was affiliated with the Foreign Missionary Society of America and was particularly interested in African missions.

8,838. Young Women's Christian Association
Records. 1912-56. 1 in.
Open. No guide.
Olmsted County Historical Society.
Treasurer's report of the Rochester YWCA for 1952, committee reports for 1944, correspondence, a chronology and a history of the local group written by Grace Nye Willson, programs, certificates, newsletters, advertisements, and clippings.

8,839. Motherhouse Archives
Records. 1877- . 30 cabinets, 36 tapes, and 6 shelves.
Access restricted. No guide.
Sisters of St. Francis, Assisi Heights Motherhouse.
Financial records, chapter proceedings, correspondence, dissertations, taped interviews, videotapes, photos, scrapbooks, community newsletters, clippings, memorabilia, and other records of the Sisters concerning their works, the founding of the community in Rochester in 1877, and members of the order.

ST. CLOUD

8,840. American Association of University Women
Records. 1922-71. 5 Hollinger boxes and 8 vols.
Open. Inventory.
Central Minnesota Historical Center.
Minutes, reports, notebooks, clippings, and bulletins of the St. Cloud branch of the AAUW, established in 1922 with 31 charter members. Comprised of St. Cloud area women who have graduated from AAUW-approved colleges and universities throughout the world, the group raises money for scholarships, charitable organizations, and social welfare campaigns.

8,841. Brenny, Bertha, and Rodemann, Emma
Oral history. 1973. 1 tape.
Open. Unpublished guide.
Central Minnesota Historical Center.
Taped and transcribed interview with Brenny (1906-) and Rodemann (1908-), who were elementary school teachers, contains descriptions of school life and teaching from the 1920s to the 1970s, as well as information about people and activities in Sauk Rapids, MN.

8,842. Brotherhood of Railroad Trainmen, Ladies Auxiliary
Records. 1921-46. 1 Hollinger box.
Open. Inventory.
Central Minnesota Historical Center.
Minutes, legislative reports, correspondence, and booklets of the Auxiliary, which was founded in 1921, provide a detailed view of St. Cloud and its community leaders during the 1930s and 1940s.

8,843. Petersen, Medora Granprey
Oral history. 1973. 1 tape.
Open. Unpublished guide.
Central Minnesota Historical Center.
In a taped interview, Petersen (ca. 1900-), the wife of Minnesota governor Hjalmar Petersen, discusses the life and activities of her husband, her own political involvement, life in Steele County, MN, and her experiences as a newspaper editor.

8,844. St. Cloud, McCarthy for President Committee
Records. 1968. 2 Hollinger boxes.
Open. Inventory.

Central Minnesota Historical Center.
Campaign material relates to the St. Cloud Democratic Farmer-Labor Party and local support for Gene McCarthy in the US presidential race. Includes information about active Committee worker Phyllis Janey and about McCarthy's wife Abigail McCarthy.

8,845. Stearns County, MN: WPA Biographical Sketches
Records. Nd. 9 Hollinger boxes.
Open. Inventory.
Central Minnesota Historical Center.
Lists and biographies pertain to women who were Stearns County residents during the late 1930s.

8,846. Sullivan, Ruth L.
Oral history. 1973. 1 tape.
Open. Unpublished guide.
Central Minnesota Historical Center.
Interview in which Sullivan, the wife of Minnesota legislator Henry Sullivan, describes her husband's political experiences during his 20 years in the state senate; Sullivan's reminiscences concern events dating from 1889 to 1959.

8,847. Minnesota Association of School Librarians
Records. 1947-76. 2.5 ft.
Open. No guide.
St. Cloud State University, Special Collections.
Founded in 1947 by women librarians, the Association merged into the Minnesota Educational Media Organization when it was formed in 1976. Minutes, annual workshop reports, and correspondence.

ST. JOSEPH

8,848. Archives
Records. 1857- . Ca. 260 cu.ft.
Access restricted. No guide.
St. Benedict's Convent.
Chapter and committee minutes, financial records, correspondence, diaries, papers of nine mother prioresses and of other members of the community, autobiographies, committee reports, chronicles, theses, dissertations, photos, family histories, newsletters, scrapbooks, memorabilia, and other official records of St. Benedict's Convent, which was founded in 1857 in St. Cloud, MN. Includes material on the schools, hospitals, foreign missions, Indian missions, and orphanages established and operated by members of the order and personal papers of Sister Inez Hilger, an anthropologist.

ST. PAUL

8,849. Baptist General Conference Archives
Records. Ca. 1850- . No size given.
Open. No guide.
Bethel Seminary Library, Archives of the Baptist General Conference.
Included in records of the Conference are correspondence of and biographical items about women who served as missionaries overseas or as church and social workers in the US, papers relating to the wives of clergymen and other women active in church work, and records of women's organizations within individual churches and within the Conference as a whole. For the period from ca. 1850 to 1920, when Conference congregations contained many Swedish immigrants, the records of church women's groups are often in Swedish.

8,850. McCarthy, Abigail Eleanor (Quigley)
Papers. Nd. 1 item.
Open. No guide.
College of St. Catherine Library.
Manuscript of *Private Faces/Public Places* by McCarthy (1916-), an author and former wife of politician Eugene McCarthy.

8,851. McHugh, Sister Antonia
Papers. 1915-42. 1 drawer.
Open. No guide.
College of St. Catherine Library.
Personal and professional papers of Sister Antonia (1873-1944), formerly Anna McHugh, who was a religious educator and the first president of the College.

8,852. Sawyer, Ruth
Papers. 1916-70. 150 items and 1 tape.
Open. Card index.
College of St. Catherine Library.
Sawyer (1880-1970) was an author of children's books and a storyteller. Consists of letters she received before 1942 from friends who were authors and letters she sent to her friends at the College.

8,853. Sisters of St. Joseph of Carondelet
Records. 1905- . 3 drawers.
Open. No guide.
College of St. Catherine Library.
Papers of members of this Order, who have taught at the College since 1905.

8,854. Smith, Sister Maris Stella
Papers. 1918- . 0.5 drawer.
Open. Unpublished guide.
College of St. Catherine Library.
Manuscripts of Smith (1899), formerly Alice Gustava, and correspondence with literary colleagues. Smith is a poet and educator.

8,855. Women
Collection. Nd. 4 drawers and 3300 items.
Open. Unpublished guide.
College of St. Catherine Library.
Print and nonprint material, collected since 1964, focuses on the psychological liberation of women in the 20th century. Includes items on the feminist movement and especially on women in religion.

8,856. Biographical File
Collection. 1839-1977. 5 drawers.
Open. No guide.
Luther Theological Seminary, Archives of the American Church.
Photos, clippings, and articles pertain to single and married women missionaries and their spouses; pastors, including two women clergy, and pastors' wives; and a few women church leaders and writers. Also included are biographies of two women who pioneered in America in 1842 with their pastor-husbands.

8,857. Board of Charities, Evangelical Lutheran Church
Records. Ca. 1918-60. 15 ft.
Open. No guide.
Luther Theological Seminary, Archives of the American Church.
Financial records, reports, and correspondence of ELC charitable agencies, including the Lutheran Girls' Home in Minneapolis, the Deaconess Hospital in New York City, and the Lutheran Maternity Home in Sioux Falls, SD.

8,858. Board of Foreign Missions, Evangelical Lutheran Church and its Antecedents
Records. 1893-1960s. 47 ft.
Partially restricted. No guide.
Luther Theological Seminary, Archives of the American Church.
In directing Lutheran mission work outside the US, the Board established congregations, schools, and hospitals. Minutes and correspondence, the earliest of which are in Norwegian, contain biographical material about women missionaries and their activities. Correspondence between the missionaries and their home congregations, organizations, and the mission office include letters from women missionaries and wives of missionaries serving in such areas as the Sudan, Madagascar, China, and Japan. Also includes diaries.

8,859. The Diaconate
Records. 1890-1960. 1.75 ft.
Open. No guide.
Luther Theological Seminary, Archives of the American Church.
Records of the Diaconate of the Evangelical Lutheran Church, which directed hospitals and social welfare institutions, include annual reports, anniversary booklets, and programs of the Deaconess Home and Hospital in Brooklyn, NY, which was founded in 1883, and annual reports, minutes, photos, booklets, leaflets, and periodicals of the Home and Hospital in Chicago, which was founded in 1897. Also contains records of the Diaconate of the Lutheran Free Church from 1890, consisting of annual reports, photos, and booklets of the Norwegian Lutheran Deaconess Institute of Minneapolis; records of the Commission on Diaconic Service, which was founded in 1946, include minutes, correspondence, mimeographed items, printed material, and programs of the annual Christian Service Institute.

8,860. Lutheran Board of Missions, Lutheran Free Church
Records. 1893-1962. 17.75 ft.
Open. No guide.
Luther Theological Seminary, Archives of the American Church.
The Board was established in 1893 to conduct mission work outside the US and to create new congregations, schools, and hospitals. Minutes of the Board contain biographical information concerning women at the time they were called to become missionaries and reports about the work of specific women. Correspondence includes letters between the mission office and missionaries, single women, and wives of pastors. Early records are in Norwegian.

8,861. Lutheran Daughters of the Reformation
Records. 1934-60. 7 ft.
Open. No guide.
Luther Theological Seminary, Archives of the American Church.
Agendas and minutes of the national board, convention reports, correspondence, handbooks, and manuals of a group organized in 1926 at St. Olaf College in Northfield, MN, to serve the needs of young, professional, and business women. Originally named Daughters of the Reformation, the LDR in 1928 became an auxiliary of the Women's Missionary Federation of the Evangelical Lutheran Church and expanded into nine national districts. The LDR sponsored missionary work in Alaska in its early years but later pursued various missionary and charitable activities; and, under the leadership of Arna Njaa from 1936 to 1961, the group became influential within the Lutheran Church. The LDR consolidated in 1961 with the WMF and other groups to form the American Lutheran Church Women.

8,862. Lutheran Deaconess Home and Hospital
Records. 1892-1960. 1.5 ft., 5 vols., and 20 items.
Open. No guide.
Luther Theological Seminary, Archives of the American Church.
The Lutheran Deaconesses operated a number of hospitals and homes for the aged in Minneapolis, Chicago, and New York City. Minutes; financial reports, including some items of the Deaconess School of Nursing in Chicago; correspondence; and photos.

8,863. Lutheran Girls' Home
Records. 1930-42. 1 folder.
Open. No guide.
Luther Theological Seminary, Archives of the American Church.
Correspondence and other records of the Home, which provided prenatal care for unwed mothers who usually put their babies up for adoption.

8,864. Lutheran Ladies' Seminary
Records. 1894-1920. 2 in. and ca. 100 items.
Open. No guide.
Luther Theological Seminary, Archives of the American Church.
A history, photos, clippings, catalogs, periodicals, memorabilia, and other items of a Red Wing, MN, Lutheran academy for girls in their late teenage years. The Seminary closed in 1920 after a fire.

8,865. Lutheran Nurses' Guild
Records. 1941-65. 2.5 ft. and 50 items.
Open. No guide.
Luther Theological Seminary, Archives of the American Church.
Constitution, minutes, legal documents, correspondence, photos, scrapbooks, periodicals, and printed material of the Guild, a national organization founded in 1940 to promote, through local branches, Christian life and fellowship among Lutheran nurses, including those who worked in Deaconess hospitals and homes. [Miss] Edith Bergquist of Chicago served as the Guild's first president.

8,866. Pioneer Pastors' Wives
Collection. 1843-1930. 2 portfolios and 100 items.
Open. No guide.
Luther Theological Seminary, Archives of the American Church.
Photos and biographical information about Norwegian Lutheran pastors' wives, chiefly in the Upper Midwest.

8,867. Women's Missionary Federation: the Evangelical Lutheran, the United Norwegian Lutheran, and the Lutheran Free Churches
Records. 1911-63. 68 ft., 3 vols., 100 items, and 10 tapes.
Open. No guide.
Luther Theological Seminary, Archives of the American Church.
The Federation was founded in 1917 following the merger of the United Norwegian Lutheran Church group and similar organizations of two other Lutheran synods; of the three antecedent bodies, only the UNLC group, formed in 1911, kept formal minutes of its activities. UNLC member Lena (Gjertsen) [Mrs. T. H.] Dahl played a prominent role in the 1917 merger and then presided over the ELC Federation. The Federation of the LFC was established in 1916; as did the ELC group, it supported Lutheran synodical foreign and domestic missions and, later, promoted education and charity work. Minutes of the national boards and district organizations; histories of national, district, and circuit groups, as well as 1500 histories of early local Ladies' Aid Societies with some biographies; tapes of the "Women's Radio Hour"; slides of pioneer churches, pastors, and their wives; photos; convention reports; account books; correspondence; scrapbooks; newsletters; pamphlets; periodicals; and published programs. Katharina Blilie, the ELC group's official historian, was responsible for the local histories.

8,868. Akins, Ethel M.
Oral history. 1976. 4 tapes and 121-page transcript.
Open. Unpublished guide.
Midwest China Oral History and Archives Collection.
Interviews with Akins (1895-), an Augustana Lutheran missionary, concern her career in northern Honan, China, from 1921 to 1949 and in southern Taiwan from 1952 to 1965.

8,869. Anderson, Alice K.
Oral history. 1976. 6 tapes and 150-page transcript.
Open. Unpublished guide.
Midwest China Oral History and Archives Collection.
Interviews with Anderson (1905-), an Augustana Lutheran missionary, focus on her evangelical and educational work in northern Honan, China, from 1935 to 1949, in Guyana from 1950 to 1952, and in Hong Kong from 1952 until 1975.

8,870. Anderson, Colena
Oral history. 1977. 1 tape and 25-page transcript.
Open. Unpublished guide.
Midwest China Oral History and Archives Collection.
An American Baptist missionary, Anderson (1891-) served at the University of Shanghai from 1918 to 1924 and at the Shanghai American School from 1923 to 1932. The interview highlights her Shanghai educational involvements.

8,871. Bright, Carrie Lena McMullen
Oral history. 1976. 1 tape and 20-page transcript.
Open. Unpublished guide.
Midwest China Oral History and Archives Collection.
Interview in which Bright (1915-), whose parents were Southern Presbyterian missionaries to Hangchow, China, and whose father was provost of Hangchow Christian College, describes her childhood in Hangchow and her schooling at the Shanghai American School. Also includes her reflections about the way in which being raised in China affected her life.

8,872. Chou, Ivy
Oral history. 1976. 3 tapes and 48-page transcript.
Open. Unpublished guide.
Midwest China Oral History and Archives Collection.
Interview with Chou (1914-), a theological educator in China for 35 years, contains information about her family's background and relationship to the Methodist church in China as well as about her own education and work through 1950.

8,873. Dahlin, Helen (DePass)
Oral history. 1976. 2 tapes and 32-page transcript.
Open. Unpublished guide.
Midwest China Oral History and Archives Collection.
Dahlin (1923-) was the daughter of US military officer M. B. DePass, who, accompanied by his family, served various tours of duty in China from 1923 to 1948. Interview concerns Colonel DePass's involvement in China and Helen DePass Dahlin's childhood in Tientsin from 1923 to 1931.

8,874. Granskou, Ella Odland
Oral history. 1977. 3 tapes and 94-page transcript.
Open. Unpublished guide.
Midwest China Oral History and Archives Collection.
Interviews with Granskou (1891-), a United Lutheran missionary, concern her career in Kwangshan and Kikungshan, China, from 1921 to 1927.

8,875. Hanson, Constance Twedt
Oral history. 1976. 1 tape and 35-page transcript.
Open. Unpublished guide.
Midwest China Oral History and Archives Collection.
Interview with Hanson (1919-), an Evangelical Lutheran church missionary to China between 1946 and 1949, pertains to her nursing work in Honan province, in Shanghai at the Holy Light Clinic, and in Kunming at opium camp clinics.

8,876. Hayes, Helen
Oral history. 1977. 3 tapes and 58-page transcript.
Open. Unpublished guide.
Midwest China Oral History and Archives Collection.
Hayes (1896-) was a Methodist missionary to China from 1921 to 1935. Interview concerns her experiences as an educator in Wuhu, Anhwei, China.

8,877. Hughes, C. Elizabeth
Oral history. 1977. 1 tape and 40-page transcript.
Open. Unpublished guide.
Midwest China Oral History and Archives Collection.
Interview with Hughes, who served as a Friends Ambulance Unit nurse in China from 1946 to 1949, pertains to her work in Kunming, Chengchow, Weihiwai, and Yenan.

8,878. Hyde, Agnes Holstad
Oral history. 1923-76. 1 tape, 15-page transcript, and other items.
Open. Unpublished guide.
Midwest China Oral History and Archives Collection.
From 1923 to 1927 Hyde (1899-) served as a Norwegian Lutheran Church in America missionary to Kikungshan in Honan, China. Interview concerns her experiences as an educator at the American School in Kikungshan. Also includes her personal correspondence from China dated 1923 and 1924.

8,879. Jarvis, Anna Moffet
Papers. 1920-77. 4 tapes, 140-page transcript, and other items.
Open. Unpublished guide.
Midwest China Oral History and Archives Collection.
Interviews, personal reports, and correspondence of Jarvis (1892-), a missionary to China and India who also worked as a missionary administrator in Nanking, Chengtu, and Foochow, China; India; and New York City. From 1920 to 1944 she served as a Presbyterian missionary to China; in 1945 she became a Methodist missionary, spending four more years in China and then working in India from 1950 to 1953. In 1954 Jarvis became an administrator for the Methodist Board of Missions' office of the medical secretary, a position she held until 1958.

8,880. Jones, Clara J.
Oral history. 1976. 3 tapes and 65-page transcript.
Open. Unpublished guide.
Midwest China Oral History and Archives Collection.
Interview with Jones (1900-) relates to her experiences as a missionary nurse, educator, and student worker for the Evangelical and American Lutheran church. She served in Honan, Hupeh, Chengtu, and Chungking, China, from 1938 to 1945 and in Taipei, Taiwan, from 1952 to 1970.

8,881. Liu, Beatrice Exner
Oral history. 1977. 3 tapes and 90-page transcript.
Open. Unpublished guide.
Midwest China Oral History and Archives Collection.
Interview with Liu (1907-) concerns her involvement as an educator and relief worker in Tientsin and southwest China from 1935 to 1945.

8,882. Martinson, Cora
Oral history. 1977. 6 tapes and 160-page transcript.
Open. Unpublished guide.
Midwest China Oral History and Archives Collection.
The daughter of Lutheran missionaries in China, Martinson (1902-) also became a missionary in Honan, China, and in Hong Kong. Interviews in which she describes the work of her mother Anna Martha Martinson in China and Hong Kong from 1902 to 1969 also include Cora's reflections on her own educational missionary service in Honan from 1937 to 1947 and the following 25 years, which she spent in Hong Kong.

8,883. Nilsen, Frida R.
Oral history. 1976. 9 tapes and 200-page transcript.
Access restricted. Unpublished guide.

Midwest China Oral History and Archives Collection. Interviews with Nilsen (1894-), a Norwegian Lutheran Church in America missionary to China from 1918 to 1925, highlight her years as a teacher and headmistress of the Lena Dahl Middle School in Sinyang, Honan Province.

8,884. Olson, Lillian A.
Oral history. 1977. 3 tapes and 62-page transcript.
Open. Unpublished guide.
Midwest China Oral History and Archives Collection. From 1936 to 1941 Olson (1907-) served as an Augustana Lutheran missionary to Hsucheng and Kiahsien in Honan, China. Interview concerns her involvement as a medical doctor in China and her subsequent internment in the Philippines from 1941 to 1945.

8,885. Russell, Maud
Oral history. 1976. 2 tapes and 51-page transcript.
Open. Unpublished guide.
Midwest China Oral History and Archives Collection. Interview with Russell (1893-), who was a member of the YWCA staff in China from 1917 to 1943, concerns her YWCA activity and women's work in China. Also includes descriptions of her visits to the People's Republic of China in 1959 and 1972.

8,886. Smythe, Margaret Garret
Oral history. 1977. 1 tape and 21-page transcript.
Open. Unpublished guide.
Midwest China Oral History and Archives Collection. The daughter of United Christian Missionary Society missionaries in China, Smythe (1901-) served as a medical missionary in Nanking and western China for the United Christian Missionary Society of the Disciples of Christ from 1928 to 1951. Interview in which Smythe discusses the underlying principles of the missionary movement and changes in the missionaries' perceptions of their task.

8,887. Sovik, Gertrude
Oral history. 1976. 3 tapes and 65-page transcript.
Open. Unpublished guide.
Midwest China Oral History and Archives Collection. Interviews with Sovik (1907-), the daughter of Lutheran missionaries to Sinyang in Honan, China, pertain to her childhood and youth in China and her own educational missionary work with the American School in Kikungshan from 1935 to 1949.

8,888. Syrdal, Borghild Roe
Oral history. 1977. 2 tapes and 60-page transcript.
Open. Unpublished guide.
Midwest China Oral History and Archives Collection. Interviews with Syrdal (1902-) focus on her service as a Norwegian Lutheran Church of America educational missionary to Hupeh and Honan, China, from 1926 to 1936.

8,889. Tack, Minnie
Oral history. 1977. 4 tapes and 130-page transcript.
Open. Unpublished guide.
Midwest China Oral History and Archives Collection. Interviews with Tack (1899-) pertain to her Augustana Lutheran evangelical and educational missionary activity in Honan, China, from 1921 to 1949 and her work in Hong Kong from 1950 to 1969.

8,890. Tesdell, Margaret Stanley
Oral history. 1977. 3 tapes and 86-page transcript.
Open. Unpublished guide.
Midwest China Oral History and Archives Collection. From 1946 to 1948 Tesdell (1919-) was a Friends Ambulance Unit nurse in Honan, Shensi, and Shansi, China. Interviews concerning her nursing activity in northern China also include her descriptions of a visit in 1972 to the People's Republic of China as part of the American Friends Service Committee delegation.

8,891. Ward, Katherine Bertha Boeye
Oral history. 1977. 2 tapes and 60-page transcript.
Open. Unpublished guide.
Midwest China Oral History and Archives Collection. Interview with Ward (1900-) pertains to her Methodist missionary work as an educational administrator in Nanking and Chungking, China, from 1925 to 1939, in western China and Shanghai from 1948 to 1950, and during the following eight years and from 1960 to 1967 in Taiwan and Hong Kong. Ward also discusses her experiences from 1948 to 1958 as wife of Ralph Ward, a Methodist bishop.

8,892. Young, Mildred Test
Oral history. 1977. 4 tapes and 100-page transcript.
Open. Unpublished guide.
Midwest China Oral History and Archives Collection. Interviews with Young (1896-), a Methodist missionary to China, relate to her educational and administrative work in Yungchun, Fukien Province, China, from 1921 to 1926.

8,893. Abbott, Howard Strickland, and Family
Papers. 1859-1948. 1 box.
Open. Unpublished guide.
Minnesota Historical Society, Archives and Manuscripts.
Abbott (1863-1944), a lawyer, railroad executive, and lecturer at the University of Minnesota, was the son of Methodist minister Abiel Howard Abbott and teacher Mary Ellen Strickland Abbott, who were early settlers in Minnesota. Includes letters to Howard Abbott while he was at the University of Minnesota from his mother and his sister Eunice "Birdie" Strickland Abbott (1870-1956), who later married David H. Mercer, giving information on the family, social events, crops, and prices for agricultural commodities; a letter of recommendation for Mary Strickland from Standing Stone, where she taught school; and Mary Strickland Abbott's teaching certificate for third grade.

8,894. Abell, James Scott, and Family
Papers. 1814-94. 1 box and 6 oversize items.
Open. Unpublished guide.
Minnesota Historical Society, Archives and Manuscripts.
Consists of letters James Abell wrote to his daughter Maggie Abell describing his experiences as a Civil War soldier, of pension claims made by his wife Cetelda F. Farward Abell after the War, and of sketches by Nida Copelin.

8,895. Adams, Andrew W., and Family
Papers. 1856. 33-page item.
Open. Unpublished guide.
Minnesota Historical Society, Archives and Manuscripts.
Diary kept by Adams's wife Susan Maria Hazeltine Adams (1831-?), who left New Hampshire to settle in Shakopee, Minnesota Territory, in 1854. She describes her daily experiences as a housekeeper and teacher, community activities, her religious beliefs, the weather, food, social life, illnesses, and deaths in the community.

8,896. Adams, Elmer Ellsworth, and Family
Papers. 1860-1951. 3 oversize folders, 62 boxes, 1 oversize bacase, and 2 items.
Partially restricted. Unpublished guide.
Minnesota Historical Society, Archives and Manuscripts.
Papers of Frances (Cowles) Adams (1859-1937), who married Elmer Adams in ca. 1888, include correspondence with her uncle Reginald M. Reynolds concerning her career as a teacher, her diaries for 1874 to 1875 and of trips abroad in 1922 and 1927, and information and printed material on groups with which she was involved, including the Women's Club of Fergus Falls, MN, the Woman Suffrage State Central Committee, the Minnesota Woman Suffrage Association, the Minnesota Anti-Saloon League, the Scandinavian Temperance Union of Fergus Falls, the National Woman's party, the LWV, the Children's Home Society, and the Literary Club of Fergus Falls. Also includes correspondence between Helen (Cowles) Reynolds and her husband Reginald M. Reynolds, her diaries for 1863 and 1875 to 1879, and her teaching certificates; letters that Dorothy Quincey Adams (1894-) wrote while attending Dana Hall and Smith College and information concerning her marriage to a Mr. Eschweiler in ca. 1920; letters by Marjorie Adams (1891-1951), who was attending Dana Hall and Wellesley College; letters of Anna Hale Adams (1923-) describing life at Wellesley College and a paper by her about her grandfather Elmer Adams; an 1871 teaching contract of Anne E. Fuller; and information concerning the marriage in 1941 of Mary Evans and Elmer Adams. Also includes correspondence by and about Minnesota educators Maria L. Sanford and Ada Comstock and Minnesota legislators Mabeth Hurd Paige and Hannah J. Kempfer.

8,897. Adams School Civic League, Minneapolis
Records. 1904-10. 1 box.
Open. Unpublished guide.
Minnesota Historical Society, Archives and Manuscripts.
Minutes of meetings, membership lists, reports on national and local current events, commencement programs, and clippings of this 8th grade civics club.

8,898. Adelphai Club
Records. 1942-49. 1 vol. and 2 items.
Open. Unpublished guide.
Minnesota Historical Society, Archives and Manuscripts.
Records of this civic, philanthropic, and educational organization, which was founded in 1899 in St. Paul and is the oldest black women's club in Minnesota. Includes a volume containing material on the 50th anniversary program, a list of those who attended, congratulatory letters, and telegrams; two histories of the Club compiled by [Mrs.] Carrie E. Lindsay; and material relating to the Club's programs.

8,899. Aiton, John Felix
Papers. 1835-88. 3 boxes.
Open. Unpublished guide.
Minnesota Historical Society, Archives and Manuscripts.
Aiton (1817-92), a Methodist missionary, married Nancy Hunter (ca. 1820-53) of Quincy, IL, in 1848. They moved to Minnesota Territory, where she taught and he ministered to the Dakota Indians. Correspondence of Nancy Aiton with her sisters Hannah Hunter, a teacher, and Jane Hunter; with John Aiton before their marriage discussing their future in mission work and after their marriage concerning women's work, church work, and operating a frontier home; from other women involved in missionary work; from Indian girls in mission schools regarding religion, their families, and schooling; and from her brother Robert Hunter and father Charles Hunter about religious reform and mission work. Also includes a recommendation for Nancy Hunter from W. Beardsley of the Mission Institute of Quincy, IL; correspondence of John Aiton with his second wife Mary Briggs Aiton concerning household matters, religious work, family and friends, the Civil War, hospital care during the War, and deaths; and John

Aiton's correspondence with his daughter Hannah Aiton regarding family news and financial matters.

8,900. Akers, Peter, and Family
Papers. 1776-1911. 1 box.
Open. Unpublished guide.
Minnesota Historical Society, Archives and Manuscripts.
Includes letters by Mrs. Peter Akers to her son Charles N. Akers and her daughter-in-law Mary Dwight Akers; an 1894 letter in which Frances Willard responded to a letter Charles Akers had written about Peter Akers, the Methodist church, and temperance work; a letter in which Phoebe Cope [Mrs. John] Stone of Saffordville, KS, describes to Charles Akers the settlement of Red Wing, MN, during the early 1850s and her feelings about her daughter's leaving home; a letter written by A. Akers, Elizabeth Akers, and Elizabeth Lytle Brodwell about Akers family history; a short essay written by an anonymous woman in ca. 1893 about women's versus men's education; and land sale documents, many of which name women owners.

8,901. All Saints Episcopal Church
Records. 1932-71. 1 microfilm reel.
Open. Unpublished guide.
Minnesota Historical Society, Archives and Manuscripts.
Parish records of this Minneapolis church include a secretary's book of the All Saints Guild for 1957 to 1960.

8,902. American Association of University Women, Minnesota Division
Records. 1889-1966. 8 boxes, 2 bacases, and 1 oversize bacase.
Open. Unpublished guide.
Minnesota Historical Society, Archives and Manuscripts.
Minutes of board meetings and annual meetings; a treasurer's book; financial statements and reports; correspondence; histories of each of the branches; scrapbooks; and other records of the Minnesota Division, which was founded in 1889. Also includes minutes and scrapbooks of the St. Paul College Club, minutes and a history of its Creative Writing Group, and records of other Division branches. The St. Paul branch, organized in 1889, and the Minneapolis branch, organized in 1905, later merged with the state division of the AAUW.

8,903. American Board of Commissioners for Foreign Missions
Papers. 1827-78. 7 boxes.
Open. Unpublished guide.
Minnesota Historical Society, Archives and Manuscripts.
Copies of correspondence with missionaries in the Ojibwe and Dakota missions, including Hester Crooks [Mrs. William] Boutwell and Jane Smith Williamson. Also includes diaries, biographies, and other records sent to the Board, the originals of which are held at the Congregational House in Boston.

8,904. American Committee for Italian War Relief
Records. 1943-48. 40 items.
Open. Unpublished guide.
Minnesota Historical Society, Archives and Manuscripts.
This organization, formed in St. Paul to aid victims of war in Italy, was composed of representatives of Italian organizations and Italian Catholic churches. Articles of incorporation, minutes of meetings about clothing and financial drives and shipments of food and clothing to Italian civilians, and clippings relating to health and living conditions in Italy. Rose Ceresi was secretary of the organization.

8,905. American Guild of Music Teachers, Inc.
Records. 1926-58. 3 boxes and 1 bacase.
Open. Unpublished guide.
Minnesota Historical Society, Archives and Manuscripts.
The Guild was founded to "unite, protect and further the interests of music teachers, to raise standards of music teaching . . . and promote the civilization of musical art." Articles of incorporation, minutes of board and membership meetings, and financial data of the American Guild, which was founded in 1928; constitution, bylaws, minutes, a list of original members, bulletins, and clippings of the Minneapolis Guild, which was founded in 1926; and minutes of executive board meetings, financial statements, membership lists, bulletins, and clippings about programs and recitals of the St. Paul Guild, which was founded in 1927. Also includes letters to congressmen concerning legislation and the arts and programs of student recitals.

8,906. American Hungarian Ladies Benevolent Society
Records. 1931-66. 1 box.
Open. Unpublished guide.
Minnesota Historical Society, Archives and Manuscripts.
Records of this Minneapolis organization of Jewish Hungarian-American women include minutes, membership account books, correspondence, and clippings relating to heart surgery performed on Miriam Revesy, which was financed by the Society, and to financial contributions the Society made to various health societies, Israeli relief organizations, and Jewish appeals in the US.

8,907. American Legion Auxiliary, Minnesota Department
Records. 1926-65. 21 boxes.
Open. Unpublished guide.
Minnesota Historical Society, Archives and Manuscripts.
Constitution; minutes of the first annual convention, held in 1920; registration cards for conferences and conventions; histories of individual units of the Auxiliary in Minnesota; biographical data on men from Minnesota who served in WWI; and scrapbooks of the St. Anthony Park post in St. Paul and the 4th district of this women's organization, which is associated with the American Legion, an organization of veterans of world wars. Part of the collection is available on microfilm.

8,908. American Red Cross, Northern Division
Records. 1915-21. 12 boxes.
Open. Unpublished guide.
Minnesota Historical Society, Archives and Manuscripts.
Form letters, reports of conferences, and other records of the national headquarters and northern division main office in Minneapolis; histories of Minnesota county chapters of the American National Red Cross; records of the Minneapolis and St. Paul chapters, including material on war fund drives, membership drives, contributions, training courses in first aid and hygiene, home nursing, and preparing relief kits; and reports and interoffice communications of the Civilian Relief Department, including material relating to After Care, care of wounded soldiers in US hospitals, and the Home Service, which provided care for WWI veterans and their families and for victims of domestic disasters.

8,909. Amherst H. Wilder Foundation
Records. Ca. 1890-1968. 10 ft.
Access restricted. No guide.
Minnesota Historical Society, Archives and Manuscripts.
The Foundation, established in St. Paul in the 1890s, was named after Amherst Wilder, a St. Paul businessman who funded many social service projects. Annual reports, reports on projects and St. Paul social agencies, a foster home study, biographies, foundation histories, statistics, research department material from WWII, a scrapbook, clippings, brochures and other publicity material, and other records.

8,910. Anderson and Blegen
Collection. 1849-1942. 3 boxes.
Open. Unpublished guide.
Minnesota Historical Society, Archives and Manuscripts.
Copies of political platforms and resolutions adopted at political conventions in Minnesota from 1849 to 1942, which were compiled by William Anderson and Theodore Christian Blegen. Also includes correspondence of Sarah A. Davidson and others working on the project with party leaders and workers, including Jessie E. Scott and Anna Dickie Olesen.

8,911. Anderson, Eugenie Moore
Papers. 1955. 14-page item.
Open. No guide.
Minnesota Historical Society, Archives and Manuscripts.
[Mrs. John P.] Anderson (1909-) was ambassador to Denmark from 1949 to 1953. Transcript of an address she delivered at the Historical Society's annual meeting on the economic, political, social, cultural, and military factors that have united America with the countries of western Europe and the importance of keeping ties with those countries intact.

8,912. Anderson, Eugenie Moore
Papers. 1890s-1973. 26.25 ft.
Access restricted. No guide.
Minnesota Historical Society, Archives and Manuscripts.
[Mrs. John P.] Anderson (1909-), a Democratic-Farmer-Labor party activist, was ambassabor to Denmark from 1949 to 1952, minister to Bulgaria from 1962 to 1964, and a member of the US delegation to the UN from 1965 to 1968. Correspondence and other papers relate to her diplomatic career; her political activities, including her primary campaign for the US Senate in 1958 and her work in the Hubert Humphrey presidential campaign of 1968; her trips to India in 1961 and to Vietnam in 1967; and the Moore family.

8,913. Anderson, William
Papers. 1912-47. 2.5 boxes.
Open. Unpublished guide.
Minnesota Historical Society, Archives and Manuscripts.
Papers of Anderson, a professor of political science at the University of Minnesota, include correspondence, proposals, reports, and the transcript of a LWV-sponsored radio show on Minneapolis city charter reform; a 1930 letter from the city clerk of Minneapolis giving the number of men and women registered to vote in the city and the votes cast by sex in 1910, 1912, 1914, 1916, and 1918 elections; a 1926 letter to Mrs. C. S. Mitchell regarding the Duluth Charter Commission, of which she was a member; minutes; resolutions; drafts of charters for the city of Minneapolis; and clippings. Correspondents include Ruth Haynes Carpenter, director and secretary of the Citizen's Volunteer Committee; Gratia Countryman, a librarian at the Minneapolis Public Library; and Jessie [Mrs. W. J.] Marcley, a member of the Minneapolis Charter Commission from 1930 to 1932.

8,914. Andrews, James Amasa, and Family
Papers. 1831-1945. 3.5 boxes, 1 vol., and 40 oversize items.
Open. Unpublished guide.

Minnesota Historical Society, Archives and Manuscripts.
Scattered diaries and cash accounts of Andrews's wife Ellen Miriam Gibson Andrews (?-1921) for the period 1894 to 1920, scattered diaries of Ruth Caroline Andrews (1878-?), a student and clubwoman, for the period 1895 to 1945; and a minute book of the Margaret Fuller Association, 1872. Among the topics discussed in the diaries are social life in Hudson, WI; the St. Croix Bible Society; the Baptist church in Wisconsin; and religion in Wisconsin.

8,915. Andrews, Sarah E.
Papers. 1864-66. 1 microfilm reel.
Open. Unpublished guide.
Minnesota Historical Society, Archives and Manuscripts.
Letters that Andrews, a resident of Hudson, WI, wrote to her brother James while he was serving in the Civil War.

8,916. Anthony, Susan Brownell
Papers. 1868. 1 item.
Open. No guide.
Minnesota Historical Society, Archives and Manuscripts.
Letter in which Anthony (1820-1906) congratulated Josephine Lapham on her entry into the ministry, noting the importance of women's activities in all phases of national life.

8,917. Arbolado Parent Teacher Association of District 33, Ramsey County
Records. 1921-58. 2 boxes.
Open. Unpublished guide.
Minnesota Historical Society, Archives and Manuscripts.
Arbolado School existed from 1926 to 1957. Minutes of the District 33 PTA for 1924 to 1957, of the Maplewood PTA for 1939 to 1957, of the Mothers' Club for 1921 to 1924, and of Coleman's Lake View Improvement Association; "School Days," a poem by Mrs. Elmer Stanke; and a program and clippings concerning the closing of Arbolado School.

8,918. Architects' Small Home Service Bureau of the United States
Records. 1920-41. 64 bacases.
Open. Partial unpublished guide.
Minnesota Historical Society, Archives and Manuscripts.
Correspondence, accounts, and clippings of this organization, which was founded and headquartered in Minneapolis. The Bureau sold plans of small houses, offered advice and counseling, and performed other professional services on a cooperative basis for people with limited incomes. Includes volumes on how to plan, finance, and build a home.

8,919. Arlington Hills Mothers' Club
Records. 1897-99. 1 vol.
Open. Unpublished guide.
Minnesota Historical Society, Archives and Manuscripts.
Minutes; a description of programs, which included discussion of raising children and music of the period; and lists of members and officers of this St. Paul group.

8,920. Arney, Maude Baumann
Papers. 1900-02. 7 items.
Open. No guide.
Minnesota Historical Society, Archives and Manuscripts.
Reminiscences of the George Baumann family written by Arney, a 15-year-old girl, include an account of a trip the family took from Waltham, MN, to Bagley, MN, in search of a homestead; photos and data on the family and homestead; and a history of School District No. 64 in Holst Township, Clearwater County, MN.

8,921. Arthur's Home Magazine
Records. 1853-64. 17 items.
Open. No guide.
Minnesota Historical Society, Archives and Manuscripts.
Transcripts from *Arthur's Home Magazine* of Philadelphia relate to Minnesota and include stories and poems by Minnie Mary Lee; notes on the upper Mississippi region, especially on the legend of Sugar Loaf Mountain in Winona, MN; and a story by Mary H. Eastman. The magazine was variously titled *Arthur's Home Magazine, The Home Magazine,* the *Lady's Home Magazine of Literature, Art and Fashion,* and *Peterson's Magazine.*

8,922. Associated Charities of St. Paul
Records. 1892-1917. 2 boxes.
Open. Unpublished guide.
Minnesota Historical Society, Archives and Manuscripts.
The Associated Charities was founded in 1892 to promote cooperation of public and private charitable agencies in St. Paul and to establish a registration office to record the charitable work of these agencies. In 1914 the group changed its name to the United Charities of St. Paul and established a relief department. Minutes, reports, registration files on families and individuals, and other records of the Associated Charities, including information on charity work of member organizations and relations between member agencies, and minutes and reports of the United Charities for 1914 to 1917, with information on visits made to applicants for relief, "friendly visiting" to the poor and needy by volunteers, thrift teaching, legal aid, child welfare, and legislation relating to children, women, and the poor.

8,923. Association of Minneapolis Jewish Women's Organizations
Records. 1936-42. 1 box.
Open. Unpublished guide.
Minnesota Historical Society, Archives and Manuscripts.
The purpose of this Minneapolis group, which was organized in 1930 and was composed of representatives from Jewish women's organizations engaged in communal, religious, philanthropic, and cultural activities, was to promote interorganizational goodwill within the Jewish community, to maintain a community calendar, to conduct educational workshops, and to be responsible for the women's division of the Minneapolis Federation for Jewish Service. Minutes containing information on finances, membership, guest speakers, anti-Semitism, educational functions, and philanthropic work and lists of members, officers, and constituent organizations.

8,924. Atwood, Edwin H., and Family
Papers. 1860-1900. 7 boxes.
Open. Unpublished guide.
Minnesota Historical Society, Archives and Manuscripts.
Atwood (1829-1900), an early settler in Stearns County, MN, was a farmer and president of the State Farmer's Alliance in 1888. Includes correspondence of Atwood with his wife Augusta Allen Atwood about his trip to California in 1897; letters from his daughters and son living in California during the 1890s; letters from his sister Jeanette Langrishe, who discusses her work, politics, and family news; and letters from female cousins in New York concerning their work and health, the family, and genealogy. Also includes a letter from Ella Paddock to Edwin Atwood, who was her legal guardian, concerning her life at St. Mary's Hall in Faribault, MN, and at St. Cloud State Teacher's College in St. Cloud, MN, during the 1880s and 1890s and estate papers of Nancy W. Allen.

8,925. Austin, Horace, and Family
Papers. 1857-1953. 1 box and 13 oversize items.
Open. Unpublished guide.
Minnesota Historical Society, Archives and Manuscripts.
Austin (1831-1905) was governor of Minnesota from 1870 to 1873. Letters to Austin from Andrew R. McGill concerning the activities of Mrs. Cushman K. Davis in 1903 after the death of her husband, 1870s letters in which Austin discusses women's suffrage with Mr. and Mrs. William Dodge, and letters to Austin's wife Helen Austin and Leonora (Austin) [Mrs. Conde] Hamlin; clippings about the Austin family, including Helen Austin and Leonora Austin; and obituaries of Horace and Helen Austin.

8,926. Ayer, Elizabeth Taylor
Papers. 1868-92. 1 microfilm reel.
Open. Unpublished guide.
Minnesota Historical Society, Archives and Manuscripts.
Ayer (1803-98) was a missionary who taught among the Ojibwe people. Letters by Ayer to her brother Jonathan recalling incidents in her missionary career and family life and to J. Fletcher Williams of the Historical Society staff describing the Chippewa Mission at Pokegama, Pine County, MN; a reminiscent account of the Belle Prairie School in Belle Prairie, MN; and a biographical sketch by Ayer of her husband Frederick Ayer.

8,927. Ayer, Harry Darius, and Family
Papers. 1787-1966. 11 boxes.
Open. Unpublished guide.
Minnesota Historical Society, Archives and Manuscripts.
Ayer (1878-1966) and his wife Janette Ora (Foster) Ayer (1884-1966) lived for 52 years on Mille Lacs Indian Reservation, where they operated a private store and then a trading post. They hired only Indians, took an interest in the Ojibwe community, and helped with Ojibwe commercial fishing and harvesting of wild rice on Mille Lacs Lake. Correspondence of Janette (Foster) Ayer to Harry Ayer, of Janette Ayer's family, and relating to the Basford, Bradbury, and Foster families; customer account statements; trading post account and charge books; deeds, contracts, and other legal papers; estate papers of Emma Bug and of other Indians whose estates Harry Ayer handled; poetry books of Lavina Bradbury; a physiology notebook and a University of Minnesota student account book, 1903-04, of Janette Foster; a 1908 wedding book of Harry Ayer and Janette Foster; genealogical data; and a memorial booklet to Janette Ayer.

8,928. Baasen, Francis, and Family
Papers. 1840-1958. 24 items.
Open. Unpublished guide.
Minnesota Historical Society, Archives and Manuscripts.
Baasen (1820-1901) was the first secretary of state of Minnesota. Includes a letter to Joseph L. Donovan in 1958 while he was secretary of state of Minnesota from Mary A. Baasen Wooldrik giving details about her family, a 1900 stock certificate made out to Louise Baasen for ownership in the Western Telegraph Typewriting Machine Company, clippings about Baasen family activities, and obituaries of Francis Baasen and Mary Belland Baasen (1842-1929).

8,929. Babcock, Willoughby, and Family
Papers. 1836-1963. 12 boxes.
Open. Unpublished guide.
Minnesota Historical Society, Archives and Manuscripts.
Letters that Babcock (1832-64) wrote to his wife Helen E. Maynard Babcock (1838-?) during his service as an officer with the Third New York Volunteers in Florida and Louisiana concerning his life in the army and his deep feeling for her; their

diaries for 1863 and 1864; a letter she wrote to her son Willoughby M. Babcock (1864-1925) at Yale; and a volume entitled *Marriage Advice*, which contains Helen and Willoughby Babcock's marriage certificate. Also includes an 1836 letter by Louisa Atwater Babcock (?-1850) of Courtland County, NY, to her husband Samuel Babcock (?-1895), a farmer; an article on Minnesota Indians by Beverly Mindrum for the Minnesota Governor's Human Rights Commission, 1962; and articles on Minnesota territorial life by Grace (Henshaw) Babcock, an author and researcher who was married to Willoughby M. Babcock II (1893-1967), curator at the Minnesota Historical Society.

8,930. Babies Home
Records. 1890-1900. 1 bacase.
Open. Unpublished guide.
Minnesota Historical Society, Archives and Manuscripts.
Articles of incorporation, minutes of the board of managers, receipts and disbursements, lists of donations, and a daily record of official visitors to the Home, which existed from 1890 to 1900 in St. Paul to care for abandoned or orphaned children under 2 years of age.

8,931. Bachmann, Charles W., and Family
Papers. 1854-1912. 1 box and 1 vol.
Open. Unpublished guide.
Minnesota Historical Society, Archives and Manuscripts.
Includes correspondence in German of Ida Mackenroth Bachmann (1837-?), a housewife, with her family in Germany in the 1860s.

8,932. Backus, Marion A.
Papers. 1918-46. 1.5 in.
Open. No guide.
Minnesota Historical Society, Archives and Manuscripts.
Correspondence, documents, and a tape recording of Backus relate primarily to her service as a nurse in France during WWI.

8,933. Bailey, Belle
Papers. Nd. 6-page item.
Open. No guide.
Minnesota Historical Society, Archives and Manuscripts.
Writing by Bailey concerns the experiences of a government surveyor Joel Bailey in 1854.

8,934. Bailey, Everett Hoskins, and Family
Papers. 1839-1954. 8 boxes.
Open. Unpublished guide.
Minnesota Historical Society, Archives and Manuscripts.
Papers of Jeannette (Jones) Bailey (1851-1923) include letters to Everett Bailey describing a trip to Europe in 1891 and a trip to Japan in 1910, letters of introduction written for her by James J. Hill and Archbishop John Ireland, indentures for St. Paul property she bought, and her will. Also includes letters from Florence Bailey Dorman to Everett Bailey concerning family and business matters; correspondence between William Timmis, Caroline B. Pier, Frank Bailey, and Everett Bailey regarding Timmis's invention of an air brake; correspondence between Everett Bailey, Stephen D. Ryan, and Gertrude W. Ryan about the bankruptcy case of Dennis Ryan; and letters about the Belgium Child Welfare Fund from Jane Henry and Louisa d'Ursel, who was the Fund's national chairman. Also includes diary entries by Delia Garlick Jones (1830-1934), the mother of Jeannette Bailey; an essay by Caroline Pier at Jamestown Academy in New York; and wills of Martha E. Bailey.

8,935. Baillif, Matilda Victorine
Papers. 1848-1930. 0.5 box and 1 vol.
Open. Unpublished guide.
Minnesota Historical Society, Archives and Manuscripts.
Correspondence of Baillif (1883-), an author and genealogist, with relatives in France and elsewhere concerning her preparation of a genealogy, a scrapbook of her 1930 trip to Europe, and an autobiographical sketch by her father, which she translated from French into English.

8,936. Bailly, Alexis
Papers. 1821-98. 7 boxes, 2 vols., and 3 microfilm reels.
Open. Unpublished guide.
Minnesota Historical Society, Archives and Manuscripts.
Letters by wives and relatives of fur traders, including Sally G. Crafte, Jane Lamont, Jane Movey, Mary E. Ortley, Peggy Pizanne, Lucy Bailly, Sophie (Hostense) Bailly, Nancy Bouske, Nancy G. Buisson, Mary Conner, Lucy Prescott, Eva Putnam, Mary Taliaferro, Nancy Jolie, Mrs. Ezra Petton, and Emily R. Faribault. Also includes a Dakota manuscript by Mary Hudson and an 1856 marriage certificate of Eliza Hoppe Duke.

8,937. Baird, Sarah G.
Papers. 1870-1918. 1 box.
Open. Unpublished guide.
Minnesota Historical Society, Archives and Manuscripts.
Includes diaries in which [Mrs. George W.] Baird (1843-1923) recorded from 1882 to 1918 her daily housekeeping chores, social events, visits from friends, and trips to California in 1892 and 1913 and to the Chicago World's Fair in 1893. She also mentions activities of the local Grange and the national Grange.

8,938. Bald Eagle Union Church
Records. 1905-35. 0.5 box.
Open. Unpublished guide.
Minnesota Historical Society, Archives and Manuscripts.
Records of the Ladies Aid Society of this church in Bald Eagle, Ramsey County, MN.

8,939. Barbeau, Rose
Papers. 1933. 5-page item.
Open. No guide.
Minnesota Historical Society, Archives and Manuscripts.
Narrative told to Charles Wright by [Mrs.] Barbeau (1844-?) of Fergus Falls, MN, who moved to Otter Tail, MN, in 1866 from the Canadian Northwest, where her father and husband had been employed by the Hudson's Bay Company.

8,940. Bassett, Joel B.
Papers. 1858-76. 86 items.
Open. Unpublished guide.
Minnesota Historical Society, Archives and Manuscripts.
Bassett (1817-1912) was a Chippewa Indian agent in Minnesota from 1865 to 1869. Includes two accounts by Ellen McArthur, wife of Chippewa leader Hole-in-the-Day, of a robbery of her home, one of which was written in 1868.

8,941. Baxter, Luther Loren, and Family
Papers. 1853-1950. 2 boxes.
Open. Unpublished guide.
Minnesota Historical Society, Archives and Manuscripts.
Baxter (1838-1915), a lawyer who was a territorial settler from Vermont, served in the Minnesota legislature from 1865 to 1881 and as judge of the 7th judicial district from 1885 to 1910. Letters to Baxter from his sister-in-law Jennie Baxter, his mother Philene Baxter (?-1902), and other family and friends in the East; from his first wife Emma Ward Baxter during the Civil War; from his sisters Lorinda Woodbury and Mary Pritchard; from prominent Minnesotans, including Harriet McKelvey of the Northwestern Freedman's Aid Commission; and from his son Chauncey Luther Baxter (ca. 1858-1927), a lawyer and entrepreneur, and Chauncey's wife Elizabeth Deuhs Baxter (?-1947), a teacher, concerning family problems, their separation, and their divorce. Also includes letters relating to Elizabeth Baxter's activities in St. Cloud, MN, where she completed her education and raised her daughter Nellie, and letters by Bertha Baxter concerning the death and division of the estate of Nellie Baxter (ca. 1879-1950), an operator of the Chaska Fairway grocery store, who was active in the Republican party in Carver County, MN.

8,942. Bayliss, Celeste Chamberlain
Papers. 1918-45. 120 items.
Open. Unpublished guide.
Minnesota Historical Society, Archives and Manuscripts.
Bayliss (1875-1935) attended the universities of Wisconsin and Minnesota and taught school in several Wisconsin communities before marrying and moving to Minnesota, where her husband Willard Bayliss was superintendent for the Oliver Iron Mining Company. The mother of six children, Celeste Bayliss was active in civic organizations and women's clubs on the Iron Range, serving from 1918 to 1935 on the St. Louis County Child Welfare Board. Letters and clippings regarding her work with and presidency from 1925 to 1929 of the Minnesota Federation of Women's Clubs, certificates, and speeches and articles relating to her interest in reforestation, clean milk, communal property rights for women, and effective organization of women for community service.

8,943. Bell, James Ford
Papers. 1916-60. 8 boxes.
Open. Unpublished guide.
Minnesota Historical Society, Archives and Manuscripts.
Bell (1879-1961) was chairman of the board of General Mills in Minneapolis. Includes correspondence between Bell and Sister Elizabeth Kenny, a nurse who developed a treatment to cure infantile paralysis; clippings; and printed material concerning the care and treatment of patients at the National Foundation for Infantile Paralysis and a copy of a speech by Queen Juliana of the Netherlands concerning the Indonesian crisis of 1949.

8,944. Bell, Robert Mowry, and Family
Papers. 1845-1933. 1 box.
Open. Unpublished guide.
Minnesota Historical Society, Archives and Manuscripts.
Correspondence between family members with news of visits to Europe and Asia; a letter to Estella Bates from Warren D. Parker of River Falls Teachers College in Wisconsin discussing her teaching career; a diary kept by Robert Bell's wife Elizabeth (Kennedy) Bell (ca. 1871-?) while her family lived in Leipzig, Germany; and diaries kept by Katharine L. Kennedy [Mrs. John H.] Barr (ca. 1863-?) in 1903 and 1904 concerning life in Ithaca, NY, and in 1914 during a trip to the Mediterranean countries of Europe.

8,945. Bell, William J.
Papers. 1837-1964. 2.5 ft.
Open. No guide.
Minnesota Historical Society, Archives and Manuscripts.
Diaries kept from 1886 to 1888 by Clara Wiley [Mrs. James Hamilton] Bell, who settled in Minnesota's Red River Valley in the 1880s, and family expense records for 1914 to 1916 kept by William Jefferson Bell (1888-), a Presbyterian minister and missionary on the Minnesota Iron Range, and by his wife Helen Mary Hunt Bell.

8,946. Benitt, Carsten, and Family
Papers. 1780-1905. 2 vols. and 19 items.
Open. Unpublished guide.
Minnesota Historical Society, Archives and Manuscripts.
The Benitts were a German Lutheran family who farmed near Cologne, Germany and later emigrated to Minnesota. Memoirs of Catherine Benitt (?-1780) and information on her death as well as an account book of Peter Benitt, the guardian of Katherine, Rebecca, and Gierdt Benitt, including monetary valuations of their personal and real property. The papers are in German.

8,947. Benitt, William A., and Family
Papers. 1930-66. 2 boxes.
Open. Unpublished guide.
Minnesota Historical Society, Archives and Manuscripts.
Linda (James) Benitt, who received a BA from the University of Minnesota and degrees in public health from Harvard and MIT, operated Apple Acres Farm in Hastings, MN, with her husband William A. Benitt and taught an adult education program for the Agricultural Adjustment Administration from 1939 to 1943. Letters from Linda Benitt to her friend Nellie M. Hubbell and others about economic conditions, rural conditions in Washington County, MN, and production of livestock, poultry, grains, and fruit on their farm; personal, farm, and household account books; a paper in which she summarizes her farming activity; and clippings.

8,948. Benjamin, John, and Family
Papers. 1840-1951. 6 boxes.
Open. Unpublished guide.
Minnesota Historical Society, Archives and Manuscripts.
John Benjamin (1823-?) emigrated from Wales to the US in 1849 and married Elizabeth Garner (1830-1900), also of Wales, in 1851. They lived in Massachusetts, Illinois, and Minnesota. Correspondence of Elizabeth Benjamin with her husband and with her brother and letters from Hattie Hutchinson and letters to the Benjamins from Richard and Mary Wait of Lawrence, Kansas Territory. Other correspondents include Richard and Marian Garner; Mary Christopherson, who describes life in Wales; Joshua and Jeanette Sweet, who write about life in Glencoe, MN; Agnes Ramsden; and Elizabeth Dawson. Papers of Blanche Grimshaw [Mrs. Arthur Edwin] Benjamin (1870-1951) consist of congratulatory letters on her 50th wedding anniversary, a diary she kept from 1908 to 1916, a history of the Grimshaw family she wrote, her wedding announcement, a stock certificate, and a clipping about her and her family. Also includes Minneapolis public school diplomas of Helen Dorcas Jordan, a US passport and DAR membership card of Mildred Salome Jordan, and a DAR membership card of Maude Grimshaw Jordan.

8,949. Benson, Elmer Austin
Papers. 1931-73. 29 boxes.
Open. Unpublished guide.
Minnesota Historical Society, Archives and Manuscripts.
Benson (1895-), a lawyer and banker, served as US senator from Minnesota in 1935 and 1936, as Minnesota governor from 1936 to 1939, and as a leader in the Farmer-Labor party and in the 1948 Progressive party. Correspondence, speeches, political literature, and clippings and publications relating to Benson's political career. Includes letters from Viena Johnson, Irene [Mrs. Henry] Paull, Susie W. Stageberg, Freda Kirchwey, Eslanda Goode [Mrs. Paul A.] Robeson, and others concerning the issue of communists in the Farmer-Labor party, WWII, the origins of the Cold War, the 1948 Progressive party, the emergence of the Democratic-Farmer-Labor party, and other subjects relating to Minnesota politics. Also includes a paper by Marian LeSueur on the liberal movement in the northern Middle West, a pamphlet on the Vera Hathaway deportation case, and publications edited by Maud Russell and Anna Louise Strong.

8,950. Bessesen, Beatrice (Gjertsen)
Papers. 1904-34. 2.33 in.
Open. Unpublished guide.
Minnesota Historical Society, Archives and Manuscripts.
Bessesen (1886-1935), born in Minneapolis and educated at the University of Minnesota, was a professional opera singer who received musical citations from Emperor William II of Germany and Queen Wilhelmina of the Netherlands. Scrapbook of letters, photos, and clippings relates to her career as a singer in the US and Europe from 1904 to 1914, her marriage to William A. Bessesen in 1915, and her efforts to organize music conservatories in Albert Lea, MN, and Minneapolis.

8,951. Bethany Congregational Church
Records. 1899-1924. 3 boxes.
Open. Unpublished guide.
Minnesota Historical Society, Archives and Manuscripts.
Minutes of the Ladies' Aid Society of this Minneapolis church for 1909 to 1913.

8,952. Bethany Lutheran Church
Records. 1911-33. 0.5 box.
Open. Unpublished guide.
Minnesota Historical Society, Archives and Manuscripts.
Record book containing minutes, accounts, and bills of the secretary-treasurer of the Ladies's Aid Society of this Remer, MN, church.

8,953. Bill, Fred Adelbert, and Family
Papers. 1793-1957. 10 boxes and 3 bacases.
Open. Unpublished guide.
Minnesota Historical Society, Archives and Manuscripts.
Correspondence of Bill with Mrs. George Hazzard concerning a lawsuit she brought against the Minnesota Territorial Pioneers, with Ida M. Tarbell about Stephen Hanks and the Lincoln family, and with Louise Phelps Kellogg, historian of the State Historical Society of Wisconsin, about the history of steamboating on the Mississippi and Chippewa rivers; poetry of Betsy Orcutt Davis [Mrs. Epaphras Chapman] Bill (1826-57); an article by Clara McMaster [Mrs. Fred] Bill (1852-1928) about the McMaster family; clippings about the Fred Bill family; and pamphlets by phrenologists describing the character of Clara Bill and Fred Bill. Papers of Clara and Fred Bill's daughter Jessie Mary (Bill) [Mrs. Harry] Clark (1878-?) include correspondence, a diary she kept in 1916, estate papers, and biographical and genealogical data.

8,954. Bishop, Judson Wade, and Family
Papers. 1856-1949. 2 boxes.
Open. Unpublished guide.
Minnesota Historical Society, Archives and Manuscripts.
Bishop (1831-1917) was a surveyor, journalist, railroad contractor, and organizer and operator of the St. Paul Trust Company. Correspondence of Bishop with his mother Elena Brown [Mrs. John F.] Bishop (1810-1903) of Lorraine, NY, and with his sisters Anna Bishop and Lena Bishop of Chatfield, MN. Also includes a letter from Bishop's wife Mary Axtell Bishop (ca. 1859-1953) to Flora M. Bishop Nuese in Santa Cruz, CA; the letter to Nuese, the widow of their son Robert Haven Bishop, is accompanied by a clipping giving information about the Bishop family. Also contains a letter from Elizabeth Van Cleve Hall, the daughter of Horatio and Charlotte Van Cleve, regarding her receipt of Judson Bishop's book about his Civil War experiences, and the first annual catalog of the Chatfield Academy, which lists students, faculty members, curriculum, objectives, fees, and tuition of this coeducational academy of which Judson Bishop was principal.

8,955. Bloomer, Samuel
Papers. 1861-1920. 1 box.
Open. Unpublished guide.
Minnesota Historical Society, Archives and Manuscripts.
Letters to Bloomer, a Minnesota soldier serving in the Civil War, from Ada Cornman, a teacher in Stillwater, MN, who describes social life, teaching, and students and gives news of the Civil War in Minnesota.

8,956. Boardman, Frances
Oral history. 1953. 2 items.
Open. No guide.
Minnesota Historical Society, Archives and Manuscripts.
Transcripts of an interview, conducted by Lucile M. Kane of the Minnesota Historical Society, with [Miss] Boardman (1879-1953), who describes her early life and schooling in St. Paul, her father's occupation, her work as a theater reporter for the *St. Paul Daily News,* her work in Winnipeg theaters, and the funeral of Archbishop John Ireland, which she covered for the St. Paul newspapers.

8,957. Bovey, Margaret (Jackson)
Papers. Nd. 31-page item.
Open. No guide.
Minnesota Historical Society, Archives and Manuscripts.
Reminiscences by [Mrs. John] Bovey (1887-) concern life in Minneapolis during the 1890s and include information on the family's summer home at Northwood, holiday celebrations, the Lafayette Hotel on Lake Minnetonka, making clothes, the conversion of the family's city home from gaslights to electricity, the installation of their first telephone, social life, and Madison School, which Margaret Jackson attended until her graduation in 1899. Bovey also describes the early life of her parents Anson Jackson and Eugenia (Adams) Jackson (ca. 1850-?). Her mother was born in Painesville, OH, and began teaching school there at the age of 17 before moving to Minneapolis in 1878. Anson Jackson, who was born in Brooklyn, NY, graduated from Hobart College and Columbia law school, came to Minneapolis in 1878, and married Eugenia Adams in 1881.

8,958. Boyd, George, and Family
Papers. 1852-1961. 20 items and 14 oversize items.
Open. Unpublished guide.
Minnesota Historical Society, Archives and Manuscripts.
Boyd (1832-79) was a territorial settler in Minnesota, a Civil War soldier, and a harness maker. Includes correspondence between his granddaughter Marian Boyd [Mrs. James D.] Winter and Kathryn Ann Johnson, assistant curator of manuscripts at the Historical Society, about the death of Boyd's first wife Nancy Williams Boyd (?-1857), the marriage of Sarah A. Williams Boyd (?-1899) to George Boyd, and the settlement of Minnesota as well as documents relating to the pension of Sarah Williams Boyd.

8,959. Breckenridge, Elizabeth E., and Family
Papers. 1863-97. 1 box.
Open. Unpublished guide.
Minnesota Historical Society, Archives and Manuscripts.
Notebooks kept by Breckenridge (1859-1942) in Baring, ME, containing short stories, lessons, and lists of classmates and autograph books she and her family kept in Baring and Pine City, MN.

8,960. Bremer, Fredrika
Papers. 1846-49. 2 items.
Open. Unpublished guide.
Minnesota Historical Society, Archives and Manuscripts.
Bremer (1801-65) was a Swede who traveled in the US during the late 1840s. Includes a letter written by Bremer in Cambridge, MA, to "My dear Miss Parks" and another in which Bremer describes Massachusetts social life and the US. Her second letter was probably written to Andrew J. Downing.

8,961. Briggs, Melissa (Chapin), and Briggs, Welcolm G.
Papers. 1859-68. 47 items.
Open. Unpublished guide.
Minnesota Historical Society, Archives and Manuscripts.
Melissa Briggs (?-1861) and her husband Welcolm Briggs (1823-?) settled in Shakopee, MN, in 1860, where they were farmers and operators of a dry goods store; she died in childbirth in 1861. Includes letters Melissa Briggs wrote to her mother Mrs. Nelson Chapin describing her life in Shakopee, social affairs, and singing at local church services as well as a farewell letter Briggs wrote to her family when she knew she was dying. After her death, her baby was cared for by a neighbor, Mandana [Mrs. Charles] Morrison. Letters by Mandana Morrison to Mrs. Chapin concern Melissa Briggs's death and continue after the death of the baby in 1862. Also includes a lineage chart that Virginia Chapin Pride, a great-granddaughter of Nelson Chapin, used to apply for membership in the Society of Colonial Dames.

8,962. Brill, Hascal Russell, and Family
Papers. 1805-1964. 18 boxes.
Open. Unpublished guide.
Minnesota Historical Society, Archives and Manuscripts.
Brill (1846-1922) was a district court judge. Papers of his wife Cora Amelia (Gray) Brill (1850-1927) include correspondence with her husband, which contains discussion of women's rights; with her mother Abby Jane Gray; and with others concerning Brill's family history for DAR membership. Also includes her diary for 1889 to 1902 and a scrapbook. The Brills' daughters Edith Brill (1876-1961) and Alice Cora Brill (1889-1968) both worked in the fields of education and social welfare. Edith Brill's papers include correspondence with her family, written while she was at Smith College from 1895 to 1898 and on European vacations, some of which concerns family genealogy; her diary for 1913; class notes; a biography of her parents and grandmother; and a genealogy of the Brill family. Alice Brill's papers include correspondence with her family while she was at Columbia University in the early 1920s and on European vacations, letters from Paul C. Raymond, correspondence for the United Charities of St. Paul, and correspondence regarding her work as director of the child study department of the Council Bluffs, IA, public schools; her diary for 1913, 1919 to 1920, and 1949 to 1955; memory books; manuscripts, including *The Graham Hall Murder;* a narrative she wrote with Edith Brill concerning one of their European trips; and articles and form letters on child study and parent education. Also includes correspondence regarding the contested inheritance of Abby Jane Gray; correspondence with publishers, research letters, diaries for 1899 to 1960, and copies of published short stories and poems of Ethel Claire Brill (1877-1962), who was the niece of Hascal Brill and an author of children's stories, articles, and poems; and correspondence in which Regina (Arthur) Caw discusses her status as sister of President Chester A. Arthur and literary, religious, and political subjects.

8,963. Brin, Fanny (Fligelman)
Papers. 1896-1958. 25 boxes, 1 bacase, and 1 oversize box.
Open. Unpublished guide.
Minnesota Historical Society, Archives and Manuscripts.
Correspondence, minutes, speeches, news releases, reports, posters, broadsides, pamphlets, articles, and clippings of Brin (1884-1961) relate to her involvement in numerous organizations concerned with peace, Jewish welfare, and women's rights, particularly the National Council of Jewish Women, but also including the National Committee on the Cause and Cure of War, the Women's Peace Party, the Minneapolis Committee for World Disarmament, the Women's Centennial Congress, the National Women's Suffrage Association, and the National Conference of Christians and Jews. Correspondents involved in the National Council of Jewish Women include its founder Hannah Solomon, president Rose Brenner, chairman of the committee on peace and arbitration Gertrude Feibleman, Blanche B. Goldman, and Cecelia Razousky. Other correspondents include Minneapolis civic leader Nina Morais Cohen, pacifists Rosika Schwimmer and Emily Hickman, Carrie Chapman Catt, and Gratia Countryman and Mrs. Elbert Carpenter, members of the Minneapolis Committee for World Disarmament. Also includes files on communism, socialism, anti-Semitism, Palestine, and refugees.

8,964. Brooks, Fern E.
Papers. 1936. 6-page item.
Open. No guide.
Minnesota Historical Society, Archives and Manuscripts.
Paper read at a meeting of the St. Louis County Historical Society concerns the activities of women of the Arrowhead region of Minnesota and mentions women's organizations of Duluth, MN.

8,965. Brown, Edward Josiah
Papers. 1879-1928. 1 box and 2 bacases.
Open. Unpublished guide.
Minnesota Historical Society, Archives and Manuscripts.
Brown (1851-1938) was a Minneapolis physician. Correspondence of Brown with women patients about their physical condition, bills, an account book kept by his wife, and medical case records containing each patient's name, address, occupation, a record of visits to the office, complaints, and treatments.

8,966. Brown, Joseph Renshaw, and Brown, Samuel J.
Papers. 1838-1916. 7.5 ft.
Open. Unpublished guide.
Minnesota Historical Society, Archives and Manuscripts.
Joseph Brown (1805-70), a trader with Dakota Indians, was associated with the development of several towns in Minnesota Territory. His wife was Susan Freniere Brown. Their son Samuel Jerome Brown (1845-1925), a teacher and real estate developer on Sisseton Reservation in Dakota Territory, was one-eighth Sisseton and considered a member of the Sisseton Dakota tribe. Correspondence of members of the Brown, Freniere, Allanson, Rice, Hines, Parker, Robertson, and Carli families; correspondence and other papers on the death of Samuel Brown's wife Phoebe Robinson Brown, ca. 1910; and estate papers of Susan Brown.

8,967. Bucklin, Abby
Papers. Nd. 69-page item.
Open. No guide.
Minnesota Historical Society, Archives and Manuscripts.
Manuscript by [Mrs. George] Bucklin concerns the pioneer experiences of her grandparents Elkanah Davis and Sarah (McCauley) Davis, who moved from Pennsylvania to Michigan and then in 1857 to Minnesota, where they homesteaded in Red Jacket near Mankato. Bucklin describes pioneer life in Michigan and Minnesota, the trip by covered wagon, making clothes and preparing food, home building, Indians, and the family's experiences in the Sioux outbreak of 1862.

8,968. Bullard, Marjorie L.
Papers. 1896-98. 10 pp.
Open. Unpublished guide.
Minnesota Historical Society, Archives and Manuscripts.
Diary in which Bullard, a young girl, describes school life, social activities, concerts, holiday celebrations, and the Spanish-American War.

8,969. Bullard, Polly Caroline
Papers. Nd. 80 pp.
Open. No guide.
Minnesota Historical Society, Archives and Manuscripts.
Letters that Bullard (1881-1949) wrote to her mother from 1908 to 1911 concern her experiences as a schoolteacher in Eveleth, MN, life on the Minnesota Iron Range, Finnish socialists, miners' homes, and Duluth. In her diary Bullard describes her activities as a young girl in St. Paul in 1897, her social life, clubs, school, friends, and musical events; she also briefly discusses family genealogy. Her reminiscences provide an account of her life in St. Paul from the time the Bullard family moved there in 1884 to the early 1900s. She discusses the neighborhoods of St. Anthony Park and Irvine Park, interior furnishings of homes, people who lived there, and her first days at Murray School in St. Anthony Park.

8,970. Bullis, Harry Amos
Papers. 1898-1963. 1 box, 13 bacases, and 12 oversize bacases.
Open. Unpublished guide.
Minnesota Historical Society, Archives and Manuscripts.
Bullis (1890-1963) was a General Mills executive and WWI veteran who was active in the Republican party and civic organizations. Consists primarily of scrapbooks, which relate to the marriage of Harry Bullis and Irme Elizabeth Alexander (1889-1947), the illness of Irme Bullis, services for her, the wedding of Harry Bullis and Countess Maria Robert Smorczewska, and activities of Maria Bullis. Scrapbooks contain letters of Irme Bullis and clippings about Countess Smorczewska. Also includes notebooks, certificates, citations, and booklets.

8,971. Burnquist, Joseph Alfred Arner
Papers. 1884-1960. 28 boxes.
Open. Unpublished guide.
Minnesota Historical Society, Archives and Manuscripts.
Burnquist (1879-1961), a lawyer and legislator, served as lieutenant governor of Minnesota from 1913 to 1915 and as governor from 1916 to 1920. Correspondence with Edith [Mrs. Charles H.] Mayo, Anna Dickie Olesen, Carrie Chapman Catt, Lenora Austin Hamlin, and Mary F. Severance concerning his work for passage of laws relating to women and child labor and to the Public Safety Commission, an executive committee created by Governor Burnquist during WWI to investigate activities of political radicals, members of ethnic groups, and others in order to determine their loyalty to the US government. Also includes clippings about such subjects as woman suffrage, wartime restrictions, and the Commission.

8,972. Business Women's Holding Company
Records. 1909-33. 12 boxes and 4 oversize items.
Open. Unpublished guide.
Minnesota Historical Society, Archives and Manuscripts.
Minutes, correspondence, and a membership list of

the Company as well as contracts, specifications, receipted bills, blueprints, and a daybook of the progress on the construction of the Business Women's Club in Minneapolis.

8,973. Butler, Eloise
Papers. 1914-31. 36 pp.
Open. No guide.
Minnesota Historical Society, Archives and Manuscripts.
Annals of the wildlife reserve at Theodore Wirth Park in Minneapolis concern [Miss] Butler's experiences as curator of the reserve in collecting, planting, and caring for the garden. Includes data on flowers, trees, ferns, shrubs, weeds, birds, and animals.

8,974. Butters, William, and Family
Papers. 1848-1916. 2.5 ft.
Open. No guide.
Minnesota Historical Society, Archives and Manuscripts.
The Butters family, after migrating to Minneapolis from Massachusetts in the 1860s, became involved in the lumbering industry and banking. Consists primarily of account books of Ella S. King Butters (?-1916), including one she kept with her husband William Butters (1849-1902) from 1885 to 1892, one for 1890 to 1908, and one for 1909 to 1916; in the books she notes activities, visitors, and letters received in addition to her daily household expenses. Also includes her journals for 1873 to 1874 before her marriage and for 1875 to 1899.

8,975. Cady and Randolph Families
Papers. 1844-1943. 1 box.
Open. Unpublished guide.
Minnesota Historical Society, Archives and Manuscripts.
Alonzo D. Cady (ca. 1823-1917) and Sabrina E. Ellis Cady moved from New York to Iowa, South Dakota, and Montana after their marriage. Correspondence between the couple while he was serving in the Civil War and she was in Iowa; letters from Jeannette Rankin, US representative from Montana, to the Cadys' daughter Emma (Cady) Randolph (ca. 1860-1940) and her husband John M. Randolph concerning the military service of their three sons and Rankin's sympathy on the death of their son Peyton Randolph in 1918; and an 1844 autograph book of Eliza Ellis of Essex County, NY.

8,976. Carey, Miriam Eliza
Papers. 1911-52. Ca. 4 in.
Open. Unpublished guide.
Minnesota Historical Society, Archives and Manuscripts.
Carey (1858-1937), a librarian, was supervisor of institutional libraries in Minnesota and Iowa and a teacher at the University of Minnesota. Correspondence between Carey, author Zona Gale, librarian Perrie Jones, and others about Carey's work with institutional libraries and the organization of libraries in army camps during WWI under the auspices of the American Library Association; a biographical sketch of Carey and correspondence relating to it by Jones; and articles and lectures pertaining to institutional libraries.

8,977. Carlson, Pehr, and Family
Papers. 1862-1906. 3.5 in.
Open. No guide.
Minnesota Historical Society, Archives and Manuscripts.
Papers of Pehr Carlson (?-1904), also known as Peter Carlson, and his wife Catharina Carlson, Swedish immigrants who settled in East Union, MN, in the 1850s, include family correspondence and a 1906 pension certificate of Catharina Carlson.

8,978. Carpenter, Mary E. Lovell, and Family
Papers. 1870-89. 48 items.
Open. Unpublished guide.
Minnesota Historical Society, Archives and Manuscripts.
Letters by Mary E. (Lovell) [Mrs. George] Carpenter (1840-1925) describing economic and social conditions on a farm in Marshall, MN, and by her mother Sylvia [Mrs. Lorenzo Orin] Lovell (ca. 1812-?) and daughter Mamie (Carpenter) [Mrs. Charles] Hurd (ca. 1864-?) describing farm life in Larrimore, Dakota Territory.

8,979. Carpenter, Sylvia Macomber, and Family
Papers. 1863-68. 8 items.
Open. Unpublished guide.
Minnesota Historical Society, Archives and Manuscripts.
Letters in which Carpenter (ca. 1845-?), a housewife on a farm in Faribault County, MN, describes to relatives life in southern Minnesota, in particular settlers from Ohio, land values, schools, prices received from the sale of produce, food, weather, and family news.

8,980. Case, George E., and Family
Papers. 1902-27. 1 box.
Open. Unpublished guide.
Minnesota Historical Society, Archives and Manuscripts.
Papers of Case, his wife Kate Hunt Case (1849-1927), and their daughters Maude (Case) [Mrs. Frank Maloy] Anderson (1871-?) and Mabel Almeria Case (1877-1933) include letters Maude Anderson wrote to her family while on a trip to Alaska in 1903; diaries in which Mabel Case describes her daily activities and social life for the period 1902-08 as a teacher in rural Minnesota, her nursing studies at St. Luke's Hospital in New York City, and her travels in Europe; a biographical sketch of Mabel Case by her sister Maude Anderson, and clippings on the death of Kate Case.

8,981. Case, John Higley
Papers. 1854-1926. 2 boxes and 1 vol.
Open. Unpublished guide.
Minnesota Historical Society, Archives and Manuscripts.
Includes a notebook kept by Jannette Case, a music and elocution teacher, containing students' names, lessons given, and prices charged; wedding invitations, Victorian valentines, calling cards, school programs, and other mementos of social life in Hastings, MN, during the last quarter of the 19th century; and articles collected by John Case about pioneers in and around Hastings, MN, including the John Brown, Henry Belland, Eli Pettijohn, Faribault, and Countryman families.

8,982. Cathcart, Alexander Henry, and Family
Papers. 1850-1921. 1.25 ft.
Open. Unpublished guide.
Minnesota Historical Society, Archives and Manuscripts.
Cathcart (1820-99) and his wife Rebecca Lowry (Marshall) Cathcart (1830-1925) were settlers in Minnesota Territory and operators of a dry goods store in St. Paul. Correspondence between the Cathcarts while he was in the East buying goods for the store; reminiscences by Rebecca Cathcart, which were published in 1915 in *Minnesota Historical Society Collections,* concerning the Marshall family's migration in 1849 to St. Paul and schools, churches, social life, St. Paul families, and political leaders; an invitation to funeral services in 1850 for Alexander Cathcart's mother Catherine Cathcart; and clippings.

8,983. Central Community House, Inc.
Records. 1938-65. 2 folders.
Open. Unpublished guide.
Minnesota Historical Society, Archives and Manuscripts.
Bylaws, minutes, and correspondence of this Jewish community center in St. Paul, which was organized in 1921. Contains information on meetings of the board of trustees and directors, fund raising, use of the House's facilities by community members, administration of the program, and disposition of the organization's funds upon its dissolution in 1965. Among the women prominent in the work of the House were Lillian Davidson [Mrs. Joseph] Paper, Faye Biederman, and Mrs. Jerome Baer.

8,984. Central Labor Union of Minneapolis and Hennepin County
Records. 1912-62. 61 boxes.
Access restricted. Unpublished guide.
Minnesota Historical Society, Archives and Manuscripts.
Records of the Minneapolis Trades and Labor Assembly, which existed from 1903 to 1925, and of the Central Labor Union, which was founded in 1925. Both groups were affiliates of the American Federation of Labor and were comprised of delegates from local AFL unions. Constitutions; bylaws; minutes; resolutions; correspondence; reports; speeches; news releases; newsletters; copies of city, state, and national legislation; campaign literature; sample ballots; pamphlets; and clippings of the glove workers, city and county employees, dental technicians, garment workers, hosiery workers, hotel and restaurant employees, office workers, retail clerks, sales clerks, telephone workers, and other unions. Also includes records of the Citizens Committee on Displaced Persons, the Minneapolis Citizen's Committee on Public Education, the Crusade for Children, the labor coordinating committee of the Minneapolis Defense Council, the LWV, the Minneapolis Labor School, the Minnesota Fair Employment Practice Commission, and the War Manpower Commission. Correspondence and other papers relate to the Central Labor Union's endorsement of Marcella Killen for the position of assistant secretary of labor. Also includes a letter and copies of records from Butforth Place, Inc., which served as a guidance center for women problem drinkers.

8,985. Central Woman's Christian Temperance Union
Records. 1906-17. 1 box.
Open. Unpublished guide.
Minnesota Historical Society, Archives and Manuscripts.
Annual reports, minutes, and other records of the WCTU.

8,986. Chambers, Alexander, and Family
Papers. 1830-1958. 2 boxes and 9 oversize items.
Open. Unpublished guide.
Minnesota Historical Society, Archives and Manuscripts.
Correspondence of Fanny Winslow Chambers and members of her family, especially Agnes Chambers Searle (ca. 1825-?) and Sarah Chambers (1801-?); correspondence of Celestia (Johnson) Sawyer (ca. 1844-?) in Owatonna, MN, with her sister Agnes (Johnson) Hansel (ca. 1841-?) and their brother Richard Z. Johnson in Boise, ID; a letter mentioning the marriage of Lucy Johnson (ca. 1850-?) to Clarke Chambers in 1875; and correspondence between Sarah Chambers and her family. Also includes the 1865 marriage license of Agnes Hansel, a report card issued by the Cleveland Female Seminary in 1859 to Celestia Johnson, and blank declaration forms for pensions of widows and children.

8,987. Chaney, Josiah B.
Papers. 1792-1916. 10 boxes and 1 vol.
Open. Unpublished guide.
Minnesota Historical Society, Archives and Manuscripts.
Letter book of Chaney (?-1908) containing letters

he wrote to his wife Melissa Chaney during the Peninsula Campaign of the Civil War; the letters contain advice on child rearing and discussion of the living conditions and diet of soldiers, other Minnesotans in the War, and life in a military hospital in Washington, DC. Also contains a letter book of Josiah Chaney's mother Abigail [Mrs. John] Chaney of Wilton, ME, with letters from her children, grandchildren, and friends; a 1909 diary in which Josiah Chaney's daughter Delia E. Chaney describes social life in St. Paul, monthly expenditures, activities of the Women's Alliance of the Unity Church in St. Paul, and the Liberal Union of Minnesota Women; and a diary kept by Frances Evelyn [Mrs. George C.] Cahoon in 1888 concerning the birth of her daughter in Carthage in Dakota Territory, the child's development, the death of Cahoon's husband, her journey back east with her baby, and the baby's first birthday.

8,988. Chapin, George A., and Family
Papers. 1847-1900. 2 boxes.
Open. Unpublished guide.
Minnesota Historical Society, Archives and Manuscripts.
Accounts of personal and household expenses kept by Chapin's wife Sarah Davis Chapin (ca. 1825-?) and records of a private school conducted in the Chapins' St. Paul home by their daughters Blanche I. Chapin (ca. 1865-?) and Sarah D. Chapin (1847-1947). The school records were kept by Blanche Chapin and her brother Walter Leeds Chapin (1863-1947), a teacher, lawyer, and St. Paul assistant city attorney.

8,989. Chatfield, Andrew Gould, and Family
Papers. 1831-1942. 2 boxes.
Open. Unpublished guide.
Minnesota Historical Society, Archives and Manuscripts.
Chatfield (1810-75), a lawyer, was born in New York and in 1836 married Eunice Beeman, also a New York native. They moved to Kenosha, WI, in 1849. He was appointed associate justice of the Supreme Court of Minnesota Territory in 1853 and justice of the 8th Judicial District in 1871. Correspondence of Andrew Chatfield with his wife; with his cousin Harriet R. Jackson of New Milford, CT, and New Canaan, CT, concerning her future and ambitions, family news, and social life; and with his brother Levi B. Chatfield relating to politics, childbirth and child rearing, wives' work, and social life. Also includes correspondence of Eunice Chatfield with her husband, with her sister Amanda Beeman concerning health and family news, from friends in Addison, NY, concerning her moving and leaving behind friends, and from her nieces relating to her work running a boardinghouse. An 1897 obituary of Mrs. John Wellendorf is also included.

8,990. Cheney, Mary Moulton, and Family
Papers. 1841-1929. 3 boxes and 7 items.
Open. Unpublished guide.
Minnesota Historical Society, Archives and Manuscripts.
Cheney (1871-1957), an artist, taught at the Minneapolis Institute of Arts from 1892 to 1927. Correspondence between Cheney and various artists and educators concerning teaching and her business in art design; personal and commercial monograms, bookplates, and greeting cards she designed; and clippings about Cheney and other local artists.

8,991. Chesley, Albert Justus
Papers. 1900-49. 1.25 ft.
Open. Unpublished guide.
Minnesota Historical Society, Archives and Manuscripts.
Chesley (1877-1955), a physician, was an official of the Minnesota department of health; he also was instrumental in helping to develop public health medicine in Minnesota. His wife was Placida (Gardner) Chesley, a physician and American National Red Cross associate during and after WWI. Correspondence between the Chesleys before their marriage; letters from members of the Gardner family; memoranda; annual reports for 1921 and 1922 of the Minneapolis LWV efficiency in government committee; treasurer's reports and records of contributions that Albert Chesley kept from 1922 to 1924 as treasurer of the Providence Foundation for Training of Normal School Teachers in Warsaw, Poland, which was a home for girls in teacher training; and clippings.

8,992. Chester-Kent, Inc.
Records. 1905-59. 12 boxes.
Open. Unpublished guide.
Minnesota Historical Society, Archives and Manuscripts.
This drug company in St. Paul manufactured and sold a laxative called Adlerika as well as liver pills and vitamin tonic. Correspondence and testimonials by Adlerika users, including many women. The testimonials consist of questionnaires concerning the effectiveness of the medicine and the general physical condition of the user before and after use; blank questionnaires were included with each package of medicine, filled out by the user, and mailed back to the company.

8,993. Child Labor Committee, Minnesota
Records. 1908-23. 1 box.
Open. Unpublished guide.
Minnesota Historical Society, Archives and Manuscripts.
Records of the Committee, which was founded in 1908 with financial support from the Minneapolis Woman's Club, include the constitution, minutes of meetings, financial reports, a membership list, and reports on labor conditions and labor legislation. The Committee sought regulations to protect working children and the enforcement of laws regarding child labor.

8,994. Christensen, Otto Augustus, and Family
Papers. 1854-1964. 3 boxes.
Open. Unpublished guide.
Minnesota Historical Society, Archives and Manuscripts.
The Christensens were Norwegian-Americans who lived on a farm in the Red River Valley in Clay County, MN. Letters to Otto Christensen (1851-1918), many of them in Norwegian, from his sister Matilda (Christensen) Bergland, Julia E. Persons, Fannie E. Metcalf, his mother Catherine Christensen Pease, and others; letters to Oscar A. Christensen, who was active in the Farmers Union, Cooperative Union Activities groups, and the Farmers Holiday Movement, and to his wife from their daughter Ethel Christensen, while she was attending the Sauk Centre School for Girls in 1933 and 1934; a manuscript by Oscar Christensen based on letters, diaries, and his own experiences of farm life in Norwegian communities in the Red River Valley and of work with farm organizations of the 1930s and 1940s; and a translation by Oscar Christensen of stories by Kristopher Janson about life in Norwegian settlements in the US.

8,995. Christie, James C., and Family
Papers. 1835-1949. 16 ft.
Open. Unpublished guide.
Minnesota Historical Society, Archives and Manuscripts.
Christie's daughter Sarah Jane (Christie) Stevens (1844-1919) was a teacher at Carleton College in Northfield, MN, from 1873 to 1875 and at Wheaton College in Wheaton, IL, from 1875 to 1877, and superintendent of public schools in Blue Earth County, MN, in 1890; she also was active in the suffrage and temperance movements. Includes correspondence of Sarah Stevens with her father, Eva (McDonald) Valesh, Mary Ghostley, and her four brothers William, Thomas, Alexander, and David Christie. Sarah Stevens had some medical knowledge and often prescribed remedies for neighbors.

8,996. Christie, Thomas, and Christie, Carmelite Brewer, and Family
Papers. 1843-1962. 16 ft.
Open. Unpublished guide.
Minnesota Historical Society, Archives and Manuscripts.
Thomas Christie and Carmelite Christie (1852-1931) were missionaries in Turkey from 1877 to 1920, where they became associated with St. Paul's Institute in Tarsus. Mary Christie Rogers Nute (1881-1975) worked in Turkey until 1959. Correspondence, diaries, oral history tapes, and photos of family members, including Carmelite Christie, Mary Nute, Jean Christie Lien (1891-), Anna Christie (1876-1910), and Agnes Christie (1887-1920). The papers concern missionary life, education, the children's feelings about being sent to school in America, Armenian massacres in Tarsus, travel, the YMCA, and gynecological problems of the Christie daughters. Includes detailed diaries Carmelite Christie kept during WWI when she was the only American in Tarsus.

8,997. Church of St. John's on the Hill
Records. 1884-1976. 1 microfilm reel.
Open. Unpublished guide.
Minnesota Historical Society, Archives and Manuscripts.
Treasurer's dues book, 1941-50; financial record book, 1940-50; and secretary's book, 1945-59, of the St. Agnes Guild of this Episcopal church in Lake Benton, Lincoln County, MN.

8,998. Church of the Messiah
Records. 1890-1909. 1 box.
Open. Unpublished guide.
Minnesota Historical Society, Archives and Manuscripts.
Reports of women's groups and other groups of this Protestant Episcopal church in St. Paul.

8,999. Citizens' Service Corps
Records. 1943-44. 1 box.
Open. Unpublished guide.
Minnesota Historical Society, Archives and Manuscripts.
The Corps was an organization of citizens whose purpose was to mobilize the populace for the transition to war. Organizational records include field reports, names of committee chairmen and field representatives, and lists of committees, among them those on child care, education, health, physical fitness, victory aides, victory gardens, and war bonds. The committee chairmen were almost always women.

9,000. Clapp, George Christopher, and Family
Papers. 1858-1968. 1 box.
Open. Unpublished guide.
Minnesota Historical Society, Archives and Manuscripts.
Clapp (1823-91) and his family moved from Massachusetts and settled in territorial Minnesota. Papers of Clapp's wife Mariette Warner Clapp (1824-1903) include letters to her son George Frederic Clapp (1867-1955) in Wisconsin; reminiscences of her early days, which she wrote for the first annual meeting of the Old Settlers Association in Kasota, MN; an account of her pioneer experiences, which was published in the *Mankato Daily Review* in 1897; and clippings from the *St. Peter Tribune* of her reminiscences of early days in Minnesota. Also includes a letter by Ella and Isabelle Clapp in Minnesota to their cousin Mary, letters to family members in Wisconsin and South Dakota from Florence Julia Tilton [Mrs. Harrie Winter] Clapp (1858-1946), papers establishing a claim to a Civil War pension for George and Mariette Clapp, and a biographical sketch of Harrie Winter Clapp (1858-1949) by his granddaughter Julia Anne Peake.

9,001. Clapp, Moses E.
Papers. 1873-1929. 1 microfilm reel.
Open. Unpublished guide.
Minnesota Historical Society, Archives and Manuscripts.
Clapp (1851-1929), who was married to Hattie Allen Clapp (1850-1924), was a US senator from Minnesota from 1901 to 1917 and a leader in the Progressive party. Letters that Moses Clapp wrote from Caracas, Venezuela, in 1895 to his daughter Katherina Clapp (ca. 1880-1903) describing the country, people, food, and customs; letters to Clapp that Jeannette Rankin, US congresswoman from Montana, wrote in 1917 thanking him for his support during her political campaign; and letters from Sarah M. Algeo, general chairman of the Woman Suffrage party of Providence, RI, who wrote in 1914 thanking him for his help. Also includes speeches by Moses Clapp about "women making laws"; programs and clippings relating to his support of woman suffrage; clippings concerning deaths, weddings, and the background of the Clapp family; and clippings on progressive political issues from *The Woman's National Weekly,* which was published in 1913 by The Woman's National Publishing Company in St. Louis.

9,002. Clarence Walworth Alvord Memorial Commission
Records. 1913-50. 3 boxes.
Open. Unpublished guide.
Minnesota Historical Society, Archives and Manuscripts.
The Commission, which was founded in memory of Alvord by the Mississippi Valley Historical Association to publish volumes of documents, existed from 1928 to 1955. Correspondence relating to the work of the Commission, including fund raising, appointment of members, securing manuscripts for publication, and marketing of *Documents Relating to Northwest Missions* by Grace Lee Nute, third and final chairman of the Commission, and *Military Life in Dakota* by Lucile Marie Kane.

9,003. Clark, Charles Asa, and Family
Papers. 1887-1966. 3 boxes and 2 oversize items.
Open. Unpublished guide.
Minnesota Historical Society, Archives and Manuscripts.
Correspondence between Cleora Clark Wheeler (ca. 1883-), a designer, and her cousin Pearl Clark (1872-1963) concerning the estate of Wheeler's uncle; letters to Wheeler from another cousin's husband Millard F. Harmon, who describes his service in the Pacific theater during WWII; letters by Pearl Clark describing her work as an army nurse in the Philippine Islands from 1903 to 1933; Clark's diary for the years 1903 to 1960; a biographical sketch of Clark by Wheeler; and an essay by Wheeler on the early history of the Philippine Islands.

9,004. Clark, Charles Henry, and Family
Papers. 1807-1964. 3 boxes.
Open. Unpublished guide.
Minnesota Historical Society, Archives and Manuscripts.
Letters to Clark from his sisters Mary, Grace, Anna, Carrie, and Eliza Clark describing dances, weddings, theatricals, lectures, sports, and other aspects of social and family life in Boston during the 1850s and 1860s; business letters of Eliza (Clark) Darrah (1829-?) and of Martha Cowper Pierce Clark (1837-?); letters that H. P. [Mrs. Samuel B.] Pierce wrote to her children and others about family and social life; a letter and brochure of Marion Craig Wentworth; an autograph album kept by Mary E. Beecher; and clippings about opera singer Louise Dilworth (Beatty) Homer. Papers of Mary Barnard Clark (1871-1963), who later married a Mr. Putnam, include correspondence and photos detailing her life as a student at Smith College in 1893, diaries of her travels in Europe in 1896-97 and 1937-38 and meeting Louise Homer on a European trip in 1899; Clark's diary of a Caribbean cruise in 1939; and her writing about her experiences housekeeping in England.

9,005. Clark, L. S., and Family
Papers. 1888-1924. 4 in.
Open. Unpublished guide.
Minnesota Historical Society, Archives and Manuscripts.
Mary Montressor Sears (ca. 1868-?), a student in Caton, CT, and Ithaca, NY, later taught school in Wisconsin before she became a housewife in Minnesota. Her notebooks from 1888 and 1890 contain class notes, poems, parlor games, jokes, riddles, and information on celebrities. Also includes an invitation to the wedding of Sears and David Francis Clark in 1897, their 35th anniversary book, and a pamphlet of quotations collected by members of the Congregational Church of Christ in Ladysmith, WI.

9,006. Clarke, Ethan Case, and Family
Papers. 1856-1903. 1 box.
Open. Unpublished guide.
Minnesota Historical Society, Archives and Manuscripts.
Correspondence of Clarke's wife Elizabeth Mickel Clarke (1826-?) includes letters from women friends in Superior, WI, discussing family and community news, social life, and their health and letters from Irwin W. Gates and George B. Hudnall about land she inherited after her husband's death in 1889, taxes and ownership of land in Minnesota and Wisconsin, and news from Duluth, MN, and Superior. Also includes tax receipts, a list of properties owned by Elizabeth Clarke in and near Superior in 1894, deeds, agreements, and other legal papers.

9,007. Club Montparnasse
Records. 1930-50. 1 vol.
Open. Unpublished guide.
Minnesota Historical Society, Archives and Manuscripts.
Records of this St. Paul club, which was organized in 1930 to "stimulate creative effort and offer opportunities for the recognition of talent in art, music, literature, the drama, and the dance," include a history of the Club by Marie T. Magee and a scrapbook of clippings pertaining to Club activities.

9,008. Cockburn, John Cassilis
Papers. 1875-1905. 1 box.
Open. Unpublished guide.
Minnesota Historical Society, Archives and Manuscripts.
Cockburn (1842-1911), a physician, served as Minneapolis city physician and health commissioner from 1882 to 1889; he also was a professor of physiology at Hamline University in St. Paul. Daybook and ledger giving patient's name, reason for visit, and price charged; physician's death records, which provide the date of death, name of deceased, age, occupation, nativity, place and cause of death, duration of disease, sex, color, marital status, names and birthplaces of parents, and physician's signature; and physician's birth records, listing name of child, sex, color, date and place of birth, full name of mother, mother's residence, full name of father, father's occupation, and nativity of parents.

9,009. Colby, Pauline
Papers. 1931. 1 vol.
Open. No guide.
Minnesota Historical Society, Archives and Manuscripts.
Account by Colby (1853-1944) of her experiences as a missionary at White Earth Indian Reservation and Leech Lake Indian Reservation in Minnesota. Also includes three letters concerning Colby and her lace making and a biographical sketch of Colby by Francis L. Palmer.

9,010. Columbian Club
Records. 1912-26. 2 vols.
Open. Unpublished guide.
Minnesota Historical Society, Archives and Manuscripts.
Constitution, bylaws, and lists of members of this women's study club, which was founded in 1891 in Minneapolis.

9,011. Communications Workers of America
Records. 1938-74. 8.25 ft.
Partially restricted. No guide.
Minnesota Historical Society, Archives and Manuscripts.
Records of this labor union, which was formed in 1947, include executive board minutes, 1950-69; memos of Joseph A. Beirne, president; proceedings and reports of CWA conventions; executive board reports; grievance case files and reports; arbitrations; agreements with Northwestern Bell Telephone Co.; a newsletter; a history; and a book on automation. Also includes records of Local 7220 of Crookston, MN, and of predecessors of Local 7200 of Minneapolis, including the Northwestern Union of Telephone Workers.

9,012. Congregational Conference of Minnesota, Minneapolis
Records. 1856-1954. 11 boxes, 1 vol., and 1 oversize item.
Open. Unpublished guide.
Minnesota Historical Society, Archives and Manuscripts.
Minutes of the Widows and Orphans Aid Society, 1885-1921; minutes for 1895 to 1913, a scrapbook of clippings, and other records of the Minnesota Woman's Home Missionary Union; and articles of incorporation and minutes of the Minnesota Congregational Woman's Missionary Society.

9,013. Consolidated Biographies File
Collection. Nd. 5.5 boxes.
Open. Unpublished guide.
Minnesota Historical Society, Archives and Manuscripts.
Includes about 40 biographical or autobiographical sketches of primarily 19th-and early 20th-century women, among them early settlers, immigrants, missionaries, teachers, suffragists, and wives of fur traders.

9,014. Cook, Edith Clemons, and Family
Papers. Ca. 1840s-1960s. 1 bacase.
Open. No guide.
Minnesota Historical Society, Archives and Manuscripts.
Diaries, family photos, portraits, clippings, Bibles, and other papers of the family of [Mrs.] Cook, who lived in Cloquet, MN.

9,015. Coolidge, Mrs. Marshall H.
Papers. 1898-1932. 8 vols.
Open. Unpublished guide.
Minnesota Historical Society, Archives and Manuscripts.
Coolidge, a state regent of the DAR and a campaign worker for the Republican party in 1920, was involved in the child welfare movement in Minneapolis. Scrapbooks of correspondence, photos, invitations, and clippings pertain to activities of Coolidge and her family.

9,016. Corbett, Harriet B.
Papers. 1853-75. 175 items.
Open. Unpublished guide.
Minnesota Historical Society, Archives and Manuscripts.
Receipts, policies, deeds, and other legal papers of Harriet B. Corbett [Mrs. Eben L.] Adams, a housewife in early St. Paul.

9,017. Cornwell, Irene
Papers. Ca. 1912-20. 0.25 ft.
Open. No guide.
Minnesota Historical Society, Archives and Manuscripts.
Papers of Cornwell, a French teacher, concern her admission to and attendance at school in Paris, her work as a teacher in France, her applications and arrangements for teaching positions in the US, and her work in France after WWI helping to establish a children's day school. Many of the papers were written in French.

9,018. Cory and Forbes
Papers. 1849-1941. 3.5 boxes, 1 bacase, and 127 oversize items.
Open. Unpublished guide.
Minnesota Historical Society, Archives and Manuscripts.
Correspondence between sisters Amanda (Cory) [Mrs. William H.] Forbes, Phoebe Frances Cory, Nancy (Cory) [Mrs. Louis] Blum, and Julia (Cory) [Mrs. Alexis] Bailly, three of whom lived in St. Paul and the fourth in New York state. Also includes an account book for 1857 of the Forbes family, receipts for purchases made by Amanda Forbes, Victorian calling cards, and social and wedding invitations.

9,019. Cotton, Helen
Papers. 1870-73. 1 vol.
Open. No guide.
Minnesota Historical Society, Archives and Manuscripts.
Diary of Cotton records social life, presumably in a suburb of Philadelphia, and contains personal accounts.

9,020. Countryman, Gratia Alta
Papers. 1871-1953. 6 boxes.
Open. Unpublished guide.
Minnesota Historical Society, Archives and Manuscripts.
Born in Hastings, MN, Countryman (1866-1953) graduated from the University of Minnesota in 1889 and then worked as head librarian at the Minneapolis Public Library from 1903 to 1936. She was active in many civic and social organizations and served as president of the American Library Association in 1932. Her personal and professional correspondence includes letters from University friends and professors, letters relating to the ALA, congratulatory letters she received at various points in her career, and letters she wrote to her family while she was in Europe in 1926 and 1935. Also includes her diaries kept periodically from 1896 to 1947, a calendar containing verses she wrote, a poetry book by Emma Belle Yourdan, a certificate, a scrapbook containing poetry by members of the Minneapolis Public Library poetry class, programs, clippings, and speeches and articles by Countryman on such topics as suffrage, schools and libraries, world peace, and adult education. Correspondence between her parents Levi Newton Countryman and Alta Chamberlain Countryman is also included.

9,021. Countryman, Gratia Alta, and Family
Papers. 1861-1939. 11 items.
Open. Unpublished guide.
Minnesota Historical Society, Archives and Manuscripts.
Diplomas of Countryman (1866-1953), who was director of the Minneapolis Public Library from the 1900s to the 1930s, and papers relating to her appointments to the State Public Library Commission in 1899, 1907, and 1913 and to the Advisory Committee on Women's Participation in the New York World's Fair in 1939. Gratia Countryman was the daughter of Levi Newton Countryman (1832-1924).

9,022. Cox, Sister Ignatius Loyola
Papers. 1894-1915. 24 items.
Access restricted. Unpublished guide.
Minnesota Historical Society, Archives and Manuscripts.
Correspondence of Sister Ignatius, a member of the Sisters of St. Joseph of Carondolet, while she was at St. Joseph's Convent in Stillwater, MN, and at St. Joseph's Academy in St. Paul, from 1894 to 1895. Letters relate to activities of other sisters of the order, the establishment of mission schools in St. Paul and Long Prairie, MN, by sisters who came to the area in 1851, building the cathedral in St. Paul, and the deaths of sisters in the order.

9,023. Craig, Austin, and Family
Papers. 1733-1956. 14 boxes.
Open. Unpublished guide.
Minnesota Historical Society, Archives and Manuscripts.
Craig (1824-81) was a teacher, minister, and president of Antioch College from 1862 to 1868. He was married to Mary Adelaide (Churchill) Craig (1828-79). Correspondence between Austin and Mary Craig, between the Craig and Churchill families, and of Josephine Craig; diaries of Austin and Mary Craig for 1865 to 1868; manuscript of a book by Josephine Craig; a genealogical notebook of Josephine Craig; a circular concerning the fall term at Miss Churchill's School at Richfield Springs, NY, and reminiscences about Clara Barton by an unidentified woman who attended school with her at Clinton Liberal Institute in Fort Plain, NY. Papers of Eunice Malvina Churchill, who operated a school for young ladies, include correspondence, diaries for 1885 to 1887 and 1903, and other material pertaining to her relationship with her sister's orphaned children, teaching, attending religious and temperance conferences, life in Richfield, NY, and the disposition of her property. Correspondence, articles, a personal property inventory, and other papers of Adelaide Craig Snyder (1870-1967) relate to her association with the Clinton Liberal Institute and Starkey College in Eddytown, NY; her marriage to Harry Snyder; their move to Minnesota from Ithaca, NY; and assistance she gave in preparing a book on Austin Craig. Also includes letters by Lucretia Mott and Charlotte (Garrigue) [Mrs. Thomas] Masaryk.

9,024. Crosby, Francis Marion, and Family
Papers. 1851-1953. 3 boxes and 4 items.
Open. Unpublished guide.
Minnesota Historical Society, Archives and Manuscripts.
Diary kept by Crosby's wife Helen Sophia Bates Crosby (?-1909) from 1905 to 1908 concerning family and social activities, correspondence and clippings on her death, correspondence and clippings about the marriage of Helen B. Crosby to a Mr. Prescott in 1896, correspondence of Marion Emma Crosby regarding the management and distribution of the property of her father Francis Crosby, an 1891 commencement program from Hastings High School listing her as a graduate, and a letter from educator Maria Louise Sanford to a Mrs. Hall concerning the lack of a major book on Venice.

9,025. Crosby, George
Papers. 1866-1930. 2 boxes.
Open. No guide.
Minnesota Historical Society, Archives and Manuscripts.
Correspondence and mementos of Crosby, who lived in Hudson, WI, including letters from his cousin Sarah Adella Crosby, Nellie P. Crosby, and Florence Crosby in Missouri concerning family news, school and farm work, and social life; from his sister Alice Crosby in Seattle and St. Paul; from his nieces Laura Palmer of Amery, WI, and Lillian Crosby of River Falls, WI; from Mamie Reynolds and her mother [Mrs.] Sarah B. Reynolds concerning St. Paul, social news, health, and Mrs. Reynolds's nursing work; and from Katie Carlin, Rose Anna Bretag, Betsy Graham, and Annie Kolstad.

9,026. Cross, William, and Family
Papers. 1876-1935. 2 boxes.
Open. Unpublished guide.
Minnesota Historical Society, Archives and Manuscripts.
Includes diaries of Ada Cross (ca. 1858-?), a housekeeper on a farm in Martin County, MN, with brief notes on daily and social activities.

9,027. Current Events Club
Records. 1899-1932. 25 items.
Open. Unpublished guide.
Minnesota Historical Society, Archives and Manuscripts.
Correspondence, programs, and clippings of this Crookston, MN, club, including correspondence of [Mrs.] Edith Webb Watts, who with [Mrs.] Clara Bircher Nebelung wrote a history of the Club.

9,028. Curtis, Mary A.
Papers. 1856-1901. 1 ft.
Open. No guide.
Minnesota Historical Society, Archives and Manuscripts.
Correspondence and financial papers of [Mrs. Gold Tompkins] Curtis date primarily from the 1890s and include letters from her son Gold Curtis, a Montana banker; her daughter Jenny, who married Henry M. Cannon; other relatives; friends; and bankers in New York and Stillwater, MN.

9,029. Daughters of the American Revolution of Minnesota
Records. 1928. 1 box.
Open. Unpublished guide.
Minnesota Historical Society, Archives and Manuscripts.
Two volumes compiled by Mrs. Henry B. Tillotson include histories of each DAR chapter in Minnesota by chapter historians and a history of geographic names of Minnesota counties, which mentions the location of DAR chapters.

9,030. Daughters of the American Revolution of Minnesota, Minneapolis
Records. 1939-41. 13 items.
Open. Unpublished guide.
Minnesota Historical Society, Archives and Manuscripts.
Records of the Minneapolis chapter include a religious survey of members, regent's reports, a report of the 1940 continental congress of the DAR, and newsletters.

9,031. Daughters of the American Revolution of Minnesota, St. Paul Chapter
Records. 1891-1959. 5 boxes, 3 bacases, and 3 oversize items.
Open. Unpublished guide.
Minnesota Historical Society, Archives and Manuscripts.
Records of the St. Paul chapter include bylaws, annual reports, minutes, a charter, treasurer's records, a secretary's record, a roll book, lineage books, directories, yearbooks, membership lists, scrapbooks, and a history with biographical sketches of regents.

9,032. Daughters of the American Revolution, Sibley House Association of Minnesota
Records. 1891-1953. 33 items.
Open. Unpublished guide.
Minnesota Historical Society, Archives and Manuscripts.
Sibley House was the home of Henry H. Sibley, first governor of the state of Minnesota. Articles of incorporation and a certificate of incorporation of the Sibley House Association, correspondence with naval officials on the disposition of relics of the battleship *Maine*, an annual report of the chairman of the house and grounds committee, a

report of a committee chaired by [Mrs.] Harriet Myrick Evans to study the teaching of Minnesota history, a history of the Sibley House by [Mrs.] Winifred Murray Deming Milne, and articles on Native American customs.

9,033. Davidson, William Fuson, and Family
Papers. 1817-1919. 134 ft.
Open. Unpublished guide.
Minnesota Historical Society, Archives and Manuscripts.
Correspondence concerning legal difficulties from 1888 to 1890 with Lotta Crabtree and a 1911 lawsuit; journals for 1892 to 1899, cashbooks, and rental records of Sarah Matilda (Davidson) [Mrs. W. P.] Davidson (1874-1945); journals for 1890 to 1897, ledgers, cashbooks, and rental records of Sarah Anne (Johnston) [Mrs. William F.] Davidson; and rental records for 1898 to 1908 of [Mrs.] Julia B. Davidson.

9,034. Day, Emma Rebecca (Hunt)
Papers. 1865-1938. 14 items.
Open. No guide.
Minnesota Historical Society, Archives and Manuscripts.
Letters to Emma Rebecca Hunt Ewing, a housewife and teacher, from her first husband John T. Ewing, who was at the gold mines of Montana; from Emma Ewing in 1869 to James Collins Day (1822-1911) concerning the possibility of their getting married; and to Emma Ewing Day from her husband James Day, who was a storekeeper at La Crescent, MN, and a legislator. Also includes reminiscences by Ann Day Lloyd, daughter of Emma and J. C. Lloyd, about labor troubles in La Crescent between Polish railroad workers and Emma and James Day.

9,035. Day, Frank Arah
Papers. 1889-1928. 5 boxes.
Open. Unpublished guide.
Minnesota Historical Society, Archives and Manuscripts.
Day (1855-1928), a newspaperman in Minnesota and Montana, served as a state legislator, lieutenant governor of Minnesota from 1895 to 1897, and secretary to Minnesota governor John A. Johnson from 1905 to 1909. Correspondence relates primarily to prohibition, woman suffrage, and Woodrow Wilson's preparedness policies. Day was a prohibitionist and supporter of woman suffrage.

9,036. Dean, William Blake, and Family
Papers. 1806-1937. 1 box.
Open. Unpublished guide.
Minnesota Historical Society, Archives and Manuscripts.
Papers of Dean contain correspondence of his father-in-law and business partner John Nichols (1812-73) with his wife Caroline (Meeker) Nichols (1813-45) of Hillsboro, MD, while he was serving in the Maryland legislature and she was living with her parents in Newark, NJ. These letters concern the births of their children; illnesses, deaths, and marriages of family and friends; social events in Annapolis, MD, during the legislative session; camp meetings; revivals; and farm harvests. Also includes letters of Caroline Nichols to her parents Obadiah Meeker (1782-1855) and Jerusha Cook Harrison Meeker (1784-1871) and letters by Jane Blair Miller Kurtz, who was preparing a family genealogy.

9,037. Dean, William Blake, and Family
Papers. 1851-1929. 2 boxes, 1 vol., and 4 oversize items.
Open. Unpublished guide.
Minnesota Historical Society, Archives and Manuscripts.
Includes papers of William Blake Dean's daughter-in-law Laura (Winter) [Mrs. William John] Dean (1870-1968), with correspondence, minutes, committee lists, a membership and subscriber list, and clippings she gathered while she was chairman of the St. Paul chapter and member of the national executive board of the Fatherless Children of France; letters by Laura Dean and her husband from France in 1919; their wedding announcement from 1894; invoices for purchases of household goods; and clippings on the Deans' marriage, marriages of their daughters, and the centennial celebration of the Sarah Porter School. Laura Dean's correspondents include Elise Jusserand, wife of the French ambassador to the US in 1918; Laura Allen, a Red Cross worker in Switzerland during WWI; and Jeanne Seligmann-Lui, secretary of the Fraternité Franco-Américaine. Also includes a treasurer's book of the St. Paul auxiliary of the American McAll Association, which Helen Dean kept from 1903 to 1919.

9,038. Delta Kappa Gamma Society
Records. 1941-68. 1 box.
Open. Unpublished guide.
Minnesota Historical Society, Archives and Manuscripts.
Consists of typescript biographical sketches of 52 women who were pioneer teachers in Minnesota compiled by members of the Society and a pamphlet containing abridged biographies of 18 teachers. Among the women represented are Harriet Bishop, Edith Graham Mayo, Sister Antonia McHugh, Mary Nolan, Hedi Oplesch, Mary (Longley) Riggs, Maria Sanford, and Stella Louise Wood.

9,039. Democratic-Farmer-Labor State Central Committee
Records. 1947-76. Ca. 244 ft.
Access restricted. No guide.
Minnesota Historical Society, Archives and Manuscripts.
Minutes; financial records; state chairperson, caucus, convention, campaign, and legislative files; clippings, and other records of the Committee. Also includes some files of the Young Democratic-Farmer-Labor party.

9,040. Democratic-Farmer-Labor State Central Committee
Records. 1944-54. 1 folder, 44 boxes, and 7 bacases.
Access restricted. Unpublished guide.
Minnesota Historical Society, Archives and Manuscripts.
Minutes, financial records, correspondence, reports, press releases, speeches, biographies, committee lists, campaign schedules, clippings, and other records of the Central Committee and of the Young Democratic-Farmer-Labor Clubs of Minnesota relate to political campaigns and appointments, special events, patronage, the relationship of right-and left-wing forces in the party, and party stands on local, state, and national issues. Includes correspondence for 1948 and 1949 of [Mrs.] Florence Frederickson, Eugenie Moore [Mrs. John P.] Anderson, and [Mrs.] Helga Nielson to Orville Freeman, then state chairman of the DFL party, and of Coya Gjesdal [Mrs. Andrew] Knutson, 9th district congresswoman from 1955 to 1958. Also includes material relating to a 1949 dinner for Eugenie Anderson on the occasion of her appointment as ambassador to Denmark and to a 1953 reception on her return from the post as well as biographies of DFL-endorsed candidates in 1950, among them Marcella Killen, who was running in the primary election for Congress from the 5th district; Mrs. A. J. McGuire, who was running for secretary of state; and Shirley Zaverl, who was running for state senator from the 30th district.

9,041. Densmore, Benjamin, and Family
Papers. 1797-1955. 6.5 boxes and 116 oversize items.
Open. Unpublished guide.
Minnesota Historical Society, Archives and Manuscripts.
Correspondence of Margaret Seaton (Hartshorn) Densmore (1776-1823), who lived on a farm in New York, and her daughter Ismena (Densmore) Bennett (1798-1887), who lived on farms in New York and Wisconsin Territory, with each other, Margaret Densmore's husband, and other family and friends; correspondence of Diana Densmore McVean (1808-56); letters from Anna McVean McLaren (1832-86) to her cousin Margaret Seaton Densmore Smith (1835-1919) about her life at Fort Snelling in Minneapolis as the wife of an army officer; correspondence of Elizabeth (Fowle) Densmore (1805-91), a housewife on farms in New York and Wisconsin, and her husband Orrin Densmore; correspondence of Susan (Fowle) Hanford (1802-72) and her husband Charles Hanford, who lived on a farm in New York; and correspondence between Martha Elizabeth Densmore (1838-1908), who later married a Mr. Hodgman, and her brothers concerning soldier and civilian life during the Civil War and visits to California. Also includes letters Betsy Ann Brockway wrote in 1839 complaining of the mistreatment of her brother, a slave, by James Fowle; graduation programs, report cards, and a teacher's certificate issued to Margaret Louise Densmore (1874-?); correspondence of Margaret Densmore Smith with her brother during the Civil War and with her son Gilman and a diary she kept from 1917 to 1919; and a confirmation certificate of Sarah Adelaide Densmore. Papers of musicologist Frances Theresa Densmore (1867-1957) include notes and portions of articles she wrote about Indian music, dances, and religion; a manuscript of "I Heard an Indian Drum"; essays; graduation programs; report cards; a citation awarded her by the Chippewa Indian Dancers of Odanah, WI; and a speech given in recognition of her work by US senator August H. Andresen.

9,042. Densmore, Frances Theresa
Papers. 1927-39. 1 box.
Open. Unpublished guide.
Minnesota Historical Society, Archives and Manuscripts.
Densmore (1867-1957) was born in Red Wing, MN, and studied music at the Oberlin Conservatory of Music from 1884 to 1886 and at Harvard University in 1889 and 1890. She began her study of American Indian music in 1893, working with the Bureau of Ethnology of the Smithsonian Institution to record the music of the US Indian nations. Manuscripts and radio addresses by Densmore concerning music, stories, industries, place names, and chiefs of the Dakota and Ojibwe Indians of Minnesota and a transcript of an interview with Good Star Woman, a Sioux, who gives an account of the uprising in Minnesota. Also includes transcripts of interviews with early settlers of Red Wing, including Pauline Colby, who describes her experiences as an Episcopal missionary to the Ojibwe at White Earth and Leech Lake reservations; Ellen Wilson [Mrs. A. F.] Andersen, who describes her family's immigration from Norway, their arrival in Minnesota in 1862, early Red Wing, and women's work during the 1870s; and Catherine [Mrs. George W.] Diepenbrock, a second-generation Belgian.

9,043. Dickson, Margarette Ball
Papers. 1900-63. 22.5 boxes.
Open. No guide.
Minnesota Historical Society, Archives and Manuscripts.
[Mrs.] Dickson (?-1963), a teacher of creative writing in Staples, MN, was president of the League of Minnesota Poets and editor of *County Bard*. Correspondence, poetry, scrapbooks, clippings, bulletins, and other papers, many of which relate to the composition of poetry in the US and in particular in Minnesota. Includes a story

from the Minneapolis *Star* about whether Dickson was named official state poet.

9,044. Dinner Gang
Records. 1893-1912. 1 vol.
Open. Unpublished guide.
Minnesota Historical Society, Archives and Manuscripts.
Records of this family dinner club in St. Paul, which was founded in 1878, include speeches, programs, place cards, and clippings relating to the annual Thanksgiving day meeting of the families of Henry A. Castle, Mark D. Flower, Henry G. Hicks, and Joseph J. McCardy.

9,045. Dodd, William B., and Family
Papers. 1854-63. 9 items.
Open. Unpublished guide.
Minnesota Historical Society, Archives and Manuscripts.
Dodd, the "first citizen" of St. Peter, MN, was second in command to Charles E. Flandrau during the Dakota War of 1862. Diary that his wife kept in 1862 and 1863 concerns the Dakota War, her husband's death in the War, his funeral, family affairs, visits to the St. Peter hospital, and early social life in St. Peter.

9,046. Dollenmayer, Albert, and Family
Papers. 1865-1938. 3 ft.
Open. Unpublished guide.
Minnesota Historical Society, Archives and Manuscripts.
Correspondence of Dollenmayer, a reporter for the Minneapolis *Tribune,* with his sister Emma (Dollenmayer) Taylor concerning family matters and her work as a teacher in Pennsylvania and as a bookkeeper in Minneapolis and San Francisco; with Katherine E. Miller, a reporter for the Minneapolis *Tribune,* concerning her writing; and with Eva (McDonald) Valesh, a political organizer for the Populist party in Minnesota, concerning politics, labor, and her work with the Farmer's Alliance. Also includes Dollenmayer's diary, a biographical sketch he wrote of Valesh, and clippings.

9,047. Dondore, Dorothy Anne
Papers. 1930-45. 1 box.
Open. Unpublished guide.
Minnesota Historical Society, Archives and Manuscripts.
Papers of Dondore (1894-1946), a professor of English at Elmira College in New York, include correspondence, an unpublished manuscript she wrote on literature pertaining to the Mormon exodus to Utah and the treatment of Plains Indians in American literature, a scrapbook of letters and clippings from her associates and students, data concerning her educational and scholarly background, and reprints of her articles.

9,048. Donnelly, Ignatius
Papers. 1856-1972. 53 ft. and 77 vols.
Open. Published guide.
Minnesota Historical Society, Archives and Manuscripts.
Donnelly (1831-1901), a newspaper editor and publisher, town site promoter, orator, and author, served as lieutenant governor of Minnesota from 1859 to 1863, as a congressman from 1863 to 1869, and as a state legislator. At various times a Democrat, a Republican, and a third party politician, he was a candidate for numerous political offices, including vice-president of the US in 1900. He was married first to Katharine "Kate" McCaffrey Donnelly (1833-94), a singer and grade school principal, and then to his secretary Marion O. Hanson Donnelly (1877-1964). Correspondence between Ignatius and Katharine Donnelly in Minnesota and their families and friends in Philadelphia; correspondence of Katharine Donnelly with Constance M. [Mrs. Henry] Pott, Philip Rohr, and Rose O'Brien; correspondence of Ignatius Donnelly with his mother Catharine Gavin [Mrs. Philip C.] Donnelly concerning his medical studies in Vienna and her correspondence with her lawyer discussing litigation following her husband's bankruptcy; diaries; financial records; household accounts; poems by Ignatius Donnelly's sister Eleanor Cecelia Donnelly (1838-1917) and a sketch of her career as a poet; a manuscript of Ignatius Donnelly's tribute to his wife Katharine Donnelly after her death; invitations and social cards; bound pamphlets; and clippings. Ignatius Donnelly's correspondents include his sisters, who tell of their experiences as Philadelphia schoolteachers; Harriet Kress [Mrs. W. J.] Arnold; Jane Grey (Cannon) Swisshelm; Antoinette V. Wakeman; Sarah Cahill Worthington; Mary Elizabeth Lease; Eva (McDonald) Valesh; Henrietta Vinton Davis; Mary B. [Mrs. William J.] Bryan; Rose Elizabeth Cleveland; and Emma Lazarus. Also includes financial reports, correspondence, programs, and other records of the Ignatius Donnelly Memorial Association, which worked to preserve the Donnelly house in Nininger, MN, to safeguard Donnelly's library and manuscripts, and to commemorate his career in various ways. Also available on microfilm. See Helen McCann White, comp., *Guide to a Microfilm Edition of the Ignatius Donnelly Papers* (St. Paul: Minnesota Historical Society, 1968).

9,049. Dougherty, John Alley
Papers. 1959-62. 1 box.
Open. Unpublished guide.
Minnesota Historical Society, Archives and Manuscripts.
Papers of the LeDuc family, territorial settlers in Hastings, MN, and of the Gardner family include a letter from Alice Sumner LeDuc (1868-1962) to Jean Brookins of the Historical Society; interviews by Dougherty with Edith Gardner, Katherine [Mrs. Augustine Vincent] Gardner (?-1966), Mabel Mary Gardner (1875-1967), and Alice LeDuc; and photos of the interior, floor plans, lists of furnishings and portraits, and sketches of the William G. LeDuc house in Hastings and the Gardner house in Minneapolis. Includes sketches by Alice LeDuc.

9,050. Dousman, Hercules Louis
Papers. 1822-1903. 3 boxes and 4 bacases.
Open. Unpublished guide.
Minnesota Historical Society, Archives and Manuscripts.
Dousman (1800-68) was a fur trader and entrepreneur. His son, also named Hercules Louis Dousman (1848-86), was a businessman who dealt in stocks and bonds, real estate, and utilities investments. Papers of the younger Dousman's wife Nina Sturgis Dousman include a letter book with correspondence relating to business and payment of bills and debts, including children's tuition and mortgages, and an account book for 1888 to 1895 with a monthly record of her major income and expenses in Prairie du Chien, WI.

9,051. Dreves, Louise M.
Papers. 1923. 1 vol.
Open. Unpublished guide.
Minnesota Historical Society, Archives and Manuscripts.
Diary kept by Dreves, the daughter of a St. Paul brokerage owner, during her trip to Germany, Switzerland, Belgium, England, Scotland, and the Netherlands.

9,052. Drew, James Meddick, and Family
Papers. 1848-1948. 5 boxes and 23 oversize items.
Open. Unpublished guide.
Minnesota Historical Society, Archives and Manuscripts.
Papers of James Drew (1863-1948), who taught blacksmithing, recreation, and crafts in agriculture extension at the University of Minnesota, contain correspondence with his cousin Jeanette Dildine [Mrs. John] Williamson concerning family news, health, and disposal of land; letters from county home agents, who were primarily women, about setting up programs, sports, and craft demonstrations; family correspondence; "resolutions" passed on the death of Drew's aunt Jeanette Drew (?-1895) by her friends in the Scranton chapter of the Epworth League of the Chicago Grace Methodist Episcopal Church; an account concerning the settlement of the estate of Jennette (Drew) [Mrs. Marcene H.] Dildine (1843-1918) of Hammondsport, NY; obituaries; and clippings. Papers of Edward Bolivar Drew (1827-1902), who settled in Winona County, MN, in the 1850s and served as a member of the Minnesota legislature, include correspondence with his mother Matilda Sherwood [Mrs. John S.] Drew (1802-67) and his sisters Jennette (Drew) Dildine and Mary Drew and his school roll book from Hammondsport, with names of students, grades, and roll call. Also includes a letter by Benjamin Franklin Drew (1831-82) to his sister Mary Drew and clippings about the careers of Elsie Salisbury [Mrs. James Meddick] Drew (1865-1945), a teacher of mathematics, and Helen Drew [Mrs. Robert] Richardson, a professor of English at Rockford College in Rockford, IL.

9,053. Druck, Rae
Papers. Ca. 1917-47. 5 in.
Open. No guide.
Minnesota Historical Society, Archives and Manuscripts.
Papers of [Mrs. Bernard] Druck include minutes, correspondence, reports, flyers, and clippings of the Child Psychology Study Circle dating from 1924 to 1947 and correspondence, reports, speeches, flyers, and other records of the National Thanksgiving Association dating from ca. 1917 to the 1940s.

9,054. Duluth Federated Trades and Labor Assembly
Papers. 1892-1942. 12 boxes.
Open. Unpublished guide.
Minnesota Historical Society, Archives and Manuscripts.
The Assembly, an affiliate of the American Federation of Labor, was formed in 1887 and was initially called the Duluth Federated Trades Assembly. Minutes; accounts of receipts, expenditures, and dues; correspondence relating to such topics as shorter work days, improved working conditions, and political, economic, and social conditions in Duluth, MN; and resolutions passed at meetings, including one passed in 1918 supporting woman suffrage.

9,055. Dunwoody, William Hood, and Family
Papers. 1837-1915. 3 boxes and 1 bacase.
Open. Unpublished guide.
Minnesota Historical Society, Archives and Manuscripts.
Papers of the family of Dunwoody (1841-1914), an entrepreneur in the grain and flour trade, who founded Dunwoody Institute, an industrial training school for young men in Minneapolis. Includes correspondence between his wife Catherine Lane (Patten) Dunwoody (1845-1914) and her brother John William Patten; letters from [Mrs.] R. A. Dunwoody Jones in Chicago to her brother John Dunwoody, a commission merchant in Philadelphia, concerning family news, the port of Chicago, and available consumer goods; and correspondence of Kate Dunwoody with her husband Frank Dunwoody and letters to her brother-in-law James Penrose Dunwoody in Pennsylvania concerning life in Minneapolis, a trip to Minnehaha Falls and St. Paul, her children, and raising chickens and a cow. Also includes a letter to William Dunwoody from Mary Theresa Mehegan [Mrs. James Jerome] Hill concerning a book he sent her.

9,056. Eastlick, Mrs. L. John
Papers. Nd. 25-page item.
Open. No guide.
Minnesota Historical Society, Archives and Manuscripts.
Narrative by Eastlick (1833-?) concerns the Sioux uprising of 1862 as it involved her small neighborhood of settlers on Lake Shetek in Murray County, MN.

9,057. Edgar, William Crowell, and Family
Papers. 1832-1949. 6 boxes, 13 items, and 1 microfilm reel.
Open. Unpublished guide.
Minnesota Historical Society, Archives and Manuscripts.
Correspondence of Edgar (1856-1932), business manager and editor of the *Northwestern Miller* from 1882 to 1924, concerns his publications and includes letters from Anne Robinson and George Rowan Robinson, the parents of his wife Anne Randolph Page (Robinson) Edgar (ca. 1860-1949); from his daughter Marjorie Edgar (1889-1960), who describes Girl Guide activities in England; and to his wife. Also includes a manuscript on Finnish folk songs and notes on folk songs by his daughter, a folklorist; a certificate and a medal presented to his wife by Queen Elizabeth for relief work in Belgium; memorabilia concerning his sister Mary (Edgar) Sill and her husband William Raymond Sill; and clippings. Correspondents include Lou Henry [Mrs. Herbert C.] Hoover, actress Beatrice (Cameron) [Mrs. Richard] Mansfield, pianist Fannie (Bloomfield) Zeisler, artist and author Mary Hallock [Mrs. Arthur De Wint] Foote, Minnie Maddern [Mrs. Harrison Guy] Fiske, Matilda Lang, Mary Custis Lee, and authors Alice French, Laura (Howe) [Mrs. Henry] Richards, and Constance Fenimore Woolson.

9,058. Edward F. Waite Neighborhood House
Records. 1922-62. 23 boxes.
Open. Unpublished guide.
Minnesota Historical Society, Archives and Manuscripts.
The mission from which this neighborhood house in Minneapolis developed was founded in 1913. Minutes, reports, and correspondence of the board of directors; financial records; reports and correspondence of various staff programs; statistics; a history of the House; group work and camp records; reports on school and home visits; publicity and publications; and a social survey of families residing in Minneapolis settlement house districts. Also includes letters from Belle Mead, Mary E. Blake, Caroline M. Crosby, and other women; information on family and community life; and minutes of the Neighborhood Affairs Council for 1947 to 1951.

9,059. Ericksen, Theresa
Papers. 1906-37. 1 box and 2 items.
Open. No guide.
Minnesota Historical Society, Archives and Manuscripts.
Ericksen (1867-?) was a nurse who served in the Spanish-American War with the 13th Minnesota regiment and in WWI; she also was a member of Women's Overseas Service League, an organization of women who served in WWI. Correspondence with others who served in the Spanish-American War, regiment papers, a scrapbook, information on the activities of Spanish-American War veterans and the Veterans of Foreign Wars in Minnesota, and bulletins of the 13th Minnesota regimental society of northern California.

9,060. Farmer, Eugenia B.
Papers. Nd. 30-page item.
Open. No guide.
Minnesota Historical Society, Archives and Manuscripts.
Sketch of Susan B. Anthony's life from 1820 to 1880 is included along with some facts about Anthony, Elizabeth Cady Stanton, and Lucy Stone and a poem entitled "All the Rights She Wants."

9,061. Farmer, Eugenia B.
Papers. 1918. 6-page item.
Open. No guide.
Minnesota Historical Society, Archives and Manuscripts.
Paper [Mrs.] Farmer read before the state convention of the Minnesota Woman Suffrage Association in 1918 concerns her reminiscences of experiences with Confederate sympathizers in Missouri during the Civil War and her efforts on behalf of woman suffrage in Kentucky.

9,062. Farmer-Labor Association of Minnesota
Records. 1918-48. 8 boxes and 4 vols.
Open. Unpublished guide.
Minnesota Historical Society, Archives and Manuscripts.
Party constitutions; convention data, including minutes, proceedings, delegate lists, resolutions, platforms, and committee membership information; correspondence; campaign material; clippings; and other records, including some relating to the Democratic-Farmer-Labor party. Numerous items concern Susie (Williamson) [Mrs. Olaf O.] Stageberg, who was active in the Farmer-Labor party.

9,063. Fast, Hermann J., and Family
Papers. 1914-20. 1 microfilm reel.
Open. Unpublished guide.
Minnesota Historical Society, Archives and Manuscripts.
Fast and his wife Aganetha Becker Fast (1865-1930) were Volga Germans who emigrated during the 1870s from Russia to Mountain Lake, MN, where they were members of a Mennonite community. Diaries of Aganetha Fast for 1914 to 1920 provide information on farming operations, social life, church activities, and local participation in WWI. Also includes an account of their trip to the US and the settlement and development of the area around Mountain Lake, MN.

9,064. Fawcett, Charles Edward
Papers. 1894-1939. 46-page item.
Open. No guide.
Minnesota Historical Society, Archives and Manuscripts.
Obstetrical chart consists of a list of births kept by Fawcett (1869-1939), a Stewartville, MN, physician.

9,065. Ferguson, William Henry, and Family
Papers. 1849-1952. 1 vol. and 1 microfilm reel.
Open. Unpublished guide.
Minnesota Historical Society, Archives and Manuscripts.
Diary kept by Ferguson (1816-57) and his wife Lydia Dale Estey Ferguson (1825-95) concerning their settlement in territorial Minnesota and William's death in 1857; a memorandum book they kept from 1853 to 1869 containing letters and stories by various family members, a letter by Lydia describing a controversy over Scripture reading in a Plymouth, MN, public school, and reminiscences of a trip from Elmira, NY, to Minnesota; an autograph book; and family data on births, marriages, and deaths between ca. 1700 and 1952 copied from the family Bible.

9,066. Ferris, Gratia F.
Papers. 1907. 14-page item.
Open. No guide.
Minnesota Historical Society, Archives and Manuscripts.
Letter by Ferris to her sister May concerns pioneer life in Minnesota from 1855 to 1903 and is accompanied by a genealogical chart.

9,067. Firkins, Oscar W., and Family
Papers. 1876-1934. 20 boxes.
Open. Unpublished guide.
Minnesota Historical Society, Archives and Manuscripts.
Papers of [Miss] Ina Ten Eyck Firkins (1866-1937), a librarian, translator, and author, include letters to her brother Oscar Firkins (1864-1932), a drama critic, teacher, and author; the letters relate primarily to her trip to Europe in 1894. Also includes diaries for 1891, 1894, and 1912-32, in which she discusses family relationships, travel, WWI, health, death, marriage, and academia; short stories and articles she wrote; notes on toasts given at various academic dinners; and a pamphlet.

9,068. First Baptist Church
Records. 1856-1942. 1 box.
Open. Unpublished guide.
Minnesota Historical Society, Archives and Manuscripts.
Minutes of and a tribute to the Baptist Women's Missionary Society. The Church, located in Northfield, MN, was founded in 1856.

9,069. First Baptist Church
Records. 1868-1913. 2 boxes.
Open. Unpublished guide.
Minnesota Historical Society, Archives and Manuscripts.
Includes a minute book kept by the secretary of the Women's Foreign Missionary Society of the First Baptist Church in Waseca, MN.

9,070. First Baptist Church, St. Paul
Records. 1851-1944. 9 boxes and 1 oversize box.
Open. Unpublished guide.
Minnesota Historical Society, Archives and Manuscripts.
Constitutions, minutes, and reports of women's groups affiliated with the Church, including the Ladies Benevolent Society, the Ladies Society, the Home Mission Circle, the Woman's Missionary Society, and the Young Woman's Tuesday Club; biographical sketches of Church members, among them Mrs. Enbert Anderson, Edith R. [Mrs. Henry C.] Mabie, Lucy Ann [Mrs. John D.] Pope, and Mrs. John G. Randall; and published Church histories, some of which were written by women. The Church was founded in 1849.

9,071. First Congregational Church, Marine, MN
Records. 1857-1909. 1 box.
Open. Unpublished guide.
Minnesota Historical Society, Archives and Manuscripts.
Includes constitution and minutes of the Marine Mite Society, 1866 and 1868-75; bylaws, minutes, and a list of members of the Ladies Church Aid Society, 1878-92; minutes and a list of members of the Ladies Union League, 1863-66; and minutes of the Marine Sewing Society, 1858.

9,072. First Swedish Methodist Episcopal Church
Records. 1854-1925. 2 boxes and 1 bacase.
Open. Unpublished guide.
Minnesota Historical Society, Archives and Manuscripts.
Records of this St. Paul church include minutes of the Ladies Aid Society, 1904-12, and of the Sunday School Board, 1894-1903. The minutes were written in Swedish until 1897.

9,073. Folk Arts Foundation of America, Inc.
Records. 1943-65. 1 box.
Open. Unpublished guide.
Minnesota Historical Society, Archives and Manuscripts.
Minutes, correspondence, programs, and reports of this St. Paul organization, which was formed in 1944 to increase the knowledge and practice of folk arts in America. Includes material relating to the

work of Frances Densmore and Marjorie Edgar in recording music and folk songs, the Finnish studies and lectures of Clara Stocker, publication of *North Star News,* folk dancing, and arts and crafts. Esther Jerabek, Mrs. Lewis R. Jones, Alice Liliequist [Mrs. Henry James] Sickels, and Marjorie Edgar were among those active in organizing and promoting the Foundation's program.

9,074. Folsom, Simeon Pearl
Papers. 1869-1903. 2 boxes.
Open. Unpublished guide.
Minnesota Historical Society, Archives and Manuscripts.
Folsom, a fur trader, railroad engineer, and lawyer in early St. Paul, served in the Mexican War and the Indian wars of the 1860s. His diaries for 1869 to 1903 contain information on social and political life, economic conditions, and business activities. Also contains a diary kept by his daughter-in-law in 1903 concerning her daily schedule, social events, sewing, piano lessons, and housework.

9,075. Folsom, W. H. C., and Family
Papers. Nd. 1 oversize folder, 12 bacases, and 2 vols.
Open. No guide.
Minnesota Historical Society, Archives and Manuscripts
Correspondence, financial records, land and legal papers, and post cards of the Folsom and Smith families date from about the 1850s to the 1920s. Includes papers of Cordelia Ayer Paine, a pianist, writer, and genealogist, which contain literary manuscripts, research notes, and family information and albums with photos of the Folsom family house, early Taylors Falls, MN, and the Dalles area near Taylors Falls.

9,076. Folsom, William Henry Carman, and Family
Papers. 1836-1944. 10 boxes and 7 oversize items.
Open. Unpublished guide.
Minnesota Historical Society, Archives and Manuscripts.
Correspondence, business records, and other papers of the family of William Folsom (1817-1900), a lumberman, general store proprietor, legislator, speculator, real estate dealer, and regional historian. Includes correspondence of his wife Mary Jane Wyman Folsom (1818-96) with her family the Wymans in Maine on such subjects as social celebrations, women's fashions, antislavery sentiments, economic conditions, the attraction of the West, labor and mining, and the anxiety of mothers and wives during the Civil War. Also includes 1893 correspondence of William Folsom, who was called in as a technical expert in litigation over lands in Itasca County once belonging to Sophia A. Lambert, a woman who was part Chippewa; an 1885 marriage certificate of Mary C. Wieck (1860-96) and Wyman X. Folsom (1844-1929); an autograph book of Mary Wieck Folsom with entries from schoolmates at Stillwater High School and Carleton College; invitations; and dance programs.

9,077. Folwell, William Watts, and Family
Papers. 1704-1945. 120 boxes and 2 bacases.
Open. Unpublished guide.
Minnesota Historical Society, Archives and Manuscripts.
Folwell (1833-1929), a lawyer, economist, historian, lecturer, and philanthropist, was president of the University of Minnesota from 1869 until 1884. Includes correspondence between members of the Folwell and Heywood families concerning life in Minnesota, women's education, family news, homesteading, libraries, and hospitals; diaries of Sarah Heywood [Mrs. William Watts] Folwell (1838-1931) for 1850 and of Mary Heywood Folwell for 1888, 1907, and 1908; family reminiscences, including those of Sarah Folwell; memo books of Sarah Folwell and Joanna Bainbridge Folwell; a clinical record book and a cookbook of Sarah Folwell; a drawing book of Mary S. Heywood; and a grade school lesson book and address book of Mary Heywood Folwell. Also includes "The General Flight," a reminiscence, which was dictated to William Folwell by [Mrs.] Mary MacMath Bainbridge, and professional correspondence of William Folwell with Maria Louise Sanford.

9,078. Forest History Foundation
Oral history. 1953-57. 1 box.
Open. Unpublished guide.
Minnesota Historical Society, Archives and Manuscripts.
Transcripts of interviews with pioneer lumbermen and women conducted by members of the Forest History Society include one in which Hope (Garlick) [Mrs. Wirt] Mineau and [Mrs.] Maud (Mullan) Carlgren describe Carlgren's uncle Smith Ellison, who was a pioneer lumberman; early lumbering activities; Indian-white relationships; and the genealogy of the Garlick family. Also includes an interview with Margaret (Orr) [Mrs. Charles] O'Neill (1872-1963), who discusses her father's logging camp in the 1880s in Wisconsin, working with her sister as a cook in the camps, the types of meals prepared, incidents in the camps, lumberjack songs, Indians, nationality groups in the camps, and wages paid to the men.

9,079. Fortun, Myrtle E.
Papers. 1941-48. 1 box.
Open. Unpublished guide.
Minnesota Historical Society, Archives and Manuscripts.
Volume of Fortun (ca. 1912-), a telephone operator in Lyle, MN, includes letters to her from servicemen during WWII, diary entries for 1941 to 1948, ration books, cards, and clippings.

9,080. Fosseen, Carrie Secelia Jorgens
Papers. 1914-51. 1 box and 1 microfilm reel.
Open. Unpublished guide.
Minnesota Historical Society, Archives and Manuscripts.
[Mrs. Manley Lewis] Fosseen (1875-1963), a leader in the Republican party, was active in the Minnesota Federation of Women's Clubs, the Republican Federation of Women, and the Dome Club, a social group she organized for wives of members of the Minnesota legislature. Correspondence relating to her political activities; speeches on such subjects as politics, Norwegian contributions to American life, and her opposition to the radical political movements of the 1920s and 1930s; scrapbooks containing letters, programs, and clippings; invitations; clippings, including some relating to the Dome Club; and other papers. Fosseen also was president of the Dome Club from 1903 to 1949.

9,081. Foster, John Burt
Papers. 1928-74. 7 boxes.
Access restricted. Unpublished guide.
Minnesota Historical Society, Archives and Manuscripts.
Foster (1911-), who was born in Faribault, MN, served as a missionary of the Protestant Episcopal church in China from 1934 to 1940. He helped operate a mission hospital in 1938 for the Eighth Route (Communist) Army in China, and then held positions in China with the US Information Service and US State Department from 1941 to 1947. Correspondence with his parents and sister Jane Foster in which he discusses Chinese society and his contact with Chou En-lai, Agnes Smedley, and Madame Sun Yat-sen; correspondence with Pearl Buck; manuscript poems by Jane Foster; impressions of his 1974 visit to China; articles; and pamphlets. Since 1952 John Foster has been professor of English at Mankato State University in Mankato, MN.

9,082. Foster, Lysander Patterson
Papers. 1877-1924. 1 box.
Open. Unpublished guide.
Minnesota Historical Society, Archives and Manuscripts.
Foster (1836-1924), a territorial settler in St. Anthony, MN, was a lawyer, doctor, and amateur photographer. Photo album with family photos and clippings about family events and handwritten physician's handbooks listing symptoms and treatments of various diseases, including many women's problems, which are identified by organ of the body and symptom.

9,083. Frankel, Hiram D.
Papers. 1873-1930. 21 ft.
Open. No guide.
Minnesota Historical Society, Archives and Manuscripts.
Frankel (1882-1931), a St. Paul lawyer and leader in the Jewish community, was president of B'nai B'rith in the Midwest and an active member of the Jewish Welfare Board. Includes correspondence of the B'nai B'rith Women's Auxiliary of Chicago; records of the Jewish Welfare Board, including an account of its general work and visits of "mother's aids" to the ghetto; and correspondence with Mrs. Nathan Rose about entertainment.

9,084. Fraser, Arvonne
Papers. 1950-74. 12.5 ft.
Access restricted. No guide.
Minnesota Historical Society, Archives and Manuscripts.
Fraser, a Democratic-Farmer-Labor party organizer and activist, is the wife and administrative assistant of Donald Fraser, US representative from Minnesota since 1963. Personal and family letters, material relating to Fraser campaigns, and speeches, reports, files, and other records of the Women's Equity Action League.

9,085. Fuller, Abby Abbe, and Family
Papers. 1840-1928. 2 boxes and 17 oversize items.
Open. Unpublished guide.
Minnesota Historical Society, Archives and Manuscripts.
Letters from members of the Fuller family in Minnesota to relatives in Connecticut and to the *Boston Times* concerning social and economic conditions in Minnesota, the early history of St. Paul, trade and annuity payments to the Winnebago people, the Dakota War, and the history and customs of the Ojibwe; deeds from the 1850s, including one relating to the sale of Fort Ripley Reservation; and clippings relating to the Fuller family.

9,086. Furber, Pierce P., and Family
Papers. 1855-80. 0.5 box.
Open. No guide.
Minnesota Historical Society, Archives and Manuscripts.
Diaries kept in 1855 by [Mrs.] Lucy Metcalfe Furber, a housewife in Maine, contain information on family and social life.

9,087. Fyffe, David Maxwell, and Fyffe, Jessie
Papers. 1931-38. 1 box.
Open. Unpublished guide.
Minnesota Historical Society, Archives and Manuscripts.
Reminiscences by Daniel Fyffe (1856-1934), a Scottish immigrant who was a ranch manager in Minnesota and Nebraska and superintendent of farm schools in Ohio and Indiana, concern early settlement days in southwestern Minnesota during the 1880s and 1890s. Reminiscences of his wife Jessie Smith Allan Fyffe (?-1946) contain information on the blizzard of 1882 and pioneer settlers in Pipestone County, MN.

9,088. Gale, Amory, and Family
Papers. 1857-1957. 3 items.
Open. Unpublished guide.
Minnesota Historical Society, Archives and Manuscripts.
Booklet that Amory Gale (1815-74), a Baptist minister in territorial Minnesota, wrote in 1857 providing instructions to his wife Caroline E. Goddard Gale for her trip from Boston to join him in Minneapolis. Also includes an account by their daughter Caroline (Gale) [Mrs. George H.] Johnston (1874-?) of Amory Gale's arrival in Minnesota.

9,089. Gale, Richard Pillsbury
Papers. 1935-45. 8 boxes.
Open. Unpublished guide.
Minnesota Historical Society, Archives and Manuscripts.
Includes letters from Mary Pillsbury [Mrs. Oswald Bates] Lord and a mailing list for the Women's International League for Peace and Freedom.

9,090. Gale, Samuel Chester, and Gale, Susan Damon
Papers. 1850-78. 2 vols.
Open. No guide.
Minnesota Historical Society, Archives and Manuscripts.
A settler in Minnesota Territory, Samuel Gale (1827-1916) returned to Massachusetts to marry and then brought his wife Susan Damon back to Minneapolis, where they became active in Plymouth Congregational Church. His journal contains frequent mentions of his wife, children, and parents. Papers of Susan Gale (1833-1908) include a diary kept in 1850 before her marriage in which she describes school, church, family, and social events; a family journal she kept from 1861 to 1879 "to record the principal events of home life," beginning with her marriage; photos of the Gale house in Minneapolis and of Susan Gale; drawings of the Damon residence in Massachusetts; and obituaries of Susan Gale. Also includes reminiscences of the last weeks of Susan Gale's life by her daughter Anna.

9,091. Garfield, Mary Elizabeth (Parker), and Family
Papers. 1868-98. 1 vol. and 5 items.
Open. Unpublished guide.
Minnesota Historical Society, Archives and Manuscripts.
Letters to friends and relatives in Potsdam, NY, and an 1869 diary of [Mrs. John P.] Garfield (1839-70), a housewife, concern her life in the Minnesota towns of Winona and Lake City, the weather, her health, and visits from family and friends. Also includes an 1898 letter in which Josephine Barnhart discusses with her cousin Florence (Garfield) [Mrs. George Milo] Russell, a housewife who was Garfield's daughter, family news and the Spanish-American War; in her letter Barnhart also forwarded letters written by Russell's mother in 1868 and 1869.

9,092. General Federation of Women's Clubs, Fifth District
Records. 1940-41. 10 items.
Open. Unpublished guide.
Minnesota Historical Society, Archives and Manuscripts.
Contains records relating to formation of the Federation's policies, resolutions on national defense policies, student membership in the Foreign Policy Association, and the teaching of Spanish in Minnesota public schools.

9,093. Gethsemane Episcopal Church
Records. 1856-1975. 6 microfilm reels.
Open. Unpublished guide.
Minnesota Historical Society, Archives and Manuscripts.
Includes minutes, 1905-13, of the Woman's Guild of the first Episcopal parish in Minneapolis west of the Mississippi River, which was founded in 1856.

9,094. Gilman, Catheryne Cooke
Papers. 1952. 3 vols.
Open. No guide.
Minnesota Historical Society, Archives and Manuscripts.
History by Gilman (1880-1954) of the Northeast Neighborhood House in Minneapolis from its founding in 1914 through 1947. The history was based upon Gilman's recollections of the development of the House and the recollections of her husband Robbins Gilman as well as upon research.

9,095. Gilman, Robbins, and Family
Papers. 1699-1952. 41 ft.
Partially closed. Unpublished guide.
Minnesota Historical Society, Archives and Manuscripts.
Papers of Gilman, a social worker, and his wife Catheryne (Cooke) Gilman (1880-1954), who taught in rural Iowa for about 10 years before becoming a social worker and social reformer. Catheryne Gilman worked at the East Side House Settlement and University Settlement in New York and at the Northeast Neighborhood House in Minneapolis, headed the Women's Cooperative Alliance in Minneapolis from 1916 to 1932, and was active in the International Council of Women, peace groups, and organizations seeking to improve the quality of motion pictures. Correspondence; a manuscript of an unpublished book she wrote; research files on juvenile delinquency, social hygiene, social problems in Minneapolis, and the movie industry; newsletters; and printed material by Catheryne Gilman and others. Papers relate to such subjects as social settlement work, prohibition, sex crimes and prostitution, child rearing, the American Friends' Service Committee, and Neighbors United. Includes correspondence of the Gilmans' son Logan Gilman and his wife Rhoda (Raasch) Gilman, of Elizabeth Drinker Paxson Gilman with her son Robbins Gilman, and of Catheryne Gilman's sisters Nira (Cook) [Mrs. Henry] Carroll and Georgia (Cook) [Mrs. Ben] Thompson, whose maiden names varied from Gilman's because she changed it. Correspondence of Robbins Gilman's sisters Frances Paxson Gilman and Helen Ives Gilman reflects the life of upper middle-class single women in Yonkers, NY, especially their financial responsibilities and arrangements.

9,096. Glaser, Emma
Papers. 1943-50. 1 box.
Open. Unpublished guide.
Minnesota Historical Society, Archives and Manuscripts.
Manuscript history of the St. Croix valley by Glaser (1883-), a writer and local historian, was written from published sources, manuscripts, and interviews with old settlers. It deals with logging camps, the life of a lumberjack, land and timber acquisition, descriptions of the St. Croix River and explorations, the establishment of the first settlements, the building and development of Stillwater, MN, the establishment of the US government and courts, and the lives of early settlers, including Lydia Ann (Brown) [Mrs. Christopher] Carli.

9,097. Gleason, Sarah
Papers. 1878-1930. 79 items.
Open. Unpublished guide.
Minnesota Historical Society, Archives and Manuscripts.
Correspondence, petitions, teaching certificates, and attendance records of Gleason (?-1930), who taught school in Chippewa, Meeker, Grant, Wright, and McLeod counties in Minnesota, as well as letters by a "Mattie" to her mother describing the 1894 forest fire in Hinckley, MN.

9,098. Glenn, Andrew William, and Family
Papers. 1842-1919. 1 box.
Open. Unpublished guide.
Minnesota Historical Society, Archives and Manuscripts.
Glenn (1852-1937) was married to Maria Frances McMillan Glenn. Letters that Aggie Wallace wrote to Maria Frances McMillan from the mission home in Nashville contain descriptions of school, southern attitudes toward Yankee teachers, and the activities of the Ku Klux Klan. Also includes a volume kept by the McMillan family from 1842 to 1870, which contains an essay by Alice McMillan; minutes for 1850 and 1851 of the Period, a literary society in Dalton, IA; honey, soap, whitewash, and other recipes; and a cure for bedbugs.

9,099. Godfrey, Ard, and Family
Papers. 1839-1945. 3 boxes.
Open. Unpublished guide.
Minnesota Historical Society, Archives and Manuscripts.
Godfrey (1813-94), a lumber businessman and entrepreneur, and his wife Harriet (Newell) Godfrey (1816-96) were territorial settlers who moved to Minnesota from Maine. Correspondence between Ard and Harriet Godfrey and between Harriet Godfrey and relatives back East; letters from their daughter Helen (Godfrey) [Mrs. Mark] Berry (1839-1902); diaries Harriet (Newell) Godfrey kept in 1858, 1872, 1888, and 1890; diaries of Helen Berry for 1860 and 1868; and clippings on the Godfrey family, their home, and early Minneapolis history. Papers of Ard and Harriet Godfrey's daughter Harriet R. Godfrey (1849-1943), a teacher and matron of a church home and the Crittenton Home, include her diaries for 1863 through 1930 with entries on family relationships and problems, her religious beliefs, financial matters, and social activities; essays she wrote; her reminiscences of Fort Snelling and St. Anthony; teaching certificates; school programs; and religious cards.

9,100. Gove, Lucy (Rogers)
Papers. 1879-88. 4 vols.
Open. No guide.
Minnesota Historical Society, Archives and Manuscripts.
Class records of the old Minneapolis High School include records of grades and a list of later addresses of pupils.

9,101. Graber, Albert, and Family
Papers. 1849-1955. 1 box and 5 oversize items.
Open. Unpublished guide.
Minnesota Historical Society, Archives and Manuscripts.
Typescript by Graber's wife Anna Erb Graber (1868-?) concerning life in Minneapolis between 1870 and 1900; six volumes containing constitutions, bylaws, membership lists, attendance records, and other records of the Young Ladies Home Mission Society of the First Methodist Church of Minneapolis and its successor the Mnemosyne Club, of which Anna Graber was a member; an article and transcript of a radio address by Evelyn Graber [Mrs. Everett Wallace] Cosandy concerning the Range Symphony Orchestra of the Minnesota Iron Range; and theater and commencement programs.

9,102. Grace Methodist Episcopal Church
Records. 1874-1933. 8.5 boxes, 1 bacase, and 1 vol.
Open. Unpublished guide.
Minnesota Historical Society, Archives and Manuscripts.
Records of this St. Paul church include minutes of the Women's Foreign Missionary Society, minutes of the Sunday school, and leaflets of Sunday school class records.

9,103. Gray, James, and Family
Papers. 1862-1960. 10 boxes.
Open. Unpublished guide.
Minnesota Historical Society, Archives and Manuscripts.
Includes papers of Gray's wife Grace (Farrington) Gray (1871-1935), a native of New York who reported on sessions of the original Chautauqua at Chautauqua, NY. She came to Minnesota in 1891 and worked as a reporter and editorial writer for the *Minneapolis Times* and associate editor of *The Farmer's Wife;* an author, she also was active in political campaigns and in the organization of the kindergarten system in the Minneapolis public schools. Correspondence of Grace Gray concerning her Chautauqua activities and with Zona Gale, Maria L. Sanford, May Waldron Robson, and Blanche Yurka; a diary fragment, poems, and a short novel by Grace Gray; her public speeches and lectures; "Forward Minneapolis" (1905), a pamphlet she wrote; her high school records from Jamestown, NY; a review of her book *Dreams and Idols* (1900); clippings; and programs of the Woman's Club of Minneapolis, the Peripatetics of Minneapolis, and the Hennepin County Sunday School Association. Also includes speeches by her daughter-in-law Sophie Stryker [Mrs. James] Gray (1901-52).

9,104. Greater St. Paul United Fund and Council, Inc.
Records. 1921-66. 10.5 ft.
Access restricted. Unpublished guide.
Minnesota Historical Society, Archives and Manuscripts.
Records of the St. Paul Community Chest, which existed from 1920 to 1961, and of the United Fund and Council, which was founded in 1962, both of which were fund-raising organizations for St. Paul social service, health, and recreational organizations. Minute books of Community Chest committees, including the budget committee, the planning and research council, the social planning committee, the health council, the leisure time council, and the group services and recreational council, which concern the Girl Scouts, the Boy Scouts, the YWCA, the International Institute, and local community centers and camp associations. Also includes correspondence and reports of the St. Paul Clothing Center relating to financial matters, meetings, monthly clothing sales, and the possibility of closing the Center.

9,105. Griffin, Abbie T.
Papers. 1882-85. 1 vol.
Open. Unpublished guide.
Minnesota Historical Society, Archives and Manuscripts.
Diary kept by Griffin (1851-?), a Minneapolis seamstress, concerns her daily life, household tasks, social activities, the weather, her art needlework projects, her health, recipes, and her marriage in 1885 to S. Clint Dike.

9,106. Grimstvedt, Abr
Papers. 1850-75. 1 vol.
Open. No guide.
Minnesota Historical Society, Archives and Manuscripts.
Letters written by Norwegian immigrants [Mrs.] Susanne Kristiansdatter, [Mrs.] Herborg Kristiansdatter (Grimstvedt) Klausson, and [Mrs.] Anne Johanne Kristiansdatter Nordby contain descriptions of pioneer life in Wisconsin, Iowa, and Dakota. The letters, written in Norwegian, were gathered and edited by Abr Grimstvedt.

9,107. Griswold, Harriet
Papers. 1856-61. 18 items.
Open. Unpublished guide.
Minnesota Historical Society, Archives and Manuscripts.
Griswold, a widow, was a territorial settler who operated a boarding house. Correspondence between Griswold, her children, and relatives in the East contains descriptions of life near Cambridge, MN; cranberry picking; the boarding house; agricultural methods; prices; the sale of land; and travel in early Minnesota.

9,108. Grout, Jane M.
Papers. 1873. 1 vol.
Open. No guide.
Minnesota Historical Society, Archives and Manuscripts.
Diary kept by Grout with annotations by Mary Ellen Lewis concerns a journey from Fountain Prairie, WI, to Luverne, MN, in 1873 by covered wagon.

9,109. Hadassah
Records. 1948-62. 1 box and 5 vols.
Open. Unpublished guide.
Minnesota Historical Society, Archives and Manuscripts.
Journal of cash receipts and disbursements and scrapbooks of the Minneapolis chapter of Hadassah, a Jewish women's organization that was founded by Henrietta Szold. Szold also helped found Youth Aliyah, through which thousands of Jewish children were transported to Palestine from Germany and other Nazi-controlled parts of Europe.

9,110. Hadassah, Virginia, Minnesota
Records. 1940-45. 62 pp.
Open. Unpublished guide.
Minnesota Historical Society, Archives and Manuscripts.
Minutes of meetings of Hadassah, a Jewish women's fund-raising and benefit organization in Virginia, a town on the Iron Range in northern Minnesota.

9,111. Hahn, Emilia
Papers. 1860. 2-page item.
Open. No guide.
Minnesota Historical Society, Archives and Manuscripts.
Letter in German by Hahn, a young woman in Germany, to her husband Ferdinand, who had come to the US, concerning their child, her sadness at their separation, and her hope to join him soon in the US.

9,112. Hale, William Dinsmore, and Family
Papers. 1819-1913. 20 Hollinger boxes, 7 bacases, 3 oversize items, and 1 microfilm reel.
Open. Unpublished guide.
Minnesota Historical Society, Archives and Manuscripts.
Letters to Hale (1836-1915) from his sister Lucie Hale in various towns in New York where she was a teacher and principal; letters from the Hammond family in Pennsylvania to Flora Annett Hammond Hale (1844-1936), a friend and coworker of Lucie Hale, who moved to Minneapolis in 1868 and two years later married Lucie's brother William Hale; and a 1908 diary of Flora Hale.

9,113. Hall, Marion Snelling, and Family
Papers. 1807-1962. 1 box.
Open. Unpublished guide.
Minnesota Historical Society, Archives and Manuscripts.
Correspondence and other papers relating to family events, marriages, property, the DAR, and Fort Snelling; genealogical charts and notes on the Hazard, Hunt, and Snelling families; obituaries of family members; clippings on Fort Snelling and Josiah Snelling, who was commandant of the Fort in Minnesota during the 1820s; and other papers of Hall (1882-), the great-granddaughter of Josiah Snelling.

9,114. Hallie Q. Brown Community House
Records. 1861-1960s. 2 bacases and 32 items.
Open. Unpublished guide.
Minnesota Historical Society, Archives and Manuscripts.
Minutes of staff and board of directors meetings, financial records, correspondence, scrapbook items, brochures, clippings, and other records of this settlement house, which was founded in 1931 to serve the black community of St. Paul. Includes correspondence relating to the visit of Hallie Quinn Brown to the House for its 18th anniversary celebration in 1947, a paper by I. Myrtle Carden with information on the St. Paul black community and the House, and a report F. J. Davis wrote in 1962 on the relocation of families who were forced to move because of construction of a freeway.

9,115. Halverson, Leila
Oral history. 1967. 47-page transcript.
Open. Unpublished guide.
Minnesota Historical Society, Archives and Manuscripts.
Interview with Halverson (1883-) conducted by Lila Johnson of the Historical Society and Leonora J. Collatz, executive secretary of the Minnesota Board of Nursing, concerns nurses and nursing.

9,116. Handel, Jensine
Papers. 1902. 1 vol.
Open. No guide.
Minnesota Historical Society, Archives and Manuscripts.
Teacher's class book kept by Handel at the First Lutheran Church Sunday school in Duluth, MN.

9,117. Hartley, Lucie Klammer
Papers. 1961. 105-page item.
Open. No guide.
Minnesota Historical Society, Archives and Manuscripts.
Manuscript history of Carver, MN, by [Mrs. Scott] Hartley (1911-) gives information on early settlers, churches, schools, the Minnesota River, railroads, the Sioux outbreak, the Civil War, holiday celebrations, and cemeteries. The history was published in the *Weekly Valley Herald* in 1961.

9,118. Hasselborg, Flora Valeria
Papers. Nd. 108-page item.
Open. Unpublished guide.
Minnesota Historical Society, Archives and Manuscripts.
Reminiscences of Hasselborg (1885-), the daughter of Swedish immigrants, cover the period up to the early 1900s and concern her childhood and education in Franconia, MN, where her father was postmaster, justice of the peace, and an odd jobber; the character and activities of her parents and siblings; the family's move to Florida in 1893 and their life there as subsistence homesteaders on a Gulf of Mexico bayou; schools, neighbors, financial hardships, and social life in Florida; her brothers' travels and employments; her sisters' work as schoolteachers; and her impressions of the Spanish-American War. Hasselborg also discusses her mother's childhood.

9,119. Hawkins, Oscar Ferdinand, and Hawkins, Madge (Ytrehus), and Family
Papers. 1888-1963. 11 boxes and 1 bacase.
Open. Unpublished guide.
Minnesota Historical Society, Archives and Manuscripts.
Hawkins (1872-1964), a teacher and principal in Minnesota and California, was active in the Farmer-Labor and Socialist parties during the 1920s and 1930s. Correspondence of Hawkins with family members, especially his sister Ruth Hawkins (1882-), concerning family activities, teaching, religion, politics, and current events; a diary that Amanda Broberg (?-1919), who probably was his first wife, kept from 1899 to 1908; correspondence and notebooks on politics kept by his second wife Madge Hawkins, who was president of the Hennepin County, MN, Farmer-Labor Women's Federation; minutes for

1941 of the Minneapolis chapter of the American Peace Mobilization, of which Madge Hawkins was secretary; speeches, newsletters, and pamphlets by Elizabeth Gurley Flynn, Ella Reeve Bloor, Anita Whitney, Maud Russell, Anna Louise Strong, and Corliss Lamont; and literature of political campaigns and organizations, including the Women's International League for Peace and Freedom.

9,120. Hawley, Augustine Boyer, and Family
Papers. 1767-1956. 2 boxes, 4 items, and 6 oversize items.
Open. Unpublished guide.
Minnesota Historical Society, Archives and Manuscripts.
Papers of Anne MacDonald Hawley (1876-?) contain letters from University of Minnesota professor [Miss] Maria Sanford, from Mabeth Hurd Paige on the death of Anne Hawley's brother Edward Hawley in 1952, and to Bishop Stephen K. Keeler, with information on Augustine Hawley's arrival in Red Wing, MN, in 1857 and his work building the Episcopal Christ Church there. Also includes her diary of a trip to Niagara Falls, NY, and the Great Lakes in 1888; her reminiscences of teaching experiences from 1898 to 1932; a letter of recommendation for her by University of Minnesota president Cyrus Northrup in 1897, the year she graduated; her University diploma; and her high school diploma. In addition, collection contains a letter in which Augustine Hawley's wife, who lived in Red Wing, describes to her aunt Ellie the interior of the Hawley home in 1863 and letters from Susan Decatur, widow of Stephen Decatur, to Richard Montgomery Boyer concerning a congressional bill to compensate members of the crew of the *Intrepid* and their families for their actions in the recapture of the *Philadelphia*.

9,121. Hazelton, Alice K.
Papers. 1941. 10-page item.
Open. No guide.
Minnesota Historical Society, Archives and Manuscripts.
Reminiscences by Hazelton of early days in Hazelton Township, Aitkin County, MN.

9,122. Heald, Sarah Thorp
Papers. 1937. 10 pp.
Open. No guide.
Minnesota Historical Society, Archives and Manuscripts.
History of old Crow Wing, MN, by Heald with quotations from interviews with early pioneers.

9,123. Hebrew Ladies' Benevolent Society
Records. 1881-99. 1 box.
Open. Unpublished guide.
Minnesota Historical Society, Archives and Manuscripts.
Minutes of this St. Paul organization, which existed from 1871 until 1925 to provide relief for needy Jewish families. The group was later known as the Jewish Relief Society of St. Paul.

9,124. Heerman, Edward Edson
Papers. 1855-1929. 2 boxes.
Open. Unpublished guide.
Minnesota Historical Society, Archives and Manuscripts.
Includes a diary kept from 1881 to 1885 by Minnie Heerman (1864-?), who was born in Reed's Landing, MN, of German immigrant parents and moved with her family to Devils Lake, ND, during the 1880s. She describes a trip to Montreal in 1881, social events, family relations, homesteading, moving, housekeepers, and her father's work running a steamboat on the Chippewa River, Lake Pepin, and Devils Lake.

9,125. Heilbron, Bertha Lion
Papers. Ca. 1920s-70. 10.5 ft.
Open. No guide.
Minnesota Historical Society, Archives and Manuscripts.
Heilbron (1895-197?) was a research assistant, editor of *Minnesota History,* and research fellow for 40 years at the Minnesota Historical Society. Correspondence, manuscripts of books and articles, note cards, printed items, and other papers relate to the publication of an English language edition of Henry Lewis's *Das Illustrirte Mississippithal,* to other works edited or written by Heilbron, and to research projects not completed.

9,126. Hemingway, Mary Welsh
Papers. Ca. 1967. 85-page item.
Access restricted. Unpublished guide.
Minnesota Historical Society, Archives and Manuscripts.
Partial draft of a projected autobiographical book "A House Is Never Finished" by Mary Hemingway, wife of author Ernest Hemingway. The manuscript contains descriptions of Mary Hemingway's childhood near Bemidji, MN, and Leech Lake, MN. Her father was a lumberman and piloted a paddle wheeler on Leech Lake.

9,127. Hendrickson, Viena Johnson
Papers. 1925-72. 12 ft.
Open. Unpublished guide.
Minnesota Historical Society, Archives and Manuscripts.
Correspondence, speeches, scrapbooks, and printed matter of [Mrs.] Hendrickson, a feminist and Farmer-Labor activist, pertain to the International Ladies' Garment Workers' Union, the Minnesota State Teachers College Board, the Finnish-American Historical Society, the Jane Addams Centennial, the Minnesota Peace Action Coalition, the Vietnam War, the Farmer-Labor party, the Democratic-Farmer-Labor party, and the Minnesota Committee for a Sane Nuclear Policy.

9,128. Hennepin County Bar Association
Papers. 1935-58. 1 box.
Open. Unpublished guide.
Minnesota Historical Society, Archives and Manuscripts.
Includes memorials for deceased members of the Association, including Alice D. Kercher, Margaret A. Young, and Sarah Roslyn Gensler Schwartz.

9,129. Hennepin County Farmer-Labor Women's Club, Minneapolis
Records. 1938-50. 1 in.
Open. Unpublished guide.
Minnesota Historical Society, Archives and Manuscripts.
Minutes for 1938 to 1946 of the Club, whose chairman was Madge (Ytrehus) [Mrs. Oscar Ferdinand] Hawkins. Also includes the constitution, bylaws, and a list of officers of the Women's Progressive Party Club, of which Hawkins was president.

9,130. Hennepin County War Finance Committee, Women's Division
Records. 1941-45. 2 boxes.
Open. Unpublished guide.
Minnesota Historical Society, Archives and Manuscripts.
The Committee was first organized to sell war bonds and stamps under the name Hennepin County War Savings Committee, Women's Division, with Dorothy (Bridgman) Atkinson as chairman and Hortense Honig [Mrs. Amos S.] Deinard as secretary. Correspondence; scripts of skits and plays to be used in schools, on the radio, and by women's clubs; bond drive statistics; a chairman's handbook; newsletters, including "Minnesota Memo to Women"; circular letters; news releases; bibliographies of US Treasury material; bulletins; and publications.

9,131. Hess, George H., and Family
Papers. 1864-1948. 27 boxes.
Open. Unpublished guide.
Minnesota Historical Society, Archives and Manuscripts.
Hess (1873-?) was a railroad executive and comptroller for Great Northern from 1920 to 1946. Correspondence between Hess and his wife Cora Ryland Hess; letters, articles, book proofs, and printed matter relating to astrology and theosophy, which Cora Hess collected; and correspondence regarding the properties and investments that George Hess handled for his niece Inez Marvin.

9,132. Hielscher, Helen Hughes
Papers. 1920-35. 31 items.
Open. Unpublished guide.
Minnesota Historical Society, Archives and Manuscripts.
[Mrs. J. A.] Hielscher (1863-1935) was a physician in Mankato, MN, and an organizer of the Mankato and Minnesota American Legion Auxiliaries; she also was active in obtaining medical care for disabled American veterans. Letters from hospitals in Minnesota providing historical data; minutes of the first meeting of the American Legion Auxiliary, 1920; a biographical sketch of Hielscher by Blanche W. Scallen; a paper by Hielscher on hospitalization in Minnesota; and articles extracted from the publication *The Minnesota Registered Nurse,* 1930-32, on the history of various hospitals in Minnesota.

9,133. Hill, Alberta (Kirchner)
Papers. 1891-1959. 1 box.
Open. No guide.
Minnesota Historical Society, Archives and Manuscripts.
Reminiscences by [Mrs. Leslie A.] Hill (1898-), whose father Albert Kirchner and grandfather Edward Kirchner operated a fleet of boats on the upper Mississippi River from 1898 to 1917, constructing dams and making other improvements. Hill describes the Kirchner family, the Kirchner contracting business, life on the houseboat, operating the boat, the crew, river scenery, and fires on boats.

9,134. Himrod, Anna
Papers. Nd. 1 vol.
Open. No guide.
Minnesota Historical Society, Archives and Manuscripts.
History of Crow Wing County, MN, by Himrod.

9,135. Holyoke, William H.
Papers. 1863-1912. 1 box.
Open. Unpublished guide.
Minnesota Historical Society, Archives and Manuscripts.
Includes a diary in which Margaret Turner Holyoke recorded books she read and plays and operas she attended from 1907 to 1912.

9,136. Home Co-op Club, Inc., Nashwauk, MN
Records. 1909-65. 21 boxes and 3 vols.
Open. Unpublished guide.
Minnesota Historical Society, Archives and Manuscripts.
Organizational records, many of them in Finnish, of this cooperative boarding home founded in 1908 in Nashwauk, MN, and of the Elanto Company, which included a co-op grocery store. Includes articles of incorporation; minutes of meetings; time book and payroll, 1917-47; financial records; accounts of boarders; sales slips; and a list of volumes in the Home Co-op library.

9,137. Hope, Virginia Mae
Papers. 1943-46. 18 items.
Open. Unpublished guide.
Minnesota Historical Society, Archives and Manuscripts.
Hope (1921-44), who was born in Minnesota and

studied at Northwestern University in Illinois, was a Women's Air Forces Service Pilot; the WASPs ferried aircraft and supplies from base to base in the US in order to free military pilots for combat duty. Hope was killed in a plane crash in Omaha in 1944. Includes a letter from Hope to her parents Robert and Adaline Hope of Winnebago, MN, reminiscing about her days at a WASP training camp in Texas, a letter to her from a friend at Patterson Field, letters of commendation and condolence, and clippings.

9,138. Hopkins, Elvira
Papers. 1849-59. 20 items.
Open. Unpublished guide.
Minnesota Historical Society, Archives and Manuscripts.
Letters in which [Mrs. Daniel] Hopkins describes to her family and friends in the East the growth of St. Paul, food prices, speculation on real estate, immigrants to the city, and the amount of game and fish brought in by hunters.

9,139. Hugy, Alice E.
Papers. 1874-1967. 1 vol. and 67 items.
Open. Unpublished guide.
Minnesota Historical Society, Archives and Manuscripts.
Papers of Hugy, a St. Paul artist, consist of personal and business correspondence, a volume containing minutes, a membership list, and a record of dues received and paid bills of the Artists' Society of St. Paul, 1914-21; a list of artists living in St. Paul; and clippings. Correspondents include Paul Manship and Samuel C. Sabean.

9,140. Humphrey, Hubert Horatio
Papers. Ca. 1946-70. 2700 ft.
Access restricted. Unpublished guide.
Minnesota Historical Society, Archives and Manuscripts.
Correspondence, research files, and clippings of Humphrey (1911-78), who was mayor of Minneapolis from 1943 to 1948, US senator from Minnesota from 1949 to 1964 and 1970 to 1978, and Vice-President of the US from 1965 to 1968. Includes correspondence of his wife Muriel (Buck) Humphrey relating to the public aspects of her life during the vice-presidential years and Hubert Humphrey's correspondence with constituents and others on such subjects as the Equal Rights Amendment, child adoption, and widows' pensions; files on child care, the LWV, and the Family Welfare Association of Minneapolis; and campaign files containing material on Minnesota Women for Humphrey. Correspondents include Eugenie Anderson, Geri Joseph, Dorothy Jacobson, Arvonne Fraser, Ann Chambers, Shirley Filiatrault, Mary Lasker, Genevieve Blatt, Agnes Meyer, and Minnesota women prominent in the Democratic-Farmer-Labor party, including Phyllis Jones, Ione Hunt, Eleanor Moen, [Mrs.] Helga Nielsen, Ruth Bye, and Marjorie Maki.

9,141. Hunt, George B., and Family
Papers. 1710-1902. 1 box, 2 vols., and 4 items.
Open. Unpublished guide.
Minnesota Historical Society, Archives and Manuscripts.
Fidelia Hunt Thayer was a teacher in Massachusetts during the 1850s and later a territorial settler in Winona, MN. Correspondence of Fidelia Hunt Thayer with Simeon O. Thayer before their marriage, with her sisters concerning marriage and teaching, and with her daughters regarding parental instructions, family news, and social events in 1894 while she was spending the summer in Massachusetts. Also includes an 1851 Massachusetts teaching certificate of Fidelia Hunt.

9,142. Hurd, Ethel Edgerton
Papers. 1899-1913. 6 items.
Open. Unpublished guide.
Minnesota Historical Society, Archives and Manuscripts.
Letters to Hurd (1845-1929), a suffragist and resident of Minneapolis, from Susan B. Anthony, Carrie Chapman Catt, and Anna Howard Shaw concerning details of the national convention of the National American Woman Suffrage Association, writing petitions to Congress supporting passage of the woman suffrage constitutional amendment, and organization of local suffrage clubs.

9,143. Inglenook Reading Club
Records. 1905-38. 1 box.
Open. Unpublished guide.
Minnesota Historical Society, Archives and Manuscripts.
Constitution and bylaws with revisions, minutes, treasurer's reports, and addresses of this St. Paul women's club.

9,144. Inter Nos Study Club
Records. 1907-16. 1 vol.
Open. Unpublished guide.
Minnesota Historical Society, Archives and Manuscripts.
Minutes of meetings of this Minneapolis women's club.

9,145. Iota Study Club
Records. Ca. 1935-42. 1 in.
Open. Unpublished guide.
Minnesota Historical Society, Archives and Manuscripts.
Scrapbook of clippings collected by this Minneapolis club relates to Minnesota and northwestern artists, including Emily Abbott, Barbara Bell, Ellen Carney, Elizabeth J. Carney, Wanda Gág, Louise Kelly, Clara Mairs, Elizabeth Olds, Alice Tenney, Cleora Wheeler, Lolita Wadman, Lucia Wiley, and Elsa Jemne, a St. Paul artist who was active in Minnesota WPA art projects.

9,146. Jacob, Frances
Papers. 1945?. 11-page item.
Open. No guide.
Minnesota Historical Society, Archives and Manuscripts.
Account by Jacob, a WAC corporal, concerns her experiences with the Los Alamos division of the Manhattan project to develop the atomic bomb from the time she was screened and selected for assignment until her discharge from the hospital after an illness of seven weeks. The illness resulted from the strain of her duties as a technician.

9,147. Jaeger, Luth, and Jaeger, Nanny (Mattson)
Papers. 1874-1933. 4 boxes.
Open. Unpublished guide.
Minnesota Historical Society, Archives and Manuscripts.
Nanny Jaeger (1859-?), who was the wife of Luth Jaeger, was a member of the Political Equality Club of Minneapolis and president of the Scandinavian Woman's Suffrage Association. Correspondence, legislation, reports, and programs include material relating to the fight for woman suffrage, suffrage activities during WWI, and the suffragists' support of the Minneapolis Council of Americanization. Correspondents include suffragist Christabel Pankhurst.

9,148. Jamison, Anne McMeans
Papers. 1780-1932. 4 items.
Open. No guide.
Minnesota Historical Society, Archives and Manuscripts.
Reminiscences written by Jamison (1744-?) in 1824 concerning a journey from Kentucky to New Orleans and then to Pennsylvania. Jamison and her family originally lived in Pennsylvania but moved to Carolina and then Kentucky because of their poor financial state. The family left Kentucky for Natchez, MS, in 1780 and lived for a time at Fort Jefferson on the Ohio River, where Jamison's husband died; she continued the journey with her children and other settlers, arriving in New Orleans in 1782. The party left New Orleans by boat and returned to Pennsylvania in 1783.

9,149. Jerome, Charles Waldron, and Family
Papers. 1855-1966. 4 boxes.
Open. Unpublished guide.
Minnesota Historical Society, Archives and Manuscripts.
Letters to Jerome from his aunt Martha Watson, between Jerome and his wife Eva (Sardeson) Jerome (1875-1966) before and after their marriage, and to Eva Jerome from her family; diaries Eva Jerome kept in 1901, 1902, and 1952; and essays and reports Eva Jerome wrote as a schoolgirl. Correspondence relating to the political and social service organizations in which Eva Jerome was involved deals with such subjects as racial discrimination, religious prejudice, equal opportunity in employment, Minnesota politics, Senator Joseph McCarthy, the Vietnamese conflict, apartheid in Africa, and mental health.

9,150. Jewish Community Relations Council of Minnesota
Records. 1922-74. 31.25 ft.
Open. Unpublished guide.
Minnesota Historical Society, Archives and Manuscripts.
The Council was organized in Minneapolis in the 1930s to investigate the activities of the alleged fascist and communist organizations in Minneapolis and St. Paul and to bring to public attention the anti-Semitic philosophies of these groups. During WWII the Council investigated and attempted to rectify some of the more overt anti-Semitic activities, which included discrimination in housing and restaurants. The Council is also involved in supporting liberal immigration policies, civil rights and civil liberties, the separation of church and state, and interreligious cooperation. Correspondence, reports, articles, clippings, and publications are filed under various subject headings, among them American War Mothers, Minute Women of America, Inc., Mothers of America, Ethel and Julius Rosenberg, Lyrl Clark Von Hyning, [Mrs.] Elizabeth Dilling, and Ruth Gage Colby, who was president of the Minnesota Save the Children Federation.

9,151. Jewish Family and Children's Service of Minneapolis
Records. 1910-63. 5 boxes.
Open. Unpublished guide.
Minnesota Historical Society, Archives and Manuscripts.
This organization was founded in 1910 as the Associated Jewish Charities of Minneapolis "to collect and distribute funds and to administer property for the benefit of Jewish sponsored charitable and educational activities and to assume custody and supervision of dependent children." Articles of incorporation; constitution; bylaws; annual reports; minutes of the board of directors, the executive committee, subcommittees, and annual meetings; financial reports; correspondence; individual relief and social work cases; brochures; clippings; and other organizational records. Also includes articles of incorporation of the Jewish Sheltering Home for Children, which was founded in 1918.

9,152. Johnson, Agnes
Papers. 1948. 2 items.
Open. No guide.
Minnesota Historical Society, Archives and Manuscripts.
A fictionalized account by [Mrs. David] Johnson (1896-) of the pioneer experiences of the Peter G. and Emma Johnson family concerns their migration from Galesburg, IL, where Agnes Johnson was

born, to Fridham, near Little Falls, MN, in 1908; lumbering activities in the Little Falls area; the topography of the area; construction of pioneer homes and churches; mail facilities; crops; and community activities. Although Daniels is the name Johnson uses for this family, it is her own family she is describing.

9,153. Johnson High School
Records. Ca. 1936-37. 1 box.
Open. Unpublished guide.
Minnesota Historical Society, Archives and Manuscripts.
Studies made by the National Youth Administration about students at Johnson High School in St. Paul include an analysis of questionnaires to determine the nature of and amount of time spent by students on recreation, work, sleep, clubs, and organizations and an analysis of nationalities, the average girl's expenses while attending Johnson, and the percentage of failures for senior high students.

9,154. Johnson, Lucia Beckius
Papers. 1963. 2 items.
Open. No guide.
Minnesota Historical Society, Archives and Manuscripts.
Account by Johnson (ca. 1893-) of the emigration to the US from Luxembourg in 1855 of the family of her grandparents Michael and Cecelia (Hammer) Beckius. The Beckius family settled in Sand Creek Township, Scott County, MN. Peter and Hanna Molitor, who were the parents of Johnson's mother Mary Molitor, also came to Minnesota in 1855 and settled in Nicollet County near St. Peter. Johnson describes family relationships, pioneer life, cloth making, farming methods, schools, weather, animals, and game. Also includes Johnson's reminiscences of county fairs held in Cass County, MN, the first of which was held at Sylvan Lake in 1898.

9,155. Johnson, Magnus
Papers. 1923-41. 4.25 ft.
Open. Unpublished guide.
Minnesota Historical Society, Archives and Manuscripts.
Johnson (1871-1936), a Swedish immigrant and Progressive farmer, served as Minnesota state representative and senator, a Nonpartisan League candidate for governor, US senator from Minnesota in 1923, and then US congressman from 1932 to 1934. Correspondence from constituents during the depression concerns New Deal legislation, economic issues, regulatory measures, and requests for government assistance. Correspondents include Isabella Greenway, a congresswoman from Arizona.

9,156. Johnston, Caroline Gale
Papers. 1951. 19-page item.
Open. No guide.
Minnesota Historical Society, Archives and Manuscripts.
Reminiscences by [Mrs. George H.] Johnston (1874-?) concerning summers she spent in the Gale family home on Huntington's Point, Lake Minnetonka, in Minnesota. She discusses other families who lived in the area, transportation facilities to Lake Minnetonka, social activities, flowers and animals, homes, and boating on the Lake.

9,157. Jones, Elizabeth McLeod
Papers. Nd. 1 microfilm reel.
Open. Unpublished guide.
Minnesota Historical Society, Archives and Manuscripts.
Reminiscences by [Mrs. Lewis R.] Jones (?-1958), a journalist and newspaper editor, concern the experiences of the McLeod family in editing country newspapers, newspaper equipment and personnel, family and friends, life in small towns, her activities at the Minneapolis School of Art, and her career in journalism.

9,158. Jones, Sarah
Papers. Nd. 9-page item.
Open. No guide.
Minnesota Historical Society, Archives and Manuscripts.
Reminiscences in which [Mrs.] Jones recalls teaching at a country school in New York from 1873 to 1875, her marriage, farming in New York from 1876 to 1881, her trip to Dodge Center, MN, in 1881 and to Waubay in Dakota Territory the following year, and life on a Dakota homestead.

9,159. Judd, Walter Henry
Papers. 1918-62. 212 boxes.
Access restricted. No guide.
Minnesota Historical Society, Archives and Manuscripts.
Correspondence, speeches, articles, campaign files, and printed matter of Judd (1898-), a physician who was a medical missionary to China from 1925 to 1937, a lecturer on China and the Far East, and a Minnesota congressman from 1942 to 1962. His papers relate to such subjects as American foreign policy, his service on the Foreign Affairs Committee, his support of the Nationalist regime in China, his fear of Communist infiltration, distrust of government intervention into the lives of the people, and his concern over taxation and inflation. Includes articles on caring for the children of working mothers and on the question of whether nurses should be drafted as well as one entitled "Women Will Win If They Work." There is information on Anna Marie Lederer [Mrs. Julius] Rosenberg and on the congressional campaigns of Judd against Marcella Fitzpatrick [Mrs. Starr] Killen. Among the correspondents are Gladys Sinclair [Mrs. Wright W.] Brooks, Marie Smorczewska [Mrs. Harry Amos] Bullis, Fleur Fenton [Mrs. Gardner] Cowles, Oveta Culp [Mrs. William Pettus] Hobby, Elizabeth Kenny, Mary Kyle, and Cornelia (Bryce) [Mrs. Gifford] Pinchot.

9,160. Kellogg, Frank Billings
Papers. 1890-1942. 54 microfilm reels.
Open. Published guide.
Minnesota Historical Society, Archives and Manuscripts.
Kellogg (1856-1937) was US senator from Minnesota from 1917 to 1923, ambassador to England in 1924 and 1925, secretary of state from 1925 to 1929, and judge on the World Court from 1930 to 1935. Correspondence of Kellogg from his wife Clara Cook Kellogg (1861-1942) regarding family news and social engagements; with his sister Jean Austin; with his niece Jean Austin [Mrs. Seabury] Stanton, who writes about her adjustments after contracting polio in 1924, coping with paralysis, and meeting Franklin Roosevelt during treatment; with Mrs. Ogden Reid, a journalist; and from the Women's International League for Peace and Freedom about the Kellogg-Briand Pact of 1927. See Deborah K. Neubeck, *Guide to a Microfilm Edition of the Frank B. Kellogg Papers* (St. Paul: Minnesota Historical Society, 1978).

9,161. Kennedy, Anna
Papers. 1896-1904. 6 items.
Open. Unpublished guide.
Minnesota Historical Society, Archives and Manuscripts.
Letters in which Kennedy (?-1949) describes to her mother life and weather conditions while she was teaching in Melrose, MN, and later while she was studying physiography at the University of Minnesota.

9,162. Kenny, Sister Elizabeth
Papers. 1942-58. 46 items.
Open. Unpublished guide.
Minnesota Historical Society, Archives and Manuscripts.
Sister Kenny (1886-1952) was an Australian-born nurse whose research work on infantile paralysis brought about a new concept of treatment. She came to the US in 1940 to present her concepts on the disease. Correspondence between Sister Kenny and officials of the Elizabeth Kenny Institute and the Sister Elizabeth Kenny Foundation, both located in Minneapolis, and reports, articles, and memoranda relating to Sister Kenny's method of treating infantile paralysis, the Institute, the Foundation, the allotment of funds to various centers practicing the Kenny method, publicity, and tributes to Kenny.

9,163. Kenwood Monday Club
Records. 1931-36. 1 vol.
Open. Unpublished guide.
Minnesota Historical Society, Archives and Manuscripts.
Minutes, treasurer's reports, and attendance records of this women's study club in Minneapolis.

9,164. Klestadt, Annie
Papers. 1948. 8-page item.
Open. No guide.
Minnesota Historical Society, Archives and Manuscripts.
Speech that Klestadt gave to the New World Club in 1948 concerns Jewish refugees who fled to Shanghai, social life and customs of the Chinese, and treatment of refugees by the Chinese.

9,165. Ladies Aid, Jewish Congregation
Records. 1908-35. 3 folders.
Open. Unpublished guide.
Minnesota Historical Society, Archives and Manuscripts.
Minute book and account books of this women's ethnic aid organization in Virginia, MN, on the Iron Range.

9,166. Ladies Christian Union of the City of St. Paul
Records. 1867-1937. 2 boxes.
Open. Unpublished guide.
Minnesota Historical Society, Archives and Manuscripts.
The Union was founded in 1867 by Harriet E. Bishop and other Protestant women of the city to provide homes for the homeless, but also to aid widows, the fatherless, and persons in prison and "to afford protection to young persons exposed to contagion from the moral evils that are rife in society." The name was changed many times and in 1935 became the Protestant Home of St. Paul. Proposed amendments to bylaws, minute books, correspondence, accounts, manager's expense book, resolutions, lists of residents of the Home and women admitted to the Home, lists of officers and board members, a register of children adopted between 1883 and 1887, an inventory of property, and a daily record.

9,167. Ladies of the Grand Army of the Republic, Department of Minnesota
Records. 1893-1924. 1 box.
Open. Unpublished guide.
Minnesota Historical Society, Archives and Manuscripts.
Minutes of meetings and proceedings of annual conventions of the organization's Minnesota department, which were kept by [Mrs.] May A. Dennis, past president and historian of the Department.

9,168. Ladies of the Grand Army of the Republic Monument Association
Records. Nd. 1 vol.
Open. Unpublished guide.

Minnesota Historical Society, Archives and Manuscripts.
Volume contains a history of the organization and a list of members and officers.

9,169. Langlie, Dorothy (Hatch)
Papers. 1963. 69-page item.
Open. No guide.
Minnesota Historical Society, Archives and Manuscripts.
Reminiscences of [Mrs. Theos A.] Langlie (1902-?), who was born in Dell Rapids, SD, concern her childhood in St. Louis Park, then a small town on the outskirts of Minneapolis where her father was superintendent of schools; her love of music; her grandparents' farm in North Dakota; church services; holidays; social clubs and musical events in Minneapolis; family activities; WWI activities; the University of Minnesota, which she and her brother Lloyd Hatch attended; her career as a violinist; and her marriage to Langlie.

9,170. Lawton, Helen Fuller
Papers. 1906-36. 1 box.
Open. Unpublished guide.
Minnesota Historical Society, Archives and Manuscripts.
A sculptor, [Mrs. Harry C.] Lawton (1895-) was a student of sculptor Lorado Taft. Letters that Taft wrote from Chicago to Helen Fuller about her work, family news, and the progress of his work; letters in which Taft's wife Ada (Bartlett) Taft congratulated Fuller on the births of her children and thanked her for her help during the Tafts' visit to the Twin Cities; a post card from the Art Institute of Chicago announcing to Fuller that her work *Emma* had been accepted for exhibition; photos; and clippings concerning the stage career of Emily Taft, a daughter of Lorado Taft, who married Paul H. Douglas, a US senator from Illinois. Also includes clippings on the work of Kathleen Robinson, another of Lorado Taft's students; wedding announcements of Lorado Taft's daughters; and a brochure of the St. Paul School of Fine Arts which contains reproductions of works by Helen Fuller.

9,171. League of Minnesota Poets
Records. Nd. 2 bacases.
Open. Unpublished guide.
Minnesota Historical Society, Archives and Manuscripts.
Scrapbooks containing biographical sketches, published and unpublished poems, and pictures of Minnesota poets, including more than 300 women.

9,172. LeDuc, William Gates, and Family
Papers. 1791-1941. 57.5 ft.
Open. No guide.
Minnesota Historical Society, Archives and Manuscripts.
Correspondence, diaries, account books, scrapbooks, and other papers of the LeDuc and Gardiner families. The LeDucs were territorial settlers in Hastings, MN.

9,173. LeDuc, William Gates, and Family
Papers. 1850s-1927. 3 folders.
Open. Unpublished guide.
Minnesota Historical Society, Archives and Manuscripts.
Papers of the LeDucs, who were early territorial settlers in Hastings, MN, include diplomas, certificates, and plans, sketches, and drawings by Alice Sumner LeDuc (1868-1962).

9,174. Leekley, Richard
Papers. 1939-40. 1 box.
Open. Unpublished guide.
Minnesota Historical Society, Archives and Manuscripts.
Correspondence relating to a rough draft of Leekley's manuscript history of the Farmer-Labor party. Includes letters from many Farmer-Labor leaders, among them Susie (Williamson) [Mrs. Olaf] Stageberg.

9,175. Lemberg, Lauri
Papers. Ca. 1920-68. 3 boxes.
Open. Unpublished guide.
Minnesota Historical Society, Archives and Manuscripts.
Lemberg (1887-1965), a printer, journalist, playwright, and theater director, emigrated from Finland to the US in 1903 and moved to Duluth, MN, in 1913, where he was active in cultural organizations sponsored by the Finnish Socialist party. His wife Sigrid Lemberg operated a booking service for Finnish language plays from 1920 to 1946 with him, worked as a translator in the Duluth courts, and was a leader in Finnish-American cultural activities and in the Finnish women's branch of the Masonic order. Includes ledgers listing plays rented to drama clubs by the Lembergs from 1922 to 1963, a biographical sketch of the Lembergs from *Siértokanson Kalenteri* (1958), and a biographical sketch of their daughter Rose (Lemberg) Salmelin.

9,176. Leonard, William Huntington, and Family
Papers. 1843-1955. 1 box and 15 items.
Open. Unpublished guide.
Minnesota Historical Society, Archives and Manuscripts.
Papers of Leonard (1825-1907), an 1853 graduate of Yale Medical School who practiced medicine in Minneapolis from 1855 until 1907, include a record of his marriage to Jane Preston in 1853; a prescription book with recipes for old cures, ointments, and extracts; and a volume of obstetrical records containing names and birthplaces of parents, the date labor commenced, sex of child, and comments on the birth. Also includes a medical scrapbook identifying birthplace, sex, occupation, and marital status of persons on whom autopsies were performed and a summary of the autopsies performed by William and Jane Leonard's son William Edwin Leonard (1855-1935), an 1879 graduate of the Hahnemann Medical College in Philadelphia who became a Minneapolis physican and professor in the college of homeopathic medicine and surgery at the University of Minnesota.

9,177. LeSueur, Arthur
Papers. Ca. 1910-54. 6 ft.
Open. Unpublished guide.
Minnesota Historical Society, Archives and Manuscripts.
LeSueur (1867-1950), a socialist, was active in the Nonpartisan League and the Farmer-Labor party; he was married to Marion Wharton LeSueur (1877-1954), also a socialist. Marion LeSueur was head of the English department at People's College in Fort Scott, KS; educational director in Minnesota for the National Nonpartisan League in 1917; and a candidate for US Senate in 1952. She also was active in the Democratic-Farmer-Labor and Progressive parties. Included with correspondence, clippings, and printed matter of Arthur LeSueur are a few items relating to his wife.

9,178. Lewis, Edwin J.
Papers. 1889-1926. 1 box.
Open. Unpublished guide.
Minnesota Historical Society, Archives and Manuscripts.
Papers of Lewis (1848-1926), a doctor in Sauk Centre, MN, and the father of author Sinclair Lewis, include cash account books of monthly household income and expenditures and a notebook in which Lewis kept an account of patients he saw each day, including obstetrical cases, with information on their period of expected confinement and the actual time and date of birth.

9,179. Lewis, Henry, and Family
Papers. 1829-1965. 2 boxes.
Open. Unpublished guide.
Minnesota Historical Society, Archives and Manuscripts.
Lewis (1819-1904) was an English-born artist who was primarily interested in the Mississippi River as a subject for his painting. He served as US consular agent in Düsseldorf, Germany, from 1867 to 1884. Includes a letter by his wife Marie Jones Lewis (?-1891) from Düsseldorf, a letter to Henry Lewis from Mary (Henderson) [Mrs. Seth] Eastman, articles from *Arthur's Home Magazine* (1853), and correspondence of and research material on Lewis and his family gathered by Bertha Lion Heilbron, a member of the Historical Society staff, for *The Valley of the Mississippi Illustrated,* which she edited.

9,180. Lewis, Russell
Papers. Nd. 94 ft.
Open. No guide.
Minnesota Historical Society, Archives and Manuscripts.
Papers relating to cooperatives, including Midland Cooperatives and health cooperatives such as Group Health. Includes files of Dorothy Jacobson and of credit unions.

9,181. Lindbergh, Charles Augustus
Papers. 1900-53. 3 boxes.
Access restricted. Unpublished guide.
Minnesota Historical Society, Archives and Manuscripts.
Correspondence, legal papers, and clippings of Lindbergh (1858-1924), a lawyer and congressman from Minnesota from 1907 to 1917; he also owned real estate in Florida and Minnesota. Includes Lindbergh's correspondence with his wife Evangeline Lodge (Land) Lindbergh (ca. 1875-1954) and with his son Charles Augustus Lindbergh, Jr. (1902-74) concerning family matters and personal finances.

9,182. Linnea Society
Records. 1904-18. 114 pp.
Open. Unpublished guide.
Minnesota Historical Society, Archives and Manuscripts.
Minute book and financial information in Swedish of the Society, which was organized by Swedish women of St. Paul to provide homes for young single Scandinavian women and elderly women. The group remained in existence until 1918.

9,183. Livingston, Britania J.
Papers. 1925. 5 pp.
Open. No guide.
Minnesota Historical Society, Archives and Manuscripts.
Notes on pioneer life in Martin County, MN, in ca. 1870 and a poem by Livingston, whose letters were published in a series of articles in the *Fairmont Daily Sentinel* in 1925.

9,184. Local Historical Societies of Minnesota
Records. Nd. 11 boxes.
Open. Unpublished guide.
Minnesota Historical Society, Archives and Manuscripts.
Constitution, annual reports, minutes of meetings, correspondence, and membership lists dating from the 19th and 20th centuries of local and county historical societies, many of which were staffed by women volunteers.

9,185. Longley, Alfred, and Longley, Mary Ann Clark
Papers. 1832-69. 1 box.
Open. Unpublished guide.
Minnesota Historical Society, Archives and Manuscripts.
Mary Longley (1813-69) was born in Hawley, MA, and taught school in Bethlehem, IN, before

marrying Stephen Return Riggs (1812-83) in 1837. She and her husband were missionaries to the Dakota nation during the 1840s and 1850s. Correspondence between Mary Ann and Stephen Riggs reflecting New England religious and moral attitudes and love letters between Mary Ann Riggs's brother Alfred Longley (?-1851) and Julia Read, whom he later married.

9,186. Lord, Lucy A.
Papers. 1838-43. 2 vols.
Open. No guide.
Minnesota Historical Society, Archives and Manuscripts.
Practice books for bookkeeping, including a daybook and ledger of a general store for 1838 with notations at the end for 1843.

9,187. Lovett, Beatrice Russel
Papers. 1960. 3 items.
Open. No guide.
Minnesota Historical Society, Archives and Manuscripts.
Reminiscences of Jane Addams and Hull-House by Lovett (1898-), who lived at Hull-House for a number of years; a copy of a proclamation of Jane Addams Month by Minnesota governor Orville L. Freeman; and a clipping about Lovett.

9,188. Lowe, Mrs. E. L.
Papers. Nd. 9 items.
Open. No guide.
Minnesota Historical Society, Archives and Manuscripts.
Brief sketches of women's clubs in Anoka County, MN.

9,189. Lund, Rhoda
Papers. 1958-73. 8 ft.
Access restricted. No guide.
Minnesota Historical Society, Archives and Manuscripts.
[Mrs. Russell] Lund of Edina, MN, was a Republican party activist during the 1950s and 1960s, serving as Republican State Chairwoman and national committeewoman. Correspondence files; research, subject, campaign, convention, and speakers files relating primarily to activities of the Minnesota Republican party and to the 1972 campaign to reelect Richard Nixon as President; and 1968 files of the Minnesota Republican Task Forces.

9,190. Lyngblomsten Retirement Center, St. Paul
Records. 1913-16. 1 item.
Open. Unpublished guide.
Minnesota Historical Society, Archives and Manuscripts.
Minute book kept in Norwegian by [Mrs.] Laura Bratager and [Mrs. Jens] Johnson, secretaries of the Residents Association of this Norwegian Lutheran retirement home.

9,191. Macalester Presbyterian Church
Records. 1889-1927. 1 box and 3 vols.
Open. Unpublished guide.
Minnesota Historical Society, Archives and Manuscripts.
Minutes and treasurer's reports of the Ladies Aid and minutes and printed programs of the Woman's Home and Foreign Missionary Society of this St. Paul church.

9,192. McCarthy, Abigail (Quigley)
Papers. 1920s-70. 51 ft.
Access restricted. No guide.
Minnesota Historical Society, Archives and Manuscripts.
Correspondence, a taped interview, scrapbooks, and other papers of [Mrs. Eugene] McCarthy relate to her involvement in politics, ecumenism and other religious movements, women's movements, and activities at the College of St. Catherine in St. Paul. Includes information on Women for McCarthy, the Church Women United, the 1968 presidential campaign in which her husband was a candidate, St. John's University, and the writing of her autobiographical book *Private Faces, Public Places.*

9,193. McCarthy, Eugene
Papers. 1948-70. 390 ft.
Access restricted. Unpublished guide.
Minnesota Historical Society, Archives and Manuscripts.
Papers of McCarthy, a US senator from Minnesota, include a scrapbook and press clippings of his wife Abigail (Quigley) McCarthy, an author and member of the board of trustees at the College of St. Catherine in St. Paul.

9,194. McConnell, Jennie A.
Papers. Nd. 1 vol.
Open. No guide.
Minnesota Historical Society, Archives and Manuscripts.
Volume on educational practices handwritten by McConnell includes discussion of the preliminary activities of a teacher in a new school, suggested lesson plans, the purposes of education, discipline, qualifications of a teacher, recitations, and philosophies of educators from the 1600s to the 1800s.

9,195. McDaniel, Orianna
Papers. 1946. 3 items.
Open. No guide.
Minnesota Historical Society, Archives and Manuscripts.
McDaniel (1872-?), a bacteriologist, was born in New Hampshire and attended the Michigan Medical School in 1890. After interning at Northwestern Hospital in Minneapolis, she became the first woman employee of the Minnesota department of health when she was hired by Charles N. Hewitt in 1896 as a bacteriologist. Notes on an interview with McDaniel conducted for the Public Health Project and a clipping about her retirement from the department of health in 1946.

9,196. McDonough, John Joseph
Papers. 1940-48. 2 boxes.
Open. Unpublished guide.
Minnesota Historical Society, Archives and Manuscripts.
McDonough (1895-1962), a Minnesota legislator from 1924 to 1934, served as chief clerk of the Minnesota house of representatives in 1937. Scrapbooks of clippings relate to events that occurred during his administration as mayor of St. Paul from 1940 to 1948 and to women serving in the armed forces, housing, school financing, teachers' salaries, the establishment of the Fair Employment Practices Commission, and city employees' salaries.

9,197. McGuire, Arthur James, and McGuire, Marie Frances (McCormick)
Papers. 1896-1964. 5.5 ft.
Open. Unpublished guide.
Minnesota Historical Society, Archives and Manuscripts.
[Mrs. Arthur] McGuire (1878-1964) was a teacher, an unsuccessful Democratic candidate for Minnesota secretary of state in 1950, and an accredited observer at the UN founding conference in 1945. She was active in the LWV and other women's organizations, the Democratic party, and organizations to promote world peace. Her correspondence, speeches, notes, and clippings relate to the New Deal Homemakers Cooperative, the LWV, the League of Nations Association of Minnesota, the Woman's Centennial Congress, the Conference on the Cause and Cure of War, her candidacy for secretary of state, and her work with the Agricultural Adjustment Administration and the Office of Price Stabilization. Also includes her desk diaries for 1928 and 1951 to 1952, an account book of the Arthur McGuire family for 1914 to 1915 containing clippings about Marie McGuire, and correspondence regarding the estate of Anna Vadnais.

9,198. Mackay, Constance D'Arcy
Papers. 1903-17. 1 vol. and 74 items.
Open. Unpublished guide.
Minnesota Historical Society, Archives and Manuscripts.
Constance Mackay [Mrs. Richard] Holt, a playwright, was born in St. Paul and attended school there and from 1903 to 1904 at Boston University. Letters from Mackay in St. Paul, Boston, and New York to Allison McKibben of St. Paul concerning her studies at Boston University, her literary career, production of her plays, and social events, as well as a volume of her plays, including *The Beau of Both,* which was produced by the Little Theatre of St. Paul in 1917 with Sinclair Lewis as a cast member.

9,199. Maher and Mates Family
Papers. 1894-1957. 75 items.
Open. Unpublished guide.
Minnesota Historical Society, Archives and Manuscripts.
Theater programs, playbills, clippings, and other papers relating to the theatrical careers of actress Bessye Maher Mates and actor Harry James Mates (1879-).

9,200. Manahan, James, and Family
Papers. 1883-1935. 3.75 ft.
Open. Unpublished guide.
Minnesota Historical Society, Archives and Manuscripts.
Manahan (1866-1932) was a lawyer in Minnesota and Nebraska and a congressman from Minnesota from 1913 to 1915. He was a progressive Democrat until 1908, when he became a progressive Republican. Correspondence of Manahan with Jeannette Rankin and others; biographical reminiscences of Manahan by his daughter Kathryn (Manahan) Hoxmeier (1896-), a St. Paul attorney; wedding announcements, including that of James and Mary Manahan; and an article on the Nonpartisan League by Kathryn Manahan.

9,201. Martin, Jenova
Papers. 1910-12. 2 items.
Open. No guide.
Minnesota Historical Society, Archives and Manuscripts.
Documents relating to the appointment of [Mrs.] Jenova Martin as delegate to the Minnesota Conservation and Agricultural Development Congress and to her activities in support of woman suffrage.

9,202. Mason, William F., and Family
Papers. 1854-1935. 10 boxes, 1 bacase, and 1 oversize item.
Open. Unpublished guide.
Minnesota Historical Society, Archives and Manuscripts.
Mason (1837-1908) was a St. Paul businessman. Papers of his daughter Rachel Mason, a teacher, include her diaries for 1883, 1889, and 1922 to 1931 concerning her social life in St. Paul; her personal expense account and household account book; her income tax papers and those of her brother Alfred Mason; and her plan book and workbook samples for the kindergarten classes. Also includes a diary of Rebecca McHarg for 1873 to 1882, which contains descriptions of household tasks and social life in Montgomery County, PA, and account books listing household expenses and profits from rents.

9,203. Maternity Hospital
Records. 1887-1956. 3 boxes.
Open. Unpublished guide.
Minnesota Historical Society, Archives and Manuscripts.
The Hospital was founded in Minneapolis in 1886 by Martha George (Rogers) Ripley, a physician, to care for unwed mothers and for married women who were unable to afford prenatal and childbirth care. In 1955 the name of the Hospital was changed to Ripley Hospital for Women; the Hospital remained in existence until 1957. Annual reports, minutes of the board of directors and of the Sarah L. Lara Auxiliary, correspondence, statistical reports, a record of donations, a list of Martha Ripley's medical books, a scrapbook, and clippings.

9,204. Mattson, Hans, and Family
Papers. 1855-1939. 3 boxes and 16 oversize items.
Open. Unpublished guide.
Minnesota Historical Society, Archives and Manuscripts.
Mattson (1832-93), a Swedish immigrant, served as Minnesota secretary of state from 1870 to 1872 and 1887 to 1891, as secretary of the state board of immigration, as US consul general in Calcutta, India, and as editor of *Stats Tidning* in Minneapolis. Contains Mattson's letters to his wife Kjersti (Perrson) Mattson (1837-1911) in Red Wing, MN, describing his Civil War experiences and letters he wrote to his wife and children while he was in Calcutta from 1881 to 1883, including one concerning his daughter Nanny's engagement to Luth Jaeger. Also includes a certificate of dismissal from the Scandinavian Evangelical Lutheran Church of Red Wing to Hans and Kjersti Mattson as well as an autograph book and a scrapbook kept by Nanny (Mattson) Jaeger (1859-?), a suffragist, which contains information on her campaign for the school board and on the suffrage movement.

9,205. Mayo, Charles Edwin
Papers. 1851-98. 1 box.
Open. Unpublished guide.
Minnesota Historical Society, Archives and Manuscripts.
Mayo (1827-99) operated a hardware store and was employed at the US Customs Office in St. Paul. Includes a handwritten literary paper and newsletter "The Penny Royal Gazette," which was edited by Mayo and his sister S. Mayo from 1856 to 1858; "The Gazette" contains information on personal matters, weather, arrivals of steamboats, births, marriages, deaths, the legislature, fires, accidents, lyceum meetings, and the founding of the YMCA and the St. Paul Public Library. Also includes three issues of "The Home Messenger," which was similar to the "Gazette" and edited by S. Mayo in Brewster, MA, in 1856 and 1857.

9,206. Meighen, John Felix Dryden, and Family
Papers. 1852-1960. 40 boxes and 1 vol.
Open. No guide.
Minnesota Historical Society, Archives and Manuscripts.
Meighen (1877-1957), who was born in Spring Valley, MN, practiced law from 1901 to 1957, was active in Democratic party politics, and was judge of the 10th judicial district of Minnesota from 1921 to 1923. In 1917 he married Katherine Trusdell [Mrs. William A.] Morin (1873-1968), a widow with two children from her first marriage. Notebook of Katherine Meighen containing information on farm land and ownership, probate proceedings of Joseph P. Meighen and Thomas V. Meighen, and a record of liberty bonds, bank accounts, and a mortgage; a wedding journal of John Meighen consisting of a daily diary, photos and calling cards with handwritten captions, notes, clippings, and mementos documenting a wedding trip to the Caribbean; and volumes of judicial decisions made by John Meighen, many of which relate to divorce, rape, carnal knowledge, and wills.

9,207. Mendenhall, Richard Junius
Papers. 1856-65. 1 box.
Open. Unpublished guide.
Minnesota Historical Society, Archives and Manuscripts.
Includes a diary that Mendenhall (1828-1906) and his wife Abby Swift Mendenhall (1832-?) kept during the years 1856 to 1861; they discuss Minnesota customs, land surveying, free blacks in Minnesota, the state fair of 1860, the Friends Library Association, Thanksgiving, the 4th of July, early Minneapolis, and Quakers in Minnesota.

9,208. Merritt, Callie
Papers. 1952. 14-page item.
Open. No guide.
Minnesota Historical Society, Archives and Manuscripts.
[Miss] Merritt (1891-), a resident of Duluth, MN, is the granddaughter of Lucien Merritt, one of the Merritt brothers who discovered the Mesabi iron range. Transcript of a speech Merritt gave during a meeting of the St. Louis County Historical Society about early settlers in Oneota (Duluth), the establishment of the first school in the area in 1856, and the six school districts that were formed in the Duluth area in 1858. Also includes extracts from a school district record book with names of early schoolteachers and lists of families with school-aged children.

9,209. Metro Clean Air Committee
Records. Ca. 1967-74. 3.75 ft.
Open. No guide.
Minnesota Historical Society, Archives and Manuscripts.
Minutes, correspondence, and other records relating to the work of this organization concerned about air pollution in the Minneapolis-St. Paul metropolitan area.

9,210. Mexican-American Community, St. Paul
Collection. 1934-75. 1 bacase.
Open. No guide.
Minnesota Historical Society, Archives and Manuscripts.
Includes invitations to weddings, baptisms, and other ceremonies in the Mexican-American community; proposals for a bilingual-bicultural education program in the St. Paul public school system; and records of the Guadalupe Area Project, the Mi Cultura Day Care Center, Our Lady of Guadalupe Catholic Church, and Torre de San Miguel Homes, Inc., all of which are located in St. Paul.

9,211. Michelet, Simon Thenistrup, and Family
Papers. 1879-1943. 3 boxes.
Open. Unpublished guide.
Minnesota Historical Society, Archives and Manuscripts.
Michelet (1871-1956) was secretary to Senator Knute Nelson of Minnesota from 1918 to 1923 and founder of the National Get-Out-The-Vote-Club. Correspondence relating to the registration of women voters in 1928 and data concerning the political activities of the LWV and other groups.

9,212. Michener, Carroll Kinsey
Papers. 1858-1970. 3.5 ft.
Open. Unpublished guide.
Minnesota Historical Society, Archives and Manuscripts.
Family correspondence of Ida Blakeslee Michener (1862-?), who was the daughter of territorial settlers in a small southern Minnesota town and the wife of legislator and judge Daniel K. Michener, concerning her teaching experiences; letters of Sarah "Sally" Spensley (1897-) to Carroll Kinsey Michener (1885-1970) and a diary of their wedding trip to South America in 1921; letters to Carroll Michener from Pauline Shore, a nurse who traveled with him when he became ill after leaving China in 1913; a diary Sally Michener kept during a trip to England and Scotland in 1950; a thesis she wrote about newspaperwomen; book reviews she wrote; and a pamphlet by Carroll Michener about the lives of Daniel Michener and Ida Blakeslee Michener.

9,213. Mickay, Elizabeth Bouchea
Papers. 1856-75. 2-page item.
Open. No guide.
Minnesota Historical Society, Archives and Manuscripts.
Account by Mickay of girlhood experiences in and around Hudson, WI.

9,214. Mills, Lucius D.
Papers. Nd. 1 vol.
Open. No guide.
Minnesota Historical Society, Archives and Manuscripts.
Reminiscences of pioneer life in Minnesota and other memoirs by Mills (1848-1936) and members of his family concern their life in Blue Earth County, MN, where they were among the first to settle. Includes photos of the family, their home, and surroundings and blueprints of their log cabin and sorghum shanty. Also includes General James Heaton Baker's memorial to [Mrs.] Permelia L. Mills and an article about Mrs. James H. Baker, a lifelong friend of Permelia Mills, which contains descriptions of the old Mills Hotel between Mankato, MN, and Garden City and the entertainment there.

9,215. Minneapolis Association Opposed to the Further Extension of Suffrage to Women
Records. Nd. 5 pp.
Open. Unpublished guide.
Minnesota Historical Society, Archives and Manuscripts.
Constitution and bylaws of the Association.

9,216. Minneapolis Audubon Society
Records. 1915-62. 14 items.
Open. Unpublished guide.
Minnesota Historical Society, Archives and Manuscripts.
Records of the Society, established in 1915 as an affiliate of the National Audubon Society which was founded in 1914 and comprised mainly of women, include a biographical sketch of Frances Stillman [Mrs. Gaylord] Davidson; remarks made at a memorial service in 1961 for Frances Andrews; histories and recollections of the Society by Mrs. R. H. Wells, Mrs. I. A. Liepient, and Gustav Swenson; and lists of presidents, honorary and life members, contributions, donations, memorials, and gifts.

9,217. Minneapolis Authors' Club
Records. 1894. 1 vol.
Open. Unpublished guide.
Minnesota Historical Society, Archives and Manuscripts.
Manuscripts of poems by Club members, 10 (or, one-half) of whom were women. A number of the poems concern temperance.

9,218. Minneapolis B'nai B'rith Women's Chapter 267
Records. 1939-63. 1 box and 3 vols.
Open. Unpublished guide.
Minnesota Historical Society, Archives and Manuscripts.
The purpose of this Minneapolis women's auxiliary to the Independent Order of B'nai B'rith was to engage in religious, civic, fraternal, educational, and social activities in the Jewish community. Founded in 1939, its name was changed in 1949 to the Bertha Rutz Fiterman Chapter. Scrapbooks and printed material relate to activities of the chapter

during WWII with the American National Red Cross, Russian war relief, war bond drives, and aid to servicemen; the group's role in organizing the Hillel Foundation on the University of Minnesota campus; its aid to postwar refugees; and its support of the formation of the country of Israel.

9,219. Minneapolis Committee on Resettlement of Japanese-Americans
Records. 1942-44. 2 boxes.
Open. Unpublished guide.
Minnesota Historical Society, Archives and Manuscripts.
Sponsored by the Federal Council of Churches of Christ in America, the YWCA, the YMCA, and the War Relocation Authority, the Committee helped find employment for loyal Japanese-Americans (Nisei) who were evacuated from their Pacific Coast homes. Correspondence, application forms giving information on Nisei evacuees, and progress reports. Correspondence is primarily between the Committee's secretary Genevieve F. [Mrs. Lawrence D.] Steefel and Nisei seeking employment, but it also includes correspondence of Committee members with US officials and the War Relocation Authority.

9,220. Minneapolis Friends Meeting
Records. 1860-1964. 3.75 ft.
Access restricted. Unpublished guide.
Minnesota Historical Society, Archives and Manuscripts.
Includes minutes of meetings of women Friends, ca. 1861-94; of the Minneapolis Preparative Meeting of Women Friends, 1863-83; of the Woman's Missionary Society, 1914-30; and of the Margaret Fell Society, 1940-42. Also includes Sunday school records. The collection is also available on microfilm.

9,221. Minneapolis Friends Meeting
Records. 1938-73. 10 boxes and 4 bacases.
Open. Unpublished guide.
Minnesota Historical Society, Archives and Manuscripts.
Minutes of the Minneapolis Society of Friends Women, 1955-61; a history of the Minneapolis Meeting that Alexina Gray wrote for the group's centennial in 1963; reports and lists of members of committees; and directories of members of the Minneapolis Meeting, which is affiliated with the Friends United Meeting and worldwide Society of Friends.

9,222. Minneapolis Humane Society
Records. 1905-28. 37 boxes and 8 vols.
Access restricted. Unpublished guide.
Minnesota Historical Society, Archives and Manuscripts.
Articles of incorporation, constitution, bylaws, annual reports, minutes, financial reports, correspondence, and scrapbooks of the Humane Society and of the Juvenile Protective League, which merged with the Society in 1917 to form the Children's Protective Society. Also includes case records of each person who received aid from the Humane Society, one of whose primary missions was to work with unmarried young mothers and other dependent or delinquent girls.

9,223. Minnesota Congress of Parents and Teachers, Eighth District
Records. 1929-50. 1 box.
Open. Unpublished guide.
Minnesota Historical Society, Archives and Manuscripts.
Minutes of meetings, financial records, budgets, correspondence, conference rules, membership lists, lists of board members, and programs of the Eighth District of the PTA, which consists of Ramsey, Washington, and Dakota counties.

9,224. Minnesota Educational Association
Records. 1861-92. 1 vol.
Open. Unpublished guide.
Minnesota Historical Society, Archives and Manuscripts.
The Association is a teachers' professional organization founded in 1876. Minutes of annual meetings of the Minnesota Teachers Association, 1861-74; financial reports; membership lists; and miscellaneous programs, speeches, and clippings. The Teachers Association was probably a predecessor of MEA.

9,225. Minnesota Equal Franchise League
Records. 1911-17. 1 box and 1 oversize item.
Open. Unpublished guide.
Minnesota Historical Society, Archives and Manuscripts.
Correspondence with the National American Woman Suffrage Association regarding lobbying with congressmen and legislators for woman suffrage and bills before the legislature granting suffrage to women, a list of Minnesota congressmen and their views, and two "traveling campaign kits."

9,226. Minnesota Federation of Business and Professional Women's Clubs, Inc.
Records. 1942-45. 77 pp.
Open. Unpublished guide.
Minnesota Historical Society, Archives and Manuscripts.
Extracts compiled by Elfrida Swenson from reports of the Federation relate to women's activities in WWII.

9,227. Minnesota Federation of Women's Clubs
Records. 1896-1947. 3 boxes and 1 oversize box.
Open. Unpublished guide.
Minnesota Historical Society, Archives and Manuscripts.
Certificate of incorporation, records of the eighth biennial convention in 1906, a register of delegates at annual meetings, memorials to members, and a scrapbook of programs and clippings of the Federation. Also includes minutes and clippings of the Pioneer Workers of the Minnesota Federation of Women's Clubs, 1912-24; minutes of the Iota Study Club of Minneapolis, 1928-45; a history of the Clio Club of Minneapolis; and items pertaining to the celebration of Susan B. Anthony Day from 1941 to 1947.

9,228. Minnesota Federation of Women's Clubs, Fifth District
Records. 1946?. 1 vol.
Open. Unpublished guide.
Minnesota Historical Society, Archives and Manuscripts.
Histories by members of 38 clubs of the fifth district, including study clubs, ethnic organizations, and homemakers' societies.

9,229. Minnesota Historical Society
Records. 1849-99. 14 boxes.
Access restricted. Unpublished guide.
Minnesota Historical Society, Archives and Manuscripts.
Correspondence of the Society includes letters from early residents of Minnesota, among them [Mrs.] Elisabeth Taylor Ayer and Charlotte Ouisconsin (Clark) Van Cleve, who recall the early history of the state.

9,230. Minnesota Historical Society Archives
Records. 1849- . 230 boxes.
Open. Unpublished guide.
Minnesota Historical Society, Archives and Manuscripts.
Records documenting the activities and interests of the Society, which was founded in 1849, include organizational records, correspondence of women who worked for the Society, manuscripts written by women and submitted for publication, and scrapbooks. Includes manuscripts by Elizabeth Taylor [Mrs. Frederick] Ayer, Jeanette Sykes, Mrs. N. D. White, Alice B. Clapp, Marjorie Edgar, Melva Lind, Maude Lindquist, and Frieda Monger. Among the Society's employees represented are Grace Lee Nute, Ethel Virtue, Bertha L. Heilbron, June D. Holmquist, Lucile M. Kane, Rhoda Gilman, A. Hermina Poatgieter, Esther Jerabek, Lila J. Goff, Viki Sand, and Patricia Harpole.

9,231. Minnesota League of Women Voters
Records. 1919-71. 37 boxes, 30 bacases, and 2 items.
Open. Unpublished guide.
Minnesota Historical Society, Archives and Manuscripts.
Constitution; bylaws; articles of incorporation; minutes of meetings of the board of directors, executive committee, and legislative council; financial records; correspondence; reports; speeches; circular mail; news releases; scrapbooks; programs; clippings; and other organizational records of the Minnesota LWV, which was founded in 1919 in Minneapolis. Also includes master's theses by Edna Honoria Akre and Barbara Stuhler on the national and Minnesota LWV and manuscripts about the emergence of the Minnesota LWV from suffrage organizations, which provide biographical information on such leaders as Clara Ueland, Mabeth Hurd Paige, Marguerite Wells, and Ethel Hurd.

9,232. Minnesota Legislature Miscellany
Collection. 1933-39. 2 boxes.
Open. Unpublished guide.
Minnesota Historical Society, Archives and Manuscripts.
Correspondence, resolutions, petitions, copies of legislative bills, and other items, including a resolution from the Hennepin County Farmer-Labor Women's Club supporting the appointment of Marion LeSueur, Florence Cook, and Paul Amidon to the State Board of Education. The three had been accused of communist and socialist sympathies.

9,233. Minnesota Library Association
Records. 1891-1949. 4 boxes and 2 vols.
Open. Unpublished guide.
Minnesota Historical Society, Archives and Manuscripts.
Constitution; a treasurer's book; financial statements; receipts; correspondence; reports, addresses, and programs of annual meetings; resolutions; list of officers; proceedings of annual meetings in 1924, 1940, and 1942 and of the St. Cloud Institute in 1941; and clippings of the MLA, which was founded in 1891. Also includes correspondence, committee reports, press releases, programs of action by libraries in other states, and proceedings of the 1932 Five State Regional Conference of the American Library Association. [Mrs.] Helen McCaine was the first vice-president of the MLA.

9,234. Minnesota Music Teachers' Association, Inc.
Records. 1913-60. 4 boxes.
Open. Unpublished guide.
Minnesota Historical Society, Archives and Manuscripts.
The Association, comprised mainly of women, was founded in 1901 to promote "the true culture of music by the interchange of ideas, to advance the interest of musical art, and to foster professional fraternity." Articles of incorporation, minutes, financial reports, convention proceedings, correspondence, a membership list, a history, examination questions and certificates given to persons applying for associate membership in the organization, and clippings about annual meetings. Correspondents include musicians Hazel Griggs, Lilia MacKinnon, and Mrs. Ernest Lachmund.

9,235. Minnesota Peace Society
Records. 1913-22. 1 box.
Open. Unpublished guide.
Minnesota Historical Society, Archives and Manuscripts.
Minutes, an account book, and correspondence of the Society, which was founded in 1913.

9,236. Minnesota School of Missions
Papers. 1907-34. 1 box.
Open. Unpublished guide.
Minnesota Historical Society, Archives and Manuscripts.
The School, which was founded in 1907, had women of eight denominations as members. Constitution, bylaws, minutes, financial reports, correspondence, programs, and clippings relating to sponsorship of an annual summer school of mission education. The School was also known as the Minnesota Summer School of Missions.

9,237. Minnesota State Advisory Council on Indian Affairs
Records. 1929. 6 pp.
Open. No guide.
Minnesota Historical Society, Archives and Manuscripts.
Minutes of a 1929 meeting of the Council and a report presented to the Council by state senator Peter Sharpe and state representative Harriet H. Weeks on the condition of the Chippewa Indians in Mahnomen County, MN.

9,238. Minnesota Territorial Pioneers Association
Records. 1897-1941. 3 boxes.
Open. Unpublished guide.
Minnesota Historical Society, Archives and Manuscripts.
Membership in the Association is made up of individuals who settled in Minnesota Territory and their descendants. The Minnesota Territorial Pioneer Guild, founded in 1927, was comprised of women and was later incorporated into the Association, which was formerly an all-male group. Bylaws, articles of incorporation, a receipt and minute book, membership rolls and receipt book, scrapbooks of clippings, a catalog of portraits in the Portrait Hall on the state fairgrounds, a volume relating to builders of the log cabin at the fairgrounds, and other records of the Association. Records of the Guild include lists of charter members and Hennepin County, MN, members, a poem by [Mrs.] Helga Treat, and minutes and a scrapbook of the Camp Lincoln Library of Washington County, MN. Also includes biographical sketches of Minnesota pioneers and secretary's reports.

9,239. Minnesota Volunteers for Stevenson-Kefauver, Minneapolis
Records. 1955-57. 2 boxes.
Open. Unpublished guide.
Minnesota Historical Society, Archives and Manuscripts.
Correspondence between state and national volunteers and officers of the Democratic National Committee; brief campaign biographies, including one of Mrs. Hale Boggs; copies of speeches by Adlai Stevenson; a report on the organization and management of national volunteers; news releases; instructions to volunteers; campaign leaflets; questionnaires; a pamphlet relating to issues of the 1956 campaign, prepared by Minnesota Women for Stevenson-Kefauver; a list of supporters; clippings; and other material relating to the Stevenson-Kefauver campaign for President and Vice-President in 1956.

9,240. Minnesota Woman Suffrage Association
Records. 1894-1919. 12 boxes, 1 bacase, and 2 oversize items.
Open. Unpublished guide.
Minnesota Historical Society, Archives and Manuscripts.
The Association, which was established in 1881 and existed until 1919, was affiliated with the National American Woman Suffrage Association. Constitution, articles of incorporation, minutes of meetings, a treasurer's book, accounts, correspondence, lists of members, reports, scrapbooks concerning such events as the suffrage parade in 1914 in Minneapolis and the Mississippi Valley Suffrage Association Convention in 1916, handbills, clippings, and printed material, including biographical sketches of suffragists, data on Minnesota congressmen and legislators, resolutions, articles by Julia B. Nelson, and information about the Minnesota bill for woman suffrage. Also includes records of the Scandinavian Suffrage Association and of the Woman's Suffrage Association of Hennepin County, MN.

9,241. Mitchell, William Bell, and Family
Papers. 1806-1957. 6 boxes, 2 vols., and 8 items.
Open. Unpublished guide.
Minnesota Historical Society, Archives and Manuscripts.
Correspondence and legal papers of the Mitchell, Swisshelm, and Cannon families. Papers of Jane Grey (Cannon) [Mrs. James] Swisshelm (1815-84), a suffragist, newspaper editor, and abolitionist, include letters from Amelia Bloomer and Frances E. Willard concerning Swisshelm's book *Half a Century,* letters from Susan B. Anthony concerning a woman suffrage convention, family letters, letters Swisshelm wrote Mary C. Mitchell about the relief of colored women and children, and legal papers, promissory notes, a scrapbook of clippings, and other papers relating to Swisshelm, the *St. Cloud Democrat,* and her support of John C. Fremont's presidential candidacy. Also includes a short manuscript by Marianne Clark about the first farms and farmers of the Upper Mississippi, autograph books of Elizabeth Ann Cannon (1821-1910) and Emily Whittlesay (1849-1926), a marriage certificate of William B. Mitchell and Emily Whittlesay, and a copy of the *St. Cloud Visiter* (1858).

9,242. Mitchell, William DeWitt, and Family
Papers. 1871-1956. 7 boxes, 1 vol., and 24 items.
Access restricted. Unpublished guide.
Minnesota Historical Society, Archives and Manuscripts.
Correspondence between William Mitchell (1832-1900), associate justice of the Minnesota Supreme Court from 1881 to 1899, and his wife Frances Smith Mitchell. Also includes diaries that Gertrude Bancroft Mitchell (?-1952) kept on a trip to Europe in 1913 with her husband William DeWitt Mitchell (1874-1955), who was solicitor general of the US from 1925 to 1929 and US attorney general from 1929 to 1933, and diaries of a family camping trip to Alberta in 1920, a journey from Duluth, MN, to Buffalo, NY, via the Great Lakes in 1921, a European tour with her sons William and Bancroft in 1928, and a trip to England in 1935 with her husband. Also includes clippings and printed material.

9,243. Monday Literary Club
Records. 1910-35. 1 box.
Open. Unpublished guide.
Minnesota Historical Society, Archives and Manuscripts.
Constitution and minutes of meetings of this women's literary club in St. Paul, which was organized in 1910 as an auxiliary to the East Side Commercial Club.

9,244. Montgomery, Sarah Ann (Purnell)
Papers. 1930. 1 microfilm reel.
Open. No guide.
Minnesota Historical Society, Archives and Manuscripts.
Reminiscences by Montgomery of her childhood days among the Indians in Minnesota from 1856 to 1862.

9,245. Moody, Kathryn Stoner Hicks
Papers. 1960. 41-page item.
Open. No guide.
Minnesota Historical Society, Archives and Manuscripts.
Narrative in which [Mrs. Lowell H.] Moody, the granddaughter of Benjamin Stoner, describes the experiences of the Stoner family on their trip from Pennsylvania to Shelbyville, MN, in 1856, population and industries in Minnesota in the 1850s, pioneer life, schools, homes, food, and the Sioux outbreak.

9,246. Morehouse, Lewis Cass
Papers. 1894-1918. 1 box.
Open. Unpublished guide.
Minnesota Historical Society, Archives and Manuscripts.
Letters to Morehouse, a Methodist minister in Minnesota and Alberta, Canada, from his daughters while they were at the University of Illinois, from his sisters, and from other family members concerning school, family news and finances, social events and mores, teaching, temperance, tent meetings, baptism, conversion, salvation, and other religious beliefs. Also includes sermons, receipts, and other papers.

9,247. Morris, William M., and Family
Papers. 1920-25. 1 box.
Open. Unpublished guide.
Minnesota Historical Society, Archives and Manuscripts.
Includes diaries in which Morris's wife Abbie Grace Morris (1875-1924) discusses daily activities, religious affiliations, and weather conditions in St. Cloud, MN, from 1920 to 1922. Abbie Morris was a clubwoman and a member of the WCTU.

9,248. Morrison, Dorilus, and Family
Papers. 1706-1913. 4 boxes, 1 vol., 10 items, and 4 oversize items.
Open. Unpublished guide.
Minnesota Historical Society, Archives and Manuscripts.
Papers of Julia K. Washburn, who married Clinton Morrison (1842-1913) in 1873, include notebooks with diary entries for 1875 to 1877 concerning social events and her daughter Ethel's christening, copies of correspondence, extracts from literature, and notes on chemistry lectures; papers relating to her property holdings before her marriage; and her marriage certificate. Also includes a volume on family travels, social events, and the progress in vocabulary, education, and pronunciation of Ethel Morrison (1876-?); an 1899 diary of Ethel (Morrison) Van Derlip of a trip to China and Japan; and marriage certificates for 1829 to 1833 of Joel Whitmore, justice of the peace in Harrison, ME.

9,249. Morrison, Dot
Papers. Nd. 108-page item.
Open. No guide.
Minnesota Historical Society, Archives and Manuscripts.
A fictional representation of events in the life of Dottie "Dot" Morrison (1845-?) from 1861 to 1864, including the Sioux uprising of 1862 and the fictional settlement of Glendale. Morrison was the daughter of O. E. Morrison, a pioneer in Pope County, MN.

9,250. Mould and McNicol
Papers. 1887. 7 items.
Open. No guide.
Minnesota Historical Society, Archives and Manuscripts.
Architectural drawings of a home designed by Mould and McNicol for Elizabeth S. [Mrs. Samuel L.] Robbins in Irvine Park, St. Paul.

9,251. Mount Zion Hebrew Congregation
Records. 1853-1958. 18 boxes.
Open. Unpublished guide.
Minnesota Historical Society, Archives and Manuscripts.
Records of the first Jewish congregation in Minnesota, which was founded in 1857 in St. Paul and which is associated with Reform Judaism, include minutes of the Sisterhood of Mount Zion Temple, 1937-56; correspondence with Bertha Lion Heilbron of the Minnesota Historical Society staff, Mady Ziegler [Mrs. Ludwig] Metzger, Mrs. Isaac L. Rypins, Mrs. Julius Austrian, and others; and annual applications for marriage.

9,252. Nance, Ethel Ray
Papers. 1920-68. Ca. 70 items.
Open. No guide.
Minnesota Historical Society, Archives and Manuscripts.
[Mrs.] Nance worked with the Minnesota Forest Fires Relief Committee from 1920 to 1922, as a stenographer for the Minnesota House of Representatives in 1923 and 1925, as a Minneapolis policewoman from 1928 to 1932, and with the Phyllis Wheatley settlement house in Minneapolis. Includes pamphlets and newsletters from Wheatley House, a program from the annual convention of the NAACP in 1956, a 1945 newsletter of the Seattle Council for Minority Rights, an article by Nance on the Harlem Renaissance in *Negro History Bulletin* (April 1968), a study of community conditions in the north district in 1925 by the Women's Co-op Alliance, a 1967 article on the lower-income Negro family in St. Paul by Robert E. Staples, clippings about black artist Henry Bannarn, and *Minnesota Negro Council News and Reviews,* 1938.

9,253. National Council of Jewish Women
Records. 1935-41. 82 pp.
Open. Unpublished guide.
Minnesota Historical Society, Archives and Manuscripts.
Minutes of board meetings and general meetings of the St. Paul chapter of the Council. A number of Jewish refugees were brought to St. Paul through Council projects.

9,254. National Council of Jewish Women, Minneapolis Section
Records. 1917-67. 3 boxes.
Open. Unpublished guide.
Minnesota Historical Society, Archives and Manuscripts.
Bylaws, annual reports, minutes of executive board meetings for 1948 to 1950, records of expenditures and contributions, correspondence, conference proceedings, committee and other reports, resolutions, news releases, programs, pamphlets, brochures, and a president's manual and other books of the Minneapolis section of the Council, which was founded in 1893 to work for the welfare of Jewish people, the rights of women, and peace. Includes news bulletins, reports, and other material on such subjects as proposed welfare and immigration legislation, contributions to charity, Bertha Weiskopf and Nina Morais Cohen scholarship funds, an overseas scholarship program, immigrant aid and Americanization, child study, social hygiene, education, music, religion, and civic and communal affairs. Theresa Beatrice [Mrs. Nathan] Berman, Ann W. [Mrs. Felix] Moses, Sadye Ascheim [Mrs. James] Kantrowitz, and Mildred G. [Mrs. Joseph M.] Welt were among the members of the Minneapolis branch of the Council.

9,255. National League of American Pen Women
Records. 1927-58. 1 box and 2 vols.
Open. Unpublished guide.
Minnesota Historical Society, Archives and Manuscripts.
Records of the Minnesota branch of the League include information on 175 women writers, including Margaret (Culkin) Banning and Sister Maris Stella; questionnaires providing biographical information and information on the writings of members; a history of the Minnesota branch by Cleora Clark Wheeler; and a scrapbook containing manuscript lists and clippings about the activities and literary and artistic productions of members.

9,256. National Society, Daughters of the British Empire in Minnesota
Records. 1918-61. 6 boxes and 17 items.
Access restricted. Unpublished guide.
Minnesota Historical Society, Archives and Manuscripts.
The organization was founded in 1918. Charters of 14 chapters; minutes of meetings of the state board; minute books, treasurers' books, a bankbook, a membership book, and a scrapbook of various chapters; correspondence between Dorothy Evans and a Mrs. Venables concerning the choice of Minnesota as national headquarters of the organization; a certificate of membership in the National Society; a covenant between societies constituting the National Society; a history of the organization; and a program of the triennial convention, held in Philadelphia in 1953.

9,257. National Society of Colonial Dames of America in the State of Minnesota
Records. 1894-1971. 1 bacase and 7 microfilm reels.
Open. Unpublished guide.
Minnesota Historical Society, Archives and Manuscripts.
Minutes containing historians' reports on social and patriotic activities and applications for membership in the National Society of Colonial Dames of America, which include genealogical information. The Minnesota organization was founded in 1894.

9,258. National Society of the Colonial Dames of America in the State of Minnesota
Records. Nd. 2 folders.
Open. Unpublished guide.
Minnesota Historical Society, Archives and Manuscripts.
Records of this women's patriotic society include information about Minnesota counties and county courthouses compiled by the Colonial Dames historical activities committee.

9,259. Neal, Eva, and Family
Papers. 1881-1963. 5 in.
Open. No guide.
Minnesota Historical Society, Archives and Manuscripts.
Correspondence, leaflets, clippings, and other papers of Eva (Bell) Neal, her parents Andrew Jackson Bell and Amanda Lee Bell, and other members of the Neal and Bell families. The material pertains largely to the black community of Minneapolis and St. Paul, the St. James African Methodist Episcopal Church in St. Paul, black newspaper editor John Q. Adams, the United Spanish War Veterans and Auxiliary, and a biography and genealogy of the Bell and Neal families. Includes reminiscences of Eva Neal as well as letters by Shirley [Mrs. W. E. B.] DuBois.

9,260. Nebelung, Clara (Bircher)
Papers. 1926? 41-page item.
Open. No guide.
Minnesota Historical Society, Archives and Manuscripts.
History of the Current Events Club of Crookston, MN, from 1899 to 1926 was written by Nebelung and Edith Weble Watts.

9,261. Neighborhood House Association
Records. 1903-68. 4 boxes.
Open. Unpublished guide.
Minnesota Historical Society, Archives and Manuscripts.
The Association, a nonprofit social service agency in St. Paul, was founded in 1897. The Neighborhood House was one of the earliest settlement houses in "the flats" on St. Paul's west side, where the inhabitants, of varying nationalities, were mostly foreign-born. Articles of incorporation, a proposed constitution, annual reports, minutes of board meetings, correspondence, financial reports, resolutions committee reports, statistical reports, policy statements, newsletters, brochures, and other records of the Association. Includes correspondence concerning the history of the House, organization and membership of the Association, cooperative projects with other local service agencies, and problems of public housing and urban development; monthly reports by the head resident detailing daily activities and social events at the House; and staff reports.

9,262. Nelson, Carrie M.
Papers. 1907-21. 4 items.
Open. No guide.
Minnesota Historical Society, Archives and Manuscripts.
Biographical data on Civil War nurses Ellen (Cantwell) Sargent, [Mrs.] Sylvia Townsend, and [Mrs.] Jennie E. Marsh, as well as two letters by Townsend.

9,263. Nelson, Knute
Papers. 1861-1934. 266 boxes, 1 item, and 13 oversize items.
Open. Unpublished guide.
Minnesota Historical Society, Archives and Manuscripts.
Nelson (1843-1923), a Norwegian immigrant, was a lawyer, governor of Minnesota, and US senator from Minnesota from 1893 to 1923. Correspondence concerning women's suffrage, child labor and child welfare legislation, the Children's Bureau, the Palmer-Owen and Keating-Owen bills, and the Sheppard Towner maternal welfare bill.

9,264. Nelson, Mary E.
Papers. 1895. 1 vol.
Open. Unpublished guide.
Minnesota Historical Society, Archives and Manuscripts.
Diary of [Mrs. B. F.] Nelson contains an account of her visit to Spain, Egypt, Italy, Palestine, Greece, Paris, and London.

9,265. Nichols, Harriet S.
Papers. 1853. 2-page item.
Open. No guide.
Minnesota Historical Society, Archives and Manuscripts.
Letter by Nichols, a teacher at Frederick Ayer's Mission School in Belle Prairie, MN, to the Newburyport, MA, Sewing Society concerns the number and kind of pupils enrolled and the type of clothing and material needed for the School. The Society had donated supplies and finances to the School.

9,266. Nielsen, Ole, and Family
Papers. 1855-1931. 1 box.
Open. Unpublished guide.
Minnesota Historical Society, Archives and Manuscripts.
Letters Gro Nielsdatter [Mrs. Ole] Svendsen wrote to her family in Norway describing her trip across the ocean in 1862 and life in Esterville, IA, and letters to family members in Norway from other relatives in Iowa, Minnesota, and the Dakotas, including Margit Opsata, Birgit Knudsdatter, Barbro Sandro, Viola Norgaard, and Ragnhild Solheim.

9,267. Nineteenth Century Club
Records. 1901-32. Ca. 2 boxes.
Open. Unpublished guide.

Minnesota Historical Society, Archives and Manuscripts.
Minutes, a treasurers' record, and a history of this Minneapolis woman's study club.

9,268. Nolan, William Ignatius
Papers. 1900-43. 8 boxes.
Open. Unpublished guide.
Minnesota Historical Society, Archives and Manuscripts.
Nolan (1874-1943) was a Minnesota legislator at various times between 1903 and 1923, lieutenant governor from 1925 to 1929, a congressman from 1929 to 1933, and a Chautauqua lecturer. Correspondence and political papers, including material on woman suffrage by Mary F. Severance and others.

9,269. Norlander, Mary Olson
Papers. Nd. 7-page item.
Open. No guide.
Minnesota Historical Society, Archives and Manuscripts.
Reminiscences by [Mrs.] Norlander (1876-?), a Swedish immigrant, of pioneer life in Mille Lacs County, MN, and in a Minnesota lumbering community.

9,270. North East Neighborhood House
Records. 1889-1961. 37 boxes.
Open. Unpublished guide.
Minnesota Historical Society, Archives and Manuscripts.
Records of the House, which was established in Minneapolis in 1915, include minutes and reports of the board of directors, minutes of staff meetings, financial records, correspondence, personnel records, a history, departmental and head workers' reports, group work records, counseling and placement records, statistical reports, clippings, and printed matter. In addition, there are correspondence, reports, and other records from such social service agencies as the Minneapolis Council of Social Agencies, the National Federation of Settlements, the Twin City Federation of Settlements, and Maternity Hospitals. Correspondents include social worker Catheryne (Cooke) Gilman, Gratia A. Countryman, and Stella Louise Wood.

9,271. Norwegian Evangelical Lutheran Churches in Clay and Becker Counties
Records. 1872-1976. 3 microfilm reels.
Open. Unpublished guide.
Minnesota Historical Society, Archives and Manuscripts.
Records of seven churches in Minnesota's Clay and Becker counties include minutes of the Ladies Aid of Buffalo River Norwegian Evangelical Lutheran Church in Hitterdal, 1913-15; religious school membership and subscription books of Atlanta Norwegian Evangelical Lutheran Church in Atlanta Township, 1896-1946; minutes of the Ladies Aid Society of the Keene Norwegian Evangelical Lutheran Church in Keene Township, 1916-30 and 1938-59; minutes, 1948-53, and a treasurer's book, 1954-62, of the Ladies Aid of Salem Lutheran Church in Hitterdal; and minutes, 1944-54, and a treasurer's book, 1922-52, of the Ladies Aid of Lysne Norwegian Evangelical Lutheran Church in Cromwell Township.

9,272. Nute, Grace Lee
Papers. 1924-57. 1 box.
Open. Unpublished guide.
Minnesota Historical Society, Archives and Manuscripts.
Papers of Nute (1895-), an archivist, historian, and member of the Historical Society staff, include correspondence and manuscripts relating to her book *Caesars of the Wilderness;* 69 manuscripts, reports, and radio addresses by Nute on the fur trade, early territorial Minnesota, pioneer women of Minnesota, and her research trips; and index cards for her calendar of events relating to Charles A. Lindbergh.

9,273. Oliver Iron Mining Company
Records. 1901-30. 5 boxes.
Open. Unpublished guide.
Minnesota Historical Society, Archives and Manuscripts.
This Duluth, MN, company is a subsidiary of US Steel Corporation, one of the largest mining companies on the Minnesota Iron Range. Consists primarily of correspondence between the Company's president W. J. Olcott, district superintendents and managers, and officers of US Steel concerning the Company's relationship to the welfare, social life, and education in the mining communities and its donations to social organizations, churches, and charities in the communities where it operated. Includes folders with material on such topics as Americanization, community affairs, charity and welfare contributions to families of men killed or disabled on the job, visiting nurses, company-sponsored recreation, public schools, employee education, garden projects, the YMCA and the YWCA, and the Olcott Rest Lodge in Half Moon Lake, MN, a convalescent home for wives of company employees.

9,274. Osmond, William R., and Family
Papers. 1743-1939. 2 boxes.
Open. Unpublished guide.
Minnesota Historical Society, Archives and Manuscripts.
Family correspondence; letters of Ann Russell, Elizabeth Stirling, and Ann Estabrook; correspondence between Mary Osmond and Ella Osmond and their brother; reminiscences of Ella Osmond Ashby; antiwar poems written in 1917 and 1918 by Mary Osmond and her brother; a teaching certificate of Mary Osmond; a copybook of Sarah Comfort, a student; and an autograph book of Mary Hampton, who also was a student. Papers of Ann Sammes Osmond (ca. 1814-93) include copybooks of her poetry, a daybook, an exercise book, and a ledger.

9,275. Oxboro Heath Community League
Records. 1920-24. 2 vols.
Open. Unpublished guide.
Minnesota Historical Society, Archives and Manuscripts.
Constitution, bylaws, and minutes of meetings of this group of women in Hennepin County, which organized in 1920 to finance a Sunday school, to raise funds for the establishment of a community church open to all denominations, and to take part in social and civic enterprises. The League disbanded in 1926 after the community church had been built.

9,276. Paige, Mabeth Hurd
Papers. 1943-58. 1 folder and 1 box.
Open. Unpublished guide.
Minnesota Historical Society, Archives and Manuscripts.
[Mrs. James] Paige (?-1961), a Minneapolis resident, was active in the woman suffrage movement and other political and social movements. Correspondence, including letters from novelist Gladys (Hasty) [Mrs. Herbert Allen] Carroll and the Governor's Interracial Commission on the lives of Minnesota Indians; speeches relating to her activities in the woman suffrage movement; bulletins of the woman's division of the Republican National Committee; a 1958 article on school desegregation; a service award given to Paige by the Minneapolis Urban League; a citation awarded to her by the Minneapolis Council of Civic Clubs; and passes to Republican National Conventions.

9,277. Park, Agnes (Morrison), and Family
Papers. 1837-1948. 1.25 ft.
Open. No guide.
Minnesota Historical Society, Archives and Manuscripts.
Correspondence of Park and members of the Babcock family. Mary Brown [Mrs. Dwight W.] Babcock (1829-1906), who was the mother of Jessica (Babcock) [Mrs. Gardner S.] Moore (ca. 1860-?) and Mary (Babcock) [Mrs. John Henry] Morrison (1857-?), was educated at the Female Academy in Albany, NY, and Mansion Square Boarding School in Poughkeepsie, NY; she moved to Minnesota in 1883. Her granddaughter Agnes [Mrs. Charles Richardson] Park (1893-), who studied at the Lycée and University of Paris, worked with the American Ambulance Hospital in France in 1916 and 1917, for the American National Red Cross in the US, and at the American Legation in Brussels. Includes letters by the Babcocks' governess Maria Fergus, who later married John Pizzini, Italian vice-consul to the US; Babcock letters relating to family activities and social events in St. Paul between 1888 and 1906; letters to Agnes Morrison while she was attending school in Michigan and France; letters by Agnes Morrison while she was secretary at the American Embassy in Brussels and then working in Paris with Delineator, a French War relief organization; letters by Mary Morrison while she was traveling in Europe and the Mediterranean; letters of introduction for Mary Morrison and Agnes Park by Frank B. Kellogg; and post cards showing housing for mill girls in Belding, MI.

9,278. Patrons of Husbandry, Pomona Grange No. 12
Records. 1881-1904. 2 microfilm reels.
Open. Unpublished guide.
Minnesota Historical Society, Archives and Manuscripts.
Minute books and correspondence relating principally to the Grange, a farm family organization in Hennepin County, MN, that worked to change the political and economic situation in favor of farmers. Women were active in the Grange from the 1860s until the 1900s. Includes correspondence of and minutes by Caroline Scofield and John D. Scofield.

9,279. Pattee, Edward Sidney, and Family
Papers. 1839-99. 1 box.
Open. Unpublished guide.
Minnesota Historical Society, Archives and Manuscripts.
Letters from Pattee's wife Dora (Jewett) Pattee (1853-1939) to her parents concern family news, school life, Minneapolis social functions, domestic activites, her job as Minneapolis post office clerk from 1877 to 1883, and her attendance at a session of the Republican National Convention in 1892. Also includes 12 letters received from women with information on soap making, blood poisoning remedies, life on a Dakota wheat farm, and riots in southern and western Ireland.

9,280. Paul, Helen M. G.
Papers. Nd. 22-page item.
Open. No guide.
Minnesota Historical Society, Archives and Manuscripts.
Detailed account of the founding of the DAR, beginning with the organization of "The Cincinnati" at Baron Steuben's home in 1783, and a partial summary of the DAR's accomplishments.

9,281. Peet, James, and Family
Papers. 1846-71. 4 boxes.
Open. Unpublished guide.
Minnesota Historical Society, Archives and Manuscripts.
Peet (1828-66), a resident of New York state, married Harriet Evens (ca. 1828-1914) in 1854 and migrated to Minnesota in 1855 as a Methodist missionary. He worked around Lake Superior until 1861, served as a chaplain in the Civil War, and then settled in Anoka, MN. Correspondence

between James and Harriet Peet about family matters, schools, religion, and life styles and of the Peets with other missionary couples in Minnesota; an 1863 circular *Little Lizzie's Letter* published by the American Tract Society in New York City; and recipes for liniment, cough drops, and hair restorer.

9,282. Pendergast, William Wirt, and Family
Papers. 1816-1956. 14 boxes, 6 bacases, and 11 oversize items.
Open. Unpublished guide.
Minnesota Historical Society, Archives and Manuscripts.
The Pendergasts were abolitionists and temperance advocates from Massachusetts and New Hampshire who settled in Minnesota. William Pendergast was a farmer, state superintendent of public instruction in 1882, and first principal and major organizer of the University of Minnesota's school of agriculture. Correspondence of his wife Abigail "Abbie" Lowe Cogswell Pendergast (1839-1917) and of their daughters Elizabeth (Pendergast) [Mrs. Henry] Greenberg (1858-1929), a teacher who was interested in reform movements and the Unitarian church; Edith Myra Pendergast (1860-78); Mary Abbie (Pendergast) [Mrs. John A.] Vye (1865-?), who was a teacher, a medical student at the University of Minnesota, and secretary to the dean of the University's college of medicine; and May (Pendergast) [Mrs. Henry A.] White, an English teacher at normal schools and the University's school of agriculture, who traveled in South America and Europe. Also includes correspondence between Lydia Pendergast Todd of Hutchinson, MN, and Jessie Pendergast; of Sophia May Pendergast [Mrs. Harry A.] White (1873-?), a resident of Hutchinson; of Ellen Myra Pendergast [Mrs. Lewis] Harrington (1836-1915) of Hutchinson; and of women of the *Gopher* staff of 1896, including Caroline Fullerton, Grace Mabel Tennant, and Alice E. Walker. In addition, the collection contains scattered diaries of Sophia Pendergast White for 1889 to 1951, her reminiscences of the Pendergast family's home life, and school certificates and diplomas.

9,283. People's Church
Records. 1890-1901. 90 items.
Open. Unpublished guide.
Minnesota Historical Society, Archives and Manuscripts.
Accounts, reports, and correspondence of the Women's Foreign Missionary Society, the Sunday school, and various other organizations within this St. Paul church.

9,284. Persons, Irene
Papers. 1937. 6-page item.
Open. No guide.
Minnesota Historical Society, Archives and Manuscripts.
Interview in Minneapolis with Sally (Brown) Dover, who was a descendant of a white man and a Negro slave from Virginia, contains information on the race problem.

9,285. Persons, Irene
Papers. 1937. 4 pp.
Open. No guide.
Minnesota Historical Society, Archives and Manuscripts.
Consists of an interview in which Margareta Holl [Mrs. Peter] Hahn describes pioneer life in Brown County, MN, and the defense of New Ulm, MN, during the Sioux uprising of 1862.

9,286. Peter, Grace Bakke
Papers. 1962-65. 102 items.
Open. Unpublished guide.
Minnesota Historical Society, Archives and Manuscripts.
[Mrs. Louis G.] Peter (1906-), a registered nurse born in Sacred Heart, MN, served in the US Navy Nurse Corps in WWII; she later worked in Veterans Administration hospitals and in a hospital in Malaysia as a Peace Corps volunteer in 1963. Correspondence and clippings, including letters describing her 1963 trip through Bali and Indonesia and official ceremonies on the establishment of the state of Malaysia, with comments on the assassinations of President John F. Kennedy and President Diem of Vietnam. Includes letters from Kennedy, Peace Corps director R. Sargent Shriver, Senator Hubert Humphrey, and Minnesota governor Karl F. Rolvaag.

9,287. Petersen, Hjalmar
Papers. 1907-68. 12.5 ft.
Open. Unpublished guide.
Minnesota Historical Society, Archives and Manuscripts.
Petersen (1890-1968) was a newspaperman and Farmer-Labor party activist who served as state representative from 1931 to 1933, as lieutenant governor from 1935 to 1936, as governor of Minnesota in 1936, and for many years as a railroad and warehouse commissioner. Correspondence, including letters of his second wife Medora Belle (Grandprey) Petersen concerning her teaching career in Morris, MN, and her activities with local, state, and national PTAs; a speech given in 1936 by Hjalmar Petersen to the Federation of Women's Clubs in Minneapolis on the status of women; a 1934 seminar report on the adolescent girl by Medora Grandprey; a scrapbook for 1936 to 1942 of the daughter of Hjalmar Petersen and his first wife Rigmor Christine Laursen (Wosgaard) Petersen, containing mementos of school trips and campus politics at the University of Minnesota and *Minnesota Daily* clippings; and printed material from the American Friends Service Committee and the Women's International League for Peace and Freedom. Correspondents include Eugenie Moore [Mrs. John P.] Anderson, Congresswoman Coya Gjesdal [Mrs. Andrew] Knutson, state Representative Mabeth Hurd [Mrs. James] Paige, columnist Vivian Stanley Thorp, Farmer-Labor party official Irene Welby, and Mrs. Charles Lundquist.

9,288. Peyton, Theresa Barbara
Papers. 1898-1917. 1 box, 1 bacase, and 3 items.
Open. Unpublished guide.
Minnesota Historical Society, Archives and Manuscripts.
Papers of Peyton (1880-1929), a suffragist and teacher, include correspondence relating to speakers and writers on suffrage, the problems of courts in domestic and juvenile cases, and a patent on a drawing table; school and student records containing information on the work of Peyton's students in a St. Paul school; scrapbooks; and a volume of clippings.

9,289. Phyllis Wheatley Settlement House
Records. 1924-63. 16 boxes.
Open. Unpublished guide.
Minnesota Historical Society, Archives and Manuscripts.
The House was founded in 1923 to serve the black community in Minneapolis. Certificate of incorporation, bylaws, annual reports, minutes and reports of the board of directors, financial records, correspondence, personnel records, a history and purposes of the House, a biography of Phyllis Wheatley, committee and house officer reports, a speech, and files containing correspondence, clippings, and printed matter on human rights, public housing, black organizations, Eslanda Robeson, and neighborhood service workers. Correspondents include the National Federation of Settlements, the Minneapolis Federation of Settlements, the Minneapolis Council of Social Agencies, the Minneapolis Urban League, and the National Association of Social Workers. Among the many women involved with the operation of the House were Louise Love Bromley, Willis Gertrude Brown, Magnolia Latimore, Mabeth Hurd Paige, Ruth Gage Thompson, and Alice Webb.

9,290. Plymouth Congregational Church
Records. 1858-1926. 5 boxes and 1 vol.
Open. Unpublished guide.
Minnesota Historical Society, Archives and Manuscripts.
Minutes for 1872 to 1898 of the Ladies Social Circle of the first Congregational church in St. Paul, which was founded in 1858.

9,291. Political Equality Club of Minneapolis
Records. 1892-1920. 2 boxes.
Open. Unpublished guide.
Minnesota Historical Society, Archives and Manuscripts.
Constitution, minutes of meetings, correspondence, a list of members, a brief organizational history, reports, lists of woman suffrage clubs of Minnesota, and other records of the Club, which was affiliated with the Minnesota Woman Suffrage Association. Includes a circular letter from Carrie Chapman Catt, a letter by Henry Brown Blackwell, reminiscences of Elizabeth (Cady) Stanton, and a history of suffrage in Minnesota by Maud C. Stockwell. Also contained are minutes of the Minneapolis Women's School and Library Organization, which was sponsored by the Club to promote election of women to the city board of education and the library board.

9,292. Political Equality Club of St. Paul
Records. 1910-17. 1 box.
Open. Unpublished guide.
Minnesota Historical Society, Archives and Manuscripts.
Minutes of meetings of the Club demonstrate its efforts to spread information about woman suffrage in Minnesota.

9,293. Pond, Agnes Carson Johnson
Papers. Nd. 21-page item.
Open. No guide.
Minnesota Historical Society, Archives and Manuscripts.
Reminiscences written by Pond (1825-?) for her granddaughter Marian Moir concern her childhood in Ohio, her marriage to Robert Hopkins, her first trip to the Northwest, life at Lac Qui Parle Mission and Traverse des Sioux, and her marriage to Gideon Hollister Pond.

9,294. Pond Family
Papers. 1833-1935. 16 boxes.
Open. Unpublished guide.
Minnesota Historical Society, Archives and Manuscripts.
Papers of Gideon Hollister Pond (1810-78) and his brother Samuel William Pond (1808-91), who were missionaries to the Dakota Indians and territorial settlers in Minnesota. Samuel Pond was married to Cordelia Eggleston Pond; their children were Jennette Cordelia Pond and Rebecca Cordelia Pond (1844-1910), who married William J. Dean. Correspondence of Gideon Pond, Samuel Pond, Rebecca (Pond) Dean, her daughter Jennette Cordelia Dean, Jennette Pond, Cordelia Eggleston Pond, Mary M. Pond, Anna Riggs, Jennie M. Eggleston, Eliza Huggins, and Mary Huggins. Many of the family members were missionaries; letters relate to churches served, religious ideas and spiritual life, family affairs, farming, the Crow Creek Agency, and the Civil War. Also includes diaries of Janet Pond for 1850 to 1856; diaries kept by Gideon Hollister Pond, Jr. (1858-?) and his wife from 1885 to 1914, which contain mentions of social life near Bloomington, MN, the weather, beekeeping, and the prices of farm products; records of the Bloomington Temperance Society for 1871 to 1875; reminiscences by and about Pond family members; a scrapbook of Rebecca Pond; and an autograph album of Sarah Poage [Mrs. Gideon H.] Pond's mother.

9,295. Pope, William Cox, and Family
Papers. 1858-1968. 1 box and 1 bacase.
Open. Unpublished guide.
Minnesota Historical Society, Archives and Manuscripts.
Pope (1841-1917) was an Episcopal minister who founded the Church of the Good Shepherd in St. Paul in 1868. Constitution, minutes, and signatures of members of the American Church Temperance Society, Minnesota branch; a scrapbook containing the articles of incorporation and clippings of the Luckey School for Girls in St. Paul; and articles on Catherine Deaver Lealtad, a Negro who graduated from Macalester College with honors in 1916.

9,296. Powell, Ransom Judd
Papers. 1769-1938. 7 boxes and 15 vols.
Open. Unpublished guide.
Minnesota Historical Society, Archives and Manuscripts.
Papers of Powell (1865-1937), who received a law degree from the University of Minnesota in 1899 and in 1907 was retained by the government to defend the Chippewa Indians of Minnesota in cases involving trespass on timberlands on Indian reservations. He later served on a commission appointed by Congress to determine the genealogy of 200 Chippewa families living on the White Earth Reservation. Correspondence concerning Indian claims to allotments on the Reservation; legal case files on Indian estate claims and land transfers and legal testimony about the "blood status" of Chippewa persons; Indian genealogies; rolls giving the name, sex, age, blood status, and property data relating to Chippewa owners of Reservation land; anthropological survey sheets; plat books showing Indian allotments; and other papers relating to Powell's work with the Chippewas of Minnesota.

9,297. Preus, Jacob Aall Otteson, and Family
Papers. 1853-1946. 38 boxes and 1 vol.
Open. Unpublished guide.
Minnesota Historical Society, Archives and Manuscripts.
Preus (1883-1961) served as governor of Minnesota from 1921 to 1925. His papers, which primarily concern his political career, include letters from Carrie Secelia Jorgens [Mrs. Manley Lewis] Fosseen and Catheryne (Cooke) [Mrs. Robbins] Gilman as well as letters urging the appointment of Carrie Fosseen and various other candidates of the US Senate after the death of Senator Knute Nelson in 1923. Also includes letters from Jacob Preus and his wife Idella Louise Haugen Preus to their sons while they were attending Luther College in Decorah, IA, and in subsequent years.

9,298. Primary Teachers' Union
Records. 1888. 1 vol.
Open. Unpublished guide.
Minnesota Historical Society, Archives and Manuscripts.
Minutes kept by Martha C. [Mrs. Cyrus W.] Wells and a membership list of this Minneapolis union of Sunday school teachers of several denominations.

9,299. Pritchard, Lydia
Papers. 1916-53. 1 box.
Open. Unpublished guide.
Minnesota Historical Society, Archives and Manuscripts.
Papers of Pritchard (1887-), a policewoman in Hibbing, MN, include correspondence, transcripts of her speeches, and reports on social workers' meetings, but they consist primarily of clippings she compiled on law enforcement, crime, social problems, prohibition, birth control, marriage laws, child welfare legislation, dance hall regulations, mental health, narcotics, sterilization of the feebleminded, and juvenile delinquency.

9,300. Protestant Episcopal Churches in Minneapolis
Records. 1886-1936. 1 microfilm reel.
Open. Unpublished guide.
Minnesota Historical Society, Archives and Manuscripts.
Parish records of five Protestant Episcopal churches in Minneapolis include a household census, ca. 1892-1912, of St. Johannes Church. The census is primarily written in Swedish.

9,301. Protestant Episcopal Churches in St. Paul
Records. 1867-1962. 1 microfilm reel.
Open. Unpublished guide.
Minnesota Historical Society, Archives and Manuscripts.
Parish records of three Protestant Episcopal churches in St. Paul include minutes, financial records, and membership material of St. Mark's Guild of St. Mark's Church in Highwood, St. Paul, 1923-32.

9,302. Quetico-Superior Council
Records. 1906-67. 109 boxes and 20 bacases.
Access restricted. Unpublished guide.
Minnesota Historical Society, Archives and Manuscripts.
Correspondence and clippings of the Council, a conservation group established in 1928 in Minneapolis to preserve the wilderness area on the Minnesota-Ontario border. Includes biographical data about correspondents, among them Jane Addams, Frances E. Andrews, Anna (Botsford) Comstock, Frances Densmore, Charlotte [Mrs. Duncan] Ferguson, Zona Gale, and Mabeth Hurd Paige, and such women's clubs as the Women's International League for Peace and Freedom.

9,303. Ramsey, Alexander, and Family
Papers. 1775-1965. 61 boxes and 57 microfilm reels.
Open. Published guide.
Minnesota Historical Society, Archives and Manuscripts.
Ramsey (1815-1903), a lawyer and real estate investor, was a Whig-Republican who served as US senator and representative, US secretary of war, the first governor of Minnesota Territory, and governor of the state of Minnesota. Letters of his wife Anna Earl Jenks Ramsey (1826-84) to their daughter Marion (Ramsey) [Mrs. Charles Eliot] Furness (1853-1935); letters and diaries concerning educational travels to Europe in 1868; diaries of Anna Ramsey for 1865 to 1884, of Marion Furness for 1869 to 1901, of Marion Furness's daughter Laura Furness (1882-1959) for 1895 and 1903, and of Rebecca and Laura Furness for 1893 and 1894; and school notebooks, scrapbooks, and recipe books of Anna Ramsey, Marion Ramsey, Laura Furness, and her sister Anna Earl Ramsey Furness (1876-1964). Also includes papers relating to the estates of Alexander Ramsey, his brother Justus Ramsey, and Anna Ramsey; reports on crime, criminal proceedings, and prisons, including the murder trial of Mary Ann Evards Wright Bilansky in the 1860s; information on the career of Alexander Ramsey's niece Pauline Nininger, a singer whose stage name was Pauline Lucca; information on the Ramseys' Negro servant Martha E. Clark [Mrs. Peter] Hall, her friends, and her social life in St. Paul and Washington, DC; and material about social life, customs, attitudes, and prejudices during the second half of the 19th century. See Helen McCann White, *Guide to a Microfilm Edition of the Alexander Ramsey Papers and Records* (St. Paul, MN: Minnesota Historical Society, 1974).

9,304. Ramsey County Historical Society Interviews
Oral history. Ca. 1948-60. 1 box.
Open. Unpublished guide.
Minnesota Historical Society, Archives and Manuscripts.
Includes interviews with members of the Reiff family and Amelia Blase, who discuss the early days of North St. Paul; with Agnes Freeman Farrar, who was a schoolteacher in Ramsey County, MN; with Mary Moulton Cheney and her brother Charles W. Cheney, who reminisce about the Cheney family and life in early Minneapolis and St. Anthony Park; with Mrs. Edward Collingwood Hall, who describes the early days of the St. Anthony Park area of St. Paul, where she moved with her husband in 1886; and with Anna E. Meili, the daughter of Charles Passavant, an early register of deeds for Ramsey County, who discusses her family, Germans in St. Paul, and early schools and churches there.

9,305. Ramsey County Sunday School Association
Records. 1915-48. 3.5 boxes.
Open. Unpublished guide.
Minnesota Historical Society, Archives and Manuscripts.
Minutes, financial reports, and correspondence of this St. Paul organization and its successor, the St. Paul Council of Churches, which was formed in 1944.

9,306. Ramsey County Women's Democratic Club
Records. 1940-49. 1 vol.
Open. Unpublished guide.
Minnesota Historical Society, Archives and Manuscripts.
Constitution and minute book of the Club.

9,307. Raudenbush, David Webb
Papers. 1952-57. 0.5 box.
Open. No guide.
Minnesota Historical Society, Archives and Manuscripts.
Correspondence between Raudenbush and Elizabeth Heffelfinger, who was a Republican national committeewoman.

9,308. Remey, Charles Mason
Papers. 1939. 35 vols.
Open. No guide.
Minnesota Historical Society, Archives and Manuscripts.
History of the family of Charles Mason (1804-82), who was chief justice of the Iowa Supreme Court, includes correspondence, diaries, Remey family genealogy, and other papers relating to such subjects as political activities, the Lincoln administration, the Civil War, the Spanish-American War, the Boxer rebellion, the slave question, Negro suffrage, woman suffrage, important court cases, Reconstruction, the Mormons, navigation, travel in Europe, and social life and customs from the early 19th to mid-20th century. Includes letters of and information about Mason's daughter Mary Josephine (Mason) Remey (1845-1938) and her husband Rear Admiral George Collier Remey (1841-1928), their son Charles Mason Remey (1874-?), and Gertrude Heim Remey (1888-1932).

9,309. Retail Clerks Union
Records. 1936-63. 14 ft.
Partially restricted. Unpublished guide.
Minnesota Historical Society, Archives and Manuscripts.
Minutes, membership and financial records, correspondence, contracts, negotiation records, grievance files, reports, and printed materials of Local No. 2, a union local for department, drug, and furniture store clerks, founded in 1936, and of Local No. 789, a union local for grocery store clerks, founded in 1944. The locals had many women members, including Grace H. Lunney, who was corresponding and financial secretary of Local No. 2. The two St. Paul locals merged in 1959.

9,310. Reynolds, Mrs. O. J.
Papers. 1929. 16-page item.
Open. No guide.
Minnesota Historical Society, Archives and Manuscripts.
Brief history by Reynolds of the Central Presbyterian Church's Woman's Missionary Society, which was formed by the merger of the Woman's Home and Foreign Missionary societies in 1912. The Church was located in St. Paul.

9,311. Rice, Henry Mower, and Family
Papers. 1824-1966. 7 boxes.
Open. Unpublished guide.
Minnesota Historical Society, Archives and Manuscripts.
Papers of Rice (1816-94), a Vermont native who served as US senator from Minnesota from 1858 to 1863, include correspondence with his wife Matilda (Whitall) Rice, her correspondence with her children, and a letter she wrote to her father about her husband's election. Also includes correspondence of Robert Rice Auerbach, who changed his name to Robert Auerbach Rice during WWI as a patriotic gesture, with members of his family, including his wife Mary Virginia (Rugg) Auerbach Rice (1881-), about marital happiness, family history, American National Red Cross nursing during WWI, the usefulness of a college education, and monuments to Henry Rice. In addition, the collection contains letters of Matilda Rice [Mrs. Maurice] Auerbach (?-1945) and Matilda (Auerbach) [Mrs. Richard] Elliott and correspondence of Rachel (Newbold) [Mrs. Gilbert] Whitall in Richmond, VA, with her brother Caleb Newbold, Jr., in Philadelphia, in which they discuss family needs, finances, and property during the 1840s.

9,312. Richards, Amasa, and Family
Papers. 1851-77. 33 items.
Open. Unpublished guide.
Minnesota Historical Society, Archives and Manuscripts.
Mary and Amasa Richards were settlers in Shakopee, Minnesota Territory. Letters from family members in Sturbridge and Plymouth, MA, most of whom were sisters and female cousins, concern family and community news, health, disease, reactions to death, crops, the Civil War, the Dakota War of 1862, the military draft, dress, land, homes, and livestock.

9,313. Richards and Breen
Papers. 1940-61. 3 boxes.
Open. Unpublished guide.
Minnesota Historical Society, Archives and Manuscripts.
Biographical and autobiographical information about Minnesota writers or nationally known writers who had Minnesota backgrounds, including about 150 women, was compiled by Genevieve Rose Breen and Carmen Nelson [Mrs. Orrin J.] Richards for two volumes of *Minnesota Writers* (1945 and 1961).

9,314. Richardson, Ahira, and Family
Papers. 1865-73. 1 vol. and 1 item.
Open. Unpublished guide.
Minnesota Historical Society, Archives and Manuscripts.
Diary and an account book in which [Mrs. Ahira] Richardson, a St. Paul housewife, comments on the weather, social life and customs, the Masonic lodge, and the Episcopal church.

9,315. Richardson, Georgia Mounts
Papers. 1862-1936. 1 box.
Open. Unpublished guide.
Minnesota Historical Society, Archives and Manuscripts.
Letters to Richardson (1858-1937) from her cousin Ella S. Sargent while on a tour of Europe in 1906 and from Ole O. Sageng in 1924 concerning a US senatorship; letters of sympathy on the death of her husband Almer O. Richardson, who was president of the Menagha, MN, village council; and two autograph albums.

9,316. Riggs, Stephen Return, and Family
Papers. 1837-1958. 4 boxes.
Open. Unpublished guide.
Minnesota Historical Society, Archives and Manuscripts.
Riggs (1812-83), a Presbyterian minister to Indian missions, went to Minnesota in 1837. Correspondence between Riggs and members of his family in Ohio and the Longley family in Massachusetts, letters from other missionaries and from Indians, letters to his daughter Martha in 1869 describing the illness and death of his wife Mary Ann Clark (Longley) Riggs (1813-69), and letters concerning the Western Female Seminary in Oxford, OH, which Martha Riggs attended. Also includes correspondence of Martha Riggs and Jane S. Williamson, a missionary to the Dakota mission; deeds; financial accounts; and a certificate of deportment issued to Anna J. Riggs by the Rockford Female Seminary in 1864. Letters from Mary Riggs to her parents Thomas Longley and Martha Anne (Taylor) Longley in Hawley, MA, concern her trip west with her husband, their arrival in Minnesota, and life at the school and mission at Lake Harriet and Lac Qui Parle. A volume by Stephen Riggs contains detailed biographical sketches of missionaries associated with the Dakota mission in the period 1835-60, among them Lucy Cornelia Stevens, Jane Smith Williamson, Lucy Jane Spooner, Mary Roche Spooner, and Anne Boke Sekley, as well as sketches of the families of other missionaries and of part-Indian and part-white children who attended the Hazelwood School at Lac Qui Parle. Also includes an account written in 1958 by Anna Amrud in which she reminisces about the early settlement of Minnesota.

9,317. Riheldaffer, John Gillan, and Family
Papers. 1848-1959. 2 boxes and 4 oversize items.
Open. Unpublished guide.
Minnesota Historical Society, Archives and Manuscripts.
John Riheldaffer (1818-93) was a Presbyterian minister, a territorial settler in Minnesota, and founder of the St. Paul Female Seminary. His papers include correspondence with his wife and daughters about family and community news, religious beliefs, and moral advice; a manuscript he wrote about his family life and childhood; and notes concerning the execution of Anne Evards [Mrs. Stanislaus] Bilansky in 1860 and Jane Grey Swisshelm's appearance before the Minnesota Senate in 1862 arguing for women's right to hold property in their own name and to have custody of minor children, about which Riheldaffer commented, "The views of this woman are in contravention with the laws of God." Also includes diaries of Martha Anna Riheldaffer (1856-1930) for 1873 to 1886 and of her sister Catherine Riheldaffer (1858-1935) for 1873 to 1891 dealing in part with their work as teachers at the Minnesota State Reform School in St. Paul; a family journal for 1876 to 1905, in which members recorded their thoughts, feelings, and descriptions of events; a diploma Catherine Riheldaffer received from the Seminary in 1876; and a 1959 Christmas letter by Helen Gould Wallace [Mrs. David Timerman] Riheldaffer (1908-) containing information on family history. Records of the Seminary, which was established in 1858, include a prospectus for 1858, a roll book for 1864 to 1870, essays and articles about the Seminary, and "Model Things," a booklet issued by the school in 1866, which contains essays on the model wife, husband, baby, schoolgirl, bachelor, old maid, minister, editor, newspaper, and church.

9,318. Ristine, Henry, and Family
Papers. 1855-1950. 3 boxes and 3 items.
Open. Unpublished guide.
Minnesota Historical Society, Archives and Manuscripts.
Correspondence, including letters from Ristine, a physician, to his wife Catherine McMaster Ristine (?-1893) concerning his Civil War experiences and letters to her from her sister in Cincinnati; manuscript essays by Bella Maria Ristine [Mrs. Oliver Cromwell] Wyman (1855-1953), a kindergarten teacher and artist; wedding announcements of the Vaughn and Wyman families; certificates awarded to Bella Ristine for completion of courses at Mrs. C. F. Mederia's Normal Training School for Kindergarteners in Cedar Rapids, IA, in 1878 and 1879; and volumes of drawing, design, and composition books of Bella Ristine, including her mat designs, geometric designs, and designs for weaving.

9,319. Roberts, Thomas Sadler
Papers. 1857-1947. 2 boxes.
Open. Unpublished guide.
Minnesota Historical Society, Archives and Manuscripts.
Roberts (1858-1946) was a Minneapolis physician, state ornithologist, and director of the Natural Science Museum at the University of Minnesota. Includes diaries in which his mother Elizabeth Jane (Sadler) [Mrs. John] Roberts describes a trip to Europe and other events that occurred between 1891 and 1903.

9,320. Robinson, Mortimer, and Family
Papers. 1859-74. 1 microfilm reel.
Open. Unpublished guide.
Minnesota Historical Society, Archives and Manuscripts.
Letters Robinson wrote while he was a drummer boy for the First Minnesota Regiment and other Civil War letters, several of which were by women. Also includes minutes of meetings of the Hennepin County Anti-Slavery Society, which urged the legislature to pass a stringent personal liberty bill and to amend the state constitution to provide for equal suffrage.

9,321. Rood, Dorothy (Bridgman) Atkinson, and Family
Papers. 1903-64. 1 box and 2 bacases.
Open. Unpublished guide.
Minnesota Historical Society, Archives and Manuscripts.
Letters to her family, diaries, scrapbooks, and clippings of [Mrs. John] Rood (1890-1965), who was active in civic affairs. Includes diaries in which she describes trips to Europe in 1903 and 1910-11; her time at Wellesley College and marriage to Frederich Atkinson, 1907-11; the births of her children and life in Minneapolis, 1912-15; and her children, 1918.

9,322. Roos, Carl, and Family
Papers. 1848-1965. 3 microfilm reels.
Open. Unpublished guide.
Minnesota Historical Society, Archives and Manuscripts.
Carl Roos (1805-89) and his family, who emigrated from Sweden, were among the first settlers in the Swedish community of Vasa Township, Goodhue County, MN. Letters to Roos from his wife Clara Sofia Persdotter Roos (1827-1910); his daughters Carolina Gustafva (Roos) [Mrs. Frank] Barnes (1853-1910), Cornelia Sophia Roos (1856-ca. 1910), Camilla Rosalia (Roos) [Mrs. John F.] Rosenfield (1860-98), Celinda Armida Roos (1866-84), and Tialender Cassandra (Roos) [Mrs. James] McNeilly (1874-1964); his two sons; and persons outside the family. Also includes financial records and a family Bible containing genealogical notes.

9,323. Rosenthal, Robert
Papers. Nd. 3.75 ft.
Open. Unpublished guide.
Minnesota Historical Society, Archives and Manuscripts.
Research notes by Rosenthal on the history of medicine in Minnesota include mention of about 40 women physicians and biographies detailing the professional careers of physicians Emma K. Ogden, [Mrs.] Mary M. S. Pratt, Mrs. M. I. Mathew, Adelaide Brunelle, Lea Murphy, Augusta Isabella True, Elizabeth Stacey, Johanna Disbro, Ellen M. Fairbanks, Fannie Allen Anderson, Martha George Ripley, Clara Ruter, Louise Marie Gruber-Dietmeier, E. Stella Perrigo, Carrol C. Carpenter, Jennie Miller Colsan, Fanny Gray Kimball Fiester, Emma Washburn Rodgers, Sarah Catherine Wilcox, Genevieve Tucker, Sara M. Ayars, Florence C. Baier, Mary A. Bassett, Ella Everett, Elizabeth Lewis, Elizabeth Mallison, Mary Ranson Strickler, Nellie N. Barsness, midwife Nellie Helmin, the Benedictine Sisters, and St. Cloud Hospital.

9,324. Rovers' Club
Records. 1903-35. 1 box.
Open. Unpublished guide.
Minnesota Historical Society, Archives and Manuscripts.
Minutes of meetings of this social club of Excelsior, MN, families, which was organized in 1901.

9,325. Rowley, Adelaide A.
Papers. 1929. 55-page item.
Open. No guide.
Minnesota Historical Society, Archives and Manuscripts.
Reminiscences by Rowley (1905-) of the pioneer experiences of her family in Nebraska, South Dakota, and Canada. She describes sod houses in Nebraska, social life, crops, schools, and other aspects of pioneer life.

9,326. Royalton Methodist Episcopal Church, Royalton, Township, MN
Records. 1889-1969. 1 box.
Open. Unpublished guide.
Minnesota Historical Society, Archives and Manuscripts.
Records of this church in Pine County, MN, are primarily in Swedish and include a treasurer's book, 1923-50, and financial statements, 1945-46, of the Ladies Aid.

9,327. Sageng, Ole O.
Papers. 1904-53. 5 boxes.
Open. Unpublished guide.
Minnesota Historical Society, Archives and Manuscripts.
Sageng (1871-1963), a Republican, was a state representative from 1900 to 1922 and state senator from 1951 to 1954. Correspondence centers around legislation and includes items relating to Sageng's interest in and support of woman suffrage, prohibition, the establishment of the Home School for Girls in Sauk Centre, MN, and teacher pensions and retirement plans. Also includes correspondence pertaining to his unsuccessful bid for the Republican nomination for US senator in 1923 and 1924; the letters indicate that he was strongly supported by leaders of the woman suffrage and prohibition movements. Correspondents include Marguerite Milton Wells, Ethel Edgerton, Eugenia B. Farmer, and Isabel Higbee.

9,328. St. Aladie, Sister
Papers. 1899. 2 microfilm reels.
Open. Unpublished guide.
Minnesota Historical Society, Archives and Manuscripts.
Manuscript history of the Little Sisters of the Poor, a Roman Catholic community of women in St. Paul dedicated to serving the poor and providing them with housing, clothing, and food. The history, which was written in French by Sister St. Aladie, a member of the order, commences with the year 1883.

9,329. St. Ansgarius Episcopal Church
Records. 1880-1936. 1 microfilm reel.
Open. Unpublished guide.
Minnesota Historical Society, Archives and Manuscripts.
Household census of parishioners of this Minneapolis church.

9,330. St. Anthony Park Association
Papers. 1897-1926. 3 boxes.
Open. Unpublished guide.
Minnesota Historical Society, Archives and Manuscripts.
Minutes, financial records, historical sketches, and reminiscences of this St. Paul study club interested in civic improvements, which was originally named the St. Anthony Park Women's Association. Also includes minutes, 1897-98, of the St. Anthony Park School Union, a group that was organized by the Women's Association to promote educational interests.

9,331. St. James Episcopal Church
Records. 1887-1975. 1 microfilm reel.
Open. Unpublished guide.
Minnesota Historical Society, Archives and Manuscripts.
Parish records of this Marshall, MN, church include records of the St. Cecelia Guild, a women's organization.

9,332. St. Mark's African Methodist Episcopal Church
Records. 1893-1957. 1 microfilm reel.
Open. Unpublished guide.
Minnesota Historical Society, Archives and Manuscripts.
Parish records of this Duluth, MN, church include financial reports of the Sarah Allen Missionary Society and Sunday school and Sunday school teachers' record books.

9,333. St. Paul and Ramsey County War History Committee
Records. 1942-46. 2 boxes and 1 vol.
Open. Unpublished guide.
Minnesota Historical Society, Archives and Manuscripts.
The Committee, which existed from 1942 to 1946, was composed of citizens interested in preserving documents pertaining to the history of St. Paul and Ramsey County, MN, during WWII; the group was under the direction of the Minnesota Office of Civilian Defense. contains interviews by the chairman of the Committee with St. Paul citizens who describe the ways in which the war affected their business or profession. Among those interviewed were Katherine Tschida, who was dean of girls at Mechanic Arts High School in St. Paul; Alice Lilliequist [Mrs. Henry Lawrence] Sickels, who worked at the International Institute; Mrs. J. E. Howe, who was active in community services; Frances Boardman, who was involved in music and the fine arts; and Sophie Hein, who worked in hospitals.

9,334. St. Paul Chamber of Commerce
Records. 1859-1945. 4 boxes, 1 vol., and 10 items.
Open. Unpublished guide.
Minnesota Historical Society, Archives and Manuscripts.
Includes minutes of meetings of the joint civic committee of the St. Paul Commercial Club, the Woman's Civic League of St. Paul, and the Twin City Municipal Exhibit Committee, groups that worked together to prepare an exhibit about the Twin Cities for the St. Louis Exposition of 1904.

9,335. St. Paul Choral Club
Records. 1898-1907. 1 vol.
Open. Unpublished guide.
Minnesota Historical Society, Archives and Manuscripts.
Scrapbook containing correspondence, financial records, tickets, programs, and clippings of the Club, which was organized in 1899.

9,336. St. Paul City Planning Board
Records. 1934-48. 13 items.
Open. Unpublished guide.
Minnesota Historical Society, Archives and Manuscripts.
Studies of the foreign-born population of St. Paul and a research project on the Minnesota Emergency Relief Administration with text by Katherine Spear.

9,337. St. Paul Ladies Auxiliary
Papers. 1901-07. 1 vol.
Open. Unpublished guide.
Minnesota Historical Society, Archives and Manuscripts.
Minutes and a membership list of this patriotic and civic organization contain descriptions of its activities, which included flower shows, programs for domestic science courses in schools, and benefit performances to raise money.

9,338. St. Paul Municipal Chorus
Records. 1920-34. 1 box and 1 vol.
Open. Unpublished guide.
Minnesota Historical Society, Archives and Manuscripts.
Minutes, correspondence, records of rehearsals, programs, and clippings of the Chorus, which included both men and women as members.

9,339. St. Paul Protestant Orphan Asylum
Records. 1883-1929. 1 bacase.
Open. Unpublished guide.
Minnesota Historical Society, Archives and Manuscripts.
Minutes of board meetings, account books, and letters written by the Asylum's corresponding secretary Katharine M. Beals.

9,340. Saint Paul Reading Circle
Records. 1872-80. 3 vols.
Open. Unpublished guide.
Minnesota Historical Society, Archives and Manuscripts.
Constitution, minutes, membership lists, and programs of this social club of men and women who read and discussed the classics and presented private theatricals.

9,341. St. Paul Resettlement Committee
Records. 1942-53. 1 box and 1 vol.
Open. Unpublished guide.
Minnesota Historical Society, Archives and Manuscripts.
The Committee was organized in 1942 to aid Japanese-Americans coming to St. Paul from the West Coast after evacuation following the outbreak of WWII; the Committee provided occupations, financial assistance, and housing facilities and helped to integrate the Japanese-Americans into the social, cultural, and economic life of the city. Bylaws; a certificate of incorporation; minutes of meetings; correspondence; a lease on the St. Paul Resettlement Hostel, which was maintained by the Committee from 1945 to 1948; a journal of expenses and a register of the Hostel; reports by Elizbeth Evans, director of the Hostel, and others; committee lists; a list of contributors; and clippings. Also includes correspondence of various women involved in the Committee, among them Ruth Gage [Mrs. Woodard] Colby, Martha [Mrs. Elliot] Magraw, Ruth [Mrs. Earl] Tanbara, and Alice Lilliequest [Mrs. Henry Lawrence] Sickels.

9,342. St. Paul Urban League
Papers. 1928-69. 2 microfilm reels.
Open. Unpublished guide.
Minnesota Historical Society, Archives and Manuscripts.
Organized in 1923, the League is "an interracial movement which aims to improve the living and working conditions among the Black population [and] to heighten understanding and cooperation between Black and White Americans." Board of directors' proceedings, a board members guide, lists, and accounts of the League, which merged with the Minneapolis Urban League in 1926. It became a separate organization again in 1937. Many of its members and officers have been women.

9,343. St. Sigfrid's Episcopal Church
Records. 1896-1932. 1 microfilm reel.
Open. Unpublished guide.
Minnesota Historical Society, Archives and Manuscripts.
Records of this St. Paul church include a household census of parishioners.

9,344. Salem Congregational Church
Records. 1855-1956. 1 microfilm reel.
Open. Unpublished guide.
Minnesota Historical Society, Archives and Manuscripts.
Sunday school record book for 1879 to 1889, a semi-centennial scrapbook from 1905, a photo, clippings, and a 75th anniversary booklet of this Welsh Presbyterian church in Cambria, Blue Earth County, MN, which merged with several other churches in the 1950s. Some of the records are in Welsh.

9,345. Salisbury, Susan E., and Family
Papers. 1805-1927. 1 box and 20 items.
Open. Unpublished guide.
Minnesota Historical Society, Archives and Manuscripts.
Correspondence of members of the Salisbury and Whipple families includes letters from Sarah Brayton (Whipple) Salisbury in Adams, NY, to her husband Hiram Salisbury, to Sarah Salisbury and her daughter Susan E. Salisbury (1854-1930) from Susan Letitia (Whipple) [Mrs. Zaccheus] Hill (1826-94) and Cornelia Whipple concerning a trip to Scotland for a church celebration and life in England and Scotland, and to Susan Salisbury from her family and friends. Also includes deeds, title abstracts, information on stock investments, and other financial and legal papers of Susan Salisbury and of Hiram Salisbury's father D'Estaing Salisbury (?-1813) relating to the administration of his estate and to the care of his four minor children.

9,346. Sanford, Edward Rollin, and Family
Papers. 1836-1954. 5 boxes.
Open. Unpublished guide.
Minnesota Historical Society, Archives and Manuscripts.
Sanford, a wholesale lumber dealer in St. Paul, was married to Charlotte L. (Mead) Sanford (1871-?), the daughter of St. Paul lawyer Warren Mead. She was a vocalist who taught language for a short time at Macalester College in St. Paul. Correspondence, diary extracts, indentures, deeds, sketches, invitations, programs, menus, photos, clippings, and other papers of family members. Letters, passports, programs, and other items relate to the travels in Europe and residence in France and Germany of Charlotte Mead and her mother Frances Hughes Mead (1841-ca. 1900) while Charlotte was attending school there from 1884 to 1893. Other papers of Charlotte (Mead) Sanford include her diaries for 1903; a friendship album; scrapbooks of notes, photos, programs, and clippings concerning her wedding, her musical performances, and her work for the Fatherless Children of France, Inc.; a guest book containing autographs, photos, and programs; information on her friend Loie Fuller, a dancer; and reminiscences of Maria Gibbs Davis. Also includes a photo album and baby book of Frances Hughes Sanford (1906-), who later married Robert Anderson, and information on her attendance at Miss Spence's School for Girls in 1922 and 1923.

9,347. Sanford, Maria Louise
Papers. 1851-1920. 6 boxes and 2 oversize items.
Open. Unpublished guide.
Minnesota Historical Society, Archives and Manuscripts.
Sanford (1836-1920) was a professor of rhetoric at Swarthmore College from 1873 to 1880 and at the University of Minnesota from 1881 to 1909. Correspondence concerning her lectures throughout the US on literary and educational subjects and her interest in reform and progressive movements such as woman suffrage, Indian education, missionary work, and civic improvement of Minneapolis. Includes letters from colleagues and from former students of Maria Sanford Junior High in Minneapolis, printed material such as clippings on her life and on reform movements from the *Woman's Journal* and the *Suffrage News*, her lectures, bulletins and programs of the Woman's Club of Minneapolis and other women's clubs, tracts on reform issues, teacher's institute catalogs and proceedings, pamphlets on Sanford family genealogy, and memorial items relating to Sanford and Nina Morais Cohen.

9,348. Sans Souci, Gertrude
Papers. Ca. 1904-13. 34 items.
Open. Unpublished guide.
Minnesota Historical Society, Archives and Manuscripts.
Manuscripts of songs written by Sans Souci (1873-1913) and published by Paul A. Schmitt Music Company of Minneapolis, an invoice from Schmitt Music listing Sans Souci's royalties on sale of songs, an obituary of Sans Souci, and a brochure about her. Sans Souci was married to William C. Toomey.

9,349. Satterlee, Frances Mae (Howe)
Papers. 1892-1968. 9.5 ft.
Open. Unpublished guide.
Minnesota Historical Society, Archives and Manuscripts.
[Mrs. August N.] Satterlee (1892-), who was born in Minnesota, worked as a music teacher, manager of a talent booking agency, producer of historical pageants, and research analyst for Munsingwear, Inc., in Minneapolis. Correspondence, radio and television scripts, financial records, minutes of meetings, reports, and clippings relate to her involvement in consumer affairs and women's clubs, including the Minnesota Federation of Women's Clubs, the Hennepin County Women's Conference for Defense, Consumer Interests of Minneapolis, the GFWC consumer division, the Defense Advisory Committee on Women in the Services, and the US Food and Drug Administration's consumer consultant program.

9,350. Satterlee, William Wilson, and Satterlee, Marion P.
Papers. 1879-1928. 1 box and file cards.
Open. No guide.
Minnesota Historical Society, Archives and Manuscripts.
William Satterlee (1837-93) was a leader of the Prohibition party in Minnesota and a professor at Grant University in Athens, TN. Includes a letter to Satterlee from Frances Willard about the Prohibition party.

9,351. Savage, Edward P.
Papers. 1903-18. 1 box.
Open. Unpublished guide.
Minnesota Historical Society, Archives and Manuscripts.
Savage (1844-1921), a minister, was officer and superintendent of the Children's Home Society of Minnesota from 1889 to 1921. Manuscript history by Savage of the Society, whose purpose was to find homes for homeless children; reports on the evolution, collections, and work of the Society, which were written and delivered by Savage as sermons; draft legislation concerning the abandonment or neglect of wives and children, foster homes, custody of the feebleminded, formation of child welfare boards, a "wet nurse" bill, and licensing of lying-in hospitals; and clippings on homeless children, child mortality, and nourishment of a normal mother.

9,352. Save the Children Federation, Minnesota Branch
Records. 1925-51. 2 boxes.
Open. Unpublished guide.
Minnesota Historical Society, Archives and Manuscripts.
Financial records, correspondence concerning child relief activities in the US and Europe and local Minnesota sponsorships and programs, fund-raising letters, reports, and circulars of the Minnesota Branch, which was located in St. Paul and existed from 1945 until ca. 1954. Includes correspondence of Ruth Gage [Mrs. Woodward L.] Colby, who was president of the Minnesota Branch, and of Mae L. [Mrs. George H.] Washburn, who was executive secretary of the Minnesota branch. Financial records of the St. Paul chapter are also included.

9,353. Scandinavian Young Women's Christian Temperance Union of Minneapolis
Records. 1885-92. 2 folders.
Open. Unpublished guide.
Minnesota Historical Society, Archives and Manuscripts.
Minutes and an account and memorandum book that contains data on the organization, meetings, taking of pledges, election of officers, appointment and functioning of committees, payment of dues, membership, and preparation of the constitution and bylaws. Members of the Union pledged to abstain from alcohol and to discourage the use of alcohol.

9,354. Schaefer, Jacob, and Family
Papers. 1855-1935. 1 box and 1 item.
Open. Unpublished guide.
Minnesota Historical Society, Archives and Manuscripts.
Diary in which Sarah (Miller) [Mrs. Jacob] Schaefer (1820-1908) describes a trip to Honduras; an essay by Mary Thayer Hale (1848-1942) concerning the arrival of the Hale family in Minneapolis from Connecticut in 1860 and the economic and cultural growth of Minneapolis between 1860 and 1930; autographs; and papers of Francesca Schaefer (1856-?), including her school report card and 1874 diploma from the Minneapolis Female Seminary, letters written to her family after her marriage to William Overton Winston about a tour through Scandinavian and western European countries, and an essay describing her trip to Honduras in 1935 to visit the village in which she was born. Also includes an essay by Elizabeth Martin Winston and her husband Donald O. Winston on the economic, political, and social history of Colombia.

9,355. Schmidt, Mary (Schwandt)
Papers. 1895-1918. 1 box.
Open. Unpublished guide.
Minnesota Historical Society, Archives and Manuscripts.
The Schwandts were German immigrants who settled in Minnesota Territory. Letters of [Mrs. William F.] Schmidt (1848-?) from Maggie Brass, who calls Schmidt her "dear adopted daughter" and discusses the times they spent together, Indian relationships and life, expenses, visits, and her desire to see Schmidt again; an 1862 photo of Brass; and articles and a newspaper story by

Schmidt relating to her journey to Minnesota, her life in Minnesota Territory, the Dakota War of 1862, her captivity, and her family. Brass, whose Dakota name was Snana, wrote to Schmidt from the Santee Agency in Nebraska.

9,356. Schoolcraft, Henry Rowe
Papers. 1806-1926. 1 vol.
Open. No guide.
Minnesota Historical Society, Archives and Manuscripts.
Volume includes correspondence between John K. West and Henry L. Schoolcraft in 1926 concerning the possibility that the volume was kept by Henry R. Schoolcraft and an extract from the diary of [Mrs.] Mary (Howard) Schoolcraft.

9,357. Schubert Club
Records. 1885-1968. 5 boxes, 7 bacases, and 1 oversize item.
Open. Unpublished guide.
Minnesota Historical Society, Archives and Manuscripts.
Founded in St. Paul in 1887, this women's club sponsors a chorus and orchestra as well as visiting artists. Includes minutes of board meetings, a treasurer's book, an account book, a financial statement, committee reports and annual reports of the president, a secretary's book, correspondence, membership lists, scrapbooks, programs, material on the Education Loan Fund, and other records. Also includes a secretary's book, 1885-88, of the Ladies Musicale, which was founded in 1882, and a 1954 manuscript by Jeannette Murray concerning a music group.

9,358. Schutz, John G., and Family
Papers. 1874-1952. 1 vol. and 35 items.
Open. Unpublished guide.
Minnesota Historical Society, Archives and Manuscripts.
Correspondence of Josephine Amy Hunt (1857-1937), before and after her marriage to Schutz, with her aunt and friends concerning social activities, schools, and teaching in Minnesota; a certificate from New York State University, which indicates that she was registered there in 1874; an 1875 contract for Josephine Hunt to teach school in Excelsior, MN; and birth, marriage, and death records of the John and Josephine Schutz family. Also includes diaries that Louise Elizabeth Schutz (1885-) kept during a tour of western Europe in 1913 and on a tour of the Caribbean, eastern Africa, South Asia, the Middle East, and the Mediterranean in 1952.

9,359. Schwyzer, Arnold, and Family
Papers. 1852-1964. 15 boxes and 15 vols.
Access restricted. Unpublished guide.
Minnesota Historical Society, Archives and Manuscripts.
Schwyzer (1864-1944), a Swiss immigrant, was professor of surgery at Hamline University in St. Paul and a lecturer at the University of Minnesota medical school. He was married to Johanna Heneggeler Schwyzer (?-1905) and then to Marguerite Mueller Schwyzer. His daughter Marguerite Schwyzer (?-1968) was a St. Paul physician who worked for the Wilder Foundation, MEDICO, and the University of Minnesota student health center. Correspondence, primarily in German, between Arnold Schwyzer and his parents and friends in Switzerland and in English between his children during their college days; diary and composition notebooks of Johanna Heneggeler; a notebook and autograph book of Marguerite Mueller; and guest books, an autograph book, and other papers of the younger Marguerite Schwyzer relating to her medical practice, her efforts to promote motor vehicle safety, and anticommunist activities.

9,360. Scott, Alma Deivia Schmidt
Papers. 1908-62. 3 boxes.
Open. Unpublished guide.
Minnesota Historical Society, Archives and Manuscripts.
Papers of [Mrs.] Scott (1892-) relate primarily to her biography of Wanda Gág, the work for which was supported by a grant from the University of Minnesota Regional Writing Fellowships. Correspondence of Scott with Gág containing notes on Scott's interviews with family and friends of Gág; correspondence of Scott with Gág's husband Earle Humphreys, with Gág's sister Stella Gág, and with Helen Clapesattle; a manuscript of the biography, which was published in 1949 by the University of Minnesota Press; an article by Scott on the history of the New Ulm, MN, Public Library; sketches and drawings by Gág; catalogs of Gág's exhibits; and clippings on Gág, her biography, and the Wanda Gág Memorial Fund. Also includes letters to Scott from Rolland T. Heywood, who was serving in the Korean War at the time.

9,361. Scott, Louis N., and Family
Papers. 1882-1943. 14 boxes, 2 oversize boxes, and 2 bacases.
Open. Unpublished guide.
Minnesota Historical Society, Archives and Manuscripts.
Scott (1859-1929) managed the New Market Theater and the Metropolitan Opera House in St. Paul and was lessee, manager, and owner of several other important theaters in St. Paul. After his death his wife Elizabeth N. Scott (ca. 1876-1955) continued his work. Correspondence concerning Eva Tanguay, Rose Kane, and other performers; letters from theatrical agencies and managers representing such performers as Gracie Emmett, Emma Abbott, Lizzie Evans, Madeline Merli, and the Jeanie Winston Opera Company; correspondence of Elizabeth Scott with civic groups about her efforts to save legitimate theater in Minneapolis; an account book, a ledger, and a journal of the Metropolitan Opera House Company in St. Paul; check stubs and cashbooks; leases and managing records for various Twin Cities theaters; invoices, statements, and contracts of Elizabeth Scott for theatrical productions; biographical sketches of actors and actresses; advertising lists; and other papers.

9,362. Scriver, Helen
Papers. 1918-19. 2 folders.
Open. Unpublished guide.
Minnesota Historical Society, Archives and Manuscripts.
Scriver (1889-), a Minneapolis native, was an American National Red Cross worker during WWI in France, where she assisted with the establishment of a social service exchange in Marseilles. Her papers include correspondence in which she describes her social life, dances for American soldiers, her relationships with French families, and conditions and life in Paris and Marseilles.

9,363. Seabury, Channing, and Family
Papers. 1854-1955. 2 folders.
Open. Unpublished guide.
Minnesota Historical Society, Archives and Manuscripts.
Seabury (1842-1910), who migrated from Massachusetts to Minnesota in 1860, was a wholesale merchandiser. Letters by Seabury and his sister Caroline Seabury to their aunt and uncle in New York City giving information on their schooling, diaries, and certificates. Diary kept by Caroline Seabury from 1854 to 1863 while she was teaching in a female seminary in Columbus, MS, contains descriptions of her journey from Jersey City to Columbus; a smallpox epidemic in 1857; her growing appreciation of southerners; hiring of and bidding for black slaves; attitudes of southerners during the Civil War; the health of her sister Martha, who came to stay with her and teach in the South; her experiences in the Columbus hospital when 800 wounded men were brought in from the battle of Shiloh; and traveling through the lines home to New York after losing her job in 1862 because she was not of southern birth.

9,364. Senkler, George Easton, and Family
Papers. 1844-1965. 0.5 ft.
Open. No guide.
Minnesota Historical Society, Archives and Manuscripts.
Papers of Senkler's wife Abigail Louise (Dickson) Senkler (1871-1961), a St. Paul physician, include letters to her mother during her wedding trip to Europe in 1902, her marriage certificate, and a cabin passenger list. Also includes letters to their daughter Ellen Burgess Senkler, who later married J. Fuller Brown, from Eleanor James concerning family history and family news.

9,365. Sharp, Mrs. Edgar E.
Papers. 1938. 6-page item.
Open. No guide.
Minnesota Historical Society, Archives and Manuscripts.
A chapter in the history of the Ladies' Union of the First Congregational Church of Moorhead, MN.

9,366. Shattuck, Eliza (Lanphear)
Papers. 1850-90. 1 box.
Open. Unpublished guide.
Minnesota Historical Society, Archives and Manuscripts.
Polly Lanphear and Mary Lanphear, who later married Frank Cummings, left Vermont with their father and brothers and settled in Minnesota Territory. Letters to their sister Eliza (Lanphear) Shattuck in Vermont concern their journey to Illinois in 1850, social life, male-female relationships, clothing, factory work, locating a homestead, health and death, boarders, homes, family events, weather, Indian wars, and crops.

9,367. Shillock, Daniel G., and Family
Papers. 1854-1914. 1 box.
Open. Unpublished guide.
Minnesota Historical Society, Archives and Manuscripts.
Shillock (1824-?) and his family emigrated from Koenigsburg, Prussia, in 1854 and lived in Texas, Connecticut, and Wisconsin before settling in New Ulm, MN, where Shillock, a lawyer and later a state senator and representative, organized a bank. Letters in German to family and friends in Koenigsburg by his wife Mathilda Shillock (1826-?), a piano teacher, chronicle the family's travels and lives. Also includes a 1914 diary in which their daughter Anna Felicia Shillock (1866-?), a math and German teacher in Minneapolis high schools, describes the outbreak of WWI and a home budget book with financial accounts for the last part of the family's journey from Prussia.

9,368. Shipstead, Henrik
Papers. 1913-53. 28 boxes, 4 bacases, and 1 oversize box.
Access restricted. Unpublished guide.
Minnesota Historical Society, Archives and Manuscripts.
Shipstead (1881-1960), US senator from Minnesota from 1922 to 1946, was a member of the Senate Foreign Relations Committee. Letters from constituents concerning legislation and personal requests and a 1945 letter and memo from Eugenie Moore [Mrs. John P.] Anderson urging him to support the proposals developed during the international monetary conference held in 1944 at Bretton Woods, NH.

9,369. Shober, George, and Family
Papers. 1811-96. 3 boxes, 1 vol., and 3 oversize items.
Open. Unpublished guide.
Minnesota Historical Society, Archives and Manuscripts.
Correspondence among members of the Shober and related families in Ohio, Iowa, Kansas, and Minnesota concerns family news, the sale of property, prices of land, crops, prices received for sale of farm produce, and the weather. Includes frequent letters by Amanda (Scott) [Mrs. Herod Jacob] Shober (ca. 1835-71), her daughter Harriet Shober (ca. 1860-?), Amanda Shober's mother Polly Scott, Mary Scott, and Elizabeth (Shober) [Mrs. William] Evans (1834-?), sister of Herod Shober (1821-?) and John H. Shober (1832-1925), who was a territorial settler and postmaster in Mantorville, MN, as well as a store owner, register of deeds, and clerk of court in Dodge County, MN.

9,370. Shumway, John P.
Papers. 1853-65. 76 items.
Open. Unpublished guide.
Minnesota Historical Society, Archives and Manuscripts.
Shumway (1830-1917), a farmer, was born in Connecticut and settled in Minnesota Territory. His wife Louisa A. (Ross) Shumway taught school in Connecticut before marrying and moving to Minnesota in the late 1850s. Letters to John Shumway from friends and relatives in Connecticut, including Louisa Ross, and correspondence between John and Louisa Shumway, while he was serving in the Civil War, about the weather, loneliness, guerrilla warfare, railroads, clothing, food, and family needs.

9,371. Sibley, Henry Hastings
Papers. 1815-1930. 15 ft. and 32 microfilm reels.
Open. Published guide.
Minnesota Historical Society, Archives and Manuscripts.
Sibley (1811-91), who began his career as a fur trade agent and partner in the American Fur Company, later served as Minnesota territorial representative to Congress. A Democrat, he was the first governor of the state of Minnesota and founder of the University of Minnesota and the Minnesota Historical Society. Correspondence, an unfinished autobiography Sibley wrote from 1884 to 1886, fur trade records, a scrapbook, and other papers. Includes papers concerning Helen Hastings (whose Indian name was Muzzah Wakon Win), the daughter of Sibley and Red Blanket Woman, a Wahpekute Dakota Indian, and Sibley's assuming financial responsibility for his daughter. Correspondence of Sarah Jane (Steele) Sibley (?-1869), whom he married in 1843, includes a letter to her sister Rachel (Steele) Johnson and letters to and from her husband while he was in Washington and during his military service from 1861 to 1865. A scrapbook by Constance Locke [Mrs. Charles F.] Sibley relates to the Sibley family and house. Letters by Henry Sibley relate to the health of Sarah Sibley and their children Augusta Ann (Sibley) [Mrs. Douglas] Pope (1844-), Sarah Jane (Sibley) [Mrs. Albert A.] Young (1851-), Charles Frederic Sibley (1860-), and Alfred Busch Sibley (1866-); to the death of one of their children in 1851; and to his concern for and desire to help victims of the Dakota War of 1862, especially Mary Schwandt and Mrs. Stephen Riggs. Includes microfilm copies of Sibley manuscripts from the Burton Historical Collection of the Detroit Public Library. See Jane Spector Davis, comp., *Guide to a Microfilm Edition of the Henry Hastings Sibley Papers* (St. Paul: Minnesota Historical Society, 1968).

9,372. Simpson, David Ferguson, and Family
Papers. 1847-1956. 1 box.
Open. Unpublished guide.
Minnesota Historical Society, Archives and Manuscripts.
Simpson, a lawyer and Minnesota Supreme Court justice, was married to Josephine Sarles Simpson (1862-1948). Correspondence; typescript of "A Talk to Women About Women," probably written by Josephine Simpson in ca. 1944; a scrapbook containing programs, clippings, and other material relating to such events as the marriage of Josephine Sarles and David Simpson and their graduation from the University of Wisconsin; a citation to Josephine Simpson from the National American Woman Suffrage Association; material relating to the appointment of Josephine Simpson as a delegate to the First Minnesota Conservation and Development Congress in St. Paul in 1910 and to the Conference on Law Enforcement in Washington, DC; an 1847 marriage certificate of William Lewis and Maria Newkirk of Montgomery County, NY; and an essay by Jessie Simpson about the Scottish ancestry of the Goodsir, Simpson, and Ferguson families and their migration to the US in the 19th century.

9,373. Sloan, Marion Louisa
Papers. 1937. 30 pp.
Open. No guide.
Minnesota Historical Society, Archives and Manuscripts.
Interview in which [Miss] Sloan (1846-?) gives information on her trip from Massachusetts to Rochester, MN, in 1856, her experiences as a schoolteacher, and Clara Barton's visit to Minnesota. Also includes reminiscences she wrote in 1926 about early Rochester schools and genealogies of the Clark and Winslow families, from which she was descended.

9,374. Smith, Dee
Papers. 1917-21. 1 box.
Open. Unpublished guide.
Minnesota Historical Society, Archives and Manuscripts.
Smith (1882-), a resident of Minneapolis, served with the American National Red Cross in France during WWI and from 1919 to 1946 was executive secretary of the Minneapolis Teachers' Retirement Association. Letters by Smith to her family concerning her decision to join the Red Cross, her training in New York City, her trip to Paris via Liverpool and London, living arrangements and social life in Paris, and her clerical work with the Red Cross; minutes of a 1921 Women's Overseas Service League meeting in Minneapolis; a poster; programs; pamphlets on the experiences of a Red Cross girl and instructions to Red Cross workers in France; and medals.

9,375. Smith, Francis Monroe
Papers. 1936-51. 3 boxes.
Open. Unpublished guide.
Minnesota Historical Society, Archives and Manuscripts.
Includes correspondence of the Minnesota Democratic Farmer-Labor Women's Study Club in St. Paul and of the Indpendent Voters of Minnesota indicating support for liberal candidates in the 1946 election, including Marcia Killen for the 5th district congressional seat, and a certificate of nomination of Susie (Williamson) [Mrs. Olaf O.] Stageberg as Progressive party candidate for lieutenant governor in 1950.

9,376. Smith, Henry Arthur, and Family
Papers. 1820-1927. 4 boxes.
Open. Unpublished guide.
Minnesota Historical Society, Archives and Manuscripts.
Correspondence, diaries, and clippings of the family of Smith (1844-?), a journalist in Dodge County, MN. Includes letters to his niece in London, MI; letters from an aunt who discusses religion, morality, family news, health, childbirth, child rearing, housework, and death; and letters to his daughter Eva Smith while she was a student at Carleton College in Northfield, MN, in 1909. Also includes correspondence between family members concerning "woman's work," social life, church activities, religion, land, marriage, health, and death and sketches by Henry Smith of a "female shower" party in the 1850s.

9,377. Smith, Mrs. Walter F.
Papers. 1954. 3 items.
Open. No guide.
Minnesota Historical Society, Archives and Manuscripts.
Manuscripts by Smith on the history of Balsam Township in Itasca County, MN, of Balsam Township schools, and of the Itasca County Farm Bureau from 1924 to 1953.

9,378. Smith, Orrin F., and Family
Papers. 1829-1932. 3 boxes and 3 oversize items.
Open. Unpublished guide.
Minnesota Historical Society, Archives and Manuscripts.
Papers of Smith include diaries, articles, a scrapbook, and other papers of Catherine McClure Fruit Goddard Smith. Includes a diary she kept during a trip from Pennsylvania to Illinois after her marriage in 1833 to Abner S. Goddard. Also includes a scrapbook and articles by and about her after her marriage to Alexander B. Smith. The scrapbook contains her reminiscences about early Winona, MN, and articles about herself, other territorial settlers, and about Helen M. Ely, who in 1875 became the first female graduate of the University of Minnesota. Also contains an article she wrote about the first Christmas dinner in Winona.

9,379. Socialist Labor Party of Minnesota, Minneapolis
Records. 1908-64. 2 boxes and 2 packages.
Open. Unpublished guide.
Minnesota Historical Society, Archives and Manuscripts.
Speeches; news releases; pamphlets issued by the national party on peace and disarmament, automation, civil rights, and other topics; *Arm and Hammer* for some years in the period 1924-35; booklets by Olive Johnson, Georgia P. Cozzini, and other authors published by the Socialist Labor party; Socialist Labor party magazines; and other records of the Socialist Labor party of Minnesota, which is located in Minneapolis.

9,380. Socialist Workers Party
Records. 1914-64. 10 boxes.
Open. Unpublished guide.
Minnesota Historical Society, Archives and Manuscripts.
Correspondence, campaign material, a scrapbook, and clippings of the party in Minneapolis relate to campaigns by party members, including that of Grace Holmes Carlson, a Minnesotan, for the US vice-presidency in 1948 and of Myra Tanner Weiss for Vice-President in 1952 and for other offices. Also includes booklets by Mary E. Marcy, Larissa Reissner, Charlotte Todes, and Myra Weiss and records, 1941-44, of the civil rights defense committee, which organized to protest the prosecution and imprisonment of 18 officers of Motor Transport and Allied Workers Industrial Union Local 544 of Minneapolis who were accused of sedition under the Smith Act.

9,381. Sollie, Allan N., and Sollie, Violet Johnson
Papers. Ca. 1928-60s. 6 bacases.
Access restricted. No guide.
Minnesota Historical Society, Archives and Manuscripts.
Violet Sollie, a tax expert who helped draft much of the Minnesota tax legislation passed by the Farmer-Labor party in the 1930s, was with her husband active in the labor movement and a leader

in the Hennepin County Farmer-Labor party. Correspondence, reports, articles, clippings, and mimeographed and printed material relate to the Sollies' political activities, Floyd B. Olson campaigns, Minnesota tax legislation, rehabilitation and employment of the handicapped, education, mental retardation, conservation, public transportation, civic issues, and labor unions, including the AFL-CIO, the Office and Professional Employees International Union, and the American Federation of State, County and Municipal Employees.

9,382. Solomon, Harrie M.
Papers. 1909. 1 vol.
Open. No guide.
Minnesota Historical Society, Archives and Manuscripts.
Consists of *The Girl Graduate, Her Own Book,* a scrapbook published by Central High School of St. Paul. Contains class photos, programs, and signatures.

9,383. Southworth, Newton, and Family
Papers. 1852-1917. 1 box.
Open. Unpublished guide.
Minnesota Historical Society, Archives and Manuscripts.
Correspondence of members of the Southworth family, who migrated from Massachusetts to Belle Plaine in territorial Minnesota, and their friends and relations. Includes letters from Rhoda Sparrow [Mrs. Newton] Southworth (1811-?) to her son Eli; letters Eli received from his sisters Sophie Wing Southworth (1840-?) and Nellie Southworth, who wrote during the Civil War giving information about family activities, crops, religion, and family hardships while the men were in the army; and letters in which Susan M. Sparrow [Mrs. Solomon] Eaton of Mattopoisett, MA, who was the sister of Rhoda Sparrow Southworth, discusses news of family and friends in Massachusetts and her reactions to the outbreak of the Civil War.

9,384. Spears, Julia A. (Warren), and Family
Papers. 1839-1923. 15 items.
Open. Unpublished guide.
Minnesota Historical Society, Archives and Manuscripts.
Letters and reminiscent articles by [Mrs. Andrew J.] Spears (1832-?), a part-Ojibwe Indian and teacher of the Ojibwe, concerning the Fairbanks family, two traders of Otter Tail Lake, frontier days, a trip to Sandy Lake in 1850 with her brother William Warren, the assassination of Hole-in-the-Day, and the history of White Earth, MN. Also includes letters to Lyman Warren from his brother James H. Warren and from Henry Adams.

9,385. Spencer, Rose Carolyn Hedlund
Papers. 1889-1967. 4 ft.
Open. Unpublished guide.
Minnesota Historical Society, Archives and Manuscripts.
[Mrs. Milton Leroy] Spencer (1891-1967), a graduate of Hamline University in St. Paul, taught speech and music; she also was active in civic, political, and charitable organizations. Correspondence, minutes, plays, reports, membership lists and cards, certificates, newsletters, clippings, and other papers relate to the AAUW; the Minnesota Mother's Committee; social welfare; dramatics; hospital auxiliaries; the UN; the Minnesota division of the American Cancer Society, of which she was president; and the Minnesota department of the American Legion Auxiliary, of which she was president. Also includes papers relating to her service as state chairwoman of the Republican party from 1939 to 1949, the women's division of the Republican State Central Committee, the Winona County Historical Society, the Winona County Public Health Nursing Advisory Committee, the Winona PTA, and the Chautauqua Club there.

9,386. Stageberg, Susie (Williamson)
Papers. 1881-1961. 3 boxes.
Open. Unpublished guide.
Minnesota Historical Society, Archives and Manuscripts.
[Mrs. Olaf O.] Stageberg (ca. 1877-1961), a leader in the Minnesota Farmer-Labor party, ran for secretary of state in 1922, 1924, and 1928 and for Congress in 1932 on the Farmer-Labor ticket; she also was executive secretary of the Women's Nonpartisan Clubs of Minnesota. Correspondence with Belle (Case) [Mrs. Robert Marion] La Follette, Selma Seestrom, Jean [Mrs. Frederick W.] Wittich, and others; articles she wrote about temperance, religion, and world peace, some of which were published in *Minnesota Leader;* campaign material; songbooks of a woman suffrage organization; and the temperance publications *Minnesota White Ribboner* (1894) and *Western Womanhood* (1896). In 1950 Stageberg ran for lieutenant governor of Minnesota on the Progressive party ticket.

9,387. Stanchfield, Bessie Mae
Papers. 1935-47. 2 boxes.
Open. Unpublished guide.
Minnesota Historical Society, Archives and Manuscripts.
Stanchfield (1901-48) was supervisor of music in the St. Cloud, MN, public schools, a summer school instructor at the University of Minnesota, and coordinator of music for the Los Angeles public schools from 1945 to 1948. Correspondence from individuals and institutions concerning an article she was writing and her progress in compiling folk music; music and lyrics of and notes on folk songs, including lumberjack songs collected by Stanchfield; radio show scripts and articles by Stanchfield on such subjects as songs of Minnesota pioneers, folk ballads of Minnesota, and musical contributions made to Minnesota by national groups; clippings; a bibliography on folk music; and a card index of Minnesota songs.

9,388. Staples, George Howard, and Family
Papers. 1882-1950. 2 boxes.
Open. Unpublished guide.
Minnesota Historical Society, Archives and Manuscripts.
Staples (1858-1944) was married to Carrie Gertrude Rodgers Staples (1864-1955). Her papers contain a letter to her cousin in Santa Cruz; congratulatory letters on her 50th wedding anniversary in 1937; her diaries for 1882 and 1944 to 1950; a transcript of an address she gave in 1938 at a testimonial dinner for Harold E. Stassen, Republican candidate for governor of Minnesota; her history of a Mendota, MN, school district; her genealogy of the Lincoln, Dayton, and Staples families; an account she wrote of Milfred Willis Staples's service in WWI, based on letters he wrote to his family; other writings; and report cards and tuition receipts from the Baldwin School in St. Paul, which she attended in 1885 and 1886. Papers of Myrtle Cole Staples (1890-1927) include her diary of a 1915 trip to Montana, where she worked on a ranch owned by relatives; a notebook of examples of sewing and mending, which she kept while attending the agriculture school at the University of Minnesota; a paper she wrote on her graduation from the University; and a remembrance card issued to her by School District No. 5 in Mendota.

9,389. Stapleton, Susan
Papers. 1964-65. 14 items.
Open. Unpublished guide.
Minnesota Historical Society, Archives and Manuscripts.
Correspondence and clippings of Stapleton, a Bemidji, MN, resident who was a Peace Corps volunteer in Guatemala. Includes letters in which she describes inhabitants, housing conditions, food, educational facilities, political situations, and her experiences in Guatemala.

9,390. Starr, Augusta
Papers. 1958. 16 pp.
Open. No guide.
Minnesota Historical Society, Archives and Manuscripts.
Manuscripts in which Starr reminisces about life on Nicollet Island in Minneapolis during the 1870s and 1880s. She describes the visit of the P. T. Barnum Circus, Chinese families in Minneapolis, the Emerson Public School, families who lived in the area, homes built on the Island, the first kindergarten, social events, and holidays.

9,391. State of North Carolina
Records. 1850. 1 p.
Open. No guide.
Minnesota Historical Society, Archives and Manuscripts.
A certificate signed by Joseph Daniel and Thomas Neville granting freedom to Margaret Smith, a slave, gives a physical description of Smith and attests to her honesty and good character.

9,392. Steefel, Genevieve (Fallon)
Papers. 1923-62. 35 boxes.
Open. Unpublished guide.
Minnesota Historical Society, Archives and Manuscripts.
Correspondence, notes, records and reports of organizations, clippings, and printed matter of [Mrs. Lawrence D.] Steefel (1899-), a social service worker and activist who received her BA from Radcliffe College and her MA from the University of Bordeaux in France before she worked as a teaching fellow at the University of Minnesota. Steefel was a member of the First Unitarian Society of Minneapolis, chairman of the Minnesota Unitarian Service Committee, president of the Minnesota AAUW from 1946 to 1948, and chairman of the Minneapolis Mayor's Council on Human Relations. She also served on the boards of the Minnesota Birth Control League, the Minneapolis Committee for the Resettlement for Japanese-Americans, and the Minnesota Mental Hygiene Society in addition to her activities with numerous other organizations, among them the NAACP and the Minnesota Council on Indian Affairs.

9,393. Steere, Isaac, and Family
Papers. 1855-97. 19 items.
Open. Unpublished guide.
Minnesota Historical Society, Archives and Manuscripts.
Letters that Steere's wife Elizabeth Steere, a Quaker farm wife who settled near Rochester, Minnesota Territory, wrote to her family in Michigan about her longing for family and friends. Also includes deeds and indentures and a military bounty land warrant.

9,394. Steffens, Charles Hammond, and Family
Papers. 1800-1948. 7 boxes and 2 oversize items.
Open. Unpublished guide.
Minnesota Historical Society, Archives and Manuscripts.
Correspondence of Steffens (1861-?), a teacher and farmer in Martin County, MN, with his daughter Charlotte M. Steffens, who discusses her basic training and work as a WAC during the 1940s; his daughter Alice M. Steffens, a teacher in Zumbrota, MN, who discusses students, classes, her educational philosophy and discipline, the Order of the Eastern Star, social events, and politics; and former students, colleagues, and community friends. Also includes a diary of Charles Steffens's mother-in-law Ella M. Felch, written perhaps in the early 1870s, which contains descriptions of the weather, housework, chores, school, and social

events and a 1944 power of attorney document from Charlotte Steffens to her sister Alice Steffens in Racine, MN.

9,395. Stone, Carl L., and Family
Papers. 1892-1920. 1 box.
Open. Unpublished guide.
Minnesota Historical Society, Archives and Manuscripts.
[Mrs.] E. Elnora Stone was the mother of Carl L. Stone (1874-1920), who was acting governor of the island of Mindoro in the Philippines in 1913. Letters Elnora Stone wrote from the Philippines to her sisters in Minnesota and to her son discussing family events, Americans in the Philippines, social life, travel, life and customs, weather, and natural disasters; a poem by Elnora Stone; reminiscences of her girlhood; and a short manuscript she composed about life on a military post in the Philippine Islands. Also includes letters to his mother and reports by Carl Stone.

9,396. Strout, Irwin Charles
Papers. 1922-39. 12 boxes, 2 vols., and 4 items.
Open. Unpublished guide.
Minnesota Historical Society, Archives and Manuscripts.
Papers of Strout (1893-1954), a Farmer-Labor party organizer and worker, are political in nature and include letters from women's coalitions within the party, among them the Women's Nonpartisan League of Minnesota, the Independent Women Olson for Governor League, and the Farmer-Labor Women's Federation of Minnesota, and from individuals active in the Farmer-Labor party structure, including Jean Wittich, Rosana C. Payne, and Susie (Williamson) Stageberg.

9,397. Superior National Forest
Records. 1903-69. 17 microfilm reels.
Open. Unpublished guide.
Minnesota Historical Society, Archives and Manuscripts.
Correspondence and clippings relating to Lynda Bird Johnson's trip to northeastern Minnesota in 1965, to a Minnesota Federation of Women's Clubs project to plant a memorial forest, and to other groups, many of which were women's organizations, that have sponsored and worked for conservation of the resources of Superior National Forest in northeastern Minnesota. Includes letters or writings by Dorothy Molter, Irene J. Dawson, Jennie S. S. Richardson, Alice W. Scheffey, Eileen Carroll, and Esther Davis.

9,398. Swisshelm, Jane Grey (Cannon), Agreement
Papers. 1858. 1 p.
Open. No guide.
Minnesota Historical Society, Archives and Manuscripts.
Agreement between George F. Brott and Swisshelm (1815-84) conveying lots in St. Cloud to Swisshelm in exchange for her furnishing paper for publishing a newspaper in that city.

9,399. Tapping, Minnie Ellingson
Papers. 1940s. 257-page item.
Open. No guide.
Minnesota Historical Society, Archives and Manuscripts.
Reminiscences of Tapping (1867-1949), who lived in the Minnesota River Valley most of her life, are entitled "Eighty Years at the Gopher Hole: 1867-1947" and provide details of home life, people who lived in the Valley, farming, education, religion, and transportation.

9,400. Teigan, Henry George
Papers. 1916-41. 51 boxes.
Open. Published and unpublished guides.
Minnesota Historical Society, Archives and Manuscripts.
Teigan (1881-1941), a Farmer-Labor activist, was secretary of the Nonpartisan League, a state senator from 1933 to 1935, a congressman from Minnesota from 1936 to 1938, and editor of the *Minnesota Leader.* Correspondence with [Mrs.] Florence Borner, who wanted the League to publish her poetry, and with local boosters and Women's Nonpartisan Clubs regarding scheduling, itineraries, publicity, and financing for meetings. Information on the Women's Nonpartisan Clubs of Minnesota is contained in correspondence, the call to the 1923 annual convention, and Susie (Williamson) Stageberg's report of the convention proceedings. See Deborah K. Neubeck, *Guide to a Microfilm Edition of The National Nonpartisan League Papers* (St. Paul: Minnesota Historical Society, 1970).

9,401. Thompson, Horace, and Family
Papers. 1845-1909. 2 boxes.
Open. Unpublished guide.
Minnesota Historical Society, Archives and Manuscripts.
Thompson (1827-80) was born in Vermont and in 1845 moved to Americus, GA, where he operated a mercantile building with his brother. In 1859 he moved to St. Paul and became a banker and railroad executive. His wife Carrie (Scarborough) Thompson (1832-?) was the daughter of an Americus judge. Letters from southern friends and relatives concerning family activities, economic conditions in the South, education, temperance, church activities, and the Civil War; to Horace Thompson from his sister Angie Thompson; and to Horace Thompson in Americus from his parents Amos Thompson and Nancy Christie Thompson in Poultney, VT. Also includes an 1875 memorandum book of Bible quotations and significant events kept by Carrie (Scarborough) Thompson, 18th-and 19th-century records in Bibles of the Thompson family, and an obituary of Mary Angelina [Mrs. James Egbert] Thompson (1830-52).

9,402. Thomson, Margaret M.
Papers. Ca. 1934-73. 2 bacases.
Open. No guide.
Minnesota Historical Society, Archives and Manuscripts.
Papers relate chiefly to Thomson's involvement in the Women's International League for Peace and Freedom. Includes correspondence files, an historical sketch, and newsletters of the Minnesota division of the WILPF; scattered issues of the national WILPF newsletter; information regarding civil rights and human rights; and religious, scientific, and labor "contacts" relating to WILPF committees.

9,403. Thomson, Mildred
Papers. 1961-62. 309-page item.
Open. No guide.
Minnesota Historical Society, Archives and Manuscripts.
Reminiscences of [Miss] Thomson (1889-), a social worker who was a supervisor in the Minnesota department of public welfare, trace the development of care of the mentally retarded in the US and Minnesota during the 19th century. Includes information concerning her activities in the field, changes in the state program for the mentally retarded, leaders in the field, citizens' organizations that dealt with the mentally retarded, changes in approach to the problem, and agencies and institutions created by the state of Minnesota.

9,404. Tourist Club
Records. 1891-1941. 2 boxes and 2 bacases.
Open. Unpublished guide.
Minnesota Historical Society, Archives and Manuscripts.
Records of this Minneapolis women's club consist of the constitution, bylaws, minutes, a treasurer's record, bills, receipts, canceled checks, reports, a diary on club activities kept from 1923 to 1924 by Mrs. J. R. Maxener, membership lists, scrapbooks containing papers read at meetings and clippings on topics that were studied, and programs. Also includes tourist notebooks Martha C. [Mrs. Cyrus W.] Wells kept in France, Spain, and Germany from 1893 to 1896.

9,405. Trinity Lutheran Church
Records. 1870-1943. 5 boxes and 1 bacase.
Open. Unpublished guide.
Minnesota Historical Society, Archives and Manuscripts.
Minutes and treasurer's record for the years 1872 to 1939 of the Ladies Aid of this Norwegian Evangelical Lutheran church in St. Paul.

9,406. Tuttle Universalist Church
Records. 1895-1947. 2 boxes.
Open. Unpublished guide.
Minnesota Historical Society, Archives and Manuscripts.
Records of the Church, which was founded in 1859, include minutes, correspondence, and reports of the Ladies Aid Society, which existed until 1928; the Women's Association, which was founded in 1928; the Women's Universalist Association of Minnesota; and the Tuttle Association of Universalist Women. Also includes minutes of the Church's Clara Barton Guild for 1923 to 1940 and clippings about Mary Garard [Mrs. Isaac R.] Andrews, a suffragist who moved to Minneapolis in 1911.

9,407. Ullmann, Mrs. Joseph
Papers. 1896. 162-page item.
Open. No guide.
Minnesota Historical Society, Archives and Manuscripts.
Reminiscent narrative by Ullmann concerning St. Paul in the period 1855 to 1865 contains details on food, housing, entertainment, and business.

9,408. United Garment Workers of America, No. 171
Records. 1909-30. 2 vols.
Open. Unpublished guide.
Minnesota Historical Society, Archives and Manuscripts.
Minutes of meetings of Local 171 of St. Paul, which was composed entirely of women, concern boycotting nonunion industries, strikes, working conditions, contributions to national labor causes, and relations with other unions, particularly the tailors' union.

9,409. United Spanish War Veterans National Auxiliary
Records. 1898-1968. 1 box and 1 bacase.
Open. Unpublished guide.
Minnesota Historical Society, Archives and Manuscripts.
Records of the Minnesota division of the Auxiliary include minutes of meetings of the administrative council; Auxiliary minute books; correspondence, primarily of Sara E. Edwards, secretary of the Minnesota division, with state and national officers; lists of officers; committee and annual convention reports; membership books; a history; and scrapbooks.

9,410. United States Census Office
Records. 1890. 4 microfilm reels.
Open. Unpublished guide.
Minnesota Historical Society, Archives and Manuscripts.
Special schedules of the 11th census, which was taken in 1890, contain data on Civil War veterans of the US Army, Navy, and Marine Corps. Includes the name of the veteran or of his widow if he did not survive, rank, company, regiment or vessel, dates of enlistment and discharge, length of service, post office address, disability incurred, and remarks.

9,411. United States Office of Indian Affairs
Records. 1797-1920. 5 boxes and 71 microfilm reels.
Open. Unpublished guide.
Minnesota Historical Society, Archives and Manuscripts.
Includes a ledger containing accounts with individual Indians kept by [Mrs.] Susan Johnston, an Indian trader in Sault Ste. Marie and mother-in-law of Henry R. Schoolcraft; monthly, quarterly, and annual school reports; maps prepared by students; and samples of handwriting.

9,412. United States Work Projects Administration, Stearns County, MN, Museum Project
Records. Nd. 4 boxes.
Open. Unpublished guide.
Minnesota Historical Society, Archives and Manuscripts.
Biographical sketches of early settlers of Stearns County and research notes and articles on St. Cloud, MN, and Sauk Centre, MN. About one-quarter of the biographical sketches are of women.

9,413. Unity Church
Records. 1860-1966. 13 boxes and 1 vol.
Open. Unpublished guide.
Minnesota Historical Society, Archives and Manuscripts.
Unity Church in St. Paul was associated with the American Unitarian Association and the Minnesota Unitarian Conference. Includes records of the Unity Guild; minutes, an account book, and correspondence of the Women's Alliance; minutes, an account book, and an order book of the Elizabeth Eliot Club; and attendance records, plays and pageants, records of teachers' meetings and committees, teacher's aids, and lessons of the Church school.

9,414. Upham, Henry Pratt, and Family
Papers. 1801-1900. 2 boxes.
Open. Unpublished guide.
Minnesota Historical Society, Archives and Manuscripts.
Upham (1837-1909) was an historian, author, and genealogist who was active in patriotic societies and the Minnesota Historical Society. Correspondence of Upham with family members about Upham genealogy and between family members about family events, schools and teaching, health, and death; the 1826 will of Jonah Howe of Shrewsbury, MA; and notes on the 1697 will in which Annis Little gave much of his property and belongings to his daughter.

9,415. Valesh, Eva (McDonald)
Papers. 1952-57. 1 item and 1 microfilm reel.
Open. Unpublished guide.
Minnesota Historical Society, Archives and Manuscripts.
[Mrs. Frank] Valesh (1866-1956) was a newspaper reporter, a labor organizer in Minneapolis during the 1890s and 1900s, and a leader of the Farmers' Alliance. Transcript of an interview in which Valesh reminisces to Wendell H. Link of the Columbia University Oral History Project about her life and reminiscences by Blanche McDonald (ca. 1870-?) about her sister Eva Valesh.

9,416. Van Cleve, Charlotte Ouisconsin (Clark)
Papers. Nd. 1 microfilm reel.
Open. Unpublished guide.
Minnesota Historical Society, Archives and Manuscripts.
Biographical sketch of Horatio Phillips Van Cleve (1809-91) by his wife Charlotte Van Cleve (1819-1907), who was the daughter of Major Nathan Clark. The sketch also contains information on her girlhood and education, her father's assignment to Fort Winnebago in Wisconsin, and her courtship and marriage to Horatio Van Cleve, who was born in Princeton, NJ, educated at Princeton and West Point, and assigned to Fort Winnebago. Also includes information on the Van Cleves' travels to Ohio, Michigan, and Missouri after he left military service in 1836; their removal to Long Prairie, MN, in 1856; Horatio Van Cleve's service in the Civil War; his work as assessor for the town of St. Anthony and as state attorney general; and his death.

9,417. Van Cleve, Horatio Phillips, and Family
Papers. 1827-1930. 1 folder, 1 box, and 12 bacases.
Open. No guide.
Minnesota Historical Society, Archives and Manuscripts.
Van Cleve (1809-91), a native of New Jersey who graduated from West Point in 1831, served in the Fifth Regiment at Fort Snelling; in 1861 he was appointed colonel of the Second Regiment. In 1836 he married Charlotte Ouisconsin Clark (1819-1907), who was born at Prairie du Chien, WI, and grew up at Fort Snelling. Correspondence of Charlotte Clark, correspondence between Horatio and Charlotte Van Cleve during the Civil War, letters by Charlotte Van Cleve to Mrs. David Secombe, letters that Elizabeth Van Cleve Hall wrote from Honolulu in 1866 and 1867, correspondence of E. M. Van Cleve's wives Sarah Adams Van Cleve and Mary Williams Van Cleve, and correspondence of the Williams family. Also includes diaries, school papers of Charlotte Clark, financial and legal papers, records of the Sisterhood of Bethany, and clippings.

9,418. Vandergon, Gertrude Braat
Papers. Nd. 138-page item.
Open. No guide.
Minnesota Historical Society, Archives and Manuscripts.
Reminiscences of pioneer days in Minnesota by [Mrs. Nicholas] Vandergon (1860-1941), who came from Holland with her family and several other families in 1867. She recalls the departure from Europe, the voyage across the Atlantic, homesteading in Wright County, and the struggle during the early years to become established in the new country.

9,419. Vigen, Helena Carlson
Papers. 1921. 3-page item.
Open. No guide.
Minnesota Historical Society, Archives and Manuscripts.
Address delivered by [Mrs. Engbret Trond] Vigen (1861-1935) of Lake Park, MN, on the 50th anniversary of the Norwegian Lutheran Church in Audubon, MN, concerns the emigration of the Carlson family from Freeborn County, MN, to Becker County, MN, in 1871, Indian attacks on whites, pioneer homes and food, and railroad construction.

9,420. Violet Study Club
Records. 1906-43. 2 items.
Open. Unpublished guide.
Minnesota Historical Society, Archives and Manuscripts.
History of this women's study club in Minneapolis contains names of members and officers and lists of topics for study.

9,421. Volstead, Andrew John, and Family
Papers. 1868-1955. 7 boxes.
Open. Unpublished guide.
Minnesota Historical Society, Archives and Manuscripts.
Volstead (1860-1947), a Minnesota congressman from 1907 to 1923, was married to Helen Mary Osler Gilruth Volstead (1868-1915), a teacher and housewife. Includes letters to Andrew Volstead from the WCTU and the anti-Saloon League, teaching certificates, and invitations received by family members.

9,422. Wait, William A., and Family
Papers. 1854-1911. 1 box.
Open. Unpublished guide.
Minnesota Historical Society, Archives and Manuscripts.
Consists primarily of letters in which Mary J. Mills [Mrs. George B.] Whipple (?-1911), who was the first headmistress of St. Mary's Hall in Faribault, MN, describes to Mary Eliza Hopkins [Mrs. William A.] Wait (1836-1930) her trip from Buffalo, NY, to Minnesota, her home, St. Mary's and the mission in Faribault, her health, her marriage, Christmas celebrations, and family matters. Also includes letters she wrote to Mary Wait from Hawaii during the 1870s discussing her husband's work as an Episcopal chaplain and their home and telling about two girls, Eva and Emma Havens, whom they adopted.

9,423. Wakefield, John L., and Family
Papers. 1862-1901. 4 items.
Open. Unpublished guide.
Minnesota Historical Society, Archives and Manuscripts.
Wakefield (1823-74), who was born in Connecticut, moved to Shakopee in Minnesota Territory in 1854 and was appointed physician of the Yellow Medicine Agency in 1861. During the uprising of 1862 his family was captured by Dakota Indians and lost all their belongings. Legal document setting forth the Wakefields' claim to the government for losses incurred during the Dakota War includes a list of household belongings, foodstuff, livestock, and Wakefield's medical equipment, along with the value of each item. Also includes an obituary of Wakefield's wife Sarah F. Wakefield (ca. 1833-1901).

9,424. Walker, Thomas Barlow, and Family
Papers. 1860-1951. Ca. 277 ft.
Closed. No guide.
Minnesota Historical Society, Archives and Manuscripts.
Papers of Walker (1840-1928) and his family, who settled in territorial Minnesota, relate primarily to their lumbering business, real estate, and philanthropic activities. Papers of Walker's wife Harriet G. Hulet Walker include correspondence, diaries kept in some years for the period 1870 to 1898, letter registers, rent ledgers, a cashbook, a ledger relating to her estate, and scrapbooks containing her writings and items on temperance, education, and social services. Also includes Harriet Walker's correspondence and other papers relating to the Bethany Home, a home in southeast Minneapolis for unwed mothers and reformed prostitutes, and a journal of Susan Rogers Walker for 1931 to 1934.

9,425. Wallace, Elizabeth
Papers. 1870-1961. 8 boxes and 4 oversize items.
Open. Unpublished guide.
Minnesota Historical Society, Archives and Manuscripts.
Wallace (1865-1960), a scholar of history and French and Spanish literature, was a graduate student, lecturer, professor, and dean at the University of Chicago. She also was the author of *Mark Twain and the Happy Island* (1912). Correspondence with her family, Lily Gillet, Maguy Bizot, Madame Gaston Paris, and Alfred Morel-Fatio; 66 diaries and notebooks, which contain entries concerning her friendship with Mark Twain; and manuscripts of her lectures and writings, including the unpublished English version of her work on Sor Juana Ines de la Cruz, which was published in Spanish in Mexico City in 1944. Wallace worked with the Rockefeller medical mission to France and with the American National Red Cross during WWI; during WWII she was a leader in American relief work for France.

9,426. Walton, Edmund, and Family
Papers. 1874-1930s. 3.5 ft.
Open. Unpublished guide.
Minnesota Historical Society, Archives and Manuscripts.
Correspondence of Walton family members, including Nell (Ingram) Walton, Audrey Walton, and Dorothy (Walton) Binder; letters Dorothy Walton wrote from France during WWI before her marriage to Carroll Binder in 1920; and a diary of Bess H. Ingram describing her trip to Minneapolis in 1898.

9,427. Walton, Edmund George, and Family
Papers. 1874-1964. 4 boxes.
Open. Unpublished guide.
Minnesota Historical Society, Archives and Manuscripts.
Walton (1865-1919), an English immigrant, sold real estate and was active in the civic and social life of Minneapolis. His wife Nell Ingram Walton (1866-1945) was a member of many Minneapolis civic and social organizations. Correspondence, invitations, programs, clippings, memorabilia, and memory books for 1905 to 1920 of Audrey Walton (1890-), a Girl Scout counselor and charity and social worker in Minneapolis and California, who was active in the Minneapolis women's suffrage movement, and of Dorothy (Walton) [Mrs. Carroll] Binder (1894-), who attended Wellesley College, worked in social service, and served as a war relief worker in France in 1918 and 1919. The memory books contain letters, diary entries, photos, clippings, and other mementos. Also included are legal papers regarding the estate of Edmund Walton's mother Sophia Peet Glaskin [Mrs. Edmund] Walton.

9,428. Wanous, Josie A.
Papers. 1902-18. 10 items and 1 oversize item.
Open. Unpublished guide.
Minnesota Historical Society, Archives and Manuscripts.
Wanous (1871-1936), who married Arthur Stuart, was the first woman pharmacist in Minnesota. Her papers include a letter, bills, her pharmacist certificate, and advertising material relating to her herb bags for shampooing hair.

9,429. Waseca County Sunday School Association
Records. 1904-23. 1 vol.
Open. Unpublished guide.
Minnesota Historical Society, Archives and Manuscripts.
Minutes and programs of annual conventions and meetings at Methodist, Congregational, and Evangelical churches and reports of individual Sunday schools.

9,430. Wellesley Club
Records. 1918. 22 items.
Open. Unpublished guide.
Minnesota Historical Society, Archives and Manuscripts.
Records of the St. Paul Wellesley alumnae club relate to its activities in support of a relief unit sent to France during WWI by Wellesley College alumnae. Fund-raising letters and other correspondence, a newsletter, cloth patterns and directions for knitting sweaters and caps, American National Red Cross articles about refugee garments, and swatches to be used for sewing and knitting garments for French children.

9,431. Wells, Edward Payson, and Family
Papers. 1861-1932. 2 boxes.
Open. Unpublished guide.
Minnesota Historical Society, Archives and Manuscripts.
Wells (1847-1936) was a businessman who dealt in insurance, real estate, banking, and railroad development; he was closely associated with many Minnesota and North Dakota business and political leaders. Correspondence between Wells and his wife Nellie March Johnson Wells (1848-1930) from the period when he was living in Dakota Territory or traveling throughout the US; letters his parents Milton and Melissa Wells wrote him while he was attending school in Allen Grove, WI, and then teaching school at Bradford, WI; and letters to Edward and Nellie Wells from their daughter Marguerite Milton Wells (1872-1959), which were written in 1894 at the time she was attending Smith College, her father was traveling in Europe, and her mother was seriously ill. Also includes reminiscences by Edward Wells of his family and career and clippings about the family after Edward Wells's retirement in 1922.

9,432. Westminster Presbyterian Church
Records. 1867-95. 1 box.
Open. Unpublished guide.
Minnesota Historical Society, Archives and Manuscripts.
Constitution and minutes of meetings of the Women's Home Missionary Society and an 1883 annual report of the Ladies Home Mission Society of this Minneapolis church, which was founded in 1857.

9,433. Weyerhaeuser Family
Papers. 1860-1961. 104 ft.
Access restricted. Unpublished guide.
Minnesota Historical Society, Archives and Manuscripts.
Frederick King Weyerhaeuser (1834-1914), who was married to Elizabeth Sarah Bloedel Weyerhaeuser, was a German immigrant who founded a lumbering, building material, and paper industry. Collection consists primarily of corporate correspondence of Frederick Weyerhaeuser and of businesses associated with Weyerhaeuser stockholdings, but it also contains correspondence, financial records, and other personal papers of his children, including Elise (Weyerhaeuser) [Mrs. W. B.] Hill (1860-1946), Margaret (Weyerhaeuser) [Mrs. J. R.] Jewett (1862-1939), and Apollonia (Weyerhaeuser) [Mrs. S. S.] Davis (1864-1953), and of his grandchildren.

9,434. Wheaton, Herbert E., and Family
Papers. 1888-1954. 2 boxes and 1 vol.
Access restricted. Unpublished guide.
Minnesota Historical Society, Archives and Manuscripts.
Wheaton was editor of the *Hokah Chief* of Hokah, MN, from 1912 to 1952. Letters to Wheaton and his wife Sophie Wheaton from their daughters Gladys (Wheaton) [Mrs. B. F.] Ahrens (1900-), a housewife in Illinois, and Marilouise (Wheaton) [Mrs. L. J.] Jackson, whose husband was a soldier stationed in Texas during WWII and later in Ohio. They discuss their husbands' work, running a household, family news and visits, politics, the Republican party, and their children. Also includes letters from Republican women, including Elenor Yorke, who was a writer of conservative political literature, and manuscript poetry sent to the *Hokah Chief* for publication.

9,435. Wheeler, Rush Benjamin, and Family
Papers. 1875-1955. 10 boxes.
Open. Unpublished guide.
Minnesota Historical Society, Archives and Manuscripts.
Wheeler (1844-1930), a Yale graduate, was in the real estate and loan business; he was director of the First National Bank in Austin, MN, from 1880 to 1883 and later served as director of the St. Paul Chamber of Commerce. Consists primarily of papers relating to his work as secretary and treasurer of the Summit Avenue Improvement Association in St. Paul. Includes research notes by his daughter Cleora Clark Wheeler (ca. 1883-), a designer, concerning her father's role in the development of St. Paul, her biographical sketches of Wheeler family members, her sample sketches of historic sites in the Twin Cities to be used for greeting cards, bookplates she designed, and notes she and Alice Andrews prepared concerning Christopher C. Andrews's activities in the Summit Avenue Association.

9,436. Wheelock, Joseph Albert, and Family
Papers. 1719-1906. 5 boxes.
Open. Unpublished guide.
Minnesota Historical Society, Archives and Manuscripts.
Wheelock (1831-1906) was an early St. Paul journalist who married Kate (French) Wheelock. Correspondence between Joseph and Kate Wheelock and letters from her family concerning social life in New Hampshire and St. Paul, the Civil War and the battlefront, the Dakota War and treaties with the Ojibwe, and newspaper development in St. Paul from the 1850s to the 1880s. Also includes household and family expense books.

9,437. Whipple and Scandrett Family
Papers. 1829-1959. 10 boxes.
Open. Unpublished guide.
Minnesota Historical Society, Archives and Manuscripts.
Correspondence of the family of Henry Benjamin Whipple (1822-1901), an Episcopal bishop of Minnesota, includes that of Whipple and his first wife Cornelia (Wright) Whipple (1816-90) and their correspondence with their children Elizabeth (Whipple) [Mrs. Charles Augustus] Farnum (1843-ca. 1918), Cornelia (Whipple) [Mrs. William Wilkins] Davis [Mrs. Francis Marion] Rose (1845-84), Frances (Whipple) [Mrs. Frank G.] Craw [Mrs. Freedom W.] Jackson, Charles Henry Whipple (1849-1932), John Hall Whipple (?-1878), and Jane "Jennie" (Whipple) Scandrett (1847-1932). Also includes correspondence of Henry Whipple and Evangeline (Marrs) [Mrs. Michael H.] Simpson (1860-1930) in 1895, the year before their marriage; letters to Evangline Whipple from her friend Rose E. Cleveland, who was the sister of President Grover Cleveland; letters to Rose Cleveland from Amelia Candles, Edna Dean Proctor, Matilda Coxe Stevenson, and others; and correspondence of Jennie Scandrett with Evangeline Whipple and with her brother and sister-in-law Charles and Evelyn Whipple. Correspondence of Jane Whipple with her future husband Henry Alexander Scandrett (1843-83); their children Henry A. Scandrett, Jr. (1876-1957), Jean Scandrett, and Benjamin Wright Scandrett (1883-1954); and Ben's wife Bertha Reid Scandrett (1883-) and children Betty Scandrett and Cornelia (Scandrett) [Mrs. Jack E.] Hanstein (1912-) is included as well. In addition, collection contains correspondence of other Scandrett family members, a memorial sermon for Cornelia Wright Whipple, clippings relating to Bishop Whipple's ministry and to Evangeline Whipple's work with Italian refugees after WWI, and a pamphlet about early citizens of Faribault, MN, by Anna Cole Theobald.

9,438. Whipple, Henry Benjamin
Papers. 1833-1934. 45 boxes.
Open. Unpublished guide.
Minnesota Historical Society, Archives and Manuscripts.
Whipple (1822-1901), who was born in New York, was the first Episcopal bishop of Minnesota and founder of Seabury Divinity School, Shattuck School for boys, and St. Mary's Hall for Girls, all of which were located in Faribault, MN. He also helped found Breck School in Wilder, MN, and served as a missionary among the Ojibwe and Dakota tribes of Minnesota. Includes correspondence with Frances (Folsom) [Mrs. Grover] Cleveland, Rose Elizabeth Cleveland, Mary [Mrs. S. L.] Coles, Helen Maria (Fiske) Hunt [Mrs. William Sharpless] Jackson, Henrietta S. Sidney Lear, Augusta M. Johnston [Mrs. Horatio Gates] Shumway, Cosima [Mrs. Richard] Wagner,

and others and a diary kept by Whipple's wife Evangeline Whipple in 1897.

9,439. Whitford, James H., and Family
Papers. 1854-83. 51 items.
Open. Unpublished guide.
Minnesota Historical Society, Archives and Manuscripts.
Includes letters to Ella Whitford from her aunt, cousins, grandmother, a friend in Langdon, MN, and her sister in Idaho Territory regarding family matters and life in Hampton and Northfield, MN. Also includes photos of homes, activities, and people in Florida, which were sent to Whitford after her marriage to Ross Phillips.

9,440. Wilcox, Hugh B., and Family
Papers. 1929-64. 2 boxes.
Open. Unpublished guide.
Minnesota Historical Society, Archives and Manuscripts.
Correspondence, minutes, memoranda, circular letters, reading lists, programs, pamphlets, articles, and other papers of Wilcox and his wife Jean M. Wilcox, who was secretary of the Minnesota Birth Control League. Includes minutes of the League and of the Motherhood Protective League for 1930 to 1934; correspondence and other papers relating to birth control legislation, Margaret Sanger, the American Birth Control League, Inc., the National Committee on Federal Legislation for Birth Control, and the Minnesota League for Planned Parenthood; and correspondence, programs, and other papers of the Minneapolis Progressive Education Association, the Citizen's Charter Committee of Minneapolis, the Women's International League for Peace and Freedom, cooperatives, and the Minneapolis Town Meeting Association, of which Jean Wilcox was program chairman.

9,441. Wilcox, Phebe Almira
Papers. 1836-40. 1 vol.
Open. No guide.
Minnesota Historical Society, Archives and Manuscripts.
Album containing verses, essays, and a newspaper notice of Wilcox's death.

9,442. Wilder, Amherst Holcomb, and Family
Papers. 1866-1937. 8 boxes and 12 bacases.
Access restricted. Unpublished guide.
Minnesota Historical Society, Archives and Manuscripts.
Wilder (1828-94) was involved in the mercantile, real estate, and transportation businesses in early St. Paul; his wife was Fanny Spencer Wilder (1837-1903). Journals, cashbooks, cash journals, ledgers, trial balances, a letterpress book, and a property inventory of Fanny S. Wilder and Cornelia Day (Wilder) [Mrs. T. E. W. Villiers] Appleby (1868-1903) relate to the Wilder family estate. Also includes cashbooks, ledgers, stock and bond registers, a letterpress book, insurance and tax records, and other financial records of the Amherst H. Wilder Charity. The Charity, a social service center that was a consolidation of three charity corporations, was established in St. Paul in 1910 by the wills of Amherst and Fanny Wilder and their daughter Cornelia (Wilder) Appleby. Includes correspondence about the Breck Mission and Farm School, which was founded at Wilder, MN, for the education of farm children, and correspondence concerning the Wilder Charity's relationship to such St. Paul groups as the Society for the Relief of the Poor, the Associated Charities of St. Paul, the St. Paul Free Medical Dispensary, and the Central Council of Social Welfare Agencies of St. Paul.

9,443. Williams, Howard Yolen
Papers. 1924-70. 28.75 ft.
Open. Unpublished guide.
Minnesota Historical Society, Archives and Manuscripts.
Williams (1889-1973), pastor of a Congregational church in St. Paul, was active in the Farmer-Labor party, the Democratic-Farmer-Labor party, and national political organizations. Correspondence, minutes, transcripts of speeches and articles, membership lists, press releases, and clippings. Includes correspondence of his wife Elizabeth (Bacon) Williams and of the Bacon and Williams families as well as his correspondence with women involved in the League for Independent Political Action, among them [Mrs.] Hannah Clothier Hull, Agnes M. Jenks, Katherine Devereaux Blake, and Eleanor G. Coit; with Estelle M. Sternberger and Lucy P. Carner, who were associated with the Farmer Labor Political Federation; and with Lillian Herstein, a member of the national executive committee of the American Commonwealth Political Federation. Other correspondents include Jane Addams, Mrs. Sherwood Anderson, Babette Deutsch, Zona Gale, Fannie Hurst, and Eleanor Roosevelt.

9,444. Williams, John, and Family
Papers. 1850-70. 36 items.
Open. Unpublished guide.
Minnesota Historical Society, Archives and Manuscripts.
Correspondence between members of the Williams family in Ohio, Illinois, Washington, DC, Connecticut, Pennsylvania, California, Iowa, and Colorado concerns family news, health, the Civil War, household management, social life, children, gardening, and crops. Includes letters by Cynthia [Mrs. Lyman] Williams and her daughters Nellie Williams, Abby Williams, and Louise Williams.

9,445. Williams, Thomas Hale, and Family
Papers. 1792-1965. 5 boxes.
Open. Unpublished guide.
Minnesota Historical Society, Archives and Manuscripts.
Williams (1813-1901), a native of Rhode Island, received a law degree from Harvard and moved to Minneapolis in 1854, where he founded the Minneapolis Athenaeum. He married Martha Wilder Williams (ca. 1814-1910). Correspondence of Williams with his parents Thomas and Ruth (Hale) Williams (1788-1867) and with his siblings Nathan, Stephen, and Mary Williams, who lived in the East, and letters from his daughter Mary Williams and his daughter Edith Williams (1863-1939), who was an art student in New York City during the 1890s. Also includes Edith Williams's journal of a visit to Lake Superior in 1871 and her notebook, sketchbook, and autograph book.

Samuel McKeehan Williams (1845-1930), a native of Pennsylvania, came to Minneapolis in 1857 and operated a book and stationery store there with Thomas Williams, whose daughter Sarah he married in 1879. Letters from Samuel and Sarah's daughter Sarah Elizabeth Williams, diaries of his wife for 1912 to 1921 and 1932 to 1936, diaries of Louise Williams (1884-) for 1899 to 1913, scattered diaries of Ruth Jewett Williams for 1911 to 1965, her expense account books, a 1900 golden anniversary book of Thomas and Martha Williams, and clippings.

9,446. Williamson, Thomas Smith, and Family
Papers. 1839-1939. 4 boxes.
Open. Unpublished guide.
Minnesota Historical Society, Archives and Manuscripts.
Williamson (1800-79), who was born in South Carolina and studied medicine and theology in Ohio and at Yale, was a Presbyterian missionary to the Dakota people at Lac Qui Parle and Kaposia from 1835 to 1862. He settled in St. Peter, MN, with his wife Margaret (Poage) Williamson (1804-72). Correspondence, financial accounts, receipts, and a biography and reminiscences of Thomas Williamson by Mary Briggs Aiton, second wife of missionary John F. Aiton. Includes letters from Thomas Williamson's sister Jane Smith Williamson (1803-?), who worked with her brother as a missionary, to members of the Aiton family; by Thomas Williamson's daughters Martha Williamson (1844-?) and Nancy Jane Williamson; and by Thomas Williamson, who describes the death of his wife to his son John Poage Williamson.

9,447. Wilson, Gilbert Livingston
Papers. 1894-1929. 8.5 boxes, 4 vols., 4 oversize items, and 1 microfilm reel.
Open. Unpublished guide.
Minnesota Historical Society, Archives and Manuscripts.
Includes a notebook of Mrs. James McLaughlin Wilson containing 20 Dakota myths and stories recorded in 1905 and information about Dakota traditions and beliefs as well as notebooks of Gilbert Wilson, which include narratives on the Hidatsa tribe of North Dakota supplied by Buffalo Bird Woman, her brother Wolf Chief, and her son Goodbird.

9,448. Winchell, Newton Horace, and Family
Papers. 1814-1958. 17 boxes and 2 bacases.
Open. Unpublished guide.
Minnesota Historical Society, Archives and Manuscripts.
Newton Winchell (1839-1914) was a teacher in New York, a superintendent of schools in Michigan, a geologist, and an archaeologist who served as Minnesota state geologist from 1872 to 1900. He was married to Charlotte Sophie (Imus) Winchell (1836-1926), who was a member of the faculty of Albion College in Albion, MI. Papers of Charlotte Winchell include correspondence with her husband while he was working on geological surveys, letters from family and friends, and letters from her niece Mabel regarding the Foreign Missionary Association; diaries Charlotte Winchell kept from 1920 to 1926; articles, essays, speeches, and notes she wrote; a biographical sketch of her; her teaching contracts; and papers relating to her involvement in the Woman's Foreign Missionary Association of the First Methodist Church in Minneapolis, the WCTU, and the Minneapolis school board and to her trip to France in 1896. Also includes correspondence between Horace Winchell (1796-1873) and his wife Caroline (McAllister) Winchell (1806-92); poems by members of the Imus family; writing books, essays, and other papers of Newton Winchell's sister Clarissa Winchell (1827-42); and a biographical sketch of Ida Belle (Winchell) [Mrs. Henry V.] Winchell (1862-?).

9,449. Winton, David Judson
Papers. 1929-67. 73 boxes.
Access restricted. Partial unpublished guide.
Minnesota Historical Society, Archives and Manuscripts.
Winton (1897-), a lumberman and head of Winton Companies, worked in government and was involved in such international committees as the US National Committee for UNESCO and the United World Federalists. Correspondence with Eugenie Moore [Mrs. John P.] Anderson, Genevieve Bridel, Adeline Fonvieille, Helen Hill Miller, Barbara Lady Jackson [Mrs. Robert Gillman Allen J.] Ward, and others; photos of "lumberjills," women working in the lumber industry in England during WWII; and other papers.

9,450. Woman Suffrage Petition
Records. 1887. 1 p.
Open. No guide.
Minnesota Historical Society, Archives and Manuscripts.
A petition to the Minnesota legislature signed by women of Atwater, Kandiyohi County, MN, to amend the Minnesota constitution to provide for woman suffrage.

9,451. Woman's Christian Association of Minneapolis
Records. 1866-1963. 3 items.
Open. Unpublished guide.
Minnesota Historical Society, Archives and Manuscripts.
The Association, which was also called the Christian Aid Society, was established in 1866 by Minneapolis churchwomen to provide food, clothing, and religious and literary instruction to needy persons regardless of class or color. Minute book for 1866 to 1867, a membership directory, and a 1960 booklet containing articles of incorporation, a brief history of the organization, programs, and a membership list.

9,452. The Woman's Journal, Boston and Chicago
Records. 1870. 8 items.
Open. No guide.
Minnesota Historical Society, Archives and Manuscripts.
Articles from *The Woman's Journal* include one on the woman suffrage bill submitted to the Minnesota legislature and one by Celia Burleigh about Jane Grey (Cannon) Swisshelm.

9,453. Woman's Missionary Society of the Synod of Minnesota
Records. 1880-1942. 4 boxes.
Open. Unpublished guide.
Minnesota Historical Society, Archives and Manuscripts.
Minutes of the administrative board of the Presbyterian Foreign Missionary Society and Home Missionary Society, which is the state administrative body for the eight Minnesota presbyterial societies; statistical reports of the corresponding secretary, budgets, fieldworker reports; yearbook files; programs; and publications.

9,454. Woman's Presbyterial Missionary Society of the St. Paul Presbytery
Records. 1877-1941. 3 boxes and 1 vol.
Open. Unpublished guide.
Minnesota Historical Society, Archives and Manuscripts.
Constitutions and minutes of the Presbyterian Home Missionary Society for 1893 to 1913 and of the Foreign Missionary Society for 1877 to 1941, minutes of executive committee meetings, treasurer's records, corresponding secretary's records, correspondence with mission stations, a history of the Presbyterial Society written by Mrs. E. C. Stringer in 1913, and programs. The Home Missionary Society and the Foreign Missionary Society of the St. Paul Presbytery united in 1913.

9,455. Women's Auxiliary to the Railway Mail Association
Records. 1898-1964. 2 boxes and 2 vols.
Open. Unpublished guide.
Minnesota Historical Society, Archives and Manuscripts.
This St. Paul group, which existed from 1898 to 1964, became affiliated with the Minnesota Federation of Women's Clubs and the district Federation in 1907. Minutes, a letter from a French war orphan who received support from the Auxiliary, letters about the erection and dedication of a statue of [Miss] Maria Sanford in the US Capitol, letters concerning the history of the Auxiliary, scrapbooks, and other items.

9,456. Women's International League for Peace and Freedom, Minnesota Branch
Records. 1924-73. 46 ft.
Access restricted. No guide.
Minnesota Historical Society, Archives and Manuscripts.
Minutes; treasurer's records; correspondence with members, legislators, and the national League; state and national reports; publicity and promotional material; organizational, financial, and membership files; subject files; fact sheets, statements, background information, and resolutions on social, political, and foreign affairs issues; material on state and national meetings and conferences; scrapbooks; and League periodicals and publications. Includes correspondence about League activities and programs, especially with relation to peace, interracial programs, education, and volunteer work camps; correspondence of Ruth Gage Colby and Jean Wilcox; and information on legislative work and on affiliated and related groups.

9,457. Women's Overseas Service League
Records. 1919-42. 1 box.
Open. Unpublished guide.
Minnesota Historical Society, Archives and Manuscripts.
Constitution, bylaws, articles of incorporation, minutes of meetings, treasurer's books, financial statements, correspondence, a history, and biographical sketches of members of the St. Paul League, an organization founded in 1919 and composed of women who served overseas in the allied forces during WWI.

9,458. Women's Progress Club, Dakota County, MN
Records. 1912-22. 1 vol.
Open. Unpublished guide.
Minnesota Historical Society, Archives and Manuscripts.
Minutes of meetings of the Society, which is now known as the PTA of School District no. 5, Mendota Township.

9,459. Women's Sewing Circle
Records. 1908-13. 1 vol.
Open. Unpublished guide.
Minnesota Historical Society, Archives and Manuscripts.
Minutes in Finnish of a Nashwauk, MN, women's sewing circle.

9,460. Women's Welfare League
Records. 1911-62. 2 boxes.
Open. Unpublished guide.
Minnesota Historical Society, Archives and Manuscripts.
The League, which existed in Minneapolis from 1911 to 1962, sponsored a resort lodge for working girls, a convalescent home, a home for mentally retarded and delinquent girls, community recreation facilities, and nursing and boarding homes for elderly women. Constitution; articles of incorporation; minutes and reports of regular and annual League meetings; correspondence concerning activities of the League, a bequest to the League by [Mrs.] Florence Barton Loring of her home and $50,000 for its maintenance; deeds; membership lists; and brochures and other printed material describing the League and its welfare program.

9,461. Woodward, Lydia
Papers. 1905. 1 vol.
Open. Unpublished guide.
Minnesota Historical Society, Archives and Manuscripts.
Diary kept by [Mrs. George] Woodward, a housewife who lived near Langdon, MN, in Washington County, contains information about her household duties, her husband's sheep business, and social events.

9,462. Work Projects Administration
Records. 1849-1942. 337 boxes and 3 bacases.
Open. Unpublished guide.
Minnesota Historical Society, Archives and Manuscripts.
Annals of Minnesota compiled as part of the WPA Writers' Project consist of transcripts of articles from Minnesota newspapers, primarily from the 19th century, on such subjects as folkways, immigration and settlement, labor, nationality groups, public welfare and health, education and culture, and social attitudes. Includes interviews with residents of the McGregor Lakes region of Minnesota for a history by Mary Gardner Pruitt, an article on the history of Sibley County, MN, by Mary Simonson, reminiscences of Julia Lobdell and Susan Bahr about the Dakota War of 1862, manuscripts by Frances Densmore on the history of Indians in Minnesota, reminiscences and biographies of four Lithuanian women in Minnesota, and interviews and biographical sketches of Finns in Minnesota and of Itasca County, MN, residents, including Nellie Bloomquist, Mrs. George Wakefield, and nine other women. Also includes a survey of historical records of counties, townships, cities, villages, school districts, organizations, churches, and cemeteries in Minnesota.

9,463. Work Projects Administration, Minnesota
Records. 1923-42. 3 boxes.
Open. Unpublished guide.
Minnesota Historical Society, Archives and Manuscripts.
Interviews and material collected in preparation for the book *The Bohemian Flats* and historical sketches of Minnesota pioneers Matilda Jane Campbell [Mrs. George F.] Wilkin, Fanny [Mrs. James] Van Dyke, and Maude Mary Van Dyke; the Vermilyea family; the Metzroth Clothing Company of St. Cloud, MN; and the Powers Mercantile Company of Minneapolis.

9,464. Wright, George Burdick, and Family
Papers. 1785-1955. 2 oversize folders and 10 Hollinger boxes.
Open. Unpublished guide.
Minnesota Historical Society, Archives and Manuscripts.
The Wright family was involved in the business and financial development of Fergus Falls, MN, especially the water power company and gas company. Correspondence between George Wright (1835-82) and Serena Marie (Ames) Wright (1840-68) before and after their marriage concerning travel, home life, territorial hardships, schools, literary figures, anti-Negro sentiment, the 1860 presidential election, and the Civil War; correspondence of Grace Tillston Clarke Wright (1874-1950) and her husband Vernon Ames Wright (1863-1938) about the early history of the water power industry, factories, and the proposed Coffer Dam in Fergus Falls, MN; an 1886 diary of Grace Clarke; and a series of letters from Grace Clarke while she was a student at Bryn Mawr College. Also includes correspondence between members of the Thomas William Clarke family relating to New England, trade, education, and family news and a marriage license of Thomas Clarke and Eliza Ann Redmond.

9,465. Young Women's Christian Association
Records. 1943-44. 12 items.
Open. Unpublished guide.
Minnesota Historical Society, Archives and Manuscripts.
Correspondence of the Minneapolis YWCA relating to the committee on resettlement of Japanese-Americans includes requests from Japanese persons in relocation areas for information about Minneapolis schools.

9,466. Zon, Raphael
Papers. 1887-1957. 15 boxes and 5 oversize items.
Open. Unpublished guide.
Minnesota Historical Society, Archives and Manuscripts.
Correspondence of Zon (1874-1956), a Russian Jewish immigrant, forester, author, and editor of the *Journal of Forestry.* Correspondence between Zon and his wife Anna Abramovna (Puzyriskaya) Zon and of Anna Zon with her friends concerns

her education in Vilna and Koyan and the birth of their sons Henry and Leo. Includes letters from Cornelia (Bryce) [Mrs. Gifford] Pinchot with family news; from Mrs. M. B. Coulston, an actress in the Wilfred Clarke company and employee of the Park Improvement Committee in San Diego, CA, who writes of her travels, her acting, and mutual friends; to Zon as director of the Lake States Forest Experiment Station from the Women's Welfare League, the Women's Cooperative Alliance, and other groups working for social improvement and in 1939 concerning a proposed constitution for the Agricultural Faculty Women's Club of the University of Minnesota; and correspondence in Russian, probably with his family.

9,467. Oral History Tapes
Oral history. Ca. 1945- . Ca. 800 items. Partially restricted. Unpublished guide.
Minnesota Historical Society, Audio-Visual Library.
Of the ca. 800 taped interviews, speeches, and other material in the Society's Oral History Collection, 114 histories clearly pertain to women in Minnesota or in the Midwest. Reminiscences relating to 19th- and early 20th-century settlement, homesteading, family life, and social activities in both rural and urban centers include those of Anna M. Cihak, who grew up in a small town during the 1910s and worked as a dental hygienist; Ruth Velzora Benson Mikulewicz (1902-), who describes girlhood entertainments and customs, refrigeration and root cellars, American National Red Cross work in WWI, and transportation by trolley and railroads; Louise D. Featherstone (1899-), who discusses farm chores, church, social life, prohibition, the Ku Klux Klan, the WCTU, and women's liberation; Anna Earl Ramsey Furness (1876-1964), who describes early St. Paul social life, the St. Paul winter carnivals, and the James J. Hill home; an anonymous Norwegian who came to North Dakota to homestead in 1905, telling about her education and employment experiences; Mrs. Annie Pederson, a North Dakota homesteader who discusses settlement life and the Nonpartisan League; and Lillie Waroe, who describes North Shore Lake Superior fisheries, the Ladies Aid Society, and life during the early 20th century.

Interviews with ethnic and racial minority women in Minnesota pertain to settlement, family and social life, culture and customs, employment, and group or race relations. Interviews with 18 Mexican-Americans are included, among them are those with Stella Alvo, who discusses the Mi Cultura Day Care Center; Maria J. Bosquez, who describes the St. Paul Mexican-American community, adjusting to life in the US, and the Mexican Revolution; Felicitas Herrera, who talks about early life in Mexico, life in the US and jobs held, and religious practices; and Carlos and Marcelina R. Urvina, who describe work in Minnesota beet fields, child rearing, education, and Mexican customs in the home. Among the black Minnesotans interviewed are Florence Hibbs Daniels, a Canadian black who came to Minneapolis in 1890, discussing black communities in Alexandria, St. Cloud, Fergus Falls, and St. Paul; Carrie L. Doyier, describing social and economic conditions of blacks in Duluth from 1920 to the 1950s, the internal structure of the black community, and NAACP activities; Nellie Stone Johnson, who was active in Farmer-Labor and Democratic-Farmer-Labor party politics and founded Local 665 of the Hotel and Restaurant International union, discussing Twin Cities union activity and blacks and the union movement; Louis Moore, Jr., and his wife Cora Moore, prominent black citizens of St. Paul for over 50 years, describing the St. Paul black community, the depression, the war years, and racial prejudice; Mrs. Ethel Ray Nance, the first black policewoman in Minneapolis in 1926 and associate head resident of the Phyllis Wheatley Center during the 1920s, discussing Duluth lynchings and that city's black community, Harlem during the 1920s, and black-Indian relations; and Mrs. Paulette Webster, whose family lived in Mendota during the 1860s, describing the early Minneapolis black community and black migration to the Twin Cities area in ca. 1920. Minnesota Indians include Elizabeth [Mrs. Harry] Lawrence, or "Morning Star," niece of Chief Little Crow, who sings and discusses Dakota songs; Lu Perkins [Mrs. Gale] Anderson, who sings "The Steal of the White Man"; Rose Whipple Bluestone, a Dakota, who describes schooling, religion, and economic problems; and Jerry and Katherine Martin, an Ojibwe couple, with Katherine (1890-) telling of her family, fishing, making maple sugar, Ojibwe games, and drums. Also includes interviews with Finnish Minnesotans: Ellen Davis, who married a black communist leader on the Iron Range, describes work, the struggles of blacks and workers, labor defense, and legal cases; Helmi Saari Dyhr, an immigrant to Ely, talks about her family background, subsistence farming, and relations with the Ojibwe; Helmi Jarvinen Gawboy, a second generation Finnish-American, discusses rural schooling, teaching, her marriage to an Ojibwe, Indian reservations and traditions, the place of women in Ojibwe society, childbirth, and Indian and white attitudes toward her and her mixed-blood children; Viena Hendrickson (1898-), an immigrant on the Iron Range, describes working for the Duluth Iron Range Railroad in order to support her education at Chicago's Busch Music Conservatory, her years at Detroit City College and Duluth State Teachers College, her membership on the Minnesota state teachers college board from 1937 to 1941, and involvement with the Democratic-Farmer-Labor party, the Industrial Workers of the World, and women and peace movements; Cecilia Kuitunen, an immigrant who ran a boarding house and public sauna in Winton, discusses life in Finland and her trip to the US, underground mining, her mother's attitude toward education, Finnish organizations, and relationships between Finns and other nationalities; and Toini Maki, wife of an organizer for the CIO Steel Workers Union and chairman for the Communist party in Minnesota, talks about Finnish cultural life on the Iron Range. Additional material about ethnic groups in Minnesota includes interviews with Mr. and Mrs. Fritz Johnson, Swedish immigrants to Minnesota's North Shore of Lake Superior, who describe early fishing at the Shore, taconite pollution, and lampreys; Anna Josephine Carson, who talks about growing up in a Swedish-Norwegian home, her relationship with her mother, training as a nurse, her husband, children, and housework; Beatrice Manessari Masnari, an Italian immigrant to the Iron Range in 1931, who discusses her trip to the US and Minnesota, settling in Ely during the depression, economic conditions, learning English, and her relationship with her sister who remained in Italy; and Mrs. Della Ulbrich, daughter of Polish immigrants, who describes work in a laundry, a shoe factory, and a twine factory as well as life in Dakota County since 1917.

Other interviews pertain to the history of private colleges and women's education in Minnesota and include tapes of Sister Camille Bowe, former president of the College of St. Teresa, and Sisters Eucharista Galvin, Antonius Kennelly, and Antonine O'Brien from the College of St. Catherine. Material about Minnesota politics, government, civic concerns, and organizational activity includes tapes of Eugenie Moore [Mrs. John P.] Anderson, who discusses her career in politics and government; politicians' wives Jane (Shields) [Mrs. Orville] Freeman and Muriel (Buck) [Mrs. Hubert] Humphrey; Sue M. Dickey Hough, a member of the Minnesota state legislature in 1923, who talks about campaigns, issues, bills, and opinions on women in the legislature; Sally Luther, a state representative from 1950 to 1962 and executive assistant to Governor Karl Rolvaag, who discusses her legislative experience, Minnesota politics, Congresswoman Coya Knutson, and the Sugar Hills meeting; Katharine Giltinan [Mrs. Trevor R.] Bowen, who reminisces about her grandfather Ignatius Donnelly and her experiences in China during WWII; Marion (Hanson) Donnelly Woltman, the second wife of Ignatius Donnelly, who provides information on her family's immigration from Norway, her education, newspaper work from 1896 to 1898, and her marriage to Donnelly; Sylvia Simonson, who discusses her role as the wife of ambassador Joseph Simonson and their residence, cooking, and social life in Ethiopia; Nellie Minor, who discusses a nursery bill enabling the state to raise trees and the role of women in the Izaak Walton League, a conservation group; and Anna Lee [Mrs. Maurice] Wolff, a pacifist and founder of a local branch of the National Council of Jewish Women, who talks about her early life in Minneapolis, public affairs, and anti-Semitism. Interviews with women involved in the state chapter of and the national Women's International League for Peace and Freedom include tapes of Madge [Mrs. Oscar] Hawkins (1882-), a Norwegian-born teacher who was active in North Dakota's Nonpartisan League and the Minnesota Farmer-Labor party; Marjorie Sibley, an Augsburg College librarian who served in the early 1950s as state WILPF president; and Gertrude Visscher (1899-), the daughter of missionaries, who was born in Japan and who also became a missionary in Japan, worked actively during the 1930s for the Minnesota YWCA and cooperative movement, and in the 1960s became involved with the WILPF. Visscher talks about pacifism, racism, the Vietnam War, structural changes in the League, and the women's rights movement. Also includes a 1954 speech by Maud C. Stockwell, organizer of the Minnesota WILPF branch in 1922 and its first president, concerning Jane Addams and the League.

Material pertaining to the arts and entertainment includes interviews with Frances Cranmer Greenman, a South Dakota native who worked as a portrait painter in Minneapolis, New York City, and Washington, DC, discussing life in New York as an artist and designer; Mrs. C. O. Kalman, a confidante of Zelda Fitzgerald, who reminisces about F. Scott and Zelda Fitzgerald; Nettie Sherman, who worked in 1924 for WLAG (later WCCO) radio in Minnesota in soap operas and also at various night clubs, discussing her early life, work in the Twin Cities and Chicago, and the St. Paul black community; and Anne Kovarik, sister of composer Antonin Dvořak's American secretary Josef J. Kovarik, describing Dvořak on his visit to the US and St. Paul in 1893 and providing details about the Dvořak and Kovarik families. Collection also includes a tape of 23 songs composed by Minnesota women between the 1850s and 1958.

Interviews with various professional women in Minnesota include Leila Halverson, a registered nurse in North Dakota and Minnesota from 1907 to 1948 who served in the American National Red Cross during WWI in France, Palestine, and Poland, describing her family, nurses' training, war work and experiences, her career on the state board of examiners of nurses, and the professionalization of nursing; Mary Blanche Lovejoy (1905-), a Hastings registered nurse, discussing her family, Hastings, hospitals, prohibition, the Ku Klux Klan, toboggan slides, and the Hastings trolley; Margaret Kelly and Nora A. Kelly, both teachers and members of the Teachers' Union, speaking about the 1946 St. Paul teachers' strike, which was the first such organized strike in the US; Mary McGough, a teachers' rights activist, retired teacher, and former member of the board of directors of the St. Paul Teachers Federation and Minnesota Education Association, talking about lobbying in the state legislature from the 1920s to the 1940s for improvements in teachers' positions, tenure, and laws regarding teachers; Allen Sollie and Violet Johnson Sollie, the latter a lawyer and labor and tax researcher, discussing their involvement in Farmer-Labor party politics and the 1934 Minneapolis truckers' strike; [Mrs.] Anita Bracy Tucker, a social worker, describing the Hallie Q. Brown Community House in the 1950s and the effect area freeway construction had on House residents; Marilyn McClure, a bilingual and bicultural social worker for Ramsey County Mental Health services who was born in New Mexico and worked in St. Paul schools, discussing her education, the Ramsey County Mental Health Spanish American Project, and Mexican-Americans; Ann Zuvekas, talking about Migrant Health Services, Inc., of which she was director; and Sister Anna Marie Meyers, a member of St. Joseph's order, discussing her personal life, the founding of Christ Child School for exceptional children in St. Paul, and case studies. Several other interviews pertain to women in industry or the labor movement: Alma Foley, who was secretary of the Minnesota branches of the International Labor Defense and American Committee for Protection of Foreign Born; Myrtle [Mrs. Helmer] Harris, chief organizer for the International Ladies' Garment Workers' Union and member of the Minneapolis Library Board and Central Labor Union; and Hokan Lind, an inspector for the North Shore Lake Superior fishing industry from 1935 to 1969, who describes the industry and life on the North Shore.

9,468. Photos
Collection. 1850- . 150,000 items.
Open. Unpublished guide.
Minnesota Historical Society, Audio-Visual Library.
Includes portraits of ca. 10,000 women and photos of Historical Society events and projects; state officials and employees; State Fair events; University of Minnesota faculty, students, and employees; sports; politics; women's organizations; the suffrage movement; politics and government; education; medicine; communications; lumbering; and mining. Women are also depicted in photos relating to pioneer lives and immigration; blacks and other ethnic groups; family life; children and youth; social and fraternal groups; and tribal life and customs, government relations and reservations, warfare, and artifacts of Dakota, Ojibwe, and other Indian tribes. Among other subjects dealt with are the depression and prohibition; US history, including photos on the American National Red Cross and nursing in war; recreation; customs and holidays; costume; social service; the performing and visual arts, such as music, dance, theater, circuses, painting, and sculpture; agriculture; commerce; industry and labor, with photos on union activities and unemployment; and various forms of transportation.

9,469. Anoka County: Agricultural Agent and Extension Service
Records. 1934-56. 1 box.
Open. Control Statement.
Minnesota Historical Society, State Archives.
Annual reports provide information on clothing projects and on girls' activities in 4-H clubs. Also contains photos of clothing exhibits.

9,470. Board of Pardons
Records. 1880s-1954. 46 boxes and 5 oversize boxes.
Open. Control statement.
Minnesota Historical Society, State Archives.
Includes applications for pardons, which provide information on disposition of the application, from women seeking pardon for a variety of crimes ranging from murder to procurement for a house of assignation.

9,471. Department of Conservation: State Land Office
Records. 1863-1944. 80 boxes.
Open. Control statement.
Minnesota Historical Society, State Archives.
Records of the State Land Office include trust fund land sale receipts, 1863-1938; memoranda of the sale of state land, 1903-44; and lists for taxation, 1913-27. Receipts of trust fund land sales, grouped by county in which the transaction took place, give the names of purchasers, many of whom were women, and indicate the amount paid for principal, interest, and penalties.

9,472. Department of Education
Records. 1867-1971. 552 boxes.
Open. Control statement.
Minnesota Historical Society, State Archives.
Includes home economics education annual reports, 1941-57; correspondence and reports of the inspector of schools, 1919-22, including some personal papers of Anna Swenson, an inspector; reports of county teachers leagues and of the Teachers Patriotic League; and school library reports, ca. 1912-54, which are arranged by county. Also contains, under the general heading of records, such material as a self-survey form for graded elementary and secondary schools, 1953-56; material on special education for the homebound and the mentally retarded, 1950-57; and records of visitations to graded schools, 1884-92.

9,473. Department of Labor and Industry
Records. 1897-1950. 39 boxes.
Open. Control statement.
Minnesota Historical Society, State Archives.
Contains correspondence, reports, and other records pertaining to minimum wage, insurance and workmen's compensation, hours, trade unions, railroads, and other matters. Includes records of the Department's Bureau of Women and Children, 1909-23 (1 box), which consist primarily of correspondence and notes on investigations of complaints made by workers against employers. Amanda Severson complained in 1913, for example, that her employer had failed to pay the balance of wages due to her; the employer responded that it was because she had failed to give proper notice when leaving his employment. Complaints and investigations dealt with schools and truancy, hours and wages, and working conditions, especially toilets.

9,474. Governor: Karl F. Rolvaag
Records. 1963-65. 64 boxes.
Open. Control statement.
Minnesota Historical Society, State Archives.
Includes material pertaining to the Governor's commission on the status of women and to the commission's employment subcommittee, which was chaired by Edna Schwartz.

9,475. Governor: Wendell R. Anderson
Records. 1971-76. 310 boxes.
Open. Control statement.
Minnesota Historical Society, State Archives.
Consists of Governor Wendell Anderson's office files, including constituent correspondence, 1971 (2 boxes), regarding proposed abortion legislation in Minnesota.

9,476. Health Department: Hospital Services Division
Records. 1917-45. 13 boxes.
Open. Control statement.
Minnesota Historical Society, State Archives.
Contains records pertaining to maternity hospitals, including statements of standards for the hospitals, with provision for committees on venereal disease; housing, staff, and equipment; leisure time, occupation, and vocational guidance; and religious training.

9,477. Legislature: House: Committee Minutes
Records. 1919-69. 77 oversize boxes.
Open. Control statement.
Minnesota Historical Society, State Archives.
Consists of minutes of committees of the house of representatives, among them committees on labor and labor legislation, education, public welfare and social legislation, temperance, cities, public health and hospitals, crime prevention, and emergency relief. Minutes for the committee on temperance in 1925, for example, when four bills concerning temperance were introduced, give the file number, title of the bill, representative introducing it, its disposition to a subcommittee, and when it was reported back to the full committee. In 1921 a witness testified before the committee that the lemon extract provision of one temperance bill would not improve conditions and would inconvenience "house-wives."

9,478. Lieutenant Governor: Rudy Perpich
Records. 1959-76. 44 boxes.
Open. Control statement.
Minnesota Historical Society, State Archives.
Correspondence, reports, subject files, clippings, campaign files, computer printouts, clippings, and published material from Perpich's terms in the Minnesota state legislature and as lieutenant governor. Includes material pertaining to the state arts council, which was chaired by Anne Marie Plunkett.

9,479. Minnesota Statehood Centennial Commission
Records. 1957-59. 54 boxes.
Open. Control statement.
Minnesota Historical Society, State Archives.
Includes correspondence, reports, scrapbooks, photos, and other records of the Commission's women's committee. Includes reports of county committees and clippings regarding women's centennial activities.

9,480. Public Examiner
Records: 1878-1970s. 249 boxes.
Open. Control statement.
Minnesota Historical Society, State Archives.
Includes audits of state departments, boards, commissions, and institutions, among them state and county hospitals, nursing homes, and sanitoriums. Includes audits of the Ladies of the G.A.R. Home, 1908-47; the Minnesota Home for Girls, 1910-50; the Women's Reformatory, 1920-48; the nursing board examiners, 1910-51; and the hairdressing and beauty culture examination board, 1927-50. An audit of the Koochiching County Nursing Home, for example, lists the members of the board of directors and their terms of office, lists of accounts receivable (from patients), and other budgetary and operating information.

9,481. Public Safety Commission
Records. 1916-1920s. 129 boxes.
Open. Control statement.
Minnesota Historical Society, State Archives.
Includes alien registration forms, 1918 (48 boxes), which are arranged by county; forms for the cities of Duluth, Minneapolis, and St. Paul are arranged by wards. The forms give the county, municipality, name, address, age, country to which the registrant claimed allegiance, information about port of entry, marital status, trade or profession, names and ages of all children attending public schools, questions regarding naturalization, ownership of real estate and personal property, possession of a safe deposit vault, and other information.

Records from the commission's "main file" include correspondence from citizens, for example, a 1918 letter from a woman who complained that she had been committed to a state hospital without a hearing and one regarding a complaint by a Red Cross worker in northern Minnesota that Finns were drinking Hoffman's Drops, which were characterized as "dope." Also contains records of the woman's committee, Minnesota division, of the Council of National Defense, a WWI organization that coordinated efforts of women.

9,482. State Board of Control
Records. Ca. 1900-40. 48 boxes.
Open. Control statement.
Minnesota Historical Society, State Archives.
Includes reports and publications of the Board and its subdivisions and store records (records of purchase of supplies) for the Shakopee Women's Reformatory, 1919-25. Also contains records pertaining to the children's bureau, 1917-39, including records of maternity homes.

9,483. State Board of Cosmetology
Records. 1927-70. 12 boxes.
Open. Control statement.
Minnesota Historical Society, State Archives.
Includes extensive minutes of the Board, 1927-70; transcripts of hearings, primarily regarding establishment of new schools or businesses; a list of shops registered, 1940-41; and other records.

9,484. State Board of Examiners of Nurses
Records. 1910-26. 2 boxes.
Open. Control statement.
Minnesota Historical Society, State Archives.
Reports and correspondence of the public examiner along with records of Board receipts and disbursements.

9,485. United States General Land Office
Records. 1847-1926. 274 boxes.
Open. Control statement.
Minnesota Historical Society, State Archives.
Contains records for Minnesota district land offices, including registers of homestead entries and of final homestead entries, records pertaining to Indian land sales, and financial and other records. Registers of homestead entries give the date of application, a legal description of the land, the names and addresses of the applicants, some of whom were women, and fees levied.

9,486. War History Committee
Records. 1940-45. 98 boxes.
Open. Control statement.
Minnesota Historical Society, State Archives.
Records of the War History Committee include a history of Minnesota civilian defense by Mary Proal Lindeke and records of groups and committees concerned with the defense effort. Contained in a family welfare section in the records are letters from citizens requesting assistance; one woman requested extra tires because she had to drive a child with a dislocated hip to school. Includes correspondence of Mrs. Blance H. Merry, head of the department of complaints and referrals in the state division of social welfare.

9,487. War Records Commission
Records. Ca. 1917-24. 163 boxes.
Open. Control statement.
Minnesota Historical Society, State Archives.
Includes records of the Council of National Defense, a WWI emergency agency established to coordinate defense efforts, and of its various committees dealing with women's concerns. Records of the woman's committee, Minneapolis division, contain a 1917 list of women's organizations in Minneapolis and reports on Americanization activities; records of the women's committee on women in industry include correspondence of Agens L. Peterson, chairman. Also contains volunteer enrollment census cards, which provide detailed information about the volunteers, including 154 categories in which the volunteer might have or wish to acquire competence; a Ramsey County council of home defense census, which describes the county block by block and includes assessments of wealth; and a detailed survey of women employed outside the home. The latter survey gives the name of the investigator; the name and nature of the firm; the total number of employees; the number of men, women, and children under 16 employed by the firm; and descriptions of hours and working conditions. It also includes extensive information about the women employees and about women who replaced men in the firm.

9,488. Minnesota Mutual Life Belles
Records. 1961-76. 1 box.
Open. No guide.
Minnesota Mutual Life Insurance Company.
Correspondence, performance schedules, photos, a recording disc, clippings, and musical scores of the Belles, a musical group formed in 1961 by 10 Minnesota Mutual Life Insurance Company employees who played 27 handbells. Directed by [Mrs.] Marilyn Shandorf of West St. Paul, MN, and accompanied by [Mrs.] Barbara Jentink, the Belles performed chiefly during the holiday season for community groups, senior citizens, and schoolchildren. The group was organized to draw public attention to the chimes that ring from the Minnesota Mutual Life building.

9,489. Archives
Records. 1945- . No size given.
Open. No guide.
St. Paul's Priory.
Legal documents, correspondence, memoirs of religious superiors and archbishops, literary manuscripts, oral history tapes, photos, diplomas, scrapbooks, newspapers, rare books, and other records of the Priory, which was established in 1948.

9,490. Province Archives
Records. 1951-. 56 drawers and 82 shelves.
Open. No guide.
Sisters of St. Joseph of Carondelet, St. Paul Province.
The order, the members of which are involved in education, nursing and social services, was established in 1851 by six sisters who moved to St. Paul from St. Louis. Minutes, financial records, correspondence, diaries, oral history tapes, files, blueprints, photos, parish bulletins, scrapbooks, pamphlets, school yearbooks, books, and other records. Includes papers relating to Sister Seraphine Ireland; Sister Antonia McHugh, president of the College of St. Catherine; Sister Anna Marie Meyers, who worked with retarded children in the 1930s; and Sister Helen Angela Hurley's research work and publications. The Sisters opened St. Joseph's Academy, the first Catholic school for girls in St. Paul, in 1851; established St. Joseph's Hospital, Minnesota's first hospital, in 1853; worked with the Winnebago Indians at Long Prairie, MN, in the 1850s; worked with unwed mothers; and did pioneer work in the establishment of two orphanages in St. Paul and Minneapolis.

9,491. Province Archives
Records. 1868- . 1 room.
Partially restricted. No guide.
Sisters of the Good Shepherd, St. Paul Provincialate.
This religious congregation, whose members are involved in social service to girls and families in difficulty, was founded in France in 1642 and established in St. Paul in 1868. Minutes, correspondence, diaries, photos, motion pictures, scrapbooks, and other records of the Province.

9,492. American Council for Nationalities Service
Records. 1918-75. 180 ft.
Partially restricted. Unpublished guide.
University of Minnesota, Immigration History Research Center.
Reports, correspondence, essays, articles, press releases, and personnel files of the ACNS include items written by women who were officers of this national organization, which has its headquarters in New York City, and its antecedent groups. Represented are Edith Terry Bremer, Elmina Lucke, Elizabeth Campbell, Hanny Cohrsen, Josephine Roche, Mary Crocetti, Mary Hurlbutt, Pauline Gardescu, Margaret M. Anderson, and Alice Stetten. Also includes correspondence of the ACNS with the nationalities division of the GFWC.

Established in 1918 as the Foreign Language Information Service and in 1940 renamed the Common Council for American Unity, the ACNS assumed its current name when the Common Council merged with the American Federation of International Institutes in 1959. Throughout its history, the ACNS has served immigrants and foreign born by conducting casework, offering legal assistance, supporting immigration legislation and organizations, working with foreign language press and radio, sponsoring folk festivals, addressing resettlement and refugee issues, studying second-generation problems, promoting adult education, and conducting a public relations campaign directed toward an understanding of immigrant culture by American society

9,493. Bambace, Angela
Papers. Ca. 1938-76. 2 in.
Open. Unpublished guide.
University of Minnesota, Immigration History Research Center.
Correspondence, speeches, photos, and clippings of Bambace (1898-1975), a union organizer, vice-president of the International Ladies' Garment Workers' Union, and women's rights advocate. She began her labor movement career in 1919. In 1932 she helped organize the Amalgamated Clothing Workers strike in Elizabeth, NJ, and one year later was involved in a walkout of 75,000 dressmakers in New York. In 1936 she founded the first women's local at a Baltimore coat factory. Bambace was also a member of the Italian American Labor Council executive board.

9,494. DuBois, Rachel Davis
Papers. Ca. 1926-58. 5.5 ft.
Open. Unpublished guide.
University of Minnesota, Immigration History Research Center.
A pioneer in the intercultural education movement, DuBois (1892-) founded and directed the Service Bureau for Intercultural Education and the Workshop for Cultural Democracy. Correspondence, writings, classroom materials, programs for the radio series "Americans All—Immigrants All," and minutes, reports, and other items pertaining to the Workshops for Cultural Democracy. DuBois was also active in the peace movement of the early 1920s and was a delegate with Jane Addams to the Women's International League for Peace and Freedom conference held in Holland in 1922.

9,495. Ets, Marie Hall
Papers. Ca. 1930s-60s. 1.5 ft.
Open. Unpublished guide.
University of Minnesota, Immigration History Research Center.
Papers of [Mrs.] Ets chiefly relate to her book *Rosa, the Life of an Italian Immigrant* (Minneapolis: University of Minnesota Press, 1970) and consist of research notes and stories told to Ets by Rosa Cassettari, an Italian immigrant who was a cleaning lady at the Chicago Commons. Cassettari and Ets became friends at the Commons and throughout their relationship, which lasted from 1918 to 1943, Cassettari told Ets stories about her life in Italy as well as folklore of the people in her native village.

9,496. Grieco, Rose
Papers. Ca. 1956-74. 1 in.
Open. No guide.
University of Minnesota, Immigration History Research Center.
Typescript of the play *Anthony on Overtime,* articles, clippings, playbills, and souvenir programs of Grieco, an Italian-American playwright whose plays and articles recount "the beauty of Italian folkways and the danger of their disappearance from our lives." Her critically acclaimed three-act

comedy *Anthony on Overtime* was produced at the Blackfriars Theatre in New York during the 1961-62 season. Her second off-Broadway play *Daddy, Come Home,* which was part of the Blackfriars's 1962-63 season, won for her the Amita Award in the field of playwriting. The Award is given annually to women of Italian origin who have achieved recognition in various fields.

9,497. Grillo, Clara (Corica)
Papers. Ca. 1928-77. Ca. 1 ft.
Open. No guide.
University of Minnesota, Immigration History Research Center.
A retired teacher, [Mrs. Dominic] Grillo (1906-) was a nationality secretary at the Nationalities Service Center of Cleveland. Includes a study by Grillo about the Italians in Cleveland and about the International Institute of Cleveland; an article she wrote comparing attitudes of first- and second-generation Italian Americans; tape transcripts; clippings; and material about theater, films, and vaudeville. Her article about Italian Americans won for her the American Italian Historical Association's Leonard Covello award for the best article in Italian-American studies.

9,498. Harju, Walter A.
Papers. Ca. 1929-73. 32 folders and 17 tapes.
Open. Unpublished guide.
University of Minnesota, Immigration History Research Center.
Correspondence and personal papers, speeches, recorded interviews, minutes, and clippings of Harju (ca. 1900-73), a Finnish-American writer and activist in American labor and cooperative movements, include short autobiographies, interviews, and a few photos of Finnish-American "pioneers." Some of the interviews, including several with women, were written in ca. 1938 while Harju worked for the WPA Writers' Project, but others were completed in the early 1960s.

9,499. Humenna, Dokia
Papers. Ca. 1928-73. 1 vol.
Open. Unpublished guide.
University of Minnesota, Immigration History Research Center.
Scrapbook of Humenna (1904-), a Ukrainian-American writer, contains correspondence, epigrams, book reviews, and publication announcements.

9,500. Kaleva, Nuoriso Chapter
Records. 1937-44. 1 vol.
Open. Preliminary guide.
University of Minnesota, Immigration History Research Center.
Ledger containing bylaws and minutes of this junior branch of the Knights and Ladies of Kaleva in Ely, MN. The Chapter promoted brotherhood and sisterhood among Finnish-American youth, the preservation of their Finnish heritage and customs, and good citizenship. Women were equal members with men in the organization and frequently held offices.

9,501. Klepachivsky, Konstantyn
Papers. 1915- . No size given.
Open. Unpublished guide.
University of Minnesota, Immigration History Research Center.
Correspondence of Klepachivsky (1887-), lawyer and banker who emigrated to the US from Poltava, Ukraine; correspondence of his wife Maria (Arkas) Klepachivska (1900-) with their daughter Mudra, who was in Prague; and records of the Ukrainian National Bank, including constitution, accounts, attestations, certificates, clippings, and maps, 1920-44. Born in Mykolaïv, Ukraine, Maria Klepachivska was a bookkeeper, home economics teacher, and secretary of the women's section of the Ukrainian Relief Committee in Chelm before she emigrated to the US. She then became active in the social and cultural activities of the Ukrainian community of Astoria, IL.

9,502. Koivisto, Edith
Papers. Ca. 1910-77. Ca. 7 ft.
Open. Preliminary guide.
University of Minnesota, Immigration History Research Center.
Correspondence, diaries and recollections, biographical sketches of Finnish Americans, unpublished and published articles, plays, minutes, photos, scrapbooks, and sheet music of Koivisto (1889-), an active playwright, director, actress, and singer in Finnish-American theater who also is a journalist and writer. Papers pertain to such topics as the Central Cooperative Wholesale, Ladies of Kaleva, Minnesota Finnish American Historical Society, the theater, art shows, and the Finnish temperance movement. Born in Kuusenkoski, Finland, Koivisto came to the US in 1910 to live with her sister in Spokane, WA. In 1912 she moved to the Duluth, MN, area and has lived in northern Minnesota since that time.

9,503. Mattson, Helmi (Lampila)
Papers. 1916-74. Ca. 2 ft.
Open. Unpublished guide.
University of Minnesota, Immigration History Research Center.
Papers of [Mrs. William] Mattson (1890-1974), a Finnish-American newspaper editor, journalist, playwright, and novelist, contain manuscripts of her autobiography and other books, scripts of her plays, poems, photos, scrapbooks, and clippings. Also included are minutes, financial records, and a history of the Northwestern Finnish Historical Society and miscellaneous newspapers. Mattson emigrated to Canada from Finland in 1911 and moved to the US several years later. She was a prolific contributor to the *Toveritar* newspaper and became its editor in 1920, a position she held for 10 years. In later years she continued to contribute to Finnish-American newspapers in addition to writing poetry, novels, and plays.

9,504. Naisyhdistys "Pyrkijä"
Records. Ca. 1923-72. Ca. 1 ft.
Open. Preliminary guide.
University of Minnesota, Immigration History Research Center.
Minutes and printed pamphlets containing a history of Pyrkijä, a Finnish-American society founded in 1893 to provide social and welfare services for newly arrived immigrant women. Members paid dues and received financial benefits from the organization when they were ill. In later years Pyrkijä became involved in fund raising for war victims, churches, and other causes. The group dissolved in 1972.

9,505. Nashwauk Finnish Socialist Chapter and Related Organizations
Records. 1906-53. 22 ledgers.
Open. Unpublished guide.
University of Minnesota, Immigration History Research Center.
Included with minutes and other records of the Chapter, a Finnish-American political and social organization, are minutes and financial records of the Nashwauk (MN) Finnish Cooperative Women's Guild from 1926 to 1953. Originally established as a sewing circle, the Guild also served as an auxiliary group to the Finnish Socialist Chapter until 1929 when it became a separate organization. The Guild existed until 1953.

9,506. Northern States Cooperative Guilds and Clubs
Records. 1930-69. Ca. 4 ft.
Open. Preliminary guide.
University of Minnesota, Immigration History Research Center.
Minutes, reports, correspondence, photos, and scrapbooks of the NSCGC, the first independently functioning cooperative women's district organization in the US. Founded in 1930, this Finnish auxiliary of Central Cooperative Wholesale encouraged social and educational activities among cooperatives by organizing summer camps and serving as a liaison between homemakers and Central Cooperative Wholesale's commodity program; it also promoted the cooperative movement through fair booths and other projects. The NSCGC operated until 1969.

9,507. Our Lady of Mount Carmel Roman Catholic Church, Ladies Society
Records. Ca. 1950-75. 4 in.
Open. Unpublished guide.
University of Minnesota, Immigration History Research Center.
Records of this Italian women's church group in Kenosha, WI, chiefly consist of financial records and membership lists but also contain a constitution, announcements, jubilee memorial booklets, and a copy of Father Tagliavia's "The Italians in Milwaukee." The Society, which was formed in ca. 1949, pursued the social and religious interests of its members.

9,508. Panchuck, John
Papers. 1933-55. 3 ft.
Open. Unpublished guide.
University of Minnesota, Immigration History Research Center.
Correspondence, memoranda, and reports of Panchuck (1904-), who was president of the United Ukrainian American Relief Committee and chairman of the Michigan Commission on Displaced Persons. Includes material pertaining to Florence Cassidy, secretary of the Michigan Commission; Julie Konick, fieldworker for four years at the European headquarters of the UUARC; and Helen Lototsky, vice-president of UUARC and also president of the Ukrainian National Women's League of America, Inc.

9,509. Pechak, Lena
Papers. Ca. 1917-67. 1.3 ft.
Open. Unpublished guide.
University of Minnesota, Immigration History Research Center.
Correspondence, programs, and clippings of Pechak, an active member of the Rochester, NY, Ukrainian community. She helped to establish the American Museum of Immigration in New York City.

9,510. Rypka, Zdeňka (Sojka)
Papers. 1825-1953. 1 ft.
Open. Preliminary guide.
University of Minnesota, Immigration History Research Center.
Correspondence, family diary, photos, post cards, and clippings of [Mrs. Walter E.] Rypka (1894-1975), a Czech schoolteacher.

9,511. Törma and Silvola Family
Papers. Ca. 1900-73. Ca. 9 ft.
Open. Preliminary guide.
University of Minnesota, Immigration History Research Center.
Family papers of Fred Törma, an early Finnish immigrant to the US who now lives in Nashwauk, MN, and of Törma's son-in-law Richard Silvola, who has served as a Minnesota state senator, contain photos, scrapbooks, and memorabilia, including items of female family members. Also contains minutes and other records pertaining to the Virginia, MN, Cooperative Women's Guilds, 1930-67.

9,512. United Ukrainian American Relief Committee
Records. Ca. 1945-60. 260 ft.
Access restricted. Unpublished guide.

University of Minnesota, Immigration History Research Center.
The UUARC was formed in 1944 to aid Ukrainian displaced persons, political refugees, and other victims of war. Financial and resettlement records, correspondence, applications, and photos include information about Joanne Draginda and Julie Konick, UUARC-International Relief Organization fieldworkers in Europe; Josephine Moroz, Mary Parazak, Julia Wenz, and Anne Crapleve, fieldworkers at the European branch of the UUARC who assisted in resettlement; Florence Cassidy, secretary of the Michigan Commission on Displaced Persons; Oksana Gengalo, who assisted in resettlement; Helen Lototsky, vice-president of UUARC and president of the Ukrainian National Women's League of America, Inc. Also contains material about resettlement aid for widows.

9,513. Wasylowsky, Philip, and Wasylowsky, Anna
Papers. Ca. 1940- . Ca. 10 ft.
Open. Unpublished guide.
University of Minnesota, Immigration History Research Center.
Philip Wasylowsky and his wife Anna were active in the American Ukrainian Republican Association and the Ukrainian National Association; Anna Wasylowsky served as an officer in both organizations. Correspondence, reports, photos, clippings, and published items.

ST. PETER

9,514. Thelander, Hulda Evelyn
Papers. 1897-1976. 1 package.
Open. No guide.
Lutheran Church in America, Minnesota Synod Archives.
Correspondence, diaries, and family history of Thelander (1896-), a physician who was the only woman graduate of the University of Minnesota medical school in 1926. She developed a children's clinic in San Francisco and also served as a missionary in China for the Augustana Synod, which combined with three other Lutheran church bodies in 1962 to form the Lutheran Church in America.

STANCHFIELD

9,515. Women's Little Remembrance Club
Records. 1974. 1 item.
Open. Unpublished guide.
Isanti County Historical Society.
Fiftieth anniversary pamphlet of this local organization, which was founded to help the needy, includes lists of officers for each year and lists of present and deceased members. In 1953 the group's name was changed from the Women's Local Relief Club to the Women's Little Remembrance Club.

WABASSO

9,516. Wabasso Woman's Civic Club
Records. 1952-64. 5 vols.
Open. No guide.
County Center Historical Society Museum.
Bylaws, articles of incorporation, minutes, financial statements, membership documents, programs, and other records of the Club, which promoted "healthy" activities for young people in the community and supported various civic improvements.

WILLMAR

9,517. Sperry, Muriel Frelander
Papers. 1892-1954. 3 boxes.
Open. Unpublished guide.
Kandiyohi County Historical Society.
Personal correspondence, school notebooks and papers, financial receipts, music papers, and other items of Sperry (1901-54), a Minneapolis native who attended a Minneapolis business college, played the piano professionally, and later managed the music department of the Minneapolis Dayton's department store. Includes her correspondence with railroad engineer Bryan Sperry while he was serving with the armed forces in Europe during WWI. The couple was married in 1924; they then moved to Willmar where she lived as a homemaker until her death.

WINDOM

9,518. Business and Professional Women
Records. 1923-41. 8 vols.
Open. No guide.
Cottonwood County Historical Society.
Scrapbooks containing histories and other records of women's organizations in Windom and the Cottonwood County area, some established as early as 1913.

WINONA

9,519. College Archives
Records. 1894- . Ca. 135 boxes and 15 files.
Open. Index files.
College of Saint Teresa Archives.
Minutes, financial records, ledgers and documents, correspondence, photos, scrapbooks, publicity material, clippings, campus bulletins and publications, and books of the College, a women's school since its founding in 1894. The records pertain to administrative, faculty, and student activities on campus.

9,520. Berry and Morey
Papers. 1846-1960. 3 ft.
Partially restricted. Unpublished guide.
Southeast Minnesota Historical Center.
Papers of Charles Henry Berry (1823-1900), a lawyer and state and federal court judge, and of his son-in-law and associate Charles Anson Morey (1851-1904), a lawyer and principal of Winona State Normal School, include correspondence, diaries for ca. 1857 to 1879, reminiscences, and an account book of Charles Berry's wife Frances Eliza (Hubbel) Berry and two scrapbooks of their daughter Kate (Berry) [Mrs. Charles] Morey. She received one of the volumes from her father in 1886; it contains programs, poems, and other items about his career. She compiled the second, which contains letters from her father and clippings about czarist Russia, between ca. 1901 and 1903.

Frances Berry, who grew up in New York state, married Charles Berry in 1850, and in 1855 they moved to Winona where he became state district judge. Their daughter Kate Morey was active in many local social clubs, serving as vice-president of the Alumni Association of Winona High School in 1884, president of the Thursday Club in 1899, and as a member of the executive committee of the Fortnightly Club in 1910 and 1911

9,521. Coleman, Mary (Haldane)
Papers. 1899-1906. 1 Hollinger box.
Open. Unpublished guide.
Southeast Minnesota Historical Center.
Correspondence, diaries, journals, and photos of Coleman (1874 or 1875-1967), who was born in Virginia and moved to Winona in 1900 with her husband George Coleman. Papers, including letters chiefly written to her mother and mother-in-law, contain information about her daily life as a housewife, local news, weather, and social functions.

9,522. Lund, Joyce Dreton
Papers. 1935-57. 2.5 in.
Open. Unpublished guide.
Southeast Minnesota Historical Center.
Papers of Lund (1909-), a journalist, state representative, and homemaker, contain correspondence, speeches, telegrams, campaign items such as nomination notices and political advertisements, programs, and clippings. After graduating from the University of Minnesota school of journalism, Lund was editor of the *Wabasha County Herald* for three years and was active in the LWV and the American Legion Auxiliary. In 1952 she ran unsuccessfully for a seat in the Minnesota House of Representatives, but in 1955 she was elected, becoming the first woman to represent Wabasha County in the Minnesota House. Lund has also served as chairman of the Wabasha County chapter of the National Foundation for Infantile Paralysis and as a member of an interim committee to study handicapped children and of the state advisory committee of the March of Dimes. She is married to Eugene Lund.

9,523. McMillan, Helen Elvira (Davis)
Papers. 1971-74. 4.5 ft.
Open. Unpublished guide.
Southeast Minnesota Historical Center.
Correspondence and legislative papers of McMillan (1909-), a housewife who served as state representative from Mower County, MN, between 1962 and 1972. The papers reflect her work as a member of the House committees on crime prevention and corrections, health and welfare, and higher education and include information on abortion, crime prevention, child services, health care, and the University of Minnesota. McMillan is married to Kenneth McMillan.

9,524. Mantorville Reminiscences
Collection. 1919. 1 in.
Open. Unpublished guide.
Southeast Minnesota Historical Center.
Consists of letters from former Mantorville, MN, pioneers to the Old Settlers Association on the occasion of their 1919 reunion; among those writing are 12 women pioneers who describe immigration experiences, community life, and town organization after 1854. Also includes clippings about the reunion.

9,525. Torgerson, Katherine Virginia Gillespie Geary
Papers. 1962-71. 4 vols.
Access restricted. Unpublished guide.
Southeast Minnesota Historical Center.
Scrapbooks containing photos, clippings, campaign cards, and other papers of Torgerson (1912-), a lawyer and homemaker who was elected to the Minnesota House of Representatives in 1963. Collection reflects her legislative campaign as well as her involvement in the Winona Taxpayers Association, the Third Judicial District Bar Association, and the Winona Art Club. Torgerson served as secretary-treasurer of the taxpayers and bar associations.

An honor graduate of the St. Paul College of Law, Torgerson began to pratice law in 1939. In 1942 she came to Winona and was part of the George, Owen, and Brehmer law firm until 1946 when she established a private practice. In 1960 she joined her husband Loren Torgerson's firm of Goldberg & Torgerson but continued to practice privately as well. In 1967 she was instrumental in the writing of the Winona city charter.

9,526. Winona State University Archives
Records. 1855- . 42.5 ft.
Open. Unpublished guide.
Southeast Minnesota Historical Center.
Reports, correspondence, enrollment records, photos, programs, bulletins, catalogs, directories, clippings, folios, maps, and books of the University, which was founded in 1860 and was known as the Normal School, Winona Normal School, and Winona State College before it achieved university status. Included is correspondence of Nels Minne with the AAUW regarding the College's membership affiliation with that organization in 1952 and other matters. Also contains speeches and other papers of kindergarten educator Louise C. Sutherland, who came to Winona in 1915 and was president of the kindergarten division of the Minnesota Education Association and chairman of both the graphic arts and the music committees of the International Kindergarten Union. Born in Brooklyn, NY, Sutherland earned her BA and MA degrees from Teachers College, Columbia University. After teaching at a private school in New York, she held teaching positions at the Horace Mann kindergarten in New York City and in the teaching department of Columbia Teachers College. At one time she was also secretary of the Teachers College Alumni Association.

9,527. Genealogy File
Collection. 1870- . Ca. 200 folders.
Open. No guide.
Winona County Historical Society.
Correspondence, manuscripts, reports, clippings, and lineage records primarily relate to Winona County area residents. Included are items about such notable local women as Gretchen Lamberton, Mabel Anderson Miller, Emma Shelton, Lorraine Cieminski, and Margaret Simpson. Gretchen Lamberton (1895-1965), a writer and newspaper columnist who graduated from Vassar College in 1917, worked during WWI in the Office of War Information publicity division in Washington, DC, and, later, for a New York City publishing house. In 1936 she was Minnesota's Democratic national committeewoman. Her concern for animals resulted in the dedication of the Gretchen Lamberton Animal Shelter in 1976. Mabel Miller, a poet, grew up in Minnesota and studied at State Teacher's College in Dickinson, ND, and at what is now Winona State University. A member of the League of Minnesota Poets, the American Poetry League, and the Winona Art Group, she received wide recognition for her poetry. [Mrs.] Emma Shelton, a prominent black resident during the 1930s, owned Winona's first beauty shop. [Mrs.] Lorraine Cieminski, the first woman elected to the Winona County board of commissioners, won her post in 1976. Margaret Simpson (1837-88), wife of Old Settler's Association president Thomas Simpson, nursed sick and wounded soldiers who passed through Winona during the Civil War. She was appointed director of the Winona State Soldier's Orphan Home after the War.

9,528. Old Settler's Scrapbook
Collection. 1840s-ca. 1920. 550 pp.
Open. Unpublished guide.
Winona County Historical Society.
Scrapbook contains correspondence, manuscript writings by early Winona residents, photos, clippings, obituaries, land titles, and marriage licenses principally of local women. Includes a document prescribing the sentence of Mary E. Surratt, one of the conspirators named by the US War Department in the assassination of President Abraham Lincoln. Surratt was hanged after being found guilty of "receiving, entertaining, harboring, and concealing" the other conspirators. Also includes material concerning "Aunt" Catharine Goddard Smith, the first permanent white woman settler in Winona. Born in Pennsylvania, Smith came to Winona in 1852 with her husband Abner Goddard and opened a shanty hotel for new settlers. Her son Orrin F. Smith was the first white child born in Winona.

MISSISSIPPI

ABERDEEN

9,529. Aberdeen Garden Club
Records. 1935- . 41 vols.
Open. Index.
Evans Memorial Library.
Founded in 1935 to further beautification in the Aberdeen area, the Club has promoted the pilgrimage (a tour of the city's antebellum homes and gardens), flower shows, the planting of flowers, and landscaping. Minute books, register, scrapbooks, yearbooks, leaflets, and miscellaneous material.

9,530. Aberdeen Woman's Club
Records. 1920- . Ca. 4 drawers.
Open. Index.
Evans Memorial Library.
The Club, organized in 1920, helped found the Aberdeen city library, staged benefits for crippled children, and worked with the local hospital. Minutes, program records, scrapbooks, and yearbooks. At the organizational meeting, the 10 members voted to require each individual to donate a book or to pay the cost of a book for a circulating library for Club members. Members then discussed the idea of a public city library; a "book shower" was held at city hall in 1921, and many books were donated for a community library. Among the Club's other projects were efforts in 1923 and 1924 to secure a home demonstration agent for Monroe County and a program in 1924 and 1925 to entertain the town's elderly women on Mother's Day.

9,531. Augustus
Papers. Ca. 1880-1946. 343 items.
Open. Index.
Evans Memorial Library.
Nicholas Augustus was a Methodist minister of Pontotoc, MS, who donated part of his library to Evans Memorial Library. Correspondence, photos, tintypes, leaflets, clippings, and miscellaneous material, including items relating to the Augustus family and to southern Methodism. Also contains women's letters and other papers, chiefly photos concerning Pontotoc women.

9,532. County Discards
Records. Ca. 1824-1943. 1641 items.
Open. Index.
Evans Memorial Library.
Family records, property lists, census sheets from 1850, county documents, land deeds, insurance policies, litigation records, and other material, the bulk of which dates from 1850 to 1900. Discarded by Monroe County courthouse officials in ca. 1950, the material includes records of divorce and guardianship proceedings, estate documents, and payroll lists for county schools dating from the 1870s and 1880s. The census records list the occupation of the head of the household and include the names of family members, places of birth, age, color, real estate owned by the household head, and information on schooling, illiteracy, and an indication, where appropriate, of family members who were "deaf and dumb, blind, insane, idiotic, pauper or convicts." The divorce records concern black and white County residents.

9,533. Dahlia Club
Records. Ca. 1935- . 52 vols.
Open. Index.
Evans Memorial Library.
Minute books, scrapbooks, and yearbooks of this Aberdeen group, founded in 1935 for the study of dahlias. Includes material on the Club's flower shows, history, and study programs.

9,534. Evans, Maria Holiday Elkin
Papers. Ca. 1830- . More than 3 drawers.
Open. Index.
Evans Memorial Library.
Aberdeen's social leader and head of the United Daughters of the Confederacy, Evans was wife of Julian Evans, Sr., who had extensive plantation holdings around Aberdeen. Correspondence, diaries, family invitations, tax and land deeds, obituaries, and clippings focus on family business activities.

9,535. Glass Negatives
Collection. Ca. 1880-1912. 14,000 items.
Open. No guide.
Evans Memorial Library.
Glass negatives of photos of families and individuals of late 19th-century Aberdeen and nearby towns. The negatives were prepared by photographer F. S. McKnight.

9,536. Junior Woman's Club
Records. 1939-50. 26 vols.
Open. Index.
Evans Memorial Library.
Minutes, club histories, reports and program material, scrapbooks, yearbooks, and certificates and ribbons of the Club, which was founded in ca. 1939 as a civic organization for younger women. Includes material about Club social service projects.

9,537. Lann-Carter
Records. Ca. 1890-1959. 1330 items.
Open. Index.
Evans Memorial Library.
Records of the Lann-Carter Hardware Store of Aberdeen illustrate business operations in a small Mississippi town. Financial statements, bills, receipts, correspondence, telegrams, leaflets, and printed material. Includes personal letters to "sister" and to male and female business clients and correspondence with such institutions as St. Katherine's School of Bolivar, TN, the Aberdeen Church of Christ, the Peabody Hotel in Memphis, and the Mississippi Children's Home. Also contains advertisements for plows and sewing machines as well as office, home, and agricultural equipment.

9,538. Milligan, Irma (Lambeth)
Papers. 1841-1910. 1 vol. and 131 items.
Open. Index.
Evans Memorial Library.
Correspondence, notes, bills and account books, speeches, poems, a scrapbook containing obituaries, clippings of local significance, photos, piano compositions, china dolls, lace, and miscellaneous material of Milligan (ca. 1900-70), who willed her house and farm to Evans Memorial Library. Included are women's Civil War letters; letters from the 1890s of Irma Lambeth, who perhaps was Irma (Lambeth) Milligan's mother; a volume begun in 1846 of farm remedies for livestock and humans, which also records births, accounts, plantings, and farm operations; a speech on aesthetic culture by Ida Lambeth; announcements for the weddings of Nellie Broyles in 1891 and Maud Adella Wilbur; pamphlets and booklets concerning education in Aberdeen schools from ca. 1890 to 1899; and a pamphlet from Aberdeen Female College that lists students, instructors, academic curriculum, tuition and "government charges," examinations, anniversaries, regulations, and dress for 1882 to 1883. Also contains a workbook, a drawing book, and a penmanship booklet.

9,539. Murff
Papers. 1825-1963. 42 items.
Open. Index.
Evans Memorial Library.
Correspondence, bills, and other papers of the family of Mayde R. Murff (ca. 1900-63), a Monroe County, MS, librarian, including letters of other women family members from the 1850s and Civil War era. Also contains land grant deeds of this farming family as well as tax receipts, bank documents, and land patents.

9,540. Photographs
Collection. Ca. 1850- . 6000 items.
Partially restricted. No guide.
Evans Memorial Library.
Tintypes, daguerreotypes, ambrotypes, and photos show families, pioneer life, and scenes of Aberdeen.

9,541. Twentieth Century Club
Records. 1946- . 42 vols. and other items.
Open. Index.
Evans Memorial Library.
Minutes, club histories, scrapbooks, yearbooks, and other records of this women's literary and community service group that was founded in 1939. Club meetings in 1947 and 1948 dealt with such topics as Mississippi, its music, composers, cotton production, art, library extension, and statewide maternal and child welfare. In 1951 and 1952 the group focused on child welfare with committees on religious and youth education, art and literature, state institutions, international relations, and library extension.

BILOXI

9,542. Local Oral History
Oral history. 1974- . 78 tapes and ca. 25 transcripts.
Access restricted. No guide.
Biloxi Public Library.
Interviews and photos of 64 local residents document the history of the Biloxi area. Among the women interviewed were Eva (Olier) Weiniewitz, Sister Mary Adrienne, and Fannie (Birch) Nichols.

Eva (Olier) Wieniewitz came to Biloxi as a young girl who spoke only French. When she was a young widow with several children, she worked in the local shrimp factory, practiced folk medicine, and served as a midwife. Known as the "Healing Lady," she took children to the doctor and paid the fee herself when she knew her treatments could not help them. She was 82 at the time of the interview.

Sister Mary Adrienne, a Biloxi native born Adrienne Curet, was in her 80s when she was interviewed. A member of the Catholic Sisters of Mercy, she opened and operated a day-care center for children of seafood industry workers. The street beside the day-care center was renamed in her honor.

Fannie (Birch) Nichols founded Nichols High School, the first school to provide secondary education for Biloxi's black children. [Mrs.] Nichols was active in the National Teachers Association and the Mississippi Teachers Association. She was 87 at the time of her interview.

BLUE MOUNTAIN

9,543. Blue Mountain College History
Records. 1873- . 12 drawers, 1 cabinet, and 4 tapes.
Open. Unpublished guide.
Blue Mountain College Alumnae Room.
Founded in 1873, Blue Mountain College is Mississippi's oldest women's college. Minutes; correspondence; tapes of programs of historical interest, including reminiscences; photos; scrapbooks; and other items of the College. Includes biographical material about the school's founder General M. P. Lowrey, his daughters Modena (Lowrey) Berry and Janie (Lowrey) Sanford Graves, and other family members. Berry was an official of the college from its founding until her death. A tape of the celebration marking her 90th birthday is included in the collection. Graves, a missionary to China, was associated with the Mo Kwong Home for Blind Girls in Canton.

CLEVELAND

9,544. Elliott, Jane Whiteside, "Lucy Somerville Howorth: Legislative Career, 1932-1935"
Papers. 1975. 91 pp.
Open. No guide.
Delta State University, W. B. Roberts Library.
Master's thesis by Elliott concerning the work of Lucy R. (Somerville) Howorth (1895-) in the Mississippi House of Representatives and her role in adoption of depression legislation. Ultimately appointed to the federal Board of Veterans' Appeals, [Mrs. Joseph M.] Howorth is an attorney who attended the University of Mississippi school of law. She was chairman of the state board of law examiners and of the Mississippi Public Lands Committee. The daughter of Nellie (Nugent) Somerville, who was the first woman elected to the Mississippi House of Representatives, Howorth pledged during her legislative campaign to oppose "nuisance taxes" imposed on Mississippians and to support measures to reduce political influence in the operation of the state's colleges and at the University.

9,545. Graves, Florence (Carson)
Papers. 1866-86. 1 folder.
Open. Card catalog.
Delta State University, W. B. Roberts Library.
Correspondence of Graves, sister of Mary (Carson) Warfield of Rosedale, MS, who married Nat Graves and lived in Phillips County, Arkansas. Most of the letters are from her father James Carson of Naphee, MS, and date from the period after her marriage; others were written by women friends before her marriage.

9,546. Howorth, Lucy R. (Somerville)
Oral history. 1895- . 20 tapes.
Open. Card catalog.
Delta State University, W. B. Roberts Library.
Legislator, federal official, judge, and longtime feminist, [Mrs. Joseph M.] Howorth (1895-) is the daughter of pioneer woman legislator and feminist Nellie (Nugent) Somerville. Interviews contain information on Howorth's youth in Greenville, MS, her education, her legislative career, her work in Washington, DC, and her concern with women's issues in Mississippi.

9,547. Merideth, Mary Louise, "The Mississippi Woman's Rights Movement, 1889-1923"
Papers. 1974. 97 pp.
Open. No guide.
Delta State University, W. B. Roberts Library.
Master's thesis by Merideth concerning the Mississippi women's rights movement and the leadership role of the city of Greenville and of Nellie (Nugent) Somerville, the first woman elected to the Mississippi House of Representatives. Focusing on the period from 1889 to 1923, Merideth notes that 19th-century Mississippians generally disapproved of women's activities away from the home and that conservatives viewed the women's rights movement with suspicion because some early suffragists had supported abolition. Thesis includes information about Somerville's activities as president of the Mississippi Suffrage Association and the state legislature's rejection of the suffrage amendment.

9,548. Myles, Harriet (Clark)
Papers. 1868-76. 3 vols.
Open. Card catalog.
Delta State University, W. B. Roberts Library.
Diaries of Myles, sister of Matilda (Clark) Sillers of the Mississippi delta town of Rosedale.

9,549. Nugent, Lucy Warfield
Papers. 1888-1908, nd. 2 folders.
Open. Card catalog.
Delta State University, W. B. Roberts Library.
Correspondence, essays, and stories of Nugent, a member of a prominent family in the Mississippi delta town of Rosedale. Revised versions of Nugent's stories are included.

9,550. Ogden, Florence (Sillers)
Papers. 1897-1972. 35.67 cu.ft.
Partially restricted. Card catalog.
Delta State University, W. B. Roberts Library.
A writer and newspaper columnist from the Mississippi delta, Ogden was active in the national Democratic party. Correspondence, manuscripts, an unpublished local history manuscript, research notes on local history, and clippings. The sister of prominent Mississippi legislator Walter Sillers, Jr., Ogden numbered national political figures and important Mississippians among her correspondents. Collection includes copies of her column "Dis N Dat," which appeared in Jackson, MS, and Greenville, MS, newspapers; descriptions of social and domestic life in Rosedale, MS; a narrative about Chinese in the Mississippi delta and their schools; and speeches she delivered before the DAR and civic groups.

9,551. Sillers, Florence (Warfield)
Papers. 1854-1958. 4 cu.ft.
Partially restricted. Card catalog.
Delta State University, W. B. Roberts Library.
Writer, historian of the Mississippi delta, and longtime member and officer of the DAR, Sillers was the mother of Florence (Sillers) Ogden and daughter of Mary Carson Warfield. Correspondence, memoirs, unpublished manuscripts, business records, historical material, organizational papers, and clippings provide information about local history. Sillers wrote about political and social life in the delta and the periodic flooding of the area's rivers. She compiled *A History of Bolivar County.* Includes DAR correspondence, material concerning the Magna Charta Dames, manuscripts relating to her history of Bolivar County as well as to the Daughters of Founders and Patriots and to the Woman's Club and Civic League of Rosedale, MS, and Warfield family genealogies and histories.

9,552. Warfield, Mary (Carson)
Papers. Ca. 1864-1919. 1 cu.ft.
Open. Card catalog.
Delta State University, W. B. Roberts Library.
A writer and member of a prominent Mississippi delta family, Warfield was the grandmother of Mississippi legislator Walter Sillers, Jr. Correspondence, unpublished manuscripts, miscellaneous papers, and a scrapbook. Mary Anderson Carson married Elisha Warfield in 1864; throughout her married life she wrote novels about her region. Contains several of her unpublished manuscripts, among them "Wanalane or Glimpses of Southern Life" and "Angola, The Story of a Country Neighborhood." Also contains pamphlets and writings of a political and social nature and an undated essay about the antebellum woman.

CLINTON

9,553. Mississippi Baptist Historical Collection
Collection. 1780- . 350 vols.
Open. Partial index.
Mississippi Baptist Historical Commission.
Official publications of Mississippi Baptists, issues of denominational papers dating from 1836 to the present, personal correspondence relating to denominational activity, and other items make up this collection, which was begun by [Mrs.] Adelia Hillman in 1888. The publications include minutes of various Mississippi Baptist churches from their founding to the present. These minutes contain information about women's organizations and individual women. Also available on microfilm.

COLUMBUS

9,554. American Association of University Women
Records. 1921-58. 1173 cu.in.
Open. No guide.
Mississippi University for Women Library.
The AAUW chapter, apparently founded in 1921, includes faculty members and others connected with the Mississippi University for Women. Constitution, minutes, financial reports, correspondence, memoranda, membership lists, a scrapbook, programs, and literature of the national AAUW.

9,555. Annual Bulletins
Records. 1885-1977. 104 vols.
Open. No guide.
Mississippi University for Women Library.
The school was founded as the Mississippi Industrial Institute and College to educate the young white women of Mississippi; the institution is now open to women from other states and countries. The bulletins reflect changes in women's education and the special educational needs of women.

9,556. Biographical Sketches
Records. Ca. 1837-98. Ca. 1 Hollinger box.
Open. Card catalog.
Mississippi University for Women Library.
Biographical sketches of women instrumental in the founding of Mississippi Industrial Institute and College in 1884, correspondence, photos, copies of petitions addressed to the state legislature in ca. 1856, clippings, and copies of "A Plea for Industrial Education," written by [Miss] Jennie Vaughn in ca. 1886. The collection provides information about [Mrs.] Annie Coleman Peyton, [Miss] Sallie Eola Reneau, and other women. Peyton, a Whitworth College graduate, began working for the establishment of a Mississippi women's college in the late 1870s. She waged an active campaign, writing editorials and columns for Mississippi newspapers. In 1891 she was appointed head of the department of history and mental and moral philosophy at MII&C, a position she held until her death in 1898. Reneau, who was educated at Holly Springs, MS, worked for more than 20 years for a women's school that would provide an education "for the underprivileged and needy as well as for the women citizens of the state in general."

9,557. Dilletanti
Records. 1954-76. 4 vols. and 4 items.
Open. No guide.
Mississippi University for Women Library.
Issues of *Dilletanti,* a literary publication of Mississippi University for Women, reflect cultural attitudes of the school's students.

9,558. Fant, John Clayton
Papers. Ca. 1880-1929. 1611 cu.in.
Open. No guide.
Mississippi University for Women Library.
Fant (1870-1929), an educator who earned the degree doctor of pedagogy at New York University, was president of Mississippi State College for Women from 1920 until 1929; his wife Mabel Beckett Fant (?-1927), a MSCW graduate, was an author. Personal and business correspondence, including that relating to the administration of MSCW during its earliest years; essays; speeches; grade reports; conference books; school contracts; diplomas; and clippings. Some of the letters concern parents' attempts to have their daughters admitted to the school; in one instance, a cow was offered in lieu of the $10 per year tuition. Other letters contain recommendations for students. Includes some material about Mabel Fant, who served as vice-president of the MSCW Alumnae Association and was active in the Ladies Reading Circle and Woman's Club in Columbus. She and her husband wrote *Mississippi History,* a public school textbook.

9,559. Industrial Institute and College and Mississippi State College for Women: Curriculum
Records. 1885-1910. Ca. 1 Hollinger box.
Open. Card Catalog.
Mississippi University for Women Library.
Mississippi Industrial Institute and College was established in 1884 as a high school, vocational training institute, and college. Correspondence, written reports, descriptions of departments, and graduation lists. Includes reports of the departments of repoussé and art needlework, millinery, dressmaking, mothercraft, home economics, education, music, art, history, infirmary, photography and printing, English, rhetoric and composition, mathematics, science, library, political economy and social studies, stenography, typewriting, telegraphy, bookkeeping, commercial law, penmanship, and mental and moral philosophy.

9,560. Industrial Institute and College and Mississippi State College for Women: History
Records. 1850-85. Ca. 1 Hollinger box.
Open. Card catalog.
Mississippi University for Women Library.
Copy of the legislative act that created the Mississippi Industrial Institute and College, the school's charter, a US Senate bill, correspondence, reports, and clippings concern the establishment in 1884 of this state-supported women's school and controversies relating to the school. Includes defenses of the school, of its curriculum, and of the education of women. The school was defended as helping to fit women for "ways of modest usefulness, for works of true benevolence," and for investing in its students "that character and those beautiful Christian graces that constitute her the charm of social life and queen of the home."

9,561. Meh Lady
Records. 1901-76. 70 vols.
Open. No guide.
Mississippi University for Women Library.
Issues of *Meh Lady,* the college's yearbook, reflect the changing appearance, activities, and interests of young women.

9,562. Mississippi Industrial Institute and College and Mississippi State College for Women: History
Records. 1884-1929. 1 Hollinger box.
Open. Card catalog.
Mississippi University for Women Library.
In its early decades Mississippi Industrial Institute and College, later called Mississippi State College for Women, functioned as a high school, vocational school, and women's college. School expense ledger, record books, a book listing students and their parents or guardians, and a clipping about the school in 1924. Contains a record ledger of the reasons students gave for leaving the school from ca. 1886 to 1890. The ledger indicates that many cited personal health problems or illnesses in their families. Others cited financial reasons, and a few said they were taking teaching positions. One left because of "parents' anxiety," while another left because of "deportment." Other records include itemized expenditures for furnishings, boilers, and other purchases.

9,563. Mississippi State College for Women: Baccalaureate Sermons and Addresses
Records. Ca. 1889-1968. Ca. 1 Hollinger box.
Open. Card catalog.
Mississippi University for Women Library.
Copies of addresses and clippings concerning graduation exercises at Mississippi State College for Women include speeches about progress in the education of women, which reflect women's roles in American society. One address by Rose Jeffries Peebles, a MSCW graduate who was head of the English department at Vassar College, was devoted to world change and expanding educational opportunities for women. Several speeches from the 1950s emphasized American freedom and the dangers of communism.

9,564. Mississippi State College for Women: Fiftieth Anniversary Celebration
Records. 1934. Ca. 1 Hollinger box.
Open. Card catalog.
Mississippi University for Women Library.
Mississippi State College for Women, now known as Mississippi University for Women, was founded in 1884 as the nation's first state-supported school for women. Then called Mississippi Industrial Institute and College, the institution included a high school and college, which offered instruction in liberal arts and vocational training. Manuscripts of *The Clock and the Fountain, A Masque in Three Parts,* a play written for the school's 50th anniversary; correspondence related to production of the play; telegrams; alumnae programs; pamphlets; and clippings. Includes descriptions of the efforts of [Miss] Sallie Eola Reneau, [Mrs.] Annie Coleman Peyton, and [Mrs.] Olivia Hastings in favor of a state-sponsored women's college in Mississippi. Reneau, a Grenada, MS, resident, began the agitation for a woman's college in 1856.

9,565. Mississippi State College for Women: Seventy-fifth Anniversary Celebration
Records. 1960. Ca. 1 Hollinger box.
Open. Card catalog.
Mississippi University for Women Library.
Mississippi State College for Women, now Mississippi University for Women, was an early leader in vocational education for women. Its early students received certificates attesting their proficiency in bookkeeping, music, or secretarial work; normal degrees; bachelor's of science or arts degrees; or other citations. Announcements, commemorative booklets, a pageant program, bulletins, and clippings concern the school's diamond anniversary and include information about the school's history.

9,566. Mississippi State College for Women Subject File
Records. Ca. 1884- . 2 drawers.
Open. Index.
Mississippi University for Women Library.
Clippings concern all aspects of Mississippi State College for Women, including academic departments, special events, honor and social societies, the alumnae association, and activities. Also contains information about prominent alumnae and faculty members as well as material on MSCW women who belonged to such organizations as the AAUW.

9,567. Mississippi Subject File: Mississippi Authors
Collection. Nd. Ca. 1.5 in.
Open. Index.
Mississippi University for Women Library.
Announcements, dust jackets, and clippings concerning the lives, work, and writings of Mississippi authors. Includes information about Frances Louise Medlin, Patsy Edwina Clark Pace, Louise Eskrigge Crump, Florence Warfield Sillers, Ann Caulfield Winston, Eudora Welty, and Elizabeth Spencer.

9,568. Pohl, Emma Ody
Papers. 1907-55. Ca. 1 Hollinger box.
Open. Card catalog.
Mississippi University for Women Library.
[Miss] Pohl (1880-post 1955), a physical education teacher, was head of her department at Mississippi College for Women from 1907 to 1955. Personal and professional correspondence, biographical sketches, photos, reprints from the student newspaper, and clippings. Pohl specialized in dance instruction, choreographing a variety of performances, among them the annual Zouave Drill. She initiated the MSCW Ballet and directed various historical pageants in Columbus. Although she never received a formal degree, Pohl studied at various dance schools and at the Chautauqua Institute for six summers.

9,569. Public Information Scrapbooks
Records. Ca. 1927-66. 66 vols.
Open. No guide.
Mississippi University for Women Library.
Scrapbooks of clippings contain descriptions of the lives of students and faculty at the college, founded in 1884.

9,570. Spectator
Records. 1904-76. 80 vols. and 9 microfilm reels.
Open. Card catalog.
Mississippi University for Women Library.
Copies of *Spectator,* which was published as a monthly literary magazine at Mississippi Industrial Institute and College from 1904 to 1916 and as the school's weekly student newspaper from 1916 to 1976. The magazine issues contain poems, historical essays, plays, short stories, written debates, meeting announcements of the 19th Century Reading Club, YWCA reports, photos, and other items. Also includes essays on such subjects as woman's suffrage, the Mississippi rural school system, and college women in the business world.

9,571. Student Handbooks
Records. 1915-77. 60 vols.
Open. No guide.
Mississippi University for Women Library.
Pamphlet-sized volumes served as guides for students in their life at this school, which was founded in 1884 and held its first classes in 1885. The school was known initially as Mississippi Industrial Institute and College and then as Mississippi State College for Women; the school's current name is Mississippi University for Women.

HATTIESBURG

9,572. De Grummond, Lena Y.
Collection. 1750- . 700 ft. and 9800 vols.
Open. Unpublished guide.
University of Southern Mississippi, William David McCain Graduate Library.
De Grummond is a former state supervisor of school libraries in Louisiana and professor of library science at the University of Southern Mississippi. Correspondence, galley proofs, drawings, paintings, and other items pertain to the writing and illustration of children's books. More than half of the 450 persons who donated material for the collection were women, many of them award-winning authors and illustrators.

HOLLY SPRINGS

9,573. Clark, Kate Freeman
Papers. 1840-1956. Ca. 18 ft.
Open. Unpublished guide.
Marshall County Historical Museum.
Correspondence, diaries and journals, financial records, photos, and scrapbooks of [Miss] Clark (1875-1956), a painter who studied at the Art Student's League in New York; her mother Cary Ann (Freeman) [Mrs. Edward D.] Clark (1849-1922) and her grandmother Margaret C. "Kate" (Walthall) [Mrs. George R.] Freeman (1828-1919); and other members of the women's families. Correspondence of the three deals primarily with family and social news but includes references to contemporary political events. Kate Freeman Clark bequeathed more than 1000 of her paintings to Holly Springs, her hometown. Her father was an assistant secretary of the US Department of the Interior. Also available on microfilm.

9,574. Marshall County Historical Society
Collection. 1834- . Ca. 6 ft.
Open. No guide.
Marshall County Historical Museum.
Correspondence, diaries, financial and club records, photos, land grants, maps, clippings, and other items collected by the Society. Includes Harriet Pegues's daybook, 1848-49, and Emma Finley's diary, 1858-59, which reflect the home and social lives of two young girls; the diary that Belle Strickland began as a girl of 9 in 1864 and kept until 1871; and the diary of Thea Alexander, 1858-76, which includes essays and notations about life at a boarding school.

JACKSON

9,575. Clippings
Collection. Nd. 4 drawers.
Open. Subject file.
Jackson State University Library, Special Collections.
Clippings and some manuscripts, photos, and pamphlets focus on blacks, Mississippians, and Jackson State University, its students, staff, and faculty. Increasing numbers of items written by whites are being added to the collection at this predominantly black university. Includes material on Florence Alexander, a black educator; Clarice Collins Harvey, a businesswoman; Margaret Walker Alexander, author and educator; Nikki Giovanni, poet; Ernestine Lipscomb, educator and librarian; Vinnie Burrows, entertainer; Dorothy Porter, librarian; Paula Giddings, editor; and educators Jane Ellen McAllister, Mildred Williams, and Cleopatra Thompson.

9,576. Jackson State University Catalogs
Records. 1886- . 54 vols.
Open. Subject file.
Jackson State University Library, Special Collections.
Founded in 1877 as a predominantly black school, Jackson State has had an increasing white enrollment since desegregation in the 1960s. Early catalogs include the names of students and their home counties or towns; descriptions of courses such as sewing, dressmaking, home economics, and domestic science; and information about Sunday school, the YWCA, literary societies, and other activities involving women.

9,577. Jackson State University Yearbooks
Records. 1925- . 54 vols.
Open. Title file.
Jackson State University Library, Special Collections.
Yearbooks depict life on the University campus. Early annuals include photos of women students, faculty, and staff members and contain photos and descriptions of the YWCA, girls' chorus, domestic science students, the dressmaking department, the women's basketball squad, beauty queens, sororities, organizations, and the school's physical plant. Also included are class photos, poems, short essays, and directories of graduating students that list the individual student's major, organization memberships, and address.

9,578. Mississippi
Collection. Nd. 1 cabinet.
Open. Subject file.
Jackson State University Library, Special Collections.
Clippings and pamphlets concern prominent residents of Mississippi, some of them women, and the state in general.

9,579. Photos
Records. Nd. Ca. 1 drawer.
Open. Subject file.
Jackson State University Library, Special Collections.
Photos of persons and activities directly related to the University. Some also include visiting dignitaries.

9,580. Adams, Mrs. William
Papers. 1835-1854. 9 items.
Open. Description.
Mississippi Department of Archives and History.
Celia A. Mortimer married William Adams of Lebanon, OH, in the mid-19th century. Correspondence to Mortimer and Adams includes letters from Mary J. Nutt at Laurel Hill and Rosemund, MS, and Mrs. C. Doherty at Clifton, MS.

9,581. Alaux, Alexander
Papers. 1928. 1 vol.
Open. Description.
Mississippi Department of Archives and History.
Notes taken by Louisa Antoinette Alaux for use by her father Alexander Alaux, a New Orleans artist, in his painting *DeSoto Discovers the Mississippi.* The painting was done for the Mississippi Department of Archives and History.

9,582. Alcorn, James L., and Family
Papers. 1839-1906. 3 vols. and 52 items.
Open. Description.
Mississippi Department of Archives and History.
Correspondence and diaries of Alcorn (1816-94), a Mississippi governor and US senator, and his second wife Amelia Walton (Glover) Alcorn (ca. 1830-post 1903) contain James Alcorn's letters to his wife. Also included is a manuscript biography of Alcorn written by his daughter. A self-made planter, Alcorn apparently improved his social position when he married Amelia Glover, daughter of an Alabama planter. They had at least seven children. Alcorn, a Whig, was pro-unionist in the secession conventions, a moderate Republican governor in 1870 and 1871, and a Republican senator from 1871 to 1877. The Alcorns lived in Coahoma County, MS.

9,583. Alexander, Margaret Walker
Papers. 1966. 1 Hollinger box.
Open. Description.
Mississippi Department of Archives and History.
Alexander (1915-), an educator, poet, and author who was born in Birmingham, AL, is director of the Institute for the Study of History, Life, and Culture of Black Studies at Jackson State University in Jackson. Galley proof of her book *Jubilee* (Boston: Houghton-Mifflin Company, 1966). Alexander received her PhD from the University of Iowa and has taught at Livingstone College in North Carolina, West Virginia State College, and, since 1949, at Jackson State University. She received the Yale Award for

younger poets in 1942 and was Rosenwald Fellow for creative writing in 1944, Ford Fellow at Yale in 1954, and Houghton-Mifflin Literary Fellow in 1966. Her books include *For My People* (1942) and *Prophets for a New Day* (1970).

9,584. Anonymous Diary
Papers. 1863-72. 1 vol.
Open. Description.
Mississippi Department of Archives and History.
Copy of a diary written by a Natchez, MS, woman during the Civil War, with the bulk of the entries dated 1863. The writer comments on life in occupied Natchez, reports on battles, and describes the manners and appearance of Yankee soldiers. The writer resumes her narrative in 1865 and comments briefly about the feeling of southerners toward their "oppressors." Contains one entry each from 1870, 1871, and 1872.

9,585. Audio Visual
Collection. Ca. 1958- . Ca. 750 tapes.
Open. Published guide and card catalog.
Mississippi Department of Archives and History.
Sound recordings, films, and videotapes gathered by the Department of Archives and History include many recordings by Leontyne Price; speeches by Charlotte Capers, former head of the Archives Department, and Mississippi Lieutenant Governor Evelyn Gandy; and interviews with writers Eudora Welty and Margaret Walker Alexander. The collection was initiated in 1958 but some material predates the project. Includes the "Ladies' Night" section of the Mississippi Folk Voices series, a group of recordings focusing on grass roots folk music and oral traditions. See H. T. Holmes, "Oral History in the Mississippi Department of Archives and History," *Journal of Mississippi History* (Feb. 1976).

9,586. Balfour Diary
Papers. 1863. 1 vol.
Open. Description.
Mississippi Department of Archives and History.
Typescript of diary kept by Emma Balfour, a Vicksburg, MS, resident, during the siege of Vicksburg.

9,587. Barber, Bette E.
Papers. 1942-1968. 5 boxes, 1 vol., and 75 items.
Open. Description.
Mississippi Department of Archives and History.
A native of Vicksburg, MS, Barber (?-1968) was an author, photographer, and newspaperwoman who married Harry Hammer of Hammer Galleries of New York City. Includes correspondence between Barber and Elbert Hilliard, curator of Jackson's Old Capitol Museum, concerning plans for her photographic exhibits "In Memorium Voor Hen Die Vielen" and "Ol' Man River Road"; typescript entitled "Vicksburg: Home Town Gibraltar" prepared by Barber for use with slides of Vicksburg in ca. 1953; ca. 600 negatives and prints and 61 photos of personnel of the Royal Netherlands Flying School, which was located at the Jackson Air Base in Jackson from 1942 until 1944; general photos of Mississippi and Louisiana; and a catalog.

9,588. Bateman, Mary E.
Papers. 1856. 1 microfilm reel and 3 microfiche.
Open. Description.
Mississippi Department of Archives and History.
Diary that Bateman, a Greenville, MS, woman, kept as a young girl while visiting relatives at Argyle Plantation located near Greenville in Washington County.

9,589. Beach, Elizabeth Jane
Papers. 1864-1957. 5 items.
Open. Description.
Mississippi Department of Archives and History.
Correspondence and photos of Beach, a resident of New Albany, MS, during the Civil War, including photos of her daughter Minnie Lee (Beach) [Mrs. Joseph C.] Parker. Contains letter in which Beach, writing to her parents Mr. and Mrs. Nathan Renfroe of Sandersville, GA, describes Civil War events in and around New Albany; she tells of thefts and arson by the Yankees and of their coming to her home. Includes a 1957 letter from Parker to the Union County, MS, Library.

9,590. Bickley, Beulah Vick
Papers. 1940. 15-page item.
Open. Description.
Mississippi Department of Archives and History.
Typescript of a poem entitled "The Romance of Vicksburg (An Epic of the South)" by Bickley of Waterloo, IA.

9,591. Bizell, Pattie
Papers. 1934-76. 9 vols.
Open. Description.
Mississippi Department of Archives and History.
Diaries of [Mrs. H.C.] Bizell of Pace, MS, include information about the area, social events, high school activities, and comments about relatives and other acquaintances.

9,592. Black, Narcissa L.
Papers. 1860-84. 35 ft. of microfilm.
Open. Description.
Mississippi Department of Archives and History.
Diaries and miscellaneous papers of Black (1810-post 1884), the wife of John L. Black (1805-65), who farmed near Corinth, MS, include complete weather information and work records of farm employees from 1860 to 1871 and infrequent entries after that date. Also contains family Bible records of John and Narcissa Black, along with those of his mother Katherine Ramsey and an incomplete letter dated 1875 to "Aunt Black" from an unidentified person in Texas.

9,593. Bodie Family
Papers. 1850-64. 4 folders.
Open. Description.
Mississippi Department of Archives and History.
Correspondence and genealogical material of a Mississippi family, including letters from Louisa Forbes Henry, Jane E. Pickett, Betsy Miller, Mary Vaughn, Mrs. S. G. Clark, and others.

9,594. Bond, Priscilla "Mittie" Munnikhuysen
Papers. 1858-1966. 17 microfiche and other material.
Open. Description.
Mississippi Department of Archives and History.
Two-volume diary of Bond, dated from 1858 to 1865, and biographical material prepared by [Mrs.] Hazel L. McNeal in 1966. Diary entries describe country life in Maryland before the Civil War and on a sugar plantation in Terrebonne Parish and in Abbeville, LA, during the War. Includes letters, poetry, clippings, and keepsakes removed from the diary.

9,595. Brown, Ann Regan
Papers. 1868-83. 31-page vol.
Open. Description.
Mississippi Department of Archives and History.
Diary of Brown, a resident of Cayuga in Hinds County, MS, contains weather observations and notes the activities of her family and helpers on the farm. Also includes clippings, household hints, and recipes from newspapers, some of which date from 1868 and 1869.

9,596. Brown, Maud (Morrow)
Papers. 1836-1938. 1 Hollinger box and 227 pp.
Open. Descriptions.
Mississippi Department of Archives and History.
[Mrs. Calvin S.] Brown was an historian of the Presbyterian Church in Mississippi, the DAR, and the Albert Sidney Johnson Chapter of the United Daughters of the Confederacy. Correspondence, reports, and manuscripts, including Brown's "At Home in Lafayette County, Mississippi, 1860-1865"; histories of the Oxford, MS, First Presbyterian Church from 1837 until 1936; her manuscript about her grandmother Nancy K. Merriam; "Some Pioneer Women of Mississippi," compiled by Brown as DAR historian; and speeches she gave on Memorial Day in 1935 and before the UDC state convention in 1938. Also contains reports and copies of letters written to Margery B. Rogers Clark from 1861 to 1863 by her husband T. G. Clark and her sons Jonathan and A. H. Clark and recollections of the Civil War in Lafayette County by [Miss] Ella F. Pegues of Oxford.

9,597. Buie Family
Papers. 1825-1940. 12 boxes and 1 vol.
Open. Descriptions.
Mississippi Department of Archives and History.
Correspondence; photos; Bible containing Buie, McRae, and Leach family records; land records; printed material; and memorabilia of Prentiss Buie and his wife Emma McRae Buie, settlers in what became Lincoln County, MS; their daughter Hallie, a missionary in Korea from 1909 to 1940; and other family members. Bulk of material concerns Hallie Buie and her activities in Korea and includes her correspondence with her sisters Mary, Estelle, and Prential, who married a minister, R. G. Rew, and lived in Texarkana, AR. One of nine children, Hallie Buie attended a Presbyterian girls school at Holly Springs, MS, a school at Lexington, MS, the Industrial Institute and College at Columbus, MS, and Scarritt College in Kansas City. After arriving in Korea in 1909, she spent five years at Wonsan; she then was transferred to Seoul where she taught school until 1940 when her health forced her to retire. She returned to Mississippi where she died in Brookhaven in 1949.

9,598. Butterfield, Frances Westgate
Papers. 1946-58. 1 vol. and 116 items.
Open. Description.
Mississippi Department of Archives and History.
A native of Brookhaven, MS, [Miss] Butterfield taught school in Korea for three years, served as a public relations officer for the WACs during WWII, wrote publicity for the New York City Board of Education, and taught at the Metropolitan Vocational School in New York. Typescripts of Butterfield's articles and drafts of her book *From Little Acorns* (New York: Renbayle House, 1951).

9,599. Capers, Charlotte
Papers. 1937-38. 1 Hollinger box.
Open. Description.
Mississippi Department of Archives and History.
An archivist and Jackson newspaper columnist, [Miss] Capers (1913-) was director of the Mississippi Department of Archives and History from 1955 until 1967 and is director of the agency's division of information and education. A scrapbook containing clippings, photos, and other items, including articles entitled "Miss Quote" that she wrote for the *Jackson Daily News*. Raised in Jackson, Capers graduated from the University of Mississippi. She was elected a fellow of the Society of American Archivists in 1967 and served as administrator of the State Historical Museum in Jackson. She has been editor-in-chief of the *Journal of Mississippi History*, secretary-treasurer of the Mississippi Historical Society, and a contributing editor of the *Delta Review*. Vice-president of the Jackson Junior League, Capers was the group's representative on the governing board of the Negro Community Hospital.

9,600. Carey, Cora E. Watson
Papers. 1855-1909. 1 vol. and 105 items.
Open. Descriptions.
Mississippi Department of Archives and History.
Born Cora E. White in Fayette, MS, Cora Watson (1843-1911) was widowed when her husband Will Watson was killed in the Civil War; she became associate editor of the *New Orleans Times*

Democrat woman's page after her marriage to S. E. Carey, a railroad man. Correspondence, literary papers, account book, and miscellaneous papers, including letters from Sherwood Bonner, Bonner's husband Edward McDowell, and New Orleans writer Grace King. Also contains resolutions of a meeting of Marshall County citizens in 1869 for the benefit of Jefferson Davis. Before her second marriage, Carey, then Cora Watson, lived with her parents-in-law Judge and Mrs. J. W. Watson in Holly Springs, MS. She died in Jackson.

9,601. Casey, Anna Z.
Papers. 1891. 1 vol.
Open. Description.
Mississippi Department of Archives and History.
A diary kept by a young woman, presumably Casey, during a European tour, which included a visit with relatives in Ireland.

9,602. Charles, Crutcher and McRaven
Papers. 1851-66. 1 box (58 items).
Open. Description.
Mississippi Department of Archives and History.
Correspondence of members of the Charles family of Liberty, IL, and the Crutcher and McRaven families of Vicksburg and Clinton, MS, includes letters from Emma C. Crutcher to Thomas C. and Ellen (McRaven) Charles and letters from Laura M. S. DeFrance, sister of Ellen Charles. Also includes a Crutcher family history.

9,603. Chateaubriand, Rene de
Papers. 1971. 1 box.
Open. No guide.
Mississippi Department of Archives and History.
Manuscript of [Mrs.] Louise Montgomery's English translation of Chateaubriand's *Les Natchez* and correspondence relating to the book, which principally deals with the French in Mississippi. The letters include two about the Department of Archives and History's acquisition of the manuscript and three from Montgomery to a potential publisher.

9,604. Chelette, Atala, and Family
Papers. 1819-1919. 4 microfiche.
Open. Description.
Mississippi Department of Archives and History.
Papers of a free Negro family of Natchitoches Parish, LA, include a copy of the act of manumission of a mulatto woman named Angelique, who was freed by Louis Fort in 1819; personal papers of Joseph Perot, a freeman of color; and personal papers and business records of Manuel and Atala Chelette.

9,605. Citizens' Council Forum Films
Records. 1955-65. 20 boxes (133 motion picture reels).
Open. Description.
Mississippi Department of Archives and History.
Films produced by the Forum, which had its headquarters in Jackson, consist principally of interviews concerning segregation, black racial characteristics, communist threats, communism and school integration, state's rights, and the Vietnam war. Persons interviewed usually were politicians, congressmen, or state officials and included US Senator Allen Ellender from Louisiana and Mrs. Harris Blyche of the US House of Representatives.

9,606. Colbert, Mrs. William B.
Papers. 1913-62. 1 box.
Open. Description.
Mississippi Department of Archives and History.
Religious correspondence, manuscript entitled "The Responsibility of a Citizen," photos, notes from an American government course, bulletins from two Jackson Episcopal churches, and printed material relating to the church.

9,607. Collums, Thelma T.
Papers. 1973. 1 vol.
Open. Description.
Mississippi Department of Archives and History.
A graduate of Blue Mountain College and the University of Mississippi, Collums taught in Calhoun City and Houlka, MS, for 14 years; in 1953 she moved to Jackson where she taught in the city's public school system for 21 years. Manuscript by Collums about Houlka's growth and development.

9,608. Colonial Dames of America
Records. 1917-23. 1 vol.
Open. Description.
Mississippi Department of Archives and History.
Volume compiled by Mrs. Walter Sillers of Rosedale, MS, listing the WWI service of male and female relatives of members of the National Society for the Colonial Dames of America of the State of Mississippi, a social, genealogical, service, and historical society.

9,609. Cook, Mrs. Jared Reese
Papers. 1855-59. 1 vol. (microfilm).
Open. Description.
Mississippi Department of Archives and History.
Diary of Minerva Hynes [Mrs. Jared Reese] Cook, a resident of Newman's Grove near Vicksburg, MS.

9,610. Cooper, Janie (Drake)
Papers. 1896-1962. 1 vol. and 9 items.
Open. Description.
Mississippi Department of Archives and History.
Granddaughter of B. M. Drake, an early Methodist minister in Mississippi, Cooper (1875-1963) was head of the English department and dean for more than 20 years at Whitworth College in Brookhaven, MS. Correspondence; manuscript; scrapbook containing letters commending Janie Drake as a student and teacher; manuscript of "A Century of Progress in the Higher Education of Women," a pageant Cooper wrote in celebration of Whitworth College's diamond anniversary; and a scrapbook of correspondence, clippings, and memorabilia. The pageant was performed at the Century of Progress Exposition in 1933 in Chicago. Her husband I. W. Cooper was president of Whitworth College and her sister [Miss] Claribel Drake lived at Mount Ararat Plantation at Church Hill, MS.

9,611. Corneil, Mrs. R. F.
Papers. Nd. 23-page vol.
Open. Description.
Mississippi Department of Archives and History.
Scrapbook containing poetry and other papers of Corneil, a resident of Vicksburg, MS, pertain principally to the War Between the States.

9,612. Crump, Louise Eskrigge
Papers. 1954. 1 vol.
Open. Description.
Mississippi Department of Archives and History.
Copy of the manuscript of *The Face of Fear* (New York, London, Ontario: Longman, Green and Co., 1954) by Crump, a Greenville, MS, resident.

9,613. Crutcher and Shannon
Papers. 1826-1929. 2257 items.
Open. Description.
Mississippi Department of Archives and History.
Papers centering around Marmaduke Shannon and Levina (Morris) Shannon of Vicksburg, MS, and seven of their 11 children: Emma (Shannon) [Mrs. William O.] Crutcher; Anne (Shannon) [Mrs. William A.] Martin; Levina (Shannon) [Mrs. Thomas] Mount; and Marmaduke, Mary, Alice, and Grace Shannon. Correspondence, business and personal account books, cancelled checks, statements of the Warren County jail and the Vicksburg Whig office, compositions, family pictures, theater programs, prescriptions, invitations, and other material. Includes letters from Emma and Anne at St. Mary's Hall in Burlington, NJ, during the 1857-58 school year, a letter to Emma begun by Anne and finished by Grace or Alice during the siege of Vicksburg in 1863, letters concerning Mississippi prison conditions in the 1890s, and genealogical information about the Morris, Crutcher, Shannon, and Stockton families. Marmaduke and Levina Shannon had four other children who died in childhood.

9,614. Darden Family
Papers. 1820-99. 2 vols. and 99 items.
Open. Description.
Mississippi Department of Archives and History.
Correspondence, diaries, land grants, and business papers of the family of Susan (Sillers) Darden, the daughter of Walter and Mourning Kane Sillers, and her husband Jesse H. Darden, a Jefferson County, MS, planter. Susan Darden's diaries cover the years 1853 to 1861 and 1865 to 1877. Other material includes records pertaining to Elizabeth Darden's estate, statements dated 1855 from Franklin Female College in Holly Springs, MS, and agreements between James T. Darden and Sarah Annette Darden regarding Moss Side Plantation and other Bolivar County, MS, property.

9,615. Daughters of Confederate Veterans
Records. 1894-1937. 5 vols. and 931 items.
Open. Description.
Mississippi Department of Archives and History.
Constitution, minute books, treasurer's reports, correspondence, essays, roll books, membership applications, resolutions, clippings, and other records.

9,616. Daughters of the American Revolution
Records. 1902-50. 4 boxes.
Open. Description.
Mississippi Department of Archives and History.
Minutes, treasurer's reports, financial statements, membership lists, scrapbooks, yearbooks, national DAR handbook, programs, portraits, and other items of the Magnolia State and Ralph Humphreys chapters, organized in 1929 and in 1902 respectively. Also contains programs of the Copiah Chapter and of the 21st state DAR conference.

9,617. Davis, Jefferson, and Davis, Varina
Papers. 1848-1961. 1 Hollinger box, 1 folder, and 25 items.
Open. Descriptions.
Mississippi Department of Archives and History.
Correspondence, speech transcripts, minutes, clippings, and papers of Davis (1808-89), president of the Confederate States of America, and his wife Varina Anne (Howell) Davis (1826-1906), including copies of letters the Davises wrote from Richmond, VA, Vicksburg, MS, Memphis, New York, and other locations. Also contains minutes that Varina Davis recorded of the sixth annual meeting of the United Daughters of the Confederacy.

9,618. Davis, Varina (Howell)
Papers. 1847-1905. 2 vols. and 71 items.
Open. Descriptions.
Mississippi Department of Archives and History.
Correspondence, notes, page proofs, and other items of Davis (1826-1906), who was wife of Jefferson Davis, president of the Confederate States of America, including a letter she wrote from Narragansett, RI, to Owen Dorsey. Concerned with the purchase of the Beauvoir residence in Biloxi, MS, the letter, signed V. Jefferson Davis, also discusses matters regarding the Dorsey family. Also contains letters Davis wrote to [Miss] Clare de Graffenried and to Davis's cousin Margaret Graham Sprague Winchester. Davis wrote to Winchester from New York as she was preparing for the final burial of her husband; the message concerns her family, illness, and financial problems. Also includes a copy of the Beauvoir deed and page proofs of Davis's *Jefferson Davis,*

Ex-President of the Confederate States of America: A Memoir (New York: Belford, 1890).

9,619. Davis, Varina (Howell), and Hayes, Margaret Howell Jefferson (Davis)
Papers. 1904-08. 10 items.
Open. Description.
Mississippi Department of Archives and History.
The reaction of Varina [Mrs. Jefferson] Davis and her daughter Margaret Hayes to Mississippians' disapproval of the burial of Jefferson Davis in Richmond, VA, is reflected in their correspondence to Colonel J. J. Hood of Meridian, MS. The letters also show that Hayes felt some southerners favored her younger sister Varina Anne "Winnie" over herself. Letters provide insight into the relationships of Davis family members and show the veneration accorded Jefferson Davis. They also describe the experiences of Margaret Davis when her father was captured by Union forces in Georgia.

9,620. DeHay, Elizabeth (Norton)
Papers. 1857-1930. 56 items.
Open. Description.
Mississippi Department of Archives and History.
Correspondence and clippings of [Mrs. P. S.] DeHay, a Houston, MS, teacher, include letters she wrote as a student at a Catholic girls school in the 1850s. Letters from the Civil War period give accounts of civilian and military life. Also contains clippings concerning the deaths of James Money Vardaman and James Kimble Vardaman.

9,621. DeLonne, Mrs. H. B.
Papers. Nd. 8 pp.
Open. Description.
Mississippi Department of Archives and History.
Manuscript of DeLonne's reminiscences about General William Sherman's march through Port Gibson, MS, in 1863.

9,622. Dixon, Annie Hughes
Papers. 1934. 1 vol.
Open. Description.
Mississippi Department of Archives and History.
This manuscript history of Greenwood, MS, was sponsored by the Junior Chamber of Commerce and the Chakchiuma DAR Chapter and supervised by [Mrs.] Dixon.

9,623. Dockery, Octavia
Papers. Nd. 6-page item.
Open. Description.
Mississippi Department of Archives and History.
Unpublished short story by Dockery, a Natchez, MS, resident, entitled "Held by the Enemy." The story was set in Champion Hill, MS, in 1863.

9,624. Dockery, Octavia
Papers. 1882-1942. 34 items.
Open. Description.
Mississippi Department of Archives and History.
[Miss] Dockery (?-1949), a Natchez, MS, resident who was the daughter of Confederate General Thomas P. Dockery of Arkansas, gained notoriety in the "Goat Castle" murder case. Correspondence, invitations, broadsides, and a copy of a 1942 Supreme Court opinion that dealt with the Glenwood ("Goat Castle") property. Dockery was guardian of Richard Dana of Natchez, the son of churchman Charles D. Dana. She and the younger Dana were accused in the 1932 slaying of [Miss] Janie Merrill. Both were acquitted. Dockery's correspondents included US Representative Alexander M. Dockery, who apparently was her cousin.

9,625. Dunbar, William
Papers. 1793-96. 32 items.
Open. Description.
Mississippi Department of Archives and History.
Correspondence of Dunbar, a Mississippi planter, scientist, and agricultural innovator, contains information about his wife Dinah Clark Dunbar (1769-1821), a native of England who managed their plantation The Forest during Dunbar's absences. The letters include instructions about crops, agricultural matters, finance, and administration and provide an indication of the duties of a plantation mistress. The Dunbars had nine children.

9,626. Easterling, Narena
Papers. 1941. 212-page vol.
Open. Description.
Mississippi Department of Archives and History.
Manuscript of a novel by [Mrs. Lamar F.] Easterling, which is entitled *Louisiana Lady* (New York: Gramercy Publishing Co., 1941). The manuscript was originally entitled "Second Marriage."

9,627. Ellzey, Maude
Papers. Nd. 42-page vol.
Open. Description.
Mississippi Department of Archives and History.
Manuscript by Ellzey entitled "Epochs in the Life of Jefferson Davis."

9,628. Foote, Helen E.
Papers. 1883-88. 2 vols.
Open. Description.
Mississippi Department of Archives and History.
Diaries of Foote, later Mrs. Charles Kent Brown of Cayuga, MS, reflect her experiences as a girl in her parents' home, as a student at Port Gibson Female College in Mississippi, and as a teacher in a rural school near Cayuga in Hinds County.

9,629. Franklin, Eulalia (Rogers)
Papers. 1951-52. 27 items.
Open. Description.
Mississippi Department of Archives and History.
Correspondence, speeches, and clippings relate to the work of Franklin, a Jackson resident, as state chairman of the National Poetry Day Committee. Also includes Governor Fielding L. Wright's proclamation declaring October 15 National Poetry Day in Mississippi.

9,630. Garrett, Louisiana (Dunlevy)
Papers. 1860-68. 20 items (microfilm).
Open. Description.
Mississippi Department of Archives and History.
Garrett was the wife of Fontaine D. Garrett who died as the result of an accident while serving as an assistant surgeon with Logan's Cavalry of the Confederate army. Correspondence from Louisiana Garrett's parents, her sister E. Wood of New Orleans, and her mother-in-law Mrs. S. D. Garrett of Canton, MS, as well as her letters to her husband, contain descriptions of civilian life during the Civil War.

9,631. Gassaway, Mary
Papers. 1940-56. 2 items.
Open. Description.
Mississippi Department of Archives and History.
Scrapbook of [Miss] Gassaway, a New Albany, MS, resident, contains clippings from 1956 issues of the *New Albany Gazette* that include transcripts of the diary kept by James Bardin during a covered wagon trip from Ripley, MS, to California in 1855. Bardin's wife was Mary Jane Collins, daughter of Moses Collins, who founded New Albany. The second scrapbook contains clippings and written information about the Gassaway and Collins families.

9,632. "Germans in the Colonial Southeast"
Papers. 1976. 1 item.
Open. Description.
Mississippi Department of Archives and History.
Manuscript prepared by Jacqueline Young deals with early German settlement, exploration, and development in the southeastern United States.

9,633. Gray, Alma (Ratliff)
Papers. 1890-91. 9 items.
Open. Description.
Mississippi Department of Archives and History.
Manuscript and copies of "Uncle Scipio's War Story" written by Gray, a Hazlehurst, MS, resident, and submitted to *The Youth's Companion* competition for the best folklore stories. Includes an addenda describing the writing of the story and biographical information about Gray.

9,634. Green, Selina Jewel (East)
Papers. 1857-1971. 3 boxes.
Open. Description.
Mississippi Department of Archives and History.
Green (1887-1971) taught in Mississippi towns including Tupelo, Crystal Springs, and Hazlehurst before marrying Theophilus Walton Green, a minister, in 1962; the Greens donated more than $50,000 to Mississippi College and Selina Green bequeathed her estate to the College, which is located in Clinton, MS. Correspondence, including that with R. A. McLemore, executor of Selina Green's estate and former director of the Department of Archives and History; tax records; deeds; wills; and insurance policies.

9,635. Greenleaf, Matilda (Beaumont)
Papers. 1822-24. 3 items.
Open. Description.
Mississippi Department of Archives and History.
Correspondence of Greenleaf, who married Daniel Greenleaf in 1822, includes a letter she wrote from Natchez, MS, to a sister discussing family matters and a later letter to [Mrs.] Margaret M. Fox, probably the sister involved in the earlier letter, describing Port Gibson, MS, and the Greenleafs' new home there.

9,636. Guyton, Pearl Vivian
Papers. 1804-1934. 1 vol. and 7 items.
Open. Descriptions.
Mississippi Department of Archives and History.
[Miss] Guyton was a teacher and head of the history department at Natchez High School in Natchez, MS. Copy of Guyton's *The History of Mississippi from Indian Times to the Present Day* (1934), magazines, newspapers, and a Civil War letter from a man in Okolona, MS, to his wife. Includes an 1810 issue of *The Hampshire Federalist,* an 1839 issue of *The New York Observer,* an 1804 issue of the *Columbian Sentinel and Massachusetts Federalist,* an 1833 copy of *The Knickerbocker,* and other newspapers.

9,637. Hardenstein, Hattie
Papers. Nd. 40-page vol.
Open. Description.
Mississippi Department of Archives and History.
Notebook in French of Hardenstein, a Jackson resident.

9,638. Hardy, Genie Steele, and Palmer, Etta Sessums
Papers. 1925. 134-page vol.
Open. Description.
Mississippi Department of Archives and History.
[Mrs.] Hardy was regent of the Barnard Romans Chapter of the DAR, while [Mrs.] Palmer was Chapter secretary. Volume assembled by the two women concerns the history of Lowndes County, MS, from its establishment in 1830 until 1925.

9,639. Harper, Annie E.
Papers. 1876. 79-page vol.
Open. Description.
Mississippi Department of Archives and History.
An account of the War Between the States and Reconstruction written by Harper for her daughter Lurline N. Harper.

9,640. Hays, Sue Brown
Papers. 1946. 223-page vol.
Open. Description.

Mississippi Department of Archives and History. Manuscript of [Mrs.] Hays's Natchez, MS, mystery novel *Go Down, Death* (New York: Charles Scribner's Sons, 1946). Hays was a New Orleans resident.

9,641. Headley, Katy (McCaleb)
Papers. 1973. 1 microfilm reel.
Closed. No guide.
Mississippi Department of Archives and History. Manuscript entitled "Claiborne County, Mississippi, The Promised Land," by Headley, a Port Gibson, MS, resident. Majority of the research for the manuscript was done from county records and the local newspaper, the *Reveille,* while Headley was crippled following an accident. Includes discussion of private schools, slavery, yellow fever, and other aspects of the county's history.

9,642. Hederman, Ellen
Papers. 1918. 4 items.
Open. Description.
Mississippi Department of Archives and History. Correspondence includes a letter in which "Widow Lansoy" of France thanks [Miss] Hederman for her support of Lansoy's son Daniel through the Fatherless Children of Europe program. Lansoy's husband was killed in WWI.

9,643. Henry, Henrietta (Mitchell)
Papers. 1917-57. 12 Hollinger boxes (2407 items).
Open. Description.
Mississippi Department of Archives and History. [Mrs. Robert H.] Henry (?-1958?), prominent in Jackson and Natchez social circles, was the first Democratic national committeewoman from Mississippi. Correspondence, recollections, genealogical data, photos, pamphlets, clippings, and other papers, including correspondence from many Democratic leaders and Democratic National Committee members. Also includes family photos and photos of Mississippi political figures, buildings, interiors, and furnishings of the early 20th century. Henry was the daughter of T. J. Mitchell, superintendent of the Mississippi State Hospital for the Insane.

9,644. Hickey, Bertie (Westbrook)
Papers. 1924-53. 5 boxes and 2 vols.
Open. Description.
Mississippi Department of Archives and History. Born in Meridian, MS, [Mrs. Charles Kennedy] Hickey organized Jackson's first Women's Civic Club after she moved to that city in ca. 1920, served as president of the Mississippi division of the United Daughters of the Confederacy and of the Frances Ewing Gordon Chapter of the King's Daughters and Sons, and was active in other civic and religious groups. Correspondence, speeches, records of various organizations with which she was associated, photos, clippings, invitations, cards, and other papers include items regarding the Jefferson Davis Shrine and the Galloway Memorial Women's Bible Class.

9,645. Hilliard, Mrs. Isaac H.
Papers. 1849-66. 3 microfiche.
Open. Description.
Mississippi Department of Archives and History. Diary of Hilliard, wife of a Chicot County, AR, planter and relative by marriage of Bishop Leonidas Polk, includes descriptions of household activities on the Hilliard plantation during a Christmas and New Year's visit of her sister-in-law Mrs. George W. Polk. Also tells of social activities and trips to Louisiana, Mississippi, and Kentucky in 1849 and 1850. Her son Isaac H. Hilliard, Jr., made diary entries in 1866 for tuition expenses at Kentucky Military Institute.

9,646. Hollingsworth, Jane, and Jones, Katherine H.
Papers. 1962. 1 microfilm reel.
Open. Description.
Mississippi Department of Archives and History. Biographical data and clippings pertaining to Mississippi artists and art and a history of the Mississippi Art Association by Jones. Hollingsworth, the wife of William R. Hollingsworth, Jr., collected data for the survey.

9,647. Howorth, Lucy R. (Somerville)
Papers. 1929-1934. Ca. 1 in.
Open. Description.
Mississippi Department of Archives and History. An attorney and proponent of women's rights, [Mrs. Joseph M.] Howorth (1895-) was general counsel for the US War Claims Commission in 1953, a judge, a state legislator, and a feminist. Correspondence, biographical information, minutes, accounts, resolutions, and clippings document Howorth's career as treasurer of the central committee for an Economic Survey of Mississippi, as a member of the Research Commission of the State of Mississippi, as director in 1934 of the Natchez Trace Highway Association, and as a judge and attorney. Born in Greenville, MS, Howorth told an interviewer in 1975 that "women have had a large part in promoting the wave of humanitarian legislation since the 1920s." Her mother was the first woman member of the Mississippi legislature. Howorth is a member of the AAUW, the DAR, the Business and Professional Women's Club, and Eastern Star.

9,648. Huff, Grace Clementine
Papers. 1956. 1 item.
Open. Description.
Mississippi Department of Archives and History. Manuscript of the historical pageant of Sylvarena in Smith County, MS, written by [Miss] Huff, a Pascagoula, MS, resident. The pageant was presented to celebrate the centennial of Sylvarena School.

9,649. Humphrey, Emily Barksdale
Papers. 1974?. 1 box.
Open. Description.
Mississippi Department of Archives and History. Pencil and carbon copies of *An Informal History of St. Clement's Episcopal Church, 1876-1976* by Humphrey, a resident of Vaiden, MS, where the Church is located.

9,650. Hunt, Sarah Ethridge, and Cain, Ethel
Papers. 1941. 1 vol.
Open. Description.
Mississippi Department of Archives and History. [Mrs.] Hunt and [Miss] Cain were faculty members at Delta State Teachers College. Manuscript of their *Games Around the World: Four Hundred Folk Games for an Integrated Program in the Elementary School* (New York: A. S. Barnes and Co., 1941).

9,651. Irion and Neilson Family
Papers. 1813-1971. 17 boxes.
Open. Description.
Mississippi Department of Archives and History. Personal correspondence, diaries, journals, transcript, photos, scrapbooks, souvenir album, sheet music, and publications; the bulk of the papers are journals and scrapbooks of Eliza Lucy (Irion) Neilson for the years 1843 to 1911. Eliza Irion married Captain John Abert Neilson of Columbus, MS, after his service in the Confederate Army's Company K, 14th Regiment of Mississippi Infantry. Includes love letters exchanged by the two in 1870 and 1871 and John Neilson's Civil War diaries. Also contains correspondence of James W. Irion to his family from 1859 to 1862 and correspondence of Mr. and Mrs. McKinney F. Irion, Jr., to Elizabeth Charlotte and Eliza Lucy Irion from 1844 to 1862.

9,652. Jackson-Thames, Frances
Papers. 1954. 268-page vol.
Open. Description.
Mississippi Department of Archives and History. Manuscript of *Girl of the Hills* (New York: Pageant Press, 1954) by Jackson-Thames, a Decatur, MS, resident.

9,653. Jacobs, Annie E. (Clark)
Papers. Nd. 252 pp.
Open. Description.
Mississippi Department of Archives and History. Jacobs was the daughter of General Charles Clark, governor of Mississippi from 1863 to 1865. Her unpublished manuscript is entitled "The Master of Dora Plantation—An Epic of the Old South."

9,654. Jones, Lulie, and Carnahan, Ann
Papers. 1844-81. 1 box.
Open. Description.
Mississippi Department of Archives and History. New Testament Bible of Carnahan and Jones's 1881 autograph book.

9,655. Kager, Mary B.
Papers. 1861-76. 1 vol.
Open. Description.
Mississippi Department of Archives and History. Scrapbook of articles primarily relating to the Civil War.

9,656. Kearney, Belle
Papers. 1865-1938. 426 items.
Open. Description.
Mississippi Department of Archives and History. The first woman to serve as a Mississippi state senator, [Miss] Kearney (1863-1939) was president of the Mississippi Woman Suffrage Association and of the state WCTU during the early 1900s. Correspondence, articles, pictures, certificates, and other papers, including two letters from World WCTU president Frances E. Willard, one in which she asks whether Kearney would undertake a world lecture tour for the group; clippings pertaining to the WCTU and woman suffrage in Mississippi; an 1865 certificate of medical examination for a slave in Canton, MS; an 1891 copy of *The Mississippi White Ribbon;* and information about Kearney, Owen, Masterson, Alston, Lindsay, and Walter genealogies. Author of two books, *A Slaveholder's Daughter* and *Conqueror or Conquered?,* Kearney was an unsuccessful candidate for the US Senate in 1921. She supported child welfare, protective legislation for women in industry, labor legislation, disarmament, and the League of Nations. A resident of Vernon, MS, she was appointed the WCTU's Round-the-World Missionary in England in 1895.

9,657. Kimbrough, A. McC., and Family
Papers. 1895-1974. 2 boxes.
Open. No guide.
Mississippi Department of Archives and History. Papers deal primarily with Mary Hunter (Southworth) Kimbrough and her efforts to establish Beauvoir, Jefferson Davis's residence at Biloxi, as a Mississippi historic site. Correspondence, articles by Kimbrough, photos, annual convention programs and other material relating to the United Daughters of the Confederacy and the Sons of Confederate Veterans, a program for ceremonies in 1920 during which the Jefferson Davis Memorial Gateway was unveiled at Beauvoir, clippings, and a 1971 issue of *The Journal of the Southern Confederacy.* Contains material from UDC conventions in 1917, 1918, and 1921.

9,658. Kimbrough, Allan McCaskell, and Family
Papers. 1868-1934. 2 boxes.
Open. Description.
Mississippi Department of Archives and History. Family correspondence of Kimbrough (1850-?), a circuit court judge, and his wife Mary Hunter (Southworth) Kimbrough, the daughter of Judge Hunter H. Southworth (?-1878) and Mary Morgan

Southworth. Allan Kimbrough, a Greenwood, MS, attorney and longtime friend of Jefferson and Varina Davis, was appointed circuit judge in 1903. Correspondence includes letters from Varina Davis and from state and national officials, among them Theodore G. Bilbo, Pat Harrison, A. H. Longino, A. J. McLaurin, J. M. Stone, James K. Vardaman, John Sharp Williams, Theodore Roosevelt, and Woodrow Wilson. Kimbrough was the son of O. L. Kimbrough (1804-81), one of the early settlers of Carrollton, MS, and Charlotte Grey Kimbrough (1825-?).

9,659. Ladies Aid Society, First Baptist Church of Jackson
Records. 1901-04. 93-page vol.
Open. Description.
Mississippi Department of Archives and History.
Minute book kept by Mrs. W. N. Campbell and Mrs. W. F. Yarborough.

9,660. Ladies Sustentation Society of the Presbyterian Church of Jackson
Records. Ca. 1870. 1 item.
Open. Description.
Mississippi Department of Archives and History.
Constitution bearing the signatures of 20 women who apparently were members of the organization.

9,661. Lauderdale, Maggie R.
Papers. 1863-64. 5 items.
Open. Description.
Mississippi Department of Archives and History.
Family correspondence written during the Civil War from Columbus and Macon, GA, and Raleigh, NC.

9,662. Lenoir, Dorothy
Papers. 1946-69. 1 box.
Open. Description.
Mississippi Department of Archives and History.
From 1948 until her retirement in 1963, [Miss] Lenoir was director of the placement bureau at the University of Southern Mississippi; in 1960 and 1961 she was on the State Education Study Committee. Correspondence and committee papers include commendatory letters Lenoir received while placement bureau director; correspondence from H. M. Ivy, superintendent of the Meridian, MS, public schools and later executive director of Associated Consultants in Education, Inc.; and correspondence and records relating to the Study Committee.

9,663. Lenoir, Mrs. Robert L.
Papers. 1900. 2 items.
Open. Description.
Mississippi Department of Archives and History.
Letters of condolence to Lenoir, a Magnolia, MS, resident, on the death of her daughter Minnie (Lenoir) Holmes, written by Mrs. J. J. White, mother of Mississippi Governor Hugh L. White, and by Julia V. L. Battles of Washington, DC.

9,664. Lindsey, Bell
Papers. 1943-45. 27 items.
Access restricted. Description.
Mississippi Department of Archives and History.
Correspondence to [Miss] Lindsey, a teacher at Copiah-Lincoln Junior College, from some of her former students. Written during WWII, the letters reflect living conditions in the military and the students' desire to return to Mississippi.

9,665. Lockhart and Weir Family
Papers. 1833-95. 50-page vol. and 584 items.
Open. Description.
Mississippi Department of Archives and History.
Correspondence, memoranda, and business and estate records of the Lockhart and Weir families of Carroll County, MS, chiefly consist of papers of Lucinda Lockhart, the widow of Samuel T. Lockhart, and her daughters Ella C. and Ophelia W. Lockhart. Business papers include Carroll County tax receipts, 1846-85, and invoices and receipts from a Vaiden, MS, doctor and druggist, New Orleans cotton factors, Memphis commission merchants, two railroad companies, and other firms.

9,666. Lowry, Kathryn Runge
Papers. 1858-85. 2 vols. and 1 item.
Open. Description.
Mississippi Department of Archives and History.
[Mrs.] Lowry was a Jackson resident. Memory books of Mary A. Norrel and Addie Watt, both of Brandon, MS, dated 1858 and 1885 respectively, and an 1861 letter from a New Orleans merchant to A. E. Martin of Brandon concerning an order for silk material.

9,667. Lowry, Mrs. J. C.
Papers. 1959. 15-page item.
Open. Description.
Mississippi Department of Archives and History.
Copy of the manuscript of "History and Stories of Old Centreville," which was compiled by Lowry and presented to the Centreville Book Club by Lowry, Mrs. C. C. Germany, Jr., and Mrs. D. N. Redhead.

9,668. Luckett, Maggie C.
Papers. 1933-35. 24 items.
Open. Description.
Mississippi Department of Archives and History.
Papers and pictures filed in Madison County Circuit Court in the suit of [Mrs.] Luckett against C. H. James and the Louisiana Oil Corporation in connection with the death of Tom Luckett.

9,669. Lyons, Mrs. R.
Papers. 1909-28. 128 items.
Open. Description.
Mississippi Department of Archives and History.
Records and speeches of Lyon, a Heidelberg, MS, resident, in connection with the Jasper County Chapter, No. 1221, of the United Daughters of the Confederacy in Heidelberg. Includes certificates stating the eligibility of some of the county's Confederate veterans for the UDC Southern Cross of Honor. Also contains three articles apparently by Mrs. J. A. McFarland of Bay Springs, MS, concerning Jasper County writers, musicians, points of interest, and "Schools of Yesterday and Today."

9,670. McLaurin, Laura Raunch
Papers. 1902. 34-page vol.
Open. Description.
Mississippi Department of Archives and History.
Recipe book of McLaurin who lived in Brandon, MS, and Washington, DC.

9,671. McLemore, Richard Aubrey
Papers. 1910-71. 37 boxes.
Open. Description.
Mississippi Department of Archives and History.
Educator, scholar, and Mississippi historian, McLemore (1903-) served as dean at Jones County Junior College in Ellisville, MS; at Judson College in Marion, AL; and at Mississippi Southern College in Hattiesburg, MS; and, from 1957 to 1968, as president of Mississippi College at Clinton, MS. Correspondence, speech manuscripts, articles and book reviews, biographical information, receipts and canceled checks, photos, clippings, and other papers include a box of letters from his mother Mrs. H. K. McLemore. McLemore wrote several books including *Mississippi Through Four Centuries,* which he co-authored with his wife Nannie Pitts McLemore, and *Our Nation's Story,* which he wrote with Everett Augspurger. A member of the Mississippi Department of Archives and History board of trustees since 1950, McLemore was chosen the Department's director in 1969.

9,672. McLemore, Richard Aubrey: McLemore, Nannie Pitts
Papers. 1910-71. 42 Hollinger boxes.
Open. Description.
Mississippi Department of Archives and History.
Correspondence, biographical information, canceled checks, photos, clippings, printed material, and other items of Nannie [Mrs. Richard A.] McLemore (1900-), a Mississippi historian and teacher. Born in Harvest, AL, McLemore is a 1921 graduate of Athens College in Alabama who received a master's degree in 1927 from Peabody Institute in Nashville. She headed the history department at McComb, MS, High School from 1925 to 1927 and later taught at Jones Junior College in Ellisville, MS, where her husband was dean. She and her husband co-authored *Outline of Mississippi History* (1941), *Mississippi Through Four Centuries* (1945), and *Our Nation's Story* and *The Mississippi Story,* both published in 1959. A Democrat and a Baptist, she is a member of the AAUW, the Mississippi Historical Society, and the Mississippi Genealogical Society.

9,673. McLemore, Richard Aubrey: Mississippi Federation of Club Women
Papers. 1915-60. 2 boxes.
Open. Description.
Mississippi Department of Archives and History.
McLemore is a Mississippi archivist and educator. Scrapbooks, yearbooks, pamphlets, and other records of the Mississippi Federation of Club Women, organized in 1898 in Kosciusko, contain material of the Woman's Club of Jackson, the Hinds County Federation of Woman's Clubs, and the Fortnightly Club, formed in 1907 as an outlet for the expression of literary taste. The Woman's Club of Jackson was organized in 1922 to focus women's strength for promotion of health, knowledge, service, and spirit in the city, while the Hinds County Federation serves as a clearinghouse for Federation activities.

9,674. McNabb, Eliza R.
Papers. 1866-76. 15 items.
Open. Description.
Mississippi Department of Archives and History.
Copies of letters from McNabb, a Pike County, MS, resident, to Mary Ott, who moved from Pike County to Louisiana in 1865.

9,675. Magruder, Eliza L.
Papers. 1846-57. 7 microfiche.
Open. Description.
Mississippi Department of Archives and History.
Diary that Magruder kept during a stay at her uncle Joseph Dunbar's Locust Plantation near Natchez, MS, contains comments on local social events; literature; treatment, and unrest of slaves; religious life, including sermon texts and names of ministers; and yellow fever epidemics.

9,676. Martin, Anne (Shannon)
Papers. 1863-64. 1 vol.
Open. Description.
Mississippi Department of Archives and History.
Diary and cash account entries of Martin, a Vicksburg, MS, resident.

9,677. Mayes, Annie
Papers. Nd. 3 boxes.
Open. Description.
Mississippi Department of Archives and History.
Two boxes and two scrapbooks of clippings compiled by [Miss] Mayes concern the Civil War and other historic events.

9,678. Miller, Emily (Van Dorn)
Papers. 1866-1907. 12 items.
Open. Description.
Mississippi Department of Archives and History.
Correspondence of Miller, a resident of New Orleans and Washington, DC, includes letters pertaining to her brother Major General Earl Van

Dorn of Port Gibson, MS, who was assassinated in 1863, and letters written by Jefferson Davis, Fitzhugh Lee, and Franklin L. Riley.

9,679. Miller, Martha "Matt" Davis
Papers. 1861-92. 9 items.
Open. Description.
Mississippi Department of Archives and History.
Collection includes letters written by Miller, a Ripley, MS, resident, to a soldier in 1861 and letters written in 1892 by Ada E. Ferris of Carpinteria, CA, concerning the Miller letters.

9,680. Miller, Mrs. J. Balfour
Papers. 1930-65. 1 microfilm reel.
Open. Description.
Mississippi Department of Archives and History.
In 1931, Miller initiated the Natchez Pilgrimage, a tour of local historic homes. Histories and photos pertaining to Pilgrimage homes and a scrapbook of clippings and pamphlets that trace the Pilgrimage's history.

9,681. Mississippi Federation of Women's Clubs
Records. 1952-56. 2 items.
Open. Description.
Mississippi Department of Archives and History.
Typescript histories of the Federation from 1952 to 1956 include information about officers, committees, contests, projects, and other activities.

9,682. Mississippi Society of the National Society of Colonial Dames, XVII Century
Records. 1968. 1 box.
Open. Description.
Mississippi Department of Archives and History.
Biographies of "Women of the Year."

9,683. Mohamed, Ethel, Stitchery Slides
Papers. 1976. 76 items.
Open. Description.
Mississippi Department of Archives and History.
Color slides of [Mrs.] Mohamed's stitchery and her explanatory narrative about them.

9,684. Montgomery, Mrs. C. W., and Family
Papers. 1862. 4 items.
Open. Description.
Mississippi Department of Archives and History.
Correspondence of members of the family of Montgomery, an Edwards, MS, resident, includes a letter from Confederate soldier T. J. Hanes, who was a prisoner of war in Nashville, to his mother and one written in Tupelo, MS, by M. P. Lowery to his wife Sarah.

9,685. Morgan, Mrs. Adlia
Papers. 1897-1946. 65 items.
Open. No guide.
Mississippi Department of Archives and History.
Correspondence consists primarily of letters to Madel (Jacobs) [Mrs. Adlia] Morgan, a Jackson resident, from her brothers Captain Charles Clark Jacobs and Private First Class Fred Clark Jacobs, who served with the Marine Corps in the Pacific during WWII. An 1897 letter, written from British Columbia, is from Morgan's father Charles Clark Jacobs.

9,686. Morris, Jane T.
Papers. 1865-70. 128 items.
Open. Description.
Mississippi Department of Archives and History.
Operator of a Jackson boarding house, Morris was the widow of John Morris (1826-65), an engineer for the Southern Railroad born in Durham County, England. Business records including contracts by which Jane Morris rented two boarding houses and receipts from three railroad companies, a banking office, and other businesses; advertising from the Jackson *Clarion* for her boarding houses; and obituaries of John Morris from the Jackson *News and Mississippian.* Also includes receipts for licenses and taxes and a receipt signed by Mayor D. N. Barrows for her husband's burial lot in City Cemetery.

9,687. Mosley, Jessie B.
Papers. 1950. 1 vol.
Open. Description.
Mississippi Department of Archives and History.
Mosley, the wife of Charles C. Mosley, Sr., was a teacher and Jackson resident. Typescript of *The Negro in Mississippi History* (Jackson: Hederman Brothers, 1950), which Mosley wrote while teaching at the Southern Christian Institute at Edwards, MS.

9,688. Musgrove, Maggie Williams
Papers. 1852-1938. 3 boxes.
Open. Description.
Mississippi Department of Archives and History.
A founder of the Irwin Russell Memorial Association at Port Gibson, MS, [Mrs.] Musgrove, later Mrs. J. M. Taylor, was a writer for the WPA Claiborne County history. Bulk of the papers consists of notes about Russell and correspondence relating to the Russell Memorial, including letters from US Representative Percy E. Quinn and Governor Theodore G. Bilbo. Notes and typescripts related to Musgrove's work for the WPA and copies of Russell's works are also included.

9,689. National Society of the Colonial Dames of Mississippi
Records. 1963-72. 1 ms. box.
Open. Description.
Mississippi Department of Archives and History.
The Mississippi division of the National Society of Colonial Dames of America was incorporated in 1900 "to collect and preserve manuscripts, traditions, relics, and mementos of bygone days" and foster young people's appreciation of the achievements of early Americans. Copies of *Review* magazine and folders from Mississippi Colonial Dames chapters, including those named for Colonel Richard Pace, John Pulliam, Elizabeth Tilley, Samuel Swayze, and John Taliaferro.

9,690. National Society United States Daughters of 1812
Records. 1907-30. 88 items.
Open. Description.
Mississippi Department of Archives and History.
Charter, constitution, correspondence, completed membership applications, and blank forms.

9,691. Navy Mothers' Club
Records. 1941-45. 1 vol.
Open. Description.
Mississippi Department of Archives and History.
Minutes and lists of officers of the Club, organized in 1941 by [Mrs.] Mary Turner during a meeting at Jackson's Robert E. Lee Hotel.

9,692. Neilson, A. Lou
Papers. 1911-32. 253 items.
Open. Description.
Mississippi Department of Archives and History.
Correspondence and notes principally relate to [Miss] Neilson's genealogical research for members of the Colonial Dames of America and the DAR as well as other persons throughout the US. An Oxford, MS, resident, she belonged to the Colonial Dames and was an officer of the David Reese Chapter of the Mississippi Society of the DAR. Also contains a four-page history of the David Reese Chapter by [Miss] Annie Boggs.

9,693. Nutt Family
Papers. 1811-66. 350 items.
Open. Description.
Mississippi Department of Archives and History.
Correspondence primarily reflects efforts of Julia Augusta Williams Nutt to maintain the holdings of her husband Haller Nutt after his death, which coincided with the end of the Civil War. The son of agricultural innovator Rush Nutt, Haller Nutt owned five plantations, of which Julie Nutt was able to retain several. Also contains material relating to the Nutts' daughters Carey and Mary.

9,694. Oral History
Oral history. 1958- . Ca. 204 interviews.
Open. Published guide and card catalog.
Mississippi Department of Archives and History.
Interviews conducted by the Department of Archives and History concern memories of Mississippians, rural folk traditions, oral traditions, and other topics. Transcripts for 54 of the interviews, tapes, and photos of ca. 60 percent of the interviewees. Women are represented in most of the project's subgroups, including Mississippi first ladies and the Governor's Mansion; natural disasters, such as the 1926 Mississippi River flood and Hurricane Camille; the Mississippi lumber industry; Mississippi literary figures; the state legislature and Edwards Hotel; and Mississippi Dalmatians. Women interviewees include Mississippi novelist Eudora Welty; Fannie Lou Hamer, a civil rights activist; artists Marie Hull and Theora Hamblett; Frances Hicks, former clerk of the Mississippi House of Representatives; Julia Starnes, state librarian for many years; Charlotte Capers, former director of the Archives Department; and women from the Dalmatian colony in Biloxi of immigrants who worked in the seafood industry. See H. T. Holmes, "Oral History in the Mississippi Department of Archives and History," *Journal of Mississippi History* (Feb. 1976).

9,695. Order of the Sisters of Mercy, Vicksburg, MS
Records. 1879-1961. 1 microfilm reel.
Open. Description.
Mississippi Department of Archives and History.
The Order of the Sisters of Mercy in Vicksburg was established in 1860 by six nuns who left Baltimore with Father Leray; the Order was founded by Mother Catherine McAuley in Dublin, Ireland, to educate children and provide "a temporary home for good women out of institutions." Typescripts about the Order's history, one of them by Mother M. Anglea Fedou about the Vicksburg Sisters' work during an 1879 yellow fever epidemic in Edwards, MS; an anonymous diary for the period 1883-86 that includes an address from Catholic Choctaw Indians in Neshoba County, MS, to Pope Leo XIII and a letter of the bishop of Natchez to the rector of the American College in Rome, Italy; and a 1961 thesis by Sister M. Ethelbert De Muth, R.S.M., entitled "Thy Mercies Will I Sing."

9,696. Otey, Martha Ann (Nolley)
Papers. 1866. 1 item.
Open. Description.
Mississippi Department of Archives and History.
Otey (1832-67) and her husband Colonel Armistead George Otey of Lexington, MS, opened a school for young ladies at Castalian Springs near Durant, MS, shortly after their marriage in 1858. Diary and correspondence assembled by Henri Gerard Noordberg with footnotes and biographical and genealogical notes he supplied. After the Confederate Army requisitioned their Castalian Springs property, the Oteys moved to Casula, where Colonel Otey died in 1863. After the war, Martha Otey attempted unsuccessfully to establish a school at Casula and then went to Texas to seek employment so she could support her parents and children. Her diary describes her trip by boat from Tchula, MS, to Vicksburg, MS, New Orleans, and Galveston, TX, and inland. Contains comment on her meeting in New Orleans with Mrs. Jefferson Davis.

9,697. Otken, Frances Powell
Papers. 1811-1960. 33 ms. boxes.
Open. Description.
Mississippi Department of Archives and History.
Born in Summit, MS, Frances Otken, the youngest daughter of Charles Otken and Emily Jane Lee Otken, was a McComb, MS, genealogist. Correspondence, diary, notes, speeches, sermons, photos, invitations, clippings, and other papers. Includes her father's diary for 1906 and 1907 and his writings on education and atonement; an address by [Miss] Mildred Lewis Rutherford, historian of the United Daughters of the Confederacy; an address at the graduation exercise of the McComb City Hospital in 1913; speeches by Mississippi legislators, including John S. Williams, W. F. Love, and Hernando Money; sermons and printed material concerning the First Baptist Church of McComb and Richard Curtis, the first Baptist preacher in Mississippi; yearbooks and magazines of the DAR and other groups; and printed material on the South, national government, local history, shorthand, and other subjects.

9,698. Patton, Laura
Papers. 1861-63. 26-page vol.
Open. Description.
Mississippi Department of Archives and History.
Autograph album of [Miss] Patton, a student at Huntsville Female College in Huntsville, AL.

9,699. Pictures
Collection. 1750- . Ca. 30,000 items.
Partially restricted. Partial card catalog.
Mississippi Department of Archives and History.
The collection, which illustrates Mississippi history, was initiated in about 1850 by the Mississippi Historical Society and came under the direction of the Department of Archives and History in 1902. Tintypes, daguerreotypes, lithographs, slides, negatives, and other pictorial material include items relating to the Old Southeast—which encompassed Florida, Georgia, the Carolinas, Alabama, Tennessee, and Louisiana—as well as Mississippi. Most of the women included in 19th-century material were associated with or related to political figures; after 1910 many of the women photo subjects were active themselves in the state's politics. More recent photos show music celebrities and women in the arts, such as Eudora Welty and Leontyne Price. Contains 19th-century photos of white and black women; photos of Mississippi-born New Deal administrator Ellen (Sullivan) Woodward; many WPA photos, including rural women and scenes of home and family life during the Depression; and institutional photos relating to Belhaven College, a Jackson coeducational college which was formerly a women's school, and Mississippi University for Women in Columbus, MS.

9,700. Pittman, Anna (Prince)
Papers. 1909-42. 27 items.
Open. Description.
Mississippi Department of Archives and History.
Correspondence and photos of Pittman, a Jackson resident.

9,701. Polk, Mr. and Mrs. James K., Jr.
Papers. 1945-68. 61 items.
Open. Description.
Mississippi Department of Archives and History.
The Polks owned Macon Plantation near Inverness, MS. Consists of correspondence written by servants and former servants; about half of this correspondence, principally from Margaret Davis, was written during the summers of 1960 and 1961 while the Polk family was in Monteagle, TN, and contains day-to-day reports of weather and crop conditions, the operation of the plantation, and routine household matters. Other letters were written to Mrs. Polk asking for assistance and reporting on family affairs.

9,702. Polk, Mrs. James K., Jr.
Papers. 1968-73. 1 folder and 7 items.
Open. Description.
Mississippi Department of Archives and History.
Correspondence written to Polk, wife of James K. Polk, Jr., an Inverness, MS, plantation owner. Some of the letters were written while she was in Monteagle, TN, and Portugal, while others were written by former servants.

9,703. Ponder, Eleanor (Fox)
Papers. 1901-63. 1 vol. and 13 items.
Open. Description.
Mississippi Department of Archives and History.
Manuscript, essays, page proof of book, and clippings of Ponder, a Jackson resident. Includes the manuscript of her book *Plantation Shadows* (New Orleans: Pelican Publishing Company, 1949), page proof of her book of poems *Glimpses of Heights and Depths,* and clippings, including the front page of a 1901 issue of *The Brandon News.*

9,704. Port Gibson Methodist Episcopal Church, South, Methodist Ladies Cooperative Association
Records. 1871-1942. 1 microfilm reel.
Open. Description.
Mississippi Department of Archives and History.
Minutes of the Ladies Association, a history of the group written in 1942 by Kate Archer Drake, and the cradle roll of the Port Gibson, MS, Church, which was organized in 1903.

9,705. Posey, Evie (Stubblefield)
Papers. 1930-42. 3 vols.
Open. Descriptions.
Mississippi Department of Archives and History.
Correspondence and diaries of [Mrs. H. A.] Posey, a Yazoo City, MS, resident, including copies of letters she wrote to her nephew William Henry McRaven of Nashville. In her diaries Posey describes trips to Europe, to the World's Fair in Chicago in 1933, and to the eastern US.

9,706. Posey, Zoe
Papers. 1888-1953. 151-page vol. and 22 items.
Open. Description.
Mississippi Department of Archives and History.
Posey was a New Orleans resident. Correspondence, including letters from Eaton J. Bowers, a US congressman in the early 1900s, to his wife Tallulah Gaines Bowers, organizer of the Gulf Coast Chapter of the DAR; letters to the Bowerses from Juliet and Nolan B. Harmon and John Sharp Williams; and letters signed by Turner Catledge, managing editor of *The New York Times,* and Randolph Ray, rector of the Church of the Transfiguration, Little Church Around the Corner in New York. Also contains a scrapbook of New Orleans clippings concerning Mississippi Gulf Coast property, official returns from the 1888 Mississippi election of presidential electors, and a brief history of Grace Episcopal Church in Canton, MS.

9,707. Powell, Susan Virginia
Papers. 1926-45. 531 items.
Open. Description.
Mississippi Department of Archives and History.
Correspondence and papers of Powell, a Jackson resident who was chairman of the Coordinating Council of Women's Organizations for War Service during WWII and president of the Mississippi WCTU in 1944 and 1945.

9,708. Powell, Susan Virginia
Papers. Nd. 1 vol.
Open. Description.
Mississippi Department of Archives and History.
[Miss] Powell (1869-1952) was a Lincoln County, MS, school teacher who became Mississippi's first home demonstration agent and state director of home economics. Pictures, clippings, programs, and yearbooks reflect her activities. She was a pioneer in 4-H Club work for girls and an active participant in the Mississippi Federation of Women's Clubs and the WCTU.

9,709. Power, Kate M.
Papers. 1936-38. 1 folder, 322 items, and 1 microfilm reel.
Open. Descriptions.
Mississippi Department of Archives and History.
A newswoman and editor of the *Jackson Clarion-Ledger,* [Miss] Power (ca. 1866-1946) volunteered for American National Red Cross work during WWI and, by the end of the war, was appointed head of Red Cross organizations in New Orleans. Narrative written in 1936 concerning her memories of Jackson's First Presbyterian Church and biographical data, correspondence, and photos gathered for a proposed book "The First Ladies of Mississippi." Educated at private schools in Jackson and at Mary Baldwin Seminary at Stanton, VA, Power began her journalistic career as the *Clarion-Ledger's* society editor. She held nearly every position on the paper, serving ultimately as city editor and editor-in-chief. Power was the only woman during WWI to be sent to the Naval Air Station in Pensacola, FL, where she attained the American National Red Cross rank of major and served for 11 years. Power's papers include material about the following Mississippi governors' wives: Amelia Walton Alcorn, Blanche (Butler) Ames, Linda (Gaddy) Bilbo, Minnie (Block) Brewer, Roberta (Young) Brown, Ann Eliza (Darden) Clark, Alma Graham Conner, Elizabeth Winter Foote, Cornelia Hall Guion, Mildred (Maury) Humphreys, Marion Buckley Longino, Louise (Powers) McKie, Elvira Raunch McLaurin, Catherine (Anderson) McWillie, Marth Ann (Jones) Matthews, Clara (Martin) Murphree, Alice (Tye) Noel, Eliza (Turner) Quitman, Ethelmary (Day) Russell, Minerva (Cage) Sharkey, Mary Gillem Stone, Sarah (McBee) Tucker, Anna (Buruson) Vardaman, Judith (Sugg) White, Mary (White) Whitfield, and Caroline (Dyer) Whitfield.

9,710. Pride, Hannah T., and Pride, William W.
Papers. 1821-26. 7 items.
Open. Description.
Mississippi Department of Archives and History.
Correspondence written by Hannah Pride at Mayhew in the Choctaw Nation and at Bethel and Elliot, MS, to Thomas Thacher of Thompson, CT, principally concerning family matters, religious thought, and their ideas concerning missionary work among the Choctaws. Pride writes of her disappointment over the results of trying to educate the Indian children before educating the adults.

9,711. Pullen and Carson
Papers. 1841-1960. 2 vols., 1 box, and 320 items.
Open. Description.
Mississippi Department of Archives and History.
An insurance man, William H. Pullen, Jr., was part, and later full, owner of the Jackson law firm of Nugent and Pullen; his wife, the former Catherine Carson of Natchez, MS, was active in Girl Scout work. Family correspondence, including letters between the Pullens before their marriage in 1919 and a letter to Catherine Pullen from her father Thomas James Carson; a herd book kept by Estelle Carson for Thomas Carson's Lexington, KY, stud farm; account journals of James Carson in Natchez for the period 1841-62; photos of the Pullen family, Girl Scouts, and WWI soldiers; clippings concerning the Pullen family; and poetry, programs, a pamphlet, maps, and other items. William Pullen was president of the Jackson school board and the town's original Kiwanis Club.

9,712. Rice, Nannie Herndon
Papers. 1923-25. 371 items.
Open. Description.
Mississippi Department of Archives and History.
Correspondence, questionnaires, and tabulations of

a survey of Mississippi libraries that [Miss] Rice (1886-1963) made in 1924 while she was a library staff member at Mississippi Agricultural and Mechanical College in Starkville.

9,713. Richey, Nancy
Papers. 1860-71. 22 items.
Open. Description.
Mississippi Department of Archives and History.
Correspondence and business papers of Nancy Richey and her husband F. N. Richey of Brownsville, MS. Six letters to Nancy Richey dated 1865 to 1867 are from John Watt and Company, her factors in New Orleans, while others pertain to the partnership of F. N. Richey and G. W. Freeman.

9,714. Roach
Papers. 1897. 1 item.
Open. Description.
Mississippi Department of Archives and History.
Correspondence written from Vicksburg, MS, by a Mrs. Roach describes Joseph Davis's plantation, The Hurricane. Addressed to "My dear son," the letter includes a description of Mrs. Jefferson Davis during the Mexican War period as "then a slight (ugly) young married woman."

9,715. Robins, Julia Pryor
Papers. 1860-72. 184-page vol.
Open. Description.
Mississippi Department of Archives and History.
Scrapbook of poetry, pictures, and Confederate material collected by [Miss] Robins.

9,716. Robinson, Nancy (McDougall)
Papers. 1832-73. 2 ms. boxes.
Open. Description.
Mississippi Department of Archives and History.
Born in Hamilton, Canada, the eldest child of Elizabeth McEvers Rouse and Judge Nicholas McDougall, Nancy McDougall (1808-?) was educated in Marietta, OH, and moved with her family to Claiborne County, MS; in 1832 she married Alfred Bassett Robinson. Correspondence, diaries, payment receipts, slave lists and accounts, from 1861 and 1862, birth and death records, photos, and recipes.

9,717. Rollins, Mrs. Roy
Papers. 1821-1951. 386 items.
Open. Description.
Mississippi Department of Archives and History.
Rollins was an Aberdeen, MS, resident. Copies of Shaw family letters from 1860 to 1890; a poem by Rollins; copies of land and marriage records, will books, and contracts between planters and freedmen; articles about Aberdeen hotels; and a clipping from the Aberdeen *Examiner* regarding General Reuben Davis.

9,718. Ross, Elizabeth Magruder
Papers. 1854-72. 28 items.
Open. Description.
Mississippi Department of Archives and History.
Correspondence of Ross, a Claiborne County, MS, resident.

9,719. Rowland, Mrs. Dunbar
Papers. 1908-38. 7 Hollinger boxes, 3 vols., and 158 items.
Open. Descriptions.
Mississippi Department of Archives and History.
Eron Opha (Moore) [Mrs. Dunbar] Rowland (ca. 1863-1951), a Jackson author and historian, was assistant and acting director of the Mississippi Department of Archives and History. Correspondence, notes, memoranda, manuscripts and revisions, and miscellaneous material relating to Rowland's historical writings. Includes notes and other material she collected for a literary history of Mississippi; correspondence and papers she compiled for a book concerning Andrew Jackson, the Creek Indians, and Mississippi Territory during the War of 1812; and manuscript of her *Life, Letters and Papers of William Dunbar of Elgin, Morayshire, Scotland and Natchez, Mississippi: Pioneer Scientist of the Southern United States* (Jackson: Press of the Mississippi Historical Society, 1930). Also contains letters from Woodrow Wilson, Belle Kearney, and Tiffany and Company of New York City; material relating to the DAR, the WCTU, the United Daughters of the Confederacy, and other groups; and manuscripts of Rowland's "Mississippi," which was the state song from 1917 until 1948.

9,720. Russell, Mary Elizabeth
Papers. 1946. 3 items.
Open. Description.
Mississippi Department of Archives and History.
Correspondence of [Miss] Russell, sister of Mississippi poet Irwin Russell, with [Mrs.] Laura D. S. Harrell of the Mississippi Department of Archives and History. Harrell sought information about Irwin Russell for articles which were to appear in the *Journal of Mississippi History.*

9,721. Ryker, Mrs. Darrell W.
Papers. 1974. 1 box and 12 items.
Open. Description.
Mississippi Department of Archives and History.
Typescripts of lectures given in Natchez, MS, with an introduction by Ryker, a Natchez resident. The lectures dealt with such subjects as the history of Natchez and Wilkinson County, the Aaron Burr conspiracy, archaeological findings and Indian culture, and early newspapers.

9,722. Sager, Sarah Knox (Harris)
Papers. 1793-1921. 6 boxes and 2 vols.
Open. Description.
Mississippi Department of Archives and History.
Descended from President James K. Polk and from a niece of Mrs. Andrew Jackson, Sager was the great-great-granddaughter of John Sevier, first governor of Tennessee. Personal and business correspondence, diary for the period 1905-08; memorandum books; financial record books; children's books, including five by Sadie Harris Sager; recipe books; and other items. Contains financial records of Mrs. J. V. Harris, Mrs. E. S. Jeffries, and Mrs. J. V. S. Harris. Also includes a genealogy of the Donelson family, of which Andrew Jackson's wife Rachel was a member.

9,723. Saint Andrew's Parish Woman's Auxiliary
Records. 1900-12. 54-page vol.
Open. Description.
Mississippi Department of Archives and History.
Constitution, minutes, rolls, and various notes about this Jackson organization's activities.

9,724. Satterfield, Ellen Steele
Papers. 1923-45. 16-page vol. and 21 items.
Open. Descriptions.
Mississippi Department of Archives and History.
Correspondence and a journal of [Miss] Satterfield, an English teacher at Laurel, MS, High School. The correspondence, written by WWII servicemen who were former students of Satterfield, describes training periods in the US and service in Europe and the Pacific. The journal contains stories Satterfield recorded based on tales she heard as a child in Port Gibson, MS, including "Miss Addie," "Windsor," "Irwin Russell," and "The War and Reconstruction Days."

9,725. Saucier, Marie Louise
Papers. 1849-1934. 1 folder.
Open. Description.
Mississippi Department of Archives and History.
Land transfer records concerning property originally owned by Pierre and Marie Saucier, descendants of John B. Saucier, who in 1712 settled near Bayou of Delisle in Harrison County, MS. Also includes a pamphlet entitled *History of Delisle and Its Missions.*

9,726. Scales, Cordelia Lewis
Papers. 1861-63. 7 items.
Open. Description.
Mississippi Department of Archives and History.
Correspondence of [Miss] Scales (1844-1915), a Virginia native who married Ben Cottrell Gray in 1866. The letters depict life and civilian morale during the War Between the States. Four of the letters were included in Percy L. Rainwater, ed., "The Civil War Letters of Cordelia Scales," *Journal of Mississippi History* (July, 1939).

9,727. Scott, Flo (Hampton)
Papers. 1969. 1 vol. and 10 items.
Open. Description.
Mississippi Department of Archives and History.
[Mrs. Charles C.] Scott was a Jackson resident. Includes typescript of her *Ghosts with Southern Accents and Evidence of Extrasensory Perception* (Birmingham, AL: Southern University Press, 1969), notes, photos of typical rural Mississippi scenes, and clippings.

9,728. Shelton, Maria L.
Papers. 1918. 24 items.
Open. Description.
Mississippi Department of Archives and History.
Correspondence and papers relate to private research by [Miss] Shelton, an employee of the Mississippi Department of Archives and History, concerning A. B. Lawrence, a Presbyterian preacher in Mississippi. The research was done for a Beaumont, TX, attorney for a US district court suit filed by Angeline Louise Bailey Dolbear and others against Gulf Production Company. Most of the material was copied from Synod of Mississippi records dating from 1846 to 1855.

9,729. Shields, Sarah
Papers. 1967. 25 ft. of microfilm.
Open. Description.
Mississippi Department of Archives and History.
Research paper by [Miss] Shields concerning John Bisland (1742-1821), a native of Scotland who came to the US in 1774 and established a merchandise store in North Carolina. In 1782 he received a Spanish grant for land in Mississippi Territory, which he developed into an extensive cotton plantation.

9,730. Shingleur, Elvira (Flewellen)
Papers. 1857-63. 37 items.
Open. Description.
Mississippi Department of Archives and History.
Family correspondence of "Elvie" [Mrs. J. A.] Shingleur, a Wymton, GA, resident; eighteen of the letters were written by Lieutenant J. A. Shingleur, a member of the Columbus City Light Rifles, before the couple's marriage in 1861. Other letters are from Elvira Shingleur's mother, her sister Lizzie, her brother Hugh, and her aunt Lea Harris.

9,731. Sillers, Mrs. Walter
Papers. 1924. 571-page vol.
Open. Description.
Mississippi Department of Archives and History.
Sillers was regent of the Mississippi Delta Chapter of the DAR, which included Rosedale and the surrounding Bolivar County. A history of Bolivar County from its establishment in 1836 through 1924 and biographical sketches of pioneer families which were compiled by Sillers and members of her DAR Chapter.

9,732. Skelton, Mrs. Allen
Papers. 1976. 75 items.
Open. Description.
Mississippi Department of Archives and History.
Thirty-nine black and white prints and 35 color slides of quilts made by Skelton, a Vicksburg, MS,

resident. Also includes a narrative Skelton wrote about her quilts.

9,733. Smith, Frank Ellis, and Warren, Audrey
Papers. 1968. 2 vols.
Open. Description.
Mississippi Department of Archives and History.
Smith, a former US representative from Mississippi, is a director of the Tennessee Valley Authority. [Mrs.] Warren, Smith's executive assistant during his congressional years, has served as editorial assistant on books he published after leaving office. Working manuscripts of *Mississippians All* (New Orleans: Pelican Publishing House, 1968) by Smith and Warren.

9,734. Sommerville, Nellie (Nugent)
Papers. 1896-1951. 1 microfilm reel.
Open. Description.
Mississippi Department of Archives and History.
Somerville (1863-1952), the mother of Judge Lucy (Somerville) Howorth, was the first female state legislator in Mississippi. Speeches, scrapbooks, and other papers pertaining to women suffrage in Mississippi, the originals of which are held at the Schlesinger Library at Radcliffe College. Also includes related papers of Catherine (Waugh) McCulloch and Ella Harrison.

9,735. Speed, Katherine Rhymes
Papers. 1967-72. 1 Hollinger box.
Open. Description.
Mississippi Department of Archives and History.
Notes, memoranda, sketches, and photos related to the sculpting by Speed, a sculptor, of the statue of Andrew Jackson that stands in front of Jackson's City Hall.

9,736. Spencer, Elizabeth
Papers. 1967. 411-page vol.
Open. Description.
Mississippi Department of Archives and History.
An author born in Carrollton, MS, [Miss] Spencer (1921-) has worked as a newspaper reporter and a teacher of English and creative writing in Mississippi and Tennessee. Manuscript of her *No Place for an Angel* (New York: McGraw-Hill Book Company, 1967). Six of Spencer's novels have been published and many of her short stories have appeared in *The New Yorker.*

9,737. Sprague, Frances
Papers. 1881-87. 100-page vol.
Open. Description.
Mississippi Department of Archives and History.
[Mrs.] Sprague, a Natchez, MS, resident, was the mother of Mrs. Josiah Winchester. Scrapbook containing clippings on general subjects as well as clippings about Winnie Davis, Margaret Howell, [Mrs.] Eliza Wilkins Fiske, [Mrs.] Mercy B. Mason, Mrs. F. B. Mosby, Mrs. Wilmer H. Shields, Jefferson Davis, and Josiah Winchester.

9,738. Stanton, Elizabeth Brandon
Papers. 1925. 3 items.
Open. Description.
Mississippi Department of Archives and History.
[Miss] Stanton, a resident of Windy Hill Manor in Natchez, MS, was the author of *Fata Morgana* (1917). Correspondence between Stanton and Henry D. Pierce of Indianapolis contains his praise for *Fata Morgana* and genealogical data about the Caldwell, Pierce, and Brandon family. Also includes a broadside advertisement with testimonials for *Fata Morgana.*

9,739. State Archives
Records. Ca. 1790s- . More than 2000 cu.ft. and 5000 microfilm reels.
Open. Published guide.
Mississippi Department of Archives and History.
The State Archives includes official records of Mississippi Territory, the state of Mississippi, and Mississippi counties and municipalities. Among the state records containing information on women are the Institutions of Higher Learning record group (RG 39), which includes records of Mississippi State College for Women and other colleges and universities, and the State Health Institutions record group (RG 56). County records are primarily those of various courts and provide information about wills, estate, property, marriage, and similar matters. See Thomas W. Henderson and Donald E. Tomlin, *Guide to Official Records in the Mississippi Department of Archives and History* (Jackson, MS: Mississippi Department of Archives and History, 1975).

9,740. Stevens, Daisy (McLaurin)
Papers. 1908-15. 20 items.
Open. Description.
Mississippi Department of Archives and History.
Correspondence and papers of Stevens (1875-1950), who was the daughter of Anselm J. McLaurin and president general of the United Daughters of the Confederacy from 1913 to 1915.

9,741. Stockwell, Eunice J.
Papers. 1939. 23 items.
Open. Description.
Mississippi Department of Archives and History.
[Miss] Stockwell was a Greenville, MS, staff member of the Historical Records Survey. Manuscripts containing information from letters, diaries, recollections, and papers from 1833 to 1913 of [Miss] Florence Burrus, [Miss] Helen Finlay, Mary Ann Hunt, [Mrs.] Myra Smith, [Mrs.] Mary A. C. Montgomery, and other individuals and families. Also includes Stockwell's manuscript concerning the Green family genealogy.

9,742. Stovall, Rosemary McLain
Papers. 1973-74. 1 box.
Open. Description.
Mississippi Department of Archives and History.
A Madison, MS, songwriter, guitarist, and singer, Stovall recorded "Rosemary" at Malaco Sound Studios in Jackson. Musical scores including "One Step at a Time," "Bubble Gum Baby," "High Hopes," "Christmas on the Farm," "Deep Repentance," "Hikin' Down the Interstate," "Live It Up Honey," and "Please Mr. Sunshine."

9,743. Strickland, Belle
Papers. 1864-77. 1 folder.
Open. Description.
Mississippi Department of Archives and History.
Diary that Strickland (1855-?), a Holly Springs, MS, resident, kept from age 9 until age 22.

9,744. Sumner, Cid (Ricketts)
Papers. 1968. 4 items.
Open. Description.
Mississippi Department of Archives and History.
Typescripts and excerpts from correspondence of Bertha (Ricketts) Sumner (1890-1970), a Duxbury, MA, author who wrote under the name Cid Ricketts. Contains manuscript reminiscences concerning Sumner's childhood in Jackson that she wrote at the request of her children. Also includes typescripts of childhood recollections of her mother Bertha Burnley Ricketts and her aunt Edwina Burnley, genealogical information on the Burnley and Ricketts families, explanatory notes, and letters exchanged by Dorothy Lenoir and Sumner.

9,745. Sumner, Cid (Ricketts)
Papers. 1915-70. 27 boxes.
Open. Descriptions.
Mississippi Department of Archives and History.
A Mississippi native, Bertha (Ricketts) Sumner (1890-1970) was an author who wrote under the name Cid Ricketts. Correspondence, notes, drafts, manuscripts, galleys, page proofs, contracts, royalty statements, photos, scrapbook, clippings, book reviews, and miscellaneous papers, among them Sumner's correspondence with publishers, agents, and others, including composer Lehman Engel. Known chiefly for her novels about Tammy Tyree, Sumner wrote poetry and numerous books. Manuscripts or typescripts of ca. 20 of her works are found in the collection, including *Tammy in Rome, Tammy Tell Me True* (a screenplay), *Traveler in the Wilderness,* and *Saddle Your Dreams.*

9,746. Sutter, Lillian
Papers. 1937. 27-page vol.
Open. Description.
Mississippi Department of Archives and History.
Typescript of Sutter's "Bibliography of Mississippi Writers," which she compiled in connection with studies in bibliography and reference at the University of Alabama.

9,747. Swanson and Yates Family
Papers. 1833-79. 83 items.
Open. Description.
Mississippi Department of Archives and History.
Correspondence and papers of Obedience Yates, wife of Ignatius Yates of Utica, MS, and of their daughter Maria (Yates) Swanson and her husband Alexander B. Swanson. Correspondence, most of which dates from the Reconstruction period, includes letters from Obedience Yates's sons Jerome Yates and Thomas Davis, from her daughter Maria, and from her grandchildren Florence "Bettie" Chunn and Lucretia Fontaine; letters exchanged by Maria and Alexander Swanson; and letters of recommendation for Alexander Swanson. Also includes lists of marriages and deaths in the Swanson and Yates families. Alexander Swanson, a naturalized Scot, was a schoolteacher who became a lawyer in Raymond, MS. He served in the state troops as a judge advocate and went to Vicksburg, where he apparently worked as a cotton agent for the Union Army.

9,748. Tamplet, Serita (Campbell)
Papers. 1892-1908. 15 items.
Open. Description.
Mississippi Department of Archives and History.
Tamplet, a Brenham, TX, resident, was the daughter of George W. Campbell, an ensign in the Tombigbee Rifles, 1st Mississippi Regiment, during the Mexican War. Correspondence and clippings regarding the flag used by her father's Mexican War unit. Cared for by her father, the flag was used in 1893 to cover the casket of Jefferson Davis when his body was moved from New Orleans to Richmond, VA, for reburial.

9,749. Thompson, Helen
Papers. 1861-1920. 38-page vol. and 18 items.
Open. Description.
Mississippi Department of Archives and History.
A Washington, DC, resident, Thompson was the daughter of Captain Frank Thompson and granddaughter of Hugh Miller Thompson. Minutes from 1861 and 1862 of the Livingston Ladies Aid Military Association, obituaries of Frank Thompson, an article entitled "Mrs. Helen S. Johnstone Harris: What She Did for the Confederacy and How She Lives in Annandale," and other papers.

9,750. Thompson, Lily Wilkinson
Papers. 1817-1959. 4 ms. boxes, 1 vol., and 25 items.
Open. Descriptions.
Mississippi Department of Archives and History.
A pioneer woman suffrage organizer, [Mrs.] Wilkinson was president of the Mississippi Woman Suffrage Association in 1912 and 1913. Personal and business correspondence, correspondence from 1817 to 1868 certifying church membership, speeches, constitution and bylaws of the Mississippi Woman Suffrage Association, and annual and quarterly reports, minutes, financial records, legal agreements, histories, pamphlets, articles, books, and other material, much of which dates from ca.

1908 to 1920 and pertains to such groups as the National American Woman Suffrage Association and the Mississippi Federation of Women's Clubs. Also includes records of the Women's Missionary Society of the Mississippi Conference, Methodist Episcopal Church, South and of Galloway Memorial Methodist Episcopal Church, South. Thompson lived in Crystal Springs, MS, and Jackson.

9,751. Timberlake, Alcinda
Papers. 1911. 2 items.
Open. Description.
Mississippi Department of Archives and History.
Manuscript of Eliza Ann Lanier's recollections of conditions in Warren County, MS, during the Civil War and a typed copy with explanatory notes prepared by Lanier's granddaughter [Miss] Timberlake.

9,752. Topp, Mildred (Spurrier)
Papers. 1948. 307-page vol.
Open. Description.
Mississippi Department of Archives and History.
Manuscript of *Smile Please* (Boston: Houghton Mifflin Co., 1948) by Topp, a Greenwood, MS, resident.

9,753. Town, Clarissa E. Leavitt
Papers. 1853-1954. 5 microfiche.
Open. Description.
Mississippi Department of Archives and History.
Typescript of "Grandma Town's Diary" prepared in 1954 by her great-granddaughter Josephine R. Devall of Prairieville, LA. Entries made by Town in 1853 pertain to trips to New Orleans and Baton Rouge, the religious and social lives of the slaves, and holiday celebrations; the entries also include mention of Leonidas Polk, Edward George Washington Butler, William Markham, and Louis Agassiz. Town, a Buffalo, NY, resident, kept the diary while she was living with her daughter and son-in-law A. H. Lamon, a Protestant Episcopal clergyman, in Devall, West Baton Rouge Parish, LA.

9,754. Trotter, Ida (Barlow)
Papers. Nd. 17 pp.
Open. Description.
Mississippi Department of Archives and History.
Manuscript reminiscences of the siege of Vicksburg, MS, by Trotter, a Winona, MS, resident who lived with her parents during the siege in 1863.

9,755. Tyner, Doris B.
Papers. 1935-41. 1 folder.
Open. Description.
Mississippi Department of Archives and History.
Tyner was postmistress in Port Gibson, MS. Eleven books of duplicate registration stubs for the purchase of US savings bonds and several loose stubs and applications for bonds.

9,756. United Daughters of the Confederacy
Records. 1896-1954. 3 ms. boxes.
Open. Description.
Mississippi Department of Archives and History.
The Mississippi Division of the United Daughters of the Confederacy held its first convention in Meridian in 1897; made up of descendants of Confederate soldiers, the organization seeks "to collect and preserve material for a true history of the War Between the States; (and) to unite with the Confederate veterans in the determination that American history shall be properly taught in public" and private Mississippi schools. Charters of incorporation, writings, correspondence, membership certificates and lists, report, yearbooks, programs, and a newspaper. Includes UDC chapter records, a report by the group's recording secretary-general, writings by UDC historians concerning Judge John Burrus and General N. B. Forrest, and a 1904 edition of the *Biloxi News* concerning the UDC's annual reunion. The organization maintains a scholarship for students who are descendants of Confederate soldiers.

9,757. United Daughters of the Confederacy
Records. 1861-1964. 6 boxes, 13 vols., and 775 items.
Open. Description.
Mississippi Department of Archives and History.
Membership records and applications, records regarding the Southern Cross of Honor bestowed by the United Daughters of the Confederacy, correspondence, and miscellaneous records of various Mississippi UDC chapters, including a scrapbook containing material dating from 1861 to 1952 of General Charles Clark Chapter No. 1144, in Beulah; lineage sheets of Stephen D. Lee Chapter No. 34, compiled from 1962 to 1964 during the presidency of Mrs. C. A. Pilkinton; and an incomplete list of Confederate veterans buried in Greenville, MS, Cemetery. Includes membership applications or other material from chapters in the following Mississippi towns: Jackson, Gulfport, Biloxi, Baldwyn, Clinton, Columbus, Greenwood, Magnolia, Natchez, Okolona, Sardis, Water Valley, West Point, Rosedale, and Raymond. The Raymond chapter was organized in 1903 and dissolved in 1950; its material includes records concerning an affiliate organization, the Carrie Johnston Gillespie Chapter of the Children of the Confederacy. Bulk of the collection material dates from ca. 1897 to ca. 1950.

9,758. United Daughters of the Confederacy, Mississippi Division, Honor Roll, World War II
Records. 1943. 1 vol.
Open. Description.
Mississippi Department of Archives and History.
Loose-leaf notebook containing biographical and statistical information about UDC members' relatives who served in WWII. Includes name of the serviceman, his relationship to a specific UDC member, and information about the serviceman's experiences and assignments.

9,759. Vaughan, Sue (Adams) Landon
Papers. 1897-1919. 8 items.
Open. Description.
Mississippi Department of Archives and History.
Vaughan, the wife of Landon Vaughan, is said to have been the first person in Jackson to decorate the graves of Confederate and Union soldiers, on April 26, 1865. Manuscript that Vaughan wrote in 1897 in which she described Decoration Day in 1865; *Biographical Sketch of Sue Landon Vaughan* (1907), by L. E. Everland of Seaglade, FL; and memorabilia.

9,760. Ventress, J. A.
Papers. 1789-1920. 1 Paige box and 1 oversize Hollinger box.
Open. Description.
Mississippi Department of Archives and History.
Papers of James Alexander Ventress (?-1867), an inventor, scientist, and cotton and sugar planter, and his wife Charlotte (1815-77), who inherited the 6000-acre LaGrange Plantation in Wilkinson County, MS, from her uncle. Correspondence including letters Charlotte Ventress wrote to her sons while they were attending the University of Virginia; photos; maps; clippings; and printed documents and journals. She served as housekeeper and hostess for her uncle from 1837 until her marriage in 1848. She retained ownership of the family's extensive holdings in Mississippi and Louisiana after her husband's death in 1867, a time of regional poverty and bankruptcy.

9,761. Waggoner, Maude
Papers. 1941-45. 7 vols.
Open. Description.
Mississippi Department of Archives and History.
Scrapbooks kept by [Mrs.] Waggoner containing clippings pertaining to WWII.

9,762. Walsh, Aimee Shands, and Family
Papers. 1825-46. Ca. 2 in. (21 items).
Open. Description.
Mississippi Department of Archives and History.
Correspondence, memoirs, genealogical material, and other papers of this Jackson family contain the memoirs of Aimee Webb Nugent, Cecile Stollenwerck Webb, and [Mrs.] Amelia Thompson Watts; biographical material about Patrick Henry's sister Elizabeth Henry and about Aimee Webb Nugent, Lucy Shands Rives, and Amelia Thompson Watts; a DAR chart of the Rosebrough family; genealogical information on the Rosebrough, Rives, Henry, and Cabell families; and seven letters written in French and dated from 1825 to 1846.

9,763. Walsh, Jean H.
Papers. 1938-43. 17 items.
Open. Description.
Mississippi Department of Archives and History.
Articles and genealogical material written or collected by Walsh, a Gulfport, MS, writer, include a brief sketch of the life of Eron Moore Rowland and an article that Walsh compiled with Clarence Kerns, entitled "The First Steamboat on Western Waters."

9,764. Watkins, Ethel
Papers, 1911-51. 10 items.
Open. Description.
Mississippi Department of Archives and History.
Diplomas, certificates, and a thesis typescript of Ethel Watkins, a schoolteacher educated in the Mississippi school and college system. Contains her thesis "Stephen, King of England" and licenses to teach in Mississippi and Alabama schools. Also includes diplomas from Industrial Institute and College at Columbus, MS, State Teachers College at Hattiesburg, MS, and Mississippi State College at State College, MS. Watkins was a resident of Cedar Bluff, MS.

9,765. Watkins, Mrs. Herbert B.
Papers. 1921-23. 10 items.
Open. Description.
Mississippi Department of Archives and History.
Miscellaneous papers of Watkins, a Jackson resident.

9,766. Watts, Amelia
Papers. 1832. 1 item and 1 microfilm reel.
Open. Description.
Mississippi Department of Archives and History.
Manuscript of "A Summer on a Louisiana Cotton Plantation in 1832" by [Mrs.] Watts.

9,767. Weaver, Gustine Nancy Courson
Papers. Nd. 1 vol. and 65 items.
Open. Description.
Mississippi Department of Archives and History.
Photos and a typescript of "Life's Nexus and Plexus" by [Mrs.] Weaver. Material relates to the Gustine and Dunbar families of Natchez, MS, and includes family portraits as well as interior and exterior scenes of homes. The Dunbar family became wealthy cotton planters during the early and middle 19th century.

9,768. Welty, Eudora
Papers. 1953-1975. 5 Hollinger boxes, 4 oversize boxes, and 2 folders.
Access restricted. Descriptions.
Mississippi Department of Archives and History.
Correspondence, articles, galley proof, reviews, photos, scrapbook, program, clippings, and other papers of [Miss] Welty (1909-), a novelist and short story writer who received the Pulitzer Prize for Fiction in 1973. Included are a galley proof of *The Ponder Heart* and scrapbooks relating to this Welty novel; a 1975 article entitled "In Memoriam" by Welty about Frank Hains, arts editor of the *Jackson Daily News;* and a program of 1975 commencement exercises at Southern Methodist

University during which Welty received the degree of doctor of humane letters.

9,769. Welty, Eudora
Papers. 1935-71. 1 Hollinger box, 4 oversize boxes, and 5 items.
Access restricted. Descriptions.
Mississippi Department of Archives and History.
Primarily correspondence of [Miss] Welty (1909-), a novelist and short story writer, including personal and business correspondence principally dating from 1935 to 1956, the period of Welty's greatest productivity. Includes a 1936 letter from *Manuscript* accepting Welty's first published short story "Death of a Traveling Salesman"; letters concerning *The Ponder Heart,* first published by *The New Yorker* in 1953 and adapted for the stage in 1955 by Fields and Chodorov; and letters from *The Southern Review,* in which many of Welty's early works were printed. Also contains a letter Welty received from Mary Elizabeth Russell, sister of Mississippi writer Irwin Russell; letters to the Internal Revenue Service; and an affidavit of Charlotte Capers concerning Welty's donation of material to the Mississippi Department of Archives and History. Correspondents include Robert Penn Warren; Cleanth Brooks; Ford Maddox Ford; Lambert Davis, editor at Harcourt Brace; Kenneth Haxton and Ben Wasson of Levee Press in Greenville, MS; Maurice Evans; Danny Kaye; Ken McCormick of Doubleday, Doran; Joseph A. Fields; and Jerome Chodorov. Also includes correspondence from John Woodburn, Welty's editor at Doubleday, Doran; at Harcourt Brace; and at Little, Brown.

9,770. Welty, Eudora
Papers. 1930-75. 7 ms. boxes, 6 Hollinger boxes, 2 oversize ms. boxes, 2 folders, and microfilm.
Access restricted. Descriptions.
Mississippi Department of Archives and History.
Manuscripts, tear and proof sheets, master's theses, speeches, photos, theater programs, and miscellaneous papers of [Miss] Welty (1909-), a Pulitzer Prize-winning novelist and short story writer. Welty, who lives in Jackson, writes of the common people of the South, particularly of the region's rural areas and small towns; she received the Pulitzer Prize for Fiction in 1973. Contains manuscripts or other material related to writing or publication of such Welty novels as *The Ponder Heart* (New York: Harcourt, Brace and Co., 1954); *The Bride of Innisfallen and Other Stories* (New York: Harcourt, Brace and Co., 1955); *Delta Wedding* (New York: Harcourt, Brace and Co., 1945, 1946); and *The Optimist's Daughter.* Also contains material concerning short stories and articles published in *The New Yorker, Harper's Bazaar,* and other magazines, including "The Fairy Tale of the Natchez Trace," "The Burning," "Going to Naples," "Spring," and "English from the Inside." Other papers include a 1954 checklist by Katherine Powell Hinds of Welty's story publications, a 1958 master's thesis by Leone P. Jordon concerning humor in Welty's works, a 1956 adaptation by Emily Helen Evans of Western Reserve University of two Welty stories "A Piece of News" and "Petrified Man," letters from Jordon and Evans, manuscript of an unpublished revue "What Year Is This?" by Welty and Hildegarde Dolson, copy of the appraisal of part of the collection, a paper Welty read in 1975 before the Mississippi Historical Society concerning her second work "The Robber Bridegroom," and material regarding *One Time, One Place,* a collection of photos that Welty took during the late 1930s and early 1940s.

9,771. Wetherill, Thomas M., and Family
Papers. 1853-1930. 26 vols. and 244 items.
Open. Description.
Mississippi Department of Archives and History.
Wetherill's papers include diaries, journals, and an autograph book from 1876 of Julia Kern (Wetherill) Baker (1857-1931), a journalist, novelist, and poet. Born in Woodville, MS, Julia Wetherill was educated in Philadelphia and in 1884 moved to New Orleans. In 1886 she married Marion A. Baker, who with his two brothers operated the New Orleans *Times-Democrat,* later called the *Times-Picayune.* Julia Baker, who served as the *Times-Picayune's* Sunday editor, also had stories published in *Lippincott's Magazine, Atlantic Monthly, Century,* and *Critic.* She wrote a book review column entitled "Literary Pathways" and a column about theater and music titled "Innocent Bystander" for New Orleans newspapers.

9,772. Whitehurst, Mary
Papers. 1875-89. 12 items.
Open. Description.
Mississippi Department of Archives and History.
Personal correspondence of Whitehurst, a resident of Washington, MS.

9,773. Williams, Eva Joor
Papers. 1939. 1 vol. and 2 items.
Open. Description.
Mississippi Department of Archives and History.
Scrapbook entitled "Earliest Protestantism in Mississippi," containing articles published in a Copiah County newspaper by Williams (?-post 1940), and two of her poems, "Ode to Mississippi" and "Mississippi."

9,774. Wilson, Margaret
Papers. 1835-37. 77-page vol.
Open. Description.
Mississippi Department of Archives and History.
Diary of Wilson of Pittsburgh, who was governess on Selma Plantation at Washington, MS, from 1834 to 1848. She later managed an academy in Washington.

9,775. Woman's Christian Temperance Union
Records. 1920-49. 1 Hollinger box.
Open. Description.
Mississippi Department of Archives and History.
Executive minutes, minutes of annual meetings, convention programs, and other material of the Mississippi WCTU.

9,776. Woman's Missionary Society
Records. 1878-90. 1 vol.
Open. Description.
Mississippi Department of Archives and History.
Minute book of this Brandon, MS, group.

9,777. Woman's Reading Club, Goodman, MS
Records. 1930-35. 6 items.
Open. Description.
Mississippi Department of Archives and History.
Yearbooks.

9,778. Wood, Jane Margaret
Papers. 1851. 1 vol. (Microfilm).
Open. Description.
Mississippi Department of Archives and History.
Diary kept by Wood, wife of Paul Tudor Jones, I.

9,779. Woodward, Ellen (Sullivan)
Papers. 1925-61. 32 Hollinger horizontal boxes and 4 oversize ms. boxes.
Open. Descriptions.
Mississippi Department of Archives and History.
Daughter of US Senator William V. Sullivan and Belle Murray Sullivan, Ellen Woodward (1887-1971) was a Mississippi legislator, New Deal administrator, and the only woman member of the wartime Social Security Board. Correspondence, memoranda, notes, articles, speeches, biographical material, minutes, photos, WPA reports, news releases, clippings, and other papers include correspondence from President and Mrs. Franklin D. Roosevelt, William Alexander Percy, Archibald MacLeish, and Frances Parkinson Keyes and papers and correspondence concerning the Mississippi State Board of Development, the White House Conference on Child Health and Protection, the Democratic National Committee, the WPA, the Social Security Board, the Federal Security Agency, American Tung Oil Association, the United Nations Relief and Rehabilitation Administration, and the Business and Professional Women's Club. Born in Oxford, MS, Ellen Sullivan earned a law degree at the University of South Carolina and in 1907 married Judge Albert Woodward (?-1925). Elected to the Mississippi legislature in 1926, she later became director of the Mississippi Board of Development. In 1933 she served as assistant administrator in charge of the Federal Emergency Relief Administration women's division, organizing a nationwide program of work projects for ca. 400,000 unemployed women who were heads of families. Woodward eventually became deputy director of the WPA. After the demise of that agency, Roosevelt appointed her to the Social Security Board. She later became an international specialist with the Federal Security Agency and an active participant in programs of the United Nations Relief and Rehabilitation Administration and UNESCO. She also was a member of the DAR, the Pilot Club, and the LWV.

9,780. Worthington and Stone Family
Papers. 1859-1951. 3 Hollinger boxes.
Open. Description.
Mississippi Department of Archives and History.
Correspondence, school papers, genealogical material, photos, scrapbooks, books, and miscellaneous material of these prominent Washington County, MS, families. Bulk of the correspondence is that of William Mason Worthington, Bettie Stone Worthington, and their daughter Mary Garland Archer. William Worthington was the brother of [Miss] Amanda Worthington, librarian in Greenville, MS, for a number of years. Contains several folders of poems and songs by [Miss] Worthington, school papers of Mary Worthington, and the prayer book of Mary G. Worthington.

9,781. Worthington Family
Papers. 1820-1911. 1 vol., 151 items, and 1 microfilm reel.
Open. Descriptions.
Mississippi Department of Archives and History.
Family correspondence, diaries, record book, "Forget-Me-Not" album, and other papers of the family of Samuel and Amanda (Dougherty) Worthington, plantation owners of Washington County, MS. Included are the Civil War diaries of their daughter Amanda Worthington (ca. 1845-?); a ledger of Samuel Worthington in which he lists names of Negroes taken from him in 1863; a "Forget-Me-Not" album containing verses and autographs of Mary Worthington, sister of [Miss] Amanda Worthington; and a paper read in 1911 by Sam Worthington before the Washington County Historical Society. Amanda (Dougherty) Worthington was the daughter of Thomas Dougherty, clerk of the US House of Representatives. An article about the school life of [Miss] Amanda Worthington, who became the Greenville, MS, librarian, appeared in *Journal of Mississippi History* (May 1972).

9,782. Wright Family
Papers. 1837-76. 2 folders.
Open. Description.
Mississippi Department of Archives and History.
A family correspondence of Eliza Abert Barry Wright and her husband David Wright, a missionary from Vermont who worked among the Mississippi Choctaws, includes letters from their children Laura E. Wright and J. W. A. Wright and a letter from J. W. Hamilton of Columbus, MS. Eliza Wright's sister was Louisa Abert Neilson of Belmont in Lowndes County, MS.

9,783. Young, Lucy Hayes, and Allen, Roberta Etheridge
Papers. 1959-72. 10 items.
Open. Description.
Mississippi Department of Archives and History.
[Mrs.] Young was the last surviving granddaughter of Jefferson Davis. Three photos of Young with her daughter and granddaughter; six clippings concerning Young, her family, and her relation to Jefferson and Varina Davis; and a genealogical chart of Young's descendants. The articles, two photos, and chart were by Allen of Little Rock, AR.

MISSISSIPPI STATE

9,784. Carroll County
Records. 1871-76. 2 microfilm reels.
Open. Unpublished guide.
Mississippi State University, Mitchell Memorial Library.
Marriage bonds from Carroll County, MS.

9,785. Chickasaw Female College
Records. 1852-1928. 1 vol.
Open. Unpublished guide.
Mississippi State University, Mitchell Memorial Library.
Minutes of meetings of the College's board of trustees.

9,786. Childs, Emma
Papers. 1875. 1 vol.
Open. Unpublished guide.
Mississippi State University, Mitchell Memorial Library.
Scrapbook of [Miss] Childs.

9,787. Clark, Lena (Simmons)
Papers. 1856-1912. 54 items and 1 microfilm reel.
Open. Unpublished guide.
Mississippi State University, Mitchell Memorial Library.
Farm records from Grenada County, MS, including accounts, receipts, financial statements, and cotton sale records; post cards; invitations; a scrapbook of clippings; almanacs; material relating to the education of children; and other items.

9,788. Cobb, Lois P. (Dowdle)
Papers. 1915-69. 45 items.
Open. Unpublished guide.
Mississippi State University, Mitchell Memorial Library.
Correspondence, clippings, publications, and other papers of Cobb, a home economist, relate primarily to establishment of the American Institute of Home Grown Fats and Oils, of which she was director from 1933 to 1935, and to her presidency of the Association of Southern Agricultural Workers.

9,789. Dowling, Nannie
Papers. 1885-87. 1 item.
Open. Unpublished guide.
Mississippi State University, Mitchell Memorial Library.
Autograph book of Dowling, a resident of Hickory, MS.

9,790. Fontaine, Edward
Papers. 1818-1923. Ca. 2000 items.
Open. Unpublished guide.
Mississippi State University, Mitchell Memorial Library.
Personal and business correspondence, daily journals, autobiographies, writings, sermons, lectures, eulogies, legal papers, biographies, church records, a scrapbook, articles, and other papers of Fontaine, an Episcopal minister and Confederate officer, and members of his family. Collection contains correspondence of Fontaine's wife Susan C. Fontaine and of his daughter Susan "Susette" (Fontaine) Sawyer, an artist and author, as well as journals of Lemuella S. Brickell Fontaine, wife of Edward Fontaine's son Lamar Fontaine.

9,791. Hic-a-sha-ba-ha DAR
Records. 1910-71. Ca. 74 items.
Open. Unpublished guide.
Mississippi State University, Mitchell Memorial Library.
Minute books, treasurer's files, correspondence, membership lists, scrapbooks, and publications of the Hic-a-sha-ba-ha DAR of Starkville, MS. Also included are miscellaneous lineage books of the National Society of the DAR.

9,792. Howell, Eliza D.
Papers. 1836. 1 item.
Open. Unpublished guide.
Mississippi State University, Mitchell Memorial Library.
Will of Howell, a resident of Alabama.

9,793. Kimbrough
Papers. 1863-1955. Ca. 800 items and 1 microfilm reel.
Partially restricted. Unpublished guide.
Mississippi State University, Mitchell Memorial Library.
Correspondence from Mrs. Jefferson Davis, a resident of Beauvoir in Biloxi, MS, and of New Orleans and New York, to members of the Kimbrough family; photos and a will of her daughter Varina Anne Jefferson Davis; accounts; a deed to Beauvoir from Sarah A. Dorsey to Jefferson Davis; and other material. Also includes correspondence of Mary Hunter (Southworth) [Mrs. A. McC.] Kimbrough, mostly concerning the United Daughters of the Confederacy and Beauvoir, and correspondence of her daughter Mary Craig (Kimbrough) [Mrs. Upton] Sinclair.

9,794. King, Edith Follett
Papers. 1956. 3 items.
Open. Unpublished guide.
Mississippi State University, Mitchell Memorial Library.
Mimeographed account of life of the King family on the Iona plantation in Madison Parish, LA, in the latter part of the 19th century. Also includes a clipping and an article concerning Edward L. King, a professor and head of the department of obstetrics at Tulane from 1928 to 1960.

9,795. McGeoy
Papers. 1901-09. 11 items.
Open. Unpublished guide.
Mississippi State University, Mitchell Memorial Library.
Letter by Margaret Howell (Davis) Hayes concerning the death of her mother Mrs. Jefferson Davis; a sympathy acknowledgement from the A. J. McLaurin family; tax receipts for the Jefferson Davis estate in Harrison County, MS; and newspapers dealing with Mary Hunter (Southworth) [Mrs. A. McC.] Kimbrough and United Daughters of the Confederacy activities relating to Beauvoir, the home of Jefferson Davis.

9,796. McRae, Sallie B.
Papers. 1862. 1 item.
Open. Unpublished guide.
Mississippi State University, Mitchell Memorial Library.
Copy of McRae's diary, which was edited by James W. Webb.

9,797. Moore, Irene (Ivy)
Papers. 1847-1931. 9-page item.
Open. Unpublished guide.
Mississippi State University, Mitchell Memorial Library.
Recollections of early settlers of northern Mississippi, primarily of Chickasaw and Pontotoc counties.

9,798. Posey, Alice (Puckett)
Papers. 1944. 12-page item.
Open. Unpublished guide.
Mississippi State University, Mitchell Memorial Library.
History of [Mrs.] Posey's life in Aberdeen, MS, and northeastern Mississippi from 1857 to 1944.

9,799. Posey, Zoë
Papers. Nd. 11 vols.
Open. Unpublished guide.
Mississippi State University, Mitchell Memorial Library.
Scrapbooks of Posey, daughter of a Confederate general, contain clippings relating to Mississippi and Louisiana history, with an emphasis on Confederate and 20th-century history. Also included are Louisiana recipes.

9,800. Preston, Zenas
Papers. 1850-53. 1 item.
Open. Unpublished guide.
Mississippi State University, Mitchell Memorial Library.
Diary in which Preston describes slaves, crops, levees and floods, diseases, prescriptions, taxes, road work, and other aspects of life on a plantation on Lake Saint Peter across the river from Natchez, MS.

9,801. Raymond, Henry Rodney
Papers. 1850-1949. 347 items and 1 microfilm reel.
Open. Unpublished guide.
Mississippi State University, Mitchell Memorial Library.
Raymond was a Presbyterian minister, Confederate chaplain, teacher, and president of the Marion Female Institute. Collection contains a diary; family correspondence and correspondence relating to his activities as a minister in Mississippi, Alabama, and Texas; a minute book and programs of the Starkville Woman's Club; minutes of the Presbyterian Synod of Alabama; genealogical and family records; scrapbooks relating to religious, church, and family matters; and other material.

9,802. Red, Abbie Bell Nicholson
Papers. 1905-06. No size given.
Open. Unpublished guide.
Mississippi State University, Mitchell Memorial Library.
Diary of [Mrs.] Red concerns daily events in the life of a college girl at Industrial Institute and College, the predecessor of Mississippi State College for Women, in Columbus, MS.

9,803. Rice, Nannie Herndon
Papers. 1824-1963. 7539 items.
Open. Unpublished guide.
Mississippi State University, Mitchell Memorial Library.
Correspondence, diaries, ledgers, deeds, claims, bills of sale of slaves, rent and labor contracts, estate papers, school reports from the 1860s, genealogical data, and other papers of [Miss] Rice (1886-1963) relate to her family; to her work as librarian at Mississippi State University; to her student days at Mississippi State College for Women, Columbia University, the Vassar College Training Camp for Nurses, and the University of Illinois; and to her work with the Mississippi women's suffrage movement. Also included are papers of Rice's father Arthur H. Rice, a physician and planter in Oktibbeha County, MS; of her grandparents John W. Rice and Augusta (Hopkins) Rice; her great-uncle John James Walker and great-aunt Maria (Hopkins) Walker; and her great-grandfather Arthur Francis Hopkins.

9,804. Stansel, Horace Sylvan
Papers. 1911-66. 2306 items.
Open. Unpublished guide.

Mississippi State University, Mitchell Memorial Library.
Correspondence, photos, clippings, and other papers of Stansel, a resident of Ruleville, MS, relate to his career as a civil and structural engineer and as a Mississippi state legislator. Also included are papers of his wife Pearl (High) Stansel (1886-), which pertain to her service in the Mississippi legislature and to the Horace S. Stansel Memorial Library in Ruleville.

9,805. Starkville Woman's Club
Records. 1932-70. 17 vols.
Open. Unpublished guide.
Mississippi State University, Mitchell Memorial Library.
Scrapbooks of the Club.

9,806. Swann and Cavett
Papers. 1884-1929. 486 items.
Open. Unpublished guide.
Mississippi State University, Mitchell Memorial Library.
Statements, receipts, legal documents, clippings, pamphlets and reprints opposing woman's suffrage, and other papers of the family of E. D. Cavett, a deputy US tax collector, Mississippi state legislator, and grand cyclops of the Noxubee, MS, Ku Klux Klan. Collection contains correspondence of Cavett's daughter Allie (Cavett) Swann and of her son Porter Swann and letters by Allie Swann and Bess Swann while they were attending Mississippi State College for Women in Columbus, MS.

9,807. Trigg, Sue Pelham
Papers. 1784-1944. 1 microfilm reel.
Open. Unpublished guide.
Mississippi State University, Mitchell Memorial Library.
Papers of [Miss] Trigg, a teacher and historian of Greenville, MS, include manuscripts of her articles about Greenville and Washington County, MS, clippings relating to local history, and letters of the Bodley family of Kentucky and Mississippi.

9,808. United Daughters of the Confederacy
Records. 1952-55. 3 vols.
Open. Unpublished guide.
Mississippi State University, Mitchell Memorial Library.
Scrapbooks of the Lyda C. Moore Chapter of the UDC in Lula, MS.

9,809. University Archives
Records. 1878-1974. 1300 ft.
Open. Unpublished guide.
Mississippi State University, Mitchell Memorial Library.
Official records of the University include minutes of meetings of the board of trustees, presidents' correspondence, a vice-president's papers for 1930 to 1932, comptrollers' office records, annual and biennial reports, and departmental records. Includes correspondence, committee reports, and other papers of Frances (Patterson) Lee, who was dean of women at the University from 1961 to 1973.

Also included are papers of other individuals who were associated with the University. Among them are the Mildred Barr papers, which include notes, essays, photos, and clippings relating to personalities and activities at the University and papers of Mary Galloway Schlater relating to her attendance in 1905 at the Mississippi Agricultural and Mechanical College, predecessor of Mississippi State University, where she was the only female student; includes Schlater's correspondence with classmates, photos, mementos, and publications.

9,810. Valiant, Margaret
Papers. 1918-78. 712 items.
Open. Unpublished guide.
Mississippi State University, Mitchell Memorial Library.
Correspondence and other papers relating to [Mrs.] Valiant's work with the special skills division of the Resettlement Administration and with the music division of the National Youth Administration. Also included is material relating to migrant workers, folk music, dramatic productions, population control, and the National Council of the Southern Negro Youth Congress. Correspondents include Eleanor Roosevelt and Margaret Sanger.

9,811. Walker, Noverta
Papers. 1847-1949. 840 items.
Open. Unpublished guide.
Mississippi State University, Mitchell Memorial Library.
Walker was a seamstress and local historian of Ripley, MS. Letters from family and friends, minute books of the Baptist Young People's Union and the Tuesday Evening Club, invitations and programs of social events in Ripley, photos of local and national figures, and clippings.

9,812. Ward, Rufus
Papers. 1837-1900. 1464 items.
Open. Unpublished guide.
Mississippi State University, Mitchell Memorial Library.
Personal and business correspondence, accounts, receipts, deeds, slave records, military orders, genealogical material, and other papers of the family of James Sykes (1810-85) of Columbus, MS. Includes letters which his grandchildren Wildie Sykes, who later married Joseph Saunders Billups, and Ida Sykes (1858-91), who later married Thomas Carlton Billups (1839-98), wrote while they were attending Patapsco Female Institute in Ellicotts City, MD. Also includes papers of James Sykes's wife Martha (Lanier) Sykes (1815-81), her mother Elizabeth Lanier, Ida and Thomas Billups, and Wildie and Joseph Billups.

NATCHEZ

9,813. Natchez Garden Club
Records. 1927- . Ca. 3 drawers and 1 bookcase.
Access restricted. No guide.
Natchez Garden Club Archives.
Minutes, correspondence, photos, scrapbooks, yearbooks, clippings, and other records of the Club, which was chartered in 1927 to promote beautification of the city and to foster the study of nature and the history of Natchez Territory. Primarily concerns events centering around the Club's work in establishing the Natchez Pilgrimage, a tour of the area's historic homes. Includes papers of Lillie Vidal [Mrs. S. A.] Boatner, who served as the Club's executive secretary during the early years of the Pilgrimage; Harriet [Mrs. Joseph] Dixon, former president and publicity chairman of the Club; Edith Wyatt Moore, an author and historian of the Club; and Roane Fleming [Mrs. Ferriday] Byrnes, who helped organize the Pilgrimage and many of the Club's historic preservation projects. In addition to Connelly's Tavern, which was built in about 1798, the Club owns the Priest's House, constructed in about 1794; the Lawyers' Lodge; the William Johnson House; and Magnolia Hall.

UNIVERSITY

9,814. Arthur Palmer Hudson Folklore Collection
Collection. 1908-63. 4.67 ft., 7 tapes, and 5 recording discs.
Open. Unpublished guide.
University of Mississippi Library.
Includes folk songs about women and their roles.

9,815. Brown, Juanita
Papers. 1801-1900. Ca. 2 ft.
Open. Unpublished guide.
University of Mississippi Library, Archives and Special Collections.
Letters that Juanita Brown, a resident of Sallis, MS, wrote to her parents Mr. and Mrs. Terrel Brown while she was away at school. Also included are letters, receipts, bills, and other business documents; deeds; land warranties; Confederate money and notes; clippings; and other material pertaining to the Browns' social life.

9,816. Daughters of the American Revolution, David Reese Chapter
Records. 1818-1936. 3 ft.
Open. Unpublished guide.
University of Mississippi Library, Archives and Special Collections.
Nearly complete set of minutes of the Chapter, which was founded in 1899; programs and reports; notes on cemeteries and antiquities; genealogical notes on the Archibald, Gaines, Harris, Armstead, BeBerry, Howery, Carter, Byrd, Reese, Rhys, Tye, Walthall, Buckner, Craig, and Isom families; lists of Revolutionary War soldiers who lived in Mississippi, their service records, and Mississippi pension rolls from 1818, 1833, and 1840 with genealogical notes on each pensioner; and information on early history of the Chapter, of Oxford, MS, and of Lafayette County.

9,817. Holly Springs Female Academy
Records. 1836-1901. 2 folders.
Open. Unpublished guide.
University of Mississippi Library, Archives and Special Collections.
Original and amended acts of incorporation, a nearly complete set of board minutes, and an agreement of the Academy, an educational institution for women in Holly Springs, MS.

9,818. League of Women Voters of Oxford
Records. 1962- . 19 vols.
Open. Unpublished guide.
University of Mississippi Library, Archives and Special Collections.
School and town surveys; a directory of Oxford public officials and voting information; press books; and volumes of *The Oxford Area Voter,* the news bulletin of this LWV chapter, which was founded in 1962.

9,819. Miscellany
Collection. Nd. 15.2 ft.
Open. No guide.
University of Mississippi Library, Archives and Special Collections.
Collections pertaining to women include those of Mrs. R. E. Price, Bobbie Gentry, Katherine Sherwood McDowell, Mrs. John Robert Rayburn, Dorothy Oldham, Sally Kate Winters, and Mrs. Dunbar Roland. Also included are manuscripts of Emilie Blackmore Stapp and minutes of the University Dames.

9,820. Oral History Project
Oral history. 1976. 3 tapes.
Open. No guide.
University of Mississippi Library, Archives and Special Collections.
Interviews in which midwives tell of their experiences.

9,821. Thompson, Lily Wilkinson
Papers. 1877-1920. 1 ft. and 1 vol.
Open. Unpublished guide.
University of Mississippi Library, Archives and Special Collections.
Personal correspondence, manuscripts, reports, clippings, magazines, scrapbooks, and miscellany of Thompson pertain to woman suffrage. Also includes material on Belle Kearney and a letter from US President Taft.

9,822. University Dames (University of Mississippi Women's Club)
Records. 1927- . 1 ft.
Open. No guide.
University of Mississippi Library, Archives and Special Collections.
The Dames, formally known as the University of Mississippi Women's Club, is a social organization open to the University's women employees and wives of employees. Constitution, amendments, and minutes.

MISSOURI

BLUE SPRINGS

9,823. Archives
Records. 1937- . 1 cabinet, 39 vols., and 3 microfilm reels.
Access restricted. No guide.
National Federation of Press Women, Inc.
Correspondence, biographical data, administrative files, a history, pamphlets, photos, and a complete run of *Press Woman* magazine of the National Federation of Press Women, a professional organization for women and men in communications founded in Chicago in 1937. Includes biographical information on past NFPW presidents, women of achievement, winners in annual contests, and recipients of the Helen Miller Malloch scholarship. Issues of *Press Woman* contain information on NFPW members, among them Eleanor Roosevelt, Clare (Boothe) Luce, Dorothy Dix, Mary Margaret McBride, Sarah McClendon, Marjorie Holmes, and Margaret Hickey.

COLUMBIA

9,824. Columbia College Archives
Records. 1851- . 1 cabinet.
Open. No guide.
Columbia College Library.
Founded in 1851 as a four-year women's school known as Christian Female College, the institution became a junior college in the early 1900s and a four-year coeducational college in the early 1970s. Annual reports; a card file on alumni; photos; scrapbooks; a compilation of course syllabi for the 1929-30 school year; class bulletins and catalogs; issues of the *Christian College Chronicle,* a student magazine, 1893-1907, and of *Christian College Microphone,* a bimonthly student newspaper, 1929- ; student yearbooks, directories, and handbooks; copies of Allean Lemmon Hale's *Petticoat Pioneer* (St. Paul, MN: North Central Publishing Co., 1968), a history of the school to 1968; and other records. A nonsectarian school that received some support from the Disciples of Christ Church, the College had a woman president during the late 1800s and two women presidents, who were responsible for its change to junior college status. In 1913 the school began to issue associate in arts rather than baccalaureate degrees, thus enabling students to transfer to four-year schools as juniors.

9,825. Stephens College Archives
Records. 1853- . No size given.
Closed. Partial card file.
Stephens College Library.
Founded as a female academy in 1833, Stephens College is a four-year women's school. Minutes, correspondence, diaries, photos, scrapbooks, catalogs, yearbooks, newspapers, and other records, including files of the Woman's Foundation, which was established in the 1940s by James Madison Wood who was president of Stephens College from 1912 to 1947. Includes ca. 188 reels of recorded musical concerts and of telephone conversations between well-known persons and Stephens faculty and students.

9,826. Keeley, Mary (Paxton)
Papers. Ca. 1955-71. 0.17 cu.ft.
Open. Unpublished guide.
University of Missouri Archives.
The first woman to graduate from the University of Missouri-Columbia journalism school, Keeley (1886-) wrote for a Kansas City newspaper and, from 1928 to 1952, taught English and journalism at Christian College in Columbia. Transcript of an interview and photos she took for an exhibit at the new Medical Center, which was located on the University of Missouri-Columbia campus. The photos show surgical operations in progress, mothers and newborn infants, hospital administrators, and other persons and activities at the Medical Center.

9,827. Lapp and Wilson
Papers. 1892-1917. 1 cu.ft.
Open. Unpublished guide.
University of Missouri Archives.
Scrapbooks of Mary Agnes Lapp and James F. Wilson, both former students of the University of Missouri-Columbia, contain photos, announcements, programs, clippings, and other items about University athletic events and schedules, fraternity and sorority functions, students, campus buildings, class schedules, a fire on campus, and other subjects.

9,828. McCurdy, Frances
Papers. 1954-73. 3.5 cu.ft.
Open. Unpublished guide.
University of Missouri Archives.
McCurdy is professor emeritus of speech and dramatic arts and former chairman of her department at the University of Missouri. Correspondence, memoranda, bylaws and minutes of committee meetings, photos, news releases, book reviews, programs, clippings, and other papers reflect McCurdy's career as a classroom teacher, a director of dramatic productions, originator and manager of the annual Hawthorn Festival, and an active member in professional speech associations. In particular, the papers show her work in promoting standards for certification of secondary speech teachers and oral interpretation programs. She retired in 1973.

9,829. Mangel, Margaret
Papers. 1952-68. 0.5 cu.ft.
Open. Unpublished guide.
University of Missouri Archives.
Speeches that Mangel, dean of the University college of home economics, gave before groups, including Phi Upsilon Omicron, Christian College students, Missouri Home Economics Association, and the Missouri and Kansas Dietetic Association, and during extension seminars, short courses, and television programs. The talks concern such subjects as nutrition, research in home economics, graduate studies, extension work, professional careers in home economics, new textiles, combined journalism-home economics curricula, women's role in the national economy, and farm surpluses. Mangel earned a PhD at the University of Chicago.

9,830. Theta Sigma Phi
Records. 1942-68. 1.5 cu.ft.
Open. Unpublished guide.
University of Missouri Archives.
The Gamma Chapter of Theta Sigma Phi, a national women's journalism fraternity, was formed in 1942. Constitution, bylaws, minutes, scrapbooks, certificates, articles and clippings by various Chapter members and about Chapter activities, and other records.

9,831. American Association of University Women, Missouri Committee on Equal Pay
Records. 1963. 2 vols.
Open. Unpublished guide.
University of Missouri Library, State Historical Society of Missouri.
Scrapbooks contain correspondence, background material, photos, pamphlets, clippings, and other material regarding the AAUW's "equal pay for equal work" campaign. Includes correspondence from clubwomen, professional women, legislators, and businessmen.

9,832. Armstrong, C. J.: "Who Is Becky Thatcher?"
Papers. Nd. 7-page item.
Open. Unpublished guide.
University of Missouri Library, State Historical Society of Missouri.
Armstrong was a minister of the First Christian Church in Hannibal, MO. Article that Armstrong submitted for publication in the *Missouri Historical Review* concerns his contention that Laura Hawkins Frazer was the model for Mark Twain's Becky Thatcher. The manuscript contains copies of correspondence between Frazer and Samuel L. Clemens and between Clemens's daughter [Mrs.] Clara C. Gabrilovich, Albert Bigelow Paine, and Armstrong.

9,833. Arrow Rock Tavern Board
Records. 1826-1923. 8 folders and 1 vol.
Open. Unpublished guide.
University of Missouri Library, State Historical Society of Missouri.
Includes correspondence of Elizabeth Gentry concerning placement of Highway 40 and Santa Fe Trail markers, a diary of Martha J. Woods for 1854 to 1860, and a scrapbook of Hugh Stephens. Wood's diary pertains to her overland journey from Virginia to Missouri with her brother, sister-in-law, and their children. After two years she returned to Virginia by train, but she retraced her path a year later to help nurse her sister-in-law and nephew. Three other children had died during her absence. The scrapbook contains clippings about Arrow Rock, MO, one of them an item about a romance between an Arrow Rock girl and an Irishman who was a side-wheeler captain on the Missouri River.

9,834. Barnes, Sarah Randleman
Papers. 1909. 3-page item.
Open. Unpublished guide.
University of Missouri Library, State Historical Society of Missouri.
Account of pioneer life in Missouri and Kentucky that Barnes (ca. 1827-?) wrote at her daughter's request. References to women include a story about a grandmother who was disinherited by her wealthy family after her marriage and hard times that followed; a 14-year-old girl who was kidnapped by the Indians but refused to leave the tribe later in her life; and a grandmother who cared for the wounded during Revolutionary War battles and who refused to give information under torture. Barnes said this same woman later was widowed and left with several children to support.

9,835. Barrows Family
Papers. 1834-49. 2 folders.
Open. Unpublished guide.
University of Missouri Library, State Historical Society of Missouri.
Correspondence between Freeman Barrows, his brother John, and his sister Sarah and between Elizabeth (Vaill) Waldo and her sister Asenath B. (Vaill) [Mrs. Freeman] Barrows. In his letters, Freeman Barrows tells of business, social, and economic conditions in Batesville and Papinville, MO, and urges his mother, brothers, and sisters to join him and his family there.

9,836. Barth Family
Papers. 1852-1907. 4 folders.
Open. Unpublished guide.
University of Missouri Library, State Historical Society of Missouri.
Family, business, and legal papers of the family of Moses Barth, a native of Germany who became a dry goods merchant in Fayette and Rocheport, MO. Correspondence, which includes many references to women, relates to recruiting for the Confederate army, deteriorating economic conditions in Rocheport during the Civil War, and skirmishes and raids in the area.

9,837. Bingham Family
Papers. 1814-1930. 27 folders.
Open. Unpublished guide.
University of Missouri Library, State Historical Society of Missouri.
Correspondence of the family of George Caleb Bingham, a portrait and landscape painter. Family members, beginning with Bingham's grandfather, lived in Virginia and, later, in Missouri and Texas. Letters include references to friends, deaths, marriages, travel, prices, estates, and family matters.

9,838. Botts, Benson
Papers. 1908. 1 vol.
Open. Unpublished guide.
University of Missouri Library, State Historical Society of Missouri.
[Miss] Benson Botts was a student at the University of Missouri summer session in 1908; a Miss Etheridge was her roommate. Handmade booklet presented to Botts by Etheridge contains poetry and illustrations concerning their experiences during the summer. The booklet was entitled "Reminiscences—A Schoolmarmian Epic."

9,839. Brashear, Margaret M.
Papers. 1868-1962. 349 folders, 1 vol., and 1 file.
Open. Unpublished guide.
University of Missouri Library, State Historical Society of Missouri.
A college educator and author of works on Missouri literature and Mark Twain, Brashear (1874-1963) was a member of the AAUP, the Modern Language Association, Pi Lambda Theta, and Delta Kappa Gamma. Correspondence; notes made in preparation for her articles, books, and classes; papers by students and Missouri authors; pamphlets; and other papers. Born in Brashear, MO, Margaret Brashear graduated from Northeast Missouri Normal School in 1892; she attended Radcliffe College in 1897-98 and summer school at Oxford. She received a BA from the University of Missouri in 1922 and a PhD from the University of North Carolina in 1930. After teaching for three years in public high schools in Missouri and Montana, she taught English at Beaver College in Pennsylvania, at Kirksville Teachers College, at the University of Idaho, and at the University of Missouri from 1919 to 1944. She then retired and moved to her father's home in Kirksville. Brashear published *Mark Twain, Son of Missouri* in 1934 and co-authored *The Art, Humor, and Humanity of Mark Twain* with Robert M. Rodney in 1959.

9,840. Breckenridge, Clarence Edward
Papers. 1897-1960. 15 folders.
Open. Unpublished guide.
University of Missouri Library, State Historical Society of Missouri.
Family correspondence, genealogical and historical notes, and clippings of Breckenridge (1877-1963). Includes correspondence with a cousin Adella Breckenridge Moore of Caledonia, MO, about the Breckenridge family and typescripts and articles of Moore concerning genealogical and historical subjects.

9,841. Breckenridge, William Clark
Papers. 1752-1927. 117 folders and 21 vols.
Open. Unpublished guide.
University of Missouri Library, State Historical Society of Missouri.
Correspondence, miscellaneous papers, and scrapbooks of Breckenridge (1862-1927), a St. Louis businessman, writer, and historian. Includes letters of Eliza Bierstadt; mention of the Patience Worth cult in St. Louis and of Worth's medium [Mrs.] Pearl Curran; a description of the autobiography of the daughter of a free Negro woman; recollections of Mrs. Wilson Primm on early St. Louis schools, social life, and fashion; recollections of [Mrs.] Lucy Sims Munday concerning overland travel and life with the Delaware Indians; biographical sketches of poets Frances Brown and "Una," who was Mary A. Ford; death notices of Kate Chopin, a writer of stories about the lives of Louisiana Creoles; and material concerning women's rights, elementary and female education for teachers, divorce, life in hotels, the Monticello Female Academy, modern women, diets, make-up, Mrs. John C. Frémont, comic actors and actresses, minstrel and opera troupes, Avonia Jones, and Maggie Mitchell.

9,842. Burris, Edith S.: "Patsy the Pioneer"
Papers. Nd. 1 folder.
Open. Unpublished guide.
University of Missouri Library, State Historical Society of Missouri.
Burris's biography of Rebecca Gregg concerns her life as a frontierswoman in Missouri from the War of 1812 until after the Civil War.

9,843. Business and Professional Woman's Club
Records. 1941-66. 5 vols.
Open. Unpublished guide.
University of Missouri Library, State Historical Society of Missouri.
Minutes, treasurer's reports, membership lists, and other items of the Columbia Business and Professional Women's Club, which was founded before 1925.

9,844. Cady, Lee D.
Papers. 1937-41. 62 folders.
Open. Unpublished guide.
University of Missouri Library, State Historical Society of Missouri.
From 1939 to 1941, Cady (1896-), a physician, was chairman of the Missouri State Medical Association's committee on the study of medical practice laws and chairman of the Missouri Social Hygiene Association legislative committee that drafted a prenatal blood test bill. Correspondence, including that with Harriet S. Cory, a physician who was executive secretary of the Missouri Social Hygiene Association; copies of premarital examination and prenatal blood test bills; and promotional publications regarding these bills. As chairman of the committee on medical practice laws, Cady studied premarital examination laws in other states and helped draft a bill requiring couples seeking a marriage license to take a blood test for syphilis. The bill did not win immediate legislative approval. Cady also helped prepare a successful bill that required pregnant women to take a blood test for syphilis.

9,845. Chilton, Octavia (Blackwell)
Papers. 1842. 2-page item.
Open. Unpublished guide.
University of Missouri Library, State Historical Society of Missouri.
Letter in which Chilton relates family news to her mother Betsey Blackwell of Fauquier County, VA, and describes the merits of Missouri.

9,846. Chrisman, L. R.
Papers. 1960. 7-page item.
Open. Unpublished guide.
University of Missouri Library, State Historical Society of Missouri.
Letter to a friend in which Chrisman of Newell, SD, describes Martha Jane "Calamity Jane" (Cannary) Burk during the late 1890s and early 1900s in Deadwood and Belle Fourche, SD. Calamity Jane died in 1903 and was buried in Deadwood.

9,847. Christopher, Adrienne Tinker
Papers. 1965. 1 folder.
Open. Unpublished guide.
University of Missouri Library, State Historical Society of Missouri.
Two articles concerning early Westport, MO, and one by Christopher about the Old Burr Oak in Kansas City. "Old Westport," published by T. S. Hough in 1920, contains descriptions of the city during the 1850s and Hough's admonition that young women of the town should take as their ideal of womanhood "the dear old mothers of Westport." Also includes a 1913 article in which Anna Elizabeth Charles Krueger recorded her memories of a two-week Westport reunion in 1912.

9,848. Christy, E. A.
Papers. 1863. 2-page item.
Open. Unpublished guide.
University of Missouri Library, State Historical Society of Missouri.
A letter in which Christy, a homemaker writing to her father, discusses the Civil War, particularly Jayhawkers and marauding bands, and mentions conscription and the health of various family members.

9,849. Collins, Charles
Papers. 1836-1954. 8 folders.
Open. Unpublished guide.
University of Missouri Library, State Historical Society of Missouri.
Correspondence and clippings regarding the Royall, Switzler, Price, and Henderson families. Includes a clipping "Anne Royall—First 'Colyumist'" by Jessie Tresham, a 1940 National Broadcasting Company radio broadcast program "The Cavalcade of America Broadcast Number 175—The People vs. Anne Newport Royall," and Mary Jane Royall Switzler's album of poetry and other items. Anne Newport, subject of both the Tresham clipping and the broadcast, was the daughter of a backwoods family who was educated by William Royall, a wealthy Virginian. She acquired the poise and manners of an upper-class woman and married Royall in 1797. After his death in 1813, Royall's relatives successfully contested his will, leaving his widow impoverished. She supported herself by writing and eventually turned to muckraking.

9,850. Colt, Miriam Davis
Papers. 1856. 1 folder.
Open. Unpublished guide.
University of Missouri Library, State Historical Society of Missouri.
Colt (1817-post 1899) traveled west from New York in 1856 with her husband William H. Colt, their two children, her husband's parents, and his sister; they were part of the expedition planned by the "Vegetarian Settlement Company," which had Fort Scott, KS, as its goal. In her account, written in diary form with editorial notes provided in 1941, Miriam Colt tells of her family's departure from New York and of their disastrous stay in Kansas. At one point the entire party with the exception of Miriam Colt was sick with fever. She and her husband decided to return east, but William and their son Willie died in Missouri. Miriam Colt provided headstones for their graves before she and her daughter returned to New York. Eventually she acquired land near Potsdam, NY, and earned her living by raising chickens and doing needlework.

9,851. Columbia Equal Suffrage Association and League of Women Voters
Records. 1912-23. 1 folder.
Open. Unpublished guide.
University of Missouri Library, State Historical Society of Missouri.
Minutes of the Association from 1912 to 1920 and of the LWV from 1920 to 1923; constitution of the LWV of Missouri, adopted in 1919; and a clipping concerning five Columbia women honored for their work in the suffrage campaign.

9,852. Cooper, Nan P.: "Mother's Trip Across the Plains"
Papers. 1901. 32-page item.
Open. Unpublished guide.
University of Missouri Library, State Historical Society of Missouri.
Arvazena Angeline Cooper's account of a journey by wagon train in 1863 from Lawrence County, MO, to Oregon. She tells of her feelings about leaving home, the hardships of camp life, antics of her young daughter, the birth of her son, and the reception the party received in the West.

9,853. Creel, Virginia Fackler
Papers. 1864-1937. 19 pp.
Open. Unpublished guide.
University of Missouri Library, State Historical Society of Missouri.
Creel (1845-1937) was a homemaker. A letter in which her son George Creel, writing to his two brothers after the death of their mother, tells of his anger that press notices assume she had "no identity except through her sons"; a brief biography of Virginia Creel written by her sons in 1937; and an 1864 diary of an overland journey west.

9,854. Davis, Anna M.
Papers. 1876-1905. 1 vol.
Open. Unpublished guide.
University of Missouri Library, State Historical Society of Missouri.
Clippings scrapbook includes women's obituaries and articles on weddings and anniversaries, information about the Marshall Female Seminary, and "Freedom for Farmers' Wives." Also contains poetry, including "The Follies of Fashion—The Fashionable Girl's Soliloquy on a Practical and Pressing Subject."

9,855. Dunaway, Mrs. B. L.
Papers. 1965. 1 folder.
Open. Unpublished guide.
University of Missouri Library, State Historical Society of Missouri.
Brief history of the role of Sarah (Barton) Murphy (ca. 1748-1817) in the settlement of Farmington, MO. The pamphlet, printed for the Old Settlement Festival in 1965, honored Murphy for her courage in moving to the Farmington area after her husband's death in 1800. He had selected the site in 1799. In 1805 she organized and taught the first Sunday school west of the Mississippi; she also raised the daughter of her brother Joab Barton and an Indian woman. Several of her descendants gained prominence; her son was a delegate to Missouri's first constitutional convention.

9,856. Federated Republican Women's Club
Records. 1934-69. 14 folders and 3 vols.
Open. Unpublished guide.
University of Missouri Library, State Historical Society of Missouri.
Minutes, a scrapbook, and an award of this local group, which was organized in 1932.

9,857. Ferris, Ruth: "Betty Ragland at Adelphai College, Boonville, MO, 1854-1855"
Papers. Nd. 29-page item.
Open. Unpublished guide.
University of Missouri Library, State Historical Society of Missouri.
In a typed paper Ferris describes Ragland's background and the circumstances that led to her work as a student and teacher at Adelphai College. Ferris also writes about the history of the school, formerly called the Female Collegiate Institute; its financial collapse; and how a Mr. Stephens and a Colonel Nelson befriended Ragland after she lost her job.

9,858. Fike, Ellie
Papers. 1879-92. 3 folders and 3 vols.
Open. Unpublished guide.
University of Missouri Library, State Historical Society of Missouri.
A teacher and secretary, Fike (1861-?) helped manage her parents' home after illness forced her to resign from her job. Diaries contain information on her student life at the State Normal School at Warrensburg, MO; her graduation; women's fashions; a railroad trip to Fort Worth, TX; the St. Louis exposition; work at the Normal School; and her social life. Collection also includes programs and clippings.

9,859. Foard, Rebecca
Papers. 1860-80. 1 vol.
Open. Unpublished guide.
University of Missouri Library, State Historical Society of Missouri.
Scrapbook of clippings, including obituaries of several women and items on such topics as marriage, motherhood, and women's health.

9,860. France, Charles B.
Papers. 1856-90. 8 folders.
Open. Unpublished guide.
University of Missouri Library, State Historical Society of Missouri.
Included with the correspondence, accounts, and other papers of France (1835-95), a St. Joseph, MO, banker, are journals of Martha McDonald and Mattie W. McDonald. Martha McDonald's journal, which dates from 1856 to 1863, tells of her schooling, home and social life, and conditions in Andrew County, MO, during the Civil War. She comments on rumors and news of the War and discusses her preference for the southern cause. Mattie McDonald's journal concerns her trip with her father in the spring of 1860 from Quincy, IL, to Washington, DC. France's family correspondence, some of it written by women, contains items about student life at various Missouri colleges and eastern schools, Reconstruction, the western gold rush of the 1860s, and letters from Colorado during the 1860s and 1870s.

9,861. French and Spanish Archives
Records. 1763-1847. 10 folders and 23 microfilm reels.
Open. Unpublished guide.
University of Missouri Library, State Historical Society of Missouri.
More than 3000 legal documents from the St. Louis area include marriage contracts with terms of the dowry and property rights, wills in which property is left to the widow, and extensive property inventories. Contains the 1803 will of Juaneta Forchet, a free Negro woman. Indexes list the documents by number, type, principal persons involved, language, and date.

9,862. Fritts, Stella
Papers. Nd. 2 folders.
Open. Unpublished guide.
University of Missouri Library, State Historical Society of Missouri.
Biographical essay in which [Mrs.] Fritts reminisces about her family and gives her thoughts on politics and religion. She also discusses dissent during the late 1960s.

9,863. Gentry, Mary E.
Papers. 1852. 1 vol.
Open. Unpublished guide.
University of Missouri Library, State Historical Society of Missouri.
Scrapbook containing correspondence and clippings of short stories, poetry, travel accounts, and other items.

9,864. Gentry, Thomas Benton
Papers. 1870-1902. 1 folder.
Open. Unpublished guide.
University of Missouri Library, State Historical Society of Missouri.
Gentry (1830-1906) was a deputy postmaster and lawyer. Four household account books covering the period and a brief biographical sketch of Gentry by his grandson William R. Gentry, Jr. The expense books itemize amounts paid for each household purchase and include references to Gentry's two wives "Molly" or "Mary" and "Eugenia" or "Eugie." The biographical sketch mentions Mary Gentry's assistance to her husband in his efforts to graduate from law school.

9,865. Geyer, Henry S.
Papers. 1829-58. 1 folder.
Open. Unpublished guide.
University of Missouri Library, State Historical Society of Missouri.
Love letters between Geyer and Johanna A. Quarles and an 1858 deed.

9,866. Gourgas Family
Papers. 1815-43. 10 folders.
Open. Unpublished guide.
University of Missouri Library, State Historical Society of Missouri.
Correspondence, some of it in French, includes letters of Adéle Gourgas, who as a young girl emigrated in 1813 to Lexington, KY, from Boston where her Swiss immigrant family had settled. She met John Dubois in Kentucky, married him, in 1819 moved with him to Cincinnati. In letters to her brother John Mark Gourgas, she discusses her daily life, her friends, her garden, and family news. A letter from Wolcott Richards, Adéle Dubois's physician, tells of her last illness and death. Also contains letters pertaining to family inheritance.

9,867. Hadley Family
Papers. 1838-69. 1 folder.
Open. Unpublished guide.
University of Missouri Library, State Historical Society of Missouri.
Elizabeth (Hadley) Wyman was a schoolteacher and, later, a homemaker. Letters of Wyman and her husband Edward to her parents Moses and Susan Hadley. In one of the earlier letters Edward Wyman requested the Hadleys to allow Elizabeth to marry him. A second letter concerns a trip from Boston to Illinois in 1839, while another pertains to the Wymans' growing family.

9,868. Hamilton, Mrs. Henry
Papers. 1885-97. 2 folders.
Open. Unpublished guide.
University of Missouri Library, State Historical Society of Missouri.
Letters of advertisement, pamphlets, and brochures concerning organs, sewing machines, and various medical items, many of which were advertised as cures for "female complaints."

9,869. Headman, Mary Hoss: Sevier
Papers. Nd. 32 pp.
Open. Unpublished guide.
University of Missouri Library, State Historical Society of Missouri.
Biographical sketches about Sarah Hawkins Sevier and Catherine Sherrill Sevier, the first and second wives of Tennessee's first governor John Sevier, by Headman, who believed that Sarah Sevier's assistance to her husband's career had been

overlooked. Sevier, the mother of 10, was buried in a wilderness grave that was left unmarked to prevent its desecration by the Indians.

9,870. Helm and Davidson Family
Papers. 1824-1970. 87 folders.
Open. Unpublished guide.
University of Missouri Library, State Historical Society of Missouri.
Correspondence, diaries, account books, genealogical records, and other papers of Mary Aileen Davidson and her ancestors. Includes Davidson's correspondence regarding the DAR, the Colonial Dames, and the First Families of Virginia and correspondence of John B. Helm, his first wife Jane Maria Pope Helm, and Sarah E. (Crump) "Crumpsie" Helm. Also includes diaries dating from 1917 to 1942 of Mary Davidson, diaries dating from 1919 to 1931 and rent books of Mrs. James Frank Davidson, and diaries dating from 1884 to 1894, notes, receipts, and clippings of Mrs. Thetis Clay Hatch.

9,871. Hobbs, Fannie P.
Papers. 1900. 1 vol.
Open. Unpublished guide.
University of Missouri Library, State Historical Society of Missouri.
Volume contains notes on Frederick Froebel's methodology of kindergarten teaching. The notes were taken in connection with an education class in Bonne Terre, MO.

9,872. Horak, Ella Lilly
Papers. Nd. 1 folder.
Open. Unpublished guide.
University of Missouri Library, State Historical Society of Missouri.
Sale bill and a detailed recipe for washday given to a young bride in Tennessee in ca. 1780. The recipe was handed down through six generations of the Epps family.

9,873. Howard Female College
Records. 1859. 1 item.
Open. Unpublished guide.
University of Missouri Library, State Historical Society of Missouri.
Rules for the boarding pupils at this Fayette, MO, school pertain to dress, manners, exercise, and other topics.

9,874. Hughes, Sarah Francis (Hickman)
Papers. 1942. 8 pp.
Open. Unpublished guide.
University of Missouri Library, State Historical Society of Missouri.
Reminiscences of Hughes (1858-?) include information about her early childhood in an army camp during the Civil War. Her father was a soldier and her mother, a cook. In 1865, the family traveled west by wagon train. She writes briefly of her family history and of her children, grandchildren, and great-grandchildren.

9,875. Hunter, Clora Twedell: "Memories and Reminiscences of Early Days at Old Siloam"
Papers. 1961. 1 folder.
Open. Unpublished guide.
University of Missouri Library, State Historical Society of Missouri.
Historical account of Siloam Springs, MO, written by Hunter, who spent her childhood there.

9,876. Ingram, Nellie Allen
Papers. 1872-1946. 2 vols.
Open. Unpublished guide.
University of Missouri Library, State Historical Society of Missouri.
An elocutionist and "young lady of breeding" from Sedalia, MO, Ingram (1866-1945) met her future husband Edmund George Walton, an English citizen, during her return voyage from Europe in 1885; the two were married in 1889 and moved to Minneapolis where Edmund Walton became a millionaire real estate dealer. Scrapbooks containing clippings, programs from Ingram's recitals and social activities, and memorabilia; theater programs and printed items from her tour of England and Europe; and letters written in response to her articles. During her tour Ingram wrote reports of her adventures, many of which were published by the *Sedalia Daily Democrat*. Nellie and Edmund Walton had three daughters. An invitation and clippings describe their eldest daughter's social debut. Collection also contains obituaries for Edmund and Nellie Walton and other family members.

9,877. Isely, Mildred
Papers. 1825-71. 1 folder.
Open. Unpublished guide.
University of Missouri Library, State Historical Society of Missouri.
Scrapbook contains correspondence, short stories, essays, poetry, and clippings on such topics as paternal rights in a daughter's marriage, stray wives, a letter from ladies of Hartford, CT, to ladies of Greece, incest, women's contribution to temperance, women's wages, acts of bravery by women, and physical education of women.

9,878. Isherwood and Coons Family
Papers. 1859-1936. 1 vol.
Open. Unpublished guide.
University of Missouri Library, State Historical Society of Missouri.
Scrapbook of Susie M. Coons Isherwood contains clippings and other papers about the two Missouri families. The clippings include obituaries for women; a reprint of a wedding notice marking the 50th anniversary of the marriage; an article about Louise Dudley [Mrs. Leslie] Carter, an actress; and an extract of Mary Pickford's article "What Religion Means to Me."

9,879. Jackson, Martha Peeler
Papers. 1953. 14-page item.
Open. Unpublished guide.
University of Missouri Library, State Historical Society of Missouri.
Autobiography in which Jackson (1863-?) describes her genealogy, her education, her job as a teacher, marriage, raising a family, trips taken, and her years as a widow.

9,880. Kramer, Herbert G.: "Sister Jerome, Hospital Sister from Osage County"
Papers. Nd. 1 folder.
Open. Unpublished guide.
University of Missouri Library, State Historical Society of Missouri.
Biography of Sister Jerome (1852-1922), a member of the Sisters of the Poor of St. Francis in Cincinnati, includes her obituary and eulogies honoring her.

9,881. Kuemmel, Cornelia A.
Papers. 1901-33. 1 vol.
Open. Unpublished guide.
University of Missouri Library, State Historical Society of Missouri.
Personal and business account book of Kuemmel (1863-?), a music instructor, includes current price information on a variety of goods and services.

9,882. Kuemmel, Natalia Wagner
Papers. 1861-69. 1 vol.
Open. Unpublished guide.
University of Missouri Library, State Historical Society of Missouri.
Volume used by [Mrs. George F.] Kuemmel (1840-?) as a letter record, notebook, and daybook. The notebook section contains jokes and stories while the daybook lists tasks and work accomplished during 1861.

9,883. Lenoir Family
Papers. 1832-60. 5 folders.
Open. Unpublished guide.
University of Missouri Library, State Historical Society of Missouri.
Correspondence of a family of early Boone County, MO, settlers includes a letter from Evelina [Mrs. Walter R.] Lenoir about the family's trip to Missouri. Other letters from the Walter R. Lenoir family concern life in Columbia and Boone County, family matters, marriages, children, finances, education, farming, land, and slaves. The family came from Tennessee and North Carolina.

9,884. Leonard, Abiel
Papers. 1786-1909. 636 folders.
Open. Unpublished guide.
University of Missouri Library, State Historical Society of Missouri.
Leonard (1796-1863) was a Whig lawyer, farmer, and landowner who served on the Missouri Supreme Court. Correspondence of the Missouri militia, the early US Army, and others; legal papers; bills; receipts; accounts; and deeds. Contains letters in which Leonard was encouraged to marry and letters relating to Leonard's daughter Mary, her husband Horace Everett, her fear of pregnancy and motherhood, and the death of their child; to Margaret Bailey's insanity and restored mental health; the terminal illness and death of Leonard's mother; the gift of a slave to Mary; a marriage of slaves of two different masters; trips to New York, Europe, and other locations; the placement of Leonard's daughter Ada in a finishing school; reactions to the Civil War and the fear of bushwhackers; the capture of Jefferson Davis and the end of the War; and the selling of Oakwood. Also contains a Supreme Court decision concerning the inheritance of property by women. Ada Leonard married Bishop C. S. Hawkes.

9,885. Lively, Mrs. Charles E.: "A History of the First Twenty Years of the Resident Wives Club, 1941-1961"
Papers. 1961. 1 folder.
Open. Unpublished guide.
University of Missouri Library, State Historical Society of Missouri.
History of the Club, a social organization formed in 1941 of wives of agricultural resident faculty members at the University of Missouri at Columbia.

9,886. Long, Martha White
Papers. 1904. 1 vol.
Open. Unpublished guide.
University of Missouri Library, State Historical Society of Missouri.
Reminiscences of Long (1829-1909) concern her early childhood, education, religious training and conversion, teaching experiences, and married life. An obituary of Cornelia C. White precedes the title page.

9,887. Lowe, Blanche Beal
Papers. 1858-1933. 1 folder.
Open. Unpublished guide.
University of Missouri Library, State Historical Society of Missouri.
Correspondence, a genealogy, and a clipping pertain to the Absalom Smith and William Fletcher Lowe families and include letters that Josephine and Lizzie Marr wrote from Carondelet, MO, to their cousin Bridget Ann Lowe in Ingersoll, Canada West, between 1858 and 1866; a letter Kittie Lowe wrote from Carondelet to her family in Bloomington, IL, in 1862; and an obituary for Mrs. Samuel Perry.

9,888. McLorn, Olive (Gilbreath)
Papers. 1915-34. 47 folders.
Access restricted. Unpublished guide.

University of Missouri Library, State Historical Society of Missouri.
Love letters written by William L. Cazalet, a British businessman living in Russia, to Gilbreath convey Cazalet's impressions of WWI, the Russian Revolution, and British refugees and creditors of Russia. The war and then the revolution prevented Gilbreath and Cazalet from meeting; eventually the two married other people.

9,889. Marsh, Susan Louise
Papers. 1920-35. 2 vols.
Open. Unpublished guide.
University of Missouri Library, State Historical Society of Missouri.
Scrapbooks containing correspondence, poems, and clippings of [Mrs.] Marsh, a writer and poet who was Missouri's first poet laureate. Marsh participated extensively in club activities and campaigned to save Eugene Field's childhood home.

9,890. Martineau, Harriet
Papers. Nd. 2-page item.
Open. Unpublished guide.
University of Missouri Library, State Historical Society of Missouri.
Letter by Martineau (1802-76) to Catherine Sheil includes discussions on the subjects of Martineau's recent book, female education, and the position of women.

9,891. Medley, Amanda Beckwith
Papers. 1924. 4 pp.
Open. Unpublished guide.
University of Missouri Library, State Historical Society of Missouri.
Memoir in which [Mrs.] Medley writes of her life as a southern sympathizer during the Civil War. She and her sister secretly moved supplies; she and her cousins made bandages; and she, her father, and brother plowed their fields.

9,892. Mermoud, Willa: "History of Barry County's Home Economics Clubs"
Papers. Nd. 1 folder.
Open. Unpublished guide.
University of Missouri Library, State Historical Society of Missouri.
[Mrs. J. Fred] Mermoud was an extension club historian. This history of Barry County, MO, 4-H and women's clubs from 1914 to 1958 contains a list of the groups, their services, and extension service officers.

9,893. Miller, Helen Guthrie
Papers. 1933. 5 pp.
Open. Unpublished guide.
University of Missouri Library, State Historical Society of Missouri.
Letter from [Mrs.] Miller in Kalispell, MT, to [Miss] Carolyn Meyer in response to Meyer's inquiry about activities of Miller and the Missouri Federation of Women's Clubs in promoting a pure food law in Missouri before 1907. The letter is quoted in Meyer's University of Missouri master's thesis.

9,894. Missouri Council of Defense
Records. 1917-19. 1177 folders.
Open. Unpublished guide.
University of Missouri Library, State Historical Society of Missouri.
Created by the governor in 1917 and disbanded in 1919, the Council sought to stimulate patriotism and to organize Missouri's resources with emphasis on food production and conservation. Correspondence, circulars, bulletins, posters, and other printed material of the US government and state and local Councils reflect the country's attitudes during WWI. Disloyalty, sedition, and problems of German minority groups in Missouri are mentioned, as are home demonstrations and recruitment of nurses. Contains material concerning Sarah Louise Arnold, Comtessa Madeline de Bryas, Ella Victoria Dobbs, Martha Nelson McCan, Mrs. William D. Steele, Clara Smith Steichen, [Mrs.] Olive B. Swan, Mina C. Van Winkle, and the WCTU.

9,895. Missouri East Conference, United Methodist Church
Records. 1800-1972. 161 folders and 1315 vols.
Open. Unpublished guide.
University of Missouri Library, State Historical Society of Missouri.
Correspondence, photos, brochures, pamphlets, periodicals, journals, and books include material of the Methodist Episcopal Church and the Methodist Episcopal Church South, which merged with the Methodist Protestant Church in 1939 to form the Methodist Church, and of the Evangelical United Brethren Church, which united with the Methodist Church in 1968 to form the United Methodist Church. Contains some photos of women and copies of *The Methodist Woman,* published by the Woman's Division of Christian Service of the Board of Missions of the Methodist Church.

9,896. Missouri Methodist Church
Records. 1906-38. 11 vols.
Open. Unpublished guide.
University of Missouri Library, State Historical Society of Missouri.
The Maria Laying Gibson Circle was a women's fellowship and service society connected with this Columbia church. Church records contain the Circle's minutes for 1919 and 1920 and other references to women's groups.

9,897. Missouri, University of
Records. 1843-1925. 3 items.
Open. Unpublished guide.
University of Missouri Library, State Historical Society of Missouri.
Charts listing the number of men and women enrolled at the University of Missouri from 1843 to 1925, names and addresses of and degrees received by the University's women graduates from 1870 to 1922, and the total number of students who received degrees from 1870 to 1924.

9,898. Missouri Women's Press Club
Records. 1937-64. 1 vol.
Open. Unpublished guide.
University of Missouri Library, State Historical Society of Missouri.
Treasurers' book lists dues-paying members.

9,899. Nagel, Elsa
Papers. 1912. 2 folders.
Open. Unpublished guide.
University of Missouri Library, State Historical Society of Missouri.
Letters written by German and Swiss girls to Missouri state food and drug commissioner William P. Cutler, a physician, in response to an article he published in German and Swiss newspapers and magazines soliciting wives for American servicemen stationed in the Philippines. A clipping in German and a translation are included.

9,900. O'Hare, Kate Richards
Papers. 1919-20. 1 vol.
Open. Unpublished guide.
University of Missouri Library, State Historical Society of Missouri.
O'Hare (1877-1948), a socialist lecturer and organizer, was sentenced to five years in prison for opposing the draft during WWI. Letters O'Hare wrote to her family during the 14 months she spent in the Missouri State Penitentiary provide a view of prison life, O'Hare's adjustment to that life, her efforts at prison reform, and her relationship with her supporters around the country. The letters contain many references to O'Hare's fellow inmate, anarchist Emma Goldman.

9,901. Pompey, Sherman Lee
Papers. 1960. 6-page item.
Open. Unpublished guide.
University of Missouri Library, State Historical Society of Missouri.
Biographical sketch of Nancie "Granny" Gore (ca. 1821-1917), an early Ozark settler who was widely known for her folk medicine.

9,902. Pope, Elizabeth Lar
Papers. 1875. 8-page item.
Open. Unpublished guide.
University of Missouri Library, State Historical Society of Missouri.
Letter in which Pope (1773-post 1875), an early settler of Kentucky whose parents were among 61 families led there by Daniel Boone, declines an invitation to attend a gathering of old settlers of Missouri during the Buchanan County Agricultural Fair but describes incidents she remembers from her childhood. She writes about Indian troubles, helping to care for the infant Abraham Lincoln, early marriage and widowhood, remarriage, and her numerous descendants.

9,903. Quitman Select School
Records. 1884-1955?. 1 folder.
Open. Unpublished guide.
University of Missouri Library, State Historical Society of Missouri.
Correspondence, reminiscence, and a list of students of the School, founded in 1882 and disbanded in 1887. Wroz Carpenter, who attended the School, wrote the reminiscence; she discusses the School's founding, its rules, where the students came from, transportation problems, students' accomplishments, and the reason the School was closed. Also includes a letter from Carpenter to another former student, Mollie LaMar, which notes that only five former students were still living. Collection also contains a program to the School's annual exhibition, dated 1884.

9,904. Randall, James J.
Papers. Nd. 3 items and 8 pp.
Open. Unpublished guide.
University of Missouri Library, State Historical Society of Missouri.
Two-page biography of Lucinda (Harris) Eagle Kennedy (1792-post 1885), a drawing of her, six pages of genealogical charts, and photos of people mentioned in the charts. The Kennedy biography is a copy of a clipping printed in 1885 marking Kennedy's 103rd birthday. The item mentions her marriage at the age of 16, the birth of 12 children, widowhood, and remarriage. Kennedy had 90 grandchildren, 30 great-grandchildren, and between 25 and 30 great-great-grandchildren.

9,905. Ritchie, Letitia
Papers. 1878. 1 vol. and 1 item.
Open. Unpublished guide.
University of Missouri Library, State Historical Society of Missouri.
Diary in which an Englishwoman who traveled from London to Chicago to visit her son, his wife, and family, describes her trip by ship and train, her stay in Chicago, and the trip home. She often compares and contrasts American and European ways. Also includes photos, post cards, and clippings.

9,906. Rogers and Banks Family
Papers. 1820-78. 3 folders.
Open. Unpublished guide.
University of Missouri Library, State Historical Society of Missouri.
A Kentucky-born physician, Lynn Stanton Banks (1830-65) had an active practice in Marion County, MO, until his death; his wife was Mary Rogers Banks (1833-1903), whose family migrated to Missouri from Kentucky. Family business and legal papers; minutes of Baptist churches in Missouri, Indiana, and Kentucky, dating from 1821

to 1841; and Lynn Banks's physician record books dating from 1854 to 1964. The record books include Banks's calendar of obstetric cases for 1858. Several of the women listed in the calendar were slaves. Also contains a half-page essay with arguments in support of equal education for women.

9,907. Roy, Nancy Rebecca: "Early Remembrances of Edgarton Junction"
Papers. 1954. 19-page item.
Open. Unpublished guide.
University of Missouri Library, State Historical Society of Missouri.
Roy's remembrance of a town of about 20 houses located in northwestern Missouri includes a description of the now defunct community, its inhabitants, incidents, and gossip. Roy spoke with other former inhabitants to add to her personal recollections.

9,908. Russell, Cornelia
Papers. 1866-71. 1 folder.
Open. Unpublished guide.
University of Missouri Library, State Historical Society of Missouri.
Letters to Russell about farming and family life from Ruth Horton and from Sallie Daniels, who apparently was Russell's niece. Also includes a grocery price list.

9,909. Schenck, Peter Voorhees
Papers. 1859-1964. 1 folder and 1 vol.
Open. Unpublished guide.
University of Missouri Library, State Historical Society of Missouri.
A physician who served in the Union army as a surgeon, Schenck (1838-85) was superintendent of St. Louis Female Hospital, health commissioner of St. Louis, and a professor at Missouri Medical College. Correspondence, including a letter in which Schenck proposed marriage to Anna McCune; biographical notes; a photo; and clippings about the McCune-Schenck wedding, the high infant mortality rate, an incident in which a nurse at St. Louis Female Hospital committed suicide after accidentally administering bed bug poison to a patient, and a charge against a nurse for practicing witchcraft at a St. Louis hospital. The clipping concerning infant mortality argued that women were brought up mentally dwarfed and physically compressed. Also contains an article by Schenck's niece Mary S. (Schenck) [Mrs. Franklin Conrad] Woolman (1860-1940), director of domestic art at Columbia University Teachers College.

9,910. Shakespeare Club
Records. 1892-1911. 3 vols.
Open. Unpublished guide.
University of Missouri Library, State Historical Society of Missouri.
Organized in 1886 in Clinton, MO, the Club was a ladies' cultural improvement group. Minutes listing members in attendance at meetings and the lesson for each session, two yearly programs, a clipping describing the Club's 25th anniversary, and the constitution and bylaws of the Missouri State Federation of Women's Clubs.

9,911. Smith, Elizabeth C., Mexican War Service
Papers. 1848. 23 pp.
Open. Unpublished guide.
University of Missouri Library, State Historical Society of Missouri.
Copies of papers supplied by the Veterans Administration and a copy of an act of Congress establishing that [Mrs.] Elizabeth "Bill" Newcom Smith was a Mexican War veteran and was entitled to pay and 160 acres of land.

9,912. Smith, Thomas Adams
Papers. 1798-1864. 7 vols. and 387 items.
Open. Unpublished guide.
University of Missouri Library, State Historical Society of Missouri.
Smith (1781-1844) was a professional soldier who resigned his military commission in 1818 to accept an appointment as receiver of public monies at Franklin, MO. Correspondence, letter books, and miscellaneous papers include references to Smith's wife and other women. Contains mention of Major and Mrs. Sibley, who founded Lindenwood College in St. Charles, MO; a request from a gentleman in Quebec that his wife be given a pass to visit her mother in Pennsylvania; a notation that "the base and brutal conduct of General Rector to his wife and his conduct to General and Mrs. Trigg is not only reprehensible, but shameful and counsel"; and several references to marriages among Smith's acquaintances.

9,913. Smoke, Margaret: "Missouri Women in Journalism"
Papers. 1931. 19-page item.
Open. Unpublished guide.
University of Missouri Library, State Historical Society of Missouri.
A term paper submitted by [Mrs. Ashe] Smoke to the University of Missouri school of journalism concerns the participation of women in journalism in Missouri.

9,914. Snell, Robert L.
Papers. 1870-1966. 56 folders and 1 vol.
Open. Unpublished guide.
University of Missouri Library, State Historical Society of Missouri.
A WWII veteran and officer of Koca-Reeder-Giddens Post No. 233 of the American Legion, Snell secured financial aid for veterans and their families. American Legion records, WWII letters, and miscellaneous items concerning residents of the El Dorado Springs, MO, area. Includes Jessie Wither's memory book from 1900, reports from 1918 of the Woman's Liberty Loan Committee, and a résumé telling about the Committee and its relationship to the Men's Committee.

9,915. Stephens College Alumnae Club
Records. 1925-59. 2 vols.
Open. Unpublished guide.
University of Missouri Library, State Historical Society of Missouri.
Minutes of the Club, which included Stephens alumnae who lived in Columbia and nearby towns, reflect topics of their meetings, one of which was the history of women's education in Columbia.

9,916. Stokes, Charles E., "Augusta Stokes Chambers, A Pioneer Missouri School Teacher"
Papers. Nd. 2-page item.
Open. Unpublished guide.
University of Missouri Library, State Historical Society of Missouri.
Biographical sketch concerns the background and education of Augusta Stokes Chambers, one of the first women schoolteachers in Missouri; her teaching career; and her marriage to Paschal H. Chambers, a physician in Dover, MO.

9,917. Terry, George F., and Terry, Ursula
Papers. 1814-43. 4 items.
Open. Unpublished guide.
University of Missouri Library, State Historical Society of Missouri.
Correspondence to Reuben and Elizabeth Terry of Millersburgh, KY, from their son George Terry, a farmer, and daughter-in-law Ursula Terry chronicles hard times, crops, and family activities. In the last letter, Ursula Terry asks her father-in-law for financial assistance, explaining that her husband "dropped dead in a field" and that she was left with a mortgaged farm and five young children to raise.

9,918. Troxell, Belle Alexander
Papers. 1857-1951. 9 folders.
Open. Unpublished guide.
University of Missouri Library, State Historical Society of Missouri.
Troxell was a clubwoman. Autobiographical sketch of Nannie Tidd, written in 1951 when she was 86; photos; advertisements for "Parisian Perfect Form" corsets and the St. Louis Button Company; club programs; and clippings. Includes programs of the Tuesday (women's) Club, the United Daughters of the Confederacy, the Missouri LWV, the Columbia Garden Club, the Alliance Woman's Club Company, and the Philalaethean Society, a woman's literary club at the University of Missouri.

9,919. United Daughters of the Confederacy, John S. Marmaduke Chapter
Records. ?-1929. 2 vols.
Open. Unpublished guide.
University of Missouri Library, State Historical Society of Missouri.
Scrapbooks containing photos, programs, and clippings include items in commemoration of the Civil War and others concerning the Chapter's members and activities. Separate clippings concern the controversy caused when a Negro woman attended a White House tea party; Belle Boyd and other female Confederate spies; Sarah King Quantrill, wife of Confederate raider William Clarke Quantrill; Lady Astor, an American-born peeress; the University of Virginia's exclusion of women; Wesleyan in Georgia, said to be the world's first chartered women's college; Lucy Mathilda Kenny, who served in the Confederate army with her husband; Nancy Coonsman Hahn, a sculptor who designed a Missouri monument for France; and Florence Nightingale, pioneer of professional nursing care.

9,920. Vanarsdale, Susan D.
Papers. 1847-55. 1 vol.
Open. Unpublished guide.
University of Missouri Library, State Historical Society of Missouri.
Diary of Vanarsdale (1824-56), written in Mexico, MO, and at various points in Illinois and Indiana, includes notes about family and personal matters, local people, and religious activities, sermons, and temperance lectures. One of the pages includes a discussion of the women's rights movement and of Lucy Stone, both of which she denounced. Also includes a genealogical introduction apparently written by a niece. Vanarsdale occasionally wrote for newspaper publication.

9,921. Watson, Catherine, and Watson, Cyrus
Papers. 1836-37. 1 vol.
Open. Unpublished guide.
University of Missouri Library, State Historical Society of Missouri.
Letters from Catherine Watson and her husband Cyrus in Louisiana, Missouri, and Springfield and Bloomington, IL, to friends and relatives include references to the illnesses and deaths of Mary Pond and Catherine Watson, medical practices during the 1830s, the frontier life of a minister, and devotional sentiments.

9,922. White, Cornelia C.
Papers. 1913-31. 1 vol.
Open. Unpublished guide.
University of Missouri Library, State Historical Society of Missouri.
Reminiscences of White (1860-1931) concern her early childhood in Cazenovia, NY, and childhood adventures and the punishments that followed. Also includes letters from White to J. Christian Bay, a photo of White, printed articles, and an obituary of White.

9,923. Women's Society of Christian Service, Methodist Church
Papers. 1879-1971. 147 folders and 248 vols.
Open. Unpublished guide.
University of Missouri Library, State Historical Society of Missouri.
Minutes, correspondence from 1940 to 1944, committee and officers' reports, programs, pamphlets, and published volumes of the state-level organization of the Society. Includes a pamphlet concerning the status of women in the Methodist church. Bulk of the material dates from 1940 to 1968.

9,924. Women's Suffrage
Papers. Ca. 1880. 6-page item.
Open. Unpublished guide.
University of Missouri Library, State Historical Society of Missouri.
Handwritten essay presents arguments against equal rights for women, contending that women would have to be "brought down" to be made equal. The essay states that eastern women who advocate equal rights do not believe in the principle but support it because their beauty has faded and they must "battle for their own support." According to the essay, the lecture circuit provides a lucrative living for such women.

9,925. Young Ladies' Philalaethean Society
Records. 1885-95. 1 vol.
Open. Unpublished guide.
University of Missouri Library, State Historical Society of Missouri.
Minutes and membership lists of this literary society.

9,926. Alvord
Papers. 1760-1962. 1452 folders, 13 boxes, and 6 vols.
Open. Unpublished guide.
University of Missouri Library, Western Historical Manuscripts Collection.
Genealogy became the primary interest of Idress Adaline (Head) Alvord (1874-?), curator of the Missouri Historical Society, following her husband's death in 1928. Correspondence, including that pertaining to her work with Missouri historian Louis Houck, her position as curator, her husband before their marriage, and her family genealogy, as well as writings and other material.

9,927. American Association of University Women
Records. 1921- . 451 folders and 1 vol.
Open. Unpublished guide.
University of Missouri Library, Western Historical Manuscripts Collection.
Records of the AAUW Missouri division, founded in 1922, make up 75 percent of the collection, while material of the AAUW Southwest central region and the International Federation of University Women constitute the remainder. Includes material of the economic and legal status of women committee and items related to the Festival of Missouri Women in the Arts, which was held in 1974.

9,928. American Council on Education, War Service Opportunities
Records. 1942-43. 1 vol.
Open. Unpublished guide.
University of Missouri Library, Western Historical Manuscripts Collection.
Newsletters containing information about the government's personnel needs during WWII and about qualifications required by various services open to young men and women.

9,929. Atchison, David Rice
Papers. 1837-1953. 19 folders and 1 microfilm reel.
Open. Unpublished guide.
University of Missouri Library, Western Historical Manuscripts Collection.
Personal and political correspondence of Atchison (1807-86), a lawyer, judge, and two-term US senator from Missouri. Includes correspondence from Elizabeth A. (Relfe) Linn, widow of Lewis Fields Linn, a physician who was a US senator from Missouri from 1834 to 1843. Elizabeth Linn's letters concern her husband and his political adversary and Senate colleague Thomas Hart Benton of Missouri. Linn wrote that she greatly resented the fact that Benton delivered the eulogy following her husband's death in 1843.

9,930. Baker, Thomas Frazier, III
Papers. 1959-67. 716 folders and 8 vols.
Open. Unpublished guide.
University of Missouri Library, Western Historical Manuscripts Collection.
From 1961 to 1966 Baker (1918-) was a Missouri state representative from Stoddard County. Correspondence from his campaign and legislative term includes letters from constituents concerning pending legislation and welfare assistance, the interim report of the Missouri Committee on the Status of Women, a letter from the LWV on reapportionment, and a pamphlet about tax-supported birth control services.

9,931. Beauchamp Family
Papers. 1832-94. 6 folders.
Open. Unpublished guide.
University of Missouri Library, Western Historical Manuscripts Collection.
Family correspondence includes a letter from Dolly Beauchamp to her son John discussing family news and difficulties, a letter describing the illness and death of Catherine Beauchamp and a trip by Dolly Beauchamp to Tennessee, letters concerning the education of Edwin and Clara Beauchamp, letters of Henrietta Dunlap and her family in Paris, TN, and material pertaining to Dolly Beauchamp's death and the settlement of her estate.

9,932. Bell, C. Jasper
Papers. 1934-48. 9022 folders.
Open. Unpublished guide.
University of Missouri Library, Western Historical Manuscripts Collection.
Correspondence and other papers of Bell (1885-1978), a US representative from Missouri from 1935 to 1949. Includes correspondence with Fannie Fox, a former orthopedic surgical supervisor, concerning her research on the culture, society, dialects, religion, and geographical conditions of Dakar, Senegal; correspondence with Margaret Chase Smith; correspondence about equal rights for women, world war widows, and dependent children; widows' pension claims; material relating to the dismissal of married persons working for the same governmental agency; and copies of the Nurses Selective Act and a House of Representatives bill to establish a national charter for US Army war mothers.

9,933. Bennett, Marion Tinsley
Papers. 1941-48. 1492 folders and 70 vols.
Open. Unpublished guide.
University of Missouri Library, Western Historical Manuscripts Collection.
Congressional correspondence and papers of Philip Allen Bennett (1881-1942), a congressman who died before he could serve his second term, and his son Marion Bennett (1914-), who succeeded his father in office. Contains information about Republican women, housewives complaining of shortages, women voters, a trust fund established by a man for his sister and his criticism of another sister for profligacy, the Fairfield divorce, and the University of Missouri women's working unit. Also contains a critique of women's organizations.

9,934. Blair, James Thomas, Jr.
Papers. 1957-61. 5152 folders and 25 vols.
Open. Unpublished guide.
University of Missouri Library, Western Historical Manuscripts Collection.
Gubernatorial papers of Blair (1902-62), governor of Missouri from 1957 to 1961, include letters from Leonor Sullivan, a US representative; material concerning the naming of Blair's mother as Missouri Mother of the Year in 1958; crank letters on topics such as eligible daughters and prostitution; items pertaining to the LWV, the National Catholic Women's Union, the Missouri Association for Social Welfare, the United Daughters of the Confederacy, the International Ladies' Garment Workers' Union, the AAUW, and the State Board of Nursing; and material concerning divorce, legal help for indigents, juveniles and parental responsibility, women's complaints about their husbands, annulments, child marriage, the women's prison at Tipton, striptease acts, marriage regulations, and the problems of hiring a woman as assistant state service officer.

9,935. Bradshaw, Doris Crump
Papers. 1930-62. 162 folders and 2 vols.
Open. Unpublished guide.
University of Missouri Library, Western Historical Manuscripts Collection.
Bradshaw, a librarian, was an active participant in civic and women's groups, particularly the AAUW, and her civic, professional, and organizational papers and scrapbooks reflect these activities. Bradshaw studied at the Los Angeles Library School and worked in several California public libraries before entering the University of Missouri in 1923. She graduated with a bachelor's degree in journalism in 1925 and in 1926 married William L. Bradshaw, a political scientist who became dean of the University's school of business and public administration. Their son William L. Bradshaw, Jr., was born in 1935. Doris Bradshaw worked as part-time cataloger at the Columbia Public Library from 1942 to 1946, and devoted the remainder of her time to various organizations. She chaired state AAUW committees from 1945 to 1951 and was a member of the Columbia LWV, the Columbia Public Library Board, the Missouri Library Association, the Fortnightly Club, the Columbia Garden Club, and the DAR.

9,936. Brady, Thomas A.
Papers. 1910-59. 958 folders.
Open. Unpublished guide.
University of Missouri Library, Western Historical Manuscripts Collection.
Brady (1902-64) was a professor of history and vice-president of the University of Missouri. Correspondence, bulletins, and reports about University affairs, including several letters from University applicants concerning the women's housing shortage, reports of the director of student affairs for women and of the committee on student housing concerning housing for men and women, a constitution of the women students' association, and a paper concerning activities of college women's Greek-letter societies.

9,937. Brannock, Lizzia E.
Papers. 1864. 6-page item.
Open. Unpublished guide.
University of Missouri Library, Western Historical Manuscripts Collection.
Letter in which Brannock, writing from Chapel Hill, MO, to her brother Edwin, describes the desolate condition of Missouri, her husband's imprisonment by the Union Army in St. Louis, and her attempts to support her family.

9,938. Cannon, Clarence A.
Papers. 1896-1964. 3300 folders and 124 vols.
Partially closed. Unpublished guide.

University of Missouri Library, Western Historical Manuscripts Collection.
Public and private papers of Cannon (1879-1964), a Democratic congressman from Missouri's ninth district from 1923 to 1964 who earlier had worked at Stephens College, a women's school in Columbia. Includes letters from Cannon to his wife and daughters, correspondence with the ninth district Women's Democratic Club, and correspondence concerning women's suffrage; notes and copies of recruitment pamphlets Cannon wrote for Stephens College from 1904 to 1908; material concerning Cannon's daughter's marriage, his attitude on public morality, a loan for a women's dormitory at Northeast Missouri State Teachers College in Kirksville, the work of Catholic nuns, and Leonor K. Sullivan; and clippings about the death in 1930 of Congressman Steadman, the last Civil War veteran to serve in Congress, and notes on Cannon's efforts to have Steadman's daughter fill his unexpired term. Also includes clippings relating to women in politics, farm life, professional careers, and the home; a legislative reference report on pioneer women; and biographical sketches of women prominent in government, women who were famous by age 30, and Democratic party women.

9,939. Carter, William R.
Collection. 1867-1917. 23 folders.
Open. Unpublished guide.
University of Missouri Library, Western Historical Manuscripts Collection.
Statistics, reports, and other material compiled by Carter on the subject of the University of Missouri, particularly the Normal School. Includes course lists and descriptions, entrance requirements, degrees and certificates, information on summer school courses and attendance, and discussion of the graduate department. "Provisions for Women" reports explain that all University departments, except military science and tactics, were open to women. Six rooms were furnished as "waiting rooms" for ladies; one of these was a gymnasium for physical culture. During lecture hours, young ladies not attending lecture sessions were required to be in the waiting rooms, the library, or at their residences. In the early years, boarding facilities were available only through arrangement with local families.

9,940. Caulfield, Henry S.
Papers. 1904-66. 117 folders.
Access restricted. Unpublished guide.
University of Missouri Library, Western Historical Manuscripts Collection.
Personal, political, and legal papers of Caulfield (1873-1966), governor of Missouri from 1929 to 1933. Includes laws regarding employment of women in dramshops, speeches delivered before the DAR, and material regarding the treatment of women prisoners in Missouri, divorce, women and their importance, and Caulfield's daughter's trip to Europe.

9,941. Chomeau, Henri
Papers. 1869-1956. 5 folders.
Open. Unpublished guide.
University of Missouri Library, Western Historical Manuscripts Collection.
Papers of Chomeau include his correspondence with Roswell M. Field concerning activities at the University of Missouri, a proposed trip to Europe, social gossip, and Eugene Field. Making frequent reference to young ladies attending school in Columbia, Chomeau and Field describe the ladies and advise each other on their social affairs. Also contains an essay against women's suffrage.

9,942. Christian College
Records. 1847-1959. 462 folders and 17 vols.
Open. Unpublished guide.
University of Missouri Library, Western Historical Manuscripts Collection.
Records of this women's college, founded in Columbia in 1851, contain minute and composition books, student publications, photos of the College, scrapbooks, bulletins, catalogs, student handbooks, directories, and clippings from the Civil War era. Specific items include biographical data about Marion Hertig and a description of her job as the College social director; clippings concerning the life and work of sculptor Vinnie Ream; samples of essays and poetry by students, including "Women's Sphere of Energy Should Be Enlarged"; faculty notes describing faculty training and positions from 1893 to 1951; a faculty article on the health of college women; notes on the relationship between Columbia Female Academy and Stephens College, which is located in Columbia; a description of the Civil War years at Christian College; a remembrance of 1880 college days; a history of the College; and copies of the school paper. Also contains information about the school's centennial, which included a speech by US Senator J. William Fulbright of Arkansas, an alumnae tea, an Ivy Chain ceremony, and a "Small Boys" reunion.

9,943. Clay Seminary
Records. 1855-64. 18 items.
Open. Unpublished guide.
University of Missouri Library, Western Historical Manuscripts Collection.
Apparently founded in 1855, the Seminary was a young ladies school located in Liberty, MO. Catalog, items concerning commencement exercises and exhibitions of the Eunomian Literary Society, and advertising circulars. The circulars and catalog describe all aspects of the students' study, schedule, and discipline. A list of students and a testimonial from the board of visitors are included in the catalog.

9,944. Cochran, Betty Holmes: "The Cecile Taylor Circle of King's Daughters, 1948-69"
Papers. 1969. 21-page item.
Open. Unpublished guide.
University of Missouri Library, Western Historical Manuscripts Collection.
A history of the Circle of King's Daughters, a service and social organization, provides details about the formation of the Circle in 1948, its membership, officers, projects, and creation of a subordinate chapter.

9,945. Columbia Female Academy
Records. 1841-53. 2 folders.
Open. Unpublished guide.
University of Missouri Library, Western Historical Manuscripts Collection.
Founded in 1833, this Columbia school was closed in 1854. Copy of an address which J. L. Yantis, a clergyman, delivered in 1841 during the examination of the Academy's pupils and an 1853 Academy catalog. The speech mentions the public's changing perspective concerning the duties of women and the education women need in order to perform their roles. The catalog lists the school's trustees, instructors, pupils and their places of residence, courses of study, and other information.

9,946. Columbia League of Women Voters
Records. 1923-74. 68 folders and 17 vols.
Open. Unpublished guide.
University of Missouri Library, Western Historical Manuscripts Collection.
Minutes of the Columbia LWV and scrapbooks of local clippings make up the bulk of the collection. Miscellaneous Columbia LWV papers and publications of the national LWV are also included. One of the topics reflected in the material is government and the legal status of women.

9,947. Columbia Women's Political Caucus
Records. 1971-77. 41 folders.
Open. Unpublished guide.
University of Missouri Library, Western Historical Manuscripts Collection.
Formed in 1972, the Caucus encourages women to participate in the political system, to seek elective and appointive office, and to support candidates and legislation to improve the status of women. Correspondence, candidate questionnaires, newsletters, pamphlets, and other items of the Caucus and its affiliated organizations, the Missouri State Women's Political Caucus and the National Women's Political Caucus, primarily focus on the Equal Rights Amendment. Questionnaires returned by Missouri legislative candidates in 1976 reflect their opinions on various women's issues.

9,948. Connaway, John Waldo
Papers. 1878-1944. 158 folders and 2 vols.
Open. Unpublished guide.
University of Missouri Library, Western Historical Manuscripts Collection.
Correspondence and papers of Connaway (1859-1947), a professor of veterinary science and comparative medicine at the Missouri University agricultural experiment station, contain letters and post cards concerning his wife Eleanor (Ficklin) Connaway and his daughter Penelope. Includes replies to Eleanor Connaway's letters urging attendance at the 1930 reunion of the University of Missouri class of 1885, a letter from John Connaway to a niece concerning his wife's death, and letters he wrote concerning Penelope's mental condition and her treatment.

9,949. Croy, Homer
Papers. 1936-64. 18 folders.
Access restricted. Unpublished guide.
University of Missouri Library, Western Historical Manuscripts Collection.
Correspondence, notes, manuscripts, anecdotes, and clippings of Croy (1883-1965), a newspaper reporter and author. Includes a draft of "The Bandit's Bride," which concerns Frank James's wife, and "The Story of Susan O. Hall," who died in 1852 during an overland journey to California and whose husband erected a monument in her honor. Also contains notes on an interview with Mrs. Jesse James, Jr.

9,950. Curtis, Thomas B.
Papers. 1950-69. 28,118 folders.
Access restricted. Unpublished guide.
University of Missouri Library, Western Historical Manuscripts Collection.
Correspondence with constituents of Curtis (1911-), Republican US representative from Missouri from 1950 to 1969, and committee records, principally items of the Ways and Means and Joint Economic committees. Includes private bills introduced by Curtis, some of which concern women, and material pertaining to deductions for child-care expenses when a wife is disabled, the Equal Rights Amendment, the LWV, the Nellie Salmon Day Nursery, and Ruth Shelby.

9,951. Dalton, John M.
Papers. 1921-65. 11,967 folders and 60 vols.
Open. Unpublished guide.
University of Missouri Library, Western Historical Manuscripts Collection.
Correspondence, personal and official papers, photos, and clippings of Dalton (1900-72), who served as governor of Missouri from 1961 to 1965 and as the state's attorney general. Includes correspondence relating to the "equal pay" movement by Southwestern Bell Telephone Company employees to abolish community wage scales; information about two women's schools, Stephens and Christian colleges; and material concerning the Missouri State Penitentiary for Women at Tipton, maternal and child care, a training school for girls, marriage and divorce, the

Missouri Commission on the Status of Women, and control of sororities and fraternities in Missouri public schools. Also includes claims of sexual and racial discrimination from 1960 to 1965 in the choosing of officers for the Department of Corrections Board of Probation and Parole and material on Gladys Gooding, longtime organist for the Brooklyn Dodgers.

9,952. Daniels, Agnes Powell Williams Jones
Papers. 1876-1955. 1 folder.
Open. Unpublished guide.
University of Missouri Library, Western Historical Manuscripts Collection.
Biography of Daniels (1827-94), an immigrant and pioneer farm wife in Missouri; copies of letters by Daniels and other family members; and a 1955 Welsh-American newspaper. The biography records that Agnes Powell married Richard Williams and emigrated with him from Wales to the US in ca. 1845. Her husband died shortly after their arrival. She married Francis Jones in 1852 in St. Louis and bore him a son in 1853. Jones died in 1855. In 1856 she married David Daniels, a widower with a daughter, and they moved to Morgan County, MO, two years later. The Danielses had six children. One of the newspaper's articles concerns women's Welsh clubs in America.

9,953. Daughters of the American Revolution
Records. 1946-71?. Several folders and 2 vols.
Open. No guide.
University of Missouri Library, Western Historical Manuscripts Collection.
Treasurers' records of the Columbia chapter of the DAR include information about receipts and disbursements, notes and post cards concerning the transfer of members from chapter to chapter and payment of dues, financial reports of the chapter to the state organization, and bank forms.

9,954. Davis, Amanda
Papers. 1895-1917. 12 folders.
Open. Unpublished guide.
University of Missouri Library, Western Historical Manuscripts Collection.
Family correspondence, tax receipts, and school material of Davis, a teacher, and sales material for "The Century Book of Facts." The correspondence contains a discussion of possible careers for young women and of schoolwork; the school material includes Davis's grades for 1897, teachers contracts, recommendations for teachers, and acceptances of positions.

9,955. Davis, Margaret (Stout)
Papers. 1952. 12-page item.
Open. Unpublished guide.
University of Missouri Library, Western Historical Manuscripts Collection.
Autobiography of Davis (1870-?), a homemaker and the daughter of Ira and Sarah Elizabeth Smith Stout. Davis describes a childhood marked by her father's shifts between farm and city work; her courtship with Will Davis, a young cattle buyer whom she married; her husband's business interests, sometimes in partnership with her father; her work in their Bakersville, MO, general store; the birth and death of children; religious conversion; and her life at 81 when she wrote the autobiography.

9,956. Dearmont, Russell L.
Papers. 1929-65. 5323 folders and 20 packages.
Access restricted. Unpublished guide.
University of Missouri Library, Western Historical Manuscripts Collection.
A Missouri state senator in 1928 and Democratic candidate for governor in 1932, Dearmont (1891-1967) was counsel to officers of the Missouri Pacific Railroad and was a member of the boards of Lindenwood and Westminster colleges, the St. Louis Police Commission, and the American Bar Association judiciary committee. Includes correspondence of Elsie Belle [Mrs. Laurence] McDaniel, the state's Democratic national committeewoman, concerning the role of women in politics; letters and testimonials in connection with McDaniel's bid for the position of collector of internal revenue for the eastern district; correspondence of Dearmont's secretary Irene Peterson concerning the National Business and Professional Women's Clubs; a national radio speech by Dorothy Thompson supporting the Roosevelt-Truman ticket in 1944; and material concerning the LWV, the National Business Woman Conference, and [Miss] Catherine Lorenz and an investigation of state hospitals.

9,957. Decker, Perl D.
Papers. 1897-1935. 53 folders and 5 vols.
Open. Unpublished guide.
University of Missouri Library, Western Historical Manuscripts Collection.
Decker (1875-1934) was a lawyer and a Democratic congressman from Missouri from 1912 to 1919. Correspondence; speeches, including a congressional speech by Decker on woman suffrage and remarks about the Arkansas apple blossom queen of 1926; and clippings.

9,958. Dickmann, Bernard "Barney" F.
Papers. 1900-71. 128 folders and 23 vols.
Access restricted. Unpublished guide.
University of Missouri Library, Western Historical Manuscripts Collection.
Dickmann (1888-1971) was mayor of St. Louis from 1933 to 1941. Correspondence, diaries, scrapbooks of newspapers covering his mayoral terms, clippings, books, and other items, including a pamphlet concerning prominent women in early St. Louis and a 1940 LWV report about the duties and organization of city government.

9,959. Dierssen, Anna
Papers. 1907-65. 6 vols.
Open. Unpublished guide.
University of Missouri Library, Western Historical Manuscripts Collection.
Papers of Dierssen (1884-1969), a homemaker, include "Missouri University and I," which describes the 1907-08 school year's social life and courses and contains handwritten themes in German and English; a diary for 1911 to 1918 concerning her membership in the Wednesday Club, a women's literary group in Cape Girardeau, MO; a novelette of remembrances of a 100-year-old woman; books of limericks and her poems; and an account of a trip to a family reunion in West Virginia in 1961.

9,960. Dobbs, Ella Victoria
Papers. 1923-61. 40 folders and 1 vol.
Open. Unpublished guide.
University of Missouri Library, Western Historical Manuscripts Collection.
A professor of applied arts at Missouri University, Dobbs (1866-1952) was a writer, artist, community and state leader, and a founder of Pi Lambda Theta, a national association for women in education. Correspondence, notebooks used in lectures, manuscript material for her book *The Creative Arts in Democratic Living,* pamphlets, and Verna M. Wulfekammer's biography of Dobbs. Includes letters from friends, other art teachers, and fellow members of Pi Lambda Theta.

9,961. Doble and Lucas
Papers. 1856-65. 1 microfilm reel.
Open. Unpublished guide.
University of Missouri Library, Western Historical Manuscripts Collection.
Correspondence between Margaret McFarland Doble and her cousin Elizabeth E. Lucas and between Lucas and Doble's brother-in-law John Doble, whom she never met. The Lucas-John Doble correspondence forms the bulk of the collection.

9,962. Donnell, Forrest C.
Papers. 1941-45. 7641 folders and 15 vols.
Access restricted. Unpublished guide.
University of Missouri Library, Western Historical Manuscripts Collection.
Files and papers generated during Donnell's term as governor of Missouri from 1941 to 1945 include correspondence of Frances Perkins, secretary of labor; the US War Department, concerning the Women's Army Auxiliary Corps; a woman who was attempting to have her husband drafted; women applying to be army hostesses and nurses; WWI widows requesting compensation; Mrs. Lee Johnston, chief investigator for the Commission for the Blind, replying to a request concerning the eleemosynary board; persons complaining about conditions at the Industrial Home for Negro Girls; [Miss] Edith Massey, a Negro seeking admission to the University of Missouri; [Miss] Marion Martin of the Republican National Committee; Carol Bates of the Missouri Welfare League; Mrs. Ira A. Jones, president of the Missouri Commission for the Blind; and Mary Rust of the Daughters of American Colonists. Also contains material pertaining to a dispute between the International Ladies' Garment Workers' Union and Weil-Kalter Manufacturing Company, information concerning the appointment of Agnes Mae Wilson to the Public Service Commission, and material concerning the WACs, prostitution, venereal disease, St. Louis's No. 1 war mother, maternal and child health, the selection of Margaret Truman over Donnell's daughter to launch a battleship, and maximum working hours for male and female workers.

9,963. Donnelly, Phil M.
Papers. 1944-57. 8235 folders, 17 boxes, and 69 vols.
Open. Unpublished guide.
University of Missouri Library, Western Historical Manuscripts Collection.
Gubernatorial files and departmental correspondence of Donnelly (1891-1961), governor of Missouri from 1945 to 1949 and from 1953 to 1957, include material regarding the death of Donnelly's mother; Mary L. Schoenheit's battle to keep a child out of public schools; Eleanor Roosevelt; women seeking designation as honorary colonels in recognition of their support for Donnelly in his political campaigns; Catholic Gold Star Mothers; the Missouri Democratic Women's Club; the Industrial Home for Girls in Chillicothe, MO; the Industrial Home for Negro Girls in Tipton, MO; transfer of Negro girls to Chillicothe; and divorce law and children.

9,964. Elliff, Joseph D.
Papers. 1906-30. 120 folders.
Open. Unpublished guide.
University of Missouri Library, Western Historical Manuscripts Collection.
Elliff (1863-1959) was an educator at Stephens College, a Columbia women's school. Correspondence, lectures, reports, bulletins, articles, and other papers contain information about work in education and vocational guidance. Includes a 1912 survey of occupations open to 14- to 16-year-old girls written by Harriet Hazen Dodge for the Girls Trade Education League in Boston, a 1912 paper regarding vocational guidance for girls in elementary schools written by Eleanor M. Colleton in Boston, and Stephens College brochures.

9,965. Ellis, Elmer
Papers. 1928-41. 122 folders.
Open. Unpublished guides.
University of Missouri Library, Western Historical Manuscripts Collection.
Correspondence and notes concerning Henry Moore Teller, a US senator from Colorado, compiled by Ellis in preparation for a book about Teller. Includes correspondence of Teller's two

surviving children [Mrs.] Emma Tyler and James H. Teller and references to Teller's young wife Harriet, women's suffrage, and Helen Hunt Jackson.

9,966. Ellis, Sallie F.
Papers. 1864-1932. 3 folders.
Open. Unpublished guide.
University of Missouri Library, Western Historical Manuscripts Collection.
Notebook and loose notes on music, recipes, remedies, accounts, and business; school reports; post cards; and clippings.

9,967. Elmwood Seminary
Records. 1911-14. 3 vols. and 59 items.
Open. Unpublished guide.
University of Missouri Library, Western Historical Manuscripts Collection.
Organized in 1885 in Farmington, MO, under the auspices of the Presbyterian Church, this female academy offered a four-year academic course and two years of college work; in 1911-12 the school consisted of 99 pupils and a faculty of eight. Expense accounts, notices of meetings, reports, correspondence, and books. [Miss] Maud Montgomery, [Miss] Lulu May Winn, and [Miss] Eudora M. Dickson were presidents of the Seminary during the three years covered by the collection. O. W. Bleeck was secretary of the board.

9,968. Fortnightly Club
Records. 1895-1971. 3 folders and 1 vol.
Open. Unpublished guide.
University of Missouri Library, Western Historical Manuscripts Collection.
Constitution, bylaws, minutes from 1964 to 1971, and annual programs of this social and service organization, which was founded in 1892 and consisted of women faculty and staff members and the wives of faculty and staff members at the University of Missouri.

9,969. Fortnightly Club, Newcomers Group
Records. 1935-57. 3 vols.
Open. Unpublished guide.
University of Missouri Library, Western Historical Manuscripts Collection.
Minute books of a division of the Club, a social and service organization founded in 1892 that included women members of the University of Missouri faculty and staff and wives of faculty and staff members.

9,970. France Family
Papers. 1889-1905. 4 vols.
Open. Unpublished guide.
University of Missouri Library, Western Historical Manuscripts Collection.
In the France family papers are Sara France's diary and a scrapbook and picture album compiled while she was at the Ogantz School in Pennsylvania from 1889 to 1892, a diary of [Mrs.] France for 1889 to 1893 containing entries about everyday life, and a scrapbook of French newspaper clippings.

9,971. Gano, John Allen, Family
Papers. 1794-1948. 128 folders and 2 microfilm reels.
Open. Unpublished guide.
University of Missouri Library, Western Historical Manuscripts Collection.
Correspondence, a diary, accounts and bills, advertisements, circulars, and publications of Gano, a Bourbon County, KY, evangelist of the early Disciples of Christ Church. Includes letters from Gano's wife Mary Catherine Gano, from Mary E. Gano at Woodford College, and from his sisters. Gano's letters pertain to his family life; his children's college days in Bethany, VA; his conversion, baptism, and life as a preacher; and other matters.

9,972. Gentry, North Todd
Papers. 1803-1947. 233 folders.
Open. Unpublished guide.
University of Missouri Library, Western Historical Manuscripts Collection.
Correspondence, legal papers, speeches, anecdotes, photos, and programs of Gentry (1866-1944), a Boone County, MO, lawyer and local historian who served as state attorney general from 1925 to 1928 and became a member of the state Supreme Court in 1928. Includes legal material relating to women, letters of his daughter Mary Gentry, and information about other women, among them Ann Gentry, a widow who raised her children while serving as postmaster and running a boardinghouse and tavern. Contains biographical information about Ann Gentry, with references to Lucy, a Negro woman who stayed with Ann Gentry after she gained her freedom. Also contains letters of Mary Gentry immediately before and after the death of her first child; North Gentry's legal opinion on whether it was a crime for an unmarried man and woman to register at a hotel as husband and wife; letters to North Gentry supporting his stand on the sex questionnaire "scandal" at the University of Missouri in 1921; material concerning [Miss] Lucy Ann Wales's employment as a preceptress of Columbia Female Academy in 1833; an obituary for Matilda (Ferguson) Todd; biographical material on Mary Todd, daughter of Roger North Todd and Matilda (Ferguson) Todd; a biography of Minnie Martin Baity; a biography of Meredith Poindexter Gentry by Susie Gentry; lists of types of legal cases North Gentry handled, including rape, assault to rape, seduction, carnal knowledge, defiling a ward, taking away a female, and bigamy; an address concerning Columbia Female Academy and Lucy Wales; a record of divorce laws in Missouri; and arguments about reasons why women should support the Republican party.

9,973. Gentry, Richard Harrison
Papers. 1837-43. 1 folder.
Open. Unpublished guide.
University of Missouri Library, Western Historical Manuscripts Collection.
Copies of love letters exchanged by Gentry of Columbia and Mary Wyatt of Pinckney, MO, before their marriage in 1843. Also includes a letter to Gentry from his sister Dorothy while he was a student at the University of Arkansas.

9,974. Gentry, William Richard, Jr.: "Ann Hawkins Gentry"
Papers. 1960. 5-page item.
Open. Unpublished guide.
University of Missouri Library, Western Historical Manuscripts Collection.
The widowed mother of nine children, Ann Gentry (1791-1870) was a pioneer woman, innkeeper, postmaster, and supporter of the University of Missouri. Collection consists of a biographical speech about Gentry, which her great-grandson William Gentry, Jr., gave during the dedication of a Gentry County, MO, roadside park named in her honor.

9,975. Gigous Family
Papers. 1875-77. 1 folder.
Open. Unpublished guide.
University of Missouri Library, Western Historical Manuscripts Collection.
Correspondence written to George Gigous and his wife Mary Gigous by her sister M. E. Wagner, his friend Amos Castle, and his cousin Daniel Stull about farming, agricultural prices, immigration, rural education, and rural life in Otter Creek, IA, and Maryville, MO. Also includes typed notes about the family.

9,976. Givens, Spencer H.
Papers. 1816-1911. 35 folders.
Open. Unpublished guide.
University of Missouri Library, Western Historical Manuscripts Collection.
Levin Cropper was a justice of the peace in Cooper County, MO, during the 1820s. Family and business correspondence, tax bills, notes, naturalization papers, a German passport, and records of county office appointments by Missouri governors, indentures for apprenticeships, and public and private land transactions. Includes correspondence of Mary and Levin Cropper from their children Sara, Vincent, Jancintha Simonton, and Mary Stephens; legal divorce papers, signed by the husband to the wife's father and given for $1; letters to Levin Cropper from grandchildren about everyday life; an indenture for an apprenticeship to Cropper, who was to instruct a girl in housewifery and housekeeping; and a notice of a sheriff's sale of one-seventh of a Negro girl's services.

9,977. Glenn Family
Papers. 1845-1930. 79 folders.
Open. Unpublished guide.
University of Missouri Library, Western Historical Manuscripts Collection.
John H. Glenn and his son Robert C. Glenn ran a mercantile business in Mound City, MO, while another son Addison N. Glenn operated a farm implement store in Falls City, NE. Included with personal and business papers are personal correspondence of Bella Mitchell Glenn, the wife of Robert Glenn, and a diary she kept in early 1877 before her marriage.

9,978. Greene, Flora Hartley
Papers. 1905-31. 216 folders.
Open. Unpublished guide.
University of Missouri Library, Western Historical Manuscripts Collection.
A special agent in the US Children's Bureau and counselor of the American Home Economics Association, [Mrs. Charles W.] Greene (1865-1948) was a Columbia resident and an officer of local, state, and national organizations. Correspondence, her master's thesis, bulletins, clippings, and other papers partially pertain to her work in the Missouri Federation of Women's Clubs, the Eugene Field Foundation, the Missouri Society for Crippled Children, and the Missouri Council of Defense. Greene earned bachelor's degrees from Indiana State Normal School and from Stanford University; she received her master's degree from the University of Missouri in 1909. Married in 1895, she and her husband Charles Greene had two sons and one daughter. Flora Greene held many offices in the Missouri Federation of Women's Clubs and served on the state boards of the LWV and the American National Red Cross. She died in Columbia.

9,979. Guthrie, Charles Claude, Sr.
Papers. 1896-1943. 199 folders.
Access restricted. Unpublished guide.
University of Missouri Library, Western Historical Manuscripts Collection.
Guthrie (1880-1963) was a physician, professor of physiology and pharmacology, inventor, and pioneer researcher in vascular surgery. His youngest sister Frances "Fannie" Virginia Guthrie (1885-) worked as his research assistant and, later, as a research and teaching assistant in pathology at the University of Missouri. Correspondence, primarily that between Charles Guthrie, his mother Fannie Hall Guthrie, and his sisters in Missouri, as well as college essays and notes and other personal papers. Fannie V. Guthrie's letters describe her life as a career woman who cared for her aging parents; those of her married sisters describe the growth of their families. Also contains a letter Charlotte Corder wrote to Fannie V. Guthrie in 1917 expressing her dissatisfaction with the female role in society and a letter in which Guthrie describes women's basketball at the University of Missouri and the unwillingness of women to play before male spectators. Fannie V. Guthrie received two

bachelor's degrees and an MA in history. She worked as her brother's research assistant at Washington University in St. Louis and at the University of Pittsburgh until she returned to Columbia in 1912 to care for her parents. She then studied physiology and pathology at the University of Missouri, where she also served as a research and teaching assistant from 1917 until 1923.

9,980. Hagerman and Hayden
Papers. 1852-93. 51 folders.
Open. Unpublished guide.
University of Missouri Library, Western Historical Manuscripts Collection.
Correspondence and papers of B. F. Hagerman, an Alexandria, MO, lawyer, include letters to family and friends from Hagerman's daughter Linnetta "Linnie" Hagerman (1852-?).

9,981. Hale, Allean Lemmon
Papers. Nd. 1 ft.
Closed. No guide.
University of Missouri Library, Western Historical Manuscripts Collection.
Hale, an author, is a member of the board of directors of the Lenoir Home, a retirement center run by the Disciples of Christ church. Correspondence between Hale and Mary Paxton Keeley, a journalist, poet, playwright, and novelist who was the first woman graduate of the University of Missouri school of journalism. Hale's principal book *Petticoat Pioneer* is a history of Christian College, which formerly was a woman's college and now is Columbia College. Hale also has been active in such projects as an historical study of Hull-House in Chicago.

9,982. Hardin, Charles Henry
Papers. 1842-92. 10 folders.
Open. Unpublished guide.
University of Missouri Library, Western Historical Manuscripts Collection.
Governor of Missouri from 1874 until 1876, Hardin (1820-92) was a lawyer and founder of Hardin College in Mexico, MO; his wife was Mary Jenkins Hardin. Correspondence, a diary, unofficial reports written by Charles Hardin, essays, speeches, and a notebook of legal cases in several Missouri counties. Includes correspondence exchanged between the Hardins from 1842 to 1854, a diary in which Mary Hardin made scattered entries from 1854 to 1860, and an essay she wrote concerning a Biblical interpretation of wealth and advice. Her diary pertains to daily activities at home in Fulton, MO, and religious subjects; it also contains recipes.

9,983. Haskell, Agnes Hadley
Papers. 1909-46. 92 folders.
Open. Unpublished guide.
University of Missouri Library, Western Historical Manuscripts Collection.
Interested in cultural and artistic activities, Haskell (1876-1946) was the wife of Herbert S. Hadley, governor of Missouri from 1908 to 1913; after his death in 1927, she married Henry C. Haskell, editor of the *Kansas City Star.* Correspondence; daybooks for the years 1909, 1912, and 1922 to 1946; travel journals; memorabilia; and clippings. Travel descriptions pertain to trips in Canada, Spain, Poland, France, Morocco, Algeria, Venice, and England. Also contains notes on the International Federation of University Women Conference in 1924.

9,984. Hay, Charles Martin
Papers. 1919-33. 442 folders.
Open. Unpublished guide.
University of Missouri Library, Western Historical Manuscripts Collection.
Correspondence, speeches, legal records, clippings, and political material of Hay (1879-1945), a St. Louis attorney; advocate of prohibition; leader in the Methodist Episcopal Church, South; and three-time unsuccessful candidate for the US Senate nomination. Includes political and personal items related to women, among them letters of the Women's Democratic State Committee of Missouri; a letter from Mrs. W. S. Baintree to Mrs. Joshua Barbee about a woman denied a political career because of her sex; letters to Hay's daughter in college; letters from [Mrs.] Laura Edwards, secretary of the Citizens School Tax Campaign Committee; and a copy of a 1932 radio address by Mrs. George Gelhorn, president of the LWV, supporting Hay in the Democratic Senate primary.

9,985. Hearnes, Warren E.
Papers. 1950-72. 686 folders.
Access restricted. Unpublished guide.
University of Missouri Library, Western Historical Manuscripts Collection.
Correspondence and other material that Hearnes (1923-), governor of Missouri from 1965 to 1973, deemed his personal papers. Includes correspondence of and biographical information about his wife Betty Cooper Hearnes.

9,986. Hennings, Thomas C., Jr.
Papers. 1934-60. 482 boxes and 45 vols.
Access restricted. Unpublished guide.
University of Missouri Library, Western Historical Manuscripts Collection.
A lawyer and circuit attorney in St. Louis, Hennings (1903-60) served as a US congressman from 1934 to 1940, as a naval officer during WWII, and as a US senator from 1950 to 1960. Focusing on his senatorial years, his papers include personal and constituent correspondence, speeches, press releases, and political and legislative material. Contains references to the Equal Rights Amendment, nursing legislation and education, the DAR, Mildred Horton, [Mrs.] Leola Breckenridge, pensions for judges' widows, [Mrs.] Ellen Knauff, Cecilia T. Tolentino, Erna and Helene Narr, Heidi G. Connelly, Marie Haddad, Helena Tomasowa, Ester Chan Lee, Ernst and Hanna Fraenkel, Princess Ilena Issarescu, Gertrude Eichorn, Martha So-Shin Hsia, and the Widow of the Month Club.

9,987. Hickman and Bryan
Papers. 1796-1920. 297 folders.
Open. Unpublished guide.
University of Missouri Library, Western Historical Manuscripts Collection.
Personal and business correspondence, legal documents, accounts, tax receipts, and other papers of these families of Louisiana and Missouri landowners and businessmen whose dealings involved slaves, stock, and land. Family members included Peter T. Hickman, Thomas J. Hickman (?-1854), and William P. Hickman (?-1842), three brothers who owned Louisiana plantations; David M., David H., John L., Thomas H., and Thaddeus B. Hickman and Sarah (Hickman) [Mrs. Arch] Young of Boone County, MO; and Morgan Bryan of Kentucky and his sons Milton and William W., who lived in Missouri. The two Hickman families intermarried, while the Bryans were related to the Hickmans of Boone County by marriage. The wives of William P. Hickman, Thomas J. Hickman, and Peter T. Hickman carried on their husbands' estates after the deaths of their spouses. Mrs. Peter T. Hickman came to live in Boone County with her daughters Naomi, Louise, and Amanda; Louise and Amanda married brothers, Thaddeus and Thomas H. Hickman. Cornelia Ann Bryan, who was educated at the Bonne Femme Academy, came from Kentucky in 1827 with her widowed mother Sarah [Mrs. Morgan] Bryan. She married David M. Hickman in 1829, and they had seven children before her husband died in 1851. Fourteen years later she married John M. Robinson, a one-time business partner of her first husband. Collection contains an 1871 agreement in Swedish in which a woman, upon sailing from Sweden, contracted to become a maid for the Thomas H. Hickman family; a book of household accounts of Cornelia (Bryan) Hickman Robinson; letters of Amanda Hickman, mostly from her sisters in New Orleans concerning family matters; and a recipe book and family correspondence of Louise Hickman, who mentions health, travels, and the dilemma of caring for an aged mother.

9,988. Hirth, William
Papers. 1925-34. 276 folders.
Open. Unpublished guide.
University of Missouri Library, Western Historical Manuscripts Collection.
Correspondence, radio speeches, and clippings of Hirth (1875-1940), a farm leader and an organizer and president of the Missouri Farmers Association. Includes a description of the Indiana Farm Board women's organization by Verna Hatch; an article, "Do We Exercise Our Right of Franchise?"; bulletins of the Women's Progressive Farmers Association of Missouri; and Hirth's "A Heart to Heart Talk with the Farm Women of Missouri."

9,989. "History of Reverend William Murphy and His Descendants, 1798-1958"
Papers. Nd. 1 folder.
Open. Unpublished guide.
University of Missouri Library, Western Historical Manuscripts Collection.
Description of Murphy's immigration from Ireland to Virginia and his family's move to the Farmington, MO, area; genealogical listing about the clergyman's second wife Sarah (Barton) Murphy, who after her husband's death moved the family to Ste. Genevieve, MO, where she helped establish the first church west of the Mississippi River; and other material.

9,990. Holeman, Nancy Nash
Papers. 1869-77. 10 folders.
Open. Unpublished guide.
University of Missouri Library, Western Historical Manuscripts Collection.
Copies of correspondence, a diary, recipes, and a clipping of Holeman (1806-?), a homesteader. Includes brief daily accounts of a woman's work, local news, sicknesses, births, deaths, visits, trading, and the weather.

9,991. Holt, Ivan Lee
Papers. 1835-1967. 1505 folders, 4 oversize folders, 12 vols., and 4 recording discs.
Access restricted. Unpublished guide.
University of Missouri Library, Western Historical Manuscripts Collection.
Papers documenting the work of Holt (1886-1967) as pastor of St. John's Methodist Church in St. Louis from 1918 to 1938, bishop of north Texas from 1939 to 1944, and bishop of Missouri from 1944 to 1956. In addition, the collection contains family correspondence and other items concerning his marriages to Leland Burks Holt, Starr B. Carrithers Holt, and Modena M. Rudiswell Holt. Also contains letters from the wife of a missionary concerning the situation in Nanking, China; a letter in which [Miss] Dolly Breitenbaugh describes a plan to colonize part of the western coast of Africa with American Negroes to prevent a racial war; a letter written by a mother to her daughter after learning that the daughter had become a Roman Catholic; data on divorce rates; and other material on the lives and work of women in the Methodist church.

9,992. Hosmer and Hubbard
Papers. 1859-1923. 11 vols.
Open. Unpublished guide.
University of Missouri Library, Western Historical Manuscripts Collection.
Diary of Almyra Hubbard provides a daily account of a high school girl's experience in a Massachusetts public school in 1859; the remaining diaries were written by Elizabeth S. (Viles) Hosmer and include an account of her tour of the British

Isles and European continent in 1881, daily accounts of the Viles-Hosmer family, and notes on the weather and local and national news events. Place designations in the diaries include Waltham, MA, Columbia, and Pasadena, CA.

9,993. Hubble Family
Papers. 1833-1937. 35 folders.
Open. Unpublished guide.
University of Missouri Library, Western Historical Manuscripts Collection.
Correspondence and documents collected by [Miss] Janie Hubble for genealogical research include bylaws of the Missouri Women's Association of Commerce for 1919 and clippings from 1910 and 1911 concerning DAR activities.

9,994. Hull, William "Bill" R., Jr.
Papers. 1954-72. 2160 folders and 15 vols. (microfilm).
Open. Unpublished guide.
University of Missouri Library, Western Historical Manuscripts Collection.
Hull (1906-77) was a US representative from Missouri's sixth congressional district in the 84th through 92nd Congresses. Personal and political papers consist principally of constituent correspondence and include material concerning the Missouri Commission on the Status of Women in 1970.

9,995. Hyde, Arthur Mastick
Papers. 1919-25. 1290 folders.
Open. Unpublished guide.
University of Missouri Library, Western Historical Manuscripts Collection.
Personal and official correspondence of Hyde (1877-1947), a Republican governor of Missouri. Includes letters from rural women recounting problems with moonshiners; resolutions from the annual convention of the Missouri LWV in 1921; letters from Lilla Day Monroe, editor of the *Kansas Woman's Journal* of Topeka, KS, which described itself as "devoted to the interests of Women, Children, and Home"; a letter from Daisy B. Calhoun, president of the Woman's Universal Alliance, concerning plans to build a temple to womanhood with the Mothers' Memorial Tower in Washington, DC; material of the Lucy Stone League, which sought public acceptance of the practice of women retaining their maiden names when they marry; and a 1922 copy of *The Woman Patriot,* which was "dedicated to the Defense of The Family and The State AGAINST Feminism and Socialism."

9,996. Hyde, Ira B.
Papers. 1856-1924. 37 folders.
Open. Unpublished guide.
University of Missouri Library, Western Historical Manuscripts Collection.
A Princeton, MO, lawyer and US representative, Hyde (1838-1926) was the father of Arthur M. Hyde, a Missouri governor, and Laurance M. Hyde, a state supreme court justice. School, speech, legal, and political papers, including lyceum material concerning celibacy and women's rights and notes and speeches about women's suffrage.

9,997. Johnston, Eva
Papers. Nd. 14 folders.
Open. Unpublished guide.
University of Missouri Library, Western Historical Manuscripts Collection.
Johnston (1865-1941) was a student and professor at the University of Missouri. Lectures on such topics as women's education and wages, popular superstitions, and Latin and Greek literature and dramatists; speeches; and translations, including one of Terence's *Hecyra.*

9,998. Johnston, Eva
Papers. 1893-1926. 4 items.
Open. Unpublished guide.
University of Missouri Library, Western Historical Manuscripts Collection.
An assistant and associate professor of Latin after 1899, Johnston (1865-1941) served as dean of women students at Missouri University from 1912 to 1923. Copy of a commencement address that Johnston gave before the 18 women of the class of 1923 at Hosmer Hall in St. Louis, a speech which [Miss] Louise Nardin gave during the dedication of a portrait of Johnston at the University in 1926, and two copybooks containing a translation of Euripides' *Medea.* In the commencement speech, Johnston told the women that the results of an educational curriculum should be development of the mind, body, and spirit. In her dedicatory speech, Nardin notes that a page about Johnston would be included in the Founder's Book of the AAUW and explains why men as well as women were allowed to contribute to a Johnston memorial.

9,999. Kaylor, Wesley
Papers. 1857-63. 32 items.
Open. Unpublished guide.
University of Missouri Library, Western Historical Manuscripts Collection.
Correspondence, including an 1857 letter from Emeline Kaylor to her daughter Margaret, who was traveling to school, about a recent illness, local news, and visitors at her home. Bulk of the collection consists of letters written by Wesley Kaylor, a Union solider, to his family in Newark, MO. Some of his letters give his opinion of various girls and what he thought their opinion of him was.

10,000. Keeley, Mary (Paxton)
Papers. Nd. 7.5 ft.
Closed. No guide.
University of Missouri Library, Western Historical Manuscripts Collection.
Born Mary Gentry Paxton, Keeley (1886-) is a journalist, poet, playwright, and novelist who was the first woman graduate of the University of Missouri school of journalism. Correspondence, diaries, articles, photos, clippings, and miscellaneous items. Includes correspondence with J. C. Penney, Harry Truman, Tom McAfee, and Rose Wilder Lane, and clippings by and about Keeley and other newspaperwomen, among them Sue Gentry and Dorothy Roe Lewis. Keeley grew up in Independence, MO, as a close friend of Bess Wallace, later Mrs. Harry Truman. After graduation from college, she was a reporter for the Kansas City *Post,* and she taught journalism for many years at Christian College, a women's school in Columbia. Keeley spent 10 months overseas as a YMCA canteen worker during WWI. She and her husband Edmund Burke Keeley (?-ca. 1921), whom she married in 1919, had one son, John Paxton Keeley.

10,001. Lemmon, C. E.
Papers. 1908-74. 1503 folders (microfilm).
Open. Unpublished guide.
University of Missouri Library, Western Historical Manuscripts Collection.
Clarence Eugene Lemmon (1888-1963) was a Disciples of Christ minister. Correspondence, lecture notes, sermon outlines and typescripts, and other papers provide information about Christian churches at Hastings, NE, St. Louis, and Columbia, and about the World Council of Churches and other church groups. Also contains material about Christian College, a women's school in Columbia; the Christian Women's Fellowship; and the United Church Women in Columbia. The originals of Lemmon's papers are located at the Disciples of Christ Historical Society in Nashville.

10,002. Lemmon, Constance Harlan
Papers. 1910-74. 80 folders (microfilm).
Open. Unpublished guide.
University of Missouri Library, Western Historical Manuscripts Collection.
Lemmon (1887-1972) was an active churchwoman and wife of C. E. Lemmon, a Disciples of Christ minister. Correspondence, diaries, notes, financial statements, canceled checks, an annual report, a genealogy, a reading list, brochures, clippings, and other material relating to her personal life and church activities. Originals are held at the Disciples of Christ Historical Society at Nashville.

10,003. Leonard, Abiel
Papers. 1769-1928. 1126 folders
Open. Unpublished guide.
University of Missouri Library, Western Historical Manuscripts Collection.
Correspondence, legal material, accounts, and deeds of Leonard (1796-1863), a Fayette, MO, landowner and lawyer elected to the Missouri Supreme Court in 1855. Includes correspondence among Leonard family women about local events, reactions to national events, and such family news as courtship, marriage, children, school, travel and visiting, clothes and fashion, religion, death, and club activities. Also includes references to women's rights and a Susan B. Anthony lecture.

10,004. Logan Family
Papers. 1836-66. 6 folders.
Open. Unpublished guide.
University of Missouri Library, Western Historical Manuscripts Collection.
Correspondence and diaries include material of Martha Logan, who traveled to California by wagon in 1864. Her diary contains information on the wagon camp's social life and entertainment, scenery, and her moods from day to day. Salt Lake City entries concern Mormon women with fruits and vegetables for sale, sightseeing in the city, a visit to the "ice cream saloon," and a Sabbath speech by Brigham Young.

10,005. Long, Fannie Blair, Family
Papers. 1834-1944. 24 folders and 1 vol.
Open. Unpublished guide.
University of Missouri Library, Western Historical Manuscripts Collection.
Correspondence and legal papers of Long's family include material relating to the settlement of the Isaac Long estate in Keswick, VA, and to the education of Carroll F. Dewees, ward of Fannie Long. Also includes a diary, a genealogy, and a memento of an unidentified woman as well as photos, some of which picture students at a female college.

10,006. Luckett, Catharine, Family
Papers. 1854-1936. 1 vol.
Open. Unpublished guide.
University of Missouri Library, Western Historical Manuscripts Collection.
Scrapbook contains correspondence, invitations, greeting cards, obituaries, poetry, short stories, clippings, a scrap of a Confederate apron, and engravings, which concern such topics as health, beauty, recipes, religion, patriotism, children, and moral lessons. Includes a page from a ledger kept during the Civil War by Catharine Luckett's grandmother Mrs. Thomas Prince Earl Ries listing property taken by Union troops in 1861 and 1862.

10,007. McBeth, Kate
Papers. Nd. 11 pp.
Open. Unpublished guide.
University of Missouri Library, Western Historical Manuscripts Collection.
Speech in which McBeth criticized the woman suffrage movement, citing Biblical texts to show that the male is the protector, "an oak for the female vine." McBeth argued that female suffrage had proved a blight to progress in Utah, Wyoming, and Washington Territory; that it was unlikely that women voters could promote temperance or improve women's wages; and that "men do not like to marry women who want to vote."

10,008. McRoberts, A. J., Family
Papers. 1862-76. 4 folders.
Open. Unpublished guide.
University of Missouri Library, Western Historical Manuscripts Collection.
Correspondence, principally consisting of letters exchanged by McRoberts and his wife Mollie Lisk McRoberts during the Civil War. McRoberts was a Union sympathizer who lived in Saline County, MO, while his wife had returned to her family in Ohio. Also contains letters to Mollie McRoberts from girl friends.

10,009. Marshall, Joseph, Family
Papers. 1852-1909. 5 folders and microfilm.
Open. Unpublished guide.
University of Missouri Library, Western Historical Manuscripts Collection.
Correspondence and land deeds of the Marshall and Lynch families. Included are a written proposal of marriage and discussions of such topics as slavery, family and local news, the treatment of illness, and school life.

10,010. Marti, Anna M. (Fritz)
Papers. Nd. 1 folder.
Open. Unpublished guide.
University of Missouri Library, Western Historical Manuscripts Collection.
Biographical sketches, one by Marti (1840-?), a homemaker, and one about her by Mrs. E. L. Gage. Marti's sketch, "How Mother Got Her Forty Acres," concerns the marriage of her parents Frances Sthamm and Philip Fritz in Switzerland. After her husband began drinking and lost everything, Frances Fritz migrated to the US in 1845 and eventually moved to Kochville, MI, where she became the first woman to buy land. The second sketch is a description of Marti's life as a farmer's wife and as a widow with 13 children. Marti learned to read both German and English from her husband and learned to write at age 70. She was buried near her mother's land.

10,011. Missouri Association for Social Welfare
Records. 1908-71. 87 ft.
Access restricted. Unpublished guide.
University of Missouri Library, Western Historical Manuscripts Collection.
Founded in 1901, the MASW was a social service organization that included many women among the social workers, nurses, lawyers, other professionals, and lay people who made up its membership. Constitutions, bylaws, minutes, bills and receipts, correspondence, speeches, reports, questionnaires, news releases, newsletters, handbooks, bulletins, pamphlets, articles, and other material.

10,012. Missouri Library Association
Records. 1900-77. 3300 folders.
Open. Unpublished guide.
University of Missouri Library, Western Historical Manuscripts Collection.
From the early 1930s until the middle 1960s, this professional and educational organization, formed in 1900, supported certification as a way to promote professionalism among librarians. Applications for MLA certification, which are included in the group's records, provide biographical and employment information about librarians. Also includes minutes, financial and administrative records, correspondence, reports, convention and organizational material, lists, scrapbooks, pamphlets of other organizations, and publications. Specific items include surveys concerning salary, rank, and promotion by the Social Responsibilities Round Table Task Force on the Status of Women in Librarianship, which concluded that sex, rather than competency, governed job classifications; endorsements of the Missouri Library Commission by the Missouri Woman's Legislative Committee, the Green County Woman's Democratic Club, and the Missouri Federation of Women's Clubs; a list of Missouri women authors of books for juveniles; notes on the founding and work of the Women's History Research Center Library; and "Woman as Nigger," an article that examines women's "place" in society.

10,013. Missouri State Council of Defense
Records. 1940-45. 3148 folders and 2 boxes.
Open. Unpublished guide.
University of Missouri Library, Western Historical Manuscripts Collection.
Minutes, budgets, correspondence, bulletins, applications, mailing lists, maps, clippings, and other records of the Council, which was formed in 1940 to promote civilian defense during WWII. Includes material on women, day care, and other means of caring for the children of working mothers; women in the armed services in WWI and WWII and the types of jobs women performed; prospects for women when war work was over; the Vassar Summer Institute for Family and Child Care Services in War Time; and statistics on an emergency maternity and infant care program. Also includes LWV broadsides on rationing and cooperation with the government and photos of the women's auxiliary fire fighters of North Kansas City, women modeling civilian defense uniforms at the Missouri Capitol, and women with babies in a contest.

10,014. Missouri, University of, Admission of Women Centennial
Records. 1967-68. 64 folders.
Open. Unpublished guide.
University of Missouri Library, Western Historical Manuscripts Collection.
Speeches, correspondence, press releases, photos, programs, posters, and other material about activities commemorating the centennial of the admission of women to the University. Also includes historical information on women at the University and biographical information about women who participated in centennial activities.

10,015. Missouri, University of, Agricultural Extension Service
Records. 1912-74. 230 microfilm reels.
Open. Unpublished guide.
University of Missouri Library, Western Historical Manuscripts Collection.
The Service helped families operate their farms more efficiently by demonstrating improved techniques in crop and livestock management and home economics, and it provided leadership for farm children in boys' and girls' clubs. Annual reports of county and district extension service agents and of extension activities at Lincoln University in Jefferson City, MO, and at the University of Missouri in Columbia, Kansas City, Rolla, and St. Louis. A significant part of the collection pertains to the Service's work with farm women. Home demonstration agents, renamed county home agents in 1947, were women trained to teach farm wives about nutrition, canning, economy and efficiency in clothing a family, child care, house planning, and home nursing. The girls' clubs helped school-age girls develop skills valuable to them as future farm wives.

10,016. Missouri, University of, Agricultural Extension Service, Home Demonstration
Records. 1915-53. 6 folders.
Open. Unpublished guide.
University of Missouri Library, Western Historical Manuscripts Collection.
Correspondence, program outlines, essays, and club records of the Service, which was established by Congress in 1914. Includes essays on the benefits of home demonstration service and early records of homemakers' clubs and home extension programs in Missouri.

10,017. Missouri, University of, Columbia, Chancellor's Committee on the Status of Women
Records. 1974-76. Several folders.
Access restricted. No guide.
University of Missouri Library, Western Historical Manuscripts Collection.
Survey forms, computer coding notes, and the Committee's final report "Background, Job Involvement, Perceived Discrimination and Job Dissatisfaction Among Academic Women at UMC, March, 1976."

10,018. Missouri, University of, Cooperative Extension Service
Records. 1920-63. 100 folders.
Open. Unpublished guide.
University of Missouri Library, Western Historical Manuscripts Collection.
Correspondence, reports, newsletters, bulletins, and other service records contain a report by Mary Ruth Rapp about county home demonstration agents and reasons the agents left their jobs. The home demonstration agent, the female counterpart of a county agent, demonstrated methods of home economics and agriculture to rural women. Also contains a 1921 US Department of Agriculture circular on home demonstration work in the northern and western states.

10,019. Missouri, University of, Cooperative Extension Service
Records. 1908-63. 101 folders.
Open. Unpublished guide.
University of Missouri Library, Western Historical Manuscripts Collection.
Correspondence, memoranda, speeches, histories, reports, photos, maps, clippings, and publications. Includes a history of home economics extension work in Missouri before the organization of home bureaus in 1917, a discussion of the homemaker's place in the economic world, a homemakers' club program for 1922 and a description of home economics extension work in Missouri, form letters from the Agricultural extension service to club presidents around the state, and photos of "more attractive homes."

10,020. Missouri, University of, Free Speech Controversy
Records. 1968-69. 2 folders.
Open. Unpublished guide.
University of Missouri Library, Western Historical Manuscripts Collection.
Correspondence, reports, resolutions, leaflets, and clippings contain material on the student rights march, the Students for a Democratic Society summer workshop, and incidents at Lincoln University that led to issuance of a temporary restraining order. Also contains "SDS New Left Notes," which includes a commemoration of International Women's Day.

10,021. Missouri, University of, Graduate School
Records. 1911-67. 2165 folders.
Open. Unpublished guide.
University of Missouri Library, Western Historical Manuscripts Collection.
Minutes of the University of Missouri graduate committees and correspondence of the graduate school's dean with administrators, graduate faculty members and students, government officials, foundation officers, and alumni. Includes a letter from Lucile H. Bluford, a Negro woman who attempted to gain admission to the graduate school, and a letter replying to her request.

10,022. Missouri, University of, President's Reports
Records. 1893-94. 2 vols.
Open. Unpublished guide.

University of Missouri Library, Western Historical Manuscripts Collection.
Reports by Richard H. Jesse, president of the University of Missouri from 1891 to 1908, to the University's board of curators and executive board. The reports, composed of administrative and enrollment information and financial statements, include some references to specific women students and women faculty members as well as to the University matron, the secretary of the University, and professors' wives. The reports reflect a decision that allowed wives of faculty and staff members to attend classes without fee if they were not pursuing a degree. The board of curators was requested to rule on uniform dress for the women students. Concerning the hiring of personnel, Jesse included an observation that "the person best qualified for the position should be elected in all places regardless of sex." If qualifications were equal, he said the board might wish "for a season at least to give the preference to the women."

10,023. Missouri, University of, School of Home Economics
Records. 1886-1927. 52 folders.
Open. Unpublished guide.
University of Missouri Library, Western Historical Manuscripts Collection.
Correspondence and other records of the School and bulletins and reports of the US Department of Agriculture extension service. Includes an 1886 cookbook; material concerning such 1918 farm home conveniences as the fireless cooker, sponge box, iceless refrigerator, flytrap, and shower bath; a 1927 US Department of Agriculture report, "Vacation Camps Give Rest and Instruction to Many Farm Women"; and obituaries of the School's faculty members.

10,024. Missouri, University of, School of Mines and Metallurgy
Records. 1870-1948. 726 folders.
Open. Unpublished guide.
University of Missouri Library, Western Historical Manuscripts Collection.
The School's executive, financial, student, and political records include a 1921 letter from a local WCTU committee to the chairman of the School's executive committee and to the student council. In the letter, WCTU members protested a freshman smoker and dances held at the School.

10,025. Mitchell, Ewing Young, Jr.
Papers. 1841-1949. 4018 folders, 4 boxes, and 7 vols.
Open. Unpublished guide.
University of Missouri Library, Western Historical Manuscripts Collection.
Personal, family, political, and professional papers of Mitchell (1873-1954), a Springfield, MO, lawyer and Democrat. Includes Mitchell's mother's writings about WWI; legal material and correspondence from family and friends about Mitchell's divorce; notes about stage performances of Julia Marlowe, Clara Morris, Sarah Bernhardt, and Maggie Mitchell; and items concerning women's suffrage in Missouri.

10,026. Moore, Mary Brown (Daniel)
Papers. 1936. 5-page item.
Open. Unpublished guide.
University of Missouri Library, Western Historical Manuscripts Collection.
Letter from [Mrs. John T.] Moore (1875-?) of Nashville reminiscing about the school days of her mother Elizabeth Gillenwaters (Brown) [Mrs. Henry Clay] Daniel (1847-). Moore describes "Lizzie" Brown's education at Independence Female College in Independence, MO, in 1860-61; at the Howard Female College in Fayette, MO, in 1862-63; and at Christian College in Columbia, beginning in 1863. She notes housekeeping arrangements, room assignments, and daily routine at Christian College, where the president, faculty, and approximately 30 students lived in one building.

10,027. Mott, Frank Luther, and Mott, Vera Ingram
Papers. 1775-1965. 2227 folders, 21 boxes, 72 vols., and 5 tapes.
Access restricted. Unpublished guide.
University of Missouri Library, Western Historical Manuscripts Collection.
A professor of journalism and dean, Frank Mott (1886-1964) was an author and editor who received the Pulitzer Prize in 1939. His wife Vera Mott (1885-1964) was an author of articles on dime novels, a teacher of high school and college English, an active clubwoman, and an assistant to her husband with his research, writing, and indexing. Frank Mott's papers include personal and professional correspondence, published and unpublished manuscripts, copies of his articles and books, photos, an autograph collection, pamphlets, clippings, awards and degrees, memorabilia, and other items. Vera Mott's papers contain one of her articles on dime novels, index cards, photos, clippings, awards, and memorabilia. Specific items include letters Frank Mott wrote to his wife from 1917 to 1920, Vera Mott's record of their family life in Iowa City, IA, and Columbia, letters and cards of condolence concerning her death, and taped interviews with the Motts' daughter Mildred (Mott) Wedel. Also includes a survey and poll of women journalists in 1944 and references to Sarah J. Hale's influence on *Godey's Lady's Book,* women's education, and *Ladies' Home Journal.*

10,028. Napton, Baily
Papers. Nd. 2 items.
Open. Unpublished guide.
University of Missouri Library, Western Historical Manuscripts Collection.
Letters to Judge Napton from his wife in which she writes of family incidents and activities and of her visit to another town.

10,029. Neihardt, John G.
Papers. 1896-1967. 14.5 ft. and 2 microfilm reels.
Open. Unpublished guide.
University of Missouri Library, Western Historical Manuscripts Collection.
Family and business correspondence, manuscripts, articles, book reviews, photos, and clippings of Neihardt (1881-1973), a poet and lecturer; his mother Alice Neihardt, who was interested in spiritualism; his wife Mona Martinsen Neihardt, a sculptor and student of Rodin; and the Neihardt children Alice, Hilda, Sigurd, and Enid, who occasionally traveled with their father to record his conversations in shorthand. Enid helped her father in his research on the Sioux Indians; information about the lives and customs of Sioux women are included in transcriptions of her shorthand notes. Also contains correspondence in which Neihardt and [Miss] Harriet Monroe, a Chicago poet and editor who published his work in her *Poetry: A Magazine of Verse,* carried on a debate about poetry. Other correspondents include Ina D. Coolbrith, a California poet; Minnie Maddern Fiske, an actress; Natalie L. B. Forsyth, widow of General Forsyth; and Mrs. T. W. Todd, whose father fought in the Indian wars. Photos include one of Mrs. Joseph La Flesche, wife of the Omaha tribal leader and mother of Susan (La Flesche) Picotte, who was reputedly the first Indian woman to become a physician.

10,030. Nelson, Earl F.
Papers. 1904-67. 244 folders.
Open. Unpublished guide.
University of Missouri Library, Western Historical Manuscripts Collection.
Personal, political, and business correspondence; journals; insurance data; tax records; and ledgers of Nelson (1884-1945), a member of the University of Missouri board of curators. Contains a report on the court case brought in 1940 by [Miss] Lucile Bluford, a Negro who sought admission to the University of Missouri. The report describes the presentation of the University's position and the jury's decision.

10,031. Overland Diary
Papers. 1857. 1 folder.
Open. Unpublished guide.
University of Missouri Library, Western Historical Manuscripts Collection.
Diary kept by an unidentified young girl as she and her family traveled by covered wagon from Concord, KY, to near Brunswick, MO, includes descriptions of traveling conditions, roads, bridges, the land, people they met, "the Hoosier" country of Indiana, coal mines in Illinois, and crossing the Mississippi River.

10,032. Park, Guy Brasfield
Papers. 1932-36. 2255 folders.
Access restricted. Unpublished guide.
University of Missouri Library, Western Historical Manuscripts Collection.
Personal and official correspondence and papers of Park (1872-1946), Democratic governor of Missouri from 1933 to 1937, include material concerning [Mrs.] Mary Edna Cruzen, state labor commissioner, and other items relating to women. Contains correspondence about Cruzen and letters from the Women's Trade Union League and others supporting her reappointment. Also contains a resolution to allow women to serve liquor; material of the National Woman's Party on the minimum wage; information about the interest of the DAR and the National Society of US Daughters of 1812 in preservation of an historic tavern at Arrow Rock, MO; a field report on the State Industrial Home for Girls at Chilicothe, MO; letters from Mrs. W. W. Henderson, director of the State Children's Bureau, and Helen Louise Purcell, owner of the newspaper *The Jimplicute,* concerning a bond issue; a letter about drunk women; and letters from women's organizations on such topics as historic markers, flag ceremonies, and banquets. Also contains material relating to the Women's Organization for National Prohibition Reform, the LWV, the Woman's City Club of Kansas City, the American War Mothers, the Federation of Democratic Women's Clubs, and the Missouri Federation of Women's Clubs.

10,033. Payne, Moses U.
Papers. 1803-1903. 403 folders and 2 vols.
Open. Unpublished guide.
University of Missouri Library, Western Historical Manuscripts Collection.
Correspondence, business papers, account books, daybooks of a mercantile firm, reports, and other papers of Payne (1807-95), a pioneer merchant, landowner, farmer, stockman, preacher, and railroad builder, include mention of Howard Female College of Fayette, MO.

10,034. Peek, George N.
Papers. 1911-47. 3088 folders and 10 boxes.
Open. Unpublished guide.
University of Missouri Library, Western Historical Manuscripts Collection.
Administrator of the War Industries Board, Peek (1873-1943) was a lobbyist for McNary-Haugen farm legislation and administrator of the Agricultural Adjustment Act. Included with Peek's papers is a journal his wife kept during part of 1927 and 1928. The journal contains descriptions of two apartments the Peeks lived in while in Washington as well as discussions of fashion, social activities, trips, and Georgia (Lindsey) [Mrs. George N.] Peek's impressions as she followed congressional debate on the McNary-Haugen farm legislation.

10,035. Rainey, Homer Price
Papers. 1919-52. 1962 folders, 3 vols., and 116 items.
Access restricted. Unpublished guide.
University of Missouri Library, Western Historical Manuscripts Collection.
Correspondence, minutes, a scrapbook of clippings, and other papers of Rainey (1896-), an educator and college administrator who served as director of the American Youth Commission, pertain to his work with the Commission, his struggle for "academic freedom" at the University of Texas, his campaign for the Democratic gubernatorial nomination in Texas, and the administration of Stephens College, a women's school in Columbia. Includes youth and educational material, Woman's Foundation minutes and correspondence, correspondence with Eleanor Roosevelt about the Youth Commission, and material regarding his presidency of Stephens College. Includes pamphlets of the Woman's Foundation, James Wood, and J. Edgar Hoover concerning mothers and their place in the war effort, employed women and the home, improved family living through better housing, and "The Place of the Family in American Life."

10,036. Rankin Family
Papers. 1834-72. 6 items.
Open. Unpublished guide.
University of Missouri Library, Western Historical Manuscripts Collection.
Financial documents and an 1872 letter to John William Rankin from his cousin Sarah Smith. In the letter, written for her father who felt too old to write, Smith mentions the dry summer and the crop situation, a recent meeting during which three sermons were preached each day for five consecutive days, and family and neighborhood news.

10,037. Raut, Irwin
Papers. 1871-1950. 19 folders and 16 vols.
Open. Unpublished guide.
University of Missouri Library, Western Historical Manuscripts Collection.
Pamphlet concerning missionaries supported by Missouri women in 1909 contains biographies of [Miss] Eva Swift, [Misses] Mary and Elizabeth Webb, [Miss] Elizabeth Torrey, and [Miss] Charlotte B. DeForest. Also contains price lists for trunks from 1874 to 1879, railway schedules, maps of St. Louis, information on Sedalia, MO, elementary school textbooks from 1882 and 1883, a personal poetry collection, and a Bible.

10,038. Read, Daniel
Papers. 1866-76. 14 folders.
Open. Unpublished guide.
University of Missouri Library, Western Historical Manuscripts Collection.
Read (1805-78) was president of the University of Missouri. Correspondence, speeches, and drafts of reports prepared by Read for the University board of curators and general assembly include material about women at the school. Contains a committee report supporting a university college for women, an article supporting university education for women, a report on the University's growth and integration of women into academic life, a report on the admission of women to the University, and a press release on the forthcoming European tour of Read's daughter Mary.

10,039. Reese, Madge Janet
Papers. 1887-1962. 67 folders.
Open. Unpublished guide.
University of Missouri Library, Western Historical Manuscripts Collection.
[Miss] Reese (1894-1955) was a state and field agent of the US Department of Agriculture from 1915 to 1955. Speeches, reports, and other items contain Reese's publications concerning home demonstration work in relation to girls' clubs, farm women, rural education, home economics, and rural families. Also contains material tracing the origin and development of agricultural extension work; addresses, broadcasts, and statements that Reese delivered from 1916 to 1955; and copies of the National Honorary Extension Fraternity yearbook.

10,040. Reick, Addie Henry
Papers. 1910. 48-page item.
Open. Unpublished guide.
University of Missouri Library, Western Historical Manuscripts Collection.
Diary in which [Mrs.] Reick (?-ca. 1952) describes her trip with her husband from Seattle to Ophir, AK. The diary, which Reick wrote for friends and relatives in Missouri, concerns scenery and people encountered and includes a map showing the route of her journey. Reick stayed in Alaska for more than 30 years before moving to Washington state. She was buried in Shannon County, MO.

10,041. Richards, Channing
Papers. 1835-63. 2 folders.
Open. Unpublished guide.
University of Missouri Library, Western Historical Manuscripts Collection.
Correspondence between Richards, a businessman, and his wife Lydia (Williamson) Richards, a homemaker, includes letters from Williamson to Richards before their marriage. These letters, dated 1835, tell about social life and family activities in Newark and Jersey City, NJ. Channing Richards's letters concern his business trips and related subjects, including grain markets and prices. Lydia Richards's later letters include news of family activities and friends in Cincinnati.

10,042. Rogers, Margaret
Papers. 1909-10. 1 folder.
Open. No guide.
University of Missouri Library, Western Historical Manuscripts Collection.
A travel diary that Rogers, a music student, kept during a two-month trip from Berlin to Russia and back. Traveling with 20 students, Rogers wrote the diary for her father, who remained in the US; her mother stayed in Berlin during her Russian tour. Diary entries include descriptions of transportation, hotels, historic sites, opera performances, churches, and church services. Rogers later married Laurence Phipps.

10,043. St. Louis Louisiana Purchase Exposition Educational Exhibit
Records. 1904. 169 folders and 43 vols.
Open. Unpublished guide.
University of Missouri Library, Western Historical Manuscripts Collection.
Copybooks from several public schools and school essays on such topics as the decline of marriage, divorce, "Education and Life Love," and women as florists.

10,044. Sappington
Papers. 1831-1939. 14 folders.
Open. Unpublished guide.
University of Missouri Library, Western Historical Manuscripts Collection.
John Sappington (1776-1856), a physician, popularized the use of quinine in the treatment of fevers. Principally material about financial provisions Sappington made for the children of his daughter; also includes a few personal papers, household accounts, and papers relating to his pill business.

10,045. Schermerhorn, John Freeman
Papers. 1809-1909. 20 folders.
Open. Unpublished guide.
University of Missouri Library, Western Historical Manuscripts Collection.
Correspondence and papers of Schermerhorn (1787-1859), a landowner, frontier preacher, and peacemaker with the Indians, including material relating to his two wives, his daughters, and other women. Contains letters from Schermerhorn to [Miss] Catherine Yates before and after their marriage in 1813; correspondence to the Schermerhorns' daughter Catherine from her father and from friends concerning Indians, a trip west in 1833, missionary work, family news, and the death of her mother; letters of Mary, Catherine, and Harriet Schermerhorn; correspondence from John Schermerhorn concerning the family and his marriage to his second wife Elizabeth L. Spottswood; and correspondence concerning Catherine's trip to Washington, DC, her health, teaching, and death. Also contains letters concerning the family's move to Indiana in 1840 and the birth of Mary's son as well as letters to Kate Ward from Union soldiers and others during the Civil War about the War, southern women, death, and personal news. Also includes compositions of Mary Y. Schermerhorn while she was at Utica (NY) Female Academy in 1838 and 1839.

10,046. Shackelford, Thomas
Papers. 1820-1908. 45 folders.
Open. Unpublished guide.
University of Missouri Library, Western Historical Manuscripts Collection.
Personal and business correspondence, memoirs, and documents of Shackelford (1822-1908), a lawyer and politician who was a member of the Missouri Convention in 1861 and the Constitutional Convention in 1875; his wife Sarah Harrison Shackelford; and their daughter Ida. Includes an 1871 letter in which Ida, writing from Hannibal, MO, tells her parents of seeing the light from the Chicago fire; an item with references to women's suffrage, to which Thomas Shackelford was opposed; a note by Shackelford concerning the death of [Miss] Mary Louise Dalton of the Missouri Historical Society; and a memorial to Sarah Shackelford.

10,047. Slusher, H. E.
Papers. 1944-58. 1676 folders.
Open. Unpublished guide.
University of Missouri Library, Western Historical Manuscripts Collection.
Correspondence and other papers generated during the tenure of Slusher (1893-) as president of the Missouri Farm Bureau Federation. Includes material concerning women's activities as well as Slusher's correspondence with the US Department of Agriculture and Missouri legislators.

10,048. Smith, Forrest
Papers. 1940-53. 6658 folders, 8 boxes, and 13 vols.
Open. Unpublished guide.
University of Missouri Library, Western Historical Manuscripts Collection.
Smith (1886-1962) was governor of Missouri from 1949 to 1953. Papers created during his term as governor include references to Margaret Truman's singing; the centennial of Christian College, a women's school; the DAR, the American Mothers Platform to Prevent War, and the St. Louis Women's Democratic Club; Dorothy J. Shofstall, the Missouri director of CARE; high school sororities; and marriage laws.

10,049. Smith, William Benjamin
Papers. Nd. 23 folders.
Open. Unpublished guide.
University of Missouri Library, Western Historical Manuscripts Collection.
Smith (1850-1934) was a member of the University of Missouri faculty from 1885 to 1893, serving first as professor of physics and then as professor of mathematics. Biographical sketch and manuscripts by Smith, including "Woman's Suffrage."

10,050. Stark, Lloyd C.
Papers. 1931-41. 12,401 folders.
Open. Unpublished guide.
University of Missouri Library, Western Historical Manuscripts Collection.
Stark (1886-1972) was the Democratic governor of Missouri from 1937 to 1941. Correspondence and papers relating to Stark's campaigns, official position, and personal affairs include references to women who participated in politics through such groups as the Women's Democratic Clubs and the Missouri LWV. Also contains several letters from husbands asking that gambling establishments be closed so their wives will stay home at night, a letter from a woman who claims her husband is in "machine" politics and is trying to kill her because she "knows too much," and a complaint about married women working when so many "breadwinners" are unemployed.

10,051. Stephens, Mrs. Lon Vest
Papers. 1897-1903. 1 vol.
Open. No guide.
University of Missouri Library, Western Historical Manuscripts Collection.
Diary in which Margaret (Nelson) Stephens (1859-1929) describes her life during the service of her husband Lawrence "Lon" Stephens as governor. She writes about family life in the governor's mansion in Jefferson City, social affairs, health problems and medical treatment, trips taken, the weather, petitions asking pardons for relatives, some aspects of politics, and her fear of strong drink.

10,052. Stratton, Pauline H.
Papers. 1841-70. 7 folders.
Open. Unpublished guide.
University of Missouri Library, Western Historical Manuscripts Collection.
Stratton (1814-87), who lived in Virginia and Missouri, was a homemaker. Daybook entries and a copy of an 1841 letter from Stratton to her husband before their marriage. Daybook entries from 1846 to ca. 1855 reflect her life in Virginia; the remainder were written in Missouri. She writes of spinning, weaving, soap making, rearing her children, trouble with Negro servants, the Civil War as it affected her daily life, and of business difficulties she encountered after her husband's death.

10,053. Sutter, Rosa Schafer
Papers. 1875-1920. 8 folders.
Open. Unpublished guide.
University of Missouri Library, Western Historical Manuscripts Collection.
Sutter (1850-1920) was a housewife who lived near Billings, MO. Notes on correspondence, diaries about home activities and family affairs, and a receipt book containing bakery recipes for cakes and pies as well as remedies for illnesses, prescriptions for rheumatism, and other information. Many of the diaries were written in memorandum books provided by commercial companies.

10,054. Travel Account of Journey from Indiana to Washington
Papers. Ca. 1850. 1 folder.
Open. Unpublished guide.
University of Missouri Library, Western Historical Manuscripts Collection.
Copy of an unidentified woman's account of a journey from Indiana to Washington state provides a record of the weather, landscape, encounters with Indians, illnesses, and territory covered each day. The diarist occasionally makes such comments as: "The men amused themselves a fishing and hunting and bathing in the pure clear stream while we women's amusement was washing and cooking in the burning sun over the hot fire." Also contains a list of provisions, charges, and expenses kept by George Royse.

10,055. U.S. Work Projects Administration, Historical Records Survey, Missouri
Records. 1935-42. 24,282 folders.
Open. Unpublished guide.
University of Missouri Library, Western Historical Manuscripts Collection.
The Survey was created to inventory those Missouri counties' records that pertained to county government; in time, the project expanded to include inventories of church records, manuscript collections, women's organizations, vital statistics, American imprints, federal archives, and the Civil Works Administration as well as inventories concerning defense, Negro education, and a space survey. The completed inventory was to be published with one volume per county, but only about one-third of the volumes were published before WWII ended the project. Correspondence, essays, research material and notes, reports, instructions, publications, and other records include material involving the following women who held positions in the Survey; Florence Kerr, assistant commissioner of the WPA; Geraldine Parker, director of Federal Writers Projects; Anita K. Hynes, director of community service programs, women's and professional projects, and professional and service projects; Lucy Latimer; Ester Marshall Greer; Alice T. Barnett; Hazel Carter Lahey; Malissa Rigdon; Clara B. Chapman; Della H. Roberts; Lena B. Small; Hazel Blair; and Mayme Ratekin.

10,056. Walker Family
Papers. 1782-1883. 5 folders.
Open. Unpublished guide.
University of Missouri Library, Western Historical Manuscripts Collection.
Family correspondence and portraits, letters of character recommendation, a bond for service, tax receipts, wills, and a clipping containing the text of [Mrs.] Nannie Jane Walker Lenoir's address to Christian College alumnae in 1883.

10,057. Weber Family
Papers. 1899-1966. 12 folders.
Open. Unpublished guide.
University of Missouri Library, Western Historical Manuscripts Collection.
Nan Winston Gardner Weber was a prominent clubwoman and participant in civic and service organizations. Correspondence, including a small amount of Nan Weber's correspondence; genealogical information; family photos; clippings concerning her activities and honors; and a silver anniversary booklet of the Federated Garden Clubs of Missouri.

10,058. Wednesday Study Club
Records. 1908-35. 1 vol.
Open. Unpublished guide.
University of Missouri Library, Western Historical Manuscripts Collection.
Minutes reflect programs, charitable projects, and routine business of this women's social and charitable organization.

10,059. Welty, Elizabeth
Papers. 1891-94. 2 items.
Open. Unpublished guide.
University of Missouri Library, Western Historical Manuscripts Collection.
Born in Wright City, MO, Elizabeth Waltemath (ca. 1870-1900) married John Welty and moved with him to Colorado where they homesteaded near Monte Vista. Letters written by Elizabeth Welty from near Monte Vista and Lockett, CO, to her sister Ida in Missouri concern household and family matters, farming, the price of fruit and cereal crops, and crop conditions. She complains of hardships and asks her sister to mail her some roses folded in a damp cloth in a shoe box because there were so few flowers in her part of Colorado.

10,060. Williams, Sara Lawrence (Lockwood)
Papers. 1885-1961. 1426 folders and 84 vols.
Open. Unpublished guide.
University of Missouri Library, Western Historical Manuscripts Collection.
A journalist, educator, and clubwoman, Williams (1891-1961) was the second wife of Walter Williams, journalist and president of the University of Missouri from 1930 until 1935. Diaries, speeches, articles, interviews, photos, clippings, books, and other papers include biographical information on the Williamses, accounts of their journalistic activities, and interviews with Adolf Hitler, Marquis Okuma, and Benito Mussolini. Diaries of Sara Williams chronicle various periods of her life, including her work as a reporter in Philadelphia, her romance with Walter Williams, and later trips to Japan and China. Sara Lockwood received her bachelor of journalism degree from Missouri University in 1913. She worked at several newspapers and taught at the University of Missouri before marrying Walter Williams in 1927. Following her husband's death in 1935, she became a visiting journalism professor at Yenching University in China. She served as national president of Theta Sigma Phi, a women's national journalism society, from 1925 to 1927 and as president of the Missouri Women's Press Club in 1953. She wrote numerous articles and two books.

10,061. Willis Family
Papers. 1843-1908. 3 folders.
Open. Unpublished guide.
University of Missouri Library, Western Historical Manuscripts Collection.
Correspondence between A. F. Willis and his wife; Willis spent several years working in the California gold fields and at other jobs in the West, while his wife stayed with their two young sons in Fayette, MO.

10,062. Wilson, Clyde
Papers. 1962-72. 255 folders.
Open. Unpublished guide.
University of Missouri Library, Western Historical Manuscripts Collection.
Wilson (1926-) is a member of the Columbia city council and of the University of Missouri anthropology department faculty; in 1970 he unsuccessfully challenged US Representative Richard H. Ichord of Missouri's 8th Congressional District. Campaign material arranged into campaign, county, research, and reference files contains clippings from local papers concerning equal rights and the status of women.

10,063. Woman's Christian Temperance Union, Columbia
Records. 1884-88. 1 vol.
Open. Unpublished guide.
University of Missouri Library, Western Historical Manuscripts Collection.
Minute book contains the group's constitution, bylaws, minutes, roll of members, and records of the organization's activities. Also contains a constitution and bylaws of the Philalaethean Society of the University of Missouri.

10,064. World War II
Collection. 1940-46. 3467 folders.
Open. Unpublished guide.
University of Missouri Library, Western Historical Manuscripts Collection.
Correspondence and poems written by American servicemen and women to friends and relatives throughout the US primarily concern family and hometown news and their immediate circumstances. Some letters reflect the author's reactions to the war. Includes about 80 letters written by women who served as WACs, WAVES, and nurses as well as letters from American women who married foreign nationals and lived in their husbands' countries during the war.

10,065. Wymore, William
Papers. 1864. 2 items.
Open. Unpublished guide.
University of Missouri Library, Western Historical Manuscripts Collection.
Correspondence between Wymore and his wife, who ran the family farm and cared for their children while her husband was away. Wymore's letter pertains to his trip from Nashville to Bridgeport, AL, and life at an army camp in the Alabama town. In her letter, Mrs. Wymore describes harvesting and sowing crops, the condition of the livestock, and trouble with hired help. She speaks of General Grant's taking Petersburg, VA, and moving on to Richmond and mentions a "butternut picnic" held at Newberg, MO.

FAYETTE

10,066. Missouri Methodist Historical Collection
Records. Ca. 1870s- . Ca. 4 cabinets and additional records.
Open. No guide.
Central Methodist College Library.
Annual reports, minutes, notes, committee reports, programs, and other records of Methodist organizations in Missouri. Includes annual reports of the Women's Society of Christian Service, Missouri Conference, and of the Conference's woman's foreign and home missionary societies; minutes of the Southwest Missouri Conference woman's home and foreign missionary societies; minutes, programs, and other records of the district Epworth League, an organization for high school students; programs, notes, and other material concerning the School of Missions, a week-long educational seminar primarily attended by women; and a history, dated 1929, of the woman's foreign and home missionary societies of the Missouri Conference, Methodist Episcopal Church, South, which deals with local organizations and includes lists of members.

FLORISSANT

10,067. Society of the Missionary Sisters of the Catholic Apostolate Archives
Records. 1912- . 10 vols.
Closed. Unpublished guide.
Society of Missionary Sisters, Pallottine Provincialate.
This religious order of women was founded in Rome, Italy, in 1838. Financial records; correspondence, including letters of mothers superior; photos; conference proceedings; scrapbooks; and items relating to the order's apostolates in the US.

GRAHAM

10,068. Local History
Collection. 1840- . More than 50,000 cards and other items.
Partially closed. Unpublished guide.
Graham Historical Society.
Land transfers; records of marriages, births, and deaths; photos; scrapbooks; clippings; and other items relating to the history of Nodaway County, MO, which was settled in 1839. Includes 50,000 genealogy cards, three taped interviews, a cookbook, a record of cemetery inscriptions from Hughes Township, a two-volume history of the township, and information about persons who have some connection with the area.

INDEPENDENCE

10,069. Adams, Lina D.
Papers. 1940-62. 1 ft.
Access restricted. Unpublished guide.
Harry S. Truman Library.
Office correspondence and memoranda, Democratic party campaign material and dinner programs, articles, and clippings collected by [Mrs.] Adams, who served on the Democratic National Committee's staff in Washington, DC, for many years.

10,070. Bontecou, Eleanor
Papers. 1938-55. 6 ft.
Access restricted. Unpublished guide.
Harry S. Truman Library.
Bontecou (1891-1976) served as a lawyer in the Department of Justice civil rights section from 1943 to 1946 and, then, in 1946 and 1947 as a legal adviser in the war crimes branch of the War Department civil affairs division. Memoranda, notes, reports, speech drafts, files pertaining to legislation and court cases, and publications relate to civil rights, the federal internal security program, and the WWII war crime trials.

10,071. Fenton, Fleur
Papers. 1946. Ca. 1 ft.
Access restricted. Unpublished guide.
Harry S. Truman Library.
Fenton (1910-) is an editor. Correspondence, memoranda, notes, reports, and radio transcripts concern Fenton's work as special consultant to the Office of War Mobilization and Reconversion media programming division for the President's Famine Emergency Campaign.

10,072. Hennock, Frieda
Papers. 1948-55. 9 ft.
Access restricted. Unpublished guide.
Harry S. Truman Library.
[Miss] Hennock was a lawyer, government official, and member of the Federal Communications Commission. Reflecting her FCC work on educational television, the collection includes general correspondence and public opinion mail; correspondence concerning Hennock's dissent from the FCC's 1954 decision on UHF television; comments, briefs, and sworn statements from academic institutions, broadcasting companies, and other groups; articles; and publications.

10,073. Keeley, Mary Paxton
Papers. 1906-63. 1 ft.
Closed. No guide.
Harry S. Truman Library.
Keeley (1886-), a college professor, was a longtime friend of Mr. and Mrs. Harry S. Truman and Charles G. Ross. Principally correspondence since 1944 from Bess (Wallace) [Mrs. Harry S.] Truman, the Trumans' daughter Margaret (Truman) [Mrs. Clifton] Daniel, Mrs. Truman's mother Madge (Gates) [Mrs. George] Wallace, and Charles G. Ross.

10,074. Laughlin, Anne
Papers. 1936-57. 2 ft.
Open. Unpublished guide.
Harry S. Truman Library.
Correspondence, reports, notes, articles, and clippings relate to Laughlin's service as UNICEF's chief of mission in Bulgaria from 1946 to 1950, as director of the United Nations Relief and Rehabilitation Administration of the Netherlands in 1946, and as state director of the National Youth Administration in Topeka, KS, from 1936 to 1941.

10,075. Long, Westray Battle Boyce
Papers. 1945-62. 2 ft.
Access restricted. Unpublished guide.
Harry S. Truman Library.
Director of the WACs from 1945 to 1947, [Mrs. Willie J.] Long (1901-72) was a government official and a businesswoman. Correspondence, memoranda, reports, publications, and clippings relate primarily to Long's work as chief of the Rural Electrification Administration insurance unit from 1934 to 1942 and as a WAC officer beginning in 1942.

10,076. Noland, Mary Ethel
Papers. 1903-71. 3 ft.
Access restricted. Unpublished guide.
Harry S. Truman Library.
Noland (1883-1971) was a teacher, genealogist, and cousin of Harry S. Truman. Correspondence from Truman to his cousins Ethel and Nellie Noland of Independence and his aunt Mrs. Joseph T. Noland; correspondence and charts pertaining to genealogy of the Truman, Noland, and related families; from Truman, his wife, and their daughter; and miscellaneous material relating to Truman and Independence.

10,077. Publicity Division of the Democratic National Committee
Records. 1943-52. 7 ft.
Open. Unpublished guide.
Harry S. Truman Library.
Memoranda, scripts, press releases, and clippings pertain to radio and television broadcasts sponsored by the women's division of the Democratic National Committee, 1948 and 1950.

10,078. Roberts, Willa Mae
Papers. 1934-56. Ca. 1 ft.
Open. Unpublished guide.
Harry S. Truman Library.
[Mrs.] Roberts was a Democratic National Committee member from 1956 to 1960. Correspondence, speeches, programs, press releases, clippings, and publications regarding Roberts's activities as a member and later vice-chairman of the Monroe County, MO, Democratic Central Committee as well as her membership on the state Democratic committee and the National Committee.

10,079. Truman, Harry S., as President of the United States
Papers. 1945-53. 2824 ft.
Access restricted. Unpublished guide.
Harry S. Truman Library.
Correspondence of Truman (1884-1972) with women's organizations and women active in public affairs and correspondence from citizens regarding public and personal matters, files relating both to the appointment of women to and their activities in federal positions, material pertaining to women's roles in the Democratic party and national political campaigns, files of speeches delivered by Truman before women's groups, memoranda, notes, reports, appointment books, clipping files, and published material.

10,080. Truman, Harry S., as United States Senator
Papers. 1934-45. 124 ft.
Access restricted. Unpublished guide.
Harry S. Truman Library.
Includes correspondence of Truman (1884-1972) with women's organizations, women constituents, and women active in Missouri's Democratic party.

10,081. Truman, Mary Martha, and Bentley, Nancy
Papers. 1882-91. 56 items.
Open. Unpublished guide.
Harry S. Truman Library.
Letters from M. M. Truman (1860-1900), schoolteacher and aunt of Harry S. Truman, to her friend and college roommate Nancy Bentley.

10,082. White House Office of Social Correspondence
Records. 1945-53. 100 ft.
Access restricted. Unpublished guide.
Harry S. Truman Library.
The Office handled correspondence of President Truman's wife Elizabeth "Bess" Virginia (Wallace) Truman and their daughter Margaret Truman. Files emanating from their national position relate to interviews, publicity, invitations, and many other White House matters; condolences on the death of Bess Truman's mother; and material on the 1948 presidential election, General Douglas MacArthur, and the March of Dimes. Also included are biographical data, poems, recipes, photos, clippings, pamphlets, and books.

Margaret Truman's files primarily relate to her interest and career in music, with correspondence about her concert, radio, and television appearances; itineraries, programs, and letters to the President about her concert debut; sheet music; and clippings. The 1952 whistle-stop campaign is also mentioned

10,083. White House Social Office
Records. 1945-53. 42 ft.
Access restricted. Unpublished guide.
Harry S. Truman Library.
The Office handled formal social correspondence of President Truman's wife Bess (Wallace) Truman and their daughter Margaret and planned formal White House social events. Correspondence, memoranda, programs, sample guest lists and invitations, and other papers, including requests for interviews, acknowledgements of gifts, and files for each formal social function (luncheons, dinners, receptions, teas, and musicales) that President and Mrs. Truman gave at the White House, the Blair House, or elsewhere in Washington, DC.

10,084. Bancroft Reading Club
Records. 1888-1961. Ca. 5 Hollinger boxes.
Open. No guide.
Jackson County Historical Society.
Records of this Kansas City study group, which was affiliated with the Federated Women's Clubs, include minutes, financial records, a scrapbook, and year books.

10,085. Independence Browning Society
Records. 1926-68. 2 Hollinger boxes.
Open. Unpublished guide.
Jackson County Historical Society.
Founded in 1926 as an outgrowth of the study of Robert and Elizabeth (Barrett) Browning by the Mary Paxton Study Class, the Society was composed primarily of women who sought to continue their education. Minutes, correspondence, membership rosters, a scrapbook, and clippings. The Society was open to men and women, but eventually men ceased seeking membership. Its leaders included [Miss] Matilda Brown and Ardella Hardin [Mrs. W. L. C.] Palmer, both of whom had taught Harry S. Truman in school, and Mary Ethel Noland. The group disbanded in 1968.

10,086. Mary Paxton Study Class
Records. 1894- . 4 Hollinger boxes.
Open. Unpublished guide.
Jackson County Historical Society.
Founded in 1894 under the leadership of Mary Gentry Paxton, the Class promotes the study of literature and history. Minutes, financial reports, correspondence, a scrapbook, a history of the club, and a biography of Paxton by her daughter Mary (Paxton) Keeley. The group, which has helped married women further their education, took its present name after the death of Paxton, a former teacher and attorney's wife, in 1903. Originally, presentations were made by Class members; now a lecturer is hired to lead Class meetings. In 1913 the members helped found the Saturday Club for their daughters. The Independence Browning Society grew from the Class's two-year study of the lives and poetry of Robert and Elizabeth (Barrett) Browning. Over the years, the three groups have presented plays, given literary benefits, and worked together on other projects.

10,087. Saturday Club
Records. 1913- . 3 Hollinger boxes.
Open. Unpublished guide.
Jackson County Historical Society.
Founded in 1913 by members of the Mary Paxton Study Class for their daughters, the Club requires its members to study a variety of subjects and present papers and book reviews. Minutes, study guides, and a scrapbook containing photos and clippings. Four of the Club's charter members remain affiliated with the organization. Recent projects included a four-year study of the women's movement. Refreshments and gift giving are banned, and emphasis is placed on a potential member's intellectual abilities. [Miss] Matilda Brown, a teacher at Independence High School, directed the group's study and gave a 30-minute lesson each week until her death in the mid-1920s. A charter member, Mary "May" Southern [Mrs. George Porterfield] Wallace, assumed leadership of the Club after Brown's death and continues to direct its activities.

10,088. Bidamon, Lewis C.
Papers. 1837-82. Ca. 0.5 Hollinger box.
Open. Card catalog.
Reorganized Church of Jesus Christ of Latter Day Saints, Library-Archives.
Bidamon (1806-91) married Emma (Hale) Smith (1804-79) after the death of her first husband Joseph Smith, Jr. Correspondence and legal papers concern Nauvoo, IL, property and the settlement of the Joseph Smith estate.

10,089. Davis, Inez (Smith)
Papers. Nd. 9 Hollinger boxes.
Open. No guide.
Reorganized Church of Jesus Christ of Latter Day Saints, Library-Archives.
Notes and research material that Davis (1889-1964), a Church member, used to write a history of the Reorganized Church of Jesus Christ of Latter Day Saints. The Library-Archives also hold Davis's diaries dating from 1920 to 1923.

10,090. Kelley, William H.
Papers. 1863-1914. 47 Hollinger boxes.
Open. Card catalog.
Reorganized Church of Jesus Christ of Latter Day Saints, Library-Archives.
Correspondence, notes, and other papers of Kelley (1841-1914), a member of the Reorganized Church hierarchy. Includes letters of his wife Ellen Kelley and his daughter Belle (Kelley) Anderson and others from Church officials, missionaries, and wives of missionaries.

10,091. Miscellany
Papers. 1829-1968. 13 Hollinger boxes.
Open. Card catalog.
Reorganized Church of Jesus Christ of Latter Day Saints, Library-Archives.
Correspondence and other papers of Joseph Smith III (1832-1914), first president of the Reorganized Church, including letters of Smith's three wives Emmeline "Emma" (Griswold) Smith, Bertha (Madison) Smith, and Ada (Clark) Smith; his daughters Carrie (Smith) Weld (1861-1944), Zaide (Smith) Salyards, Emma (Smith) McCallum, and Mary Audentia (Smith) Anderson; and other women. The correspondence reflects church and family concerns. Correspondence of Mary Audentia Anderson, daughter of Joseph Smith III and Bertha Smith, includes letters to her father, two brothers, and Church members and missionaries. Anderson, who was prominent in Church affairs, wrote *Ancestry and Posterity of Joseph Smith and Emma Hale.*

10,092. Smith, Emma (Hale)
Papers. 1842-1937. 1 document box.
Open. Card catalog.
Reorganized Church of Jesus Christ of Latter Day Saints, Library-Archives.
Smith (1804-79) was the wife of Joseph Smith, Jr., and, after his death, of Lewis C. Bidamon. She was active in Church affairs. Papers consist chiefly of correspondence and include letters to Bidamon, her son Joseph Smith III, and others. Also includes correspondence with Governor Thomas Carlin of Illinois concerning the prison term of Joseph Smith, Jr.

10,093. Weld, Carrie (Smith)
Papers. 1875-1938. 5 document boxes.
Open. Card catalog.
Reorganized Church of Jesus Christ of Latter Day Saints, Library-Archives.
The daughter of Joseph Smith III and Emma (Griswold) Smith, Weld (1861-1944) was a housewife. Correspondence with her father and her daughter Rebecca (Weld) Nolan reflects family concerns.

10,094. Women's Organization
Records. Ca. 1893-1955. No size given.
Open. No guide.
Reorganized Church of Jesus Christ of Latter Day Saints, Library-Archives.
Minute books, treasurer's records, and other records of the women's organization within the Reorganized Church. The group, which has been called the Daughters of Zion, Women's Department, and the Women's Auxiliary, sponsors retreats and workshops, prepares study materials, and conducts other programs. Includes material of the Women's Council, the executive committee for women's activities.

JEFFERSON CITY

10,095. Lincoln
Records. 1890- . 4 cabinets.
Open. No guide.
Lincoln University Library.
Lincoln University, a coeducational institution, was founded in 1864 to provide education for Negroes. School catalogs, commencement announcements, a history of the school, pamphlets, clippings, and other ephemera.

10,096. State Archives
Records. Nd. No size given.
Open. Published guide.
Missouri State Archives.
The State Archives houses records of counties, cities, special districts, and other local government units of Missouri as well as official state records. Material about women can be found, for example, in records of the Secretary of State (RG 3), which include the pollbook used by Marie L. [Mrs. Morris] Byrum, the first woman to vote in Missouri (in 1920); in records of the Judiciary (RG 8), which contain the Dred Scott case and include a petition, approved by the St. Louis Circuit Court, which permitted Scott to sue his owner Mrs. Irene Emerson for his freedom; in records of Consumer Affairs, Regulation, and Licensing (RG 11), which contain records of the commission on human rights and studies of race and sex discrimination, 1958-73, as well as records of the division of professional registration, which contain material about registered nurses, 1910-11 and 1941-53; and in records of Labor and Industrial Relations (RG 15), which include material on the commission on the status of women, 1970-73. See *A Guide to the Missouri State Archives: 1975* (Jefferson City, MO: State of Missouri, Office of the Secretary of State, 1975).

KANSAS CITY

10,097. Bureau of Indian Affairs: Canton Asylum for Insane Indians (RG 75)
Records. 1910-34. 4 ft.
Open. Unpublished guide.
Federal Archives and Records Center, Kansas City Archives Branch.
Correspondence and ledgers of the Asylum, which was established in Canton, SD, in 1901 and about half of whose patients were women. Includes employment data such as age, marital status, salary, and employment history for women employees, who were laundresses, matrons, attendants, and laborers. Also contains information on women patients and YWCA work for the Asylum.

10,098. Bureau of Indian Affairs: Cheyenne River Agency (RG 75)
Records. 1868-1953. 310 cu.ft.
Open. No guide.
Federal Archives and Records Center, Kansas City Archives Branch.
Includes correspondence relating to the capture of Mary Jordan by Indians in 1872.

10,099. Bureau of Indian Affairs: Potawatomi Indian Agency (RG 75)
Records. 1850-1955. 164 cu.ft.
Open. Unpublished guide.
Federal Archives and Records Center, Kansas City Archives Branch.
General mission and relief correspondence; school records; community payroll lists; heirship and death record book; birth, death, and marriage lists; education records; general welfare records; records of land allotments; and material pertaining to law enforcement and general health.

10,100. Bureau of Indian Affairs: Rosebud Agency (RG 75)
Records. 1878-1952. 680 cu.ft.
Open. Unpublished guide.
Federal Archives and Records Center, Kansas City Archives Branch.
Correspondence and reports of the Rosebud Agency, which was established in 1878. The general correspondence file (decimal file), 1930-50, contains annual reports with vital statistics; reports of social workers, school supervisors, nurses, supervisors of nurses, and others; personnel information and information about applicants for positions as clerks, laundresses, matrons, nurses, teachers, and social workers; material about schools, runaway wives, suicides, divorce, births and deaths, and family support; and other records.

10,101. Bureau of Indian Affairs: Winnebago Agency (RG 75)
Records. 1861-1955. 201 cu.ft.
Open. Unpublished guide.
Federal Archives and Records Center, Kansas City Archives Branch.
Correspondence and other records of this Indian reservation, which was founded in 1848, provide information about marriage and divorce, women as witnesses in liquor cases, women in the Peyote cult, and the GFWC and the Nebraska Federation of Women's Clubs, which were promoting anti-Peyote legislation. Correspondents include Jeannette [Mrs. O. A.] Nickman and Mrs. C. H. England.

10,102. Bureau of Indian Affairs: Yankton Indian Agency (RG 75)
Records. 1926-33. 9 ft.
Open. No guide.
Federal Archives and Records Center, Kansas City Archives Branch.
General correspondence file (decimal file) of this Indian reservation, which was established in 1859, includes annual reports with narrative and statistical sections; school census material; and scattered financial records pertaining to women who were recipients of educational loans and pension checks. Contains information about indigent Indians and destitute persons, medical examinations, divorces, polygamy, boys and girls clubs, and education, including commercial courses, enrollment and attendance, and other school records. Also contains a letter from and a pamphlet by the GFWC and a report of a white woman's trip to Yankton.

10,103. United States Attorneys and Marshals (RG 118)
Records. 1856-ca. 1950. 120 cu.ft.
Open. Unpublished guides.
Federal Archives and Records Center, Kansas City Archives Branch.
Contains records of Attorneys and Marshals in Iowa, Kansas, Nebraska, North Dakota, South Dakota, Minnesota, and Missouri. Includes records pertaining to civil and criminal cases in which women appeared as plaintiffs and defendants, among them records (1 box), 1917-18, relating to the trial of Kate Richards O'Hare in the North Dakota District for sedition. There are unpublished guides for portions of the records.

10,104. United States District Courts (RG 21)
Records. 1828-ca. 1920. 18,000 cu.ft.
Open. Unpublished guides.
Federal Archives and Records Center, Kansas City Archives Branch.
Contains records of the Courts for Iowa, Kansas, Nebraska, North Dakota, South Dakota, Minnesota, and Missouri, whose jurisdictions include admiralty, bankruptcy, civil, criminal, equity, and law cases. Includes 29 cases for the North Dakota District, 1861-1945, for example, in which women were plaintiffs or defendants in cases involving railroads, especially the Great Northern Railway, as well as life insurance companies, Standard Oil, and other organizations and corporations. North Dakota court records also include material (1 box) pertaining to Kate Richards O'Hare, who was tried for sedition. There are unpublished guides for some portions of the records.

10,105. Buck, Luella
Papers. 1887-90. 1 vol.
Open. Unpublished guide.
Kansas City Museum of History and Science.
Journal of Buck concerns her experiences during her first years as a teacher in a one-room school in Atchison, KS.

10,106. Fike, Ellie
Papers. 1871-90. 5 vols.
Open. Unpublished guide.
Kansas City Museum of History and Science.
Diaries in which [Miss] Fike describes life in her hometown of Warrensburg, MO. She includes comments about the activities of her mother Lucy Cimbaline Fike.

10,107. Fike, Lucy Cimbaline
Papers. 1871-1905. 30 vols.
Open. Unpublished guide.
Kansas City Museum of History and Science.
Diaries of [Mrs.] Fike, a Warrensburg, MO, housewife who was active in church affairs. She was the wife of a school superintendent and the mother of Ellie Fike.

10,108. Kansas City Mothers' Union
Records. 1895-1903. 5 vols.
Open. Unpublished guide.
Kansas City Museum of History and Science.
Minutes of the Union, a voluntary organization formed in about 1895 by mothers who were interested in children's education. Mrs. Edwin Weeks, president of the Union, became one of the first officers of the national PTA.

10,109. Daughters of the American Revolution
Records. 1892-1940s. No size given.
Open. No guide.
Kansas City Public Library, Missouri Valley Room.
Scrapbooks and miscellaneous files of the Kansas City and Elizabeth Benton chapters of the DAR. Also includes minute books dating from 1910 to 1943 of the James S. Kearney chapter of the United States Daughters of the War of 1812.

10,110. Greenwood, Josephine M.
Papers. Nd. Ca. 2 cu.ft.
Open. No guide.
Kansas City Public Library, Missouri Valley Room.
An early principal in the Kansas City school system, Greenwood (?-1920s) was the second wife of James Greenwood, local superintendent of schools. Correspondence, speeches she gave about a school principal's activities, and notes for her classes. Part of the correspondence concerns school matters and dates from the 1880s and 1890s; other letters concern her husband and more general subjects.

10,111. Hale Sisters
Papers. Ca. 1890s. 2 vols.
Open. No guide.
Kansas City Public Library, Missouri Valley Room.
Scrapbooks kept by dancers Martie and Sadie Hale contain clippings, broadsides, and assorted items related to theatrical entertainment in Kansas City. The two were daughters of George Hale, a Kansas City fire chief.

10,112. Kansas City and Missouri Organizations
Collection. Late 1800s- . No size given.
Open. No guide.
Kansas City Public Library, Missouri Valley Room.
Annual reports, newsletters, program books, and other items of social and civic organizations, including the Kansas City Quill Club, the Needlework Guild of America, the Kansas City Book Chat Club, the Citizen's League, the Women's Swope Park Civic Club, The 81 Club, Friends In Council, the Woman's City Club of Kansas City, the Greenwood Society, the Kansas City AAUW, the state DAR, and Mayflower Descendants. The Friends In Council records date from 1881 to 1908 and those of the Citizen's League, a reform organization, from 1918 to 1938.

10,113. McLaughlyn, Ada (Greenwood)
Papers. Nd. No size given.
Open. No guide.
Kansas City Public Library, Missouri Valley Room.
A teacher at Kansas City's Westport High School, McLaughlyn was the daughter of Kansas City's first superintendent of schools James M. Greenwood. Correspondence reflects her travels with her husband and her involvement in the Harris Home Association, a movement to save an historic home in the Westport area. Also includes notes from the high school classes she taught and genealogical notes.

10,114. Missouri Valley Historical Society
Records. 1890s-1930s. No size given.
Open. No guide.
Kansas City Public Library, Missouri Valley Room.
Founded in the 1890s as the Early Settlers Association, the organization became the Kansas City Historical Society and later the Missouri Valley Historical Society. Women made up the bulk of the membership of the Society, which was discontinued in 1933. Minutes, treasurer's books, and annual volumes of reminiscences. The Society collected artifacts and manuscripts and maintained a small museum.

10,115. Native Sons of America
Records. Nd. 70 vols. and other items.
Open. No guide.

Kansas City Public Library, Missouri Valley Room.
Scrapbooks of the Native Sons of America, an historical organization founded in 1878 to save a Union cementery. Some of the scrapbooks contain correspondence, photos, clippings, and memorabilia about important Kansas City women and about women in such fields as music and education. One scrapbook concerns Mrs. Johnston Lykins, who was instrumental in the establishment of the Kansas City Widows and Orphans Home.

10,116. Woman's Christian Temperance Union, McDonald Union
Records. 1901-09. 4 vols.
Open. No guide.
Kansas City Public Library, Missouri Valley Room.
Minute books and a cash book of the McDonald Union, which was named for Almena Parker McDonald. The Union represented the Kansas City District.

10,117. Gallager
Papers. 1920-72. 4 vols.
Open. No guide.
Kansas City Public Library, West Branch, Mexican American Archives.
[Mrs.] Dorothy Gallager collected notes, photos, pamphlets, clippings, and memorabilia concerning Mexican Americans in Kansas City. Some of the material contained in her four scrapbooks relates to the Guadalupe Center, a service agency for Mexican Americans.

10,118. Beach, Amy Marcy (Cheney)
Papers. Nd. 35 items.
Access restricted. Unpublished guide.
University of Missouri-Kansas City, Conservatory Library.
Musical manuscripts that Beach (1867-1944), a composer, wrote as a child and later in life. The wife of Henry Harris Aubrey Beach, Amy Beach was known as Mrs. H. H. A. Beach.

10,119. Kettering, Eunice Lea
Papers. Nd. 2 ft.
Access restricted. No guide.
University of Missouri-Kansas City, Conservatory Library.
Musical manuscripts and tape recordings of compositions by Kettering (1906-), an Ohio-born composer and music teacher.

10,120. Lichtenwalter, Geneve
Papers. 1890s-1920s. 3 ft.
Open. No guide.
University of Missouri-Kansas City, Conservatory Library.
[Miss] Lichtenwalter (1867-1951) was a Kansas City music teacher and pianist. Scrapbooks of programs and program books of local musical events. Lichtenwalter was the teacher of composer Virgil Thomson, a native of Kansas City.

10,121. Weaver, Mary Watson
Papers. Nd. 2 ft.
Access restricted. No guide.
University of Missouri-Kansas City, Conservatory Library.
Correspondence, musical manuscripts, drawings, and paintings of Weaver, a composer and piano teacher. She is the widow of composer Powell Weaver (1890-1951). Correspondents include Mrs. H. H. A. Beach, Mrs. Edward MacDowell, and others involved in music.

LAWSON

10,122. Carrau
Papers. Late 1800s-early 1900s. 2 boxes.
Open. Card catalog.
Watkins Mill Historic Site.
Correspondence, photos, documents, and artifacts of Catherine (Watkins) Carrau (1887-), the granddaughter of Waltus Watkins, owner of a woolen mill.

10,123. Frass
Papers. Late 1800s-early 1900s. 3 boxes.
Open. Catalog cards.
Watkins Mill Historic Site.
Correspondence, documents, magazines, books, and artifacts of Henry Frass and his daughter Teresa (Frass) Weber, who owned the Watkins farm from 1945 to 1958. The papers and artifacts had been owned previously by the Watkins family.

10,124. Mason
Papers. Ca. 1855-1945. 7 boxes.
Open. Catalog cards.
Watkins Mill Historic Site.
Correspondence, documents, and artifacts donated by Emelia (Frass) Mason (?-ca. 1969), who lived in and cared for the Watkins home from 1945 to 1958. She willed the papers and objects, which had belonged to the Watkins family, to the Watkins Mill Association.

10,125. Watkins, Waltus
Papers. 1800-1958. No size given.
Partially restricted. Card catalog.
Watkins Mill Historic Site.
Correspondence, photos, documents, maps, artifacts, and other items of the family of Watkins (1806-84), who ran a woolen mill. Includes letters of his daughters Martha (Watkins) [Mrs. W. D.] Scruggs, Katherine (Watkins) [Mrs. Jehu B.] Atchison, Mary Elizabeth "Lizzie" (Watkins) [Mrs. William] Atchison, and Caroline Watkins.

MARYVILLE

10,126. Dykes, Mattie
Papers. 1910-70. Ca. 1 ft.
Open. Unpublished guide.
Northwest Missouri State University Library, Missouriana Room.
Correspondence, diaries, photos, and scrapbooks of Dykes (1890-), a writer who belonged to the Missouri Press Association. She wrote a history of Northwest Missouri State University.

10,127. Ford, Beatrice
Papers. 1880-1976. 2 ft.
Open. Unpublished guide.
Northwest Missouri State University Library, Missouriana Room.
Correspondence, diaries, photos, and scrapbooks of Ford (1881-1975), a writer and political organizer. She was a member of the Missouri Press Association during the 1940s and was active in the Democratic party.

NEVADA

10,128. P.E.O. Sisterhood
Records. 1909- . 4 ft. and 2 boxes.
Access restricted. Unpublished guide.
Cottey College Archives.
Records of this educational and philanthropic women's organization, founded in 1869, principally consist of the *P.E.O. Record,* the Sisterhood's monthly magazine, and scrapbooks of the local chapter. Also includes the Sisterhood's constitution, bylaws, copies of the standing rules, the creed, and souvenir programs.

O'FALLON

10,129. Convent Archives
Records. 1845- . 40 ft.
Access restricted. Unpublished guide.
Sisters of the Most Precious Blood Convent.
Constitution; custom books; correspondence and biographies of superiors general; histories of the order; lists of superiors general, chaplains, members, jubilarians, and missions; photos; maps; cemetery guide; descriptions of paintings in the chapel; and clippings of this religious order of women, whose members are teachers, nurses, artists, and makers of vestments.

PERRY

10,130. Family and Friends of Mark Twain
Collection. 1835- . No size given.
Access restricted. No guide.
Mark Twain Research Foundation, Inc.
Letters written by Samuel L. Clemens, whose pen name was Mark Twain, and by Twain's family and friends, including Laura H. Frazer, who was the model for Twain's character Becky Thatcher; Helen K. Garth; Annie Moffett Webster; and others. The letters, which are published in the Foundation's bimonthly newspaper *The Twainian,* deal with matters related to the Missouri-born author but also reflect events and society of the period in which they were written.

POINT LOOKOUT

10,131. McCord, May Kennedy
Papers. 1880- . 10 items and 67 tapes.
Open. No guide.
Ralph Foster Museum.
Articles and photos of McCord (1880-), a folk singer, composer, writer, lecturer, and radio personality who collected folklore for the National Archives in 1930. Also includes tapes of air checks of her radio broadcasts from the early 1960s.

10,132. Mahnkey, Mary Elizabeth
Papers. 1878-1948. 11 items.
Open. No guide.
Ralph Foster Museum.
A storekeeper and postmaster in Mincey, MO, Mahnkey (1878-1948) was a poet and writer who was named the state's poet laureate. Articles, poems, photos, and other items.

10,133. O'Neill, Rose Cecil
Papers. Nd. 177 items.
Open. No guide.
Ralph Foster Museum.
O'Neill (1874-1944) was a writer, artist, and sculptor who created the Kewpie doll. Correspondence, photos of O'Neill and her Kewpie dolls, books by Harry Leon Wilson with illustrations by O'Neill, calendars, cards, Kewpie dolls, statues, dishes, paintings, doll clothes, and other items.

ST. CHARLES

10,134. Clippings
Collection. 1950s-60s. Ca. 10 binders.
Open. No guide.
St. Charles County Historical Society.
St. Charles *Journal* clippings, chiefly written by [Mrs.] Edna McElhiney Olson, include items about Mary (Easton) Sibley, who with her husband George Champlin Sibley founded Linden Wood Female College (now Lindenwood College) in

1827; Mother General M. Augusta Volk, who established the motherhouse of the Sisters of the Most Precious Blood in O'Fallon, MO, in 1873; Mother Mary Odilia, who, with six other sisters, came to St. Louis from Germany and helped nurse local residents through various epidemics; Sina Simmonds, a free mulatto who used money she gained by buying and selling property to purchase and then free slaves; [Mrs.] Catherine Collier who opened a free common school in 1830 and taught white and Negro children in a Methodist Church building; and Mother Rose Philippine Duchesne, who helped establish the Sacred Heart school for girls in 1818. In 1824, Mother Duchesne opened a school for Indian girls.

10,135. Olson, Edna McElhiney
Papers. Nd. 16 drawers.
Open. No guide.
St. Charles County Historical Society.
A founder of the St. Charles County Historical Society, [Mrs.] Olson (?-1969) was the County's unofficial historian. Research notes, programs, clippings, and other papers accumulated by Olson and her mother, who was a genealogist. Olson wrote several books and articles as well as a regular historical series for the St. Charles *Journal.*

10,136. Woman's Relief Corps
Records. Nd. No size given.
Open. No guide.
St. Charles County Historical Society.
Records of the local Corps unit, an auxiliary of the Grand Army of the Republic, Department of Missouri, and of a soldiers home, a residence the Corps supported in St. James, MO.

ST. CLAIR

10,137. Hearst, Phoebe (Apperson)
Papers. 1800- . 4 ft. and 2 tapes.
Open. No guide.
Phoebe Apperson Hearst Historical Society, Inc.
A philanthropist, Hearst (1842-1919) was the wife of US senator George Hearst and the mother of William Randolph Hearst. Correspondence about the Hearst family and about the founding of the National Congress of Mothers and the PTA. Also includes papers of her husband, son, and grandson William Randolph Hearst, Jr.; correspondence and studies about the early life of Phoebe Hearst; research material on the Hearst family; oral history tapes; and other items. The collection is housed at the Hearst Historical Schoolhouse at Anaconda, MO.

ST. LOUIS

10,138. Congregation Archives
Records. 1874- . 64 drawers.
Partially restricted. Unpublished guide.
Benedictine Convent of Perpetual Adoration.
Constitutions, correspondence, history of foundations made and discontinued, retreat notes, photos of persons and buildings, souvenir booklets, records of conferences of prioresses, and other records of the Congregation, which was founded in 1874 at Maryville, MO, and moved to Conception, MO, and Clyde, MO. Includes correspondence of the foundress with sisters in Switzerland; correspondence of sisters establishing new foundations; material about such topics as the Benedictine Institute of Sacred Theology in Collegeville, MN, and the Benedictine Superiors' Retreat and Novitiate Workshop, held in 1953; records of day and boarding students and catalogs listing subjects offered at St. Joseph's Academy from 1882 to 1934; items concerning changes within the Congregation from 1874 to the present; and issues, on microfilm, of the magazine *Tabernacle and Purgatory,* later called *Spirit and Life.*

10,139. Lutheran Church—Missouri Synod: Board of Missions
Records. 1878-1976. 341.2 feet.
Open. Partial unpublished guide.
Concordia Historical Institute.
The original mission board of the Lutheran Church—Missouri Synod was founded in 1878. The current Board, organized in 1967, has carried on the original purpose of propagation of the Gospel at home and abroad. Board minutes, correspondence, personnel records, and photos contain information about women who served in the Church's missionary effort.

10,140. Lutheran Women's Missionary League
Records. 1929-75. 32 ft.
Open. Partial unpublished guide.
Concordia Historical Institute.
The League was founded in 1942 to support mission activities of the Lutheran Church—Missouri Synod and to promote the Christian growth of its members. Constitutions, minutes, treasurer's reports and invoices, convention proceedings, histories, and scrapbooks of photos and clippings of the Women's Missionary League and of the Lutheran Women's League, a predecessor group formed in 1930. Includes correspondence of such officers as Bertha (Graebner) [Mrs. R. H. C.] Meyer, Clara (Senninger) [Mrs. Otto F.] Schmitt, and Florence (Stolte) [Mrs. C. R.] Montz.

10,141. Lutheran Women's Missionary League, Western District
Records. 1932-68. 3.5 ft.
Open. Partial unpublished guide.
Concordia Historical Institute.
Organized in 1943, the League raised funds among its members to support mission congregations in the Western District of the Luthern Church—Missouri Synod; it also fostered its members' Christian growth. Minutes, financial records, convention proceedings, correspondence, a history, and booklets of this women's organization and its predecessors, the Lutheran Women's League of Greater St. Louis and the Lutheran Women's League of the Western District. The first predecessor was formed in 1932 and the second, in 1941. Includes correspondence of officers, particularly the group's first president Clara (Senninger) [Mrs. Otto F.] Schmitt, and a history of the organization from 1929 to 1963. This division of the League was disbanded in 1968 when the Western District was divided into the Missouri and Mid-South districts.

10,142. Personal Collections
Collection. 1839-1976. No size given.
Partially restricted. Partial unpublished guide.
Concordia Historical Institute.
Included with the correspondence, diaries, and photos of a large number of individuals are papers of women who were missionaries, lay leaders in church organizations, teachers in parochial schools, or who played other important roles in the Church.

10,143. Thode, Frieda Oelschlaeger
Papers. Nd. 0.5 ft.
Open. No guide.
Concordia Historical Institute.
[Mrs. E. H.] Thode and her husband were missionaries in Hong Kong and China. Autobiography and an account, with photos, of the Thodes' missionary work.

10,144. West Central Province Archives
Records. 1809- . 57 boxes and 1558 vols.
Open. Card index.
Daughters of Charity of St. Vincent de Paul, Marillac Provincial House.
The order was founded in the US in 1809 by Mother Elizabeth Ann Seton, who is known as the founder of the parochial school system. Minutes, financial records, correspondence, diaries concerning WWII, missionary activities, sermons, conferences, biographies, travelogues, photos, scrapbooks, clippings, publications by community members, and other records of the Province. Includes material about the leprosarium in Carville and the work of the sisters in education, health, social ministry, and wartime and disaster activities. Also includes the Catholic Americana Collection, which contains books and historical magazines relating to the development of the Catholic Church in the US, biographies of foundresses of religious orders, and histories of religious communities.

10,145. Guild of St. Barnabas for Nurses, St. Louis Chapter
Records. 1915-23. 1 vol.
Open. No guide.
Episcopal Diocese of Missouri.
Minute book of the Guild, an Episcopalian organization for women in the nursing profession, which was founded in 1890.

10,146. Sisterhood of the Good Shepherd
Records. 1875-1935. Ca. 1 carton and 2 tapes.
Access restricted. No guide.
Episcopal Diocese of Missouri.
The Sisterhood moved to St. Louis in 1872 to staff St. Luke's Hospital; in 1875 its members founded the School of the Good Shepherd, a school for girls. Scrapbook, school catalogs, and interviews with former students of the School, which closed in 1915. The order became defunct in 1935.

10,147. Woman's Auxiliary
Records. 1881-1976. 3 ft.
Access restricted. No guide.
Episcopal Diocese of Missouri.
Minute books of the executive board, yearbooks, and other records of the group, the membership of which includes every woman in the Episcopal Church. Founded in 1881 as an auxiliary to the Board of Missions, the group was known after 1919 as the Woman's Auxiliary to the National Council of the Episcopal Church. It became the Episcopal Churchwomen of the Diocese of Missouri in about 1960.

10,148. Field, Eugene
Papers. 1850-1936. 20 Hollinger boxes.
Closed. No guide.
Eugene Field House and Toy Museum.
Correspondence, financial records, photos, and other papers of Field (1850-95), a poet and journalist, and his wife Julia (Comstock) Field (1857-1937), a homemaker. Also includes memorabilia.

10,149. Harris Teachers College and St. Louis Public Schools
Records. 1854- . Ca. 563 vols.
Access restricted. Unpublished guide.
Harris-Stowe College Library.
Records of the St. Louis public schools, which were organized in 1854, and Harris Teachers College, which was founded in 1857 as a two-year normal school, include *Reports* and *Proceedings* of the St. Louis Board of Education, the *Public School Messenger,* the *Western,* and archival material of Harris Teachers College and Stowe Teachers College, which was founded in 1890. Also includes works of Susan Blow, the founder of the kindergarten movement in the US, and William Torrey Harris, superintendent of St. Louis schools and later US commissioner of education. Harris and Stowe colleges merged in 1954; the name of the combined school was changed to Harris-Stowe College in 1977.

10,150. Anderson, Edgar
Papers. Ca. 1900-69. 27 boxes.
Closed. No guide.

Missouri Botanical Garden.
Papers of Anderson, a taxonomist, ethnobotanist, and director of the Missouri Botanical Garden, include correspondence and diaries of his wife Dorothy (Moore) Anderson, which reflect their social and professional lives.

10,151. Biographical File
Collection. Nd. Ca. 1050 folders.
Open. No guide.
Missouri Botanical Garden.
Collection contains information about such women as Kathleen Bever Blackburn, Diane Mary Bridson, Mary Agnes Chase, Maureen Elizabeth Church, Ethel Katherine Crum, Clara E. Cummings, Alice Eastwood, Joanna G. Erasmus, Katharine Esau, Dallas Fawdry, Victoria Gordon, Adele Lewis Grant, Patricia Halliday, Mireille Kramer, Mary Maxine Larisey, Joanna Asquith Lowe, Margaret Ursula Mee, Margaret Meen, Elena Elektra Megaw, Ynes Enriquetta Julietta Mexia, Mary Farnham Miller, Marie C. Neal, Dorothea F. M. Pertz, Stella Ross-Craig, Mathilda Smith, Lilian Snelling, E. Margaret Stones, Kasumi Teshigahara, Harriet Anne Thiselton-Dyer, Rosa M. Towne, Elsie Maud Wakefield, Ann V. Webster, Heather Wood, and Tomoe Yokoi.

10,152. Historical Manuscripts
Collection. Ca. 1780s- . Ca. 525 folders.
Closed. No guide.
Missouri Botanical Garden.
Limited amounts of correspondence and botanical research data of women, including Agnes (Robertson) Arber, a botanist and natural historian; Estelle Brodman, a medical librarian; Mary Agnes (Merrill) Chase, an agrostologist and botanist; Mary Anna Day, a botanical librarian and bibliographer; Alice Eastwood, a taxonomist and plant collector; Adele Gerard (Lewis) Grant, a plant morphologist, taxonomist, and plant collector; Bertha Marion [Mrs. Charles E.] Lahman; Esther Louise Larsen, a botanical historian and taxonomist; Mildred E. Mathias, a taxonomist and horticulturist; Norma Etta Pfeiffer, a taxonomist and plant morphologist; Sarah Frances "Sadie" Price, a pteridologist, taxonomist, plant collector, and artist; Caroline Thomas Rumbold; and Elizabeth F. Sprague.

10,153. Shaw, Henry
Papers. 1820s-89. Ca. 100 boxes.
Closed. No guide.
Missouri Botanical Garden.
Papers of Shaw (1800-99), founder of the Missouri Botanical Garden, include letters from his mother and two sisters as well as his sister Sarah's travel diary from ca. 1840. Also includes articles about the breach of promise suit that [Miss] Effie Carstang filed against Shaw in 1857, alleging that he had promised to marry her in 1856. She won $100,000 in damages at the first trial, but she lost the subsequent appeal.

10,154. Bernays, Thekla Mary
Papers. 1870-1930. 300 items.
Open. Card catalog.
Missouri Historical Society.
Bernays (1856-1931) was a writer, speaker, and supporter of women's rights. Translations, usually from German to English; correspondence; and clippings scrapbooks relate principally to literary figures in St. Louis in the early 20th century. Correspondents include Zoë Akins, George S. Johns, William Marion Reedy, and Sara Teasdale.

10,155. Blake, Lillie (Devereux)
Papers. 1847-1910. 1200 items.
Open. Card catalog.
Missouri Historical Society.
[Mrs. Grinfill] Blake (1833-1913) was an author, lecturer, reformer, and suffragist. Correspondence, journals, speeches, autobiography for the period 1873-1903, scrapbooks concerning the organization of the women's rights movement, brochures, and handbills. Included are letters of such suffragists as the Blackwells, Carrie Chapman Catt, and Elizabeth Cady Stanton. The journals and scrapbooks cover the antebellum period, the Civil War years, and Lillie Blake's activities in the women's rights and woman suffrage movements, including the National Woman Suffrage Association. Before her marriage to Grinfill Blake, she was married to Frank Geoffrey Quay Umsted.

10,156. Blow Family
Papers. 1840-1911. Ca. 175 items.
Open. Card catalog.
Missouri Historical Society.
Correspondence and other papers of Henry Taylor Blow, his wife Minerva Grimsley Blow, and his daughter Susan Elizabeth Blow (1843-1916), an educator credited with founding the first kindergarten west of the Mississippi. Includes correspondence concerning family and business matters, the Civil War, and national and state politics. Also contains lectures delivered by Susan Blow from about 1890 to 1900. After studying the works of Friedrich Froebel and observing his kindergartens while traveling in Germany in the 1860s, she founded her kindergarten with the approval of the St. Louis superintendent of schools.

10,157. Bulkley Family
Papers. 1848-65. Ca. 70 items.
Open. Card catalog.
Missouri Historical Society.
Family correspondence, biographical data, and a typescript entitled "Grandmother, Mother, and me" by Mary E. Bulkley, which describes the lives of the three women named in the title. Also includes letters from the Civil War period and biographical data on Caroline Thomas Rumbold, a noted plant pathologist.

10,158. Chopin, Kate (O'Flaherty)
Papers. 1870-1902. No size given.
Partially closed. Card catalog.
Missouri Historical Society.
Chopin (1851-1904) was a writer whose published works included *At Fault, Bayou Folk, A Night in Acadie,* and *The Awakening.* Correspondence with readers and friends, manuscripts of about 40 poems and 20 stories, translations of Guy de Maupassant, extracts from works by other authors, and lists of the stories she sold, fees she received, and dates of rejections and acceptances. Chopin, who married Oscar Chopin in 1870, also wrote magazine articles and stories for young people.

10,159. Cook, Fannie (Frank)
Papers. 1881-1949. Ca. 4 ft.
Open. Card catalog.
Missouri Historical Society.
An author and lecturer, [Mrs. Jerome E.] Cook (1893-1949) was interested in southeast Missouri sharecroppers, racial problems, and relief conditions. Correspondence, notebooks, literary papers, biographical data, scrapbooks, pamphlets, clippings, periodicals, and other printed material reflect her interests, among them racial problems involved in the Franklin School controversy in St. Louis in 1930. Includes manuscripts of her *Mrs. Palmer's Honey* (1946), *Storm Against the Wall* (1948), *The Long Bridge* (1949), the unpublished "William Beaumont," and numerous short stories.

10,160. Couzins, John E. D.
Papers. 1825-1950. Ca. 100 items.
Open. Card catalog.
Missouri Historical Society.
Couzins (1813-86) was St. Louis chief of police and US marshal for the eastern district of Missouri, while his daughter Phoebe Wilson Couzins (?-1913) was Missouri's second woman lawyer and the first woman US marshal. Correspondence, receipts of ordnance stores, a genealogy, clippings, and other papers of John Couzins, his wife, and Phoebe Couzins contain information about the Civil War Sanitary Commission in which the three were involved. Phoebe Couzins's papers include correspondence and other material regarding her work and writings. She received her law degree from Washington University in St. Louis in 1871 and served as a deputy to her father. When his health failed, she assumed his duties and became US marshal in 1887. A supporter of woman's suffrage, Phoebe Couzins lectured on the topic and belonged to the Woman's Franchise Organization.

10,161. Eliot, Henry Ware
Papers. Nd. No size given.
Open. Card catalog.
Missouri Historical Society.
Family correspondence, poetry manuscripts, and notes and printed matter of Eliot and his wife Charlotte Champe (Stearns) Eliot (1843-1929). Includes material from 1900 to 1903 concerning Charlotte Eliot's support for legislation to regulate the treatment of neglected and delinquent children, notes she wrote about a slave named Archer Alexander, and three notebooks of her poetry.

10,162. Field, Eugene
Papers. Nd. No size given.
Open. Card catalog.
Missouri Historical Society.
Portions of the correspondence and other papers of Field (1850-95), a poet and journalist, relate to Mary Katherine "Kate" Keemle Field (1838-96), a lecturer and journalist who supported such causes as Hawaiian annexation, temperance, and the abolition of Mormon polygamy. Contains some of Kate Field's writings about women and some of her lectures on Mormonism. Letters by Kate Field, included in the Society's Ludlow-Field-Maury collection, tell of her attempts to popularize the position of women as lecturers and to dispel the assumption that they must act or sing. Other letters refer to Field or to her speaking tours.

10,163. Green, John
Papers. 1855-1956. 5 ft.
Open. Card catalog.
Missouri Historical Society.
Green (1835-1913) was an eye doctor and physician; his daughter Elizabeth Green (1878-1965) was a St. Louis patron of the arts. Correspondence of John Green, his wife Hattie (Jones) Green, and Elizabeth Green; medical notes; and records, notes, writings, and pamphlets of John Green. The correspondence of Hattie and Elizabeth Green provides information about St. Louis social life. Elizabeth Green worked with artists connected with the WPA in St. Louis, with the Professional Workers' Program which sponsored the People's Art Center for Negroes in St. Louis, and with other art projects in the city.

10,164. Hayward, Florence
Papers. 1862-1913. 4 vols.
Open. Card catalog.
Missouri Historical Society.
Scrapbooks of Hayward, a newspaper columnist, include correspondence, clippings of her newspaper columns and about a trip to London, Civil War sketches, photos, theater programs, autographs, and other memorabilia.

10,165. Heath, Anna Barnes
Papers. 1869-1951. 25 items.
Open. Card catalog.
Missouri Historical Society.
Heath, a friend of Julia [Mrs. Ulysses] Grant, was invited to the Grant inaugurations and balls; dinners at the White House during the Grant, Hayes, and Cleveland administrations; and to the Grant-Sartoris wedding. Souvenirs of White House social life during the Grant administration, clippings about various events, menus, and place cards.

10,166. Kalkman, Adelaide
Papers. Ca. 1860-97. No size given.
Open. Card catalog.
Missouri Historical Society.
Correspondence, diaries, and notes of Kalkman, a St. Louis singer who toured in Europe. Kalkman kept her financial accounts and diaries in account books of a firm called Kalkman and Wessels located in Nebraska City, Nebraska Territory. The books include the firm's accounts for 1860 to 1864 as well as Kalkman's accounts, diary, and expenses from a European trip from 1895 to 1897. Another diary records an 1892 tour of London, Paris, Lucerne, Milan, Munich, the Rhine, and other points in Europe.

10,167. Lamb, Harriet
Papers. 1847-52. 4 vols.
Open. Card catalog.
Missouri Historical Society.
Diaries in which Lamb, an Illinois housewife, writes about the weather, her children, her work, and other aspects of her daily life.

10,168. Langsdorf, Alexander S.
Papers. 1922-44. No size given.
Open. Card catalog.
Missouri Historical Society.
Correspondence, diaries, notebooks, minutes, scrapbooks, and legislative bills of Alexander S. Langsdorf and of his wife Elsie (Hirsch) Langsdorf, a Missouri state representative who was also active in child welfare work. Her papers include minutes and organizational correspondence of Chapter 65 of the National Federation for Child Study, of which she was a member; a notebook containing entries on social and cultural topics and suggestions for additional reading; a scrapbook relating to her campaign in 1942 for election to the Missouri House of Representatives from the 4th District and her work from 1942 to 1944 as a state legislator; and legislative bills which she annotated. Her scrapbooks and letters reflect her interest in child welfare, the St. Louis Council for Child Study and Parent Education, and the Urban League.

10,169. Lindenwood College
Records. Nd. No size given.
Open. Card catalog.
Missouri Historical Society.
Lindenwood College, a girls school, was founded in 1827 in St. Charles, MO, by George C. Sibley and his wife Mary Smith Easton Sibley. Includes letters of Mary Sibley with inquiries about the education of the correspondents' daughters, the problems of conducting schools in competition with Catholics, tuition payments, and concern about the continuation of a Protestant school in St. Charles. School circulars are also included.

10,170. Linn, Lewis F.
Papers. 1814-61. Ca. 150 items.
Open. Card catalog.
Missouri Historical Society.
Correspondence and scrapbooks of Linn (1795-1843), a physician who served in the Missouri Senate in 1827 and in the US Senate from 1833 to 1843, primarily consist of letters to his wife Elizabeth A. (Relfe) Linn. These letters concern politics, gossip about political figures and events in St. Genevieve, MO, and the personal life of her husband. James Buchanan, John C. Calhoun, Charles Dickens, Jane Means Pierce, Martin Van Buren, and prominent Missourians were among her correspondents. The two scrapbooks contain letters, autographs, and memorabilia.

10,171. Loeb, Therese "Tess"
Papers. 1943-44. 1 item.
Open. Card catalog.
Missouri Historical Society.
[Mrs. Virgil] Loeb was an active member of the LWV. List of the dates of articles that Loeb wrote for the St. Louis *Star-Times* concerning the Missouri Constitutional Convention of 1943-44 held in Jefferson City.

10,172. McConnell, Genevieve Knapp
Papers. 1876-ca. 1915. 3 vols.
Open. Card catalog.
Missouri Historical Society.
Manuscript of the autobiography of McConnell, an author of children's stories, who was best known for her *The Seeing Eye*. See Knapp Family Papers elsewhere in the repository for McConnell's 1890 diary.

10,173. Markham, Mary (McKittrick)
Papers. 1897-1943. 3 vols.
Open. Card catalog.
Missouri Historical Society.
[Mrs. George D.] Markham was a St. Louis society woman and philanthropist. Scrapbooks containing handwritten entries, programs, clippings, and mementos provide day-by-day information about Markham's activities and reflect her interests, including support for the "dry law" crusade. Markham collected items relating to balls, weddings, parties, charity events, and other social functions.

10,174. Missouri Welfare League
Records. 1920-49. No size given.
Open. Card catalog.
Missouri Historical Society.
[Miss] Carol Bates served as executive secretary of the League, which sought to improve conditions in Missouri prisons and to promote legislation for penal reforms. Correspondence, speeches, and reports Bates wrote in connection with her work for the League.

10,175. Moore, Missouri (Bishop)
Papers. 1859. 1 vol.
Open. Card catalog.
Missouri Historical Society.
Copy of the journal in which Martha "Missouri" Moore (1837-81), a housewife, describes her six-month journey to California with James Preston Moore, whom she married in 1858. The copy was made by Frances Bishop Sweany, a sister of the author.

10,176. Neilson, Lillian Adelaide
Papers. Nd. 1 vol.
Open. Card catalog.
Missouri Historical Society.
Scrapbook contains correspondence, programs, portraits, press notices, and clippings regarding the career of Neilson, a St. Louis actress.

10,177. O'Hare, Frank P.
Papers. 1918-52. No size given.
Open. Card catalog.
Missouri Historical Society.
Correspondence, typescript reports, and miscellaneous papers of O'Hare primarily relate to his wife Kate (Richards) O'Hare (1877-1948), a socialist and pacifist imprisoned under the Espionage Act after entry of the US into WWI. Correspondence, some of it between the O'Hares, pertains to her imprisonment in 1919 and 1920, during which she suffered heat prostration, complained about conditions, and succeeded in forcing a report (also included) on conditions in the Missouri State Penitentiary. In addition, the collection contains letters, reports, and other material about the Kate Richards O'Hare Appeal Fund, the Liberty Defense Union, the Children's Crusade to Free Political Prisoners, and the Children's Crusade for Amnesty. Also includes letters O'Hare wrote to her children and letters reflecting her interest in Llano Colony, Newllano, LA; her speaking tours; and her growing differences with her husband. Their marriage ended in divorce, and she married Charles C. Cunningham.

10,178. O'Neill, Rose Cecil
Papers. Nd. Ca. 200 items.
Open. Card catalog.
Missouri Historical Society.
An illustrator for *Puck* and *Life* magazines and a writer, O'Neill (1874-1944) created the Kewpie doll cartoon, which was syndicated by newspapers and serialized by four national magazines. Correspondence, notes, drawings, memorabilia, and a typescript chapter of her autobiography. O'Neill was married to Gray Latham and, in 1902, to Harry Leon Wilson.

10,179. Petri, Anna Louise
Papers. 1892-1942. 11 vols.
Open. Card catalog.
Missouri Historical Society.
A St. Louis musician, Petri participated in musical programs for the Missouri Federation of Music Clubs, the Rubenstein Music Club, and the Morning Etude. Scrapbooks containing programs of musical and organ recitals, programs in which Petri participated, clippings and articles which include information about music, and clippings about the Missouri Federation of Music Clubs.

10,180. Rumbold, Charlotte
Papers. 1928-44. No size given.
Open. Card catalog.
Missouri Historical Society.
Correspondence, diaries, notes, photos, and clippings of Rumbold, a feminist and director of playground recreation in St. Louis for many years, and her sister Caroline Thomas Rumbold, a noted plant pathologist who held a doctoral degree. Includes Caroline Rumbold's diaries of a trip around the world in 1928.

10,181. Scovel, Sylvester
Papers. Nd. No size given.
Open. Card catalog.
Missouri Historical Society.
Collection of Scovel, a correspondent for the New York *World,* includes an account by his wife Frances Cabanne Scovel of her expedition to the Yukon during the gold rush of 1897. She described her trip along an "almost impassable" trail from Lake Bennett to Skagway. She later married W. F. "Bill" Saportas, who served as her guide during the Yukon expedition.

10,182. Smith, Sol
Papers. 1830s-1900. No size given.
Open. Card catalog.
Missouri Historical Society.
Smith was a theatrical agent. Correspondence and miscellaneous material relating to the theater include ca. 42 letters dating from the 1830s to 1877 from Ellen (Tree) Kean, an entertainer. Her letters concern theatrical affairs in England and the US; other letters concern Kean's performances, schedules of her American tours, revenues, and problems with noisy audiences. Also included are letters from Kean's husband Charles Kean, which refer to his wife.

10,183. Teasdale, Sara
Papers. 1910-31. 254 items.
Closed. Card catalog.
Missouri Historical Society.
Consists primarily of the letters of Teasdale (1884-1933), a poet, to her husband Ernst B. Filsinger, but includes articles and clippings as well. In the correspondence, Teasdale and Filsinger discuss her relationships with and evaluations of her contemporaries in literature and the arts. Some of the letters reflect the formative stages of her poetry, while others concern publication of poems.

10,184. Worth, Patience
Papers. 1913-37. Ca. 29 vols.
Open. Card catalog.
Missouri Historical Society.
Worth was said to be a 17th-century girl contacted

by Pearl [Mrs. John W.] Curran and a friend through the use of a Ouija board. Curran transcribed 29 volumes of stories and other literary efforts she attributed to Worth. Some of Curran's transcripts were published by the Patience Worth Publishing Company. Other collections at the Society describe seances during which Worth was contacted, a doctor's concern for Curran's health, and inconsistencies in Worth's writings.

10,185. Archives of Pi Beta Phi
Records. 1867- . No size given.
Open. No guide.
Pi Beta Phi Fraternity.
Minutes, correspondence, histories, scrapbooks, photos, clippings, and memorabilia of Pi Beta Phi, a national women's fraternity founded in 1867 by 12 college women at Monmouth College in Monmouth, IL. Contains information on national meetings, individual chapters, and women who were officers of or workers for the fraternity. Founders included Emma (Brownlee) Kilgore, Margaret Campbell, Libbie (Brook) Gaddis, Ada (Bruen) Grier, Rosa Moore, Clara (Brownlee) Hutchinson, physician Jennie Nichol, Inez (Smith) Soule, Fannie (Whitenack) Libbey, Jennie (Horne) Turnbull, Fannie Thomson, and Nancy (Black) Wallace.

10,186. Province Archives
Records. 1929-77. No size given.
Access restricted. No guide.
Sisters of Mercy Provincialate.
Correspondence, scrapbooks, photos, and other records of the Province, which was established in 1929. The Sisters work in hospitals, schools, and colleges and perform various ministries.

10,187. Generalate Archives
Records. 1836- . 65 ft.
Partially restricted. No guide.
Sisters of St. Joseph of Carondelet.
This congregation of religious women dedicated to works of charity was founded in France and established in the US in 1836 in Carondelet, MO. Minutes of general chapters, general councils, and other meetings; financial and administrative records; correspondence; diaries and other personal papers of sisters; oral history tapes; photos; annals of the congregation; necrologies; proceedings of an educational conference; scrapbooks; and books relate to the Sisters' work in colleges, schools, hospitals, and homes and with Indian tribes in Michigan and Arizona during the 19th and 20th centuries.

10,188. Province Archives
Records. 1836-1977. 150 Hollinger boxes.
Access restricted. Unpublished guide.
Sisters of St. Joseph of Carondelet, St. Louis Province Archives.
The order was first established in the US in 1836 at Carondelet, MO. Its members are involved in education, social welfare, and nursing. Minutes; financial records; property deeds; correspondence; diaries; literary manuscripts; histories of convents, hospitals, colleges, orphanages, elementary and secondary schools, and schools for deaf children; tapes; photos; scrapbooks; and other records.

10,189. Archives
Records. 1872- . No size given.
Closed. No guide.
Sisters of St. Mary of the Third Order of St. Francis, Motherhouse.
Correspondence, retreat notes, photos, scrapbooks, and memorabilia of this religious community of women, which was founded in 1872 in St. Louis by Mother Mary Odilia Berger. The principal activity of the community is health care; the Sisters own and operate a number of hospitals and clinics in Missouri and elsewhere.

10,190. University Archives
Records. 1957- . 188 cu.ft.
Open. Unpublished guide.
University of Missouri-St. Louis Archives.
Correspondence and publications of the University administration, faculty, and staff; studies for the affirmative action office regarding salary, promotion, and tenure for women; and material about the following organizations that promote women's interests at UMSL: the UMSL Women's Group, an organization of faculty and staff women that holds informational meetings on campus and monitors affirmative action; the Feminist Alliance, a group of students, faculty, and staff women that monitors course offerings and promotes women's studies; the ad hoc committee for women's studies; and the UMSL Women's Center, which provides programs for women and establishes links to community women's groups. The collection also contains material regarding the professional activities of women faculty and staff members.

10,191. Alpha Kappa Alpha
Records. 1974-75. 1 ft.
Open. No guide.
University of Missouri-St. Louis, Western Historical Manuscript Collection-St. Louis.
Alpha Kappa Alpha, the oldest black sorority in the US, was established in 1909 at Howard University; the St. Louis Chapter is called Gamma Omega. Biographies and photos of prominent St. Louis black women collected as part of the Chapter's black heritage activities. Among the women included are attorneys Doris (Gregory) Black, Rita Montgomery, Peggy Thompson, and Wyvetter H. Younge; journalists Sheila (Rule) Boyd and Ellen (Sweets) Dunning; DeVerne Lee Calloway, state representative; Julia Davis, historian; Nettie Cunningham, co-owner of Cunningham and Moore Funeral Home; Sylvia (Brent) Elliot, retail shop owner; Pearlie I. Evans, district assistant to US Representative William H. Clay; Merdean Fielding, staff producer and announcer, KTVI-TV; Ruth (Payne) Flowers, president and founder of the Ruth Flower Institute of Cosmetology; Gwen Giles, commission of human relations for St. Louis; Lola (Wallace) Harris, cosmetologist and teacher; Betty Lee, editor of *Proud Magazine;* Leah (Brock) McCartney, municipal judge; Lucille McClelland, professor and dean of the school of nursing at South Illinois University at Edwardsville; Bertha Mason, florist and owner of Mason's Flowers; Charlotte (Wilson) Smith, city treasurer in East St. Louis, IL; Florence A. Spotts, educator; Melba A. Sweets, associate editor and columnist for the *St. Louis American;* and Brenda Williams, a member of the news and public affairs staff of KSD-TV.

10,192. Aurora Club
Records. 1958-75. 0.5 ft.
Open. No guide.
University of Missouri-St. Louis, Western Historical Manuscript Collection-St. Louis.
The Aurora Club was formed in the early 1940s when the Phillis Wheatley Branch of the St. Louis YWCA, the black women's branch, suggested that employers of Negro women establish clubs for working women. Club scrapbook with photos, programs, and clippings. The Club, the only club sponsored by the employed women's committee of the St. Louis Metropolitan YWCA, has done volunteer work at the USO, delivered food to the needy at Christmas time, and donated toothbrushes and washcloths to patients at one of the city hospitals. The group was organized by women who worked in a dress shop owned by David Portney.

10,193. Bliss, Florence, and Bliss, Marie
Papers. 1832-1972. 5 ft.
Open. Unpublished guide.
University of Missouri-St. Louis, Western Historical Manuscript Collection-St. Louis.
Marie Bliss (1887-1972), an editorial secretary at the St. Louis *Post-Dispatch,* worked with the Civil Liberties Committee in the early 1940s and was involved in the peace movement during WWII and the Vietnam War; she and her sister Florence Bliss (1890-) were active in the Fellowship of Reconciliation, a peace group with religious ties. Correspondence, diaries, manuscripts of stories and plays, articles, clippings, serials, books, and issues from 1837 to 1845 of the *Youth's Cabinet,* which was devoted to liberty, peace, temperance, purity, and truth. Includes Marie Bliss's diaries for 1933 to 1947 and 1951 to 1971, which reflect her work for peace; earlier entries describe her difficulties in retaining her job at the newspaper. Many of the collection's books date from the 1800s and early 1900s and are typical of gifts given to children for perfect Sunday school attendance. Contained in the book *The Jews* is an essay written by Cynthia B. Bliss, Florence and Marie's grandmother.

10,194. Calloway, DeVerne
Papers. 1963- . 3 ft.
Open. Unpublished guide.
University of Missouri-St. Louis, Western Historical Manuscript Collection-St. Louis.
General correspondence, memos, reports, minutes, and clippings of Calloway (ca. 1918-), Missouri state representative from the 81st District, document her work in education, public welfare, and issues involving women. Elected in 1962, Calloway has sponsored bills to establish equal pay for equal work and the Missouri Commission on the Status of Women. In 1967 she participated in the effort to establish a St. Louis congressional district with a black majority and has supported increased state aid for public education, for reforming and improving welfare grants, and for services for dependent children, the blind, the disabled, and the elderly. She is chairperson of the Committee on State Institutions and Properties and has served on the First State Capitol Restoration Commission, Goals for Missouri Commission, and the State Records Commission. In addition she has served on legislative committees concerned with elections, insurance, welfare, and medicaid. Information on Calloway's 1962 election campaign and photos of her are included in the Ernest and DeVerne Calloway collection.

10,195. College Club
Records. 1921-43. 3 ft.
Open. No guide.
University of Missouri-St. Louis, Western Historical Manuscript Collection-St. Louis.
Scrapbooks containing programs, press notices, flyers, and clippings of the College Club, which is the local chapter of the AAUW. The Club, one of the oldest continuing women's organizations in the St. Louis area, was founded in about 1900 by socially active women, including Edna Gellhorn. It conducts study action programs and sponsors annual AAUW fellowships for women.

10,196. Dyson, Bell, and Sans Souci
Papers. 1850-80. 1 ft.
Open. Unpublished guide.
University of Missouri-St. Louis, Western Historical Manuscript Collection-St. Louis.
Correspondence of Absalom Roby Dyson (1832-64), a postmaster, schoolteacher, and part-time farmer from Franklin County, MO, who joined the 5th Missouri Volunteers of the Confederate Army; his wife Louisa (Johnson) Dyson (1833-98), who ran the family farm in his absence; and [Mrs.] Amanda Robertson of Raymond, MS, who cared for Absalom Dyson in her home after he was wounded in the fighting. About half of the collection's correspondence was written before the Civil War. The wartime letters include those that Absalom wrote to Robertson from 1863 until his death in 1864 and a letter from Robertson telling Louisa Dyson of Absalom's death. The correspondence between Louisa Dyson and Robertson extended to 1868 and shows the

war's impact on the two women. Also contains two photos of Louisa Dyson and the Dysons' daughter Cornelia (1860-?).

10,197. Hickey, Margaret

Papers. 1928-76. 25 ft.
Open. Unpublished guide.
University of Missouri-St. Louis, Western Historical Manuscript Collection-St. Louis.
A lawyer, businesswoman, and senior public affairs editor of *Ladies Home Journal,* Hickey (1902-) served on several federal committees. She was active in volunteer work and was an officer of the American National Red Cross, of the League of Red Cross Societies beginning in 1946, and of the National Conference on Social Welfare and International Council on Social Welfare beginning in 1956. Correspondence, speeches dating from the 1940s, interviews and transcription, scrapbooks, and photos. Includes letters from governmental, Red Cross, and social welfare officials, including Henry Kissinger, Eleanor Roosevelt, Nelson Rockefeller, Ellen Winston, George M. Elsey, Erich Fromm, Lyndon B. Johnson, John F. Kennedy, Nathan M. Pusey, Leonor Sullivan, and W. Willard Wirtz. As a businesswoman, Hickey founded and ran the Margaret Hickey School for Secretaries from 1933 to 1969. She also served on a succession of governmental panels: from 1942 to 1945 she chaired the Woman's Advisory Committee of the War Manpower Commission, from 1950 to 1952 she was a member of the International Development Advisory Board that studied President Truman's Point Four Program, in 1954 she became a member of the Citizen's Advisory Committee on Voluntary Foreign Aid, in 1955 she was a member of the President's Committee on the White House Conference on Education, from 1961 to 1963 she was a member of Kennedy's Commission on the Status of Women, and later she chaired the Citizen's Advisory Council on the Status of Women under President Johnson. In addition Hickey was national president of the Business and Professional Women's Clubs from 1944 to 1946 and an international vice-president from 1946 to 1948.

10,198. Hickey School

Records. 1960-65. 12 ft.
Open. No guide.
University of Missouri-St. Louis, Western Historical Manuscript Collection-St. Louis.
The School, founded in 1933 as the Margaret Hickey School for Secretaries, retrained women with college degrees and those with some working experience for secretarial, clerical, or statistical jobs or careers in fashion merchandising. Financial records, correspondence, memos, reports, school records, brochures, and clippings. The School, which was directed by Margaret Hickey until 1969, maintains a successful placement service for its graduates, most of whom are women.

10,199. League of Women Voters of Missouri

Records. 1911-76. 33 ft. and 1 microfilm reel.
Open. Unpublished guide.
University of Missouri-St. Louis, Western Historical Manuscript Collection-St. Louis.
The state LWV, founded in 1919, is a "non-partisan volunteer organization dedicated to promoting political responsibility through informed and active participation of citizens in government." Its records include minutes and treasurer's reports of the Missouri Equal Suffrage Association, founded in 1911 and disbanded in 1919. Divided into four series, LWV records contain constitutions; minutes and reports of state and national LWV conventions and council and program meetings; correspondence; records of the finance, organization, membership, voters services, and publications committees and of the LWV's research and education arm, the Overseas Education Fund; taped interviews with early LWV leaders; and material related to the LWV's legislative interests, including civil and women's rights, individual liberties, civil service, legislative reorganization, reapportionment, the Missouri constitutional convention of 1943 and 1944, voting procedures, taxes, the Missouri Valley Authority, ecology, and education. Also includes biographical data sheets, photos, scrapbooks, early handbills and pamphlets, clippings, and microfilm copies of *The Missouri Woman,* the official publication of the Suffrage Association.

10,200. Metropolitan League of Women Voters

Records. Ca. 1930-75. Ca. 20 ft.
Open. No guide.
University of Missouri-St. Louis, Western Historical Manuscript Collection-St. Louis.
Records of the St. Louis area LWV include correspondence from Edna Gellhorn, Tess Loeb, Maud Wood Park, Mrs. Aaron Fischer, Helen Guthrie Miller, Luella St. Clair Moss, and Mrs. J. Hardin Smith.

10,201. Metropolitan Young Women's Christian Association of St. Louis

Records. 1904-72. 60 ft.
Open. No guide.
University of Missouri-St. Louis, Western Historical Manuscript Collection-St. Louis.
The local YWCA dates from the St. Louis World's Fair of 1904 when a committee of concerned women organized a home for young women who came to the Fair with little money and no family in the area. Financial records, correspondence, memos, reports, photos, scrapbooks, and publications. Includes correspondence of Fannie (Barrier) Williams, a black journalist and clubwoman from Chicago, and Eva Bowles and Cordella Winn, two sisters who both served as secretary and administrator for the national board for the Council on Colored Work.

10,202. Mulligan, Mary Margaret

Papers. 1942-46. 0.5 ft.
Open. No guide.
University of Missouri-St. Louis, Western Historical Manuscript Collection-St. Louis.
A five-year diary kept by the mother of Mary Mulligan during the first five years of Mary's life. The diary reflects family life during WWI and child rearing methods in the 1940s.

10,203. National Council of Negro Women, St. Louis Section

Records. 1964-72. 1 ft.
Open. No guide.
University of Missouri-St. Louis, Western Historical Manuscript Collection-St. Louis.
Minutes, correspondence, reports, photos, interviews, brochures, clippings, and other items are focused upon this local group's former president, Mrs. John Peoples. A civic leader and anti-poverty worker, Peoples sponsored the women's committee for Mayor Alfonso J. Cervanties in 1965 and was chairwoman of the Committee for Completion of the Riverfront Memorial. The National Council of Negro Women, which was founded by Mary (McLeod) Bethune in 1935, encourages black women to assume leadership roles and to promote social change. The group fights racism, inadequate and substandard housing, hunger and malnutrition, insufficient child care centers, drug abuse, inhumane detention centers and prisons, exploitation of the poor, and demeaning work for household employees.

10,204. National Organization for Women in Missouri

Records. 1971-76. 1 ft.
Open. No guide.
University of Missouri-St. Louis, Western Historical Manuscript Collection-St. Louis.
Founded in 1966, NOW supports full equality for women and seeks to end prejudice and discrimination in government, industry, professions, churches, politics, and other areas. Bylaws, correspondence, memos, reports, statistics, pamphlets, newspapers, and other records, including material from North County, Columbia, and St. Louis NOW chapters and a folder regarding the Equal Rights Amendment drive of 1972 to 1974.

10,205. St. Louis Association of Colored Women's Clubs

Records. 1965-76. 0.5 ft.
Open. No guide.
University of Missouri-St. Louis, Western Historical Manuscript Collection-St. Louis.
An affiliate of the National Association of Colored Women's Clubs, Inc., the St. Louis group was formed in 1904 by Susan (Paul) Vashon to unite black women's organizations to solve the city's racial problems. Reports, histories, lists of officers, yearbooks, programs of the annual fellowship breakfasts, and catalogs. The national and local organizations viewed themselves as united club movements working for social uplift of the Negro and for racial development.

10,206. Women's International League for Peace and Freedom.

Records. 1963-76. 1.5 ft.
Open. Unpublished guide.
University of Missouri-St Louis, Western Historical Manuscript Collection-St. Louis.
A branch of the national organization founded in 1915 by Jane Addams, the St. Louis WILPF operated a peace center that provided a focus for local activities in opposition to the Vietnam War and for counseling draft resisters. Minutes, correspondence, memos, position papers, reports, resolutions, and monthly bulletins. Includes correspondence and other items donated by Yvonne Logan, president of the local WILPF, which strongly opposed US intervention in Vietnam. The national group works for political, economic, social, and psychological conditions that could assure peace and freedom.

10,207. Graham, Helen (Tredway)

Papers. 1898-1971. 8 ft. and 1 reel.
Open. Unpublished guide.
Washington University, School of Medicine Library Archives.
Graham (1890-1971) was professor of pharmacology at Washington University School of Medicine from 1954 to 1959 and professor emeritus from 1959 to 1971. Correspondence, notebooks, papers documenting her civic concerns, photo albums, scientific reprints, clippings, and memorabilia. Also includes an oral history interview about Graham by one of her colleagues. Graham's career began in 1918-19 when she worked as an assistant in pharmacology at Johns Hopkins University. Her research centered on the physiology and pharmacology of peripheral nerves and on the role of histamines and their relationship to allergies. She held various faculty positions at Washington University School of Medicine from 1925 until 1971. She was married from 1916 to 1957 to Evarts Ambrose Graham, a physician who was a professor and head of the department of surgery at Washington University. The collection is also available on microfilm.

10,208. Silberberg, Martin, and Silberberg, Ruth

Papers. 1959-ca. 1975. 5.75 ft.
Open. No guide.
Washington University, School of Medicine Library Archives.
Martin Silberberg (1895-1966) was associate professor of pathology at Washington University School of Medicine where he worked from 1937 to 1941 and from 1944 to 1966. His wife Ruth Silberberg (1906-) is professor emeritus of pathology and lecturer in pathology at Washington University School of Medicine. Notebooks contain electron microscope prints from cartilage research

and an oral history interview in which Ruth Silberberg discusses changes in medical education and pathology research. The Silberbergs studied the changes that occur in joint cartilage during an individual's life span and the effects of diabetes on cartilage tissue.

10,209. Smith, Margaret G.
Papers. 1933-69. 11 ft.
Open. Unpublished guide.
Washington University, School of Medicine Library Archives.
A professor of pathology at Washington University School of Medicine from 1929 to 1964, Smith (1896-1970) was noted for her research in pediatric pathology. Correspondence, lecture notes, case studies, notebooks, photos, scientific reprints, and memorabilia. Smith became a full professor in 1957. She isolated the St. Louis encephalitis virus and the salivary gland virus. She was the first to propagate the *Herpes Seniplex* virus in a mouse and the first to discover the cytomegetic inclusion disease virus. The collection is also available on microfilm.

10,210. Suntzeff, Valentina
Papers. 1923-73. 1.7 ft.
Open. Unpublished guide.
Washington University, School of Medicine Library Archives.
Autobiographical sketch, reprints of scientific articles, photos, certificates, and clippings of Suntzeff (1891-1975), a research associate in cancer research at Washington University School of Medicine. After receiving her MD degree in 1917 from the Women's Medical Institute in Petrograd, Suntzeff practiced medicine in Russia from 1918 to 1920 and in Manchuria from 1920 to 1923. In 1948, Suntzeff and an associate analyzed the difference between cancerous tissue and normal tissue. She was research associate professor emeritus in cancer research and lecturer in anatomy at Washington University from 1960 to 1975.

WARRENSBURG

10,211. Local History
Collection. 1835- . No size given.
Open. Card catalog.
Johnson County Historical Society, Heritage Library.
Manuscripts, 23 tapes, photos, scrapbooks, marriage and cemetery records, clippings, books, and other material document the history of Johnson County. Includes more than 1000 clippings by or about women; special material pertaining to Mary Miller Smiser, Lizzie Grover, Lulu Simmerman, Lisa Spickard, Nellie Wells, Virginia Gilkeson Hedges, Monia Morris, Mary X. Ferguson, Verna Rush, and other women; records of the Study Club, DAR, Centennial Club, and of local churches; and records and a scrapbook of women in county extension clubs. Also contains records of the Arts, Books and Crafts Club.

WEBSTER GROVES

10,212. Women in the German Evangelical Synod of North America
Records. Ca. 1880-1930. No size given.
Open. Unpublished guide.
Eden Archives and Library.
Minutes, published accounts, denominational and local publications, and other records of the German Evangelical Synod of North America, a Protestant denomination formed along lines similar to those of the Prussian Evangelical Church of the Union. Includes information about the Deaconess Order of the Synod, a nursing and parish order similar to Catholic orders of religious women, and about the "Frauenfrage," the question of the role of women in the Synod. Some of the material is in German. The Synod became a part of the United Church of Christ.

MONTANA

BILLINGS

10,213. Custer, Elizabeth (Bacon)
Papers. 1856-1933. 48 ft. and 8 microfilm reels.
Access restricted. Partial card catalog.
Eastern Montana College Library.
Military and personal correspondence, telegrams, notes, orders, reports, and photos of General George A. Custer (1839-76), a US Army officer killed at the Battle of the Little Big Horn, and of his wife Elizabeth Custer (1842-1933). The material dating from after his death pertains to her efforts to perpetuate her husband's memory.

BOZEMAN

10,214. Associated Women Students
Records. 1922- . 3 cu.ft.
Open. No guide.
Montana State University Archives.
Founded in 1917 under the direction of Una B. Herrick, who was dean, the AWS is primarily involved in campus political activities. Includes scrapbooks, 1924-65; Women's Day Programs; and Co-ed Codes. Each fall AWS published a Co-ed Code for new women students, and each spring they sponsored Women's Day, an honors assembly.

10,215. Cushman, Harriette E.
Papers. 1922-54. 1 cu.ft.
Open. Unpublished guide.
Montana State University Archives.
Contains annual reports and publications of [Miss] Cushman (1890-), an extension service poultry specialist from 1922 to 1954. Cushman organized the first cooperative turkey marketing association in the US and was the first federal turkey grader. In addition, she researched and wrote numerous publications on poultry raising.

10,216. Dean of Women
Records. 1920-75. 3 cu.ft.
Open. Inventory.
Montana State University Archives.
Includes minutes, correspondence, memos, and reports of the Dean of Women's office, which began administering the affairs of female students on campus in 1910. Also includes records of committees concerned with housing, counseling, scholarships, and vocational guidance; student employees; and the women's clubs. Una B. Herrick, Ethelyn Harrison, Esther Brown, and Marjorie (Flaherty) Paisley are among those who served as dean. Also contains Herrick's unpublished manuscript "Twenty Years at Montana State College."

10,217. Extension Service
Records. 1915-73. 104 cu.ft.
Open. Inventory.
Montana State University Archives.
Organized in 1915, the Service was involved in dispensing services and research to improve home management and agriculture. Includes annual reports, 1915-73; home demonstration agents' newsletters, 1929-67; and records and reports from the agents at large, 1918-50. Also includes records relating to child development, clothing, family life, food and nutrition, 4-H programs, home management, and home demonstration leaders.

10,218. Physical Education Department
Records. 1930-73. 2.5 cu.ft.
Partially restricted. Card catalog.
Montana State University Archives.
Contains grade books, 1937-73; scrapbooks, 1930-50 and 1964-65; and Play Day regulations and other items, 1937-57, of the Women's Physical Education Department, which was organized in ca. 1920 by Una B. Herrick, dean of women. Records relate to many women's sports and recreational activities, women's physical education classes, women coaches, extramural competition, and the Women's Athletics Association, which Herrick organized to promote women's sports. The Association sponsored a Play Day every spring, inviting teams from other schools.

10,219. School of Home Economics
Records. 1922-75. 11 cu.ft.
Partially restricted. Inventory.
Montana State University Archives.
Includes annual reports, 1931-43; financial and budget records, 1926-47; Home Economics extension and student files and grade books; and records related to the nursery school and the Home Management House. Since 1894 when the first class was offered, the professors, instructors, and students of the School—nearly all of whom were women—have focused their attention on household economy, cooking, sewing, sanitation, child care, and other domestic duties.

10,220. School of Nursing
Records. 1939-75. 3 cu.ft.
Partially restricted. Inventory.
Montana State University Archives.
The School was founded in 1938 to meet the demands for advanced work for nurses. Originally offering only one course, the School now offers a full nursing program. Includes annual reports, 1939-56; minutes of faculty meetings, 1946 to the present; staff meeting minutes from hospitals where the students worked, including the Bozeman Deaconess Hospital, the Montana State Hospital, and the Montana State Tuberculosis Sanitorium; correspondence of the executive director, ca. 1960-69; general office correspondence; grade books; and items related to the accrediting service, workshops, and conferences.

10,221. Spurs
Records. 1922- . 12.5 cu.ft.
Access restricted. Inventory.
Montana State University Archives.
Records of Spurs, a sophomore honorary service for women that was founded at the University in 1922, include financial and membership records, officers' files, correspondence with the central office, histories and reports of the local chapters, scrapbooks of activities of the local and national chapters, and issues of *The Spur,* their newspaper.

10,222. Student Affairs
Records. 1948-70. 2.5 cu.ft.
Open. Inventory.
Montana State University Archives.
Includes annual reports, 1949-63; budget records, 1954-63; student health records, 1951-64; and residence halls' office files of the Student Affairs department, which began administering student activities in ca. 1944. Also includes minutes of meetings of the Associated Women Students, 1965-70; records of meetings and activities of Alpha Lamda Delta, 1948-63; and records of meetings of the Women's Residence Hall Association, 1965-69.

10,223. Alderson Family
Papers. 1896-1916. 0.5 ft.
Open. Card catalog.
Montana State University Library, Special Collections.
Correspondence, pictures, and publications of Mary (Long) Alderson (1860-1940), who was active in

the WCTU and the Montana suffrage movement. She was the wife of Bozeman newspaperman Matthew W. Alderson.

10,224. Beall, Mrs. William J.
Papers. 1838-1929. 1 vol.
Open. Card catalog.
Montana State University Library, Special Collections.
Beall was the first white woman to reside in Bozeman. Scrapbook of clippings regarding Montana pioneers and certificates, programs, and ephemera pertaining to Beall's social activities.

10,225. Brainard, Laura Russell
Oral history. 1966. 1 tape.
Open. No guide.
Montana State University Library, Special Collections.
Interview in which [Mrs.] Brainard describes her trip to Montana in 1888 and ranch life near Spring Hill in Gallatin County, MT.

10,226. Busick, Mary Ann
Papers. 1908. 1 item.
Open. Published guide and card catalog.
Montana State University Library, Special Collections.
Reminiscences of Elizabeth E. O'Neil regarding the experiences of her mother Mary Ann Busick in Virginia City and Diamond City, MT, in 1865. See Brian Cockhill and Dale L. Johnson, comps. and eds., *Guide to Manuscripts in Montana Repositories* (Missoula, MT: University of Montana, 1973).

10,227. Buzell, Mrs. R. L.
Papers. 1913. 5 items.
Open. Published guide and card catalog.
Montana State University Library, Special Collections.
Correspondence of Buzell, a Conrad, MT, homesteader, regarding farm credit. See Brian Cockhill and Dale L. Johnson, comps. and eds., *Guide to Manuscripts in Montana Repositories* (Missoula, MT: University of Montana, 1973).

10,228. Campbell Family
Papers. 1836-1920. 0.2 ft.
Open. Published guide and card catalog.
Montana State University Library, Special Collections.
Correspondence of Major James B. Campbell concerning his real estate interests in Chicago, where he lived prior to moving to Gallatin City, MT, in 1863; correspondence from 1866 to 1877 of his son Gordon Campbell regarding the family trading post, which provided supplies for Indians and miners; and the papers from 1870 to 1920 of James Campbell's daughter Fannie Thornburg, a schoolteacher and homesteader. See Brian Cockhill and Dale L. Johnson, comps. and eds., *Guide to Manuscripts in Montana Repositories* (Missoula, MT: University of Montana, 1973).

10,229. Carey, Mary
Papers. 1864-1950. 6 in.
Open. Card catalog.
Montana State University Library, Special Collections.
Carey (1857-1950), an Adobetown, MT, merchant and postmistress from 1905 to 1907, came to Montana in 1864. Photos from ca. 1870 to 1910 of Carey's family, friends, and local sites; business records; and ledgers entitled "Carey and O'Brien, dealers in groceries, liquors, miner's supplies and clothing."

10,230. Childers, Mrs. John
Oral history. 1970. 1 tape.
Open. Card catalog.
Montana State University Library, Special Collections.
Interview with Childers, who came from England to Montana where she joined a cousin in Miles City. She was then chaperoned to Toronto, Canada, by a branch of the Church of England. Later she married a Mr. Boyce, and in 1904 they moved to Powderville, a road ranch in Powder River County, MT. In 1908 they became homesteaders. After marrying John Childers in 1948, she moved to Arizona.

10,231. Chowning, Jennie Ennis
Papers. 1930-50. 0.2 ft.
Open. Card catalog.
Montana State University Library, Special Collections.
Member of a Madison Valley, MT, pioneer family, Chowning (1863-1951) was active in community affairs, and for a short time she served as Madison Valley postmistress. Correspondence relating to efforts of Chowning and [Mrs.] Winifred Jeffers to collect information on local history. Also included are articles written for presentation to Ennis, MT, community groups interested in Madison Valley history and clippings.

10,232. Coates, Grace Stone
Papers. Nd. 0.2 ft.
Open. Card catalog.
Montana State University Library, Special Collections.
Coates, a Martinsdale, MT, resident, was an historical columnist and author. Correspondence from 1933 to 1937 between Coates and other local authors and research notes for Montana newspaper feature stories.

10,233. Considine, Mrs. M. H.
Papers. 1918-63. 6 in.
Open. Card catalog.
Montana State University Library, Special Collections.
Diaries of Considine, wife of a Biddle, MT, rancher, contain information on ranch life, Biddle, and gardening, including planting times and watering procedures.

10,234. Cowan, Mrs. Arthur
Papers. 1895. 1 vol.
Open. Card catalog.
Montana State University Library, Special Collections.
Diary in which Cowan, a Woody Island, MT, homesteader, discusses her loneliness, hard work, harsh weather, and illness in the family.

10,235. DeHaven, Mary (Redfield) Lindsey
Papers. 1943-64. 0.1 ft.
Open. Card catalog.
Montana State University Library, Special Collections.
DeHaven (1892-1972) was a mother, schoolteacher, practical nurse, and newspaper feature writer; she also was active in Methodist church and community affairs. Research notes for DeHaven's articles and clippings.

10,236. Doane, Gustavus C.
Papers. 1875-92. 0.3 ft.
Open. Card catalog.
Montana State University Library, Special Collections.
Correspondence, commissary records, and official reports of Doane (?-1892), a lieutenant in the US Army and military explorer who came to Montana in 1869. Includes correspondence documenting the attempt of his wife Mary (Hunter) Doane to copyright her husband's 1870 Yellowstone expedition report.

10,237. Doane, Mary (Hunter)
Papers. Ca. 1930-55. 4 items.
Open. Card catalog.
Montana State University Library, Special Collections.
Doane (1859-1952) was a schoolteacher, historical researcher and writer, and wife of Lieutenant Gustavus C. Doane, a US Army officer and military explorer. Correspondence with friends, letters regarding her research, reminiscences of life at Hunter's Hot Springs and with the US Army during the Indian wars, a history of St. Vincent's Academy in Helena, MT, where Doane taught, and a scrapbook of material pertaining to the pioneers of Madison and Gallatin counties in Montana.

10,238. Dot S Dot Ranch
Records. 1835-1965. 4.6 ft.
Open. Inventory.
Montana State University Library, Special Collections.
Correspondence, diaries, and pictures of [Mrs.] Anne Hart (1909-64) document the activities of the dude ranch that she operated on the family cattle and horse ranch. Prior to this, Hart was an instructor and administrator at the woman's branch of the Carnegie Institute of Technology.

10,239. Ennis, Fannie (Davis)
Papers. Nd. 4 items.
Open. Card catalog.
Montana State University Library, Special Collections.
Ennis (1867-1955) was a Montana pioneer. Notes for speeches and a manuscript entitled "Early Days in Virginia City."

10,240. Ferris, Mrs. Eddy R.
Papers. 1874-84. 0.1 ft.
Open. Card catalog.
Montana State University Library, Special Collections.
Margaret Ferris (?-1889) was the wife of Eddy R. Ferris, a member of Sebree, Ferris, and White, a firm that provided material for the Utah and Northern Railroad as it was constructed from Utah into Montana. Correspondence of Ferris contains descriptions of living conditions and social life in terminal towns during the railroad construction period.

10,241. Flaherty, Marie
Oral history. 1966. 1 item and 1 tape.
Open. Card catalog.
Montana State University Library, Special Collections.
Flaherty (1874-) was a Montana ranch wife and mother; she later worked at the girls correctional institution in Helena, MT. Interview and transcript about her early life in Willow Creek and Three Forks, MT, particularly her education, family life, social conditions, and community growth.

10,242. Flanagan, May G.
Papers. Nd. 0.2 ft.
Access restricted. Card catalog.
Montana State University Library, Special Collections.
Flanagan (1874-1958) was a Fort Benton, MT, schoolteacher. Diary of 1903 trip to Yellowstone Park and reminiscences regarding I. G. Baker, T. C. Power, the Conrad brothers, steamboating on the upper Missouri River, transportation by stagecoach, and other topics. The reminiscences pertain to events from 1819 to 1952.

10,243. Fletcher, Ellen Louise
Papers. 1866-70. 1 in.
Open. Card catalog.
Montana State University Library, Special Collections.
Correspondence of [Mrs.] Fletcher (1841-?), a Madison Valley, MT, resident and mother, includes a typescript regarding her trip in 1865 from Cuba, NY, to Virginia City, MT, and letters concerning life in a mining camp and on a ranch.

10,244. Gates, Eva
Papers. Nd. 1 item.
Open. Card catalog.

Montana State University Library, Special Collections.
A local historian, Gates (1888-1968) was the daughter of Montana pioneers and a longtime state resident. Copy from 1963 of an unpublished manuscript containing a history of the Mineral County, MT, area where gold was discovered; the manuscript includes histories of Alberton, Fish Creek, Saltese, Taft, Iron Mountain, Superior, Cedar Creek, Carter, Keystone, Amador, and Deborgia.

10,245. Harper, Jewell
Oral history. 1967. 1 tape and other items.
Open. Card catalog.
Montana State University Library, Special Collections.
[Mrs.] Harper (ca. 1900-) is a Montana rancher. Interview and transcripts containing her reminiscences regarding her father, a rancher who was once an owner of the Two Dot Wilson ranch, and photos of the ranch.

10,246. Herndon, Sarah (Raymond)
Papers. 1866-99. 1 folder.
Open. Card catalog.
Montana State University Library, Special Collections.
Herndon was a Virginia City, MT, public school teacher. Copy of an 1866 diary in which she describes her teaching experiences and letters she wrote in 1899 to a friend on her views of classroom discipline.

10,247. Houston, Elizabeth Lena (Alderson)
Papers. 1926-38. 2 vols.
Open. Card catalog.
Montana State University Library, Special Collections.
Houston (1860-1933), who came to Montana in 1866, was the daughter of William W. Alderson, one of the founders of Bozeman. Scrapbooks of clippings about Bozeman.

10,248. Jackson, Mercy
Papers. 1880-1935. 0.1 ft.
Open. Card catalog.
Montana State University Library, Special Collections.
Typescript of reminiscences of Jackson, a Lewistown, MT, pioneer and schoolteacher, regarding her journey by wagon train to Bozeman in 1880, activities in Bozeman, and her move to Lewiston.

10,249. Jeffers, Susie L.
Papers. 1865. 1 item.
Open. Card catalog.
Montana State University Library, Special Collections.
Reminiscences of Susan Lois Switzer Jeffers (1859-1955), wife of a wealthy cattle owner, concern her wagon train journey from Victor, IA, to Virginia City, MT, with her parents.

10,250. Kerr, Electra (Padden)
Papers. Ca. 1940. 8-page item.
Open. Card catalog.
Montana State University Library, Special Collections.
Reminiscences of Kerr (1874-1953), a Baker, MT, resident, pertain to her experiences from ca. 1885 to 1908. Entitled "My Early Dakota Life," the manuscript contains information about the severe winter of 1885-86, the isolation of families, the rise of the area cattle industry, and the Indians and their meat hunts.

10,251. Kraenzel, Margaret Powell
Papers. Nd. 6 items.
Open. Card catalog.
Montana State University Library, Special Collections.
Kraenzel is an author and wife of Carl Kraenzel, a professor of agricultural economics. Manuscripts for *The House on Center Street, Weight Lifter of Iron, Iran's Most Valued Citizen,* and other books.

10,252. McDonald, Marie
Papers. Nd. 0.1 ft.
Open. Card catalog.
Montana State University Library, Special Collections.
Interviews, 200 photos of homesteads, and maps of McDonald, an author, which she used in her *After Barbed Wire* (1963).

10,253. McGill, Caroline
Papers. 1910-58. 0.5 ft.
Open. Card catalog.
Montana State University Library, Special Collections.
McGill (1879-1959) was a physician and diagnostician who practiced in Butte, MT; she also owned a dude ranch in Gallatin Canyon, where she retired. Correspondence with friends regarding historical interests, publications, and family affairs; reminiscences; an autobiography; research notes for a west Gallatin Canyon history; museum notes; photos; a scrapbook of clippings about pioneers of Madison and Gallatin counties; printed material on dude ranches; and tourist information. McGill obtained her PhD in 1908 and her medical degree in 1914 from Johns Hopkins University.

10,254. Madison Valley Woman's Club
Records. Nd. 1 item.
Open. Card catalog.
Montana State University Library, Special Collections.
History of the Club, which was organized in 1920 to promote community service and personal betterment. The Club's predecessor the Priscilla Embroidery Club was disbanded during WWI when members became involved in American National Red Cross work. The history, which was compiled by [Mrs.] Pauline Clark and [Mrs.] Jo Jeffers, covers the period from 1920 to 1964.

10,255. Matovick, John
Papers. 1956. 1 item.
Open. Card catalog.
Montana State University Library, Special Collections.
Letter written by John Matovick's mother (1884-) contains reminiscences and her family history from 1884 to 1956. She describes coming to Regina, MT, in 1911 as a Yugoslav immigrant, the raising of 10 children, the joy of buying their first "Chevy truck," and building their own home.

10,256. Miller, Grace
Oral history. Nd. 1 tape and other items.
Open. Card catalog.
Montana State University Library, Special Collections.
A member of the group that established dude ranches in the US in 1923, Miller (ca. 1896-), with her husband, owned and operated the Elkhorn Dude Ranch in Gallatin Canyon, MT. Tape of an interview recorded in 1973 and 1974 and reminiscences regarding the history of the Elkhorn Dude Ranch and Miller's experiences as a Montana State University staff member in 1922.

10,257. Moore Women's Club
Records. 1904-64. 1 item.
Open. Card catalog.
Montana State University Library, Special Collections.
The Club was organized in ca. 1904 for community service and personal betterment. Manuscript of a history of Moore, MT, includes an account of its founding, community members, businesses, and growth.

10,258. Packer, Martha Suckow
Papers. 1880-1970. 10 in.
Open. Card catalog.
Montana State University Library, Special Collections.
Correspondence, reminiscences, business records, and photos of Packer (1880-1970), an Inverness, MT, homesteader, and her daughter Dorothy (Packer) Duncan.

10,259. Park County Poultry Producers Association
Records. 1923-40. 1.3 ft.
Open. Inventory.
Montana State University Library, Special Collections.
Correspondence and other records of the Association, which was founded in 1923 and which provided income for ranch women during the 1930s. It was disbanded in 1940.

10,260. Parks, Lucia (Darling)
Papers. Nd. 1 microfilm reel and other items.
Open. Card catalog.
Montana State University Library, Special Collections.
Parks (1839-1905) was an early Montana schoolteacher. Copy of an 1863 diary regarding her journey from Tallmadge, OH, to Bannack City, MT, letters of transmittal, clippings, and microfilm of interviews with people who knew Parks. The microfilm represents a collection compiled in 1942 by the Dillon, MT, branch of Delta Kappa Gamma, an international teachers organization.

10,261. Phelps, Mrs. W. G.
Papers. 1914-26. 3 vols.
Open. Card catalog.
Montana State University Library, Special Collections.
Cassandra [Mrs. W. G.] Phelps (?-1964) was a home economics extension worker. Scrapbook of clippings regarding the Montana Extension Service's efforts from 1924 to 1926 to improve state farm economy and home life and two scrapbooks from 1914 and 1919 containing clippings on various topics.

10,262. Place, Marian T.
Papers. 1953-63. 1.6 ft.
Open. Inventory.
Montana State University Library, Special Collections.
Place (ca. 1910-) is an author of young adult fiction, who sometimes writes under the pseudonyms Dale White and R. D. Whitinger; she also was a winner of the Western Writers of America award. Correspondence with her publisher and manuscripts for books about Montana, including *The Mouse-Gray Stallion* (1957), *Lotta Crabtree, Gold Rush Girl* (1958), *Steamboat up the Missouri* (1958), and *John Wesley Powell; Canyon's Conqueror* (1963).

10,263. Powers, Mary Johnstone
Papers. Nd. 1 in.
Open. Card catalog.
Montana State University Library, Special Collections.
Reminiscences of Powers regarding her experiences as a Fort Benton, MT, schoolteacher from 1883 to 1887 and as Choteau County superintendent of education.

10,264. Smith and Mendenhall Family
Papers. 1855-80. 0.2 ft.
Open. Card catalog.
Montana State University Library, Special Collections.
Correspondence and a scrapbook of Mary Sue Mendenhall (?-1933), whose first husband Robert Henry Smith, a Confederate soldier, was killed in 1863. She joined her sister in Montana in 1869 and married John S. Mendenhall sometime after

1873. Affectionate correspondence between Mary Sue and Robert Smith, 1855-63; with relatives, including her sister Fannie and Harvey Oliver, 1858-73; and with John Mendenhall, 1878-80. Correspondence contains discussions of the Civil War, family and local news, and Mendenhall's journey west.

10,265. Stewart, Lou Stocking
Papers. Nd. 9 ft.
Open. Inventory.
Montana State University Library, Special Collections.
The first white child born in Fort Benton, MT, Stewart married a Choteau, MT, sheep rancher and lived in Great Falls, MT. Correspondence, diaries of Stewart's mother and her grandmother [Mrs.] Lucy Stocking regarding steamboat travel into Montana during the 1870s, photos of Fort Benton from the 1880s, and scrapbooks. A diary of Lucy Stocking concerns a steamboat trip up the Missouri River to Fort Benton and daily activities while living on a ranch in the area.

10,266. Talboys, Millie
Papers. Nd. 1 item.
Open. Card catalog.
Montana State University Library, Special Collections.
Reminiscences of a covered wagon journey from Missouri to Montana in 1898, as told by Estelle C. Lauhlin and recorded by Talboys.

10,267. Trumper, May
Papers. 1954. 62 pp.
Open. Card catalog.
Montana State University Library, Special Collections.
Reminiscences of Trumper, a Montana schoolteacher from 1899 to 1929, Flathead County superintendent, and Montana superintendent of public instruction from 1916 to 1929, reveal the attitudes of men toward women in politics.

10,268. Vincent, Mrs. T. H.
Papers. 1882. 1 item.
Open. Card catalog.
Montana State University Library, Special Collections.
Diary in which Lora Richter [Mrs. T. H.] Vincent (?-1948), who came to Montana in 1864, describes her trip through Yellowstone Park and the Park's geysers, falls, and geological phenomena.

10,269. Zook, Laura (Brown)
Papers. 1869-1944. 2 items.
Open. Card catalog.
Montana State University Library, Special Collections.
Reminiscences and a biography of Zook (1868-1944), who was a teacher at the Lame Deer, MT, Cheyenne Indian school and later Custer County, MT, superintendent of schools. Her reminiscences concern Indian affairs; tensions in Miles City, MT; living conditions; recreation; diet; and Indian celebrations. Zook's biography contains information on her youth, education, family, and career working in the community and with the Indians.

HELENA

10,270. Abbott, Mary (Stuart), and Mueller, Oscar O.
Oral history. 1958. 1 tape.
Open. Catalog card.
Montana Historical Society.
Talks given by Abbott and Mueller at the Montana Institute of the Arts tour meeting in Lewistown, MT. Abbott, who was the daughter of Montana pioneer Granville Stuart and the wife of cattleman and author E. C. "Teddy Blue" Abbott of Giltedge, MT, reminisced about her childhood days on the DHS ranch near Lewistown; she also told stories about her father. Mueller, a lawyer, amateur historian, and archaeologist of Lewistown, commented on his research on the central Montana vigilante raids in 1884.

10,271. Alderson, Mrs. Matt W.
Papers. 1934. 81-page item.
Open. Catalog card.
Montana Historical Society.
Manuscript history of the movement for women's rights in Montana that Alderson, a pioneer resident of Twin Bridges, MT, wrote on the basis of her own experiences as well as research.

10,272. Allard, Lulu Spurgeon
Papers. 1929-46. 1 folder.
Open. Published guide and card catalog.
Montana Historical Society.
Correspondence and legal documents of Allard, wife of Charles Allard, a western Montana rancher and bison preservationist. Includes material pertaining to land allotments on the Flathead Indian reservations. See Brian Cockhill and Dale L. Johnson, comps. and eds., *Guide to Manuscripts in Montana Repositories* (Missoula, MT: University of Montana, 1973).

10,273. American Association of University Women, Montana Division
Records. 1931-73. 6.5 ft.
Open. Published guide and catalog card.
Montana Historical Society.
Minutes, organizational records, financial records, correspondence, reports, bulletins, photos, and publications of the Montana AAUW. Includes files of the AAUW historian. See Brian Cockhill and Dale L. Johnson, comps. and eds., *Guide to Manuscripts in Montana Repositories* (Missoula, MT: University of Montana, 1973).

10,274. Attix, Frederick F.
Papers. 1899-1948. 4 microfilm reels.
Open. Published guide and card catalog.
Montana Historical Society.
Diaries and financial records of Attix, a Fergus County, MT, physician, including a diary kept by his wife Ruth Attix in 1902. See Brian Cockhill and Dale L. Johnson, comps. and eds., *Guide to Manuscripts in Montana Repositories* (Missoula, MT: University of Montana, 1973).

10,275. Bangs, Mrs. William
Papers. Nd. 4-page item.
Open. Catalog card.
Montana Historical Society.
Reminiscences by Bangs, who homesteaded and taught school at Inverness, MT, before retiring to Havre, MT. She discusses her experiences as a single woman homesteading in Montana's Hi Line area from 1910 to 1914.

10,276. Barrett, Alice E.
Papers. Nd. No size given.
Open. Catalog card.
Montana Historical Society.
Reminiscences by Barrett concerning her experiences crossing the plains in 1867, her life on the Montana prairie near Boulder from the 1860s to 1885, and her husband Martin Barrett.

10,277. Benjamin, Lulu
Papers. 1915-21. 53 items.
Open. No guide.
Montana Historical Society.
[Mrs. E. E.] Benjamin (1864-?) describes her life on a Montana homestead in letters sent to friends in the East.

10,278. Bruce, Ida Lovell, and Lourie, Emma (Keene)
Oral history. Nd. 1 tape.
Open. Catalog card.
Montana Historical Society.
Interviews with [Mrs.] Bruce, a resident of Broadwater County, MT, who reminisces about her childhood in Diamond City, and with Lourie, the daughter of pioneer rancher Flavins J. Keene and wife of Joseph H. Lourie, a rancher at Sheep Creek, MT. Lourie's reminiscence covers the period from the 1880s to the 1920s and concerns her family and her childhood on a ranch in Broadwater County.

10,279. Canfield, Andrew N., and Canfield, Sarah E.
Papers. 1866-68. 1 microfilm reel.
Open. Published guide and card catalog.
Montana Historical Society.
Diaries of Andrew Canfield and his wife Sarah contain descriptions of conditions in Montana Territory. See Brian Cockhill and Dale L. Johnson, comps. and eds., *Guide to Manuscripts in Montana Repositories* (Missoula, MT: University of Montana, 1973).

10,280. Citizens Committee on the State Legislature
Records. 1966-73. 1 ft.
Open. Catalog card.
Montana Historical Society.
Minutes, correspondence, reports, and clippings of C. W. Cooley, chairman of this committee appointed by the Legislative Council, the administrative office for the state legislature, to study and recommend ways to improve the state's legislative process. The Committee had women members.

10,281. Clarke, Helen P.
Papers. 1872-1913. 0.1 ft.
Open. Catalog card.
Montana Historical Society.
Correspondence and writings of [Miss] Clarke, who was superintendent of schools in Helena and a teacher for the Bureau of Indian Affairs. Clark was the daughter of E. Malcolm Clarke and his Blackfoot wife.

10,282. Collins, Fannie Belle
Papers. Ca. 1950. 38-page item.
Open. Card catalog.
Montana Historical Society.
Biography of Collins (1867-?), a pioneer schoolteacher and resident of Great Falls, MT, concerns her childhood, settling in Montana, her teaching career, and other events.

10,283. Connelly, Michael, and Connelly, Bridget
Papers. 1952. 1 item.
Open. Catalog card.
Montana Historical Society.
Family history and reminiscences about Michael Connelly (1848-1944) and his wife Bridget Connelly (1853-1952) by their granddaughter Helena Sullivan Pennell contain details about their arrival in Montana and their life and experiences in early Montana communities from 1848 to 1952.

10,284. Conner, B. Pearl
Oral history. 1970. 1 tape and 1 transcript.
Open. Catalog card.
Montana Historical Society.
In an interview conducted by her son Stuart W. Conner, [Mrs.] Conner discusses her homestead experiences between ca. 1900 and 1905 in the Camp Creek area north of Bozeman, MT.

10,285. Constitutional Convention Commission
Records. 1970-72. 10 ft.
Open. Catalog card.
Montana Historical Society.
Minutes, administrative correspondence and subject files, studies, reports, and clippings of this study and planning group created by the 1971 Montana Legislative Assembly to prepare for the convening

and operation of the 1972 constitutional convention. A number of women served in administrative posts on the Commission and as members of various committees.

10,286. Constitutional Revision Commission
Records. 1969-71. 3 ft.
Open. Catalog card.
Montana Historical Society.
Minutes, executive director's administrative files, reports, promotional and public information files, and other records of this commission created by the 1969 Montana Legislative Assembly to determine the need for constitutional revision and to begin preparations for a convention.

10,287. Cowan, Emma Carpenter
Papers. 1902. 79-page item.
Open. Catalog card.
Montana Historical Society.
Reminiscences by Cowan, a resident of Boulder, MT, and the wife of attorney George F. Cowan, in which she describes crossing the plains to Montana by wagon in 1864 and a trip to Yellowstone Park in the summer of 1877 with a party that was captured by the Nez Percé.

10,288. Cox, Mary Peachy
Oral history. 1957. 12-page transcript.
Open. Catalog card.
Montana Historical Society.
Interview in which Cox, a pioneer in Miles City, MT, reminisces about her early life in Miles City during the 1880s and 1890s. Cox's nephew Floyd Alderson conducted the interview.

10,289. Craig, Genieve Woodruff
Papers. Ca. 1912. 10-page item.
Open. Catalog card.
Montana Historical Society.
Talk given by Craig to the Society of the Daughters of the US Army concerning her life as an Army child and wife. Craig was the wife of General Nalin Craig, US Army Chief of Staff.

10,290. Culver, Lillian E. H.
Papers. 1884-1928. 1 ft.
Open. Catalog card.
Montana Historical Society.
Correspondence, financial records, and other papers of Culver and her husband William N. Culver, a Centennial Valley rancher and mail contractor. The Culvers' home Picnic Springs Ranch was near Elk Lake, MT.

10,291. Daems, Marie L.
Papers. 1901. 1 item.
Open. Card catalog.
Montana Historical Society.
Letter in which Daems (?-1904) describes traveling from Belgium to New York in 1856, living in Denver, moving to Montana in 1863, and supporting herself and adjusting to hardships after the death of her husband in 1874.

10,292. Danniel, Pearl Sparks
Papers. 1960. 1 item.
Open. Catalog card.
Montana Historical Society.
Reminiscences by Danniel (1885-), a McCone County, MT, homesteader and author, concern her homesteading experiences.

10,293. Darling, Lucia A.
Papers. 1863. 128-page vol.
Open. No guide.
Montana Historical Society.
Diary in which Darling, one of Montana Territory's first school teachers, describes an overland journey to Montana with the family of her uncle Sidney Edgerton, first governor of the Territory. Diary is also available on microfilm.

10,294. Daughters of the American Revolution, Black Eagle Chapter
Records. 1931-62. 2 ft.
Open. Catalog card.
Montana Historical Society.
Scrapbooks of photos, programs, clippings, and other material of this Great Falls, MT, branch of the DAR.

10,295. Daughters of the American Revolution, Oro Fino Chapter
Records. 1938-54. 1 ft.
Open. Catalog card.
Montana Historical Society.
Scrapbooks of this Helena chapter of the DAR contain correspondence, programs, and material on lineage research.

10,296. Davidson, Sallie Davenport
Papers. 1928. 5-page item.
Open. Card catalog.
Montana Historical Society.
Memoirs in which Davidson (1857-1935) describes traveling to Montana with her parents in 1864; hardships, including measles and encounters with Indians; and settling in Montana.

10,297. Day, Mrs. James C.
Papers. 1856-75. 1 microfilm reel.
Open. Published guide and card catalog.
Montana Historical Society.
Letters to Day, the wife of a Montana miner, from her husband in the goldfields. See Brian Cockhill and Dale L. Johnson, comps. and eds., *Guide to Manuscripts in Montana Repositories* (Missoula, MT: University of Montana, 1973).

10,298. De Lacy, Walter Washington
Papers. 1855-96. 0.4 ft.
Open. Catalog card.
Montana Historical Society.
De Lacy (1819-92) was a Helena surveyor and cartographer who served as an official in the US Surveyor's Office. Correspondence concerning family matters, professional activities, and conditions in Helena and Montana. Among the correspondents are William de Lacy and Fannie de Lacy.

10,299. Department of Institutions: Children's Center
Records. 1894-1975. 13.5 cu.ft.
Open. Catalog card.
Montana Historical Society.
Executive board minutes, financial records, statistical registers and indexes, and other records of the Center, which was established in 1894 as the State Orphans Home. The Center closed in 1975.

10,300. Edgerton Family
Papers. 1859-84. 0.5 ft.
Open. Unpublished guide.
Montana Historical Society.
Correspondence in which Martha "Mattie" A. Edgerton, Mary [Mrs. Sidney] Edgerton, and Mary Pauline Edgerton, pioneer women of the family of Montana's first territorial governor Sidney Edgerton, describe conditions encountered while crossing the plains and life in Bannack, Montana Territory. Letters also provide information on road agents and vigilantes and offer opinions on the political organization of Montana's new government.

10,301. Erickson, Grace Vance
Papers. 1889-1932. 0.5 ft.
Open. Catalog card.
Montana Historical Society.
Correspondence, diaries, a family photo album, and other papers of Erickson, who was the wife of Montana governor John E. Erickson.

10,302. Erickson, Grace Vance
Papers. 1930-45. 0.1 ft.
Open. Catalog card.
Montana Historical Society.
Correspondence, notes, and other papers of [Mrs. John E.] Erickson, an amateur historian from the Helena area, relate to early historic sites and their preservation.

10,303. Erwin, Meryl
Oral history. 1969. 2 tapes.
Open. Catalog card.
Montana Historical Society.
Interview in which Erwin (1883-), a Dillon, MT, resident and secretary for various Beaverhead County attorneys, reminisces about her life in Dillon, her association with community residents, and her work as secretary for Montana governor Edwin L. Norris.

10,304. First Presbyterian Church
Records. 1887-1924. 0.2 ft.
Open. Catalog card.
Montana Historical Society.
Annual reports, correspondence, membership lists, and other records of the Ladies Aid Society of this Helena church.

10,305. Fisk Family
Papers. 1859-1901. 5.4 ft.
Open. Unpublished guide.
Montana Historical Society.
Correspondence, diaries, speeches, writings, scrapbooks, photos, and pencil sketches of the family of Robert E. Fisk, *Helena Herald* publisher, and his wife Elizabeth (Chester) Fisk (1846-1927). Robert Fisk, together with his brothers Andrew J., James L., and Van Hayden Fisk, guided wagon trains in the 1860s from Minnesota to Montana, mined gold, and later entered the newspaper profession. Bulk of collection consists of Elizabeth Fisk's correspondence with her family in Connecticut about frontier life, politics, and business activities in Helena. Also includes diaries of Andrew J. Fisk chronicling the Fisk expeditions of 1862, 1863, and 1866 from Minnesota.

10,306. Flanagan, May G.
Papers. Nd. 8-page item and 2 tapes.
Open. Catalog cards.
Montana Historical Society.
Flanagan (1874-1958), the daughter of druggist and postmaster Michael A. Flanagan of Fort Benton, MT, was a pioneer and an elementary school principal in Great Falls, MT. Reminiscences of a childhood journey in 1887 down the Missouri River from Fort Benton to Bismarck, ND, on the steamboat *Eclipse* and tapes of a speech she gave about the history and early residents of Fort Benton and Montana's fur trade era.

10,307. Fogarty, Kate Hammond
Papers. Nd. 0.5 ft.
Open. Published guide and card catalog.
Montana Historical Society.
Research notes of Fogarty, a Butte, MT, author, regarding the history of the Summit Valley mining district near Butte, include lists of mines and their locations, who found them, and who owned them. See Brian Cockhill and Dale L. Johnson, comps. and eds., *Guide to Manuscripts in Montana Repositories* (Missoula, MT: University of Montana, 1973).

10,308. Gardner, Flora
Papers. 1879. 1 item.
Open. Catalog card.
Montana Historical Society.
Reminiscences by [Mrs. Edward M.] Gardner (1839-1910), who was a resident of Bozeman, MT, concern a journey from Fort Benton, MT, to Bozeman in 1879. The reminiscences were written in the form of a letter to Mr. and Mrs. D. M. Vinsonhaler.

10,309. Gilmore, Grace Marron
Papers. 1884-1943. 0.2 ft.
Open. Catalog card.
Montana Historical Society.
Correspondence, writings, legal documents, and other papers of Gilmore, who was first married to Edward Marron, a cattle rancher in eastern Montana, and after Marron's death married James W. Gilmore, a sheep rancher in Glendive, MT. Also includes a 1916 diary by an unidentified person.

10,310. Great Falls, MT, Newspaper Guild No. 81
Records. 1974-75. 0.1 ft.
Open. Catalog card.
Montana Historical Society.
Minutes, correspondence, contract offers, strike papers, and other material relating to the 1974 strike by this union, a local of the National Newspaper Guild, against the *Great Falls Tribune*. Newspaperwoman Carla Beck was president of the local Guild at the time of the strike.

10,311. Greenfield, Marguerite
Papers. 1865-1960. 6 ft.
Open. Catalog card.
Montana Historical Society.
Correspondence, writings, subject files, photos, clippings, and other papers of Greenfield.

10,312. Hannah Family
Papers. 1947. 4 items.
Open. Catalog card.
Montana Historical Society.
Reminiscences concerning childhood days in Big Timber, MT, and later working experiences of Robert Bruce Hannah (1901-), an engineer for the Mountain Bell Telephone Company in Denver, and his sister Aloha Margaret (Hallah) Alvara, a Montana schoolteacher and later a professor at the University of Helsinki in Finland. Also includes a biography of their father William James Hannah and a speech read by Jerome G. Locke at William Hannah's funeral in 1947.

10,313. Hard Ground, Patricia, and Standing Elk, Fannie
Oral history. 1957. 4-page transcript.
Open. Catalog card.
Montana Historical Society.
Interviews with Hard Ground and Standing Elk, who were eyewitnesses to the deaths of Head Chief and Young Mule on the Northern Cheyenne Reservation.

10,314. Harris, Fanny
Papers. 1908-09. 59 pp.
Open. Catalog card.
Montana Historical Society.
Diaries Harris kept on trips by wagon to northern Idaho from Pueblo, CO, via Yellowstone Park. Also includes biographical material.

10,315. Hedges Family
Papers. 1828-1945. 4.6 ft.
Open. Unpublished guide and catalog card.
Montana Historical Society.
Correspondence, diaries of a trip from Massachusetts to Montana, writings and speeches, financial records, legal documents, and other papers of Cornelius Hedges (1831-1907), a lawyer, miner, and pioneer in Montana, and of other family members.

10,316. Helena Business Women's Suffrage Club
Records. 1894-1917. Ca. 1 in.
Open. Published guide and catalog card.
Montana Historical Society.
Minutes, correspondence, speeches, and clippings of this group founded in 1894. Jeannette Rankin, who later became Montana's first congresswoman, was prominent in the Club. See Brian Cockhill and Dale L. Johnson, comps. and eds., *Guide to Manuscripts in Montana Repositories* (Missoula, MT: University of Montana, 1973).

10,317. Herndon, Sallie Raymond
Papers. 1866-99. 1 microfilm reel.
Open. Catalog card.
Montana Historical Society.
Diary kept in 1866 by Herndon, a seamstress and schoolteacher in early Virginia City, MT, and two 1899 letters from Herndon to a Mrs. Howey discussing the history of education in Virginia City.

10,318. Howells, Joseph, and Howells, Sue
Papers. 1972. 56-page item.
Open. Catalog card.
Montana Historical Society.
Reminiscences by Joseph Howells and his wife Sue Howells concerning their experiences as homesteaders in the Graceville, MT, area. They filed on their land in 1910 and remained on the land until 1915, when they gave up farming. They later settled in Kalispell.

10,319. Howey, Laura E.
Papers. 1892-93. 1.5 ft.
Open. Published guide and card catalog.
Montana Historical Society.
Correspondence of Howey regarding the Montana State Board of World's Fair Managers, of which she was a member. See Brian Cockhill and Dale L. Johnson, comps. and eds., *Guide to Manuscripts in Montana Repositories* (Missoula, MT: University of Montana, 1973).

10,320. Ingalls, Emma
Papers. 1924-37. 0.5 ft.
Open. No guide.
Montana Historical Society.
Correspondence, clippings, and other papers of Ingalls, a Flathead County, MT, legislator, primarily concern state and national Republican party politics.

10,321. Jones, Mrs. Lee A.
Papers. Nd. 14-page item.
Open. Catalog card.
Montana Historical Society.
Reminiscences by Jones, a Montana pioneer, concern early days in Havre, MT, from 1893 to 1920.

10,322. Kelley, Mary L.
Papers. 1920. 7-page item.
Open. Card catalog.
Montana Historical Society.
Reminiscences of [Mrs. R. S.] Kelley, a Deer Lodge, MT, resident, regarding her overland journey to Montana in 1864, dangers encountered along the way, longing for her home in Missouri, and her reunion with her husband, who had arrived earlier to participate in placer mining.

10,323. Kirkpatrick, Alma Coffin
Papers. Ca. 1920. 27-page item.
Open. Card catalog.
Montana Historical Society.
Reminiscences in which [Mrs. James] Kirkpatrick describes her trip up the Missouri River to Montana in 1878; the mining camp of Glendive; religious, educational, and social life of Beaverhead Valley, MT, residents; and living conditions in the area.

10,324. Leavens, Ella Lamport
Oral history. 1971. 1 tape.
Open. Catalog card.
Montana Historical Society.
Leavens, the widow of cowboy, stageline operator, engineer, and politician Robert Leavens, reminisces about early Bearcreek and Billings, MT.

10,325. Legislative Assembly
Records. 1905. 0.2 cu.ft.
Open. Catalog card.
Montana Historical Society.
Records of the 9th Montana Legislative Assembly include petitions to the legislature calling for the passage of women's suffrage.

10,326. Lewis and Clark Heritage Foundation
Records. 1975. 2 tapes.
Open. Catalog card.
Montana Historical Society.
Speeches by Vivian Paladin of Helena and Wilbur P. Werner of Cut Bank, MT, given at a seminar at Great Falls, MT, on Lewis and Clark and Sacajawea.

10,327. Linderman, Frank B.
Papers. 1903-38. 2.5 ft.
Open. Published guide and card catalog.
Montana Historical Society.
Papers of Linderman (1869-1938) include correspondence with Grace Stone Coates from 1934 to 1937 and with Jane Wall in 1911. See Brian Cockhill and Dale L. Johnson, comps. and eds., *Guide to Manuscripts in Montana Repositories* (Missoula, MT: University of Montana, 1973).

10,328. Logan, Frances D.
Papers. 1947-72. 10 ft.
Open. No guide.
Montana Historical Society.
Logan (1899-) was secretary of the Committee for Paradise Dam Project from 1947 to 1964 and Montana Democratic national committeewoman from 1964 to 1967. Bulk of the collection consists of correspondence, hearings transcripts, subject files, photos, clippings, maps, printed material, and publications concerning the proposed construction of Paradise and Knowles dams in western Montana. Also included is correspondence relating to Logan's work in the Montana Democratic party and her environmental concerns.

10,329. Lott, Melvina J.
Papers. 1880. 1 microfilm reel.
Open. Catalog card.
Montana Historical Society.
Diary kept by Lott, a pioneer in Sheridan, MT, on a trip to the geysers of Yellowstone in 1880.

10,330. McCartney, Maida
Oral history. 1975. 1 tape.
Open. No guide.
Montana Historical Society.
Interview with McCartney, a Chinook, MT, radio broadcaster, contains reminiscences of her work from 1948 to 1968 on KOJM's "Chinook Hour," a local news roundup in Havre, MT. The interview was made for an oral history project carried out by American Women in Radio and Television.

10,331. McKay, Alexander
Papers. 1856-1942. 1.5 ft.
Open. No guide.
Montana Historical Society.
Papers of McKay, a pioneer Montana miner, miller, and businessman, include official records of women's clubs maintained by his wife Caroline McKay (1837-1917) and daughter Flora (McKay) McNulty (1861-1945). Contains minutes, monthly cash books, rolls, and other material from 1896 to 1924 of the Ladies of the Maccabees, founded in 1896 as a financial assistance group for the Maccabees of Virginia City, MT; constitution, minutes, and financial records from 1895 to 1898 of the Ladies Guild of the St. Paul's Mutual Improvement Society, which promoted and provided financial assistance for community activities of Virginia City's St. Paul Episcopal Church; and minutes and financial entries of the Union Circle of King's Daughters, founded in 1892 to support the Virginia City library.

10,332. MacLean, Eva
Papers. 1936-38. 0.4 ft.
Open. No guide.
Montana Historical Society.
MacLean was a WPA writer and author. Writings, plays, poems, children's stories, historical manuscripts, and histories of Dawson, Richland, and Wibaux counties, MT.

10,333. Manix Family
Papers. 1932-68. 2 items.
Open. Catalog card.
Montana Historical Society.
Autobiographical writings by Margaret Manix Furman (1864-1932) and her daughter Mable Manix Pings (1884-1968) about the St. Peters Mission and their experiences in the Augusta, MT, area.

10,334. Mansfield, Rachell K.
Papers. 1971-72. 3 ft.
Open. No guide.
Montana Historical Society.
Correspondence, speeches, photos, clippings, published material, and ephemera of Mansfield, a Democratic delegate to the 1972 Montana Constitutional Convention from Choteau County, District 14, and a member of the Bill of Rights Committee.

10,335. Mardis, Mrs. James
Papers. Ca. 1910. 1 folder.
Open. Card catalog.
Montana Historical Society.
Biographical sketch written by Mrs. M. W. Alderson about Mardis (1845-?), who traveled to Montana in 1864. Contains descriptions of the journey's hardships, encounters with Indians, health problems, and social activities engaged in by Montana pioneers.

10,336. Melvin, Eva (Strode)
Papers. 1967-69. 0.1 ft.
Open. Catalog card.
Montana Historical Society.
Papers of Melvin, who was the daughter of Thomas P. Strode, an early cattleman of the Sweet Grass Hills, MT, area include letters and writings on Shelby area pioneers that appeared in the *Shelby Promoter.*

10,337. Meredith, Emily R.
Papers. Nd. 1 vol.
Open. Catalog card.
Montana Historical Society.
Meredith's reminiscences "By Wagon from Bannack City to the Bitter Root Valley" regarding her trip in Idaho Territory in 1862 and 1863.

10,338. Montana-American Mothers Bicentennial Project
Records. 1975. 0.1 ft.
Open. Catalog card.
Montana Historical Society.
Biographical sketches of 38 pioneer Montana women written as part of a national Bicentennial project reflect pioneer and homestead life.

10,339. Montana Cowbelles, Inc.
Records. 1952-77. 2 ft.
Open. Catalog card.
Montana Historical Society.
Membership lists and scrapbooks containing constitutions, bylaws, historical sketches, photos, clippings, project and promotional material, and memorabilia of each unit of this statewide women's organization, which serves as an auxiliary to the Montana Stockgrowers Association, a promoter of Montana beef products.

10,340. Montana League of Women Voters
Records. 1951-76. 11 ft.
Open. No guide.
Montana Historical Society.
Minutes, financial records, organizational material, correspondence, subject files, scrapbooks, clippings, and other material of the state chapter and local affiliates of the LWV.

10,341. Montana Legislative Wives Club
Records. 1943-65. 0.5 ft.
Open. Catalog card.
Montana Historical Society.
Minute books, financial records, scrapbooks, and other records of this social organization for wives of members of Montana's legislative assembly.

10,342. Montana State Archives, Attorney General
Records. 1896-1969. 255 ft.
Open. No guide.
Montana Historical Society.
Correspondence, subject files, case files, investigation reports, legal briefs, opinions, and dockets of the state legal officer whose position was created in 1889 when Montana became a state. The 1908 to 1920 subject files contain material on nurses, prostitution, rape, the legal age of women, and woman suffrage.

10,343. Montana State Archives, Board of World's Fair Managers
Records. 1891-94. 1 ft.
Open. No guide.
Montana Historical Society.
Organizational and membership records, correspondence, and other material of the group that was Montana's representative to the Chicago World's Columbian Exposition. Laura E. Howey of Helena acted as coordinator, liaison, and state representative for the group's auxiliary, the board of lady managers.

10,344. Montana State Archives, Constitutional Convention
Records. 1972. 23 ft.
Open. Unpublished guide.
Montana Historical Society.
Committee minutes, administrative and financial records, procedural publications, photos, and clippings of this 100-member body that rewrote Montana's constitution in 1972. Approximately 20 percent of the Convention delegates were women and many administrative positions were filled by women.

10,345. Montana State Archives, Legislative Assembly
Records. 1905- . 100 ft.
Open. No guide.
Montana Historical Society.
Minutes, fiscal notes, committee reports, bills, resolutions, recorded votes, and witness testimony of the legislative branch of the state government of Montana, which became a state in 1889. Contains material on women state representatives and senators and on such issues as woman suffrage in 1905 and abortion and the Equal Rights Amendment in the 1970s.

10,346. Montana State Archives, Superintendent of Public Instruction
Records. 1930-68. 20 ft.
Open. No guide.
Montana Historical Society.
Statistical records, reports, correspondence, and subject files of the state educational officer. The post has been held primarily by women since Montana became a state.

10,347. Moore, Merle (Jordan)
Oral history. Nd. 1 tape.
Open. Catalog card.
Montana Historical Society.
Interview in which Moore, who was the daughter of Montana minister Walter M. Jordan and a resident of Seattle, reminisces about her childhood in Cascade, MT, and Helena and remarks about her mother's acquaintance with Western artist Charles M. Russell.

10,348. Nagle, Margaret
Papers. 1933-62. 1 ft.
Open. Catalog card.
Montana Historical Society.
Correspondence, notes, photos, clippings, and printed material of Nagle, a resident of Helena, relate to promotion of the restoration of the Montana governor's mansion. Also includes files containing printed material on similar projects in other states.

10,349. Nave Family
Papers. 1865-90. 0.1 ft.
Open. Catalog card.
Montana Historical Society.
Correspondence primarily of Jacob Nave, who came with other members of his family to Montana Territory as a farmer and prospector and later ranched near Lewistown, MT. Also includes a diary of Elizabeth Nave for 1867.

10,350. Nichols, Lucy Ann
Papers. 1912-15. 8 items.
Open. Catalog card.
Montana Historical Society.
Letters from Nichols, the wife of a homesteader in Mildred, MT, to her children in Waupaca, WI, contain descriptions of life on a homestead.

10,351. O'Neal, Evelena O. Marsh
Papers. 1955. 0.1 ft. and 5-page item.
Open. Card catalog.
Montana Historical Society.
Reminiscences by O'Neal (1874-1962), a native of Michigan who moved to Montana, concern her steamboat journey to Montana in 1883 on the Missouri River and her life in Montana at Fort Carroll, Rocky Point, Big Sandy, and Chinook.

10,352. Oneal, Marion Sherrard
Papers. 1916-59. 2 in.
Open. Catalog card.
Montana Historical Society.
Correspondence, clippings, and periodicals containing published articles and poetry of Oneal (1884-), a Montana author and poet.

10,353. O'Neil, Elizabeth E. (Busick)
Papers. Ca. 1910. 1 item.
Open. Catalog card.
Montana Historical Society.
Reminiscences by O'Neil, the wife of an East Helena rancher, concern her wagon journey from Omaha to Virginia City, MT, in 1863 and her experiences in that community and in Diamond City, MT, between 1864 and 1877.

10,354. People's Voice
Records. 1904-67. 6.9 ft.
Open. Unpublished guide.
Montana Historical Society.
A Helena-based cooperative newspaper, the *People's Voice* was backed by labor leaders and farm cooperatives. Primarily correspondence and subject files on Montana politics, farm organizations, labor, and power development, the collection also contains financial records, legal documents, court records, and photos. The editor's wife Gretchen G. Billings was a staff writer who advocated protection of public lands, promoted public power districts, supported farmers' cooperatives, and opposed capital punishment in Montana. Founded in 1939, the newspaper was discontinued in 1969.

10,355. Pike, Martha Ellen Goforth Fox
Papers. 1945. 1 folder.
Open. Card catalog.
Montana Historical Society.
Autobiographical account of [Mrs.] Pike (1861-?)

regarding her travels from Tennessee to Nevada, Utah, and Idaho and her arrival in Montana, where she settled in 1897. Contains descriptions of the hardships of her journeys, confrontations with Indians, army camps, mining, lumbering, and Irish immigrants.

10,356. Plassmann, Martha Edgerton
Papers. Nd. 3 ft.
Open. Preliminary inventory.
Montana Historical Society.
Plassmann (?-1936) was an historian and newspaper columnist. Manuscripts of historical articles she submitted for publication in various Montana newspapers during the 1920s include biographies of Montana pioneers, descriptions of pioneer life, and reminiscences of early Montana residents.

10,357. Porter, Mae (Reed)
Phonotape. 1953. 1 tape.
Open. Catalog card.
Montana Historical Society.
Speech given in Anaconda, MT, by Porter, a Kansas City, MO, author and historical researcher, about her experiences buying 1000 Alfred Jacob Miller sketches and her search for artifacts of George Ruxton in Scotland.

10,358. Powers, Mary Johnstone
Papers. 1947. 10-page item.
Open. Catalog card.
Montana Historical Society.
Talk given by Powers to the Corozon Club in Los Angeles concerning the Samuel Johnstone family in Minnesota from 1866 to 1875, the family's covered wagon journey from Kansas to Fort Benton, MT, in 1882 and 1883, and her experiences as Chouteau County school superintendent from 1883 to 1887.

10,359. Ragen, Mary Ellen
Oral history. Nd. 1 tape.
Open. Catalog card.
Montana Historical Society.
Reminiscences by Ragen (1867-1961), who was the wife of Broadwater County, MT, rancher Edward Ragen, concern her early life in Broadwater County. She also gives an account of her parents' journey across the plains from Omaha to Virginia City, MT, in 1864.

10,360. Rankin, Jeannette
Papers. 1936-50. 0.1 ft.
Open. Published guide and card catalog.
Montana Historical Society.
Papers and memorabilia of Rankin (1880-1973), the first female member of Congress, an advocate of women's rights, and an antiwar protester during WWI, WWII, and the Vietnam War. See Brian Cockhill and Dale L. Johnson, comps. and eds., *Guide to Manuscripts in Montana Repositories* (Missoula, MT: University of Montana, 1973).

10,361. Reeder, Adelaide Staves
Papers. 1886-1902. 0.5 ft.
Open. Catalog card.
Montana Historical Society.
Correspondence, biographical material, and clippings of Reeder, a teacher and suffragist.

10,362. Reeder, Irma Brown
Papers. 1927-63. 1 ft.
Open. No guide.
Montana Historical Society.
Diaries of Reeder (1898-1971) detail her work and activities as a Big Sandy, MT, schoolteacher and later as a motel owner in Livingston, MT, near Yellowstone National Park. Also contains correspondence, broadsides, and other material.

10,363. Renner, Fred, and Renner, Ginger
Phonotape. 1974. 1 tape.
Open. Catalog card.
Montana Historical Society.
Lectures given at the 3rd Annual Rendezvous of Western Art at the Historical Society by Fred Renner, a retired consultant on western art and an authority on the works of Charles M. Russell, and by his wife Ginger Renner. The Renners own western art studios in California and Wyoming. Fred Renner talked about dispelling certain myths concerning Russell, while Ginger Renner commented on the importance of contemporary western art and gave a slide show on art criticism.

10,364. Russel, Fannie Forbes Irvine
Papers. Nd. 2 items.
Open. Card catalog.
Montana Historical Society.
Reminiscences written in 1920 by [Mrs. James R.] Russel (?-1934), a native of Missouri and a Butte, MT, resident, regarding her journey by wagon train to Montana in 1864, diet along the way, encounters with Indians, building of her home, mining for gold, vigilante groups, and other pioneer activities. Also includes an account by Russel of her first year in Montana Territory as a resident of Virginia City and Race Track.

10,365. Sanders, Harriet Peck Fenn
Papers. 1863-89. 0.5 in. and 1 microfilm reel.
Open. Card catalog.
Montana Historical Society.
Diaries, writings, an 1889 membership certificate for the Society of Montana Pioneers, biographical material, and clippings of Sanders, who was the wife of W. F. Sanders, a Helena lawyer and politician. Includes a diary from 1863 regarding a trip from Omaha to Bannack, MT, and a diary from 1888 concerning domestic activities; the notebook containing the 1888 diary also includes a history of Italy in Sanders's handwriting.

10,366. Sanders, Helen Fitzgerald
Papers. 1886-1955. 0.4 ft.
Open. Catalog card.
Montana Historical Society.
Correspondence, galley proofs, and clippings of Sanders, an author, historian, and resident of Helena and Butte, MT. Also includes drafts of reminiscences about John X. Beidler, which were used in *X. Beidler: Vigilante,* a book compiled and edited by Sanders and William Bertsche, Jr.

10,367. School District No. 10, Glasgow, MT
Records. 1915-24. 1 microfilm reel.
Open. Catalog card.
Montana Historical Society.
Clerk's record book containing minutes of school board meetings, receipts and expenditures, records of school board elections, a school census, teachers' reports, and lists of textbooks used, library books, and teachers employed in this Valley County school district.

10,368. Schultz, Julia
Oral history. Nd. 1 microfilm reel.
Open. Catalog card.
Montana Historical Society.
Transcript of a taped interview with Schultz, a mixed-blood Gros Ventre Indian who was a pioneer of Phillips County, MT. She reminisces about tribal life, her experiences with Indians, and the Lost Keyes Mine.

10,369. Schultz, Julia, and Long Horse, Peter
Oral history. 1961. 1 tape.
Open. Catalog card.
Montana Historical Society.
Interviews with Schultz, a mixed-blood Gros Ventre Indian and resident of Dodson, MT, who was a pioneer in Phillips County, and Long Horse, a Gros Ventre Indian. They reminisce about Gros Ventre Indian life, customs, and stories. Part of the interview is spoken in the Gros Ventre tongue.

10,370. Sedgwick, Mollie
Papers. 1964. 7-page item.
Open. Catalog card.
Montana Historical Society.
[Mrs.] Sedgwick, a resident of Kalispell, MT, reminisces about her experiences on Montana's Territorial Centennial Train during its journey to New York City and the 1964 World's Fair.

10,371. Sherlock, W. A., and Sherlock, Mary
Oral history. Nd. 2 tapes.
Open. Catalog card.
Montana Historical Society.
The Sherlocks were cattle and sheep owners in Broadwater County, MT. Interviews with W. A. Sherlock about his ranching experiences and incidents in Broadwater County and with Mary Sherlock concerning the establishment of Crow Creek community.

10,372. Sizer, Linda Pyle
Papers. Nd. 2 items.
Open. Catalog card.
Montana Historical Society.
Reminiscences by Sizer, a Montana pioneer, of a steamboat trip she made down the Missouri to the "States" in 1880 when she was 14 years old and a biographical sketch and reminiscences concerning her uncle William Patterson of Keokuk, IA.

10,373. Small, Cecillia Gibson
Papers. Nd. 25-page item.
Open. Catalog card.
Montana Historical Society.
Biographical manuscript by Grace E. Doorenbos about Small, a Cut Bank, MT, teacher who had earlier taught in Washington, and about their friendship from 1908 to 1954.

10,374. Smith, Ella F. Levengood
Papers. Ca. 1920. 3-page item.
Open. Card catalog.
Montana Historical Society.
Reminiscences of Smith regarding her journey by steamboat to Montana in 1867, relations with the Indians, and the hardships of settling in Montana.

10,375. Smith, Veva
Oral history. Nd. 1 tape.
Open. Catalog card.
Montana Historical Society.
Interview in which [Mrs. Charles W.] Smith (1878-1969), who was the daughter of Townsend, MT, businessman James Rufus Marks, reminisces about her childhood in Townsend.

10,376. Southeastern Montana Cowbelles
Records. 1955-66. 0.4 ft.
Open. Catalog card.
Montana Historical Society.
Correspondence and clippings relating to the activities of this social organization made up of women cattle ranchers or wives of cattle ranchers who were interested in promoting the cattle-raising industry.

10,377. Stewart Family
Papers. 1910-78. 3 items.
Open. Catalog card.
Montana Historical Society.
Letter by Addie Osborn [Mrs. Carry E.] Stewart, a homesteader in Ismay, MT, to Emma Milnor of Rome, IN, describing her first six months on the family homestead. Also includes reminiscences by Addie Stewart which were completed by her son Charles A. Stewart as a family history.

10,378. Stewart, Mrs. Paul A.
Papers. Nd. 1 ft.
Open. Catalog card.
Montana Historical Society.
Clippings, other papers, and books of Stewart.

10,379. Stiefvator, Anne Calwell
Papers. 1954. 6-page item.
Open. Card catalog.

Montana Historical Society.
Reminiscences of Stiefvator regarding ranching in eastern Montana contain descriptions of homesteading on 320 acres in 1917, diet, chores, gardening, washing, and hardships. She also describes working in Chicago sweatshops during her youth for two and one-half cents per hour and the effects of the child labor laws.

10,380. Stocking, Lucy
Papers. 1871-82. 0.1 ft.
Open. Catalog card.
Montana Historical Society.
Diary of Stocking, the daughter of a pioneer who had a ranch on the Teton River in Montana, contains details of a trip up the Missouri River and her life on her father's ranch.

10,381. Story, Mrs. Nelson
Papers. 1908. 1 folder.
Open. Card catalog.
Montana Historical Society.
Ellen Trent Story (1846-?) was a resident of Bozeman, MT, and the wife of Nelson Story, a prominent businessman. Clippings and a biographical account written by Mrs. M. W. Alderson regarding Ellen Story's travels up the Missouri River to Montana, her life in a mining camp, her residency in Bozeman from 1866 to 1908, and her strengths as a wife and mother.

10,382. Stuart, Granville
Papers. 1863-1918. 1 ft.
Open. Card catalog.
Montana Historical Society.
Correspondence, a diary of a trip to France in 1894, biographical material, an account ledger for the DHS Ranch, an historical sketch of Deer Lodge County, MT, scrapbooks, and other papers of Stuart (1834-1918), a pioneer miner and cattleman in Montana. Includes letters to Stuart from May Crosby and Julia A. Hall and letters Nancy C. Stuart wrote to her sons.

10,383. Sturgis Family
Papers. 1862-67. 5 items.
Open. Catalog card.
Montana Historical Society.
Papers of members of the Sturgis family, who were pioneer residents of Bannock, MT, include letters to William Sturgis describing conditions in Minnesota and the trip to Montana by steamboat; letters by Rosanna Sturgis; and 1866 affidavits crediting William Sturgis with work on the Red Rock and Beaverhead Canyon Road.

10,384. Sullivan, Kathryn
Papers. 1906-29. 0.3 ft.
Open. Catalog card.
Montana Historical Society.
Sullivan was a Marysville, MT, store operator. Correspondence of the Sullivan family and legal correspondence and documents of L. L. Lush, a Marysville attorney.

10,385. Supreme Court
Records. 1868-1967. 962 cu.ft.
Open. Catalog card.
Montana Historical Society.
Territorial case files for 1868 to 1890 and case files, opinions, filings, exhibits, and other records of the Montana Supreme Court for 1890 to 1967.

10,386. Talbot, Susan A.
Papers. 1973. 19-page item.
Open. Catalog card.
Montana Historical Society.
Reminiscences and a history by Talbot, a resident of Missoula, MT, concerning her grandparents the Charles B. Andersons and the Walter Aitkens and her family's early experiences in Bozeman and other parts of Montana. The history was written for presentation at the Missoula Cosmos Club.

10,387. Topping, Lucille
Oral history. 1968. 1 tape.
Open. Catalog card.
Montana Historical Society.
Topping was the wife of Helena realtor Tom Topping and the daughter of Montana pioneer Ralph Dyas. In her interview she reminisces about her life in Montana and tells stories about her father and her grandfather William F. Wheeler.

10,388. Turner, Sally
Papers. Nd. 1 vol.
Open. Catalog card.
Montana Historical Society.
Manuscript by Turner, a homesteader in the Yaak River Valley of northwestern Montana, provides a history of the area and its settlers the Yaakers.

10,389. Turpin, Frances Lynn
Papers. 1895. 40-page item.
Open. Catalog card.
Montana Historical Society.
Diary kept by Turpin, a resident of St. Louis, during a tour of Yellowstone National Park.

10,390. Tyler, Elizabeth Ruth
Papers. 1954. 1 folder.
Open. Card catalog.
Montana Historical Society.
Reminiscences of Tyler, a Glendive, MT, resident, regarding hardships and other aspects of homesteading in the Glendive area after 1906. Also includes a nurse's and a teacher's certificate from Des Moines College in Iowa.

10,391. Tyler, Jane
Papers. Nd. 3-page item.
Open. Catalog card.
Montana Historical Society.
Autobiographical sketch by [Mrs. C. J.] Tyler.

10,392. Wade Family
Papers. 1793-1926. Ca. 2 ft.
Open. Unpublished guide.
Montana Historical Society.
Decius S. Wade (1835-1905) served as chief justice of the Montana Territorial Supreme Court. The collection is primarily correspondence of Wade, his wife Bernice (Galpin) Wade, their daughter Clare L. (Wade) Safford, Decius Wade's sister Lucia, and his first cousin Nellie Colfax, wife of US Vice-President Schuyler Colfax. Material reflects the attitudes of women prominent in Helena's social and political circles.

10,393. Williams, Della Johnson
Oral history. Nd. 1 tape.
Open. Catalog card.
Montana Historical Society.
Interview in which Williams, a resident of Radersburg, MT, and mother of actress Myrna Loy, reminisces about her life in Radersburg and the Crow Creek Valley area and her children David and Myrna.

10,394. Wilson, Elise Munser Beck
Oral history. 1967. 1 tape.
Open. Catalog card.
Montana Historical Society.
Interview with Wilson (1881-), who reminisces about the early history of Basin, MT, where she resided.

10,395. Wilson, Nettie Emery
Papers. 1865. 13-page item.
Open. Catalog card.
Montana Historical Society.
Narrative by Wilson about life in Virginia City, MT, in 1865.

10,396. Women's Helena for the Capital Club
Records. 1894. 1 vol.
Open. No guide.
Montana Historical Society.
Organizational material, financial reports, correspondence, speeches, resolutions, clippings, broadsides, and other records of this Helena-based group organized in 1894 to encourage statewide women's participation in an effort to establish Helena as the state capital.

10,397. Young Women's Christian Association
Records. 1918-43. 0.1 ft.
Open. Catalog card.
Montana Historical Society.
Records documenting the Second War Fund Campaign of the Flathead County, MT, chapter of the YWCA include correspondence between Grace V. Erickson, Blanche D. Walker, and Nellie D. Sadler.

10,398. Zook, Laura (Brown)
Papers. 1953-64. 2 folders.
Open. Card catalog.
Montana Historical Society.
Biographical sketches about Zook (1868-1944), a Miles City, MT, pioneer, a teacher at the Cheyenne Indian school at Lame Deer, MT, and superintendent of schools for Custer County, MT.

MISSOULA

10,399. Johnson, Dorothy M.
Papers. Nd. No size given.
Open. Published guide.
University of Montana Library.
Manuscripts and other material concerning *Beulah Bunny Tells All, Flame on the Frontier, Difficult Courtship,* and other books by Johnson (1905-). See Brian Cockhill and Dale L. Johnson, comps. and eds., *Guide to Manuscripts in Montana Repositories* (Missoula, MT: University of Montana, 1973).

10,400. Labrie, Rene J.
Papers. Nd. No size given.
Open. Published guide.
University of Montana Library.
Papers of Labrie, a pioneer in Harlowton, MT, contain information on steamboats, the fur trade, and Indian trails. See Brian Cockhill and Dale L. Johnson, comps. and eds., *Guide to Manuscripts in Montana Repositories* (Missoula, MT: University of Montana, 1973).

10,401. Patterson, Ida S.
Papers. Nd. 1 folder.
Open. Published guide.
University of Montana Library.
Reminiscences of [Mrs.] Emma H. Magee, (1866-1950), a resident of western Montana. See Brian Cockhill and Dale L. Johnson, comps. and eds., *Guide to Manuscripts in Montana Repositories* (Missoula, MT: University of Montana, 1973).

VIRGINIA CITY

10,402. McNulty, Flora (McKay)
Papers. 1883-1945. Ca. 6 cu.ft.
Access restricted. No guide.
Historic Landmark Society of Montana.
A physician, McNulty (1861-1945) was the wife of a dentist. Correspondence, notes, financial papers, scrapbooks, photos, clippings, and records of women's clubs, including minutes, financial records, and other items. McNulty belonged to a variety of organizations, including the Medical Association of Montana, the Montana Society of Pioneers, the WCTU, the Ladies Literary Circle, and the Ancient Order of United Workmen. She also was involved in the women's suffrage movement.

NEBRASKA

CHADRON

10,403. Northwest Nebraska's Voices of History
Oral history. Ca. 1976. 40 tapes and other items.
Access restricted. Published guide and index.
Chadron State College, Mari Sandoz Heritage Society.
Interviews with and photos of 12 northwestern Nebraska pioneer residents include reminiscences of Marie (Surber) Hare (1887-), who became a schoolteacher at the age of 17; Jennie Broadhurst [Mrs. George] Lawrence (1884-), a farm woman; and Grace Francis Pollard (1893-), who as a teenager took part in social activities at Fort Robinson, NE. Pollard describes social events at the fort and comments that the cavalry officers regarded themselves as royalty among the area's settlers and homesteaders. In her interview Lawrence comments that her family's first home was in a cellar. Hare, who came to the US with her family from Switzerland in the 1890s, taught in many Sheridan County schools. See *Northwest Nebraska's Voices of History* (Chadron: Chadron State College and The Mari Sandoz Heritage Society, 1976).

DORCHESTER

10,404. Blue Valley Transportation, Inc.
Records. Ca. 1968-76. 1 box.
Open. No guide.
Saline County Historical Society, Inc.
Founded in about 1968 and reorganized in 1973, this program provides bus transportation for senior citizens who live in rural areas and small towns. Articles of incorporation, minutes of board meetings, financial records, correspondence, public transportation survey, records of trips and stops, membership file, schedules, clippings, and other records. Organized in Fairbury, NE, as a private, non-profit organization, the program was designed to help elderly persons who needed transportation for shopping or for visiting their doctors. Women helped organize the project, which received Office of Economic Opportunity funds to purchase a van. [Miss] Helen Storms is manager of the bus and secretary of the organization. Marlene [Mrs. Don] Bartels is the driver.

10,405. Bray, Avis
Papers. Ca. 1952-60. 4 in.
Open. No guide.
Saline County Historical Society, Inc.
Bray, a medical doctor, moved to Dorchester after local residents conducted a search for a physician for their Community. She left after two years because of family problems. Correspondence, minutes, financial records, and clippings document the town's search, which was led by the Dorchester Community Medical Fund. Many women participated in the work of the Fund, which was organized in 1955, to raise money to establish and equip an office for the doctor. Much of the correspondence was written to [Mrs.] Rosa Dusanek by the Nebraska State Medical Association.

10,406. Dorchester Woman's Club
Records. 1936-74. Ca. 4.5 in.
Open. No guide.
Saline County Historical Society, Inc.
Constitution, minutes, financial records, programs, yearbooks, pamphlet, clippings, and other records of this local woman's social club, which was organized in 1936 and disbanded in 1974. Includes articles of incorporation and bylaws of the Nebraska Federation of Women's Clubs, Inc.; programs of annual conventions of the Nebraska Federation's fourth district; and a program for a convention of the Seward-Saline Inter-County Federation of Women's Clubs.

10,407. Miller, Florence (Hazen)
Papers. Ca. 1923-60s. Ca. 11 in.
Open. No guide.
Saline County Historical Society, Inc.
[Mrs. B. G.] Miller was a local philanthropist and member of the DAR. Scrapbook about Miller's philanthropic activities, which included gifts to Doane College in Crete, NE, and four memorial albums concerning Revolutionary War soldiers. The albums, sponsored by the Nebraska DAR, were compiled by Miller.

GRAND ISLAND

10,408. American Legion Auxiliary, Grand Island Post 53
Records. 1933-34. 1 in.
Open. No guide.
Stuhr Museum of the Prairie Pioneer.
Organized in 1920, the group was the auxiliary of American Legion Grand Island Post 53. History of the local auxiliary with a list of members, program of the state auxiliary's 14th annual convention, delegates report from the state convention, and issues of the *Veterans News,* a monthly publication of the Grand Island Legion post.

10,409. Business and Professional Women's Club
Records. 1934-35. 1 item.
Open. No guide.
Stuhr Museum of the Prairie Pioneer.
Yearbook of the local Club, which was organized in 1915.

10,410. Daughters of the American Revolution in Nebraska
Records. 1943-45. 2 items.
Open. No guide.
Stuhr Museum of the Prairie Pioneer.
Yearbooks of the Betsey Hager Chapter of the DAR. This Grand Island group was founded in 1926.

10,411. Rebekah Assembly, I.O.O.F. of the State of Nebraska
Records. Ca. 1919-43. 6 items.
Open. No guide.
Stuhr Museum of the Prairie Pioneer.
Constitution of the Assembly of the Nebraska Independent Order of Odd Fellows; minutes of the Assembly's 36th Annual Session, held in 1919 at York, NE; and programs from annual sessions held by units located in Wood River, Grand Island, Shelton, Hastings, and other Nebraska towns.

10,412. Royal Neighbors of America, Fifth and Sixth Districts
Records. Ca. 1917-33. Ca. 0.5 in.
Open. No guide.
Stuhr Museum of the Prairie Pioneer.
Programs and pamphlets of these two Nebraska districts of the Royal Neighbors of America, including programs from annual conventions in the central Nebraska towns of Grand Island, Hastings, Kearney, St. Paul, and Ravenna and a pamphlet concerning the organization's rituals.

10,413. Truth Circle
Records. 1937-39. 2 items.
Open. No guide.
Stuhr Museum of the Prairie Pioneer.
Program booklets of this women's club.

10,414. Woman's Relief Corps, District No. 3
Records. Ca. 1916-48. 9 items.
Open. No guide.
Stuhr Museum of the Prairie Pioneer.
Constitution, list of members, and programs of the Woman's Relief Corps, Auxiliary to the Grand Army of the Republic, District No. 3, in Nebraska. Includes programs from the district's annual conventions in Grand Island, Central City, and Shelton, NE, and programs from encampments in 1927 and 1935 of the state GAR and allied organizations, including the Woman's Relief Corps.

HASTINGS

10,415. George Eliot Club
Records. 1889-1974. 1 Hollinger box.
Open. Unpublished guide.
Adams County Historical Society Archives.
Correspondence and programs of this women's study club, described as the oldest and most prestigious in a Great Plains county seat.

10,416. Round Table Club
Records. 1901-47. 1 Hollinger box.
Open. Unpublished guide.
Adams County Historical Society Archives.
Programs of a women's study club, which was organized in 1893.

10,417. Women in Adams County
Records. 1871- . 1 Hollinger box.
Open. Unpublished guide.
Adams County Historical Society Archives.
Collection includes diaries of pioneer women from the first settlement in ca. 1871 in Adams County, biographies of individuals compiled for newspaper series, correspondence, photos, and scrapbooks.

LINCOLN

10,418. International Fiddlers and Fiddling
Collection. Nd. 29 drawers, 400 recording discs, and tapes.
Access restricted. No guide.
American Old Time Fiddlers Association.
Correspondence, printed music, discs, sound tapes, photos, magazines and periodicals, clippings, and books collected by DeLores DeRyke as research for *The Complete Book of Fiddling.* The Fiddlers Association, founded by DeRyke in 1965, seeks to preserve and promote old-time fiddling and related arts and skills. Material contains letters by and biographies of women fiddlers.

10,419. Abbott, Grace
Papers. 1917-39. 0.33 ft.
Open. No guide.
Nebraska State Historical Society.
Scrapbook contains copies of correspondence, addresses, congressional hearing reports, and clippings of [Miss] Abbott (1878-1939), director of the US Department of Labor Children's Bureau. Also contains items compiled by her niece Charlotte Abbott of Grand Island, NE. The daughter of a Nebraska family, Grace Abbott graduated from the University of Nebraska and then moved to Chicago where she worked to improve immigration legislation. She later became executive secretary of the Immigration Commission of Massachusetts. In 1921 President Warren Harding named her director of the Children's Bureau.

10,420. Aldrich, Benton
Papers. 1873-1918. 11 ft.
Open. Unpublished guide.
Nebraska State Historical Society.
Correspondence, notebooks, notes, manuscripts, minutes, clippings, and other papers of Aldrich (1831-1918), a horticulturist, include a constitution, amendments, bylaws, and minutes of the Clifton Women's Club, founded in 1894. Bulk of

collection concerns horticulture and farm life during the early years of Nebraska statehood.

10,421. Aldrich, Bess (Streeter)
Papers. 1907-54. 11 ft.
Open. Unpublished guide.
Nebraska State Historical Society.
General and business correspondence, telegrams, notes, manuscripts, legal and financial files, scrapbooks, art, newspapers, clippings, and other printed matter of [Mrs. Charles S.] Aldrich (1881-1954), an author. Includes correspondence from agents, producers, and publishers. Manuscript and note files arranged alphabetically by story reveal the sources of her short stories and novels. Bulk of the collection is printed material.

10,422. Allen, Katherine Fay (Worley)
Papers. 1916-61. 5 cu.ft.
Open. Unpublished guide.
Nebraska State Historical Society.
[Mrs. Charles] Allen (1876-1971), a newspaperwoman, served as chairman of the Nebraska Board of Control of State Institutions. Includes correspondence and clippings concerning her work on the Board of Control, clippings about activities of the Omaha Woman's Club, a copy of *Victory: Report of the Women's Liberty Loan Committee Tenth Federal Reserve District* (1919), and scrapbooks. Appointed to the Board of Control in 1920, Allen became chairman in 1921. She resigned in 1923 to return to Omaha to manage her press-clipping service.

10,423. Altrusa International Club
Records. 1922-60. 1.5 ft.
Open. Unpublished guide.
Nebraska State Historical Society.
Minutes, correspondence, biographies of members, histories, reports, photos, and other records of Altrusa districts 6 and 7 in Nebraska and of the national organization, formed in 1917. The group, which included business and professional women, sought to promote character and citizenship.

10,424. American Association of University Women
Records. 1930-69. 3 ft.
Open. Unpublished guide.
Nebraska State Historical Society.
Minutes, histories of state and local branches, reports, membership lists, and scrapbooks of the state AAUW, formed in 1900.

10,425. American Association of University Women
Records. 1920-65. 2 cu.ft.
Open. Unpublished guide.
Nebraska State Historical Society.
Charter, constitution, bylaws, minutes, correspondence, reports, scrapbooks containing clippings, and printed material of the Lincoln AAUW branch, founded in 1900. Includes papers regarding Louise Pound, a vice-president of the national AAUW. Records reflect activities of the group that sought improved conditions for women students at the University of Nebraska.

10,426. American Women's Overseas Service Legion
Records. 1921-60. 5 ft.
Open. Unpublished guide.
Nebraska State Historical Society.
Correspondence, rosters, personnel records, and miscellany of the Marion Crandell unit of the Legion, founded in 1921 by women who served overseas in WWI. The Legion was associated with the American Legion and other veterans' groups.

10,427. Anderson, Helen Marie (Nance)
Papers. 1871-1966. 11.5 ft.
Open. Unpublished guide.
Nebraska State Historical Society.
Anderson (1877-1966) was the daughter of Nebraska governor Albinus Nance. Correspondence, journals, financial and legal records, scrapbooks, printed matter, and other items primarily pertaining to legal affairs of Anderson and her husband Walter L. Anderson. Includes discussion of their travel and farm property. The journals reflect incidents that occurred during Helen Anderson's trips to Europe; one account includes her observations at the outbreak of WWI. Also contains a journal pertaining to the European voyage of Lina S. Merchant and material concerning the Republican party.

10,428. Aspinwall Family
Papers. 1808-1960. 5 cu.ft.
Open. Unpublished guide.
Nebraska State Historical Society.
Bulk of the collection pertains to [Miss] Nan J. Aspinwall (1880-), an expert horsewoman, lariatist, and sharpshooter, who replaced Annie Oakley in Buffalo Bill's Wild West Show. Correspondence, manuscripts, financial records, scrapbook, photos, printed matter, and other papers provide information about Nan Aspinwall's early life, her cross-country round-trip ride on horseback in 1911 from San Francisco to New York, and the vaudeville troupe that she and her husband Frank Gable owned.

10,429. Athenea Club
Records. 1892-1936. 12 items.
Open. Unpublished guide.
Nebraska State Historical Society.
Minutes and programs of a Lincoln women's group, founded in 1892, which discussed historical, literary, and political topics.

10,430. Avery, May (Bennett)
Papers. 1880-1930. 3 in.
Open. Unpublished guide.
Nebraska State Historical Society.
Manuscripts, a diary, and miscellany of [Mrs. Samuel] Avery (1870-1960) consist primarily of book reviews, speeches, and essays. Also includes an account of Avery's trip to Europe in 1930 and the manuscript "Memories of Pioneer Days," in which Eva (Hendrickson) Klepper of Wilsonville, NE, recalls her trip from Illinois to Nebraska during the 1880s and pioneer life in a sod house until 1903.

10,431. Ballantine, David Coulter
Papers. 1870-1960. 2 cu.ft. and 1 microfilm reel.
Open. Unpublished guide.
Nebraska State Historical Society.
Correspondence and diaries of Ballantine (1877-1960), a rancher, and poetry and fiction of his mother Anna Eliza Ena Palmer Raymonde Ballantine McClary (1848-84), a frontierswoman and author.

10,432. Baptist, Julia
Papers. 1885-88. 1 ft.
Open. Unpublished guide.
Nebraska State Historical Society.
Correspondence concerns pioneer life, personal matters, and weather in Phelps County, NE.

10,433. Bettelyoun, Susan Bordeaux
Papers. 1840-1940. 1 cu.ft. and 1 microfilm reel.
Open. Unpublished guide.
Nebraska State Historical Society.
Bettelyoun (1857-?) was a teacher on the Rosebud Indian Reservation and at Fort Laramie, WY. Correspondence, manuscripts, and autobiographical information that Bettelyoun told to [Mrs.] Josephine Waggoner. Includes descriptions of the experiences of the Bordeaux family and data about Fort Laramie, Crazy Horse, the Oglala Sioux Indians, the Battle of Ash Hollow, the fur trade, the Crow Butte legend, and Indian-military history.

10,434. Birkley, Hannah (Vatteng)
Papers. 1957. 5.5 ft.
Open. Unpublished guide.
Nebraska State Historical Society.
Memorabilia and an interview in which Birkley recalls her solitary trip in 1875 from Norway to be with an uncle in South Dakota. In 1882 she married Iver Birkley, a harness maker, and moved with him to Nebraska.

10,435. Brady, John David
Papers. 1922-69. 1 cu.ft.
Open. Unpublished guide.
Nebraska State Historical Society.
Brady's papers contain material of [Miss] Flora Crumley, a retired Lincoln art teacher who lived with the Brady family. Her papers include poetry and diaries concerning daily weather, her personal schedule, and other topics.

10,436. Bressler Family
Papers. 1881-1961. 2 ft.
Open. Unpublished guide.
Nebraska State Historical Society.
Correspondence, poetry, and songs of Julia (Nelson) [Mrs. Calvin] Bressler (1881-), a Geneva, IL, native who moved with her family to Nebraska in 1887. Family correspondence includes items between Bressler and her son Allen from 1955 to 1957 while she was a patient at the Nebraska State Hospitals. Julia Bressler a housewife, wrote songs, including "When Your Two Lips Smile at Me," "My Home Is a Heaven to Me," "The Cowboy on the Plain," and "Just Like a Morning Glory."

10,437. Bruner Family
Papers. 1869-1956. 4 cu.ft.
Open. Unpublished guide.
Nebraska State Historical Society.
The Bruners were a Nebraska pioneer family. Collection includes school material and personal papers of Amelia Phoneta (Bruner) [Mrs. James W.] Monroe (1854-?); personal items of Lillie C. Bruner (1864-1957); correspondence, notebooks, and a cookbook of Ellen Judith (Bruner) Debell (1868-1936); personal items and poetry of Ida M. (Bruner) [Mrs. J. J.] King; and a news release of Amy Celeste (Bruner) [Mrs. John Edwin] Almy (1875-1943). The five sisters were pioneers, authors, and builders. Collection also includes material pertaining to women of West Point, NE, the Elkhorn Valley, and the Omaha area.

10,438. Bullock, Flora
Papers. 1913-62. 1 ft.
Open. Unpublished guide.
Nebraska State Historical Society.
A teacher, author, and composer, Bullock (1871-1962) taught at the Nebraska School for the Blind; she also was an extension employee of the University of Nebraska college of agriculture. Correspondence, manuscripts, printed material, personal items, and miscellany.

10,439. Cameron, Anna M.
Papers. 1939. 0.1 ft.
Open. No guide.
Nebraska State Historical Society.
Cameron served as editor for the North Loup Valley, NE, Historical Society during the June 1939 celebration of Trail of the Loup Days. Manuscript of edited conversations of men and women reminiscing about their early lives as settlers in the late 19th century in north central Nebraska.

10,440. Carns, Margaret Jane (Burke)
Papers. 1865-1952. 2 cu.ft.
Open. Unpublished guide.
Nebraska State Historical Society.
An attorney, [Mrs. Edmund C.] Carns (1859-1952) was the first woman member of the American Bar Association and a leader in women's activities in the US and abroad. Correspondence, notes,

manuscripts, documents, certificates, printed matter, and memorabilia relate primarily to her activities with the ABA, the National Association of Women Lawyers, and the Nebraska Prison Board.

10,441. Carter, Susan Ophelia
Papers. 1887. 3.1 ft.
Open. No guide.
Nebraska State Historical Society.
Diary and a transcribed manuscript of Carter (1860-1946), a Nebraska pioneer and schoolteacher. Born in Gardner, IL, Carter moved to Odebolt, IA, with her parents and later migrated with her family to Nebraska, where they lived near the Custer-Loup county line. Information in the diary was transcribed in 1965 by Carter's granddaughter Colleen Switzer and apparently dealt with a year during Carter's teaching career.

10,442. Cather Family
Papers. 1870-95. 1 microfilm reel.
Open. Unpublished guide.
Nebraska State Historical Society.
The Cathers were pioneers in Virginia and Nebraska. Personal and family correspondence concerns the lives of pioneer women in Webster County, NE.

10,443. Cather, Willa Sibert
Papers. 1875-1955. 0.5 cu. ft. and 2 microfilm reels.
Open. Unpublished guide.
Nebraska State Historical Society.
Correspondence, articles, stories, research material, photos, scrapbooks, clippings, and other papers of [Miss] Cather (1873-1947), an author, contain her theatrical columns from the *Lincoln Courier* and the *Nebraska State Journal*. Includes information about Cather's early career.

10,444. Chmiel, Elizabeth McKinney
Papers. 1951-58. Less than 1 cu.ft.
Open. Unpublished guide.
Nebraska State Historical Society.
Correspondence, clippings, and other papers of Chmiel chiefly concern her cousin Mary Frances Ford (ca. 1854-1956), children's page editor for the *Chicago Daily News*. Ford, who began her newspaper career at age 60, is said to have been the author of the children's story *The Little Engine That Could*. She was one of the first women to conduct a radio program. After retiring at the age of 76, she moved to Philadelphia.

10,445. Clark, John Calvin
Papers. 1852-63. 1 microfilm reel.
Open. Unpublished guide.
Nebraska State Historical Society.
Personal correspondence between John Clark (1829-?) and his wife Arianna Clark during his service in the Civil War. Arianna Clark's letters primarily relate to her management of the family farm in Iowa during her husband's absence.

10,446. Clements, Edith Gertrude (Schwartz)
Papers. 1911-49. 2 ft.
Open. Unpublished guide.
Nebraska State Historical Society.
In 1908, [Mrs. Frederick E.] Clements (?-1971), an ecologist from Omaha, became the first woman to earn a PhD from the University of Nebraska. Correspondence, biographical data, photos, clippings, and printed material consist for the most part of letters of Clements and her husband, a professor of botany at the University of Nebraska, containing descriptions of an Atlantic crossing and travels through England and Europe. Clements received her PhD under her husband's direction.

10,447. Cole, Nellie Wurtsmith
Papers. 1932-53. 5.5 in.
Open. Unpublished guide.
Nebraska State Historical Society.
Diaries of Cole (1864-1955), a Beatrice, NE, resident; minutes and reports of the Altar Guild of Beatrice's Christ Episcopal Church; household accounts, and printed material.

10,448. Correll, Erasmus Michael
Papers. 1869-91. 0.5 cu.ft.
Open. Unpublished guide.
Nebraska State Historical Society.
A Nebraska editor and state senator, Correll (1846-95) fought an unsuccessful legislative battle in 1881 for woman's suffrage and established the *Western Women's Journal* in 1882. Correspondence, notes, speech drafts, pamphlets, and clippings relating to Correll's legislative campaign and woman suffrage in Nebraska; information regarding the 1881 Nebraska Woman Suffrage Convention in Omaha; records of Hebron, NE, and Thayer County; and miscellany.

10,449. Crawford, Harry Love
Papers. 1934-58. 0.5 ft.
Open. Unpublished guide.
Nebraska State Historical Society.
Correspondence, manuscripts, notes, printed material, and Nebraska history miscellany of Crawford (1879-1959), a furniture dealer, mortician, and amateur historian and biographer. Includes biographical sketches of Lucy Sizer Hull, who came to Kearney, NE, as a young child in 1872 and taught piano there for 48 years; Cordelia M. Waite, who came to Elm Creek, NE, during the 1870s and died in 1881; Mrs. John Davis; and Emily M. Carpenter, a Bristol, NH, native who in 1872 moved to Gibbon, NE, where she taught school. Carpenter's home served as the Majors, NE, post office.

10,450. Crittenden, Cornelia Williams
Papers. 1855-1920. 5.5 in.
Open. Unpublished guide.
Nebraska State Historical Society.
Correspondence, diaries, family photos, clippings, and personal books, including a baby book, a Book of Common Prayer, and a New Testament of Crittenden (1895-1959), a Nebraska homemaker. Correspondence regarding settlement of an estate in 1902 is addressed to Crittenden's mother Marion Brown Crittenden of Lincoln from an uncle Charles B. Loomis.

10,451. Daughters of the American Revolution
Records. 1903-64. 12 ft.
Open. Unpublished guide.
Nebraska State Historical Society.
Correspondence, files, genealogies, histories, scrapbooks, yearbooks, printed matter, and other records of Nebraska and national DAR groups. The state's first chapter, the Deborah Avery Chapter of Lincoln, was founded in 1896.

10,452. Davis, Margaret
Papers. 1836-1956. 5.5 in.
Open. Unpublished guide.
Nebraska State Historical Society.
[Miss] Davis (1875-1958) was a teacher and Lincoln resident. Minutes of the British War Relief Society of Lincoln from 1942 to 1945; Winslow and Davis family records, which consist of military warrants, deeds, mortgages, and Cass County tax receipts; clippings concerning Cass County history; scrapbooks containing reminiscences by Davis's mother Kate (Winslow) Davis of Jane Thompson, who died in 1882; limited records of the University of Nebraska class of 1901; and memorabilia of Margaret Davis's years as a history teacher.

10,453. Delta Kappa Gamma, Zeta Chapter
Records. 1928-48. 5.5 in.
Open. Unpublished guide.
Nebraska State Historical Society.
Correspondence; research, biographical, and autobiographical data; committee reports; and printed matter generated by the Lincoln chapter of Delta Kappa Gamma, a professional honorary teaching fraternity, in connection with its Pioneer Women Teacher Research Project. Bulk of the material deals with such pioneer Nebraska teachers as Susan R. Frazier and Olga F. Stastny. The Zeta Chapter was founded in 1929.

10,454. DeWeese, Alice Christine (Towne)
Papers. 1798-1950. 2 ft.
Open. Unpublished guide.
Nebraska State Historical Society.
Correspondence, manuscripts, genealogical material, photos, printed matter, and miscellany of [Mrs. Fred M.] DeWeese (1884-), a Lincoln genealogist, include letters and genealogical manuscripts she wrote about the Seabury, Towne, Galbraith, Trumbull, and Lindsey families. Also contains address books, a portion of a cookbook, a University of Nebraska songbook from 1921, souvenir pamphlets, and printed matter about Nebraska ornithology.

10,455. Dodge, Caroline E. (Marshall)
Papers. 1800-1926. 0.5 ft.
Open. Unpublished guide.
Nebraska State Historical Society.
Correspondence, financial records, essays, histories, newspapers, and miscellany of [Mrs. George A.] Dodge, who was born in the early 1800s. Bulk of collection consists of correspondence to her concerning domestic matters in Maine and Illinois. Also includes a Marshall family history from 1750 to 1800 and newspapers from Omaha and Fremont, NE, and Maryville, MO.

10,456. Duncombe, Frances E.
Papers. 1891-1957. 3 in.
Open. Unpublished guide.
Nebraska State Historical Society.
Correspondence, a diary, clippings, and printed matter of [Miss] Duncombe (1870-1958) relate to her experiences at the University of Nebraska from 1897 to 1901 and as an English teacher at Lincoln High School for 37 years.

10,457. Edgar, NE, Woman's Foreign Missionary Society
Records. 1892-1903. 1 vol.
Open. Unpublished guide.
Nebraska State Historical Society.
Minutes of monthly meetings of the Woman's Foreign Missionary Society of the Methodist Episcopal Church. The Edgar Church was organized in 1873 and the local Society chapter, in ca. 1885.

10,458. Elliott, Lillian A.
Papers. 1947-54. 17 items.
Open. Unpublished guide.
Nebraska State Historical Society.
Written reminiscences of [Miss] Elliott (1880-), a pioneer, relate to early settlement of the Elkhorn River Valley and to the grasshopper plague of the early 1870s.

10,459. Fletcher, Alice Cunningham
Papers. 1886-91. 3 microfilm reels.
Open. Unpublished guide.
Nebraska State Historical Society.
Correspondence of [Miss] Fletcher (1838-1923), an archaeologist and ethnologist who served in 1896 as national vice-president of the American Academy for the Advancement of Science and as president in 1905 of the Folklore Society. Born in Havana, Cuba, Fletcher grew up in New York City. She became interested in the plight of Indians and toured the East fighting for Indian reform. She lived with the Omaha tribe in Nebraska, became a tribal member in 1881, and supported passage in 1887 of the Dawes Act. Her studies of Indian culture led to her publication in 1911 of *The Omaha Tribe*. Fletcher maintained close ties with the La Flesches, a Nebraska Omaha

family, and Francis La Flesche, son of Omaha leader Joseph La Flesche, assisted her in her research. She spent her final years in Washington, DC.

10,460. Fremont, NE, First Congregational Church, UCC
Records. 1880-1945. 1 microfilm reel.
Open. Unpublished guide.
Nebraska State Historical Society.
Memoir, reports, rosters, manuals, and printed matter of the Church, founded in 1857, include manuscript material regarding the work of a member, [Miss] Ruth Mulliken, who was a missionary in China from 1910 until 1942. Also contains records of the Women's Missionary Society.

10,461. Friend, NE, First Congregational Church
Records. 1875-1960. 2 microfilm reels.
Open. Unpublished guide.
Nebraska State Historical Society.
Records of the Church, founded in 1875, include the constitution and minutes of the Women's Fellowship, which earlier was known as the Women's Missionary Society and the Dorcas Federated Missionary Society.

10,462. Gerrard, Elizabeth Caroline (Weaver)
Papers. 1879-1913. 3 ft.
Open. Unpublished guide.
Nebraska State Historical Society.
Correspondence, legal notices, and orders of [Mrs. Leonard] Gerrard (1852-1924) relate to her activities as an officer in the Women's Suffrage Association and the WCTU in Columbus, NE.

10,463. Gilmore, George Harrison
Papers. 1852-1955. 17 cu. ft.
Open. Unpublished guide.
Nebraska State Historical Society.
Gilmore (1866-1955) was a physician and historian. Correspondence, diaries, archaeological data, research material, legal records, biographies, autobiographies, scrapbooks, clippings, printed matter, and other papers include reports and journals of the Woman's Relief Corps, an auxiliary to the Grand Army of the Republic founded in Massachusetts in 1883 and established in Nebraska in 1884. The reports and journals concern Nebraska and national conventions. Also contains a scrapbook pertaining to weddings, deaths, clubs, and other events around Plattsmouth, NE, from 1894 to 1935.

10,464. Grant, NE, First Congregational Church
Records. 1887-1970. 1 microfilm reel.
Open. Unpublished guide.
Nebraska State Historical Society.
Annual reports, general correspondence, registers, history, and miscellany of the Church, founded in 1887, include a constitution, membership records, and reports of the Ladies' Aid Society.

10,465. Green, Norma Kidd
Papers. 1900-69. 25 cu.ft.
Access restricted. No guide.
Nebraska State Historical Society.
[Mrs. Roy M.] Green (1893-1975), a native of Beatrice, NE, was an author, civic leader, collector, and historian. Correspondence, manuscripts, genealogical material, scrapbooks, printed matter, and miscellany, including manuscripts of some of Green's publications, such as *Books and You; A Forgotten Chapter in American Education: Jane Andrews of Newburyport;* and *Iron Eye's Family: The Children of Joseph LaFlesche.* Green spent her adult life in Lincoln.

10,466. Gregory Family
Papers. 1870-1945. 3.5 ft.
Open. Unpublished guide.
Nebraska State Historical Society.
Autobiography, genealogy diaries, research notes, temperance handbills and tracts, scrapbooks, music, and miscellany of George Albert Gregory (1851-1945), an educator and farmer. Contains papers of his daughter Annadora Foss Gregory (1893-), who earned a doctorate from the University of Nebraska in 1932. Her papers include correspondence, dissertation research notes, and the final manuscript of her dissertation on the history of Crete, NE, from 1870 to 1888.

10,467. Gund, Ida May
Papers. 1880-1915. Less than 1 cu. ft.
Open. Unpublished guide.
Nebraska State Historical Society.
Personal and family correspondence of Gund (1868-1951), a teacher, and her mother Josephine Gund, a Lincoln resident, concerns camping, investments, illnesses, children, school studies, social activities, and other subjects.

10,468. Harpster, Mary Margaret (Pike)
Papers. 1885-89. 1 microfilm reel.
Open. Unpublished guide.
Nebraska State Historical Society.
Diary of [Mrs. William A.] Harpster (1852-?), a homemaker, contains notes on the weather, social life, birthdays, marriages, and deaths of relatives and residents of the Blue Springs, NE, area.

10,469. Harrison, Agnes (Schmitt)
Papers. 1929-68. 1.5 cu. ft.
Open. Unpublished guide.
Nebraska State Historical Society.
Scrapbooks, certificates, and diplomas of Harrison (1894-1966), a cosmetologist and civic leader. Scrapbooks contain photos, printed matter, clippings, and memorabilia related to her career and activities with civic and service groups. Harrison served on the State Board of Cosmetology Examiners from 1930 to 1941.

10,470. Harrison, NE, Ladies Community Club
Records. 1967. Less than 1 ft.
Open. Unpublished guide.
Nebraska State Historical Society.
Manuscript and research material used in preparation of the book *Sioux County—Memoirs of Its Pioneers* consists of individual reminiscences, anecdotes, and miscellaneous history. The Club was a service organization.

10,471. Hartzell, Laura Belle
Papers. 1845-1943. 1.5 ft.
Open. Unpublished guide.
Nebraska State Historical Society.
Correspondence, journals, account books, and family genealogical material of Hartzell (1881-1956), a businesswoman and homemaker, consist principally of diaries and daily record books of Mr. and Mrs. J. L. Walter concerning operation of their Butler County, NE, farm, including the sale and purchase of grain, horses, and other goods. Also includes a folder pertaining to the Lincoln Business and Professional Women's Club.

10,472. Hill, Ruth (Davis)
Papers. 1954-65. 2.5 cu.ft.
Open. No guide.
Nebraska State Historical Society.
Correspondence, personal notes, speeches, conference records, committee material, and other papers of [Mrs. Roscoe] Hill (1914-67), a school board member, civic leader, and clubwoman, include items relating to her activities with the Lincoln Foundation and her involvement in 1964 with the Governor's Regional Conference on Education in Lincoln.

10,473. Hinman, Eleanor Hamlin
Papers. 1930-43. Less than 1 cu.ft.
Open. Unpublished guide.
Nebraska State Historical Society.
Bulk of the correspondence, interviews, and other papers of [Miss] Hinman (1899-), an educator, relates to her research concerning Crazy Horse. Includes interviews she conducted in 1930 with acquaintances of the Oglala Sioux leader, who speak about his life and his death in 1877 at Fort Robinson, NE.

10,474. Hoerger, Minnie V.
Papers. 1917-48. Less than 1 cu. ft.
Open. Unpublished guide.
Nebraska State Historical Society.
Records of the Sutton, NE, chapter of the American National Red Cross, treasurer's files of the Nebraska WCTU, Bible study lessons, and other material of [Miss] Hoerger (1882-1970), a Sutton teacher who was secretary of the local Red Cross chapter.

10,475. Hollingworth, Leta Anna (Stetter)
Papers. 1914-39. 0.5 cu.ft.
Open. Unpublished guide.
Nebraska State Historical Society.
Manuscripts, biographical material, and printed matter of [Mrs. Harry Levi] Hollingworth (1886-1939), an educator and psychologist who was born on her grandfather's homestead near Chadron, NE. Bulk of collection consists of her publications regarding the gifted child and other aspects of educational psychology. After her marriage, Hollingworth lived with her husband in New York, where she earned her doctorate and taught at Columbia University.

10,476. Humboldt, NE, United Methodist Church
Records. 1860-1968. 1 microfilm reel.
Open. Unpublished guide.
Nebraska State Historical Society.
Records and printed matter of the Church, founded in 1858, include minutes of the Women's Foreign Missionary Society from 1932 to 1940. Also contains records of the Humboldt Methodist Church, the German Methodist Church, and the Pleasant View Methodist Church.

10,477. Johnson, John Reuben
Papers. 1939-73. 3.5 cu. ft.
Open. Unpublished guide.
Nebraska State Historical Society.
Correspondence, manuscripts, book reviews, articles, college course material, clippings, and other items of Johnson (1897-1973), an educator and historian at Wayne State Teachers' College in Wayne, NE. Includes correspondence and research notes his daughter Janice Johnson compiled for her graduate thesis about the Nebraska unicameral legislature as well as material pertaining to her college education.

10,478. Keller, John F.
Papers. 1932-60. 0.5 cu.ft.
Open. Unpublished guide.
Nebraska State Historical Society.
Keller (1885-) was a homesteader in Cherry County, NE. Correspondence, manuscripts, and recording discs, including recordings of songs he wrote with Verna S. Broad, among them "The Cowboy's Return" and "N-E-B-R-A-S-K-A." Also includes three songs by Broad, "Valentine,""I Tried to Tell You," and "One Who Cares." The bulk of the collection is material written by Keller.

10,479. Kellie, Luna E. (Sanford)
Papers. 1876-ca. 1881. 148-page item.
Open. Unpublished guide.
Nebraska State Historical Society.
Memoir of [Mrs. James T.] Kellie (1857-1940), state secretary for a political farm organization, concerns experiences that she and her husband had farming after their trip from Illinois to Adams County, NE, during the mid-1870s. The memoirs contain descriptions of building their sod house,

family life, and social activities; they also include brief reference to the early political involvement of Luna Kellie, who became state secretary of the Nebraska Farmers' Alliance.

10,480. Kidder, Electa Emeline (Morse)
Papers. 1854-84. 0.5 ft.
Open. Unpublished guide.
Nebraska State Historical Society.
[Mrs. Thomas B.] Kidder (1864-1929), a teacher, was a resident of New York until 1920, when she married and moved to Lincoln. Diary, certificates, and other material including a diary, apparently of Mary Ann Morse of Troy, NY, for the year 1862. Remainder of the material relates to life in New York state during the 19th century.

10,481. Kinscella, Hazel Gertrude
Papers. 1918-39. 11 in.
Open. Unpublished guide.
Nebraska State Historical Society.
An Iowa native, [Miss] Kinscella (?-1960) was a professor, composer, and piano teacher known primarily for her ability as a pianist and for development of the Kinscella method of instruction. Manuscripts, notes, published compositions and arrangements, sheet music, printed material, and player piano rolls relate to Kinscella's career, particularly to music education. She taught at the University of Nebraska and lived in Lincoln.

10,482. Kizer Family
Papers. 1899-1954. 3 cu.ft.
Open. No guide.
Nebraska State Historical Society.
Family papers of Jacob R. Kizer (1833-1910) of Lincoln, a pioneer Nebraska businessman, contain records of his granddaughter Charlotte Elizabeth Kizer, who was supervisor of art for the Lincoln Public Schools before she moved to Scarsdale, NY. Family and business correspondence, diaries, business and sorority records, a scrapbook, printed matter, and other material. Charlotte Kizer's papers include diaries, notebooks, records of the Alpha Kappa chapter of Sigma Kappa at the University of Nebraska-Lincoln, a scrapbook, and other items.

10,483. La Flesche Family
Papers. 1859-1939. 1.5 cu.ft. and 1 microfilm reel.
Open. Unpublished guide.
Nebraska State Historical Society.
Correspondence, diaries, manuscripts, a libretto, memorabilia, and other items of the family of Omaha Indian leader Joseph La Flesche, whose Indian name was Iron Eye. Includes papers of his daughters Susette (La Flesche) [Mrs. Thomas] Tibbles (1854-1903), a spokesman for Indian rights; Susan (La Flesche) [Mrs. Henry] Picotte (1865-1915), who by graduating from the Women's Medical College in Philadelphia in 1889 was the first Indian woman to earn a medical degree; Rosalie (La Flesche) Farley, who with her husband managed the financial affairs of several Omaha tribal members as well as funding received from philanthropic organizations; and Marguerite (La Flesche) [Mrs. Walter T.] Diddock. Also includes papers of Alice Cunningham Fletcher and Sara T. Kinney of the Connecticut Women's Indian Association and the libretto and notes for *Da-O-Ma,* an opera that was based on an Omaha Indian legend and composed by Joseph La Flesche's son Francis La Flesche, Nelle Richmond Eberhart, and Charles W. Cadman. The La Flesche family gained acclaim as educators, Indian leaders, and ethnologists. Alice Fletcher, an ethnologist, was a friend and biographer of the La Flesche family.

10,484. Larsen, Hannah
Papers. 1939-54. 1 ft.
Open. Unpublished guide.
Nebraska State Historical Society.
Correspondence, manuscripts, scrapbooks, and other material of [Miss] Larsen (1887-1955), a Lincoln civic leader, reflect her activities in the YWCA, the Outlook Club, Goodwill Industries, and the Southwest Community Center.

10,485. Lincoln Council of Church Women
Records. 1930-66. 5 cu.ft.
Open. No guide.
Nebraska State Historical Society.
Minutes, financial reports, reports, scrapbooks, and newsletters of this local group, a part of the Lincoln Council of Churches, which promotes interdenominational activities.

10,486. Lincoln General Hospital School of Nursing
Records. 1928-76. 3 cu.ft.
Open. Unpublished guide.
Nebraska State Historical Society.
The School was organized in 1925 and graduated its first students in 1928. Minutes, reports, scrapbooks, student handbooks, nurses' examinations, and clippings. Includes minutes of the School's student association, records of the Nebraska State Student Nurses Association, minutes of the School's nursing faculty, and lists of the School's students and graduates.

10,487. McKelvie, Martha (DeArnold)
Papers. 1917-61. 2.5 cu.ft.
Open. No guide.
Nebraska State Historical Society.
McKelvie (1887-1976), a Valentine, NE, rancher, newspaperwoman, and author, was the wife of Nebraska governor Sam R. McKelvie. Published books and scrapbooks containing personal correspondence and White House correspondence to the McKelvies as well as information about her husband's term as governor, visits of President Herbert Hoover and Governor Thomas Dewey to their ranch, the Pershing family and other military figures, family activities, and publicity of the McKelvies. Also includes articles about movie stars that she wrote while she was a newspaperwoman in California. McKelvie also wrote *The Hills of Yesterday,* vignettes about the Black Hills of South Dakota; *The Fenceless Range,* tales about cowboy Buckskin Jim Bullis; and *The Empty Sleeve,* the story of Zereld James, mother of outlaws Jessie and Frank James.

10,488. McPhee, Clare Mary, and McPhee, Marguerite Cameron
Papers. 1904-60. 1 cu.ft.
Open. Unpublished guide.
Nebraska State Historical Society.
Publications, scrapbooks, music, and other items of the sisters Clare McPhee (?-1960) and Marguerite McPhee (?-1970), both of whom were educators and cultural leaders in Lincoln. Includes copies of Clare McPhee's publications about teaching language arts and a scrapbook of memorabilia collected during her tenure as principal of Lincoln's Capitol School and supervisor of the English program. The scrapbook of Marguerite McPhee concerns her work as a faculty member of the University of Nebraska English department and her participation in the AAUW and, during WWII, in the British War Relief Society. Also contains two texts that the sisters co-authored and material about the Capitol School's involvement with the United War Work Campaign during WWI.

10,489. Magee, Nellie (Throop)
Papers. 1865-1936. 1 microfilm reel.
Open. Unpublished.
Nebraska State Historical Society.
Manuscripts of [Mrs. Oliver N.] Magee (1874-1962), a Lincoln resident, contain stories relating to social customs and the lives of early Nebraska settlers.

10,490. Meachem, Chell (Crozier)
Papers. 1950s. 1 cu.ft.
Open. Unpublished guide.
Nebraska State Historical Society.
The daughter of a Polk County, NE, homesteader, [Mrs. Colo W.] Meachem (1884-) taught in Polk County and in Las Vegas. Scrapbooks pertain to a tour of Germany she took in conjunction with the Great Books Foundation; the volumes include information on sightseeing and prominent people of the late 1950s in Germany, Switzerland, Austria, and Italy.

10,491. Mears, Louise Wilhelmina
Papers. 1927-57. Less than 1 cu.ft.
Open. Unpublished guide.
Nebraska State Historical Society.
[Miss] Mears (1874-1925) was an author and teacher. Biographical manuscripts, historical and biographical sketches, clippings, printed material, and other items relate largely to her literary efforts. Includes an original manuscript regarding Bess (Streeter) Aldrich's *Lantern in Her Hand;* a narrative about Carroll G. Pearse, a Nebraska homesteader and educator; a manuscript about old homes located near Peru State College in Peru, NE; a poem about Auburn, NE; and financial records and printed matter pertaining to Judge Samuel Maxwell of Fremont, NE.

10,492. Meredith, Mamie Jane
Papers. 1917-66. 6 cu.ft.
Access restricted. Unpublished guide.
Nebraska State Historical Society.
Papers of [Miss] Meredith (1888-1966), an English teacher at the University of Nebraska from 1923 to 1956 and the writer of numerous articles, include correspondence, manuscripts, and printed matter about Nebraska writers, artists, and organizations. Born in Illinois, Meredith received her college education at the University of Nebraska. She studied the development of the English language and belonged to professional organizations. The editor of three journals, Meredith was a friend of several Nebraska authors.

10,493. Military Waiting Wives Club of Lincoln
Records. 1967-74. 0.5 cu.ft.
Open. Unpublished guide.
Nebraska State Historical Society.
The group, founded in 1967, promoted programs to provide companionship, social activity, sympathy, and understanding for its members whose spouses were serving abroad. Records, scrapbooks, printed matter, and other papers relate to members and include information about men who became prisoners of war or were listed as missing in action during the Vietnam conflict.

10,494. Miller, Annie Louise
Papers. 1889-1941. 1.5 ft.
Open. Unpublished guide.
Nebraska State Historical Society.
[Miss] Miller (1860-1945), a journalist, worked for the *Nebraska State Journal* from 1898 to 1931. Correspondence, manuscripts, scrapbooks, publications, and other material; primarily consists of programs and clippings concerning artists and their performances in Lincoln between the late 1890s and the 1920s.

10,495. Minick, Alice Ann (Lockwood)
Papers. 1897-1938. 2 ft.
Open. Unpublished guide.
Nebraska State Historical Society.
Correspondence, manuscripts, scrapbooks, pamphlets, clippings, and other papers of [Mrs. John S.] Minick (1844-1939), a writer, temperance leader, and lawyer. Material primarily relates to the history of Brownville, where Minick lived, and Nemaha County. Also includes manuscripts she wrote.

10,496. Morton, Nancy Jane Fletcher
Papers. 1860-68. 200 pp. (microfilm).
Open. Unpublished guide.
Nebraska State Historical Society.
Edited and personal account of the capture of Morton (1845-1912), a pioneer, in 1864 by Cheyenne Indians. Traveling across Nebraska with her husband Thomas Frank Morton, Nancy Morton was captured in what came to be known as the Plum Creek Massacre near Fort Kearny, NE. Her husband, brother, and cousin were killed. She later married George W. Stevens.

10,497. National League of American Pen Women
Records. 1949-56. Less than 1 ft.
Open. No guide.
Nebraska State Historical Society.
Minutes, newsletters, and convention information of the Lincoln branch, which was founded in 1950 to encourage and support its members' creative endeavors. The National League was founded in 1897.

10,498. National League of American Pen Women
Records. 1957-76. Less than 1 ft.
Open. No guide.
Nebraska State Historical Society.
Minutes, newsletters, and clippings pertaining to the Chadron, NE, chapter of this organization, which sought to support the acceptance and publication of its members' works. The Chadron branch was founded in 1957, while the National League was organized in 1897.

10,499. Nebraska Baptist State Convention
Records. 1824-1956. 1 microfilm reel.
Open. Unpublished guide.
Nebraska State Historical Society.
Annual reports, minutes, church histories, programs, clippings, and other material of the Convention, formed in 1824, including folders concerning the life of Jannie Clare Adams, a martyred Baptist missionary nurse. Born in Chambers, NE, Adams served in the Philippines. Collection also contains material regarding the state Woman's Baptist Mission Society and local societies at Sheridan Baptist in Lincoln and at First Baptist in Omaha.

10,500. Nebraska Board of Nursing
Records. 1904-73. 15 cu.ft.
Open. Unpublished guide.
Nebraska State Historical Society.
An independent board was established in 1915 to administer a law, passed in 1909, that required licensing of nurses in Nebraska; the Board, which had different names and different positions in the governmental structure, has been in existence since that time. Correspondence and reports of the Board, records of students in nurses training schools, and reports of nursing schools to the Board.

10,501. Nebraska Conference of the United Church of Christ
Records. 1857-1963. 9 microfilm reels.
Open. Unpublished guide.
Nebraska State Historical Society.
Minutes, clippings, and other records of this religious denomination, founded in 1857, contain minutes for periods between 1878 and 1927 of the Women's Home Missionary Society and the Women's Home Missionary Union of Nebraska.

10,502. Nebraska Department of Public Institutions, Girls' Training School
Records. 1891-1909. 0.5 cu.ft.
Open. Unpublished guide.
Nebraska State Historical Society.
Established in 1891 in Geneva, NE, as an institution for female juvenile delinquents, the School has admitted both boys and girls since 1973. Monthly and special reports on admissions, discharges, and general conditions; correspondence; and rules and regulations.

10,503. Nebraska Department of Public Institutions, Nebraska Industrial Home
Records. 1889-94. 0.25 cu.ft.
Open. Unpublished guide.
Nebraska State Historical Society.
Established by law in 1887 and opened at Milford, NE, in 1889, the Home was to provide shelter, protection, employment, and "means of self support to penitent women and girls, with a view to aid in the suppression of prostitution." Minute books contain records of the Home while it was under the administration of a private group, the Woman's Associated Charities of the State of Nebraska. The 1887 law provided that the state would reimburse the group for running the Home. Sometime between 1896 and 1898 the Charities gave control of the facility to the state, which ran the Home until it was abolished in 1951.

10,504. Nebraska Farmer
Records. 1957-58. 3 in.
Open. Unpublished guide.
Nebraska State Historical Society.
Correspondence that this farming periodical received in response to a request for information about pioneer experiences in the late 19th and early 20th centuries. Bulk of the letters were written by women about Nebraska locations. The *Nebraska Farmer,* published in Lincoln, was established in 1859.

10,505. Nebraska Farmers' Alliance
Records. 1887-1901. 6 ft. and 1 microfilm reel.
Open. Unpublished guide.
Nebraska State Historical Society.
Correspondence, reports, and miscellaneous papers of the Alliance, which was founded in 1881 to improve the social, educational, financial, and political status of farmers; it became one of the most prominent protest groups of the last two decades of the 19th century. Material relates to the Alliance's development in Nebraska and includes manuscripts and notes of Luna E. Kellie, the organization's state secretary.

10,506. Nebraska Federation of Women's Clubs
Records. 1919-20. 0.5 ft.
Open. Unpublished guide.
Nebraska State Historical Society.
Reports, programs, and other material, the bulk of which consists of reports of correspondence regarding Nebraskans in WWI. The Nebraska Federation was formed in 1894.

10,507. Nebraska Legislative Ladies League
Records. 1915-56. 1 ft.
Open. Unpublished guide.
Nebraska State Historical Society.
Correspondence, scrapbooks, yearbooks, and publicity and other material of the group, a social and civic organization of governors' and legislators' wives.

10,508. Nebraska Society of Radiological Technologists
Records. 1930-76. 8 cu.ft.
Open. Unpublished guide.
Nebraska State Historical Society.
Founded in 1931 at St. Joseph Hospital in Omaha by Sister M. Liberia, O.S.F., Helena McCloud, Mary Mulcahey, and Erminda R. Clarke, the group promotes the professional interests of radiologists and informs its members about theoretical and practical aspects of radiology. Financial records, correspondence of state officers, committee files, scrapbooks, periodicals, and other records, including copies of *The X-Ray Technician,* the journal of the American Society of Radiologic Technologists. Clarke, a president of the Nebraska Society, was an editor of and contributor to the journal.

10,509. Nebraska State Council of Defense
Records. 1917-19. 50 cu.ft.
Open. Unpublished guide.
Nebraska State Historical Society.
The Council was organized in 1917 to support the war effort through such activities as stimulating food production and conservation, helping to supply farm labor, and by cooperating in Liberty Loan drives and in American National Red Cross and Home Guard work; it also investigated the loyalty of Nebraska residents, particularly German-Americans. Minutes, financial records, and correspondence of the Council women's committee comprise about half of the Council records. A number of statewide women's groups coordinated their work with that of the women's committee. The Council went out of existence in 1919.

10,510. Nebraska Women's State Invitational Golf Association
Records. 1916-72. 1.5 cu.ft.
Open. Unpublished guide.
Nebraska State Historical Society.
The Association, founded in 1916, promotes interest in golf in Nebraska and stages the annual state women's golf tournament. Minutes, correspondence, membership rolls, reports, photos, scrapbooks, brochures, and clippings include a 1956 letter in which Louise Pound summarized her athletic activities.

10,511. Nebraska Women's Suffrage Association
Records. 1910-40. 2.5 ft.
Open. Unpublished guide.
Nebraska State Historical Society.
Founded in 1910, the Association sought to secure the vote for Nebraska women prior to passage of the 19th Amendment to the US Constitution; the group also supported laws to improve the condition of women and children in the state. Minutes, correspondence, printed matter, and other records.

10,512. Nebraska Writers Guild
Records. 1926-67. 1 cu.ft.
Open. Unpublished guide.
Nebraska State Historical Society.
Correspondence, manuscripts, scrapbooks, and printed matter of the Guild, which was founded in 1925 to encourage Nebraska writers to produce professional writing. Bulk of the collection consists of scrapbooks and clippings about Nebraska authors, among them Mari Sandoz and Louise Pound.

10,513. Norris, George William
Papers. 1886-1967. 14 cu.ft.
Open. Unpublished guide.
Nebraska State Historical Society.
Correspondence, manuscripts, congressional records, biographical data, scrapbooks, printed matter, and other papers of Norris (1861-1944), a US representative and US senator from Nebraska. Contains correspondence of his second wife Ella Leonard Norris, whom he married in 1903.

10,514. North, Frank Joshua
Papers. 1864-77. 1 cu.ft.
Open. Unpublished guide.
Nebraska State Historical Society.
Correspondence, diaries, manuscripts, records, clippings, books, and other papers of North (1840-85), an early Pawnee scout from Platte County, NE. Includes a diary kept by his mother Mrs. Jones A. North describing her tasks; the diary also contains family news, recipes, and comments on friends, social activities, and deaths.

10,515. Noxon, Hannah (Shaw)
Papers. 1858-1933. 1 cu.ft.
Open. Unpublished guide.

Nebraska State Historical Society.
Family correspondence of Noxon (1834-1920?), a merchant and postmistress in Leona and Adams, NE, and of her husband George constitutes the bulk of the collection, while the remainder consists of manuscript material, ledgers, autograph books, clippings, and Bibles. George and Hannah Noxon farmed near Adams until his death in 1870. She then opened a small mercantile business in Leona and received an appointment as postmistress. In 1880 she moved to Adams, opened a general store, and received a new postmistress appointment. Operation of the Adams store is described in the correspondence.

10,516. Oblinger, Uriah Wesley
Papers. 1862-1959. 1 ft.
Closed. No guide.
Nebraska State Historical Society.
Family correspondence, a diary, family and genealogical records, autograph albums, books and other printed matter, and memorabilia of Oblinger (1842-1901), a Fillmore County, NE, pioneer, and his wife Martha "Mattie" Thomas Oblinger, including letters they exchanged during their courtship and after their marriage as well as Martha Oblinger's letters to her parents, brothers, and sisters in Indiana. Also contains personal items of the Oblingers' daughters Maggie (Oblinger) Sandon, who moved to Denver as an adult, and Neta (Oblinger) Lennemann and Ella (Oblinger) Roesch, who remained in Nebraska. Family correspondence concerns the establishment of a Nebraska homestead between 1872 and 1880, frontier family life, and economic conditions.

10,517. Omaha Woman's Press Club
Records. 1918-35. 0.5 ft.
Open. Unpublished guide.
Nebraska State Historical Society.
The Omaha Club was founded in 1914 to encourage women in literary work and to promote fellowship among newspaperwomen and writers. Minutes, correspondence, a scrapbook, printed matter, and other records primarily relate to women's literary societies during the 1930s.

10,518. Omaha Young Women's Christian Association
Records. 1893-1973. 20 cu.ft.
Open. No guide.
Nebraska State Historical Society.
Founded in 1893, this Omaha group joined the national YWCA in 1906. Minutes, financial records, correspondence, reports, membership lists, photos, scrapbooks, blueprints, pamphlets, and publications document such Omaha YWCA activities as maintaining a lunchroom for working girls from 1893 until 1933, opening Omaha-area summer camps in 1910 and 1913 and a women's residence in 1919, and becoming a charter member of the Omaha Community Chest in 1923. Collection contains blueprints and other records concerning construction of the Omaha YWCA headquarters building. [Mrs.] Emma F. Byers was general secretary during the organization's early years, and Louise Pound was active in the group's physical education programs.

10,519. Overholser Family
Papers. 1919-44. 0.5 ft.
Open. Unpublished guide.
Nebraska State Historical Society.
Correspondence, manuscripts, orders, and a memorial of Colonel Forrest E. Overholser, a career army officer who served in WWI and WWII; his daughter Frances Overholser, who was a WAC in WWII; and his wife Winnie Overholser. Bulk of the material pertains to Forrest and Frances Overholser. The family lived in Lincoln.

10,520. Phillips, Laurie Kent
Papers. 1953-63. 0.3 ft.
Open. No guide.
Nebraska State Historical Society.
Manuscripts, rejections, and payment records of publications of Phillips, a Lincoln short story writer. Includes manuscripts of stories she wrote that were published by religious magazines.

10,521. Pound, Laura Biddlecombe
Papers. 1890-1928. 1 cu.ft.
Open. Unpublished guide.
Nebraska State Historical Society.
A native of Phelps, NY, and descendant of English immigrants of 1630, Pound (1841-1928), a community leader and cultural historian, moved to Lincoln after her marriage to Judge Stephen Pound in 1869. Correspondence, manuscripts, photos, and scrapbooks. Includes historical and biographical sketches that she wrote, a Biddlecombe family genealogy, and her husband's scrapbooks. Laura Pound was the mother of Roscoe, Louise, and Olivia Pound.

10,522. Pound, Louise
Papers. 1890-1958. 17 cu.ft. and 1 microfilm reel.
Open. Unpublished guide.
Nebraska State Historical Society.
[Miss] Pound (1872-1958) was a University of Nebraska professor, scholar, folklorist, athlete, and civic leader. Correspondence, lecture notes, notebooks, manuscripts, folklore and folk songs, organizational records, photos, scrapbooks, pamphlets, periodicals, and other material reflect her interest in folklore, linguistics, and noted authors and her activities in University of Nebraska organizations. A native of Lincoln, Pound was educated by her mother along with her brother Roscoe and sister Olivia. She attended the preparatory school of the University of Nebraska and the University itself, earning her bachelor's and master's degrees. Pound completed her doctoral work in two semesters at the University of Heidelberg in Germany.

10,523. Pound, Olivia
Papers. 1897-1961. 3.5 cu.ft.
Open. Unpublished guide.
Nebraska State Historical Society.
[Miss] Pound (1874-1961) was a teacher, author, and community leader who spent most of her life in Lincoln. Correspondence, articles, estate and biographical material, printed matter, and other items. She attended Columbia, Harvard, and Chicago universities.

10,524. Price, Sarah Jane
Papers. 1878-95. 0.5 cu.ft.
Open. Unpublished guide.
Nebraska State Historical Society.
Price (1841-1922) was a public school teacher in Phillips, NE. Diaries recording her daily life as a teacher, recollections of her mother, and an account of a summer trip to Italy. Also contains school notes and other material.

10,525. The Quill
Records. 1921-63. 0.5 cu.ft.
Open. Unpublished guide.
Nebraska State Historical Society.
Minutes and scrapbook of clippings of this group of women writers, founded in 1921 in Lincoln. Originally known as the Happy Venture Club, the group meets each month to hear members read their works and report on their manuscripts and to stage dramatic sketches.

10,526. Reeder, Hazel Perin: "Amelia"
Papers. 1976. 0.1 ft.
Open. No guide.
Nebraska State Historical Society.
Manuscript biography by [Mrs.] Reeder about her grandmother, who is identified only as Amelia. Born in 1834, Amelia was a Nebraska pioneer housewife who apparently lived in Custer County.

10,527. Rosicky, Rose
Papers. 1921-33. 1 ft.
Open. Unpublished guide.
Nebraska State Historical Society.
A Crete, NE, writer and editor, Rosicky (1875-1954) was the daughter of a well-known Nebraska Czech pioneer. Correspondence, manuscripts, scrapbooks, and other papers pertaining to publication of her *History of the Czechs (Bohemians) in Nebraska* (Omaha: Czech Historical Society of Nebraska, 1929).

10,528. Round Table Club
Records. 1884-1935. 0.5 ft.
Open. Unpublished guide.
Nebraska State Historical Society.
This Crete, NE, group, founded in 1884 to improve women's literary knowledge, was one of the earliest women's organizations in the state. Constitution, minutes, correspondence, history, and other records.

10,529. Sandoz, Mari Susette
Papers. 1934-66. 10 in.
Open. No guide.
Nebraska State Historical Society.
[Miss] Sandoz (1896?-1966) was an author from Gordon, NE, whose works dealt with the settlement of the Great Plains. Correspondence, manuscripts by and about her, notes pertaining to her book *Old Jules,* draft television scripts, publicity and comment about *Old Jules* and *Slogum House,* biographical and bibliographical information, and book reviews and clippings about Nebraskans.

10,530. Scott, Emily D. (Freeman)
Papers. 1852-68. Less than 1 ft.
Open. Unpublished guide.
Nebraska State Historical Society.
The wife of Presbyterian minister George Scott, Emily Scott was born in Pennsylvania and lived with her husband in Texas and Illinois. Diaries relate to her life as a schoolgirl at Pleasant Hill Seminary in Washington, PA, and as a minister's wife in Texas.

10,531. Scrimsher, Lila
Papers. 1926-48. 2.5 cu.ft.
Open. No guide.
Nebraska State Historical Society.
An author and Lincoln schoolteacher who lived in Nebraska throughout her life, Scrimsher (1900-76) wrote *General Pershing, Strong Man,* and *The Pumpkin Flood at Harper's Ferry* as well as the unpublished "Black, Cool and Collected: The Story of George A. Maston." Correspondence, manuscripts, sketches, photos, scrapbooks, clippings, and magazines primarily contain material regarding Maston, John J. Pershing, Missouri River exploration, and the frontier experience.

10,532. Seward, NE, Frieden German Evangelical Church
Records. 1878-1973. 1 cu.ft. and 1 microfilm reel.
Open. Unpublished guide.
Nebraska State Historical Society.
Services of the Church, organized in 1878 by immigrants of German descent, were conducted in German until the early 1920s. Church records include the constitution and minute book from 1894 to 1922 of the Women's Society.

10,533. Shaw Family
Papers. 1850-92. 4.5 ft.
Open. Unpublished guide.
Nebraska State Historical Society.
Correspondence, diaries, journals, and other papers of Stephen P. Shaw (1801-63) and his wife Hannah Hicks Shaw (?-1886), who established a homestead in Gage County, NE, after a trip by ox team from Wisconsin in 1857. Other family members followed the Shaws westward. Correspondence

includes letters from women family members concerning their frontier travel and experiences.

10,534. Sheldon, Margaret (Thompson)
Papers. 1908-42. 2 cu.ft.
Open. No guide.
Nebraska State Historical Society.
A lifelong resident of Lincoln, Sheldon (?-1942) was an historian, author, naturalist, and state and national women's club official. Correspondence, personal notes, manuscripts and lecture notes about birds, women's club records, Congregational Church bulletins, and clippings. Sheldon was president of the Nebraska Federation of Women's Clubs and a member of the GFWC board of directors. Her husband Addison E. Sheldon was a Nebraska historian, author, and director of the Nebraska State Historical Society.

10,535. Sim Family
Papers. 1856-80. 1 microfilm reel.
Open. Unpublished guide.
Nebraska State Historical Society.
Correspondence and a genealogy chart of Sarah (Clarke) Sim (1824-80) and her husband Francis Sim (1821-1907), pioneers in Camp Creek, NE. Sarah Sim, who moved to Nebraska Territory from Middletown, CT, in 1856, died of breast cancer. Correspondence includes letters from Sarah and her husband to her family in Connecticut and from her sister and niece, Wealthy and Eugenie Hathaway, who cared for her during her last illness.

10,536. Sorosis Club
Records. 1889-1966. 1 ft.
Open. Unpublished guide.
Nebraska State Historical Society.
Scrapbooks, yearbooks, programs, clippings, and other records of this women's social and literary group, founded in 1889 in Lincoln.

10,537. Stanley, Ruth (Moore)
Papers. 1926-56. 0.5 in.
Open. Unpublished guide.
Nebraska State Historical Society.
Correspondence, including letters to Stanley, an Oklahoma City educator, from Louise Pound, a Lincoln educator, author, and civic leader, contains information about the University of Nebraska.

10,538. Stastny, Olga Frances (Sadilek)
Papers. 1892-1953. 1 ft.
Open. Unpublished guide.
Nebraska State Historical Society.
[Mrs. Charles] Stastny (1878-1952), an Omaha physician, attended the University of Nebraska college of medicine after her husband's death in 1907; during WWI she was decorated by the French government for service in France. Correspondence, manuscripts, records, certificates, memorials, printed matter, and other items concern her medical career, with emphasis on her work in Europe from 1918 to 1924. Born in Wilber, NE, Stastny interned in New England and began her practice in Omaha in 1914.

10,539. "Stella"
Papers. 1866. 1 item.
Open. Unpublished guide.
Nebraska State Historical Society.
Letter signed "Stella" from Nebraska City concerns life in the southeastern Nebraska town. The letter is apparently written to the author's sister in the East.

10,540. Stevens, Doris
Papers. 1920-72. 0.5 cu.ft.
Open. No guide.
Nebraska State Historical Society.
Stevens (1892-1963) was a composer and suffragist who wrote *Jailed For Freedom,* a book about woman suffrage efforts from 1913 to 1919. Copy of Stevens's book, recording discs, and sheet music that Stevens wrote about her Omaha childhood, including "I Was Teaching in Nebraska," "My Little Brother," "I Tied My Kitty to a Wild Plum Tree," "He Was Never Seen Again (or Husband's Folly)," "On the Prairie," and "When Father Made Root Beer."

10,541. Swanson, Mary Nellie (Peterson)
Papers. 1895-1940. 1 ft.
Open. Unpublished guide.
Nebraska State Historical Society.
Scrapbooks of [Mrs. Gust E.] Swanson, a teacher in Wausa in Knox County, NE, contain material concerning events in her personal life.

10,542. Syford Family
Papers. 1856-1965. 23.5 ft.
Open. Unpublished guide.
Nebraska State Historical Society.
Correspondence, diaries, manuscripts, records, a biography, a genealogy, records of organizations, and other items of Amanda O. (Bean) Syford (1843-1930), her husband DeWitt N. Syford (1847-1926), and their daughters Ethel Corrine Syford (1881-1955) and Constance Miriam Syford (1887-1965), members of an early Nebraska cattle-raising family, who also were cultural and civic leaders. Dewitt and Amanda Syford came to Lancaster County, NE, from Illinois in 1879. Correspondence relates to the family's work and studies and travels of the children, who became Lincoln residents. Diaries contain travel information of Constance Syford; her notes, poems, and short stories also are included.

10,543. Throop, Ellen M. (Johnson)
Papers. 1901-27. 0.75 ft.
Open. Unpublished guide.
Nebraska State Historical Society.
Throop (1843-1927) was a Valparaiso, NE, homesteader. Her account book for 1901 to 1903, a pamphlet of reminiscences she wrote about pioneer life, and a manuscript by Nellie J. Magee about family history and the history of Valparaiso.

10,544. Turner, Martha Margaret
Papers. 1896-1946. 1 cu.ft.
Open. Unpublished guide.
Nebraska State Historical Society.
[Miss] Turner (1868-1946) was an historian, newspaperwoman, artist, author, and curator of newspapers and photos for the Nebraska State Historical Society. Essays and stories by Nebraska schoolchildren about pioneer days, general Nebraska history stories and notes compiled by Turner, and clippings about Columbus, NE.

10,545. Ulmer, Laura M. (White)
Papers. 1924-38. 1 microfilm reel.
Access restricted. Unpublished guide.
Nebraska State Historical Society.
Diaries of [Mrs. Walter P.] Ulmer (1896-1974), a missionary, relate to her service in China. Ulmer and her husband settled in Dawson, NE, after their return to the US in 1948.

10,546. Unadilla, NE, Christian Church
Records. 1873-1971. 1 microfilm reel.
Open. Unpublished guide.
Nebraska State Historical Society.
Minutes and other records of the Church, established in 1873, contain minutes and records of the Christian Women's Board of Missions from 1885 to 1925.

10,547. United Spanish War Veterans, Nebraska Department
Records. 1907-62. 11 cu.ft.
Open. Unpublished guide.
Nebraska State Historical Society.
The Nebraska Department of this national association of veterans of the Spanish-American War and the Philippine Insurrection had a women's auxiliary that grew from the support the veterans received from women's organizations. Financial records, correspondence, reports, and other records of the Nebraska Department, founded in 1907. Includes minute books, correspondence, and reports of the women's auxiliary, 1926-52. The national USWV was founded in 1904.

10,548. Van Wyck, Charles Henry
Papers. 1860-1929. Less than 1 cu.ft.
Open. Unpublished guide.
Nebraska State Historical Society.
Van Wyck (1824-95), a US senator from Nebraska from 1881 to 1887, was the topic of a master's thesis by [Miss] Marie Harmer, a graduate student at the University of Nebraska in 1929. Correspondence, Harmer's thesis, manuscripts, biographical data, and material gathered by Harmer and J. L. Sellers for an article in *Nebraska History.*

10,549. Vold, Margaret Anna (Bryan)
Papers. Nd. 0.75 ft.
Open. Unpublished guide.
Nebraska State Historical Society.
Correspondence and poetry primarily related to the work of Vold, a poet from Lincoln.

10,550. Weeping Water, NE, First Congregational Church
Records. 1860-1924. 1 microfilm reel.
Open. Unpublished guide.
Nebraska State Historical Society.
Minutes and other records of the Church, founded in 1860, including records of the Woman's Missionary Society, 1873-89.

10,551. Wentz, Elizabeth (Lemen)
Papers. 1922-27. Less than 1 cu.ft.
Open. Unpublished guide.
Nebraska State Historical Society.
Essays, minutes, reports, printed matter, and other papers of [Mrs. George H.] Wentz (1869-1956) relate to her work as president of the Nebraska Congress of Parents and Teachers.

10,552. Wesner, Lulu (Nuckolls)
Papers. 1785-1958. 1.5 ft.
Open. Unpublished guide.
Nebraska State Historical Society.
[Mrs. Joy E.] Wesner (1880-1959) was a teacher. Correspondence, diaries, manuscripts, personal documents and records, clippings, and other papers, including Nuckolls family correspondence from their home in the Nebraska City, NE, area. Bulk of the collection pertains to the history of the Nuckolls family from 1889 to 1957.

10,553. Whisenand, Margaret Eleanor (Long)
Papers. 1903-40. 1 cu.ft.
Open. Unpublished guide.
Nebraska State Historical Society.
Scrapbooks, clippings, printed matter, and memorabilia of Whisenand (1893-), a resident of Illinois and Nebraska, consist of material relating to her life and that of her family in Madison, NE.

10,554. Williams, Hattie (Plum)
Papers. 1884-1959. 30.9 ft.
Open. Unpublished guide.
Nebraska State Historical Society.
[Mrs. Thomas] Williams (1878-1963) was a professor of sociology at the University of Nebraska. Correspondence, research notes, speeches, lectures, and printed matter relating primarily to Williams's position as a University professor and to her affiliation with public welfare agencies. Research notes deal particularly with immigration of German-Russians to Nebraska.

10,555. Williams, Nettie Leona
Papers. 1890-1940. Less than 1 cu.ft.
Open. Unpublished guide.
Nebraska State Historical Society.
Family records and diary for 1936 to 1940 of [Miss] Williams (1883-1959), a member of a family that apparently lived near Mead, NE.

10,556. Wilson, Everett Pitt
Papers. 1931-44. 1.5 cu.ft.
Open. Unpublished guide.
Nebraska State Historical Society.
Correspondence, research material, records, and other items chiefly concerning research projects done from 1931 to 1934 by students of Wilson (1868-1956), a history teacher at Chadron State Teachers College in Chadron, NE. Among the authors were some 100 women. Material pertains to western Nebraska history, the frontier cattle industry, and reminiscences for the period 1803 to 1891.

10,557. Winne, Caroline (Frey)
Papers. 1874-99. Ca. 125 items (microfilm).
Open. Unpublished guide.
Nebraska State Historical Society.
Winne (1841-1922) was the wife of army surgeon Charles K. Winne. Correspondence she wrote from forts Sidney, McPherson, and Crook in Nebraska and Fort Washakie, WY, pertains to life at the posts during Indian wars and includes comments on army officials, government policies, Indians and their ceremonies, conferences between Indians and army officers, medical facilities, housing, social events, food supplies, transportation, weather, and other topics. Winne's correspondence is part of the Frey papers, the originals of which are housed at the New York Historical Society.

10,558. Woman's Bi-Metallic League
Records. 1898-1900. Less than 1 cu.ft.
Open. Unpublished guide.
Nebraska State Historical Society.
Minutes and a membership list of this Lincoln women's group, organized in 1898 to promote bimetallism and general education on political questions. The League was disbanded in 1900.

10,559. Woman's Christian Temperance Union
Records. 1874-1958. 0.5 ft.
Open. Unpublished guide.
Nebraska State Historical Society.
Records, history, programs, and clippings of the Nebraska WCTU and of activities of local chapters in Lincoln, Kearney, Omaha, Bethany, Blue Springs, and Hastings. The state organization was in existence from 1874 to 1958.

10,560. Woman's Relief Corps, Department of Nebraska U. S. Grant Chapter
Records. 1908-47. 2 cu.ft.
Open. Unpublished guide.
Nebraska State Historical Society.
Records, correspondence, general orders, membership applications, reports, printed matter, and other records of the Omaha chapter, which was open to all "loyal women" but was chiefly composed of mothers, wives, daughters, and sisters of Union soldiers. The chapter was organized in 1883.

10,561. Wood, Elias M.
Papers. 1864-92. Less than 1 ft.
Open. Unpublished guide.
Nebraska State Historical Society.
Correspondence, a diary, and certificates of Wood (1830-?), an Illinois and Merrick County, NE, homesteader. Includes family letters from Eliza A. L. Reed to her sister-in-law Marcia Wood. Among the diary entries are ones signed "Miss A. L. Reed," which deal with the weather in Albion, NE, during the late 1880s.

10,562. Wright, Elizabeth
Papers. Nd. 2 cu.ft.
Open. Unpublished guide.
Nebraska State Historical Society.
Journals, a genealogy, and scrapbooks of [Miss] Wright (1888-), a Lincoln educator and genealogist, include photos and documents of Nebraska and out-of-state families.

10,563. Zetetic Club
Records. 1874-1917. 1 ft.
Open. Unpublished guide.
Nebraska State Historical Society.
Records, correspondence, and printed matter of this woman's literary society in Weeping Water, NE, which was organized in 1884 and disbanded in 1919.

10,564. Curtis, Nellie M.
Papers. Ca. 1909-27. Ca. 6 in.
Open. No guide.
Nebraska Wesleyan University, United Methodist Church Archives.
A teacher and Methodist Episcopal church deaconess, Curtis (1865-1943) was superintendent of the Deaconess Home in Portland, OR, in the 1920s. Correspondence; manuscripts, including an eight-page item entitled "The Ideal Deaconess"; reports she wrote about the Deaconess Home; religious lectures; clippings; and deaconess diploma, license, and hat. Curtis attended the University of Nebraska and taught in Fillmore County, NE, schools and at the Girls Training School at Geneva, NE. She also attended the Chicago Training School for City, Home and Foreign Missions and served as a deaconess in Chicago churches before becoming head of the Deaconess Home.

10,565. Deaconess Board, Nebraska Conference, Methodist Church
Records. 1914-39. 3 in.
Open. No guide.
Nebraska Wesleyan University, United Methodist Church Archives.
Minutes for 1914 to 1925 and later records and correspondence.

10,566. Dorcas Methodist Episcopal Ladies Aid, LaSalle St. Methodist Episcopal Church, Beatrice, NE
Records. 1899-1940. 7.5 in.
Open. No guide.
Nebraska Wesleyan University, United Methodist Church Archives.
Financial and other records.

10,567. Frauen Mission Verein, Hastings, NE
Records. 1910-22. 1.25 in.
Open. No guide.
Nebraska Wesleyan University, United Methodist Church Archives.
Secretary's books containing minutes in German of this women's missionary society.

10,568. Hopper, Phoebe May
Papers. Ca. 1945-67. Ca. 6 in.
Open. No guide.
Nebraska Wesleyan University, United Methodist Church Archives.
Diaries, lectures, and radio talks of Hopper (1867-1967), a teacher at Nebraska Wesleyan University. Subjects of the lectures range from religious and geographical to literary topics. Also includes the certificate of membership in the Together Magazine Century Club that Hopper received when she reached her 100th birthday.

10,569. Ladies Aid Society, Pleasant Valley, NE
Records. 1914-18. 0.5 in.
Open. No guide.
Nebraska Wesleyan University, United Methodist Church Archives.
Constitution, bylaws, minutes, and financial records of this Evangelical church organization.

10,570. Ladies Seminary Society, York, NE
Records. 1880-81. 1 item.
Open. No guide.
Nebraska Wesleyan University, United Methodist Church Archives.
Report of the secretary of a group organized in 1880 to raise construction funds for the foundation of a Methodist seminary building in York.

10,571. Magee, Nellie T.
Papers. 1878-1955. 10 in.
Open. No guide.
Nebraska Wesleyan University, United Methodist Church Archives.
[Mrs.] Magee, a prominent Methodist churchwoman, developed Bible study games in 1906 that were still in use in 1954. Collection includes Magee's study games; a Junior Epworth League Workers notebook she compiled; sermons; notes on the history of Chautauqua and the Society of the Hall in the Grove, a Chautauqua literary and scientific circle organized in 1888 in Chautauqua, NY; Chautauqua study books and yearbooks; and minutes of the Graduate Circle of Alethean Chautauqua of Lincoln, a woman's organization with a prescribed four-year course of study.

10,572. Mission Band, Nebraska Branch of the Woman's Missionary Society of the Evangelical Church
Records. 1935-48. 2.5 in.
Open. No guide.
Nebraska Wesleyan University, United Methodist Church Archives.
Records of a children's group that was a division of the Woman's Missionary Society of the Evangelical Church.

10,573. Mission Band, Winslow, NE
Records. 1944-45. 1 item.
Open. No guide.
Nebraska Wesleyan University, United Methodist Church Archives.
Minutes of a children's group, organized in 1944, that was a division of the Woman's Missionary Society of the Evangelical Church.

10,574. Turner, Martha
Papers. Nd. 3 in.
Open. No guide.
Nebraska Wesleyan University, United Methodist Church Archives.
Notes on early Methodist churches in Lincoln.

10,575. Wesleyan Service Guild, Epworth Methodist Church, Lincoln
Records. 1941-68. 4 in.
Open. No guide.
Nebraska Wesleyan University, United Methodist Church Archives.
Records of this women's church organization.

10,576. Wesleyan Service Guild, Nebraska Conference, Methodist Church
Records. 1931-73. 18 in.
Open. No guide.
Nebraska Wesleyan University, United Methodist Church Archives.
Scrapbooks, assorted newsletters, reports, and programs of this women's church organization, including reports on the cultivation of spiritual life as well as historical material.

10,577. Woman's Foreign Missionary Society, First Methodist Episcopal Church, Lincoln
Records. 1902-40. 4.5 in.
Open. No guide.
Nebraska Wesleyan University, United Methodist Church Archives.
Secretary's reports of 1902 to 1911 and 1919 to 1940.

10,578. Woman's Foreign Missionary Society, First United Evangelical Church, Omaha
Records. 1910-18. 1 in.
Open. No guide.
Nebraska Wesleyan University, United Methodist Church Archives.
Minutes of the Society and of the Woman's Home and Foreign Missionary Society.

10,579. Woman's Foreign Missionary Society, Methodist Episcopal Church, Topeka, KS, Branch
Records. 1921-40. 9.75 in.
Open. No guide.
Nebraska Wesleyan University, United Methodist Church Archives.
Scrapbooks concerning annual meetings of the Topeka Branch, which includes churches in Kansas and Nebraska, and issues of the Topeka *Branch Herald,* the group's newspaper.

10,580. Woman's Foreign Missionary Society, Nebraska Conference, Methodist Episcopal Church
Records. 1899-1919. Ca. 1.5 in.
Open. No guide.
Nebraska Wesleyan University, United Methodist Church Archives.
Pamphlets on the Society and its history include a 1908 report on the Margaret Eliza Nast Memorial Hospital in Sing Iu, Fukien Province, China, which was directed by physicians Emma J. Betow and Frances L. Draper, and *Our Work for the Church,* compiled by Mrs. W. F. McDowell in 1913.

10,581. Woman's Home and Foreign Missionary Society, United Evangelical Church, Naponee, NE
Records. 1917-18. 1 item.
Open. No guide.
Nebraska Wesleyan University, United Methodist Church Archives.
Secretary's book.

10,582. Woman's Home and Foreign Missionary Society, United Evangelical Church, York, NE
Records. 1916-26. 1 in.
Open. No guide.
Nebraska Wesleyan University, United Methodist Church Archives.
Minutes.

10,583. Woman's Home Missionary Society, First Methodist Episcopal Church, Lincoln
Records. 1924-40. 4.75 in.
Open. No guide.
Nebraska Wesleyan University, United Methodist Church Archives.
Nearly complete set of secretary's reports and three calendars.

10,584. Woman's Home Missionary Society, Nebraska Conference, Methodist Episcopal Church
Records. 1886-1940. 9.5 in.
Open. No guide.
Nebraska Wesleyan University, United Methodist Church Archives.
Collection of annual reports, minutes, financial records, convention programs, and perpetual membership roll contains minutes of the annual conventions and executive board meetings between 1917 and 1940, as well as records of the corresponding secretary from 1886 to 1892 and of the Nebraska Conference Contingent Fund from 1906 to 1913. Also included is material concerning the national WHMS, such as a pamphlet of the group's first annual report in 1882 and a printed address in which Bishop I. W. Wiley supported the national organization.

10,585. Woman's Home Missionary Society, North Nebraska Conference, Methodist Episcopal Church
Records. 1899-1900. 1 item.
Open. No guide.
Nebraska Wesleyan University, United Methodist Church Archives.
Record of the corresponding secretary.

10,586. Woman's Missionary Association of the Church of the United Brethren in Christ, Nebraska Branch
Records. Ca. 1902-41. 5.5 in.
Open. No guide.
Nebraska Wesleyan University, United Methodist Church Archives.
Annual and quarterly reports, financial records, treasurer's books, and pamphlets and books on the group's history, one of which is entitled *History of the Woman's Missionary Association of the United Brethren in Christ, Jubilee Edition* (Dayton, OH: 1921), by Mrs. L. R. Harford and Alice E. Bell.

10,587. Woman's Missionary Society, Beaver Crossing, NE
Records. 1933-56. 1.5 in.
Open. No guide.
Nebraska Wesleyan University, United Methodist Church Archives.
The name of the group, associated with an Evangelical church, was changed in 1947 to Woman's Society of World Service. Treasurer's book, statistical reports, and secretary's books of minutes.

10,588. Woman's Missionary Society, Evangelical Association
Records. Ca. 1916. 4 items.
Open. No guide.
Nebraska Wesleyan University, United Methodist Church Archives.
Pamphlets include information on women missionaries, the Society, and "prayer cycles."

10,589. Woman's Missionary Society, First Church, Omaha
Records. 1916-24. 1 item.
Open. No guide.
Nebraska Wesleyan University, United Methodist Church Archives.
Minutes of the group known until 1921 as the Frauen Mission Verein, after which time it changed its name to WMS. Initially, the minutes were kept in German. The organization's church was a member of the Evangelical Association of Evangelical Churches.

10,590. Woman's Missionary Society, Ithaca Church, Ithaca, NE
Records. 1910-42. 4.5 in.
Open. No guide.
Nebraska Wesleyan University, United Methodist Church Archives.
Originally called Der Ithaca Frauen Mission Verein, Ithaca Bezirk, members of this Evangelical Church woman's group changed its name in 1924 and began recording their minutes in English rather than in German. Secretary's books for the entire period and financial records.

10,591. Woman's Missionary Society, Nebraska Branch, Evangelical Church
Records. Ca. 1917-47. 17 in.
Open. No guide.
Nebraska Wesleyan University, United Methodist Church Archives.
Minutes, treasurer's and auditor's reports, missionary records, reports of conventions, historical material, and other records include pamphlets tracing the group's history from 1890 to 1923; the pamphlet *A Chaplet of Memories,* which is about four WMS members, Emma M. Dubs, Mary M. T. Fouke, Martha Alice Remer, and Ida M. Haefele; and a 1927 book *History of the Ohio Branch of the Woman's Missionary Society of the Evangelical Church,* edited by Margaret S. Hudson. Also contains 1917-23 records of the Nebraska and Platte River conferences of the Woman's Missionary Society of the United Evangelical Church.

10,592. Woman's Missionary Society Rally, Lincoln District, Nebraska
Records. 1932-46. 0.75 in.
Open. No guide.
Nebraska Wesleyan University, United Methodist Church Archives.
Secretary's book, program, and attendance records of a rally held in the Lincoln District of the Evangelical Church.

10,593. Woman's Missionary Society, St. Paul's Evangelical Church, Clay Center, NE
Records. 1908-47. 2.5 in.
Open. No guide.
Nebraska Wesleyan University, United Methodist Church Archives.
Secretary's books containing minutes that were written in German through 1919.

10,594. Woman's Missionary Society, Salem Evangelical Church, Platte River Conference, Lincoln
Records. 1906-17. 1.25 in.
Open. No guide.
Nebraska Wesleyan University, United Methodist Church Archives.
Minutes of the Society and of the Miriam Circle of the Young Women's Missionary Society.

10,595. Woman's Missionary Society, United Brethren Church of Prairie Gem, NE
Records. 1909-62. 4.25 in.
Open. No guide.
Nebraska Wesleyan University, United Methodist Church Archives.
Minutes, financial records, and annual, quarterly, and mid-year secretary's reports. The name of the organization was changed in 1947 to Women's Society of World Service of the Evangelical United Brethren Church of Prairie Gem.

10,596. Woman's Missionary Society, Zion Evangelical Church, Harvard, NE
Records. 1928-59. 2.5 in.
Open. No guide.
Nebraska Wesleyan University, United Methodist Church Archives.
Minutes, treasurer's book, and other financial records of the group known as the Woman's Society for World Service after 1947. The local church's name was changed to the Zion Evangelical United Brethren Church in the same year, marking the merger of the Evangelical Church and the United Brethren in Christ.

10,597. Woman's Society of Christian Service and Wesleyan Service Guild, First Methodist Church, Lincoln
Records. 1948-73. 1 ft.
Open. No guide.
Nebraska Wesleyan University, United Methodist Church Archives.
Minutes, financial records, correspondence, membership records, and a complete set of yearbooks.

10,598. Woman's Society of Christian Service, Nebraska Conference, Methodist Church
Records. 1939-69. 41.25 in.
Open. No guide.
Nebraska Wesleyan University, United Methodist Church Archives.
Annual reports; minutes; financial reports; scrapbooks concerning WSCS officers, missionaries, and deaconesses; membership lists; programs of the School of Missions and annual meetings; an incomplete set of the Nebraska *Conference News WSCS,* the group's newspaper; and other records.

10,599. Woman's Society of World Service, Nebraska Conference, Evangelical United Brethren Church
Records. 1946-69. 24.25 in.
Open. No guide.

Nebraska Wesleyan University, United Methodist Church Archives.
Annual reports, minutes, treasurer's and auditor's reports, correspondence, publicity material, plans of work, convention programs, and other records of the WSWS and of its Christian Service Guild, including separate minutes of these women's groups of the Evangelical and United Brethren in Christ churches, joint minutes, and then minutes of the merged group. Also includes a booklet containing pictures and biographies of missionaries and records of district officer training conferences of the Nebraska WSWS.

10,600. Woman's Wesleyan Educational Council of Nebraska
Records. Ca. 1889-1974. 5 ft.
Open. No guide.
Nebraska Wesleyan University, United Methodist Church Archives.
Founded in 1896, this organization seeks to interest Methodist women and others in the welfare of Nebraska Wesleyan University. Constitution and bylaws, annual reports, minutes, financial reports, records of student loans and scholarships, correspondence, historian's reports, photos, yearbooks, and other material, including a paper by Mrs. L. O. Jones on the Council's early history.

10,601. Women's Organizations of the Districts of the Nebraska Conference, Methodist Episcopal Church
Records. 1890-1973. Ca. 29 in.
Open. No guide.
Nebraska Wesleyan University, United Methodist Church Archives.
Annual reports, minutes, membership rolls, programs, some biographical sketches, photos, and miscellaneous records of the women's foreign and home missionary societies and the Woman's Society of Christian Service of the Beatrice, Lincoln, Geneva and Hastings, McCook, Norfolk, Northwest, and Southwest districts. Annual reports of the Woman's Home Missionary Society, Lincoln District, date from 1890 to 1940.

10,602. White, Ellen Gould (Harmon)
Papers. 1851- . No size given.
Open. Card catalog.
Union College Library.
Cofounder of the Seventh-day Adventist church, [Mrs. James Springer] White (1827-1915) was a writer, lecturer, and counselor to her church. Correspondence, articles and published works by White, photos, and scrapbooks.

10,603. Abbott, Grace, and Abbott, Edith
Papers. 1897-1954. 6 cu.ft.
Open. Unpublished guide.
University of Nebraska-Lincoln Archives.
Grace Abbott (1878-1939) was chief of the Children's Bureau of the US Department of Labor, while Edith Abbott (1876-1957) was a professor of social work and dean of the University of Chicago's school of social service administration. General and family correspondence; lecture notes and material relating to such topics as child labor, juvenile delinquency, housing, immigration, poor laws, social welfare, and the status of women; biographical material; and scrapbooks and photos concerning the Abbott sisters' family life. Grace Abbott also served as director of the Labor Department's child labor division and of the Immigrants Protective League and as a Hull House associate.

10,604. Associated Women Students
Records. 1942-70. 1 cu.ft.
Open. No guide.
University of Nebraska-Lincoln Archives.
This governing body for women students at the University was founded in 1911. Minutes of executive board meetings, files on special activities sponsored by the organization, correspondence, handbooks, and other material. Also included are records of "court" proceedings on regulations and hours in living units.

10,605. Fedde, Margaret
Papers. 1928-70. Ca. 0.4 cu.ft.
Open. No guide.
University of Nebraska-Lincoln Archives.
Fedde (1883-) was chairman of the University's department of home economics from 1919 until 1949. Personal and professional correspondence, biographical material, notes on the department's history, a list of home economics graduates, photos, and collected material on home economics. Fedde began teaching home economics at the University in 1914.

10,606. Mortar Boards (Black Masque)
Records. 1905-70. 3 cu.ft.
Open. Unpublished guide.
University of Nebraska-Lincoln Archives.
This women's senior honorary society was founded in 1905 as the Black Masque and affiliated with the national society Mortar Boards in 1921. Nearly complete set of presidents' reports, minutes, files on events sponsored by the society, scrapbooks, and photos of members.

10,607. Rokahr, Mary A.
Papers. 1902-68. 5 cu.ft.
Open. Unpublished guide.
University of Nebraska-Lincoln Archives.
Rokahr (1892-1972) directed the home economics section of the University of Nebraska's mission to Turkey from 1956 to 1958; she also was head of the University of Connecticut's home economics department in 1953 and an extension specialist for the US Department of Agriculture, the University of Nebraska, and the state of Wyoming. Family correspondence, journals and diaries describing the world travels of Rokahr and her sister, speeches, reference material, articles, scrapbooks, and memorabilia. Among topics represented are family economics, the status of women in a changing world, and the education and role of women.

10,608. Sandoz, Mari
Papers. 1925-66. Ca. 210 ft.
Open. Unpublished guide.
University of Nebraska-Lincoln Archives.
Sandoz (1896?-1966) was a writer, historian, and educator. Files containing ca. 25,000 letters that include information on Sandoz's life and career, creative writing, the Plains Indians, and western American history; her personal library; manuscript and published copies of her 21 published books, articles, and short stories; and her resource file, research and reading notes, maps, photos, clippings, cassette tapes, and microfilm reels. Collection contains information about pioneer and Indian women and letters from many leading female contemporaries.

10,609. Young Women's Christian Association
Records. 1884-1961. Ca. 2.5 cu.ft.
Open. Unpublished guide.
University of Nebraska-Lincoln Archives.
Records of the University and city branches of the YWCA contain minutes, fiscal records, office files on the groups' activities, circulars and brochures, and photo and clippings scrapbooks. Included are biographical sketches of outstanding members of the University YWCA, a history of the school's YWCA, a biography of Grace Coppock, and material on the Nebraska YWCA's work in China between 1921 and 1935.

NORFOLK

10,610. Archives
Records. 1923- . 2 boxes and 1 vol.
Open. No guide.
Missionary Benedictine Sisters, Immaculata Convent.
Correspondence, school and hospital reports, chronicles, unpublished manuscripts, photos, scrapbooks, obituaries, and tracts of the American priory, which was founded in 1923 in Raeville, NE. Records relate to the founding and operation of mission stations in Nebraska, Minnesota, and Kentucky as well as in other countries.

OMAHA

10,611. Religious Women
Collection. Ca. 1855-1951. Ca. 15.5 in.
Open. No guide.
Catholic Archdiocese of Omaha Archives.
Correspondence, a treatise, and other documents and records concern Catholic religious women in Nebraska and other states. Includes records of the following convents and orders: the Convent of the Holy Child Jesus, Lincoln, NE; the Convent of the Holy Child Jesus, Cheyenne, WY; the Dominican Sisters of St. Catherine, KY; the Missionary Benedictine Sisters of Raeville, Norfolk, Lynch, and Madison, NE; the Order of Carmel; the Precious Blood Sisters; the Sisters of Mercy; the Parish Visitors of Mary Immaculate; the Poor Clares; the Poor Sisters of St. Francis Seraph of Perpetual Adoration; the Sisters of the Blessed Sacrament at the Winnebago Indian Mission at Winnebago, NE; the Sisters of Divine Providence; the Sisters of the Good Shepherd-Magdalenes; the Sisters of Notre Dame in Omaha; the Ursulines in Louisville and Maple Mount, KY; and the Servants of Mary. Most of the orders' records consist of letters to the bishops of Omaha, including Bishop James O'Connor. Correspondence concerns the establishment of the Convent of the Holy Child Jesus in Lincoln and teaching boys in a parochial school; the establishment of the Convent of the Holy Child Jesus in Cheyenne in ca. 1886; Margaret M. Chambers, who wished to enter the order of the Parish Visitors of Mary Immaculate, 1939-41; an investigation of complaints about the St. Clare Convent of the Poor Clares in Omaha in 1888; and other topics.

10,612. Joslyn, Sarah Hannah Selleck
Papers. 1851-1975. Ca. 1 ft.
Open. No guide.
Joslyn Art Museum Library.
Joslyn (1851-1940), a philanthropist, established the Joslyn Art Museum in 1931 as a memorial to her husband George A. Joslyn (1848-1916), who was president of the Western Newspaper Union from 1896 to 1916. Correspondence, manuscripts, clippings, and Museum publications concern the Museum's opening and include information about the Joslyn family genealogy, the Joslyns' home, and Sarah Joslyn's personal business. Born in Vermont, she came to Omaha with her husband in 1879.

10,613. Archives
Records. 1875- . 4 drawers.
Access restricted. Unpublished guide.
Monastery of St. Clare.
Financial records, legal records, handwritten annals, correspondence, photos, and clippings of this Monastery of the Order of St. Clare, a religious order of women whose foundresses came to the US in 1875 and to Omaha in 1878.

10,614. Archives
Records. 1893- . 2 files.
Open. No guide.
Servants of Mary Motherhouse.
This religious order of women was established in the US in 1893 in Mount Vernon, IN. Originally devoted to teaching, the Sisters are now involved in various apostolates. Correspondence, diaries, reminiscences, photos, scrapbooks, community newsletters, books, and other records. Includes the daily diaries of the foundress Sister Mary Gertrude

Guinan from the time she arrived to found the American mission at Mount Vernon until her return to England in 1926.

10,615. Province Archives
Records. 1831- . 30 drawers and 42 shelves.
Access restricted. Unpublished guide.
Sisters of Mercy Provincialate, Omaha Province.
Minutes of the provincial council and its advisory board; financial records; correspondence; provincial chapter books and general chapter books; chronicles; files of novitiate houses and of schools, nursing homes, hospitals, and other institutions operated by the Sisters; novitiate and profession records of sisters; reports; construction plans; blueprints; tapes; slides; photo albums; programs; school annuals; newsletters; clippings; custom books; directories; prayer books; and vow books of this religious order of women which was founded in Dublin, Ireland, in 1831.

10,616. Nebraska Medical History
Collection. 1850- . 52 drawers.
Open. Card index.
University of Nebraska Medical Center, Library of Medicine.
Published and unpublished historical records of medical practice in Nebraska, photos, and records of the Omaha Medical College, which existed from 1869 to 1902, and of the University of Nebraska Medical Center, which opened in 1902. Included are manuscripts and daily records of women who practiced medicine in the state from 1850 to 1900. Records of the College and the Center include minutes of the schools, their faculties, and auxiliaries; reports; catalogs; and clippings. The Medical Center comprises the colleges of medicine, nursing, and pharmacy and the school of allied health professions.

RED CLOUD

10,617. Cather, Willa Sibert
Papers. 1873- . 350 vols., 5860 items, and 210 reels.
Access restricted. Partial card index.
Willa Cather Historical Center.
Cather (1873-1947) was a short story writer and novelist. Correspondence from Cather to residents of Red Cloud, manuscripts about Cather, book reviews, photos, periodicals, clippings, and museum items related to Cather's life and writing.

WAVERLY

10,618. Archives
Records. 1952- . No size given.
Closed. No guide.
Marian Sisters Motherhouse.
Minutes, diaries, photos, and scrapbooks of the community, which was founded in 1854. The Sisters are involved in teaching and nursing.

YORK

10,619. Daughters of Union Veterans, Clara Barton Tent, No. 5
Records. Ca. 1919-50. 0.5 in.
Open. No guide.
Anna Palmer Museum.
Scrapbook contains a list dated 1919 of charter members of the Tent and clippings about members and their fathers.

10,620. Kline, Christine
Papers. Ca. 1950s. 2 in.
Open. No guide.
Anna Palmer Museum.
Correspondence of [Mrs. Emery] Kline includes letters from Nebraska politicians and national figures such as Ivy (Baker) Priest and items concerning flood relief efforts in Topeka, KS, in 1951. Also contains a scrapbook, certificates, awards, and letters of commendation for Kline.

10,621. Mothers' Jewels Home
Records. Ca. 1892-1941. 2 in.
Open. No guide.
Anna Palmer Museum.
Located in York, the Home is an orphanage supported by the Woman's Division of the Board of Global Ministries of the United Methodist Church. Photos, bulletins, brochures, circulars, and a 1941 program for dedication services for a new building at the Home, which originally was supported by the Methodist Episcopal Church, a predecessor of the United Methodist Church. The name of the Home was changed to Epworth Village in 1961.

10,622. National Alliance of the Daughters of Veterans, United States of America
Records. 1894. 1 item.
Open. No guide.
Anna Palmer Museum.
Constitution of the organization, which was founded in 1885.

10,623. Pleasant Hill Recorder
Records. Ca. 1860. 0.5 in.
Open. No guide.
Anna Palmer Museum.
The *Recorder,* a semimonthly journal prepared for Pleasant Hill School, was devoted to "amusement and literature." Volume containing the magazine's first seven issues; [Miss] Mary A. Bennett is listed as "editress" of the first issue. The journal records the thoughts of various persons at the school, which apparently was coeducational, and includes several articles by women.

10,624. United Spanish War Veterans, Walter Poor Auxiliary, No. 16
Records. Ca. 1932-50. 1.5 in.
Open. No guide.
Anna Palmer Museum.
The women's auxiliary to the Walter Poor Camp, United Spanish War Veterans, was organized in York in 1932. Scrapbook contains a list of the Auxiliary's charter members, information about the Walter Poor Camp, and clippings concerning the Auxiliary's activities.

10,625. Woman's Relief Corps, No. 5
Records. Ca. 1880-83. 2 items.
Open. No guide.
Anna Palmer Museum.
Organized in about 1880, this local group was the woman's auxiliary of the Robert Anderson Post, No. 32, Department of Nebraska, Grand Army of the Republic. Roster of the members of the Post and the women's auxiliary; a pamphlet containing a short history of Woman's Relief Corps, No. 5; and a list of its members.

10,626. York County Women
Collection. Nd. No size given.
Open. No guide.
York County Historical Association.
Contains clippings and other papers about local women including [Miss] Alice Florer, who was York County superintendent of schools; [Miss] Grace Moore (1871-1957), who was a newspaper publisher; and Marion [Mrs. O. M.] Moore (1880s-late 1940s), a music publisher and composer.

NEVADA

CARSON CITY

10,627. Future Homemakers of America, Nevada
Records. 1949-76. 2 ft.
Open. No guide.
Nevada State, County, and Municipal Archives.
Scrapbooks contain clippings concerning the activities of the Nevada chapter of Future Homemakers.

ELKO

10,628. Gardner, Alice (Brewer)
Papers. Nd. 4-page item.
Open. No guide.
Northeastern Nevada Museum.
Biography of Gardner, which was written by a student for a local history writing contest, contains information about her work as an early schoolteacher in Nevada, assisting her husband with the family sheep business in 1914, and managing the business after his death in 1936.

10,629. Knemeyer, Bertha C.
Papers. Ca. 1963. 22-page item.
Open. No guide.
Northeastern Nevada Museum.
A biography of Knemeyer (1885-1963), who entered the University of Nevada at Reno at the age of 15 after skipping high school because of her mathematical abilities. She taught school for two years and then worked as an educational administrator for nearly 30 years. After her retirement, Knemeyer traveled across the US and through 35 foreign countries.

10,630. Nelson, Estella (Bish)
Papers. Ca. 1960. 8-page item.
Open. No guide.
Northeastern Nevada Museum.
Biography by Sadie Davidson about Nelson (1887-1960), an educator, mining camp cook, and homesteader who assisted her husband with cattle ranching. Nelson also served as an American National Red Cross worker during WWI.

10,631. Peterson, Theresa (Alphin) Wilkinson Taber
Papers. Ca. 1962. 6-page item.
Open. No guide.
Northeastern Nevada Museum.
A biography of Peterson (1877-1954) reviewing her work as a nurse with the Shoshoni Indians, the introduction of such health practices as using soap and toothbrushes, and her close association as an advisor of the tribe over a period of 50 years. Peterson, who was also a painter and poet, was made a member of the Indian tribe.

10,632. Pioneer Women of Nevada
Collection. Ca. 1975. 5 in.
Open. No guide.
Northeastern Nevada Museum.
Collected by the AAUW, these essays are about various Nevada women pioneers, including [Mrs.] Anna Licking, who took in children after they lost their parents or needed assistance; Nevada (Hardesty) Griswold, daughter of a roving miner and named after his location of work, who describes the hardships of pioneer life, the difficulties of obtaining an education, and community activities she engaged in after her marriage; Virginia Boitano Guisti (1860-1948), an Italian who came to the US to be married and who later served as nurse and doctor for the Cortez, NV, area; Jane Elizabeth Crosson (1847-1927), who discusses difficulties of pioneer life that arose

because of Indians, the weather, and the lack of goods; Mrs. A. D. Geer (1846-1936), an early settler in White Pine County; Gertrude (Lang) Garrecht (1844-?), born in Switzerland, who recalls Indian raids near Shasta, CA, which she experienced before mining work brought her and her husband to Nevada in 1869; and Anna Christine (Brown) Glaser.

10,633. Sharp, Florence Beatrice (Wines)
Papers. Ca. 1964. 16-page item.
Open. No guide.
Northeastern Nevada Museum.
Autobiographical reminiscences in which [Mrs. Lewis, Sr.] Sharp (1884-?) describes her childhood, family, and community. She also mentions Chinese laborers she saw, her association with Indians, the San Francisco earthquake, and her first experiences with automobiles and radios.

10,634. Smith, Eva (Byrne) Rizzi
Papers. Ca. 1945. 1 folder.
Open. No guide.
Northeastern Nevada Museum.
Autobiography in which Smith, an early resident of Nevada, describes the trek westward her parents made for the California gold rush and her own experiences as a child in small Nevada communities, her fear of Indians, dependence on the weather, and homesteading.

10,635. Westfall, Elizabeth Bird
Papers. Ca. 1962. 8-page item.
Open. No guide.
Northeastern Nevada Museum.
Biography by Bea Wagner about Westfall (1878-1958) concerns her experiences as a teacher, nurse, and seamstress and her travels in the US. Also includes details about Westfall's activities with social clubs and community organizations.

10,636. Wines, Margaret Taylor
Papers. Ca. 1956. 5-page item.
Open. No guide.
Northeastern Nevada Museum.
Biography by Florence Wines Sharp about [Mrs. Ira D.] Wines (1846-1908), an early settler of Lehi, UT, who moved to the Ruby Valley, NV, in 1865, concerns her move, conflicts with Indians, and difficulties she experienced.

RENO

10,637. Addenbrooke, Alice Baltzell
Papers. 1934-57. 1 carton.
Open. Published guide.
Nevada Historical Society.
Correspondence and other papers of Addenbrooke, an author and civic leader who was largely responsible for the preservation and restoration of Fort Churchill and Bowers' Mansion. Material relates primarily to her books about the Fort and the Mansion. See L. James Higgins, *A Guide to the Manuscript Collections at the Nevada Historical Society* (Reno, NV: Nevada Historical Society, 1975).

10,638. Allen, Robert A.
Papers. Nd. 12 Paige boxes.
Open. Published guide.
Nevada Historical Society.
Allen (1886-1968) was Nevada state engineer from 1922 to 1927, state highway engineer from 1925 to 1947, and chairman of the Public Service Commission from 1947 to 1959. A collector of material relating to Nevada history, Allen enlisted the aid of [Miss] Mary L. Ream and Herbert Hamblin, who traveled throughout the western US visiting libraries, interviewing descendants of pioneers, and securing or copying pertinent material. Contains pioneer diaries, including a diary of Phoebe Twerwilliger, and information relating to trails, the Pony Express, Mormons, mining, milling, agriculture, railroads, parks, and other topics. Taken from L. James Higgins, *A Guide to the Manuscript Collections at the Nevada Historical Society* (Reno, NV: Nevada Historical Society, 1975).

10,639. American Association of University Women
Records. 1916- . 2 boxes.
Open. Card catalog.
Nevada Historical Society.
Bylaws, chapter minutes, treasurer's reports, correspondence, membership lists, and national, state, and Reno chapter periodicals of the Reno chapter of the AAUW. Contains items of past presidents, including Edith Kast Hartman, Effie Mona Mack, and Clara Smith Beatty.

10,640. American Association of University Women, Nevada Division
Records. 1952-72. 2 cartons.
Open. Published guide.
Nevada Historical Society.
Minutes, correspondence, scrapbooks, and other records of the Nevada AAUW, including reports from chapters within Nevada and from state officers. See L. James Higgins, *A Guide to the Manuscript Collections at the Nevada Historical Society* (Reno, NV: Nevada Historical Society, 1975).

10,641. American Association of University Women, Sparks Branch
Records. 1953-74. 1 box.
Open. Published guide.
Nevada Historical Society.
Financial and membership records and correspondence of the Sparks, NV, AAUW. See L. James Higgins, *A Guide to the Manuscript Collections at the Nevada Historical Society* (Reno, NV: Nevada Historical Society, 1975).

10,642. Anti-Saloon League
Records. 1910-23. 19 items.
Open. Published guide.
Nevada Historical Society.
Correspondence and other records of the League, founded in ca. 1910, concern legislation and prohibition. See L. James Higgins, *A Guide to the Manuscript Collections at the Nevada Historical Society* (Reno, NV: Nevada Historical Society, 1975).

10,643. Austin Literary Association
Records. 1878-80. 1 vol.
Open. No guide.
Nevada Historical Society.
Constitution, bylaws, minutes, and other records of this social club.

10,644. Beatty, Clara Smith
Papers. 1914-69. Ca. 3 in.
Open. Published guide.
Nevada Historical Society.
Correspondence and other papers of [Mrs.] Beatty (1890-1967), executive secretary of the Nevada Historical Society, pertain to her speeches, legislation, and preservation of Nevada's history. Contains a monograph concerning Nevada legislation and a history of the Rebaleati-Merialdo family, who were Italian settlers in Nevada, with information about Mary Romando Rebaleati. See L. James Higgins, *A Guide to the Manuscript Collections at the Nevada Historical Society* (Reno, NV: Nevada Historical Society, 1975).

10,645. Bender, Flora I.
Papers. 1863. 25-page item.
Open. Published guide.
Nevada Historical Society.
Diary of Bender concerns a wagon train journey from Nebraska to Virginia City, NV. Taken from L. James Higgins, *A Guide to the Manuscript Collections at the Nevada Historical Society* (Reno, NV: Nevada Historical Society, 1975).

10,646. Biggs, Londa
Papers. 1961. 20-page item and ca. 30 cards.
Open. Published guide.
Nevada Historical Society.
An essay and note cards of Biggs pertain to Marjorie Mead Downs, a Fallon, NV, resident, and Downs's arrival in Nevada, education, teaching, activities as a legislative attaché, her marriage, and welfare work. Taken from L. James Higgins, *A Guide to the Manuscript Collections at the Nevada Historical Society* (Reno, NV: Nevada Historical Society, 1975).

10,647. Blume, Julius, and Blume, Nettie
Papers. 1870-79. 12 items.
Open. Published guide.
Nevada Historical Society.
Collection includes three letters from Nettie Blume, a resident of Reno, to her mother and sister. See L. James Higgins, *A Guide to the Manuscript Collections at the Nevada Historical Society* (Reno, NV: Nevada Historical Society, 1975).

10,648. Boak, Cada Castolas
Papers. 1902-28. 121 items.
Open. Published guide.
Nevada Historical Society.
Correspondence, a document, and other papers of Boak (1870-1954) regarding his campaign to erect a monument to Mr. and Mrs. James L. Butler; Mrs. Butler was a founder of Tonopah, NV. Also includes 18 letters from Boak to his wife. See L. James Higgins, *A Guide to the Manuscript Collections at the Nevada Historical Society* (Reno, NV: Nevada Historical Society, 1975).

10,649. Boyle, Emmet Derby
Papers. 1915-27. 1 box and 2 vols.
Open. Published guide.
Nevada Historical Society.
Correspondence and other papers of Boyle (1879-1927), governor of Nevada from 1915 to 1923, and some of his wife's papers from after his death. While in office Boyle endorsed the 19th Amendment, which passed during his term. See L. James Higgins, *A Guide to the Manuscript Collections at the Nevada Historical Society* (Reno, NV: Nevada Historical Society, 1975).

10,650. Breedlove, Mildred
Papers. 1940-76. 1 box.
Open. No guide.
Nevada Historical Society.
Breedlove (1904-) was Nevada's poet laureate from 1957 to 1966. The collection consists of correspondence, primarily with her mother in Oklahoma; other letters regard requests for her works "Those Desert Hills and Other Poems" and *Nevada,* which commemorated the state's centennial. Breedlove, who married Crongy P. Breedlove (1900-1957) in 1920, was also a real estate broker and ranch owner.

10,651. Browder, Mary P.
Papers. 1892-1920. 1 carton.
Open. Published guide.
Nevada Historical Society.
Correspondence and scrapbooks containing clippings about 19th-century literary and theatrical figures and a pamphlet on women composers. Includes clippings about prima donnas Emma Eames, Lillian Nordica, Emma Abbott, and Susan Stron; singer Ellen Beach Yaw; actress Mary Anderson; and Adelina Patti, Florence Nightingale, Jenny Lind, Blanch Walsh, Clara Morris, Emma Nevada, and Sarah Bernhardt. See L. James Higgins, *A Guide to the Manuscript Collections at the Nevada Historical Society* (Reno, NV: Nevada Historical Society, 1975).

10,652. Cagwin, Eunice Adelaide, and White, Florence Evelyn
Papers. 1913-14. Ca. 1 in.
Open. Published guide.
Nevada Historical Society.
Correspondence of Cagwin and White concerns their research on county jails in Nevada and a monograph regarding penal administration in Nevada. See L. James Higgins, *A Guide to the Manuscript Collections at the Nevada Historical Society* (Reno, NV: Nevada Historical Society, 1975).

10,653. Cahlan, Florence Lee Jones
Papers. 1959. 1 item.
Open. Published guide.
Nevada Historical Society.
A history of the Cahlan-Edmunds family of Nevada, including information about Charlotte Farley Cahlan and Gertrude Barron Edmonds. See L. James Higgins, *A Guide to the Manuscript Collections at the Nevada Historical Society* (Reno, NV: Nevada Historical Society, 1975).

10,654. Cerveri, Doris
Papers. 1964-72. 95 items.
Open. Published guide.
Nevada Historical Society.
Correspondence and notes of Cerveri concern her research regarding the grave of Lucinda Duncan and the uses of peyote. See L. James Higgins, *A Guide to the Manuscript Collections at the Nevada Historical Society* (Reno, NV: Nevada Historical Society, 1975).

10,655. Clapp, Hannah Keziah, and Babcock, Elizabeth Celicia
Papers. 1859-1906. 1 box.
Open. Published guide.
Nevada Historical Society.
Correspondence and other papers of [Miss] Clapp (1824-1908) and [Miss] Babcock (?-1899), who were longtime friends, pertain to establishment of the Babcock Kindergarten in Reno, Clapp's teaching at the University of Nevada, and condolences extended to Clapp at the death of Babcock. Correspondents include Miriam Michelson, J. E. Church, Jr., and Jeanne E. Wier. See L. James Higgins, *A Guide to the Manuscript Collections at the Nevada Historical Society* (Reno, NV: Nevada Historical Society, 1975).

10,656. Clasen, Jeannie M.
Papers. Nd. 16-page item.
Open. Published guide.
Nevada Historical Society.
Monograph regarding the history of prostitution in Nevada. Taken from L. James Higgins, *A Guide to the Manuscript Collections at the Nevada Historical Society* (Reno, NV: Nevada Historical Society, 1975).

10,657. Cohn, Amy
Papers. 1908. 21-page item.
Open. Published guide.
Nevada Historical Society.
Text of a lecture presented by [Mrs. Abraham] Cohn on Indian arts in the Washoe region of Nevada, particularly the basketry of Dat-So-La-Lee. See L. James Higgins, *A Guide to the Manuscript Collections at the Nevada Historical Society* (Reno, NV: Nevada Historical Society, 1975).

10,658. Cohn, Felice
Papers. 1902-60. 4 cartons.
Open. Published guide.
Nevada Historical Society.
Correspondence, scrapbooks, and other papers of [Miss] Cohn (1884-1961), a Reno attorney and author of the woman suffrage amendment adopted by the Nevada legislature. She also was an American National Red Cross chapter chairman, vice-president of the National Association of Women Lawyers, and an active participant in the Business and Professional Women's Club, the Nevada Federation of Women's Clubs, the Nevada Historical Society, the women's suffrage movement, and various civic organizations. She received her education at the University of Nevada, Stanford University, and Washington Law School. Correspondents include Carrie Chapman Catt, Mary Sumner Boyd, Miles N. Pike, and Florence B. Bovett. See L. James Higgins, *A Guide to the Manuscript Collections at the Nevada Historical Society* (Reno, NV: Nevada Historical Society, 1975).

10,659. Concert Girls
Records. Ca. 1907. 2 items.
Open. Catalog card.
Nevada Historical Society.
Dodgers that claim that the Unique and Adobe concert halls in Rhyolite are unfair houses and request that all union men stay away from the establishments.

10,660. Crisler, Clara M.
Papers. Ca. 1890-1957. 41 boxes.
Open. No guide.
Nevada Historical Society.
Correspondence of and several hundred scrapbooks containing information about Nevada collected by [Miss] Crisler (1882-1957), a descendant of Nevada pioneers and collector since childhood of material regarding the state's history. In 1923 she was appointed a land office registrar by President Harding, a post she held until 1934. Active in Carson City, NV, civic and social affairs, she organized the first Nevada Day parade.

10,661. Dangberg, Grace M.
Papers. 1938-73. Ca. 1.5 in.
Open. Published guide.
Nevada Historical Society.
Collection of [Miss] Dangberg, a local historian, includes correspondence and notes relating to her study of Jack Wilson, whose Indian name was Wovoka; a letter detailing the holdings of the Dangberg Land and Live Stock Company; a speech given by Dangberg regarding Nevada history sources; and a monograph describing the Washo Indian language. See L. James Higgins, *A Guide to the Manuscript Collections at the Nevada Historical Society* (Reno, NV: Nevada Historical Society, 1975).

10,662. Daughters of the American Revolution
Records. 1763-1974. 6 cartons.
Open. No guide.
Nevada Historical Society.
Correspondence and other records from 1943 to 1974 of the Nevada state society of the DAR and of the John C. Fremont Chapter of the DAR in Nevada. Contains minutes, financial records, correspondence, scrapbooks, family genealogies, cemetery census records from various Nevada towns, Episcopal church records, and the records of the Bowers' Mansion restoration group. Also includes an early family Bible.

10,663. Delta Kappa Gamma
Records. 1942-72. Ca. 1.5 ft.
Open. Published guide.
Nevada Historical Society.
Minutes, financial and membership records, and other material of the Alpha chapter, a local Nevada chapter of this society, which was organized to unite women educators. The Alpha chapter is part of the Alpha Chi State chapter. See L. James Higgins, *A Guide to the Manuscript Collections at the Nevada Historical Society* (Reno, NV: Nevada Historical Society, 1975).

10,664. Doten Family
Papers. 1858-1945. 3 cartons.
Open. No guide.
Nevada Historical Society.
Correspondence and other papers of the Doten family, including a diary kept by Mary Stoddard from 1858 to 1870 and poetry scrapbooks of Elizabeth Doten and Mary Stoddard; articles regarding Nevada and the Comstock Lode, several of which were written by family members; and photos of family and friends. Collection also contains material pertaining to education.

10,665. Doughty, Nanelia S.
Papers. 1970. 71 items.
Open. Published guide.
Nevada Historical Society.
Collection of [Mrs.] Doughty, a local historian, includes a letter from her to Hugh A. Shamberger about the water supply for Candelaria, NV, and bibliographic newspaper references for her research on the history of central Nevada. Also includes a summary that mentions several local women. See L. James Higgins, *A Guide to the Manuscript Collections at the Nevada Historical Society* (Reno, NV: Nevada Historical Society, 1975).

10,666. Douglas, Ida A. (Cooper)
Papers. 1927?-42. Ca. 6 in.
Open. Published guide.
Nevada Historical Society.
Correspondence and other papers of [Mrs. Thurlow] Douglas concern her activities with the DAR and the WCTU in Reno. Also includes a scrapbook containing articles Douglas wrote about pioneer families. See L. James Higgins, *A Guide to the Manuscript Collections at the Nevada Historical Society* (Reno, NV: Nevada Historical Society, 1975).

10,667. Earl, Phillip Irving
Papers. Nd. 1 box, 1 card file, and 1 tape.
Access restricted. Published guide.
Nevada Historical Society.
Tape of lecture presented by Earl in 1974 on women's suffrage; an information card file kept by Earl concerning suffrage in Nevada; broadsides and campaign material, 1910-14; and an article Earl wrote about the woman suffrage movement in northeastern Nevada. The article was published in the *Northeastern Nevada Historical Society Quarterly* (Elko, NV: 1976). See L. James Higgins, *A Guide to the Manuscript Collections at the Nevada Historical Society* (Reno, NV: Nevada Historical Society, 1975).

10,668. Eichelberger, Bessie Reese
Papers. 1863-1948. 1 box.
Open. Published guide.
Nevada Historical Society.
Correspondence and other papers of Eichelberger regarding personal finances, Reno civic organizations, and the women's suffrage movement. Correspondents include Anne Henrietta Martin. See L. James Higgins, *A Guide to the Manuscript Collections at the Nevada Historical Society* (Reno, NV: Nevada Historical Society, 1975).

10,669. Evans, Ida Suella Elliott
Oral history. Nd. 1 tape.
Open. No guide.
Nevada Historical Society.
Interview with Evans, a Reno resident, concerns the finding and rearing of Johnson Sides, who was known as the "Paiute Peacemaker"; Evan's memories of Sides and of her uncle Emanuel Penrod; and the ways in which Reno changed during her lifetime.

10,670. Fulstone, Maggie
Oral history. 1955. 1 tape.
Open. No guide.
Nevada Historical Society.
Interview in which [Mrs. Joseph H.] Fulstone, a Nevada resident, discusses her childhood, her father's career as a stone mason in California and Nevada, the history of Carson City, NV, moving to

Ash Valley and Indian conflicts there, ranching, and shopping for supplies in Susanville, CA.

10,671. Gastanaga Family
Papers. 1800-1973. 28 boxes.
Access restricted. No guide.
Nevada Historical Society.
Collection of this Nevada family includes papers of Lola Jimella Harvey Gastanaga regarding her activities in civil defense, the Business and Professional Women's Club, and other organizations. Also contains photos, slides, and motion picture films of family members and Lola Gastanaga's world travels.

10,672. Grey, Jessie
Papers. 1889-91. 1 vol.
Open. No guide.
Nevada Historical Society.
Correspondence from [Miss] Grey in Verdi, NV, to Charles Carter, a railroad employee in Wadsworth, NV, concerns their friendship and growing romance.

10,673. Hershiser, Nettie P.
Papers. 1903-30. 1 box.
Open. No guide.
Nevada Historical Society.
Correspondence and other papers of [Mrs. Anthony Emmett] Hershiser primarily pertain to her activities as president of the Nevada WCTU chapter. Also contains two essays written by her daughter Beulah Hershiser about the California/Nevada boundary dispute and the development of communal settlements in the western US. Correspondents include Margaret Dye Ellis, Tasker L. Oddie, Hannah J. Baily, Robert Shaw Oliver, John P. Jones, D. C. Van Duzer, Francis G. Newlands, George R. Nixon, James S. Sherman, and Robert M. La Follette.

10,674. Leavitt, Mary Luella Abbott
Papers. 1938-46. 34-page item.
Open. Published guide.
Nevada Historical Society.
Monograph of [Mrs. Thomas Dudley, Sr.] Leavitt, a Mormon and plural wife, contains reminiscences regarding life in Utah and Bunkerville, NV, polygamy, the United Order, and caring for the sick. The United Order was conceived by Brigham Young in the 1870s as a system of economic cooperation involving common ownership of property and the sharing of work and proceeds. It operated at various locations until abandoned in the early 1880s. Taken from L. James Higgins, *A Guide to the Manuscript Collections at the Nevada Historical Society* (Reno, NV: Nevada Historical Society, 1975).

10,675. Lockhart, Edith A.
Papers. 1861. 1 vol.
Open. Card catalog.
Nevada Historical Society.
Diary in which Lockhart, who later married a Mr. Humphrey, describes her trip from Clay County, MO, to Honey Lake Valley, CA. The diary was transcribed by Freda Humphrey Schuyler.

10,676. Lyman, Marguerite Rice
Papers. 1955-67. Ca. 1 in.
Open. Published guide.
Nevada Historical Society.
Historical sketches, articles, journals, and research material of [Mrs. Bert] Lyman (1893 or 1894-), an historical researcher, relate to southern Nevada history. Includes biographical information about Mormon pioneers Asaph Rice and his wives Louisa Busenbark and Mary Busenbark, who were sisters; Elizabeth Claridge McCune; and Melissa Jane Lambson Davis. See L. James Higgins, *A Guide to the Manuscript Collections at the Nevada Historical Society* (Reno, NV: Nevada Historical Society, 1975).

10,677. Mack, Effie Mona
Papers. 1917-69. 6 cartons.
Open. Published guide.
Nevada Historical Society.
Correspondence and other papers of Mack (1888-1969), an educator in Reno schools and at the University of Nevada, who also was an author concerned with Nevada government and history. She was educated at the University of Nevada and Smith College and received a PhD from the University of California, Berkeley. Contains correspondence regarding Mack's activities with the silver and statehood centennials; correspondence and notes concerning her research on the Comstock Lode, Mark Twain, and the Theodore Winters family; and grade books from her teaching years. Correspondents include Florence Bovett, Eva B. Adams, Hal Holbrook, Herb Caen, William Randolph Hearst, Jr., George P. Hammond, Donald Culross Peattie, Edwin H. Carpenter, Jr., Jordon J. Crouch, and Lucius Beebe. See L. James Higgins, *A Guide to the Manuscript Collections at the Nevada Historical Society* (Reno, NV: Nevada Historical Society, 1975).

10,678. Mack, Margaret M.
Papers. 1859-1930. 1 box.
Open. Published guide.
Nevada Historical Society.
Collection of [Miss] Mack (1871-1945) contains photos and other papers regarding the Comstock Lode; photos of the University of Nevada; a scrapbook kept by William R. Armstrong, an early Nevada County, CA, legislator, regarding early California and Storey County, NV, political campaign material and obituaries; poetry; a recipe book, possibly kept by Elizabeth Mack; and a history of the Mack family in Nevada with an emphasis on Thomas Porter Mack, a civil engineer in Dayton, and his descendants. See L. James Higgins, *A Guide to the Manuscript Collections at the Nevada Historical Society* (Reno, NV: Nevada Historical Society, 1975).

10,679. Mack, Sarah Emeline
Papers. 1911-46. 1 carton.
Open. Published guide.
Nevada Historical Society.
Correspondence and other papers of [Mrs. O. H.] Mack concern her involvement as a member or officer of the Washoe county unit, Nevada state chapter of the Pro-America Republican Women's Club; the Equal Franchise Society of Nevada; the Reno LWV; the Nevada LWV; the DAR; and the Women Citizens' Club. Contains correspondence with local, state, and national leaders of these organizations and minutes and other records of the Reno LWV, the Nevada LWV, and the Women Citizens' Club. Correspondents include Elva H. Carpenter, Mrs. A. C. Mattei, Charles A. Cantwell, J. LaRue Robinson, Mrs. William E. Steinbach, Key Pittman, Julia K. Jaffrey, Theodore R. Hofer, Mina C. Van Winkle, and Sam S. Arentz. See L. James Higgins, *A Guide to the Manuscript Collections at the Nevada Historical Society* (Reno, NV: Nevada Historical Society, 1975).

10,680. Manuscripts
Collections. Early 1800s- . No size given.
Partially restricted. Published guide.
Nevada Historical Society.
These ca. 600 collections pertaining to women contain ca. 350 essays written primarily by high school students in response to contests sponsored by such organizations as the AAUW. The essays relate to journeys west by wagon train; homesteading and building cabins in Nevada; Indians; mining; ranching; farming; prospecting; the development of towns; Mormon settlements, the Episcopal church, and Spanish missions in Nevada; histories of place names, such as Maiden's Grave and Susan's Bluff; and pioneer women who were civic leaders, educators, and businesswomen. Also included are correspondence, diaries, family papers and histories, records of Bishop Whitaker's School for Girls, a teacher's scrapbook, an 1871 teaching contract, autograph books, marriage and divorce records, baptism certificates, land transfer deeds, dance programs, and other papers. Represented in the collections are Dat-So-La-Lee, a Washo Indian basket weaver; singer Emma Nevada; Fanny Hazlett, who founded the Helping Hand Club in Dayton, NV, to instruct girls in domestic arts and crafts; Mrs. James Ellis, a pioneer who, in the absence of a minister, drew up the first marriage contract in Nevada Territory; the National Woman's Liberty Loan Committee; and the Roosevelt Women's Democratic Labor Club. Taken from L. James Higgins, *A Guide to the Manuscript Collections at the Nevada Historical Society* (Reno, NV: Nevada Historical Society, 1975).

10,681. Martin, Anne Henrietta
Papers. 1889-1951. 1 carton.
Open. Summary.
Nevada Historical Society.
[Miss] Martin (1875-1951) was president of the Nevada Equal Franchise Society in 1911 and an executive committee member of the Women's Congressional Union, the National American Woman Suffrage Association, and the National Woman's Party; she also taught European history at Nevada State University and ran for the US senate in 1918 and 1920. Personal correspondence; correspondence and other papers regarding venereal disease, family health, and prenatal care; reminiscences and sketchbooks from her years as a student at Bishop Whitaker's School for Girls in Reno; a poem she wrote; reports and pamphlets pertaining to prostitution, the white slave traffic, and obscene publications; printed material concerning the woman suffrage movement, pacifism, and Martin's senatorial campaigns; papers regarding the League of Nations and the Women's International League for Peace and Freedom; and other items. Correspondents include Edna Martin Parratt.

10,682. Mason Family
Papers. 1880-1917. 104 items.
Open. Card catalog.
Nevada Historical Society.
Correspondence details the personal lives and associations of the Mason family, which resided in Reno. The letters are primarily between [Miss] Abby E. Mason (1865-1958), a schoolteacher in Ione City and later Poeville, and John Uerquhart, a miner who worked in Esmerelda County. Also includes letters of her parents Elma Briggs Mason (1842-1934) and Levi S. Mason (1837-1912) and her sisters Harriet "Hattie" Sophia (Mason) [Mrs. William] Mohr (1878-1975) and Edna (Mason) [Mrs. William Henry] Eickbush (1870-1918). Abby Mason later married Orrin Webster McAlpin.

10,683. Moffat, Emma Louise Presser
Papers. 1907-59. 2 folders and 1 vol.
Open. No guide.
Nevada Historical Society.
Correspondence, reminiscences, photos, and other papers of [Mrs. John Andrew] Moffat, the first schoolteacher in Rhyolite, NV, concern her marriage and life in Rhyolite.

10,684. Molan, Libbie
Papers. 1889-1928. 193 items.
Open. Published guide.
Nevada Historical Society.
Correspondence and other papers of Hannah Elizabeth "Libbie" [Mrs. Ed M.] Emmons [Mrs. Thomas] Molan (1843?-1935) concern financial matters, mine holdings in central Nevada, and her divorce from Ed M. Emmons and subsequent division of property. Taken from L. James Higgins, *A Guide to the Manuscript Collections at the Nevada Historical Society* (Reno, NV: Nevada Historical Society, 1975).

10,685. Near and Far Folk Dance Club
Records. 1953-70. 1 carton.
Open. No guide.
Nevada Historical Society.
Constitution, minutes, treasurer's book, correspondence, membership lists, publicity records, scrapbooks, and a guest book of this Reno group, founded in 1953 and dissolved in 1970.

10,686. Nenzel, Ora Adelaid
Oral history. 1963. 1 tape.
Open. No guide.
Nevada Historical Society.
Interview in which [Mrs. Joseph] Nenzel discusses the founding of Rochester, NV, and its development into a mining community, the flood at Seven Troughs, NV, and Mazuma, NV, and life in Jessup, NV.

10,687. Nevada Equal Franchise Society
Records. 1909-19. 1 carton.
Open. No guide.
Nevada Historical Society.
Bylaws, annual reports, a president's report, minutes, correspondence, manuscripts, press releases, history, invitations, articles, clippings, published items, and other records of the Society pertain to woman suffrage, the Society's successor the Nevada Women's Civic League, and various state and national organizations, such as the National Woman's party, the Nevada Voter's Club, the Men's League for Woman Suffrage of the State of Nevada, and the Nevada Association of Women Opposed to Equal Suffrage. Includes correspondence with and records concerning Anne H. Martin, [Miss] Jeanne E. Wier, Anna Howard Shaw, Katherine Mackay, Felice Cohn, the Society's first president Margaret Stanislawsky, and Carrie Chapman Catt.

10,688. Nevada Federation of Business and Professional Women's Clubs
Records. 1929-75. 45 cartons.
Open. Published guide.
Nevada Historical Society.
Minutes, reports, financial and membership records, and other material of this organization founded in 1929 to promote education in industrial, scientific, and vocational areas for women in business and the professions. Also includes reports and other records from local chapters in Nevada. The membership records specify the occupations of members. See L. James Higgins, *A Guide to the Manuscript Collections at the Nevada Historical Society* (Reno, NV: Nevada Historical Society, 1975).

10,689. Nevada Federation of Women's Clubs
Records. 1913-72. 11 cartons and 4 vols.
Open. No guide.
Nevada Historical Society.
The Federation was founded in 1913 to unite for combined action all clubs in Nevada concerned with literary, artistic, musical, philanthropic, civic, scientific, or educational purposes; it included such groups as the Twentieth Century Club of Reno, the Ely Women's Club, the Sparks PTA, the Carson City Leisure Hour Club, and the Toyiabe Literary Club. Contains minutes, reports, correspondence, scrapbooks, publications, and other records of the Federation, including reports from individual groups and correspondence between Federation officers and member groups. The Federation sponsored high school essay contests, an educational traffic safety program, art contests, and the publication of Nevada poetry. In addition, the Federation promoted conservation of natural resources and restoration of usable or historic sites.

10,690. Nevada Native Daughters
Oral history. 1956. 1 tape.
Open. Published guide.
Nevada Historical Society.
Interviews with members of the organization about their early lives in Nevada. See L. James Higgins, *A Guide to the Manuscript Collections at the Nevada Historical Society* (Reno, NV: Nevada Historical Society, 1975).

10,691. Nevada State Children's Home
Records. 1870-1900. 1 box.
Open. Published guide.
Nevada Historical Society.
Correspondence, a list of residents, and other records of the Home pertain to its operation and the education of children living there. See L. James Higgins, *A Guide to the Manuscript Collections at the Nevada Historical Society* (Reno, NV: Nevada Historical Society, 1975).

10,692. Nevada State Council of Defense
Records. 1918-46. 22 boxes.
Open. Published guide.
Nevada Historical Society.
Minutes, correspondence, and other records of the two Nevada agencies created during WWI and WWII to coordinate civil defense programs on a state and county level. Contains information regarding civilian mobilization, evacuation contingency plans, farm labor programs, the abolition of prostitution during WWII, victory gardens, child care, conscientious objectors, and the American National Red Cross. Correspondents include Florence B. Bovett and Clara S. Beatty. See L. James Higgins, *A Guide to the Manuscript Collections at the Nevada Historical Society* (Reno, NV: Nevada Historical Society, 1975).

10,693. Nevers, Henrietta
Papers. 1885. 2-page item.
Open. Published guide.
Nevada Historical Society.
Letter that Nevers wrote to her cousin Sarah Josephine Evans Burton about family matters and the winter in Carson City, NV, as well as her support for women's suffrage. Taken from L. James Higgins, *A Guide to the Manuscript Collections at the Nevada Historical Society* (Reno, NV: Nevada Historical Society, 1975).

10,694. Newspapers
Collection. Nd. No size given.
Open. No guide.
Nevada Historical Society.
Microfilm of newspapers from every county in Nevada.

10,695. Ormsby, Augusta
Papers. 1868. 10 pp.
Open. Published guide.
Nevada Historical Society.
Diary of Ormsby concerning her journey by wagon train from Arkansas through Kansas and New Mexico to Los Angeles contains an historical sketch of the Ormsby family. Taken from L. James Higgins, *A Guide to the Manuscript Collections at the Nevada Historical Society* (Reno, NV: Nevada Historical Society, 1975).

10,696. Patrick, Mrs. Edward Thomas
Papers. 1904-17. 1 box.
Open. Published guide.
Nevada Historical Society.
Scrapbook that Patrick kept at Goldfield and during trips to Los Angeles and Illinois. See L. James Higgins, *A Guide to the Manuscript Collections at the Nevada Historical Society* (Reno, NV: Nevada Historical Society, 1975).

10,697. Patton, Arrilla
Papers. 1889. 2 items.
Open. Published guide.
Nevada Historical Society.
Family correspondence of Patton and her discharge certificate from the Woman's Relief Corps. Taken from L. James Higgins, *A Guide to the Manuscript Collections at the Nevada Historical Society* (Reno, NV: Nevada Historical Society, 1975).

10,698. Peterson, Mrs. Edward C.
Oral history. 1967. 1 tape.
Open. Published guide.
Nevada Historical Society.
Interview in which Peterson, a Nevada resident, discusses the family of George Washington Gale Ferris, Sr., in Illinois and Nevada, the invention of the Ferris wheel, and Carson Valley history. See L. James Higgins, *A Guide to the Manuscript Collections at the Nevada Historical Society* (Reno, NV: Nevada Historical Society, 1975).

10,699. Photographs
Collection. Nd. 39 drawers (ca. 117 ft.).
Open. No guide.
Nevada Historical Society.
Photos regarding Nevada and its history include family photos and photos of miscellaneous women.

10,700. Protestant Episcopal Church in the U.S.A.
Records. 1862-1969. 27 boxes.
Open. Published guide.
Nevada Historical Society.
Collection of the Nevada diocese of this church contains administrative records; cash receipts; registers of services, births, burials, confirmations, marriages, and baptisms; correspondence; photos; scrapbooks; Church histories; and Church literature representing 32 Nevada towns, including Carson City, Ely, Goldfield, Las Vegas, Reno, Sparks, Tempuite, Tonopah, Winnemucca, and Virginia City. Also includes material pertaining to the bishop of the diocese, Camp Galilee and other Church groups, and annual meetings. See L. James Higgins, *A Guide to the Manuscript Collections at the Nevada Historical Society* (Reno, NV: Nevada Historical Society, 1975).

10,701. Purdy, Bertha
Papers. Nd. 1 tape.
Open. Published guide.
Nevada Historical Society.
Two songs that [Mrs.] Purdy composed and performed to express her admiration for Nevada pioneers. See L. James Higgins, *A Guide to the Manuscript Collections at the Nevada Historical Society* (Reno, NV: Nevada Historical Society, 1975).

10,702. Rader, Iva
Oral history. 1962. 1 tape.
Open. Published guide.
Nevada Historical Society.
Interview in which [Mrs.] Rader describes her grandmother Lucinda Duncan's trip west in 1863, her illness, her death, and the legend surrounding the Maiden's Grave. See L. James Higgins, *A Guide to the Manuscript Collections at the Nevada Historical Society* (Reno, NV: Nevada Historical Society, 1975).

10,703. Red Cross Society
Records. 1898. 1 item.
Open. Published guide.
Nevada Historical Society.
Letter in which Captain Charles H. Stoddard, commander of Company C of the Nevada Volunteers, was asked to help establish a curfew for young girls visiting the temporary base at Carson City. The letter was signed by Amy Cohn, Jennie Keyser, and Martha E. Schulz, and endorsed by the Society's state president Hedley F. Lemmon. See L. James Higgins, *A Guide to the Manuscript Collections at the Nevada Historical Society* (Reno, NV: Nevada Historical Society, 1975).

10,704. Reno, Sparks, and Carson City Garden Clubs
Records. 1948-69. 3 vols.
Open. Published guide.
Nevada Historical Society.
Scrapbooks of these Nevada clubs contain clippings and ephemera pertaining to flower shows and

improved methods of horticulture. See L. James Higgins, *A Guide to the Manuscript Collections at the Nevada Historical Society* (Reno, NV: Nevada Historical Society, 1975).

10,705. Reno Women's Civic Club
Records. 1944-59. 2 folders and 1 vol.
Open. Published guide.
Nevada Historical Society.
Articles of incorporation, constitution, bylaws, minutes, and correspondence of the Club, founded in 1944. See L. James Higgins, *A Guide to the Manuscript Collections at the Nevada Historical Society* (Reno, NV: Nevada Historical Society, 1975).

10,706. Republican Party
Records. 1952-72. 3 boxes and 2 vols.
Open. Published guide.
Nevada Historical Society.
Minutes, delegate election certificates, voter registration lists, lists of financial supporters, a scrapbook of clippings, and other records of the Republican party in Nevada. Includes records of state conventions and of the central committees of Washoe and Storey counties. See L. James Higgins, *A Guide to the Manuscript Collections at the Nevada Historical Society* (Reno, NV: Nevada Historical Society, 1975).

10,707. Retired Teachers of Nevada, Washoe Unit, Incorporated
Records. 1863-1973. 5 cartons and 2 vols.
Open. Published guide.
Nevada Historical Society.
Tapes of interviews, correspondence, scrapbooks, and other records of this organization founded in 1863 to record the history of education in Nevada, particularly in Washoe County. Contains reminiscences of pioneer educators in Nevada and a manuscript written by Mildred L. Swift on the history of home economics at the University of Nevada. Also includes records pertaining to the formation, finances, and membership of the Retired Teachers of Nevada, the Western Nevada Teachers' Association, and the Nevada Education Association as well as minutes, financial records, and census and attendance records from ca. 1863 to 1907 of the Anderson school district and the Glendale School, both in Truckee Meadows. See L. James Higgins, *A Guide to the Manuscript Collections at the Nevada Historical Society* (Reno, NV: Nevada Historical Society, 1975).

10,708. Roberts, Belle
Oral history. 1965-67. 2 tapes.
Open. Published guide.
Nevada Historical Society.
Interviews in which [Mrs.] Roberts discusses her family's history; her parents' settlement at Austin, NV; ranching near Austin; memories of Emma Wixom, known as Emma Nevada, and her father W. W. Wixom, a physician; social life in Austin; and historical landmarks in the area. See L. James Higgins, *A Guide to the Manuscript Collections at the Nevada Historical Society* (Reno, NV: Nevada Historical Society, 1975).

10,709. Rose Garden Club
Records. 1951-69. 1 carton.
Open. Published guide.
Nevada Historical Society.
Minutes, correspondence, and other records of the Reno and Sparks, NV, chapters of the Club, which sponsored flower shows and studied new trends in horticulture. Also includes records of the Petal Pushers Club. See L. James Higgins, *A Guide to the Manuscript Collections at the Nevada Historical Society* (Reno, NV: Nevada Historical Society, 1975).

10,710. Sawyer, Byrd Wall
Papers. 1958-60. 264 items.
Open. Published guide.
Nevada Historical Society.
Correspondence and other papers of Sawyer, a midwife, pertain to her research into Nevada history and the history of midwifery in the state. Includes an MA thesis from the University of Nevada at Reno regarding labor conditions in Tonopah, NV, and Goldfield, NV, particularly the strikes of the Industrial Workers of the World and the Western Federation of Miners, state intervention, and the results of these events. See L. James Higgins, *A Guide to the Manuscript Collections at the Nevada Historical Society* (Reno, NV: Nevada Historical Society, 1975).

10,711. Sermon
Papers. Nd. 6-page item.
Open. Published guide.
Nevada Historical Society.
A religious sermon concerning the history of divorce, gambling, and prostitution in Nevada and prostitution's effects on the state's economy and commonwealth. Taken from L. James Higgins, *A Guide to the Manuscript Collections at the Nevada Historical Society* (Reno, NV: Nevada Historical Society, 1975).

10,712. Shannon, Phillip E.
Papers. 1876. 3 items.
Open. Published guide.
Nevada Historical Society.
Deed by which Shannon (1827-95) sold his interest in the Victoria Mining Company, Virginia Mining District, to [Miss] Martha Jackson, together with an explanatory note concerning Jackson. Taken from L. James Higgins, *A Guide to the Manuscript Collections at the Nevada Historical Society* (Reno, NV: Nevada Historical Society, 1975).

10,713. Sharp, Lewis, and Sharp, Florence Beatrice Wines
Papers. Ca. 1964. 45 items.
Open. Published guide.
Nevada Historical Society.
Lewis Sharp and his wife Florence Beatrice Wines Sharp are authors. Monographs contain reminiscences and biographical sketches of Lewis Sharp's parents Lewis Sharp, Sr., and his wife (1884-) and Margaret Taylor Wines (1846-?) and her husband Ira Dern Wines, all of whom were pioneer ranchers in Ruby Valley. Also includes essays Florence Sharp wrote about the Paiute and Shoshoni Indians. See L. James Higgins, *A Guide to the Manuscript Collections at the Nevada Historical Society* (Reno, NV: Nevada Historical Society, 1975).

10,714. Silver State Historical Society
Oral history. Nd. 11 tapes.
Open. Published guide.
Nevada Historical Society.
Interviews containing reminiscences of older residents of Tonopah and Goldfield, NV. Women interviewed include Elizabeth Williams Barndt, Mary McCann Sharp, Ella Humphrey, Winefred Eason, Charlotte Stimler Nay, Emma Bowler Welsch, Lida Gilbert, Vassie Cline, Rose Walters, and Imogene Irwin Vanover. See L. James Higgins, *A Guide to the Manuscript Collections at the Nevada Historical Society* (Reno, NV: Nevada Historical Society, 1975).

10,715. Smith, Ida Sauer
Oral history. 1957. 2 tapes.
Open. Published guide.
Nevada Historical Society.
Interview in which Smith discusses Sauer family history, life in Washoe City and Washoe Valley, ranching, lumbering, her marriage, the Smith family brick business in Reno, and early Reno. See L. James Higgins, *A Guide to the Manuscript Collections at the Nevada Historical Society* (Reno, NV: Nevada Historical Society, 1975).

10,716. Society of Nevada Pioneers
Records. 1911-15. Ca. 0.5 in.
Open. Published guide.
Nevada Historical Society.
Correspondence and membership records of the Society. Includes letters in which early pioneers describe their journeys to and settlement in Nevada. See L. James Higgins, *A Guide to the Manuscript Collections at the Nevada Historical Society* (Reno, NV: Nevada Historical Society, 1975).

10,717. Soldo, Betty Lougaris
Papers. 1974. 95-page item.
Open. Published guide.
Nevada Historical Society.
MA thesis that Soldo wrote for California State College at Fullerton regarding female entertainers on the Comstock Lode in Virginia City, NV, from 1865 to 1880. Includes information concerning Caroline Chapman, Sarah Winnemucca, Lotta Crabtree, Annie Yeamans, Blanche Chapman, Ella Chapman, Emma Nevada, and Mazeppa. See L. James Higgins, *A Guide to the Manuscript Collections at the Nevada Historical Society* (Reno, NV: Nevada Historical Society, 1975).

10,718. Stark, Elizabeth
Papers. Nd. 10 items.
Open. Published guide.
Nevada Historical Society.
Essay by Stark about Mary Stanton, an Ely Indian healer, and a statement by Stanton concerning her powers of communication with spirits and the ways in which she used spirits to heal the sick. Also contains clippings concerning Stanton and copies of Velma Stevens Truett's "The Sun God Smiled." Taken from L. James Higgins, *A Guide to the Manuscript Collections at the Nevada Historical Society* (Reno, NV: Nevada Historical Society, 1975).

10,719. Stewart, Helen Jane Wiser
Papers. 1869-1948. 1 box.
Open. Published guide.
Nevada Historical Society.
Personal and business papers, including correspondence, of Stewart (1854-1926) concern the death of her husband Archibald Stewart, raising her family, and operating a cattle ranch. Known as "the First Lady of Las Vegas," she was active in the establishment of that town and its early government. See L. James Higgins, *A Guide to the Manuscript Collections at the Nevada Historical Society* (Reno, NV: Nevada Historical Society, 1975).

10,720. Summerfield, Marie Louise
Papers. 1919-37. 1 carton.
Open. Published guide.
Nevada Historical Society.
Correspondence, scrapbooks, theater and concert programs, and other papers of [Mrs.] Summerfield, who was active in the Republican party and the Order of the Eastern Star; she also was a member of the American National Red Cross and the Nevada Federation of Women's Clubs. Includes a history of her grandparents Henry Douglas and Margaret (Blackburn) Douglas. See L. James Higgins, *A Guide to the Manuscript Collections at the Nevada Historical Society* (Reno, NV: Nevada Historical Society, 1975).

10,721. Toogood, Mona Keig Lake
Oral history. 1968. 1 tape.
Open. Published guide.
Nevada Historical Society.
Interview in which [Mrs.] Toogood discusses her memories of Virginia City, [Miss] Julia Bulette, the hanging of Jean Millean for the murder of Bulette, Toogood's husband's medical career, and Mona Toogood's earlier marriage to Myron Charles Lake, Jr. See L. James Higgins, *A Guide to the Manuscript Collections at the Nevada Historical*

Society (Reno, NV: Nevada Historical Society, 1975).

10,722. Truett, Velma Stevens
Papers. 1861-1966. 2 cartons and 2 vols.
Open. Published guide.
Nevada Historical Society.
Correspondence, research notes, source material, and other papers of [Miss] Truett (1901-67) relating to her study of the livestock industry and cattle brands in Nevada. See L. James Higgins, *A Guide to the Manuscript Collections at the Nevada Historical Society* (Reno, NV: Nevada Historical Society, 1975).

10,723. U.S. Decennial Census
Records. 1850-1900. No size given.
Open. Published guide.
Nevada Historical Society.
All available US census records pertaining to the Nevada area beginning with the 1850 census for Utah Territory and the New Mexico Territorial counties that later became part of Nevada. Includes the 1890 special schedule for Nevada Union Civil War veterans and widows. See L. James Higgins, *A Guide to the Manuscript Collections at the Nevada Historical Society* (Reno, NV: Nevada Historical Society, 1975).

10,724. Voice of America
Oral history. 1972. 6 tapes.
Open. Published guide.
Nevada Historical Society.
Interviews with Nevada residents include discussion with Myrtle Tate Myles about her grandfather's stage line business in central Nevada, Nevada history anecdotes, the writing of the Harold's Club series of *Pioneer Nevada,* the Lost Murphy Mine, social life in various early mining camps, and the decline of Belmont, NV. See L. James Higgins, *A Guide to the Manuscript Collections at the Nevada Historical Society* (Reno, NV: Nevada Historical Society, 1975).

10,725. Webster, Stella N.
Papers. 1885-1919. 21 items.
Open. Published guide.
Nevada Historical Society.
Correspondence and other papers of [Miss] Webster primarily concern her work in education and temperance. Includes correspondence from Frances E. Willard, president of the WCTU. Taken from L. James Higgins, *A Guide to the Manuscript Collections at the Nevada Historical Society* (Reno, NV: Nevada Historical Society, 1975).

10,726. Wheat, Margaret M.
Papers. 1960-67. 2 cartons.
Open. Published guide.
Nevada Historical Society.
Correspondence, minutes, reports, and other papers of Wheat, an anthropologist, archaeologist, and geologist, concern her involvement in the Nevada State Park Advisory Commission and particularly work on the Ichthyosaur Paleontological State Monument, Lake Tahoe, and Lake Lohontan. See L. James Higgins, *A Guide to the Manuscript Collections at the Nevada Historical Society* (Reno, NV: Nevada Historical Society, 1975).

10,727. Wier, Jeanne Elizabeth
Papers. 1893-1950. 25 boxes.
Open. Published guide.
Nevada Historical Society.
Correspondence, business records, and other papers of [Miss] Wier (1870-1950) relate to the women's suffrage movement in Nevada and to her positions as executive secretary of the Nevada Historical Society from 1904 to 1950 and as chairman of the history and political science department of the University of Nevada for nearly 40 years. Includes papers pertaining to Nevada history, archaeology, and anthropology that Wier collected on her travels within the state on behalf of the Historical Society. Wier was born in Iowa and attended Stanford University. Active in the suffrage movement, she also was instrumental in the formation of the Historical Society. See L. James Higgins, *A Guide to the Manuscript Collections at the Nevada Historical Society* (Reno, NV: Nevada Historical Society, 1975).

10,728. Williams, Frances E.
Papers. 1905-46. 34 items.
Open. Card catalog.
Nevada Historical Society.
Williams (1844?-1909) was a physician and a mining pioneer. Includes a letter from Williams to [Miss] Jeanne Elizabeth Wier in which Williams outlines her activities in Nye and Esmeralda counties in Nevada and mentions her property at Gold Mountain, which Wier, the director of the Historical Society, claimed was the "Lost Breyfogle." Also includes reports, 1908-37, on the Royal Flush Mine in Gold Mountain, Esmeralda County, and a letter from Addison N. Clark to Jeanne Wier in which he discusses the history of the property and Wier's assertion that the mine was the "Lost Breyfogle." Also includes a clipping from *The Pueblo Chieftain* from Pueblo, CO, concerning Williams's life.

10,729. Wixom, Emma
Papers. Nd. No size given.
Open. Published guide.
Nevada Historical Society.
Biographical notes, photos, a 20-page scrapbook, and clippings of Wixom (1859-1940), who was known as Emma Nevada. Wixom was married to Raymond S. Palmer, a physician. Taken from L. James Higgins, *A Guide to the Manuscript Collections at the Nevada Historical Society* (Reno, NV: Nevada Historical Society, 1975).

10,730. Women's International League for Peace and Freedom
Records. 1932-35. 161 items.
Open. Published guide.
Nevada Historical Society.
Correspondence, brochures, and other records of the WILPF include the annual and monthly reports of Dorothy Detzer and Mildred Scott Olmsted. See L. James Higgins, *A Guide to the Manuscript Collections at the Nevada Historical Society* (Reno, NV: Nevada Historical Society, 1975).

10,731. Wright, Edgar
Papers. 1930-78. 8 pp.
Open. Card catalog.
Nevada Historical Society.
Consists of "Sandy Bowers' Wife, Queen of the Comstock," a manuscript chapter from Wright's memoirs in which he reminisces about Eilley (Orrum) Bowers (1826-1903) and her activities in 1889 at Camp Alamo in the Baja California region of Mexico. A convert to Mormonism, Bowers eventually married Lemuel Sanford "Sandy" Bowers (1830-68) and, with her husband, owned a mine that became one of the Comstock Lode's richest producers. Eilley Bowers, who died in poverty, earned her living during her last years by telling fortunes.

10,732. Archives
Records. Ca. 1907-?. Ca. 10 in.
Open. No guide.
Saint Mary's Hospital.
Archives of the Hospital, which was founded in 1907, include bylaws; minutes of doctors' staff meetings, 1922-59; registers of patients, 1908-59; research notes; typescript dissertations about the Hospital, which were written by Sister Mary Gerald La Voy and Sister Mary Carl Otten; a history of the Dominican Sisters of Reno from 1877 to 1906; photos; clippings; and other records. Collection also contains other information about the history of the Hospital and those associated with it, including Sister M. Gerard, a registered nurse and supervisor of the obstetrics department for 10 years; Sister Mary Xavier, a registered nurse who served St. Mary's for 50 years in a variety of capacities, including director of nurses and supervisor of surgery; Sister M. Seraphine, who was administrator of the Hospital from 1931 to 1965; and Sister M. Dominga, who was Hospital administrator from 1965 to 1971. The sisters listed above are or were members of the Dominican Nuns of Perpetual Adoration.

10,733. Binion, L. B.
Oral history. 1973. 95-page transcript.
Open. Card catalog.
University of Nevada, Reno, Library, Oral History Project.
Interview with Binion (1904-), a prominent casino owner in Las Vegas, contains a detailed discussion of women card dealers in the casinos.

10,734. Edwards, Elbert
Oral history. 1966. 252-page transcript.
Open. Card catalog.
University of Nevada, Reno, Library, Oral History Project.
Interview in which Edwards (1907-), a teacher, school superintendent, and amateur historian, reminisces about his family's settlement in southern Nevada; he gives a detailed description of his mother's life on a ranch.

10,735. Gardella, Louie A.
Oral history. 1973. 479-page transcript.
Open. Card catalog.
University of Nevada, Reno, Library, Oral History Project.
Interview with Gardella (1908-), a descendant of Italian pioneer farmers who spent his early years on a ranch near Wadsworth, NV. After graduating from college in agriculture, he had a long career with the agricultural extension service. Includes a detailed discussion of the women who engaged in extension service work throughout the state from 1934 to 1968.

10,736. Hug, Procter R., Sr.
Oral history. 1971. 330-page transcript.
Open. Card catalog.
University of Nevada, Reno, Library, Oral History Project.
Interview with Hug (1902-), a teacher, school administrator, and more recently a Nevada state legislator, includes a detailed discussion about the abortion law in Nevada, which he researched while he was a legislator.

10,737. Johnson, Cecyl (Allen)
Oral history. Ca. 1966. 199-page transcript.
Open. Card catalog.
University of Nevada, Reno, Library, Oral History Project.
Interview with [Mrs. James W.] Johnson (1890-1966), a rancher, contains information from family papers about the early pioneers of St. Clair district, where the Allens settled, and includes an Allen genealogy, anecdotes, and historical notes about politics, ranching, and industries in the Fallon, NV, area. Also contains accounts of Johnson's activities and social and cultural events in Churchill county, NV, as well as anecdotes about women teachers and civil servants, including one about Daisy (Allen) White, a Nevada state assemblywoman.

10,738. Kofoed, Leslie S.
Oral history. 1971. 362-page transcript.
Open. Card catalog.
University of Nevada, Reno, Library, Oral History Project.
Interview with Kofoed (1909-), a Lovelock, NV, public relations director for Harolds Club, a Reno gambling casino; head of the Gaming Industry Association of Nevada; a state senator in 1941; and

US marshal for Nevada from 1942 to 1946. Kofoed discusses the point at which women were allowed to become card dealers in the casinos and his recollections of a woman US marshal.

10,739. Lawlor, Glenn Joseph
Oral history. 1970-71. 316-page transcript.
Open. Card catalog.
University of Nevada, Reno, Library, Oral History Project.
Interview with "Jake" Lawlor (1907-), an outstanding athlete who became a high school athletic coach and director of athletics at the University of Nevada, Reno; includes comments on Marion Motley, a man who coached a women's football team. Lawlor also tells an anecdote about women's intercollegiate athletics.

10,740. Miller, Thomas Woodnutt
Oral history. 1965. 251-page transcript.
Open. Card catalog.
University of Nevada, Reno, Library, Oral History Project.
Interview with Miller (1886-1973), who was secretary of state in Delaware from 1913 to 1915 and a member of the US House of Representatives from 1915 to 1917. Includes his comments on Mabel (Walker) Willebrandt, an assistant attorney general who prosecuted him for alien property violation during the Harding administration scandals. Also includes a discussion of his support of women's suffrage legislation in 1915 and the criticism he received from some of his colleagues for his stand, as well as his recollections of Mabel Vernon, a suffragist.

10,741. Nelson, Dwight A.
Oral history. 1970-71. 377-page transcript.
Open. Card catalog and index.
University of Nevada, Reno, Library, Oral History Project.
Interview with Nelson (1911-), who was an educator, a juvenile probation and detention officer in Washoe County, NV, and a Washoe County commissioner. Includes anecdotes about women as juvenile offenders and a description of Helen (Gerbich) [Mrs. Ralph K.] Wittenberg, for whom the juvenile detention facility in Reno was named. Nelson also remarks on his impression of the women who assisted in building the detention center and the ways in which their work made it possible to construct the center.

10,742. Sanford, John
Oral history. 1971. 561-page transcript.
Open. Card catalog.
University of Nevada, Reno, Library, Oral History Project.
Interview in which Sanford (1906-), a newspaperman from 1925 to 1968, comments on women he knew during his career.

10,743. Semenza, Edwin S.
Oral history. 1971. 411-page transcript.
Open. Card catalog.
University of Nevada, Reno, Library, Oral History Project.
Interview with Semenza (1910-), a founder of the Reno Little Theater and theatrical performer, includes anecdotes about women who worked at the Theater. Semenza also was a part-time member of the faculty at the University, served a term on the Reno city council, and later worked in the insurance business.

10,744. White, W. Wallace
Oral history. 1970. 236-page transcript.
Open. Card catalog.
University of Nevada, Reno, Library, Oral History Project.
Interview with White (1905-), a sanitary engineer in the division of public health engineering for the Nevada state department of health, who inspected houses of prostitution prior to WWI. Includes a detailed discussion of legalized prostitution.

10,745. Wooster, Earl
Oral history. 1965. 142-page transcript.
Open. Card catalog.
University of Nevada, Reno, Library, Oral History Project.
Interview with Wooster (1893-1977), an educator in Nevada, includes an account of a woman who in the 1950s became the first black student teacher in Reno schools.

10,746. American Association of University Women
Records. 1917-57. 15 in.
Open. No guide.
University of Nevada, Reno, Library, Special Collections.
Board minutes, scrapbooks, printed programs, bulletins, and invitations of the Reno AAUW, which was founded in 1917.

10,747. American Women's Volunteer Service
Records. 1942-66. 20 in.
Open. No guide.
University of Nevada, Reno, Library, Special Collections.
Board minutes, photos, and scrapbooks containing clippings and memorabilia of the Service's Nevada chapter, which was established in 1942 to recruit and train women for patriotic work.

10,748. Blair, Minnie P. (Nichols)
Papers. 1864-1967. 1 folder and 152-page vol.
Open. Card catalog.
University of Nevada, Reno, Library, Special Collections.
Blair (1886-1973) was a banking and farming partner with her husband Ernest W. Blair in Goldfield, Tonopah, and Fallon, NV. Business and personal correspondence from 1961 to 1964 of the Blairs and a transcript of an interview conducted by Mary Ellen Glass in 1966 and 1967, in which Blair describes her early life in Folsom and Placerville, CA; marrying and moving to Goldfield in 1909; the social, economic, and political affairs of the area; poultry and truck farming on the Atlanta Ranch near Fallon; her husband's banking association with George Wingfield; and business ventures, civic activities, and political affairs. Also contains a copy of an 1864 letter signed by President Abraham Lincoln admitting Nevada to the Union.

10,749. Boyer, Florence M. (Squires) Doherty
Oral history. 1966. 189-page transcript.
Open. Card catalog.
University of Nevada, Reno, Library, Special Collections.
Interview conducted by Mary Ellen Glass with Boyer (1890-), who was the clerk of Clark County, NV, a schoolteacher, and a newspaperwoman. Includes family history and descriptions of the founding, growth, and political figures of Las Vegas; Clark County pioneers, including her father Charles P. Squires; family life in Las Vegas; southern Nevada economics and society; and Boyer's career as county clerk.

10,750. Boyle, Vida Margaret (McClure)
Oral history. Nd. 24 pp.
Open. Card catalog.
University of Nevada, Reno, Library, Special Collections.
Typescript of an interview with Boyle (1880-?), wife of Nevada governor Emmet D. Boyle, conducted by Grace Dangberg with interjections by her mother Mrs. John Dangberg. Contains recollections of hardships while living in the governor's mansion in Carson City.

10,751. Bruns, Eugenia "Jennie" May
Oral history. Nd. 37-page transcript.
Open. Card catalog.
University of Nevada, Reno, Library, Special Collections.
Interview conducted in 1965 and 1966 of Bruns (1877-1970), a schoolteacher in Lander and Lyon counties, NV, and in Alpine County, CA, where she was also superintendent. Includes reminiscences about her girlhood in Empire, NV, life at the University of Nevada (Reno) during the 1890s, her teaching experiences, a trip to Yosemite Valley in 1896, and practices in the rural community where she lived for more than 60 years.

10,752. Coffin, Trenmor
Papers. 1864-1927. 7 ft.
Open. Card catalog.
University of Nevada, Reno, Library, Special Collections.
Correspondence and legal and political papers of Coffin (1848-1904), a lawyer, businessman, Nevada state assemblyman, Republican state central committee member from 1892 to 1898, and resident of Carson City. Contains correspondence from 1891 to 1917 of Coffin's wife Marie Louise Coffin regarding family news and her horoscope.

10,753. Dickerson Family
Papers. 1898-1965. 1 microfilm reel.
Open. Card catalog.
University of Nevada, Reno, Library, Special Collections.
Scrapbook containing correspondence, photos, and clippings of Denver S. Dickerson (1872-?), governor of Nevada from 1908 to 1910 and owner of the *White Pine News,* and of his wife Una Reiley Dickerson, state law librarian. Material relates to Denver Dickerson when he was lieutenant governor and acting governor, to Una Dickerson, and to other family members.

10,754. General Federation of Women's Clubs
Records. 1935. 60-page item.
Open. No guide.
University of Nevada, Reno, Library, Special Collections.
Review of the GFWC's 1935 triennial convention held in Detroit contains reports on the GFWC departments of American citizenship, American home, education, fine arts, international relations, juniors, legislation, press and publicity, and public welfare. The first GFWC triennial convention was held in Chicago in 1892.

10,755. Glass, Mary Ellen (Miller)
Papers. 1967. 1 folder.
Open. Card catalog.
University of Nevada, Reno, Library, Special Collections.
Typescript of Glass (1927-), director of the oral history program at the University of Nevada, Reno, since 1964, contains her account of the founding of the Reno AAUW based on an interview with [Mrs.] Myrtle Hawkins, one of the original members. A list of Reno AAUW presidents from 1917 to 1967 is also included.

10,756. Godbey, Erma O. (Drumm)
Oral history. Nd. 129-page transcript.
Open. Unpublished guide.
University of Nevada, Reno, Library, Special Collections.
Interview conducted in 1966 by Mary Ellen Glass with Godbey (1905-), a housewife and civic leader, describing her early life in Colorado mining camps and in Boulder City, NV, where in 1931 she was the first permanent female resident. Contains biographical information on her husband Thomas Godbey, including accounts of his activities in the state legislature.

10,757. Goldfield Women's Club
Records. 1907-22. 1 vol.
Open. Card catalog.
University of Nevada, Reno, Library, Special Collections.
Minutes of the board of directors of the now defunct Goldfield, NV, Club, founded in 1907 to promote community service and personal betterment through the study of literature, music, art, and the social sciences.

10,758. Gosse, Marguerite H.
Papers. 1960. 1 folder.
Open. Card catalog.
University of Nevada, Reno, Library, Special Collections.
Biography of Gosse, whose later married name was Clark, written by Grace E. Puddington. Puddington was a Nevada legislator who introduced the bill that resulted in the Nurse Practice Act of 1923. The biography includes photos.

10,759. Gould, Margaret (Douglass)
Papers. 1953-67. 1 folder and 8 pp.
Open. Card catalog.
University of Nevada, Reno, Library, Special Collections.
Account written in 1953 by [Mrs. Warren H.] Gould, a civic leader and author, regarding her mother-in-law Prudence Ermina (Hymers) Gould (1867-?), a Nevada pioneer, and Prudence Gould's journey west, business ventures with her husband William Gould, and community activities in later years. Also includes accounts of other Gould family members who came west from Maine in 1869 and settled in Reno in 1876 as well as descriptions of the activities of some of their descendants; these accounts were written for the 1964 Nevada Centennial Committee and include a 1967 postcript.

10,760. Griffen, Gloria Grace
Papers. Nd. 4 boxes.
Open. No guide.
University of Nevada, Reno, Library, Special Collections.
Gloria Grace (Griffen) Cline Harrison (1929-73) was an historian, author, and teacher. Manuscripts and notes for her *Exploring the Great Basin* and *Peter Skene Ogden* and teaching material. She was nominated for a Pulitzer Prize for her first book.

10,761. Gulling, Amy (Thompson)
Oral history. 1965. 131-page transcript.
Open. Card catalog.
University of Nevada, Reno, Library, Special Collections.
Interview with Gulling (1899-), a member of Reno's oldest family; worked for the Republican party from the precinct level to the national committee. Reminiscences regarding Gulling's pioneer grandmother Mrs. Lake and Gulling's mother Mrs. Thompson; school days in Franktown and Reno; Reno buildings and streets at the turn of the century; Gulling's sister Alice Thompson, a physician; Reno social, cultural and political activities; Gulling's participation in national Republican politics; and her title of Nevada Mother of the Year. Gulling retired from political activity in 1964.

10,762. Hazlett, Fanny
Papers. Nd. 1 folder.
Open. Card catalog.
University of Nevada, Reno, Library, Special Collections.
Several historical and reminiscent sketches of Dayton, NV, by Hazlett, a suffrage and civic leader who came to Nevada in 1865.

10,763. Hewes, Clair (Hofer)
Papers. Nd. 1 folder and 17-page vol.
Open. Card catalog.
University of Nevada, Reno, Library, Special Collections.
Reminiscences and transcript of an interview conducted in 1965 of Hewes (1898-), the daughter of western Nevada pioneers Flora Evelyn (Kingsley) Hofer and Theodore R. Hofer. Contains descriptions of the 1852 overland journey of her grandfather Henry Kingsley, his gold mining activity near Placerville, CA, his move to Nevada, and early gold miners in the Comstock area, as well as information about her father, who was superintendent of the US Mint at Carson City, NV. In her interview Hewes discusses her grandmother Marietta Hungerford Dana, who came to Nevada in 1852; her mother; her childhood and social life in Carson City; and the Chinese, Indians, and Jews who resided in the area.

10,764. Lander, Frederick Charles, Family
Papers. Ca. 1858-70. 1 folder.
Open. No guide.
University of Nevada, Reno, Library, Special Collections.
Photos, clippings, and other papers of the family of Frederick W. Lander (?-1863), chief civil engineer for the US government. Contains photos, a program, and clippings regarding an 1859 statue of Virginia Dare, the first child born to English parents in the New World. The statue was sculpted in Rome by Lander's sister Louisa Lander. Frederick Charles Lander later changed his name to Frederick West Lander.

10,765. League of Women Voters
Records. 1951-67. Ca. 6 ft.
Open. Card catalog.
University of Nevada, Reno, Library, Special Collections.
Annual reports, board minutes, financial records, correspondence and communications of the national LWV, correspondence from state and local LWV chapters, research reports, printed material, and local election information.

10,766. Lewers, Robert, and Lewers, Louise
Papers. 1885-1951. 3 in.
Open. No guide.
University of Nevada, Reno, Library, Special Collections.
Correspondence, financial records, photos, certificates, clippings, and printed material concerning primarily the profession, interests, and awards of Robert Lewers (1862-1922), a professor and vice-president of the University of Nevada at Reno from 1906 to 1922. Includes family correspondence of his wife Louise Lewers from ca. 1900 to 1951.

10,767. McFarlin, Mary Ann
Papers. 1923-46. 1 box.
Open. Card catalog.
University of Nevada, Reno, Library, Special Collections.
Records of the estate of McFarlin (1838-1929) include financial records, bank accounts, monthly statements, receipts of spending, and a will written in 1923.

10,768. Martin, Anne Henrietta
Papers. Ca. 1946. 1 folder.
Open. Card catalog.
University of Nevada, Reno, Library, Special Collections.
An 1894 graduate of the University, Martin (1875-1951) later taught history at that institution; she also was involved in suffrage activities from 1909 to 1911, president of the Nevada Equal Franchise Society from 1911 to 1914, and in 1918 the first woman to run for the US Senate, although she was defeated. Manuscript of Martin's recollections of her work in the campaign that resulted in equal suffrage for Nevada in 1914.

10,769. National League of American Pen Women
Records. 1946-71. 5 in.
Open. No guide.
University of Nevada, Reno, Library, Special Collections.
Board minutes, correspondence, manuscripts, scrapbooks, certificates and awards, contest entries, and printed material of the Reno branch of the League, an organization of women involved commercially in writing and the fine arts.

10,770. Nevada Federation of Women's Clubs
Records. 1920-64. 1 box.
Open. Card catalog.
University of Nevada, Reno, Library, Special Collections.
Constitution, bylaws, financial records, correspondence, convention programs, and directories of the state Federation, which was founded in 1908.

10,771. Nevada Federation of Women's Clubs
Records. 1919-55. 2 in.
Open. No guide.
University of Nevada, Reno, Library, Special Collections.
Correspondence from 1920 and printed material of the Federation, which was founded in 1908 for community service and the personal betterment of its members.

10,772. Order of the Eastern Star, Electra Chapter No. 2
Records. 1904-41. 3 vols.
Open. Unpublished guide.
University of Nevada, Reno, Library, Special Collections.
Minutes, a register of members, and a brief history of this Austin, NV, women's auxiliary of the Masonic Order; the Chapter was founded in 1877.

10,773. Priest, Ellen Goodrich
Papers. 1915-68. 18 in.
Open. No guide.
University of Nevada, Reno, Library, Special Collections.
Correspondence, photos, two DAR scrapbooks, certificates, clippings, and printed material of Priest (1894-) relate primarily to her activities as a DAR member. Priest was author of *My Memories of Carson City* (1974).

10,774. Requa, Amy
Papers. 1891-93. 1 folder and 1 vol.
Open. No guide.
University of Nevada, Reno, Library, Special Collections.
Requa (1895?-), a resident of White Pine County, NV, and Reno, was the daughter of Mark Requa, who developed the White Pine Copper industry. Handwritten book of songs, which were not composed by Requa.

10,775. Riegelhuth, Katharine M.
Oral history. Nd. 57-page transcript.
Open. Card catalog.
University of Nevada, Reno, Library, Special Collections.
Interview conducted by Mary Ellen Glass in 1966 and 1967 with Riegelhuth (1876-1973), a teacher of German and English at the University of Nevada, Reno, from 1905 to 1943. Riegelhuth came to the US and Nevada from Germany when she was 4 years old. Reminiscences of her mother Katharina and stepfather Frank Riegelhuth, who was a musician and early resident of Eureka, NV, and descriptions of music and culture in Eureka, student life and educational practices at the University of Nevada (Reno), and the founding of Reno's first maternity home.

10,776. Rives, Henry Macon
Papers. Ca. 1878-1940. 15 in.
Open. No guide.
University of Nevada, Reno, Library, Special Collections.
Correspondence, diaries, financial records, photos, certificates, clippings, and other papers of four generations of the family of Henry M. Rives (1883-1952), a Nevada mining magnate and member of the state tax commission. Contains papers of Margaret Muldoon Morris (1828?-93), wife of James Morris; correspondence of Annie Morris (1860?-?), ca. 1920s; correspondence, 1914-37, of Marguerite Raycraft Rives (1893-), who was involved in dance and elocution and taught grace and culture; correspondence and certificates of Dorothy Raycraft (1898-), ca. 1900-30; and papers, 1878-1918, of Madge Morris Raycraft, mother-in-law of Henry M. Rives, including correspondence, an autograph book, and a report card.

10,777. Rousseau Family
Papers. 1847-1924. 1 box.
Open. Unpublished guide.
University of Nevada, Reno, Library, Special Collections.
Correspondence, financial records, legal documents, photos, albums, certificates, bills, receipts, and clippings of three generations of the Cottle and Rousseau families. Includes correspondence, documents, and certificates of Barzelia Cottle, Rebecca Rich Cottle, Margaret Elizabeth Cottle Rousseau, and Solomon Rousseau. Also contains correspondence, a diploma, University of Nevada (Reno) programs, and an obituary of Margaret Elizabeth Cottle Rousseau's daughter Margaret Elizabeth "Bessie" Rousseau, who died shortly after receiving her degree from the University. Most of the material was generated in Nevada and California.

10,778. Sauer, Alice Edmunds
Oral history. Nd. 2 transcripts (50 pp. each).
Open. Card catalog.
University of Nevada, Reno, Library, Special Collections.
Interviews taped in 1966 and 1967 of Sauer (1877-1972), a teacher. The first contains reminiscences of her childhood in Virginia City, NV, an account of her University of Nevada (Reno) student days, and her subsequent teaching career in Nevada and Montana, as well as biographical sketches of her children. The second interview concerns life, schools, and community members in Virginia City and Washoe Valley, NV.

10,779. Sawyer, Byrd Wall
Papers. 1948-65. 3 in.
Open. No guide.
University of Nevada, Reno, Library, Special Collections.
Sawyer was an author, schoolteacher, historian, and stepmother of Nevada governor Grant Sawyer. Includes correspondence, research notes, biographies of women she compiled along with local histories, 1958 financial records, and a biography of Hannah Keziah Clapp, who was an early Nevada schoolteacher.

10,780. Shellenberger, Frances Jane (Horsley)
Papers. 1963. 66 pp.
Open. Card catalog.
University of Nevada, Reno, Library, Special Collections.
Biography, including a genealogical chart, of Shellenberger (1884-?), an early Nevada resident, was written by her daughter Hope (Shellenberger) Dukes. Shellenberger was born in Ferron, UT, of Mormon immigrants from England. She spent her childhood in Ferron and in Lund and Preston, NV, married in 1904 and moved to Ruth and then Ely, NV, in 1906, ranched in the Snake Valley, and then returned to Ely in 1924. Shellenberger raised 10 daughters.

10,781. Squires, Charles Pemberton
Papers. Nd. 1 microfilm reel.
Open. Card catalog.
University of Nevada, Reno, Library, Special Collections.
Squires (1865-1958), the owner and editor of the *Las Vegas Age,* was instrumental in the building of the Hoover Dam. His wife Delphine (Anderson) Squires (1868-1961) wrote for the *Las Vegas Age,* the *Las Vegas Review-Journal,* and the *Las Vegas Sun.* Consists of Charles and Delphine Squires' manuscript "Las Vegas, Nevada: Its Romance and History," which was written in 1955 and concerns Las Vegas particularly since 1905 when the Squireses arrived in the city.

10,782. Taylor, Maude Sawin
Papers. 1910-64. 1 Hollinger box.
Open. No guide.
University of Nevada, Reno, Library, Special Collections.
Correspondence, certificates, and other papers of Taylor (?-1974), a writer and clubwoman, regarding the Nevada Federation of Women's Clubs and Taylor's title as Nevada Mother of the Year in ca. 1959.

10,783. Twentieth Century Club of Reno
Records. 1931-65. 2 folders.
Open. No guide.
University of Nevada, Reno, Library, Special Collections.
Correspondence, a history, and yearbooks of the Club, which was founded in 1894 to promote culture, education, and the general welfare and to disseminate historical, scientific, and practical knowledge.

10,784. Walsh, Phyllis J.
Oral history. Nd. 144-page transcript.
Open. Card catalog.
University of Nevada, Reno, Library, Special Collections.
Interview taped in 1971 with Walsh (1897-), who attended private schools in New England, enlisted in the French Army during WWI, played tennis professionally, and wrote a sports column for a New York newspaper. She also became a stockbroker, opposed prohibition, and assisted in managing a Nevada ranch during the 1940s and 1950s. Contains her reminiscences of childhood, early days at the S Bar S Ranch, and experiences in Reno, as well as descriptions of her work with the American Women's Volunteer Service, the USO, the American National Red Cross, and other groups.

10,785. White Pine District of the Nevada Library Association
Oral history. 1967. 9 tapes.
Open. No guide.
University of Nevada, Reno, Library, Special Collections.
History of White Pine County as told by several women who are longtime residents of the area includes reminiscences of schoolteaching, social life, and community members.

10,786. Woman's Relief Corps, Department of California and Nevada
Records. 1886-1908. 6 in.
Open. Card catalog.
University of Nevada, Reno, Library, Special Collections.
Minutes, receipt stubs, and a printing block with the seal of this now defunct auxiliary to the Grand Army of the Republic, founded in Carson City, NV, in 1884 to assist the needy.

10,787. Woods, Josie Alma
Papers. 1973. 1 folder.
Open. No guide.
University of Nevada, Reno, Library, Special Collections.
Letters to Mary Ellen Glass written by Woods (1892-), a teacher, dental technician, and Nevada legislator in 1943 and 1945, contain biographical information gathered in preparation for an oral history interview.

NEW HAMPSHIRE

ASHLAND

10,788. Richardson, Mary Fletcher
Papers. 1837-42. 127-page item.
Open. No guide.
Ashland Historical Society.
Journal of Richardson, a Westford, MA, resident, in which she describes trips to Anson, ME, and to Cleveland and Manhattan, OH, where her family lived until her brother's business failed. She also records her family's return to Westford and her marriage, following a courtship of "an hour or two," to Thomas Richardson.

CANAAN

10,789. Local History
Collection. Ca. 1800- . Ca. 5 ft.
Open. No guide.
Canaan Historical Museum.
Correspondence, legal documents, financial ledgers and records, manuscript material of a Civil War soldier, record books, pamphlets, photos, scrapbooks, and clippings document the history of the town of Canaan, which was founded in 1761. Included is an 1844 inventory of property for assessing town school taxes, which shows women as property owners; a receipt book, 1893-94, for a local school, which records women cleaning, teaching, and running boarding houses; individual portrait photos of women; class pictures for the local high school and grammar schools; a group photo taken in ca. 1890 of Mascoma Overalls Factory workers, which included 30 women; and a photo of mica rifters, some of whom were women, employed in local mining during WWI.

CLAREMONT

10,790. Tolles, Mary
Papers. 1871-86. 14 vols.
Open. No guide.
Claremont Historical Society.
Diaries of Tolles (ca. 1840-90), a farmwife, in which she describes her daily routine, including cooking, keeping house, darning, and knitting, and writes about the daily work of the men in the family.

CONCORD

10,791. American Association of University Women, NH Division
Records. 1927-70. 2 ft.
Open. Unpublished guide.
New Hampshire Historical Society.
Minutes, attendance records, a scrapbook containing clippings, and printed items of this division of the AAUW, which was founded in 1927

to provide social and educational activities for women.

10,792. Ayer, Sarah Connell
Papers. 1805-35. 5 vols.
Open. No guide.
New Hampshire Historical Society.
Diary in which [Mrs.] Ayer (1791-1835) describes her daily life in Concord and Bow, NH, and Portland, ME, and her religious feelings. Only two of her six children survived birth or childhood. She became a widow in 1832. The diary was published as *Diary of Sarah Connell Ayer* (Portland: Lefavor-Tower Co., 1910).

10,793. Bartlett, Caroline Gardner
Papers. 1891-1930. 5 boxes.
Access restricted. No guide.
New Hampshire Historical Society.
Papers of [Mrs.] Bartlett (1868-1934?), who was also known as Sister Beatrice. Correspondence pertains to her training and career as a concert singer and voice teacher and is primarily with Madame Lillian Nordica Young and Colonel Henry Mapleson, who was her agent in London. Also contains correspondence and other papers relating to Bartlett's activities in raising funds and obtaining supplies for field hospitals in France during WWI. She was also active in Serbian relief. Other papers from English, French, Canadian, and US sources were collected to disprove the charge that she was a German spy.

10,794. Bartlett, Josiah
Papers. 1761-94. 700 items.
Open. Published and unpublished guides.
New Hampshire Historical Society.
Papers of Bartlett include correspondence of his wife Mary Bartlett, in which she seeks advice from him on business and farm matters while he is at the Continental Congress, gives news of family and friends, and comments on problems in New Hampshire and a runaway slave. Also available on microfilm. See Frank Mevers, ed., *Guide to the Microfilm Edition of the Papers of Josiah Bartlett, 1729-1795* (Concord: New Hampshire Historical Society, 1976).

10,795. Beacham, Sarah
Papers. 1863-1906. 5 items.
Open. No guide.
New Hampshire Historical Society.
Scattered diaries of Beacham (1843-1909), who did piecework in a mill near Ossipee, NH.

10,796. Blair, Mary E.
Papers. 1854-64. 11 items.
Open. No guide.
New Hampshire Historical Society.
Letters to Blair, an author, from poets John Greenleaf Whittier and Lucy Larcom.

10,797. Blake, Effie A.
Papers. Ca. 1870. 1 vol.
Open. No guide.
New Hampshire Historical Society.
Journal of Blake, a schoolteacher in Concord, contains notes on arithmetic and the geography and history of New Hampshire as well as receipts.

10,798. Bridgman, Laura
Papers. 1876-93. 12 items.
Open. No guide.
New Hampshire Historical Society.
Correspondence and clippings of Bridgman (1829-89), a deaf, mute, and blind woman, who was the first pupil at Perkins Institution for the Blind in Watertown, MA. Bridgman's family lived in Aetna, NH.

10,799. Burgum Family
Papers. 1839-1922. Ca. 250 items.
Open. Unpublished guide.
New Hampshire Historical Society.
Family papers include those of Emma Gannell Burgum (1826-1923), who was the adopted daughter of Sarah Thompson, countess of Rumford, and who married John Burgum. Includes her correspondence, scattered diaries dating from 1894 to 1922, a volume of reminiscences, and an autograph album containing poetry.

10,800. Chandler, William E.
Papers. 1829-1917. 22 ft.
Open. Unpublished guide.
New Hampshire Historical Society.
Papers of Chandler, a US senator from New Hampshire, include letters from his wife Lucy L. (Hale) Chandler (1842-1915), the daughter of John Parker Hale who was a US congressman and minister to Spain, to her mother, sister, and friends. Also includes her journals, 1854 and 1867-69. Also contained in the collection is a diary kept by William Chandler's mother Mary Ann Tucker Chandler, 1829-79, in which she recorded births, deaths, trips, and household inventories. Chandler's papers also include correspondence of Mary Baker Eddy, the founder of the First Church of Christ, Scientist, as well as legal papers relating to law suits over the settlement of her estate. Other correspondence of Eddy is located in the Streeter Collection at the Historical Society.

10,801. Chase, Charles
Papers. 1830-74. 300 items.
Open. Unpublished guide.
New Hampshire Historical Society.
Family papers of Chase include pocket diaries of his wife Hannah Chase, which date from 1856 to 1874, and her household accounts. In her diaries she describes family life in Keene, NH. Other papers include letters from Hannah Abby (Chase) [Mrs. George Franklin] Goodnow (1833-?) written to her family in Keene, NH, from Pecatonica and Rockford, IL.

10,802. Clark, Betsey Brickett
Papers. 1846-85. 27 vols.
Open. No guide.
New Hampshire Historical Society.
Collection includes the diary of [Mrs. Nathaniel] Clark, 1855-85. In her diary she comments on family life, the church, weddings, and funerals in Plaistow, NH.

10,803. Corning, Charles R.
Papers. 1861-1921. Ca. 300 items.
Open. No guide.
New Hampshire Historical Society.
Includes a diary kept by Lizzie M. Corning from 1861 to 1873, in which she describes her activities in Concord, NH, and her occasional visits to army camps during the Civil War.

10,804. Cram Family
Papers. 1795-1892. Ca. 300 items.
Open. No guide.
New Hampshire Historical Society.
Letters to Anna Brown Cram (1756-1849), a widow who lived in Exeter, NH, from her children. Also includes the deed and indentures to land in Exeter and Stratham, NH, as well as receipts, notes, and inventories.

10,805. Diary
Papers. 1880. 1 vol.
Open. No guide.
New Hampshire Historical Society.
Diary of a schoolteacher who resided in Milton Mills, NH.

10,806. Diary
Papers. 1860. 1 vol.
Open. No guide.
New Hampshire Historical Society.
Diary of a young girl, who was the daughter of Ephraim Nelson Hidden, a Congregational minister who lived in Candia, NH. In her diary she writes about family matters, visits, and her reading and comments on her poor health.

10,807. Dolloff Family
Papers. 1867-1933. 12 vols.
Open. Unpublished guide.
New Hampshire Historical Society.
Diary in which Myra E. Dolloff (1864-ca. 1933) describes the life of a young girl on a farm and at school in Bridgewater, NH. Also includes an essay Clarice May Elliott, the granddaughter of Myra Dolloff, wrote at age 12 about Elm Farm in Bridgewater.

10,808. Eddy, Mary (Baker)
Papers. 1861-1907. Ca. 500 items.
Open. Unpublished guide.
New Hampshire Historical Society.
Correspondence of [Mrs. Asa Gilbert] Eddy (1821-1910), the founder of the First Church of Christ, Scientist, with her son George Glover and her adopted son E. J. Foster Eddy. Also includes correspondence with George Moses, editor of the *Concord Monitor* in New Hampshire, concerning publications in the newspaper.

10,809. Foster, John Harold
Papers. 1838-1966. 700 items.
Open. Unpublished guide.
New Hampshire Historical Society.
Courtship correspondence of Mary Elliot Foster (?-ca. 1920) while she was at a summer resort in Waterville, NH, and at a winter residence in Plymouth, NH. In the letters, which date from 1908 to 1913, she describes visits to Boston and Chicago and her wedding preparations.

10,810. Giddings, Mary Coult
Papers. 1851-54. 2 vols.
Open. No guide.
New Hampshire Historical Society.
Diary of Giddings, a schoolteacher in Auburn, NH, in which she describes the death of her parents, her marriage, her visits, and her removal to Connecticut.

10,811. Goddard, E.
Papers. Nd. 1 vol.
Open. No guide.
New Hampshire Historical Society.
Diary Goddard kept during the mid-19th century, in which she describes her illness and how she was taken to Concord, NH, to recuperate. She also includes detailed descriptions of the countryside. Another diary by an unknown author is contained in the back of the volume and includes descriptions of traveling.

10,812. Grimes Family
Papers. 1851-65. 100 items.
Open. Unpublished guide.
New Hampshire Historical Society.
Includes letters from Sarah Grimes Smith, a physician's wife who probably lived in De Kalb, IL, to her family in Keene, NH, in which she describes her family life, house, and the Baptist Church.

10,813. Hall, Mary
Papers. 1821-36. 1 vol.
Open. Unpublished guide.
New Hampshire Historical Society.
Diaries Hall, a mill girl, kept in Concord and in Lowell, MA. In the volumes she writes about visits with friends and relatives, deaths, sermons, and the weather in Concord and about her work as a weaver for the Merrimac Corp. in Lowell from 1831 to 1836.

10,814. Ham, Maria G.
Papers. 1839. 8-page item.
Open. No guide.

New Hampshire Historical Society.
Reminiscences that Ham, a resident of Canterbury, NH, wrote about Shakers she had known.

10,815. Hopkins, Marion
Papers. 1851-55. 1 vol.
Open. No guide.
New Hampshire Historical Society.
Diary in which Hopkins, a mill girl from Sunapee, NH, describes family visits, deaths and illnesses, and trips to Boston and Charlestown, MA. Hopkins worked in a textile mill in Manchester, NH, and boarded in Amoskeag Foundation #12. She also did leather piecework at home.

10,816. Hutchins, Ephraim
Papers. 1777-1919. Ca. 1000 items.
Open. Unpublished guide.
New Hampshire Historical Society.
Includes correspondence of Elizabeth Hutchins [Mrs. Augustus] Schutz, a resident of Concord, dating from 1864 to 1871. Her letters describe her life and the country around Coquimbo, Chile, where her husband had been appointed US consul.

10,817. Kelly, John
Papers. 1736-1860. Ca. 142 items.
Open. Unpublished guide.
New Hampshire Historical Society.
Includes diaries kept by Lavina Bayley Kelly Cilley, 1829-38, when she was a young girl in New Hampshire.

10,818. Ladies Anti-Slavery Society of Dover
Records. 1835-66. 2 vols.
Open. No guide.
New Hampshire Historical Society.
Constitution and minutes of this Dover, NH, antislavery group, which was founded in ca. 1835. In 1840 the Society reorganized and became the Dover Anti-Slavery Sewing Circle. Also includes volumes pertaining to the Loudon Village Anti-Slavery Sewing Circle and the South New Market Anti-Slavery Society.

10,819. Livermore, Elizabeth A.
Papers. 1862-66. 2 vols.
Open. No guide.
New Hampshire Historical Society.
Diary in which Livermore (1818-?) describes life in Milford, NH, during the Civil War, her work for the Soldiers Aid Society, and news of the war and politics. She also expresses interest in letters from her brother Leonard, who was a minister in Cambridge, MA, and her nephew Captain Thomas Leonard Livermore of the 5th New Hampshire Volunteers.

10,820. New Hampshire Federation of Women's Clubs
Records. 1895-1971. 9 ft.
Open. Unpublished guide.
New Hampshire Historical Society.
Minutes and bulletins of the New Hampshire Federation.

10,821. Niles
Papers. 1905-35. 4 vols.
Open. No guide.
New Hampshire Historical Society.
Diaries of Bertha and Mary Niles, residents of Concord who were the daughters of William W. Niles, Episcopal bishop of the diocese of New Hampshire from 1832 to 1914. In the volumes they describe their art lessons, household activities, and visits.

10,822. Parrott
Papers. 1792-1878. 2500 items.
Open. Unpublished guide.
New Hampshire Historical Society.
Includes correspondence of Sarah Parrott (?-1886), a resident of Portsmouth, NH, chiefly letters to her father John Fabyan Parrott when he was in Washington, DC, in 1817. In her letters she writes about family matters, social life in Portsmouth, and political gossip.

10,823. Pierce, Franklin
Papers. 1820-1974. 6 ft.
Open. Published and unpublished guides.
New Hampshire Historical Society.
Includes letters from Jane Means (Appleton) Pierce (1806-63), who was married to President Franklin Pierce (1804-69), to her husband and family, especially the Aikens in Andover, MA. In her letters she describes family matters, her health, and occasionally Franklin Pierce's political activities and life in Washington, DC. Also includes correspondence and memorabilia of Mary Pierce (1883-1971) and Susan Pierce (?-1974), grandnieces of Franklin Pierce, which pertain to President Pierce and the Pierce homestead in Hillsborough, NH. Also available on microfilm. See *Index to the Franklin Pierce Papers* (Washington, DC: The Library of Congress, Presidents' Papers, Index Series, Manuscript Division, 1962).

10,824. Piper, Lizzie H.
Papers. 1866-67. 2 vols.
Open. No guide.
New Hampshire Historical Society.
Notebooks of Piper, a schoolteacher, contain a diary, accounts, and a school register.

10,825. Proctor, Edna Dean
Papers. 1845-1922. 424 items.
Open. Unpublished guide.
New Hampshire Historical Society.
Correspondence of [Miss] Proctor (1829-1923), a poet, chiefly relates to her poetry. Correspondents include Henry Ward Beecher, Henry Wadsworth Longfellow, John Greenleaf Whittier, and William E. Chandler, a New Hampshire politician.

10,826. Rawson, Marion Nicholl
Papers. 1937-56. 30 items.
Open. No guide.
New Hampshire Historical Society.
Letters from [Mrs.] Rawson, an author, to George Marsh, a pastor, and his wife Jean Marsh, who were residents of East Alstead, NH, where Rawson had a summer home. In the letters she discusses the activities of the church, her family, and the historical society. The letters contain poems she wrote for the Marshes.

10,827. Spooner, Mrs. J. Walter
Papers. 1862-70. 1 vol.
Open. No guide.
New Hampshire Historical Society.
Journal of Spooner, a resident of Concord, in which she records things her baby Maud said and Christmas presents she received.

10,828. Stewart, Helen Augusta
Papers. 1871-90. 7 vols.
Open. No guide.
New Hampshire Historical Society.
Diary of Stewart (1849-1935), a teacher in Concord, in which she describes concerts, lectures, church matters, visits, and trips. Stewart details her studies and activities at Wellesley College, from which she graduated with the first graduating class in 1879. Later she traveled west.

10,829. Sturvant
Papers. 1861-1953. 50 items.
Open. Unpublished guide.
New Hampshire Historical Society.
Includes a diary kept in 1890 by Lucy Johnson [Mrs. Henry C.] Sturvant (?-1919 or 1920), in which she tells about summer camping in tents on Lake Sunapee, NH. In order to get to Sunapee she traveled by train, steamer, and row boat. Includes a photo.

10,830. Thaxter, Celia
Papers. 1870-91. 15 items.
Open. Unpublished guide.
New Hampshire Historical Society.
Correspondence and poems of Thaxter (1835-94), a poet. The correspondence, which concerns publications and invitations, is from the period when she lived on the Isles of Shoals, NH.

10,831. Thompson, Benjamin
Papers. 1747-1852. Ca. 350 items.
Open. Unpublished guide.
New Hampshire Historical Society.
Includes papers of Sarah Thompson (1774-1852), countess of Rumford, who was the daughter of Sir Benjamin Thompson, count of Rumford, a scientist and inventor who became a Loyalist and moved to London and the Continent. Sarah Thompson later returned to Concord. Contains letters from Sir Charles Blagden and Comtesse de Nogarola, extracts from her father's letters, an inventory of possessions, and business papers.

10,832. Webster, Daniel
Papers. 1798-1852. 3 boxes and 20 vols.
Open. Unpublished guide.
New Hampshire Historical Society.
Contains correspondence of Grace (Fletcher) Webster (1781-1828), who was married to Daniel Webster, a lawyer and secretary of state, concerning such personal matters as her family, children, and health. The Websters were residents of New Hampshire and Marshfield, MA.

10,833. Wheeler, Martha A.
Papers. 1900-01. 3 items.
Open. No guide.
New Hampshire Historical Society.
Letters written to Wheeler from China relating to conditions there and the siege of Tientsin.

10,834. Wilson, James, Jr.
Papers. 1835-73. 12 ft.
Open. Unpublished guide.
New Hampshire Historical Society.
Contains correspondence of Mary Elizabeth (Wilson) Sherwood (1826-1903), an author and social arbiter, who was the daughter of James Wilson, Jr. The oldest of Wilson's children, she assumed the position of the lady of the house after her mother died in 1848. In some letters she describes daily family life in Keene, NH, and the family's financial difficulties. After her marriage in 1851, her letters concern her social position and personal life in New York City. Sherwood published poems and short stories in periodicals and books.

10,835. Beach, Amy Marcy (Cheney)
Papers. 1929-32. 19 items.
Open. No guide.
New Hampshire State Library.
Letters from [Mrs. Henry Harris Aubrey] Beach (1867-1944), a composer and pianist, to [Miss] Ruth Whittier. Beach played with the Boston Symphony and later gave concerts of her own works in many large cities.

10,836. International Order of the King's Daughters and Sons, New Hampshire Branch
Records. 1897- . 3 vols.
Access restricted. No guide.
New Hampshire State Library.
Record books of the secretary of the Order.

10,837. League of Women Voters, New Hampshire
Records. Nd. 1 drawer.
Access restricted. No guide.
New Hampshire State Library.
Records of the League.

10,838. New Hampshire Federation of Garden Clubs
Records. 1944-51. 5 vols.
Access restricted. No guide.
New Hampshire State Library.
Scrapbooks of the Federation.

10,839. New Hampshire League of Nursing Education
Records. 1920-34. 1 vol.
Access restricted. No guide.
New Hampshire State Library.
Record book.

DOVER

10,840. Daughters of the American Revolution, Margery Sullivan Chapter
Records. 1896- . Ca. 110 items.
Open. Unpublished guide.
Dover Public Library.
Program booklets containing a constitution; bylaws; regent's, membership, and state officers' lists; a chapter calender; annual conference booklets; yearbooks; and continental congress booklets of the New Hampshire DAR, which was founded in 1896.

10,841. Dover Women's Club
Records. 1899- . Ca. 150 items.
Open. Unpublished guide.
Dover Public Library.
Constitution, bylaws, a history, notes, scrapbooks, committee and membership lists, calendars, and programs of the Club, which was founded in 1899 to allow its members to explore historical, cultural, literary, musical, and artistic interests through monthly meetings and lectures.

10,842. Garden Clubs of Dover
Records. 1928-43. 16 items.
Open. Unpublished guide.
Dover Public Library.
Program booklets and a 1932 scrapbook of this organization, which was founded in 1928 to promote gardening and flower cultivation and to improve the community through horticulture.

10,843. Lesbian Club
Records. 1901-02. 1 item.
Open. Unpublished guide.
Dover Public Library.
Program booklet of the Club, a women's social organization which promoted cultural knowledge through the presentation of monthly programs on foreign lands. The 1901-02 topic was French art, history, literature, and music.

10,844. Ricker, Marilla Marks (Young)
Papers. 1895-1920. 10 items.
Open. Unpublished guide.
Dover Public Library.
Papers of [Mrs. John] Ricker (1840-1920), a teacher, lawyer, and suffragist, include photos, biographical sketches, clippings of articles by and about her, and her books *The Four Gospels* (East Aurora, NY: 1911) and *I Don't Know—Do You?* (East Aurora, NY: 1916). Ricker attempted to vote for city selectmen in 1870 and tried each election day for the next 30 years. She was admitted to the bar in Washington, DC, in 1882 and worked for prisoners' rights. In 1890 she became the first woman to be admitted to the bar in New Hampshire. She was a candidate for the New Hampshire governorship in 1910, vice-president of the National Legislative League, and president of the New Hampshire Woman Suffrage Association.

10,845. Tuesday Club
Records. 1892-1937. 46 items.
Open. Unpublished guide.
Dover Public Library.
Rules and bylaws, secretary's and treasurer's book, and membership lists of the Club, a women's social organization founded in 1892 to broaden the education of the Dover woman through the exploration of such topics as Africa, South America, notable books, modern poetry, the Presidents, and the Bible.

10,846. Women of Dover
Collection. Ca. 1900. 3 items.
Open. Unpublished guide.
Dover Public Library.
Manuscripts given to the Northam colonists by historian John Scales, a resident of Dover. One manuscript pertains to Christine Otis Baker (1689-1773), a tavern owner who escaped from "Romish" priests in French Canada who wanted her to become a nun. She traveled 160 miles by canoe to reach Dover where she married Colonel Baker and ran the local tavern for nearly 40 years. Another relates to Margery Sullivan (1714-1801), the wife of General John Sullivan and mother of a governor of New Hampshire. She is described as a shrewish woman who drove her husband out of his home in the summer of 1742, but then placed an advertisement in the Boston papers pleading for him to return. The local chapter of the DAR is named after her. The other manuscript relates to Quaker women and gives an account of Alice Ambrose, Mary Tomkins, and Ann Coleman, Quaker preachers who were tied to the back of a cart and whipped for their faith. Also includes an account of Elizabeth Hooton (1611?-68?), a Quaker preacher driven from Dover.

DURHAM

10,847. Thompson, Mary Pickering
Papers. 1825-94. No size given.
Open. Unpublished guide.
Durham Historic Association Museum.
Correspondence, family biographies, articles, and other papers of Thompson (1825-94), a teacher, writer, traveler, and scholar. Includes pressed plants and flowers from all over the world, items pertaining to local history, and clipped signatures of famous people.

10,848. Barker, Shirley
Papers. Ca. 1956-60. 1.5 ft.
Open. Unpublished guide.
University of New Hampshire Library, Special Collections.
Manuscripts and proofs of Barker (1911-65), a New Hampshire author, editor, and librarian, of her novels *Liza Bowe* (1956), *Swear By Apollo* (1958), and *The Last Gentleman* (1960).

10,849. Durham Tuesday Afternoon Club
Records. 1910-74. 0.5 ft.
Open. No guide.
University of New Hampshire Library, Special Collections.
Constitutions, minutes of meetings, and programs of the Club, a women's social group.

10,850. Hubbard, Margaret Carson
Papers. Ca. 1934-74. 8 ft.
Open. Unpublished guide.
University of New Hampshire Library, Special Collections.
Correspondence, manuscript items, scrapbooks, clippings, and maps of Hubbard (ca.1907-), a journalist, traveler, and writer who specializes in African culture. Hubbard raised a family alone while pursuing her own career interests.

10,851. Lamson
Collection. 1817-1978. 1450 vols.
Open. Unpublished guide.
University of New Hampshire Library, Special Collections.
Manuscripts, books, pamphlets, and other items collected by the Piscataqua Pioneers, a genealogical association of persons descended from settlers of the Piscataqua River basin in southeastern New Hampshire and southwestern Maine. The group emphasizes the study of New Hampshire genealogy and local history. Also includes genealogies, histories, and clippings in proceedings books of the Pioneers. The collection is named for Albert Henry Lamson (1862-1941), a judge who was a founder of the organization and its secretary from 1905 to 1941.

10,852. Manton-MacDowell Colony
Collection. 1880-1957. 3 ft.
Access restricted. Unpublished guide.
University of New Hampshire Library, Special Collections.
MacDowell Colony, an artists' colony in Peterborough, NH, was established by Marian Griswold (Nevins) MacDowell (1857-1956) in 1907 as a memorial to her husband Edward MacDowell, a composer. Contains correspondence, essays about the Colony, music manuscripts, photos, and clippings, which pertain primarily to the MacDowells. Includes letters from Marian MacDowell to composer Robert Manton.

10,853. New Hampshire Women Writers
Collection. 1877- . 2 ft.
Open. Unpublished guide.
University of New Hampshire Library, Special Collections.
Correspondence and literary manuscripts of women authors who have some association with the state of New Hampshire, including Alice Brown, Willa Cather, Annie Fields, Teresa Foley, Sarah Josepha Hale, Sarah Orne Jewett, Maxine Kumin, Amy Lowell, May Sarton, Celia Thaxter, and Elizabeth Yates.

10,854. Oates, Joyce Carol
Papers. 1968-76. 1 ft.
Open. Unpublished guide.
University of New Hampshire Library, Special Collections.
Correspondence of Oates (1938-), an author, relates primarily to the publication of *Dreaming America* (1973) and *The Spider Monkey* (1976).

10,855. Thompson, Mary P.
Papers. Ca. 1723-1893. 18 ft.
Open. No guide.
University of New Hampshire Library, Special Collections.
Thompson (1825-94) was a teacher, writer, historian, and resident of New Hampshire. Includes correspondence; ledgers; notes from her historical research; scrapbooks; papers of her great-grandfather, who was a New Hampshire judge, and other family members; Durham and Dover, NH, town records; and genealogical records.

10,856. Women's Club of Durham
Records. 1896-1974. 1 ft.
Open. No guide.
University of New Hampshire Library, Special Collections.
Minutes, yearbooks, and scrapbooks of the Club, a social, civic, and literary group that was founded in 1896.

HANOVER

10,857. Adams, Eliza
Papers. 1800-70. 2 ft.
Open. No guide.
Dartmouth College Library, Special Collections.
Family correspondence, volumes of poems and

essays, clippings, and pamphlets of Eliza (Adams) Young (1810-88), who married Ira Young, a Dartmouth College faculty member. Also includes ledgers, probably belonging to her father Ebenezer Adams, and her husband's passport.

10,858. Appleton Family
Papers. 1798-1972. 7.5 ft.
Open. Unpublished guide.
Dartmouth College Library, Special Collections.
Correspondence, diaries, writings, genealogical papers, and wills of this Boston family. Consists of copies of material used by [Mrs.] Louise Hall Tharp for her book *The Appletons of Beacon Hill* (Boston, 1973). Includes papers on Frances "Fanny" Elizabeth Appleton Longfellow (1817-61); Nathan Appleton (1779-1861), a cotton manufacturer and congressman; Samuel Appleton (1766-1853), a merchant and philanthropist; William Appleton (1786-1862), a congressman; and Thomas Gold Appleton (1812-84), an author.

10,859. Blackjack, Adda
Papers. 1923. 2 vols.
Open. No guide.
Dartmouth College Library, Special Collections.
Diary in which Blackjack describes her experiences as an assistant on and as the only survivor of the Wrangel Island Expedition in 1923.

10,860. Crane, Stephen
Papers. 1895-1963. 99 items.
Open. No guide.
Dartmouth College Library, Special Collections.
Correspondence and books by and about Crane (1871-1900), an author. Includes letters from Amy Leslie and from James B. Pinker to Crane's wife Cora (Howarth) Crane (1865-1910). Also includes "Stephen Crane's Lost Helen," an article Anne Allison wrote about Nancy Crouse Carpenter.

10,861. Dow, Margaret Elder, and Kane, Elisha Kent
Papers. 1835-1962. 6 ft.
Open. Unpublished guide.
Dartmouth College Library, Special Collections.
Dow (?-1962) was a collector, researcher, and writer. Contains Kane family correspondence, clippings, and research material on Kane; writings by Dow on Kane, as well as articles about him by other writers; Kane's logbooks; and a portfolio of pictures and maps.

10,862. Hale and Chandler
Papers. 1777-1959. 2.5 ft.
Open. Unpublished guide.
Dartmouth College Library, Special Collections.
Parker family genealogy, Hale family records, and correspondence of both families. Includes letters from William Eaton Chandler (1835 -1917), secretary of the navy, member of the New Hampshire House of Representatives, and US senator, to his wife Lucy Lambert Hale Chandler (1842-1915). Also includes correspondence of Samuel Hale, a Tory, and his wife Lydia P. Hale, as well as of their son John Parker Hale (1806-73), a senator, congressman from New Hampshire, an 1852 presidential nominee on the Free Soil ticket, and US minister to Spain.

10,863. Hovey, Richard
Papers. 1878-1961. 10 ft.
Open. Unpublished guide.
Dartmouth College Library, Special Collections.
Correspondence, manuscripts, and other papers of Hovey (1864-1900), a poet, playwright, and lecturer who graduated from Dartmouth College in 1885. Includes correspondence with his mother and his wife Henriette Russell Hovey, who was a pupil of Francois Delsarte and a lecturer.

10,864. Hubbard and Haslam
Papers. 1935-60. Ca. 140 items.
Open. No guide.
Dartmouth College Library, Special Collections.
Correspondence between Greville Haslam, a headmaster, and [Mrs.] Mina Benson Hubbard Ellis, an explorer and author, primarily relates to the placing of a tombstone at the unmarked grave of Ellis's first husband Leonidas Hubbard, Jr. Also includes later correspondence relating to the gift of these letters to the Library and clippings. In 1905 Ellis became the first woman to lead an expedition into the interior of Labrador.

10,865. Hubbard, Faith (Silliman)
Papers. 1829-73. Ca. 150 items.
Open. No guide.
Dartmouth College Library, Special Collections.
Family correspondence of Hubbard (1812-87), who ran a school in Hanover. She was married to Oliver P. Hubbard, a Dartmouth College faculty member.

10,866. Huneker, James Gibbons
Papers. 1867-1951. Ca. 1860 items.
Access restricted. No guide.
Dartmouth College Library, Special Collections.
Correspondence, manuscripts, notebooks, family and legal papers, and scrapbooks of Huneker (1857-1921), an essayist and music critic. Correspondents include Frida Ashforth, Madeleine Elise (Reynier) Boyd, Josephine (Lasca) Huneker, Rosalind Lohrfinck, and Lola Lorme.

10,867. Laing, Dilys (Bennett)
Papers. 1914-60. 4 ft. and 1 tape.
Closed. No guide.
Dartmouth College Library, Special Collections.
[Mrs. Alexander Kinnan L.] Laing (1906-60) was an author and poet. Includes correspondence, a diary, drafts of her novels *Corazon* and *The Great Year,* published and unpublished manuscripts of poetry and articles, notebooks, notes, a phonotape of an interview with Ramon Guthrie, clippings, and drawings.

10,868. MacKaye Family
Papers. 1853-1956. 138 ft.
Access restricted. Unpublished guide.
Dartmouth College Library, Special Collections.
Personal and business correspondence, poetry, notes, scrapbooks, photos, clippings, playbills, and books of four generations of the MacKaye family. Family members, who were actors, authors, designers, playwrights, or artists, include Sarah MacKaye Alling (1809-1904), Emily MacKaye Von Hesse (1838-?), Sarah MacKaye Warner (1840-76), Mary Medbery [Mrs. Steele] MacKaye (1845-1924), Marion Morse [Mrs. Percy] MacKaye (1872-1939), Arvia MacKaye (1902-), Christy MacKaye (1909-), and Hazel MacKaye (1880-1944).

10,869. McWilliams, Vera Seeley
Papers. Ca. 1946-56. Ca. 150 items.
Open. No guide.
Dartmouth College Library, Special Collections.
Correspondence of McWilliams, a writer, with Herbert F. West, a writer, book collector, and faculty member at Dartmouth College. In their letters and post cards they discuss their personal difficulties. McWilliams was the author of *Lafcadio Hearn* (Boston, 1946).

10,870. Marsh, Elizabeth
Papers. 1898-ca. 1957. Ca. 2 ft.
Open. No guide.
Dartmouth College Library, Special Collections.
Correspondence, typescripts of radio plays, notebooks, photos, address books, and copyright information of Marsh (1873-1964), an author of radio plays. Correspondence relates to her attempts to publish the radio plays.

10,871. Mencken, Henry Louis
Papers. 1921-51. 7 boxes, 458 items, and 28 drawers of cards.
Closed. No guide.
Dartmouth College Library, Special Collections.
Correspondence and manuscripts of Mencken (1880-1956), an author, journalist, and critic. Correspondents include Madeleine Elise (Reynier) Boyd, his secretary Rosalind Lohrfinck, and a Miss Osborne.

10,872. Nelson, Elba Chase
Papers. 1908-67. 2.5 ft.
Open. Unpublished guide.
Dartmouth College Library, Special Collections.
[Mrs.] Nelson (1891-1967), secretary of the Communist party in New Hampshire from 1933 to 1961, ran for governor of New Hampshire in 1936, 1938, and 1940. Contains correspondence, primarily letters to US senators, congressmen, attorneys general, and editors of New Hampshire newspapers about controversial topics; speeches; radio scripts; and clippings. Much of the material relates to the period from 1947 to 1954. Also contains information on the trial of such Communist leaders as Elizabeth Gurley Flynn.

10,873. Sanborn Family
Papers. 1794-1910. 2 boxes.
Open. Unpublished guide.
Dartmouth College Library, Special Collections.
Correspondence of the Sanborn and Webster families. Includes letters of Katherine "Kate" Abbott Sanborn (1839-1917), an author, teacher, and lecturer, and her notes for lectures on Longfellow, Italian art, and other topics.

10,874. Shoner, Sarah Augusta
Papers. 1948-59. Ca. 130 items.
Open. No guide.
Dartmouth College Library, Special Collections.
Correspondence, articles, and clippings of Shoner, a newspaper columnist and director of a children's singing group. Correspondence is primarily to Herbert F. West, a Dartmouth College faculty member.

10,875. Taggard, Genevieve
Papers. 1910-74. 8 ft.
Open. No guide.
Dartmouth College Library, Special Collections.
Manuscripts, book reviews, music, published poems, and anthologies of Taggard (1894-1948), a poet and author.

HOPKINTON

10,876. Sampson, Deborah
Papers. 1876-77. Ca. 99 pp.
Access restricted. No guide.
New Hampshire Antiquarian Society.
Manuscript of "Life of Deborah Sampson, the Female Soldier of the Revolution" by John Adams Vinton of Winchester, MA, as well as correspondence relating to research for and correction of the work. Sampson enlisted under the name of Robert Shurtleiff. Following her military service, she lectured in Massachusetts on her experiences.

10,877. Walker
Papers. Nd. 1 item.
Access restricted. No guide.
New Hampshire Antiquarian Society.
Diary evidently written by Mrs. Walker, the wife of Thomas Walker who did personal service with the Continental Army during the Revolution. In the diary she describes conditions during the American invasion of Canada in 1775 and provides information about the American army. The Society published the account as the "Diary of the Invasion of Canada."

HUDSON

10,878. Hudson Fortnightly Club
Records. 1926-76. 47 vols.
Open. No guide.
Hudson Historical Society, Inc.
Scrapbooks of yearly activities of the Club, which seeks to promote friendship and sponsors community activities. Organized in 1910 and federated in 1914, the Club was involved in establishing a baby clinic in 1924 and in organizing the 1976 Bicentennial activities. A member of the GFWC and the New Hampshire Federation of Women's Clubs, the Club was involved in the founding of the Hudson Historical Society in 1966.

LEBANON

10,879. Lovejoy, Julia Louisa (Hardy) [Mrs. Charles H.]
Papers. 1828-64. 149-page vol.
Open. No guide.
Lebanon Historical Society.
Diary of Lovejoy (1812-82), a teacher, newspaper correspondent, and author of magazine articles. Lovejoy recorded events of her youth and teaching career in Lebanon and wrote about trials she encountered as the wife of an itinerant Methodist minister in New Hampshire, Vermont, and Maine. Lovejoy bore six children; two of them died at birth. In 1855 she and her husband went west to Kansas Territory and helped to lay out the town of Manhattan. She advocated freedom for slaves, and her writings for newspapers in the East attracted the attention of William Quantrill, a Confederate guerilla leader who tried to kill her. She escaped by hiding in a cornfield.

MANCHESTER

10,880. Community Archives
Records. 1933- . Ca. 13 vols. and 2 cabinets.
Access restricted. No guide.
Sisters of the Presentation of Mary, Provincial House.
Correspondence, biographical data on community members, transcripts, questionnaires, and a history of the foundings of and principal events at convents and schools where the sisters have lived and served. This religious order of women, dedicated primarily to education, was founded in France in 1796. The New England province was founded in 1933.

NEWMARKET

10,881. Newmarket Manufacturing Company
Records. 1826-29. 2 vols.
Open. No guide.
New Market Historical Society.
Payroll ledgers of the Company, which spun and wove cotton cloth and, later, rayon. Established in 1823 in New Market, the Company moved to Lowell, MA, in about 1929. The volumes contain lists of names of the workers, many of whom were women; their wages; and their duties.

10,882. Shackford, Martha (Boardman)
Papers. 1848-58. 1 vol.
Open. No guide.
New Market Historical Society.
Diary of Shackford (1789-1863), daughter of William and Martha (Lane) Boardman, who married Seth Ring Shackford and resided in New Market. In the volume she describes village life, mills, illnesses, deaths, local history, early train travel, and a visit to a family in Maine; she also lists financial transactions. Shackford's grandfather Lane was a tanner in Stratham, NH, and her brother was a shipbuilder at Lamprey River in New Market. She and her husband had nine children, some of whom worked in the early cotton mills.

ROCHESTER

10,883. Haven Hill Garden Club
Records. 1933- . 17 vols.
Open. No guide.
Rochester Public Library.
Minutes and scrapbooks of this horticultural women's organization, which was founded in 1933 in Rochester. The group beautified the town with plantings, cooperated with the library in building up a collection of books on gardening, sponsored lectures and flower shows, decorated the hospital and other public buildings, and worked with local schools; in addition, the Club sponsored many social events for its members.

10,884. Monday Club
Records. 1896-1936. Ca. 4 in.
Open. No guide.
Rochester Public Library.
Minutes, annual programs, correspondence, clippings, and memorabilia of the Club, a women's social and literary study group which was founded in 1896, reflect their meetings to discuss current events, literature, and historical topics, as well as their dinners, parties, and excursions to nearby sites.

10,885. Rochester Republican Women's Club
Records. 1959. 1 vol.
Open. No guide.
Rochester Public Library.
Scrapbook containing programs, campaign literature, photos, clippings, and memorabilia documents the campaign and educational activities of this political group.

10,886. Rochester Woman's Club
Records. 1899- . Ca. 4 ft.
Open. No guide.
Rochester Public Library.
Minutes, lists of members, treasurer's account books, programs, scrapbooks, and histories of the Club, a social, philanthropic, educational, and civic group founded in 1899. In 1900 the Club joined the New Hampshire Federation of Women's Clubs and in 1937 the GFWC. The group was responsible for a curfew law, the first public rest room, early waste removal efforts, and tree planting in the Common, among other things. It raised funds for scholarships, music and domestic science departments in local schools, needy families, and the hospital. From the beginning until 1957, Club meetings included tea. Book reviews and musical and dramatic entertainment have also been frequent features. During WWII, members engaged in American National Red Cross work.

10,887. Worcester, Millie A.
Papers. 1887-1912. 1 vol.
Open. No guide.
Rochester Public Library.
Scrapbook of [Mrs. Horace L.] Worcester (?-1911), a Rochester clubwoman, contains correspondence, telegrams, programs, memorabilia, and clippings concerning personal and local events. Also included is documentation of the early history of the Mary Torr Chapter of the DAR, the Rochester Woman's Club, and other groups to which Worcester belonged.

WINDHAM

10,888. Archives
Records. 1839- . 6 files, 4 cabinets, 2 display cases, 120 tapes, 28 motion pictures, and 30 sets of slides.
Access restricted. No guide.
Sisters of Mercy, Motherhouse.
The Manchester, NH, community was founded by Mother Frances Xavier Warde in 1858 to work with the poor, sick, and ignorant. Financial records, papers of superiors, letters from foundresses in Ireland dating from 1839, other correspondence, retreat notes, tapes of community government meetings and lectures, oral history tapes, photos, blueprints, slides, scrapbooks, and other records of the community. Includes material relating to missions, deceased sisters, and institutions staffed by the Sisters and a 1918 stereopticon lecture with glass slides of Mercy communities in Ireland, England, and the US. Also includes audio-video programs, scrapbooks, yearbooks, publications, and other records of the recently closed Mount Saint Mary College in Hooksett, NH, and a complete set of the magazine *Magnificat* for 1907 to 1967.

NEW JERSEY

BLOOMFIELD

10,889. Bloomfield Organizations During WW II
Records. Ca. 1947. Ca. 10 items.
Open. Published guide.
Bloomfield Public Library.
Reports or summaries of the accomplishments during the war of local organizations, several of which were women's groups. Includes a history of the MOM's Club by Mrs. John J. Higgins, a description of library activities by Janet F. Melvain, and information on the work of the Bloomfield Women's Club, the Girl Scouts, the Bloomfield Jewish community, the Bloomfield Federation of Music, and the Bloomfield Art League. See Paul A. Stellhorn et al., eds., *Directory of New Jersey Historical Manuscripts* (Trenton, NJ: New Jersey Historical Commission, forthcoming).

CALDWELL

10,890. Archives
Records. 1872- . No size given.
Closed. No guide.
Sisters of St. Dominic Motherhouse.
Constitutions, minutes, correspondence, necrologies, building plans, photos, scrapbooks, records of apostolic activities, and other records of the congregation. Includes papers of major superiors, personal information on sisters, information on three private academies and one college, and registries of entrance, reception, profession, and death or departure from the congregation. This religious order of women was founded in New Jersey in 1872 and gained its status as an independent congregation in 1881. Its chief activity until recent years was classroom teaching.

CAMDEN

10,891. Women's Club of Camden
Records. 1894-1960. 1 cu.ft.
Open. No guide.

Camden County Historical Society.
President's report, 1931-32; a list of officers, 1894-97 and 1910-17; a list of members with place of residence, 1894-1910; a complete membership roll book; photo albums; and scrapbooks of the Club. Also includes a 17-page article by Abby Perrin [Mrs. Edward] Damon, a Club member, on political and literary developments in the US.

CONVENT STATION

10,892. College of St. Elizabeth
Records. 1899-1976. 19 drawers, ca. 28 boxes, 2 vols., and 5 glass cases.
Open. Published guide.
College of St. Elizabeth Archives.
Founded in 1899 by Mother Mary Xavier Mehegan and the Sisters of Charity of St. Elizabeth, this Catholic liberal arts school was the first four-year college for women in New Jersey. Complete records of the board of trustees, administration, and academic departments; president's reports, 1940-77; financial records; complete admission records; alumnae records, including correspondence and other material pertaining to fund raising; student organizations' constitutions; curriculum outlines and proposals; catalogs; College publications; photos; and other items. The College's first baccalaureate degrees were granted in 1903. It is accredited by the Association of American Universities and Middle States Association of Colleges and Secondary Schools.

DENVILLE

10,893. Archives
Records. 1895- . Ca. 3 boxes and 3 vols.
Closed. No guide.
Sisters of the Sorrowful Mother, Our Lady of Sorrows Convent.
Minutes, financial records, correspondence, chronicles, photos, scrapbooks, and other records date from the beginning of the St. Francis Health Resort in 1895 in Denville. Includes information concerning the sisters of the Denville province and their apostolates.

ELIZABETH

10,894. Woody, Regina (Jones)
Papers. 1912-72. 5 boxes and 1 tape.
Open. Unpublished guide.
Elizabeth Free Public Library.
Galleys, articles, lectures, scrapbooks, ephemera, and an interview of Woody (1894-), a stage dancer and author of such books as *Student Dancer* (1951), *One Day at a Time* (1968), and *The Young Medics* (1968). After studying ballet in London from 1910 to 1912, Regina Jones made her debut at the Folies Bergère in Paris before she became part of a vaudeville song and dance routine with Eva Gauthier. The team toured the US for a year. In 1918 Jones married physician McIver Woody and in 1920 sold her first article, which described the correct way to wash dishes, to *Hygeia* magazine, now *Today's Health.* She also wrote articles for *Collier's, Dance Magazine, Parents, Reader's Digest,* and other magazines. From 1946 to 1950 she taught juvenile writing at New York University.

FREEHOLD

10,895. Davison, Ada Clark
Papers. 1927. 1 vol.
Open. No guide.
Monmouth County Historical Association.
Diary in which Davison, a housewife, comments on daily activities, her Sunday school class, family, and the weather.

10,896. Freehold Sewing Association
Records. 1825-33. 1 vol.
Open. No guide.
Monmouth County Historical Association.
This women's organization was founded for the instruction of indigent inhabitants of the pine barrens area in New Jersey. Constitution, minutes, and a list of officers.

10,897. Freehold Young Ladies' Seminary
Records. 1845-1976. 2 boxes.
Open. No guide.
Monmouth County Historical Association.
The Seminary was founded in 1845 to provide young women instruction in languages, mathematics, natural science, and physical education. Girls aged approximately 8 through 23 attended the school until ca. 1904 when, after changes in ownership and administration, the Seminary became the Freehold Military Academy. Seminary catalogs with lists of courses and pupils, 1845-97; commencement and anniversary programs; records of the art and music department concerning examinations, rehearsals, and concerts; assorted student newspapers; tuition bills and receipts; photos; and clippings. Also includes papers of Annie Seabrook and other students, including notebooks, essays, a school diary, a spelling test, and report cards; correspondence of G. L. Barrows, another student; and a student term paper by Gail Mezey with slides, entitled "The Freehold Young Ladies Seminary: A Justifiable End to an Era."

10,898. Hosach
Papers. 1815-16. 1 vol.
Open. No guide.
Monmouth County Historical Association.
Detailed notes on the physical development and treatment of women during pregnancy and childbirth appear to have been recorded during the training of a physician named Hosach.

10,899. Keyport Literary Club
Records. 1892-1932. 1 folder and 1 box.
Open. No guide.
Monmouth County Historical Association.
The Club was founded in 1892 as the Ladies' Parlor Reading Circle for "self-improvement through systematic and choice reading." Constitution and bylaws, minutes from a few meetings, meeting programs, yearbooks, notebooks of selections read at meetings between 1897 and 1904, a scrapbook, and clippings.

10,900. Lake, Ida
Papers. 1915. 3 pp.
Open. No guide.
Monmouth County Historical Association.
A typescript history by Lake of the Ladies' Aid Society of the First Baptist Church of Shrewsbury-Red Bank.

10,901. Lesson Books
Collection. 1801-36. 8 vols.
Open. No guide.
Monmouth County Historical Association.
Includes a penmanship book of Ada Brokaw and a ciphering book, which consists of arithmetic rules, formulae, tables, and problems, of Elizabeth Murphy, 1801. Also contains arithmetic books of Sinechy Conover, 1822; Eleanor Hendrickson, 1808; Elizabeth Smith, 1810-14; Mary Conover, 1821; Mary Conover, 1836; and Maria Flinn, 1829-32.

10,902. Scott, Elizabeth Chadwick Roberts
Papers. 1814. 2 items.
Open. No guide.
Monmouth County Historical Association.
Autobiography of Scott (1784-1847) contains information on her marriage in 1798 to a mate on a ship, who was named Roberts; her premonitions of the death of a loved one and the events that confirmed her fears; her early interest in books and writing; and her feeling that she was deprived of an education, which she felt would have enabled her to correct some of the evils of life.

HACKETTSTOWN

10,903. Cummins, George Wyckoff, and Cummins, Annie Blair (Titman)
Papers. Ca. 1838-1945. Ca. 10 boxes.
Open. Published guide.
Centenary College Library.
Both George Cummins (1865-1942) and Annie Cummins (1867-1952), whom he married in 1890, were graduates of Centenary Collegiate Institute and local historians. George Cummins also was a physician, and Annie Cummins was founder of the William Maxwell chapter of the DAR in 1931 and the piano and organ player for local churches and other groups. Family correspondence; correspondence and other records of the DAR chapter; deeds, indentures, and other legal papers collected by the Cumminses; and manuscript histories by the Cumminses of Warren County, NJ, with particular emphasis on the Revolutionary War, soldiers, and their wives and daughters. Also includes a 98-page diary of Annie Cummins's mother Margaret Elizabeth Roseberry [Mrs. William Blair] Titman (1844-1940). Centenary College was known as Centenary Collegiate Institute from 1874 to 1929. See Paul A. Stellhorn et al., eds., *Directory of New Jersey Historical Manuscripts* (Trenton, NJ: New Jersey Historical Commission, forthcoming).

HIBERNIA

10,904. Malone, Katherine D.
Papers. Ca. 1900-50. Ca. 1 box.
Open. No guide.
Historical Society of the Rockaways.
Papers relating to the career of Malone (1881-) as an elementary school teacher and principal in Rockaway Township public schools for 44 years. Includes correspondence; student work, such as art, poems, and penmanship exercises; a daily plan book; school register; teaching certificates; photos; clippings; and textbooks.

LIVINGSTON

10,905. Local History
Oral history. 1974-75. 10 tapes.
Access restricted. Description.
Free Public Library of Livingston.
Interviews of local residents reminiscing about the past, including Edith [Mrs. Ralph] DeCamp, a founder of the Library, who moved to Livingston Township with her husband in 1907; [Mrs.] Amy Vincent Hamilton, a founder of the Library and of the first local PTA in 1916, whose mother Ada Vincent was the first woman to serve on the Livingston School Board, 1906-10, and whose grandfather Thomas Vincent, Jr., owned and operated milk and produce farms in the area; [Mrs.] Edith Squier Muller, a descendant of Jonathan Squier, one of the first settlers to purchase land in the Township (in 1744) in the section that came to be known as Squiertown because generations of the Squier family had lived there; Florence [Mrs. William] Rathburn, whose husband was head of the Township water department until his death, at which time she

succeeded him in that position; and [Mrs.] Bernice (Burnet) Taylor, whose ancestors the Burnets, Meekers, and Edwardses were early settlers in the Township and founders of the Northfield Baptist Church. Also includes interviews with [Mrs.] Renie Collins Slater, who describes her childhood in Livingston and memories of her Collins family relatives and their activities; with [Miss] Olive "Girlie" Youngjohn, who was born and raised in Livingston and who tells about her childhood and her experiences as a teacher in the Central and Collins schools for 40 years; and with [Mrs.] Grace Dusenbury, a descendant of early land owners Jonathan Squier and Nathaniel Crane, who discusses her memories of the West Livingston area where for many years the Crane family owned and operated a large dairy farm.

10,906. Women's Club of Livingston
Records. 1936-74. 4 folders and 5 vols.
Open. Published guide.
Free Public Library of Livingston.
Founded in 1932, the Club, whose motto is "Not for ourselves—but for all," is affiliated with the state Federation of Women's Clubs and the GFWC. Lists of officers and committee chairmen, correspondence, and scrapbooks. The Club has been involved in a variety of philanthropic and civic activities such as donating funds to the Library, the local hospital, and a college scholarship fund. See Paul A. Stellhorn et al., eds., *Directory of New Jersey Historical Manuscripts* (Trenton, NJ: New Jersey Historical Commission, forthcoming).

MADISON

10,907. Butler, Clementina (Ware)
Papers. 1848. 2 items.
Open. Description.
Drew University Library.
Letters of Butler (1820-1913), a leader in the Women's Foreign Missionary Society of the Methodist Episcopal Church for half a century.

10,908. Garrettson, Catherine (Livingston)
Papers. 1787-1848. Ca. 2 vols. and 400 items.
Open. Description.
Drew University Library.
Papers of Garrettson (1752-1849), wife of clergyman Freeborn Garrettson, who was a Methodist circuit rider, consist of correspondence with her husband and other members of her family, a diary for 1787 to 1827, and her autobiography.

10,909. Lind, Johanna "Jennie" Maria
Papers. 1851-52. 2 items.
Open. Description.
Drew University Library.
Letters of Jennie Lind (1820-87), a singer, are addressed to clergyman Olaf G. Hedstrom and concern Methodist missions to Swedish immigrants in New York City.

10,910. Northern New Jersey Conference of the United Methodist Church
Records. 1800-1976. Ca. 17 folders, 19.5 drawers, and 99 vols.
Open. Published guide.
Drew University Library.
Minutes, financial and membership records, journals, reports, church record books, and other primarily 19th-century records of the Northern New Jersey Annual Conference, which was formerly known as the Newark Annual Conference. Includes records of the Women's Society of Christian Service (now known as the United Methodist Women), which was the principal organization for women's work in developing fellowship and concepts of mission within the church, 1939-76; records of the Jersey City, NJ, Summit Avenue Methodist Church, Women's Society of Christian Service, 1940-49; and records of the Paterson, NJ, Wesley Methodist Church, Women's Society of Christian Service, 1965-70. Also includes a minute book of the Female Missionary Society of the Methodist Episcopal Church of Newark, NJ, 1834-47. See Paul A. Stellhorn et al., eds., *Directory of New Jersey Historical Manuscripts* (Trenton, NJ: New Jersey Historical Commission, forthcoming).

10,911. Palmer, Phoebe (Worrall)
Papers. 1854-83. 11 items.
Open. Description.
Drew University Library.
Correspondence of Palmer (1807-74), an evangelist who married Walter Clark Palmer in 1827, relates to holiness meetings and others of her activities. Palmer held Tuesday Meetings for the Promotion of Holiness, which drew crowds for many years; her religious beliefs were influenced by John Wesley and the perfectionist movement.

10,912. Willard, Frances Elizabeth
Papers. 1865-97. 22 items.
Open. Description.
Drew University Library.
Correspondence of Willard (1839-98), a woman's suffrage advocate and temperance reformer who was president of the WCTU for ca. 20 years.

10,913. Oral History
Oral history. 1959-73. 7 tapes.
Open. No guide.
Madison Historical Society.
Tapes of interviews about the history of the Madison area include reminiscences of a Miss Martin, a physician's daughter who lived in Madison for most of her life, and of sisters Mrs. A. B. Churchill, whose maiden name was Pierson, and Helen (Pierson) Brower, who recall the town, school, and events from their youth as well as parties at the estate of Frank Fuller, the inventor of shredded wheat cereal. The sisters are granddaughters of Louis Noe, a Madison businessman whose ancestors have lived in the Madison area since before the Revolutionary War.

10,914. Redmond, Anna G.
Papers. 1869-83. 3 vols.
Open. No guide.
Madison Historical Society.
Diaries of Redmond (1852-?), a schoolgirl, contain descriptions of her daily and social life during a period when she apparently lived with aunts in Burlington, NJ.

MATAWAN

10,915. Public Libraries in Matawan
Oral history. 1971. 4 tapes.
Open. Synopsis.
Aberdeen-Matawan Public Library.
Interviews concern the founding and history of the Public Library and its predecessors. [Miss] J. Mabel Brown (ca. 1880s-), editor of local newspapers *Matawan Journal* and the *Keyport Weekly,* was a member of the Library's board of trustees for more than 40 years and president of the board for much of that time; she discusses the early building, services, employees, funds, and operating procedures of the Library. Her father Benjamin Brown helped found the Library. [Mrs.] May Dominick (ca. 1890s-), librarian of the Library from 1922 to 1963, discusses the Literary Society, which operated a circulating library from 1870 to 1920; she also discusses her work in the Library and important Library events. [Mrs.] Helen J. Enterline (ca. 1920s-), a member of the Library staff for many years and co-author of an unpublished history of public libraries in Matawan, gives an account of her work with the Library and her research on the Library's history. [Mrs.] Evelyn Carter (ca. 1920s-), a member of the Library's board of trustees and president from 1963 to 1969, discusses the changes that expansion and growth of the Township of Matawan caused for the Library, including construction of a new building.

MENDHAM

10,916. Convent Archives
Records. 1873- . 48 drawers and 5 cabinets.
Access restricted. No guide.
Sisters of Christian Charity Convent.
This religious order of women is engaged in education, health services, and retreat work. The American province was founded in 1873 in Wilkes-Barre, PA. Financial records; correspondence of the superior general, the provincial superior, and other members; data on each sister; yearly annals of each of the ca. 60 houses; photos; scrapbooks; works on the foundress; and files on deceased members and former members of the congregation, on the Sisters' role in education, and on the general and provincial chapters.

METUCHEN

10,917. Borough Improvement Society
Records. 1901-76. 16 vols.
Access restricted. Published guide.
Metuchen Public Library.
Minute books, programs, and scrapbooks of this women's association, founded in 1900 to improve and beautify the borough and to awaken "in the minds of the general populace a deeper interest in the general welfare." The Society sponsors study groups, card parties to raise funds for scholarships, and other activities. See Paul A. Stellhorn et al., eds., *Directory of New Jersey Historical Manuscripts* (Trenton, NJ: New Jersey Historical Commission, forthcoming).

10,918. Quiet Hour Club
Records. 1895-1976. Ca. 2.25 drawers.
Access restricted. Published guide.
Metuchen Public Library.
Treasurer's reports, minutes, yearly programs, and papers read at meetings of the Club, a women's group founded in 1895 to bring women together "for mental culture, social interchange, and a sympathetic understanding of whatever women are doing along the best lines of Progress." The group chooses a study topic for each year and then members prepare papers on the subject. See Paul A. Stellhorn et al., eds., *Directory of New Jersey Historical Manuscripts* (Trenton, NJ: New Jersey Historical Commission, forthcoming).

MONTCLAIR

10,919. Montclair Local History
Collection. 1900s- . Ca. 12 drawers.
Open. Published guide.
Montclair Public Library.
Collection of correspondence, manuscripts, pamphlets, photos, and clippings includes a two-volume memory book that [Miss] Elizabeth B. French kept during her junior and senior years at Montclair High School in ca. 1910. Also includes the 465-page reminiscences of Sarah J. (Starkweather) Churchill in which she describes her life, family, travels, and work teaching music in local schools from 1869 to 1894; she dictated these reminiscences to [Miss] Gladys L. Roosevelt in ca. 1910 after losing her sight. Churchill tells of studying music in 1850 so she could help support her family, which was beset by financial uncertainties because of the beliefs of her father

John Starkweather, a Second Adventist prophet who predicted the end of the world in 1843. After moving to Montclair from Brooklyn, NY, Churchill supported her family by singing in a church choir and by teaching. She also speaks of trips she took to Europe and the Orient with her husband, who was an importer, and of the births of five children and the deaths of two of them. After she became blind in 1907, she devoted her time to improving the lives of other blind people and helped found the New Jersey State Commission for the Blind. The collection also contains the constitution and membership rolls of the Woman's Town Improvement and Health Protection Association of Montclair, a community welfare group of women organized in ca. 1900 by Sarah Churchill and others. See Paul A. Stellhorn et al., eds., *Directory of New Jersey Historical Manuscripts* (Trenton, NJ: New Jersey Historical Commission, forthcoming).

MORRISTOWN

10,920. Vail, Stephen

Papers. 1825-64. Ca. 8 vols., 22 folders, and 3 microfilm reels.
Open. Published guide and inventory.
The Speedwell Village.
Family correspondence, business papers, journals, and other material of Vail (1780-1864), a businessman, owner of the Speedwell Iron Works, and judge; his son Alfred Vail helped perfect Samuel F. B. Morse's telegraph at the Vail farm in 1837 and 1838. Includes correspondence in which Stephen Vail's daughter Sarah D. (Vail) Cutler Hurd (1811-87), whose second husband Whitfield Hurd operated a mill for Stephen Vail in Sparta, NJ, writes to him about mill activities, the weather, household chores, and her concern for the welfare of each of the six children of her first marriage, whom her father was supporting. Also includes letters to him from Sarah Hurd's daughter Sarah Cecelia Cutler (1842-83) describing household chores, female arts such as fashioning jewelry from human hair, and parties, church socials, and Fourth of July celebrations and correspondence in which Jane Elizabeth Cutler (1837-1915), who kept house for her brother Augustus on a farm that their grandfather Stephen Vail owned near Hackettstown, NJ, writes about nursing ill members of the family, helping the dressmaker, struggling to control flies, and such household activities as churning butter, tending ducks, and processing meat after it had been butchered. Collection also contains correspondence that Harriet Vail Canfield (1849-?), a student at the Moravian Seminary in Bethlehem, PA, in 1863, wrote to her great-grandfather Stephen Vail, who was paying for her schooling, about her progress in school; the few diversions available, such as walking, skating, and sleighing; and attending church fairs, concerts, and lectures. See Paul A. Stellhorn et al., eds., *Directory of New Jersey Historical Manuscripts* (Trenton, NJ: New Jersey Historical Commission, forthcoming).

NEPTUNE

10,921. Goodrich, Margaret "Peggy" Day (Taintor)

Papers. 1962- . 7 vols., 5 files, and 2 tapes.
Closed. Unpublished guide.
Neptune Historical Museum.
Literary manuscripts, files of building plans for the new Neptune Public Library, photos, and scrapbooks on the Neptune Historical Museum of [Mrs. Robert R.] Goodrich (1921-), curator of the Museum and an author and columnist. Goodrich wrote *History of Shark River Hills* (1963); *Ike's Travels* (1976), which is a biography of Neptune resident Navy Commodore Isaac Schlossbach; and other works.

10,922. Hopper, Kathryn

Phonotape. 1973. 1 tape and 8-page transcript.
Open. Unpublished guide.
Neptune Historical Museum.
Speech by [Mrs.] Hopper (ca. 1902-74), a teacher, local historian, and lecturer, concerns the history and traditions of Ocean Grove in Neptune Township. Ocean Grove was founded in 1869 as a Methodist camp meeting association. Hopper describes the association grounds, auditorium, Victorian homes, and the ways in which Ocean Grove still observed "blue laws" by closing its streets to traffic and allowing no swimming or business to be transacted on Sundays.

10,923. Mauch, Margaret

Phonotape. 1974. 1 tape and 4-page transcript.
Open. Unpublished guide.
Neptune Historical Museum.
Discussion by [Mrs. Rowland C.] Mauch (ca. 1905-), former librarian of the Neptune Public Library, of the history of the Library after 1955. The Neptune Public Library was started in 1924 in the Ocean Grove Woman's Club as a bookmobile stop of the Monmouth County Library. Collection also contains four scrapbooks on the history of the Library.

NEW BRUNSWICK

10,924. Daughters of the American Revolution

Records. 1890-1920. 158 vols.
Open. No guide.
New Brunswick Public Library.
Genealogical tracings contain information on the birthplaces and lineage of members of the DAR.

10,925. Reformed Church in America, Women's Board of Foreign Missions

Records. Ca. 1850s-1950s. 6 ft.
Open. No guide.
New Brunswick Theological Seminary, Archives of the Reformed Church in America.
Annual reports, financial records, articles, and other records document the activities of the Board, which was founded in 1832.

10,926. Thoms, May De Pree

Papers. Ca. 1910-40. 1 folder.
Open. No guide.
New Brunswick Theological Seminary, Archives of the Reformed Church in America.
Correspondence and photos of Thoms (1878-1952), a missionary in Arabia and founder in 1920 of the Baghdad School for girls. After receiving a BA from Butler University and studying at the Hartford School of Missions, De Pree went to Arabia, where in 1906 she married Sharon J. Thoms, a medical missionary. When he died in 1913, she took his children by his previous wife back to the US for their education. In 1918 she returned to work in the field.

10,927. Van Ess, Dorothy Firman

Papers. Ca. 1910-50. Ca. 2 folders, 1 vol., and 1 microfilm reel.
Open. No guide.
New Brunswick Theological Seminary, Archives of the Reformed Church in America.
Correspondence, miscellaneous manuscripts, photos, and a book of [Mrs. John] Van Ess (1885-1975), a missionary for the Reformed Church in America from 1909 to 1957 in Arabia; she founded the first modern school for girls in Basrah, Arabia (now Iraq). In addition to work with the school, she conducted evangelistic meetings, study classes, and a Sunday school; she visited the poor; and she had access to the secluded quarters of Arab female society, where she observed and participated in a variety of social functions, including the day-long ceremonial bath and all-night tea parties of the Moslem month of fasting (Ramahdan). She was also the author of *Fatima and Her Sisters* and *Pioneers in the Arab World.* She received a bachelor's degree from Mount Holyoke College and an MA from Wellesley College in English and literature.

10,928. Demarest, William H. S.

Records. 1904-24. Ca. 12 cartons.
Open. Published guide and description.
Rutgers University Archives.
Correspondence and other papers of Demarest, president of Rutgers University from 1906 to 1924, contain letters about the founding and early days of the New Jersey College for Women, which was renamed Douglass College in 1955. Also includes a personal letter in which Mabel (Smith) Douglass thanks Demarest for her appointment as dean, describes her love for the students, and mentions an illness from which she suffered. See Herbert F. Smith, *A Guide to the Manuscript Collection of the Rutgers University Library* (New Brunswick, NJ: The Rutgers University Press, 1964).

10,929. Presidents John Martin Thomas, Phillip M. Brett, and Robert Clarkson Clothier

Records. 1925-52. Ca. 150 boxes and 7 cartons.
Open. Published guide and description.
Rutgers University Archives.
Papers of these Rutgers University presidents contain judicial proceedings at the New Jersey College for Women and notes of Clothier concerning the choice of a successor for Mabel (Smith) Douglass as dean of the College. See Herbert F. Smith, *A Guide to the Manuscript Collection of the Rutgers University Library* (New Brunswick, NJ: The Rutgers University Press, 1964).

10,930. Rutgers University Board of Directors

Records. 1911-33. Ca. 3.5 cartons and 4 vols.
Open. Description.
Rutgers University Archives.
Minutes and correspondence of the Board concern the establishment in 1918 of New Jersey College for Women, a coordinate college of Rutgers, and the administration of the College. Includes reports of the committee on relations with the woman's college and information on College faculty and staff appointments, financial matters, candidates for degrees, and difficulties in the relationship of Rutgers, the College, and other Rutgers colleges with the state of New Jersey. Also includes correspondence in which students, administrators, and the New Jersey State Federation of Women's Clubs protest a reorganization through which the College would have been made coeducational and material relating to a substantial College budget cut in 1932, the appointment of five women to the board of trustees, and the leave of absence, resignation, and death of Mabel (Smith) Douglass, dean of the College. In 1955 the New Jersey College for Women was renamed Douglass College.

10,931. Douglass, Mabel (Smith)

Papers. 1877-1968. 14 boxes, 1 oversize box, 1 folder, and 1 vol.
Open. Description.
Rutgers University, Douglass College Library.
[Mrs. William Shipman] Douglass (1877-1933) was the founder and first dean of the New Jersey College for Women, an affiliate of Rutgers, which later was renamed Douglass College. Her personal papers and official files from her tenure as dean contain correspondence, speeches, financial records, reports, catalogs, yearbooks, campus and faculty publications, motion pictures, photos, clippings, and memorabilia pertaining to the establishment, development, and history of the College. Also includes material about her failing health and resignation as dean, her disappearance and death in

1933, and the discovery and burial of her body in 1963. Correspondence of her daughter Edith (Douglass) Roth (?-1948), who willed her mother's papers to the College, is also contained.

Material concerning the College includes Douglass's correspondence with Rutgers president William H. S. Demarest about the establishment of the school and with other colleges and universities about women's schools and students, statistical analyses of college programs for women, records of fund raising and building dedications, and interviews with people reminiscing about Douglass and the College during its early years.

10,932. English, Ada
Papers. Ca. 1911-47. 16 folders.
Open. Description.
Rutgers University, Douglass College Library.
A librarian and historian of the New Jersey College for Women, [Mrs.] English collected these letters, minutes, reports, manuscript articles, and other material to document the history of the College. Contains items by or concerning Mabel (Smith) Douglass and material documenting support of the College by the New Jersey State Federation of Women's Clubs, including Federation minutes, correspondence between the Federation and trustees of Rutgers, and papers of Mrs. Frank Pattison, who was Federation president between 1919 and 1921. Also includes correspondence, interviews, reports English received in response to her request for reminiscences from persons active in the early history of the College, and the program of events, addresses, and a booklet pertaining to the College's 25th anniversary.

10,933. Stanton, Elizabeth (Cady)
Papers. Ca. 1851-1915. 18 in.
Open. Unpublished guide.
Rutgers University, Douglass College Library.
Stanton (1815-1902) was a woman's rights leader and writer. Correspondence; manuscripts of several of her works, including *Fashionable Women Shipwreck, Marriage and Divorce,* and *An Epistolary Autobiography* (New York, 1906), edited by Harriot (Stanton) Blatch and Theodore Stanton; and pamphlets, broadsides, and photos concerning her lecture tours and woman suffrage.

10,934. Abeel, Gustavus
Papers. 1821-23. 20 items.
Open. Accession card.
Rutgers University Libraries, Special Collections.
Letters Mary Stille Abeel received from Gustavus Abeel, a student at the New Brunswick Theological Seminary.

10,935. Anonymous Honeymoon Journal
Papers. 1956. 42 pp.
Open. Accession card.
Rutgers University Libraries, Special Collections.
Diary of Marilyn and David, who apparently were from New Jersey, contains observations and accounts of touring and entertainment while they were staying at the Coral Island Club Hotel in Bermuda.

10,936. Appleton, Agnes Morgan (Reeves)
Papers. 1856-64. 2 vols. (microfilm).
Open. Accession card.
Rutgers University Libraries, Special Collections.
Diary of Agnes Reeves (1839-1901), who was the daughter of Samuel Morgan Reeves (1790-1886), a Haddonfield, NJ, merchant of Quaker antecedents. During 1856 and 1857 she was a student at the Moravian Seminary for Young Ladies in Bethlehem, PA. In later sections of the diary she describes family, social, and Baptist religious activities in Haddonfield and vicinity. In 1865 she married clergyman James H. Appleton.

10,937. Atkinson Family
Papers. 1793-1955. 3 oversize folders, 22 boxes, 7 vols., and 1 bundle.
Open. Accession card.
Rutgers University Libraries, Special Collections.
Papers of this New Brunswick family include correspondence of Sarah Atkinson (1861-1956), a translator for the American delegation to the Paris peace conference of 1898; correspondence and diaries of Mary Josephine Atkinson (1854-1933), a teacher and tutor; and diaries of Florence Atkinson (1863-89), a teacher. The scattered diaries of Mary Atkinson for 1876 to 1925 contain information on her travels in the US and Europe as well as her life in New Brunswick. The diaries of Florence Atkinson for 1883 to 1886 concern her trip to and from Argentina where she worked for two years as a faculty member at the Escuela Normal de San Juan. She had been recruited by the Argentine government along with other women teachers to serve as instructors in women's normal schools.

10,938. Bartine, Mary Oakley
Papers. 1897. 18 pp.
Open. Accession card.
Rutgers University Libraries, Special Collections.
Diary of [Miss] Bartine (1879-) provides a detailed picture of the life and social activities of the daughter of a well-to-do family. The only unpleasant experiences she mentions are visits to a dentist in Plainfield, NJ.

10,939. Bayles, Sarah (Staats)
Papers. 1835-51. 32 pp.
Open. Unpublished guide.
Rutgers University Libraries, Special Collections.
Diary of Bayles (1787-1870), who after three years of a difficult marriage left her husband in 1817 and returned to the Staats farm near South Bound Brook, NJ. The diary includes notes about sermons she heard at Bound Brook Presbyterian Church and comments about neighborhood marriages, deaths, births, visits, and domestic activities, such as candlemaking. Also includes poetry, formulas and receipts, and records of servants, including two Negro slaves. Bayles lived at her family's farm throughout the remainder of her life.

10,940. Beggs, Vera W.
Papers. 1928-42. 2 boxes.
Open. Accession card.
Rutgers University Libraries, Special Collections.
A civic leader, [Mrs. Frederic] Beggs was an officer of the international relations department of the GFWC and of the New Jersey Committee on the Cause and Cure of War, a group with headquarters in Newark, NJ, which was dedicated to preventing war through education and discussion. Correspondence, reports, articles, pamphlets, and other papers relate to the Committee and to the department, particularly the department's concern over Pan-American relations.

10,941. Bleecker, Leonard
Papers. 1777-78. 6 items.
Open. Accession card.
Rutgers University Libraries, Special Collections.
Letters to Bleecker, an army captain, from his sister Ann Eliza Bleecker of Albany, NY, concern her social activities in Albany.

10,942. Bronson, Miles
Papers. 1849-57. 22 items.
Open. Accession card.
Rutgers University Libraries, Special Collections.
Letters that Bronson and his wife Ruth M. Lucas Bronson, missionaries in Nowgong, India, received from fellow missionaries in Assam, India, including clergyman Ira J. Stoddard and his wife Druscilla Allen Stoddard and clergyman Nathan Brown and his wife. The letters contain detailed information about missionary activities and conditions and events in Assam.

10,943. Burnett, Virginia Stiles
Papers. ?-1947. 6 boxes.
Open. Accession card.
Rutgers University Libraries, Special Collections.
Ordered by subject, this historical material on New Jersey was collected by Burnett (1903-47) in connection with her work as curator of Special Collections at Rutgers. Compilations and notes on 17th- and 18th-century New Brunswick, transcripts and bibliographic information on travel diaries, note cards consisting of brief biographical notes on outstanding New Jersey women, 17th-century newspapers, early New Jersey almanacs, and records of the First Presbyterian Church and cemetery in Morristown, NJ.

10,944. Butler, Francis E.
Papers. 1830-1900. 2 boxes and 6 vols.
Open. Accession card.
Rutgers University Libraries, Special Collections.
Correspondence, diaries, a book of manuscript poems, scrapbooks, and a photo album of the Butler family. Includes letters from 1862 and 1863 and a diary of Francis Butler for 1846 to 1862. Also includes a diary of Julia Colt Butler (1872-?), daughter of Paterson, NJ, manufacturer Henry V. Butler. Her diary, which she kept in 1889 and 1890, contains detailed information about her social and family visits, games, her interest in such sports as football, church attendance, the theater, concerts, and trips to Washington and New England. Much of the diary concerns a six-month trip she made with other girls and a chaperone to Europe, with short stays in Antwerp and Brussels, and her three-month residence in a Paris hotel where she was tutored daily in French and music.

10,945. Buttenheim, Mrs. Harold S.
Papers. 1915-21. 2 vols.
Open. Accession card.
Rutgers University Libraries, Special Collections.
Correspondence, reports, and other papers relating to Buttenheim's work as New Jersey state chairman of child welfare.

10,946. City Improvement Society of New Brunswick
Records. 1895-1927. 3 folders and 4 vols.
Open. Accession card.
Rutgers University Libraries, Special Collections.
Complete minutes, correspondence, notes, and clippings of the Society, a women's group founded in 1895 to improve and beautify the city. Working first to promote clean streets and lots, members later became involved in such social problems as prison welfare and child labor legislation.

10,947. Clarissa D. Spaulding Girls' School
Records. 1851-88. 1 vol.
Open. Accession card.
Rutgers University Libraries, Special Collections.
A register of students of this Elizabeth, NJ, school for 1851 to 1861 and clippings.

10,948. Clark, Frances (Beardsley)
Papers. 1837-50. 152 pp.
Open. Accession card.
Rutgers University Libraries, Special Collections.
Diary of Clark (1822-?), who was the daughter of Samuel Beardsley (1790-1860), a lawyer, New York state attorney general, state supreme court justice, and congressman. During the early period of the diary Frances Beardsley was attending a local female seminary in Utica, NY. Later she lived with her parents and engaged in domestic chores, visits to friends and relatives, and church attendance. In the final period her life as a housewife married to Erasmus Clark is depicted. Throughout the diary she frequently expresses religious thoughts and anxieties.

10,949. Clark, Margaret Miller (Davidson)
Papers. 1868-1916. 2 vols. and 1 item.
Open. Accession card.

Rutgers University Libraries, Special Collections. Diary in which Clark describes her voyage from New York to Japan and residence in Yokohama tutoring Japanese children during 1871 and 1872. Also includes a commonplace book, verse, an 1868 letter from her brother in Yokohama, and family obituaries.

10,950. Condict, Marion Angevine (Freeman)
Papers. 1897-1906. 253 pp.
Open. Unpublished guide.
Rutgers University Libraries, Special Collections. Diary of Condict (1876-?), the daughter of an Orange, NJ, lawyer. The scattered entries record events in her personal, family, and social life. The final entry reports her engagement to John H. N. Condict, a local man of whom her family disapproved. She married him in 1908.

10,951. Conner, Virginia
Papers. 1857-60. 73-page vol.
Open. Accession card.
Rutgers University Libraries, Special Collections. Diary of Conner, an 1857 graduate from the Wesleyan Female College in Macon, GA, concerns her teaching a small class of children, living with her family, and household and church activities. Diary also contains several compositions.

10,952. Connett, Cornelia Ett (Thompson)
Papers. 1888-1917. 41 vols. and 1 item.
Open. Accession card.
Rutgers University Libraries, Special Collections. Diaries of Connett (1836-1919), wife of Earl Fairchild Connett (1826-1914), who operated a sawmill and lumberyard, contain particularly detailed accounts of household, family, business, and neighborhood activity in Brookside, NJ. Also includes a compilation by her granddaughter Helen Martha Wright of a volume-by-volume analysis of the diaries' contents and biographical and other data.

10,953. Consumers League of New Jersey
Records. 1913-75. 18 folders, 46 boxes, 6 vols., and 13 cartons.
Open. Accession card.
Rutgers University Libraries, Special Collections. Established in 1900 to improve the working conditions of women and children in industry, the League attempted to reform working conditions through child labor laws; minimum wage and maximum hour laws; regulation of factory, retail, household, and migrant working conditions; and improvement of health standards and safety. By 1960, however, the group was involved in such consumer interests as the use of pesticides and food additives, consumer fraud, food prices, national health insurance, and pollution. Organizational records, minutes, financial and membership records, correspondence, reports, clippings, and biographical material on officials of the New Jersey and National Consumers Leagues. Includes correspondence of New Jersey League presidents, including Mary L. Dyckman, 1942-75, and information concerning the reorganization of the New Jersey health department.

10,954. Cook, George Hammell
Papers. Ca. 1835-1905. Ca. 9000 items.
Open. Accession card.
Rutgers University Libraries, Special Collections. Papers of Cook, New Jersey state geologist, include a diary his daughter Sarah Cook (1849-78) kept in 1864 and 1865 while she was a student at the Troy Female Seminary in Troy, NY, the school Emma Willard founded. In 1874 Sarah Cook married Nicholas Williamson, a New Brunswick physician.

10,955. Cowdrey, Mary Bartlett
Papers. 1910-71. 6 cartons, 1 box, and 1 bundle.
Open. Accession card.
Rutgers University Libraries, Special Collections. An art historian, [Miss] Cowdrey (1910-74) was assistant curator of the Smith College art museum. Correspondence; published writings, articles, reviews, and clippings; an inventory of books and art works she acquired; and information about gifts to Rutgers University. Also includes autographs of prominent artists, 1783-1955, and correspondence concerning women to be included in *Notable American Women, 1607-1950* (Cambridge, MA: Harvard University Press, 1975). Cowdrey specialized in 19th-century painting and co-authored a book on painter William Sidney Mount.

10,956. Cranbury, NJ, First Presbyterian Church
Records. 1739-1954. 3 microfilm reels.
Open. Accession card.
Rutgers University Libraries, Special Collections. Constitution; minutes of session, of congregation and corporation meetings, and of the trustees of the Church; accounts; subscriptions; and records of communicants, baptisms, marriages, funerals, and deaths. Also includes minutes, accounts, lists of officers and members, and other records of the Female Charitable Society of Cranbury, 1817-37; the Ladies Benevolent Society of the First Presbyterian Church of Cranbury, 1882-83; and the Female Benevolent Society of the First Presbyterian Congregation of Cranbury, 1840-68. Includes as well an 1817 constitution of the Female Charitable Society, which defines the group's purpose as aiding the Western Missionary Society of New Jersey and Princeton Theological Seminary, purchasing tracts for distribution, and helping the indigent and distressed.

10,957. Crane, Elizabeth "Betsey" (Mulford)
Papers. 1824-28. 132 pp.
Open. Accession card.
Rutgers University Libraries, Special Collections. Diary in which Crane (1775-1828), a resident of New Providence, NJ, and wife of farmer John Crane (1764-1843), describes farming, church, domestic and social activities, family events, and visits. A transcript of the diary, which is available on microfilm, contains interspersed explanatory notes, genealogical data, and an index of personal names.

10,958. Culp, Cordie Jacob
Papers. 1902-45. 13 vols.
Open. Accession card.
Rutgers University Libraries, Special Collections. Travel journal of a trip made in 1932 by Culp (1872-1952), a Presbyterian minister, and scattered diaries of his wife Florence M. (Burns) Culp (1874-?). In her diaries Florence Culp describes in detail life as a clergyman's wife, particularly church services, funerals, the choir, Sunday school classes, and church society meetings. She also discusses household and family events as well as vacation trips.

10,959. Darcy, Timothy Johnes
Papers. 1811-1900. 15 vols. and 320 items.
Open. Accession card.
Rutgers University Libraries, Special Collections. Papers of Darcy (1790-1878), a farmer, include an 1876 diary in which his daughter [Miss] Eliza Darcy (1835?-?) of Wayne Township, NJ, wrote of living with her sister and their elderly parents, housekeeping, visits with relatives and friends, simple entertainments, and church. Also includes her household accounts, 1841-76.

10,960. Daughters of the American Revolution, Camp Middlebrook Chapter
Records. 1805-1965. 23 vols.
Open. Accession card.
Rutgers University Libraries, Special Collections. Records of this New Jersey chapter of the DAR consist of minutes of meetings, accounts, deeds, membership rosters, and scrapbooks of correspondence, programs, circulars, photos, and clippings.

10,961. Daughters of the American Revolution, General Frelinghuysen Chapter, Somerville, NJ
Records. 1759-1938. 1 box.
Open. Accession card.
Rutgers University Libraries, Special Collections. Historical notes, correspondence, clippings, and other papers of Helen Rawson Cook, DAR Chapter regent, include information on the observance of Constitution Week in 1955 and 1956. Also includes a deed and correspondence of the Whitehouse Chapter of the DAR in Hunterdon County, NJ.

10,962. Davidson Family
Papers. Ca. 1800-80. 1 box.
Open. Accession card.
Rutgers University Libraries, Special Collections. Personal and family correspondence of Lucretia Maria Davidson (1808-25), [Miss] Margaret Miller Davidson, and other family members; verses of Lucretia Davidson; genealogical items; miscellany; and a narrative of a trip Margaret Miller Clark, a precocious 10-year-old, made in 1833 with her family from Lake Champlain to their home in Plattsburg, NY, and then to Saratoga Springs and New York City. Margaret Clark's poems were published posthumously in 1841 with a biography by Washington Irving.

10,963. Davis, Elizabeth S.
Papers. Ca. 1922. 8 pp.
Open. Accession card.
Rutgers University Libraries, Special Collections. A manuscript history of the Jersey Blue Chapter of the DAR from 1906 to 1922. The Chapter was located in New Brunswick.

10,964. Demarest, David D.
Papers. 1835-93. 7 folders.
Open. Accession card.
Rutgers University Libraries, Special Collections. Personal and theological papers of Demarest include papers of his wife Catharine Louisa (Nevius) Demarest.

10,965. Dorcas and Day Nursery Society of New Brunswick
Records. 1813-1929. 1 folder and 7 vols.
Open. Accession card.
Rutgers University Libraries, Special Collections. Originally named the New Brunswick Dorcas Society, this women's group gave clothing and financial assistance to the sick and needy; in 1897 the group also established a day nursery. Minutes, 1813-1900 and 1928-29; accounts, 1869-97; and miscellaneous records.

10,966. Duncan, Susan (Lear)
Papers. 1788. 43 pp.
Open. Accession card.
Rutgers University Libraries, Special Collections. Diary of a journey by Susan Lear (1770?-?) from Philadelphia to Providence, RI, Boston, and back. Lear later married James Duncan.

10,967. Durham, Ruth
Papers. 1930-32. 1 folder.
Open. Accession card.
Rutgers University Libraries, Special Collections. Correspondence and legal papers relate to the successful attempt of Durham to be reinstated as senior clerk-bookkeeper in the Middlesex County treasurer's office. Apparently she had been replaced by a man who was not as well qualified for the position as she was.

10,968. Eddy, Lucy H.
Papers. 1830. 1 vol.
Open. Accession card.

Rutgers University Libraries, Special Collections.
Diary of [Miss] Eddy (1796-?), who lived in a well-to-do household with her widowed mother; her brother Thomas, a New York merchant; her sister; and an orphaned niece. Her diary concerns household and social life, religious activities with the Society of Friends, a New York monthly meeting school of which she was a committee member, visits to Hyde Park and to her childhood home in Elizabeth, NJ, and a fire in New York.

10,969. Elizabeth Town Female Humane Society
Records. 1810-29. 1 vol.
Open. Accession card.
Rutgers University Libraries, Special Collections.
This New Jersey women's group was founded in 1810 to assist the poor and unfortunate by "relieving the distresses" and educating their children. District managers administered the program. Constitution, minutes of the board of directors and the membership, and accounts.

10,970. Elmer, William
Papers. 1808-79. 2 boxes.
Open. Accession card.
Rutgers University Libraries, Special Collections.
Papers of Elmer, a physician, contain the constitution and accounts of the Young Female Religious Tract Society of Bridgeton, NJ, 1816-20.

10,971. Fisher, Gustavus
Papers. Nd. 6 items.
Open. Accession card.
Rutgers University Libraries, Special Collections.
Writings of Fisher (1815-93), a professor of modern languages at Rutgers College from 1859 to 1869, include a narrative on the many civic activities of "patriotic" New Jersey women.

10,972. Florence Mission
Records. 1889-98. 7 folders.
Open. Accession card.
Rutgers University Libraries, Special Collections.
Founded in 1889, the Mission was associated with the WCTU; it promoted temperance, evangelism, the rehabilitation of "human derelicts," nightly gospel meetings, and a Sabbath school. Accounts, a sketchy Mission journal, an inventory of furnishings, historical notes, clippings, and correspondence, much of which is addressed by persons served by the Mission to Ellen Kilburn, who seems to have been a worker at the Mission.

10,973. Freeman, Ginevra
Papers. 1869-1916. 29 vols.
Open. Unpublished guide.
Rutgers University Libraries, Special Collections.
Diary of Freeman (1839-?), an unmarried woman who lived with her parents Alexander H. Freeman (?-1883) and Lucinda Crane Freeman (?-1889); her brother Wilberforce Freeman (?-1907); his wife Katharine M. Kirtland Freeman (?-1912); and their daughter Marion (1876-?), who married John H. N. Condict in 1908. A trustee of the Orange Orphan's Home, Ginevra Freeman was active in the Orange Orphan Society, of which her mother was a founder; the Woman's Benevolent Society; and the Second Presbyterian Church, where she taught a Sunday school class. Her diary tells of her domestic chores, her visits with relatives and friends, of trips to Newark, NJ, and New York, and of a seven-month trip to England and the Continent she took with her sister-in-law in 1909.

10,974. Grieve, Lucia Catherine Graeme
Papers. 1878-1937. 3 folders and 39 vols.
Open. Accession card.
Rutgers University Libraries, Special Collections.
The daughter of clergyman David Graeme Grieve, [Miss] Grieve (1862-1946) was a student, lecturer, and teacher. Diaries, notebooks, programs of temperance and Methodist meetings, stories, a play, an outline of a novel, and articles. Her diaries, which cover most of the period, contain detailed entries about her life as a student at Wellesley College, 1880-83, and as a teacher at the Staunton Female Seminary in Staunton, VA, 1883-84; the Frederick Female Seminary in Frederick, MD, 1884-85; the Freehold Young Ladies Seminary in Freehold, NJ, 1885-86; the Maury Institute in Holly Springs, MS, 1886-88; and the Young Female College in Thomasville, GA, 1888-91. Her diaries also contain information about her travels in the British Isles during 1889, in India and the British Isles during 1904, and in Ireland during 1907. Educated in art and archaeology, Grieve earned a PhD from Columbia University in 1898. She lived in New York, Martindale Depot (NJ?), Westerleigh, NY, and Ocean Grove, NJ. She lectured on geography in New York, farmed between 1911 and 1922 at Martindale Depot, wrote poetry that was published in newspapers and minor anthologies, and was an active church worker.

The collection also includes diaries in which her mother Martha Lucy (Kinkead) Grieve (1838-?) comments on family and personal matters as well as her extensive welfare activity among the needy of New York and Staten Island. Visiting 200 homes each month, Martha Grieve distributed tracts, Bibles, bedding, clothing, and financial aid. Her work was influenced by Helen Louisa Phelps Stokes, wife of financier Anson Phelps Stokes, to whom she reported monthly.

10,975. Griffis, William Elliot
Papers. 1805-1964. 71 boxes and 21 vols.
Open. Accession card.
Rutgers University Libraries, Special Collections.
Papers of Griffis (1843-1928), a clergyman, educator, writer, and authority on Japan, contain diaries of his first wife Katharine Lyra (Stanton) Griffis (1856-98), a teacher whom he married in 1879; of his second wife Sarah Frances King Griffis (1868-1959), a teacher whom he married in 1900; and of his sister [Miss] Margaret Quandril Clark Griffis (1838-1913), who was also a teacher.

During part of the period covered by Katharine Griffis's diaries for 1873 to 1876, she taught at the Union Classical Institute, a school of which her father Benjamin Stanton was headmaster. An 1877 graduate of Vassar College, she then taught at a girls school in Albany, NY, until her marriage to Griffis.

Sarah Griffis was also a Vassar graduate (in 1890), and she taught school for a few years prior to her marriage to Griffis. Her diaries, scattered between 1900 and 1925, contain brief entries; some concern trips she made to Europe with her husband.

Diaries of Margaret Griffis from 1858 to 1913 contain detailed information about working between 1857 and 1860 as a tutor or governess for the children of plantation owners in Virginia and Tennessee, her observations of the South and plantation life, the period she spent between 1872 and 1874 with her brother William Griffis in Tokyo employed as an assistant principal and teacher in the Takehashi girls high school (Jo-Gakkō), and the years following 1899 when she lived with her brother in Ithaca, NY, assisting him with the clerical details of his work as a lecturer and writer.

10,976. Griggs, Oliver
Papers. 1841-54. 49 items.
Open. Accession card.
Rutgers University Libraries, Special Collections.
Correspondence of Griggs chiefly consists of letters from his daughter [Miss] Anne Helen Griggs, a teacher in Millville, NJ. Also included are letters from physician E. B. Richman, who was the self-appointed guardian of Anne Griggs.

10,977. Gwinnup Family
Papers. 1799-1916. 3 boxes, 1 envelope, and 1 container.
Open. Accession card.
Rutgers University Libraries, Special Collections.
Papers of the Gwinnup family include papers and medical instruments of Jabez Gwinnup (1799-1881), a physician, and diaries of [Miss] Laura Gwinnup (1832-1916) and her sister [Miss] Emma Gwinnup (1835?-68), who lived on the farm of their father Alfred Gwinnup (1808-88) in Blairstown Township, NJ. Emma Gwinnup's 1855 diary contains accounts of household work, sewing, visiting, church attendance, occasional entertainment, family and neighborhood events, and references to the westward migration. During part of 1855 she attended a school operated by H. Johnson; in 1868 she died of tuberculosis. The lengthy diaries of Laura Gwinnup for 1854 to 1916 contain details about farm and country life, church attendance, visiting and other social activities, and neighborhood events.

10,978. Hahm, Elmira H.
Papers. 1892. 2 items.
Open. Accession card.
Rutgers University Libraries, Special Collections.
Hahm was a midwife. Collection consists of a New Jersey state license to practice midwifery and a circular about state regulations on midwifery.

10,979. Halsey, Ezra
Papers. 1823-24. 1 item.
Open. Accession card.
Rutgers University Libraries, Special Collections.
Records of attendance of female scholars in an unidentified school, which were kept by Halsey of Mine Hill, NJ.

10,980. Hardenbergh Family
Papers. 1749-1927. Ca. 280 items.
Open. Accession card.
Rutgers University Libraries, Special Collections.
Papers of members of this New Brunswick family include papers of Catherine L. Hardenbergh (1794-1873) and diaries of Ann "Nancy" Maria Hardenbergh (1828-60) and of Catherine Low Hardenbergh (1852-1902). The journal kept in 1840 and 1841 by Nancy Hardenbergh, daughter of attorney Cornelius L. Hardenbergh (1790-1860), seems to have been part of a school assignment while she was a student at the Raritan Seminary in Perth Amboy, NJ; it also contains school compositions. The diary kept in 1869 and 1870 by Catherine Hardenbergh, teen-age daughter of real estate and insurance broker Jacob Rutsen Hardenbergh (1824-92), contains information about her daily life, sewing, visits, a few household chores, reading, family matters, and Second Reformed church activities.

10,981. Henderson, Alfred R.
Papers. 1905-51. 2 folders.
Open. Accession card.
Rutgers University Libraries, Special Collections.
Personal papers and material relating to the estate of Mabel (Smith) Douglass, who founded the New Jersey College for Women, which later became Douglass College. Henderson was a beneficiary of the estate.

10,982. Heroy, Anne Pluymert
Papers. 1912-26. 4 vols.
Open. Unpublished guide.
Rutgers University Libraries, Special Collections.
Travel journals of Heroy (1855-1939), a Newark, NJ, native who became totally deaf before the age of 20, include her records of European cruises in 1912, 1922, and 1926. During the trips she visited Italy, Switzerland, Germany, the Netherlands, England, Monaco, and the French Riviera. Her diary entries tell of sightseeing, shopping, visits to museums, historic sites, antiquities, and social contacts with other travelers. Heroy became adept at lip reading and was able to communicate despite her handicap. At the time of the 1912 trip she was living in New York with her sisters and her

widowed mother. By 1922 her mother and a sister were dead and she was living with a younger sister.

10,983. Hobart, Elizabeth Wills (Rutter)
Papers. 1863. 1 microfilm reel.
Open. Accession card.
Rutgers University Libraries, Special Collections.
Diary of Elizabeth Rutter (1839-1918), daughter of Pottstown, PA, resident Charles Rutter, contains details about her daily life, family, social visits, church, and such Civil War activities as soldiers' aid meetings. Rutter later married William Mintzer Hobart.

10,984. Housman, Ida E.
Papers. 1914-64. 10 items.
Open. Accession card.
Rutgers University Libraries, Special Collections.
A teacher and activist, Housman also ran for Hoboken, NJ, city commissioner in 1951. Collection consists of a constitution, bylaws, and minutes of the Equal Franchise Society of New Jersey; 1914 and 1920 correspondence from woman suffrage associations; literature, photos, and clippings relating to her campaign; a typescript article on politics in Hoboken; and information on pensions for teachers.

10,985. Howell, Asher
Papers. Ca. 1800-1956. 1 oversize folder, 3 boxes, and ca. 65 items.
Open. Accession card.
Rutgers University Libraries, Special Collections.
Family correspondence; biographical sketches; genealogical notes on the Howell, Atkinson, and related families; and other papers. Includes diaries of Bertha (Wilson) [Mrs. William] Howell and correspondence and diaries, 1894 and 1906, of [Miss] Eliza Dunham Howell (1834-1916), who was daughter of New Brunswick banker and industrialist Martin A. Howell. Her diaries contain comments on stocks and other investments and information about a trip she made to Europe.

10,986. Hulsizer, Mary Burr
Papers. 1957. 163 pp.
Open. Catalog card.
Rutgers University Libraries, Special Collections.
Travel journal of [Miss] Hulsizer (1889-) describes sightseeing, shopping, and social contacts during a trip through England, Italy, Germany, Switzerland, France, Spain, and five other countries. From 1928 until her retirement in 1955, Hulsizer was supervisor of health and nursing in the Newark, NJ, public school system.

10,987. Jarnagin, Emily L. (Murrell)
Papers. 1850. 144 pp.
Open. Accession card.
Rutgers University Libraries, Special Collections.
Diary of a visit young Emily Murrell made with relatives and friends in the Cherokee Nation in what is now the northeastern section of Oklahoma. The social life, local trips, and visits she describes primarily concern members and affiliates of the Nation. In 1852 she married Milton Preston Jarnagin.

10,988. Kidder, Harriette (Smith)
Papers. 1831-1902. 6 vols.
Open. Accession card.
Rutgers University Libraries, Special Collections.
Diaries and a commonplace book of Kidder (1816-1915), who was born in Connecticut and in 1842 married clergyman Daniel P. Kidder (1815-91), an editor of Methodist Sunday school publications, a professor at the Garrett Bible Institute in Evanston, IL, from 1856 to 1871, and at the Drew Theological Seminary in Madison, NJ, from 1871 to 1881. Before she began these diaries, Harriette Smith was a teacher and principal at the Worthington (Ohio) Female Seminary. The diaries contain detailed retrospective narratives, family sketches, and reminiscences, as well as information about her involvement in Methodism as a minister's wife and independently; her theological, moral, and social concerns; her interest in temperance; and accounts of travel with her husband in the US, England, and Europe. The diaries also contain a few copies of letters and clippings.

10,989. Kirkpatrick, Andrew
Papers. 1788-1834. 1 vol. and 4 items.
Open. Accession card.
Rutgers University Libraries, Special Collections.
Kirkpatrick (1756-1831) was a New Brunswick attorney, New Jersey Supreme Court justice and chief justice, trustee of Princeton University, and president of the Princeton Theological Seminary. Correspondence he received and a diary in which his wife Jane (Bayard) Kirkpatrick (1772-1851) details domestic and social activities, local events, and news about her children, friends, and relatives.

10,990. Kite, Elizabeth Sarah
Papers. 1840-1962. 3 boxes and 23 items.
Open. Accession card.
Rutgers University Libraries, Special Collections.
Kite (1864-1954) was an author, historian, and archivist of the American Catholic Historical Society. Correspondence, notes, an autobiography, articles and other writings, genealogical material, photos, and clippings. Born in Philadelphia, Kite was trained as a teacher and worked in ca. 1910 at the Vineland, NJ, Training School for Mental Defectives, where she conducted psychological research. She then became interested in the French contribution and aid to America during the American Revolution. Collection contains material from her writing and research on these subjects, the feeble-minded and mental degeneracy, and on residents of the Pine Barrens region in New Jersey.

10,991. Knox, Aletta V. (Van Doren)
Papers. 1828-31. 2 vols.
Open. Accession card.
Rutgers University Libraries, Special Collections.
Diary of Aletta Van Doren (1816-52) contains details about her life at the Van Doren Collegiate Institute in Brooklyn Heights, NY, and vacation visits to her home on a farm in Raritan, NJ. Van Doren later married John P. Knox (1811-83), a Reformed and Presbyterian clergyman.

10,992. Kriendler Memorial
Collection. Mid-20th century. 7 boxes.
Open. Accession card.
Rutgers University Libraries, Special Collections.
Literary manuscripts of recent fiction and nonfiction include works by Faith Baldwin, Vina Delmar, Edna Ferber, Fannie Ferber Fox, Lillian Hellman, Alva Johnston, Louise Kennedy Mable, and Mary Roberts Rinehart.

10,993. La Tourrette, Cornelius Wyckoff
Papers. 1849-51. 9 items and 64 pp.
Open. Unpublished guide.
Rutgers University Libraries, Special Collections.
A California gold rush diary of La Tourrette (1814-1902) and correspondence of La Tourrette with his wife Margaret, who remained in South Bound Brook, NJ, with their children during her husband's two-year trip to California. The diary contains entries about Cornelius La Tourrette's sea and land journey from the Caribbean side of Panama to the Sacramento River in California. His letters to his wife supplement his diary, while her letters contain local and family news. They also indicate her impatience with his California mining venture, which yielded modest success.

10,994. Ladies Book Club
Records. 1896-1903. 1 vol.
Open. Accession card.
Rutgers University Libraries, Special Collections.
A list of several hundred books read or reviewed by members of the Club, which may have been a New Brunswick group.

10,995. Larison, Mary Jane (Sergeant)
Papers. Ca. 1855-57. 231 pp.
Open. Accession card.
Rutgers University Libraries, Special Collections.
Abridged copy of a diary in which Mary Sergeant (1837-1917), a member of the first class of the New Jersey State Normal School in Trenton, discusses lessons, classroom instruction, analyses of lectures, educational method, philosophy, and other matters. Sergeant became a teacher in various Hunterdon County, NJ, schools. In 1863 she married Cornelius Wilson Larison, a Ringoes, NJ, physician.

10,996. League of Women Voters of New Brunswick
Records. 1936-53. 2 boxes and 3 vols.
Open. Accession card.
Rutgers University Libraries, Special Collections.
Records of this local affiliate of the LWV contain a constitution, bylaws, annual reports, minutes, budgets, membership lists, newsletters, and clippings.

10,997. LeFetra, Elizabeth Rylee
Papers. 1837-54. 31 items.
Open. Accession card.
Rutgers University Libraries, Special Collections.
Correspondence, a diary, receipts, and verses by [Miss] LeFetra, who probably was a Quaker. In her diary she describes daily social activities, religious sewing meetings, funerals, and family visits. In 1846 she was a boarding student at the Eatontown Institute in Eatontown, NJ; from 1851 to 1853 she was a teacher in Manasquan, NJ. She also had numerous friends and relatives in Eatontown, Manasquan, and New York City, whom she wrote or visited frequently.

10,998. McCoy, Emma
Papers. 1902-18. 4 vols.
Open. Accession card.
Rutgers University Libraries, Special Collections.
Contains records of the New Jersey Teachers Retirement Fund, New Brunswick department, 1902-03; minutes of the Middlesex County Women Teacher's Association; and volumes of clippings.

10,999. Magee, Abbie Eliza
Papers. 1905. 122 pp.
Open. Accession card.
Rutgers University Libraries, Special Collections.
Diary in which [Miss] Magee (1847-1909), daughter of Captain James J. R. Magee of Marlboro Township, NJ, describes living with relatives in Monmouth County, NJ, domestic and farm chores, visits, family events, the weather, and sewing, some of which she seems to have done professionally.

11,000. Minor, Julia
Papers. 1946-49. 2 folders.
Open. Accession card.
Rutgers University Libraries, Special Collections.
Minor was executive secretary of the Family and Children's Society. Collection contains records relating to the activities of the child welfare committee of the New Jersey Welfare Council and its effort to form a separate agency for child welfare in the state, correspondence in which other child welfare agencies comment on the policies in their states, and articles on unwed mothers.

11,001. Morrogh, Mary F.
Papers. 1828-50. 7 items.
Open. Accession card.
Rutgers University Libraries, Special Collections.
Letters of Mary Richmond, who was wife and then widow of George Richmond, are addressed to her uncles John Brown of Philadelphia and Isaac B. Parker of Philadelphia and Burlington, NJ. Her

last letter primarily concerns her prospective second husband C. T. Morrogh, a New Brunswick physician.

11,002. Mott, Sarah "Sallie"
Papers. 1803-04. 102-page vol.
Open. Accession card.
Rutgers University Libraries, Special Collections.
Copy of a journal that [Miss] Mott, a Trenton, NJ, resident, kept for her cousin [Mrs.] Martha Lowry of a trip from Philadelphia to Portugal aboard the *Richmond* in the company of a Dr. Thompson and Edward Tilghman of Philadelphia. Mott stayed in Lisbon for some time; she also visited Cintia.

11,003. National Board of Prisons and Prison Labor
Records. 1926. 1 vol.
Open. Accession card.
Rutgers University Libraries, Special Collections.
A survey report on the work girls performed in selected reformatories was compiled by Anna Lalor Burdick for the Board. Superintendents of the following institutions contributed information: Andrews Institute in Willoughby, OH; the Women's Prison and the Indiana Girls School in Indianapolis; the New York Reformatory for Women in Bedford, NY; the Correctional School for Women in Muncy, PA; the Clinton Farms in New Jersey; and other schools of correction in New Jersey.

11,004. Naughright, Anna De Yoe
Papers. 1902-03. 2 vols.
Open. Accession card.
Rutgers University Libraries, Special Collections.
Journal of a trip Naughright, a Morris County, NJ, resident, made with a Mrs. Graves and Graves's children to Ireland, the Isle of Man, Scotland, England, Paris, Monte Carlo, Naples, and Rome.

11,005. Neilson Family
Papers. 1690-1937. Ca. 80 cu.ft.
Open. Accession card.
Rutgers University Libraries, Special Collections.
Family papers of Colonel John Neilson and Colonel James Neilson chiefly concern their activities in New Jersey during the Revolutionary War. Also includes a travel journal in which Catharine (Bleecker) Neilson (1809-93), widow of businessman James Neilson (1784-1862), describes the voyage she made with her son James Neilson (1844-1937) to England and Europe during 1866 and 1867. A travel journal of her daughter-in-law Mary Putnam (Woodbury) Neilson (1846-1914), wife of businessman and philanthropist James Neilson, concerns trips to the British Isles and Europe, one of which she made before her marriage. Her diary for 1898 and 1902 contains entries about the weather, birds, gardening, and social life.

11,006. New Brunswick Board of Recreation
Records. 1936-55. 2 vols.
Open. Accession card.
Rutgers University Libraries, Special Collections.
Minutes, reports, and other records of the Board and the city department of recreation. Also includes reports, correspondence, and other material of the New Brunswick Woman's Club committee of public recreation.

11,007. New Brunswick City Committee on Public Recreation
Records. 1922-51. 1 box.
Open. Accession card.
Rutgers University Libraries, Special Collections.
Reports, correspondence, notes, and other records of the Committee. Also included are reports about public recreation that Mrs. Walter T. Marvin prepared for the City Improvement Society and the New Brunswick Woman's Club.

11,008. New Brunswick First Reformed Church Ladies Foreign Missionary Society
Records. 1839-45. 1 vol.
Open. Accession card.
Rutgers University Libraries, Special Collections.
Constitution, minutes of meetings, and subscribers and donors lists of the Society.

11,009. New Jersey Federation of Business and Professional Women's Clubs
Records. 1919- . Ca. 45 boxes, 5 vols., and 3 bundles.
Open. Accession card.
Rutgers University Libraries, Special Collections.
Founded in 1919, the Federation seeks to extend opportunities to women in professions and business through activities and education. Constitution, bylaws, minutes, financial records, correspondence, reports, membership applications and lists, Club charters, directories, clippings, and printed matter.

11,010. New Jersey Federation of Business and Professional Women's Clubs, New Brunswick Club
Records. 1923-76. 8 boxes and 10 vols.
Open. Accession card.
Rutgers University Libraries, Special Collections.
A women's voluntary association, the New Brunswick Club is an affiliate of the state Federation of Business and Professional Women's Clubs. Bylaws, minutes of the executive board and of membership meetings, treasurers' reports, budgets, records of the scholarship and loan fund, insurance documents, correspondence, committee and convention reports, histories, membership rosters, news releases, photos, scrapbooks, and other material.

11,011. New Jersey Governor's Task Force on Migrant Farm Labor
Records. 1950-68. 4 boxes.
Open. Accession card.
Rutgers University Libraries, Special Collections.
Many women were active on the Task Force, which was associated with the Consumers' League of New Jersey. Minutes, correspondence, reports, pamphlets, and clippings contain data on migrant workers and working conditions and information concerning migrant labor legislation. Also includes a bibliography the League compiled of material on migrant workers.

11,012. New Jersey Home Economics Association
Records. 1950-64. 6 boxes.
Open. Accession card.
Rutgers University Libraries, Special Collections.
Records of this Newark, NJ, professional organization, associated with the American Home Economics Association in Washington, DC, contain constitution, bylaws, minutes, committee and financial reports, correspondence, newsletters, programs, and articles.

11,013. New Jersey Welfare Council, Newark
Records. 1919- . 10 cu.ft.
Open. Accession card.
Rutgers University Libraries, Special Collections.
The Council was founded in 1919. Treasurer's statements, accounts, minutes, proceedings, papers read before annual conferences, questionnaires, case studies, surveys on such topics as the Negro in New Jersey, and records of the Emergency Relief Association, 1922-33.

11,014. Newell, Julia (Florance)
Papers. 1916. 71-page vol.
Open. Accession card.
Rutgers University Libraries, Special Collections.
Diary of a trip that Julia Florance (1898-), daughter of New Brunswick attorney, public official, insurance executive, and bank director William E. Florance, made with her parents and others in a Cadillac from New Brunswick to New Hampshire and back. She later married Duncan H. Newell.

11,015. Newkirk, Sarah Cordelia (Miller)
Papers. 1887-88. 1 vol.
Open. Accession card.
Rutgers University Libraries, Special Collections.
Diary in which [Mrs. Thompson] Newkirk (1817-97), a widow living with two sons and a daughter-in-law near Spokane, WA, describes the hardships of farm life. Oppressed by her domestic situation, Newkirk moved to Philadelphia to live with others of her children.

11,016. Norton, Mary T.
Papers. 1920-60. 10 boxes and 11 vols.
Open. Accession card.
Rutgers University Libraries, Special Collections.
Norton (1875-1959) was a US congresswoman. Correspondence, speeches and writings, political subject file, biographical data, tributes, photos, and clippings. Also includes drafts of her unpublished memoir "Madame Congressman."

11,017. Olden, Marion S.
Papers. 1934-70. 2 boxes.
Open. Accession card.
Rutgers University Libraries, Special Collections.
Olden (1888-?) was a proponent of compulsory sterilization for 20 years. Pamphlets she wrote, reports, surveys, articles, scrapbooks, and clippings contain information on genetics, birth control, and sterilization.

11,018. Pell, Orlie
Papers. Ca. 1920-60. Ca. 22 cartons.
Access restricted. Accession card.
Rutgers University Libraries, Special Collections.
Correspondence and other papers of Pell (? ca. 1975), a wealthy Flemington, NJ, resident, reflect her interests in pacifism, the UN, and the LWV of Hunterdon County.

11,019. Pierson, William
Papers. 1827-61. 1 vol.
Open. Accession card.
Rutgers University Libraries, Special Collections.
The obstetrical register of Pierson (1796-1882), an Orange, NJ, physician, includes selected case notes.

11,020. Place, Anna Miller (Newkirk)
Papers. 1909-18. 3 vols.
Open. Accession card.
Rutgers University Libraries, Special Collections.
The travel journal of Place (1841-1918), daughter of Thompson and Sarah Cordelia (Miller) Newkirk, concerns her voyage in 1909 and 1910 from New York to Queenstown (Ireland?) and travel in the British Isles, France, and other places. Also includes a diary of the period when she was living with her daughter Cordelia and son-in-law Robert C. Eddy, a physician, in New Rochelle, NY. The diary contains references to Place's visits to her daughters in New York City, Worcester, MA, and Pittsburgh. Anna Miller Newkirk married James W. Barker in 1859 and James Keyes Place in 1872.

11,021. Potter, Ellen Culver
Papers. 1932-57. 4 boxes.
Open. Accession card.
Rutgers University Libraries, Special Collections.
A social worker and physician, Potter helped found the Rutgers graduate school of social work; she also was a member of the board of directors of the American Association of Social Workers. Correspondence, reports, pamphlets, and other publications. Also includes material on the care and treatment of the aged.

11,022. Rahway Association for the Relief of Sick Poor
Records. 1818-1957. 3 vols.
Open. Accession card.

Rutgers University Libraries, Special Collections. Records of the Association, an organization of women who dispensed charity to the sick and poor, consist of minutes, disbursements, subscription lists, and other items. Formerly the group was known as the Female Association of Bridge Town, NJ. It was dissolved in 1957 because of declining membership and out of the belief that other organizations could better help the sick and poor.

11,023. Readington, NJ, Reformed Church
Records. 1719-1959. 2 microfilm reels.
Open. Accession card.
Rutgers University Libraries, Special Collections. Church records include consistory minutes, 1721-96 and 1827-1939; accounts, 1849-1925; scattered membership records; baptism records, 1720-1958; marriage records, 1833-53 and 1871-1959; and death records, 1834-1959; a history; and an anniversary scrapbook of the Church. Also includes minutes of the Ladies' Missionary Society, 1875-1901, and minutes for the Raritan Valley "Great Consistory," as well as information about the area surrounding Readington.

11,024. Reynolds, Mary Ann (Guest)
Papers. 1817. 7 pp.
Open. Accession card.
Rutgers University Libraries, Special Collections. Travel journal of Reynolds (1797-1855) concerns her move from New Brunswick to Cincinnati with her sisters and parents. She describes leaving their home, proceeding to Philadelphia where they embarked on a "Pennsylvania ship" drawn by horses, and traveling through the Pennsylvania counties of Philadelphia, Chester, Lancaster, Dauphin, Cumberland, and Franklin. Her narrative ends at Strawsburg (Strasburg).

11,025. Ruttkay, Louise (Kossuth)
Papers. 1875-97. 79 items.
Open. Accession card.
Rutgers University Libraries, Special Collections. Correspondence to [Miss] Eliza Elvira Kenyon from Ruttkay, sister of Louis Kossuth, concerns his exile in Turin, Italy, as well as the transcendental movement in the US, Hungarian politics, and women's rights.

11,026. Schanck, Jane Ann
Papers. 1871-81. 132 items.
Open. Accession card.
Rutgers University Libraries, Special Collections. Letters Schanck wrote while she was a student at Miss Bucknall's Seminary in New Brunswick to her parents in Holmdel, NJ, correspondence from them, and letters of condolence on her death.

11,027. Schenck, Henrietta
Papers. 1918-19. 4 folders.
Open. Accession card.
Rutgers University Libraries, Special Collections. Miscellaneous papers of Schenck, a resident of New Brunswick, relate to her volunteer work on home front activities with the American National Red Cross, the War Camp Community Service, and Liberty Loan campaigns.

11,028. Schulze, Edith
Papers. 1938-71. 1 box.
Open. Accession card.
Rutgers University Libraries, Special Collections. Schulze was a member of Free Acres, a single-tax, utopian community, and head of its forestry committee. Minutes of monthly meetings, financial memoranda and other records of the committee, newsletters, clippings, and other material.

11,029. Schureman, John
Papers. 1799-1891. 47 items.
Open. Accession card.
Rutgers University Libraries, Special Collections. Correspondence of Schureman (1778-1818), a minister in New Jersey and New York City and a professor at Queens College, contains letters he wrote his wife Julia Ann (Conover) Schureman (1781-1834) of Middletown, NJ. Also includes a diary she kept from 1828 to 1834 after his death.

11,030. Sheltering Arms
Records. 1852-1966. Ca. 117 Paige boxes and 21 oversize vols.
Access restricted. Inventory.
Rutgers University Libraries, Special Collections. Sheltering Arms was founded in 1864 by clergyman Thomas McClure Peters to provide a home for children who were not eligible for admission to any other existing institutions. In 1944 the Sheltering Arms Children's Service was created from the merger of Sheltering Arms with the New York Child's Foster Home Service; the new group's purpose was to provide foster home care for children. Organizational records; annual reports, 1865-1961; minutes, 1864-1944; financial records, 1880-1953; case histories, registers, and other information on the backgrounds of children admitted to Sheltering Arms, 1864-1955; foster homes files, 1917-66; and Sheltering Arms magazines. Also includes records of the New York Child's Foster Home Service, 1852-1956; the Howard Mission Home for Little Wanderers, ca. 1860-1945; the Children's Fold, 1870-1905; the Shepherd's Fold, 1894-1904; and the Katy Ferguson Home, 1925-53.

11,031. Smith, Rescarrick Moore
Papers. 1759-1910. 37 vols. and ca. 2000 items.
Open. Accession card.
Rutgers University Libraries, Special Collections. Papers of Smith (1804-?), a Hightstown, NJ, businessman and treasurer of the state of New Jersey, include correspondence and bills of Sara B. Smith, 1843-72, and a diary of his sister [Miss] Anna Maria Smith (1811-?) for 1827 to 1849. She lived on the family homestead and then later with relatives in Mercer County, NJ, either as a working guest or an employee. Her diary contains information on a prolonged but unhappy love affair. Her main preoccupations are religious anxieties and death.

11,032. Society of Friends, New York Yearly Meetings
Records. 1728-1886. 5 microfilm reels.
Open. Accession card.
Rutgers University Libraries, Special Collections. Records of the New York Society consist of minutes of monthly and yearly women's meetings, 1728-80 and 1828-70; minutes of yearly men's meetings, 1746-1872; and meetings of monthly meetings for sufferings, 1758-1886.

11,033. Society of Friends, Rancocas Preparative Meeting
Records. 1775-1835. 35 items.
Open. Accession card.
Rutgers University Libraries, Special Collections. Correspondence from the women's meeting of a local Rancocas, NJ, Society of Friends and from the London yearly meeting, extracts from the Philadelphia yearly meeting, a membership list, subscription lists, and other material.

11,034. Somerset County Prosecutor's Office: Hall-Mills Murder Case
Records. 1922-24. 8 folders.
Open. Accession card.
Rutgers University Libraries, Special Collections. Records of the case concerning the murder of Episcopal minister Edward Wheeler Hall and choir singer Eleanor Reinhardt Mills consist of correspondence, copies of the autopsy report, court pleas, and other items. Most of the correspondence is addressed to prosecutor Azariah M. Beekman and special prosecutor Wilbur A. Mott. The 1922 murder was never solved officially; Edward Hall's wife and her two brothers were tried but released because of insufficient evidence. At the trial it was revealed that Hall and Mills had been involved in an affair that had scandalized area residents for some time.

11,035. Southwick, Mary Ferguson (Page)
Papers. 1872-76. 35 pp.
Open. Accession card.
Rutgers University Libraries, Special Collections. Diary entries of [Mrs. Philip R. V.] Southwick, a Flemington and Trenton, NJ, housewife, are inscribed in the volume her father Edward Page (1787-1867), a Methodist circuit rider, used to record marriages, sermon outlines, and the like.

11,036. Stanton, Theodore
Papers. Ca. 1800-1925. Ca. 6000 items.
Open. Accession card.
Rutgers University Libraries, Special Collections. Correspondence, literary manuscripts, and other material received by Stanton (1851-1925), a European literary agent for the *North American Review,* Harper Brothers, and other firms, from such authors as Jeannette Leonard Gilder, Mary Jane Holmes, Sara Jane (Clarke) Lippincott, Amy Lowell, Elizabeth Robins Pennell, and Jessie Bell Rittenhouse.

11,037. Stevens, Catharine Clarkson (Crosby)
Papers. 1833-35. 24 pp.
Open. Accession card.
Rutgers University Libraries, Special Collections. Travel journals of Catharine Crosby (1812-82), daughter of New York banker William B. Crosby, concern trips with relatives from New York City to Buffalo, NY, Niagara Falls, Montreal, Quebec, and Albany, NY, and south to Philadelphia, Richmond, and Washington. The author later married Henry H. Stevens.

11,038. Stillwell, Laura Jean (Libbey)
Papers. 1886-1925. 3 boxes.
Open. Accession card.
Rutgers University Libraries, Special Collections. A novelist, playwright, and columnist, [Mrs. Van Mater] Stillwell (1862-1924) always gave her stories happy endings. Correspondence; manuscripts of *Estranged—But They Still Love, In an Unguarded Moment,* and others of her plays; business and legal papers; installment payment receipts for publications; advertisements; clippings of a personal advice column she wrote; and other papers.

11,039. Stoddard Family
Papers. 1809-1919. 8 boxes.
Open. Accession card.
Rutgers University Libraries, Special Collections. Papers of clergyman Ira Joy Stoddard and his wife Druscilla Chapman (Allen) Stoddard (1821-1913), educators and Baptist missionaries in India from 1848 to 1873, contain material about their missionary work and about the Allen, Stoddard, Whitney, and other related families. Also includes information pertaining to Madison (now Colgate) University, Central University in Pella, IA, and the Troy (New York) Female Seminary. Collection includes papers of Charlotte Joy Stoddard as well.

11,040. Stokes, Helen Louisa Phelps
Papers. 1883-84. 226 pp.
Open. Accession card.
Rutgers University Libraries, Special Collections. Stokes (1846-?) was the wife of Anson Phelps Stokes (1838-1913), a New York banker and financier; she also was active in charitable work. Her diary contains full entries about household and social life, particularly servants, the Stokeses' yacht, and vacation camping trips.

11,041. Strong, Alan Hartwell
Papers. 1800-1931. 4 boxes.
Open. Accession card.
Rutgers University Libraries, Special Collections. Legal papers of Garret A. Vroom and papers of his

widow are included with the diaries for 1879 to 1928 of Susan de Lancey Cullen (Van Rensselaer) Strong (1851-1931), who was wife of New Brunswick and Philadelphia attorney Alan Hartwell Strong. Irregular diary entries, some of which are long, indicate that she was active socially and in historical and hereditary society work. Also includes an 1889 diary of Cornelia Josepha (Codwise) Van Rensselaer (1810-90) containing brief household and personal accounts and details about servants.

11,042. Ten Eyck Family
Papers. 1725-1899. 11 boxes and 19 vols.
Open. Accession card.
Rutgers University Libraries, Special Collections.
Business papers and diaries of Jacob Ten Eyck (1733-94) and other family members, including a diary of [Miss] Margaret Ten Eyck (1766-1850), a professional seamstress who lived with relatives and customers. The diary covers the period from 1834 to 1844 and contains brief entries concerning visits, finances, and sewing and quilting work.

11,043. Thomas, Ada R.
Papers. 1893-94. 2 items.
Open. Accession card.
Rutgers University Libraries, Special Collections.
Medical diplomas of Thomas, a physician, are from the Women's Medical College of the Pennsylvania Hospital of Philadelphia. One represents her award of a doctorate in medicine; the other certifies that she has completed her internship.

11,044. Thomson, Sarah
Papers. 1809. 10 pp.
Open. Accession card.
Rutgers University Libraries, Special Collections.
Diary in which Thomson, a young woman apparently from Philadelphia, describes daily social activities during a visit she made with her mother and brother to the family of Judge Ebenezer Tucker in Tuckerton, NJ.

11,045. Travellers' Club
Records. 1916-46. 1 box.
Open. Accession card.
Rutgers University Libraries, Special Collections.
Both men and women were members of this New Brunswick club. Collection consists of papers on historical or other topics read at meetings. One paper, presented by Elizabeth S. Davis in 1928, concerns New Jersey women during the Revolutionary War.

11,046. Trevett, Cyrus C.
Papers. 1879-90. 1 vol.
Open. Accession card.
Rutgers University Libraries, Special Collections.
Diary in which Trevett's mother Rebecca Angeline (Clark) [Mrs. Sewell S.] Trevett (1832-?) describes farm activities, family and neighborhood social events, and the weather. Cyrus Trevett had earlier written a diary in the same volume.

11,047. U.S. Office of Education, Federal Board for Vocational Education
Records. Ca. 1921-30s. 2 boxes.
Open. Accession card.
Rutgers University Libraries, Special Collections.
Correspondence, reports, and other material from the personal files of [Mrs.] Anna L. Burdick, special agent for the girls and women division of the Trade and Industrial Education Service of the Board.

11,048. Vail, Rebecca (Warden)
Papers. 1847. 1 folder.
Open. Accession card.
Rutgers University Libraries, Special Collections.
Diary in which [Mrs. Emmor K.] Vail (?-1872), a young Quaker housewife, discusses her daily activities and visits with friends and relatives, most of whom were Quakers, in Green Brook and Rahway, NJ.

11,049. Van Dyke, Mary Dix (Strong)
Papers. 1849-50. 48 pp.
Open. Accession card.
Rutgers University Libraries, Special Collections.
Diary of Van Dyke (1819-75), wife of John Van Dyke, a Whig congressman from New Jersey, contains entries about family and social life in Washington and observations on political events. Some longer accounts concern a White House dinner in 1850, the deaths of John C. Calhoun and President Taylor, and the text of a letter she wrote urging George E. Badger, a US senator from North Carolina, to remove the pistol he reputedly kept in his Senate desk. On her husband's advice, she did not send the letter.

11,050. Van Dyke, Rachel
Papers. 1810-12. 31 diary sections.
Open. Unpublished guide.
Rutgers University Libraries, Special Collections.
Diary in which Van Dyke (1793-?), the daughter of a well-to-do New Brunswick gentleman, wrote about her social and home activities, her studies, and her feelings for Ebenezer Grosvenor, a Yale graduate who tutored her in Latin. During the period covered by her diary, her father died, she studied with Grosvenor, and she wrote to him after he returned to Connecticut because of ill health. Van Dyke's studies included Latin, chemistry, and eventually botany. Prior to the period during which she kept the diary, she had attended a local girls school.

11,051. Voorhees, Sarah Rutgers (Neilson)
Papers. 1891-92. 1 vol.
Open. Accession card.
Rutgers University Libraries, Special Collections.
Diary of Voorhees (1853-?) concerns her social and personal activities with her husband Willard P. Voorhees (1851-1914), an attorney and then New Jersey Supreme Court justice. After her first husband died, she married Albert J. Jones.

11,052. Voorhees, Tracy Stebbins
Papers. 1948-74. 13 boxes, 16 cartons, 13 vols., and 4 bundles.
Open. Catalog card.
Rutgers University Libraries, Special Collections.
Papers of Voorhees (1890-1974), who was appointed assistant and undersecretary of the army by President Truman, include ca. 100 letters of condolence his widow Josephine Ludlow Palmer Voorhees received after his death.

11,053. Wendover, Jessie May
Papers. 1881-1953. 73 vols.
Open. Accession card.
Rutgers University Libraries, Special Collections.
Diaries detail the life of [Miss] Wendover (1872-?), daughter of Newark grocer William Wendover (?-1900), from childhood to old age. After graduating from Barnard College in 1896, she lived in Newark and Metuchen, NJ. In her diaries she describes household chores, recreation, studies and reading, music lessons, social life, visits, shopping, and vacations. She also occasionally mentions national and world events.

11,054. Werner, Adelaide
Papers. 1906-07. 1 vol.
Open. Accession card.
Rutgers University Libraries, Special Collections.
Diary of Werner, the daughter of Louis Werner, concerns a trip to England and her experiences as a student near Columbia University in New York City. Werner appears to have been a teen-ager when she wrote the diary.

11,055. Whitlock, Sarah O.
Papers. Ca. 1914. 1 folder.
Open. Accession card.
Rutgers University Libraries, Special Collections.
Essays by Whitlock, an historian, concern the history of New Brunswick and apparently were intended to be chapters in a book, for a preface on the history and future of New Brunswick is included as well. Also contains miscellaneous papers.

11,056. Whitney Family
Papers. 1861-1921. 1 box.
Open. Accession card.
Rutgers University Libraries, Special Collections.
Family papers consist of correspondence of Bennett Whitney and his wife, primarily letters from their son Eben Whitney, 1861-73; letters Henry Whitney and his wife Bertha (Stoddard) Whitney (1850-?) received from her parents and from clergyman Ira Joy Stoddard and his wife Druscilla Chapman (Allen) Stoddard, former missionaries in India who were then living at the George Nugent Home for Baptists in Germantown, PA; and a diary Bertha Stoddard kept before her marriage to Henry Whitney. During the period of the diary she was a student at Kalamazoo College in Michigan who lived with relatives (in 1868), a student at the Troy Female Seminary in Troy, NY (in 1871), and a public school teacher in Pella, IA (in 1875). In her diary she mentions frequent church activity as well as visits to relatives in Cortland and Erie counties in New York.

11,057. Whitney, Susan
Papers. 1856-57. 20 pp.
Open. Accession card.
Rutgers University Libraries, Special Collections.
Diary that probably belonged to Whitney (1839-?) reveals her interest in activities at the Perth Amboy, NJ, Baptist Church where she taught a small class of Negro children. Her diary also contains regular entries about household, family, and local affairs.

11,058. Wilcox, Anna B.
Papers. 1852-1956. 191 items.
Open. Accession card.
Rutgers University Libraries, Special Collections.
Papers of [Mrs. Albert] Wilcox include a journal she kept of her trip to France and Italy during 1905, a letter, funeral cards, and a diary of a 1956 honeymoon taken in Bermuda by a New Jersey couple.

11,059. Williamson, Julia B.
Papers. 1886-1945. 3 boxes.
Open. Accession card.
Rutgers University Libraries, Special Collections.
Williamson (1894-1945) was president of the New Brunswick branch of the Needlework Guild of America, a women's group that provided garments to the needy. Directors' and financial reports, annual meeting minutes, a 50-year history, garment reports, and other records of the Guild. Also includes personal and family papers, a school notebook, photos, and clippings.

11,060. Wilson, Woodrow
Papers. 1896-1927. 28 items.
Open. Accession card.
Rutgers University Libraries, Special Collections.
Correspondence of President Wilson, his wife Edith (Bolling) Galt Wilson (1872-1961), and others.

11,061. Wister, Sarah
Papers. 1777-78. 16 pp.
Open. Accession card.
Rutgers University Libraries, Special Collections.
Diary of Wister (1761-1804), a Quaker living with her family in North Wales (Gwynedd), PA, approximately 15 miles from British-occupied Philadelphia. Wister followed local military activity with interest and was a friend of young American officers. Her diary was edited by Albert Cook Myers and published as *Sally Wister's Journal; a True Narrative* (1902). The collection's

manuscript copy of Wister's diary was made from the original in 1837 by John F. Watson, a Philadelphia historian, but the texts of Watson's and Myers's copies vary.

11,062. Woman's Christian Temperance Union, Middlesex County
Records. 1886-1948. 1 box, 22 vols., and 2 oversize vols.
Open. Accession card.
Rutgers University Libraries, Special Collections.
Organizational records, minutes, treasurers' accounts, clippings, and printed matter of local New Jersey units of the WCTU, including the New Brunswick, Sayreville, Metuchen, and Middlesex County branches.

11,063. Wood, Janet Margaret
Papers. 1936-53. 3 vols. and 19 items.
Open. Accession card.
Rutgers University Libraries, Special Collections.
[Miss] Wood (1907-) was captain of an American National Red Cross "clubmobile" that dispensed doughnuts, coffee, cigarettes, and candy to military units near Cheltenham, NJ, during WWII; later she became a social worker. Her 1943 diary contains lists of supplies and other memoranda as well as descriptions of her work with the clubmobile. Also includes notes on Scottish heraldry, clippings, and articles on social work, the care of crippled children, and the relationship of mental hygiene to public health nursing, some of which she wrote.

11,064. Zwemer, Susanna (Peirce)
Papers. 1939-48. 3 boxes.
Open. Accession card.
Rutgers University Libraries, Special Collections.
Zwemer worked with various groups, including the LWV, the New Jersey Committee on Constitutional Revision, and the New Jersey Constitution Foundation, promoting the revision of the New Jersey constitution; she also was president of the New Jersey Consumers' League. Speeches, notes, reports, publicity releases, leaflets, clippings, and other material. Also includes correspondence of the Westfield, NJ, Committee on Constitutional Revision and Federal Writers' Project monographs on Union County government and officials and on the County park system.

NEW PROVIDENCE

11,065. Mason, Mary Mellow
Papers. 1905-64. 44 vols.
Open. No guide.
New Providence Historical Society.
Diaries in which [Mrs. Frank] Mason (?-ca. 1967), a housewife, mentions her daily, family, and social activities as well as her training as a nurse before marriage in 1906, her caring for those who were ill, and her work as a saleswoman during the depression.

NEWARK

11,066. Monastery Archives
Records. 1880- . No size given.
Access restricted. No guide.
Monastery of St. Dominic.
Minutes, financial records, correspondence, and photos record the history of this cloistered contemplative community. Founded in 1880, the community was the first monastery in the US of Nuns of the Order of Preachers, commonly known as Dominican Nuns.

11,067. Abeel, C. R.
Papers. 1871-76. 12 items.
Open. Published guide.
The New Jersey Historical Society.
Historical sketches by Abeel and data on the size and purpose of Newark women's organizations and charitable institutions, including the Newark Female Charitable Society, the Home for Respectable Aged Women, the Women's Christian Association of Newark, the First Ward Industrial School, the Women's Board of Foreign Missions of the Presbytery of Newark, the Ladies' Benevolent Association of the North Reformed Church, and the Ladies of Orange Orphan's Society. See *Guide to the Manuscript Collections of The New Jersey Historical Society* (forthcoming).

11,068. Academy of Medicine of New Jersey
Records. 1775-1968. 16 ft.
Open. Published guide.
The New Jersey Historical Society.
Records of the Academy from 1911; records of several other local and state medical associations; lectures T. Gaillard gave on gynecology at the Columbia University College of Physicians and Surgeons during 1872 and 1873; the pharmacopoeia of Gertrude M. Watson, ca. 1898-99; and a casebook of Charles L. Ill concerning caesarian section. See *Guide to the Manuscript Collections of The New Jersey Historical Society* (forthcoming).

11,069. Allen, Adaline Y.
Papers. 1856-59. 4 vols.
Open. Published guide.
The New Jersey Historical Society.
Lecture notes of Allen, a student at the Spingler Institute in New York City, concern courses in aesthetics, the philosophy of history, and elements of mental philosophy. Also includes a diary in which she recorded her daily school and social activities. Formerly, the Institute was known as Abbott's Institute for the Education of Young Ladies. See *Guide to the Manuscript Collections of The New Jersey Historical Society* (forthcoming).

11,070. Ashfield, Isabella, and Ashfield, Elisabeth
Papers. 1720-51. 1 vol.
Open. Published guide.
The New Jersey Historical Society.
Cookbook with approximately 200 recipes compiled by the Ashfields and by a daughter of Lewis Morris (1671-1746), governor of New Jersey from 1738. See *Guide to the Manuscript Collections of The New Jersey Historical Society* (forthcoming).

11,071. Barton, Sally Ann
Papers. 1822-23. 1 vol.
Open. Published guide.
The New Jersey Historical Society.
Book of Barton contains practice exercises in penmanship and arithmetic as well as poetry. See *Guide to the Manuscript Collections of The New Jersey Historical Society* (forthcoming).

11,072. Beach, Joseph W., and Beach, Phebe Ann
Papers. 1831-56. 45 items.
Open. Published guide.
The New Jersey Historical Society.
Educational papers and material of Phebe Beach, a teacher in Cherry Valley, now South Orange, NJ, and records her husband Joseph Beach kept as superintendent of a Sabbath school. See *Guide to the Manuscript Collections of The New Jersey Historical Society* (forthcoming).

11,073. Biggs, Frankland
Papers. 1902-17. 5 ft.
Open. Published guide.
The New Jersey Historical Society.
Personal papers of Biggs (1877-1944), vice-president and general counsel for the New Jersey Bell Telephone Company, include a list of potential recruits for the New Jersey Association Opposed to Woman Suffrage. See *Guide to the Manuscript Collections of The New Jersey Historical Society* (forthcoming).

11,074. Blair, John Insley
Papers. 1830-96. 16 ft.
Open. Published guide.
The New Jersey Historical Society.
Personal and business papers of Blair (1802-99), a railroad magnate, contain genealogical material on the Blair, Vail, and other related families; estate papers of Margaret Hankinson, for whom Blair served as executor; records of various schools and churches in Blairstown and Warren County, NJ; and correspondence or other papers of Anne Blair, Aurelia Blair, Emma Blair, Euphenia Hunt, and Anne Carol Reiley. See *Guide to the Manuscript Collections of The New Jersey Historical Society* (forthcoming).

11,075. Boudinot Family
Papers. 1775-1875. 33 items.
Open. Published guide.
The New Jersey Historical Society.
Correspondence and other papers of this New Jersey family, including correspondence of Elisha Boudinot and his daughter Catherine (Boudinot) Atterbury. See *Guide to the Manuscript Collections of The New Jersey Historical Society* (forthcoming).

11,076. Bradley, Joseph P.
Papers. 1836-1936. 15 ft.
Open. Published guide.
The New Jersey Historical Society.
Miscellaneous papers of Bradley (1813-92), US Supreme Court justice, contain correspondence and business papers of Caroline Bradley Hornblower. See *Guide to the Manuscript Collections of The New Jersey Historical Society* (forthcoming).

11,077. Braithwaite, William Stanley
Papers. 1916-33. 35 items.
Open. Published guide.
The New Jersey Historical Society.
Papers of Braithwaite, an editor who worked with the B. J. Brimmer Company in Boston, consist of correspondence with and poetry of New Jersey poets, including Dorothy C. Alyea, Lydia C. Bowne, Alice E. Crane, Caroline Fritter, Caroline Fuller, Ethel Woodruff Macy, Portia Martin, Harriet Rowsell, Helena Ruth Sterry, and Lucia Trent. See *Guide to the Manuscript Collections of The New Jersey Historical Society* (forthcoming).

11,078. Brinckerhoff, Catherine
Papers. Ca. 1786. 1 vol.
Open. Published guide.
The New Jersey Historical Society.
Commonplace book of Brinckerhoff includes her poem "Lavinia—at Pastoral." See *Guide to the Manuscript Collections of The New Jersey Historical Society* (forthcoming).

11,079. Brokaw, Cornelia
Papers. 1870-71. 1 vol.
Open. Unpublished guide.
The New Jersey Historical Society.
Recipes for cakes, wines, and domestic medicinal remedies compiled by Brokaw, a Bound Brook, NJ, resident.

11,080. Burlington, NJ, Women's Newspapers
Collection. 1835. 1 vol.
Open. Published guide and description.
The New Jersey Historical Society.
Manuscript copies of the *Burlington Starry Journal* and *La pleine lune, or, Mysterious Visitor,* both of which contain poetry and prose by or about women. See *Guide to the Manuscript Collections of The New Jersey Historical Society* (forthcoming).

11,081. Casterline, Jennie (Allen)
Papers. 1867-74. 1 vol.
Open. Published guide.
The New Jersey Historical Society.
Diary of Casterline (?-1881), a resident of Morris County, NJ, includes some poetry. The daughter of Robert P. Allen of Mount Freedom, now Randolph Township, she married John Andrew Casterline in 1868. See *Guide to the Manuscript Collections of The New Jersey Historical Society* (forthcoming).

11,082. Churchill, Sarah J.
Papers. 1890-94. 5 vols.
Open. Published guide.
The New Jersey Historical Society.
A music teacher from Montclair, NJ, Churchill (ca. 1836-?) taught at schools in Montclair, Newark, and Orange, NJ. Her diaries contain brief entries about daily events and philosophical comments on life; also contained are clippings of inspirational items that have been pasted into the diaries. See *Guide to the Manuscript Collections of The New Jersey Historical Society* (forthcoming).

11,083. Cipher Books
Collection. 1805-26. 6 vols.
Open. Published guide.
The New Jersey Historical Society.
Includes cipher books of Elizabeth Susan Brinckerhoff, New York, and of Almira Parkhurst. See *Guide to the Manuscript Collections of The New Jersey Historical Society* (forthcoming).

11,084. Colles, Julia Keese
Papers. Ca. 1900. 284 pp.
Open. Published guide.
The New Jersey Historical Society.
Colles was an author and chairman of social science at the Rutgers Female College in New York City. Contains bibliographical sketches of female and male authors from Newark and an autobiographical sketch of Jeanette L. Gildez. See *Guide to the Manuscript Collections of The New Jersey Historical Society* (forthcoming).

11,085. Condict, Jemima
Papers. 1772-78. 1 vol.
Open. Published guide.
The New Jersey Historical Society.
Diary of [Miss] Condict (1757-79), a resident of Orange, NJ, which has been published as *Jemima Condict: Her Book, Being a Transcript of the Diary of an Essex County Maid During the Revolutionary War* (Newark, 1930).

11,086. Condict, Ruth W.
Papers. 1815. 10 vols.
Open. Published guide.
The New Jersey Historical Society.
Condict (1798-1815) was the daughter of Ira Condict, pastor of the Dutch Reformed Church in New Brunswick, NJ. In her diaries she discusses daily life, social activities, family, friends, and the weather. See *Guide to the Manuscript Collections of The New Jersey Historical Society* (forthcoming).

11,087. Cooke, Sarah M.
Papers. 1854. 1 vol.
Open. Published guide.
The New Jersey Historical Society.
Diary kept by Cooke, a boarding school student. See *Guide to the Manuscript Collections of The New Jersey Historical Society* (forthcoming).

11,088. Corey, Mr. and Mrs. Ashbel
Papers. 1820-95. 2 ft.
Open. Published guide.
The New Jersey Historical Society.
Correspondence, most of it to Mrs. Corey; legal and financial records; documents concerning leases and rents for properties the Coreys owned; religious essays by Mrs. Corey; and travel accounts of her trips to Cuba and the West Indies during the 1830s. See *Guide to the Manuscript Collections of The New Jersey Historical Society* (forthcoming).

11,089. Dickinson, Mary
Papers. Ca. 1868. 2 vols.
Open. Published guide.
The New Jersey Historical Society.
Cookbooks of Dickinson contain recipes for food, medicine, and various household uses. See *Guide to the Manuscript Collections of The New Jersey Historical Society* (forthcoming).

11,090. Dickinson, Rebecca
Papers. 1809-20. 1 vol.
Open. Published guide.
The New Jersey Historical Society.
A book of personal and household accounts of Dickinson, widow of Philemon Dickinson (1739-1809), includes notes on European history and a letter from Samuel Dickinson. See *Guide to the Manuscript Collections of The New Jersey Historical Society* (forthcoming).

11,091. Douglas, Amanda Minnie
Papers. Ca. 1866-1916. 2 ft.
Open. Published guide.
The New Jersey Historical Society.
A Newark author of writings for young readers, [Miss] Douglas (1831-1916) also was a member of the Ray Palmer Club and of the New Jersey Woman's Press Club. Manuscript and printed poetry, essays, articles, a novel, and stories, including "Eunice Richmond's Confirmation" and "The Princess Amber and Her Three Tasks." Also includes literary scrapbooks and material relating to her invention of a mosquito net frame, as well as manuscript poems of her sister Annie (Douglas) Bell. See *Guide to the Manuscript Collections of The New Jersey Historical Society* (forthcoming).

11,092. Emery, John R., and Emery, Alla M.
Papers. 1862-1921. 29 items.
Open. Unpublished guide.
The New Jersey Historical Society.
Correspondence and other papers of John Emery, a Civil War lieutenant who became an attorney, and his wife Alla. Includes letters John Emery wrote in 1862 and 1863 while he was a lieutenant in Company A, 15th New Jersey Volunteers; records of the 15th Regiment New Jersey Volunteer Veterans Association and its Women's Auxiliary; and records of memorial proceedings held in 1916 by the Lawyer's Club of Essex County to honor John Emery. After receiving his discharge in 1863, John Emery studied law and was admitted to the bar in 1865.

11,093. Everett Family
Papers. 1844-73. 8 vols.
Open. Published guide.
The New Jersey Historical Society.
Miscellaneous family papers include an autograph and verse book of Hannah Martin and diaries of Anna Everett and Lizzie L. Everett of Lafayette, NJ. See *Guide to the Manuscript Collections of The New Jersey Historical Society* (forthcoming).

11,094. Female Union School Association
Records. 1822-50. 1 vol.
Open. Published guide.
The New Jersey Historical Society.
Constitution, bylaws, minutes, and a subscription list of the Association, a Newark charitable institution founded in 1822 to establish a free school for the "promotion of learning, industry, morality, and piety" among indigent girls. The Association also cooperated with the Priscilla Society, which was devoted to teaching indigent girls to knit and sew. In 1850 ownership of the Female Union School was transferred to the Protestant Foster Home Society of the City of Newark. See *Guide to the Manuscript Collections of The New Jersey Historical Society* (forthcoming).

11,095. First United Methodist Church, Newark
Records. 1839-1960. 10 ft.
Open. Published guide.
The New Jersey Historical Society.
Formerly the Wesley Chapel and the Halsey Street Methodist Episcopal Church, the First United Methodist Church was formed as the result of a merger with the Central Methodist Episcopal Church and the Union Street Methodist Episcopal Church. Business and financial records, church registers, correspondence, and printed matter. Also includes minutes of the board of control of the Newark Deaconess Home, 1923-48, and financial records and reports of the Ladies Aid Society of the Halsey Street Church, 1925-37. See *Guide to the Manuscript Collections of The New Jersey Historical Society* (forthcoming).

11,096. Foster, Flora Shaw
Papers. 1891-1905. 4 vols.
Open. Unpublished guide.
The New Jersey Historical Society.
Diaries and a daybook kept by [Mrs. Charles E.] Foster, wife of a Newark hardware dealer. She was the mother of Agnes Perry Foster and Sarah Shaw Foster.

11,097. Gildersleeve Family
Papers. 1797-1887. 29 items.
Open. Published guide.
The New Jersey Historical Society.
Correspondence, deeds, and other papers of the Gildersleeve and related families in New Jersey and New York. Includes school compositions that Anna Maria Gildersleeve wrote in 1849 while she was a student in Jefferson Village, now Maplewood, NJ. See *Guide to the Manuscript Collections of The New Jersey Historical Society* (forthcoming).

11,098. Goose, Cornelia F.
Papers. 1911-15. 1 vol.
Open. Published guide.
The New Jersey Historical Society.
Book of sentiments contains brief poems by Goose. See *Guide to the Manuscript Collections of The New Jersey Historical Society* (forthcoming).

11,099. Halsted, Mr. and Mrs. N. Norris
Papers. 1852-91. 3 ft.
Open. Published guide.
The New Jersey Historical Society.
Personal and business papers of N. Norris Halsted (1816-84), a partner in the dry goods firm of Halsted, Brokaw and Company of New York, and of his wife Nancy Marsh Halsted, who was active in church and hospital work and the Mount Vernon Ladies Association. Includes her commonplace books; poetry; genealogical notes; notes on sermons preached by Elijah R. Craven, pastor of the Third Presbyterian Church of Newark, between 1869 and 1872; an 1876 minute book of the New Jersey Washington Aid Society; and correspondence and legal papers of her relatives. See *Guide to the Manuscript Collections of The New Jersey Historical Society* (forthcoming).

11,100. Hart, Anne
Papers. 1804-11. 11 items.
Open. Published guide.
The New Jersey Historical Society.
Letters that Hart, widow of clergyman Oliver Hart of Hopewell, Mercer County, NJ, wrote from Burlington, NJ, to clergyman John Stanford in New York. See *Guide to the Manuscript Collections of The New Jersey Historical Society* (forthcoming).

11,101. Hoffman Family
Papers. 1870-1964. 70 items.
Open. Published guide.

The New Jersey Historical Society.
Horace J. Hoffman served in the 10th Wisconsin Infantry Regiment during the Civil War; in 1896 he and his family moved to Jersey City, NJ, where he established a metal fixture shop and printing office. Legal documents and genealogical data pertain to him and his wife Dora Hoffman and other family members. Also includes letters written by various family members to Helen Martha Wright, the genealogist who assembled this collection. See *Guide to the Manuscript Collections of The New Jersey Historical Society* (forthcoming).

11,102. Kenney Family
Papers. 1854-1904. 1 vol.
Open. Published guide.
The New Jersey Historical Society.
Correspondence of clergymen Edward J. Kenney and Edward T. Kenney and of Elizabeth Kenney Myers concerns personal, family, and religious matters. Some of the letters pertain to religious activities in Ocean Grove, NJ. See *Guide to the Manuscript Collections of The New Jersey Historical Society* (forthcoming).

11,103. Kinney Family
Papers. 1783-1900. 8 ft. and 1 vol.
Open. Published guide.
The New Jersey Historical Society.
Papers of this Newark family include correspondence and verse of Elizabeth Clementine Kinney (1810-89), a poet and essayist who was wife of William B. Kinney (1799-1880), a lawyer and publisher of the *Newark Daily Advertiser*, and mother of Thomas T. Kinney (1821-1900), editor and publisher of the *Advertiser*. Also includes papers of and a casebook that her mother-in-law Hannah Burnet Kinney (1761-1832) kept as an officer of the Newark Female Charitable Society. Dorothea L. Dix is one of the correspondents. See *Guide to the Manuscript Collections of The New Jersey Historical Society* (forthcoming).

11,104. Knowland, Josephine
Papers. 1883. 1 vol.
Open. Unpublished guide.
The New Jersey Historical Society.
Diary of Knowland (1862-1949) includes her account of an Easter trip to Atlantic City, NJ. Knowland lived in Plainfield, NJ, until her marriage to Louis Ellsworth Laflin in 1885.

11,105. Kramer, George W., and Kramer, Harriet Estelle Blackman
Papers. 1849-1931. 150 items.
Open. Unpublished guide.
The New Jersey Historical Society.
Correspondence, diaries, poetry, and scrapbooks of George Kramer (1847-1938), an architect, and Harriet Blackman Kramer, whom he married in 1870. Includes his scrapbook concerning domestic, civil, and ecclesiastical architecture and papers about the Kramer and Blackman families. From 1879 to 1894 George Kramer was a partner in an Akron, OH, architectural firm; he then moved to New York City, where he founded his own firm.

11,106. Kress, Idabelle Haughey
Papers. 1881-83. 1 vol.
Open. Published guide.
The New Jersey Historical Society.
Diary that Kress, a soprano from Vancouver, OR, kept during a European voyage and singing tour she made with her parents. Kress later married and settled in Newark. In 1921 she copied and illustrated her diary with memorabilia. See *Guide to the Manuscript Collections of The New Jersey Historical Society* (forthcoming).

11,107. Ladies Missionary Society of the North Reformed Church
Records. 1889-1904. 2 vols.
Open. Published guide.
The New Jersey Historical Society.
Constitution, annual reports, minutes, and membership lists of this Passaic, NJ, organization. See *Guide to the Manuscript Collections of The New Jersey Historical Society* (forthcoming).

11,108. Lake Hopatcong Public School
Records. 1865-85. 22 pp.
Open. Published guide.
The New Jersey Historical Society.
Manuscript newspaper entitled *Our Port Folio*, which was edited by the young ladies of a public school in Morris County, NJ. See *Guide to the Manuscript Collections of The New Jersey Historical Society* (forthcoming).

11,109. Lambert, Isabel St. George
Papers. 1863-66. 1 vol.
Open. Published guide.
The New Jersey Historical Society.
Autograph album of Lambert, a resident of Morristown, NJ, contains signatures and sentiments by persons living in Morristown and in Geneseo, IL. See *Guide to the Manuscript Collections of The New Jersey Historical Society* (forthcoming).

11,110. Literary Clubs
Records. 1772-78. 1 vol.
Open. Published guide.
The New Jersey Historical Society.
Constitutions, bylaws, minutes, and membership list of three Newark women's literary clubs: the Belles-lettres Society, the Union Society, and the Minerva Society. See *Guide to the Manuscript Collections of The New Jersey Historical Society* (forthcoming).

11,111. McDowell Family
Papers. 1792-1966. 46 ft.
Open. Published guide, description, and inventory.
The New Jersey Historical Society.
Personal papers of William Anderson McDowell (1789-1851), a Presbyterian minister, and of other family members. While serving as a clergyman in Charlestown, SC, between 1823 and 1832, McDowell became an intimate friend and spiritual confidant of abolitionist Angelina Grimké. Collection includes their correspondence and papers of Rachel K. McDowell (1880-1949), a reporter for *The Newark Evening News* and *The New York Herald* and religious editor for *The New York Times* from 1920 to 1948. See *Guide to the Manuscript Collections of The New Jersey Historical Society* (forthcoming).

11,112. Moorfield, Amelia Berndt
Papers. 1913-23. 1 ft.
Open. Unpublished guide.
The New Jersey Historical Society.
Papers chiefly consisting of official photos and printed material collected by Moorfield, a Newark suffragist who was secretary-treasurer of the Women's Political Union of New Jersey. Includes broadsides of the New Jersey Association Opposed to Women Suffrage and other antisuffrage groups.

11,113. New Jersey Historical Society
Records. 1845- . Ca. 125 ft.
Open. Published guide.
The New Jersey Historical Society.
Financial and other records, official correspondence, lectures, scrapbooks, and other items of the Society, which was founded in 1845, and of its women's branch, which was primarily involved in fund raising and social functions. Susan B. Anthony is among the correspondents. See *Guide to the Manuscript Collections of The New Jersey Historical Society* (forthcoming).

11,114. New Jersey Woman Suffrage Association
Records. 1894-98. 1 vol.
Open. Published guide.
The New Jersey Historical Society.
Constitution with amendments and minutes of the Association, which met principally in Essex County. Members included Ella B. Carter, Florence Hall Howe, Kate B. Lippincott, Mary Philbrook, and Mary D. Hussey. See *Guide to the Manuscript Collections of The New Jersey Historical Society* (forthcoming).

11,115. New Jersey Women Authors
Collection. 1900. 379 pp.
Open. Published guide.
The New Jersey Historical Society.
This unpublished biographical dictionary of 19th-century women authors contains information on the family background and education of many of these women as well as lists of their writings. See *Guide to the Manuscript Collections of The New Jersey Historical Society* (forthcoming).

11,116. Newark Academy, Sabbath School for Coloured People, Female Department
Records. 1819-22. 4 items.
Open. Published guide.
The New Jersey Historical Society.
Monthly and annual reports of the Female Department of this Sabbath school. See *Guide to the Manuscript Collections of The New Jersey Historical Society* (forthcoming).

11,117. Newark Alms House
Records. 1854-58. 1 vol.
Open. Published guide.
The New Jersey Historical Society.
Records kept by House superintendent Jonathan B. Shay of male and female paupers include dates of entrance and discharge or death, age, and notations concerning disease. See *Guide to the Manuscript Collections of The New Jersey Historical Society* (forthcoming).

11,118. Newark Board of Education
Records. 1839-1932. 18 ft.
Open. Published guide.
The New Jersey Historical Society.
Includes records of graduates, examinations, and school statistics, 1839-1913; minutes of principals' meetings, 1860s-90s, as well as those of the Committee on Teachers and the Teacher's Monthly Institute; accounts of Vailsburg school district no. 29, 1890-94; correspondence of the city superintendent, 1881-1901; and records of the Newark Teachers' Institute. Also includes volumes of student compositions and artwork, which were bound for the Newark Educational Exhibit at the Pan-American Exposition of 1901. See *Guide to the Manuscript Collections of The New Jersey Historical Society* (forthcoming).

11,119. Newark Female Charitable Society
Records. 1803-1937. 4 ft.
Open. Published guide.
The New Jersey Historical Society.
Constitution, minutes, financial records, and correspondence of the Society, which was founded in 1803. Also includes records of several committees of the Crazy Jane Society, an auxiliary of the Society, founded in 1874. See *Guide to the Manuscript Collections of The New Jersey Historical Society* (forthcoming).

11,120. Nicholson, Ann
Papers. 1819. 1 vol.
Open. Published guide.
The New Jersey Historical Society.
Commonplace book of Nicholson contains selected verse and notes on Quaker meetings in Philadelphia and Salem, NJ. See *Guide to the Manuscript Collections of The New Jersey Historical Society* (forthcoming).

11,121. Pell, Charles H.
Papers. 1853-1906. 2 ft.
Open. Published guide.

The New Jersey Historical Society.
Professional papers of Pell (1853-1906), a lawyer who represented minister Hannibal Goodwin in his litigation with the Eastman Kodak Company over the invention of flexible celluloid photographic film. Also includes correspondence for 1906 and 1907 in which Ethelwyn A. Pell lobbied on behalf of the College Women's Club of Essex County and its interest in civic improvement. See *Guide to the Manuscript Collections of The New Jersey Historical Society* (forthcoming).

11,122. Pennington Family
Papers. 1799-1885. 1 ft.
Open. Published guide.
The New Jersey Historical Society.
Diaries, legal and financial papers, and other manuscripts of this New Jersey family include information on Samuel Pennington (1765-1835), cofounder of the Newark *Centinel of Freedom,* and his son Jabez Pennington (1827-73), a Newark lawyer. Also includes a diary that Caroline W. Condit (1830-?) kept between 1844 and 1847. See *Guide to the Manuscript Collections of The New Jersey Historical Society* (forthcoming).

11,123. Philbrook, Mary
Papers. 1899-1958. 3 ft.
Open. Published guide.
The New Jersey Historical Society.
[Miss] Philbrook (1872-1958) was a women's rights leader and lawyer. Correspondence; legal, historical, and genealogical papers; a manuscript autobiography; and scrapbooks. The first woman lawyer to be admitted to the New Jersey bar, in 1895, Philbrook then became active nationally and on the state level in the women's suffrage and the Equal Rights Amendment campaigns. She was also chairman of the archives committee of the National Woman's party and was involved in the New Jersey Center for Women's Archives. Correspondents include Marguerite MacDonald Carpenter, Florence Bayard Hilles, Mary M. Lyons, Alice Paul, Frances Perkins, Congresswoman Mary T. Norton, historians Carles A. and Mary (Ritter) Beard, and Beatrice Winser, librarian of the Newark Public Library. See *Guide to the Manuscript Collections of The New Jersey Historical Society* (forthcoming).

11,124. Pope, Elizabeth
Papers. 1910-20. 1 vol.
Open. Published guide.
The New Jersey Historical Society.
Scrapbook kept by Pope, press chairman of the New Jersey Woman Suffrage Association, contains correspondence, speeches, articles, leaflets, pamphlets, broadsides, and clippings. See *Guide to the Manuscript Collections of The New Jersey Historical Society* (forthcoming).

11,125. Raritan Bay Union and Eagleswood Military Academy
Records. 1849-1973. 1 ft.
Open. Published guide.
The New Jersey Historical Society.
Correspondence, printed matter, and other documents concern the Raritan Bay Union, founded in 1853 by educators Marcus and Rebecca Buffum Spring (1811-1911), and the Union's successor, the Eagleswood Military Academy. Includes correspondence of Rebecca Spring on the utopian and antislavery movements as well as correspondence of Frederika Bremer, Lydia Maria Child, Margaret Fuller, Ellen Wright Garrison, Mary Hewitt, and Mary Mann. See *Guide to the Manuscript Collections of The New Jersey Historical Society* (forthcoming).

11,126. Ray Palmer Club
Records. 1888-1952. 3 ft.
Open. Published guide.
The New Jersey Historical Society.
Minutes, accounts, correspondence, scrapbooks, and other records of this Newark women's association founded in 1886 for the pursuit of literary and educational interests. Between 1888 and 1892 the Club functioned as a Chautauqua circle. Newark author Amanda M. Douglas was an early Club member and officer. See *Guide to the Manuscript Collections of The New Jersey Historical Society* (forthcoming).

11,127. Rogers, Mary E.
Papers. 1933-53. 13 vols.
Open. Published guide.
The New Jersey Historical Society.
Brief diaries in which Rogers, an East Orange, NJ, housewife, mentions household, family, and social activities. See *Guide to the Manuscript Collections of The New Jersey Historical Society* (forthcoming).

11,128. Rutherfurd Family
Papers. 1815-22. 14 items.
Open. Unpublished guide.
The New Jersey Historical Society.
Correspondence between John Rutherfurd (1760-1840), Robert Walter Rutherfurd (1788-1852), and Sabina Morris Rutherfurd (1789-1857) concerns Sabina Rutherfurd's mental illness and management of the family estates in Newton, NJ, and Edgerston (now Rutherford), NJ.

11,129. Schley, Reeve, Sr.
Papers. 1904-44. 25 ft.
Open. Published guide and description.
The New Jersey Historical Society.
Business papers of Schley (1881-1960), a banker and lawyer who was mayor of Far Hills, NJ, contain correspondence of his wife Kate Prentice Schley. See *Guide to the Manuscript Collections of The New Jersey Historical Society* (forthcoming).

11,130. Smith Family
Papers. 1667-1960. 60 ft.
Open. Published guide.
The New Jersey Historical Society.
Papers of the Smith, Cobb, Dodd, Green, MacLaren, and Waddell families, including material relating to Alice Waddell Smith and Isabella MacLaren Smith. See *Guide to the Manuscript Collections of The New Jersey Historical Society* (forthcoming).

11,131. Smith, Rebecca D.
Papers. Ca. 1846-70. 1 vol.
Open. Published guide.
The New Jersey Historical Society.
A book of poems, most of which were dedicated to Smith and either written into the book by their authors or copied by her with notes of explanation; a number of authors of the poems were women. The book also contains anecdotes and verse dated Washington, DC, concerning Senator John Jorden Crittenden of Kentucky. See *Guide to the Manuscript Collections of The New Jersey Historical Society* (forthcoming).

11,132. Sons of Union Veterans of the Civil War, Hugh C. Irish Camp No. 8
Records. 1861-1946. 1 vol.
Open. Published guide.
The New Jersey Historical Society.
Cemetery records and historical sketches of this veterans association, including a sketch of its Ladies Auxiliary No. 3, which was founded in 1866. See *Guide to the Manuscript Collections of The New Jersey Historical Society* (forthcoming).

11,133. South Orange, NJ, Female Organizations
Records. 1861-68. 1 vol.
Open. Published guide.
The New Jersey Historical Society.
Bylaws, treasurer's reports, minutes, and membership lists of the School Girls Circle of South Orange, 1861, and of the Ladies Benevolent Association of South Orange, 1864-68. See *Guide to the Manuscript Collections of The New Jersey Historical Society* (forthcoming).

11,134. Stevens Family
Papers. 1663-1959. 60 ft.
Open. Published guide and calendar.
The New Jersey Historical Society.
The male members of this New Jersey family were sea captains, merchants, and soldiers; one of the best known was Colonel John Stevens (1749-1838), a lawyer, inventor, founder of the town of Hoboken, NJ, and builder of the first ocean steamship, the *Phoenix,* and of one of the first American steam locomotives. Includes estate papers of Mary Alexander and genealogical notes on Ann Campbell, Elizabeth Alexander, Rachel Cox, and Martha Dod. Also includes papers of [Mrs.] Caroline Bayard Stevens Alexander, a feminist, social worker, and Democratic committeewoman who later married Mayor Otto Wittpen of Jersey City, NJ. The collection is also available on microfilm. See *Guide to the Microfilm Edition of the Stevens Family Papers* (Newark, 1968).

11,135. Sutton, Emma L.
Papers. 1896-98. 2 vols.
Open. Published guide.
The New Jersey Historical Society.
Scrapbooks kept by Sutton, a young Mendham Township, NJ, girl. She pasted the material over the daybook of a Newark shoemaker and the sales book for the Morris and Essex Railroad Company's Dover Station. See *Guide to the Manuscript Collections of The New Jersey Historical Society* (forthcoming).

11,136. Swinton, Marion
Papers. 1922-36. 74 items.
Open. Published guide.
The New Jersey Historical Society.
A Hackensack, NJ, artist, Swinton (?-1938) painted historical scenes and portraits, including one of Woodrow Wilson. Correspondence, lists of exhibited works, and a clipping contain reference to her service as local chairman of the League of Nations Non-Partisan Association. See *Guide to the Manuscript Collections of The New Jersey Historical Society* (forthcoming).

11,137. Thomas, Anna A.
Papers. 1834-35. 1 vol.
Open. Published guide.
The New Jersey Historical Society.
Commonplace book kept by Thomas, a student at the Newark Young Ladies Institute. See *Guide to the Manuscript Collections of The New Jersey Historical Society* (forthcoming).

11,138. Van Ness Family
Papers. 1787-1875. 14 items.
Open. Published guide.
The New Jersey Historical Society.
Miscellaneous papers of this family include a book of verse, ca. 1841, of Phebe Williams Condict. See *Guide to the Manuscript Collections of The New Jersey Historical Society* (forthcoming).

11,139. Williams, Sarah
Papers. 1787-1851. 58 items.
Open. Published guide.
The New Jersey Historical Society.
Correspondence, deeds and indentures, and receipts pertain to the Elizabeth, NJ, estate of [Mrs.] Williams. See *Guide to the Manuscript Collections of The New Jersey Historical Society* (forthcoming).

11,140. Winser Family
Papers. 1806-1963. 1 ft.
Open. Unpublished guide.

The New Jersey Historical Society.
Papers contain correspondence, journals, scrapbooks, and memorabilia of Winser family members; Henry Jacob Winser (1823-96), a journalist and diplomat; Beatrice Winser (1869-1947), director of the Newark Public Library and Newark Museum; and Natalie Winser, a deaconess of Trinity Cathedral in Newark.

11,141. Woman's Club of Orange, NJ
Records. 1872-1974. 15 ft.
Open. Published guide and inventory.
The New Jersey Historical Society.
Annual reports, minutes, membership records, scrapbooks, and other records of the Club and of the Junior Woman's Club of Orange. Founded in 1872 in reponse to the early women's club movement, the Woman's Club became part of the GFWC in New Jersey. Originally its purpose was discussion of topics of social and general importance in order to "awaken in its members a more vital interest in such topics." After many years of declining membership, the Woman's Club disposed of its assets and dissolved in 1977. See *Guide to the Manuscript Collections of The New Jersey Historical Society* (forthcoming).

11,142. Woodruff, Marietta H. Crane
Papers. 1874-1900. 1 vol.
Open. Published guide.
The New Jersey Historical Society.
Casebook of Woodruff, an obstetrician who worked in the Boonton, NJ, area. See *Guide to the Manuscript Collections of The New Jersey Historical Society* (forthcoming).

11,143. Work Project Administration, Federal Writers' Project, New Jersey, Women's Archives
Records. Ca. 1840-1940. 3 ft.
Open. Published guide and inventory.
The New Jersey Historical Society.
Organizational files, correspondence, typescripts of newspaper articles, and other records of the New Jersey branch of the World Center for Women's Archives, an organization founded by Mary (Ritter) Beard to collect and preserve the papers of prominent American women; in 1940 the Federal Writers' Project in New Jersey agreed to continue the work of the Archives' New Jersey branch. Material, primarily relating to New Jersey women, includes records of the World Center, 1937-40, and of the New Jersey Center for Women's Archives; personal correspondence from Mary Philbrook, a women's rights leader and the first woman lawyer admitted to the New Jersey bar; general correspondence of the New Jersey Consumers' League, 1933-40; and scattered records of the National Woman's Party and the Committee to Eliminate Discrimination against Women. See *Guide to the Manuscript Collections of The New Jersey Historical Society* (forthcoming).

11,144. Autographs
Collection. Ca. 1750s-1950s. 712 items.
Open. No guide.
Newark Public Library, Art and Music Department.
Correspondence and other papers of persons prominent in history, politics, and the arts, particularly in New Jersey. Includes material of Beatrice Winser, Newark Library librarian; Julia Sabine, Library art historian and curator; Lillian M. Gilbreth, efficiency expert and author of *Cheaper by the Dozen;* Olive Sanford, New Jersey assemblywoman; and authors Anne Parrish, Antoinettea Scudder, Jane Dann Tallman, and Adrianna Tuttle. Also includes material of Helen Keller, Pearl S. Buck, Mary (Mapes) Dodge, and Eleanor Roosevelt.

11,145. Ryan, Anne
Papers. Ca. 1925-50. Ca. 300 pp.
Open. Published guide.
Newark Public Library, Art and Music Department.
Ryan (1889-1954) was an artist, poet, and writer. Manuscripts of and graphic works relating to some of her poems, including "For a Grand Child"; short stories, among them "Clowns at the Inn at Deya" and "The Kiss"; and novellas, such as "The Weavers." See Paul A. Stellhorn et al., eds., *Directory of New Jersey Historical Manuscripts* (Trenton, NJ: New Jersey Historical Commission, forthcoming).

OLD BRIDGE TOWNSHIP

11,146. Browntown PTA
Records. 1946-69. 2 folders and 1 vol.
Open. Index.
Madison Township Historical Society.
President's reports, minutes, treasurer's records, a bankbook, photos, a scrapbook, clippings, and a 90-page history of the Browntown-Madison Township PTA, which was founded in 1946. The majority of the members and officers of the group were women.

PATERSON

11,147. General Archives
Records. 1909- . No size given.
Closed. No guide.
Missionary Sisters of the Immaculate Conception of the Mother of God.
Financial records, official documents, correspondence, films, photos, and printed material of the order, which is engaged in education, health services, and social services in the US, Germany, China, Brazil, southwest Africa, and Bolivia. Includes papers of four superiors general and correspondence, a diary, and conference notes of the foundress.

11,148. Provincial Archives
Records. 1958- . No size given.
Closed. No guide.
Missionary Sisters of the Immaculate Conception of the Mother of God.
The Province of the Immaculate Conception was founded in 1958 in West Paterson, NJ, and is involved in education, health services, and social services. Financial records, official documents, correspondence, photos, films, and printed matter of the Province, including institutional records of elementary schools, hospitals, culinary departments, and individual apostolates.

11,149. Paterson General Hospital
Records. 1871-1966. 2 vols. and 34 items.
Open. No guide.
Paterson Public Library.
Annual reports containing statistical medical reports, financial reports, reports of the secretary, and lists of officers and contributors of the Hospital, which was founded in 1871 as the result of efforts of the Ladies Hospital Association of Paterson, an organization that changed its name in 1887 to the Paterson General Hospital Association. Originally, the idea of a nonsectarian general hospital came from the Ministers Association of Paterson. Women were the early leaders of the Hospital Association, management of which was eventually dominated by men.

PRINCETON

11,150. Archives
Records. 1900- . 500 cu.ft.
Partially closed. Unpublished guides.
Educational Testing Service Archives.
The Archives contains correspondence, memoranda, reports, tapes, publications, and other records and papers pertaining to ETS instructional, testing, and research areas. Topics represented include sex bias in educational testing; sex differences in academic aptitude, achievement tests, and cognitive styles; sex discrimination; and other topics concerning women, education, and learning. For example, one record series contains correspondence, tests, a television script draft, questionnaires, reports, publicity, and other items relating to an ETS project, conducted in 1953 and 1954 for the American National Red Cross, to evaluate the use of television to teach a course in home nursing.

11,151. Women Students
Records. 1968-76. 2 boxes.
Open. No guide.
Princeton University Archives.
Miscellaneous material pertaining to the admission of undergraduate women to the University includes questionnaires on the education of women at Princeton distributed to faculty members and an analysis of responses as well as special committee and other reports. Also contains records of the Women's Center at Princeton, including newsletters and news releases, and Princeton University Women's Organization bylaws, minutes, and a report on employment practices at the University.

11,152. Audubon, John James
Papers. 1785-1851. 9 boxes and 1 oversize box.
Open. Card catalog.
Princeton University Library, Manuscript Division.
Papers relating to the work of Audubon (1785-1851), an artist who was known for his drawings of birds in naturalistic settings, include a few letters his wife Lucy Bakewell Audubon (1788-1874) wrote over a period of 35 years. In her letters she describes settling with her family in New Haven, CT, when she was 15 years old, meeting Audubon, their honeymoon trip, the death of her father, and the travels and publications of her husband.

11,153. Beach, Sylvia
Papers. Ca. 1900-62. 288 boxes.
Partially restricted. Check list.
Princeton University Library, Manuscript Division.
[Miss] Beach (1887-1962) was the proprietor of Shakespeare and Company, a Paris bookshop and lending library specializing in English and American books, which was a meeting place for French, English, Irish, and American writers during the 1920s and 1930s. She also was the publisher of James Joyce's *Ulysses* (1922), which she distributed as long as it was banned in England and the US. Family and personal papers, diaries, Shakespeare and Company records and publications, pamphlets, photos, paintings, drawings, phonograph records, memorabilia, and Beach's published writings, including her memoirs *Shakespeare and Company* (New York: Harcourt, Brace and Co., 1956). Her correspondents included Joyce, Hilda Doolittle, Ezra Pound, Gertrude Stein, Alice B. Toklas, Ernest Hemingway, Marianne Craig Moore, Katherine Anne Porter, D. H. Lawrence, Paul Valéry, and André Gide. Beach was the daughter of Eleanor Orbison Beach and Sylvester Woodbridge Beach, minister of the First Presbyterian Church in Princeton.

11,154. Blair and Lee
Papers. Ca. 1733-1916. Ca. 300 boxes, 11 cartons, and 5 vols.
Open. Checklist.
Princeton University Library, Manuscript Division.
Papers of these families, the male members of which were active in the navy and politics, include boxes of papers, 1839-94, of Elizabeth (Blair) Lee, wife of Admiral Samuel Phillips Lee (1812-97) and a close friend of Mary (Todd) Lincoln. Includes correspondence with her husband, her father Francis Preston Blair, other relatives and friends,

the DAR, and the Washington City Orphan Asylum; notebooks containing poetry; memoranda; bills; recipes; and clippings.

11,155. Bogan, Louise
Papers. Nd. 4 boxes.
Open. Card catalog.
Princeton University Library, Manuscript Division.
An author and poet, Bogan (1897-1970) was noted for her lyric poetry. Correspondence and manuscripts of prose writings.

11,156. Charles Scribner's Sons, Publishers
Records. Ca. 1854-1960. 419 boxes and 1 carton.
Open. Checklist.
Princeton University Library, Manuscript Division.
Correspondence, legal documents, manuscripts, and other records pertain to the publication by Scribner's of the works of hundreds of authors, including Willa Cather, Edith Wharton, Katherine Anne Porter, and Zelda Fitzgerald.

11,157. Dodge, Mary Elizabeth (Mapes)
Papers. Ca. 1865-1900. Ca. 17 boxes and 2 cartons.
Open. Card catalog.
Princeton University Library, Manuscript Division.
[Mrs. William] Dodge (1831-1905) was editor of *St. Nicholas Magazine* and author of such children's books as *Hans Brinker; or the Silver Skates* (1865). Correspondence, miscellaneous papers, and an autograph album of letters, cards, and photos of eminent Americans, 1771-1904, compiled by Robert Stockton Pyne.

11,158. Dulles, Edith Foster
Papers. 1934. 1 vol.
Open. No guide.
Princeton University Library, Manuscript Division.
The autobiography of Dulles (1863-1941), mother of US Secretary of State John Foster Dulles, was written for her grandchildren.

11,159. Dulles, John Foster
Papers. Ca. 1891-1959. 621 boxes.
Partially closed. Checklist.
Princeton University Library, Manuscript Division.
Papers of Dulles (1888-1959), US secretary of state between 1953 and 1959, include letters to his wife Janet Pomeroy (Avery) Dulles and boxes of her papers.

11,160. Fitzgerald, Zelda (Sayre)
Papers. Ca. 1900-48. 14 boxes.
Partially restricted. Checklist.
Princeton University Library, Manuscript Division.
Fitzgerald (1900-48) was an author and wife of author F. Scott Fitzgerald. Letters to her husband; correspondence with their daughter Frances Scott Fitzgerald and others; manuscripts of her novel *Save Me the Waltz,* her play *Scandalabra,* short stories, and articles; notes; bills; photos; clippings; and other items.

11,161. Freeman, Mary Eleanor (Wilkins)
Papers. Nd. Ca. 17 items.
Open. Card catalog.
Princeton University Library, Manuscript Division.
An author of short stories and novels, [Mrs. Charles M.] Freeman (1852-1930) was awarded the Howells Medal for fiction by the American Academy of Arts and Letters in 1925. Correspondence and manuscript poems, including "Camillia's Snuff Box."

11,162. Gerould, Katharine Elizabeth (Fullerton)
Papers. 1907-36. 7 items.
Open. Card catalog.
Princeton University Library, Manuscript Division.
Correspondence of [Mrs. Gordon Hall] Gerould (1879-1944), a writer of short stories, novels, and essays.

11,163. Gordon, Caroline
Papers. Ca. 1930-76. 24 boxes.
Partially restricted. Card catalog.
Princeton University Library, Manuscript Division.
A novelist who explored southern value systems in her works, Gordon (1895-) was married for a time to poet, novelist, and critic Allen Tate. Correspondence with Tate, Katherine Anne Porter, and former students; correspondence of the Wood, Meriwether, and Gordon families; background notes for her writing; typescripts of *The Malefactors* (1956), *None Shall Look Back* (1937), and others of her novels, plays, and short stories; book reviews; photos of family and friends; clippings; and other items.

11,164. Hamilton, Edith
Papers. Ca. 1930-65. 3 boxes.
Open. Card catalog.
Princeton University Library, Manuscript Division.
An educator, classical scholar, and author, Hamilton (1867-1963) worked as headmistress of the Bryn Mawr Preparatory School for Girls in Baltimore and then in her 60s began her literary career with *The Greek Way;* she also wrote essays, criticism, book reviews, and translations of the works of others. Correspondence, including letters of Storer B. Lunt, president of W. W. Norton Company, about her literary activities and correspondence with John Mason Brown, who wrote a biographical essay about her; manuscripts of books such as *The Ever-Present Past;* notes; speeches; and clippings.

11,165. Harold Ober Associates, Inc.
Records. 1927-40. 118 boxes.
Open. Inventory.
Princeton University Library, Manuscript Division.
Author files of these literary agents in New York contain correspondence, legal documents, and other material of Catherine Bowen, Nancy Hale, Pearl Buck, Margaret Millar, Nancy Ross, Elizabeth Fenwick, Josephine Bentham, Pauline de Rothschild, Diana Cavallo, Victoria Lincoln, Olive Higgins Prouty, and other authors.

11,166. John Day Company, Publishers
Records. Ca. 1926-63. 52 boxes, 126 cartons, and 37 cases.
Partially restricted. Card catalog.
Princeton University Library, Manuscript Division.
Editorial files and correspondence of this publishing firm with various authors, some of whom were women.

11,167. Livermore, Mary Ashton (Rice)
Papers. Ca. 1846-1905. 7 boxes.
Open. Checklist.
Princeton University Library, Manuscript Division.
[Mrs. Daniel Parker] Livermore (1820-1905) was an organizer and fund raiser for the Chicago Sanitary Commission during the Civil War, a temperance and suffrage leader, editor of the *Woman's Journal* and of her own suffrage journal *Agitator,* and a lecturer. Correspondence; memorandum books; drafts of ca. 190 lectures, including "Equal Rights" and "Superfluous Women"; articles; issues of various periodicals; photos; and clippings. Correspondents include Mary (Mapes) Dodge and [Miss] Adelaide Withington.

11,168. MacInnes, Helen
Papers. Nd. Ca. 34 boxes, 2 cartons, and 7 packages.
Open. Card catalog.
Princeton University Library, Manuscript Division.
MacInnes (1907-) is an author and the widow of Gilbert Highet. Background notes and manuscripts with corrections of *Above Suspicion, Decision at Delphi,* and others of her novels. Also includes clippings and miscellaneous papers.

11,169. Madison, James, and Madison, Dolley
Papers. 1788-1836. 9 boxes and 1 carton.
Open. Checklist.
Princeton University Library, Manuscript Division.
Papers of James Madison (1751-1836), fourth US President, include correspondence, quotations, poems, and pictures of his wife Dorothea "Dolley" (Payne) [Mrs. John, Jr.] Todd Madison (1768-1849).

11,170. Marquand, Allan
Papers. Nd. 44 boxes, 7 cartons, and 1 shelf.
Open. Card catalog.
Princeton University Library, Manuscript Division.
Correspondence and miscellaneous and family papers of Marquand (1853-1924), a professor of art and archaeology at Princeton University, and his wife Eleanor Cross Marquand (1874-1950), an amateur botanist and civic worker in Princeton. Although her special interest was the study and identification of flowers and other flora as they appeared in paintings, illuminated manuscripts, tapestries, and mosaics, she was also active in University affairs, the Village Improvement Association and other civic groups, and in the reorganization of the police department.

11,171. Moore, Marianne Craig
Papers. Nd. 8 folders.
Open. Card catalog.
Princeton University Library, Manuscript Division.
A poet who wrote free verse, Moore (1887-1972) won the National Book Award and the Pulitzer Prize for poetry in 1952. Correspondence, manuscripts of "What Are Years?" (1941) and others of her poems, autograph changes in the text of her translation of *The Fables of La Fontaine,* and photos taken of her at Harvard University. Correspondents include a Mrs. Latimer, [Mrs.] Mildred Kienbusch, Carl O. von Kienbusch, a Thurairajah Tambimuttu, and a Mr. Mass.

11,172. Smith, Samuel Stanhope
Papers. 1779-1812. 1 box.
Open. Card catalog.
Princeton University Library, Manuscript Division.
Letter book of Smith (1750-1819), the seventh president of Princeton University, contains his correspondence with his cousin and close friend Susan (Shippen) Blair, a resident of Germantown, PA, whose father William Shippen was a founder of Princeton, whose brother William Shippen was a surgeon, and whose cousin Peggy Shippen was the wife of Benedict Arnold. The letter book contains correspondence, poems, and poetic epigrams, many of which were written by Blair.

11,173. Stockton, Annis Boudinot
Papers. Ca. 1769-90. Ca. 4 vols. and 3 folders.
Open. Card catalog.
Princeton University Library, Manuscript Division.
Stockton (1736-?) was a poet and the wife of Richard Stockton, a signer of the Declaration of Independence; a friend of George Washington, she wrote poetry about him and about political and domestic themes. Correspondence, including one letter from her husband; manuscript poems; a book of colonial and Revolutionary War verse; a recipe book, with comments; and commonplace books of Mary S. Harrison and Caroline Stockton, which contain some of Annis Stockton's poetry.

11,174. Torrence, Frederick Ridgely
Papers. Ca. 1833-1958. Ca. 117 boxes, 3 cartons, 2 vols., and 1 package.
Open. Checklist.
Princeton University Library, Manuscript Division.
Papers of Torrence (1874-1950), an author, playwright, poet, and editor, and of his wife Olivia (Dunbar) Torrence (1873-1953), an author. Her 14 boxes of material include a typescript of *Life of William Vaughn Moody,* other writings, correspondence, and notes. Her husband's

correspondence with various writers includes letters of Moody.

11,175. Wharton, Edith Newbold (Jones)
Papers. Ca. 1903-27. 1 box.
Open. Card catalog.
Princeton University Library, Manuscript Division.
An author of novels and short stories, [Mrs. Edward Robbins] Wharton (1862-1937) was the first woman to receive two Pulitzer Prizes. Letters to Mr. and Mrs. Alfred Austin and literary manuscripts, including typescripts of what appear to be chapters of *The Writing of Fiction.*

11,176. Wilson, Margaret Woodrow
Papers. Ca. 1915-44. 3 boxes.
Open. Card catalog.
Princeton University Library, Manuscript Division.
[Miss] Wilson (1882-1944) was a professional singer and daughter of President Woodrow Wilson. Correspondence, including letters of Edith (Bolling) Wilson; a diary and notebook, which Margaret Wilson's accompanist Elizabeth Ruggles David used in writing *I Played Their Accompaniments* (New York: D. Appleton Century Company, Inc., 1940); proofs and a printed copy of the book; photos; clippings; and memorabilia. Wilson toured in Europe before WWI and, in addition, she gave benefit concerts for social welfare projects in the US. In ca. 1940 she moved to the religious retreat of Sri Aurobindo in Pondicherry, India, and lived there until her death.

11,177. Wilson, Woodrow
Papers. 1875-1925. Ca. 106 boxes and 2 cartons.
Open. Checklist.
Princeton University Library, Manuscript Division.
Personal papers of Wilson (1856-1924) contain material primarily from the period before he became President. Correspondence; manuscript memoranda, speeches, and articles; photos; clippings; and memorabilia. Includes 16 boxes of correspondence with his first wife Ellen Louise (Axson) Wilson (1860-1914) between 1883 and 1914, with his second wife Edith (Bolling) Galt Wilson (1872-1961), his mother Jeanie Woodrow Wilson, and his cousins Helen Woodrow Bones and Harriet Woodrow.

11,178. American Civil Liberties Union
Records. Ca. 1912-74. Ca. 911 cartons.
Open. Published guide and unpublished inventories.
Princeton University, Seeley G. Mudd Manuscript Library.
The ACLU was founded in 1920 to protect such civil liberties as the freedom of belief, expression, and association; equality before the law; and due process under the law. Legal briefs, correspondence, reports, clippings, and other records relate to civil liberties cases and other activities of the ACLU and its predecessor organizations. Includes subject files on birth control, equal rights, a married woman teacher's case, academic freedom, censorship, segregation, welfare benefits, obscenity, and other topics. Also includes files of the national office's legal department, 1945-60, and general files of the Washington office, 1938-62. Prominent women are among the correspondents. See Alex Baskin, *The American Civil Liberties Union Papers: A Guide to the Records of the American Civil Liberties Union Cases, 1912-1946* (Stony Brook, NY: Archives of Social History, 1971).

11,179. Gibbons, Herbert Adams
Papers. 1908-34. 14 boxes.
Open. Description.
Princeton University, Seeley G. Mudd Manuscript Library.
Papers of Gibbons (1880-1934), a foreign correspondent who was particularly interested in foreign policy and international affairs. Includes papers of his wife Helen Davenport (Brown) Gibbons (1882-1960), an author who wrote about her experiences in France and in Turkey during the Armenian massacre; she also translated such works as *The Radiant Story of Jesus.* Also includes correspondence documenting her personal efforts to provide relief or homes for needy children during WWI and scrapbooks concerning the Gibbonses' careers during the war.

SOMERS POINT

11,180. Doughty and Clark
Papers. 1792-1856. 200 items.
Open. No guide.
Atlantic County Historical Society.
Includes 55 letters, 1841-57, of female members of the Clark family concerning social activities, illnesses, deaths, births, weddings, financial problems, and other subjects. Also includes 20 letters, 1837-53, of female members of the Doughty family, including letters in which Emma Hillman [Mrs. Daniel] Doughty (1790-1851), a native of Absecon, NJ, wrote home about moving to Ohio in 1837, the death of her husband in a steamboat explosion in 1838, and difficulties she encountered in raising her three sons and four daughters. In other letters, Doughty family members ask those in Absecon for financial assistance because of their desperate circumstances.

SUCCASUNNA

11,181. Local History
Oral history. 1970-71. 9 tapes.
Open. No guide.
Roxbury Public Library.
Interviews with residents who reminisce about Roxbury Township, including Annie (Stelce) [Mrs. Benjamin] Hosking, an elementary school teacher in Roxbury Township, local historian, author of histories about the area, and officer of the Roxbury Township Historical Society; [Miss] Florence Harvey, a teacher in Roxbury Township schools and former president of the Library's board of trustees; Catherine (Carter) [Mrs. Cook] Conkling, a teacher in Roxbury schools who is active in the Roxbury Township Historical Society; and [Miss] Harriet Meeker, a teacher in Roxbury schools, local historian, author of histories about the area, and president of the Roxbury Township Historical Society. In her interview Catherine (Fancher) [Mrs. Frank] Vleit, a lifelong resident of Roxbury, discusses the blizzard of 1888 and the heyday of Lake Hopatcong as a resort for celebrities. Vleit's daughter Edith [Mrs. Dayton] McNair, who taught the area's first class for mentally handicapped children, also participated in Vleit's interview.

11,182. Thompson, Mary Franklin (Wolfe)
Papers. 1886-1970. 3 folders, ca. 1 box, 30 vols., and 2 tapes.
Access restricted. Published guide.
Roxbury Public Library.
[Mrs. Charles] Thompson (1886-1970) was a teacher in the Succasunna area and an author of biographies of her parents and children's fiction based on the history of New Jersey and New England; at age 82, she received the Dorothy Canfield Fisher Children's Book Award. Correspondence with Annie S. Hosking and others, diaries for 1936 to 1960, tapes of reminiscences, a Wolfe family genealogy she compiled, and clippings. Includes her books *The Wag on the Wall,* which is about her mother Gertrude Franklin Wolfe; *Theodore Frelinghuysen Wolfe,* about her father, a physician who practiced only a few years before becoming literary editor of *Lippincott's Magazine; My Grandpa's Farm* (Stokes, 1931); and *Two in the Wilderness* (McKay, 1967). Thompson was an only child. She received a degree from a New Jersey teachers college but taught school only briefly. See Paul A. Stellhorn et al., eds., *Directory of New Jersey Historical Manuscripts* (Trenton, NJ: New Jersey Historical Commission, forthcoming).

TRENTON

11,183. Trenton College Club
Records. 1911-72. 11 vols.
Open. No guide.
Free Public Library of the City of Trenton.
Founded in 1911, the Club is an affiliate of the AAUW. Minutes; reports of the treasurer, secretary, and publicity, ways and means, and scholarship committees; a brief history; and lists of charter members and early presidents.

11,184. Trentonia
Collection. 1721-1968. 5 drawers and 10 microfilm reels.
Open. Published guide and card catalog.
Free Public Library of the City of Trenton.
Miscellaneous material relating to the history of Trenton includes papers of the founders and early mayors of Trenton, of New Jersey governors, of colonial printers, and of Revolutionary War generals as well as records of the Trenton Library Company, 1799-1855. Also includes a letter in which Jane Ewing of Trenton describes to her brother in Philadelphia a celebration given by the ladies of Trenton in honor of General Washington's visit in 1789; papers of Ellen Clementine Howarth, a Trenton poet who signed her poems Clementine, including manuscripts of poems and correspondence with William S. Yard, her friend, publisher, and literary agent; and a late 19th-century petition from 46 women in Burlington County, NJ, to the state legislature favoring the prohibition of liquor sales on Sunday, fewer liquor licenses, and more rigid licensing procedures. In addition, the collection contains a constitution, minutes of annual meetings from 1816 to 1880, and lists of officers and subscribers of the Trenton Female Tract Society, founded in 1816 to promote "the cause of our Redeemer by adopting some plans for circulation of Religious tracts." Also includes microfilm records of the Chesterfield Friends from 1675 to 1920, including minutes of men's meetings, 1684-1917, and of women's meetings, 1688-1824 as well as records of births and deaths, 1675-1750, of marriages, 1675-1847, of removals, and of other matters. See Paul A. Stellhorn et al., eds., *Directory of New Jersey Historical Manuscripts* (Trenton, NJ: New Jersey Historical Commission, forthcoming).

11,185. New Jersey Historical Sites Inventory
Collection. Ca. 1960- . 4000 items.
Open. No guide.
New Jersey Department of Environmental Protection.
Between 30 and 40 items documenting the residences of historic women, the most notable of whom are Clara Barton, Dorothea Dix, Elizabeth (Cady) Stanton, Lotta Crabtree, Patience (Lovell) Wright, Molly Pitcher, Tempe Wicke, Lucy Stone, and Carolyn Keene.

11,186. Batsto Furnace
Records. Ca. 1770-1909. 69 vols. and microfilm.
Open. Unpublished guide.
New Jersey State Library, Bureau of Archives & History.
Records of the iron furnace and glassworks that supported a small town in an isolated area of New Jersey. Includes Wharton tract deeds and information about women.

11,187. Chancery Court
Records. 1743-1824. 46 cu.ft.
Open. Unpublished guide.

New Jersey State Library, Bureau of Archives & History.
Records of the Court include divorce cases and other legal actions brought by or against women.

11,188. Department of State: Deeds and Marriages
Records. 1664-1878. 153 vols.
Open. Published and unpublished guides.
New Jersey State Library, Bureau of Archives & History.
Marriage deeds. See *Calendar of New Jersey Records for Deeds, 1664 to 1703,* series I, vol. 21 (Trenton, New Jersey Archives).

11,189. Department of State: Wills
Records. 1663- . Ca. 191,450 items.
Open. Unpublished guide.
New Jersey State Library, Bureau of Archives & History.
Wills and inventories concerning estates settled throughout the period. Also includes intestate and guardianship papers, renunciations, and other material concerning the administration of the estates of men and women in each of the 21 counties in New Jersey. Includes the will of Elizabeth C. White, a Burlington County resident who was a pioneer in the "agri-production" of blueberries and cranberries.

11,190. Hall and Mills Murder Trial
Records. 1926. 14 vols.
Open. No guide.
New Jersey State Library, Bureau of Archives & History.
Court reporters' transcriptions of the proceedings, photos, and clippings pertaining to the trial for the murder in 1922 of Edward Wheeler Hall, an Episcopal minister in New Brunswick, NJ, and [Mrs.] Eleanor Reinhardt Mills, a choir singer in his church. Charged with the crime but found not guilty were the rector's wife Frances (Stevens) Hall, her brother Willie Carpenter Stevens, and a cousin, Henry Stevens.

11,191. Inquisitions of the Dead
Records. 1688-1798. 4 vols.
Open. Index.
New Jersey State Library, Bureau of Archives & History.
Records consist of inquiries into the unknown or violent deaths of 348 men and women.

11,192. Insolvent Debtors
Records. 1747-1818. 3 vols.
Open. Index.
New Jersey State Library, Bureau of Archives & History.
Material relating to 502 debtors, some of whom were women.

11,193. Marriage Bonds
Records. 1665-1800. Ca. 125 vols.
Open. Published guide.
New Jersey State Library, Bureau of Archives & History.
Records of approximately one-quarter of the marriages that took place during the period. See William A. Nelson, *New Jersey Marriage Records, 1665-1800* (Baltimore: Genealogical Publishing Company, 1967).

11,194. Military Records of the Civil War
Records. 1865-76. 200 cu.ft.
Open. Unpublished guide.
New Jersey State Library, Bureau of Archives & History.
Some of the material concerns pension claims of Civil War soldiers and their wives or widows as well as a soldiers' children's home in Trenton.

11,195. Military Records of the Revolutionary War
Records. 1774-1824. 15,701 items.
Open. Unpublished guide.
New Jersey State Library, Bureau of Archives & History.
Correspondence, governmental and personal financial records, and other manuscripts pertaining to the Revolutionary War. Includes two letters General William Irvine wrote to Ann Irvine in 1780, two letters from Lady Theresa Asgill to the Count De Vergennes, and a letter from Asgill to Major Gordon.

11,196. Military Records of the Revolutionary War: Forfeited Estates
Records. 1776-95. 168 items.
Open. Unpublished guide.
New Jersey State Library, Bureau of Archives & History.
Depositions, notes, accounts, receipts, orders, lists, certificates, and other records pertaining to the forfeiture of estates in Bergen, Burlington, Cape May, Essex, Hunterdon, Middlesex, Monmouth, Morris, and Sussex counties in New Jersey. Includes a 1777 deposition by Ann Farr against Monmouth County Loyalists.

11,197. Military Records of the Spanish American War
Records. Nd. 18 cu.ft.
Open. Unpublished guide.
New Jersey State Library, Bureau of Archives & History.
Includes pension records containing information on the wives and widows of soldiers who took part in the Spanish American War of 1898.

11,198. Military Records of the War of 1812
Records. 1800-14. 18 cu.ft.
Open. Unpublished guide.
New Jersey State Library, Bureau of Archives & History.
Some of the records pertaining to the War contain information on women.

11,199. Mount, Charles Wright
Papers. 1862-65. 91 items.
Open. Unpublished guide.
New Jersey State Library, Bureau of Archives & History.
Many of the letters Mount received while serving in the US Navy are from his wife and other women living in the Hightstown, NJ, area.

11,200. Municipal Records: Tax Ratables
Records. Ca. 1773-1822. 60 cu.ft.
Open. No guide.
New Jersey State Library, Bureau of Archives & History.
Township tax assessor books list the names of individual landowners, at least five percent of whom were women; the amount of improved and unimproved land; livestock; carriages; houses; money on loan; and other data. Those women who owned property could vote in the state of New Jersey between 1776 and 1807.

11,201. Records of the Governor: Livingston, William
Records. 1776-90. 1 cu.ft.
Open. Unpublished guide.
New Jersey State Library, Bureau of Archives & History.
Correspondence of Livingston (1723-90), governor of New Jersey from 1776 to 1790, contains letters he wrote to and received from women.

11,202. Records of the Governors
Records. 1878-1975. 1826 cu.ft.
Partially restricted. Unpublished guide.
New Jersey State Library, Bureau of Archives & History.
Material of New Jersey governors, some of which pertains to women, is arranged by name of the individual governors.

11,203. Secretary of State: Legislative Records
Records. 1703-1845. 2 cu.ft. and 22 vols.
Open. Unpublished guide.
New Jersey State Library, Bureau of Archives & History.
Minutes of proceedings and votes, committee reports, and other records of the New Jersey General Assembly contain information about matters of concern to women during the 18th century. Records also include petitions for naturalization by 896 male and female immigrants, 1749-1842, and two petitions Rachel Wells presented to the legislature for the repayment of a substantial loan she made the state during the Revolutionary War. Wells, the sister of sculptor Patience (Lovell) Wright, owned a waxworks in Trenton from after the War until her death in 1796.

11,204. Secretary of State: Loan Office Mortgages
Records. 1724-86. 7 vols.
Open. Index.
New Jersey State Library, Bureau of Archives & History.
Organized by county and by name of individual, these records contain information on mortgages obtained by more than 1300 men and women in the following New Jersey counties: Burlington, 1724-50; Gloucester, 1786; Hunterdon, 1737-48; and Somerset, 1786.

11,205. Supreme Court
Records. Ca. 1705-1818. 201 cu.ft. and 4 boxes.
Open. Unpublished guide.
New Jersey State Library, Bureau of Archives & History.
Records on actions at law, judgment rolls, docket books, and minutes include information on cases involving women.

11,206. Tavern Licenses
Records. ?-1895. 43 cu.ft. and 14 vols.
Open. Unpublished guide.
New Jersey State Library, Bureau of Archives & History.
Petitions from men and women for legal permission to operate a tavern for the next year, some of which include information on the exact location of the tavern and the length of operation to date as well as a number of signatures of local inhabitants. The petitions are for taverns in Camden, Essex, Hunterdon, Mercer, Ocean, Somerset, and Sussex counties, NJ.

WOODBURY

11,207. County Documents
Records. 1686-1900. Ca. 70,000 items.
Open. Unpublished guide.
Gloucester County Historical Society Library.
Records pertaining to court and legal matters in old Gloucester County, which until 1837 included the present counties of Camden, Atlantic, and Gloucester. Women figure prominently in tavern licenses, petitions, and recognizances where they are often listed as owners and granted yearly licenses; in marriage reports for 1783 to 1880 filed by county justices of the peace and ministers, which name the bride, groom, official, date of marriage, and, often, residence of couple; and in examinations, many of which pertain to young girls and women who either were raped or bore illegitimate children. Women are also named giving testimony, paying bond money, and standing trial. Other material includes accusations of larceny; affidavits; election returns; narratives; records of slave births, manumissions, and trials;

warrants; writs; and Revolutionary and Civil War documents.

11,208. Genealogical Files
Collection. 18th century- . 30 drawers.
Open. No guide.
Gloucester County Historical Society Library.
Collection includes correspondence, family histories, genealogical charts, Bible records, baptismal and death certificates and notices, marriage licenses, military service discharge papers, pension applications, clippings, silhouettes, tintypes, daguerreotypes, and photos.

11,209. Howell, Anna (Blackwood)
Papers. 1739-1890. 1 drawer.
Open. No guide.
Gloucester County Historical Society Library.
Correspondence, daybooks, account books, invoices, receipts, household memoranda, and indentures of [Mrs. Joshua Ladd] Howell (1769-1855), who was a housewife and owner and manager of the Howell Shad Fisheries after her husband's death in 1818. Daybooks and account books detail the operations between 1820 and 1853 of the Howell homestead and of the Fisheries. Other material is ordered by names of individual family members, ranging from Howell's father-in-law John Ladd Howell (1739-85) to her grandchildren.

11,210. Reading Club
Records. 1887- . 1 folder.
Open. No guide.
Gloucester County Historical Society Library.
Minutes, correspondence, membership lists, programs, and other records of this Woodbury, NJ, women's group, founded in 1887 for the promotion of civic projects, scholarships, and literature. The Club was responsible for organizing a branch of the American National Red Cross in Gloucester County.

11,211. Turner, Rebecca (Bee)
Papers. 1877-89. 166-page vol.
Open. No guide.
Gloucester County Historical Society Library.
Diary of [Mrs. John C.] Turner (1815-98), a housewife, describes daily life in Gloucester County with references to hog killings, quilting bees, church services, and neighborhood births, deaths, and marriages.

11,212. Vital Statistics
Collection. 1700-1972. Ca. 250,000 cards.
Open. No guide.
Gloucester County Historical Society Library.
Data on births, deaths, and marriages, extracted primarily from local South Jersey newspapers and old Bibles.

NEW MEXICO

ALBUQUERQUE

11,213. Biography File
Collection. Early 1900s- . 8 ft.
Open. No guide.
Albuquerque Public Library, Southwest Room.
Clippings on New Mexico women, particularly of the Albuquerque area, include information about Ina Sizer Cassidy, Louise Coe, Natachee Scott Momaday, and Pablita Velarde.

Ina Sizer Cassidy (1869-1965) wrote a monthly column entitled "Art and Artists" for *New Mexico Magazine* from 1931 to 1960. Both she and her husband Gerald Cassidy were instrumental in development of Santa Fe's art colony. Ina Cassidy wrote prize-winning poetry, and Gerald Cassidy was a painter and lithographer. Before coming to New Mexico in 1912, she campaigned for women's suffrage in Detroit and New York, then continued this work in New Mexico. Ina and Gerald Cassidy were married from 1912 to 1934

Louise Coe (1896-), who at age 28 became the first woman elected to the New Mexico state senate, was the youngest person at that time to hold state office. While serving from 1925 to 1941, she was influential in the passage of bills aimed at improving education through free textbooks, larger libraries, higher salaries for teachers, and allocation of sales and severance taxes as sources of school finance

Natachee Scott Momaday (1913-) is an educator, writer, and artist who wrote *Owl in the Cedar Tree* (1956). In 1946 she and Al Momaday, a Kiowa artist whom she married in 1933, took over operation of the Jemez Pueblo Day School near Jemez Springs, NM. They taught art to the Pueblo children; exhibits of the children's works have been displayed nationwide. Natachee's mother was a Cherokee, and her father was white

Pablita Velarde (1918-) is a Pueblo Indian artist whose paintings depict the traditions, culture, and daily life of her people. She is known for her earth paintings, where stone-ground pigments of sand, earth, and clay, mixed with water and glue, are applied in layers to a coated masonite board. Her daughter Helen Hardin Craddoc, known professionally as Tsa-sah-wee-eh, is also a painter

11,214. Fergusson, Erna
Papers. 1920s-50s. 5 in.
Open. No guide.
Albuquerque Public Library, Southwest Room.
Focusing on the Southwest and Latin America, Fergusson (1888-1964) was an author of biographies, histories, and studies of Southwest Indian culture. Fergusson's notes on her biography of Clyde Tingley, an Albuquerque mayor; articles by Fergusson; summaries of lectures she delivered; photos; reviews of her works; and clippings about the Southwest and Fergusson, including some that relate to the controversy surrounding her study of the Jicarilla Apache people.

11,215. Garrett, Elizabeth
Papers. 1915-50s. 0.5 in.
Open. No guide.
Albuquerque Public Library, Southwest Room.
A musician and composer, Garrett (?-1947) was the daughter of Pat Garrett, who shot Billy the Kid. Although blind from birth, she wrote the lyrics and music for "O, Fair New Mexico," the state song, in 1915. Original score of that song; correspondence regarding attempts to transpose the state song to a lower, more usable key for general audiences; and clippings. Garrett was chairman of the folk music section of the New Mexico General Federation of Women's Clubs department of fine arts. She performed her compositions nationwide.

11,216. Hunning, Henrika Bush
Papers. 1876-80s. 0.25 in.
Open. No guide.
Albuquerque Public Library, Southwest Room.
A native of Germany, [Mrs.] Hunning (1853-1921) was the daughter of a pioneer New Mexico forester. Hunning's notes and reminiscences of her arrival in the US in 1876 and her life in New Mexico, a manuscript by Laurel Drew giving background information on Hunning and her family, and Drew's editorial comments on Hunning's notes.

11,217. Women in New Mexico
Oral history. 1975. No size given.
Open. Biographical booklet.
Museum of Albuquerque.
Tapes of interviews with eight notable New Mexico women: Louise Coe, Bertha Pauline Dutton, Grace Thompson Edmister, Fabiola Cabeza de Baca Gilbert, Laura Gilpin, Concha Ortiz y Pino de Kleven, Natachee Scott Momaday, and Pablita Velarde.

Louise Coe (1896-), who at age 28 became the first woman elected to the New Mexico state senate, was the youngest person to hold state office at that time. She served from 1925 to 1941

Bertha Pauline Dutton (1903-) is a noted scholar whose interests range from research on the history of Indians of the Southwest to interpretation and preservation of their contemporary culture and crafts. She served on the staff of the Museum of New Mexico from 1937 to 1965

Grace Thompson Edmister (1893-), who founded the Albuquerque Symphony Orchestra and organized the University of New Mexico music department, was probably the first woman in the US to direct a city orchestra. She is a Christian Scientist. In 1942 she married William R. Edmister, who died in 1957

Fabiola Cabeza de Baca Gilbert (1898-) was the first agent for the New Mexico Cooperative Extension Service to work among Pueblo Indian women and girls. For 30 years she taught the Pueblos and others skills to improve their daily lives. She also wrote books on the traditions, customs, and daily life of the descendants of the conquistadores as well as a weekly column for the Santa Fe *New Mexican* for 20 years

Laura Gilpin (1891-), a photographer of the Southwest and its people, has published several books of her photos

Concha Ortiz y Pino de Kleven (1914-) was a member of the New Mexico House of Representatives from 1936 to 1942 and the only woman to be majority whip in a state legislature. She sponsored legislation for bilingual education and the right of women to serve on juries and was particularly concerned with improving conditions for the disabled, juveniles in trouble, and penitentiary inmates. She was married to Victor Kleven from 1943 to 1956

Natachee Scott Momaday (1913-) is an educator, writer, and artist. In 1946 she and Al Momaday, whom she married in 1933, took over operation of the Jemez Pueblo Day School where they taught art to Pueblo children. Some of their students' work has been exhibited nationwide. Natachee Momaday wrote *Owl in the Cedar Tree* (1956) and also published a textbook on Indian authors. The Momadays' son Scott received the 1969 Pulitzer prize for his novel *House Made of Dawn.*

Pablita Velarde (1918-) is a Pueblo Indian artist whose paintings depict the traditions, culture, and daily life of her people. She is known for her earth paintings, where pigments of sand, earth, and clay, mixed with water and glue, are applied in layers to a coated masonite board. Her daughter Helen Hardin Craddoc, known professionally as Tsa-sah-wee-eh, is also a painter

11,218. Edmister, Grace Thompson
Papers. 1923-56. 2 folders.
Open. No guide.
University of New Mexico, Fine Arts Library.
Scrapbooks containing correspondence, photos, and clippings of [Mrs.] Edmister (1893-), founder and head of the University of New Mexico music department and founder of the Albuquerque Symphony Orchestra and the local chapter of Sigma Alpha Iota. Material concerns Edmister's personal life, musical events in the Southwest during the 1930s and 1940s, and public attitudes toward a woman conductor, arranger, and teacher.

11,219. Kettering, Eunice Lea
Papers. Nd. 40 items.
Open. No guide.
University of New Mexico, Fine Arts Library.
Manuscript compositions for voice, brass quintet, organ, and other instruments by Kettering (1906-), who is a composer.

11,220. Austin, Mary (Hunter)
Papers. 1901-29. 1.5 ft.
Open. Unpublished guide.
University of New Mexico General Library, Special Collections.
Correspondence, manuscripts, articles, book reviews, photos, paintings, and books of [Mrs. Stafford Wallace] Austin (1868-1934), an essayist, poet, novelist, and playwright. An opponent of the Americanization of Indians, Austin married a registrar of an Indian Agency and lived for 17 years among the Shoshones and the Paiutes, who eventually made her a member of their tribe. Founder of a literary colony in Carmel, CA, Austin later settled in Santa Fe, NM, with a group of artists, writers, and photographers, including Witter Bynner, Frank Applegate, and Ansel Adams.

11,221. Black Sparrow Press
Records. 1973-75. 8 ft.
Open. Unpublished guide.
University of New Mexico General Library, Special Collections.
Correspondence, manuscripts, page and galley proofs, photos, graphics, and finished books of the Press, founded in 1966 to publish limited editions of new and unusual works in American literature, particularly poetry. Includes works by Joyce Carol Oates, a novelist and professor of English at the University of Windsor in Canada, among them *The Hungry Ghosts* and *The Hostile Sun;* Rochelle Owens, a poet, avant-garde playwright, and founder and member of the New York Theatre Strategy & Women's Theatre Council; Diane Wakoski, a teacher of English at a junior high school in New York and a poet whose works were featured in *Four Young Lady Poets,* edited by Le Roi Jones; and Sherril Jaffe, a California writer of ironic stories and vignettes about "modern, enlightened" men and women. Jaffe's works include *Scars Make Your Body More Interesting.*

11,222. De Huff, Elizabeth
Papers. 1901-51. 25 items.
Open. Unpublished guide.
University of New Mexico General Library, Special Collections.
Correspondence, a diary, a ledger, theater programs, and clippings of De Huff (1892-), a teacher, lecturer, and author of books, short stories, verse, plays, and articles. An art teacher at the Santa Fe Indian School, De Huff founded a project wherein her students depicted Pueblo Indian dances and ceremonies in watercolor paintings, which were exhibited in New York City in 1919. Fred Kabotie, a Hopi Indian who was one of her students, became the illustrator for some of De Huff's books on Pueblo Indians and New Mexico, including the Indian children's stories *Tay Tay's Tales* (1922), *Five Little Kachinas* (1930), and *Say the Bells of Old Missions* (1943), which consists of legends about New Mexico churches. De Huff is also a member of the DAR, the Santa Fe Players, the New Mexico Association of Indian Affairs, and the Santa Fe Women's Club.

11,223. Fergusson, Erna
Papers. 1846-1964. 24 ft.
Open. Unpublished guide.
University of New Mexico General Library, Special Collections.
Personal and professional correspondence, notebooks, manuscripts, research material, family papers, photos, drawings, clippings, and other papers of Fergusson (1888-1964), a writer, lecturer, teacher, and founder of and guide for tours of Indian pueblos during the 1920s. A specialist in the history of New Mexico and Indians, Fergusson also worked to promote greater autonomy for Indians throughout the US. Her books included *Dancing Gods* (1931), *Our Southwest* (1940), and *Fiesta in Mexico* (1934). She also was a book reviewer for the New York *Herald Tribune* during the 1930s and 1940s. Collection contains histories of New Mexico women, interviews, and other sources of information about local history.

11,224. Lawrence, Frieda (von Richthofen)
Papers. 1933-58. 1 box.
Open. Unpublished guide.
University of New Mexico General Library, Special Collections.
The wife of D. H. Lawrence, Frieda Lawrence (1879-1956) was a writer and compiler of her husband's papers. Correspondence, notebooks, chronologies, biographical notes and comments on the Lawrences, programs, brochures, photos of paintings, and clippings provide information on her life once she returned after her husband's death to the Taos, NM, ranch they purchased and had lived in from 1922 to 1925. In 1950 she married Angelino Ravagli, an Italian who came to the US during the 1930s.

11,225. New Mexico Health Foundation
Records. 1940-65. 2 archival boxes.
Open. Unpublished guide.
University of New Mexico General Library, Special Collections.
Correspondence, photos, clippings, and other records of the Foundation, organized in 1946 by Katarina (McCormick) Barnes and the Simms family to establish public health clinics in rural areas of New Mexico and to provide medical and dental services to persons of limited means. Although successful in founding community clinics and health centers in Albuquerque, Cuba, Taos, Catron County, Roy, and Springer, NM, the Foundation was dissolved in 1965 because of depleted funds, but its services were then taken over by the New Mexico Department of Public Health. Katarina Barnes, who was the daughter of Ruth (Hanna) McCormick Simms, a US congresswoman from Illinois who after her second marriage became active in politics in New Mexico, also tried to provide money for Indian and Spanish-American students who desired to pursue careers in medicine or nursing.

11,226. Pillsbury, Dorothy (Pinckney)
Papers. 1922-67. 2 ft.
Open. Unpublished guide.
University of New Mexico General Library, Special Collections.
Correspondence, fan mail, notes, manuscripts, articles, photos, and clippings of Pillsbury (1896-1967), a social worker in Los Angeles from 1920 to 1935, who once vacationed in and then moved to New Mexico where she wrote essays, articles, and vignettes on Spanish-Americans and Indians and the countryside of New Mexico and the Southwest for *The Christian Science Monitor.* Her books, among them *Roots in Adobe* (1959), were based on these writings for the *Monitor.* In addition, Pillsbury wrote articles and short stories for a variety of other publications.

11,227. Pioneers Foundation Inc.
Records. 1865-1952. 40 ft.
Open. Unpublished guide.
University of New Mexico General Library, Special Collections.
The Foundation functioned between 1951 and 1965 to obtain tapes of the recollections of pioneers of New Mexico and the Southwest. Collection contains these tapes and transcripts, correspondence, a book manuscript, and outlines. Approximately 20 of the pioneers taped were women, including [Mrs.] Marietta Wetherill, wife of the archaeologist who discovered the Mesa Verde ruins. She describes travels by wagon across most of the Southwest, Alaska, Florida, and Missouri; being kidnapped by Paiute Indians and later adopted by Navajos; the culture and customs of the Navajo, Hopi, Acoma, and Isleta pueblos; and running a ranch later in life in the Jemez Mountains. Also includes interviews of Isabel Lancaster Eckles, a schoolteacher in Silver City, NM, who later became state superintendent of public instruction and Agnes Meador Snider, who discusses early life in Arizona and Texas, Indian customs and raids, and episodes involving Billy the Kid.

11,228. Shelton, Wilma Loy
Papers. 1869-1967. 10 ft.
Open. Unpublished guide.
University of New Mexico General Library, Special Collections.
Correspondence, itineraries of foreign visitors, official agency reports, guest books with descriptions and photos, and clippings of Shelton (1889-1972), a librarian and professor of library science at the University of New Mexico from 1920 to 1950. She also was supervisor and dean of women at the University and a member of various professional organizations, including the AAUW. During her first years in Albuquerque, she organized 20 small, traveling libraries, often transporting the book collections herself by car to nearby villages. After retirement from the University, she spent the next 15 years as official hostess in New Mexico for the US Department of State.

11,229. Spiegelberg, Flora (Langerman)
Papers. 1919-39. 49 items.
Open. Unpublished guide.
University of New Mexico General Library, Special Collections.
Correspondence, recollections, and clippings of [Mrs. Willi] Spiegelberg (1857-1943), an author of children's stories, educator, and civic reformer. The first Jewish woman in New Mexico, where she moved with her husband in 1874 from Colorado, Spiegelberg organized Sante Fe's first nonsectarian school for girls, which emphasized vocational education in addition to regular studies; she taught the courses on needlework, gardening, and nature study. Later, she and her husband moved to New York City, and she suggested a garbage collection and incineration plan there that was adopted by the City's sanitation department in 1911.

11,230. Van Dyke, May
Papers. Ca. 1900-63. No size given.
Closed. No guide.
University of New Mexico, Jonson Gallery.
Correspondence, manuscripts of compositions, programs, and a tape recording of two-piano compositions by Van Dyke (1888-1963), a pianist and composer. Van Dyke was the wife of Arthur Johnson, but she was known almost exclusively as May Van Dyke.

CHURCH ROCK

11,231. Archives
Records. 1922-78. No size given.
Access restricted. No guide.
Inter-Tribal Indian Ceremonial Association.
Minutes, financial records, correspondence, diaries, photos, scrapbooks, and oral history tapes and transcripts of the Inter-Tribal Indian Ceremonial Association, which was founded in 1922 by civic leaders to present Indian culture through annual dances and other activities in Gallup, NM, and to stimulate Indian arts and crafts. Includes information on Indian women who have taken part in the organization and its presentations, including Kay Bennett, a Navajo writer, singer, and craftswoman, and Maria Martinez, a potter in San Ildefonso, NM.

RIO RANCHO

11,232. Archives
Records. 1855- . Ca. 2 files and 3 shelves.
Access restricted. No guide.
Felician Sisters, Assumption of Our Lady Provincial House.
The Province was established in Ponca City, OK, in 1953. Minutes, financial records, correspondence, biographies of Sisters, histories of the motherhouse and of Felician communities in several states, statistical reports, photo albums, scrapbooks, guest books, clippings, a published history of the Province, and other records of the Province. Also includes constitutions, customs, statistical information, and books dating from the founding of the order in 1855.

SANTA FE

11,233. Cassidy, Ina (Sizer)
Papers. Ca. 1952-65. 2 in.
Open. No guide.
Museum of New Mexico.
Cassidy (1869-1965), a writer, poet, and lecturer on the Southwest, Indians, and history, was the wife of Gerald Cassidy, a painter and lithographer, from 1912 to 1934. Includes correspondence, handwritten verse by Cassidy, her notes on Gerald Cassidy's life and work, and clippings about Ina and Gerald Cassidy.

11,234. Oral History
Oral history. Nd. 6 tapes.
Open. No guide.
Museum of New Mexico.
Taped reminiscences of [Miss] Helen Blumenschein regarding her father Ernest L. Blumenschein, an early artist in Taos, NM; of Ina (Sizer) [Mrs. Gerald] Cassidy in 1955 and 1959; of A. F. [Mrs. Paul] Walter in 1959; of Ruth [Mrs. James L.] Seligman in 1959; and of others.

11,235. Photos
Collection. 1840s- . 80,000 items.
Open. No guide.
Museum of New Mexico.
Represented in this collection of photos, negatives, and glass slides are numerous women, primarily from the New Mexico Territory, including Laura Gilpin, photographer of the Southwest; sculptress Eugenie Shonnard; artist Georgia O'Keeffe; arts patron Ina (Sizer) [Mrs. Gerald] Cassidy; Pueblo Indian artist Pablita Velarde; Sadie Orchard, a madam and stage coach owner and driver; Katherine Stinson Otero, an aviator who flew a mail route and helped develop an airline corporation; Mary (Hunter) Austin; and Mabel (Ganson) Dodge.

11,236. New Mexico Federation of Women's Clubs Archives
Records. 1911-67. 8 ft.
Open. No guide.
New Mexico Federation of Women's Clubs.
Constitution and bylaws, annual reports, minutes, treasurers' records, correspondence, membership lists, speeches, resolutions, transcripts of radio broadcasts, photos, programs, bulletins, clippings, yearbooks, copy of state senate bill, and periodicals of this New Mexico organization, which was organized in 1911 at Las Cruces and admitted that same year to the GFWC, which was founded in 1890. Originally the NMFWC served a primarily social purpose, but it soon established departments and divisions to deal with such concerns as the American home and family, community affairs, conservation of natural resources, education, fine arts, citizenship and the status of women, veterans, Indian affairs, national defense, international affairs, and world religions. Highlighted in the collection is Julia Brown Asplund (1875-1958), who from 1911 to 1929 was a member of NMFWC's library extension committee, except for the period from 1914 to 1916 when she was NMFWC president. Asplund, who married Rupert Asplund in 1905, was concerned with social legislation, including women's suffrage, and with bringing library service to all New Mexicans. She was instrumental in establishing a girls reform school in 1919 and was chairman of the first Girls Welfare Board. She was also the first woman regent of the University of New Mexico. Her material includes a 1916 telegram from Woodrow Wilson's staff soliciting the NMFWC's support for Wilson's reelection and her correspondence with GFWC regarding her opposition to the GFWC's progovernment stand on the Pueblo Indian rights question in 1923. The collection's clippings deal with such topics as women's suffrage, children's rights, juvenile delinquency, women's role during WWI and WWII, and the Americanization of immigrants. Material on the war years includes resolutions criticizing WWII domestic programs as insufficient and urging placement of women in administrative positions to help run federal war programs.

11,237. Avery, Jennie M.
Papers. 1836-1972. 5 cu.ft.
Open. No guide.
New Mexico State Records Center and Archives.
[Miss] Avery (1888-1976) was a bonded abstractor for property titles who came to Santa Fe in 1914. Records from Avery's abstracting business, the Avery-Bowman Company, and a small amount of personal correspondence and notes include material by and about [Miss] Grace Bowman, Avery's lifelong business partner. Both women graduated from the University of Michigan and were members of the Santa Fe Business and Professional Women, the Altrusas, and the AAUW. Bowman was president of the New Mexico BPW and chairman of the BPW's western central region.

11,238. Boyd, E.
Papers. 1933-74. 6 cu.ft.
Partially restricted. Inventory.
New Mexico State Records Center and Archives.
Correspondence, manuscripts, field notebooks, working files, collected archival manuscripts, original drawings, and photos of Boyd, an artist, author, scholar of Spanish colonial culture, and curator of Spanish colonial arts for the Museum of New Mexico. Her full name was Elizabeth Boyd, but she always used E. Boyd.

11,239. Cline, Dorothy I.
Papers. 1912-70. 10 cu.ft.
Open. Inventory.
New Mexico State Records Center and Archives.
Cline was a political science professor at the University of New Mexico from 1946 until her retirement in 1971; she also was active in state politics and the New Mexico Committee on the Status of Women. Correspondence, manuscripts of published works, notes, tables of figures, student papers, political documents and speeches, state agency pamphlets, and clippings include material on New Mexico secretaries of state, who were often women, and on the state LWV, particularly the state constitutional revision issue of 1968.

11,240. Dietrich, Margretta (Shaw)
Papers. 1915-61. 6 in.
Open. Inventory.
New Mexico State Records Center and Archives.
Correspondence, biographical material, photos, and clippings of [Mrs. Charles H.] Dietrich (1881-), the wife of a Nebraska governor, a suffrage leader, and president of the Nebraska LWV during the 1920s. She moved to Santa Fe in 1929 after her husband's death. For the next thirty years she was active in many organizations, including the New Mexico Association of Indian Affairs and the Old Santa Fe Association.

11,241. Getty Family
Papers. 1846-70. 2 in.
Open. Inventory.
New Mexico State Records Center and Archives.
Correspondence and clippings of the family of George W. Getty, a US Army officer during the Mexican War who later became a military commander in New Mexico. Includes letters written by his daughter Annie Getty (?-1926) to her friends regarding life in Santa Fe and her marriage to Colonel Charles McClure and clippings announcing her wedding and death.

11,242. Long Family
Papers. 1856-1929. No size given.
Open. Inventory.
New Mexico State Records Center and Archives.
In 1885 Elisha V. Long (1836-1928), an attorney, postmaster, and court commissioner, was appointed chief justice of the New Mexico Territorial Supreme Court by President Cleveland; he resigned the post in 1890. Public and professional papers, family correspondence, publications by Long, speeches, articles, clippings, and obituaries include Long's articles and letters to the editor. Among his articles is one written in 1915 on the ideal wife, which was rejected for publication; one on Mary Lennon McElroy, a pioneer; and one on the household. In 1873 Long married Alice R. Walton, his second wife; they had four children, Alfred, Boaz, Mary, and Teresa. Also included are the Long children's school grades and some musical material.

11,243. Lusk, Georgia Lee
Papers. 1939-late 1950s. 5 cu.ft.
Open. No guide.
New Mexico State Records Center and Archives.
Correspondence, speeches, photos, and scrapbooks of Lusk (1893-), who served as New Mexico superintendent of public instruction from 1930 to 1934, from 1942 to 1946, and from 1954 to 1956. She also was a delegate to the Democratic National Convention in 1928 and a US congresswoman for one term after her election in 1946. In addition, she engaged in the family ranching business. Also included are minutes and reports of the New Mexico War Claims Commission, of which Lusk was a member from 1951 to 1953.

11,244. Pope Wallis, Marie
Papers. 1940-72. 3.5 cu.ft.
Open. Inventory.
New Mexico State Records Center and Archives.
Correspondence, diaries, manuscripts, published material, and other personal papers of Pope Wallis, who after an active career in the theater and social service in California came in 1939 to the University of New Mexico where she received a doctorate in Latin American literature and served as a member of the faculty from 1939 to 1942 and from 1945 to 1950. During WWII she saw active service with the Women's Army Corps and then remained briefly in Europe as a welfare officer for the UN Relief and Rehabilitation Administration. After 1950 she continued to teach and later worked as a librarian.

11,245. Spanish-Mexican Families
Papers. 1696-1952. 10 ft.
Open. Item index.
New Mexico State Records Center and Archives.
Personal papers, business records, correspondence, poems, legal documents, land conveyances, wills, military records, photos, funeral notices, and genealogies of 22 Spanish-Mexican families. The land conveyances are of particular interest because women maintained individual property rights during the Spanish-Mexican period from 1598 through 1846.

11,246. Woodward, Dorothy
Papers. 1685-1950s. 15 cu.ft.
Partially restricted. Inventory.

New Mexico State Records Center and Archives.
Woodward (1895-1961) was a history professor, and later a regent, at the University of New Mexico; she assisted in establishing the New Mexico State Records Center and Archives. Correspondence, manuscripts of Woodward's writings, and her personal papers. Also included is archival material Woodward collected, which contains correspondence providing a daily chronicle of the life of Harriet Cornelia Bidwell Shaw as wife of a Baptist minister and family activities in New Mexico Territory from 1850 to 1861.

NEW YORK

ALBANY

11,247. Albany Army Relief Bazaar
Records. 1864-1908. 2 boxes.
Open. Unpublished guide.
Albany Institute of History and Art Library.
The Bazaar was organized in 1864 by the Albany Army Relief Association, which was composed primarily of local women, to aid Civil War soldiers and to raise money for the US Sanitary Commission, a precursor of the American National Red Cross. Includes correspondence concerning participants in the Bazaar, photos, clippings, a catalog of the exhibits, and copies of *The Canteen,* the Bazaar's official newspaper.

11,248. Dana Natural History Society
Records. 1868- . Ca. 8 ft.
Open. No guide.
Albany Institute of History and Art Library.
Founded in 1868 by faculty and students of the Albany Female Academy, the Society is among the oldest women's scientific organizations in America. Includes minutes, rosters, programs, papers presented, and lists of officers, speakers, and field activities. The primary activity of the Society was to awaken an interest in the study of nature for both practical and scientific purposes. The Albany Society began as one of several chapters throughout the nation, but, since 1876, it has been the only active chapter in the country.

11,249. Hamlin, Huybertie Lansing (Pruyn)
Papers. 1878-1957. 46 boxes and 60 vols.
Open. Partial unpublished guide.
Albany Institute of History and Art Library.
Papers of [Mrs. Charles Sumner] Hamlin (1873-1964), an author of numerous articles about life in Albany and about the social class of which she was a member, consist of correspondence, diaries, journals, manuscript memoirs, manuscript articles, scrapbooks, clippings, and other papers. Includes 57 volumes of her diaries, 1881-1956, as well as correspondence with her mother Anna Fenn (Parker) Pruyn; with Florence Gardiner Hall, an American missionary in China and Japan; and with and about President and Mrs. Grover Cleveland, President Woodrow Wilson and his wife Edith Bolling (Galt) Wilson, Franklin and Eleanor Roosevelt, the Democratic Convention of 1924, the Women's National Democratic Club in Washington, DC, and the League of Nations. Also contains the correspondence of Anna Pruyn with her daughter Harriet Langdon (Pruyn) [Mrs. William Gorham] Rice and her diaries for the period 1878-89.

Hamlin's correspondence, diaries, and memoirs deal with the social life and history of Albany, Boston, Washington, DC, and Europe; the antisuffrage movement in Albany and the Anti-Suffrage Association of Albany; and visits to the White House. Also contains photos, clippings about Eleanor Roosevelt and about Franklin Roosevelt's political career, invitations to White House functions, and political pamphlets

11,250. Rice, Harriet Langdon (Pruyn)
Papers. 1879-1939. 41 vols.
Open. No guide.
Albany Institute of History and Art Library.
Correspondence, journals, and guest books of Rice (1868-1939), a prominent hostess in Albany who was among those involved in developing the concept of the League of Nations. Rice was married to William Gorham Rice, Sr., a US civil service commissioner under President Cleveland. Her papers include information on the League of Nations and descriptions of yearly trips abroad and Albany social life.

11,251. College of St. Rose
Records. 1920- . No size given.
Access restricted. Unpublished guide.
College of St. Rose Archives.
Annual reports, minutes, curriculum records, reports, correspondence, photos, a tape, clippings, catalogs, yearbooks, and faculty publications of the College, which was founded in 1920. The school was a women's college until 1970 when it became a coeducational institution. Includes files on College presidents and a history of the College's first 25 years, which was written by Sister Catherine Francis Soulier, a former president of the school.

11,252. Abbott, Bérénice
Papers. 1935-39. 40 items.
Open. Catalog cards.
Division of Historical Services-New York State Museum.
Photos by Abbott (1898-) of New York City scenes during the depression. The photos were taken for her book *Changing New York,* the text of which was written by Elizabeth McCausland.

11,253. Women's Organization for National Prohibition Reform
Records. 1929-33. 50 items.
Open. Unpublished guide.
Division of Historical Services-New York State Museum.
Clippings and circulars of the Organization, which was founded in 1929 to work toward repeal of the 18th Amendment. The Organization was founded by Mrs. Charles Sabin and disbanded in 1933 after the ratification of the 21st Amendment.

11,254. Department of Correctional Services and Department of Mental Hygiene
Records. 1840-1971. 500 cu.ft.
Partially restricted. Unpublished guide.
New York State Archives.
Approximately half of the records pertain to women, including those who were incarcerated in state penal institutions and state mental hospitals. Contains extensive information about the inmates and clients as well as about the administration of state institutions and programs for the criminal or insane person. Among the records is material relating to the Western House of Refuge in Albion, NY, a state-supported institution established in 1893 as one of the first reformatories for women in the US. Amy Lowell was instrumental in founding the House.

11,255. New York State Factory Investigating Committee
Records. 1911-15. 50 cu.ft.
Open. Unpublished guide.
New York State Archives.
The Committee, which was chaired by Robert F. Wagner, was commissioned by the New York state legislature after the Triangle Shirtwaist fire in 1911. It issued published reports each year from 1912 to 1915. Approximately half of the records consists of employee information cards giving demographic and employment data on women who worked in New York City factories at the time. Also includes reports by Committee field workers who interviewed women factory workers.

11,256. Temporary State Commission for Widowed Mothers
Records. 1913-14. 5 cu.ft.
Open. Unpublished guide.
New York State Archives.
Includes transcripts of committee hearings, reports of meetings, correspondence, and the Commission's final report, which was published in 1914.

11,257. Albany Female Seminary
Records. 1827-61. 5 vols.
Open. No guide.
New York State Library, Manuscripts and Special Collections.
The Seminary was founded in 1828 to educate young women of Albany. Includes articles of association with a list of the original stock subscribers, reports to the regents, a trustees' minute book for 1827 to 1849, a stock certificate book, student rosters, a class book, a deed to the school property, a title search, and a fire insurance policy.

11,258. Albany Woman's Suffrage Society
Records. 1882-83. 1 vol. and 8 items.
Open. Unpublished guide.
New York State Library, Manuscripts and Special Collections.
Minute book, copies of legislation, notes, and brochures of the Society, which was founded in 1880.

11,259. Canfield, Malcolm
Papers. 1815-95. 6 ft.
Open. Unpublished guide.
New York State Library, Manuscripts and Special Collections.
Correspondence, a diary, a travel journal, account books, and other papers of Canfield (1822-92), an agent in a freight transportation business who had a farm homestead in Sunderland, VT. Also contains papers of his wife Harriet Augusta Graves Canfield, whom he married in 1855, including her correspondence, 1839-66, with relatives, friends, and her husband who, as a freight agent, spent April to December in New York City. In her letters she writes about family news, farm business, weather, purchases to be made, the draft, elections, and the Civil War. Also includes a diary, for 1850 and 1851, in which she describes farm life in Vermont, and letters to Malcolm Canfield from his sister Mary Ann, who gives him the family news in Sunderland and Arlington, VT.

11,260. Cherry Hill
Collection. Ca. 1700-1960. 70 ft.
Open. Unpublished guide.
New York State Library, Manuscripts and Special Collections.
Papers of families that resided at or were related to families residing at Cherry Hill in Albany. Contains correspondence, diaries, writings, legal and land papers, business records, recipe books, publications, and maps of the Van Rensselaer, Bonney, Elmendorf, Gould, Rankin, and other families. Includes correspondence, diaries, manuscripts of a Van Rensselaer family history, notebooks, business and legal papers, estate papers, and photos of Catherine Visscher (Van Rensselaer) Bonney, a daughter of General Solomon Van Rensselaer, who served with her husband Samuel W. Bonney as a missionary to China in the 1850s and 1860s. Other papers relate to Harriet Van Rensselaer, who was married to General Solomon Van Rensselaer; her daughters Elizabeth, Margaretta, and Maria; Harriet Maria Elmendorf and her daughter Harriet (Elmendorf) Gould; Catherine Bonney's daughter Emma; Catherine Woodworth; Catherine Livingston Gould; and Emily Rankin.

11,261. Colles, Gertrude
Papers. 1895-1909. 1 ft.
Open. Unpublished guide.
New York State Library, Manuscripts and Special Collections.
Papers of Colles, an artist, include correspondence for 1901 to 1908, broadsides, suffrage meeting notices, pamphlets, and other papers, along with a handwritten constitution of the National Progressive Women Suffrage Union and suffrage buttons. Papers relate to the women's suffrage movement in New York City around the turn of the century. Colles was a member of the executive committee of the Civic Council of New York City in 1901.

11,262. Hall, James
Papers. 1830-1930. 90 ft.
Open. Unpublished guide.
New York State Library, Manuscripts and Special Collections.
Includes correspondence, journals, diaries, financial records, and other papers of Hall (1811-1898), a geologist and paleontologist, as well as correspondence for 1895 to 1916, business records, notes, and printed items of his daughter Josephine (Hall) Bishop (1841-1917).

11,263. Leonard, Elizabeth F. (Wilson)
Papers. 1875-1906. 1 ft.
Open. Unpublished guide.
New York State Library, Manuscripts and Special Collections.
Correspondence, invitations, and autograph cards of Leonard (1862-?), who was active in Albany civic and social functions and who was the wife of Edgar Cotrell Leonard, who with his brothers ran the firm of Cotrell and Leonard, Furriers, in Albany. Elizabeth Leonard was a member and president of the Albany Fresh Air Guild for Children during the early 1900s.

11,264. Morss, Caroline Amelia (Kirtland)
Papers. 1829-41. 1 ft.
Open. Unpublished guide.
New York State Library, Manuscripts and Special Collections.
Letters from Morss (1810-80), a housewife and mother who married Burton G. Morss in 1831; her sister Julia (Kirtland) Sayre; and others to Frederick W. Kirtland, brother of Amelia Morss and Julia Sayre. The letters concern family life in Greene County, NY.

11,265. Pettit, Elsie de Witt (Norton)
Papers. 1893-97. 4 vols.
Open. No guide.
New York State Library, Manuscripts and Special Collections.
Scrapbooks of Pettit containing clippings, cards, programs, and brochures relate primarily to foreign theater, cultural, sporting, and other events. Also includes a recipe book.

11,266. World's Columbian Exposition, Board of Lady Managers
Records. Nd. 1 ft.
Open. Unpublished guide.
New York State Library, Manuscripts and Special Collections.
The Board, which was created by an act of Congress in 1890, was recognized as "the official channel of communication through which all women, or organizations of women may be brought into relation with the Exposition." It was authorized to award prizes for exhibits produced by women, managed the Woman's Building at the exhibit, and approved all activities relating to women's interests at the Exposition. Contains official records of the national board and various state boards, including correspondence, prospectuses, circulars, and illustrations concerning organizational and administrative matters.

11,267. University Archives
Records. 1844- . 1600 cu.ft., 80 ft., 46 vertical file drawers, 20 plan file drawers, 2750 vols., and 62 tapes.
Open. Unpublished guide.
State University of New York at Albany, University Archives.
Minutes, financial records, correspondence, student transcripts, scrapbooks, photos, clippings, maps, and publications of the University, which was founded in 1844 as the State Normal School, Albany. Seventy-five percent of the students between 1844 and the early 1960s were women. Few of the Archives' records predate 1906, when some of the University buildings burned.

ALBION

11,268. Achilles, Lillian A.
Papers. 1890-1941. 1 ft.
Access restricted. No guide.
Swan Library Local History Archives.
Correspondence, diaries, annual reports, photos, and memorabilia of [Miss] Achilles (1871-1941), who was a librarian at the Free Town Library from 1891 to 1899 and at Swan Library from 1899 to 1941. Includes correspondence with publishers and material on her involvement with the state library association.

11,269. Rodden, Donna (Strickland)
Papers. 1969-77. 1 ft.
Open. Unpublished guide.
Swan Library Local History Archives.
Correspondence, photos, scrapbooks, and memorabilia of Rodden (1926-), who in 1973 became the first woman mayor of Albion. The daughter of an attorney, Rodden received her bachelor's degree in radio journalism from Syracuse University in 1946, an MS in journalism from New York University in 1948, and another master's degree from Brockport State Teachers College in New York in 1962. Rodden has been radio and television director for Cayton, Inc.; editor of the *Lyndonville Enterprise* in Lyndonville, NY; chairman of the board of mental hygiene for Orleans County; and president of the Orleans County Council on the Arts.

ALDEN

11,270. Alden Liberal Club
Records. 1914-56. 6 vols.
Open. No guide.
Alden Historical Society Museum
Minutes of the board of directors and of Club meetings. The Club was organized in 1902, federated in 1903, incorporated in 1908, and is still in existence. The group's aim is to promote literary culture and to advance the interests of the local Alden Ewell Library. Club members were responsible for many village improvements, including supplying benches, street markers, and a watering trough as well as sponsoring money-making projects. In 1913 Mrs. Charles Ellers, a Club member, became president of the Western New York Federation of Women's Clubs.

ALFRED

11,271. Alfred University Archives
Records. 1836- . Ca. 110 ft.
Open. No guide.
Alfred University Library.
Includes minutes and programs of early women's literary lyceums and other social and charitable organizations, correspondence, diaries, scrapbooks, autograph books, privately published biographies and memorials, faculty and alumni biographical and publications file, a newspaper and clipping file, University serial publications, and Seventh-Day Baptist yearbooks and histories. Alfred University was founded as a coeducational Select School in 1836. Records cover the topics of suffrage, abolition, temperance, education, and the Seventh-Day Baptist work and philosophy. People represented include missionaries, doctors, church workers, poets, educators, nurses, artists, engineers, and persons involved in business.

ALLEGANY

11,272. Motherhouse Archives
Records. 1859- . Ca. 200 boxes, 87 items, and 14 tapes.
Open. Unpublished guide.
Franciscan Sisters of Allegany, New York, St. Elizabeth Motherhouse.
The Motherhouse was founded in 1859 by the Franciscan Sisters of Allegany, NY, a congregation of religious women involved in education, health care, and social work. Includes records of the congregation and its membership, directives sent from general superiors to the congregation, correspondence of members, biographies of various general superiors, accounts of the work of the Sisters in various ministries, photos, a film about a Tampa, FL, hospital now used as a residence for senior sisters and laypersons, material describing historical celebrations, yearbooks of schools conducted by the Sisters, booklets, pamphlets, artwork, religious objects, and other items. Contains a tape-recorded account of the death of a general superior, taped recollections of sisters about former general superiors and other sisters, and tapes concerning archival policy and organization, confidentiality, and the relation of archives to the congregation.

AMITYVILLE

11,273. Motherhouse Archives
Records. 1853- . 20 drawers.
Open. Unpublished guide.
Sisters of the Order of St. Dominic, Queen of the Rosary Motherhouse.
Financial records, correspondence, retreat notes, photos, and scrapbooks of the Sisters, a religious order of women founded in Brooklyn, NY, in 1853. Records pertain to the government and growth of the congregation and include annals of individual missions and ministries.

AUBURN

11,274. Cayuga County Cemetery
Records. 1800s-1900s. 10 vols.
Open. Unpublished guide.
Cayuga County Historical Research Center.
Records that local DAR members compiled from tombstones dating from the early 1800s to the mid-1900s. Records are also available on microfilm.

11,275. Slade, Betsey
Papers. 1781-1882. 1 folder.
Open. Unpublished guide.
Cayuga County Historical Research Center.
Correspondence, poems and other writings, an address by a church pastor, and clippings of [Mrs. Peleg] Slade (1781-1882), a homemaker, relate to her 100th birthday.

11,276. Tracy, Deborah Woodworth
Papers. Nd. 8-page item.
Open. Unpublished guide.

Cayuga County Historical Research Center.
Reminiscence that [Mrs.] Tracy (1772-1854), a homemaker, wrote about herself, her family, and their migration from New England to central New York.

11,277. Tubman, Harriet (Ross)
Papers. Ca. 1870- . 1 folder.
Open. Unpublished guide.
Cayuga County Historical Research Center.
Biography, deeds, a will, an obituary, clippings, and census data of Tubman (ca. 1815-1913), a slave, nurse, and Civil War spy, who was a leader in the underground railroad. Papers relate to her work with slaves during the Civil War, her establishment of a home for the aged in Auburn, NY, and her friendship with William H. Seward. She was married to John Tubman.

AURORA

11,278. Hollcroft, Temple Rice
Papers. Ca. 1825-80s. 9 ft.
Open. Unpublished guide.
Wells College Archives.
Papers of Hollcroft (1889-1967), a mathematics professor at Wells and the official College historian, consist of correspondence and historical research material relating to the history of the College and Aurora and to local business affairs and the business interests of Henry Wells and Edwin Barber Morgan, particularly the American Express Company and Wells, Fargo & Company. Also contains papers concerning Alonzo Delano, a friend and business associate of Edwin B. Morgan, who traveled to California in 1849 and wrote several books about his experiences and gold rush miners. Included are Hollcroft's notes and drafts of a partially completed biography of Delano and correspondence from Delano and his wife Mary Burt Delano to Edwin Morgan. Mary Delano's letters pertain to financial arrangements for her daughter Harriet Delano, who was institutionalized at a state hospital.

11,279. Howland, Emily
Papers. Nd. Ca. 20 ft.
Open. Unpublished annotated bibliography.
Wells College Archives.
Articles, speeches, and printed proceedings of Howland (1827-1929), an educator, reformer, and philanthropist who resided near Wells College in Sherwood, NY. Papers pertain to woman suffrage, Indians, antislavery, temperance, the Unitarian Church, and other topics. Includes volumes of copied notes from the Emily Howland papers at Swarthmore College as compiled by [Miss] Phebe King in 1969 and notes made from Howland's diaries by Mrs. Kenneth Coulson. Represented in these notes are Howland's correspondence, ca. 1857-70; a journal, a report, reminiscences, and letters from a contraband camp; speeches about temperance, woman suffrage, and peace; and diary excerpts and commencement speeches given at Sherwood Select School, 1849-1927.

11,280. Morgan, Edwin Barber
Papers. Ca. 1834-89. Ca. 6 ft., 23 vols., and ca. 130 items.
Open. Unpublished guide.
Wells College Archives.
A boyhood friend and business associate of Henry Wells as well as a politician and philanthropist, Morgan (1806-81) was a charter trustee and benefactor of Wells College. Diaries, 1862-81; account books for the period; and correspondence chiefly between Lewis Henry Morgan and William H. Seward. Also includes books owned by Edwin B. Morgan.

11,281. Publications and Local History
Records. Ca. 1864- . No size given.
Open. Unpublished guide.
Wells College Archives.
Consists chiefly of college and student publications at Wells, such as the Wells College *Catalog*, the *Alumnae News* and its successor the *Express*, the student newspaper *Courier*, the student yearbook *Cardinal*, and the student literary journal *Chronicle;* publications of faculty, alumnae, and local residents; local history publications; and files of photos and pamphlets related to the school and the Aurora area.

Also contains account books, autograph books, scrapbooks, and miscellaneous records relating to the College community, including scattered minutes, correspondence, and other items of the local chapter of the AAUP

11,282. Smith, Helen Fairchild
Papers. 1864-1930s. Ca. 6 ft. and 30 vols.
Open. Unpublished guide.
Wells College Archives.
Smith (1837-1926) taught English literature and history at Wells College, also serving as the school's lady principal and then dean from 1875 to 1905. Personal and family correspondence, including her letters to her niece Katharine Ledyard Hill of Newport, RI, in which Smith discusses her opinions on ministers and religion and recounts her daily activities, and extensive diaries, 1864-1926, in which she comments on the weather, personal experiences, and College events.

11,283. Wellsiana
Records. Ca. 1828-1908. Ca. 10 ft.
Open. Unpublished guide.
Wells College Archives.
The Wellsiana collection pertains to administration and activities of Wells College, established in 1868 as Wells Seminary for the Higher Education of Young Women; to College founder and benefactor Henry Wells (1805-78); and to Henry Wells's business interests in Wells, Fargo & Company. Constitution and minutes of the school's collegiate association; secretary's reports and correspondence of the Wells College Missionary Society, 1871-99; missionary correspondence of the local YWCA, 1900-05; minutes of the class of 1908; notes and programs of the Wells College Philharmonic Club, 1895-1901; and examination questions in all academic subjects offered, 1871-74.

Also contains correspondence of Henry Wells, a philanthropist and partner in and president of Wells & Company, American Express Company, and Wells, Fargo & Company. Includes family correspondence of his daughter Mary E., who spelled her surname Welles, and his second wife Mary Prentice Wells (1829-1908), whom he married in 1861

BELLPORT

11,284. The Pigskin Book
Papers. 1699-1707 or 1708. 1 vol.
Open. No guide.
Bellport-Brookhaven Historical Society Museum.
Volume of "Lady Martha" (Tunstall) Smith, who was married to William Tangier Smith, the owner of St. George's Manor in Mastic, NY. In the volume she describes their Indian crew's whaling excursions, the barrels of "oyle," and the pounds of "boane." The book also contains estate accounts.

BINGHAMTON

11,285. ACUNY Archives
Records. Ca. 1946-53. 35 cu.ft.
Closed. No guide.
State University of New York at Binghamton Library.
Transcripts of committee meetings, administrative records, records of academic departments, correspondence, manuscripts, catalogs, directives, promotional literature, and publications of the Associated Colleges of Upper New York, which comprise Mohawk, Sampson, and Champlain colleges as well as the Middletown Center. Includes papers of Amy M. Gilbert, professor emeritus of SUNY at Binghamton, who served as head of the history and political science departments for the ACUNY campuses and as dean of Champlain College from 1952 to 1953.

11,286. Colum
Papers. Ca. 1900-60s. 18 ft.
Partially restricted. Partial published guide.
State University of New York at Binghamton Library.
Chiefly incoming correspondence but also diaries, manuscripts, tapes of interviews and readings, notebooks, and photos of Padraic Colum (1881-1972), a writer, and his wife Mary (Maguire) Colum (1887-1956), a literary critic. Mary Colum's correspondence includes letters from such literary figures as Maxwell Perkins and Van Wyck Brooks and concerns both professional and personal matters. See Zack Bowen, *Annotated Catalog and Bibliography for the Colum Collection of the Library at State University of New York at Binghamton* (Binghamton, NY: State University of New York at Binghamton, 1969).

11,287. Lavin
Papers. 1940s-60s. 250 items.
Open. Published guide.
State University of New York at Binghamton Library.
Correspondence and tapes of interviews of Mary (Walsh) Lavin (1912-), a writer. Letters and cards are chiefly from Lord Edward and Lady Beatrice Dunsany and concern mutual literary interests. Lavin later married Michael MacDonald Scott. See Zack Bowen, et al., *Annotated Catalog and Bibliography for the Lavin Collection of the Library at State University of New York at Binghamton* (Binghamton, NY: State University of New York at Binghamton, 1973).

11,288. Link
Papers. 1940s-60s. Ca. 20,000 items.
Access restricted. No guide.
State University of New York at Binghamton Library.
Correspondence, reports, financial documents, plans, drawings, and other papers of Edwin A. Link (1904-), a pioneer in aviation and underwater archaeology and engineering, and his wife Marion (Clayton) Link, a writer. Marion Link has been involved in her husband's underwater work and has published books and articles, including *Sea Diver: A Quest for History under the Sea* (Coral Gables, FL: University of Miami Press, 1964) and *Windows in the Sea* (Washington, DC: Smithsonian Institution Press, 1973).

11,289. Williams and Chambers
Papers. 1840s-1960s. 5 cu.ft.
Open. Unpublished guide.
State University of New York at Binghamton Library.
Correspondence, diaries, transcripts, manuscripts, and photos of William Frederic Williams (1818-71), a Protestant missionary from central New York who worked in Iraq and Turkey from 1848 to 1871. Much of the collection consists of the papers of Williams's four wives and his children.

BROCKPORT

11,290. College Archives
Records. 1841- . 80 ft.
Open. No guide.
State University of New York College at Brockport, Library.
Minutes of governing bodies and faculty, student

academic records, histories of the college, scrapbooks, photos, clippings, college catalogs, yearbooks, student magazines and newspapers, alumni newsletters, and programs from campus events of the College, which was founded in 1841 as Brockport Collegiate Institute. Until 1960 Brockport was primarily a teacher's college. After that time it became a liberal arts college with strong emphasis on education and professional programs in social work, nursing, and other fields. From the beginning women faculty members were included on the staff of the female department. During much of the school's existence, women made up the majority in the student body.

BRONX

11,291. Hutchinson, Anne
Phonotapes. Nd. No size given.
Open. No guide.
Bronx County Historical Society Research Library.
Radio tapes from the Society's "Out of the Past" program, which recreates through interviews the lives of such historical figures as Anne Hutchinson.

11,292. Archives
Records. 1889- . 2 boxes and 7 vols.
Closed. No guide.
Dominican Nuns of Perpetual Adoration, Corpus Christi Monastery.
Annals of the foundation of the Monastery, the second Dominican cloister in the US with perpetual adoration, describe the daily life and problems of the members. Also includes short biographical items concerning several of the sisters in the early days of the foundation, lists of entrances and professions, obituaries, and photos of the Monastery, grounds, the foundresses and early sisters, and the family of Mother Mary of Jesus, who was the principal foundress.

11,293. Du Bois, Constance Goddard
Papers. 1897-1909. 3 boxes.
Access restricted. No guide.
Library Museum of the American Indian.
Correspondence, field notes, articles, and clippings of Du Bois relate to her interest in Diegueno and Luiseno Indians on the Mesa Grande, Campo, and Pala reservations in southern California around 1905.

11,294. Gilbert, Mary
Papers. 1803. 16-page item.
Access restricted. No guide.
Library Museum of the American Indian.
Letter of Gilbert, in which she describes a visit Penrose Wily, John Letchworth, Mary Bell, and others made to the Seneca Indians settled on the Allegheny River.

11,295. Magill, Margaret W.
Papers. 1887. 185-page vol. and 47-page item.
Access restricted. No guide.
Library Museum of the American Indian.
Diary of [Miss] Magill, who was the first wife of Frederick W. Hodge and the sister-in-law of Frank H. Cushing. Diary relates to part of the Hemenway expedition to a Hawkiuh, NM, Zuni site excavated by Cushing and Hodge. Also includes a typescript of the diary.

11,296. Wa-Wa-Chaw Nunez
Papers. Nd. 1 box.
Access restricted. No guide.
Library Museum of the American Indian.
Diaries, journals, and sketches of Nunez, an Indian princess, relate to paintings in the Museum.

11,297. Archives and Manuscripts
Collection. 1891-1976. 225,000 items.
Open. Published guide.
Library of the New York Botanical Garden.
The history of the Botanical Garden, founded in 1891 to foster botanical and horticultural research and education, is documented in correspondence and other manuscripts relating to the Garden's development and programs. Included are papers of Elizabeth G. (Knight) Britton and Ynes Enriquetta Julietta Mexia, botanists; Elizabeth C. Hall and Anna Murray Vail, librarians; Helen Morganthau Fox, an educator and horticulturist; Jane Loring Gray, wife of botanist Asa Gray; and Emily Lovira Gregory, a naturalist. See Sara Lenley et al., *Catalog of the Manuscript and Archival Collections and Index to the Correspondence of John Torrey* (Boston: G. K. Hall, 1973).

11,298. Archives
Records. 1817- . Ca. 150 cu.ft.
Partially restricted. Unpublished guide.
Sisters of Charity of New York Archives.
Records of this religious order of women, which was founded in 1809 in Emmitsburg, MD. Includes correspondence, retreat notes, photos, and scrapbooks. Papers relate to several mothers superior, the activities of the congregation, and the founding of the congregation, the Foundling Hospital, St. Vincent's Hospital, various educational institutions, and child care and social work agencies.

BRONXVILLE

11,299. Dannett, Sylvia G. L., and Randall, Mercedes
Papers. 1940-59. 2 Hollinger boxes.
Open. No guide.
Sarah Lawrence College Archives.
Correspondence, clippings, pamphlets, and other papers of Dannett and Randall, who wrote about American history during the 1950s. Includes material on black women during the Civil War and Jane Addams and the Women's International League for Peace and Freedom.

11,300. History of the College
Records. 1926- . 159 drawers, 618 vols., and 196 tapes.
Partially restricted. Unpublished guide.
Sarah Lawrence College Archives.
Sarah Lawrence was founded in 1926 as a women's college devoted to a special type of women's education. Includes reports of the president to the board of trustees; correspondence; tapes of Constance Warren, the first president; syllabi; class assignments; handbooks; and records relating to the College's history and founding, presidents and deans, faculty, center of continuing education, black studies, campus events, faculty committees, Upward Bound, the Early Childhood Center, coeducation, and the library. Also includes tapes and photos of the Lawrence family.

11,301. Sarah Lawrence College Archives
Records. 1926- . 40 drawers, 618 vols., and 190 tapes.
Partially restricted. Partial unpublished guide.
Sarah Lawrence College Archives.
Records of the College, which was founded in 1926 as a women's college and sought to help women use learning as a vehicle for growth and self-sufficiency, include correspondence, tapes and films, speeches, educational studies, work study reports, photos, reviews, newspapers, and other material.

11,302. Student Activities and Publications
Records. 1928- . 70 drawers, 158 vols., and 20 tapes.
Open. Unpublished guide.
Sarah Lawrence College Archives.
Includes tapes, interviews, questionnaires, photos, reviews, journals, and newspapers related to student activities and publications of the College, which was founded in 1928. Contains copies of the newspapers *The Campus* and *The Tribune,* literary magazines such as *The Literary Review* and *The Alumnae Magazine,* and the yearbook.

11,303. Student Theses and Honor Papers
Records. Nd. 1 drawer, 10 boxes, 126 vols., and 6 tapes.
Open. Unpublished guide.
Sarah Lawrence College Archives.
Student papers related to anthropology, history, literature, philosophy, psychology, sociology, genetics, the performing arts, and women's studies. Includes papers on Dorothea Lynde Dix, Emma Goldman, and New York City female antislavery societies between 1834 and 1840. Also includes a teacher's guide for women's history, anthologies, books by alumnae, and an alumnae directory.

11,304. Women's Magazines
Collection. 1895-1955. No size given.
Open. Unpublished guide.
Sarah Lawrence College Archives.
Includes copies of the *Delineator, Good Housekeeping, Home Needlework Magazine, Ladies' Home Journal, McClure's, Modern Priscilla, Pictorical Review, Vogue,* and the *Women's Home Companion.*

11,305. Women's History
Collection. Nd. 10,000 vols., 50 princeton files, and 106 microfilm reels.
Open. Unpublished guide.
Sarah Lawrence College Library.
Contains items not listed in bibliographic sources, which the library at the College collected after the women's history program was started in 1971. Includes a complete set of the US Women's Bureau bulletins; autobiographies of Mary Anderson, Elizabeth Gurley Flynn, Emma Goldman, Agnes Nestor, and Rose Pesotta; correspondence; personal accounts, diaries, and travel journals of such women as Marie Thérèse (de Solms) Blanc, Mary Boykin Chesnut, Frances Anne Kemble, Harriet Martineau, Anne (Newport) Royall, Jane Grey (Cannon) Swisshelm, Frances (Milton) Trollope, and Sarah Wister; a book about a woman's duties in the marriage relation by William A. Alcott; and the *Mother's Book* (1831) by Lydia Maria Child. Also includes issues of *Godey's Lady's Book,* 1840-52, and other periodicals on women and women's rights, among them the *Forerunner, Lily,* the *Lowell Offering, The Revolution,* and *Una.*

11,306. Faculty Publications
Papers. 1928- . Ca. 300 vols. and 100 tapes.
Open. Unpublished guide.
Sarah Lawrence College Library and Archives.
Correspondence, tapes, speeches, essays, research papers, work study reports, educational studies, papers from symposiums, essays, reviews, and photos concerning College faculty publications. Includes Esther Raushenbush's "Literature for an Individual Education" and "Psychology for an Individual Education," Ruth Munroe's "Teaching the Individual," Lois B. Murphy's "Emotional Factors in Learning," Helen Merrell Lynd's "Field Work in College Education," B. J. Loewenberg and R. Bogin's "Black Women" and "American Women Speak," Melissa Richter's "A Revolution in the Education of Women," Constance Warren's "A New Design for Women's Education," and an oral history of Bessie (Schonberg) Varley.

11,307. Taggard, Genevieve, and Dickinson, Emily
Papers. 1935-46. Ca. 300 vols. and 3 microfilm reels.
Open. Unpublished guide.
Sarah Lawrence College Library and Archives.
Papers that Taggard (1894-1948), a poet and teacher, collected in preparation for a biography of the poet Emily Dickinson. Consists of

correspondence and poems of Dickinson along with other items concerning her life, friends, and her social and literary background. Some books contain notes in Taggard's hand.

BROOKLYN

11,308. Bender, Lauretta
Papers. 1926-73. 3 drawers.
Open. Unpublished guide.
Brooklyn College Library, Special Collections.
Correspondence, scrapbooks, and photos of Bender (1897-), a psychiatrist and author. Bender was particularly interested in child psychiatry and in visual motor gestalt. She became senior psychiatrist at Bellevue Hospital in New York City in 1930 and was in charge of the children's service there until 1956. In 1959 she became director of research for child psychiatry at the New York state department of mental hygiene. Includes letters from Karl Menninger.

11,309. Benét, Laura
Papers. 1944-59. 2 boxes.
Open. No guide.
Brooklyn College Library, Special Collections.
Correspondence, a diary for 1944 to 1955, and manuscripts of Benét, a poet who was the sister of Stephen Vincent and William Rose Benét. Includes letters from poet Marianne Moore and manuscript and galley proofs of Laura Benét's *Famous American Humorists* (1959). Benét received a medal as honor poet at the National Poetry Center in 1936 and was invited to record her poems for the Library of Congress in 1958. Benét was a settlement house worker in New York from 1915 to 1919; she wrote for the *New York Evening Post* and the *New York Evening Sun* from 1928 to 1929 and *The New York Times* in 1930. She was the author of books of fiction and biography.

11,310. Davis, Dorothy Salisbury
Papers. 1949-65. 2 boxes.
Open. No guide.
Brooklyn College Library, Special Collections.
Manuscripts and research notes of [Mrs.] Davis (1916-), a mystery novelist and short-story writer. Manuscripts include her novels *Men of No Property* (1956) and *The Evening of the Good Samaritan* (1961); her short stories "Home to the Hills" (1963) and "Sweet William" (1954); an unproduced play *Cry of Winter* (1965), with comments by and letters from Clifford Odets; and review articles for the *New Republic* (1954). Born in Chicago, Davis now lives in Palisades, NY.

11,311. Brooklyn Daily Eagle
Collection. 1841-1955. Ca. 200 cabinets and microfilm reels.
Access restricted. No guide.
Brooklyn Public Library, Brooklyn Collection.
Clipping morgue of the *Brooklyn Daily Eagle*, a daily newspaper, consists of photos, clippings, and microfilm reels.

11,312. Hoffman, Gertrude
Papers. Ca. 1900-39. 1 folder and 3 boxes.
Access restricted. Unpublished guide.
Brooklyn Public Library, Brooklyn Collection.
Correspondence, dance notations, photos, clippings, and playbills of Hoffman, a dancer and choreographer.

11,313. Archives
Records. 1845- . Ca. 30 vols.
Partially restricted. No guide.
Franciscan Sisters of the Poor, Community Service Center.
Correspondence, annals, photos, slides, motion pictures, scrapbooks, and other records of the congregation, which was founded in Aachen, Germany, in 1845; members of the congregation came to the US in 1858. The Brooklyn office is the international center of the congregation.

11,314. Bishop Family
Papers. 1828-79. 1 Hollinger box.
Open. Unpublished guide.
Long Island Historical Society.
Contains papers of Susan Holmes Bishop (1817-47) before her marriage to A. Hamilton Bishop (1810?-79), a minister who lived on Long Island. Includes a travel diary she kept from 1838 to 1839 during a trip to Europe, Asia Minor, and Africa. Also includes family letters written from Astoria, NY, to New Haven, CT, and Poughkeepsie, NY.

11,315. Blake, Euphemia Vale Smith
Papers. Ca. 1880-1900. 1 Hollinger box.
Open. No guide.
Long Island Historical Society.
[Mrs.] Blake (1830?-1905) was a Brooklyn Heights, NY, socialite and the author of the books *History of the Polaris Expedition* (New York, 1874) and *History of Newburyport, Mass.* (Newburyport, 1854). Contains unpublished manuscripts concerning North American and Central American Indian folklore, the noble families of Europe with emphasis on great medieval women, and an index of quotations from Shakespeare with a supplemental index to Shakespearean subjects.

11,316. Bound Manuscripts
Collection. Ca. 1650-1956. Ca. 9 ft.
Open. Unpublished guide.
Long Island Historical Society.
Includes a journal, 1839-41, of Lucy Hooper (1814-41) containing her poetry, much of which was published in periodicals such as *Ladies' Companion* and *The New Yorker;* a letter copybook, 1856-71, of Ann Chase, the wife of the US consul at Tampico, Mexico, which contains letters and notes about personal and official life at Tampico; and a volume, 1825-28, of the New York City Female Union Society for the Promotion of Sabbath Schools, which contains a constitution, rules, and records of the distribution of Bibles to women.

11,317. Brooklyn Society of New England Women
Records. 1905-54. 5 ft.
Open. No guide.
Long Island Historical Society.
Constitution, bylaws, notes, material about events, membership lists, and records of deaths and resignations of members of this branch of the Society, which existed from 1905 to 1954 "to form a bond of sympathy between all women of New England ancestry in the Brooklyn community and to instill pride and love for the traditions of New England." The National Society was founded in 1895.

11,318. Cruikshank
Collection. 1712-1890. 1 Hollinger box.
Open. Unpublished guide.
Long Island Historical Society.
Includes a letter of Ann Van Horn, which she wrote in Quebec, Canada, 1776; a will of Rachel Ferris for her Westchester, NY, estate, 1834; a mortgage of Jane Robert to Roelf and Phoebe Wiggins, 1844; deeds of Abigail and Leffert Llyod of Flatbush for land conveyed by Aguila and Eliza Giles to Bateman Llyod through Catherine Duryee, 1827; a mortgage of Louisa and William Ellsworth to Abraham Vanderveer, 1838; receipts of Mrs. Evert Augustus Duyckinck to Peter Signton and of John White to Mrs. Brockhost, 1712; and a power of attorney of Mary Park, a resident of Liverpool, England, granting Edmond Jenney and David Van Horn authority to collect from Roper Dawson, a resident of New York, 1763.

11,319. Daughters of the American Revolution
Records. 1905- . 1 Hollinger box.
Open. No guide.
Long Island Historical Society.
Bylaws, an account book, correspondence, address books, addenda, souvenir books, photos, pamphlets, and other items of the Brooklyn Battle Pass Chapter of the DAR, which was founded in 1905 to perpetuate the memory and spirit of those men and women who achieved American independence. The DAR sponsored acquisition and protection of historical sites, erection of monuments, encouragement of historical research, publication, preservation of documents and relics, and promotion of patriotic events and celebrations.

11,320. Huntington, Edna
Papers. 1930-60. 2 Hollinger boxes.
Open. Unpublished guide.
Long Island Historical Society.
Huntington (1895-1965), chief librarian for the Historical Society from 1936 to 1960, was author of *Monuments and Markers.* Includes correspondence; manuscripts of "The Mills of Long Island," "Authors Who Have Lived in Brooklyn, Dates and Places," and others of her works; scrapbooks; and notes.

11,321. Lasar, Clementine
Papers. 1870-79. 1 Hollinger box.
Open. No guide.
Long Island Historical Society.
Scrapbook of Lasar, an opera soprano, actress, organist, and reader in Brooklyn Heights, NY. Contains clippings pertaining to her stage, musical, and singing career. She performed in small church halls and light opera companies in Brooklyn and toured in New York City, New Haven and Hartford, CT, and Boston. Also includes programs and press reviews.

11,322. Lott Family
Papers. 1717-1868. 1 Hollinger box.
Open. Unpublished guide.
Long Island Historical Society.
Papers of this late 18th- and early 19th-century family which had extensive land holdings in Brooklyn. Includes an Erasmus Hall School report for [Miss] Abby, [Miss] Maria S., and John F. Lott, 1850; an appraisal and inventory of the personal property of Cathrintie Lott, 1841; a deed of Jane Ditmars to John Galloways for a farm in Brooklyn, 1821; a release granted to Lydia Lott from Catharine Duryee, Leffert W. Llyod, Sara Llyod, and Abigail Llyod, 1825; and a copy of a surrogate's order to Jeremiah Lott to publish for claims on the estate of Margaret Bogert of Montgomery, NJ, 1832.

11,323. Ludlow Family
Papers. 1701-1867. 1 Hollinger box.
Open. Unpublished guide.
Long Island Historical Society.
Includes papers of [Miss] Elizabeth Ludlow (1785?-1867), a socialite in Brooklyn Heights, NY, who speculated in land and the stock market. Includes her correspondence, an 1867 will, receipts, and a power of attorney and letters of administration, 1828, as well as a stock cancellation of Cornelia A. Willink and Elizabeth Ludlow and a release of Cornelia and Gabriel Ludlow from Charles, John, and Mary Ludlow.

11,324. Miscellaneous Certificates
Collection. 1811-1962. 2 Hollinger boxes.
Open. Unpublished guide.
Long Island Historical Society.
Includes a certificate of Annie E. Morgan for her first Holy Communion, 1880; a certificate of citizenship of Margaret Scunet, 1851; a certificate of [Miss] Adelaide Mudgely stating her qualifications to teach primary school, 1878; a certificate of membership for Rachel Smith to the United Daughters of Rechab, 1846; a receipt for

the sale of a Negro slave named Mary in Petersburg, VA, 1864; a graduation diploma for Carrie Crane granted by the board of education of Brooklyn, 1874; a certificate to Amy Meireis from the YMCA at completion of a dressmaking course, 1915; a Brooklyn Fire Insurance Company policy on the house of a Miss Williams, who lived in Brooklyn, 1829; a certificate of good standing awarded to the Long Island Federation of Women's Clubs by the Urban Club, 1895; a membership approval for Mrs. L. F. Robbins Naylor from the DAR, 1922; a certificate of life membership of Julia Pierrepont from the Historical Society, 1882; a certificate of highest honors from the trustees of the Packer Collegiate Institute to Clara Corinne Naylor; and education degrees and certificates of merit and award of Emily Rueger, 1879-95.

11,325. Miscellaneous Manuscripts
Collection. 1675-1900. 2 Hollinger boxes.
Open. Unpublished guide.
Long Island Historical Society.
Includes a will of Adriana Magaw, a resident of Greavesend, NY, 1831; a marriage certificate of Peter Anderson and Maria Nelson, 1847; a deed of Garrit and Ann Margaret Van Horne for land in Newtown, 1785; a deed of Elizabeth and E. P. Parvin for property in Brooklyn to Jane W. Webb, 1882; an indenture of Cornelia and Garrett Middafgh for land, 1758; a permit from William Walton to [Mrs.] Deborah Covenhoven enabling her to pass to Staten Island on her way to New Jersey, 1782; inventories of goods and chattels of Margaret Eldert, a resident of Brooklyn, 1817; and a petition to the US Congress by Eliza, Teresa, and Americus Vespucius asking for citizenship, along with a grant of land written in Spanish with an English translation, ca. 1850.

11,326. Neuman, Fannie
Papers. 1939-40. 1 Hollinger box.
Open. No guide.
Long Island Historical Society.
Photograph album of Neuman (1900-), a Brooklyn Heights, NY, socialite and amateur photographer, contains photos of the 1939-40 World's Fair, which was held in New York City.

11,327. Stryker-Rodda, Harriet
Papers. 1903-65. 1 Hollinger box.
Open. Unpublished guide.
Long Island Historical Society.
Papers of Stryker-Rodda (1910-), a librarian and researcher for the Historical Society, includes her correspondence with John D. Scott and Edward Van Altena; notes of John Ripley concerning Anita Stewart, Norma Talmage, and other women; and items concerning John Scott and Edward Van Altena, manufacturers of hand-colored song slides in Brooklyn, with color slides of Norma Talmage, Alice Joyce, and Anita Stewart. The song slides were used to project lyrics and descriptive photos onto the movie screen during reel changes at early motion pictures.

11,328. Toedteberg, Emma, and Toedteberg, Augustus
Papers. 1849-1936. 1 Hollinger box.
Open. No guide.
Long Island Historical Society.
Emma Toedteberg (1857-1936), chief librarian of the Historical Society from 1886 to 1936, was the daughter of Augustus Toedteberg (1825-1909) and Catharine Lagere Toedteberg (1821-1905). Includes a funeral book in memory of Emma Toedteberg; the 1849 marriage certificate of Augustus Toedteberg and Catharine Toedteberg; baptismal certificates of August Frederich, Louisa, Emma, and Augusta Toedteberg from the United German Evangelical Lutheran Church in Brooklyn; photos; daguerreotypes; and other items relating to Emma Toedteberg.

11,329. Trommer, Marie
Papers. 1900?-66. 1 Hollinger box.
Open. No guide.
Long Island Historical Society.
Papers of Trommer, an artist and schoolteacher, include a credit book from a Brooklyn grocery store, unpublished short stories by Trommer, catalogs of 1932-33 art exhibitions that included Trommer's works, photos, drawings, sketches, a public school science textbook, block prints, and naturalization papers of Bertha Trembisky.

11,330. Willink Family
Papers. 1825-51. 1 Hollinger box.
Open. Unpublished guide.
Long Island Historical Society.
Family papers include those of John A. Willink (ca. 1805-65), a gentleman farmer, and of his wife Cornelia Ann (Ludlow) Willink (ca. 1805-65). Includes a deed of John and Cornelia Willink to Mathew K. Couzens for land in Livingston's Landing, 1851; a deed for land in Brooklyn owned by John and Cornelia Willink and Elizabeth Ludlow, 1833; a receipt from Cornelia Livingston to John William Willink, 1834; and a power of attorney from Cornelia Willink and Elizabeth Ludlow to William D. Sherman, 1839.

11,331. Wood, Alice L.
Papers. 1955-67. 1 Hollinger box.
Open. No guide.
Long Island Historical Society.
Papers of Wood, a publisher, author, and editor of *Bookniks* and *Friendly World,* which are privately published pamphlet magazines devoted to the cause of world peace. Includes letters to subscribers concerning the UN, UNESCO, and the peace movement; her published and unpublished works; articles; pamphlets; circulars; and paper cutouts.

11,332. Long Island University Archives
Records. 1911- . 192 ft.
Open. No guide.
Long Island University-Brooklyn Center, Libraries.
Minutes, financial records, correspondence, photos, scrapbooks, and publications of the University, which was founded in 1926. Women were founders of the school and have been trustees, benefactors, faculty members, administrators, and students of the University.

11,333. Library and Library School
Records. 1887- . Ca. 4 ft.
Open. Unpublished guide.
Pratt Institute Archives.
Annual reports, departmental records, correspondence, handbooks, publications, and memorabilia of the Library and Library School dating from the founding of Pratt Institute in 1887. Also includes manuscripts, scrapbooks, photos, and memorabilia of the publications department and correspondence and memorabilia of librarians Anne Carroll Moore, Mary Wright Plummer, and Julia Rathbone, who also served as instructors.

BUFFALO

11,334. Amherst Book Club
Records. 1941-73. 1 vol.
Open. Unpublished guide.
Buffalo and Erie County Historical Society.
A history of the Club written by Virginia McKinley. Members of this women's group, founded in 1941, studied current books and presented book reviews.

11,335. Bartlett, George F. Hunter
Papers. 1867-1919. 20 boxes.
Open. Unpublished guide.
Buffalo and Erie County Historical Society.
Family photos of Bartlett (1836-1931), who was trained as a physician but became a businessman and amateur photographer in Buffalo. He photographed civic, cultural, and social events, as well as his business activities. Also includes family business records.

11,336. Benedict, Vida Grenville Meister
Papers. 1894-1912. 11 vols.
Open. Unpublished guide.
Buffalo and Erie County Historical Society.
Diary and scrapbooks of Benedict, a Buffalo socialite, contain pictures, photos, clippings, and theater programs.

11,337. Beston, Mrs. Henry
Papers. Nd. 4 items.
Open. Unpublished guide.
Buffalo and Erie County Historical Society.
Recollections of Buffalo and notes in which Elizabeth (Coatsworth) Beston (1893-) comments on the Coatsworth family, Buffalo families, places near Buffalo, and her travels.

11,338. Boll, Luellan H.
Papers. 1890-1973. 11 Hollinger boxes and 2 vols.
Open. Unpublished guide.
Buffalo and Erie County Historical Society.
Correspondence, poems, photos, and scrapbooks of [Miss] Boll (1890-1973), a poet. Much of Boll's work dealt with current events and documented local history. She also wrote a series of poems about famous people.

11,339. Cary
Papers. 1836-1923. 8 folders and 1 Hollinger box.
Open. Unpublished guide.
Buffalo and Erie County Historical Society.
Correspondence of Julia Love Cary (1826 or 1827-1915); Maria M. Love (1839 or 1840-1931), her sister Elizabeth Love Cary (1841 or 1842-1924), and other members of the Cary family with Frances (Folsom) Cleveland Preston (1863 or 1864-1947), who was married to President Grover Cleveland, and Rose Elizabeth Cleveland, a White House hostess and the sister of President Grover Cleveland. Maria Love was chairman of the board of the Fitch Creche nursery for more than 50 years.

11,340. Cleveland, Grover
Papers. Nd. 1 Hollinger box.
Open. Unpublished guide.
Buffalo and Erie County Historical Society.
Includes photos of Cleveland's wife Frances (Folsom) Cleveland (1864-1947).

11,341. Coatsworth
Papers. Nd. 1 Hollinger box.
Open. Unpublished guide.
Buffalo and Erie County Historical Society.
Photos of Coatsworth family members.

11,342. Costumes
Collection. Nd. 3 Hollinger boxes.
Open. Unpublished guide.
Buffalo and Erie County Historical Society.
Collection contains prints and photos of men's, women's, and children's dress from the 1800s to the present.

11,343. Crawford, Annie I.
Papers. Nd. 1 folder.
Open. Unpublished guide.
Buffalo and Erie County Historical Society.
Poems by Crawford (1857-1942), a Buffalo artist and author.

11,344. DeForest, Marian
Papers. 1916-61. 2 Hollinger boxes.
Open. Unpublished guide.
Buffalo and Erie County Historical Society.
Correspondence, scripts of plays, legal contracts and agreements, clippings, and theater programs of [Miss] DeForest (1864-1935), a playwright, author, and journalist who lived in Buffalo. DeForest

served as editor of the women's department of the *Buffalo Evening News* and in 1919 was a founder of the Zonta Club of Buffalo, an organization for women business executives. Her works include *Little Women,* a play in which Katharine Cornell starred, and a biography of Louisa May Alcott.

11,345. Fillmore, Millard
Papers. 1809-74. 120 Hollinger boxes.
Open. Published and unpublished guides.
Buffalo and Erie County Historical Society.
Correspondence of Fillmore (1800-74), thirteenth President of the US and a resident of Buffalo, includes letters from writer Anna Ella Carroll, social reformer Dorothea L. Dix, his first wife Abigail (Powers) Fillmore, his daughter Mary Abigail Fillmore, and his sisters Julia Harris and Olive Johnson. Also includes photos of portraits and prints of Fillmore's two wives, Abigail and Caroline Fillmore. Collection is also available on microfilm. See Lester W. Smith, ed., and Arthur C. Detmers, asst. ed., *Guide to the Microfilm Edition of the Millard Fillmore Papers* (Buffalo: Buffalo and Erie County Historical Society and State University College at Oswego, NY, 1975).

11,346. Fox, Anna Barlett
Papers. 1907-48. 3 folders.
Open. Unpublished guide.
Buffalo and Erie County Historical Society.
Correspondence, financial papers, and clippings of [Mrs.] Fox (1870 or 1871-1959), who was active in social work in the Buffalo area; in 1924 she was the first woman elected president of the New York Conference of Social Work. Includes papers and booklets about social work as well as information on the Library Loan Committee, the Buffalo Foundation, the Old Buffalo Pageant and Bazaar, service to families, and relief needs in Erie County.

11,347. Glenny, Esther Ann (Burwell)
Papers. 1836-99. 11 folders.
Open. Unpublished guide.
Buffalo and Erie County Historical Society.
Personal correspondence and other papers of Glenny, the daughter of Bryant Burwell; of her family and her husband William H. Glenny (?-1882), a Buffalo businessman; and of his family. Includes a eulogy and diary about the death of Mary Burwell, which her mother wrote.

11,348. Herox, Susan Stafford, and Brunck, Catharine L.
Papers. 1859-67. 3 vols.
Open. Unpublished guide.
Buffalo and Erie County Historical Society.
Diary that Brunck, the wife of local physician Francis C. Brunck, kept in 1867 as well as diaries for 1859 and 1863 of Herox, who knew the Brunck family.

11,349. Inter-Club Council of Western New York
Records. 1939-62. 4 Hollinger boxes and 1 vol.
Open. Unpublished guide.
Buffalo and Erie County Historical Society.
Constitution, minutes, and treasurer's reports of the Council, an organization of women's clubs. Also includes reports, programs, rosters, résumés, and histories of the various member clubs, including the National Secretaries Association, Hadassah, the Business and Professional Women's Club, the YWCA, and the AAUW. In addition, the collection contains biographical sketches of Susan B. Anthony, Ruth Stopper, Alice (Koller) Leopold, Madge Taggert, Mary A. Lane, Catherine Rowley Lautz, Norma M. Wedlake, and Dorothy McCullough Lee. Also includes a scrapbook of photos, clippings, and programs relating to the Council and to Susan B. Anthony.

11,350. Judd, Harriet Stewart
Papers. 1903-05. 341-page item.
Open. Unpublished guide.
Buffalo and Erie County Historical Society.
Autobiography of Judd (1822-1907), who was the widow of Orange Judd, the publisher of *The American Agriculturist* and a benefactor of Wesleyan University. Harriet Judd assisted in building up the circulation of her husband's magazine. She was also treasurer of the New York branch of the Women's Foreign Missionary Society and secretary of the Methodist Women's Foreign Missionary Society during the early 1870s.

11,351. Keyes, Bertha A.
Papers. 1915-48. 1 folder.
Open. Unpublished guide.
Buffalo and Erie County Historical Society.
Personal letters from former students, texts of graduation talks, and prize day awards lists of [Miss] Keyes (1868-1959), an educator. In 1899 Keyes joined the faculty of the Franklin School in Buffalo; from 1925 until her retirement in 1938, she was headmistress of the School. Keyes was an organizer of the Headmistress Association of the Middle West, a member of the National Association of Principals of Schools for Girls, and a founder of the Smith College Club in Buffalo.

11,352. Larke
Papers. 1858-1926. 3 Hollinger boxes.
Open. Unpublished guide.
Buffalo and Erie County Historical Society.
Diaries of the Larke family. Margaret Larke and her husband Alfred Larke moved from Texas to Buffalo in 1879. Their daughter Janet (1839-?) was married to a Mr. Hatchard in 1866.

11,353. McKinley, William
Papers. Nd. 3 Hollinger boxes.
Open. Unpublished guide.
Buffalo and Erie County Historical Society.
Includes photos of McKinley's wife Ida (Saxton) McKinley (1847-1907) at 16 and 18 years of age and photos of her with President McKinley at the Pan American Exposition.

11,354. Moore, Augusta C.
Papers. 1850-60. 1 Hollinger box.
Open. Unpublished guide.
Buffalo and Erie County Historical Society.
Diaries and poetry notebooks of Moore (1841 or 1842-1925), who was married to General John Card Moore, a soldier, lawyer, and public official.

11,355. Mulligan, Charlotte
Papers. 1861-1912. 1 folder and 1 Hollinger box.
Open. Unpublished guide.
Buffalo and Erie County Historical Society.
Letters that Mulligan (?-1900), a music critic for the *Buffalo-Courier* and a Buffalo Sunday school teacher, received from former Sunday school pupils, who wrote about the ways in which her teaching influenced their lives. Also includes an autobiography and financial reports of the Guard of Honor Society.

11,356. Sidway Family
Papers. 1864-1926. 1 folder.
Open. Unpublished guide.
Buffalo and Erie County Historical Society.
Papers of the Sidway family include correspondence of Charlotte Spaulding Sidway and certificates relating to the 40th, 45th, and 50th reunions of the Buffalo Seminary Graduates' Association, class of 1861.

11,357. Viele, Anne
Papers. 1909-67. 1 folder.
Open. Unpublished guide.
Buffalo and Erie County Historical Society.
Correspondence, clippings, membership certificates, and medical conference programs of Viele (1884-1967), a physician who graduated from the University of Buffalo medical school in 1922. Papers pertain to her work as a school physician in Niagara Falls and Hornell, NY. She also served as a staff member of E. J. Meyer Memorial Hospital, a special consultant at the Warsaw, NY, hospital, and a presiding physician in charge of women at the Buffalo State Hospital during WWII.

11,358. Williams, Olive
Papers. 1860-1925. 1 Hollinger box.
Open. Unpublished guide.
Buffalo and Erie County Historical Society.
Includes photos of [Miss] Williams (1890-1971) and other members of her family. Williams helped organize the Allentown Association.

11,359. Williamsville, NY: Women's Auxiliary, Calvary Episcopal Church
Records. 1913-18. 1 folder.
Open. Unpublished guide.
Buffalo and Erie County Historical Society.
Minute book of the Women's Auxiliary, of the Calvary Episcopal Church in Williamsville, which was founded in 1913.

11,360. Witmer Family
Papers. Ca. 1850-1911. 30 vols.
Open. Unpublished guide.
Buffalo and Erie County Historical Society.
Diaries of the Tobias and Christian Witmer families include a diary of Anna Witmer.

11,361. Women's Teachers' Association of Buffalo
Records. 1894-1965. 2 Hollinger boxes and 10 vols.
Open. Unpublished guide.
Buffalo and Erie County Historical Society.
Constitution, bylaws, minutes, correspondence, a ledger, and reports of this organization for women teachers. Also includes scrapbooks containing clippings and pamphlets, which Adelaide Graybiel and Elizabeth Leary kept, and a thesis.

11,362. Archives
Records. 1854- . Ca. 20 boxes, 8 vols., and ca. 20 tapes.
Access restricted. No guide.
Sisters of St. Joseph Generalate.
Minutes; financial records, including the founders' personal records; records of governmental chapter meetings; photos; and scrapbooks of the Sisters, a religious order of women involved in teaching, nursing, and social work. The Buffalo congregation was founded in 1854. Includes records relating to the achievements of the general superiors, the houses, and the community.

11,363. Bacon, Gertrude M.
Papers. 1870-1937. No size given.
Open. Unpublished guide.
State University College at Buffalo, E. H. Butler Library.
Papers and clippings of Bacon (1866-1937), a teacher, principal, and professor of elementary education at the State Normal School, which became the state teachers college at the University. Also includes a biographical sketch of her in the unpublished booklet "These Were Builders" by Sister Martin Joseph Jones. A building on the University campus is named in her honor.

11,364. Cassety, Louise M.
Papers. 1870-1931. No size given.
Open. Unpublished guide.
State University College at Buffalo, E. H. Butler Library.
Papers and clippings of Cassety (1873-1931), a teacher and principal of the kindergarten department at the State Normal School at the University. Also includes a biographical sketch of her in the booklet "These Were Builders" by Sister Martin Joseph Jones. Cassety worked for the advancement of the education program at the Normal School. A building on the University campus is named in her honor.

11,365. Caudell, Myrtle Viola
Papers. 1870-1936. No size given.
Open. Unpublished guide.
State University College at Buffalo, E. H. Butler Library.
Papers and clippings of Caudell (1878-1963), who was director of the home economics department at the State Normal School and the college of education at the University from 1919 to 1936. Also includes a biographical sketch of her in the unpublished booklet "These Were Builders" by Sister Martin Joseph Jones. During Caudell's tenure, home economics became a four-year program that granted a BA degree. A building on the University campus is dedicated to her.

11,366. Chase, Susan Frances
Papers. 1870-1927. No size given.
Open. Unpublished guide.
State University College at Buffalo, E. H. Butler Library.
Papers and clippings of Chase (1859-1927), a professor of philosophy. Also includes a biographical sketch of her in the unpublished booklet "These Were Builders" by Sister Martin Joseph Jones. Chase, a PhD, joined the staff of the State Normal School at the University in 1899 and remained on the faculty until 1926. She also was involved with a training class at the University of West Virginia and worked as an instructor at the University of Buffalo for three years. A lecturer on topics in education in several states, she also contributed to education publications and was an active member of many civic organizations. A building on the University campus is named in her honor.

11,367. Fronczak, Francis Eustachius
Papers. 1874-1955. Ca. 18 ft.
Open. Published guide.
State University College at Buffalo, E. H. Butler Library.
Papers of Fronczak (1874-1955), a physician and Polish-American leader. Includes correspondence with his wife Lucy R. Fronczak (1880-1933), a housewife; with their daughter Eugenia (Fronczak) Bukowska, a physician; and with their son and other family members. Although she spent some time in a tuberculosis sanitorium, Lucy Fronczak supported her husband in his numerous projects, especially those related to Polish affairs, and her letters reflect her in-depth knowledge of political matters. See Sister Martin Joseph Jones, comp. and ed., *The Francis E. Fronczak Collection* (Buffalo: State University College at Buffalo, 1976).

11,368. Lenski, Lois
Papers. 1894-1974. Ca. 38 ft.
Open. Published guide.
State University College at Buffalo, E. H. Butler Library.
Manuscripts, notes, research material, illustrations, photos, and first editions of Lenski (1893-1974), an author and illustrator of children's books. Among Lenski's numerous books are *Arabella and Her Aunts* (1932) and *Strawberry Girl* (1945). Lenski won the Newbery and Caldecott awards in children's literature. See Carolyn Giambra, comp., *The Lois Lenski Children's Collection in the Edward H. Butler Library* (Buffalo: State University College at Buffalo, 1972).

11,369. Albrecht, Milton C.
Papers. 1946-75. 5.9 ft.
Open. Unpublished guide.
State University of New York at Buffalo, Archives.
Personal and professional papers of Albrecht (1904-), a sociologist and dean of the University college of arts and sciences. Includes papers reflecting the involvement of his wife Evelyn Albrecht with social issues in Buffalo between 1946 and 1955. Also includes minutes and membership lists of the Buffalo chapter of the National Union of Consumers.

11,370. Alumnae Association
Records. 1933-57. 0.5 ft.
Open. Unpublished guide.
State University of New York at Buffalo, Archives.
Scrapbook contains correspondence, clippings, programs, and announcements concerned with the University's Alumnae Association and its social activities.

11,371. Bartholomew, Ruth
Papers. 1922-63. 9.7 ft.
Open. Unpublished guide.
State University of New York at Buffalo, Archives.
Correspondence, a subject file, and account and memoranda books of Bartholomew (1899-1969) pertain to her career as a librarian at the University from 1922 to 1964.

11,372. Capen, Samuel Paul
Papers. 1898-1956. 14.5 ft.
Open. Unpublished guide.
State University of New York at Buffalo, Archives.
Personal and professional papers of Capen (1878-1956), an educator who was the first director of the American Council on Education and first full-time chancellor of the University. Includes letters, 1904-22, to his wife Grace Duncan (Wright) Capen (1874-1951), who was the daughter of Colonel Carroll D. Wright, the first president of Clark College. In their letters, which were written before and after their marriage in 1908, they discuss Samuel Capen's work, educational concerns, and personal matters.

11,373. The Colleges
Records. 1968-76. 17 ft.
Partially restricted. Unpublished guide.
State University of New York at Buffalo, Archives.
Administrative records, faculty and student records, reports, catalogs, and other records of the Colleges, which are residential and nonresidential academic units made up of students, faculty, and members of the community. Each College develops its own academic focus. Included are records pertaining to the Women's Studies College, which was established in 1971, with material related to the controversy over the exclusion of men from certain courses.

11,374. Land, Adelle H.
Papers. 1920-68. 88.5 ft.
Closed. Unpublished guide.
State University of New York at Buffalo, Archives.
Papers of Land (1901-69), a professor of education at the University from 1923 to 1969. Includes papers relating to the unified program in teacher education, the Professional Unit, which was developed and taught by Land at the University; notes, correspondence, and papers from her doctoral work at Teachers College, Columbia University, from 1932 to 1937; and other material reflecting her career as a progressive educator and early advocate of preparation for teaching in higher education.

11,375. Norton Union
Records. 1923-69. 16.4 ft.
Access restricted. Unpublished guide.
State University of New York at Buffalo, Archives.
Minutes, reports, correspondence, and other records of this student union at the University, which was organized in 1933. Contains records of Union staff members responsible for administering the student activities program, student program committees that were involved in planning and evaluating the activities, advisors to student groups, and orientation programs. Includes records of the advisor to the Panhellenic Council and a file on individual sororities, which was kept by Lillias Macdonald, dean of women. Many of the Union's administrative positions were filled by women, including Dorothy Hass, who was director from 1944 to 1969.

11,376. Phi Psi
Records. 1928-46. 0.5 ft.
Open. Unpublished guide.
State University of New York at Buffalo, Archives.
Minutes of the active chapter of the sorority, which was established at the University of Buffalo in 1923 and became inactive in 1943; minutes of the passive or alumnae chapter, which was established in 1928; a scrapbook containing a brief history of the University, sketches of faculty members, and personal histories of sorority members; and photos of sorority members.

11,377. School of Nursing
Records. 1967-68. 0.2 ft. and 4 tapes.
Open. Unpublished guide.
State University of New York at Buffalo, Archives.
History of the School written by [Mrs.] Anne Walker Sengbusch, its first dean. Also includes tapes and a transcript of a 1968 interview with Sengbusch, which professor of nursing education A. Margaret Larsen conducted, concerning the development of the School. A degree program in nursing was established at the University in 1930; the division of nursing was established in 1936; and the School of Nursing was established in 1940.

11,378. School of Pedagogy
Records. 1895-98. 1 ft. and 1 microfilm reel.
Open. Unpublished guide.
State University of New York at Buffalo, Archives.
Minute book of the board of trustees, a school register, catalogs, and printed material of the School, which was established at the University in 1895, changed its name to Teacher's College in 1897, and dissolved in 1898. The majority of the student body was female. Two women, Ida C. Bender, an instructor in primary education, and Natalie Mankell, an instructor in gymnastics, were members of the School's faculty.

11,379. Secretarial Training Program
Records. 1967-69. 1 ft.
Open. Unpublished guide.
State University of New York at Buffalo, Archives.
Minutes, correspondence, monthly reports, program proposals, data on trainees, tests, and other records of the Program, which was established at the University in 1967 to train inner-city women in Buffalo for secretarial employment. The Program provided training to help women pass civil service tests and supervised on-the-job experience in University offices. It was phased out in 1969.

11,380. State University of New York at Buffalo, University Archives
Records. 1846-1976. Ca. 3300 ft.
Access restricted. Unpublished guide.
State University of New York at Buffalo, Archives.
Official records of the University, its offices, schools, and departments; professional and personal papers of administrators, faculty members, and others connected with the University; and publications, tape recordings, news clippings, photos, and other material documenting the University, its staff, and students. Includes records pertaining to the University from its establishment as the University of Buffalo in 1846, including material on the school of medicine, founded in 1846; the school of law, founded in 1887; the school of social work, founded in 1936; and the school of health-related professions, founded in 1965. Although women were not excluded from the University, no woman graduated from it until 1876. Beginning in 1880, there have been women in most graduation classes in all departments, with the exception of the school of engineering, which has had few women graduates. Women have often been in the majority of students in the schools of pedagogy, education, social work, nursing, and the college of arts and sciences.

11,381. State University of New York at Buffalo Women's Club
Records. 1945-75. 6 ft.
Open. Unpublished guide.
State University of New York at Buffalo, Archives.
Organizational records, minutes, annual reports of officers and committees, correspondence, scrapbooks of clippings, photos, newsletters, yearbooks, and other records of the Club, which was founded in 1946. Composed of women members and wives of faculty members, the Club's aim is to encourage social and educational activities among its members. Club activities include providing scholarships and loans for students and volunteer labor for the community and the University, organizing special interest study groups, and producing a radio program for patients at a local veteran's hospital.

11,382. State University of New York Librarians Association
Records. 1967-75. 1.2 ft.
Open. Unpublished guide.
State University of New York at Buffalo, Archives.
Minutes, committee reports, correspondence, membership lists, newsletters, and other records of the Association, which was established in 1969 to advance the professional status of librarians within the State University of New York system, to develop standards of librarianship, and to encourage individual and collective professional development.

11,383. Thorn, Katherine
Papers. 1940-69. 2 ft. and 14 tapes.
Access restricted. Unpublished guide.
State University of New York at Buffalo, Archives.
Papers of Thorn (1907-77), a professor of speech pathology and director of the speech clinic at the University. Includes papers pertaining to the curriculum in speech therapy, working papers of the University's committee on the evaluation of the student constitution, and tape recordings that illustrate speech disorders.

11,384. University Organizations
Records. 1926-73. 5.6 ft.
Open. Unpublished guide.
State University of New York at Buffalo, Archives.
Records of organizations associated with the University but not part of the academic or administrative structure. Includes records of the University Dames, a social club established in 1964 for the wives of students.

11,385. Watson, Evelyn M.
Papers. 1921-50. 7 ft.
Open. Unpublished guide.
State University of New York at Buffalo, Archives.
Correspondence and manuscript poems, essays, and plays of Watson (1886-1954), a poet and author. Papers pertain to western New York as well as to her numerous works on metaphysics and Christian mysticism. Watson was called the poet laureate of the Niagara Frontier.

11,386. Webster, Emily H.
Papers. 1952-69. 1.2 ft.
Open. Unpublished guide.
State University of New York at Buffalo, Archives.
Correspondence, memoranda, and notes of Webster (1902-), assistant vice-president for business affairs at the University from 1963 to 1968, pertain to University memorials and ceremonies, gifts, and scholarship funds. Includes a copy of her *Eastern States Association of College and University Business Officers: Fifty Years in Review* (1969). Webster was assistant to the treasurer at the University from 1923 to 1930 and assistant treasurer from 1930 to 1962. She was also a member of the University of Buffalo Council from 1940 to 1952.

11,387. White, Marian E.
Papers. 1942-75. 6 ft. and 14 tapes.
Open. Unpublished guide.
State University of New York at Buffalo, Archives.
Papers of White (1921-75), an anthropologist, concern her work on the archaeology of Late Woodland period Indians of New York state, especially the Iroquois, and her involvement with the preservation of archaeological sites. Also includes her course notes from graduate study in anthropology at the University of Michigan and tape recordings. White was a faculty member of SUNY at Buffalo, president of the Eastern States Archaeological Federation and the New York State Archaeological Council, and a member of the New York State Preservation Board.

11,388. Women's Honor Societies
Records. 1924-64. 1 ft.
Open. Unpublished guide.
State University of New York at Buffalo, Archives.
Scrapbooks that Jeannette Scudder, dean of women at the University, kept. Includes minutes, reports, correspondence, photos, clippings, and memorabilia of Cap and Gown, a University women's honor society founded in 1924, and of the Buffalo chapter of Alpha Lambda Delta, a scholastic honor society founded in 1958 for freshmen women.

11,389. Women's International League for Peace and Freedom
Records. 1960-73. 6.5 ft.
Open. Unpublished guide.
State University of New York at Buffalo, Archives.
Minutes, correspondence, and newsletters pertain to the activities and organizational affairs of the Buffalo branch of WILPF, which was established in ca. 1960 to support international peace and nonviolent solutions to social problems. The branch dissolved in ca. 1973. Also includes subject files on activities, including support of civil rights, the United Nations, disarmament and opposition to selective service and the Vietnam War, along with correspondence with the US section of WILPF and printed material pertaining to peace and human rights.

11,390. Wright, Lydia T.
Papers. 1883-1968. 8 ft.
Open. Unpublished guide.
State University of New York at Buffalo, Archives.
Correspondence, speeches, clippings, and other papers of Wright (1922-), a pediatrician, relate to her civic and school board activities. Includes minutes of the Buffalo school board, research material on school integration, papers pertaining to the issue of quality integrated education, and family papers. Wright was the first Negro member of the Buffalo board of education.

CANTON

11,391. Brown, Olympia
Papers. 1863-1930. No size given.
Open. No guide.
St. Lawrence University Archives.
Brown (1835-1926) was an ordained minister and suffrage worker. Includes correspondence and other papers as well as numerous articles about her. Brown, who graduated from the Theological School of St. Lawrence University in 1863, was the first woman to be ordained to the ministry by full denominational authority. During the time she was minister in a church in Weymouth Landing, MA, she met John Henry Willis, whom she married in 1873. In 1868 she founded the New England Woman Suffrage Association. From 1884 to 1912 she was president of the Wisconsin Woman Suffrage Association. In 1887 she relinquished her pastoral duties in her last regular parish, Racine, WI, but continued to preach in the Racine area.

11,392. Browning Society
Records. 1876-1915. No size given.
Open. No guide.
St. Lawrence University Archives.
The principal aim of members of the Society, which existed from 1876 to 1915, was to improve themselves so that they might demonstrate "woman's equal capacity and fitness for intellectual advancement." Records include correspondence, biographies, essays, and photos. Clara Weaver, Campbellina "Cammie" Woods, Georgietta "Ettie" Bacheller, Inez Jones, Lucia Heaton, Emily Eaton, Florence Lee, and Jessie Stearns were among the members.

11,393. Church, Isabel
Papers. 1882-1934. No size given.
Open. No guide.
St. Lawrence University Archives.
Correspondence, photos, and clippings of Church (1862-1941), a physician who was head of the New York State Society of Rural Women and secretary of the State Council of Agriculture and Markets and of the State Federation of Home Bureaus.

11,394. Gaines Family
Papers. 1870-1976. No size given.
Open. No guide.
St. Lawrence University Archives.
Lectures, poems, novels, and college programs of the family, including items of Cammie Pendleton Gaines (1863-1920), a poet involved in community events, and Chloe S. Gaines (1880-1944), a musician.

11,395. Heaton Family
Papers. 1821-1930. No size given.
Open. No guide.
St. Lawrence University Archives.
Papers of the family include correspondence, books, essays, and medical instruments of Lucia Heaton (ca. 1856-1944), the first woman physician in St. Lawrence County.

11,396. Hepburn Family
Papers. 1886-1955. No size given.
Open. No guide.
St. Lawrence University Archives.
Includes correspondence, articles, and biographical books of Emily (Eaton) Hepburn (1886-1955), a suffrage worker and philanthropist, and of her husband A. Barton Hepburn, a chairman of the Chase Bank in New York City.

11,397. McCormick, Helen P.
Papers. 1936-37. No size given.
Open. No guide.
St. Lawrence University Archives.
Clippings concern McCormick (1889-1937), a lawyer who was the first assistant district attorney of Brooklyn, NY, and founder of the Catholic Big Sisters.

11,398. St. Lawrence University
Records. 1868-1900. No size given.
Open. No guide.
St. Lawrence University Archives.
Contains diplomas from the College of Letters and Sciences and the Universalist Theological School at the University, which was founded in 1856. Originally women earned Laureate in Science degrees. Later they were allowed to earn BS degrees.

11,399. Shaw, Annette Jane
Papers. 1873-1920. No size given.
Open. No guide.
St. Lawrence University Archives.
Correspondence and clippings of Shaw (1853-1920), a physician, Universalist preacher, and charity worker. Shaw practiced medicine in Wisconsin and became interested in a home for unmarried mothers. She gave most of her money and time to the home and died penniless.

11,400. Sherman, Emma Powell
Papers. 1876-1938. No size given.
Open. No guide.
St. Lawrence University Archives.
Letter and articles of Sherman (1856-1938), a gynecologist and pediatrician. Sherman stated that her public interests were the "raising, training, and education of all children; equal rights of women; closer bonds of friendship and mutual understanding among all nations; the cessation of war; and the continuance of our great legislative and judicial institutions, national and international." She was involved in organizations concerned with these interests.

11,401. Swain, Reba
Papers. 1915-30. No size given.
Open. No guide.
St. Lawrence University Archives.
Correspondence and articles of Swain (1895-ca. 1935), a lawyer and poet who became deputy attorney general of New York state. She later retired to private practice.

11,402. Taylor, Marian Young
Papers. Ca. 1930-60. No size given.
Open. No guide.
St. Lawrence University Archives.
Articles of Taylor (1909-75), who was a radio commentator for the "Martha Deane Show" on station WOR in New York City. She conducted interviews with authors, scientists, and statesman and is reported to have won more awards than any other woman on the air at that time.

11,403. Whitney, Mary Traffarn
Papers. 1872-1940. No size given.
Open. No guide.
St. Lawrence University Archives.
Correspondence, clippings, and a publication about eugenics of Whitney (1852-1940), a Universalist minister, who did early work in eugenics and was editor of the first American publication on the subject.

CASTLETON-ON-HUDSON

11,404. Provincial Archives
Records. 1891- . 6 files.
Access restricted. No guide.
Sisters of the Resurrection of Our Lord Jesus Christ, Saint Joseph Province.
Financial records, scholastic records, correspondence, circular letters of the superiors general, chronicles, albums, photos, and newsletters of the Sisters in the Saint Joseph Province, which was established in 1928. The American congregation of the Sisters was founded in 1900 in Chicago.

COOPERSTOWN

11,405. Photos
Collection. Nd. No size given.
Open. No guide.
National Baseball Hall of Fame and Museum.
Includes photos of a women's baseball team, which was organized by Joe Engel, owner of the Chattanooga Southern Association Club, ca. 1930; Julia St. Clair, who was a female pitcher, probably during the 1880s or 1890s; Jackie Mitchell with Lou Gehrig and Babe Ruth, both of whom she struck out during a 1931 exhibition game; Ladies Day in the 1880s; Gladys Gooding at the Ebbets Field console organ in the 1940s and 1950s; and Eleanor Engle, whose effort to join the Harrisburg Senators, a minor league team, was blocked in 1952.

CORNING

11,406. Corning Clionian Circle
Records. Nd. Ca. 2 boxes.
Access restricted. No guide.
Corning Clionian Circle Archives.
Minutes, reports, and other records of the Circle, which was founded in 1881 and is still in existence. Primarily a women's study group, the Circle is also active in civic matters. Includes Chautauqua study material used by Circle members during the group's early years.

11,407. Miscellany
Papers. 1885-1966. 3 items.
Open. Catalog card.
Corning Community College Library.
Manuscript for *Mrs. Catherine Dineen: Her Life and Contributions* (Syracuse, NY, 1966), which was written by Eleanor B. Gibson about Catherine Dineen [Mrs. William] Mack, technical librarian at Corning Glass Works for many years; "Little Red Schoolhouse," an article by [Mrs.] Helen Ives Lyon, a long-time schoolteacher in north central Pennsylvania; and copies of the *Young Women's Banner,* 1895-97, which was published by Banner Publishing Co. in Elmira, NY. Lyon's article, written in the 1920s for the Friday Club of Wellsboro, PA, was published in 1960 in an abridged form by *Reader's Digest.*

11,408. Corning Glass Works Archives
Records. 1851- . 1500 cartons, 151,000 items, 150 microfilm reels, 550 tapes, 210 motion pictures, and other items.
Access restricted. Unpublished guides.
Corning Glass Works.
Financial, personnel, purchasing, legal, product development, stockholder, research, and other records of Corning Glass Works. Includes operating and personal papers of Corning executives, scientists, and employees; 150,000 photo negatives; 2,200 cans of high-speed film; 500 audiotape cassettes; 50 videotape cassettes; and 1000 blueprints.

CORTLAND

11,409. Daughters of the American Revolution, Tioughnioga Chapter
Records. 1900- . 2.33 ft.
Open. No guide.
Cortland County Historical Society.
Minutes, treasurer's records, scrapbooks, programs, and photos of this chapter of the DAR, which was founded in 1900 to preserve the memory of the American Revolutionary War patriots who settled in Cortland County and to promote education and good citizenship.

11,410. King's Daughters
Records. 1900-68. 3.25 ft.
Open. No guide.
Cortland County Historical Society.
Minutes, financial records, and correspondence of King's Daughters, a charitable organization, as well as minutes, financial records, children's medical records, correspondence, and children's home register photos relating to the King's Daughters Home for Children, which existed from 1906 to 1957.

11,411. Ladies Literary Club
Records. 1880- . 1.25 ft.
Open. Unpublished guide.
Cortland County Historical Society.
Constitution, bylaws, minutes, treasurer's reports, papers delivered at meetings, Club histories, and membership lists and programs of the Club, a Cortland literary club founded in 1880. The group was primarily concerned with literature but also had an interest in city, state, and world affairs.

11,412. Mudge and Collins Families
Papers. 1821-ca. 1897. 5 in.
Open. Unpublished guide.
Cortland County Historical Society.
Primarily correspondence, poetry, and memorabilia of Mary (Mudge) Collins (1841-89), a poet and civic leader. Papers concern her intellectual interests; leadership in the Cortland Library Association, the WCTU, and the Ladies Literary Club; life in rural central New York; slavery; abolition; and the Union Army. Included is a letter in which Gerrit Smith, a reformer and abolitionist, describes to Collins the arrival at his home of Sojourner Truth, a freed slave who advocated emancipation and women's rights.

11,413. Twentieth Century Club
Records. 1903- . 4 ft.
Open. No guide.
Cortland County Historical Society.
Minutes, treasurer's records, yearbooks, and clippings of the Club, a women's organization which was founded in 1904 to help women to help one another and to be useful to society.

COXSACKIE

11,414. Borthwick, William S.
Papers. 1800-1950. Ca. 3 ft.
Open. No guide.
Greene County Historical Society.
Correspondence, diaries, photos, and other papers of Borthwick's family, residents of Greene County, who were farmers, millers, and housewives. Includes diaries of Hannah Bushnell for 1849 to 1858 and a diary of Mary Frances Borthwick for 1904.

11,415. Bronck Family
Papers. 1650-1939. Ca. 4 ft.
Open. Unpublished guide.
Greene County Historical Society.
Diaries, manuscripts, record books, and printed material of the family, which included Greene County farmers, land developers, investors, and political figures. Includes family correspondence of female members of the family, including that of Maria Bronck Lampman. Also includes Lampman's account book of expenses during the time she attended Ogontz School in Pennsylvania in 1895 and photos of her School activities. The Bronck family settled in Coxsackie in 1663. Bronx Borough in New York City was named after Jonas Bronck, a first-generation family member. Some family papers have been published in *Letters from a Revolution* (1974-75), edited by Raymond Beecher.

11,416. Bronck, Susannah
Papers. 1800-14. 1 folder and other items.
Open. No guide.
Greene County Historical Society.
Personal and estate papers of Bronck (?-1814), a wealthy housewife and the second wife of Jan Leonard Bronck. Papers relate to her leaving her home and considerable property to her slaves.

11,417. Catskill Travel Club
Records. 1916-17. 0.3 ft.
Open. No guide.
Greene County Historical Society.
Record book of a group of Catskill, NY, women who were interested in traveling.

11,418. Conine, Eytje
Papers. Ca. 1820. 1 folder.
Open. No guide.
Greene County Historical Society.
Estate papers of Conine, a housewife, include an

inventory of her personal property with provisions to nieces of sets of silver spoons.

11,419. Decker, Katharine M.
Papers. Ca. 1859-1900. 1.25 ft.
Open. No guide.
Greene County Historical Society.
Scattered diaries of [Mrs.] Mary Allen Stone, who was the wife of Benjamin Stone, a Hudson River artist who lived in Catskill, NY, contain descriptions of life in Catskill. Also includes some art material.

11,420. Friday Club
Records. 1909-12. 1 vol.
Open. No guide.
Greene County Historical Society.
Record book of the Club, which was located in Leeds, NY, contains the constitution, bylaws, and minutes. The Club concerned itself with doing good deeds.

11,421. Friendship Albums
Collection. Nd. Ca. 1.5 ft.
Open. No guide.
Greene County Historical Society.
Albums contain friendship verses with signatures.

11,422. Greene County WCTU
Records. 1885. 1 vol.
Open. No guide.
Greene County Historical Society.
Record book contains information relating to the organization of this branch of the WCTU in 1885.

11,423. Greene, Jeanette
Papers. 1890s- . 2 folders.
Open. No guide.
Greene County Historical Society.
Family and personal papers of Greene, a pioneer female physician, relate to her preparation for the medical profession. The Greene family were residents of Catskill, NY.

11,424. Howard, Mrs. George A.
Papers. 1890. 4 vols.
Open. No guide.
Greene County Historical Society.
Travel diaries in which Howard, the wife of a Presbyterian minister in Catskill, NY, describes a trip to Europe and England.

11,425. Howland Family
Papers. 1880-1935. 1.25 ft.
Open. No guide.
Greene County Historical Society.
Correspondence, accounts, and photos of the family relate to family life, travel, and art. Includes correspondence of Emily Howland Sherwood, a resident of central New York, who was an activist in women's rights groups; papers of Edith Howland, an artist; and papers of her sisters, who traveled extensively.

11,426. Riewe, Fred, and Riewe, Harriet
Papers. 1928. 1 folder.
Open. No guide.
Greene County Historical Society.
Letters that Fred Riewe, a marine, and his wife Harriet Riewe wrote to her father George W. Hood describing life in the Marine Corps in the South and in Central America.

11,427. Van Gelder, Fiero, Pine, and Wardle
Papers. Nd. 6 ft.
Open. No guide.
Greene County Historical Society.
Correspondence, contracts, photos, and programs of this Greene County family as well as papers related to family history dating from the early 1800s to just before WWI. Includes papers concerning Constance Wardle, who was a professional singer in New York City prior to WWII.

11,428. Vedder, Jessie Van Vechten
Papers. 1926-33. Ca. 0.75 ft.
Open. No guide.
Greene County Historical Society.
Diaries and related papers of Vedder (1859-1952), a teacher, historian, and author, contain her notes on local historical events. Vedder was the first Greene County historian.

11,429. Vosburgh, Hattie Jansen
Papers. 1903-25. Ca. 0.75 ft.
Open. No guide.
Greene County Historical Society.
Diaries of Vosburgh (1865-1957), a housewife, who describes her family, local activities, and farm work. Also includes a description of men in the family who harvested ice from the Hudson River during the winter.

11,430. WCTU
Records. 1881-1932. Ca. 0.75 ft.
Open. No guide.
Greene County Historical Society.
Record books of the Coxsackie chapter of the WCTU, which was probably founded in 1881, include minutes, financial data, and a description of the group's activities.

11,431. Wilkinson, Florence
Papers. 1899-1902. Ca. 2 in.
Open. No guide.
Greene County Historical Society.
Diaries Wilkinson kept of her travels abroad. Includes photos and printed material.

11,432. Woodworth, Olive Newell
Papers. Nd. 6 in.
Open. No guide.
Greene County Historical Society.
Woodworth, a historian, was concerned with local history near her home in Hensonville, NY. Papers relate to her research on the Revolutionary War records of early heads of families who settled in the local mountains. Also includes scrapbooks containing clippings of social and religious events in the area.

DOBBS FERRY

11,433. Archives of the New York Province
Records. 1846- . Ca. 52 drawers, 151 vols., 2 cabinets, and other items.
Partially restricted. Inventory.
Sisters of Mercy of the Union, New York Province Archives.
Financial records, correspondence of administrators, cassettes, motion pictures, photos, clippings, and other items of this order of religious women, which was founded in 1846. Includes papers relating to the Province's history.

EAST AURORA

11,434. Archives: Price, Margaret (Evans)
Papers. 1930-76. 1 folder.
Open. No guide.
East Aurora Town Hall.
Papers and clippings of Price (1889-1973), an artist, author, and civic leader who was the wife of Irving Price, one of the founders of Fisher-Price Toys. Margaret Price, a portrait artist who wrote and illustrated children's books, is said to have designed the first toys made by Fisher-Price. She held evening meetings in her home to provide culture, music, and drama for local high school girls and gave scholarships for camp, dance, music lessons, and college tuition to deserving young women. Through her efforts the Millard and Abigail Fillmore house was saved and became a national monument.

11,435. Elbert Hubbard Library Museum
Papers. 1855-1977. No size given.
Open. Unpublished guide.
East Aurora Village Hall.
Manuscripts, photos, and published works of Alice (Moore) [Mrs. Elbert] Hubbard (1861-1915), a teacher, author, and business partner in Roycroft Enterprises. Alice Hubbard was a leading force in the Roycroft movement, a suffragist, and a musician. Papers pertain to her and to Roycroft artisans and craftsmen.

11,436. Millard Fillmore National Landmark House
Papers. 1850-1975. No size given.
Open. No guide.
Fillmore Museum.
Papers, files, books, and possessions of the Fillmore family. Includes items of Mary Abigail Fillmore (1832-54), the daughter of President Millard Fillmore; she became official White House hostess when her mother became ill.

EAST DURHAM

11,437. Catskill Valley Grange, No. 1557
Records. 1937- . 8 vols.
Open. No guide.
Durham Center Museum, Inc.
Ledgers of this local unit of the Grange contain minutes and historical material. The Catskill Valley Grange was founded in 1937 and still exists.

11,438. Meeting House Hill Chapter NSDAR
Records. 1960- . 1 drawer.
Open. No guide.
Durham Center Museum, Inc.
Charter, minutes, research papers, personal records of members' families, and books on genealogy of this DAR branch, which was founded in 1960 and is still active.

EDEN

11,439. Town of Eden and Eden Historical Society
Records. 1808- . 3 drawers and 1 walk-in safe.
Open. No guide.
Eden Historical Society.
Includes minutes, financial records, correspondence, diaries, scrapbooks, and photos.

ELMIRA

11,440. Biography Files
Collection. 1700s- . 11 ft.
Open. Card file.
Chemung County Historical Society.
This collection of correspondence, biographies, genealogies, photos, and clippings consists primarily of genealogical information on hundreds of families, but it also contains a family history from the 1600s to 1954 of the Ketcham family; a Swain family history; biographical material on Laura Pitcher Hill; articles about Mr. and Mrs. Brayton's Himalayan mountain climb; an account of Elmira Teall and the city's being named after her; a story about the Tuthill family and the actions of Jenny Strong, "a supposedly content slave who was well loved by the community"; and an autobiography of [Mrs.] Emma Sayles McAtee, who describes her life during the mid-1800s, the people around her, her travels, and her experiences.

Biographical material consisting primarily of photos and clippings describes the lives of many women, including the following: Mary "Molly" Brant (ca. 1736-96), a Mohawk Indian who was consort of Sir William Johnson, superintendent of

Indian Affairs for the Northern Colonies, and who became a high society hostess; Ruth Blackman, a female parachutist during the 1920s; Mrs. William H. Breeden, a Seneca Indian who worked as an art teacher in the Elmira area; Helen L. Bullock, who was active in the WCTU and manager of a home for girls during the late 19th century and early 20th; Rita B. Church (1838-1928), a physician who founded the Williamsport Hospital; Clara Gilbert, head of the New York State Employment Bureau during the 1920s; Mary Leavitt, an American National Red Cross worker; Catherine Loonie, who pleaded guilty to forging deeds in 1900; Helen Mallory, a banker who was chosen to be a member of the national women's committee of the American Institute of Banking in 1929; [Mrs.] Fannie Monroe, founder of the county WCTU and a Bible school teacher; "Mother" Elizabeth Paine, an Elmira black woman noted for her cooking and for speaking several languages; [Mrs.] Kate Warn, a female detective and superintendent of the Female Department of Pinkerton's National Police Agency during the 1860s; and Jemima Wilkinson, founder of a colony of early settlers, which was called Friend's Society.

Also includes correspondence on daily life between members of the Elijah Griswald family and between James A. Rodburn family members; letters concerning the work of Margaret [Mrs. James] Buckley with deaf children; correspondence and other personal papers of Sarah Smith, a missionary to Japan; and correspondence between William Lowman and his wife, including an 1848 letter in which she wrote about how much she missed him, as well as an 1857 letter to Mrs. Lowman from her sister, who describes her illness and her wish that Mrs. Lowman visit her; school notes and essays by Amelia Monroe, an Elmira Academy student, on causes of the American Revolution, loving one's school, and the use of words; a sermon by Olivia Lewis Langdon (1810-90); poems by and biographical information about poet Amira Carpenter Thompson (ca. 1800-?); articles on the death of Mrs. R. B. Hargrove, whose drowning in the Chemung River in 1926 was believed to be the result of suicidal mania, as well as analyses of her death; and biographical material, recital programs, reviews, and discussions of the performances of Jennie Jewell [Mrs. Thomas W.] Hotchkiss, a noted 19th-century elocutionist.

In addition, the collection contains biographical material on the Bird, Breese, Clark, Collin, Diven, Fitch, Hutchinson, Montour, Perry, William and Mary Streeter, Todd, and Westlake families.

11,441. Cemetery Records

Collection. Ca. 1770s- . Ca. 27 ft.
Open. Card file.
Chemung County Historical Society.
Index cards for nearly every person born in Chemung County since the late 18th century contain information on birth and death dates, names of spouses, and burial places. Also included are cards on burials in Schuyler County cemeteries and cards on the burial places of American Revolution soldiers.

11,442. Family Papers

Collection. 1850s-1900s. 5 Hollinger boxes.
Open. Card catalog.
Chemung County Historical Society.
Correspondence, diaries, biographies, manuscripts, financial and business papers, medical reports, articles, clippings, and other material of various families include articles and papers on Catharine Beecher, who founded several schools for girls; papers of Julia (Jones) Beecher, who is noted for her "Beecher dolls," including her 1890s letter to Cora Derby about the education of young girls; and correspondence of female members of the Wright family, with letters wherein Eliza Wright writes to her son about family matters and faith in God.

11,443. Miscellany

Collection. 1796- . Ca. 77 ft.
Open. Card catalog.
Chemung County Historical Society.
Trade cards for household products and medicines, and grocery and drug ads and prices from the late 19th through the early 20th century; cookbooks; folders of vital statistics; volumes of local and county newspapers; photos; and other material. Includes correspondence between Mrs. Benjamin Manning and her husband, a Union soldier, during the Civil War; diaries of Effie M. Forsythe discussing daily life and the health and affairs of those close to her; an 1869 diary of Carrie Manning, a 13-year-old school girl from Ithaca, NY; an 1853 letter of Julia Griswald to her siblings; surveys wherein women residents in neighborhoods that are about to undergo urban renewal reminisce about their neighborhoods' history; poetry by local poets, among them Alice Corey; and histories and articles on regional Indian tribes. The collection also contains records of Elmira College, Elmira Free Academy, the Elizabeth Guild of the First Presbyterian Church, and a young women's magazine *Christianity Culture Civism,* including a few issues of that magazine from 1895 to 1897; material on the WCTU, consisting mainly of letters to Mrs. Taylor concerning the Bullock Home for Girls in Elmira, which she managed; correspondence from 1915 between members of the state Women's Suffrage Association; records of the Arnot Ogden Memorial Hospital and copies of its women's auxiliary magazine *Cheery Chatter;* and material on the Elmira Water Cure, which was practiced at the Gleason Health Resort from the mid- to late 1800s.

11,444. Scrapbooks

Collection. Nd. 47 ft.
Open. Card file.
Chemung County Historical Society.
Scrapbooks of clippings from local newspapers and maps and atlases are arranged by subject and include information on such topics as Anchorage, a girls school; the *Elmira Women's News Magazine;* the American National Red Cross; women's charitable activities; and the YWCA.

11,445. Vertical files

Collection. Nd. 21 ft.
Open. Card file.
Chemung County Historical Society.
Arranged by subject, the collection consists of files on such topics as art, education, hospitals, women's work during WWI and WWII, music, politics, prohibition, and the Historical Society. Includes material on the American Cancer Society, the Home for the Aged, the Blind Association, the LWV, the Neighborhood House, the Audubon Society, the Elmira Business and Professional Women's Club, the Volunteers of America, the DAR, and the Women's Relief Corps. Also contains a copy of *Queen Catherine of Montour,* a play by Catherine Connelly; material on beauty contests; an article and photo of a Mrs. Spellman, who became a motion picture actress in Hollywood in 1927; biographical information on Indian Queen Esther and a narrative of Jane Strope White, who during the late 18th century was captured by Indians; a list of women who were electrocuted in New York between ca. 1890 and 1963; material on pension cuts for widows of policemen and firemen; an article on a Mrs. Marshall, who in 1926 was proprietor of a drug store in Elmira; letters from a soldier on Sullivan's Expedition to his sweetheart; information about a 1925 archery contest for women; an article in which a Miss Ahn describes her experiences as a telephone switchboard operator in 1928; and a 1970 article on Miss Scott, a black registered nurse. A minute book for 1878 to 1885 of the Ladies Temperance and Benevolent Union of Elmira and a minute book for 1908 to 1929 of the Industrial School and Free Kindergarten Association of Elmira, a temperance and charitable association, are included as well.

11,446. Elmira College Archives

Records. 1853- . 231 ft., 241 folders, 3 drawers, 37 boxes, and 56 items.
Open. No guide
Elmira College Archives.
Charters, bylaws, minutes of various organizations, financial records, correspondence, photos, newspapers, newsletters, catalogs, manuals, programs for school events, magazines, yearbooks, biographies, films, and other records of the College, a women's college founded in 1855 by a small group of clergymen and laymen in Albany, NY, to provide women with an education equal to that available at men's colleges. The College became coeducational in 1969.

11,447. New York State Federation of Women's Clubs

Records. 1899-1962. 9 ft.
Open. Inventory.
Elmira College Archives.
The Federation was founded in 1894 to provide mutual assistance for clubs throughout New York state and to help them achieve their literary, scientific, professional, industrial, and philanthropic goals. The Federation's predecessor, Sorosis, was a women's club founded in 1868 in reaction to discriminatory practices against women. Executive board minutes; minutes and reports related to annual state conventions; financial records; correspondence, speeches, and clippings of the Federation's presidents; histories; an honor roll; yearbooks; and magazines.

ESOPUS

11,448. Diary

Papers. 1957-77. Ca. 1000 pp.
Access restricted. No guide.
Redemptoristine Nuns, Mother of Perpetual Help Monastery.
Diary of daily events at the Monastery, which was established in 1857. This order of contemplative nuns was founded in 1731 in Italy.

FLUSHING

11,449. Benedict, Mrs. Elliott S.

Papers. 1889-1958. 16 vols.
Open. No guide.
Queens College, Paul Klapper Library.
Collection of scrapbooks donated by Benedict consists of theater programs, playbills, and clippings and mentions such actresses as Anne Bancroft, Ethel Barrymore, Beatrice Lillie, Lena Horne, and Gena Rowlands.

11,450. Chancery Court

Records. 1683-1847. Ca. 500,000 items.
Open. Unpublished guide.
Queens College, Paul Klapper Library.
The Court dealt with cases concerning such matters as land transactions, foreclosures, libel, boundary disputes, and guardianship cases. Includes bills of foreclosure, idiot papers, habitual drunkard papers, enrollments, decrees, and master reports. Approximately 50,000 items pertain to women who appear to be involved in all types of cases originating in the Court.

11,451. City Vouchers and Warrants

Records. 1701-1790. 500,000 items.
Open. Unpublished guide.
Queens College, Paul Klapper Library.
Records generated in the common council, a forerunner of the New York city council, which served as the legislative branch of the city. The

vouchers authorize payment for work related to street repairs, ferryboats, city hall surveys, and other work. Approximately 50,000 items deal with women. The bulk of the records is from the 19th century.

11,452. Coroner Reports and Books
Records. 1784-1817, late 19th and early 20th centuries. No size given.
Open. Unpublished guide.
Queens College, Paul Klapper Library.
Reports and books from the office of the comptroller, the fiscal agency of New York City, provide information on the cause of death, age, sex, and ethnic origin. Approximately 0.3 feet of the coroner's records, 1784-1817, deal with women.

11,453. Montgomery, George P.
Papers. 1889-1932. 12 vols.
Open. Unpublished guide.
Queens College, Paul Klapper Library.
Scrapbooks containing autographs, playbills, programs, and clippings document the history of the theater from 1889-1932. Some of the women represented are Maude Adams, Janet Alexander, May Irwin, Pauline Chase, Nester Neilson, Anna Held, Ethel Barrymore, Eleanora Duse, and Billie Burke. The scrapbooks were compiled by Montgomery.

11,454. New York City and Albany Insolvency Assignments
Records. 1754-1897. 190 ft.
Open. Unpublished guide.
Queens College, Paul Klapper Library.
Records of the New York court of appeals, which heard appeal cases dealing with equity procedures in bankruptcy hearings. In the indexes, ledgers, bankruptcy papers, and insolvent papers are descriptions of real and personal property. Approximately 19 feet of records deal with women.

11,455. New York Inventories
Records. 1666-1844. Ca. 10,000 items.
Open. Unpublished guide.
Queens College, Paul Klapper Library.
Inventories of the surrogate courts of New York County, which probate wills and administer estates. Consists of detailed lists of personal property with the value of the estate set. Approximately 1000 items deal with women.

11,456. New York Wills
Records. 1658-1978. Ca. 10,000 items.
Open. Unpublished guide.
Queens College, Paul Klapper Library.
Wills of the surrogate courts of New York County, which probate wills and administer estates. Approximately 1000 items deal with women.

11,457. Rood-Scanlan
Collection. 1839-47. 5 vols.
Open. Unpublished guide.
Queens College, Paul Klapper Library.
Unpublished typescripts, photos, and playbills pertaining to James A. Herne (1839-1901) and his daughters Chrystal Herne (1882-1950) and Julie Herne, members of a family of actors and actresses. James Herne, one of the pioneers of realism in the theater, wrote plays such as *Shore Acres* and *Sag Harbor* and acted with Edwin Booth, Junius Brutus Booth, and others. Chrystal Herne made her debut in her father's play *Griffith Davenport* in 1899; her autobiography *I Remember Me* describes her acting career, roles in such plays as *Candida* and *Roseanne,* and her friendship with other actresses, among them Josephine Hull and Sally Jane Crothers. Also includes Julie Herne's biography of her father, *A Man Named Herne (What They Told Me and What I Remember).* One of the photos is of Chrystal Herne's mother Catherine Corcoran.

11,458. Safe Deposit Company
Records. 1865-1907. More than 13 reels.
Open. Unpublished guide.
Queens College, Paul Klapper Library.
Records of the Company, which rents safe deposit boxes, include a renters' index, 1865-1875. The index contains at least 190 pages of descriptions of depositors, including names, addresses, signatures, and physical descriptions that include age, height, complexion, color of hair, color of eyes, and distinguishing marks such as scars or moles. Also includes information on deputies, persons who had access to the safe deposit box; the information includes the deputy's name, address, signature, and physical description. Also includes the names of references, the persons who introduce the depositors to the Company. Approximately 260 of 1800 depositors are women and 210 of 1400 deputies are women. Most of the references are men.

11,459. Scherr, Amy Lay Hall
Collection. 1887-1953. 68 vols.
Open. No guide.
Queens College, Paul Klapper Library.
Scrapbooks include playbills, programs, clippings, and photos providing information about such actresses as Sarah Bernhardt, Judith Anderson, and Beatrice Straight. The collection was donated in honor of [Mrs.] Scherr.

11,460. Supreme Court
Records. 1691-1847. 133 ft.
Open. Unpublished guide.
Queens College, Paul Klapper Library.
Court ledgers, docket of judgment books, and minute books of the Court, which was a trial court with original jurisdiction in civil and criminal cases. Minute books, 1692-1840, summarize judicial records of the Court while the docket of judgment books, 1785-1847, are an alphabetical listing of people for and against whom judgments were made. These books also list damages, debts, expenses, the dates of enrolling the judgments and the attorneys' names. Approximately 13 feet of records pertain to women.

11,461. Sweyd, Lester
Papers. Ca. 1920s-50s. No size given.
Open. No guide.
Queens College, Paul Klapper Library.
Movie scripts, movie stills, playbills, programs, publicity material, posters, and other papers of Sweyd, a theatrical actor and theatrical agent. Includes movie scripts for such films as *The Women;* clippings about such actresses as Annette Funicello and Delores Del Rio; movie stills of Shelley Winters, Heddy Lamar, and Greta Garbo; and other material pertaining to theater and movie actresses during the period.

11,462. Tax Assessment Rolls
Records. 1699-1841. 20 ft. and microfilm.
Open. Unpublished guide.
Queens College, Paul Klapper Library.
Approximately two feet of records deal with women.

11,463. Town Records
Records. 1644-1892. 11 ft. and 14 reels.
Open. No guide.
Queens College, Paul Klapper Library.
Town records from Flushing, Hempstead, Jamaica, Newtown, and Westchester, approximately one foot of which deals with women.

FORT PLAIN

11,464. Lipe Family
Papers. Nd. Ca. 1 Hollinger box.
Open. No guide.
Fort Plain Museum.
Correspondence, daybooks, financial records, wills, and inventories of the family, the members of which were involved in farming and mercantile enterprises on the Erie Canal.

GARRISON

11,465. Convent Archives
Records. 1895- . Ca. 52 boxes and 5 cabinets.
Open. No guide.
Franciscan Sisters of the Atonement, St. Francis Convent.
Financial records, correspondence, diaries, and photos of the Sisters, a missionary community that serves in the US, Canada, Italy, Ireland, Japan, and Brazil. The Society of the Atonement was founded in 1898 within the Anglican Church at Graymoor in Garrison. The community was incorporated into the Roman Catholic Church in 1909. Includes correspondence between the two founders prior to the community's foundation as well as records concerning the history of the community, missions staffed by its members, and houses that have closed.

GENESEO

11,466. Wadsworth Family
Papers. 1789-1952. 145 ft. and 7 microfilm reels.
Access restricted. No guide.
State University College at Geneseo, Milne Library.
Includes correspondence of Elizabeth (Wadsworth) Murray (1815-1851) and of other female family members, business records of Emmeline (Austin) Wadsworth (1808-85), and photos that Martha (Blow) Wadsworth (1864-1934), an amateur photographer, took from about 1900 to 1910 of trips to Europe, a Great Lakes boat trip, the Panama Canal under construction, the Alaska-Canada border survey, western Indians, western park lands, and horseback tours from Washington, DC, to Geneseo.

GENEVA

11,467. Blackwell, Elizabeth
Papers. 1848- . Ca. 150 items.
Open. Card catalog.
Hobart and William Smith Colleges, Warren Hunting Smith Library.
Photos, clippings, a copy of a diploma of Blackwell (1821-1910), a physician. After trying to enter other medical schools, Blackwell was admitted to the Geneva Medical School, which was connected with Hobart College. She was the only female in the class and in 1849 became the first woman to graduate from an American medical school.

11,468. William Smith College
Records. 1908- . Ca. 400 items.
Open. Card catalog.
Hobart and William Smith Colleges, Warren Hunting Smith Library.
Financial records, correspondence, scrapbooks, and photos pertain to the founding in 1908 and early history of this women's college.

GERMANTOWN

11,469. St. Teresa's Motherhouse and Novitiate
Records. 1929- . No size given.
Closed. No guide.
St. Teresa's Motherhouse and Novitiate.
This Carmelite motherhouse and novitiate was

founded in 1929 by Mother M. Angeline Teresa, a native of Ireland, to care for the aged and infirm. Includes papers concerned with the mother foundress, the opening of houses, the golden jubilee of the foundress, and the silver jubilee of the congregation as well as photos.

GILBERTSVILLE

11,470. Bushnell, Rosetta (Hammond)
Papers. 1857-66. No size given.
Access restricted. Unpublished guide.
Gilbertsville Free Library.
Diaries that Bushnell (1842-1915) kept in 1857, 1859, and 1864-66 relate to her teaching in a local school at the age of 16, her marriage to a farmer at 17, and her early married life.

11,471. Cope
Papers. 1833-49. 373-page vol.
Access restricted. Unpublished guide.
Gilbertsville Free Library.
Correspondence of Emily (Kilbourn) Cope (1808-1901), a teacher and missionary who was married to a missionary. Includes letters from former students of the Clinton Domestic Seminary in Clinton, NY; letters describing teaching at "coloured" schools and at Oberlin College, which had recently admitted women; and letters about missionary work in Madura, India, and Jaffna, Barricotta, and Oodoopitty, Ceylon. The items were compiled by Cope's granddaughter Dorothy Cope Howard.

11,472. Cox
Papers. 1855-73. No size given.
Access restricted. Unpublished guide.
Gilbertsville Free Library.
Correspondence of Hannah (Gilbert) Cox (1830-85), a resident of Albany, NY, with her husband James Cox, a physician; her daughter Caroline; her sisters and sisters-in-law; and friends.

11,473. Francke, Katharine (Gilbert)
Papers. 1927. 96-page vol.
Access restricted. Unpublished guide.
Gilbertsville Free Library.
Booklet of Francke (1860-1956), who attended Radcliffe College and married Harvard College professor Kuno Francke, in which she describes her childhood in Gilbertsville.

11,474. Gilbert, Caroline (Chapman)
Papers. 1854-61?. 22-page vol.
Access restricted. Unpublished guide.
Gilbertsville Free Library.
Letters of Gilbert (1793 or 1794-1868), the second wife of Joseph T. Gilbert, primarily to her step-daughter Hannah Gilbert Cox.

11,475. Gilbert, Elizabeth (Lathrop)
Papers. 1901-08. No size given.
Access restricted. Unpublished guide.
Gilbertsville Free Library.
Diary of Gilbert (1825-1910), who married John Henry Gilbert, in which she describes family life in a village.

HAMBURG

11,476. Convent Archives
Records. 1897- . 106 boxes and 36 tapes.
Access restricted. No guide.
Franciscan Sisters of St. Joseph, Immaculate Conception Convent.
Minutes, financial reports, correspondence, tapes, photos, scrapbooks, prayer books, emblems, and religious articles of the Sisters, a religious order of women founded in 1897 in Trenton, NJ, by Mother Mary Colette Hilbert. The Convent's primary apostolates are teaching and health care. Also includes records of former mothers superior and of all the convents and institutions established and operated by the Franciscan Sisters of St. Joesph.

11,477. Archives
Records. 1855- . 1 file and 2 items.
Access restricted. No guide.
Sisters of Our Lady of Charity Convent.
Correspondence, photos, scrapbooks, clippings, and brochures of this religious order of women, which works to rehabilitate girls. Includes letters from the first sisters who came to the US to sisters in Rennes, France, describing their trip and settlement. The first US foundation of the order, which originated in France in 1641, was made in Buffalo, NY, in 1855.

HYDE PARK

11,478. Blackburn, Katherine C. "Casey"
Papers. 1913-46. Less than 1 ft.
Open. Registration statement.
Franklin D. Roosevelt Library.
[Miss] Blackburn (1892-1972) was a government employee during the New Deal and WWII. Correspondence, clippings, and souvenirs relate to her personal and professional life. Associated with the Woodrow Wilson Foundation from 1926 until 1932, she entered government service as special assistant to the assistant secretary of state in 1933. She held National Emergency Council and State Department posts in press intelligence and information dissemination until 1939, when she was named assistant director of the Office of Government Reports. From 1943 to 1945 she served as chief of special services for the Office of War Information's domestic branch and in 1946 as chief of the Bureau of the Budget's government information service. In 1947 she was acting chief of the Office of Government Reports.

11,479. Crooks, Heléne
Papers. 1921-62. 175 pp.
Open. No guide.
Franklin D. Roosevelt Library.
Copies of correspondence, Christmas cards, invitations, notes accompanying gifts, and memorabilia relating to [Mrs.] Eleanor Roosevelt, a personal friend of [Miss] Crooks, are included. The originals of Crooks's papers are held at the Colby College Library in Waterville, ME.

11,480. Davis, Hallie (Ferguson) Flanagan
Papers. 1935-39. 17 microfilm reels.
Open. Unpublished guide.
Franklin D. Roosevelt Library.
Davis (1890-1969), a drama professor at Vassar College, was founder and from 1925 to 1942 director of its experimental theatre. From 1935 to 1939 she also served as director of the WPA Federal Theatre Project. Correspondence, memoranda, reports, drafts of speeches and articles, clippings, and printed material relate to Davis's work with the Theatre Project.

11,481. Delano Family
Papers. 1833-1919. 21.6 ft.
Open. Unpublished guide.
Franklin D. Roosevelt Library.
The family is descended from Phillippe de la Noye, who arrived in Plymouth, MA, in 1621 and was involved in New England sea trade. Personal, business, financial, and legal correspondence; post cards; scrapbooks; clippings; and the log of the *Phillippe de la Noye* are included. Female correspondents include President Franklin D. Roosevelt's mother Sara (Delano) Roosevelt (1857-1941), Catherine Robbins Lyman Delano, Laura Astor Delano, Sarah Alvey Delano, Annie (Delano) Hitch, and Dora (Delano) Forbes.

11,482. Delano, Frederic Adrian
Papers. Ca. 1840-1953. 8 ft.
Open. Unpublished guide.
Franklin D. Roosevelt Library.
Delano (1863-1953), the uncle of President Franklin D. Roosevelt, was a member of the National Capital Park and Planning Commission as well as chairman of the National Resources Planning Board. Papers include a journal his mother Catherine Robbins [Mrs. Warren, II] Delano kept on a voyage from New York to Hong Kong in 1862; diaries of his parents and sister Annie (Delano) Hitch (1849-1926); a scrapbook compiled by Hitch, which concerns her educational and philanthropic interests in and around Newburgh, NY; and a scrapbook by his sister Dora (Delano) Forbes (1847-1940), which contains clippings concerning family matters during the 1920s and 1930s.

11,483. Dewson, Mary "Molly" M. Williams
Papers. 1924-60. 10 ft.
Open. Unpublished guide.
Franklin D. Roosevelt Library.
[Miss] Dewson (1874-1962) was active in Democratic party politics. Correspondence, a diary, notebooks, speeches, scrapbooks, campaign material, and clippings. She was in charge of the midwestern regional headquarters of the Democratic National Committee in 1928, director of the women's division of the Committee from 1931 to 1934, and vice-chairman of the full Committee from 1936 to 1937. She was appointed to the Social Security Board in 1937. After retiring from active politics, Dewson corresponded with Democratic party leaders and others concerning party matters and current political issues. Her correspondents included Eleanor Roosevelt, Frances Perkins, Ruth (Bryan) Owen, Emma Miller, Ellen Woodward, Margaret Chase Smith, and India Edwards.

11,484. Ellickson, Katherine Pollack
Papers. 1935-37. 14-page item and 6 microfilm reels.
Open. Registration statement and accession record.
Franklin D. Roosevelt Library.
Ellickson (1905-) was assistant to the director of the CIO from 1935 to 1937. Office files contain papers related to her work with the CIO in its formative years; a memoir entitled "Mrs. Eleanor Roosevelt's Contribution to the Status of Women" is also included. Ellickson later worked for the National Labor Relations Board and the Social Security Board and was appointed to the President's Commission on the Status of Women and the President's Commission on Equal Opportunity.

11,485. Ferris, Helen
Papers. 1944-64. Less than 1 ft.
Open. Registration statement.
Franklin D. Roosevelt Library.
[Miss] Ferris (1891-1969) was an author and editor of children's books. Collection consists of correspondence from Eleanor Roosevelt and her secretary Maureen Corr to Ferris as well as articles concerning Roosevelt and the Junior Literary Guild. Ferris served as editor-in-chief of the Guild from 1929 to 1959 and with Roosevelt co-authored the book *Partners: The United Nations and Youth.*

11,486. Forbush, Gabrielle
Papers. 1932-67. Ca. 126 pp. and 1 tape.
Open. Registration statement.
Franklin D. Roosevelt Library.
[Mrs.] Forbush was a member of the secretarial staff for Louis Howe, manager of Franklin D. Roosevelt's 1932 campaign. Correspondence with Franklin and Eleanor Roosevelt, Franklin Roosevelt's draft of a form letter, resolutions approved by state legislatures following an assassination attempt in Miami in 1933, clippings,

and memorabilia. Also included is a taped interview with Forbush, who worked as a Treasury Department staff member until her retirement in 1966.

11,487. Hall Family
Papers. 1842-1930. Less than 1 ft.
Open. Registration statement.
Franklin D. Roosevelt Library.
Correspondence, deeds, contracts, bills, leases, court judgments, and maps of such family members as Valentine Hall and Mary Hall, residents of Tivoli, NY, and their daughter Anna (Hall) Roosevelt, who was the mother of Eleanor Roosevelt.

11,488. Halsted, Anna (Roosevelt)
Papers. Ca. 1886-1973. 25 ft.
Open. Unpublished guide.
Franklin D. Roosevelt Library.
Halsted (1906-75) was the eldest child and only daughter of Franklin and Eleanor Roosevelt. Papers dealing with Roosevelt family matters, Eleanor Roosevelt's activities, White House events, and Halsted's personal, business, and public concerns are included with correspondence from Eleanor Roosevelt. Halsted, a writer, broadcaster, and journalist, lived in the White House during the 1930s and in the last part of WWII. Serving as an aide to her father, Halsted accompanied him to the Yalta Conference in 1945.

11,489. Hickok, Lorena
Papers. 1932-62. 15 cu.ft.
Open. No guide.
Franklin D. Roosevelt Library.
Personal correspondence of [Miss] Hickok (1893-1968), an Associated Press reporter. Assigned to cover Franklin Roosevelt's first presidential campaign, she became a close friend of Eleanor Roosevelt. During the New Deal she became a confidential aide to Harry Hopkins, head of the WPA. She was the author of several biographies and children's books and collaborated with Eleanor Roosevelt in writing *Ladies of Courage.*

11,490. Joseph, Nannine
Papers. 1931-62. Less than 1 ft.
Open. Unpublished guide.
Franklin D. Roosevelt Library.
Joseph (1889-1976) headed her own literary agency from 1930 until her death. Correspondence with Franklin and Eleanor Roosevelt, drafts, and published material. Joseph was an executive secretary for a music publisher and a contributor to the *Ladies Home Journal* before she became head of the nonfiction department for the literary agent firm Brandt and Brandt in 1925. She was also a lecturer at Columbia University graduate school of journalism and the New School for Social Research. The Roosevelts were among her literary clients.

11,491. Kleeman, Rita Halle
Papers. 1854-1946. 1 ft.
Open. Unpublished guide.
Franklin D. Roosevelt Library.
Kleeman (1887-1971) was an author and a friend of the Roosevelt family. Papers consist of the manuscript of her book *Gracious Lady: The Life of Sara Delano Roosevelt,* with corrections made by Franklin Roosevelt, and Roosevelt family papers she used for her book *Young Franklin Roosevelt.* Kleeman served as an officer of many Latin American organizations, was chairman of the western hemisphere solidarity committee of the National Council of Women, and served on the Writers War Board during WWII. She contributed to *The Saturday Evening Post, Good Housekeeping,* and other national magazines.

11,492. Livingston Family
Papers. 1630-1900. 14 ft. (13 microfilm reels).
Open. Unpublished guide.
Franklin D. Roosevelt Library.
Papers include letters, many of which are in Dutch, to Alida (Schuyler) Van Rensselaer Livingston (1656-1729) from family members in Albany, NY, Kingston, NY, New York City, and London. Papers of the descendants of Alida Livingston and her husband Robert Livingston, who figured prominently in the social, political and economic history of the Hudson Valley, relate to family matters, the situation in New York under British colonial rule and after independence, the American Revolution, Jacob Leisler's rebellion, trade and commerce of the Hudson Valley, privateers such as Captain Kidd, and Indian affairs.

11,493. Mrs. Roosevelt's Press Conference Association
Records. 1942-45. 2 ft.
Open. Unpublished guide.
Franklin D. Roosevelt Library.
An unofficial organization of women journalists who attended Eleanor Roosevelt's White House press conferences, the Association, in cooperation with the Secret Service, restricted conference participants to reporters from daily newspapers or weekly news magazines, press associations, and broadcasting companies. Among those who served as officers of the Association's standing committee were Ann Cottrell of the New York *Herald-Tribune;* Edith Gaylord of the Associated Press; Isabel K. Griffin of the Springfield, MA, *Union;* Mary Hornaday of the *Christian Science Monitor;* Elinor Lee of CBS; Mary Mason of NBC; Eulalie G. McDowell of the United Press; Ruth S. Montgomery of the New York *Daily News;* and Martha Strayer of the Washington *Daily News.*

11,494. Murray, Pauli
Papers. 1939-62. Less than 1 ft.
Open. No guide.
Franklin D. Roosevelt Library.
Correspondence between Eleanor Roosevelt and [Miss] Murray, who was a WPA teacher, an officer of the National Sharecropper's Union, a black activist during the 1930s, a lawyer, and a writer.

11,495. Olds, Leland
Papers. 1848-1960. 132 ft.
Open. Unpublished guide.
Franklin D. Roosevelt Library.
Olds (1890-1960), a government worker, served from 1940 to 1945 and again in 1947 as chairman of the Federal Power Commission. His papers include correspondence with his wife Maud Olds, his children, and his mother Marion Olds. Also included is a school notebook of Mary P. Adams, his maternal grandmother. Olds's other papers relate to his career and reflect his interest in conservation, electric power, and ecology.

11,496. Roosevelt, Anna Eleanor: Radio Show
Papers. 1937-40. 2 ft.
Open. Registration statement.
Franklin D. Roosevelt Library.
Correspondence generated by two radio programs broadcast by Eleanor Roosevelt. In the absence of Roosevelt, Mrs. Ernest K. Lindley responded to incoming letters.

11,497. Roosevelt, Anna Eleanor (Roosevelt)
Papers. 1877-1964. 1330 ft.
Open. Unpublished guide.
Franklin D. Roosevelt Library.
Correspondence, diaries, memoranda, engagement calendars, school notebooks, speeches, articles, and clippings of Roosevelt (1884-1962), who married her fifth cousin Franklin Delano Roosevelt. Her career was linked with that of her husband for 40 years. After Franklin Roosevelt's death, she was appointed to the US delegation to the United Nations General Assembly, a post she held from 1945 to 1953 and again in 1961. Her other activities included lecturing, writing, conducting a television series "Prospects of Mankind," and participating in state and national politics.

11,498. Roosevelt Family
Papers. 1706-1941. 32 cu.ft.
Open. Unpublished guide.
Franklin D. Roosevelt Library.
Papers of antecedent members and branches of the Roosevelt family include diaries of Rebecca Howland Roosevelt (1831-76), who was the first wife of Franklin D. Roosevelt's father James Roosevelt; correspondence, diaries for 1880 to 1941, a guest book, and a recipe book of Franklin Roosevelt's mother Sara (Delano) Roosevelt; family papers of John A. Roosevelt and Mary Rebecca (Aspinwall) Roosevelt, the uncle and aunt of Franklin Roosevelt; and diaries of Mary Roosevelt's sister Louisa E. Aspinwall concerning her travels in Europe.

11,499. Roosevelt Family
Papers. Ca. 1800-1945. 19 ft.
Access restricted. Unpublished guide.
Franklin D. Roosevelt Library.
Consists primarily of family correspondence, 1864-1945, including letters exchanged by Franklin D. Roosevelt, his mother Sara (Delano) Roosevelt, and his wife Eleanor Roosevelt. Also contains letters by Roosevelt children to their parents and grandmother, correspondence of Eleanor Roosevelt with her mother-in-law, and correspondence of other members of the Theodore Roosevelt and Hall families. Also includes diaries Eleanor Roosevelt's cousin Susan Ludlow Parish kept from 1880 to 1910; papers of Ludlow family members, among them Eleanor Roosevelt's great-grandparents Edward Ludlow and Elizabeth Livingston Ludlow; and estate and legal papers of James Roosevelt and Sara (Delano) Roosevelt.

11,500. Roosevelt, Franklin D.: Naval and Marine Manuscripts
Collection. 1731-1942. 36 ft.
Open. Unpublished guide.
Franklin D. Roosevelt Library.
Roosevelt began collecting manuscripts concerning naval history during his undergraduate days at Harvard. Collection includes correspondence between an American naval commander David Conner, who served in the War of 1812 and the Mexican War, and Susan Syng Physick before and after their marriage in 1828. Also includes a journal relating to the Conners' courtship, marriage, and early married life. Letters of Rear Admiral John J. Almy to his wife Sarah Almy during his command of US gunboats on blockade duty off southern ports during the Civil War are also included.

11,501. Smith, Hilda Worthington
Papers. 1922-47. 14 ft.
Open. Unpublished guide.
Franklin D. Roosevelt Library.
Born in New York, [Miss] Smith (1888-) is a specialist in public housing and programs to aid the elderly and a pioneer in the development of worker's education. Correspondence, memoranda, reports, clippings, and published material relate to Smith's interests in worker education. A graduate of Bryn Mawr College and the New York School of Social Work, she became dean of Bryn Mawr and organized the first summer school for working women there in 1921. She served as director of the WPA Workers Education Service, which hired unemployed teachers to re-educate wage earners, and directed camps across the country for 8000 unemployed women. During WWII Smith worked for the Federal Public Housing Administration. She later served as a consultant with the Office of Economic Opportunity.

11,502. Thompson, C. Mildred
Papers. 1928-62. Less than 1 ft.
Open. Registration statement.
Franklin D. Roosevelt Library.
Thompson (1882-1975) was dean of Vassar College from 1923 to 1948. Correspondence with her friend Eleanor Roosevelt and with Franklin Roosevelt is included along with campaign material. Thompson was active in President Roosevelt's re-election campaign in 1936 and headed an educators' committee for him.

11,503. Women's Division of the Democratic National Committee
Records. 1932-44. 89 ft.
Open. Unpublished guide.
Franklin D. Roosevelt Library.
Correspondence with the Democratic national chairmen and other party leaders as well as with leaders of Democratic women's organizations at the state and county levels is included with material relating to arrangements for speakers and radio broadcasts, the preparation and publication of the *Democratic Digest* and other campaign literature, and to the Division's reporter plan for accumulating and distributing data on New Deal programs and projects for use by party workers. Division heads included [Miss] Mary Dewson, Mrs. James H. Wolfe, Mrs. Thomas McAllister, and Mrs. Charles W. Tillett. The records relate primarily to the 1936 and 1940 campaigns.

11,504. Perkins, Frances
Papers. 1932-44. Less than 1 ft.
Open. No guide.
Franklin D. Roosevelt Library.
[Miss] Perkins (1882-1965) began her government career in 1912 as executive secretary of the New York Commission of Safety; she held other state government positions until President Roosevelt named her secretary of labor in 1933. Correspondence with labor leaders about labor's participation in the National Defense Program, a report summarizing her first 10 years as labor secretary, material concerning a 1932 conference on unemployment, speeches, press conferences, radio forums, and published articles. After resigning her Labor Department post in 1945, Perkins served as a member of the Civil Service Commission for six years.

ITHACA

11,505. Abbe, Elfriede Martha
Papers. 1939-68. 1 vol. and 470 items.
Open. Unpublished guide.
Cornell University, Department of Manuscripts and University Archives.
Papers of Abbe (1919-), a sculptor, printer, printmaker, and scientific illustrator who graduated from Cornell in 1940, include correspondence with people and organizations who commissioned her sculpture, suppliers of sculptures and casting firms, the publisher of her books, other artists, admirers, and others; lectures; notes; manuscripts and proofs of books she illustrated; photos; a catalog of her sculpture; clippings; and announcements. Correspondents include Cornelia Van A. Chapin, Katherine Thayer Hobson, Alison Mason Kingsbury, Carolyn and Lewis Knudson, and Alice and Rolla Tryon.

11,506. Abbe, George Waldo, and Abbe, Charlotte (Colgate)
Papers. 1840-83. 37 items.
Open. Unpublished guide.
Cornell University, Department of Manuscripts and University Archives.
Correspondence between George Abbe (1811-79), a New York City merchant, abolitionist, and a founder of the American Bible Union, and Charlotte Abbe (1817-85), whom he married in 1837. The letters were written while he was traveling in the Midwest. Also includes a letter from his mother Talitha Waldo Abbe (1789-?).

11,507. Allen, Elsa Guerdrum
Papers. 1899-1968. Ca. 31 ft.
Access restricted. Unpublished guide.
Cornell University, Department of Manuscripts and University Archives.
Allen (1888-1969), an ornithologist and a research associate at the laboratory of ornithology at Cornell, married Arthur Augustus Allen, a professor of ornithology at Cornell, in 1913. The Allens collaborated in teaching, writing, and fieldwork. Contains Elsa Allen's professional papers, which primarily consist of correspondence, research and field notes, drafts, reprints, and photos concerning her publications and lectures about ornithology and the history of ornithology. Also includes a manuscript of her unpublished biography of John Abbot, an early American ornithologist. Personal papers include family correspondence with her mother, her aunt, her husband, and her five children as well as letters concerning the Guerdrum family, diaries, a manuscript of her unpublished novel "Minerva's Daughters," student papers, and notes.

11,508. Alumni Association and Services
Records. 1868-1965. Ca. 260 ft.
Partially restricted. Published and unpublished guides.
Cornell University, Department of Manuscripts and University Archives.
Primarily contains records of deceased alumni and deceased WWII servicemen, including correspondence, biographical data, photos, and clippings. Other records include Alumni secretaries' and field secretaries' records concerning reunion activities, the maintenance of class records, and contributions to the Alumni fund; correspondence of alumnae secretary Pauline J. Schmid with the officers of the alumnae classes concerning related financial matters; and records concerning the activities of individual men's clubs, women's clubs, and combined Alumni clubs throughout the US, including the Federation of Cornell Women's Clubs. The Federation recommended that the position of advisor of women be established and given faculty status at Cornell. Correspondence of [Miss] Kate M. Schutt concerning the duties and status of deans of women at other American universities and the selection of the women's advisor is included with a file on annual conferences on fields of work for women held at Cornell from 1935 to 1942. Also includes correspondence of Schutt, Agda Swenson Osborn, and others concerning the Alumni trustee candidacies of Anna Botsford Comstock, Mary Merritt Crawford, and Mary H. Donlon; Cornell Women Graduates' Association accounts; minutes and reports of the administrative board of the Cornell University Council; and minutes, constitutions, correspondence, and other papers of individual clubs. Officers and alumnae represented include Bessie DeWitt Beahan, Helen E. Bullard, Isabel Howland, Ruth F. Irish, Helen Holme Mackie, and Orpha Spicer Zimmer. Taken from *Cornell University Collection of Regional History and the University Archives, Report of the Curator and Archivist* (Ithaca, NY: Cornell University Department of Manuscripts and University Archives, 1974).

11,509. Alward, Emily Wight (Babcock)
Papers. 1806-1919. 6 in.
Open. Published guide.
Cornell University, Department of Manuscripts and University Archives.
Papers primarily concern a journey Emily Babcock (1836-1919) took to England to marry Dennis R. Alward, assistant secretary of the US legation in London, and the couple's life in diplomatic and court society. Includes letters to her mother Mary (Potter) Babcock, with descriptions of Emily Alward's presentation to Queen Victoria and comments on the status, personality, appearance, and costumes of the Queen, members of the royal family, English noblewomen, and others; schoolgirl poetry and compositions, including one that gives a description of Buffalo as it appeared in 1848; her London engagement book; and a scrapbook of invitations, announcements, and similar items. Also includes Mary Babcock's letters to her husband and children and a diary in which she describes her impressions of her trip to England with her daughter and her return trip. Taken from *Cornell University Collection of Regional History and the University Archives, Report of the Curator and Archivist* (Ithaca, NY: Cornell University Department of Manuscripts and University Archives, 1959).

11,510. American Association of University Women
Records. 1918-70. 1.2 cu.ft.
Open. Published guides.
Cornell University, Department of Manuscripts and University Archives.
Incomplete minute books, correspondence, membership lists, calendars, newsletters, and programs of the Ithaca branch of the AAUW and programs of meetings of regional, national, and international AAUW groups. Records reflect the active participation of such Ithaca women as Helen Magill [Mrs. Andrew Dickson] White, [Mrs.] Anna Botsford Comstock, and Margaret K. (Carleton) [Mrs. Livingston] Farrand. Also includes a history of the Ithaca AAUW by Edith Anna Ellis. Taken from *Cornell University Collection of Regional History and the University Archives, Report of the Curator and Archivist* (Ithaca, NY: Cornell University Department of Manuscripts and University Archives, 1959); *Cornell University Collection of Regional History and the University Archives, Report of the Curator and Archivist* (Ithaca, NY: Cornell University Department of Manuscripts and University Archives, 1963).

11,511. American Medical Women's Association
Records. 1895-1970. 20 cu.ft.
Open. Unpublished guide.
Cornell University, Department of Manuscripts and University Archives.
Constitution; bylaws; annual reports and minutes, 1915-61; financial records; correspondence of Association presidents; correspondence of the executive secretary and the editor, including that of Elizabeth Kittridge who held both offices from 1937 to 1947; records of regional groups; and printed items, including publications of the Association and biographical information collected for publication of the *Directory of Medical Women* (1949), which was edited by Elizabeth Mason-Hohl. Founded in 1915, the Association proposed to "further the art and science of medicine; to promote interests common to women physicians and the public; to aid and encourage pre-medical, medical and post-graduate medical studies; to foster medical relief projects; and to cooperate with other organizations having comparable interests." Although at its inception membership was open to all women with medical interests, the Association is now limited to women physicians and women medical students. Includes questionnaires, 1895, containing biographical sketches of women in medicine and information concerning the fight for equal status for women doctors in the armed forces during WWII. Most of the material dates from after 1912.

11,512. Ayres, Sidney
Papers. 1779-1919. 1 ft.
Open. Published guide.
Cornell University, Department of Manuscripts and University Archives.
Includes early 20th-century letters to D. C. Ayres,

a publisher of the Penn Yan *Chronicle,* from W. H. Samson, editor of the Rochester *Post Express,* concerning Jemima Wilkinson's will and signature as well as a 1783 eulogy to Wilkinson, the "public universal friend." Taken from *Cornell University Collection of Regional History and the University Archives, Report of the Curator and Archivist* (Ithaca, NY: Cornell University Department of Manuscripts and University Archives, 1959).

11,513. Badger Family
Papers. 1843-83. 1 vol.
Open. Published guide.
Cornell University, Department of Manuscripts and University Archives.
Record book of the Badger family, residents of Steuben County, NY, includes legal, farm, and household accounts; daily weather records; an inventory of farm property; and directions for making medical and household preparations and treating animal and human diseases. Taken from *Cornell University Collection of Regional History and the University Archives, Report of the Curator and Archivist* (Ithaca, NY: Cornell University Department of Manuscripts and University Archives, 1963).

11,514. Bancroft, George
Papers. 1811-1941. 7 ft.
Open. Published guides.
Cornell University, Department of Manuscripts and University Archives.
Papers of Bancroft (1800-91), an historian and diplomat, consist primarily of correspondence, including that of Bancroft with his first wife Sarah (Dwight) Bancroft (?-1837); his second wife Elizabeth (Davis) Bliss Bancroft; his father Aaron Bancroft; his sister Eliza (Bancroft) Davis; her husband John Davis, governor of Massachusetts; another sister Lucretia (Bancroft) Farnum; and his two sons George Bancroft, Jr., and John Chandler Bancroft during their school days and their travels abroad. Other family letters are from other sisters and brothers, members of the Dwight family, Bancroft's two stepsons, nieces, nephews, and other relatives. Also includes correspondence of or about Ann Bancroft, Mary Bancroft, Louisa Bancroft, Sarah Bancroft, and Jane Putnam Bancroft Gherardi. Also available on microfilm. See Herbert Finch, ed., *George Bancroft Papers at Cornell University, 1811-1901* (Ithaca, NY: Collection of Regional History and University Archives, John M. Olin Library, 1965). See also *Cornell University Collection of Regional History and the University Archives, Report of the Curator and Archivist* (Ithaca, NY: Cornell University Department of Manuscripts and University Archives, 1955); *Cornell University Collection of Regional History and the University Archives, Report of the Curator and Archivist* (Ithaca, NY: Cornell University Department of Manuscripts and University Archives, 1963).

11,515. Beard, Mary
Papers. 1926-ca. 1940. 16 in.
Open. Unpublished guide.
Cornell University, Department of Manuscripts and University Archives.
Papers of Beard (1876-1946), a nurse, include a diary for 1926 to 1940, manuscripts of papers she delivered as well as her published papers, notes for talks she gave, and pamphlets relating to nursing and public health. Beard graduated from the New York Hospital School of Nursing in 1903. From 1912 to 1922 she served as instructive director of the District Nursing Association and the Community Health Association; from 1924 to 1938 she was associate director for the international health division of the Rockefeller Foundation; and from 1938 to 1944 she was director of nursing service for the American National Red Cross in Washington, DC.

11,516. Beaumont, Jane Lightfoot
Papers. 1921-70. 3.8 ft. and 2 microfilm reels.
Open. Unpublished guide.
Cornell University, Department of Manuscripts and University Archives.
Consists of family papers and material [Mrs. Charles] Beaumont collected on the history of Penn Yan, NY, and Yates County, NY. Includes correspondence, scrapbooks, and articles of [Miss] Winifred Graville (1939-70), a distant cousin of Beaumont, concerning her activities, lectures, and prospects for coming from England to the US to lecture. Also includes letters from Sidney Clarke to Beaumont; correspondence, photos, clippings, and pamphlets of Edson S. Lott, a local historian and author of Yates County, NY; a scrapbook kept by Louella D. Everett (?-1967), an associate editor of the 11th edition of Bartlett's *Familiar Quotations;* Beaumont's research papers on Victorian silver; and 10 scrapbooks concerning her family and local history.

11,517. Bedell, Alice
Papers. 1915. 8 items.
Open. Published guide.
Cornell University, Department of Manuscripts and University Archives.
Letters and subscription receipts of [Mrs.] Bedell, a resident of Savona, NY, from the Explorations Holding Company in California. Taken from *Cornell University Collection of Regional History and the University Archives, Report of the Curator and Archivist* (Ithaca, NY: Cornell University Department of Manuscripts and University Archives, 1947).

11,518. Bennett, Mary
Papers. 1866-74. 1 vol. and 21 items.
Open. Published guide.
Cornell University, Department of Manuscripts and University Archives.
Diaries, accounts, and other personal papers of Bennett, a resident of Interlaken, NY. Taken from *Cornell University Collection of Regional History and the University Archives, Report of the Curator and Archivist* (Ithaca, NY: Cornell University, 1946).

11,519. Berkshire: 80 Years Ago
Papers. 1935. 4-page item.
Open. Published guide.
Cornell University, Department of Manuscripts and University Archives.
Essay by Elizabeth Marsh, a resident of Tioga County, NY. Taken from *Cornell University Collection of Regional History and the University Archives, Report of the Curator and Archivist* (Ithaca, NY: Cornell University Department of Manuscripts and University Archives, 1951).

11,520. Berry Family
Papers. 1812-1917. 3 boxes and 35 vols.
Open. Published guide.
Cornell University, Department of Manuscripts and University Archives.
Contains correspondence, diaries, accounts, and other papers, which relate to the activities of the related Berry, Nearing, and Osborn families of Onondaga County, NY, and the Waterbury family of Livingston County, NY. Includes correspondence relating to a smallpox epidemic; temperance meetings; prices of crops; a lady's seminary exhibition in Lima, NY; farming conditions; politics; and new settlement and emigration from New York to High Forest, Minnesota Territory. Also includes diaries of Mary Nearing, who reflects on her life as a teacher in Pompey and Lafayette; diaries of her sister Alicia Nearing, who describes her teaching life at Williamsville Institute in Erie County, NY, 1863-64; and diaries of Alicia's husband W. W. Hayden, who wrote about his senior year at Williams College, his disagreement with College president Mark Hopkins's views on doctrine, a speech by Elihu Burritt on the extermination of slavery, and various college activities, 1860-63. Taken from *Cornell University Collection of Regional History and the University Archives, Report of the Curator and Archivist* (Ithaca, NY: Cornell University Department of Manuscripts and University Archives, 1951).

11,521. Betten, Beatrice Argetsinger
Papers. Nd. 13-page item.
Open. Published guide.
Cornell University, Department of Manuscripts and University Archives.
Reminiscences of Betten concern her husband Cornelius Betten, dean of the University faculty; dictation he gave to her when she was Mrs. Argetsinger, his secretary; and statements he made to her following their marriage. She also describes the contributions made by John McFarlane Howie, a hotel owner; Beulah Blackmore, Flora Rose, and Martha Van Rensselaer, professors of home economics; her husband; Howard B. Meek; and others to the establishment of the school of hotel administration at Cornell. She also discusses the way in which Leonard Elmhirst's friendship with Dorothy Straight led to the founding of Willard Straight Hall. Taken from *Cornell University Collection of Regional History and the University Archives, Report of the Curator and Archivist* (Ithaca, NY: Cornell University Department of Manuscripts and University Archives, 1974).

11,522. Bibbens Family
Papers. 1766-1961. 2 items and 1 microfilm reel.
Open. Published guide.
Cornell University, Department of Manuscripts and University Archives.
Contains a diary in which Susan (Bibbens) Fox (1803-90) describes her religious feelings and gives accounts of revival meetings. Diary also contains genealogical data and obituaries of Fox and her husband Jonathan Fox. Also includes Bible records of births, deaths, and marriages of members of the Bibbens family, residents of Weedsport, NY, and of the related Hall, Miller, Shepherd, and Wright families as well as a report on the Bibbens family prepared by Weedsport town historian Howard J. Finley. Taken from *Cornell University Collection of Regional History and the University Archives, Report of the Curator and Archivist* (Ithaca, NY: Cornell University Department of Manuscripts and University Archives, 1963).

11,523. Bishop, Della
Papers. 1893-1921. 0.2 ft.
Open. Unpublished guide.
Cornell University, Department of Manuscripts and University Archives.
Account book in which Bishop listed mortgages and mortgage payments for property in Ithaca and surrounding counties.

11,524. Boardman, Douglass
Papers. 1877-91. 8 in.
Open. Published guides.
Cornell University, Department of Manuscripts and University Archives.
Letters from Jennie (McGraw) Fiske to Boardman (1822-91), a judge and executor of her father John McGraw's estate, relate primarily to the estate and to her European travels, but they also concern the future of Cornell University without Andrew D. White as president and other matters. Also includes receipts for personal property, a volume containing an inventory of art objects, other inventories, and other items pertaining to Jennie Fiske's estate. Taken from *Cornell University Collection of Regional History and the University Archives, Report of the Curator and Archivist* (Ithaca, NY: Cornell University Department of Manuscripts and University Archives, 1959); *Cornell University Collection of Regional History and the University Archives, Report of the Curator and Archivist* (Ithaca, NY: Cornell University

Department of Manuscripts and University Archives, 1963).

11,525. Boardman, Emily
Papers. 1888-1903. 79 items.
Open. Published guide.
Cornell University, Department of Manuscripts and University Archives.
Contains a will of [Miss] Boardman, (?-1898), a resident of Trumansburg, NY, who was the sister of Douglass Boardman, a judge, and correspondence, accounts, receipts, and other legal papers pertaining to the settlement of Emily Boardman's estate. Also includes correspondence referring to the estates of Maria S. Blakeslee and Riley Spence. Taken from *Cornell University Collection of Regional History and the University Archives, Report of the Curator and Archivist* (Ithaca, NY: Cornell University Department of Manuscripts and University Archives, 1963).

11,526. Bohannon, Mary Elizabeth
Papers. Ca. 1930-63. 5 ft.
Open. Published and unpublished guides.
Cornell University, Department of Manuscripts and University Archives.
Correspondence, diaries, account books, notes, transcripts, and maps that Bohannon (1905-63), an historian, compiled for her study of the 17th-century English Barrington family, which she began as a doctoral dissertation at Cornell and later expanded under fellowships from the AAUW and the Folger Shakespeare Library. Also includes related research she conducted while she was a member of the faculty of Wells College in Aurora, NY; correspondence with Carl Becker and other scholars concerning her research; drafts of her thesis; and articles. Taken from *Cornell University Collection of Regional History and the University Archives, Report of the Curator and Archivist* (Ithaca, NY: Cornell University Department of Manuscripts and University Archives, 1974).

11,527. Bond and Grayston
Papers. 1870-99. 28 items.
Open. Published guide.
Cornell University, Department of Manuscripts and University Archives.
Includes letters in which Catherine (Grayston) Bond comments to relatives in England about the growth of her family, about living and working conditions, and about the master, a Philadelphia businessman to whom she and her husband were engaged as farm helpers. Also includes letters Bond wrote while she was living in Bunker Hill, Russell County, KS, about her family, living conditions, land prices, wages, and other matters and letters James Grayston wrote from Grafton, WV, concerning the railroad strike, lack of work, and land that was rent-free for the clearing. Taken from *Cornell University Collection of Regional History and the University Archives, Report of the Curator and Archivist* (Ithaca, NY: Cornell University Department of Manuscripts and University Archives, 1951).

11,528. Botsford, Frank, Family
Papers. 1792-1970. 13 ft.
Open. Unpublished guide.
Cornell University, Department of Manuscripts and University Archives.
Primarily family correspondence of Frank and Alice Ansley Botsford with their children Anna, Elizabeth, Franklin, Mary, Myrtie, Kathleen, and Samuel and other relatives. Also includes diaries and notebooks that document the interests and daily lives of family members; Alice Botsford's poetry, short stories, and scrapbooks; account books and other financial records, which relate to the family farm, to occupations of various family members, and to the settlement of estates; deeds, mortgages, leases, promissory notes, and insurance policies; genealogies of the Ansley, Bostford, and Spangler families; photos; clippings and other printed items relating to family members and local history; and memorabilia.

11,529. Brayton Family
Papers. 1829-73. 0.3 cu.ft.
Open. Published guide.
Cornell University, Department of Manuscripts and University Archives.
Includes a poetry album of Cynthia Brayton, 1829; a diary of Ellen M. Brayton (1836-?), 1850-51, and her composition book, 1851-54; and a scrapbook of Katy C. Brayton, begun in 1873. See *Cornell University Collection of Regional History and the University Archives, Report of the Curator and Archivist* (Ithaca, NY: Cornell University Department of Manuscripts and University Archives, 1949).

11,530. Bride's Club
Records. 1926-50. 4 vols.
Open. Published guide.
Cornell University, Department of Manuscripts and University Archives.
Minutes, accounts, correspondence, clippings, and programs of the Bride's Club of Cornell, which was organized in 1908 and disbanded in 1950. Taken from *Cornell University Collection of Regional History and the University Archives, Report of the Curator and Archivist* (Ithaca, NY: Cornell University Department of Manuscripts and University Archives, 1951).

11,531. Brown, Mary R.
Papers. 1953. 9-page item.
Open. Published guide.
Cornell University, Department of Manuscripts and University Archives.
Includes Brown's anecdotes about Henry W. Sage, housing for women students, and other aspects of life for college women from 1888 to 1893. See *Cornell University Collection of Regional History and the University Archives, Report of the Curator and Archivist* (Ithaca, NY: Cornell University Department of Manuscripts and University Archives, 1955).

11,532. Bryant, Laura
Papers. Ca. 1895-1961. 37 ft.
Open. Published guide.
Cornell University, Department of Manuscripts and University Archives.
Includes personal correspondence, diaries, and notebooks of Bryant (1878-1961), a music teacher and supervisor of singing in the Ithaca public schools from 1906 to 1950. Also contains professional correspondence with colleagues, publishers, and others concerning the textbooks on which she collaborated with Hollis Dann and later with Katherine Knapp; scrapbooks pertaining to her activities and those of former students and others; albums; photos; and items relating to her teaching in Ithaca schools and in summer sessions at Cornell and other colleges. Taken from *Cornell University Collection of Regional History and the University Archives, Report of the Curator and Archivist* (Ithaca, NY: Cornell University Department of Manuscripts and University Archives, 1963).

11,533. Camp Family
Papers. 1817-1953. 4 ft.
Open. Published guides.
Cornell University, Department of Manuscripts and University Archives.
Includes correspondence between Elizabeth Francis Osborn Camp (1835-1920) and her husband Jacob Andrus Camp (1823-1900), an 1852 diary Elizabeth Camp kept before and after her marriage, and her household expense accounts. Also includes *Out of Old Virginia and New England—The Family Story of Jacob Andrus Camp 1823-1900 [and] Elizabeth Francis Osborn Camp 1835-1920,* by Anna Rachel (Camp) [Mrs. Richard Henry] Edwards, a daughter of Jacob Camp. Taken from *Cornell University Collection of Regional History and the University Archives, Report of the Curator and Archivist* (Ithaca, NY: Cornell University Department of Manuscripts and University Archives, 1949); *Cornell University Collection of Regional History and the University Archives, Report of the Curator and Archivist* (Ithaca, NY: Cornell University Department of Manuscripts and University Archives, 1951); *Cornell University Collection of Regional History and the University Archives, Report of the Curator and Archivist* (Ithaca, NY: Cornell University Department of Manuscripts and University Archives, 1959).

11,534. Cantine, Christina M.
Papers. 1819-87. 4 in.
Open. Published guide.
Cornell University, Department of Manuscripts and University Archives.
Letters to members of the related Cantine and Williams families, who resided in Ithaca, especially to Christina Cantine, and to members of the related Van Buren family, who resided in Kinderhook, NY. Includes a letter in which Martin Van Buren wrote about the life of his brother-in-law, close friend, and political supporter Moses I. Cantine (1774-1823), who was editor of the *Albany Argus* and a New York state senator; letters from Moses Cantine to his daughter Christina; and letters from Henry Shaler Williams and Roger B. Williams to their mother about life at Yale College, with comments on their religious activities and the "tyranny" of the faculty. Other correspondents include Ruth Croswell, Jane L. Hardy, Louisa Hardy, Mary Seymour Montgomery, Susan Walker, Louise Williams, and Angelica (Singleton) Van Buren. Taken from *Cornell University Collection of Regional History and the University Archives, Report of the Curator and Archivist* (Ithaca, NY: Cornell University Department of Manuscripts and University Archives, 1959).

11,535. Case, Laura Abigail
Papers. 1832. 2-page item.
Open. Published guide.
Cornell University, Department of Manuscripts and University Archives.
Letter of Case (1815-94), who describes her journey from Tompkins County, NY, to Pekin, IL. Taken from *Cornell University Collection of Regional History and the University Archives, Report of the Curator and Archivist* (Ithaca, NY: Cornell University Department of Manuscripts and University Archives, 1963).

11,536. Case, Mary Ann Humble
Papers. 1867-1951. 5-page item.
Open. Published guide.
Cornell University, Department of Manuscripts and University Archives.
Unpublished memoirs of [Mrs.] Case (1867-?), the daughter of a Mormon blacksmith from Mount Emmons, UT. Case, who married a farmer and homesteader, describes their efforts to settle in various places in Utah, her loneliness when her husband was away, her encounters with Indians, the births of eight of her nine children without the aid of a doctor or midwife, her work in the Mormon Church, and her visit to the Salt Lake Temple. Taken from *Cornell University Collection of Regional History and the University Archives, Report of the Curator and Archivist* (Ithaca, NY: Cornell University Department of Manuscripts and University Archives, 1959).

11,537. Castle, Irene (Foote)
Papers. 1916-46. 0.4 cu.ft.
Open. Published guide.
Cornell University, Department of Manuscripts and University Archives.
Papers of Castle (1893-1969), an actress and a dancer, pertain to her film career and to the early motion picture industry in Ithaca. Includes the certificate of incorporation for Cayuga Pictures and

the certificate of incorporation and other legal documents, accounts, and correspondence of the Hol-Tre Producing Company of Ithaca and the W. W. Hodkinson Corporation, with which Edwin L. Hollywood, Charles H. Blood, Sid Schlager, Ernest I. White, and Castle's second husband Robert Elias Treman were associated. The companies made and distributed films starring Irene Castle. Also includes financial accounts of the Mrs. Vernon Castle Management and the Castle Club, an establishment where Castle and her first husband Vernon Castle (?-1918) danced; scrapbooks of clippings concerning Castle and her films; publicity galleys for the movie *French Heels;* and clippings, some of which concern her influence on women's fashions and her later years in retirement. Irene and Vernon Castle were married in 1911; she married Treman in 1919. After their marriage ended in divorce in 1923, she married Frederic McLaughlin (?-1944). She married George Enzinger (?-1959) in 1946 or 1947. See *Cornell University Collection of Regional History and the University Archives, Report of the Curator and Archivist* (Ithaca, NY: Cornell University Department of Manuscripts and University Archives, 1974).

11,538. Challenge to University Governance
Records. 1969-71. 6.7 ft.
Access restricted. Unpublished guide.
Cornell University, Department of Manuscripts and University Archives.
Includes transcripts of interviews with 16 women for an oral history project at Cornell on the challenges to governance at the University. Also includes reports, position papers, and other items.

11,539. Church, Mary Jane
Papers. 1864-65. 13 items.
Open. Published guide.
Cornell University, Department of Manuscripts and University Archives.
Letters that [Miss] Church (1847-?) wrote to her brother while she was attending Rutgers' Female College in New York City concern their relatives, friends, and schoolwork. The letters also contain sisterly advice, descriptions of places visited in the City, impressions of Henry Ward Beecher, and comments on the progress of the Civil War and the reaction in New York to Lincoln's assassination. Taken from *Cornell University Collection of Regional History and the University Archives, Report of the Curator and Archivist* (Ithaca, NY: Cornell University Department of Manuscripts and University Archives, 1974).

11,540. Claassen, Evelyn
Oral history. 1962. 26-page transcript.
Open. Published guide.
Cornell University, Department of Manuscripts and University Archives.
Interview with Claassen, a faculty wife, concerns her experiences during the 1924-25 academic year during which she accompanied her husband Peter Walter Claassen, an entomologist, to China and her impressions of that country and its people. Taken from *Cornell University Collection of Regional History and the University Archives, Report of the Curator and Archivist* (Ithaca, NY: Cornell University Department of Manuscripts and University Archives, 1974).

11,541. Cline, Carolynne Helen
Papers. 1939-64. 2.67 ft. and 4 tapes.
Access restricted. Published guide.
Cornell University, Department of Manuscripts and University Archives.
Includes correspondence, memoranda, photos, programs, pamphlets, and memorabilia of [Miss] Cline, secretary of the women in the class of 1937, which pertain to class reunions. Cornell women graduates elect class officers as do their male counterparts. Also includes questionnaires and other biographical information for each of these reunions and tapes of the women's reunion banquet and a midnight dormitory party. Correspondents include Rachel Louise Fitch, Pauline J. Schmid, and Margaret K. Farrand. Also includes a diary Cline kept during her trip to the Soviet Union in 1956 and tapes of her interviews with Frances Perkins, Perry Gilbert, and others. Taken from *Cornell University Collection of Regional History and the University Archives, Report of the Curator and Archivist* (Ithaca, NY: Cornell University Department of Manuscripts and University Archives, 1974).

11,542. Coad, Pauline Corson
Oral history. 1958. 3 tapes.
Open. Published guide.
Cornell University, Department of Manuscripts and University Archives.
Reminiscences of [Mrs.] Coad concern her grandfather Hiram Corson and her summer visits to Ithaca in the early 1900s; they include memories of Cornell and faculty members during that period and remarks on Hiram Corson's belief in and practice of spiritualism. Also contains reference to visits by the noted spiritualist Madame Helena Petrovna Blavatsky. Taken from *Cornell University Collection of Regional History and the University Archives, Report of the Curator and Archivist* (Ithaca, NY: Cornell University Department of Manuscripts and University Archives, 1963).

11,543. Comstock, John Henry, and Comstock, Anna (Botsford)
Papers. 1874-1955. 1 ft.
Open. Published guide.
Cornell University, Department of Manuscripts and University Archives.
Papers of John Comstock (1849-1931), a professor of entomology and nature study, and of his wife Anna Comstock (1854-1930), a professor of nature study who was closely associated with her husband in his work. Includes letters from Anna Comstock's mother Phoebe Botsford to Anna, then Miss Botsford, while she was a student at Sage College, Cornell University; letters to Anna Botsford from Cornell president Andrew D. White and Jennie Bartlett, a former student, who discuss student accommodations in Ithaca; and letters Anna Comstock wrote to a Mrs. Crocker outlining the Comstocks' plans for a European trip and enclosing a copy of "the only novel I ever wrote or ever shall write," *Confessions to a Heathen Idol* (1906). Also includes a draft of Anna Comstock's autobiography; her drawings, which were intended as illustrations for writings on nature study; printed nature study syllabi and glass slides she used in her teaching; photos of the Comstocks, their relatives, and their home; her drawings of scenes in Ithaca and Europe; and notes apparently for a speech Anna Comstock gave on wood engraving. Taken from *Cornell University Collection of Regional History and the University Archives, Report of the Curator and Archivist* (Ithaca, NY: Cornell University Department of Manuscripts and University Archives, 1974).

11,544. Coney, Delphine
Papers. 1866-76. 11 vols.
Open. Published guide.
Cornell University, Department of Manuscripts and University Archives.
Diaries of Coney (1853-95), a resident of Clarkson, NY, chiefly concern her school, church, social, and domestic activities. Taken from *Cornell University Collection of Regional History and the University Archives, Report of the Curator and Archivist* (Ithaca, NY: Cornell University Department of Manuscripts and University Archives, 1974).

11,545. Cook, Alice Hanson
Papers. 1962-69. 3 items and 3 tapes.
Partially restricted. Published and unpublished guides.
Cornell University, Department of Manuscripts and University Archives.
[Mrs.] Cook (1903-), a professor of industrial and labor relations, served as ombudsman at Cornell. Includes her account of a year she spent on a Fulbright grant at the institute of labor-management studies at Keio University in Tokyo, her research and teaching there, her impressions of Japan and the Japanese, and life and the labor movement in Okinawa, Taiwan, the Philippines, Hong Kong, and Korea. Also includes tapes of an interview in which Cook discusses her work as ombudsman and as a delegate to the Democratic National Convention as well as a tape and transcript of a lecture by Cook. See *Cornell University Collection of Regional History and the University Archives, Report of the Curator and Archivist* (Ithaca, NY: Cornell University Department of Manuscripts and University Archives, 1974).

11,546. Cook, Constance Knowles Eberhardt
Papers. 1947-74. 150 ft.
Access restricted. Unpublished guide.
Cornell University, Department of Manuscripts and University Archives.
Working files of Cook (1919-), an attorney and New York assemblywoman for Tompkins and Tioga counties from 1962 to 1966, include topical, legislative, constituent, and chronological files and files relating to Tompkins and Tioga counties. Cook received her bachelor of laws degree from Cornell in 1943. She was in private practice until 1949 and then served as a law assistant to Governor Thomas E. Dewey. She married Alfred P. Cook in 1955 and had two children.

11,547. Cooper, Sarah Brown (Ingersoll)
Papers. 1842-1910. 13 ft. and 2 microfilm reels.
Open. Published guide.
Cornell University, Department of Manuscripts and University Archives.
Papers of [Mrs. Halsey Fenimore] Cooper (1835-96), an educator and social reformer, relate to the Golden Gate Kindergarten Association in San Francisco, which Cooper founded, and to woman suffrage, temperance, and other reform movements. Includes correspondence, diaries, reports, and other papers of Cooper and her daughter Harriet Cooper (1856-96); letters from Susan B. Anthony and Frances Willard; scattered accounts and papers pertaining to the settlement of the estates of Cooper and her daughter; photos; and printed items. Correspondents include Ella Adams, Philip D. Armour, Rachel G. (Foster) Avery, Earl Barnes, Sophia L. Boardman, Nicholas E. Boyd, Lucy Brinkerhoff, Charles O. Browne, F. C. Clarke, Henry C. Dane, John Eaton, Nellie B. Eyster, Helen G. Fairchild, George T. Gaden, Minna V. Gaden, Caroline T. Haven, Phoebe (Apperson) Hearst, Ellen M. Henrotin, Robert G. Ingersoll, David Starr Jordan, Miranda W. Lux, Irena Ingersoll Rawlings, Emma B. Ryder, Caroline Maria (Seymour) Severance, William E. Sheldon, Anna Howard Shaw, Harriet Ingersoll Skilton, Jane L. Stanford, Charlotte Perkins Stetson, Sarah A. Stewart, Ada van Pelt, E. G. Waite, and Yung Wing. Taken from *Cornell University Collection of Regional History and the University Archives, Report of the Curator and Archivist* (Ithaca, NY: Cornell University Department of Manuscripts and University Archives, 1955).

11,548. Cornell, Dorothy
Papers. 1941. 4 items.
Open. Published guide.
Cornell University, Department of Manuscripts and University Archives.
Letters from Cornell, a resident of Ithaca, to Eva Thomas, a resident of Owego, NY, relate primarily to the history of Ithaca families. Taken from *Cornell University Collection of Regional History and the University Archives, Report of the Curator and Archivist* (Ithaca, NY: Cornell University

Department of Manuscripts and University Archives, 1951).

11,549. Cornell, Ethel Letitia
Papers. 1906-64. 4 ft.
Open. Published guide.
Cornell University, Department of Manuscripts and University Archives.
Correspondence, articles, reports, proceedings of meetings, bibliographies, and other papers of Cornell (1892-1963), a psychologist, pertain to intelligence testing and the nature of intelligence, exceptional children, growth studies, the characteristics of high school students, language usage of high school students, early secondary education in New York state, mental health, the certification and role of the school psychologist, the New York State Psychological Intern Training Program, the activities of the American Psychological Association and the New York State and American Associations of Applied Psychology, and other related topics. Also includes Cornell's notes from college courses, her creative writing, and other nonscientific manuscripts. Taken from *Cornell University Collection of Regional History and the University Archives, Report of the Curator and Archivist* (Ithaca, NY: Cornell University Department of Manuscripts and University Archives, 1974).

11,550. Cornell, Ezra
Papers. 1806-1943. 28 cu.ft. and 5 microfilm reels.
Open. Published guides.
Cornell University, Department of Manuscripts and University Archives.
Papers of Cornell (1807-74), a businessman, mechanic, and philanthropist, include letters to his wife Mary Ann Cornell and their son Alonzo B. Cornell. Correspondence relates to Cornell family genealogy; telegraphy; the production of coal oil; state and national politics; the Tompkins County and New York State Agricultural Society; his philosophy of education; the founding, staffing, and equipping of Cornell University; and conditions of travel. Also includes correspondence of the Cornell family, of Elizabeth (Cady) Stanton, and of Maria Mitchell (1818-89). Taken from *Cornell University Collection of Regional History and the University Archives, Report of the Curator and Archivist* (Ithaca, NY: Cornell University, 1946); *Cornell University Collection of Regional History and the University Archives, Report of the Curator and Archivist* (Ithaca, NY: Cornell University Department of Manuscripts and University Archives, 1949); *Cornell University Collection of Regional History and the University Archives, Report of the Curator and Archivist* (Ithaca, NY: Cornell University Department of Manuscripts and University Archives, 1951); *Cornell University Collection of Regional History and the University Archives, Report of the Curator and Archivist* (Ithaca, NY: Cornell University Department of Manuscripts and University Archives, 1955); *Cornell University Collection of Regional History and the University Archives, Report of the Curator and Archivist* (Ithaca, NY: Cornell University Department of Manuscripts and University Archives, 1959); *Cornell University Collection of Regional History and the University Archives, Report of the Curator and Archivist* (Ithaca, NY: Cornell University Department of Manuscripts and University Archives, 1974).

11,551. Corson, Hiram
Papers. 1852-1946. 7 ft.
Open. Published guide.
Cornell University, Department of Manuscripts and University Archives.
Scrapbooks of Corson (1828-1911) relate to his travels, life, and career as a professor at various colleges. Includes correspondence between Corson and colleagues concerning Shakespeare, Chaucer, Tennyson, and Browning; correspondence with friends and family members dealing chiefly with personal matters; a scrapbook devoted to spiritualism, including letters from and about Madame Helena Petrovna Blavatsky, confounder of the American Theosophical Society; and accounts of the travels of Corson, his wife Caroline, and their son Eugene and of their daily work and activities. Correspondents include Mary Cowden Clarke. Taken from *Cornell University Collection of Regional History and the University Archives, Report of the Curator and Archivist* (Ithaca, NY: Cornell University Department of Manuscripts and University Archives, 1959).

11,552. Coulter, Margaret Elizabeth
Papers. 1907-08. 8 items.
Open. Unpublished guide.
Cornell University, Department of Manuscripts and University Archives.
Letters Coulter (1881-1939) wrote to "Charlie" while she was a student at Cornell. In her letters she describes her train trip to Ithaca, her studies, her family, her loneliness, and her need for money.

11,553. Crangle, Roland, and Crangle, Emily Elkus
Papers. 1898-1955. 1.8 cu.ft.
Open. Published guide.
Cornell University, Department of Manuscripts and University Archives.
Scrapbooks of Roland Crangle (1862-1945), a Buffalo, NY, attorney, and of his wife Emily Crangle (1878-?), both of whom were prominent in Buffalo social and political life, include correspondence, speeches, clippings, and other items. Papers pertain to Emily Crangle's activities in the Erie County chapter of the LWV, her appointment to the board of visitors of the New York State Agricultural and Industrial School at Industry, NY, her social work, and her interest in state politics as well as to Roland Crangle's legal career, his candidacy for the US House of Representatives on the Democratic ticket, and his interests in the future of Ireland and New York state politics. Correspondents include Frances Perkins, Grace A. Reavy, and Eleanor Roosevelt. Taken from *Cornell University Collection of Regional History and the University Archives, Report of the Curator and Archivist* (Ithaca, NY: Cornell University Department of Manuscripts and University Archives, 1959).

11,554. Crawford, Ada L.
Papers. 1862. 1 item.
Open. Published guide.
Cornell University, Department of Manuscripts and University Archives.
Letter from [Miss] Crawford, a resident of Fulton, NY, to L. P. Storms, a lieutenant in the 1st Engineers Corps d'Afrique in New Orleans. She discusses local social activities and the return of Captain Fox, an officer who had been seriously wounded at the second battle of Bull Run. Taken from *Cornell University Collection of Regional History and the University Archives, Report of the Curator and Archivist* (Ithaca, NY: Cornell University Department of Manuscripts and University Archives, 1963).

11,555. Crawford, Charlotte Holmes
Papers. 1908-66. 1 vol., 84 items, and 23 ft. of microfilm.
Open. Published guide.
Cornell University, Department of Manuscripts and University Archives.
Crawford (1885-1971) was an actress, a nurse during WWI, chairman of the French department at Erasmus Hall High School, and an author. Contains a diary in which she describes her trip to Italy and Greece with Mr. and Mrs. Lewis Leaming Forman and Mabel Virginia Root in 1908, with observations on people and places and numerous mythological references; reminiscences of her years at Cornell; her poetry; speeches, press releases, pamphlets, and broadsides concerning the Fight for Freedom Committee, a group she belonged to that campaigned for US participation in WWII; a 1966 letter that refers to Crawford's opposition to the House Un-American Activities Committee; and her biography of Sidney A. Reeve, a thermodynamics engineer and author who attempted to organize a social and political movement called the "consumerists." Taken from *Cornell University Collection of Regional History and the University Archives, Report of the Curator and Archivist* (Ithaca, NY: Cornell University Department of Manuscripts and University Archives, 1974).

11,556. Crawford, Mary Merritt
Papers. 1903-64. 33 items and 2 tapes.
Open. Published guide.
Cornell University, Department of Manuscripts and University Archives.
Papers of Crawford, a physician and alumni trustee who was married to Edward Schuster, include published letters that Crawford wrote while she was house surgeon at the American Ambulance Hospital in Neuilly-sur-Seine, France, from 1914 to 1915; tapes and transcripts of interviews with Crawford concerning her life as a Cornell student, her career as a doctor, and her service on the board of trustees at Cornell; correspondence, notes, photos, and printed items concerning alumni affairs, including biographical data on Cornell women; and campaign material and reports to the Cornell Alumni Corporation upon completion of each of her terms as alumni trustee. Taken from *Cornell University Collection of Regional History and the University Archives, Report of the Curator and Archivist* (Ithaca, NY: Cornell University Department of Manuscripts and University Archives, 1974).

11,557. Curtis, Charles William, and Curtis, Stephanie (Marx)
Papers. 1883-1916. 1 ft.
Open. Published guide.
Cornell University, Department of Manuscripts and University Archives.
Includes correspondence between the Curtises before their marriage, letters of recommendation that various Cornell professors wrote for Stephanie Marx, and scrapbooks the Curtises kept while they were students at Cornell. Taken from *Cornell University Collection of Regional History and the University Archives, Report of the Curator and Archivist* (Ithaca, NY: Cornell University Department of Manuscripts and University Archives, 1959).

11,558. Curtiss, Charles
Papers. 1870-1901. 1 ft. and 2 vols.
Open. Published guide.
Cornell University, Department of Manuscripts and University Archives.
Includes letters to Cornelia Curtiss from Mrs. C. W. Fiske, the mother of Willard Fiske, and from Caroline [Mrs. Hiram] Corson, which contain detailed descriptions of their European travels as well as references to Jennie McGraw and other residents of Ithaca. Taken from *Cornell University Collection of Regional History and the University Archives, Report of the Curator and Archivist* (Ithaca, NY: Cornell University Department of Manuscripts and University Archives, 1955).

11,559. Dalley Family
Papers. 1883-1908. 4 in.
Open. Published guide.
Cornell University, Department of Manuscripts and University Archives.
Papers include an autograph book of Gretta M. Dalley for 1883 and photos. Taken from *Cornell University Collection of Regional History and the University Archives, Report of the Curator and Archivist* (Ithaca, NY: Cornell University Department of Manuscripts and University Archives, 1959).

11,560. Davenport Family
Papers. 1800-1949. 34 ft. and 29 vols.
Open. Published guides.
Cornell University, Department of Manuscripts and University Archives.
Includes correspondence, deeds and land contracts, photos, and other papers concerning land the Davenports and related families owned in western New York, Michigan, Nebraska, and elsewhere. Also includes such records of the Davenport Home for Female Orphan Children as bylaws; minutes of trustees' meetings; reports of the secretary-treasurer and the supervisor; construction, operating, and investment management accounts; and records of admissions and dismissals. Includes correspondence relating to legacies received by Fanny Davenport MacVeagh, Christina Davenport Sedgwick Marquand, Lily Cameron Sedgwick, Elizabeth C. Whitney Smith, Fanny C. Whitney Smith, and Christina C. Whitney. Taken from *Cornell University Collection of Regional History and the University Archives, Report of the Curator and Archivist* (Ithaca, NY: Cornell University Department of Manuscripts and University Archives, 1949); *Cornell University Collection of Regional History and the University Archives, Report of the Curator and Archivist* (Ithaca, NY: Cornell University Department of Manuscripts and University Archives, 1955); *Cornell University Collection of Regional History and the University Archives, Report of the Curator and Archivist* (Ithaca, NY: Cornell University Department of Manuscripts and University Archives, 1959); *Cornell University Collection of Regional History and the University Archives, Report of the Curator and Archivist* (Ithaca, NY: Cornell University Department of Manuscripts and University Archives, 1963).

11,561. Dean of Women
Records. 1916-53. 5 ft.
Open. Published guide.
Cornell University, Department of Manuscripts and University Archives.
Business and financial records of the dean of women's office, correspondence with the president and the board of trustees of Cornell, and correspondence and printed items pertaining to counseling activities, financial aid and employment for students and alumnae, housing, student conduct, student and alumnae activities and associations, and the history and activities of the Women's Self-Government Association. Taken from *Cornell University Collection of Regional History and the University Archives, Report of the Curator and Archivist* (Ithaca, NY: Cornell University Department of Manuscripts and University Archives, 1959).

11,562. Decision Making in Farm Families
Oral history. 1967-78. Ca. 200 tapes and ca. 310 vols.
Access restricted. Unpublished guide.
Cornell University, Department of Manuscripts and University Archives.
Tapes and transcripts of a documentation project conducted with the cooperation of a panel of 20 farm families. The goals of the project are "to obtain source material . . . to chronicle the evolution of individual farm families and to . . . support research on decision making in farm families." Information was gathered at two-year intervals from family members who were over 7 years old.

11,563. Decker, Aurelia
Papers. 1862. 1 item.
Open. Published guide.
Cornell University, Department of Manuscripts and University Archives.
Letter from Decker to relatives about the welfare of her husband Henry Decker, whose regiment was reported to have been at New Madrid, MO, and about other matters. Taken from *Cornell University Collection of Regional History and the University Archives, Report of the Curator and Archivist* (Ithaca, NY: Cornell University Department of Manuscripts and University Archives, 1959).

11,564. Department of Household Economics and Management
Records. Ca. 1917-62. 5.33 ft.
Open. Published guide.
Cornell University, Department of Manuscripts and University Archives.
Home economics extension records concern Buffalo, Rochester, and Syracuse, NY, and all New York counties. Includes annual reports and summaries of home economics and household management programs carried on by home demonstration agents; field trip reports by extension specialists from Cornell; counties' requests to the college of home economics for assistance with their extension program; reports from household study clubs, "kitchen conferences," and extension speakers; extension leaders' lesson plans; and related items. Taken from *Cornell University Collection of Regional History and the University Archives, Report of the Curator and Archivist* (Ithaca, NY: Cornell University Department of Manuscripts and University Archives, 1974).

11,565. Department of Household Economics and Management
Records. 1913-61. 60 ft.
Access restricted. Unpublished guide.
Cornell University, Department of Manuscripts and University Archives.
Survey records of the Department contain information on such topics as management of family finances by 195 families in Livingston County, NY; the cost of living for farm families in Tompkins County, NY; management of finances by 40 women graduate students; food shopping practices of families; acceptance of the mechanical dishwasher by 295 homemakers in Rochester, NY; decision making about household activities, as reported by 77 homemakers in New York state; and the daily activities of homemakers confined to wheelchairs, according to 10 homemakers in Ithaca. See *Documentation Newsletter,* vol. I, no. 1 (May 1975).

11,566. Department of Institution Management
Records. 1929-66. 1.67 ft.
Open. Published guide.
Cornell University, Department of Manuscripts and University Archives.
Includes minutes, correspondence, reports, plans, and other papers pertaining to projects such as the development of a moderately priced mobile kitchen for feeding large groups of people in emergencies, of training schools for industrial nutritionists, of school lunch programs, and of extension work in feeding migrant workers. Includes speeches and articles by Katharine W. Harris and other Cornell professors of home economics as well as correspondence of [Miss] Kathleen L. Cutlar, professor of institution management and manager of the home economics cafeteria, relating to cooking and institutional management problems. Taken from *Cornell University Collection of Regional History and the University Archives, Report of the Curator and Archivist* (Ithaca, NY: Cornell University Department of Manuscripts and University Archives, 1974).

11,567. Department of Speech and Drama
Records. 1893-1965. Ca. 15 ft.
Open. Published guide.
Cornell University, Department of Manuscripts and University Archives.
Includes a scrapbook containing correspondence, photos, programs, clippings, announcements, and broadsides relating to the Cornell Women's Dramatic Club, which merged with the Cornell Dramatic Club in 1925. Includes a letter from Georgia Laura White, a dean, to [Miss] Florence Dahme, president of the Cornell Women's Dramatic Club, in answer to Dahme's request for advice concerning the merging of the clubs and reminiscences that Dahme wrote in 1963. Taken from *Cornell University Collection of Regional History and the University Archives, Report of the Curator and Archivist* (Ithaca, NY: Cornell University Department of Manuscripts and University Archives, 1974).

11,568. Devereux, Mary D.
Papers. 1835-76. 6 in.
Open. Published and unpublished guides.
Cornell University, Department of Manuscripts and University Archives.
Scrapbooks of Devereux, a resident of Utica, NY, contain family correspondence, greeting cards, social announcements, fashion plates, and clippings. Includes letters pertaining to the election of 1840 and to the Roman Catholic missionary effort in America as well as correspondence of Nicholas Devereux and William Constable Pierrepont. Taken from *Cornell University Collection of Regional History and the University Archives, Report of the Curator and Archivist* (Ithaca, NY: Cornell University Department of Manuscripts and University Archives, 1955).

11,569. Donlon, Mary Honor
Oral history. 1966. 1 vol.
Access restricted. Unpublished guide.
Cornell University, Department of Manuscripts and University Archives.
Interview with Donlon (1893-), a judge and a Cornell trustee.

11,570. Dutchess County
Collection. 1806-65. 34 items.
Open. Published guide.
Cornell University, Department of Manuscripts and University Archives.
Includes a diary Mary T. Doty kept from April until October of 1865. Taken from *Cornell University Collection of Regional History and the University Archives, Report of the Curator and Archivist* (Ithaca, NY: Cornell University, 1946).

11,571. Eddy, Martha H.
Papers. 1934-48. 2 in.
Open. Published guide.
Cornell University, Department of Manuscripts and University Archives.
Correspondence, reports, circulars, questionnaires, and other printed items of Eddy (1881-1957), a home economics extension and administration specialist, pertain to public health, particularly pneumonia control, and the public health activities of the New York state department of health and the New York state home bureaus. Includes correspondence of Alexander D. Langmuir, Burt R. Rickards, Edward S. Rogers, and V. A. Van Volkenburgh. Taken from *Cornell University Collection of Regional History and the University Archives, Report of the Curator and Archivist* (Ithaca, NY: Cornell University Department of Manuscripts and University Archives, 1959).

11,572. Edwards, Richard Henry, Family
Papers. Ca. 1897-1953. 30 ft.
Open. Published guide.
Cornell University, Department of Manuscripts and University Archives.
Primarily the papers of Richard Edwards (1877-1954), a clergyman and religious educator. Includes his correspondence and diaries; personal correspondence of his wife Anna Rachel (Camp) Edwards (1876-1956); her examination books from Western Reserve University; items pertaining to the John Dewey Practice School at the University of Chicago, where she taught from 1897 to 1902; correspondence with her sister Katherine (Camp) Mayhew concerning the writing and publication of

their book on the School; and reminiscences of participants in this educational experiment, which were collected for use in their book. Collection also includes notes, outlines, drafts, and printed items reflecting the interest of Richard and Anna Edwards in the history of their respective families and of Lisle, the town in which they lived. Correspondents include Jane Addams, John Childs, Evelyn Dewey, John Dewey, Sherwood Eddy, Galen M. Fisher, Harriet Harding, Paul S. Livermore, Shailer Mathews, James A. G. Moore, John R. Mott, Walter Rauschenbusch, Vida Scudder, and Frank M. Sheldon. Taken from *Cornell University Collection of Regional History and the University Archives, Report of the Curator and Archivist* (Ithaca, NY: Cornell University Department of Manuscripts and University Archives, 1959).

11,573. Eells and Young
Papers. 1863-74. 2 vols.
Open. Published guide.
Cornell University, Department of Manuscripts and University Archives.
Consists of personal accounts and recipes of Mrs. H. B. Eells and farm and labor accounts of W. S. Young, both of whom were residents of Tompkins County, NY. Taken from *Cornell University Collection of Regional History and the University Archives, Report of the Curator and Archivist* (Ithaca, NY: Cornell University Department of Manuscripts and University Archives, 1951).

11,574. Eliot, Mabel
Papers. 1859-1932. 1 ft.
Open. Published guide.
Cornell University, Department of Manuscripts and University Archives.
Consists of Eliot family correspondence, handbills, pamphlets, a collection of maps, souvenirs of Bloomington, IL, and miscellaneous papers, which relate primarily to railroads and land development in the Midwest and to the sale of Indian reservation lands in 1904. Taken from *Cornell University Collection of Regional History and the University Archives, Report of the Curator and Archivist* (Ithaca, NY: Cornell University Department of Manuscripts and University Archives, 1947).

11,575. Elliott, Ellen Coit Brown
Papers. 1953-54. 30 items.
Open. Published guide.
Cornell University, Department of Manuscripts and University Archives.
Reminiscences of Ellen Brown (1860-1957), who married Orrin Leslie Elliott, include descriptions of Cornell president Andrew D. White and professor George Lincoln Burr, whom Brown assisted in White's library. Also includes a description of the activities and attitudes of women students at Cornell. Taken from *Cornell University Collection of Regional History and the University Archives, Report of the Curator and Archivist* (Ithaca, NY: Cornell University Department of Manuscripts and University Archives, 1955).

11,576. Ellis, Edith M.
Papers. 1924-33. 2 vols.
Open. Published guide.
Cornell University, Department of Manuscripts and University Archives.
Scrapbooks containing correspondence, clippings, and other papers of [Mrs. Willard W.] Ellis, a resident of Ithaca. Papers relate to her activities on the Democratic State Committee, the Democratic Union, the New York Federation of Women's Clubs, and other organizations. Correspondents include James A. Farley, Helen Keller, Herbert H. Lehman, [Mrs.] Caroline Love (Goodwin) O'Day, Eleanor Roosevelt, Franklin D. Roosevelt, and others. Taken from *Cornell University Collection of Regional History and the University Archives, Report of the Curator and Archivist* (Ithaca, NY: Cornell University Department of Manuscripts and University Archives, 1949).

11,577. Elsbree, Anna
Papers. 1788-1953. 4 ft.
Open. Published guide.
Cornell University, Department of Manuscripts and University Archives.
Correspondence of Elsbree, former librarian of the Cornell Public Library, relates to genealogy. Also includes Elsbree family correspondence dating from 1941 to 1951 and other Elsbree papers; an account and recipe book; notes and clippings on the history of Ithaca and of other towns in Tompkins County and elsewhere in the state; notebooks, notes, and clippings on the genealogy of numerous families; cemetery records of 14 towns in Tompkins County; a photograph of Llewellyn Elsbree; family and other photos; an autograph album; and pamphlets and broadsides. Taken from *Cornell University Collection of Regional History and the University Archives, Report of the Curator and Archivist* (Ithaca, NY: Cornell University Department of Manuscripts and University Archives, 1959).

11,578. Emerson, Alice Edwards
Papers. 1862-1933. 389-page item.
Open. Published guide.
Cornell University, Department of Manuscripts and University Archives.
Unpublished manuscript "A Mythology for Musicians: Ancient Greece and Modern Music" by Emerson (1862-1933), a musician and lecturer who married Alfred Emerson, a Cornell professor of archaeology. Also includes a letter from their daughter Edith about her mother's musical studies in Munich and her career as a piano teacher at Wellesley and at the Ithaca Conservatory, as a lecturer on music history at the University of Chicago, and as a lecturer on musical forms at Cornell and in Ithaca. The letter also relates to Alfred Emerson's professional activities and to the family's studies and travels in Europe and elsewhere. Taken from *Cornell University Collection of Regional History and the University Archives, Report of the Curator and Archivist* (Ithaca, NY: Cornell University Department of Manuscripts and University Archives, 1974).

11,579. Evans, Alice Catherine
Papers. 1908-65. 565 items.
Open. Published and unpublished guides.
Cornell University, Department of Manuscripts and University Archives.
Papers of [Miss] Evans (1881-), a bacteriologist, include letters from Carrie Chapman Catt, Paul de Kruif, Marie Dressler, Elmer V. McCollum, Veranus A. Moore, Henry Morgenthau, Jr., Bela Schick, Luther Terry, Martha Van Rensselaer, Hans Zinsser, and others in medicine, science, or public life. Also includes Evans's memoirs, scientific speeches, articles, reports, clippings, photos, and other papers relating to her participation in the first and second international congresses for microbiology; to a Cornell conference concerning fields of work for women, which Evans addressed in 1935; to her research on brucellosis, on other diseases, and on the problem of human infection through the milk of animals, which she conducted during her years as a dairy bacteriologist for the US Public Health Service. Taken from *Cornell University Collection of Regional History and the University Archives, Report of the Curator and Archivist* (Ithaca, NY: Cornell University Department of Manuscripts and University Archives, 1974).

11,580. Ewer, Mary Anita
Papers. 1922-36. 1.33 ft.
Partially restricted. Published guide.
Cornell University, Department of Manuscripts and University Archives.
Includes correspondence between [Miss] Ewer (1892-1961) and Cornell professor Edward L. Nichols, Tutomu Tanaka, and others concerning her work in preparing physics research for publication, together with charts, notes, and reports. Also includes letters from Ernest Merritt and D. T. Wilber, with whom she worked, and from editors of scientific publications; correspondence with Julia K. Sommer, clergymen, and others concerning theosophy and the activities of the Theosophical World-University; and Ewer's drafts and outlines on mystic symbolism. Taken from *Cornell University Collection of Regional History and the University Archives, Report of the Curator and Archivist* (Ithaca, NY: Cornell University Department of Manuscripts and University Archives, 1974).

11,581. Faculty Organizations
Records. 1900-76. 3 ft.
Open. Published guide.
Cornell University, Department of Manuscripts and University Archives.
Includes constitutions, bylaws, annual reports, minutes, financial records, committee reports, correspondence, questionnaires, historical sketches, and membership lists of the following organizations, all of which were composed chiefly of faculty wives: the Agricultural Circle, the Brides' Club, the Campus Book Club, the Campus Club, the Campus Club Choral Group, the Engineering Women's Club, and the Sibley Faculty Wives Society. See *Cornell University Collection of Regional History and the University Archives, Report of the Curator and Archivist* (Ithaca, NY: Cornell University Department of Manuscripts and University Archives, 1959); *Cornell University Collection of Regional History and the University Archives, Report of the Curator and Archivist* (Ithaca, NY: Cornell University Department of Manuscripts and University Archives, 1963); *Cornell University Collection of Regional History and the University Archives, Report of the Curator and Archivist* (Ithaca, NY: Cornell University Department of Manuscripts and University Archives, 1974).

11,582. Fairley and Stevens Families
Papers. 1837-1907. 8 in.
Open. Published guide.
Cornell University, Department of Manuscripts and University Archives.
Correspondence, diaries, accounts, and estate settlement papers of William D. Fairley (?-1871) and his wife Catherine Fairley, who later married Melvin James Stevens. Includes correspondence of Catherine Fairley's sister Mrs. Hugh Moore, a resident of Nashua, IA; her son Charles Fairley, who lived in Nebraska; the Copeland family; other relatives; and friends. Also includes diaries of Fannie Fairchild (Fairley), who married John L. Dillon, and of her brothers along with papers relating to Catherine Fairley's guardianship of her minor children. Taken from *Cornell University Collection of Regional History and the University Archives, Report of the Curator and Archivist* (Ithaca, NY: Cornell University Department of Manuscripts and University Archives, 1963).

11,583. Ferris
Collection. 1834-98. 2 in.
Open. Published guide.
Cornell University, Department of Manuscripts and University Archives.
Includes letters to [Mrs.] Mary Seymour, a resident of Dansville, NY, that John Todd of Tarrytown, NY, wrote from 1887 to 1898 concerning settlement of the estate of two sisters Mary and Carolina Masterton of Tarrytown. Also includes deeds, bills, agreements, maps, and other papers concerning the settlement of William Reed's estate. Taken from *Cornell University Collection of Regional History and the University Archives, Report of the Curator and Archivist* (Ithaca, NY:

Cornell University Department of Manuscripts and University Archives, 1947).

11,584. Ferry, Priscilla
Papers. 1957. 6-page item.
Open. Published guide.
Cornell University, Department of Manuscripts and University Archives.
Reminiscences that [Miss] Ferry wrote about her grandfather Andrew D. White and the Cornell campus. Taken from *Cornell University Collection of Regional History and the University Archives, Report of the Curator and Archivist* (Ithaca, NY: Cornell University Department of Manuscripts and University Archives, 1959).

11,585. Field, William R.
Papers. 1851-81. 1 box.
Open. Published guide.
Cornell University, Department of Manuscripts and University Archives.
Contains correspondence of Field, a resident of Pittstown, NY, and Mary Hyde, a resident of New York, who later married Field. Also includes a diary that Hyde kept. Taken from *Cornell University Collection of Regional History and the University Archives, Report of the Curator and Archivist* (Ithaca, NY: Cornell University Department of Manuscripts and University Archives, 1947).

11,586. Finch, Harriet
Papers. Ca. 1912. 2 vols.
Open. Published guide.
Cornell University, Department of Manuscripts and University Archives.
Photo albums of Finch contain photos of the Finch family, their home, the Cornell campus, Ithaca and the surrounding area, Atlantic City, and other subjects. Taken from *Cornell University Collection of Regional History and the University Archives, Report of the Curator and Archivist* (Ithaca, NY: Cornell University Department of Manuscripts and University Archives, 1959).

11,587. First Baptist Church of Ithaca
Records. 1811-1959. 9.5 ft.
Open. Published guide.
Cornell University, Department of Manuscripts and University Archives.
Includes annual Church letters; minutes of the board of trustees, the board of deacons and deaconesses, and business meetings; weekly reports of Church activities; and minutes and other records of the Northrup Circle, the Woman's Union, the Young People's Society of Christian Endeavor, and the Woman's Mission Circle and Missionary Society. Also includes historical sketches, photos, and lists of baptisms, dismissions, and deaths as well as records of the Danby Baptist Church and the First Baptist Church of Christ of Ithaca. Taken from *Cornell University Collection of Regional History and the University Archives, Report of the Curator and Archivist* (Ithaca, NY: Cornell University Department of Manuscripts and University Archives, 1963).

11,588. Fiske, Jennie (McGraw)
Papers. 1862-1913. 5 vols. and 169 items.
Open. Published guide.
Cornell University, Department of Manuscripts and University Archives.
Correspondence, accounts, and records pertaining to administration of the estate of [Mrs. Willard] Fiske (1840-81), a resident of Ithaca. Also includes a letter that Fiske, who then was Jennie McGraw, wrote to her uncle Thomas McGraw while she was visiting in Detroit in 1862. In the letter she describes the impact of the Civil War on Detroit. See *Cornell University Collection of Regional History and the University Archives, Report of the Curator and Archivist* (Ithaca, NY: Cornell University, 1946); *Cornell University Collection of Regional History and the University Archives, Report of the Curator and Archivist* (Ithaca, NY: Cornell University Department of Manuscripts and University Archives, 1951).

11,589. Fitch, Asa
Papers. 1831-ca. 1957. 75 items.
Open. Published guides.
Cornell University, Department of Manuscripts and University Archives.
Papers of Fitch (1809-79), an entomologist, include a narrative concerning Fitch's daughter Sarah Elizabeth (Fitch) Poates and her life as a schoolmistress and plantation wife near Bolton, MS, before and during the Civil War, with mentions of the Fitch household during her early girlhood in Salem, NY. Using the pseudonym May Agnes Marston, Poates's granddaughter [Mrs.] May Beattie Johnson, a Salem resident, wrote the narrative in the form of correspondence to "Amy," a fictitious character. Also includes Poates's notes on her grandfather John Lemuel Poates and a photo of her. Taken from *Cornell University Collection of Regional History and the University Archives, Report of the Curator and Archivist* (Ithaca, NY: Cornell University Department of Manuscripts and University Archives, 1951); *Cornell University Collection of Regional History and the University Archives, Report of the Curator and Archivist* (Ithaca, NY: Cornell University Department of Manuscripts and University Archives, 1974).

11,590. Fowler and Wells
Papers. 1848-87. 263 items.
Open. Published guide.
Cornell University, Department of Manuscripts and University Archives.
Letters to members of the Wells and Fowler families, who were on the staff of *The Phrenological Journal,* which was published in New York. Correspondents include Susan B. Anthony, Antoinette Brown, and Sarah Grimké. Taken from *Cornell University Collection of Regional History and the University Archives, Report of the Curator and Archivist* (Ithaca, NY: Cornell University, 1946).

11,591. Fraser, Helen Anderson
Papers. 1918-66. 10.17 ft.
Open. Published guides.
Cornell University, Department of Manuscripts and University Archives.
Correspondence, diaries for 1918 to 1961, reports, newsletters, press releases, programs, posters, and other items of [Miss] Fraser (1902-), a medical librarian and 1925 graduate of Cornell, pertain to her interest in the Albany Inter-Racial Council, the New York State Commission Against Discrimination, Unitarian church work, health insurance plans, folklore studies, and many other civic and cultural activities. Correspondents include Mary R. Fraser and Helen R. Gilmore. Taken from *Cornell University Collection of Regional History and the University Archives, Report of the Curator and Archivist* (Ithaca, NY: Cornell University Department of Manuscripts and University Archives, 1963); *Cornell University Collection of Regional History and the University Archives, Report of the Curator and Archivist* (Ithaca, NY: Cornell University Department of Manuscripts and University Archives, 1974).

11,592. Gannett, Caroline Werner
Papers. 1947-63. 5.5 ft.
Open. Published and unpublished guides.
Cornell University, Department of Manuscripts and University Archives.
Correspondence of [Mrs. Frank E.] Gannett (1894-), a civic leader who was a resident of Rochester, NY, mainly concerns her work as a member or supporter of the New York State Board of Regents, the White House Conference on Children and Youth, the Syracuse University Youth Development Center, the Republican party, the Gannett Newspaper Foundation, the Gannett Youth Center, the Gannett Company board, and the Frank Gannett Newspaperboy Scholarship, Inc. Correspondents include Thomas E. Dewey, Howard A. Dillingham, Edward R. Eastman, Deane W. Malott, Richard M. Nixon, and Nelson A. Rockefeller. Also includes material concerning her awards and honorary degrees and printed items relating to conferences on youth. Taken from *Cornell University Collection of Regional History and the University Archives, Report of the Curator and Archivist* (Ithaca, NY: Cornell University Department of Manuscripts and University Archives, 1974).

11,593. Gardiner, Elizabeth Greene
Papers. 1847-1968. 2.7 ft.
Open. Inventory.
Cornell University, Department of Manuscripts and University Archives.
Correspondence, diaries, reports, student essays, photos, clippings, pamphlets, and memorabilia of Gardiner (1890-), a social worker and professor. Collection consists primarily of letters Gardiner wrote to her family about her personal and professional life; she describes her service during WWI as a nurses' aid with the Italian Red Cross, her medical social work on Ellis Island from 1919 to 1922, her assistant professorship at the University of Minnesota, her service as a welfare officer for the UN Relief and Rehabilitation Administration in Egypt, Italy, and Germany from 1944 to 1946, and many other activities. Also includes family correspondence, with letters from Gardiner's mother Eliza Doane Gardiner to Ellen Parkman Vaughan.

11,594. Gaskill, Gussie Esther
Papers. 1931-59. 38 items.
Open. Published guide.
Cornell University, Department of Manuscripts and University Archives.
Correspondence of Gaskill (1898-), librarian of the President White Historical Library and curator of the Wason Collection, with Roland H. Bainton, George Lincoln Burr, and others pertaining to her position as librarian, her expertise on the Far East, and her association with Burr and Carl L. Becker, both as a student and a friend. Taken from *Cornell University Collection of Regional History and the University Archives, Report of the Curator and Archivist* (Ithaca, NY: Cornell University Department of Manuscripts and University Archives, 1974).

11,595. Gates and Moore Family
Papers. 1847-1913. 1.2 cu.ft.
Open. Published guide.
Cornell University, Department of Manuscripts and University Archives.
Correspondence, accounts, and other papers of Lillian Gates and Katherine [Mrs. M. J.] Moore, residents of Savona, NY, relate to investments in land and tenancy in Michigan, North Dakota, Illinois, and Oklahoma and to investments in the East Lynn Railroad and other eastern enterprises. Also includes a diary of a trip to New Orleans in 1897, bills, bankbooks of Katherine Moore, clippings, and items relating to a transatlantic cruise. Taken from *Cornell University Collection of Regional History and the University Archives, Report of the Curator and Archivist* (Ithaca, NY: Cornell University Department of Manuscripts and University Archives, 1949).

11,596. George Junior Republic
Records. 1807-1966. 59.8 cu.ft.
Partially restricted. Published and unpublished guides.
Cornell University, Department of Manuscripts and University Archives.
Records relate to William Reuben George (1866-1936), founder of the Republic, which was an experiment in youthful self-government

established in 1895 with a group of boys from the slums of New York; the Republic operated on the principle of "nothing without labor." To oppose the Child Labor Amendment, which also contradicted the principles of the Republic, George also formed the League of Adult Minors to combat the threat of the Amendment as well as communism, socialism, pacifism, and the welfare state. Records of the Republic include a constitution, articles on the farm scheme and on relations with outside business organizations, early sketches concerning a social sanitarium idea adopted in 1915, work schedules and plans, notes on the children as census takers, records of applicants, case studies, and correspondence regarding the establishment of a vocational bureau for alumni. Also includes records relating to George's work with the National Association of Junior Republics and to his contacts with leaders of welfare and fraternal organizations. Correspondents include Juliet Baldwin, Mrs. Thomas Broadhurst, Mrs. Harry Emerson, Ida Minerva Tarbell, Harriet Amelia Boyer, Iva Ellis, Kate Fowler, Agnes Hocking, Josephine MacLeod, Pauline Brooks McClelland, Susan Dixwell Miller, Vera Cober Rockwell, and Helen Tripp. Also includes family correspondence, including letters George wrote to his wife Esther Ide Brewster George (1872-1962) and his daughter Edith George Freeborn; papers of Esther George, including correspondence with friends and former citizens, a diary, her notebooks on the Republic, guest books, and address books; correspondence of Edith Freeborn with former citizens and friends; and a George family genealogy. Taken from Douglas A. Bakken, ed., *The William R. George and George Junior Republic Papers* (Ithaca, NY: Collection of Regional History and University Archives, Cornell University, 1970). Also taken from *Cornell University Collection of Regional History and the University Archives, Report of the Curator and Archivist* (Ithaca, NY: Cornell University Department of Manuscripts and University Archives, 1951); *Cornell University Collection of Regional History and the University Archives, Report of the Curator and Archivist* (Ithaca, NY: Cornell University Department of Manuscripts and University Archives, 1959); *Cornell University Collection of Regional History and the University Archives, Report of the Curator and Archivist* (Ithaca, NY: Cornell University Department of Manuscripts and University Archives, 1963); *Cornell University Collection of Regional History and the University Archives, Report of the Curator and Archivist* (Ithaca, NY: Cornell University Department of Manuscripts and University Archives, 1974).

11,597. Gibson, Margaret Purdy

Papers. 1890-91. 2 vols.
Open. Published guide.
Cornell University, Department of Manuscripts and University Archives.
Scrapbook of [Mrs.] Gibson (1849-?), a factory inspector who resided in Syracuse, NY, contains clippings concerning her periodic inspections of fire escapes, sanitation facilities, and the general working conditions in factories employing women and young people in Syracuse, Rochester, Oswego, and elsewhere in a 10-county area of central New York. Papers also refer to the dismissal of another inspector Mrs. Alexander Bremer and to the policies of chief factory inspector James Connolly. Taken from *Cornell University Collection of Regional History and the University Archives, Report of the Curator and Archivist* (Ithaca, NY: Cornell University Department of Manuscripts and University Archives, 1974).

11,598. Girls' Friendly Society

Records. 1893-1924. 1 vol.
Open. Published guide.
Cornell University, Department of Manuscripts and University Archives.
Minutes of the western New York diocesan organization of the Society. Taken from *Cornell University Collection of Regional History and the University Archives, Report of the Curator and Archivist* (Ithaca, NY: Cornell University Department of Manuscripts and University Archives, 1951).

11,599. Gould, Hannah (Wright)

Papers. 1834-1913. 1 vol., 97 items, and 1 microfilm reel.
Open. Published guides.
Cornell University, Department of Manuscripts and University Archives.
Includes letters to Gould (1819-1912) from her father Thomas Wright; correspondence of her brother Thomas Wright concerning family finances and statements of account; and letters from John Stanton Gould, whom she married in 1849, who discusses his travels to the New York towns of Utica, Syracuse, Rochester, and Niagara Falls as well as to Washington, DC, and other locations. In his letters John Gould also describes his lectures at Cornell, the hostility that he felt faculty wives exhibited toward women students, and a visit to Union Springs, where he called on Susanah Howland and attended a Quaker meeting. Also includes letters to Hannah Gould from a friend in Germantown, PA, referring to the need for assistance in caring for the wounded after the battle of Gettysburg; social correspondence of Hannah Gould, her daughters, and other women relatives; correspondence pertaining to Gould's interest in Barbara (Haver) Frietchie; Gould's diary, in which she describes her life in Hudson, NY, and reflects upon religion; Gould family genealogical charts and notes, which Gould's granddaughter Dorothy C. Abbott compiled; and data on the related Atterbury, Bakewell, Gilpin, Gregg, Lawton, Newton, Parker, Rodman, Wanton, and Wright families. Gould's diary is available on microfilm. Taken from *Cornell University Collection of Regional History and the University Archives, Report of the Curator and Archivist* (Ithaca, NY: Cornell University Department of Manuscripts and University Archives, 1963); *Cornell University Collection of Regional History and the University Archives, Report of the Curator and Archivist* (Ithaca, NY: Cornell University Department of Manuscripts and University Archives, 1974).

11,600. Gould, John Stanton

Papers. 1823-1914. 5 vols. and 164 items.
Open. Published guides.
Cornell University, Department of Manuscripts and University Archives.
Papers of Gould (1812-74), a New York state assemblyman, agriculturist, and Cornell trustee and nonresident faculty member, include letters in which his mother Hannah (Rodman) Gould mentions Quaker meetings and refers to lectures held in Newport, RI, on phrenology, magnetism, Millerism, and other subjects; the influx of summer visitors to the town; smallpox and whooping cough epidemics; the death of John Gould's first wife Mary Ashby Gould (1817-43); and other matters. Also includes letters from John Gould to his daughter Mary (Gould) Baldwin concerning the history and genealogy of the Goulds and the related Mott, Rodman, Stanton, and Wanton families as well as the Newport of his boyhood, his interest in the antislavery and temperance movements and in scientific agriculture, his views on religion and politics, and his marriage to Mary (Gould) Baldwin's mother Sarah Ashby Gould and annotations of the letters by his granddaughter Dorothy C. Abbott. Also includes John Gould's journal for 1847 to 1850, in which he refers to the antislavery movement, prison reform, the need for improvement in agricultural and medical education, the care of the insane, temperance, and other issues of the day. Taken from *Cornell University Collection of Regional History and the University Archives, Report of the Curator and Archivist* (Ithaca, NY: Cornell University Department of Manuscripts and University Archives, 1963); *Cornell University Collection of Regional History and the University Archives, Report of the Curator and Archivist* (Ithaca, NY: Cornell University Department of Manuscripts and University Archives, 1974).

11,601. Harmon Association for the Advancement of Nursing

Records. 1926-51. 11 ft.
Open. Inventory.
Cornell University, Department of Manuscripts and University Archives.
Minutes of trustees meetings from 1926 to 1948, of executive committee meetings from 1927 to 1948, and of corporation meetings from 1926 to 1950; treasurer's reports; correspondence; a scrapbook containing publicity material; and printed items of the Association, which was affiliated with the Harmon Foundation in New York City.

11,602. Hatheway Family

Papers. 1788-ca. 1900. 5.5 ft.
Open. Published and unpublished guides.
Cornell University, Department of Manuscripts and University Archives.
Includes family papers of Samuel Gilbert Hatheway or Hathaway (1780-1867), a resident of Bristol County, MA, and a US congressman from 1833 to 1835. Contains letters from his first wife Sarah Emerson and letters by their eldest daughter Sarah (1811-72) and her husband Benajah T. Whitney, which they wrote during a stay in Clarksville, TN, concerning the town's society and their reactions to the institution of slavery. Also contains correspondence of their second daughter Welthea Hannah Boyd (1817-55), who married John W. Boyd, a resident of Wisconsin; of their third daughter Lavinia Matilda (1819-85), primarily with her younger sister concerning her reading of Swedenborg, other literary subjects, and domestic matters; and of their fourth daughter Elizabeth Dorothea (1823-1908) who, after her father's marriage to Catherine Saxton, resumed her studies at Miss Spafard's school in Philadelphia.

Elizabeth Hatheway wrote home about her social life; fashions; customs in Philadelphia; her teachers and fellow students; her studies in literature, languages, and drawing; her visits to Mount Vernon and Washington, where she made observations on the demeanor of Cass, Clay, Seward, and Webster in the US Senate; and matters of current interest, such as mesmerism. Elizabeth Hatheway's other letters concern her teaching at boarding schools; her work as a governess to Helen Johnstone on a plantation in Madison County, MS; her observations of slaves and the religious instructions she gave them; yellow fever epidemics; camp meetings; and her travels with her niece Caroline Boyd (1848-82) in the British Isles, western Europe, and the Near East. Elizabeth Hatheway's correspondents include Mary A. (Holland) Ryan, a governess in Tennessee, who describes her duties and the monotony and isolation of plantation life; Annie Devlin, a teacher at the Utica Female Seminary, who writes about the lectures of professor Orson Squire Fowler, her own phrenological analyses, and her views on women's rights and other issues; Mary Lockhart (Lawson) Birckhead, poet and onetime secretary of the Mount Vernon Association, who describes her work, literary tastes, and the position of independent women; and Henry Sanson of Canton, MS, who details the postwar fortunes of mutual friends and the condition of the freed Negro. Also includes Elizabeth Hatheway's scrapbooks, which contain annotated papers relating to travel, literature, and history. Additional correspondents and others represented in the papers include Marianna Arnot, Mary Elizabeth (Thropp) Cone, and Kate F. (Miller) Peabody. Taken from *Cornell University Collection of Regional History and the University Archives, Report of the Curator and Archivist* (Ithaca, NY: Cornell University

Department of Manuscripts and University Archives, 1974).

11,603. Hauck, Hazel Marie
Papers. 1924-60. 2.67 ft.
Open. Published guide.
Cornell University, Department of Manuscripts and University Archives.
Hauck (1900-64) was a professor of food and nutrition, a nutrition specialist for the Cornell-in-Thailand Project, and a field consultant for the Village Improvement and Leadership Training Program of the Unitarian Service Committee in Awo Amamma, Eastern Nigeria, in 1959 and 1960. Includes correspondence with former students and Cornell administrators; her Nigerian diaries; notes, statistical reports, and pamphlets concerning nutrition and disease in Thailand, Nigeria, and elsewhere; her articles concerning her work in these countries; photos showing children suffering from malnutrition; and notes, syllabi, reading lists, and other material relating to courses she taught at Cornell. Taken from *Cornell University Collection of Regional History and the University Archives, Report of the Curator and Archivist* (Ithaca, NY: Cornell University Department of Manuscripts and University Archives, 1974).

11,604. Hauser, Rita E.
Phonotape. 1970. 1 tape.
Open. Unpublished guide.
Cornell University, Department of Manuscripts and University Archives.
Tape of a lecture given at Cornell University by Hauser (1934-), an attorney and US representative to the UN Commission on Human Rights.

11,605. Hazzard, Florence (Woolsey)
Papers. 1819-1966. 1.4 cu.ft. and 2 microfilm reels.
Partially restricted. Published and unpublished guides.
Cornell University, Department of Manuscripts and University Archives.
Papers of Hazzard (1903-), a writer and psychologist, deal chiefly with her studies of eminent American women. Includes letters from Mary (Ritter) Beard concerning the disposition of the Emily Howland papers, the World Center for Women's Archives, and writing and publishing problems; from Marjorie White concerning the dissolution of the Women's Archives and Hazzard's research; from Carrie Chapman Catt concerning Howland and her papers and commenting on the history of the women's rights movement in the US and her own part in it; and from Isabel Howland concerning Hazzard's interest in the career of her aunt Emily Howland. Also includes correspondence with relatives and associates of Lillie (Devereux) Blake and Katherine Devereux Blake, Rachel Brooks Gleason, Angelina and Sarah Grimké, and Cornelia Hancock. In addition, collection contains copies of or excerpts from an 1819 letter from Emma (Hart) Willard, correspondence of Eliza Mosher and her family, and an unpublished manuscript "Woman Pioneers in Democracy," which includes essays on Abigail (Smith) Adams, Susan B. Anthony, Lydia Maria Child, Margaret Fuller, the Grimké sisters, Lucretia (Coffin) Mott, Elizabeth (Cady) Stanton, and Emma Willard. Also contains two unpublished biographies of Eliza Mosher; short sketches of Cornelia Hancock, Julia Ward Howe, Alice Freeman Palmer, Lucy Stone, and Harriet Tubman and of physicians Elizabeth Blackwell, Amanda Sanford Hickey, and Eliza Maria Mosher; notes, transcripts, bibliographies, pamphlets, offprints, or clippings concerning Mary Sheldon Barnes, Prudence Crandall, Harriet May Mills, and May Preston Slosson; and photos of many women, including those who attended the Woman Suffrage Convention in Washington, DC, in 1891 and Harriet (Ross) Tubman with a number of Negroes. Also includes letters from various professors relating to Hazzard's course work and experiments on the psychology of odor perception, correspondence relating to her marriage, photos, and other papers of the Hazzard family. Taken from *Cornell University Collection of Regional History and the University Archives, Report of the Curator and Archivist* (Ithaca, NY: Cornell University Department of Manuscripts and University Archives, 1974).

11,606. Helm, Elizabeth Sager
Papers. 1913. 1 item.
Open. Published guide.
Cornell University, Department of Manuscripts and University Archives.
Letter in which Helm (1837-1925), an adopted daughter of Marcus Whitman, describes the circumstances of her adoption and Whitman. Taken from *Cornell University Collection of Regional History and the University Archives, Report of the Curator and Archivist* (Ithaca, NY: Cornell University Department of Manuscripts and University Archives, 1947).

11,607. Hennessy, Mame
Papers. 1915-65. 0.3 cu.ft.
Open. Inventory.
Cornell University, Department of Manuscripts and University Archives.
Papers of Mary L. Hennessy, an actress whose stage name was Mame Hennessy, include correspondence, post cards, photos, clippings, and printed items. Relating primarily to her career, the collection also contains items concerning activities of the movie industry in Ithaca in the early 20th century. Hennessey and other actresses acted for the Essanay Movie Company, which shot films in Ithaca at Cayuga Lake and several nearby gorges. Collection includes photos of such actresses as Irene Castle and Pearl White as well.

11,608. Hicks, Mabel Claudia
Papers. 1892-1915. 4 in.
Open. Published guide.
Cornell University, Department of Manuscripts and University Archives.
Correspondence of Hicks concerns her employment as a teacher from 1908 to 1913. Also includes copies of examinations, undated essays, and school notebooks. Taken from *Cornell University Collection of Regional History and the University Archives, Report of the Curator and Archivist* (Ithaca, NY: Cornell University Department of Manuscripts and University Archives, 1963).

11,609. Hight, Mary A.
Papers. 1876-83. 4 vols.
Open. Published guide.
Cornell University, Department of Manuscripts and University Archives.
Diaries of Hight, a resident of Bradford, NY. Taken from *Cornell University Collection of Regional History and the University Archives, Report of the Curator and Archivist* (Ithaca, NY: Cornell University, 1946).

11,610. Hill, May Ashmore Thropp
Papers. Ca. 1916-64. 1 ft.
Open. Unpublished guide.
Cornell University, Department of Manuscripts and University Archives.
Papers of [Mrs. William Holcombe] Hill (1899-1967), an attorney and New Jersey assemblywoman from 1924 to 1927, include correspondence pertaining to a defense appropriation bill in the New Jersey legislature and to the New Jersey State Hospital at Trenton, where she served on the board of managers from 1949 to 1957; photo albums and a scrapbook pertaining to Hill when she was a student at Cornell; clippings; and printed items. Hill also served on the joint appropriations committee, the commission investigating women's working conditions, and the board of directors of the Trenton YWCA. She also was a member of the Women's Republican League.

11,611. Hitchcock, Martha L.
Papers. 1899-1944. 4 in.
Open. Unpublished guide.
Cornell University, Department of Manuscripts and University Archives.
Papers of [Miss] Hitchcock (1869-1966) primarily pertain to her career as principal of the Campus School in Ithaca from 1896 to 1923. Includes correspondence relating to Hitchcock's efforts to obtain a teaching certificate from New York state and letters to her from students and others, an account book, school accounts, a notebook of students' names, and a record book, which lists student names and ages by grade and summarizes the teaching program in reading, arithmetic, spelling, geography, and English. Also includes a tribute book presented to Hitchcock by her students' parents in 1944 when she retired as principal of the Cayuga Heights School in Ithaca, where she had served since 1923. The volume contains a biography of Hitchcock that was written by her nephew.

11,612. Hochbaum, Elfrieda
Papers. Ca. 1906-63. 3.5 ft. and 26 ft. of microfilm.
Open. Published and unpublished guides.
Cornell University, Department of Manuscripts and University Archives.
Primarily manuscripts of published and unpublished novels, short stories, and other writings by [Miss] Hochbaum (1877-1962), who received her PhD in 1903. Hochbaum was married to Paul Russel Pope, a professor of German at Cornell. Taken from *Cornell University Collection of Regional History and the University Archives, Report of the Curator and Archivist* (Ithaca, NY: Cornell University Department of Manuscripts and University Archives, 1974).

11,613. Holbrook, Frederick
Papers. 1863. 3-page item.
Open. Published guide.
Cornell University, Department of Manuscripts and University Archives.
Fair copy of letter to Holbrook (1813-1909), a governor of Vermont, from Roxy [Mrs. Abram] Holmes, a resident of Kents Corners, VT, who requests that her three sons, all Civil War casualties, be transferred to the military hospital at Brattleboro, VT. Taken from *Cornell University Collection of Regional History and the University Archives, Report of the Curator and Archivist* (Ithaca, NY: Cornell University Department of Manuscripts and University Archives, 1959).

11,614. Hopkins, Emma Santee
Papers. 1912. 2 items.
Open. Unpublished guide.
Cornell University, Department of Manuscripts and University Archives.
Letter in which [Mrs. Alva A.] Hopkins, a passenger on the S.S. *Mauretania,* describes the reaction of the passengers and crew to the news of the sinking of the S.S. *Titanic.* She notes that she and her husband had changed their booking from the *Titanic* to the *Mauretania* at the last moment and describes the rough weather.

11,615. Hopper, Arvilla
Papers. 1865-1915. 27 items.
Open. Published guide.
Cornell University, Department of Manuscripts and University Archives.
Includes correspondence and receipts of the Hopper family, residents of Ithaca, as well as a scrapbook, clippings, and a portfolio of items pertaining to Abraham Lincoln. Taken from *Cornell University Collection of Regional History and the University Archives, Report of the Curator and Archivist* (Ithaca, NY: Cornell University

Department of Manuscripts and University Archives, 1947).

11,616. Howland, Emily

Papers. 1797-1932. 5.6 cu.ft. and 15 microfilm reels.
Open. Published and unpublished guides.
Cornell University, Department of Manuscripts and University Archives.
[Miss] Howland (1827-1929) was an educator, reformer, and philanthropist. Primarily includes incoming letters about alleged fraudulent solicitations for support of the Negro refugees in Canada, the misuse of Quaker aid to "contrabands" in the US, the trials of those attempting to establish schools for escaped slaves and freedmen in the South, and life at Oberlin College, including a recounting of President Charles Grandison Finney's opinion of John Brown and other abolitionists. Also includes correspondence regarding a northerner's scheme for colonizing Northumberland County, VA; the woman suffrage movement in New York; the temperance crusade; the Universal Peace Union and National Arbitration League of Washington; and women's higher education in Great Britain. Correspondents include Caroline F. Putnam, Lillie Devereux Blake, Mary E. Bowman, Emma V. Brown, Phoebe Hathaway, Sallie Holley, Elizabeth Palmer Peabody, and Julia A. Wilbur.

The only daughter of a prosperous Quaker family, Howland grew up in Sherwood, NY. At the age of 30 she went to Washington, DC, to teach black girls in a normal school. She nursed and taught in refugee slave camps near Washington during the Civil War and raised funds for the refugees. After the War she started a school in Heathsville, VA, on land her father helped her purchase. She supported this school for 50 years. After her parents' death she contributed funds from her inheritance to normal and industrial schools in the South. She also worked for woman suffrage, the temperance cause, and in her later years for international peace. Also includes papers of the related Howland and Tallcot families. Taken from Patricia H. Gaffney, ed., *The Emily Howland Papers at Cornell University: A Guide to the Microfilm Publication* (Ithaca: Department of Manuscripts and University Archives, Cornell University Libraries, 1975). Also taken from *Cornell University Collection of Regional History and the University Archives, Report of the Curator and Archivist* (Ithaca, NY: Cornell University Department of Manuscripts and University Archives, 1974).

11,617. Hoyt, Julia A.

Papers. 1819?. 3 vols.
Open. Published guide.
Cornell University, Department of Manuscripts and University Archives.
Accounting textbooks of Hoyt, a resident of Oneida County, NY. Taken from *Cornell University Collection of Regional History and the University Archives, Report of the Curator and Archivist* (Ithaca, NY: Cornell University Department of Manuscripts and University Archives, 1951).

11,618. Hubbell, Henry Salem

Papers. 1800-1954. 4.8 ft.
Open. Published and unpublished guides.
Cornell University, Department of Manuscripts and University Archives.
Includes family correspondence of Hubbell (1869-1949), a portrait artist and head of the school of painting and decoration at the Carnegie Institute of Technology in Pittsburgh; letters from Hubbell and his wife Nellie Rose (Strong) Hubbell to his benefactor [Mrs.] Lydia Arms Avery Coonley Ward; typescripts and proofs of the journals, plays, short stories, articles, and verse of Nellie Hubbell, including *If I Could Fly* (New York and London, 1917), a group of stories in free verse for children; and papers concerned with the history and genealogy of the Hubbell (sometimes Hubbels or Hubbel), Gleason, Rockwell, and related families. Taken from *Cornell University Collection of Regional History and the University Archives, Report of the Curator and Archivist* (Ithaca, NY: Cornell University Department of Manuscripts and University Archives, 1963); *Cornell University Collection of Regional History and the University Archives, Report of the Curator and Archivist* (Ithaca, NY: Cornell University Department of Manuscripts and University Archives, 1974).

11,619. Hull, Charles H.

Papers. 1733-1945. 5 ft., 4 in., 1 box, and 22 items.
Open. Published guides.
Cornell University, Department of Manuscripts and University Archives.
Papers of Hull, a professor of American history at Cornell, include correspondence and other papers of his sister [Miss] Mary J. Hull, one-time treasurer of the Ithaca Children's Home. Her papers pertain to the 1934 and 1937 annual reports of the Home, which were sent to the New York state department of social welfare. Also includes financial accounts, correspondence, and other items of the Ithaca Children's Home and the Ladies Union Benevolent Society. Taken from *Cornell University Collection of Regional History and the University Archives, Report of the Curator and Archivist* (Ithaca, NY: Cornell University Department of Manuscripts and University Archives, 1947); *Cornell University Collection of Regional History and the University Archives, Report of the Curator and Archivist* (Ithaca, NY: Cornell University Department of Manuscripts and University Archives, 1951); *Cornell University Collection of Regional History and the University Archives, Report of the Curator and Archivist* (Ithaca, NY: Cornell University Department of Manuscripts and University Archives, 1959); *Cornell University Collection of Regional History and the University Archives, Report of the Curator and Archivist* (Ithaca, NY: Cornell University Department of Manuscripts and University Archives, 1963).

11,620. Humphreys, Robert

Papers. 1845-92. 43 items.
Open. Published guide.
Cornell University, Department of Manuscripts and University Archives.
Letters to Humphreys, a carpenter in Dublin, Ireland, and Windsor, England, from his aunt and uncle Honora and John Fleming, residents of Philadelphia; cousins; and a friend in the US, all of whom urge him to immigrate to America. In their letters they mention the wages offered in the US in his trade, and they keep him informed about family matters. Also includes letters to his mother Sarah Humphreys from her sister Honora Fleming about family matters. Taken from *Cornell University Collection of Regional History and the University Archives, Report of the Curator and Archivist* (Ithaca, NY: Cornell University Department of Manuscripts and University Archives, 1959).

11,621. Hyde Family

Papers. 1863-1960. 3.6 cu.ft.
Open. Published guides.
Cornell University, Department of Manuscripts and University Archives.
Correspondence, clippings, and other papers of [Miss] Florence Elise Hyde, the daughter of Orange Percy Hyde, chiefly concern her literary activities, her support of the repeal of the 18th Amendment, her interest in national politics and American foreign policy, and Ithaca social and civic life. Also includes papers of her father and family correspondence of her brother Walter Woodburn Hyde, much of it from the years when he was teaching at the Northampton, MA, high school and Princeton University, traveling in Great Britain, and studying in Athens, Rome, Halle, and other European cities. Correspondents include George Lincoln Burr, Alfred M. Landon, Frances Folsom Cleveland Preston, Pauline Morton Sabin, Grace Alvana Seeley, Jouett Shouse, and Robert A. Taft. See *Cornell University Collection of Regional History and the University Archives, Report of the Curator and Archivist* (Ithaca, NY: Cornell University Department of Manuscripts and University Archives, 1959); *Cornell University Collection of Regional History and the University Archives, Report of the Curator and Archivist* (Ithaca, NY: Cornell University Department of Manuscripts and University Archives, 1963).

11,622. Intercollegiate Bureau of Occupations

Records. 1914-15. 9 items.
Open. Published guide.
Cornell University, Department of Manuscripts and University Archives.
The Bureau was founded in 1911 by the Cornell Women's Club of New York and alumnae of various women's colleges with the fourfold aim of finding positions outside the teaching field for women with college educations, professional or technical training, or valuable experience; placing both men and women social workers; providing vocational counseling; and performing research concerning vocational problems. Includes an annual report, a letter sent to members asking for contributions, committee reports, a report concerning the work of the Bureau since its origin, and lists of the board of directors and committees. Taken from *Cornell University Collection of Regional History and the University Archives, Report of the Curator and Archivist* (Ithaca, NY: Cornell University Department of Manuscripts and University Archives, 1974).

11,623. Ithaca City Federation of Women's Organizations

Records. 1920-49. 5 ft.
Access restricted. Inventory.
Cornell University, Department of Manuscripts and University Archives.
Includes constitutions; minutes of executive committee meetings, 1910-65, along with minutes of executive board and organization meetings; and items pertaining to the Federation, which was formed in 1910 by the Ithaca Women's Club, the WCTU, and the Political Study Club. The group now includes more than 50 women's organizations. Also includes records concerning the Women's Community Building in Ithaca, which the Federation built and maintains.

11,624. Ithaca Methodist Church

Records. 1821-1963. 12 ft.
Open. Published and unpublished guides.
Cornell University, Department of Manuscripts and University Archives.
Records of the Church, which since has been renamed St. Paul's United Methodist Church, include trustees' minutes and correspondence, treasurer's reports, accounts of the Sabbath School Society, and records of marriages and baptisms. Also includes secretary's minutes and attendance books of the Loyal Daughters' Class; minutes of the Ladies' Social Union, the Ladies' and Pastor's Christian Union, and the Ladies' Aid Society; minutes, treasurer's reports, accounts, and attendance books of the Woman's Home Missionary Society, the Foreign Missionary Society, the India Missionary Society, and the Young Woman's Foreign Missionary Society; and minutes, a scrapbook, and other papers of the Women's Society of Christian Service, which was formed in 1940 through the merger of the earlier women's organizations. Taken from *Cornell University Collection of Regional History and the University Archives, Report of the Curator and Archivist* (Ithaca, NY: Cornell University Department of Manuscripts and University Archives, 1974).

11,625. Ithaca Woman's Club
Records. 1895-1963. 4 in.
Open. Unpublished guide.
Cornell University, Department of Manuscripts and University Archives.
Includes minutes taken in 1902, account books, a scrapbook containing a history of the Club, speeches, a list of charter and early members, photos, and programs, historical notes, and outlines of talks of the home economics section of the Club, a women's social and service organization in Ithaca, which was founded by Mrs. William H. Riley in 1895.

11,626. Ives, Eliza
Papers. 1849-68. 2 in.
Open. Published guide.
Cornell University, Department of Manuscripts and University Archives.
Letters to Ives, a schoolgirl who lived in Salisbury, NY, from friends and relatives who describe social life in a small town and problems in teaching there. Includes printed items and papers relating to the Mount Pleasant Presbyterian Church in Raymilton, PA. Taken from *Cornell University Collection of Regional History and the University Archives, Report of the Curator and Archivist* (Ithaca, NY: Cornell University Department of Manuscripts and University Archives, 1955).

11,627. Jean, Sally Lucas
Papers. 1948-72. 1 vol. and 11 items.
Open. Unpublished guide.
Cornell University, Department of Manuscripts and University Archives.
Papers of [Miss] Jean (1878-1971), a health educator, consist of her correspondence with her cousin John Sellman Woolman, correspondence concerning Jean, a 1948 testimonial from the American School Health Association, a 1949 article from *The Journal of School Health,* and a dissertation Marguerite Vollmer wrote about Jean in 1970. Jean graduated from the Maryland Hospital Training School for Nurses in 1898. She served as director of the Child Health Organization of America from 1918 to 1923 and as director of the health education division of the American Child Health Association from 1923 to 1924.

11,628. Jenkins, Anna Eliza
Papers. 1908-61. 1 vol. and 69 items.
Open. Published guide.
Cornell University, Department of Manuscripts and University Archives.
Papers of Jenkins (1886-), a mycologist for the US Department of Agriculture, include professional correspondence; class and laboratory notes and drawings from courses in rural social conditions, botany, and plant pathology; a thesis entitled "Lettuce Drop and Its Control in the Greenhouse"; and certificates and awards. Taken from *Cornell University Collection of Regional History and the University Archives, Report of the Curator and Archivist* (Ithaca, NY: Cornell University Department of Manuscripts and University Archives, 1974).

11,629. Jenkins, Minnie Kimball
Papers. 1903-30. 1.25 ft.
Open. Published guide.
Cornell University, Department of Manuscripts and University Archives.
Papers of [Miss] Jenkins (1883-), a bacteriologist. Includes notes from graduate work she undertook at George Washington University and printed matter from the US Department of Agriculture, the New York State College of Agriculture, and the New York State Agricultural Experiment Station concerning dairy cows, eggs, milk, and storage. Taken from *Cornell University Collection of Regional History and the University Archives, Report of the Curator and Archivist* (Ithaca, NY: Cornell University Department of Manuscripts and University Archives, 1963).

11,630. Jones, Sarah
Papers. 1865-1933. 9-page item.
Open. Published guide.
Cornell University, Department of Manuscripts and University Archives.
Description that Jones wrote about life in Madison County, NY; Minnesota; and Dakota Territory. Taken from *Cornell University Collection of Regional History and the University Archives, Report of the Curator and Archivist* (Ithaca, NY: Cornell University Department of Manuscripts and University Archives, 1947).

11,631. Kelly-Gadol, Joan
Phonotape. 1969. 1 tape and 1 transcript.
Open. Unpublished guide.
Cornell University, Department of Manuscripts and University Archives.
Tape and transcript of a lecture given by Kelly-Gadol (1928-), a professor of European history at the City College of New York.

11,632. Kingsley, Carter Robie
Papers. 1887-1951. 60 ft.
Open. Published guide.
Cornell University, Department of Manuscripts and University Archives.
Papers of Kingsley, a lawyer, include those of his mother Mary (Robie) Kingsley, who was the daughter, wife, and mother of Bath, NY, attorneys. Her papers (ca. 1 box) include social correspondence; announcements of births, deaths, marriages, and funerals; invitations to social affairs in Bath and surrounding towns; family photos and records; and photos taken on a trip to Europe and trips to the western US. See *Cornell University Collection of Regional History and the University Archives, Report of the Curator and Archivist* (Ithaca, NY: Cornell University Department of Manuscripts and University Archives, 1955).

11,633. Kitchelt, Florence Ledyard (Cross)
Papers. 1896-1954. 26 items.
Open. Published guide.
Cornell University, Department of Manuscripts and University Archives.
Papers of Cross (1874-1961), who married Richard Kitchelt, include letters from Susan Dixwell [Mrs. Gerrit Smith] Miller concerning Cross's settlement house work in Brooklyn; correspondence, notes, and reminiscences concerning the beginnings of the George Junior Republic; and family correspondence and printed items. Taken from *Cornell University Collection of Regional History and the University Archives, Report of the Curator and Archivist* (Ithaca, NY: Cornell University Department of Manuscripts and University Archives, 1963).

11,634. Knox, Helen M.
Papers. 1945. 1 vol.
Open. Published guide.
Cornell University, Department of Manuscripts and University Archives.
Notebook, probably owned by Knox, contains information about early Forest Home at Ithaca, with reminiscences by [Mrs.] Charlotte Edwards and [Miss] Mary E. McKinney. Taken from *Cornell University Collection of Regional History and the University Archives, Report of the Curator and Archivist* (Ithaca, NY: Cornell University Department of Manuscripts and University Archives, 1947).

11,635. Ladies' Auxiliary to the Sage Infirmary
Records. 1966-70. 0.3 ft.
Open. Unpublished guide.
Cornell University, Department of Manuscripts and University Archives.
Records of the Auxiliary, which supported the infirmary at Cornell; the Auxiliary was organized in 1966 by Jean Bredin Perkins, who was the wife of James A. Perkins, president of Cornell from 1963 to 1969. Includes reports of the treasurer, correspondence of the president and treasurer, executive board and membership rosters, and other subject files. The Auxiliary organized volunteers to help distribute flowers and messages, transport patients, and solicit funds for magazines and general support.

11,636. Ladies Union Benevolent Society
Records. 1921-47. 6 vols. and 20 items.
Open. Published guide.
Cornell University, Department of Manuscripts and University Archives.
Miscellaneous financial records of this Ithaca group. Taken from *Cornell University Collection of Regional History and the University Archives, Report of the Curator and Archivist* (Ithaca, NY: Cornell University Department of Manuscripts and University Archives, 1955).

11,637. Langdon, Ida
Papers. 1902-64. 43 items.
Open. Published guide.
Cornell University, Department of Manuscripts and University Archives.
[Miss] Langdon (1880-1964) was a professor and chairman of the English department at Elmira College. Papers pertain to Langdon's uncle Samuel Clemens, also known as Mark Twain, in particular to his life in Elmira, NY. Includes letters to her from Henry Nash Smith, Orville Prescott, and others regarding her speeches on Twain; articles by Langdon and others on Twain; speeches she gave on Twain; and clippings. Taken from *Cornell University Collection of Regional History and the University Archives, Report of the Curator and Archivist* (Ithaca, NY: Cornell University Department of Manuscripts and University Archives, 1974).

11,638. Legg, Mary
Papers. 1915-47. 33 items.
Open. Published guide.
Cornell University, Department of Manuscripts and University Archives.
Notes on the history of Speedsville, NY, and clippings, which were compiled by Legg, a local historian. Taken from *Cornell University Collection of Regional History and the University Archives, Report of the Curator and Archivist* (Ithaca, NY: Cornell University Department of Manuscripts and University Archives, 1959).

11,639. Loomis, Augustus Ward, Family
Papers. 1803-97. 123 items.
Access restricted. Published guide.
Cornell University, Department of Manuscripts and University Archives.
Letters by Loomis and his wife Mary Ann Loomis, Presbyterian missionaries to Chekiang Province in China, to Indians in the US, and to the Chinese in San Francisco. The letters concern such topics as their religious views and activities, their impressions of the places they visited, and their evaluation of the Chinese and the Creek and Cherokee Indians. Taken from *Cornell University Collection of Regional History and the University Archives, Report of the Curator and Archivist* (Ithaca, NY: Cornell University Department of Manuscripts and University Archives, 1974).

11,640. Loomis, Elisha
Papers. 1816-59. 32 items and 84 ft. of microfilm.
Open. Published and unpublished guides.
Cornell University, Department of Manuscripts and University Archives.
Papers of Loomis (1799-1836), a printer, missionary, linguist, and educator, include letters from his wife Maria Sartwell Loomis and others in Rushville and Rochester, NY, and an 1816 journal concerning his family's life in Rushville, into which Maria Loomis added entries in 1835 and 1836 concerning her husband's death and the later history of herself and their children. She also included a list of family birth and death dates.

Taken from *Cornell University Collection of Regional History and the University Archives, Report of the Curator and Archivist* (Ithaca, NY: Cornell University Department of Manuscripts and University Archives, 1974).

11,641. Lyon, Katherine
Papers. 1912-29. 0.3 ft.
Open. Unpublished guide.
Cornell University, Department of Manuscripts and University Archives.
Primarily letters that Lyon (1893-) wrote to her parents Mr. and Mrs. Stephen J. Lyon, residents of Hudson, NY, while she was a student at Cornell. She describes her activities, her classes, and her financial needs. The recipient of a state scholarship, Lyon graduated from Cornell in 1916. She later married Arthur J. Mix.

11,642. Lyons, Helen M.
Papers. 1957. 58 items.
Open. Published guide.
Cornell University, Department of Manuscripts and University Archives.
Letters to [Miss] Lyons, a stenographer, from faculty members, students, alumni, and fellow employees paying tribute to her for her 57 years of service to the Cornell physics department. Taken from *Cornell University Collection of Regional History and the University Archives, Report of the Curator and Archivist* (Ithaca, NY: Cornell University Department of Manuscripts and University Archives, 1974).

11,643. MacDonald Farm
Papers. 1793-1967. 4.67 ft., 1 vol., and 1 tape.
Open. Partial published guide.
Cornell University, Department of Manuscripts and University Archives.
Family correspondence, legal papers, wills, deeds, indentures, mortgages, inventories, photos, and household, farm, and mill accounts of the farm, which was located near Delhi, NY. Includes a tape and transcript of an interview in 1967 with two sisters who ran the farm. See *Cornell University Collection of Regional History and the University Archives, Report of the Curator and Archivist* (Ithaca, NY: Cornell University Department of Manuscripts and University Archives, 1955).

11,644. McDonald, Ruth Seely (Berry)
Papers. 1850-1959. 1.17 ft.
Open. Published guides.
Cornell University, Department of Manuscripts and University Archives.
Includes letters to McDonald (1913-) from her father Romeyn Berry concerning his writing for the *Ithaca Journal;* McDonald's positions in New York City, primarily with the publishing firm Walter J. Black, Inc.; Berry's daughter Hilda's service with the WACs during WWII; McDonald's marriage to William Naylor McDonald III; and the family history she wrote. Also includes letters from Hilda to her sister and father concerning the wartime situation in France and England; letters from Hendrik Willem van Loon to Ruth McDonald concerning his illustrating and writing; letters from Katharine "Kip" Fuertes concerning her brother Louis Agassiz Fuertes; and correspondence of the McDonald family of Jacksonville, FL, and Nashville and the related Hicks family. Other papers include a family history McDonald prepared, which contains historical, biographical, and genealogical information on William Bogardus Berry; his wife Elizabeth Wright (Gould) Berry; their children Romeyn and Harriet Esselstyn Berry, who later married James Wood Tyson; and other members of the Berry family and the family of Elizabeth Gould's father John Stanton Gould. Includes extracts from family correspondence, diaries, clippings, and photos. Taken from *Cornell University Collection of Regional History and the University Archives, Report of the Curator and Archivist* (Ithaca, NY: Cornell University Department of Manuscripts and University Archives, 1963); *Cornell University Collection of Regional History and the University Archives, Report of the Curator and Archivist* (Ithaca, NY: Cornell University Department of Manuscripts and University Archives, 1974).

11,645. McGraw Family
Papers. 1854-1956. 3 vols. and 114 items.
Open. Published guide.
Cornell University, Department of Manuscripts and University Archives.
Includes letters from Douglass Boardman to Jennie McGraw (1840-81) and later to Jennie and her husband Willard Fiske, whom she married in 1880. The letters concern financial matters, mutual friends, and local events. Also includes letters that Jennie Fiske wrote to her cousin Mary Celestia "Lettie" McGraw [Mrs. John C.] Gauntlett, Minna Gauntlett, and others from France, Italy, Germany, Russia, and Egypt, in which she gives her impressions of these and in particular of Moscow and Cairo; letters Harrison B. McGraw wrote to [Mrs.] Anna Gauntlett Whitcomb in 1941 concerning McGraw family genealogy; photos; and clippings. In addition, the collection contains diaries for 1875 and 1877 in which Jennie McGraw describes her travels to Philadelphia, New York, Detroit, Chicago, other American cities, England, and the Continent; her social life at home; her numerous callers and correspondents from among prominent Ithaca families and the Cornell University faculty; and her father's death and estate settlement problems. Taken from *Cornell University Collection of Regional History and the University Archives, Report of the Curator and Archivist* (Ithaca, NY: Cornell University Department of Manuscripts and University Archives, 1974).

11,646. Malott, Eleanor S.
Papers. 1958. 1 vol.
Open. Published guide.
Cornell University, Department of Manuscripts and University Archives.
Journal that Malott kept of her impressions of Russia and the Russian people during a two-week stay in the Soviet Union with her husband. Taken from *Cornell University Collection of Regional History and the University Archives, Report of the Curator and Archivist* (Ithaca, NY: Cornell University Department of Manuscripts and University Archives, 1959).

11,647. Mandeville Family
Papers. 1845-1934. 8 in.
Open. Published guide.
Cornell University, Department of Manuscripts and University Archives.
Papers of Emma L. (Underhill) Mandeville, whose father was an editor of the Bath, NY, *Advocate,* and of her husband Frederick Austin Mandeville, a physician. The Mandevilles were residents of Rochester, NY. Includes announcements and programs of voice recitals and concerts Emma Mandeville gave before and after her marriage and of recitals that both she and her husband gave after their marriage, especially while they were members of St. Peter's Presbyterian Church in Rochester. Taken from *Cornell University Collection of Regional History and the University Archives, Report of the Curator and Archivist* (Ithaca, NY: Cornell University Department of Manuscripts and University Archives, 1959).

11,648. Mansfield
Papers. 1825-69. 3 items.
Open. Published guide.
Cornell University, Department of Manuscripts and University Archives.
Consists of a composition and entry book and a Castle Hall Seminary notebook of Maria Mills Mansfield (?-1888) as well as a journal of a trip to Florida in 1868 and 1869. Mansfield married Hugh White (1798-1870) before 1833, the year in which their elder son William Mansfield White was born. See *Cornell University Collection of Regional History and the University Archives, Report of the Curator and Archivist* (Ithaca, NY: Cornell University Department of Manuscripts and University Archives, 1949).

11,649. Mekeel Family
Papers. 1839. 3-page item.
Open. Published guide.
Cornell University, Department of Manuscripts and University Archives.
Includes a letter in which Amy Quinby Mekeel (1785-1845) describes to Aaron Mekeel a trip in 1839 from Tompkins County to New York City to attend a yearly meeting of the Society of Friends. Taken from *Cornell University Collection of Regional History and the University Archives, Report of the Curator and Archivist* (Ithaca, NY: Cornell University Department of Manuscripts and University Archives, 1947).

11,650. Merritt, Bessie
Papers. 1874-1912. 7 items.
Open. Published guide.
Cornell University, Department of Manuscripts and University Archives.
Collection includes accounts, bills, fair programs for western New York, and a Fredonia State Normal School publication, which concern Merritt's mother Alice Jane Tooke [Mrs. Nelson G.] Merritt, Merritt herself, the Agricultural Society of Northern Chautauqua, the Farmers Institute, and the Sinclairville Fair Grounds Association. Includes a bill, dated 1874, for Alice Merritt's wedding dress. Bessie Merritt was on the staff that produced the Normal School publication. Taken from *Cornell University Collection of Regional History and the University Archives, Report of the Curator and Archivist* (Ithaca, NY: Cornell University Department of Manuscripts and University Archives, 1955).

11,651. Milhan, Mabel A.
Papers. Ca. 1913-63. 3 vols. and 60 items.
Open. Published guide.
Cornell University, Department of Manuscripts and University Archives.
Scrapbooks of [Miss] Milhan, a home demonstration agent in Rensselaer County, NY, contain clippings used to illustrate talks she gave during her 25 years in home demonstration work. Papers pertain to the history of food, clothing, customs, and home economics as well as to people who were active in home demonstration extension work. Also includes unmounted clippings and pamphlets. Taken from *Cornell University Collection of Regional History and the University Archives, Report of the Curator and Archivist* (Ithaca, NY: Cornell University Department of Manuscripts and University Archives, 1974).

11,652. Miller, Mary Rogers
Papers. 1954. 1 item.
Open. Published guide.
Cornell University, Department of Manuscripts and University Archives.
Letter in which Miller reminisces about her activities as a student at Cornell during the 1890s. Taken from *Cornell University Collection of Regional History and the University Archives, Report of the Curator and Archivist* (Ithaca, NY: Cornell University Department of Manuscripts and University Archives, 1955).

11,653. Mitchell Family
Papers. 1799-1900. 14 items.
Open. Published guide.
Cornell University, Department of Manuscripts and University Archives.
Includes letters to Eunice (Barney) Mitchell primarily from her daughters and other relatives concerning family matters, a scarlet fever epidemic,

a shipwreck off Nantucket, and whaling voyage preparations; poetry; a genealogy; Eunice and Benjamin Mitchell's 1799 marriage certificate; and a photo. Correspondents include Jane Barney and Nehemiah and Anna Mitchell Merritt. Taken from *Cornell University Collection of Regional History and the University Archives, Report of the Curator and Archivist* (Ithaca, NY: Cornell University Department of Manuscripts and University Archives, 1974).

11,654. Moore Family

Papers. 1751-1939. 0.4 cu.ft.
Open. Published guide.
Cornell University, Department of Manuscripts and University Archives.
Papers of the family include a corrected transcript of recollections written by the wife of an aide to General Jacob Brown about Lafayette, President Monroe, Mrs. Monroe, Louisa Catherine (Johnson) [Mrs. John Quincy] Adams, Rachel (Donelson) [Mrs. Andrew] Jackson, Henry Clay, and other people involved in Washington society during the winter of 1824-25. Taken from *Cornell University Collection of Regional History and the University Archives, Report of the Curator and Archivist* (Ithaca, NY: Cornell University Department of Manuscripts and University Archives, 1947).

11,655. Morehouse and Lang Families

Papers. 1843-1954. 1.33 ft.
Open. Published guide.
Cornell University, Department of Manuscripts and University Archives.
Includes papers of Emma Margaret Lang, who married Herbert H. Morehouse, including invitations to dances, a letter from Walter F. Willcox congratulating her on her approaching marriage, her notes from an English literature course, a copy of her thesis "The Tenement Poor of New York City," and room, board, and tuition receipts. Also includes letters of thanks from Hiram Corson to Emma's sister Rosa Christine Lang and notes of Sarah Tracy Barrows from a course on Goethe's life and works. Taken from *Cornell University Collection of Regional History and the University Archives, Report of the Curator and Archivist* (Ithaca, NY: Cornell University Department of Manuscripts and University Archives, 1974).

11,656. Morey, Nancy Booker

Papers. 1933-44. 1 ft.
Open. Unpublished guide.
Cornell University, Department of Manuscripts and University Archives.
Correspondence and pamphlets of [Mrs. Donald R.] Morey (1903-), a professor of food and nutrition at Cornell. Papers pertain primarily to her studies of nutrition and include correspondence and articles on the value of diets. Also includes some personal correspondence and reprints of articles on economics. Correspondents include Sybil L. Smith, administrator of Purnell Funds for Research, which provided support for Morey's research; Helen Atwater, editor of the *Journal of the American Home Economic Association;* and nutritionists Francis G. Benedict, Thorne M. Carpenter, and E. P. Cathcart.

11,657. Morris, Jacob

Papers. 1791-1935. 6 in.
Open. Published guide.
Cornell University, Department of Manuscripts and University Archives.
Papers of Morris (1755-1844), a lawyer, New York state senator, and resident of Butternuts, NY, contain correspondence primarily relating to family matters or Morris's activities as a land agent. Includes letters from his mother Mary Morris and from other family members. Also includes correspondence of Elizabeth (Schuyler) [Mrs. Alexander] Hamilton. Taken from *Cornell University Collection of Regional History and the University Archives, Report of the Curator and Archivist* (Ithaca, NY: Cornell University Department of Manuscripts and University Archives, 1959).

11,658. Morse Family

Papers. 1903-38. 1 vol. and 11 items.
Open. Published guide.
Cornell University, Department of Manuscripts and University Archives.
Includes a letter to Effie Dallas [Mrs. Virgil D.] Morse from Ellen M. Mitchell concerning a lecture Mitchell was to give in Ithaca on her "Beloved friend, Julie Ward Howe"; to Morse from her son Robert V. Morse concerning the anti-American attitude he had recently observed in Germany; and to Virgil Morse, a friend and benefactor of the Ithaca Reconstruction Home, from Governor Franklin D. Roosevelt, who expressed his regrets at being unable to attend the opening of the Home. Also includes scrapbooks of the Morses' daughter Dorothea Clara (Morse) Coors concerning her years at Ithaca High School, from which she graduated in 1908, and at Randolph-Macon Woman's College, 1903-09; remarks Martin D. Hardin, Jr., made upon the death of Effie Morse, emphasizing the contributions she made to the welfare of the Ithaca community; and pamphlets concerning the literary and civic interests of the family. Taken from *Cornell University Collection of Regional History and the University Archives, Report of the Curator and Archivist* (Ithaca, NY: Cornell University Department of Manuscripts and University Archives, 1974).

11,659. Murray, Elsie

Papers. Ca. 1896-1965. 43 ft.
Open. Published guide.
Cornell University, Department of Manuscripts and University Archives.
Murray (1878-1965) was a psychologist and a professor. Includes personal correspondence; scattered diaries from 1919 to 1940; manuscripts and notes pertaining to her interest in music, poetry, and social psychology; manuscripts of her unpublished fiction; accounts; her journal as secretary of the Cornell University music department from 1926 to 1927; notes from classes in which she was a student and a professor; photos; and clippings. Also includes correspondence, test forms and material, research testing notes, drafts of scientific writings, and printed matter pertaining to the studies and publications of Murray and fellow psychologists on color blindness and various aspects of color vision. Taken from *Cornell University Collection of Regional History and the University Archives, Report of the Curator and Archivist* (Ithaca, NY: Cornell University Department of Manuscripts and University Archives, 1974).

11,660. Nelson, Gertrude Jane, and Nelson, Ruth Augusta

Papers. 1891-97. Ca. 115 items.
Open. Published guide.
Cornell University, Department of Manuscripts and University Archives.
Letters that Gertrude Nelson (1872-1950) and Ruth Nelson (1876-?) wrote to their parents while they were residing at Sage College for Women concern activities at Sage College, courses and examinations, dating, parties, football games, clubs, Bible classes, Sage Chapel attendance, and the prices of clothing in Ithaca; their letters also contain observations on various Cornell figures. Also includes letters from their father Charles Alexander Nelson (1839-1933), a librarian at Columbia University, about family and friends. Taken from *Cornell University Collection of Regional History and the University Archives, Report of the Curator and Archivist* (Ithaca, NY: Cornell University Department of Manuscripts and University Archives, 1974).

11,661. New York State College of Home Economics

Oral history. 1962-66. 2787 pp.
Partially restricted. Published guide.
Cornell University, Department of Manuscripts and University Archives.
Includes interviews with Beulah Blackmore, a College teacher, concerning the development of curriculum in textiles and design at Cornell; with Sarah Gibson Blanding, a College president, relating to problems of college administration; with Orilla Butts, a College extension leader, pertaining to urban extension work in home economics; with Ellen Ann Dunham, a businesswoman, about her career at General Foods and the role of the home economist in business; with Mary Ford, a psychologist, concerning problems associated with placing a department of child development and family relationships in a college of home economics; with Clara Browning Goodman, a housewife, relating to her student and faculty experiences at Cornell in the department of home economics; with Mabel Rollins, an economist, pertaining to the program in home management at Cornell; and with Catherine Sharp, a housewife, about her experiences in the first class in home economics at Cornell. Taken from *Cornell University Collection of Regional History and the University Archives, Report of the Curator and Archivist* (Ithaca, NY: Cornell University Department of Manuscripts and University Archives, 1974).

11,662. New York State College of Home Economics

Records. 1877-1966. Ca. 45 cu.ft.
Open. Published and unpublished guides.
Cornell University, Department of Manuscripts and University Archives.
Contains records of the College as well as of the New York State Federation of Home Bureaus. College records include financial statements, correspondence, reports, studies, data, manuscripts, radio transcripts, speeches, photos, clippings, printed items, and other records. Subjects include resident teaching; research; international, national, state, and local public relations efforts; all-College activities; administration and personnel; departments and divisions of the College; buildings and equipment; and the history of the College, including items relating to Martha Van Rensselaer and Flora Rose. Correspondents include Katherine Rogers Adams, Clara M. Brown Arny, Liberty Hyde Bailey, Sarah Gibson Blanding, Mary Phillips Bleeker, Alice May Blinn, Janet H. Clark, Jeannette P. Davis, Mary H. Donlon, Mary F. Henry, Edith H. MacArthur, Catherine J. Personius, Eleanor Roosevelt, Virginia True, Florence J. B. Ward, and Mary B. Wood.

Records relating to the Federation include a constitution; bylaws; minutes of the organizational meeting, annual meetings, board of directors' meetings, and district meetings; programs and notes concerning citizenship leader training schools; reports and correspondence concerning the work of the Home Bureau, the resignations of the various local Home Bureaus from the New York State Home Bureau Federation, and the impending separation of the Federation from the New York Cooperative Extension Service, which was made official by legislation in 1956; and related clippings and photos. Also includes files of the Associated Country Women of the World, the New York State Council of Rural Women, home demonstration work, older rural youth, farm and home week, and the nutrition institute and nutrition committee. Correspondents include Mildred C. Aldridge, Orilla Wright Butts, Helen Canon, Helen G. Canoyer, Ruth Day, Anna Dickerson, Florence Freer, Beverly Tucker Galloway, Blanche Kelsey, Frances C. Ladd, Elizabeth McDonald, Cecile Perkins, Mary G. Phillips, Flora Rose, Frances Scudder, Ruby Green Smith, Frances R. Todd, Martha Van Rensselaer, Elizabeth Lee Vincent, Florence E.

Ward, and Carrie Williams. Taken from *Cornell University Collection of Regional History and the University Archives, Report of the Curator and Archivist* (Ithaca, NY: Cornell University Department of Manuscripts and University Archives, 1955); *Cornell University Collection of Regional History and the University Archives, Report of the Curator and Archivist* (Ithaca, NY: Cornell University Department of Manuscripts and University Archives, 1963); *Cornell University Collection of Regional History and the University Archives, Report of the Curator and Archivist* (Ithaca, NY: Cornell University Department of Manuscripts and University Archives, 1974).

11,663. New York State College of Home Economics: "Women Today"
Records. 1969. 8 transcripts.
Open. Unpublished guide.
Cornell University, Department of Manuscripts and University Archives.
Transcripts of tape recordings from a conference "Women Today," which was organized by Sheila Tobias, assistant to the vice-president for academic affairs at Cornell, and sponsored by the New York State College of Home Economics. Kate Millett, Betty Friedan, and other national women's leaders attended the conference to discuss topics, including "How Do Men Look at Women? How Do Women Look at Themselves?"; "The Political Dimension: Is This a Political Question?"; "Childbearing, Child Rearing, Abortion, and Contraception"; "Future of Women in America"; "The Psychological Differences Between Men and Women"; and "The Black Woman in America."

11,664. New York State Farm Bureau Women's Committee
Records. 1967. 1 tape and 1 vol.
Open. Unpublished guide.
Cornell University, Department of Manuscripts and University Archives.
Includes Committee members' discussions of the satisfaction found in farm life.

11,665. Nice, Margaret Morse
Papers. 1917-68. 5.8 ft.
Open. Unpublished guide.
Cornell University, Department of Manuscripts and University Archives.
Papers of Nice (1883-), an ornithologist who married Leonard Blaine Nice in 1909. Includes correspondence, manuscripts and reprints of her publications and scholarly articles, bird observation notes and notebooks, abstracts, excerpts, and files relating to her activities as associate editor of *Wilson Bulletin* and of *Bird Banding.* Nice was a member and president from 1937 to 1939 of the Wilson Ornithological Society.

11,666. North Family
Papers. 1814-82. 16 in.
Open. Published guide.
Cornell University, Department of Manuscripts and University Archives.
Personal and business papers of North family members and various relatives, most of whom resided in Walton or Unadilla, NY. Includes correspondence and accounts of Mary North and her first husband Roswell Wright, 1814-66; papers pertaining to the settlement of his estate and the guardianship of their children Elizabeth and Henry; and personal correspondence of the family, including letters to Henry Metzger from his mother, sister, and stepfather concerning the 1844 presidential campaign and election and the New York City winter social season. Also includes letters from Henry E. Bartlett, Mary North's second husband who was a physician and a Democratic politician, to his wife. Collection also includes correspondence or other papers of Delia Searing and Gertrude L. Vanderbilt. Taken from *Cornell University Collection of Regional History and the University Archives, Report of the Curator and Archivist* (Ithaca, NY: Cornell University Department of Manuscripts and University Archives, 1959).

11,667. Osborn, Agda Teoline Swenson
Papers. 1930-64. 1 vol. and 474 items.
Open. Published guide.
Cornell University, Department of Manuscripts and University Archives.
Includes letters to [Mrs.] Osborn (1898-), secretary of the women's class of 1920, from classmates concerning reunions and their personal activities; minutes, financial records, newsletters, and address lists for the class of 1920; accounts, reservations, and programs for various reunions; a scrapbook containing photos, biographical data, and clippings; and minutes from the Cornell Association of Class Secretaries. Taken from *Cornell University Collection of Regional History and the University Archives, Report of the Curator and Archivist* (Ithaca, NY: Cornell University Department of Manuscripts and University Archives, 1974).

11,668. Ostrander Family
Papers. 1877-ca. 1912. 10 items.
Open. Published guide.
Cornell University, Department of Manuscripts and University Archives.
Correspondence between the wife and children of John B. Ostrander (1810-79), residents of Dryden, NY, who discuss John Ostrander's death and family matters. Also includes photos with accompanying genealogical data. Taken from *Cornell University Collection of Regional History and the University Archives, Report of the Curator and Archivist* (Ithaca, NY: Cornell University Department of Manuscripts and University Archives, 1974).

11,669. Ostrander, John, Family
Papers. 1827-65. 1.3 cu.ft.
Open. Published guide.
Cornell University, Department of Manuscripts and University Archives.
Consists of letters that John Ostrander, a resident of Kennedyville, now Kanona, NY, wrote to his wife Eveline Ostrander describing his travels by stage, packet, foot, or raft in lower New York state, where he was selling lumber and cattle; an inventory of John Ostrander's effects; papers relating to Eveline Ostrander's suspension from the Second Presbyterian Church of Bath for embracing the doctrine of Universalism; and Civil War papers of Clinton N. and Dwight H. Ostrander, sons of Eveline and John Ostrander. Taken from *Cornell University Collection of Regional History and the University Archives, Report of the Curator and Archivist* (Ithaca, NY: Cornell University Department of Manuscripts and University Archives, 1959).

11,670. Palmer, Maud Alice
Papers. 1954-55. 23 items.
Open. Unpublished guide.
Cornell University, Department of Manuscripts and University Archives.
Correspondence between Harry Letsche and Emerson Hinchliff and others regarding requests for information about Palmer, (1869-1951), whose will established scholarships for Pittsburgh area students who wished to attend Cornell. Palmer, who became a schoolteacher at age 18, did not have enough money to attend college immediately after graduating from high school. She finally began college at the age of 41, and in 1918 she received an MA in English from Columbia University. Her will provided $160,000 for scholarships.

11,671. Palmer, Sarah Cornelia
Papers. 1813-97. 0.2 cu.ft.
Open. Published guide.
Cornell University, Department of Manuscripts and University Archives.
Family and business correspondence and other papers of Palmer (1844-?), a resident of Monterey, NY. Taken from *Cornell University Collection of Regional History and the University Archives, Report of the Curator and Archivist* (Ithaca, NY: Cornell University, 1946).

11,672. Peck Family
Papers. 1808-83. 2 in. and 2 vols.
Open. Published guide.
Cornell University, Department of Manuscripts and University Archives.
Contains letters that Mary Hopkinton wrote to Lucetta Abbott, 1832-41, mentioning Universalism in St. Lawrence County and describing McConnellsville, OH; correspondence, 1841-49, of members of the Olin family of Bloomingdale, WI, who discuss the conflict of religious sentiment with the realities of land speculation, the weather, prices, and the progress of settlement; and correspondence for 1851 of W. Abbott from Nevada City and Placerville, which relates to mining conditions. Also includes account books, 1843-83, of the Peck family, the members of which resided in Potsdam, NY. Taken from *Cornell University Collection of Regional History and the University Archives, Report of the Curator and Archivist* (Ithaca, NY: Cornell University Department of Manuscripts and University Archives, 1947).

11,673. Perception of Change in the Ithaca City School District
Oral history. 1966-74. 26 tapes and 18 vols.
Access restricted. Unpublished guide.
Cornell University, Department of Manuscripts and University Archives.
Tapes and transcripts include interviews with 12 women concerning the operation of and teaching in the Ithaca schools. From 1956 to 1961 voters in the Ithaca public school district rejected the appeal of the board of education for new school buildings, and in 1962 the board of education dismissed the superintendent of schools. Between 1966 and 1974, 22 persons, including six members of the board of education, the dismissed superintendent, and his successor, were interviewed to identify and consider the relationships between issues, individuals, and events associated with the rejection of the referendum, the superintendent's dismissal, and the subsequent development of alternative education in Ithaca.

11,674. Percy, Alice
Papers. 1888-1901. 55 items.
Open. Published guide.
Cornell University, Department of Manuscripts and University Archives.
Includes a letter from Jacob Gould Schurman denying [Miss] Percy (1871-1920) permission to leave Sage College at the beginning of the spring term, letters various professors wrote recommending Percy for a teaching position, photos, and programs. Percy later married Alton Winslow Leighton. Taken from *Cornell University Collection of Regional History and the University Archives, Report of the Curator and Archivist* (Ithaca, NY: Cornell University Department of Manuscripts and University Archives, 1974).

11,675. Perkham, Phila M.
Papers. 1854-75. 1 vol. and 2 items.
Open. Published guide.
Cornell University, Department of Manuscripts and University Archives.
Volume of Perkham, a resident of Wilton, IL, contains a diary for part of 1854, a copy of a poem, a list of books read, and notations on household expenses for 1862. Also includes a legal document. Taken from *Cornell University Collection of Regional History and the University Archives, Report of the Curator and Archivist*

(Ithaca, NY: Cornell University Department of Manuscripts and University Archives, 1951).

11,676. Perkins, Frances
Papers. 1958-65. 1 item and 1 tape.
Open. Partial published guide.
Cornell University, Department of Manuscripts and University Archives.
Letter in which [Miss] Perkins (1882-1965), US secretary of labor from 1933 to 1945, thanked Dorothy M. Gibson and her husband Anson Wright Gibson, a professor at Cornell, for the pleasant day she spent with them at church and at their home. Also includes a tape of a lecture given by Perkins in 1965. Taken from *Cornell University Collection of Regional History and the University Archives, Report of the Curator and Archivist* (Ithaca, NY: Cornell University Department of Manuscripts and University Archives, 1974).

11,677. Personius, Catherine Jane
Papers. 1930-67. 9.5 ft.
Open. Unpublished guide.
Cornell University, Department of Manuscripts and University Archives.
Papers of Personius (1904-), a professor of food and nutrition at Cornell, include articles and papers relating to home economics.

11,678. Political Equality Society of Bath
Records. 1898-1906. 1 vol.
Open. Published guide.
Cornell University, Department of Manuscripts and University Archives.
Journal of the Society, a Steuben County, NY, organization concerned primarily with women's suffrage but also interested in social improvement. Taken from *Cornell University Collection of Regional History and the University Archives, Report of the Curator and Archivist* (Ithaca, NY: Cornell University Department of Manuscripts and University Archives, 1951).

11,679. Pratt Family
Papers. 1885-1935. Ca. 370 items.
Open. Published guide.
Cornell University, Department of Manuscripts and University Archives.
Contains papers of Hortense Louise Black, who later married Schuyler Pratt, including letters from her family and a friend who was on a motorcycle tour of Europe, a letter from Martha Van Rensselaer concerning the use of a room in Prudence Risley Hall as a resting or guest room during Farmers' Week, and a scrapbook of photos, letter fragments, invitations, grade cards, and programs. Taken from *Cornell University Collection of Regional History and the University Archives, Report of the Curator and Archivist* (Ithaca, NY: Cornell University Department of Manuscripts and University Archives, 1974).

11,680. Prudence Risley Hall
Records. 1910-21. 1 vol.
Open. Published guide.
Cornell University, Department of Manuscripts and University Archives.
Scrapbook contains correspondence pertaining to the financing and construction of the Hall; correspondence, reports, clippings, and programs concerning operation of the women's dormitory and student-sponsored social activities; and reports on women's student government. Includes correspondence of Gertrude Nye, Mrs. Russell Sage, and Andrew D. White. Taken from *Cornell University Collection of Regional History and the University Archives, Report of the Curator and Archivist* (Ithaca, NY: Cornell University Department of Manuscripts and University Archives, 1959).

11,681. Quinby, Moses
Papers. 1810-63. 2 in.
Open. Published guide.
Cornell University, Department of Manuscripts and University Archives.
Consists of a diary Quinby kept of a journey in 1831 to Massilon, OH, and to the Zoar community as well as correspondence of Quinby's parents William and Hannah Quinby. The Quinby family was connected with an Owenite colony at Coxsackie, NY. Taken from *Cornell University Collection of Regional History and the University Archives, Report of the Curator and Archivist* (Ithaca, NY: Cornell University, 1946).

11,682. Rahn, Otto
Papers. 1952. 1 vol.
Open. Published guide.
Cornell University, Department of Manuscripts and University Archives.
Illustrated family history that Rahn (1881-), a professor of bacteriology, and his wife prepared for their children and grandchildren. The volume, which relates to Rahn family life in the US and Germany, includes reminiscences of both their families, their childhood experiences, their education, and their early careers in science as well as descriptions of Rahn's work as a teacher and research bacteriologist. Taken from *Cornell University Collection of Regional History and the University Archives, Report of the Curator and Archivist* (Ithaca, NY: Cornell University Department of Manuscripts and University Archives, 1959).

11,683. Randall, Henry Stephens
Papers. Ca. 1844-76. 1 microfilm reel.
Open. Published and unpublished guides.
Cornell University, Department of Manuscripts and University Archives.
Papers of Randall (1811-76), an agriculturist, educator, and author, include correspondence of his wife Jane Rebecca Polhemus Randall. Taken from *Cornell University Collection of Regional History and the University Archives, Report of the Curator and Archivist* (Ithaca, NY: Cornell University Department of Manuscripts and University Archives, 1974).

11,684. Rankin, Louise Spieker
Papers. 1937-52. 42 items.
Open. Published guide.
Cornell University, Department of Manuscripts and University Archives.
Letters from Rankin (1897-1951), an author, primarily to her mother concerning social life, household management, and travels in India where her husband Everett H. Rankin was a Standard Oil representative; her diary for 1939 to 1943; her unfinished biography of Liberty Hyde Bailey; and a notebook of information she collected on Indian trees. Taken from *Cornell University Collection of Regional History and the University Archives, Report of the Curator and Archivist* (Ithaca, NY: Cornell University Department of Manuscripts and University Archives, 1974).

11,685. Reed, Bertha (Wilder)
Papers. 1955. 8-page item.
Open. Published guide.
Cornell University, Department of Manuscripts and University Archives.
Reminiscences of [Mrs. Robert R.] Reed (1874-?) concern Cornell during the 1880s and 1890s. Includes anecdotes and brief commentaries about her father Burt Green Wilder, a professor, and other campus personalities; the campus social life; and living conditions at Cascadilla Place. Taken from *Cornell University Collection of Regional History and the University Archives, Report of the Curator and Archivist* (Ithaca, NY: Cornell University Department of Manuscripts and University Archives, 1959).

11,686. Richardson, Cora A. Chapman
Papers. 1906-14. 30 pp.
Open. Published guide.
Cornell University, Department of Manuscripts and University Archives.
Includes [Mrs.] Richardson's accounts of trips to Washington, DC, from Hornellsville, NY, in 1906; through New York and Canada during the summer of 1910; and to Rochester, Montreal, Quebec, Lake Champlain, Albany, and back to Hornell in 1913. Also includes a speech she made before the Girls' Friendly Society in 1914 in which she speaks about the Society's origin and purpose, about her hopes that women would enter politics, and about the recent appointment of a police matron. Taken from *Cornell University Collection of Regional History and the University Archives, Report of the Curator and Archivist* (Ithaca, NY: Cornell University Department of Manuscripts and University Archives, 1951).

11,687. Riley, Julia (Mack)
Papers. 1957. 1 vol.
Open. No guide.
Cornell University, Department of Manuscripts and University Archives.
Reminiscences of Riley (1879-1962), a 1901 graduate of Cornell and the daughter of Horace Mack, an assistant to the treasurer at Cornell, pertain to her early life in Cascadilla Building, the official student and faculty dormitory at Cornell, and to a display of the aurora borealis in Ithaca in ca. 1890.

11,688. Rivoire, Alice Cecilia (Sanderson)
Papers. 1925-48. 2.67 ft.
Open. Published guide.
Cornell University, Department of Manuscripts and University Archives.
Includes scrapbooks of Rivoire, who graduated from Cornell in 1941, containing manuscripts, notes, reports, and printed items concerning her school life, travel in the US and abroad, and her teaching career. Also includes letters written from Europe by her parents Cecilia Blandford Sanderson and Dwight Sanderson, a professor, and their cousin and traveling companion Flora (Grace) Prince; diaries Cecilia Sanderson kept while her husband was on sabbatic leave; a guest book from the Sanderson home; and photos. Taken from *Cornell University Collection of Regional History and the University Archives, Report of the Curator and Archivist* (Ithaca, NY: Cornell University Department of Manuscripts and University Archives, 1963).

11,689. Rochester Lyceum Theatre
Records. 1888-1934. 14 ft.
Open. Published and unpublished guides.
Cornell University, Department of Manuscripts and University Archives.
Owned by Abe E. Wollf and members of his family, the Theatre, which opened in 1888, presented drama, musical comedy, minstrel shows, summer stock productions, and silent films; it was host to such performers as Sarah Bernhardt, Helen Hayes, and the Barrymores. Includes financial records, correspondence with the manager Hattie Lutt concerning booking arrangements and Theatre operations, scrapbooks of clippings and press releases, and photos. Taken from *Cornell University Collection of Regional History and the University Archives, Report of the Curator and Archivist* (Ithaca, NY: Cornell University Department of Manuscripts and University Archives, 1974).

11,690. Root, Mabel Virginia
Papers. 1908. 17 items.
Open. Published guide.
Cornell University, Department of Manuscripts and University Archives.
Letters from Root (1870-1965) to her family concern a summer visit to Italy and Greece with Charlotte Holmes Crawford and Mr. and Mrs. Lewis Leaming Forman. Taken from *Cornell University Collection of Regional History and the*

University Archives, Report of the Curator and Archivist (Ithaca, NY: Cornell University Department of Manuscripts and University Archives, 1974).

11,691. Rose, Flora
Papers. 1923-53. 6.25 ft. and 1 tape.
Open. Published and unpublished guides.
Cornell University, Department of Manuscripts and University Archives.
Interview with [Miss] Rose (1874-1959), a professor and director of the New York State College of Home Economics, in which she reminisces about the establishment and growth of the college of home economics at Cornell and comments on the contributions of Liberty Hyde Bailey, Lillian Galbraith, Martha Van Rensselaer, Eleanor Roosevelt, and others. Also includes statistical data Rose collected during her study of the nutrition of Belgian schoolchildren following WWI. Taken from *Cornell University Collection of Regional History and the University Archives, Report of the Curator and Archivist* (Ithaca, NY: Cornell University Department of Manuscripts and University Archives, 1959); *Cornell University Collection of Regional History and the University Archives, Report of the Curator and Archivist* (Ithaca, NY: Cornell University Department of Manuscripts and University Archives, 1963).

11,692. Rose, Mabel
Papers. 1896-1915. 24 items.
Open. Published guide.
Cornell University, Department of Manuscripts and University Archives.
Includes an undergraduate scrapbook of Rose, who was a member of the Cornell University class of 1900; a Wayside-Aftermath Club scrapbook with photos and lists of members; items relating to the activities of the Cornell Women's Club; and other papers. Taken from *Cornell University Collection of Regional History and the University Archives, Report of the Curator and Archivist* (Ithaca, NY: Cornell University Department of Manuscripts and University Archives, 1951).

11,693. Rosenbloom
Papers. 1905-34. 11 vols.
Open. Published guide.
Cornell University, Department of Manuscripts and University Archives.
Accounts of Clara, Marcus, and Isaac Rosenbloom, residents of Syracuse, NY, relate to real estate. Taken from *Cornell University Collection of Regional History and the University Archives, Report of the Curator and Archivist* (Ithaca, NY: Cornell University Department of Manuscripts and University Archives, 1949).

11,694. Sage College Building
Records. 1871-85. 1 box.
Open. Published guide.
Cornell University, Department of Manuscripts and University Archives.
Contains records and accounts relating to the planning and construction of Sage College, the women's college at Cornell. Includes letters from George Kosmer, president of Antioch College, and James Fairchild, president of Oberlin College, relating to coeducation. Taken from *Cornell University Collection of Regional History and the University Archives, Report of the Curator and Archivist* (Ithaca, NY: Cornell University Department of Manuscripts and University Archives, 1951).

11,695. St. George, Katharine Price Collier
Papers. 1939-64. 84 ft.
Access restricted. Published and unpublished guides.
Cornell University, Department of Manuscripts and University Archives.
[Mrs.] St. George (1896-) was a US congresswoman from New York from 1947 to 1964. Papers primarily deal with her service in the House and include correspondence with her constituents in Rockland, Orange, Sullivan, and Delaware counties; with other citizens; and with her congressional colleagues concerning specific legislation and such issues as appropriations, agriculture, alien property, civil rights, conservation, flood control, foreign affairs and aid, the space program, health insurance, housing, poverty, and the administration of public welfare in the city of Newburgh, NY. Also includes speeches, bills, reports, and remarks pertaining to her effort to eliminate sex discrimination through the proposed Equal Rights Amendment; correspondence and memoranda concerning her tour of Spain and her visits to US military and naval bases in that country; bills introduced by St. George; motion pictures; tapes; photos; and clippings. Taken from *Cornell University Collection of Regional History and the University Archives, Report of the Curator and Archivist* (Ithaca, NY: Cornell University Department of Manuscripts and University Archives, 1974).

11,696. Salem Village
Collection. Ca. 1780-1959. 0.3 cu.ft.
Open. Published guide.
Cornell University, Department of Manuscripts and University Archives.
Includes scattered correspondence, accounts, legal papers, and other papers, three items of which relate to Laura B. Crane, a resident of Chimney Point, VT. Also includes reminiscences, historical and biographical sketches, photos, and programs, some of which pertain to the Salem Woman's Club. Taken from *Cornell University Collection of Regional History and the University Archives, Report of the Curator and Archivist* (Ithaca, NY: Cornell University Department of Manuscripts and University Archives, 1963).

11,697. Sandy Creek Congregational Church
Records. 1859-75. 1 vol.
Open. Published guide.
Cornell University, Department of Manuscripts and University Archives.
Contains records of the Ladies' Sewing Society and of the Sociable Society in Oswego County, NY. Taken from *Cornell University Collection of Regional History and the University Archives, Report of the Curator and Archivist* (Ithaca, NY: Cornell University Department of Manuscripts and University Archives, 1949).

11,698. Sanford, Hilda Truslow (Berry)
Papers. 1929-44. 1 vol.
Open. Published guide.
Cornell University, Department of Manuscripts and University Archives.
Scrapbook of Sanford (1916-) chiefly relates to her school days at Ithaca High School, Kent Place School, and Barnard College as well as to her service in the WACs during WWII. Taken from *Cornell University Collection of Regional History and the University Archives, Report of the Curator and Archivist* (Ithaca, NY: Cornell University Department of Manuscripts and University Archives, 1963).

11,699. Sarnoff, Dorothy
Papers. 1941-72. 29 ft.
Open. Unpublished guide.
Cornell University, Department of Manuscripts and University Archives.
Papers of Sarnoff (1914-), a singer and speech consultant, primarily relate to her professional singing career. Includes correspondence, contracts, research notes, galleys for her book *Speech Can Change Your Life*, photos, clippings, scrapbooks, songbooks, and sheet music, much of which was annotated by Sarnoff. Sarnoff, who graduated from Cornell in 1935, was chairman of and a speech consultant with Speech Dynamics, Inc., in New York City.

11,700. Schaeffer, Evelyn (Schuyler)
Papers. Nd. 98-page item.
Open. Published guide.
Cornell University, Department of Manuscripts and University Archives.
Incomplete autobiography by Schaeffer, the daughter of George W. Schuyler, an Ithaca businessman and a charter trustee of Cornell University, is entitled *From Sunrise to Sunset.* Taken from *Cornell University Collection of Regional History and the University Archives, Report of the Curator and Archivist* (Ithaca, NY: Cornell University Department of Manuscripts and University Archives, 1947).

11,701. Scheetz, Virginia deMorat Smith
Papers. 1941-68. 2.67 ft.
Access restricted. Inventory.
Cornell University, Department of Manuscripts and University Archives.
Papers of Scheetz (1901-), an amateur ornithologist and horticulturist, who was married to Francis Harley Scheetz, Jr. (1894-1968), an attorney and a trustee of Cornell, include correspondence; minutes and balance sheets, including those of the advisory council of the laboratory of ornithology at Cornell; notes for speeches; class notes and notebooks; tapes; articles; and photos. The major portion of her papers relate to Cornell's laboratory of ornithology, where she was a member of the advisory council and editor of the laboratory's newsletters, but the collection also contains papers relating to her speaking engagements about ornithology and her interest and activities in horticulture, including minutes of the executive board, correspondence, newsletters, and yearbooks of the Pennsylvania Horticultural Society.

11,702. Schmid, Pauline Johanna
Papers. 1908-60. 2 in.
Open. Unpublished guide.
Cornell University, Department of Manuscripts and University Archives.
Correspondence, photos, clippings, and printed items of Schmid (1903-), who was alumnae secretary at Cornell in 1944, primarily pertain to her student days at Cornell, from which she graduated in 1925, and to her career as a school librarian.

11,703. Schmukler, Joan
Oral history. 1969. 2 transcripts.
Open. Unpublished guide.
Cornell University, Department of Manuscripts and University Archives.
Transcripts of an interview with Schmukler (1949-), a student at the New York State College of Agriculture in the class of 1970, concerning reform of the College.

11,704. Scott, Matthew T.
Papers. 1831-1930. 4.9 cu.ft.
Open. Published guide.
Cornell University, Department of Manuscripts and University Archives.
Correspondence, business diaries, rental agreements, deeds, and other papers relate to the establishment and development of frontier estates in Illinois and Iowa by Matthew T. Scott, Jr. (?-1891), a resident of Lexington, KY. The estates consisted of 55,000 acres in McLean, Livingston, Ford, Piatt, Coles, Champaign, Iroquois, Vermilion, Woodford, LaSalle, and Macon counties in Illinois and 5600 acres in Mills, Monona, Montgomery, Calhoun, and Cass counties in Iowa. Includes correspondence concerning Matthew Scott's wife Julia (Green) Scott (?-1923) and her management of the land after her husband's death as well as letters concerning her work with the DAR from 1909 to 1913. Upon her death the original holdings, which had been reduced to 8650 acres, became the property of her two daughters Mrs. Carl S. Vrooman and Mrs. Charles S. Bromwell.

Taken from *Cornell University Collection of Regional History and the University Archives, Report of the Curator and Archivist* (Ithaca, NY: Cornell University Department of Manuscripts and University Archives, 1947).

11,705. Selden Family
Papers. 1785-1857. 0.4 cu.ft. and 38 items.
Open. Published guides.
Cornell University, Department of Manuscripts and University Archives.
Includes correspondence of Abigail Jones Selden, Eliza Selden, and Charles Selden, residents of Lansingburgh, NY; of Harriet Yvonnet Gale (1823-?), the daughter of George W. Gale, who was a founder of the Oneida Institute and Knox College; and of Harriet (Selden) Gale (?-1840), Margaret Gale Hitchcock, and Mary Selden. Taken from *Cornell University Collection of Regional History and the University Archives, Report of the Curator and Archivist* (Ithaca, NY: Cornell University, 1946); *Cornell University Collection of Regional History and the University Archives, Report of the Curator and Archivist* (Ithaca, NY: Cornell University Department of Manuscripts and University Archives, 1959).

11,706. Severance, Lena Lillian Hill
Papers. 1903-16. 23 items.
Open. Unpublished guide.
Cornell University, Department of Manuscripts and University Archives.
Correspondence of Severance (1854-1942), a teachers' pension lobbyist who was married to Frank H. Severance, a Buffalo, NY, historian, relates primarily to salaries and pensions for teachers and to the improvement of normal schools in New York. Lena Severance is said to have been responsible for adoption of a pension law for New York state normal school teachers. A graduate of Cornell, she served on the national educational committee of the Association of Collegiate Alumnae and was a member of the AAUW, the New York Historical Association, and the American Institute of Archaeology.

11,707. Shaw, Adelaide Taber (Young)
Papers. 1887-1911. 2 ft.
Open. Published and unpublished guides.
Cornell University, Department of Manuscripts and University Archives.
Includes letters that [Mrs. Farnham Horatio] Shaw (1877-1964) wrote to her mother during her college days at Cornell about student life, sorority matters, social activities, fellow students and professors; correspondence with family and friends in her hometown of Wellsboro, PA; a letter from George Lincoln Burr, thanking her for a New Year's gift book; her American history notes; scrapbooks containing photos, clippings, programs, and other items pertaining to her undergraduate years at Cornell, to Elmira College where she taught biology and physiology, and to her sister Sara Louise, an Elmira College graduate; and photos of trees, friends and relatives, and other subjects. Taken from *Cornell University Collection of Regional History and the University Archives, Report of the Curator and Archivist* (Ithaca, NY: Cornell University Department of Manuscripts and University Archives, 1963); *Cornell University Collection of Regional History and the University Archives, Report of the Curator and Archivist* (Ithaca, NY: Cornell University Department of Manuscripts and University Archives, 1974).

11,708. Sheafe, Nathaniel Tracy
Papers. 1813-76. 4 in.
Open. Published guide.
Cornell University, Department of Manuscripts and University Archives.
Papers of Sheafe include letters from his sister Margarette Sheafe, who comments on the faculty, curriculum, examinations, and social life at Canandaigua Academy in Ontario County, NY. Taken from *Cornell University Collection of Regional History and the University Archives, Report of the Curator and Archivist* (Ithaca, NY: Cornell University Department of Manuscripts and University Archives, 1951).

11,709. Shelton
Papers. 1783-1934. 0.4 cu.ft.
Open. Published guide.
Cornell University, Department of Manuscripts and University Archives.
Consists in part of correspondence between members of the related Bennett, Tappan, Brewster, Tomlinson, and Shelton families concerning religious, missionary, educational experiences, and family matters. Includes letters from Anne Tappan, who was at Catharine Beecher's School in Hartford, CT; from Lucy Tappan, a teacher at a religious academy in Detroit, about local conditions, [Miss] Beecher, and nativist fears; and from a woman teacher at the Brainard Cherokee Mission School. Collection also contains wills, deeds, receipts, and other papers. Taken from *Cornell University Collection of Regional History and the University Archives, Report of the Curator and Archivist* (Ithaca, NY: Cornell University Department of Manuscripts and University Archives, 1951).

11,710. Sheppard, George S.
Papers. 1717-1933. 0.6 cu.ft.
Open. Published guide.
Cornell University, Department of Manuscripts and University Archives.
Correspondence of Sheppard, a lawyer, businessman, and amateur historian of Penn Yan County. Includes letters from Mrs. Stafford Canning Cleveland and others concerning the manuscript and printed sheets of the unfinished second volume of Cleveland's husband's *Yates County History.* Taken from *Cornell University Collection of Regional History and the University Archives, Report of the Curator and Archivist* (Ithaca, NY: Cornell University Department of Manuscripts and University Archives, 1947).

11,711. Shipman, Ellen
Papers. Nd. 30 ft.
Open. Published guide.
Cornell University, Department of Manuscripts and University Archives.
Notes, sketches, and plans of Shipman, a landscape architect. Taken from *Cornell University Collection of Regional History and the University Archives, Report of the Curator and Archivist* (Ithaca, NY: Cornell University Department of Manuscripts and University Archives, 1955).

11,712. Sigma Kappa and Chi Gamma
Records. 1921-64. Ca. 3 ft.
Access restricted. Partial published guide.
Cornell University, Department of Manuscripts and University Archives.
Includes records of the Alpha Zeta Chapter of the national Sigma Kappa sorority and of Chi Gamma, a local sorority formed by Sigma Kappa members after the Alpha Zeta Chapter was suspended from the national organization in 1956. Alpha Zeta records contain a manuscript history of the Chapter, including its petition for a charter and photos of the founders in ca. 1922, leases for the chapter house, scholarship reports, photos of members, menus, invitations, and clippings as well as correspondence, reports, minutes, clippings and other items concerning the Chapter's suspension and the 1958 national Sigma Kappa convention at which the suspension was discussed. Records of Chi Gamma include president's and secretary's notebooks, bills and accounts, correspondence, membership lists, notes pertaining to pledging and initiation ceremonies, certificates, pins, and other items. See *Cornell University Collection of Regional History and the University Archives, Report of the Curator and Archivist* (Ithaca, NY: Cornell University Department of Manuscripts and University Archives, 1974).

11,713. Skillen, Melita Hamilton
Papers. 1932-60. 42 items.
Open. Published guide.
Cornell University, Department of Manuscripts and University Archives.
Papers of [Miss] Skillen (1887-), a dramatics teacher and director, include autobiographical sketches, certificates, and clippings concerning her life and work as director of drama at Senn High School in Chicago, from which she retired in 1952. Also includes items relating to the Cornell Women's Club of Chicago, such as a sketch of the Club and some of its prominent members and incomplete lists of officers and activities. Skillen was a member and officer of the Club, which was founded in 1911. Taken from *Cornell University Collection of Regional History and the University Archives, Report of the Curator and Archivist* (Ithaca, NY: Cornell University Department of Manuscripts and University Archives, 1974).

11,714. Slingerland, Effie Brown Earll
Papers. Ca. 1900. 142 items.
Open. Published guide.
Cornell University, Department of Manuscripts and University Archives.
Lantern slides that Slingerland (1868-1950) made of butterflies, moths, and worms. She made the slides, some of which are in color, at the request of her husband Mark Vernon Slingerland, a professor, and John Henry Comstock and Anna Botsford Comstock. Effie Slingerland believed that she was the first person to make color slides. Taken from *Cornell University Collection of Regional History and the University Archives, Report of the Curator and Archivist* (Ithaca, NY: Cornell University Department of Manuscripts and University Archives, 1974).

11,715. Smith, Lovina
Papers. 1841-53. 11 items.
Open. Published guide.
Cornell University, Department of Manuscripts and University Archives.
Correspondence between Smith and her husband Joseph H. Smith, residents of Erie County, NY, chiefly concerns family matters, the weather, and the difficulty of travel between western New York and other states. Also contains clippings. Taken from *Cornell University Collection of Regional History and the University Archives, Report of the Curator and Archivist* (Ithaca, NY: Cornell University Department of Manuscripts and University Archives, 1959).

11,716. Society of Cornell Dames
Records. 1922-55. 3 vols.
Open. Published guide.
Cornell University, Department of Manuscripts and University Archives.
Constitution, bylaws, minutes, reports, correspondence, lists of members and officers, and clippings pertain to the activities of the Society. Taken from *Cornell University Collection of Regional History and the University Archives, Report of the Curator and Archivist* (Ithaca, NY: Cornell University Department of Manuscripts and University Archives, 1974).

11,717. Starkweather, Elizabeth
Papers. 1809-ca. 1930. 0.8 cu.ft.
Open. Published guide.
Cornell University, Department of Manuscripts and University Archives.
Papers of the related Ayres, Chase, Kerfoot, King, Leal, Shankland, Starkweather, and Tuttle families include letters from Ebenezah Maxwell Leal, a clerk in the post office department in Washington, DC, to his wife Lucy Buell (King) Leal, who later married William Henry Shankland; correspondence of other family members; diaries of Lucy

Shankland, 1868-1900; genealogical tables and notes; photos; and clippings. Includes photos and papers of Hannah Tuttle King Brown, Lillian Brown, Ethel Bull, Hazel Columbia, Mary Ann Kerfoot, Molly Knight, Mary Ayres Leal, and Lucina Tuttle. Taken from *Cornell University Collection of Regional History and the University Archives, Report of the Curator and Archivist* (Ithaca, NY: Cornell University Department of Manuscripts and University Archives, 1959).

11,718. Stebbins, Amanda

Papers. 1832-40. 11 items.
Open. Published guides.
Cornell University, Department of Manuscripts and University Archives.
Correspondence in which Stebbins describes Ithaca and the surrounding area. In one unsigned letter, thought to have been written by Stebbins, she comments on a smallpox epidemic, her religious experience, temperance, health foods, an execution and grave robbery, the schoolhouse, local stores, prices of provisions, tuition, and general expenses. Several of the letters were written to Sally Stebbins in Wilbraham, MA. Taken from *Cornell University Collection of Regional History and the University Archives, Report of the Curator and Archivist* (Ithaca, NY: Cornell University, 1946); *Cornell University Collection of Regional History and the University Archives, Report of the Curator and Archivist* (Ithaca, NY: Cornell University Department of Manuscripts and University Archives, 1951).

11,719. Stoddard, Hannah Gould (Johnson)

Papers. 1564-1943. 1.5 ft.
Open. Published and unpublished guides.
Cornell University, Department of Manuscripts and University Archives.
Contains Gould, Johnson, and Stoddard family papers, including 1832 religious correspondence of Sarah Sherman; letters to Julia E. Sanford, who later married Goodwin Stoddard, written while she was a student at the Brooklyn Heights Seminary in the early 1870s; a letter Hannah Gould Johnson wrote in ca. 1900, which provides details about a Yale prom she attended with Sanford Stoddard, along with notes to her on her engagement to Stoddard; travel letters, including those Johnson wrote when she accompanied her parents Benoni Johnson and Annie (Gould) Johnson and her sister Hilda Johnson to Europe, giving her impressions of Gibraltar, Venice, and places in Switzerland, England, and Scotland; letters in which Mary B. Lewis discusses a tour of Japan and China in 1902, including her excursion by mule litter to the Great Wall; and letters from Hannah (Johnson) Stoddard's aunt Elizabeth Wright (Gould) Berry (1851-1920) and her cousin Harriet, which were written chiefly from Florence, Lausanne, and Munich. Also includes round-robin letters written by former members of the White Lodge at Smith College about their activities following graduation; these letters contain opinions on such issues as woman suffrage and the position of women, the League of Nations, and progressive education and document the graduates' involvement in American National Red Cross work and food conservation during WWI and in social betterment groups. Some of the letters are from Anna Speck Thomson concerning her teaching at the settlement school in Hindman, KY, and at Oklahoma College for Women in Chickasha. Collection also contains printed items pertaining to Stoddard's devotion to child training and welfare, literary studies, and other educational and civic matters. Taken from *Cornell University Collection of Regional History and the University Archives, Report of the Curator and Archivist* (Ithaca, NY: Cornell University Department of Manuscripts and University Archives, 1974).

11,720. Straight, Willard D.

Papers. 1857-1922. 90 ft.
Open. Published and unpublished guides.
Cornell University, Department of Manuscripts and University Archives.
Correspondence of Straight (1880-1918), a diplomat, financier, and philanthropist who was an American diplomat in Korea and Manchuria and an American business group's representative in China. Straight married Dorothy Payne Whitney in 1911, and after 1912 they lived in New York City where he was associated with the J. P. Morgan Company. Dorothy Straight was an active social reformer, and in 1914 she joined her husband in establishing the *New Republic*, a magazine of political comment. After Willard Straight's death, the correspondence was addressed to Dorothy Straight, although most of it concerns him. Also includes his diaries and scrapbooks relating to his work during WWI. Correspondents include Laura Newkirk and Emma Straight. See Patricia H. Gaffney, ed., *The Willard Straight Papers at Cornell University, Guide to a Microfilm Edition* (Ithaca: Department of Manuscripts and University Archives, 1974). See also *Cornell University Collection of Regional History and the University Archives, Report of the Curator and Archivist* (Ithaca, NY: Cornell University Department of Manuscripts and University Archives, 1955).

11,721. Student Clubs

Records. 1868-1951. 3 ft.
Open. Published guide.
Cornell University, Department of Manuscripts and University Archives.
Includes records of the Biological Society, 1902-05; the Classical Association, 1887-95; the Cornell University Presbyterian Union, 1885-94; the Cornell University Teachers' Association, 1885; the Wayside-Aftermath Literary Club, 1892-1951; and the Women's Southern Club of Cornell, 1900-02. Taken from *Cornell University Collection of Regional History and the University Archives, Report of the Curator and Archivist* (Ithaca, NY: Cornell University Department of Manuscripts and University Archives, 1959).

11,722. Swartwout, Mrs. Benjamin C.

Papers. 1884-1925. 1 vol.
Open. Published guide.
Cornell University, Department of Manuscripts and University Archives.
Accounts of Swartwout, a resident of Huguenot, NY. Taken from *Cornell University Collection of Regional History and the University Archives, Report of the Curator and Archivist* (Ithaca, NY: Cornell University, 1946).

11,723. Taylor, Charles L., and Taylor, Lillian Horton

Papers. 1805-1963. 24 vols. and 49 items.
Open. Unpublished guide.
Cornell University, Department of Manuscripts and University Archives.
Includes diaries for 1934 to 1945 of Charles Taylor, a farmer, and a daybook for 1946 to 1952, diaries for 1952 to 1963, and a cashbook for 1939 to 1949 of his wife Lillian Taylor. Also contains deeds, auction receipts, bonds, and other records.

11,724. Thatcher, Elizabeth

Papers. 1882-84. 1 vol.
Open. Published guide.
Cornell University, Department of Manuscripts and University Archives.
Lecture notes on teaching methods that [Miss] Thatcher, a rural schoolteacher, kept while she was at teachers' institutes in Mayville, Jamestown, and Chautauqua, NY. Also includes attendance records. Taken from *Cornell University Collection of Regional History and the University Archives, Report of the Curator and Archivist* (Ithaca, NY: Cornell University Department of Manuscripts and University Archives, 1955).

11,725. Thayer, Abby E.

Papers. 1880. 1 vol.
Open. Published guide.
Cornell University, Department of Manuscripts and University Archives.
Physiology notebook of Thayer contains sketches. Taken from *Cornell University Collection of Regional History and the University Archives, Report of the Curator and Archivist* (Ithaca, NY: Cornell University Department of Manuscripts and University Archives, 1951).

11,726. Throop, George A.

Papers. 1803-1939. 2 in.
Open. Published guide.
Cornell University, Department of Manuscripts and University Archives.
Correspondence of the Throop family and Deborah Goldsmith contains comments about a Fourierist colony in Madison County, NY, the Millerites, and the temperance movement. Some of the correspondence was published in Olive C. Smith, *The Old Travelling Bag: Ancestral Charts of George Addison Throop, Deborah Goldsmith* (East St. Louis, 1934). Taken from *Cornell University Collection of Regional History and the University Archives, Report of the Curator and Archivist* (Ithaca, NY: Cornell University, 1946).

11,727. Tjomsland, Anne

Papers. Ca. 1918-64. 7 ft.
Open. Unpublished guide.
Cornell University, Department of Manuscripts and University Archives.
Papers of Tjomsland (1890-1968), a physician, include correspondence and case histories related to her general medical and anesthesiology practice. She served as a contract surgeon in Vichy, France, during WWI, and she published *Bellevue in France, Anecdotal History of Base Hospital #1* (1941). She also is the author of a history of American and Scandinavian medicine, and she translated a work about the life of a 13th-century Icelandic physician.

11,728. Todd Family

Papers. 1758-1959. 2.33 ft. and 10.5 ft. of microfilm.
Open. Published guide.
Cornell University, Department of Manuscripts and University Archives.
Includes letters that Sarah M. Todd, a resident of Pultneyville, NY, wrote to her daughter Ellen Todd, who was at the Fairfield Seminary; an essay and photos of Ellen Todd; and poetry of Sarah Todd. Also contains letters from Laura McLouth West and her husband John West, residents of New York City, to the McLouth family in Walworth, NY; the 1758 will of Sarah (Pierpont) [Mrs. Jonathan] Edwards, a resident of Stockbridge, MA; and valentines from the 1840s. Taken from *Cornell University Collection of Regional History and the University Archives, Report of the Curator and Archivist* (Ithaca, NY: Cornell University Department of Manuscripts and University Archives, 1974).

11,729. Todd, Jane Hedges

Papers. 1920-66. 5 ft.
Open. Unpublished guide.
Cornell University, Department of Manuscripts and University Archives.
Todd (1890-1966) was a New York state assemblywoman from Westchester County from 1935 to 1944. Includes personal and professional correspondence, scrapbooks, clippings, reports, pamphlets pertaining to her political career, press releases, and articles about the New York State Women's Council. Todd was deputy state commerce commissioner of New York from 1945 to 1955 and from 1959 to 1960 and a consultant to the Women's Bureau of the US Department of

Labor from 1955 to 1959. She retired in 1960. During her career Todd sponsored laws to require licensing of all nurses and to establish the principle of equal pay for equal work.

11,730. Tooke
Papers. 1819-1963. Ca. 0.6 cu.ft., 21 items, and 19 ft. of microfilm.
Open. Published guides.
Cornell University, Department of Manuscripts and University Archives.
Family correspondence, diaries, notebooks, account books, bills, receipts, photos, legal documents, post cards, greeting cards, and other papers of members of the Tooke family, some of whom spelled the surname Tuke. Includes an 1882 letter from Mary E. Tooke, a resident of Oneida Castle, NY, to her brother Manley J. Tooke in which she discusses the extensive local growing of hops, the high prices being paid for them, and the use of migrant labor, especially of Belgians; Civil War letters; Mary E. Tooke's recipe and remedy book; birth, death, and marriage records, 1839-1930, of members of the Burns, Martin, Meginnis, and Tooke families; seamstress accounts, 1830-33; a sketch that Helen (Tooke) Butler, who collected much of the material in the collection, wrote in 1963 about the Tooke homestead in Madison County. See *Cornell University Collection of Regional History and the University Archives, Report of the Curator and Archivist* (Ithaca, NY: Cornell University Department of Manuscripts and University Archives, 1951); *Cornell University Collection of Regional History and the University Archives, Report of the Curator and Archivist* (Ithaca, NY: Cornell University Department of Manuscripts and University Archives, 1959); *Cornell University Collection of Regional History and the University Archives, Report of the Curator and Archivist* (Ithaca, NY: Cornell University Department of Manuscripts and University Archives, 1974).

11,731. Traxel, Emma J.
Papers. 1905-31. 4 in.
Open. Published guide.
Cornell University, Department of Manuscripts and University Archives.
Diary that [Miss] Traxel (1869-1953), a resident of Rome, NY, kept of a trip to Switzerland and other European countries. Also includes post cards and family photos. Taken from *Cornell University Collection of Regional History and the University Archives, Report of the Curator and Archivist* (Ithaca, NY: Cornell University Department of Manuscripts and University Archives, 1959).

11,732. Treman, Elizabeth Lovejoy
Papers. 1889-94. 2 vols.
Open. Published guide.
Cornell University, Department of Manuscripts and University Archives.
Diaries that [Mrs. Elias] Treman, a resident of Ithaca, kept during vacation trips by rail and steamer to Massachusetts, Maine, and Nova Scotia. Taken from *Cornell University Collection of Regional History and the University Archives, Report of the Curator and Archivist* (Ithaca, NY: Cornell University Department of Manuscripts and University Archives, 1963).

11,733. Tunnell Family
Papers. 1894-95. 6 items.
Open. Published guide.
Cornell University, Department of Manuscripts and University Archives.
Letters that Byron Tunnell and his wife Bella Tunnell wrote to his mother Mrs. M. F. Tunnell, a resident of Oakland, CA, describing life on a coffee plantation in Guatemala from the viewpoint of a North American overseer; they also comment on wages, living conditions, earthquakes, scenery and wildlife, the status of the Indian population, and family matters. Also includes letters to Mrs. M. F. Tunnell from California friends. Taken from *Cornell University Collection of Regional History and the University Archives, Report of the Curator and Archivist* (Ithaca, NY: Cornell University Department of Manuscripts and University Archives, 1959).

11,734. Tyson, Harriet Esselstyn (Berry)
Papers. 1490-1960. 290 items.
Open. Published and unpublished guides.
Cornell University, Department of Manuscripts and University Archives.
Papers of the Gould and Berry families collected by Tyson (1883-), the granddaughter of John Stanton Gould and Hannah (Wright) Gould and sister of Romeyn Berry. Includes letters to Tyson's mother Elizabeth Wright (Gould) [Mrs. William Bogardus] Berry (1851-1921) from her parents, sisters, and her husband and correspondence of Tyson, including one letter she wrote while she was en route to France to serve with the American National Red Cross. Also includes letters Elizabeth Berry wrote to her daughter-in-law Olive (Nutting) Berry from several European cities, Elizabeth Berry's journal of her children's infancy, and legal, business, and land papers. Taken from *Cornell University Collection of Regional History and the University Archives, Report of the Curator and Archivist* (Ithaca, NY: Cornell University Department of Manuscripts and University Archives, 1963); *Cornell University Collection of Regional History and the University Archives, Report of the Curator and Archivist* (Ithaca, NY: Cornell University Department of Manuscripts and University Archives, 1974).

11,735. Upton, George Burr
Papers. 1845-1942. 2 in.
Open. Published guide.
Cornell University, Department of Manuscripts and University Archives.
Papers of Upton (1882-1942), a professor of mechanical engineering and a naturalist, include his mother's correspondence and excerpts from her letters, which concern incidents from his boyhood and life in the Colorado grain country during the 1880s and 1890s. Also includes genealogical notes on the Burr family. Taken from *Cornell University Collection of Regional History and the University Archives, Report of the Curator and Archivist* (Ithaca, NY: Cornell University Department of Manuscripts and University Archives, 1959).

11,736. Van Cleef Family
Papers. 1900-24. 20 in.
Open. Published guide.
Cornell University, Department of Manuscripts and University Archives.
Includes scrapbooks for 1900 to 1913 of [Miss] Eugenia and [Miss] Jeannette Van Cleef, residents of Ithaca, containing personal mementos of social life in Ithaca, student life at Ithaca High School, and student life at Cornell University. Also includes correspondence of their father Mynderse Van Cleef and related clippings pertaining to his donation of a bandstand to the village of Seneca Falls, NY. Taken from *Cornell University Collection of Regional History and the University Archives, Report of the Curator and Archivist* (Ithaca, NY: Cornell University Department of Manuscripts and University Archives, 1959).

11,737. Van Schaick
Papers. 1732-1826. 0.2 cu.ft.
Open. Published guide.
Cornell University, Department of Manuscripts and University Archives.
Includes land deeds; accounts and receipts; the will of Christina van Schaick, 1799; deeds for the sale of female slaves in 1736, 1758, and 1787; and other papers. The land deeds include a deed of sale signed by Elisabeth van Corlaer, 1735-36, and rental deeds of Christina van Schaick of Isle Cohoes in Albany County, 1784; Maria van Schaick of Albany, NY, 1785; and Anna van Schaick of Albany County, 1813. See *Cornell University Collection of Regional History and the University Archives, Report of the Curator and Archivist* (Ithaca, NY: Cornell University Department of Manuscripts and University Archives, 1947).

11,738. Wall Family
Papers. 1857-81. 4 in.
Open. Published guide.
Cornell University, Department of Manuscripts and University Archives.
Includes letters in which Jane Middleton tells about her work among indigent women in New York City. Taken from *Cornell University Collection of Regional History and the University Archives, Report of the Curator and Archivist* (Ithaca, NY: Cornell University Department of Manuscripts and University Archives, 1963).

11,739. Waring, Ethel Bushnell
Papers. Ca. 1925-56. 86 ft.
Open. Published guide.
Cornell University, Department of Manuscripts and University Archives.
Papers of Waring (1887-), a professor emeritus of child development and family relationships, include correspondence, research reports, motion pictures, nursery school records, and other papers. The papers document the history of the department of child development and family relationships from its origin as a group of courses in child guidance in the 1924 summer school to its present status as an independent department of the New York State College of Home Economics. Taken from *Cornell University Collection of Regional History and the University Archives, Report of the Curator and Archivist* (Ithaca, NY: Cornell University Department of Manuscripts and University Archives, 1963).

11,740. Waterbury Family
Papers. 1830-1903. 2 vols.
Open. Published guide.
Cornell University, Department of Manuscripts and University Archives.
Includes personal accounts of Lucy and Mary Waterbury, residents of Delaware County, NY; notations concerning the Ladies' Aid Society and Women's Missionary Society of a Presbyterian church; and music lesson accounts. Taken from *Cornell University Collection of Regional History and the University Archives, Report of the Curator and Archivist* (Ithaca, NY: Cornell University Department of Manuscripts and University Archives, 1963).

11,741. Wells, Charlotte (Fowler)
Papers. 1838-1901. 42 items.
Open. Published guide.
Cornell University, Department of Manuscripts and University Archives.
Includes a letter of sympathy and admiration from Susan B. Anthony to a niece of [Mrs. Samuel Robert] Wells (1814-1901); a report Wells wrote about spiritualist meetings held in New York City during 1850, including comments on the participation of Horace Greeley and others; a sketch by professor L. N. Fowler, including facts about mesmerism; and photos of Wells, Fowler, and various associates as well as of the office of Fowler and Wells. Taken from *Cornell University Collection of Regional History and the University Archives, Report of the Curator and Archivist* (Ithaca, NY: Cornell University Department of Manuscripts and University Archives, 1951).

11,742. White, Andrew D., and White, Mary Amanda (Outwater)
Papers. 1845-1918. Ca. 102 ft.
Open. Published guides.
Cornell University, Department of Manuscripts and University Archives.
Papers of Andrew White (1832-1918), educator,

diplomat, and first president of Cornell, and his first wife Mary (Outwater) White (1836-87) include letters she wrote to him during their courtship; her letters to her mother Lucia Outwater; letters to Andrew White from Mary White's friend Maria H. Wilkinson; correspondence of Andrew White's second wife Helen (Magill) White (1853-1944), his daughter Clara (White) Newberry, and his mother Clara Dickson [Mrs. Horace] White (1810-82); and letters from prominent women, including Elizabeth Cabot (Cary) [Mrs. Jean Louis Rodolfe] Agassiz, Susan Brownell Anthony, Catharine Esther Beecher, Anne Charlotte (Lynch) [Mrs. Vincenzo] Botta, Anna (Botsford) [Mrs. John Henry] Comstock, Abby (Morton) [Mrs. Manuel A.] Diaz, Ellen Coit (Brown) [Mrs. Orrin L.] Elliott, Annie A. [Mrs. James T.] Fields, Julia (Ward) [Mrs. Samuel Gridley] Howe, Elizabeth Palmer Peabody, Margaret Olivia (Slocum) [Mrs. Russell B.] Sage, Jane Eliza Lathrop [Mrs. Leland] Stanford, Elizabeth (Cady) [Mrs. Henry Brewster] Stanton, Ida Minerva Tarbell, Martha Carey Thomas, Helen Frances "Fanny" (Garrison) [Mrs. Henry] Villard, and Emma (Hart) [Mrs. John] Willard. See *Cornell University Collection of Regional History and the University Archives, Report of the Curator and Archivist* (Ithaca, NY: Cornell University Department of Manuscripts and University Archives, 1955); *Cornell University Collection of Regional History and the University Archives, Report of the Curator and Archivist* (Ithaca, NY: Cornell University Department of Manuscripts and University Archives, 1959).

11,743. White, George Leonard
Papers. 1891. 1 item.
Open. Published guide.
Cornell University, Department of Manuscripts and University Archives.
Letter in which White (?-1895) tells [Miss] Rhoda E. Mead, a resident of Waterbury, CT, about the Cornell campus, Ithaca, and Cayuga Lake as well as about the work he and Mrs. White performed to assist her brother E. P. Gilbert in the management of Sage College for Women. He mentions the electrification of the building for the 1891-92 school year and adds that he would not want his daughter Georgia Laura White, then a student at Lake Erie Seminary in Painesville, OH, to enter the University as an undergraduate, despite its superior educational opportunities, because "it is the survival of the fittest, with the balance against what we would call right development." Georgia White later became dean of women at Cornell. Taken from *Cornell University Collection of Regional History and the University Archives, Report of the Curator and Archivist* (Ithaca, NY: Cornell University Department of Manuscripts and University Archives, 1974).

11,744. White House Conference on Children and Youth
Records. 1958-60. 3 ft.
Open. Unpublished guide.
Cornell University, Department of Manuscripts and University Archives.
Material generated by Margaret Kirkwood [Mrs. J. Lanning] Taylor, a consultant on arrangements for the 1960 Conference, includes work sheets, plans for the physical arrangements for the meeting and hotel accommodations for the delegates, President Eisenhower's call of the Conference, and publications about children and youth.

11,745. Whiteside
Papers. 1769-1938. 0.4 cu.ft. and 1 microfilm reel.
Open. Published guide.
Cornell University, Department of Manuscripts and University Archives.
Papers relate to the activities of Phineas and John Whiteside, pioneer farmers in Washington County, NY, who acted as agents handling 3756 acres of land for Henrietta Maria Colden and her son. Includes deeds to Phineas Whiteside from Alexander Colden and Richard Nicholas Colden along with Henrietta Maria Colden's rent roll, which contains detailed information about the lots, names, rents, and terms. Taken from *Cornell University Collection of Regional History and the University Archives, Report of the Curator and Archivist* (Ithaca, NY: Cornell University Department of Manuscripts and University Archives, 1949).

11,746. Wilkinson, Jemima
Papers. 1768-1872. 2 microfilm reels.
Open. Published and unpublished guides.
Cornell University, Department of Manuscripts and University Archives.
Papers of Wilkinson (1752-1819), who was known as the "universal friend"; her followers; and their descendants. Relates primarily to the migration of Wilkinson and her followers at the close of the American Revolution from Rhode Island to what is now Yates County, NY; the development of their settlement; their conflict and litigation over land; and their religious life. Includes minutes, deeds, correspondence, the last will of Wilkinson and others, journals, sermons, accounts, and records relating to the Boston and Massachusetts Pre-emptions, the Gore Land Case, the Yates County Bank, the Second National Bank, President Andrew Jackson, temperance, and other subjects. Correspondents include Sarah Richards, Ruth Richards, Rachel Malin, members of the Malin family, Alice Hazzard, and Ruth Spencer. Taken from *Cornell University Collection of Regional History and the University Archives, Report of the Curator and Archivist* (Ithaca, NY: Cornell University Department of Manuscripts and University Archives, 1947); *Cornell University Collection of Regional History and the University Archives, Report of the Curator and Archivist* (Ithaca, NY: Cornell University Department of Manuscripts and University Archives, 1959).

11,747. Willcox, Walter Francis
Papers. 1818-1963. 22 ft. and 31 items.
Open. Published and unpublished guides.
Cornell University, Department of Manuscripts and University Archives.
Papers of Willcox (1861-1964), a professor of economics and statistics, chief statistician of the US Census from 1899 to 1901, and an officer and honorary president of the International Statistical Institute, include family papers, which chiefly consist of correspondence of his father William Henry Willcox, his mother Anna Holmes (Goodenow) Willcox, and earlier relatives and genealogical and biographical information pertaining to the Willcox and Work families. Also includes letters to him from Alice Eloise Work, whom he married in 1892; she describes her life as a student of literature at Wellesley College in the late 1880s, as a young woman living with her family in Akron, OH, where she taught Sunday school and studied language and literature with a circle of friends and pupils, and as a wife and mother. In addition, the collection contains correspondence with his daughter Mary G. Willcox, who married Alexander Wiley; with his sister Mary Alice Willcox (1856-?), a zoologist, concerning family matters; and with other relatives and friends. Also includes family photos. Taken from *Cornell University Collection of Regional History and the University Archives, Report of the Curator and Archivist* (Ithaca, NY: Cornell University Department of Manuscripts and University Archives, 1959); *Cornell University Collection of Regional History and the University Archives, Report of the Curator and Archivist* (Ithaca, NY: Cornell University Department of Manuscripts and University Archives, 1963); *Cornell University Collection of Regional History and the University Archives, Report of the Curator and Archivist* (Ithaca, NY: Cornell University Department of Manuscripts and University Archives, 1974).

11,748. Williams and Craddock Family
Papers. 1844-1921. 4 in.
Open. Published guide.
Cornell University, Department of Manuscripts and University Archives.
Papers relate primarily to the school and teaching activities of the Williams and Craddock families of Weedsport, NY. Includes letters from Samuel Craddock, who describes his experiences at Geneva Medical College and the attempt to steal a cadaver from the graveyard; correspondence of Diana Craddock Williams and her daughters Ida and Alice relating to student, teaching, and social activities at Oswego Normal and Training School, Ann Arbor, and the School for Girls in New York City; letters from [Mrs.] Helen Campbell relating to her appointment at the University of Wisconsin and her lecturing career. Also includes letters from Mary Sheldon relating to Oswego Normal School and Wellesley College; life in Clay County, KY; and activities at Cornell and Stanford universities. Taken from *Cornell University Collection of Regional History and the University Archives, Report of the Curator and Archivist* (Ithaca, NY: Cornell University Department of Manuscripts and University Archives, 1949).

11,749. Williams Family
Papers. 1836-1924. 0.4 cu.ft.
Open. Published guide.
Cornell University, Department of Manuscripts and University Archives.
Consists primarily of correspondence of Mary Gilmare Williams, a resident of Corning, NY, which relates to her activities as a student at Mount Holyoke College and as a teacher at Kalamazoo College. Includes school attendance records for Pulteney and Urbana, NY. Taken from *Cornell University Collection of Regional History and the University Archives, Report of the Curator and Archivist* (Ithaca, NY: Cornell University Department of Manuscripts and University Archives, 1949).

11,750. Williams, Josiah Butler, Family
Papers. 1778-1941. 83 cu.ft.
Open. Published guide.
Cornell University, Department of Manuscripts and University Archives.
Contains papers of Mary (Hardy) Williams (1824-1911), the wife of Josiah Williams (1810-83), a banker, lawyer, businessman, and New York state senator. Includes correspondence with family members and friends, a diary, invitations and announcements, household account books, and canceled checks; the papers chiefly concern activities of the Presbyterian church of Ithaca and missionary work. Also includes correspondence, receipted bills, and bank slips of the Williamses' children Charlotte, Jane, Ella, and Otis; of Mary Williams's sisters Louisa and Jane Hardy; and of their father Charles Elias Hardy, the cofounder of a hardware store in Ithaca. Jane Hardy's papers chiefly concern her position on the board of trustees and as an officer of the Ithaca City Hospital. Also contains printed items about Williams family genealogy. Correspondents include A. S. and Zoe Fiske, Jane Smith, Anna Walker, Susan Walker, and Louise Williams. Taken from *Cornell University Collection of Regional History and the University Archives, Report of the Curator and Archivist* (Ithaca, NY: Cornell University Department of Manuscripts and University Archives, 1959).

11,751. Women's Festival
Phonotape. 1971. 2 tapes.
Open. Unpublished guide.
Cornell University, Department of Manuscripts and University Archives.
Tapes of events held during the Festival, which was held at Cornell in 1971.

11,752. Women's Judiciary Board
Records. 1917-62. 1.33 ft.
Access restricted. Inventory.
Cornell University, Department of Manuscripts and University Archives.
Includes minutes of the Board, a student government organization at Cornell; scattered minutes of the women's judiciary committee; records relating to Board cases and sorority and dormitory cases; records from a fraternity and sorority survey; manuals; and pamphlets.

11,753. Women's Medical College of Baltimore
Records. 1882-1942. 0.2 ft.
Open. Unpublished guide.
Cornell University, Department of Manuscripts and University Archives.
Contains correspondence, including several letters to [Miss] Bessie Grigg, managing editor of the *Medical Woman's Journal* during the 1940s; a history of the College; histories of the Woman's Medical Society of Baltimore; copies of the College bulletin; and photos.

11,754. Women's Medical Society of New York State
Records. 1907-72. 1.8 cu.ft.
Open. Published guide.
Cornell University, Department of Manuscripts and University Archives.
Includes minutes, financial accounts, accounts of the medical education committee, reports, newsletters, membership lists, a scrapbook, photos, and clippings of the Society. Also includes correspondence of women doctors concerning the Society's business and letters from the United Board for Christian Colleges in China; officials of medical schools in China, Korea, and India; student recipients of medical scholarships; and medical missionaries concerning their activities and financial support that the Society gave to Christian women medical students in these countries. Among the correspondents are physicians Emily (Dunning) Barringer, Mary Theresa Greene, Rosetta Sherwood Hall, Jennie H. Harris, Harriet Hosmer, M. Pauline Jeffery, and Sherwood Hall. Taken from *Cornell University Collection of Regional History and the University Archives, Report of the Curator and Archivist* (Ithaca, NY: Cornell University Department of Manuscripts and University Archives, 1974).

11,755. Women's Self-Government Association
Records. Ca. 1915-68. 20 ft.
Open. Unpublished guide.
Cornell University, Department of Manuscripts and University Archives.
Minutes of the executive committee, executive council, and the house of representatives; correspondence; reports; scrapbooks; clippings; and pamphlets of the Association, a self-governing association of undergraduate women with regulatory authority and disciplinary jurisdiction, which existed from 1917 to 1970. Records, which are primarily subject files, relate to applications, banquets, dormitories, dining, faculty committees, and freshman orientation as well as to the Association's publications. Correspondence pertains to the history, constitution, and bylaws of the Association.

11,756. Wylie, Margaret
Papers. 1926-63. 69 ft.
Open. Published and unpublished guides.
Cornell University, Department of Manuscripts and University Archives.
Wylie (1889-1964), a professor of child development and family relationships, was largely responsible for establishing Cornell's extension program in family life. Includes correspondence, reports, and printed items pertaining to home economics extension work throughout New York and to conferences, workshops, and committees relating to family life. Also includes letters Flora Rose wrote to her friends in the college of home economics while she was in Berkeley, CA; course outlines and cards giving dates of meetings, attendance, records, and topics discussed at Cornell Child Study Clubs throughout the state; report forms from her trips as a home demonstration extension specialist; questionnaires, study data, and other records pertaining to the Cornell Twin Study Club of Jamestown, for which Wylie, who made studies of twins, was an advisor; annual reports of the department of child development and family relationships extension service, 1926-50; minutes, correspondence, memoranda, and reports of the department of child development and family relationships and the evaluation steering committee of the college of home economics; motion pictures; scripts and recordings from a series of radio broadcasts entitled "The Family Grows Up"; and recording discs from the 1950 White House Conference on Children and Youth. Taken from *Cornell University Collection of Regional History and the University Archives, Report of the Curator and Archivist* (Ithaca, NY: Cornell University Department of Manuscripts and University Archives, 1963); *Cornell University Collection of Regional History and the University Archives, Report of the Curator and Archivist* (Ithaca, NY: Cornell University Department of Manuscripts and University Archives, 1974).

11,757. Yates, Martha F.
Papers. 1894-1904. 1 vol.
Open. Published guide.
Cornell University, Department of Manuscripts and University Archives.
Scrapbook of [Miss] Yates, a resident of Slaterville Springs, NY, contains correspondence and clippings concerning the "New York," a prize-winning giant strawberry she developed. Taken from *Cornell University Collection of Regional History and the University Archives, Report of the Curator and Archivist* (Ithaca, NY: Cornell University Department of Manuscripts and University Archives, 1974).

11,758. The Young Women's Hospital Aid
Records. 1912-67. 0.4 ft.
Open. Unpublished guide.
Cornell University, Department of Manuscripts and University Archives.
Includes minutes of the general meeting, 1946-63, and minutes of board meetings, 1957-63; correspondence; reports of the charity ball, which was the annual fund-raising activity; newsletters; and items related to the history of the Young Women's Hospital Aid, a social organization of Ithaca area women whose prime function was fund raising for the Tompkins County Memorial Hospital. The organization existed from 1913 to 1964, when it was absorbed into the Hospital's department of volunteer services.

11,759. Zeller, Adelheid Bertha Marie Zoe, and Zeller, Cornelia Pauline Hedwig
Papers. 1911-18. 1 ft.
Open. Published guide.
Cornell University, Department of Manuscripts and University Archives.
Includes a diary for 1913 to 1918 of Adelheid Zeller (1892-), who married Ilbert O. Lacy; notes Cornelia Zeller (1894-) took in bibliography, biology, German, history, philosophy, and psychology classes at the University; an account book listing the income and expenses of the sisters while they were undergraduates at Cornell; and photos, concert and play programs, party souvenirs, post card views of Cornell, and other memorabilia pertaining to their student days. Taken from *Cornell University Collection of Regional History and the University Archives, Report of the Curator and Archivist* (Ithaca, NY: Cornell University Department of Manuscripts and University Archives, 1974).

11,760. American Association for Labor Legislation
Records. 1905-43. 60 microfilm reels.
Open. Published guide.
Cornell University, New York State School of Industrial and Labor Relations, Labor-Management Documentation Center.
Contains correspondence of the Association, a lobbying organization, with Irene Osgood Andrews, assistant Association secretary and head of the Association's committee on women's work, as well as with Irene Sylvester Chubb, the Association's lobbyist in Albany, NY, and Washington, DC, between 1916 and 1924. Other women involved in the organization include Jane Addams, Elizabeth Brandeis, Mary Dreier, Alice Hamilton, Florence Kelley, and Frances Perkins. Maternity benefits, the organization of women's unions, old age and mothers' pensions and insurance, women's working hours, minimum wages for women, health and social insurance, industrial poisons, diseases and accidents, working conditions and workmen's compensation are topics covered in the papers.

11,761. American Federation of Teachers, Local 2
Records. 1925-57. 26.3 ft.
Open. Unpublished guide.
Cornell University, New York State School of Industrial and Labor Relations, Labor-Management Documentation Center.
Office files of Local 2 of the AFT document the Local's historical development and issues related to communism and socialism. Includes legislative material and various committees' correspondence and other records.

11,762. American Labor Education Service
Records. 1927-62. 167.6 ft.
Open. Unpublished guide.
Cornell University, New York State School of Industrial and Labor Relations, Labor-Management Documentation Center.
Records of the Service, which organized education programs for workers, include school catalogs, curriculum, material, and letters to various schools for women workers, including the Bryn Mawr Summer School for Women Workers, the Summer School for Women Workers in Industry, the Southern Summer School, and the Vineyard Shore School of Women Workers in Industry.

11,763. Consumers League of New York
Records. 1920-60. 20 ft.
Open. Unpublished guide.
Cornell University, New York State School of Industrial and Labor Relations, Labor-Management Documentation Center.
Minutes, correspondence, reports, surveys, research material, photos, and publications of the League, a lobbying organization. Women have been prominent in the administration of the League's activities, which primarily concern migrant labor. The organization made legislative efforts toward improving conditions for farm workers through education and better wages and hours, health standards, and housing. Records also cover the League's work on disability insurance, unemployment insurance, and night work for women.

11,764. Cook, Alice Hanson
Papers. 1952- . 53.9 ft.
Access restricted. Unpublished guide.
Cornell University, New York State School of Industrial and Labor Relations, Labor-Management Documentation Center.
Correspondence of Cook, an author and professor emerita, as well as research material, course material, committee records, books, term papers, and student files and publications relating to her career at the New York State School of Industrial and Labor Relations. Cook served as Cornell University's first ombudsman. In 1972 she left for

a year-long tour of socialist and nonsocialist countries to study child care and other support for working mothers in industry. Her most recent book is *The Working Mother.*

11,765. Donnelly, Betty Hawley
Papers. 1930-70. 2.7 ft.
Open. Unpublished guide.
Cornell University, New York State School of Industrial and Labor Relations, Labor-Management Documentation Center.
Correspondence, subject files, photos, clippings, publications, and certificates of Donnelly, who served as vice-president of the New York State AFL-CIO for 50 years and as chairman of its committee on education. She also worked with the New York City board of education for 40 years and served as a member of the President's and governor's committees for the physically handicapped.

11,766. Ellickson, Katherine Pollak
Papers. 1935-37. 3 microfilm reels.
Open. Unpublished guide.
Cornell University, New York State School of Industrial and Labor Relations, Labor-Management Documentation Center.
[Mrs.] Ellickson (1905-) was assistant director of the CIO while John Brophy was director. Includes speeches, notes on meetings and conferences, field reports, articles, and plans and procedures for the establishment and organization of local unions.

11,767. Grant, Alice
Papers. Nd. 5 ft.
Open. Unpublished guide.
Cornell University, New York State School of Industrial and Labor Relations, Labor-Management Documentation Center.
Correspondence of Grant, a teacher and member of the American Arbitration Association and the fact-finding panel for the New York State Public Employment Relations Board. Also includes reports and clippings relating to public employment activities in New York.

11,768. Leslie, Mabel
Papers. Nd. 5 in.
Open. Unpublished guide.
Cornell University, New York State School of Industrial and Labor Relations, Labor-Management Documentation Center.
Includes files of [Miss] Leslie, an arbitrator, relating to mediation and arbitration cases that she handled as a member of the New York State Board of Mediation and as an impartial arbitrator for building maintenance cases.

11,769. McDonald, Grace
Papers. 1936-69. 4 in.
Open. Unpublished guide.
Cornell University, New York State School of Industrial and Labor Relations, Labor-Management Documentation Center.
Reports and publications of [Mrs.] McDonald, who worked closely with her husband on the railroad unity movement of the 1930s. She organized the California Farmer-Labor Association and issued a monthly bulletin *Farmer Consumer Reporter.* McDonald also was a lobbyist and organizer on issues of small farmer welfare and labor cooperation.

11,770. McKelvey, Jean T.
Papers. Nd. 30.8 ft.
Access restricted. Unpublished guide.
Cornell University, New York State School of Industrial and Labor Relations, Labor-Management Documentation Center.
Papers of McKelvey, a professor emerita, arbitrator, and author, relate to her career as a teacher, author, former president of the National Academy of Arbitrators, and member of the arbitration panel of the American Arbitration Association, the New York State Board of Mediation, the public review board of the UAW, the special advisory panel to the President's review committee on federal employee-management relations, emergency boards appointed by the President under the Railway Labor Act, and other organizations.

11,771. National Consumers League
Records. 1911-47. 2 ft.
Open. Unpublished guide.
Cornell University, New York State School of Industrial and Labor Relations, Labor-Management Documentation Center.
Minutes, correspondence, reports, research material, and publications of the League, a lobbying organization. Women involved in the League included Florence Kelley, Josephine Roche, Lucy R. Mason, Mary Dublin, Elizabeth Magee, Frances Perkins, Clara Beyer, Mary Dewson, Dorothy Kenyon, and Josephine Goldmark. Through legislation the League effected the passage, enforcement, and defense of laws having to do with safety, sanitation, night work, child labor, maximum hours, minimum wages, social security, migrant camp conditions, and fair employment practices.

11,772. Retail, Wholesale and Department Store Union, Local 1199
Records. 1933-68. 135 ft.
Open. Unpublished guide.
Cornell University, New York State School of Industrial and Labor Relations, Labor-Management Documentation Center.
Contains minutes, correspondence, reports, clippings, releases, publications, and agreements relating to all aspects of the Union's activities, including grievances, strikes, arbitration cases, organizing, legislative matters, and civil rights. A number of members were women.

11,773. Schneider, Anna Weinstock
Papers. Nd. 10 in. and 22 items.
Open. Unpublished guide.
Cornell University, New York State School of Industrial and Labor Relations, Labor-Management Documentation Center.
Correspondence, transcripts of interviews, a scrapbook, photos, and clippings of Schneider (1898-), who in 1922 became the first woman appointed commissioner of conciliation for the US Department of Labor. She was a member of several minimum wage boards in Massachusetts, a lobbyist for labor legislation there, and an organizer for the Massachusetts Suffrage Association. President of the Boston Women's Trade Union League, she also was an organizer for the International Ladies' Garment Workers' Union.

11,774. Teachers Union of the City of New York
Records. 1916-64. 38.9 ft.
Open. Unpublished guide.
Cornell University, New York State School of Industrial and Labor Relations, Labor-Management Documentation Center.
Papers of the Union, which had a long history of radical involvement. Includes substantial material on the Lusk Commission and teachers' dismissals for unpopular political views during the 1950s. Women involved in the Union as officers and as defendants in cases involving academic freedom include Leonna Abrams, Dorothy Albert, Elaine Berlin, Dorothy Bloch, Minna Finkelstein, Mildred Flacks, Mildred Grossman, Minnie Gutride, Lillian Lipowsky, Gladys Mann, Dorothy Rand, Rose Russell, and Celia Zitron.

11,775. Watson, Amy
Papers. 1928-42. 6.3 ft.
Open. Unpublished guide.
Cornell University, New York State School of Industrial and Labor Relations, Labor-Management Documentation Center.
Watson was an executive secretary of the National Council on Household Employment, Inc. Includes correspondence, organizational records of the Council, publications, and a topical file on aspects and conditions of household employment.

11,776. Wolfson, Theresa
Papers. Nd. 53.9 ft.
Open. Unpublished guide.
Cornell University, New York State School of Industrial and Labor Relations, Labor-Management Documentation Center.
Papers of [Miss] Wolfson (1897-1972) document her career as a professor, social activist, feminist, and labor arbitrator. Also includes papers she collected as part of her research on Frances Wright.

11,777. Cowdry, Belle
Papers. 1858-1926. 1 Hollinger box.
Open. Unpublished guide.
DeWitt Historical Society of Tompkins County.
Scattered journals of Cowdry (1838-1922), a philanthropist and trustee of the City Hospital, date from 1858 to 1863. Cowdry, who apparently was a recluse, discusses her philosophy of life and her thoughts in the earlier journals. She also gives accounts of school friends, school and household duties, music lessons, family events, social happenings, Civil War activities, Frederick Douglass's mass meeting, the reaction to news that Richmond, VA, had been taken by the Union, and other local and national events. Also includes clippings relating to Cowdry's death and the Cowdry home and estate.

11,778. Dorn, Juliett Georgia
Papers. 1864-65. 2 vols.
Open. No guide.
DeWitt Historical Society of Tompkins County.
Diaries of Dorn (1843-?), who in 1861 married Seth Dorn, a farmer, in which she describes her marriage; her daily life in Danby, NY; her son Eugene Dorn; and the birth of her second son Augustus Dorn in 1865. All subjective references to her husband in the diaries have been erased or crossed out.

11,779. Manning, Carrie
Papers. 1869. 1 item.
Open. Published guide.
DeWitt Historical Society of Tompkins County.
Diary of Manning (1856-75), who lived on a farm in Ithaca, NY, in which she describes chores, games, religious practices, genealogy, and home and school activities. See William Heidt, Jr., ed., *Carrie Manning's Diary: 1869* (Ithaca: DeWitt Historical Society, 1962).

11,780. Smiley, Addie
Papers. 1870-94. 62 items.
Open. Published guide and inventory.
DeWitt Historical Society of Tompkins County.
Letters from Permelia Adelaide "Addie" Weed Smiley (1847-86), who married John G. Smiley (?-1894), a sheep farmer, to [Mrs.] Julia Brady and other friends and relatives. Also includes correspondence of John Smiley with relatives and George Barber as well as letters to Barber from Laura Bergen. The Smileys were married in 1871 and moved westward from Etna, NY, in the 1880s. The letters provide information about women's roles; the duties of a wife; social customs, including dress and dancing; domestic relationships; and the Smileys' experiences in the West, including a letter in which Addie Smiley describes the first time she saw a woman vote. The Smileys lived in Fort Steele, WY, and in Omaha; John Smiley died in Nebraska. See William Heidt, Jr., ed., *Addie Smiley's Letters from the West 1882-1886* (Ithaca: DeWitt Historical Society, 1955).

11,781. Ithaca College Archives
Records. 1893- . 100 cu.ft.
Open. Unpublished guide.
Ithaca College Library.
Primarily made up of faculty and student publications, the Archives also includes council and committee minutes, photos, scrapbooks, handbooks, directories, class lists, and catalogs. The College was founded in 1852 as a music conservatory. The curriculum now includes physical education, recreation, drama, communications, health, and business courses as well as a liberal arts program.

11,782. Peters, Roberta
Papers. Nd. 75 cu.ft., 70 tapes, and 150 recording discs.
Open. Unpublished guide.
Ithaca College Library.
Peters (1930-) is an opera singer. Includes personal correspondence and fan mail; diaries of her tours in the US and abroad; tapes and recording discs of live performances, radio and television shows, sessions with her singing coach, and musical sessions with her children; photos; scrapbooks; picture albums; clippings; and programs. Peters made her debut at the Metropolitan Opera in 1950. She grew up in the Bronx, NY, and began studying voice seriously at the age of 10. In 1955 she married Bertram Fields, a New York hotel executive. Peters and her husband have two sons, Paul Adam Fields (1957-) and Bruce Eric Fields (1959-); they live in Scarsdale, NY.

JAMAICA

11,783. Amory, Martha
Papers. 1830-50. Ca. 90 items.
Open. Unpublished guide.
Queens Borough Public Library.
Receipted bills, especially tax bills, and rental agreements of Amory, who owned some property in lower and mid-Manhattan during the 19th century.

11,784. Cook Family
Papers. 1791-1934. 900 items.
Open. Unpublished guide.
Queens Borough Public Library.
Includes correspondence of Anna Rose Cook (ca. 1847-1920s), who was active in political and social circles and was the wife of Addison Melville Cook, a surveyor and real estate agent. The letters, which are primarily from her daughter Carol Halsey (Cook) Stoots and other family and friends, relate to personal matters. Also includes correspondence of Carol Stoots, who married William D. Stoots near the turn of the century; letters to [Miss] Betsey Cook from friends and family, 1830s to the 1840s; and albums and copybooks, which contain literary passages, of Caroline Halsey [Mrs. Allanson Melville] Cook.

11,785. Devan, Irene (Sanford)
Papers. 1880s-90s. Ca. 90 items.
Open. Unpublished guide.
Queens Borough Public Library.
School attendance records, merit cards, and school certificates of Devan (1882-1964) from the years when she was a young girl and of her sister Edith Sanford. The papers were issued by the Corona public school and Miss Jennie Lee's School, a small private school in Corona, NY.

11,786. Hagner Family
Papers. 1790s-1880s. 485 items.
Open. Unpublished guide.
Queens Borough Public Library.
Includes financial papers and receipted bills of Elizabeth Hagner (1779-1844), who was married to Henry Hagner, Jr., a general merchant in Herricks, NY. Includes medical bills, school bills for her daughter Phebe Hagner, and bills for merchandise Elizabeth Hagner purchased. Also includes similar papers of Phebe Hagner.

11,787. Ladies Employment Society of Flushing
Records. 1866-1923. 6 vols.
Open. Unpublished guide.
Queens Borough Public Library.
Minute books of the Society, a charitable organization that existed from 1866 to 1923 for the purpose of furnishing "sewing to the needy women of Flushing who may be duly recommended."

11,788. Meury, John, and Meury, Emily Jane
Papers. 1863-1912. 18 vols.
Open. Unpublished guide.
Queens Borough Public Library.
Includes diaries and notebooks of Emily Meury (1865-1912), a probation officer who was the daughter of John Meury (?-1890), a minister of the Hopkins German Presbyterian Church in Brooklyn, NY. The notebooks are similar to address books, and only occasional entries refer to her work in court-related activities. At the time of her death, Emily Meury was termed the "oldest Probationary officer in point of service in Brooklyn."

11,789. Miller, John Hamlin, and Miller, Frances Higbie
Papers. 1851-88. 3 cu.ft.
Open. Unpublished guide.
Queens Borough Public Library.
Includes diaries and notebooks of Frances Miller, who with her husband John Miller farmed in West Islip, NY. Her diaries primarily contain lists of financial transactions. Also includes diaries her daughter Fannie Miller kept from 1866 to 1868 while she was a student at a school, which was probably in Elmira, NY.

11,790. Prince Family
Papers. 1784-1918. 4 cu.ft.
Open. Unpublished guide.
Queens Borough Public Library.
Correspondence, diaries, and financial papers of the family, members of which were primarily horticulturists. Includes correspondence of Charlotte (Prince) [Mrs. Edwin] Henry (1827-1920s), the daughter of William Robert Prince (1795-1869), a nurseryman. Also available on microfilm.

11,791. Rose Family
Papers. 1825-1931. 0.5 cu.ft.
Open. Unpublished guide.
Queens Borough Public Library.
Correspondence of this Bridgehampton, NY, family includes letters to [Miss] Charlotte "Lottie" Rose dating from the 1840s to the 1920s. The letters are from relatives in various parts of New York and contain information about family matters.

11,792. Smith, Ruth Newey
Papers. 1878-1915. 9 vols.
Open. Unpublished guide.
Queens Borough Public Library.
Diaries of [Mrs.] Smith (1835-1917), who owned the Smithport Hotel in Patchogue, NY. In the diaries she writes about family matters, visits to friends, and weather conditions. Also includes her 1915 commonplace book, which contains literary passages and articles copied from the *Patchogue Advance.* Smith also was the owner of the Lake View Cemetery in Patchogue.

11,793. Talbot and Perkins, Mrs. R. C.
Papers. 1913-15. 50 items.
Open. Unpublished guide.
Queens Borough Public Library.
Perkins, a resident of Brooklyn, NY, was a leader in the women's suffrage movement. Her letters, which concern the suffrage movement in Brooklyn and Long Island, are from people connected with such groups as the New York State Woman Suffrage Association, the New York State Federation of Women's Clubs, and the Men's League for Woman Suffrage.

11,794. Women's Club of Forest Hills
Records. 1913-59. 3 cu.ft.
Open. Unpublished guide.
Queens Borough Public Library.
Annual reports, minute books, account books, and scrapbooks of the Club, a philanthropic and social club, in Forest Hills, NY, which was organized in 1913 and is still extant.

KATONAH

11,795. Jay Family
Papers. 1697- . Ca. 4500 items.
Open. Unpublished guide.
John Jay Homestead.
Papers of the ancestors and descendants of John Jay (1745-1829), first chief justice of the US and twice governor of New York, include correspondence of female family members; an 1829 diary of Maria (Jay) [Mrs. Goldsborough] Banyer (1782-1856), in which she describes a train trip through Pennsylvania; the commonplace book of Augusta (McVickar) [Mrs. William] Jay (1790-1857); the diary of Eleanor Kingsland (Field) [Mrs. John] Jay (1819-1909), describing a trip to Europe in 1848; the diaries of Eleanor (Jay) [Mrs. Arthur] Iselin (1882-1953), 1900-01, in which she describes a trip to Spain, Algiers, and Italy and her impressions of great works of art as well as life at Bedford House, which now is the John Jay Homestead; a scrapbook of congratulatory mail on Eleanor Jay's engagement to Arthur Iselin in 1904; and a scrapbook containing clippings on the illness, death, and burial of Eleanor (O'Donnell) Iselin (1820-97), a philanthropist who was married to financier Adrian Iselin. Also includes published diaries and letters of female family members.

LATHAM

11,796. Province Archives
Records. 1838- . 146 cu.ft., 15 tapes, and 1 motion picture.
Open. Unpublished guide.
Sisters of St. Joseph of Carondelet, Provincial House.
Minutes, account books, reports, correspondence, chronicles, diaries, memoirs, parish histories, photos, scrapbooks, community publications, and published histories and research of the congregation, a Roman Catholic order of women who are primarily involved in education, health care, and orphanages. The congregation was established in the US in Carondelet, MO, in 1836; the Albany, NY, province was founded in 1858.

LOCKPORT

11,797. Census
Records. 1800-75. No size given.
Open. No guide.
Niagara County Historian.
Consists of the census of Niagara County for the years 1800, 1810, 1820, 1830, 1840, 1850, 1855, 1860, 1865, and 1875.

11,798. General Biographical File
Collection. 1808- . Ca. 2200 folders.
Opan. No guide.
Niagara County Historian.
Contains correspondence, diaries, photos, and clippings of various Niagara County, NY, families.

11,799. Seven Sutherland Sisters
Papers. Ca. 1850-1938. 2 boxes.
Open. No guide.
Niagara County Historian.
Correspondence, photos, and clippings of the daughters of Fletcher Sutherland, who lived in Cambria, NY. Sutherland is said to have developed a formula known as Seven Sutherland Sisters Hair Restorer. He toured the US and Europe with his daughters, whose hair was floor-length, to sell the product. The family made more than a million dollars, but the company went bankrupt when short hair came into fashion during WWI.

11,800. Vital Records
Records. 1808-ca. 1920. 40,000 items.
Access restricted. No guide.
Niagara County Historian.
Index file of tombstone inscriptions; marriage, birth, and church records; and obituaries from newspapers.

11,801. Woman's Christian Temperance Union
Records. Nd. Ca. 24 vols.
Open. No guide.
Niagara County Historian.
Volumes contain minutes, financial reports, accounts, notes, and attendance records of the Niagara County branch of the WCTU.

LYNDONVILLE

11,802. Conference Archives
Records. 1797- . 120 ft.
Open. Unpublished guide.
Western New York Conference of the United Methodist Church.
Includes annual conference minutes, records of defunct churches, foreign mission records, histories of active churches, seminary records, denominational newspapers, pastoral lists and appointments, and Conference publications on Methodism.

MARYKNOLL

11,803. Maryknoll Sisters Archives
Records. 1912-76. Ca. 500 ft.
Access restricted. No guide.
Maryknoll Sisters Center.
The Congregation is a Roman Catholic sisterhood of more than 1000 members, which was founded in the US in 1912 by Mother Mary Joseph (Mary Josephine Rogers) to perform foreign mission service. The Sisters are involved in educational, social, medical, and pastoral mission work in Africa, Asia, Latin America, the Pacific Islands, and in the US. In addition to the administrative records of the foundress and those of subsequent administrations, the Congregation's records contain annual reports, minutes, financial records, correspondence, personal files for each member, historical accounts, diaries, tapes of conferences, motion pictures, photos, newsletters, clippings, and other items. Also includes such creative works of sisters as theses, books, articles, and tape recordings.

MOUNT VERNON

11,804. Campbell, Persia Crawford
Papers. 1906-74. 120 ft.
Access restricted. Unpublished guide.
Consumers Union, Center for the Study of the Consumer Movement.
[Mrs. Edward Rice, Jr.] Campbell (1898-1974) was an economist, consumer advocate, feminist, author, and a director of the Consumers Union of the United States, Inc. Includes correspondence, journals, drafts, speeches, work files, photos, scrapbooks, and her personal library. Campbell, a professor of economics at Queens College, served as the first consumer counsel for the state of New York from 1954 to 1958. She also was appointed by President Kennedy to serve on his Consumer Advisory Council. A founder of the International Organization of Consumers Unions, she was a delegate to the International Federation of University Women and an officer of the AAUW. She was involved in UN programs, particularly those dealing with the Pacific and Southeast Asia.

11,805. Center for the Study of the Consumer Movement
Records. 1900-67. Ca. 500 ft.
Partially restricted. Finding aids.
Consumers Union, Center for the Study of the Consumer Movement.
Board minutes, editorial files, personal and official correspondence, drafts, unpublished speeches, oral history interviews, diaries, films, videotapes, statistical data, photos, scrapbooks, clippings, and published books and pamphlets of the Center date primarily from 1927 to 1967. The records relate to the development of the consumer movement and consumerism, including the role of women in the consumer movement, the development of domestic protest, and the effect of changing patterns of production and distribution on the welfare of consumers. Includes items relating to the careers of early consumer advocates, including Helen Canoyer, Persia Campbell, Mildred Brady, Helen Nelson, Colston E. Warne, and Henry Harap as well as records of major consumer organizations, including Consumers Union of the United States, Inc.; the National Association of Consumers; the International Organization of Consumers Unions; the Intermountain Consumers' Service; and others. Also contains material relating to the development of home economics, consumer education, food and drug regulation, consumer protection, public health movements, safety, and environmental reform.

11,806. Warne, Colston E.
Papers. 1927-77. 90 ft.
Partially restricted. Unpublished guide.
Consumers Union, Center for the Study of the Consumer Movement.
Personal and official correspondence, oral history interviews, articles, speeches, testimony, monographs, drafts, photos, pamphlet collection, and personal library of Warne (1900-), an economist, consumer advocate, and reformer, who was a founder of Consumers Union of the United States, Inc., and who has served as president of the organization since its inception. Includes correspondence with women engaged in governmental and social welfare activities, including Persia Campbell, Helen Canoyer, Esther Peterson, and Caroline Ware; correspondence with such organizations as the National Association of Consumers, the Consumer Federation of America, the League for Mutual Aid, the American Home Economics Association, the League of Women Shoppers, the LWV, the International Ladies' Garment Workers' Union, the Bryn Mawr Summer School for Women Workers, the AAUW, and the YWCA; and correspondence with government agencies, including the wartime Office of Price Administration, the Food and Drug Administration, the Federal Communications Commission and the Bureau of Standards.

NEW ROCHELLE

11,807. College of New Rochelle
Records. 1904- . Ca. 250 Hollinger boxes, 7 tapes, and 21 motion picture reels.
Access restricted. Unpublished guide.
College of New Rochelle Archives.
Annual reports, minutes of trustees' meetings and college committees, budget records, reports, correspondence, studies, photos, scrapbooks, faculty publications, yearbooks, newspapers, literary magazines, and other records of the College, which was founded in 1904 as a women's liberal arts college under the auspices of the Catholic Church. Also contains records of the Alumnae Association, the Ursuline Guild, and student organizations as well as papers of the foundress Mother Irene Gill, who served as the first academic dean from 1904 to 1918; other academic deans, most of whom were Ursuline nuns; women presidents, including Sister Dorothea Dunkerley; and women professors, including Mary Dora Rogick.

11,808. Ursuline
Records. 1535- . 28 ft.
Access restricted. Unpublished guide.
College of New Rochelle Archives.
Books and pamphlets dealing with the history of the Ursuline Order, founded in 1535 for the education of women by St. Angela Merici. Includes rule books, novices' manual, histories of the foundations of the Order throughout the world, books on Ursuline methods of education, biographies of famous Ursulines, issues of the Order's official newsletter through the 1930s, and official statements of various prioresses general.

NEW YORK

11,809. Amalgamated Clothing and Textile Workers Union
Records. 1914- . 27 file drawers.
Open. No guide.
Amalgamated Clothing and Textile Workers Union Archives.
From its inception in 1914, this labor organization of workers in the male apparel industries has had a high proportion of women members. Financial statements, correspondence, convention proceedings, clippings, and other records, including limited material on specific women leaders, among them Bessie Hillman.

11,810. Women Members
Records. Nd. No size given.
Access restricted. No guide.
American Academy and Institute of Arts and Letters.
Business correspondence, manuscripts, photos, and clippings of many women who were members of the Academy and Institute, including Georgia O'Keeffe, Djuna Barnes, Marchette Chute, Lillian Hellman, Margaret Mead, Katherine Anne Porter, May Swenson, Eudora Welty, Hannah Arendt, Rachel Carson, Ellen Glasgow, Edith Hamilton, Helen Keller, Carson McCullers, Edna St. Vincent Millay, Marianne Craig Moore, Dorothy Parker, Dorothy Thompson, and others.

11,811. American Foundation for the Blind
Records. 1921- . 1012 ft.
Access restricted. Unpublished guide.
American Foundation for the Blind.
Legal records, correspondence with private and public agencies serving the blind, photos, and clippings of the Foundation, which was founded in 1921 as a national consultative agency concerned with problems related to blindness and severe visual handicaps. Records deal with services for the blind; legislation beneficial to blind persons; research projects concerning the technological, educational, and socio-economic aspects of blindness; and the problems and achievements of blind women. The Foundation manufactures "talking books" for the blind and physically handicapped and maintains the M. C. Migel Library, one of the largest collections of print material on blindness in the world.

11,812. Keller, Helen Adams
Papers. 1887- . 71,500 items.
Access restricted. Unpublished guide.
American Foundation for the Blind.
Keller (1880-1968) was a deaf and blind author, lecturer, and counselor on national and international relations for the American Foundation for the Blind and the American Foundation for the Overseas Blind. Correspondence, speeches, literary manuscripts, legal and genealogical papers, clippings, sound recordings, a film *Helen Keller In Her Story,* and transcribed braille material. Subjects include work on behalf of the blind, the deaf-blind, children and women in factories, suffrage, planned parenthood, labor movements, and peace. Extensive papers on Keller's teacher Anne (Sullivan) Macy and on Keller's secretary-companion, [Miss] Mary Agnes "Polly" Thomson. Papers on Mary McLeod Bethune, Pearl Buck, Carrie Chapman Catt, Genevieve Caulfield, Katharine Cornell, Edna Ferber, Elizabeth Gurley Flynn, Emma Goldman, Fannie Hurst, Alice Hegan Rice, Mary Roberts Rinehart, Eleanor Roosevelt, Margaret Sanger, Edith Jones Wharton, and women of other countries.

11,813. Autobiographies
Collection. 1964-65. 28 pp.
Open. No guide.
American Institute of Physics.
Includes manuscript autobiographies of Elizabeth Laird, Maria Goeppert Mayer, and Gail Preston Smith, all of whom were physicists.

11,814. Laird, Elizabeth Rebecca
Papers. 1897-1959. Ca. 100 items.
Open. Finding aid.
American Institute of Physics.
Correspondence of Laird (1874-1969), a physicist, concerns experimental physics research, education, publications, visitors to Mount Holyoke College, and other matters. Correspondents include Niels Bohr, Arthur Holly Compton, Arthur J. Dempster, Theodore Lyman, Arthur Stanley Mackenzie, Dayton Clarence Miller, and Robert Andrews Millikan. Also includes Laird's student notebooks on Edgar Buckingham's lectures on thermodynamics and A. S. Mackenzie's lectures on physics; annotated manuscripts; reprints, including Laird's doctoral dissertation; photos; and clippings concerning dielectrics, soft x-rays, discharge rays, chlorine spectra, Raman effect, and thermal conductivity.

11,815. Oral History
Oral history. 1962-68. More than 4 tapes and 315 pp.
Open. No guide.
American Institute of Physics.
Includes interviews with Betty Compton, wife of the physicist Arthur Holly Compton, 1968; Cecilia Payne-Gaposchkin, an astronomer, 1968; Mary L. Shane, an astronomer, 1967; Maria Goeppert Mayer, a physicist, 1962; and Lise Meitner, a physicist, 1963.

11,816. Whiting, Sarah Frances
Papers. 1883-1914. 20 items.
Open. No guide.
American Institute of Physics.
Correspondence of Whiting (1847-1927), who was a physicist, astronomer, and educator.

11,817. Oral Memoirs
Oral history. 1969- . 98 tapes and 4843 pp. of transcripts.
Access restricted. Unpublished guides.
American Jewish Committee, William E. Wiener Oral History Library.
Tapes and transcripts reflect the American Jewish experience in the 20th century and include interviews with Elizabeth Holtzman, US congresswoman; Roberta Peters and Beverly Sills, opera stars; Molly Picon and Celia Adler, Yiddish theater stars; Sigrid Schultz, overseas correspondent; Beatrice [Mrs. Judah L.] Magnes; Bela Schick, pediatrician, scientist, and author; Dorothy I. Height, president of the National Council of Negro Women; Patricia Roberts Harris, an attorney who was chairman of the credentials committee for the 1972 Democratic National Convention; Rita E. Hauser, an attorney who was cochairman of the Committee to Re-elect the President; Brigette Altman, who was sheltered by Lithuanian peasants during WWII; Kitty Carlisle; Grace LeBoy Kahn; Bel Kaufman; Minnie Marcus; Bess Myerson; Dorothy Rodgers; and Iphigene Ochs Sulzberger.

11,818. Archives of American Art
Collection. Nd. No size given.
Open. Published guide.
Archives of American Art, New York Area Center.
Many of the collections described in the guide for the Smithsonian Institution, Archives of American Art in Washington, DC, are available on microfilm at the New York Area Center as well as at the New England, Midwest, and West Coast Area centers. See *Archives of American Art, Smithsonian Institution: A Checklist of the Collection,* 2nd ed. rev. (1977), which identifies the collections that are available on microfilm, and Garnett McCoy, *Archives of American Art: A Directory of Resources* (New York: R. R. Bowker Company, 1972).

11,819. College Archives
Records. 1917- . Ca. 520 items.
Open. No guide.
Bank Street College of Education.
Founded in 1916, the College offers a four-year degree program in teaching, trains other school personnel, and operates education centers for children and their families. Reports; a scrapbook containing items related to the College's founding and development, including staff memoranda, work schedules, lists of workshops and courses taught by women, fund-raising appeals, philosophical statements on education by the school's teachers and comments by other New York City educators; clippings consisting primarily of book reviews and articles on child development and activities held at the College; typescripts; an alumni directory; publications; reprints; and other items. Records primarily relate to child development, elementary school teaching techniques, and the language of children. Lucy Sprague Mitchell organized the Bureau of Educational Experiments in 1916; the Bureau became the Bank Street College in 1951. Other prominent women connected with the project in its early years included Harriet Mitchell Johnson, who served as director of the Nursery School, and Jessie Stanton, who joined the Bureau staff in 1930.

11,820. Barnard College Archives
Records. 1880s- . 300 ft.
Open. Unpublished guide.
Barnard College Archives.
Minutes, correspondence, oral history tapes and transcripts, scrapbooks, photos, memorabilia, and other records of the College, an undergraduate women's liberal arts college founded in 1889. Records were generated by College faculty, administrators, trustees, and students.

11,821. Overbury, Bertha (Van Riper)
Collection. 1877-1957. Ca. 1000 items.
Open. Unpublished guide.
Barnard College Library.
The collection, assembled by [Mrs. Frederick] Overbury, consists of correspondence and manuscripts of American feminists, authors, political figures, social workers, and other women. Those represented include Abigail Adams, Louisa May Alcott, Gertrude Atherton, Mary Austin, Pearl Buck, Lydia Maria Child, Rebecca (Harding) Davis, Margaret Deland, Emily Dickinson, Zona Gale, Julia Ward Howe, Helen Hunt Jackson, Sarah Orne Jewett, Edna St. Vincent Millay, Harriet Monroe, Marianne Moore, Louise (Chandler) Moulton, Julia Peterkin, Anne Ritchie, Anne Royall, Catherine Maria Sedgwick, Harriet Spofford, Gertrude Stein, Harriet Beecher Stowe, Sara Teasdale, Celia (Laighton) Thaxter, Edith Wharton, Ella Wheeler Wilcox, Frances Willard, and Elinor Wylie.

11,822. Butterick Archives
Records. 1854- . 2000 cu.ft.
Access restricted. Unpublished guide.
Butterick Fashion Marketing Company Library.
Minutes, financial records, correspondence, publications, scrapbooks, photos, and sample products of the Butterick Company, producer of paper dress patterns and related books and magazines. From its early days, Butterick has employed women as writers, designers, artists, fashion consultants, models, and executives. Artists have included Maude Humphreys Bogart, the mother of actor Humphrey Bogart; editors and writers included Marie Mattingly Meloney and Honore Willsie.

11,823. Papers Read Before Cayuga County Historical Society
Records. 1791-mid 1800s. 1 vol.
Open. Unpublished guide.
Cayuga County Historical Research Center.
Includes [Mrs.] Deborah Bronson's and Mrs. S. Benton Hunt's recollections of their early lives in Auburn, NY.

11,824. Avery Family
Papers. 1890-1914. Ca. 75 items.
Open. No guide.
Columbia University, Avery Architectural Library.
Correspondence of Avery family members, chiefly to E. R. Smith, the first librarian of the Avery Architectural Library at Columbia University. The letters primarily concern the contributions of the family to the University and the establishment and early growth of Avery Library.

11,825. Columbiana Library
Collection. 1754- . 15,000 vols. and 24 cabinets.
Open. No guide.
Columbia University, Columbiana Library.
The Library collects material dealing with students, faculty, staff, donors, winners of honorary degrees, and other people connected with the University and its predecessors King's College and Columbia College. Includes manuscripts, photos, clippings, biographies, autobiographies, books, yearbooks, course catalogs, and memorabilia. Also included are clipping files concerning Margaret Mead; Marjorie Hope Nicolson, the first woman appointed as a full professor at the Columbia graduate school; Isadore Gilbert Mudge; Lillian Hellman; Virginia C. Gildersleeve; Mamie (Doud) Eisenhower; and Winifred H. Edgerton as well as files on such subjects as women's liberation, Barnard College, the school of nursing, the Women's Graduate Club, and the Women's Counseling Project.

11,826. Moore, Charity (Clarke), and Moore, Clement Clarke
Papers. 1767-1863. 1 vol. and 44 items.
Open. No guide.
Columbia University, Columbiana Library.
Letters from Charity Moore, wife of Bishop Benjamin Moore (1748-1816), to her sister Lady Affleck, other family members, and friends. Also includes an 1840 letter from her son Clement Clarke Moore (1779-1863), author of *A Compendious Lexicon of the Hebrew Language* and *'Twas the Night Before Christmas,* to his cousin Lady Lilford and his diary for 1856 to 1863. The letters are personal and deal with family matters and daily events. Benjamin Moore was president of Columbia College from 1801 to 1811.

The collection is housed in the Columbia University Rare Book and Manuscript Library.

11,827. Adlai E. Stevenson Project
Oral history. 1966-70. 5326 pp.
Access restricted. Published guide.
Columbia University, Oral History Collection.
Tapes and transcripts of interviews in which friends and associates of Stevenson describe his life and career, particularly as governor of Illinois from 1949 to 1953, as Democratic nominee for the presidency in 1952 and 1956, and as ambassador to the UN from 1961 to 1965. Stevenson's sister Elizabeth (Stevenson) Ives recalls their childhood, their family homes in Libertyville and Bloomington, family anecdotes, the last year of Stevenson's life, and her impressions of his relationships with John F. Kennedy, Robert Kennedy, Hubert Humphrey, Richard J. Daley, and others; she also evaluates Stevenson's biographers. [Mrs.] Marietta Tree, who was US representative to the UN Human Rights Commission and a member of the US mission to the UN under Stevenson, discusses Stevenson, his relationship with Lyndon Johnson, press representation during the 1950s, the last weeks of his life, and his funeral. [Mrs.] Jane Dick talks about Stevenson's religious beliefs and views on capital punishment, her reaction to the Cuban missile crisis, and Ellen Borden Stevenson. Other women interviewed include Katherine Clark Gibbons, Mrs. Warwick Anderson, Lauren Bacall, Elizabeth Beale, Mrs. John Carpenter, Carol Evans, [Mrs.] Margaret M. Farwell, [Mrs.] Ruth Field, Phyllis Gustafson, [Mrs.] Marian Heiskell, Juanda Higgins, [Mrs.] Alicia Hoge, Barbara Kerr, Doris Fleeson Kimball, Kathryn Lewis, Mrs. Glen Alfred Lloyd, [Mrs.] Katie Scofield Louchheim, [Mrs.] Katherine McDougal, Nan McEvoy, Kay McQuaid, Mrs. Paul Budd Magnuson, [Mrs.] Elizabeth Paepcke, Viola Reardy, Mrs. Lawrence Rust, Mrs. Herman Dunlap Smith, [Mrs.] Nancy Anderson Stevenson, Mrs. Chalmer C. Taylor, Mrs. Clifton Maxwell Utley, Mrs. A. L. Voight, and [Mrs.] Harriet Welling. Taken from Elizabeth B. Mason and Louis M. Starr, eds., *The Oral History Collection of Columbia University* (New York: New York Times Company, 1973).

11,828. Allan Nevins Project
Oral history. 1966- . 599 pp.
Access restricted. Published guide.
Columbia University, Oral History Collection.
Associates of historian Nevins recall his career at Columbia from 1928 to 1958 and at the Huntington Library and his later years. Included are interviews with his wife Mary Fleming Nevins, Lillian Bean, and [Mrs.] Jean Stone. Taken from Elizabeth B. Mason and Louis M. Starr, eds., *The Oral History Collection of Columbia University* (New York: New York Times Company, 1973).

11,829. American Cultural Leaders
Oral history. 1968. 1510 pp.
Access restricted. Published guide.
Columbia University, Oral History Collection.
Transcripts of interviews conducted by [Mrs.] Joan Simpson Burns for a study of patterns in American cultural life, which focus on family backgrounds, early exposure to the arts, and the contributions to American culture of those interviewed. Burns's experimental interviewing method encouraged free association and frequent digressions. Includes an interview with Mrs. Marshall Thompson. Taken from Elizabeth B. Mason and Louis M. Starr, eds., *The Oral History Collection of Columbia University* (New York: New York Times Company, 1973).

11,830. Association for the Aid of Crippled Children
Oral history. 1972. 575 pp.
Access restricted. Published guide.
Columbia University, Oral History Collection.
The Association provided services to handicapped children in metropolitan New York for 50 years until its reorganization in 1948. Tapes and transcripts of interviews with staff and board members concern the Association's transition to a foundation; its support of research in prenatal and perinatal problems, genetics, and embryology; conferences on prematurity, the placenta, limb morphology, and teratology; studies of learning disabilities, mental retardation, and accident prevention; and the Association's international collaborative studies. Included are interviews with [Mrs.] Jessie Emmet, [Mrs.] Alice FitzGerald, and [Mrs.] Emily McFarland. Taken from Elizabeth B. Mason and Louis M. Starr, eds., *The Oral History Collection of Columbia University* (New York: New York Times Company, 1973).

11,831. Aviation
Oral history. 1961. 5264 pp.
Partially closed. Published guide.
Columbia University, Oral History Collection.
Transcripts of interviews with designers, engineers, pilots, executives, stunt flyers, and barnstormers concern the development of aviation, beginning with accounts by associates of the Wright brothers and other pioneers of aviation in the US and abroad. Subjects discussed include the development of aerial warfare in WWI; commercial aviation; air mail; exploits of the US air forces, the Royal Air Force, and the Luftwaffe in WWII; and development of rockets and missiles. Jacqueline Cochran, who was married to Floyd B. Odlum, talks about receiving her pilot's license in 1932, the Australian race, ferry flights during WWII, women pilots in the air force, the use of jet planes, and Amelia Earhart. Harry A. Bruno discusses the contribution of women to world aviation. Also interviewed were Adrienne Bolland, Georgia T. Brown, Ellen Church, Jerrie Cobb, [Mrs.] Esther C. Goddard, Mathilde Moisant, Muriel E. Morrissey, Blanche Noyes, Ruth Law Oliver, Hanna Reitsch, Katherine Stinson, and Ruth Rowland Nichols. Taken from Elizabeth B. Mason and Louis M. Starr, eds., *The Oral History Collection of Columbia University* (New York: New York Times Company, 1973).

11,832. Baker, Dorothy
Oral history. 1962. 146-page transcript.
Open. Published guide.
Columbia University, Oral History Collection.
Baker (1907-68) was the author of *Young Man With a Horn, Trio,* and *Cassandra at the Wedding.* Interview concerns her early life, her beginnings as a writer, her reactions to writing and criticism, and her impressions of Robert Frost, Robert Penn Warren, Carson McCullers, F. O. Matthiessen, and May Sarton. Taken from Elizabeth B. Mason and Louis M. Starr, eds., *The Oral History Collection of Columbia University* (New York: New York Times Company, 1973).

11,833. Benedum and the Oil Industry
Oral history. 1951. 1085 pp.
Open. Published guide.
Columbia University, Oral History Collection.
Tapes and transcripts of interviews with Michael Late Benedum (1869-1959) and his associates record the development of the Benedum oil interests from 1890 to 1950. Among the subjects discussed are oil and gas production; transportation, marketing, and refining; oil exploration within and outside the US; geology; legal and tax problems; development of companies and corporate holdings; a US income tax claim against Benedum and Foster B. Parriott in 1925 and the 1937 Supreme Court decision in their favor; and early life and political activities of Benedum. Included are interviews with Sophie and Pearl Benedum and Margaret E. Davis. Taken from Elizabeth B. Mason and Louis M. Starr, eds., *The Oral History Collection of Columbia University* (New York: New York Times Company, 1973).

11,834. Bishop, Isabel
Oral history. 1956. 107-page transcript.
Partially restricted. Published guide.
Columbia University, Oral History Collection.
Bishop (1902-), an artist, is the wife of Harold G. Wolff. Interview relates to her early life and training, the life of an artist, her philosophy of art, the creative process, painting techniques and commentary on her own work, the production of an effective painting through etchings and drawings, and abstract art. Taken from Elizabeth B. Mason and Louis M. Starr, eds., *The Oral History Collection of Columbia University* (New York: New York Times Company, 1973).

11,835. Blake, Mrs. William H.
Oral history. 1975. 6 tapes and 211-page transcript.
Open. Index.
Columbia University, Oral History Collection.
Blake, an artist, discusses activities of the National Association of Women Artists, her life in Paris, art classes in the 1920s in New York City, her work at the Tiffany Foundation, activities at Riverside Church, establishment of the Women's Archives, faculty functions at Columbia University, and her impressions of Cecilia Beaux, F. Luis Mora, Louis Tiffany, and others. Also included are lecture notes from the Art Students League.

11,836. Boas, Franziska
Oral history. 1972. 3 tapes and 76-page transcript.
Partially restricted. Published guide.
Columbia University, Oral History Collection.
Boas reminisces about her father Franz Boas (1858-1942). Taken from Elizabeth B. Mason and Louis M. Starr, eds., *The Oral History Collection of Columbia University* (New York: New York Times Company, 1973).

11,837. Book-of-the-Month Club
Oral history. 1955. 1124 pp.
Open. Published guide.
Columbia University, Oral History Collection.
The founding and development of the Club from 1926 to 1955 is described in interviews with founders, including Harry Scherman; with members of the selection committee; and with executive and technical personnel. Transcripts relate to the reader system of culling books submitted by publishers, attempts by outsiders to influence selection, relationships with publishers, characteristics of subscribers, the preparation and testing of advertisements, other book clubs, opposition of booksellers, the corporate structure of the company, and personnel relations. Includes interviews with Helen R. Feil, Edwina Kohlman, Amy Loveman, Edith Walker, and with Dorothy Canfield Fisher, an author and member of the first selection committee, who comments on committee members, book selection policies, notable books reviewed, and the relationship of the selection committee to the management of the Club. Taken from Elizabeth B. Mason and Louis M. Starr, eds., *The Oral History Collection of Columbia University* (New York: New York Times Company, 1973).

11,838. Boole, Ella Alexander
Oral history. 1950. 28-page transcript.
Open. Published guide.
Columbia University, Oral History Collection.
Interview with [Mrs. William H.] Boole (1858-1952), a church and temperance worker, concerns Prohibition and the development, political activities, and personnel of the WCTU. Taken from Elizabeth B. Mason and Louis M. Starr, eds., *The Oral History Collection of Columbia University* (New York: New York Times Company, 1973).

11,839. Bowles, Dorothy Stebbins
Oral history. 1963. 89-page transcript.
Partially restricted. Published guide.
Columbia University, Oral History Collection.
Bowles describes political events in Connecticut and elsewhere in the life of her husband Chester Bowles, a diplomat and government official; she also talks about John Bailey and William Benton. Taken from Elizabeth B. Mason and Louis M. Starr, eds., *The Oral History Collection of Columbia University* (New York: New York Times Company, 1973).

11,840. Braden, Anne
Oral history. Nd. 1 tape.
Closed. Published guide.
Columbia University, Oral History Collection.
Tape and transcript of an interview with Braden (1924-), a journalist and civil rights activist, concerning her girlhood and education in Alabama; her work as a reporter in Birmingham, AL, and Louisville; postwar race relations in the South, especially in Louisville; the arrest of Braden and her husband Carl Braden for sedition in 1954; and the Southern Conference Educational Fund. Taken from Elizabeth B. Mason and Louis M. Starr, eds., *The Oral History Collection of Columbia University* (New York: New York Times Company, 1973).

11,841. Bunzl, Mrs. Walter
Oral history. 1949. 24-page transcript.
Partially restricted. Published guide.
Columbia University, Oral History Collection.
Bunzl (1907-68), a research assistant to New York City mayor Fiorello La Guardia, discusses New York City politics, the Citizens Union, and La Guardia. Also includes some of her papers. Taken from Elizabeth B. Mason and Louis M. Starr, eds., *The Oral History Collection of Columbia University* (New York: New York Times Company, 1973).

11,842. Burke, Agnes
Oral history. 1969. 50-page transcript.
Partially restricted. Published guide.
Columbia University, Oral History Collection.
Interview with Burke (?-1974), an educator, concerns her childhood in Winona, MN; attending normal school in Winona, the Miss Wheelock Kindergarten Training School in Boston, and Teachers College in New York City; and her experiences as a tutor, reading consultant, and teacher. Taken from Elizabeth B. Mason and Louis M. Starr, eds., *The Oral History Collection of Columbia University* (New York: New York Times Company, 1973).

11,843. Cahill, Holger
Oral history. 1957. 622-page transcript.
Partially restricted. Published guide.
Columbia University, Oral History Collection.
Cahill (1893-1960), a writer and art director, describes his early life in North Dakota, newspaper work in New York City, the New York art world during the 1920s, folk art, the Federal Arts Project, Mrs. John D. Rockefeller, Jr., and art, especially abstract expressionism, since 1943. Included are brief interviews with Cahill's wife Dorothy Canning Miller and with Clair Laning. Taken from Elizabeth B. Mason and Louis M. Starr, eds., *The Oral History Collection of Columbia University* (New York: New York Times Company, 1973).

11,844. Carnegie Corporation
Oral history. 1966-70. 9948 pp.
Access restricted. Published guide and index.
Columbia University, Oral History Collection.
Tapes and manuscripts of interviews with officers, staff members, and grant recipients trace the first 58 years of this philanthropic organization whose purpose is to promote the advancement and diffusion of knowledge and understanding. Interviews concern the corporation's administrative history and its work in such areas as adult education, art and music education, library science, and national security and with independent agencies that received funding from the Corporation. A 656-page transcript of an interview with Florence Anderson (1910-), a foundation officer, relates her experiences with the Corporation beginning in 1934. She discusses major programs undertaken by the Corporation and their impact, trustees and staff members, the Corporation's relationship with the federal government, congressional investigations, and her impressions of Andrew Carnegie, John Gardner, and other educators and public figures. Roberta Capers discusses her work as arts adviser for the Corporation from 1926 to 1934 and as chairman of the Arts Department at Tulane University, museum programs, the American Federation of Arts, the Metropolitan Museum of Art in New York City, and her impressions of Corporation officials. Also included are interviews with Katherine Ford, Alice Hoctor, [Mrs.] Guion Griffis Johnson, Dorothy Rowden Loemker, Constance McCue, Margaret Mahoney, Lois Murkland, and Isabelle C. Neilson. Taken from Elizabeth B. Mason and Louis M. Starr, eds., *The Oral History Collection of Columbia University* (New York: New York Times Company, 1973).

11,845. Children's Television Workshop
Oral history. 1972. 164 pp.
Open. Published guide.
Columbia University, Oral History Collection.
Tapes and transcripts of interviews relate to the founding and staffing of the Workshop; discussions in 1966 of how television might be made to serve preschool children; the roles of the Carnegie Corporation, the Ford Foundation, and US Commissioner of Education Harold Howe II in advancing and helping to finance the concept; the emergence of the "Sesame Street" format; and the relationship of the Workshop with National Educational Television, from which it became independent. Included are interviews with Joan Ganz Cooney and Barbara Finberg. Taken from Elizabeth B. Mason and Louis M. Starr, eds., *The Oral History Collection of Columbia University* (New York: New York Times Company, 1973).

11,846. China Missionaries
Oral history. 1969-71. 3023 pp.
Open. Published guide.
Columbia University, Oral History Collection.
Tapes and transcripts of interviews conducted as part of a project by the Oral History Program at Claremont Graduate School in Claremont, CA, to assess the influence of the missionary movement in China between 1900 and 1950. Christian workers, including educators, medical administrators, teachers, ministers, authors, and translators, discuss local conditions in rural and urban China, their experiences in China, and interaction between American residents and Chinese communities. Women interviewed include Netta Powell Allen, Helen Dizney, Mary Fairfield, Lyda Suydam Houston, Lydia Johnson, [Mrs.] Lucile Williams Jones, Alice Clara Reed, Marjorie Rankin Steurt, Martha Wiley, Pearl Fosnot Winans, Mildred Welch Cranston, Mary Lee Latimer, Ethel Lacey Hylbert, Grace May Rowley, Agnes (Kelly) Scott, Margaret Timberlake Simkin, Margaret (Garrett) Smythe, Louise Hathaway Stanley, Katherine Ward, and Sister Mary Colmcille McCormick. Taken from Elizabeth B. Mason and Louis M. Starr, eds., *The Oral History Collection of Columbia University* (New York: New York Times Company, 1973).

11,847. Columbia Crisis of 1968
Oral history. 1968. 2426 pp.
Access restricted. Published guide.
Columbia University, Oral History Collection.
Tapes and transcripts of interviews conducted for the most part on the Columbia University campus in May 1968 with conservative, independent, and radical student activists; faculty members; administrators; supporting staff; and parents concerning the crisis that resulted in the occupation of five Columbia buildings by students in April 1968; suspension of classes; police interventions; a campuswide strike; and restructuring of the University. Among those interviewed were Cathleen Cook and Barbara and David Nasaw. Taken from Elizabeth B. Mason and Louis M. Starr, eds., *The Oral History Collection of Columbia University* (New York: New York Times Company, 1973).

11,848. Columbia Television Lectures
Oral history. 1962-63. 217 pp.
Open. Published guide.
Columbia University, Oral History Collection.
Tapes and transcripts of lectures by Columbia scholars on current world issues include one by J. E. Kimmy about US foreign policy and the US image abroad. Taken from Elizabeth B. Mason and Louis M. Starr, eds., *The Oral History Collection of Columbia University* (New York: New York Times Company, 1973).

11,849. Columbiana
Oral history. 1955-71. 186 pp.
Open. Published guide.
Columbia University, Oral History Collection.
Tapes and transcripts of interviews with Virginia C. Gildersleeve, Isadore Gilbert Mudge, E. Berthol Sayre, and others who have either made significant contributions to the development of Columbia University or have observed its development over the years. Included are recollections of Nicholas Murray Butler, president of the University from 1902 to 1945, by members of his administration. Taken from Elizabeth B. Mason and Louis M. Starr, eds., *The Oral History Collection of Columbia University* (New York: New York Times Company, 1973).

11,850. Commins, Dorothy Berliner
Oral history. 1962. 181-page transcript.
Closed. Published guide.
Columbia University, Oral History Collection.
Commins discusses the editorial career of her husband Saxe Commins at Liveright, Random House, and Modern Library and her impressions of her husband's relationships with authors, especially Eugene O'Neill and William Faulkner. The interview is closed during her lifetime. Taken from Elizabeth B. Mason and Louis M. Starr, eds., *The Oral History Collection of Columbia University* (New York: New York Times Company, 1973).

11,851. Continental Group Project
Oral history. 1974-75. 21,306 pp.
Access restricted. Index.
Columbia University, Oral History Collection.
Tapes and transcripts of interviews record the experiences of a number of persons who worked at Continental Group, also known as Con Can. Mary F. Clair, a personnel manager in the New York office, describes desirable qualities of women employees in the first few decades of the 20th century. Mary T. Daly talks about her first job with the Conway Company, her career as administrative assistant to the general manager in Con Can's overseas department, and expansion of the export business after WWII. Mary Ellen Tewksbury discusses her childhood and family life during the Depression; her employment with Con Can, first as a clerk typist and eventually as an employment supervisor; relations with the union; changing employee attitudes; and expanding opportunities for women. Gladys Gallagher talks about the position of women in the early 20th century, her training and work as a secretary for Con Can, and management personalities. Secretary and contract clerk Vera R. Oehlberg describes family work for Con Can, career opportunities in

business for women, and women's wardrobes and salaries in the 1930s. Anne Siroky talks about her work as a stenographer for White Cap, union agitation and a wildcat strike in the 1940s, Con Can's acquisition of White Cap, and her work as editor of a weekly newspaper at Con Can. Evelyn Norton Seiler describes early canning processes, the formation of Con Can Company, and her personal recollections of Edwin Norton and of Carle Conway, who was one of the founders of Con Can. Genevieve Kuzma, an hourly worker at White Cap and then Con Can, discusses the piecework and bonus system versus salaries, working as a packer, operating a press, health hazards on the job, and morale of workers. Mary H. Kalamar describes her early life in Hungary and her experiences as a pieceworker from 1922 to 1958 at Con Can. Frances A. Tyler describes her employment as an hourly worker for 46 years in the folding and taping department, employment of women in that department, attitudes toward the union, industrial accidents, and working the night shift. David and Patricia Wilson, relatives of Carle C. Conway, discuss the development of Con Can from 1904 to 1970 and their personal recollections of family and corporate life.

11,852. Corbin, Hazel
Oral history. 1970. 1 tape and 78-page transcript.
Partially restricted. Published guide.
Columbia University, Oral History Collection.
Corbin (1895-), a nurse, discusses health legislation and federal agencies, the World Health Organization, and her work with the Maternity Center Association, founded in 1918, in the areas of prenatal care, maternity institutes, training public health nurses, a certification program for nurse-midwives, and teaching aids. Taken from Elizabeth B. Mason and Louis M. Starr, eds., *The Oral History Collection of Columbia University* (New York: New York Times Company, 1973).

11,853. Dickerman, Marion
Oral history. 1971. 345-page transcript.
Access restricted. Published guide.
Columbia University, Oral History Collection.
Interview with Dickerman (1890-), an educator, concerns her friendship with Franklin and Eleanor Roosevelt; reminiscences of Hyde Park, Campobello, and Warm Springs; Eleanor Roosevelt's childhood and her interest in woman's suffrage and West Virginia mine workers; and the deaths of the Roosevelts. Also relates to WWI; the Todhunter School; Valkill Industries; Alfred E. Smith; opposition to Tammany Hall; the Democratic conventions of 1924 to 1932; the 74th Congress, 1935-36; visiting royalty; international conferences; and recollections of the Roosevelt children and of Louis Howe, Sumner Welles, Marguerite LeHand, Harry Hopkins, and others. Taken from Elizabeth B. Mason and Louis M. Starr, eds., *The Oral History Collection of Columbia University* (New York: New York Times Company, 1973).

11,854. Duer, Caroline King
Oral history. 1950. 76-page transcript.
Partially restricted. Published guide.
Columbia University, Oral History Collection.
Duer (1865-1956), a poet and writer, discusses New York society, her hospital work in WWI and WWII, and personal recollections of Henry James, Edith Wharton, and other writers. Also included are letters from France during WWI on microfilm. Taken from Elizabeth B. Mason and Louis M. Starr, eds., *The Oral History Collection of Columbia University* (New York: New York Times Company, 1973).

11,855. Durr, Virginia Foster
Oral history. 1974. 1 tape and 373-page transcript.
Partially restricted. Index.
Columbia University, Oral History Collection.
Durr (1903-), a civil rights worker, discusses her family history, her childhood with blacks in the South, Birmingham society, attending finishing school, her marriage to Clifford Durr, their move to Washington, DC, the poll tax fight, the movement to unionize the South, and her husband's law practice after 1951 in Montgomery, AL. She reminisces about her sister's courtship and marriage to Hugo Black, Black's campaign for the Senate, and his appointment to the Supreme Court. She also discusses activities of the Southern Conference for Human Welfare in Birmingham, AL; the Ku Klux Klan; civil rights activities; the bus boycott and [Mrs.] Rosa Parks; the Selma march; Martin Luther King, Juliette Morgan, clergymen, and freedom riders; the black power movement; directions in race relations; southern issues; southern women; and Lyndon Johnson, Justice Brandeis, and others.

11,856. Earle, Genevieve Beavers
Oral history. 1950. 126-page transcript.
Partially restricted. Published guide.
Columbia University, Oral History Collection.
Earle (1883-1956), a social worker and politician, was the wife of William P. Earle. She discusses New York City politics from 1917 to 1950, the New York City Charter Revision Committee of 1935, and Fiorello H. La Guardia. Taken from Elizabeth B. Mason and Louis M. Starr, eds., *The Oral History Collection of Columbia University* (New York: New York Times Company, 1973).

11,857. Eisenhower Administration
Oral history. 1962-72. 30,275 pp.
Partially closed. Published guide.
Columbia University, Oral History Collection.
Tapes and transcripts of interviews with persons who played major roles in the Eisenhower administration, including a number of women. Frequent topics of discussion are the Republican party, the Republican National Committee, the 1952 and 1956 Republican conventions and Eisenhower campaigns, and impressions of and anecdotes about President and Mrs. Eisenhower. Anne W. Wheaton, who served as assistant chief of press relations and head of publicity for the women's division of the Republican National Committee from 1939 to 1957 and as associate press secretary to the President, describes Eisenhower's press conferences, cabinet meetings, and the White House staff. [Mrs.] Mary Pillsbury Lord discusses the North Atlantic Treaty Organization, her years with the UN, refugee problems, the Planned Parenthood Association, political and social conditions in Africa and the Middle East, her experiences in Iron Curtain countries, the Atlantic Institute, the 1960 uprising in Ethiopia, student riots in Paris, and her impressions of prominent women. [Mrs.] Clare Boothe Luce discusses the foreign service, her years as ambassador to Italy and Brazil, and John Foster Dulles. Economist Eleanor Lansing Dulles describes her family background and childhood in New York state; her undergraduate work at Bryn Mawr College and teaching there from 1932 to 1936; her refugee work in Paris from 1917 to 1919; her graduate training, including study at the London School of Economics; the Social Security Board; the Board of Economic Warfare; the UN Relief and Rehabilitation Administration; currency reform and monetary conversion; and her impressions of Robert Lansing, John Foster Dulles, Allen Dulles, and others. Also included are interviews with [Mrs.] Katherine Graham Howard, deputy civil defense administrator and delegate to the NATO civil defense committee; Ilene Slater, secretary of Citizens for Eisenhower and secretary to Sherman Adams in the White House; physician Leonard Andrew Scheele, who gives his impressions of Oveta Culp Hobby; Bertha Adkins, who talks about women in government; [Mrs.] Vivion Brewer; Patricia House; Elizabeth Huckaby; [Mrs.] Irene Samuel; Mrs. Thomas E. Stephens; Mrs. Abbot McConnell Washburn; and [Mrs.] Jessie Willock Thornton. Interviews with Mrs. Robert J. Long and Lelia Grace Picking were conducted by the staff of the Eisenhower Library in Abilene, KS, and deposited at Columbia. Long discusses the establishment of Belle Springs Creamery, her work there as bookkeeper, and her relationship with Eisenhower, while Picking describes her family background, church affiliation, attending Abilene High School with Dwight D. Eisenhower, social activities at the School, her teaching experiences, Eisenhower's 1945 homecoming celebration and later visits, and the 50th reunion of the class of 1909. Taken from Elizabeth B. Mason and Louis M. Starr, eds., *The Oral History Collection of Columbia University* (New York: New York Times Company, 1973).

11,858. Erskine, Helen W.
Oral history. 1957. 223-page transcript.
Closed. Published guide.
Columbia University, Oral History Collection.
Interview with Erskine (1896-), an author, relates to her early life in Denver and in New York City, Paris in 1925, her work for the New York *World* and *World-Telegram* from 1926 to 1931, and her first husband John Erskine, a professor. She later married W. H. H. Cranmer. The interview is closed during her lifetime. Taken from Elizabeth B. Mason and Louis M. Starr, eds., *The Oral History Collection of Columbia University* (New York: New York Times Company, 1973).

11,859. Federated Department Stores
Oral history. 1965. 2911 pp.
Access restricted. Published guide.
Columbia University, Oral History Collection.
Tapes and transcripts of interviews with Fred Lazarus, Jr., founder and board chairman; with his family and friends and with others who contributed to the development of Federated, the largest department store organization in the US. Participants discuss the evolution of the organization; changes in its policies, methods, and objectives; and changes in consumer tastes and buying habits over the years. Women interviewed include his wife Celia Rosenthal Lazarus; Eleanor and Margaret Lazarus; Irma Mendelson Lazarus, the wife of Fred Lazarus III; Mrs. Ralph Lazarus; Mrs. Gray Hussey; Mrs. Jesse Evans Ross; Ann Lazarus Schloss; and Ann Visconti. Taken from Elizabeth B. Mason and Louis M. Starr, eds., *The Oral History Collection of Columbia University* (New York: New York Times Company, 1973).

11,860. Ferrell, Conchata
Oral history. 1974. 1 tape and 59-page transcript.
Partially restricted. Index.
Columbia University, Oral History Collection.
Ferrell, an actress, describes her childhood in West Virginia, attending Marshall University in Huntington, WV, her experiences with the Circle Repertory Theatre Company in New York, receiving the Theatre World Award, and her impressions of various actors and actresses.

11,861. Flying Tigers
Oral history. 1962. 583 pp.
Partially restricted. Published guide.
Columbia University, Oral History Collection.
Tapes and transcripts of interviews conducted at a Flying Tiger reunion in Ojai, CA, wherein pilots, mechanics, radiomen, administrators, and ground crew personnel reminisce about their experiences during and after WII with army officer Claire Lee Chennault's American Volunteer Group in Burma and with the China National Aviation Corps. Interviews tell of retreating over the Burma Road, flying P-40s against Japanese bombers, and operating the Mukden shuttle before the fall of Shanghai in 1949. Also includes anecdotes and impressions of Claire Chennault and interviews of [Mrs.] Anna Chennault and Doreen Davis. Taken

from Elizabeth B. Mason and Louis M. Starr, eds., *The Oral History Collection of Columbia University* (New York: New York Times Company, 1973).

11,862. Fordyce, Alice
Oral history. 1964-74. 142 pp.
Partially restricted. Published guide.
Columbia University, Oral History Collection.
In a 1964 interview, Fordyce (1905-), a foundation officer, discusses the use of BCG vaccine for tuberculosis in the US and other countries, isoniazid as a treatment for tuberculosis, and Lasker Foundation Awards for Medical Journalism. In a separate interview conducted in 1974, she discusses the medical profession's continued resistance to the use of BCG. Taken from Elizabeth B. Mason and Louis M. Starr, eds., *The Oral History Collection of Columbia University* (New York: New York Times Company, 1973).

11,863. Forest History Society
Oral history. 1957. 237 pp.
Open. Published guide.
Columbia University, Oral History Collection.
Tapes and transcripts of interviews underwritten by the Society concern forestry, conservation, woods safety, fire fighting, the development of protective associations, old Minnesota logging camps, logging methods and machinery, the development of the Paul Bunyan legends, and impressions of H. L. Mencken, George S. Long, and various lumbermen. Included is an interview with Maggie Orr O'Neill. Taken from Elizabeth B. Mason and Louis M. Starr, eds., *The Oral History Collection of Columbia University* (New York: New York Times Company, 1973).

11,864. Garrison, Charlotte
Oral history. 1967. 58-page transcript.
Partially restricted. Published guide.
Columbia University, Oral History Collection.
Garrison (1881-1972), an educator, discusses studying at Teachers College from 1906 to 1908, her work at the Horace Mann kindergarten where she was director from 1906 to 1928, parents' associations, educational toys, progressive education, the Manhattanville Nursery, a visit to Russia in 1929, and her impressions of James E. Russell, Grace Dodge, Patty Hill, Agnes Burke, and John Dewey. Taken from Elizabeth B. Mason and Louis M. Starr, eds., *The Oral History Collection of Columbia University* (New York: New York Times Company, 1973).

11,865. Gellhorn, Edna
Oral history. 1959-64. 23-page transcript.
Open. Published guide.
Columbia University, Oral History Collection.
In separate interviews [Mrs. George] Gellhorn discusses the LWV from 1919 to 1954, in particular its organization, leaders, and concern with federal and state laws; organizing the Women's Suffrage League of St. Louis in 1919; and working with prominent suffragists. Taken from Elizabeth B. Mason and Louis M. Starr, eds., *The Oral History Collection of Columbia University* (New York: New York Times Company, 1973).

11,866. Gibson, Mary Bass
Oral history. 1975. 13 tapes and 549-page transcript.
Access restricted. Index.
Columbia University, Oral History Collection.
Gibson (1905-), who was an executive editor of *Ladies Home Journal,* discusses her family background; her childhood in Mexico during the early 1900s; evacuation to the US; college life; work at the Hispanic Society of America and publicity work; the careers and influences on her of her four husbands; her marriages, motherhood, and career; the problems and rewards of career women; her career at *Ladies Home Journal* from 1939 to 1962; her work with Bruce and Beatrice Gould; "What the Women of America Think" polls; the Kinsey report; WWII coverage and feature articles; book editing for *Seventeen* magazine; and the *Family Circle* series on careers at home.

11,867. Gilman, Mildred
Oral history. 1969. 82-page transcript.
Partially restricted. Published guide.
Columbia University, Oral History Collection.
Gilman, the wife of Robert Wohlforth, discusses Heywood Broun's activities in the 1920s and 1930s; the Sacco-Vanzetti case; her work at the New York *World* as secretary to Broun; the Algonquin Round Table; Broun, his attempts to unionize reporters, and the Newspaper Guild; the newspaper *Connecticut Nutmeg;* and such figures as Ruth Hale, Sherwood Anderson, Robert Benchley, and H. L. Mencken. Also includes some papers of Gilman. Taken from Elizabeth B. Mason and Louis M. Starr, eds., *The Oral History Collection of Columbia University* (New York: New York Times Company, 1973).

11,868. Goell, Theresa
Oral history. 1965. 1 tape and 54-page transcript.
Access restricted. Published guide.
Columbia University, Oral History Collection.
Interview of Goell, an archaeologist, concerns her early life and education; an archaeological expedition to Turkey, Numrad Dag; and Hartley Lehman. Taken from Elizabeth B. Mason and Louis M. Starr, eds., *The Oral History Collection of Columbia University* (New York: New York Times Company, 1973).

11,869. Guion, Connie Myers
Oral history. 1956. 260-page transcript.
Partially restricted. Published guide.
Columbia University, Oral History Collection.
Guion (1882-1971), a physician, describes her family background and childhood, education, internship at Bellevue Hospital, experiences as an assistant to physicians James Babcock and Frank S. Meara, work at the Cornell Pay Clinic from 1922 to 1932 and at Cornell Medical College from 1932 to 1941, and the Family Comprehensive Care Program. Taken from Elizabeth B. Mason and Louis M. Starr, eds., *The Oral History Collection of Columbia University* (New York: New York Times Company, 1973).

11,870. Hagen, Beulah W.
Oral history. 1976. 3 tapes and 235-page transcript.
Partially restricted. Index.
Columbia University, Oral History Collection.
Interview with Hagen concerns her family background; her teaching experiences; her marriage and life in New York during the Depression; her work at Harper and Brothers from 1935 to 1975 and relationships with authors there; her duties as assistant to Cass Canfield; wartime projects, problems, and memories; Harper fellowships and prizes; publishing policies at Harper; employee unionization; and archival work.

11,871. Halsted, Anna (Roosevelt)
Oral history. 1973. 2 tapes and 55-page transcript.
Access restricted. Index.
Columbia University, Oral History Collection.
Halsted (1906-75), the daughter of Franklin Delano and Eleanor Roosevelt, describes her childhood in Hyde Park, family life and relationships, family associates, the years when her father was governor of New York, Yalta, and Franklin D., Eleanor, Sara, and Elliot Roosevelt.

11,872. Harriman, Florence Jaffray
Oral history. 1950. 40-page transcript.
Partially restricted. Published guide.
Columbia University, Oral History Collection.
Interview with Florence "Daisy" Jaffray (Hurst) Harriman (1870-1967), a politician and diplomat who was married to J. Borden Harriman, concerns Democratic party politics from 1912 to 1945. Taken from Elizabeth B. Mason and Louis M. Starr, eds., *The Oral History Collection of Columbia University* (New York: New York Times Company, 1973).

11,873. Hart Crane Project
Oral history. 1963. 201 pp.
Access restricted. Published guide.
Columbia University, Oral History Collection.
Transcripts of interviews with [Mrs.] Margaret Babcock, Peggy Baird, Fredrica Crane Lewis, and others concern Hart Crane and the literary world in Ohio and New York City during the 1920s. Taken from Elizabeth B. Mason and Louis M. Starr, eds., *The Oral History Collection of Columbia University* (New York: New York Times Company, 1973).

11,874. Henry H. Arnold Project
Oral history. 1959-60. 1726 pp.
Access restricted. Published guide.
Columbia University, Oral History Collection.
Tapes and transcripts of interviews with associates of General Arnold (1886-1950), first commander of the Army Air Forces, concern his role in the Air Forces, his contributions to the development of military aviation, and his work as a member of the Combined Chiefs of Staff during WWII. Includes an interview with Arnold's widow Eleanor Pool Arnold, who describes Henry Arnold's family background; their engagement and marriage in 1913; his work with forest patrols and air mail for the Army Air Corps; the trial, reprimand, and exile of William L. Mitchell; effects of the Depression; and her impressions of Douglas MacArthur, George C. Marshall, and others. Taken from Elizabeth B. Mason and Louis M. Starr, eds., *The Oral History Collection of Columbia University* (New York: New York Times Company, 1973).

11,875. Herbert H. Lehman Project
Oral history. 1959. 1184 pp.
Partially restricted. Published guide.
Columbia University, Oral History Collection.
Transcripts of interviews with Lehman, a businessman and New York senator, and with persons who were closely associated with him through various stages of his career, including [Mrs.] Helen Altschul, Carolin A. Flexner, [Mrs.] Eleanor Roosevelt, and Anna Marie (Lederer) Rosenberg. Taken from Elizabeth B. Mason and Louis M. Starr, eds., *The Oral History Collection of Columbia University* (New York: New York Times Company, 1973).

11,876. Holm, Jeanne
Oral history. 1973. 80-page transcript.
Open. Index.
Columbia University, Oral History Collection.
Holm, a brigadier general, was interviewed as part of the US Air Force Project; she discusses the role of women in the armed services from WWI to the present, the differences between the branches of the services in the acceptance of women, Air Force policies, the Reserve Officers Training Corps for women, and the Equal Rights Amendment.

11,877. Independence National Historical Park
Oral history. 1970. 574 pp.
Access restricted. Published guide.
Columbia University, Oral History Collection.
Tapes and transcripts of interviews with persons involved in the development of the Park and in the Independence Hall Association concern urban redevelopment; historic preservation and restoration in Philadelphia; legal, financial, architectural, and procedural problems and how they were surmounted; and the role of the National Park Service. Included are interviews with Lysbeth Boyd Borie and Mrs. Joseph Carson. Taken from Elizabeth B. Mason and Louis M. Starr, eds., *The*

Oral History Collection of Columbia University (New York: New York Times Company, 1973).

11,878. Jackson Hole Preserve
Oral history. 1966. 1080 pp.
Access restricted. Published guide.
Columbia University, Oral History Collection.
Tapes and transcripts of interviews with some of the Jackson Hole residents who have experienced the transformation of the area since it became part of the National Park System in the 1940s. Among the subjects discussed are the history of the Jackson Hole Preserve, the Rockefeller family's interest in preserving and protecting the area, and difficulties in acquiring the land for the Park System. Includes an interview with Katharine Newlin Burt. Taken from Elizabeth B. Mason and Louis M. Starr, eds., *The Oral History Collection of Columbia University* (New York: New York Times Company, 1973).

11,879. James B. Duke Project
Oral history. 1966. 2907 pp.
Access restricted. Published guide.
Columbia University, Oral History Collection.
Transcripts of interviews with associates of Duke (1857-1925) concern the Duke family; the development of the Duke Power Company; life in the Piedmont region of North Carolina and economic and social changes brought by industrialization; Duke's interest in southern education, in particular Trinity College, which later became Duke University; and the Duke Endowment. Mary Reamey Thomas Few describes her family background in Virginia, her education at Trinity College where she received a BA in 1902, her friendship with the Duke family, her graduate work at Columbia University, her life as the wife of Trinity College and Duke University president William Preston Few, the founding of the University in 1924, her impressions of various academic and political figures, and her work as a Republican national committeewoman. Also included are interviews with Mildred Baldwin, [Mrs.] Mary Glassen, Mrs. E. C. Marshall, Mr. and Mrs. E. R. Merrick, [Mrs.] Mary Duke Biddle Trent Semans, and Mrs. John Williams. Taken from Elizabeth B. Mason and Louis M. Starr, eds., *The Oral History Collection of Columbia University* (New York: New York Times Company, 1973).

11,880. John Robert Gregg Project
Oral history. 1956. 168 pp.
Access restricted. Published guide.
Columbia University, Oral History Collection.
Transcripts of interviews with friends and associates of Gregg (1867-1948), who developed the Gregg shorthand system, including one with Margaret Richards Shimko. Taken from Elizabeth B. Mason and Louis M. Starr, eds., *The Oral History Collection of Columbia University* (New York: New York Times Company, 1973).

11,881. Joseph M. Proskauer Project
Oral history. 1966. 299 pp.
Access restricted. Published guide.
Columbia University, Oral History Collection.
Transcripts of Judge Proskauer's reminiscences and anecdotes and recollections by his family, friends, and associates, including Kate Pantell and Ruth Proskauer Smith. Taken from Elizabeth B. Mason and Louis M. Starr, eds., *The Oral History Collection of Columbia University* (New York: New York Times Company, 1973).

11,882. Kennedy, Elsie (Parsons)
Oral history. 1962. 1 tape and 58-page transcript.
Partially restricted. Published guide.
Columbia University, Oral History Collection.
Kennedy (1903-66), who was the daughter of anthropologist Elsie Clews Parsons, recalls her parents and grandparents, Newport and New York society, the Republican Convention of 1920, and real estate developments during the 1920s in New York City. Taken from Elizabeth B. Mason and Louis M. Starr, eds., *The Oral History Collection of Columbia University* (New York: New York Times Company, 1973).

11,883. Kerr, Florence
Oral history. 1974. 1 tape and 110-page transcript.
Partially restricted. Index.
Columbia University, Oral History Collection.
Kerr (1890-1975) served from 1935 to 1938 as Chicago Midwest regional director and in 1938 as Washington assistant commissioner of the Women's and Professional Projects of the WPA and from 1942 to 1945 as assistant commissioner of the Federal Works Agency. She describes unskilled women's projects, the Arts Project and appropriations for it, Russian missions, Harry Hopkins, and her relations with and impressions of Franklin Roosevelt and other New Dealers.

11,884. La Guardia, Marie M.
Oral history. 1950. 56-page transcript.
Partially restricted. Published guide.
Columbia University, Oral History Collection.
La Guardia (1896-) gives personal reminiscences of her husband Fiorello H. La Guardia, mayor of New York City. Taken from Elizabeth B. Mason and Louis M. Starr, eds., *The Oral History Collection of Columbia University* (New York: New York Times Company, 1973).

11,885. Lasker, Mary
Oral history. 1965-72. 14 tapes and 1525-page transcript.
Closed. Published guide.
Columbia University, Oral History Collection.
Interviews with Lasker (1900-), a philanthropist and the widow of Albert D. Lasker, concern her family background, education at the University of Wisconsin and Radcliffe College, study at Oxford University, interest in fine arts and the performing arts, her Hollywood dress pattern business, and promotion of medical research. She discusses the US Public Health Service; the National Science Foundation, fund-raising activities for the American Cancer Society and the American Heart Association, her promotion of the Planned Parenthood Federation, activities of the Lasker Foundation to promote health through medical research, attempts to secure appropriations to implement existing legislation for medical research, federal aid to medical education, the development of regional medical centers, health insurance, her interest in psychoanalysis, and the development of national institutes for cancer, heart disease, arthritis, mental health, neurological diseases, and blindness. Taken from Elizabeth B. Mason and Louis M. Starr, eds., *The Oral History Collection of Columbia University* (New York: New York Times Company, 1973).

11,886. Lee, Percy Maxim
Oral history. 1973. 2 tapes and 559-page transcript.
Partially restricted. Index.
Columbia University, Oral History Collection.
Interview with [Mrs. John Glessner] Lee concerns the origin and development of the LWV, the Carrie Chapman Catt Memorial Foundation, Lee's presidency of the LWV and her experiences in Washington, DC, and her impressions of other LWV members, including Anna Lord Strauss, Katharine Ludington, and Marguerite Wells.

11,887. Longwood Gardens Project
Oral history. 1974-75. No size given.
Access restricted. Index.
Columbia University, Oral History Collection.
[Mrs.] Wilhelmina du Pont Ross reminisces about her childhood at Longwood Gardens, her uncle and aunt Mr. and Mrs. Pierre S. du Pont, and her service on the advisory committee for Longwood Gardens after Pierre du Pont's death. [Mrs.] I. Sophie du Pont May describes Pierre du Pont's involvement in planning and constructing the Gardens, the history of the buildings and garden, and entertaining there.

11,888. Lynd, Helen M.
Oral history. 1973. 4 tapes and 290-page transcript.
Access restricted. Index.
Columbia University, Oral History Collection.
Lynd, an educator and writer, describes her early life, background, and education; her married life; working with her husband Robert Lynd on *Middletown;* her children; teaching at Sarah Lawrence College; and the McCarthy hearings.

11,889. McGraw-Hill, Inc.
Oral history. 1956. 4170 pp.
Access restricted. Published guide.
Columbia University, Oral History Collection.
The development of McGraw-Hill and its part in educational, industrial, and technical development in the US and abroad from 1886 to 1964 are traced in a series of interviews with persons associated with the company. Associates of James H. McGraw and John A. Hill recall the careers of these two men, the merger of the two publishing companies in the early 20th century, and the continued expansion of McGraw-Hill. Editors of trade, educational, and business publications discuss editorial and circulation policy, standards of responsibility vis à vis readers and advertisers, and new fields for publications and instructional materials. Other topics discussed include the writing and publishing of college and vocational education textbooks, elementary and high school instructional material, technical writing, and the international aspects of book publishing. Women interviewed include Lillian Charlton, Maud Clark, Helene Frye, Elizabeth Gile, Alice E. Kraft, Mrs. Donald C. McGraw, Alice McMullin, and Margaret Richards. Taken from Elizabeth B. Mason and Louis M. Starr, eds., *The Oral History Collection of Columbia University* (New York: New York Times Company, 1973).

11,890. McIntosh, Millicent Carey
Oral history. 1966. 13 tapes and 695-page transcript.
Access restricted. Published guide.
Columbia University, Oral History Collection.
Interview with McIntosh (1898-), an educator, concerns her family and youth, education at Bryn Mawr School and Bryn Mawr College, work at Brearley School, graduate work at Johns Hopkins University, her presidency of Barnard College, and the development of religion and education programs at Barnard. She also discusses changes in curriculum and methodology, women's education, trends in progressive education, her attitudes toward advanced placement, her impressions of prominent educators, social work and community activities, changes in manners and morals, and the generation gap. Taken from Elizabeth B. Mason and Louis M. Starr, eds., *The Oral History Collection of Columbia University* (New York: New York Times Company, 1973).

11,891. Macy, Helen
Oral history. 1974. 17 tapes and 605-page transcript.
Access restricted. Published guide.
Columbia University, Oral History Collection.
Tapes of interview in which Macy discusses the career of her husband George Macy (1900-56), founder of the Limited Editions Club. Taken from Elizabeth B. Mason and Louis M. Starr, eds., *The Oral History Collection of Columbia University* (New York: New York Times Company, 1973).

11,892. Marshall, John
Oral history. 1974. 22 tapes and 1053-page transcript.
Access restricted. Index.
Columbia University, Oral History Collection.
Marshall, a Rockefeller Foundation officer, recalls his childhood and education, his associations with the Foundation, and his travels in the Middle East and Europe for the Foundation. Also included is an account by Marshall's wife of her participation in the management of the Villa Serbelloni.

11,893. Massee, May
Oral history. 1966. 8 tapes and 96-page transcript.
Partially restricted. Published guide.
Columbia University, Oral History Collection.
Interview in which Massee (1889-1966), an editor, discusses her early library work, attending the Wisconsin library school, her work at Armour Institute and Buffalo Library, her work as organizer and editor of the children's book department at Doubleday, and her impressions of such publishers as Frank Doubleday. Taken from Elizabeth B. Mason and Louis M. Starr, eds., *The Oral History Collection of Columbia University* (New York: New York Times Company, 1973).

11,894. Masters, Ellen Coyne
Oral history. 1971. 2 tapes and 208-page transcript.
Access restricted. Published guide.
Columbia University, Oral History Collection.
Masters (1899-) discusses her girlhood in Kansas City, Panama, and the Missouri Ozarks; her education at the University of Chicago; work at the Abbey Theatre in 1924; recollections of literary figures such as Theodore Dreiser, Vachel Lindsay, and H. L. Mencken; her courtship and marriage to Edgar Lee Masters during the 1920s in New York City; anecdotes about her husband's early life; her husband's personality and creative approach; and works by her husband, including *Spoon River Anthology* and *Domesday Book.* Taken from Elizabeth B. Mason and Louis M. Starr, eds., *The Oral History Collection of Columbia University* (New York: New York Times Company, 1973).

11,895. Max, Pearl
Oral history. 1961. 185-page transcript.
Partially restricted. Published guide.
Columbia University, Oral History Collection.
[Mrs. Louis W.] Max (1904-) was an administrator on the New York City board of higher education from 1938 to 1961. She discusses relationships between city administrations and city colleges, policies and personalities in New York City higher education, the Bertrand Russell case, investigation of higher education in New York City by the Rapp-Coudert and Strayer committees, and her impressions of mayors Fiorello La Guardia, Vincent Impellitteri, and Robert F. Wagner. Taken from Elizabeth B. Mason and Louis M. Starr, eds., *The Oral History Collection of Columbia University* (New York: New York Times Company, 1973).

11,896. Meyer, Eugene
Oral history. 1953. 1 tape and 938-page transcript.
Partially restricted. Published guide.
Columbia University, Oral History Collection.
Interview with Meyer (1875-1959), a financier and newspaper executive, concerns his childhood and education, financial operations, the Reconstruction Finance Administration and the Federal Reserve System during the banking crisis of 1933, and his work with the Washington *Post* from 1933 to 1953. Also included are excerpts from a diary by Meyer's wife Agnes Meyer describing the Washington scene during the 1920s and 1930s. Taken from Elizabeth B. Mason and Louis M. Starr, eds., *The Oral History Collection of Columbia University* (New York: New York Times Company, 1973).

11,897. Miscellany
Oral history. Nd. No size given.
Partially closed. Published guide.
Columbia University, Oral History Collection.
A number of interviews in the Oral History Collection pertain to women although the participants are not women. Among these are the Abraham Kazan and Solomon Barkin interviews, both of which touch on the International Ladies' Garment Workers' Union; the interview with labor organizer Benjamin McLaurin, who speaks of the International Ladies Auxiliary; and the John W. Edelman interview, in which Edelman relates his impressions of women prominent in the labor movement. The Labor Seminar, part of the University Seminars collection, contains discussions of job discrimination against women, women in unions, and pay scales. Author-journalist George Samuel Schuyler speaks of Socialist party activities, the NAACP, and interracial marriage. The New York Political Studies collection includes discussions by Mrs. Fiorello H. La Guardia and Jane H. Todd about the New York election of 1949 and a study of the office of deputy mayor of New York, in which the Women's City Club participated.

Homer Folks and Lawrence Veiller speak of social work in New York City, Veiller describing reforms in the children's and domestic relations courts and Folks discussing children's aid and American social work in general. Attorney George William Alger gives his observations of social reformers Lillian Wald and Florence Kelley, while Judge Joseph Aloysius Cox describes notable cases, including those of Ida Wood and Mabel Greer. Nicholas Kelley speaks of his family background and mother Florence Kelley, a social worker and reformer who was active at Hull House, the Henry Street Settlement, and in the National Consumers' League.

Physician Clarence E. de la Chapelle speaks of women in medicine, and educator James Madison Wood discusses women's activities in junior colleges, the women's rights movement, and the Women's Foundation. As professor and later head of Teachers College, Hollis Caswell set patterns which influence women teachers throughout the country; he discusses the College, which still has a preponderance of women teachers in graduate training there. [Miss] Anna T. Jeanes supplied a fund for training teachers, most of them women, for Negro educational institutions; educator J. Curtis Dixon talks about Jeanes teachers in his interview.

There are comments on such women as Eleanor Roosevelt, Margaret Sanger, Edith Wharton, Edna St. Vincent Millay, Mary Calderone, and Jacqueline Kennedy in interviews with Roger Nash Baldwin, Will Winton Alexander, Charles Ascher, Cass Canfield, and Edward Bernays. Margaret Mead and Marya Mannes participated in forums assessing American journalism in the 1960s; transcripts of the forums are in the Journalism Lectures collection. Alfred A. Knopf, William Stanley Beaumont Braithwaite, Carl Van Vechten, and John Hall Wheelock speak of American women prominent in the literary field, including Gertrude Stein, Amy Lowell, Willa Cather, and Sara Teasdale. Bennett Cerf talks about the Miss America pageant, his marriages to Sylvia Sidney and Phyllis Fraser, and well-known personalities in literary and entertainment fields. Paul Joseph Sachs, a professor of fine arts, discusses women as patrons of the arts, as students in the Harvard Museum course, and as professional curators and museum assistants. Actor, producer, and director Eddie Dowling comments on people in the theater and Hollywood, among them Sarah Bernhardt. Actor Richard Gordon relates his impressions of Maude Adams, Mary Emerson, Anne Sutherland, Frances Ring, and Mildred Holland. Taken fromElizabeth B. Mason and Louis M. Starr, eds., *The Oral History Collection of Columbia University* (New York: New York Times Company, 1973).

11,898. Mitchell, Lucy Sprague
Oral history. 1960. 167-page transcript.
Partially restricted. Published guide.
Columbia University, Oral History Collection.
Interviews conducted by the Regional Oral History Office of the University of California at Berkeley with Mitchell (1878-1967), an educator, concern her position as dean of women at the University of California in 1906, her marriage to Wesley Clair Mitchell and move to New York in 1912, her interest in experimental education, founding the Bank Street School, and teaching and writing for children. Taken from Elizabeth B. Mason and Louis M. Starr, eds., *The Oral History Collection of Columbia University* (New York: New York Times Company, 1973).

11,899. Murphy, Katherine Prentis
Oral history. 1957. 50-page transcript.
Open. Published guide.
Columbia University, Oral History Collection.
Random reflections by Murphy (1882-1969), a collector of early American furnishings. Taken from Elizabeth B. Mason and Louis M. Starr, eds., *The Oral History Collection of Columbia University* (New York: New York Times Company, 1973).

11,900. New School Lectures
Oral history. 1959. 58 pp.
Open. Published guide.
Columbia University, Oral History Collection.
Lectures from the Wisdom of Life series delivered at the New School primarily concern management of human resources; one of the lectures was by Lillian M. Gilbreth. Taken from Elizabeth B. Mason and Louis M. Starr, eds., *The Oral History Collection of Columbia University* (New York: New York Times Company, 1973).

11,901. Nobel Laureates on Scientific Research
Oral history. 1964. 1525 pp.
Access restricted. Published guide.
Columbia University, Oral History Collection.
Interviews in which Nobel laureates in science each describe their relations with coworkers, the contributions of others and events leading up to their discoveries, and their associations with Nobel prize winners and with other eminent scientists. This project, which was supported by the National Science Foundation, includes an interview with Maria Goeppert Mayer, who received the Nobel prize for physics in 1963. Taken from Elizabeth B. Mason and Louis M. Starr, eds., *The Oral History Collection of Columbia University* (New York: New York Times Company, 1973).

11,902. Occupation of Japan
Oral history. 1960-61. 1488 pp.
Partially restricted. Published guide.
Columbia University, Oral History Collection.
Transcripts of interviews with persons who participated in the occupation of Japan relate to occupation programs and policies; accounts of social, economic, agricultural, educational, and cultural developments; purges; and problems of civil rights. Also included are descriptions of the drafting of the new constitution, of steps leading to the change in the role of the Emperor of Japan, and of leading figures of the Supreme Commander for Allied Powers and the Far Eastern Commission. Women interviewed include Esther Crane, Madame Ai Kume, Josephine McKean, and Lulu Holmes, who was adviser to the SCAP on higher education for women in Japan. Taken from Elizabeth B. Mason and Louis M. Starr, eds., *The Oral History Collection of Columbia University* (New York: New York Times Company, 1973).

11,903. Oppenheim, Adelaide
Oral history. 1976. 1 tape and 50-page transcript. Open. Index.
Columbia University, Oral History Collection.
Oppenheim, an engineer, describes her education at Cornell University from 1930 to 1934 and at the State University of New York from 1934 to 1935, her work in 1941 as a heat transfer laboratory supervisor at the General Electric engineering lab, her work at the Knolls Atomic Power Lab, and courses on women in program management and the program evaluation review technique in 1974 at the graduate school and in continuing education at Union College in Schenectady, NY.

11,904. Paul, Alice
Oral history. 1973. 648-page transcript. Partially restricted. Index.
Columbia University, Oral History Collection.
In a series of interviews conducted by the Regional Oral History Office of the University of California at Berkeley, Paul (1885-1977), a feminist, describes her Quaker background, her education at Swarthmore College, study and social work in New York City, study and work with the Pankhurst movement in England, and her return to the US, where she received a PhD in economics in 1912. Paul discusses her involvement with the woman suffrage movement as head of the National American Woman Suffrage Association congressional union; her split with NAWSA following a dispute over the Shafroth-Palmer Amendment; lobbying, the policy of holding the party in power responsible, and other methods of campaigning for suffrage; her imprisonment; and the formation of the National Woman's Party. She also talks about selecting the wording of the Equal Rights Amendment, lobbying for the ERA, opposition to the ERA by the AAUW and the Women's Bureau, passage of the ERA with a change in enforcement and a seven-year limit, an attempted insurrection within the NWP and its effect on the ERA campaign, and other concerns of the NWP.

11,905. Perkins, Frances
Oral history. 1955. 3 tapes and 5566-page transcript.
Partially restricted. Published guide.
Columbia University, Oral History Collection.
Perkins (1882-1965), a government official, discusses her education at Mount Holyoke College; social work in Chicago and Philadelphia; her work for woman's suffrage; the Consumers' League of New York; New York mayors and their administrations; Democratic National Conventions and elections of 1920 to 1940; unemployment in the period 1929 to 1932; workmen's compensation; labor unions and labor legislation; the New York labor department; migrant labor; her position as secretary of labor from 1933 to 1945; the National Labor Relations Board; the background of the National Recovery Administration; various strikes, including the General Motors strike of 1937 and the San Francisco longshoremen's strike; the International Labor Office; WWI; WWII; women and careers; and art and literature. Also included are papers of Perkins. Taken from Elizabeth B. Mason and Louis M. Starr, eds., *The Oral History Collection of Columbia University* (New York: New York Times Company, 1973).

11,906. Phillips, Kathryn Sisson
Oral history. 1962. 1 tape and 98-page transcript. Partially restricted. Published guide.
Columbia University, Oral History Collection.
Interview with Phillips (1879-1968), an educator, concerns her childhood in Kansas and Nebraska, her education at Ohio Wesleyan, her work as secretary of the YWCA, her early experiences as dean of women at a state teachers' college in Chadron, NE, formation of the National Association of Deans of Women, her educational opinions and theories, and the Phillips Foundation. Taken from Elizabeth B. Mason and Louis M. Starr, eds., *The Oral History Collection of Columbia University* (New York: New York Times Company, 1973).

11,907. Popular Arts Project
Oral history. 1958-60. 7819 pp.
Partially restricted. Published guide.
Columbia University, Oral History Collection.
The development of the performing arts in the 20th century is depicted in interviews with actors and actresses, producers, directors, playwrights, composers, lyricists, dancers, journalists, critics, advertising men, and others. Included are recollections of nickelodeon days, early studios and equipment in New York and New Jersey, the Hollywood mythology, the emergence of slapstick comedy, state censorship, the origin of the Motion Picture Code, silent films, and the effects of the introduction of sound. Also discussed are the social structure of Hollywood in the 1930s, the life of a child actor, and the impact of television and of charges of communism upon the entertainment industry. Interviews about popular music concern Tin Pan Alley; the vaudeville circuits; effects of the player piano, phonograph, and radio; the era of the big bands; and recent trends. Discussions of the stage relate to the stock company as training ground, the road, new methods of acting and directing, the role of the legitimate theater in contemporary life, artistic freedom, comparisons of stage with screen techniques, and the concentration of theater in New York City. Women interviewed include Jean Aberbach, Betty Comden, Katharine Cornell, Glenda Farrell, Betty Field, Dorothy Fields, Gracie Fields, Janet Gaynor, Sheilah Graham, Bonita Granville, Julie Harris, Celeste Holm, [Mrs.] Katherine Handy Lewis, Anita Loos, Myrna Loy, Jeanette MacDonald, Aline MacMahon, Frances Marion, Mae Marsh, Mae Murray, Nita Naldi, Geraldine Page, Evelyn Pain, Dorothy Rothschild Parker, Louella O. Parsons, Mary Pickford, Blanche Ring, Bella Loebel Spewack, Kim Stanley, Maureen Stapleton, Gloria Swanson, Joanne Woodward, Teresa Wright, and Lila Lee. Taken from Elizabeth B. Mason and Louis M. Starr, eds., *The Oral History Collection of Columbia University* (New York: New York Times Company, 1973).

11,908. Psychoanalytic Movement
Oral history. 1963-66. 1802 pp.
Partially restricted. Published guide.
Columbia University, Oral History Collection.
Pioneers of the movement, including leading representatives of major schools of psychoanalytic theory, associates of Sigmund Freud, and others closely related to the movement discuss the early history of psychoanalysis and its subsequent ramifications. Included is an interview in which Margaret Mahler discusses her youth and education in Hungary and Germany, her work with the von Pirquet clinic in Vienna and the Moll Well-baby Clinic, undergoing analysis, her association with second generation psychoanalysts, her acceptance in the Vienna Psychoanalytic Institute in 1933, Rorschach studies, the establishment of the first psychoanalytically oriented child guidance clinic in 1933, her escape to New York during the Nazi takeover, her work at the New York Psychiatric Institute, and child development, analysis, and psychosis studies. Taken from Elizabeth B. Mason and Louis M. Starr, eds., *The Oral History Collection of Columbia University* (New York: New York Times Company, 1973).

11,909. Radio Pioneers
Oral history. 1950- . 4765 pp.
Partially restricted. Published guide.
Columbia University, Oral History Collection.
Tapes and transcripts of interviews with engineers, station and network executives, government officials, writers, directors, and performers present a comprehensive record of the early history of radio. Among the topics discussed are early experiments with radio, engineering problems, broadcast ethics, the growth of networks, the impact of television on the radio business, the Federal Radio Commission, the FCC, radio law and legislation, censorship during WWII, and programming. Included are interviews with Rosaline Greene, Ruth Lyons, Sybil True, and Dorothy Gordon, who discusses her childhood and education, her marriage, her early experience in radio, her work on radio programs for children, and her impressions of radio personalities and public figures. Taken from Elizabeth B. Mason and Louis M. Starr, eds., *The Oral History Collection of Columbia University* (New York: New York Times Company, 1973).

11,910. Raushenbush, Esther
Oral history. 1973-74. 1 tape and 658 pp.
Partially restricted. Index.
Columbia University, Oral History Collection.
Interview with [Mrs.] Raushenbush (1898-) concerns her family history, educational background, marriage, professional career at Wellesley and Barnard, her presidency of Sarah Lawrence College, progressive education, implementation of social change, scholarship programs for minority group members, the Center for Continuing Education at Sarah Lawrence, the McCarthy era, and her impressions of various people connected with Sarah Lawrence, including Beatrice Doerschuk and Constance Warren. In a separate interview Raushenbush discusses the beginnings, development, and present status of continuing education for women at Sarah Lawrence.

11,911. Rhind, Flora Macdonald
Oral history. 1969. 31 tapes and 1520-page transcript.
Access restricted. Published guide.
Columbia University, Oral History Collection.
Interview with Rhind (1904-), a foundation officer, concerns her background and education and her work with the General Education Board and the Rockefeller Foundation from 1933 to 1964. In particular, she discusses evaluating programs; her responsibilities as secretary of the Rockefeller Foundation; the social science program; fellowships and grants-in-aid; the evolution of the general education program; the American Youth Commission; development of the southern program, including the Southern Fellowships Fund, the Southern Regional Education Board, the state agents for rural schools; the European program; and congressional investigations. Rhind also discusses her impressions of John D. Rockefeller, Jr., John D. Rockefeller, 3rd, and others. Taken from Elizabeth B. Mason and Louis M. Starr, eds., *The Oral History Collection of Columbia University* (New York: New York Times Company, 1973).

11,912. Richard Hofstadter Project
Oral history. 1972. 238 pp.
Partially restricted. Published guide.
Columbia University, Oral History Collection.
Hofstadter, author of *The Age of Reform* and *The American Political Tradition,* was a professor of American history at Columbia from 1946 to 1970. Tapes and transcripts of interviews with students, colleagues, and others who knew Hofstadter concern his character, intellectual development, teaching, and writing. Includes an interview with Elisabeth Earley. Taken from Elizabeth B. Mason and Louis M. Starr, eds., *The Oral History Collection of Columbia University* (New York: New York Times Company, 1973).

11,913. Robert A. Taft Project
Oral history. 1967-70. 1471 pp.
Access restricted. Published guide.
Columbia University, Oral History Collection.
Tapes and transcripts of interviews with colleagues,

friends, and family of Taft (1889-1953), a US senator from Ohio who was a Republican, describing his development as a lawyer, his political growth, his activities in Ohio and Washington, DC, and his family relationships. Included are interviews with Mrs. Robert L. Black, Katharine Kennedy Brown, [Mrs.] Eugenie Mary Davie, Marjorie Hein, [Mrs.] Helen Herron (Taft) Manning, Mrs. Stanley Rowe, and [Mrs.] Barbara Taft. Taken from Elizabeth B. Mason and Louis M. Starr, eds., *The Oral History Collection of Columbia University* (New York: New York Times Company, 1973).

11,914. Rosenman, Dorothy (Reuben)
Oral history. 1976. 2 tapes and 65-page transcript.
Open. Index.
Columbia University, Oral History Collection.
Rosenman (1900-), who was active in housing reform during the 1930s and 1940s, discusses the Citizens' Housing Council; the housing committee of United Neighborhood Houses of New York; the National Committee on Housing; the National Urban League; a New York state constitutional amendment on housing; her husband Samuel I. Rosenman, a judge; and their political and social contacts, including Fiorello La Guardia, Bob Moses, Franklin and Eleanor Roosevelt, Harry Truman, and Belle Moskowitz.

11,915. Skirball, Sheba
Oral history. 1976. 2 tapes and 105-page transcript.
Open. Index.
Columbia University, Oral History Collection.
Interview with Skirball, a librarian, concerns her Jewish immigrant parents; graduating from Brown University in 1955 and receiving a degree from Columbia University in 1970, her husband Henry Skirball, a rabbi, and his directorship of an Israeli youth movement; her emigration to Israel with her family; and her library career in the film archives of the Institute for Contemporary Jewry at Hebrew University in Jerusalem.

11,916. Social Security
Oral history. 1965-68. 10,649 pp.
Partially closed. Published guide.
Columbia University, Oral History Collection.
The origins and early years of Social Security and Medicare are described in tapes and transcripts of interviews with persons involved. Attorney Barbara Armstrong, a consultant in 1934 on unemployment and old-age insurance for the Committee on Economic Security, gives a detailed account of work done in preparation for Social Security legislation. Bernice Bernstein, who served as regional attorney for the Federal Security Agency in 1947 discusses the old-age insurance program and Wisconsin unemployment legislation. Economist Eveline Mabel Burns, who served on the board of Consumers' League of New York and on the Committee on Economic Security, describes her studies of social security programs and impressions of Mary W. Dewson. Martha May Eliot, a physician, discusses the origins of the Public Health Service and the Children's Bureau, the American Medical Association's role in medical care and insurance programs, and public health legislation. The efforts of organized labor to enact federal old-age, survivors, and Medicare legislation are discussed by Katherine Ellickson. Lavinia Engle, who was field secretary of the National American Woman Suffrage Association and executive director of the Maryland LWV, talks about decentralization of Social Security programs and about Anna Rosenberg, while Jane Margueretta Hoey describes her experiences as federal director of Public Assistance from 1936 to 1954. Katharine Fredrica Lenroot, a social worker who was employed by the Children's Bureau beginning in 1915, discusses studies of infant mortality and child labor; early Mother's Aid laws; and her impressions of Emma Octavia Lundberg, Frances Perkins, and Eleanor Roosevelt. Also included are interviews with Maurine Mulliner, who was technical adviser to the Social Security Board in 1936, and with Lisbeth Bamberger Schorr, who talks about the role of the AFL-CIO in health insurance and social security programs. [Mrs.] Elizabeth Raushenbush discusses her work in unemployment and Social Security, including administration of Wisconsin's state unemployment compensation program. Elizabeth Wickenden discusses her work as a representative for the American Public Welfare Association and as a consultant on health insurance to John F. Kennedy, Lyndon Johnson, and others. Also included are interviews with Loula Friend Dunn, Kathryn Goodwin, Marjorie Hunter, Dorothy McCamman, and Gerel Rubien. Taken from Elizabeth B. Mason and Louis M. Starr, eds., *The Oral History Collection of Columbia University* (New York: New York Times Company, 1973).

11,917. Socialist Movement
Oral history. 1965. 1141 pp.
Open. Published guide.
Columbia University, Oral History Collection.
Interviews with persons involved in the Socialist party describe its origin and development; the relationship of the party to unions, the American Labor party, the Trotskyist movement, the Communist party, and other groups; and the role Socialists have played in civil rights activities. Interviewees also analyze the failure of the Party to thrive in this country and the impact of Franklin Roosevelt and the New Deal on the Party; they also give their recollections of Eugene V. Debs, Samuel Gompers, Upton Sinclair, Norman Thomas, and others. Includes an interview with Pauline Newman. Taken from Elizabeth B. Mason and Louis M. Starr, eds., *The Oral History Collection of Columbia University* (New York: New York Times Company, 1973).

11,918. Stewart, Isabel Maitland
Oral history. 1960. 1 tape and 459-page transcript.
Partially restricted. Published guide.
Columbia University, Oral History Collection.
Interview with Stewart (1878-1963), a professor of nursing, concerns her nursing education at the end of the 19th century at Winnipeg General Hospital in Canada, the beginning of graduate nursing education at Teachers College in New York, attempts to standardize curricula and improve nursing education, nurses in WWI, travel in Europe and Asia, the Goldmark Commission, Lillian Wald, and the Rockefeller Commission's investigation of curricula in 1927 and after. Also included are papers of Stewart. Taken from Elizabeth B. Mason and Louis M. Starr, eds., *The Oral History Collection of Columbia University* (New York: New York Times Company, 1973).

11,919. Stone, Mrs. William S.
Oral history. 1973. 43-page transcript.
Access restricted. Index.
Columbia University, Oral History Collection.
Interview with Myra M. Stone conducted as part of the US Air Force Academy Project concerns her recollections of Academy life as a superintendent's wife, their house and furnishings, and entertainment habits.

11,920. Strauss, Anna Lord
Oral history. 1972. 17 tapes and 571-page transcript.
Partially restricted. Published guide.
Columbia University, Oral History Collection.
Interview with Strauss (1899-), a civic leader, concerns her girlhood in New York City, Lucretia Mott and woman's suffrage, New York City politics, her involvement with the New York City and state LWV from 1934 to 1943, and her presidency of the national LWV from 1944 to 1950. She discusses LWV positions on the Equal Rights Amendment, the Tennessee Valley Authority, civil service reform, and civil rights; foreign affairs programs; atomic energy control; the International Alliance of Women; postwar anti-Communist agitation; her service in 1951 and 1952 as a UN delegate; the position of women in the US and abroad; and her impressions of colleagues in government and the LWV. Taken from Elizabeth B. Mason and Louis M. Starr, eds., *The Oral History Collection of Columbia University* (New York: New York Times Company, 1973).

11,921. Szladits, Lola L.
Oral history. 1974. 1 tape and 67-page transcript.
Open. Index.
Columbia University, Oral History Collection.
Interview with Szladits, curator of the Berg Collection at the New York Public Library, was conducted as part of the Rare Book Project. She speaks of her background and experiences in acquiring rare books and mentions the Berg Collection, Columbia's Rare Book Collection, and museum collections.

11,922. Theodore Roosevelt Association
Oral history. 1953-55. 515 pp.
Partially restricted. Published guide.
Columbia University, Oral History Collection.
Tapes and transcripts of reminiscences by family, friends, and associates about Roosevelt, his family and circle, his impact on American life, and the Bull Moose campaign. Included are interviews with Alice Lee Roosevelt Longworth and Helen R. Roosevelt Robinson. Taken from Elizabeth B. Mason and Louis M. Starr, eds., *The Oral History Collection of Columbia University* (New York: New York Times Company, 1973).

11,923. Thomas Alva Edison Project
Oral history. 1972. 119 pp.
Access restricted. Published guide.
Columbia University, Oral History Collection.
Tapes and transcripts of interviews with family members and associates of Edison (1847-1931) concern his character, personality, and motivation; the family home and his laboratory in West Orange, NJ; and specific projects carried on in the laboratory. Included are interviews with [Mrs.] Madeleine Edison Sloane and Lillian P. Warren and recordings prepared by the Edison National Historic Site. Taken from Elizabeth B. Mason and Louis M. Starr, eds., *The Oral History Collection of Columbia University* (New York: New York Times Company, 1973).

11,924. Thorne, Florence Calvert
Oral history. 1957. 165-page transcript.
Partially restricted. Published guide.
Columbia University, Oral History Collection.
Thorne (1878-1973), an aide to Samuel Gompers, describes her education at the University of Chicago, the AFL and Gompers, prominent US labor leaders before WWI, and the growth of the research movement in the AFL during the 1920s. Taken from Elizabeth B. Mason and Louis M. Starr, eds., *The Oral History Collection of Columbia University* (New York: New York Times Company, 1973).

11,925. Towle, Katherine A.
Oral history. 1967. 296-page transcript.
Open. Index.
Columbia University, Oral History Collection.
Towle (1898-) was dean of women in 1953 and dean of students from 1961 to 1965 at the University of California at Berkeley; in 1945 she was director of the US Marine Corps Women's Reserve. In interviews conducted by the Regional Oral History Office of the University of California at Berkeley, she discusses her education at Berkeley, where she received her BA in 1920 and

her MA in 1935; her position as dean and then headmistress at the Miss Ransom and Miss Bridges School from 1927 to 1932; her employment at the University of California Press from 1935 to 1943; her position as administrative assistant and as assistant dean of women at Berkeley from 1946 to 1948; and her work as director of women of the US Marine Corps Regulars from 1948 to 1953.

11,926. Valesh, Eva McDonald
Oral history. 1952. 228-page transcript.
Partially restricted. Published guide.
Columbia University, Oral History Collection.
Interview with Valesh (1866-1956), a journalist, labor leader, and civic worker, concerns her education, her labor work and journalism in Minnesota and New York, the AFL, Samuel Gompers and the *AFL Magazine*, her social work in New York, the Democratic National Committee, and persons in labor and social work. Taken from Elizabeth B. Mason and Louis M. Starr, eds., *The Oral History Collection of Columbia University* (New York: New York Times Company, 1973).

11,927. Vorse, Mary Heaton
Oral history. 1957. 73-page transcript.
Open. Published guide.
Columbia University, Oral History Collection.
[Mrs.] Vorse (1881-1966), who was married to Albert White, was an author. She discusses the Lawrence, MA, strike; the Elizabethton, TN, textile strike; anarcho-syndicalism; Soviet Russia; and the International Workers of the World. Taken from Elizabeth B. Mason and Louis M. Starr, eds., *The Oral History Collection of Columbia University* (New York: New York Times Company, 1973).

11,928. Warner, Emily (Smith)
Oral history. 1967. 3 tapes and 118-page transcript.
Partially restricted. Published guide.
Columbia University, Oral History Collection.
[Mrs. John] Warner discusses her father Alfred E. Smith, his boyhood and education, his career in the New York State Assembly, his terms as governor, the 1928 campaign, his civil rights stands, his differences with Franklin D. Roosevelt, Prohibition, Tammany Hall, and her impressions of Belle Moskowitz, Robert Moses, William Randolph Hearst, and mayors James Walker and Fiorello La Guardia. Taken from Elizabeth B. Mason and Louis M. Starr, eds., *The Oral History Collection of Columbia University* (New York: New York Times Company, 1973).

11,929. Wickens, Aryness Joy
Oral history. 1957. 94-page transcript.
Partially restricted. Published guide.
Columbia University, Oral History Collection.
[Mrs. David L.] Wickens (1901-), a government official and economist, discusses the US Department of Labor from the Coolidge administration to the Eisenhower administration and the Bureau of Labor Statistics and its relation to the labor movement. Taken from Elizabeth B. Mason and Louis M. Starr, eds., *The Oral History Collection of Columbia University* (New York: New York Times Company, 1973).

11,930. Winchell, Constance Mabel
Oral history. 1963. 246-page transcript.
Partially restricted. Published guide.
Columbia University, Oral History Collection.
Winchell (1896-), a librarian, describes her education, her experiences as a student at the New York Public Library School in 1919, working at the University of Michigan from 1920 to 1923, reference work and interlibrary loans, her work at the American Library in Paris in 1924, her work in the reference department at the Columbia University Library beginning in 1925, library school, the American Library Association, and her impressions of [Miss] Isadore G. Mudge and Columbia University president Nicholas Murray Butler. Taken from Elizabeth B. Mason and Louis M. Starr, eds., *The Oral History Collection of Columbia University* (New York: New York Times Company, 1973).

11,931. Witherspoon, Frances, and Mygatt, Tracy
Oral history. 1966. 1 tape and 53-page transcript.
Partially restricted. Published guide.
Columbia University, Oral History Collection.
Pacifists Witherspoon (1886-1973) and Mygatt (1885-1973) describe their girlhoods in New England and the South, their education at Bryn Mawr College, their support of pacifism and racial equality and opposition to US participation in WWI, the War Resisters' League, their book *The Glorious Company,* and the New York Bureau of Legal Advice and its defense of conscientious objectors and persons charged under the Espionage Act. Papers of Witherspoon and Mygatt are also included. Taken from Elizabeth B. Mason and Louis M. Starr, eds., *The Oral History Collection of Columbia University* (New York: New York Times Company, 1973).

11,932. Women's History and Population Issues
Oral history. 1973-76. 2012 pp.
Partially restricted. Index.
Columbia University, Oral History Collection.
Transcripts of interviews conducted by the staff of the Schlesinger Library at Radcliffe College, Cambridge, MA, concern such subjects as public health, maternal and child health care, family planning, marriage counseling, and medical and missionary work. Patricia Maginnis describes her childhood in Oklahoma, her Catholic and convent schooling, her experiences in the WACs, events leading to her involvement in the abortion reform movement, the founding and subsequent activities of the Society for Humane Abortion, establishment of free pre- and post-abortion care clinics, and the formation of the National Association for Repeal of Abortion Laws in 1969. Lana Clarke Phelan also discusses the Society for Humane Abortion and the NARAL. Helen Brooke Taussig, a cardiologist, talks about her medical training at Johns Hopkins University, establishment of the Cardiac Clinic, her work with congenital malformations and pediatric heart surgery, American Heart Association activities, study of thalidomide deformities, and her concern for abortion legislation and fetal research. Lawyer and legislator Sarah Weddington discusses her family and educational background, Supreme Court arguments and the 1973 decision on abortion, the Medicaid coverage issue, the trimester approach to abortion regulation, NARAL activities, and her experiences of discrimination. Other interviews with women conducted for this project are housed at the Schlesinger Library.

11,933. Zorach, William
Oral history. 1957. 348-page transcript.
Partially restricted. Published guide.
Columbia University, Oral History Collection.
Zorach (1887-1966), a sculptor and painter, talks about his early life in Cleveland, studying at the National Academy and in Europe, commissioned monuments, his work habits and artistic philosophy, and citizenship difficulties. Also included is an interview with his wife Marguerite Zorach. Taken from Elizabeth B. Mason and Louis M. Starr, eds., *The Oral History Collection of Columbia University* (New York: New York Times Company, 1973).

11,934. Abzug, Bella Savitsky
Papers. 1970-76. Ca. 1000 boxes.
Partially closed. Unpublished guide.
Columbia University, Rare Book and Manuscript Library.
Papers of Abzug (1920-) include correspondence, memoranda, speeches, reports, photos, and printed items relating to her tenure as Congresswoman from New York City's 19th and 20th Congressional Districts from 1971 to 1976. Contains general correspondence and administrative files, extensive subject files on many topics with which Abzug was involved while in Congress, and legislative files containing background material for legislation considered on the House floor and printed versions of legislation by Abzug and others.

11,935. Allen, Arthur J.
Papers. 1938-54. 110 items.
Open. Unpublished guide.
Columbia University, Rare Book and Manuscript Library.
Correspondence of Allen (1891-1954) and his wife Netta Powell Allen, Episcopal missionaries to China from the 1930s to 1951, includes their letters to friends and relatives in the US in which they describe social, cultural, and political conditions in China as well as their ministerial activities. Also included are letters from their son Walter Allen, who taught in various schools in China and later joined the US Army.

11,936. American Library Association, Board of Education for Librarianship
Records. 1945-54. Ca. 4200 items.
Open. No guide.
Columbia University, Rare Book and Manuscript Library.
The files of two Board members Richard H. Logsdon and Francis R. St. John include correspondence, primarily between Anita N. Hostetter, secretary of the Board, and other Board members; reports; and other material concerning library school programs, curricula, course outlines, exams, accreditation, and related matters.

11,937. American Library Association, International Relations Committee
Records. 1941-67. Ca. 7000 items.
Open. No guide.
Columbia University, Rare Book and Manuscript Library.
Minutes, agenda, reports, memoranda, correspondence, and printed material concern the programs of the Committee, which existed from 1941 to 1967. Office files of the Committee, of chairman Florabelle Ludington, and of Jack Dalton, the director of the Association's International Relations Office are also included. The Committee sought to foster an exchange of ideas and methods between American and foreign librarians through visits by librarians both to and from the US, through technical assistance of American librarians to librarians in Asia and Latin America, and through participation in international library organizations such as the International Federation of Library Associations, Fédération Internationale de Documentation, and UNESCO.

11,938. American Library Association, Training Class Section
Records. 1917-31. Ca. 600 items.
Open. No guide.
Columbia University, Rare Book and Manuscript Library.
Files and correspondence of the Section, which was concerned with the education of library staff members through training and apprentice classes given by individual libraries and with the dissemination of information on classes and class methods. Among the correspondents are Marie A. Newberry, Carrie E. Scott, Faith L. Allen, and Vera S. Cooper.

11,939. Association for the Relief of Respectable, Aged, Indigent Females
Records. 1863-1928. 7 vols.
Open. No guide.
Columbia University, Rare Book and Manuscript Library.
Minutes, cash books, and a donations book of this

New York City group, which provided housing and pensions for poor, elderly women.

11,940. Authors' Manuscripts
Collection. Ca. 1940- . No size given.
Open. Unpublished guide.
Columbia University, Rare Book and Manuscript Library.
Collection consists of manuscripts of published works by authors who were connected with Columbia University. Female authors include Jane Belo, Dorothea C. Blaisdell, Elizabeth Coatsworth, Alice Tisdale Hobart, Elizabeth Metzger Howard, Edna Mason Kaula, Winifred B. Linderman, Henrietta Mason, Helen E. Smith, Anne B. Tufts, Grace Faulkner Ward, and Charlotte Chandler Wycoff.

11,941. Bard, Samuel
Papers. 1817-21. Ca. 300 items.
Open. Unpublished guide.
Columbia University, Rare Book and Manuscript Library.
Family correspondence includes letters of Bard, a physician and professor of medicine at Columbia College, to his grandson Francis V. Johnston, a medical student at Columbia and house doctor at New York Hospital. Female correspondents include Caroline Bard, Sally Bard, Sarah Barton, Mary (Sands) Griffin, Magdalena Muirson, Henriett Elizabeth de Normandie, Susannah Pendleton, Frances Ridgeway, Fanny Sands, and Susan (Bard) Sands.

11,942. Barrell Family
Papers. 1791-1846. 254 items.
Open. Unpublished register.
Columbia University, Rare Book and Manuscript Library.
Correspondence between family members in London, the US, Barbados, and British Guiana includes letters of Abigail Barrell and Charlotte (Barrell) Forbes, as well as letters from Walter Barrell in London to his son Theodore Barrell, a merchant in America. The letters reveal the events, philosophy, and social practices of the day. Also included are family chronicles, a diary cash book, autograph albums, photos, and other papers.

11,943. Bartlett, Willard
Papers. 1855-1924. Ca. 3000 items.
Open. Unpublished guide.
Columbia University, Rare Book and Manuscript Library.
Papers of Bartlett (1846-1925), a New York lawyer and judge, include correspondence of Mary (Buffum) Bartlett as well as letters by and relating to the Bartlett and Buffum families. Also contains poems written by Willard Bartlett for Mary Bartlett.

11,944. Belmont, Eleanor (Robson)
Papers. 1853-1960. Ca. 4000 items.
Open. Unpublished guide.
Columbia University, Rare Book and Manuscript Library.
Correspondence, manuscripts, and other papers of [Mrs. August B.] Belmont (1879-), an actress. Her correspondence reflects her interest in the theatrical, musical, philanthropic, and social worlds and includes letters from Theodore Roosevelt, George Bernard Shaw, Frances (Hodgson) Burnett, Edith Wharton, Herbert Hoover, Anatole France, Mary Austin, Stephen Vincent Benét, Calvin Coolidge, Dwight David Eisenhower, John Galsworthy, Ellen Glasgow, Yvette Guilbert, Amy Lowell, Archibald MacLeish, Edgar Lee Masters, John J. Pershing, William Howard Taft, and William Butler Yeats. Also included are a manuscript for her autobiography *Fabric of Memory* and correspondence, notes, and reports relating to the organizations to which Belmont belonged, including the American Shakespeare Festival Foundation, the Educational Dramatic League, the Metropolitan Opera Association, the Motion Picture Research Council, and the American National Red Cross.

11,945. Benjamin, Park
Papers. 1645-1925. 15 boxes.
Open. Unpublished guide.
Columbia University, Rare Book and Manuscript Library.
Papers of Benjamin include personal and family correspondence, manuscript poems and lectures, family papers, financial papers, monographs, photos, and clippings. Also provides genealogical information about the Benjamin and related families from the 16th century to the present. Correspondents include Mary Brower (Western) Benjamin, Mary Gladding (Wheeler) [Mrs. Nathan] Benjamin, and Mary Judith (Gall) Benjamin [Mrs. James] Lanman (1777-1848).

11,946. Black, Algernon David
Papers. Ca. 1932-75. Ca. 14,000 items.
Open. Unpublished guide.
Columbia University, Rare Book and Manuscript Library.
Correspondence, speeches, memoranda, minutes, and publications of Black (1900-), a writer, lecturer, and leader of the New York Society for Ethical Culture. Included are radio talks and platform addresses given at the Society, records of several housing committees on which Black served, and subject files documenting his participation in many organizations and social causes. His female correspondents include Dorothy Parker, Eleanor Roosevelt, and Margaret Sanger.

11,947. Blackwell
Papers. Ca. 1850-84. 152 items.
Open. Unpublished guide.
Columbia University, Rare Book and Manuscript Library.
Letters from Elizabeth Blackwell (1821-1910), the first woman to graduate from medical school in modern times, to her close friend Barbara (Smith) Bodichon, in which she describes her fight against prejudice towards women in the medical profession, her work in the Civil War, and her efforts to improve sanitary conditions. Also included is correspondence of her sister Emily Blackwell (1826-1910), who was also a physician.

11,948. Blunden, Edmund Charles
Papers. 1922-68. 104 items.
Open. Unpublished guide.
Columbia University, Rare Book and Manuscript Library.
Papers of Blunden (1896-1974), an English poet, include correspondence with Pauline Francis Stephens and Dorothy Hewlett Kilgour.

11,949. Bonsall Family
Papers. Ca. 1751-1905. Ca. 350 items.
Open. No guide.
Columbia University, Rare Book and Manuscript Library.
Correspondence dealing with personal and business matters and topics of contemporary interest, notes, poetry journals, memoranda, genealogical material, indentures, marriage certificates, deeds and other legal papers, photos, tintypes, and silhouettes. Other papers relate to the family, which resided primarily in Germantown, PA, and to Ellen C. Bonsall. Richard Bonsall came to America with William Penn and settled in Philadelphia about 1683. His descendants were chiefly associated with transportation, the law, teaching, and real estate. Correspondents include Anna Bonsall and Lydia Bonsall.

11,950. Boudin, Louis B.
Papers. Ca. 1900-50. Ca. 500 items.
Open. Unpublished guide.
Columbia University, Rare Book and Manuscript Library.
Papers of Boudin, a lawyer, authority on socialists and socialism, and author of works related to socialism and law, include correspondence with European and American socialists and with Anna P. Boudin and Leah Boudin.

11,951. Bourne, Randolph Silliman
Papers. Ca. 1910-66. 20 boxes.
Open. Unpublished guide.
Columbia University, Rare Book and Manuscript Library.
Papers of Bourne (1886-1918) chiefly relate to education, government, and Bourne's publications and include personal and business correspondence as well as correspondence from Alyse Gregory, Dorothy Teall, and Agnes De Lima regarding possible publication of Bourne's letters. Also included are letters from his mother Sara Randolph (Barrett) Bourne to Esther Cornell.

11,952. Brooks, Van Wyck
Papers. 1934-63. 60 items.
Open. Unpublished guide.
Columbia University, Rare Book and Manuscript Library.
Papers of Brooks, a critic, include correspondence of his wife Gladys Brooks.

11,953. Broughton, Sarah (Summer)
Papers. 1823-80. 94 items.
Open. Unpublished guide.
Columbia University, Rare Book and Manuscript Library.
Correspondence of Broughton (1802-53), a pioneer woman who wrote poems and stories for women's magazines, includes that with her daughter Celeste Broughton and other family members and friends. Also included are manuscript poems by Sarah Broughton and a manuscript essay by Celeste Broughton. Shebuel and Sarah Broughton married in Massachusetts; later they moved to New York, Michigan, and then farther westward. Only two of their 11 children survived early middle age. The collection primarily documents Sarah Broughton's later life and the family's move to Michigan.

11,954. Brown, James Oliver
Papers. Ca. 1927-70. 87,000 items.
Access restricted. Unpublished guide.
Columbia University, Rare Book and Manuscript Library.
Papers of Brown, a literary agent, and his predecessor George T. Bye include letters and manuscripts of Fannie Hurst, Katherine Anne Porter (1890-), Eleanor Roosevelt, Jean Stafford, and Rebecca West. Also included are financial records and files on agents and publishers.

11,955. Brown, K.: New York State Library School Register
Records. 1955-60. Ca. 1500 items.
Open. No guide.
Columbia University, Rare Book and Manuscript Library.
File of biographical data on the School's alumni, kept by editor Kark Brown (1895-) as preparation for the 1959 revised edition of the *New York State Library School Register.*

11,956. Burgess Family
Papers. Ca. 1850-1950. 9 boxes, 1 vol., and other items.
Open. Unpublished guide.
Columbia University, Rare Book and Manuscript Library.
Correspondence, photos, portraits, and other papers of this family. Includes correspondence and memorabilia of John William Burgess (1844-1931), a professor of public law at Columbia University, and papers of his wife Ruth Payne (Jewett) Burgess (?-1934), including a song she wrote, a sketchbook, notices and catalogs of her painting exhibitions

from 1928 and 1934, and a booklet concerned with the National Association of Women Painters and Sculptors, of which she was president from 1905 to 1910. Papers of Ruth Burgess's family include a Bible of Captain Nathan Jewett (1767-1861) containing family births, deaths, and marriages as well as daguerreotypes of his wife Ruth Payne Jewett (1769 or 1770-1828); genealogy of the Field family, including Ruth Burgess's grandfather Charles Kellogg Field; letters from Ruth Burgess's father Elisha Payne Jewett to her and her son Elisha Payne Jewett Burgess; and letters from her son's wife Annette Louise (Curnen) Burgess. Also contains correspondence from US senator John Foster Dulles and a post card from George Bernard Shaw to Annette Burgess, who was the daughter of Mr. and Mrs. James Francis Curnen of New York City and who received her AB from Barnard College in 1918. Papers of Ruth Payne Jewett Burgess II, the daughter of Elisha and Annette Burgess, include a letter from Kaiser Wilhelm II; photos taken during her society debut in 1941; clippings concerning her 1945 marriage to Walter E. A. Jaeggi, the first secretary of legation of Switzerland; and clippings concerning the birth of her daughter Marie Anna Ruth Annette "Mara" Jaeggi in 1951.

11,957. Burgess, John William
Papers. Ca. 1873-1930. 26 file boxes.
Open. Partial guide.
Columbia University, Rare Book and Manuscript Library.
Correspondence of Burgess (1844-1931), professor of political science at Amherst College and Columbia University, with friends, associates, and scholars in political science deals with academic and scholarly subjects, publication of his writings, his teaching career, and business and personal matters. Also included is a diary of his wife Ruth Payne Burgess.

11,958. Burns, Eveline Mabel (Richardson)
Papers. 1931-70. Ca. 35,000 items.
Open. Unpublished register.
Columbia University, Rare Book and Manuscript Library.
Papers of [Mrs.] Burns (1900-), an economist, include correspondence, 1939-70; unpublished papers; subject files relating to social work and economics; book reviews; and material for two unfinished books on unemployment. Burns has served as a consultant to various agencies, including the National Resources Planning Board, the Social Science Research Council, and the Social Security Board. She was on the faculty of the New York School of Social Work from 1946 to 1967. Also includes files on the American Public Welfare Association; the Federal Advisory Council; the US Department of Health, Education, and Welfare; the National Conference on Social Work, later the National Conference on Social Welfare; and the New York School of Social Work, later the Columbia University School of Social Work.

11,959. Cable, George Washington
Papers. 1887-1908. 412 items.
Open. Unpublished guide.
Columbia University, Rare Book and Manuscript Library.
Papers of Cable (1844-1925), a writer who started the Home Culture Clubs, include correspondence of his wife, her daughter, and [Miss] Adeline Moffat, the secretary of the Clubs. Material relating to the Clubs, Moffat's resignation, and Cable's writing are also included.

11,960. Calvert Family
Papers. 1795-1820. 91 items.
Open. Unpublished guide.
Columbia University, Rare Book and Manuscript Library.
Correspondence of George Henry Calvert (1803-89), an author and mayor of Newport, RI, who was descended from Lord Baltimore; Calvert's mother Rosalie Stier, a daughter of a Belgian émigré who had temporarily settled in Maryland; and of other family members. Calvert's letters are in French.

11,961. Chandler, Charles Frederick
Papers. Ca. 1864-1915. 234 boxes.
Open. Unpublished guide.
Columbia University, Rare Book and Manuscript Library.
Papers of Chandler (1836-1925), a legal and industrial chemist, include the papers of his second wife Augusta Berard Chandler. Her correspondence with her husband is included with correspondence, notebooks, and scrapbooks relating to the opera, the family, and dinner guests. Miscellaneous financial records are also included. Chandler's first wife Anna Craig Chandler died in 1895.

11,962. Chapman, Mary (Sumner)
Papers. 1859-91. 106 items.
Open. Unpublished guide.
Columbia University, Rare Book and Manuscript Library.
Correspondence of Chapman to her daughter Mary Adelaide and from her sons Oscar and Croydon. The sons' letters were written from army posts during the Civil War and were passed from one family member to another, each adding a note for the next. Also included is Chapman's 1862 diary and a diary of B. F. Watkins, a descendant of Chapman's niece Laura Broughton Watkins.

11,963. Child, Lydia Maria (Francis)
Papers. 1829-70. 35 items.
Open. Unpublished guide.
Columbia University, Rare Book and Manuscript Library.
Correspondence of [Mrs. David Lee] Child (1802-80), who was an author, reformer, teacher, and journalist, deals with events in her personal life, her writing career, and her work in the antislavery movement. Besides writing novels and working with *Juvenile Miscellany,* the first American periodical for children, Child wrote pamphlets and books on slavery and edited the *National Anti-Slavery Standard* from 1841 to 1843. Also included are manuscripts of maxims and poems.

11,964. Chute, Charles Lionel
Papers. 1899-1913. 100 items.
Open. Unpublished guide.
Columbia University, Rare Book and Manuscript Library.
Chute (1882-1953) fought to obtain effective child labor legislation. Biographical material, reports, articles, leaflets, announcements, photos, and clippings pertain to the movement for child labor laws. Papers include "Women and Children in the Glass Industry," which was a review of a government report about the condition of women and children, and Orren B. Booth's "The White Slave Traffic," which contained information from cases and records of houses of prostitution.

11,965. Civic Legislative League
Records. 1949-52. 16 boxes and 4 card files.
Open. Unpublished guide.
Columbia University, Rare Book and Manuscript Library.
Minutes, financial records, reports, registers of individuals and organizations, publications, and correspondence of the League, which existed from 1950 to 1952. The group was concerned with securing effective social welfare legislation for New York. Its files contain information about family welfare, correction, education, health, child labor, day care, mentally retarded children, the placement of children in free homes, and migrant labor.

11,966. Clark, Donald Lumen
Papers. 1927-46. 7 items.
Open. Unpublished guide.
Columbia University, Rare Book and Manuscript Library.
Correspondence of Clark (1888-1966), an English professor at Columbia University, includes letters from such writers as Susan Ertz, Ellen Glasgow, and T. S. Stribling.

11,967. Clemens, Samuel L.
Papers. 1900-09. 1 box.
Open. Unpublished guide.
Columbia University, Rare Book and Manuscript Library.
Correspondence of Clemens (1835-1910), an author, includes personal letters to his niece by marriage Mary Benjamin [Mrs. H. H.] Rogers and letters to Dorothy Sturgis relating to the Angel-Fish Aquarium club. Also includes photos and clippings.

11,968. Cole, Dorothy Ethlyn
Papers. 1953-55. Ca. 500 items.
Open. Unpublished guide.
Columbia University, Rare Book and Manuscript Library.
Files of Cole (1907-), editor of the third edition of *Who's Who in Library Service* (1955), contain material relating to publication of the book. Cole was a library science professor.

11,969. Columbia University English Department
Records. 1896-1961. Ca. 1150 items.
Open. Unpublished guide.
Columbia University, Rare Book and Manuscript Library.
Correspondence primarily relating to lectureships and courses given under the auspices of the English department. Correspondents include Amy Lowell, Marjorie Nicolson, Marchette Chute, T. S. Eliot, Robert Frost, Thomas Mann, Theodore Roosevelt, and Robert Penn Warren.

11,970. Columbia University Institute of Arts and Sciences
Records. 1930-45. 79 items.
Open. Unpublished guide.
Columbia University, Rare Book and Manuscript Library.
The Institute was a nonacademic division of University Extension at Columbia University from 1913 to 1957. It provided evening lectures for adults who were interested in current thought in the arts. Correspondence includes letters, some of a personal nature, from Gertrude Stein, Edna Ferber, Robert Frost, Al Smith, and others.

11,971. Columbia University Libraries, Library Office
Records. 1890-1948. Ca. 38,500 items.
Open. Unpublished guide.
Columbia University, Rare Book and Manuscript Library.
Office files of the Library include annual reports, financial records, memoranda, and correspondence of the administrative staff.

11,972. Columbia University Libraries, Reference Department
Records. 1904-59. Ca. 1000 items.
Open. Unpublished guide.
Columbia University, Rare Book and Manuscript Library.
Office files, annual reports, and correspondence of the Department. Included are the files of two heads of the Department, Constance Mabel Winchell, who served from 1940 to 1945 and 1947 to 1959, and Isadore Mudge, who served from 1930 to 1937 and in 1940.

11,973. Columbia University Libraries, Staff Association
Records. 1949-50. 1000 items.
Open. Unpublished guide.
Columbia University, Rare Book and Manuscript Library.
Files contain constitution, minutes, reports, memoranda, correspondence, and ballots of the Association.

11,974. Connolly, Vera Leona
Papers. 1913-45. Ca. 7500 items.
Open. Unpublished guide.
Columbia University, Rare Book and Manuscript Library.
Correspondence, notes, manuscripts, and clippings of Connolly (1888-1964), a journalist, relate to her writing, which included articles on such topics as juvenile delinquency, marital conditions in the US, prisons and reformatories, and Indians. Her articles and stories appeared in numerous newspapers and magazines, including the *Delineator, Collier's, Good Housekeeping, Reader's Digest,* and *Woman's Home Companion.*

11,975. Cowles Family
Papers. 1832-70. 40 items.
Open. Unpublished guide.
Columbia University, Rare Book and Manuscript Library.
Correspondence from George Cowles, a resident of Rygate, VT, to Mary Bradley, his fiancée, who resided in Peacham, VT; letters from Mary (Bradley) Cowles to her children Jennie and Francie; and letters of Laura Bradley, S. H. Cowles, and Noah Worcester. The letters pertain to personal and family matters.

11,976. Craigie, Dorothy
Papers. 1960-66. Ca. 80 items.
Open. Unpublished guide.
Columbia University, Rare Book and Manuscript Library.
Correspondence, notes, and proofs relate to publication of *Victorian Detective Fiction: A Catalogue of the Collection* (1966) compiled by Graham Greene, Eric Osborne, and Craigie (1901-), who wrote under the name of Dorothy Glover. Also includes correspondence and notes of Green's secretary Josephine Reid.

11,977. Craigie, Pearl Mary Teresa (Richards)
Papers. 1896-1904. 1 box and 1 vol.
Open. Unpublished guide.
Columbia University, Rare Book and Manuscript Library.
Correspondence of Craigie (1867-1906), an Anglo-American novelist and dramatist who wrote under the pseudonym John Oliver Hobbes. Includes a manuscript of her novel *The Serious Wooing.*

11,978. Crane, Cora (Howarth)
Papers. 1886-1910. Ca. 1800 items.
Open. Unpublished guide.
Columbia University, Rare Book and Manuscript Library.
Correspondence, financial records, and other papers of Crane (1865-1910), who was the common-law wife of author Stephen Crane. The papers relate primarily to the operation of her brothel, The Court; her marriage to her last husband Hammon P. McNeil; and her work on the invention of a new army canteen.

11,979. Crane, Stephen
Papers. Ca. 1895-1908. 1269 items.
Open. Unpublished guide.
Columbia University, Rare Book and Manuscript Library.
Correspondence to Crane (1871-1900), an author, and his wife Cora (Howarth) Crane (1865-1910) from such literary figures as Joseph Conrad, Henry James, H. G. Wells, George Bernard Shaw, Hamlin Garland, Elbert Hubbard, and Rider Haggard, as well as from Crane and Howarth family members. The letters relate to life at Brede Place in Sussex, England, and to Cora Crane's activities after her husband's death. Stories, articles, photos, pictures, and memorabilia of Cora Crane are also included.

11,980. Crary, Catherine S.
Papers. 1724-1826. 3 oversize folders and 31 items.
Open. Unpublished guide.
Columbia University, Rare Book and Manuscript Library.
Correspondence, manuscripts, and other papers Crary, an author, collected primarily for use in the writing of her book on American Tories, *The Price of Loyalty* (1973).

11,981. Dawson, Nancy
Papers. 1955-65. Ca. 650 items.
Access restricted. Unpublished guide.
Columbia University, Rare Book and Manuscript Library.
Correspondence between Herman Wouk, an author, and his secretary and assistant for 11 years, [Mrs. Ralph Burk] Dawson (1920-). Material contains biographical and critical information.

11,982. Dewey, John
Papers. 1930-50. 151 items.
Open. Unpublished guide.
Columbia University, Rare Book and Manuscript Library.
Letters from Dewey (1859-1952), a professor and philosopher, to [Mrs.] Corinne Chesholm Frost concern philosophical problems.

11,983. Dorfman, Elsa
Papers. 1960-69. 58 items.
Open. Unpublished guide.
Columbia University, Rare Book and Manuscript Library.
Correspondence of [Miss] Dorfman, a poet, photographer, and free-lance writer, includes letters from such poets as Allen Ginsberg, Philip Whalen, Frank O'Hara, Edward Field, and Robert Creeley. Also includes a few of Dorfman's poems with critical comments by Ginsberg.

11,984. Dragonette, Jessica
Papers. 1936-67. Ca. 300 items.
Open. Unpublished guide.
Columbia University, Rare Book and Manuscript Library.
Manuscripts, photos, clippings, posters, and programs of [Miss] Dragonette, an author and singer, as well as her books *Faith Is A Song* and *Your Voice and You.*

11,985. Dramatic Museum
Records. 1732-1970. More than 65,000 items.
Open. Unpublished guide.
Columbia University, Rare Book and Manuscript Library.
Correspondence, manuscripts, scrapbooks, photos, clippings, pamphlets, prints, programs, and playbills relate to such aspects of the American and English theater as drama, opera, dance, movies, puppets, and spectacles. Included are letters and manuscripts of [Miss] Charlotte Cushman, an actress; letters of William Charley Macready, an actor with whom she toured for many years; correspondence thought to be written by Eliza Vestris, a singer, actress, and manager; correspondence and manuscripts of other actors, actresses, and theatrical managers; and photos and autographs collected by Anne Jane Gilbert.

11,986. Dunning, William A.
Papers. 1781-1922. 7 boxes.
Open. Unpublished guide.
Columbia University, Rare Book and Manuscript Library.
Correspondence, photos, and clippings relate to Dunning (1857-1922), a professor at Columbia University, and to members of his family. Includes letters to Matilda M. Dunning and a journal kept by Charlotte Dunning from 1899 to 1915.

11,987. Earle, Genevieve Beavers
Papers. 1935-50. 2879 items.
Open. Unpublished guide.
Columbia University, Rare Book and Manuscript Library.
[Mrs.] Earle (1883-1956) was a member of the New York City Council and other municipal government agencies. Correspondence, notes, minutes, memoranda, and copies of legislation relate to her work with the Bureau of Municipal Research, the Child Welfare Board, the Mayor's Committee on the plan and survey of New York City, the Emergency Unemployment Committee, the New York City Charter Revision Commission, and the City Council, of which she was a member beginning in 1937 and a minority leader from 1940 to 1946. A memoir of Earle's career and activities based upon an interview with her is located in the files of the Oral History Research Project at the Library.

11,988. Eaton, Anne Thaxter
Papers. 1917-69. 12 boxes and 1 package.
Open. Unpublished guide.
Columbia University, Rare Book and Manuscript Library.
[Miss] Eaton (1881-1971) was the librarian at the Lincoln school of Columbia University Teachers' College from its creation in 1917 until 1946; after her retirement from Columbia, she was a professor of librarianship at St. John's University and a reviewer of children's books. Correspondence; manuscripts of children's works, including poetry anthologies; lecture notes; reports; articles; book reviews; and clippings are included.

11,989. Evans, Ernestine
Papers. 1930-65. Ca. 600 items.
Open. Unpublished guide.
Columbia University, Rare Book and Manuscript Library.
Correspondence and manuscripts of Evans (1889-1967), a journalist, news correspondent, and editor for Coward-McCann and for J. B. Lippincott, relate to her editorial work and to her friendship with the family of film director Robert J. Flaherty.

11,990. Farrar, Clarissa Palmer
Papers. Nd. Ca. 22,000 items.
Open. Unpublished guide.
Columbia University, Rare Book and Manuscript Library.
Card files compiled by Farrar (1899-1963), who assisted Columbia University professor Paul O. Kristeller in a project to provide bio-bibliographical information on Latin writers active between 1300 and 1600.

11,991. Follett, Barbara Newhall
Papers. 1919-1939. Ca. 2000 items.
Open. Unpublished guide.
Columbia University, Rare Book and Manuscript Library.
Correspondence and manuscripts of Follett (1914-?), an author who was the daughter of authors Wilson Follett and Helen (Thomas) Follett. She began writing at the age of 4, and as she grew older, she developed a private language based on her view of nature. Her first book *The House Without Windows* was published when she was 12. In 1939 Follett walked out of her apartment and was never seen again. Includes manuscripts for *The House Without Windows, Lost Island,* and other works as well as material relating to a biography of Follett by Harold Grier McCurdy.

11,992. Follett, Helen (Thomas)
Papers. Ca. 1919-70. Ca. 1500 items.
Open. Unpublished guide.
Columbia University, Rare Book and Manuscript Library.
Correspondence, manuscripts, photos, and printed material of Follett (?-1970), an author. Her works include *Mrs. Flowers' Dog Days; Magic Portholes,* which was written with her daughter Barbara Newhall Follett (1914-?); and numerous magazine articles.

11,993. Frank, Maude Morrison
Papers. 1853-1953. 100 items.
Open. Unpublished guide.
Columbia University, Rare Book and Manuscript Library.
[Miss] Frank (1870-1956) was a textbook author and contributor to literary magazines. Correspondence includes letters to her from Walter de la Mare and letters she collected that were written by various literary figures. Correspondents include members of William Makepeace Thackeray's family, John Galsworthy, Sydney Cockerell, and Virginia Woolf. Also includes Frank's book *Great Authors in Their Youth.*

11,994. Franken, Rose
Papers. 1925-66. 42 boxes, 46 vols., 1000 items, 200 recording discs, and 6 motion pictures.
Open. Unpublished guide.
Columbia University, Rare Book and Manuscript Library.
Correspondence, manuscripts, recordings, clippings, and other material of Franken (1895-), a novelist and playwright. Includes drafts, typescripts, and proofs of her short stories; novels; plays; and radio, film, and television scripts. Her first novel *Pattern* was published in 1925, and her latest novel *You're Well Out of a Hospital* was published in 1966. Many of the manuscripts relate to her most famous characters Claudia and David.

11,995. Franklin, Christine (Ladd), and Franklin, Fabian
Papers. Ca. 1900-39. Ca. 7000 items.
Open. Unpublished guide.
Columbia University, Rare Book and Manuscript Library.
Correspondence and other papers of Christine Franklin (1847-1930) and her husband Fabian Franklin (1853-1939) relate to their work in psychology and logic. A lecturer at Columbia University from 1914 to 1927, Christine Franklin was known for her method of reducing all syllogisms to a single formula and for her contributions ot knowledge relating to color vision. Included are letters to her from Bertrand Russell.

11,996. Freeman, Mary Eleanor (Wilkins)
Papers. 1893-1901. 54 items.
Open. Unpublished guide.
Columbia University, Rare Book and Manuscript Library.
Correspondence of [Mrs. Charles M.] Freeman (1852-1930), who wrote novels and short stories, to Harper Brothers and *Century* magazine relates chiefly to publication of her works in serial and book form. Includes letters to Richard Watson Gilder, Robert Underwood Johnson, and Colonel George B. Harvey.

11,997. Freuh Theatrical Cartoons
Papers. Ca. 1905-25. 22 items.
Open. Unpublished guide.
Columbia University, Rare Book and Manuscript Library.
Woodcuts of cartoons drawn by cartoonist Alfred Freuh (1880-1968) include pictures of Maude Adams, Ethel Barrymore, Katharine Cornell, Yvette Gilbert, Annette Kellerman, Julia Marlowe, Olga Petrova, and Sophie Tucker.

11,998. Gay, Sydney Howard
Papers. Ca. 1770-1900. 86 boxes.
Open. Unpublished guide.
Columbia University, Rare Book and Manuscript Library.
Gay (1814-88), a journalist and author who was the son of Ebenezer Gay and Mary Allyne (Otis) Gay, was an active abolitionist who edited the *Anti-Slavery Standard* before the Civil War and served as managing editor of the *New York Tribune* during the War. In 1845 he married Elizabeth Neall, a resident of Philadelphia who was also active in abolitionist work and the women's rights movement. Papers include correspondence between Elizabeth and Sydney Gay; letters to them from family, friends, and business associates; and other family correspondence, including letters of Sarah Gay. In 1867 Sydney Gay became managing editor of the *Chicago Tribune;* he later served on the editorial board of the *Saturday Evening Post.* Part of collection is available on microfilm.

11,999. Gildersleeve, Virginia Crocheron
Papers. 1898-1962. Ca. 7500 items.
Open. Unpublished guide.
Columbia University, Rare Book and Manuscript Library.
Correspondence, notes, speeches, reports, and articles of Gildersleeve (1877-1965), who was dean of Barnard College from 1911 to 1947 and a member of the US delegation to the Charter Conference of the UN in 1945. Material relates to Barnard, the Charter Conference, the Dumbarton Oaks Conference, the International Federation of University Women, the AAUW, the American Council on Education, and the Near East College Association. Includes a letter from President Franklin Roosevelt appointing Gildersleeve to the Charter Conference delegation.

12,000. Given
Papers. 1845-70. 50 items.
Open. Unpublished guide.
Columbia University, Rare Book and Manuscript Library.
Correspondence to Captain John O. Given from business associates and family members and letters from his wife Annie Rachel Given to her sister describing events that occurred during a voyage with her husband. Many of the letters describe life at sea. Also includes an account, thought to have been written by Annie Given, concerning an incident at sea.

12,001. Gramercy Bookshop: Wilbur, Lorraine, and Wilbur, Robert
Records. Ca. 1931-54. 1 box.
Open. Unpublished guide.
Columbia University, Rare Book and Manuscript Library.
Correspondence of the Wilburs, owners of this New York City bookshop, with writers and critics pertains primarily to the purchase of books. Among the correspondents are John Ciardi, Leon Edel, Wallace Fowlie, Robert McAlmon, Alfred E. Smith, William Carlos Williams, and Edmund Wilson.

12,002. Granniss, Ruth Shepard
Papers. 1911-15. 60 items.
Open. Unpublished guide.
Columbia University, Rare Book and Manuscript Library.
Correspondence of [Miss] Granniss (1872-1954), a librarian at the Grolier Club in New York City, relates to the preparation of her book *An American Friend of Southey* (1913), which was a sketch of Maria (Gowen) Brooks. Also includes a copy of the book, two copperplates used to illustrate it, and a copy of "Zóphiël" (1825), a poem by Brooks.

12,003. Griffing
Papers. 1862-72. 53 items.
Open. Unpublished guide.
Columbia University, Rare Book and Manuscript Library.
Correspondence of Josephine Sophia (White) [Mrs. Charles Stockman Spooner] Griffing (1814-72), a social reformer, relates to her interest in the emancipation of Negroes, temperance, and women's suffrage. Correspondents include Charles Sumner, Horace Greeley, Henry Ward Beecher, Anna Dickinson, Lucretia Mott, William H. Seward, and John Greenleaf Whittier. Also includes a scrapbook of clippings that pertain to her life and an autograph book of a relative George T. Driggs, which contains signatures of prominent political and military figures of the late 1860s.

12,004. Gumby, L. S. Alexander
Collection. Ca. 1800-1960. 16 boxes and 161 vols.
Open. Unpublished guide.
Columbia University, Rare Book and Manuscript Library.
Collection, which was compiled by Gumby (1885-1961), concerns Negro life in America. Correspondence, manuscripts, photos, pictures, clippings, pamphlets, extracts from periodicals, and signatures. Included are scrapbooks concerned with Marian Anderson, Florence Mills, Ethel Walters, Josephine Baker, and with such subjects as intermarriage of Negroes and whites, libraries, dancers, Negroes in drama, and Negro entertainers, religions, and schools. Clippings deal with Eleanor Roosevelt and Althea Gibson as well as such subjects as crimes, music, and theater. Part of collection is available on microfilm.

12,005. Haggard, H. Rider
Papers. 1866-1941. Ca. 350 items.
Open. Unpublished guide.
Columbia University, Rare Book and Manuscript Library.
Papers of Haggard, a writer, include correspondence to family members, primarily his sister-in-law Agnes Barber Haggard, who had been his secretary. Other correspondents include Mrs. Patrick Campbell, Marie Corelli, and A. Conan Doyle.

12,006. Hards, Ira A.
Papers. 1895-1937. 72 items.
Open. Unpublished guide.
Columbia University, Rare Book and Manuscript Library.
Hards (1873-1938), a theatrical producer, and his wife Ina (Hammer) Hards, who was an actress and playwright, organized a stock company in Mount Vernon, NY, which lasted from 1911 to 1918. Correspondence from people involved in literature or the theater, including letters from George W. Cable and Mary Austin, both of whom collaborated with the Hardses on dramatic works. Also includes one-act plays, of which Ina Hards was the author and leading actress; works by such authors as John Kendrick Bangs, Harry Kemp, and Evelyn Greenleaf Sutherland; scrapbooks; programs; and other papers.

12,007. Hazeltine, Alice Isabel
Papers. Ca. 1929-35. Ca. 75 items.
Open. No guide.
Columbia University, Rare Book and Manuscript Library.
Correspondence, notes, and bibliographical lists and descriptions concerning children's magazines of [Miss] Hazeltine (1878-1959), who was assistant professor of library work for children at the Columbia University school of library service from 1927 to 1943. Correspondence includes letters from libraries answering Hazeltine's inquiries about their children's periodical holdings.

12,008. Helen Hall Settlement Collection
Papers. 1928-61. Ca. 100 items.
Open. Unpublished guide.

Columbia University, Rare Book and Manuscript Library.
Reports and surveys of Helen Hall and others who worked at the Henry Street Settlement House in New York City. Material centers on community studies, especially unemployment. Hall succeeded Lillian Wald as headworker at the Settlement House in 1933.

12,009. Hellman, C. Doris
Papers. Ca. 1925-73. Ca. 27,000 items.
Open. Unpublished guide.
Columbia University, Rare Book and Manuscript Library.
Clarisse Doris Hellman (1910-73) was a professor of social studies at Pratt Institute from 1951 to 1956 and professor of history at Queens College from 1957 to 1973. Correspondence, notes, manuscripts, speeches, printed material, and other papers concern her study of 16th- and 17th-century astronomers; astronomy; and ancient, medieval, and Renaissance science. Her professional correspondence includes letters from George Sarton and Lynn Thorndike. Notes and research material also concern her teaching, research, and lectures at New York University, Cornell, and the Columbia University renaissance seminar, as well as her participation in professional organizations such as the History of Science Society. Also included are family correspondence, photos, and papers on the Jewish Foundation for the Education of Girls. Hellman received her AB from Vassar College in 1930, her AM from Radcliffe College in 1931, and her PhD from Columbia University in 1933. She was married to Morton Pepper.

12,010. Hill, Frank Ernest
Papers. 1941-45. 88 items.
Open. No guide.
Columbia University, Rare Book and Manuscript Library.
Letters to Hill and his wife Ruth Nickel Hill from paratroopers and servicewomen who served in North Africa, Italy, and other places during WWII.

12,011. Hitchcock, Ripley
Papers. Ca. 1885-1935. Ca. 10,000 items.
Open. Unpublished guide.
Columbia University, Rare Book and Manuscript Library.
James Ripley Wellman Hitchcock (1857-1918) was an art critic, editor, and historian. Papers include letters to his second wife Helen Sanborn (Sargent) Hitchcock from people involved in literature and art in New York. Material relating to the American Art Alliance, in which Helen Hitchcock was interested, is also included.

12,012. Holubnychy, Lydia
Papers. Ca. 1923-75. Ca. 4000 items.
Open. Unpublished guide.
Columbia University, Rare Book and Manuscript Library.
Correspondence, notes, manuscripts, and clippings of Holubnychy, a Sino-Soviet scholar who was studying at Columbia University at the time of her death. Collection chiefly consists of research material she had compiled for her unfinished dissertation.

12,013. Hope, Constance
Papers. 1931-75. 17 boxes and 1 oversize box.
Open. Unpublished guide.
Columbia University, Rare Book and Manuscript Library.
Correspondence, photos, contracts, and printed material of Hope (1908-), a public relations specialist and artists' representative, relate to her association with the artists for whom she acted as agent. Correspondents include Fannie Hurst, Lotte Lehmann, Erich Leinsdorf, Lily Pons, Bruno Walter, Grace Moore, Leopold Stokowski, and Leonard Bernstein. Hope is the wife of Milton Lionel Berliner.

12,014. Hoyt Family
Papers. 1865-1920. Ca. 1000 items.
Open. No guide.
Columbia University, Rare Book and Manuscript Library.
Correspondence, manuscripts, and other papers of this New York City family. Most of the letters are to Mr. and Mrs. James Otis Hoyt and are of a personal nature.

12,015. Hubbard Family
Papers. 1849-1950. Ca. 500 items.
Open. No guide.
Columbia University, Rare Book and Manuscript Library.
Correspondence of Lucius Lee Hubbard (1849-1933), an author and geologist; his wife; their three daughters; and other relatives in Cambridge, MA, and Houghton, MI. Most of the letters are to his daughter Frances (Hubbard) Flaherty, who married and worked with film director Robert J. Flaherty. Correspondence of Mrs. Hubbard's parents and relations, the Lambard family of Georgia, is also included.

12,016. Hull, Helen Rose
Papers. Ca. 1900-63. 17 boxes and 1 vol.
Open. Unpublished guide.
Columbia University, Rare Book and Manuscript Library.
Hull (1888-?), a novelist and editor, taught English and creative writing at Columbia University from 1916 to 1958. Correspondence; manuscripts of her novels, short stories, and essays; notes and outlines for stories; clippings; and printed items are included. Among Hull's novels are *Hawk's Flight, A Tapping on the Wall,* and *Close Her Pale Blue Eyes.* She edited *The Writers Book* and *Writer's Roundtable.*

12,017. Hutchinson, Dorothy
Papers. Ca. 1943-55. Ca. 800 items.
Open. Unpublished guide.
Columbia University, Rare Book and Manuscript Library.
Notes and outlines for courses, notes for papers presented at conferences, case records, and printed material of Hutchinson (1895-1956), who taught at the New York School of Social Work. Hutchinson's primary areas of interest were adoption, foster parents, and unwed mothers.

12,018. Irving, John Treat
Papers. 1807-1936. 312 items.
Open. Unpublished guide.
Columbia University, Rare Book and Manuscript Library.
Family correspondence of Irving (1812-1906), an author and a nephew of Washington Irving, includes the letters of his mother Abigail Spicer (Furman) Irving and father John Treat Irving, Sr., other family members, and friends.

12,019. Irving, John Treat
Papers. 1781-1858. 49 items.
Open. Unpublished guide.
Columbia University, Rare Book and Manuscript Library.
Correspondence of Irving (1778-1838), a judge who was the brother of Washington Irving, and his wife Abigail Spicer (Furman) Irving to members of the Irving and Furman families. Most of the letters are personal and relate to family matters.

12,020. Jay Family
Papers. 1828-1943. 14,678 items.
Open. Unpublished guide.
Columbia University, Rare Book and Manuscript Library.
Family correspondence includes letters of the related Bruen, Butterworth, Chapman, Clarkson, Dawson, Du Bois, Field, Iselin, McVickar, Mortimer, O'Kill, Pellew, Pierrepont, Prime, Robinson, Schieffelin, Von Schweinitz, Sedgwick, and Wurts families. In addition to family and personal matters, the correspondence deals with antislavery feelings, New York civil service, repeal of the Missouri Compromise, the Civil War, international affairs, and New York City and state politics and government.

12,021. Jewett, Sarah Orne
Papers. Ca. 1870-79. 120 items.
Open. Unpublished guide.
Columbia University, Rare Book and Manuscript Library.
Correspondence of Jewett (1849-1909), an author, includes letters to Louise Droesel and from William Dean Howells, Ellen Emerson, James R. Osgood, Horace Scudder, Charles C. Hoyt, Jewett's family, and other friends. Most of the letters are personal, but a few relate to publication of her works.

12,022. Johnson, Robert Underwood
Papers. 1848-1937. Ca. 1600 items.
Open. Unpublished guide.
Columbia University, Rare Book and Manuscript Library.
Johnson (1853-1937) was editor of *Century Magazine* and American ambassador to Italy in 1920 and 1921. Business correspondents include Annie Fields, Mary (Mapes) Dodge, and Helen Hunt Jackson. Personal correspondence between Johnson and his wife Katharine (McMahon) Johnson also concerns literary and business matters. Included in manuscripts of poetry and prose are works of Katharine Johnson, Mary (Mapes) Dodge, and Mrs. Humphrey Ward.

12,023. Joy, Eleanor
Papers. 1882-91. 17 items.
Open. Unpublished guide.
Columbia University, Rare Book and Manuscript Library.
Joy (1868-1936) was a daughter of Charles Joy, professor of chemistry at Columbia University. In her diaries she describes traveling with her family in the US, England, and on the Continent. Also includes a description of the diaries of her son Sir Douglas Busk.

12,024. Kaiser, John Boynton
Papers. 1928-71. Ca. 4000 items.
Open. Unpublished guide.
Columbia University, Rare Book and Manuscript Library.
Papers of Kaiser (1887-1973), a professor of library science, deal with many aspects of the library profession, including administration and teaching.

12,025. Kane-Hand Family
Papers. 1770-1940. 14 file boxes.
Open. Unpublished guide.
Columbia University, Rare Book and Manuscript Library.
Included are the family correspondence, accounts, and personal papers of Oliver Kane-Hand, who lived in Albany, NY, and the household account books of the wife of Thomas Jennings Hand, a resident of New York. Family members also resided in Baltimore and Ossining, NY.

12,026. Kelley Family
Papers. 1681-1936. Ca. 1800 items.
Open. Unpublished guide.
Columbia University, Rare Book and Manuscript Library.
Correspondence, photos, and other papers of this Philadelphia family, which included Florence Kelley (1859-1932), her parents William Darrah Kelley (1814-90) and Caroline B. Kelley, Albert Kelley, John Bartram Kelley, Margaret Dana Kelley, and Nicholas Kelley. Florence Kelley promoted social legislation and was a resident of Hull House in Chicago and the Henry Street Settlement in New York City. Letters to her from Jane Addams are included.

12,027. Kemble, Frances "Fanny" Anne
Papers. 1848-60. 29 items.
Open. Unpublished guide.
Columbia University, Rare Book and Manuscript Library.
Collection consists of personal correspondence from Kemble (1809-93) to Charles Sedgwick and his wife.

12,028. Kent Family
Papers. 1785-1901. 398 items.
Open. Unpublished guide.
Columbia University, Rare Book and Manuscript Library.
Included are diaries and notebooks of Mary Kent [Mrs. John Seely] Stone. One of the volumes is a journal she kept during a trip to Europe in 1826. Also includes correspondence and other material collected by the Kent, Pinckney, and Webster families while they were in London during the 1790s and 1830s. The bulk of the papers was generated by James Kent (1763-1847), first professor of law at Columbia College, and by his great-grandson William Kent (1858-1910), a Harvard professor.

12,029. Kenton, Edna
Papers. 1903-36. 146 items.
Open. Unpublished guide.
Columbia University, Rare Book and Manuscript Library.
Correspondence of [Miss] Kenton (1876-1954), an author, contains letters from such literary figures as Theodore Dreiser, Carl Van Vechten, Charles Hanson Towne, George Cram Cook, Henry L. Mencken, Richard Watson Gilder, and Witter Bynner. Primarily consists of letters from editors of the magazines in which Kenton's stories were published. Also includes some personal letters and some concerning the Provincetown Players.

12,030. Kerr, Sophie
Papers. 1916-64. 473 items.
Access restricted. Unpublished guide.
Columbia University, Rare Book and Manuscript Library.
Includes drafts and manuscripts of Kerr (1880-1965), who was a novelist and short story writer. Her career spanned six decades; she published 23 volumes and several hundred short stories and essays.

12,031. Lawrence, Vivian Shirley
Papers. 1960-69. Ca. 50 items.
Open. Unpublished guide.
Columbia University, Rare Book and Manuscript Library.
Lawrence (1918-74) was a faculty member of the school of general studies at Columbia University and later a research writer in residence at the school of library service at Columbia. Includes notes, miscellaneous material, and manuscripts of her books, among them *Dialect Mixture in Three New England Pronunciation Patterns* (1960), *A Brief Historical Rhetoric* (1969), and *The Portmanteau One* (1968).

12,032. Lazarus, Emma
Papers. 1868-87. 86 items.
Open. Unpublished guide.
Columbia University, Rare Book and Manuscript Library.
[Miss] Lazarus (1849-87) was a poet and essayist. Correspondence contains letters from Ralph Waldo Emerson, James Bryce, John Burroughs, Henry James, Tomaso Salvini, and others. The letters are personal and contain references to Lazarus's poetry.

12,033. Lenroot, Katharine Fredrica
Papers. 1919-71. Ca. 12,500 items.
Open. Unpublished guide.
Columbia University, Rare Book and Manuscript Library.
Lenroot (1891-) was a child care social worker. Correspondence, reports, and memoranda concern her work with the Children's Bureau of the US Department of Labor from 1915 to 1951, with UNICEF, and with other social welfare organizations. Included in her files are correspondence and other papers of Grace Abbott and Josephine Brown.

12,034. Leverich Family
Papers. 1820-70. Ca. 600 items.
Open. Unpublished guide.
Columbia University, Rare Book and Manuscript Library.
Correspondence of this New York family includes the letters of Charles P. Leverich, a merchant; his wife Matilda Leverich; Elizabeth N. Bevan; Sarah E. Blaine; Margaret Gustine; Sarah Leaming; Kate L. Minor; and Joanna M. Shepard. The letters are primarily personal in nature.

12,035. Loveman, Amy
Papers. 1935-43. 28 items.
Open. Unpublished guide.
Columbia University, Rare Book and Manuscript Library.
Loveman (1881-1955), cofounder of the *Saturday Review of Literature,* was head of the reading department and a member of the board of judges for the Book-of-the-Month Club. Her correspondence includes letters from Leonard Bacon, Charlotte Bassett, Herschel Brickell, Hermann Broch, Witter Bynner, Carl Carmer, George Catlin, Mary Ellen Chase, George Dangerfield, Marcia Davenport, Babette Deutsch, John Gould Fletcher, Ellen Glasgow, George S. Hellman, Gilbert Highet, and M. A. De Wolfe Howe.

12,036. Low, Seth
Papers. 1870-1930. 43,000 items.
Open. Unpublished guide.
Columbia University, Rare Book and Manuscript Library.
Papers of Low (1850-1916), who was mayor of New York City and president of Columbia College, and his wife Annie Low include her business and financial correspondence, invitations, requests for donations, and bills.

12,037. Lundberg, Emma Octavia
Papers. Ca. 1909-54. 3300 items.
Open. Unpublished guide.
Columbia University, Rare Book and Manuscript Library.
Lundberg (1880 or 1881-1954) was a social worker who served with the Children's Bureau of the Department of Labor. Notes, notebooks, speeches, articles, and clippings concern her work in child welfare and child labor.

12,038. MacDowell, Edward Alexander
Papers. 1876-1908. More than 78 items.
Open. Unpublished guide.
Columbia University, Rare Book and Manuscript Library.
Papers of MacDowell (1861-1908), a composer, musician, and professor of music, include a diary and letterbook of his wife Marian Nevins MacDowell containing copies of letters to Nicholas M. Butler and others concerning Edward MacDowell's controversial career at Columbia.

12,039. Machiz, Herbert
Papers. 1956-69. 25 items.
Open. Unpublished guide.
Columbia University, Rare Book and Manuscript Library.
Correspondence of Machiz (1923-76), a theatrical director in New York, includes letters from actors and authors, among them Julie Harris.

12,040. Macy, George
Papers. 1916-60. Ca. 3500 items.
Open. Unpublished guide.
Columbia University, Rare Book and Manuscript Library.
Papers of Macy (1900-56), founder of the Limited Editions Club and the Heritage Press, include letters from Lillian Gish (1896-) and Florence March. Also includes a pencil drawing by Carlotta Petrina.

12,041. Marquis, Don
Papers. Ca. 1910-37. Ca. 350 items.
Open. Unpublished register.
Columbia University, Rare Book and Manuscript Library.
Manuscripts, typescripts, proofs, and published versions of the articles, stories, novels, poems, and dramas of Marquis (1878-1937), who was an author and humorist. Includes correspondence with his drama agent Ethel C. Taylor and with Mrs. William Brown Meloney as well as correspondence of his wife Marjorie (Vonnegut) Marquis and Fola La Follette.

12,042. Marshall, Lenore Guinzburg
Papers. Ca. 1921-70. Ca. 3500 items.
Access restricted. Unpublished guide.
Columbia University, Rare Book and Manuscript Library.
Marshall (1897-1971) was a poet and novelist. Letters from Irwin Edman to her and her husband James Marshall; letters to her from Robert Penn Warren, Edward Weeks, Klaus Mann, and others; diaries; notes, drafts, manuscripts, and proofs of her novel *The Hill Is Level;* manuscripts of her short stories and poems; notebooks; and miscellaneous notes and school papers. Also includes correspondence, memoranda, reports, clippings, and printed material, which deal with the origins of the National Committee for a Sane Nuclear Policy (SANE), the Committee for Nuclear Responsibility, and peace and anti-war organizations in which Marshall was active, and a scrapbook pertaining to economic aid for western Europe. Marshall received her AB from Barnard College in 1919.

12,043. Matthews, James Brander
Papers. 1877-1929. Ca. 14,260 items.
Open. Unpublished guide.
Columbia University, Rare Book and Manuscript Library.
Correspondence of Matthews (1852-1929), a professor, with his literary contemporaries and others includes letters of Mrs. Frank Tracy, Mrs. Harold G. Henderson, Rudyard Kipling and his family, and Mr. and Mrs. Theodore Roosevelt and their family.

12,044. Meloney, Marie (Mattingly)
Papers. 1915-43. Ca. 4730 items.
Open. Unpublished guide.
Columbia University, Rare Book and Manuscript Library.
Correspondence of [Mrs.] Meloney (1883-1943), who was editor of *The Delineator* from 1920 to 1926, of the *New York Herald Tribune Sunday Magazine* from 1926 to 1943, and of *This Week Magazine* from 1934 to 1943. Correspondence from cabinet ministers, diplomats, jurists, authors, journalists, editors, educators, soldiers, and socialites, including Jane Addams, Anna (Roosevelt) Boettiger, Pearl S. Buck, Willa Cather, Carrie Chapman Catt, Ethel C. Roosevelt [Mrs. Richard] Derby, Helen Keller, Frances Perkins, Mary Roberts Rinehart, Abby (Aldrich) [Mrs. John D., Jr.] Rockefeller, Eleanor Roosevelt, and Dorothy Thompson. Manuscripts of Meloney's writings are included as are those of Mrs. Belloc Lowndes.

12,045. Meloney, William, and the Curies
Papers. 1920-43. 400 items.
Open. Unpublished guide.

Columbia University, Rare Book and Manuscript Library.
Correspondence of Marie (Mattingly) [Mrs. William Brown] Meloney (1883-1943), the editor of the *Herald Tribune Sunday Magazine,* with Marie Curie and her daughters Eve and Iréne concerns campaigns for funds for more radium for Curie's experiments and details of arrangements for her visit to the US to solicit funds in person. Also includes manuscripts; photos; printed material, including articles by Frederic and Iréne Joliot-Curie; and other papers, which concern Curie and her work.

12,046. Meloney, William: Mitchel
Papers. Ca. 1830-1918. 1912 items.
Open. Unpublished guide.
Columbia University, Rare Book and Manuscript Library.
Correspondence, a diary, manuscripts, scrapbooks, a biography, and other papers of John Mitchel (1815-75), an Irish nationalist; his wife Jane Verner Mitchel; his grandson John Purroy Mitchel (1879-1918); James Mitchel and his wife Mary Purroy Mitchel; John B. Purroy and the American Atlantic and Pacific Ship Canal Company; and other family members.

12,047. Mespoulet, Marguerite
Papers. Ca. 1925-64. Ca. 13,000 items.
Access restricted. Unpublished guide.
Columbia University, Rare Book and Manuscript Library.
Correspondence, notes, lectures, and clippings of Mespoulet (1880-1965), who was a professor of French at Barnard College, relate to her work and writings on 19th- and 20th-century French literature, with emphasis on Charles Baudelaire, Paul Claudel, and Max Jacob. Correspondence and manuscripts of Paul Claudel and Max Jacob and correspondence of Pierre Reverdy are also included.

12,048. Mitchell, Lucy (Sprague)
Papers. 1878-1967. 6700 items.
Open. Unpublished guide.
Columbia University, Rare Book and Manuscript Library.
Papers of Mitchell (1878-1967), an advocate of experimental education, founder of the Bank Street College of Education, and author of numerous books for children. The collection consists primarily of correspondence, manuscripts, and notes pertaining to her books, but it also includes personal correspondence with friends, family, and her husband Wesley Clair Mitchell before and after their marriage; diaries; and speeches.

12,049. Moers, Ellen
Papers. 1972-74. Ca. 100 items.
Open. No guide.
Columbia University, Rare Book and Manuscript Library.
Correspondence, notes, printed material, and drafts of Moers (1928-), an English professor at Barnard College, pertain to an article she published in the *New York Review of Books* (May 3, 1973) after a two-year study of the financial crisis of the New York Public Library.

12,050. Moore, Douglas Stuart
Papers. 1907-63. Ca. 5400 items.
Open. Unpublished guide.
Columbia University, Rare Book and Manuscript Library.
Moore (1893-1969) was a composer, music professor, and music department chairman at Columbia University from 1926 to 1962. Correspondence concerning his musical compositions; his membership in the Century Club, the MacDowell Association, and the National Institute of Arts and Letters; and his editorship of the Prentice Hall Music Series includes letters from Eleanor Robson Belmont, Peggy Glanville-Hicks, Martha Graham, and Marian Nevins [Mrs. Edward] MacDowell.

12,051. Moore, Samuel
Papers. 1777-1867. 236 items.
Open. Unpublished guide.
Columbia University, Rare Book and Manuscript Library.
Correspondence of Moore, postmaster at Steuben, ME, and others with local and state politicians and friends. The letters deal with political, personal, and family matters. Also included are deeds, bills, receipts, and other papers from Steuben and Sidney, ME. Correspondents include Martha Gallison, Sarah Stevens, and Mary Upton.

12,052. Morgan Family
Papers. 1811-1956. 50 items.
Open. Unpublished guide.
Columbia University, Rare Book and Manuscript Library.
Correspondence, land deeds, clippings, and other papers of this Aurora, NY, family, which was descended from Christopher Morgan, a Groton, CT, resident who served in Congress with Edwin Barber Morgan during the Civil War. Correspondents include family members and others, among them Kate (Morgan) [Mrs. William] Brookfield, Cornelius N. Bliss, Charles Foster, Benjamin Harrison, Temple R. Hollcroft, Herbert Hoover, Levi P. Morton, and William H. Seward.

12,053. Mott Family
Papers. 1840-1954. Ca. 300 items.
Open. Unpublished guide.
Columbia University, Rare Book and Manuscript Library.
Papers of three generations of the Mott family, which lived at Mott Haven in New York City. Correspondence, deeds, leases, and other papers of Jordan Lawrence Mott (1799-?), an inventor and industrialist, pertain to the subdivision, improvement, and letting of Mott Haven. Letters from prominent members of English society to industrialist Jordan Lawrence Mott II (1829-1915), who was known as J. L. Mott, Jr., and his wife Katharine Jerome Purdy, who was a cousin of the Jerome sisters, Lady Randolph Churchill, Lady Constance Leslie, and Mrs. Moreton Frewen. Also included are correspondence with publishers, manuscripts, and financial papers of Jordan Lawrence Mott III (1881-ca. 1913), who was known as Lawrence Mott, a novelist who married Caroline Pitkin.

12,054. Mudge, Isadore Gilbert
Papers. Ca. 1914-41. 4000 items.
Open. No guide.
Columbia University, Rare Book and Manuscript Library.
Mudge (1875-1957), reference librarian at Columbia University from 1911 to 1941, collected children's magazines. Correspondence, invoices and receipts from American and English bookdealers from whom she purchased periodicals, and letters from librarians answering her queries about their children's periodical holdings. Also included is a card file indexing magazine titles.

12,055. Munroe, Henry Smith
Papers. 1855-99. Ca. 300 items.
Open. No guide.
Columbia University, Rare Book and Manuscript Library.
Munroe (1850-1933), born Henry Munroe Smith, was professor of mining at Columbia University from 1877 to 1915. Contains correspondence from family members, including his father Horatio Southgate Smith, his mother Susan Dwight (Munroe) Smith, and his brother Edmund "Ned" Munroe Smith, a professor of international law at Columbia. Also includes business and professional correspondence, letters from friends, and letters from Munroe's paternal grandparents to his father while he attended Dartmouth College and Bowdoin medical school from 1837 to 1844.

12,056. New York City League of Women Voters
Records. 1919-60. Ca. 1500 items.
Open. Unpublished guide.
Columbia University, Rare Book and Manuscript Library.
Minutes, correspondence, and scrapbooks containing LWV publications relate to the League's work in obtaining permanent personal registration.

12,057. New York City League of Women Voters
Records. 1920-69. Ca. 11,000 items.
Open. Unpublished guide.
Columbia University, Rare Book and Manuscript Library.
Files of the New York City and state LWV contain reports, memoranda, correspondence, and printed material concerning such interests as voters service, personal registration, city affairs, and water resources.

12,058. New York State League of Women Voters
Records. 1921-63. 19 vols. and ca. 25,000 items.
Open. Unpublished guide.
Columbia University, Rare Book and Manuscript Library.
Minutes of the LWV record the proceedings of state conventions and various state executive groups. Also included are memoranda, agenda, and correspondence.

12,059. New York Woman Suffrage
Records. 1869-1919. 14 vols. and ca. 1000 items.
Open. Unpublished guide.
Columbia University, Rare Book and Manuscript Library.
Constitutions, minutes, correspondence, membership lists, photos, pamphlets, and clippings of the Suffrage Association of New York state, which existed from 1869 to 1917, and the Woman Suffrage party of New York City, which existed from 1910 to 1919.

12,060. Newman, Philip C., and Newman, Ruth
Papers. Ca. 1949-64. Ca. 1000 items.
Open. Unpublished guide.
Columbia University, Rare Book and Manuscript Library.
Correspondence, notes, reports, and miscellaneous papers relate to the work of Philip Newman (1914-), a labor economist and consultant, and to that of his wife Ruth Newman, a clinical psychologist.

12,061. Norman, Dorothy Stecher
Papers. 1923-71. Ca. 17,000 items.
Open. Unpublished guide.
Columbia University, Rare Book and Manuscript Library.
Correspondence, reports, pamphlets, and clippings of [Mrs.] Norman (1905-), a columnist for the *New York Post* who was active in a wide range of social and political movements, pertain to health, population control, civil liberties, refugees, exiled governments and people of WWII, the UN, education, delinquency, race relations, emerging nationalities, censorship, and foreign aid. Much of the correspondence in the collection centers around Norman's column in the *Post* during the 1940s. Organizations represented include the American Civil Liberties Union, the New York Civil Liberties Union, the Americans for Democratic Action, the American Citizens Committee for Economic Aid Abroad, the Women's City Club, the American Emergency Food Committee for India, the New York Urban League, the Liberal party, the Free Germany Movement, and the Free China Movement.

12,062. O'Shaughnessy, Arthur William Edgar
Papers. 1869-79. 62 items.
Open. Unpublished guide.
Columbia University, Rare Book and Manuscript Library.
Papers of O'Shaughnessy (1844-81), a poet, include correspondence with his wife Eleanor Kyme (Marston) O'Shaughnessy before and after their marriage as well as her letters to others.

12,063. Page, Curtis Hidden
Papers. Ca. 1870-1948. 9 boxes.
Open. Unpublished guide.
Columbia University, Rare Book and Manuscript Library.
Page (1870-1948) was a professor of French and English at Harvard, Dartmouth, and Columbia. Family correspondence includes letters to his grandmother [Mrs.] Mary E. Hidden.

12,064. Pa'lante
Records. 1959-69. Ca. 600 items.
Open. Unpublished guide.
Columbia University, Rare Book and Manuscript Library.
Publication of the magazine *Pa'lante* was halted in 1962 after distribution of the first issue; the magazine was published by Howard Schulman in association with Elizabeth Sutherland and Jose Yglesias for the League of Militant Poets. Files include correspondence and manuscripts of such writers as William Burroughs, Diane di Prima, Allen Ginsberg, Anselm Hallo, Walter Lowenfels, Michael McClure, Gerald Malanga, and John Wieners. The League published guerrilla writings from Latin America and new works from socialist nations.

12,065. Parker, Katherine H.
Collection. 1861-1944. 7 boxes and 14 vols.
Open. Unpublished guide.
Columbia University, Rare Book and Manuscript Library.
Correspondence, photos, printed material, and memorabilia collected by [Mrs. George W.] Parker principally deals with Edward Hugh Sothern, his wife Julia Morlowe Sothern, and Daniel Frohman. Material also pertains to American and English theater.

12,066. Parris, Guichard Auguste Bolivar
Papers. Ca. 1910-75. Ca. 44,520 items.
Open. Unpublished guide.
Columbia University, Rare Book and Manuscript Library.
Personal and professional files of Parris (1903-), who was director of public relations for the National Urban League, include correspondence with Mary (McLeod) Bethune from the period when he was affiliated with the National Youth Administration, with Ruth Standish (Bowles) Baldwin, and with Evangeline Stokowska.

12,067. Parsons, Elsie (Clews)
Papers. 1883-94. 34 items.
Access restricted. Unpublished guide.
Columbia University, Rare Book and Manuscript Library.
Field notebooks in which anthropologist [Mrs. Herbert] Parsons (1875-1941) details the customs and ceremonies of the Hopi Indians. Also included are notebooks in which Alexander M. Stephen, a US Army officer, and Jeremiah Sullivan describe life among the Hopi during the 1880s, Hopi and Navaho relations, and the Tewa and Hokya Indians.

12,068. Payne, John Howard
Papers. Ca. 1780-1952. Ca. 7000 items.
Open. Unpublished guide.
Columbia University, Rare Book and Manuscript Library.
Papers of Payne, who was an actor, playwright, US consul in Tunis, and a champion of Indian rights, include correspondence and manuscripts of his sister Eloise Richards Payne (1787-1819), which portray the social, cultural, and political life of the time. Also includes family correspondence as well as biographical material concerning the Shippen, Lynch, Luquer, and Lea families.

12,069. Lehman, Herbert H.
Papers. 1895-1976. Ca. 1,250,000 items, 250 microfilm reels, 250 recording discs, and 20 motion pictures.
Open. Published guide.
Columbia University, School of International Affairs, Herbert Lehman Papers.
Papers of Lehman (1878-1963), a government official and banker, contain material relating to his mother Babette Newgass Lehman and his wife Edith Altschul Lehman (?-1976), including Edith Lehman's correspondence with national political and philanthropic leaders after her husband's death. Herbert Lehman's correspondents include New York philanthropist Dorothy Lehman Bernhard; New York political leaders Mary W. Dewson, Mary Dreier, Elinore (Morehouse) Herrick, Frieda S. Miller, and Mary K. Simkhovitch; Congresswoman Helen (Gahagan) Douglas; economist and journalist Barbara Ward; New York lawyer and political leader Dorothy Kenyon; New York judge and social worker Anna Moskowitz Kross; Israeli prime minister Golda Meir; cabinet officer Frances Perkins; New York judge Justine (Wise) Polier, who was the daughter of Rabbi Stephen Wise; government official Anna M. Rosenberg; New York political leader and social worker Rose Schneiderman; and social worker Lillian Wald. See *Herbert H. Lehman Papers: Introduction, Checklist, and Guide* (New York: Columbia University School of International Affairs, 1968).

12,070. McDonald, James G.
Papers. 1909-64. 20 ft.
Open. Unpublished guide.
Columbia University, School of International Affairs, Herbert Lehman Papers.
Papers of McDonald (1886-1964), a journalist and diplomat who was League of Nations high commissioner for refugees and first US ambassador to Israel, include correspondence with his wife, his daughters Mrs. Halsey V. Barrett and Mrs. Archibald Stewart, New York hotel keeper Jennie Grossinger, Israeli prime minister Golda Meir, Eleanor Roosevelt, and journalist Dorothy Thompson.

12,071. Poletti, Charles
Papers. 1921-75. 28 ft.
Open. Unpublished guide.
Columbia University, School of International Affairs, Herbert Lehman Papers.
Papers of Poletti (1903-), a politician, lawyer, and US Army officer, include correspondence with his wife Jean Ellis Poletti, his daughters Joanna Shattuck and Carla Knox Poletti, his parents and relatives in Italy, New York philanthropist Edith Altschul Lehman, New York state government official Frieda S. Miller, and Eleanor Roosevelt.

12,072. Ward, Barbara
Papers. 1970-71. 3 ft.
Open. No guide.
Columbia University, School of International Affairs, Herbert Lehman Papers.
Notes and drafts for *Only One Earth: The Care and Maintenance of a Small Planet* (New York: W. W. Norton, 1972), which was co-authored by Ward (1914-), an economist and journalist, and René Dubos.

12,073. Adelaide Nutting Historical Nursing Collection. 1613-1920s. 128 ft.
Open. Partial published guide.
Columbia University, Teachers College Library, Archives and TCana.
Correspondence, personal papers, articles, books, and documents pertain to nursing and to the history of medicine and hospitals. Includes correspondence, articles, and books by and about Florence Nightingale. See *The Adelaide Nutting Historical Nursing Collection* (New York: Bureau of Publications, Teachers College, 1929).

12,074. Archives of the Department of Nursing Education
Records. 1899-ca. 1965. 145 ft.
Open. No guide.
Columbia University, Teachers College Library, Archives and TCana.
Founded in 1899, the nursing education department at Teachers College was the first institution to provide college preparation for registered nurses and advanced preparation for teaching and administration in nursing. Included are letters, diaries, family papers, photos, and annotations on personal copies of books of Mary Adelaide Nutting, a nurse educator who was offered the first professorship in nursing by Teachers College, and the papers of several nurse educators, among them Lavinia Dock, Isabel Stewart, R. Louise McManus, and Isabel (Hampton) Robb. Also included are papers of Josephine Goldmark, a sociologist involved in nursing studies; Florence Sabin, a physician; and Lillian Wald, who was involved in the fields of public health and nurse administration. Their papers contain correspondence, minutes, and records; reports of studies done by the department of nursing and by national organizations; government reports on health and nursing, particularly during both world wars; and a biographical file of prominent nursing leaders, with pamphlets, obituaries, and clippings. In addition, the collection contains an audio tape and videotape of R. Louise McManus and an oral history of Isabel Stewart. In their correspondence the women discuss education, professional licensure, physician-nurse relationships, and public health. Other material relates to such organizations as the Cosmopolitan Club, the American Nurses Association, the National League of Nursing Education, and the American Society of Superintendents of Training Schools.

12,075. Dodge, Grace Hoadley
Papers. 1897-1914. Ca. 1002 items.
Open. No guide.
Columbia University, Teachers College Library, Archives and TCana.
Correspondence, diaries, and personal record books of [Miss] Dodge (1856-1914), a social welfare worker, educator, and philanthropist. Most of the Dodge papers are included within the Teachers College presidential papers.

12,076. National Kindergarten Association
Records. 1900-75. 3 boxes and 1 package.
Open. No guide.
Columbia University, Teachers College Library, Archives and TCana.
Annual reports, correspondence, memoranda, children's art and posters, and miscellaneous records of the Association, which was founded in 1909 to promote the opening of kindergartens operated by trained kindergarten teachers in public schools.

12,077. Spaulding, Eugenia K.
Papers. Ca. 1915-68. 8 drawers.
Open. No guide.
Columbia University, Teachers College Library, Archives and TCana.
Correspondence; speeches; notes for courses taught in 1957, from business meetings, and regarding the National League of Nursing; pictures; clippings; and articles of Spaulding, a nurse and nursing educator. Contains material on the National League

of Nursing Education and the National League for Nursing, 1954-58; the American Nurses Association committee on ethical standards, ?-1944; Association of Collegiate Schools of Nursing committee on guidance, 1944; and the National Organization for Public Health Nursing joint committee on postgraduate education, 1949-50.

12,078. Archive
Records. 1939- . 7 cabinets and shelves in safe.
Open. No guide.
Community Service Society.
Minutes, reports, service statistics, correspondence, press releases, photos, clippings, and pamphlets of the Society, which was formed in 1939 by the merger of the Association for Improving the Condition of the Poor and the Charity Organization Society. The Society focuses on issues that affect families, youth, and the aged, such as social and health services, family counseling, financial aid, public health nursing, technical assistance to neighborhood groups, integrating neighborhood services for persons in need, home economics consultation, camps, residences for the aged, and aid for single parents. Women connected with the Society are Eleanor (Robson) Belmont, a chairman; Eveline Mabel (Richardson) Burns, an economist; Lucy H. Gillett, a nutritionist; Ollie A. Randall, an old-age specialist; Clare M. Tousley, a social worker and executive publicist; Marion Sulzberger [Mrs. Andrew] Heiskell, chairman of the board of trustees; Elinor (Coleman) [Mrs. Randolph] Guggenheimer, a trustee; Mary Pillsbury [Mrs. Oswald B.] Lord, a trustee; Alice McCabe, a social welfare specialist; and Jean Wallace Carey, a specialist in aging.

12,079. Association for Improving the Condition of the Poor
Records. 1843-1939. Ca. 3 cabinets and shelves in safe.
Open. Unpublished guide.
Community Service Society.
Minutes, reports, correspondence, photos, clippings, and pamphlets of the Association, which was founded in 1843 and was involved in such community action programs as family social service, financial aid, public health nursing, nutrition counseling, dental and health maintenance clinics, camps, and residences for the aged. Women involved in the Association include Eleanor (Robson) [Mrs. August B.] Belmont, a committee leader; Alta Dines, director of educational nursing; Lucy H. Gillett, a nutritionist; and Ollie A. Randall, an old-age specialist.

12,080. Charity Organization Society
Records. 1882-1939. 5 cabinets and shelves in safe.
Open. Unpublished guide.
Community Service Society.
Minutes, reports, correspondence, photos, clippings, and pamphlets of the Charity Organization Society, which was founded in 1882. At first, society members, and then professional staff workers, were involved in visiting the needy, social casework, education for social workers, financial aid to families, and community action, especially concerning the courts and housing. Women involved in the Society included Josephine (Shaw) Lowell, the founder; Joanna Carver Colcord, a social work administrator; Clare M. Tousley, a social worker and executive publicist; and Mary Lord, a volunteer case aide.

12,081. Photos
Collection. 1910-18. 80 items.
Open. No guide.
Community Service Society.
Photos by Jessie Tarbox [Mrs. A. Tennyson B.] Beals (1870-1942), a professional photographer, depict the life of poor children and families on the streets and in the tenement dwellings of Manhattan. The photos were commissioned by the New York Association for Improving the Condition of the Poor for publication in its reports.

12,082. Diocese Archives
Records. 1785- . Ca. 1000 cu.ft.
Open. Unpublished guide.
Episcopal Diocese of New York.
Includes administrative, financial, and legal records; correspondence; diaries; photos; and scrapbooks of the Diocese, which was founded in 1785. Includes records of various bishops, proceedings of diocesan organizations and administrative bodies, and daily records.

12,083. Convention Proceedings
Records. 1785- . 14 cu.ft.
Open. Unpublished guide.
Episcopal Diocese of New York Archives.
Transcripts, reports, correspondence, and published proceedings of the Diocesan Convention, the annually convened governing body of the diocese. Membership consists of clergy associated with and ministering in the diocese and lay delegates from each congregation within the diocese. The issue of women's ordination to the Episcopal priesthood was first aired officially at Convention. The collection includes records of the Committee on Ordination of Women to the Priesthood and Episcopacy.

12,084. Episcopal Churchwomen
Records. 1894- . 15 cu.ft.
Open. No guide.
Episcopal Diocese of New York Archives.
Minutes, reports, correspondence, membership lists, photos, and newsletters of the Churchwomen, which was founded in 1874 as the Women's Auxiliary to the Board of Missions and is still in existence. The organization was formed to support the missionary activity of the Church through raising funds and collecting items such as clothing and books. Its activities have expanded, however, and it now also serves as a forum for women in the Church. In 1958 the group's name was changed to Episcopal Churchwomen, Diocese of New York.

12,085. Standing Committee Proceedings
Records. 1785- . 18 cu.ft.
Access restricted. No guide.
Episcopal Diocese of New York Archives.
Minutes, financial records, reports, legal documents, and correspondence of the Committee, which acts as an advisory council to the bishop, approves candidates for ordination, approves the formation and dissolution of parishes, judges complaints between a rector and his parish, and authorizes the sale or mortgage of property. Includes records relating to women's ordination and correspondence from parishes in the Diocese and other areas of the country reacting to the ordinations of women, especially the ordination of Ellen Marie Barrett.

12,086. The Fashion Group, Inc.
Records. 1931- . Ca. 6 ft. and 2 drawers.
Open. No guide.
The Fashion Group, Inc.
An organization of women executives in the fashion industry, the Group began in 1929 with 15 members. Minutes, reports to members on activities, correspondence and written accounts of founding members, photos, and slides. The Group was incorporated in 1931 and has since grown to include 32 regional groups throughout the world. Made up of women involved in retail sales, the news media, schools, and advertising, the Group has included among its members such women as Edna Woolman Chase of *Vogue,* Carmel Snow of *Harper's Bazaar,* Dorothy Shaver of Lord & Taylor, Geraldine Stutz of Henri Bendel, and designer Adele Simpson.

12,087. Manning, Bishop W. T.
Papers. 1846-1954. 71 boxes.
Open. Unpublished guide.
General Theological Seminary, St. Mark's Library.
Manning (1866-1949) was bishop of the Episcopal archdiocese of New York from 1921 to 1946. Includes correspondence with Mrs. W. T. Manning, Eleanor Roosevelt, Mrs. Andrew Carnegie, Mrs. Ogden Reid, and other women concerning such topics as sex, morality, divorce, and remarriage. Also includes a 1926 address on marriage and divorce, a 1934 address to the women's auxiliary, and articles from church publications on the role of women in the Episcopal church.

12,088. Miscellany
Papers. Ca. 1780s-1940s. 2 boxes.
Open. Unpublished guide.
General Theological Seminary, St. Mark's Library.
Includes correspondence of women, some of which concerns the Female Missionary Society of St. Paul's Chapel. Also contains letters to Mrs. Morris P. Ferris on the meaning of Holy Communion, 1889-1913; records of the Corporation for the Relief of Widows and Orphans in New York, 1850-98; and an 1847 brochure from Miss Snow's Boarding School for Young Ladies.

12,089. Robbins
Papers. 1784-1932. 39 boxes.
Open. Unpublished guide.
General Theological Seminary, St. Mark's Library.
Howard C. Robbins (1879-1952) was dean of the Cathedral of St. John the Divine in New York City from 1917 to 1929 and a collector of historical documents. Includes correspondence of the wives and daughters of bishops and ministers, 1834-1932; an 1855 address given to a group of women; a girl's 1823 confirmation certificate; and an 1801 marriage certificate.

12,090. Seminary Archives
Records. 1824-1942. 6 boxes.
Open. Unpublished guide.
General Theological Seminary, St. Mark's Library.
Dean's office records, correspondence, information on scholarships, sermons, essays, lists of students, and examination schedules of the Seminary, which was founded in 1794 to train seminarians for the priesthood and other vocations in the Protestant Episcopal church. Includes correspondence of some women. Records of women students admitted after 1971 are housed in the registrar's office.

12,091. Anniversaries
Records. 1926- . 1.25 ft.
Open. Unpublished guide.
Girl Scouts of the USA Library and Archives.
Correspondence, memoranda, scrapbooks, personal notebooks and messages, clippings, and publications relate to the yearly anniversaries of the Girl Scouts. Includes extensive files on the 25th and 50th anniversaries in 1937 and 1962 and material on Silver Jubilee Camp, Girl Scout week and Girl Scout day celebrations, the 1948 commemorative stamp, and founder's day celebrations.

12,092. Association of Girl Scout Professional Workers
Records. 1939- . 1 folder.
Open. Unpublished guide.
Girl Scouts of the USA Library and Archives.
Constitution, bylaws, correspondence, memoranda, a directory, and publications of the Association, which was founded in 1939 and is devoted to the professional development of executive Girl Scout personnel. According to the constitution and bylaws, the Association is not limited to women; it functions separately from, but cooperates with, the national Girl Scout organization.

12,093. Baden-Powell, Olave, and Baden-Powell, Robert
Papers. 1919- . 1.17 ft.
Open. Unpublished guide.
Girl Scouts of the USA Library and Archives.
Correspondence, speeches, memoranda, photos, clippings, and publications of the Baden-Powells. Lady Baden-Powell (1889-1977) was head of Girl Guides; Lord Baden-Powell (1857-1941) was founder of Boy Scouts in England. Contains papers related to Lady Baden-Powell's relationship with and influence on GSUSA, including records of her visits to the US and to various Girl Scout councils and correspondence containing her opinions on GSUSA activities. Also includes writings, speeches, and messages of an inspirational nature. Lady Baden-Powell continued to be an important figure in Boy Scouting and Girl Guiding and Scouting after her husband's death.

12,094. Bee-Hive Girls
Records. 1916-39. 1 folder.
Open. No guide.
Girl Scouts of the USA Library and Archives.
Correspondence, publications, and a description of this group, which was founded in ca. 1912. Correspondence deals with the proposed amalgamation of the Bee-Hive Girls and the Girl Scouts.

12,095. Book of Memory
Records. 1945- . 0.15 ft. and 6 vols.
Open. Unpublished guide.
Girl Scouts of the USA Library and Archives.
Books contain posthumous tributes and photos honoring women and men who contributed to Girl Scouting. Also includes minutes of special committees, correspondence, memoranda, and other records concerning preparation of tributes and maintenance of the books. Honored staff, leaders, presidents, and executive directors include Juliette (Gordon) Low, founder of the Girl Scouts; Edith Carpenter Macy, a contributor of land and money; Jane Deeter Rippin, an early national executive director; Lou (Henry) [Mrs. Herbert C.] Hoover, twice the president and once the honorary president; Nina Anderson Pape, the leader of the first Girl Scout troop; program contributor Lillian (Moller) Gilbreth; and Ray Mitchell, an early advisor of the Brownies.

12,096. Boy Scouts of America Controversy
Records. 1918-41. 0.5 ft.
Access restricted. Unpublished guide.
Girl Scouts of the USA Library and Archives.
Reports, questionnaires, and correspondence concerned with the controversy over the name "Scouts" and with the existence of Boy Scouts and Girl Scouts in the same areas. Reports from local Scout officials describe the degree of cooperation between the groups. Also includes comments from national leaders.

12,097. Brownie Girl Scouts
Records. 1919-51. 0.5 ft.
Open. Unpublished guide.
Girl Scouts of the USA Library and Archives.
Minutes, conference reports, correspondence, memoranda, clippings, and publications trace the development of the Brownie Scouts, a program of Girl Scouting for younger girls. Includes material relating to camp programs, experimental packs, training courses, source stories, and conferences. The program was not adopted officially until 1935.

12,098. Camp Fire Girls
Records. 1916- . 0.25 ft.
Access restricted. Unpublished guide.
Girl Scouts of the USA Library and Archives.
Official statements, reports, correspondence, and memoranda concern the amalgamation controversy between the Girl Scouts and the Camp Fire Girls, another organization for girls.

12,099. Campus Girl Scouts
Records. 1914- . 3 ft.
Open. No guide.
Girl Scouts of the USA Library and Archives.
Reports, correspondence, memoranda, clippings, photos, and publications of adult volunteers on college campuses who were active in Girl Scouting. The women who came into Girl Scouting as college students in the 1920s tended later to become troop, council, committee, and national leaders.

12,100. Conferences
Records. 1935- . 3 ft.
Open. No guide.
Girl Scouts of the USA Library and Archives.
Reports, correspondence, memoranda, publications, and printed material of conferences held on subjects relevant to Girl Scouting. Includes material from conferences on child guidance, 1935; handicapped Girl Scouts, 1935; international exchange program evaluation, 1959; camp administration, 1960; scouting for black girls, 1970; and scouting for Mexican-American girls, 1971.

12,101. Conventions
Records. 1915- . 43 ft.
Open. No guide.
Girl Scouts of the USA Library and Archives.
Correspondence, memoranda, kits, programs, clippings, publications, and press releases of the Girl Scouts National Council meetings. Records reflect preparation for and action taken at all conventions. The 1975 convention considered whether boys should be admitted to membership in Girl Scouts.

12,102. General History of the Girl Scouts
Records. 1912- . 0.5 ft.
Open. Unpublished guide.
Girl Scouts of the USA Library and Archives.
National secretary's reports from 1912 to 1926, information sheets, and clippings of the Girl Scouts. Also includes personal accounts by women involved in the early stages of the movement in Savannah, GA; Washington, DC; and New York City. The organization was known as Girl Scouts until 1915 when it became Girl Scouts, Inc. The name was changed to Girl Scouts of the USA in 1950 when the organization received a congressional charter.

12,103. Girl Guide Histories
Records. 1910- . 0.75 ft.
Open. No guide.
Girl Scouts of the USA Library and Archives.
Reports and publications document the founding and activities of international guide and scout organizations. Includes annual reports, periodicals, handbooks, and songbooks from countries, including Argentina, Costa Rica, Denmark, Ghana, Iceland, India, Japan, Lichtenstein, Malaysia, the Netherlands, Pakistan, Panama, Poland, Sierra Leone, Sri Lanka, Uganda, Vietnam, and Zambia.

12,104. Girl Guides of America
Records. 1911. 1 folder.
Open. No guide.
Girl Scouts of the USA Library and Archives.
Handbooks and publications of an early girls' and women's organization, which was formed about the same time as the Girl Scouts but offered a different type of program.

12,105. Girl Pioneers of America
Records. 1920-27. 1 folder.
Open. No guide.
Girl Scouts of the USA Library and Archives.
Correspondence, memoranda, and publications of a girls' and women's group, which was formed in 1912.

12,106. Girl Scout Board Meetings
Records. 1915- . 150 ft.
Access restricted. Unpublished guide.
Girl Scouts of the USA Library and Archives.
Minutes of board meetings, which are held three times a year. The minutes cover such issues as children's rights, the Kerner Report, and the Equal Rights Amendment.

12,107. Girl Scouts of America
Records. 1915-20. 1 folder.
Open. No guide.
Girl Scouts of the USA Library and Archives.
Correspondence, memoranda, and publications reflect the purpose and activities of the Girl Scouts of America, an organization for girls and women formed at about the same time as the Girl Scouts.

12,108. Lisetor-Lane, Clara A.
Papers. 1913-62. 0.14 ft.
Access restricted. Unpublished guide.
Girl Scouts of the USA Library and Archives.
Primarily correspondence between [Miss] Lisetor-Lane, Juliette (Gordon) Low, and Lou (Henry) Hoover regarding Lisetor-Lane's contention that she founded the Girl Scouts before Juliette Low.

12,109. Low, Juliette Magill Kinzie (Gordon)
Papers. 1860- . 2.5 ft.
Open. Unpublished guide.
Girl Scouts of the USA Library and Archives.
Business and personal correspondence, diaries, speeches, writings, memoranda, drawings, clippings, and other papers of [Mrs. William Mackay] Low (1860-1927), founder of the organization that became Girl Scouts of the USA. Also includes files on the Juliette Low Museum, the Juliette Gordon Low birthplace, and Juliette Low World Friendship Fund.

12,110. Memorabilia
Collection. 1912- . No size given.
Open. Card catalog.
Girl Scouts of the USA Library and Archives.
Objects reflecting the history of Girl Scouting and the people involved with it, including photos, clothing, uniforms, filmstrips, tapes, discs, scrapbooks, publications, sculpture, and paintings.

12,111. Personalities
Records. 1912- . 9 ft.
Open. Unpublished guide.
Girl Scouts of the USA Library and Archives.
Files of more than 1150 individuals connected with the Girl Scouts include correspondence, memoranda, biographies, notebooks, clippings, press releases, publications, and memorabilia. People represented include national presidents Juliette (Gordon) Low, Anne Hyde Choate, Gloria D. Scott, and Lou (Henry) [Mrs. Herbert] Hoover; national executive directors Edith D. Johnston and Frances R. Hesselbein; national and local staff members; and celebrities Lucille Ball and Debbie Reynolds. Others represented include Leonid Brezhnev, Dorothy Canfield Fisher, and Queen Elizabeth. Also includes an oral history of several long-time staff members who were interviewed in the 1960s as part of an historical project.

12,112. Photo Files
Records. 1912- . 11 ft.
Open. Unpublished guide.
Girl Scouts of the USA Library and Archives.
Includes photos of persons associated with girl scouting world conferences, program areas, camp and camping, international girl guides and scouts, national centers, and uniforms.

12,113. Publications
Records. 1912- . Ca. 81 ft.
Open. Partial catalog.
Girl Scouts of the USA Library and Archives.
Includes copies of all publications of GSUSA, including annual reports, administrative manuals, handbooks, films, kits, and the organization's periodicals *American Girl, Girl Scout Leader,* and

Daisy (formerly the *Brownie Reader).* Also includes files dealing with development of the publications.

12,114. War and Post-War Activities
Records. 1918-49. 0.66 ft.
Open. No guide.
Girl Scouts of the USA Library and Archives.
Reports, correspondence, memoranda, clippings, and publications of the GSUSA reflect efforts of the Girl Scouts to aid in the war effort. Contains files on such subjects as plans for displaced persons; activities in various countries, including Australia, the Balkans, Russia, and Switzerland; farm aide and victory garden projects; and Liberty Loan campaigns.

12,115. World Association of Girl Guides and Girl Scouts
Records. 1926- . 9.83 ft.
Open. No guide.
Girl Scouts of the USA Library and Archives.
Reports, correspondence, memoranda, and publications of the Association, which was founded in 1928 to promote unity in the principles and purposes of the worldwide Girl Guide and Girl Scout movements.

12,116. World Conferences
Records. 1920- . 4 ft.
Open. Unpublished guide.
Girl Scouts of the USA Library and Archives.
Reports, agendas, correspondence, memoranda, clippings, and publications concern the meetings of the World Association of Girl Guides and Girl Scouts and reflect the international problems and concerns of the associations and members.

12,117. Archives
Records. 1912- . 600 ft.; 3000 microfilm reels, tapes, and motion pictures; and 100,000 items.
Open. Partial unpublished guide.
Hadassah, Women's Zionist Organization of America.
Correspondence, reports, speeches, photos, slides, pamphlets, booklets, and other records relate to the founding of Hadassah in 1912 and to its efforts to set medical and health standards in Palestine and Israel and to foster Jewish ideals and education in America. Hadassah works through two corporations: Hadassah, the Women's Zionist Organization of America, Inc., and the Hadassah Medical Relief Association. The former administers the American program and the latter, the Israel program. The records also concern the history of Hadassah's chapters, its founders and early leaders, and its first president Henrietta Szold. Other early leaders included Zip Szold, Jessie Sampter, Irma Lindheim, Alice Seligsberg, Madeline Lewin-Epstein, Emma L. Gottheil, Sophie Berger, Lotte Levensohn, Julia Dushkin, and Rosalie Phillips. Also includes records of such projects as the American Zionist Medical Unit, Junior Hadassah, and Hadassah Israel Education Services as well as information on Hadassah's relationship with the US government, the British mandate government in Palestine, and Israel and Arab-Jewish relations.

12,118. Szold, Henrietta
Papers. 1890- . 15 ft. and 1 motion picture.
Open. Unpublished guide.
Hadassah, Women's Zionist Organization of America.
Correspondence, speeches, minutes, tapes, transcripts, motion pictures, pictorial albums, and photos of Szold (1860-1945), founder and organizer of Hadassah. Includes correspondence with family and friends and letters to members of the national board of Hadassah, world leaders, and Jewish and Zionist leaders concerning the organization and purpose of Hadassah, Youth Aliyah, and political matters. Also includes tributes to her and correspondence and other papers relating to an honorary doctorate she received from Boston University in 1944. Szold was a cofounder and organizer of Youth Aliyah, a child rescue movement, and established vocational education programs in Palestine.

12,119. Correspondence
Records. 1883-1920. Ca. 7 ft.
Open. No guide.
The Huguenot Society of America Library.
Correspondence of the Society, which was founded in 1883 to promote the cause of religious freedom and perpetuate the memory of the Huguenot settlers in America, includes letters from women requesting genealogical tracings and membership information. Includes official correspondence of E. M. A. [Mrs. James M.] Lawton, secretary of the Society from 1900 to 1919.

12,120. Official Files
Records. 1919-62. 1 drawer.
Open. No guide.
The Huguenot Society of America Library.
Minutes, 1927-1962, and membership lists of the Society, which was founded in 1883 to promote the cause of religious freedom, to perpetuate the memory of the Huguenot settlers in America, and to commemorate the principal events in the history of the Huguenots by discovering, collecting, and preserving all existing monuments, memorabilia, and documents relating to Huguenot history and genealogy. Many women were members, and Society secretaries included [Miss] Margaret A. Jackson and [Miss] Lorraine Sherwood.

12,121. Proceedings
Records. 1884-1933. 7 vols.
Open. No guide.
The Huguenot Society of America Library.
Includes published minutes of committee and general meetings and membership lists of the Society, which was founded in 1883 to promote the cause of religious freedom and to perpetuate the memory of the Huguenot settlers in America. Contains the minutes of the Ladies Committee, a special subcommittee founded in 1887 to communicate with various Huguenot groups across the country and to try to enlarge the society's membership by writing letters to potential members. The original members of the Committee included Mrs. Henry C. Stimson and [Miss] Catherine G. Van Rensselaer.

12,122. Hunter College Archives
Records. 1870- . 345 boxes and 5 tapes.
Open. Card file.
Hunter College of the City University of New York.
One of the first schools to offer tuition-free higher education to women, Hunter College was founded in 1870 to educate teachers for the New York City school system; in 1964 it became coeducational, and in 1976 it began charging tuition. Annual reports of the presidents, minutes of the board of trustees, financial and social records, College and alumnae publications, complete sets of College bulletins and commencement programs, photos, clippings, records of the alumnae association, and other material about students and alumnae.

12,123. Photos of Women in History
Collection. 1840- . No size given.
Open. No guide.
Janet Lehr, Inc.
Includes portraits of feminists, photos of women photographers, and photos of the Pankhurst movement.

12,124. The Juilliard School
Records. 1905- . 375 vols.
Open. No guide.
The Juilliard School, Lila Acheson Wallace Library.
Faculty minutes, class records, scrapbooks containing clippings, school catalogs and magazines, and master's theses of the School, which was founded as the Institute of Musical Art in 1905. The institution provides musical education on a precollege and college level, education for dance performance, and education for dramatic performance. Many prominent women musicians have been associated with the School.

12,125. Metropolitan Opera Association Archives
Records. 1833- . Ca. 1000 ft. and 165 drawers.
Access restricted. Unpublished guide.
Metropolitan Opera Association Archives.
Financial records, artists' contracts, correspondence, opera and artist performance index cards, photos, clippings, biographies, programs, *Opera News* magazines, and set designs of the Opera Association. The Metropolitan Opera was founded in 1883. Mrs. August Belmont organized the Metropolitan Opera Guild in 1935 and the National Council of the Metropolitan Opera Association in 1952. [Miss] Lucrezia Bori was production chairman of the Metropolitan Opera from 1936 to ca. 1960.

12,126. Department of Photography
Collection. Ca. 1850- . No size given.
Access restricted. No guide.
The Museum of Modern Art.
Ca. 10,000 original photos include works by such photographers as Diane Arbus, Gertrude Käsebier, and Imogen Cunningham. Also includes biographical files on the artists containing correspondence, clippings, and exhibition announcements.

12,127. Byron, Joseph, and Byron, Percy
Papers. 1885-1930. Ca. 10,000 items.
Open. Unpublished guide.
Museum of the City of New York.
Photos and negatives of Joseph Byron (1844-1923) and his son Percy Byron (1878-1959), professional photographers. Includes photos of women in ballet rehearsals, kitchen scenes, family scenes, classes, almshouses, and gym classes and women sewing, working in offices, and working as nurses in hospitals.

12,128. Manuscripts
Collection. 1640- . Ca. 8000 items.
Open. Unpublished guide.
Museum of the City of New York.
Collection concerns the history of New York City and contains correspondence, wills, receipts of deeds, copybooks, receipts for goods purchased, autograph albums, wedding certificates, and tickets to social balls. Includes a letter written by Mrs. Peter DeLancey, 1742; a letter from Abigail Adams, 1786; an account book kept by a Mrs. Strauss, 1877-85; and an autograph album from the Rutgers Female Institute, 1860.

12,129. Photos
Collection. 1614-1939. Ca. 500,000 items.
Open. Unpublished guide.
Museum of the City of New York.
Includes photos of individual women as well as women taking part in a suffragist street meeting, involved in various occupations and activities, and posing with their families. Also includes photos relating to the theater, including pictures of Ethel Barrymore, Mary Pickford, Fanny Brice, Sarah Bernhardt, Joan Crawford, Greta Garbo, Ingrid Bergman, Helen Hayes, Marlene Dietrich, Katherine Hepburn, Judy Garland, and Isadora Duncan.

12,130. Riis, Jacob
Papers. 1877-1910. 790 items.
Open. Unpublished guide.
Museum of the City of New York.
Riis (1849-1914) was a journalist, writer, and photographer. Contains photos, negatives, and lantern slides, including pictures of women in tenements, family scenes, police stations, oyster canneries, and a female almshouse on Blackwell's Island. Also includes pictures of women sewing

and women vagrants. Includes some photos taken by other photographers.

12,131. National Academy of Design
Records. 1825- . No size given.
Access restricted. No guide.
National Academy of Design.
Architectural photos, prints, paintings, and sculpture of the Academy, which was founded in 1825. Female artists have been elected to membership in the Academy since 1833.

12,132. Cockett, Marguerite Standish
Papers. 1915-19. Ca. 1 ft.
Open. No guide.
National Board of Young Men's Christian Associations.
Papers of Cockett (1878-?), a physician, include correspondence, reports, photo albums and photos, and scrapbooks. Cockett served with the American Fund for French Wounded and, beginning in 1917, with the Women's Bureau of the YMCA in Paris. She took part in war relief work, particularly in setting up canteens for soldiers. An important figure in the management of the Women's Bureau, she worked for equal recognition for YMCA women war workers from the International Committee, the YMCA's governing body.

12,133. Women's Auxiliaries of the International Committee of YMCAs
Records. 1887-1917. Ca. 2 ft.
Open. No guide.
National Board of Young Men's Christian Associations.
Annual reports, correspondence, speeches, scrapbooks, and pamphlets of the women's auxiliaries, which were formed in ca. 1885; the groups' members taught Bible classes and Sunday school, visited the sick, decorated the reading rooms of local associations, and raised funds. Most of the auxiliaries functioned under the supervision of the male general secretary of the YMCA with which they were affiliated.

12,134. World War I—Women's Work
Records. 1917-21. Ca. 1 ft.
Open. No guide.
National Board of Young Men's Christian Associations.
Records relate primarily to the work of the Women's Bureau of the YMCA, which was responsible for supervising women's war relief work and women canteen personnel. Includes a record book, reports, correspondence, histories, and pamphlets.

12,135. YMCA Work with Women and Girls
Records. 1939-68. Ca. 8 ft.
Open. No guide.
National Board of Young Men's Christian Associations.
Minutes, reports, correspondence, and pamphlets reflect the ways in which the YMCA met the needs of women and girls in education, religion, personality development, and physical activities. Women were brought into YMCA activities and previously all-male facilities were opened to them.

12,136. YMCA—YWCA Relationships
Records. Ca. 1917- . Ca. 3 ft.
Open. No guide.
National Board of Young Men's Christian Associations.
Minutes, reports, surveys, memoranda, and correspondence concern the relationship between the YWCA and the YMCA.

12,137. Central Files
Records. 1893- . Ca. 1500 ft., 1000 vols., 9000 items, 370 microfilm reels, and 3600 microfiche.
Access restricted. Partial unpublished guide.
National League for Nursing.
Includes annual reports, minutes, financial and legal records, correspondence, convention tape recordings, reports, surveys, biographical information, photos, scrapbooks, periodicals, pamphlets, and publications of the League, which was formed when five other organizations combined in 1952. The League is dedicated to meeting the health needs of the people by improving nursing education and nursing services. The group's activities include accreditation of programs in basic nursing education, graduate nursing, and continuing education; consultation services for education programs; testing for and licensing of registered and practical nurses; and publishing research. Includes information on such nursing leaders as Isabel H. Robb, Linda Richards, and Mary Roberts, editor of the *American Journal of Nursing*.

12,138. Bellevue Hospital
Records. 1881-82. 316 pp.
Open. Published guide.
New York Academy of Medicine.
Case histories of the women's wards at Bellevue Hospital in New York City. See *New York Academy of Medicine, Author Catalog of the Library, First Supplement,* 4 vols. (Boston: G. K. Hall & Co., 1974).

12,139. Campbell, Jane
Papers. 1901. 51-page item.
Open. Published guide.
New York Academy of Medicine.
Sketch by Campbell about the life of Hannah E. Myers Longshore, a pioneer woman physician who lived in Philadelphia. See *New York Academy of Medicine, Author Catalog of the Library, First Supplement,* 4 vols. (Boston: G. K. Hall & Co., 1974).

12,140. Guion, Ferebe E.
Papers. 1891-92. 89-page vol.
Open. Published guide.
New York Academy of Medicine.
Record book Guion kept while she was a student at St. Luke's Hospital Training School for Nurses and also during a course of instruction in obstetrical nursing, which was provided at Sloane Maternity Hospital for the St. Luke's students. See *New York Academy of Medicine, Author Catalog of the Library, First Supplement,* 4 vols. (Boston: G. K. Hall & Co., 1974).

12,141. Midwifery
Records. 1842-43. 71 pp.
Open. Published guide.
New York Academy of Medicine.
Reports of cases attended by students of New York University Medical College and physicians of the New York Asylum for Lying-In Women. See *New York Academy of Medicine, Author Catalog of the Library,* 43 vols. (Boston: G. K. Hall & Co., 1969).

12,142. Stimson, Philip Moen
Papers. 1941-67. 19-page item.
Open. Published guide.
New York Academy of Medicine.
Scrapbook of correspondence, photos, clippings, and pamphlets pertaining to Sister Elizabeth Kenny, which Stimson (1888-1971), a physician, compiled. See *New York Academy of Medicine, Author Catalog of the Library,* 43 vols. (Boston: G. K. Hall & Co., 1969).

12,143. Walker, Emma Elizabeth
Papers. 1894-99. 45-page vol.
Open. Published guide.
New York Academy of Medicine.
Scrapbook of correspondence, calling cards, clippings, schedules of classes, and commencement programs of Walker pertain to the Johns Hopkins Medical School and Hospital in Baltimore. See *New York Academy of Medicine, Author Catalog of the Library, First Supplement,* 4 vols. (Boston: G. K. Hall & Co., 1974).

12,144. Austin, Joyce P.
Papers. 1960-64. 1 cu.ft.
Open. Unpublished guide.
New York City Municipal Archives.
Financial statements, reports of meetings, and publicity releases of Austin, who was an assistant to Mayor Robert F. Wagner of New York.

12,145. Earle, Genevive Beavers
Papers. 1909-49. 2 cu.ft.
Open. Unpublished guide.
New York City Municipal Archives.
[Mrs. William P.] Earle (1883-1956) was the first woman member of the New York City council. Includes correspondence, scrapbooks, clippings, and memorabilia as well as official papers generated before and during her tenure as councilwoman.

12,146. Farbman, Ruth
Papers. 1960-65. 17 cu.ft.
Open. Unpublished guide.
New York City Municipal Archives.
Farbman was a special assistant to Mayor Robert Wagner of New York from 1960 to 1964. Contains correspondence, memos, and general files, including the mayor's annual report for 1963, the mayor's speeches for 1963 and 1964, executive orders and memos, press releases, and items concerned with the Columbus Day Purple Line, the Mobile Unit Information Center, public officials, and other topics.

12,147. Gallant, Ceil
Papers. 1968. 2 cu.ft.
Open. Unpublished guide.
New York City Municipal Archives.
General files of Gallant, who was an assistant to Mayor John Lindsay of New York, include correspondence and memoranda.

12,148. Holtzman, Elizabeth
Papers. 1968-69. 5 cu.ft.
Open. Unpublished guide.
New York City Municipal Archives.
Papers of Holtzman, who was an assistant to Mayor John Lindsay of New York, relate to abandoned cars, model cities, and the Economic Development Administration.

12,149. Kelly, Ann
Papers. 1959-61. 2 cu.ft.
Open. Unpublished guide.
New York City Municipal Archives.
Correspondence and other papers of Kelly, who was deputy commissioner of the department of commerce under Mayor Robert Wagner of New York from 1959 to 1961, relate to the economic development of New York City.

12,150. McCray, Bernice Melae
Papers. 1963-65. 3 cu.ft.
Open. Unpublished guide.
New York City Municipal Archives.
McCray was secretary to Mayor Robert Wagner of New York. Consists of official files created during her tenure, which include correspondence, memoranda, reports, and other papers.

12,151. Rankin, Rebecca B.
Papers. 1930-50. 5 cu.ft.
Open. Unpublished guide.
New York City Municipal Archives.
Correspondence, memoranda, and other records of Rankin, a librarian for the Municipal reference library, were created during her tenure as reference librarian.

12,152. Abbott's Institution
Records. 1847-49. 1 item and 35 pp.
Open. No guide.

New-York Historical Society.
Diary in which a boarding student describes her activities in school and in New York. John S. C. Abbott (1805-77) was headmaster of the school, which was located on Bleecker Street in New York City. Also includes [Miss] Sarah Johnson's report card.

12,153. Adams, Abigail (Smith)
Papers. 1787-1815. 16 items.
Open. No guide.
New-York Historical Society.
Correspondence of Adams (1744-1818), who was the wife of President John Adams, pertains to the activities of Congress in 1789, Shays' Rebellion, and other political and family matters. Also includes her letters to Cotton Tufts, a Boston physician and legislator.

12,154. Allen, Sarah Elizabeth
Papers. 1838-42. 11 items.
Open. No guide.
New-Yorian Historical Society.
Correspondence of Allen from Little Neck, Long Island, NY, includes letters from her friends Mary Dayton of Sag Harbor, Long Island, and Mary Louisa Thayer writing from Cartagena, Spain.

12,155. Anderson, Alexander
Papers. Ca. 1791-1870. 3 vols. and 122 items.
Open. No guide.
New-York Historical Society.
Anderson (1775-1870) was a physician and engraver in New York City. His papers include correspondence with his daughter Julia Malvina Halsey and others, wood engravings of his daughter Ann (Anderson) Maverick, and a list of yellow fever patients at Bellevue Hospital in 1795.

12,156. Association for the Relief of Respectable Aged and Indigent Females in New York City
Records. 1814-82. 8 vols.
Open. No guide.
New-York Historical Society.
From its founding in 1814, the women of the Association met regularly and visited dependent pensioners with gifts of clothing, groceries, and cash. In 1838 they established an asylum for the pensioners. Records include a journal in which Association members describe in detail conditions and activities they observed in visits to the asylum, a list of deaths of asylum inmates, and lists of pensioners the Association relieved in its early years, which include pensioners' religious affiliation, the names of members responsible for visiting them, and pensioners' death dates. Also includes advisory committee minutes, some of which concern the financial management of the Association's investments, and records of expenditures and receipts.

12,157. Bacon, Lydia
Papers. Ca. 1811-12. 78-page vol.
Open. No guide.
New-York Historical Society.
Bacon's journal, which she kept while traveling in Vincennes and Detroit with her husband Josiah Bacon, a lieutenant in the US infantry, has been published in *Indiana Magazine of History* (December 1944 and March 1945).

12,158. Banfield Family
Papers. Ca. 1851-74. 23 items.
Open. No guide.
New-York Historical Society.
Letters to Prudence (Osborn) Hadden Vanderbeck of New York from her daughter Mary Ann Banfield, her son-in-law John Banfield, and their children concern their 1851 voyage to Panama, life in California, and their family and social life in San Francisco.

12,159. Barnard Club of the City of New York
Records. 1894-1947. 2 vols.
Open. No guide.
New-York Historical Society.
Constitution, bylaws, minutes of annual meetings and of the board of managers, and membership lists of the Club, which was formed to promote the welfare of Barnard College. Also includes a book listing candidates for admission to the Club and the names of their sponsors.

12,160. Beach, Elizabeth T. Porter
Papers. Ca. 1860-67. 31 items.
Open. No guide.
New-York Historical Society.
Papers of [Mrs.] Beach, a resident of New York City, include correspondence with E. T. Throup. Also includes manuscript music for voices and piano entitled "The Evening Prayer," which was dedicated to Beach by the composer Fernando Andrillon, and a prose translation and accompanying letter by Charles E. Sprague.

12,161. Bell, Andrew
Papers. 1793-1843. 4 vols. and 234 items.
Open. No guide.
New-York Historical Society.
Papers of Bell (1757-1843), a merchant in Perth Amboy, NJ, include correspondence of his wife Susannah Bell. Also included are letters from their niece Jane E. Paterson of Morristown, NJ, and from Sarah Nelson, who lived in Norfolk, VA.

12,162. Bledsoe, Mary C.
Papers. 1867-70. 27 items.
Open. No guide.
New-York Historical Society.
Correspondence of Bledsoe, a resident of Madison County, LA, includes letters she wrote to Thomas Jefferson Durant, her attorney, regarding her claim against the US government for property losses at Milliken's Bend, LA, during General Grant's stay in the area. She valued the property at more than $125,000.

12,163. Bliss, George
Papers. 1876-95. 3 vols.
Open. No guide.
New-York Historical Society.
Papers of Bliss (1830-97), a New York City lawyer, include correspondence he and his wife Anais Bliss (?-1920) wrote while they were in Europe from 1894 to 1895. These letters to Florence L. Hanson, George Bliss's sister Sarah Walder, and Anna Walder contain information on the Blisses' experiences and people they met. Also includes Anais Bliss's account of the two years before her husband's death, a eulogy for Anais Bliss, and her husband's autobiography.

12,164. Bloomingdale, New York: Hopkins, Mary Clark
Papers. Nd. 11 pp.
Open. No guide.
New-York Historical Society.
Personal history [Mrs.] Hopkins wrote about her childhood in the Bloomingdale district of New York City. She describes houses in the area, such as the Livingston house, and reminisces about Mrs. Coventry Waddell. Notes to Mrs. W. H. Coventry Waddell from Washington Irving and William M. Thackeray are also included.

12,165. Blunt, Sarah R.
Papers. 1862-65. 31 items.
Open. No guide.
New-York Historical Society.
Correspondence of Blunt, a Civil War nurse. Writing to her parents and sister in Brooklyn, NY, she describes her personal sentiments, living conditions, duties, fellow personnel, and the wounded in hospitals at Point Lookout, MD, and Harpers Ferry, WV.

12,166. Boggs Family
Papers. 1800-78. 47 items.
Open. No guide.
New-York Historical Society.
Correspondence of this family includes letters from Mary L. Boggs (1777-?) of Bedford, NY, to her daughter Mary (Boggs) Blauvelt of New Brunswick, NJ, and letters Boggs wrote from Paris and England to her son Charles Stuart Boggs (1811-72). Also includes a letter from Robert Boggs (1766-1831) to [Miss] Maria Brenton at the Mansion of Truth in Harlem, NY, a school run by Brenton's sister [Miss] Fanny Brenton.

12,167. Booth, Mary Louise
Papers. 1859-88. 19 items.
Open. No guide.
New-York Historical Society.
[Miss] Booth (1831-89) was an author and editor. Includes correspondence to Henry B. Dawson concerning publication of his articles and books and a letter in which Booth comments on the adverse reaction of Bostonians to publication of a history book.

12,168. Botta, Anne Charlotte (Lynch)
Papers. 1835-55. 19 items.
Open. No guide.
New-York Historical Society.
Correspondence of [Mrs. Vincenzo] Botta (1815-91), who was a New York author and hostess, includes letters from Lydia Sigourney and [Mrs.] Lizzie Sherwood and personal letters from Senator John McPherson Berrien.

12,169. Brady, Mary A.
Papers. 1862-65. 32-page vol.
Open. No guide.
New-York Historical Society.
A philanthropist, Brady was a resident of Philadelphia. Biographical sketch concerns her activities as president of the Ladies Association for Soldiers Relief, among them her visits to sick and wounded soldiers near the front lines.

12,170. Brasher, Helen (Kortwright)
Papers. 1802-08. 47-page item.
Open. No guide.
New-York Historical Society.
In her diary [Mrs. Abraham] Brasher (1739-1819) reminisces about her youth in New York City; her social life and beaux; a sermon by George Whitefield; the coming of the Revolutionary War; moving to Paramus, NJ; raids by the British; difficulties her family experienced as refugees; absences of her husband, who was a member of the New York State Assembly; his death; and details of her life.

12,171. Brooks, Charles
Papers. 1858-59. 2 vols.
Open. No guide.
New-York Historical Society.
Brooks (1795-1872) was a Unitarian clergyman and educator. Included are letters he wrote to his wife Charlotte Brooks while he was traveling through Savannah, GA, Charleston, SC, Raleigh, NC, Washington, DC, Philadelphia, and New York. He describes a chewing tobacco factory in Richmond, VA, and an asylum for the deaf, dumb, and blind in Raleigh. He also writes about Mrs. Henry C. King of Charleston and his experiences worshipping at various churches. Correspondence his daughter Elizabeth Brooks wrote him describing persons, places, and life in San Francisco is included.

12,172. Brown, James Wright
Papers. 1789-1951. 600 items.
Open. No guide.
New-York Historical Society.
Papers of Brown (1873-1959), an editor and publisher, include correspondence from Lucy Stone and Kate Field about routine matters in the literary and newspaper professions.

12,173. Burke, Annie Elizabeth
Papers. 1885-1924. Ca. 40 items.
Open. No guide.
New-York Historical Society.
[Mrs. Russell W.] Burke was a playwright in New York City. Her correspondence includes personal letters from actor and playwright Ramsay Morris, actress Julia Marlowe, and other prominent actors and producers.

12,174. Burr, Aaron
Papers. 1755-1836. Ca. 15,000 items (27 microfilm reels).
Open. Published guide.
New-York Historical Society.
Burr (1756-1836) was a lawyer, politician, and western adventurer. His family correspondence includes that with his sister Sarah (Burr) [Mrs. Tapping] Reeves, his wife Theodosia Prevost Burr, and his daughter Theodosia (Burr) [Mrs. Joseph] Alston (1783-1813). Burr's personal and business correspondents include Rebecca Smith [Mrs. Samuel] Blodgett, Isabella Mix, and Rachel Maltbie [Mrs. Medcef] Eden and her daughters Sally Ann Maltbie [Mrs. Benjamin] Waldron, Elizabeth Maltbie (Eden) [Mrs. Isadore] Guillet, and Rebecca Maltbie (Eden) [Mrs. John Lyde] Wilson. Burr was a confidante to these women as well as a legal and business adviser on such matters as the recovery of real property, divorce, and child custody. Also included are numerous letters from indigent women seeking his aid. In correspondence to friends and wards, he makes many comments about women's education. See *Guide and Indexes to the Papers of Aaron Burr* (Glen Rock, NJ: Microfilming Corporation of America, 1978).

12,175. Butler, Rose
Papers. 1819. 20 pp.
Open. No guide.
New-York Historical Society.
A resident of New York City, Butler was executed after being convicted of arson. Affidavits, a confession, a pamphlet containing a statement of the case and a description of her conduct, and other papers relate to Butler's trial and death.

12,176. California Gold Rush: Annis, Isaac
Papers. 1849-51. 13 items.
Open. No guide.
New-York Historical Society.
Correspondence between Annis and his daughter Nancy Russell of Port Gibson, NY. She describes local events, and he describes his trip to California and his attempts at prospecting and setting up a business.

12,177. Canaan, Columbia County, New York: Hall, Lucretia Warner
Papers. 1832-46. 130-page vol.
Open. No guide.
New-York Historical Society.
Diary in which [Mrs. Benjamin] Hall (1785-1847) describes the weather, chores, local events, visitors, family matters, and her neighbors in Canaan.

12,178. Carey and Hart
Records. 1829-48. Ca. 80 items.
Open. No guide.
New-York Historical Society.
Correspondence of these Philadelphia publishers and booksellers includes letters from Lydia H. Sigourney.

12,179. Chambers, Frank Ross
Papers. 1853-ca. 1947. Ca. 200 items.
Open. No guide.
New-York Historical Society.
Correspondence and other papers of Chambers (1850-1940), a partner of Rogers, Peet and Company of New York; his wife Kate Waller Chambers (?-1947); and other members of the Chambers and Waller families. Also includes photos of family members and of the Chamberses' home Crow's Nest in Bronxville, NY.

12,180. Chanler, William Astor
Papers. 1897-1929. 25 boxes.
Open. No guide.
New-York Historical Society.
Correspondence, memoranda, brochures, photos, and clippings of Beatrice Winthrop Ashley Chanler (1886-1946), a playwright and author, are contained in the papers of her husband William Chanler (1867-1934), a businessman, explorer, and congressman from New York state. Her papers pertain to her career; her involvement in efforts to save Kenmore, the home of George Washington's sister; child welfare work; the role of Spanish women during the Spanish Civil War; the Committee for Defending America; the Lafayette Fund for the relief of children of French soldiers and the Fund's WWII successor, the Committee of Mercy; and the Friends of Greece. She served as president of the latter two groups.

12,181. Child, Lydia Maria (Francis)
Papers. 1844-78. 16 items.
Open. No guide.
New-York Historical Society.
[Mrs. David Lee] Child (1802-80) was an antislavery writer. Her correspondence deals with her publications, the reactions of other women to her, her unwillingness to speak in public, and her love of seclusion. A manuscript article "The Colored Mammy and her White Foster-Child, A True Story" signed by "Dolly Dixie" is also included.

12,182. Chrystie, Mary
Papers. 1801-06. 320-page vol.
Open. No guide.
New-York Historical Society.
Receipt book of Chrystie, a china and glassware dealer in New York City, contains records of her payments on numerous accounts, including purchases of china and glassware.

12,183. Clarkson, Catharine
Papers. 1833-35. 27 pp.
Open. No guide.
New-York Historical Society.
Diaries in which [Miss] Clarkson, a resident of New York City, details her trips through northern New York, Virginia, and West Virginia. She describes the sights, travel conditions, accommodations, pastimes, and other travelers and friends she met, among them Henry Stevens, whom she later married.

12,184. Cleveland, Grover
Papers. 1905-1940. 4 items.
Open. No guide.
New-York Historical Society.
Papers of Cleveland include a letter from his widow Frances (Folsom) Cleveland Preston (1864-1947) to Mrs. Robert James Malone concerning the publication of letters between Malone's father George M. Eckels and Grover Cleveland about fishing.

12,185. Coan, Titus
Papers. 1830-72. Ca. 840 items.
Open. No guide.
New-York Historical Society.
Correspondence, poems, and other papers of Coan (1801-82), a Presbyterian missionary in Hawaii; his wife Fidelia Church Coan (1810-72); their son Titus Munson Coan (1836-1921), a physician, editor, and author; and Sarah Eliza Coan (1843-1916). Correspondence between Titus and Fidelia Coan extends from 1830 when he was a seminary student in New York state, through his first missionary trip to Patagonia, to their separations from 1835 to 1872 while he served as a missionary throughout the Hawaiian Islands and she lived in Hilo, HI. Also includes a 1903 diary of Sarah Coan and a letter from Fidelia Coan to Mrs. William Little Lee.

12,186. Corbett, Marion
Papers. 1837-41. 14 vols.
Open. No guide.
New-York Historical Society.
Letter books, notes on literary projects, poetry, and other items of Corbett, an English author, are included with a diary she kept during her residence in Washington, DC, and her stay in New York City. She comments on prominent people she met, places she visited, and her impressions of local customs.

12,187. Corse, Israel
Papers. 1858-1909. 125 items.
Open. No guide.
New-York Historical Society.
Papers of Corse (1819-85), a leather merchant in New York City, include friendly letters from former mayor Smith Ely to Corse's great-granddaughter [Miss] Lena Cadwallader Evans. Also includes an address Evans delivered in 1933 at a freedom of the press celebration in Mount Vernon, NY.

12,188. Crosby, Mary
Papers. 1842-92. 1 vol.
Open. No guide.
New-York Historical Society.
Diary in which Crosby (1822-?), the daughter of William Bedlow Crosby, describes and later reminisces about her activities as a young girl in New York City.

12,189. Daughters of the Military Order of the Loyal Region
Records. 1905-43. 2 vols. and 17 items.
Open. No guide.
New-York Historical Society.
Constitution, bylaws, a minute book, and a treasurer's book of this organization. Also includes correspondence of Mrs. E. K. Waterbury, who was treasurer from 1925 to 1943.

12,190. Davis, Jefferson
Papers. 1841-1902. 74 items.
Open. No guide.
New-York Historical Society.
Correspondence of Davis (1808-89), who was president of the Confederacy, includes correspondence with his wife Varina Anne (Howell) Davis (1826-1906). Her other correspondents incluce Mrs. Howell Cobb and [Mrs.] Justine Van Rensselaer Townsend.

12,191. De Camp Family
Papers. 1805-77. Ca. 100 items.
Open. No guide.
New-York Historical Society.
Correspondence and memorabilia of this Saratoga Springs and Albany, NY, family primarily concern family matters. Correspondents include Samuel G. J. De Camp, who was a US Army surgeon during the Civil War; his mother Susan (Grandin) De Camp; his son John De Camp (1812-75), a rear admiral in the US Navy; John De Camp's sisters Sarah Canfield (De Camp) Brandegee and Anna Maria Jackson (De Camp) Morris, who married Gouverneur Morris; John De Camp's daughter Mary A. G. De Camp (1843-?), who in 1866 married Edwin Weld Corning (?-1871); and Mary Augusta (Green) Tudor. Correspondence of Edwin Corning's parents Erastus Corning (1794-1872) and Harriet (Weld) Corning is also included.

12,192. De Groot Family
Papers. 1837-1965. 7 ft.
Open. No guide.
New-York Historical Society.
Correspondence, diaries, notebooks, stories, and other papers of this New York family and of the Hawley family, particularly of Elizabeth King

Hawley, who married William De Groot. Included are letters Elizabeth and Marianna Hawley wrote during a visit with Elizabeth (Schuyler) Hamilton, widow of Alexander Hamilton, describing their social life in Washington, DC. Also included is correspondence concerning the authenticity of paintings by Renoir, Cezanne, and Corot, which Adelaide Milton De Groot purchased.

12,193. De Peyster Family
Papers. 1677-1881. 5 ft.
Open. No guide.
New-York Historical Society.
Correspondence and legal and business papers of this and related families. Accounts, bonds, and miscellaneous papers of Eve De Peyster; tradesmen's accounts and bills of Cornelia De Peyster; and correspondence written by Margaret James in London to her brother Frederick De Peyster (1758-1834) are included. A daybook kept by a member of the family in New York City from 1723 to 1733 contains records of sales of a wide variety of merchandise to various customers.

12,194. Decatur, Stephen
Papers. Ca. 1804-35. 28 items.
Open. No guide.
New-York Historical Society.
Among the correspondence of Decatur (1779-1820), a naval officer, are letters of his wife Susan Decatur.

12,195. Delafield, Emily (Prime)
Papers. 1890s. 100 items.
Open. No guide.
New-York Historical Society.
Correspondence of [Mrs. Lewis Levingston] Delafield (1840-1909), a New York City resident, includes letters concerning her travels in Japan, Hong Kong, India, Europe, and California, which she wrote to her sister-in-law Julia Delafield. Also included are Emily Delafield's letters to her daughter Emily Delafield about family, personal, and female matters.

12,196. DePeyster, Elizabeth Van Rensselaer
Papers. 1874. 57-page vol.
Open. No guide.
New-York Historical Society.
In her diary DePeyster describes her daily activities and personal impressions during a trip through Italy, Turkey, Greece, France, and England with her mother and two other persons.

12,197. Dryer Family
Papers. 1839-1938. 166 items.
Open. Unpublished guide.
New-York Historical Society.
Correspondence of this Stockport and Stuyvesant, NY, family includes letters from Harriet L. Dryer while she was attending the Friend's Boarding School in Washington, NY, during the 1840s. Letters to her from her mother and from her sister Mary are also included. Harriet Dryer was a daughter of Horatio N. Dryer (1805-87), a clergyman who in 1856 became steward of the State Lunatic Asylum in Utica, NY.

12,198. DuBois, Henry Osgood
Papers. 1876-1944. 118 items.
Open. No guide.
New-York Historical Society.
Correspondence between DuBois, a clergyman in New York City, and his fiancée Emily Stuart Meier Smith in 1876. Other letters were written while DuBois was in Europe in 1908.

12,199. Dunwell, Amelia L.
Papers. 1847-54. Ca. 80 items.
Open. No guide.
New-York Historical Society.
Correspondence, valentines, and miscellaneous papers of Dunwell, who married Benjamin H. Streeter (1826-69), a farmer, merchant, and New York state assemblyman from Clyde, NY. Includes letters from family and friends concerning social activities, schooling, employment, family matters, and the musical talents of the Dunwell family.

12,200. Durell Family
Papers. 1794-1887. 9 vols., 2300 items, and 1074 pp.
Open. No guide.
New-York Historical Society.
Family papers include correspondence of Fanny Poor and Elizabeth S. Durell. Also includes correspondence of Mary Seitz Gebhart with her fiancé Edward Henry Durell and a diary she kept during their honeymoon in Montreal in 1875.

12,201. Dutch Rhymes: Ferris, Mrs. Morris P.
Papers. 1889. 16 pp.
Open. No guide.
New-York Historical Society.
Dutch rhymes Ferris collected and translated into English; she dedicated them to the Holland Society in 1889.

12,202. Dyckman, Fannie Fredericka
Papers. 1896. No size given.
Open. No guide.
New-York Historical Society.
Wedding book, which Dyckman, a resident of Inwood, NY, kept on the occasion of her marriage to Alexander McMillan Welch. Her account of their honeymoon is included with photos of the bridal party, clippings, signatures of guests, and invitations.

12,203. Fairchild, Charles Stebbins
Papers. 1873-1924. Ca. 2100 items.
Open. No guide.
New-York Historical Society.
Fairchild (1842-1924) was US secretary of the treasury, a banker, and a New York reformer. His papers include the correspondence, writings, memoranda, photos, and clippings of his wife Helen (Lincklaen) Fairchild (1845-ca. 1931). Also contains her genealogical material about her ancestors, including the Freneau, Seymore, Forman, and Van derKemp families. Her correspondents include Susan M. Edmund, George L. Schuyler, Mrs. John Field, Emily N. Trevor, and Grover Cleveland. Charles Fairchild was president of the New York Security and Trust Co. and a leader of the independent Democratic movement in New York state.

12,204. Female Charitable Society
Records. 1816-1908. 4 vols.
Open. No guide.
New-York Historical Society.
Founded in Bedford, NY, the Society provided for the education of children, made and distributed clothing, and donated Bibles. Minutes; treasurer's report and account book; a list of members, their donations, and expenses; and other reports.

12,205. Fenno, Mary Eliza
Papers. 1803-13. 29 items.
Open. No guide.
New-York Historical Society.
Correspondence of Fenno, who later married Gulian C. Verplanck, includes letters from her friend Rebecca Gratz and letters to Verplanck.

12,206. Fenwick Family
Papers. Ca. 1798-1852. Ca. 200 items.
Open. No guide.
New-York Historical Society.
Family papers include correspondence of Elizabeth [Mrs. John] Fenwick (1767-1840), some of which was written to Mary Hays from England, Barbados, and America and published in [Miss] A. F. Wedd's work *The Fate of the Fenwicks* (1927). Also includes correspondence between Alexander Duncan Savage (?-1935) and Wedd concerning the introduction to her book and correspondence of Fenwick's granddaughter Elizabeth (Rutherford) Savage (1817-99). Elizabeth Rutherford married clergyman Thomas Stoughton Savage in 1844 while serving as an Episcopal missionary in Africa.

12,207. Field, Susan Kilteridge
Papers. 1818-34. 40 items.
Open. No guide.
New-York Historical Society.
Correspondence of Susan Kilteridge (Osgood) [Mrs. Moses] Field of New York concerns social affairs, local news, and family matters. Among her correspondents were her sister Julian (Osgood) Putnam, Hannah Clinton, Julia M. Tallamadge, and Mary Hamilton.

12,208. The Fraternity
Records. Ca. 1869-77. 7 vols.
Open. No guide.
New-York Historical Society.
Essays, fiction, poems, pen sketches, and watercolors of this New York City literary and social group, which existed from 1869 to 1877. Female contributors and editors included Sara Coan, Mrs. J. W. Bigelow, Mrs. Ogden N. Rood, Mrs. John Hopper, Mrs. Haven Putnam, and Julia Gould.

12,209. Gay, Horace
Papers. 1835-90. 24 items and 21 pp.
Open. No guide.
New-York Historical Society.
Letters of Gay, a resident of Rochester, NY, and a member of the New York state Assembly, include correspondence with his wife Fidelia Thompson Gay. The letters contain personal sentiments, family news, and information about his business and other activities. Also included are Fidelia Gay's reminiscences of Riga, NY, in the early 19th century.

12,210. Genet, Edmund Charles
Papers. 1792-1842. 2 vols. and 264 items.
Open. No guide.
New-York Historical Society.
Papers of Genet (1763-1834), French minister to the United States, include correspondence of Cornelia Tappen Clinton, who was his first wife and the daughter of New York governor George Clinton. Also includes correspondence of Genet's second wife Martha B. Osgood and an account book pertaining to his children and to the estate of Sharen Clinton.

12,211. Gilman Family
Papers. Ca. 1863-93. Ca. 400 items.
Open. No guide.
New-York Historical Society.
Correspondence of this family includes letters from Caroline E. [Mrs. Charles F.] Park of Palisades, NY, to her daughters Caroline Hoskins (Park) [Mrs. Charles K. W.] Strong of Washington, DC, and Anna Canfield (Park) [Mrs. Winthrop S., Jr.] Gilman, of Des Moines, IA, and Santa Barbara, CA. Also included is correspondence of Caroline E. Park and her then husband William Mulligan regarding the estate of her previous husband Charles F. Park as well as letters with a publisher concerning volumes of poetry and prose by Caroline Gilman.

12,212. Goldsmith, Hannah
Papers. 1842-49. 19 items.
Open. No guide.
New-York Historical Society.
A resident of Southold, NY, Goldsmith (1823-77) later married a Mr. Williams. Correspondence with her nephew Jeremiah Goldsmith Tuthill and other family members is included with her autograph album.

12,213. Goold, Sarah C.
Papers. 1818-29. 85 items.
Open. No guide.
New-York Historical Society.
Business correspondence, notes, receipts, and miscellaneous papers of Goold, a resident of St. Croix, West Indies, concern her commercial trade between New York and St. Croix.

12,214. Gould, Helen Miller
Papers. 1880-1936. 1 vol. and ca. 350 items.
Open. No guide.
New-York Historical Society.
Correspondence with family and friends of Gould (1868-1938), daughter of Jay Gould and a resident of New York City who married Finley S. Shepard, is included with a diary in which she describes a trip through the Mediterranean on the family yacht *Atlanta*. Also included are papers relating to her many charitable activities and interests, reminiscences she collected about her father, and six school notebooks.

12,215. Grant, Anne MacVicar
Papers. 1818-33. 15 items.
Open. No guide.
New-York Historical Society.
Correspondence of Grant (1755-1838), a Scottish author, with Jeremiah Van Rensselaer of New York. The letters concern intellectual life in Scotland, mutual friends, other writers and poets, and invitations to social functions. In one letter Grant claims it is no longer fashionable to be frivolous because "there is a new seriousness everywhere."

12,216. Griffin, Walter Burley
Papers. Nd. 8 vols.
Open. No guide.
New-York Historical Society.
Griffin (1876-1937) was an architect in the United States and Australia. Collection consists of "The Magic of America," an account of his career by his wife Marion Mahony Griffin (1871-1962). The account deals primarily with his architectural work and includes drawings, photos, and other illustrations.

12,217. Guion, Mary
Papers. 1800-52. 387-page vol.
Open. No guide.
New-York Historical Society.
Diary in which Guion (1782-?) of Northcastle, NY, recorded daily activities, local news, her courtship, personal reflections, and visits to family and friends. Entries following her marriage in 1807 to Samuel Brown are scattered.

12,218. Hall, Bolton
Papers. 1882-1933. Ca. 211 items.
Open. No guide.
New-York Historical Society.
Papers of Hall (1854-1932), who was a New York City lawyer and reformer, include correspondence and other papers of his wife, letters to his daughter Mrs. Gerard Herrick, and indentures and legal papers pertaining to New York City property owned by the Herrick family.

12,219. Harper Family
Papers. 1799-1951. 66 vols. and ca. 1500 items.
Open. No guide.
New-York Historical Society.
Family papers include correspondence, diaries, notes, and a sketchbook of Christina A. Harper, a New York artist who married Samuel B. Harper in 1799. Also includes correspondence of writer Mabel Helen Urner Harper concerning her serialized "Helen and Warren" stories, diaries, a financial account book of her and her husband Lathrop Colgate Harper (1867-1950), and a book of her verse. In addition, collection contains a diary Althea Harper kept during her trip to Europe in 1901 and correspondence of James Philip Harper, a New York merchant, to Margaret (Perego) Harper, whom he married in 1853.

12,220. Hawkes Family
Papers. 1820-1900. 3 ft.
Open. No guide.
New-York Historical Society.
Includes correspondence of Ann (Laurance) Bolton, who was the daughter of John Laurance of New York City, widow of George Wright Hawkes, and wife of Daniel Bolton. Some of the correspondence concerns Ann Bolton's claim that her brother John McDougall Laurance was dishonest in handling their father's estate and in other matters. Also included are papers pertaining to the extensive acreage she held with her husband Bolton, correpondence of her sister Elizabeth Laurance, and papers of Charlotte L'Aignoux, Addie L. Forbes, Eliza D. Forbes, and other members of these related families.

12,221. Hawley, Mary
Papers. 1864. 180-page vol.
Open. No guide.
New-York Historical Society.
Diary in which Hawley, an elderly woman, wrote about her daily activities in Poughkeepsie, NY, and current war news.

12,222. Highet, Isabella Boudinot
Papers. Ca. 1926. 92 items.
Open. No guide.
New-York Historical Society.
Telegrams and letters of condolence sent to Frank Brewster Highet on the death of his wife Isabella Highet (1859-1926).

12,223. Hill, Eunice
Papers. 1814-37. 11 items.
Open. No guide.
New-York Historical Society.
Correspondence of Hill, a resident of Chatham, NY, pertains primarily to family matters and local events. In one letter she advises her son Noadiah M. Hill to get a smallpox vaccination.

12,224. History of the Society of Friends in New York City
Records. 1880. 111 pp.
Open. No guide.
New-York Historical Society.
Account of the Society contains documents and photos of members, compiled by Mary S. [Mrs. William] Wood.

12,225. Howe, Fisher
Papers. 1820-98. 5 vols. and ca. 10 items.
Open. No guide.
New-York Historical Society.
Letterpress book, account books, and miscellaneous papers of Howe (1798-1871), a merchant in New York City and Brooklyn, and of his wife Elizabeth Leavitt Howe (1815-99).

12,226. Howland, Mrs. John Hicks
Papers. 1818-22. 28-page vol.
Open. No guide.
New-York Historical Society.
Diary in which Sarah (Hazard) Howland (1781-1847) describes her travels through New York, New Jersey, Connecticut, and Pennsylvania, indicating travel distances, places visited, and the cost of meals and accommodations.

12,227. Indentures of Apprenticeship
Collection. 1792-1891. 38 vols. and 1 folio.
Open. No guide.
New-York Historical Society.
Collection consists of indentures for apprenticeship of New York City children.

12,228. Ireland, Juliet S.
Papers. 1828-31. 84 pp.
Open. No guide.
New-York Historical Society.
Commonplace book of Ireland, a New York City resident, contains a few drawings and poems written by friends, relatives, and such acquaintances as W. H. Ireland, Loisa Clinch, and Helena Tutus.

12,229. Jennings Family
Papers. 1844-1957. 24 vols. and 57 items.
Open. No guide.
New-York Historical Society.
Papers of the Jennings and Allen family include correspondence and diaries of Caroline Jerusha (Allen) Jennings. In her diaries she describes daily events and personal feelings. Caroline Allen married musician Arthur Bates Jennings in 1881.

12,230. John Brown Family
Papers. 1761-1835. 140 items.
Open. No guide.
New-York Historical Society.
Family correspondence includes letters of Susannah Brown, Betsey Brown Maunsell, and John Brown, all of whom were residents of New Providence, Bahama Islands.

12,231. Johnson Family
Papers. 1796-1870. 1 folder and 49 items.
Open. No guide.
New-York Historical Society.
Papers of this and related families primarily concern the management of property inherited from William Walton Woolsey and Nicholas Bayard by [Mrs.] Sarah D. Johnson (1805-70) and others. Distribution and property lists, statements of account, and correspondence with R. C. McCormick, an accountant.

12,232. Jones, Samuel W.
Papers. 1816-51. 78 items.
Open. No guide.
New-York Historical Society.
Correspondence includes letters which Hannah Amelia Jones wrote her brother Samuel Jones prior to her marriage to Samuel Seabury, a minister. She describes family news; events in Cold Spring, Long Island; and visits to New York City.

12,233. Judd, Harriet Stewart
Papers. 1822-72. 341-page vol.
Open. No guide.
New-York Historical Society.
Autobiography in which [Mrs. Orange] Judd (1822-1907) wrote of her birth in New Jersey, moving to Hartland, NY, her schooling, and her duties as a teacher in Rockford, IL. She also wrote about her marriage in 1855, her husband's activities with the US Sanitary Commission during the Civil War, her travels in Europe and the US, and her husband's gift of a hall of science to Wesleyan University.

12,234. Jumel, Eliza (Bowen)
Papers. Ca. 1850-65. Ca. 275 items.
Open. No guide.
New-York Historical Society.
Jumel (1775-1865) was married to Stephen Jumel and then to Aaron Burr. Her correspondence includes letters from Stephen Jumel and Nelson Chase, a lawyer. Other papers relate primarily to her property and business activities. Also included is [Miss] Anna Parker's account of a visit to the Jumel mansion. She describes the house, Eliza Jumel's appearance and reminiscences, and other details of their conversation.

12,235. Kellogg Family
Papers. 1805-1946. 159 vols.
Open. No guide.
New-York Historical Society.
Family diaries include an 1805 journal Tryphena Ely White (1784-1816) kept before her marriage in 1813 to Frederick Kellogg (1766-1832). She describes life in a frontier community in New

York, which was later named Belle Isle. Also includes a 1905 printed edition of her journal with an introduction and notes by her granddaughter Fanny Kellogg (1848-1947). In her diaries Fanny Kellogg, who lived in Brooklyn and Port Kent, NY, describes her daily activities from 1861 to 1946. Also included are the diaries for 1863 to 1902 of her sister Gertrude Kellogg (1843-1903), a prominent New York actress. She describes her debut with Augustin Daly, her performances with such actors as Edwin Forrest, and her portrayal of the Queen opposite Edwin Booth in *Hamlet.* Diaries of Charles White Kellogg (1815-1896), a Brooklyn resident who was the father of Fanny and Gertrude Kellogg, contain information concerning his activities in the fancy livestock business and reveal his interest in spiritualism. His daughter-in-law Julia Burwell (Snow) Kellogg (1842-92), a resident of Brooklyn who was married to Peter Comstock Kellogg, writes of daily activities and family relationships.

12,236. La Farge, John
Papers. 1899-1952. 4 ft.
Open. No guide.
New-York Historical Society.
Correspondence of La Farge (1880-1963), a Jesuit priest and author, with family members including his mother Margaret M. La Farge and others. The letters pertain to family matters, the background of the La Farge and related families, John La Farge's work in Ridge, MD, the Negro school he established there, his efforts to improve race relations, and his activities as editor of *America.*

12,237. Ladies Benevolent Society of St. Mark's Protestant Episcopal Church
Records. 1861-87. Ca. 3 vols.
Open. No guide.
New-York Historical Society.
Minutes and treasurer's accounts of the Society, which contributed clothing to missionaries and soldiers and made and sold garments for the benefit of the poor in the parish. Mrs. Hamilton Fish, Mrs. Charles Easton, Mrs. James B. Harrick, Mrs. James Barrow, Jr., Mrs. John Winthrop Chanler, and Mrs. Robert Watts were Society officers. Also included are treasurer's accounts of the Ladies Auxiliary Missionary Society.

12,238. Ladies Industrial School Association
Records. 1854-61. 134-page vol.
Open. No guide.
New-York Historical Society.
Minutes of general meetings and of the board of managers of the Association, which was founded to help neglected children in Chicago and to prepare them for public school. Mrs. Timothy Write, Anna R. Bentley, Mrs. D. J. Ely, Mrs. Henry Farnam, and Martha Joanna Lamb were Association officers.

12,239. Lamb, Agnes Treat
Papers. 1826-39. 19 items.
Open. No guide.
New-York Historical Society.
Lamb (1811-?), a resident of New York City and Newburgh, NY, was the daughter of Anthony Lamb and the wife of Timothy P. Richards. Her correspondence with her sister Matilda [Mrs. Robert K.] Richards deals with personal, family, and social matters.

12,240. Lamb, Martha Joanna Reade (Nash)
Papers. 1878-93. 1000 items.
Open. No guide.
New-York Historical Society.
An historian, [Mrs. Charles A.] Lamb (1826-93) was editor of the *Magazine of American History.* Business and personal correspondence, a diary, manuscript articles submitted for publication, her works "The Van Rensselaer Manor" and "Lion Gardiner," and samples of her poetry are included with minutes, correspondence, and other records of the Huguenot Society.

12,241. Langzettel, Marian B.
Papers. 1904-35. Ca. 215 items.
Open. No guide.
New-York Historical Society.
[Mrs.] Langzettel (1861-1929) was founder of the Froebel League School in New York City. Her correspondence and papers pertain to the Froebel League and to a fund in her memory for educating a young boy.

12,242. Leonard, Robert Woodward
Papers. 1862-63. 68 items.
Open. No guide.
New-York Historical Society.
Correspondence of Leonard (1843-1929), who was adjutant and major in the 162nd Regiment of New York, includes letters from his mother Camilla Davis [Mrs. William H.] Leonard, his sister Camilla (Leonard) [Mrs. Walter] Edwards, his cousin Camilla Woodward, Alice Minturn, and Martha B. Stevens.

12,243. Lester, Andrew
Papers. 1836-88. 16 vols.
Open. No guide.
New-York Historical Society.
Diaries of Lester (1813-89), who was a dry goods merchant in New York City, and his wife Mary (Harris) Lester. Mary Lester's diaries date from just before their marriage in 1847 to 1849. In addition to describing her wedding, she wrote about personal and family activities.

12,244. Levy, Florence Nightingale
Papers. 1899-1946. 1 vol. and 147 items.
Open. No guide.
New-York Historical Society.
Levy (1870-1947) was editor of the *American Art Annual.* Her correspondence includes personal letters from James P. Haney, director of art education in New York high schools, which he wrote from Europe between 1908 and 1923. Also included are letters of appreciation for Levy's service from people in the arts and an autograph album her mother gave her.

12,245. Lewiston, Maine: Libby, A. M.
Papers. 1871-1900. 231-page vol.
Open. No guide.
New-York Historical Society.
[Miss] Libby was a schoolteacher in Lewiston. In her diary she writes about personal, family, and local matters.

12,246. Life in Springfield, Illinois: Hubbard, Mary Hedges
Papers. 1857-59. 6 items.
Open. No guide.
New-York Historical Society.
Correspondence that Hubbard wrote to her family in the East while she was living in Springfield. In letters to Ellen Sterling Hubbard, Cornelia Hubbard, and Mrs. Ward Hubbard, she observed that towns in the Midwest were not as clean and fresh as those in the East and that there were many bank failures. She describes social activities, including a party during which she played euchre with Abraham Lincoln, and also comments about books she read.

12,247. Lincklaen, Mr. and Mrs. Ledyard
Papers. 1857. 1 vol. and 47 pp.
Open. No guide.
New-York Historical Society.
Travel diary and correspondence of the Lincklaens, who were residents of Cazenovia, NY. They describe places they visited in Virginia, South Carolina, Florida, Havana, and Trinidad; people they met; local gossip; and personal sentiments. Also included is correspondence to their daughter Helen Lincklaen, later Mrs. Charles Stebbins Fairchild.

12,248. Lintz, Maria (Sneckner)
Papers. Nd. 1 vol.
Open. No guide.
New-York Historical Society.
Recipe book of Lintz (1818-89), a resident of New York, contains recipes for pies, cakes, puddings, and other foods.

12,249. Lockley, Fred
Papers. 1920-58. 800 items.
Open. No guide.
New-York Historical Society.
Correspondence and 1930s diaries of Lockley (?-1958), a journalist and book dealer in Portland, OR, and of his wife Laura Simpson Lockley are included with sketches of interviews with early Oregon residents and articles on the history of Oregon.

12,250. Lockwood, Sarah S.
Papers. 1811-15. 71-page vol.
Open. No guide.
New-York Historical Society.
Receipt book of [Mrs.] Lockwood of New York City lists payments for rent, schooling, bread, meat, and other groceries. It also contains autographs of many early residents of the City.

12,251. Lowe Peter
Papers. 1785-94. 9 items.
Open. No guide.
New-York Historical Society.
Lowe (1764-1818) was a minister in the Reformed Dutch Church in Flatbush, NY. His correspondence includes letters in Dutch with his mother Maria Lowe of Kingston, NY.

12,252. Lowell, Josephine (Shaw)
Papers. 1877-94. 29 items.
Open. No guide.
New-York Historical Society.
Correspondence of [Mrs. Charles Russell] Lowell (1843-1905), a social reformer, with Mr. or Mrs. Charles Stebbins Fairchild about the New York State Board of Charities and other reform and political topics. Also included is a letter from Louisa Lee Schuyler.

12,253. Lyell, Lorain
Papers. 1792-95. 1 vol.
Open. No guide.
New-York Historical Society.
Ledger of Lyell, who was a milliner from Perth Amboy, NJ, contains records of hat sales and charges for dressing hats.

12,254. MacLaren, Mrs. Finley
Papers. 1880-1910. 23 vols.
Open. No guide.
New-York Historical Society.
MacLaren lived in New York City. In her pocket diaries, she writes of her personal activities, visits from friends, and trips to Europe in 1880 and 1882, and to the Bahamas in 1886. Also included are three notebooks.

12,255. Madison, Dolley (Payne) Todd
Papers. 1805-48. 35 items.
Open. No guide.
New-York Historical Society.
Correspondence of Madison (1768-1849), wife of President James Madison, includes letters in which she describes to Hannah (Nicholson) Gallatin her husband's illness and deplores the Senate's action regarding Gallatin's mission. Others of Madison's letters, which deal with family news, social gossip, and the prospect of peace, are located in the Gallatin Collection at the Historical Society.

12,256. Madison Square Presbyterian Church
Records. Ca. 1880-85. Ca. 45 items.
Open. No guide.
New-York Historical Society.
Constitution, minutes, reports, correspondence, and membership lists pertain to this New York City church's philanthropic organizations. Included are records of the Loan Relief Society, which were kept by Mary Hartley Brown and Martha Joanna Lamb.

12,257. Mason, Myra (Peters)
Papers. 1824-29. 69 pp.
Open. No guide.
New-York Historical Society.
Letter book of Mason (1797-1862) includes correspondence with her sister Mary Peters of New Haven, CT. Mason describes her wedding journey to Niagara Falls, Detroit, and Mackinac, MI, and life in Mackinac.

12,258. Maude, Jenny
Papers. 1926-33. 14 items.
Open. No guide.
New-York Historical Society.
Correspondence of Maude, the daughter of Jenny Lind, with Leonidas Westervelt concerns his requests for Jenny Lind souvenirs and manuscripts.

12,259. Maxson, Lydia Harriett (Yates)
Papers. 1861-1902. 21 items.
Open. No guide.
New-York Historical Society.
Under the pseudonym Josepha, [Mrs. Thaddeus W.] Maxson (1839-1902) wrote a column for Iowa newspapers, "Advice for the Young Folk." Poems, clippings of her column, a report card, a photo, and programs and announcements from the New York Conference Seminary in Charlottesville, NY.

12,260. Mayo, Margot
Papers. Nd. Ca. 4 ft.
Open. No guide.
New-York Historical Society.
Research notes of [Miss] Mayo, a New York City resident, concern the history of dance and dancing instruction in New York City and the nation. Also includes material concerning such topics as the Shakers, religion, taverns, and ethnic settlers.

12,261. Metropolitan Fair for the Benefit of the U.S. Sanitary Commission
Records. 1864. 1 ft.
Open. No guide.
New-York Historical Society.
Correspondence, lists of contributions, photos, circulars, catalogs, and other records of the Commission include correspondence of Ellen R. Strong, the Commission's treasurer.

12,262. Miller, S. Lou
Papers. Nd. 64-page vol.
Open. No guide.
New-York Historical Society.
The 19th-century recipe book of [Miss] Miller includes recipes for puddings, cakes, cookies, and breads.

12,263. Monday Sewing Class
Records. 1872-ca. 1957. No size given.
Open. No guide.
New-York Historical Society.
Founded in 1872 by prominent New York City women, the Class made garments for the needy. A record book contains bylaws, minutes, and accounts of donations of money and cloth; it also lists finished garments, which were donated to such organizations as the Children's Aid, the American National Red Cross, the Navy League, and the American Friends. Also includes a membership and attendance book and a 70th anniversary memorial volume. Correspondence and other records of this organization are included in the Robinson Collection at the Historical Society.

12,264. Montgomery, Janet (Livingston)
Papers. 1787-1806. 30 items.
Open. No guide.
New-York Historical Society.
Correspondence and other papers of Montgomery (1743-1828), the widow of General Richard Montgomery, concern her petition to the legislature of New York for bounty lands owed to her husband, her business and family affairs, and news of her friends. Also included are many letters between Montgomery and her brother Robert R. Livingston, which pertain to her low opinion of Lord and Lady Ranelagh.

12,265. Moore, Abel Buell
Papers. 1933-35. 30 items.
Open. No guide.
New-York Historical Society.
Moore (1806-79) was an artist. Correspondence of the Historical Society with his granddaughter Helen M. Cross and of [Mrs.] Mary C. Munson relates to his life and work.

12,266. Morgenstern, Louise, and Morgenstern, Birdie
Papers. 1909-28. Ca. 425 items.
Open. No guide.
New-York Historical Society.
Papers of these New York City residents relate to their activities as members of the Riverside branch of the Woman's Municipal League, the Committee on Municipal Affairs, and the Committee on Streets. The street committee's responsibilities included maintenance, mail drop lighting, provision of refuse disposals, and dealing with violations by landlords.

12,267. Morrell Family
Papers. 1808-1909. 250 items.
Open. No guide.
New-York Historical Society.
Family papers include correspondence of Anna B. Morrell (1785-1855), her husband Charles Horton Morrell (1779-1837), Charlotte (Morrell) Boyer (1816-1901), her husband Augustine C. Boyer (?-1884), Louisa (Morrell) Cuyler (1802-?), her husband Benjamin Ledyard Cuyler (1802-?), and Maria Comegys Boyer. Includes a letter in which Charlotte Boyer provides a detailed description of a child's clothing.

12,268. Murray, Hannah, and Murray, Mary
Papers. 1808-25. 7 vols.
Open. No guide.
New-York Historical Society.
Hannah Murray and Mary Murray (1737-1808) were daughters of John Murray, a New York merchant. In the diaries they kept during their summer vacation trips, they describe their sentiments, places they visited, accomodations, modes of travel, people met, and other experiences. Among the places they visited were upper New York state, the Canadian side of Niagara Falls, Philadelphia, and Bethlehem, PA.

12,269. Nestell, Ann R.
Papers. 1828-34. 1 vol.
Open. No guide.
New-York Historical Society.
Album of sentimental verses written by friends and acquaintances of Nestell, who was a resident of Litchfield, CT.

12,270. Nevins, Elizabeth West
Papers. 1850. 130-page vol.
Open. No guide.
New-York Historical Society.
Diary that Nevins kept while traveling from her home in Philadelphia to Baltimore; Wilmington, DE; Washington, DC; Charleston, SC; and Havana. She writes about the discomfort of traveling, social social life in Charleston and Havana, prejudice between northerners and southerners, and secessionist feelings in the South.

12,271. New York House and School of Industry
Records. 1868-1954. 6 vols. and 100 items.
Open. No guide.
New-York Historical Society.
The School, located in New York City, helped employ needy women by teaching them to sew. After merging with Greenwich House in 1951, the School helped elderly people prepare for modern employment through teaching secretarial skills. Annual reports, minutes, and a copy of the act of incorporation relating to the merger. Mrs. Thomas C. Doremus, Mrs. R. M. Blatchford, Mrs. Whitelaw Reid, Mrs. Benjamin Knower, and Mrs. William M. Kingsland were among the organization's presidents. Members included many prominent New York City women.

12,272. New York Nursery and Child's Hospital
Records. 1880-1934. 14 vols. and 565 items.
Open. No guide.
New-York Historical Society.
Account books, medical reports, rules and regulations, city and county reports, and other records of this New York City hospital. Also included is correspondence of the Hospital's first directress [Mrs.] Mary A. Dubois; scrapbooks of reports, circulars, pamphlets, clippings, and other papers pertaining to the Hospital's charity balls held between 1900 and 1934, which were assembled by ball officials Mary Mildred (Hammond) Sullivan and her son George Hammond Sullivan; and material on other benefits sponsored for the Hospital.

12,273. Newel, Helen F.
Papers. 1897-1901. 4 vols.
Open. No guide.
New-York Historical Society.
Diary Newel kept while her husband Stanford Newel was US minister to the Netherlands. She writes of their voyage from New York; social life in The Hague, Paris, London, and Brussels; the coronation and marriage of Queen Wilhelmina; and a peace conference in 1899.

12,274. Newton, Gilbert Stuart
Papers. 1831-37. 37 items.
Open. No guide.
New-York Historical Society.
Correspondence of Newton (1794-1835), who was a painter; his wife; and their friend William Sullivan of Boston with Thomas Aspinwall, the US consul in London. Many of the letters pertain to Newton's death and to the arrangement of his affairs.

12,275. Nutter, Valentine
Papers. 1798-1834. 65 items.
Open. No guide.
New-York Historical Society.
Correspondence of Nutter, a New York City resident, includes letters from his daughter "Matty" and his granddaughter Catherine Cleveland.

12,276. Osborn, Henry Fairfield
Papers. Ca. 1832-1936. Ca. 5000 items.
Open. No guide.
New-York Historical Society.
Papers of the Osborn and the related Cady and Sturges families. Included are numerous letters between Henry Osborn (1857-1935), his parents William Henry Osborn (1820-94) and Virginia R. Osborn (1830-1902), his wife Lucretia "Loulu" Perry Osborn (1858-94), and their children. Also includes his mother's diaries for 1850, 1851, 1871, and 1875. Material relating to Henry Osborn's career as a paleontologist and as president of the American Museum of Natural History in New York City was partially arranged and annotated by his secretary [Miss] Florence Milligan; it contains correspondence from Edith Roosevelt.

12,277. Osgood, Joseph Otis
Papers. 1865-1916. 3 ft.
Open. No guide.
New-York Historical Society.
Correspondence of Osgood (1848-1916), who was a civil engineer, includes letters of his parents Joseph Osgood and Ellen Devereux Sewall Osgood of Cohasset, MA, his wife Sarah Eva Littlefield Osgood, and his daughters Ellen and Laura Osgood.

12,278. Overmann, Mrs. Henry John
Papers. 1837-66. 77 pp.
Open. No guide.
New-York Historical Society.
Diary which Mary Lorrain Peters Overmann (1822-1907) kept while she was a young girl in New Haven, CT, New York City, and Philadelphia. Also included are notes of her travels in Europe and America, genealogical information on the Covell and Peters families, and two poems written by her aunt Mary Peters [Mrs. Samuel] Wilkeson.

12,279. Parker, Mary Ann (Coit)
Papers. 1849-50. 134-page vol.
Open. No guide.
New-York Historical Society.
A resident of New York City, Parker married Willard Parker, a surgeon. In her diary she discusses household and family matters, community events, her husband's activities, literature, and religion.

12,280. Parsons Family
Papers. 1889-1939. 4 boxes and 300 items.
Open. No guide.
New-York Historical Society.
Correspondence of various members of the family, particularly Mary Parsons (1864-1940) of New York City and Lenox, MA. Her letters detail her travels in Europe and her experiences in Lenox; she recounts anecdotes about many friends and acquaintances, some of whom were socially prominent. Correspondence of her father John E. Parsons (1849 or 1850-93), Edith Parsons Morgan, Gertrude Parsons, and Constance Parsons Hare is also included.

12,281. Peck Family
Papers. 1833-90. 22 items.
Open. No guide.
New-York Historical Society.
Papers of this New York City and Bridgeport, CT, family include correspondence of Henry W. Peck, his wife Joanna W. (Platt) Peck, their son Henry W. Peck, Jr., C. Isabel Peck, and John A. Peck. The letters concern such family matters as trips, marriages, deaths, and personal relationships. Also includes the 1881 will of Joanna Peck and an inventory of her estate.

12,282. Pennell, Joseph
Papers. 1903-36. 54 items.
Open. No guide.
New-York Historical Society.
Correspondence of Pennell (1857-1926), an etcher, includes letters of his wife Elizabeth (Robins) Pennell (1855-1936), many of which were to Gertrude Hills.

12,283. Pierce, Mrs. Henry M.
Papers. 1864-72. 37 items.
Open. No guide.
New-York Historical Society.
Mary Jane Church, a student at Rutgers Female College in New York City, married Henry M. Pierce, the president of the College, in 1866. In letters to her parents, sister, and brother, she writes of family matters, her studies, her anti-Union sentiments, setting up her new household, and social events. Also included are letters she wrote to her husband during visits to her family's home in Riga, NY.

12,284. Plumer Family
Papers. 1810-78. 130 items.
Open. No guide.
New-York Historical Society.
Family papers include correspondence to Margaret Plumer from her husband William Plumer, Jr. (1789-1854), a congressman from New Hampshire. He writes of personal and family matters, his living conditions, and his social activities in Washington, DC.

12,285. Poor, Caroline A.
Papers. 1857-58. 1 vol.
Open. No guide.
New-York Historical Society.
A Boston resident, Poor kept a diary while traveling through England, France, Italy, Germany, Switzerland, and Scotland. She writes of sights that interested her, people she met, and her other experiences.

12,286. Post, Mary Minturn
Papers. 1806. 6 pp.
Open. No guide.
New-York Historical Society.
Description of the wedding journey of [Mrs. Henry] Post, a resident of New York City. Traveling through New York, the couple took a Hudson River sloop to Albany, a carriage to Ballston Spa and Canandaigua, and a plantation wagon to Buffalo and Niagara Falls.

12,287. Presbyterian Home for Aged Women
Records. 1866-1961. 18 vols.
Open. No guide.
New-York Historical Society.
Founded in New York City in 1866, the Home continues to exist at its original location. Treasurer's accounts, records of the financial secretary, cash and inmate accounts, a list of contributors, an 1888 scrapbook, and other records.

12,288. Prince Family
Papers. Ca. 1818-90. Ca. 880 items.
Open. No guide.
New-York Historical Society.
Letters and business papers of this New York City family include correspondence of Charlotte Collins Prince, who was the daughter of Rhode Island governor John Collins and wife of merchant William Robert Prince (1795-1869).

12,289. Putnam, Mrs. George
Papers. 1880. 116-page item.
Open. No guide.
New-York Historical Society.
Diary S. B. Putnam kept while traveling in Germany, Switzerland, and France with her husband George Putnam, their children, and Mr. and Mrs. Thompson. She writes about places they visited and their personal activities.

12,290. Ramsay, Andrew
Papers. 1880-84. 21 items.
Open. No guide.
New-York Historical Society.
Ramsay, also known as J. R. Ramsay, was a Canadian poet. His correspondence includes personal letters from [Miss] Vida Moss Near, a resident of Brooklyn, NY; she refers to mutual friends in Brooklyn.

12,291. Rannefeld, Herrmann
Papers. 1879-1939. 58 vols. and ca. 140 items.
Open. No guide.
New-York Historical Society.
Papers of Rannefeld, an organist in New York City, include correspondence with his fiancée Amelia R. Koenig, who later became his wife. Her correspondence with her brother Henry Koenig is also included.

12,292. Redpath, James
Papers. 1863-89. 36 items.
Open. No guide.
New-York Historical Society.
Redpath (1833-91) was a journalist, lecture promoter, and editor. His correspondence includes several letters from Louisa May Alcott.

12,293. Reich, Jacques
Papers. 1887-1923. 1 vol. and 98 items.
Open. Unpublished guide.
New-York Historical Society.
Reich (1852-1923) was an artist and portrait etcher. His papers include correspondence with Abby (Aldrich) Rockefeller and Mr. and Mrs. Frederick Dent Grant.

12,294. Reynolds, Marjorie Richards
Papers. 1908-42. 12 vols. and 51 items.
Open. No guide.
New-York Historical Society.
A New York City resident, [Mrs.] Reynolds wrote to various women's colleges in 1942 asking them whether they were preparing students to assist in postwar reconstruction. Replies from about 40 colleges are included. Also included are diaries Reynolds kept from 1908 to 1919 describing her daily activities, social life, and interests.

12,295. Richard, Mrs. George
Papers. 1883-1937. 34 vols.
Open. No guide.
New-York Historical Society.
Diaries in which Richard (?-1939) describes homelife in New York City and the New Jersey suburbs and in Litchfield, CT, during the summers. Diaries of her sister Marjorie Reynolds are also held by the Historical Society.

12,296. Robinson Family
Papers. 1801-1917. 2 boxes.
Open. No guide.
New-York Historical Society.
Legal and business papers of this New York City and Ossining, NY, family relate to James W. Robinson, his wife Hannah Robinson, and their sons Edward, Augustus, and William Henry Robinson.

12,297. Robinson Family
Papers. Ca. 1869-1945. 3 ft. and 37 vols.
Open. No guide.
New-York Historical Society.
Papers of Beverley Robinson and her husband, a physician; their children Pauline, Herman, and Beverley Randolph Robinson (1876-1951); and of relatives such as Anna E. Foster. Included is correspondence concerning Beverley Randolph Robinson's bid for election as a New York City alderman in 1903, public school recreation centers, the Monday Sewing Club, and the Children's Aid Society; records of the Monday Sewing Club from 1877; and social scrapbooks of Pauline Robinson, which contain invitations, programs, menus, and clippings. Also included are diaries Anna E. Foster kept while traveling in Europe between 1869 and 1871.

12,298. Rogers Family
Papers. 1818-1955. 1000 items.
Open. No guide.
New-York Historical Society.
Papers of the Rogers family include 1846 correspondence in which Clara Rogers provides Ellen Rogers with family news, details of her visits, and a description of seeing volunteers march into Boston. Also includes 1865 letters in which Harriet M. Francis Rogers describes to Sarah Ellen Derby Rogers the sights in England and gives some personal reflections; a genealogy of the Rogers and Bromfield families and sketches of family members by Katherine P. Rogers; and a folder of poems by Elizabeth Schip, which were inspired by a sculptor, John Rogers, Jr.

12,299. Roosevelt, Theodore
Papers. 1888-1918. Ca. 80 items.
Open. No guide.
New-York Historical Society.
Papers of President Roosevelt (1858-1919) include correspondence of his wife Edith Kermit (Carow) Roosevelt (1861-1948) with Mrs. Laurent Oppenheim, Mrs. Richard Derby, Mrs. Douglas Robinson, Andrew Murray Williams, Jr., and others. Also includes Theodore Roosevelt's manuscript articles "The Conservation of Womanhood and Childhood" and "No Pigtails for Uncle Sam."

12,300. Rose Family
Papers. 1772-1918. 300 items.
Open. No guide.
New-York Historical Society.
Correspondence and other papers of this and the related Strong families, residents of Blooming Grove and Mastick, NY. Included are papers of Sarah (Strong) Rose and family correspondence of Nathan Strong, Temperance Strong, Joseph Strong, Nancy Rose, Esther Rose, Anna Rose, and Elihu Rose.

12,301. Royal School of Art Needlework and School of Applied Design
Records. 1894-1902. 2 vols.
Open. No guide.
New-York Historical Society.
Princess Helena Christian worked with [Mrs.] Ellen Dunlap Hopkins, founder of the New York School of Applied Design for women, to establish the Royal School for women in England. Records contain correspondence, much of it between Hopkins and the Princess, and clippings.

12,302. Saltonstall, Mary Susan
Papers. 1824-47. 50 items.
Open. No guide.
New-York Historical Society.
Premarital correspondence to Saltonstall (1807-69), who was a resident of New Brunswick, NJ, New York City, and Coldenham, NY, from Thomas Marston Beare of New York City. He discusses his new job in a bank, social life, and the activities of their friends.

12,303. Satterlee Family
Papers. 1857-65. 34 items.
Open. No guide.
New-York Historical Society.
Correspondence of this Brooklyn, NY, family includes letters from Kate Satterlee Boyle from St. Louis, MO, telling of daily events, the monetary crisis of 1857, and Union refugees and letters of Emily Satterlee, which also relate to current events.

12,304. A School for Young Ladies
Records. 1827-29. 60-page vol.
Open. No guide.
New-York Historical Society.
Account book kept by the proprietor of a school in New York City contains the names of students, their date of entry, and their expenses for such things as writing books, lead pencils, textbooks, stationery, fuel, and carriage hire.

12,305. Schuyler and Jones Families
Papers. 1789-1842. Ca. 80 items.
Open. No guide.
New-York Historical Society.
Correspondence of the Schuyler family of Rhinebeck, NY, and the Jones family, including letters between Mary Ann Schuyler Jones; her husband Samuel Jones (1770-1853), who was a judge; and his daughter. Also includes correspondence of Sarah Schuyler and Catherine Rutsen Suckley.

12,306. Scotch and American Cookbook: Moffat Family
Papers. 1790-1819. 180 pp.
Open. No guide.
New-York Historical Society.
Cookbook started in Glasgow and Dalkeith, Scotland, and then brought to New York City by David Moffat; recipes were added to this cookbook by various members of the family. It contains recipes for desserts, sauces, meats, pastries, and other foods, as well as commentary about the book by Susanna Myers, a descendant.

12,307. Scott, Margaret
Papers. 1855-77. Ca. 100 items.
Open. No guide.
New-York Historical Society.
Correspondence of Scott, a resident of New York City, with her sons William Scott, Jr., and John Scott, other relatives, and friends. Many of the letters detail the experiences and deaths of her sons, who served with the Army of the Potomac.

12,308. Selby Family
Papers. 1830-77. 33 items.
Open. No guide.
New-York Historical Society.
Correspondence of this Baltimore family was generated primarily by John S. Selby (1803-77), his wife Margaret Selby, and their sons James and Joseph Selby, who were Confederate soldiers. Joseph was captured and interned in Fort Delaware.

12,309. Shakers
Collection. 1841-78. 2 vols. and 136-page item.
Open. No guide.
New-York Historical Society.
Consists of correspondence containing religious and sentimental reflections of a Shaker woman whose initials were E. B. and Eldress Sarah Ann Grover's account of the visits or "rides" made by members of the Shaker colony at Harvard, MA. Also included are names of members of the Harvard Community and a book of divinely inspired instruction or "rolls" given to Mary H. Grosvenor and other members of the Second Family in Harvard.

12,310. Sharland, Emily
Papers. 1820-51. 28 items.
Open. No guide.
New-York Historical Society.
Correspondence of Sharland, a resident of Evansville, IN, includes letters from her husband Edward while he was traveling through the US looking for work. Also includes letters from her brother William D. Greenwood, who lived in the Southwest.

12,311. Shipman Family
Papers. 1823-92. 581 items.
Open. No guide.
New-York Historical Society.
Correspondence and other papers of this New Jersey and New York family include the letters of Caleb H. Shipman; his wife Harriett Holden Shipman (1797-1867); her children Emma, Henry, William, Mary, and Elizabeth Shipman; and other relatives. The principal correspondent is Emma Shipman, who in 1852 married Charles H. Hedges, a physician from Flushing, NY. Correspondence primarily concerns family matters.

12,312. Sigourney, Lydia Howard (Huntley)
Papers. 1825-62. 1 vol. and 50 items.
Open. No guide.
New-York Historical Society.
Correspondence and other papers of [Mrs. Charles] Sigourney (1791-1865), an author. Includes several letters to her publisher and a volume of manuscript prose and poetry collected for her by Sarah B. Sigourney.

12,313. Smith, Eliza Leaycraft
Papers. Ca. 1880. 109 pp.
Open. No guide.
New-York Historical Society.
Memoirs in which Smith (1802-93) reminisces about her family's New York City residence, Rose Hill; her visits to Europe; the death of her father Gamaliel Smith; her marriage to Antoine Lentilhon; her relatives; and other families.

12,314. Smith Family
Papers. Ca. 1762-1904. 8 ft.
Open. No guide.
New-York Historical Society.
Included with the papers of this Connecticut family are correspondence and other papers of Helen Evertson Smith, an historical writer. Includes her articles on American colonial history, the Revolutionary War, loyalists, and social customs and chapters from her study "Rebels and Royalists." This study relates to the Gallup, Worthington, Livingston, Everston, L'Estrange (Strang), Kent, Kane, Russell, Morris, and Bloom families.

12,315. Society for the Relief of Poor Widows with Small Children of New York City
Records. 1799-1932. 8 vols.
Open. No guide.
New-York Historical Society.
Minutes of the board of directors and of the Society, which was first proposed in 1797. Among its members were Isabella Graham, Catharine Wilkinson, Jane H. Harrison, Sarah Goold, Sarah Mills, Sarah Hoffman, Eliza Ann Seton, Mary Hosack, Helen Rogers, Susan Bogert, Frances Burrall, Ann Pierce, Mary Wyckoff, Mary Watts, Mary Murray, Mary Bird, Catharine Few, and Susan Pendleton.

12,316. Society of the New York Asylum for Lying-In Women
Records. 1823-31. 2 vols.
Open. No guide.
New-York Historical Society.
The Society was founded in 1823 for the "medical treatment, nursing, and necessary care of mothers and infants during confinement." Minutes of the visiting committee; an account of the Society by one of its founders, Mrs. T. Mason; and records containing such information as requests for admission, names of the patients, comments on the background of some patients, dates of admission, births, deaths, discharges, and the children's names. Members of the visiting committee included Eliza Chester, Magdalena Hughes, Elizabeth Cock, Catherine Bostwick, Julia E. Hyde, Ann McCready, Harriet H. Peters, and Elizabeth W. Blake.

12,317. South Carolina
Papers. Nd. No size given.
Open. No guide.
New-York Historical Society.
Included are three letters in which [Miss] H. F. Clarkson details to Harriet Aston [Mrs. William Bedlow] Crosby her rough voyage from New York to Charleston, SC, in 1810. Clarkson also describes events in Charleston and Wadmalaw, SC, the wedding of Eliza Legare, and the treatment of Negroes.

12,318. Stimson, Henry Albert
Papers. Ca. 1858-1936. 12 ft.
Open. No guide.
New-York Historical Society.
Papers of Stimson (1842-1936), who was a Congregational clergyman, include correspondence from his wife Alice W. (Bartlett) Stimson, his mother and father, his grandmother Catherine A. Atterbury, and his brother John Ward Stimson.

12,319. Sutro, Florence Clinton
Papers. 1899-1906. 104 items.
Open. No guide.
New-York Historical Society.
[Mrs.] Sutro (1865-1906) was a musician and a social leader in New York City. Her papers consist of letters acknowledging Mr. Sutro's and her invitation to their crystal wedding anniversary in 1899; a scrapbook concerning the National Federation of Musical Clubs, which she founded before her marriage; and clippings of death notices.

12,320. Tallmadge, Matthias Burnet
Papers. 1800-50. 1 vol. and ca. 900 items.
Open. No guide.
New-York Historical Society.
Tallmadge (1774-1819) was a jurist in New York City. Included is frequent correspondence with his wife Elizabeth Tallmadge, who was the daughter of New York governor George Clinton. Also includes a memorandum book Matthias Tallmadge kept while visiting the southeastern states, which contains a map of Charleston, SC, drawn by Jane Bacot.

12,321. Thomas, Fannie Edgar
Papers. 1902-10. 15 items.
Open. No guide.
New-York Historical Society.
[Miss] Thomas was an author. Her correspondence includes letters from Geraldine Ferrar, Maurice Grau, and Ellan Wheeler Wilcox.

12,322. Thursby, Emma Cecilia
Papers. Ca. 1870-1932. Ca. 6 ft.
Open. No guide.
New-York Historical Society.
A vocalist who gave concerts in the US, Europe, China, and Japan, Thursby (1845-1931) was a voice teacher in New York City from 1898 on. Correspondence, diaries, business papers, singing contracts, clippings, and other papers pertain to travels and activities. Includes correspondence of her sisters Alice and Ina Thursby, Maurice Strakosch, Emma Thursby's many students, and people prominent in the social and cultural life of New York and Europe. Also contains a testimonial to her which was signed by Grover Cleveland and by members of the cabinet and diplomatic corps.

12,323. Thursday Evening Club
Records. 1878-1965. 4 boxes and 13 vols.
Open. No guide.
New-York Historical Society.
Minutes, memoranda, checkbooks, membership and nomination lists, a record of entertainments, photos, scrapbooks, and other records of the Club, which was founded in New York City in 1878.

12,324. Todd, Maria C. Duffie
Papers. 1837-54. 4 vols.
Open. No guide.
New-York Historical Society.
Diaries in which [Mrs. William W.] Todd (1787-1857), a resident of New York City, describes personal religious sentiments, family matters, local events, funerals, meetings, the Female Bible Society, and the activities of the Oliver Street Baptist Church.

12,325. Tomlinson, Lizzie
Papers. Ca. 1852. 23-page vol.
Open. No guide.
New-York Historical Society.
Correspondence of Tomlinson, who resided in Northville, CT. Apparently writing to her family or friends, she describes her journey through New York and Michigan to Wisconsin.

12,326. Townsend, Caroline Parrish
Papers. 1865-66. 65-page vol.
Open. No guide.
New-York Historical Society.
Diary of Townsend, who was the daughter of New York City merchant Peter Townsend. She writes of a trip to Italy, Paris, and London and her voyage to New York on the *Australasian.* She comments about her social life and about meeting General U. S. Grant, Jennie Jerome, and the Jerome family.

12,327. Townsend Family
Papers. 1793-1912. Ca. 440 items.
Open. No guide.
New-York Historical Society.
Papers of this Albany, NY, family include correspondence of Justine Van Rensselaer Townsend pertaining to the activities of her husband Howard Townsend (?-1867), a physician, and of her son Howard Townsend, Jr. (1858-1935). Also includes a letter from Varina Anne Jefferson Davis, the daughter of Jefferson Davis, expressing her interest in Mount Vernon and letters of Sarah, Hannah, Mary, and Harriet Townsend.

12,328. Trotter, Matthew
Papers. 1798-1830. 70 items.
Open. No guide.
New-York Historical Society.
Correspondence and other papers of Trotter, a resident of Albany, NY, include material pertaining to his business with Alexander, William, and Maria Alexander.

12,329. Turner, Helen Maria
Papers. 1904-57. 6 vols.
Open. No guide.
New-York Historical Society.
Turner (1858-1957) was an artist. Her papers include a pocket diary she kept on a trip in Europe in 1904, another diary she kept during 1926, and scrapbooks containing correspondence, notes, invitations, photos, memorabilia, and clippings relating to her career, genealogy, and the social organizations to which she belonged.

12,330. A Vacation Trip in New York State: Sipple Family
Papers. 1821. 140 pp.
Open. No guide.
New-York Historical Society.
Travel diary in which Mr. and Mrs. Sipple of Milford, DE, describe their trip through New York, including their steamboat ride up the Hudson River.

12,331. Vache and Cox Families
Papers. 1802-1936. 250 items.
Open. No guide.
New-York Historical Society.
Papers of these families include correspondence and other papers of Isabella Vache Cox (1857-1947). Included is material pertaining to her membership in the Primrose League and a greeting card to her from [Miss] Faustina H. Hodges.

12,332. Van Rensselaer, Emily Denning
Papers. 1821-95. 1 vol.
Open. No guide.
New-York Historical Society.
Album of Van Rensselaer contains recollections and photos of people and scenery at Presqu'Ile, the Denning home near Beacon-on-Hudson, NY.

12,333. Van Rensselaer, Sallie B. Pendleton
Papers. 1862-69. 87-page vol.
Open. No guide.
New-York Historical Society.
Diary in which Van Rensselaer wrote about the activities of Union and Confederate forces near her home at Berkeley Springs and Martinsburg, WV, her antisecession sentiments, her removal to the family of her cousin John Pendleton Kennedy in Baltimore, her courtship with and marriage to Eugene Van Rensselaer, and her residence in the Van Rensselaer home in Albany, NY.

12,334. Van Schaack, Catherine
Papers. 1802-36. 21 items.
Open. No guide.
New-York Historical Society.
A resident of Kinderhook, NY, Van Schaack was the daughter of Peter Van Schaack. Includes correspondence to Sarah Louisa Jay about family and friends, daily activities, religion, and moral questions; family correspondence; a diary Catherine Van Schaack kept while attending school in Litchfield, CT; an account book that lists dressmakers' names and traveling, schooling, and other personal expenses; and a composition she wrote on "politeness."

12,335. Vanderbilt Family
Papers. 1821-1915. 3 vols. and 36 items.
Open. No guide.
New-York Historical Society.
Papers pertaining to the Vanderbilts include diaries of Mrs. Vanderbilt (1839-85), who was the wife of "Commodore" Cornelius Vanderbilt (1843-99), which center on her husband's illness and a visit to Europe with Mrs. E. Crawford, Mr. and Mrs. R. L. Crawford, and their three children. Also includes a story written by Rosa Pendleton Chiles in 1890 about Locust Grove, the Virginia homestead of Mrs. Vanderbilt's family.

12,336. Vanderpoel, James
Papers. 1808-22. 16 items.
Open. No guide.
New-York Historical Society.
Correspondence and other papers of Vanderpoel, a resident of Kinderhook, NY, include letters from Margaret Hoog, a resident of Coxsackie, NY, concerning her financial distress after the death of her mother.

12,337. VanKeuren, Maria D.
Papers. 1826-30. 72 pp.
Open. No guide.
New-York Historical Society.
Keepsake book of VanKeuren, a Kingston, NY, resident, contains poems inscribed to her by Mary R. C. Sudam, Sarah Ann Brink, and other friends.

12,338. Visit of Indians to Bethlehem, PA
Papers. Ca. 1792. 8-page item.
Open. No guide.
New-York Historical Society.
Account written by Mary Magdalen Flagg, a member of the Moravian settlement at Bethlehem, of a stop made there by 50 Indians from the Six Nations, who were on their way to visit Congress. The minister of the group was Samuel Kirkland.

12,339. Wendell, Sarah (Packard)
Papers. 1810-29. 2 vols.
Open. No guide.
New-York Historical Society.
Household and expense books of [Mrs. Philip] Wendell, a housewife who lived in Albany, NY, lists expenditures for groceries, household items, servants, washing, chimney sweeps, and church donations.

12,340. Wheeler, Mary Ann
Papers. 1848-54. 161-page vol.
Open. No guide.
New-York Historical Society.
Account book in which Wheeler, who was a dressmaker in Greenwich Village, NY, recorded the dresses she made for local women and the prices of accessories.

12,341. Whitcher, Frances Miriam (Berry)
Papers. 1846-51. 80 items.
Open. No guide.
New-York Historical Society.
An author, Whitcher (1811-52) wrote satirical sketches "Widow Bedott" and "Aunt Magwire" about small-town society, which were published in Neal's *Gazette* and *Godey's Lady's Book.* In her

detailed correspondence to her husband Benjamin W. Whitcher, a clergyman, and to her sister Kate, she remarks on the creation and publication of and often adverse reaction to her sketches. Her letters also concern religion, health, and local and family matters.

12,342. White, Campbell Patrick
Papers. Ca. 1820-55. Ca. 6 ft. and 20 vols.
Open. No guide.
New-York Historical Society.
Papers of White (1787-1859), a merchant and Democratic congressman from New York City, include correspondence and other papers of the White family of New York City and Baltimore and of the related LeRoy and Banyar families. Papers of Joseph White, Ann White, Mary John White, Robert White, Henry White, John Campbell White, and Harriet Banyar White are included as is a letter from Charlotte S. Cushman concerning her proposal to erect a theater on the site of the Washington Hotel.

12,343. White, Stanford
Papers. Ca. 1873-1920. Ca. 2 ft.
Open. No guide.
New-York Historical Society.
Papers of White (1853-1906), an architect, include correspondence of his mother Alexina Mease White, his wife Bessie Smith White, and Janet Scudder.

12,344. Willowbrook: Martin, Cornelia Eliza
Papers. 1837-70. 1 vol.
Open. No guide.
New-York Historical Society.
Album containing reminiscences, verse, miscellaneous writings, and photos relating to activities and persons connected with Willowbrook, the home of Enos Thompson Throop Martin on Owasco Lake near Auburn, NY. The material was collected by his daughter Cornelia Eliza Martin.

12,345. Wilson Family
Papers. Ca. 1786-1900. Ca. 1 ft.
Open. No guide.
New-York Historical Society.
Correspondence and other papers of this Clermont, NY, family relate to William Wilson, a physician, judge, and postmaster; Ann Wilson; Frances Wilson; Harold Wilson; and Mary E. L. Wilson. Also included are papers relating to the Ten Broeck Monument erected at Clermont in 1900 through the efforts of Mary E. L. Wilson and material concerning the related Sanders family of Schenectady, NY.

12,346. Women's Centennial Union
Records. 1876. 55-page vol.
Open. No guide.
New-York Historical Society.
The Union, which existed from February until May of 1876, collected funds to make a banner for the women's pavilion at the Grand Exposition in Philadelphia and to aid in completion of the pavilion. A report of the New York City organization lists members and subscribers.

12,347. Women's League for the Protection of Riverside Park
Records. 1916-30. 4 ft. and 9 boxes.
Open. No guide.
New-York Historical Society.
Minutes, accounts, correspondence, reports, and other records of the League, which concerned itself with beautification and extension of Riverside Drive in New York City. The League's projects included covering the New York Central railroad tracks, planting and preserving trees, placing memorials and plaques in parks, and maintaining public safety in the City. Included are numerous letters of Mrs. John Clappertus Kerr, League president.

12,348. Women's Patriotic Relief Association
Records. 1898-99. 173-page vol.
Open. No guide.
New-York Historical Society.
Minutes of the Association, which was founded in 1898 in New York City to relieve destitute families of those who entered the armed services and to provide hospital service and supplies. The officers included Mrs. Howard Carroll, Mrs. Frank C. Loveland, [Miss] Emma A. Egan, Mrs. Egbert Guernsey, and Mrs. H. Gardner Wetherbee.

12,349. Wood, William Halsey
Papers. 1889-97. Ca. 4 in. and 67 items.
Open. No guide.
New-York Historical Society.
Correspondence of Wood (1855-97), an architect, includes letters with his fiancée Florence Hemsley, many of which pertain to their forthcoming marriage. Also includes Florence Wood's work "Memories of William Halsey Wood."

12,350. Youmans, Edward Livingston
Papers. 1852-94. Ca. 210 items and 200 pp.
Open. No guide.
New-York Historical Society.
Papers of Youmans (1821-87), editor of *Popular Science Monthly,* include correspondence that his wife Catherine Newton Lee Youmans received while she was married to William Little Lee and after her marriage to Youmans. Her correspondents include her former brother-and sister-in-law Mr. and Mrs. Charles Dudley Warner of Hartford, CT, her friend Mary S. Turril of Oswego, NY, and Los Gatos, CA, and Josephine Curtis Jenner. Also contains a lecture about Herbert Spencer and other writings in Catherine Youmans's handwriting and a telegram announcing the revolution in Hawaii. Correspondence from Eliza A. Youmans to her brother Edward L. Youmans is also included.

12,351. Cornell University-New York Hospital School of Nursing
Records. 1877- . 160 ft.
Access restricted. Published and unpublished guides.
New York Hospital-Cornell Medical Center.
Includes minutes, financial records, correspondence, office files, student records, oral history transcripts, reports, curriculum material, alumni association records, records of individual students and faculty members, photos, and memorabilia of the School, which was established by the Society of the New York Hospital in 1877; it was one of the earliest schools in America based on the Florence Nightingale method of nursing. In 1942 the School became a part of Cornell University. Student records include items on Lillian Wald, Julia Stimson, Clara Weeks, Annie Goodrich, and Mary Beard. Among the former deans and associate deans whose records are included are Irene Sutliffe, Virginia M. Dunbar, Muriel Carbery, Veronica Lyons, and Lydia B. Anderson. See Adele A. Lerner, *An Introduction to the Medical Archives, The New York Hospital-Cornell Medical Center* (New York: The New York Hospital-Cornell Medical Center, 1976).

12,352. Guion, Connie Myers
Papers. 1913-71. 4.5 ft.
Open. Unpublished guide.
New York Hospital-Cornell Medical Center.
Guion (1882-1971) was a physician and medical educator at the Hospital and the Center. Includes correspondence with friends, family, and medical colleagues; speeches; medical and case notes; student notebooks; reports on out-patient care programs; papers related to fund-raising activities; reports of the Cornell medical college alumni association; photos; scrapbooks; clippings; and memorabilia. Guion, who was a graduate student at Cornell in 1913, later became honorary governor of the Society of the New York Hospital and emeritus clinical professor of Cornell University Medical College. She was particularly concerned with the care of ambulatory patients. The Dr. Connie Guion Building, which houses many of the Hospital's out-patient clinics, was dedicated to her in 1963.

12,353. Manhattan Maternity and Dispensary
Records. 1901-47. 130 ft.
Open. Published and unpublished guides.
New York Hospital-Cornell Medical Center.
Annual reports, minutes, financial reports, and medical case records of the Maternity and Dispensary, which from 1901 to 1947 cared for women during childbirth, providing an alternative to at-home care or the City hospitals. Pay and charity cases were accepted, and the social service department taught mothers about proper child care. The facility also housed a training program for nurses and an internship program for physicians and medical students. Medical case records contain information about in-hospital deliveries, out-patient service, and different methods of childbirth. See Adele A. Lerner, *An Introduction to the Medical Archives, The New York Hospital-Cornell Medical Center* (New York: The New York Hospital-Cornell Medical Center, 1976).

12,354. New York Asylum for Lying-In Women
Records. 1823-99. 2.5 ft.
Open. Published and unpublished guides.
New York Hospital-Cornell Medical Center.
Annual reports, minutes, admission records, reports, and a history of the Asylum, which functioned from 1823 to 1899 for the care of "destitute respectable women in confinement." Patients were screened for admission by the board of managers, and the minutes of the board contain numerous character references. The outdoor department, which opened in 1831, had a more lenient admissions policy. In an 1894 history, Elizabeth F. Cock, the first directress, reminisces about the Asylum. See Adele A. Lerner, *An Introduction to the Medical Archives, The New York Hospital-Cornell Medical Center* (New York: The New York Hospital-Cornell Medical Center, 1976).

12,355. New York Infant Asylum
Records. 1865-1910. 8.25 ft.
Open. Published and unpublished guides.
New York Hospital-Cornell Medical Center.
Annual reports, minutes, adoption records, and medical case histories of the Asylum, which was chartered in 1865 to care for foundlings and destitute children. In 1871 the program was expanded to include lying-in care and child-care training for mothers. Includes information on unwed mothers, unwanted children, and persons who were willing to care for such children. See Adele A. Lerner, *An Introduction to the Medical Archives, The New York Hospital-Cornell Medical Center* (New York: The New York Hospital-Cornell Medical Center, 1976).

12,356. New York Nursery and Child's Hospital
Records. 1910-34. 29.75 ft.
Open. Published and unpublished guides.
New York Hospital-Cornell Medical Center.
Annual reports, minutes, financial records, medical records, legal records, scrapbooks, and real estate data of the Hospital, which existed from 1910 to 1934 and maintained a lying-in hospital, a hospital for sick children, a nursery and home for destitute children, a placement service to board children in homes, and a training program for nurses. See Adele A. Lerner, *An Introduction to the Medical Archives, The New York Hospital-Cornell Medical Center* (New York: The New York Hospital-Cornell Medical Center, 1976).

12,357. Nursery and Child's Hospital
Records. 1854-1910. 3.5 ft.
Open. Published and unpublished guides.
New York Hospital-Cornell Medical Center.
Annual reports, minutes, medical case histories, adoption records, scrapbooks, and real estate records of the Hospital, which existed from 1854 to 1910 and provided day care for children. By 1857 the medical care of children and pregnant women became a major function of the Hospital. Records also reflect the changing focus of charitable concern and the nature and cost of health care. See Adele A. Lerner, *An Introduction to the Medical Archives, The New York Hospital-Cornell Medical Center* (New York: The New York Hospital-Cornell Medical Center, 1976).

12,358. Society of the Lying-In Hospital of the City of New York
Records. 1798- . 102 ft.
Open. Published and unpublished guides.
New York Hospital-Cornell Medical Center.
Annual reports, minutes, financial records, correspondence, medical case records, scrapbooks, and real estate records of the Hospital, which was founded in 1799 to care for poor women during childbirth. Early records of the board of governors contain information about social concern for women and attitudes toward unwed mothers and broken marriages. The ladies auxiliary to the board instituted social welfare programs for women and children. The Hospital has expanded its concerns to include research in gynecology and human fertility. See Adele A. Lerner, *An Introduction to the Medical Archives, The New York Hospital-Cornell Medical Center* (New York: The New York Hospital-Cornell Medical Center, 1976).

12,359. Craig and Duncan
Papers. 1901-57. Ca. 400 items.
Access restricted. Published guide.
New York Public Library at Lincoln Center, Performing Arts Research Center, Dance Collection.
Papers of Edward Gordon Craig (1872-1966), a theater artist and author, and of Isadora Duncan (1878-1927), a dancer, include their correspondence and correspondence with Augustin Duncan, Elizabeth Duncan, Irma Duncan, Raymond Duncan, and Ellen Terry. Also includes Craig's sketchbooks and notebooks relating to Duncan as well as photos and programs. Correspondence between Craig and Duncan provides insights into their relationship, her intellectual and emotional life, her financial situation, and her work creating and performing dances. See Nicki N. Ostrom, "The Gordon Craig-Isadora Duncan Collection, a register," *Bulletin of the New York Public Library* (1972).

12,360. De Mille, Agnes
Papers. 1918- . Ca. 95 folders.
Access restricted. Folder list.
New York Public Library at Lincoln Center, Performing Arts Research Center, Dance Collection
Correspondence, choreographic notes, scenarios, writings, and television scripts of de Mille (1908-), a dancer, choreographer, and writer. Correspondents include Lily Bess Campbell, Lucia Chase, Allan Devoe, Beulah Flebbe, Carmelita Maracci, Oliver Smith, and Joseph Welch. De Mille worked with such groups as Ballet Theatre, Ballet Russe de Monte Carlo, and the Theatre Guild. Musical comedies that she choreographed include *Bloomer Girl* and *Carousel.* Collection contains manuscripts for her work *Lizzie Borden: A Dance of Death* and notes for the "Russian Journals," her published notes on the 1966 American Ballet Theatre Russian tour and the 1969 International Ballet Competition in Moscow.

12,361. Duncan, Irma
Collection. Nd. Ca. 300 items.
Access restricted. Register and folder list.
New York Public Library at Lincoln Center, Performing Arts Research Center, Dance Collection.
Correspondence, manuscripts, clippings, and memorabilia of Isadora Duncan (1878-1927), which were compiled by and also relate to Irma Duncan Rogers. Isadora Duncan, a modern dance pioneer, married Sergei Esenin in 1922. Includes correspondence of Isadora Duncan with her husband, Irma Duncan, Anatolii Lunarcharskii, Gordon Craig, Fernand Divoire, Eleonora Duse, Walter Morse Rummel, and Ellen Terry. Also includes autobiographical writings, notebooks, and material relating to programs. Isadora Duncan was born in San Francisco but spent most of her career in Europe. She established a dancing school for children at Grünewald, Germany, in 1904; she also opened a school in Moscow. Her autobiography is entitled *My Life.* A large portion of the manuscripts and correspondence in the collection has been published in *Duncan Dancer* by Irma Duncan, *Isadora Duncan's Russian Days* by Irma Duncan and Allan Ross Macdougall, and *Isadora* by Macdougall.

12,362. Enters, Angna
Papers. 1933-46. Ca. 105 items.
Access restricted. Register and folder list.
New York Public Library at Lincoln Center, Performing Arts Research Center, Dance Collection.
Letters that Enters (1907-), a mime dancer, choreographer, composer, writer, and designer, wrote to her English friend Edward L. Berman about her careers, travels, and political thoughts during her involvement in wartime activities. Her books include *First Person Plural* (1937), *Love Possessed Juana* (1939), and *Silly Girl* (1944). In 1934 Enters was awarded a Guggenheim fellowship; her paintings and sculptures were exhibited in New York and London.

12,363. Humphrey, Doris
Papers. 1811-1958. Ca. 7000 items.
Access restricted. Published guide.
New York Public Library at Lincoln Center, Performing Arts Research Center, Dance Collection.
Humphrey (1895-1958) was a dancer and choreographer who married Charles F. Woodford in 1932. Includes correspondence with her parents Horace and Julia Humphrey, Mary Walker, Charles Weidman, Pauline Lawrence, José Limon, Ian Wolfe, Helen Mary Robinson, Eleanor Frampton, and Eleanor King. Also includes manuscripts of articles, essays, and her major published works; personal financial papers; and business records relating to Humphrey-Weidman Company. Involved in the modern dance movement, Humphrey enrolled in the Denishawn School in 1917. In 1928 she started her own school with Charles Weidman. Also includes miscellaneous papers concerning Humphrey's schoolwork, the career of Mary Wood Hinman, and the Shakers. See Andrew Mark Wentink, "The Doris Humphrey Collection, an Introduction and Guide," *Bulletin of the New York Public Library* (Autumn 1973).

12,364. Moore, Lillian
Papers. Ca. 1936-67. 24 drawers.
Partially closed. No guide.
New York Public Library at Lincoln Center, Performing Arts Research Center, Dance Collection.
Correspondence, manuscripts and manuscript material, notes and notebooks, photos, clippings, programs, and printed items of Moore (1911-67), a dancer, writer, and teacher. Papers relate to her research on dancers in 18th- and 19th-century America, Auguste Bournonville, Erik Bruhn, and ballet. Includes letters from Walter Toscanini, Ivor Guest, Ifan Kyrle Fletcher, Ted Shawn, and Clive Barnes. Other correspondence is with art councils, libraries, dance companies, and a number of American and Danish dancers. Moore studied under Balanchine, Alexandra Fedorova-Fokine, and Charles Weidman. After retiring in 1954 she devoted her time to teaching and dance research. A contributor to *Dance News* and the *Dance Encyclopedia,* she wrote such books as *Artists of the Dance* and with Erik Bruhn co-authored *Bournonville and Ballet Technique.*

12,365. Shawn, Ted
Papers. Ca. 1920-70. 28 drawers.
Partially closed. Published guide.
New York Public Library at Lincoln Center, Performing Arts Research Center, Dance Collection.
Born Edwin M. Shawn, Ted Shawn (1891-1972) married Ruth St. Denis (1878-1968), born Ruth Dennis, in 1914; the couple separated in 1930. Personal correspondence between Shawn and St. Denis and Shawn's business correspondence, which includes letters from important figures in the dance world; holographs; and typescripts. Also includes route books and ledgers along with yearbooks of Ted Shawn and His Men Dancers, which was organized in 1933; the Jacob's Pillow Dance Festival; and the Denishawn School, which Shawn and St. Denis organized first in Los Angeles and later in New York. Also includes a manuscript of *Thirty Years of American Dance,* a study by Christena Schlundt.

12,366. Tamiris, Helen
Papers. Ca. 1939-66. Ca. 1000 items.
Access restricted. Published guide.
New York Public Library at Lincoln Center, Performing Arts Research Center, Dance Collection.
Correspondence, manuscripts, notebooks, and business papers of Tamiris (1905-66), a modern dancer and choreographer, as well as papers relating to musical shows, concert dances, conferences, and summer workshops. Also includes material on her husband Daniel Nagrin, also a dancer, and on the development of their company the Tamiris-Nagrin Dance Company. Tamiris choreographed numerous Broadway productions, among them *Annie Get Your Gun.*

12,367. Theatre on Film and Tape
Collection. 1970- . 82 films and videotapes.
Partially restricted. Unpublished guide.
New York Public Library at Lincoln Center, Performing Arts Research Center, Theatre Collection.
Films and videotapes of live performances of theatrical productions, special theater events, and dialogues between people prominent in theater. Includes dialogues with Geraldine Fitzgerald and Arvin Brown, who discuss the directional approach to *Long Day's Journey into Night* and interpretations of the role of Mary Tyrone (1971); Lotte Lenya and George Voskovec, who reminisce about the European theater in the early 1930s, Kurt Weill, Berthold Brecht, and their own careers (1972); Street Theatre producers Geraldine Fitzgerald, Hazel Bryant, Mical Whitaker, and Brother Jonathan, who talk about the origins of the Street Theatre Festival at Lincoln Center and other aspects of this special form of theater (1973); Liza Minnelli, Fred Ebb, and John Kander, who talk about their admiration for each other's talents, which led to the development of a three-way collaboration (1974); Lehman Engel and Wesley Addy, associated with Margaret Webster on several productions, who reflect on [Miss] Webster's wide range of talents as an actress, director, and lecturer on the theater (1975); Eva LeGallienne, an actress, who reminisces with Josephine Hutchinson and Staats Cotsworth about her theatrical career and her struggle to establish a permanent repertory theater in the US (1975); and Mrs. Sean O'Casey, who converses with Brendan Gill about her life with her husband, an Irish author and playwright, as well as about her own careers as an actress and writer (1976).

Also includes films and videotapes of such productions as *Now Is the Time for All Good Men,* book and lyrics by Gretchen Cryer and music by Nancy Ford (1971); *Long Day's Journey into Night* by Eugene O'Neill, starring Geraldine Fitzgerald and Robert Ryan (1971); *Everyman and*

Roach by Geraldine Fitzgerald and Brother Jonathan (1972); *Blind Junky,* a rock musical with book, lyrics, and music by Peter Copani, who depicts a cross section of slum streets, junkies, prostitutes, and pushers and their effects on their community (1972); highlights from *F. Jasmine Addams* by Carson McCullers and G. Wood (1972); *Liza,* a performance for the Actors' Fund of America in which Liza Minnelli sang and danced (1974); *Something About Yesterday,* a one-act play by Susan H. Schulman (1972); excerpts from Rodgers and Hart musicals, including *Too Many Girls* and *No Strings; Cat on a Hot Tin Roof* by Tennessee Williams, starring Elizabeth Ashley and Keir Dullea (1974); three one-act plays, *Schubert's Last Serenade, The Final Analysis,* and *The Super Lover,* written and directed by [Miss] Julie Bovasso and performed at the LaMama Experimental Theatre; *In Gay Company,* a musical review and parody of both the homosexual scene and society's attitude toward it (1975); *Juno and the Paycock,* starring Maureen Stapleton, Jack Lemmon, and Walter Matthau (1974); *Pictures in the Hallway* by Sean O'Casey, produced and recorded by the Library as a memorial to Margaret Webster (1975); *Ah, Wilderness!* by Eugene O'Neill, starring Geraldine Fitzgerald, Teresa Wright, and other members of the Long Wharf resident theater (1975); *The Royal Family* by George S. Kaufman and Edna Ferber, starring Ellis Rabb, Rosemary Harris, and Eva LeGallienne (1976); films of five television shows featuring Aline MacMahon; and "The Ford Anniversary Show," a CBS television show featuring Ethel Merman, Mary Martin, and others

12,368. Ackley, Louisa Maria
Papers. 1831-32. 1 vol.
Open. No guide.
The New York Public Library, Manuscripts and Archives.
Diary in which Ackley, who was a student at the Geneva, NY, Female Seminary, describes her arrival at school, visits from her family, her academic life, and the other girls. The basic religious policy of the school is reflected in her writings and those of her teachers, who inscribed wishes for her at the end of her year's study.

12,369. Adams, John
Papers. 1795-1893. 1 box.
Open. No guide.
The New York Public Library, Manuscripts and Archives.
Correspondence of Adams (1735-1826), second President of the US, includes letters of his wife Abigail (Smith) Adams, [Miss] A. M. Clark, Susanna Boylston Clark, and Louisa Catherine Smith. The Adams family letters have been edited by L. H. Butterfield and published in *Adams Family Archives* (Cambridge: Belknap Press of Harvard University Press, 1963).

12,370. Adams, Susan
Papers. 1809-67. 1 box.
Open. No guide.
The New York Public Library, Manuscripts and Archives.
Correspondence of Adams (?-1839); her sister Charlotte (Adams) Slocum and her husband Christopher Slocum, residents of Medway, MA; and of Esther (Slocum) [Mrs. Lewis] Pennell, a schoolteacher. Includes a letter to Charlotte Slocum from William A. Harrison, colporteur of the American Tract Society in Virginia. Material contains information concerning the social and economic conditions of women in Massachusetts and Rhode Island who worked in private homes as spinners, weavers, and housekeepers; of women who were shopkeepers, mantua-makers, and schoolteachers; and of mezzotint painting teachers. The letters also reflect religious life in Malden, MA, in 1820, when "above an hundred souls were born in a week" at a revival.

12,371. Alms House, Commissioners, New York City
Records. 1822-25. 1 vol.
Open. No guide.
The New York Public Library, Manuscripts and Archives.
Indentures of girls who were minors sent out as servants and infants who were adopted. The forms were filled in, signed by the principals, and endorsed by the commissioners. The terms of the contracts were that the master must teach the child to read and write and give her a new suit of clothing and a new Bible when the term of service was over. The girls ranged in age from 5 to 14, and the length of the indenture was from 4 to 12 years.

12,372. American Play Company
Records. 1940-50. 1 carton.
Open. Unpublished guide.
The New York Public Library, Manuscripts and Archives.
The Company is a literary agency in New York City. Included are typescripts of novels and short stories from such authors as Lida Rose McCabe, Edith Reader, Marguerite Veiller, and Rita Weimar.

12,373. Arnold, Benedict; Arnold, Margaret (Shippen); and Family
Papers. 1800-75. 1 folder.
Open. Unpublished guide.
The New York Public Library, Manuscripts and Archives.
Letters written from England by the Arnolds to their son Edward Arnold offering him advice and comfort while he was in India and letters in which Margaret Arnold (1760-1804) provided Edward Arnold with details of his father's death and information about financial and family matters and the fear of an invasion by Bonaparte. Also includes letters from Edward Arnold about the provenance of the letters from his parents, family letters written by William Arnold, and a genealogical chart for the Arnolds. Letters from Benedict and Margaret Arnold are published in John George Tayloe's *Some New Light on the Later Life and Last Resting Place of Benedict Arnold and of his Wife Margaret Shippen* (London, 1931).

12,374. Ashmore, Grace Eulalie (Matthews)
Papers. 1829-1972. 5 boxes.
Open. No guide.
The New York Public Library, Manuscripts and Archives.
Diaries for 1896 to 1972 in which Ashmore (1885-1972), a New York society woman, describes her daily activities in New York City and environs and in Europe, her family and social life, schooling, travels, marriage, and volunteer work during WWI. Also included are letters to Ashmore that Ernst de Weerth wrote from Rome between 1956 and 1966 commenting on the theatrical and operatic world, transcripts of Matthews family ledgers from 1829 to 1870, and a genealogical table and notes.

12,375. Baker, Thomas Barwick Lloyd
Papers. 1877-83. 28 items.
Open. No guide.
The New York Public Library, Manuscripts and Archives.
Consists primarily of letters from Baker (1807-86), an Englishman who established the reformatory school system, to [Mrs.] Josephine (Shaw) Lowell concerning crime and criminals, prisons, and charities.

12,376. Balmanno, Robert
Papers. 1852-68. 59 items.
Open. No guide.
The New York Public Library, Manuscripts and Archives.
Letters from Balmanno (1780-1861), an author and collector who lived in New York City, to John Sartain, an engraver in Philadelphia, concerning literary and artistic matters and his attempts to publish *Pen and Pencil* (New York: D. Appleton, 1858), a book by his wife Mary Balmanno. Also includes correspondence from Mary Balmanno to Sartain concerning the disposal of her husband's collection of books, engravings, and autographs.

12,377. Bancker, Van Vleck, and King
Papers. 1753-ca. 1900. 3 in.
Open. No guide.
The New York Public Library, Manuscripts and Archives.
Papers of this family of landholders in Lansingburg, NY, which later engaged in business, include correspondence of Peter B. King and his wife Sarah Van Vleck King from before and after their marriage, between 1856 and 1882, and during his service with the Union Army in the Civil War. Also contains letters to Sarah King from other family members and from John Chipman, a friend of the family, and bills and business papers of the Kings. Also contains a will, inventory of estate, and power of attorney of Martha Bancker, the widow of Flores Bancker; an acknowledgement of receipt by Elizabeth Vantarlingh and Mary Brown from Adrian Bancker for legacies left them by their grandfather Flooris Van Taerlingh; and an inventory of the estate and list of survivors of Catherine Van Vleck.

12,378. Baptist Church, Hunterdon County, NJ
Records. 1742-1824. 0.5 in.
Open. No guide.
The New York Public Library, Manuscripts and Archives.
Minutes of proceedings and lists of persons who were baptized or married.

12,379. Barnes Family
Papers. 1817-1934. 5 items.
Open. No guide.
The New York Public Library, Manuscripts and Archives.
Papers of this pioneer family of Fairfield, NY, include correspondence of Philinda Barnes, who became Mrs. John Bucklin; a letter from James Barnes to Harriet Briggs giving a history of the Barnes family in England and America; and a pedigree of the family compiled between 1932 and 1934.

12,380. Barrus, Clara
Papers. 1906-29. 1 in.
Open. No guide.
The New York Public Library, Manuscripts and Archives.
Letters to Barrus (1864-1931), a physician and writer, from Charles F. Lummis regarding his work, health, and personal affairs and from R. W. Gilder and others, some of which concern John Burroughs, for whom she was literary executor and official biographer. Also included are poems and a diary of Barrus, in which she describes her travels in France and Switzerland in 1929.

12,381. Baxley, Catherine Virginia
Papers. 1865. 1 in.
Open. No guide.
The New York Public Library, Manuscripts and Archives.
Diary and notebook [Mrs.] Baxley, a resident of Baltimore, kept after her arrest as a blockade runner for the Confederacy and during her confinement at the Old Capitol Prison in Washington, DC. Written in a copy of Alfred Tennyson's *Enoch Arden,* her diary contains a list of women prisoners and the causes for which they were arrested. She also describes the death of her son, a Confederate soldier, in the same prison. Baxley had been previously arrested as a spy in 1861 and was one of the first women confined in the Old Capitol Prison.

12,382. Beach Family
Papers. 1833-1909. 2 boxes.
Open. No guide.
The New York Public Library, Manuscripts and Archives.
Correspondence and other papers of Joseph Wickliff Beach (1822-91); his wife Mary A. (Walkley) Beach (1824-97); their children David Nelson, Lucy N., Harlan Page, and Anna S. Beach; and other members of the Beach and Walkley families. Correspondence deals chiefly with family and personal matters and reflects everyday life in New Jersey, Connecticut, Massachusetts, Vermont, Maine, and Colorado.

12,383. Belmont, August
Papers. 1853-87. 7 in.
Open. No guide.
The New York Public Library, Manuscripts and Archives.
Papers of Belmont (1816-89), a banker and US Chargé d'Affaires and Minister to the Netherlands who resided in New York City, include letters to his wife Caroline Slidell (Perry) Belmont from European figures as well as family memorabilia.

12,384. Benners, John
Papers. 1863-68. 29 items.
Open. No guide.
The New York Public Library, Manuscripts and Archives.
Letters from Benners, a publisher who resided in Brooklyn, NY, and the US Virgin Islands, written from the Virgin Islands to his daughters in Brooklyn, concerns news of local friends, social matters, epidemics, earthquakes, and advice on family problems.

12,385. Bennett, Augustus P.
Papers. 1868-1928. 1 box.
Open. No guide.
The New York Public Library, Manuscripts and Archives.
Correspondence of Bennett and members of his family, including his wife Genie F. (Carey) Bennett, their daughter Thelma, and various members and friends of the Bennett and Carey families. In their letters they describe family matters and events in and around Greenville and Jersey City, NJ.

12,386. Bennett, Elizabeth H.
Papers. 1943-46. Ca. 200 items.
Open. No guide.
The New York Public Library, Manuscripts and Archives.
Papers of Bennett, who was an English teacher at Machine and Metal Trades High School in New York City, consist of letters from former students who were at training camps and active duty stations, photos, clippings, and armed forces newspapers.

12,387. Bens, Gwendolyn T.
Papers. 1916-18. Ca. 350 items.
Open. No guide.
The New York Public Library, Manuscripts and Archives.
Correspondence, press releases, public statements, and other papers of [Mrs.] Bens relate to the New York State Woman Suffrage Party and her activities as 2nd Assembly District leader, from Utica, NY, and as press chairman. Includes party papers of Carrie Chapman Catt, Harriet B. Laidlaw, and Vivian (Boarman) Whitehouse.

12,388. Bense Family
Papers. 1885-93. 16 vols.
Open. Unpublished guide.
The New York Public Library, Manuscripts and Archives.
Diaries [Miss] J. Anne Bense and [Miss] Evangeline Isabelle Bense kept during their travels through Europe, Africa, and the Near East, along with notes used for studying German and French.

12,389. Bevier, Henrietta Cornelia
Papers. 1809. 0.5 in.
Open. No guide.
The New York Public Library, Manuscripts and Archives.
Journal kept by Bevier, who lived in Rochester, NY, while she was attending Miss Sarah Pierce's school in Litchfield, CT. In her journal she recorded at the end of each week current events, a synopsis of the weekly sermon and the name of the preacher, and other matters.

12,390. Bliss, George Theodore
Papers. 1873-1919. 3 boxes.
Open. No guide.
The New York Public Library, Manuscripts and Archives.
Household and family accounts of the Bliss homes in New York City, Ridgefield, CT, and Bayshore, Long Island, NY include itemized bills for food, clothing, liquor, furniture, art objects, boarding horses, harnesses, and stable equipment. Also includes household accounts of Amos T. Dwight.

12,391. Bliss, Mrs. George T., and Bliss, Susan D.
Papers. 1908-37. 1 box.
Open. No guide.
The New York Public Library, Manuscripts and Archives.
Correspondence of the Blisses, who were residents of New York City, with French children who were recipients of their financial aid; with family members of these children; and with American Ouvroir Funds in New York City, M. Hanotte of Paris, and others relating to the welfare of the children.

12,392. Bliss, Susan Dwight
Papers. 1903-38. 6 boxes.
Open. No guide.
The New York Public Library, Manuscripts and Archives.
Business correspondence and brokerage accounts of Bliss and household, farm, and garden accounts for her New York City home and New Canaan, CT, farm. Includes itemized bills for household goods, seeds, livestock, hardware and plumbing, machinery, taxes and insurance, utilities, and labor.

12,393. Bogan, Louise
Papers. Ca. 1944. 29 pp.
Open. No guide.
The New York Public Library, Manuscripts and Archives.
Draft and notes of Bogan (1897-1970) for her review of F. O. Matthiessen's *Henry James: The Major Phase.*

12,394. Bonner, Robert
Papers. 1860-99. 18 boxes.
Open. Unpublished guide.
The New York Public Library, Manuscripts and Archives.
Correspondence of Bonner (1824-99), a newspaper publisher, proprietor of the *New York Ledger,* and a turfman, is primarily from contributors and includes letters from authors Mary E. (Clemmer) Ames and Lydia Howard Huntley Sigourney, as well as from journalist, author, lecturer, actress, and reformer Mary Katherine "Kate" Keemle Field.

12,395. Bowker, Richard Rogers
Papers. 1859-1953. 171 boxes, 29 vols., and 5 packages.
Open. Unpublished guide for part of collection.
The New York Public Library, Manuscripts and Archives.
Papers of Bowker (1848-1933), an editor, publisher, industrial director, and journalist, relate to his residency in England as a representative of *Harper's magazine* and his relationships with Americans and English people involved in the arts; *Publishers Weekly,* of which he became proprietor and editor; his founding and editing of *Library Journal;* his activities as a member of the American Library Association, the Authors League of America, and the American Copyright League; his presidency of the Economist Press; his vice-presidency of the Edison Electric Illuminating Company; his inventions; and his numerous other activities. Also includes correspondence of Rose Weinberg of R. R. Bowker, a publishing company, with E. McClung Fleming, relating to a biography of Bowker.

12,396. Briffault, Herma (Hoyt)
Papers. Ca. 1951-73. 1 package.
Open. No guide.
The New York Public Library, Manuscripts and Archives.
Briffault (1898-) is an author and translator. Typescript of "To the Yukon and Beyond," a story of the Russian-American telegraph expedition to the arctic region of Alaska and Siberia, as well as correspondence regarding its publication, copies of source material relating to the expedition, and other papers. Includes letters from Vilhjalmur Stefansson.

12,397. Bristol, Fanny L.
Papers. 1838. 4-page item.
Open. No guide.
The New York Public Library, Manuscripts and Archives.
Letter Bristol, a resident of New Haven, CT, wrote to her brother Louis in Quincy, IL, in which she describes two trips to New York City; seeing the Murdock family sail for England, visits to the Hudson River homes of the James family, William B. Astor, and Mrs. Robert Donaldson; meeting Abby Howland and others on a return trip to New York; a Loco Foco procession; and local church and family matters.

12,398. Bronson Family
Papers. 1790-1875. 58 ft.
Open. Unpublished guide.
The New York Public Library, Manuscripts and Archives.
Correspondence, accounts of loans and mortgages, deeds, maps, and other land, business, and personal papers of Isaac Bronson (1760-1838), a resident of New York City and Greenfield, CT, and of his sons Arthur Bronson (1801-44), Fredric Bronson (1802-68), and Oliver Bronson (1799-1875), who aided him in his business. Also contains papers of female members of the family, including correspondence and accounts of [Mrs.] Anna Olcott Bronson, Ann Bronson, Harriet Bronson, Mary Bronson, and [Mrs.] Ann Eliza Bailey Bronson; correspondence and land papers of Louisa Troup Brinckerhoff and Charlotte Troup (Brinckerhoff) Bronson (1818-61); correspondence, accounts, and other papers of Caroline Bronson Willett; and account books of Ethel Bronson (1765-1825) as agent for Isaac Bronson, including a statement of Isaac Bronson's claims against representatives of Ethel Bronson.

12,399. Brooks, Maria (Gowen)
Papers. 1833-43. 13 folders and 1 vol.
Open. No guide.
The New York Public Library, Manuscripts and Archives.
Correspondence of [Mrs. John] Brooks (ca. 1794-1845), a poet called "Maria del Occidente," relating to her works and to personal matters, as well as poems and other papers. Correspondents include W. B. Force, Rufus Griswold, Fitz-Greene Halleck, Robert Southey, George Ticknor, and E. P. Whipple. Brooks was a member of a group called the Lake poets.

12,400. Brooks, Rachel
Papers. Nd. 380-page item.
Open. No guide.
The New York Public Library, Manuscripts and Archives.
Typescript of an unpublished manuscript by Brooks (1884-), a YMCA fieldworker in China, includes bibliographical notes and a preface by Bertrand Russell. In the book she writes of her experiences as a fieldworker China and her activities with the Central Christian (Disciples) Church in New York working with the Chinese.

12,401. Brown, William Adams
Papers. Ca. 1850-1939. 8 cartons.
Open. Unpublished guide.
The New York Public Library, Manuscripts and Archives.
Correspondence and other papers of Brown (1865-1943), a Presbyterian minister and professor of theology, and his wife Helen Gilman (Noyes) Brown, their children, and various other members of the Brown and Noyes families. Papers relate chiefly to family matters.

12,402. Bruce, Charles K.
Papers. 1826. 18 pp.
Open. No guide.
The New York Public Library, Manuscripts and Archives.
Letters of Bruce, a resident of Staten Island, NY, to his brother Upton Bruce and his sister Mrs. E. B. Scott, who resided in Maryland. The letters relate to financial matters, farming and cattle sales in Maryland, yellow fever, failure of New York banks, land transactions in Virginia, construction of a canal through Maryland, and other matters.

12,403. Bryant and Godwin
Papers. 1804-1913. 17 boxes.
Open. Unpublished guide.
The New York Public Library, Manuscripts and Archives.
Letters to William Cullen Bryant (1794-1878), a poet and editor of the *New York Evening Post;* to his son-in-law Parke Godwin (1816-1904), an author and editor of the *New York Evening Post* and the *Commercial Advertiser;* and to family members from people who were distinguished in literature, the arts, science, politics, philanthropy, and religion. Includes correspondence with authors Lydia Maria Francis Child, Julia Caroline Ripley Dorr, Eliza Wood (Burhans) Farnham, Helen Maria (Fiske) Hunt Jackson, Martha Joanna Reade (Nash) Lamb, Elizabeth Palmer Peabody, Carolina Coronado Perry, and Lydia Howard (Huntley) Sigourney. Also includes letters of Caroline Howard; painter and author Catharine Ann Janvier regarding social engagements, health, and the death of her son; dramatic soprano Clara Louise Kellogg regarding social activities; author Annie (Adams) [Mrs. James Thomas] Fields regarding social visits and charity work; philanthropist and reformer Josephine (Shaw) Lowell regarding the Woman's Municipal League, Citizen's Union, and other matters; Eliza Robbins regarding friends and traveling; author, translator, and philologist Therese Albertine Louise Von Jakob Robinson regarding social engagements and servants; and author Catherine Maria Sedgwick primarily concerning personal matters.

12,404. Bryant Family
Papers. 1824-1906. 1000 items.
Open. No guide.
The New York Public Library, Manuscripts and Archives.
Correspondence, school compositions, legal and land papers, and an autograph album of this Illinois pioneer family. Correspondents include William Cullen Bryant (1794-1878), John Howard Bryant (1807-1902), and Parke Godwin, whose letters relate to Illinois and Kansas in the Civil War, pioneer life, family matters, finances, and slavery. Also includes letters of Sarah (Snell) Bryant, whose sons were William Cullen, Cyrus, and John H. Bryant, to her brother Thomas Snell concerning her journey to Illinois and pioneer life in Princeton, IL, and letters of Julia S. Bryant, who was the daughter of William Cullen Bryant, to her uncle John Bryant concerning personal affairs, finances, her father, and her travels to Europe.

12,405. Buehermann, Elizabeth
Papers. Ca. 1904-55. 1.5 in.
Open. Unpublished guide.
The New York Public Library, Manuscripts and Archives.
Letters to Buehermann, a photographer, from persons in literary, art, and photographic fields relates to her work and is primarily from clients upon receipt of photos. Correspondents include Alfred Stieglitz, Carl Sandburg, and Elbert Hubbard. Also includes letters to Blancharel d'Aoust from Alexis Carel, Mrs. Ralph Stockman, and others regarding his essay, "Man's Destiny."

12,406. Burge, Marie Louise
Papers. 1849-1947. 1 box and 3 vols.
Open. No guide.
The New York Public Library, Manuscripts and Archives.
Correspondence, manuscripts, photos of Wickford (RI) clippings, printed items, and other papers of [Miss] Burge, an author who lived in Rhode Island. Includes papers relating to the Burge family, letters to the press, her lectures, woman suffrage, and her father J. H. Burge, a physician.

12,407. Burgess Family
Papers. 1799-1925. 13 boxes, 5 vols., and 1 portfolio.
Open. Unpublished guide.
The New York Public Library, Manuscripts and Archives.
Correspondence, diaries, accounts, genealogical chart, and legal and other papers of three generations of the Burgess family of England, New York City, and Scarsdale, NY. Includes correspondence of Henry Burgess, an inventor, economist, partner in Baring Bros. and Co., and editor of "The Bankers Circular," and his wife Frances Burgess; correspondence of his sons Charles Henry, Edward, Joseph, and George Burgess, including information on British trade and diplomacy in Persia and Afghanistan; notes from an interview with Anna [Mrs. Edward] Burgess in 1880; correspondence of George Burgess, who came to America in 1840 and later became an importer in New York City and Dundee, Scotland, and his wife Valeria Burgess, including that with Lucy [Mrs. John James] Audubon; and letters from Mme. Fanny Burgess Bottin to her cousin Thomas Foljambe Burgess.

12,408. Burlingham, Elizabeth
Papers. 1821-36?. 68-page vol.
Open. No guide.
The New York Public Library, Manuscripts and Archives.
Ledger of Burlingham, probably the owner of a general store in Newport, RI, contains records of sales of merchandise, copies of letters she wrote concerning family and religion, notes on sermons, and memoranda.

12,409. Burnett, Frances Eliza (Hodgson)
Papers. Ca. 1897-1901. 1 vol. and ca. 115 pp.
Open. No guide.
The New York Public Library, Manuscripts and Archives.
Manuscript and typescripts of [Mrs. Swan Moses] Burnett (1849-1924) an author, include "The Proud Little Grain of Wheat"; "One Woman of the 19th Century," a memorial to Queen Victoria; and *The First Gentleman of Europe,* a play by Burnett and George Hemming, which was produced in 1897. Burnett was the author of numerous short stories, plays, and novels, including *Little Lord Fauntleroy* (1886). Burnett later married Stephen Townesend.

12,410. Burr, Aaron
Papers. Nd. 1 in.
Open. Unpublished guide.
The New York Public Library, Manuscripts and Archives.
Correspondence, clippings, and documents of Burr (1756-1836), who was a lawyer and the third vice-president of the US. Includes a letter to Burr from Theodosia (Barton) Prevost Burr (?-ca. 1800), who married Burr in 1782, concerning children and her love for her husband. Also contains correspondence between Theodosia (Burr) Alston (1783-1813) and her husband Joseph Alston, governor of South Carolina, concerning their absence from each other.

12,411. Callister, Henry
Papers. Ca. 1741-88. 5 vols.
Open. Unpublished guide.
The New York Public Library, Manuscripts and Archives.
Papers of Callister (1716?-1768?), a merchant and planter in Maryland, include correspondence relating to economic, political, social, and cultural matters; family papers; and papers of his wife Sarah Trippe Callister concerning her school for girls in Baltimore and Chestertown, MD, and other matters. The school was operated by Sarah Callister and Mrs. E. Peale.

12,412. Carruth, Hayden
Papers. 1853-1961. 80 vols. and 19 boxes.
Open. Unpublished guide.
The New York Public Library, Manuscripts and Archives.
Papers of Fred Hayden Carruth (1862-1932), a journalist and author, include diaries of his grandmother Louisa Usher Shaw [Mrs. Uriah] Veeder, 1859-64 and 1866-67, and pocket diaries of his mother Mary (Veeder) Carruth, who married Oliver Powers Carruth in 1859, in which she describes social conditions in central New York state, 1853-59 and 1875. Also included are pocket diaries Hayden Carruth kept in Lake City, MN, and Minneapolis from 1879 to 1885, including entries he copied from his grandmother's diary about the sickness and death of his mother and earlier family notes going back to 1858; pocket diaries of Helen E. Kimball, a resident of Lake City who was a friend of Carruth's parents, 1877-78; and papers related to Carruth's editorship of "The Postcript," a feature in the *Woman's Home Companion.*

12,413. Carstarphen, Frank Ellice
Papers. 1897-1951. 1 box.
Open. No guide.
The New York Public Library, Manuscripts and Archives.
Papers of Carstarphen (1871-1952), a lawyer and dramatist, include correspondence with Anne Warwick concerning the dramatization of her novel *The Chalk Line* (1915) and its production in Woodstock, NY, in 1935, as well as correspondence with Margery Lawrence relating to Carstarphen's play *Maddalena,* which was based on her novel, *The Maddonna of Seven Moons* (1933). Family correspondence is also included.

12,414. Cather, Willa Sibert
Papers. 1926-40. 4 slipcases and 1 vol.
Open. No guide.
The New York Public Library, Manuscripts and Archives.
Typescripts with revisions of works by Cather (1873-1947), an author, consist of *A Chance Meeting, Lucy Gayheart* (1935), *My Mortal Enemy* (1926), and *Shadows on the Rock* (1931). Also contains revised galley proofs of *Sapphira and the Slave Girl* (1940).

12,415. Catt, Carrie Clinton (Lane) Chapman
Papers. 1887-1947. 2.5 ft.
Open. No guide.
The New York Public Library, Manuscripts and Archives.
[Mrs. George William] Catt (1859-1947) was a lecturer, woman suffrage leader, and peace worker. Correspondence; addresses, articles, and other writings; scrapbooks; photos; and other papers relate to woman suffrage, the peace movement, and temperance. Correspondence with notable contemporaries; correspondence of the International Alliance of Women for Suffrage and Equal Citizenship; papers of the National American Woman Suffrage Association, of which Catt was president, including questionnaires Catt sent to the presidents of auxiliaries prior to campaigning for the suffrage amendment; a scrapbook of clippings about woman suffrage; papers relating to the Empire State Campaign Committee; material relating to the Woman's Centennial Congress in 1940; and photos of Catt's trip to Panama in 1923.

12,416. Chapin, Barbara
Papers. 1948-55. Ca. 14 items.
Open. No guide.
The New York Public Library, Manuscripts and Archives.
Correspondence and other papers of Chapin relating to "Carnival Caravan," a mobile cultural "circus" which toured some rural towns in New York. It later became Artmobile, Inc.

12,417. Charities, New York City
Records. 1876. Ca. 30 items.
Open. No guide.
The New York Public Library, Manuscripts and Archives.
Correspondence and reports concerning various charities and social welfare agencies in New York City are addressed to Mrs. Aubrey H. Smith of the Women's Centennial Executive Committee, which worked on the 1876 Centennial Exposition in Philadelphia.

12,418. Chauncey Family
Papers. 1744-1857. 67 items.
Open. No guide.
The New York Public Library, Manuscripts and Archives.
Correspondence, deeds, legal papers, and other papers of this Connecticut family. Family members include Charles Chauncey (1747-1823), a jurist; his son Charles Chauncey (1777-1849), a lawyer in Philadelphia; Wolcott and Ann (Brown) Chauncey; their son Isaac Chauncey (1772-1840), a naval officer; and his wife Catharine Sickles Chauncey.

12,419. Child, Lydia Maria (Francis)
Papers. 1838-78. Ca. 100 items.
Open. No guide.
The New York Public Library, Manuscripts and Archives.
[Mrs. David Lee] Child (1802-80) was an author, reformer, and abolitionist. Letters to antislavery lawyer Ellis Gray Loring concerning the antislavery movement, contemporary politics, social life and conditions in New York City, the abolishment of capital punishment, well-known contemporary people, and her difficulties in editing the *National Anti-Slavery Standard.* Also contains letters to Loring from Sarah Moore Grimké, requesting counsel in her project of writing a digest of the laws respecting women, and from D. L. Child, Wendell Phillips, William Lloyd Garrison, Theodore Parker, James Freeman Clark, and John F. Webb. Other correspondence and manuscripts include a letter from Child to a Mrs. Archibald explaining why she gave up her projected biography of John Brown, her admiration for him and for Kansas, and the progress of the abolition movement. Child conducted a private school in Watertown, MA; started a periodical for children, *Juvenile Miscellany;* served on the executive committee of the American Anti-Slavery Society from 1840 to 1843; and edited its weekly *National Anti-Slavery Standard.*

12,420. Church, Maria Trumbull (Silliman)
Papers. 1829-58. 2 boxes.
Open. Published guide.
The New York Public Library, Manuscripts and Archives.
Correspondence of Church (1810-80) includes that with her husband John Barker Church; her mother Harriet (Trumbull) Silliman (1783-1850); her father Benjamin Silliman (1779-1864), a professor of chemistry and natural history at Yale College; her sister Faith (Silliman) [Mrs. Oliver Payson] Hubbard, a resident of Hanover, NH; her sister Henrietta, who later married James Dwight Dana, a resident of New Haven, CT; and her aunt Mrs. Daniel Wadsworth, a resident of Hartford, CT. The letters relate to the life of the Church family at Triana, near Angelica, NY, their daily domestic routine, the rearing and education of the seven children, the improvement of their farm, the operation of John Church's lumber company, and the removal of the family to New Haven, CT, and subsequently to New York in 1849. Other subjects include the attendance of women at Benjamin Silliman's lectures and in his laboratory. See *Dictionary Catalog of the Manuscript Division, The New York Public Library* (New York: G. K. Hall and Company, 1967).

12,421. Clark, Mary
Papers. 1865-72. Ca. 125 items.
Open. No guide.
The New York Public Library, Manuscripts and Archives.
Correspondence of [Miss] Mary "Mollie" Clark, a resident of West Chazy, NY, to Willie Franklin, to whom she was engaged for a time, and to George S. Purdy. In her letters she comments on the state of her health and emotions, local events, family economic position, her visits to Canada and Mackinac Island, MI, in 1871, and the 17th Connecticut Volunteers, Grand Army of the Republic.

12,422. Cohn, Fannia Mary
Papers. 1919-62. 16 boxes.
Open. Unpublished guide.
The New York Public Library, Manuscripts and Archives.
Correspondence; writings; speeches, including "Women's Place in the Labor Movement"; and printed material of [Miss] Cohn (1885-1962), a labor official and educator. Cohn graduated from the University of Chicago in 1914 and took a position in the education department of the International Ladies' Garment Workers' Union. Later she became vice-president of the Union and secretary of their educational department. Cohn also helped found Brookwood Labor College and the Workers' Education Bureau of America.

12,423. Commissioners for Alms House and Bridewell, New York City
Records. 1791-97. 130-page item.
Open. No guide.
The New York Public Library, Manuscripts and Archives.
Minutes of the almshouse and prison, recorded by Samuel Dodge, the keeper of the Alms House, relate to general relief of the poor; care of infants; schooling and binding out of children; distribution of food and firewood; contracts for supplies, physicians, midwives, apothecaries, and keepers; and quarterly accounts of costs.

12,424. Committee of 15, New York City
Records. 1900-01. 49 boxes and 1 vol.
Open. Unpublished guide.
The New York Public Library, Manuscripts and Archives.
Minutes of meetings, testimony, affidavits, reports, correspondence, membership lists, and clippings of the Committee. Includes reports and affidavits concerned with prostitution and gambling in New York City.

12,425. Cowing, Julia Radcliffe
Papers. Ca. 1895. 42 pp.
Open. No guide.
The New York Public Library, Manuscripts and Archives.
Typescripts of Cowing relate to Colorado.

12,426. Cowl, Jane
Papers. 1907-45. 3 boxes and 1 vol.
Open. No guide.
The New York Public Library, Manuscripts and Archives.
Cowl (1883-1950) was an actress and playwright. Personal correspondence and correspondence concerning "Hervey House" and radio programs; material for her autobiography, which was to be written with F. Morse, including a draft concerned with her difficulties with Actors Equity; a diary Cowl kept in 1907 during her first trip to Europe, in which she describes the sights of England, plays she saw, and actors she met; play contracts and agreements; and papers relating to plays and controversies with producers and agents. Born in Boston as Grace Bailey, Cowl gave her family name as Cowles. In 1906 Cowl married theatrical producer Adolph Klauber (1879-1933). Cowl starred in such plays as *Smilin' Through, Romeo and Juliet,* and *Antony and Cleopatra.*

12,427. Cowles, James Lewis
Papers. 1897-1919. 5 boxes.
Open. Box list.
The New York Public Library, Manuscripts and Archives.
Papers of Cowles (1843-1922), an author, include correspondence of his daughter Genevieve Almeda Cowles, an artist, lecturer, and writer, as well as correspondence from Edith Cowles and Marian Cowles Wyatt, notebooks, addresses, articles, and portraits.

12,428. Cushing, Stella Marek
Papers. 1928-34. 1 box.
Open. No guide.
The New York Public Library, Manuscripts and Archives.
Correspondence and journals of Cushing, in which she describes her trips to Europe in 1928, 1930, and 1934. While there she collected folksongs, dances, and costumes for lecture and concert programs in the US. Some correspondence relates to her success in this endeavor; program notes are included. Countries she visited include Czechoslovakia, Albania, Russia, Poland, Yugoslavia, Germany, Austria, Hungary, and Rumania.

12,429. Dahlgren, John Adolphus Bernard
Papers. 1829-95. 3 vols.
Open. No guide.
The New York Public Library, Manuscripts and Archives.
Journal and letter book of Dahlgren (1809-70), a naval officer, are included with a daily record of household expenses that his wife Sarah Madeleine (Vinton) Dahlgren (1825-98) kept from 1877 to 1885. Also includes a few accounts from her summer home in South Mountain, MD, and a personal register of callers the Dahlgrens received in their home in Washington, DC.

12,430. Daly, Charles Patrick
Papers. 1716-1899. 48 boxes and 20 vols.
Open. Partial unpublished guide.
The New York Public Library, Manuscripts and Archives.
Correspondence and manuscripts of Daly (1816-99), a New York City jurist and author. Includes addresses, lectures, and other writings on

English female novelists, Jews in New York City, and welfare work for women and others. Correspondence relates to women's war relief work and social matters. Also includes diaries his wife Maria (Lydig) Daly (1824-94) kept from 1861 to 1893, where she commented on the Dalys' social life and events and personalities during the Civil War, especially meeting Union officers. A portion of her diaries was published as *Diary of a Union Lady 1861-65* (New York: Funk and Wagnall's, 1962), edited by Harold Earl Hammond.

12,431. Daly, Maria (Lydig)
Papers. 1857-94. 3 boxes.
Open. No guide.
The New York Public Library, Manuscripts and Archives.
Born in New York City, Daly (1824-94) married jurist and author Charles Patrick Daly (1816-99). Letters from the Lydig, Otto, and Hoyt families; from Louise [Mrs. George] Jeffries of Charleston, WV; and from G. W. Armstrong regarding Judge Daly's lands in Minnesota, which were under the management of Maria Daly. Also includes social letters from Charlotte Cushman, [Mrs.] Jessie B. Fremont, [Mrs.] Virginia Farragut, [Mrs.] Anabella Barlow, [Mrs.] Ruth Dana Draper, and [Mrs.] Laura A. Delano and correspondence relating to the establishment of a kindergarten in New York, the New York Botanical Garden, the Women's Central Association for Relief for the Army, the US Sanitary Commission, the Women's Patriotic Association for Diminishing the Use of Foreign Luxuries, and the Union Home and School for the Children of Volunteers, of which Mrs. Daly was president.

12,432. Darnley Family
Papers. 1843-84. 33 items.
Open. No guide.
The New York Public Library, Manuscripts and Archives.
Letters from William Darnley, a carpenter, to his wife and family while he was working in New York City and Canada. Letters from other members of the family are also included.

12,433. D'Auliffe
Papers. 1800-01. 6 vols.
Open. No guide.
The New York Public Library, Manuscripts and Archives.
Letters d'Auliffe wrote in French from the family home Chevilly in Bloomingdale, New York City, primarily to his daughters at Adderley's boarding school. In his letters he describes attending the theater; he also discusses religion, study, manners and conduct, health, duty to family, and his love for his native France.

12,434. Davis, Gherardi
Papers. 1828-40. 6 boxes and 6 vols.
Open. No guide.
The New York Public Library, Manuscripts and Archives.
Papers of Davis (1858-1941), who was a lawyer in New York City, a state legislator, third deputy police commissioner, and ambassador to Germany, include a letter [Mrs.] Lucretia Bancroft wrote to her daughter [Mrs.] Jane Putnam (Bancroft) Gherardi in 1828.

12,435. Davis, Mary Gould
Papers. 1927-59. Ca. 38 items.
Open. Unpublished guide.
The New York Public Library, Manuscripts and Archives.
[Miss] Davis (1882-1956) was a children's librarian and storyteller. Letters from authors and illustrators and others relating to children's books and storytelling, clippings, and other material. Also includes letters to her sister Purley B. Davis.

12,436. Davis, Robert Hobart
Papers. 1901-42. 26 boxes.
Open. Unpublished guide.
The New York Public Library, Manuscripts and Archives.
Letters to Davis (1869-1942), an editor, author, poet, dramatist, journalist, and amateur photographer who lived in New York City, from Geraldine Farrar, Fannie Hurst, Katherine D. Osbourne, and Mary (Roberts) Rinehart.

12,437. Deland, Margaretta "Margaret" Wade (Campbell)
Papers. 1898-1911. 1 folder.
Open. No guide.
The New York Public Library, Manuscripts and Archives.
Letters from Deland (1857-1945), an author, poet, and industrial design teacher in New York City, to [Mrs.] Frances Anderson concerning a lecture and to H. E. Rood regarding galleys and proofs of several articles and books. Deland was born in Allegheny, PA; she married Lorin Fuller Deland in 1880.

12,438. Deming, Edwin Willard
Papers. 1880-1921. 1 box.
Open. Unpublished guide.
The New York Public Library, Manuscripts and Archives.
Letters that Deming (1860-1942), an artist, wrote to his family while he was attending The Art Students' League in New York City and while he was in Chicago, Mexico, and Paris. Also includes letters to his wife dating from 1896 to 1921.

12,439. Denslow, Dwight B., and Denslow, Louise A.
Papers. 1861-62. 312-page vol.
Open. No guide.
The New York Public Library, Manuscripts and Archives.
Diary in which the Denslows describe their travels by land and sea from Brooklyn, NY, to Europe, the Mediterranean, Egypt, and the Holy Land. They comment on highlights of their trip, including a visit to a salt merchant at Hyères, Cairo and the pyramids, and meeting with a Mrs. Leider, wife of a Coptic missionary and one-time tutor to the children of Mohammed Ali.

12,440. Depew, Chauncey Mitchell
Papers. Ca. 1887-1922. Ca. 190 items.
Open. Unpublished guide.
The New York Public Library, Manuscripts and Archives.
Correspondence, calling cards, and autographs of Depew (1834-1928), a lawyer, legislator, railroad executive, orator, and US senator from New York. Primarily letters to Depew from people prominent in American and English political and social life. Correspondents include Alice I. Andre, C. Olivia Brice, Mary Goelet, Emily Ladenberg, Nellie Melba, Penelope Monk, and Theresa Shrewsbury.

12,441. Deutsch, Babette
Papers. 1923-41. 1 vol. and 1 package.
Open. No guide.
The New York Public Library, Manuscripts and Archives.
Correspondence, notes, a poem, and typescripts of Deutsch (1895-), a poet, critic, and author. Papers relate to preparation of the book *Contemporary German Poetry* (1923) by Deutsch and Avrahm Yarmolinsky. Also includes galley proofs of her *Mask of Solomon* (1933); typescripts with corrections of *The Poor Thief's Legacy, This Modern Poetry* (1935), and *Walt Whitman, Builder for America* (1941); and typescripts of *Brittle Heaven* and *In Such a Night.*

12,442. Diary of a New York Woman
Papers. 1929-37. 2 vols.
Open. No guide.
The New York Public Library, Manuscripts and Archives.
Diaries in which a New York woman describes her social and personal activities while in Pennsylvania, New York City, Nashville, Atlantic City, NJ, Wyckoff, NJ, and a New York City suburb.

12,443. Dickinson, Emily
Papers. Nd. 1 slipcase.
Open. No guide.
The New York Public Library, Manuscripts and Archives.
Copy of a bread-and-butter letter from [Miss] Dickinson (1830-86), a poet, to Mr. and Mrs. Josiah G. Holland. The original letter is in the Houghton Library at Harvard University.

12,444. Dillingham, Charles Bancroft
Papers. 1905-27. 23 cartons.
Open. No guide.
The New York Public Library, Manuscripts and Archives.
Correspondence and account books of Dillingham (1868-1934), owner and manager of the Globe Theatre, who also was associated with the Knickerbocker and Hippodrome theaters in New York City. The papers, included with those of his associate Bruce Edwards, relate to production of various shows in New York and road tours. Stage personalities mentioned include Elsie James, Ina Claire, Bessie McCoy, and Julia Sanderson.

12,445. Dix, Dorothea Lynde
Papers. 1848-52. 39 items.
Open. Unpublished guide.
The New York Public Library, Manuscripts and Archives.
Letters that [Miss] Dix (1802-87), a reformer of mental hospitals and prisons, wrote to William E. Hacker in Philadelphia describing her philanthropic activities and personal family matters. Also includes notes and clippings of reviews of a biography of Dix by Francis Tiffany (Boston: Houghton Mifflin, 1890). Dix was born in Maine, moved to Boston, and lived there until 1830.

12,446. Donlevy, Alice Heighes
Papers. 1860-1911. 9 boxes.
Open. Unpublished guide.
The New York Public Library, Manuscripts and Archives.
[Miss] Donlevy (1846-1929) was an art teacher and lecturer. Correspondence, notes, memorabilia, and other papers of the Ladies' Art Association, which was founded to aid the art-industrial education of women; the Woman's Memorial Fund; the Woman's South African League; and the Woman's Auxiliary League of the Boer Relief Fund. Also includes a notebook of [Mrs.] Eliza F. Verplanck Richards, who was president of the Woman's South African League. Donlevy was secretary of the Ladies' Art Association and of the Woman's Memorial Fund as well as an executive committee member of the Woman's Auxiliary League of the Boer Relief Fund.

12,447. Donovan, John
Papers. 1852. 1 folder.
Open. No guide.
The New York Public Library, Manuscripts and Archives.
Papers of Donovan, a master tailor in Brooklyn, NY, include correspondence between Mrs. Donovan and a Mrs. Cary, who discuss local and family news.

12,448. Doty-Dubois Family
Papers. 1846-65. 6 folders.
Open. No guide.
The New York Public Library, Manuscripts and Archives.
Correspondence between Elihu Doty (1809-64), a missionary for the Dutch Reformed church, and his daughter [Miss] Amelia C. Doty-Dubois, including

many letters in which he describes life as a missionary in Amoy, China. Also includes letters to John Dubois, who adopted Amelia Doty, and a letter that Amelia Doty-Dubois, who was in Wurtsboro, NY, received from her cousin Robert, at or near Memphis, TN, who describes conditions near the close of the Civil War.

12,449. Dowden, Elizabeth Dickinson (West)
Papers. 1913-31. Ca. 80 items.
Open. No guide.
The New York Public Library, Manuscripts and Archives.
Letters from Dowden, who lived in Dublin, Ireland, to Clara Barrus in West Park, NY, relate to personal and literary matters, especially to the writings of her husband Edward Dowden (1843-1913), an Irish editor and critic, and to Barrus's friend John Burroughs. Includes references to Walt Whitman and current events, especially WWI.

12,450. Drake, Benjamin
Papers. Ca. 1820-30. 1 folder.
Open. No guide.
The New York Public Library, Manuscripts and Archives.
Papers of Drake, a 19th-century physician who lived in New York City, include a letter recommending that another doctor attend the midwife at a birth and a funeral notice of Ellcana Wood's wife.

12,451. Dransfield, Jane
Papers. Ca. 1918-31. 2 folders.
Open. No guide.
The New York Public Library, Manuscripts and Archives.
Correspondence of Dransfield (1875-1957), who was a playwright, poet, and lecturer on drama, with actors, authors, stage directors, producers, theater workshop groups, and literary agents about drama and poetry. Correspondents include Theresa Helburn, Edna St. Vincent Millay, and Harriet Monroe.

12,452. Draper, Henry, and Draper, Anna (Palmer)
Papers. 1869-1914. 3 boxes.
Open. No guide.
The New York Public Library, Manuscripts and Archives.
Correspondence, clippings, photos, and other papers of Anna Draper (ca. 1845-1914) relate to her collection of antiques. In 1867 she married Henry Draper (1837-82), an astronomer and pioneer in astronomical photography, who lived in New York City. After her husband's death Anna Draper gave funds and his equipment to the Harvard College Observatory.

12,453. Draper, Muriel
Papers. Ca. 1930s. 14 pp.
Open. No guide.
The New York Public Library, Manuscripts and Archives.
Account by Draper (1886-) of her airplane trip from New York to Boston.

12,454. Du Bois, Marguerite Delavarre
Papers. 1907-08. 1 vol.
Open. No guide.
The New York Public Library, Manuscripts and Archives.
Diary that Du Bois (?-1947?) kept in 1907 contains descriptions of her study of Franch and German, her painting, attendance at theaters, and visits to Saratoga, Lake George, Plattsburgh, and Albany, NY, and Montreal and the Catskills.

12,455. Dunkley, Ferdinand L.
Papers. Nd. 4 boxes.
Open. No guide.
The New York Public Library, Manuscripts and Archives.
Papers of Dunkley (1869-?), a musician, teacher, and author, include some poetic compositions by his wife. Dunkley was a resident of New Orleans near the end of his life.

12,456. Dunn, Gertrude
Papers. 1865. 1 vol. and 1 item.
Open. No guide.
The New York Public Library, Manuscripts and Archives.
Diary in which Dunn describes a visit to Washington, DC, where she saw President Lincoln shot. Also includes a letter about the event.

12,457. Dunn, Julia Elizabeth
Papers. 1876-1925. 1 box.
Open. No guide.
The New York Public Library, Manuscripts and Archives.
Letters to Dunn, a resident of Boston, from her German music teachers and from others, including Charles Timothy Brooks, Robert Franz, Ellen Frothingham, Benjamin J. Lang, Marie Leonhardi, Marie Von Lindeman, Gustav Merkel, Madeline Schiller, Clara Schumann, E. Schwigger-Seidel, and A. Wintzer. Also includes the original manuscript of Percy Wallace MacKaye's poem "With a Rose," letters and cards from him to Sara Anna Dunn, letters to Sara Dunn from E. Risler, printed stanzas by Mary Medbery MacKaye, and clippings about Percy MacKaye.

12,458. Dunstan, Caroline A.
Papers. 1856-70. 14 vols.
Open. No guide.
The New York Public Library, Manuscripts and Archives.
Diaries of Dunstan, a housewife in New York City, who describes household activities, social life, and the health of family members; she also comments on current events, including Civil War news.

12,459. Durand, Asher Brown
Papers. 1812-83. Ca. 1200 items.
Open. Unpublished guide.
The New York Public Library, Manuscripts and Archives.
Letters that Durand (1796-1886), an engraver and printer, wrote to his wife Mary Durand, his sister Caroline, and his son.

12,460. Duyckinck
Papers. 1768-1890. Ca. 39 ft.
Open. Unpublished guide.
The New York Public Library, Manuscripts and Archives.
Papers of the Duyckinck family include correspondence and accounts of Margaret Wolfe Duyckinck; correspondence, notes, and accounts of her husband Evert Augustus Duyckinck (1816-78), a New York City author, historian, lawyer, and biographer; correspondence, journals, and accounts of his father Evert Duyckinck; papers of the Wolfe and Panton families; and correspondence of Sophia Roorbach. Also includes an 1860s photo album of Evert Augustus Duyckinck's friends.

12,461. Dwight Family
Papers. 1789-1866. 2 boxes.
Open. No guide.
The New York Public Library, Manuscripts and Archives.
Letters that Theodore Dwight, Sr. (1764-1846), a lawyer, editor, and author, wrote to his wife Abigail Dwight before and after their marriage in 1792 and to Sally Dwight concerning family matters; letters to Abigail Dwight from her sister concerning the illness of female members of the family, her mother and cousin, and local religious matters; and correspondence of Theodore Dwight, Jr. (1796-1850), an author and educator, with his mother Abigail Dwight, his sister, and Lydia Howard Huntley Sigourney. Also includes letters William R. Dwight wrote to his mother mentioning and describing cousin Mary, letters he addressed to his grandmother, letters Theodore Dwight, Jr.'s wife wrote to her aunt, correspondence between Marianne and Sally Dwight concerning a love affair between mutual acquaintances, and correspondence between Theodore and Abigail Dwight and Mary Alsop concerning the Dwights' move to Hartford, the offer of their house to Alsop, and family matters.

12,462. Eddy, Martha
Papers. 1814-29. 1 vol.
Open. No guide.
The New York Public Library, Manuscripts and Archives.
Verses Eddy wrote and collected while she was in Providence, RI, and Charleston, MA. Also included are drawings for embroidery patterns.

12,463. Embury, Emma Catherine (Manley)
Papers. 1736-1893. 6 boxes and 261-page vol.
Open. No guide.
The New York Public Library, Manuscripts and Archives.
Papers of Embury (ca. 1806-63), a writer who was married to Daniel Embury, a banker in Brooklyn, NY, include correspondence and contracts with her publishers; letters from Charles Fenns Hoffman; her prose and poetry writings, including "Guido, a Tale, and Other Poems" dedicated to her husband; a listing of her writings, with the titles of magazines in which they appeared, dates sent, and payments received; notebooks; clippings of her writings; and an autograph album. Also includes a certificate of membership in the Parthenian Society of the Baltimore Female College, a cookbook, a notebook containing a list of persons to whom [Mrs.] Anna K. Sheldon gave copies of *The Poems of Emma C. Embury* (New York, 1869) and *Selected Prose Writings of Mrs. Emma C. Embury* (New York, 1893), letters received by Anna Sheldon with reviews of the poems, and portraits of Embury and her friend Lucy Hooper. Collection also contains papers of the Manley and Embury families relating to ownership of real estate in New York City and accounts for 1736 and 1754, correspondence of Daniel Embury, prose and poetry he wrote, a journal he kept in 1861 of a trip from New York to St. Paul, MN, and papers relating to the death of his son Philip Augustus Embury in 1861.

12,464. Emerson Family
Papers. 1847-1948. 27 boxes, 11 vols., and 1 slipcase.
Open. Unpublished guide.
The New York Public Library, Manuscripts and Archives.
Correspondence, diaries, account books, poetry, and other papers of Edwin Emerson, a minister and professor of literature; his wife Mary Ingham Emerson; and their children Alfred Edwin, Jr., George Harrington, Samuel, and Margaret Emerson (1863-1948), who taught school in Tokyo at Peer's Middle School. Included are correspondence between Margaret Emerson and Hilda Rose; Margaret Emerson's diaries, 1886-88; and Mary Emerson's diaries, 1865-78. The family lived in such places as Greencastle, PA; Troy, NY; Ithaca, NY; Denver; New York City; Paris; Japan; and Dresden and Munich, Germany.

12,465. Ensign, Mary W.
Papers. 1903-04. 91-page vol.
Open. No guide.
The New York Public Library, Manuscripts and Archives.
Diary that [Mrs. Horace S.] Ensign kept while she and her husband served as Mormon missionaries in Japan. She recorded current events, personal and family matters, and activities of the Mormons and visitors.

12,466. Everts, Lillian
Papers. 1933-56. 2 boxes and 5 cartons.
Open. Box list.
The New York Public Library, Manuscripts and Archives.
Everts (1898-1960), born Lillian Epstein and wife of a Mr. Levine, was a poet and writer who contributed to *The New York Times,* the *Herald Tribune,* and the *American Mercury.* Correspondence with poets, editors, publishers, writers, organizations, friends, and members of her family; clippings of her poems; articles by and about her; and memorabilia. Among her writings is "Journey to the Future."

12,467. Fales, De Coursey
Collection. Nd. 9 boxes and 9 vols.
Open. No guide.
The New York Public Library, Manuscripts and Archives.
Correspondence, manuscripts, and other papers compiled by Fales (1888-1966), a collector, lawyer, banker, and yachtsman. Dating from the 18th to the 20th century, the collection includes correspondence of author [Mrs.] Frances Eliza Hodgson Burnett, author and reformer Julia (Ward) Howe, and Charlotte Yonge. Also includes a poem "From Reflection," by Jean Ingelow.

12,468. Farrar, Geraldine
Papers. 1952-56. 47 items.
Open. No guide.
The New York Public Library, Manuscripts and Archives.
Letters from [Miss] Farrar (1882-1967), a singer, to Lawrence and Alice McFadden Brinton Eyre, in which she reminisces about people involved in the field of music, musical events, and personal matters.

12,469. Fenno Family
Papers. Nd. 3 vols.
Open. No guide.
The New York Public Library, Manuscripts and Archives.
Poetry and other writings of the family consist largely of the work of authors August and Henry Fenno. Also includes a commonplace book of Ann M. Fenno (1839-81?).

12,470. Ferris, Isaac
Papers. Ca. 1856. 20 pp.
Open. No guide.
The New York Public Library, Manuscripts and Archives.
Address of Ferris (1798-1873) on resigning the presidency of Rutgers Female Institute in New York. Also includes an historical sketch of the Institute and a school notebook. Founded by Ferris, a Reformed Dutch clergyman, Rutgers Female Institute provided free education for schoolteachers. Ferris was also associated with the Albany Female Seminary and was later chancellor of New York University.

12,471. Fischer, Alice
Papers. Ca. 1867-1923. 3 in.
Open. No guide.
The New York Public Library, Manuscripts and Archives.
Correspondence, telegrams, clippings, and other papers of [Miss] Fischer (1869-1947), an actress, relate to her career and that of her husband William Harcourt King (1866-1923), an actor. Also includes correspondence, pocket diaries, and other papers of Frank Mayo.

12,472. Fishbein, Frieda
Papers. 1926-31?. 57 items.
Open. No guide.
The New York Public Library, Manuscripts and Archives.
Correspondence of Fishbein, a literary agent, with actors, producers, playwrights, and others associated with the theater.

12,473. Fisher, Dorothy Frances (Canfield)
Papers. Nd. Ca. 500 pp.
Open. No guide.
The New York Public Library, Manuscripts and Archives.
Correspondence, manuscripts, and clippings of Fisher (1879-1958), an author and translator. Includes manuscripts of "An Escape-thought," a short sketch of the career of Emma (Hart) Willard; a fragment of a novel; "The Knothole," a short story that won the O. Henry award in 1943; and her story "Getting Ready to Be an Old Maid." Fisher was a supporter of woman suffrage, adult education, internationalism, and the rights of children and minority groups.

12,474. Fiske, Minnie Maddern (Davey)
Papers. 1913-41. 96 items.
Open. No guide.
The New York Public Library, Manuscripts and Archives.
Letters from Maria Augusta "Minnie Maddern" Fiske (1865-1932), an actress, producer, and director, to Lawrence Eyre chiefly relate to productions and proposed production of Eyre's plays by Fiske and her husband Harrison Grey Fiske, editor of the *New York Dramatic Mirror.* Also includes an introductory explanation Eyre wrote describing his relationship with the Fiskes and a manuscript "Mrs. Fiske's Definition of Art." Minnie Fiske was known as "Little Minnie Maddern" as a child actress.

12,475. Fitzhugh, Mary Darby
Papers. Nd. 3 folders.
Open. No guide.
The New York Public Library, Manuscripts and Archives.
Poems; typescripts of articles, including several about the history of Washington, DC, and the city's growth; scripts for radio; and clippings of Fitzhugh.

12,476. Ford, Harriet
Papers. 1888-1948. 9 in.
Open. No guide.
The New York Public Library, Manuscripts and Archives.
Correspondence of [Miss] Ford (1868-1949), an author and playwright, with people prominent in the theater and in literature; poems; a play *Cupid and Psyche;* clippings; and autographs. Correspondents include Winthrop Ames, David Belasco, Mary Johnston, Elisabeth Marbury, Sinclair Lewis, Chauncy Olcott, Otis Skinner, Laurette (Cooney) Taylor, and Walker Whiteside.

12,477. Foster, Jeanne Robert
Papers. 1924-59. 19 items.
Open. No guide.
The New York Public Library, Manuscripts and Archives.
Correspondence of [Mrs.] Foster (1884-1970), an international literary and art figure, primarily letters from Henri-Pierre Roché regarding John Quinn and literary, artistic and personal matters. Other correspondents include Mme. Henri-Pierre Roché and Gwen John. The letters are in English and French.

12,478. Fowler Family
Papers. 1818-70. Ca. 80 items.
Open. No guide.
The New York Public Library, Manuscripts and Archives.
Primarily correspondence of William Chauncey Fowler (1793-1881), a clergyman, educator at Middlebury and Amherst Colleges, and a politician, and his wife Harriet (Webster) Fowler, who was the daughter of Noah Webster. Includes other correspondence of the Fowler family of New England as well.

12,479. Freeman, Marilla Waite
Papers. Nd. 0.5 in.
Open. No guide.
The New York Public Library, Manuscripts and Archives.
Correspondence of Freeman (1870-1961), a librarian, including one letter from Mrs. D. H. Lawrence. Also includes a testimonial from the Goodwyn Institute in Memphis, TN, of which she was head librarian. At first head librarian of the Cleveland Public Library, Freeman later organized and headed public libraries in Michigan City and Davenport, IN. During WWI she became head librarian of Camp Dix. Admitted to the bar in Tennessee, she became head of the foreign law department at Harvard University Library. Freeman also served as vice-president of the American Library Association.

12,480. Freeman, Mary Eleanor (Wilkins)
Papers. Nd. 9 items.
Open. No guide.
The New York Public Library, Manuscripts and Archives.
Manuscripts of short stories, including "The Coronation" and "The Witch's Daughter," by [Mrs. Charles M.] Freeman (1852-1930), an author who sometimes used her maiden name in her work. Also includes clippings from the *Pictorial Review* of some of her short stories. Freeman wrote primarily about New England.

12,481. Frémont, John Charles
Papers. Nd. 1 in.
Open. No guide.
The New York Public Library, Manuscripts and Archives.
Correspondence, manuscripts, and clippings of Frémont (1813-90), an explorer, politician, and soldier, and his wife Jessie Ann (Benton) Frémont (1824-1902), a writer who was the daughter of Thomas Hart Benton, a US senator. The Frémonts were residents of California and Washington. Includes Jessie Benton's correspondence with George Bancroft, B. P. Poore, and Parke Godwin, as well as personal letters to Anne Charlotte (Lynch) Botta and letters objecting to Lincoln's treatment of her husband during the Civil War. Jessie Frémont began contributing travel and historical sketches to periodicals after her husband suffered financial reverses. Among her works are *A Year of American Travel* (1878) and *Far West Sketches* (1890).

12,482. Frizzell, Lodisa
Papers. 1852. 64-page item.
Open. No guide.
The New York Public Library, Manuscripts and Archives.
Journal of Frizzell, a pioneer who traveled from Effington County, IL, to Cañon Creek, CA. In her journal she describes the journey on the Little Wabash River, to St. Louis and St. Joseph, MO, over the St. Joseph and Oregon Trails, to the Pacific Springs in Fremont County, WY. Frizzell wrote the diary from notes and memory and illustrated it with several drawings and maps. An edited version of the journal appeared in the New York Public Library *Bulletin,* vol. 19.

12,483. Fuller, Hattie
Papers. 1855-56. 1 vol.
Open. No guide.
The New York Public Library, Manuscripts and Archives.
Autograph album of Fuller, resident of Beaufort, SC, and Baltimore, contains poetic sentiments her friends inscribed to her.

12,484. General Federation of Women's Clubs, Department of Literature
Records. 1917. 1 vol.
Open. No guide.
The New York Public Library, Manuscripts and Archives.
Correspondence of Martha Foot Crowe, advisor for poetry, with various women's clubs in the US relating to a poetry prize competition and similar matters.

12,485. George, Henry
Papers. 1854-1916. 18 boxes and 2 cases.
Open. Unpublished guide.
The New York Public Library, Manuscripts and Archives.
Correspondence, diaries, manuscripts, lectures, speeches, notes, and other papers of George (1839-97), an economist and reformer, and correspondence of his wife Annie (Fox) George with William Lloyd Garrison, Seth Low, Edwin R. A. Seligman, Samuel Gompers, and Helen Taylor, who was the stepdaughter of John Stuart Mill. Papers of George's son Henry George (1862-1916), a journalist and US representative from New York City, include material relating to the Fennell, Pratt, Shaw, and Vallance families and letters of condolence on the death of his mother.

12,486. Gibbs, Lillian
Papers. 1931-59. 1 box.
Open. No guide.
The New York Public Library, Manuscripts and Archives.
Correspondence, notes, and other papers of Gibbs, a housewife and citizen, relate to the distribution of a scrapbook.

12,487. Goldman, Emma
Papers. 1906-40. 2 boxes and 1 microfilm reel.
Open. No guide.
The New York Public Library, Manuscripts and Archives.
[Miss] Goldman (1869-1940) was an immigrant, an anarchist, and the founder and editor of the journal *Mother Earth.* Correspondence, address books, and other papers relate to anarchism, labor, war and militarism, conditions in Germany and Russia after WWI, the Spanish Civil War, and other topics. Correspondents include Stella Ballantine, Bayard Boyesen, Mabel C. Crouch, Harry Kelly, Ethel Mannin, and Frances Perkins. Also included are typescripts for Alexander Berkman's *The Russian Myth,* an index for Goldman's autobiography *Living My Life* (1931), and condolences on the occasion of her death. Goldman was arrested for inciting to riot in 1893 in Union Square, New York City; she was deported from the US to Russia in 1919.

12,488. Grant, Ethel (Watts) Mumford
Papers. 1900-34. 9 boxes.
Open. Box list.
The New York Public Library, Manuscripts and Archives.
Correspondence, short stories, plays, musical lyrics, poetry, articles, contracts and agreements, sketches, watercolors, and clippings of Grant (1878-1940), an author of short stories, novels, and plays, including *His Majesty the Queen, Sick-A-Bed,* and *It Pays to Smile.* She studied art at the Julian Academy in Paris.

12,489. Gray, Ethel Huyler
Papers. Nd. 2 boxes.
Open. No guide.
The New York Public Library, Manuscripts and Archives.
Letters to Gray (1877-?) from Walter Owne, a British author and publisher living in Buenos Aires, Argentina, concerning his writing from 1941 to 1947; manuscripts of her short poems and articles concerning such subjects as unicorns, British archaeology, and the history of St. Mark's Episcopal Church in New York City; and a summary of her career.

12,490. Grinnell, Helen (Lansing)
Papers. 1859-67. 1 vol.
Open. No guide.
The New York Public Library, Manuscripts and Archives.
Diary of Grinnell, who was married to banker George Blake Grinnell and a resident of Audubon Park in New York City. She kept the diary for her son Frank Lansing Grinnell in order that he might view his childhood as seen through his mother's eyes. While describing family life and Frank Grinnell's upbringing from age 6 to 14, she comments on George Bird Grinnell (1849-1938); the Civil War; the draft riots in New York City; the assassination of President Lincoln; an 1862 visit to Brattleboro, VT, and neighboring towns such as Greenfield and Gill, MA; and details of family illnesses, in particular scarlet fever.

12,491. Griswold, Florence (Kressler)
Papers. 1903-28. 50 items.
Open. No guide.
The New York Public Library, Manuscripts and Archives.
Correspondence, notes, manuscripts, articles, clippings, and printed material of Griswold (1851-1937), a sociologist, lecturer, author, and patron of the arts who directed an artist's colony at her home in Old Lyme, CT. She entertained, supported, and encouraged many artists, including Ellen Louise Wilson, the first wife of President Woodrow Wilson.

12,492. Groff, Florence
Papers. Nd. 1 vol.
Open. No guide.
The New York Public Library, Manuscripts and Archives.
Souvenir album of [Miss] Groff, who was the sister of William N. Groff, an Egyptologist, contains items she apparently collected while traveling abroad.

12,493. Gross, Marie Bertrand
Papers. 1883-1935. 200 items.
Open. No guide.
The New York Public Library, Manuscripts and Archives.
Correspondence of Gross chiefly with [Miss] Nora Archibald Smith, an author and educator, relates to their common interest in kindergarten work, books and plays for children, and personal matters. Also included are references and letters to Smith's sister Kate Douglas Wiggin.

12,494. Hall, Sophie C.
Papers. 1879. 1 vol.
Open. No guide.
The New York Public Library, Manuscripts and Archives.
Diary [Mrs. George W.] Hall kept during a visit to New York contains descriptions of stores, museums and their collections, churches and preachers, companions at her boarding house, Greenwood Cemetery, the general appearance of the city, and other sights.

12,495. Hamilton, Alexander
Papers. 1775-1806. 1 box.
Open. No guide.
The New York Public Library, Manuscripts and Archives.
Family correspondence of Hamilton (1757-1804), a statesman, including notes on his affair with a Mrs. Reynolds.

12,496. Hamilton, Clayton Meeker
Papers. 1899-1946. 12 boxes.
Open. Unpublished guide.
The New York Public Library, Manuscripts and Archives.
Correspondence of Hamilton (1881-1946), an author and drama critic, includes letters to his wife Gladys Coates Hamilton and from Gertrude Atherton, Eleanor (Robson) Belmont, Alice Blaine Damrosch, Minnie Maddern Fiske, Lillian Kalich, and Cornelia Otis Skinner.

12,497. Hapgood, Isabel Florence
Papers. 1886-1922. 5 boxes.
Open. Unpublished guide.
The New York Public Library, Manuscripts and Archives.
[Miss] Hapgood (1850-1928) was an author and translator. Letters from Lucy (Maude) Alexayeff, Elizabeth C. Lovering of Somerville, MA, and others relate to the Kate Marsden case. Papers relating to the history of education of women in Russia include letters from Grand Duchess Marie Pavlovna and Emperor and Empress Nikolai Alexandrovitch and Alexandra Feodorovna as well as reports and biographies. Also included are family papers of Hapgood and a report "Experiences with Miss Clara Barton."

12,498. Harkness, Edward Stephen, and Harkness, Mary Emma (Stillman)
Collection. Nd. 29 vols.
Open. Published guide.
The New York Public Library, Manuscripts and Archives.
Collection that Mary Harkness (1874-1950) and her husband Edward Harkness (1874-1940) assembled consists of a letter signed by Harriet Stowe and a manuscript of Frances (Hodgson) Burnett's *The Proud Little Grain of Wheat.* See the *New York Public Library Bulletin,* vols. 54-55 (Dec. 1950-May 1951).

12,499. Harper & Brothers
Records. 1929-35. 9 items.
Open. No guide.
The New York Public Library, Manuscripts and Archives.
Correspondence of Harper & Brothers, a publishing house that was founded in 1833. Includes correspondence of Mr. Saxton, an editor, with author Stella Benson concerning her new book and of Saxton with Edna Ferber; Saxton suggested that Ferber write a book about "the fundamental decency and importance of the motives and emotions and background of the people of the United States." Because Ferber found this suggestion abhorrent, she threatened to switch publishers and later to stop writing.

12,500. Harper, Ida A. (Husted)
Papers. 1898-1926. No size given.
Open. No guide.
The New York Public Library, Manuscripts and Archives.
[Mrs. Thomas Winans] Harper (1851-1931) was a journalist and author in Indiana. Correspondence, a scrapbook on women's suffrage, clippings, leaflets, portraits, views, programs, and menus. Managing editor of the Terre Haute *Daily News* and department editor of the New York *Sunday Sun* and *Harper's Bazaar,* Harper wrote a biography of Susan B. Anthony. In 1899 Harper was a delegate to the International Council of Women.

12,501. Hartshorn Family
Papers. 1828-75. 1 box.
Open. No guide.
The New York Public Library, Manuscripts and Archives.
Daybooks, ledgers, copybooks, classbooks, and invitations of Charles W., George F., Martha E., and Mary L. Hartshorn. Also includes an 1844 letter of Jessie Hartshorn.

12,502. Haste, Gwendolen
Papers. 1900-66. 6 boxes.
Open. Unpublished guide.
The New York Public Library, Manuscripts and Archives.
Papers of Haste (1889-), a poet, include personal and family correspondence; a diary for 1909 to 1912; literary notebooks; travel journals; reminiscences about Harriet Monroe, Jeannette Rankin, Burton K. Wheeler, and Billings, MT; scrapbooks; and other papers.

12,503. Hawthorne, Sophia Amelia Peabody
Papers. 1863. 1 folder.
Open. No guide.
The New York Public Library, Manuscripts and Archives.
Letter that Hawthorne (1809-71), who married Nathaniel Hawthorne, wrote to a Dr. Loring requesting autographs of General Butler, President Jefferson Davis, and other Civil War figures.

12,504. Hawxhurst Family
Papers. 1821-70. 1 folder.
Open. No guide.
The New York Public Library, Manuscripts and Archives.
Correspondence of James Hawxhurst (1775-1854) includes a letter from Mrs. Louis Carhart concerning the death of his aunt Penelope Hawxhurst; a letter his niece Susan C. Hawxhurst wrote introducing herself on the occasion of the reading of the will and estate of her father Stephen Hawxhurst, who was James's brother; and a letter in which James's mother Sarah Hawxhurst describes a trip she took to New York City for reasons of health. Also includes letters in which Penelope Fancher tells her brother about her illnesses and gossip and another in which she asks her sister to visit her because she is in ill health.

12,505. Hay, Mary Garrett
Papers. 1896-1928. 1 vol.
Open. No guide.
The New York Public Library, Manuscripts and Archives.
Hay (1857-1928), the daughter of a physician who was active in politics, was a civic worker. Correspondence, including letters of condolence after her death; "Some Incidents in the Life of Mary Garrett Hay, A Wonderful Boss and a Gallant Fighter," a scrapbook that records her work for woman suffrage, better citizenship, and law enforcement; a tribute written on the occasion of her death and addressed primarily to Carrie Chapman Catt and to Hay's sister Katherine (Hay) Humphreys; photos; clippings; and programs. Hay was a state officer of the WCTU, an organizer of the New York City Women's Suffrage party, chairman of the Republican Women's National Executive Committee, and a member of the New York City LWV.

12,506. Heller, Eugenie M.
Papers. 1890-1936. 2 boxes.
Open. No guide.
The New York Public Library, Manuscripts and Archives.
Correspondence, primarily bread-and-butter notes, of [Miss] Heller, an artist in New York City, with artists and writers, including Jeanne Baraduc, Terese Boissiere-Roumanille, Mary Cassatt, Elizabeth (William) Chomperey, and Catherine Anne (Drinker) Janvier. Also includes correspondence with people involved in WWI and papers relating to Heller's American National Red Cross work at Willard Parker and other New York City hospitals.

12,507. Heyman, Gertrude
Papers. 1928-53. 2 boxes.
Open. No guide.
The New York Public Library, Manuscripts and Archives.
Heyman (?-1958) was a humanitarian and civic rights organizer. Correspondence with New York City, New York state, and federal officials as well as with civic groups, peace organizations, and others relates to the improvement of living conditions in New York City and state, federal legislative issues, world peace, and other matters. Also includes reminiscences and copies of the Bahai burial service.

12,508. Hoe Family
Papers. Nd. 1 folder.
Open. No guide.
The New York Public Library, Manuscripts and Archives.
Wedding announcements for Elizabeth Woodbridge Hoe and Caroline Phelps Hoe and clippings of the double wedding of Olivia and Laura Hoe, which took place "without notice, it is said, to their family." Also includes papers of Robert Hoe (1784-1833), a printing equipment manufacturer in New York, and his grandson Robert Hoe (1839-1909), a printing equipment manufacturer and inventor in New York.

12,509. Holmes, John
Papers. 1803-38. 95 items.
Open. No guide.
The New York Public Library, Manuscripts and Archives.
Correspondence of Holmes (1773-1843), a lawyer and US senator from Maine, includes a letter from his mother and one from his wife Sally Holmes concerning family matters.

12,510. Holmes, Samuel Leek, and Bouton, Huldah
Papers. 1821. 37 items.
Open. No guide.
The New York Public Library, Manuscripts and Archives.
Courtship letters and biographical notes of Holmes and Bouton, schoolteachers in Bedford, NY, who married in 1821.

12,511. Hooglandt, Anna
Papers. Nd. 4 pp.
Open. No guide.
The New York Public Library, Manuscripts and Archives.
Inventory of the estate of Hooglandt, a widow who lived in New York City.

12,512. Horsfield and Kummer Family
Papers. 1747-1873. 2 boxes and 2 vols.
Open. No guide.
The New York Public Library, Manuscripts and Archives.
Memoirs of Sister Elizabeth Horsfield, written by her children; a journal and ledger of Timothy Horsfield; and letters to Joseph Kummer, a resident of St. Croix, Danish West Indies, from his father Jacob Kummer and other members of the family, all of whom were members of the United Brethren (Moravian) church and residents of Bethlehem and Nazareth, PA.

12,513. Howard, Francis Gilman
Papers. 1894-1936. 1 box.
Open. No guide.
The New York Public Library, Manuscripts and Archives.
Papers of Howard (1869-1937), an architect, include letters from Gertrude B. Clark, a psychic, concerning Howard's wife Lucy Howard, who was in the hospital; from an aunt Lizzie concerning Lucy Howard's health; and from Louisa Tarkington to Lucy Howard. Also includes correspondence of Elizabeth Emmons and Mary Talbot, bread-and-butter notes from Cornelia Cheston, and an I.O.U. from Virginia Vaughan for $85.

12,514. Hudson Family
Papers. 1659-1862. 7 boxes and 4 vols.
Open. Unpublished guide.
The New York Public Library, Manuscripts and Archives.
Letters that Anna (Rogers) Hunter, a resident of Halifax, wrote to her brother John Rogers regarding family, friends, and visits with mutual acquaintances; that Anna (Rogers) [Mrs. Henry, Sr.] Hudson wrote to her sister regarding her son's smallpox, having the President as a neighbor, a yellow fever epidemic in New York, some dress goods that were available in New York, and an apology for the behavior of Nancy Balch at a family gathering; that Louise C. [Mrs. Henry, Jr.] Hudson wrote to her mother-in-law Anna Hudson concerning general family matters and Hudson estate monies; that Anna Hudson wrote to her mother Mary [Mrs. John, Jr.] Rogers about family illnesses and a young woman who came to stay and "treats me ill"; that Mary Rogers wrote to her mother Mary Rogers, some of which concern Mrs. Hudson's having "putrid fever"; and that Hannah Hudson, wife of John Rogers Hudson (1784-?), wrote thanking her sister for clothes and about Lucy E.'s sickness and the weather. Also includes correspondence between John Rogers and his sister Mary Rogers regarding the difficulty of finding a house that would suit his wife and items sent by ship, which were thankfully received.

12,515. Hunt, Mary Hannah (Hanchett)
Papers. 1890-1918. 8 boxes.
Open. No guide.
The New York Public Library, Manuscripts and Archives.
Correspondence of [Mrs. Leander B.] Hunt (1830-1906), who was an educator and temperance reformer in Massachusetts, dates from the period of her service as superintendent of the department of scientific temperance instruction of the National and International WCTU and editor of *The School Physiology Journal.* Also includes correspondence of the Scientific Temperance Federation of Boston, which continued Hunt's work in collecting and supplying scientific facts about the nature and effects of alcoholic drinks and other narcotics and in editing the physiology journal under the title *Scientific Temperance Journal.*

12,516. Ingersoll and Farrell Family
Papers. 1878-1940. 3 boxes.
Open. No guide.
The New York Public Library, Manuscripts and Archives.
Correspondence and drafts of speeches and newspaper articles of Robert Green Ingersoll (1833-99), a lawyer and lecturer; social and family correspondence of the children and female members of the Ingersoll and Farrell families; and correspondence of Mrs. Clinton P. Farrell, president of the Vivisection Investigation League of New York, dealing with efforts to abolish vivisection and with movements for humane treatment of animals and for combating enforced inoculation of children, soldiers, and others.

12,517. Inter-Municipal Research Committee
Records. Ca. 1906. 150-page item.
Open. No guide.
The New York Public Library, Manuscripts and Archives.
Confidential report on the conditions of immigrants after arrival in the US, including suggestions for their protection. The Committee began investigations of social conditions in 1906. Some material was gathered by the Department of Commerce and Labor, and later the Committee worked in cooperation with the National Civic Federation.

12,518. International Committee for Political Prisoners
Records. 1923-42. 7 boxes.
Open. Unpublished guide.
The New York Public Library, Manuscripts and Archives.
Minutes of meetings of the executive committee, correspondence of Roger Baldwin as chairman, reports, membership lists, press releases, and printed material of the Committee, which was concerned with the conditions and treatment of political prisoners around the world, especially in Canada, China, France, India, and the Soviet Union. Includes correspondence with Jane Addams and Emma Goldman concerning prisoners in the Soviet Union, the Women's International League for Peace and Freedom concerning prisoners in Cuba and Switzerland, and the Women's International Matteotti Committee concerning Matteotti in Italy.

12,519. Jackson, Helen Maria (Fiske) Hunt
Papers. Nd. 2 folders.
Open. No guide.
The New York Public Library, Manuscripts and Archives.
[Mrs. William Sharpless] Jackson (1830-85), a writer who was primarily interested in Indians in the West, was the author of *Ramona.* Incomplete manuscript of her unpublished novel "Elspeth Dynor"; clippings, primarily of book reviews from *The New York Times* concerning a biographical work about Jackson; and sales catalogs, including some of her works and work in which she was interested.

12,520. Jacob A. Riis Neighborhood Settlement
Records. 1898-1962. 11 boxes, 26 vols., and 1 package.
Open. Unpublished guide.
The New York Public Library, Manuscripts and Archives.
Minutes and reports of the board of managers and the executive committee, annual reports, and correspondence of headworkers Florence Clendenning, Helen H. Jessup, Margaret Gibson, Helene Nelson, and Charlotte Waterbury with benefactors, volunteer workers, staff members, officials of charitable organizations, and others. The settlement house was founded in 1890 in New York City by The King's Daughters, an Episcopal church women's group, and by Jacob Riis. After Riis's death, the house was run by his wife Mary A. Phillips Riis (1877-1967), a social worker and financier, and later by his son Roger William Riis (1895-1953), an author. Includes correspondence of Mary Riis, who later became honorary chairman of Riis House.

12,521. Jarvis, Anna
Papers. 1929. 4 items.
Open. No guide.
The New York Public Library, Manuscripts and Archives.
Papers of Jarvis (1864-1948), owner and director of the Mother's Day International Association, consist of a clipping relating to Jarvis, a program from a pageant for famous women of the US at Mackinac Island in 1929, a Mother's Day button, and material relating to acting New York governor H. H. Lehman's proclamation making May 12, 1929, Mother's Day.

12,522. Jay, John
Papers. 1793-1826. Ca. 12 items.
Open. No guide.
The New York Public Library, Manuscripts and Archives.
Correspondence of Jay (1745-1829), first chief justice of the US Supreme Court and a governor of New York, includes letters to his mother and his aunt.

12,523. Jeannette Rankin Brigade
Records. 1967-68. 2 vols. and 1 box.
Open. No guide.
The New York Public Library, Manuscripts and Archives.
Minutes, reports, correspondence, press releases and other papers of the Brigade, a peace organization, relate to the Woman's March on Washington in 1968 to end the Vietnam War. Includes papers of the National Women's Emergency Coalition, which succeeded the Brigade, and clippings about Jeannette Rankin.

12,524. Johnson, Helen Louise (Kendrick)
Papers. 1844-1917. 8 boxes.
Open. Box list.
The New York Public Library, Manuscripts and Archives.
[Mrs. Rossiter] Johnson (1844-1917) was an author, editor, and lecturer who lived in New York City and Amagansett, NY. Letters to her daughter Florence Kendrick Johnson, aunt Georgia (Avery) Kendrick, sister Ann (Kendrick) Benedict, and sister Caroline (Kendrick) Cooper. Also includes personal accounts and royalty statements, 1871-1916; announcements of meetings, 1886-1902, and other records of the Meridian, which she founded in 1886 to discuss social and literary topics; discussion papers about literary matters; and records relating to the Guidon Club, the National League for Civic Education of Women, the National League for Opposing Woman Suffrage, the National Society for Maintaining American Institutions, and the New York State Association Opposed to Women's Suffrage. Her works include the "Roddy Books" and the "Nutshell Series."

12,525. Johnson, Rossiter
Papers. 1881-1929. 9 boxes.
Open. Box list.
The New York Public Library, Manuscripts and Archives.
Correspondence of Johnson (1840-1931), an author, editor, and lecturer who lived in New York City and Amagansett, NY, includes letters to his wife Helen Louise (Kendrick) Johnson (1844-1917); to his daughter Florence Kendrick Johnson during the time she was a student; to his sister and brother-in-law Eva (Johnson) O'Connor and Joseph O'Connor; to Georgia (Avery) Kendrick, lady principal of Vassar College; to Marguerite Merington concerning a proposed dramatization of *Phaeton Rogers;* and to Dora Knowlton Ranoue, Elizabeth Akers Allen, and Mary Virginia Terhune. Also included are records concerning the Guidon Club, the Man-Suffrage Association Opposed to Political Suffrage for Women, and the National Association Opposed to Woman Suffrage.

12,526. Jones, Ada Alice
Papers. 1881-1939. 9 boxes.
Open. No guide.
The New York Public Library, Manuscripts and Archives.
Correspondence, diaries, journals from 1900 and 1924 to 1939 of Jones (1874-1943), a librarian and teacher at the New York State Library School. She attended Wellesley College from 1878 to 1882 and worked as a cataloger at Wellesley. Jones later became assistant librarian for the YWCA in New York City and then a cataloger for Columbia University. She was a librarian for the World's Columbian Exposition in Chicago in 1893, a cataloging instructor at the New York Library School from 1889 to 1911, and secretary of the Library School's faculty from 1891 to 1924. A member of the American Library Association and the New York Library Association, Jones also was president of the New York Library School Association from 1898 to 1899.

12,527. Jones, George
Papers. 1837-78. 1 box.
Open. No guide.
The New York Public Library, Manuscripts and Archives.
Letters to Jones (?-1878), an actor and lecturer also known as "Count Joannes," from his wife Eliza Jones concerning his next performance and her improving health; from his daughter Emma Bouney upon the death of her grandfather, his father; and from his sister Abbie Maria Jones. In one of her letters Abbie Jones offers to lend George Jones her legacy so that he might pursue his career. Also includes a letter of introduction that a Mrs. Walker of Ithaca, NY, wrote for him, thank-you letters from a Mrs. Morrison and Lizzie Foye, and a letter from [Mrs.] Susan V. Mears concerning a lecture she attended.

12,528. Jones, Mrs. W. G.
Papers. 1841-96. 2 vols.
Open. No guide.
The New York Public Library, Manuscripts and Archives.
Papers of Julia A. Wagstaff Jones include a diary for 1859, an autobiography for 1875, and notes primarily relating to drama and the stage.

12,529. Jordan, Elizabeth Garver
Papers. 1891-1946. 2 boxes and 1 vol.
Open. No guide.
The New York Public Library, Manuscripts and Archives.
Correspondence of Jordan (1865-1947), an author, editor, journalist, playwright, and woman suffrage leader, includes letters from Susan B. Anthony, Gertrude Atherton, John Kendrick Bangs, Alice Brown, Frances (Hodgson) Burnett, Samuel L. Clemens, Margaret Deland, Julia Ward Howe, Henry James, Kate Douglas Wiggin Riggs, Effie Shannon, Anna Howard Shaw, Otis Skinner, Henry Van Dyke, Elizabeth S. P. Ward, Ella Wheeler Wilcox, and Mary E. Wilkins. Also includes a typescript of *The Sturdy Oak,* a novel about American politics written by 14 authors and edited by Jordan.

12,530. Kane, Whitford
Papers. 1913-15. 1 box.
Open. Unpublished guide.
The New York Public Library, Manuscripts and Archives.
Correspondence of Kane (1882-), an actor, with American, English, and Irish theater and literary figures, including Katharine Hepburn.

12,531. Katz, Gertrude Price
Papers. Nd. 2 binders.
Open. No guide.
The New York Public Library, Manuscripts and Archives.
Genealogical papers collected and edited by [Mrs. Alexander J.] Katz relate to the Mourne family and the allied Blair, Dickey, James, Jones, McKinney, Mays, Nickolls, Pugh, Scott, Smith, and Thomas families.

12,532. Katz, Mr. and Mrs. Alexander J.
Papers. 1962-71. 9 folders.
Open. No guide.
The New York Public Library, Manuscripts and Archives.
Correspondence, notes, and other papers compiled by the Katzes relate to a variety of subjects, including Cuban prisoners of war, the death of Martin Luther King, Jr., genealogical information on southern families, the northern Bourne family, the DAR, and the National Council on the Arts. Includes letters from [Mrs.] F. Antoinette Cox, a resident of Northampton, MA; [Miss] Virginia Quisinberry, of Danville, KY; and [Mrs.] Linnie H. Bourne. Also includes applications to the National Society of the DAR from Willa Mae Dill Moore, a resident of Kansas City, MO; Bertha Bourne, of Franklin, TN; Ruby Wilson Eskew, of Winstown, KY; and Gladys Elizabeth Moller, of Wellington, MO.

12,533. Kaufman, Bel
Papers. Nd. 2 cartons.
Open. Unpublished guide.
The New York Public Library, Manuscripts and Archives.
Born in Berlin, [Miss] Kaufman was an author and a teacher in New York City. Correspondence, a typescript, working notes, galley and page proofs, clippings, source material, and other papers relate to her book *Up the Down Staircase* (1964).

12,534. Kelley, Nicholas
Papers. 1870-1967. 67 boxes and 5 packages.
Open. Unpublished guide.
The New York Public Library, Manuscripts and Archives.
Papers of Kelley (1885-1965), a New York City lawyer, and of his mother Florence Kelley (1859-1932), a social worker. Includes letters she wrote to colleagues, among them Jane Addams, Grace Abbott, Emily G. Balch, Louis D. Brandeis, Carrie C. Catt, Friedrich Engles, Felix Frankfurter, Alice Hamilton, Julia Clifford Lathrop, Lola M. Lloyd, and Lillian Wald. Also includes a few of her writings and other papers.

12,535. Kester, Paul
Papers. 1880-1933. 28 ft.
Open. No guide.
The New York Public Library, Manuscripts and Archives.
Correspondence, literary manuscripts, and personal papers of Kester (1870-1933); his brother Vaughan Kester (1869-1911), a journalist and novelist; and their mother Harriet Watkins Kester (?-1926). The papers concern their work as dramatists and authors, their relations with actors and actresses, and their homes in New York, England, Canada, and Virginia. Correspondents include Margaret Anglin, Minnie Maddern Fiske, Fanny Janauschek, and Julia Marlowe. Also includes papers relating to Edith Louisa Cavell and to gypsies.

12,536. Kippen, Manart
Papers. 1886-1947. 1 box.
Open. No guide.
The New York Public Library, Manuscripts and Archives.
Correspondence of Kippen (1892-1947), an actor, with Pauline Lord, Julia Marlowe, Florence Stewart, and others. Also includes papers of Minna Eveline Smith.

12,537. Knopf, Alfred A.
Papers. 1919-51. 3 boxes.
Open. Unpublished guide.
The New York Public Library, Manuscripts and Archives.
Correspondence of Knopf (1892-), a publisher, relates to literary matters. Authors Katharine Anthony, Marjorie Flack [Mrs. William Rose] Benét, Margaret [Mrs. Morris L.] Ernst, Zona Gale, Helen Hedrick, and May Merrill Miller are among his correspondents.

12,538. Knox, Henry
Papers. 1719-1835. 55 vols.
Open. No guide.
The New York Public Library, Manuscripts and Archives.
Papers of Knox (1750-1806), an officer and secretary of war, include papers of his wife Lucy (Flucker) Knox (?-1824), daughter of Thomas Flucker, who was royal secretary of Boston Province. The collection, which is also available on microfilm, also contains Flucker family papers.

12,539. Langtry, Lillie
Papers. 1882-1901. 59 items.
Open. No guide.
The New York Public Library, Manuscripts and Archives.
Letters that Langtry (1853-1929), an actress, wrote from London, Paris, the provinces, and America to Clement Scott, a dramatic critic, asking for advice on various theatrical ventures, discussing plays in which she was appearing or intended to appear, and mentioning such actors as the Bancrofts, Sarah Bernhardt, Arthur Bouchier, and Ellen Terry.

12,540. Langworthy, Isaac Pendleton
Papers. 1829-89. 7 boxes.
Open. Unpublished guide.
The New York Public Library, Manuscripts and Archives.
Langworthy was a Congregational clergyman in Chelsea, MA. Includes his correspondence, accounts, sermons, and other papers; correspondence of his wife Sarah (Williams) Langworthy, a daughter of Cyrus Williams, including letters she received while she was a student at the female academy in Andover, MA; and a journal for 1839 of her sister Martha (Williams) Sherman, a missionary in the Near East.

12,541. Lay, Julia Anna Hartness
Papers. 1851-78. 3 vols.
Open. No guide.
The New York Public Library, Manuscripts and Archives.
Diaries that Lay (1819-78) kept in New York City contain discussions of family matters, her church, sermons she heard, weather conditions, social activities, concerts, lectures, vacations to Albany, NY, and elsewhere, the laying of the Atlantic cable, Civil War incidents, and other current events. Also includes family memorabilia.

12,542. Le Roy
Papers. 1815-56. 3 in.
Open. No guide.
The New York Public Library, Manuscripts and Archives.
Correspondence and financial and legal papers of the Le Roy family, who were landowners in Genessee County, NY, Michigan, Ohio, and Pennsylvania. Includes an item related to the payment of Caroline Le Roy Webster's $5,000 dowry to her husband Daniel Webster (1797-1885), whom she married in 1827. Also contains correspondence and other papers removed from *Mr. W. and I.* (1942), a diary Caroline Webster kept during a trip to Europe in 1839, which was published by Ives Washburn.

12,543. Lea, Anna M.
Papers. 1875-78. 1 vol.
Open. No guide.
The New York Public Library, Manuscripts and Archives.
Letters from [Miss] Lea (1844-1930), a painter, to J. E. Gawthorne, probably a resident of Ireland, relate to his purchase of her painting "St. Cecilia" from the Royal Academy in 1875. Also includes clippings and notes concerning the painting and a review of two volumes Lea wrote about her late husband Henry Merritt, an English painter.

12,544. Levy, Florence Nightingale
Papers. 1890-1947. 2 boxes.
Open. No guide.
The New York Public Library, Manuscripts and Archives.
Correspondence, manuscripts, radio scripts, magazine articles, and other writings of [Mrs.] Levy (1870-1947), an art editor and educator who lived in New York City. Also includes papers of the Federated Council of Art Education, for which Levy served as supervisor.

12,545. Lewis, Margaret Lynn
Papers. Nd. 1 vol.
Open. No guide.
The New York Public Library, Manuscripts and Archives.
Diary in which Lewis describes her life in Loch Lynn, Scotland, and later in Augusta County, VA, after she came to America with her husband John Lewis in 1730. She tells about pioneer life, building a home in the wilderness, developing thousands of acres of farm land, social and religious life, building the town of Staunton, VA, troubles with the Indians, and the capture of her daughter by Indians and her detention in a "palace under the earth," probably Lurey Caverns.

12,546. Libbey, Laura Jean
Papers. 1892-1903. 6 vols.
Open. No guide.
The New York Public Library, Manuscripts and Archives.
Diaries that Libbey (1862-1924), an author, kept during tours through Egypt, Europe, the West Indies, and Bermuda.

12,547. Lion, Oscar
Papers. 1914-55. 3 boxes.
Open. No guide.
The New York Public Library, Manuscripts and Archives.
Correspondence of Lion, a businessman in New York City, with [Mrs.] Anne (Montgomerie) Traubel, a resident of Germantown, PA, relates to personal matters, their interest in Walt Whitman, and Traubel's work as an advertising consultant to the Lion Rubber Company.

12,548. Livingston, Philip, and Livingston, Peter Van Brugh
Papers. 1541-1859. 3 vols.
Open. No guide.
The New York Public Library, Manuscripts and Archives.
Correspondence of Peter Livingston with [Mrs.] Harriet Houston, his fiancée and later his wife. Peter Livingston was the son of Philip Livingston, a New York City merchant.

12,549. Lockhart, Dorothy
Papers. 1930s-50s. 3 boxes.
Open. Unpublished guide.
The New York Public Library, Manuscripts and Archives.
Correspondence of [Miss] Lockhart, a theatrical producer, with such theater and literary figures as Norman Bel Geddes, Annie Russell, Gilbert Seldes, and Oswald Yorke. The letters relate to Lockhart's work at Rollins College, FL, and her association with the Annie Russell Theatre and the Town Hall Series.

12,550. Lovell Family
Papers. 1834-61. 11 items.
Open. No guide.
The New York Public Library, Manuscripts and Archives.
Correspondence of Martha B. Lovell, a schoolteacher in Fall River, MA, with her sister Laura Lovell and their friends and letters to other members of the Lovell family.

12,551. Low, Josiah Orne
Papers. 1837-84. 58 items.
Open. No guide.
The New York Public Library, Manuscripts and Archives.
Letters to Low (1821-95), a merchant in Brooklyn, NY, from his sister Harriet [Mrs. John] Hillard, who was in London; his sister Sarah; Maria H. Daniels, in Manila; and from a cousin Margaret Huntington, in Charleston, SC.

12,552. McBlair Family
Papers. 1793-1874. 12 folders.
Open. No guide.
The New York Public Library, Manuscripts and Archives.
Correspondence and other papers of this Maryland family, including Captain Charles H. McBlair, a US Confederate Naval officer; his wife Fanny (Duncan) McBlair; her mother Margaret S. Duncan, a resident of Carlisle, PA, and Baltimore;

his brother Thomas McBlair (?-1857), a purser in the US Navy; and Alexander McDonald, a merchant in Baltimore. Included in Fanny McBlair's correspondence are letters from friends, who wrote while traveling through Europe in 1867, and a letter from Lizzie Avery Meriweather on the event of the death of McBlair's nephew.

12,553. McCormick, Anne (O'Hare)
Papers. 1936-54. 16 boxes.
Open. Unpublished guides.
The New York Public Library, Manuscripts and Archives.
An editor and journalist born in Yorkshire, England, McCormick (1882-1954) was the first woman to win the Pulitzer Prize. Correspondence, lectures, articles, dispatches, and editorials, columns, and other contributions to *The New York Times.* Correspondents include theater critic Brooks Atkinson; M. L. G. Balfour; Franklin Roosevelt's business advisor Bernard Baruch; economist and advisor to Franklin Roosevelt, A. A. Berle; author Pearl Buck; the president of Columbia University, Nicholas Murray Butler; Secretary of State John Foster Dulles; and President Herbert Hoover. Correspondence pertains to such subjects as postwar Europe, Germany, France, Greece, Russia, Ireland, and Italy. McCormick began doing free-lance work for *The New York Times* in 1921, and in 1936 she became a member of the editorial staff of *The Times.* She won the Pulitzer Prize in 1937. During 1944 she was a war correspondent, and in 1946 she was the US delegate to the UNESCO conference.

12,554. McDonald, Elizabeth DeHart Bleecker
Papers. 1799-1806. 218-page vol.
Open. No guide.
The New York Public Library, Manuscripts and Archives.
Diary of [Mrs. Alexander] McDonald, a resident of New York, contains descriptions of social activities, current events, births, marriages, deaths, launchings of warships, fires, the Burr and Hamilton duel and other duels, the annual flu epidemic, business failures, the laying of the cornerstone of city hall, and visits to Bedford, NY. She frequently mentions distinguished residents.

12,555. Mackay, Annie A.
Papers. 1883-90. 1 vol.
Open. No guide.
The New York Public Library, Manuscripts and Archives.
Commonplace book of Mackay, a resident of Bazile Mills, NE, contains reflections on music, religion, character, her mother, and on her reading of national and racial tracts.

12,556. McKelway, St. Clair
Papers. 1863-1948. 19 boxes and 4 packages.
Open. Box list.
The New York Public Library, Manuscripts and Archives.
Correspondence, speeches, editorials, book reviews, and other papers of McKelway (1845-1915), editor of the Albany *Argus* and then the *Brooklyn Eagle* and chancellor of the State University of New York. Includes correspondence of his wife Virginia Brooks Thompson McKelway and his niece Flora Hale Foster, letters to them from Minnie Maddern Fiske, letters to Flora Foster concerning the papers of St. Clair McKelway, and a photographic portrait of St. Clair and Virginia McKelway.

12,557. Major, Clare Tree
Papers. 1912-54. 3 boxes and 20 vols.
Open. No guide.
The New York Public Library, Manuscripts and Archives.
Major (1880-1954), the founder and director of the Children's Theatre, was married to John D. Kenderdine. Correspondence; diaries she kept during her trips to England in 1934 and in 1949 and her trip to California in 1938; bylaws and minutes of the National Threshold Theatre Association from 1925 to 1927; financial records from 1921 to 1943, including expenses for costumes, scenery, programs, publicity, royalties, and salaries; and a registry of students enrolled in training classes.

12,558. Malverne, Gladys
Papers. Nd. 1 package.
Open. No guide,
The New York Public Library, Manuscripts and Archives.
Typescripts of fictional and biographical writings.

12,559. Mansfield, Richard
Papers. 1888-1940. 13 boxes.
Open. Box list.
The New York Public Library, Manuscripts and Archives.
Correspondence and other papers of Mansfield (1854-1907) and his family, who were actors and performers. Includes letters from Mansfield to his family and friends; correspondence of his wife Beatrice (Cameron) Mansfield with her family and people prominent in the theater, including Booth Tarkington, Clyde Fitch, Walter Hampden, and William Winter; papers relating to Beatrice Mansfield's work in Syria and Mesopotamia with the American Committee for Relief in the Near East; scattered diaries; and her writings. The Mansfields performed works by Gilbert and Sullivan, Ibsen, Shaw, Shakespeare, and Molière.

12,560. Mars, Carmelia
Papers. Nd. No size given.
Open. No guide.
The New York Public Library, Manuscripts and Archives.
Typescripts of "Michal, the Romance of a King's Daughter" and "Herschella."

12,561. Marshall, Margaret
Papers. 1895-99. 1 slipcase.
Open. No guide.
The New York Public Library, Manuscripts and Archives.
Testimonials from the Fourth Presbyterian Church, the Grace Methodist Church, and the West End Presbyterian Church in New York City to Marshall after she presented these churches with memorials to her parents Robert and Ann Marshall.

12,562. Mencken
Papers. Nd. 1 item.
Open. No guide.
The New York Public Library, Manuscripts and Archives.
Letter to H. L. Mencken from Mrs. Paul Armstrong, which accompanied a typescript of the play *The Vanity of Man* by Paul Armstrong, and a contribution of her own, which she wished to submit to *Smart Set.*

12,563. Meredith, Reese
Papers. 1722-76. 13 items.
Open. No guide.
The New York Public Library, Manuscripts and Archives.
Papers of Meredith (1708-99), a merchant in Philadelphia, contain accounts of Martha Carpenter, who later became his wife; of her sister Hannah Carpenter, including one with William Fishbourn for wharfage and storage; Reese's 1722 indenture of apprenticeship; a bond; a deed poll for lands in Northampton, Northumberland, and Westmoreland counties in Pennsylvania; a statement of accounts; and papers relating to the settlement of Meredith's estate.

12,564. Merington, Marguerite
Papers. 1890s-1940. 6 boxes and 1 package.
Open. No guide.
The New York Public Library, Manuscripts and Archives.
Correspondence, drafts of writings on General George Custer, short stories, collected essays, and dramatic works of Merington (1861?-1951), an author.

12,565. Meyer, Gladys Eleanor
Papers. Nd. 2 items.
Open. No guide.
The New York Public Library, Manuscripts and Archives.
Original and corrected typescripts of Meyer's *The Magic Circle.*

12,566. Might-Have-Been-Letters
Papers. 1907. 199-page vol.
Open. No guide.
The New York Public Library, Manuscripts and Archives.
Diary thought to have been written by an American woman and her husband, who describe to a cousin a brief journey they made to the markets of the Netherlands.

12,567. Mitchel, Jane Verner
Papers. 1851-55. 1 vol.
Open. No guide.
The New York Public Library, Manuscripts and Archives.
Letters that Mitchel, who was married to a Fenian leader John Mitchel (1815-75), wrote to Mary Thompson in Ireland about the life of the Mitchel family as political prisoners in Van Diemens Land (Tasmania) and their escape to and life in the US.

12,568. Mitchell, Margaret "Maggie" Julia
Papers. 1854-90. 30 items.
Open. No guide.
The New York Public Library, Manuscripts and Archives.
Letters to actress Mitchell (1832-1918) and her husband and manager Henry T. Paddock and other papers.

12,569. Montgomery, Janet (Livingston), and Gates, Horatio
Papers. Ca. 1775-99. 7 items.
Open. No guide.
The New York Public Library, Manuscripts and Archives.
Correspondence between [Mrs. Richard] Montgomery (1743-1828) and Horatio Gates, including her refusal of Gates's proposal of marriage. Also includes a ca. 1775 letter from Richard Montgomery to Janet Montgomery.

12,570. Moore, Anne Carroll
Papers. 1900-60. 6 boxes.
Open. No guide.
The New York Public Library, Manuscripts and Archives.
[Miss] Moore (1871-1961) was a librarian and author of children's books. Letters from authors, illustrators, publishers, and friends relate to Moore's books, in particular *The Art of Beatrix Potter* (1955) and *Nicholas and the Golden Goose* (1932). Correspondents include Rhoda Brooks Balfour, Margery Bianco, L. Leslie Brooke, Sybil D. Brooke, James H. Daugherty, Walter De La Mare, Eleanor Farjeon, Dorothy Canfield Fisher, Beatrix Potter, and Carl Sandburg. Moore was superintendent of work with children in the New York Public Library; she received the Constance Lindsay Skinner gold medal at the first annual Women's National Book Association and the Booksellers League of New York for outstanding work in improving children's literature. She was an 1896 graduate of the Pratt Institute School of Library Science, and as library director of the children's department at Pratt, she made storytelling part of the library schedule.

12,571. Morgan, Angela
Papers. 1940s-50s. 1 vol. and 25 cartons.
Open. Carton list.
The New York Public Library, Manuscripts and Archives.
[Miss] Morgan (?-1957) was a poet. Includes correspondence; manuscripts and typescripts of poems, short stories, and articles; addresses and lectures; notes and notebooks; financial and publicity papers; photos; recording discs of Morgan's voice; and a scrapbook of memorabilia.

12,572. The Nation
Records. 1873-1906. 5 vols. and 1 box.
Open. No guide.
The New York Public Library, Manuscripts and Archives.
Ledgers, correspondence, lists of contributors, records of books sent for review, lists of articles, and other papers of *The Nation,* which was founded in 1865 by Wendell Phillips Garrison. Letters Garrison received as literary editor include those from Georgina G. Buckler, Alice Hayes, newspaper correspondent Lucy Hamilton Hooper, Helen M. Judd, relatives of Jessie White Mario, Clara B. Martin, author Lady Blanche Murphy, Pauline B. de Ruiz, and Lina Vickers. Their letters primarily concern employment with the magazine or articles the women had written or wished to write.

12,573. National American Woman Suffrage Association
Records. 1896-1922. 8 boxes.
Open. Unpublished guide.
The New York Public Library, Manuscripts and Archives.
Letters from members of Congress to Ellen Powell Thompson and Susan Brownell Anthony, of the Association, regarding woman suffrage; correspondence and other papers regarding state ratification of the suffrage amendment and other aspects of woman suffrage, international war relief, and national defense activities of women during WWI; press releases; and clippings. The National and American Woman Suffrage Associations were joined in 1890.

12,574. National Civic Federation
Records. 1876-1948. 219 boxes.
Open. Unpublished guide.
The New York Public Library, Manuscripts and Archives.
Minutes, financial records, subject files, and correspondence of various departments of the Federation, which was founded in 1900 by Ralph M. Easley (1856-1939). Includes material on annual, executive council, and executive committee meetings, as well as on the American Civic Alliance, the Chicago Civic Federation, communism and subversion, employee welfare, child care during wartime, child labor, nurseries, public health and education, stewardesses on steamships, textile industry, welfare work and workers, and woman suffrage. Also includes papers of Ralph Easley and his wife Gertrude Brackenridge Beeks Easley (1867-1950). Gertrude Easley, a sociologist, was successively president of the National Association of Business Women, head of the sociology department at McCormick Harvesting Machine Co., and director of the welfare department of the National Civic Federation.

12,575. National Woman's Party
Records. 1919-39. 75 items and 150 pp.
Open. No guide.
The New York Public Library, Manuscripts and Archives.
Correspondence and clippings of the campaign Mabel R. [Mrs. Frank] Putnam directed for adoption of the 1921 Wisconsin law, "The First Bill of Rights for Women," as well as correspondence and clippings relating to Putnam's work in the National Woman's Party to extend the law nationally. Includes letters from Mrs. O. H. P. Belmont, Governor John G. Blaine, Zona Gale, Senators I. Lenroot and R. M. La Follette, and Alice Paul.

12,576. New York Prison Association
Records. 1845-52. 2 vols.
Open. No guide.
The New York Public Library, Manuscripts and Archives.
Records Isaac T. Hopper (1771-1852), a philanthropist and abolitionist, kept of the Association, including records of casework with male and female discharged prisoners, gifts of money and books, the Association's home for females, and financial and other matters. Includes some correspondence.

12,577. New York School of Applied Design for Women
Records. 1892-1939. 1 folder.
Open. No guide.
The New York Public Library, Manuscripts and Archives.
Letters to [Mrs.] Ellen Dunlap Hopkins (1858-1939), founder of the School, and to her assistant and cousin [Miss] Ellen Pond concern the School and Hopkins's part in it. Also includes clippings and other papers. An author and philanthropist, Hopkins received the Michael Friedsam Gold Medal for outstanding contribution to art in industry in 1936; she was the first woman to receive the prize.

12,578. Nicholson and Burwell
Papers. 1698-1704. 1 vol.
Open. No guide.
The New York Public Library, Manuscripts and Archives.
Photostats of correspondence and memoranda between Francis Nicholson (1655-1728), governor of Virginia; Colonel Lewis Burwell (?-1710); his daughter Lucy Burwell (1683-1716); and others concern Nicholson's love for Lucy Burwell. The original papers are housed in Colonial Williamsburg in Virginia.

12,579. Nillson, Carlotta
Papers. 1900-51. 2 boxes.
Open. No guide.
The New York Public Library, Manuscripts and Archives.
Correspondence of Nillson, an actress, relates to her activities in the theater and to business matters. Also includes notes for a play, notes on her reading, and a receipted bill.

12,580. Olcott, Euphemia M.
Papers. 1850-1921. 6 vols. and 8 items.
Open. No guide.
The New York Public Library, Manuscripts and Archives.
Papers of Olcott include correspondence; a diary of a trip to Europe, 1902-03; school notebooks and compositions; and commonplace books she kept in New York City, 1850-1921. Olcott was probably the daughter of John Nathaniel Olcott (?-1887) and Euphemia Helen (Knox) Olcott (?-1909), who lived in New York City.

12,581. Parsons, Anna Reed
Papers. 1930-32. 143 items.
Open. No guide.
The New York Public Library, Manuscripts and Archives.
Correspondence of [Mrs. William B.] Parsons (18??-1958) relates to her activities as chairman of the library committee of the Monmouth County Historical Association.

12,582. Paterson, Isabel (Bowler)
Papers. 1924-60. Ca. 65 items.
Open. No guide.
The New York Public Library, Manuscripts and Archives.
Letters that Paterson (1886-1961), an author and columnist who lived in New York City, wrote while she was a member of the staff of the New York *Herald Tribune* to her friend Lillian Fischer, who was a fashion model and Paris editor of *Harper's Bazaar* and who was married to Frank Farley. In her letters Paterson comments on literary personalities and her social life in New York.

12,583. Payne, John Howard
Papers. Ca. 1813-18. 1 box.
Open. No guide.
The New York Public Library, Manuscripts and Archives.
Summary of events and circumstances of the friendship of Payne (1791-1852) with Emilia Von Harten as well as copies he made of their letters.

12,584. Peace Now Movement
Records. 1936-44. 6 boxes.
Open. No guide.
The New York Public Library, Manuscripts and Archives.
Accounts, correspondence, reports, and other records of the national organization, located in New York City, which was devoted to ending WWII. Correspondents include Dorothy M. Hutchinson.

12,585. Peck and Colby Family
Papers. 1840-1904. 1 folder.
Open. No guide.
The New York Public Library, Manuscripts and Archives.
Letters Hannah M. Colby and her relatives wrote from Lima, Albany, and Rochester, NY; Janesville, WI; and Bainbridge, IN. Also includes family papers of Williams Peck and Sibyl Short.

12,586. Peck, Florence C.
Papers. 1898-1903. 4 vols.
Open. No guide.
The New York Public Library, Manuscripts and Archives.
Diaries that Peck, a kindergarten teacher, kept in Rochester, NY, and Boston about her daily life in high school and college and her activities as a kindergarten teacher. Also includes memoranda concerning books she read.

12,587. Peck, Helen Maude (Ames)
Papers. Ca. 1899-1929. 1 folder.
Open. No guide.
The New York Public Library, Manuscripts and Archives.
Papers and memorabilia of Peck, who was a physical culturist in New York City.

12,588. Penfield, E. Z.
Papers. 1851-93. 1 box.
Open. No guide.
The New York Public Library, Manuscripts and Archives.
Correspondence of Penfield, secretary of the Panama Railroad Company, relates to the operations of the Company, political conditions in Panama, and the Panama Canal. Includes a letter to Mrs. Penfield from Anna Howard Shaw.

12,589. Pesotta, Rose
Papers. 1922-65. 45 boxes and 3 packages.
Open. Unpublished guide.
The New York Public Library, Manuscripts and Archives.
[Miss] Pesotta (1896-1965) was a labor union official. Correspondence and other papers concerning her career as an official of the International Ladies' Garment Workers' Union and as an organizer of garment workers in various cities in the US, Canada, and Puerto Rico; family correspondence and papers; correspondence with

Emma Goldman and correspondence, speeches, and lectures relating to Goldman; correspondence with Mollie Steimer Flechine concerning refugees; diaries for 1934 to 1949; speeches and writings, including drafts of Pesotta's books *Bread upon the Waters* (1944) and *Days of Our Lives* (1958); and a biographical sketch of a woman in industry, Susan D. Adams.

12,590. Peters Family
Papers. 1807-11. 16 items.
Open. No guide.
The New York Public Library, Manuscripts and Archives.
Letters that Anna Marie and Harriet Peters, who were in New Orleans, wrote to their father in New York discussing personal matters, social life in New Orleans, traveling conditions, and a slave insurrection.

12,591. Phelps, John Wolcott
Papers. 1833-84. 6 boxes and 48 vols.
Open. No guide.
The New York Public Library, Manuscripts and Archives.
Personal and family correspondence of Phelps (1813-85) includes correspondence of Helen Philips.

12,592. Phillips, Adelaide
Papers. 186?-81. 76 items.
Open. No guide.
The New York Public Library, Manuscripts and Archives.
Letters from [Miss] Phillips (1833-82), an opera singer, are primarily to Emily (Ellsworth) Ford about Phillips's career and travels.

12,593. Pilling, James Constantine
Papers. 1895-97. Ca. 600 items.
Open. No guide.
The New York Public Library, Manuscripts and Archives.
Correspondence of Pilling (1864-95), an ethnologist, includes letters from his wife to Wilberforce Eames, a bibliographer.

12,594. Pitman, Benn
Papers. 1864-1912. 1 folder.
Open. No guide.
The New York Public Library, Manuscripts and Archives.
Correspondence and a clipping of Pitman (1822-1910), originator of the shorthand technique, relate to the trial of [Mrs.] Mary Surratt and others for their alleged complicity in the assassination of President Lincoln.

12,595. Pocahontas Memorial Association
Records. Nd. No size given.
Open. No guide.
The New York Public Library, Manuscripts and Archives.
Records of the incorporation and activities of the Association were collected by the vice-regent at large, Mrs. George Wilson Smith.

12,596. Potter, Maud
Papers. 1882-92. 1 vol.
Open. No guide.
The New York Public Library, Manuscripts and Archives.
Commonplace book in which Potter details her activities in Saratoga Springs, NY.

12,597. Putnam, Mabel R.
Papers. 1919-39. 1 folder.
Open. No guide.
The New York Public Library, Manuscripts and Archives.
Correspondence and clippings of [Mrs. Frank] Putnam, a feminist, relate to a campaign she directed for adoption of a 1921 Wisconsin law, "The First Bill of Rights for Women," and to her work with the National Woman's party to extend the law nationally. Correspondents include Mrs. O. H. P. Belmont, Zona Gale, Alice Paul, and Senator R. M. La Follette.

12,598. Ray Palmer Club
Records. 1892. 1 vol.
Open. No guide.
The New York Public Library, Manuscripts and Archives.
Historic scroll the Club historian [Miss] Charlotte E. Crane wrote. An organization devoted to reading and studying literature, the Club was founded in 1888 in Newark, NJ, to give members the chance to associate with other women, improve themselves, and become aware of the special characteristics of women. Also includes excerpts from members' papers on such topics as music, Greek sculpture, and microbes as well as certificates of membership in the GFWC and the New Jersey State Federation of Women's Clubs.

12,599. Reeve, Sidney Armor
Papers. Nd. 29 pp.
Open. No guide.
The New York Public Library, Manuscripts and Archives.
Biographical sketch of Reeve (1866-1941), an engineer, and a record of [Miss] Charlotte Holmes Crawford's association with him, as well as poems presumably written by Crawford.

12,600. Remsen, Henry, Jr.
Papers. 1730-1846. 6 in.
Open. No guide.
The New York Public Library, Manuscripts and Archives.
Family and business correspondence and other papers of Remsen, a financier in New York City, president of the Manhattan Bank, and private secretary to Thomas Jefferson, relate to family matters, family estates, current events, social gossip and customs, the Manhattan Co., and Highland Turnpike Co. Also includes correspondence from Charles Willson Peale regarding his wife's inheritance.

12,601. Rent Control, New York City
Records. 1945-64. 143 items.
Open. No guide.
The New York Public Library, Manuscripts and Archives.
Correspondence and other related papers of Ira J. Belmont and his wife concern service and rent increases at the Essex House Hotel, Inc., and illustrate practices and problems of rent control in New York City.

12,602. Ripley, Louisa Augusta (Schlossberger)
Papers. Ca. 1873-90. 46 items.
Open. No guide.
The New York Public Library, Manuscripts and Archives,
Letters from Ripley to a Mr. Ford, editor of the *New York Tribune,* and his wife deals primarily with social and business matters but also with her loneliness after the death of her first husband George Ripley, a literary critic for the *New York Tribune.* After his death Ripley married Alphonse Pinède.

12,603. Roach, Emeline
Papers. 1875-77. 1 vol.
Open. No guide.
The New York Public Library, Manuscripts and Archives.
Album of Roach, a resident of Chester, NY, and New York City, contains autographs and verses by her friends in both cities.

12,604. Robinson, Ellie Bond
Papers. 1871-74. 56 pp.
Open. No guide.
The New York Public Library, Manuscripts and Archives.
French notebook and miscellaneous dictées notebook of Robinson, a resident of New York City.

12,605. Rodman and Harvey Family
Papers. 1777-1850. 6 in.
Open. No guide.
The New York Public Library, Manuscripts and Archives.
Correspondence and household and business accounts of Washington Hendrix Rodman (1792-?) and his wife Mary (Harvey) Rodman, who were residents of Brooklyn, NY, and New York City. Includes correspondence with Lucy A. Rodman referring to members of the Whistler family, with Mary Rodman's mother Elizabeth (Mackaness) Harvey, and with relatives in Stonington, CT, Ohio, and Michigan. Also contains correspondence of Elizabeth Harvey with her other children and with her father Thomas Mackaness, a merchant in New York City, while she was at school in England. Correspondence is primarily religious in tone.

12,606. Rogers, Matilda Livingston
Papers. Ca. 1850. 1 vol.
Open. No guide.
The New York Public Library, Manuscripts and Archives.
Notebook consists of a recipe book compiled by Rogers and a French exercise book.

12,607. Ronalds, Mary Lorillard
Papers. 1836-37. 168-page vol.
Open. No guide.
The New York Public Library, Manuscripts and Archives.
Diary kept by Ronalds (?-1840), a resident of New York and the daughter of Thomas A. Ronalds, during a trip through France and Italy with her uncle and aunt Mr. and Mrs. John David Wolfe. She describes the journey by boat from Marseilles to Leghorn and includes notes on the art and architecture of the places listed on their itinerary. She mentions attending the theater and opera, visiting artists' studios, the execution of busts of her uncle and aunt by Thomas Crawford, and seeing the Brinckerhoffs, Morgans, and others at Rome.

12,608. Rose Temperance Society
Records. 1829-36. 1 in.
Open. No guide.
The New York Public Library, Manuscripts and Archives.
Constitution, minutes, and list of members of the Society, which was auxiliary to the Wayne County Temperance Society in New York. Members were predominantly women; the officers were men.

12,609. Rosenthal, Virginia
Papers. 1902. 146-page vol.
Open. No guide.
The New York Public Library, Manuscripts and Archives.
Travel diary in which Rosenthal describes scenery and points of interest in England, France, Italy, Switzerland, Germany, and Holland.

12,610. Row, Arthur William
Papers. Ca. 1945-52. 5 boxes.
Open. No guide.
The New York Public Library, Manuscripts and Archives.
Writings and notebooks of Row (1878-1961), an actor, include his recollections of the theater; essays on John Barrymore, Sarah Bernhardt, actress and producer Katharine Cornell, and Ellen Terry; and a typescript of his work "Sarah the Divine." Also includes personal accounts, photos, clippings, and other papers.

12,611. Ruggles, Charles Herman
Papers. 1821-55. 3 in.
Open. No guide.
The New York Public Library, Manuscripts and Archives.
Papers of Ruggles (1789-1865), a jurist and congressman who lived in Poughkeepsie, NY, and became chief justice of the New York Court of Appeals. Includes correspondence with his sister-in-law Sarah Colden [Mrs. David] Ruggles, Samuel B. Ruggles, and other relatives concerning family, personal, and business matters; Sarah Ruggles's sons; the Washington social and political scene; mulberry trees; and real estate in New York City.

12,612. Russell, Annie
Papers. 1874-1936. 7 boxes.
Open. No guide.
The New York Public Library, Manuscripts and Archives.
[Miss] Russell (1864?-1936) was an actress. Includes correspondence, diaries, writings, notes, poems, notebooks of road tour statistics from 1898 to 1904, address book, and papers concerned with the settlement of her St. Petersburg, FL, estate and with her marriage to and divorce from Oswald Yorke. Primarily correspondence from theater and literary figures concerned with Russell's performances in New York, London, and elsewhere and her work in the 1930s as director of the Annie Russell Theatre at Rollins College, Winter Park, FL. Correspondents include G. B. Shaw and Dorothy Lockhart, an associate in the Annie Russell Theatre. Also includes correspondence of earlier celebrities that Russell collected.

12,613. Sabin, Dorothy Virginia (Forbes)
Papers. Nd. 7 pp.
Open. No guide.
The New York Public Library, Manuscripts and Archives.
Family papers compiled in 1947 by Sabin, who was married to Joseph Percy Sabin.

12,614. Sage, Elizabeth Manning
Papers. 1910. 1 vol.
Open. No guide.
The New York Public Library, Manuscripts and Archives.
Schoolbook of Sage primarily contains history notes.

12,615. Schieffelin, Hannah (Lawrence)
Papers. 1780. 5-page item.
Open. No guide.
The New York Public Library, Manuscripts and Archives.
Letter from Schieffelin to her father John Lawrence, a resident of New York City, concerns a trip she took from Quebec through LaChine, the Cedars, Oswegatchie, and Carleton Island to Fort Niagara. She mentions meeting Molly Brant and several Revolutionary War captains.

12,616. Schroeder, Theodore
Papers. 1846-ca. 1940. 3 boxes.
Open. No guide.
The New York Public Library, Manuscripts and Archives.
Papers relating to Mormonism, including letters to Brigham Young from his wives, were compiled by Schroeder (1864-1953), a lawyer, author, and psychologist.

12,617. Schwimmer and Lloyd
Papers. Nd. 6 trays.
Open. Unpublished guide.
The New York Public Library, Manuscripts and Archives.
Manuscripts, papers, books, and ephemera relate to the careers of Lola Maverick Lloyd (?-1944) and Rosika Schwimmer (1877-1948), who in 1911 married a Mr. Bédy and in 1913 divorced him.

12,618. Sedgwick Family
Papers. 1812-99. 1 box and 2 vols.
Open. No guide.
The New York Public Library, Manuscripts and Archives.
Commonplace book Grace Sedgwick kept and a volume of poetry written by Susan Anne Sedgwick, who was married to Theodore Sedgwick. The Sedgwicks resided in Stockbridge, MA.

12,619. Seitz, Don Carlos
Papers. 1882-1934. 4 boxes and 2 vols.
Open. No guide.
The New York Public Library, Manuscripts and Archives.
Letters to Seitz (1862-1935), an author and journalist living in Brooklyn, NY, relate to his books. Correspondents include editors, publishers, authors, journalists, public officials, political leaders, diplomats, university presidents, clergymen, bankers, feminists, artists, theater producers, explorers, and others.

12,620. Shakers, Union Village, Franklin County, OH
Records. 1821-69. 1 folder.
Open. No guide.
The New York Public Library, Manuscripts and Archives.
Letter of Betsey Blake to "my beloved Eldress Ann" and a list of members of the religious community.

12,621. Shaw Family
Papers. 1862-76. 18 items.
Open. No guide.
The New York Public Library, Manuscripts and Archives.
Papers of the Shaw family include letters from author Lydia Maria Child, who lived in New York City, to Francis G. Shaw and his wife.

12,622. Skinner, Constance Lindsay
Papers. 1899-1939. 34 boxes and 11 vols.
Open. No guide.
The New York Public Library, Manuscripts and Archives.
Correspondence, writings, a scrapbook, and clippings of Constance Skinner (1877-1939), a New York City author. Includes family correspondence and letters from her mother Annie Lindsay Skinner (?-1925), a public school teacher in Vancouver, BC, and from publishers, editors, literary agents, authors, journalists, artists, actresses, theater producers, explorers, university professors, learned societies, librarians, book dealers, and radio broadcasting stations.

12,623. Skinner, Neil McFee
Papers. 1929-44. 2 boxes and 1 package.
Open. No guide.
The New York Public Library, Manuscripts and Archives.
Correspondence and other papers of Skinner, an actor and theater manager, and his wife Edith Warman Skinner relate to the Warf Theatre in Provincetown, MA, the Martha's Vineyard Playhouse in Massachusetts, and family matters.

12,624. Smith, Elizabeth Oakes (Prince)
Papers. 1852-91. 3 boxes and 2 vols.
Open. No guide.
The New York Public Library, Manuscripts and Archives.
Correspondence and a diary of Smith (1806-93), an author, suffragist, and lyceum lecturer in Portland, ME, New York City, and Hollywood, NC.

12,625. Smith Family
Papers. 1769-1907. 2 boxes.
Open. Published guide.
The New York Public Library, Manuscripts and Archives.
Family correspondence and political speeches on peace, temperance, abolition of slavery, women's suffrage, and other topics and printed circular letters. Includes correspondence of Elizabeth (Smith) Miller, philanthropist and reformer Gerrit Smith (1797-1874), and Susan B. Anthony. See *Dictionary Catalog of the Manuscript Division,* vol. 2 (Boston: G. K. Hall and Co., 1967).

12,626. Smith, William
Papers. 1848-93. Ca. 150 items.
Open. No guide.
The New York Public Library, Manuscripts and Archives.
Correspondence of Smith, a master mechanic in Massachusetts, including letters of his wife Caroline Cobb Smith and their children about family and social matters.

12,627. Society of Friends
Records. 1671-1703. 150-page vol.
Open. No guide.
The New York Public Library, Manuscripts and Archives.
Minutes of monthly, quarterly, and yearly meetings of the Friends held at Flushing, NY, which became known respectively as the Flushing meeting, Westbury meeting, and New York meeting. Reputed to be the earliest extant minutes of a Quaker meeting in the US, the volume contains marriage records and a disciplinary document George Fox inscribed, which may have been the earliest dogma issued or adopted.

12,628. Society of Friends, Rhode Island
Records. 1755-1866. Ca. 75 items.
Open. No guide.
The New York Public Library, Manuscripts and Archives.
Extracts from reports of quarterly and monthly meetings of the Friends held at Newport, South Kingston, and Smithfield, RI, and at Dartmouth and other towns in Massachusetts. Includes correspondence of Isaac Lawton of Portsmouth, RI, and Stephen Gould and others of Newport; testimonial biographies of deceased members; and papers relating to Peter Davis and Samuel Fotheringill.

12,629. Sothern and Marlowe
Papers. 1859-1950. No size given.
Open. No guide.
The New York Public Library, Manuscripts and Archives.
Letters that Julia Marlowe Sothern (1866-1950) and her husband Edward H. Sothern, an early 20th-century Shakespearean acting team, exchanged while they were on tour. In their letters they discuss the theater, plans for work, mutual finances, world affairs, her health, and her activities. Also includes correspondence between Julia Sothern and Mary Daly, her lifelong friend and companion, and family papers of Edward Sothern.

12,630. Sothern, Julia Marlowe
Papers. 1934-46. 90 items.
Open. No guide.
The New York Public Library, Manuscripts and Archives.
Correspondence of Sothern (1866-1950), who with her husband Edward H. Sothern made up an early 20th-century Shakespearean acting team. Includes letters to Mr. and Mrs. Robert Davis, which were written from Lausanne, Florence, Paris, Egypt, New York City, and other places in the US, concerning world affairs.

12,631. Sothern, Julia Marlowe, and Sothern, Edward Hugh
Papers. 1924-46. 68 items.
Open. No guide.
The New York Public Library, Manuscripts and Archives.
Letters that Julia Sothern (1866-1950) and her

husband Edward Sothern, an early 20th-century Shakespearean acting team, wrote from Lausanne, Paris, Florence, and various places in New York and Massachusetts to Mr. and Mrs. Lawrence Veiller concerning Julia Sothern's health, their plans for travel, the theater, and world affairs.

12,632. Speranza, Florence (Colgate)
Papers. 1899-1935. 4 boxes and 2 vols.
Open. No guide.
The New York Public Library, Manuscripts and Archives.
Speranza (1873-1951) was an educator and administrator who lived in New York City and Irvington, NY. Diary notes and commonplace books from 1935 containing her impressions of political conditions in Italy and the Ethiopian War; correspondence as a trustee of Barnard College; minutes of meetings, treasurer's reports, correspondence, and other records of the Scuola d'Industrie Italiane, which was organized at Richmond Hill House in New York City; material on Italian immigrants in Texas, a letter from Lillian (Vernon) de Bosis to an Aunt Margaret and an Aunt Katharine; and clippings relating to de Bosis's arrest and trial on the charge of anti-Fascist activities.

12,633. Squire, Ally
Papers. 1815-16. 1 vol.
Open. No guide.
The New York Public Library, Manuscripts and Archives.
Diary that [Mrs. Alvin] Squire (1788-?) began on the occasion of the death of her son Alvin A. Squire (?-1815). A record of her religious life for a year, the book was given to her by her "nearest earthly friend" and was intended for his eye only. She relates her personal standards of conduct, mentions joining the Presbyterian church, and gives her views on Christian unity.

12,634. Stage Women's War Relief
Records. 1918-38. 2 boxes.
Open. No guide.
The New York Public Library, Manuscripts and Archives.
Correspondence, press releases, and publicity material of this organization. Includes letters to the Actor's Fund.

12,635. Stanton, Robert Brewster
Papers. 1846-1909. 1 box.
Open. No guide.
The New York Public Library, Manuscripts and Archives.
Reminiscences that Stanton (1846-1922) wrote on the Stanton, Moore, Garnet, and Stone families include notes about Elizabeth Cady Stanton.

12,636. Stephens, Anna Sophia (Winterbotham)
Papers. 1847-1937. 1 box and 1 vol.
Open. No guide.
The New York Public Library, Manuscripts and Archives.
Letters from Stephens (1813-86), an author, to her daughter concern family matters.

12,637. Sterner, Albert E.
Papers. 1899-1945. 2 folders.
Open. Unpublished guide.
The New York Public Library, Manuscripts and Archives.
Correspondence of Sterner (1863-1946), a painter, etcher, and lithographer, and his wife primarily relates to art and cultural matters. Correspondents include Constance Collier, Elsie Ferguson, Eva LaGallienne, Julia Marlowe, Mary Augusta [Mrs. Humphrey] Ward, and Edith Wharton.

12,638. Storrs, George
Papers. 1814-54. 1 box.
Open. No guide.
The New York Public Library, Manuscripts and Archives.
Correspondence of Storrs (1796-1879), a Methodist clergyman and antislavery agitator, includes letters from his wife Lucinda Storrs.

12,639. Story, William Cumming
Papers. 1867-70. 1 vol.
Open. No guide.
The New York Public Library, Manuscripts and Archives.
Diary in which Story (1851-?), an usher at Crosby's Opera House in Chicago, comments on a women's rights convention held at Library Hall in Chicago on February 23, 1869.

12,640. Stoughton, Mary
Papers. 1878-79. 2 vols.
Open. No guide.
The New York Public Library, Manuscripts and Archives.
Diary of Stoughton, who was married to Edwin Wallace Stoughton, a US minister to Russia, contains descriptions of their travels in Spain, France, and England and the events of their official life at the Russian court in St. Petersburg.

12,641. Taggard and Conkling
Papers. 1924-29?. 8 items.
Open. No guide.
The New York Public Library, Manuscripts and Archives.
Letters from Genevieve Taggard (1894-1948) to [Mrs.] Grace Walcott Hazard Conkling (1878-1958) relate chiefly to Conkling's poetry.

12,642. Taggard, Genevieve
Papers. 1920-48. 8 ft.
Access restricted. Shelf list.
The New York Public Library, Manuscripts and Archives.
Taggard (1894-1948) was an author and teacher. Personal correspondence; correspondence with editors and publishers; letters, notes, drafts, galley proofs, and transcripts of writings by or about the poet Emily Dickinson; miscellaneous manuscripts of Taggard's writings and of others; notes for teaching at Mount Holyoke and Sarah Lawrence College; and phonograph and tape recordings of Taggard's voice. Correspondents include Maxwell Anderson, William Rose Benét, Alexander Calder, Padraic Colum, Max Eastman, Edgar Lee Masters, and Katherine Anne Porter. Taggard wrote *The Life and Mind of Emily Dickinson* (1930) and founded *The Measure, A Journal of Verse.* Besides teaching at Mount Holyoke and Sarah Lawrence College, she taught at Bennington College.

12,643. Taylor, John
Papers. 1805-13. 49 items.
Open. No guide.
The New York Public Library, Manuscripts and Archives.
Accounts of Ann DeLancey, daughter of Taylor and administrator of his estate, include partition papers listing the shares allotted to DeLancey and other partition deeds and patents for land in New York state.

12,644. Thomas, Dorothy
Papers. Nd. 1 envelope.
Open. No guide.
The New York Public Library, Manuscripts and Archives.
Typescripts of Thomas's short stories "Fire Guard," "Happiness Insurance," and "The Parting." Also includes a book of sketches and a copy of Edna St. Vincent Millay's "Wine from These Grapes."

12,645. Thompson, Mrs. Almon Harris
Papers. 1872-73?. 132-page vol.
Open. No guide.
The New York Public Library, Manuscripts and Archives.
Diary that Thompson kept while on a trip to the Colorado River with her husband Almon Thompson. Also includes his diary for 1875.

12,646. Tisdale, Phebe Alden
Papers. Nd. 2 items.
Open. No guide.
The New York Public Library, Manuscripts and Archives.
Copies of the original manuscript of Tisdale's *All Seasons Around the Sun, A Telescopic View of the First Centuries* and the typeset copy of her work *Allow for the Skeleton (Dry Though It May Be)—and the Rest Revines,* a 2000-year survey.

12,647. Toldridge, Elizabeth Barnet
Papers. Nd. 1 envelope.
Open. No guide.
The New York Public Library, Manuscripts and Archives.
Correspondence, genealogical notes, and photos of Toldridge are included with a folder marked "Winnings," which contains poems probably written between 1900 and 1930.

12,648. Towne, Charles Hanson
Papers. 1922-46. 13 boxes and 14 vols.
Open. No guide.
The New York Public Library, Manuscripts and Archives.
Papers of Towne (1877-1949), a poet and editor, include letters from Gertrude Atherton, Royal Cortissoz, Theodosia Faulks, Ellen Glasgow, Fannie Hurst, and others prominent in the fields of literature and drama.

12,649. Tucker, Silvia R., and Stoddard, Nancy Cooley
Papers. 1834. 17-page vol.
Open. No guide.
The New York Public Library, Manuscripts and Archives.
Writing book of Stoddard, a resident of Hanover, MA, containing poems she copied in 1834. The book was used previously by Maria Augusta Fuller at a boarding school in Providence, RI, and by Tucker, a resident of Dartmouth, MA.

12,650. Tufts, Mrs. D. A. M. T.
Papers. 1907-14. 1 vol.
Open. No guide.
The New York Public Library, Manuscripts and Archives.
Diary kept by Tufts, primarily while she was on a European tour, deals chiefly with social matters.

12,651. Unger, Gladys Buchanan
Papers. Nd. 1 package.
Open. No guide.
The New York Public Library, Manuscripts and Archives.
Unger (1885-1940) was a playwright and screenwriter. Manuscripts of her plays *High C* and *California Cousins* and a notebook of ideas and themes for new plays.

12,652. United World Federalists, New York State Branch
Records. Ca. 1942-50. 11 cartons.
Open. Unpublished guide.
The New York Public Library, Manuscripts and Archives.
Financial papers, correspondence, and ephemera of the United World Federalists, which was founded in 1941 as the World Federalists. Includes correspondence of executive directors Oliver A. Quayle III and of William H. Wells and of chairman Mary Coffin (Ware) Dennett. Dennett, who was a suffragist, pacifist, birth control and sex education advocate, was also corresponding secretary of the National American Woman Suffrage Association.

12,653. Upson Family
Papers. 1815-1906. 1 box.
Open. No guide.
The New York Public Library, Manuscripts and Archives.
Correspondence of members of the Upson, Painter, and Stevens families, particularly of William and Polly Painter, concerning their move from Connecticut to Ohio in 1817 and living conditions in Medina, OH. Also includes correspondence between parents and children of the Upson family of New Haven, CT, primarily letters Minnie Upson McLendon wrote shortly before and during the Civil War, in which she describes social life and customs and war conditions in Alabama. Also contains letters from Harvey Upson, who was in London, to his wife; a diary of Sam W. Upson for 1833 to 1834; a copybook of Chloe Painter; and genealogical notes.

12,654. US Air Force, Libraries: Gilliam, Beverly
Papers. 1953-58. 22 items.
Open. No guide.
The New York Public Library, Manuscripts and Archives.
Letters that Gilliam, a special services librarian in the US Armed Forces, wrote from London and Korea to Mr. and Mrs. William H. Matthews and others who were friends on the staff of the Aguilar Branch of the New York Public Library. In her letters she describes working conditions, social activities, and daily life in both locations.

12,655. Wadsworth, Alice Colden
Papers. 1819. 1 vol.
Open. No guide.
The New York Public Library, Manuscripts and Archives.
Sketch Wadsworth wrote about her parents, her parents' families, and her own life.

12,656. Wainwright Family
Papers. 1781-1845. 3 boxes.
Open. No guide.
The New York Public Library, Manuscripts and Archives.
Correspondence of Peter Wainwright, Sr., a tobacconist in Boston, and of his wife Elizabeth (Mayhew) Wainwright and their children Peter Wainwright, Jr., a treasurer of the Provident Loan and Trust Company in Boston, and his wife Charlotte (Lumbert) Wainwright; Eliza (Wainwright) Channing; and Jonathan Mayhew Wainwright, a bishop of the Protestant Episcopal church, and his wife Amelia Maria Wainwright. Also includes letters Elizabeth Wainwright's sister Mrs. H. C. Howard wrote from Havana to her sisters in Boston.

12,657. Wald, Lillian D.
Papers. Ca. 1918-40. Ca. 60 items.
Open. No guide.
The New York Public Library, Manuscripts and Archives.
Letters, notes, and telegrams to Wald (1867-1940), a public health nurse and settlement house founder, from Naomi Deutsch as well as correspondence and other papers relating to the Henry Street Visiting Nurse Society.

12,658. Walsh, Frank P.
Papers. 1913-37. 4 boxes.
Open. No guide.
The New York Public Library, Manuscripts and Archives.
Correspondence of Walsh (1864-1939), a lawyer, labor representative, and public official, with his wife Katherine O'Flaherty Walsh; his daughters Celia (Walsh) Bradley, Catherine Louise Walsh, Sister Francis Marie, and Virginia Walsh; his sisters Katherine (Walsh) Webb and Madame M. Walsh; his nieces Grace Walsh and Sara Walsh Elsey; his sister-in-law Mrs. James W. Walsh; and his daughter-in-law Pauline Altman Walsh.

12,659. Walsh, Townsend
Papers. 1914-35. 11 boxes.
Open. No guide.
The New York Public Library, Manuscripts and Archives.
Correspondence of Walsh (?-1941), a press agent who wrote about the theater, includes correspondence with Minnie Maddern Fiske.

12,660. Ward, Henry Dana
Papers. 1850-57. 1 vol.
Open. No guide.
The New York Public Library, Manuscripts and Archives.
Diary of Ward, rector of St. Jude's Protestant Episcopal Church in New York City, includes material on his family and a school for young ladies.

12,661. Ward, Mary Augusta
Papers. 1899-1945. 2 folders.
Open. No guide.
The New York Public Library, Manuscripts and Archives.
Letters that [Mrs. Humphrey] Ward (1851-1920), an author, wrote to Albert Steiner of Harper and Bros. publishers in New York concern two illustrations for her novels and other editorial and personal matters.

12,662. Ward, Samuel
Papers. 1647-1883. 3 boxes.
Open. No guide.
The New York Public Library, Manuscripts and Archives.
Correspondence of Ward (1814-84), a lobbyist and author, contains family correspondence, including letters from Julia (Ward) Howe (1819-1910).

12,663. Washburn, Hannah Blaney Thatcher
Papers. 1861-70. No size given.
Open. No guide.
The New York Public Library, Manuscripts and Archives.
Diaries of Washburn, who was the mother of Peter Blaney Thatcher, a resident of Woodstock, NY. In her diaries she comments on social life at home, books she read, church meetings, gardening, apple picking and drying, other home occupations, weather and road conditions, death and funerals, Civil War events, and President Grant's stop at a local depot.

12,664. Washburn, Mrs. Samuel B.
Papers. 1862. No size given.
Open. No guide.
The New York Public Library, Manuscripts and Archives.
Diary in which Washburn, who was married to a US naval officer, describes domestic matters in Bethany, NY, a trip to New York City, and military events.

12,665. Waters, Amy L.
Papers. 1907-10. 1 vol.
Open. No guide.
The New York Public Library, Manuscripts and Archives.
Diary Waters kept during a tour of Europe.

12,666. Watkins, Abiathar, and Watkins, Emily
Papers. 1836-94. No size given.
Open. No guide.
The New York Public Library, Manuscripts and Archives.
Family correspondence; letters from Emily Watkins's friends regarding local news in Oxford, Norwich, Cherry Valley, Cooperstown, and Brooklyn, NY, and her treatment in sanatoria of James C. Jackson in Daneville, NY; her journals for 1840 to 1863; and domestic accounts for 1847 to 1870.

12,667. Webster, Noah
Papers. 1764-1843. 10 boxes and 12 vols.
Open. No guide.
The New York Public Library, Manuscripts and Archives.
Papers of Webster (1758-1843), a lexicographer, include correspondence with his wife Rebecca Greenleaf Webster and writing on suffragism.

12,668. Weeks, Marian E.
Papers. 1942-44. 1 vol.
Open. No guide.
The New York Public Library, Manuscripts and Archives.
Diary of Weeks (?-1968), who was a Library staff member, contains descriptions of her experiences as an air-raid warden in New York City.

12,669. Whipple, Charlotte Lambert
Papers. 1849-88. 1 slipcase.
Open. No guide.
The New York Public Library, Manuscripts and Archives.
Diaries of Whipple (18??-88), a pioneer, who describes family, social, and school life in the Catskill region of New York; a wagon train journey from Batavia, IL, to Oregon; and life at the home the family established on the Columbia River near Portland, OR. Includes correspondence of the Whipple family with friends and relatives about life in Oregon, family welfare, and other matters.

12,670. Whistler, Anna Matilda (McNeill)
Papers. 1843-48. 2 vols.
Open. No guide.
The New York Public Library, Manuscripts and Archives.
Journal that [Mrs. George] Whistler (1804-81), the mother of artist James Whistler, kept in St. Petersburg. Includes notes her sister Eliza A. Winstanley made of a journey from Preston and photos of portraits of Whistler's grandparents, parents, and maternal aunt.

12,671. Whiting, Elizabeth F. P.
Papers. 1924-70. 36 items.
Open. No guide.
The New York Public Library, Manuscripts and Archives.
Diaries in which Whiting recounts her personal and day-to-day activities.

12,672. Whittemore Family
Papers. 1796-1858. 322 items.
Open. No guide.
The New York Public Library, Manuscripts and Archives.
Papers of the Whittemore family, who were industrialists in West Cambridge, MA, include correspondence of Eliza Ann (Cutter) Whittemore, who married Henry Whittemore.

12,673. Wick, Blachly, and Colles Family
Papers. 1688-1925. 3 boxes.
Open. No guide.
The New York Public Library, Manuscripts and Archives.
Includes a journal Mary A. Colles kept while she was traveling in Belgium at the outbreak of WWI.

12,674. Williams, Cyrus
Papers. 1823-42. 1 box.
Open. No guide.
The New York Public Library, Manuscripts and Archives.
Papers of Williams (1783-1863) include correspondence and a writing exercise book of his daughter Martha Williams, who married C. S. Sherman, a missionary in the Holy Land. Also includes correspondence of another of Williams's daughters, Joanna Williams.

12,675. Williams, Tirzah M.
Papers. 1821-47. 1 box.
Open. No guide.
The New York Public Library, Manuscripts and Archives.
Letters to Williams, an 1843 graduate of Mount Holyoke Female Seminary and the daughter of Cyrus Williams (1783-1863), a resident of North Stonington and New Haven, CT, were written by teachers and friends at Mount Holyoke and by Mary Lyon. Also includes Tirzah Williams's diary for 1838 to 1841.

12,676. Winthrop, Rogers, Parkin, and Moore Families
Papers. 1781-1846. No size given.
Open. No guide.
The New York Public Library, Manuscripts and Archives.
Includes correspondence of Augusta Temple Winthrop dating from 1807 to 1828.

12,677. Women's Peace Union
Records. 1920-41. 9 boxes.
Open. No guide.
The New York Public Library, Manuscripts and Archives.
Minutes, financial records, correspondence, reports of committees, petitions, lists of names, an address book, publicity material, and other records of this pacifist organization. Includes items relating to a proposed amendment to the Constitution making war and all preparation for war illegal.

12,678. Yezierska, Anzia
Papers. Nd. 8-page item.
Open. No guide.
The New York Public Library, Manuscripts and Archives.
Typescript of "Shut Out," a short story by Yezierska (1885-), which was probably not published.

12,679. Zemser, Marion (Shomer)
Papers. Ca. 1900-07. 1 box and 1 package.
Open. No guide.
The New York Public Library, Manuscripts and Archives.
Journal of Zemser (?-1951), an author, contains descriptions of her European travels. Also includes reminiscences of her mother's family in Russia during the 19th century.

12,680. Adams, Wilhelmina
Papers. 1926-62. 2000 items.
Open. Unpublished guide.
The New York Public Library, Schomburg Center for Research in Black Culture.
Correspondence, speeches, programs, pamphlets, broadsides, photos, and clippings of Adams (ca. 1900-), a social worker, politician, and florist. Adams, a black woman who was active in New York politics and in the Harlem community, was involved in such organizations as the Aeolian Ladies of Charity, the National Council of Negro Women, the NAACP, and the New York Urban League. Elected chairman of the women's division of the Democratic National Committee, she was the first black woman delegate to a Democratic convention. In 1941 she ran for Democratic leader of the 17th assembly district in New York.

12,681. Bearden, Bessye
Papers. 1923-44. 2 in.
Open. No guide.
The New York Public Library, Schomburg Center for Research in Black Culture.
Bearden (?-1943) was active in New York social and political matters. Incoming correspondence relates to organizations in which she was involved, among them the YWCA and the National Council of Negro Women, and includes letters from Mary (McLeod) Bethune. Also included are letters of condolence to her husband Howard Bearden and her son Romare Bearden, who was an artist, on the occasion of her death.

12,682. Civil Rights Congress
Records. 1946-55. 56 ft.
Open. Unpublished guide.
The New York Public Library, Schomburg Center for Research in Black Culture.
Correspondence, speeches, press releases, bulletins, periodicals, and other printed material of the Congress, which resulted from the cooperative efforts in 1946 of the National Federation for Constitutional Liberties, the International Labor Defense, and the National Negro Congress. The Civil Rights Congress was dedicated to the defense of the rights of labor; of Negro, Mexican, and other national groups; and of political minorities. Its records consist largely of case files, many of which concern women. Included are records of the case of Rosa Lee Ingram, a black woman tenant farmer who in 1948 was convicted with her two sons for the murder in 1947 of their white tenant farmer neighbor John Ethron Stratford in Schley County, GA. The death sentence for the three defendants was later commuted to life imprisonment. Records document the publicity and fund-raising campaign initiated in Ingram's behalf by the Congress. Also available on microfilm.

12,683. Conrad and Tubman
Papers. 1839-1941. 3 ft.
Open. Unpublished guide.
The New York Public Library, Schomburg Center for Research in Black Culture.
Research material compiled by Earl Conrad, a journalist and historian, for use in writing biographical works about Harriet (Ross) Tubman (ca. 1821-1913), who was a black nurse, spy, scout, and conductor on the underground railroad. Research and publisher's correspondence, research notes, statements of and transcripts of interviews with people who knew or worked with Tubman and with members of her family, a bibliography, photos, clippings, programs, pamphlets, and drafts and typescripts of Conrad's books and articles on Tubman. Also available on microfilm.

12,684. Cosmé, Eusebia
Papers. 1930-68. 2 cu.ft.
Open. No guide.
The New York Public Library, Schomburg Center for Research in Black Culture.
Correspondence, contracts, photos, posters, reviews, clippings, programs, and scripts of Cosmé (1911-), a black Cuban actress and dramatic reader. She collaborated with Langston Hughes, participated in numerous poetry readings of the work of Cuban poet Nicolás Guillén, and appeared in the film *The Pawnbroker.* Material is primarily in Spanish.

12,685. Davis, Ruby Sheppard
Papers. 1940-75. 2 in.
Open. No guide.
The New York Public Library, Schomburg Center for Research in Black Culture.
Scrapbooks containing photos, clippings, programs, one-act plays, poems, jokes, gags, and fables of Davis, a 20th-century black woman who was an actress, dancer, singer, poet, and songwriter. Davis was involved in the Negro Actor's Guild of America, Inc., and the New York Guild of the National Negro Opera Company; she also was private secretary to composer Leigh Whipper.

12,686. Dawson, Mary Cardwell
Papers. 1937-59. 2 in.
Open. No guide.
The New York Public Library, Schomburg Center for Research in Black Culture.
Dawson, a musician and teacher, founded the National Negro Opera Company in 1941. Booklet concerning the history and activities of the Company includes biographical information on Dawson, certificates commending her for her achievements and contributions to various organizations, and programs.

12,687. Herbert, Rietta Hines
Papers. 1948-64. 1.5 cu.ft.
Open. Unpublished guide.
The New York Public Library, Schomburg Center for Research in Black Culture.
Herbert (1911-73) was a black social worker and teacher in the New York City school system. Correspondence, notes, field reports and memoranda, bibliographies and other study material, reports from seminars and institutes, photos, social work pamphlets and periodicals, and memorabilia. Herbert was particularly interested in child abuse.

12,688. Lyons and Williamson
Papers. 1830-1957. 5 cu.ft.
Open. Unpublished guide.
The New York Public Library, Schomburg Center for Research in Black Culture.
Correspondence, articles, sketches, photos, clippings, contracts, deeds, receipts, certificates, diplomas, and other papers of these families. Letters from Pauline Lyons Williamson to her parents and to Maritcha (Remond) Lyons concern her life in California and the progress of her son Harry Williamson. Also includes a 1928 autobiography of Maritcha Lyons (1848-1929), who was a teacher in New York, and papers related to Harry A. Williamson's research on the Black Freemason's movement.

12,689. McInnis, Alice
Papers. 1938-74. 9 cu.ft.
Open. No guide.
The New York Public Library, Schomburg Center for Research in Black Culture.
Correspondence, notes, financial papers, photos, clippings, programs, periodicals, books, and other printed material of McInnis, an actress, writer, astrologer, and dress designer. Material primarily relates to astrology and includes notes for individual horoscopes, but it also concerns her theatrical career.

12,690. Miscellaneous
Collection. 1792-1968. 9 cu.ft.
Open. Unpublished guide.
The New York Public Library, Schomburg Center for Research in Black Culture.
Correspondence, speeches, articles, photos, clippings, programs, and printed material of black Americans involved in such fields as the performing arts, literature, politics, education, and civil rights. Includes personal and professional correspondence and photos, 1933-39, of actor Ira Aldridge and his daughter Amanda Ira Aldridge, a composer and singer; correspondence of Estelle Massey Riddle concerning an interracial forum in 1943; and correspondence, photos, articles, clippings, and programs, 1933-55, of Isabelle Taliaferro Spiller, whose papers relate to her career as a musician, music teacher, and orchestra leader in New York and to her participation in the Federal Music Project.

12,691. National Association of Colored Graduate Nurses
Records. 1908-51. 1 cu. ft.
Open. Unpublished guide.
The New York Public Library, Schomburg Center for Research in Black Culture.
Minutes, correspondence, conference and meeting programs, newsletters, photos, scrapbooks, and articles concern the Association, an organization of black nurses, which was founded in 1908 and incorporated in 1920. The Association provided guidance to women entering the profession and strove to eliminate discrimination against black nurses and to increase placement and promotion possibilities for them. The organization was also

concerned with improving standards of nursing training and hospital care. Correspondence and other material relate to individual nurses such as Mabel K. Staupers. Also available on microfilm.

12,692. Prince, Lucy Terry
Papers. 1967-72. 2 cu.ft.
Open. No guide.
The New York Public Library, Schomburg Center for Research in Black Culture.
Research files of Jonathan and Bernard Katz contain correspondence, research notes, typescripts, galley proofs, articles, and other material concerned with Prince (1730-1821), a black pioneer woman and former slave who lived in western Massachusetts. Their book *Black Woman: A Fictionalized Biography of Lucy Terry Prince* (Pantheon, 1973), aimed at an adolescent audience, concerns both Prince's life and New England history.

12,693. Slavery and Abolition
Collection. 1700-1890. 1 cu.ft.
Open. Published guide.
The New York Public Library, Schomburg Center for Research in Black Culture.
Correspondence, speeches, wills, slave sales, papers, certificates of registry, manumission papers, and passes relate to slavery and the abolition of the slave trade. Material pertains to women as slaves, slave owners, and abolitionists. See *Calendar of the Manuscripts in the Schomburg Collection* (New York: Historical Records Survey, Work Projects Administration, 1942).

12,694. Smythe, Hugh
Papers. 1942-64. 5 ft.
Open. Unpublished guide.
The New York Public Library, Schomburg Center for Research in Black Culture.
Smythe (1913-77), a teacher, author, and diplomat, was married to Mabel Murphy Smythe (1918-), who taught economics and wrote about economics and education. Her papers include correspondence, short story manuscripts, notes for a school segregation study, and a personal scrapbook. Mabel Smythe was a member of the US Advisory Commissions on Education Exchange, International Education, and Cultural Affairs. Also available on microfilm.

12,695. Women's Miscellany
Collection. Nd. No size given.
Open. Card index.
New York Society Library.
Collection contains correspondence, manuscript poetry and other writings, scrapbooks, autographs, clippings, and published works of women in the 18th, 19th, and 20th centuries. Contains letters to Benjamin Goodhue from his daughters Frances (Goodhue) [Mrs. William] Ashton, Sarah Goodhue, and Mary (Goodhue) [Mrs. Benjamin, Jr.] Shreve; correspondence of Benjamin Goodhue's son Jonathan Goodhue, Jonathan Goodhue's wife Catharine Rutherfurd (Clarkson) Goodhue and their sons Henry and Charles, Catharine Goodhue's father Matthew Clarkson, and her sister Elizabeth Clarkson; and correspondence of Susan Brownell Anthony, Anna Howard Shaw, Marion (Morrison) [Mrs. Frederick Gore] King, Rosemary (Carr) [Mrs. Stephen Vincent] Benét, and others. Includes letters to Matthew Clarkson from Elizabeth (Schuyler) [Mrs. Alexander] Hamilton, Catharine Livingston [Mrs. Matthew] Ridley [Mrs. John] Livingston, and Sarah Browne [Mrs. Edward] Hall and letters to Jonathan Goodhue from Maria (Weston) Chapman, his stepmother Anna Willard [Mrs. Benjamin] Goodhue, and his sister Martha Hardy (Goodhue) [Mrs. Gideon] Tucker. Also includes a speech about the history of old Greenwich Village by Susan Farley (Nichols) [Mrs. Harold Trowbridge] Pulsifer, 1953; scrapbooks of poetry that Marion (Morrison) King compiled for Mrs. Theodore Roosevelt, 1930-33; and poetry scrapbooks of Marion King containing letters of Maude Adams, Willa Cather, and Sara Teasdale Filsinger.

12,696. Robins, Elizabeth
Papers. Ca. 1890-1940. Ca. 10,000 items.
Open. No guide.
New York University, Fales Library, Elmer Holmes Bobst Library.
Correspondence, diaries, manuscripts, and photos of [Miss] Robins (1862-1952), an actress and author who was involved in the Alaska gold rush of the 1890s. Papers relate to all phases of her career and her published works.

12,697. Livingston, William
Papers. 1776-90. Ca. 5000 items.
Access restricted. Card file.
New York University, Papers of William Livingston.
Official and family correspondence, newspaper and magazine contributions, military records, and other papers of Livingston (1723-90), the first governor of New Jersey. Includes correspondence with his wife Susannah "Sukey" (French) Livingston; his daughters Catherine "Kitty" and Susan Livingston and Sarah (Livingston) [Mrs. John] Jay; and his sister Alida Hoffman. Also includes Livingston's correspondence with George Washington and others about British treatment of women and items pertaining to widows' claims and requests to him as governor.

12,698. Bailie, Helen Tufts
Papers. 1879-1906. 1 Hollinger box.
Open. Unpublished guide.
New York University, Tamiment Library.
Correspondence, manuscripts, and printed items of Bailie (1874-1962), a writer and social activist who married William Bailie (1867-1957). Also includes papers of William Bailie, Helena Born, and Miriam Daniell, all of whom were anarchists and contributors to Benjamin R. Tucker's *Liberty*. Helen Bailie's correspondence is with prominent people regarding the publication of works in the *Atlantic Monthly*, where she was employed as an editor, as well as with her husband on the occasion of the death of Born. Contains a biography of Born and other papers reflecting the labor activities of Born and Daniell while they were involved in the Bristol Socialist Society in England prior to their removal to Cambridge, MA, in 1890. Includes manuscripts of Daniell and Born's writing on Walt Whitman.

12,699. Berkman, Alexander
Papers. 1917-19. 2 Hollinger boxes.
Open. Unpublished guide.
New York University, Tamiment Library.
Primarily court transcripts and legal papers of Berkman (1870-1936), an anarchist and author, which relate to his involvement with the No Conscription League, his fight against extradition to California in connection with the Mooney-Billings bombing case, and his and Emma Goldman's trial for violating the Draft Act and their unsuccessful attempts to prevent deportation. Also includes a transcript of a speech Emma Goldman gave in 1919 in honor of Kate Richards O'Hare.

12,700. Caylor, George N.
Papers. 1903-73. 2 Hollinger boxes.
Open. Unpublished guide.
New York University, Tamiment Library.
Papers of Caylor (1885-1974), a socialist who was born George N. Cohen, include sketches of socialist and labor figures, among them Elizabeth Gurley Flynn, Frances Perkins, and Bettina Borrman Wells. Also includes the manuscript of Caylor's autobiography *If My Memory Serves Me Right*, in which he discusses his early years in Philadelphia, the socialist movement, his brother Joseph E. Cohen, Frances Perkins, Rose Schneiderman, Pauline Newman, and others.

12,701. Goldman, Emma
Papers. 1924-40. 6 Hollinger boxes.
Open. Unpublished guide.
New York University, Tamiment Library.
Papers of Goldman (1869-1940), an anarchist, focus on publication of her autobiography *Living My Life* (1931); a tour of the US in 1934, which was her first since she returned after her deportation in 1919; and other matters. Includes correspondence with Arthur Leonard Ross, Alfred A. Knopf, Roger Baldwin of the American Civil Liberties Union, Bertrand Russell, Rebecca West, Havelock Ellis, Israel Zangwill, Peter Kropotkin, Eugene V. Debs, Herbert Read, M. Eleanor Fitzgerald of the Provincetown Playhouse, Norman Thomas, and Upton Sinclair. Also contains transcripts of addresses and press conferences of her 1934 tour; notes for articles on Hitler, Mussolini, and China; and Jeanette Levey's unpublished manuscript "Emma Goldman Speaks," which contains correspondence, addresses, and articles about national and international politics and current events, political theory, developments in Russia, reports on the Spanish Civil War, literature, and drama.

12,702. Lewis, Lena Morrow
Papers. 1899-1949. 4 Hollinger boxes.
Open. Unpublished guide.
New York University, Tamiment Library.
Correspondence of [Mrs. Arthur Morrow] Lewis (1862-1950), a socialist activist and journalist, primarily with Warren K. Billings during 17 of his 23 years in prison. An active trade unionist, Billings, along with Tom Mooney, was convicted in connection with a bombing at a 1916 Preparedness Day parade in San Francisco in which nine persons were killed. The letters protest his innocence and concentrate on his efforts to win his release. Other correspondents include Theodore Debs, James H. Maurer, James Oneal, Iva Ettor, Eugene V. Debs, Norman Thomas, and Charles Edward Russell. Scrapbooks focus on the Lewises, Lena Lewis's experience as a journalist and political candidate in Alaska, worldwide communism, and the Socialist party in California and contain articles she edited for *Labor World*. Other items include WEVD radio scripts and speech notes touching on the Social Democratic Federation, in which she was active, and on other contemporary issues.

12,703. New York Bureau of Legal Advice
Records. 1917-19. No size given.
Open. Unpublished guide.
New York University, Tamiment Library.
Case histories, correspondence, press releases, and clippings of the Bureau, which existed from 1917 to 1919 to "furnish legal advice and counsel free of charge" to people who came into conflict with wartime laws. Attorney Charles Recht conducted much of the legal work, while Fannie M. Witherspoon was secretary. Correspondents include Ella Reeve "Mother" Bloor and M. Eleanor Fitzgerald of the League for the Amnesty of Political Prisoners. The Bureau provided information, investigative assistance, publicity, and free legal aid. The most common areas they dealt with were selective service exemption, draft evasion, conscientious objector status, military discharge, desertion, evasion, amnesty, civil liberties, and deportation. Also includes a report from a US district attorney following a government investigation of the Bureau and the National Civil Liberties Bureau as well as the former's response to the report.

12,704. Schneiderman, Rose
Papers. 1904-67. 5 Hollinger boxes.
Partially restricted. Unpublished guide.
New York University, Tamiment Library.
Correspondence, manuscripts, photos, and clippings of Schneiderman (1882-1972), a feminist, trade unionist, president of the National Women's Trade Union League from 1926 to 1950, and New York

state secretary of labor in 1937. Letters to her concern women's suffrage and trade union activities. Correspondents include family members; Margaret (Dreier) Robins; Joseph E. Cohen; Pauline M. Newman, who was involved in organizing the activities of the International Ladies' Garment Workers' Union; Franklin and Eleanor Roosevelt; and Frances Perkins. Also includes committee and executive board minutes; reports from organizers; reports on factory and sanitary conditions; correspondence and clippings concerning a training school for women organizers of the National Women's Trade Union League; remarks on the National Recovery Administration labor advisory board, on which Schneiderman served, and a manuscript of its history; addresses; and clippings about Schneiderman, Eleanor Roosevelt, and the women's trade union movement. Part of collection is also available on microfilm.

12,705. Stokes, Rose Pastor
Papers. 1905-33. 6 Hollinger boxes.
Open. Unpublished guide.
New York University, Tamiment Library.
Correspondence, manuscripts, and clippings of Stokes (1879-1933), a socialist and communist activist and writer, who was born Rose Harriet Weislander but adopted Pastor, her stepfather's name. Born in Poland, she moved in 1890 to Cleveland, where she worked in garment and cigar factories before becoming a part-time columnist for *New York Daily Jewish News.* In 1903 she married James Graham Phelps Stokes, a wealthy resident of University Settlement House. Correspondents include James Stokes, Harry Laidler, Elizabeth Gurley Flynn, Patrick L. Quinlan, Margaret Sanger, Leonard D. Abbott, Olive Tilford Dargan, Ann (Kaplan) Williams Feinberg, Kahlil Gibran, Daniel Kiefer, J. Edward Morgan, Scott Nearing, Vladamir Resnikoff, Upton Sinclair, Lincoln Steffens, Rose Strunsky, and family members. The letters relate to the Intercollegiate Socialist Society, which James Stokes helped found in 1905; the New York restaurant and hotel workers' strike in 1912, which Rose Stokes helped to organize; Quinlan's conviction and imprisonment for his role in the Paterson silk workers' strike; the National Birth Control League; her plays, which were produced by the Washington Square Players; her poems; her literary sketches of Moscow; the Women's Peace party; the Communist party; and her visit to the USSR in 1922 as a delegate to the fourth congress of the Communist International, at which time she adopted the pseudonym "Sasha." She divorced Stokes in 1925 and married communist activist Jerome I. Romaine, also known as Victor J. Jerome.

12,706. The Salvation Army
Records. 1865-1977. 392 ft., 469 microfilm reels, and 45 motion picture reels.
Open. Preliminary inventory.
The Salvation Army Archives and Research Center.
Founded as The Christian Mission in 1865 by William Booth, the organization was renamed The Salvation Army in 1878; its mission was to serve the temporal and spiritual needs of the public. Includes annual reports, minutes, legal and financial records, correspondence, diaries, periodicals containing statistical and biographical information, tapes and transcripts, photos, pamphlets, brochures, and programs, which document the work of women in all branches of Salvation Army work, including that as officers, administrators, doctors, nurses, teachers, editors, literary agents, and overseas agents during peace and war. In the early days of the Army, women initiated projects to ameliorate poor social conditions by door-to-door visitation and by offering child care, aid to unwed mothers, and settlement house services. Also includes records of and about Evangeline Cory Booth, the daughter of William Booth. Evangeline Booth was national commander of the Army in the US from 1904 to 1934 and general from 1934 to 1939.

12,707. International Women's Year Conference
Records. Ca. 1969-76. 90 tapes.
Open. Unpublished guide.
United Nations Archives.
Recordings of meetings held at the Conference in Mexico City as well as of preparatory sessions for the Conference. Includes tapes of meetings of the Commission on the Status of Women, 1969-76; of meetings about an international law to eliminate discrimination against women, 1974; of meetings of a working group concerned with the activities of the International Women's Year, 1974; and of meetings of the consultative committee for the world conference of the International Women's Year, 1975.

12,708. United Negro College Fund, Greater New York Women's Division
Records. 1946-57. 6 cu.ft.
Access restricted. Unpublished guide.
United Negro College Fund Archives.
Founded in 1944, the UNCF is a fund-raising consortium of 41 predominantly black colleges and universities. The Women's Division was created in 1946 to solicit funds from women and groups in New York City and Westchester, NY. Consists primarily of correspondence, including solicitation letters, but also contains clippings and press releases. The Women's Division, which helped to make people aware of the plight of the black colleges, sponsored teas, dinner parties, and an annual symposium at Hunter College. Cochairmen of the Division were Catherine (Hughes) [Mrs. Chauncey] Waddell, a daughter of Charles Evans Hughes, and Margery [Mrs. Richard O.] Loengard. They were assisted by [Miss] Betty Stebman, who handled technical aspects of the Division's operations. The Division's sponsors have included Mrs. Winthrop W. Aldrich, [Miss] Tallulah Bankhead, Mrs. Edward L. Bernays, Mrs. Lucius R. Eastman, Mrs. Bernard Gimbel, [Miss] Ruth Gordon, Mrs. Walter Hoving, [Mrs.] Clare Boothe Luce, Margaret Mead, Mrs. Thomas A. Morgan, [Mrs.] Dorothy H. Paley, [Miss] Cornelia Otis Skinner, Mrs. Arthur Hays Sulzberger, and Mrs. Wendell L. Willkie.

12,709. Whitney, Gertrude (Vanderbilt)
Papers. 1914-45. 13 microfilm reels.
Open. Unpublished guide.
Whitney Museum of American Art Library.
[Mrs. Harry Payne] Whitney (1875-1942) was a sculptor and art patron who founded the Whitney Museum. Includes biographical material, scrapbooks on the Whitney Studio Club and the early years of the Museum, reviews of her work, photos, clippings, and exhibition catalogs.

12,710. Carner, Lucy Perkins
Papers. 1922-76. 34 items.
Open. Unpublished guide.
Young Women's Christian Association, Archives of the National Board.
Carner (1886-) was the industrial secretary for the National Board from 1920 to 1935. An excerpt from her 1922 diary; notes and quotations from courses given by Florence Simms, the first industrial secretary of the National YWCA; an unpublished biography about Simms; speeches; articles, including some from *The Woman's Press;* and clippings. Carner also worked on local YWCA staffs in Pittsburgh and Wilkes Barre, PA.

12,711. Cratty, Mabel
Papers. 1904-28. 0.5 ft.
Open. Unpublished guide.
Young Women's Christian Association, Archives of the National Board.
[Miss] Cratty (1868-1928) served from 1906 to 1928 as the first executive director of the National Board. Correspondence, devotional notes, case studies of YWCA problems for a course in leadership, and clippings. Cratty was a former staff member of the American committee of the YWCA, a predecessor of the National Board.

12,712. Dodge, Grace Hoadley
Papers. 1889-1956. 1 vol. and 25 items.
Open. Unpublished guide.
Young Women's Christian Association, Archives of the National Board.
[Miss] Dodge (1856-1914), a philanthropist, was the first president of the National Board. Correspondence to girls clubs, commemorative letters and speeches, speech notes, biographical data, lists of club members, a commemorative issue of the *Association Monthly,* and other papers. President of the National Board from 1906 to 1914, Dodge also served as treasurer of Columbia University Teachers College and as a vice-president of the Constantinople College board of trustees in Turkey.

12,713. French, Eleanor
Papers. 1935-40. 22 items.
Open. Unpublished guide.
Young Women's Christian Association, Archives of the National Board.
French (1904-71) was an executive of the student YWCA at Ohio State University. Notes, outlines, and evaluations of the student YWCA programs are included. Also contains material concerning the YWCA's problems competing for membership with other college activities, racial integration of college activities, and the position of religion in higher education.

12,714. Fulton, Christine (Zduleczna)
Papers. 1922-72. 12 items.
Open. Unpublished guide.
Young Women's Christian Association, Archives of the National Board.
During WWI Fulton (1898?-) was a member of the Polish Grey Samaritans, a YWCA project made up of women volunteers of Polish background. Trained in New York City, 20 of the women did relief work in Poland. Correspondence includes letters from former Samaritans evaluating the program. Published items describe the work of the PGS.

12,715. Harrison, Agatha
Papers. 1924-54. 60 items.
Open. Unpublished guide.
Young Women's Christian Association, Archives of the National Board.
Harrison (?-1954), a pacifist, was hired by the YWCA in 1921 to do an industrial study of the status of women in China. Later she became involved in India's struggle for freedom and nonviolence. Correspondence includes letters to Margaret Ernestine Burton, a colleague on the National YWCA staff, concerning Harrison's support for peace in India. Also includes reviews of Irene Harrison's biography of her sister. Agatha Harrison was a friend of Gandhi, literary executor of C. F. Andrews, and a member of the India Conciliation Group and the Women's International League for Peace and Freedom. She also gave lectures about India to British audiences.

12,716. Hendee, Elizabeth (Russell)
Papers. 1918-33. 0.1 ft., 2 vols., and 1 item.
Open. Unpublished guide.
Young Women's Christian Association, Archives of the National Board.
Hendee served on the national staff of the YWCA from 1919 to 1934 and worked in the training school for Old Country Service of the National War Work Council. Correspondence, reports and evaluations of the Polish Grey Samaritans and the Old Country Service training school, accounts of the programs, lists of students, schedules, and a cookbook. Hendee was also director of the

nationality program at the YWCA's Fletcher farm in Vermont.

12,717. Industrial Work: Buffalo, NY, YWCA
Records. 1922-28. 0.1 ft.
Open. Unpublished guide.
Young Women's Christian Association, Archives of the National Board.
Collected by Buffalo YWCA staff members Eleanor Coit and Ethlyn Christensen, the records consist of studies of the background of industrial women, outlines for industrial courses offered by the YWCA, and statements about the YWCA's commitment to unionism.

12,718. Irving, Ruth (Beane)
Papers. 1919. 15 items.
Open. Unpublished guide.
Young Women's Christian Association, Archives of the National Board.
Diaries of Irving, who worked in the YWCA war brides program during WWI. She writes about her work in France and her trip back to the US with French war brides. Printed literature concerning American YWCA work in France during WWI is also included.

12,719. James, Genevieve
Papers. 1919-42. 1 vol. and 3 items.
Open. Unpublished guide.
Young Women's Christian Association, Archives of the National Board.
James (?-1958) was an assistant supervisor of YWCA hostess houses in the southeastern department of the US Army during WWI. During WWII she organized and administered USOs in California. Unpublished manuscripts about her experiences during the wars and a scrapbook about YWCA hostess houses are included.

12,720. Job Corps; YWCA
Records. 1966-75. 8 cu.ft.
Access restricted. No guide.
Young Women's Christian Association, Archives of the National Board.
The YWCA's Job Corps program began in 1967 when the National Board contracted with the US Office of Economic Opportunity to provide employment training in urban areas for disadvantaged girls. Files of the YWCA's Job Corps headquarters include administrative records, financial material, correspondence, reports, evaluations, memoranda, handbooks, directories, newsletters, and manuals. The YWCA Job Corps program ended in 1975.

12,721. Long, Lillian Louise
Papers. 1908-13. 13 items.
Open. Unpublished guide.
Young Women's Christian Association, Archives of the National Board.
Long was the mill village secretary of the National Board in the South and industrial and extension secretary in Pittsburgh. Correspondence, manuscripts, scrapbook, programs, newsletters, and a cookbook reflect the YWCA's attempts to improve working conditions and provide recreational activities for women working in industry in the rural South.

12,722. Lowrie, Helen (Ogden)
Papers. 1917-19. 19 items.
Open. Unpublished guide.
Young Women's Christian Association, Archives of the National Board.
Correspondence of Lowrie to her family concerns her trip to Russia and her YWCA work there.

12,723. National Association of Employed Officers of the YWCA
Records. 1920-55. 0.75 ft.
Open. Unpublished guide.
Young Women's Christian Association, Archives of the National Board.
The Association was founded in 1911 to educate professional YWCA personnel about the importance of their work with women and girls, to set standards of professional performance, to stimulate continuing education, and to add to their experience in training social workers. Constitution, committee minutes, dissolution proceedings, speeches, and publications. Material primarily concerns a counseling program the Association offered from 1933 to 1941 for unemployed YWCA professional workers, including questionnaires sent to the workers during the 1930s and correspondence with them. The Association, later called the National Association of Employed Officers, dissolved in 1955 when professional social worker associations came into being.

12,724. National Board
Records. 1876-1964. 280 microfilm reels.
Access restricted. Published guide.
Young Women's Christian Association, Archives of the National Board.
Founded in 1906, the National Board is the chief accrediting and consulting organization for YWCA member associations. Files contain minutes of Board and committee meetings; financial records; financial, statistical, staff, program, and conference reports; studies of communities, associations, members, and programs; case records; biographical information about Board members; and material printed by the Board to aid member associations. The files reflect the YWCA's activities in such areas as education; employment; family relations; human relations; health care and health education; immigration; industrial work and labor relations; leadership training for women; the peace movement; racial justice; rural, student, and teen work; social work; vocational guidance; and war work. Also included is material concerning fieldwork in Europe, Africa, South America, Asia, and especially China. See Louisa Bowen, comp., *Inventory to the Records Files Collection, Accession No. 1* (New York: National Board YWCA, 1978).

12,725. National Board Photos
Records. 1890-1973. Ca. 3000 items.
Open. No guide.
Young Women's Christian Association, Archives of the National Board.
Photos taken by the publicity department of the YWCA and snapshots and group photos donated by former board and staff members. The photos depict YWCA work during WWI, hostess houses in the US and France, women working in industrial or day-care settings, and women engaging in recreational activities. Also included are pictures of the Polish Grey Samaritans; the USO; the Job Corps; YWCA rural work in the South during the Depression; activities in China, the Near East, South America, and Eastern Europe; the national staff and board members; and YWCA buildings.

12,726. Pierce, Florence
Papers. 1926-62. 0.1 ft.
Open. Unpublished guide.
Young Women's Christian Association, Archives of the National Board.
Pierce (1891-1974) was the executive of student work in China and Singapore from 1925 to 1937 and from 1946 to 1950. Correspondence concerning the challenge of missionary work makes up the bulk of the collection. Includes descriptions of travel through China, of YWCA programs there in the 1930s, and of the Chinese political situation during 1949 and 1950.

12,727. Rice, Anna Virena
Papers. 1931-61. 27 items.
Open. Description.
Young Women's Christian Association, Archives of the National Board.
Rice (1888-1966) was executive director of the National Board from 1928 to 1938. Notes, speeches, devotional texts, worship service outlines, and quotations and other material compiled from speakers, conferences, and meetings.

12,728. United Service Organizations: YWCA
Records. 1949-77. 16 cu.ft.
Access restricted. No guide.
Young Women's Christian Association, Archives of the National Board.
The YWCA was affiliated with the USO from 1941 to 1947 and from 1949 to March 1977. Files include minutes, correspondence, reports, and studies. The YWCA was the only women's agency of six agencies who cooperated to form the USO, which provides civilian services for military personnel.

12,729. War Work Council of the National Board, YWCA
Records. 1917-22. 0.1 ft. and 2 vols.
Open. Unpublished guide.
Young Women's Christian Association, Archives of the National Board.
The Council, established in 1917 and dissolved in 1920, trained women for leadership roles; its activities included establishing hostess houses, relief work in liberated Europe, and arranging for the transportation of European war brides to the US. Included are financial statements of the YWCA, the YMCA, and the United War Work Campaign and program material from the volunteer workers bureau. Also includes scrapbooks containing material relating to an Ellington Airfield, TX, hostess house, the Polish Grey Samaritans, and the training school for Old Country Service. The YMCA, the YWCA, the National Catholic War Council, the Jewish Welfare Board, the War Camp Community service, the American Library Association and The Salvation Army were the original members of the general committee of the United War Work Campaign.

12,730. Wygal, Winnifred
Papers. 1928-71. 0.5 ft.
Open. Description.
Young Women's Christian Association, Archives of the National Board.
National Board and a lecturer on religious topics. Correspondence primarily from YWCA colleagues, diary excerpts from a trip to a Gandhi ashram, autobiographical material, speech and conference notes, published and unpublished articles, and devotional readings are included.

12,731. Young, Louise
Papers. 1930-35. 0.1 ft.
Open. Unpublished guide.
Young Women's Christian Association, Archives of the National Board.
Young (1892-1974) was a member of the National Board staff during the 1930s and a professor at Scarritt College. Correspondence relates to her involvement in the organization of the Southern Council on Women and Children in Industry and to the Association of Southern Women for the Prevention of Lynching.

12,732. The YWCA of China
Records. 1912-52. 0.5 cu.ft.
Open. Unpublished guide.
Young Women's Christian Association, Archives of the National Board.
Annual reports of the national committee of the YWCA of China, reports on the status of women in China and the progress of the YWCA work there, surveys of the associations, and correspondence of the American field staff concerning their adjustment to work in China, including travel narratives and descriptions of the life style, cultural habits, and political climate of

the country. Newsletters, posters, pamphlets, and material concerning rural and industrial programs offered by the YWCA are also included.

NEWBURGH

12,733. Congregation Archives
Records. 1869- . 8 boxes and 15 vols.
Access restricted. No guide.
Dominican Sisters, Congregation of the Most Holy Rosary.
Minutes, financial records, school records, correspondence, and photos of the Congregation, a religious order of women founded in 1869 in New York City. Includes correspondence of mothers general, reminiscences of several sisters, and items related to the Saint Nicholas School in New York City, which was established and operated by members of the order.

NIAGARA FALLS

12,734. History of Niagara Falls and the Niagara Frontier
Collection. 1669- . More than 10,000 vols. and items.
Access restricted. No guide.
Niagara Falls Public Library.
Correspondence, diaries, financial papers, minutes, genealogical material, scrapbooks, pamphlets, and books pertain to Niagara Falls and the Niagara Frontier. Includes correspondence and other papers of the Porter family, the first permanent settlers in the region; scrapbooks and papers of the Parkhurst Whitney family; pictures and descriptions of women who did rope walking and barrel riding on the Niagara River; items concerned with local women's experiences during the War of 1812; programs of The Study Club, a women's group of the early 20th century; clippings containing birth, death, and marriage information; cemetery records; and family Bibles.

12,735. Niagara Falls Area History
Collection. 1678- . Ca. 15,000 items and 534 microfilm reels.
Open. Catalog and newspaper index.
Niagara Falls Public Library.
Correspondence, manuscripts, minutes, financial records, scrapbooks, photos, clippings, newspapers, iconography, and books concern Niagara Falls, the city of Niagara Falls, area residents, and communities and activities along the lower Niagara River.

NORTH TARRYTOWN

12,736. Bureau of Social Hygiene
Records. 1911-40. 32 cu.ft.
Open. Unpublished guide.
Rockefeller University, Rockefeller Archive Center.
Founded in 1911 and disbanded in 1940 after six years with no appropriations, the Bureau sought to study, improve, and prevent "those social conditions, crimes, and diseases which adversely affect the well-being of society, with special reference to prostitution and the evils associated therewith." Annual reports, minutes, financial records, and correspondence re projects concerning prostitution, white slave traffic, birth control, population, maternal health, and policewomen. Included are a few folders on each of the following: the American Birth Control League, the American Social Hygiene Association, the British Social Hygiene Council, and the Committee on Maternal Health. Katharine B. Davis served as the Bureau's general secretary from 1918 to 1928.

12,737. General Education Board
Records. 1902-56. Ca. 350 cu.ft.
Open. Unpublished guide.
Rockefeller University, Rockefeller Archive Center.
The Board, founded in 1903, sought to give "assistance to education in the US without distinction of race, sex, or creed." Minutes, financial and administrative records, correspondence, diaries, surveys, reports, studies, and conference proceedings. Includes information on grant-making activities and studies concerning child study, 4-H clubs, home economics, and homemakers clubs, as well as direct grants to colleges and universities, with a few folders on Barnard, Bennington, Bryn Mawr, Connecticut College for Women, Goucher, Huntingdon (Alabama), Mount Holyoke, North Carolina College for Women, Radcliffe, Sarah Lawrence, Simmons, Skidmore, Smith, Vassar, Wells, Wellesley, Western College for Women (Ohio), and Wheaton. Nine folders on Wesleyan College for Women (Georgia) are also included.

12,738. Laura Spelman Rockefeller Memorial
Records. 1918-41. 58 cu.ft.
Open. Unpublished guide.
Rockefeller University, Rockefeller Archive Center.
Founded in 1918 in memory of Laura (Spelman) [Mrs. John D.] Rockefeller and disbanded in 1929, this philanthropic organization attempted to achieve concrete improvements in living conditions and to contribute to public welfare. Minutes, administrative papers, financial records, correspondence, reports, charts, maps, pamphlets, and clippings. Correspondence relates to projects sponsored or aided by the Memorial for public health, religion, emergency relief, leisure, child study and parent education, social studies, interracial relations, and general education. Correspondents include Mabel Choate, Orie L. Hatcher, Emma P. Hirth, Kate Burr Johnson, Lucy Peabody, Florence Read, Emma B. Speer, Elizabeth Woodward, Sydnor H. Walker, Elizabeth Walton, and Edna N. White. Included are a few folders on each of the following: the American Association for Adult Education; the Bureau of Vocational Information, New York; the Camp Fire Girls; the Girl Scouts; Merrill-Palmer School; the National Organization for Public Health Nursing; the Philadelphia Bureau of Occupations for Trained Women; the Public School Athletic League, Girls Branch; Smith College, Institute for Coordination of Women's Interests; Spelman College; University of North Carolina, State Board of Charities; the Women's American Baptist Foreign Mission Society; and the Women's Educational and Industrial Union. Also included are a substantial number of folders on the American Home Economics Association; the Child Study Association; the Maternity Center Association, Manhattan and Brooklyn; the Neighborhood Teachers Association—National Education Committee for Non-English-Speaking Women; the Southern Women's Educational Alliance; and the YWCA.

12,739. Rockefeller Foundation
Records. 1913-41. Ca. 1255 cu.ft.
Open. Unpublished guide.
Rockefeller University, Rockefeller Archive Center.
Minutes, financial records, reports, and correspondence concerning projects sponsored or aided by this philanthropic organization, which was founded in 1913. Most material relating to women appears in the child study and nursing files. Mary Beard, Elizabeth W. Brackett, F. Elizabeth Crowell, Persis Putnam, and Mary Elizabeth Tennant were officers of the nursing program, while Sydnor H. Walker was an officer in social sciences. Correspondents include Esther W. Bates, Vera (Micheles) Dean, Marion M. Dilts, and Ethel Johns. Includes a few folders each for the American Female Guardian Society and Home for the Friendless, the Child Research Council, the Institute of Women's Professional Relations, Johns Hopkins University (obstetrical records), Wellesley College (building and endowment), the Working Women's Protective Union, and the YWCA national board.

12,740. Rockefeller, John D.
Papers. 1839-1937. Ca. 200 cu.ft. and 4000 microfiche.
Open. Unpublished guide.
Rockefeller University, Rockefeller Archive Center.
Rockefeller (1839-1937) was a businessman and philanthropist. Collection contains correspondence with female leaders in education, temperance, and suffrage, including Jennie F. Duty, J. E. Foster, Harriet E. Giles, Mary E. Ingersoll, Mrs. F. D. Mather, Sophia B. Packard, Louise S. Patterson, and Lucy H. Washington. Schools and colleges represented include Barnard, Lake Erie Seminary, Mount Holyoke, Rutgers Female College, Smith, Spelman, Vassar, and Wellesley.

ONEIDA

12,741. Oneida Woman's Christian Temperance Union
Records. 1914-56. 4 vols.
Open. Unpublished guide.
Madison County Historical Society.
Minute books of the Oneida WCTU, which campaigned for temperance and prohibition. The group also assisted needy area families, helped with community programs, and supported foreign missionaries.

12,742. Perkins, Mary
Papers. 1846-88. 5 vols.
Open. No guide.
Madison County Historical Society.
Scattered diaries of [Mrs. Reuben] Perkins, a farmwife who lived in Canastota, NY.

12,743. Political Equality Club, Oneida Chapter
Records. 1896-1914. 2 vols.
Open. Unpublished guide.
Madison County Historical Society.
Minute books of this chapter of the Club, which was founded in 1896 to work for women's suffrage and other rights for women. Members met with legislators to discuss pending legislation and studied political matters.

12,744. Smith, Gerrit, Family
Papers. 1839-74. 115 items.
Open. Unpublished guide.
Madison County Historical Society.
Includes family correspondence of Smith (1797-1874), a philanthropist, politician, and resident of Peterboro, NY, who crusaded for abolition, temperance, and women's rights. The letters are primarily from his wife Ann Fitzhugh Smith (1805-75) and daughter Elizabeth (Smith) [Mrs. Charles Dudley] Miller (1822-1911) and were written while the women were on a European tour in 1862. Elizabeth Miller later became an active suffragist.

ONEONTA

12,745. Hartwick College
Records. 1928- . No size given.
Open. No guide.
Hartwick College Archives.
Records of Hartwick College, a coeducational school that was established in 1928, include faculty minutes; Women's Club minutes and programs; a transcript of an oral history interview; a 1929 circular for women students; house rules for 1935; class registers; a nursing newsletter; photos of

faculty, students, sororities, the alumni association, clubs, and college events; a college newspaper; press releases; sorority magazines; faculty publications; clippings; and other items.

12,746. Hartwick Seminary Archives
Records. 1797-1941. No size given.
Open. No guide.
Hartwick College Archives.
The Seminary was established in 1797 and first admitted women in 1851; after 1929 it was called Hartwick Academy. Transcripts of oral history interviews; constitution, bylaws, rules of order, a history, a song, and programs of the Zetasophian "Zeta" Society, a women's group; photos of faculty members, students, families, basketball teams, the choir, a husking bee, the Zeta Society, the Hartwick Seminary Association, and C. G. Hall prize winners; and Seminary publications, including issues of the *Monthly* and *The Hartwickian.* Also includes correspondence and manuscripts, some of which may refer to women faculty or students such as Alice Whitbeck, who in 1881 was the first woman to receive a diploma in classics from the Seminary.

12,747. Saxton, Andrew B.
Papers. 1882-1929. 142 items.
Open. No guide.
Hartwick College Archives.
Includes letters from women to Saxton, a poet and newspaper editor, concerning literary matters as well as personal letters to his family and poems by Saxton.

12,748. Yale Collection
Collection. 1796-1801. 36 items.
Open. No guide.
Hartwick College Archives.
Papers relating to John Christopher Hartwick include a 1797 letter from Janet Montgomery of the Hartwick Patent (a land grant) to John C. Kunze concerning the college Hartwick wanted to establish.

OSSINING

12,749. Center House Archives
Records. 1876- . No size given.
Closed. No guide.
Dominican Sisters of the Sick Poor, Center House.
Financial records, correspondence, photos, and clippings of the Sisters, a religious order of women first recognized by the Catholic Church in 1910. Includes items on the establishment of the congregation, which concern the foundress's efforts to meet the needs of New York City's sick and poor. Also includes reports of major superiors and directives of the congregation's assemblies.

12,750. Ossining School for Girls
Records. 1874-ca. 1932. Ca. 2 ft.
Open. No guide.
Ossining Historical Society Museum.
The School, founded in 1869, admitted both boarders and day pupils for classes from kindergarten through high school. Includes academic records and files of alumnae, records of social events and cultural programs, photos of buildings and students, copies of the yearbook *The Quill,* and diaries of [Miss] Clara C. Fuller, principal from ca. 1894 to 1932, when the school closed.

12,751. Redway, Virginia Larkin
Papers. Ca. 1937-65. Ca. 2 ft.
Open. No guide.
Ossining Historical Society Museum.
Family papers, including photos, clippings, and portraits of [Mrs. Laurance D.] Redway (1886-1975), who was Museum curator from 1938 to 1950, president of the Ossining Historical Society from 1951 to 1955, and an active participant in many civic organizations. Also contains Ossining Historical Society records, including correspondence, scrapbooks, photos, clippings, pamphlets, and copies of the annual *Intelligencer* as well as records of the Ossining War Council, formed during WWII, and of the Ossining Council of Social Agencies. Other records and clippings relate to Redway's participation in the local branch of the American National Red Cross, the Women's Auxiliary of the Medical Society of Westchester County, the Ossining Music Guild, the Ossining Children's Center, and the Ossining Recreation Commission.

OSWEGO

12,752. Church and Douglass Families
Papers. 1815-1935. 1.5 ft.
Open. Published guide.
Oswego County Historical Society.
Papers of these families, which were closely associated with the development of the Oswego public schools and the Oswego Normal School, date primarily from 1850 to 1870. Includes correspondence of Amanda Church, Eliza Church, Julia Church, Carrie Church Douglass, and others about family matters. Also includes a journal and a book of lesson plans that Frances Weed kept. Taken from Monica Taller and Kurt Toback, *Sources Relating to Women's History in Special Collections, Penfield Library, State University College and Oswego County Historical Society* (Oswego, NY: State University College and Oswego County Historical Society).

12,753. Coates, Aurora (Walker)
Papers. 1886-1900. 3 vols.
Open. Published guide.
Oswego County Historical Society.
Scattered diaries kept by Coates (1826-1900), who was born and lived all her life on a farm in Oswego. In her diaries she describes her daily life, including her home and church activities; her personal philosophy of life; and local people, including her sister Mary Edwards Walker (1832-1919), a physician. The diaries also contain poems, which Coates may have written. Taken from Monica Taller and Kurt Toback, *Sources Relating to Women's History in Special Collections, Penfield Library, State University College and Oswego County Historical Society* (Oswego, NY: State University College and Oswego County Historical Society).

12,754. Walker, Mary Edwards
Papers. 1860-1918. 1 ft.
Open. Published guide.
Oswego County Historical Society.
Walker (1832-1919) was a physician, Civil War surgeon, dress reformer, and the first woman to win the Congressional Medal of Honor. Includes correspondence concerning her speaking engagements in England and other business and personal matters. Also includes her Congressional Medal of Honor, her medical diploma, and photos. Taken from Monica Taller and Kurt Toback, *Sources Relating to Women's History in Special Collections, Penfield Library, State University College and Oswego County Historical Society* (Oswego, NY: State University College and Oswego County Historical Society).

12,755. Burt, Bradley Benedict
Papers. 1745-1899. 18 in.
Open. Published guide.
State University College at Oswego Library, Special Collections.
Burt (1814-98), a lawyer and law partner of his brother-in-law William Curtis Noyes, was interested in local history and genealogy. Family papers include letters to Burt from Mary Elizabeth Burt (1850-1918), Libbie Burt, John Burt, and James Burt regarding family matters; correspondence of female family members about the family business; letters to William Noyes and his sister Martha (Noyes) Williams, dealing primarily with family and genealogical matters; and letters relating to genealogy. Also includes a family history by William Noyes and a poem that Emma Burt probably wrote. Taken from Monica Taller and Kurt Toback, *Sources Relating to Women's History in Special Collections, Penfield Library, State University College and Oswego County Historical Society* (Oswego, NY: State University College and Oswego County Historical Society).

12,756. Coye, Laura Parker
Papers. 1840-64. 6 in.
Open. Published guide.
State University College at Oswego Library, Special Collections.
Letters to Coye, a resident of Gilbertsville, NY, are from relatives and friends, especially female cousins and sisters. Also includes Coye's school essays and poems. Taken from Monica Taller and Kurt Toback, *Sources Relating to Women's History in Special Collections, Penfield Library, State University College and Oswego County Historical Society* (Oswego, NY: State University College and Oswego County Historical Society).

12,757. Fillmore, Millard
Papers. 1824-89. 20 ft.
Open. Published guide.
State University College at Oswego Library, Special Collections.
Papers of Fillmore (1800-74), President of the US from 1850 to 1852, include correspondence with his first wife Abigail Powers Fillmore; his second wife Caroline C. Fillmore; Anna Ella Carroll, who stated that she had determined northern military strategy in the Civil War; Dorothea Dix, a crusader for better mental hospitals; and other women. Taken from Monica Taller and Kurt Toback, *Sources Relating to Women's History in Special Collections, Penfield Library, State University College and Oswego County Historical Society* (Oswego, NY: State University College and Oswego County Historical Society).

12,758. Hayes Textile Company
Records. 1913-29. 8 ft.
Open. Published guide.
State University College at Oswego Library, Special Collections.
The Company manufactured knitted goods in Oswego from 1906 to 1929, when it shut down because of lack of business. Primarily ledger books and other business records, including a payroll ledger listing names of workers, many of them women, by job category with hours worked, rate of pay, and total pay per week. Taken from Monica Taller and Kurt Toback, *Sources Relating to Women's History in Special Collections, Penfield Library, State University College and Oswego County Historical Society* (Oswego, NY: State University College and Oswego County Historical Society).

12,759. Marshall Family
Papers. 1762-1908. 125 ft.
Open. Published guide.
State University College at Oswego Library, Special Collections.
Papers of five generations of the Holmes, Marshall, DeAngelis, and other related families, who settled in central and western New York during the early 19th century. Includes correspondence, diaries, meditations, a reminiscence, financial and admittance records relating to the Buffalo Orphan Asylum, and an obituary of Ruth Holmes Marshall (1790-1878). Ruth Marshall was a resident of Sherburne, NY, and Chautauqua County, NY, until her marriage to John Ellis Marshall (1785-1838), a

physician who practiced in Mayville, NY. Ruth Marshall served as chief directress of the Buffalo Orphan Asylum for many years. After her husband's death she lived with their son Orsamus Holmes Marshall (1812-?), who was married to Millicent Ann (DeAngelis) Marshall (1813-87). Papers of Millicent Marshall, whose parents were Elizabeth Webb DeAngelis and Pascal Charles Joseph DeAngelis, include letters from relatives, her husband, and their daughter Elizabeth Coe Marshall (1847-92) as well as a journal she kept in Europe in 1860 and financial papers. Elizabeth Marshall's papers include correspondence with close friends, diaries, and financial papers. Educated at Miss Sheldon's school in Buffalo, NY, and at Miss Porter's in Farmington, CT, Elizabeth Marshall was an active member of the First Presbyterian Church in Buffalo, an organizer of the Buffalo District Nurses' Association, and a member of the executive board of Buffalo General Hospital. Other papers relate to Octavia Simpson Marshall (?-1894), who married John Ellis Marshall (1839-1900) and resided in Cincinnati, OH; these include correspondence with her husband, Millicent Marshall, her grandfather J. A. Simpson, and Emma Coburn. Octavia Marshall had no children. Taken from Monica Taller and Kurt Toback, *Sources Relating to Women's History in Special Collections, Penfield Library, State University College and Oswego County Historical Society* (Oswego, NY: State University College and Oswego County Historical Society).

12,760. Oral Histories
Oral history. Nd. 24 tapes.
Open. Published guide.
State University College at Oswego Library, Special Collections.
Interviews with various Oswego County women relate to women and factory work; women on the farm, in the home, and as teachers; women's clubs and club leaders; and black women on campus. Taken from Monica Taller and Kurt Toback, *Sources Relating to Women's History in Special Collections, Penfield Library, State University College and Oswego County Historical Society* (Oswego, NY: State University College and Oswego County Historical Society).

12,761. Scrapbooks
Collection. Nd. No size given.
Open. Published guide.
State University College at Oswego Library, Special Collections.
Scrapbooks containing obituaries of 19th-century Oswego residents, including many women. Also available on microfilm. Taken from Monica Taller and Kurt Toback, *Sources Relating to Women's History in Special Collections, Penfield Library, State University College and Oswego County Historical Society* (Oswego, NY: State University College and Oswego County Historical Society).

12,762. Sheldon, Edward Austin
Papers. 1819-97. 12.5 in.
Open. Published guide.
State University College at Oswego Library, Special Collections.
Papers of Sheldon (1823-97), who founded the Oswego Primary Teachers' Training School in 1861, which eventually became the State University College at Oswego. Includes letters from Margaret E. M. Jones, Elizabeth Mayo, Lucy Larcom, and other women involved in education and teacher training; notebooks containing Sheldon's notes on the instructional techniques of Margaret E. M. Jones, who was brought from England in 1861 to demonstrate the application of Pestalozzian methods; a report on compensation of women teachers; and Sheldon family papers, including family correspondence and a few papers relating to Mary Downing (Sheldon) [Mrs. Earl] Barnes (1850-98), Laura Austin Sheldon, and Elizabeth Sheldon. Taken from Monica Taller and Kurt Toback, *Sources Relating to Women's History in Special Collections, Penfield Library, State University College and Oswego County Historical Society* (Oswego, NY: State University College and Oswego County Historical Society).

12,763. Shepard Family
Papers. 1838-1936. 7 boxes.
Open. Published guide.
State University College at Oswego Library, Special Collections.
Includes letters from Hannah (DeAngelis) Lemoyne Wells (1802-90), the daughter of Pascal DeAngelis, to her sisters, brother, and daughter Elizabeth Shepard about family matters. Born in Holland Patent, NY, Hannah married Chester Wells in 1825, and they settled on a farm near New Haven, NY, which later became the Shepard estate, LaBergerie. Also contains letters from Elizabeth DeAngelis (Wells) Shepard (1830-1922), the daughter of Elizabeth and Chester Wells, to family members, among them her uncle Orsamus Marshall. In 1851 she married Sidney Shepard, a wealthy factory owner, and they resided both in Buffalo, NY, and at her summer home in New Haven. Other papers include correspondence of Florence Wells, the daughter of William Wells, regarding business matters and details of family and home life and of the administration of the family estate in New Haven, which she inherited. The letters are primarily from Grant Lindsley, secretary to the family. Taken from Monica Taller and Kurt Toback, *Sources Relating to Women's History in Special Collections, Penfield Library, State University College and Oswego County Historical Society* (Oswego, NY: State University College and Oswego County Historical Society).

12,764. Skinner Family
Papers. 1815-76. 2.5 in.
Open. Published guide.
State University College at Oswego Library, Special Collections.
Includes letters from Cynthia (Skinner) Walker (1792-?), who married Hiram Walker in 1827, to her parents Timothy and Ruth Skinner and her friend Charlotte Stebbins. The letters deal primarily with her home life in Union Square, NY, and her memories of her parents, but they also contain some discussion of religious attitudes and references to anti-Masonry. Also includes correspondence of Charlotte (Stebbins) Skinner, who married Avery Skinner after the death of his first wife. Her letters, primarily to her husband while he was in the state government, provide insight into their marriage and family life. Taken from Monica Taller and Kurt Toback, *Sources Relating to Women's History in Special Collections, Penfield Library, State University College and Oswego County Historical Society* (Oswego, NY: State University College and Oswego County Historical Society).

12,765. Snyder, Charles McCool
Papers. ?-1972. 8 ft.
Open. Published guide.
State University College at Oswego Library, Special Collections.
Papers of Snyder, a former history professor at the College, include notes, photos, and the manuscript for his biography of Mary Edwards Walker, a 19th-century dress reformer, feminist, physician, and winner of the Congressional Medal of Honor. The book was published as *Dr. Mary Walker: The Little Lady in Pants* (New York: Vantage Press, 1962). Taken from Monica Taller and Kurt Toback, *Sources Relating to Women's History in Special Collections, Penfield Library, State University College and Oswego County Historical Society* (Oswego, NY: State University College and Oswego County Historical Society).

OWEGO

12,766. Smith, Fannie (Sackett)
Oral history. 1966. 1 tape.
Open. Unpublished guide.
Tioga County Historical Society Museum.
Interview with [Mrs. William B.] Smith (1865-1972), a teacher, in which she relates her early teaching experiences in Owego and Candor, NY.

PEEKSKILL

12,767. Archives
Records. 1865- . No size given.
Open. No guide.
Franciscan Missionary Sisters of the Sacred Heart.
Papers of mothers superior, correspondence, photos, scrapbooks, and other records, including material relating to St. Joseph's Home for Orphans, which was established and operated by members of the order. The order was founded in Italy in 1860 and established in the US in New York City in 1865.

PENN YAN

12,768. Wilkinson, Jemima
Papers. 1788-1831. Ca. 1 ft.
Access restricted. No guide.
Yates County Genealogical and Historical Society.
Wilkinson (1752-1819) was the leader of a religious group and a pioneer settler in Yates County. Includes correspondence, diaries, sermon notes, poems, deeds, and inventories.

PLATTSBURGH

12,769. Delord Family
Papers. 1799-1914. 8 boxes (773 items).
Open. Published guide.
State University College, North Country History Center.
Personal correspondence and financial papers of Henry Delord (1764-1825), a merchant, postmaster, justice of the peace, judge, and county supervisor, and of his wife Elizabeth (Ketchum) Delord. Her correspondence, some of which is with her husband, also relates to invitations and social life in Plattsburgh during and after the War of 1812. Also includes correspondence of their daughter Frances Henrietta Delord with her mother and friends while she was at school in Champlain, NY, as well as letters written before her marriage in 1832. Additional family correspondence is included. See G. Glyndon Cole, *Manuscripts for Research: Report of the Director of the North Country History Center, 1961-1974* (Plattsburgh, NY: State University College, 1975).

12,770. Hall Family
Papers. 1861-1909. 6 boxes (1002 items).
Open. Published guide.
State University College, North Country History Center.
Papers of Frances Delord (Webb) Hall (1834-1913), a temperance leader and charity worker, and her husband Francis Bloodgood Hall (1827-1903), pastor of the Peristrome Presbyterian Church in Plattsburgh, an inventor, and a US Army chaplain during the Civil War who was awarded the Congressional Medal of Honor. Includes correspondence between them and Francis Hall's mother Margaret Hall; papers related to their charity work and to the Cumberland Bay Works, a family corporation that manufactured an ointment for women known as Fanoline; scrapbooks; and

printed items. See G. Glyndon Cole, *Manuscripts for Research: Report of the Director of the North Country History Center, 1961-1974* (Plattsburgh, NY: State University College, 1975).

12,771. Hall, Frances Delord (Webb)
Papers. 1848-1917. 11 boxes (1091 items).
Open. Published guide.
State University College, North Country History Center.
Hall (1834-1913), a leader in the New York temperance movement and a self-styled physician, was married to Francis B. Hall, pastor of the Peristrome Presbyterian Church in Plattsburgh. Contains personal correspondence, including a large number of letters of condolence after her husband's death; a journal and correspondence pertaining to a trip abroad with her husband; essays and poems she wrote before her marriage; business and legal papers; and obituaries of and tributes to her husband. See G. Glyndon Cole, *Manuscripts for Research: Report of the Director of the North Country History Center, 1961-1974* (Plattsburgh, NY: State University College, 1975).

12,772. Porter, Marjorie Lansing
Papers. Nd. 45 boxes.
Open. Published guide.
State University College, North Country History Center.
A newspaper columnist, writer, lecturer, and collector of folk songs and folklore, Porter (1891-1973) was an historian for Essex and Clinton counties and for the city of Plattsburgh. Contains correspondence; oral history tapes and transcripts; manuscripts of published books, stories, and articles; photos; prints; and personal memorabilia. Includes items Porter collected during her research on the history of northern New York. See G. Glyndon Cole, *Manuscripts for Research: Report of the Director of the North Country History Center, 1961-1974* (Plattsburgh, NY: State University College, 1975).

12,773. Swetland Family
Papers. 1829-84. 7 boxes (891 items).
Open. Published guide.
State University College, North Country History Center.
Correspondence and financial papers of William Swetland (1782-1864) and his wife Elizabeth (Ketchum) Delord Swetland. The letters contain information about Elizabeth Swetland's raising of her granddaughter after the child's mother died, church and community matters, activities of friends and neighbors, travel conditions, living conditions, and state and national events. Before her marriage to Swetland, Elizabeth Ketchum was married to Henry Delord. See G. Glyndon Cole, *Manuscripts for Research: Report of the Director of the North Country History Center, 1961-1974* (Plattsburgh, NY: State University College, 1975).

POTSDAM

12,774. Hosmer, Helen
Papers. 1927-65. 6 drawers.
Open. No guide.
State University of New York College at Potsdam Archives.
Correspondence, course outlines, class notes and schedules, and concert programs of Hosmer relate to her years as a teacher at the Crane School of Music at the College.

RIVERHEAD

12,775. Cleveland
Papers. ?-1972. 6 ft. and 2 drawers.
Open. No guide.
Suffolk County Historical Society.
Notes and transcriptions of records, including cemetery records, that Loie (Burr) [Mrs. Walter H.] Cleveland (1905-72) made while doing research on her ancestry. Cleveland was a charter member of the genealogy section of the Historical Society.

12,776. Daughters of the Revolution
Records. 1919-73. 1 Hollinger box.
Open. No guide.
Suffolk County Historical Society.
Secretary's books, treasurer's books and receipts, an historian's book containing clippings from local newspapers, and books of the Yennicott chapter of the Daughters, a hereditary society that was founded in 1891. This chapter was organized in 1919 and disbanded in 1973. The group, which was similar to the DAR, held regular meetings to talk about the patriots' roles in the Revolution. Also includes two pamphlets by the Woman's Board of Missions, "Dr. Kate Woodhull—Pioneer Doctor for Women in Foochow" and "The Hospital on Peace Street, Foochow China." These refer to Catherine C. Woodhull and Hannah C. Woodhull, missionaries to China and charter members of the Yennicott chapter. They were the daughters of Noah Hallock Woodhull and Hannah (Conklin) Woodhull of Wading River, NY.

12,777. Dickinson, Irene Hallock
Papers. Nd. 3 vols.
Open. No guide.
Suffolk County Historical Society.
Notebooks of [Miss] Dickinson (1888-) contain reminiscences, poetry, photos, and clippings about her family and its history.

12,778. Long Island Forum: Strong, Kate W.
Papers. 1938-77. 3 ft.
Open. Unpublished guide.
Suffolk County Historical Society.
[Miss] Strong (1879-1977) was a regular contributing editor to the *Long Island Forum.* Contains stories she wrote for the magazine, including "True Tales of Long Island," which she wrote from memory and from family papers.

12,779. Luce and Howell Families
Papers. 1773-1861. 1 document case.
Open. Unpublished guide.
Suffolk County Historical Society.
Letters to Abraham Luce (ca. 1789-ca. 1865), a minister, and his wife Abigail (Howell) Luce from their nieces H. Harriet Hudson Ogden, Abigail Howell, and Eliza Howell; a sister Mehetable W. Reeve; a friend Phebe Hudson; and other relatives and friends. In their letters the women describe their family and friends, illnesses, deaths, visits, and travels.

12,780. Riverhead Lecture Association
Records. 1893-1924. 1 document case.
Open. No guide.
Suffolk County Historical Society.
Programs of the Association, which organized lectures and entertainment for the winter months, contain descriptions of the lectures and other events. Also includes photos and reviews. The Association was founded in 1890.

12,781. Westhampton Presbyterian Church
Records. 1798-1975. 1 vol.
Open. No guide.
Suffolk County Historical Society.
Church records of births, baptisms, deaths, and weddings. The Church was founded in 1742 and is still in existence.

12,782. Young, Ida May (Dayton)
Papers. 1910-50. 10 vols.
Open. Partial unpublished guide.
Suffolk County Historical Society.
Scrapbooks of Young (1872-?) contain clippings, many of which relate to family reunions, weddings, births, and marriages. Also contains a birthday book in which she listed people's birthdays, often including as many as 20 people to a day.

ROCHESTER

12,783. American Baptist Foreign Mission Society and Woman's American Baptist Foreign Mission Society
Records. 1830-1969. Ca. 500,000 items.
Access restricted. No guide.
American Baptist Historical Society.
Records of the Society.

12,784. Crawford, Isabel Alice Hartley
Papers. 1880-1916. 6 ft.
Open. No guide.
American Baptist Historical Society.
Papers of Crawford (1865-1961), a missionary who lived among American Indians.

12,785. Judson, Emily Chubbuck
Papers. Nd. 7 items.
Open. No guide.
American Baptist Historical Society
Correspondence of [Mrs. Adoniram] Judson (1817-54).

12,786. Rauschenbusch, Pauline E. Rother
Papers. 1900-40. 12 ft.
Closed. No guide.
American Baptist Historical Society.
Personal correspondence of [Mrs. Walter] Rauschenbusch.

12,787. Swain, Anna Canada
Papers. 1930-60. 11 boxes.
Open. No guide.
American Baptist Historical Society.
Papers of [Mrs. Leslie] Swain (1889-), who was involved in the American Baptist ecumenical movement.

12,788. Traver, Edith Grace
Papers. 1910-30. 11 boxes.
Open. No guide.
American Baptist Historical Society.
Correspondence and diaries of [Miss] Traver, who was a missionary in China.

12,789. International Museum of Photography at George Eastman House
Collection. 1839- . Ca. 450,000 items.
Open. Published guide.
International Museum of Photography at George Eastman House, Archives.
Primarily consisting of photos, the collection also includes correspondence, tapes and transcripts of oral history interviews, and other items pertaining to the history and aesthetics of photography. Includes correspondence and other manuscripts of Barbara Morgan, Imogen Cunningham, Nancy Newhall, and other women; transcripts of interviews with Bérénice Abbott and Dorothea Lange; and a master's thesis by Gerda Peterich about French calotypes. The Museum is in the former home of George Eastman, the founder of Eastman Kodak Company. A part of the Archives collection is described in each issue of the Eastman House's publication *Image.*

12,790. Monroe County Women
Collection. 1856-1968. 1 drawer and tapes.
Open. No guide.
Monroe County Historian's Office.
Contains letters, 1860-1926, from Maggie Brownyard in Kent County, MI, to her sister in Penfield, NY, as well as a Brownyard genealogy; a letter of Eliza Burgess Rust in Chili, NY, to her family in England comparing life and farm customs in England and America, ca. 1852; an 1878 diary of Mary Jane "Jennie" Brownyard that she wrote in

Rochester; an autobiography of Emma Willard, who was born in Monroe County and was a founder of the WCTU; an autobiography of Antoinette Brown Blackwell, a resident of Henrietta, NY, who was a Congregational and Unitarian minister; memoirs and genealogical material of Virginia Gruppe concerning her childhood in Henrietta, NY, in the early 20th century; a tape of remarks by aviator Blanche Stuart Scott; remarks by Caroline K. Simon, secretary of state in New York, concerning women in government; articles, booklets, cartoons, and a portrait of Susan B. Anthony; clippings concerning Congresswoman Jessica Weis, Caroline [Mrs. Frank] Gannett, New York state regent Helen Power, Sister Hieronymo, Martha Taylor Howard, and other women; WCTU files on county chapters; and a scrapbook of the Rochester Republican Women's Organization.

12,791. Anthony, Susan Brownell
Papers. 1837-1947. 1 box.
Open. Unpublished guide.
Rochester Museum and Science Center Library.
[Miss] Anthony (1820-1906) was a women's suffrage leader. Includes Anthony family letters, scrapbooks prepared by Anthony's personal secretary concerning the woman suffrage movement, and photos.

12,792. American Association of University Women
Records. 1930-36. 5 vols.
Open. No guide.
Rochester Public Library, Local History Division.
Founded as the College Women's Club in 1897, this Rochester group became affiliated with the AAUW in 1916. Scrapbooks contain clippings and programs concerning projects, teas, style shows, study groups, and activities designed to benefit the scholarship fund. Members of the AAUW listened to speeches, participated in discussions, and cooperated with other organizations.

12,793. Badger, Ella Louise (Smith)
Papers. 1877-84. 1 package.
Open. No guide.
Rochester Public Library, Local History Division.
Diaries in which [Mrs. Robert A.] Badger (1859-1949) describes friendships, parties, social activities, schooling, and family life from 1877 until four days before her marriage in 1884. Badger's activities included riding, singing and painting lessons, and attending church. Also includes an 1876 autograph album, school themes and exercises, and parlor games.

12,794. Belinson, Florence (Fenyvessy)
Papers. 1949-66. 1 folder and 2 vols.
Open. No guide.
Rochester Public Library, Local History Division.
Belinson and her husband Benjamin Belinson were owners and managers of the Little Theatre, a Rochester movie theater, for 35 years. Correspondence, telegrams, photos, theater programs, and clippings pertain to the Theatre. Florence Belinson came from a family which had been active in theater ownership and management in Rochester. The Belinsons acquired the Theatre in 1931; she managed the business alone from the time of her husband's death in 1957 until her retirement in 1966.

12,795. DeKroyft, Susan Helen (Aldrich)
Papers. 1848-1913. 19 vols. and 6 items.
Open. No guide.
Rochester Public Library, Local History Division.
[Mrs. William] DeKroyft (1818-1915) was a blind author. Included are manuscripts of her published works *Mortara* and *Story of Little Jakey* and of unpublished autobiographical and religious works such as "A Remarkable Exposition of the Position of Woman in the Human Family from Bible Times to the Present Century." Personal account books are also included.

12,796. Klinzing, Ernestine M.
Papers. 1907-63. 6 vols.
Open. No guide.
Rochester Public Library, Local History Division.
Scrapbooks of Klinzing (1891-1977), who was a piano and music history teacher at the Eastman School of Music in Rochester, contain musical programs, photos, clippings, and other papers from Rochester, New York City, several European cities, and from Baltimore, where she studied and taught at the Peabody Conservatory for six months.

12,797. Knox, Helena (Langslow)
Papers. 1914-46. 2 vols.
Open. No guide.
Rochester Public Library, Local History Division.
Scrapbooks of [Mrs. Paul] Knox (1888?-1969), who did war relief work in Rochester, contain correspondence, telegrams, photos, clippings, and other items. The material concerns such activities as collecting clothing, raising money, and making bandages. Knox received a bronze medal from the French government for her work in WWII. In 1941 she helped found the Maple Leaf Fund's Rochester branch.

12,798. O'Connor, Evelyn
Papers. 1887-1943. 81 vols.
Open. No guide.
Rochester Public Library, Local History Division.
Scrapbooks of O'Connor (1879-1953) contain theater and concert programs and pictures of actors and actresses performing in Rochester and New York City. Actresses such as Ethel Barrymore, Sarah Bernhardt, Fanny Brice, Mary Garden, and Helena Modjeska are represented.

12,799. Political Equality Club of Rochester
Records. 1887-1906. 1 folder and 11 vols.
Open. No guide.
Rochester Public Library, Local History Division.
The Club was founded in 1873 as the Women Taxpayers Association; in 1891 it became the Political Equality Club, and men were admitted to membership for the first time. Constitution, bylaws, annual reports, recording secretary's reports, scrapbooks, programs, publicity material, and a European travel diary are included. The Club's primary aim was to secure the right to vote, but it also became involved in other areas such as working to open the University of Rochester to women. Susan B. Anthony figures prominently in the material. The Club apparently dissolved in ca. 1915.

12,800. Rawlings, Marjorie (Kinnan)
Papers. 1926-28. 188-page item.
Open. No guide.
Rochester Public Library, Local History Division.
Poems by Rawlings (1896-1953), an author, entitled "Songs of a Housewife," which were published in the *Times-Union* during the time she lived in Rochester. The verse describes her attitude toward homemaking. Divorced from her husband Charles A. Rawlings in 1933, she married Norton Baskin in 1941.

12,801. Rochester Female Academy
Records. 1836-88. 2 folders and 18 vols.
Open. No guide.
Rochester Public Library, Local History Division.
The Academy was founded in Rochester in 1835 as the Rochester Female Seminary. Trustees reports list stock subscriptions and costs for purchasing the lot and for constructing and furnishing the school building. Also included are tuition books, treasurer's account book, and class books listing students and their completed courses. Aside from deportment, grammar, spelling, and composition, the young women studied a wide range of academic subjects, including philosophy, astronomy, literature, geography, French, botany, rhetoric, theology, ancient and contemporary history, algebra, geometry, technology, and constitutional law. The school was incorporated as the Rochester Female Academy in 1837 and was called the Misses Nichols' School from 1892 until it closed in 1903.

12,802. Rochester Female Charitable Society
Records. 1828-1923. 2 folders and 40 vols.
Open. No guide.
Rochester Public Library, Local History Division.
Founded in 1822 to provide aid to the destitute and sick, the Society is Rochester's oldest charitable organization. Constitution; minutes; treasurer's books; record books; records of clothing and aid distributed and received; relief workers' books; lists of officers, directresses, trustees, and committee members; and publicity circulars. The Society collected and distributed food and clothing and performed other services for those who had lost their income because of illness or related domestic emergencies. Aid was originally distributed through a network of women reponsible for knowing the needs of residents within their visiting districts. The Society also raised funds for the Rochester General Hospital and served as the Hospital's board of managers from 1864 to 1934. Fund-raising events included a concert by Jenny Lind in 1851. The Society now assists other agencies.

12,803. Rochester Picture File
Collection. Ca. 1800- . 16 drawers.
Open. Unpublished guide.
Rochester Public Library, Local History Division.
Visiting cards, cabinet photos, glossy photos, and drawings and engravings from books are included. Material contains pictures of actresses, authors, businesswomen, librarians, teachers, professors, women in community service, and other local residents, including Susan B. Anthony.

12,804. Roundabout Club
Records. 1885-1945. 5 folders and 30 vols.
Open. No guide.
Rochester Public Library, Local History Division.
Founded in 1885 by Mrs. B. O. Hough, the Club selected a topic of study every year, and each member gave a paper on a different aspect of this theme. Constitution, bylaws, minutes, financial records, papers presented, correspondence, and programs.

12,805. Woman's Christian Temperance Union, Fairport, NY
Records. 1877-1941. 11 vols.
Open. No guide.
Rochester Public Library, Local History Division.
Minutes and the corresponding secretary's records of the Fairport WCTU, which was founded in 1877. The members sang hymns, prayed, and listened to lectures. They eventually shifted their concern to narcotics.

12,806. Woman's Christian Temperance Union of Monroe County, NY
Records. 1895-1934. 9 vols.
Open. No guide.
Rochester Public Library, Local History Division.
Minutes of executive committee meetings and records of the recording and corresponding secretaries of this WCTU branch, which was founded in 1874. The records include details on all WCTU units in the County, including dates of organization, number of members, and kinds of activities. After passage of the 18th Amendment, the WCTU continued with such activities as promoting alcohol education in schools and petitioning against repeal of the Amendment. Other concerns such as purity in literature and art and the evils of tobacco also emerged.

12,807. Woman's Ethical Club
Records. 1889-1906. 2 folders and 6 vols.
Open. No guide.
Rochester Public Library, Local History Division.
The Club was founded in 1889 to discuss ethics and philanthropy and to cultivate spirit, liberality, and cooperation among members of various churches. Annual reports, minutes, financial records, correspondence, an address book of members, programs, and clippings are included. The Club, which met in local churches, discussed such topics as women's dress, college coeducation, self-culture, use of time, charity, thrift, business ethics, child rearing, working women, ethics in the arts, women in municipal affairs, and problems of modern life. Two notable speakers were Julia (Ward) Howe and Kate (Gannett) Wells.

12,808. Women's Educational and Industrial Union
Records. 1893- . 1 box, 4 vols., and 31 envelopes.
Open. No guide.
Rochester Public Library, Local History Division.
Founded in 1893, the Union wished to increase fellowship among women and to promote practical methods for securing their educational, industrial, and social advancement. Minutes of board meetings and annual meetings, thrift shop reports, tracts, programs, clippings, and other printed material. Members heard lecturers speak on various aspects of the fine arts and humanities, government, labor, politics, economics, social welfare, modern society, and gardening. Programs operated or supported by the Union included college scholarships for young women, occupational therapy and manual industrial training workshops, employment bureaus, services for the aged, and inexpensive school lunches. Many of the Union's public service programs were assumed by federal or state agencies.

12,809. Archives
Records. 1857- . 73 boxes, ca. 135 microfilm reels, and 10 tapes.
Access restricted. Unpublished guide.
Sisters of Mercy Motherhouse.
Minutes of organizations connected with the community, accounts of institutions operated by the Sisters, financial records, papers of sisters superior, governmental procedures, correspondence, 25 theses, photos, scrapbooks, and clippings of the community, which was established in 1857.

12,810. Congregation Archives
Records. 1836- . Ca. 11 boxes and 60 tapes.
Open. Inventory.
Sisters of St. Joseph Motherhouse.
Minutes, financial records, correspondence, diaries, oral history tapes and transcripts, teachers' class notes, photos, and scrapbooks of the Congregation, which was established in the US in 1836 in St. Louis. The Sisters are active primarily in education and social services, especially health care, care of the elderly, and care of orphans. Also includes records of mothers general, items pertaining to institutions of learning and health care established and conducted by the order, unpublished poems, music compositions, theses, historical annals, and other records.

12,811. Anthony and Avery
Papers. 1882-1908. Ca. 280 items.
Open. Unpublished guide.
University of Rochester Library.
Consists of letters primarily from [Miss] Susan Brownell Anthony (1820-1906) to Rachel Foster [Mrs. Cyrus Miller] Avery (1858-1919), who served as corresponding secretary of the National American Woman Suffrage Association. The letters reflect many facets of the suffrage movement, including plans for national conventions, strategies for adding women's suffrage amendments to the states' constitutions, the problems of winning new converts to the cause and of raising money, preparation of Anthony's biography by Ida (Husted) Harper, and the personal relationship between Anthony and Avery. Other letters to Anthony and Avery are from Elizabeth Cady Stanton, Carrie Chapman Catt, May Eliza (Wright) Sewall, Harriet (Taylor) Upton, Isabel Howland, Lillie (Devereux) Blake, Anna Howard Shaw, Lucretia (Longshore) Blankenburg, Elizabeth Blackwell, and Mary Garrett Hay.

12,812. Anthony, Susan Brownell
Papers. 1846-1904. 1 ft.
Open. Unpublished guide.
University of Rochester Library.
Letters from [Miss] Anthony (1820-1906), a suffragist, are primarily addressed to Harriet (Taylor) Upton and concern Upton's efforts to secure congressional support for the cause of women's suffrage. Also includes photos, ephemera, and memorabilia.

12,813. Broke, Frederica Sophia (Mure)
Papers. 1834. 1 vol.
Open. Card catalog.
University of Rochester Library.
Travel journal of Broke, who was the daughter of James Mure of Cecil Lodge, Herfordshire, England. In 1825 she married Horatio George Broke (1790-1860), who served as quartermaster general in Nova Scotia from 1830 to 1834. In 1834 the Brokes, their son Horace, Frederica Broke's sister, and three servants left Nova Scotia to tour the US. They visited Boston, Niagara Falls, Quebec, New York City, Philadelphia, Baltimore, and Washington, DC. In her journal Frederica Broke describes places, people, and events, and briefly lists the expenses of the trip. The portion of the diary that contains descriptions of Broke's experiences in upstate New York was published in *The University of Rochester Library Bulletin,* 4, no. 2 (Winter 1949).

12,814. Clarke, Freeman, Family
Papers. 1812-1929. 10 ft.
Open. Unpublished guide.
University of Rochester Library.
Correspondence and financial and legal records of Clarke (1809-87), a businessman and congressman from Rochester. Also includes letters Clarke wrote to his wife Henrietta Jaquelina (Ward) Clarke (1814-90) while he was in Washington as a congressman; letters from her sisters Susan W. Seldon and Siba Hand Smith, which relate to personal affairs and domestic matters such as the health of family members and arrangements for visits; and letters from her sons Edward Smith Clarke and Sherman Clarke. Other correspondence is between Henrietta Clarke's daughter Caroline (Clarke) Allen and her two daughters Henrietta (Allen) Mills and Mary Percival Allen. Also contains correspondence and a journal of Mary Allen concerning her experiences as a nurse in France in 1918 and 1919 and in Newfoundland in 1920.

12,815. Crapsey, Adelaide
Papers. 1878-1934. 2 ft.
Open. Unpublished guide.
University of Rochester Library.
[Miss] Crapsey (1878-1914) was a poet. Includes letters from Crapsey to her parents; letters Crapsey wrote to Esther Lowenthal, her teaching colleague at Smith College, while Crapsey was receiving tuberculosis treatment at a Saranac Lake, NY, nursing home in 1913 and 1914; manuscript and typed copies of Crapsey's poems and her study of English metrics; published and unpublished articles about Crapsey; photos; and memorabilia. Crapsey's posthumously published book of poetry *Verses* (1915) has gone through five editions. Many of her poems are written in the verse form she invented, the cinquain, which is a poem of five short lines of unequal length. Also published posthumously was Crapsey's analysis of English prosody *A Study in English Metrics* (1918).

12,816. Duncan, Barbara
Papers. 1878-1955. 0.5 ft.
Open. Unpublished guide.
University of Rochester Library.
[Miss] Duncan (1882-1965), music librarian at the Boston Public Library, became the first librarian for the Sibley Music Library at the Eastman School of Music at the University of Rochester, where she worked from 1922 until her retirement in 1950. Includes family correspondence, letters Duncan wrote to her mother during trips she took abroad to build the Music Library's collections, an essay Duncan wrote about her trips, and other essays she wrote.

12,817. Frost, Elizabeth (Hollister)
Papers. 1927-50. 0.5 ft.
Open. Unpublished guide.
University of Rochester Library.
Correspondence, biographical material, photos, and newspaper reviews of Frost (?-1958), an author. In her first book of poetry *The Lost Lyrist* (1928), Frost eulogizes her husband Elliott Park Frost (1884-1926), a professor of psychology at the University. Frost's other works include two books of poetry and three novels.

12,818. Gannett, William Channing
Papers. 1841-1956. 18 ft.
Open. Unpublished guide.
University of Rochester Library.
Gannett (1840-1923) was a Unitarian minister in St. Paul, MN, and in Rochester, NY. He and his wife Mary Thorn (Lewis) Gannett (1854-1952) were prominent civic leaders in Rochester, and both were active supporters of the women's rights movement. Includes correspondence, diaries, financial papers, manuscript and printed copies of sermons and articles, and printed articles on Unitarianism and women's suffrage. Also includes diaries, 1882-1944, of Mary Gannett, who was a member and officer of Rochester's Political Equality Club and the Woman Suffrage party of Monroe County, Inc. Also contained are letters to William Gannett from his sister Kate (Gannett) Wells (1838-1911), a Boston author, educator, philanthropist, and antisuffragist, and letters to the Gannetts from Susan B. Anthony, who, with her sister Mary S. Anthony, was a member of Gannett's congregation and a close personal friend of the Gannetts.

12,819. Green, Sylvina Maria (Dewey)
Papers. Ca. 1890-1900. 1 vol.
Open. Card catalog.
University of Rochester Library.
Scrapbook of Green (1832-?), who was active in the women's suffrage movement, contains clippings pertaining to the movement, which include speeches of Susan B. Anthony, Elizabeth Cady Stanton, Mary Livermore, Carrie Chapman Catt, Lucy Stone, Lucretia Mott, and others.

12,820. Harper, Margaret Cook (Durbin)
Papers. 1878-85. 0.5 ft.
Open. Unpublished guide.
University of Rochester Library.
Papers of Harper (1830-86), a philanthropist who was married to Fletcher Harper, Jr., of Harper Brothers. In the summer of 1878, Margaret Harper opened the Sea Shore Cottage at Atlanticville, NJ, "to afford a Summer Resort for the young working women of New York, who are in need of rest and recreation, with but a limited time to spare and insufficient means to pay the charges at the usual resorts." Includes letters from Julia F. Thompson, superintendent of the Cottage; well-wishers; and a few of the women who stayed at the Cottage. Also includes a scrapbook containing clippings about the resort, pictures, and printed items.

12,821. Harvey, Dorothy (Dudley)
Papers. 1917-52. 1 ft.
Open. Unpublished guide.
University of Rochester Library.
Correspondence and manuscripts and typescripts of poems and stories of [Mrs. Henry Blodgett] Harvey (1884-1962), an author. Includes correspondence and typescript poems of Theodore Dreiser and Carl Sandburg as well as letters from Alfred Stieglitz, Sherwood Anderson, Edgar Lee Masters, Harriet Monroe, H. L. Mencken, Marianne Moore, Gertrude Stein, Henri Matisse, Henry Miller, and J. Cowper Powys. Dorothy Dudley was involved in a Chicago literary group centered around Harriet Monroe. Dudley published poems and reviews in *Poetry: A Magazine of Verse,* the *American Magazine of Art,* and the *Nation;* she also published a biography of Theodore Dreiser, *Forgotten Frontiers: Dreiser and the Land of the Free* (1932). The Harveys and their two children lived in France for many years.

12,822. Hebrew Ladies Aid Society
Records. 1870-1924. 3 vols.
Open. Card catalog.
University of Rochester Library.
Records of the Society, which was founded in 1870 "to assist poor and needy women and orphans and to maintain an interest in the Rochester City Hospital." Consists of a president's book, which gives an inventory of the sewn goods made by members; a donation and reception committee account book containing lists of goods and money that members donated to the Society as well as lists of the number of members who attended each meeting; and the relief committee account book, which catalogs the clothes that members sewed.

12,823. The History Class
Records. 1890-1976. 0.5 ft.
Open. Unpublished guide.
University of Rochester Library.
The History Class, which was founded in 1890 as The American History Class, was established for the study of history through presentation of papers and discussion. Includes histories of the group that members wrote, papers members presented, membership lists, book lists, and printed programs. In 1901 the group changed its focus from American history to world history, and the name became The History Class.

12,824. Irving, Julia A. (Granger)
Papers. 1870-84. 1 vol.
Open. Card catalog.
University of Rochester Library.
Journals of Irving (1822-97), who was married to Sanders Irving (1813-84), a nephew of Washington Irving. Apparently the Irvings lived with Mr. and Mrs. John Greig, relatives of Julia Irving, at their home in Canandaigua, NY, from 1870 to 1884. During that time Julia Irving wrote descriptions in her journals of social engagements, travels, visitors, and visits. The volume also contains photos and clippings.

12,825. Jones, Ambrose
Papers. 1834-79. 1 vol.
Open. Card catalog.
University of Rochester Library.
Journal of Jones (1809-83), a physician in Farmersville, Knowlesville, Newfane, and Charlotte, NY. For each child he delivered, Jones listed the father's name, the weight of the baby, whether the birth was difficult or natural, the time of delivery, the duration of labor, and the baby's sex.

12,826. Judson, Emily (Chubbuck)
Papers. Nd. 1 folder and 1 vol.
Open. Unpublished guide.
University of Rochester Library.
[Mrs. Adoniram] Judson (1817-54) was an author and missionary. Consists of a volume of manuscript poems and loose poems removed from the volume.

12,827. McElroy, Nellie L.
Papers. 1913-19. 1 item.
Open. Card catalog.
University of Rochester Library.
Official police journal of McElroy (?-1937), who became Rochester's first policewoman in 1913. The volume contains descriptions of her daily activities, including the names, addresses, and nationalities of offenders and the final disposition of each case. McElroy's duties included patrolling dance halls and theaters; arresting prostitutes, vagrants, and other women lawbreakers; investigating cases involving missing girls; checking home conditions of delinquent or potentially delinquent girls and finding them new homes or jobs if necessary; serving as a parole officer; and mediating domestic problems.

12,828. Montgomery, Ella (Sargent)
Papers. Ca. 1870-80. 1 vol.
Open. Card catalog.
University of Rochester Library.
Scrapbook of Montgomery, who was the daughter of Aaron Augustus Sargent, a US senator from California, and of Ellen (Clark) Sargent, who was a suffragist and treasurer of the National American Woman Suffrage Association. The volume contains a letter Susan B. Anthony wrote to Montgomery discussing Lucretia Mott, who had died recently; sentiments Mott and Elizabeth Cady Stanton autographed; and clippings on women's rights and other topics. Anthony was a friend of Montgomery's parents and often stayed in their home.

12,829. Planned Parenthood of Rochester and Monroe County
Records. 1932-74. 0.5 ft.
Open. Unpublished guide.
University of Rochester Library.
Consists of minutes of executive board meetings and reminiscences early members wrote in 1973. This branch of Planned Parenthood was founded in 1932 as the Birth Control League of Monroe County. The organization disseminated birth control information and operated a birth control clinic.

12,830. Rochester Female Charitable Society
Records. 1882-89. 1 vol.
Open. Card catalog.
University of Rochester Library.
Financial records containing lists of monies received and spent by members of the Society, which was founded in 1822 to relieve "indigent persons and families in cases of sickness and distress" and to establish a charity school. Members solicited funds for their work and visited the poor in their assigned district, distributing food and clothing as needed. Among the members were Mrs. Henry M. Montgomery, Mrs. M. M. Lane, Mrs. A. S. Lane, Mrs. A. Prentice, Jr., and Mrs. G. C. Harmm.

12,831. Rochester Female Seminary
Records. 1835-36. 1 vol.
Open. Card catalog.
University of Rochester Library.
Contains minutes of stockholders' meetings, financial records, an agreement with the contractor to construct the building, and a list of the subscribers to the building fund for the Seminary, which was founded in 1836.

12,832. Russell, Lillian (Leonard)
Papers. 1878-86. 80 items.
Open. Unpublished guide.
University of Rochester Library.
Correspondence of Russell (1861-1922), an actress, contains letters from Russell and her second husband Edward Solomon to Constance DuFlon, a resident of New York City, most of which were written during Russell's tour with a company in 1885 and 1886. The letters relate to daily occurrences, conditions, bookings, financial problems, and personality conflicts in the touring company. Also includes letters to DuFlon from Fred Solomon, Fanny Davenport, and Jesse Millward, all of whom were members of the company.

12,833. Seward, William Henry
Papers. 1776-1921. 230 ft.
Open. Unpublished guide.
University of Rochester Library.
Correspondence, diaries, financial papers, and scrapbooks of Seward (1801-72), governor of New York from 1839 to 1842, a US senator from 1849 to 1861, and secretary of state from 1861 to 1869. Public correspondence includes letters from Elizabeth Cady Stanton, Sarah Josepha Hale, Charlotte Cushman, Myrtilla Miner, and Emma Willard. Family correspondence includes correspondence of Seward with his wife Frances Adeline (Miller) Seward (1805-65), Frances Seward's letters to her children and to her sister Lazette Marie (Miller) Worden, and letters from the Sewards' daughter Frances "Fanny" Adeline Seward (1844-66) to her aunt Lazette Worden. Also includes Frances Seward's diary of a trip through Pennsylvania, Virginia, and Maryland, 1835; her household account books, 1839-64; Fanny Seward's diaries, which provide an account of a young woman in Washington society during the Civil War; a scrapbook and Civil War reminiscences of Janet McNeil (Watson) [Mrs. William Henry, Jr.] Seward; and financial papers of William Henry Seward's adopted daughter Olive Risley Seward. Part of Fanny Seward's Civil War diaries were edited for an unpublished PhD dissertation.

12,834. Susan B. Anthony Memorial, Inc.
Records. Ca. 1870-1925. 2.5 ft.
Open. Unpublished guide.
University of Rochester Library.
The Memorial was established in 1945 as a tribute to [Miss] Anthony and as a depository for material relating to Anthony and the suffrage movement. At the encouragement of Carrie Chapman Catt, Anthony's successor as president of the National American Woman Suffrage Association, suffragists donated manuscripts and memorabilia. Includes letters dating from 1870 to 1905 that Anthony wrote to her housekeeper, friend, and occasional secretary Anne E. (Dann) Mason and Mason's reminiscences about Anthony. Also includes letters Genevieve Lel Hawley wrote to her aunt Eliza H. Hawley between 1897 and 1902 describing the daily routines and her work assisting [Mrs.] Ida Husted Harper in the preparation of *The Life and Work of Susan B. Anthony* (1898) and *The History of Woman Suffrage* (1902); letters from Anthony and Harper to Genevieve Hawley; and correspondence of Ella (Hawley) Crossett, a resident of Warsaw, NY, who was elected president of the New York State Woman Suffrage Association in 1902, including letters from Anthony, Anna Howard Shaw, Carrie Chapman Catt, Harriet (Stanton) Blatch, and Jean Brooks Greenleaf, who was Crossett's predecessor as president of the state Suffrage Association. Other papers include those of Carrie Chapman Catt, Catherine (Fish) Stebbins, and Fanny (Garrison) Villard; a report to the Warsaw, NY, Suffrage Club about the 1898 convention of the National American Woman Suffrage Association; minutes of the Rochester Political Equality Club from 1894 to 1896; photos; and early feminist newspapers.

12,835. Sweet, Emma (Biddlecom)
Papers. 1808-1951. 3 ft.
Open. Unpublished guide.
University of Rochester Library.
Correspondence, photos, clippings, pamphlets,

broadsides, and memorabilia of [Mrs. Fred G.] Sweet (1862-1951), a suffragist and distant cousin of Susan B. Anthony. Sweet served as Anthony's personal secretary intermittently between 1895 and 1906 and held executive positions in the Political Equality Club of Rochester and its successor the Woman Suffrage party of Monroe County, Inc. Includes letters from Carrie Chapman Catt, a personal friend of Sweet, and letters from Susan B. Anthony, Mary S. Anthony, William Channing Gannett, Charlotte (Perkins) Gilman, Anna Howard Shaw, Maud Nathan, Lucy E. Anthony, and Harriet (Stanton) Blatch.

12,836. University of Rochester Archives
Records. 1845- . Ca. 500,000 items.
Partially restricted. Unpublished guides.
University of Rochester Library.
The University, which was founded in 1850, admitted women in 1900. Includes trustee minutes; president's reports and correspondence; official correspondence of Annette Gardner Munro, Helen Bragdon, and Janet H. Clark, who were deans of women, and of other administrative officials of the College for Women; records related to the Susan B. Anthony Memorial Association, which raised funds for Anthony Memorial Hall; analyses of occupations of the graduates of the College for Women for 1930 through 1950; reminiscences; photos; scrapbooks; memorabilia; and printed items. Susan B. Anthony played an integral part in the admittance of women to the University. The University became coeducational in 1955 when the men's and women's colleges merged.

12,837. Wile, Ira Solomon
Papers. 1894-1943. 10 ft.
Open. Unpublished guide.
University of Rochester Library.
Correspondence, manuscripts and printed copies of articles and speeches, and reports of Wile (1877-1943), a physician, author, and lecturer. Contains material on the birth control movement in America, including letters Margaret Sanger wrote between 1929 and 1937 and speeches and articles by Wile on birth control, sex education, public health, and hygiene.

12,838. Woman's Christian Temperance Union of Allegany County, NY
Records. 1880-90. 1 vol.
Open. Card catalog.
University of Rochester Library.
Secretary's book of this WCTU branch, which was founded in 1880 as the Allegany County Woman's Temperance Union, contains a constitution, minutes, a membership list, clippings, and programs.

12,839. Women's City Club
Records. 1929-35. 0.5 ft.
Open. Unpublished guide.
University of Rochester Library.
Financial papers and correspondence of the Club, which was founded in 1911 in Rochester and which worked for such civic reforms as the campaign for a city manager charter, a central library, smoke abatement, and pasteurized milk. Includes treasurer's reports, a financial ledger, bills and statements, bankbooks and statements, and business correspondence, all of which relate to the Club primarily from the time of its disbandment in 1930 to the final disposition of its property in 1935.

12,840. Dolley, Sarah Read (Adamson)
Papers. 1870-1909. 2 cartons.
Closed. No guide.
University of Rochester School of Medicine and Dentistry, Edward G. Miner Library.
Correspondence of [Mrs. Lester Clinton] Dolley (1829-1909), a physician, primarily with her son Charles Sumner Dolley, a physician and marine biologist who lived in Philadelphia, but also with family members and others. The letters primarily concern family matters. Also includes Dolley family genealogy.

12,841. Potter, Marion Craig
Papers. 1886-1925. 1 box.
Closed. No guide.
University of Rochester School of Medicine and Dentistry, Edward G. Miner Library.
Records collected or generated by Potter, an early Rochester woman physician, include incorporation records, minute and account books, correspondence, membership lists, photos, and clippings of the Provident Dispensary, which existed from 1886 to ca. 1925. The Dispensary, an outpatient clinic for indigent women and children, was one of the first clinics organized and run by women physicians. Also includes records of the Practitioner's Society, later renamed the Blackwell Medical Society, which existed from 1887 to ca. 1913 as an organization of physicians who provided continuing education and were active in the community, and records, 1913-23, of the Women's Medical Society of New York State, which was founded in 1907.

12,842. Research Center
Records. Ca. 1840- . No size given.
Open. Unpublished guide.
Visual Studies Workshop.
Includes informational files on artists, museums, and galleries; audio and videotapes; prints, including daguerreotypes, tintypes, ambrotypes, stereographs, lantern slides, and glass plates as well as photos, slides, albums, cartes de visite, and post cards; and periodicals, including experimental publications along with standard art and photography magazines. Records relate to photographers, photo-printmakers, and writers within the field of photography.

ROSLYN

12,843. Mackay, Clarence H.
Papers. 1895-1975. 30 ft.
Open. No guide.
Bryant Library.
Scrapbooks of the family of Clarence Mackay, who laid the Pacific cable and was president of the Postal Telegraph Company. The volumes contain clippings from international newspapers, articles, ephemera, and memorabilia. In 1898 Mackay married Katherine Duer Mackay (?-1930), a member of a prominent New York family. During her marriage to Clarence Mackay, Katherine Mackay ran for and was elected to the Roslyn, NY, school board; worked for divorce reform in New York; founded the Equal Franchise Society in New York; and wrote a number of articles and books. The Mackays were the parents of John Mackay and Ellen (Mackay) Berlin, who married songwriter Irving Berlin. In 1914 Katherine Mackay divorced her husband and married Joseph Blake, a physician. She accompanied Blake to France, where she drove an ambulance, worked in army hospitals, and assisted her husband.

ROUND LAKE

12,844. Miscellany
Collection. Nd. No size given.
Open. No guide.
Village of Round Lake.
Contains portions of the diaries of Elizabeth King Ames, a summer resident of Round Lake, and of Emma Winans, a resident of Round Lake; tapes of reminiscences of Emma De Garmo McKean, a lifelong resident of Round Lake, and of Dorothy Powers Northup, a long-time resident and former librarian; a constitution, bylaws, minutes, history, and programs of the Woman's Round Lake Improvement Society; minute books and correspondence of the WCTU; minute books of the Round Lake Association; a photograph collection; and scrapbooks.

SARANAC LAKE

12,845. Monastery Archives
Records. 1952- . 8 drawers and 1 cabinet.
Access restricted. No guide.
Carmelite Monastery.
Constitutions and customs, minutes, financial records, community diary, cassettes and tapes, correspondence, photos, and scrapbooks of the Discalced Carmelite order, a contemplative order of women that is more than 400 years old. The Saranac Lake monastery was founded in 1952. Records pertain to the community's growth from a group of seven sisters to 17 and to the manner in which the members live out their vows.

SARATOGA SPRINGS

12,846. Britten, Evelyn (Barrett)
Papers. 1910-69. 4 vols.
Open. No guide.
Historical Society of Saratoga Springs Museum.
Scrapbooks relating to [Mrs. Walter] Britten (1891-1969), who was a civic worker, reporter, historian, and author who also wrote under the name Jean McGregor.

12,847. Walworth
Papers. 1850s-1915. 36 ft., 3 drawers, and 1 tape.
Open. Card catalog.
Historical Society of Saratoga Springs Museum.
Correspondence, journals, books, and published articles of three generations of the Walworth family. Includes papers of Reuben Hyde Walworth (1788-1867), a chancellor of the state of New York who was defeated in a campaign for governor by Free Soil candidate Martin Van Buren; Walworth's first wife Maria Averill Walworth (1795-1847), a Presbyterian who performed charitable works and reared six children; and his second wife Sarah E. Hardin (1811-74), a widow whom he married in 1851. Sarah Hardin previously was married to John J. Hardin, a lawyer from Illinois who served in Congress and died in the Mexican War. The Walworths' children were Mary Elizabeth (1812-75), Sarah Simonds (1815-87), Ann Elizabeth (1817-95), Francis DeLord (1834-39), Clarence Agustus (1820-1900), and Mansfield Tracy (1830-73). John and Sarah Hardin's children were Lemuel, Martin D., and Ellen Hardin (1832-1915).

Ellen Hardin, who cofounded the DAR in 1890, married her stepbrother Mansfield Walworth in 1852, and they had eight children. Ellen Walworth eventually divorced him, and after further disputes, their eldest son Frank killed him. Ellen Walworth supported her family by opening a boarding school in the family home at Pine Grove, NY. In 1880 she became one of the first women elected to the Saratoga Board of Education. A trustee of the Saratoga Monument Association, she also was involved in fund raising for the restoration of Mount Vernon.

12,848. County Archives
Records. 1791- . No size given.
Open. No guide.
Saratoga County Historian's Office.
Includes a tape concerning the life of Orra Phelps, a physician, geologist, botanist, lecturer, and mountain climber; items concerning Catherine "Sweet Kitty" Schuyler, the wife of General Philip Schuyler, a Revolutionary War general; and the published diary of Frederika Reidesel, the wife of General Frederick Reidesel, a general in the British

army, who accompanied her husband and stayed nearby while he fought in the Battle of Saratoga.

12,849. Assessment and Tax Records
Records. 1823-1915. 215 vols.
Open. Unpublished guide.
Saratoga Springs City Archives.
Incomplete property assessment and tax records for the town and village of Saratoga Springs.

12,850. Miscellany
Collection. Nd. No size given.
Open. No guide.
Saratoga Springs City Historian.
Includes an oral history interview with Gertrude Hodgman, a retired nurse; biographical files; photos; records of cemetery inscriptions; and city directories.

12,851. Women's Organizations in Saratoga Springs
Records. 1892-43. No size given.
Open. No guide.
Saratoga Springs City Historian.
Minutes, reports, scrapbooks, and other records of the American Legion Auxiliary, the Girl Scouts, the Katrina Trask Alliance, the Katrina Trask Garden Club, the Mother's Club, the Practice Club, the Study Club, the Travellers-at-Home-Club, the Travellers Aid, and the Saratoga Women's Association, which later became the Women's Civic League.

12,852. City Directories
Records. 1868- . No size given.
Open. No guide.
Saratoga Springs Public Library.
Directories for the city of Saratoga Springs.

12,853. Lester, Lucy (Cooke)
Papers. 1839-50. Ca. 5.5 in.
Open. No guide.
Saratoga Springs Public Library.
Letters that [Mrs. Charles] Lester (1827-1921), a housewife and civic worker, wrote to her parents in Milford, NY, concerning her life in Saratoga Springs where she was living with relatives and attending Miss Wayland's School. Includes letters she wrote to her husband during the time she returned to Milford to have her first child and other correspondence concerning her marriage.

SENECA FALLS

12,854. Bloomer, Amelia (Jenks)
Papers. 1852-54. 18 items.
Access restricted. No guide.
Seneca Falls Historical Society.
Manuscripts of [Mrs. Dexter Chamberlain] Bloomer (1818-94), a temperance activist, writer, newspaper editor, orator, and suffragist, are of speeches and treatises relating to temperance, right to property, woman suffrage, employment, and female education. Also includes copies of *The Lily*, a periodical edited and published by Bloomer. Written by women for women, the publication was Bloomer's primary vehicle for expressing her opinions on temperance.

12,855. Convention Anniversaries and Celebrations
Records. 1908-78. 1 drawer.
Open. No guide.
Seneca Falls Historical Society.
Minutes, financial records, correspondence, speeches, photos, clippings, memorabilia, and souvenirs of the anniversaries and celebrations of the 1848 Seneca Falls Women's Rights Convention, the purpose of which was to awaken women and men to the inequality of the sexes and to promote the idea of enfranchisement of women. Some of the recent celebrations were held in connection with the International Women's Year.

12,856. National Woman's Party and Other Women's Associations
Records. 1884-1974. 4 folders.
Open. No guide.
Seneca Falls Historical Society.
Annual reports, statements of purpose, speeches, photos, clippings, and published items of the party, which was founded in 1913; of the New York State Woman Suffrage Association, which was founded in 1868; and of the Women's National Indian Association, which was founded in 1880. All the organizations were devoted to eliminating discrimination against women.

12,857. Women's Rights Convention
Records. 1848-70. 5 items.
Open. No guide.
Seneca Falls Historical Society.
Original proceedings of the first women's rights convention, which was held in Seneca Falls in 1848, and of a Rochester, NY, convention that was also held in 1848. Also contains an 1870 publication of the minutes of these conventions. Includes references to Elizabeth Cady Stanton, Susan B. Anthony, Lucretia Mott, and Frederick Douglass. The Rochester Convention was called to air the grievances of women and to discuss the Declaration of Sentiments introduced at the Seneca Falls Convention. Reports were read and resolutions were offered on the laboring classes, the condition of women, and other topics. One hundred seven persons signed the Declaration of Sentiments during the Rochester Convention.

SOMERS

12,858. Rowell, Hugh Grant
Collection. 1800-1940. 4 drawers and 1 map case.
Open. Unpublished guide.
Somers Historical Society.
Correspondence, route books, photos, scrapbooks, lithographs, posters, and pamphlets of the early American circus, which Rowell collected. Includes items pertaining to women circus curiosities, performers, and owners.

SPARKILL

12,859. Convent Archives
Records. 1876- . 40 drawers, 4 cabinets, 1 microfilm reel, and 112 tapes.
Open. Unpublished guide.
Dominican Convent of Our Lady of the Rosary.
Correspondence of the mothers general; correspondence with archdiocesan and diocesan officials, school superintendents, architects, and builders; school records; plans, surveys, and specifications; photos; scrapbooks; and clippings of the Convent, which was founded by Mother Catherine Mary Antoninus Thorpe in New York City in 1876. Originally the community was engaged primarily in social work; later the members focused on education in elementary and secondary schools and in colleges. Presently, the sisters work in various ministries.

STATEN ISLAND

12,860. American Committee on Italian Migration
Records. 1952-73. 221 boxes, 7 cartons, and 4 vols.
Open. Published and unpublished guides.
Center for Migration Studies Archives.
General records of the Committee contain records of the women's division, including minutes, memoranda, reports, correspondence, speeches, notes, programs, and printed items, which deal with the division's fund-raising activities. See Olha della Cava, *A Guide to the Archives,* vol. 1 (New York: Center for Migration Studies, Inc., 1974).

12,861. Italian American Labor Movement
Records. 1900-75. 6 boxes, 11 vols., and 21 microfilm reels.
Open. Published and unpublished guides.
Center for Migration Studies Archives.
Minutes of International Ladies' Garment Workers' Union locals, many of of the members of which were women. Contains minutes of Local 48 of the Italian Cloak, Suit, and Skirt Makers Union, 1920-74, and minutes of Local 89 of the Italian Dress and Waist Makers Union, 1919-75. Also contains *L'Operaia,* a newspaper published by the ILGWU, 1917-18, and *Il Lavoro,* which was published by the Amalgamated Clothing Workers of America, 1922-30. Also includes books, pamphlets, and souvenir journals. See Olha della Cava, *A Guide to the Archives,* vol. 1 (New York: Center for Migration Studies, Inc., 1974).

12,862. Italian Welfare League, Inc.
Records. 1914-71. 22 boxes, 25 cartons, and 1 microfilm reel.
Open. Published and unpublished guides.
Center for Migration Studies Archives.
General records of the national office of the League, a social service organization established in 1920 by women active in relief work. The organization continues to be directed and staffed by women. Includes minutes, financial records, personal and business correspondence, reports, photos, clippings, programs and printed materials of the League; records concerning the Ellis Island branch office; port and dock committee reports, 1955-71, giving statistical data for each passenger assisted and each ship met; records pertaining to immigrants assisted; and correspondence with other US organizations that deal with immigrants. See Olha della Cava, *A Guide to the Archives,* vol. 1 (New York: Center for Migration Studies, Inc., 1974).

12,863. Abbott, Mabel
Papers. 1942-56. 4 files.
Open. No guide.
Staten Island Institute of Arts and Sciences Library.
Letters to [Miss] Abbott (1874-1973), a journalist, historian, and genealogist, concern activities on Staten Island. Abbott wrote for many newspapers, including the *Tacoma Times* in Washington state, *Chicago Herald, Chicago Daily News, Detroit News, Wichita Beacon* in Kansas, and *The New York Morning World.* In 1925 she moved to Staten Island. Interested in local history, she became curator of history and literature at the Institute. After her retirement in 1952, she studied the piano and remained active in the Belles Lettres Society.

12,864. Curtis, George William
Papers. 1826-92. 1 cabinet.
Open. Published guide.
Staten Island Institute of Arts and Sciences Library.
Papers of Curtis (1824-92), a writer, editor, abolitionist, supporter of women's suffrage, political reformer, and civil service reformer. Includes correspondence with suffragists, manuscripts of published speeches, galleys for published books, scrapbooks, and books. His wife and his sister-in-law Josephine (Shaw) Lowell are mentioned in the collection. See *Proceedings, Staten Island Institute of Arts and Sciences,* vol. 12, no. 3 (1950) and vol. 13, no. 3 (1951).

12,865. Poole
Papers. 1900-67. 4 Hollinger boxes.
Closed. No guide.

Staten Island Institute of Arts and Sciences Library.
Correspondence, journals, notes for speeches on black history, photos, programs, and books on black history, religion, and nursing of Drusilla Poole (ca. 1900-67) and of her husband Archibald Poole. Poole, a black woman, concerned herself with the health, education, and culture of black people. She was secretary of the Negro Library Association, an organizer of a local Helping Hand Club, a leader in the New York state Negro women's Republican organization, and a founder of the local NAACP.

STELLA NIAGARA

12,866. Archives
Records. 1874- . 15 boxes.
Open. No guide.
Sisters of St. Francis of Penance and Christian Charity, Provincialate.
Account books, correspondence of provincial superiors, photos, scrapbooks, and books concern the congregation, the foundress, and communities founded in the US, especially the Holy Name Province. This religious order of women was founded in 1835 in the Netherlands. Members came to the US in 1874, settling in Buffalo, NY.

STILLWATER

12,867. Fillmore, Abigail (Powers)
Papers. 1798-1853. 1 file.
Open. No guide.
Stillwater Town Historian.
Fillmore (1798-1853) was a teacher and the wife of President Millard Fillmore. Includes correspondence of Fillmore written during her husband's public service; correspondence and research notes of Mrs. Earl G. Hayner and Elizabeth Abel, town historians, concerning researchers and those interested in Fillmore genealogy; and excerpts from published works on the Powers and Leland families. The correspondence consists of photocopies of items at the State University of New York at Oswego.

STONY BROOK

12,868. Dean, Mary Ann
Papers. 1838-46. 1 vol.
Open. No guide.
State University of New York at Stony Brook Library, Special Collections.
Poems, quotations, and notes to [Miss] Dean from an unknown author.

12,869. Fletcher, Mary T. (MacMurray)
Papers. Ca. 1957-76. 5 ft.
Open. No guide.
State University of New York at Stony Brook Library, Special Collections.
Correspondence, files, scrapbooks, meeting reports, and notices of [Mrs. Donald A.] Fletcher, a retired biology teacher who was active in Nassau County organizations concerned with environmental matters, including the Federated Garden Clubs of New York, the Baldwin Bird Club, and the Audubon Club.

12,870. Gordon, Edith
Papers. Ca. 1963-68. 1 ft.
Open. No guide.
State University of New York at Stony Brook Library, Special Collections.
Correspondence, notes, leaflets, and flyers of [Mrs. Barry M.] Gordon, a schoolteacher, artist, and oral historian, who was president of the LWV of North Brookhaven, NY. Gordon was involved in open housing and civil rights activities and town planning as well as in the consolidation of the Setauket and Stony Brook school districts.

12,871. Jacobs, Helen Hull
Papers. 1943-45. 4 vols.
Open. No guide.
State University of New York at Stony Brook Library, Special Collections.
Scrapbooks of Jacobs (1908-), a tennis champion, naval officer, and author, contain clippings, programs, and ephemera related to WAVES training on the Hunter College campus in Bronx, NY.

12,872. League of Women Voters of Brookhaven South, NY
Records. Ca. 1950-75. 5 ft.
Open. Unpublished guide.
State University of New York at Stony Brook Library, Special Collections.
Minutes, files, correspondence, notes, and scrapbooks of this chapter of the LWV, which was founded ca. 1950 and is still in existence.

12,873. League of Women Voters of North Brookhaven
Records. 1941-75. 5 ft.
Open. Unpublished guide.
State University of New York at Stony Brook Library, Special Collections.
Minutes, committee files, correspondence, and clippings of this chapter of the LWV.

12,874. League of Women Voters of Riverhead and Southold, NY
Records. 1950-ca. 1971. 3.5 ft.
Open. Unpublished guide.
State University of New York at Stony Brook Library, Special Collections.
Minutes, files, correspondence, reports, newsletters, and other records of this branch of the LWV, which was founded in 1950.

12,875. Long Island Environmental Council, Inc.
Records. 1969-74. 5 ft.
Open. Unpublished guide.
State University of New York at Stony Brook Library, Special Collections.
Correspondence, a telephone register, and reading files of the Council, which was founded in 1969 by [Mrs.] Claire Stern, a New York state environmentalist who served as the Council's executive director until 1977. A coalition of environmental groups organized for lobbying and political action, the Council also conducts research on environmental issues.

12,876. Long Island NOW, Nassau Chapter
Records. Ca. 1970-74. 1.5 ft.
Open. No guide.
State University of New York at Stony Brook Library, Special Collections.
Correspondence and files of this chapter of the National Organization for Women.

12,877. Miscellaneous Manuscripts
Collection. Nd. No size given.
Open. Card catalog.
State University of New York at Stony Brook Library, Special Collections.
Contains letters from many authors, including Diane Di Prima, Denise Levertov, Susan Brownell Anthony, Annie (Wood) Besant, Janet Chance, and Elga (Liverman) Duval.

12,878. Parkway Nursery School
Records. 1957-75. 7 ft.
Open. Unpublished guide.
State University of New York at Stony Brook Library, Special Collections.
Bylaws; minutes; business, financial, and tax records; correspondence; school rosters and bulletins; plot and house plans; and a scrapbook of the School, a cooperative nursery school in which parents participated. The School was founded in the late 1940s in Levittown, NY.

12,879. Perishable Press Limited
Records. 1964-73. 11.5 ft.
Open. Unpublished guide.
State University of New York at Stony Brook Library, Special Collections.
Correspondence, manuscripts, and drawings of the Press, a private enterprise founded in 1964 that publishes original poetry, prose, and literature on handmade paper. The Press is run by Walter Hamady, who handles the correspondence, and his wife Mary (Laird) Hamady, who serves as typesetter. Records relate to women in the paper business, women binders, women authors, and authors' wives, among them author Denise Levertov, bookbinder Elizabeth Kner, artist and illustrator Ellen Lanyon, and Mrs. Loren Eiseley.

12,880. Söderberg, Eugenia (Riwkin)
Papers. 1903-73. 39 ft.
Closed. No guide.
State University of New York at Stony Brook Library, Special Collections.
Correspondence, diaries, journals, manuscripts, and notebooks in Russian, Swedish, German, and English of Söderberg (1903-73). Söderberg, the author of numerous books, reviewed American theater and films and interviewed literary personalities in her work as a correspondent for Swedish and Finnish newspapers. During the 1930s she was associated with a group of literary radicals, who worked for *Spektrum,* an avant-garde Swedish magazine founded by her brother Josef Riwkin. Contains correspondence of many authors involved in the magazine, including Karin Boye, Gunnar Ekelof, and Harry Martinson. Söderberg married Hugo Perls, but she continued to use her first married name in her work.

12,881. Woman's History Ephemera
Collection. Ca. 1970- . 2 cu.ft.
Open. Card catalog and shelflist.
State University of New York at Stony Brook Library, Special Collections.
Bibliographies, clippings, newsletters, flyers, broadsides, and newspapers concerned with women and their activities and publications.

12,882. Women's Club of the State University of New York at Stony Brook
Records. 1958-75. 5 ft.
Open. No guide.
State University of New York at Stony Brook Library, Special Collections.
Historian's records of the Club, which was founded in 1958 and still exists, include memoranda, correspondence, pictures, and programs. The purposes of the organization are to bring together faculty wives and faculty women, to support university projects, and to sponsor events.

12,883. Women's International League for Peace and Freedom, Central Suffolk Branch
Records. 1965-73. 1 ft.
Open. No guide.
State University of New York at Stony Brook Library, Special Collections.
Scrapbooks, pamphlets, posters, and other papers of this branch of WILPF, which was primarily concerned with opposing American involvement in the Vietnam War. Papers also relate to such activities as UNICEF collection and George S. McGovern's 1972 Democratic presidential campaign.

12,884. Johnson, Oakley C.
Papers. 1890-1976. 30 ft.
Open. Unpublished guide.

State University of New York at Stony Brook, Special Collections.
Correspondence, diaries, manuscripts, photos, offprints, and memorabilia of Johnson (1890-1976), a professor, book reviewer, and member of the Communist party. Includes letters of his first wife Mary (Olmsted) Johnson (1890-1950), a painter and art teacher, that were written to her husband in New York while she was on a farm in Michigan with her children as well as correspondence of his daughters, sisters, and other relatives. Other correspondents include Hallie (Ferguson) Flanagan Davis, Dorothy Day, Bella (Visono) Dodd, Shirley Lola (Graham) Du Bois, Elizabeth Gurley Flynn, Freda Kirchwey, Suzanne La Follette, Meridel Le Sueur, Helen Gertrude Lynch, Helen Sobel, Anna Louise Strong, and Helen (Wagenknecht) Winter.

SUFFERN

12,885. Convent Archives
Records. 1880s- . 6 boxes.
Closed. No guide.
Sisters of Our Lady of Christian Doctrine, Marydell Convent.
Correspondence, retreat notes, and newsletters of the Sisters, a religious order of women founded in 1910 in New York City. Includes correspondence of the founder and photos of the Convent.

SYRACUSE

12,886. Miscellany
Collection. 1820-1920. 4 drawers.
Open. No guide.
Canal Museum.
Includes correspondence of women, a diary that mentions women on the Erie Canal, a will, and stock notices and passenger lists containing the names of women.

12,887. Photographs
Collection. 1840-1976. 5000 items.
Open. No guide.
Canal Museum.
Photos of groups of people in street scenes, of women on canal boats, and of family life on canal boats.

12,888. Bacon, Peggy
Papers. 1893-1964. 3.5 ft.
Open. Unpublished guide.
Syracuse University, George Arents Research Library, Manuscript Collections.
[Miss] Bacon (1895-) is an artist and author. Correspondence; manuscript sketches, designs, notes, poems, and short stories; awards; press releases; photos; clippings; and published items. After working as an artist and book illustrator, Bacon began writing and contributed articles to such magazines as *The New Yorker* and *Saturday Review.* She also served as vice-president of the National Institute of Arts and Letters.

12,889. Bates, Gladys E.
Papers. 1913-62. 3.5 ft.
Open. Unpublished guide.
Syracuse University, George Arents Research Library, Manuscript Collections.
Correspondence, sketchbooks, scrapbooks, exhibition programs, and clippings of [Mrs. Kenneth] Bates (1895-), a sculptor. Includes professional correspondence with other artists and invitations to assist on exhibition juries.

12,890. Berg, Gertrude (Edelstein)
Papers. 1932-60. 55 ft.
Open. Unpublished guide.
Syracuse University, George Arents Research Library, Manuscript Collections.
[Mrs. Lewis] Berg (1899-1966) was an actress, producer, and author. Correspondence, subject file, and published items are included with many radio and television scripts and scrapbooks.

12,891. Bourke-White, Margaret
Papers. 1929-64. Ca. 54.5 ft. and tapes.
Partially restricted. Unpublished guide.
Syracuse University, George Arents Research Library, Manuscript Collections.
Bourke-White (1904-71) was a photojournalist. Business and personal correspondence, notes, taped interviews, production orders, clippings, photos and negatives, and published items. As a *Life* photographer, Bourke-White covered WWII, the German concentration camps, and the partition of India. She produced some of her photo essays, such as *You Have Seen Their Faces,* in collaboration with her husband Erskine Caldwell.

12,892. Caeser, Doris (Porter)
Papers. 1920-65. 2.5 ft.
Open. Unpublished guide.
Syracuse University, George Arents Research Library, Manuscript Collections.
A sculptor, [Mrs. Harry I.] Caeser (1892-1971), exhibited internationally in one-woman shows; one of her fortes was designing art for institutions, particularly churches. Correspondence, biographical material, notes on sculpture, poems, photos, and published material. She was a member of the Federation of Modern Painters and Sculptors, the Sculptors Guild, the Architecture League of New York, the Society of Women Artists, and the Audubon Artists.

12,893. Crow, Martha (Foote)
Papers. 1884-1921. 3.5 ft.
Open. Unpublished guide.
Syracuse University, George Arents Research Library, Manuscript Collections.
[Mrs. John M.] Crow (1854-1924) was a poet and author. Correspondence, biographical data, lecture notes, writings, photos, and published material relate primarily to her work with the Poetry Society of America and the GFWC.

12,894. Di Prima, Diane
Papers. 1948-71. 2.5 ft. and 4 tapes.
Open. Unpublished guide.
Syracuse University, George Arents Research Library, Manuscript Collections.
Correspondence, writings, and taped readings of Di Prima (1934-), a poet and author, including letters from Lawrence Ferlinghetti, Alan Marlowe, Kenneth Patchen, and William Burroughs. Also included are 1961-68 copies of *Floating Bear* and manuscripts submitted to that newsletter by LeRoi Jones and Frank O'Hara.

12,895. Fenton, Beatrice
Papers. Nd. 0.5 ft.
Open. Unpublished guide.
Syracuse University, George Arents Research Library, Manuscript Collections.
Correspondence, clippings, published items, and photos of the work of Fenton (1887-), a sculptor.

12,896. Fraser, James Earle, and Fraser, Laura (Gardin)
Papers. 1892-1967. 57 ft.
Open. Unpublished guide.
Syracuse University, George Arents Research Library, Manuscript Collections.
Papers of Laura Fraser (1889-1966), a sculptor, consist of correspondence; writings; business documents; models, sketches, blueprints, and photos of her work; and memorabilia. Included are letters from Edward Arlington Robinson.

12,897. Frishmuth, Harriet D.
Papers. 1924-63. 6.5 ft. and 11 tapes.
Access restricted. Unpublished guide.
Syracuse University, George Arents Research Library, Manuscript Collections.
An award-winning sculptor, Frishmuth (1880-) exhibits internationally. Correspondence, tapes in which she describes her work, financial papers, photos of her and her work, clippings, and awards. A student of Rodin, Frishmuth is noted for her lyric style.

12,898. Gershoy, Eugenie
Papers. 1914-65. 2 ft.
Open. Unpublished guide.
Syracuse University, George Arents Research Library, Manuscript Collections.
Correspondence, manuscripts, subject file, personal photos, published matter, and photos of the work of Gershoy (1905-), a sculptor and painter who developed polychrome, which is a composition of dextrine, glue, and plastic.

12,899. Hager, Alice Rogers
Papers. 1801-1964. 2 ft.
Access restricted. Unpublished guide.
Syracuse University, George Arents Research Library, Manuscript Collections.
[Mrs. John Mansfield] Hager (1894-1969), an author who served as a special agent for the US Department of Labor in 1918 and a reporter for various newspapers and an area office of the US Information Agency from 1953 to 1957. Correspondence, autobiographical data, manuscripts, family documents, publicity items, and clippings are included.

12,900. Hansl, Eva Elise (vom Baur)
Papers. 1935-67. 22.5 ft.
Open. Unpublished guide.
Syracuse University, George Arents Research Library, Manuscript Collections.
Hansl (1889-) was an author and a radio commentator. Radio scripts and programming and research material contain information on women's roles and attitudes, power, education, and counseling.

12,901. Huntington, Anna Vaughn (Hyatt)
Papers. 1887-1966. 34.5 ft.
Access restricted. Unpublished guide.
Syracuse University, George Arents Research Library, Manuscript Collections.
Correspondence, personal notes, manuscripts, scrapbooks, sculpture lists, photos of works, and published items of Huntington (1876-1973), a sculptor, who was the second wife of Archer Milton Huntington. She created monumental works which have appeared in the Metropolitan Museum of Art in New York City and in more than 200 other museums across the country. Material relating to Brookgreen Gardens, a sculpture garden and land preserve donated to the state of South Carolina by the Huntingtons is included. She was a member of the National Academy of Design, the National Sculpture Society, and the American Academy of Arts and Letters.

12,902. Huntington, Arabella Duval
Papers. 1888-1925. 1.5 ft.
Open. Unpublished guide.
Syracuse University, George Arents Research Library, Manuscript Collections.
Correspondence; legal papers; bills and receipts; inventories of jewelry, real estate, and paintings; and other material of Huntington (1851-1924), a philanthropist who assisted in building the collection of the Henry E. Huntington Library and Art Gallery in California. She was the widow both of Collis P. Huntington and of his nephew Henry E. Huntington.

12,903. Lenski, Lois
Papers. 1932-62. 8.5 ft.
Open. Unpublished guide.
Syracuse University, George Arents Research Library, Manuscript Collections.
Lenski (1893-1974) was an author and illustrator of many children's books. Notebooks, biographical data, manuscripts of poems and songs, page proofs and publisher's copies of books, correspondence from children, photos, children's blocks designed by Lenski, and published items. She received many awards, including the Newbery Medal in 1946. Lenski was married to Arthur Covey.

12,904. McGinley, Phyllis
Papers. 1897-1967. 13.5 ft.
Open. Unpublished guide.
Syracuse University, George Arents Research Library, Manuscript Collections.
Correspondence, manuscripts, scrapbooks, awards, photos, and published matter of [Mrs. Charles] McGinley (1905-), a poet and author of children's fiction, whose work appears frequently in women's magazines.

12,905. Norman, Dorothy
Papers. 1937-67. 33 ft.
Open. Unpublished guide.
Syracuse University, George Arents Research Library, Manuscript Collections.
Correspondence, manuscripts, and published material of [Mrs.] Norman (1905-), an author, relate to her research and her book *Nehru: The First Sixty Years.*

12,906. Parsons, Alice (Beal)
Papers. ?-1966. 9 ft.
Open. Unpublished guide.
Syracuse University, George Arents Research Library, Manuscript Collections.
Correspondence, manuscript short stories, and articles of [Mrs. Hugh Graham] Parsons (1886-1962), who was an author and book reviewer. She also was a member of the Committee for Cultural Freedom and honorary vice-chairman of the executive committee of the New York state Liberal party.

12,907. Peale, Ruth (Stafford)
Papers. 1950-65. 23 ft.
Closed. Unpublished guide.
Syracuse University, George Arents Research Library, Manuscript Collections.
Peale (1906-) is a leader in church activities and business manager for her husband Norman Vincent Peale. Correspondence, sermons, manuscripts, and articles are included with correspondence, reports, published material, and other records of the the National Council of Churches. A graduate of Syracuse University, Ruth Peale is vice-president of the Council.

12,908. Robertson, Constance Pierrepont (Noyes)
Papers. 1837-66. 8 ft.
Open. Unpublished guide.
Syracuse University, George Arents Research Library, Manuscript Collections.
Correspondence, writings, speeches, and memorabilia of [Mrs. Miles] Robertson (1897-), who is an author and the granddaughter of John Humphrey Noyes of the Oneida Community. Her novel *Fire Bell in the Night* concerns the Jerry Rescue, an antislavery action which took place in Syracuse, NY.

12,909. Sipprell, Clara E.
Papers. 1915-63. 2 ft.
Open. Unpublished guide.
Syracuse University, George Arents Research Library, Manuscript Collections.
Material of Sipprell (1886-1975), a photographer, consists of 240 original photos, some of famous people, landscapes, and still lifes. She used only natural light in her work and did not enlarge or crop her photos.

12,910. Taylor, Mildred (Frick)
Papers. 1921-60. 8.5 ft.
Access restricted. Unpublished guide.
Syracuse University, George Arents Research Library, Manuscript Collections.
[Mrs. E. Paul] Taylor (1905-) was an assemblywoman for the New York state legislature-assembly from 1946 to 1960. Correspondence, blueprints, bills introduced, and published items, including material relating to Rose Resolution no. 106, a bill she introduced to make the rose the national flower. Taylor served on the state ways and means committee and was a member of the National Order of Women Legislators.

12,911. Thompson, Dorothy
Papers. 1918-61. 68.5 ft.
Open. Unpublished guide.
Syracuse University, George Arents Research Library, Manuscript Collections.
Papers of Thompson (1894-1961), a journalist and columnist, include correspondence, notes, manuscripts by Thompson and others, subject file, research material, "On the Record" articles, *Ladies Home Journal* material, and family papers. Thompson married Josef Bard, then Sinclair Lewis, and then Maxim Kopf.

12,912. Turnbull, Grace Hill
Papers. 1914-60. 3 ft.
Open. Unpublished guide.
Syracuse University, George Arents Research Library, Manuscript Collections.
Correspondence, manuscripts, subject file, photos, and published material of Turnbull (1880-1976), a sculptor, artist, and author. She has exhibited in the Delphic Studio, NY; the Corcoran Gallery, Washington; the Art Institute of Chicago; the Salon des Beaux Arts; and the International Art Union.

12,913. Walker, Mary
Papers. 1799-1919. 2 ft. and 1 microfilm reel.
Open. Unpublished guide.
Syracuse University, George Arents Research Library, Manuscript Collections.
Correspondence, writings, legal and financial material, pension documents, and memorabilia of Walker (1832-1919), a physician, reveal her interest in women's rights, dress reform, the health of women and children, treatment of prisoners of war, and camp conditions during the Civil War. Married and divorced, she never took her husband's name. She was awarded the Congressional Medal of Honor by President Andrew Johnson in 1865; it was rescinded in 1916 but finally re-awarded in 1977.

12,914. Weschler, Anita
Papers. 1902-60. 25.5 ft.
Closed. Unpublished guide.
Syracuse University, George Arents Research Library, Manuscript Collections.
[Miss] Weschler (1903-) is a sculptor, painter, interior decorator, and author. Correspondence, writings, financial papers, artwork, photos, memorabilia, and exhibition catalogs are included. Weschler is represented in several permanent art collections across the US and has exhibited in one-woman and traveling shows.

12,915. Widdemer, Margaret
Papers. 1923-62. 6 ft. and 1 microfilm reel.
Closed. Unpublished guide.
Syracuse University, George Arents Research Library, Manuscript Collections.
Correspondence, manuscripts, poems set to music, scrapbooks, clippings, and published material of [Miss] Widdemer, who is a poet and author. She has been writing since childhood, and in 1919 she shared the American Poetry Society's America Prize with Carl Sandburg.

12,916. Association of Women Students
Records. 1908-64. 14 Hollinger boxes.
Open. Unpublished guide.
Syracuse University, George Arents Research Library, University Archives.
Subject files of this women's student government group and of its predecessors consist of constitutions, bylaws, minutes of meetings of the organizations and of their committees, budgets and other financial material, correspondence, rules and regulations governing student life, reports, evaluations, petitions, clippings, and other items. Also included are records of the Independent Women's Association, which dissolved in 1953; of the Men's Student Government; of the Joint Student Government; and of 313 student groups which were active between 1932 and 1961. The Association of Women Students was founded in 1908 as the Women's League.

12,917. Comfort Family
Papers. 1776-1944. 7.5 ft.
Open. Unpublished guide.
Syracuse University, George Arents Research Library, University Archives.
Contains correspondence, biographical material, writings, medical records, photos, memorabilia, clippings, and printed matter of Anna (Manning) Comfort (1845-1931), a physician. After several years of practice, she specialized in gynecology; she also was active in women's rights throughout her life. Comfort graduated in 1865 in the first class of the New York Medical College for Women, which was founded by her aunt Clemence Lozier, a physician and friend of Susan B. Anthony. Comfort was the first woman to practice medicine in Connecticut. In 1871 she married George Fisk Comfort, who was the first dean of the College of Fine Arts at Syracuse University.

12,918. Davis, Laura
Papers. 1913-17. 174 items.
Open. Unpublished guide.
Syracuse University, George Arents Research Library, University Archives.
Consists of letters Davis wrote home while she was a student at the University.

12,919. Dean of Women's Office, Director of Social Activities
Records. 1923-69. 29 Hollinger boxes.
Open. Unpublished guide.
Syracuse University, George Arents Research Library, University Archives.
Subject files including minutes, financial material, correspondence, reports, memoranda, programs, photos, sketchbooks, and clippings relate to social activities at the University, such as orientation, dances, and special events.

12,920. Hartley, Helene (Willey)
Papers. 1911-65. 12 Hollinger boxes.
Open. Unpublished guide.
Syracuse University, George Arents Research Library, University Archives.
Hartley (1893-1963) was a PhD and a professor of education. Correspondence, biographical data, writings, and publications relate to her professional and civic activities. She was a member of the AAUW, the National Council of Teachers of English, the LWV, the YWCA, and many other groups.

12,921. Hilton, Eunice M.
Papers. 1920-71. 46 Hollinger boxes.
Open. Unpublished guide.
Syracuse University, George Arents Research Library, University Archives.
Correspondence, speeches, articles, lecture notes, financial papers, files, photos, and printed matter of Hilton (1899-1975), an educator and administrator

who married John Freeland in 1959 and later a Mr. Vreeland. Dean of women and a teacher at a Nebraska junior college, Hilton later went to Syracuse University to earn a PhD. At Syracuse she was dean of women from 1935 to 1949 and from 1948 to 1959 dean of the College of Home Economics, in addition to serving as director of the graduate program in student personnel administration. She also developed a course there on the status and responsibility of women. In 1959 she became coordinator of a graduate internship program in student personnel and a professor of education at the University of Denver. Hilton was president of the National Association of Women Deans and Counselors between 1955 and 1957, a trustee of the Foundation of the National Federation of Business and Professional Women, and a delegate to the Mid-Century White House Conference on Children and Youth, in addition to other professional activities.

12,922. Lugg, M. Jean
Papers. 1908-15. 1 Hollinger box.
Open. Unpublished guide.
Syracuse University, George Arents Research Library, University Archives.
Papers of Lugg, a student at Syracuse University, consist of essays on her first impressions of the school, letters she wrote home, and financial documents.

12,923. Macleod, Annie L.
Papers. 1928-48. 8 Hollinger boxes.
Open. Unpublished guide.
Syracuse University, George Arents Research Library, University Archives.
Correspondence and subject files of Macleod (1883-), who was dean of the College of Home Economics at Syracuse University from 1928 to 1948, after teaching at Vassar College for 14 years as a professor of chemistry and director of euthenics. She expanded the College of Home Economics's program to include applied arts, child development, foods and nutrition, euthenics, and home economics in business. She was a member of the American Home Economics Association, the AAUW, the AAUP, the American Association for the Advancement of Science, and the American Academy of Political and Social Science. She was also honorary vice-president of the American Humane Society.

12,924. Smith, Marjorie C.
Papers. 1932-70. 19 ft.
Open. Unpublished guide.
Syracuse University, George Arents Research Library, University Archives.
A specialist in student housing, Smith (?-1972) was director of women's residences at the University from 1935 to 1936, then assistant dean of women until 1949, and then dean of women until 1969. Her subject files include correspondence, minutes, reports, scrapbooks, and printed matter. Smith served as president of the Business and Professional Women's Clubs of New York state and of the central New York branch of the National League of American Pen Women; she was also a member of the Syracuse Girl Scout Council and the National Association of Deans of Women.

12,925. Stanicki, Jane M.
Papers. 1969-75. 4 ft.
Access restricted. Unpublished guide.
Syracuse University, George Arents Research Library, University Archives.
Subject files including correspondence, speeches, minutes, and memoranda of Stanicki, vice-president for the office of residential life, reflect her interest in the individual rights of students and in the "living-learning center" concept of collective living.

TARRYTOWN

12,926. College Archives
Records. 1907- . Ca. 432 ft.
Access restricted. Unpublished guide.
Marymount College Archives.
Constitutions; bylaws; minutes of the board of trustees; history of the College, including biographical material on the founders and presidents; correspondence; photos; scrapbooks; newspapers; clippings; and publications of the College, a resident liberal arts college for women founded in 1919. Courses in women's studies are offered, and the College has initiated conferences and workshops about various aspects of women's roles in contemporary society. The College gives particular attention to career development for women.

TROY

12,927. Emma Willard School Archives
Records. 1814- . 130 cu.ft. and 20 ft.
Open. No guide.
Emma Willard School.
Emma (Hart) Willard founded this institution in 1814 in Middlebury, VT, to educate girls and young women. Annual reports, financial and student records, correspondence, curriculum material, records concerning physical plant development, photos, student publications, alumnae records and publications, clippings, and catalogs of the School and its predecessor the Troy Female Seminary. The school moved to Waterford, NY, in 1819 and to Troy, NY, in 1821.

12,928. Manuscripts
Papers. 1814- . 22 cu.ft.
Open. No guide.
Emma Willard School.
Personal correspondence, diaries, writings, photos, souvenir albums, diplomas, and mementos of administrators, faculty, and students associated with the School and its predecessor the Troy Female Seminary.

WATERLOO

12,929. Waterloo Female Temperance Society
Records. 1841-?. 1 vol.
Access restricted. No guide.
Waterloo Library and Historical Society.
Minute book of the Society, which was founded in 1841, contains minutes regarding the adoption of the group's constitution and bylaws as well as the names of officers and members. Members of the Society pledged to abstain from the use of all intoxicating liquors, both as a beverage and in culinary preparations, and to discourage, in all suitable ways, traffic in them.

WEST POINT

12,930. Warner House
Papers. 1800-1915. 8 drawers.
Closed. Unpublished guide.
Constitution Island Association, Inc.
Correspondence, manuscripts, diaries, essays, account books, scrapbooks, photos, drawings, recipes, and other papers of the Warner family, the members of which lived on Constitution Island near West Point, NY, from 1836 to 1915. Also includes family possessions and the family library. Contains papers of Susan Bogert Warner (1819-85) and her sister Anna Bartlett Warner (1824-1915), both of whom began writing to help support the family after financial losses. Susan Warner took the pen name Elizabeth Wetherell; Anna Warner used the name Amy Lothrop. Separately and in collaboration the sisters wrote 85 novels, short stories, essays, biographies, and religious treatises.

WEST SAYVILLE

12,931. Ship Wrecks and Groundings
Collection. 1657-1952. No size given.
Partially restricted. Unpublished guide.
Suffolk Marine Museum.
Includes information on Della Prince, who operated Horton's Point Lighthouse on the north shore of Long Island in 1903 and 1904; the Women's National Relief Association; the Blue Anchor Society; the League of Coast Guard Women; and Aid for the Shipwrecked.

WHITE PLAINS

12,932. Convent Archives
Records. 1869- . No size given.
Access restricted. No guide.
Sisters of the Divine Compassion, Good Counsel Convent.
The order was founded in 1886 by Mother M. Veronica Starr, the president of the Association for Befriending Children and Young Girls and the directress of the House of the Holy Family. Before the order's establishment, Starr was Mary Caroline (Dannat) [Mrs. Walter] Starr. Reports, records of institutions, correspondence, notes, histories of works of the order, diaries, biographies of sisters, photos, scrapbooks, articles, and books. Also includes items on Starr's family, life, and work as well as records of the Good Counsel Training School.

WILLIAMSVILLE

12,933. Motherhouse Archives
Records. 1927- . 1 drawer.
Access restricted. No guide.
Franciscan Missionary Sisters of the Divine Child, Motherhouse.
Correspondence; personnel data on sisters; history of the community; records of the founding fathers, of ministerial involvements, and of entrance dates and departures; photos; and scrapbooks of the Motherhouse of the Sisters, a religious order of women founded in 1927 in Buffalo, NY. Members of the order engage in ministries to meet the needs of the Catholic Church and of society. The order's founding fathers included the Right Reverend Monsignor Joseph Gambino, pastor of Holy Cross Parish in which the order was founded, and the Most Reverend Bishop William Turner, bishop of the Buffalo diocese, who granted permission for establishment of the community.

YONKERS

12,934. Monastery Archives
Records. 1912- . 1 cabinet and 1 motion picture.
Closed. No guide.
Blessed Sacrament Monastery.
Minutes of community meetings, financial records, correspondence, photos, and scrapbooks of the Monastery of the Religious of the Order of the Blessed Sacrament and of Our Lady. The Yonkers house of the order, the members of which are known as Sacramentine Nuns, was founded in 1912 for the perpetual adoration of the Sacrament in the context of monastic and contemplative life. Includes items relating to the mothers superior,

sisters, the building of the Monastery and a related academy, and the operation of the two facilities.

NORTH CAROLINA

CHAPEL HILL

12,935. Adams, Agatha (Boyd)
Papers. 1938. 126-page vol.
Open. Published and unpublished guides.
University of North Carolina Library, Southern Historical Collection.
Diary and memoranda of Adams (?-1950), a librarian at the University of North Carolina, that she kept on a journey to Mexico. Contains a few entries about Havana, Cuba. Taken from Susan Sokol Blosser and Clyde Norman Wilson, Jr., *The Southern Historical Collection: A Guide to Manuscripts* (Chapel Hill, NC: University of North Carolina Library, 1970).

12,936. Allensworth, Emma H.
Papers. 1893. 1 vol.
Open. Published and unpublished guides.
University of North Carolina Library, Southern Historical Collection.
Diary of Allensworth, a young Nashville woman, gives a detailed account of her visit to the Chicago World's Fair. Taken from Susan Sokol Blosser and Clyde Norman Wilson, Jr., *The Southern Historical Collection: A Guide to Manuscripts* (Chapel Hill, NC: University of North Carolina Library, 1970).

12,937. American Alliance for Health, Physical Education and Recreation, Southern District
Records. 1927-72. 8 vols. and ca. 700 items.
Open. Unpublished guide.
University of North Carolina Library, Southern Historical Collection.
The Southern Division of the Alliance, originally called the American Association for Health, Physical Education and Recreation, was formed in 1927 to disseminate knowledge about and promote physical and health education programs. The organization is a department of the National Education Association. Constitutions; minutes and reports; financial reports; correspondence; lists of members, officers, and convention delegates; convention programs; clippings; and publications. Also includes dissertations and papers on Emma W. Plunkett, Jessie Reid Garrison Mehling, the development of physical education in Tennessee, and a history of the Florida Association for Health, Physical Education and Recreation.

12,938. American Association of University Women
Records. 1923-73. 1.5 ft. and 18 vols.
Open. Published and unpublished guides.
University of North Carolina Library, Southern Historical Collection.
Annual reports of activities, minutes, correspondence, membership information, scrapbooks, programs submitted at conventions of the North Carolina division, and other records of the Chapel Hill branch of the AAUW. Taken from Everard H. Smith III, *The Southern Historical Collection: Supplementary Guide to Manuscripts, 1970-1975* (Chapel Hill, NC: The University of North Carolina Library, 1976).

12,939. Ames, Jessie (Daniel)
Papers. 1920-63. 2 ft.
Open. Published and unpublished guides.
University of North Carolina Library, Southern Historical Collection.
Ames (1883-), who lived in Texas, Georgia, and North Carolina, was an officer of the Texas Interracial Commission and the Commission on Interracial Cooperation in Atlanta and a founder of the Association of Southern Women for the Prevention of Lynching. Papers relate to her involvement in these organizations and include correspondence, reports, memoranda, clippings, and articles on such subjects as education, lynchings, domestic servants, conferences and public opinion in various states, war morale, Negroes, and race relations. Taken from Susan Sokol Blosser and Clyde Norman Wilson, Jr., *The Southern Historical Collection: A Guide to Manuscripts* (Chapel Hill, NC: University of North Carolina Library, 1970).

12,940. Archbell, Lillie (Vause)
Papers. 1900-23. 2 vols. and 98 items.
Open. Published and unpublished guides.
University of North Carolina Library, Southern Historical Collection.
Papers written, compiled, and collected by Archbell (1854?-1946), a leader of the United Daughters of the Confederacy, pertain to Civil War events on the North Carolina coast and include historical articles, reminiscences dictated to Archbell, notes, words to Confederate songs, clippings, and a diary kept by a young girl in 1900 in Kinston and New Bern, NC. Taken from Susan Sokol Blosser and Clyde Norman Wilson, Jr., *The Southern Historical Collection: A Guide to Manuscripts* (Chapel Hill, NC: University of North Carolina Library, 1970).

12,941. Arrington, Mary Jones
Papers. 1707-1955. 34 vols. and 691 items.
Open. Published and unpublished guides.
University of North Carolina Library, Southern Historical Collection.
Correspondence, wills, Bible records, and other papers of [Miss] Arrington (1874-1950) of Rocky Mount, NC, relate to family and local history in Nash and Edgecombe counties, NC. Also includes minutes, 1916-21, of the Rocky Mount Women's Club and correspondence of James Perry Drake, a US land official in Indiana; Benjamin Michael Drake, a Methodist minister and college president in Mississippi; and other members of the Drake family. Taken from Susan Sokol Blosser and Clyde Norman Wilson, Jr., *The Southern Historical Collection: A Guide to Manuscripts* (Chapel Hill, NC: University of North Carolina Library, 1970).

12,942. Bailey, Mary E.
Papers. 1869-82. 2 vols.
Open. Published and unpublished guides.
University of North Carolina Library, Southern Historical Collection.
Diary kept by Bailey (1845-1922), a resident of Gainesville, FL, in 1869 in which she recorded daily household activities, visits, readings, and the weather. Also includes a book of accounts of her personal expenses. Taken from Susan Sokol Blosser and Clyde Norman Wilson, Jr., *The Southern Historical Collection: A Guide to Manuscripts* (Chapel Hill, NC: University of North Carolina Library, 1970).

12,943. Baker, Blanche
Papers. 1675-1937. 835 items.
Open. Published and unpublished guides.
University of North Carolina Library, Southern Historical Collection.
Correspondence, compilations, wills, and other papers pertaining to the history of the Baker family and related families who resided in southern Virginia and northeastern North Carolina. The papers date from the 17th to the 20th centuries and were collected by [Miss] Baker (1855-1943). Includes correspondence and a diary of her father William J. Baker of Gates County, NC, while he was studying law in Raleigh, NC, in 1841 and then while he was a Confederate officer in Virginia and a diary of her mother Sarah (Collins) Baker in Portsmouth, VA, in 1841. Taken from Susan Sokol Blosser and Clyde Norman Wilson, Jr., *The Southern Historical Collection: A Guide to Manuscripts* (Chapel Hill, NC: University of North Carolina Library, 1970).

12,944. Baldwin, Lucy (Hull)
Papers. Ca. 1905. 14 items.
Open. Published and unpublished guides.
University of North Carolina Library, Southern Historical Collection.
Belles lettres and an autobiography by [Mrs. George Johnson] Baldwin (?-1923) in which she describes her childhood in Atlanta during the Civil War, plantation life, and life in New York and Savannah, GA. Taken from Susan Sokol Blosser and Clyde Norman Wilson, Jr., *The Southern Historical Collection: A Guide to Manuscripts* (Chapel Hill, NC: University of North Carolina Library, 1970).

12,945. Barringer, Susanna Elisabeth
Papers. 1784-88. 6 items.
Open. Published and unpublished guides.
University of North Carolina Library, Southern Historical Collection.
Testimonials relating to [Mrs.] Barringer's attempt to secure aid in returning to her home in Germany. Barringer was a resident of Cabarrus County, NC. Taken from Susan Sokol Blosser and Clyde Norman Wilson, Jr., *The Southern Historical Collection: A Guide to Manuscripts* (Chapel Hill, NC: University of North Carolina Library, 1970).

12,946. Bateman, Mary E.
Papers. 1856. 1 vol.
Open. Published and unpublished guides.
University of North Carolina Library, Southern Historical Collection.
Diary kept by Bateman in which she describes her family life and leisure activities on a plantation near Greenville, MS. Taken from Susan Sokol Blosser and Clyde Norman Wilson, Jr., *The Southern Historical Collection: A Guide to Manuscripts* (Chapel Hill, NC: University of North Carolina Library, 1970).

12,947. Beale, Maria (Taylor)
Papers. 1895. 1 item.
Open. Published and unpublished guides.
University of North Carolina Library, Southern Historical Collection.
Letter by Beale (1849-?), a North Carolina author, concerns her writing and personal matters. Taken from Susan Sokol Blosser and Clyde Norman Wilson, Jr., *The Southern Historical Collection: A Guide to Manuscripts* (Chapel Hill, NC: University of North Carolina Library, 1970).

12,948. Beall, Mary (Harper)
Papers. 1858. 1 item.
Open. Published and unpublished guides.
University of North Carolina Library, Southern Historical Collection.
Letter by Beall in which she describes a journey through North Carolina, South Carolina, and Georgia, with detailed accounts of Columbia, SC, and Wilmington, NC. Taken from Susan Sokol Blosser and Clyde Norman Wilson, Jr., *The Southern Historical Collection: A Guide to Manuscripts* (Chapel Hill, NC: University of North Carolina Library, 1970).

12,949. Beard, Grace Pierson (James)
Papers. Nd. 15-page item.
Open. Published and unpublished guides.
University of North Carolina Library, Southern Historical Collection.
Reminiscences by Beard in which she describes her experiences while managing a plantation in the Fairfield District of South Carolina during the passage of Sherman's army. Taken from Susan Sokol Blosser and Clyde Norman Wilson, Jr., *The Southern Historical Collection: A Guide to Manuscripts* (Chapel Hill, NC: University of North Carolina Library, 1970).

12,950. Beck, Sarah G.
Papers. 1863-65. 7 items.
Open. Published and unpublished guides.
University of North Carolina Library, Southern Historical Collection.
Letters and passes received by [Mrs.] Beck, who worked with the US Sanitary Commission in the District of Columbia, Pennsylvania, and North Carolina. Taken from Susan Sokol Blosser and Clyde Norman Wilson, Jr., *The Southern Historical Collection: A Guide to Manuscripts* (Chapel Hill, NC: University of North Carolina Library, 1970).

12,951. Berry, Eliza (Usher)
Papers. 1830-43. 7 items (microfilm).
Open. Published and unpublished guides.
University of North Carolina Library, Southern Historical Collection.
Berry, a resident of North Carolina, was the wife of US Army doctor William Augustus Berry. Physician's accounts and a travel diary of her sister Francenia Usher, a Roman Catholic who journeyed from Maryland to Louisiana in 1830 and 1831 by way of the Ohio and Mississippi rivers. In her diary, she particularly noted churches, convents, and coreligionists she encountered. Also includes letters from Eliza Berry's brother Patrick Usher between 1839 and 1843 while he was a member of the congress of the Texas Republic and while he was in a Mexican prison. Taken from Susan Sokol Blosser and Clyde Norman Wilson, Jr., *The Southern Historical Collection: A Guide to Manuscripts* (Chapel Hill, NC: University of North Carolina Library, 1970).

12,952. Berry, Harriet Morehead
Papers. 1914-62. 3 ft.
Open. Published and unpublished guides.
University of North Carolina Library, Southern Historical Collection.
[Miss] Berry (1877-1940), a resident of Orange County, NC, was secretary of the North Carolina Geological and Economic Survey from 1901 to 1921 and of the North Carolina Good Roads Association. Correspondence, speeches, circulars, press releases, articles, and clippings relate to her activities in the Good Roads movement and to her promotion of state roads legislation as well as to her work with the North Carolina Credit Union Association from 1923 to 1931, with the Democratic national convention of 1924, and with state and national party campaigns. Also includes minutes of the North Carolina Good Roads Association for 1916 to 1923 and material for a history of the Good Roads movement and for a biography of Berry. Taken from Susan Sokol Blosser and Clyde Norman Wilson, Jr., *The Southern Historical Collection: A Guide to Manuscripts* (Chapel Hill, NC: University of North Carolina Library, 1970).

12,953. Berry, Mrs. John
Papers. 1841-1944. 30 items.
Open. Published and unpublished guides.
University of North Carolina Library, Southern Historical Collection.
Papers of the family of Mary (Strayhorn) Berry (?-1934) include letters from a Civil War soldier who was serving in Virginia and Pennsylvania, correspondence of Berry's daughters, and Berry's recollections of her childhood near Hillsborough, NC, before the Civil War. Taken from Susan Sokol Blosser and Clyde Norman Wilson, Jr., *The Southern Historical Collection: A Guide to Manuscripts* (Chapel Hill, NC: University of North Carolina Library, 1970).

12,954. Bethell, Mary (Jeffreys)
Papers. 1853-73. 1 vol.
Open. Published and unpublished guides.
University of North Carolina Library, Southern Historical Collection.
Intermittent diary of Bethell (1821-?), a resident of Rockingham County, NC, contains entries about family matters, the education of her children, Methodist activities, and daily life. Taken from Susan Sokol Blosser and Clyde Norman Wilson, Jr., *The Southern Historical Collection: A Guide to Manuscripts* (Chapel Hill, NC: University of North Carolina Library, 1970).

12,955. Blanchard, Elizabeth Amis Cameron (Hooper)
Papers. 1694-1954. 3 ft. and 16 vols.
Open. Published and unpublished guides.
University of North Carolina Library, Southern Historical Collection.
Family and personal correspondence, a manuscript, and other papers of Blanchard (1873-1956), a resident of New York City, relate to the book *The Life and Times of Sir Archie: The Story of America's Greatest Thoroughbred* (University of North Carolina Press, 1958), which Blanchard co-authored with Manly Wade Wellman. Also contains correspondence of Blanchard, including that with artists and with others interested in the arts; of her husband John Osgood Blanchard; of her mother Mary (Amis) Hooper, who published a book of verse in 1926 at age 83; of her mother's three sisters; and of other relatives and friends. The letters of Sarah (Davis) Amis describe plantation life in Columbus, MS, between 1836 and 1852. A few legal papers pertain to mining interests in New Mexico, Arizona, and California. Taken from Susan Sokol Blosser and Clyde Norman Wilson, Jr., *The Southern Historical Collection: A Guide to Manuscripts* (Chapel Hill, NC: University of North Carolina Library, 1970); Everard H. Smith III, *The Southern Historical Collection: Supplementary Guide to Manuscripts, 1970-1975* (Chapel Hill, NC: The University of North Carolina Library, 1976).

12,956. Bondurant, Emily (Morrison)
Papers. 1864-1925. 15 items.
Open. Published and unpublished guides.
University of North Carolina Library, Southern Historical Collection.
Reminiscences by Bondurant (1837-1926), who was the daughter of Presbyterian minister James Morrison, concern her childhood in Rockbridge County, VA, and her life as a wife and mother in Buckingham County, VA, after her marriage to Alexander Joseph Bondurant in 1859. Also includes a manuscript by her husband about his family background and childhood in Virginia, bylaws of Buckingham County agriculture clubs, and other papers. Taken from Susan Sokol Blosser and Clyde Norman Wilson, Jr., *The Southern Historical Collection: A Guide to Manuscripts* (Chapel Hill, NC: University of North Carolina Library, 1970).

12,957. Bonebrake, Jeanette E.
Papers. 1862-66. 59 items.
Open. Published and unpublished guides.
University of North Carolina Library, Southern Historical Collection.
Civil War letters received by [Miss] Bonebrake of Indiana from her brother and other Federal soldiers serving with the 125th Illinois Regiment in Tennessee, Kentucky, and Georgia and from a woman friend in Indiana. Taken from Susan Sokol Blosser and Clyde Norman Wilson, Jr., *The Southern Historical Collection: A Guide to Manuscripts* (Chapel Hill, NC: University of North Carolina Library, 1970).

12,958. Bradwell, Annie (Campbell)
Papers. 1936-40. 1 vol. and 39 items.
Open. Published and unpublished guides.
University of North Carolina Library, Southern Historical Collection.
Letters, notes, biographical sketches, articles, and other papers of Bradwell relate to the 19th-century history of Bainbridge, GA, and Decatur County, GA. Taken from Susan Sokol Blosser and Clyde Norman Wilson, Jr., *The Southern Historical Collection: A Guide to Manuscripts* (Chapel Hill, NC: University of North Carolina Library, 1970).

12,959. Bridgers, Ann Preston
Papers. 1936. Ca. 26 items.
Open. Unpublished guide.
University of North Carolina Library, Southern Historical Collection.
Scripts of three apparently unpublished plays by Bridgers, "This Throne of Kings," "Miss Sally," and "This Beautiful Structure, A Play of John S. Calhoun," as well as material about Calhoun collected in preparation for the play, photos of Bridgers and members of her family, and a program from a pageant in Fort Hill, SC, in 1936 during which the play about Calhoun was presented.

12,960. Broidrick, Annie Laurie (Harris)
Papers. 1893. 24-page item.
Open. Published and unpublished guides.
University of North Carolina Library, Southern Historical Collection.
Recollections by Broidrick of plantation life just before the Civil War and an account of the war experiences and flight of the women and children of the Harris family from their Vicksburg, MS, home. Taken from Susan Sokol Blosser and Clyde Norman Wilson, Jr., *The Southern Historical Collection: A Guide to Manuscripts* (Chapel Hill, NC: University of North Carolina Library, 1970).

12,961. Brumby, Ann Eliza
Papers. 1858. 1 item.
Open. Published and unpublished guides.
University of North Carolina Library, Southern Historical Collection.
Letter to Brumby from her father Richard Trapier Brumby (1804-75), a South Carolina professor and geologist, in which he advises her about the education of a lady. Taken from Susan Sokol Blosser and Clyde Norman Wilson, Jr., *The Southern Historical Collection: A Guide to Manuscripts* (Chapel Hill, NC: University of North Carolina Library, 1970).

12,962. Bryan, Mary Biddle (Norcott)
Papers. Ca. 1820-1921. 243-page vol.
Open. Published and unpublished guides.
University of North Carolina Library, Southern Historical Collection.
Scrapbook compiled by Bryan (1841-1925), the wife of Henry Ravenscroft Bryan (1836-1919), a judge in New Bern, NC, contains her reminiscences of her family and correspondence between the Norcott, Biddle, and Bryan families. Taken from Susan Sokol Blosser and Clyde Norman Wilson, Jr., *The Southern Historical Collection: A Guide to Manuscripts* (Chapel Hill, NC: University of North Carolina Library, 1970).

12,963. Buffington, Mrs. W. R.
Papers. 1618-1864. 42 items (microfilm).
Open. Published and unpublished guides.
University of North Carolina Library, Southern Historical Collection.
Consists primarily of family correspondence, 1804-43, of Magdalene Hutchins [Mrs. Ferdinand Leigh] Claiborne of Natchez, MS, including letters from her brother-in-law William Charles Coles Claiborne, who was governor of Louisiana, and her son-in-law John Hazelhurst Boneval Latrobe, a Baltimore lawyer, author, and artist. Taken from Susan Sokol Blosser and Clyde Norman Wilson, Jr., *The Southern Historical Collection: A Guide to Manuscripts* (Chapel Hill, NC: University of North Carolina Library, 1970).

12,964. Butler, Lucy (Wood)
Papers. 1859-63. 178 pp.
Open. Published and unpublished guides.
University of North Carolina Library, Southern Historical Collection.
Letters to Butler, a resident of Charlottesville, VA, from her fiancé in Fernandina, FL, and a diary she

kept from 1861 to 1863. Taken from Susan Sokol Blosser and Clyde Norman Wilson, Jr., *The Southern Historical Collection: A Guide to Manuscripts* (Chapel Hill, NC: University of North Carolina Library, 1970).

12,965. Butler, Mrs. Marion
Papers. 1895-1918. 176 items.
Open. Published and unpublished guides.
University of North Carolina Library, Southern Historical Collection.
Family and social correspondence of Florence (Faison) Butler, clubwoman and wife of US senator Marion Butler, in Raleigh, NC, and Washington, DC. Taken from Susan Sokol Blosser and Clyde Norman Wilson, Jr., *The Southern Historical Collection: A Guide to Manuscripts* (Chapel Hill, NC: University of North Carolina Library, 1970).

12,966. Buttrick, Caroline I.
Papers. 1946-65. 473-page item.
Open. Published and unpublished guides.
University of North Carolina Library, Southern Historical Collection.
Biography by Buttrick, a physician, of her mother and of her father Wallace Henry Buttrick (1853-1926), a New York Baptist clergyman who was secretary and president of the General Education Board and director of the China Medical Board of the Rockefeller Foundation. In the biography Caroline Buttrick also discusses her own experiences and observations about the Rockefeller Foundation, the China Medical Board, life in the Orient, changes in the practice of medicine over 40 years, and social work and social movements of her parents' time. Taken from Susan Sokol Blosser and Clyde Norman Wilson, Jr., *The Southern Historical Collection: A Guide to Manuscripts* (Chapel Hill, NC: University of North Carolina Library, 1970).

12,967. Cannon, Mrs. Charles Albert
Papers. 1830-1953. 2 ft.
Open. Published and unpublished guides.
University of North Carolina Library, Southern Historical Collection.
Papers of Ruth Louise (Coltrane) Cannon (1891-1966), a clubwoman, include correspondence relating to the Roanoke Island Historical Society; correspondence and photos relating to the publication of *Old Homes and Gardens of North Carolina* (1939), which Cannon compiled; typescripts of interviews with old inhabitants for the Roanoke Farms Resettlement Administration Project in Halifax, NC; essays and pictures of old North Carolina churches; and pictures of Confederate leaders and battle scenes. Taken from Susan Sokol Blosser and Clyde Norman Wilson, Jr., *The Southern Historical Collection: A Guide to Manuscripts* (Chapel Hill, NC: University of North Carolina Library, 1970).

12,968. Capehart, Meeta (Armistead)
Papers. 1668-1868. 144 items.
Open. Published and unpublished guides.
University of North Carolina Library, Southern Historical Collection.
Letters to Capehart of Granville County, NC, during the Civil War from her husband Captain B. A. Capehart, quartermaster of the 15th North Carolina Battalion, in which he describes his activities and duties in Virginia and North Carolina and advises his wife on management of their farm. Also includes scattered Armistead and Capehart family papers and colonial land grants in the Albemarle Sound region. Taken from Susan Sokol Blosser and Clyde Norman Wilson, Jr., *The Southern Historical Collection: A Guide to Manuscripts* (Chapel Hill, NC: University of North Carolina Library, 1970); Everard H. Smith III, *The Southern Historical Collection: Supplementary Guide to Manuscripts, 1970-1975* (Chapel Hill, NC: The University of North Carolina Library, 1976).

12,969. Carmouche, Annie (Jeter)
Papers. 1853-1915. 50 items (microfilm).
Open. Published and unpublished guides.
University of North Carolina Library, Southern Historical Collection.
Family correspondence and reminiscences of Carmouche (1843-?), who was the daughter of Pointe Coupée, LA, sugar planter John Tinsley Jeter (1799-1862) and the wife of Emile A. Carmouche (?-1885) of St. Landry and Shreveport, LA. She recalls family, plantation, and social life before and after the Civil War and life in New Orleans during the War. Includes letters written by her husband and brother from the Confederate army and federal prisons. Taken from Susan Sokol Blosser and Clyde Norman Wilson, Jr., *The Southern Historical Collection: A Guide to Manuscripts* (Chapel Hill, NC: University of North Carolina Library, 1970).

12,970. Carney, Kate S.
Papers. 1859-62. 1 vol.
Open. Published and unpublished guides.
University of North Carolina Library, Southern Historical Collection.
Diary kept by Carney (1842-?), the daughter of a Murfreesboro, TN, merchant, in which she describes antebellum life in Murfreesboro; travel in the Southeast, Northeast, Middle West, and Canada; her schooling in Philadelphia; a stay with her sister in Yazoo County, MS; and life at home under US army occupation. Taken from Susan Sokol Blosser and Clyde Norman Wilson, Jr., *The Southern Historical Collection: A Guide to Manuscripts* (Chapel Hill, NC: University of North Carolina Library, 1970).

12,971. Carr, Laura Noell
Papers. 1942-48. More than 375 items.
Open. Unpublished guide.
University of North Carolina Library, Southern Historical Collection.
Laura Noell, a resident of Danville, VA, married Austin Heaton Carr (?-1942) in 1918. After his death she married Robert Hett Chapman. Letters to Laura Carr from her sons Austin Heaton Carr, Jr., who served in the Air Force during WWII and lived in New York after the war, and Charles Noell Carr, a student at Woodberry Forest, VA, and Cambridge, MA. Also includes issues of the Woodberry Forest student newspaper and clippings.

12,972. Chamberlain, Hope (Summerell)
Papers. 1888-1951. 25 items.
Open. Published and unpublished guides.
University of North Carolina Library, Southern Historical Collection.
Correspondence, a biographical sketch, and clippings of Chamberlain (1870-1960), a Raleigh, NC, clubwoman and author of works about local history. Includes letters she wrote as a schoolgirl and letters about her grandfather Elisha Mitchell and North Carolina history. Taken from Susan Sokol Blosser and Clyde Norman Wilson, Jr., *The Southern Historical Collection: A Guide to Manuscripts* (Chapel Hill, NC: University of North Carolina Library, 1970).

12,973. Chapel Hill Bird Club
Records. 1941-76. 2 vols. and ca. 244 items.
Open. Unpublished guide.
University of North Carolina Library, Southern Historical Collection.
Constitution, bylaws, minutes, treasurer's reports and other financial records, correspondence, membership lists, notices, advertisements, bird lists, bulletins, catalogs, clippings, and other records of the Club. Includes material relating to activities of the Audubon Society and the constitution, minutes, and announcements of the North Carolina Bird Club, of which Mrs. O. F. Jensen of Chapel Hill was president.

12,974. Chapel Hill Business and Professional Women's Club
Records. 1943-48. 28 items.
Open. Published and unpublished guides.
University of North Carolina Library, Southern Historical Collection.
Bylaws, minutes, membership rolls, and other records of the Club. Taken from Susan Sokol Blosser and Clyde Norman Wilson, Jr., *The Southern Historical Collection: A Guide to Manuscripts* (Chapel Hill, NC: University of North Carolina Library, 1970).

12,975. Chisholm, Mrs. W. S.
Papers. 1866-68. 1 vol.
Open. Published and unpublished guides.
University of North Carolina Library, Southern Historical Collection.
Account book of Chisholm, a resident of Savannah, GA, records household and other expenditures. Taken from Susan Sokol Blosser and Clyde Norman Wilson, Jr., *The Southern Historical Collection: A Guide to Manuscripts* (Chapel Hill, NC: University of North Carolina Library, 1970).

12,976. Chotard, Eliza William
Papers. 1868. 1 vol. (microfilm).
Open. Published and unpublished guides.
University of North Carolina Library, Southern Historical Collection.
Autobiography of Chotard (1798-?) covers the period to 1825 and concerns her early life in Natchez, MS, with her father, an emigré from Santa Domingo; her experiences in accompanying her mother to New Orleans; and settling on the family lands in Tuscaloosa County, AL. Chotard later married William Proctor Gould. Taken from Susan Sokol Blosser and Clyde Norman Wilson, Jr., *The Southern Historical Collection: A Guide to Manuscripts* (Chapel Hill, NC: University of North Carolina Library, 1970).

12,977. Claiborne, Magdalene (Hutchins)
Papers. 1813-80s. 14 items.
Open. Published and unpublished guides.
University of North Carolina Library, Southern Historical Collection.
Letters received by [Mrs. Ferdinand Leigh] Claiborne, who lived near Natchez, MS, from relatives in Louisiana and Virginia; other family correspondence; and printed funeral notices. Some of the letters are on microfilm. Taken from Susan Sokol Blosser and Clyde Norman Wilson, Jr., *The Southern Historical Collection: A Guide to Manuscripts* (Chapel Hill, NC: University of North Carolina Library, 1970).

12,978. Clay, Mary
Papers. Ca. 1783. 1 item.
Open. Published and unpublished guides.
University of North Carolina Library, Southern Historical Collection.
Letter from Clay (1766-1803), a young girl in Camden, SC, to her sister in Savannah, GA, in which she describes a dance she attended and refers to the British. Taken from Susan Sokol Blosser and Clyde Norman Wilson, Jr., *The Southern Historical Collection: A Guide to Manuscripts* (Chapel Hill, NC: University of North Carolina Library, 1970).

12,979. Cleveland, Zuleika Haralson
Papers. Nd. 1 item.
Open. Published and unpublished guides.
University of North Carolina Library, Southern Historical Collection.
Poem written by [Miss] Cleveland during Reconstruction in which she prays for deliverance from Republican control. Taken from Susan Sokol Blosser and Clyde Norman Wilson, Jr., *The Southern Historical Collection: A Guide to Manuscripts* (Chapel Hill, NC: University of North Carolina Library, 1970).

12,980. Clitherall, Eliza Carolina (Burgwin)
Papers. 1751-1860. 17 vols.
Open. Published and unpublished guides.
University of North Carolina Library, Southern Historical Collection.
Combined diary, autobiography, and family history of Clitherall (1784-1863), who spent her childhood on a plantation near Wilmington, NC, and at school in England; lived with her husband George Campbell Clitherall on plantations in South and North Carolina; and, after 1836, lived in Alabama. In addition to raising her children, her grandchildren, and orphans, Eliza Clitherall taught school, traveled, ran a boarding house, and lived through the yellow fever epidemics of the 1850s. Taken from Susan Sokol Blosser and Clyde Norman Wilson, Jr., *The Southern Historical Collection: A Guide to Manuscripts* (Chapel Hill, NC: University of North Carolina Library, 1970).

12,981. Clotworthy, Mrs. John B.
Papers. 1736-1931. 2.5 ft.
Open. Published and unpublished guides.
University of North Carolina Library, Southern Historical Collection.
Correspondence and genealogical data of about 15 southern families collected by Clotworthy, a Georgia resident. Items from the 18th century are primarily wills. Taken from Susan Sokol Blosser and Clyde Norman Wilson, Jr., *The Southern Historical Collection: A Guide to Manuscripts* (Chapel Hill, NC: University of North Carolina Library, 1970).

12,982. Cobb Family
Papers. 1853-1975. Ca. 10 ft.
Open. Unpublished guide.
University of North Carolina Library, Southern Historical Collection.
Personal and professional papers of Collier Cobb (1862-1934), a geologist who was a geology professor at the University from 1892 to 1933, include family letters, correspondence with friends and professional associates, notes and writings, students' papers, genealogical notes, bills and receipts, photos, programs, invitations, and clippings. Also includes letters of Cobb's parents; his brothers and sisters, particularly Lucy Cobb and Penelope Cobb; his three wives, Mary Battle Cobb (1864-1900), Lucy Battle Cobb (1861-1905), and Mary Gatlin Cobb (1875-1973), whom he married in 1910; his children William Battle Cobb (1891-1933), Collier Cobb, Jr. (1893-), and Mary Louisa Cobb (1899-1976); and grandchildren, cousins, nieces, and nephews.

12,983. Collier, Elizabeth
Papers. 1862-65. 1 vol.
Open. Published and unpublished guides.
University of North Carolina Library, Southern Historical Collection.
Diary of Collier (ca. 1844-?), who lived near Goldsboro, NC, and Hillsborough, NC, in which she writes primarily of her reactions to the Civil War. Taken from Susan Sokol Blosser and Clyde Norman Wilson, Jr., *The Southern Historical Collection: A Guide to Manuscripts* (Chapel Hill, NC: University of North Carolina Library, 1970).

12,984. Comer, Laura (Beecher)
Papers. 1862-73. 3 vols.
Open. Published and unpublished guides.
University of North Carolina Library, Southern Historical Collection.
Comer (1817-1900), a Connecticut native, was the niece of Henry Ward Beecher and the wife of James Comer (1797-1864) of Georgia. In her diaries she records her daily life in Columbus, GA; her religious sentiments; and trips to Europe and the North. Taken from Susan Sokol Blosser and Clyde Norman Wilson, Jr., *The Southern Historical Collection: A Guide to Manuscripts* (Chapel Hill, NC: University of North Carolina Library, 1970).

12,985. Conner, Juliana Margaret (Courtney)
Papers. 1827. 89-page vol.
Open. Published and unpublished guides.
University of North Carolina Library, Southern Historical Collection.
Diary by Conner concerns a trip with her husband Henry Workman Conner of Charleston, SC, to the home of his father James Conner, a planter in Mecklenburg County, NC. They visited the Conner home and places in the vicinity; then went to Salem, NC; traveled through Tennessee to Nashville; visited the Andrew Jacksons; and returned through Cherokee territory and northern Georgia. Taken from Susan Sokol Blosser and Clyde Norman Wilson, Jr., *The Southern Historical Collection: A Guide to Manuscripts* (Chapel Hill, NC: University of North Carolina Library, 1970).

12,986. Connor, Otelia Carrington (Cuningham)
Papers. 1888-1968. 480 items.
Open. Published and unpublished guides.
University of North Carolina Library, Southern Historical Collection.
Papers of [Mrs. David M.] Connor (1894-1969), a clubwoman and feature writer of Chapel Hill and Durham, NC, include family letters, typescripts of her articles, and papers relating to her activities with several women's patriotic and historical clubs, hospitals, and a Durham school. Also includes correspondence and other papers of her mother Mrs. John S. Cuningham of Durham and Greensboro, NC, relating to her activities in the women's suffrage movement, the Democratic party, Episcopal church organizations, and social service and educational groups. Taken from Susan Sokol Blosser and Clyde Norman Wilson, Jr., *The Southern Historical Collection: A Guide to Manuscripts* (Chapel Hill, NC: University of North Carolina Library, 1970).

12,987. Cornwall, Susan
Papers. 1857-66. 1 vol.
Open. Published and unpublished guides.
University of North Carolina Library, Southern Historical Collection.
Volume of [Miss] Cornwall (1825-1905), a resident of Burke County, GA, who later married Oscar Lassiter Shewmake, contains original poetry and occasional diary entries about her personal life and thoughts, her literary aspirations, and her reactions to war and public events. Taken from Susan Sokol Blosser and Clyde Norman Wilson, Jr., *The Southern Historical Collection: A Guide to Manuscripts* (Chapel Hill, NC: University of North Carolina Library, 1970).

12,988. Cotten, Elizabeth (Henderson)
Papers. 1926-74. 4.5 ft.
Open. Published and unpublished guides.
University of North Carolina Library, Southern Historical Collection.
Correspondence and other papers of [Mrs. Lyman A.] Cotten (1875-1975), who for many years was curator of the Southern Historical Collection, relate to old homes and gardens and the early architecture of North Carolina; the Edwards-Tryon-Nash house in Hillsborough, NC; her committee work for the Tryon Palace restoration at New Bern, NC; the restoration of St. John's Episcopal Church in Williamsboro, NC; and to the placement of a statue commemorating Virginia Dare on Roanoke Island. Taken from Susan Sokol Blosser and Clyde Norman Wilson, Jr., *The Southern Historical Collection: A Guide to Manuscripts* (Chapel Hill, NC: University of North Carolina Library, 1970); Everard H. Smith III, *The Southern Historical Collection: Supplementary Guide to Manuscripts, 1970-1975* (Chapel Hill, NC: The University of North Carolina Library, 1976).

12,989. Cox, Miriam (Bishop)
Papers. 1832. 1 item.
Open. Published and unpublished guides.
University of North Carolina Library, Southern Historical Collection.
Letter to Cox in North Carolina from her daughter, a Quaker who had moved recently to New Garden, IN, to be in a free state. Taken from Susan Sokol Blosser and Clyde Norman Wilson, Jr., *The Southern Historical Collection: A Guide to Manuscripts* (Chapel Hill, NC: University of North Carolina Library, 1970).

12,990. Cozens, Marianne (Bull)
Papers. 1830. 10-page vol.
Open. Published and unpublished guides.
University of North Carolina Library, Southern Historical Collection.
Diary kept by Cozens in December 1830 in which she describes a sea journey from New York to Charleston, SC, and a visit of a few days in Charleston. Taken from Susan Sokol Blosser and Clyde Norman Wilson, Jr., *The Southern Historical Collection: A Guide to Manuscripts* (Chapel Hill, NC: University of North Carolina Library, 1970).

12,991. Craig, Marjorie
Papers. 1934-35. 45 items.
Open. Published and unpublished guides.
University of North Carolina Library, Southern Historical Collection.
Letters from southern librarians, editors, novelists, and local historians that [Miss] Craig (?-1955) received in response to inquiries she made while preparing a master's thesis for the University of North Carolina on "The Survival of the Chivalric Tournament in Southern Life and Literature." Taken from Susan Sokol Blosser and Clyde Norman Wilson, Jr., *The Southern Historical Collection: A Guide to Manuscripts* (Chapel Hill, NC: University of North Carolina Library, 1970).

12,992. Dargan, Olive (Tilford)
Papers. 1934-47. 17 items.
Open. Published and unpublished guides.
University of North Carolina Library, Southern Historical Collection.
Papers of Dargan (1868-1968), an author and poet of Asheville, NC, who sometimes used the pen name Fielding Burke, include a typescript for part of her novel *A Stone Came Rolling* (1935). Taken from Everard H. Smith III, *The Southern Historical Collection: Supplementary Guide to Manuscripts, 1970-1975* (Chapel Hill, NC: The University of North Carolina Library, 1976).

12,993. Dashiell, Margaret (May)
Papers. 1921-48. 120 items.
Open. Published and unpublished guides.
University of North Carolina Library, Southern Historical Collection.
[Mrs. John Parker] Dashiell (1869-1958), a resident of Richmond, VA, was a businesswoman, an importer of French fashion prints, and an illustrator of Richmond, Charleston, and New Orleans scenes and people. Correspondence with literary and artistic people, poems, her watercolor illustrations, and sketches. Taken from Susan Sokol Blosser and Clyde Norman Wilson, Jr., *The Southern Historical Collection: A Guide to Manuscripts* (Chapel Hill, NC: University of North Carolina Library, 1970).

12,994. Daughters of the American Revolution, Davie Poplar Chapter
Records. 1928-71. 1 ft.
Open. Published and unpublished guides.
University of North Carolina Library, Southern Historical Collection.
Minutes, membership data, and scrapbooks of letters, photos, and items relating to WWII activities of this Orange County organization. The Chapter is located in Chapel Hill. Taken from Susan Sokol Blosser and Clyde Norman Wilson, Jr., *The Southern Historical Collection: A Guide*

to Manuscripts (Chapel Hill, NC: University of North Carolina Library, 1970); Everard H. Smith III, *The Southern Historical Collection: Supplementary Guide to Manuscripts, 1970-1975* (Chapel Hill, NC: The University of North Carolina Library, 1976).

12,995. DeMilly, Marie Louise (Morris)
Papers. Nd. 2-page item.
Open. Published and unpublished guides.
University of North Carolina Library, Southern Historical Collection.
Recollections by DeMilly of her early life in France and her immigration to Florida after the revolution of 1830. Taken from Susan Sokol Blosser and Clyde Norman Wilson, Jr., *The Southern Historical Collection: A Guide to Manuscripts* (Chapel Hill, NC: University of North Carolina Library, 1970).

12,996. Devereux, Margaret (Mordecai)
Papers. 1837-56. 60 items.
Open. Published and unpublished guides.
University of North Carolina Library, Southern Historical Collection.
Correspondence of Margaret Mordecai with her sister Ellen Mordecai while they were at school in Philadelphia and Petersburg, VA, and as married women on a Bertie County, NC, plantation and a Raleigh, NC, estate. Margaret Mordecai married John Devereux, and Ellen Mordecai married Samuel Fox Mordecai. The sisters were nieces of author Ellen Mordecai. Taken from Susan Sokol Blosser and Clyde Norman Wilson, Jr., *The Southern Historical Collection: A Guide to Manuscripts* (Chapel Hill, NC: University of North Carolina Library, 1970).

12,997. Dixon, Marian (Homes)
Papers. 1950. 6-page item.
Open. Published and unpublished guides.
University of North Carolina Library, Southern Historical Collection.
Short history by Dixon of the town of Boydton, VA, and reminiscences of her life there in about 1900. Taken from Susan Sokol Blosser and Clyde Norman Wilson, Jr., *The Southern Historical Collection: A Guide to Manuscripts* (Chapel Hill, NC: University of North Carolina Library, 1970).

12,998. Dolan, Margaret (Baggett)
Papers. 1936-74. 8 ft., 7 tapes, and 1 recording disc.
Access restricted. Published and unpublished guides.
University of North Carolina Library, Southern Historical Collection.
Dolan (1914-74), a resident of Chapel Hill, was a public health nurse and a professor and head of the department of public health nursing in the School of Public Health at the University of North Carolina from 1959 to 1974. She served as president of the North Carolina State Nurses Association, as president of the American Nurses Association from 1962 to 1964, as president of the National Health Council in 1969 and 1970, and as president of the American Public Health Association in 1973. Includes administrative files relating to the professional organizations for which she worked, especially the ANA and APHA; correspondence; committee documents; speeches; reports; publications; photos; citations; awards; and clippings. Taken from Everard H. Smith III, *The Southern Historical Collection: Supplementary Guide to Manuscripts, 1970-1975* (Chapel Hill, NC: The University of North Carolina Library, 1976).

12,999. Dudley, Marion
Papers. 1927-66. 4 vols. and 16 items.
Open. Published and unpublished guides.
University of North Carolina Library, Southern Historical Collection.
Letters by Dudley (1895-), a resident of Wilmington, NC, in which she describes her life and social work for the YWCA in China from 1927 to 1931, 1938 to 1942, and 1943 to 1947; photos, scrapbooks, and clippings about China; and a scrapbook concerning the theatrical career of her brother John Stuart Dudley (1893-1966). Taken from Everard H. Smith III, *The Southern Historical Collection: Supplementary Guide to Manuscripts, 1970-1975* (Chapel Hill, NC: The University of North Carolina Library, 1976).

13,000. Duffee, Mary Gordon
Papers. 1909-10. 4 items.
Open. Published and unpublished guides.
University of North Carolina Library, Southern Historical Collection.
Letters concerning De Soto Fort by Duffee, an author of books on the Fort, which is located in De Kalb County, AL, and was supposedly built by the Spanish explorer De Soto. Taken from Susan Sokol Blosser and Clyde Norman Wilson, Jr., *The Southern Historical Collection: A Guide to Manuscripts* (Chapel Hill, NC: University of North Carolina Library, 1970).

13,001. Eagan, Julia Goode
Papers. 1932-44. 24 items.
Open. Unpublished guide.
University of North Carolina Library, Southern Historical Collection.
Eagan (1888-1963), a native of Atlanta, married Henry E. Eagan in 1912. She studied at Columbia University, was social editor of the *Salisbury Post* from 1915 to 1920, wrote feature articles for the *Charlotte Observer* and *Atlanta Journal,* and worked for the North Carolina Employment Office. Correspondence between Julia Eagan and Archibald Henderson, a professor of mathematics at the University of North Carolina; typescript of an article she wrote about Henderson; biographical data on Julia Eagan; and a photo of her. Julia Eagan was co-author of *The Prophet of Zion-Parnassus* with James F. Hurley.

13,002. Eaton, Harriet H. A.
Papers. 1853-64. 5 vols.
Open. Published and unpublished guides.
University of North Carolina Library, Southern Historical Collection.
Diary kept in 1853 and 1854 by [Mrs.] Eaton, a resident of Portland, ME, concerning a sea voyage to Mobile, AL, and her stay there and a diary she kept from 1862 to 1864 while she was a nurse with the US army. She recorded her thoughts and activities as she visited various camps in Virginia to leave supplies and aid the sick and wounded. Also includes an undated record of hospital supplies distributed to Maine regiments. Taken from Susan Sokol Blosser and Clyde Norman Wilson, Jr., *The Southern Historical Collection: A Guide to Manuscripts* (Chapel Hill, NC: University of North Carolina Library, 1970).

13,003. Edmondson, Belle
Papers. 1864. 1 vol.
Open. Published and unpublished guides.
University of North Carolina Library, Southern Historical Collection.
Diary kept by [Miss] Edmondson of Shelby County, TN, during the Civil War contains accounts of news from the front, local skirmishes and rumors, troop movements, running contraband through Federal lines, her family, slaves, and a trip to Mississippi, where she visited two generals. Taken from Susan Sokol Blosser and Clyde Norman Wilson, Jr., *The Southern Historical Collection: A Guide to Manuscripts* (Chapel Hill, NC: University of North Carolina Library, 1970).

13,004. Egleston, Sophie (Lyon)
Papers. 1933. 8-page item.
Open. Published and unpublished guides.
University of North Carolina Library, Southern Historical Collection.
Reminiscences by Egleston (1856-?) of life in Alabama and in a colony of southerners in the San Joaquin valley of California after the Civil War. Taken from Susan Sokol Blosser and Clyde Norman Wilson, Jr., *The Southern Historical Collection: A Guide to Manuscripts* (Chapel Hill, NC: University of North Carolina Library, 1970).

13,005. Elmore, Grace B.
Papers. 1861-72. 6 vols.
Open. Published and unpublished guides.
University of North Carolina Library, Southern Historical Collection.
Diary kept intermittently by [Miss] Elmore (1839-?) is primarily introspective but contains a detailed account of life and events in Columbia, SC, from September 1864 to January 1865. Also includes notebooks containing drafts of a novel and other literary material. Taken from Susan Sokol Blosser and Clyde Norman Wilson, Jr., *The Southern Historical Collection: A Guide to Manuscripts* (Chapel Hill, NC: University of North Carolina Library, 1970).

13,006. Enfield, Gertrude (Dixon)
Papers. 1744-1964. 12 items.
Open. Published and unpublished guides.
University of North Carolina Library, Southern Historical Collection.
Unpublished biography by Enfield (?-1969) of her ancestor Christopher Houston (1744-1837), a Revolutionary War soldier and early settler of Maury County, TN. Includes other related material. Taken from Susan Sokol Blosser and Clyde Norman Wilson, Jr., *The Southern Historical Collection: A Guide to Manuscripts* (Chapel Hill, NC: University of North Carolina Library, 1970).

13,007. Eppes, Mrs. Nicholas Ware
Papers. 1847-1933. 40 items.
Open. Published and unpublished guides.
University of North Carolina Library, Southern Historical Collection.
Letters to Susan (Bradford) Eppes, a Tallahassee, FL, author, from James L. Rodgers of Miami concerning her writings on the Old South and the Confederacy. Also includes antebellum correspondence of the Bradford family. Taken from Susan Sokol Blosser and Clyde Norman Wilson, Jr., *The Southern Historical Collection: A Guide to Manuscripts* (Chapel Hill, NC: University of North Carolina Library, 1970).

13,008. Eugenia Rawls and Donald Seawell Theatre Collection
Papers. 1916-74. 23 ft., 110 vols., 7 tapes, 5 recording discs, and 1 motion picture.
Open. Published and unpublished guides.
University of North Carolina Library, Southern Historical Collection.
[Miss] Rawls (1913-) is a Broadway and television actress; her husband Donald Seawell (1912-) is a lawyer, former army officer, and a theatrical producer of Denver and New York City. Correspondence of Rawls with her children, relatives, colleagues, and friends and with her husband while he was stationed in England and France during WWII as an army counterintelligence officer; radio plays and other writings by Rawls, including drafts of her one-woman shows on Fanny Kemble and Tallulah Bankhead; notebooks of her activities as a drama student at the University of North Carolina; photos; posters; seven videotapes; two audiotapes; recording discs; radio, television, and theatrical scripts for productions in which she appeared; and scrapbooks of clippings. Also includes Seawell's office files relating to his business and theatrical affairs and to the production of several plays in the 1960s. Taken from Everard H. Smith III, *The Southern Historical Collection: Supplementary Guide to Manuscripts, 1970-1975* (Chapel Hill,

NC: The University of North Carolina Library, 1976).

13,009. Fisher, Julia (Johnson)
Papers. 1864. 15-page item.
Open. Published and unpublished guides.
University of North Carolina Library, Southern Historical Collection.
Diary kept by Fisher (1814-85), a native of Massachusetts, while she was living with her husband William Fisher and their children in an isolated area in Camden County, GA, near the Florida border. She writes of conditions and incidents of daily life, family and neighborhood news, personal thoughts, and reports of military activity in the region. Taken from Susan Sokol Blosser and Clyde Norman Wilson, Jr., *The Southern Historical Collection: A Guide to Manuscripts* (Chapel Hill, NC: University of North Carolina Library, 1970).

13,010. Fisher, Susan
Papers. 1838-41. 13 items.
Open. Published and unpublished guides.
University of North Carolina Library, Southern Historical Collection.
Letters to [Miss] Fisher in Augusta, ME, from her sisters, who had gone to Augusta, GA, to establish a drygoods and ladies' clothing store. The sisters describe their lives in the South, with frequent comparisons to Maine, and concentrate on social activities and business conditions. Also includes letters from a nephew working in a law office in Georgia; he comments on politics and local activities. Taken from Susan Sokol Blosser and Clyde Norman Wilson, Jr., *The Southern Historical Collection: A Guide to Manuscripts* (Chapel Hill, NC: University of North Carolina Library, 1970).

13,011. Floyd, Letitia (Preston)
Papers. 1843. 41-page vol.
Open. Published and unpublished guides.
University of North Carolina Library, Southern Historical Collection.
Reminiscences by Floyd, who was the wife of Virginia governor John Floyd (1783-1837), concern 18th-century pioneers of western Virginia and Kentucky, including her father William Preston. She writes of incidents with Indians and of the history and genealogy of the Preston and Floyd families. Taken from Susan Sokol Blosser and Clyde Norman Wilson, Jr., *The Southern Historical Collection: A Guide to Manuscripts* (Chapel Hill, NC: University of North Carolina Library, 1970).

13,012. Foster, Elmina
Papers. 1917. 21-page item.
Open. Published and unpublished guides.
University of North Carolina Library, Southern Historical Collection.
Recollections by Foster (1827-1917) of her childhood and plantation life in Guilford County, NC. Taken from Susan Sokol Blosser and Clyde Norman Wilson, Jr., *The Southern Historical Collection: A Guide to Manuscripts* (Chapel Hill, NC: University of North Carolina Library, 1970).

13,013. Franck, Maria (Miller) Hill
Papers. 1828-79. 225 items.
Open. Published and unpublished guides.
University of North Carolina Library, Southern Historical Collection.
Personal correspondence of Franck, a Quaker who was the wife of John Martin Franck (?-1868) of Onslow County, NC, includes letters from relatives and friends in eastern North Carolina towns, Carthage, IN, and Galesburg, IL, giving household news and alluding to the contested will of Maria Franck's first husband Samuel Hill (?-1859). Taken from Susan Sokol Blosser and Clyde Norman Wilson, Jr., *The Southern Historical Collection: A Guide to Manuscripts* (Chapel Hill, NC: University of North Carolina Library, 1970).

13,014. Garretson, Anna Maria (Deans)
Papers. 1807-93. 48 items.
Open. Published and unpublished guides.
University of North Carolina Library, Southern Historical Collection.
Correspondence of Garretson, a resident of Gloucester and Mathews counties in Virginia, with her friends and relatives. The items are dated 1807 to 1829 and 1893. Taken from Everard H. Smith III, *The Southern Historical Collection: Supplementary Guide to Manuscripts, 1970-1975* (Chapel Hill, NC: The University of North Carolina Library, 1976).

13,015. Gilson, Mary Barnett
Papers. 1909-59. 14 items.
Open. Published and unpublished guides.
University of North Carolina Library, Southern Historical Collection.
Papers of [Miss] Gilson (1877-1969), an economist at the University of Chicago from 1931 to 1942 and with various government agencies, include diary-memorandum books from her trips to Europe in 1909, 1926, and 1959 and letters from Sir Herbert G. Williams, Neville Chamberlain, Henry L. Stimson, and others. Taken from Susan Sokol Blosser and Clyde Norman Wilson, Jr., *The Southern Historical Collection: A Guide to Manuscripts* (Chapel Hill, NC: University of North Carolina Library, 1970).

13,016. Graves, Louis, and Graves, Mildred
Papers. 1876-1976. 8 ft.
Open. Unpublished guide.
University of North Carolina Library, Southern Historical Collection.
Family and professional correspondence, notes and writings, bills, receipts, genealogical notes, a map, clippings, and other papers of Louis Graves (1883-1965), a writer, journalist, and founder of the *Chapel Hill Weekly,* and his wife Mildred "Mim" (Moses) Graves (1892-1976). Includes correspondence of Louis Graves's mother Julia Charlotte Hooper Graves and of his sister Mary (Graves) Rees (1886-1953). Professional and business correspondence pertains to the *Weekly* and to activities of such Graves and Claywell family members as Mildred Graves's sister Mary (Moses) Claywell and her niece Allen (Claywell) Irvine.

13,017. Graydon, Nell (Saunders)
Papers. 1878-1959. 10 items.
Open. Published and unpublished guides.
University of North Carolina Library, Southern Historical Collection.
Correspondence and other papers of Graydon, a South Carolina author, concern real persons who were the basis for her novel about a woman Federal spy in South Carolina during the Civil War. The items are dated 1878, 1908, and 1959. Taken from Susan Sokol Blosser and Clyde Norman Wilson, Jr., *The Southern Historical Collection: A Guide to Manuscripts* (Chapel Hill, NC: University of North Carolina Library, 1970).

13,018. Greeley, Floretta Elmore
Papers. 1906-09. 1 vol.
Open. Published and unpublished guides.
University of North Carolina Library, Southern Historical Collection.
Letters from Greeley, a student at Radcliffe College, to her parents in Milwaukee. Taken from Susan Sokol Blosser and Clyde Norman Wilson, Jr., *The Southern Historical Collection: A Guide to Manuscripts* (Chapel Hill, NC: University of North Carolina Library, 1970).

13,019. Grimball, Margaret Ann "Meta" (Morris)
Papers. 1860-66. 1 vol.
Open. Published and unpublished guides.
University of North Carolina Library, Southern Historical Collection.
Diary kept by [Mrs. John Berkley] Grimball (?-1881), primarily in 1860 and 1861, pertains to her life on a Colleton District plantation; in wartime Charleston, SC; and as a refugee in Spartanburg, SC. Taken from Susan Sokol Blosser and Clyde Norman Wilson, Jr., *The Southern Historical Collection: A Guide to Manuscripts* (Chapel Hill, NC: University of North Carolina Library, 1970).

13,020. Gurley, Jane
Papers. 1830-41. 25 items.
Open. Published and unpublished guides.
University of North Carolina Library, Southern Historical Collection.
Letters to [Mrs.] Gurley of Windsor, NC, from friends and relatives in La Grange, TN, and various North Carolina towns, concern family affairs. Also includes two letters from a former slave in Brownsville, TX. Taken from Susan Sokol Blosser and Clyde Norman Wilson, Jr., *The Southern Historical Collection: A Guide to Manuscripts* (Chapel Hill, NC: University of North Carolina Library, 1970).

13,021. Habersham, Josephine C.
Papers. 1863. 1 vol.
Open. Published and unpublished guides.
University of North Carolina Library, Southern Historical Collection.
Diary of Habersham, who lived near Savannah, GA, concerns family and social life, war hardships, and hospital work. The diary was published as *Ebb Tide,* (1958). Taken from Susan Sokol Blosser and Clyde Norman Wilson, Jr., *The Southern Historical Collection: A Guide to Manuscripts* (Chapel Hill, NC: University of North Carolina Library, 1970).

13,022. Hall, Anne (Troy)
Papers. 1821-88. 19 items.
Open. Published and unpublished guides.
University of North Carolina Library, Southern Historical Collection.
Correspondence of Hall (?-1873) and her children is concerned primarily with family matters and social life in Fayetteville, NC, before the Civil War. Taken from Susan Sokol Blosser and Clyde Norman Wilson, Jr., *The Southern Historical Collection: A Guide to Manuscripts* (Chapel Hill, NC: University of North Carolina Library, 1970).

13,023. Hamblen, Maria Florilla (Flint)
Papers. Nd. 7-page item.
Open. Published and unpublished guides.
University of North Carolina Library, Southern Historical Collection.
Excerpts from the reminiscences of Hamblen, a young New York woman, concern her life in Warrenton, NC, from September 1860 to June 1861, where she was a teacher in a girls' academy. Taken from Susan Sokol Blosser and Clyde Norman Wilson, Jr., *The Southern Historical Collection: A Guide to Manuscripts* (Chapel Hill, NC: University of North Carolina Library, 1970).

13,024. Hardeman, Elle (Goode)
Papers. 1917-46. 8 vols.
Open. Published and unpublished guides.
University of North Carolina Library, Southern Historical Collection.
Scrapbooks of letters, photos, programs, and clippings relating to servicemen at Camp Greene in Charlotte, NC, during and after WWI and Chapel Hill activities during WWII. Also includes WWI sheet music and clippings. Taken from Susan Sokol Blosser and Clyde Norman Wilson, Jr., *The Southern Historical Collection: A Guide to Manuscripts* (Chapel Hill, NC: University of North Carolina Library, 1970).

13,025. Hardie Family
Papers. 1937-51. 3 items (microfilm).
Open. Published and unpublished guides.
University of North Carolina Library, Southern Historical Collection.
Memoirs by Lucita (Hardie) Wait of her childhood in Brazil after the Civil War. Also includes a genealogy. Taken from Susan Sokol Blosser and Clyde Norman Wilson, Jr., *The Southern Historical Collection: A Guide to Manuscripts* (Chapel Hill, NC: University of North Carolina Library, 1970).

13,026. Harrington, Edith (Russell)
Papers. 1933-73. 3 ft.
Open. Published and unpublished guides.
University of North Carolina Library, Southern Historical Collection.
Harrington (1898-1967) and her husband Herschel R. Harrington owned the firm Harrington-Russell Studios, Complete Pageant Service and Stage Equipment. Correspondence, plans, notes, outlines, and other papers regarding Edith Harrington's work in the 1930s with outdoor dramas and festivals in the South and scripts written and directed by her and by others between 1964 and 1973 for the Children's Civic Theatre in Atlanta, of which she was cofounder and her husband technical director. Also includes correspondence; scripts; programs; set, lighting, and costume designs; and other production data, 1940-54, of the Harrington-Russell Studios in Asheville, NC, and Orlando, FL. Taken from Susan Sokol Blosser and Clyde Norman Wilson, Jr., *The Southern Historical Collection: A Guide to Manuscripts* (Chapel Hill, NC: University of North Carolina Library, 1970); Everard H. Smith III, *The Southern Historical Collection: Supplementary Guide to Manuscripts, 1970-1975* (Chapel Hill, NC: The University of North Carolina Library, 1976).

13,027. Harris, Corra May (White)
Papers. 1920-21. 3 items.
Open. Published and unpublished guides.
University of North Carolina Library, Southern Historical Collection.
Letters from [Mrs. Lundy Howard] Harris (1869-1935), a Georgia author, to Arthur Turner Vance, editor of *Pictorial Review,* concerning publication of some of her work. Taken from Susan Sokol Blosser and Clyde Norman Wilson, Jr., *The Southern Historical Collection: A Guide to Manuscripts* (Chapel Hill, NC: University of North Carolina Library, 1970).

13,028. Hawes, Maria (Southgate)
Papers. 1914. 27-page item.
Open. Published and unpublished guides.
University of North Carolina Library, Southern Historical Collection.
Reminiscences by Hawes (1836-1918), who was the wife of Confederate general James Morrison Hawes, concern her early life in Kentucky, her antebellum years as the wife of an army officer, and her experiences during the Civil War when she lived in Kentucky, Tennessee, Louisiana, Arkansas, and Texas. Taken from Susan Sokol Blosser and Clyde Norman Wilson, Jr., *The Southern Historical Collection: A Guide to Manuscripts* (Chapel Hill, NC: University of North Carolina Library, 1970).

13,029. Haynsworth, Maria L.
Papers. 1865. 15-page item.
Open. Published and unpublished guides.
University of North Carolina Library, Southern Historical Collection.
Letter by Haynsworth in which she describes the days that Federal troops passed through the Camden, SC, area. Taken from Susan Sokol Blosser and Clyde Norman Wilson, Jr., *The Southern Historical Collection: A Guide to Manuscripts* (Chapel Hill, NC: University of North Carolina Library, 1970).

13,030. Heustis, Rachel (Lyons)
Papers. 1859-65. 26 items.
Open. Published and unpublished guides.
University of North Carolina Library, Southern Historical Collection.
Papers of Rachel Lyons, a resident of South Carolina who later married James Fountain Heustis, include letters from Alabama novelist Augusta Jane (Evans) Wilson, poems from Henry Timrod, and love letters from soldiers. Taken from Susan Sokol Blosser and Clyde Norman Wilson, Jr., *The Southern Historical Collection: A Guide to Manuscripts* (Chapel Hill, NC: University of North Carolina Library, 1970).

13,031. Hill, Rebecca
Papers. 1827-1930. Ca. 275 items.
Open. Unpublished guide.
University of North Carolina Library, Southern Historical Collection.
Hill, the daughter of Thomas B. Hill, Jr. (1813-88), moved to Hillsborough, NC, in 1854. Correspondence from her relatives in the Norfleet, Graham, and other families; letters concerning her genealogical searches to establish her eligibility for various societies; notes; references; pamphlets; and clippings. Also includes letters to Alice [Mrs. Joseph Cheshire, Sr.] Webb on the death of her husband in 1913; a legal memo by J. W. Graham about the will of Rebecca Hill; and other family letters and papers.

13,032. Hinton, Mary Hilliard
Papers. 1883-1929. 266 items.
Open. Published and unpublished guides.
University of North Carolina Library, Southern Historical Collection.
Letters received by [Miss] Hinton (?-1961) of Raleigh, NC, a clubwoman and editor of the *North Carolina Booklet,* a quarterly of historical articles, from former classmates at St. Mary's School in Raleigh. Taken from Susan Sokol Blosser and Clyde Norman Wilson, Jr., *The Southern Historical Collection: A Guide to Manuscripts* (Chapel Hill, NC: University of North Carolina Library, 1970).

13,033. Hooper, Caroline (Mallett)
Papers. 1835-80. 66 items (microfilm).
Open. Published and unpublished guides.
University of North Carolina Library, Southern Historical Collection.
Family correspondence of Hooper includes letters from her father Charles Peter Mallett of Fayetteville, NC; her fiancé and then husband George DeBerniere Hooper, a lawyer in La Fayette, AL; and other relatives. Taken from Susan Sokol Blosser and Clyde Norman Wilson, Jr., *The Southern Historical Collection: A Guide to Manuscripts* (Chapel Hill, NC: University of North Carolina Library, 1970).

13,034. Horner, Julia E.
Papers. 1880-82. 35 items.
Open. Published and unpublished guides.
University of North Carolina Library, Southern Historical Collection.
Essays by Horner concerning her experiences and ideas while she was attending school in Hillsborough, NC. Taken from Susan Sokol Blosser and Clyde Norman Wilson, Jr., *The Southern Historical Collection: A Guide to Manuscripts* (Chapel Hill, NC: University of North Carolina Library, 1970).

13,035. Huggins, Rosa
Papers. 1853-55. 14-page item.
Open. Published and unpublished guides.
University of North Carolina Library, Southern Historical Collection.
Excerpts from a diary kept by Huggins of Appleton, TN, while on trips by boat to New Orleans in 1853 and by railroad to Charleston in 1855. Entries relate chiefly to incidents of travel and sightseeing with friends and relatives. Taken from Susan Sokol Blosser and Clyde Norman Wilson, Jr., *The Southern Historical Collection: A Guide to Manuscripts* (Chapel Hill, NC: University of North Carolina Library, 1970).

13,036. Hume, Fannie Page
Papers. 1860-62. 3 vols.
Open. Published and unpublished guides.
University of North Carolina Library, Southern Historical Collection.
Diary in which [Miss] Hume (1838-65), a resident of Orange County, VA, made daily entries about her household, her social life, Civil War news from the front, and neighborhood activities. Taken from Susan Sokol Blosser and Clyde Norman Wilson, Jr., *The Southern Historical Collection: A Guide to Manuscripts* (Chapel Hill, NC: University of North Carolina Library, 1970).

13,037. Hunley, Mary T.
Papers. 1861-64. 5-page item.
Open. Published and unpublished guides.
University of North Carolina Library, Southern Historical Collection.
Part of a Civil War diary kept by [Mrs.] Hunley of Gwynns Island, VA, in which she discusses the lawlessness and violence in the area, including property burning, killings, and desertion by Union and Confederate soldiers. Taken from Susan Sokol Blosser and Clyde Norman Wilson, Jr., *The Southern Historical Collection: A Guide to Manuscripts* (Chapel Hill, NC: University of North Carolina Library, 1970).

13,038. Hutchison, Susan Davis (Nye)
Papers. 1815-1962. 2 items.
Open. Published and unpublished guides.
University of North Carolina Library, Southern Historical Collection.
Extracts from the diary of Hutchison (1790-1867), a schoolteacher from Amenia, NY, who came to Raleigh, NC, in 1815 to teach and then moved to Augusta, GA, where she married Adam Hutchison, a widower with children. She returned to New York with her children and stepchildren after her husband's death and later returned to North Carolina to teach in Raleigh, Salisbury, and Charlotte. Her papers date from 1815 to 1841; the collection also includes material compiled about her in 1962. Taken from Susan Sokol Blosser and Clyde Norman Wilson, Jr., *The Southern Historical Collection: A Guide to Manuscripts* (Chapel Hill, NC: University of North Carolina Library, 1970).

13,039. Hyde, Anne (Bachman)
Papers. 1826-1937. 50 items.
Open. Published and unpublished guides.
University of North Carolina Library, Southern Historical Collection.
Correspondence, notes, writings, clippings, and other material collected by [Mrs. Charles R.] Hyde of Chattanooga, TN, pertain to historical incidents, particularly the Civil War. Includes an account of Sherman's men in Sumter, SC, in 1865 and correspondence and writings about the actions of Union general Gouverneur Kemble Warren at the battle of Five Forks and the subsequent court of inquiry. Taken from Susan Sokol Blosser and Clyde Norman Wilson, Jr., *The Southern Historical Collection: A Guide to Manuscripts* (Chapel Hill, NC: University of North Carolina Library, 1970).

13,040. Inman, Myra
Papers. 1859-66. 1 vol.
Open. Published and unpublished guides.
University of North Carolina Library, Southern Historical Collection.
Diary of Inman (1845-1914), a teenager in Cleveland, TN, in which she records daily household and social activities, war news, local activities, and postwar poverty. Taken from Susan Sokol Blosser and Clyde Norman Wilson, Jr., *The Southern Historical Collection: A Guide to*

Manuscripts (Chapel Hill, NC: University of North Carolina Library, 1970).

13,041. Iredell, Helen Blair
Papers. Nd. 1 vol.
Open. Published and unpublished guides.
University of North Carolina Library, Southern Historical Collection.
Notebook containing brief compositions by Iredell, the daughter of James Iredell, governor of North Carolina. Taken from Susan Sokol Blosser and Clyde Norman Wilson, Jr., *The Southern Historical Collection: A Guide to Manuscripts* (Chapel Hill, NC: University of North Carolina Library, 1970).

13,042. Jones, Anne Catherine "Kate" (Boykin)
Papers. 1851. 186-page vol.
Open. Published and unpublished guides.
University of North Carolina Library, Southern Historical Collection.
Diary kept by [Mrs. J. R.] Jones of Columbus, GA, while she was on a trip to England and the Continent. Taken from Susan Sokol Blosser and Clyde Norman Wilson, Jr., *The Southern Historical Collection: A Guide to Manuscripts* (Chapel Hill, NC: University of North Carolina Library, 1970).

13,043. Jones, Kate (Harben)
Papers. 1917-49. 56 items.
Open. Published and unpublished guides.
University of North Carolina Library, Southern Historical Collection.
Published and unpublished poems in manuscript form with notes by author [Mrs. Archibald A.] Jones (1866-?), a native of Georgia and a founder of the Academy of American Poets. Also includes some correspondence. Taken from Susan Sokol Blosser and Clyde Norman Wilson, Jr., *The Southern Historical Collection: A Guide to Manuscripts* (Chapel Hill, NC: University of North Carolina Library, 1970).

13,044. Jones, Margaret (Hathaway)
Papers. 1694-1953. 1 vol. and 15 items.
Open. Published and unpublished guides.
University of North Carolina Library, Southern Historical Collection.
Papers of the Hathaway and Jones families of Edenton, NC, including 17th-and 18th-century legal papers and bills and a merchandise ledger for 1838 to 1839. Taken from Susan Sokol Blosser and Clyde Norman Wilson, Jr., *The Southern Historical Collection: A Guide to Manuscripts* (Chapel Hill, NC: University of North Carolina Library, 1970).

13,045. Kealhofer, Lutie
Papers. 1863-1943. 1 vol. and 5 items.
Open. Published and unpublished guides.
University of North Carolina Library, Southern Historical Collection.
Pocket diary kept by Kealhofer (1841-76) in 1863 while she was living in Hagerstown, MD; she described her activities during the Civil War and a journey she made to Canada and upstate New York. Also includes letters written in 1943 about the diary. Taken from Susan Sokol Blosser and Clyde Norman Wilson, Jr., *The Southern Historical Collection: A Guide to Manuscripts* (Chapel Hill, NC: University of North Carolina Library, 1970).

13,046. Kearney, Belle
Papers. Nd. 17-page item.
Open. Published and unpublished guides.
University of North Carolina Library, Southern Historical Collection.
Essay by Kearney (1863-1939) in which she describes Madison County, MS, before the Civil War and gives an account of the War's effects. Taken from Susan Sokol Blosser and Clyde Norman Wilson, Jr., *The Southern Historical Collection: A Guide to Manuscripts* (Chapel Hill, NC: University of North Carolina Library, 1970).

13,047. Ker, Mary Susan
Papers. 1785-1923. 6 ft.
Open. Published and unpublished guides.
University of North Carolina Library, Southern Historical Collection.
Correspondence of [Miss] Ker (1838-1923) with relatives in Texas, Louisiana, and Mississippi while she was a governess in Vicksburg, MS, and a teacher in Natchez, MS; traveling in Europe and the US; and spending the summer at Pass Christian, MS. Also includes her daily diaries for 1886 to 1923 and correspondence and land grants of her father John Ker, a Natchez planter and physician, and her mother Mary (Baker) Ker. Taken from Susan Sokol Blosser and Clyde Norman Wilson, Jr., *The Southern Historical Collection: A Guide to Manuscripts* (Chapel Hill, NC: University of North Carolina Library, 1970).

13,048. Kerr, Alice Spencer
Papers. 1872-87. 332 items.
Open. Published and unpublished guides.
University of North Carolina Library, Southern Historical Collection.
Personal letters received by Kerr (1858-79), the daughter of geologist Washington Caruthers Kerr, while she was a student and teacher in Raleigh, NC, and in Chapel Hill. Includes a volume of notes she made while she was a student at Peace Institute in Raleigh. Taken from Susan Sokol Blosser and Clyde Norman Wilson, Jr., *The Southern Historical Collection: A Guide to Manuscripts* (Chapel Hill, NC: University of North Carolina Library, 1970).

13,049. Keyes, Julia Louisa (Hentz)
Papers. 1867-74. 102 pp. (microfilm).
Open. Published and unpublished guides.
University of North Carolina Library, Southern Historical Collection.
Letters, diary, and reminiscences compiled in about 1874 by Keyes, who was the wife of a Montgomery, AL, physician, concern their experiences in Brazil after the fall of the Confederacy. Keyes was the daughter of novelist Caroline Lee Hentz. Taken from Susan Sokol Blosser and Clyde Norman Wilson, Jr., *The Southern Historical Collection: A Guide to Manuscripts* (Chapel Hill, NC: University of North Carolina Library, 1970).

13,050. Killian, Eliza C.
Papers. 1856-86. 1 microfilm reel.
Access restricted. Published and unpublished guides.
University of North Carolina Library, Southern Historical Collection.
Correspondence of [Miss] Killian, a resident of Killian's Mill, NC, includes letters from relatives in South Carolina, Tennessee, and Maine and from friends in the Confederate army in Virginia, North Carolina, and Tennessee. Taken from Everard H. Smith III, *The Southern Historical Collection: Supplementary Guide to Manuscripts, 1970-1975* (Chapel Hill, NC: The University of North Carolina Library, 1976).

13,051. King Family
Papers. 1836-1932. 100 items.
Open. Published and unpublished guides.
University of North Carolina Library, Southern Historical Collection.
Papers of this New Orleans family include letters from [Miss] Nina King while she was traveling in Europe from 1906 to 1908 to Mrs. Charles Gayarre, the typescript of a story by [Miss] Annie Ragan King, and a scrapbook of author Grace King containing clippings on New Orleans, the Civil War, and other historical topics. Also includes five microfilm reels of papers of Grace Elizabeth King (1853?-1932), the originals of which are housed at Louisiana State University. Taken from Susan Sokol Blosser and Clyde Norman Wilson, Jr., *The Southern Historical Collection: A Guide to Manuscripts* (Chapel Hill, NC: University of North Carolina Library, 1970).

13,052. King, Florence
Papers. 1860-88. 13 items.
Open. Unpublished guide.
University of North Carolina Library, Southern Historical Collection.
King (1859-1939), a teacher in Sweet Home, NC, married John Wilson Lawrence in 1890. Correspondence between King and her cousin Davis Foute Eagleton (1861-1916) in which he describes his experiences as a teacher in Ladonia, TX; his travels to Indian territory; and his trip through Arizona and New Mexico in 1888 to attend the National Education Association convention in San Francisco. Also includes an address in English and Latin by a student at Concord, NC, Female College; an 1860 history of Statesville, NC, by A. Hortense Cowan; and a history of the Hall family by Mary Adams. Also available on microfilm.

13,053. Ladies Memorial Association
Records. 1878-79. 7 items.
Open. Published and unpublished guides.
University of North Carolina Library, Southern Historical Collection.
Correspondence and other records concerning a memorial statue to the Confederate soldier in Savannah, GA. Taken from Susan Sokol Blosser and Clyde Norman Wilson, Jr., *The Southern Historical Collection: A Guide to Manuscripts* (Chapel Hill, NC: University of North Carolina Library, 1970).

13,054. Lanier, Mary T.
Papers. 1862-88. 6 items.
Open. Published and unpublished guides.
University of North Carolina Library, Southern Historical Collection.
Personal letters received by [Mrs.] Lanier of Alabama, including two from Jefferson Davis, two from her nephew Sidney Lanier, and one from General John H. Morgan during the Civil War. Taken from Susan Sokol Blosser and Clyde Norman Wilson, Jr., *The Southern Historical Collection: A Guide to Manuscripts* (Chapel Hill, NC: University of North Carolina Library, 1970).

13,055. Latshaw, Sylvia Louise Arrowood
Papers. 1959-76. 20 items and 1 tape.
Open. Unpublished guide.
University of North Carolina Library, Southern Historical Collection.
Correspondence, photos, and clippings relating to author Olive Tilford Dargan collected by [Mrs. Harry F.] Latshaw, a friend and neighbor of Dargan in Almond, NC. Letters from Dargan to Latshaw in which she describes her mountain cabin and gives personal news and her reflections on the state of the world; a portrait of Dargan; photos of Dargan, her house, and the Cherokee Indians of the region; and clippings about poetry awards Dargan received. Also includes a taped conversation of Latshaw with her sister Julia [Mrs. Charles] Mason, Carolyn Wallace, and Ellen Neal in 1976. Latshaw discusses her studies at the University of North Carolina, her work teaching reading to disturbed and handicapped children, her husband's teaching career, her relationship with Dargan and her husband Peagram Dargan, the effect of Peagram Dargan's suicide on her life, and the Dargans' friendship with mountain people. Mason recalls her education at Boston University School of Medicine, from which she graduated in 1933; her career as an anesthesiologist at Massachusetts General Hospital and with the United Mine Workers hospital system in Kentucky; and early life with her father, a Presbyterian minister.

13,056. Laurens, Caroline Olivia
Papers. 1823-27. 42-page vol.
Open. Published and unpublished guides.
University of North Carolina Library, Southern Historical Collection.
Laurens was the wife of John B. Laurens, a planter near Charleston, SC. Diary contains monthly entries in which she wrote about her health, personal activities, and her children's development. Taken from Susan Sokol Blosser and Clyde Norman Wilson, Jr., *The Southern Historical Collection: A Guide to Manuscripts* (Chapel Hill, NC: University of North Carolina Library, 1970).

13,057. Le Conte, Emma
Papers. 1864-65. 1 vol.
Open. Published and unpublished guides.
University of North Carolina Library, Southern Historical Collection.
Diary kept by Le Conte, the daughter of scientist Joseph Le Conte and a resident of Columbia, SC, in which she recorded her reflections and activities. The diary was published as *When the World Ended: The Diary of Emma Le Conte* (1957). Taken from Susan Sokol Blosser and Clyde Norman Wilson, Jr., *The Southern Historical Collection: A Guide to Manuscripts* (Chapel Hill, NC: University of North Carolina Library, 1970).

13,058. League of Women Voters of Chapel Hill
Records. 1951-73. 3 ft.
Open. Published and unpublished guides.
University of North Carolina Library, Southern Historical Collection.
Correspondence and other papers of several presidents and committee chairmen of the Chapel Hill LWV and circular letters, reports, and other mailings received from the state and national headquarters of the LWV. Taken from Everard H. Smith III, *The Southern Historical Collection: Supplementary Guide to Manuscripts, 1970-1975* (Chapel Hill, NC: The University of North Carolina Library, 1976).

13,059. McCorvey, Mrs. Thomas Chalmers
Papers. 1861-65. 15 items.
Open. Published and unpublished guides.
University of North Carolina Library, Southern Historical Collection.
Letters to McCorvey, a resident of Alabama, from two cousins who were Confederate cavalry soldiers in Virginia and Alabama. Taken from Susan Sokol Blosser and Clyde Norman Wilson, Jr., *The Southern Historical Collection: A Guide to Manuscripts* (Chapel Hill, NC: University of North Carolina Library, 1970).

13,060. McDowall, Sallie D.
Papers. 1860. 2 vols.
Open. Published and unpublished guides.
University of North Carolina Library, Southern Historical Collection.
Composition book and notes on European history kept by McDowall while she was a student in Camden, SC. Taken from Susan Sokol Blosser and Clyde Norman Wilson, Jr., *The Southern Historical Collection: A Guide to Manuscripts* (Chapel Hill, NC: University of North Carolina Library, 1970).

13,061. McGimsey, Laura Cornelia
Papers. 1856-68. 113 items.
Access restricted. Published and unpublished guides.
University of North Carolina Library, Southern Historical Collection.
Correspondence of [Miss] McGimsey (1840-1920), a resident of Burke County, NC, is primarily with Lewis Warlick, whom she married during the Civil War. Lewis Warlick was with Confederate troops in eastern North Carolina and Virginia, in a federal hospital in New York after being wounded and captured, and in Confederate hospitals in Virginia and North Carolina. Also includes letters of courtship written to Laura Warlick from 1866 to 1868 after she was widowed. Taken from Susan Sokol Blosser and Clyde Norman Wilson, Jr., *The Southern Historical Collection: A Guide to Manuscripts* (Chapel Hill, NC: University of North Carolina Library, 1970).

13,062. McGuire, Judith (Brockenbrough)
Papers. 1861-65. 1 vol.
Open. Published and unpublished guides.
University of North Carolina Library, Southern Historical Collection.
Excerpts from the diary of McGuire, who was the wife of John P. McGuire, principal of Episcopal High School in Alexandria, VA, with an introduction and comments by an unidentified editor. Taken from Susan Sokol Blosser and Clyde Norman Wilson, Jr., *The Southern Historical Collection: A Guide to Manuscripts* (Chapel Hill, NC: University of North Carolina Library, 1970).

13,063. MacKenzie, Ella (Noland)
Papers. 1841-86. 438 items.
Open. Published and unpublished guides.
University of North Carolina Library, Southern Historical Collection.
Family and personal correspondence of MacKenzie, who was the daughter of Lloyd and Elizabeth Noland of Glen Ora near Leesburg, VA, while she was in school in Virginia and Baltimore, while she was visiting her aunt Sarah (Hollingsworth) [Mrs. William] Gibson in Philadelphia, and after her marriage in 1852 to John Carrerre MacKenzie (?-1866), a Baltimore physician. Includes letters from the Nolands and other relatives in Virginia and from members of the MacKenzie family and friends in Baltimore pertaining chiefly to social conditions and women's activities. Also includes letters illustrating the difficulties of southern sympathizers in Philadelphia, Baltimore, and northern Virginia. The MacKenzies were the parents of John Noland MacKenzie (1853-1925), a noted laryngologist. Taken from Susan Sokol Blosser and Clyde Norman Wilson, Jr., *The Southern Historical Collection: A Guide to Manuscripts* (Chapel Hill, NC: University of North Carolina Library, 1970).

13,064. McKimmon, Jane (Simpson)
Papers. 1917-19. 175 items.
Open. Published and unpublished guides.
University of North Carolina Library, Southern Historical Collection.
Family correspondence of McKimmon (1867-1957) includes letters she wrote to her sons from Raleigh, NC; letters from her son W. S. McKimmon in aviation school at the Georgia School of Technology, at Park Field in Memphis, and in France; and letters from other sons in Ensley, AL, Chapel Hill, and Plattsburg, NY. Taken from Susan Sokol Blosser and Clyde Norman Wilson, Jr., *The Southern Historical Collection: A Guide to Manuscripts* (Chapel Hill, NC: University of North Carolina Library, 1970).

13,065. McLaurin, Anna Blue
Papers. 1860-71. 93 items.
Open. Published and unpublished guides.
University of North Carolina Library, Southern Historical Collection.
Consists primarily of Civil War letters to McLaurin, a resident of Griffin, GA, from her brother and another man serving with the Confederate army in Virginia and coastal North Carolina. Taken from Susan Sokol Blosser and Clyde Norman Wilson, Jr., *The Southern Historical Collection: A Guide to Manuscripts* (Chapel Hill, NC: University of North Carolina Library, 1970).

13,066. Manigault, Morris, and Grimball Family
Papers. 1795-1832. 135 items.
Open. Published and unpublished guides.
University of North Carolina Library, Southern Historical Collection.
Consists primarily of letters to Elizabeth (Manigault) Morris in Charleston, SC, from her mother Margaret (Izard) Manigault in Philadelphia with detailed descriptions of the activities and concerns of Philadelphia society. Also includes letters containing family news from Harriet (Manigault) Wilcocks of Philadelphia to her niece Meta (Morris) Grimball (?-1881) in Charleston. Taken from Susan Sokol Blosser and Clyde Norman Wilson, Jr., *The Southern Historical Collection: A Guide to Manuscripts* (Chapel Hill, NC: University of North Carolina Library, 1970).

13,067. Martin, Elizabeth S.
Papers. 1841-49. 21 items.
Open. Published and unpublished guides.
University of North Carolina Library, Southern Historical Collection.
Letters to Martin from a deaf-mute cousin in New Orleans concerning her schooling, travels to the North, attempted cures, local events, and family news. Taken from Susan Sokol Blosser and Clyde Norman Wilson, Jr., *The Southern Historical Collection: A Guide to Manuscripts* (Chapel Hill, NC: University of North Carolina Library, 1970).

13,068. "Mary Valentine"
Papers. 1854-58. 6 items.
Open. Published and unpublished guides.
University of North Carolina Library, Southern Historical Collection.
Poems written to John R. Reston, a Wilmington, NC, bachelor, on five successive February 14ths by an unidentified woman who signed herself "Mary Valentine." Taken from Susan Sokol Blosser and Clyde Norman Wilson, Jr., *The Southern Historical Collection: A Guide to Manuscripts* (Chapel Hill, NC: University of North Carolina Library, 1970).

13,069. Miller, Letitia D.
Papers. 1926. 21-page item.
Open. Published and unpublished guides.
University of North Carolina Library, Southern Historical Collection.
Recollections by Miller (1852-?) of her childhood in Raymond, MS, before and during the Civil War. Taken from Susan Sokol Blosser and Clyde Norman Wilson, Jr., *The Southern Historical Collection: A Guide to Manuscripts* (Chapel Hill, NC: University of North Carolina Library, 1970).

13,070. Moffitt, Elvira Evelyna (Worth)
Papers. 1853-1930. 1150 items.
Open. Published and unpublished guides.
University of North Carolina Library, Southern Historical Collection.
Correspondence, club records, scrapbooks, autograph albums, and other papers of [Mrs.] Moffitt (1836-1940), the thrice-widowed daughter of North Carolina governor Jonathan Worth, relate to her club work and civic, cultural, and historical projects in Raleigh, NC, and Richmond, VA. Among the groups with which she was involved were the Raleigh Woman's Club, the North Carolina Peace Society, Women's Association for the Betterment of Public Schools, the DAR, the United Daughters of the Confederacy, Colonial Dames, and the Roanoke Colony Memorial Association. Also includes records of family property and estate settlements. Taken from Susan Sokol Blosser and Clyde Norman Wilson, Jr., *The Southern Historical Collection: A Guide to Manuscripts* (Chapel Hill, NC: University of North Carolina Library, 1970).

13,071. Moore, Genevieve Pearce
Papers. 1917-67. 20 vols.
Open. Published and unpublished guides.
University of North Carolina Library, Southern Historical Collection.
Diary kept intermittently by [Miss] Moore (1889-), a native of High Point, NC, who was an

elementary school teacher and counselor in North Carolina, Florida, and New Jersey. She wrote about her work with schoolchildren, especially in music; her social, church, volunteer, and club activities; and her vacation trips. Taken from Everard H. Smith III, *The Southern Historical Collection: Supplementary Guide to Manuscripts, 1970-1975* (Chapel Hill, NC: The University of North Carolina Library, 1976).

13,072. Moore, Harriet Ellen
Papers. 1863. 1 vol. (microfilm).
Open. Published and unpublished guides.
University of North Carolina Library, Southern Historical Collection.
Diary kept by [Miss] Moore while she was in Nashville during its occupation by Federal troops concerns the weather, social events, army and civilian relations, and Negroes who joined the US Army. Moore later married Thomas P. Weakley. Taken from Susan Sokol Blosser and Clyde Norman Wilson, Jr., *The Southern Historical Collection: A Guide to Manuscripts* (Chapel Hill, NC: University of North Carolina Library, 1970).

13,073. Moore, Idora (McClellan) Plowman
Papers. 1882-1939. Ca. 25 items.
Open. Published and unpublished guides.
University of North Carolina Library, Southern Historical Collection.
Moore (1843-1929), a resident of Talladega County, AL, wrote humorous articles under the pen name Betsy Hamilton in the dialect of the backwoods people of Alabama or of antebellum Negroes. Correspondence from editors, readers, and friends as well as clippings of her writings. Taken from Susan Sokol Blosser and Clyde Norman Wilson, Jr., *The Southern Historical Collection: A Guide to Manuscripts* (Chapel Hill, NC: University of North Carolina Library, 1970).

13,074. Mordecai Family
Papers. 1783-1947. 1870 items.
Open. Published and unpublished guides.
University of North Carolina Library, Southern Historical Collection.
Family correspondence of Jacob Mordecai (1762-1838), a merchant of Warrenton, NC, who was married twice and conducted a female seminary from 1809 until 1819 when he moved to Richmond, VA. Correspondence between Mordecai, his wives, and their six sons and seven daughters concerns the school at Warrenton; family and social events; summer travels; problems regarding religious belief and family tradition in this part-Jewish, part-gentile family; and publication of the works of [Miss] Ellen Mordecai (1790-1884) in the 1840s. Also includes diaries, reminiscences, and writings of Ellen Mordecai and Emma Mordecai; an 1880s scrapbook; and Samuel Mordecai's 1815 travel diary. Taken from Susan Sokol Blosser and Clyde Norman Wilson, Jr., *The Southern Historical Collection: A Guide to Manuscripts* (Chapel Hill, NC: University of North Carolina Library, 1970).

13,075. Morgan, Minnie (Buerbaum)
Papers. 1840-61. 3 vols.
Open. Published and unpublished guides.
University of North Carolina Library, Southern Historical Collection.
Account books, written in Gloucester County, VA, including one containing a list of slaves hired out and rates at which they were hired, and a lawyer's fee book. Taken from Susan Sokol Blosser and Clyde Norman Wilson, Jr., *The Southern Historical Collection: A Guide to Manuscripts* (Chapel Hill, NC: University of North Carolina Library, 1970).

13,076. Morrison, Sarah Varick (Cozens)
Papers. 1832-74. 1 vol. (microfilm).
Open. Published and unpublished guides.
University of North Carolina Library, Southern Historical Collection.
Scattered diary entries by Morrison (1814-?), a native of New York and the wife of North Carolina minister William N. Morrison, concern her personal feelings and devotions. Taken from Susan Sokol Blosser and Clyde Norman Wilson, Jr., *The Southern Historical Collection: A Guide to Manuscripts* (Chapel Hill, NC: University of North Carolina Library, 1970).

13,077. Morton, Matilda (Lamb)
Papers. Nd. 8-page item.
Open. Published and unpublished guides.
University of North Carolina Library, Southern Historical Collection.
Reminiscences by Morton (ca. 1857-?), from her own and family recollections, of life at Tarboro, NC, and Williamston, NC, during the Civil War. Taken from Susan Sokol Blosser and Clyde Norman Wilson, Jr., *The Southern Historical Collection: A Guide to Manuscripts* (Chapel Hill, NC: University of North Carolina Library, 1970).

13,078. Moseley, Daisy Haywood
Papers. 1915-62. 4 vols. and 55 items.
Open. Published and unpublished guides.
University of North Carolina Library, Southern Historical Collection.
[Miss] Moseley (1892-) is a Catholic laywoman and writer from Glen Ridge, NJ, and Chapel Hill. Correspondence with other authors, editors, and friends; writings; a diary of meditations; and travel descriptions of Rome, the Holy Land, and southern Europe. Taken from Everard H. Smith III, *The Southern Historical Collection: Supplementary Guide to Manuscripts, 1970-1975* (Chapel Hill, NC: The University of North Carolina Library, 1976).

13,079. Moses, Miriam Gratz
Papers. 1824-64. 340 items.
Open. Published and unpublished guides.
University of North Carolina Library, Southern Historical Collection.
Correspondence of this close-knit Jewish family includes letters from Rebecca Gratz (1781-1869), a Philadelphia philanthropist, to her niece Miriam Gratz Moses [Mrs. Solomon] Cohen, a resident of Charleston, SC, and Savannah, GA; letters to Cohen from her son in Confederate army camps, at the Georgia Military Institute, and at the University of Virginia; letters by British Hebrew author Grace Aguilar concerning doctrine, literature, and personal news; and letters written after Grace Aguilar's death by her mother Sarah Aguilar. Also includes commonplace and poetry books of Miriam Moses, who was raised by her aunt Rebecca Gratz, and other family papers. Taken from Susan Sokol Blosser and Clyde Norman Wilson, Jr., *The Southern Historical Collection: A Guide to Manuscripts* (Chapel Hill, NC: University of North Carolina Library, 1970).

13,080. Nicholson, Caroline (O'Reilly)
Papers. 1894. 43-page item.
Open. Published and unpublished guides.
University of North Carolina Library, Southern Historical Collection.
Nicholson (1812-?) was the wife of Alfred Osborn Pope Nicholson (1808-76), US senator and chief justice of Tennessee. Her reminiscences concern social activities, religious life, and town events in Columbia, SC, and Nashville; Washington, DC, society; and her husband's political activities, including his friendship and political association with James Knox Polk. Taken from Susan Sokol Blosser and Clyde Norman Wilson, Jr., *The Southern Historical Collection: A Guide to Manuscripts* (Chapel Hill, NC: University of North Carolina Library, 1970).

13,081. O'Brien-Moore, Annette Erin Eileen
Papers. Ca. 1910-50. 1 ft. and 2 vols.
Open. Published and unpublished guides.
University of North Carolina Library, Southern Historical Collection.
Correspondence, telegrams, photos, playbills, and clippings of [Miss] O'Brien-Moore (1908-), a Broadway and Hollywood actress who is a native of Tucson, AZ. Taken from Everard H. Smith III, *The Southern Historical Collection: Supplementary Guide to Manuscripts, 1970-1975* (Chapel Hill, NC: The University of North Carolina Library, 1976).

13,082. O'Hanlon, Margaret Langdon
Papers. 1856-57?. 2 items.
Open. Published and unpublished guides.
University of North Carolina Library, Southern Historical Collection.
Talks made by O'Hanlon in presenting a flag to the Fayetteville militia and in accepting her selection as May Queen. Taken from Susan Sokol Blosser and Clyde Norman Wilson, Jr., *The Southern Historical Collection: A Guide to Manuscripts* (Chapel Hill, NC: University of North Carolina Library, 1970).

13,083. Oxford Women's Literary Club
Records. 1919-24. 1 vol. and other items.
Open. Published and unpublished guides.
University of North Carolina Library, Southern Historical Collection.
Minutes of this Oxford, NC, group include subjects of papers presented by members and the secretaries' comments on the proceedings. Taken from Susan Sokol Blosser and Clyde Norman Wilson, Jr., *The Southern Historical Collection: A Guide to Manuscripts* (Chapel Hill, NC: University of North Carolina Library, 1970).

13,084. Parham, Mollie A.
Papers. 1863-73. 6 vols. and 1 item.
Open. Published and unpublished guides.
University of North Carolina Library, Southern Historical Collection.
[Miss] Parham, a resident of Virginia, was a teacher of the children of the Palmer family of Shelby County, TN. Includes a schoolgirl essay she wrote and a diary she kept in 1872 and 1873 in which she describes teaching, life with the family, social activities, and a visit to an exposition in Memphis. Taken from Susan Sokol Blosser and Clyde Norman Wilson, Jr., *The Southern Historical Collection: A Guide to Manuscripts* (Chapel Hill, NC: University of North Carolina Library, 1970).

13,085. Parsley, Eliza Hall (Nutt)
Papers. 1802-1922. 600 items.
Open. Published and unpublished guides.
University of North Carolina Library, Southern Historical Collection.
Correspondence and papers received or collected by [Mrs. W. M.] Parsley of Wilmington, NC, as president of the North Carolina Division of the United Daughters of the Confederacy; Civil War letters and memoranda by her husband William Murdoch Parsley (1840-65), lieutenant colonel in the 3rd North Carolina Regiment, while he was serving in Virginia and as a prisoner at Fort Delaware and Hilton Head; club records; historical sketches; a portfolio of amateur plays and pageants presented in Wilmington in the 1890s; scrapbooks; and clippings. Taken from Susan Sokol Blosser and Clyde Norman Wilson, Jr., *The Southern Historical Collection: A Guide to Manuscripts* (Chapel Hill, NC: University of North Carolina Library, 1970).

13,086. Patterson, Mary (Fries)
Papers. 1863-1911. 2 vols.
Open. Published and unpublished guides.
University of North Carolina Library, Southern Historical Collection.
Diary kept in 1863 and 1864 by Mary Fries (1844-1927), a resident of Salem, NC, during her

engagement to Rufus Lenoir Patterson (1830-79), a manufacturer. She writes of visits from her fiancé, friends, and relatives; activities at the Presbyterian and Moravian churches; meetings of the Relief Society; news of Confederate soldiers; and her wedding preparations. Also includes her diary for 1911. Fries was the daughter of Francis Fries, a manufacturer. Taken from Susan Sokol Blosser and Clyde Norman Wilson, Jr., *The Southern Historical Collection: A Guide to Manuscripts* (Chapel Hill, NC: University of North Carolina Library, 1970).

13,087. Pember, Phoebe Yates (Levy)
Papers. 1861-1920. 150 items.
Open. Published and unpublished guides.
University of North Carolina Library, Southern Historical Collection.
[Mrs. Thomas] Pember (1823-1913), a resident of Georgia, was a Confederate hospital nurse and a writer. Letters she wrote from Chimborazo Hospital in Richmond, VA, between 1861 and 1865 and later letters containing comments on political events, social and economic conditions, personal finances and living arrangements, her reading, religion, visitors, relatives, and daily life in Mendham, NJ; Savannah, GA; and elsewhere. Letters from the period 1895-99 concern her travels, accommodations, prices, health, acquaintances, and the social life of American expatriates in Germany, Italy, and Switzerland. Taken from Susan Sokol Blosser and Clyde Norman Wilson, Jr., *The Southern Historical Collection: A Guide to Manuscripts* (Chapel Hill, NC: University of North Carolina Library, 1970).

13,088. Perry, Elizabeth Frances (McCall)
Papers. 1837-88. 1 vol.
Open. Published and unpublished guides.
University of North Carolina Library, Southern Historical Collection.
Scattered diary entries by Perry, who was married to Benjamin Franklin Perry and was a resident of Greenville, SC, relate to family and personal matters. Taken from Susan Sokol Blosser and Clyde Norman Wilson, Jr., *The Southern Historical Collection: A Guide to Manuscripts* (Chapel Hill, NC: University of North Carolina Library, 1970).

13,089. Person, Alice (Morgan)
Papers. 1872-1972. 5 vols. and 10 items.
Access restricted. Published and unpublished guides.
University of North Carolina Library, Southern Historical Collection.
Manuscript autobiography of Person (1840-1913), a resident of Franklin County, NC, who manufactured "Mrs. Joe Person's Remedy," a proprietary medicine. Also includes her account book for 1910 to 1911, a scrapbook of clippings, and diaries of her sister Lucy (Morgan) Beard, a schoolteacher in Hickory, NC, for 1872 to 1873 and 1913 to 1916. Taken from Everard H. Smith III, *The Southern Historical Collection: Supplementary Guide to Manuscripts, 1970-1975* (Chapel Hill, NC: The University of North Carolina Library, 1976).

13,090. Phillips, Sarah Ellen
Papers. 1865. 6-page item.
Open. Published and unpublished guides.
University of North Carolina Library, Southern Historical Collection.
Reminiscences by Phillips of her experiences as a girl living near Selma, AL, during General J. H. Wilson's Federal cavalry raid in April 1865. Taken from Susan Sokol Blosser and Clyde Norman Wilson, Jr., *The Southern Historical Collection: A Guide to Manuscripts* (Chapel Hill, NC: University of North Carolina Library, 1970).

13,091. Pilsbury, Rebecca S. C.
Papers. 1848-51. 80-page vol. (microfilm).
Open. Published and unpublished guides.
University of North Carolina Library, Southern Historical Collection.
Diary kept by Pilsbury, a native of New England, in which she discusses managing her household, plantation, and slaves while her husband Timothy Pilsbury (1780-1858) was in the District of Columbia as a member of Congress in 1848 and 1849 or away from home for other reasons. Taken from Susan Sokol Blosser and Clyde Norman Wilson, Jr., *The Southern Historical Collection: A Guide to Manuscripts* (Chapel Hill, NC: University of North Carolina Library, 1970).

13,092. Plant, Martha
Papers. 1954. 10-page item.
Open. Published and unpublished guides.
University of North Carolina Library, Southern Historical Collection.
Reminiscences by Plant of family life in Macon, GA, and Mount Airy, GA, in the 1890s and early 1900s. She describes family events, leisure activities, and the local social environment. Taken from Susan Sokol Blosser and Clyde Norman Wilson, Jr., *The Southern Historical Collection: A Guide to Manuscripts* (Chapel Hill, NC: University of North Carolina Library, 1970).

13,093. Polhill, Emily Hines (Nisbet)
Papers. 1823-97. 18 items.
Open. Published and unpublished guides.
University of North Carolina Library, Southern Historical Collection.
Scattered family correspondence of the Polhills of Macon, GA, and Milledgeville, GA. All but one item was written before the Civil War. Taken from Susan Sokol Blosser and Clyde Norman Wilson, Jr., *The Southern Historical Collection: A Guide to Manuscripts* (Chapel Hill, NC: University of North Carolina Library, 1970).

13,094. Pollard, Emily Louise
Papers. Nd. 8 vols. and ca. 100 items.
Open. Unpublished guide.
University of North Carolina Library, Southern Historical Collection.
Correspondence, travel diaries, writings, photos, clippings, and printed matter of Pollard (1896-1972).

13,095. Porcher, Charlotte
Papers. 1825-75. 7 items.
Open. Published and unpublished guides.
University of North Carolina Library, Southern Historical Collection.
Family letters received by Porcher, a resident of Charleston, SC. Taken from Susan Sokol Blosser and Clyde Norman Wilson, Jr., *The Southern Historical Collection: A Guide to Manuscripts* (Chapel Hill, NC: University of North Carolina Library, 1970).

13,096. Power, Ellen Louise
Papers. 1862-63. 1 vol.
Open. Published and unpublished guides.
University of North Carolina Library, Southern Historical Collection.
Diary of Power (1841-1917), a resident of East Feliciana Parish, LA, in which she wrote chiefly about domestic matters and Civil War news. Taken from Susan Sokol Blosser and Clyde Norman Wilson, Jr., *The Southern Historical Collection: A Guide to Manuscripts* (Chapel Hill, NC: University of North Carolina Library, 1970).

13,097. Pratt, Mary (Bayley)
Papers. 1899-1929. 159 items.
Open. Published and unpublished guides.
University of North Carolina Library, Southern Historical Collection.
Consists primarily of letters from Pratt (?-1929) to her parents, to the William Bayleys of Springfield, OH, and to her brothers and their wives giving personal, family, and community news from the time she went to Chapel Hill as the bride of University of North Carolina professor Joseph Hyde Pratt until her death. Taken from Susan Sokol Blosser and Clyde Norman Wilson, Jr., *The Southern Historical Collection: A Guide to Manuscripts* (Chapel Hill, NC: University of North Carolina Library, 1970).

13,098. Prescott, Helen M.
Papers. 1835-1944. 1 ft.
Open. Published and unpublished guides.
University of North Carolina Library, Southern Historical Collection.
Correspondence and notes of an Atlanta genealogist, antebellum letters of the Prescott and Slade families of Fort Gaines, GA, and occasional diaries of [Miss] Prescott and her mother for 1944. In the diaries the two women wrote of their daily domestic activities. Taken from Susan Sokol Blosser and Clyde Norman Wilson, Jr., *The Southern Historical Collection: A Guide to Manuscripts* (Chapel Hill, NC: University of North Carolina Library, 1970).

13,099. Preston, Margaret (Junkin)
Papers. 1812-1938. 2 vols. and 160 items.
Open. Published and unpublished guides.
University of North Carolina Library, Southern Historical Collection.
Preston (1820-97), a poet and author, was married to John Thomas Lewis Preston of Lexington, VA. Letters by editors, writers, and Confederate leaders collected or received by Margaret Preston include letters from the wife of English author Charles Kingsley and her daughter Rose Kingsley and from Thomas Jonathan Jackson. Also includes Margaret Preston's workbook containing drafts and revisions of her poems on Confederate, historical, and religious topics as well as her commonplace and recipe books. Taken from Susan Sokol Blosser and Clyde Norman Wilson, Jr., *The Southern Historical Collection: A Guide to Manuscripts* (Chapel Hill, NC: University of North Carolina Library, 1970); Everard H. Smith III, *The Southern Historical Collection: Supplementary Guide to Manuscripts, 1970-1975* (Chapel Hill, NC: The University of North Carolina Library, 1976).

13,100. Prince, Lillian (Hughes)
Papers. 1938-61. 300 items.
Open. Published and unpublished guides.
University of North Carolina Library, Southern Historical Collection.
Correspondence and scrapbooks of [Mrs. William Meade] Prince (?-1962), who was active with the Carolina Playmakers for more than 20 years. Includes letters, photos, playbills, and clippings relating to her roles in the outdoor drama *The Lost Colony* at Manteo, NC; in various productions by the Playmakers; and in *Dark of the Moon* in New York and on tour in 1945 and 1946. Taken from Susan Sokol Blosser and Clyde Norman Wilson, Jr., *The Southern Historical Collection: A Guide to Manuscripts* (Chapel Hill, NC: University of North Carolina Library, 1970).

13,101. Pritchard, Catherine McAlpin (Wray)
Papers. 1829-99. 2 vols. and 20 items.
Open. Published and unpublished guides.
University of North Carolina Library, Southern Historical Collection.
Diary kept by Pritchard (1811-88), a resident of New Orleans, during a trip to Scotland and England in 1829 and papers regarding a claim against the federal government for damages during the Civil War occupation. Taken from Susan Sokol Blosser and Clyde Norman Wilson, Jr., *The Southern Historical Collection: A Guide to Manuscripts* (Chapel Hill, NC: University of North Carolina Library, 1970).

13,102. Race, Olivia Corinne (Kittredge)
Papers. 1870-73. 2 vols. (microfilm).
Open. Published and unpublished guides.

University of North Carolina Library, Southern Historical Collection.
Diary of Race (1835-1916) relates to family and social life in New Orleans and Pass Christian, MS. Race and her husband George Wesley Race were active in civic affairs and the Episcopal church. Taken from Susan Sokol Blosser and Clyde Norman Wilson, Jr., *The Southern Historical Collection: A Guide to Manuscripts* (Chapel Hill, NC: University of North Carolina Library, 1970).

13,103. Rankin, Emma Lydia
Papers. 1865-1908. 5 vols.
Open. Published and unpublished guides.
University of North Carolina Library, Southern Historical Collection.
Brief diary of Rankin (1838-1908), a Lenoir, NC, schoolteacher, in which she recorded the weather and daily activities. Also includes her reminiscences of Stoneman's Federal cavalry raid in western North Carolina in 1865. Taken from Susan Sokol Blosser and Clyde Norman Wilson, Jr., *The Southern Historical Collection: A Guide to Manuscripts* (Chapel Hill, NC: University of North Carolina Library, 1970).

13,104. Ravenel, Beatrice (Witte)
Papers. 1892-1948. 2.5 ft. and 6 vols.
Open. Published and unpublished guides.
University of North Carolina Library, Southern Historical Collection.
Papers of Ravenel (1870-1956), a writer and poet of Charleston, SC, include correspondence with authors, poets, and publishers; manuscripts of her writings; published stories and poems; an unpublished chapter from a biography of Eliza Lucas Pinckney; scrapbooks of letters and clippings; a sketchbook of her charcoals and watercolors; and reviews. Taken from Everard H. Smith III, *The Southern Historical Collection: Supplementary Guide to Manuscripts, 1970-1975* (Chapel Hill, NC: The University of North Carolina Library, 1976).

13,105. Raymond, Clara (Compton)
Papers. 1930s. 1 vol.
Open. Published and unpublished guides.
University of North Carolina Library, Southern Historical Collection.
Reminiscences by Raymond (1857-?) concerning her life as a girl on plantations in Rapides Parish, LA, and her education in Germany and Switzerland from 1865 to 1868. Taken from Susan Sokol Blosser and Clyde Norman Wilson, Jr., *The Southern Historical Collection: A Guide to Manuscripts* (Chapel Hill, NC: University of North Carolina Library, 1970).

13,106. Ready, Alice
Papers. 1860-62. 120-page vol.
Open. Published and unpublished guides.
University of North Carolina Library, Southern Historical Collection.
Diary kept by Ready (?-1890) while she was at school in Maryland, visiting New York, and at home in Murfreesboro, TN, during the Civil War. Taken from Susan Sokol Blosser and Clyde Norman Wilson, Jr., *The Southern Historical Collection: A Guide to Manuscripts* (Chapel Hill, NC: University of North Carolina Library, 1970).

13,107. Reeves, Elizabeth, and Reeves, Andrew J.
Papers. 1857-92. 28 items.
Open. Unpublished guide.
University of North Carolina Library, Southern Historical Collection.
Letters to Elizabeth and Andrew Reeves of Bowdon, GA, and their children Mollie and John M. Reeves from friends and relatives in Georgia, Louisiana, and Alabama concerning family news, health, crops, livestock, social events, marriages, church meetings and church sings, schools, and religious feelings. Includes a letter by John Reeves to his parents in 1862 in which he describes his experiences in the army.

13,108. Reston, James Barrett, Jr.
Papers. 1975-76. Ca. 84 items.
Open. Unpublished guide.
University of North Carolina Library, Southern Historical Collection.
Reston (1941-) covered the trial of Joan Little for *The New York Times* and wrote a book on the subject. Records relating to the trial, including transcripts of testimony by such persons as Little and criminologist Hubert Leon MacDonnell, who testified for the defense; arguments to the jury; tapes made by Little, Celine Chenier, Marjorie Wright, and inmates Jacquatta Davis and Marie Hill; transcripts of the lower court case and two appeals; and clippings about the trial. Little's first name was also spelled Joann.

13,109. Reston, Marie Louise (DuBrutz)
Papers. 1926. 16-page item.
Open. Published and unpublished guides.
University of North Carolina Library, Southern Historical Collection.
Memoirs of Reston in which she describes her life as the daughter of an antebellum Alabama doctor, a trip to England in 1850, her life in North Carolina during the Civil War, and a few later events. Taken from Susan Sokol Blosser and Clyde Norman Wilson, Jr., *The Southern Historical Collection: A Guide to Manuscripts* (Chapel Hill, NC: University of North Carolina Library, 1970).

13,110. Ricks, Mary Bynum (Holmes)
Papers. 1943-45. 167 items.
Open. Published and unpublished guides.
University of North Carolina Library, Southern Historical Collection.
Letters to Ricks from officers of southern colleges and universities answering an inquiry about the status of graduate education in the South, graduate study among Negroes, and southerners trained in Europe before 1900. Taken from Susan Sokol Blosser and Clyde Norman Wilson, Jr., *The Southern Historical Collection: A Guide to Manuscripts* (Chapel Hill, NC: University of North Carolina Library, 1970).

13,111. Riddick, Elsie
Papers. 1855-1954. 4 vols. and ca. 150 items.
Open. Unpublished guide.
University of North Carolina Library, Southern Historical Collection.
Riddick (1879-) attended the Normal and Industrial School in Greensboro, NC, and worked for the Public Utilities Commission for 50 years. She was active in the woman's suffrage movement, the Business and Professional Women's Club, the Democratic party, and other organizations. Correspondence, post cards, photos, scrapbook, an autograph album of Anna I. Jones, mementos, clippings, and other papers.

13,112. Riddick, Ivey
Papers. Ca. 1917-64. 2 boxes.
Open. Unpublished guide.
University of North Carolina Library, Southern Historical Collection.
Correspondence, photos, a scrapbook, and printed matter of Ivey Riddick, who was a representative of the American Tobacco Company in China and elsewhere in the Orient; his wife Margaret Riddick; and their daughter Frances Riddick. Also includes correspondence, deeds, bank books, essays, wills, awards, a biographical sketch of Wallace Carl Riddick, and genealogical material of other members of the Riddick family.

13,113. Rives, Mary Elizabeth (Carter)
Papers. 1865-99. 360-page vol. (microfilm).
Open. Published and unpublished guides.
University of North Carolina Library, Southern Historical Collection.
Diary of Rives (1829-1900) concerns family and household events in Shreveport, LA; visits to New Orleans and Mansfield, LA; and a sojourn from 1868 to 1870 in Gilmer, TX, where her children were in school. Taken from Susan Sokol Blosser and Clyde Norman Wilson, Jr., *The Southern Historical Collection: A Guide to Manuscripts* (Chapel Hill, NC: University of North Carolina Library, 1970).

13,114. Robertson, Eliza Ann (Marsh)
Papers. 1849-72. 1 vol.
Open. Published and unpublished guides.
University of North Carolina Library, Southern Historical Collection.
Diary kept by Robertson (?-1878) from 1849 to 1856, probably while she was living at New Iberia, LA, in which she describes the weather and household activities such as cooking and sewing. Six letters are also enclosed. Taken from Susan Sokol Blosser and Clyde Norman Wilson, Jr., *The Southern Historical Collection: A Guide to Manuscripts* (Chapel Hill, NC: University of North Carolina Library, 1970).

13,115. Rockwell, Loula (Ayres)
Papers. 1953-59. 2 items.
Open. Published and unpublished guides.
University of North Carolina Library, Southern Historical Collection.
Recollections of the election of 1876 by Rockwell (1866-1959), who at the time was a child in Marion County, SC. Also includes an autobiographical letter by her son Paul Ayres Rockwell (1889-) of North Carolina, who volunteered for the French army in 1914. Taken from Susan Sokol Blosser and Clyde Norman Wilson, Jr., *The Southern Historical Collection: A Guide to Manuscripts* (Chapel Hill, NC: University of North Carolina Library, 1970).

13,116. Rogers, Louisa H.
Papers. 1824. 4-page item.
Open. Published and unpublished guides.
University of North Carolina Library, Southern Historical Collection.
Letter by Rogers to friends in which she describes the scenery and her personal experiences in the mountains of western North Carolina around Asheville. Taken from Susan Sokol Blosser and Clyde Norman Wilson, Jr., *The Southern Historical Collection: A Guide to Manuscripts* (Chapel Hill, NC: University of North Carolina Library, 1970).

13,117. Root, Anne (Gales)
Papers. 1821-94. 44 items.
Open. Published and unpublished guides.
University of North Carolina Library, Southern Historical Collection.
Root was the daughter of Raleigh, NC, editor Weston Raleigh Gales (1803-48) and the wife of Charles B. Root (1818-?), a native of Massachusetts who became a businessman in Raleigh. Correspondence of Anne Root and her daughter. Taken from Susan Sokol Blosser and Clyde Norman Wilson, Jr., *The Southern Historical Collection: A Guide to Manuscripts* (Chapel Hill, NC: University of North Carolina Library, 1970).

13,118. Ryan, Martha
Papers. 1781. 1 vol.
Open. Published and unpublished guides.
University of North Carolina Library, Southern Historical Collection.
Homemade cipher book with hand-drawn text and illustrations includes patriotic mottoes and symbols. Taken from Susan Sokol Blosser and Clyde Norman Wilson, Jr., *The Southern Historical Collection: A Guide to Manuscripts* (Chapel Hill, NC: University of North Carolina Library, 1970).

13,119. Scales, Cordelia Lewis
Papers. 1861-98. 1 item.
Open. Published and unpublished guides.
University of North Carolina Library, Southern Historical Collection.
Letters from [Miss] Scales (1844-1915) of Holly Springs, MS, to a former schoolmate during and immediately after the Civil War. Also includes a few letters by Ben Cottrell Gray, who became Scales's husband, and her brother. Taken from Susan Sokol Blosser and Clyde Norman Wilson, Jr., *The Southern Historical Collection: A Guide to Manuscripts* (Chapel Hill, NC: University of North Carolina Library, 1970).

13,120. Schofield, Martha
Papers. 1865-69. 3 items.
Open. Published and unpublished guides.
University of North Carolina Library, Southern Historical Collection.
Diaries kept in 1865 and 1869 by Schofield (1839-1916), a northern teacher-missionary among the Negroes of the Sea Islands and at Aiken, SC. Also includes a farewell speech given by Lydia A. Schofield at St. Helena Island in 1868. Taken from Susan Sokol Blosser and Clyde Norman Wilson, Jr., *The Southern Historical Collection: A Guide to Manuscripts* (Chapel Hill, NC: University of North Carolina Library, 1970).

13,121. Service, Emma Maria
Papers. 1803-92. 400 items.
Open. Published and unpublished guides.
University of North Carolina Library, Southern Historical Collection.
Family correspondence of [Miss] Service, a resident of Augusta, GA; her parents John Hugh James Service and Martha (Stackhouse) Williford Service; and their children from previous marriages, including William S. Williford, a commission merchant at Macon, GA, and Martha Williford, a teacher at Montpelier Institute near Macon and a missionary in Africa beginning in 1850. Martha Williford worked there with Episcopal Bishop John Payne, whom she married. Also includes letters from the Stackhouse family of Hinds County, MS. Taken from Susan Sokol Blosser and Clyde Norman Wilson, Jr., *The Southern Historical Collection: A Guide to Manuscripts* (Chapel Hill, NC: University of North Carolina Library, 1970).

13,122. Shaw, Ruth Faison
Papers. 1913-68. Ca. 10,000 items.
Open. Unpublished guide.
University of North Carolina Library, Southern Historical Collection.
[Miss] Shaw (1887-1969) taught school in North Carolina and, after WWI, taught English and American children in Rome, where she developed the art of finger painting. Correspondence, writings, notebooks, photos, her will, Shaw family genealogy, scrapbooks, drawings, articles concerning her work with finger painting, clippings, and printed matter. Also includes her personal financial records and financial records of the Shaw Finger Paint Studio. After leaving Rome in 1932, Shaw taught finger painting at the Mac Jennet School in Paris and became affiliated with the Dalton School of Art in New York City. She organized the Shaw Finger Paint Studio in New York City and in the 1960s served as a consultant on the use of finger painting in psychiatric therapy at the North Carolina Memorial Hospital and at the Murdock Center at Umstead Park in Butner, NC. She was the author of several books.

13,123. Sheppard, Louisa (Campbell)
Papers. 1892. 70-page vol. (microfilm).
Open. Published and unpublished guides.
University of North Carolina Library, Southern Historical Collection.
Recollections by Sheppard (1848-?) of her childhood, primarily the period 1860-65, in Springfield, MO, and then in Mississippi, Arkansas, and Texas. She writes of slaves, the 1863 Vicksburg, MS, campaign, and the heroism of Confederate women. Taken from Susan Sokol Blosser and Clyde Norman Wilson, Jr., *The Southern Historical Collection: A Guide to Manuscripts* (Chapel Hill, NC: University of North Carolina Library, 1970).

13,124. Sigourney Club
Records. 1848-52. 39-page vol.
Open. Published and unpublished guides.
University of North Carolina Library, Southern Historical Collection.
Minutes, subjects of programs, a list of books purchased, and other records of this literary society at a girls' school near Gaffney, SC. Taken from Susan Sokol Blosser and Clyde Norman Wilson, Jr., *The Southern Historical Collection: A Guide to Manuscripts* (Chapel Hill, NC: University of North Carolina Library, 1970).

13,125. Simpson, Leah, and Simpson, Rebecca
Papers. 1797-1883. 125 items.
Open. Published and unpublished guides.
University of North Carolina Library, Southern Historical Collection.
Descriptive letters received by Leah Simpson (1798-?) and Rebecca Calhoun Simpson (1800-?), sisters who were residents of Pensacola, FL, from their male relatives who traveled widely in the South and to New York. Taken from Susan Sokol Blosser and Clyde Norman Wilson, Jr., *The Southern Historical Collection: A Guide to Manuscripts* (Chapel Hill, NC: University of North Carolina Library, 1970).

13,126. Singleton, Anne Hinman (Broun)
Papers. 1822-1935. 90 items.
Partially restricted. Published and unpublished guides.
University of North Carolina Library, Southern Historical Collection.
Consists primarily of letters received by Singleton (1848-1932) from the 1860s through the 1880s from her parents and other relatives in Sumter and Kershaw counties of South Carolina and in Georgia. Also includes other family papers. Taken from Susan Sokol Blosser and Clyde Norman Wilson, Jr., *The Southern Historical Collection: A Guide to Manuscripts* (Chapel Hill, NC: University of North Carolina Library, 1970).

13,127. Sivley, Jane
Papers. 1862-67. 81 items.
Open. Published and unpublished guides.
University of North Carolina Library, Southern Historical Collection.
Letters received by Sivley while she was a girl at school in Alabama from her parents in Hinds County, MS, and relatives in Confederate Army units from Tennessee. Taken from Susan Sokol Blosser and Clyde Norman Wilson, Jr., *The Southern Historical Collection: A Guide to Manuscripts* (Chapel Hill, NC: University of North Carolina Library, 1970).

13,128. Sloop, Mary (Martin)
Papers. 1945-46. 5 items.
Open. Published and unpublished guides.
University of North Carolina Library, Southern Historical Collection.
Letters by Sloop (1873-1962) concern the work of the Crossnore School for mountain children in Avery County, NC. Taken from Susan Sokol Blosser and Clyde Norman Wilson, Jr., *The Southern Historical Collection: A Guide to Manuscripts* (Chapel Hill, NC: University of North Carolina Library, 1970).

13,129. Smedes, Emilie Rose
Papers. 1905-10. 13 items.
Open. Published and unpublished guides.
University of North Carolina Library, Southern Historical Collection.
Consists primarily of letters that [Miss] Smedes (?-1950) received from John Simcox Holmes (1868-?) in October 1909; the letters concerned their wedding, which occurred during the following month. Holmes, a forester at Asheville, NC, later became state forester. Taken from Susan Sokol Blosser and Clyde Norman Wilson, Jr., *The Southern Historical Collection: A Guide to Manuscripts* (Chapel Hill, NC: University of North Carolina Library, 1970).

13,130. Smedes, Susan (Dabney)
Papers. 1860-1930. 2 items and partial microfilm reel.
Open. Published and unpublished guides.
University of North Carolina Library, Southern Historical Collection.
Papers of Smedes (1840-1913), who was an author, a teacher in the West, and a daughter of a Mississippi planter, include her diary and memoranda written in Helena, MT, in 1888 and 1889; letters she wrote from England in 1908; an account of her life written in 1930; and an 1860 recipe and household hint book. Taken from Susan Sokol Blosser and Clyde Norman Wilson, Jr., *The Southern Historical Collection: A Guide to Manuscripts* (Chapel Hill, NC: University of North Carolina Library, 1970).

13,131. Smith, Betty
Papers. 1909-72. 16 ft., 10 vols., and 1 tape.
Partially restricted. Published and unpublished guides.
University of North Carolina Library, Southern Historical Collection.
[Miss] Smith (1896-1972), an author, lived in Brooklyn, NY; Ann Arbor, MI; and Chapel Hill. Letters from her husbands Joseph Piper Jones and Robert Voris Finch (1909-59), from relatives and friends, and from fans, other writers, publishers, and literary collaborators; manuscripts of plays, articles, short stories, an unfinished autobiography, and novels by Smith and other writers; photos; posters; and clippings. Taken from Everard H. Smith III, *The Southern Historical Collection: Supplementary Guide to Manuscripts, 1970-1975* (Chapel Hill, NC: The University of North Carolina Library, 1976).

13,132. Smith, Mary Ruffin
Papers. 1750-1903. 115 items.
Open. Published and unpublished guides.
University of North Carolina Library, Southern Historical Collection.
Papers of an Orange County, NC, family include correspondence of [Miss] Smith, primarily in the 1880s, concerning her financial affairs and her gift of lands to the University of North Carolina; deeds for Illinois lands granted for military service and deeds for North Carolina lands; and papers of her brother, a physician, recording his patients' medical treatments and charges. Taken from Susan Sokol Blosser and Clyde Norman Wilson, Jr., *The Southern Historical Collection: A Guide to Manuscripts* (Chapel Hill, NC: University of North Carolina Library, 1970).

13,133. Spalding, Ella Barrow
Papers. Ca. 1800-1912. 2 vols. and 98 items.
Open. Published and unpublished guides.
University of North Carolina Library, Southern Historical Collection.
Circulars and broadsides of academies, factors, and orchards; historical sketches; scrapbooks; and other items collected by Spalding pertain primarily to Georgia. Taken from Susan Sokol Blosser and Clyde Norman Wilson, Jr., *The Southern Historical Collection: A Guide to Manuscripts* (Chapel Hill, NC: University of North Carolina Library, 1970).

13,134. Spencer, Cornelia Ann (Phillips)
Papers. 1833-1975. 4.5 ft.
Open. Published and unpublished guides.
University of North Carolina Library, Southern Historical Collection.
[Mrs. James Monroe] Spencer (1825-1908), an author, was the daughter of James Phillips, a professor at the University of North Carolina. Extensive correspondence with her family and others pertaining to life in Chapel Hill, to the University's struggle to remain open during Reconstruction, and to contemporary events in North Carolina; her diary for 1906 to 1908; manuscripts of her historical writings for newspapers and magazines; commonplace books; scrapbooks; writings about her; and other papers. Also includes astronomy, mathematics, and natural philosophy lecture notes of her father and family letters of her daughter June (Spencer) Love, which were written while she was studying and traveling in England and Germany in 1884 and residing in Cambridge, MA, from 1890 to 1894 while her husband James Lee Love was a professor of mathematics at Harvard. Taken from Susan Sokol Blosser and Clyde Norman Wilson, Jr., *The Southern Historical Collection: A Guide to Manuscripts* (Chapel Hill, NC: University of North Carolina Library, 1970); Everard H. Smith III, *The Southern Historical Collection: Supplementary Guide to Manuscripts, 1970-1975* (Chapel Hill, NC: The University of North Carolina Library, 1976).

13,135. Springs Family
Papers. Ca. 1772-1924. 4511 items.
Access restricted. Unpublished guide.
University of North Carolina Library, Southern Historical Collection.
Correspondence, bills, receipts, land grants and surveys, and printed material of the Springses and related families of Mecklenburg County, NC, and of York District, SC, and correspondence of the related Baxter family of Hancock County, GA, and later Cherokee County, TX. Includes papers of John Springs III (1782-1853) of Springfield Plantation near Fort Mill, SC; of his son Andrew Baxter Springs (1819-86); and of Andrew Springs's wife (and cousin) Julia Blandina "Blandie" (Baxter) Springs (1827-1902). Both John Springs III and Andrew Baxter Springs were members of the South Carolina legislature and were stockholders and directors of various banks and railroads and of the Graniteville Manufacturing Company.

13,136. Stamps, Mary
Papers. 1863-83. 36 items.
Open. Published and unpublished guides.
University of North Carolina Library, Southern Historical Collection.
Letters to [Mrs.] Stamps, a resident of New Orleans, from her uncle Jefferson Davis after 1869 concerning personal matters and two wartime letters, including one written in January 1865 about problems of the Confederate government. Taken from Susan Sokol Blosser and Clyde Norman Wilson, Jr., *The Southern Historical Collection: A Guide to Manuscripts* (Chapel Hill, NC: University of North Carolina Library, 1970).

13,137. Stewart, Mrs. Francis B.
Papers. 1745-1918. 72 items (microfilm).
Open. Published and unpublished guides.
University of North Carolina Library, Southern Historical Collection.
Personal correspondence of the Pinckney, Rutledge, Middleton, and Horry families of South Carolina includes a letterbook for 1763 to 1771 of Harriott (Pinckney) Horry and correspondence of her mother Eliza (Lucas) Pinckney. Taken from Susan Sokol Blosser and Clyde Norman Wilson, Jr., *The Southern Historical Collection: A Guide to Manuscripts* (Chapel Hill, NC: University of North Carolina Library, 1970).

13,138. Stone, Olive Matthews
Papers. 1932-76. Ca. 500 items.
Partially restricted. Unpublished guide.
University of North Carolina Library, Southern Historical Collection.
Correspondence concerning a sabbatical trip to the Orient by Stone (1897-) in 1932 and her association with the Southern Conference for Human Welfare, the League for Industrial Democracy, and the Southern League for People's Rights; typescript of an outline for a research project on the Alabama farmer under the direction of the sociology department of the Woman's College of Alabama; material relating to the Orient; printed matter; and other papers. Stone earned a PhD in 1939.

13,139. Street, Rebecca (Wilkinson)
Papers. Nd. 18-page item.
Open. Published and unpublished guides.
University of North Carolina Library, Southern Historical Collection.
Sketch about the intellectual life of Street (1780-1833), a poet and the wife of a planter, includes some of her verse. Taken from Susan Sokol Blosser and Clyde Norman Wilson, Jr., *The Southern Historical Collection: A Guide to Manuscripts* (Chapel Hill, NC: University of North Carolina Library, 1970).

13,140. Strudwick, Annie
Papers. 1862-64. 4 ft. of microfilm.
Open. Published and unpublished guides.
University of North Carolina Library, Southern Historical Collection.
A letter and a diary kept in 1862 by [Miss] Strudwick (?-ca. 1870) of Marengo County, AL, containing entries about teaching, reading, relatives and friends, and daily life. Taken from Susan Sokol Blosser and Clyde Norman Wilson, Jr., *The Southern Historical Collection: A Guide to Manuscripts* (Chapel Hill, NC: University of North Carolina Library, 1970).

13,141. Stubblefield, Mary
Papers. 1916. 1 item.
Open. Published and unpublished guides.
University of North Carolina Library, Southern Historical Collection.
Letter by Stubblefield as an elderly woman to her niece in which she describes the antebellum home industries of weaving and dyeing cotton cloth and candlemaking. Taken from Susan Sokol Blosser and Clyde Norman Wilson, Jr., *The Southern Historical Collection: A Guide to Manuscripts* (Chapel Hill, NC: University of North Carolina Library, 1970).

13,142. Summey, Polly Mira (Avery)
Papers. 1830-56. 13 items.
Open. Unpublished guide.
University of North Carolina Library, Southern Historical Collection.
Correspondence of Summey (1779-1857), a resident of Hendersonville, NC, and her granddaughter Delia Annie Spann (?-1910), who married a man named Patton in 1854. The letters relate to news of family and friends, health, crops, the weather, and community events, particularly deaths and marriages. Includes letters written by Spann to her grandmother while she was traveling to New York and then back to Athens, GA, in 1852 and from North Carolina through Tennessee to her parents' home in Mississippi in 1853 by train, stage, and boat. Also includes letters to Summey from her mother Leah Avery and from Leah Caroline Spann to her daughter.

13,143. Sutton, Maude (Minish)
Papers. 1921-22. 3 vols. and 1 item.
Open. Published and unpublished guides.
University of North Carolina Library, Southern Historical Collection.
Papers of Sutton (?-1936), a teacher, writer, and folklorist who lived in Caldwell County, NC, include a literary typescript, a notebook of her poems and collected ballads, a brief diary, and a scrapbook of clippings of her articles about the people of the Blue Ridge Mountains and their traditions. Taken from Everard H. Smith III, *The Southern Historical Collection: Supplementary Guide to Manuscripts, 1970-1975* (Chapel Hill, NC: The University of North Carolina Library, 1976).

13,144. Talley, Elizabeth (Furman)
Papers. 1776-1931. 5 vols. and 257 items.
Open. Published and unpublished guides.
University of North Carolina Library, Southern Historical Collection.
Consists primarily of Talley's 20th-century correspondence and papers concerning the genealogy of the Le Conte, Furman, and related families. Also includes family correspondence of Farish Carter, Georgia governor Charles James McDonald, South Carolina Baptist minister Richard Furman (1755-1825), and the Le Conte family of Georgia and California and a manuscript autobiography and philosophical essays of geologist Joseph Le Conte. Taken from Susan Sokol Blosser and Clyde Norman Wilson, Jr., *The Southern Historical Collection: A Guide to Manuscripts* (Chapel Hill, NC: University of North Carolina Library, 1970).

13,145. Terrell, Marjory
Papers. 1918-19. 50 items.
Open. Published and unpublished guides.
University of North Carolina Library, Southern Historical Collection.
Letters [Miss] Terrell, a resident of Raleigh, NC, received from soldiers in the US, England, and France to whom she had sent letters or packages. Taken from Susan Sokol Blosser and Clyde Norman Wilson, Jr., *The Southern Historical Collection: A Guide to Manuscripts* (Chapel Hill, NC: University of North Carolina Library, 1970).

13,146. Trist, Elizabeth (House)
Papers. 1783-85. 23-page vol.
Open. Published and unpublished guides.
University of North Carolina Library, Southern Historical Collection.
Diary by [Mrs. Nicholas] Trist in which she describes parts of a trip from Philadelphia to New Orleans. She went overland from Carlisle, PA, to Pittsburgh and by river from Pittsburgh to Natchez, MS. Trist was the grandmother of diplomat Nicholas Philip Trist. Taken from Susan Sokol Blosser and Clyde Norman Wilson, Jr., *The Southern Historical Collection: A Guide to Manuscripts* (Chapel Hill, NC: University of North Carolina Library, 1970).

13,147. Tutwiler, Ida
Papers. 1836-72?. 3 items.
Open. Published and unpublished guides.
University of North Carolina Library, Southern Historical Collection.
Letter to Tutwiler from her sister Julia Strudwick Tutwiler (1841-1916), a college president and pioneer in women's higher education, concerns her educational experiences. Also includes some family papers. Taken from Susan Sokol Blosser and Clyde Norman Wilson, Jr., *The Southern Historical Collection: A Guide to Manuscripts* (Chapel Hill, NC: University of North Carolina Library, 1970).

13,148. Ulmer, Margaret Anne
Papers. 1857-58. 1 vol. and 1 item.
Open. Published and unpublished guides.
University of North Carolina Library, Southern Historical Collection.
Detailed letter to Ulmer from her brother in which he describes a horseback journey in northeast Texas and Indian territory and a brief diary she kept while attending Tuskegee Female Academy in Alabama. Taken from Susan Sokol Blosser and

Clyde Norman Wilson, Jr., *The Southern Historical Collection: A Guide to Manuscripts* (Chapel Hill, NC: University of North Carolina Library, 1970).

13,149. Vogler, Lisetta Maria
Papers. 1831. 19-page vol.
Open. Published and unpublished guides.
University of North Carolina Library, Southern Historical Collection.
Diary kept by Vogler (1820-1903) in which she described a journey from Salem, NC, to New York and back and a stay with Moravian coreligionists in Pennsylvania. Vogler later married Francis Fries (1812-63). Taken from Susan Sokol Blosser and Clyde Norman Wilson, Jr., *The Southern Historical Collection: A Guide to Manuscripts* (Chapel Hill, NC: University of North Carolina Library, 1970).

13,150. Voorhees, Julia A.
Papers. 1867-72. 2 vols.
Open. Published and unpublished guides.
University of North Carolina Library, Southern Historical Collection.
Brief record of daily activities of a woman in New York City. Taken from Susan Sokol Blosser and Clyde Norman Wilson, Jr., *The Southern Historical Collection: A Guide to Manuscripts* (Chapel Hill, NC: University of North Carolina Library, 1970).

13,151. Waddell, Susanna (Gordon)
Papers. 1863-65. 2 vols.
Open. Published and unpublished guides.
University of North Carolina Library, Southern Historical Collection.
Diary of Waddell (1824-?), a resident of Monroe County, WV, who was the wife of James Alexander Waddell, a physician, in which she describes her placid life, which was interrupted by Federal army raids. Includes poems and recipes. Taken from Susan Sokol Blosser and Clyde Norman Wilson, Jr., *The Southern Historical Collection: A Guide to Manuscripts* (Chapel Hill, NC: University of North Carolina Library, 1970).

13,152. Wadley, Sarah Lois
Papers. 1859-86. 5 vols. and 1 item.
Open. Published and unpublished guides.
University of North Carolina Library, Southern Historical Collection.
Diary kept by [Miss] Wadley (1844-?), the daughter of a planter near Monroe, LA, in which she describes visits to New Orleans and Vicksburg, MS; a trip to a Georgia resort; and a journey before the Civil War to New Hampshire to visit relatives by way of St. Louis, Chicago, and Niagara Falls. She also writes about shorter trips and about her thoughts, experiences, and family life. Includes her essay on manners. Taken from Susan Sokol Blosser and Clyde Norman Wilson, Jr., *The Southern Historical Collection: A Guide to Manuscripts* (Chapel Hill, NC: University of North Carolina Library, 1970).

13,153. Walker, Hermione (Ross)
Papers. 1830-1942. 50 items.
Open. Published and unpublished guides.
University of North Carolina Library, Southern Historical Collection.
Correspondence, diaries, and memoirs of related families from the Macon, GA, area. Includes diaries of Anne Rose (1851-?) for 1861, 1867, and 1869; a biographical sketch and travel diary of Macon editor Simri Rose (1799-1869); and Reconstruction memoirs by Edgar A. Ross (1850-1929). Taken from Susan Sokol Blosser and Clyde Norman Wilson, Jr., *The Southern Historical Collection: A Guide to Manuscripts* (Chapel Hill, NC: University of North Carolina Library, 1970).

13,154. Wallace, Frances (Woolfolk)
Papers. 1864. 1 vol.
Open. Published and unpublished guides.
University of North Carolina Library, Southern Historical Collection.
Diary of Wallace (1835-?) in which she describes her experiences during a journey to and from her Kentucky home to visit her husband, a Confederate officer in Alabama; a two months' stay at Tuskegee, AL; and shorter stays along the route. Taken from Susan Sokol Blosser and Clyde Norman Wilson, Jr., *The Southern Historical Collection: A Guide to Manuscripts* (Chapel Hill, NC: University of North Carolina Library, 1970).

13,155. Wallace, Lillian Frances (Parker)
Papers. 1907-25. 2 vols.
Open. Published and unpublished guides.
University of North Carolina Library, Southern Historical Collection.
Diary kept intermittently by Lillian Parker while she was a student at the University of Denver in 1907 and a daybook of her father George S. Parker of Marietta, GA, in which he recorded farm wages and accounts. Taken from Everard H. Smith III, *The Southern Historical Collection: Supplementary Guide to Manuscripts, 1970-1975* (Chapel Hill, NC: The University of North Carolina Library, 1976).

13,156. Wayside Home Register
Records. 1862-64. 2 vols.
Open. Published and unpublished guides.
University of North Carolina Library, Southern Historical Collection.
Register of names and units of men who visited this home operated by women in Greene County, GA, to provide food and lodging for traveling Confederate soldiers. Taken from Susan Sokol Blosser and Clyde Norman Wilson, Jr., *The Southern Historical Collection: A Guide to Manuscripts* (Chapel Hill, NC: University of North Carolina Library, 1970).

13,157. Weakley, Eliza (Bedford)
Papers. 1832-1904. 2 vols. and 27 items.
Open. Published and unpublished guides.
University of North Carolina Library, Southern Historical Collection.
Brief diary of daily activities kept by [Mrs. S. D.] Weakley in 1864, 1865, and 1869 at Florence, AL, and family correspondence, bills, and receipts. Taken from Susan Sokol Blosser and Clyde Norman Wilson, Jr., *The Southern Historical Collection: A Guide to Manuscripts* (Chapel Hill, NC: University of North Carolina Library, 1970).

13,158. Weber, Margaret Isabella (Walker)
Papers. 1904. 34-page vol.
Open. Published and unpublished guides.
University of North Carolina Library, Southern Historical Collection.
Recollections by Weber (1824-?) of growing up in an antebellum North Carolina planter family and teaching in South Carolina, Tennessee, and in other places with her husband, who was a German immigrant. Taken from Susan Sokol Blosser and Clyde Norman Wilson, Jr., *The Southern Historical Collection: A Guide to Manuscripts* (Chapel Hill, NC: University of North Carolina Library, 1970).

13,159. Welborn, Mrs. John Scott
Papers. 1777-1937. 0.75 ft.
Open. Published and unpublished guides.
University of North Carolina Library, Southern Historical Collection.
Correspondence of Welborn relating to her efforts to collect genealogical and historical material as an officer of the DAR and United Daughters of the Confederacy; letters relating to North Carolina history and particularly to Randolph and Gulford counties; 18th-and 19th-century deeds, estate papers, circulars, and clippings; and genealogical and historical material concerning events from colonial times through the Civil War. Taken from Susan Sokol Blosser and Clyde Norman Wilson, Jr., *The Southern Historical Collection: A Guide to Manuscripts* (Chapel Hill, NC: University of North Carolina Library, 1970).

13,160. Wells, Martha P.
Papers. 1831. 1 vol.
Open. Published and unpublished guides.
University of North Carolina Library, Southern Historical Collection.
Album of verse with hand-painted illustrations belonging to Wells, a resident of Suffolk, VA. Taken from Susan Sokol Blosser and Clyde Norman Wilson, Jr., *The Southern Historical Collection: A Guide to Manuscripts* (Chapel Hill, NC: University of North Carolina Library, 1970).

13,161. Wentz, Alice K.
Papers. 1943. 1 item.
Open. Published and unpublished guides.
University of North Carolina Library, Southern Historical Collection.
Letter by Wentz in which she describes her experiences as a US Army nurse in England. Taken from Susan Sokol Blosser and Clyde Norman Wilson, Jr., *The Southern Historical Collection: A Guide to Manuscripts* (Chapel Hill, NC: University of North Carolina Library, 1970).

13,162. Westerfield, Peggy
Papers. 1938-45. 9 items.
Open. Published and unpublished guides.
University of North Carolina Library, Southern Historical Collection.
Letters by Westerfield in which she describes life and the local history of the isolated mountain community of Epperson, TN. Taken from Susan Sokol Blosser and Clyde Norman Wilson, Jr., *The Southern Historical Collection: A Guide to Manuscripts* (Chapel Hill, NC: University of North Carolina Library, 1970).

13,163. Westfeldt, Martha (Gasquet)
Papers. 1875-1936. 350 items.
Open. Published and unpublished guides.
University of North Carolina Library, Southern Historical Collection.
Correspondence of Westfeldt (1883-1960), a resident of New Orleans, concerns women's groups and organizations that opposed Huey Pierce Long in Louisiana and sought his expulsion by the US Senate. Also includes campaign material of various state and local candidates who opposed Long in the 1930s. Taken from Susan Sokol Blosser and Clyde Norman Wilson, Jr., *The Southern Historical Collection: A Guide to Manuscripts* (Chapel Hill, NC: University of North Carolina Library, 1970).

13,164. White, Sarah (Caldwell)
Papers. 1770-1918. 208 items.
Open. Published and unpublished guides.
University of North Carolina Library, Southern Historical Collection.
Family correspondence of White; antebellum correspondence, deeds, and land surveys of the Caldwell family of Mecklenburg County, NC; and bills, receipts, and accounts for household purchases. Taken from Susan Sokol Blosser and Clyde Norman Wilson, Jr., *The Southern Historical Collection: A Guide to Manuscripts* (Chapel Hill, NC: University of North Carolina Library, 1970).

13,165. Whitman, Angelia (Smith)
Papers. 1839-40. 3 items.
Open. Published and unpublished guides.
University of North Carolina Library, Southern Historical Collection.
Two letters written home and one received by Whitman, a Maine woman who was teaching school in Clarksville, TN. Taken from Susan Sokol Blosser and Clyde Norman Wilson, Jr., *The Southern Historical Collection: A Guide to Manuscripts* (Chapel Hill, NC: University of North Carolina Library, 1970).

13,166. Williams, Anne (Jackson)
Papers. 1880-1950. 1400 items.
Open. Published and unpublished guides.
University of North Carolina Library, Southern Historical Collection.
Williams, a resident of Raleigh, NC, was a newspaper feature writer and secretary to farm leader and editor Clarence Poe. Correspondence with her mother and sister in Forsyth, GA, and letters from other relatives. Taken from Susan Sokol Blosser and Clyde Norman Wilson, Jr., *The Southern Historical Collection: A Guide to Manuscripts* (Chapel Hill, NC: University of North Carolina Library, 1970); Everard H. Smith III, *The Southern Historical Collection: Supplementary Guide to Manuscripts, 1970-1975* (Chapel Hill, NC: The University of North Carolina Library, 1976).

13,167. Williams, Nannie (Haskins)
Papers. 1869-90. 1 vol.
Open. Published and unpublished guides.
University of North Carolina Library, Southern Historical Collection.
Intermittent diary of Williams, who lived on a farm in Todd County, KY, in which she records family concerns, everyday life and difficulties, thoughts and interests, religious life, her efforts to write a novel, and news of the county and adjacent Montgomery County, TN. Taken from Susan Sokol Blosser and Clyde Norman Wilson, Jr., *The Southern Historical Collection: A Guide to Manuscripts* (Chapel Hill, NC: University of North Carolina Library, 1970).

13,168. Williams, Sarah Frances (Hicks)
Papers. 1838-68. 110 items.
Open. Published and unpublished guides.
University of North Carolina Library, Southern Historical Collection.
Letters Sarah Hicks (1827-?) wrote to her parents in New Hartford, NY, while she was a student in Albany, NY; while visiting relatives in New York, Ohio, and New Hampshire; and after her marriage in 1853 to Benjamin F. Williams, a North Carolina state legislator, railroad stockholder, and owner of turpentine properties in North Carolina and Georgia. Letters contain detailed accounts of her daily life as a wife, mother, and the northern daughter-in-law of a southern family. Some of the letters were published in the *North Carolina Historical Review* (July and Oct. 1956). Taken from Susan Sokol Blosser and Clyde Norman Wilson, Jr., *The Southern Historical Collection: A Guide to Manuscripts* (Chapel Hill, NC: University of North Carolina Library, 1970).

13,169. Wilson, Mary Ann (Covington)
Papers. 1850-75. 60 items.
Open. Published and unpublished guides.
University of North Carolina Library, Southern Historical Collection.
Papers of [Mrs. Thomas M.] Wilson, a resident of Cleveland County, NC, include letters and poems from Thomas Wilson during their engagement; letters from her husband while he was partially disabled and on limited military service during the Civil War; antebellum and Civil War correspondence from unionist cousins in east Tennessee; and postbellum correspondence from various relatives who were schoolteachers, laborers, and farm tenants in Tennessee, Kentucky, Illinois, and Arkansas. Taken from Susan Sokol Blosser and Clyde Norman Wilson, Jr., *The Southern Historical Collection: A Guide to Manuscripts* (Chapel Hill, NC: University of North Carolina Library, 1970).

13,170. Wilson, Mrs. Wins F.
Collection. Ca. 1880-1902. 1 vol. and 18 items.
Open. Published and unpublished guides.
University of North Carolina Library, Southern Historical Collection.
Photos of faculty groups and buildings at various southern colleges, of private houses, of leisure scenes, and of L. R. Hamberlin, who was a poet and professor at colleges in Texas and elsewhere. Also includes an autograph album of a Virginia girl. Taken from Susan Sokol Blosser and Clyde Norman Wilson, Jr., *The Southern Historical Collection: A Guide to Manuscripts* (Chapel Hill, NC: University of North Carolina Library, 1970).

13,171. Withers, Anita (Dwyer)
Papers. 1860-65. 1 vol.
Open. Published and unpublished guides.
University of North Carolina Library, Southern Historical Collection.
Diary of Withers, who was the wife of US and Confederate army officer John Withers, contains entries about her life in the Confederate capital of Richmond, VA; her concern for her husband and children; social visits; the Catholic church; news from battles; rumors and threats of approaching Union troops; and temporary visits away from the city. Anita Withers lived in San Antonio, TX, and briefly in Washington, DC, before the war and returned to Texas after the conflict. Taken from Susan Sokol Blosser and Clyde Norman Wilson, Jr., *The Southern Historical Collection: A Guide to Manuscripts* (Chapel Hill, NC: University of North Carolina Library, 1970).

13,172. Wootten, Mrs. Bayard
Papers. Ca. 1870s. 3 items.
Open. Published and unpublished guides.
University of North Carolina Library, Southern Historical Collection.
Manuscripts of a story by Mary D. Morgan, of a poem, and of an unpublished novel about Creole life in Louisiana by Mary Bayard (Devereux) Clarke, a poet and novelist of North Carolina and Texas. Taken from Susan Sokol Blosser and Clyde Norman Wilson, Jr., *The Southern Historical Collection: A Guide to Manuscripts* (Chapel Hill, NC: University of North Carolina Library, 1970).

13,173. Worthington, Amanda (Dougherty)
Papers. 1819-78. 97 items (microfilm).
Open. Published and unpublished guides.
University of North Carolina Library, Southern Historical Collection.
Family correspondence and a Civil War diary of Worthington (1805-?), who was the daughter of Thomas Dougherty, clerk of the US House of Representatives, and wife of Samuel Worthington, a planter in Washington County, MS. Includes letters with political and social news from her family in Washington, DC; from relatives in Danville, KY, describing the cholera epidemic of 1833; to her son at the University of Virginia in 1857 and 1858; and from her son while he was in the Confederate Army of Tennessee. Also includes a diary for 1863 to 1865 of her daughter Amanda (ca. 1845-?) concerned primarily with social life at the plantation. Taken from Susan Sokol Blosser and Clyde Norman Wilson, Jr., *The Southern Historical Collection: A Guide to Manuscripts* (Chapel Hill, NC: University of North Carolina Library, 1970).

13,174. Young, Rachel (Barry) Burnap
Papers. 1735-1925. 81 items.
Open. Published and unpublished guides.
University of North Carolina Library, Southern Historical Collection.
Family correspondence of Young of Onslow County, NC, includes letters before and during the Civil War from her three brothers who lived in Texas near the frontier line and from her son at school and working in Texas in the 1870s. Also includes some deeds. Taken from Susan Sokol Blosser and Clyde Norman Wilson, Jr., *The Southern Historical Collection: A Guide to Manuscripts* (Chapel Hill, NC: University of North Carolina Library, 1970).

13,175. Industrialization of the Southern Piedmont
Oral history. Ca. 1978- . No size given.
Closed. Unpublished guide.
University of North Carolina, Southern Oral History Program.
Tapes and transcripts of interviews concerning the transition of Piedmont towns from agricultural to urban industrial centers include ca. 20 interviews with North Carolina women who worked in the textiles, tobacco, and other industries. Events discussed in the interviews stretch from the late 19th century to the present.

13,176. Southern Women after Suffrage
Oral history. 1972-76. Ca. 4000 pp.
Closed. Unpublished guide.
University of North Carolina, Southern Oral History Program.
Interviews with 60 women, including writers Edith (Mitchell) Dabbs, Harriette Arnow, Cornelia Spencer Love, and Dorothy Markey, who used the pen name Myra Page. Also includes interviews with sociologists Harriet Herring, Katharine DuPre Lumpkin, and Olive Stone and civil rights activists Ella Baker, Virginia (Foster) Durr, Modjeska (Montieth) Simkins, Septima (Poinsetta) Clark, Alice Spearman Wright, Daisy Bates, and Vivion Brewer. A number of women discuss the Bryn Mawr Summer School and the Southern Summer School for Women Workers in Industry, among them Alice Hanson Cook, professor emeritus at Cornell University; Miriam Bonner Camp, who taught at both schools; Brooks Spivey Creedy; Lois MacDonald, who founded the Southern Summer School; Brownie Lee Jones, former director of the Southern Summer School; Vesta Finley and Polly Hayden Robkin, students at the Southern Summer School; Hilda Worthington Smith; and Bessie Edens, a mill worker who attended the Southern Summer School.

Also includes interviews with Eleanor Copenhaver Anderson, who worked with the YWCA and participated in the workers' education movement; Anne Queen, who was director of the YMCA and YWCA at the University of North Carolina at Chapel Hill; Eleanor Coit, who was director of the American Labor Education Service; Eula McGill, an organizer for the Textile Workers' Organizing Committee and the Amalgamated Clothing Workers' Union; and Evelyn Smith Munro, a socialist who worked for the Southern Tenant Farmers' Union. There are interviews with several women who were active in the women's suffrage movement, among them Mabel Pollitzer of Charleston, SC; Eulalie Salley, who was the first woman real estate agent in South Carolina; Gladys (Avery) Tillett, who is the former president of ERA United of North Carolina; and Adelle Clark, an artist and president of the Virginia LWV.

Also includes interviews with Mississippi lawyer and judge Lucy (Somerville) Howorth, the daughter of suffrage leader Nellie Nugent Somerville; author, lawyer, and Episcopal priest Pauli Murray; educators Louise Young, Rosamund R. Boyd, and Marguerite Tolbert; Ellen (Black) Winston, who served as US and North Carolina commissioner of welfare; Mary (Price) Adamson, former director of the Committee for North Carolina, Southern Conference for Human Welfare; North Carolina historian Guion (Griffis) Johnson; Thelma Stevens, who served from 1940 to 1968 as executive director of Christian Social Relations, Women's Division, Board of Missions of the United Methodist Church; and Frances Pauley, who served as president of the Georgia LWV and director of the Georgia Council on Human Relations.

CHARLOTTE

13,177. Burwell, Margaret Anna (Robertson)
Papers. 1831-71. 2 folders and other items.
Open. No guide.
Queens College Library.
[Mrs. Robert] Burwell (1810-71) was a faculty member at Charlotte Female Institute, which became Queens College, and was in charge of a girls academy at Hillsboro, NC. Correspondence, photos, clippings, and other papers reflect Burwell's activities as an educator, as the wife of an educator, and as a mother.

13,178. Harrell, Rena
Papers. 1926-56. 1 box and other items.
Open. No guide.
Queens College Library.
[Miss] Harrell (1882-1973) was a librarian associated with the English department at Queens College. Correspondence, notes, and manuscripts show her interests in history, archival material for Queens, authenticating historical facts, genealogy, and other topics. Also includes material collected for a history of the College.

13,179. Long, Lily Webb
Papers. 1890-1910. 1 folder and other items.
Open. No guide.
Queens College Library.
[Miss] Long (1847-1929) was the first president, or principal, of Presbyterian College for Women, a predecessor of Queens College. Correspondence concerning Long, a manuscript, genealogy, photos, and clippings. Long was a teacher of modern languages at Charlotte Female Institute until it closed in 1891; she continued to operate the Institute under the title Charlotte Seminary for Girls, serving as principal until the Seminary was incorporated into the Presbyterian College for Women in 1896. She became president of the College and then principal during the presidency of J. R. Bridges. From 1901 to 1910 she was the College's dean.

13,180. Queens College
Records. 1771- . 48 ft., 29 drawers, and 35 boxes.
Open. No guide.
Queens College Library.
Founded in 1771, this women's college was known initially as Queens Museum. Annual reports, ledger books, correspondence, charters, photos, scrapbooks, literary magazines, catalogs, programs, invitations, and other records. The school's name was changed to Liberty Hall in 1777, to Charlotte Female Academy in 1821, and then to Charlotte Female Institute in 1857. When the Institute closed in 1891, [Miss] Lily Long opened Charlotte Seminary for Girls and acted as its president until it was incorporated into Presbyterian College for Women in 1896. In 1912 the school became Queens College and in 1920, Queens-Chicora College. The current name was adopted in 1939.

13,181. Charlotte Board of School Commissioners
Records. 1890-1960. 14 vols.
Open. Descriptive inventory.
University of North Carolina at Charlotte, Atkins Library.
Minutes of the Board reflect the expansion of the Charlotte school system during a time of economic growth, racial tension, and integration.

13,182. Charlotte Unitarian Church
Records. 1946-67. 15 Hollinger boxes and 1 vol.
Open. No guide.
University of North Carolina at Charlotte, Atkins Library.
Minutes, financial records, photos, bulletins, and clippings of the Church. Includes records of activities of the Church's women, particularly of the Woman's Alliance and the Sunday school.

13,183. Charlotte Unitarian Church, Woman's Alliance
Records. Ca. 1947-67. 2 Hollinger boxes.
Open. No guide.
University of North Carolina at Charlotte, Atkins Library.
Minutes, reports, and other records of the group, which was involved in volunteer work in Charlotte and in support of service projects abroad. Among the Alliance's projects were collection of garments for the American Service Committee, sewing garments, adoption of a European child in 1947, making stuffed animals for the Sunday school, holding a bazaar in 1948, and seeking a solution for the "school lunch problem" in 1959. The local group was a branch of a national organization that, by 1963, was known as the General Alliance of Unitarian-Universalist Women.

13,184. Mecklenburg County Board of Education
Records. 1885-1960. 15 vols.
Open. Descriptive inventory.
University of North Carolina at Charlotte, Atkins Library.
The school systems of Mecklenburg County, NC, and the city of Charlotte were separate until 1960 when they came under a single administration. Minutes contain material relating to management of a school system in an area that was becoming increasingly urbanized. Also includes records of the Board's receipts and expenditures from 1928 to 1931.

13,185. President, Charlotte College: General
Records. 1949-65. 34 Hollinger boxes.
Access restricted. Descriptive inventory.
University of North Carolina at Charlotte, Atkins Library.
Institutional records, reports, evaluations, and classroom records generated while [Miss] Bonnie Ethel Cone was president of Charlotte College. Includes grade and examination reports for specific students as well as building plans, curricula, and financial records. Cone became vice-chancellor for student affairs in 1965 when Charlotte College was integrated into the University of North Carolina system. She also was a mathematics professor and leader in educational organizations.

13,186. President, Charlotte College: Subject Files
Records. 1960-65. 48 Hollinger boxes.
Access restricted. Descriptive inventory.
University of North Carolina at Charlotte, Atkins Library.
Correspondence and other records generated from 1946 to 1965 while [Miss] Bonnie Ethel Cone was president of Charlotte College. The papers document the College's operation as well as Cone's activities in Charlotte and in the state. Includes information about adult education, concerts, English, extension courses, the faculty, nursing, and scholarships, as well as grade distribution surveys, instructors' applications, and name files on instructors. Departmental papers reflect the development and expansion of degree-granting programs at Charlotte College. The College became part of the University of North Carolina system in 1965.

13,187. Student Affairs and Community Relations, Vice-Chancellor
Records. 1965-70. 40 Hollinger boxes.
Access restricted. Descriptive inventory.
University of North Carolina at Charlotte, Atkins Library.
Correspondence, notes, photos, clippings, and other records related to the work of [Miss] Bonnie Ethel Cone as vice-chancellor for student affairs and community relations at the University of North Carolina at Charlotte. Includes material about the AAUW, the Civinette Club, a community college conference, counseling, the Health Services Training Center, the Junior Woman's Club, residence halls, student unrest, talented underprivileged students, and the Young Americans for Freedom. Also includes faculty minutes and evaluations. A mathematics professor, leader of education organizations, and church worker, Cone served as vice-chancellor from 1965 to 1970. Earlier she was president of Charlotte College.

13,188. Young, Sarah
Papers. Ca. 1831-60. 47 items.
Open. Descriptive inventory.
University of North Carolina at Charlotte, Atkins Library.
Business records of [Miss] Young and other members of the Young and Tate families of North Carolina include account ledgers, receipts, records of slave purchases and sales, land papers, and loan notes. Slave records provide prices quoted at various dates: Amanda was purchased for $500 in 1853; Rose, for $100; Milly, for $250; Nate, for $866; and Martin, for $1037. Sarah Young's personal records contain itemized lists of expenditures.

DURHAM

13,189. Baldwin, Alice Mary
Papers. 1877-1960. 12.5 ft.
Access restricted. Detailed index.
Duke University Archives.
Baldwin (1879-1960) was dean of the Woman's College and professor of history at Duke University from 1924 to 1947. Correspondence, scrapbooks, clippings, photos, writings, and research notes from her career as a student at Cornell University and Chicago University and as a college administrator. Correspondents include Meta Glass, Harriet C. Greve, Orie Latham Hatcher, Claudia Watkins Hunter, Louise Leonard McLaren, and Belle Rankin. Subjects include higher education for women, women's business and professional associations, the Southern School for Workers, the Alliance for Guidance of Rural Youth, the AAUW, the Institute of Women's Professional Relations, the LWV, the Southern Association of Colleges for Women, the World Center for Women's Archives, and the proposed racial integration of the WAVES during WWII. Includes a diary kept from 1877 to 1885 by Baldwin's mother Sarah L. Baldwin describing life in New England.

13,190. Bevington, Helen Smith
Papers. 1965-76. 2 ft.
Open. Unpublished guide.
Duke University Archives.
Bevington (1906-) is professor emerita of English at Duke University, author, and poet. Typescripts, galley, and page proofs of some of her published works, including *A Book and a Love Affair, The House Was Quiet and the World Was Calm,* and *Along Came the Witch.*

13,191. Brinkley, Roberta Florence
Papers. 1938-67. 1 Hollinger box.
Open. Unpublished guide.
Duke University Archives.
Brinkley (1893-1967) was dean of the Woman's College and professor of English at Duke University from 1947 to 1963. Correspondence, writings, and typescript of her unpublished work "Milton's Poems Adapted for Music."

13,192. Brown, Frances Campbell
Papers. 1932-74. Ca. 2500 items.
Open. Unpublished guide.
Duke University Archives.
Brown (1906-) was professor of chemistry at Duke University and a member at local and national levels of the AAUP. Correspondence, printed material, and AAUP files.

13,193. Bullard, Lucille M.
Papers. 1918-20. Ca. 100 items.
Open. Unpublished guide.
Duke University Archives.
Bullard was a volunteer worker and director of the alumnae war work committee at Trinity College (now Duke University), which raised money for WWI American National Red Cross activities in Europe and to send a "woman worker" to France. Correspondence, financial records, and photos.

13,194. Duke University Archives Miscellaneous Holdings
Records. 1838- . No size given.
Open. Unpublished guide.
Duke University Archives.
Office files, photos, volumes, and publications of Duke University, which grew from a one-room schoolhouse opened in 1838. Includes *Bulletins,* 1858- ; *The Archive,* the campus literary magazine, 1887- ; *Chronicle,* the student newspaper, 1905- ; *Chanticleer,* the University's yearbook, 1912- ; and *Alumni Register,* 1915- , as well as deactivated files of the Bureau of Public Information, which contain folders for individuals and organizations. *Alumni Register* provides information about alumnae affairs, faculty, staff, and student activities, while *Bulletins* contain general information about entrance requirements, curriculum, faculty, and academic regulations.

13,195. Duke University Campus Club
Records. 1938-75. 10 ft.
Open. Unpublished guide.
Duke University Archives.
Records of a social organization for faculty wives that later expanded to include female faculty and staff at Duke University. Includes minutes, correspondence, scrapbooks, and printed and other material. Club activities such as sponsorship of a lecture series, study groups, and a newcomers' club are reflected.

13,196. Duke University Career Development and Continuing Education Program
Records. 1969-75. 2 folders.
Open. Unpublished guide.
Duke University Archives.
Minutes, printed material, and clippings of a program established to assist women by academic and career counseling.

13,197. Duke University Divinity Dames
Records. 1963-74. 1 Hollinger box.
Open. Unpublished guide.
Duke University Archives.
Minutes and printed and other material of this service and social organization of women students and wives of students at the Duke divinity school.

13,198. Duke University Law Dames
Records. 1951-73. 1 box.
Open. Unpublished guide.
Duke University Archives.
Reports, scrapbooks, and other records of this social organization of wives of students at Duke law school.

13,199. Duke University Order of the White Duchy
Records. 1925-68. 350 items.
Access restricted. Unpublished guide.
Duke University Archives.
Surviving records of a secret honorary leadership sorority at the Woman's College of Duke University include the constitution, minutes, financial records, correspondence, and other material. Each year seven women were "tapped" for membership because of their academic achievement and social prominence and especially because of their service to the University community.

13,200. Duke University Physical Education for Women
Records. 1935-74. 1 box.
Open. Unpublished guide.
Duke University Archives.
Records and printed material of the department of physical education at the Woman's College of Duke University, including departmental annual reports issued since the 1935-36 school year.

13,201. Duke University Woman's College
Records. 1930-72. Ca. 15 drawers and 15 Hollinger boxes.
Access restricted. Unpublished guide.
Duke University Archives.
The Woman's College was the resident liberal arts college for women at Duke University from 1930 to 1972 when it merged with the men's college to form Trinity College of Arts and Sciences. Minutes, files of several deans, correspondence, admissions data, academic and social regulations, alumnae newsletters, and other material.

13,202. Duke University Women's Student Government Association
Records. 1919-72. 19 Hollinger boxes.
Open. Unpublished guide.
Duke University Archives.
Minutes, resolutions, financial records, correspondence, and office files of this representative assembly for undergraduate women at Trinity College and at Trinity's successor, the Woman's College of Duke University, before the group was absorbed by the Associated Students of Duke University in 1967. Records document the changing concerns of women students over social regulations, governance, and student activism.

13,203. Duke University Young Women's Christian Association
Records. 1917-68. 1 box.
Open. Unpublished guide.
Duke University Archives.
Records of the Duke chapter of the YWCA include minutes, financial records, correspondence, printed material, and a history of the chapter's founding.

13,204. Griggs, Lillian Baker
Papers. 1930-49. 1 drawer.
Open. Unpublished guide.
Duke University Archives.
[Mrs.] Griggs (1876-1955) was librarian of the Duke University Woman's College library from 1930 to 1949, developer of public libraries and bookmobile services in North Carolina, and a member of the North Carolina and the American Library Associations. Correspondence, minutes, and reports present a general view of library administration; other material concerns a special women's symposium held in 1939 as part of Duke's centennial observation. One letter from Alice Stone Blackwell contains personal remembrances of Elizabeth Blackwell, Antoinette Brown Blackwell, and Lucy Stone.

13,205. Grout, Julia Rebecca
Papers. 1947-70. Ca. 100 items.
Open. Unpublished guide.
Duke University Archives.
[Miss] Grout was director of physical education at the Woman's College of Duke University. Correspondence, printed material, and typescripts include Grout's writings about physical education for women, her history of women's physical education at Duke University from 1924 to 1964, and her history of Durham's Altrusa Club.

13,206. Ingles, Thelma
Papers. 1933-75. Ca. 200 items.
Open. Unpublished guide.
Duke University Archives.
Ingles was professor of nursing education at Duke University's school of nursing and a consultant on nursing for the Rockefeller Foundation. Correspondence, including letters written between 1945 and 1948 from Turkey where Ingles served as a Navy nurse; copies and reprints of her articles and writings; and items relating to her five years of work in Cali, Colombia, with a Rockefeller medical project.

13,207. Sandeen, Muriel Ione
Papers. 1950-63. 8 Hollinger boxes.
Open. Unpublished guide.
Duke University Archives.
Sandeen (1924-63) was professor of zoology at Duke University. Correspondence, typescripts, and research notes relating primarily to her research on the physiology of marine crustaceans.

13,208. Trinity College Coordinate College for Women
Records. Ca. 1915-20. 6 items.
Open. Unpublished guide.
Duke University Archives.
Printed items document efforts to establish a separate liberal arts college for women at Trinity (now Duke University), which were not successful until 1930 when the Woman's College was founded. Achievements of women at the predominantly male Trinity College are chronicled in a booklet about women at Trinity.

13,209. Wilson, Mary Grace
Papers. 1933-69. 4 Hollinger boxes.
Open. Unpublished guide.
Duke University Archives.
Wilson (?-) was dean of undergraduate women at the Woman's College of Duke University. Correspondence, reports, minutes, and printed material provide information about social regulations, campus organizations, student activities, and the racial integration of the college in the 1960s.

13,210. Iredell, James, Sr., and Iredell, James, Jr.
Papers. 1724-1890. 6 vols. and 1046 items.
Open. Published and unpublished guides.
Duke University, William R. Perkins Library, Manuscript Department.
Correspondence and legal memoranda of James Iredell, Sr. (1751-99), statesman and associate justice of the US Supreme Court, and of James Iredell, Jr. (1788-1853), governor of North Carolina and US senator. Includes correspondence of Hannah (Johnston) Iredell, wife of the senior Iredell, containing material about the status and activities of socially prominent women in the 18th century, and of other female family members about domestic and social matters. Political subjects are discussed from the Revolution through the Jacksonian era and, to a lesser degree, through the term of President John Tyler. See partial description in Nannie M. Tilley and Noma Lee Goodwin, *Guide to the Manuscript Collections in the Duke University Library* (Durham, 1947).

13,211. King, Carl Howie, and King, Mary (Eskridge)
Papers. 1918-73. 1 vol. and 3993 items.
Open. Unpublished guide.
Duke University, William R. Perkins Library, Manuscript Department.
Carl King (1898-1967) was a Methodist clergyman and educator, and Mary King (1901-73) was a Methodist laywoman. Correspondence and printed material relate to women's activities in the Methodist and United Methodist churches. Mary King's papers consist principally of ephemeral printed material regarding women's organizations in the United Methodist church during the 1960s and the early 1970s and items relating to missionary work and race relations.

13,212. Mason, Lucy Randolph
Papers. 1917-54. 4 vols. and 6528 items.
Open. Unpublished guide.

Duke University, William R. Perkins Library, Manuscript Department.
A social activist, Mason (1882-1959) was general secretary of the National Consumers' League from 1932 until 1937 and, later, public relations representative for the CIO in the Southeast. Correspondence, memoranda, speeches, clippings, and miscellaneous papers relate to Mason's efforts to improve the status of factory workers, women, and blacks and to involve women in the labor movement and in political and social concerns. Much of the material deals with the period from 1937 to 1954 during which Mason lived in Atlanta and was associated with the CIO.

13,213. Thomas, Ella Gertrude (Clanton)
Papers. 1848-89. 13 vols.
Open. Unpublished guide.
Duke University, William R. Perkins Library, Manuscript Department.
Diaries of Thomas (1834-?) record her life from girlhood as a popular debutante through her years as an elderly woman who took in boarders to supplement the family's financial resources, which were depleted during the Civil War and Reconstruction. Thomas discusses the status of women, popular literature, plantation management, education, southern and national politics, the Civil War and its effect on civilians in the South, Reconstruction, and domestic concerns.

GREENSBORO

13,214. Afro-American Women
Collection. Nd. No size given.
Open. No guide.
Bennett College Library.
Photos, pamphlets, clippings, books, recording discs, and other items concern the achievements of Afro-American women from the 18th century to the present. Includes a first edition of *Poems* (1773) by Phillis Wheatley.

13,215. Bennett College
Records. 1873- . 120 in.
Open. No guide.
Bennett College Library.
Founded in 1873 as a Methodist high school and college, Bennett was operated later as a seminary and then became a four-year black women's college in 1926. Minutes, reports of the College's president, teacher self-study material, photos, handbooks, bulletins, and other records of the College and summer institutes held at the school provide information about the education of black women.

13,216. Scrapbooks
Records. 1929-50s. Ca. 16 vols.
Open. No guide.
Bennett College Library.
Founded in 1873, Bennett College became a four-year college for black women in 1926. Scrapbooks include correspondence, photos, clippings, and related items kept by students and faculty members as a chronicle of the school's history.

13,217. Vertical File
Collection. Nd. 2 drawers.
Open. No guide.
Bennett College Library.
Correspondence, scrapbooks, and clippings include information on women involved in art, business and industry, education, literature, the military, and civil defense. Women represented include Mrs. William Amey, a florist; Letha Artis, a bus driver; Mildred Blount, a hat designer and window dresser; the Caldwell sisters, who operated a butcher shop; Olivia Clarke, who operated a beauty salon; Jackie Ormes, who was involved in the manufacturing of dolls; and educators Gertrude Ayers, [Mrs.] Mary Bethune, Charlotte Brown, and Nannie Burroughs. Also contains clippings about religious denominations in North Carolina.

13,218. American National Red Cross, Greensboro, NC, Chapter
Records. Ca. 1917-18. 1 vol.
Open. No guide.
Greensboro Public Library.
History of work done by the Greensboro Chapter during WWI with a roster of Chapter volunteers, most of whom were women. Includes names of workers in war fund campaigns and those who provided emergency service during the 1918 influenza epidemic.

13,219. Bell, Martha McFarlane McGee
Papers. Ca. 1770s-1840s. 1 envelope.
Open. No guide.
Greensboro Public Library.
Correspondence, legal documents, and other papers, including the will of Colonel John McGee (?-1774), a planter, in which he says his wife Martha McFarlane McGee (?-1820) was to receive "the back room bed and furniture" before his estate was divided. Martha McGee married William Bell in 1779. Also includes Martha Bell's will with precise gifts, including slaves, for specific children and grandchildren; family letters containing family news and commentary on child raising; and the will of Jane Wilborn in which she bequeathes slaves and goods to her son.

13,220. Guilford County Literary and Historical Association
Records. 1906-07. 1 vol.
Open. No guide.
Greensboro Public Library.
The Association was organized in 1906 as a literary group with the additional purpose of preserving historic relics. Constitution; minutes; list of 82 charter members, most of whom were women; publicity material; and other records. Women held most of the Association offices, but men often chaired the standing committees, which were concerned with such subjects as history, literature, and an historical museum.

13,221. Binford Family
Papers. 1900-52. Ca. 28 Hollinger boxes.
Open. No guide.
Guilford College, Quaker Collection.
A teacher, housewife, and mother, Helen [Mrs. Raymond] Binford (1885-1952) was active in the national PTA and with her husband, who served as president of Guilford College from 1918 to 1934, directed a civilian public service camp in North Carolina during WWII. The Binfords later directed an American Friends Service Committee camp in Mexico. Correspondence, diaries, notebooks, speeches, articles, scrapbooks, and calendars include information on child development, family life, education, and international relations. Helen Binford held a national PTA post during the 1930s and was active in the North Carolina Yearly Meeting throughout her adult life.

13,222. Cox, Clara I.
Papers. 1929-32. 1 Hollinger box.
Open. No guide.
Guilford College, Quaker Collection.
A Friends pastor in High Point, NC, Cox (1879-1939) held offices in various Friends groups that sought interracial cooperation. Correspondence, papers of organizations, and reports contain information about the Friends Interracial Committee, the Committee on Interracial Cooperation, and the North Carolina Commission on Interracial Cooperation.

13,223. Guilford College
Records. 1834- . Several Hollinger boxes and 50 vols.
Open. Index.
Guilford College, Quaker Collection.
Chartered in 1834 as New Garden Boarding School, this institution was a coeducational Quaker primary and secondary school until 1888 when it became Guilford College, a coeducational liberal arts institution. Minutes of the board of trustees, faculty, alumni association, and, from 1962 to 1966, of the student government; financial records, which include faculty pay lists and salaries; registrar's records of students' names and hometowns, their purchases at Guilford, and the name of the person paying their bills; and alumni association records. Also includes material on Mary (Mendenhall) Hobbs and the girls aid committee of Guilford. The number of women faculty members at Guilford has been approximately equal to that of men.

13,224. Guilford College: Bulletin, Alumni Issue
Records. 1937- . 11 vols.
Open. Index.
Guilford College, Quaker Collection.
The *Alumni Journal* includes information about the activities of Guilford College students, faculty, and graduates. The bulletins include such articles as "Guilford's Contribution to Education," consisting of photos and biographical notes on Guilford alumni who became prominent in education, and "With Guilfordians Everywhere," containing information on travel, employment, honors, and activities of Guilford graduates, about half of whom were women.

13,225. Guilford College: Bulletins, Catalogs
Records. 1888- . 30 vols.
Open. Holdings list.
Guilford College, Quaker Collection.
Catalogs of a coeducational Quaker liberal arts school, established in 1888, include information about faculty, students, and curriculum. The catalogs show that women were members of the faculty during the school's early years and taught Latin, history, literature and rhetoric, shorthand, and typewriting. Women also were active on the advisory committee and the committee on endowment. The bulletin for the 1891-92 school year notes that, while the school was under the control of the Friends, it was nonsectarian. The curriculum included Latin language and literature, Greek, German, English literature, mathematics, natural science, a normal department, and departments for commercial courses and shorthand. Each issue includes lists of alumni and their hometowns.

13,226. Guilford College: The Guilford Collegian
Records. 1888-1914. 26 vols.
Open. Holdings list.
Guilford College, Quaker Collection.
Initiated in 1888, the *Collegian* was a student newspaper and literary magazine that was replaced by the *Guilfordian* in 1914. The publication's articles, many of them written by women, reflect the intellectual life of a coeducational institution. An 1889 issue features a report on the North Carolina WCTU convention, an article about the work of a Quaker woman missionary in Mexico, essays, personal columns, and officer lists for the women's Philagorean Debating Society, the YWCA, and the senior class. The personals column included the notation that Rodema E. Wright was not with the senior class that year, but that her classmates were "sure that while at home with her feeble mother she is doing the duty which is nearest."

13,227. Guilford College: The Guilfordian
Records. 1914- . 19 vols.
Open. No guide.
Guilford College, Quaker Collection.
Copies of the College's student newspaper, established in 1914, provide information about the

academic and social lives of women at a coeducational Quaker college. *Guilfordian* issues in 1914 include notes about the YWCA, alumni, music, the Philomathean Society, and social events. Women served as editors in chief and as writers on the *Guilfordian.*

13,228. Hobbs, Mary (Mendenhall)
Papers. 1908-23. Ca. 12 items.
Open. No guide.
Guilford College, Quaker Collection.
Hobbs (1852-1930) was a teacher, housewife, mother, and writer and lecturer in the cause of women's education. Her correspondence includes letters from Charles McIver regarding establishment of a state college for women at Greensboro and letters concerning controversial issues among Quakers, especially their relation to war. Also includes an announcement of the awarding of an honorary doctorate in literature in 1921 from the University of North Carolina at Chapel Hill. Correspondents include Joe Cannon, speaker of the US House of Representatives, and Josephus Daniels, who wrote concerning Hobbs's article of ca. 1922 about a Carolina woman's view of the President.

13,229. Hockett Family
Papers. Ca. 1855-63. 1 Hollinger box.
Open. No guide.
Guilford College, Quaker Collection.
A farmer in Randolph County, NC, William H. Hockett was held prisoner by the Confederacy for refusing military service. Collection primarily consists of correspondence between Hockett and family members, including his wife Rachel Branson Hockett and his daughters, during his two-year incarceration.

13,230. Martin and Haworth Family
Papers. 1875-1967. Ca. 1300 items.
Open. Card catalog.
Guilford College, Quaker Collection.
Correspondence, diaries, class and lecture notes, genealogical information, photos, clippings, and other papers of Susanna (Janeway) Martin (1853-1930); her husband Zenas Martin (?-1931), who directed the Friends Mission in Cuba; their daughter Evelyn (Martin) Haworth (1877-1967); and Evelyn's husband, Samuel Lee Haworth (1868-1957), professor of religion at Wilmington and Guilford colleges. Contains correspondence between Zenas and Susanna Martin and between Evelyn and Samuel Haworth, Susanna Martin's diaries, and poems of Samuel Haworth. Also contains Samuel Haworth's files on conscientious objectors, the Friends World Conference in 1937, the North Carolina Council of Churches, and the World Council of Churches.

13,231. Mendenhall and Hobbs Family
Papers. Ca. 1790-1933. 9 Hollinger boxes.
Open. No guide.
Guilford College, Quaker Collection.
Mary (Mendenhall) Hobbs (1852-1930) was a teacher, housewife, mother, and writer and lecturer in the cause of women's education. Gertrude Mendenhall (1861-1926) was a mathematics teacher at a North Carolina women's college. Correspondence, writings, deeds, wills, estate records, other family papers, and photos. Includes Mary Hobbs's writings, school notebooks, biographical and historical studies, essays on inspirational subjects, and copies of weekly lectures she delivered to Guilford women on such topics as hygiene, social graces, and religion. Also includes papers relating to Gertrude Mendenhall's mathematics studies. Mary Hobbs was instrumental in establishing a scholarship fund and a cooperative dormitory for women at Guilford College.

13,232. Mendenhall, Delphina
Papers. Ca. 1850-80. 1 Hollinger box.
Open. No guide.
Guilford College, Quaker Collection.
Mendenhall (1811-post 1880), a writer and poet, was a member of the Mendenhall family of Guilford County, NC. Correspondence, poems, and papers dealing with estate matters. Includes letters to church groups that Mendenhall wrote in her capacity as clerk of the North Carolina Women's Yearly Meeting, letters from 1860 describing her husband's death, and drafts of letters to individuals, including John Greenleaf Whittier.

13,233. Meredith, Mary Moon
Papers. Ca. 1879-80. 1 Hollinger box.
Open. Card catalog.
Guilford College, Quaker Collection.
A Quaker minister from the Midwest, Meredith (1845-1924) served in North Carolina in 1879 and 1880. Correspondence, photos, and a clipping book trace her North Carolina work traveling from parish to parish inspiring revivalism.

13,234. New Garden Boarding School
Records. 1834-88. Ca. 6 Hollinger boxes and 20 vols.
Open. No guide.
Guilford College, Quaker Collection.
Trustee minutes, financial records, correspondence, and bulletins of this coeducational Quaker primary and secondary boarding school, which existed from 1834 until 1888. Bulletins include names and hometowns of students in the Female Department and report that the course work of students of both sexes was substantially the same. Women taught in the Female Department, and one was named superintendent as early as 1855.

13,235. North Carolina Yearly Meeting, Society of Friends
Records. Ca. 1678- . 628 vols. and other items.
Open. Index.
Guilford College, Quaker Collection.
Minutes of business meetings and birth, death, and membership lists of the North Carolina Society of Friends reflect the activities of Quaker women and include reports of quarterly and monthly meetings of local Quaker groups. Also contains records and reports of the Foreign Mission Board of the North Carolina Women's Missionary Union, ca. 1874-1914, and of the United Society of Friends Women, ca. 1949-71. Includes records of separate women's meetings held from the early 1700s through the late 1800s. The women's business meetings concerned membership, marriage, and the moral and spiritual state of the Quakers.

13,236. Oral History Project
Oral history. Ca. 1971- . 30 tapes.
Open. No guide.
Guilford College, Quaker Collection.
Interviews with North Carolina Quakers concern various subjects dating from the late 1880s to the present.

13,237. Peck Family
Papers. 1837-39. 1 Hollinger box.
Open. Card catalog.
Guilford College, Quaker Collection.
Harriet Peck (1815-40) and her fiancé Peren Peck were teachers at New Garden School. Correspondence of the Peck family, a group of Rhode Island Quakers, includes that between Harriet and Peren Peck during the last months of her life.

13,238. Reynolds, Catherine
Papers. 1841-49. 50 items.
Open. Card catalog.
Guilford College, Quaker Collection.
Correspondence of Reynolds, a teacher at the New Garden Boarding School from 1841 to 1849, concerns daily life at the School; includes letters from her sister Hannah (Reynolds) Watkins and one photo. Reynolds married after teaching at the School.

13,239. Smiley, Sarah F.
Papers. 1865-67. 2 vols.
Open. No guide.
Guilford College, Quaker Collection.
A representative of the Baltimore Association for the Relief of Friends in the South, Smiley came to Goldsboro in Wayne County, NC, an area devastated during the Civil War. Journals in which she recorded her observations concerning the conditions of Quaker families in Goldsboro and the region's cultural life. Smiley investigated the relief needs of each Quaker family in Goldsboro.

13,240. Thorne, Dorothy Lloyd Gilbert
Papers. Ca. 1922-71. 5 Hollinger boxes.
Open. Card catalog.
Guilford College, Quaker Collection.
A writer and historian, [Mrs. Howard Harlan] Thorne (1902-76) taught English at Guilford College. Correspondence, much of it referring to the Friends World Committee, an international group designed to promote cooperation among Quaker organizations. Thorne began teaching at Guilford in 1924. She married Thorne in 1955 and moved to Ohio where she lived until about 1967. She then returned to Guilford and taught until 1971. She was a representative to the Friends World Committee from the North Carolina Yearly Meeting.

13,241. Elliott, Harriet Wiseman
Papers. 1900-72. 7 ft.
Open. Unpublished guide.
University of North Carolina at Greensboro, Library, Archives.
Dean of women at State Normal and Industrial School in 1935, [Miss] Elliott (1884-1947) was consumer commissioner on the Council of National Defense advisory commission in 1940 and 1941 and chairman of the women's division of the War Finance Committee from 1942 to 1946. Correspondence, speeches, minutes, reports, photos, news releases, clippings, publications, and other papers. Includes personal papers relating to her school days at Park College in Missouri, letters she wrote to her family in 1920 while she was visiting in England and France, and correspondence concerning her work as consumer commissioner. Correspondents include Franklin and Eleanor Roosevelt, Judge Florence Allen, and Mary "Molly" Dewson. Also includes minutes and records of UNESCO meetings in 1945 and 1946. Elliott was deputy director of the Office of Price Administration and US delegate to a UNESCO conference in 1945 in London.

13,242. Foust, Julius Isaac
Papers. 1906-67. 42 ft.
Open. Unpublished guide.
University of North Carolina at Greensboro, Library, Archives.
Correspondence, speeches, invoices, receipts, photos, clippings, publications, and other papers of Foust (1865-1946), who was president of the State Normal and Industrial College (now the University of North Carolina at Greensboro) from 1902 until 1934. Foust's papers document the institution's evolution from a normal school to a women's liberal arts college. Contains information about the addition of new departments, such as sociology and economics, hygiene and public health, and vocal and school music; regulations for the school's students; coordination of programs with other state-supported schools; public controversies that occurred during Foust's administration; and student affairs.

13,243. Gove, Anna Maria
Papers. 1892-1948. 4.75 ft.
Open. Unpublished guide.

University of North Carolina at Greensboro, Library, Archives.
[Miss] Gove (1867-1948) was resident physician, director of the department of health, and professor of hygiene at the State Normal and Industrial School (now the University of North Carolina at Greensboro) from 1893 until her retirement in 1937. Photos, post cards, and albums collected by Gove during personal and professional trips throughout the US and in Europe, Africa, Central America, and the Orient. The first of the trips was the result of Gove's medical study in Vienna in 1896 and 1897. Some of the other photos relate to her work as an American National Red Cross volunteer in France during WWI. Also included are photos of the Greensboro area and of local blacks.

13,244. Lathrop, Virginia Terrell
Papers. 1942-74. 3 ft. and 1 archival box.
Open. Unpublished guides.
University of North Carolina at Greensboro, Library, Archives.
A 1923 graduate of North Carolina College for Women, [Mrs. Albert H.] Lathrop (1900-74) was a journalist, author, and head of the Woman's College news bureau. Correspondence, manuscripts, memos, notes, informational material, and printed items. Includes manuscripts of Lathrop's *Educate a Woman* (Chapel Hill, NC: University of North Carolina Press, 1942); a history of Woman's College; and *Bricks and People* (1973), which she wrote with Marguerite Schumann. Lathrop worked as a journalist for the Raleigh, NC, *News and Observer;* the *Asheville Citizen* in Asheville, NC; the *New York Post;* and the London and Paris offices of the *New York Herald Tribune.* From 1937 to 1941 she headed the Woman's College news bureau. She served on the board of trustees of Consolidated University of North Carolina from 1949 until her death. A large portion of her papers is related to the work of this board, which oversaw the operation of all public institutions of higher education in North Carolina. She and her husband had one son, George Terrell Lathrop.

13,245. McIver, Charles Duncan, and McIver, Lula (Martin)
Papers. 1872-1906. Ca. 43.25 ft.
Open. Unpublished guides.
University of North Carolina at Greensboro, Library, Archives.
Correspondence, diaries, speeches, school notebooks, invoices, receipts, photos, publications, and other papers of Charles McIver (1860-1906), founder and first president of State Normal and Industrial School, and his wife Lula McIver (1864-1944), a teacher who played a major role in the School's development. Lula Martin graduated from Salem Academy in 1881 and taught in public schools and at an orphanage; at Peace Institute at Raleigh, NC; and at Presbyterian Female College in Charlotte, NC. She married Charles McIver in 1885. Their personal correspondence reveals their belief in shared responsibilities. Charles McIver's papers provide a chronicle of the early years of State Normal and Industrial School and provide information about the status of education in the South. Included are daily letters that his secretary Laura Coit wrote during his absences to tell him of events at the School. Also includes correspondence and various items of the McIvers' daughters Annie and Lula Martin McIver and of their son Charles D. McIver and letters of condolence sent to Lula McIver following her husband's death. Lula Martin McIver later married John Dickinson.

13,246. Shaw, Anna Howard
Papers. 1917-18. 6 items.
Open. Unpublished guide.
University of North Carolina at Greensboro, Library, Archives.
A reformer, minister, and physician, [Miss] Shaw (1847-1919) was chairman of the women's committee of the Council of National Defense during WWI. Correspondence between Shaw and students of the State Normal and Industrial College at Greensboro and photos of Shaw and Susan B. Anthony. Shaw's letters to the students include exhortations to the young women to value themselves as human beings and as distinct individuals. She delivered the commencement address at the College in 1919.

13,247. Woman's Association for the Betterment of Public School Houses
Records. 1902-44. 1.5 ft.
Open. Unpublished guide.
University of North Carolina at Greensboro, Library, Archives.
The Association was founded in Greensboro in 1902 by Charles D. McIver, president of the State Normal and Industrial College, to organize local groups of parents and teachers to improve the state's public schools. Minutes, correspondence, speech notes, county reports, photos, clippings, and other records. Includes papers of McIver's wife Lula (Martin) McIver, who served as the Association's field secretary. Also includes papers of Mary Taylor Moore and Mrs. W. R. Hollowell. The organization merged with the North Carolina Congress of Parents and Teachers in 1919.

13,248. Archives
Records. 1880- . 300 ft.
Open. Unpublished guide.
University of North Carolina at Greensboro, Library, Special Collections.
Founded as State Normal and Industrial School in 1891, the institution was for a time the largest state-supported residential women's college in the US. Minutes, financial records, correspondence, diaries, oral history tapes and transcripts of interviews with early graduates, reports, photos, scrapbooks, clippings, memorabilia, and other records. Founded by Charles Duncan McIver as North Carolina's first state-supported institution of higher learning for women, the school became State Normal and Industrial College for Women in 1896, North Carolina College for Women in 1919, and Woman's College of the University of North Carolina in 1931. The school remained all white until 1954. The institution became coeducational in 1962, the year in which the current name was adopted.

13,249. Ferguson, Sue Ramsey (Johnston)
Papers. 1945-47. 0.33 ft.
Open. Unpublished guide.
University of North Carolina at Greensboro, Library, Special Collections.
A 1918 graduate of State Normal and Industrial College who received her MS at Columbia University, [Mrs. Raymond S.] Ferguson (1897-) was an educational and Democratic party leader in North Carolina. Correspondence and clippings pertain to education in the state. Ferguson was a trustee of the University of North Carolina, a member of the North Carolina State Board of Education, and a state senator from 1947 to 1949. During her legislative term, she proposed that a committee be established to investigate the state's schools; the State Education Commission was formed as a result. Much of her correspondence is concerned with her proposal for an investigating committee, while other items deal with teachers' salaries and the school lunch program. Ferguson and her husband, who live in Taylorsville, NC, were married in 1934.

13,250. Howard Family
Papers. 1829-68. 14 items.
Open. Unpublished guide.
University of North Carolina at Greensboro, Library, Special Collections.
Correspondence and a broadside of the family of Jacob Howard, who apparently was a merchant in Lebanon, TN. Consists primarily of letters to his daughter Elizabeth "Lizzie" R. (Howard) [Mrs. Sam] Milligan, particularly from her mother and from her brother John Howard. The correspondence concerns family news and activities with references to a visit at the home of Judge Ewing, the chief justice of Kentucky; a cholera epidemic in Nashville; the price of slaves in the area; and Mammoth Cave in Kentucky. Civil War letters tell of the family's fear of Yankee troops and their feeling of isolation from the rest of the South. The 1829 broadside is an advertisement for Mrs. Howard's School for Young Ladies in Jonesborough, TN.

13,251. Johns, Annie E.
Papers. 1846-1909. 17 items.
Open. Unpublished guide.
University of North Carolina at Greensboro, Library, Special Collections.
Correspondences, poems, articles, and clippings of [Miss] Johns (1831-89), an author and Civil War nurse. The correspondence was chiefly from other authors concerning literary matters. She was the author of a novel *Cooleemee,* poems, and magazine articles. In the South, she was best known for her work as assistant matron of hospitals in Danville, VA, during the Civil War.

13,252. Lenski, Lois
Papers. 1916-72. 12 ft.
Open. Unpublished guide.
University of North Carolina at Greensboro, Library, Special Collections.
An artist and author, Lenski (1893-1974) won the 1946 Newbery Medal for her self-illustrated book *Strawberry Girl.* Manuscripts, illustrated writing books, and other volumes. Lenski received a BS in education from Ohio State University in 1915 and married Arthur Covey, a mural painter, in 1921. She received an honorary doctorate from the University in 1962.

13,253. North Carolina Council of Women's Organizations, Inc.
Records. 1955-75. Ca. 10 ft.
Open. Unpublished guides.
University of North Carolina at Greensboro, Library, Special Collections.
Organized in 1952 as the North Carolina Woman's Council, this group served as a clearinghouse for women's organizations to prevent duplication of effort and to allow groups to work together in areas of special interest to women. Minutes, financial and committee reports, correspondence, photos, annual directories, printed items, and other records. In 1955, the agency's name was changed to North Carolina Council of Women's Organizations. In 1956, it became a cooperative service of the University of North Carolina Extension Division; in 1959 it was chartered and its concerns were extended to include safety, continuing education, and implementation of the status of women report. By 1970 the Council included 39 affiliated organizations with a membership of more than 500,000 persons.

13,254. Southern Association for Physical Education of College Women
Records. 1928-74. 4.5 ft.
Open. Unpublished guide.
University of North Carolina at Greensboro, Library, Special Collections.
The Association was founded in 1935 to study problems pertaining to departments of women's physical education in colleges and universities of the southern district of the American Association for Health, Physical Education and Recreation. Biennial reports, correspondence, indexes, newsletters, directories, a history of the

organization, and other records including material related to the National Association for the Physical Education of College Women.

13,255. Winston, Ellen Engelman (Black)
Papers. 1891-1973. 20 ft. and 3 tapes.
Open. Unpublished guide.
University of North Carolina at Greensboro, Library, Special Collections.
Commissioner of public welfare for the state of North Carolina from 1944 to 1963, Winston (1903-) was the first US commissioner of welfare in the Department of HEW. Correspondence, speeches, taped interview, photos, scrapbooks, invitations, clippings, copies of Winston's publications, and other papers. Includes information about the AAUW, the American Public Welfare Association, the Child Welfare League of America, international conferences on social work, the National Conference on Social Welfare, the National Social Welfare Assembly, the Southern Regional Education Board, and other organizations and conferences. A Bryson City, NC, native who received her MA and PhD from the University of Chicago, Winston was a social economist and technical editor for several federal agencies during the 1930s. She taught in the Raleigh, NC, city schools and from 1940 to 1944 headed the Meredith College department of economics and sociology. She assumed her HEW post in 1963 but resigned in 1967 to return to Raleigh to devote full time to her study of social welfare policy. She is the author of numerous publications. Her husband Sanford Winston was head of the North Carolina State University sociology department for many years.

GREENVILLE

13,256. Barlow, Della
Papers. 1866-72. 65 items.
Open. Unpublished guide.
East Carolina University, East Carolina Manuscript Collection.
Correspondence of [Miss] Barlow of Tarboro, NC, with her suitor Colonel John Perry of Beaufort, NC, reflects life in North Carolina during Reconstruction.

13,257. Beck, Cora Warren
Papers. 19th century. 22 pp.
Open. Unpublished guide.
East Carolina University, East Carolina Manuscript Collection.
Memoir in which [Mrs.] Beck recounts her life in antebellum and Civil War Georgia. Includes descriptions of plantation life, weddings, and the coming of the Civil War. During the war her family lived in Atlanta; the memoir contains accounts of wartime shortages, fast days, volunteer hospital work, slavery, the capture of Atlanta by Union forces, and Southerners' efforts to secure their valuables from the invaders as well as comments on slave emancipation, Union prison camps, Confederate emigration to Mexico, and life at a Georgia women's college.

13,258. Bost, Ethel W.
Papers. 1925. Partial microfilm reel.
Open. Unpublished guide.
East Carolina University, East Carolina Manuscript Collection.
Diary of [Miss] Bost, a Mooresville, NC, native who served as a Methodist missionary in China from 1925 to 1943 and in Japan from 1949 to 1969. The diary covers her voyage from Vancouver, British Columbia, to China and reflects the experiences of a young missionary. Bost was repatriated in 1943 as an exchange prisoner from a Japanese concentration camp. She returned to Japan in 1949.

13,259. Bowman, Frances Willard
Papers. 1957-72. 307 items.
Open. Unpublished guide.
East Carolina University, East Carolina Manuscript Collection.
An authority on sterility testing of drugs, [Mrs.] Bowman joined the Food and Drug Administration division on antibiotics in 1946. Her research consisted of studies of the stability of various antibiotics and the development of assays for antibiotic testing. Correspondence, committee and conference minutes, and scientific articles relating to her FDA work make up the bulk of the collection. Included are programs, notes, and reports on the Round Table Conference on Sterility Testing in London in 1963, the American Society of Microbiologists Convention in Detroit in 1968, and the International Symposium on Industrial Sterilization in Amsterdam in 1972. Also contains information about her projects relating to ointment sterility and penicillinase cellulase. Bowman received the FDA's Award of Merit in 1966, the East Carolina University Alumni Award in 1957, and was nominated for the Federal Woman's Award in 1969 and 1971.

13,260. Callahan, Ola Eugene
Papers. 1948-57. 8 items.
Open. Unpublished guide.
East Carolina University, East Carolina Manuscript Collection.
A North Carolina native, [Miss] Callahan served for nearly 30 years as a Methodist missionary in Mexico. Newsletters from a Methodist school in Pueblo, Mexico, include comments on the life of girls at the school, social conditions in Mexico, religious training, conversions of the girls, and normal work routine.

13,261. Charles, Lucile Marie Hoerr
Papers. 1930-63. 179 items.
Open. Unpublished guide.
East Carolina University, East Carolina Manuscript Collection.
Correspondence, essays, and articles of Charles (1903-65), who was coordinator of a dramatic series for CBS radio during the 1930s; a Fulbright Fellow at the Jung Institute in Zurich, Switzerland, from 1953 to 1955; and a teacher and director of dramatic arts at East Carolina College from 1946 to 1953 and from 1955 to 1965. Correspondence pertains primarily to the CBS radio series "The Land of Plenty," which centered around dramatic presentations concerning food, education, public health, and housing. Also contains an essay on Restoration drama; suggestions regarding drama and dramatic arts at East Carolina College and at New College, Columbia University; and Charles's article "Drama among Primitives and in Our Schools." Charles earned a PhD at Yale University.

13,262. Cooper, Kate (Wheeler)
Papers. 1833-1912. 165 items.
Open. Unpublished guide.
East Carolina University, East Carolina Manuscript Collection.
Cooper (1833-1912) was the daughter of Samuel Jordan Wheeler, a Murfreesboro, NC, physician, and the niece of John Hill Wheeler, an historian, diplomat, and politician. Correspondence pertains to the founding in 1851 of Chowan College in North Carolina; antebellum farm work; life in Baltimore from 1856 to 1858; a religious revival; college life in Washington, DC; social events at the White House during the Buchanan administration; and an attempted Negro uprising in eastern North Carolina in 1860. Postwar correspondence includes references to conditions in New Bern, NC, Washington, DC, and Murfreesboro in 1866; problems with freed slaves; labor shortages; a trip to Washington, DC, and Baltimore; and family activities. Also includes diaries recording school life in Raleigh, NC, in 1854 and life on the home front during the Civil War; financial, family, school, and medical records; and genealogical material.

13,263. Cox, Venetia
Papers. 1917-58. 196 items.
Open. Unpublished guide.
East Carolina University, East Carolina Manuscript Collection.
A native of Pitt County, NC, [Miss] Cox was an Episcopal missionary in China from 1917 to 1950; she taught music at a mission school in Hupei Province until 1937 when the Japanese invasion forced the school to relocate to Kwangsi Province. Correspondence and a diary in which Cox describes her travels in China, missionary work, living conditions, and the war's effect on her work; a narrative recounting the removal in 1938 of Cox's school from Wuchang to western China; photos; a music course book written in Chinese; and clippings concerning Cox's activities. From 1937 to 1950, Cox was forced to wander through the interior of China, traveling at times along the Burma Road.

13,264. Crisp, Lucy Cherry
Papers. 1848-1969. Ca. 2000 items.
Open. Unpublished guide.
East Carolina University, East Carolina Manuscript Collection.
[Miss] Crisp (1899-1977) was a poet, newspaper columnist, and director of the North Carolina State Art Gallery, now the North Carolina Museum of Art. Correspondence with George Washington Carver along with interview notes, clippings, and drafts for a Carver biography; complete file of her newspaper columns; and correspondence, reports, and publications dealing with the North Carolina Museum of Art, art activities in North and South Carolina, and literary works. Correspondents include Carver, Lloyd C. Douglas, Frank Porter Graham, Francis Speight, Claude Howell, Philip Moose, and William Fields.

13,265. End of the Century Book Club
Records. 1899-1968. 95 items.
Open. Unpublished guide.
East Carolina University, East Carolina Manuscript Collection.
Founded in 1899 as the first civic club in Greenville, this women's group helped establish Sheppard Memorial Library and supported other city improvements. Constitution, minutes, correspondence, notes, yearly programs, scrapbook of club activities, eulogies, and miscellaneous items.

13,266. Everett, Sallie Baker
Papers. 1941-61. 512 items.
Open. Unpublished guide.
East Carolina University, East Carolina Manuscript Collection.
Correspondence of [Mrs.] Everett (1888-1975), Democratic national committeewoman from North Carolina from 1952 to 1960, relates to her political and agricultural activities, Democratic Woman's Day in 1946, the 1952 presidential and North Carolina gubernatorial campaigns, plans for Democratic party meetings, and the 1956 and 1960 national Democratic conventions. Also contains discussion of Hurricane Diane, public welfare, and a White House conference on education. Everett was president of the Sir Walter Cabinet for legislators' wives, chairman of the Associated Women of the North Carolina Farm Bureau from 1942 to 1952, vice-chairman of the North Carolina Democratic Executive Committee from 1942 to 1948 and in 1950, manager of the women's campaign for gubernatorial candidate William B. Umstead in 1952, and delegate to the Democratic national conventions in 1952, 1956, and 1960.

13,267. Fletcher, Inglis
Papers. 1883-1964. 33 ft.
Open. No guide.

East Carolina University, East Carolina Manuscript Collection.
Fletcher (1888-1969) was a novelist, lecturer, and world traveler as well as a wife, mother, and grandmother. Correspondence, financial records, notes and drafts for her books, literary manuscripts, galley proofs, articles, speeches, photos, genealogical material, address and day books, clippings, maps, and other papers. Includes items about her literary activities in California, North Carolina, and Washington State; the writing and publication by Bobbs-Merrill Company of her "Carolina Series" of historical novels; travels to Africa and Europe in 1928 and 1929; her participation in the North Carolina Literary and Historical Association, the Roanoke Island Historical Association, and the Tryon Palace Commission; and about her private life.

13,268. Grant, Martin Smith
Papers. 1860-61. 1 vol.
Open. Unpublished guide.
East Carolina University, East Carolina Manuscript Collection.
Diary and observations by Ada Amelia Costin, a 13-year-old schoolgirl, recorded as an exercise in composition, deal primarily with schoolwork, weather, and newspaper accounts. Included are notes on militia organization in Wilmington, NC; troop movements; siege of Fort Sumter; sighting of Union naval vessels at Charleston, SC, and Savannah, GA; battles and skirmishes in Virginia and North Carolina; attempted sabotage of the Wilmington-Weldon Railroad; and Wilmington speeches by Jefferson Davis and Alexander H. Stephens.

13,269. Griffin, Elizabeth Gordan
Papers. 1809-1968. 2 microfilm reels.
Open. Unpublished guide.
East Carolina University, East Carolina Manuscript Collection.
Personal files of [Miss] Griffin, an Episcopal missionary in the Philippines, reflect her missionary work and her internment by the Japanese at Manila during WWII. Other files contain correspondence of the Murphy, Cook, and Griffin families and reminiscences concerning Norfolk, VA, and Elizabeth City, NC. Also includes an Elizabeth City tax book from 1861 to 1866, slave reminiscences, poems, and obituaries.

13,270. Hanks, Clarrisa Phelps
Papers. 1854-64. 2 vols.
Open. Unpublished guide.
East Carolina University, East Carolina Manuscript Collection.
Diaries of Hanks (1822-post 1890) are concerned almost entirely with religious activities in New Bern, NC, particularly with comments relating to church attendance, Bible reading, prayers, and efforts to convert others.

13,271. Hardison, Janice
Papers. 1960-69. 1 cu.ft.
Closed. No guide.
East Carolina University, East Carolina Manuscript Collection.
[Miss] Hardison, an assistant professor of English at East Carolina University, has been active in state Democratic party activities since 1960. Correspondence, reports, clippings, and other items contain material pertaining to state and national election campaigns in North Carolina and include correspondence with most of the state's Democratic party leaders. Hardison was a delegate to the 1960 Democratic National Convention, vice-president of the North Carolina Young Democrats Club in 1960 and 1961, president of the Democratic Women of Pitt County, director of North Carolina Democratic Women's Activities for the First Congressional District, and a member of the party's state executive committee.

13,272. Hoffman, Alice (Green)
Papers. 1911-45. Ca. 12,000 items.
Open. Unpublished guide.
East Carolina University, East Carolina Manuscript Collection.
Daughter of A. W. Green of Green-Joyce Company and a resident of Paris, New York, and Carteret County, NC, Hoffman had business interests in midtown Manhattan and was involved in development of a large dairy herd and other agricultural interests near Bogue Banks, NC. Correspondence, financial records, and other papers document her business activities. Includes correspondence from Paris and Bogue Banks and that relating to her travels to Puerto Rico, China, Egypt, Italy, and other countries. Correspondents include members of the Theodore Roosevelt, Jr., family; various New York legal and financial associates; Edward G. Mathias; Elihu Root; Josiah W. Bailey; and Graham A. Barden. Hoffman was the aunt of Mrs. Theodore Roosevelt, Jr., and a cousin of Ohio Supreme Court Justice Edward G. Mathias.

13,273. Jenkins, Mamie E.
Papers. 1896-1946. 703 items.
Open. Unpublished guide.
East Carolina University, East Carolina Manuscript Collection.
Jenkins (1875-1957) was an English professor at East Carolina College from 1909 to 1946 and served as director of the school's news agency. Correspondence, primarily from members of her family, reflects difficulties during the depression; political patronage of the Roosevelt administrations; life in Harlan, KY; a coal strike in Kentucky in 1931; and shortages of consumer goods because of WWII rationing policies.

13,274. Jerman, Cornelia (Petty)
Papers. 1911-67. 2 vols. and 51 items.
Open. Unpublished guide.
East Carolina University, East Carolina Manuscript Collection.
Correspondence, clippings, and other papers of Jerman (1874-1946), who was assistant collector of internal revenue for North Carolina from 1934 to 1939, a Democratic party officer, and a women's club official. Correspondence deals with women's suffrage, the 1928 Democratic National Convention, Jerman's selection for the Democratic National Committee in 1928, and her support for the presidential campaign of Alfred E. Smith. Scrapbooks contain clippings relating to her life, particularly to women's suffrage, women's club administration, politics, internal revenue, and honors she received. Jerman was president of the North Carolina Federation of Women's Clubs, the State Legislative Council, and the Wake County LWV; organizer of the Raleigh, NC, Equal Suffrage League in 1920; delegate to national Democratic conventions in 1924 and 1928; and a member of the Democratic National Committee from 1928 to 1934.

13,275. Johnson, Kate Ancrum (Burr)
Papers. 1919-68. 37 items.
Open. Unpublished guide.
East Carolina University, East Carolina Manuscript Collection.
[Mrs.] Johnson (1881-1968) served as director of child welfare of the North Carolina Board of Charities and Public Welfare from 1919 to 1921, as North Carolina commissioner of public welfare from 1921 to 1930, as superintendent of the New Jersey State Home for Girls from 1930 to 1948, and as a member of the North Carolina Prison Advisory Committee from 1948 to 1953. Correspondence, speeches, and articles reflect her work in the North Carolina Federation of Women's Clubs and her interest in public works, state homes for girls, delinquency among girls, state welfare programs, the North Carolina prison system, and the Lindbergh kidnap case.

13,276. Kelly, Lorena
Papers. 1922-69. Ca. 450 items.
Open. Unpublished guide.
East Carolina University, East Carolina Manuscript Collection.
A Methodist missionary to the central Congo for more than 30 years, [Miss] Kelly was dean of the home economics department at Congo Polytechnique Institute; she established a home economics school and a junior high school while she was stationed at Lodja and at Wembo Nyama. Correspondence, reports, pamphlets, newsletters, clippings, and oral history tapes provide detailed descriptions of her passage to Belgium; life in Brussels and Antwerp; African villages, their people, and food; native customs; mission schools; and travels in Africa. Contains information concerning the Congolese rebellion of 1960 to 1963 with accounts of the evacuation of the Central Congo Conference to Rhodesia, mission work in Rhodesia, and conditions in Leopoldville from 1961 to 1963 following the missionaries' return to the Congo. An expert in the Otetela language, Kelly wrote a textbook in the language. She was a native of Mount Mourne, NC.

13,277. Knox, Dorothy Rapiton
Papers. 1917-72. 6 cu.ft.
Open. Unpublished guide.
East Carolina University, East Carolina Manuscript Collection.
[Miss] Knox (1896-) was an American National Red Cross volunteer in Charlotte, NC, during WWI who later became a journalist and columnist for the *Charlotte Observer.* Correspondence, columns, photos, scrapbook pamphlets, clippings, cartoons, and magazines. Includes WWI correspondence describing camp life, training, and diseases in the US; the voyage across the Atlantic; Army camps in England and France; airplane flights; the death of Baron Von Richthofen; medical treatment of the wounded; combat area experiences near Verdun; the occupation of Germany; and impressions of the German people. Later files deal primarily with Knox's work at the *Charlotte Observer* and include columns written over a 40-year period, which depict social life in the Carolinas.

13,278. Littleton College Memorial Association
Records. 1906-69. 112 items.
Open. Unpublished guide.
East Carolina University, East Carolina Manuscript Collection.
Littleton College in Littleton, NC, was a private Methodist female college that operated from 1882 until 1919 when it was destroyed by fire. Includes correspondence of students and former students, alumnae lists, news releases, bulletins, programs, and clippings concerning the college, the Association, class reunions, and alumnae. Included are letters from a missionary in Japan who tells of her missionary life there.

13,279. Murray, Katie
Papers. 1927-63. 357 items.
Open. Unpublished guide.
East Carolina University, East Carolina Manuscript Collection.
A native of Duplin County, NC, [Miss] Murray was a missionary to China from 1927 to 1950 and to Taiwan from 1954 to 1959. Correspondence, diaries, reports, and other papers document Murray's career; the largest segment consists of annual evangelistic reports for the Chengchow mission field and correspondence of Murray with the Foreign Mission Board. Includes references to Chinese social practices and customs, individual and group conversions, and religious activities of Protestant missionaries. Other letters and diaries describe the Japanese invasion and occupation of Tsining, Kaifeng, and Chengchow; the Chinese civil war; conditions under the Chinese Communists in Kwangsi Province; and life on Formosa. Murray

was involved in refugee relief work from 1938 until 1944 when she fled to Siam. She returned to China in 1946 and worked there until the Chinese Communists forced her to leave in 1950. She completed her missionary service on Taiwan.

13,280. Parham, Catherine
Papers. 1920-72. Ca. 550 items.
Open. Unpublished guide.
East Carolina University, East Carolina Manuscript Collection.
[Miss] Parham (1901-) of Durand, GA, worked in church-centered social work in West Virginia's coal region from 1925 to 1931 before beginning 28 years of service as a Methodist missionary in the Belgian Congo. Correspondence, reports, and newsletters reflect missionary activities in the Congo with detailed descriptions of travel in Africa, native life, chieftains, villages, customs, and dress. Also included is Parham's master's thesis concerning Christian education for the Central African community, which was written in 1944 at Hartford Seminary in Hartford, CT, and commentaries concerning the impact of international problems on missionary work, the attitude of the Belgian government toward US missionaries, conditions in the Congo during the independence turmoil of 1960 and 1961, and African political developments during the entire period. Stationed at Elizabethville from 1945 until 1958, Parham headed a teacher-training program for young women. She returned to the Congo in 1968 and 1969 while translating a children's Bible into Swahili.

13,281. Parker, Minnie B.
Papers. 1839-1934. 34 items.
Open. Unpublished guide.
East Carolina University, East Carolina Manuscript Collection.
Collection centers around a WWI scrapbook of Parker, a US Army nurse. The scrapbook includes letters, military orders, Army forms, poems, a list of patients, work permits, and other items relating to American forces in France.

13,282. Pratt, Jane
Papers. 1946. 1 microfilm reel.
Open. Unpublished guide.
East Carolina University, East Carolina Manuscript Collection.
The only woman to represent North Carolina in the US Congress, [Miss] Pratt was elected from the Eighth District to complete the term of William O. Burgin, who died in 1946; she had been the secretary for the district's congressmen since 1924. Scrapbooks reflect her year in Congress and include letters of congratulation, press releases, photos, and clippings. Correspondents include Robert Lee Doughton, Clyde R. Hoey, Josiah W. Bailey, John W. McCormack, W. Kerr Scott, and William B. Umstead. Pratt was a native of Anson County, NC.

13,283. Reid, Sabrie W.
Papers. 1943-70. 2 cu.ft.
Open. Unpublished guide.
East Carolina University, East Carolina Manuscript Collection.
Involved in the public school lunch program from its earliest days, [Mrs.] Reid was director of special food services for the North Carolina state department of public instruction food services division from 1947 to 1970. Correspondence, evaluation records, reports, manuals, regulations, and other papers pertain to the state's public school lunchroom program.

13,284. Reitz, Beulah M.
Papers. 1922-36. Ca. 275 items.
Open. Unpublished guide.
East Carolina University, East Carolina Manuscript Collection.
[Miss] Reitz, a native of Kansas and graduate of Baker University in Baldwin City, KS, served from 1922 to 1955 as a Methodist missionary in South Rhodesia. Correspondence written from Umtali and Mutambara from 1922 to 1926 makes up the bulk of the collection. Included are detailed descriptions of native life and customs and the operation of missionary schools, a dispensary, and an orphanage. Contains accounts of incidents involving mission children, the tribal practice of selling daughters into marriage, witchcraft, illnesses, wedding ceremonies, camp meetings, and problems with missionaries of the Church of England.

13,285. Rives, Blanche Hardee
Papers. 1905-73. Ca. 500 items.
Open. Unpublished guide.
East Carolina University, East Carolina Manuscript Collection.
Rives (1887-1973) was a civic, cultural, religious, and club leader. Correspondence, minutes, photos, programs, pamphlets, and clippings pertain to home demonstration work; Littleton College, a private Methodist-related women's college that burned in 1919; the Methodist Protestant Church; the United Daughters of the Confederacy; and other topics.

13,286. Spilman, Johnetta Webb
Papers. 1932-69. 452 items.
Open. Unpublished guide.
East Carolina University, East Carolina Manuscript Collection.
A native of Chowan County, NC, [Mrs.] Spilman has held various state government positions, including commissioner of the North Carolina Unemployment Compensation Commission. Correspondence pertaining to Democratic party politics in the 1930s, the 1936 presidential and North Carolina gubernatorial elections, and the influence of women in these campaigns; speeches concerning the Unemployment Compensation Commission, social security, and North Carolina women; scrapbooks containing correspondence dealing with Spilman's career and Democratic party work; oral history tapes; and miscellaneous items, including press releases, invitations, and banquet programs. Spilman served as assistant treasurer of East Carolina College, commissioner of the Unemployment Compensation Commission from 1936 to 1941, manager of the Greenville Employment Security Commission from 1942 to 1944, executive director of the Pitt County Tuberculosis Association from 1950 to 1957, director of the North Carolina Mental Health Association from 1957 to 1968, and vice-chairman of the state Democratic executive committee.

13,287. Stanley, Abigail Brothers
Papers. Nd. 25-page item.
Open. Unpublished guide.
East Carolina University, East Carolina Manuscript Collection.
Memoir of Stanley concentrates on the social and cultural history of Pasquotank County, NC, during the last half of the 19th century. Includes Civil War information concerning the hiding of men in swamps and woods and information about education, religion, attitudes toward witchcraft and ghosts, economic activities, horse stealing, and Brothers family genealogy.

13,288. Taynton, Susan (Herring) Jeffries
Papers. 1896-1964. 270 items.
Open. Unpublished guide.
East Carolina University, East Carolina Manuscript Collection.
Born in China, Taynton was the daughter of David Wells Herring (1858-1940), a Baptist missionary considered controversial and outspoken; Taynton wrote a biography *Papa Wore No Halo* (1960) dealing with her father's career in China. Correspondence, photos, pamphlets, and clippings concerning missionary work in China and publication of the biography. Included are commentaries on theology, the Southern Baptist Foreign Missionary Board, Australia, the Boxer Rebellion, and the problems of writing and publishing.

13,289. Utterback, Elizabeth
Papers. 1923-65. 161 items.
Open. Unpublished guide.
East Carolina University, East Carolina Manuscript Collection.
An educator, poet, and short story writer, Martha Elizabeth Utterback (1904-66) was a member of the East Carolina College English faculty from 1950 until her death. More than 100 of her poems, short stories, and plays; manuscript for an unpublished novel; various reports, including a study of the regional elements in 11 plays of the south; book reviews; and college themes and essays. Utterback's poems and short stories were published in several US periodicals. She earned a doctorate in education at Columbia University.

13,290. Wolcott, Jessie L.
Papers. 1939-50. 90 items.
Open. Unpublished guide.
East Carolina University, East Carolina Manuscript Collection.
An Iowa native, [Miss] Wolcott was a Methodist missionary in Nanking, China, for most of the period from 1922 to 1951. Correspondence, travel accounts, and other papers. The bulk of the correspondence, dating from 1939 to 1942, contains descriptions of mission-related activities, economic conditions in and around Nanking, and conditions under Japanese occupation. From 1946 to 1950, Wolcott wrote letters describing the effect of growing inflation under the Nationalists and the US Army's impact on missionary activities. Also included are travel accounts from 1948 that provide information about areas untouched by the Sino-Japanese War and those that were under Japanese control. Wolcott was forced to leave Nanking in 1937, returned in 1939, and was evacuated again in 1941. She returned to Nanking for the last time in 1946 and remained there until the Chinese Communists occupied the city in 1951.

13,291. Zicafoose and O'Toole
Papers. 1931-35. 3 vols. and 16 items.
Open. Unpublished guide.
East Carolina University, East Carolina Manuscript Collection.
[Miss] Myrtle Zicafoose and [Miss] Ruth O'Toole are Methodist missionaries who served in a leper colony in the Congo from 1931 until 1960. Correspondence and reports include discussions of native life and customs, the Wembo Nyama school, efforts to Christianize the natives, missionary educational activities, and the work at the Minga Leper Colony; albums contain photos illustrating the life of African women, African scenes, missionary work, and illnesses that afflicted the natives.

HIGH POINT

13,292. Dalton, Frances
Papers. Nd. No size given.
Open. No guide.
High Point Museum.
Family photo album, a daguerreotype, First Presbyterian Church mementos and furniture collected by Dalton, the granddaughter of Presbyterian minister Pleasant Hunter Dalton (1821-96), the first minister to live in High Point.

13,293. High Point Garden Club
Records. 1900-75. 6 boxes.
Closed. No guide.
High Point Museum.
Founded in 1900, the Club was the city's first chartered garden club. Minutes of monthly meetings; photos of members, many of whom were

prominent in the community; scrapbooks; and clippings. Also includes personal announcements concerning births, marriages, and deaths in members' families.

LAKE JUNALUSKA

13,294. Board of Global Ministries, Division of World Missions
Records. 19th and 20th centuries. Ca. 4,000,000 items.
Partially restricted. Unpublished guide.
United Methodist Church, Commission on Archives and History.
Founded in 1819 as the Board of Missions of the Methodist Episcopal Church, the Board sponsors missionaries in more than 60 countries. Minutes, financial reports, correspondence, photos, and other records. Includes correspondence and other papers of married and single women missionaries. Among the many women represented are Anna King, missionary in North Africa, 1948-49; [Miss] Mellony Turner, missionary in Bulgaria, 1937-49; [Miss] Ellen Bjorklund, missionary in Rhodesia, 1917-31; [Miss] Bertha Griffin, missionary in Brazil, 1922-25; [Miss] Edith J. Christensen, missionary in Burma, 1926-27; and Mrs. Lyman Hale, who with her clergyman husband was a missionary in China, 1915-39.

13,295. Evangelical United Brethren Church, Board of Missions
Records. 1850-1968. Ca. 250,000 items.
Access restricted. No guide.
United Methodist Church, Commission on Archives and History.
Minutes, fiscal records, missionaries' correspondence, reports, and other records of the Board include records of the Woman's Society of World Service. The Board assigned single and married women missionaries to the mission field. Contains records of similar organizations in the following predecessors of the EUB Church: United Brethren in Christ, Evangelical Association, United Evangelical, and the Evangelical churches.

13,296. Women and Women's Work
Collection. Ca. 1850- . Ca. 450 vols.
Open. Unpublished guide.
United Methodist Church, Commission on Archives and History.
Consists primarily of books and periodicals but also includes minutes, histories, reports, and other records of agencies within the United Methodist Church and its predecessor denominations that were concerned with women's missionary work. The denominations represented include Methodist Protestant, Methodist Episcopal, Methodist Episcopal (South), Methodist Church, United Brethren in Christ, Evangelical Association, United Evangelical, Evangelical Church, Evangelical United Brethren, and United Methodist.

MARS HILL

13,297. Baptist History
Collection. 1835- . 70 boxes.
Open. Unpublished guide.
Mars Hill College Library.
Minutes, roll books, correspondence, and scrapbooks of Baptist associations of western North Carolina. Includes minutes and a scrapbook of the Women's Missionary Society of the Mars Hill Baptist Church; minutes of the Women's Missionary Union of the French Broad Baptist Association, 1911-46; a program from the 1887 convention of the WCTU of North Carolina; a scrapbook of the Mars Hill WCTU, 1954; and scattered issues of guidebooks of the Women's Missionary Union of North Carolina.

13,298. Lunsford, Bascom Lamar
Papers. 1900- . 20 Hollinger boxes.
Open. Published guide.
Mars Hill College Library.
Correspondence, diaries, typescripts, manuscripts, photos, and scrapbooks of Lunsford (1882-1973), a collector and performer of folk music. Includes correspondence of his daughters Azalea Lunsford and Jennie Louise Lunsford (1875-1966), a diary for 1903 to 1907 of Jennie Lunsford and a biography of Jennie Edwards, a mother, teacher, and missionary. See *North Carolina Folklore Journal,* vol. XXV, no. 1 (May 1977).

13,299. Madison County
Collection. Ca. 1880- . 3 boxes, 6 tapes, and other items.
Access restricted. No guide.
Mars Hill College Library.
Personal papers, college records, oral history tapes, notes, and other papers of Madison County women, including teachers, businesswomen, housewives, a college dean of women, and others. The papers deal with the women's individual experiences and contributions to the community.

13,300. Mars Hill College Archives
Records. 1856- . 48 Hollinger boxes.
Open. Unpublished guide.
Mars Hill College Library.
Founded in 1856, the College was a Baptist-affiliated junior college until 1962 when it began to offer a full four-year program. Correspondence, roll books, manuscripts, photos, clippings, and other records of the College. Includes minutes, photos, and programs of Clio, a women's literary society; papers of Ella J. Pierce concerning descendants of the College's founders; an unpublished manuscript on the life of Jesus by Abbie Benton Bonsteel; an unpublished master's thesis by Margaret Bridges about the educational philosophy of Southern Baptists as reflected at Mars Hill College; papers of Caroline Biggers, a housemother who in 1922 led students in prayer to obtain additional land for the College; and correspondence of Gladys Johnson from 1938 to 1944 concerning the establishment of a public library in Madison County.

13,301. Paxton, Nina Llyr Margaret
Papers. 1937-70. 1 Hollinger box.
Open. Unpublished guide.
Mars Hill College Library.
Correspondence, clippings, and other papers of Paxton, a nurse and amateur radio operator in Ashland, KY, who reported that she received radio distress calls from Amelia Earhart in 1937. Paxton asserted that Earhart landed safely on an island and remained alive for at least a month. Her statements brought little response from the news media.

NEWTON

13,302. Eaton, Dorothy Ervin
Papers. 1920-70. 4 ft.
Open. Unpublished guide.
Catawba County Historical Museum.
[Mrs.] Eaton (1920-70) was an educator, musician, historian, and civic leader in Chicago and in Catawba County, NC. Correspondence, writings, and scrapbooks mirror her interests in opera, literature, North Carolina wildflowers, local history, and fashion. Includes correspondence with her pupils and family.

13,303. Garden Clubs
Records. 1944-65. 3 ft.
Open. No guide.
Catawba County Historical Museum.
Minutes of various garden clubs in the Newton-Conover, NC, area and scrapbooks of photos and clippings about completed projects.

13,304. Thursday Book Club
Records. 1939-60. 2 ft.
Open. No guide.
Catawba County Historical Museum.
The Club was a Newton-Conover, NC, area literary study society that existed from 1939 to 1960. Minutes and scrapbooks.

RALEIGH

13,305. Abrahams, Grace C.
Papers. Nd. 5 items.
Open. Published guide.
North Carolina Division of Archives and History.
Poems by [Mrs.] Abrahams. Taken from Catherine E. Thompson, *A Selective Guide to Women-Related Records in the North Carolina State Archives* (Raleigh, NC: North Carolina Division of Archives and History, 1977).

13,306. African Twins
Papers. 1855-1912. 15 items.
Open. Published guide.
North Carolina Division of Archives and History.
Letter, notes, photo, broadsides, and clippings concerning Mille-Christine, Negro Siamese twins born in Columbus County, NC, and exhibited in the US and abroad. The twins were vocalists. Taken from Catherine E. Thompson, *A Selective Guide to Women-Related Records in the North Carolina State Archives* (Raleigh, NC: North Carolina Division of Archives and History, 1977).

13,307. Albers, Anni
Papers. 1937-66. 30 items.
Open. Published guide.
North Carolina Division of Archives and History.
[Mrs. Josef] Albers was a textile designer and from 1933 to 1949 assistant professor of art at Black Mountain College near Black Mountain, NC. Biographical notes; speeches on the founding of Black Mountain College and on weaving and textile work there; booklets, leaflets, and articles on the art of pictorial weaving as seen in Albers's work; and clippings on her exhibitions and her views on design. Taken from Catherine E. Thompson, *A Selective Guide to Women-Related Records in the North Carolina State Archives* (Raleigh, NC: North Carolina Division of Archives and History, 1977).

13,308. Albright and Dixon
Papers. 1789-1933. 36 items.
Open. Published guide.
North Carolina Division of Archives and History.
Collection contains letters, 1838-48, of Hannah and Sarah Dixon from Ohio and Indiana to William Albright in North Carolina concerning education and finances, an 1843 article of agreement by Sarah Hubbard to teach "common English school," and an article entitled "Stages of a Woman's Life from the Cradle to the Grave." Taken from Catherine E. Thompson, *A Selective Guide to Women-Related Records in the North Carolina State Archives* (Raleigh, NC: North Carolina Division of Archives and History, 1977).

13,309. Alderman, Jacob Oliver
Papers. 1907-54. 8 items.
Open. Published guide.
North Carolina Division of Archives and History.
Includes an essay by teacher Kate Fleetwood describing Moonlight schools, a program for illiterate adults in the 1910s, and commenting on the changing sentiments about the importance of education for women. Taken from Catherine E. Thompson, *A Selective Guide to Women-Related Records in the North Carolina State Archives*

(Raleigh, NC: North Carolina Division of Archives and History, 1977).

13,310. Allen Family
Papers. 1756-1877. Ca. 235 items.
Open. Published guide.
North Carolina Division of Archives and History.
Includes medical recipes attributed to Rachel Stout Allen for curing cancer, consumption, and other diseases. Collection is also available on microfilm. Taken from Catherine E. Thompson, *A Selective Guide to Women-Related Records in the North Carolina State Archives* (Raleigh, NC: North Carolina Division of Archives and History, 1977).

13,311. Allison, Panthea Sharpe
Papers. 1818-56. 1 item.
Open. Published guide.
North Carolina Division of Archives and History.
Record of babies delivered in Iredell County, NC, from 1818 to 1856 by Allison, a midwife. Taken from Catherine E. Thompson, *A Selective Guide to Women-Related Records in the North Carolina State Archives* (Raleigh, NC: North Carolina Division of Archives and History, 1977).

13,312. Alston and DeGraffenried Family
Papers. 1773-1970. Ca. 375 items.
Open. Published guide.
North Carolina Division of Archives and History.
Family correspondence; early 19th-century accounts of Mrs. John DeGraffenried for food, household, and farm expenses; and issues of *Frank Leslie's lady's Magazine* for 1867 to 1869 and of *Lady's Friend, A Monthly Magazine of Literature and Fashion* for 1867. Taken from Catherine E. Thompson, *A Selective Guide to Women-Related Records in the North Carolina State Archives* (Raleigh, NC: North Carolina Division of Archives and History, 1977).

13,313. American Association of Social Workers
Records. 1932-62. 25 boxes.
Open. Published guide.
North Carolina Division of Archives and History.
Constitution, charter, minutes, correspondence, membership lists, reports, committee material, program summaries, newsletter, bulletins, and other records of the North Carolina chapter of the organization. Taken from Catherine E. Thompson, *A Selective Guide to Women-Related Records in the North Carolina State Archives* (Raleigh, NC: North Carolina Division of Archives and History, 1977).

13,314. American Association of University Women
Records. 1915-67. 6 boxes.
Open. Published guide.
North Carolina Division of Archives and History.
Constitution, bylaws, minutes, financial records, membership lists, a history, publicity material, state convention material, scrapbook, newsletters, and yearbooks of the Raleigh branch of the AAUW. Taken from Catherine E. Thompson, *A Selective Guide to Women-Related Records in the North Carolina State Archives* (Raleigh, NC: North Carolina Division of Archives and History, 1977).

13,315. American Legion Auxiliary
Records. 1919-42. 12 boxes and 3 vols.
Open. Published guide.
North Carolina Division of Archives and History.
Charters, minutes, membership applications, a history, citations, and other records of Raleigh Post No. 1 of the Auxiliary. Taken from Catherine E. Thompson, *A Selective Guide to Women-Related Records in the North Carolina State Archives* (Raleigh, NC: North Carolina Division of Archives and History, 1977).

13,316. American War Mothers
Records. 1919-26. 9 boxes and 1 vol.
Open. Published guide.
North Carolina Division of Archives and History.
Registration books, membership applications, and scrapbooks of the organization. Taken from Catherine E. Thompson, *A Selective Guide to Women-Related Records in the North Carolina State Archives* (Raleigh, NC: North Carolina Division of Archives and History, 1977).

13,317. Anna Jackson Book Club
Records. 1900-68. 3 boxes.
Open. Published guide.
North Carolina Division of Archives and History.
Minutes, a scrapbook, and a book of this Lincolnton, NC, club. Taken from Catherine E. Thompson, *A Selective Guide to Women-Related Records in the North Carolina State Archives* (Raleigh, NC: North Carolina Division of Archives and History, 1977).

13,318. Arendell, Banks
Papers. 1917-20. 44 items.
Open. Published guide.
North Carolina Division of Archives and History.
Includes a speech urging a committee to support equal suffrage and broadsides asking women to vote for Cox and Roosevelt. Taken from Catherine E. Thompson, *A Selective Guide to Women-Related Records in the North Carolina State Archives* (Raleigh, NC: North Carolina Division of Archives and History, 1977).

13,319. Ashe, Samuel A'Court
Papers. 1735-1940. Ca. 700 items.
Open. Published guide.
North Carolina Division of Archives and History.
Includes correspondence of the Miller and Land families, an 1884 letter from Cornelia (Phillips) Spencer to Ashe, and letters from Adelaide L. Fries to Ashe in 1894 concerning her work on prominent North Carolina colonial women. Taken from Catherine E. Thompson, *A Selective Guide to Women-Related Records in the North Carolina State Archives* (Raleigh, NC: North Carolina Division of Archives and History, 1977).

13,320. Athenian Literary Society and Young Tar Heel Farmers
Records. 1912-30. 1 box.
Open. Published guide.
North Carolina Division of Archives and History.
Includes minutes of the Literary Society of Troy High School in Montgomery County, NC, for the years 1914 to 1919. Taken from Catherine E. Thompson, *A Selective Guide to Women-Related Records in the North Carolina State Archives* (Raleigh, NC: North Carolina Division of Archives and History, 1977).

13,321. Atkins, James W.
Papers. 1814-1909. 3 vols. and 37 items.
Open. Published guide.
North Carolina Division of Archives and History.
Diaries of Atkins, who taught at Asheville Female College in Asheville, NC, from 1879 to 1894 and at Athens Female College in Athens, TN, from 1898 to 1899, contain information about the schools and students. Also included are annual catalogs of Asheville Female College, 1879-96. Taken from Catherine E. Thompson, *A Selective Guide to Women-Related Records in the North Carolina State Archives* (Raleigh, NC: North Carolina Division of Archives and History, 1977).

13,322. Audiovisual
Collection. Nd. No size given.
Open. Published guide.
North Carolina Division of Archives and History.
Includes a movie on ladies' fashions from the 1770s to the 1930s; a movie of an interview with parachutist Tiny Broadwick; and a videotape on the General Assembly, which contains a segment on the defeat of the Equal Rights Amendment in the North Carolina Senate in 1977 with scenes of women opponents arguing with Senator Carl D. Totherow, an interview with Senator John Winters, and excerpts from speeches on the Senate floor in support of the ERA. Sound recordings include public hearings held in 1971 by the Joint Committee on Higher Education with remarks by Cathy Sterling, former student body president of North Carolina State University and testimony, public hearings, and statements by opponents and proponents of the ERA in 1977 before the Constitutional Amendments Committees of the North Carolina House and Senate. Tapes of interviews with elderly North Carolinians about the history and growth of the state include several conducted in 1958 and 1959 with such persons as Aunt Harriet Parker, who was born in slavery and discusses plantation life; with [Mrs.] Ivey Allen, a graduate of Louisburg College and former teacher; with [Mrs.] Elvira T. White, who recites poems and discusses the Civil War, 19th-century life, and Quaker schools and churches in the Albemarle region; with [Mrs.] Narcissa Nicholson Rickman, who talks of schools, farming, religion, social life, and the Civil War; with Mrs. Sterling Gary, who describes her childhood and the Civil War era; and with Mrs. J. L. Gilbert, who talks about the early home life of her mother [Mrs.] Margaret Tucker. Also included is a 1969 interview with Mrs. John R. May concerning carding and spinning cotton. Taken from Catherine E. Thompson, *A Selective Guide to Women-Related Records in the North Carolina State Archives* (Raleigh, NC: North Carolina Division of Archives and History, 1977).

13,323. Aycock, Charles Brantley
Papers. 1880-1959. 5 vols. and ca. 900 items.
Open. Published guide.
North Carolina Division of Archives and History.
Papers of Aycock's wife include a letter from Governor Broughton concerning her appointment as president of the board of directors of the North Carolina Railroad Company. Charles Aycock was governor of North Carolina from 1901 to 1905. Taken from Catherine E. Thompson, *A Selective Guide to Women-Related Records in the North Carolina State Archives* (Raleigh, NC: North Carolina Division of Archives and History, 1977).

13,324. Badgett
Papers. 1777-1889. 394 items.
Open. Published guide.
North Carolina Division of Archives and History.
Letters by Thomas J. Badgett, 1859-61, while at the University of Pennsylvania include comments on the attitude there toward women medical students. Taken from Catherine E. Thompson, *A Selective Guide to Women-Related Records in the North Carolina State Archives* (Raleigh, NC: North Carolina Division of Archives and History, 1977).

13,325. Baker Family
Papers. 1847. 1 item.
Open. Published guide.
North Carolina Division of Archives and History.
Recollections of the Baker family by physician Simmons Jones Baker include accounts of the marriages of his daughters. Taken from Catherine E. Thompson, *A Selective Guide to Women-Related Records in the North Carolina State Archives* (Raleigh, NC: North Carolina Division of Archives and History, 1977).

13,326. Ballentine, L. Y.
Papers. 1941-66. Ca. 3000 items.
Open. Published guide.
North Carolina Division of Archives and History.
Includes material relating to the 1959 expansion program for Meredith College, a women's college in Raleigh, NC. Taken from Catherine E. Thompson, *A Selective Guide to Women-Related Records in the North Carolina State Archives*

(Raleigh, NC: North Carolina Division of Archives and History, 1977).

13,327. Barringer, Paul B.
Papers. 1800-65. 1 item.
Open. Published guide.
North Carolina Division of Archives and History.
Reminiscences of Barringer include recollections of family member Mrs. Thomas J. "Stonewall" Jackson. Taken from Catherine E. Thompson, *A Selective Guide to Women-Related Records in the North Carolina State Archives* (Raleigh, NC: North Carolina Division of Archives and History, 1977).

13,328. Bauman, Mrs. Albert
Papers. 1754-1855. 1 box.
Open. Published guide.
North Carolina Division of Archives and History.
Includes an 1868 commencement program from Louisburg Female College in Louisburg, NC. Taken from Catherine E. Thompson, *A Selective Guide to Women-Related Records in the North Carolina State Archives* (Raleigh, NC: North Carolina Division of Archives and History, 1977).

13,329. Bell, J. E.
Papers. 1809-71. 1 microfilm reel.
Open. Published guide.
North Carolina Division of Archives and History.
Accounts of Bell, principal of Lincolnton Female Academy, include records of school expenses, tuition fees, payments in merchandise and services by parents and guardians, and a list of books lent. Taken from Catherine E. Thompson, *A Selective Guide to Women-Related Records in the North Carolina State Archives* (Raleigh, NC: North Carolina Division of Archives and History, 1977).

13,330. Bell, Thomas
Papers. 1836-1909. 419 items.
Open. Published guide.
North Carolina Division of Archives and History.
Includes letters, 1880-94, to Minnie Bell from schoolmates at Oxford Female Seminary in Oxford, NC, containing reminiscences and reports of current activities. Bell later married a Mr. Ballentine. Taken from Catherine E. Thompson, *A Selective Guide to Women-Related Records in the North Carolina State Archives* (Raleigh, NC: North Carolina Division of Archives and History, 1977).

13,331. Besson and Linehan Family
Papers. 1849-1967. 250 items.
Open. Published guide.
North Carolina Division of Archives and History.
Family correspondence, much of it in French; reminiscences by Babette Zeigler of her journey to America and marriage; photos; reports from schools in Raleigh and France; and a brochure concerning Mrs. Crosby Adams, a musician. Includes an 1866 letter from Caroline to her mother Babette Besson concerning management of the family business and letters to Marie Besson Linehan from her sister Caroline Besson Neatherry in South Carolina. Also included are minutes, 1915-17, and bulletins of the Alliance Francaise of Raleigh, a branch of La Federation de l'Alliance Francaise aux Etats-Unis et au Canada which was organized in 1915 to encourage study of the language, literature, art, and history of France. Taken from Catherine E. Thompson, *A Selective Guide to Women-Related Records in the North Carolina State Archives* (Raleigh, NC: North Carolina Division of Archives and History, 1977).

13,332. Bishop, W. D.
Papers. 1861-71. 11 items.
Open. Published guide.
North Carolina Division of Archives and History.
Includes a poem by Pauline Elders "composed for a friend in affliction" in 1871. Taken from Catherine E. Thompson, *A Selective Guide to Women-Related Records in the North Carolina State Archives* (Raleigh, NC: North Carolina Division of Archives and History, 1977).

13,333. Black Mountain College.
Records. 1933-56. 157 boxes, 21 vols., and 1 microfilm reel.
Partially restricted. Published guide.
North Carolina Division of Archives and History.
The College was an independent, four-year coeducational college near Black Mountain, NC, which was founded in 1933 and closed in 1956. Certificate of incorporation, bylaws, minutes, treasurer's files, financial records, correspondence, subject files, photos, a history of arts at the College, and student records, including admission material, transcripts, evaluations, rejected and withdrawn files, fees material and correspondence about financial matters, and cards reporting students' work in individual classes. Faculty files contain correspondence and records concerning faculty members, including Mary Gregory, who taught art and woodworking, designed furniture, and managed the college farm; Natasha Goldowski, a former ballet dancer and acrobat who became an internationally known physicist; Flola Shepard, linguistics specialist who was active in civil rights causes; and Nell Rice, college librarian and first wife of John Rice. Parts of the collection are available on microfilm. Taken from Catherine E. Thompson, *A Selective Guide to Women-Related Records in the North Carolina State Archives* (Raleigh, NC: North Carolina Division of Archives and History, 1977).

13,334. Blair, John Jay
Papers. 1923-27. 2 boxes.
Open. Published guide.
North Carolina Division of Archives and History.
Includes letters from Ruth Huntington Moore and [Mrs.] Katherine Pendleton Arrington concerning their interest in and activities relating to art and a resolution from the Raleigh Woman's Club giving support to the North Carolina Art Society. Taken from Catherine E. Thompson, *A Selective Guide to Women-Related Records in the North Carolina State Archives* (Raleigh, NC: North Carolina Division of Archives and History, 1977).

13,335. Blair, Roberta
Papers. 1944. 23 items.
Open. Published guide.
North Carolina Division of Archives and History.
Letters from Blair, a summer student at Black Mountain College near Black Mountain, NC, to her mother relate her impressions of the College, students, and professors. Also included are photos and slides of herself, professors, and students. Taken from Catherine E. Thompson, *A Selective Guide to Women-Related Records in the North Carolina State Archives* (Raleigh, NC: North Carolina Division of Archives and History, 1977).

13,336. Blake, Bennett T.
Papers. 1863-1919. 108 items.
Open. Published guide.
North Carolina Division of Archives and History.
Includes letters to her family from Laura Doub, a WWI army nurse, relating to hospital life and social activities in France and Germany. Taken from Catherine E. Thompson, *A Selective Guide to Women-Related Records in the North Carolina State Archives* (Raleigh, NC: North Carolina Division of Archives and History, 1977).

13,337. Blaylock, J. B.
Papers. Nd. 1 microfilm reel.
Open. Published guide.
North Carolina Division of Archives and History.
Material relates to United Daughters of the Confederacy memorials. Taken from Catherine E. Thompson, *A Selective Guide to Women-Related Records in the North Carolina State Archives* (Raleigh, NC: North Carolina Division of Archives and History, 1977).

13,338. Blount, John Gray
Papers. 1706-1933. Ca. 9000 items.
Open. Published guide.
North Carolina Division of Archives and History.
Family correspondence includes a few letters from Ann Harvey discussing family news, farming, finances, and social events. Taken from Catherine E. Thompson, *A Selective Guide to Women-Related Records in the North Carolina State Archives* (Raleigh, NC: North Carolina Division of Archives and History, 1977).

13,339. Bolles, Charles Pattison
Papers. 1845-1922. Ca. 575 items.
Open. Published guide.
North Carolina Division of Archives and History.
Papers of Bolles, a Wilmington, NC, banker, include family correspondence, a letter from astronomer Maria Mitchell concerning scientific instruments and equations, and reminiscences by his wife Maria DuBrutz Reston Bolles about her activities as the young wife of a banker during the Civil War. Taken from Catherine E. Thompson, *A Selective Guide to Women-Related Records in the North Carolina State Archives* (Raleigh, NC: North Carolina Division of Archives and History, 1977).

13,340. Boner, John Henry
Papers. 1869-1914. 15 items.
Open. Published guide.
North Carolina Division of Archives and History.
Includes a poem by Henry Jerome Stockard concerning women and the Civil War, which was read at the 1914 unveiling of a monument to women of the Confederacy on the state capitol grounds. Taken from Catherine E. Thompson, *A Selective Guide to Women-Related Records in the North Carolina State Archives* (Raleigh, NC: North Carolina Division of Archives and History, 1977).

13,341. Bonitz, Fred W.
Papers. 1917-21. 1 microfilm reel.
Open. Published guide.
North Carolina Division of Archives and History.
Diary of [Mrs.] Mary E. Bonitz of Goldsboro, NC. Taken from Catherine E. Thompson, *A Selective Guide to Women-Related Records in the North Carolina State Archives* (Raleigh, NC: North Carolina Division of Archives and History, 1977).

13,342. Boon, James
Papers. 1829-53. 192 items.
Open. Published guide.
North Carolina Division of Archives and History.
Includes letters to Boon, a free Negro, from his common-law slave wife Sarah in Raleigh concerning his business at home, family matters, and her feelings about the free woman of color Boon later married. Taken from Catherine E. Thompson, *A Selective Guide to Women-Related Records in the North Carolina State Archives* (Raleigh, NC: North Carolina Division of Archives and History, 1977).

13,343. Branch, Lawrence O'Bryan
Papers. 1805-62. Ca. 75 items.
Open. Published guide.
North Carolina Division of Archives and History.
Collection contains a letter from Mrs. C. C. Lee to Branch during the Civil War asking for the return of her husband from the army because of a sick child at home. Taken from Catherine E. Thompson, *A Selective Guide to Women-Related Records in the North Carolina State Archives* (Raleigh, NC: North Carolina Division of Archives and History, 1977).

13,344. Branch, Mrs. Lawrence O'Bryan
Papers. 1791-1884. Ca. 165 items.
Open. Published guide.
North Carolina Division of Archives and History.
Correspondence of Nancy (Blount) Branch from various family members before her marriage, from her husband Lawrence O'B. Branch while he was in Congress and a general in the Civil War, and from Jefferson and Varina Davis. Also included are letters by Nancy Branch while she was president of the Ladies Memorial Association in 1866; a DAR history scrapbook; and a note from Mildred Lee, daughter of Robert E. Lee, concerning a Confederate monument. Correspondence of Lawrence O'B. Branch includes letters from his sister Susan and from his daughter Nannie. Taken from Catherine E. Thompson, *A Selective Guide to Women-Related Records in the North Carolina State Archives* (Raleigh, NC: North Carolina Division of Archives and History, 1977).

13,345. Branson
Papers. 1848-1925. 2 boxes.
Open. Published guide.
North Carolina Division of Archives and History.
Includes pre-Civil War letters concerning religion and education written or received by Marinda Branson Moore, a teacher and founder of Margarita Seminary in Valley Home, Rockingham County, NC, and letters by other women in the Branson family. Also included are poems by Marinda Moore and Ada Moore and prose writings by Emily Branson at Greensboro Female College in Greensboro, NC, and by Marinda and Grace Branson. Taken from Catherine E. Thompson, *A Selective Guide to Women-Related Records in the North Carolina State Archives* (Raleigh, NC: North Carolina Division of Archives and History, 1977).

13,346. Brayton, Patience
Papers. 1771-72. 1 item.
Open. Published guide.
North Carolina Division of Archives and History.
Excerpts from a travel diary kept by Brayton, a resident of Swansea, MA, include impressions of her visits to North Carolina and remarks on religious meetings. The diary was published in 1801 by Isaac Collins and Sons, New York. Taken from Catherine E. Thompson, *A Selective Guide to Women-Related Records in the North Carolina State Archives* (Raleigh, NC: North Carolina Division of Archives and History, 1977).

13,347. Brevard, Alexander
Papers. 1751-1911. Ca. 300 items.
Open. Published guide.
North Carolina Division of Archives and History.
Includes an 1827 diary by Juliana Margaret [Mrs. Henry W.] Conner with descriptions of life on a Mecklenburg County, NC, plantation, slavery conditions, and travels in North Carolina, South Carolina, and Tennessee; correspondence of Mrs. R. R. Brevard McDowell to her family from 1840 to 1852 commenting on women's education; and records of Harriet Brevard's expenses at Salem Boarding School in 1816. Taken from Catherine E. Thompson, *A Selective Guide to Women-Related Records in the North Carolina State Archives* (Raleigh, NC: North Carolina Division of Archives and History, 1977).

13,348. Brickell, James B.
Papers. 1862-65. 6 items.
Open. Published guide.
North Carolina Division of Archives and History.
Includes a letter to the Brickell family in 1865 from Harriet R. Greentree, who nursed Brickell during the war, inquiring about him and describing conditions in military hospitals after the Battle of Antietam. Taken from Catherine E. Thompson, *A Selective Guide to Women-Related Records in the North Carolina State Archives* (Raleigh, NC: North Carolina Division of Archives and History, 1977).

13,349. Bridgers, Robert P.
Papers. Ca. 1888-1966. Ca. 300 items.
Open. Published guide.
North Carolina Division of Archives and History.
Includes correspondence, diary notes, and a scrapbook of Ann Preston Bridgers relating to her experiences in 1919 in Europe with the YWCA. Also included is a copy of her play *Coquette.* Taken from Catherine E. Thompson, *A Selective Guide to Women-Related Records in the North Carolina State Archives* (Raleigh, NC: North Carolina Division of Archives and History, 1977).

13,350. Briggs, Willis G.
Papers. 1794-1955. Ca. 3500 items.
Open. Published guide.
North Carolina Division of Archives and History.
Family correspondence, poetry, and programs and magazines from Meredith College in Raleigh. Includes letters to Briggs from his mother while he was a student from 1893 to 1896 at Wake Forest College in Wake Forest, NC; letters from his daughter Sarah while she was a graduate student at Cornell University from 1931 to 1935 and then a teacher, dean, and president of Penn Hall in Chambersburg, PA; and a 1920 letter by Briggs to Warren G. Harding stating that North Carolinians oppose the Susan B. Anthony Amendment. Also included are letters to Mrs. Willis Briggs from her husband and children and material concerning her farm and War Production and Farm Defense Programs; letters, 1874-83, to Willis Briggs's father Thomas Henry Briggs, Jr., from his wife Sarah (Grandy) Briggs; and letters, 1896-1902, by Eliza Pool, a schoolteacher in Raleigh, concerning studies and travels. Papers of Sarah Elizabeth Ferebee, an 1841 graduate of Wesleyan Female Collegiate Institute in Wilmington, DE, who later married a Mr. Lamb and then a Mr. Grandy, include letters from her parents while she was at school, a diary describing a return visit to the school and travels in the Northeast, and a diploma from the Institute. Other Grandy family papers include notes, poetry, articles, stories, letters to the editor, and scrapbooks of clippings apparently belonging to Sarah (Ferebee) Lamb Grandy. Taken from Catherine E. Thompson, *A Selective Guide to Women-Related Records in the North Carolina State Archives* (Raleigh, NC: North Carolina Division of Archives and History, 1977).

13,351. Broadwick, Tiny
Papers. 1902-75. Ca. 200 items.
Open. Published guide.
North Carolina Division of Archives and History.
Photos, clippings, and promotional material relate to Broadwick, a balloon aerialist and parachutist from Henderson, NC, whose given name was Georgia Ann Thompson, and to her mentor Charles Broadwick. Taken from Catherine E. Thompson, *A Selective Guide to Women-Related Records in the North Carolina State Archives* (Raleigh, NC: North Carolina Division of Archives and History, 1977).

13,352. Brooks, E. C.
Papers. 1925-31. 702 items.
Open. Published guide.
North Carolina Division of Archives and History.
Material on the Commission on County Government includes letters by Commission member Mrs. Thomas O'Berry and reports from the GFWC. Taken from Catherine E. Thompson, *A Selective Guide to Women-Related Records in the North Carolina State Archives* (Raleigh, NC: North Carolina Division of Archives and History, 1977).

13,353. Brown, Henry C.
Papers. 1896-1929. Ca. 300 items.
Open. Published guide.
North Carolina Division of Archives and History.
Includes an 1876 autograph book of Mollie E. Merritt, who became Mrs. Henry C. Brown, from her student days at Greensboro Female College in Greensboro, NC. Taken from Catherine E. Thompson, *A Selective Guide to Women-Related Records in the North Carolina State Archives* (Raleigh, NC: North Carolina Division of Archives and History, 1977).

13,354. Brown, S. Janie
Papers. Nd. 2 items.
Open. Published guide.
North Carolina Division of Archives and History.
Poem by and biographical sketch of [Miss] Brown. Taken from Catherine E. Thompson, *A Selective Guide to Women-Related Records in the North Carolina State Archives* (Raleigh, NC: North Carolina Division of Archives and History, 1977).

13,355. Brown, W. Vance
Papers. 1794-1894. 4 vols. and 652 items.
Open. Published guide.
North Carolina Division of Archives and History.
Letters of Mary Taylor [Mrs. William John] Brown to her stepson John Evans Brown beginning in 1864 discuss her negative feelings towards southerners, difficulties in renting a farm, building a home, mortgage worries, and the deterioration of the house as her husband's health fails. Taken from Catherine E. Thompson, *A Selective Guide to Women-Related Records in the North Carolina State Archives* (Raleigh, NC: North Carolina Division of Archives and History, 1977).

13,356. Bryan, John Herritage
Papers. 1716-1907. Ca. 2300 items.
Open. Published guide.
North Carolina Division of Archives and History.
Nineteenth-century correspondence of the Bryan family includes letters between Mary Shepard Bryan and her husband John H. Bryan concerning family news, social and political events, and local occurrences. Additional correspondence of Mary Bryan includes letters from Isabel [Mrs. A. P.] Bryan describing her life as a schoolgirl in Philadelphia; letters from Mary Bryan Speight regarding teachers, schoolmates, and plantation life; and letters to and from children and relatives concerning plantation life, local news, child rearing, politics, the war, and religion. Also included are letters by James West Bryan describing local activities in which women participated and referring to New Bern, NC, merchants keeping Negro mistresses, and a letter to John H. Bryan from his niece Mary Bryan Pettigrew discussing school and social life. Taken from Catherine E. Thompson, *A Selective Guide to Women-Related Records in the North Carolina State Archives* (Raleigh, NC: North Carolina Division of Archives and History, 1977).

13,357. Bryan, Richard Dobbs Spaight
Papers. 1766-1952. 30 items.
Open. Published guide.
North Carolina Division of Archives and History.
Includes a letter by Sarah Adams Bulkley to her mother in 1873 pertaining to a shipwreck. Taken from Catherine E. Thompson, *A Selective Guide to Women-Related Records in the North Carolina State Archives* (Raleigh, NC: North Carolina Division of Archives and History, 1977).

13,358. Bryant, H. E. C.
Papers. 1933-67. Ca. 10 items.
Open. Published guide.
North Carolina Division of Archives and History.
Includes a newspaper story about Adelaide Williams, who was city editor of the Charlotte *Observer* in ca. 1897; she later married Joseph Caldwell. Taken from Catherine E. Thompson, *A Selective Guide to Women-Related Records in the North Carolina State Archives* (Raleigh, NC:

North Carolina Division of Archives and History, 1977).

13,359. Burgwyn, William Hyslop Sumner
Papers. 1803-1936. Ca. 415 items.
Open. Published guide.
North Carolina Division of Archives and History.
Correspondence and papers of Mrs. W. H. S. Burgwyn for 1913 to 1936 concern business matters after her husband's death, including the sale of land, pension problems, and business agreements. Also included are letters from Cornelia (Phillips) Spencer to William Burgwyn concerning his military career and reminiscing about Chapel Hill and letters to William Burgwyn and Miss Burgwyn from Varina Howell [Mrs. Jefferson] Davis in 1867 expressing gratitude for their friendship and noting her husband's current difficulties. Taken from Catherine E. Thompson, *A Selective Guide to Women-Related Records in the North Carolina State Archives* (Raleigh, NC: North Carolina Division of Archives and History, 1977).

13,360. Burton, Robert
Papers. 1772-85. 8 items.
Open. Published guide.
North Carolina Division of Archives and History.
Letters from Agatha Burton to her father relate news of home. Taken from Catherine E. Thompson, *A Selective Guide to Women-Related Records in the North Carolina State Archives* (Raleigh, NC: North Carolina Division of Archives and History, 1977).

13,361. Busbee, Juliana
Papers. Nd. 4 items.
Open. Published guide.
North Carolina Division of Archives and History.
Reminiscences by Busbee concern her efforts to establish a pottery industry in Jugtown, NC, with her husband. Taken from Catherine E. Thompson, *A Selective Guide to Women-Related Records in the North Carolina State Archives* (Raleigh, NC: North Carolina Division of Archives and History, 1977).

13,362. Bush, Lewis
Papers. 1810-11. 1 item.
Open. Published guide.
North Carolina Division of Archives and History.
Consists of a manuscript extolling the beauties and virtues of women. Taken from Catherine E. Thompson, *A Selective Guide to Women-Related Records in the North Carolina State Archives* (Raleigh, NC: North Carolina Division of Archives and History, 1977).

13,363. Cannor, Emma F.
Papers. 1863-64. 1 item.
Open. Published guide.
North Carolina Division of Archives and History.
Composition book containing poems and sketches used by Carrie Clement while she was a student at Aberfoyle Academy in Wake County, NC. Taken from Catherine E. Thompson, *A Selective Guide to Women-Related Records in the North Carolina State Archives* (Raleigh, NC: North Carolina Division of Archives and History, 1977).

13,364. Carolina College
Records. Ca. 1906-?. 1 box.
Open. Published guide.
North Carolina Division of Archives and History.
Correspondence, a composition, clippings, and other records of the College, a girls school in Maxton, NC, which was authorized in 1906. Also included is *Carolina Echoes,* a history of the College covering the period 1912 to 1926. Taken from Catherine E. Thompson, *A Selective Guide to Women-Related Records in the North Carolina State Archives* (Raleigh, NC: North Carolina Division of Archives and History, 1977).

13,365. Carraway, Gertrude Sprague
Papers. 1948-56. 6 vols. and 1 item.
Open. Published guide.
North Carolina Division of Archives and History.
Scrapbooks of activities of the National Society of the DAR. Taken from Catherine E. Thompson, *A Selective Guide to Women-Related Records in the North Carolina State Archives* (Raleigh, NC: North Carolina Division of Archives and History, 1977).

13,366. Carroway, Daphne
Papers. 1902-34. 256 items.
Open. Published guide.
North Carolina Division of Archives and History.
[Miss] Carroway was a teacher who was known as the "Dixie Story Lady." Correspondence, bulletins, pamphlets, and clippings relate to her career, American National Red Cross work, and the Radcliffe Chatauqua. Correspondents include editors of the *Story Teller's Magazine* and *American Childhood* and Marjorie F. Webster, head of a school of expression and physical education and founder of the Ann Tillery Renshaw School of Speech. Taken from Catherine E. Thompson, *A Selective Guide to Women-Related Records in the North Carolina State Archives* (Raleigh, NC: North Carolina Division of Archives and History, 1977).

13,367. Catawba County
Records. 1860-1901. 1 microfilm reel.
Open. Published guide.
North Carolina Division of Archives and History.
Catawba County school registers kept by [Mrs.] Huldah Maybell Hubbard Rockett and her daughter [Miss] Hulda Maybell Rockett. Taken from Catherine E. Thompson, *A Selective Guide to Women-Related Records in the North Carolina State Archives* (Raleigh, NC: North Carolina Division of Archives and History, 1977).

13,368. Chamberlain, Hope (Summerell)
Papers. 1790-1950. 10 items.
Open. Published guide.
North Carolina Division of Archives and History.
Family letters and typescripts of such books by [Mrs.] Chamberlain (1870-1960) as *What's Done and Past, Oh Call Back Yesterday,* and *Among Those Present: Fifty Years in the Old Home Town.* Taken from Catherine E. Thompson, *A Selective Guide to Women-Related Records in the North Carolina State Archives* (Raleigh, NC: North Carolina Division of Archives and History, 1977).

13,369. Chandler, Alban B.
Papers. 1856-1944. Ca. 50 items.
Open. Published guide.
North Carolina Division of Archives and History.
Includes an 1856 diploma of Emily Branson from Greensboro Female College in Greensboro, NC; a report card of Mary Chandler from the Fred Olds School in Raleigh, 1937-38; and a memorial biographical sketch of educator Marinda Branson Moore. Taken from Catherine E. Thompson, *A Selective Guide to Women-Related Records in the North Carolina State Archives* (Raleigh, NC: North Carolina Division of Archives and History, 1977).

13,370. Chatham, Thurmond
Papers. 1776-1956. Ca. 50 cu.ft.
Open. Published guide.
North Carolina Division of Archives and History.
Includes letters from Sarah E. Smith at Greensboro Female College and Methodist College in 1847 and 1848 discussing life at school, academics, examinations, and her enjoyment of chemistry; a letter to Sarah from Bennett Blake at Greensboro Female College, in Greensboro, NC, relating school news; a Hugh Chatham Memorial Hospital Auxiliary annual report, 1953-54; and a book of poems compiled by Eva M. Young in memory of her mother. Taken from Catherine E. Thompson, *A Selective Guide to Women-Related Records in the North Carolina State Archives* (Raleigh, NC: North Carolina Division of Archives and History, 1977).

13,371. Cherry, R. Gregg
Papers. 1891-1957. Ca. 66,000 items.
Partially restricted. Published guide.
North Carolina Division of Archives and History.
Includes letters to Cherry, governor of North Carolina from 1945 to 1949, in which his wife Mildred describes her frustrations as the wife of a busy politician; material of the State Democratic Committee, including lists of women's Democratic organizations and women vice-chairmen; and material on male and female prisoners working in the executive mansion. Taken from Catherine E. Thompson, *A Selective Guide to Women-Related Records in the North Carolina State Archives* (Raleigh, NC: North Carolina Division of Archives and History, 1977).

13,372. Children of the American Revolution
Records. Nd. 2 boxes.
Open. Published guide.
North Carolina Division of Archives and History.
Genealogical records of the Samuel A. Ashe chapter and membership records of the Hunter-Hinton chapter. Taken from Catherine E. Thompson, *A Selective Guide to Women-Related Records in the North Carolina State Archives* (Raleigh, NC: North Carolina Division of Archives and History, 1977).

13,373. Chowan College
Records. 1848-1961. 1 microfilm reel.
Open. Published guide.
North Carolina Division of Archives and History.
Minutes of meetings of board of trustees of the College, which was founded in Murfreesboro, NC, in 1848 as the Chowan Baptist Female Institute. The school enlarged its curriculum in 1881 to include college as well as high school courses and later became a coeducational junior college. Taken from Catherine E. Thompson, *A Selective Guide to Women-Related Records in the North Carolina State Archives* (Raleigh, NC: North Carolina Division of Archives and History, 1977).

13,374. Civil War
Collection. Ca. 1861-65. 17 boxes.
Open. Published guide.
North Carolina Division of Archives and History.
Includes a letter in which [Miss] Janie Smith describes the Battle of Averasboro and her personal circumstances; a diary of Melinda Ray of Fayetteville, NC, 1861-65; reminiscences of North Carolina women; memo of treasurer's account with the Ladies' Aid Society in Raleigh in 1864; correspondence of the Quartermaster Department, including a few personal letters commenting upon the hardships suffered by widows and soldiers' families; and correspondence, essays, reports, and scrapbooks of the United Daughters of the Confederacy. Also included are correspondence, affidavits, resolutions, a scrapbook, pamphlets, and clippings collected by [Miss] Jessica Randolph Smith in support of Major Orren Randolph Smith's claim to be the designer of the Confederate flag. Taken from Catherine E. Thompson, *A Selective Guide to Women-Related Records in the North Carolina State Archives* (Raleigh, NC: North Carolina Division of Archives and History, 1977).

13,375. Clark, Henry Toole
Papers. 1860-1920. 2 vols.
Open. Published guide.
North Carolina Division of Archives and History.
Scrapbooks of Clark contain material relating to DAR activities. Taken from Catherine E. Thompson, *A Selective Guide to Women-Related Records in the North Carolina State Archives*

(Raleigh, NC: North Carolina Division of Archives and History, 1977).

13,376. Clark, Walter
Papers. 1693-1920. Ca. 4000 items.
Open. Published guide.
North Carolina Division of Archives and History.
Correspondence of Clark contains discussion of woman's suffrage, proposed legislation improving property rights of married women, and other subjects relating to women. Also included are post cards and telegrams on the suffrage issue, which was the topic of a number of articles and speeches by Clark. Correspondents include Helen Hamilton Gardener, Julia Lathrop, Lida T. Rodman, and Adelaide Fries. Letters by Mrs. Thomas J. "Stonewall" Jackson request legal advice, while Louisa H. Kendall writes of her experiences during the war and of her mother's life. Also included is Clark family correspondence. One item dates from 1693; the remainder of the collection dates from 1783 to 1920. Taken from Catherine E. Thompson, *A Selective Guide to Women-Related Records in the North Carolina State Archives* (Raleigh, NC: North Carolina Division of Archives and History, 1977).

13,377. Clinard, L. N.
Papers. 1871-80. Ca. 280 items.
Open. Published guide.
North Carolina Division of Archives and History.
Includes a letter in which Frank A. Clinard describes in 1873 the Statesville Female Seminary in Statesville, NC. Taken from Catherine E. Thompson, *A Selective Guide to Women-Related Records in the North Carolina State Archives* (Raleigh, NC: North Carolina Division of Archives and History, 1977).

13,378. Collins, Josiah
Papers. 1761-1892. 16 boxes and 10 vols.
Open. Published guide.
North Carolina Division of Archives and History.
Includes a ledger of Ann C. Blount's private accounts, 1839-61; a memorandum book of [Mrs.] Mary Collins, 1860s; a pardon given to Mary Collins by President Andrew Johnson in 1865 for her participation in a rebellion; and plantation accounts, including a list of household and kitchen furnishings. Taken from Catherine E. Thompson, *A Selective Guide to Women-Related Records in the North Carolina State Archives* (Raleigh, NC: North Carolina Division of Archives and History, 1977).

13,379. Colonial Dames of America
Records. 1936. 1 box.
Open. Published guide.
North Carolina Division of Archives and History.
Charter and 42nd annual report of the North Carolina Society of the Dames. Taken from Catherine E. Thompson, *A Selective Guide to Women-Related Records in the North Carolina State Archives* (Raleigh, NC: North Carolina Division of Archives and History, 1977).

13,380. Colonial Dames of the 17th Century
Records. 1950-61. 1 box.
Open. Published guide.
North Carolina Division of Archives and History.
History and a yearbook of the North Carolina Society of the Colonial Dames. Taken from Catherine E. Thompson, *A Selective Guide to Women-Related Records in the North Carolina State Archives* (Raleigh, NC: North Carolina Division of Archives and History, 1977).

13,381. Colton, Elizabeth Avery
Papers. 1915. 4 items.
Open. Published guide.
North Carolina Division of Archives and History.
Letter and cards from Colton, president of the Southern Association of College Women, to [Miss] Daisy Bailey Waitt, a member of the Greenville branch, and an address given to high school students about colleges for women in the South, particularly those in North Carolina which fulfill standard requirements. Taken from Catherine E. Thompson, *A Selective Guide to Women-Related Records in the North Carolina State Archives* (Raleigh, NC: North Carolina Division of Archives and History, 1977).

13,382. Coltrane, David S.
Papers. 1931-69. Ca. 1450 items.
Open. Published guide.
North Carolina Division of Archives and History.
Includes letters and clippings of Mrs. Coltrane concerning civic activities and honors, a typescript about the Wake County "woman of the week" in 1954, and a sketch for *Who's Who in American Education.* Taken from Catherine E. Thompson, *A Selective Guide to Women-Related Records in the North Carolina State Archives* (Raleigh, NC: North Carolina Division of Archives and History, 1977).

13,383. Cook, James P.
Papers. 1891-1956. 1 item.
Open. Published guide.
North Carolina Division of Archives and History.
Scrapbook of Cook, founder and chairman of the board of Stonewall Jackson Manual Training and Industrial School, contains letters from Margaret C. D. Burgwyn concerning the King's Daughters organization and its relation to the school. Taken from Catherine E. Thompson, *A Selective Guide to Women-Related Records in the North Carolina State Archives* (Raleigh, NC: North Carolina Division of Archives and History, 1977).

13,384. Cooke, William W.
Papers. 1852. 1 item.
Access restricted. Published guide.
North Carolina Division of Archives and History.
Letter by Cooke to his parents in Franklin County, NC, concerns difficulties encountered while traveling the Oregon Trail, sickness, the burial of [Mrs.] Nellie Osborne, his wife's poor health, and delivery of a premature daughter during the trip. Taken from Catherine E. Thompson, *A Selective Guide to Women-Related Records in the North Carolina State Archives* (Raleigh, NC: North Carolina Division of Archives and History, 1977).

13,385. Corbitt, David Leroy
Papers. 1923-66. 1 vol. and ca. 750 items.
Open. Published guide.
North Carolina Division of Archives and History.
Collection contains note files with information on Adelaide Lizetta Fries and speeches and addresses with material on the life of Varina Howell [Mrs. Jefferson] Davis. Taken from Catherine E. Thompson, *A Selective Guide to Women-Related Records in the North Carolina State Archives* (Raleigh, NC: North Carolina Division of Archives and History, 1977).

13,386. County Records
Records. 17th century- . More than 10,000 cu.ft., 5000 vols., and 20,000 microfilm reels.
Open. Published and unpublished guides.
North Carolina Division of Archives and History.
County records are held by county and grouped therein by series: bonds, corporations and partnerships, court, election, estates, land, marriage and vital statistics, military and pension, officials, roads and bridges, schools, tax and fiscal, wills, and miscellaneous. Most of the records originated in the offices of the clerks of county and superior courts and registers of deeds, but others were created in the offices of tax supervisors, boards of county commissioners, health departments, social services directors, and boards of education. Many of the series on marriage, divorce, and vital statistics include marriage and divorce registers and registers of the maiden names of divorced women; some include records of cohabitation and some separate "white" from "colored" records. Estate records series occasionally contain records of dower, that part of an intestate husband's estate to which his widow was legally entitled. See *Guide to Research Materials in the North Carolina State Archives: Section B: County Records* (Raleigh, NC: North Carolina Divison of Archives and History, 1978, 6th edition, revised).

13,387. Cowles, Calvin J.
Papers. 1817-85. Ca. 23,000 items.
Open. Published guide.
North Carolina Division of Archives and History.
Collection contains letter and notes from 1882 by Kate Blackiston, a 30-year-old Maryland resident, concerning her desire to persuade northern capitalists to develop Cowles's land and thus help recoup her family fortune. Also included is financial advice Cowles gave his widowed sister-in-law Mary (Evans) Cowles during the Civil War. Taken from Catherine E. Thompson, *A Selective Guide to Women-Related Records in the North Carolina State Archives* (Raleigh, NC: North Carolina Division of Archives and History, 1977).

13,388. Cozart, Toccoa Page
Papers. 1787-1907. 2 items.
Open. Published guide.
North Carolina Division of Archives and History.
Papers of Cozart, historian of the DAR and the United Daughters of the Confederacy, include a 1907 letter to Edward O. Dorman, editor of the *Journal of American History,* concerning the success of prohibitionists the previous day in Alabama and an article in which Cozart gives a brief sketch of three generations of women in her family. Taken from Catherine E. Thompson, *A Selective Guide to Women-Related Records in the North Carolina State Archives* (Raleigh, NC: North Carolina Division of Archives and History, 1977).

13,389. Crichton, Frances E.
Papers. 1820. 1 item.
Open. Published guide.
North Carolina Division of Archives and History.
Honorary certificate from the Female Department of Raleigh Academy. Taken from Catherine E. Thompson, *A Selective Guide to Women-Related Records in the North Carolina State Archives* (Raleigh, NC: North Carolina Division of Archives and History, 1977).

13,390. Crittenden, Christopher
Papers. 1915-61. 20 boxes.
Access restricted. Published guide.
North Carolina Division of Archives and History.
The collection includes correspondence of Ethel Taylor Crittenden, mother of Christopher Crittenden and a librarian at Wake Forest College in Wake Forest, NC, which concerns her work, travels, life in Wake Forest, and later life with her sister in Richmond. Correspondence and other papers of Janet Quinlan Crittenden, wife of Christopher Crittenden, concern her college days at Peace Institute in Raleigh, at Randolph-Macon in Virginia, and at the University of North Carolina at Chapel Hill; her reasons for wanting a career in social work; her master's thesis; work experiences; marriage; participation in her husband's activities; and her interest in the American National Red Cross, church, the AAUW, and St. Agnes Hospital. Also included are letters of Ann Lane (Crittenden) Griffiths Witt to her parents and grandmothers about childhood experiences, school days, college life at Wake Forest College, and her marriage; clippings of her column in the Raleigh *News and Observer;* and a marriage contract. Taken from Catherine E. Thompson, *A Selective Guide to Women-Related Records in the North Carolina State Archives* (Raleigh, NC: North Carolina Division of Archives and History, 1977).

13,391. Current, Ruth
Papers. 1926-67. Ca. 800 items.
Open. Published guide.
North Carolina Division of Archives and History.
Correspondence, telegrams, notebook, speeches, news releases, tributes, photos, awards, subject files on committees and workshops, programs of home demonstration club meetings and a convocation at Peace College in Raleigh, clippings of her column in *Southern Planter,* extension service and other publications, material for the Delta Kappa Gamma Society, and other papers of Current. Current was a local, district, and state home demonstration agent in North Carolina between 1928 and 1958, and from 1958 to 1961 she was assistant director of the North Carolina State University extension service in charge of home economics programs. Correspondents include Pearl Buck, Juliana Busbee, Georgia Neese Clark, Jane (Simpson) McKimmon, and Eleanor Roosevelt. Taken from Catherine E. Thompson, *A Selective Guide to Women-Related Records in the North Carolina State Archives* (Raleigh, NC: North Carolina Division of Archives and History, 1977).

13,392. Darden, Annie "Nannie"
Papers. 1855-67. 3 vols.
Open. Published guide.
North Carolina Division of Archives and History.
Diaries of Darden contain references to children, neighbors, friends, household chores, religious activities, social activities, events at the Institute of Murfreesboro, community reaction to the dissolution of the Union, war items, and women's work in the Soldier's Aid Society. Taken from Catherine E. Thompson, *A Selective Guide to Women-Related Records in the North Carolina State Archives* (Raleigh, NC: North Carolina Division of Archives and History, 1977).

13,393. Daughters of Colonial Wars
Records. 1936. 1 box.
Open. Published guide.
North Carolina Division of Archives and History.
Charter of the North Carolina division of the Daughters. Taken from Catherine E. Thompson, *A Selective Guide to Women-Related Records in the North Carolina State Archives* (Raleigh, NC: North Carolina Division of Archives and History, 1977).

13,394. Daughters of the American Revolution
Records. 1911-47. 22 boxes.
Open. Published guide.
North Carolina Division of Archives and History.
Bylaws, minutes, financial records, correspondence, speeches, membership material, reports, memory books, programs, yearbooks, and other records of the Caswell-Nash DAR chapter in Raleigh; a scrapbook of the Colonel Polk chapter in Raleigh; a registration book and autograph book of the General Davie chapter in Durham, NC; and financial statements, ledgers, and scrapbooks of the North Carolina branch of the national DAR. Taken from Catherine E. Thompson, *A Selective Guide to Women-Related Records in the North Carolina State Archives* (Raleigh, NC: North Carolina Division of Archives and History, 1977).

13,395. Daughters of the Revolution
Records. Nd. 13 boxes.
Partially restricted. Published guide.
North Carolina Division of Archives and History.
Constitutions, bylaws, correspondence, membership material, and reports of the national and North Carolina societies and minutes and financial records of state and local chapters. Also included are amendments, resolutions, a history, proceedings, delegate lists for annual meetings, an address book, programs, and circulars of the national society; correspondence, membership material, scrapbooks, ancestral register, yearbooks, invitations, clippings, printed matter, and publications of local chapters; minutes of the Bloomsbury chapter; and items concerning the Hooper-Hewes chapter. Taken from Catherine E. Thompson, *A Selective Guide to Women-Related Records in the North Carolina State Archives* (Raleigh, NC: North Carolina Division of Archives and History, 1977).

13,396. Davidson, Allen T., and Davidson, Theodore F.
Papers. 1769-1931. Ca. 4300 items.
Open. Published guide.
North Carolina Division of Archives and History.
Collection contains a letter by Theodore Davidson in 1898 concerning married women's contracts. Also included is an 1870 letter concerning the qualifications of a 53-year-old widow being considered for a wife. Taken from Catherine E. Thompson, *A Selective Guide to Women-Related Records in the North Carolina State Archives* (Raleigh, NC: North Carolina Division of Archives and History, 1977).

13,397. Davis, Jefferson
Papers. 1851-1906. 16 items.
Open. Published guide.
North Carolina Division of Archives and History.
Family correspondence includes letters from Davis's wife Varina Howell Davis (1826-1906) to J. A. Briggs in Raleigh recalling the time she spent in that city during the Civil War. Taken from Catherine E. Thompson, *A Selective Guide to Women-Related Records in the North Carolina State Archives* (Raleigh, NC: North Carolina Division of Archives and History, 1977).

13,398. Denmark, Leonidas Polk
Papers. 1861-1965. Ca. 2000 items.
Open. Published guide.
North Carolina Division of Archives and History.
Collection contains WWI letters to Denmark from his mother and sister describing local news, gossip, family activities, and the interest of Nell Battle Lewis, Ruth Faison Shaw, and Mrs. Thomas Bickett in war work overseas. Collection also contains a 1917 letter in which Denmark describes to his sister the cool reception given suffragists in Raleigh, a booklet by [Miss] Leonita Denmark reflecting feminine attitudes toward war, and letters to L. Polk Denmark from girl friends, including several written from Agnes Scott College in Decatur, GA, and from Meredith College in Raleigh. Also includes an account by L. Polk Denmark's mother Juanita (Polk) Denmark of watching Halley's comet in 1910; her reminiscences with additional comments by her daughter "Nita"; minutes of the 1880 Baptist Convention, which included arguments for women's education; a 1904 letter concerning the WCTU; and an article on feminism from a 1919 copy of *Wake Forest Student.* Taken from Catherine E. Thompson, *A Selective Guide to Women-Related Records in the North Carolina State Archives* (Raleigh, NC: North Carolina Division of Archives and History, 1977).

13,399. Denson
Papers. 1858-1937. 4 boxes.
Open. Published guide.
North Carolina Division of Archives and History.
Family correspondence includes a 1921 letter in which [Miss] Daisy Denson, secretary of the Board of Public Charities, protests to a Board member the appointment of Kate (Burr) [Mrs. Clarence A.] Johnson to commissioner of public welfare. Also included are items concerning women's clubs in Raleigh. Taken from Catherine E. Thompson, *A Selective Guide to Women-Related Records in the North Carolina State Archives* (Raleigh, NC: North Carolina Division of Archives and History, 1977).

13,400. Dodd, Lillian
Papers. 1779-1945. 30 boxes.
Open. Published guide.
North Carolina Division of Archives and History.
Papers of Dodd, a teacher, include correspondence, manuscripts of her poetry, invitations, programs, magazines, cookbooks, schoolbooks, material from St. Mary's College in Raleigh, a book entitled *The Young Housewife's Counsellor and Friend* by a Mrs. Mason, and an 1862 issue of *Demorest's Magazine,* "the ladies' literary conservator." Also includes letters she wrote her mother S. C. [Mrs. James] Dodd about student life, studies, travel, teaching, and upkeep of her mother's property and letters from her daughter Ceyce Dodd concerning family property, business affairs, and personal news. Correspondence of Ceyce (Dodd) Eastman includes letters from her mother Lillian Dodd and from friends and business associates. Taken from Catherine E. Thompson, *A Selective Guide to Women-Related Records in the North Carolina State Archives* (Raleigh, NC: North Carolina Division of Archives and History, 1977).

13,401. Duke University Centennial Celebration
Records. 1937-39. Ca. 73 items.
Open. Published guide.
North Carolina Division of Archives and History.
Includes symposia programs on women and contemporary life. Taken from Catherine E. Thompson, *A Selective Guide to Women-Related Records in the North Carolina State Archives* (Raleigh, NC: North Carolina Division of Archives and History, 1977).

13,402. Dunn, Anna
Papers. 1837-45. 2 vols.
Open. Published guide.
North Carolina Division of Archives and History.
Ledger of Dunn's blacksmith accounts in Franklin County, NC. Taken from Catherine E. Thompson, *A Selective Guide to Women-Related Records in the North Carolina State Archives* (Raleigh, NC: North Carolina Division of Archives and History, 1977).

13,403. Edmonston, Catherine Ann
Papers. 1860-66. 4 vols.
Open. Published guide.
North Carolina Division of Archives and History.
Diaries of [Mrs.] Edmonston portray plantation life in Halifax County, NC, during the Civil War and include accounts of disturbances preceding the War, descriptions of home affairs and battles, and lists of casualties. Taken from Catherine E. Thompson, *A Selective Guide to Women-Related Records in the North Carolina State Archives* (Raleigh, NC: North Carolina Division of Archives and History, 1977).

13,404. Equal Rights Amendment
Collection. 1975-77. 8 boxes.
Access restricted. Published guide.
North Carolina Division of Archives and History.
Correspondence and literature from constituents of several members of the North Carolina House of Representatives; papers of A. Hartwell Campbell and John R. Gamble, Jr., who were chairmen of the House Constitutional Amendments Committee in 1975 and 1977 respectively; and literature from various sources. Taken from Catherine E. Thompson, *A Selective Guide to Women-Related Records in the North Carolina State Archives* (Raleigh, NC: North Carolina Division of Archives and History, 1977).

13,405. Equal Suffrage Amendment
Collection. 1920. 1 box.
Open. Published guide.
North Carolina Division of Archives and History.
Letters to legislators and campaign material of the Equal Suffrage Association and the Southern League for the Rejection of the Susan B. Anthony amendment. Taken from Catherine E. Thompson, *A Selective Guide to Women-Related Records in the North Carolina State Archives* (Raleigh, NC:

North Carolina Division of Archives and History, 1977).

13,406. Evans, May (Thompson)
Papers. 1871-1975. Ca. 31 cu.ft.
Open. Published guide.
North Carolina Division of Archives and History.
Personal and professional correspondence, papers relating to college student work, speeches, articles, organization files, photos, sound recordings, her mother's thesis, subject files relating to specific women and women in general, and other material of [Mrs.] Evans (1901-), a speaker, editor, writer, teacher, administrator, and information officer who held various government and political positions. Correspondents include Oveta (Culp) Hobby, Cornelia (Petty) Jerman, Clare Boothe Luce, Helen Douglas Mankin, Margaret Mead, Perle Mesta, Mary T. Norton, Edith Nourse Rogers, Eleanor Roosevelt, Susie Sharp, Margaret Chase Smith, and Bess W. Truman. Included is material on Westhampton College of the University of Richmond; Mortar Board, a national collegiate honorary society; the American Newspaper Women's Club; the Democratic National Committee women's division, of which Evans was assistant director from 1937 to 1941; Young Democratic Clubs of North Carolina, of which she was president; the US and North Carolina Employment Service; the War Manpower Commission; the Public Health Service; and HEW. Also included is a research paper by Kay Hamilton on Evans's work with the Young Democratic Clubs of North Carolina and the Democratic National Committee women's division. Taken from Catherine E. Thompson, *A Selective Guide to Women-Related Records in the North Carolina State Archives* (Raleigh, NC: North Carolina Division of Archives and History, 1977).

13,407. Falkener, William
Papers. 1809. 1 item.
Open. Published guide.
North Carolina Division of Archives and History.
Advertisement describes Mrs. Falkener's Young Ladies Boarding School in Warrenton, NC. Taken from Catherine E. Thompson, *A Selective Guide to Women-Related Records in the North Carolina State Archives* (Raleigh, NC: North Carolina Division of Archives and History, 1977).

13,408. Farmers State Alliance
Records. 1887-1928. 12 boxes and 12 vols.
Open. Published guide.
North Carolina Division of Archives and History.
Minutes, financial records, proceedings, membership lists, and other records of the Alliance, in which a number of women, including Jane (Simpson) McKimmon, served as delegates and committee members during the Alliance's later years. Taken from Catherine E. Thompson, *A Selective Guide to Women-Related Records in the North Carolina State Archives* (Raleigh, NC: North Carolina Division of Archives and History, 1977).

13,409. Fleming, John Giles
Papers. 1863-65. 3 items.
Open. Published guide.
North Carolina Division of Archives and History.
Letters between Fleming and his wife Margaret concern her loneliness, crops, and the management of home affairs. Taken from Catherine E. Thompson, *A Selective Guide to Women-Related Records in the North Carolina State Archives* (Raleigh, NC: North Carolina Division of Archives and History, 1977).

13,410. Fortnightly Review Club
Records. 1899-1945. 1 box.
Open. Published guide.
North Carolina Division of Archives and History.
Minutes, correspondence, and programs of the Club and a program of the Johnsonian Book Club. Taken from Catherine E. Thompson, *A Selective Guide to Women-Related Records in the North Carolina State Archives* (Raleigh, NC: North Carolina Division of Archives and History, 1977).

13,411. Fries, Adelaide Lizetta
Papers. 1861-95. 14 items.
Open. Published guide.
North Carolina Division of Archives and History.
Papers of Fries, an archivist and historian of the Moravian Church in Salem, NC, include correspondence concerning her search for illustrations of Revolutionary War heroines and sketches of Mrs. Jesse Franklin, Elizabeth Steele, and Mary Haynes Daves. Taken from Catherine E. Thompson, *A Selective Guide to Women-Related Records in the North Carolina State Archives* (Raleigh, NC: North Carolina Division of Archives and History, 1977).

13,412. Futch
Papers. 1861-63. Ca. 66 items.
Open. Published guide.
North Carolina Division of Archives and History.
Correspondence between Martha Futch and her husband John, who was court-martialed and shot for desertion during the Civil War. Taken from Catherine E. Thompson, *A Selective Guide to Women-Related Records in the North Carolina State Archives* (Raleigh, NC: North Carolina Division of Archives and History, 1977).

13,413. Gales
Papers. 1794-1864. 1 vol. and 49 items.
Open. Published guide.
North Carolina Division of Archives and History.
Letters from Winifred Gales, author of *Matilda Berkely, or Family Anecdotes* (1804), to Jared Sparks, editor of the *North American Review,* concern Unitarianism, the relationship of church and state, their common literary interests, and family news. Taken from Catherine E. Thompson, *A Selective Guide to Women-Related Records in the North Carolina State Archives* (Raleigh, NC: North Carolina Division of Archives and History, 1977).

13,414. Gash, Mary, and Family
Papers. 1816-98. Ca. 350 items.
Open. Published guide.
North Carolina Division of Archives and History.
Family correspondence, primarily to Mary Gash, depicts life in western North Carolina communities in the 19th century and relates to family history, education, social life, temperance, religion, transportation, emigration to Missouri, travel in the South and West, the effects of the Civil War on the family and community, and the families' attempts to reestablish themselves in North Carolina, Missouri, and Texas. Included is material on a proposed school in which Mary Gash was to teach. Taken from Catherine E. Thompson, *A Selective Guide to Women-Related Records in the North Carolina State Archives* (Raleigh, NC: North Carolina Division of Archives and History, 1977).

13,415. Good Samaritan Hospital, Inc.
Records. 1892-1960. 1 box.
Open. Published guide.
North Carolina Division of Archives and History.
Bylaws, amendments to bylaws, minutes, certificate of amendment to the charter, and annual reports of this Charlotte, NC, hospital. Also includes material relating to the nursing school and medical staff. Taken from Catherine E. Thompson, *A Selective Guide to Women-Related Records in the North Carolina State Archives* (Raleigh, NC: North Carolina Division of Archives and History, 1977).

13,416. Graham, William Alexander
Papers. 1779-1918. Ca. 2050 items.
Open. Published guide.
North Carolina Division of Archives and History.
Collection contains correspondence between Graham, who was governor of North Carolina from 1845 to 1849, and his wife Susan Graham concerning their children, health, management of home affairs, and current events and correspondence with Cornelia (Phillips) Spencer. Taken from Catherine E. Thompson, *A Selective Guide to Women-Related Records in the North Carolina State Archives* (Raleigh, NC: North Carolina Division of Archives and History, 1977).

13,417. Graves, Calvin
Papers. 1833-64. 1 vol. and 27 items.
Open. Published guide.
North Carolina Division of Archives and History.
Includes an 1848 letter from Graves's daughter Caroline at school in Salem, NC, and his journal with accounts of tuition, room, and board at Oxford Female Academy. Taken from Catherine E. Thompson, *A Selective Guide to Women-Related Records in the North Carolina State Archives* (Raleigh, NC: North Carolina Division of Archives and History, 1977).

13,418. Green, Mrs. H. Clifford
Papers. 1866-1912. 1 item.
Open. Published guide.
North Carolina Division of Archives and History.
Manuscript by Mildred Edmundson contains sketches based on episodes in the life of her grandmother "Miss Sue," who taught school in Wayne, Greene, and Johnston counties in North Carolina from after the Civil War until her death in 1912. Taken from Catherine E. Thompson, *A Selective Guide to Women-Related Records in the North Carolina State Archives* (Raleigh, NC: North Carolina Division of Archives and History, 1977).

13,419. Greenhow, Rose O.
Papers. 1863-64. 3 items.
Open. Published guide.
North Carolina Division of Archives and History.
Journal, cipher, and address book of Greenhow, a Confederate spy who drowned in 1864 while trying to reach shore after the blockade runner *Condor* grounded off Fort Fisher. Her journal traces her travels from Wilmington, NC, to Bermuda, Britain, and France and describes meetings with leading European figures. Taken from Catherine E. Thompson, *A Selective Guide to Women-Related Records in the North Carolina State Archives* (Raleigh, NC: North Carolina Division of Archives and History, 1977).

13,420. Gregory, John T.
Papers. 1849-1910. 4809 items.
Open. Published guide.
North Carolina Division of Archives and History.
Family correspondence includes letters to Gregory from Mollie Lowe and Mollie Ellis at Chowan Female College in Murfreesboro, NC, from his daughters Maude and Jessica concerning their studies in New York, from his daughter Bettie concerning her studies at St. Mary's College in Raleigh, and from his daughters later in life. Also included are correspondence of Bettie Clark, a teacher at Granville Female Institute, with W. H. S. Burgwyn regarding financial aid for the purchase of Henderson Female College and receipts from the early 1800s of Bettie Clark and [Miss] Sue Carroway for the tuition of Gregory's children. Taken from Catherine E. Thompson, *A Selective Guide to Women-Related Records in the North Carolina State Archives* (Raleigh, NC: North Carolina Division of Archives and History, 1977).

13,421. Guion, Owen Haywood
Papers. 1787-1937. Ca. 364 items.
Open. Published guide.
North Carolina Division of Archives and History.
Includes clippings of historical sketches by Gertrude Carraway and Mary Bayard Clarke.

Taken from Catherine E. Thompson, *A Selective Guide to Women-Related Records in the North Carolina State Archives* (Raleigh, NC: North Carolina Division of Archives and History, 1977).

13,422. Hale, Edward Jones
Papers. 1850-67. Ca. 350 items.
Open. Published guide.
North Carolina Division of Archives and History.
Collection contains an 1862 letter from Maggie B. Smith to Hale and his son, who were printers, asserting that country women should be aroused to help soldiers in the army; letters by Cornelia (Phillips) Spencer in 1866 to Hale and his son concern a literary publication. Taken from Catherine E. Thompson, *A Selective Guide to Women-Related Records in the North Carolina State Archives* (Raleigh, NC: North Carolina Division of Archives and History, 1977).

13,423. Hall of History
Collection. Nd. No size given.
Open. Published guide.
North Carolina Division of Archives and History.
Includes indenture of Jane Mooney in 1798 as a servant to William Forrest in return for her passage to New York and an honorary certificate from Raleigh Academy in 1815 to [Miss] Sarah Littlejohn of Granville County, NC. Taken from Catherine E. Thompson, *A Selective Guide to Women-Related Records in the North Carolina State Archives* (Raleigh, NC: North Carolina Division of Archives and History, 1977).

13,424. Hamilton
Papers. 1861-64. 22 items.
Open. Published guide.
North Carolina Division of Archives and History.
Collection contains a letter from O. C. Hamilton to Lizzie Garner concerning their relationship and the disadvantages of being engaged in wartime. Taken from Catherine E. Thompson, *A Selective Guide to Women-Related Records in the North Carolina State Archives* (Raleigh, NC: North Carolina Division of Archives and History, 1977).

13,425. Hamlin, Wood Jones
Papers. 1762-1835. Ca. 300 items.
Open. Published guide.
North Carolina Division of Archives and History.
Collection contains material from 1826 on the Warrenton Female Academy. Taken from Catherine E. Thompson, *A Selective Guide to Women-Related Records in the North Carolina State Archives* (Raleigh, NC: North Carolina Division of Archives and History, 1977).

13,426. Hardin, Mary B.
Papers. 1817. 1 item.
Open. Published guide.
North Carolina Division of Archives and History.
Letter written from Boston by Jane A. Blakeley to Edward Jones of Chatham County, NC, concerns provisions made by the North Carolina General Assembly for the education of her daughter. Blakeley was the widow of Captain Johnston Blakeley, who served in the War of 1812. Taken from Catherine E. Thompson, *A Selective Guide to Women-Related Records in the North Carolina State Archives* (Raleigh, NC: North Carolina Division of Archives and History, 1977).

13,427. Harrell
Papers. Nd. 1 item.
Open. Published guide.
North Carolina Division of Archives and History.
Autobiography of Bernard Harrell contains references to his mother, "Black Mama," his stepmother, social activities, courtship customs, marriage, and several girls schools. Taken from Catherine E. Thompson, *A Selective Guide to Women-Related Records in the North Carolina State Archives* (Raleigh, NC: North Carolina Division of Archives and History, 1977).

13,428. Harris, James Henry
Papers. 1848-1967. 29 items.
Open. Published guide.
North Carolina Division of Archives and History.
Collection contains marriage bonds of free Negroes James Henry Harris and Isabella Hinton, 1851, and James Boon and Mahaly Buffaloe, 1854; receipts from Isabella Hinton Harris for the tuition of [Miss] Mahalia Buffalow's children in 1851; and a 1967 biographical sketch of James Henry Harris by [Mrs.] Elizabeth Balanoff, a student at the University of Chicago. Taken from Catherine E. Thompson, *A Selective Guide to Women-Related Records in the North Carolina State Archives* (Raleigh, NC: North Carolina Division of Archives and History, 1977).

13,429. Hatch, Cullen B.
Papers. 1832-85. 4 items.
Open. Published guide.
North Carolina Division of Archives and History.
Letters in which Martha H. Hatch describes to her grandmother [Mrs.] Frances Hill of Wrightsville, NC, a journey from North Carolina to Alabama and her plans for settling in Alabama. Taken from Catherine E. Thompson, *A Selective Guide to Women-Related Records in the North Carolina State Archives* (Raleigh, NC: North Carolina Division of Archives and History, 1977).

13,430. Hawkins, Marmaduke James
Papers. 1809-1909. Ca. 1450 items.
Open. Published guide.
North Carolina Division of Archives and History.
Collection contains a letter from a doctor in 1893 concerning the unavailablity of birth control information and his opinions on birth control and its meaning for women; a letter from Emilie W. McVea to Mrs. Hawkins concerning school policies and the progress of her daughter at St. Mary's College in Raleigh; high school academic reports from the 1890s for Janet and Lula Hawkins; and a bulletin of the Chevy Chase French and English School for Girls. Taken from Catherine E. Thompson, *A Selective Guide to Women-Related Records in the North Carolina State Archives* (Raleigh, NC: North Carolina Division of Archives and History, 1977).

13,431. Hawthorne, Sally
Papers. Nd. 1 item.
Open. Published guide.
North Carolina Division of Archives and History.
Reminiscences of Hawthorne concern experiences she and her family had near Fayetteville, NC, before, during, and after the Civil War. Taken from Catherine E. Thompson, *A Selective Guide to Women-Related Records in the North Carolina State Archives* (Raleigh, NC: North Carolina Division of Archives and History, 1977).

13,432. Haynes Family
Papers. 1869-1966. 110 items.
Open. Published guide.
North Carolina Division of Archives and History.
Collection contains photos and letters by Alice (Haynes) Grow concerning her work as a teacher at a school for the deaf in Kentucky. Letters are addressed primarily to her mother Louisa (Bunker) Haynes, who was the daughter of Siamese twin Chang Bunker, and to her sister Carrie Haynes in Raleigh or at a school for the deaf in Morganton, NC. Taken from Catherine E. Thompson, *A Selective Guide to Women-Related Records in the North Carolina State Archives* (Raleigh, NC: North Carolina Division of Archives and History, 1977).

13,433. Haywood, Martha
Papers. 1916-32. 20 items.
Open. Published guide.
North Carolina Division of Archives and History.
Collection of [Miss] Haywood includes a 1916 letter from Susan F. Hunter, secretary of the North Carolina Equal Suffrage League, and a 1919 news release by the National American Woman Suffrage Association. Taken from Catherine E. Thompson, *A Selective Guide to Women-Related Records in the North Carolina State Archives* (Raleigh, NC: North Carolina Division of Archives and History, 1977).

13,434. Heck, J. M.
Papers. 1761-1947. Ca. 261 items.
Open. Published guide.
North Carolina Division of Archives and History.
Includes religious leaflets by Fannie E. S. Heck printed by the Baptist Woman's Missionary Union and an 1891 clipping referring to Barbara Heck as the mother of Methodism in the US and Canada. Taken from Catherine E. Thompson, *A Selective Guide to Women-Related Records in the North Carolina State Archives* (Raleigh, NC: North Carolina Division of Archives and History, 1977).

13,435. Henries
Papers. 1807-77. 21 items.
Open. Published guide.
North Carolina Division of Archives and History.
Collection contains a guardian's report for 1868 for Rachel A. Johnston and Mary A. Johnston. Taken from Catherine E. Thompson, *A Selective Guide to Women-Related Records in the North Carolina State Archives* (Raleigh, NC: North Carolina Division of Archives and History, 1977).

13,436. Hill, Daniel Harvey, Jr.
Papers. 1808-1967. Ca. 1250 items.
Open. Published guide.
North Carolina Division of Archives and History.
Hill was a member of the board of trustees of the Peace Institute in Raleigh. Material relates to the resignation of the Institute's president Mary O. Graham in 1918, the possibility of combining Peace Institute with the Flora Macdonald College in Red Springs, NC, the expulsion in 1921 of a student after her graduation and entrance into another institution, and other matters. Taken from Catherine E. Thompson, *A Selective Guide to Women-Related Records in the North Carolina State Archives* (Raleigh, NC: North Carolina Division of Archives and History, 1977).

13,437. Hill, John W.
Papers. 1782-1947. Ca. 25 items.
Open. Published guide.
North Carolina Division of Archives and History.
Contains an 1845 letter from Ellen Cromartie at Floral College to her sister concerning school life and a letter to Ellen from Mary Robeson reminiscing about Floral College in Robeson County, NC. Taken from Catherine E. Thompson, *A Selective Guide to Women-Related Records in the North Carolina State Archives* (Raleigh, NC: North Carolina Division of Archives and History, 1977).

13,438. Hines, Wait, and Hines, Leone
Papers. 1839-98. 3 vols. and 498 items.
Open. Published guide.
North Carolina Division of Archives and History.
Accounts of John Peebles, 1854-85, for the schooling of daughters at the Misses Skinner School in New Bern, NC, and at St. Mary's College in Raleigh. Taken from Catherine E. Thompson, *A Selective Guide to Women-Related Records in the North Carolina State Archives* (Raleigh, NC: North Carolina Division of Archives and History, 1977).

13,439. Hodges, John M., and Hodges, Ruth
Papers. 1735-1966. Ca. 675 items.
Open. Published guide.
North Carolina Division of Archives and History.
Papers of the Worth, McNeill, and Hodges families contain correspondence of Roxana Worth McNeill, including an 1846 letter by her sister Flora describing Floral College in Robeson County, NC;

letters concerning social life in New York and a horseback trip taken by a young Quaker girl; an 1869 letter in which McNeill's father Jonathan Worth gives his opinion of Miss Frances Haywood's School in Raleigh; and a letter by the wife of McNeill's nephew James Worth describing life in Geneva, Switzerland, in 1911. Letters of Elvira (Worth) Moffitt from Richmond relate to social life, her involvement with the American Peace Society, the GFWC, the DAR, her concern over the possibility of war with Mexico, and an account of a trip to Yellowstone Park. Also included are letters to John McNeill, Sr., from his daughters Sarah and Flora, an 1888 report card of Clara Hodges from Little River Academy; and a 1910 letter in the Hodges family papers from "cousin Cattie," a Presbyterian missionary in China. Taken from Catherine E. Thompson, *A Selective Guide to Women-Related Records in the North Carolina State Archives* (Raleigh, NC: North Carolina Division of Archives and History, 1977).

13,440. Holland, George
Papers. 1720-1958. 500 items.
Open. Published guide.
North Carolina Division of Archives and History.
Includes two letters by Maude [Mrs. J. E.] Latham in 1944 and 1945 concerning the Society for Preservation of Antiquities and the Tryon Palace Commission and a 1905 booklet by Emma H. Powell about New Bern, NC. Taken from Catherine E. Thompson, *A Selective Guide to Women-Related Records in the North Carolina State Archives* (Raleigh, NC: North Carolina Division of Archives and History, 1977).

13,441. Holt, L. B.
Papers. Nd. 1 item.
Open. Published guide.
North Carolina Division of Archives and History.
A history of ophthalmology in North Carolina covers the period 1873 to 1963 and contains a section with biographical material on women ophthalmologists, among them Louise A. Merriman, who in 1904 became the first woman to practice ophthalmology in North Carolina. Taken from Catherine E. Thompson, *A Selective Guide to Women-Related Records in the North Carolina State Archives* (Raleigh, NC: North Carolina Division of Archives and History, 1977).

13,442. Horne Committee on the Memorial to the North Carolina Women of the Confederacy
Records. 1912-14. 1 box.
Open. Published guide.
North Carolina Division of Archives and History.
Minutes of the Committee and an agreement with a sculptor. Taken from Catherine E. Thompson, *A Selective Guide to Women-Related Records in the North Carolina State Archives* (Raleigh, NC: North Carolina Division of Archives and History, 1977).

13,443. Howell House
Records. 1871-96. 2 vols.
Open. Published guide.
North Carolina Division of Archives and History.
Accounts for monthly board, labor, and food purchases of Mrs. N. G. Howell's boarding house in Raleigh. Taken from Catherine E. Thompson, *A Selective Guide to Women-Related Records in the North Carolina State Archives* (Raleigh, NC: North Carolina Division of Archives and History, 1977).

13,444. Hunter, Aaron Burtis
Papers. 1831-1937. 69 vols. and ca. 425 items.
Open. Published guide.
North Carolina Division of Archives and History.
Hunter was the white principal of St. Augustine's School, a Negro college in Raleigh. Collection reflects the role of his wife Sarah Lothrop Taylor Hunter in establishing the St. Agnes Hospital on the St. Augustine campus. Also included are diaries for 1899 to 1927 with accounts, photos, and post cards concerning her life and travels in Europe. Taken from Catherine E. Thompson, *A Selective Guide to Women-Related Records in the North Carolina State Archives* (Raleigh, NC: North Carolina Division of Archives and History, 1977).

13,445. Hutchison, Susan Davis Nye
Papers. 1815-41. 3 items.
Open. Published guide.
North Carolina Division of Archives and History.
Diaries of Hutchison contain biographical information and entries about her trip from New York to Raleigh, teaching, religion, moral and cultural values, social life, her concern for female slaves, her unstable married life, students, difficulties with child rearing, and her life in North Carolina after her husband's death. The diaries are also available on microfilm. Taken from Catherine E. Thompson, *A Selective Guide to Women-Related Records in the North Carolina State Archives* (Raleigh, NC: North Carolina Division of Archives and History, 1977).

13,446. Iconography
Collection. Nd. No size given.
Open. Published guide.
North Carolina Division of Archives and History.
Photographic negatives and prints, engravings, etchings, lithographs, drawings, paintings, posters, charts, and other illustrations from publications include works by such North Carolina artists as Isabelle Bowen Henderson, Primrose McPherson, and Lena B. Davis and by students at the Ferree School of Art in Raleigh; drawings by John White of Indian women; and photos of paintings by Mary Lydia Hicks Williams depicting Negro life. Also included are scenes of dances, debutantes, parties, and weddings; of teachers, students, buildings, and school activities at East Carolina University and at Peace, St. Mary's, Flora Macdonald, and Black Mountain colleges; of women smugglers in the Civil War period; of women making pottery; and of the 1939 governor's Christmas party for the Women's Prison. Other subjects include women's clothing and fashion; home utilities and appliances; nursing; pregnancy, childbirth, and maternal mortality; DAR and Confederate women monuments; the state Supreme Court with Chief Justice Susie Sharp; and the swearing-in of [Mrs.] Grace J. Rohrer as secretary of art, culture, and history. Among the individual women depicted are midwife Amanda Jane Bunch, Tiny Broadwick, Dorothea L. Dix, Rose Greenhow, Nell Battle Lewis, Flora Macdonald, Carrie Nation, Frances Perkins, and Harriet (Espy) Vance. Also included are illustrations of a number of women's organizations, including the American Legion Auxiliary, the Girl Scouts, the YWCA, the AAUW, the American War Mothers, the Business and Professional Women's Club, the Future Homemakers, Girl's State, Hadassah, the Colonial Dames of America, the DAR, the Home Demonstration Club, the Junior League, the Negro auxiliary of the Needlework Guild of America, the North Carolina Press Women, the Raleigh Woman's Club, the Postal Auxiliary, the Women's Pressure Group for Safety, the Rainbow Girls, the Spinsters Club, and the North Carolina Equal Suffrage Association. Taken from Catherine E. Thompson, *A Selective Guide to Women-Related Records in the North Carolina State Archives* (Raleigh, NC: North Carolina Division of Archives and History, 1977).

13,447. Iden, Susan
Papers. 1855-1928. 1 microfilm reel.
Open. Published guide.
North Carolina Division of Archives and History.
Includes a letter to Iden from novelist Elizabeth Stanley Payne concerning writing as a career and women's experiences; landscape photos by Bayard Wootten and a photo of a class reunion; an article by Iden on [Miss] Mabel Pugh, head of the art department at Peace Junior College in Raleigh, NC; clippings; and a 1934 copy of *The Acorn,* a literary publication of Meredith College in Raleigh. Clippings of newspaper stories by Iden, some of which are accompanied by photos, relate to Jacques and Juliana Busbee of Jugtown; Samarcand Manor, a home for delinquent girls; Hope (Summerell) Chamberlain and her etching shop; a Raleigh policewoman; and the Raleigh Woman's Club. Also included are letters to "Ellen," 1855-96, by Virginia Royster, who later married a Mr. Howell. Taken from Catherine E. Thompson, *A Selective Guide to Women-Related Records in the North Carolina State Archives* (Raleigh, NC: North Carolina Division of Archives and History, 1977).

13,448. Indians
Collection. Nd. No size given.
Open. Published guide.
North Carolina Division of Archives and History.
Official state and county records from North Carolina contain various documents relating to Indians. County marriage registers beginning in ca. 1853 give residence, age, and race of bride and groom and list a number of persons as Indian or "Red." Colonial court records include a 1720 document from Currituck precinct with entries for taxes paid on Sue, an Indian woman. Records of state Supreme Court cases relating to Indians include the 1870 case of *State v. Tachanatah,* which ruled that Cherokees residing in North Carolina were subject to its criminal laws and that cohabitation among Indians according to tribal law is not marriage, so partners could be compelled to testify against each other. A number of deeds for sale of land by or to Indians are included, among them an 1855 deed of conveyance of a 640-acre tract from Coalachy, an Indian woman, to John C. Morris, and an 1856 deed for sale of land by W. H. Thomas to Quateh, a Cherokee woman. Among the governors' records are an 1864 letter by Margaret Love to Governor Vance describing the destitute condition of Indian families whose men were away fighting. Papers of William Williams Stringfield contain a letter by Sister Mollie in 1863 concerning a rumor that Colonel Thomas and Indians were captured by Yankees, and a letter of the same year by Sister Mary concerning the escape of Thomas and Indian troops before the arrival of the Federals. See Donna Spindel, *Introductory Guide to Indian-Related Records (To 1876) in the North Carolina State Archives* (Raleigh: North Carolina Division of Archives and History, 1977).

13,449. Jackson, Mrs. Thomas J.
Papers. 1907. 1 item.
Open. Published guide.
North Carolina Division of Archives and History.
Letter in which Mary Anna Morrison [Mrs. Thomas J.] Jackson of Charlotte, NC, expresses to Major John W. Graham her appreciation for a bill introduced in the North Carolina legislature granting her a pension; she suggests that it be appropriated for the relief of destitute widows of Confederate veterans. Taken from Catherine E. Thompson, *A Selective Guide to Women-Related Records in the North Carolina State Archives* (Raleigh, NC: North Carolina Division of Archives and History, 1977).

13,450. Jacocks, Charles W.
Papers. 1819-46. 104 items.
Open. Published guide.
North Carolina Division of Archives and History.
Collection contains correspondence of Mary Caroline (Jacocks) Reed, including letters from Oxford Female Academy about grades and progress reports. Also included are letters to Charles Jacocks from Mary [Mrs. Thomas] Potter concerning property administration, marriage, and descriptions of Tennessee and letters from Martha

E. (Webb) Mitchell concerning property, the hardships of widowhood, providing for her family, and marriage. Taken from Catherine E. Thompson, *A Selective Guide to Women-Related Records in the North Carolina State Archives* (Raleigh, NC: North Carolina Division of Archives and History, 1977).

13,451. Jefferson, Martha
Papers. 1781. 1 item.
Open. Published guide.
North Carolina Division of Archives and History.
Letter by Martha (Wayles) Jefferson (1748-82), who was first married to Bathurst Skelton and then to Thomas Jefferson, is addressed to Sarah Tate Madison, whose husband James Madison was a Protestant Episcopal bishop in Virginia and president of the College of William and Mary in Williamsburg, VA; the letter concerns a proposal by Pennsylvania ladies to promote the patriot cause. Taken from Catherine E. Thompson, *A Selective Guide to Women-Related Records in the North Carolina State Archives* (Raleigh, NC: North Carolina Division of Archives and History, 1977).

13,452. Jeffreys, William Andrew, and Family
Papers. 1786-1883. Ca. 775 items.
Open. Published guide.
North Carolina Division of Archives and History.
Contains material relating to Raleigh Female Academy, 1804-21, including correspondence about tuition and financial and business papers. Taken from Catherine E. Thompson, *A Selective Guide to Women-Related Records in the North Carolina State Archives* (Raleigh, NC: North Carolina Division of Archives and History, 1977).

13,453. Jerman, Mrs. Palmer
Papers. 1920. 1 item.
Open. Published guide.
North Carolina Division of Archives and History.
Telegram from former governor James M. Cox of Ohio, the Democratic nominee for president, to Jerman denying a report that he had sent an emissary to work against ratification of the 19th amendment in North Carolina. Taken from Catherine E. Thompson, *A Selective Guide to Women-Related Records in the North Carolina State Archives* (Raleigh, NC: North Carolina Division of Archives and History, 1977).

13,454. Johnson, Charles E.
Papers. 1694-1875. 28 boxes.
Open. Published guide.
North Carolina Division of Archives and History.
Correspondence of the James Iredell, Sr., family spans the years 1772 to 1806 and includes Hannah Iredell's letters to her husband James, who was a US Supreme Court justice from 1790 to 1799, concerning travel plans, social activities in North Carolina, and a difficult move from New York to Philadelphia with her children and mother-in-law; letters to Hannah Iredell from her niece Penelope Swann regarding her responsibilities at home resulting from her mother's poor health; and letters to James Iredell, Sr., from Mrs. P. Dawson in 1789 describing the early days of the federal government and outstanding personalities. Letters from Jane Blair to her daughter Nelly relate social, family, and local news, while her letters to Hannah and James Iredell concern her feelings about the Revolutionary War, flight from the British, difficulties of housekeeping for an extended family in wartime, rumors of abuse of women by soldiers, and plantation affairs in the postwar period. Also included are letters to James Iredell, Jr., who was governor of North Carolina in 1827 and 1828, from his wife Fanny Iredell concerning babies, children's education, business matters, household problems, and their daughter Annie going to Philadelphia to study; from his sister Annie concerning her studies; from his mother, giving advice, family news, and political opinions; and from his daughter Annie at school in Philadelphia and after her marriage. Taken from Catherine E. Thompson, *A Selective Guide to Women-Related Records in the North Carolina State Archives* (Raleigh, NC: North Carolina Division of Archives and History, 1977).

13,455. Jones, Crabtree
Papers. 1771-1934. Ca. 1250 items.
Open. Published guide.
North Carolina Division of Archives and History.
Includes an 1850 letter of [Mrs.] Martha Green to her daughter at school and an 1851 letter of [Mrs.] Mary W. Jones to her daughter at school. Taken from Catherine E. Thompson, *A Selective Guide to Women-Related Records in the North Carolina State Archives* (Raleigh, NC: North Carolina Division of Archives and History, 1977).

13,456. Joyner, James Yadkin
Papers. 1873-1919. 1211 items.
Open. Published guide.
North Carolina Division of Archives and History.
Collection contains a letter in which Mrs. R. J. Reynolds asks Joyner for advice about establishing a rural community school. Taken from Catherine E. Thompson, *A Selective Guide to Women-Related Records in the North Carolina State Archives* (Raleigh, NC: North Carolina Division of Archives and History, 1977).

13,457. Knox, Eliza Heritage Washington
Papers. 1816-93. 1 microfilm reel.
Open. Published guide.
North Carolina Division of Archives and History.
Scrapbook of [Mrs.] Knox contains letters, manuscripts, drawings, and clippings. Taken from Catherine E. Thompson, *A Selective Guide to Women-Related Records in the North Carolina State Archives* (Raleigh, NC: North Carolina Division of Archives and History, 1977).

13,458. Koonce, Lizzie
Papers. 1857. 2 items.
Open. Published guide.
North Carolina Division of Archives and History.
A report of [Miss] Koonce's progress at Goldsboro Female College. Taken from Catherine E. Thompson, *A Selective Guide to Women-Related Records in the North Carolina State Archives* (Raleigh, NC: North Carolina Division of Archives and History, 1977).

13,459. Lacy, Benjamin Rice
Papers. 1850-1929. 1427 items.
Open. Published guide.
North Carolina Division of Archives and History.
Correspondence in 1916 to Lacy, who was seeking re-election as state treasurer, concerns the woman suffrage movement and various organizations. Also includes letters to Lacy in 1921 from United Daughters of the Confederacy representatives regarding an antisouthern history textbook in the public schools. Taken from Catherine E. Thompson, *A Selective Guide to Women-Related Records in the North Carolina State Archives* (Raleigh, NC: North Carolina Division of Archives and History, 1977).

13,460. Lacy, Drury
Papers. 1856-83. 40 items.
Open. Published guide.
North Carolina Division of Archives and History.
Includes a letter from Charles Phillips to Lacy in 1881 concerning general conditions at Peace College. Taken from Catherine E. Thompson, *A Selective Guide to Women-Related Records in the North Carolina State Archives* (Raleigh, NC: North Carolina Division of Archives and History, 1977).

13,461. Ladies' Memorial Association of Wake County
Records. 1866-1919. 2 boxes.
Open. Published guide.
North Carolina Division of Archives and History.
Constitution, minutes, deeds, correspondence, speeches, membership lists, a history, reports, Confederate Memorial Day addresses, clippings, and other records of the Association. Taken from Catherine E. Thompson, *A Selective Guide to Women-Related Records in the North Carolina State Archives* (Raleigh, NC: North Carolina Division of Archives and History, 1977).

13,462. Lamberston
Papers. 1828-72. 7 items.
Open. Published guide.
North Carolina Division of Archives and History.
Reports from 1872 for Mary and Margaret Lamberston from Wesleyan Female College in Murfreesboro, NC. Taken from Catherine E. Thompson, *A Selective Guide to Women-Related Records in the North Carolina State Archives* (Raleigh, NC: North Carolina Division of Archives and History, 1977).

13,463. Lambeth, W. B., and Family
Papers. 1851-1908. Ca. 235 items.
Open. Published guide.
North Carolina Division of Archives and History.
Bell family correspondence includes letters from Nannie Bell, later Mrs. A. G. Atkins, to Susan Bell, later Mrs. Baldwin, and letters from relatives in Mississippi and Alabama discussing family news, school, and social life. Also included are Lambeth family correspondence, an advertisement for Greensboro Female College in Greensboro, NC, and recipes. Taken from Catherine E. Thompson, *A Selective Guide to Women-Related Records in the North Carolina State Archives* (Raleigh, NC: North Carolina Division of Archives and History, 1977).

13,464. League of American Pen Women
Records. 1926. 1 box.
Open. Published guide.
North Carolina Division of Archives and History.
Auxiliary certificate of the North Carolina branch. Taken from Catherine E. Thompson, *A Selective Guide to Women-Related Records in the North Carolina State Archives* (Raleigh, NC: North Carolina Division of Archives and History, 1977).

13,465. LeConte, Emma Florence
Papers. 1864-65. 1 item.
Open. Published guide.
North Carolina Division of Archives and History.
Civil War journal kept by LeConte when she was 17 contains reflections and a detailed account of the burning of Columbia, SC. The journal was published in 1957. Taken from Catherine E. Thompson, *A Selective Guide to Women-Related Records in the North Carolina State Archives* (Raleigh, NC: North Carolina Division of Archives and History, 1977).

13,466. Lewis, K. H.
Papers. 1834-1907. 42 items.
Open. Published guide.
North Carolina Division of Archives and History.
Collection contains letters to Bettie Bryan, daughter of John Herritage Bryan, from various correspondents, including a former schoolmate at St. Mary's Junior College in Raleigh; an 1879 letter describing activities at St. Mary's; and an 1876 report card for Annie Lewis from St. Mary's. Taken from Catherine E. Thompson, *A Selective Guide to Women-Related Records in the North Carolina State Archives* (Raleigh, NC: North Carolina Division of Archives and History, 1977).

13,467. Lewis, McDaniel
Papers. 1861-1972. 118 items.
Open. Published guide.
North Carolina Division of Archives and History.
Collection contains a brief history of Lewis School, a coeducational institution conducted by physician Richard Lewis and his wife from 1877 to 1902 in

Kinston, NC. Taken from Catherine E. Thompson, *A Selective Guide to Women-Related Records in the North Carolina State Archives* (Raleigh, NC: North Carolina Division of Archives and History, 1977).

13,468. Lewis, Nell Battle
Papers. 1862-1956. 53 boxes and 1 microfilm reel.
Open. Published guide.
North Carolina Division of Archives and History.
Lewis was a lawyer and for 25 years author of the column "Incidentally" in the Raleigh *News and Observer*. Collection dates primarily from 1920 to 1956 and includes correspondence, speeches on the peace movement, articles, lecture material, photos, book reviews, campaign material, microfilm of her "Incidentally" columns and Raleigh *Times* editorials, and other items. Personal correspondence includes a letter in which her brother R. H. Lewis expresses displeasure at her candidacy for the General Assembly in 1928, while other correspondence relates to her law practice, her graduate work, her connection with St. Mary's College in Raleigh, politics, social reform, communism, segregation, and other subjects. Among the correspondents are Ellen B. Winston, Gertrude Weil, and Hope (Summerell) Chamberlain. Material for her column relates to such topics as woman's suffrage, the feminist movement, laws regarding working women, women's prisons, women's education, female labor leaders, the first woman elected to the North Carolina senate, and women's work in clubs in North Carolina. Also included are articles on various women, a survey of women in industry, and correspondence and other information relating to the Samarcand arson case of 1931, wherein Lewis defended Virginia Hayes. In an 1865 letter a St. Mary's student describes the passage of Johnson's and Sherman's armies by the school. Taken from Catherine E. Thompson, *A Selective Guide to Women-Related Records in the North Carolina State Archives* (Raleigh, NC: North Carolina Division of Archives and History, 1977).

13,469. Liles, Meta
Papers. 1935. 1 item.
Open. Published guide.
North Carolina Division of Archives and History.
Typescript of a play by Liles entitled *Echoes from the Houseboat on the Styx*. Taken from Catherine E. Thompson, *A Selective Guide to Women-Related Records in the North Carolina State Archives* (Raleigh, NC: North Carolina Division of Archives and History, 1977).

13,470. Lilly
Papers. 1785-1863. 1 microfilm reel.
Open. Published guide.
North Carolina Division of Archives and History.
Letters of Mary Allen to her grandmother [Mrs.] Rachel Marshall, 1845-48, include one from Floral College near Red Springs, NC, with a brief description of life at the school, which was founded in 1841 and closed in 1878. Taken from Catherine E. Thompson, *A Selective Guide to Women-Related Records in the North Carolina State Archives* (Raleigh, NC: North Carolina Division of Archives and History, 1977).

13,471. Little and Mordecai
Papers. 1713-1959. 26 ft.
Open. Published guide.
North Carolina Division of Archives and History.
Correspondence of the Little family includes letters from Thomas Little to his mother Ann Hawkins Little, which indicate that she assumed operation of a farm after her husband's death, and letters from Margaret Little to her husband George concerning social life and customs of upper-class Raleigh in the 19th century. Papers of the family of Jacob Mordecai, who operated Warrenton Female Academy from 1809 to 1819, include correspondence, 1824-84, of his daughter Ellen Mordecai (1790-1884), chiefly from her sister Caroline in Mobile, AL; typescript of a novel written by Ellen; a register of Warrenton Academy students; journals; scrapbooks; almanacs; and textbooks. Correspondence of the Haywood family depicts family life in Raleigh. Taken from Catherine E. Thompson, *A Selective Guide to Women-Related Records in the North Carolina State Archives* (Raleigh, NC: North Carolina Division of Archives and History, 1977).

13,472. Litwack, Charlotte
Papers. 1976. 8 items and 6 tapes.
Open. Published guide.
North Carolina Division of Archives and History.
Manuscript of Litwack's book *Recollections: Conversations about House of Jacob,* which was based on synagogue minutes from 1913 and interviews with orthodox Jews in Raleigh who had been members of the House of Jacob until it was replaced in 1951 by the new synagogue, Beth Meyer. Tapes of some of the interviews are included. Taken from Catherine E. Thompson, *A Selective Guide to Women-Related Records in the North Carolina State Archives* (Raleigh, NC: North Carolina Division of Archives and History, 1977).

13,473. London, Isaac Spencer
Papers. 1769-1964. Ca. 10 cu.ft.
Open. Published guide.
North Carolina Division of Archives and History.
Collection contains a 1946 letter about congressional legislation from US representative Eliza Jane Pratt, who was more commonly known as Jane Pratt, a subject file on Flora Macdonald, and a series of clippings on Methodism in Richmond County and Rockingham, NC, written by Lillie (Moore) Everett. Taken from Catherine E. Thompson, *A Selective Guide to Women-Related Records in the North Carolina State Archives* (Raleigh, NC: North Carolina Division of Archives and History, 1977).

13,474. Long, William
Papers. 1804-1972. 3 microfilm reels.
Open. Published guide.
North Carolina Division of Archives and History.
Recipes and an 1890 program for a musical soirée at Peace Institute, which later became Peace Junior College, in Raleigh. Taken from Catherine E. Thompson, *A Selective Guide to Women-Related Records in the North Carolina State Archives* (Raleigh, NC: North Carolina Division of Archives and History, 1977).

13,475. Luria, Albert Moses
Papers. 1861-62. 1 item.
Open. Published guide.
North Carolina Division of Archives and History.
Luria's journal discusses several female friends and relatives and contains remarks on his attitudes toward women. Taken from Catherine E. Thompson, *A Selective Guide to Women-Related Records in the North Carolina State Archives* (Raleigh, NC: North Carolina Division of Archives and History, 1977).

13,476. M. W. H.
Papers. 1862. 2 items.
Open. Published guide.
North Carolina Division of Archives and History.
Letters from "M. W. H." to her husband concern war news, her fears, managing home affairs, and finances. Taken from Catherine E. Thompson, *A Selective Guide to Women-Related Records in the North Carolina State Archives* (Raleigh, NC: North Carolina Division of Archives and History, 1977).

13,477. Mack, Mary
Papers. 1873-90. 1 item.
Open. Published guide.
North Carolina Division of Archives and History.
Autograph book given to Mack by a schoolmate contains inscriptions by classmates at Salem Female Academy and by other friends. Taken from Catherine E. Thompson, *A Selective Guide to Women-Related Records in the North Carolina State Archives* (Raleigh, NC: North Carolina Division of Archives and History, 1977).

13,478. McKay and Cromartie Family
Papers. 1749-1861. 40 items.
Open. Published guide.
North Carolina Division of Archives and History.
Microfilm copy of Eliza McKay's account book for 1802 to 1854. Taken from Catherine E. Thompson, *A Selective Guide to Women-Related Records in the North Carolina State Archives* (Raleigh, NC: North Carolina Division of Archives and History, 1977).

13,479. McKimmon, Jane (Simpson)
Papers. 1910-45. 32 boxes.
Open. Published guide.
North Carolina Division of Archives and History.
McKimmon (1867-1957), a home demonstration agent for North Carolina from 1911 to 1925 and assistant director of extension for North Carolina State University from 1922 to 1936, developed a program for improvement of the lives of rural women and their families through education in home economics. Collection contains letters from friends, home demonstration agents, and heads of various divisions of the USDA extension service; desk calendars; speeches; articles; biographical sketches of McKimmon; scrapbooks; conceit books; reports; bulletins; pamphlets; Home Demonstration annual reports; booklets; clippings concerning McKimmon, home demonstration work, and rural girls and women; and other material. Also included is a diary in which Ellen Brewer records the activities of the North Carolina Home Economics Association. McKimmon received an honorary degree from the University of North Carolina at Chapel Hill. Taken from Catherine E. Thompson, *A Selective Guide to Women-Related Records in the North Carolina State Archives* (Raleigh, NC: North Carolina Division of Archives and History, 1977).

13,480. McKimmon, Kate
Papers. 1841-72. Ca. 300 items.
Open. Published guide.
North Carolina Division of Archives and History.
Letters to [Miss] McKimmon at St. Mary's College in Raleigh from former classmates and students contain reminiscences of school days and comments on Raleigh and Hillsborough, NC, residents and their activities. Also included are recipes and letters from James McKimmon in Baltimore containing comments on women and feminine styles. Taken from Catherine E. Thompson, *A Selective Guide to Women-Related Records in the North Carolina State Archives* (Raleigh, NC: North Carolina Division of Archives and History, 1977).

13,481. McLauchlin, Mrs. J. W.
Papers. Ca. 1912. 1 item.
Open. Published guide.
North Carolina Division of Archives and History.
McLauchlin's account of a skirmish at Munroe Farm in Hoke County, NC, in 1865. Taken from Catherine E. Thompson, *A Selective Guide to Women-Related Records in the North Carolina State Archives* (Raleigh, NC: North Carolina Division of Archives and History, 1977).

13,482. Macon, Nathaniel
Papers. 1773-1848. 117 items.
Open. Published guide.
North Carolina Division of Archives and History.
Includes 19th-century letters of Seigniora [Mrs. William] Eaton to her sons in Chapel Hill, NC, and the petition of a female slave to a court

concerning her husband's freedom. Taken from Catherine E. Thompson, *A Selective Guide to Women-Related Records in the North Carolina State Archives* (Raleigh, NC: North Carolina Division of Archives and History, 1977).

13,483. Madison, Dolley Payne
Papers. 1849. 1 item.
Open. Published guide.
North Carolina Division of Archives and History.
Copy of the will of Madison (1768-1849), who was first married to John Todd, Jr., and then to James Madison, US President. Taken from Catherine E. Thompson, *A Selective Guide to Women-Related Records in the North Carolina State Archives* (Raleigh, NC: North Carolina Division of Archives and History, 1977).

13,484. Mangold, Frederick R.
Papers. 1933-72. 450 items.
Open. Published guide.
North Carolina Division of Archives and History.
Collection of Mangold and his wife contains correspondence, articles, and publications concerning Black Mountain College near Black Mountain, NC, with several items by and about Anni and Josef Albers. Taken from Catherine E. Thompson, *A Selective Guide to Women-Related Records in the North Carolina State Archives* (Raleigh, NC: North Carolina Division of Archives and History, 1977).

13,485. Mangum, Willie Person
Papers. 1809-94. Ca. 2000 items.
Open. Published guide.
North Carolina Division of Archives and History.
Affectionate letters between Willie and Charity Mangum concern their children, health matters, family news, politics, and their daughters' activities, education, and later lives. Taken from Catherine E. Thompson, *A Selective Guide to Women-Related Records in the North Carolina State Archives* (Raleigh, NC: North Carolina Division of Archives and History, 1977).

13,486. Michaux and Randolph
Papers. 1745-1902. Ca. 500 items.
Open. Published guide.
North Carolina Division of Archives and History.
Includes a 1769 letter in which Mary Scott Randolph of England advises her children on marriage, friendships, and finances, and correspondence and legal papers regarding a suit filed by Joseph Michaux on behalf of his first wife's widow's dower from her first husband. Taken from Catherine E. Thompson, *A Selective Guide to Women-Related Records in the North Carolina State Archives* (Raleigh, NC: North Carolina Division of Archives and History, 1977).

13,487. Middleton, Lucy B.
Papers. 1877. 1 item.
Open. Published guide.
North Carolina Division of Archives and History.
Diploma of [Mrs. Leonidas] Middleton from the Raleigh Female Seminary in Raleigh, NC. Taken from Catherine E. Thompson, *A Selective Guide to Women-Related Records in the North Carolina State Archives* (Raleigh, NC: North Carolina Division of Archives and History, 1977).

13,488. Miscellany
Papers. 1697-1912. Ca. 650 items.
Open. Published guide.
North Carolina Division of Archives and History.
Includes an abstract of a letter describing Governor Dobbs's marriage to 15-year-old Justina Davis, whose second husband was Governor Abner Nash, and letters to and from women regarding personal matters, pension claims, local news, and other subjects. Taken from Catherine E. Thompson, *A Selective Guide to Women-Related Records in the North Carolina State Archives* (Raleigh, NC: North Carolina Division of Archives and History, 1977).

13,489. Moffitt, Elvira
Papers. 1911-23. 4 items.
Open. Published guide.
North Carolina Division of Archives and History.
Includes a letter to [Mrs.] Moffitt from Captain J. J. Laughinghouse, superintendent of the North Carolina State Prison in Raleigh, commenting on suffrage and extolling the success of the state prison farm; a prospectus of the Virginia Dare Manual Training School; and a bulletin of Fredericksburg Normal School for women. Taken from Catherine E. Thompson, *A Selective Guide to Women-Related Records in the North Carolina State Archives* (Raleigh, NC: North Carolina Division of Archives and History, 1977).

13,490. Moore, Bartholomew F.
Papers. 1791-1899. 1 microfilm reel.
Open. Published guide.
North Carolina Division of Archives and History.
Letters of Moore to his daughter Lucy Catherine "Katie," 1851-77, concern education, advice, the duties of an eldest daughter, and other subjects. Also included are letters from a mother to her daughter, 1876-82, and a clipping of maxims entitled "Some Opinions of Women." Taken from Catherine E. Thompson, *A Selective Guide to Women-Related Records in the North Carolina State Archives* (Raleigh, NC: North Carolina Division of Archives and History, 1977).

13,491. Mordecai, Pattie
Papers. 1796-1876. 173 items.
Open. Published guide.
North Carolina Division of Archives and History.
Correspondence of the family of Jacob Mordecai, who in 1809 established Mordecai Female Seminary in Warrenton, NC, includes letters of his daughters Rachel and Ellen, who assisted with the school; of Emma, a religious and educational worker; and of Caroline, who continued the school. Subjects discussed include family affairs, the school, trips, and current events. Taken from Catherine E. Thompson, *A Selective Guide to Women-Related Records in the North Carolina State Archives* (Raleigh, NC: North Carolina Division of Archives and History, 1977).

13,492. Murphey, Archibald D.
Papers. 1797-1852. 511 items.
Open. Published guide.
North Carolina Division of Archives and History.
Collection contains letters by Cornelia Anne Murphey in 1818 and 1821 to her father Archibald Murphey pertaining to her educational experiences and to management of affairs at home during his absence. Taken from Catherine E. Thompson, *A Selective Guide to Women-Related Records in the North Carolina State Archives* (Raleigh, NC: North Carolina Division of Archives and History, 1977).

13,493. Myers, Thomas J.
Papers. 1865-99. 2 items.
Open. Published guide.
North Carolina Division of Archives and History.
Typescript reminiscence describes the experiences of Floride Cantey, who later married John Johnson, and her mother with marauders from invading forces at their home near Camden, SC, during the Civil War. Taken from Catherine E. Thompson, *A Selective Guide to Women-Related Records in the North Carolina State Archives* (Raleigh, NC: North Carolina Division of Archives and History, 1977).

13,494. Nash, Francis
Papers. 1757-1864. Ca. 225 items.
Open. Published guide.
North Carolina Division of Archives and History.
Includes an 1863 circular of the boarding school of Misses Nash and Kollock in Hillsborough, NC. Taken from Catherine E. Thompson, *A Selective Guide to Women-Related Records in the North Carolina State Archives* (Raleigh, NC: North Carolina Division of Archives and History, 1977).

13,495. Neal
Papers. Nd. 1 microfilm reel.
Open. Published guide.
North Carolina Division of Archives and History.
Family memo books containing recipes. Taken from Catherine E. Thompson, *A Selective Guide to Women-Related Records in the North Carolina State Archives* (Raleigh, NC: North Carolina Division of Archives and History, 1977).

13,496. Newby, J. B.
Papers. 1846. 1 item.
Open. Published guide.
North Carolina Division of Archives and History.
Letter from Newby to Horace Mann concerns new schools with women students in Wilmington, NC, and Fayetteville, NC. Taken from Catherine E. Thompson, *A Selective Guide to Women-Related Records in the North Carolina State Archives* (Raleigh, NC: North Carolina Division of Archives and History, 1977).

13,497. Newton, Mrs. Scott R.
Papers. 1793-1859. 11 items.
Open. Published guide.
North Carolina Division of Archives and History.
Includes an 1858 letter to D. W. Shaw from his sister C. A. Shaw concerning school and an upcoming examination. Taken from Catherine E. Thompson, *A Selective Guide to Women-Related Records in the North Carolina State Archives* (Raleigh, NC: North Carolina Division of Archives and History, 1977).

13,498. Norcum, James, and Family
Papers. 1805-73. Ca. 275 items.
Open. Published guide.
North Carolina Division of Archives and History.
Family correspondence and other papers provide a history of this eastern North Carolina family through three generations and, additionally, reveal information about courtship and marriage customs and the treatment of disease. Included are letters of James Norcom to [Miss] Mary Harvey discussing the status of women and letters to Mary Matilda Norcom from her father concerning health, religion, social behavior, reading, letter writing, and the use of vacation time. Taken from Catherine E. Thompson, *A Selective Guide to Women-Related Records in the North Carolina State Archives* (Raleigh, NC: North Carolina Division of Archives and History, 1977).

13,499. Norman
Papers. 1811-1911. 400 items.
Open. Published guide.
North Carolina Division of Archives and History.
Family correspondence includes letters from S. S. Norman's daughters, who were attending school in Red Springs, NC, and at Yadkin College in Davidson County, NC, and letters between Ellen Norman and her daughters, who write about their children, and her sons, who write about their work. Taken from Catherine E. Thompson, *A Selective Guide to Women-Related Records in the North Carolina State Archives* (Raleigh, NC: North Carolina Division of Archives and History, 1977).

13,500. North Carolina Association of Jewish Women
Records. Nd. 1 box.
Open. Published guide.
North Carolina Division of Archives and History.
A history of the Association, which was founded in 1921 in Goldsboro, NC. Early leaders of the group included Sarah (Einstein) [Mrs. Sol] Weil and [Mrs.] Mina Weil. Taken from Catherine E. Thompson, *A Selective Guide to Women-Related*

Records in the North Carolina State Archives (Raleigh, NC: North Carolina Division of Archives and History, 1977).

13,501. North Carolina College Conference, Committee on Cooperative Research
Records. 1937-65. 5 boxes.
Open. Published guide.
North Carolina Division of Archives and History.
Minutes; agendas; correspondence; membership lists; subcommittee reports; reports on college and university research; programs; issues of *Proceedings,* the official record of Conference meetings; and other material of the Committee, which was active until 1965. Lillian Parker Wallace served as permanent secretary of the Committee from 1933 through 1963. Taken from Catherine E. Thompson, *A Selective Guide to Women-Related Records in the North Carolina State Archives* (Raleigh, NC: North Carolina Division of Archives and History, 1977).

13,502. North Carolina Committee on Patient Care
Records. Nd. 1 vol. and microfiche.
Open. Published guide.
North Carolina Division of Archives and History.
Constitution, bylaws, minutes, financial records, joint statement of purpose, correspondence, history, annual report, material concerning committee appointments, pamphlets, and other items of the Committee, which was formed in 1962 by the merger of the North Carolina Commission on Patient Care and the North Carolina Committee on Nursing and Nursing Education. Taken from Catherine E. Thompson, *A Selective Guide to Women-Related Records in the North Carolina State Archives* (Raleigh, NC: North Carolina Division of Archives and History, 1977).

13,503. North Carolina Committee to End the War in Indochina
Records. 1971-73. 1 box.
Open. Published guide.
North Carolina Division of Archives and History.
Correspondence, interviews, statements of position, speeches, clippings, and other records of the steering committee of the Raleigh chapter of this organization, which was a grass roots effort to end the war by encouraging citizens to write or visit congressmen, by providing information on pending legislation, and by inviting informed speakers to Raleigh. Taken from Catherine E. Thompson, *A Selective Guide to Women-Related Records in the North Carolina State Archives* (Raleigh, NC: North Carolina Division of Archives and History, 1977).

13,504. North Carolina Conference for Social Service
Records. 1922-59. 16 boxes.
Open. Published guide.
North Carolina Division of Archives and History.
Constitution, minutes, financial reports, president's and executive secretary's correspondence, membership material, speeches, reports, and other records of the Conference, which was formed in 1912 by [Miss] Daisy Denson and five men to improve social conditions in North Carolina. The Conference helped to enact legislation establishing a mothers' aid system and providing state aid for Efland School for Negro girls. Included is correspondence of Mrs. Hugh Waddell and of Gertrude Weil from 1930 to 1933 while she was serving as executive secretary of the Conference. Taken from Catherine E. Thompson, *A Selective Guide to Women-Related Records in the North Carolina State Archives* (Raleigh, NC: North Carolina Division of Archives and History, 1977).

13,505. North Carolina Council of Churches, United Church Women
Records. Nd. 8 boxes, 1 vol., and 1 microfilm reel.
Open. Published guide.
North Carolina Division of Archives and History.
Constitution, bylaws, minutes, financial records, correspondence, membership lists, reports, state assembly material, pamphlets, newsletters, directories, information and correspondence concerning local and state councils and weekday religious education in schools, clippings, and other material. Taken from Catherine E. Thompson, *A Selective Guide to Women-Related Records in the North Carolina State Archives* (Raleigh, NC: North Carolina Division of Archives and History, 1977).

13,506. North Carolina Family Life Council
Records. 1948-72. 4 boxes.
Open. Published guide.
North Carolina Division of Archives and History.
Bylaws, minutes, financial records, correspondence, membership lists, a history, reports, material concerning the work of the Council, programs, awards material, and printed literature of the Council. Taken from Catherine E. Thompson, *A Selective Guide to Women-Related Records in the North Carolina State Archives* (Raleigh, NC: North Carolina Division of Archives and History, 1977).

13,507. North Carolina Federation of Music Clubs
Records. Nd. Ca. 60 boxes and vols.
Open. Published guide.
North Carolina Division of Archives and History.
Constitutions, minutes, presidents' papers and reports, treasurers' reports, a history, material concerning state districts and departments, scrapbooks, publications, and other records of the Federation. Taken from Catherine E. Thompson, *A Selective Guide to Women-Related Records in the North Carolina State Archives* (Raleigh, NC: North Carolina Division of Archives and History, 1977).

13,508. North Carolina Federation of Women's Clubs, Raleigh Woman's Club
Records. 1904-65. 9 boxes and 5 vols.
Open. Published guide.
North Carolina Division of Archives and History.
The Club was organized in 1904 to work for intellectual, philanthropic, social, civic, and domestic improvement of the city. Includes constitution, minutes, financial records, tax records, correspondence, scholarship and other applications, a history, reports, nominating committee material, scrapbooks, awards, programs, club news, yearbooks, handbook, clippings, tributes to former presidents of the Club and to physician Delia Dixon Carroll, a 1912 report to the city planning committee of the Club, and issues of the newsletter "Tell a Woman," 1963-64. Also includes material of the state Federation. Taken from Catherine E. Thompson, *A Selective Guide to Women-Related Records in the North Carolina State Archives* (Raleigh, NC: North Carolina Division of Archives and History, 1977).

13,509. North Carolina Home Economics Association
Records. 1919-45. 2 boxes.
Open. Published guide.
North Carolina Division of Archives and History.
Minutes, financial records, membership lists, transmittals, programs, and material concerning agricultural and domestic activities of the Association. Also included are papers of Margaret Jones, who was treasurer of the Association from 1944 to 1945. Taken from Catherine E. Thompson, *A Selective Guide to Women-Related Records in the North Carolina State Archives* (Raleigh, NC: North Carolina Division of Archives and History, 1977).

13,510. North Carolina League of Women Voters
Records. 1920-75. 34 boxes.
Open. Published guide.
North Carolina Division of Archives and History.
Records of the state LWV and of the Durham, Greensboro, Raleigh-Wake County, and Winston-Salem chapters include bylaws; financial records; correspondence; board meeting information; reports; memos; calendar; resource material on various subjects; voter service material; biographical information on candidates; material on the nominating committee and conventions and on the national LWV; information about the North Carolina Council of Women's Organizations; pamphlets; a directory; publications; and other items. Taken from Catherine E. Thompson, *A Selective Guide to Women-Related Records in the North Carolina State Archives* (Raleigh, NC: North Carolina Division of Archives and History, 1977).

13,511. North Carolina Literary and Historical Association
Records. 1900-71. 56 boxes.
Open. Published guide.
North Carolina Division of Archives and History.
Collection consists of records of secretaries of the Association. Past presidents include Adelaide Fries, Alice Baldwin, Inglis Fletcher, Bernice Kelly Harris, Gertrude Carraway, and Margaret Harper. The Association has presented literary awards to a number of women, including Olive (Tilford) Dargan, Winifred Kirkland, Bernice (Kelly) Harris, Josephine Niggli, Inglis Fletcher, Helen Bevington, and Betty Smith. Taken from Catherine E. Thompson, *A Selective Guide to Women-Related Records in the North Carolina State Archives* (Raleigh, NC: North Carolina Division of Archives and History, 1977).

13,512. North Carolina Mental Health Association
Records. 1913-61. 3 boxes.
Open. Published guide.
North Carolina Division of Archives and History.
Constitution, bylaws, minutes, correspondence, committee material, reports, membership lists, a history, a photo, programs, newsletters, information on Dorothea Dix, items concerning mental health week and the National Association for Mental Health, and other records of the Association. [Miss] Daisy Denson was elected vice-president at the Association's organizational meeting. Taken from Catherine E. Thompson, *A Selective Guide to Women-Related Records in the North Carolina State Archives* (Raleigh, NC: North Carolina Division of Archives and History, 1977).

13,513. North Carolina Public Health Association
Records. 1911-69. 6 boxes.
Open. Published guide.
North Carolina Division of Archives and History.
Constitution; bylaws; annual reports; minutes; financial records; correspondence; membership records; minutes, speeches, and programs of annual conventions; material on committees, sections, and awards; newsletters; handbooks; and other records of the Association, which was known as the North Carolina Health Officers' Association until 1922. Taken from Catherine E. Thompson, *A Selective Guide to Women-Related Records in the North Carolina State Archives* (Raleigh, NC: North Carolina Division of Archives and History, 1977).

13,514. North Carolina Society for the Preservation of Antiquities
Records. 1932-70. 19 boxes and 1 microfilm reel.
Open. Published guide.

North Carolina Division of Archives and History. Certificate of incorporation, constitution, bylaws, amendments, minutes, agendas, financial records, correspondence, information about members and officers, project files, committee material and reports, news releases, information concerning branch and local units, proceedings of annual meetings, photos, scrapbook, programs, pamphlets, clippings, awards material relating to Mrs. Horace P. Robinson, and other records of the Society, which was organized in 1939 to aid and publicize preservation of historic sites, houses, and other antiquities in North Carolina. Adelaide Fries and Mrs. Ernest Ives were instrumental in the Society and [Mrs.] Ruth Coltrane Cannon served as president from 1945 until her death in 1966. Taken from Catherine E. Thompson, *A Selective Guide to Women-Related Records in the North Carolina State Archives* (Raleigh, NC: North Carolina Division of Archives and History, 1977).

13,515. North Carolina State Mothers Association
Records. 1942-74. 2 vols.
Open. Published guide.
North Carolina Division of Archives and History. Memory books of the Association. Taken from Catherine E. Thompson, *A Selective Guide to Women-Related Records in the North Carolina State Archives* (Raleigh, NC: North Carolina Division of Archives and History, 1977).

13,516. Nunn, Romulus A.
Papers. 1757-1963. Ca. 300 items.
Open. Published guide.
North Carolina Division of Archives and History. Correspondence for the period 1898 to 1940 by prominent North Carolina women opposing the 19th amendment includes a 1920 letter by Mary Hilliard Hinton, president of the North Carolina branch of the Southern League for the Rejection of the Susan B. Anthony Amendment. Also includes literature opposing the Amendment. Taken from Catherine E. Thompson, *A Selective Guide to Women-Related Records in the North Carolina State Archives* (Raleigh, NC: North Carolina Division of Archives and History, 1977).

13,517. O. Henry Book Club
Records. 1923-63. 1 box.
Open. Published guide.
North Carolina Division of Archives and History. History and yearbooks of the Club, clippings, and a paper on Shakespeare. Taken from Catherine E. Thompson, *A Selective Guide to Women-Related Records in the North Carolina State Archives* (Raleigh, NC: North Carolina Division of Archives and History, 1977).

13,518. Ogletree, Julia C.
Papers. 1861-62. 2 items.
Open. Published guide.
North Carolina Division of Archives and History. Letters from Ogletree to her father concern family matters and early Civil War activities in Alabama and northern Florida. Taken from Catherine E. Thompson, *A Selective Guide to Women-Related Records in the North Carolina State Archives* (Raleigh, NC: North Carolina Division of Archives and History, 1977).

13,519. Olds, Fred A.
Papers. 1884-1929. 173 items.
Open. Published guide.
North Carolina Division of Archives and History. Includes a biography of Emma Lydia Rankin (1838-1908) containing her account of Stoneman's Raid in 1865. Taken from Catherine E. Thompson, *A Selective Guide to Women-Related Records in the North Carolina State Archives* (Raleigh, NC: North Carolina Division of Archives and History, 1977).

13,520. Oliver, Frances Motley
Papers. 1942. 1 item.
Open. Published guide.
North Carolina Division of Archives and History. Pamphlet written and published by Oliver is entitled *Poems.* Taken from Catherine E. Thompson, *A Selective Guide to Women-Related Records in the North Carolina State Archives* (Raleigh, NC: North Carolina Division of Archives and History, 1977).

13,521. Olla Podrida Club
Records. 1902-47. 1 box.
Open. Published guide.
North Carolina Division of Archives and History. Programs and yearbooks of this book club. Taken from Catherine E. Thompson, *A Selective Guide to Women-Related Records in the North Carolina State Archives* (Raleigh, NC: North Carolina Division of Archives and History, 1977).

13,522. O'Neal, Hettie Tom
Papers. 1964. 1 item.
Open. Published guide.
North Carolina Division of Archives and History. Letter by W. S. Wahab to state archivist H. G. Jones concerns his great grandmother Hettie Tom O'Neal, a well-known midwife on Ocracoke Island in the latter half of the 19th century. Taken from Catherine E. Thompson, *A Selective Guide to Women-Related Records in the North Carolina State Archives* (Raleigh, NC: North Carolina Division of Archives and History, 1977).

13,523. Outlaw, Albert Timothy
Papers. 1749-1968. 4 microfilm reels.
Open. Published guide.
North Carolina Division of Archives and History. Biographies and clippings concern Duplin County, NC, personalities, including Jean Cebrou Thompson, Mrs. John D. Robinson, and Mrs. Harvey Boney. Taken from Catherine E. Thompson, *A Selective Guide to Women-Related Records in the North Carolina State Archives* (Raleigh, NC: North Carolina Division of Archives and History, 1977).

13,524. Owen, John
Papers. 1806-1953. 6 items.
Open. Published guide.
North Carolina Division of Archives and History. Autograph album of Margaret Owen for the period 1836 to 1851 contains messages from friends in New York and in Wilmington, Fayetteville, and New Bern, NC. Taken from Catherine E. Thompson, *A Selective Guide to Women-Related Records in the North Carolina State Archives* (Raleigh, NC: North Carolina Division of Archives and History, 1977).

13,525. Parsons, Lucretia West
Papers. 1843-1948. 1 microfilm reel.
Open. Published guide.
North Carolina Division of Archives and History. Scrapbook of [Mrs.] Parsons contains letters, pictures, clippings, and other items. Taken from Catherine E. Thompson, *A Selective Guide to Women-Related Records in the North Carolina State Archives* (Raleigh, NC: North Carolina Division of Archives and History, 1977).

13,526. Partridge, Sophia
Papers. 1834-1937. 7 items.
Open. Published guide.
North Carolina Division of Archives and History. Consists of letters from [Miss] Partridge, a teacher at the Select School for Young Ladies in Raleigh, to [Miss] Ellen Colburn during the Civil War concerning politics, war, and family affairs; a 1937 clipping describing the school and Partridge; and an album of pupils' verses. Taken from Catherine E. Thompson, *A Selective Guide to Women-Related Records in the North Carolina State Archives* (Raleigh, NC: North Carolina Division of Archives and History, 1977).

13,527. Pate, Burwell S.
Papers. 1815-98. 1588 items.
Open. Published guide.
North Carolina Division of Archives and History. Includes papers, poetry, and tuition accounts of various female members of the Pate family. Taken from Catherine E. Thompson, *A Selective Guide to Women-Related Records in the North Carolina State Archives* (Raleigh, NC: North Carolina Division of Archives and History, 1977).

13,528. Patterson
Papers. 1765-1925. Ca. 2000 items.
Open. Published guide.
North Carolina Division of Archives and History. Correspondence of this wealthy, socially prominent, and educated family consists primarily of letters between Mary Fries Patterson and her six sons from 1880 to 1903. A letter from her son Sam in 1897 implies that there is a female labor shortage in his textile mill business. Also included are letters between Rufus Lenoir Patterson and Mary Patterson before their marriage; an 1866 letter from Cornelia (Phillips) Spencer to Patterson concerning Stoneman's Raid during the Civil War; an historical sketch of the Salem Female Academy by Adelaide L. Fries and other material relating to the Academy; an 1880 issue of *Godey's Lady's Book;* and various fashion catalogs. Taken from Catherine E. Thompson, *A Selective Guide to Women-Related Records in the North Carolina State Archives* (Raleigh, NC: North Carolina Division of Archives and History, 1977).

13,529. Patterson, Robert A.
Papers. 1862. 5 items.
Open. Published guide.
North Carolina Division of Archives and History. Letter from "Lucy" to "Brother Rob" gives news of family and friends, food shortages, high prices, and war rumors. Taken from Catherine E. Thompson, *A Selective Guide to Women-Related Records in the North Carolina State Archives* (Raleigh, NC: North Carolina Division of Archives and History, 1977).

13,530. Pettigrew
Papers. 1772-1912. Ca. 3500 items.
Open. Published guide.
North Carolina Division of Archives and History. Includes extensive family correspondence which provides a view of southern plantation life and an 1863 letter from Cornelia (Phillips) Spencer to Mr. Pettigrew about personal matters. Taken from Catherine E. Thompson, *A Selective Guide to Women-Related Records in the North Carolina State Archives* (Raleigh, NC: North Carolina Division of Archives and History, 1977).

13,531. Pickel, J. M.
Papers. 1896-1920. 62 items.
Open. Published guide.
North Carolina Division of Archives and History. Collection contains a letter of application for the position of assistant feeds chemist in the State Department of Agriculture in 1918 by Katherine M. Schoene, who received an MA in chemistry in 1911. Taken from Catherine E. Thompson, *A Selective Guide to Women-Related Records in the North Carolina State Archives* (Raleigh, NC: North Carolina Division of Archives and History, 1977).

13,532. Poe, Clarence H.
Papers. 1860-1963. Ca. 18 cu.ft.
Open. Published guide.
North Carolina Division of Archives and History. Collection contains information on funds for salaries of home economics teachers; material of the North Carolina Constitutional Commission, including letters to prominent state women in 1934

seeking support for proposed changes in the state constitution; speeches and articles, including one from 1915 entitled "What May Women Do for Development of South" and one from 1939 entitled "What Sort of North Carolina Rural Civilization Should Farm Women Develop?"; and letters by Eleanor Roosevelt. Taken from Catherine E. Thompson, *A Selective Guide to Women-Related Records in the North Carolina State Archives* (Raleigh, NC: North Carolina Division of Archives and History, 1977).

13,533. Political Campaign Literature
Collection. Nd. 3 boxes.
Open. Published guide.
North Carolina Division of Archives and History.
The 1920 platform of the Prohibition party with sections on women and woman suffrage, material on the suffrage and race issue in the 1920 gubernatorial campaign, an editorial from Greensboro, NC, in 1928 defending Mrs. Alfred E. Smith, material concerning the repeal of the 18th Amendment and an antirepeal tract; material on Annie Bickett Ashcraft's congressional campaign in 1930, an appeal for women's votes in the presidential campaign of 1932, and a card of Mrs. E. L. Shearon, a 1936 candidate for the state legislature or US Congress. Taken from Catherine E. Thompson, *A Selective Guide to Women-Related Records in the North Carolina State Archives* (Raleigh, NC: North Carolina Division of Archives and History, 1977).

13,534. Polk
Papers. 1730-1897. Ca. 1300 items.
Open. Published guide.
North Carolina Division of Archives and History.
Collection portrays the life of the affluent class in the South during the 19th century. Correspondence, circulars, and other papers pertain to Warrenton Female College in Warrenton, NC. Correspondence of Lucy Eugenia Williams [Mrs. William H.] Polk concerns her social life while single, life with her husband in Tennessee, life as a widow in Warrenton, NC, war news, the education of her sons, and her attempts to overcome poverty. Also includes recipes. Taken from Catherine E. Thompson, *A Selective Guide to Women-Related Records in the North Carolina State Archives* (Raleigh, NC: North Carolina Division of Archives and History, 1977).

13,535. Poole, Eliza Anne
Papers. 1926. 3 items.
Open. Published guide.
North Carolina Division of Archives and History.
Pamphlet contains a biographical sketch of Poole, who was given an award at the Sesqui-Centennial International Exhibition in Philadelphia for being a representative teacher from North Carolina, and biographical sketches of girls who won the American Youth Award in each state for best exemplifying American ideals. Taken from Catherine E. Thompson, *A Selective Guide to Women-Related Records in the North Carolina State Archives* (Raleigh, NC: North Carolina Division of Archives and History, 1977).

13,536. Potter, Henry
Papers. 1795-1861. 115 items.
Open. Published guide.
North Carolina Division of Archives and History.
Collection contains Mary Ann Potter's account with S. T. Hawley and Son for the years 1859 to 1861. Taken from Catherine E. Thompson, *A Selective Guide to Women-Related Records in the North Carolina State Archives* (Raleigh, NC: North Carolina Division of Archives and History, 1977).

13,537. Potter, Robert A.
Papers. 1836-ca. 1875. 1 item and 1 microfilm reel.
Open. Published guide.
North Carolina Division of Archives and History.
Colonel Potter was an elected official in North Carolina and Texas. Reminiscences written by his widow Harriet A. Ames, ca. 1893, concern her unhappy first marriage, apparently to a Mr. Page; a trip from New Orleans to the prairie; her loneliness on the prairie with her children; her desertion by her husband and the approach of starvation; her move to Texas and marriage to Potter; contacts with Indians; the violent deaths of Potter and her daughter; and dealings with an outlaw named "Old Rose." Included on microfilm are Texas Supreme Court records from *Lewis and McGinnis vs. Harriet Ames,* which concern Potter's will. Taken from Catherine E. Thompson, *A Selective Guide to Women-Related Records in the North Carolina State Archives* (Raleigh, NC: North Carolina Division of Archives and History, 1977).

13,538. Powell
Papers. 1839-41. 2 items.
Open. Published guide.
North Carolina Division of Archives and History.
Letter in which Elizabeth Carter describes to her family in North Carolina earning a living in Arkansas. Taken from Catherine E. Thompson, *A Selective Guide to Women-Related Records in the North Carolina State Archives* (Raleigh, NC: North Carolina Division of Archives and History, 1977).

13,539. Powell, Jane K.
Papers. 1853-75. 1 item.
Open. Published guide.
North Carolina Division of Archives and History.
Album contains poems and messages. Taken from Catherine E. Thompson, *A Selective Guide to Women-Related Records in the North Carolina State Archives* (Raleigh, NC: North Carolina Division of Archives and History, 1977).

13,540. Powell, William S.
Papers. 1739-1928. 3 vols. and 512 items.
Open. Published guide.
North Carolina Division of Archives and History.
Includes letters from M. A. Reddick to his wife during the Civil War with instructions for planting and harvesting crops during his absence and a 1911 letter to Mr. and Mrs. C. S. Powell from their niece Lillian describing her summer as a kindergarten teacher in a Pueblo Indian village in New Mexico. Taken from Catherine E. Thompson, *A Selective Guide to Women-Related Records in the North Carolina State Archives* (Raleigh, NC: North Carolina Division of Archives and History, 1977).

13,541. Purvis
Papers. 1859-1938. 12 items.
Open. Published guide.
North Carolina Division of Archives and History.
Letters to family members apparently living in Mississippi from Eliza J. W. Purvis in Wilkesboro, Olin, Snow Creek in Iredell County, and Chatham, NC, and letters in which she mentions attending school in Olin. Taken from Catherine E. Thompson, *A Selective Guide to Women-Related Records in the North Carolina State Archives* (Raleigh, NC: North Carolina Division of Archives and History, 1977).

13,542. Queen's College
Records. 1821-1955. 2 items.
Open. Published guide.
North Carolina Division of Archives and History.
Typescript and a letter trace the deeds and name of this women's college in Charlotte, NC, from its early years to the mid-20th century. Taken from Catherine E. Thompson, *A Selective Guide to Women-Related Records in the North Carolina State Archives* (Raleigh, NC: North Carolina Division of Archives and History, 1977).

13,543. Quinlan, Betsey Lane
Papers. 1941-47. Ca. 500 items.
Open. Published guide.
North Carolina Division of Archives and History.
Letters, telegrams, poems, radio script, photos, service newsletter, clippings, and other material relate primarily to [Miss] Quinlan's American National Red Cross service in Iceland, New Guinea, and the US during WWII. Taken from Catherine E. Thompson, *A Selective Guide to Women-Related Records in the North Carolina State Archives* (Raleigh, NC: North Carolina Division of Archives and History, 1977).

13,544. Raleigh Kiwanis Scholarship Foundation, Inc.
Records. 1924-67. 1 box.
Open. Published guide.
North Carolina Division of Archives and History.
The Foundation was chartered in 1924 to aid boys and girls in continuing their education. Includes applications for loans and letters by and about girls needing money for education. Taken from Catherine E. Thompson, *A Selective Guide to Women-Related Records in the North Carolina State Archives* (Raleigh, NC: North Carolina Division of Archives and History, 1977).

13,545. Raleigh Music Club
Records. 1929-60. 7 boxes.
Open. Published guide.
North Carolina Division of Archives and History.
Constitution, bylaws, minutes, financial reports, correspondence, notes, scrapbooks, programs, and yearbooks of the Club. Taken from Catherine E. Thompson, *A Selective Guide to Women-Related Records in the North Carolina State Archives* (Raleigh, NC: North Carolina Division of Archives and History, 1977).

13,546. Ramsey, J. G. M.
Papers. 1868. 1 item.
Open. Published guide.
North Carolina Division of Archives and History.
Family history contains an account of the exile of Ramsey's wife and two daughters during the Civil War. Taken from Catherine E. Thompson, *A Selective Guide to Women-Related Records in the North Carolina State Archives* (Raleigh, NC: North Carolina Division of Archives and History, 1977).

13,547. Reavis Family
Papers. 1817-1933. 3 items.
Open. Published guide.
North Carolina Division of Archives and History.
Includes an 1867 letter from Mary Reavis Goodrich in Arkansas to Hilliard Reavis concerning her opinions on religion, crops, and money. Taken from Catherine E. Thompson, *A Selective Guide to Women-Related Records in the North Carolina State Archives* (Raleigh, NC: North Carolina Division of Archives and History, 1977).

13,548. Recipe Books
Collection. 1802-60. 1 microfilm reel.
Open. Published guide.
North Carolina Division of Archives and History.
Recipe books include one of M. Lewis with recipes for dyes, paint, pickles, yeast, cakes, jelly, and wines. Taken from Catherine E. Thompson, *A Selective Guide to Women-Related Records in the North Carolina State Archives* (Raleigh, NC: North Carolina Division of Archives and History, 1977).

13,549. Reconstruction
Collection. 1868-1959. 23 items.
Open. Published guide.
North Carolina Division of Archives and History.
Includes a statement in 1959 of the role [Mrs.] Alice Denny Lea played in the death of John Walter "Chicken" Stephens at the hands of the Ku

Klux Klan. Taken from Catherine E. Thompson, *A Selective Guide to Women-Related Records in the North Carolina State Archives* (Raleigh, NC: North Carolina Division of Archives and History, 1977).

13,550. Reid, David S.
Papers. 1803-80. Ca. 820 items.
Open. Published guide.
North Carolina Division of Archives and History.
Includes an 1852 letter by Sarah J. Hale of *Godey's Lady's Book* concerning the establishment of a permanent Thanksgiving Day. Taken from Catherine E. Thompson, *A Selective Guide to Women-Related Records in the North Carolina State Archives* (Raleigh, NC: North Carolina Division of Archives and History, 1977).

13,551. Renn, Euticus
Papers. 1967-68. 327 items.
Open. Published guide.
North Carolina Division of Archives and History.
Includes a few issues of *Women for McCarthy,* which relate to Eugene McCarthy's 1968 presidential campaign. Taken from Catherine E. Thompson, *A Selective Guide to Women-Related Records in the North Carolina State Archives* (Raleigh, NC: North Carolina Division of Archives and History, 1977).

13,552. Rewis, Mrs. Millard
Papers. 1899-1903. 2 items.
Open. Published guide.
North Carolina Division of Archives and History.
Biology notebook of a student at the Baptist Female University in Raleigh. Taken from Catherine E. Thompson, *A Selective Guide to Women-Related Records in the North Carolina State Archives* (Raleigh, NC: North Carolina Division of Archives and History, 1977).

13,553. Rex Hospital School of Nursing
Records. 1896-1967. 2 boxes.
Open. Published guide.
North Carolina Division of Archives and History.
The School was established in 1894 with Mary Lewis Wyche as its first director. Records of the Alumnae Association include minutes, reports to the board of trustees of Rex Hospital, a scholarship letter, and lists of officers and alumnae. Also included are letters concerning the history of the school, lists of graduates, a history of Rex Hospital and the School of Nursing, historical sketches, scrapbook material, photo albums, student handbooks, leaflets, bulletins, yearbook, clippings, other material. Taken from Catherine E. Thompson, *A Selective Guide to Women-Related Records in the North Carolina State Archives* (Raleigh, NC: North Carolina Division of Archives and History, 1977).

13,554. Richmond Temperance and Literary Society
Records. 1855-75. 1 microfilm reel.
Open. Published guide.
North Carolina Division of Archives and History.
Constitution, bylaws, minutes, a speech, and the roll of members of this Richmond County organization. Taken from Catherine E. Thompson, *A Selective Guide to Women-Related Records in the North Carolina State Archives* (Raleigh, NC: North Carolina Division of Archives and History, 1977).

13,555. Roberson, Joseph I.
Papers. 1751-1845. 209 items.
Open. Published guide.
North Carolina Division of Archives and History.
Letters to Roberson from his mother Elizabeth Roberson in 1842 concern a child's sickness and death and her grief. Taken from Catherine E. Thompson, *A Selective Guide to Women-Related Records in the North Carolina State Archives* (Raleigh, NC: North Carolina Division of Archives and History, 1977).

13,556. Roberts, Mrs. F. C.
Papers. 1896-1933. 1 microfilm reel.
Open. Published guide.
North Carolina Division of Archives and History.
Records of the Ladies Memorial Association compiled by Roberts of New Bern, NC, include manuscripts, speeches, pamphlets, clippings, and printed publications such as *What "Our Women in the War" Did and Suffered Within the Lines.* Taken from Catherine E. Thompson, *A Selective Guide to Women-Related Records in the North Carolina State Archives* (Raleigh, NC: North Carolina Division of Archives and History, 1977).

13,557. Rodman Family
Papers. 1835-1919. Ca. 6000 items.
Open. Published guide.
North Carolina Division of Archives and History.
Correspondence, reports, broadsides, and other papers of Lida T. Rodman relate to the Equal Suffrage League, the DAR, the Colonial Dames, and North Carolina women in the Revolution, and to her activities as chairman of the Beaufort County unit of the National Defense Committee during WWI and the Woman's Liberty Loan Committee. Also included are family correspondence, account books, and receipts of Mrs. W. B. Rodman; receipts and recipe books of Mary O. Rodman, 1843; and account books of Camille B. Rodman, 1870s-80s. Taken from Catherine E. Thompson, *A Selective Guide to Women-Related Records in the North Carolina State Archives* (Raleigh, NC: North Carolina Division of Archives and History, 1977).

13,558. Rogers, Mary Jeffreys
Papers. 1782-1965. Ca. 170 items.
Open. Published guide.
North Carolina Division of Archives and History.
Includes a brochure of Salem College in Winston-Salem, NC, from ca. 1920. Taken from Catherine E. Thompson, *A Selective Guide to Women-Related Records in the North Carolina State Archives* (Raleigh, NC: North Carolina Division of Archives and History, 1977).

13,559. St. Agnes Service Board
Records. 1952-60. 1 box.
Open. Published guide.
North Carolina Division of Archives and History.
Minutes, correspondence, membership list, and other records of the Board, which was established in 1952 under the sponsorship of the Raleigh Council of United Church Women to serve as a ladies auxiliary to St. Agnes Hospital, a general hospital for Negroes. Taken from Catherine E. Thompson, *A Selective Guide to Women-Related Records in the North Carolina State Archives* (Raleigh, NC: North Carolina Division of Archives and History, 1977).

13,560. St. Mary's School
Records. 1851. 1 item.
Open. Published guide.
North Carolina Division of Archives and History.
Account of Miss S. E. Harvey for tuition and incidental expenses at St. Mary's School in Raleigh, which is now known as St. Mary's College. Taken from Catherine E. Thompson, *A Selective Guide to Women-Related Records in the North Carolina State Archives* (Raleigh, NC: North Carolina Division of Archives and History, 1977).

13,561. Saunders, William Laurence
Papers. 1775-1890. 656 items.
Open. Published guide.
North Carolina Division of Archives and History.
Includes letters from Laura Saunders and reports from Oxford Female Seminary in Oxford, NC, in 1884 concerning her. Also included are letters from Cornelia (Phillips) Spencer to Saunders in 1888 expressing enthusiasm for his work as editor of the *Colonial Records of North Carolina.* Taken from Catherine E. Thompson, *A Selective Guide to Women-Related Records in the North Carolina State Archives* (Raleigh, NC: North Carolina Division of Archives and History, 1977).

13,562. Savage, Pamela
Papers. 1825-27. 1 item.
Open. Published guide.
North Carolina Division of Archives and History.
Diary in which Savage describes her departure from Champlain, NY, in 1825 and her trip to Oxford, NC, where she taught in an academy; it contains observations on travels, classes, and her trip home two years later. Taken from Catherine E. Thompson, *A Selective Guide to Women-Related Records in the North Carolina State Archives* (Raleigh, NC: North Carolina Division of Archives and History, 1977).

13,563. Sawyer
Papers. 1829-1919. 126 items.
Open. Published guide.
North Carolina Division of Archives and History.
Letters to Ellen Pritchard in Murfreesboro, NC, and from Sarepta Gregory at Chowan Female Institute in Murfreesboro to her aunt Pernelah Gregory concern the life of a schoolgirl during 1850s and 1860s. Also included are commencement programs from 1892 for Southern Female College in Petersburg, VA. Taken from Catherine E. Thompson, *A Selective Guide to Women-Related Records in the North Carolina State Archives* (Raleigh, NC: North Carolina Division of Archives and History, 1977).

13,564. Scott, Robert W.
Papers. 1868-1963. 24 boxes.
Open. Published guide.
North Carolina Division of Archives and History.
Family correspondence and photos, including letters between Robert Scott (1861-1929), a legislator and agricultural leader, and Lizzie J. (Hughes) Scott after their marriage about farm and neighborhood activities and letters from their daughter Margaret, who became Mrs. L. M. Smith, and their daughter-in-law Matrena [Mrs. Robert W., Jr.] Scott. Also included is correspondence of Robert Scott's sister Francis Josephine with sisters at school in Statesville, NC, and at home in Melville and Haw River, NC, with her cousin Lizzie Kerr in Raleigh and teaching in Statesville, and from her fiancé W. G. Smith. Taken from Catherine E. Thompson, *A Selective Guide to Women-Related Records in the North Carolina State Archives* (Raleigh, NC: North Carolina Division of Archives and History, 1977).

13,565. Scott, Robert W., II
Papers. 1957-68. 125 boxes.
Access restricted. Published guide.
North Carolina Division of Archives and History.
Papers of Scott, who was governor of North Carolina from 1969 to 1973, include files on the Select Committee on the Status of Women; letters relating to Mothers of the Year; gubernatorial campaign material from 1968, including a subject file on women; material on the Poultry Princess Contest and on appointments for the Commission on the Education and Employment of Women; clippings on the Democratic Women's Convention in 1964; and other material. Taken from Catherine E. Thompson, *A Selective Guide to Women-Related Records in the North Carolina State Archives* (Raleigh, NC: North Carolina Division of Archives and History, 1977).

13,566. Scott, W. Kerr
Papers. 1896-1972. Ca. 67 cu.ft.
Access restricted. Published guide.
North Carolina Division of Archives and History.
Papers of Scott, who was governor of North Carolina from 1949 to 1953, include

correspondence, clippings, and printed material on home demonstration clubs, 4-H clubs, and temperance organizations; gubernatorial campaign correspondence, including political letters written by [Miss] Myrtha Fleming, secretary to Scott while he was commissioner of agriculture; and a file on Mary M. Stanford, who was women's manager in Scott's 1954 campaign. Papers of Scott's wife Mary White Scott include personal correspondence, with letters from Margaret Truman, Bess Truman, and Lady Bird Johnson; correspondence concerning Mrs. Dan K. Moore's history of North Carolina governors' wives; an autobiography; and clippings. Taken from Catherine E. Thompson, *A Selective Guide to Women-Related Records in the North Carolina State Archives* (Raleigh, NC: North Carolina Division of Archives and History, 1977).

13,567. Settle, Thomas
Papers. 1863-64. 2 items.
Open. Published guide.
North Carolina Division of Archives and History.
Letter from Settle to Governor Vance protests the inhumane treatment of women and others by state militia attempting to extort information on deserters from the army. Taken from Catherine E. Thompson, *A Selective Guide to Women-Related Records in the North Carolina State Archives* (Raleigh, NC: North Carolina Division of Archives and History, 1977).

13,568. Shaffner
Papers. 1845-67. 1 vol. and 299 items.
Open. Published guide.
North Carolina Division of Archives and History.
Collection contains letters of Carrie Fries, including those to John E. Shaffner during the Civil War. Taken from Catherine E. Thompson, *A Selective Guide to Women-Related Records in the North Carolina State Archives* (Raleigh, NC: North Carolina Division of Archives and History, 1977).

13,569. Shaw
Papers. 1735-1883. Ca. 800 items.
Open. Published guide.
North Carolina Division of Archives and History.
Includes orphans' apprentice indentures of Jane and Margaret McIntyre for 1821 to 1823. Taken from Catherine E. Thompson, *A Selective Guide to Women-Related Records in the North Carolina State Archives* (Raleigh, NC: North Carolina Division of Archives and History, 1977).

13,570. Shober
Papers. 1858-1921. 68 items.
Open. Published guide.
North Carolina Division of Archives and History.
Guardian records of Charles E. Shober for his sister Addie include accounts for schooling at Oakland Female Institute in Norristown, PA, and expenditures for clothing and travel. Taken from Catherine E. Thompson, *A Selective Guide to Women-Related Records in the North Carolina State Archives* (Raleigh, NC: North Carolina Division of Archives and History, 1977).

13,571. Shuford, Lowery
Papers. 1862-1919. Ca. 100 items.
Open. Published guide.
North Carolina Division of Archives and History.
Reminiscences, articles, and clippings on the Civil War and the Confederacy gathered by Shuford, a resident of Gastonia, NC, and historian of the North Carolina Division of the United Daughters of the Confederacy. Taken from Catherine E. Thompson, *A Selective Guide to Women-Related Records in the North Carolina State Archives* (Raleigh, NC: North Carolina Division of Archives and History, 1977).

13,572. Siamese Twins
Papers. 1829-1962. 75 items and 1 microfilm reel.
Open. Published guide.
North Carolina Division of Archives and History.
Includes a biography of the Siamese twins Chang and Eng Bunker with material on love, courtship, their marriage to North Carolina sisters named Yates, housekeeping arrangements, birth, children, and education; a journal and photo album kept by Nancy "Nannie" Bunker while on a tour of England and Scotland in 1868 and 1869 with her father Chang Bunker, her uncle, and her cousin Kate to recoup family finances; a letter Nannie wrote to her brother; an itinerary of their travels; and accounts of purchases and money received. Taken from Catherine E. Thompson, *A Selective Guide to Women-Related Records in the North Carolina State Archives* (Raleigh, NC: North Carolina Division of Archives and History, 1977).

13,573. Simpson and Biddle Family
Papers. 1721-1944. 900 items.
Open. Published guide.
North Carolina Division of Archives and History.
Family correspondence includes an 1854 letter by Mary Biddle Norcott while she was in school in Murfreesboro; post-Civil War letters to Rosa Biddle from suitors and girl friends, including Ellie Montgomery at Louisburg College in Louisburg, NC, and Sue Pescud in Raleigh; letters from Rosa to her fiancé Samuel P. Smith in 1879; and a letter from a minister in Alabama concerning the education of young women. Also included are tuition receipts from various schools and other guardian papers of Mary B. Norcott; an indenture arranged by the Freedmen's Bureau in 1865 for an orphan girl in Franklin County, NC, to be taught domestic duties, reading, and writing; and a printed letter by Georgia Sears [Mrs. Thomas] Meredith offering a home and the *Biblical Recorder* for sale. Taken from Catherine E. Thompson, *A Selective Guide to Women-Related Records in the North Carolina State Archives* (Raleigh, NC: North Carolina Division of Archives and History, 1977).

13,574. Sir Walter Cabinet
Records. 1920-69. 2 boxes and 11 vols.
Open. Published guide.
North Carolina Division of Archives and History.
Constitution, bylaws, minutes, treasurers' records, correspondence, lists of officers and members, a history, scrapbooks, yearbooks, and other records of this organization, which was established in 1920 with membership consisting of wives of present and former General Assembly members and wives of certain ranking officers of state government. Taken from Catherine E. Thompson, *A Selective Guide to Women-Related Records in the North Carolina State Archives* (Raleigh, NC: North Carolina Division of Archives and History, 1977).

13,575. Slocumb, Mary
Collection. 1776; 1961-62. 7 items.
Open. Published guide.
North Carolina Division of Archives and History.
Includes a manuscript about the legend of Slocumb's ride to Moores Creek at the height of battle with an analysis of the truth of the story as well as correspondence in 1961 and 1962 between Christopher Crittenden, director of the North Carolina Department of Archives and History, and the National Park Service concerning the authenticity of the ride. Taken from Catherine E. Thompson, *A Selective Guide to Women-Related Records in the North Carolina State Archives* (Raleigh, NC: North Carolina Division of Archives and History, 1977).

13,576. Smith, Jessica Randolph
Papers. 1871-1934. 122 items.
Open. Published guide.
North Carolina Division of Archives and History.
Collection relates primarily to the United Daughters of the Confederacy, the Civil War, and claims by Smith's father to be the designer of the Confederate flag. Also included is material on the DAR and Colonial Dames. Taken from Catherine E. Thompson, *A Selective Guide to Women-Related Records in the North Carolina State Archives* (Raleigh, NC: North Carolina Division of Archives and History, 1977).

13,577. Smith, William Lay
Papers. 1798-1920. 53 items.
Open. Published guide.
North Carolina Division of Archives and History.
Includes letters of Nancy Smith Yancey to her son William N. H. Smith at Yale in 1834. Taken from Catherine E. Thompson, *A Selective Guide to Women-Related Records in the North Carolina State Archives* (Raleigh, NC: North Carolina Division of Archives and History, 1977).

13,578. Smoot, James Edward
Papers. 1843-1947. Ca. 10 cu.ft.
Open. Published guide.
North Carolina Division of Archives and History.
Includes a history of Cabarrus County, NC, containing family histories, photos, and recollections of [Mrs.] E. Adeline Allison White Odell. Taken from Catherine E. Thompson, *A Selective Guide to Women-Related Records in the North Carolina State Archives* (Raleigh, NC: North Carolina Division of Archives and History, 1977).

13,579. Snell, Mrs. Holt
Papers. 1867-97. 2 items.
Open. Published guide.
North Carolina Division of Archives and History.
Diploma of Bessie Bernard from Wesleyan Female College in Murfreesboro, NC, in 1867 and a flyer from Littleton Female College in Littleton, NC. Taken from Catherine E. Thompson, *A Selective Guide to Women-Related Records in the North Carolina State Archives* (Raleigh, NC: North Carolina Division of Archives and History, 1977).

13,580. Society of Mayflower Descendants
Records. 1924-70. 8 boxes.
Open. Published guide.
North Carolina Division of Archives and History.
Charter, minutes, financial records, correspondence, lists and other membership material, publicity releases, reports, an awards file, photos, notices of annual meetings, programs, yearbooks, clippings, printed material relating to the Society, records of the Central Carolina Colony, and several volumes of *Mayflower News of North Carolina*. Taken from Catherine E. Thompson, *A Selective Guide to Women-Related Records in the North Carolina State Archives* (Raleigh, NC: North Carolina Division of Archives and History, 1977).

13,581. Spencer, Cornelia Ann (Phillips)
Papers. 1857-1905. Ca. 500 items.
Open. Published guide.
North Carolina Division of Archives and History.
Correspondence of [Mrs. James Monroe] Spencer (1825-1908) relates to the University of North Carolina, politics, history, education, literature, society, personal friendships, and her published works. Correspondents include Governor Zebulon B. Vance, Governor William A. Graham, Edward J. Hale, Kemp P. Battle, Eleanor (White) [Mrs. David L.] Swain, and Mary Bayard Clarke. Taken from Catherine E. Thompson, *A Selective Guide to Women-Related Records in the North Carolina State Archives* (Raleigh, NC: North Carolina Division of Archives and History, 1977).

13,582. Steele and Ledbetter
Papers. 1756-1873. 1 microfilm reel.
Open. Published guide.
North Carolina Division of Archives and History.
Includes a list of articles laid aside for a one-year's allowance to widow Elizabeth Ledbetter. Taken from Catherine E. Thompson, *A Selective Guide to Women-Related Records in the North Carolina State Archives* (Raleigh, NC: North Carolina Division of Archives and History, 1977).

13,583. Steele, John
Papers. 1777-1831. Ca. 400 items.
Open. Published guide.
North Carolina Division of Archives and History.
Collection contains letters by Elizabeth Steele to Ephriam Steele and Robert Gillespie describing the Battle of King's Mountain in 1780 and a visit of the British to Salisbury, NC, in 1781. Taken from Catherine E. Thompson, *A Selective Guide to Women-Related Records in the North Carolina State Archives* (Raleigh, NC: North Carolina Division of Archives and History, 1977).

13,584. Stewart, Francis E.
Papers. 1918-25. 34 items.
Open. Published guide.
North Carolina Division of Archives and History.
Correspondence and other items relating to the presentation of a memorial stone at Flora Macdonald College in Red Springs, NC, a 1925 commencement program from the College, and College bulletins. Taken from Catherine E. Thompson, *A Selective Guide to Women-Related Records in the North Carolina State Archives* (Raleigh, NC: North Carolina Division of Archives and History, 1977).

13,585. Stokes, Montfort
Papers. 1783-1819. 55 items.
Open. Published guide.
North Carolina Division of Archives and History.
Letters from Mrs. William Phillips to her husband in the Salisbury jail concern his business at home, family news, and her distress at his absence. Taken from Catherine E. Thompson, *A Selective Guide to Women-Related Records in the North Carolina State Archives* (Raleigh, NC: North Carolina Division of Archives and History, 1977).

13,586. Stone, David
Papers. 1793-1942. 76 items.
Open. Published guide.
North Carolina Division of Archives and History.
Collection contains a memorandum book for 1824 to 1827 of Stone's second wife Sarah (Dashiell) Stone with aphorisms, quotations, and travel entries included. Taken from Catherine E. Thompson, *A Selective Guide to Women-Related Records in the North Carolina State Archives* (Raleigh, NC: North Carolina Division of Archives and History, 1977).

13,587. Stowe, Harriet Beecher
Papers. 1853. 2 items.
Open. Published guide.
North Carolina Division of Archives and History.
Includes a letter by [Mrs.] Stowe explaining her motivation for writing *Uncle Tom's Cabin* and a clipping of a newspaper story about the book by southern abolitionist Daniel R. Goodloe. Taken from Catherine E. Thompson, *A Selective Guide to Women-Related Records in the North Carolina State Archives* (Raleigh, NC: North Carolina Division of Archives and History, 1977).

13,588. Street, Richard
Papers. 1770-1922. 330 items.
Open. Published guide.
North Carolina Division of Archives and History.
Includes receipts from teacher Margaret Marin, 1821; an 1886 brochure and an 1893 commencement invitation for Jonesboro High School; and a 1922 commencement invitation for the Flora Macdonald College in Red Springs, NC. Taken from Catherine E. Thompson, *A Selective Guide to Women-Related Records in the North Carolina State Archives* (Raleigh, NC: North Carolina Division of Archives and History, 1977).

13,589. Strickland
Papers. 1822-82. 16 items.
Open. Published guide.
North Carolina Division of Archives and History.
Record of the allowance of food supplies by county commissioners to widow Charity Strickland in 1867. Taken from Catherine E. Thompson, *A Selective Guide to Women-Related Records in the North Carolina State Archives* (Raleigh, NC: North Carolina Division of Archives and History, 1977).

13,590. Stringfield, William Williams
Papers. 1860-92. 37 items.
Open. Published guide.
North Carolina Division of Archives and History.
Letters to Stringfield from his sister Mary Stringfield, who later became Mrs. J. W. Ray, describe life at home during the Civil War; an 1864 letter discusses having to teach school for food during the War. Collection is also available on microfilm. Taken from Catherine E. Thompson, *A Selective Guide to Women-Related Records in the North Carolina State Archives* (Raleigh, NC: North Carolina Division of Archives and History, 1977).

13,591. Strother, William H.
Papers. 1847. 1 item.
Open. Published guide.
North Carolina Division of Archives and History.
Certificate of application of Alisa Medlin, a Franklin County, NC, resident, for a government pension for her father's Revolutionary War services includes a brief biographical sketch of her family. Taken from Catherine E. Thompson, *A Selective Guide to Women-Related Records in the North Carolina State Archives* (Raleigh, NC: North Carolina Division of Archives and History, 1977).

13,592. Sugg, Jane A.
Papers. 1865. 1 item.
Open. Published guide.
North Carolina Division of Archives and History.
Letter in which Sugg relates to her brother and sister war news and rumors. Taken from Catherine E. Thompson, *A Selective Guide to Women-Related Records in the North Carolina State Archives* (Raleigh, NC: North Carolina Division of Archives and History, 1977).

13,593. Swain, David Lowry
Papers. 1763-1895. Ca. 1200 items.
Open. Published guide.
North Carolina Division of Archives and History.
Includes letters to Cornelia (Phillips) Spencer from prominent North Carolinians relating events that took place during the Civil War, a letter from Dorothea L. Dix to Swain concerning North Carolina geology and an institution for mental health care, and a sketch of [Miss] Esther Wake by Joseph Seawell Jones. Taken from Catherine E. Thompson, *A Selective Guide to Women-Related Records in the North Carolina State Archives* (Raleigh, NC: North Carolina Division of Archives and History, 1977).

13,594. Tiernan, Frances Christine (Fisher)
Papers. Nd. 2 vols.
Open. Published guide.
North Carolina Division of Archives and History.
Frances Fisher (1846-1920), who used the pen name Christian Reid, was a Salisbury, NC, novelist of the post-Civil War period who was married to James Marquis Tiernan. Poems and the first outline of her novel *Geraldine.* Taken from Catherine E. Thompson, *A Selective Guide to Women-Related Records in the North Carolina State Archives* (Raleigh, NC: North Carolina Division of Archives and History, 1977).

13,595. Travis, E. L.
Papers. 1800-1948. Ca. 100 items.
Open. Published guide.
North Carolina Division of Archives and History.
Contains an 1806 letter from "Ariana" at school in Salem, NC, to her mother, an 1827 letter by May Stanford concerning religion, and DAR magazines for 1925 and 1926. Taken from Catherine E. Thompson, *A Selective Guide to Women-Related Records in the North Carolina State Archives* (Raleigh, NC: North Carolina Division of Archives and History, 1977).

13,596. Tuesday Afternoon Book Club
Records. 1904-57. 2 boxes.
Open. Published guide.
North Carolina Division of Archives and History.
Minutes and yearbooks of the Club, which was organized in 1903 in Raleigh. Taken from Catherine E. Thompson, *A Selective Guide to Women-Related Records in the North Carolina State Archives* (Raleigh, NC: North Carolina Division of Archives and History, 1977).

13,597. United Daughters of the Confederacy
Records. 1895-1946. 13 boxes and 1 microfilm reel.
Open. Published guide.
North Carolina Division of Archives and History.
Records of the UDC include reminiscences, articles, and clippings of [Miss] Georgia Hicks, historian of the UDC; war journals; a Confederate portrait album; scrapbooks; and other material. Also contains records of the North Carolina UDC, including applications and certificates for the Southern Cross of Honor; records of the education committee, including essays and applications and correspondence concerning scholarships; and records of the Bessie Beall Reid bed fund committee. These latter records contain correspondence of various women, among them committee chairman Mrs. Victor R. Johnson; letters of appreciation from patients; a contract with a sanitorium; reports; and a history. In addition there are minutes, correspondence, a history, a memory book, pamphlets, and a scrapbook of the General James Johnston Pettigrew chapter in Raleigh and minutes, lists of soldiers, and lists of members of the Caswell Chapter. Taken from Catherine E. Thompson, *A Selective Guide to Women-Related Records in the North Carolina State Archives* (Raleigh, NC: North Carolina Division of Archives and History, 1977).

13,598. Vance, Zebulon Baird
Papers. 1827-1916. Ca. 3200 items.
Open. Published guide.
North Carolina Division of Archives and History.
Family correspondence, including letters between Vance and his wife during the Civil War years, and letters from women soliciting aid from Vance in procuring food or asking for the return of or exemption of husbands and sons from the army because of desperate home situations. Also included are letters to Vance from Cornelia (Phillips) Spencer for the period 1864 to 1879 concerning local news, education, advice, opinions, and her manuscript of *The Last Ninety Days of the War.* Taken from Catherine E. Thompson, *A Selective Guide to Women-Related Records in the North Carolina State Archives* (Raleigh, NC: North Carolina Division of Archives and History, 1977).

13,599. Vance, Zebulon Baird, and Vance, Harriet N. (Espy)
Papers. 1851-78. 285 items.
Open. Published guide.
North Carolina Division of Archives and History.
Love letters of Zebulon Vance and Harriet Vance (?-1878), which were published in 1971 in *My Beloved Zebulon;* letters between the Vances concerning family affairs and hard times; letters from family and friends, including Cornelia (Phillips) Spencer; and letters by Harriet Vance in 1874 to her son Zebbie at school. Also included are letters containing references to Vance's sister teaching at Burnsville Academy and to students and faculty of Western Carolina Female College. Taken from Catherine E. Thompson, *A Selective Guide to Women-Related Records in the North*

Carolina State Archives (Raleigh, NC: North Carolina Division of Archives and History, 1977).

13,600. Vann, John
Papers. 1765-1888. Ca. 1000 items.
Open. Published guide.
North Carolina Division of Archives and History.
Includes guardianship records from the early 1800s for Elizabeth Howell, Elizabeth Landen, and Mary Pipkin and a notation of questions to a legal advisor about a husband's rights over his wife's slaves. Taken from Catherine E. Thompson, *A Selective Guide to Women-Related Records in the North Carolina State Archives* (Raleigh, NC: North Carolina Division of Archives and History, 1977).

13,601. Waddell
Papers. 1755-1919. 103 items.
Open. Published guide.
North Carolina Division of Archives and History.
Includes [Miss] Sarah Moore's accounts for 1837 to 1839. Taken from Catherine E. Thompson, *A Selective Guide to Women-Related Records in the North Carolina State Archives* (Raleigh, NC: North Carolina Division of Archives and History, 1977).

13,602. Webb, Mrs. Thomas H.
Papers. 1865-77. 3 items.
Open. Published guide.
North Carolina Division of Archives and History.
Correspondence of Janie (Smith) [Mrs. R. R.] Robeson includes a letter describing the Battle of Averasboro, which occurred near her home Lebanon Plantation, and an 1877 letter from Bladen County, NC, concerning her wedding plans. Taken from Catherine E. Thompson, *A Selective Guide to Women-Related Records in the North Carolina State Archives* (Raleigh, NC: North Carolina Division of Archives and History, 1977).

13,603. Webster, T. C.
Papers. 1823-1905. 77 items.
Open. Published guide.
North Carolina Division of Archives and History.
Collection contains an undated extract from a schoolgirl's diary giving a brief review of school days. Taken from Catherine E. Thompson, *A Selective Guide to Women-Related Records in the North Carolina State Archives* (Raleigh, NC: North Carolina Division of Archives and History, 1977).

13,604. Weil, Gertrude
Papers. 1856-1970. 42 cu.ft.
Open. Published guide.
North Carolina Division of Archives and History.
Correspondence, expense accounts, photos, biographical and subject files, and other papers of Weil (1879-1971), the daughter of Henry and Mina (Rosenthal) Weil and a 1901 graduate of Smith College. Weil was a leader in social, civic, religious, and political projects, including woman suffrage, and was active in the GFWC and the LWV. Correspondence includes letters by Gertrude Weil while attending Horace Mann School in New York, Smith College, and summer school at Cornell University, and while traveling abroad and in North Carolina. Also included are letters between Mina Weil, her daughters Gertrude and Janet, and two sons; from Janet while attending North Carolina State Normal and Industrial College in Greensboro and Smith College; from Mina's sister Mattie Rosenthal; and from Mina's mother Eva Rosenthal to her grandchildren at school. Also included are letters from [Miss] Henrietta Szold, founder of Hadassah, a women's Zionist organization in the 1920s and 1930s; from Harriet Elliot, dean of women at the University of North Carolina at Greensboro; from Martha Boswell describing teaching at Brevard in the North Carolina mountains during the Depression; from Harriet L. Payne concerning life as the operator of a tea room and inn, American National Red Cross work in France during WWI, and social work in Philadelphia; and from numerous other women. Included in the collection is material relating to organizations in which Mina Weil and Gertrude Weil were interested, among them the National American Woman Suffrage Association and state and local suffrage associations, national and state divisions of the LWV and the GFWC, Chatauqua Circle, the North Carolina Conference for Social Service, the North Carolina Committee on Interracial Cooperation, the North Carolina Council on Human Relations, birth control organizations, and various Jewish organizations, including the North Carolina Association of Jewish Women. Taken from Catherine E. Thompson, *A Selective Guide to Women-Related Records in the North Carolina State Archives* (Raleigh, NC: North Carolina Division of Archives and History, 1977).

13,605. Wheeler, Samuel Jordan
Papers. 1832-79. 2 items.
Open. Published guide.
North Carolina Division of Archives and History.
Medical daybook includes recipes and accounts of boarders, some of whom were young ladies attending Chowan Baptist Female Institute, later called Chowan College, in Murfreesboro, NC. Taken from Catherine E. Thompson, *A Selective Guide to Women-Related Records in the North Carolina State Archives* (Raleigh, NC: North Carolina Division of Archives and History, 1977).

13,606. Whistler, Anna Matilda (McNeill)
Collection. 1930-45. 5 items.
Open. Published guide.
North Carolina Division of Archives and History.
Sketch by [Mrs.] Kate R. McDiarmid of North Wilkesboro, NC, entitled "North Carolina's Claim to Whistler's Mother" and an account of an address before the State Literary and Historical Association tracing Whistler's ancestry and describing her life in Wilmington and Bladen County, NC, as well as in Russia and England. Taken from Catherine E. Thompson, *A Selective Guide to Women-Related Records in the North Carolina State Archives* (Raleigh, NC: North Carolina Division of Archives and History, 1977).

13,607. Wilder, Gaston Henry
Papers. 1798-1915. 212 items.
Open. Published guide.
North Carolina Division of Archives and History.
Includes letters, 1874-79, about personal matters addressed to "Fannie" from her former classmates at Salem Female Academy. Taken from Catherine E. Thompson, *A Selective Guide to Women-Related Records in the North Carolina State Archives* (Raleigh, NC: North Carolina Division of Archives and History, 1977).

13,608. Wiley, Calvin H.
Papers. 1775-1925. Ca. 2200 items.
Open. Published guide.
North Carolina Division of Archives and History.
Family correspondence; correspondence of Wiley, including letters from 1859 and 1860 about Peace College in Raleigh and women's education; speeches by Wiley on women's education; and a 1900 letter to Mary Wiley from D. C. Rankin concerning her literary ambitions and mentioning novelist Mary Johnston. Speeches also available on microfilm. Taken from Catherine E. Thompson, *A Selective Guide to Women-Related Records in the North Carolina State Archives* (Raleigh, NC: North Carolina Division of Archives and History, 1977).

13,609. Wiley, Mary C.
Papers. 1949. 1 item.
Open. Published guide.
North Carolina Division of Archives and History.
Speech in which Wiley describes to the Association of County Historians in Raleigh the work of Adelaide Fries and others in writing the history of Forsyth County, NC. Taken from Catherine E. Thompson, *A Selective Guide to Women-Related Records in the North Carolina State Archives* (Raleigh, NC: North Carolina Division of Archives and History, 1977).

13,610. Williams and Dameron
Papers. 1804-1968. 2 microfilm reels.
Open. Published guide.
North Carolina Division of Archives and History.
Family correspondence concerns home, school and social activities, religion, dressmaking, and fashion and includes letters by the wife of Senator Clement Clairborne Clay describing her efforts to persuade President Andrew Johnson to release her husband from prison. Also includes letters from Salem Academy in 1833, from St. Mary's Hall in Burlington, NJ, and to a student at Warrenton Female College in 1854, 1855, and 1862. Also contained are a number of letters by Julia Mangum Dameron while she was a student at the State Normal School in Greensboro, NC, in the 1890s concerning courses, teachers, social life, and the school physician Anna M. Gove; 20th-century letters by her when she was a teacher at the School and a prominent businesswoman and clubwoman in Warren County, NC; clippings about her; a tribute to her with comments on her efforts to achieve equal pay for women's work; and letters by her sister Josie Dameron, a missionary to Korea. Taken from Catherine E. Thompson, *A Selective Guide to Women-Related Records in the North Carolina State Archives* (Raleigh, NC: North Carolina Division of Archives and History, 1977).

13,611. Williams, Archibald D.
Papers. 1844-64. 1 microfilm reel.
Open. Published guide.
North Carolina Division of Archives and History.
Plantation journal with references to the work of slave women. Taken from Catherine E. Thompson, *A Selective Guide to Women-Related Records in the North Carolina State Archives* (Raleigh, NC: North Carolina Division of Archives and History, 1977).

13,612. Williamson, James E.
Papers. 1854-1936. 1 microfilm reel.
Open. Published guide.
North Carolina Division of Archives and History.
Contains a 1936 letter from [Mrs.] Nettie N. Sheppard, a widow, to W. H. Williamson concerning her personal living conditions and tax assessment of her property. Taken from Catherine E. Thompson, *A Selective Guide to Women-Related Records in the North Carolina State Archives* (Raleigh, NC: North Carolina Division of Archives and History, 1977).

13,613. Wilson, Fannie
Papers. 1900-18. 19 items.
Open. Published guide.
North Carolina Division of Archives and History.
Includes photos of students and a building at Baptist University for Women in Raleigh, which in 1909 became Meredith College. Taken from Catherine E. Thompson, *A Selective Guide to Women-Related Records in the North Carolina State Archives* (Raleigh, NC: North Carolina Division of Archives and History, 1977).

13,614. Winston, Ellen (Black)
Papers. 1931-73. 8 microfilm reels.
Open. Published guide.
North Carolina Division of Archives and History.
Speeches with index, photos, and clippings of Winston, who held a PhD and was commissioner of public welfare for North Carolina from 1944 to 1963 and for the US from 1963 to 1967. Taken from Catherine E. Thompson, *A Selective Guide to Women-Related Records in the North Carolina*

State Archives (Raleigh, NC: North Carolina Division of Archives and History, 1977).

13,615. Women-in-Action for the Prevention of Violence and Its Causes, Inc.
Records. 1968-73. 2 boxes.
Open. Published guide.
North Carolina Division of Archives and History.
Articles of incorporation, bylaws, minutes, agendas, financial records, committee records, correspondence, reports, information on members and officers, material relating to workshops and projects, guidelines, a kick-off message, statements, addresses, awards, programs, literature, a bibliography, newsletters, clippings, and other records of the organization, which was founded in 1968 by Elna B. [Mrs. Asa] Spaulding as a civic coalition of Negro and white women to work toward prevention of violence. Taken from Catherine E. Thompson, *A Selective Guide to Women-Related Records in the North Carolina State Archives* (Raleigh, NC: North Carolina Division of Archives and History, 1977).

13,616. Wood, Horace McGuire
Papers. 1933-72. Ca. 325 items.
Open. Published guide.
North Carolina Division of Archives and History.
Material relating to Black Mountain College includes Wood's correspondence with his assistant Molly Gregory, with faculty member Hazel (Frieda) Larson, and with newspaperwoman Dorothy Mattison, who later became director of the College news bureau. Also includes a notebook listing staff and faculty wives who were involved in community work. Collection also available on microfilm. Taken from Catherine E. Thompson, *A Selective Guide to Women-Related Records in the North Carolina State Archives* (Raleigh, NC: North Carolina Division of Archives and History, 1977).

13,617. World War I
Collection. Nd. 354 boxes, 14 vols., and 2 card file drawers.
Open. Published guide.
North Carolina Division of Archives and History.
This collection of World War I material includes correspondence, sketches, news releases, posters, forms, county files with chapter histories, clippings, bulletins, and other material of the American National Red Cross; correspondence and reports of the DAR; yearbooks and publications of the American Legion Auxiliary; material of the Food Administration on canners, college food conservation courses, home economics, rationing at home, and women workers; correspondence, photos, posters, and printed material of the North Carolina Council of Defense; and miscellaneous material on the YWCA. County war records include a letter by Mrs. N. Buckner concerning her war work, a manuscript by Helen Brooks on the war work of Guilford County, NC, women, a list of war work done by Girl Scouts, a photo of working girls at Wiscassett Mills in Stanley County, NC, United Daughters of the Confederacy records, and newspaper columns by women. Also included are accounts of army nursing and hospitals by [Mrs.] May Greenfield Watson, [Miss] Odessa Chambers, and [Mrs.] Ione Branch Bain; correspondence, reports, photos, and bulletins from women's clubs and colleges, including the North Carolina College for Women and the East Carolina Teachers Training School; Navy recruiting, Liberty Loan, YWCA, Victory Girls, and other posters depicting women; material of the Woman's Liberty Loan Committee; pamphlets on thrift and related items by Mary G. Shotwell, director of the education division of the savings division of the 5th Federal Reserve District; a suffrage poem; and other material. Papers of Elizabeth Jones, a Red Cross nurse in London, and her sister May F. Jones, a YMCA worker in France, include correspondence, post cards, photos, a ration card, an identification card and tag, worker's permit, a program, clippings, a booklet, a report of the Buncombe County, NC, Committee of Colonial Dames, and other material. Taken from Catherine E. Thompson, *A Selective Guide to Women-Related Records in the North Carolina State Archives* (Raleigh, NC: North Carolina Division of Archives and History, 1977).

13,618. World War II
Collection. 1909-47. 194 boxes.
Open. Published guide.
North Carolina Division of Archives and History.
The collection relates to the part played by North Carolina citizens in WWII and includes correspondence of the DAR, the Committee on Conservation of Cultural Resources, the state PTA, and civic clubs; reports and historical records of the USO; family histories; recruiting propaganda for women's military organizations; booklets and bulletins concerning Negro life and war participation; and scrapbooks of the DAR, the American Legion Auxiliary, the Wake County, NC, Civilian Defense Council, the Raleigh Citizens' Defense Corps, and women's clubs. Also included are recruiting posters for the WACs, WAVES, US Cadet Nurse Corps, Army Nurse Corps, Marines, and other groups; magazine covers depicting women farming, working in power plants, and doing navy nursing; and various other posters. Records of the Office of Civilian Defense include correspondence and files relating to such subjects as the American National Red Cross, victory gardens, the WACs, American War Mothers, the Children's Bureau, and child care; a speech by Mrs. Walter Craven, director of the Citizens Service Corps, concerning work for women volunteers in civilian defense; pamphlets on the war effort at home; national and state civilian defense publications; correspondence, reports, and statistics on nurses, nutrition, and day nurseries; and material on the YWCA, the Girl Scouts, and family security. Other material relates to home demonstration; 4-H club work from 1909 to 1939; the Cadet Nurse Corps at Cabarrus County hospital, Salem College; St. Mary's College and Meredith College in Wake County; and Appalachian State Teachers College in Watauga County, NC. Taken from Catherine E. Thompson, *A Selective Guide to Women-Related Records in the North Carolina State Archives* (Raleigh, NC: North Carolina Division of Archives and History, 1977).

13,619. Worth, Jonathan
Papers. 1813-89. Ca. 5300 items.
Open. Published guide.
North Carolina Division of Archives and History.
Personal correspondence of Worth, governor of North Carolina from 1866 to 1868, relates to management and financial difficulties of his daughter Roxana (Worth) McNeill's plantations during and after the Civil War and to his attempt to arrange a marriage for his widowed sister-in-law. Worth's gubernatorial correspondence includes a letter from Mrs. George C. Badger seeking a position for her son, a letter from Lydia Maxwell concerning the whipping of prisoners, and letters concerning a proposed school for female orphans of veterans. Other letters concern clothing for Civil War soldiers. Taken from Catherine E. Thompson, *A Selective Guide to Women-Related Records in the North Carolina State Archives* (Raleigh, NC: North Carolina Division of Archives and History, 1977).

13,620. Worthington, Samuel Wheeler
Papers. 1841-1928. 17 items.
Open. Published guide.
North Carolina Division of Archives and History.
Letters to Lieutenant Colonel Yellowby from his sister H. A. Yellowby in 1864 concern the war, family, finances, and politics; an 1864 letter from Sophia A. Newby requests the release of her son from the army. Taken from Catherine E. Thompson, *A Selective Guide to Women-Related Records in the North Carolina State Archives* (Raleigh, NC: North Carolina Division of Archives and History, 1977).

13,621. Yarrell, Bell
Papers. 1867. 1 vol.
Open. Published guide.
North Carolina Division of Archives and History.
Notebook of prose and poetry of Yarrell, a student at Louisburg Female College in Louisburg, NC. Taken from Catherine E. Thompson, *A Selective Guide to Women-Related Records in the North Carolina State Archives* (Raleigh, NC: North Carolina Division of Archives and History, 1977).

13,622. Yates, Eliza Moring
Papers. 1847. 1 item.
Open. Published guide.
North Carolina Division of Archives and History.
Letter from [Mrs. Matthew T.] Yates, a foreign missionary, to Sarah C. Merritt concerns her travels, and religious convictions. Taken from Catherine E. Thompson, *A Selective Guide to Women-Related Records in the North Carolina State Archives* (Raleigh, NC: North Carolina Division of Archives and History, 1977).

13,623. Young Democratic Club of North Carolina
Records. 1964. 1 box.
Open. Published guide.
North Carolina Division of Archives and History.
Miscellaneous records of the Club, including a handbook and directory. Taken from Catherine E. Thompson, *A Selective Guide to Women-Related Records in the North Carolina State Archives* (Raleigh, NC: North Carolina Division of Archives and History, 1977).

13,624. Young, John Graham
Papers. 1861-64. 9 items.
Open. Published guide.
North Carolina Division of Archives and History.
Young's Civil War diary includes references to "secesh" (secession) ladies who attended the wounded and volunteered as guides and couriers. Taken from Catherine E. Thompson, *A Selective Guide to Women-Related Records in the North Carolina State Archives* (Raleigh, NC: North Carolina Division of Archives and History, 1977).

13,625. Zollicoffer
Papers. 1741-1913. 27 items.
Open. Published guide.
North Carolina Division of Archives and History.
Letters from Cornelia Webb at Shocco Academy in Warren County, NC, in 1826 to her father regarding examinations and letters to Cornelia at school. Taken from Catherine E. Thompson, *A Selective Guide to Women-Related Records in the North Carolina State Archives* (Raleigh, NC: North Carolina Division of Archives and History, 1977).

13,626. McKimmon, Jane (Simpson)
Papers. 1928-66. 104 items.
Open. No guide.
North Carolina State University Archives.
McKimmon (1867-1957), who received an honorary doctor of laws degree from the University of North Carolina in 1934, was North Carolina's first state home demonstration agent. Correspondence, biographical sketches, reports, news releases, photos, radio script, clippings, and other papers relate chiefly to her work as a home demonstration agent from 1911 until her retirement in 1946. Includes material relating to a National Broadcasting Company program, which was presented in 1949 on the "Cavalcade of America" series based on McKimmon's book *When We're Green We Grow;* items concerning a loan fund set up in McKimmon's name in 1928 by the State Home Agents Association to provide financial help

for rural girls who wanted to study home economics at college; and historical material concerning the director's office of the extension home economics section of North Carolina State University's school of agriculture and life sciences.

13,627. Peace College Archives and History
Records. 1857- . No size given.
Access restricted. No guide.
Peace College.
Founded in 1857, the College offered its first classes in 1872. Correspondence; photos; yearbooks, 1904- ; catalogs, 1872- ; student handbooks; programs; invitations; and other items.

13,628. St. Mary's College Archives
Records. 1837- . No size given.
Closed. No guide.
St. Mary's College Library.
Minutes, financial records, correspondence, diaries, photos, scrapbooks, and other records of the College, a women's college founded in 1837.

WADESBORO

13,629. Anson County
Collection. 1750-1950. Ca. 11 boxes.
Partially restricted. No guide.
Anson County Library.
Minutes, publications of various organizations, family histories, photos, articles, and clippings of Anson County families and of such local women's organizations as the DAR, the United Daughters of the Confederacy, and the Colonial Dames. Also includes papers of [Miss] Mary Louise Medley and material about pensions of North Carolina widows of Confederate soldiers.

WILMINGTON

13,630. James Walker Memorial Hospital School of Nursing
Records. 1903-62. 1 vol.
Open. No guide.
New Hanover County Museum.
The School was founded in 1902. Notebook containing a brief history of the school, class photos, and a diploma issued to [Miss] Florence Hayes. In 1903 Hayes became the first person to obtain a certificate of registration as a trained nurse from a North Carolina school.

WINSTON-SALEM

13,631. Catalog of Early Southern Decorative Arts, Manuscript Data Files
Collection. Nd. No size given.
Open. Unpublished guide.
Museum of Early Southern Decorative Arts.
Excerpts from manuscripts, court records, and newspapers contain references to decorative arts in Maryland, Virginia, the Carolinas, Georgia, Tennessee, and Kentucky from the 17th to early 19th centuries. Of the 45,000 references assembled to date, about 500 to 600 pertain to women and their activities.

13,632. Lehman, Emma Augusta
Papers. Ca. 1880-1970. 7 Hollinger boxes and 12 vols.
Open. Card catalog.
Salem College, Siewers Room.
Lehman (1841-1922) was a botanist and an English teacher at Salem College for more than 50 years. Correspondence, reading and travel diaries, lectures and lecture notes, notebooks, book lists, poetry, samples of dried plants and herbs, and other items. Her letters and essays about Salem Academy include notes about the school's first three students in 1772. She notes that these girls learned geography, astronomy, botany, hygiene, and other subjects although most people "thought women were fitted only to sew, to wash, cook and bake . . . and be a domestic drudge." Her travel diaries chronicle a tour of the British Isles and European continent by Academy teachers in 1889. A native of Bethania, NC, Lehman was a Salem Academy alumna.

13,633. Salem College
Records. 1772- . 16 drawers.
Open. No guide.
Salem College, Siewers Room.
Initially called the Girls School, Salem College was founded in 1772 for the education of young women and girls. The school's records, many of which are written in German, include trustees minutes, 1927- ; annual financial statements to the elders of the Moravian Church, 1806- ; correspondence of school administrators, parents, and students; records of the Salem College endowment campaign, 1910-21; public examination records, 1800-20, which include student responses to graduation exams; student accounts, ca. 1800-1900, listing money received for students and precise descriptions of students' expenditures; account books of the Alumnae Association, 1890-1931; registration books for students, 1804-89; photos, primarily of college buildings; instructions for teachers, 1844-66; student notebooks; college catalogs; lists of library holdings, 1805-1911; inventories of the school's assets and holdings, 1805-11; and other records. The school became known as the Girls Boarding School after 1802; it was called Salem Female Academy from 1866 until 1907 when the name was changed to Salem Academy and College.

13,634. Salem College Publications
Records. Ca. 1852- . 7 shelves.
Open. No guide.
Salem College, Siewers Room.
Published material of this institution, a women's college and academy founded in 1772 by Moravians, includes *The Academy* and its successor *The Alumnae Record,* 1878- , publications for the school's alumnae and friends which provide information about the school's policy, students, faculty, and procedures; *The Salem Catalog,* 1852- ; *The Ivy* and *The Hesperian,* literary magazines, 1898-1917; announcements of graduations and music department recitals; *Sights and Insights,* the school's yearbook, 1905- ; and *The Salemite,* the school newspaper, 1920- .

13,635. North Carolina Baptist Historical Collection
Collection. 1770- . 235 ft., 7632 vols., and 300 microfilm reels.
Open. Unpublished guides.
Wake Forest University Library.
Manuscripts, church records, publications, and other records of organizations of North Carolina Baptists, black Baptists, Southern Baptists, Primitive Baptists, Wake Forest alumni, and other groups. Also includes collections of private individuals and institutions; membership lists, marriage records, and other documents of ca. 420 local Baptist churches; records of the Woman's Missionary Union and women's missionary societies; and papers about Baptist women missionaries. Specific portions of the Collection are described in the following Wake Forest University entries.

13,636. Bruington Memorial Baptist Church
Records. 1853-74. 1 vol.
Open. Card catalog and guide.
Wake Forest University Library, North Carolina Baptist Historical Collection.
Minutes of Church conferences contain lists of white and Negro members of this Gaston County, NC, church.

13,637. Cates, John Wesley
Papers. 1890-1919. 6.8 ft.
Open. No guide.
Wake Forest University Library, North Carolina Baptist Historical Collection.
Correspondence and financial records of Cates (1847-1918), a lumber and coal entrepreneur in Burlington, NC. Includes correspondence of Cates's wife Sarah Elizabeth Cates and of their daughters Tulah (Cates) Perry and Verna (Cates) Stackhouse.

13,638. East Carolina University Baptist Student Union
Records. 1928-47. 7 items.
Open. No guide.
Wake Forest University Library, North Carolina Baptist Historical Collection.
Correspondence, an historical sketch, and other records of the Union. Includes letters from Cleo Mitchell, Mrs. W. R. Farmer, Jr., and others who mention the Union's history.

13,639. Garner, Stella Wheelock
Papers. 1867-1963. 10 items.
Open. Unpublished guide.
Wake Forest University Library, North Carolina Baptist Historical Collection.
[Mrs.] Garner (1887-) is a Baptist worker with the Yadkin County, NC, prison unit. Correspondence, a history of the Yadkin Baptist Association Woman's Missionary Union, a biographical sketch about Garner, and other papers. Includes letters of appreciation for her work.

13,640. Hardaway, Anna Jane (Hunter)
Papers. 1881-83. 9 items.
Open. Unpublished guide.
Wake Forest University Library, North Carolina Baptist Historical Collection.
Hardaway (?-1941) was a student and music teacher at the Oxford Female Seminary in Oxford, NC. A letter from Charles E. Taylor to Anna Hunter's future husband John Steger Hardaway (1852-1925) about their coming marriage, photos of Hunter and school friends, an autograph book, a commencement invitation and program, and diplomas from Oxford Female Seminary.

13,641. Heck, Fannie Exile Scudder
Papers. 1878-1924. 394 items.
Open. No guide.
Wake Forest University Library, North Carolina Baptist Historical Collection.
Heck (1862-1915) was the first president of the North Carolina Woman's Missionary Union, president of the Southern Baptist Convention Woman's Missionary Union, and a founder of the Woman's Missionary Union Training School in Louisville. Letters from WMU leaders, poems and other writings, addresses before WMU groups, notebooks of poems, biographical information, a scrapbook of pamphlets, clippings and articles about her activities as North Carolina WMU president from 1886 until her death in 1915, WMU programs, and other papers. Heck served as president of the Southern Baptist Convention WMU from 1892 to 1894, from 1895 to 1899, and from 1906 to 1915. Under her guidance the WMU adopted a definite course of mission study for women and young people. The WMU Training School she helped to found is now known as the Carver School of Missions and Social Work.

13,642. Lanneau, Sophie Stephens
Papers. 1907-50. Ca. 2122 items.
Open. No guide.
Wake Forest University Library, North Carolina Baptist Historical Collection.
Lanneau (1880-1963) was a Southern Baptist educational missionary in China for about 40 years. Correspondence, writings, photos, scrapbooks, printed material, and other papers. Lanneau founded the Wei Ling Girls' Academy in Soochow, China, in 1911, serving as principal, teacher, dean,

and treasurer. She taught English, singing, gymnastics, the Bible, science, history, and geography. After 1927 she relinquished the post of principal to a Chinese successor but continued her teaching. She served on the University of Shanghai board of directors and for 30 years as a deaconess of Soochow Baptist Church. She was captured by the Japanese in 1942 and repatriated to the US in late 1943. She returned to Wei Ling Girls' Academy in 1946, but the school was handicapped by China's economic inflation, food shortages, subversive activities by the students, and communist attacks. Lanneau retired in the fall of 1950 and returned to Wake Forest, NC, where she lived with her sisters until her death.

13,643. North Carolina Baptist Convention, Woman's Missionary Union
Records. 1881-1969. 68 vols.
Open. Card catalog.
Wake Forest University Library, North Carolina Baptist Historical Collection.
Minutes, guidebooks, programs, and a history of the North Carolina WMU reflect the group's foreign missionary work, which included the gathering of donations for missions, developing programs for specific foreign countries, and receiving and responding to missionaries' reports. The history of the state WMU was written by Foy Johnson Farmer in 1952. Also includes reports of the Woman's Central Committee for Missions, 1913-14.

13,644. North Carolina Baptist State Sunday School Convention
Records. 1873-1927. 23 vols.
Open. Card catalog.
Wake Forest University Library, North Carolina Baptist Historical Collection.
The Convention was organized by North Carolina's Negro Baptists in about 1873 "to prosecute Sunday School missions; to cooperate with the American Baptist Publication Society . . . and to establish an orphan asylum for the protection and care of colored orphans of North Carolina." Minute books of the annual meetings of the Convention, which was composed chiefly of young women. The group supported the Grant Colored Orphan Asylum and the Girls' Education Fund, raising several hundred dollars each year to support as many as 20 girls in Baptist schools throughout the state. The Convention operated a bookstore in Raleigh, the proceeds of which went to missionary work.

13,645. North Carolina Women's Missionary Organizations
Collection. Nd. No size given.
Open. Unpublished guide.
Wake Forest University Library, North Carolina Baptist Historical Collection.
Consists of records of Woman's Missionary Union and Woman's Missionary Society units in various North Carolina Baptist churches. The collection includes minutes of the WMU units in the following Baptist Associations: Gaston, 1922 and 1927; Pee Dee, 1930; Roanoke, 1911, 1914, and 1923; South Yadkin, 1967 and 1968; and Tar River, 1909 and 1911. It also includes histories of the WMU in the following Associations: Beulah, Bladen, Brunswick, Eastern, Johnston, Robeson, Sandhills, Sandy Run, Three Forks, Tuckaseigee, and West Chowan.

13,646. Oxford Female Seminary
Records. 1897-1925. 9 vols. and 4 items.
Open. No guide.
Wake Forest University Library, North Carolina Baptist Historical Collection.
Gradebooks, photos, annuals, and catalogs of this Oxford, NC, women's school, which opened in 1850 and closed during the 1930s.

13,647. University of North Carolina at Greensboro: Baptist Student Union
Records. 1922-59. 19 vols.
Open. Accession sheet.
Wake Forest University Library, North Carolina Baptist Historical Collection.
Scrapbooks reflect the projects, programs, and concerns of members of the Baptist Student Union at the University of North Carolina at Greensboro, then an all-women's college.

NORTH DAKOTA

BISMARCK

13,648. Anderson, Elizabeth (Preston)
Papers. 1893-1954. 1 in. and 1 vol.
Open. No guide.
State Historical Society of North Dakota.
[Mrs. James] Anderson (1861-1954) was president of the North Dakota WCTU from 1893 to 1933 and held office in the national WCTU. She was also an active supporter of the suffrage movement and the Prohibition party. Speeches, scrapbook, clippings, and WCTU publications.

13,649. Bismarck Civic Improvement League
Records. 1908-18. 1 vol. and 13 items.
Open. No guide.
State Historical Society of North Dakota.
Record book containing constitution, bylaws, and minutes of the League; correspondence and bills of acquisition and landscaping of Custer Park; articles of incorporation of the Bismarck Civic League; and constitution and bylaws of the Bismarck Federation of Women's Societies.

13,650. Boley, Sarah
Papers. 1877-1918. 3 vols.
Open. No guide.
State Historical Society of North Dakota.
Diaries of Sarah (Lewallan or Llewelyn) Boley, a farmer and wife of Elijah Boley, regarding daily life, weather, and agricultural conditions in Morton County, ND.

13,651. Canfield, Sarah Elizabeth (Haas)
Papers. 1866-67. 30-page item.
Open. No guide.
State Historical Society of North Dakota.
Diary in which [Mrs. Andrew Nahum] Canfield describes her journey up the Missouri River and life at Fort Berthold and Camp Cooke, MT. Published in *North Dakota History* (Oct. 1953), the diary was used by Bess (Streeter) Aldrich in *The Lieutenant's Lady.*

13,652. Cavileer, Lulah Belle
Papers. 1886-1930. Ca. 3 in. and 3 items.
Open. No guide.
State Historical Society of North Dakota.
[Miss] Cavileer was a Pembina, ND, resident and daughter of Charles Cavileer. Diaries; personal correspondence from A. L. Larpenteur, Mary T. [Mrs. James J.] Hill, L. B. Hanna, Tracy R. Bangs, W. C. Wardwell, G. B. Winship, and others; notebook containing copies of Charles Cavileer's letters; and clippings, some of which concern Charles Cavileer's death.

13,653. Heath, Fannie (Mahood)
Papers. 1922-30. 1 vol.
Open. No guide.
State Historical Society of North Dakota.
[Mrs. Frank Arnold] Heath (1864-1931) was a horticulturist. Correspondence regarding horticulture, a biography, articles, photos, and clippings.

13,654. Historical Data Project
Records. 1937. Ca. 30 ft.
Open. No guide.
State Historical Society of North Dakota.
The Project was sponsored by the State Historical Society of North Dakota under the auspices of the WPA to compile county and local historical data and biographical material on the state's pioneer families. Questionnaires include information on genealogy, the type of housing, furnishings, schools, churches, social institutions, farming, and home life.

13,655. Ladies Auxiliary
Records. 1917-18. 1 vol. and 10 items.
Open. No guide.
State Historical Society of North Dakota.
Minutes, letters from servicemen, and lists of members of this Mandan, ND, group. Also included are minutes of the organizational meeting of the Bismarck Auxiliary.

13,656. National League of American Pen Women
Records. 1927-54. 0.5 ft. and 12 vols.
Open. No guide.
State Historical Society of North Dakota.
The League was established in the 1920s to bring together women who contribute creatively to the fields of the arts, letters, and music. Records of several North Dakota chapters, including annual reports, correspondence, publications, and memorabilia.

13,657. Nelson, Deborah Ann
Papers. 1918-19. 25 items.
Open. No guide.
State Historical Society of North Dakota.
Letters from Nelson, a nurse, in New York and France to her family in Cooperstown, ND. Also included is other material relating to WWI.

13,658. Palmer, Bertha Rachel
Papers. Ca. 1900-60. Ca. 5 ft.
Open. No guide.
State Historical Society of North Dakota.
[Miss] Palmer was superintendent of public instruction in North Dakota from 1927 to 1933 and a fieldworker for the national WCTU. Correspondence and speeches regarding the WCTU, temperance, and Palmer's work as director of the Bureau of Scientific Temperance Investigation, a unit of the national WCTU; original prose and poetry; a biography; and yearbooks of the North Dakota Federation of Women's Clubs.

13,659. Pioneer Daughters of America
Records. 1934-56. 4 vols.
Open. No guide.
State Historical Society of North Dakota.
Ledger of receipts and notebooks containing photos, reports, membership lists, and clippings of the Bismarck chapter of the Daughters.

13,660. Quain, Fannie (Dunn)
Papers. 1875-1947. 0.5 ft. and 9 vols.
Open. No guide.
State Historical Society of North Dakota.
Both Quain (1876-1950) and her husband Eric P. Quain were physicians who helped found the Quain-Ramstad Clinic. Autobiography, historical material by Quain on Bismarck and Burleigh County, ND, a record of officers of Bismarck, a secretary's book of the Original Club, Fortnightly Club records, programs of the North Dakota Federation of Women's Clubs, a biographical sketch of James W. Foley, scrapbooks of photos and cards, autograph albums, clippings, and other items. Also contains papers of Quain's parents Mr. and Mrs. John Piatt Dunn.

13,661. Slaughter, Linda (Warfel)
Papers. 1870-1929. Ca. 5 in.
Open. No guide.

State Historical Society of North Dakota.
[Mrs. Benjamin Franklin] Slaughter (1850-1911) was a pioneer of Bismarck and Fort Rice, Dakota Territory. Letters from Roman Catholic priest Jean Baptiste Marie Genin, J. P. Kidder, I. E. West, W. H. H. Beadle, A. Sheridan Jones, M. H. Jewell, C. A. Lounsberry, Belva Lockwood, and others regarding personal matters, woman suffrage, the Woman's Relief Corps, the Knights of Labor, the Burleigh County Pioneers, and the Ladies Historical Society. Also included is a receipt for fees paid for a homestead declaratory statement of Charles Cavileer and minutes of the first Board of Commissioners in Pembina County, ND.

13,662. Stickney Family
Papers. Nd. 33 items.
Open. No guide.
State Historical Society of North Dakota.
Correspondence, articles, pamphlets, and clippings of this Dickinson, ND, pioneer family pertain to Victor Hugo Stickney, a physician, and to actress Dorothy Stickney and her acting career in New York.

13,663. War History Commission
Records. 1917-24. Ca. 1 ft.
Open. No guide.
State Historical Society of North Dakota.
The Commission was formed under the direction of the State Historical Society of North Dakota to document the state's WWI service. American National Red Cross county chapter records and chapter histories, reports of Liberty Loan drives, and reports of organizations including The Salvation Army and the YWCA.

13,664. Western Womanhood
Records. 1890-98. Ca. 1 in. and 1 vol.
Open. No guide.
State Historical Society of North Dakota.
This journal was the official organ of the North Dakota WCTU and the North Dakota Equal Suffrage Association from 1894 to 1898. Its stated purpose was to discuss such topics as philanthropy, business and professional life, and home duties. Published monthly by May Hewitt Tousley of Buffalo, ND, and Mary Allen Whedon of Fargo, ND, the journal included articles on women's activities, fashion, health, and etiquette, as well as transcripts of debates on important political questions. Also contains copies of the *North Dakota White Ribbon,* the predecessor of *Western Womanhood.*

13,665. White Ribbon Bulletin
Records. 1899-1969. Ca. 5 in.
Open. No guide.
State Historical Society of North Dakota.
Successor to *Western Womanhood,* the official organ of the North Dakota WCTU, the *White Ribbon Bulletin* strove to advance WCTU work in the state and to promote observance of the Golden Rule. Elizabeth Preston Anderson was editor-in-chief of the *Bulletin* and president of the North Dakota WCTU. [Mrs.] Mattie Van deBogert was the managing editor.

FARGO

13,666. Amenia Church Ladies' Aid
Records. 1914-37. 2 vols.
Open. No guide.
North Dakota State University, North Dakota Institute for Regional Studies.
Minute books of the Ladies' Aid contain minutes, 1925-32, and financial records, 1914-37.

13,667. American Association of University Women, Fargo
Records. 1931-59. 23 items.
Open. Card catalog and list entry.
North Dakota State University, North Dakota Institute for Regional Studies.
Yearbooks, reports, and programs of the Fargo branch of the AAUW.

13,668. Anderson, Elizabeth (Preston)
Papers. 1889-1956. Ca. 9 in.
Open. Unpublished guides.
North Dakota State University, North Dakota Institute for Regional Studies.
An active supporter of the suffrage movement and Prohibition party, [Mrs. James] Anderson (1861-1954) was president of the North Dakota WCTU from 1893 to 1933 and held office in the national organization. Correspondence, including an 1893 letter from Susan B. Anthony regarding women's suffrage; Anderson's unpublished autobiography "Under the Prairie Winds"; speeches; articles; a photo; and pamphlets on the WCTU and the state prohibition law. Also contains copies of *Western Womanhood,* 1894-99, and *White Ribbon Bulletin,* 1899-1956; the papers were official organs of the North Dakota WCTU.

13,669. Brennan, Angela Juanita (Stott)
Papers. 1920-77. 5 boxes.
Open. Shelflist.
North Dakota State University, North Dakota Institute for Regional Studies.
Brennan (1919-), who has been married four times and had six children, managed the Midway Service Station in Adrian, ND, with her second husband. Contains family correspondence, including letters from Brennan's son James Murray while he was in Vietnam from 1969 to 1970; files on each of her children; pedigree charts and family work sheets pertaining to the North Dakota Curleys, McManns, McDonoughs, Fords, Farresters, and Connerys, all of whom came from Ireland; North Dakota State University freshman papers written by Brennan and her daughter Debra (Connery) Lockwood; scrapbooks; clippings; dance bills of Karen Murray from the 1950s; and pamphlets. The daughter of Frank E. Stott and Mary Ellen (Schenecker) Stott of Montpelier, ND, Brennan attended Dakota Business College in Fargo. In 1939 she married Berton Colling of Jamestown, ND; they were divorced in 1940. In the same year she married James Murray (?-1949) of Fargo, and they had three children, Mary Margaret (Murray) [Mrs. George] Thomas, Karen Anne (Murray) Thompson, and James Alan Murray. In 1952, she married James Arthur Connery (?-1959), a resident of Gackle, ND, and a part owner of Midway Service Station in Adrian, ND. They had three children Debra Kaye (Connery) Lockwood, Kevin Michael Connery, and Kimberley Francine Connery. After James Connery's death, Brennan and her children continued the business until 1968. In 1969 Brennan married Don Brennan and moved to Fargo, where she worked for Western Products, Sunset Memorial, and Silverline, Inc. The Brennans were divorced in 1973. Angela Brennan then attended the Veteran's Upward Bound program for six months, later entering North Dakota State University with her daughter Debra Lockwood.

13,670. Craig, Minne D. (Davenport)
Papers. 1904-55. 3 in. and 2 vols.
Open. Unpublished guides.
North Dakota State University, North Dakota Institute for Regional Studies.
In 1922 [Mrs. Edward O.] Craig (1883-1966) became one of the first two women elected to the North Dakota legislature; she also was the first woman in the US to be elected speaker of a state House of Representatives. Correspondence, autobiography, genealogical information, scrapbooks, and two pamphlets by Craig on politics for women. Craig also was a member of the Nonpartisan League, president of the state League Women's Club, and a member of the national Republican committee.

13,671. Faculty Women's Club, North Dakota State University
Records. 1944-54. 2 in. and 1 vol.
Open. Card catalog and list entry.
North Dakota State University, North Dakota Institute for Regional Studies.
Constitution, minute book-scrapbook, meeting notes, correspondence, membership lists, programs, yearbooks, and clippings.

13,672. Gumb, Katherine (Hughes)
Papers. Nd. 2 boxes.
Open. Shelflist.
North Dakota State University, North Dakota Institute for Regional Studies.
[Mrs. Daniel J.] Gumb (1873-1963) was a local historian. Manuscripts concerning Steele County, ND, history, including biographical sketches of early settlers, and records of the Old Settlers Association of Griggs and Steele Counties, consisting primarily of a minute book, 1906-18; financial records; and correspondence. Daughter of Mr. and Mrs. Andrew C. Hughes, Gumb resided in Hope, ND, where she was active in the Women's Club, the library, the American Legion Auxiliary, the Hope Community Club, and local government.

13,673. Hollister, Joanna (Randolph) Kelley
Papers. 1908-55. 4 in.
Open. Card catalog and list entry.
North Dakota State University, North Dakota Institute for Regional Studies.
Correspondence, writings, passport, biography, and clippings of Hollister (1870-?), a teacher at the State School for the Deaf in Olatha, KS, and at the State School for the Deaf in Devils Lake, ND. She was married to Clark W. Kelley and then to George H. Hollister.

13,674. Kelsey, Vera
Papers. 1944-58. 5 boxes.
Open. Unpublished guide.
North Dakota State University, North Dakota Institute for Regional Studies.
Kelsey (ca. 1891-1961), the daughter of William H. Kelsey and Isabel Oliver (Woods) Kelsey, was a writer. Includes primarily manuscripts and research notes for her last four books *British Columbia Rides a Star, Red River Runs North!, Tomorrow Is for You,* and *Young Men So Daring* but also contains scattered correspondence dealing primarily with research information requests, clippings concerning publication of her books, and sheet music for the songs "Assiniboine Lullaby" and "My Prairie Rose" by Andrew Mulligan as well as for other songs about the Red River Valley. Born in Winnipeg, Canada, Kelsey moved to Grand Forks, ND, with her family. A 1914 graduate of the University of North Dakota, she received her MA in sociology from Brown University. From 1920 to 1922 she was a feature writer for the *North China Daily News* in Shanghai. Later she traveled extensively in Europe, Japan, and South and Central America; while there she wrote several books about her travels. After WWII she returned to Grand Forks where she wrote mystery novels and began her works on regional history. Kelsey also served as assistant editor of the *Theater Arts* magazine and was director of public relations for the American Woman's Association and the American Woman's Club. She was a member of the Author's League of America and the Fargo branch of the National League of American Pen Women. In her later years Kelsey resided in Minneapolis, MN.

13,675. Kroeze, Nettie
Papers. Nd. 3 items.
Open. No guide.
North Dakota State University, North Dakota Institute for Regional Studies.
Contains "The Woman Musicians of North Dakota," a paper by Jeannette "Nettie" Gray Kroeze (1874-), who was married to Barend H.

Kroeze (1868-1960), the first president of Jamestown College in Jamestown, ND. Also includes clippings.

13,676. League of Women Voters, Fargo
Records. Ca. 1951-59. Ca. 5 in.
Open. Card catalog and list entry.
North Dakota State University, North Dakota Institute for Regional Studies.
Bylaws, budgets, correspondence, agendas, news releases, membership lists, and national, state, and local publications, pamphlets, and leaflets.

13,677. Lobben, Clara
Papers. 1924-57. 13 vols.
Open. Card catalog and list entry.
North Dakota State University, North Dakota Institute for Regional Studies.
Lobben was a member of the World Federation of Education Associations and of the Fargo WCTU. Diaries, 1944-54; a notebook of the National WCTU Plan of Work Institute, 1947-48; and a scrapbook of clippings regarding the National Education Association.

13,678. North Dakota Federation of Music Clubs
Records. 1921-24. Ca. 1 ft.
Open. Card catalog and list entry.
North Dakota State University, North Dakota Institute for Regional Studies.
Correspondence between the Federation and local music clubs.

13,679. North Dakota Nurses Association
Records. 1912-17. Ca. 3 in.
Open. Unpublished guides.
North Dakota State University, North Dakota Institute for Regional Studies.
Correspondence regarding American National Red Cross preparation for WWI, financial records, bankbook, canceled checks, programs, and clippings.

13,680. North Dakota State Nurses' Association
Records. 1912-17. 1 box.
Open. Shelflist.
North Dakota State University, North Dakota Institute for Regional Studies.
The Association was established in 1911 when a group of graduate nurses formed an affiliate of the American Nurses' Association to protect the interests and improve the education of nurses in North Dakota. Consists of records of the American National Red Cross Nursing Service, including semi-annual reports, 1913-17, and of the North Dakota State Nurses' Association, including instructions to nurses in preparation for war, 1917, as well as bank statements, deposit books, bills, checks, receipts, and ballots. Also includes a letter and program from the Association's annual meeting in Minot, ND, in 1916, and letters concerning the dispute over formation of a rival nurses' group, the North Dakota Association of Registered and Graduate Nurses.

13,681. North Dakota State University YWCA
Records. Ca. 1904-65. 2.5 ft.
Open. Inventory.
North Dakota State University, North Dakota Institute for Regional Studies.
Constitution, bylaws, annual reports, club minutes, financial records, correspondence, roll calls, and publications.

13,682. Pearce, Gladys M.
Papers. 1936-57. 1 box.
Open. Unpublished guide.
North Dakota State University, North Dakota Institute for Regional Studies.
Correspondence of [Miss] Pearce (1893-1966), a writer, with Hazel Pearce Halvorson and Leonard Sackett of the Institute for Regional Studies and the manuscript for Pearce's unpublished work "Claimed by the Prairies," which pertains to the life of Bismarck, ND, pioneer Winnie Nicholls from 1830 to 1914. Mentioned in the work are Alexander McKenzie, Dennis Hannifin, Calamity Jane, General Custer, William Latimer, and Linda (Warfel) Slaughter. Also includes information about Comanche Indians, travel by covered wagon, Fort Seward at Jamestown, gambling halls, the removal of the North Dakota capital to Bismarck, the fire in 1898, Negro settlements, statehood, Camp Hancock, early schools, and social life in Bismarck.

13,683. Pioneer Daughters
Records. Ca. 1920. Ca. 1 ft.
Open. Card catalog and list entry.
North Dakota State University, North Dakota Institute for Regional Studies.
Minutes, correspondence, notes, clippings, and pamphlets of this North Dakota organization. Also included are biographical correspondence and sketches of Mrs. E. B. Butler, Mrs. Charles Finney, Mrs. Frederic Wilder, Mrs. W. J. Lane and Mrs. S. S. Lyon of Fargo, Mrs. Robert Morrison of Casselton, Mrs. Henry C. Simmons of Tombs, and Mrs. Theodore L. Williams of Arthur.

13,684. Raaen, Aagot
Papers. Ca. 1915-53. 1.5 ft.
Open. Unpublished guides.
North Dakota State University, North Dakota Institute for Regional Studies.
Correspondence, notes, clippings, and manuscript of *Measure of My Days,* a 1952 autobiographical novel by Raaen (1878-1957), an author and Norwegian pioneer in Steele County, ND. Also includes the manuscript for her genealogy of the Hamarsbon family.

13,685. Rich Valley Homemaker's Club
Records. Ca. 1928-69. Ca. 1 ft.
Open. Card catalog and list entry.
North Dakota State University, North Dakota Institute for Regional Studies.
Minutes, record books, correspondence, project record books, lists of officers, recipes, and household hints of this Benson County Club that was associated with the University of North Dakota extension division and affiliated with the National Home Demonstration Council and the Associated Country Women of the World.

13,686. Richards, Clara Alida
Papers. 1924-60. 1 box.
Open. Unpublished guide.
North Dakota State University, North Dakota Institute for Regional Studies.
[Miss] Richards (1884-1960) was librarian of the Fargo Masonic Grand Lodge Library from 1915 to 1956 and was noted in 1950 as being the only female Masonic librarian. Biographical information; manuscripts regarding utopian social thought, equality before the law in France, the Jew in relation to modern culture, the League of Nations, and other topics; book reviews; and notes by Richards. She was president of the North Dakota library association, helped organize the Fargo Community Welfare Association, and was a member of the Orpha Chapter of the Eastern Star. Richards graduated from the University of Wisconsin in Madison in 1906.

13,687. Round Table Club
Records. 1972. 12 items.
Open. No guide.
North Dakota State University, North Dakota Institute for Regional Studies.
Records of this Fargo study group, which was founded in 1897, contain a collection of talks and clippings from its "Women in America" study series. Includes items about women in Fargo to 1940 and in the state of North Dakota, women in state politics, and contributions of women in medicine, poetry, music, education, and art.

13,688. Trinka, Zdena Irma
Papers. 1940s. 1 box.
Open. Unpublished guide.
North Dakota State University, North Dakota Institute for Regional Studies.
Consists of "Colorful Czechoslovakia," an unpublished manuscript of Trinka (1893-1967), an author; a draft of her book *Medora* was written on the back of the manuscript. Trinka and her family came to the US from Bohemia when she was a child and lived for a short time in Idaho before settling in Lidgerwood, ND, where her father Anton Trinka worked as a tailor. Following her education Trinka became a librarian at the Lidgerwood Public Library, served as head librarian in Dickinson, ND, and in 1925 began work with the Tulare County Free Library in California. From 1936 to 1938 she was on a journalistic assignment in Europe, dividing her time between Paris and Prague. She returned to North Dakota just prior to the German invasion of Czechoslovakia and then devoted her time to writing several books.

13,689. Tyler, Annie A. (Dwight)
Papers. Nd. Ca. 0.5 ft. and 50 vols.
Open. Inventory.
North Dakota State University, North Dakota Institute for Regional Studies.
Correspondence, business records, ledgers, legal documents, deeds, stock shares, and biographical information of [Mrs. Richard] Tyler (?-1936), who came to North Dakota from New York in 1879 and became a Fargo businesswoman, owning property and operating a loan and real estate business.

13,690. Vogel, Lois (Fluetsch)
Papers. 1963-72. 3 cu.ft.
Open. Unpublished guide.
North Dakota State University, North Dakota Institute for Regional Studies.
Papers of [Mrs. Mort R.] Vogel (1914-) relate to her involvement in the North Dakota constitutional convention in 1972 as delegate, executive committee member, and convention secretary.

13,691. Votes for Women League of North Dakota
Records. 1912-19. 1 vol. and 17 items.
Open. No guide.
North Dakota State University, North Dakota Institute for Regional Studies.
Constitution, minute book dating from 1912 to 1919, correspondence, a clipping, programs, and pamphlets of the League, which was organized in Fargo in 1912.

13,692. Walters, Thorstina (Jackson)
Papers. 1918-58. Ca. 4 ft.
Open. Unpublished guides.
North Dakota State University, North Dakota Institute for Regional Studies.
An author and writer, [Mrs. Emile] Walters (?-1959) was active during WWI in the YWCA in France. Correspondence, manuscripts, lectures, biographical sketch, pamphlets, and clippings. An employee of the New York City Department of Welfare from 1933 to 1942, she was known primarily for her writings which appeared in the *Christian Science Monitor* and *The New York Times,* for her book *Modern Sagas, the Story of the Icelanders in North America* (1954), and for her interest in Iceland.

13,693. Wink, Helena Knauf
Papers. 1915-54. 21 items.
Open. No guide.
North Dakota State University, North Dakota Institute for Regional Studies.
Wink (1854-1936) was a pioneer physician in

Jamestown, ND. Includes correspondence with her brother John Knauf, condolences upon the occasion of Wink's death, clippings related to Wink and other members of the Knauf family, an address of John Knauf before the affairs committee of the North Dakota State Senate, an historical booklet on Osward T. Denny, and a program of the annual banquet for the 1915 North Dakota Bar Association. Wink was married to Mathias Wink (1854-1904).

13,694. Woman's Christian Temperance Union
Records. 1887-1921. 2 vols.
Open. No guide.
North Dakota State University, North Dakota Institute for Regional Studies.
Minute books of the Amenia, ND, chapter of the WCTU contain minutes of meetings between 1903 and 1909, receipts and expenditures from 1888 to 1921, and membership lists from 1887 to 1903.

13,695. Woman's Literary Club of Carrington, ND
Records. 1897-1925. 4 vols.
Open. Unpublished guides.
North Dakota State University, North Dakota Institute for Regional Studies.
Secretary's books of the Club, established in 1897 to unite women for their mutual improvement.

13,696. Woman's Relief Corps, Department of North Dakota, John F. Reynolds Corps No. 1
Records. 1885-1965. 6 boxes.
Open. Inventory.
North Dakota State University, North Dakota Institute for Regional Studies.
Organized in 1885 in Fargo as the auxiliary of the John F. Reynolds Post of the Grand Army of the Republic, the Corps, whose first president was Irene Hadley, participated in Memorial Day observances, contributed to the Soldiers Home at Lisbon, ND, presented flags to various institutions, entertained Company B of the state national guard in 1898 and 1917, donated money and materials during WWI, worked with the American National Red Cross, and assisted in the adoption of war orphans. Minutes; annual reports from 1936 to 1945; secretary's, treasurer's, and patriotic instructor's reports; financial records; correspondence; membership rolls; photos; scrapbook containing historical information; publications; and other records. Also contains minutes of the Past Presidents Club, records of the Col. Carroll Junior Club for young girls founded by the Corps in 1935, and minutes of the Woman's Relief Corps of Mayville in Dakota Territory. Primary correspondents were Anna Pannebaker and Louisa Goodman. The John F. Reynolds Corps was disbanded in 1965.

13,697. Woodward, Catherine Martha, Family
Papers. Ca. 1873-94. Ca. 30 items.
Open. No guide.
North Dakota State University, North Dakota Institute for Regional Studies.
Members of the Woodward family were early English pioneers in Hawley, MN. Includes correspondence of the children; diaries of Adelia Woodward, 1874, and of Lucy Louisa Woodward, 1876; financial papers; genealogical material; almanacs for 1888, 1890, and 1893-94; and a clipping pertaining to the local school.

GRAND FORKS

13,698. Aldrich, Vernice
Papers. 1926-47. 2 ft.
Open. Published and unpublished guides.
University of North Dakota, Orin G. Libby Manuscript Collection.
Aldrich (1901-59) was a teacher at the University of North Dakota, registrar at Wesley College, and editor of the *North Dakota Wheat Grower,* official publication of the Wheat Growers' Association. Correspondence, poetry by Aldrich and others, business records, manuscripts, articles, brochures, clippings, and other material relating to the institutions with which she was affiliated. See John B. Davenport, comp., *Guide to the Orin G. Libby Manuscript Collection and Related Research Collections* (Grand Forks, ND: University of North Dakota, 1975).

13,699. American Association of University Women
Records. 1930-64. 8 ft.
Open. Published guide.
University of North Dakota, Orin G. Libby Manuscript Collection.
Minutes, correspondence, state and local reports, and other material relating to the history and activities of the North Dakota chapter of the AAUW. See John B. Davenport, comp., *Guide to the Orin G. Libby Manuscript Collection and Related Research Collections* (Grand Forks, ND: University of North Dakota, 1975).

13,700. Baldwin, Elizabeth Bratt
Papers. 1899-1901. 41 items.
Open. Published and unpublished guides.
University of North Dakota, Orin G. Libby Manuscript Collection.
Correspondence, notes, speech, biography, and photos of Baldwin (?-1954), a librarian and teacher. See John B. Davenport, comp., *Guide to the Orin G. Libby Manuscript Collection and Related Research Collections* (Grand Forks, ND: University of North Dakota, 1975).

13,701. Baumgartner, Florence Eikenberry
Papers. 1925-39. 3 ft.
Open. Unpublished guide.
University of North Dakota, Orin G. Libby Manuscript Collection.
Papers of Baumgartner (ca. 1900-76), a rural North Dakota schoolteacher, contain correspondence, notebooks, workbooks, study guides, and pamphlets relating to teaching in elementary and secondary schools in such rural areas as Rock Lake.

13,702. Bjorlie, Liv
Papers. 1960-69. 4.5 ft.
Open. No guide.
University of North Dakota, Orin G. Libby Manuscript Collection.
Bjorlie was state Democratic committeewoman for North Dakota from 1964 to 1972. Campaign files, particularly for North Dakota; election material; and convention files and documents from the national Democratic party.

13,703. Eagles, Aloha
Papers. 1969-73. 1.5 ft.
Access restricted. Published and unpublished guides.
University of North Dakota, Orin G. Libby Manuscript Collection.
Correspondence of [Mrs.] Eagles (1916-), a North Dakota state representative, concerning abortion reform, the Equal Rights Amendment, and other women's rights issues. See John B. Davenport, comp., *Guide to the Orin G. Libby Manuscript Collection and Related Research Collections* (Grand Forks, ND: University of North Dakota, 1975).

13,704. Equal Rights Amendment
Records. 1973-74. 51 items.
Open. Published guide.
University of North Dakota, Orin G. Libby Manuscript Collection.
Includes 17 pamphlets produced by the North Dakota Coordinating Council for the Equal Rights Amendment. See John B. Davenport, comp., *Guide to the Orin G. Libby Manuscript Collection and Related Research Collections* (Grand Forks, ND: University of North Dakota, 1975).

13,705. Faculty Wives and Womens' Association
Records. 1947-75. 1 item.
Open. Unpublished guide.
University of North Dakota, Orin G. Libby Manuscript Collection.
Minutes of business sessions of this University of North Dakota group, 1947-69, and a short history of the Association, written in 1975.

13,706. Fox, Nita
Papers. 1964-75. 1.3 ft.
Open. Unpublished guide.
University of North Dakota, Orin G. Libby Manuscript Collection.
Papers of Fox, who was president of the Federation of North Dakota Business and Professional Women's Clubs from 1973 to 1974, pertain to the Federation, the North Dakota Commission on the Status of Women, the North Dakota Coordinating Council for the Equal Rights Amendment, and the national ERA campaign.

13,707. Goodwater, Leroy, Family
Papers. 1850-1926. 0.7 ft.
Open. Unpublished guide.
University of North Dakota, Orin G. Libby Manuscript Collection.
Correspondence between Goodwater family members in Grand Forks, Chattanooga, TN, and Palmyra, WI, includes that with Leroy Goodwater's mother Mamie Goodwater, 1884-1904 and 1926, about family news. Also contains earlier letters of Warren and William Coss and other family members.

13,708. Grand Forks Federation of Women's Clubs
Records. 1897-1904. 2 vols.
Open. Published and unpublished guides.
University of North Dakota, Orin G. Libby Manuscript Collection.
Constitution and minute books. See John B. Davenport, comp., *Guide to the Orin G. Libby Manuscript Collection and Related Research Collections* (Grand Forks, ND: University of North Dakota, 1975).

13,709. Heath, Fannie Mahood
Papers. 1921-31. 3 vols. and 53 items.
Open. Published and unpublished guides.
University of North Dakota, Orin G. Libby Manuscript Collection.
Known as "the flower woman of North Dakota," [Mrs.] Heath (1864-1931) was an expert on wild, domestic, and rare plant life. Correspondence, including that with the National Horticultural Society and English botanical gardeners; manuscript of *Gardening in North Dakota;* writings relating to her life and career; and photos. See John B. Davenport, comp., *Guide to the Orin G. Libby Manuscript Collection and Related Research Collections* (Grand Forks, ND: University of North Dakota, 1975).

13,710. Hunter, Alice M.
Papers. 1879-1973. 15 ft.
Open. Unpublished guide.
University of North Dakota, Orin G. Libby Manuscript Collection.
Correspondence, diaries, financial papers, photos, and scrapbooks of Hunter (1891 -1975), a Grand Forks physician who took over her father's various business interests and managed them throughout her lifetime.

13,711. Icelandic Immigration
Collection. 1853-1922. 12 items and 1 tape.
Open. Published and unpublished guides.

University of North Dakota, Orin G. Libby Manuscript Collection.
Correspondence, diaries, Icelandic manuscript, and tape containing 21 interviews of Icelandic immigrants to the US, including several women. Anna G. Johannsson's 1895-1922 diary and most of the correspondence are in Icelandic. See John B. Davenport, comp., *Guide to the Orin G. Libby Manuscript Collection and Related Research Collections* (Grand Forks, ND: University of North Dakota, 1975).

13,712. Kilander, Ellie
Papers. 1971-75. 0.75 ft.
Open. Unpublished guide.
University of North Dakota, Orin G. Libby Manuscript Collection.
Correspondence, subject files, and newsletters of Kilander, an equal opportunity officer for North Dakota State University. Includes information on the national campaign for passage of the Equal Rights Amendment and ERA activity in North Dakota.

13,713. Kraft, Ruby
Papers. 1921-49. 25 items.
Open. Unpublished guide.
University of North Dakota, Orin G. Libby Manuscript Collection.
Correspondence and other papers of Kraft relate to her involvement as a member and president of the North Dakota Federation of Nonpartisan League Women's Clubs.

13,714. North Dakota Dames Club
Records. 1916-58. 8 vols. and other material.
Open. Published and unpublished guides.
University of North Dakota, Orin G. Libby Manuscript Collection.
Minute books, membership rosters, and history of the Club since 1909. See John B. Davenport, comp., *Guide to the Orin G. Libby Manuscript Collection and Related Research Collections* (Grand Forks, ND: University of North Dakota, 1975).

13,715. North Dakota Immigrants
Collection. 1937-38. 8 items.
Open. Published and unpublished guides.
University of North Dakota, Orin G. Libby Manuscript Collection.
Eight WPA Historical Data Project interviews with Scandinavian and Canadian immigrants to North Dakota include such information as birth date, birthplace, family history, details of immigration, number and names of children, value and description of household goods, and religion. See John B. Davenport, comp., *Guide to the Orin G. Libby Manuscript Collection and Related Research Collections* (Grand Forks, ND: University of North Dakota, 1975).

13,716. North Dakota League of Women Voters
Records. 1950-72. 21 ft.
Open. Published and unpublished guides.
University of North Dakota, Orin G. Libby Manuscript Collection.
Correspondence, policy statements, programs, material regarding national and state conventions, and national, state, and local publications of the Grand Forks and Fargo, ND, chapters of the LWV. Issues discussed include public education, welfare and social services, and the environment. See John B. Davenport, comp., *Guide to the Orin G. Libby Manuscript Collection and Related Research Collections* (Grand Forks, ND: University of North Dakota, 1975).

13,717. O'Hare, Kate (Richards)
Papers. 1917-65. 0.33 ft.
Open. Published and unpublished guides.
University of North Dakota, Orin G. Libby Manuscript Collection.
O'Hare (1877-1948) was a socialist journalist and organizer. Transcript of O'Hare's 1917 sedition trial in Bismarck, ND; other documents relating to the trial; and manuscript of "Red Kate: A Case of Midwestern Socialism" by James J. Wood. See John B. Davenport, comp., *Guide to the Orin G. Libby Manuscript Collection and Related Research Collections* (Grand Forks, ND: University of North Dakota, 1975).

13,718. Simpson, Carrie B.
Papers. 1930-64. 0.5 ft.
Open. No guide.
University of North Dakota, Orin G. Libby Manuscript Collection.
Papers of Simpson, an author and teacher who also served as supreme president of the PEO Sisterhood, include her PEO speeches and related items, original stories and poems, "Mother and Daughter Talks," articles she wrote on education in North Dakota, and biographical material.

13,719. State Defense Council of North Dakota: "Women's Service Bulletins"
Records. 1942-44. 52 items.
Open. Unpublished guide.
University of North Dakota, Orin G. Libby Manuscript Collection.
Issues of an irregularly published newsletter about the role of women in the war effort.

13,720. Talbott Family
Papers. 1937-61. 22 ft.
Open. Published and unpublished guides.
University of North Dakota, Orin G. Libby Manuscript Collection.
Correspondence, minutes, files, and reports include material relating to [Mrs.] Gladys Talbott Edwards, director of the Farmers Union Cooperative Education Service for the northwestern states. This organization was the educational arm of the National Farmers Union. In 1937 Edwards became director of the National Farmers Union's National Department of Junior Education. See John B. Davenport, comp., *Guide to the Orin G. Libby Manuscript Collection and Related Research Collections* (Grand Forks, ND: University of North Dakota, 1975).

13,721. Votes for Women Club
Records. 1912-19. 2 vols.
Open. Published and unpublished guides.
University of North Dakota, Orin G. Libby Manuscript Collection.
Minutes of this Grand Forks women's suffrage organization, which was led by [Mrs.] Clara Darrow. See John B. Davenport, comp., *Guide to the Orin G. Libby Manuscript Collection and Related Research Collections* (Grand Forks, ND: University of North Dakota, 1975).

13,722. Wasik, Anita (Anker)
Papers. Nd. 0.33 ft.
Open. No guide.
University of North Dakota, Orin G. Libby Manuscript Collection.
Wasik (1949-) was chairwoman of the North Dakota Women's Coalition. Correspondence, financial records, speeches, Equal Rights Amendment material, files, mailing lists, newsletters, and clippings of the Coalition. Wasik later readopted her maiden name.

13,723. Young Woman's Christian Association
Records. 1917-63. 3 ft.
Open. Published and unpublished guides.
University of North Dakota, Orin G. Libby Manuscript Collection.
Minutes, financial records, correspondence, scrapbook, and other material of the University of North Dakota chapter of the YWCA. See John B. Davenport, comp., *Guide to the Orin G. Libby Manuscript Collection and Related Research Collections* (Grand Forks, ND: University of North Dakota, 1975).

HOPE

13,724. Gumb, Katie (Hughes)
Papers. 1900-45. 2 folders.
Open. Unpublished guide.
Steele County Historical Society.
Papers of [Mrs. Dan] Gumb (1873-1963), a housewife, local historian, and playwright and producer, contain correspondence, her handwritten biographies of area residents and histories of townships in Steele County, records of civic activities in which she participated, and photos. Includes correspondence relating to her work as local chairman of the 1937 George Washington bicentennial celebration. Gumb settled in Broadlawn Township in Steele County in 1880.

13,725. Hope Woman's Club
Records. 1904-45. 2 folders.
Open. Unpublished guide.
Steele County Historical Society.
Correspondence, program booklets, tickets and playbills, and clippings of this study group, founded in 1904, which sponsored lyceum programs, presented plays, and established and maintained the local city library. Program booklets reveal that Club members studied such topics as the impact of coal development in 1918, divorce, and birth control. The Club dissolved in 1945.

RICHARDTON

13,726. Priory Archives
Records. 1910- . 1 cabinet.
Closed. No guide.
Benedictine Sisters, Sacred Heart Priory.
Founded in 1910 in Elbowoods, ND, on an Indian reservation, this religious order of women continues to engage in teaching, nursing, and pastoral work. Financial records; papers of superiors' corporate affairs; correspondence, including letters to families and exchanges with bishops; retreat notes; journals and chronicles; photos; and artifacts.

OHIO

AKRON

13,727. Convent Archives
Records. 1923- . Ca. 5 drawers.
Partially restricted. Unpublished guide.
Sisters of St. Dominic, Our Lady of the Elms Convent.
The Dominican Sisters of Caldwell, NJ, first came to Akron in 1893. The first school facilities were established at Our Lady of the Elms Convent in 1923 and a separate congregation was formed in Akron in 1929. Chapter proceedings, financial reports, legal documents, correspondence, statistical records, annals of the community, photos, scrapbooks, records of community-owned schools, books, and other records. Mother M. Beda Schmid was the congregation's first mother general.

13,728. Dobbs, Catherine R.
Papers. 1932-73. 3 cu.ft.
Open. Inventory.
University of Akron, American History Research Center.
Dobbs (1909-74) was an Ohio state senator in 1949 and 1950, the mayor of Barberton, OH, from 1955

to 1961, and a local historian. Correspondence, speeches and writings, minutes taken during her tenure as mayor, financial reports, ordinances, resolutions, and other material principally deal with her work as a public official and local historian.

13,729. Gladwin, Mary
Papers. 1898-1939. 1 cu.ft.
Open. Inventory.
University of Akron, American History Research Center.
Gladwin (1861-1939) was a nurse. Correspondence, a diary, memoirs, photos, and clippings primarily relate to her work as an American National Red Cross nurse during the Spanish-American War and the Philippine Insurrection in 1898 and 1899, the Russo-Japanese War in 1904, and the Ohio flood in Dayton in 1913 and to her WWI service in Serbia from 1914 to 1916.

13,730. Hower Family
Papers. 1849-ca. 1940. 25 cu.ft.
Open. Preliminary inventory.
University of Akron, American History Research Center.
Family correspondence, financial records, photos, and scrapbooks principally relate to Blanche (Bruot) Hower (1862-1953) and her activities as a member of the Akron Board of Education from 1929 to 1934 and the Ohio House of Representatives in 1935 and 1936. Also contains papers concerning her personal and household finances and social life.

13,731. League of Women Voters of Akron
Records. 1940-73. 2 cu.ft.
Open. Inventory.
University of Akron, American History Research Center.
Minutes, financial records, correspondence, scrapbooks, reports, and printed material of the Akron LWV, founded in 1940.

13,732. League of Women Voters of Canton, OH
Records. 1920-71. 2 cu.ft.
Open. Inventory.
University of Akron, American History Research Center.
Minutes, financial records, correspondence, reports, and printed material of the Canton LWV, founded in 1920.

13,733. Summit County, OH, Woman Suffrage Association
Records. 1917-18. 1 vol.
Open. Catalog card.
University of Akron, American History Research Center.
Minute book.

13,734. Tuesday Musical Club, Akron
Records. 1893-1973. 2 ft.
Open. Catalog card.
University of Akron, American History Research Center.
Scrapbooks containing programs and clippings regarding cultural activities and events supported by the Club, a women's group founded in 1887.

13,735. Allen, Doris Twitchell
Papers. 1944-66. 3.75 ft.
Access restricted. Unpublished guide.
University of Akron, Archives of the History of American Psychology.
A psychologist who holds a PhD, Allen (1901-) is interested in international psychology, primarily the work of the International Council of Psychologists. Bylaws, minutes, correspondence, committee reports, directories of the International Council of Psychologists, and International Council of Women Psychologists newsletters dating from 1947 to 1965.

13,736. Bowman, Lillie Lewin
Papers. 1915-66. 1.25 ft.
Access restricted. Unpublished guide.
University of Akron, Archives of the History of American Psychology.
Bowman (1899-1968?) was a psychologist who worked in educational research, particularly in the identification of gifted children. Professional papers, course outlines, conference programs, photos, grade transcripts, class lists, teaching certificates, reprints, and clippings. She had a PhD.

13,737. Bregman, Elsie Oschrin
Papers. 1918-69. 4 ft.
Open. Unpublished guide.
University of Akron, Archives of the History of American Psychology.
Bregman (1896-1969) was a psychologist who worked in development of industrial psychology and employee selection. Correspondence, clinical records, New York public schools education and vocational test surveys, selection and placement tests, published tests, and reprints. Includes tests used at the R. H. Macy Co. from 1919 to 1921, which illustrate Bregman's work. She held a PhD degree.

13,738. Curti, Margaret
Papers. 1921-64. 5 in.
Open. Unpublished guide.
University of Akron, Archives of the History of American Psychology.
Correspondence, note cards concerning laboratory experiments of Pavlov and others, and reprints of Curti (1891-1961), a psychologist who earned a doctorate, reflect her work with preschool play groups in 1935 and her work with racial difference and intelligence tests, particularly with racial difference studies performed in Jamaica. Also includes her notes on early laboratory experiments concerning conditioned reflexes.

13,739. Fein, Leah Gold
Papers. 1959-75. 1.25 ft.
Access restricted. Unpublished guide.
University of Akron, Archives of the History of American Psychology.
Correspondence, annual reports, minutes, treasurers' reports, and programs of Fein (1910-), a psychologist, reflect her work in the International Council of Psychologists. Fein earned a PhD degree.

13,740. Flinn, Helen
Papers. 1930-59. 5 in.
Access restricted. Unpublished guide.
University of Akron, Archives of the History of American Psychology.
Clinic report sheets, probation reports, registration forms, and test blanks reflect the work of Flinn (1895-?) as chief clinical psychologist for the recorder's court psychiatric clinic in Detroit from 1925 until 1961. She held a master's degree.

13,741. Friedline, Cora L.
Papers. 1894-1948. 1.25 ft.
Open. Unpublished guide.
University of Akron, Archives of the History of American Psychology.
Friedline (1893-1975) was a psychologist. Correspondence and typewritten exams as well as notes of interviews in 1917 with E. B. Titchener and others concerning early laboratory experiments. The notes document Friedline's graduate study at Cornell; she earned a PhD.

13,742. Hollingsworth, Leta Anna (Stetter)
Papers. 1913-39. 4 ft.
Access restricted. Unpublished guide.
University of Akron, Archives of the History of American Psychology.
Transcripts of staff meetings, early publications, student records, photos, reprints, and memorabilia of [Mrs. Harry Levi] Hollingsworth (1886-1939), a psychologist who earned a PhD at Columbia University, pertain principally to a class for gifted children held from 1937 to 1939 at Speyer School, P.S. 500, in New York City.

13,743. Ives, Margaret
Papers. 1934-73. 8 ft.
Access restricted. Unpublished guide.
University of Akron, Archives of the History of American Psychology.
Correspondence, minutes, committee and auditors' reports, membership applications, programs, newsletters, and pamphlets of Ives (1903-), a psychologist with a doctoral degree. Bulk of the material reflects Ives's active role in international affairs, particularly in the activities of the National Council of Women Psychologists, later known as the International Council of Women Psychologists and, most recently, as the International Council of Psychologists. Also contains material on her work in two divisions of the American Psychological Association, the division of consulting psychologists and the division of psychologists in public service.

13,744. Rethlingshafer, Dorothy
Papers. 1926-66. 4 ft.
Open. Unpublished guide.
University of Akron, Archives of the History of American Psychology.
Rethlingshafer (1900-69) was a professional psychologist who held a PhD degree. Personal and professional correspondence, class notes, and material relating to publication of two books, *Motivation as Related to Personality* and *Principles of Comparative Psychology*.

13,745. Ross, Josephine
Papers. 1953-62. 5 in.
Open. Unpublished guide.
University of Akron, Archives of the History of American Psychology.
Ross (1906-72), a psychologist who earned a PhD degree, participated actively in the International Council of Psychologists, which was earlier called the International Council of Women Psychologists. Correspondence, manuscripts, speeches, transcripts of tape recordings of therapy sessions, programs, and reprints chiefly concerning her work in psychoanalysis.

13,746. Stogdill, Emily L.
Papers. 1923-66. 1.25 ft.
Open. Unpublished guide.
University of Akron, Archives of the History of American Psychology.
Lecture and reading notes, early publications, examinations, and reprints document the association of Stogdill (1893-1976), a psychologist, with the Ohio State University psychology department. She began as a graduate student, earned her PhD, joined the faculty there, and on her retirement was named professor emeritus. Includes notes from lectures by Edgar A. Doll, H. A. Toops, and H. H. Goddard.

ATHENS

13,747. American Association of University Women
Records. 1927-69. 3 boxes.
Open. Description.
Ohio University Archives.
Minutes, historian's records, a newsletter, clippings, a scrapbook, programs, calendars, rosters, and other records including the personal files of Edith Wray, a PhD and English professor who was president of the Ohio district of the AAUW.

13,748. Athens Woman's Music Club
Records. 1914-73. 3 boxes.
Open. Inventory.

Ohio University Archives.
Constitutions, minutes, treasurer's records for 1914 to 1938, membership records, achievement record scrapbooks, yearbooks, and clippings.

13,749. Boyd, Margaret
Papers. 1873. 1 vol.
Open. No guide.
Ohio University Archives.
The first woman to graduate from Ohio University, Boyd (1846-?) became principal of a Martinsville, IN, high school and a teacher at Cincinnati Wesleyan College for Young Women. Her diary from her senior year at Ohio University concerns her work and feelings. A native of rural Athens County, Boyd attended Coolville Seminary before her family moved to Athens in 1867. In 1869 she entered Ohio University as a freshman; she graduated in 1873. In 1886 she returned to teach at Athens, but resigned in 1889. A scholarship was established in her honor at Ohio University.

13,750. League of Women Voters
Records. 1949-67. 7 boxes.
Open. Inventory.
Ohio University Archives.
Annual reports, minutes, treasurer's reports, a candidates bulletin, LWV handbooks, economics pamphlets, publications, clippings, and other records of the local LWV chapter. Includes a history of the national LWV and a national LWV board report.

13,751. Pallas Club
Records. 1895-1971. 1.5 ft.
Open. Finding aid.
Ohio University Archives.
The Club was organized in 1895 in Athens to "promote culture by systematic work along literary lines." Constitutions; minute books; receipts and expense records; correspondence; lists of officers, trustees, and members; a poem; certificates of membership; clippings; and other records, including a typescript by Mrs. A. E. Price concerning 50 years of the group's history and a letter by Mary D. Means containing reminiscences about the Club's founding.

13,752. Saint Aloysius Academy
Records. 1864-1969. 5 boxes.
Open. No guide.
Ohio University Archives.
Founded in 1876 in New Lexington, OH, by the Sisters of the Order of Saint Francis, the Academy operated as a Catholic girls school until 1938 when it joined with a military academy to become a coeducational institution. Minutes of local council meetings from 1946 to the present; names, birthplaces, and other information about nuns; a history of Saint Aloysius from 1876 to 1924; deeds and legal papers; handbooks written in German; student publications; and other records, including a survey of the development of St. Aloysius Military Academy, photos, and clippings. The Sisters of the Order of Saint Francis came to the US from Holland in 1871 to avoid persecution.

13,753. Social Literary Club
Records. 1918-73. 1 ft.
Open. Inventory.
Ohio University Archives.
Organized in 1911 in Athens, the Club's programs consisted of presentations by members about literary, cultural, and current events topics. Constitution; minutes; a treasurer's book; a tape recording, a program, and photos of the 60th anniversary tea; a membership certificate in the GFWC; and yearbooks.

13,754. Voigt, Irma E.
Papers. Ca. 1927-49. 4 boxes.
Open. Inventory.
Ohio University Archives.
Voigt (1882-1953), the first dean of women at Ohio University, was president of the National Association of Deans of Women from 1935 to 1937, chairman of the American Council of Guidance and Personnel Associations in 1938 and 1939, and a state and national officer of the AAUW. Correspondence, speeches concerning college women, photos, membership cards, autographs, and clippings. Born in Quincy, IL, Voigt graduated from the State Normal University in Normal, IL, in 1902. She received a BA from the University of Illinois in 1910 and a PhD in German from that institution in 1913. She began her work as dean of women at Ohio University in 1913 and held that position until 1949. She was president of the local AAUW branch, president of the state AAUW, and a member of the national AAUW board. Author of *Life and Works of Mrs. Theresa Robinson,* Voigt was a member of the Sherwood Eddy Seminar and of the Summer School for American Women at Oxford, England.

13,755. Women's Faculty Club
Records. 1925-74. 1 box.
Open. Description.
Ohio University Archives.
Annual reports, minutes, financial records, correspondence, and other records of this social organization for female members of the Ohio University faculty. The group was founded in 1925.

13,756. Women's League
Records. 1916-60. 4 boxes.
Open. Description.
Ohio University Archives.
The League was an intercollegiate association of women. Minutes, a budget, committee records, correspondence, a handbook, clippings, publications, and other records, including minutes and standards of the Intercollegiate Association.

BLUFFTON

13,757. African Inland Mennonite Mission
Records. 1911- . Ca. 25 drawers.
Access restricted. Unpublished guide.
Bluffton College, Mennonite Historical Library.
Financial records, correspondence, reports, photos, and other records of the Mission, which was founded in 1911 to promote mission work in the Congo. A number of the mission workers were women.

13,758. Bluffton College Archives
Records. 1900- . Ca. 100 ft.
Open. No guide.
Bluffton College, Mennonite Historical Library.
Minutes, financial records, correspondence, diaries, oral history tapes, photos, scrapbooks, and other records of the College, which was founded in 1900. Women have served on the faculty since the College's earliest years.

13,759. Central District of the General Conference Mennonite Church
Records. 1888- . Ca. 30 ft.
Open. No guide.
Bluffton College, Mennonite Historical Library.
Minutes, financial records, correspondence, oral history tapes and transcripts, photos, publications and other records describe church activities, including mission and peace work, service projects, and camp work. Women played a significant role in these activities.

BOWLING GREEN

13,760. Faculty Dames
Records. 1930-64. 1 box.
Open. Inventory.
Bowling Green State University Archives.
Secretary's books and membership lists of the Dames, an organization of wives of faculty members and other University women. The group was founded in about 1930.

13,761. Ohio College Association, Women's Physical Education Section
Records. 1924-75. 1 box.
Open. Inventory.
Bowling Green State University Archives.
The Section was formed in 1924 to promote cooperation among the physical education departments of the state's colleges and to study pertinent questions. Constitutions, minutes of business meetings and of the executive board, correspondence, biographies written in 1973, historical data, membership lists, athletic policies, clippings, and other records.

BUCYRUS

13,762. Schimmoler, Lauretta
Papers. 1931-70. No size given.
Open. No guide.
Bucyrus Historical Society.
[Miss] Schimmoler (1900-) helped found and managed the Bucyrus airport from 1929 to 1933, was a member of the WACs during WWII, and worked for the Los Angeles County sheriff's department from 1950 to 1964. Photos, clippings, and other papers trace Schimmoler's career in aviation. Also includes her uniforms. In 1932 she founded the Aerial Nurse Corps of America in Cleveland. In 1942 she was technical director and an actress in *Parachute Nurses,* a Columbia film. Failing eyesight forced her to retire from her sheriff's department position in 1964. She lives in Glendale, CA.

CHARDON

13,763. Archives
Records. 1874- . 16 drawers and 1 vol.
Access restricted. No guide.
Notre Dame Educational Center.
Members of the Sisters of Notre Dame are involved in teaching children from kindergarten through college as well as at a school for slow learners. The order was founded in Germany in 1850 and established in Cleveland in 1874. Annals of activities of each school and convent written by the sisters, photos, and books used in the schools.

CINCINNATI

13,764. Association for the Relief of Jewish Widows and Orphans
Records. 1854-1938. 3.4 ft.
Open. Unpublished guide.
American Jewish Archives.
Records of this charitable organization, which was founded in 1854 in New Orleans to establish and maintain an asylum for poor Jewish widows and orphans, consist of minutes of the board of officers and of annual meetings and lists of officers.

13,765. Bernstein, Jeannette
Papers. 1957. 1 folder.
Open. Unpublished guide.
American Jewish Archives.
Family journal written by [Mrs.] Bernstein includes information on Arkansas, Cheyenne, WY, St. Louis, and immigrants and immigration.

13,766. Bloomfield-Zeisler, Fannie
Papers. 1882-1925. 3.4 ft.
Open. Unpublished guide.

American Jewish Archives.
Correspondence, recital programs, clippings, and articles concern the career of Fannie (Bloomfield)-Zeisler (1863-1927), a concert pianist. Also included is an unfinished biography of her, which was written by her husband Sigmund Zeisler.

13,767. B'nai Abraham Ladies Auxiliary
Records. 1943-50. 0.5 in.
Open. Unpublished guide.
American Jewish Archives.
Ledger of the Terre Haute, IN, Auxiliary.

13,768. B'nai B'rith Women's Lodge: Annie Weinberg Lodge No. 567
Records. 1947-56. 3 in.
Open. Unpublished guide.
American Jewish Archives.
Minutes, correspondence, and other records of this social and charitable organization located in Blytheville, AR.

13,769. B'nai Israel Congregation Sisterhood
Records. 1909-50. 2.5 in.
Open. Unpublished guide.
American Jewish Archives.
Minutes and other records of the Sisterhood, which was founded as the Ladies Auxiliary Association in 1909 in Parkersburg, WV, to provide personal and financial aid to the congregation as well as to foster the ideals of Judaism and worthy causes. In 1925 the group's name was changed.

13,770. B'nai Israel Congregation (Virginia Street Temple) Sisterhood
Records. 1917-41. 2 in.
Open. Unpublished guide.
American Jewish Archives.
Minute book of this social and charitable organization, which was founded in 1917 in Charleston, WV.

13,771. Brandon, Emma
Papers. 1846-48. 1 folder.
Open. Unpublished guide.
American Jewish Archives.
Letters, notes, essays, and memoranda of Brandon, the daughter of a prominent New York merchant, were written from New York.

13,772. Congregation Anshe Emeth Sisterhood
Records. 1924-31. 0.5 in.
Open. Unpublished guide.
American Jewish Archives.
Minutes of a social and charitable organization of Piqua, OH.

13,773. Congregation B'nai Israel Ladies Temple Aid Society
Records. 1893-1912. 2 in.
Open. Unpublished guide.
American Jewish Archives.
Minute books of this charitable organization, which was founded in 1893 in Little Rock, AR.

13,774. Congregation Emanu-El Sisterhood
Records. 1921-59. 3 Hollinger boxes.
Open. Unpublished guide.
American Jewish Archives.
Constitution, bylaws, minutes, financial records, and correspondence of this Welch, WV, organization the purpose of which was to promote religious, educational, and charitable endeavors.

13,775. Congregation Emanuel Sisterhood
Records. 1925-52. 5 in.
Open. Unpublished guide.
American Jewish Archives.
The Grand Rapids, MI, Sisterhood was established to assist in the general welfare of the Temple and of the religious school, to foster the ideals of Judaism, and to promote fellowship among its members in religious, social, and educational activities. Constitution, annual reports, and minutes.

13,776. Congregation Rodeph Shalom Sisterhood
Records. 1906-12. 1 in.
Open. Unpublished guide.
American Jewish Archives.
Minute book of the Sisterhood, which was founded in 1906 in Pittsburgh by 131 congregation women to develop social and charitable interests of its members and to conduct related activities for the community. Committees formed by the Sisterhood include those for sewing, dramatic and choral services, workers' meetings, civic services, a library association, and pulpit aid societies.

13,777. Council of Jewish Women
Records. 1926-31. 0.5 in.
Open. Unpublished guide.
American Jewish Archives.
Minute book of the Selma, AL, branch of the Council.

13,778. Council of Jewish Women
Records. 1905-27. 1.5 in.
Open. Unpublished guide.
American Jewish Archives.
Minute book of the local Marion, OH, branch of the National Council of Jewish Women. The local Council was established in 1896 as a social and charitable organization and in 1924 it merged with the Temple Israel Sisterhood.

13,779. Council of Jewish Women
Records. 1905-12. 0.5 in.
Open. Unpublished guide.
American Jewish Archives.
Minute book of the Toledo, OH, Council, whose chief activities were maintenance of the synagogue, philanthropy, organization of study circles for its members, and publication of surveys and reports, by means of which the Council sought to improve city government and bureaucracy.

13,780. Diamond, Ruby
Papers. 1891-1965. 1 microfilm reel.
Open. Unpublished guide.
American Jewish Archives.
Diamond was a philanthropist. Correspondence, biographical material, and clippings concern the activities of the Diamond family, Jewish pioneers in Florida, and the history of Tallahassee, FL.

13,781. Female Hebrew Benevolent Society
Records. 1868-1907. 2.5 in.
Open. Unpublished guide.
American Jewish Archives.
Minute book of this social and charitable organization, which was founded in 1868 to provide aid to poor, sick, or needy Jewish women in Norfolk, VA.

13,782. First Benevolent Association of Hebrew Ladies
Records. 1893-1913. 0.5 in.
Open. Unpublished guide.
American Jewish Archives.
Minute book of a charitable organization located in Quincy, IL.

13,783. Friedberg, Lillian A.
Papers. 1913-70. 9 Hollinger boxes.
Open. Unpublished guide.
American Jewish Archives.
From 1921 to 1965 Friedberg was the executive director of the Jewish Community Relations Council of Pittsburgh. Correspondence, diary, lecture notes, awards from her term in office, and minutes of the Council.

13,784. Friedman, Sophie G.
Papers. 1897-1953. 1 Hollinger box.
Open. Unpublished guide.
American Jewish Archives.
Correspondence and clippings of Friedman (1880-1957), a Memphis lawyer.

13,785. Gerstley, Jennie R.
Papers. 1859-1934. 1 folder.
Open. Unpublished guide.
American Jewish Archives.
Reminiscences of [Mrs. Henry M.] Gerstley, the founder of the Chicago Woman's Aid, and notes by Sarah Nunes Falter describing her trip across the Atlantic Ocean in the 1850s.

13,786. Gold, Rose Bogen
Papers. 1905-41. 1 folder.
Open. Unpublished guide.
American Jewish Archives.
Autobiography of Gold (1881-1947), a nurse, and her naturalization papers, marriage license, and nursing certificates.

13,787. Goldstein, Fanny
Papers. 1933-61. 10 Hollinger boxes.
Open. Unpublished guide.
American Jewish Archives.
Correspondence, reports, book reviews, and pamphlets of [Miss] Goldstein (1895-1961), a librarian, relate to her work at the West End branch of the Boston Public Library. Includes material on her published reading list "Judaica" and on Nazi book burnings.

13,788. Grossman, Jeanette
Papers. 1816-1956. 1 folder.
Open. Unpublished guide.
American Jewish Archives.
Family history, clippings, and printed items from Cambridge, OH.

13,789. Hebrew Ladies Aid Society
Records. 1915-27. 0.5 in.
Open. Unpublished guide.
American Jewish Archives.
Minute books and financial records of this Welch, WV, charitable organization which was founded in 1915.

13,790. Hebrew Ladies Aid Society
Records. 1889-1923. 1 ft.
Open. Unpublished guide.
American Jewish Archives.
Minute books and financial records of the Trinidad, CO, Society, which was established to maintain Temple Aaron and to perform philanthropic services.

13,791. Hebrew Ladies Aid Society
Records. 1896-1910. 0.5 in.
Open. Unpublished guide.
American Jewish Archives.
Minute book of the Society, which was founded in 1896 in Piqua, OH, to advance the goals of the Piqua Hebrew Association and to act jointly with Association members; to visit the sick, cheer the distressed, and assist the needy; and to ensure proper religious training for children.

13,792. Hebrew Ladies Benevolent Society
Records. 1878-1957. 5 in.
Open. Unpublished guide.
American Jewish Archives.
Records of this social and charitable organization, which was founded in 1878 in Albany, GA, consist of minute books and a 1942 Golden Jubilee and Memorial Fund booklet.

13,793. Hostess League
Records. 1917-20. 0.5 in.
Open. Unpublished guide.
American Jewish Archives.
Minute book of the League, which was founded in 1917 in Tacoma, WA, to promote the welfare of Jewish soldiers serving in WWI.

13,794. Isaacs, Hannah
Papers. 1812-1945. 1 microfilm reel.
Open. Unpublished guide.
American Jewish Archives.
Scrapbook from Cincinnati.

13,795. Jewish Family and Children's Service
Records. 1924-51. 34.2 ft.
Access restricted. Unpublished guide.
American Jewish Archives.
The Service was established in Denver for family and child welfare work, child placement and adoption, and refugee service and relief. Financial, employee, and membership records; correspondence; and extensive case files, about one-half of which pertain to women in connection with welfare assistance, employment, and immigration. Supporting biographical data and reports of interviews with case file subjects are also included.

13,796. Jewish Ladies Aid Society
Records. 1914-25. 0.5 in.
Open. Unpublished guide.
American Jewish Archives.
Minute book of the Kokomo, IN, Society.

13,797. Jewish Ladies Aid Society
Records. 1874-1927. 1.5 in.
Open. Unpublished guide.
American Jewish Archives.
Minute book of this Columbus, GA, charitable organization.

13,798. Jewish Maternity Association
Records. 1873-1913. 1 in.
Open. Unpublished guide.
American Jewish Archives.
Established in 1873 as the Society Esrath Nashim by Esther Amram, who also served as its first president, this Philadelphia group assisted poor Jewish mothers who suffered privation during their confinement. Minute books from 1873 to 1894 and a 1913 annual report.

13,799. Kallen, Horace M.
Papers. 1902-1975. 90 Hollinger boxes.
Open. Unpublished guide.
American Jewish Archives.
Correspondence of Kallen (1882-1974), an educator and philosopher, contains letters with Rachael Brooks, a Christian missionary in China, and her photos depicting life in China; manuscripts; speeches; reports; clippings; and other papers. Also included is correspondence of Kallen's sister Deborah Kallen about family matters and her work as a teacher in Palestine.

13,800. Koch, Mrs. Morris
Papers. 1940-65. 50 pp.
Open. Unpublished guide.
American Jewish Archives.
Scrapbook compiled by Koch concerns her activities and those of her family in Louisville.

13,801. Kuhn, Setty S.
Papers. 1903-48. 8 Hollinger boxes and 1 vol.
Open. Unpublished guide.
American Jewish Archives.
Kuhn was a philanthropist who lived in Cincinnati. Correspondence includes letters with her husband Simon Kuhn and other family members, Jane Addams, Albert Einstein, Harold Laski, Judah L. Magnes, and Rudolf Serkin; also included are diaries, testimonials, and photos. Material relates to political, educational, sociological, literary, and musical matters; Zionism; Palestine; revolutions in India; and the Foreign Policy Association.

13,802. Ladies Aid Society (Temple Sisterhood of Tree of Life Synagogue)
Records. 1901-30. 17 items.
Open. Unpublished guide.
American Jewish Archives.
Constitution, history, and membership applications for this charitable organization located in Columbia, SC, whose purpose was to assist the Sunday school, help maintain the Synagogue, and plan benevolent projects.

13,803. Ladies Auxiliary Society
Records. 1904-17. 0.5 in.
Open. Unpublished guide.
American Jewish Archives.
Minute book of the Vicksburg, MS, Society, which was organized in 1904 at the suggestion of Rabbi Kory to promote the interests of Judaism, generally, and the congregation, specifically. The Society sponsored fund-raising events, gave parties for children, and donated books to the Sunday school.

13,804. Ladies Benevolent Society
Records. 1907-13. 0.5 in.
Open. Unpublished guide.
American Jewish Archives.
Bylaws and minutes of the Society, which was founded in 1907 in Alpena, MI, to extend moral and financial aid to all needy and deserving persons.

13,805. Ladies Hebrew Association
Records. 1871-1923. 4.5 in.
Open. Unpublished guide.
American Jewish Archives.
Minute books and ledgers of the Association, founded in 1871 in Baton Rouge, LA, to help build a synagogue.

13,806. Ladies Hebrew Benevolent Association
Records. 1909-45. 0.5 in.
Open. Unpublished guide.
American Jewish Archives.
Minute book of the Association of Selma, AL.

13,807. Ladies Hebrew Benevolent Society
Records. 1861-1919. 3.5 in.
Open. Unpublished guide.
American Jewish Archives.
Minute books, cashbooks, and a ledger, all of which are written in German, of the Society which was founded in 1861 in Fort Wayne, IN.

13,808. Ladies Hebrew Benevolent Society
Records. 1873-1913. 2 in.
Open. Unpublished guide.
American Jewish Archives.
Established in 1873, this Grand Rapids, MI, charitable organization assisted the needy and "worthy poor" of all denominations. Constitution, bylaws, and minutes.

13,809. Lazard, Desirie Marks, and Harris, Harry
Papers. 1897-1959. 1 microfilm reel.
Open. Unpublished guide.
American Jewish Archives.
Scrapbooks contain clippings reflecting the careers of Lazard, a Broadway actress, and her husband Harris, a boxer.

13,810. Manner, Jane
Papers. 1887-1954. 2 Hollinger boxes.
Open. Unpublished guide.
American Jewish Archives.
Formerly known as Jennie Mannheimer, [Miss] Manner was a drama interpreter who served as speech instructor at Hebrew Union College before she founded the Cincinnati School of Expression. Correspondence; 1939 diaries; photos, including one in which Manner is teaching Vilma Banky, and a picture of a window ventilator invented and patented by Louise Mannheimer; programs and advertisements she collected; scrapbooks; clippings; a booklet and address memorializing her by her brother Rabbi Eugene Mannheimer of Des Moines; and other material.

13,811. Meyer, Annie (Nathan)
Papers. 1858-1950. 10.4 ft.
Open. Unpublished guide.
American Jewish Archives.
A New York City social activist and writer, Meyer (1867-1951) helped found Barnard College, the first women's college in the city; she also was active in the antisuffrage movement and the WWI home economics movement. Correspondence, including letters with Benjamin N. Cardozo, Robert Nathan, Eleanor Roosevelt, Herbert Hoover, and John Haynes Holmes; manuscripts; photos; clippings; and other material. Meyer was author of "Vorbei" (1893), *Robert Annys, Poor Priest* (1901), and *Advertising of Kate* (1911).

13,812. Mount Sinai Hospital Ladies Auxiliary
Records. 1912-17. 1 in.
Open. Unpublished guide.
American Jewish Archives.
Minute book of the Auxiliary, which was founded in 1912 in Boston to help with Hospital fund-raising and other Jewish charitable activities in the community.

13,813. National Council of Jewish Women, Minneapolis Section
Records. Ca. 1958. 0.5 in.
Open. Unpublished guide.
American Jewish Archives.
Established in 1894 to provide preventive and constructive philanthropy in addition to charity for "immediate relief," this organization began by conducting a girls religious school and a girls sewing circle, but later expanded its activities to include study circles in 1899, fund raising, and social work. Interested in being politically aware, the Council also conducted surveys and published bulletins and yearbooks. A history of the Council contains biographies of its presidents and descriptions of changes in Council objectives.

13,814. Netter, Amy
Papers. 1890-1906. 53 pp.
Open. Unpublished guide.
American Jewish Archives.
Scrapbook of personal papers and other items from Cincinnati.

13,815. Ohev Sholom Sisterhood
Records. 1870-1925. 1 Hollinger box.
Open. Unpublished guide.
American Jewish Archives.
Originally called the Ladies Hebrew Social Circle, this benevolent organization of Harrisburg, PA, adopted its present name in 1913. Minutes of the board of directors; minutes of Sisterhood meetings, some of which were recorded in German; and membership records. The Sisterhood helped maintain the Temple Ohev Sholom and organized Temple projects and celebrations.

13,816. Pioneer Women, Women's Labor Zionist Organization, Cincinnati Chapter No. 3
Records. 1957-66. 3 in.
Open. Unpublished guide.
American Jewish Archives.
Minutes, membership lists, correspondence, and clippings of this local chapter of the Pioneer Women's Labor Zionist Organization, a national body founded in the US in 1905 to assist the working women of Palestine by providing vocational training and educational opportunities for youth in Israel. Chapter No. 3 was part of the larger Cincinnati Pioneer Women's chapter established by Esther Ida Schmidt, which by 1957 split into three separate units with a combined membership of ca. 300 women. The Chapter conducted monthly social and business meetings, often with current events lectures, but its primary purpose was the organization of local fund-raising events which netted $3,000 annually for the national office.

13,817. Purvin, Jennie (Franklin)
Papers. 1868-1958. 7 ft.
Open. Unpublished guide.
American Jewish Archives.
Purvin (1873-1958) was a business executive of Mandel Brothers Department Store in Chicago. Correspondence, including family letters; writings; and other personal material.

13,818. Robi, Josephine H.
Papers. 1859-1965. 1 in.
Open. Unpublished guide.
American Jewish Archives.
Diary of Robi, which gives her impressions during a trip from St. Louis to Salt Lake City in 1881; family letters; and other items about family activities.

13,819. Rohrheimer, Rena M.
Papers. 1936-50. 1 Hollinger box.
Open. Unpublished guide.
American Jewish Archives.
Correspondence of Rohrheimer includes exchanges with relatives, friends, and refugee organizations from Germany and Nazi-occupied countries. Also included are descriptions of her travels in America, Egypt, England, France, Germany, Israel, Switzerland, and Turkey.

13,820. Rosenbaum, Jeanette W.
Papers. 1951-53. 15 in.
Open. Unpublished guide.
American Jewish Archives.
Papers of Rosenbaum contain correspondence, writings, articles, items on the life and career of Myer Myers and on Rosenbaum's publication *Myer Myers—Goldsmith,* programs of art exhibitions, and magazines.

13,821. Ruleville Drew Sisterhood
Records. 1921-51. 2.5 in.
Open. Unpublished guide.
American Jewish Archives.
Minute book of the Sisterhood, a charitable organization in Ruleville, MS.

13,822. Sisterhood of Congregation B'nai Israel
Records. 1925-33. 1.5 in.
Open. Unpublished guide.
American Jewish Archives.
Established as the Jewish Ladies Aid Society of East Liverpool and Wellsville, OH, this organization adopted its present name in 1925. Constitution, minutes, reports, and correspondence. By collecting dues and sponsoring fund-raising events, the Sisterhood helped the unemployed find work, offered financial assistance to those in need of relief, and "instilled hope and cheer into the hearts of the worthy unfortunate."

13,823. Stern, Frances
Papers. 1921-67. 15 items.
Open. Unpublished guide.
American Jewish Archives.
Correspondence, reports, and articles of [Miss] Stern (1873-1947), a nutritionist, relate to her professional activities and work with the Frances Stern Food Clinic.

13,824. Temple Beth Israel Sisterhood
Records. 1890-1948. 4 in.
Open. Unpublished guide.
American Jewish Archives.
Founded as the Judith Montefiore Society in 1890 in Tacoma, WA, the Sisterhood adopted its present name in 1920; its goals were advancement of Judaism, maintenance of the Sabbath school, and cooperation with the rabbi and the congregation to encourage cultural and social growth. Minute books and other records.

13,825. Temple Emanuel Ladies Aid Society
Records. 1910-21. 1 folder.
Open. Unpublished guide.
American Jewish Archives.
Correspondence of this Duluth, MN, social and charitable organization pertains to such Society activities as aid to orphans, immigrants, the poor, the sick, and the homeless.

13,826. Temple Emanuel Sisterhood
Records. 1912-63. 1 folder.
Open. Unpublished guide.
American Jewish Archives.
Letters to the Duluth, MN, Sisterhood from such organizations as the National Federation of Temple Sisterhoods.

13,827. Temple Etz Ahayem Sisterhood
Records. 1958-66. 1 in.
Open. Unpublished guide.
American Jewish Archives.
Minutes of this social and charitable organization, which was founded in 1919 in Montgomery, AL, to perform practical social work for the community, encourage and support the Temple Hebrew school, and promote good citizenship.

13,828. Temple Israel Sisterhood
Records. 1931-40. 1.5 in.
Open. Unpublished guide.
American Jewish Archives.
Minute books of the Sisterhood, located in Gary, IN.

13,829. Temple Israel Sisterhood
Records. 1891-93. 1 in.
Open. Unpublished guide.
American Jewish Archives.
Minute book of this organization, which was founded in New York City in 1891 to help the Jewish poor in Harlem and to foster sociability among congregation members.

13,830. Temple Israel Women's Auxiliary
Records. 1911-29. 2 in.
Open. Unpublished guide.
American Jewish Archives.
Minute books and financial and membership records of the Auxiliary, which was founded in 1911 in Gary, IN, to raise funds for the Temple and social activities.

13,831. Temple Rodef Sholom Sisterhood
Records. 1922-31. 2 in.
Open. Unpublished guide.
American Jewish Archives.
Minutes of this Waco, TX, charitable organization which helped maintain the Temple and its Sunday school.

13,832. Tucker, Sophie
Papers. 1911-66. 6 ft.
Open. Unpublished guide.
American Jewish Archives.
Tucker (1887-1966) was a singer. Correspondence, speeches, photos, plaques, and other material relate to her 1947 jubilee dinner and her activities in the American Federation of Actors.

13,833. Ullman, Amelia
Papers. 1896. 166 pp.
Open. Unpublished guide.
American Jewish Archives.
Memoir of [Mrs. Joseph] Ullman is entitled *Saint Paul Forty Years Ago, A Personal Reminiscence.*

13,834. Weiss-Rosmarin, Trude
Papers. 1962-75. 2 ft.
Open. Unpublished guide.
American Jewish Archives.
Correspondence and manuscripts of Weiss-Rosmarin (1908-), a Jewish scholar, author, and editor of *The Jewish Spectator.*

13,835. Young Ladies Cooperative Society
Records. 1901-25. 0.5 in.
Open. Unpublished guide.
American Jewish Archives.
Minute books and membership records of this religious and charitable organization, founded in 1901 in Albany, GA, by Mrs. David Brown.

13,836. Cincinnati Artists
Collection. Late 1800s-1900s. 173 folders.
Open. No guide.
Cincinnati Art Museum Library.
Photos of artists' work, exhibition announcements, and clippings relate to artists who lived or worked in Cincinnati. Includes a few scrapbooks about individual artists. Women represented in the collection include Louise Abel, Isabel Bishop, Julie Morrow De Forest, Caroline Lord, Mary Louise McLaughlin, Emma Mendenhall, Elizabeth Nourse, Dixie Selden, and Lilly (Martin) Spencer.

13,837. Rookwood Pottery
Records. Mostly 1900s. Ca. 150 items.
Open. No guide.
Cincinnati Art Museum Library.
Rookwood, a pottery manufacturing company, was founded in 1880 in Cincinnati by [Mrs.] Maria (Longworth) Nichols. The name also was associated with a style of pottery developed in the late 1800s. Photos, catalogs, brochures, articles, and clippings about the company and the pottery. An outgrowth of the women's ceramic arts movement that followed the 1876 Philadelphia Exposition, Rookwood pottery was characterized by floral decorations placed asymmetrically on a subtle earth-colored background. The style influenced other American art potteries. Rookwood had ceased to be a distinctive style by 1916.

13,838. Rookwood Pottery Drawings
Records. 1903-30s. Ca. 200 items.
Open. No guide.
Cincinnati Art Museum Library.
Architectural renderings of tiles, fireplaces, bathrooms, fountains, mantels, and facade ornaments manufactured by Rookwood Pottery, a pottery manufacturing firm founded in 1880 in Cincinnati by [Mrs.] Maria (Longworth) Nichols. The firm instituted an architectural department in the early 1900s, but the department's products remained secondary to the firm's art pottery line.

13,839. Allen, Alfred M., Family
Papers. 1839-1928. 2 boxes.
Open. Inventory.
Cincinnati Historical Society.
Consists primarily of correspondence of Alfred Allen (1860-1927), a lawyer, and Hannah (Smith) Allen (1861-1941) before their marriage in 1885; the letters provide information on the customs of well-to-do families in the last decades of the 19th century. Hannah Smith, the daughter of Erastus M. and Mary (McAlpin) Smith, was a well-educated woman who began teaching Latin and algebra at Hughes High School at the age of 20. The Allens had four children. Hannah Allen participated in civic activities and in women's club work on the local and state levels.

13,840. Bateman, Ella Louise (Trowbridge)
Papers. 1869-1907. 3 folders.
Open. Description.
Cincinnati Historical Society.
Ella Trowbridge (ca. 1848-1906), a pianist who studied for two years in Germany, was the second wife of Warner M. Bateman, a politician and lawyer. Correspondence, canceled checks, a post card, clippings, and other items. Includes correspondence between Ella Bateman and her sister Mary, who was the wife of Wilber F. Nutten of Newark, NY, and the Bateman children concerning clothes, current prices, travel, and approved baby care. Ella Trowbridge studied from 1874 to 1876 at the Conservatorium in Stuttgart, Germany. She married Bateman, then 49, shortly

after her return from Germany; the couple lived in Glendale, OH.

13,841. Cincinnati Crafters Co.
Records. 1931-55. 6 in.
Open. Unpublished guide.
Cincinnati Historical Society.
Organized and operated by women, the Crafters was founded in 1911 to sell nonessential items consigned by artist-craftsmen, many of them women, and to present at least five educational programs each year. Correspondence, reports, a history of the firm, pamphlets, and clippings. The group's organizers included many prominent Cincinnati citizens.

13,842. Cincinnati League of Women Voters
Records. 1920-66. 5 ft.
Open. Inventory.
Cincinnati Historical Society.
Minutes, account books, speeches, correspondence, reports, policy statements, membership directories, pamphlets, and other records of the Woman's Suffrage Committee, a forerunner of the LWV dedicated to gaining the vote for women, and of the local LWV, which was founded in 1920. Includes minutes and membership lists of the Suffrage Committee but primarily reflects political issues that concerned the LWV.

13,843. Colvin, Winifred Marie
Papers. 1919-55. Ca. 150 items.
Open. Unpublished guide.
Cincinnati Historical Society.
An English and Latin teacher in the College Hill, OH, schools, [Miss] Colvin (?-1965), president of a local YWCA chapter in 1908 and 1909, went to France in 1919 as a YWCA worker. Principally correspondence to Colvin's friends; diaries, published and unpublished articles, poetry, and prose are included also. Material deals primarily with Colvin's time abroad, her work with the YWCA, and her writings about postwar Europe. Colvin remained abroad after finishing her YWCA work, writing prose, poetry, and articles about her travel. She returned to the US and taught school in Cincinnati and Buffalo.

13,844. Elliston, George
Papers. 1901-42. 4 quarto boxes and 1 folio box.
Open. Description.
Cincinnati Historical Society.
[Miss] George Elliston (1883-1946) was a Cincinnati newspaper woman, poet, magazine editor, and clubwoman. Correspondence, photos, scrapbooks, music, and cartoons. Associated with the Cincinnati *Times-Star* for 40 years, Elliston was a reporter, syndicated feature writer, and from 1909 to 1929 the society editor. Her poetry was published in several volumes, in her feature called "Every Day Poem," and as music lyrics and greeting card verses. She was editor of *The Gypsy,* a poetry magazine, from 1925 to 1937.

13,845. Garden Club of Cincinnati
Records. 1914-71. 3 ft.
Open. No guide.
Cincinnati Historical Society.
Organized in ca. 1913, the Club, an affiliate of the Garden Club of America, promotes horticultural interests in Cincinnati and maintains gardens at several museums, including the Cincinnati Art Museum and the Taft Museum. Minutes, correspondence, reports, photos, pamphlets, and other records of the group, which was founded and run by women. The Club's membership consists mainly of the wives of prominent men in Cincinnati.

13,846. Gholson, William Yates
Papers. 1807-70. 5 ft.
Open. Unpublished guide.
Cincinnati Historical Society.
Correspondence, bills, checks, receipts, and miscellaneous legal documents of Gholson (1807-70), a lawyer who served as judge of the Superior Court of Cincinnati and from 1859 to 1863 as justice of the Ohio Supreme Court. Includes personal papers willed to Gholson by [Miss] Frances Wright, a Scottish reformer, freethinker, author, and friend of Marquis de Lafayette. Wright's papers deal chiefly with her business affairs, especially with her estate at Nashoba, but also include letters about her daughter, her divorce, and her personal affairs. Also contains a printed document from Wright's husband Guillaume Sylvan Casimir Phiquepal D'Arusmont, which provides a history of their unsuccessful marriage.

13,847. Girls' Week Advisory Council
Records. 1930-72. 2 ft.
Open. No guide.
Cincinnati Historical Society.
The Council organized the annual Girls' Week program to emphasize girls' activities; to show how local people could "make the lives of girls bigger, finer, and more useful; and to demonstrate to the girls how . . . to lead these finer, more interesting and useful lives." Scrapbooks, which include minutes, correspondence, programs, clippings, and other material, reflect attitudes toward women's roles in society and the ways in which these roles were presented to teen-aged girls.

13,848. Greene and Roelker
Papers. 1818-81. 3 ft.
Open. Unpublished guide.
Cincinnati Historical Society.
Correspondence, diaries, account books, sketchbooks, and other papers of William Greene (1797-1883), a Cincinnati lawyer; Greene's wife Abby Lyman Greene; and their daughter Catherine Ray Greene, who married Frederick Roelker. Their papers reflect social customs and religious beliefs in Ohio during the early 1880s.

13,849. Harrison
Papers. 1792-1893. 1 ft.
Open. Unpublished guide.
Cincinnati Historical Society.
Correspondence of Learner B. Harrison (1815-1902), a Cincinnati merchant and banking figure during the last half of the 19th century, contains correspondence of his wife Fanny Goodman Harrison with her daughter Margaret Harrison concerning social and cultural events around Cincinnati from 1891 to 1893.

13,850. Junior Woman's City Club
Records. 1946-59. 6 in.
Open. No guide.
Cincinnati Historical Society.
Board meeting minutes, financial records, correspondence, clippings, and other records of this civic and social club, which sought to provide a forum for discussion of ideas of civic importance.

13,851. Kellogg, Elizabeth R.
Papers. 1940-60. 2 ft.
Open. No guide.
Cincinnati Historical Society.
An author and artist, Kellogg (1870-1961) was a librarian at the Cincinnati Art Museum for 20 years and one of the founders of the Cincinnati Crafters. Correspondence, sketches, paintings, pamphlets, clippings, and other papers contain material about her contributions to local arts and crafts.

13,852. McLaughlin, Mary Louise
Papers. 1906-33. 6 in.
Open. No guide.
Cincinnati Historical Society.
Diaries of [Miss] McLaughlin (1848-1939), a pioneer in ceramic art who also was interested in wood carving, jewelry making, etching, plastic sculpture, and tapestry work. McLaughlin's works were exhibited in the US, France, Italy, and Germany. She wrote seven books, made her own clothes, and upholstered household furniture.

13,853. Newton, Clara Chipman
Papers. 1803-1937. 1 ft.
Open. Unpublished guide.
Cincinnati Historical Society.
[Miss] Newton (1848-1937), a local artist, was associated with Rookwood Pottery Co. of Cincinnati; she also taught art classes at the Thane Miller School and was a cofounder of the Cincinnati Pottery Club. Correspondence, diaries, financial records, articles, clippings, and other items contain material about pottery, especially Rookwood Pottery, and women's groups to which Newton belonged, including the Woman's Art Club, the Porcelain League, the Crafters Company, and the DAR. She was a charter member and director of the Cincinnati Women's Club.

13,854. Nourse, Elizabeth
Papers. 1880-1939. 1.5 ft.
Open. Unpublished guide.
Cincinnati Historical Society.
A Cincinnati-born painter, Nourse (ca. 1860-1938) lived in Paris, where she was elected to the Associée des Beaux Arts in 1895; she also received the Laetare Medal in 1922. Correspondence, a sketchbook, photos, articles, reproductions of paintings, and other material primarily concerning Nourse's painting but also dealing with her charitable works for other artists and war orphans during WWI.

13,855. Pitman Family
Papers. 1850-1954. 2 ft.
Open. Unpublished guide.
Cincinnati Historical Society.
Family papers of Benjamin Pitman (1822-1910), who came to Cincinnati as a shorthand reporter and became a professor at the Cincinnati Art Academy, and his daughter Melrose Pitman (1889-), a poet and member of the Anthroposophical Society of America. Correspondence, spiritual and religious notes, sketchbooks, biographical and genealogical material, pamphlets, clippings, wood carvings, home decorations, and other material. Includes many of Melrose Pitman's poems, some of which were choreographed and set to music, as well as information about her religious views. Benjamin Pitman founded the Phonographic Institute and in 1906 was elected president of the National Shorthand Reporters' Association.

13,856. Rookwood Pottery Co.
Records. 1880-1969. 5 ft.
Open. Unpublished guide.
Cincinnati Historical Society.
Rookwood Pottery Co. was founded in 1880 by [Mrs.] Maria Longworth Nichols to foster ceramic art free of foreign influence and original in concept. Many members of the Cincinnati Women's Pottery Club joined in the work of the Company. Correspondence, notebooks, photos, catalogs, price lists, shape cards, pamphlets, articles, clippings, and other items.

13,857. Taft, Anna Sinton
Papers. 1892-1930. 11 ft.
Open. No guide.
Cincinnati Historical Society.
[Mrs. Charles P.] Taft (?-1931) was an active philanthropist who supported local cultural organizations, particularly the Cincinnati Art Museum, the Cincinnati Symphony Orchestra, and the University of Cincinnati. Cashbooks, day journals, house accounts, property records, and other financial records.

13,858. University of Cincinnati Dames
Records. 1921-74. 1 ft.
Open. Unpublished guide.

Cincinnati Historical Society.
Organized in 1929, this social organization for the wives of University of Cincinnati students was the local chapter of the National Organization of University Dames. Constitutions, bylaws, minutes, correspondence, records of elections and scholarship winners, pamphlets, clippings, and other material.

13,859. Walker, Susan
Papers. 1853-76. 6 in.
Open. No guide.
Cincinnati Historical Society.
A philanthropist, politician, mathematician, and abolitionist, Walker (1811-87) was a leader in the care of soldiers during the Civil War and in the education of freedmen. Correspondence, journals, reports, song lyrics, clippings, and other papers primarily concerning her wartime activities and her later work with the freedmen in South Carolina and with the Bureau of Refugees, Freedmen and Abandoned Lands.

13,860. Wherry, Marie (Nast)
Papers. 1857-1966. 2 ft.
Open. Inventory.
Cincinnati Historical Society.
Wherry (1880-1971) graduated from Women's College in Baltimore (later Goucher College) and received a medical degree from Johns Hopkins University in 1906. In addition to her Cincinnati medical practice, Wherry became a well-known painter; she also was active in local groups, including the American National Red Cross, the Babies Milk Fund, the Professional Art Club, and the Woman's Art Club. Correspondence, diaries, financial records, genealogical material, scrapbooks, clippings, and diplomas.

13,861. Woman's Christian Temperance Union
Records. 1886-1901. 6 in.
Open. No guide.
Cincinnati Historical Society.
Minutes, financial records, correspondence, petitions, resolutions, statements, clippings, and other printed material of the Hartwell, OH, chapter founded in 1886, which sought "to educate public sentiment up to the standard of total abstinence, train the young, save the inebriate, and secure the legal prohibition and complete banishment of the liquor traffic."

13,862. Woman's Christian Temperance Union of Madisonville
Records. 1929-48. 2 vols.
Open. No guide.
Cincinnati Historical Society.
Minutes of monthly meetings and financial records.

13,863. Woman's Columbian Exposition of Cincinnati
Records. 1892-93. 1 ft.
Open. No guide.
Cincinnati Historical Society.
This group, organized in 1892 primarily by women, developed displays documenting women's work for the Columbian Exposition. Minutes, treasurer's reports, membership lists, clippings, and other records reflect activities considered women's work in the 1890s.

13,864. Woman's Liberation Movement
Collection. 1969-70. 15 items.
Open. No guide.
Cincinnati Historical Society.
Correspondence, articles on women's rights, news releases, and pamphlets of two groups, the National Organization for Women and the Federally Employed Women. Also includes a recording of a speech given at a Cincinnati women's rally. The material, collected by Edith Parkey, documents the women's liberation movement and some of the problems discussed by its supporters.

13,865. Women's Union Missionary Society, Cincinnati Branch
Records. 1881-91. 1 vol.
Open. No guide.
Cincinnati Historical Society.
Minutes of monthly meetings of the Society, which raised money to support missionaries in Asia.

13,866. Archives
Records. 1842- . 4 drawers and ca. 20 vols.
Access restricted. No guide.
Good Shepherd Provincial Convent.
The order of the Sisters of the Good Shepherd was founded in France in 1641; the order's first convent in the US was founded in 1842 in Louisville. Members of the Good Shepherd Provincial Convent are involved chiefly in the rehabilitation of girls and women. Includes annals of the establishment of the order in Louisville, Cincinnati, Indianapolis, and Toledo, OH; bulletins; and artifacts.

13,867. Archives of Cincinnati Ursulines
Records. 1908- . 6 boxes, 4 cabinets, and several vols.
Access restricted. No guide.
St. Ursula Convent and Academy.
Minutes, financial and legal records, correspondence, diaries, notes on spiritual conferences, educational records, unpublished literary and historical poems, manuscripts by sisters, and photos of the Convent, which was founded in 1910 in Cincinnati. Includes records of the executive councils; notes on the foundress, cofoundress, and members of the community; and information on the history of the Convent and Academy. The chief activity of members of this order is education.

13,868. Province Archives
Records. 1804- . Ca. 600 cu.ft.
Open. Published guide.
Sisters of Notre Dame de Namur, Ohio Province Archives.
Records of the Ohio Province, officially founded in 1840, document the work of the Sisters in the Christian education of youth. Includes annals, financial records, correspondence of mothers general and provincial superiors, community council minutes, scholastic records, cemetery records for deceased sisters, registers of personnel and other statistics, programs, clippings, thousands of photos, an extensive slide collection, and other records. See *Ohio Province Archives, Sisters of Notre Dame de Namur* (Cincinnati, OH: Provincial House of the Sisters of Notre Dame de Namur, 1978).

13,869. Allen, Doris Twitchell
Papers. Nd. Ca. 130 ft.
Closed. No guide.
University of Cincinnati Library, Special Collections.
Allen (1901-) is a psychologist and a professor emeritus of the University of Cincinnati. Correspondence, reports, publications, and other papers relate to her work at the University and to other personal and professional activities. Includes records of the Organization of Children's International Summer Villages, which she founded in 1946. Allen also worked at Longview State Hospital.

13,870. Arlitt, Ada Hart
Papers. 1933-34. 1 ft.
Open. Inventory.
University of Cincinnati Library, Special Collections.
Professor of child care and training at the University of Cincinnati, Arlitt (1890-) was chairman of the parent education division of the national PTA and associate editor of *Child Welfare Magazine.* Correspondence, including letters from Martha Sprague Mason, Alice Sowers, Isa Compton, and Ralph P. Bridgman, and a typescript and galley proofs of *Adolescent Psychology* (1933).

13,871. Brett, Dorothy
Papers. 1916-48. 300 items.
Open. Inventory.
University of Cincinnati Library, Special Collections.
Correspondence of Brett (1883-), biographer of D. H. Lawrence and a painter, includes letters from Lawrence, Frieda Lawrence, Virginia Woolf, Muriel Draper, Siegfried Sassoon, J. M. Keynes, J. M. Barry, and others.

13,872. Dolbey, Dorothy
Papers. 1947-73. 7.5 ft.
Access restricted. Inventory.
University of Cincinnati Library, Special Collections.
The first woman chairman of the Cincinnati Human Relations Committee, Dolbey (1908-) was a Cincinnati city councilwoman from 1953 to 1957, vice-mayor in 1955 and 1956, acting mayor in 1954, a member of the University of Cincinnati board of directors, and an officer of the United Church Women. Personal papers, speeches, photos, scrapbooks, and other papers concerning Dolbey's political activities and her work with United Church Women.

13,873. Juettner, Estelle Bode
Papers. 1885-1950. 9 ft.
Open. Inventory.
University of Cincinnati Library, Special Collections.
Correspondence, diaries, scrapbooks, and other personal papers of Juettner (1878-1970), the wife of physician Otto Juettner (1865-1922). Includes diaries of her trips to Europe during the 1930s.

13,874. Ohio Network, Hamilton County Court of Domestic Relations
Records. 1900-40s. 35 ft.
Closed. Inventory.
University of Cincinnati Library, Special Collections.
Court records concerning divorce and juvenile cases and mothers' pensions, primarily dating from 1920 to 1930. Prior to 1915 divorce cases were handled by Hamilton County Common Pleas Court; in 1914 the juvenile and domestic relations courts were combined.

13,875. Ransohoff, Martha
Papers. 1948-66. 35 ft.
Access restricted. Preliminary inventory.
University of Cincinnati Library, Special Collections.
A teacher for 35 years, Ransohoff (1894-1973) was a founder of the University of Cincinnati's child care department and an early proponent of preschool education. Lecture notes, articles on preschool education, television scripts, and Ransohoff's personal files on child care. Ransohoff was a children's programs advisor for WCPO-TV during the 1950s.

13,876. University Archives, Association of Women Administrators
Records. 1974-75. 0.5 ft.
Open. Shelf list.
University of Cincinnati Library, Special Collections.
Minutes, reports to the public, newsletters, and office files.

13,877. University Archives, College of Nursing and Health
Records. 1910-74. 45 ft.
Open. Preliminary inventory.
University of Cincinnati Library, Special Collections.
Files from the dean's office, minutes from graduate and undergraduate organizations, histories, newsletters, and catalogs.

13,878. University Archives, Office of University Commitment and Human Resources
Records. 1972-75. 1.5 ft.
Open. Shelf list.
University of Cincinnati Library, Special Collections.
The Office administered the University's affirmative action programs. Minutes of the

Affirmative Action Commission and affirmative action reports.

CLEVELAND

13,879. Arbuthnot, May H.
Papers. 1938-66. 0.13 in.
Open. Unpublished guide.
Case Western Reserve University Archives.
Arbuthnot was an associate professor of education at Western Reserve University from 1927 to 1950. Speeches and other papers concerning primary education, particularly books for children; biographical data; faculty information; a photo; and clippings about Arbuthnot's career and about her husband C. C. Arbuthnot, an economics professor at Western Reserve University.

13,880. Buell, Ellen L.
Papers. 1932-51. 2 boxes.
Open. Unpublished guide.
Case Western Reserve University Archives.
[Mrs.] Buell was chairman of the Western Reserve University department of public health nursing from 1945 to 1953. Correspondence, agenda, minutes, and reports relating to the National Organization for Public Health Nursing and, particularly, to the Organization's education and ad interim committees, on which Buell served.

13,881. Case Institute of Technology, Fortnightly Club
Records. 1894-1966. 6 boxes.
Open. Unpublished guide.
Case Western Reserve University Archives.
Founded in 1894, the Club was a social group for faculty wives. Minutes of the Club and executive board; treasurer's committee reports; correspondence concerning Club activities, particularly contributions for fatherless children in France during WWI; histories of the Club to 1937; memorial tributes to Ellen and Mary Case, Kate Holcomb Staley, Abbey Waite Howe, and others; a manuscript of a talk Minna Case gave in 1900; photos; programs; and other items. Also includes a notebook with expenses of graduation receptions from 1915 to 1927 and the Club president's book dating from 1953 to 1956.

13,882. Coyle, Grace
Papers. 1928-62. 9 boxes.
Open. Unpublished guide.
Case Western Reserve University Archives.
Coyle was a professor of social work at the School of Applied Social Sciences of Western Reserve University. Correspondence, lectures, speeches, and course material concerning the development and teaching of social work, unionization of social workers, training of recreation workers, and the role of the YWCA.

13,883. Faddis, Margene O.
Papers. 1914-54. 2 boxes.
Open. Unpublished guide.
Case Western Reserve University Archives.
Faddis was a professor of nursing at Frances Payne Bolton School of Nursing of Western Reserve University from 1929 to 1964. Correspondence, photos, clippings, diplomas, and draft material for two histories she wrote about the School of Nursing.

13,884. Flora Stone Mather College Advisory Council
Records. 1888-1968. 4 boxes.
Open. Unpublished guide.
Case Western Reserve University Archives.
The College for Women of Western Reserve University was established in 1888; the College's name was changed to Flora Stone Mather College in 1931. Minutes; reports of the dean, historian, and Guilford House committee; financial statements; correspondence; membership lists; material on the history of Mather College and the Council; and other records.

13,885. Flora Stone Mather College Alumnae Association
Records. 1968-72. 11 boxes.
Access restricted. Unpublished guide.
Case Western Reserve University Archives.
Survey questionnaires of Association members provide information on the graduates' further education, family background, employment, reading habits, and other activities. Includes computer coding instructions and computer tape.

13,886. Flora Stone Mather College Student Life
Records. 1888-1971. Ca. 40 vols.
Open. Unpublished guide.
Case Western Reserve University Archives.
Scrapbooks containing correspondence, class exercises, photos, dance and athletic event programs, invitations, place cards, and other material concerning student life at Flora Stone Mather College, the women's college of Western Reserve University and now of Case Western Reserve University.

13,887. Lakeside Hospital Training School for Nurses
Records. 1897-1946. 12 boxes.
Open. Unpublished guide.
Case Western Reserve University Archives.
Established in 1898, the School was the predecessor of the Frances Payne Bolton School of Nursing of Case Western Reserve University. Reports of the School and its committees, examinations, applications, and historical material concerning the nursing corps in WWI and WWII.

13,888. Lakeside Hospital Unit
Records. 1942-46. 1 box.
Open. Unpublished guide.
Case Western Reserve University Archives.
Memoranda, correspondence, reports, circulars, clippings, and other WWII records of the Unit, which was affiliated with the Frances Payne Bolton School of Nursing of Western Reserve University, concern the American National Red Cross, the War Manpower Commission, and the senior cadetship program.

13,889. Latimer, Frances P.
Papers. 1918-37. 3 boxes.
Open. Unpublished guide.
Case Western Reserve University Archives.
A 1906 graduate of the Lakeside Hospital Training School for Nurses, [Miss] Latimer served with the Lakeside Hospital Unit in France during WWI. Correspondence, diaries, speeches, scrapbooks, clippings, and memorabilia concerning battles, the American National Red Cross nursing service, the American National Red Cross military hospital, the American Ambulance Service, and the American Memorial Hospital in Paris.

13,890. Mather College Alumnae
Records. 1897-1951. 3 boxes.
Restricted. Unpublished guide.
Case Western Reserve University Archives.
Flora Stone Mather College was the women's college of Western Reserve University, now Case Western Reserve University. Clippings, publications, and other material concerning such alumnae as Gladys Bush, class of 1929; Agnes R. Gehr, class of 1947; Etta C. Gillman, class of 1914; Mildred P. Harrington and Harriet-Louise H. Patterson, both class of 1926; Dorothy Hart, class of 1943; Bernie Frances Pierson, class of 1928; Grace Preyer Rush, class of 1915; Alice D. Seagrave, class of 1905; Janis Carter Stilman, class of 1935; Florence Waterman, class of 1897; Grace Stone McClure Zorbaugh, class of 1898; and Abel Heinrich, class of 1951.

13,891. Meier, Elizabeth B.
Papers. 1962-67. 10 in.
Open. Unpublished guide.
Case Western Reserve University Archives.
Meier was a professor of social work at the School of Applied Social Science of Western Reserve University from 1962 to 1967. Professional papers, including master's theses; papers written during doctoral study; and course material used in teaching, seminars, and research projects, primarily in the field of child welfare and children's services.

13,892. Porter, Elizabeth Kerr
Papers. 1938-55. 1 box.
Open. Unpublished guide.
Case Western Reserve University Archives.
[Mrs.] Porter was dean of Frances Payne Bolton School of Nursing at Western Reserve University from 1953 to 1960 and president of the American Nurses' Association in 1953. Notes, speeches, minutes, and reports relate to Porter's activities outside the University, particularly to the Nurses' Association and economic security programs for nurses.

13,893. St. Barnabas Guild for Nurses
Records. 1912-75. 9 boxes.
Open. Unpublished guide.
Case Western Reserve University Archives.
Minutes, correspondence, scholarship records, plates, and photos of the Guild, a nurses' association formed in 1912.

13,894. Smith, Helen Wilkinson
Papers. 1958-75. 3 boxes.
Open. Unpublished guide.
Case Western Reserve University Archives.
Smith was chairman of the Flora Stone Mather College physical education department from 1958 to 1970. Correspondence, class notes, photos, and publications concerning the teaching of physical education classes.

13,895. Tyler, Alice Sarah
Papers. 1913-27. 2 folders.
Open. Unpublished guide.
Case Western Reserve University Archives.
[Miss] Tyler (1859-1944) was head of the Western Reserve University library school from 1913 to 1929 and professor of library organization and administration from 1915 to 1929. Personal and office correspondence, a biographical sketch about Tyler for *Notable American Women,* a thesis about Tyler by Cora Ella Richardson, pamphlets, and clippings.

13,896. Werner, Ruth M.
Papers. 1938-77. 7 record storage boxes.
Open. Unpublished guide.
Case Western Reserve University Archives.
Werner was a professor of social work and assistant dean of the School of Applied Social Science of Western Reserve University. Correspondence, records of professional participation outside the University, lectures, teaching material, memorabilia, and other items.

13,897. General Landmarks Files
Records. 1796- . More than 200 files.
Access restricted. No guide.
Cleveland Landmarks Commission.
Written material and photos principally relating to persons associated with Cleveland and Western Reserve historic sites.

13,898. Women's History Clippings
Collection. 1920- . No size given.
Closed. No guide.
Cleveland *Plain Dealer* Newspaper Library.
Clippings from the *Plain Dealer* and *Cleveland News* concern women's associations, rights, suffrage, careers, education, and legislation as well as women in the peace movements, politics, and

civic affairs. Most of the clippings concern Ohio events and personalities.

13,899. Federation of Jewish Women's Organizations
Records. 1941-57?. 6 ft.
Access restricted. No guide.
Jewish Community Federation of Cleveland.
Minutes and scrapbooks of the Federation, which was founded in 1941 and which coordinated the work of Jewish women's groups within the city and their efforts with similar groups outside the local area. The Federation's work was assumed by the Women's Organization, a department of the Jewish Community Federation, in 1957.

13,900. Women's Committee
Records. 1946- . 6 ft.
Access restricted. No guide.
Jewish Community Federation of Cleveland.
The Committee is the coordinating body for women's fund-raising activities within the Jewish Community Federation of Cleveland.

13,901. Women's Organization
Records. 1957- . 6 ft.
Access restricted. No guide.
Jewish Community Federation of Cleveland.
Minutes and scrapbooks of the Women's Organization, a department of the Jewish Community Federation that took up the work of the Federation of Jewish Women's Organizations in 1957.

13,902. Community Archives
Records. 1877- . No size given.
Closed. No guide.
Monastery of Poor Clares.
Financial records, community chronicles in German and English, correspondence, and other records of this community of cloistered contemplative nuns, which was founded in 1877 in Cleveland by Mother Mary Veronica von Elmendorff.

13,903. Motherhouse Archives
Records. 1872- . 4 drawers and other items.
Access restricted. Unpublished guide.
Sisters of St. Joseph Motherhouse.
This religious community was founded in 1872 in Painesville, OH. Financial records, correspondence, personal files, a history of the community, papers and publications of mothers general, photos, records of all ministries in which the community has been engaged, scrapbooks, and data regarding the St. Therese and Nazareth academies, which were operated by the Sisters, and St. Joseph Academy, which is still operated by the Sisters.

13,904. Allen, Florence Ellinwood
Papers. 1896-1966. 29 boxes and 1 package.
Open. Published guide and register.
Western Reserve Historical Society.
A journalist, attorney, and suffragist, [Miss] Allen (1884-1966) was the first woman elected to the Ohio Supreme Court; in 1934 President Franklin D. Roosevelt appointed her to the US Circuit Court of Appeals. Correspondence, diaries, speeches, articles by and about Allen, biographical and genealogical material, photos, scrapbooks, clippings, certificates, and awards. Born in Salt Lake City, Allen attended Salt Lake Academy and New Lyme Institute in Ashtabula County, OH. In 1904 she received her BA with honors from Western Reserve University; she received her MA in political science and constitutional law from the same school in 1908. After graduating with honors from the New York University Law School in 1913, Allen was admitted to the Ohio bar and maintained a private practice until 1919 when she was appointed assistant county prosecutor for Cuyahoga County. When it became evident that the woman suffrage amendment would be approved, Allen ran for and was elected judge of the county's court of common pleas. In 1922, she was elected to the Ohio Supreme Court. Allen served on the federal appellate court from 1934 until 1959 when she resigned her active duties and became a senior judge. She worked extensively with leaders of the woman suffrage movement and the peace movement after WWI. She also ran for the Senate but failed to win the Democratic party nomination. See Kermit J. Pike, *A Guide to the Manuscripts and Archives of The Western Reserve Historical Society* (Cleveland: The Western Reserve Historical Society, 1972).

13,905. Altenheim
Records. 1876- 1975. 2 ft.
Open. Register.
Western Reserve Historical Society.
The Altenheim Home for the Aged was founded in 1890 by a Cleveland German women's group, the West Seite Frauenverein (West Side Women's Society). Financial records, an income and expense ledger, scrapbooks, and Altenheim publications relate to German immigration to Cleveland, activities of German immigrants, the role of ethnic women in American society, and other subjects. The Frauenverein was founded in 1876 to sponsor women who wanted to enter the German Teachers' Seminary in Milwaukee. In 1880 the group joined with a similar organization on Cleveland's east side to open a needlework school. In 1886, the two groups were unable to agree on a second project because the Frauenverein wanted to open a home for the aged, while the second group wanted to establish a children's home. The Frauenverein decided to undertake its project alone, purchased property for the home in 1889, and supported construction of the building in 1890.

13,906. American Polish Women's Club
Records. 1933-72. 1 ft.
Open. Card catalog.
Western Reserve Historical Society.
The Club, part of a larger movement to bring European immigrants into US society, was founded in 1922 by [Mrs.] Helen Piotrowski, former secretary to the wife of Ignace Paderewski. Minutes, membership records, a scrapbook, and programs. The Club helped immigrants study English, attempted to preserve Polish customs, and raised money for welfare and civic projects.

13,907. Ashtabula County Female Anti-slavery Society
Records. 1835-37. 1 vol.
Open. Published guide.
Western Reserve Historical Society.
An auxiliary of the Ohio Anti-Slavery Society, this Ashtabula, OH, group sought to disseminate information about slavery and to promote the advancement of colored people. Constitution, a preamble, minutes, a list of members, a list of names of memorialists for 1836, and music notes for various songs. See Kermit J. Pike, *A Guide to the Manuscripts and Archives of The Western Reserve Historical Society* (Cleveland: The Western Reserve Historical Society, 1972).

13,908. Bedford Female Benevolent Sewing Society
Records. 1848-51. 1 vol.
Open. Published guide.
Western Reserve Historical Society.
Founded as a women's sewing society in Bedford, OH, this group was opened to male membership soon after its founding. Constitution, dues records, membership lists, and results of frequent elections of officers. See Kermit J. Pike, *A Guide to the Manuscripts and Archives of The Western Reserve Historical Society* (Cleveland: The Western Reserve Historical Society, 1972).

13,909. Bell, Myrtle (Johnson)
Papers. 1907-70. 0.5 box and 3 vols.
Open. Card catalog description.
Western Reserve Historical Society.
[Mrs.] Bell (1895-), a teacher, was the first black woman to serve as an assistant high school principal in the Cleveland public schools. Correspondence, a syllabus for a human relations course for teen-agers, photos, scrapbooks, school and club programs, a school centennial pamphlet, dinner programs and guest lists, testimonials, clippings, and other material. Bell was appointed to the Cleveland Advisory Board of Playgrounds and Recreation in 1936 and served on the city's Community Relations Board from 1945 to 1949. She was an assistant high school principal from 1938 to 1966.

13,910. Bickham, William D., Family
Papers. 1831-1917. 2 boxes.
Open. Published guide.
Western Reserve Historical Society.
Includes some personal correspondence and an autograph album of Maria Bickham. Also includes a "Book of Literary Memoranda," dating from 1846 to 1860, by Elizabeth A. Strickle at Hygiea Female Athenaeum, which was located near Cincinnati. See Kermit J. Pike, *A Guide to the Manuscripts and Archives of The Western Reserve Historical Society* (Cleveland: The Western Reserve Historical Society, 1972).

13,911. Bolton, Frances Payne (Bingham)
Papers. Ca. 1940-69. Ca. 400 boxes.
Open. Published guide.
Western Reserve Historical Society.
Primarily papers relating to the activities of [Mrs.] Bolton (1885-) as US representative from Ohio's 22nd district from 1940 to 1969. See Kermit J. Pike, *A Guide to the Manuscripts and Archives of The Western Reserve Historical Society* (Cleveland: The Western Reserve Historical Society, 1972).

13,912. Brodnik, Cecilia
Papers. Ca. 1887-1973. 0.5 container.
Open. No guide.
Western Reserve Historical Society.
Selected as the first president of the First Altar Guild of Annunciation Church in 1924, Brodnik (1880-1974) also organized citizenship classes for Slovenian immigrants in the Cleveland area. Photos, documents, programs, and clippings. Brodnik was an active supporter of the West Park Slovenian National Home, and she organized branch 21 of the Slovenian Women's Union in 1928.

13,913. Brooklyn Congregational Church, Woman's Missionary Society
Records. 1875-83. 1 vol.
Open. Published guide.
Western Reserve Historical Society.
Constitution, minutes, treasurer's annual reports, and names of the members of this Brooklyn, OH, group, which raised money for missionary activities. See Kermit J. Pike, *A Guide to the Manuscripts and Archives of The Western Reserve Historical Society* (Cleveland: The Western Reserve Historical Society, 1972).

13,914. Canton Ladies Anti-slavery Society
Records. 1836. 1 vol.
Open. Published guide.
Western Reserve Historical Society.
Preamble, constitution, and minutes of three meetings of this Canton, OH, group, which was founded in 1836. See Kermit J. Pike, *A Guide to the Manuscripts and Archives of The Western Reserve Historical Society* (Cleveland: The Western Reserve Historical Society, 1972).

13,915. Cleveland Section, National Council of Jewish Women
Records. 1894-1967. 23 ft.
Closed. Register.
Western Reserve Historical Society.
Records of this social service organization.

13,916. Cleveland Sorosis
Records. 1897-1974. 3 containers.
Open. Register.
Western Reserve Historical Society.
The Cleveland Sorosis, a personal and social improvement organization, was founded in 1891 when members of the Western Reserve Club, a women's group formed in 1882, decided to disband and reorganize following the model of the New York Sorosis. Annual report book, minutes of executive board and regular business meetings, correspondence, membership registration and pledge books, a club history, a scrapbook, guest books, and an annual for 1894 of the Cleveland Sorosis. Also contains minute books, membership books, and yearbooks of Junior Sorosis, which was founded in 1899 for women between the ages of 16 and 25. The Western Reserve Club was reorganized at the urging of a member who had attended a New York Sorosis meeting; the membership of the new group grew from 17 to 145. In 1892, the Cleveland Sorosis affiliated with the GFWC. The Club emphasized culture, responsibility, and service, with departments devoted to literature, art, house and home, businesswomen, philanthropy, temperance, drama, science, manual training, suffrage, physical culture, and dress reform.

13,917. Cleveland Writers' Club
Records. 1895-1972. 0.8 ft.
Open. Register.
Western Reserve Historical Society.
Founded in 1886 as the Cleveland Woman's Press Club, this group, the first of its kind in Ohio, brought members together to encourage writing and publication, offer criticism and advice, exchange experiences, and study literary models. Minutes, financial statements, literary works, members' biographies, membership rosters, scrapbooks, contest notices, annual programs, newsletters, clippings, and other material. The Cleveland Woman's Press Club joined with a similar group founded in Cincinnati in 1888 to form the Ohio Woman's Press Association. The Cincinnati branch later withdrew, and in 1912 the first group reassumed its original name. The Club affiliated with the city and state Federations of Women's Clubs and in 1922 adopted a new constitution as well as its current name. The group has sponsored lectures, public readings, and an annual writing contest.

13,918. Conversational Club
Records. 1898-1964. 1.5 boxes.
Open. Published guide.
Western Reserve Historical Society.
The Club was a local women's literary group founded in 1878 and disbanded in 1964. Minutes; financial accounts; membership rolls; reports of the Club's 50th, 60th, and 70th anniversary celebrations; and other records. See Kermit J. Pike, *A Guide to the Manuscripts and Archives of The Western Reserve Historical Society* (Cleveland: The Western Reserve Historical Society, 1972).

13,919. Converse, Amelia
Papers. 1839-90. 0.5 box.
Open. Published guide.
Western Reserve Historical Society.
Letters to Converse, daughter of John Phelps Converse and a Parkman, OH, resident, from friends and relatives, including Martha Converse, Mary M. Farwell, and Francis Parkman. Also includes Amelia Converse's diary, which deals primarily with illness, death, and other personal tragedies but also touches on conditions of Ohio asylums and trips she made around the state, primarily during the 1860s. See Kermit J. Pike, *A Guide to the Manuscripts and Archives of The Western Reserve Historical Society* (Cleveland: The Western Reserve Historical Society, 1972).

13,920. Daughters of the American Revolution, Ohio
Records. 1891-1917. 1 box.
Open. Published guide.
Western Reserve Historical Society.
Minutes of meetings of the Western Reserve chapter of the DAR and meetings of the committee in charge of collections for the War Emergency Relief Board; a record book of the committee of safety for 1897 and 1898; correspondence and a report concerning the promotion of patriotism in public schools; and the historian's report, consisting of genealogical records of local members. See Kermit J. Pike, *A Guide to the Manuscripts and Archives of The Western Reserve Historical Society* (Cleveland: The Western Reserve Historical Society, 1972).

13,921. Dwight, Margaret Van Horn
Papers. 1810. 1 vol.
Open. Published guide.
Western Reserve Historical Society.
Manuscript journal of Dwight (1790-1834) concerning a trip by wagon from New Haven, CT, to Warren, OH. The journal, edited by Max Farrand, was published as *A Journey to Ohio in 1810* (New Haven: Yale University Press, 1913). See Kermit J. Pike, *A Guide to the Manuscripts and Archives of The Western Reserve Historical Society* (Cleveland: The Western Reserve Historical Society, 1972).

13,922. Federation of Women's Clubs of Greater Cleveland
Records. 1902-74. 10 ft.
Open. Register.
Western Reserve Historical Society.
Annual reports, photos, and scrapbooks.

13,923. First Baptist Church, Women's Baptist Home Mission Society
Records. 1887-1900. 2 vols.
Open. Published guide.
Western Reserve Historical Society.
The goal of this Elyria, OH, group was to "cultivate a missionary spirit in this Church" and to aid "in . . . Christianizing the country." Minutes and an 1888 list of members. See Kermit J. Pike, *A Guide to the Manuscripts and Archives of The Western Reserve Historical Society* (Cleveland: The Western Reserve Historical Society, 1972).

13,924. Fleming, Leathia (Cousins)
Papers. 1914-59. 3 boxes.
Open. Card catalog description.
Western Reserve Historical Society.
Fleming (1876-1963), the wife of Cleveland councilman Thomas W. Fleming, was active in local and national Negro organizations. Correspondence, financial record books, legal papers, photos, awards, certificates, clippings, and printed matter.

13,925. Garfield, Eliza (Ballou)
Papers. 1881. 1 vol.
Open. Published guide.
Western Reserve Historical Society.
Garfield (1801-88) was the mother of President James A. Garfield. Diary that she kept during the last year of her son's life includes comments on incidents relating to herself and other family matters at Lawnfield, the President's home in Mentor, OH, and at the White House, where she lived from March until June. See Kermit J. Pike, *A Guide to the Manuscripts and Archives of The Western Reserve Historical Society* (Cleveland: The Western Reserve Historical Society, 1972).

13,926. Garfield, James Abram
Papers. 1857-1936. 9 boxes, 1 vol., and 1 package.
Open. Published guide and register.
Western Reserve Historical Society.
Correspondence and scrapbooks containing letters and clippings of Garfield (1831-81), a teacher, soldier, US representative, and President. Includes correspondence of his wife Lucretia (Rudolph) Garfield (1832-1918). See Kermit J. Pike, *A Guide to the Manuscripts and Archives of The Western Reserve Historical Society* (Cleveland: The Western Reserve Historical Society, 1972).

13,927. Gilbert, Mary Lukens
Papers. 1824-43. 17 items.
Open. Published guide.
Western Reserve Historical Society.
An abolitionist and teacher in a Negro school, Gilbert lived in Wilmington and Smithfield, OH. Consists of correspondence, primarily that with her brother Barclay Gilbert in La Porte, IN, and minutes of a meeting of antislavery advocates in Boston in 1843 about the *Liberator.* See Kermit J. Pike, *A Guide to the Manuscripts and Archives of The Western Reserve Historical Society* (Cleveland: The Western Reserve Historical Society, 1972).

13,928. Green, Ann Maria (Stockwell)
Papers. 1877-78. 3 vols.
Open. Card catalog description.
Western Reserve Historical Society.
Green (1840-1904) was the wife of George Green of Boston. Her diaries include a description of an extended European tour with entries about Glasgow, Edinburgh, London, Brussels, Amsterdam, Cologne, Strasbourg, Bern, Geneva, Paris, Rome, and other Italian cities. Green was in Rome when Victor Emmanuel II and Pius IX died in 1878.

13,929. Gregory, Sarah (Mumford)
Papers. Ca. 1920-50. 2 vols.
Open. Published guide.
Western Reserve Historical Society.
Gregory (1855-1950) was the wife of Edgar B. Gregory, publisher and editor of *The Independent* of Jonesville, MI. Scrapbooks containing correspondence, photos, and clippings, including Sarah Gregory's memoirs, which appeared in *The Independent* in 1949. See Kermit J. Pike, *A Guide to the Manuscripts and Archives of The Western Reserve Historical Society* (Cleveland: The Western Reserve Historical Society, 1972).

13,930. Guilford, Linda Thayer
Papers. 1843-1910. 1 box and 1 oversize vol.
Open. Published guide.
Western Reserve Historical Society.
[Miss] Guilford (1823-1911), who settled in Cleveland in 1848, taught at the Cleveland Female Seminary and the Cleveland Academy; she also was active in the temperance movement. Correspondence, writings, speeches, notes on early Cleveland schools, a scrapbook, and clippings concern Guilford's work as a teacher. Collection also contains letters and a secretary's book of the Young Ladies Temperance League and minutes and clippings of the Young Ladies League for Temperance Education of Cleveland. See Kermit J. Pike, *A Guide to the Manuscripts and Archives of The Western Reserve Historical Society* (Cleveland: The Western Reserve Historical Society, 1972).

13,931. Herrick, Caroline (Parmerly)
Papers. 1900. 1 vol.
Open. Published guide.
Western Reserve Historical Society.
Herrick (?-1918) was the wife of Ambassador Myron T. Herrick. Diary she kept during a Mediterranean cruise with her husband and friends includes photos taken during the voyage. See Kermit J. Pike, *A Guide to the Manuscripts and Archives of The Western Reserve Historical Society* (Cleveland: The Western Reserve Historical Society, 1972).

13,932. Hughes, Adella (Prentiss), Family
Papers. 1801-1904. 9 boxes and 1 vol.
Open. Register.
Western Reserve Historical Society.
A music impresario and civic worker, [Mrs. Felix] Hughes (1869-1950) was founder and manager of the Cleveland Orchestra. Correspondence, music programs, religious tracts, genealogical data, land deeds, poems, photos, calling cards, social invitations, broadsides, clippings, and other papers. Includes material of Hughes's maternal grandparents Benjamin Rouse (1795-1871), Cleveland agent for the American Sunday School Union, and Rebecca C. [Mrs. Benjamin] Rouse (1799-1887), president of the Cleveland branch of the US Sanitary Commission during the Civil War, and of Hughes's mother Ellen R. Prentiss. Also includes letters from Adella Prentiss, while a student at Vassar College, to her mother and correspondence and memorabilia of Ellen Prentiss and her daughter during a European tour in 1890 and 1891. Adella Hughes helped found the Cleveland Music School Settlement in 1912, and in 1915 she led in the establishment of the Musical Arts Association, which brought visiting artists, choruses, and operas to Cleveland and began to organize the city's orchestra. Hughes was a member of the Ohio Federation of Clubs, the Fortnightly Musical Club, the Vassar Alumnae, Mid-Day College, the Women's City Club, and the Polish Relief Benefit. In addition, she was decorated by the Polish government.

13,933. Hungarian Ladies Charity Club
Records. 1932-60. 0.5 ft.
Open. Card catalog description.
Western Reserve Historical Society.
Minutes and clippings, in Hungarian, of the Charity Club, which was formed in 1932 to help unemployed persons in the Hungarian community; after the depression, the Club raised money for hospitals, rest homes, and other charities.

13,934. Hunter, Jane E.
Papers. Ca. 1930-69. 1 box and 1 oversize package.
Open. Card catalog description.
Western Reserve Historical Society.
[Miss] Hunter (1882-1971) was the founder of the Phillis Wheatley Association, which sought to help unmarried black girls. Correspondence, speeches, miscellaneous writings, biographical material, clippings, and printed items.

13,935. Huntington, Hannah
Papers. 1791-1811. 51 items.
Open. Published guide.
Western Reserve Historical Society.
Huntington (1770-1818) was the wife of Samuel Huntington (1765-1817), a jurist, legislator, and governor of Ohio from 1808 to 1810. Letters from Hannah Huntington to her husband primarily concerning family matters. See Kermit J. Pike, *A Guide to the Manuscripts and Archives of The Western Reserve Historical Society* (Cleveland: The Western Reserve Historical Society, 1972).

13,936. Judson, Katherine B.
Papers. Ca. 1920s. 3 boxes.
Open. Published guide.
Western Reserve Historical Society.
Drafts of articles, notes, and copies of letters and documents used by Judson in her research on such topics as the Pacific Northwest and the exploration and settlement of America. See Kermit J. Pike, *A Guide to the Manuscripts and Archives of The Western Reserve Historical Society* (Cleveland: The Western Reserve Historical Society, 1972).

13,937. Ladies Aid Society of Brocton, OH
Records. 1866. 1 vol.
Open. Published guide.
Western Reserve Historical Society.
An auxiliary of the New York National Freedman's Relief Association, the Society was established "to furnish physical, moral, and intellectual aid to the colored people, who have recently been in bondage." Minutes, a list of members, and poems by Society members. See Kermit J. Pike, *A Guide to the Manuscripts and Archives of The Western Reserve Historical Society* (Cleveland: The Western Reserve Historical Society, 1972).

13,938. Ladies' Literary Circle
Records. 1849-50. 1 vol.
Open. Published guide.
Western Reserve Historical Society.
Constitution, bylaws, minutes, and lists of members of this Bloomington, OH, society, which sought to cultivate "pure morals" and help its members improve their minds. See Kermit J. Pike, *A Guide to the Manuscripts and Archives of The Western Reserve Historical Society* (Cleveland: The Western Reserve Historical Society, 1972).

13,939. League of Women Voters of Cleveland
Records. 1918-72. 4.3 ft.
Open. Register.
Western Reserve Historical Society.
The Cleveland LWV was formed by Cuyahoga County suffragists who, upon ratification of the 23rd Amendment in 1920, decided to disband their Woman Suffrage Party and organize a local LWV chapter. Minutes, correspondence, committee reports and recommendations, membership records, a scrapbook concerning water pollution in Cuyahoga County, scrapbooks of clippings, voter service and other LWV publications, and material relating to the history of the woman suffrage movement, including minutes of 1918 and 1919 Woman Suffrage Party conventions in Cleveland.

13,940. League of Women Voters of East Cleveland, OH
Records. 1946-72. 1 ft.
Open. Register.
Western Reserve Historical Society.
This LWV chapter was founded in 1946. Bylaws, minutes, correspondence, reports and recommendations of committees concerned with local issues, lists of members and boards of directors, national and state annual reports, East Cleveland and county LWV bulletins, voter service publications, and clippings.

13,941. MacDonald, Harriet M.
Papers. 1918-20. 1 folder.
Open. Published guide.
Western Reserve Historical Society.
Letters written by [Miss] Macdonald during her work as an American National Red Cross nurse in France in WWI. See Kermit J. Pike, *A Guide to the Manuscripts and Archives of The Western Reserve Historical Society* (Cleveland: The Western Reserve Historical Society, 1972).

13,942. Magee, Elizabeth S.
Papers. 1882-1972. 6 boxes and 2 vols.
Open. Card catalog description.
Western Reserve Historical Society.
[Miss] Magee (1899-?) was executive secretary of the Consumers League of Ohio for 20 years and general secretary of the National Consumers League for 15 years. Personal and professional correspondence, including correspondence with her father William A. Magee, Mrs. Newton D. Baker, and others; diaries, including two volumes of her sister Anna May Magee; a speech given by Emily (Taft) Douglas at a luncheon honoring Magee on her retirement in 1958 from the National Consumers League; family papers; scrapbooks, including one concerning Magee's year at Oberlin College; a temperance pledge; a White House invitation; a register of persons present at a memorial service for Magee; and other material.

13,943. Mather, Samuel, Family
Papers. Ca. 1872-1945. Ca. 30 boxes.
Open. Published guide.
Western Reserve Historical Society.
Samuel Mather (1851-1931) was an iron merchant, financier, and, with his wife Flora Stone Mather (1852-1909), a philanthropist. Correspondence, diaries, genealogical data, photos, scrapbooks, and other material, including Flora Mather's papers and letters from Constance Fenimore Woolson. The Mathers were married in 1881. See Kermit J. Pike, *A Guide to the Manuscripts and Archives of The Western Reserve Historical Society* (Cleveland: The Western Reserve Historical Society, 1972).

13,944. Methodist-Episcopal Church, Woman's Missionary Society
Records. 1871-88. 1 vol.
Open. Published guide.
Western Reserve Historical Society.
Constitution, bylaws, minutes, and lists of members of this Bucyrus, OH, group, which was an auxiliary to the Cincinnati branch of the Woman's Foreign Missionary Society of the Methodist-Episcopal Church. See Kermit J. Pike, *A Guide to the Manuscripts and Archives of The Western Reserve Historical Society* (Cleveland: The Western Reserve Historical Society, 1972).

13,945. Mitchell, L. Pearl
Papers. 1875-1974. 2.5 boxes.
Open. Card catalog description.
Western Reserve Historical Society.
Mitchell (?-1974), a social worker, was president of the Cleveland branch of the NAACP. Correspondence; biographical material about Mitchell; sermons; speeches; minutes, financial reports, pamphlets, or other material relating to the NAACP, the Alpha Kappa Alpha Society, the Mount Zion Congregational Church, the Ohio Soldiers and Sailors' Orphans Home, the women's council to the Cleveland Mental Health Association, and the Cleveland Job Corps for Women; issues of the *Wilberforce Graduate; A Half Century of Freedom of the Negro in Ohio* (1915), compiled by W. A. Joiner; and *The Long Moment* (1950) by Jo Sinclair.

13,946. Moore, Marion Louise
Papers. 1831-60. 1 vol.
Open. Published guide.
Western Reserve Historical Society.
Journal kept by Moore, a Williamsfield, OH, resident, includes entries concerning her domestic problems and religious ideas. See Kermit J. Pike, *A Guide to the Manuscripts and Archives of The Western Reserve Historical Society* (Cleveland: The Western Reserve Historical Society, 1972).

13,947. Morris, Mrs. Gouverneur
Papers. Ca. 1910-20. 2 vols.
Open. Published guide.
Western Reserve Historical Society.
Miscellaneous papers include a typescript of journal kept during a canoe trip along the north shore of Lake Superior in ca. 1910. See Kermit J. Pike, *A Guide to the Manuscripts and Archives of The Western Reserve Historical Society* (Cleveland: The Western Reserve Historical Society, 1972).

13,948. National Society of the Colonial Dames of America in the State of Ohio
Records. Ca. 1891-1952. 2 boxes.
Open. Published guide.
Western Reserve Historical Society.
Minutes of the Cleveland Circle of the National Society, correspondence, and printed material, which makes up the bulk of the collection. Printed items include meeting reports, directories, yearbooks, pamphlets, copies of *The Messenger*, and other material relating to the national organization. See Kermit J. Pike, *A Guide to the Manuscripts and Archives of The Western Reserve*

Historical Society (Cleveland: The Western Reserve Historical Society, 1972).

13,949. Parsons Family
Papers. 1860-1910. 2 boxes.
Open. Published guide.
Western Reserve Historical Society.
Personal and family papers, including compositions, copybooks, report cards, tuition receipts, examination papers, and booklets of poetry and autographs of Emma and Myrta Parsons and other family members who attended Burton Academy in Burton, OH, during the 1860s and Hiram College in Hiram, OH, in the 1880s and 1890s. Includes letters to Myrta Parsons from [Miss] Adelaide Gail Frost, a Hiram College graduate, who was serving as a missionary in Mahoba, N.W.P., India. Frost supervised a girls' orphanage. See Kermit J. Pike, *A Guide to the Manuscripts and Archives of The Western Reserve Historical Society* (Cleveland: The Western Reserve Historical Society, 1972).

13,950. Phillis Wheatley Association
Records. 1914-60. 15.5 ft.
Open. Register.
Western Reserve Historical Society.
The Working Girls Home Association, later renamed the Phillis Wheatley Association, was organized by Jane Edna Hunter in 1911 to help black women find housing and employment and adjust to city life. Minutes, financial statements, correspondence, speeches, financial and committee reports, insurance policies, brochures and clippings. With a budget of $1500, the Association maintained a boarding home for 22 girls. A larger building was purchased with $37,000 in donations in 1917 to meet the need for additional housing. In 1919, aided by the Cleveland Welfare Federation, the Phillis Wheatley Association bought an adjoining building and established the Stephen School of Music, an educational and social center.

13,951. Presbytery of Cleveland, The Women's Foreign Missionary Society of the Presbytery and City of Cleveland
Records. 1872-1914. 4 vols.
Open. Published guide.
Western Reserve Historical Society.
This group, which helped send and sustain female missionaries in foreign countries, was formally united with the Woman's Home Missionary Society in 1914. Constitution, minutes of quarterly and special meetings, names of members, and reports from sections located throughout Ohio. See Kermit J. Pike, *A Guide to the Manuscripts and Archives of The Western Reserve Historical Society* (Cleveland: The Western Reserve Historical Society, 1972).

13,952. Presbytery of Cleveland, Woman's Missionary Society
Records. 1886-1935. 2 boxes.
Open. Published guide.
Western Reserve Historical Society.
Constitution, bylaws, annual reports, minutes, correspondence, and other records of the Society, which supported home and foreign missionary work. See Kermit J. Pike, *A Guide to the Manuscripts and Archives of The Western Reserve Historical Society* (Cleveland: The Western Reserve Historical Society, 1972).

13,953. Ptak Family
Papers. 1919-74. 1.25 ft.
Open. No guide.
Western Reserve Historical Society.
Marus (Hlavacek) Ptak (1908-66) was an officer and member of Czechoslovakian cultural and fraternal groups. Personal correspondence, correspondence of the Cultural Gardens Association, correspondence and other material related to the American National Red Cross, reports and proceedings from the 1954 convention of the Czechoslovakian Society of America, programs of the Czechoslovakian Singing Society, memorabilia, and other papers. Born in Louny, Czechoslovakia, Marus Hlavacek graduated from Lycée Jeanne D'Arc in Orleans, France, and from the Czechoslovakian Academy of Commerce in Prague. In 1929 she married Victor G. Ptak in Czechoslovakia and later immigrated with him to Cleveland. She was secretary of the Czechoslovakian Cultural Gardens group from 1953 to 1965, a member of the Nationalities Services Center board of trustees from 1953 to 1966, director of the Nationalities Services Center from 1960 to 1966, and an active member of the Czechoslovakian Society of America, the Czechoslovakian Singing Society, Sokol Tyrs, and numerous civic organizations.

13,954. Rudolph, Adelaide
Papers. 1885-1950. 2 boxes.
Open. Published guide.
Western Reserve Historical Society.
A teacher and librarian at Columbia University, [Miss] Rudolph (1858-1953) was a niece of President and Mrs. James A. Garfield. Correspondence, journal for the years 1900 to 1907 and 1928 to 1937, and genealogical data and clippings concerning the Garfields and Rudolphs. After her retirement, Rudolph worked on a history of Hiram, OH, at the Cleveland Public Library. See Kermit J. Pike, *A Guide to the Manuscripts and Archives of The Western Reserve Historical Society* (Cleveland: The Western Reserve Historical Society, 1972).

13,955. Shakers
Collection. 1774-ca. 1921. 122 ft.
Open. Published guide.
Western Reserve Historical Society.
The Shakers, a communal and religious group with the formal title United Society of Believers in Christ's Second Appearing, developed in the US after the arrival of their leader Mother Ann Lee in 1774. Correspondence, which touches upon Shaker principles of communal property, celibacy, separation from the world, equality of the sexes, pacifism, and sanctity of labor; journals and diaries, including many kept by Shaker women; biographies and autobiographies; testimonies and inspired writings; archives of various communities; financial and legal records; birth, death, and statistical records; sermons; photos; scrapbooks; instructional texts; covenants; lyrics and musical compositions; recipes; prescriptions; and other material. See Kermit J. Pike, *A Guide to Shaker Manuscripts in the Library of The Western Reserve Historical Society* (Cleveland: The Western Reserve Historical Society, 1974).

13,956. Smith, Catharine B.
Records. 1843-53. 2 vols.
Open. Published guide.
Western Reserve Historical Society.
Poems written by or addressed to Smith, a Quaker resident of Mount Pleasant, OH. See Kermit J. Pike, *A Guide to the Manuscripts and Archives of The Western Reserve Historical Society* (Cleveland: The Western Reserve Historical Society, 1972).

13,957. Smyth, Sarah Lanman
Papers. 1842-57. 1 vol.
Open. Published guide.
Western Reserve Historical Society.
A journal kept for Smyth (1842-?) by her parents during the first 15 years of her life. During this period the family lived in New Haven and Milford, CT, while Sarah's father, an ordained Baptist minister, traveled to New York, Ohio, and Michigan. See Kermit J. Pike, *A Guide to the Manuscripts and Archives of The Western Reserve Historical Society* (Cleveland: The Western Reserve Historical Society, 1972).

13,958. Sterling, Emma (Betts)
Papers. 1872-92. 19 vols.
Open. Published guide.
Western Reserve Historical Society.
Sterling (1837-?), the wife of Cleveland merchant and banker Frederick A. Sterling, was active in charity work. Diaries in which she describes trips to Europe in 1872, 1879, and 1886 and at least annual trips to New York, Boston, and other eastern cities. The Sterlings spent part of almost every summer at East Coast resorts. The diaries contain descriptions of entertainments in each place the Sterlings visited and reflect upper middle-class life during the late 19th century. See Kermit J. Pike, *A Guide to the Manuscripts and Archives of The Western Reserve Historical Society* (Cleveland: The Western Reserve Historical Society, 1972).

13,959. Strong, Eleanor (Painter)
Papers. Ca. 1941. 0.5 box.
Open. Published guide.
Western Reserve Historical Society.
Typescript and galley proofs of *Spring Symphony* (New York and London: Harper and Brothers, 1941), a novel by Eleanor Painter, a writer. See Kermit J. Pike, *A Guide to the Manuscripts and Archives of The Western Reserve Historical Society* (Cleveland: The Western Reserve Historical Society, 1972).

13,960. Swidzinska, Halina
Papers. 1958-74. 0.5 box and 5 vols.
Open. No guide.
Western Reserve Historical Society.
[Miss] Swidzinska is a writer and teacher. Articles written by Swidzinska in Polish; papers including commentaries on current events in Poland; articles, essays, and stories published in Poland from 1935 to 1939 and in the emigré Polish press; and scrapbooks.

13,961. Taylor, Benjamin F., Family
Papers. 1839-1925. 1 box.
Open. Published guide.
Western Reserve Historical Society.
Taylor (1819-87) was a Cleveland journalist, artist, and poet. Correspondence, poems, speeches, and manuscript of the novel *Theophilus Trent* (1887). Includes letters touching on the career of Lucy E. L. Taylor, a member of the Cleveland Board of Education during the early 20th century, and speeches by Lucy Taylor on such topics as history, education, and culture. See Kermit J. Pike, *A Guide to the Manuscripts and Archives of The Western Reserve Historical Society* (Cleveland: The Western Reserve Historical Society, 1972).

13,962. Thomas, Wheeler, and White Families
Papers. 1832-72. 0.5 box.
Open. Published guide.
Western Reserve Historical Society.
Correspondence and sermon notes of Susan A. Thomas, a student at Mount Holyoke Female Seminary during the early 1840s, and of Homer Wheeler, who attended Indiana University in 1844-45. See Kermit J. Pike, *A Guide to the Manuscripts and Archives of The Western Reserve Historical Society* (Cleveland: The Western Reserve Historical Society, 1972).

13,963. Thompson and Tuttle Families
Papers. Ca. 1812-1915. 11 boxes.
Open. Published guide and register.
Western Reserve Historical Society.
Correspondence, legal and business papers, speeches, biographical and genealogical data, photos, pamphlets, clippings, and other material of Eliza Jane (Trimble) [Mrs. James Henry] Thompson (1816-1905), an author who was a founder and leader of the temperance movement; Mary McArthur (Thompson) Tuttle (1849-1916), an artist, author, and lecturer; and other members of these Hillsboro, OH, families. Bulk of the material consists of correspondence of Thompson

and Tuttle with representatives of the state, national, and international WCTU and of two temperance publications, *The Union Signal* and the *National W.C.T.U.* Other material relates to Thompson's *Hillsboro Crusade Sketches and Family Records* (1896), her two daughters, Frances E. Willard, and the visit of 500 WCTU delegates to Hillsboro in 1903. See Kermit J. Pike, *A Guide to the Manuscripts and Archives of The Western Reserve Historical Society* (Cleveland: The Western Reserve Historical Society, 1972).

13,964. Travelers Aid Society
Records. 1913-72. 2.4 ft.
Open. Register.
Western Reserve Historical Society.
The Cleveland Travelers Aid Society was founded in 1920 after a study showed the need for specialized service to travelers; during the early 1920s, Society workers provided assistance around-the-clock at five local railroad stations, an interurban station, and a boat dock. Minutes and correspondence make up the bulk of the collection, which also includes annual reports, financial and budget data, membership rosters, convention material, newsletters, and clippings. The Cleveland Society, with funds from the Community Chest, provided workers to help travelers and assumed a protective role toward traveling females until 1925, when the latter function was assumed by the Cleveland Police Department's new women's bureau.

13,965. Tuma, Maria
Papers. Ca. 1915-73. 0.7 ft.
Open. Register.
Western Reserve Historical Society.
[Mrs.] Tuma (1895-) has been active in Czechoslovakian fraternal and political groups, including the Czechoslovakian-American National Alliance, known in Cleveland as the Alliance of Thomas Masaryk. Correspondence, receipts, petitions, membership lists, congressional bills, leaflets, clippings, and other material relating to organizations of which Tuma was a member. In 1936 Tuma began work for the Cuyahoga County welfare department's program of aid for the aged. In 1963 she joined Jednota Cesky Vlastenek, the first independent Czechoslovakian women's fraternal union.

13,966. U.S. Sanitary Commission, Cleveland Branch: Soldier's Aid Society of Northern Ohio
Records. 1860-78. 41 boxes, 41 vols., and 1 package.
Open. Published guide and register.
Western Reserve Historical Society.
Founded in April 1861 under the leadership of Mrs. Benjamin Rouse, Mrs. John Shelley, Mrs. William Melhinch, Mary Clark Brayton, and Ellen F. Terry, the Cleveland Branch was the first of more than 500 permanently organized branches of the US Sanitary Commission; members of the Soldier's Aid Society helped the Commission by improving camp hygiene and soldiers' diet, collecting and disbursing hospital stores, inspecting hospitals and other medical facilities, caring for sick and wounded soldiers, registering and burying the dead, building and supporting a soldiers' home, and conducting a special relief program and an employment service. Abstracts of weekly and monthly reports, acknowledgements of equipment received, bank drafts, correspondence, memoranda, reports, insurance policies, clippings, and other records include items concerning the Sanitary Commission; the Soldier's Aid Society; and the Free Claim Agency, the Bureau of Information and Employment, the Special Relief Department, and the Northern Ohio Sanitary Fair of 1864, all of which were related to the Society. Also includes a memoir of Caroline Younglove Abbott concerning the work of the Society. See Kermit J. Pike, *A Guide to the Manuscripts and Archives of The Western Reserve Historical Society* (Cleveland: The Western Reserve Historical Society, 1972).

13,967. Upton, Harriet (Taylor)
Papers. 1893-1916. 1 folder.
Open. Published guide.
Western Reserve Historical Society.
Correspondence, telegrams, broadsides, and other documents of [Mrs. George Whitman] Upton (1853-1945) concern activities of the Ohio Association Opposed to Woman's Suffrage, the Ohio Woman Suffrage Association and the National Anti-Suffrage Association. Also contains a manuscript copy of an 1893 article that [Mrs.] Carolyn McCullough Everhard, president of the Ohio Woman Suffrage Association, wrote in conjunction with the passage of a school suffrage law. See Kermit J. Pike, *A Guide to the Manuscripts and Archives of The Western Reserve Historical Society* (Cleveland: The Western Reserve Historical Society, 1972).

13,968. War Emergency Relief Board
Records. 1898. 2 folders and 6 vols.
Open. Published guide.
Western Reserve Historical Society.
The Board was established in Cleveland under the auspices of the DAR to help provide supplies for hospitals caring for American men wounded during the Spanish-American War. Letters to various Board members, receipt book of the committee on appropriations, and lists of contributions, work done and returned, and auxiliary societies. See Kermit J. Pike, *A Guide to the Manuscripts and Archives of The Western Reserve Historical Society* (Cleveland: The Western Reserve Historical Society, 1972).

13,969. Wellington Literary Society
Records. 1847-48. 3 items.
Open. Published guide.
Western Reserve Historical Society.
Manuscript copies of literary periodicals "The Visitant," "The Casket," and "The Garland," which were prepared by members of this Wellington, OH, group. See Kermit J. Pike, *A Guide to the Manuscripts and Archives of The Western Reserve Historical Society* (Cleveland: The Western Reserve Historical Society, 1972).

13,970. Williamson, Katharine (Porter)
Papers. 1929-64. 1 box, 2 oversize vols., and 2 vols.
Open. Card catalog description.
Western Reserve Historical Society.
[Mrs. Harvey] Williamson (1910-64) was chief of the Ohio state division of social administration. Correspondence, reports, awards, certificates, printed items, and clippings relating to her activities as administrative assistant for the Cuyahoga County child welfare division. The correspondence includes congratulatory messages concerning awards Williamson won and messages of condolence sent to her husband after her death. Also includes her thesis, which dealt with cases not accepted by the Cleveland Humane Society during 1929.

13,971. Wilson, Ella (Grant)
Papers. Ca. 1900-39. 14 ft.
Open. No guide.
Western Reserve Historical Society.
Papers relate to the career of Wilson (1854-1939) as a florist and author and include information concerning compilation of her book *Famous Old Euclid Avenue.*

13,972. Wing, Marie R.
Papers. 1920-69. 4 boxes.
Open. Card catalog description.
Western Reserve Historical Society.
A feminist who campaigned for women's voting rights, [Miss] Wing (ca. 1884-) was a government attorney in Cleveland for 17 years and was elected to two terms on the Cleveland city council. Files concerning her campaigns for the city council and for proportional representation in Cleveland make up the bulk of the collection. Also contains correspondence, speeches, memoranda, photos, and scrapbooks relating to unemployment insurance, the Consumers League, Roosevelt's election, and antipoverty programs in Lake County, OH. Wing enrolled in law school at the age of 37.

13,973. Woman's Christian Temperance Union
Records. 1909-34. 3 vols.
Open. Published guide.
Western Reserve Historical Society.
Minutes, financial accounts, and lists of members of the Lakewood, OH, chapter of the WCTU. See Kermit J. Pike, *A Guide to the Manuscripts and Archives of The Western Reserve Historical Society* (Cleveland: The Western Reserve Historical Society, 1972).

13,974. Woman's Christian Temperance Union
Records. 1916-24. 1 vol.
Open. Published guide.
Western Reserve Historical Society.
Minutes of annual, business, and regular meetings; financial records; and a 1922 membership list of the Lake County, OH, branch of the WCTU. See Kermit J. Pike, *A Guide to the Manuscripts and Archives of The Western Reserve Historical Society* (Cleveland: The Western Reserve Historical Society, 1972).

13,975. Woman's Christian Temperance Union
Records. 1887-1932. 14 vols.
Open. Published guide.
Western Reserve Historical Society.
Secretaries' books containing minutes, financial accounts and reports, officers' reports, correspondence, and convention programs of the Cuyahoga County, OH, branch of the WCTU. See Kermit J. Pike, *A Guide to the Manuscripts and Archives of The Western Reserve Historical Society* (Cleveland: The Western Reserve Historical Society, 1972).

13,976. Woman's Christian Temperance Union
Records. 1874-1951. 2 boxes.
Open. Published guide.
Western Reserve Historical Society.
Founded in 1874, this Cleveland group was incorporated in 1880 as the Woman's Christian Temperance League of Ohio, an auxiliary to the WCTU. Constitution, articles of incorporation, minutes of board and committee meetings, financial records, and correspondence. Includes records of the Non-Partisan National Woman's Christian Temperance Union from 1886 to 1932 and of the Woman's Philanthropic Union from 1933 to 1951. In addition to the group's advocacy of temperance, the records document the organization's social, civic, and charitable activities, including sponsorship of the Central Friendly Inn, a social settlement. See Kermit J. Pike, *A Guide to the Manuscripts and Archives of The Western Reserve Historical Society* (Cleveland: The Western Reserve Historical Society, 1972).

13,977. Woman's Temperance Society of Morgan County, OH
Records. 1853-56. 1 vol.
Open. Published guide.
Western Reserve Historical Society.
Constitution and minutes of the Society, which sought "to encourage . . . Total abstinence" and disseminate temperance principles "in every laudable way." See Kermit J. Pike, *A Guide to the Manuscripts and Archives of The Western Reserve Historical Society* (Cleveland: The Western Reserve Historical Society, 1972).

13,978. Women's American Organization for Rehabilitation Training
Records. 1965-75. 1.5 boxes.
Open. No guide.
Western Reserve Historical Society.
Newsletters, reports, fund-raising manuals, brochures, a 90th anniversary yearbook printed in 1970, histories for the period 1881 to 1939, greeting cards used for fund raising, clippings, and copies of *Spotlight.*

13,979. Women's City Club
Records. 1916-65. 5.75 ft.
Open. Register.
Western Reserve Historical Society.
Founded in 1916 by suffragists and Cleveland's female social leaders, the Club takes positions on political and social issues but does not endorse candidates. Minute books, correspondence, committee files, histories, scrapbooks, clippings, and publications. Founded partially in response to the establishment of an all-male City Club in 1911, the Women's City Club was led in its early days by [Miss] Belle Sherwin, Mrs. Charles F. Thwing, and Judge Florence E. Allen. The group is concerned with county home rule, welfare, mental health care, education, and public recreation; it also performs various civic functions, including the sale of war bonds during both world wars.

13,980. Women's Missionary Union of the Cleveland Churches
Records. 1895-1915. 2 vols.
Open. Published guide.
Western Reserve Historical Society.
Secretaries' books contain a constitution, minutes, reports, and a history of this local organization, which sought to increase its members' knowledge of missionary work of all denominations and to stimulate missionary activity. See Kermit J. Pike, *A Guide to the Manuscripts and Archives of The Western Reserve Historical Society* (Cleveland: The Western Reserve Historical Society, 1972).

13,981. Women's Rights Society of Cleveland
Records. 1934-46. 1 folder.
Open. No guide.
Western Reserve Historical Society.
Constitution, correspondence, and speeches.

13,982. Young Women's Christian Association
Records. 1878-1960. 12 boxes.
Open. Published guide and register.
Western Reserve Historical Society.
Founded in 1869, the Cleveland YWCA provided recreational facilities and instruction in women's trades and domestic and office work; by the turn of the century, the group helped women find employment and maintained a residence, retreats, and rest homes for the aged or incurably ill. Minutes of the local YWCA, its advisory board, and the board of trustees; correspondence; rosters; attendance records; histories; scrapbooks; bulletins; broadsides; and other material reflect the group's involvement in a post-WWI movement to outlaw war as well as in programs to ease race relations and immigrant problems and to aid the unemployed during the depression. See Kermit J. Pike, *A Guide to the Manuscripts and Archives of The Western Reserve Historical Society* (Cleveland: The Western Reserve Historical Society, 1972).

13,983. Young Women's Christian Temperance Union
Records. 1889-91. 1 vol.
Open. Published guide and register.
Western Reserve Historical Society.
The Salem, OH, branch of the WCTU was formed in 1889 and disbanded in 1891. Secretary's book includes constitution, minutes, a pledge, and a list of members. See Kermit J. Pike, *A Guide to the Manuscripts and Archives of The Western Reserve Historical Society* (Cleveland: The Western Reserve Historical Society, 1972).

COLUMBUS

13,984. Archives
Records. Ca. 1850s- . No size given.
Access restricted. Unpublished guide.
Dominican Sisters, St. Mary of the Springs Motherhouse.
This community of religious women, who are involved primarily in education, was established in Columbus in 1868. Several dozen boxes contain financial records, correspondence, council books, annals from all of the community's missions, files of individual sisters, photos, and records of the institutions staffed by the Sisters.

13,985. Altrusa Club of Columbus
Records. 1920-73. 6.25 ft.
Open. No guide.
Ohio Historical Society.
Founded in 1918, the Club was a professional women's service group which was particularly interested in improving job opportunities for women. Minutes of directors' and Club meetings, financial records, correspondence, Club recommendations, membership lists, yearly meeting schedules, scrapbooks, and clippings.

13,986. American Association of University Women
Records. 1903-75. 4 ft.
Open. Unpublished guide.
Ohio Historical Society.
Constitution, bylaws, minutes, budgets, branch reports, history, and scrapbooks of the Columbus AAUW, which was founded in 1903. Branch reports record and evaluate study groups, workshops, and community projects relating to continuing education for women, the status of women, mental health, college faculty programs, and other subjects.

13,987. American Association of University Women, Ohio Division
Records. 1924-74. 24 ft.
Access restricted. Unpublished guide.
Ohio Historical Society.
The AAUW's Ohio Division was founded in 1924. Minutes, division reports, correspondence, scrapbooks, and clippings reflect the organization's work in advancing educational opportunities and in seeking to solve community and world problems. At the state level, the Ohio AAUW supported programs relating to juvenile courts and public health.

13,988. Big Sisters Association
Records. 1912-73. 1 ft.
Access restricted. No guide.
Ohio Historical Society.
The Association's Columbus branch, founded in 1912, maintained a home for troubled and needy girls. Minutes, supervisor's reports of the home and Association, histories of the group, photos, an Association yearbook, and clippings. In 1913 Virginia Murray, chief probation officer in the newly organized juvenile court, sought the help of Mrs. Andre Crotte, Mrs. Rutherford H. Platt, and Mrs. William M. Ritter for young girls who came into court, not because of personal misdeeds, but as victims of broken homes and bad companions.

13,989. Camp Fire Girls
Records. 1926-65. 5 ft.
Open. Unpublished guide.
Ohio Historical Society.
The Columbus area Camp Fire Girls Council was chartered in 1925 to provide a recreational program through which girls could develop spiritually, mentally, and physically and to provide opportunities for them to know and cooperate with each other. Annual reports to the National Council, board minutes, scrapbooks, and printed material, including national handbooks. Executive board minutes contain information about public relations, camp programs and activities, adult membership, finances, personnel, and training.

13,990. Casement, Frances Jennings: Suffrage
Papers. 1840-1928. 2.5 ft.
Open. Inventory.
Ohio Historical Society.
Casement was president of the Ohio Woman Suffrage Association from 1884 to 1888. Correspondence from residents of various Ohio cities; letters of Susan B. Anthony; a diary Casement kept from 1883 to 1885; financial and other records of the Ohio Woman Suffrage Association, the National Woman Suffrage Association, the Equal Rights Association, and other suffrage groups; speeches on woman suffrage; a copy of "Random Recollections by Harriet Taylor Upton"; scrapbooks, including a suffrage scrapbook kept by Mrs. William Neil King; blank petitions to the Ohio General Assembly; a pamphlet concerning the education of women in the Western Reserve; copies of *The Woman's Journal, The Woman's Tribune, The Union Signal, The New Northwest, The Philanthropist,* and other periodicals; and other material. On permanent loan to the Historical Society, this collection is the property of the Martha Kinney Cooper Ohioana Library Association.

13,991. Columbus Federation of Business and Professional Women's Clubs
Records. 1920-73. 3 ft.
Open. No guide.
Ohio Historical Society.
The Columbus FBPWC was formed in 1920 from a nucleus provided by the YWCA business girls club; in addition to striving for the betterment of working women, the early club supported establishment of the Columbus Symphony Orchestra and other civic projects. Constitution, president's files, minutes, treasurer's books and reports, membership applications, a history, local programs, photos, clippings, songbooks, and other material.

13,992. Columbus Federation of Women's Clubs
Records. 1898-1976. 3.5 ft.
Partially closed. Unpublished guide.
Ohio Historical Society.
The Federation, which was founded in 1898, promotes friendships among clubwomen and secures their cooperation in educational, civic, and welfare work. Minutes, directories, and yearbooks describe joint and individual club work in projects such as the American National Red Cross, playground recreation, and manual training.

13,993. Columbus Section of The National Council of Jewish Women
Records. 1919- . 10.67 ft.
Open. Inventory.
Ohio Historical Society.
The Columbus Section of the Council, the world's first major Jewish women's group, was founded in 1917, 24 years after Hannah Greenebaum Solomon founded the National Council during the World's Columbian Exposition in Chicago; during its formative years, the Section was involved in activities related to WWI, first aid and Americanization classes, Jewish refugees, the League of Nations, the World Court, and the farm and rural work program. Constitutions, bylaws, advisory board and executive committee minutes and reports, budgets and other financial records, correspondence, speeches, Senate testimony, essays, newsletters, kits of story and broadcast ideas for Council publicity chairmen, and other records. Council members have participated in programs supporting civil rights, community service, national and international relief, public welfare, and women's rights.

13,994. Community Health and Nursing Service
Records. 1898- . 10 ft.
Access restricted. No guide.
Ohio Historical Society.
The Service began as the Instructive District Nursing Association, the first district nursing service in Ohio. Minutes, financial data, a summary of the activities of the State Medical Board nurses examining committee from 1898 to 1960, records of the Columbus Baby Camp from 1908 to 1966, speeches, correspondence, nurses' time books, records of nurses on duty, a history, photos, a scrapbook, and other material. The Nursing Association was founded in 1898 by 18 women who solicited funds and supplies to provide home nursing care for needy families. The association became part of the Columbus Health Department after the city discontinued an appropriation it had given the group for several years.

13,995. Florence Crittenton Services of Columbus
Records. 1908-50. 1 ft.
Open. Unpublished guide.
Ohio Historical Society.
Organized in 1901 as a shelter for unmarried mothers and their children, the agency now emphasizes casework and related social welfare services. Trustees' minutes and a statistical volume, which includes the number of girls in the home, meals served, the number of births, and other information. Originally the agency's program was designed to keep the mother and her child together.

13,996. Hannah Neil Home for Children
Records. 1872-1938. 6 ft.
Access restricted. No guide.
Ohio Historical Society.
Formed in 1858 with Hannah Neil as its first president, the Columbus Female Benevolent Society founded the Hannah Neil Home for Children to help friendless women and children. Executive reports; minutes of the board of managers, corresponding secretary, and recording secretary; treasurer's reports; matron's reports from 1912 to 1935; listing of children proposed for admission; case disposition records; a hostess roster; a membership roll; photos; and a history of the Home. Four women and eight needy children were involved when the Society began its work. In 1862 the group began to meet with poor women to teach them how to keep their homes clean and to offer instruction in religion, morals, manners, and useful work for children. In 1868 the Society raised money for the Hannah Neil Mission and Home of the Friendless, which provided clothing and shelter for destitute local women.

13,997. Hayden, Gillette
Papers. 1917-27. 0.75 ft.
Open. List.
Ohio Historical Society.
An early woman dentist and national president of the Altrusa Club in 1924 and 1925, Hayden (?-1929) maintained a dental practice in Columbus; she also helped introduce methods for the prevention and treatment of periodontic disease in Europe. Her papers contain financial records, correspondence, histories, membership lists, surveys, photos, and clippings of the Altrusa Club, a woman's service club which included one woman from each of the professions; issues of *The Chronicle,* published by the Columbus Business and Professional Women's Club; National Woman's Party records, including constitution, disbursement records, correspondence, membership lists, and clippings; material of the Ohio Council on Women in Industry; maps; and other papers. Hayden graduated from Ohio State University in 1902 and from the graduate dental school at Northwestern University. She opened her practice in Columbus and taught in Europe from 1905 until 1908. Hayden helped organize the American Academy of Periodontology in 1914 and served as its president in 1916; she was president of the Federation of Woman Dentists in 1923 and 1924, as well as an early member of the National Woman's Party.

13,998. Hillsboro Crusade
Records. 1874-82. 1 microfilm reel.
Open. No guide.
Ohio Historical Society.
Minutes of the WCTU of Ohio.

13,999. Hopley Family
Papers. 1860-1957. 65 ft.
Open. Inventory.
Ohio Historical Society.
Correspondence, diaries, and business account books of John Prat Hopley (1821-1904), an Ohio educator, lawyer, postmaster, and editor of the *Bucyrus Evening Telegraph;* his son John Edward Hopley, a prominent Republican who also was editor of the *Telegraph;* and Georgia E. Hopley (1858-1944), a journalist and political worker, who was the daughter of John E. and Georgiana Rochester Hopley. Georgia Hopley worked for the Columbus *Daily Times* for several years and wrote syndicated articles from England from 1908 to 1910. In 1900 and 1901 she was selected to represent Ohio women at the Paris Exposition and on the board of lady managers of the Pan American Exposition in Buffalo, NY. She also worked as chief agent for the Ohio Bureau of Vital Statistics, during which time she attempted to improve conditions for women and children. After her stay in England, Hopley directed women workers in the campaign of Columbus mayor James J. Thomas. She managed the women's campaign for Warren G. Harding in 1920 and became a member of the Ohio State Advisory Committee during Coolidge's presidential campaign. From 1921 to 1924 Hopley was a federal prohibition agent. Her main interests, however, were woman suffrage and temperance; as a journalist and delegate, she attended state, national, and international conventions on these subjects.

14,000. Janney Family
Papers. 1796-1905. 5 ft.
Open. Inventory.
Ohio Historical Society.
Correspondence, diaries, essays, business records, minutes, petitions, and other papers of John Jay Janney (1812-1907), a banker, Republican politician, and Quaker reformer who had antislavery and pro-woman suffrage sentiments; his wife Rebecca Anne Smith Janney (1814-86); and their daughter Frances Janney, later Mrs. Samuel C. Derby. Rebecca Janney called a state suffrage convention that met in Columbus in 1884. Her papers include correspondence with her father, husband, children, other relatives, friends, and fellow reformers such as Julia Ward Howe; letters to the editor; a diary and other personal accounts; records of the state Woman's Suffrage and Temperance Union; an 1872 petition to the Ohio legislature supporting woman suffrage; and other material. Her correspondence concerns family matters and her participation in prison reform, woman suffrage, and other reform movements. Frances (Janney) Derby's papers include a medical certificate dated 1881 from the Homeopathic Medical Society of Ohio, personal and physician's diaries dating from 1878 to 1884, and lecture notebooks.

14,001. Junior League of Columbus
Records. 1926-75. 11 ft.
Open. Unpublished guide.
Ohio Historical Society.
Organized in 1923, the Columbus League coordinated the volunteer service of its members and sought to foster their interest in the community's social, economic, educational, cultural, and civic conditions. Board minutes, project records, program files, membership and attendance records, and scrapbooks contain information about the League's annual fund-raising activity, known as the Bargain Box, and about organizations to which the proceeds were given. Also includes copies of material given to provisional League members.

14,002. League of Women Voters of Metropolitan Columbus
Records. 1919-70. 11 ft.
Open. Unpublished guide.
Ohio Historical Society.
Board minutes, voter information bulletins, scrapbooks, news releases, and other records of the local LWV, the first officers of which were chosen in 1920. Includes files about such topics as investigation of communist activities in northern Ohio, the married woman and her job, child welfare, smoke abatement, the environment, and pollution control.

14,003. League of Women Voters of Ohio
Records. 1903-58. 15 ft.
Open. No guide.
Ohio Historical Society.
The Ohio LWV, founded in 1920, had its headquarters in Columbus. State board minutes, state programs and convention material, platforms, national studies, scrapbooks, yearbooks, and other material.

14,004. Lee, Mary E. (Brown)
Papers. 1893-1948. 2.5 ft.
Open. Inventory.
Ohio Historical Society.
Correspondence of Lee (1869-1952), a politician, chiefly concerns her work for the *Republican Women's Gazette;* politics at the state and local level; her activities as an officer of the Ohio State Grange, the Ohio Landowners' League, the Fish and Game Protective Association, and the League of Ohio Sportsmen; and her friendship with Warren G. and Florence K. Harding.

14,005. Mark, Clara Gould
Papers. 1858-1965. 1 ft.
Open. Unpublished guide.
Ohio Historical Society.
A geologist and paleobotanist, Mark (1882-1966) taught at a number of colleges and universities. Correspondence, lecture notes, geological papers, genealogy, and printed material. Contains Mark's reports on such Ohio topics as the physiography and geology of Fayette County, OH; her lecture notes on such subjects as fossils and evolution, plant and animal classification, erosion, and geological formations; DAR lineage records; information on the history of Westerville, OH; and other historical material.

14,006. Mark, Mary Louise
Papers. 1903-68. 1.5 ft.
Open. No guide.
Ohio Historical Society.
A sociologist, statistician, and author, [Miss] Mark (1878-1975) was a professor of sociology at Ohio State University and in 1927 a staff member of the Brookings Institution Survey of Indian Affairs. Correspondence, Indian Survey notes, financial records, income tax information, charitable contributions, sermons by Mark's father Peter Lewis Mark, coding maps, contracts, and publications. Mark received her BA from Ohio State in 1903 and her MA from Columbia University in 1907. She was a research worker for the US Immigration Commission, the US Bureau of the Census, and the US Bureau of Labor and served as a statistician for the Ohio State Board of Health before joining the Ohio State University faculty in 1914. She attained the rank of full professor in 1923 and was an organizer of the University's school of social administration. During WWI, she was acting chairman of the Ohio Women's Council of Defense committee of women

in industry. She was author or co-author of *Immigrants in the Cities* (1911), *Negroes in Columbus* (1923), *Ten Years of Birth Registration in Ohio* (1926), and *The Problems of Indian Administration* (1928).

14,007. Meekison, Vadae (Harvey)
Papers. 1912-70. 0.5 ft.
Open. Unpublished guide.
Ohio Historical Society.
Correspondence and clippings of [Mrs. George] Meekison (1884-), an attorney who was a longtime friend of Judge Florence Allen and who worked with Allen in the women's suffrage movement in northeastern Ohio. Consists chiefly of correspondence with Allen, which describes the two women's suffrage efforts and Meekison's work for Allen's election to the Ohio Supreme Court in 1922. Other correspondence relates to Allen's appointment to the US Circuit Court of Appeals in 1934, to the appointment of other women to judicial positions, and to meetings of the National Association of Women Lawyers. Also includes biographical material about Meekison and Allen.

14,008. Morrey, Grace (Hamilton)
Papers. 1893-1930. 1 ft.
Open. Unpublished guide.
Ohio Historical Society.
[Mrs. Charles] Morrey (1877-1962) was a concert pianist. Correspondence, biographical material, scrapbook, concert programs, and other papers, including reviews and critiques of her performances. Also contains catalogs for the Grace Hamilton Morrey School of Music and piano instruction material.

14,009. National Organization for Women: Equal Rights Amendment
Records. 1971-74. 1 ft.
Open. Unpublished guide.
Ohio Historical Society.
Newsletters and other publications of the National Organization for Women reflect the group's strategy in support of the Equal Rights Amendment in Ohio. Includes legislation reports, newsletters and literature from state and county NOW chapters, NOW ERA information kits, and other material. The Ohio legislature approved the amendment in 1974.

14,010. Nelson, Amalie (Kraushaar)
Papers. 1930-74. 0.25 ft.
Open. Unpublished guide.
Ohio Historical Society.
[Mrs. George I.] Nelson (1895-), a child psychologist who earned a PhD, was among the founders of Buckeye Boys Ranch, an institution for male offenders, and Friends in Action, an association to help female first offenders. Speeches, biographical data, minutes, honors, awards, and *The Behavior of the Newborn Infant* (ca. 1930) by Nelson, K. Pratt, and K. Sun. Includes board minutes from the Boys Ranch.

14,011. Ohio Coalition for Equal Rights Amendment
Records. 1972-74. 1 ft.
Open. No guide.
Ohio Historical Society.
Correspondence, voting records of state legislators, statements and testimony in support of the Equal Rights Amendment, material from the Ohio Commission on the Status of Women, promotional items, and clippings.

14,012. Ohio Commission on the Status of Women
Records. 1970. 0.5 ft.
Open. No guide.
Ohio Historical Society.
President's reports, minutes, corporation and financial records, publications, and other material of the Commission.

14,013. Planned Parenthood of Central Ohio
Records. 1932-69. 3.5 ft.
Access restricted. No guide.
Ohio Historical Society.
The group was founded in ca. 1932 as the Mother's Health Association, Planned Parenthood of Central Ohio. Incorporation records; minutes of Planned Parenthood, Region IV; correspondence; subject files for the Region, many of which concern family planning in Ohio's Appalachian area; mothers' letters requesting birth control information; and scrapbooks containing clippings and early Planned Parenthood publications.

14,014. Reynolds, Clara (Geer)
Papers. 1924-49. 1 ft.
Open. Unpublished guide.
Ohio Historical Society.
The first woman to sell real estate in Ohio, [Mrs. Clyde] Reynolds (1893-1976) was active in the Republican Women's Club and the National Woman's party; she also worked as a secretary for Viola Romans. Correspondence, scrapbooks, and clippings relate to her activities in the Republican party, to her interest in animals, and to other subjects.

14,015. Romans, Viola (Doudna)
Papers. 1901-46. 2 ft.
Open. Unpublished guide.
Ohio Historical Society.
[Mrs. C. D.] Romans (1863-1946), a public speaker, lecturer, and traveler, was a state assemblywoman from 1924 to 1928, president of the Women's Republican Club of Ohio in 1931, and president of the Ohio WCTU from 1932 to 1937. Speeches, annual programs, radio scripts, pamphlets, clippings, and scattered correspondence concerning the WCTU, women's suffrage, and the Women's Republican Club. Also includes some family correspondence and documents, including genealogical information. Romans, who promoted women's suffrage and temperance, authored important welfare legislation. She secured an appropriation for expansion of the Woman's Reformatory at Marysville, OH, and passage of a law providing educational and vocational training for women there.

14,016. Schildhouse, Ruth
Papers. 1961-73. 6 ft.
Open. Unpublished guide.
Ohio Historical Society.
Schildhouse (1927-) is active in the LWV, education groups, and the International Program for Social Workers. Correspondence, minutes, reports, resolutions, and printed material deal with the LWV, mass transit, urban education, tax revision, and governmental reform.

14,017. Scientific Temperance Federation
Records. 1881-ca. 1936. 25 ft.
Access restricted. Published guide.
Ohio Historical Society.
Organized in 1906 to centralize temperance education in the US, the Federation gathered scientific data about alcohol and its effect on the human body and disseminated the information through articles, pamphlets, books, and instruction in the schools. National and state officers' files, correspondence, biographical data, scientific temperance instruction surveys, and scrapbooks. Includes papers of several women active in the temperance movement, among them Anna A. Gordon, Mary Hannah Hunt, Lillian M. N. Stevens, Cora Frances Stoddard, Emma L. Transeau, Frances E. Willard, and Annie Wittenmyer. Also available on microfilm. See R. C. Jimerson, F. X. Blouin, and C. A. Isetts, eds., *Guide to the Microfilm Edition of Temperance and Prohibition Papers* (Ann Arbor, MI: University of Michigan, 1977).

14,018. Thompson, Delia
Papers. 1884-87. 28 items.
Open. No guide.
Ohio Historical Society.
A WCTU missionary in Columbus from 1884 to 1888, Thompson (?-1918) was a founder of the Sunday school that grew into the Union Grove Baptist Church of Columbus. Papers include Thompson's missionary reports to the WCTU.

14,019. Webb, Tessa (Sweazy)
Papers. 1925-76. 1.5 ft.
Open. Unpublished guide.
Ohio Historical Society.
Correspondence, poetry pamphlets, clippings, and printed matter of [Mrs. Reuben H.] Webb (1885-), a poet who was the founder of Ohio Poetry Day. Includes material describing procedures and legislation involved in the establishment in 1938 of Ohio Poetry Day.

14,020. West Side and Ohio Avenue Day Care Centers
Records. 1892-1964. 4 ft.
Open. No guide.
Ohio Historical Society.
The Centers were founded after the Women's Education and Industrial Union decided in 1889 that a nursery was needed for children whose mothers could not care for them properly. Annual reports, board minutes, financial records, photos, a history of day nurseries written by Mrs. David Beggs, and a constitution and reports of the Women's Union. A new organization with Beggs as its president was formed in ca. 1892 to manage the day-care centers. In 1902 the Ohio Avenue Day Nursery was founded after a teacher reported that many neighborhood children had to stay home from school to care for younger children while their mothers worked. A new nursery, made possible by a bequest from [Miss] Catherine Tuttle, was built in 1917.

14,021. Women's Action Collective
Records. 1971-74. 0.25 ft.
Open. Unpublished guide.
Ohio Historical Society.
The Collective was founded in the Ohio State University area in 1971 to create women's task forces for community action projects. Minutes, a history, newsletters, and broadsides provide information about such groups as the Women's Cooperative Garage, the Women's Health Action Collective, the Women's Libraries and Publishing Group, Women Against Rape, the Women's Creative Arts Cooperative, the Legal Action Group, the Share-a-Job Committee, and the Women's Prison Solidarity Committee. A report describes the activities of the groups, their projected budgets, and their potential for becoming self-sufficient.

14,022. Women's Association of Commerce
Records. 1930-63. 0.25 ft.
Open. Unpublished guide.
Ohio Historical Society.
Minutes and financial records of the Association, which was founded in 1912 and was the oldest service club in Columbus. The business and professional women who made up the group's membership sought to help the city solve its civic, industrial, and governmental problems and to assist women in business and the community. The organization was involved in the Community Fund, the Civic Center, the Columbus Motion Picture Council, and other projects. The Association was disbanded in 1963.

14,023. Women's Equity Action League
Records. 1968-74. 3 ft.
Open. Unpublished guide.
Ohio Historical Society.
Founded in Cleveland in 1968, WEAL is dedicated to improving economic opportunities for women, to

combating job discrimination against women, and to gathering and disseminating information and educational material. Bylaws, board records, subject files, correspondence, and other records relate to the group's work in affirmative action, careers for women, civil rights, day care, divorce reform, education, employment, the Equal Rights Amendment, and other areas. Some of the material reflects women's changing attitudes toward such issues as abortion.

14,024. Women's Music Club
Records. 1882-1974. 3 ft.
Open. No guide.
Ohio Historical Society.
Organized in 1882 by trained musicians at the home of [Miss] Mary Failing, this group was known initially as the Ladies' Musical Club. Board minutes, financial records, correspondence, a history of the group, yearbooks concerning the group's programs for 1882, Club calendars, programs, clippings, and copies of the Club's official bulletin, *The Newsletter.* The Club assumed its current name in 1905.

14,025. Women's State Committee of Ohio for Public Welfare, Health and Education
Records. 1937-74. 0.75 ft.
Open. Unpublished guide.
Ohio Historical Society.
Created in 1928 and disbanded in 1974, the Committee provided its member groups and individuals with information about state legislation and programs concerning public welfare, health, and education. Minutes, correspondence, and a history of the Committee. The minutes include notes on guest speakers and focus on prison reform, juvenile institutions, mental health care, and other topics.

14,026. Worrell, Ruth Mougey, Family
Papers. 1815-1965. 3 ft.
Open. Inventory.
Ohio Historical Society.
Worrell (1882-?), a writer and producer of pageants, was among the founders of the national United Council of Church Women in 1941. Files on pageant productions, a copy of Worrell's pageant about the struggle of women, source material, reminiscences, a genealogy, a scrapbook, family portraits, and a teaching certificate. Also includes manuals and executive secretary's reports of the United Council of Church Women, for which Worrell served as executive secretary from 1942 to 1947, and items concerning the Women's Home Missionary Society's work in the South during Reconstruction. Worrell graduated from King's School of Oratory in 1901 and became a teacher of public speaking at Ohio University. She married Charles Peters Worrell, a banker. In 1910, Ruth Worrell became a pioneer in religious pageantry, writing and producing pageants for many denominations and groups. She worked as an American National Red Cross staff member in Washington, DC, from 1920 to 1922; was employed by the Methodist Church board of foreign missions from 1924 to 1932; and served as a hostess in the Hall of Religion at the Century of Progress International Exposition in Chicago in 1934.

14,027. Young Women's Christian Association
Records. 1869-1969. 22 ft.
Open. Unpublished guide.
Ohio Historical Society.
Annual reports, minutes, budget reports, historical records, inventories, scrapbooks, and menus of the Columbus YWCA, formed in 1910, reflect local, national, and international YWCA activities, including day-care and senior citizens programs and work of the religious resources committee.

14,028. Alpha Lambda Delta
Records. 1945-71. 1 cu.ft.
Open. Inventory.
Ohio State University Archives.
Constitution; annual reports, 1945-69; minutes; four financial reports; a history of the group; photos; scrapbooks; a handbook from 1970; and newsletters of this freshmen women's scholastic honorary society. Includes information about national and district officers.

14,029. Chimes
Records. 1917-66. 1 cu.ft.
Open. Inventory.
Ohio State University Archives.
Organized in 1918, Chimes is an honorary society made up of women in their junior year of college. Members are selected on the basis of leadership, service, and personality. Constitution, treasurer's reports, financial statements, correspondence, a history of the organization at Ohio State University from 1929 to 1958, convention reports, and other records of the OSU chapter. Also contains a constitution, annual reports, president's reports, financial statements, correspondence, publications, other material of the national Chimes organization and material of the following individual chapters: Bradley University in Peoria, IL; Butler University in Indianapolis; Idaho State College in Pocatello, ID; the Iowa State Teacher's College in Cedar Falls, IA; Kansas State University in Manhattan, KS; Temple University in Philadelphia; the University of Arizona in Tucson, AZ; the University of California, Los Angeles; the University of California, Santa Barbara College; the University of Minnesota; the University of Southern California; Washington University in St. Louis; and West Virginia University in Morgantown, WV.

14,030. Mortar Board
Records. 1914-69. 4 cu.ft.
Open. Inventory.
Ohio State University Archives.
Mortar Board is a senior women's scholastic, leadership, and service society that was organized secretly on the Ohio State University campus in 1914. OSU was among the founding chapters of the national Mortar Board organization in 1918. Annual reports, minutes, treasurer's reports, financial statements, expense accounts, correspondence, convention reports and proceedings, a history of the group in 1914, photos of alumnae and others, songs, and Ohio State University annual reports and alumnae meetings information. Also includes information about the national Mortar Board organization; Mortar Board chapters at the universities of Wisconsin, Louisville, and Connecticut; racial equality in Mortar Board; charter members; and initiation ceremonies.

14,031. Ohio State University Mother's Association
Records. 1939-69. 2 cu.ft.
Open. Inventory.
Ohio State University Archives.
Constitution; constitutional revisions; annual reports, 1954-67; minutes; correspondence of state and local officers; monthly letters; student survival kit material, 1962-67; and other records of this social and service organization. Includes information about alumni workshops, scholarships, speakers, a winter workshop in 1967, and officers.

14,032. Ohio Women's Club
Records. 1895-1960. 1 cu.ft.
Open. Inventory.
Ohio State University Archives.
The Club, organized in about 1895, was a social organization that undertook some service activities. Constitution; bylaws; minutes; financial reports, 1926-30 and 1935; correspondence; historical material; records of the student loan fund, 1934-47; scrapbooks; and programs. Contains information about a 1933 minstrel show.

14,033. Paterson Hall
Records. 1956-68. 2 cu.ft.
Open. Inventory.
Ohio State University Archives.
The Hall was a women's dormitory at Ohio State University. Reports of Hall presidents, treasurer's reports, research studies using Paterson students as subjects, maintenance reports, notes and other material for journalism and other classes, student theses, residence hall manuals, brochures, pamphlets, and other items. Contains information about medical technology, nursing programs, the Peace Corps, personnel conferences, placement service, scholarships, standards committee, occupancy statistics for 1958, student assistants and advisees, student government, the student personnel assistant program, and new student meetings. Also includes material of the student senators who deal with public relations, religion, and sports.

14,034. Philomathean Literary Society
Records. 1894-1971. 2 cu.ft.
Open. Inventory.
Ohio State University Archives.
The organization, a woman's literary society, was founded on the Ohio State University campus in 1894. Constitution; minutes; financial records; general correspondence; a history of the Society, written in 1933; initiation records, 1917-44; membership lists, 1894-1945; essays; autobiographies; short stories; poetry; tryout material; a yearbook; book reviews; and clippings.

14,035. University Dames
Records. 1912-74. 3 cu.ft.
Open. Inventory.
Ohio State University Archives.
Constitution; reports of the chairperson; minutes; finance committee and treasurer's reports; receipts and disbursements; correspondence of presidents and others; reports concerning charity work, interest groups, teas, and the sewing group; a history of the group, written in 1912; scrapbooks of the scholarship committee; lists of names and addresses for officers from 1961 to 1972; directories; "Dames Digest," 1955-71; a cookbook; programs; publicity; clippings; and other records of this women's social organization. Contains information about elections, the nomination committee, initiation, installation, parliamentary procedures, secretary's duties, and the Dames' sports activities. Also contains yearbooks and other material of the National Association of University Dames.

14,036. University Women's Club
Records. 1895-1973. 3 cu. ft.
Open. Inventory.
Ohio State University Archives.
The Club was a social and service organization founded in about 1895. Constitution, amendments, and bylaws; treasurers' annual reports, from 1941-68, and other treasurer's reports, 1923-65; reports of the officer coordinator and publicity chairman; reports concerning 1971 art shows; daily logs, 1971-73; calendars of the drama, literature, and music groups; photos; newsletters; obituaries; clippings; and other records.

14,037. Women's Panhellenic Association
Records. 1915-67. 2 cu.ft.
Open. Inventory.
Ohio State University Archives.
Annual reports, minutes, secretary and treasurer's reports, correspondence, reports, and other records. Includes information on fall sorority recruitment, financial charges, Greek Week, human relations in Panhellenic, international students, organization and administration of the student leadership recognition dinner, the Panhellenic commission,

and the Panhellenic council. Also includes sorority news articles.

14,038. Women's Self Government Association
Records. 1914-67. 3 cu.ft.
Open. Inventory.
Ohio State University Archives.
The Association, founded in about 1908, oversaw the self-government of Ohio State University's women students. Constitution, minutes, correspondence, reports, and pamphlets. Includes a history of the Association from 1908 to 1957; a survey and report concerning academic honesty; big sister committee, Coed Week, and organizational reports; records of the dean of women, 1938-45; information concerning the continuing education of women and University promotion committees, the Women's Council, and the WSGA Club, a group related to a cooperative house on campus; handbooks and manuals for women students and freshmen; and programs of the May Fete.

14,039. Mosher, Cynthia
Papers. 1865-68. No size given.
Access restricted. No guide.
Ohioana Library Association.
Letters exchanged by Mosher of Cardington, OH, and Alden Moore, a Civil War soldier, during the period before their marriage.

14,040. Woman's Press Club of Cincinnati
Records. 1890-1918. No size given.
Access restricted. No guide.
Ohioana Library Association.
Programs.

14,041. Sharp, Thelma Fern
Papers. 1960-66. 2 ft.
Open. No guide.
Public Library of Columbus and Franklin County, Columbus and Ohio Division.
Fern Sharp (1898-1975) was a commentator for Ohio's first radio program devoted exclusively to women; she was associated with the program from 1937 to 1967. She also worked as a television commentator and as a columnist for the Columbus *Dispatch.* Consists of program schedules for "Sharp Comments" and "Round Robin Review."

DAYTON

14,042. Woman's Suffrage Association
Records. 1912-18. 1 box and 1 vol.
Open. No guide.
Dayton and Montgomery County Public Library.
Minutes, financial records, and a scrapbook of the Association, which was founded in 1912. The Association branch in Dayton and Montgomery County later became a unit of the LWV.

14,043. Young Women's League
Records. 1895-1952. 2 ft.
Open. Unpublished guide.
Montgomery County Historical Society.
Formed in 1895 and incorporated in 1898, the League was a social club designed to promote the spiritual, moral, mental, and physical welfare of Dayton women, particularly young working women. Financial records, photos, scrapbooks, and publications of the group, which was open to all women regardless of religion. Dues were $1 per year. Many joined the League for its classes, which included French, sewing, art, and other subjects, while others enjoyed the use of the League's library, living room, rest rooms, and bath facilities or wanted "to be part of a good piece of work." The League provided a tea room, summer vacation camp, gymnasium, and boarding house for its members as well as a public cafeteria. The League supported a halfway house to help city policewomen handle women who were on parole; the house later came under the control of the city welfare department. The League ceased operation in 1970.

14,044. Salem Heights Archives
Records. 1834- . Ca. 100 ft.
Open. No guide.
Sisters of the Precious Blood.
This order, the members of which are involved in education and social work, was founded in 1834 in Switzerland and established in the US in 1844. Administrative and financial records, correspondence, biographical and historical accounts, notes, tapes, photos, reports, slides, memorabilia, and other records.

14,045. American Legion Woman's Auxiliary Post 330
Records. 1921-24. 1 folder.
Open. No guide.
Wright State University Archives and Special Collections.
Minutes of this Auglaize County women's group.

14,046. Cox, James M.
Papers. 1913-60. 20 ft.
Open. No guide.
Wright State University Archives and Special Collections.
Correspondence, clippings, and other papers of Cox (1870-1957), a newspaper publisher, member of the US House of Representatives, Ohio governor, and Democratic presidential candidate in 1920, and of his wife Margaretta Cox (?-1960). Includes information about Margaretta Cox's contributions to charities as well as clippings and correspondence about her death. Also includes letters from many women involved in journalism, literature, and politics, among them Charlotte Reeve Conover, an historian; Betty Dietz, a journalist; Alice M. Doren of the League of Nations Non-Partisan Association; Charlotte Emmons of the Dayton *Daily News;* Helen Douglas Mankin, a congresswoman; Anne Mergen, a cartoonist; Margaret Mitchell, an author; and Eleanor Roosevelt.

14,047. Dayton Ballet Company and Dayton Civic Ballet
Records. 1924-74. 15 ft.
Open. No guide.
Wright State University Archives and Special Collections.
The Dayton Ballet Company, the second oldest regional ballet company in the US, grew from the Experimental Group for Young Dancers, which was founded in 1931 by Josephine and Hermene Schwarz. Minutes, financial records, correspondence, recital programs and records, tour records, scrapbooks, costume sketches, and other records. The Schwarzes also own the Schwarz School of the Dance, the official school for the Ballet Company. The Company's troupe is made up of about 30 individuals who are selected through auditions. Organized in 1937, the Company is supported by the Dayton Civic Ballet, Inc., a nonprofit corporation.

14,048. Montgomery County Probate Court, Record of Midwives Certificates
Records. 1896-1917. 1 vol.
Open. Card catalog.
Wright State University Archives and Special Collections.
Volume includes names of Montgomery County women who received midwife certificates from the State Board of Medical Registration and Examination.

14,049. Montgomery County Probate Court, Record of Registered Nurses
Records. 1916-45. 2 vols.
Open. No guide.
Wright State University Archives and Special Collections.
Records of Montgomery County women who were registered as nurses by the state medical board.

14,050. Newberry: League of Women Voters
Papers. 1955-72. 4 records center boxes.
Open. No guide.
Wright State University Archives and Special Collections.
[Mrs.] Jane Newberry was the chairman of the Dayton LWV. Notes, membership lists, fact sheets, programs, pamphlets, meeting notes from newspapers, and other papers.

14,051. Public Health Nursing Service
Records. 1898-1970. 12 vols.
Open. Index.
Wright State University Archives and Special Collections.
Founded in 1898 as the Fruit and Flower Mission to furnish gifts for hospital patients, the group became involved in public health nursing in Dayton and Montgomery County after changing its name to the Visiting Nurses Association in 1913. Articles of incorporation, board of directors' reports, historical material, photos, and clippings.

14,052. Thompson, Glenn
Papers. 1952-74. 9 ft.
Open. Unpublished guide.
Wright State University Archives and Special Collections.
Correspondence, records of organizations, memoranda, speeches, photos, news releases, and other papers of Thompson, retired editor of the Dayton *Journal Herald.* Includes minutes, memoranda, correspondence, committee membership lists, reports, and other records of the LWV. The LWV material concerns the Ohio Conservation Association, a workshop on air quality standards, a survey of the Ohio River basin, and other ecology-related topics and projects.

14,053. United Spanish War Veterans Auxiliaries 8 and 40
Records. 1904-49. 1 Hollinger box.
Open. No guide.
Wright State University Archives and Special Collections.
Bylaws, minutes, and a roster of officers of the auxiliaries, which were founded in 1904 to aid veterans and their families and to promote patriotism.

14,054. Woman's Relief Corps
Records. 1902-33. 1 Hollinger box.
Open. Unpublished guide.
Wright State University Archives and Special Collections.
Minutes, treasurer's reports, a cashbook, a ledger, and general orders of Kyle Corps No. 195 in Wapakoneta, OH, which was organized in 1902 and disbanded in 1933. A chapter of the national Woman's Relief Corps (organized in 1882), the Kyle Corps was open to all women who supported the Grand Army of the Republic in its effort to foster patriotism and perpetuate the memory of those who died in the Civil War. The Corps supported placement of American flags in all schools and daily flag salutes in each schoolroom.

14,055. Wright Brothers
Papers. 1857-1969. 36 ft.
Open. Unpublished guide.
Wright State University Archives and Special Collections.
Correspondence, diaries, financial records, photos, pamphlets, clippings, and other papers of the family of Wilbur Wright (1867-1912) and Orville Wright (1871-1948), co-inventors of the airplane. Includes letters from the brothers' mother Susan Koerner Wright to her husband Milton Wright.

FREMONT

14,056. Abbey, Matilda Ormond (Taylor) Birchard
Papers. 1888-89. 4 items.
Open. Inventory.
Rutherford B. Hayes Library.
Letters from Abbey, an author, to Rutherford B. Hayes concerning her books on Tracy family genealogy.

14,057. American Association of University Women
Records. 1934-76. 1 box.
Open. Inventory.
Rutherford B. Hayes Library.
Minute books, correspondence, booklets, and books of this local AAUW chapter.

14,058. Ames, Mary (Clemmer)
Papers. 1859-81. 0.5 ft.
Open. Inventory.
Rutherford B. Hayes Library.
[Mrs. Daniel] Ames (1831-84) was an author of biographies, novels, poems, and newspaper columns. Correspondence, including letters from Mary Louise Booth, Sarah M. V. Dahlgren, and Nora Perry; manuscripts of her poem "Something Beyond" and other works; biographical data; and clippings. Ames wrote a column from Washington, DC, for the New York City *Independent* from 1869 to 1884 and a column for the *Brooklyn Daily Union* from 1869 to 1872. Her other works include *Eirene, or a Woman's Right* (1871); *Memorial of Alice and Phoebe Cary* (1873); *Outlines of Men, Women, and Things* (1873); and *Ten Years in Washington* (1873).

14,059. Belden, Anne E., Family
Papers. 1826-1904. 3.33 ft.
Open. Inventory.
Rutherford B. Hayes Library.
Correspondence includes letters from members of the Allerton, Belden, Belding, Crosby, DeForest, Green, Ketchan, Mabbett, Perry, Powers, Stanton, and Stevens families.

14,060. Bigelow, Hayes, Family
Papers. 1842-1923. 7.5 ft.
Open. Inventory.
Rutherford B. Hayes Library.
Correspondence, diaries, photos, scrapbooks, pamphlets, books, and memorabilia of Bigelow (1879-1956), a citrus grower from 1890 to 1926 and a photographer from 1926 to 1956; his mother Mary Ann (Hayes) Bigelow (1838-1925), who was a cousin of Rutherford B. Hayes; Russell A. Bigelow; Jennie (Hayes) Field; Russell Hayes; Rutherford Hayes, Sr.; and the Pomeroy family.

14,061. Billau, Harriet
Papers. 1896-1948. 6 ft.
Open. Inventory.
Rutherford B. Hayes Library.
Billau (1868-1956), an officer of Fremont women's clubs, collected material about art, music, literature, life in Fremont, and other subjects. Manuscripts, scrapbooks, clippings, and memorabilia.

14,062. Claflin, William
Papers. 1831-1905. 12 ft.
Open. Inventory.
Rutherford B. Hayes Library.
Claflin (1818-1905) was a Massachusetts state senator, governor, and US congressman; his wife Mary Bucklin (Davenport) Claflin (1825-96) was an author. Correspondence, chiefly relating to business, political, literary, and religious matters, includes letters from Lyman Abbott, Henry W. Beecher, Sarah O. Jewett, Harriet Beecher Stowe, [Miss] Clara Barton, Kate N. Doggett, Margaret Deland, [Miss] Kate Field, Julia Ward Howe, Helen Hunt Jackson, Lucy Larcom, Mary A. Livermore, Louise (Chandler) Moulton, Lucy Stone, and Elizabeth Stuart (Phelps) Ward.

14,063. Congenial Circle of King's Daughters, Mary Fitch Circle
Records. 1914-70. 0.5 ft.
Open. Inventory.
Rutherford B. Hayes Library.
Records of activities of the Circle, a member of the Ohio branch of the International Order of the King's Daughters and Sons. The Circle was formed in 1914 and was concerned with welfare.

14,064. Cosmopolitan Club
Records. 1895-1975. 1 ft.
Open. Inventory.
Rutherford B. Hayes Library.
Secretary's and treasurer's reports, reminiscences, and programs of the Club, a local women's literary group founded in 1895.

14,065. Coterie Club
Records. 1917-75. 1 ft.
Open. Inventory.
Rutherford B. Hayes Library.
Secretary's books and program booklets of the Club, a local women's literary group organized in 1895.

14,066. Daughters of the American Revolution, George Croghan Chapter
Records. 1900-70. 3 ft.
Open. Inventory.
Rutherford B. Hayes Library.
Secretary's and treasurer's reports, programs, and a history of the local Chapter, which was founded in 1900.

14,067. Fremont Federation of Women's Clubs
Records. 1903-75. 10 boxes.
Open. No guide.
Rutherford B. Hayes Library.
Founded in 1903, the Federation is an organization of local women's clubs. Correspondence, photos, scrapbooks, programs, yearbooks, and clippings provide information about a number of local women's organizations and activities. The Federation provides the clubhouse for meetings of various groups. Membership is open to individuals and clubs.

14,068. Fremont Garden Club
Records. 1932-66. 0.75 ft.
Open. Inventory.
Rutherford B. Hayes Library.
Secretary's reports, a scrapbook, and programs of the Club, which was organized in 1932.

14,069. Fremont Matinee Musical Club
Records. 1919-35. 1 ft.
Open. No guide.
Rutherford B. Hayes Library.
The Club was founded in 1895 by [Miss] Ellouise Waters to improve the musical knowledge of members and to advance musical interests in Fremont. Minute books, scrapbooks of clippings and programs, and yearbooks.

14,070. Grand Army of the Republic, Department of Ohio, Woman's Relief Corps, C. G. Eaton Corps No. 188
Records. 1887-1958. 1.33 ft.
Open. Inventory.
Rutherford B. Hayes Library.
Minutes, accounts, and membership rolls of the Clyde, OH, unit of the Corps, a welfare organization. The Clyde chapter was formed in 1887.

14,071. Grant, Dickinson, and Butman Family
Papers. 1833-1914. 0.75 ft.
Open. Inventory.
Rutherford B. Hayes Library.
Correspondence of Statira (Dickinson) Grant and her family in New York with Sarah Jane Grant and Sardis Birchard provides information on family incidents and contemporary social, travel, and business interests. Also includes photos and memorabilia.

14,072. Harrington, Purnell F.
Papers. 1879-1920. 0.5 ft.
Open. No guide.
Rutherford B. Hayes Library.
Correspondence of Harrington (1844-1937), a naval officer from 1863 to 1906; his wife Maria (Ruan) Harrington; and their children. Harrington held the rank of rear admiral from 1903 to 1906.

14,073. Hayes, Chloe Smith
Papers. 1824-45. 2 vols.
Open. No guide.
Rutherford B. Hayes Library.
Diaries of Hayes (1762-1847), the grandmother of Rutherford B. Hayes.

14,074. Hayes, Frances
Papers. 1878-1950. 2 ft.
Open. Inventory.
Rutherford B. Hayes Library.
Papers of Hayes (1867-1950), daughter of President Rutherford B. Hayes, contain correspondence; diaries; notebooks and school records; account, address, and autograph books; photos; scrapbooks; and clippings.

14,075. Hayes, Lucy Ware (Webb)
Papers. 1841-90. 8 ft.
Open. Inventory.
Rutherford B. Hayes Library.
[Mrs. Rutherford B.] Hayes (1831-89), a civic leader and philanthropist, was the first President's wife to hold a college degree. Correspondence, account books, school essays, tributes, photos, and clippings. Many of the letters concern Hayes's interest in women's missionary societies of the Methodist Episcopal Church, the WCTU, the Ohio Soldiers' and Sailors' Orphans Home in Xenia, and other benevolent organizations.

14,076. Hayes, Mary (Miller)
Papers. 1878-1935. 9 ft.
Open. Inventory.
Rutherford B. Hayes Library.
Hayes (1856-1935), the wife of Webb C. Hayes I, was a civic leader and philanthropist. Correspondence and other papers concern family matters, her business investments, her American National Red Cross work, and her philanthropies.

14,077. Hayes, Rutherford B.
Papers. 1835-93. 170 ft.
Open. Card catalog.
Rutherford B. Hayes Library.
Papers of Hayes (1822-93), a lawyer, soldier, US congressman, Ohio governor, and President, include correspondence with women and provide information on women in prisons, suffrage, the WCTU, women's medical colleges, and other topics. Correspondence; speeches; account books and financial records; campaign and political notebooks; school and college notes; real estate, military, and estate records; photos; scrapbooks; maps; and other items.

14,078. Hayes, Sophia Birchard
Papers. 1846-66. 2 vols.
Open. No guide.
Rutherford B. Hayes Library.
Correspondence, diaries, and other papers of Hayes (1792-1866), the mother of Rutherford B. Hayes.

14,079. Heyl, Elizabeth (Mitchell)
Papers. 1837-1949. 3 ft.
Open. Inventory.
Rutherford B. Hayes Library.
Heyl (1864-1956) was the niece of Rutherford B. Hayes. Correspondence dealing with family

matters includes letters from her mother Laura (Platt) Mitchell, Fanny Hayes, Fanny Heyl, and her grandmother. Also includes photos.

14,080. Howells, William D.
Papers. 1856-1947. 3 ft. and 3 microfilm reels.
Open. Inventory.
Rutherford B. Hayes Library.
Correspondence, manuscripts, a genealogy, biographical material, and photos of Howells (1837-1920), an author, editor, and journalist. Includes correspondence of Howells's wife Elinor Gertrude (Mead) Howells, his sister Annie (Howells) Frechette, Hayes family members, and others. Also includes letters from Richard S. Hinton to Aurelia and Victoria Howells and literary manuscripts of Howells's sister-in-law Mrs. Joseph Howells. Howells edited the *Atlantic Monthly* from 1871 to 1881.

14,081. Izant, Grace Goulder
Papers. 1964. 0.33 ft.
Open. No guide.
Rutherford B. Hayes Library.
Izant was an author and columnist for the Cleveland *Plain Dealer*. Manuscript of her book *This Is Ohio* (Cleveland: World Publishing Company, 1964).

14,082. Keeler, Lucy Elliot
Papers. 1879-1931. 6 ft.
Open. Inventory.
Rutherford B. Hayes Library.
Keeler (1864-1930) was a journalist associated with *Youth's Companion* from 1896 to 1911, a secretary at the Birchard library in Fremont from 1915 to 1930, and a local historian. Correspondence, diaries from 1879 to 1929, notebooks, local historical and genealogical notes and papers, manuscripts of her writings, photo albums, and obituaries.

14,083. Ladies' Relief Society
Records. 1878-1953. 0.25 ft.
Open. Inventory.
Rutherford B. Hayes Library.
Accounts and other records of the Society, a local welfare group organized in 1855.

14,084. Leech, Margaret K.
Papers. 1959. 2 boxes.
Open. No guide.
Rutherford B. Hayes Library.
Manuscript and galley proofs of *In the Days of McKinley* (New York: Harper and Brothers, 1959) by Leech, an author.

14,085. Lossing, Benson J.
Papers. 1838-91. 12 ft.
Open. Inventory.
Rutherford B. Hayes Library.
Correspondence, diaries, notes, accounts, scrapbooks, artwork, and albums of Lossing (1813-91), an editor, publisher, author, and illustrator. Includes correspondence and a bankbook of Lossing's wife Helen (Sweet) Lossing.

14,086. McCandless, Lucy (Cook)
Papers. 1880-98. 1 box.
Open. Inventory.
Rutherford B. Hayes Library.
McCandless (1851-1902), the cousin of Lucy (Webb) Hayes, was the granddaughter of Ohio's first governor Edward Tiffin. Correspondence, a partial diary, legal records, accounts, and photos.

14,087. McClintock, Helen A.
Papers. 1922-54. 2 boxes.
Open. No guide.
Rutherford B. Hayes Library.
McClintock, who lived in Fremont, was a local historian. Notes and clippings about local history and residents.

14,088. McCulloch Family
Papers. 1785-1906. 3 ft.
Open. Inventory.
Rutherford B. Hayes Library.
Correspondence, school notes, photos, recipes, music, Christmas and valentine cards, clippings, and other items; most of the papers were collected by the children of C. R. McCulloch (1825-1912), a Fremont druggist, and his wife Rhoda McCulloch (1826-1905). The children, Fannie, Margaret, Rollin S., Josephine, and Julia, collected memorabilia relating to family friends and events and to their personal interests.

14,089. Ohlinger, Franklin
Papers. 1862-1919. 2.33 ft. and 4 microfilm reels.
Open. Inventory.
Rutherford B. Hayes Library.
Ohlinger (1845-1919) and his wife Bertha (Schweinfurth) Ohlinger (1856-1934) were missionaries to China from 1876 to 1886 and from 1895 to 1911 and to Korea from 1887 to 1893. Correspondence, sermons, photos, clippings, and books provide an account of these missionaries' lives in China. The Ohlingers established the Trilingual Press in Korea and the Anglo-Chinese College in Foochow, China.

14,090. Platt, Fanny Arabella (Hayes)
Papers. 1837-56. 2 vols.
Open. Index.
Rutherford B. Hayes Library.
Platt (1820-56) was the sister of President Rutherford B. Hayes. School notebook and a volume of her letters that Rutherford Hayes compiled following his sister's death.

14,091. Schwartz, Frances E.
Papers. 1907-33. 3 boxes.
Open. No guide.
Rutherford B. Hayes Library.
Correspondence, notes, and accounts of Schwartz (1877-1937), who was secretary to Webb C. Hayes I and his wife Mary (Miller) Hayes.

14,092. Scott, Anna Margaret (Tressler)
Papers. 1880-1953. 0.5 ft.
Open. Inventory.
Rutherford B. Hayes Library.
Scott (1850-1922) was secretary of the Illinois State Testimonial Committee, which commended Lucy (Webb) Hayes for not serving alcoholic beverages at the White House. Correspondence, minutes, accounts, photos, pamphlets, clippings, and memorabilia consist primarily of Committee records. A few pamphlets on the Tressler and Scott families are included.

14,093. Snead, Fayette C., and Snead, Maria Austine
Papers. 1873-89. 7 boxes and 4 vols.
Open. No guide.
Rutherford B. Hayes Library.
Fayette Snead was a journalist for the *Louisville Courier Journal.* Her daughter Maria Austine Snead (?-1888) was a journalist who worked for the *New York Daily Graphic,* the *Washington Star,* the *Louisville Courier Journal,* the *Boston Globe,* and other newspapers. Magazine and newspaper articles by Fayette and Maria Austine Snead. Also includes letters written to Rutherford B. Hayes.

14,094. Sorosis Club
Records. 1897-1955. 2 boxes.
Open. No guide.
Rutherford B. Hayes Library.
Correspondence, programs, speeches, and other papers read before the Club, a local women's literary group founded in 1894.

14,095. Sprunk, Mrs. Raymond
Papers. 1857-1929. 10 vols.
Open. Inventory.
Rutherford B. Hayes Library.
Iva Sprunk, a local historian, is active in projects concerning the heritage of Fremont. Manuscripts, photos, pamphlets, books, and memorabilia. Includes manuscripts of Lucy Elliot Keeler.

14,096. Thomas, Katherine Garford
Papers. 1949. 1 box.
Open. No guide.
Rutherford B. Hayes Library.
An author, Thomas (1883-) has been active in cultural and civic affairs in Elyria, OH. Manuscript of her book *Auntie Kate* (Columbus, OH: Ohio History Press, Ohio State Archaeological and Historical Society, 1949), which concerns her aunt Katherine Moody Smith. Thomas has published poems in various periodicals and in a poetry volume.

14,097. United States Daughters of 1812
Records. 1900-67. 10 boxes.
Open. Inventory.
Rutherford B. Hayes Library.
The Ohio chapter of the National Society of United States Daughters of the War of 1812 was organized in 1892 and incorporated in 1901. Minutes, reports, chapter histories, scrapbooks, and newsletters. Includes records of the Major John Boggs Chapter of Circleville, OH.

14,098. Whitaker, James, and Whitaker, Elizabeth
Papers. 1788-1970. 40 items.
Open. Inventory.
Rutherford B. Hayes Library.
James Whitaker (17??-1804) and his wife Elizabeth Whitaker (1765-1833), who were held captive for a time by the Wyandot Indians, were the first permanent white settlers in Sandusky County, OH. Correspondence, biographical sketches, and clippings. Originals of some of the correspondence are held in the Solomon Sibley Collection at the Detroit Public Library, Burton Historical Collection.

14,099. Wright, Dorothy Edgerton
Papers. 1923-28. 1 folder.
Open. Inventory.
Rutherford B. Hayes Library.
Correspondence, primarily concerning business matters, of Wright, librarian of the Rutherford B. Hayes Library.

GARFIELD HEIGHTS

14,100. Provincial Archives
Records. 1925- . No size given.
Access restricted. No guide.
Sisters of St. Joseph, Marymount Provincial Home.
This religious order of women, the members of which are involved in teaching and in hospital administration and care, was founded in 1901. The Province was established in 1925 in Garfield Heights. Collection consists primarily of correspondence of the past nine provincial superiors in the provincial administration files, but it also includes minutes of meetings, financial records, photos, and scrapbooks. Marymount Hospital was founded by the Sisters.

GREENVILLE

14,101. Oakley, Annie
Papers. 1880s-1976. 1 tape and other items.
Open. No guide.
Darke County Historical Society.
Correspondence, photos, scrapbooks, wills, guns, medals, and other memorabilia of Oakley (1860-1926), a Darke County native who traveled with Buffalo Bill's wild west show from 1884 to

1901. An accomplished horsewoman, Oakley also won many awards as a sharpshooter. Includes a tape recording about her life narrated by Lowell Thomas.

KENT

14,102. Cowles, Betsey Mix
Papers. 1832-1950. 1.33 cu.ft.
Open. Unpublished guide.
Kent State University, American History Research Center.
[Miss] Cowles (1810-76) was an educator, abolitionist, and women's rights advocate from Austinburg, OH. Correspondence, diaries, and publications document Cowles's work in Ohio and in other states throughout the nation.

14,103. Cowles, Myra G.
Papers. 1902-44. 0.33 cu.ft.
Open. Folder description.
Kent State University, American History Research Center.
Correspondence of Cowles (1878-1966), who taught in the Austinburg, OH, area, in the southern US, and in Puerto Rico.

14,104. Fuller Family
Papers. 1841-1946. 2 cu.ft.
Open. Folder description.
Kent State University, American History Research Center.
Papers contain correspondence of Jeannette Fuller (1868-1952), who worked as a WCTU fieldworker from 1896 to 1914 in Ohio, Pennsylvania, West Virginia, Wisconsin, and Michigan.

14,105. Mahoning County Probate Court, Girls Industrial School
Records. 1896-99. 1 vol.
Open. No guide.
Kent State University, American History Research Center.
Records of court proceedings resulting in commitment of individuals to the School.

14,106. Youngstown, OH, League of Women Voters
Records. 1923-63. 2.5 cu.ft.
Open. Folder description.
Kent State University, American History Research Center.
Subject files, state convention material, and publications of the state organization.

14,107. Kent-Ravenna Branch of the American Association of University Women
Records. 1935-65. 0.5 ft.
Open. No guide.
Kent State University Archives.
Correspondence, pamphlets, and yearbooks of this local chapter of the AAUW.

14,108. Kent State University Faculty Wives Club
Records. 1945-64. 0.5 ft.
Open. No guide.
Kent State University Archives.
Document concerning this social group's history, scrapbooks, program books, and a guest book.

14,109. Kent State University Faculty Women's Club
Records. 1913-65. 0.5 ft.
Open. No guide.
Kent State University Archives.
Minutes, treasurer's record for 1951-52, correspondence, scrapbooks, yearbooks, and clippings.

14,110. University Women of Kent State University
Records. 1964-72. 0.5 ft.
Open. No guide.
Kent State University Archives.
Scrapbooks and yearbooks of this social group.

MARIETTA

14,111. Cutler
Papers. 1748-1925. More than 5000 items.
Open. Published guide.
Marietta College Library.
Correspondence, diaries, histories, poetry, scrapbooks, clippings, and other papers of Manasseh Cutler (1742-1823); his son Ephraim Cutler (1767-1853); William Parker Cutler (1812-89) and Julia Perkins Cutler (1814-1904), the children of Ephraim Cutler; and William Parker's daughter Sarah Jane Cutler (1856-1933). Julia Cutler's papers include Civil War diaries, recollections about early Ohio history, scrapbooks, and genealogical material as well as some correspondence concerning her published histories and biographies. Sarah Cutler's papers include correspondence, a diary of a trip to Chicago in 1871, histories, and poetry. See George Jordan Blazier, *The Cutler Collection of Letters and Documents* (Marietta, OH: Marietta College, 1962).

MARTINS FERRY

14,112. Betty Zane Frontier Days
Collection. 1967- . Ca. 50 items.
Open. No guide.
Martins Ferry Public Library.
Frontier Days is an annual celebration that commemorates the contributions of [Miss] Elizabeth "Betty" Zane (1766?-1831?) and her family to the settling of Martins Ferry and the surrounding area. Pamphlets issued by the Martins Ferry Area Historical Society, photos, brochures, clippings, and other items. Betty Zane, an early settler in the Ohio Valley, was the heroine of the Battle of Fort Henry, which took place in 1782 near present-day Wheeling, WV.

MARYSVILLE

14,113. Archives
Records. 1933- . Ca. 6 ft.
Access restricted. No guide.
American Woman's Society of Certified Public Accountants.
The Society was formed in 1933 to further the professional advancement of women accountants, to publicize the achievements of women certified public accountants within the accounting profession, and to increase the number of women involved in technical accounting organizations. Annual reports, minutes, administrative files, biographical data about and photos of presidents, newsletters, and professional journals.

MASSILLON

14,114. Everhard, Carolyn (McCullough)
Papers. 1853-1902. 1 ft.
Open. Unpublished guide.
Massillon Museum.
[Mrs.] Everhard (1834-1902), the president of Ohio Woman Suffrage Association, was the first woman bank director in Ohio. Correspondence, drafts of speeches and bills, minutes of the Ohio Woman Suffrage Association and the Friends of Temperance in Massillon, photos, and scrapbooks of clippings concerning the woman suffrage movement, the humane society, and nationally prominent women.

14,115. Johnson, Belle
Papers. Ca. 1890-1975. Ca. 1 document box.
Open. Unpublished guide.
Massillon Museum.
Photos, ca. 1890-1910, including many that won awards at national and international photo shows, taken by Johnson (?-1945), a photographer. Also includes a few letters, 1969-75, about Johnson that were written by her assistant.

MOUNT SAINT JOSEPH

14,116. China
Records. 1927-49. 3 ft. and 4 tapes.
Open. Unpublished guide.
Sisters of Charity of Cincinnati, Motherhouse.
Financial reports, correspondence, diaries, oral history tapes, and photos relating to the missions in China of the Sisters of Charity. The Sisters were involved primarily in hospital care and care of the elderly and orphans. The material relates to life in pre-Communist China, the gradual occupation of China by communists, internment by the Japanese, and the gradual absorption of the religious community's property by the People's Republic. Includes a few diaries kept by sisters during their internment by the Japanese.

14,117. Reilly, Maryanne
Papers. 1823-80. 2 ft.
Open. No guide.
Sisters of Charity of Cincinnati, Motherhouse.
Diaries and journals kept by Reilly, who describes social life and her family. Also includes some of her correspondence with Archbishop John B. Purcell of Cincinnati, OH.

NEW CONCORD

14,118. Archives
Records. 1851- . 15 boxes and 5 vols.
Open. Unpublished guide.
Muskingum College Archives.
Minutes, financial records, membership lists, photo albums, scrapbooks, and other records of the College, which was founded in 1837. Includes minutes of the Aretean Literary Society, 1894-1923; constitution, minutes, and membership list of the Erodelphian Literary Society, 1860-1922; records of New Concord Female Seminary, 1851-53; minutes and programs of the Federated Club, a local women's club; material of four social clubs, the Women's Interclub, Wawyin Club, Kona Club, and Kianu Club; and a master's thesis by Elizabeth Sue Cook of Miami University concerning the history of women's physical education at Muskingum College. Cook's thesis was written in 1968.

OBERLIN

14,119. Davis, Lydia (Lord)
Papers. 1862-1944. 1.67 cu.ft.
Open. Unpublished guide.
Oberlin College Archives.
A young teacher in Ravenna, OH, Davis (?-1952) married Francis W. Davis in 1889 and went with him as a missionary to China; she was credited with founding the first girl's school in Shansi Province under the auspices of the American Board of Commissioners for Foreign Missions. Correspondence, memoranda, photos, and printed material. Includes letters Lydia Davis wrote to her

parents Mr. and Mrs. Eleazer Lord and letters Davis received from other missionaries. Her letters contain descriptions of life in China and the birth and rearing of her children; her sons William and John were born in China, while her son Lewis was born after she and her husband returned to the US on furlough in 1897. Francis Davis returned to China in 1899 and died during the Boxer uprising of 1900. Lydia Davis moved to Oberlin in 1903, where she became a speaker and fund raiser for Congregational mission work. She visited China in 1924 and supported the work of the Shansi Memorial Association, serving as its executive secretary from 1929 to 1941. Davis was particularly interested in the education of Chinese girls.

14,120. Estabrook, Helen
Papers. 1923-50s. 2.5 in.
Open. Unpublished guide.
Oberlin College Archives.
[Miss] Estabrook served after 1928 as secretary of the Order of the Pearls, which had been founded in 1923 by 35 women in Oberlin College's Talcott Hall who wanted to keep in touch with each other and the College as alumnae and brides. Correspondence and a scrapbook containing a constitution and information about the Order and its gift for the purchase of art books. Members of the Order voted to disband in 1971.

14,121. Finitimi Society
Records. 1902-23. 5 vols.
Open. Unpublished guide.
Oberlin College Archives.
Minutes of this Oberlin ladies' literary and social group, which was established in 1902.

14,122. Fitch, Florence M.
Papers. 1807-1951. 4.67 cu.ft.
Open. Unpublished guide.
Oberlin College Archives.
Fitch (1875-1959) served as dean of college women at Oberlin from 1904 until 1920 and taught philosophy, Biblical literature, and comparative religion at the school from 1904 until her retirement in 1940. Correspondence, diaries, writings, lectures, notes, photos, diplomas, clippings, and other material consist principally of Fitch's family correspondence. Includes letters from her mother Anna Haskell to her father Frank Fitch while he was at Yale from 1870 to 1873, but the majority of the correspondence comprises letters Florence Fitch wrote while she was a student at Oberlin, a student in Germany from 1900 to 1903, and a member of the Oberlin staff before her father's death in 1917. Also includes letters and clippings about her books for children, including *One God, Their Search for God,* and *Allah and the Daughter of Abd Salam.* Fitch received her bachelor's degree from Oberlin in 1897 and her PhD from the University of Berlin in 1903; she worked as secretary for the Oberlin dean in 1903 and 1904.

14,123. Hosford, Frances Juliette
Papers. 1925-35. 0.33 cu.ft.
Open. Unpublished guide.
Oberlin College Archives.
Student, teacher, dean of women, and historian, [Miss] Hosford (1853-1937) was associated with Oberlin College for 40 years. Correspondence constitutes the bulk of the collection, which also contains source material for her articles in the *Oberlin Alumni Magazine* and for her book *Father Shipherd's Magna Carta* (1937), a history of coeducation at Oberlin. Includes information concerning Antoinette (Brown) Blackwell and Betsey Mix Cowles. James T. Fairchild, W. G. Frost, Emma Monroe Fitch, W. B. Gerrish, Helen Keep, Julia Finney Monroe, Margaret Maltby, Edward S. Steele, Eloise Steele, and Florence M. Snell were among her correspondents. After graduating from Lake Erie College in Painesville, OH, in 1872, Hosford received her bachelor's and master's degrees from Oberlin in 1891 and 1896, respectively. She taught Latin at Oberlin and served as assistant dean and, then, acting dean of women from 1916 until she retired in 1920.

14,124. Kellogg, Lucy Fletcher
Papers. Ca. 1835-1900. 2.25 in.
Open. Unpublished guide.
Oberlin College Archives.
A homemaker who lived in Massachusetts, Louisiana, and Oberlin, Kellogg (1793-1891) was the mother of Mary Fairchild, who married J. H. Fairchild, president and trustee of Oberlin College. Correspondence, notebooks, legal papers, and printed material. Includes family letters that provide information about conditions in Minden, LA, and New Orleans from 1836 to 1851. One of the notebooks contains a manuscript of Kellogg's life story; a printed account of her life to 1879 is included as well.

14,125. League of Women Voters of Oberlin
Records. 1924-74. 1.33 cu.ft.
Open. Box list.
Oberlin College Archives.
Minutes, correspondence, and scrapbooks of the Oberlin LWV, which probably was founded in 1923.

14,126. Mickey, M. Portia
Papers. 1914-40. 0.67 cu.ft.
Open. Unpublished guide.
Oberlin College Archives.
[Miss] Margaret Portia Mickey, who received her bachelor's degree from Oberlin in 1912, traveled as a missionary in northern China from 1914 to 1920. Consists principally of letters she wrote from Peking and other cities in northern China but also includes letters written by her mother during a 1917-18 trip to visit Mickey. Also contains essays by Mickey on such subjects as medical work, floods, women's work, work in rural areas, and schools; programs; Oriental writings; and other items. In later years, besides working in Oberlin and other places in the US, Mickey spent additional time in China and Japan.

14,127. Oberlin Woman's Christian Temperance Union
Records. 1874-1976. 1 cu.ft.
Open. Unpublished guide.
Oberlin College Archives.
Minutes, treasurer's records, correspondence, membership lists, and programs of the Oberlin WCTU, which was founded in 1874.

14,128. Root, Azariah Smith
Papers. 1881-1931. 5.33 cu.ft.
Open. Unpublished guide.
Oberlin College Archives.
Correspondence, diaries, memoranda, writings, and blueprints of Root (1862-1927), Oberlin College librarian from 1887 to 1927 and professor of bibliography from 1890 to 1927, and of his wife Anna Metcalf Root. Anna Root's diaries for 1883, 1884, and 1904-29 record her family's life. Also includes correspondence exchanged between Azariah and Anna Root.

14,129. Williams, George L., and Williams, Mary Alice Moon
Papers. 1890-1912. 2 cu.ft.
Open. Unpublished guide.
Oberlin College Archives.
George Williams (1858-1900) and Alice Williams (1860-1952) were married in 1891, shortly before they went to China to work as missionaries; they served in Shansi Province until 1899, when she returned to the US with their three daughters. Her husband was killed during the Boxer uprising. Correspondence, a diary, memoranda, photos, printed matter, and other items. Includes letters that Alice Williams wrote from China between 1891 and 1900 and a diary covering her visit to China from 1909 to 1912. She returned to China in 1935 and remained there until 1937.

RICHFIELD

14,130. Motherhouse Archives
Records. 1851- . No size given.
Access restricted. Unpublished guide.
Sisters of Charity of St. Augustine, Motherhouse.
This religious congregation of women engaged in health services, social services, and teaching was founded in 1851 in Cleveland, which was then known as Ohio City. Constitutions, minutes of governing bodies, financial records, correspondence, histories of the congregation, audiovisual material, photos, scrapbooks and clippings relating to institutions established or staffed by the Sisters, prayer books, sacred vessels and other articles used in liturgical worship, and memorabilia.

TIFFIN

14,131. Convent Archives
Records. 1869- . 6 drawers.
Open. No guide.
Sisters of St. Francis Convent.
Minutes, correspondence, photos, and other records of this religious order of women that was founded in 1869 in Tiffin to care for children and the aged. Includes letters of the founder and memoirs and photos of the early sisters.

TOLEDO

14,132. Best, Margaret
Papers. 1857-1910. 4 vols.
Open. Inventory.
Toledo-Lucas County Public Library.
Diaries and a volume of poetry and essays by Adelia Haughton [Mrs. Michael] Best (1838-1911), the grandmother-in-law of Margaret Best. Adelia Best was the daughter of a prominent Lucas County farmer and local official. A schoolteacher for a short time, she also was active in the temperance movement. Her diaries date from 1857 to 1861 and chronicle her early adulthood, including her conflict with her father over the choice of a husband. Her poetry and essays deal with the Civil War, temperance, and self-improvement.

14,133. Colton, Olive A.
Papers. 1931-43. 4 ft.
Open. Inventory.
Toledo-Lucas County Public Library.
Colton (1874-1972), a suffrage leader, was active in the LWV. Scrapbooks contain material concerning politics, city government, the Ku Klux Klan, education, and other topics.

14,134. Cook, Louisa
Papers. 1862-65. 6 items.
Open. Inventory.
Toledo-Lucas County Public Library.
Cook (1833-?) lived in Lucas County until 1862 when she moved with her aunt and uncle to Placerville, Idaho Territory. Letters she wrote to her sister Emma (Cook) Crane in Lucas County in which she described her journey west in a covered wagon and her life in Placerville.

14,135. Dahn, Adelaide H.
Papers. 1860-1972. 2 ft.
Open. Inventory.
Toledo-Lucas County Public Library.
[Miss] Dahn (1882-1974), who taught school in Toledo from 1904 to 1946, also was an amateur

historian. Correspondence, articles and speeches, papers about and by students, family papers, play scripts, and Hathaway School, PTA, and family memorabilia. Dahn graduated from the Toledo Polytechnical School in 1902 and the Toledo Normal School in 1904. She did graduate work at the University of Wisconsin and Columbia University. Her fifth-grade class visited many locations throughout Toledo over the years and conducted oral history interviews.

14,136. Foster, May Phoebe
Papers. 1918-19. 0.5 ft.
Open. Inventory.
Toledo-Lucas County Public Library.
Foster (?-1942) worked for the Toledo public schools from 1907 until 1941. Letters that she wrote to her family and friends while she was serving as an American National Red Cross volunteer in Dijon, France. She describes her attitudes toward the war, the role of the Red Cross, and the bravery of the soldiers.

14,137. Genealogical Organizations
Records. 1896-1965. 14 ft.
Open. No guide.
Toledo-Lucas County Public Library.
Minutes, treasurers' reports, rolls of honor, and other records of the Peter Navarre Chapter of the Daughters of 1812, the Fort Industry and Ursula Wolcott Chapters of the DAR, the Toledo Colony of the New England Women, and the Toledo Colony of the Society of Mayflower Descendants. The Daughters of 1812 records, 1903-63, include minutes, correspondence, a chapter history, photos, and scrapbooks. The DAR records, 1896-1965, include minutes of board and regular meetings, treasurer's records, correspondence, scrapbook, pamphlets, yearbooks, and other material. The New England Women records, 1906-56, include a chapter history and rosters. The Society of Mayflower Descendants records, 1938-57, include publicity and scrapbooks.

14,138. Grand Army of the Republic
Records. 1883-1942. 1 ft.
Open. Inventory.
Toledo-Lucas County Public Library.
Records of the Woman's Relief Corps, 1887-1902; the Forsyth Relief Corps, 1883-1942; and the Forsyth Post Ladies Society, 1879-83. The three GAR women's auxiliaries sought to promote patriotism and to care for soldiers' widows and orphans. The WRC material includes rules and an almanac. The Forsyth Relief Corps records contain annual reports, minutes, a roster of officers and members in 1901, and minutes of the group's Past Presidents Association. The Forsyth Post Ladies Society records contain a constitution, minutes, and a membership roster.

14,139. Jones, Samuel Milton
Papers. 1897-1904. 15 ft.
Open. Published guide.
Toledo-Lucas County Public Library.
Correspondence, speeches, articles, publications, and other papers of Jones (1846-1904), Progressive mayor of Toledo from 1897 to 1904. Includes his correspondence with local and state suffrage leaders, among them Harriet (Taylor) Upton. Also available on microfilm. See Morgan J. Barclay and Jean W. Strong, *The Samuel Milton Jones Papers: An Inventory to the Microfilm Edition.*

14,140. Lanier, Bette C.
Papers. 1906-70. 1 ft.
Open. Inventory.
Toledo-Lucas County Public Library.
Scrapbook donated by Lanier concerns the activities of blacks in Toledo during the 1920s and 1930s, particularly the work of [Mrs.] Drusilla Clemens. Clemens, an active churchwoman and community leader, was involved in religious and educational functions. The scrapbook contains programs of cultural events, church and school bulletins, and clippings.

14,141. Music
Collection. 1869-1964. 4 ft.
Open. Inventory.
Toledo-Lucas County Public Library.
Records of the Eurydice Club, founded in 1891, and the Monday Musicale, founded in 1913, and scrapbooks concerning the career of Corinne Kelsey-Rider Reed, an opera singer. The two music groups promoted the appreciation of music, particularly choral singing. The Eurydice Club records include a history of the Club from 1891 to 1951 and two scrapbooks of clippings and programs. Monday Musicale records include a constitution; bylaws; minute books; notebooks containing reports, correspondence, and other records; roll books and membership lists; scrapbooks; programs; and other items.

14,142. Segur Family
Papers. 1859-77. 3 ft.
Open. Inventory.
Toledo-Lucas County Public Library.
Correspondence, business records, account books, and other papers of Daniel Segur, Sr. (1812-76), a hotel operator who served on the city council and as county commissioner, and his wife Rosa L. Klinge Segur (1833-1906), an early Toledo suffragist and schoolteacher. Includes records of the Wabash and Erie canals.

14,143. Toledo District Nurses Association
Records. 1901- . 3 ft.
Open. No guide.
Toledo-Lucas County Public Library.
Minutes and scrapbooks of the Association, which was founded in 1901 to promote public health activities, particularly in the schools, and to encourage nursing as a profession.

14,144. Woman's Movement
Collection. 1877- . 2 ft. and 1 microfilm reel.
Open. Published and unpublished guides.
Toledo-Lucas County Public Library.
Histories of the LWV and papers of woman's movement figures, including Carrie Chapman Catt; [Miss] Olive A. Colton, a local suffragist and LWV leader; Rosa L. Segur, a schoolteacher and author who helped found the Toledo Woman's Suffrage Association in 1869; Susan B. Anthony; Mary Locke Hurin, a Toledo lecturer on political affairs; Amy Grace Maher, a local consumer advocate and supporter of compulsory education and labor laws; and Sarah Kaufman, a Toledo social and juvenile court worker who helped found Banner Boys for boys who were in trouble. Also includes issues of the *National Citizen and Ballot Box,* a suffrage newspaper founded in Toledo in 1875 by Sarah S. L. Williams; publications on wages and conditions by the Ohio Council on Women in Industry, 1924-26; and publications about wages and industrial problems, particularly those relating to women and children, by the Toledo Consumers League, 1918-32. See Mara Ann Pinto Oess, *An Index to the National Citizen and Ballot Box* (Toledo: Toledo-Lucas Public Library, 1976).

14,145. Archives
Records. 1854- . 3 files and 5 cabinets.
Access restricted. No guide.
Ursuline Convent of the Sacred Heart.
The Convent was founded in 1854 in Toledo. Financial records, correspondence, annals, tapes, slides, and scrapbooks contain accounts of the founding of the Convent, the opening of a school on the Convent grounds, teaching in various parishes, imposition of cloister and its removal, the relocation of six sisters to Montana in 1884 to teach Indians, the founding of a military school for boys, staffing of parochial schools, and the merger of the Tiffin, OH, Ursuline Convent with the Toledo Convent in 1913.

TROY

14,146. Brown, Belle
Papers. 1902-10. 1 vol.
Open. No guide.
Troy-Miami County Local History Room.
Brown (1846-1924), whose given name was Mary Belle Brown, was a physician in New York City from 1880 to 1911; she served as dean of the Women's Medical College there. Scrapbook compiled by [Miss] Helen Van Wagenen contains a short note to Brown for each day of 1910, Brown's last year in New York City. The notes are written and signed by Brown's friends and well-wishers. Also includes clippings, one of which contains a description of the 1902 graduation exercises of the Women's Medical College. Brown died in Troy.

14,147. Current Events Club of Troy
Records. 1924-74. 0.5 ft.
Partially restricted. No guide.
Troy-Miami County Local History Room.
Meetings of the Club, founded in 1924, included presentation of an article about current news by each member and discussion. Bylaws, secretary's minute books, a list of charter members, a membership list from 1974, and a souvenir program for a luncheon marking the group's 50th anniversary. The minute books report all articles presented at each meeting.

14,148. Fortnightly Club
Records. 1900-52. 1 box.
Open. No guide.
Troy-Miami County Local History Room.
Founded in 1900, the Club was a women's literary society. Constitution; secretary's minutes; correspondence, including items from WWI soldiers thanking Club members for sweaters and wristlets and some from French war orphans, ca. 1920; an historical data book about the group through 1946; an undated manuscript about contemporary college women by Jessie McCullough, a Club member; a register; a group photo, ca. 1908; yearbooks, 1901-52; and clippings.

14,149. Home Circle
Records. 1918-37. 8 items.
Open. No guide.
Troy-Miami County Local History Room.
Yearly programs of the Circle, a women's literary society founded in about 1918. The Circle met in the women's homes to discuss papers, speeches, current events, book reviews, and other subjects.

14,150. Hunkins, Eusebia (Simpson)
Papers. Nd. 1 box.
Open. No guide.
Troy-Miami County Local History Room.
A pianist and composer, Hunkins (1902-) is a member of the American Society of Composers, Authors, and Publishers; she also served as bicentennial chairman of American music for the National Federation of Music Clubs. Music and librettos for five folk operas by Hunkins, a list of her compositions, photos, and clippings. Hunkins is a graduate of the Juilliard School of Music in New York City and the great-granddaughter of Eusebia (Blodgett) Harris Meeks.

14,151. Meeks, Eusebia (Blodgett) Harris
Papers. 1821-89. No size given.
Open. No guide.
Troy-Miami County Local History Room.
A descendant of Huguenot immigrants, Meeks (1821-89) was born in Jefferson County, NY, but traveled with her family by covered wagon to Lebanon, OH, by ca. 1835. Manuscript books of her remembrances, a biography, genealogy charts concerning Meeks's parents' families, and a photo of Meeks's daughter Roxanna Davenport Harris. The daughter of a minister, Meeks attended the female seminary in Centerville, OH. In her

remembrances, she describes the seminary, the town of Lebanon, and her family's home in Lowville, NY. Meeks contributed articles to newspapers. Her first husband was William Harris. Isaac Meeks, her second husband, received an MD degree at Ohio Medical College at Cincinnati in 1850.

14,152. Orbison, Hannah D. (Jones)
Papers. 1829-78. 3 ft.
Open. No guide.
Troy-Miami County Local History Room.
An 1844 graduate of Mount Holyoke Female Seminary, Hannah Jones (1820-78) taught in Massachusetts and New Hampshire high schools until 1846 when she moved to Troy to teach. She married David W. Orbison, Sr., in Troy in 1847. Correspondence between Hannah Orbison and her family in New Hampshire reveals the family's initial objection to her marriage to a man they presumed to be "an ignorant farmer." Also includes letters to Hannah from Mary Lyon, the founder of Mount Holyoke; Hannah's letters to her family through 1878; compositions she wrote while in college; account books she kept after her marriage; manuscripts by her husband and sons; school record books and other papers she accumulated as a teacher; Mount Holyoke catalogs; a history of Mount Holyoke, written to mark the school's 25th anniversary; and other papers. Also contains pamphlets, 1844-46, which were written by O. S. Fowler concerning such subjects as the use of phrenology and physiology in choosing a marriage partner, "Intemperance and Tight Lacing considered in relation to the Laws of Life," and the "evils and remedies of excessive and perverted sexuality."

14,153. Pioneer Women of Piqua
Papers. 1896. 76-page item.
Open. Unpublished guide.
Troy-Miami County Local History Room.
Published in 1896 by the Piqua, OH, chapter of the DAR, the booklet contains biographical sketches of 12 pioneer women and historical information about Piqua. Events described in the booklet date from 1797 to about 1891.

14,154. Sorosis Club
Records. 1898-1938. 1 box.
Open. No guide.
Troy-Miami County Local History Room.
Yearbooks list the officers, members, and subjects of the programs of this women's literary group, which was founded in 1893. Programs consisted of papers on various subjects, discussions, readings from famous authors, book reviews, and other activities.

14,155. Troy Altrurian Club
Records. 1894-1977. 2 ft.
Open. No guide.
Troy-Miami County Local History Room.
Founded in 1894, the Club has helped establish a free public library in Troy, raised money for the antituberculosis society, conducted sales of articles made by blind persons, and participated in other civic projects. Programs; a history of the Club, which was written by Estella Baird Broomhall, one of the founders; and cookbooks issued by the Club in 1902 and 1910. Broomhall's account deals with the group's history from 1893 through 1934. The Club's programs consist of presentations of papers, music, book reviews, current events, and guest speakers.

14,156. Troy Music Club
Records. 1919-78. 1 box.
Open. No guide.
Troy-Miami County Local History Room.
Founded in 1915, the Club sought to encourage young musicians; the group's programs consisted of musical presentations by members and guests. Minute books, a list of former members prepared for the group's 50th anniversary, correspondence received in response to invitations to the anniversary celebration, photos, programs, and clippings.

14,157. Troy Music Study Club
Records. 1937-74. 0.5 ft.
Open. No guide.
Troy-Miami County Local History Room.
Constitution and programs of this group, which was founded in 1935. The name of the organization was changed to the Musicians' Club in 1965. The group's meetings included musical performances by members and guests.

WESTERVILLE

14,158. Cleiorhetia Society
Records. 1870-1933. 2 ft.
Open. No guide.
Otterbein College Library.
Constitution, bylaws, secretary's and treasurer's records, censors books, library record books, membership rolls, and other records of the Society, which was founded in 1870 to enable members to hear literary presentations and study parliamentary procedure.

14,159. Philalethea Society
Records. 1852-1933. 2.5 ft.
Open. No guide.
Otterbein College Library.
Constitution; bylaws; secretary's, treasurer's, and librarian's records; censors books; photo album; programs; and library catalog of the Society, which was formed in 1852 and became defunct in 1933. Sessions consisted of literary presentations and discussions of parliamentary procedure.

WOOSTER

14,160. Viola Thorne Club
Records. 1923-54. 2 vols.
Open. No guide.
Ohio Agricultural Research and Development Center Library.
Minutes of monthly meetings of the Club, a social group for wives of Center employees. The organization was founded in 1914.

WRIGHT-PATTERSON AIR FORCE BASE

14,161. Women Air Force Service Pilots (WASPs)
Records. 1942-44. 2.5 ft.
Open. No guide.
Air Force Museum.
Correspondence, rosters, photos, slides, medical reports, and histories of various commands where women trained and served, as well as personal papers donated by WASPs. Reunion material also included.

XENIA

14,162. Hamilton, Elizabeth Gwinn
Papers. 1854. 21-page item.
Access restricted. Unpublished guide.
Greene County District Library.
Journal of "Lizzie" Hamilton (1833-56) tells of her daily activities, including sewing, cooking, cleaning, church attendance, helping care for a neighbor's sick child, helping to dress the body of a dead child, the apprehension of a man who had killed another, attending a fair, the Fourth of July, meeting boy friends, and other subjects. Hamilton also mentions members of her family and other people and places.

14,163. Patzig, Cynthia: Xenia School Board Election of 1895
Papers. 1973. 57-page item.
Access restricted. No guide.
Greene County District Library.
Master's thesis by Patzig chiefly concerns the sociological aspects of the local school board election in 1895 in which two women defeated three prominent men. Entitled "Pietism as a Motivating Factor in Women's Participation in the School Board Election of 1895, Xenia, OH," the thesis describes the women candidates, the community, its churches, and other subjects. Information for the thesis was taken from interviews, scrapbooks, church records, and newspapers, many of them found in the Greene County District Library.

14,164. WCTU
Records. 1874-1945. 2 vols.
Access restricted. No guide.
Greene County District Library.
Scrapbooks contain correspondence, lists, articles, clippings, and other items relating to the history of the WCTU and women's temperance work in Xenia and Greene County. Specific items include a list of Xenia women's temperance workers in 1874, a letter from poet John G. Whittier endorsing the WCTU's efforts, a list and description of the various WCTU units in Greene County, and sections of *Union Signal*.

YELLOW SPRINGS

14,165. Peabody, Mann, and Hawthorne Families
Papers. 1790-1938. 14 vols.
Open. Unpublished guide.
Antioch College, Olive Kettering Library, Antiochiana.
Collection of correspondence of these and other related families includes papers of Elizabeth Palmer Peabody (1804-94), Mary Tyler (Peabody) [Mrs. Horace] Mann (1806-87), and Sophia (Peabody) [Mrs. Nathaniel] Hawthorne (1809-71), all of whom engaged in education, writing, lecturing, and art. Their correspondence concerns the education of women, coeducation, women's rights, and Indian leader Sarah Winnemucca.

YOUNGSTOWN

14,166. Arms
Papers. 1864. 30 items.
Open. Unpublished guide.
Mahoning Valley Historical Society, Arms Museum.
Correspondence between Myron Israel Arms and his wife Emaline Warner Arms during his service in the Union Army includes information about family hardships caused by the war.

14,167. DAR
Records. 1873-1976. 2 folders.
Open. Unpublished guide.
Mahoning Valley Historical Society, Arms Museum.
Bylaws, yearbooks, pamphlets, programs, and clippings of the local DAR and an application form and certificate of membership from the national DAR. The yearbooks date from 1908 to 1938 and the programs, from 1896 to 1901.

14,168. Edwards, Louisa M.
Papers. 1868-1939. 5 vols.
Open. Unpublished guide.
Mahoning Valley Historical Society, Arms Museum.
Scrapbooks of photos and clippings collected by [Miss] Edwards (1859-1941), a descendant of

Western Reserve pioneers, include information about social, political, and cultural aspects of the period. Contains articles about the Mahoning County branch of the Ohio Suffrage Association, the Suffragette Meeting House in Salem, OH, and other topics relating to woman suffrage in the Youngstown area.

14,169. In Memoriam: Pauline Jones
Papers. 1965. 1 envelope.
Open. Unpublished guide.
Mahoning Valley Historical Society, Arms Museum.
A Youngstown native, Jones (1896-1965) was president of the Wells College Alumnae from 1921 to 1931 and from 1942 to 1949. Memorial service programs, *Wells College Alumnae News,* and clippings concern her leadership in campus affairs, her dedication to civil defense, and her civic, charitable, and religious activities. A scholarship was established in her honor at Wells College.

14,170. Journey to Ohio
Papers. 1810. 1 vol.
Open. Unpublished guide.
Mahoning Valley Historical Society, Arms Museum.
Account by Margaret (Van Horn) Dwight Bell (1790-?), a descendant of Jonathan Edwards and the mother of 13 children, of her trip from New Haven, CT, to Warren, OH, in 1810.

14,171. Junior League of Youngstown
Records. 1963-76. 2 folders.
Open. Unpublished guide.
Mahoning Valley Historical Society, Arms Museum.
The Youngstown League, founded in 1929 to promote and channel volunteer efforts of women, is one of more than 200 Leagues in the US, Canada, and Mexico. Photos, "News Sheets," brochures, and clippings.

14,172. Ku Klux Klan
Records. 1890s-1940s. 25 items.
Open. Unpublished guide.
Mahoning Valley Historical Society, Arms Museum.
Correspondence, photos, pamphlets, and clippings of the Klan contain the constitution and laws of the Order of the Women of the Ku Klux Klan, photos of women Klan members, and other items concerning women in the organization. The constitution and laws of the women's Klan group were adopted in 1927.

OKLAHOMA

BARTLESVILLE

14,173. Bartlesville Women
Collection. Nd. No size given.
Open. No guide.
Bartlesville Public Library, History Room.
Slide program contains items and information about 28 local women, including Sarah Ann (Rogers) Carr, wife of the first white man in Bartlesville; Jane (Sosha) Journeycake, wife of Chief Journeycake of the Delawares and the first person to introduce Christianity to the Delawares; Nannie (Journeycake) Bartles, wife of the cofounder of Bartlesville and founder of the First Baptist Church of Dewey, OK; Patiacow, a Delaware woman who rode horseback at night with her son from Texas to Kansas to be with her people; Widow Whiteturkey, a Delaware woman who was the mother of a large family and who died in 1912 at the age of 76; Josie (Gilstrap) [Mrs. George B.] Keeler, mother of nine cildren and a leader of Methodism in Bartlesville; Lillie A. (Armstrong) [Mrs. William] Johnstone, wife of the cofounder of Bartlesville and early leader of the Baptist church; Nora (Lookout) Standing Bear and Julia Lookout, two Osage women; Helen (Bailey) [Mrs. Loren C.] Twyford, one of the earliest graduates of Bartlesville High School; and Julia (Johnson) Whiteturkey Gilstrap Lewis Dalton, a woman outlaw.

14,174. Early Pioneer Women
Collection. 1930s. 36 pp.
Open. No guide.
Bartlesville Public Library, History Room.
Allene McDowell wrote biographies of area pioneer women and their children as part of the work of the WPA. Included are biographies of Matilda Ballard, the wife of an early doctor in Indiana Territory; Leona (Brooks) Morgan, the wife of Bartlesville postmaster Arthur Morgan and the mother of eight children, who came to Indian Territory in 1884 and taught in the region; Frances Sarcoxie, the wife of John Sarcoxie, a Baptist preacher who was a Delaware Indian; Dova L. Suagee, who came to Bartlesville in a covered wagon in 1902 and was adopted by the Cherokees after her marriage to Joel Suagee; and Evelyn Maharas, the daughter of Joel Suagee. The biography of Sarcoxie includes information about the Delaware Indians, while the Dova Suagee biography provides information about the Cherokees.

14,175. History of the Delaware People
Collection. 1867- . 1 cabinet.
Access restricted. Unpublished guide.
Bartlesville Public Library, History Room.
Historical data about the Delawares includes interviews with individual Delawares; biographical card files; biographical stories about most of the Delaware families that came to the Bartlesville area in 1867; Delaware rolls of 1858, 1862, 1867, 1898, and 1904; censuses of the Cherokee Nation, taken in 1880 and 1890; land allotment maps and records; records of the Delawares in Kansas; copies of Delaware treaties with the US government and with the Cherokee nation; clippings; and other items.

14,176. Pioneer Biographies
Collection. 1920s-?. 1 vol.
Open. No guide.
Bartlesville Public Library, History Room.
Scrapbook of biographies compiled from clippings, obituaries, and other sources provides information about persons who came to the Bartlesville area before statehood was achieved in 1907.

14,177. Tuesday Club
Records. Nd. 1 drawer.
Open. No guide.
Bartlesville Public Library, History Room.
Minutes, correspondence, diaries, photos, and scrapbooks of the Club, a musical and literary society organized in 1904.

CHICKASHA

14,178. University Archives
Records. 1908- . Ca. 31 ft., 10 boxes, and 1 cabinet.
Open. Card catalog.
University of Science and Arts of Oklahoma Library.
Founded in 1908 as the Industrial Institute and College for Girls, the institution became Oklahoma College for Women in 1916, Oklahoma College of Liberal Arts in 1965, and the University of Science and Arts of Oklahoma in 1974. College catalogs, yearbooks, issues of the school newspaper, photos, programs, and other records. Men were admitted as full-time students for the first time in 1965. The institution offers bachelor's degrees in ca. 27 subject areas and preprofessional training in dentistry, medicine, nursing, pharmacy, veterinary medicine, other health fields, and law.

GOODWELL

14,179. Neill
Papers. 1909. No size given.
Access restricted. No guide.
No Man's Land Historical Museum.
Diary and correspondence of a housewife. The diary chronicles a trip by covered wagon from the Oklahoma panhandle to Coffeeville, KS.

14,180. Oral History
Oral history. 1972-78. 20 reels.
Open. No guide.
No Man's Land Historical Museum.
Interviews with teachers and homemakers include reminiscences about their growing up and establishing homes in No Man's Land, the Dust Bowl days, learning the art of handwork, quilting, chores, and other topics. The interviewees speak of events dating from 1890 to 1960.

14,181. Pioneer Queens
Records. 1941- . No size given.
Open. No guide.
No Man's Land Historical Museum.
Personal accounts and photos of women who were honored as Pioneer Queens of No Man's Land. The women, who included housewives, community leaders, and county officials, arrived in the area from 1882 to 1910. The program to honor the women began in 1941. The women's accounts speak of their arrival and growing up in No Man's Land.

LAWTON

14,182. Chrisman, Mildred Douglas
Papers. 1910-55. 1 Hollinger box.
Access restricted. No guide.
Museum of the Great Plains.
Photos of Chrisman (1895-), a film, rodeo, and circus entertainer, show her performing in rodeos and circuses. Also includes photos of her husband Pat Chrisman in movie scenes with Tom Mix.

14,183. Vestal, Ophelia D.
Papers. 1937-38. 1 Hollinger box.
Open. Unpublished guide.
Museum of the Great Plains.
Vestal was a fieldworker for the WPA Indian-Pioneer Project. Interviews and other records provide information about pioneer and Indian history in Oklahoma Territory in the late 19th and early 20th centuries. Vestal collected the information from surviving pioneers.

14,184. Wickham, Ola Forbes
Papers. 1880-1965. 2 Hollinger boxes.
Open. Unpublished guide.
Museum of the Great Plains.
Correspondence, diaries, biographical material, art work, and other papers of Wickham (1889-), an artist who in 1914 received the first art degree issued by Oklahoma University.

MEDFORD

14,185. Allen, Catherine Ward
Papers. Nd. 1 vol. and other items.
Open. No guide.
Grant County Museum.
A book *Chariots of the Sun* and clippings by Allen (1883-), a Pond Creek and Newkirk, OK, resident. Her book deals with the race for land in the Cherokee Strip in 1893.

14,186. Amick, Georgia
Oral history. Nd. 1 tape.
Open. No guide.

Grant County Museum.
Interview with Amick (1903-), a teacher who was professor of food and nutrition at the University of Missouri in Columbia, MO. Amick, who lives in Medford, also taught in the Pond Creek, OK, schools; she is a pianist, organist, and gardener.

14,187. Boyer, Edith Mayse
Oral history. Nd. 1 tape and 1 item.
Open. No guide.
Grant County Museum.
Interview and clipping of Boyer (1900-), who taught school for 10 years and raised six sons; she also has been active in local women's organizations and served as an officer in veterans auxiliary groups. Her sons served in the armed forces during WWII.

14,188. Ellis, Ella Neuman
Oral history. Nd. 1 tape.
Open. No guide.
Grant County Museum.
Interview with Ellis (1903-), a Medford resident who worked as a legal secretary for 20 years. Ellis is treasurer of the Grant County Historical Society and a member of Medford Progress and the Veterans of Foreign Wars Auxiliary; she also participates in other community activities.

14,189. Hardy, Ida
Oral history. Nd. 1 tape and 1 item.
Open. No guide.
Grant County Museum.
Interview and clipping of [Mrs. I. V.] Hardy (ca. 1880-1965), who taught music in Grant County for 50 years. Her husband was a physician.

14,190. McMahan, Helen
Papers. 1920-50. 3 vols. and other items.
Open. No guide.
Grant County Museum.
McMahan (ca. 1877-1947) was a Pond Creek, OK, housewife and poet. Scrapbooks contain her poems and pages of a house organ she edited for women.

14,191. Pitcher, Hazel
Oral history. Nd. 1 tape.
Open. No guide.
Grant County Museum.
Interview in which [Mrs. Charles] Pitcher (1909-), a teacher in rural and city schools, discusses her life.

14,192. Pond, Nina L.
Oral history. 1 tape and other items.
Open. No guide.
Grant County Museum.
Interview of [Mrs. J. C.] Pond (1905-), a newspaperwoman in Grant County for 47 years and a Methodist church Sunday school teacher who helped establish several libraries in the county, the Grant County Historical Society, and the Medford Free Art Fair. She is co-author of *Showers for Brides and Babies,* and she has been active in the Cherokee-Oklahoma-Kansas Gateway Association, the March of Dimes, the Oklahoma Lung Association, veterans auxiliaries, and other groups. She was the editor of the *Oklahoma Clubwoman* for 20 years.

NORMAN

14,193. American Association of University Women, Norman Chapter
Records. 1930-49. Ca. 12 items.
Open. Unpublished guide.
University of Oklahoma Library, Western History Collections.
Minutes, treasurer's ledger, correspondence, yearbooks, programs, and bulletins of the Norman chapter. Also includes printed material from national, regional, and state AAUW offices.

14,194. Badger, Ina
Papers. 1890s. 5 items.
Open. Unpublished guide.
University of Oklahoma Library, Western History Collections.
Correspondence shows problems faced by pioneer women on the Oklahoma frontier.

14,195. Baker, Frances
Papers. 1673-1927. 2 items.
Open. Unpublished guide.
University of Oklahoma Library, Western History Collections.
[Mrs. Frank] Baker, an author, feature writer, and columnist for area newspapers, has published poems, short stories, and articles on a range of topics. Booklet by Baker entitled "The Quapaw County" concerns northeastern Oklahoma. Also includes a copy of an appeal syllabus from a personal injury suit filed with the Industrial Commission of the State of Oklahoma.

14,196. Barnes, Sudie (McAlester)
Papers. 1875-1920. 143 items.
Open. Unpublished guide.
University of Oklahoma Library, Western History Collections.
Diary, personal letters, and manuscript journal of Barnes depict early life in McAlester, OK, which was founded by her father J. J. McAlester. Also included are McAlester family photos.

14,197. Bass, Althea
Papers. 1847-1955. 30 items.
Open. Unpublished guide.
University of Oklahoma Library, Western History Collections.
As an Indian historian, [Mrs. John Harvey] Bass preserved Cherokee and Creek history in her manuscripts "Essays of Sarah Worcester," which she wrote between 1847 and 1850, and "Inheritance of Alice Robertson," a biography of Oklahoma's first congresswoman.

14,198. Blachly, Lucile (Spire), and Blachly, Charles Dallas
Papers. 1883-1959. 7 ft.
Open. Unpublished guide.
University of Oklahoma Library, Western History Collections.
Lucile Blachly, a physician who specialized in obstetrics and pediatrics, was appointed director of the Oklahoma Health Department bureau of maternity and infancy in 1924. She wrote extensively on health and nutrition for Oklahoma mothers and preschool children. Correspondence, manuscripts, notes, published articles by Blachly and her physician husband Charles Blachly, scrapbooks, postcards, photos, and publications collected during their medical careers in Oklahoma.

14,199. Chouteau, Yvonne
Papers. 1932-50. 200 items.
Open. Unpublished guide.
University of Oklahoma Library, Western History Collections.
[Miss] Chouteau (?-), artist in residence at the University of Oklahoma, was prima ballerina with the Ballet Russe de Monte Carlo and is a member of the Oklahoma Hall of Fame. Clippings and magazine articles about Chouteau's career and her family. She is the great-great-granddaughter of Major Auguste P. Chouteau, an Oklahoma Indian trader.

14,200. Coldiron, Daisy (Lemon)
Papers. 1920-50. 500 items.
Open. Unpublished guide.
University of Oklahoma Library, Western History Collections.
An Oklahoma poet, Coldiron (1876-1946) settled in Grant County in 1894, taught school for 11 years, attended summer classes at the University of Oklahoma, and married physician D. F. Coldiron in 1905. Political, historical, and personal correspondence; manuscripts of unpublished poems; scrapbooks; clippings; and books of her poetry. Three volumes of her poetry, *Songs of Oklahoma* (1935), *There Was a Garden* (1940), and *Who Touches This* (1950), have been published while other Coldiron works have appeared in such publications as *Harlow's Weekly, American Author,* and *Kaleidograph.*

14,201. Coleman, Emma A.
Papers. 1889-1927. Ca. 1000 photos.
Open. Unpublished guide.
University of Oklahoma Library, Western History Collections.
Emma Coleman and her husband A. E. Coleman operated a photographic gallery in the new town of Norman after participating in the 1889 Run into Oklahoma. Photos from the gallery files show early scenes of Norman, the University of Oklahoma, Indians, and farming; also included are business and personal correspondence and 319 photographic dry plates.

14,202. Douglas, Helen (Gahagan)
Papers. 1920-52. Ca. 100 ft.
Open. Unpublished guide.
University of Oklahoma Library, Western History Collections.
Douglas (1900-) was an actress, opera singer, and congresswoman from California. Correspondence; files from the 79th, 80th, and 81st Congresses; and a special file containing legislation Douglas introduced during the 81st Congress and pertaining to her participation in presidential and congressional campaigns and her unsuccessful US Senate race in 1950. Also includes speeches; biographical material; scripts, scrapbooks, and other theatrical material; contracts; and photos. Wife of actor Melvyn Douglas, she began her career acting in Broadway plays, then turned to opera in 1927. She worked on migratory labor problems with the Farm Security Administration, was appointed in 1939 to the National Advisory Committee of the WPA and the California State Advisory Committee of the National Youth Administration, and was elected member of the House of Representatives in 1944. She cosponsored the bill that placed administration of atomic energy under civilian control.

14,203. Freudenthal, Elsbeth Estelle
Papers. 1900-53. 1.5 ft.
Open. Unpublished guide.
University of Oklahoma Library, Western History Collections.
[Miss] Freudenthal (1902-53) was an economist, securities analyst, and author of books and articles on aviation. Correspondence, manuscripts, printed material on Latin American and Caribbean aviation and Pan American airways, aviation bibliography and notes, research notes for an unfinished biography of Santos-Dumont, and photos regarding early aviation. Freudenthal earned a master's degree in economics from Harvard in 1924, managed a small Wall Street investment company for six years, and worked as an associate economist for the government during WWII. She wrote two books on aviation history and served as adjutant of the New Mexico Civil Air Patrol.

14,204. Funk, Rose [Mrs.]
Papers. 1865-90. 435 items.
Open. Unpublished guide.
University of Oklahoma Library, Western History Collections.
Picture post cards depicting early railroads, Colorado mountain scenes, and Indians comprise the bulk of the collection. Cook books and recipe guides used by Oklahoma frontier women and samples of calendar art for the period 1865 to 1900 are also included.

14,205. Gardner, Florence (Guild) Bruce
Papers. 1918-55. 156 items.
Open. Unpublished guide.
University of Oklahoma Library, Western History Collections.
Gardner, an Oklahoma author, wrote short stories and feature articles on local, national, and human interest subjects. Literary correspondence and manuscripts including "Six-Shooter Junction."

14,206. Grisso, Walker D.
Papers. 1872-1956. 21 items.
Open. Unpublished guide.
University of Oklahoma Library, Western History Collections.
Papers regarding Cherokee Indian history include photos of Judge Parker's court, Indian dances and ceremonies, the Crazy Snake uprising, and General Stand Watie; a printed report on the Cherokee Outlet Case; and a postal route map of Oklahoma. Also included are autograph letters by Susan B. Anthony, Hamlin Garland, Horace Greeley, Henry W. Longfellow, Lucy (Webb) Hayes, Eliza B. Garfield, U. S. Grant, Wendell Phillips, G. D. Abbott, and Chester A. Arthur.

14,207. Hertzog, Ann Brisky
Papers. 1904-48. 2 items.
Open. Unpublished guide.
University of Oklahoma Library, Western History Collections.
Hertzog was a pioneer teacher and civic leader who with her husband William settled on the Kiowa-Comanche Reservation in 1901. Manuscript about pioneer life and an account book that served as a scrapbook and family diary contains a description of a mining boom in the Wichita Mountains and minutes of early school board meetings in Comanche country.

14,208. Hisel, Mrs. O. R.
Papers.. 1890-1950. 3 items.
Open. Unpublished guide.
University of Oklahoma Library, Western History Collections.
Manuscript histories by Hisel regarding the Missionary Federation of Muskogee, OK, the Oklahoma Federation of Music Clubs, and Presbyterian pioneers.

14,209. Jarboe, Mrs. W. C.
Papers. 1890-1913. 1 item.
Open. Unpublished guide.
University of Oklahoma Library, Western History Collections.
Jarboe settled with her husband and family near Altus, OK, in 1891. Her manuscript, written in 1913 and entitled "Early Incidents in Oklahoma as We Remember Them," describes Fort Sill, the Kiowa-Comanche Reservation, Greer County, Altus, Indians encountered by the Jarboes, hunting and fishing, and the family's adjustment to life on the frontier.

14,210. Johnson, Edith Cherry
Papers. 1915-51. 3 ft.
Open. Unpublished guide.
University of Oklahoma Library, Western History Collections.
[Miss] Johnson (1879-) was a newspaper feature writer, columnist, author, and lecturer. Correspondence; letters of endorsement for John Golobie as US minister to the Kingdom of the Serbs, Croats, and Slovenes; papers of the Oklahoma City secretary of Goodwill Industries; invitations and programs; and three scrapbooks containing clippings, biographical data, and brochures and pamphlets. Johnson is the author of two books, *Illusions and Disillusions* (1920) and *To Women of the Business World* (1922). She was chosen Oklahoma's delegate to the Women's World Fair in 1927 and in 1935 was elected to the Oklahoma Hall of Fame.

14,211. Kibler, Nell
Papers. 1828-1907. 9 items.
Open. Unpublished guide.
University of Oklahoma Library, Western History Collections.
[Miss] Kibler was a Ramona, OK, school teacher. Manuscripts relate to her early life in Missouri, the Civil War, and the Provost Guards.

14,212. Korn, Anna (Brosius)
Papers. 1860-1938. 20 items.
Open. Unpublished guide.
University of Oklahoma Library, Western History Collections.
Poems by [Mrs. Frank] Korn, her manuscript on the development of Missouri after 1860, biographical sketches of Anne Mary Bentley and Judge Thomas H. Doyle, photo of Osage Chief Fred Lookout, and clippings pertaining to Oklahoma statehood.

14,213. Lahman, Marion (Sherwood)
Papers. 1950. 87 items.
Open. Unpublished guide.
University of Oklahoma Library, Western History Collections.
Manuscripts regarding the ethnobotany of the Southwest. Includes [Mrs. Charles] Lahman's "Southwestern Wild Flowers" and 67 of her original drawings of western wild flowers.

14,214. LeFlore, Carrie
Papers. 1853-92. 13 items.
Open. Unpublished guide.
University of Oklahoma Library, Western History Collections.
Correspondence and papers of Carrie LeFlore, wife of Choctaw Indian tribal leader Basil LeFlore who was known as Governor LeFlore, document the career of her husband. He served as the tribe's chief three times.

14,215. Lenski, Lois
Papers. 1893-1958. 33 ft.
Open. Unpublished guide.
University of Oklahoma Library, Western History Collections.
Lenski (1893-), an author and illustrator of children's books, studied art education at Ohio State University and graduated from the Westminister School of Art. Correspondence, book manuscripts and galley proofs, drawings, photos, brochures, and notes. Lenski, the wife of Arthur Covey, uses her maiden name in her work.

14,216. Maguire, Grace Adeline (King)
Papers. 1892-1950. 3 ft.
Open. Unpublished guide.
University of Oklahoma Library, Western History Collections.
Maguire headed the University of Oklahoma school of music from 1895 to 1901, helped organize Norman's first library, served for many years as a board member of that library, and wrote a column for the *Norman Transcript* which contained historical and other information about the University and Norman. Documents and printed material regarding the US Land Office at Lawton, OK, scrapbooks of historical clippings, and photos of early Oklahoma Territory. Maguire left the University faculty to marry James D. Maguire in 1901.

14,217. Marable, Mary Hays
Papers. 1932-51. 3.5 ft.
Open. Unpublished guide.
University of Oklahoma Library, Western History Collections.
A faculty member of the University of Oklahoma library school for many years, [Mrs.] Marable specialized in children's literature and in the bibliography of Oklahoma history. Research and biographical notes gathered for her book *Handbook of Oklahoma Writers* and bibliographical material.

14,218. Marriott, Alice Lee
Papers. 1811-1957. 21 ft.
Open. Unpublished guide.
University of Oklahoma Library, Western History Collections.
[Miss] Marriott (1910-), an author and former Guggenheim and Rockefeller Foundation Fellow, served as a consultant on Indian lore, arts, and crafts to museums and the US government. Personal and professional correspondence, arts and crafts papers, field notes on Indian tribes including the Kiowas, and Indian photos. Marriott's published works include *The Ten Grandmothers, Winter-Telling Stories,* and *Indians on Horseback,* as well as popular and scholarly articles.

14,219. Mountain View Twentieth Century Club
Records. 1904- . 2 ft.
Open. Unpublished guide.
University of Oklahoma Library, Western History Collections.
Organized in Mountain View, OK, in 1902, the Club later affiliated with the GFWC. Correspondence, minutes, account and minute books of the Round Table Section, and program calendars.

14,220. Nieberding, Velma
Papers. 1842-1957. 184 items.
Open. Unpublished guide.
University of Oklahoma Library, Western History Collections.
[Mrs.] Nieberding was a Miami, OK, author and Indian folklorist. Includes interviews with early settlers and Indians of northeastern Oklahoma, manuscripts on General Stand Watie, and a typescript of a John Rollin Ridge letter.

14,221. Oklahoma Planned Parenthood Association
Records. 1936-58. 2.5 ft.
Open. Unpublished guide.
University of Oklahoma Library, Western History Collections.
Correspondence, reprints of articles from periodicals and professional journals, manuscript signature, clippings, and a bibliography of articles on planned parenthood.

14,222. Oklahoma State Federation of Women's Clubs
Records. 1941- . No size given.
Open. Unpublished guide.
University of Oklahoma Library, Western History Collections.
The Clubs, among the first Oklahoma organizations, promote libraries, social welfare, and community beautification. Yearbooks, scrapbook of clippings and histories of individual clubs, pamphlets, programs, and club publications.

14,223. Pearson, Lola (Clark)
Papers. 1890-1950. 10 ft.
Open. Unpublished guide.
University of Oklahoma Library, Western History Collections.
A prominent club woman, editor, writer, and lecturer, Pearson was founder and for 10 years president of the Marshall, OK, Woman's Club. Minutes, reports, convention programs, directories, and other records of the Oklahoma Federation of Women's Clubs and the GFWC. Also includes correspondence, speeches, notebooks, photos, scrapbooks, travel folders, clippings, maps, and correspondence of her husband John C. Pearson as town mayor, businessman, and member of Methodist Episcopal churches in Marshall and Oklahoma City. Lola Pearson was vice-chairman of the Republican State committee from 1921 to 1928 and was active in the WCTU. She was editor of the "Women's Page" of the *Oklahoma Farmer* and of the "Good Cheer" page of the *Oklahoma Farmer-Stockman.*

14,224. White, Lida
Papers. 1891-1952. 7 ft.
Open. Unpublished guide.
University of Oklahoma Library, Western History Collections.
A teacher in the Norman, OK, schools for more than 40 years, [Miss] White collected information on Oklahoma and Indians as part of a WPA project. Personal and business correspondence, Oklahoma Indian lore notes, interviews about post-1889 western Oklahoma, bibliographical notes, a master's degree English thesis, maps, teaching certificates, books of poetry, novels, *Women and Missions* (1933), and other material.

14,225. Wyatt, Rose M.
Papers. 1886-1943. 12 items.
Open. Unpublished guide.
University of Oklahoma Library, Western History Collections.
[Mrs.] Wyatt attended school at St. Mary's Convent of the Sacred Heart Mission on Oklahoma's Pottawatomie Reservation. Letters from Catholic nuns reflecting religious life in Indian Territory in 1886 and 1887, speeches by US Senator Robert L. Owen of Oklahoma, and photos.

OKLAHOMA CITY

14,226. Archives
Records. 1916- . 2 drawers and 49 vols.
Access restricted. No guide.
Carmelite Sisters of St. Therese, Villa Teresa Convent.
Financial records, correspondence, notebooks, photos, mementos, clippings, and other records of the congregation, which was founded in 1917 at Bentley, OK. Its members are engaged in educational and social work. Includes correspondence and other papers of Mother Agnes Teresa Cavanaugh, the first superior general of the congregation; photos and clippings about Villa Teresa Nursery and School, which was founded by Mother Agnes and is still in operation; and photos and clippings about the now defunct Holy Child School for the Retarded and a Guatemala mission school and clinic, which were founded by Mother Celine Carter, the second superior general.

14,227. Oklahoma Living Legends
Oral history. 1964- . 950 tapes.
Open. Published and unpublished guides.
Oklahoma Christian College.
Interviews with ca. 2000 individuals, about 40 percent of whom were women, deal with each interviewee's personal experiences and reflect aspects of Oklahoma history from 1889 to the present. The interviews were done for the Oklahoma Historical Society. Names of interviewees are listed in John Stewart and Kenny A. Franks, *State Records, Manuscripts, and Newspapers at the Oklahoma State Archives and Oklahoma Historical Society* (Oklahoma City: Oklahoma Department of Libraries and Oklahoma Historical Society, 1975).

14,228. Oklahoma Biography
Collection. 1940s- . 100-200 items.
Open. Card index.
Oklahoma City University Library.
Chiefly clippings about Oklahomans. Also includes speeches, articles, and other items about these individuals.

14,229. Women Faculty
Collection. 1940s- . 75-100 folders.
Open. Card index.
Oklahoma City University Library.
Photos, clippings, and articles by and about women faculty members at Oklahoma City University.

14,230. Browne, Maimee Lee Robinson
Papers. 1938-63. 1 folder.
Open. No guide.
Oklahoma Heritage Association.
[Mrs. Virgil] Browne, an active clubwoman, originated the practice of public participation in naturalization proceedings while she was in New Orleans in 1922. Biography by her daughter Alice (Browne) Quan, a photo, and clippings. Elected Oklahoma "mother of the year" in 1951, Browne was a member of the DAR, the General Society of Mayflower Descendants, the National Society of Daughters of the Colonial Wars, the Order of First Families of Virginia, the National Society of the American Colonists, the Magna Charta Dames, the United Daughters of the Confederacy, and the Oklahoma Art League.

14,231. Bryant, Anita
Papers. 1953-77. 1 folder.
Open. No guide.
Oklahoma Heritage Association.
Biographies, photos, and clippings of Bryant (1941-), an Oklahoma-born singer and author. Bryant, who began singing on Oklahoma City television station WKY at the age of 10, has made world tours with the Billy Graham Crusade and USO tours with Bob Hope. Her books include *Mine Eyes Have Seen the Glory, Bless This House,* and *Light My Candle.* Bryant is married to Bob Green.

14,232. Calvert, Maude Richman
Papers. Nd. 1 folder.
Open. No guide.
Oklahoma Heritage Association.
Director of the Oklahoma Council of Child Development and Parent Education, [Mrs. George E.] Calvert (1893-) was a teacher in Oklahoma public schools until 1915 and in colleges and universities in the state from 1916 until 1920. Biography, photos, and clippings. Maude Calvert served as state superintendent of home economics from 1921 to 1925. She was vice-president of the Oklahoma Safety Council, state president of the PTA Council from 1935 to 1940, president of the Oklahoma Pen Women in 1930 and 1931, and vice-president of the national pen women organization in 1931 and 1932. In 1939 she helped establish the Oklahoma Family Life Institute at the University of Oklahoma. Calvert was married in 1923.

14,233. Cobb, Jerrie
Papers. 1946-76. 1 folder.
Open. No guide.
Oklahoma Heritage Association.
Correspondence, photos, articles, and clippings of Cobb (1931-), an aviator who flies supplies to isolated villages in Colombia, Venezuela, Brazil, and other South American countries. Born in Norman, OK, Cobb made her first solo flight at age 16, received her pilot's license at 17, and obtained her commercial pilot's license at 18. She was the first woman to undergo testing in the astronaut's program. She carries doctors', missionaries', and anthropologists' supplies on her flights into the South American interior.

14,234. Davis, Alice (Brown)
Papers. Nd. 1 folder.
Open. No guide.
Oklahoma Heritage Association.
The daughter of a Scottish physician and a Seminole woman, Davis (1852-1935) managed a ranch, trading post, and post office after the death of her husband. She was the mother of 11 children. Biographical sketch by her daughter Mrs. W. S. Key, photos, articles, and clippings. Educated at home and in schools in the Indian Territory, she married George Rollin Davis, an area rancher and businessman, in 1874. She was appointed chief of the Seminoles by President Warren G. Harding in 1922, the only woman to hold the post. She disbursed federal payments to Seminoles who had served in the army, acted as an interpreter in state and federal courts, and helped in the work of the Dawes Commission.

14,235. Fisher, Te Ata (Thompson)
Papers. 1927-76. 1 folder.
Open. No guide.
Oklahoma Heritage Association.
An actress and Indian dancer, Fisher (1895-) is the daughter of the last treasurer of the Chickasaw Nation. Biography, photos, articles, and clippings. Born Mary Thompson, she was given the name Te Ata, which means Bearer of the Morning. She earned a BA from Oklahoma College for Women in Chickasha, OK, and did graduate work at the theater school of Carnegie Institute of Technology in Pittsburgh. Her late husband Clyde Fisher, who earned a PhD at Johns Hopkins University, was curator of the American Museum of Natural History in New York and was director of the Hayden Planetarium. A member of the Society of Woman Geographers, the National Congress of American Indians, the Oklahoma Historical Society, and the Zeta Phi Eta national speech fraternity, Te Ata Fisher conducted extensive research on Indian folklore and culture.

14,236. Latting, Patience (Sewell)
Papers. 1958-77. 1 folder.
Open. No guide.
Oklahoma Heritage Association.
[Mrs. Trimble B.] Latting (1918-), currently serving her second four-year term as mayor of Oklahoma City, was the first woman elected to the Oklahoma City council and the first woman elected mayor. Correspondence, biographies, and clippings. A magna cum laude mathematics graduate of Oklahoma University, Latting received an MA in economics and statistics from Columbia University. She was elected to the Oklahoma City council in 1967 and to the office of mayor in 1971. She has served on advisory committees for Oklahoma's governors and on the advisory board and the board of trustees of the US Conference of Mayors.

14,237. Mesta, Perle Skirvin
Papers. 1951-75. 1 folder.
Open. No guide.
Oklahoma Heritage Association.
Mesta (1892-1975) was a Washington, DC, hostess and, from 1950 to 1955, ambassador to Luxembourg. Correspondence, photos, and clippings. After studying voice and piano at Sherwood School of Music in Chicago, she married George Mesta in 1916. A delegate to the UN from the Woman's party, she also wrote a syndicated column for the *New York Herald Tribune* about her three-month tour of the USSR. She also provided financial assistance to foreign students.

14,238. Metcalfe, Augusta
Papers. 1911-71. 1 folder.
Open. No guide.
Oklahoma Heritage Association.
A homesteader in western Oklahoma, [Mrs.] Metcalfe (1881-1971) painted pictures of the horses and scenery she saw around her. Biographies, photos, and clippings. Her works were exhibited during one-woman shows in Oklahoma in 1949 and 1967 and in New York City in 1958.

14,239. Tallchief, Maria
Papers. 1947-72. 1 folder.
Open. No guide.
Oklahoma Heritage Association.
Biographies, photos, articles, and clippings of Tallchief (1925-), a ballerina who joined the Ballet Russe de Monte Carlo at the age of 17; she was a guest ballerina with the Paris Opera Ballet in 1947 and prima ballerina with the New York City Ballet in 1954 and 1955. The daughter of Alexander

Joseph Tallchief, an Osage Indian, and Ruth Mary Porter Tallchief, who was of Scotch-Irish ancestry, Maria Tallchief spent her early life on an Oklahoma Indian reservation. She made her ballet debut at the age of 15 in California. She married Henry Paschen in Chicago in 1956.

14,240. Terekhov, Yvonne (Chouteau)
Papers. 1947-76. 1 folder.
Open. No guide.
Oklahoma Heritage Association.
Biography, photos, and clippings of Terekhov (1929-), a ballerina who joined the Ballet Russe de Monte Carlo in 1943. Born in Vinita, OK, Terekhov performed with the Ballet Russe for 14 years. She and her husband Miguel Terekhov are artists in residence at the University of Oklahoma. They initiated ballet courses in 1961, which now are part of a degree program.

14,241. Indian Archives
Collection. Ca. 1860-1930s. 4905 vols., 2,788,138 pp., and 44 drawers.
Open. Published guide.
Oklahoma Historical Society.
Executive, legislative, and court records; operating records of federal Indian agencies; records of Indian schools; and interviews pertain to the Five Civilized Tribes (Cherokee, Chickasaw, Choctaw, Creek, and Seminole) and to the Cheyenne, Arapaho, Cantonment, Kiowa, Pawnee, Quapaw, Sac, and Fox-Shawnee tribes. Contains interviews made for the WPA in the 1930s and histories and reminiscences by Oklahoma Indians, pioneers, and blacks. Many of the records pertain to women. See John Stewart and Kenny A. Franks, *State Records, Manuscripts, and Newspapers at the Oklahoma State Archives and Oklahoma Historical Society* (Oklahoma City: Oklahoma Department of Libraries and Oklahoma Historical Society, 1975).

14,242. Lewers, Eva Zerline
Papers. 1930-56. 3 cu.ft.
Open. No guide.
Oklahoma Historical Society.
Lewers (1895-1956) taught at and was superintendent of the Rosebud Indian Agency from 1929 to 1934 and then served as superintendent of the Indian Boarding School at Eufaula, OK, from 1934 to 1956. Correspondence of Lewers and others involved in Indian education, manuscripts by Lewers regarding curriculum in Indian schools, and manuscripts by others concerning Indian education. Lewers primarily taught music.

14,243. Merriman, Grace, and Robertson, Ann Eliza (Worcester)
Papers. 1860-1907. 2 cu.ft.
Open. No guide.
Oklahoma Historical Society.
Family correspondence and miscellaneous papers of [Mrs. William Schenck] Robertson (1826-1905), a missionary among the Creek Indians who translated the New Testament and sections of the Old Testament into the Creek language. Robertson became known as the foremost linguist of Creek-English. Her daughter Alice Mary Robertson (1854-1931) taught for many years in the Cherokee Nation in Oklahoma.

14,244. Mitchell, Katie (Edwards) Bemo
Papers. 1865-1911. 0.75 cu.ft.
Open. No guide.
Oklahoma Historical Society.
Diaries of Mitchell (1848-1933), who began to teach in the Creek Nation in 1870. The diaries record her initial travels into Indian country; her experience as a teacher; and her marriages to John Douglas Bemo, a Creek Indian who was the son of a teacher and preacher, and to L. S. Mitchell. She was married to Bemo from 1873 to 1898 and to Mitchell from 1904 to 1929. Katie Mitchell taught principally at the Tullahassee Manual Labor Boarding School.

14,245. Photos
Collection. Ca. 1870- . 13,000 items.
Open. No guide.
Oklahoma Historical Society.
Photos and negatives that illustrate Oklahoma and Indian history include some that pertain to women.

14,246. Robertson, Alice Mary
Papers. 1805-1923. 1 cu.ft.
Open. No guide.
Oklahoma Historical Society.
A teacher in the Oklahoma Cherokee Nation, [Miss] Robertson (1854-1931) served as postmaster of Muskogee, OK, from 1906 to 1911. Correspondence, annual reports, manuscripts, pamphlets, clippings, and other papers. Much of the collection is official and personal correspondence related to Robertson's work as postmaster. Also included are manuscripts about missionary work of her parents and others among the Cherokee and Creek Indians and about Indian life and schools, annual reports of the American National Red Cross from 1921 to 1923 and other documents concerning Red Cross activities in Oklahoma during the early 1900s, a copy of the Gospel of John in the Creek language, and a typescript of Robertson family reminiscences about the Civil War.

14,247. Constitutional Convention: Speeches and Discussion of Women's Suffrage
Records. 1907. No size given.
Open. Published guide.
Oklahoma State Archives.
Minutes of the Convention, which was called to write the constitution for the state of Oklahoma. Includes speeches by those who were not delegates. Part of the minutes are available on microfilm. See Thomas W. Kremm, *Guide to the Oklahoma State Archives* (Oklahoma City, OK: Oklahoma Department of Libraries).

14,248. Department of Charities and Corrections
Records. 1907-45. 26 cu.ft.
Partially restricted. Published guide.
Oklahoma State Archives.
Administrative files of the Department, which was created in 1907, when Oklahoma became a state, under the leadership of Kate Barnard, who became its first commissioner. Correspondence and other records pertain to meetings, inspections, and investigations of county jails, the state penitentiary, and other state institutions. The bulk of the records document the work of Barnard, who served as commissioner of charities and corrections until 1914. See Thomas W. Kremm, *Guide to the Oklahoma State Archives* (Oklahoma City, OK: Oklahoma Department of Libraries).

14,249. Governor's Commission on the Status of Women
Records. 1949-69. 3 folders.
Open. Published guide.
Oklahoma State Archives.
Minutes, reports, correspondence, and pamphlets of the Commission, which was created to study the status of women, specifically employment policies, social insurance, tax laws, legal treatment, education and vocational training, and leadership opportunities in both the public and private sectors. See Thomas W. Kremm, *Guide to the Oklahoma State Archives* (Oklahoma City, OK: Oklahoma Department of Libraries).

14,250. Office of the Governor: Administrative Subject Files
Records. 1907-75. Several folders.
Open. Published guide.
Oklahoma State Archives.
In the files, which consist primarily of correspondence, is material that deals with the subject of women. See Thomas W. Kremm, *Guide to the Oklahoma State Archives* (Oklahoma City, OK: Oklahoma Department of Libraries).

14,251. Oklahoma Legislature: Bills, Resolutions, and Journals
Records. 1907- . Several folders.
Open. Published guide.
Oklahoma State Archives.
Bills and resolutions, including introduced, engrossed, and enrolled versions as well as versions amended in committee. See Thomas W. Kremm, *Guide to the Oklahoma State Archives* (Oklahoma City, OK: Oklahoma Department of Libraries).

14,252. Oklahoma State Election Board: Election Returns
Records. 1907- . 42 ft.
Open. Published guide.
Oklahoma State Archives.
Returns for all primary, special, and general elections by county and precinct. Records votes for all candidates and on state questions. Microfilm of returns from 1907 to 1970 is also available. See Thomas W. Kremm, *Guide to the Oklahoma State Archives* (Oklahoma City, OK: Oklahoma Department of Libraries).

14,253. Secretary of State: State Questions and Petitions
Records. 1907- . Several folders.
Open. Published guide.
Oklahoma State Archives.
Ballot titles, briefs, and hearings on state questions affecting women's rights. See Thomas W. Kremm, *Guide to the Oklahoma State Archives* (Oklahoma City, OK: Oklahoma Department of Libraries).

14,254. Vansant, Irene Allen
Papers. 1893-1911. 4 vols.
Open. Published guide.
Oklahoma State Archives.
Volumes of visions, transcriptions, letters, and commentaries of Vansant. Much of the material pertains to Vansant's husband Henry Garrison Carson and to his evangelical efforts during the 1880s and 1890s. See Thomas W. Kremm, *Guide to the Oklahoma State Archives* (Oklahoma City, OK: Oklahoma Department of Libraries).

STILLWATER

14,255. Dusch, Willa Adams
Papers. 1887-97. 3 vols.
Open. No guide.
Oklahoma State University Library, Special Collections.
Scrapbook and autograph and photo albums of Dusch (ca. 1880-1957) relate chiefly to her years as a student at Oklahoma Agricultural and Mechanical College, now Oklahoma State University.

14,256. Hunter, Ella Ewing
Papers. 1885-ca. 1918. 1 folder and 1 vol.
Open. No guide.
Oklahoma State University Library, Special Collections.
Correspondence, biographical material, and scrapbook of Hunter (1870-1935) relate primarily to her work as the first woman faculty member at Oklahoma Agricultural and Mechanical College, now Oklahoma State University.

14,257. Johnston, Henry S.
Papers. 1888-1965. 114.6 cu.ft.
Open. Unpublished guide.
Oklahoma State University Library, Special Collections.
Correspondence, notes, speeches, legal papers, subject files, photos, clippings, and other papers of Johnston (1867-1965), a lawyer elected governor of Oklahoma in 1926 and then impeached in 1929.

Includes a manuscript by Mamie [Mrs. O. O.] Hammonds, who was Johnston's secretary during his gubernatorial term and who was said to have been influential in his administration. In her unpublished manuscript, she sought to vindicate Johnston. Also includes other papers of Hammonds.

14,258. Roe, Vingie Eve
Papers. 1879-1958. 1 folder and 33 vols.
Open. No guide.
Oklahoma State University Library, Special Collections.
Roe (1879-1958) was an Oklahoma author. Typescripts of some of Roe's poems, articles about her, and a scrapbook of items concerning publication of her first poems and other aspects of her career through the publication of her first book. Also includes her personal library of books.

TULSA

14,259. Archives
Records. 1845- . 45 drawers, 2 cabinets, and 1 seven-shelf bookcase.
Access restricted. Unpublished guide.
Benedictine Sisters, St. Joseph Convent.
Mother Paula O'Reilly founded this community of Benedictine Sisters in 1879 in Creston, IA; the community moved to Guthrie in Oklahoma Territory in 1889. Correspondence; diaries; records of the Sisters' work in education, health services, and parish ministry; financial records; records of living and deceased sisters; photos; scrapbooks; volumes of diocesan and archdiocesan newspapers; and other records. Includes manuscripts and printed material of the Tulsa Deanery Council of the National Council of Catholic Women, which was founded in 1928.

14,260. American History Forum
Records. 1954-68. 1 box.
Open. No guide.
Tulsa County Historical Society.
Minutes of the Forum, which was founded in 1954.

14,261. Civic Music Association
Records. 1940-55. 2 cu. ft.
Open. No guide.
Tulsa County Historical Society.
Scrapbooks of the Association, which was founded in 1940 to promote music appreciation.

14,262. History and Literature Club
Records. 1915-64. 1 box.
Open. No guide.
Tulsa County Historical Society.
Scrapbooks of the Club, which was organized in 1915 to promote the study of classics and history.

14,263. Pythian Sisters, Tulsa Temple
Records. 1923-73. 1 box.
Open. No guide.
Tulsa County Historical Society.
Scrapbooks of the Sisters, an auxiliary of the Knights of Pythias, founded in 1923.

14,264. Smedley O. Butler Unit, Marine Corps League Auxiliary
Records. 1943-46. 1 box.
Open. No guide.
Tulsa County Historical Society.
Minutes and scrapbooks of the Unit, which was formed in 1943 to assist in the war effort by supporting the Marine Corps.

14,265. Tulsa Federation of Women's Clubs
Records. 1926-64. 1 box.
Open. No guide.
Tulsa County Historical Society.
Scrapbooks of the Federation, which was established in 1926 to promote interest in civic and cultural activities.

14,266. Tulsa Town Club
Records. 1919-71. 2 boxes.
Open. No guide.
Tulsa County Historical Society.
Minutes, journals, a lecture series file, radio scripts, scrapbooks, and yearbooks of the Club, which was founded in 1919. Also includes a history of the group from its inception to 1964. The Club's interests included lectures, preservation of history, and radio broadcasts.

14,267. Women's Dinner Club
Records. 1963-70. 1 box.
Open. No guide.
Tulsa County Historical Society.
Minutes and scrapbooks of the Club, which was organized in 1963 to promote social activities.

OREGON

AURORA

14,268. Aurora Colony
Records. 1855-?. Ca. 40 ft. and 6 tapes.
Access restricted. Unpublished guide.
Aurora Colony Historical Society.
Correspondence, account books, ledgers, and other personal papers; oral history interviews; and published accounts, articles, theses, and books concerning Aurora Colony, a religious communal society that flourished in Oregon from 1856 to 1883 and in Bethel, MO, from 1845 to 1883.

BEAVERTON

14,269. Archives
Records. 1886- . No size given.
Open. No guide.
Sisters of St. Mary of Oregon Motherhouse.
The order was founded in 1886 in Sublimity, OR, by William Gross, a Redemptorist priest who was archbishop of Portland. Correspondence, memoirs of foundresses, chronicles, historical information, theses about the early days of the order, photos, scrapbooks about important events, and other records of the Sisters, who are involved in teaching and nursing.

COOS BAY

14,270. Living History Series
Oral history. 1972-75. 102 tapes and other items.
Open. Index.
Southwestern Oregon Community College Library.
Interviews contain reminiscences of pioneers regarding Coos County, OR. The interviews with women relate to such topics as the WCTU, women's clubs, and women's employment. Also includes slides of old photos.

CORVALLIS

14,271. Board of Regents
Records. 1886-1929. 6 microfilm reels.
Open. Unpublished guide.
Oregon State University Archives.
Minutes, correspondence, reports, salary schedules, contracts, and other records of OSU's Board of Regents, including correspondence from ca. 1900 regarding Margaret Comstock Snell, a physician and founder of OSU's school of home economics, who protested to the Board about her low salary.

14,272. Clark, Ava Milam
Papers. Ca. 1911-50s. Ca. 8 cu.ft.
Open. No guide.
Oregon State University Archives.
Correspondence, manuscripts, research notes, speeches, poetry, clippings, and ephemera of Clark, a professor and dean of OSU's school of home economics, who wrote an autobiography and a book regarding home economics in China. Includes correspondence with the Food and Agriculture Organization of the United Nations and with home economists around the world as well as letters Clark wrote from the Far East.

14,273. Gilkey, Helen
Papers. Ca. 1911-50s. Ca. 3 cu.ft.
Open. No guide.
Oregon State University Archives.
Correspondence, MA thesis, notes, writings and talks, illustrations, and teaching material of Gilkey, a professor of botany at OSU and an expert on truffles. Papers concern mycology and her research on truffles.

14,274. Miscellaneous
Collection. Nd. 1 drawer.
Open. No guide.
Oregon State University Archives.
Correspondence, clippings, and other material, including a one-page list of women graduates in engineering from 1923 to 1962; histories, alumnae material, an internal evaluation from 1960, and ephemera of OSU's school of home economics; and Laura B. Fry's home economics notebook from 1895, which contains notes on a Margaret Comstock Snell lecture on etiquette and other lectures, quotations, and poetry. Also includes correspondence, memorabilia, and clippings regarding Margaret Comstock Snell, founder of OSU's school of home economics, as well as a letter she wrote in 1902 to the board of regents requesting an explanation for the lowering of her salary when the salaries of all other department heads were increased.

14,275. Office of the Dean of Women
Records. 1923-65. 6 microfilm reels.
Open. Unpublished guide.
Oregon State University Archives.
Correspondence, committee records, and other records of the Office regarding the military, the Panhellenic committee, employment, student personnel and counseling, honorary and service clubs, living arrangements for women other than sororities, and the Mother's Club.

14,276. Oregon State College Pan-Hellenic Association
Records. 1957-60. 1 microfilm reel.
Open. Unpublished guide.
Oregon State University Archives.
Constitution, minutes, correspondence, programs, handbooks, and other records of this administrative organization for the College's sororities.

14,277. Oregon State University Library
Records. 1908-69. 55 microfilm reels.
Open. Unpublished guide.
Oregon State University Archives.
Minutes, correspondence, personnel records, lectures, clippings, and other records of the Library. Includes biographical information about Margaret Snell, founder of the University's school of home economics, and personal and business correspondence, correspondence with the US Army's Camp Lewis during WWI, biographical notes, articles, and an obituary of Ida Angeline Kidder, a librarian from 1908 to 1920.

14,278. School of Home Economics, Department of Clothing, Textiles, and Related Arts
Records. 1931-61. 1 microfilm reel.
Open. Unpublished guide.
Oregon State University Archives.
Biennial reports, committee records, correspondence, curriculum material, research notes, and enrollment statistics of the Department. Includes items concerning Joan Patterson's research on Oregon flax.

14,279. School of Home Economics, Department of Family Life and Home Management
Records. 1919-65. 4 microfilm reels.
Open. Unpublished guide.
Oregon State University Archives.
Financial records, correspondence, reports, student papers and records, bulletins, and other records relating to the functions and policies of the Department's home management houses, which were used for demonstrations.

14,280. School of Home Economics, Office of the Dean
Records. 1943-63. 1 microfilm reel.
Open. Unpublished guide.
Oregon State University Archives.
Correspondence of the Dean relates to her work and the committees on which she served.

EUGENE

14,281. ABC Club
Records. 1939-59. 14 pp.
Open. No guide.
Lane County Museum.
Papers delivered to this Eugene woman's study club on topics such as early transportation and early schools in Lane County.

14,282. Abrams, Mary Isabella
Papers. 1972. 53-page item.
Open. No guide.
Lane County Museum.
Manuscript of Abrams's reminiscences about her family's history, dating back to her great-grandfather John Stewart who came to Oregon with the Lost Wagon Train of 1853. Her grandmother was Elizabeth Young (Stewart) Warner. The manuscript has been published.

14,283. Barette, Leonore Gale
Papers. 1895. 1 vol.
Open. No guide.
Lane County Museum.
Diary of Barette (1880-?) regards daily life in Olympia, WA, and in Eugene where she was a student at the University of Oregon. She writes of books, clothing, and study.

14,284. Bristow Family
Papers. Ca. 1820-1940. 6 oversize boxes.
Open. No guide.
Lane County Museum.
Correspondence, reminiscences, speeches and writings, business records, genealogical material, legal documents, photos, clippings, and books of the Bristows, the first family to settle in Lane County. Lisette "Lizzie" (Bristow) Stephens (1867-1962), a writer and wife of US Congressman John H. Stephens of Texas, was granddaughter of Elijah Bristow (1788-1872), the first settler in Lane County, and half sister of Darwin Bristow (1862-1951), a prominent area banker. Lisette Stephens's papers include manuscripts of her stories and historic narratives about her family and early Lane County, transcripts of a notebook containing family letters, a manuscript on the life of her stepmother Mary Jane Wells, and a scrapbook of clippings. Collection also contains clippings and correspondence of Elizabeth Coffey Bristow; Evelyn Bristow, a singer; and Helen Bristow, a civic leader.

14,285. Chambers, Edith Kerns
Papers. 1940s. 1 Hollinger box.
Open. Unpublished guide.
Lane County Museum.
Correspondence, diary, manuscripts, research notebooks, genealogy, photos, clippings, and other papers of Chambers (1876-1962), a writer of historical articles. Includes typescript of "Eugene Houses," with notes on 19th-century houses and builders; a typescript about 19th-century schools and teachers in Eugene; and letters and a diary regarding the 1948 rendezvous, trek, and convention of Old Oregon Trail, Inc.

14,286. Eakin, Jane Paul
Papers. 1866. 33-page vol.
Open. No guide.
Lane County Museum.
Diary of Eakin (ca. 1850-?), a 16-year-old girl who crossed the plains with her father Stewart Bates Eakin, Sr., and her mother.

14,287. Eugene Fortnightly Club
Records. 1953-54. 0.5 in.
Open. No guide.
Lane County Museum.
Founded in 1893, this women's club was interested in Oregon history. Scrapbook includes biographies of Club charter members and clippings regarding Club events.

14,288. Goltra, Elizabeth Julia
Papers. 1853. 30-page vol.
Open. No guide.
Lane County Museum.
Journal kept by [Mrs. Nelson] Goltra (ca. 1831-?), a pioneer, while crossing the continent. Written for the benefit of friends who would follow the next year, it contains detailed information on such matters as mileage, Indians, grass, water, and weather and indicates her trust in God. The journal has been published.

14,289. Harpham, Josephine Evans
Papers. Ca. 1959-62. Ca. 60 pp.
Open. No guide.
Lane County Museum.
Manuscripts of articles on historic houses of Eugene by Harpham, an author. She later published a book on the subject, *Doorways into History.*

14,290. Lane County Archives
Records. 1852-1963. Ca. 100 vols.
Open. Records transmittal list.
Lane County Museum.
Marriage, election, 1854 census, and court (civil, criminal, probate) records; assessment rolls; tax receipt books; register of married women's personal estates; register of widows' pensions; and records of contagious diseases. Includes demographic data on women.

14,291. Lane County Historical Society Oral History Project
Oral history. Ca. 1970s. 43 tapes and 18 items.
Open. No guide.
Lane County Museum.
Tapes and transcripts of interviews with pioneer-settlers of Lane County about life from the 1880s into the twentieth century.

14,292. Lane County Residents
Collection. 1840s-1970s. 1 drawer.
Open. No guide.
Lane County Museum.
Obituaries and other clippings, ephemera, and miscellany on Lane County residents.

14,293. Love, Helen Marne (Stewart)
Papers. 1853. 27-page vol.
Open. No guide.
Lane County Museum.
Diary which Helen Stewart (1835-73), a pioneer, kept while traveling from Pennsylvania to Oregon with her parents. The Stewarts were part of the Lost Wagon Train of 1853 in which 1000 people, attempting to make a new trail through eastern Oregon and the Cascade Mountains, became lost and suffered great hardships. Also includes a description of the steamer trip from Pittsburgh to St. Joseph, MO. Stewart later married David S. Love. The diary has been published.

14,294. Lyman, Esther, and Lyman, Joseph
Papers. 1853. 15 pp.
Open. No guide.
Lane County Museum.
The Lymans, Esther (1826-1917) and Joseph (?-1871), were part of the Lost Wagon Train of 1853, a group of pioneers that left the Oregon Trail near Fort Boise to make a new trail through the desert of eastern Oregon, the Cascade Mountains, and down the middle fork of the Willamette River. Copies of their letters, which began as a journal of the crossing of the continent. Joseph Lyman was a widower with three children when he married Esther in 1850. The letters have been published.

14,295. Native Daughters of Oregon, Martha Mulligan Cabin No. 3
Records. 1899-1904. 2 vols.
Open. No guide.
Lane County Museum.
Minute book and treasurer's book of this Eugene historic and social club for women.

14,296. Newton, Kathleen Mitchell
Papers. 1927. 9-page vol.
Open. No guide.
Lane County Museum.
Diary in which Newton (ca. 1900-) relates experiences on a hunting trip to Swift Creek Camp.

14,297. Patterson, Ida
Papers. 1843. 11-page item.
Open. No guide.
Lane County Museum.
An account of an 1843 wagon train with which the mother of Patterson (1866-1944) traveled.

14,298. Pengra, Charlotte Sterns
Papers. 1853. 56-page vol.
Open. No guide.
Lane County Museum.
Diary kept by [Mrs. B. J.] Pengra (1827-?), a pioneer, traveling on the Oregon Trail. The diary has been published.

14,299. Potter, Anna Patterson
Papers. 1885-90. 0.25 in.
Open. Preliminary inventory.
Lane County Museum.
Correspondence of Potter (1861-?) concerning her wedding; an essay for the 1885 University of Oregon commencement exercises, entitled "Act Well Your Part"; and memorabilia.

14,300. Romane, Elizabeth
Papers. Ca. 1915-68. Ca. 35 boxes and 4 vols.
Open. No guide.
Lane County Museum.
Romane was an Oregon photographer. Photo negatives and scrapbooks containing portrait photos taken by Romane and clippings, some of which she annotated, of her photos. Also includes articles on historic topics, women's clubs, and personalities.

14,301. Skaggs, Lucinda "Lulu"
Papers. 1883-84. 6 items.
Open. No guide.
Lane County Museum.
Correspondence of Skaggs (1867-84) to her cousin

Ida (Hendricks) Chambers relating her experiences as a young school teacher in rural Oregon near Eugene.

14,302. Smith, Evelyn Stewart
Papers. 1935-47. 1 vol.
Open. No guide.
Lane County Museum.
Diary of Smith (1871-?) relates daily routine, family and financial matters, and Baptist Church activities in Eugene.

14,303. Star of Hope Lodge No. 7
Records. 1865-79. 3 vols.
Open. No guide.
Lane County Museum.
Minute books and a copybook of the Eugene chapter of the International Order of Good Templars, a temperance organization.

14,304. Stewart, Eliza Seelye
Papers. 1863. 1 vol. and 1 item.
Open. No guide.
Lane County Museum.
Diary in which Stewart (1841-1911) records the daily life of a 22-year-old single woman in St. Anthony, MN. She later moved to Oregon with her husband David Stewart.

14,305. Stewart, Jessie Hills
Papers. 1913-63. 1 vol. and 48 pp.
Open. No guide.
Lane County Museum.
Diary of Stewart (1887-1972), written in 1913, describes her role in John and Jasper Hills's log drive down Fall Creek. Also included are autobiographical manuscripts regarding her spiritual life and high points of her 55 years of marriage.

14,306. Walton, Ellen Pauline
Papers. 1896-1963. 2 Hollinger boxes.
Open. No guide.
Lane County Museum.
Member of a prominent Eugene family, Walton (1879-1966) was a teacher and amateur historian who received an MA from Northwestern University in 1906. Correspondence, diary, autobiographical information, addresses and writings, diploma, 1914 teachers certificate, and clippings. Included are texts of her talks on early churches, schools, teachers, and transportation in Oregon and Eugene; speeches to the WCTU, the Pioneer Historical Society, and other groups in the 1950s and 1960s; and material on the early library association.

14,307. Warner, Agnes (Stewart)
Papers. 1853. 21 pp.
Open. No guide.
Lane County Museum.
Diary of Agnes Stewart [later Warner] (1832-1905), pioneer, contains her account of the journey to Oregon known as the Lost Wagon Train of 1853. Also included is a letter by Elizabeth Young (Stewart) Warner about the same journey. The diary has been published.

14,308. Watts, J. O., Family
Papers. Ca. 1891-1909. 1 folder.
Open. No guide.
Lane County Museum.
Family correspondence written between Montana and Oregon contains letters by Mrs. J. O. Watts, Mary Wallace, and Bess Watts. Includes love letters and a letter reflecting marital troubles.

14,309. Williams, Irena Dunn
Papers. 1853-1934. Ca. 20-page vol.
Open. No guide.
Lane County Museum.
Scrapbook of Eugene *Register-Guard* clippings of the memoirs of Williams (1856-?) concerning her life in Eugene.

14,310. Adair Family
Papers. 1848-52. 180 pp.
Open. Published guide.
University of Oregon Library, Special Collections.
Copies of letters that Mary Ann (Dickinson) Adair, a pioneer, wrote en route from Kentucky to Astoria, OR. See Martin Schmitt, *Catalogue of Manuscripts in the University of Oregon Library* (Eugene, OR: University of Oregon Press, 1971).

14,311. Aitken Family
Papers. 1874-1969. 7 ft.
Open. Supplement to published guide.
University of Oregon Library, Special Collections.
Correspondence, diaries, memory books, class notes, a diploma and mementos of Carrie Fidelia (Johnson) [Mrs. Alvord] Aitken (1860-1947) and her daughters Frances Alva Aitken (1889-1970) and Geraldine Lee Aitken. Diaries of Carrie Aitken from 1874 to 1884 concern her student days at Mills Seminary and teaching experiences in Arizona Territory mining camps from 1880 to 1884. Her diaries of 1909 to 1913 were written in Portland, OR, after the death of her husband. Her letters to her daughters from 1915 to 1946 contain family news and information on Portland's Unitarian community and its patriarch Thomas Lamb Eliot. Frances Aitken's papers include diaries from 1909 to 1969 and letters to her mother and sister from 1908 to 1951. She attended Oregon Agricultural College (now Oregon State University) from 1908 to 1910; taught home economics to children in Salem, OR, and Portland from 1910 to 1918; and was thereafter a stenographer in Portland, where she lived with her mother. She was active in the Unitarian church. Geraldine Aitken's correspondence with her mother and sister from 1909 to 1951 contains descriptions of her experiences as a student at a Boston music school in 1909, as a music teacher at Oahu College in Honolulu from 1916 to 1927 and at the Seymour School of Musical Reeducation in New York in 1927, as the operator of a private piano school in New Jersey, and as a teacher in a Honolulu private piano school from 1935. Includes letters written from Honolulu during and after the attack on Pearl Harbor in 1941.

14,312. Allen, Don B.
Papers. 1951-67. 4.5 ft.
Open. Published guide and inventory.
University of Oregon Library, Special Collections.
Correspondence with publishers and manuscripts of Allen, a writer of fiction for juveniles, include papers of his wife Thelma Diener Allen, who wrote with her husband under the joint name of T. D. Allen. See Martin Schmitt, *Catalogue of Manuscripts in the University of Oregon Library* (Eugene, OR: University of Oregon Press, 1971).

14,313. Allen, Ida (Elliot)
Papers. 1906-43. 3 ft.
Open. Published guide and inventory.
University of Oregon Library, Special Collections.
Allen (1880-1943), whose professional name was Sally Allen, was a writer and playwright in Washington and Oregon. Correspondence with literary agents; manuscripts, including one of her best-known plays, *What the Gulls Knew;* and published works. See Martin Schmitt, *Catalogue of Manuscripts in the University of Oregon Library* (Eugene, OR: University of Oregon Press, 1971).

14,314. Applegate, Oliver Cromwell
Papers. 1842-1938. 6 ft.
Open. Published guide and calendar.
University of Oregon Library, Special Collections.
Correspondence of Applegate (1845-1938), including correspondence with Frances (Fuller) Victor, a leader in the Oregon women's rights movement. See Martin Schmitt, *Catalogue of Manuscripts in the University of Oregon Library* (Eugene, OR: University of Oregon Press, 1971).

14,315. Arvonen, Helen
Papers. 1947-70. 1 box.
Open. Published guide.
University of Oregon Library, Special Collections.
Manuscripts of novels and short stories by Arvonen (1918-) and letters from Edith Margolis of the Lenniger Literary Agency. See Martin Schmitt, *Catalogue of Manuscripts in the University of Oregon Library* (Eugene, OR: University of Oregon Press, 1971).

14,316. Atwood, Hazel M.
Papers. 1933-50. 1 box.
Open. Supplement to published guide.
University of Oregon Library, Special Collections.
Correspondence and documents of Atwood, a Congregational missionary nurse in Foochow, China, include material on the Willis F. Pierce Memorial Hospital, formerly Foochow Christian Union Hospital, as well as missionary matters.

14,317. Ayer, Margaret
Papers. 1944-64. 1.5 ft.
Open. Published guide.
University of Oregon Library, Special Collections.
Manuscripts and original and published illustrations of Ayer, an illustrator and wife of Alfred Babington Smith. See Martin Schmitt, *Catalogue of Manuscripts in the University of Oregon Library* (Eugene, OR: University of Oregon Press, 1971).

14,318. Bates, Kate (Stevens)
Papers. 1860-1941. 4.5 ft.
Open. Published guide and inventory.
University of Oregon Library, Special Collections.
Correspondence, diaries, and manuscripts of Bates (1852-1941), a Portland, OR, socialite and amateur writer. Daughter of the first territorial governor of Washington Isaac I. Stevens, she was married to Edward Wingard Bingham from 1886 until his death in 1904 and then to James H. S. Bates in 1913. Diaries from 1880 to 1936 provide information on her early life in Newport, RI, and Dorchester, MA, where her family lived; the years in Portland, where she moved following her first marriage; and her life in Massachusetts after her second marriage and at Cloverfield Farms near Olympia, WA, after 1918. In Portland, Bates was a member of the Unitarian Society and an amateur writer for magazines and newspapers. Her diaries contain descriptions of social life among Portland's prominent families and her visits to Olympia. Manuscripts of her travel and historical articles are also included. Her correspondence concerns family matters, business, and social affairs. See Martin Schmitt, *Catalogue of Manuscripts in the University of Oregon Library* (Eugene, OR: University of Oregon Press, 1971).

14,319. Beatty, Hetty Burlingame
Papers. 1947-69. 8 ft.
Open. Published guide and inventory.
University of Oregon Library, Special Collections.
Beatty (1907-71) was an author and illustrator of books for children and young people. Correspondence with editors and publishers, particularly Houghton-Mifflin Co., and manuscripts and illustrations for 12 books. See Martin Schmitt, *Catalogue of Manuscripts in the University of Oregon Library* (Eugene, OR: University of Oregon Press, 1971).

14,320. Benary-Isbert, Margot
Papers. 1950-67. 1.5 ft.
Open. Published guide and inventory.
University of Oregon Library, Special Collections.
Born in Germany, Benary-Isbert (1889-), a writer, became a naturalized US citizen in 1957. Manuscripts and correspondence with German friends, readers, and Harcourt, Brace and Co. See Martin Schmitt, *Catalogue of Manuscripts in the University of Oregon Library* (Eugene, OR: University of Oregon Press, 1971).

14,321. Bendick, Jeanne
Papers. 1950-65. 3 ft.
Open. Published guide and inventory.
University of Oregon Library, Special Collections.
Manuscripts and original artwork of Bendick (1919-), an author and illustrator. See Martin Schmitt, *Catalogue of Manuscripts in the University of Oregon Library* (Eugene, OR: University of Oregon Press, 1971).

14,322. Bishop, Elizabeth
Papers. 1948-49. 24 items.
Open. Published guide.
University of Oregon Library, Special Collections.
Bishop (1911-), a poet, was a consultant in poetry at the Library of Congress from 1949 to 1950; in 1956 she won the Pulitzer Prize for poetry for *Poems: North and South* (Boston: 1955). Consists of letters to Carley Dawson regarding poetry, poets, and personal matters. See Martin Schmitt, *Catalogue of Manuscripts in the University of Oregon Library* (Eugene, OR: University of Oregon Press, 1971).

14,323. Blackwood, Lillian Caldwell
Papers. 1877-1906. 65 items.
Open. Published guide.
University of Oregon Library, Special Collections.
Letters to Blackwood, a Jacksonville, OR, resident, from her brother Richard Blackwood of Tombstone, AR; Kate Murray of Murfreesboro, TN; and Mrs. M. S. Courtney regarding family and social matters. See Martin Schmitt, *Catalogue of Manuscripts in the University of Oregon Library* (Eugene, OR: University of Oregon Press, 1971).

14,324. Blocklinger, Peggy Jeanne (O'More)
Papers. 1927-65. 6 ft.
Open. Published guide and inventory.
University of Oregon Library, Special Collections.
Correspondence, photos, scrapbooks, clippings, and books of Blocklinger (1897-1970), an author, journalist, and novelist in Texas, California, and Oregon. Also includes manuscripts of 37 books, together with synopses and alternate versions; short stories; poetry; essays; and teleplays. Correspondents include agent Adeline Alvord, E. Wartels, Alice Sachs of Crown Publishers, and Charles S. Strong of the Fact Feature Syndicate. See Martin Schmitt, *Catalogue of Manuscripts in the University of Oregon Library* (Eugene, OR: University of Oregon Press, 1971).

14,325. Boucher, Mae
Papers. 1926-49. 1 box.
Open. Published guide.
University of Oregon Library, Special Collections.
Boucher was a missionary nurse for the Methodist Episcopal church in Yenping in Fukien Province, China. Diary for 1926 and letters to her family, 1926-30, and from Frank T. Cartwright and Frederick Bankhardt. See Martin Schmitt, *Catalogue of Manuscripts in the University of Oregon Library* (Eugene, OR: University of Oregon Press, 1971).

14,326. Brann, Esther
Papers. 1924-60. 1 box.
Open. Published guide.
University of Oregon Library, Special Collections.
Brann, the wife of Richard Schorr, was an author and illustrator of children's books. Correspondence with Macmillan Co., manuscripts of books, and artwork. See Martin Schmitt, *Catalogue of Manuscripts in the University of Oregon Library* (Eugene, OR: University of Oregon Press, 1971).

14,327. Bratton, Helen
Papers. 1962-69. 1.5 ft.
Open. Inventory and supplement to published guide.
University of Oregon Library, Special Collections.
Bratton (1899-) was an author of novels for teen-age girls. Correspondence with publishers, particularly David McKay Co., and manuscripts, including drafts, final copies, and research material.

14,328. Brentano, Lowell
Papers. 1917-52. 6 ft.
Open. Inventory and supplement to published guide.
University of Oregon Library, Special Collections.
Correspondence and manuscripts of Brentano (1895-1950), a publisher, and his wife Frances Isabella (Hyams) Brentano, a writer and editor in the Brentano firm. Includes professional correspondence with writers, publishers, and agents. Correspondents include Dorothy Armbruster.

14,329. Brooks, Anne (Tedlock)
Papers. 1939-50. 2 ft.
Open. Published guide.
University of Oregon Library, Special Collections.
Correspondence and manuscripts of Brooks (1905-), an author of novels for young people. Includes correspondence with agents and editors, particularly Willis Wing, May Cameron of Samuel Curl, Inc., and Arcadia House. See Martin Schmitt, *Catalogue of Manuscripts in the University of Oregon Library* (Eugene, OR: University of Oregon Press, 1971).

14,330. Brown, Ella H.
Papers. 1920-21. 9 pp.
Open. Published guide.
University of Oregon Library, Special Collections.
Reminiscences of Brown, who describes her position as a rural Douglas County, OR, school supervisor. See Martin Schmitt, *Catalogue of Manuscripts in the University of Oregon Library* (Eugene, OR: University of Oregon Press, 1971).

14,331. Calbreath Family
Papers. 1843-1939. 3 ft.
Open. Published guide and inventory.
University of Oregon Library, Special Collections.
Correspondence, diaries, manuscripts, and financial records of John Calbreath, a Yamhill County, OR, physician and superintendent of the Oregon Insane Asylum from 1899 to 1908; his wife Irene (Smith) Calbreath of Oregon; and their daughters Helen and Evelene. Collection consists primarily of correspondence of members of the Smith and Calbreath families, with 368 letters that Helen and Evelene Calbreath wrote together while studying music in Berlin from 1907 to 1909. Also includes an 1870 diary of Irene Calbreath, manuscripts of her prose and poetry, and a diary of Evelene Calbreath for 1898. See Martin Schmitt, *Catalogue of Manuscripts in the University of Oregon Library* (Eugene, OR: University of Oregon Press, 1971).

14,332. Carson, Luella Clay
Papers. 1889-1916. 1 ft.
Open. Published guide.
University of Oregon Library, Special Collections.
Carson (1856-1938) was a professor of rhetoric at the University of Oregon from 1888 to 1909 and president of Mills College in California from 1909 to 1913. Official correspondence regarding her work, letters from former students, and teaching material. See Martin Schmitt, *Catalogue of Manuscripts in the University of Oregon Library* (Eugene, OR: University of Oregon Press, 1971).

14,333. Case, Victoria
Papers. 1938-62. 3 ft.
Open. Published guide and inventory.
University of Oregon Library, Special Collections.
Case (1897-1973) was an Oregon author and free-lance writer. Correspondence with an agent; manuscripts of articles and stories; source material for her books *We Called It Culture* (New York, 1947) about Chautauqua and *The Quiet Life of Mrs. General Lane* (New York, 1952); and published items. See Martin Schmitt, *Catalogue of Manuscripts in the University of Oregon Library* (Eugene, OR: University of Oregon Press, 1971).

14,334. Chamberlain, Hazel
Papers. 1922-25. Ca. 46 items.
Open. Published guide.
University of Oregon Library, Special Collections.
Correspondence and photos of Chamberlain, a missionary teacher in Paraguay for the Inland South American Missionary Union of New York. Includes letters she wrote to her mother and friends describing her experiences. See Martin Schmitt, *Catalogue of Manuscripts in the University of Oregon Library* (Eugene, OR: University of Oregon Press, 1971).

14,335. Chase, Mary (Coyle)
Papers. 1947-68. 1 ft.
Open. Published guide and inventory.
University of Oregon Library, Special Collections.
Chase (1907-) was a Colorado author and playwright. Correspondence and manuscripts of plays and books, including early versions and revisions of *Bernadine* and *Harvey* and the screen treatment of *Harvey*. See Martin Schmitt, *Catalogue of Manuscripts in the University of Oregon Library* (Eugene, OR: University of Oregon Press, 1971).

14,336. Cheney, Monona L.
Papers. 1918-30. Ca. 266 items.
Open. Published guide.
University of Oregon Library, Special Collections.
Letters that Cheney wrote to her family describing her experiences as a missionary teacher for the Methodist Episcopal church at Keen School in Tientsin, China, in 1920, at the Gamewell School in Peking from 1924 to 1926, and at Yenching University from 1926 to 1930. Photos are also included. See Martin Schmitt, *Catalogue of Manuscripts in the University of Oregon Library* (Eugene, OR: University of Oregon Press, 1971).

14,337. Cloran, Mrs. Timothy
Papers. 1911-54. 41 vols.
Open. Published guide.
University of Oregon Library, Special Collections.
Diaries of Cloran, a University of Oregon professor's wife, list social events, menus, entertainments, and local news. See Martin Schmitt, *Catalogue of Manuscripts in the University of Oregon Library* (Eugene, OR: University of Oregon Press, 1971).

14,338. Collins, Mary (Garden)
Papers. 1941-53. 1 ft.
Open. Published guide.
University of Oregon Library, Special Collections.
Correspondence, notes, contracts, and scrapbooks of reviews of Collins, a California mystery story writer. Includes correspondence with Gertrude Atherton and with agents, particularly Margot Johnson of A. S. Lyons, Inc. See Martin Schmitt, *Catalogue of Manuscripts in the University of Oregon Library* (Eugene, OR: University of Oregon Press, 1971).

14,339. Colman, Hila
Papers. 1963-73. 1.5 ft.
Open. Supplement to published guide.
University of Oregon Library, Special Collections.
Professional correspondence and manuscripts of Colman, a writer of books for and about "suffering" adolescents.

14,340. Congregational Church, Women's Missionary Society
Records. 1889-97. 1 vol.
Open. Published guide.
University of Oregon Library, Special Collections.
Constitution and minutes of this Albany, OR, group. See Martin Schmitt, *Catalogue of Manuscripts in the University of Oregon Library* (Eugene, OR: University of Oregon Press, 1971).

14,341. Cooper, Arvazena Angeline Spillman
Papers. 1901. 31 pp.
Open. Published guide.
University of Oregon Library, Special Collections.
Reminiscences of [Mrs. Daniel Jackson] Cooper (1845-1929), a settler at The Dalles, OR, concern her journey with her husband from Missouri to Oregon in 1863. See Martin Schmitt, *Catalogue of Manuscripts in the University of Oregon Library* (Eugene, OR: University of Oregon Press, 1971).

14,342. Corbett, Elizabeth Frances
Papers. 1928-57. 1 box.
Open. Published guide.
University of Oregon Library, Special Collections.
Corbett (1887-) is an author and novelist. Manuscripts of short stories and a play, most of which include explanatory notes by Corbett. See Martin Schmitt, *Catalogue of Manuscripts in the University of Oregon Library* (Eugene, OR: University of Oregon Press, 1971).

14,343. Cormack, Maribelle
Papers. 1931-61. 10 ft.
Open. Published guide and inventory.
University of Oregon Library, Special Collections.
Cormack (1902-), an author of science books for adults and juveniles, was director of the Roger Williams Park Museum in Providence, RI. Manuscripts and related correspondence for 18 books. See Martin Schmitt, *Catalogue of Manuscripts in the University of Oregon Library* (Eugene, OR: University of Oregon Press, 1971).

14,344. Craig, Mary Francis
Papers. 1958-66. 2 ft.
Open. Published guide and inventory.
University of Oregon Library, Special Collections.
Craig (1923-) writes short stories and articles for religious magazines, romances for confession magazines, and books for children and young people. Manuscripts of books, stories, and articles and correspondence with publishers and agents. Craig's early pen name was Mary Francis Shura. See Martin Schmitt, *Catalogue of Manuscripts in the University of Oregon Library* (Eugene, OR: University of Oregon Press, 1971).

14,345. Crain, Lucille Cardin
Papers. 1938-70. 8 ft.
Open. Inventory and supplement to published guide.
University of Oregon Library, Special Collections.
Correspondence and ephemera of Crain (1901-), an author, editor, and publisher in New York City, who joined and supported various conservative organizations, served on committees to promote conservative political action, and wrote regularly to newspapers. In 1948 she became editor and publisher of *Educational Reviewer,* a publication financed by William F. Buckley, Sr. Includes correspondence with conservative individuals and organizations and issues of *The Individualist* from 1938 to 1953.

14,346. Cummins, Lucile
Papers. 1910-35. 311 items.
Open. Supplement to published guide.
University of Oregon Library, Special Collections.
Correspondence in which Cummins (?-1975) describes her experiences teaching piano in The Dalles, OR, and Portland and attending the Juilliard School of Music in New York City in 1935.

14,347. Cunningham, Julia Woolfolk
Papers. 1957-72. 1.5 ft.
Open. Supplement to published guide.
University of Oregon Library, Special Collections.
Cunningham (1916-), an author of children's books and a poet, was associate editor for *Screen Stories.* Personal and professional correspondence, manuscripts of books, and poems.

14,348. D'Arcy, Marianne (Hunsaker)
Papers. 1846-70. 168 pp.
Open. Published guide.
University of Oregon Library, Special Collections.
Manuscript reminiscences of D'Arcy (1842-?), a pioneer who settled in Oregon City, OR, relate to her early life in Illinois, family history, an overland journey to Oregon in 1846, housing, food and drink, medicines, Oregon City during the 1840s and 1850s, social life, courting customs, the funding of McMinnville College (presently Linfield College), and schools in early Oregon. See Martin Schmitt, *Catalogue of Manuscripts in the University of Oregon Library* (Eugene, OR: University of Oregon Press, 1971).

14,349. Daughters of the American Revolution, OR
Records. 1917-36. 2 folders.
Open. Published guide.
University of Oregon Library, Special Collections.
Correspondence of Anne M. Lang, a resident of The Dalles, OR, and vice-president and state regent of the Oregon DAR. See Martin Schmitt, *Catalogue of Manuscripts in the University of Oregon Library* (Eugene, OR: University of Oregon Press, 1971).

14,350. Davies, Mary Carolyn
Papers. 1919-34. 1.5 ft.
Open. Published guide.
University of Oregon Library, Special Collections.
Manuscripts of stories and poems as well as published books and articles of Davies, a writer and poet. See Martin Schmitt, *Catalogue of Manuscripts in the University of Oregon Library* (Eugene, OR: University of Oregon Press, 1971).

14,351. Dawson, Carley (Robinson)
Papers. 1921-68. 1.5 ft.
Open. Inventory and supplement to published guide.
University of Oregon Library, Special Collections.
Correspondence of Dawson, who was active in the Mary Chess cosmetics business of London and New York, founded in 1932 by her mother Grace Chess Robinson. During the 1960s Dawson was ordained into the ministry of Divine Science. Bulk of the collection is correspondence of the Robinson and Chess families with writers, musicians, artists, and the "socially ubiquitous."

14,352. Desmond, Alice Curtis
Papers. 1931-71. 6 ft.
Open. Inventory and supplement to published guide.
University of Oregon Library, Special Collections.
Professional correspondence and manuscripts of Desmond (1897-), a writer of fiction and nonfiction for young people, includes correspondence with Dorothy Bryant of Dodd, Mead, and Co. and Doris Patee of Macmillan Co.

14,353. Dowell, Benjamin Franklin
Papers. 1848-80. 23 vols.
Open. Published guide and calendar.
University of Oregon Library, Special Collections.
Dowell (1826-97) was a Jacksonville, OR, attorney and owner and publisher of the *Oregon Sentinel.* Scrapbooks of correspondence, clippings, and ephemera that include 1134 letters exchanged by Dowell and his wife; the letters contain gossip and information on business matters. Dowell spent much of his time in Washington, DC, on behalf of Oregon clients with claims against the government for "Indian depredations" and military expenses. Dowell's wife and the printers ran the *Oregon Sentinel* in Jacksonville from 1864. See Martin Schmitt, *Catalogue of Manuscripts in the University of Oregon Library* (Eugene, OR: University of Oregon Press, 1971).

14,354. Dun, Marie de Nervaud
Papers. 1958-68. 2 ft.
Open. Inventory and supplement to published guide.
University of Oregon Library, Special Collections.
Correspondence and manuscripts of novels and stories of Dun (1884-1973), a writer of gothic novels and western adventure and romance novels and stories. Dun produced two short stories per month for 30 years for the *Chicago Tribune-New York News* syndicate; her novels were published in *Ranch Romances.*

14,355. Dunbar, Elizabeth G. Lewis
Papers. Nd. 109-page item.
Open. Supplement to published guide.
University of Oregon Library, Special Collections.
Autobiography of Dunbar (1886-1960), who was educated at the University of California medical school and who was a missionary in India from 1916 to 1947.

14,356. Dunbar, Sadie Orr
Papers. 1923-58. 42 vols.
Open. Published guide.
University of Oregon Library, Special Collections.
Diaries of Dunbar (1889-1960), a social worker, contain notations of meetings attended, persons seen, and observations. Dunbar was active in the Oregon Tuberculosis Association, the Oregon Federation of Women's Clubs, and the Oregon public nursing movement; she also served on many regional and national health and welfare committees. See Martin Schmitt, *Catalogue of Manuscripts in the University of Oregon Library* (Eugene, OR: University of Oregon Press, 1971).

14,357. Eberle, Irmengarde
Papers. 1937-68. 1.5 ft.
Open. Published guide and inventory.
University of Oregon Library, Special Collections.
Correspondence, manuscripts and related material for three books, and foreign language editions of Eberle (1898-), an author of children's books. See Martin Schmitt, *Catalogue of Manuscripts in the University of Oregon Library* (Eugene, OR: University of Oregon Press, 1971).

14,358. Ehrlich, Bettina
Papers. 1959. 1 folder.
Open. Supplement to published guide.
University of Oregon Library, Special Collections.
Correspondence, manuscripts, and illustrations of Ehrlich (1903-), a writer and illustrator. Bulk of the collection is the original and revised text and illustrations for her book *For the Leg of a Chicken* (London, 1960).

14,359. Emery, Anne McGuigan
Papers. 1941-67. 6 ft.
Open. Published guide and inventory.
University of Oregon Library, Special Collections.
Correspondence, manuscripts, notes, source material, and published items of Emery (1907-), an author of books for children and young people. Includes correspondence with agent Leslie G. Phillips and publishers. See Martin Schmitt, *Catalogue of Manuscripts in the University of Oregon Library* (Eugene, OR: University of Oregon Press, 1971).

14,360. Erickson, Ruth
Papers. 1924-70. 3 ft.
Open. Inventory and supplement to published guide.
University of Oregon Library, Special Collections.
Correspondence of Erickson (?-1970) and Eleanor Stevenson, radical political activists who lived together from the 1930s to 1970 in a small house near New Milford, CT.

14,361. Eugene City Temperance Alliance
Records. 1886-87. 1 vol.
Open. Published guide.

University of Oregon Library, Special Collections. Minute book. See Martin Schmitt, *Catalogue of Manuscripts in the University of Oregon Library* (Eugene, OR: University of Oregon Press, 1971).

14,362. Faubion, Nina (Lane)
Papers. 1887-1938. 1 box.
Open. Published guide.
University of Oregon Library, Special Collections. Faubion (1884-1945) was a writer, secretary to her father Senator Harry Lane of Oregon, and an amateur mycologist. Correspondence with Nan (Wood) Honeyman from 1936 to 1938 and with others; manuscripts, including her unpublished "Undiplomatic Relations," which concerns her view of Washington, DC, from 1915 to 1917; and a scrapbook. See Martin Schmitt, *Catalogue of Manuscripts in the University of Oregon Library* (Eugene, OR: University of Oregon Press, 1971).

14,363. Fear, William H.
Papers. 1865-1931. 3 ft.
Open. Published guide.
University of Oregon Library, Special Collections. Correspondence from 1881 to 1906 concerning the courtship and marriage of Fear and Lucia Drum, and correspondence from 1905 to 1918 written primarily by the Fear children Lyle and Lois to their parents. Also included are the case books of Lois Fear, who was a student at the University of California, Berkeley, and at Wellesley College in Massachusetts from 1906 to 1910; Lois Fear was trained as an osteopath and practiced in Portland, OR. Also found in the collection are correspondence and other files of Nora B. Green, a Portland teacher and spiritualist. See Martin Schmitt, *Catalogue of Manuscripts in the University of Oregon Library* (Eugene, OR: University of Oregon Press, 1971).

14,364. Fetter, Elizabeth Head
Papers. 1926-72. 7.5 ft.
Open. Inventory and supplement to published guide.
University of Oregon Library, Special Collections. Fetter (1904-72), whose pseudonym was Hannah Lees, was an author of detective and mystery stories as well as books that showed a concern for social problems. Correspondence with publishers and magazines; personal correspondence, including letters from readers seeking advice; and manuscripts of published and unpublished works.

14,365. Fitch, Rachel Louise
Papers. 1918. 13 items.
Open. Published guide.
University of Oregon Library, Special Collections. Letters from France written by Fitch (1878-), a social worker, to members of the Delta Delta Delta sorority describe her investigation of working conditions of French women. Her published report is entitled *Madame France* (New York, 1919). See Martin Schmitt, *Catalogue of Manuscripts in the University of Oregon Library* (Eugene, OR: University of Oregon Press, 1971).

14,366. Flebbe, Beulah Marie (Dix)
Papers. 1885-1961. 10 ft.
Open. Published guide and inventory.
University of Oregon Library, Special Collections. [Mrs. Georg Heinrich] Flebbe (1876-1970) was an author and playwright. Professional and personal correspondence; 20 volumes of her diary, which are most detailed for the period 1885-1890; manuscripts of novels, plays, and stories, some of which were made into motion pictures; financial records; contracts; photos; scrapbooks of playbills and reviews containing Flebbe's critical comments; memorabilia; and published works. Educated at Radcliffe, Flebbe wrote plays for the Radcliffe Idler Club and became the first woman to win the George B. Sohier Prize at Harvard. She joined the Boston Author's Club where she collaborated with playwright [Mrs.] Evelyn Greenleaf Sutherland. In 1910 she married book importer Georg Heinrich Flebbe and moved to Los Angeles during WWI. There she worked for Cecil B. DeMille and Jesse L. Lasky, writing screenplays and adaptations. Correspondents include publishers, Paramount Pictures, Ann Watkins, Gladys G. Holmes, Carrie A. Harper, and R. Golding Bright. See Martin Schmitt, *Catalogue of Manuscripts in the University of Oregon Library* (Eugene, OR: University of Oregon Press, 1971).

14,367. Florence Crittenton Refuge Home
Records. 1903-06. 1 vol.
Open. Published guide.
University of Oregon Library, Special Collections. Board of managers minute book of this Portland, OR, home for delinquent females. See Martin Schmitt, *Catalogue of Manuscripts in the University of Oregon Library* (Eugene, OR: University of Oregon Press, 1971).

14,368. Fortner, Ethel Nestell
Papers. 1963-73. 4.5 ft.
Open. Inventory and supplement to published guide.
University of Oregon Library, Special Collections. Fortner (1907-) was a poet, book reviewer, and poetry and book review editor for *Human Voice,* a poetry quarterly. Correspondence relating to her position as editor, manuscripts of her poetry, and ephemera.

14,369. Franchere, Ruth Myers
Papers. 1958-69. 1.5 ft.
Open. Published guide and inventory.
University of Oregon Library, Special Collections. Franchere was an English teacher and author of books for young people. Correspondence with Elizabeth M. Riley of Thomas Y. Crowell Company, manuscripts of Franchere's books, research notes, and galley proofs. See Martin Schmitt, *Catalogue of Manuscripts in the University of Oregon Library* (Eugene, OR: University of Oregon Press, 1971).

14,370. Friermood, Elisabeth (Hamilton)
Papers. 1951-63. 1.5 ft.
Open. Published guide and inventory.
University of Oregon Library, Special Collections. Manuscripts and related material for nine books by Friermood (1903-), an author and public librarian in Marion, IN. See Martin Schmitt, *Catalogue of Manuscripts in the University of Oregon Library* (Eugene, OR: University of Oregon Press, 1971).

14,371. Fuller, Cordelia Ellen
Papers. 1839-73. 3 vols.
Open. Published guide.
University of Oregon Library, Special Collections. Journal kept by Fuller (1833-1916) during an 1873 round-trip journey by train from Three Rivers, MA, to Montreal, Canada, in which she describes scenes, towns, and her traveling companions. Also included are two composition books, one from 1853 by Cordelia Fuller and one from 1839 by Hiram Fuller, both probably produced in Chicopee Falls, MA. See Martin Schmitt, *Catalogue of Manuscripts in the University of Oregon Library* (Eugene, OR: University of Oregon Press, 1971).

14,372. Goltra, Elizabeth Julia
Papers. 1853. 21 pp.
Open. Published guide.
University of Oregon Library, Special Collections. Journal describing a journey across the plains from Missouri to Oregon. See Martin Schmitt, *Catalogue of Manuscripts in the University of Oregon Library* (Eugene, OR: University of Oregon Press, 1971).

14,373. Gordon, Wyona Eliza
Papers. 1963. 103 pp.
Open. Published guide.
University of Oregon Library, Special Collections. Memoirs of Gordon describing an 1883 wagon trip from Topeka, KS, to Oregon City, OR. She attended Philomath College in Oregon and taught school in Portland, OR. See Martin Schmitt, *Catalogue of Manuscripts in the University of Oregon Library* (Eugene, OR: University of Oregon Press, 1971).

14,374. Gorman, Mary
Papers. 1940-65. 3 ft.
Open. Published guide.
University of Oregon Library, Special Collections. Gorman (1908-) was the author of romance and confession stories. Correspondence with publishers and the Lenniger Literary Agency, manuscripts of stories, and published items, which have appeared in such magazines as *True Confessions* and *Modern Romances.* See Martin Schmitt, *Catalogue of Manuscripts in the University of Oregon Library* (Eugene, OR: University of Oregon Press, 1971).

14,375. Gragg, Joseph
Papers. 1859-1930. 1 ft.
Open. Published guide and calendar.
University of Oregon Library, Special Collections. Papers of Gragg, a pioneer who settled in Monroe, OR, include a diary and letters from Gragg's sister Huldah (Gragg) Brickett who lived in Pleasantville, IL, from 1854 to 1874 and in Truckee, CA, from 1874 to 1881. Also contains letters of Gragg's daughter Bettie M. Gragg who was a student at Philomath College from 1883 to 1884; was an Alpine, OR, schoolteacher in 1887; and married William H. McLain in 1894. Topics covered include family relationships, farm life, church affairs, schools and teaching, social life, the United Brethren Church in Oregon, and Philomath College and the controversy over its control in the 1880s. See Martin Schmitt, *Catalogue of Manuscripts in the University of Oregon Library* (Eugene, OR: University of Oregon Press, 1971).

14,376. Grand Army of the Republic, Department of Oregon, Woman's Relief Corps, Meade Corps no. 18
Records. 1889-1916. 5 vols.
Open. Published guide.
University of Oregon Library, Special Collections. Minutes, ledger, and cash book of this patriotic organization. See Martin Schmitt, *Catalogue of Manuscripts in the University of Oregon Library* (Eugene, OR: University of Oregon Press, 1971).

14,377. Grant, Jane
Papers. 1918-69. 7.5 ft.
Open. Inventory and supplement to published guide.
University of Oregon Library, Special Collections. Grant (1892-1972) was a journalist and publisher who, together with her husband Harold Ross, founded *The New Yorker;* in 1921 with Ruth Hale she founded the Lucy Stone League. Personal and professional correspondence, manuscripts of books and plays, material relating to *The New Yorker,* and records of the Lucy Stone League, primarily from 1950 to 1960. Correspondents include Wilbur J. Holleman, Harold Ross, Alexander Woollcott, Janet Flanner, Raoul Fleischman, Hawley Truax, Pearl Buck, Sophie Drinker, Doris E. Fleischman, Alma Lutz, Emma (Guffey) Miller, and Doris Stevens. In 1912 Grant began working for *The New York Times,* where she became the first woman reporter in the city room. During WWI she went to France with the entertainment department of the YMCA; there she met Harold Ross.

14,378. Greenbie, Sydney
Papers. 1909-58. 16 ft.
Open. Published guide and inventory.
University of Oregon Library, Special Collections. In 1919 Greenbie (1889-1960), a lecturer, publisher, writer, and adult educator, married

Marjorie Barstow, an editor and writer whom he had met in Japan. They traveled extensively while Sydney Greenbie was associated with the Floating University and various lecture circuits. Together they wrote *My Dear Lady, the Story of Anna Ella Carroll* (New York, 1940). Correspondence between the Greenbies concerning their careers, the lecture circuits of the 1920s, and personal matters, 1918-55; correspondence regarding the University of Tampa Open Sky Players, a drama group with which Marjorie Greenbie was associated, 1948-53, and regarding the Greenbies' Traversity Press, 1950-58; Marjorie Greenbie's diaries, 1947-54; and literary manuscripts. Correspondents include Maxwell and Ruth Aley, Edna E. Allen, Nilla Cook, Sophie Drinker, Ellen Fulton, and Ann Watkins. See Martin Schmitt, *Catalogue of Manuscripts in the University of Oregon Library* (Eugene, OR: University of Oregon Press, 1971).

14,379. Gress, Ruth A.
Papers. 1939-58. Ca. 1 cu.ft.
Open. Published guide.
University of Oregon Library, Special Collections.
Gress was a Methodist missionary who went to China in 1939, spent a year in a Shanghai language school, and then went to Nanping in Fukien Province where she taught at the Chien Ching Middle School. Letters from Gress to her family in North Dakota 1939-42; letters from Ethel Wallace in Nanping; printed letters from Nanping missionaries; and a report on the experiences of Christian missions in China. See Martin Schmitt, *Catalogue of Manuscripts in the University of Oregon Library* (Eugene, OR: University of Oregon Press, 1971).

14,380. Groff-Smith, Mrs. Everitt
Papers. 1890-1941. 306 pp.
Open. Published guide.
University of Oregon Library, Special Collections.
Autobiography of Groff-Smith (1892-), whose father Henry F. Merrill and husband were commissioners in the China Maritime Customs Service, contains information on Chinese politics and customs. See Martin Schmitt, *Catalogue of Manuscripts in the University of Oregon Library* (Eugene, OR: University of Oregon Press, 1971).

14,381. Hader, Elmer Stanley
Papers. 1944-58. 8 ft.
Open. Published guide and inventory.
University of Oregon Library, Special Collections.
Manuscripts, original illustrations, proofs, and other related papers of Hader (1889-) and his wife Berta Hoerner Hader, both of whom wrote and illustrated magazine feature pages and books for children. They had attended the California School of Design in San Francisco and were married in 1919. See Martin Schmitt, *Catalogue of Manuscripts in the University of Oregon Library* (Eugene, OR: University of Oregon Press, 1971).

14,382. Hall, Grace E. (Adams)
Papers. 1892-1939. 3 ft.
Open. Inventory and supplement to published guide.
University of Oregon Library, Special Collections.
Hall (?-1939), a poet and writer in Illinois and Oregon, was poet in residence for the Portland *Oregonian* for 12 years. Her verse was syndicated, and two volumes of her collected works were published by Dodd, Mead. Correspondence, primarily professional, and manuscripts of poems and essays. Includes letters from Guy Fitch Phelps, Albert R. Wetjen, and Merrill A. Yothers.

14,383. Hamilton, Eloise
Papers. 1948-63. 1 box.
Open. Published guide.
University of Oregon Library, Special Collections.
Correspondence, manuscripts of articles, photos, and clippings of Hamilton, an Oregon poet and free-lance writer. Correspondents include Ethel Romig Fuller, Alice [Mrs. William] Rush, and Staton Coblentz. See Martin Schmitt, *Catalogue of Manuscripts in the University of Oregon Library* (Eugene, OR: University of Oregon Press, 1971).

14,384. Hargreaves, Sheba May
Papers. 1928-35. 1.5 ft.
Open. Published guide.
University of Oregon Library, Special Collections.
Manuscripts of books and articles of Hargreaves (1882-1960), an Oregon journalist and author who was a feature writer for the Portland newspapers *Oregon Journal* and the *Oregonian.* See Martin Schmitt, *Catalogue of Manuscripts in the University of Oregon Library* (Eugene, OR: University of Oregon Press, 1971).

14,385. Henry, Vera
Papers. 1949-67. 1 box.
Open. Published guide.
University of Oregon Library, Special Collections.
Henry (1909-) was a writer for confession magazines in 1943 and for other women's magazines in 1944. Correspondence with Edith Margolis of Lenniger Literary Agency and manuscripts of short stories. See Martin Schmitt, *Catalogue of Manuscripts in the University of Oregon Library* (Eugene, OR: University of Oregon Press, 1971).

14,386. Hensolt, Edith Ashmore
Papers. 1896-1954. 3 ft.
Open. Supplement to published guide.
University of Oregon Library, Special Collections.
Correspondence and diaries of Hensolt (1882-1975), a librarian from 1908 to 1916 at the Rochester Theological Seminary in New York, the University of Chicago, and the John Crerar Library. She married Charles Elder in 1916 and moved to Boulder, CO. Elder died in 1935, and she moved to Albany, OR, where she married Fred Hensolt in 1944. Hensolt's letters to her parents extend from 1896 to 1951 and include letters from Vassar, 1902-06; from Simmons College, 1908-09; and from Chicago, 1909-16. Her diaries date from 1912 to 1954.

14,387. Hill Family
Papers. 1850-1938. 3 ft.
Open. Published guide.
University of Oregon Library, Special Collections.
Correspondence of a pioneer family that settled in Independence, OR, describes family members' personal lives, pioneer life, social contacts, business affairs, and educational and cultural experiences. Papers of Nelle May Hill (1868-1900), daughter of Henry Hill (1847-1905) and student at Stanford University from 1892 to 1894, include five letters from Herbert C. Hoover, written while he was a student at Stanford. The Hoover letters have been published. See Martin Schmitt, *Catalogue of Manuscripts in the University of Oregon Library* (Eugene, OR: University of Oregon Press, 1971).

14,388. Hobart, Alice Tisdale (Nourse)
Papers. 1917-63. 4 ft.
Open. Published guide and inventory.
University of Oregon Library, Special Collections.
Hobart (1882-1967) was a novelist who wrote *The Cup and the Sword, Innocent Dreamers, Venture into Darkness,* and other works. Collection includes correspondence with publishers and readers, publicity material and reviews, first editions, reprints, and translations for all of her books. A file of correspondence with the publisher Longmans, Green is also included. See Martin Schmitt, *Catalogue of Manuscripts in the University of Oregon Library* (Eugene, OR: University of Oregon Press, 1971).

14,389. Hobart, Emily
Papers. 1884-1928. 63 items.
Open. Published guide.
University of Oregon Library, Special Collections.
Hobart was the wife of William Hatfield Hobart, Methodist missionary in Peking and Tsun Hua, China. Letters to her parents, brother, and sisters describe Chinese occupations and scenes. See Martin Schmitt, *Catalogue of Manuscripts in the University of Oregon Library* (Eugene, OR: University of Oregon Press, 1971).

14,390. Holberg, Ruth (Langland)
Papers. 1923-68. 4 ft.
Open. Published guide and inventory.
University of Oregon Library, Special Collections.
Holberg (1889-) was an author of books for children and young people. Correspondence with editors and publishers, particularly Jean Poindexter Colby, Thomas Y. Crowell Co., and Houghton Mifflin Co.; journal from the 1920s and 1930s; and manuscripts of books, articles, and stories. See Martin Schmitt, *Catalogue of Manuscripts in the University of Oregon Library* (Eugene, OR: University of Oregon Press, 1971).

14,391. Honeyman, Nan (Wood)
Papers. 1932-50. 114 items.
Open. Published guide.
University of Oregon Library, Special Collections.
Honeyman (1881-1970) was a US Democratic congresswoman from Oregon's Third District from 1937 to 1939. Correspondence concerning her political campaigns, Sandy River improvement, and other district improvement projects. Includes two personal notes from Eleanor Roosevelt. See Martin Schmitt, *Catalogue of Manuscripts in the University of Oregon Library* (Eugene, OR: University of Oregon Press, 1971).

14,392. Howe, Herbert Crombie
Papers. 1855-1940. 9 ft.
Open. Published guide.
University of Oregon Library, Special Collections.
Howe (1872-1940) was an author, lecturer, and English professor and administrator at Cornell University and professor of English at the University of Oregon. Correspondence, diaries, manuscripts, lectures, student papers, autobiography of Howe, genealogical data, photos, and other items. Papers of Howe's sister Lillian Howe include her letters to Herbert Howe, 1874-1916, and her diaries, 1874-89. She was a student at the Academy of Mount St. Vincent in West Albany, NY, from 1879 to 1881 and at Houghton Academy in Clinton, NY, from 1882 to 1884; worked in the Boston Public Library; was on the editorial staff of the *Mentor,* a literary magazine; and was a secretary for the National Association of Woolen Manufacturers in Boston. Papers relating to Howe's father Henry Clay Howe, a Fulton, NY, attorney and Republican member of the New York Assembly, include letters to Henry Howe from his wife Letitia Crombie Howe and her diaries 1860-73. See Martin Schmitt, *Catalogue of Manuscripts in the University of Oregon Library* (Eugene, OR: University of Oregon Press, 1971).

14,393. Hutchins, Grace
Papers. 1898-1954. 1.5 ft.
Open. Inventory and supplement to published guide.
University of Oregon Library, Special Collections.
Correspondence of Hutchins (1885-1969) and material on St. Hilda's School in Wuchang, China, of which Hutchins was the principal from 1915 to 1916. During the 1920s she was active in the Fellowship of Reconciliation. In 1927 Hutchins, along with Anna Rochester and others, founded the Labor Research Association. She also was editor of *Labor Fact Book* and author of books and articles on labor issues, particularly working women. Includes letters Hutchins wrote while touring the world from 1898 to 1899 with her parents, letters written while touring the Far East and Russia in 1926 and 1927 with Anna Rochester, and

correspondence with Rochester and Ella Reeve Bloor.

14,394. Ingerson, Vera Frances
Papers. 1916-65. 1.5 ft.
Open. Published guide.
University of Oregon Library, Special Collections.
From 1916 to 1942 Ingerson (1890-) was in Korea, first as a Presbyterian mission station nurse in Syenchun and later as a teacher at the Girl's Academy in Syenchun. Annual letters, diaries from 1916 to 1965, reports, photos, and mementos. See Martin Schmitt, *Catalogue of Manuscripts in the University of Oregon Library* (Eugene, OR: University of Oregon Press, 1971).

14,395. Jackson, Jean
Papers. 1953-67. 1 box.
Open. Published guide.
University of Oregon Library, Special Collections.
Manuscripts of confession stories by Jackson, her correspondence with Edith Margolis of Lenniger Literary Agency, and manuscript of a published article concerning factors that make a confession story salable. See Martin Schmitt, *Catalogue of Manuscripts in the University of Oregon Library* (Eugene, OR: University of Oregon Press, 1971).

14,396. Jacquet, Myra Anna
Papers. 1913-43. 1 folder.
Open. Published guide.
University of Oregon Library, Special Collections.
Jacquet was a teacher and principal at the Methodist mission's Gamewell School in Peking, China. Interned by the Japanese she returned to the US on the *Gripsholm* in 1943. Correspondence, including a letter about the *Gripsholm* voyage; notebooks describing the work of a mission teacher; and mementos. See Martin Schmitt, *Catalogue of Manuscripts in the University of Oregon Library* (Eugene, OR: University of Oregon Press, 1971).

14,397. Jarvis, Bruce W.
Papers. 1927-28. 1.5 ft.
Open. Published guide and inventory.
University of Oregon Library, Special Collections.
Jarvis (1885-1970) was a physician in China from 1923 to 1949. Correspondence, personal narratives, manuscript reports, documents, photos, clippings, and publications contain material about the experiences of Anna Moffet, a missionary administrator in China from 1920 to 1945, specifically regarding Nanking in 1927 to 1928 where there were battles between the Nationalists and the South Chinese. See Martin Schmitt, *Catalogue of Manuscripts in the University of Oregon Library* (Eugene, OR: University of Oregon Press, 1971).

14,398. Jensen, Gertrude Glutsch
Papers. 1951-70. 3 ft.
Open. Inventory and supplement to published guide.
University of Oregon Library, Special Collections.
Correspondence, minutes, and organizational material of Jensen, a Portland, OR, conservation leader. Includes correspondence with politicians; 40 letters from 1951 to 1957 from Kathleen Eloisa Rockwell, who was known as Klondike Kate; and material from the Columbia River Gorge Commission, 1951-70, and the Oregon Roadside Council, 1960-70.

14,399. Jones, Elizabeth Orton
Papers. 1925-68. 5 ft.
Open. Published guide and inventory.
University of Oregon Library, Special Collections.
Jones (1910-) is a writer and illustrator, primarily of children's books. Correspondence; original illustrations, some utilizing drypoint with aquatint; and a scrapbook relating to Jones's illustrations for Rachel Field's *Prayer for a Child* (New York, 1944). Jones is the daughter of Mrs. George Jones, a writer. See Martin Schmitt, *Catalogue of Manuscripts in the University of Oregon Library* (Eugene, OR: University of Oregon Press, 1971).

14,400. Jones, Mary Alice Lange
Papers. 1943-65. 1.5 ft.
Open. Published guide and inventory.
University of Oregon Library, Special Collections.
Manuscripts of stories by Jones published in romance and confession magazines, correspondence with Edith Margolis of Lenniger Literary Agency, and tear sheets. See Martin Schmitt, *Catalogue of Manuscripts in the University of Oregon Library* (Eugene, OR: University of Oregon Press, 1971).

14,401. Kerr, Alexander
Papers. 1855-1917. 1.5 ft.
Open. Published guide.
University of Oregon Library, Special Collections.
Correspondence, diary, manuscripts, and published works of Kerr (1828-1919), a public school administrator and professor of Greek at the University of Wisconsin. Includes correspondence, 1855-56, between Kerr and his future wife Katherine Brown while she was a student at Rockford Female Seminary in Rockford, IL, and he was a student at Beloit College in Wisconsin and then a teacher at Houston Academy in Houston, GA. See Martin Schmitt, *Catalogue of Manuscripts in the University of Oregon Library* (Eugene, OR: University of Oregon Press, 1971).

14,402. Kirk, William Elwood
Papers. 1854-1938. 1 ft.
Open. Published guide.
University of Oregon Library, Special Collections.
Correspondence and family mementos of Kirk (1868-1937), a professor of ancient languages at Willamette University in Salem, OR, from 1906 to 1937. Includes correspondence beginning in 1898 between Kirk, then a student at Nebraska Wesleyan University, and Iva May Howard, whom he married in 1901. Between 1916 and 1929 Iva Kirk often visited her parents in Pioneerville, ID, and wrote to her husband while she was there. See Martin Schmitt, *Catalogue of Manuscripts in the University of Oregon Library* (Eugene, OR: University of Oregon Press, 1971).

14,403. Krautter, Elisa Bialk
Papers. 1947-68. 4.5 ft.
Open. Published guide.
University of Oregon Library, Special Collections.
Krautter (1912-) was a journalist and author of books for children and young people. Manuscripts; correspondence with editors, agents, illustrators, and publishers; and fan letters from children. See Martin Schmitt, *Catalogue of Manuscripts in the University of Oregon Library* (Eugene, OR: University of Oregon Press, 1971).

14,404. Lacy, Henry Veere
Papers. 1909-50. 1 ft.
Open. Published guide.
University of Oregon Library, Special Collections.
Lacy (1886-) was a missionary teacher, evangelist, and administrator in Fukien Province, China, from 1912 to 1952 and in Singapore from 1949 to 1952. His wife Jessie (Ankeny) Lacy was a missionary teacher in Fukien from 1909 to 1949. Includes Jessie Lacy's correspondence with parents and relatives in York, NE, and Prescott, IA; missionary friends; and her sister Louise Ankeny, a teacher in China. The Lacys were married in 1913 and worked for the Methodist Episcopal Church. See Martin Schmitt, *Catalogue of Manuscripts in the University of Oregon Library* (Eugene, OR: University of Oregon Press, 1971).

14,405. Lampman, Evelyn (Sibley)
Papers. 1948-69. 3 ft.
Open. Published guide and inventory.
University of Oregon Library, Special Collections.
Manuscripts of the writings of Lampman (1907-) include Portland, OR, radio scripts, short stories, and children's books. Correspondence with J. B. Lippincott Co., Naomi Burton of Curtis Brown, Margaret Lesser of Doubleday & Co., and Ed Kuhn of McGraw-Hill. See Martin Schmitt, *Catalogue of Manuscripts in the University of Oregon Library* (Eugene, OR: University of Oregon Press, 1971).

14,406. Lee, Borghild Lundberg
Papers. 1908-62. 1.5 ft.
Open. Inventory.
University of Oregon Library, Special Collections.
Lee (1892-), who lived in Minnesota, North Dakota, and Portland, OR, was a poet and an author of short stories and confession stories. Manuscripts and correspondence with editors and writers. Includes a letter from Edna St. Vincent Millay in which she gives advice on writing poetry.

14,407. Lee, Manning de Villeneuve
Papers. 1926-61. 6 ft.
Open. Published guide and inventory.
University of Oregon Library, Special Collections.
Lee (1894-) was an artist and illustrator and his wife Eunice S. "Tina" Lee was an author of children's books and art editor of *Jack and Jill*. Correspondence with publishers, including Doubleday and Co., Margaret Grossett of Grossett Studio, and Rand McNally Co.; manuscripts of books and articles; and original illustrations for books and magazines. See Martin Schmitt, *Catalogue of Manuscripts in the University of Oregon Library* (Eugene, OR: University of Oregon Press, 1971).

14,408. Leighton, Margaret (Carver)
Papers. 1937-60. 2 ft.
Open. Published guide and inventory.
University of Oregon Library, Special Collections.
Correspondence, manuscripts, and galley proofs of Leighton (1896-), a writer of stories for young people. Includes correspondence with Wilma K. McFarland, editor of *The Portal* and *Child Life*. See Martin Schmitt, *Catalogue of Manuscripts in the University of Oregon Library* (Eugene, OR: University of Oregon Press, 1971).

14,409. Leland, Bernice
Papers. 1909-10. 1 box.
Open. Published guide.
University of Oregon Library, Special Collections.
In 1909 and 1910 Leland, a botanist, and Winifred B. Chase were in Tahiti and New Zealand collecting botanical specimens, particularly algae, for Josephine E. Tilden of the University of Minnesota botanical department. Includes letters from Tilden to Leland regarding the project, descriptive and personal diary, and other items, among them descriptions of various botanical trips. See Martin Schmitt, *Catalogue of Manuscripts in the University of Oregon Library* (Eugene, OR: University of Oregon Press, 1971).

14,410. Lenniger Literary Agency
Records. 1926-66. 15 ft.
Open. Inventory.
University of Oregon Library, Special Collections.
Correspondence of August Lenniger, who founded the Agency in New York City in 1923, and of Edith Margolis with publishers and Agency clients, many of whom were women. The letters concern editing and sales of manuscripts, requirements and house rules of publishers, the state of the literary market, and personal problems of the writers. Also included are company ledgers.

14,411. Littell, Robert
Papers. 1901-63. 8 ft.
Open. Published guide and inventory.
University of Oregon Library, Special Collections.
Littell (1896-1963) was associate editor of *New Republic* in the 1920s, drama critic for New York newspapers, and associate and senior editor for *Reader's Digest* from 1942 to 1961.

Correspondence, manuscripts, and scrapbooks. Includes letters that his wife Anita (Damrosch) Littell wrote to the Littell and Damrosch families while she and her husband were in Europe from 1949 to 1963. See Martin Schmitt, *Catalogue of Manuscripts in the University of Oregon Library* (Eugene, OR: University of Oregon Press, 1971).

14,412. McCall, Virginia Nielsen
Papers. 1935-65. 3 ft.
Open. Published guide and inventory.
University of Oregon Library, Special Collections.
McCall (1909-) was an author. Correspondence with writers, publishers, and agents and manuscripts of novels and short stories. See Martin Schmitt, *Catalogue of Manuscripts in the University of Oregon Library* (Eugene, OR: University of Oregon Press, 1971).

14,413. McConnell, Frederic Charles
Papers. 1913-68. 4.5 ft.
Open. Published guide and inventory.
University of Oregon Library, Special Collections.
In 1926 McConnell (1890-1968), who was stage director and consultant at the Cleveland Play House from 1921 to 1962, married Katherine Wick Kelly (1887-1937), an actress and playwright with the Play House. Correspondence; Kelly's diaries, 1906-26; manuscripts of plays, including those by Kelly; and records and notes of the Cleveland Play House. Includes Kelly's letters to McConnell, 1923-26 and 1936-37; letters from Peter Munro Jack; and correspondence with Max Beerbohm, Ruth Gordon, and Theresa Helburn concerning the dramatization of *Zuleika Dobson.* See Martin Schmitt, *Catalogue of Manuscripts in the University of Oregon Library* (Eugene, OR: University of Oregon Press, 1971).

14,414. McGraw, Eloise Jarvis
Papers. 1949-66. 3 ft.
Open. Published guide and inventory.
University of Oregon Library, Special Collections.
McGraw (1915-) was an author of stories for children and young people. Correspondence; manuscripts of novels, plays, short stories, biographies, and radio scripts; notes; outlines; and synopses. Contains correspondence with editors and publishers, including A. S. Burack of *The Writer Magazine,* Naomi Burton, Emilie Jacobson, Marilyn Marlow, Marion Kieckhoff, Dorothy Starr, and Alice Torrey. See Martin Schmitt, *Catalogue of Manuscripts in the University of Oregon Library* (Eugene, OR: University of Oregon Press, 1971).

14,415. Machetanz, Sara Burleson
Papers. 1954-61. 1 folder.
Open. Published guide.
University of Oregon Library, Special Collections.
Together with her husband Frederick Machetanz, Sara Machetanz (1918-) has written books and produced films about Alaskan Eskimos. Correspondence, manuscripts, and a diary kept from 1954 to 1955 in Unalakleet, AK, describing experiences in an Eskimo village. See Martin Schmitt, *Catalogue of Manuscripts in the University of Oregon Library* (Eugene, OR: University of Oregon Press, 1971).

14,416. McLelland, Isabel Couper
Papers. 1941-62. 1.5 ft.
Open. Published guide and inventory.
University of Oregon Library, Special Collections.
McLelland was a teacher and author of books for juveniles. Correspondence with Henry Holt & Co., epistolary diary kept by McLelland on her 1956 trip around the world, and manuscripts of books. See Martin Schmitt, *Catalogue of Manuscripts in the University of Oregon Library* (Eugene, OR: University of Oregon Press, 1971).

14,417. MacLeod, Ruth D.
Papers. 1953-65. 1.5 ft.
Open. Published guide and inventory.
University of Oregon Library, Special Collections.
MacLeod was a writer of romance and true confession stories. Manuscripts and correspondence with Edith Margolis of Lenniger Literary Agency and publisher Julian Messner, Inc. See Martin Schmitt, *Catalogue of Manuscripts in the University of Oregon Library* (Eugene, OR: University of Oregon Press, 1971).

14,418. McMinnville Ladies Sanitary Aid Society, OR
Records. 1864-65. 2 vols. and other items.
Open. Published guide.
University of Oregon Library, Special Collections.
Correspondence; secretary's book, including constitution, bylaws, and minutes; and treasurer's book containing receipts, expenditures, annual report, and final report of the Society, which was founded in 1864 to assist the US Sanitary Commission and the US Christian Commission. The group disbanded in 1865. Includes letters from Mrs. Addison C. Gibbs, George C. Chandler, and E. D. Shattuck, secretary of the Oregon board of the US Sanitary Commission. Officers of the Society were Mrs. George C. Chandler, Mrs. G. W. Burnett, Mrs. D. J. Yeargain, and Mrs. H. V. V. Johnson. See Martin Schmitt, *Catalogue of Manuscripts in the University of Oregon Library* (Eugene, OR: University of Oregon Press, 1971).

14,419. Main, Ida Belle (Lewis)
Papers. 1910-49. 1 ft.
Open. Published guide.
University of Oregon Library, Special Collections.
Main (1887-1969) was a Methodist missionary teacher in China. Letters to her family, 1911-49; diaries kept in 1910 and from 1935 to 1941; photos; and printed material on Hwa Nan College in Foochow. Main went to Tientsin, China, in 1910, and in 1923 she went to Shanghai as assistant secretary of education for the Methodist Church in China. In 1926 she became president of Hwa Nan College, returned to Shanghai in 1930 as secretary of the China Christian Education Association, and worked with refugees in Shanghai from 1937 to 1941. In 1946 she returned to Foochow where she served as president of Hwa Nan College until 1949. She married William A. Main in 1932. See Martin Schmitt, *Catalogue of Manuscripts in the University of Oregon Library* (Eugene, OR: University of Oregon Press, 1971).

14,420. Mallery, Bell
Papers. 1866-68. 3 vols.
Open. Published guide.
University of Oregon Library, Special Collections.
Diary of Mallery who in 1866 and 1867 lived in Sharon, PA, and Wellesville, NY, where she attended school, earned a teaching certificate, and taught. In 1868 she left New York and sailed to Salem, OR, via Panama. She taught school in Salem and Union, OR, and later married W. T. Wright of Union. See Martin Schmitt, *Catalogue of Manuscripts in the University of Oregon Library* (Eugene, OR: University of Oregon Press, 1971).

14,421. Mansfield, Norma Bicknell
Papers. 1929-60. 4.5 ft.
Open. Inventory and supplement to published guide.
University of Oregon Library, Special Collections.
Correspondence and manuscripts of Mansfield (1906-), writer of children's books and wife of writer and journalist Robert S. Mansfield. Contains correspondence with agents and editors, including Elizabeth L. Gilman of Farrar & Rinehart and Anne Stoddard of *American Girl.*

14,422. Monroe, Anne Shannon
Papers. 1902-19. 2 vols.
Open. Published guide.
University of Oregon Library, Special Collections.
A journalist, Monroe (1877-1942) wrote feature stories for the Tacoma, WA, *News.* In 1900 she went to Chicago and wrote feature essays for the Chicago *News* and the *Tribune.* She returned to Oregon in 1907 and, except for a brief stay in New York City, remained there. Scrapbooks of published stories, features, and reviews from Chicago papers. See Martin Schmitt, *Catalogue of Manuscripts in the University of Oregon Library* (Eugene, OR: University of Oregon Press, 1971).

14,423. Moore, Rosalie
Papers. 1935-70. 1.5 ft.
Open. Inventory and supplement to published guide.
University of Oregon Library, Special Collections.
Moore (1910-) is a poet, writer, and playwright who helped found the Activist Group of poets. Correspondence with poets, publishers, and award committees; manuscripts of poems, a play, and juvenile fiction; and scrapbooks of reviews and mementos. Moore's major publication is *The Grasshopper's Man* (New Haven, 1939) in the Young Poets Series, with an introduction by W. H. Auden.

14,424. Moores, Althea
Papers. 1877. 1 vol.
Open. Published guide.
University of Oregon Library, Special Collections.
Diary of Moores, who lived in Salem, OR, and attended Willamette University there. After graduating in 1877 she continued to live at home, doing housework, taking piano lessons, and participating in the social life of the community. See Martin Schmitt, *Catalogue of Manuscripts in the University of Oregon Library* (Eugene, OR: University of Oregon Press, 1971).

14,425. Morse, Esther
Papers. 1929-63. 3 ft.
Open. Inventory and supplement to published guide.
University of Oregon Library, Special Collections.
Correspondence, photos, mementos, newsletters, and ephemera of Morse (1898-), a physician who, after medical training at the University of Nebraska, worked as a Presbyterian missionary doctor at the Hainan Mission in China from 1930 to 1943 and from 1946 to 1953, at the Miral Medical Center in India from 1944 to 1945, and at Lahore in West Pakistan from 1954 to 1963. A general practitioner, she engaged in obstetric work. Bulk of the collection is Morse's descriptive letters to her family; the *Hainan Newsletter* series, 1929-36, which was the publication of the American Presbyterian Mission; and various mission pamphlets.

14,426. Moses, Mathilde R.
Papers. 1916-49. 141 items.
Open. Published guide.
University of Oregon Library, Special Collections.
Correspondence of Moses (1887-), a missionary teacher in India with the Woman's Foreign Missionary Society of the Methodist Episcopal Church. Moses went to India in 1916; from 1917 to 1919 she taught at Girls' High School in Cawnpore; and from 1920 to 1921 was principal of the Hudson Memorial School in Cawnpore. In 1922 she returned to the US on a Cook's tour, via the Near East and Europe. Returning to India in 1923, she taught at the Sawtelle Girls' School in Arrah, Bihar. During the 1930s she was with the Adams Girls' School in Almora, Uttar Pradesh, and with Methodist girls schools in Roorkee and Bareilly. The correspondence is most descriptive from 1916 to 1923 and for 1935 and deals with life in India and internal mission affairs. See Martin Schmitt, *Catalogue of Manuscripts in the University of Oregon Library* (Eugene, OR: University of Oregon Press, 1971).

14,427. Nathan, Dorothy Goldeen
Papers. 1961-66. 1 box.
Open. Published guide.

University of Oregon Library, Special Collections. Nathan was a social worker, teacher, and author of books for young people. Includes correspondence with her publisher Random House and readers concerning the books *Women of Courage* (New York, 1964) and *The Shy One* (New York, 1966). See Martin Schmitt, *Catalogue of Manuscripts in the University of Oregon Library* (Eugene, OR: University of Oregon Press, 1971).

14,428. Nelson, Vera Joyce
Papers. 1939-72. 3 ft.
Open. Inventory and supplement to published guide.
University of Oregon Library, Special Collections. Nelson (1903-), an Oregon poet, was an officer in the Verseweavers, a Portland, OR, group. Personal and professional correspondence, manuscripts, records of poetry organizations, clippings, and magazines.

14,429. Neuberger, Maurine (Brown)
Papers. 1950-67. 54 ft. plus tapes.
Open. Published guide and inventory.
University of Oregon Library, Special Collections. Neuberger (1907-) was the representative from Multnomah County, OR, to the Oregon state legislature from 1950 to 1955. When her husband Richard L. Neuberger, a US senator from Oregon, died in 1960, she served the remainder of his Senate term and was elected to a full term from 1960 to 1967. Office files from her two Senate terms include correspondence, speeches, tape recordings, press releases, statements, documents, scrapbooks, and newsletters and deal with such topics as conservation projects, public health, and social security. Material on the 1960 campaign is also included. See Martin Schmitt, *Catalogue of Manuscripts in the University of Oregon Library* (Eugene, OR: University of Oregon Press, 1971).

14,430. New England Conservatory Club
Records. 1902-42. 3 vols.
Open. Supplement to published guide.
University of Oregon Library, Special Collections. Minute books containing minutes, programs, and announcements of this women's club, founded by former pupils of the New England Conservatory of Music in Boston to promote musical interests in Portland, OR.

14,431. O'Connor, Hugh
Papers. 1918-67. 3 ft.
Open. Inventory and supplement to published guide.
University of Oregon Library, Special Collections. O'Connor (1894-1967) was a New York City journalist, National Association of Manufacturers public relations officer from 1943 to 1948, and US Office of Civil Defense public information officer from 1951 to 1964. Correspondence, including 470 letters written from 1928 to 1939 by author Katherine Ursula Parrott.

14,432. O'Hare, Kate Richards
Papers. 1919. 31 items.
Open. Published guide.
University of Oregon Library, Special Collections. Copies of letters from O'Hare to her husband from the Missouri State Penitentiary in Jefferson City. A pacifist, she was convicted of violating the Espionage Act and sentenced to prison in 1919. Copies of the letters were distributed to friends and sympathizers. See Martin Schmitt, *Catalogue of Manuscripts in the University of Oregon Library* (Eugene, OR: University of Oregon Press, 1971).

14,433. Pennell, Joseph Stanley
Papers. 1924-61. 5 ft.
Open. Published guide and inventory.
University of Oregon Library, Special Collections. Correspondence, diary, and manuscripts of Pennell (1908-63), a novelist and short story writer. Includes correspondence of Martha Gellhorn, Marion Ives, and Elizabeth Horton. Also included are a diary from 1927 to 1928 and other papers of Pennell's wife Elizabeth (Horton) Pennell written while she was living in Paris and North Africa. See Martin Schmitt, *Catalogue of Manuscripts in the University of Oregon Library* (Eugene, OR: University of Oregon Press, 1971).

14,434. Raymond, Almira Adeline David
Papers. 1849-70. 11 items.
Open. Published guide.
University of Oregon Library, Special Collections. In 1849 Raymond, the wife of pioneer missionary and mission farmer William W. Raymond, arrived in Oregon aboard the *Lausanne* as part of mission reinforcement. Letters to her parents and a sister from the Willamette mission and from Tansy Point, OR, reflect hardships of mission life and the ambivalent attitude of the missionaries about the Indians. See Martin Schmitt, *Catalogue of Manuscripts in the University of Oregon Library* (Eugene, OR: University of Oregon Press, 1971).

14,435. Reik, Elsie I.
Papers. 1922-27. 227 items.
Open. Published guide.
University of Oregon Library, Special Collections. Reik was a missionary teacher at Hwa Nan College in Foochow, China. Letters to her family in Milwaukee describing her work and experiences. See Martin Schmitt, *Catalogue of Manuscripts in the University of Oregon Library* (Eugene, OR: University of Oregon Press, 1971).

14,436. Robbins, Kate L. (Pratt)
Papers. 1855-86. 99 items.
Open. Published guide.
University of Oregon Library, Special Collections. In 1859 Robbins (1834-?) journeyed by sea with her husband Abner Robbins to Indian Creek, CA. In about 1868 they moved to Ochoco, OR, where Abner raised sheep, cattle, and horses. Letters of Kate Robbins to her parents and brother describing the journey to and life in Indian Creek and letters from 1869 to 1886 to her mother and brother and from her daughter Eunice to her grandmother describing living conditions in Ochoco and Prineville, OR, with references to Indian uprisings, feuds between cattle and sheep ranchers, politics, and social life. See Martin Schmitt, *Catalogue of Manuscripts in the University of Oregon Library* (Eugene, OR: University of Oregon Press, 1971).

14,437. Rochester, Anna
Papers. 1880-1965. 2 ft.
Open. Inventory and supplement to published guide.
University of Oregon Library, Special Collections. Rochester (1880-1966) was a social worker, editor, and labor organizer. Correspondence, a journal about her life that was kept from 1880 to 1918 by her mother, records of the Community House, book reviews, and printed works. Includes correspondence with Ella R. Bloor, Edith McGrath, and Vida Scudder. Rochester was a social worker in Boston, an executive board member of the New Jersey Consumers League, and a board member of the New Jersey Child Labor Committee. She wrote and edited reports and pamphlets for the National Child Labor Committee in New York from 1912 to 1915, and then she began working for the Children's Bureau. In 1920, Rochester, Grace Hutchins, and four other women established a commune in New York City, which operated for two years. She edited *The World Tomorrow* from 1922 to 1926, and in 1927 she helped found the Labor Research Association. Rochester also wrote books and pamphlets on the labor movement.

14,438. Royal, Denise
Papers. 1967-69. 1.5 ft.
Open. Supplement to published guide.
University of Oregon Library, Special Collections. Correspondence and manuscripts of Royal (1935-), an author of books for young people, primarily relate to the research, writing, and publishing of her biography of J. Robert Oppenheimer, which was published in 1969 by St. Martin's Press.

14,439. St. Paul's Episcopal Church, Oregon City, OR, Women's Guild
Records. 1877-1908. 2 vols.
Open. Published guide.
University of Oregon Library, Special Collections. Minutes of the Guild. See Martin Schmitt, *Catalogue of Manuscripts in the University of Oregon Library* (Eugene, OR: University of Oregon Press, 1971).

14,440. Seely, Nell
Papers. 1939-65. 5 ft.
Open. Inventory and supplement to published guide.
University of Oregon Library, Special Collections. Seely (1878-1968) was a songwriter whose compositions include "Blue Night" (New York, 1944). Correspondence with music publishers, other composers, and lyricists; musical manuscripts; and published music.

14,441. Simester, Edith Winifred
Papers. 1945-46. 1 vol. and 15 items.
Open. Published guide.
University of Oregon Library, Special Collections. Simester was a missionary teacher at the Anglo-Chinese College in Foochow, China. Correspondence, including letters from former students, and a letter book containing transcriptions of letters from Simester to her mother. See Martin Schmitt, *Catalogue of Manuscripts in the University of Oregon Library* (Eugene, OR: University of Oregon Press, 1971).

14,442. Skinner, James Edwards
Papers. 1889-1956. 2 ft.
Open. Published guide and inventory.
University of Oregon Library, Special Collections. Correspondence, diaries, reports, memoranda, photos, and newspapers of Skinner (1867-1959), a medical missionary in China. In 1896 he married Susan Lawrence (1871-1952), a graduate of Chicago Women's Medical College, and in 1897 they went to China as medical missionaries for the Methodist Episcopal Church. After a short stay in Kutien, they were transferred to Yenping, where they remained for most of the next 30 years. In 1944 they fled China via the interior for India. Included is correspondence of Susan Skinner from 1922 to 1948 and her diaries from 1903 and from 1920 to 1942. See Martin Schmitt, *Catalogue of Manuscripts in the University of Oregon Library* (Eugene, OR: University of Oregon Press, 1971).

14,443. Smith, Charles Eugene
Papers. 1922-68. 9 ft.
Open. Published guide and inventory.
University of Oregon Library, Special Collections. Correspondence, diaries, historical and administrative material, records, periodicals, and books of Smith (1890-) and his wife Viola Leora (Ziegler) Smith, who were missionaries with the American Baptist Foreign Mission Society in the Congo from 1923 into the 1960s. Included is correspondence with the Mission Society; with Ben Armstrong, a minister, and his wife Rhoda Armstrong, primarily from Leopoldville and Kikongo, describing the personal and professional problems of missionaries; and mimeographed missionary letters regarding the problems of the missions during political upheavals in the Congo. The diaries are primarily from the Smiths' early years in Africa. Viola Smith attended the Kennedy School of Missions and earned a diploma from the School of Tropical Medicine in Brussels, Belgium. She worked as a general missionary with emphasis on education, medicine, and women and children. In 1966 she wrote a history of the Congo Baptist

missions for the Congolese. See Martin Schmitt, *Catalogue of Manuscripts in the University of Oregon Library* (Eugene, OR: University of Oregon Press, 1971).

14,444. Smith, Myrtle A.
Papers. 1921-47. 111 items.
Open. Published guide.
University of Oregon Library, Special Collections.
Correspondence of Smith, a Methodist missionary teacher in Kutien in Fukien, China, in which she describes her experiences to her family and friends. Also included are a few letters from other teachers and photos. See Martin Schmitt, *Catalogue of Manuscripts in the University of Oregon Library* (Eugene, OR: University of Oregon Press, 1971).

14,445. Snow, Myra L.
Papers. 1928-44. 14 items.
Open. Published guide.
University of Oregon Library, Special Collections.
Correspondence of Snow, a missionary teacher at the Methodist mission in Tientsin, China, describes her school experiences and her reactions to the Chinese. Also included is a 1937 letter from Lora Battin and a 1944 letter from Myra Jacquet describing the Japanese invasion and life in a concentration camp. See Martin Schmitt, *Catalogue of Manuscripts in the University of Oregon Library* (Eugene, OR: University of Oregon Press, 1971).

14,446. Soule, Isobel Walker
Papers. 1916-72. 4.5 ft.
Open. Inventory and supplement to published guide.
University of Oregon Library, Special Collections.
Organizational records and personal, family, and professional correspondence of Soule (1898-1972), a social worker, editor, and journalist. After her marriage to *New Republic* editor George H. Soule in 1923, Isobel Soule became active in social causes and committees. She was on the editorial board of *Woman Today.* She worked on the Vermont quarry workers strike of the late 1930s and visited Russia during the 1930s as a journalist. Organizational records include those of the United Committee to Aid Vermont Marble Workers.

14,447. Speare, Dorothy
Papers. 1914-48. 6 ft.
Open. Published guide and inventory.
University of Oregon Library, Special Collections.
Speare (1898-1951) was an opera singer from 1926 to 1930, a scenario writer in Hollywood from 1931 to 1934, a writer and lecturer from 1935, and a teacher of creative writing at Boston University from 1948 to 1951. Correspondence with her first husband Franklin B. Christmas; her second husband Charles J. Hubbard; her father Edward Ray Speare; Russell Davenport; Joseph H. Goodspeed, Jr.; Dorothy Heyward; Vincent Lawrence; Richard L. Mealand; Robert Nathan; Dorshka Raphaelson; and Carl Van Doren. Manuscripts of novels, short stories, and plays, including the play "Prima Donna," which became the motion picture *One Night of Love,* and manuscript and published copies of student writings. See Martin Schmitt, *Catalogue of Manuscripts in the University of Oregon Library* (Eugene, OR: University of Oregon Press, 1971).

14,448. Stangland, Arthur G.
Papers. 1929-54. 3 ft.
Open. Published guide and inventory.
University of Oregon Library, Special Collections.
Correspondence, manuscripts, and published items of Stangland (1908-), a science fiction writer. Included are papers of his wife, which consist of manuscript and published copies of feature articles for women's magazines and true confession stories, some of which were written with Edith Warner, and correspondence with publishers and agents, particularly Edith Margolis of Lenniger Literary Agency. See Martin Schmitt, *Catalogue of Manuscripts in the University of Oregon Library* (Eugene, OR: University of Oregon Press, 1971).

14,449. Stearns, Daniel Warren
Papers. 1843-1906. 1 box.
Open. Published guide.
University of Oregon Library, Special Collections.
Correspondence and business records of Stearns (1821-1911), a trader, storekeeper, packtrain operator, and farmer in California, Oregon, and Idaho. Includes letters to Stearns from his wife Almira Stearns from 1861 to 1864 while she was living on the family farm in Elkton, OR, and he was a trader in the Idaho mines near Elk City and Florence. See Martin Schmitt, *Catalogue of Manuscripts in the University of Oregon Library* (Eugene, OR: University of Oregon Press, 1971).

14,450. Steffan, Alice Jacqueline (Kennedy)
Papers. 1956-66. 3 ft.
Open. Published guide and inventory.
University of Oregon Library, Special Collections.
Manuscripts of books and correspondence with agents and publishers of Steffan (1907-), a writer of books, particularly biographies, for young people. See Martin Schmitt, *Catalogue of Manuscripts in the University of Oregon Library* (Eugene, OR: University of Oregon Press, 1971).

14,451. Sterling, Dorothy
Papers. 1923-50. 3 ft.
Open. Published guide.
University of Oregon Library, Special Collections.
A journalist, Sterling (1913-) was an employee of Time, Inc., from 1936 to 1949 and then became a free-lance writer. Includes a history of Time, Inc., entitled "The Luce Empire," and supporting manuscript and published sources for the history, including correspondence, interviews, and files on subjects important to the history of the company, among them Whittaker Chambers, communism, editorial policy, labor, Henry R. Luce, personnel, and personnel policy. See Martin Schmitt, *Catalogue of Manuscripts in the University of Oregon Library* (Eugene, OR: University of Oregon Press, 1971).

14,452. Sterling, Philip
Papers. 1947-69. 5 ft.
Open. Inventory and supplement to published guide.
University of Oregon Library, Special Collections.
Correspondence, manuscripts, and research material of Sterling, an author. Includes material on Rachel Carson, author of *Silent Spring.*

14,453. Sterne, Emma (Gelders)
Papers. 1927-70. Ca. 3 ft.
Open. Published guide and inventory.
University of Oregon Library, Special Collections.
Sterne (1894-) was a writer, editor, and pacifist. Correspondence with Artists and Writers Guild, Inc.; publishers; Marjory Lacy-Baker, Edith Margolis, and Gilda Tommasi of Lenniger Literary Agency; and letters to Sterne in 1967 while she was interned at the Santa Rita, CA, Rehabilitation Center for participation in a 1967 antidraft demonstration. Manuscripts and supporting material for books and plays; a report on the 1963 peace march to Washington, DC; and files on civil rights organizations and movements and the Communist party of California, including material on the Student Non-Violent Coordinating Committee, Santa Clara Valley Friends of SNCC, Congress of Racial Equality, Council of Federated Organizations, and the Mississippi Freedom Democratic party. Sterne was educated at Smith College in Massachusetts and Columbia University in New York. She sold her first story in 1923. During WWII she wrote for the Office of War Information and later for the UN. She became editor of the Aladdin Books series of American Heritage. Some of her later books, particularly the Kathy Martin Series, were written in collaboration with her daughter Barbara Lindsay under the shared pseudonym Josephine James. See Martin Schmitt, *Catalogue of Manuscripts in the University of Oregon Library* (Eugene, OR: University of Oregon Press, 1971).

14,454. Stevens, Hazard
Papers. 1676-1918. 14 ft.
Open. Published guide and inventory.
University of Oregon Library, Special Collections.
Stevens (1842-1918) was an Army officer, railroad attorney in Washington Territory and Boston, and collector of internal revenue for Washington Territory from 1868 to 1871. Correspondence; diaries; Stevens and Hazard family papers, including genealogical notes; legal documents; essays; internal revenue papers; railroad documents; Indian treaties; scrapbooks; and other material. The family papers include correspondence of Elizabeth Barker Stevens Campbell from 1830 to 1849 and Margaret Hazard [Mrs. Isaac I.] Stevens from 1838 to 1867. Also included are the pension papers from 1863 to 1910 of Hazard Stevens's father Isaac Ingalls Stevens, an Army officer and first governor of Washington Territory who was killed in the Civil War; the papers document the fight of family members, particularly Isaac Stevens's wife Margaret Stevens, for a pension from the War Department following Isaac Stevens's death. See Martin Schmitt, *Catalogue of Manuscripts in the University of Oregon Library* (Eugene, OR: University of Oregon Press, 1971).

14,455. Stevenson, Janet
Papers. 1929-66. 4 ft.
Open. Published guide and inventory.
University of Oregon Library, Special Collections.
Stevenson (1913-) was a writer, playwright, and lecturer. Correspondence and documents relating to her dismissal from the University of Southern California Faculty in 1952; correspondence with agent Berthold Fles, Millen Brand of Crown Publishers, and Helen K. Taylor of Viking Press; letters to Mrs. John Marshall of Hubbard Woods, IL, that Stevenson wrote while on a world tour and attending the 1961 World Council of Peace in New Delhi, India; and manuscripts of short stories, articles, biographies, plays, teleplays, and poems. Examples of her work include the play *Counterattack,* which was written with her husband Philip Stevenson, and the novel *The Ardent Years.* See Martin Schmitt, *Catalogue of Manuscripts in the University of Oregon Library* (Eugene, OR: University of Oregon Press, 1971).

14,456. Stoughton, A. Ella
Papers. 1881-86. 3 vols.
Open. Published guide.
University of Oregon Library, Special Collections.
Diary of Stoughton (1857-1944), daughter of a Washington pioneer from New England, regarding her trip around the world. In 1881 she left Portland, OR, on a wheat ship to Liverpool and Belfast; from England she sailed to Singapore, Shanghai, Nagasaki, and Hong Kong; and in 1883 she arrived in New York. She visited relatives in New England and returned to Vancouver, Washington Territory, by railroad in 1884. The final part of the diary concerns Stoughton's position as the Washington territorial legislature's house enrolling clerk and her courtship with her future husband Doran H. Stearns, who later founded the Portland *Bee.* In later years A. Ella Stearns was active in Portland civic affairs and occasionally wrote articles for the Portland *Oregonian.* See Martin Schmitt, *Catalogue of Manuscripts in the University of Oregon Library* (Eugene, OR: University of Oregon Press, 1971).

14,457. Teagarden, Lyrel G.
Papers. 1921-56. 1 ft.
Open. Supplement to published guide.

University of Oregon Library, Special Collections. Teagarden (1894-) was a missionary teacher for the Disciples of Christ at Luchowfu in China from 1920 to 1951, in Jamaica, and at the Yakima Indian mission in Washington. Correspondence, which was addressed to her mother and a friend and relates primarily to her China experiences, and a 614-page manuscript fictionalized account of her stay in China.

14,458. Uchida, Yoshiko
Papers. 1949-51. 1 box.
Open. Published guide.
University of Oregon Library, Special Collections. Uchida (1921-) is a writer of children's books whose stories are primarily based on Japanese folk tales. Correspondence with Harcourt, Brace and Co. and Charles Scribner's Sons; manuscripts; and galley proofs. See Martin Schmitt, *Catalogue of Manuscripts in the University of Oregon Library* (Eugene, OR: University of Oregon Press, 1971).

14,459. Wakeman, Letha Evangeline (Ward)
Papers. 1908-74. 3 ft.
Open. Supplement to published guide.
University of Oregon Library, Special Collections. Wakeman (1898-1974) was a Baptist missionary in the Congo from 1922 to 1926 and a worker with the Oregon Migrant Ministry from 1955 to 1974. Personal correspondence from 1934 to 1974, Wakeman's diaries for 1921 to 1961, a memoir, records of the Oregon Migrant Ministry, a biographical manuscript, and ephemera. Wakeman was the daughter of Thomas and Effie Ward, missionaries to Lagos in Nigeria, and wife of Andrew Vergil Wakeman, a Baptist missionary to the Congo, who contracted filariasis and returned to the US. In the Oregon Migrant Ministry, she became director of the Gleaners Chapel in the Yamhill County mission known as Eola Village. The correspondence contains letters from missionaries in Africa, the US, and Alaska; correspondence with her children and husband; and a letter Effie Ward wrote from Lagos in 1908. Also includes Effie Ward's memoir, a manuscript biography of Wakeman by Colena M. Anderson, and various Congo mission publications.

14,460. Waldo, Mary Jane
Papers. 1948-65. 3 ft.
Open. Published guide and inventory.
University of Oregon Library, Special Collections. Correspondence, manuscripts of stories and poems, and published items of Waldo (1915-67), a Portland, OR, writer and instructor. Includes correspondence with her agent Howard Moorpark and personal correspondence from Lucile V. Payne. Waldo wrote feature stories for the Portland *Oregonian,* wrote romance and confession stories, and taught creative writing at Lewis and Clark College in Portland. See Martin Schmitt, *Catalogue of Manuscripts in the University of Oregon Library* (Eugene, OR: University of Oregon Press, 1971).

14,461. Walton, Pauline
Papers. 1927-63. 18 vols.
Open. Supplement to published guide.
University of Oregon Library, Special Collections. Diaries of Walton (1879-1966), who was the daughter of Joshua J. Walton, secretary of the University of Oregon board of regents.

14,462. Warner, Mason Young
Papers. 1853-1944. 4 ft.
Open. Published guide.
University of Oregon Library, Special Collections. Family correspondence, diaries, and genealogical data of Warner (1868-1957), a member of a Pleasant Hill, OR, pioneer family. Includes letters from 1918 to 1943 from Warner's daughter Claire (Warner) Churchill, an Oregon writer who taught school from 1920 to 1925 at Cloverdale, OR; Prosser, WA; and Wheeler, OR. From 1936 to 1939 she worked for the Oregon Writers' Project. Her letters describe teaching experiences, social life of Wheeler, and her writing. Also included are two 1853 diaries kept by Agnes Stewart, who later married Mason Warner, and Helen Stewart, later Helen Love, while traveling from St. Louis to Oregon by wagon train. Agnes Stewart's diary was edited by Claire Churchill and published in the *Oregon Historical Quarterly* (March 1928). See Martin Schmitt, *Catalogue of Manuscripts in the University of Oregon Library* (Eugene, OR: University of Oregon Press, 1971).

14,463. Watson, Jane Werner
Papers. 1958-73. 1.5 ft.
Open. Inventory and supplement to published guide.
University of Oregon Library, Special Collections. Watson (1915-) is a publisher and writer of books for children and young people. Correspondence with publishers and with Robert E. Switzer, a physician at the Menninger Clinic, regarding the writing of the Learning to Know Yourself Series, published by the Golden Press, and a manuscript of the Series.

14,464. Way, Isabel Stewart
Papers. 1931-66. 3 ft.
Open. Published guide and inventory.
University of Oregon Library, Special Collections. Way (1904-) was a writer. Correspondence, primarily with Edith Margolis of Lenniger Literary Agency; manuscripts of short stories, novelettes, and novels; and tear sheets of stories from pulp magazines. See Martin Schmitt, *Catalogue of Manuscripts in the University of Oregon Library* (Eugene, OR: University of Oregon Press, 1971).

14,465. Werner, Vivian Lescher
Papers. 1961-71. 1.5 ft.
Open. Inventory.
University of Oregon Library, Special Collections. Werner was a free-lance writer, novelist, and author of books for children and young people. Correspondence, primarily with publishers and with agents Rosica Colin and the Lenniger Literary Agency; manuscripts; and source material.

14,466. Wheeler, Laura Maude
Papers. 1903-48. 1.5 ft.
Open. Published guide and inventory.
University of Oregon Library, Special Collections. From 1903 to 1948 Wheeler (1874-1966) was a missionary teacher in northern China supported by the Woman's Society of Christian Service of the Methodist Episcopal Church. Primarily reminiscences based on personal diaries, a 1938 diary, photos and slides depicting life in China and Wheeler's travels, mementos, and a booklet by Wheeler entitled *Recollections of My Chinese Days* (Pasadena, CA, 1947). She worked at the Keen School in Tientsin and the Gamewell and Union Bible Schools in Peking. In 1943 she was interned at the Civilian Civic Center in Shantung and released in 1945. See Martin Schmitt, *Catalogue of Manuscripts in the University of Oregon Library* (Eugene, OR: University of Oregon Press, 1971).

14,467. White, Anne Terry
Papers. 1963-68. 1.5 ft.
Open. Published guide.
University of Oregon Library, Special Collections. White (1896-) was a writer of children's books and translator of Russian children's books. Correspondence with publishers, manuscripts of books and translations, and White's published translations. See Martin Schmitt, *Catalogue of Manuscripts in the University of Oregon Library* (Eugene, OR: University of Oregon Press, 1971).

14,468. Whiteley, Opal Stanley
Papers. 1911-18. 3 ft.
Open. Published guide.
University of Oregon Library, Special Collections. Whiteley (1897-) was the author of *The Fairyland Around Us* (Los Angeles, 1918) and *The Story of Opal* (Boston, 1920). Correspondence; notes; material relating to work with Christian Endeavor, an organization for young Christians; memoranda; photos; mementos; and other items. Whiteley attended the University of Oregon from 1916 to 1918. An article by Inez Fortt based on these papers was published in the University of Oregon Library *Call Number,* vol. 23, no. 1 (Fall 1961). See Martin Schmitt, *Catalogue of Manuscripts in the University of Oregon Library* (Eugene, OR: University of Oregon Press, 1971).

14,469. Williams, Jean
Papers. 1941-57. 1 box.
Open. Published guide and inventory.
University of Oregon Library, Special Collections. Williams (1876-1965) was a composer and music teacher in the US and Canada. Correspondence with music publishers and manuscript piano sheet music. See Martin Schmitt, *Catalogue of Manuscripts in the University of Oregon Library* (Eugene, OR: University of Oregon Press, 1971).

14,470. Wilson, Eleanor
Papers. 1925-51. 253 items.
Open. Supplement to published guide.
University of Oregon Library, Special Collections. Letters that Wilson (1891-1972) wrote to her family describing her missionary work. A Congregational church missionary, she was affiliated with Kobe Theological Seminary for Women in Japan from 1925 to 1932. Intermittently Wilson taught and lectured in the US for the American Board of Foreign Missions. She was a missionary to the Caroline Islands in Micronesia from 1935 to 1941 and in the Marshall and Caroline Islands from 1946 to 1950. In 1945 Wilson was ordained a Christian church minister, and from 1950 until her retirement in 1961 she was captain of the missionary ship *Morning Star VI.* A biography of Wilson, *The Lady Was a Skipper* (New York, 1956), was written by Maribelle Cormack.

14,471. Woman's Christian Temperance Union
Records. 1889-1910. 1 vol.
Open. Published guide.
University of Oregon Library, Special Collections. Treasurer's book of the Gardiner, OR, WCTU chapter. See Martin Schmitt, *Catalogue of Manuscripts in the University of Oregon Library* (Eugene, OR: University of Oregon Press, 1971).

14,472. Woman's Republican Patriotic League
Records. 1899-1902. 1 vol.
Open. Published guide.
University of Oregon Library, Special Collections. Minutes of this local organization, which was primarily a social and literary club. See Martin Schmitt, *Catalogue of Manuscripts in the University of Oregon Library* (Eugene, OR: University of Oregon Press, 1971).

14,473. Women Miscellany
Papers. 1905-15. 3 items.
Open. Published guide.
University of Oregon Library, Special Collections. Three letters, one from Abigail (Scott) Duniway of Portland, OR, to Barbara M. Booth of Eugene describing early education in Illinois and teaching experiences in Oregon, 1915; one from Eva (Emery) Dye of Oregon City, OR, to a Mrs. Colby in which Dye declines the presidency of a suffrage group and instead recommends [Mrs.] Ada Unruh, 1906; and one from A. E. Stewart in Genoa, OH, to Ella K. Dearborn, a physician in Portland, relating that she has read Dearborn's article on euthanasia and requesting a prescription for her father, 1905. See Martin Schmitt, *Catalogue of Manuscripts in the University of Oregon Library* (Eugene, OR: University of Oregon Press, 1971).

14,474. Women's Emergency Corps
Records. 1898. 1 vol.
Open. Published guide.
University of Oregon Library, Special Collections.
Daily membership and activity records of the Corps, which was organized to help Spanish-American War soldiers. See Martin Schmitt, *Catalogue of Manuscripts in the University of Oregon Library* (Eugene, OR: University of Oregon Press, 1971).

14,475. Wyndham, Lee
Papers. 1947-68. 4.5 ft.
Open. Published guide and inventory.
University of Oregon Library, Special Collections.
Wyndham was a writer of books for children and young people and of articles on how to write for this audience. Correspondence with editors and publishers, manuscripts of books and articles, notes, galley proofs, and published works. Correspondents include Dorothy M. Bryan of Dodd, Mead Co.; Margaret Lesser of Doubleday and Co.; Bertha Gunterman of Alfred A. Knopf, Longmans, Green and Co.; Arnold Madison; Teri Martini; Julian Messner; and Gertrude Blumenthal. Also included are three taped interviews done at the 1962 Christian Writers and Editors Conference, two with Wyndham and one with Phyllis A. Whitney, author of *Willow Hill.* See Martin Schmitt, *Catalogue of Manuscripts in the University of Oregon Library* (Eugene, OR: University of Oregon Press, 1971).

14,476. Yaukey, Grace (Sydenstricker)
Papers. 1934-66. 3 ft.
Open. Published guide and inventory.
University of Oregon Library, Special Collections.
Yaukey (1899-) was a writer of books for young people and adults, primarily about China. Manuscripts of books and articles and correspondence with publishers John Day Co.; Alfred A. Knopf; J. B. Lippincott; Macrae-Smith Co.; and Row, Peterson and Co. See Martin Schmitt, *Catalogue of Manuscripts in the University of Oregon Library* (Eugene, OR: University of Oregon Press, 1971).

FOREST GROVE

14,477. Brown, Tabitha (Moffat)
Papers. 1799-ca. 1950s. Ca. 5 in.
Open. No guide.
Pacific University Library, Rare Book Room.
Correspondence, journal, memoir, clippings, and ephemera of Brown (1780-1858), a pioneer who traveled to Oregon in 1846; her husband, a clergyman, had died in 1817. An educator, she founded the Forest Grove boarding school that became Pacific University. Includes correspondence of Brown with her husband, brother and sister, grandchildren, and friends, some of which concerns life in Oregon, crossing the plains, Indians, and her boarding school and clippings regarding the Brown family and the settlement of Washington County, OR.

14,478. Walker, Mary (Richardson)
Papers. 1850-56. 18-page vol.
Open. No guide.
Pacific University Library, Rare Book Room.
Book of Walker (1811-97) containing the constitution and minutes of the Maternal Association in Forest Grove, which was founded by women for the purpose of prayer and mutual counsel in reference to maternal duties. When a member of the Association died, the others were pledged to look after her children. Includes lists of children born to and adopted by members. Tabitha Brown and Myra F. Eells were members of this group.

14,479. Wilson, Elizabeth Miller
Papers. 1899. 14-page item.
Open. No guide.
Pacific University Library, Rare Book Room.
Memoir of Wilson, a pioneer schoolteacher, regarding crossing the plains to Oregon in 1851, Indians, life in Oregon, and her experiences teaching on the frontier.

JACKSONVILLE

14,480. Chase, Emma (Wendt)
Papers. 1974. 7 pp.
Open. Card catalog.
Southern Oregon Historical Society.
Reminiscences of Chase (1890-), an Oregon settler, concern her parents' emigration to Oregon and their homesteading experiences. Also includes notes by Anna Louise (Neidemeyer) Wendt.

14,481. Grand Army of the Republic, Women's Relief Corps, Burnside Post No. 24
Records. Ca. 1899-1931. Ca. 3 Hollinger cases.
Closed. No guide.
Southern Oregon Historical Society.
Minute books, correspondence, journals, ledgers, and other records of this Medford, OR, post.

14,482. Greaves, Pauline E.
Papers. 1917-19. 1 folder.
Open. Card catalog.
Southern Oregon Historical Society.
Photos and other papers of Greaves relating to her service in the US Navy during WWI.

14,483. Hadley, Amelia E.
Papers. 1851-ca. 1937. 57-page vol. and other items.
Open. Card catalog.
Southern Oregon Historical Society.
An 1851 diary of Hadley (1825-86), a pioneer, regarding her journey from Illinois to Oregon. Also includes two interviews conducted in 1936 or 1937 with her daughter Melvina F. (Hadley) Hayes shortly after her 80th birthday.

14,484. Luy, Minnie Ida (Bybee)
Papers. 1890-93. 2 vols.
Open. No guide.
Southern Oregon Historical Society.
Diaries of Luy (1871-1952) concern her experiences at St. Mary's boarding school in Portland, OR; social life in Jacksonville, including musical and theatrical events, lodge meetings, and parties; and her courtship and marriage to Fred Luy, Jr.

14,485. Methodist Episcopal Church
Records. 1886-92. 2 vols.
Open. Card catalog.
Southern Oregon Historical Society.
Minute books of the Ladies' Union and the Sunday School Board of the Church in Grants Pass, OR.

14,486. Miller, Elizabeth Ann (Awbry)
Papers. Ca. 1880-1904. 1 vol.
Open. Card catalog.
Southern Oregon Historical Society.
[Mrs. John Napper Tandy] Miller (1832-1920) was the first worthy matron of Adarel Chapter No. 3, Order of the Eastern Star; the Chapter was founded in 1880. Consists of her notebook, which contains notes, addresses, toasts, and other information.

14,487. Sherman, Mary Jane
Papers. Ca. 1860-1941. 1 vol.
Open. Card catalog.
Southern Oregon Historical Society.
Scrapbook containing notes and clippings of [Mrs. Salisbury] Sherman (1832-1926), a pioneer, regarding her husband's journey from Dakota Territory to Oregon in 1877. Also contains information about the Stearns family.

14,488. Skeeters, Grace Jane (Simpson)
Papers. Nd. 17-page item.
Open. No guide.
Southern Oregon Historical Society.
Memoirs of Skeeters (1839-?), a pioneer, concern her journey across the plains and ranch life in Josephine and Jackson counties in Oregon.

14,489. Taylor, Rachel
Papers. 1853. 34-page vol.
Open. Card catalog.
Southern Oregon Historical Society.
Journal of Taylor (ca. 1839-?), a pioneer, regarding her overland journey from Rockford, IL, to the Rogue River Valley in Oregon.

14,490. Walker, Millie Pearl (Hodges)
Papers. 1910-20. 8 vols.
Open. No guide.
Southern Oregon Historical Society.
Diaries in which Walker (1893-1964) describes her daily activities as a schoolgirl and young wife in the Gold Hill area of rural Jackson County, OR. Millie Hodges married Lee O. Walker in 1916.

14,491. Walrad, Jane H. (Mullen)
Papers. 1861-67. 1 folder and 8 vols.
Open. Unpublished guide.
Southern Oregon Historical Society.
Diaries of [Mrs. David P.] Walrad (1823-1900) contain descriptions of the daily life of a farm wife and family during the pioneer period in northern Sacramento Valley, CA, and the Emigrant Creek and Jacksonville areas in Oregon. The Walrads moved from Illinois in 1860 and engaged in farming and mining in California and southern Oregon.

14,492. Woman's Relief Corps
Records. Ca. 1895-1920s. Ca. 1 cu.ft.
Open. No guide.
Southern Oregon Historical Society.
Minute books, financial records, application forms, and ephemera of the Chester A. Arthur Chapter no. 34 of the Corps in Ashland, OR. Includes national as well as local records of this patriotic, social, and service club, which was an auxiliary to the Grand Army of the Republic.

MARYLHURST

14,493. Sisters of the Holy Name, Oregon Province
Records. 1832- . 38 ft.
Open. Unpublished guide.
Holy Name Sisters, Oregon Province Archives.
The order was established in Oregon in 1859; its members are involved in education and social services. Financial records, correspondence, journals, chronicles, biographies of sisters, tapes, photos, slides, motion pictures, maps, architectural drawings and plans, artifacts, and other records. The Sisters established St. Mary's Academy in Portland, OR, in 1859 and numerous other schools in Oregon during subsequent years.

MOUNT ANGEL

14,494. Priory Archives
Records. 1882- . No size given.
Access restricted. No guide.
Benedictine Sisters, Queen of Angels Priory
Financial records, correspondence, theses, memoirs, photos, scrapbooks, diplomas, and other records of this order of religious women who administer and nurse in a long-term health center and teach in day-care centers, kindergartens, elementary and

secondary schools, and colleges. Mother Mary Bernardine Wachter was foundress of the order.

PORTLAND

14,495. Museum Archives
Records. 1700s- . 250 cu.ft.
Access restricted. No guide.
Georgia-Pacific Historical Museum.
Photos, films, artifacts, and other records concerning the history of the wood products industry include photos of women in early lumber camps.

14,496. Lutheran Women's Missionary League
Records. 1942- . 12 in.
Open. No guide.
Lutheran Church—Missouri Synod, Northwest District Archives.
Minutes, convention reports, and quarterly newsletters of the League, founded in 1942 to coordinate activities of local Lutheran women's groups.

14,497. Oregon Jewish Oral History and Archive Project
Records. Ca. 1890- . No size given.
Open. No guide.
Mittleman Jewish Community Center.
In order to preserve the history of Jews in Oregon, the project has conducted ca. 70 interviews, about half of which are with women. Interviewees discuss their origins, the passage to America, settlement in Oregon, neighborhoods, Jewish institutions, religious life, early family history, business, and changes in the Jewish community over the years. Women interviewees also discuss their options as women and the ways in which they were circumscribed. Includes interviews with Gertrude Sweet, a labor organizer for the Bartenders and Waitresses Union; Laddie Trachtenberg, a Neighborhood House worker; Joanna Menashe, who was married by arrangement on the Isle of Rhodes to an older American Sephardic Jew who had returned there for that purpose; several survivors of the Holocaust in Europe, among them Rochella Meekcom, Diana Golden, and Lydia Lax Brown; [Miss] Molly Blumenthal, who worked in the shipyards during WWII; and Gertrude Feves, a Neighborhood House worker and member of the Jewish Women's Sewing Society. A copy of the interview with Sweet is also available at the University of Michigan's Women in Labor History project; copies of the interviews with survivors of the Holocaust are available at the William E. Wiener Oral History Library in New York City.

Collection also contains a slide-tape show giving an overview of Jewish history in Oregon and some videotaped interviews with residents of the old Jewish "ghetto" in South Portland. Minute books and albums of the Jewish Women's Sewing Society, a charitable and social group; the Jewish Service Organization, 1938-44; the Opportunity Bake Shop, 1935-41; the Jewish Shelter Home, 1921-31; and other organizations are included as well

14,498. Abbett Family
Papers. 1865-1968. 64 items.
Open. Card catalog.
Oregon Historical Society.
Family papers of John C. Abbett, a Portland businessman and flutist. Correspondence, including an 1865 Civil War letter; diaries, including the diary of Mrs. J. T. Abbett for 1911 to 1915; a history of women's foreign missionary work in the Pacific Northwest, including the organization of the Columbia River branch; papers of Myra Leanne (Abbett) Adams (?-1968), including correspondence, diaries for the period 1908-63, a 1963 autobiography, short stories, poetry, letters to the editor, and an autograph book; and other material.

14,499. Adams, Cecilia Emily McMillen
Papers. Nd. No size given.
Open. Card catalog.
Oregon Historical Society.
Adams (1829-67) was an Oregon pioneer who settled in Hillsboro, OR. Diary of an 1852 overland journey from Missouri to Oregon and a biography of Cecilia Adams by her husband William Adams, which contains information on her twin sister Parthenia E. Blank and brother-in-law Stephen Blank.

14,500. Aitken Family
Papers. 1843-1970. 1 ft.
Open. Card catalog.
Oregon Historical Society.
Correspondence, diaries, journals, an autobiography, genealogical material, and documents of a family whose members spelled their name Aitken, Akin, Aiken, or Aitkens. Genealogy of Aitkin, Johnson, and Richey families with reference to Alvord Aitken (1854-90), his wife Carrie Fidelia (Johnson) Aitken (1860-1947), their children Geraldine Lee and Frances Alva Aitken (1889-1970); John William Douglas Aitken (1824-1914); Maria Morrison Aitken (1834-83); Stuart Richey (1812-89); Catherine Aikins McElmon (1816-92); and the Stratford Johnson family. Also included are minutes for 1900 and 1901, poetry, and essays of the Fagot Club in Portland.

14,501. Alaska
Collection. 1937-70. 1 folder.
Open. Card catalog.
Oregon Historical Society.
Isobel Wylie Hutchinson was an author and explorer. A 1937 article by Hutchinson entitled "A Paradise in the Bering Sea" from *The Glasgow Herald* and letters written in 1970 between Kenneth Holmes and Marjorie Gardner regarding Hutchinson.

14,502. Albers, Hermina Charlotte
Papers. 1916. 1 vol.
Open. Card catalog.
Oregon Historical Society.
Scrapbook compiled while Albers (1899-) was a student at St. Mary's Academy in Portland contains photos, programs, and memorabilia.

14,503. Allen, Maryland
Papers. 1910-27. 2 boxes.
Open. Card catalog.
Oregon Historical Society.
Manuscripts of short stories, novels, essays, plays, and book reviews of Allen, a Portland author. Also included are correspondence with publishers and agents and letters containing observations on the Industrial Workers of the World and WWI, clippings, ephemera, and papers of Allen's husband Edward T. Tyson.

14,504. Americana
Collection. Nd. No size given.
Open. Card catalog.
Oregon Historical Society.
Correspondence and manuscript material include 1946 correspondence of Marion T. Weatherford with Eleanor Roosevelt and Senator Wayne Morse concerning labor strikes, a 1964 thank-you note from Marina N. Oswald to Ada M. Davis in Rainier, OR, and letters to Robert F. Beck regarding his recording "The Grotto Organs in Reverie" from Congresswoman Edith Green, Eunice Shriver, Fulton J. Sheen, Wayne Morse, and the White House.

14,505. Anderson, Mrs. William E., Sr.
Papers. 1963. 4-page item.
Open. Card catalog.
Oregon Historical Society.
Letter from Anderson to the Oregon Historical Society concerns the shelling of the Fort Stevens, OR, vicinity by a Japanese submarine in 1943.

14,506. Applegate Family
Papers. 1840-1930. 1 box.
Open. Card catalog.
Oregon Historical Society.
Papers of Oliver Cromwell Applegate and Lillian Gertrude Applegate; correspondence and manuscripts of Sallie (Applegate) Long regarding Jesse Applegate, Cynthia [Mrs. Jesse] Applegate, and the Applegate genealogy; a manuscript by [Mrs.] Emma Miller about Jesse Applegate entitled "Memory of the Sage of Yoncalla"; a poem by Bessie Bell Applegate; reminiscences by Virginia (Watson) Applegate of her childhood in Illinois and the Sanford Watson family's overland journey to Oregon in 1849; and articles.

14,507. Atiyeh, Victor
Papers. 1961- . No size given.
Open. Card catalog.
Oregon Historical Society.
Atiyeh (1923-), a Portland businessman and Oregon state senator since 1965, was an Oregon state representative from 1959 to 1963 and Republican gubernatorial candidate in 1974. Correspondence, primarily from constituents regarding abortion and other issues; legislative material, including reports, notes, and minutes of the Columbia Interstate Compact Commission; gubernatorial campaign material; and memorabilia.

14,508. Atkinson, George Henry
Papers. 1847-78. 2 boxes.
Open. Card catalog.
Oregon Historical Society.
A missionary, educator, scientist, and publicist, Atkinson (1819-89) was founder of Clackamas Female Seminary, cofounder of Pacific University, and pastor of the First Congregational Church in Portland; he also was considered the father of Oregon's public school system. Correspondence, including letters written by him and other family members to his wife Nancy (Bates) Atkinson; journals; and speeches.

14,509. Bailey, Maida Rossiter
Papers. 1901-62. 2.5 ft.
Open. Card catalog.
Oregon Historical Society.
Bailey (?-1973) and her husband Meredith Bailey, Jr., were ranch owners near Sisters, OR. Personal correspondence; business correspondence regarding agriculture, logging, and the Deschutes Farmer's Co-op; expense records; legal documents, including loans, contracts, receipts, permits, and agreements; and a biography of Voltaire.

14,510. Bailey, Margaret Jewett (Smith)
Papers. Ca. 1852-1971. 1 folder.
Open. Card catalog.
Oregon Historical Society.
[Mrs. William J.] Bailey was a missionary and author of *The Grains, or, Passages in the Life of Ruth Rover, with Occasional Pictures of Oregon, Natural and Moral;* Ruth Rover was her pseudonym. Includes her divorce proceedings in 1852 and those of M. J. Waddell and Francis Waddell in 1858 as well as articles about Ruth Rover by Herbert B. Nelson in 1959 and Janice K. Duncan in 1971.

14,511. Baird, R. Bruce
Papers. 1918-19. 75 items.
Open. Card catalog.
Oregon Historical Society.
Correspondence of Baird (1891-1971), a WWI soldier, includes letters to "My Dear Eva" concerning his war experiences in France and personal and family matters.

14,512. Baldwin, Eleanore Florence
Papers. 1909-27. 14 items.
Open. Card catalog.
Oregon Historical Society.
Correspondence of Baldwin, a journalist, regarding her column "Woman's View Point" in the Portland *Telegram*. Poetry is also included.

14,513. Ball, John
Papers. Nd. 1 microfilm reel and other material.
Partially restricted. Card catalog.
Oregon Historical Society.
Correspondence, an 1832 diary, lectures, and an 1874 biography of Ball (1794-1884), a lawyer and amateur scientist, contain information concerning the American Society for Encouraging the Settlement of the Oregon Territory, Ball's overland journey to Oregon in 1832 with Nathaniel Jarvis Wyeth, meteorological observations, and family affairs. Also contains correspondence of Ball's daughters Lucy Ball and Kate (Ball) Powers, including letters to Eva Emery Dye, F. G. Young, and George H. Himes regarding publication of their father's papers, and the *Autobiography of John Ball,* the material for which was compiled by his daughters Lucy, Kate, and Flora (Ball) Hopkins.

14,514. Bancroft and Trevett Families
Papers. 1835-1918. 10 folders and 10 vols.
Open. Card catalog.
Oregon Historical Society.
Correspondence and diaries of Theodore Brooks and Mary Melissa (Bancroft) Trevett (1838-); correspondence of Hubert Howe Bancroft, Albert Little Bancroft, and Emily (Bancroft) Palmer Pierce and that of Azariah Ashley and Lucy Damaris (Howe) Bancroft to their children; diary of Katherine Lucy Trevett; and diary and notebook of Emily Bancroft (Trevett) Nunn.

14,515. Barker and Adair Family
Papers. Ca. 1847-1922. 4 boxes.
Open. Card catalog.
Oregon Historical Society.
Correspondence, documents, scrapbook, copybook, school mementos, and ephemera of Mr. and Mrs. George R. Barker; an 1872 diary of Mrs. John Adair; correspondence of Anna Morris Barker, Belle B. Barker, Samuel and Ellen M. Booth, Mary L. Ferguson, S. M. [Mrs. John] Guernsey, Mary W. Lourey, Anna M. Holstein, Anna Morris, Annie Morris, Charles and Lizzie Morris, Louisa Morris, Mary R. Morris, Rachel W. Morris, Sarah E. Morris, Mary Palmer, Sophie G. Putnam, and Mary B. Rodney; correspondence and documents of William Morris Barker; diaries, notebook, school notebook from St. Helen's Hall, and autograph book of Laura Pindall Adair [Mrs. William M.] Barker; and other material.

14,516. Beaverton Band of Hope, No. 6
Records. Ca. 1882-87. 3 vols.
Open. Card catalog.
Oregon Historical Society.
Minutes and record books of the Beaverton, OR, Band and of the Beaverton WCTU.

14,517. Beckham, Nellie
Papers. Nd. 25 pp.
Open. Card catalog.
Oregon Historical Society.
Material regarding the 1867 journey to Oregon of Mr. and Mrs. Jehue Barnes.

14,518. Bellinger, Katie
Papers. 1886-88. 1 folder.
Open. Card catalog.
Oregon Historical Society.
Love letters from Bellinger to William Deueff.

14,519. Benson, Pamelia Frances (Loomis)
Papers. 1878. 1 vol.
Open. Card catalog.
Oregon Historical Society.
A diary kept by Pamelia Loomis (1865-1945) during her journey from Nebraska to Colfax, WA, when she was 13 years old. Loomis later married Simon Benson.

14,520. Birchman, Anna
Papers. 1890-91. 112-page vol.
Open. Card catalog.
Oregon Historical Society.
Diary in Swedish of Birchman (1872-?) concerns her first trip to the US at age 18. The diary is arranged as daily letters to her family. An English translation is included.

14,521. Boyd, Mary Brown (Sumner)
Papers. 1916-19. 1 folder.
Open. Card catalog.
Oregon Historical Society.
Correspondence, notes, clippings, and other material regarding woman suffrage and prohibition in Oregon.

14,522. Brockway, Margaret Rice
Papers. 1869-75. 4 items.
Open. Card catalog.
Oregon Historical Society.
Correspondence from Brockway to her cousins Gary and Mary Barnes describing family life, farming and economic conditions, weather, immigration, and Brockway's remarriage.

14,523. Burbank, Minerva
Papers. 1853-59. 1 folder.
Open. Card catalog.
Oregon Historical Society.
Correspondence from Burbank in Independence, OR, to her siblings Nancy and John Spaulding regarding family matters.

14,524. Bussard, Nettie
Papers. Nd. No size given.
Open. Card catalog.
Oregon Historical Society.
Reminiscences of Bussard, a teacher in Baker County, OR, from about 1890 to 1900, and notes gathered from old settlers concerning early events in the County.

14,525. Bussey, Minnie
Papers. Ca. 1950. 1 folder.
Open. Card catalog.
Oregon Historical Society.
Reminiscences of experiences during the difficult winter of 1889-90 in Klamath County, OR, as told to Florence Ogle by Minnie and Ella Bussey.

14,526. Calbreath, John Franklin
Papers. 1858-1903. 1 box.
Open. Card catalog.
Oregon Historical Society.
Calbreath (1854-1939) was a physician and Oregon state senator. Correspondence and genealogical material of the Calbreath and Smith families, including letters of Sidney and Mianda Smith, John U. Smith, Irene (Smith) Calbreath, and of John Calbreath's mother, sisters, and cousins. Also includes political correspondence from John H. Mitchell and George W. McBride and business and family papers of John Calbreath.

14,527. Calbreath, Mary Evelene
Papers. 1864-1962. 1 folder and 5 vols.
Open. Card catalog.
Oregon Historical Society.
Correspondence, diaries for 1900 to 1902, daybook, musical programs, genealogy, articles, a landscape album, and ephemera of Calbreath (?-1972), a Portland music teacher.

14,528. Carter, Orpha Lankton
Papers. Ca. 1812-42. 1 microfilm reel.
Open. Card catalog.
Oregon Historical Society.
Correspondence and diary of Carter, a missionary, concern her experiences aboard the *Lausanne* with Jason Lee and at Willamette Mission. Also included are financial records and poems.

14,529. Castor, Laura Rice
Papers. 1884-99. 1 vol.
Open. Card catalog.
Oregon Historical Society.
Diary describing daily events in Douglas County, OR.

14,530. Church, Mary Louise (Crane)
Papers. 1909-10. 1 vol.
Open. Card catalog.
Oregon Historical Society.
Correspondence from Church (1861-1949) to her family while she was on a world tour.

14,531. Clarke, Harriet T. (Buckingham)
Papers. Nd. No size given.
Open. Card catalog.
Oregon Historical Society.
Diary of [Mrs.] Clarke (1832-90) describing her 1851 overland journey, correspondence to Clarke, and letters and notes regarding the Buckingham family genealogy.

14,532. Coe Family
Papers. 1821-92. 3 boxes.
Open. Card catalog.
Oregon Historical Society.
Nathaniel Coe (1788-1868) and his wife Mary White Coe (1801-92) were involved in farming and manufacturing. Correspondence, primarily between Nathaniel and Mary Coe; Nathaniel Coe's personal notebook for 1821 to 1822; journal Mary Coe kept during a voyage from the Isthmus of Panama to Oregon in ca. 1854; Mary Coe's personal notebooks, which include poetry, essays, a journal, photos, and memorials; her autograph album; farm journals and accounts; records of Hood River Manufacturing Company; documents; and miscellaneous correspondence and reminiscences.

14,533. Cook, Ola Delight (Lloyd)
Papers. 1900-58. 6 boxes and 1 vol.
Open. Card catalog.
Oregon Historical Society.
Cook (1880-1958) was a railroad telegrapher and charter member of the Commercial Telegraphers Union. Correspondence, constitutions, minutes, and financial reports relating to railroad unions; the AFL, for which Cook worked; the Portland Labor Temple and the YWCA; Oregon political campaigns; and the Portland Central Labor Council, of which Cook was an honorary trustee. Also included are diaries, appointment books, and ephemera.

14,534. Cooper, Arvazena Angeline
Papers. 1901. 1 folder.
Open. Card catalog.
Oregon Historical Society.
Reminiscences written in 1901 by [Mrs.] Cooper regarding an 1863 trip from Missouri to Polk County, OR, a move which was necessitated in part by the Civil War.

14,535. Cooper, Jacob Calvin
Papers. 1896-1907. 18 folders.
Open. Card catalog.
Oregon Historical Society.
Correspondence of Cooper (1845-1937), a civic leader, contains material on the Oregon Girls' Drill Company, which was organized in 1907 to represent the state at the Jamestown Exposition. Correspondence with applicants is included.

14,536. Cornell Family
Papers. 1859-1941. 1 box.
Open. Card catalog.

Oregon Historical Society.
Correspondence and memorabilia of William Cornell (1812-91), a Methodist minister, and his family in Salem, OR. Included are the papers of Emily (Castle) Cornell (1820-88), Edward W. Cornell, Samantha Cornell McAlister (1839-96), Emma Cornell Royal, and other members of the Castle and Parmenter families. References to the Methodist Episcopal church in Oregon and to Harvey K. Hines, a minister, are also included.

14,537. Crandall, Amanda
Papers. Ca. 1850. 4 pp.
Open. Card catalog.
Oregon Historical Society.
Compositions written by Crandall as a student regarding spiritualism, letter writing, the legislature at Silverton, OR, and desirable characteristics in boys.

14,538. Crawford, Amanda Melvin (Morgin)
Papers. Nd. 1 vol.
Open. Card catalog.
Oregon Historical Society.
Notebook containing poems by Crawford, Mary E. Reed, and Morgan Ward and clippings.

14,539. Crouch, Malinda (Sutherlin)
Papers. Nd. 11 pp.
Open. Card catalog.
Oregon Historical Society.
Reminiscences of Crouch (1835-1930) regarding the Rogue River Indian wars.

14,540. Cummings, Mildred (Francis)
Papers. 1912-19. 1 folder and 39 items.
Open. Card catalog.
Oregon Historical Society.
Cummings was an Oregon schoolteacher. Report cards and reports of the Oregon Normal School in Monmouth, OR; Oregon state teacher's certificates; and a class history of Drain High School.

14,541. Deady Family
Papers. 1850-93. No size given.
Open. Card catalog.
Oregon Historical Society.
Journals, addresses, and lectures of Matthew Paul Deady (1824-93), an Oregon jurist and political leader. Also included is an account in which Deady's wife Lucy Ann (Henderson) Deady (1835-1923) describes her 1846 journey across the plains to Oregon and Oregon's early settlements, family life, and government; Lucy Deady's correspondence, including letters and telegrams of sympathy received at her husband's death; and invitations, menus, greeting cards, and other material.

14,542. Diaries and Reminiscences
Collection. Nd. 4 boxes.
Open. Card catalog.
Oregon Historical Society.
Women represented in this collection of papers of Oregon pioneers include Helen M. Warren from 1824; Mary (Richardson) Walker, 1838; Mrs. B. P. Cardwell, 1849-53; Maria Cable, 1851-52; Alta June [Mrs. John T.] Able, 1851-54; Melissa Clawson Stroud, 1852; Caroline Gale Budlong, 1856-1939; Margaret Elizabeth Irvin, 1864; Mrs. Isaac L. Bryson, 1865; Polly Mckean Bell, 1881; Grace Ruth Smith, 1905; Alice Gertrude Bretherton, 1906; and Sarah A. Cone and Mary Hamblet, undated.

14,543. Downing, Jennie
Papers. 1879-1923. 1 folder and 3 items.
Open. Card catalog.
Oregon Historical Society.
Correspondence to a cousin Cymbre regarding family matters and a description of Oregon.

14,544. Drake, June
Papers. Nd. 2 boxes.
Open. Card catalog.
Oregon Historical Society.
Drake (1881-1969) was a portrait and landscape photographer, historical preservationist in Silver Creek Falls, and local historian of the Silverton, OR, area. Historical sketches, poems, and ephemera.

14,545. Duniway, Abigail Jane (Scott)
Papers. Nd. 11 vols.
Open. Card catalog.
Oregon Historical Society.
Diary written by Duniway (1834-1915) from notes taken during her 1852 journey from Illinois to Oregon; an 1872 constitution, minute book, correspondence, and membership and account books of the Oregon State Woman's Suffrage Association; and ledger, account, cash, and subscription books of the Duniway Publishing Company. Duniway's diary is also available on microfilm.

14,546. Dunlap, Caroline Cock
Papers. Ca. 1853. No size given.
Open. Card catalog.
Oregon Historical Society.
Reminiscences of Dunlap entitled *Ancotty (Long Ago)* regarding an overland journey in 1853 and life in Olympia, WA.

14,547. Dunn, Berry Walker
Papers. 1875. 1 item.
Open. No guide.
Oregon Historical Society.
Letter in which Dunn (1823-98) in North Yamhill, OR, expressed to Mrs. M. F. Cook, corresponding secretary of the Yamhill County Woman Suffrage Association, his support of woman suffrage.

14,548. Dunn, Mary Margaret (Masterson)
Papers. 1860s-1950s. 5 pp.
Open. Card catalog.
Oregon Historical Society.
Account written by Dunn (1859-?) of her childhood and life in Eugene, OR.

14,549. Dye, Eva (Emery)
Papers. Ca. 1879-1936. Ca. 2 ft.
Open. Card catalog.
Oregon Historical Society.
Dye (1855-1947) was an author and suffragist. Correspondence, manuscripts of Dye's books, notes, and memorabilia relating to Dye's research about Pacific Northwest pioneers; Lewis and Clark; John McLoughlin; Ranald Macdonald; the Applegate, Curry, and Boone families; the Hudson's Bay Company in Oregon; and the overland journey to Oregon and pioneer life. Also contains information about Dye's work in the woman's suffrage movement from 1904 to 1913 and for the *Oregon City Chataqua* from 1901 to 1930, publication of her books, the Lewis and Clark Exposition in 1904 in Portland, the Sacajawea Statue Association, and her husband Charles Henry Dye. Included are copies of pre-1879 letters of Lewis and Clark, John Jacob Astor, and Thomas Jefferson. Correspondents include Lillian Gertrude and Oliver C. Applegate, Alphonse D. and Luther D. Boone, George L. Curry, Anne E. K. and Edward Huggins, Ranald Macdonald, David McLoughlin, John Minto, and Silas B. Smith.

14,550. Eells, Cushing
Papers. 1838-83. 1 microfilm reel and other material.
Open. Card catalog.
Oregon Historical Society.
Correspondence of Cushing and Myra (Fairbanks) Eells (1805-78), Protestant missionaries, and their sons Myron and Edwin. Also included is Myra Eells's journal describing her journey across the Rocky Mountains in the spring and summer of 1838.

14,551. Ethnology, Women
Collection. Nd. No size given.
Open. Card catalog.
Oregon Historical Society.
Essays on western women edited in 1905 by Mary Osburn Douthit of Portland; a Child Welfare Week notice of the Oregon Congress of Mothers and PTA; a program of the Portland Women's Union; two 1937 items of the Oregon Women's Industrial Forum; a 1905 article by Ben B. Lindsay on child labor legislation and its enforcement in the West; a 1912 article by Edwin V. O'Hara on welfare legislation for women and minors; an *Oregon Daily Journal* clipping concerning women opposed to child labor; a 1967 brochure of the Parry Center for Children in Portland; and "Voice of American Women," a program for KALE radio in Portland.

14,552. Failing, Henry
Papers. 1851-98. 6 ft.
Open. Card catalog.
Oregon Historical Society.
Failing (1834-98) was a pioneer merchant, banker, mayor, civil leader, and benefactor in Portland. Correspondence diary, notebook, bills, receipts, and other material include papers relating to the estates of Josiah Failing of Portland, John A. Hatt and his wife Emma M. Hatt of New York City, and John B. Price of Walla Walla, WA. Also includes correspondence, financial statements, and guest book of Henrietta Ellison Failing, WWII military papers of Henry F. Cabell, correspondence of Emily Corbett (Failing) Cabell and an 1887 diary she wrote before her marriage, a scrapbook which Mary (Malarckey) Cartwright [Mrs. Henry Failing] Cabell compiled in ca. 1910 and 1911 while she was a student at Portland Academy, a 1919 certificate of service to Miss Failing from the American Field Service in France, and photos of Failing and Cabell family members. Other correspondents include Jesse Applegate, J. W. Carhart, Melinda Forbush Failing, William Henry Cleveland, Mary Forbush Failing, Emma M. Hatt, John A. Hatt, Henry F. Merrill, and Mary (Failing) Merrill.

14,553. Fear, Lucia S. (Drum)
Papers. 1882-1900. No size given.
Open. Card catalog.
Oregon Historical Society.
Fear and her husband William H. Fear were advocates of women's rights. Includes an 1882 journal entitled "The Day of My Advent in the Legal Profession," a speech on the GFWC, and "A Climb up Mount Hood," written in 1894.

14,554. Fenton, Henry Lee
Papers. 1880-1940. No size given.
Open. Card catalog.
Oregon Historical Society.
Fenton (1863-1930) was a merchant, stock raiser, and Polk County, OR, treasurer. Includes personal, family, and business correspondence of Fenton; business papers; deeds, indentures, contracts, and other legal papers; and a diary of Henrietta "Retta" Coad from 1890 and 1891.

14,555. Fisher, Guy
Papers. 1907-65. 1 box.
Open. Card catalog.
Oregon Historical Society.
WWI correspondence of Fisher (1892-1965?), correspondence with the Veteran's Administration, and letters written during Fisher's work as a grain inspection supervisor at the Portland docks. Also included are diaries of Fisher for 1945 to 1963 and a 1907 diary of his wife Ida A. Graham Wart Fisher.

14,556. Flanders Family
Papers. 1876-1952. No size given.
Open. Card catalog.
Oregon Historical Society.
Correspondence of Caroline W. Flanders (1873-1970), Maria Louise Flanders (?-1958), and the Minott family with the Oregon State Highway Commission concerning their gift of coastal property to the state; a diary of Maria Louise Flanders describing her 1876 trip to Europe; an 1892 memorial tribute to Captain George Hall Flanders (1821-92); and a house design, ca. 1930, by Jamieson Parker for the Flanders sisters.

14,557. Fletcher Family
Papers. 1845-1945. 1 box.
Open. Card catalog.
Oregon Historical Society.
Many members of the Fletcher family were schoolteachers in Salem, Silverton, and other parts of Marion County, OR. Includes scrapbooks of Ellsworth Benjamin Fletcher containing articles by him, genealogical data, clippings, and ephemera; teaching records and certificates of Ellsworth Fletcher's daughter Lois Lorraine Fletcher; an account of an 1864 overland journey to Oregon by Benjamin F. Fletcher; and other papers of Emaline Fletcher Hobart and Ellsworth Fletcher.

14,558. Fletcher, John Elliot
Papers. 1849-51. No size given.
Open. Card catalog.
Oregon Historical Society.
Correspondence to Ruth Fletcher in Missouri from John Fletcher in California and Nevada where he was engaged in mining, baking, and raising hay.

14,559. Gaines Family
Papers. 1857-64. No size given.
Open. Card catalog.
Oregon Historical Society.
Correspondence of Abner P., Archibald, and Anna Gaines in Homestead, AR, and Oregon City, OR, primarily concerns family matters.

14,560. Gardner, Charlotte (Coffin)
Papers. 1852-55. 33-page item.
Open. Card catalog.
Oregon Historical Society.
Journal of a voyage from Nantucket, MA, to San Francisco and the Washington Territory.

14,561. Garrison, Martha Ellen Rogers
Papers. Nd. 32-page item.
Open. Card catalog.
Oregon Historical Society.
Reminiscences of [Mrs. Pliny] Garrison about an overland journey from Iowa to Oregon in 1845.

14,562. Gauntlett, Anna (Winsor)
Papers. 1899. 1 folder.
Open. Card catalog.
Oregon Historical Society.
Letter from Gauntlett in Unalaska, AK, to her family regarding family matters; she also describes Alaska.

14,563. Geer, Elizabeth (Dixon) Smith
Papers. 1847-48. 1 folder.
Open. Card catalog.
Oregon Historical Society.
Reminiscences of an overland journey to Oregon and a description of Portland. The narrative was published in *Oregon Pioneer Association Transactions* in 1907.

14,564. Gilbert, Joseph Lucien
Papers. 1861-90. 26 items.
Open. Card catalog.
Oregon Historical Society.
Correspondence of Gilbert, a schoolmaster and minister in Oakland, OR, and Eugene, OR, includes letters to his wife Adelia F. Gilbert from the mines in Idaho and Washington Territory, from Adelia Gilbert to her husband in the fields, and from friends. Also included are school accounts; a constitution of the Ladies' Sanitary Society of Eugene; a pocketbook account of a trip to mines in Florence, Washington Territory; and material concerning the lawsuit *Gilbert vs. Parsons Bros., Linn Company.*

14,565. Gilbert, Wells Smith
Papers. 1897-1965. 3 boxes.
Open. Card catalog.
Oregon Historical Society.
Gilbert (1870-1965) was an early Oregon timberman and music patron whose wife Page Morris Gilbert founded the Portland Opera Guild and pro-America organizations. Family correspondence and correspondence of Wells Gilbert regarding lumber and personal matters; of Page Gilbert, including letters to her husband; and of the Oregon Industrial Editors Association. Also included are seven diaries of Page Gilbert; a 1902 diary of Wells Gilbert; information about Page Gilbert's ideas on spiritualism; business documents; financial and tax records; household expense ledger; land sale and expense journals; minutes, financial records, resolutions, and other material of the National Organization of Republican Women, Inc.; scrapbooks regarding the Drew Timber Co., the Wilson River Lumber Co., and the Oregon chapter of Pro-America; Portland Pro-Musica programs; a membership list; biographical material on the Gilbert family; and ephemera. Collection contains material regarding anti-fluoridation, the Colonial Dames, the Oregon Civil War Round Table, the Portland Beautification Association, Pro-America, the National Association of Pro-America, and the Town Club.

14,566. Gray, William Henry
Papers. Nd. No size given.
Open. Card catalog.
Oregon Historical Society.
Correspondence, diaries, documents, and other papers of Gray (1810-89) and his wife Mary Augusta (Dix) Gray (1810-81) include an 1836-37 journal about a journey from the settlement of H. H. Spalding, a minister, on the Columbia River to Utica, NY; her diary for 1840 to 1842; and documents concerning the Gray-J. L. Parrish controversy.

14,567. Greer, George, Family
Papers. Nd. 1 folder and 2 vols.
Open. Card catalog.
Oregon Historical Society.
Notebook of hymns copied by George Greer, his commonplace book, reminiscences by Cornelia Jane (Spencer) Greer regarding her family's first Christmas in Oregon in 1852, and a letter to her from William Valentine Spencer.

14,568. Griffin, Desire Smith
Papers. 1839-40. 1 folder.
Open. Card catalog.
Oregon Historical Society.
Diary of Griffin.

14,569. Hadley, Amelia E.
Papers. Ca. 1851. 1 item and other material.
Open. Card catalog.
Oregon Historical Society.
Diary of Hadley (1825-86) describes an overland journey in 1851 from Illinois to Oregon via the Barlow Road. Family genealogical material is also included.

14,570. Hallock, Homer H.
Papers. 1879-95. 1 folder.
Open. Card catalog.
Oregon Historical Society.
Correspondence between Hallock (1856-1906) and his wife Nannie Nellie Bernardi Hallock (1861-?), correspondence regarding family matters, and a diary for the period 1879-85.

14,571. Hallock, Joseph H., Family
Papers. 1901-20. No size given.
Open. Card catalog.
Oregon Historical Society.
Includes correspondence and other papers of Joseph Hallock's sister Ahlma (Hallock) [Mrs. Stewart] McDonald.

14,572. Hanna, Esther Bell
Papers. 1852. 38-page item.
Open. Card catalog.
Oregon Historical Society.
Diary of [Mrs. Joseph A.] Hanna's overland migration from Pittsburgh to Oregon.

14,573. Harding, George A., Family
Papers. 1895-1940. 6 boxes and 1 vol.
Open. Card catalog.
Oregon Historical Society.
Harding (1843-1926) was director of the Willamette Valley Southern Railway, a drugstore operator, and a soldier. Correspondence of Harding, his wife Margaret Jennie (Barlow) Harding, and his family; diaries; personal and business papers of George Harding; a family genealogy; and ephemera of the Harding, J. L. Barlow, and H. J. Murray families. Correspondents include Helene (Ferrer) Harding, Helene (Harding) Rigger, Jennie Imogene (Harding) Brodie (1878-1956), and Nieta Natalie Harding.

14,574. Hargreaves, Sheba May
Papers. Nd. No size given.
Open. Card catalog.
Oregon Historical Society.
Hargreaves (1882-1960) was an author. Manuscript of her book *Heroine of the Prairies; A Story of the Oregon Trail* (Harpers, 1930), originally titled "Sour Gal," and of her *Pioneer Home-makers of the 1840's.*

14,575. Harris, Esther
Papers. Nd. 1 folder.
Open. Card catalog.
Oregon Historical Society.
Drafts of short stories and playlets written by Harris and manuscript of her playlet *Walulah.*

14,576. Hawkins, Caroline (Norton)
Papers. 1874-83. 30 pp.
Open. Card catalog.
Oregon Historical Society.
Letters from Hawkins to her brother Tolbert Norton in Benton County, OR, regarding family matters and personal views.

14,577. Hecht, Irene W. D.
Papers. Nd. 1 vol., 66 pp., and 3 tapes.
Open. Card catalog.
Oregon Historical Society.
Hecht was a professor at Lewis and Clark College in Portland. Under the direction of Hecht, Martha Rice conducted these interviews with Antone Van Grunsven, Anna N. Krieger, and William Meeuwsen regarding Verboort, OR. Also included is material on Pacific Northwest history seminars conducted by Hecht on Verboort as a demographic isolate and on migration, kinship, and community, specifically vis à vis the founding and maintenance of an isolated community in Oregon's Willamette Valley.

14,578. Helm, Elizabeth Sager
Papers. 1865-1915. 1 folder.
Open. Card catalog.
Oregon Historical Society.
Helm (1837-1925) was a survivor of the Whitman massacre of 1847. Family letters, primarily from Helm's in-laws William and Martha Helm and their children.

14,579. Heney, Francis J.
Papers. 1910-12. 3 items.
Open. Card catalog.

Oregon Historical Society.
Letters from Heney to Vivian Flexner in Portland regarding legal cases and woman suffrage.

14,580. Hill, Mollie (Watson)
Papers. 1865-85. 2 vols.
Open. Card catalog.
Oregon Historical Society.
Scrapbooks containing personal records, notes, recipes, clippings, and ephemera concerning current business and political and social events.

14,581. Hill, William Lair
Papers. 1833-1973. 3 boxes.
Open. Card catalog.
Oregon Historical Society.
Hill (1838-1924) was a lawyer, judge, and editor of the *Oregonian* from 1872 to 1877. Business correspondence, speeches and writings, legal papers, bills and receipts, biographical information, and other material of Hill. His family papers are primarily letters and memorabilia of his wife Julia (Chandler) Hill (1844-1932); her parents Persis Warren Heald Chandler (1814-1906) and George Clinton Chandler (1807-81); her children Margaret (Hill) Smith (1877-1973), Reuben Chandler Hill, Heald William Lair Hill, and Edward Coke Hill (1866-1961) and his wife Ella "Billie" (Wilson) Hill (1877-1962). Included in these letters are personal accounts of early missionary experiences in the Willamette area in Oregon.

14,582. Hobson, Dorothy Ann
Papers. 1936-41. 2 boxes.
Open. Card catalog.
Oregon Historical Society.
Correspondence, financial records, radio scripts, school papers, mailing lists, clippings, and ephemera Hobson (1928-) collected while she was child editor of the *Valsetz Star*, a mimeographed paper in Valsetz, OR.

14,583. Hockersmith, Martha J. (Gale)
Papers. 1853. 1 folder.
Open. Card catalog.
Oregon Historical Society.
Reminiscences of Hockersmith (1826-1903) regarding her overland journey to Medford, OR, with the Lost Wagon Train of 1853.

14,584. Hodgdon, Mary A.
Papers. 1903. 1 folder.
Open. Card catalog.
Oregon Historical Society.
Letter from Hodgdon to George H. Himes regarding her teaching experiences in the Pacific Northwest from 1861 to 1870.

14,585. Holder, Eva
Papers. 1878-1962. 1 box.
Open. Card catalog.
Oregon Historical Society.
Correspondence, reminiscences of an 1853 overland journey as told to Holder by Horace A. and Deborah G. Kent, school records, and documents relating to the Theosophical Society of America.

14,586. Holmes, Mrs. William L.
Papers. Nd. 9 pp.
Open. Card catalog.
Oregon Historical Society.
Memoir of Mary Louise Campbell Holmes by [Mrs.] Elizabeth Lovejoy.

14,587. Honeyman, Nan (Wood)
Papers. 1900-65. 1 box and 9 vols.
Open. Card catalog.
Oregon Historical Society.
Honeyman (1881-1970) was Oregon state senator from 1934 to 1936, a US congresswoman for one term beginning in 1936, and customs collector from 1942 to 1953. Personal correspondence, including letters from Eleanor Roosevelt and leading Democratic party figures; speeches Honeyman made as a congresswoman; abstracts; mementos, including those she collected as a delegate to Democratic conventions; scrapbooks on political campaigns and Franklin Delano Roosevelt's death; voting records; customs documents; and clippings.

14,588. Hosford, Asenath (Glover)
Papers. Nd. 1 folder.
Open. Card catalog.
Oregon Historical Society.
Biography of Hosford (?-1896), a Clatsop, OR, pioneer, a resident of Mt. Tabor, OR, and wife of Chauncey O. Hosford, a minister.

14,589. Houghton, Janice G.
Papers. 1956-60. 2 folders.
Open. Card catalog.
Oregon Historical Society.
Business and personal correspondence of Houghton concerns possible restoration of the Peter Britt house and other historic structures in Jacksonville, OR.

14,590. Huddle, Mildred
Papers. 1912. 1 vol.
Open. Card catalog.
Oregon Historical Society.
Child's diary of a 1912 train trip from Oberlin, KS, to McMinnville, OR.

14,591. Isom, Mary Frances
Papers. Nd. 1 folder.
Open. Card catalog.
Oregon Historical Society.
Isom (1865-1920) was a librarian, library scientist, founder of libraries, and organizer and president of the Portland National Library Association. An interview with Cornelia Marvin Pierce as transcribed by Hazel E. Mills and "Mary Frances Isom: Creative Pioneer in Library Work in the Northwest" by Bernard Van Horne of the Library Association.

14,592. James, Cheryl
Papers. Nd. 1 vol.
Open. Card catalog.
Oregon Historical Society.
The Cheryl James Defense Committee was formed in 1971 to protest the criminal trial of James and to publicize the alleged injustice of her treatment by FBI agents and the courts. At the age of 17, James was charged with assaulting an FBI agent and was subsequently sentenced to 18 months in a correctional institution. Correspondence of the Committee; notes by Arthur C. Spencer III, [Mrs.] Julia Godman Ruuttila, Ann C. Campbell, Samuel H. Swarm, and others; summaries; clippings; and other material.

14,593. Jewett, Harriet Kimball
Papers. 1850-54. 1 folder.
Open. Card catalog.
Oregon Historical Society.
Correspondence of Jewett (1809-?) includes a letter from her sister Betsy Willey in Sutton, VT, regarding the Whitman massacre, a letter from Jane Emeline Jacobs to "Aunt" Harriet asking for her assistance in traveling to Oregon because she was earning only $1.00 per week doing housework and thought she could make more in Oregon, and a letter from Nelson and Sophia Ruitter in St. Armond, Canada, about family matters and their hope of joining her in Oregon.

14,594. Johansen, Dorothy O.
Papers. 1827-1967. 2 boxes.
Open. Card catalog.
Oregon Historical Society.
Research notes, drafts, and galley proofs of the second edition of *Empire on the Columbia* (ca. 1967); articles, speeches, and papers regarding Samuel Terry McKean and Polly Hicks McKean, Eliza Jane McKean Hustler, Anna Crocker, John T. Simpson, and Sylvester Pennoyer; a letter to Governor Walter M. Pierce concerning former governor James Withycombe; correspondence, diary, and notes of Robert Newell; correspondence and survey reports of J. Nielson Barry; Joseph L. Meek's land claim; and a Hudson's Bay Company transcript of a "Snake County Journal, 1827-28."

14,595. Johnson, Ada (Stanley)
Papers. 1904-10. 1 vol.
Open. Card catalog.
Oregon Historical Society.
Scrapbook of notes and ephemera includes material on women's political and social activities and programs of Chautauqua, Epworth League, Baptist, and other organizations.

14,596. Judson, Lewis Hubbell
Papers. 1837-1964. 1 microfilm reel.
Open. Card catalog.
Oregon Historical Society.
Judson (1809-80) was a Methodist missionary and pioneer who migrated to Oregon with the Great Reinforcement in 1840; he also was involved in formation of the provisional government in 1843. Correspondence of Judson, including family correspondence and letters to his sister Adelia (Judson) Olley Leslie; poems, including those of Adelia Leslie; correspondence and documents of David Leslie; speeches; sermons; articles about Judson; and bills and receipts.

14,597. Kellogg, Jane (Davies)
Papers. Nd. 10-page item.
Open. Card catalog.
Oregon Historical Society.
Memoirs of Kellogg (1830-1922) regarding her journey across the plains in 1852.

14,598. Kelly, Albert, Family
Papers. 1833-1950. No size given.
Open. Card catalog.
Oregon Historical Society.
Correspondence from ca. 1865 to 1900 of Nira C. Bingham Kelly, wife of Albert Kelly, with her children and relatives and a scrapbook of ephemera of Nira Kelly. Diaries and notebooks of Kelly's son Silas G. Kelly; her son-in-law O. P. S. Plummer, husband of Mattie E. (Kelly) Plummer; and J. Harold Povey, son-in-law of O. P. S. Plummer and husband of Marion Plummer. Also included are diplomas, marriage and missionary society membership certificates, and land title papers.

14,599. Lane, Harry
Papers. 1891-1920. 1 box.
Open. Card catalog.
Oregon Historical Society.
Lane (1855-1917) was mayor of Portland and a US senator. Collection primarily consists of a transcript of material gathered by the Oregon Writers Project for a proposed Lane biography, personal papers and genealogy of Lane, and clippings about Lane. Also includes notes and writings of his daughter Nina (Lane) [Mrs. Isaac] McBride, who was active in the Socialist party from ca. 1912 to 1920.

14,600. Latourette, Lyman Daniel Cornwall, Family
Papers. 1859-1930. 2 boxes.
Open. Card catalog.
Oregon Historical Society.
Lyman Latourette (1825-86) was a pioneer schoolteacher and merchant of Oregon City, OR. He married Lucy Jane Grey (1831-64) and after her death her sister Ann Eliza Fisher (1839-?). Family and business correspondence, primarily of Lyman Ezra Latourette (1872-1963), who was the third son of Lyman Daniel Latourette and a Portland lawyer and city attorney. Contains correspondence to L. E. Latourette from his mother, his sister Freda Latourette, and Kenneth

and Ruth Latourette; between L. E. Latourette and his wife; to Mrs. L. E. Latourette; and to Nellie Edith Latourette. Also included are poems of Nellie Latourette, financial records, and ephemera.

14,601. Lee, Anna Green
Papers. 1847. 1 folder.
Open. Card catalog.
Oregon Historical Society.
Letter from [Mrs. Philander] Lee to her sister concerns her overland journey in 1847.

14,602. Lee, Daniel
Papers. 1833-95. No size given.
Open. Card catalog.
Oregon Historical Society.
Lee (1806-95) was a Methodist missionary and nephew of Jason Lee. Correspondence of Daniel Lee, a diary for 1847 and 1848, an agreement with J. H. Frost to publish "Ten Years in Oregon," a biographical sketch of Jason Lee, documents, and articles. Also included are papers of Maria T. (Ware) Lee, which contain a letter to her from Jason Lee; her journal for 1840 to 1842; and a booklet of handwritten poems, some of which she wrote.

14,603. Lee, George H., Family
Papers. 1870-1960. No size given.
Open. Card catalog.
Oregon Historical Society.
Diaries and pastor's journals, commonplace and account books, and school notebooks of George Hewit Lee (1859-1951), a minister; commonplace books, accounts, school composition books, and a scrapbook of Lee's wife Nattie Anna (Cooke) Lee, a schoolteacher; a diary of their daughter Ruth Lee for 1904 and 1905; and correspondence, documents, Sunday school books, scrapbooks, genealogical information, and ephemera. Included are papers of George Lee's parents William B. and Elizabeth Payson Howe Lee; his brothers Edmund Trumbull Lee, Wallace Howe Lee, and Lewis Earle Lee, all of whom were ministers; Nattie Lee's parents Joseph and Belle W. Cooke; her brothers Charles Clyde Benton Cooke, Clinton Tyng Cooke, and Gaylord W. Cooke; and George and Nattie Lee's children Louisa, Charles, Marston, Ruth, Walter C., Arthur T., Harold N., and Florence Lee.

14,604. Leslie, David, and Leslie, Adelia (Judson) Olley
Papers. 1829-86. 16 folders.
Open. Card catalog.
Oregon Historical Society.
David and Adelia Leslie were Protestant missionaries. Correspondence, including letters written to Adelia before their marriage, letters from family and friends in the East, letters regarding mission affairs in Oregon, and letters of David Leslie's first wife; an account of Adelia Leslie's voyage to Oregon in 1840 on the ship *Lausanne;* David Leslie's account book; financial records; and biographical material.

14,605. Lewis, Alan J.
Papers. 1968-74. 3 boxes.
Open. Card catalog.
Oregon Historical Society.
Minutes, reports, memoranda, proposals, press releases, and newsletters of Oregon community action and social service agencies, particularly in Multnomah County. Includes material of the Bureau of Human Resources, the Day Care and Child Development Council of Oregon, the Housing Authority of Portland, the Multnomah County Community Action Agency, Headstart, the Office of Economic Opportunity, the Portland Metropolitan Steering Committee, the Portland Planning Commission, and the Youth Services Bureau.

14,606. Lindsley and Ross Families
Papers. 1773-1953. 2 boxes.
Open. Card catalog.
Oregon Historical Society.
Aaron Ladner Lindsley was a Presbyterian missionary and pastor of the First Presbyterian Church of Oregon. Notebook dating from 1773 to 1812, accounts, and inventories of William Henderson; correspondence, sermons, and quotations of Aaron Lindsley; papers of Lindsley's wife Julia (West) Lindsley; papers of Emily (Lindsley) Ross; legal documents; and ephemera. Julia Lindsley's papers contain correspondence, including letters to John West; an 1889 diary; poetry; biographical sketches; and West and Lindsley family records she compiled. Emily Ross's papers contain correspondence, including letters from James Thorburn Ross before their marriage; an 1880 diary; her writings; a family history; guest books of Emily and James Ross; and Thorburn and Ross family genealogies.

14,607. Lord, William Paine, Family
Papers. 1865-1914. 2 boxes.
Open. Card catalog.
Oregon Historical Society.
Lord (1839-1911) was chief justice of the Oregon Supreme Court from 1880 to 1894, governor of Oregon from 1895 to 1899, and US minister to the Argentine from 1899 to 1902. Correspondence includes letters between Lord and his wife Juliette (Montague) Lord; letters between their children Montague, Elizabeth, and William Paine Lord, Jr., and from the children to their parents; and letters from Juliette Lord to her aunt Fanny Stockbridge.

14,608. Lowell, Leslie M.
Papers. Nd. 1 folder.
Open. Card catalog.
Oregon Historical Society.
Manuscripts of articles by Lowell, a writer, on Robert Newell; James Sinclair; Umpqua Valley, OR, geology and settlement; and her trip in 1863 from Washoe, NV, to Douglas County, OR.

14,609. Luckey, Eunice Waters (Robbins)
Papers. Ca. 1871-92. 1 folder.
Open. Card catalog.
Oregon Historical Society.
Letters of Luckey, an Ochoco, OR, schoolteacher, to Ira and Ella regarding an overland journey with her husband. Also includes a dictionary Luckey compiled while teaching at the Warm Spring Indian Reservation from 1888 to 1892.

14,610. McCall, Dorothy Lawson
Papers. 1963-70. 2 folders.
Access restricted. Card catalog.
Oregon Historical Society.
McCall (1888-) was an author and mother of Oregon Governor Tom McCall. Correspondence; manuscripts of the books *Khaki Pants and a Tall, Silk Hat* and *Prineville;* and the McCall family newspaper.

14,611. McClain, Martha Ann (Tuttle)
Papers. Nd. 1 folder.
Open. Card catalog.
Oregon Historical Society.
Reminiscences of McClain (1827-?) regarding her overland journey to Oregon in 1853 via the Applegate trail.

14,612. McClintock, Margaretta Faber
Papers. 1865-66. 1 folder.
Open. Card catalog.
Oregon Historical Society.
Journal of McClintock concerns her overland journey in 1866 from St. Louis to Salt Lake City with the 3rd Battalion, 18th US Infantry.

14,613. McLean, Mildred Evans
Papers. 1913. 72-page item.
Open. Card catalog.
Oregon Historical Society.
Diary of McLean, a schoolteacher, pertains to her teaching experiences in 1913 in Deep River, WA.

14,614. McLench Family
Papers. Nd. 1 folder.
Open. Card catalog.
Oregon Historical Society.
Letters to Benjamin Franklin McLench from Samuel R. Thurston and Wilson Blain; notes of McLench's wife Mary Almira (Gray) McLench, an early schoolteacher in Polk County, OR, concerning her trip to Oregon in 1851 with four other teachers sent to Oregon by the National Board of Popular Education; and biographical information about Mary McLench.

14,615. Metschan, Phil, Family
Papers. 1862-1930. 1 box and 1 vol.
Open. Card catalog.
Oregon Historical Society.
Phil Metschan (1840-1920) was Oregon state treasurer from 1891 to 1899 and proprietor of the Imperial Hotel in Portland from 1899 to 1920. Correspondence of Metschan, including letters of condolence regarding the death of his wife Maria C. Metschan in 1895; Phil Metschan's diaries for 1908 and 1915 to 1918; a letter, post cards, autograph books, and a scrapbook of Anna (Metschan) Cattanach, daughter of Maria and Phil Metschan; papers of a second Metschan daughter Lillian (Metschan) Flanders and her husband Jesse Evan Flanders; an account record; fraternal and other certificates of Phil Metschan; a 1910 *Oregon Journal* article about the Imperial Hotel; menus and programs from the Hotel; and ephemera, including pamphlets in German.

14,616. Mickle, Alice Shaw
Papers. 1884. 1 folder and 9 pp.
Open. Card catalog.
Oregon Historical Society.
Letter in which Mickle in Vancouver, Washington Territory, described to Ada Hiller in San Francisco her travels in the Northwest, including trips to Seattle, Portland, and Tacoma, WA.

14,617. Mills, Rachel (Joy) Fisher
Papers. 1847-59. 1 folder.
Open. Card catalog.
Oregon Historical Society.
Letters of Mills (?-1868) to her family in Iowa concern her overland journey to Oregon in 1847 and subsequent events.

14,618. Miscellaneous Correspondence
Collection. Nd. 3 boxes.
Open. Card catalog.
Oregon Historical Society.
Women represented in this collection of personal correspondence include Minerva Burbank, Letitia A. Chambers, Elizabeth Elledge, Harriet Kimball Jewett, and Mary Mutton, who wrote during the 1850s; Phebe Leake and Jane B. Poole, 1860s; Margaret Rice Brockway, 1860s-70s; Sybel A. Collier, 1860s-80s; Emily L. Burrows and Margaret Reimers, 1870s; Caroline Norton Hawkins, 1870s-80s; Katie Bellinger, Maria L. Daley, Mrs. Thomas A. Hendricks, Mary L. Joslyn, Alice Shaw Mickle, and Mahala Moore, 1880s; Katie Barclay, 1880s-90s; Rosa Frazar Burrell, Virginia Crooks, Olive Stanton England, and Anna (Winsor) Gauntlett, 1890s; Mary Phelps Montgomery, 1890s-1900s; Amelia Davis, Mrs. J. S. Higgins, Mildred Raymond, and Harriet Thayer, 1900s; Mrs. G. A. R. Steiner and Dorothy O. Stringer, 1910s; Louise (Von Behren) Smith and Sylvia (Williams) Thompson, 1920s; Mrs. Thomas McAllister Knox and Susie Fannell Pipes, 1930s; Ava Baltimor Reid, Carrie (Buchman) Roberts, and Caroline Vatter, 1960s; and Sarah A. Willis, undated.

14,619. Moody, Zenus Ferry, Family
Papers. 1820-1950. 3 boxes and 27 vols.
Open. Card catalog.
Oregon Historical Society.
Moody (1832-1917) was governor of Oregon from 1882 to 1887, a merchant in The Dalles, OR, and surveyor of the Umatilla Indian Reservation. In 1853 he married Mary Stephenson and they had five children: Zenus A., William H., Ralph E., Drusilla (Moody) West, and Malcolm A. (1854-1925), who later became a Dalles city councilman, mayor, and US congressman from Oregon. Correspondence, financial records, and deeds of Zenus F. Moody and correspondence, speeches, financial records, and court trial records of Malcolm A. Moody. Also contained are family correspondence and papers, including correspondence and financial records of Anne and Elizabeth Lang, sisters who were longtime friends and employees of Malcolm Moody; correspondence and diaries of Thomas and Mary Lang, who were the parents of the Lang sisters; and a Lang family genealogy.

14,620. Morse Family
Papers. 1870-1919. 1 folder.
Open. Card catalog.
Oregon Historical Society.
Manuscript of the family diary of Add and Nellie Morse printed in memory of Percy Mulford Morse (1876-1963) of Eugene, OR. Contains genealogy, an account of a move from the Midwest to Portland, in 1888 and 1889, and notes of Rex L. Morse.

14,621. Native Daughters of Oregon
Records. 1902-04. 1 vol.
Open. Card catalog.
Oregon Historical Society.
Minute book containing bylaws, minutes, a roster of members, and a motto of the Tabitha Brown Cabin Number 24, founded in 1902. Agnes Himes was the secretary.

14,622. Neuburger, Richard Lewis, and Neuburger, Maurine (Brown)
Papers. 1954-66. 13 boxes.
Open. Card catalog.
Oregon Historical Society.
Office files of US Senators Richard Neuburger (1912-60) and Maurine Neuburger (1907-) contain material on agriculture; commerce; conservation, including billboard and Oregon Dunes legislation; social security; and public lands. Also included are files on the congressional intern program, Neuberger speeches from the *Congressional Record,* statements, press releases, and the Neuburgers' newsletter entitled *Washington Calling.*

14,623. Old Ladies' Home of Portland
Records. 1892-1912. 1 folder and 1 vol.
Open. Card catalog.
Oregon Historical Society.
Ledger containing constitution, bylaws, and minutes; house rules; and application blanks of this retirement home and sanatorium.

14,624. Orchard Family
Papers. 1851-98. 24 items.
Open. Card catalog.
Oregon Historical Society.
Correspondence regarding relatives, personal matters, and family connections and miscellany of John G. and Amelia Mandaville Orchard.

14,625. Oregon Children's Aid Society
Records. 1866-1960. 1 box and 3 vols.
Access restricted. Card catalog.
Oregon Historical Society.
The Society's function is the care and placement of orphans and the facilitation of adoptions. Incorporation papers, board of managers and annual meeting minute books, account books, receipts, correspondence and documents relating to children in the Society's care, reports of admissions, legal documents, legislation, material relating to Salem Hospital and the Home Scholarship Fund, and household accounts of the Ladies Aid Society. Most of the Society's board of managers and other officials were women.

14,626. Oregon League of Democratic Women
Records. 1936-52. 2 boxes.
Open. Card catalog.
Oregon Historical Society.
Correspondence, scrapbooks relating to political campaigns of 1948 and 1952, and other material.

14,627. Oregon Native Daughters, Odell Cabin No. 8
Records. 1899-1901. 1 folder and 1 vol.
Open. Card catalog.
Oregon Historical Society.
Constitution, bylaws, minutes, organizational correspondence, a membership list, and other records of this branch of the Native Daughters of Oregon.

14,628. Overland Journeys to the Pacific
Collection. Ca. 1830-1934. 1 box and 1 microfilm reel.
Open. Card catalog.
Oregon Historical Society.
Diaries, journals, and reminiscences of pioneers who journeyed to the Pacific Coast Territory. Persons represented in the collection (with their year of travel) include Nancy A. Hunt in 1830; Sarah and Almoron Hill in 1843; Betsy Bayley and Sarah J. Cummins in 1845; Maria and Stephen King in 1846; Mary Jane Hayden in 1850; Margaret White Chambers, Martha Ann Gay, and Lucy Preston in 1851; Maria Cable in 1851-52; Cecilia Emily McMillen Adams, Mrs. L. A. Bozarth, [Mrs.] Sarah Frances Dudley, Esther Bell Hanna, Adrietta Applegate Hixon, Mary Jane Long, Harriet Scott Palmer, Mary Collins Parsons, and Alice and Caleb Richey in 1852; Maria A. Belshaw, Susan Isobel (Biles) Drew, Mrs. E. J. Farrington Goltra, and Agnes Stewart in 1853; Emeline L. Fuller in 1860; Elizabeth Lee Porter in 1864; Armeda Jane Parker in 1878; Sarah J. Wiseman Seeley in 1882; and Grace Raymond Hebard, undated. Also includes Elizabeth Irvin's account of her 1863 journey, as told to Myra Leanne (Abbett) Adams in 1934.

14,629. Owens-Adair, Bethenia Angelina
Papers. 1840-1926. 1 folder.
Open. Card catalog.
Oregon Historical Society.
Bethenia (Owens)-Adair (1840-1926) was a physician and educator. Correspondence, including letters from Jesse Applegate; a speech on woman suffrage; and material about human sterilization from ca. 1885.

14,630. Owens, John W.
Papers. 1880-82. 2 folders and 46 items.
Open. Card catalog.
Oregon Historical Society.
Correspondence, clippings, and a notebook containing quotations, anecdotes, addresses, and the like of Owens, a lecturer in phrenology. Correspondents include his sisters Lydia and Mollie Owens, other family members in Melrose, KS, Hazel Wylde, W. E. Showers, and several female suitors. Newspaper articles by Wylde entitled "Correspondence" are also found in the collection.

14,631. Parents' and Teachers' Association, Russelville, OR
Records. 1924-57. 7 vols.
Open. Card catalog.
Oregon Historical Society.
Minutes, scrapbook of clippings regarding the PTA and school activities, and other material. Contains no records for the period between 1931 and 1942.

14,632. Patterson, Laura A. (Hawn)
Papers. Nd. No size given.
Open. Card catalog.
Oregon Historical Society.
Recollections of an overland journey in 1843 and descriptions of a bateau trip from The Dalles, OR, to Fort Vancouver, WA; of the Whitman grist mill; and of other Oregon mills built by Laura Patterson's father Jacob Hawn.

14,633. Patton Home
Records. 1887-1903. 4 vols.
Open. Card catalog.
Oregon Historical Society.
Organizational records, including constitution and bylaws; minutes of board meetings; financial records; and donation lists of the Home, the oldest operating retirement home in Oregon. Founded in 1887 as the Ladies Union Relief Society of Albina, the name was changed to Patton Home in 1893 after a donation of land by Mathew Patton.

14,634. Patton, Thomas McFadden
Papers. 1861-84. 1 folder and 11 items.
Open. Card catalog.
Oregon Historical Society.
Correspondence of Patton (1829-?), an Oregon legislator from 1872 to 1876 and US consul to Japan in 1884. Letters from Patton's wife Francis "Frank" M. (Cook) Patton of Salem, OR, regarding family matters, from Rockey P. Earhart requesting settlement of financial affairs in order to save his reputation, and from Thomas and Francis Patton in Japan to family members.

14,635. Pennsylvania Women's Club of Portland, OR
Records. 1917-48. 1 folder and 5 vols.
Open. Card catalog.
Oregon Historical Society.
The Club was founded in 1917 to bring Pennsylvania women together, to cultivate fellowship among them, to study Pennsylvania history and its current progress, and to extend hospitality to Pennsylvanians coming to Oregon. Constitution, bylaws, minutes, treasurer's records, account books, correspondence, a scrapbook, a program, publicity about Pennsylvania, pamphlets, and other material.

14,636. Peters, Lucy Preston (Wilson)
Papers. Nd. 1 vol.
Open. Card catalog.
Oregon Historical Society.
Diary of Peters (1867-1950) concerns her childhood and early years of marriage in The Dalles, OR.

14,637. Politics and Political Organizations
Collection. Nd. No size given.
Open. Card catalog.
Oregon Historical Society.
Manuscripts; ephemera, including pamphlets; and other material regarding women in politics and issues such as labor, peace, equal rights, birth control, health, education, and welfare. Includes material on political women's groups supporting suffrage, temperance, feminism, women's liberation, and socialism.

14,638. Portland Academy and Female Seminary
Records. 1854-1961. 1 folder, 1 vol., and 1 microfilm reel.
Open. Card catalog.
Oregon Historical Society.
Minutes, including those of the board of trustees; financial records; indentures; instructor and student rosters; a school catalog; a reunion program; and other records of the Academy, which was founded in 1889 to prepare women for college by making

college requirements the basis of the courses of instruction.

14,639. Portland Junior Symphony
Records. 1916-65. 1 box.
Open. Card catalog.
Oregon Historical Society.
Correspondence, programs, clippings, and other records of the Symphony and its predecessor the Sagebrush Symphony Orchestra, founded in 1916 in Burns, OR, by [Mrs.] Mary Bourne Thompson Dodge. Dodge moved to Portland in 1918, and the Portland Junior Symphony Orchestra performed its first concert in 1924. Included are correspondence of Dodge and photos of both orchestras, their conductors, and Dodge and Robert Robinson, who was a master violin maker of Portland.

14,640. Portland Women's Club
Records. 1895-1925. 2 folders.
Open. Card catalog.
Oregon Historical Society.
Organized in 1895, the Club was concerned with public health, human welfare, and education. In the minutes, annual announcements, and Club history are a constitution, a financial secretary's report, fund disbursements, a list of executive and department leaders, a membership directory, and Club symbols and mottoes.

14,641. Portland Women's Research Club
Records. 1916-67. 2 boxes.
Open. Card catalog.
Oregon Historical Society.
Constitution, bylaws, minutes of the executive board and program and business meetings, financial and business records, membership records, scrapbooks, programs, and a history of the Club, which was devoted to the study of national, state, and municipal government, economics, current issues, and parliamentary law. The Club donated land and money to the Children's Farm Home in Corvallis, OR; the Pilot Education Program, School for Mentally and Physically Handicapped Children in Portland; the Oregon Historical Society; and the University of Oregon.

14,642. Portland Women's Union
Records. 1887-1965. 2 boxes.
Open. Card catalog.
Oregon Historical Society.
This philanthropic group was organized for the benefit of self-supporting women. Articles of incorporation; constitution; bylaws; president's annual reports; minutes; financial reports; receipt books; education, finance, household, and special committee reports; Women's Exchange and building reports; notes on the Union's history; scrapbooks; brochures on the Martha Washington boarding house; and other material.

14,643. Pottsmith, Marie M.
Papers. Nd. 90-page item.
Open. Card catalog.
Oregon Historical Society.
Autobiographical sketch of [Mrs. William F.] Pottsmith (1882-), a schoolteacher, is entitled "Life Story of an Oregon Immigrant—1905."

14,644. Prichard, Hattie Valentine
Papers. 1901-32. 1 box.
Open. Card catalog.
Oregon Historical Society.
Correspondence, speeches, and autobiographical notes of Prichard (1862-?), director of the People's Institute in Portland, a nonsectarian service organization for women and children founded in 1904. Records of the Institute include articles of incorporation; constitution and revisions; annual reports; minutes; correspondence; agency, class, and club reports; and clippings.

14,645. Putnam Family
Papers. 1842-62. 3 folders and 3 ft. of microfilm.
Open. Card catalog.
Oregon Historical Society.
Correspondence between Putnam family members: Charles F., Nathan J., Rozelle (Applegate), Joseph, and Susan. Includes an 1853 letter from L. Wheeler to Joseph Putnam regarding a proposed trip to Oregon and a copy of a letter from Margaret Jewett (Smith) Bailey to Mrs. William T. Vault regarding Charles Putnam.

14,646. Randle Family
Papers. 1836-1973. 13 boxes.
Open. Card catalog.
Oregon Historical Society.
Samuel Arnold Randle (1839-1933) was a professor at Santiam Academy in Lebanon, OR. Correspondence of Randle and his wife Ellen Taggert Randle; their children Henry Carlyle (1875-1936), George Havelock (1876-1937), Nellie Olivia (1878-), Alola Faye (1880-1952), Margaret (1882-1956), Sarah Agnes (1885-), Bertha Mary (1886-1919), and Hattie Carol Randle (1887-); and other family members, including Edith Randle. Also included are diaries of Ellen Randle and of all her daughters with the exception of Nellie; personal documents of Nellie Randle and Ruthe E. Jones; notes of Hattie Randle, Audubon Society notes of Faye Randle, and school notes of Margaret Randle; financial accounts and autograph books of Agnes Randle; ledgers; and photos.

14,647. Redford, Sarah Buell
Papers. Nd. 21-page item.
Open. Card catalog.
Oregon Historical Society.
A description of Oregon pioneer days by Redford (1848-?) in honor of her parents and grandparents, who were pioneers.

14,648. Reed, John, Family
Papers. 1805-53. 5 folders.
Open. Card catalog.
Oregon Historical Society.
Reed (1786-1850) was a Carlyle, PA, judge. Correspondence and poetry of Reed and his wife Sarah Ann McDowell Reed (1787-1853) and their son John Henry "Hal" Reed (1824-84), a Portland lawyer. Also included is a journal kept by Sarah Reed concerning early Pennsylvania settlements, particularly Pittsburgh, and a history of the Case family.

14,649. Renshaw, Maria Jane
Papers. 1858. 1 folder and 1 vol.
Open. Card catalog.
Oregon Historical Society.
Diary of Renshaw, a resident of Eugene, OR.

14,650. Roberts, Ephraim Peters
Papers. 1775-1930. 2 ft. and 5 microfilm reels.
Open. Card catalog.
Oregon Historical Society.
Roberts (1825-93) was a missionary in Shalong, Ponape, in the Caroline Islands. Correspondence of Roberts and his wife Myra (Farrington) Roberts (1835-1912) includes letters between Ephraim and Myra Roberts before they were married; to Myra Roberts from American Board of Commissioners of Foreign Missions wives, including Sarah W. Doane, Charlotte C. Dole, Louisa L. Gulick, Sarah G. Lyman, Lucia G. Lyons, and Nancy A. Pierson; correspondence of the Robertses while in Micronesia from 1857 to 1861; and family correspondence, including letters to Myra Roberts from her brother Daniel Farrington in California. Also included are journals of Ephraim and Myra Peters, Myra Peters's reminiscences and school compositions, Ephraim Roberts's will, and genealogical notes on the Roberts and Farrington families.

14,651. Robertson Family
Papers. 1831-1900. 9 folders.
Open. Card catalog.
Oregon Historical Society.
Correspondence of the Robertson family, pioneers in Polk County, OR, includes letters from family and friends, primarily in Illinois but also in New Jersey, Missouri, and Oregon. Correspondents include Thomas J. Riggs, James P. and Mary Ann (Riggs) Robertson, Amanda "Mandy" Robertson, Elizabeth L. Hutt, V. G. Smith, Libbie Tuple, E. R. Metcalf, Davis family members, and other Robertson and Riggs family members.

14,652. Robinson, Corinne (Roosevelt)
Papers. 1891-1927. 5 folders and 30 ft. of microfilm.
Open. Card catalog.
Oregon Historical Society.
Correspondence, including manuscript poems, to Robinson (1861-1933) from C. E. S. Wood.

14,653. Robinson, Edward G.
Papers. 1927-29. 30 items.
Open. Card catalog.
Oregon Historical Society.
Correspondence of Robinson, owner of an electric company in Aurora, OR, and expert on the flax industry. Letters primarily to Robinson and his wife Frances Robinson from friends and business associates in Oregon and Tennessee.

14,654. Robinson, Helene
Papers. 1905-08. 1 vol.
Open. Card catalog.
Oregon Historical Society.
Scrapbook containing photos and memorabilia collected while Robinson was a student at the University of Oregon. Also included are numerous journal entries.

14,655. Rumbaugh, Nora
Papers. 1945-60. 1 box and 40 items.
Open. Card catalog.
Oregon Historical Society.
Correspondence, research notes, articles, clippings, and other papers of Rumbaugh, a Hood River, OR, journalist and historian. Includes material on Camp Drum and Fort Dalles in the Hood River Valley area, cemetery and land claimant information, and census statistics for Wasco County, OR.

14,656. Ruuttila, Julia (Godman) Bertram Eaton
Papers. Nd. 1 folder.
Open. Card catalog.
Oregon Historical Society.
Ruuttila (1907-), whose pen name is Kathleen Cronin, is a writer, poet, and civil rights, peace, and labor movement worker. Correspondence, manuscripts, clippings, and articles about Ruuttila. Ruuttila's articles, some of which are about history, and poetry appear in numerous newspapers and political and labor movement periodicals. She has worked with the Industrial Workers of the World, the International Longshoremen's and Warehousemen's Union, the Women's International League for Peace and Freedom, and several civil rights defense committees. Included are two 1955 letters, one from Irvin Goodman and the other from William Chester of the ILWU, concerning problems of the blacks; a manuscript regarding civil rights; and an article on the Vanport, OR, flood.

14,657. Sexton, Caroline
Papers. Nd. 14-page item.
Open. Card catalog.
Oregon Historical Society.
Biographical sketch of Sexton (1826-1911), a pioneer, includes an account of incidents during the Rogue River Indian wars.

14,658. Shattuck School
Records. 1913-24. 1 vol.
Open. Card catalog.
Oregon Historical Society.
Minutes of the Shattuck School PTA, which was organized in Portland in 1913.

14,659. Shumway, Mary R.
Papers. 1865-83. 4 items.
Open. Card catalog.
Oregon Historical Society.
Letters to Shumway from Harriet W. Williams describing Portland, money in circulation, and personal matters.

14,660. Silcott, Jane
Papers. Nd. 1 folder.
Open. Card catalog.
Oregon Historical Society.
Manuscript of [Mrs. John] Silcott (1842-95), a Nez Percé Indian guide and explorer-adventurer. The daughter of Chief Timothy, "Princess Jane" attended the Ft. Lapwai mission school of clergyman Henry H. Spalding. Also includes a letter regarding Silcott's grave near Lewiston, ID.

14,661. Sisters of Notre Dame
Records. 1843-61. 10-page item.
Open. Card catalog.
Oregon Historical Society.
Historical manuscript of the Sisters in San Francisco regarding a colony of Sisters at St. Paul, OR; the order included Roman Catholic nuns, missionaries, and teachers.

14,662. Smith Family
Papers. 1846-1916. 1 folder.
Open. Card catalog.
Oregon Historical Society.
Reminiscences of Angelina (Smith) Crews (?-1886) regarding an 1846 overland journey by the William Smith family to Oregon via the Applegate Trail. The sketch was continued after her death by other family members; it is also available on microfilm.

14,663. Smith, Genevieve (Thompson)
Papers. 1892-1928. 2 boxes.
Open. Card catalog.
Oregon Historical Society.
Smith (1883-1974) was an author, playwright, and attorney in Portland. Manuscripts of 15 of her stories and plays, correspondence with her mother Mary Thompson and an Aunt Bessie, a diary, a memo book regarding a European trip, a production account, a 1901 diploma from Portland Academy, academic records, a scrapbook, a bride's book, a guest list, personal horoscope for 1921, invitations, programs, and clippings. Among the manuscripts are "The Feud," "Heart of an Artichoke," "The Oregon Trail—1849," and "Frail Emma."

14,664. Smith, Louise (Von Behren)
Papers. 1926-27. 1 folder.
Open. Card catalog.
Oregon Historical Society.
Correspondence of Smith (1890-1964), wife of Dorsey B. Smith, a Portland travel promoter and land proprietor of Cloud Clap Inn at Mt. Hood, OR, who was involved with railways. Includes letters in which Louise Smith describes to her parents in Evansville, IN, her world cruise with her husband. The Smiths were prominent in Portland cultural and business affairs and in the Presbyterian church.

14,665. Smith, Lucinda
Papers. 1865-70. 1 folder and 15 items.
Open. Card catalog.
Oregon Historical Society.
Correspondence of Smith in Portland to her sister Mary Sophia [Mrs. J. W.] Campbell and diaries and estate papers of her husband Ferdinand C. Smith.

14,666. Sons and Daughters of Oregon Pioneers
Records. 1945-69. 1 folder.
Open. Card catalog.
Oregon Historical Society.
Founded in 1901, this organization seeks to perpetuate the memory of pioneers who established the government and basic industries of Oregon and to preserve and restore historic sites. Constitution, bylaws, minutes, financial records, correspondence, a membership application, programs, newsletters, and memorabilia.

14,667. Spalding, Henry Harmon
Papers. 1835-74. 1 box.
Open. Card catalog.
Oregon Historical Society.
A Protestant missionary, Spalding (1803-74) worked in conjunction with the American Board of Commissioners of Foreign Missions. Correspondence of Spalding, his first wife Eliza Hart Spalding (1807-51), and his second wife Rachel J. Spalding; diaries of Eliza Spalding from 1836 to 1840 and of Henry Spalding; reports; documents; and a memorial address delivered at Eliza Spalding's grave in Spalding, ID.

14,668. Spencer Family
Papers. 1835-75. 1 box and 10 feet of microfilm.
Open. Unpublished guide and card catalog.
Oregon Historical Society.
Correspondence, diary, autobiography, school land sale papers, and other papers of John Spencer (1802-84), a Methodist minister, farmer, and superintendent of Yamhill County schools. Papers of William Valentine Spencer (1835-1923) contain correspondence, diary with an account of an 1852 overland journey from Ohio to Oregon, and his military papers from the Washington Territory Infantry (volunteers). Also includes correspondence of Cornelia Jane (Spencer) Greer (1841-1930), a housewife and teacher, and of Cecilia and Manlius Spencer.

14,669. Splawn, Margaret Larsen
Papers. Nd. 1 folder.
Open. Card catalog.
Oregon Historical Society.
Correspondence, several versions of reminiscences, and notes of [Mrs. A. J.] Splawn, a pioneer, contain anecdotes and information on Indians, Columbia River myths, roads and trails, and the meaning of place-names.

14,670. Steers, Lois
Papers. 1908-45. 43 items.
Open. Card catalog.
Oregon Historical Society.
Steers was a theatrical promoter and partner in the Steers and Coman firm in Portland. Correspondence; autographed photos of musicians such as Yehudi Menuhin, Efrem Zimbalist, and Sergei Rachmaninoff; scrapbook of the 1933-34 Portland theater season as arranged by Steers and Coman; clippings; and memorabilia.

14,671. Stella Maris House
Records. 1940-71. 10 ft. and 8 boxes.
Open. Card catalog.
Oregon Historical Society.
This Roman Catholic social work center and organization was founded in 1951 as a "friendship house" by the Dominican Fathers. Correspondence, receipts, surveys, periodicals, brochures, and other material. Includes information regarding Albina neighborhood; the Church-Community Action Program; civic and civil rights groups; education; employment; urban renewal; freeway relocation; housing; migrants, particularly the Valley Migrant League; model cities; and the US Office of Economic Opportunity. Also contains material on child care organizations, equal employment opportunity groups, the Women's Prison Council, the LWV, the National Council of Catholic Women, Planned Parenthood, and the Family Counseling Service.

14,672. Sutherland Family
Papers. 1832-1902. No size given.
Open. Card catalog.
Oregon Historical Society.
Business and personal correspondence and other papers of Alice Mary (1849-?), Mary E., Roderick (?-1896), James, and George Sutherland and of Alice M. Masters. Also included are papers and financial records of the McKenzie family.

14,673. Sutton, Sarah
Papers. 1854. 1 vol.
Open. Card catalog.
Oregon Historical Society.
Diary of an overland journey from Illinois to Oregon.

14,674. Swigert, Charles F.
Papers. 1901-35. 1 box.
Open. Card catalog.
Oregon Historical Society.
Correspondence and business records of Swigert (1862-?), president of the Pacific Bridge Company and the Electric Steel Foundry Company and chairman of the board of directors of Willamette Iron and Steel Company. Correspondence includes letters between Charles and his wife Celia Swigert, from Maryland Casualty to Celia, and leases from Celia Swigert.

14,675. Teal, Joseph Nathan
Papers. 1879-1950. 16 boxes.
Open. Card catalog.
Oregon Historical Society.
Correspondence, diaries, and business and legal papers of Teal (1858-1929), an attorney. Includes correspondence and other material of Teal's wife Bessie Teal and his sisters Clara and Helen Teal and correspondence of his daughter Ruth (Teal) Betts.

14,676. Thomas, Eloise
Papers. 1922-59. 1 box.
Open. Card catalog.
Oregon Historical Society.
Thomas (1876-?) was a schoolteacher from Walla Walla, WA. Autobiography; photos of the Thomas family; documents and scrapbooks regarding the Daughters of Pioneers of Washington, of which Thomas was an officer; documents regarding the Walla Walla Pioneer Association; historical articles; and other material.

14,677. Thompson, Lewis Thomas
Papers. 1861-63. No size given.
Open. Card catalog.
Oregon Historical Society.
Reminiscences of Thompson (1842-?) regarding an 1861 cattle drive from Douglas County, OR, to Virginia City, NV. Also included is an account of an 1863 trip from Washoe, NV, to Douglas County, OR, by Louisa A. (Thompson) Evans (?-1912), widow of Samuel D. Evans who was killed by the Pitt River Indians while on the cattle drive with Thompson.

14,678. Tomita, Saku
Papers. 1942-75. 1 folder and 1 vol.
Open. Card catalog.
Oregon Historical Society.
Fifty-page wartime relocation diary in Japanese of [Mrs.] Tomita (1900-). Also included is an English translation of the diary and a 1975 letter in which Tomita's son Hideto Tomita refers to the diary.

14,679. Tracy, Regina Jeanette (Olson)
Papers. Ca. 1910-65. 1 folder and 2 vols.
Open. Card catalog.
Oregon Historical Society.
Poetry, prose, clippings, and periodicals of Tracy (1885-1971), a poet. Includes published and

unpublished works regarding nature, religion, and pioneering.

14,680. Victor, Frances Auretta (Fuller)
Papers. 1865-97. 3 folders and 1 item.
Open. Card catalog.
Oregon Historical Society.
[Mrs. Henry Clay] Victor (1826-1902) was an historian, biographer, poet, and novelist who wrote approximately six volumes of *Bancroft's Works* (San Francisco, The History Co.) dealing with Oregon, Washington, Idaho, Montana, Colorado, Wyoming, and Nevada. Correspondence with Jesse Applegate, Walter Crowninshield, and J. Q. Thornton; poetry; a scrapbook containing biographical data on Victor, reviews, and information regarding a controversy over historical data Victor used in her account of Indian wars in Oregon; a booklet by Victor about the temperance movement in Portland and Oregon; clippings; and other material.

14,681. Walker, Elkanah
Papers. 1828-85. 1 box.
Open. Card catalog.
Oregon Historical Society.
Correspondence, diaries, and documents of Elkanah Walker (1804-77) and his wife Mary (Richardson) Walker (1811-97), Protestant missionaries. Elkanah Walker was also a subagent of Indian affairs in 1851. One of his diaries is also available on microfilm.

14,682. Walker, Mae Ross
Papers. 1876-1970. 132-page item.
Open. Card catalog.
Oregon Historical Society.
Manuscript of the autobiography of Walker (1876-1970), a Portland musician and schoolteacher. Contains an epilogue by Kathleen Walker Turner.

14,683. Washburn, Robert Charles
Papers. 1884-1944. 1 box.
Open. Card catalog.
Oregon Historical Society.
Washburn (?-1938) was a journalist and Washington state politician who later became a Portland resident and owner of an apple ranch near Central Point, OR; he was married to Mary Louise (Savier) Washburn (1867-1963), a Portland resident and benefactor of St. Mark's Episcopal Church in Portland. Political and personal correspondence of the Washburns, including letters from Senators Thomas B. Reed and Charles L. McNary regarding Washington politics and Seattle history; diaries of Mary Washburn's 1884-85 European trip; speeches and poetry concerning the Republican party, the 1916 presidential election, and apple growers; family recipes; clippings; and memorabilia.

14,684. Whiteley, Opal Stanley
Papers. 1915-63. 2 folders.
Open. Card catalog.
Oregon Historical Society.
Correspondence and clippings of Whiteley (1897-), an Oregon author. Includes correspondence with Nellie Harriet Hemenway Price and of Price with the editor of *Atlantic Monthly* concerning Whiteley's claim that she is the daughter of French prince Henry d'Orleans.

14,685. Whitman, Marcus, and Whitman, Narcissa (Prentiss)
Papers. Ca. 1834-?. 1 box.
Open. Card catalog.
Oregon Historical Society.
Marcus and Narcissa Whitman (1808-47) were Protestant missionaries; Narcissa also taught at their mission school. Correspondence of the Whitmans, including letters to the Prentiss family; Narcissa Whitman's journal of her 1836 overland journey; documents and accounts of the 1847 Whitman massacre in which both Whitmans were killed; and other material. Some of their correspondence is also available on microfilm.

14,686. Wick, Grace M.
Papers. 1917-58. 2 boxes.
Open. Card catalog.
Oregon Historical Society.
Wick (1888-1958) was an actress and political figure. Correspondence, poetry and prose, clippings, ephemera, and other papers regarding her acting career, politics, the occult, and religious groups. During her youth Wick toured the US and Canada as a member of the Forbes-Robertson Company, an English dramatic group. She later had a short-lived movie career in Hollywood. In 1927 Wick moved to Portland where she remained until her death. In 1928 she became chairman of the Oregon women's club that supported Al Smith's presidential candidacy. She ran for Congress unsuccessfully in 1934 as a Democrat and again in 1936 as an independent. In 1937 Wick became chairman of the Auxiliary of Sons of Union Veterans, an anti-immigration group, and in 1944 joined the National Gentile League. She joined the America First party and corresponded with right-wing activists who shared her views about Roosevelt, Eisenhower, integration, conscription, the UN, and Jews. In 1951 Wick became state chairman of the American Women's party. During the 1950s she became interested in local issues, campaigning against fluoridation, the zoo, and improving old-age assistance. Included are letters from Agnes Water; Lyrl Clark Van Hyning, editor of *Women's Voice;* Marilyn Allen; Peter Xavier; Adelaida Pelley Pearson; and Syd Pierce, editor of the Free Press.

14,687. Wien, Ada (Bering)
Papers. 1953-69. 1 folder.
Open. Card catalog.
Oregon Historical Society.
Before her marriage to Noel Wien, Ada Bering was legal secretary and court reporter. Correspondence, biographical material, a speech regarding early aviation in Alaska, and photos.

14,688. Williams, John T.
Papers. 1814-39. 1 folder.
Open. Card catalog.
Oregon Historical Society.
Family correspondence, including letters from William Rogers to his wife, from Mary Ann Rogers to her mother Hannah Choate, and of Sarah (Ball) Williams Matthews with her husband John Matthews and her mother Catherine Grant Ball. Also included is a genealogy.

14,689. Wilson, Elizabeth Davison (Millar)
Papers. 1851-91. 2 folders.
Open. Card catalog.
Oregon Historical Society.
Reminiscences of Wilson (1830-1913) regarding her 1851 voyage from South Argyle, NY, to Albany, OR, via Panama; a manuscript, "Copied from My Mother's Writings—Elizabeth Millar Wilson," by Wilson's daughter Lucy (Wilson) Peters; and a letter to Mrs. James C. Luckey.

14,690. Woman's Christian Temperance Union, Clatskanie, OR
Records. 1908-13. 1 vol.
Open. Card catalog.
Oregon Historical Society.
Constitution, bylaws, minutes, membership list, and a list of dues paid and outstanding.

14,691. Women's International League for Peace and Freedom
Records. Ca. 1965-77. 2 boxes.
Open. Card catalog.
Oregon Historical Society.
Constitution, bylaws, minutes, correspondence, membership lists, a WILPF history, programs, publicity literature, newsletters, articles, and clippings contain information on various Oregon peace action groups, human rights, the Jeanette Rankin brigade, disarmament and the draft, Angela Davis, civil liberties, the US-China Friendship Association, the Giese-Cronin defense, and the Peace Council.

14,692. Women's Temperance Prayer League
Records. 1874. 2 vols.
Open. Card catalog.
Oregon Historical Society.
Record book contains a roster of women members and a day-by-day account of their efforts to close Portland saloons.

14,693. York, Sarah Elizabeth (Slagle)
Papers. 1852. 1 folder.
Open. Card catalog.
Oregon Historical Society.
Reminiscences of York's 1852 overland journey.

14,694. Young Women's Christian Association
Records. 1926-61. 1 box.
Open. Card catalog.
Oregon Historical Society.
Minutes, agendas, statistical reports, correspondence, surveys, special studies, study workbook, and material on 1948 flood refuge work of the Williams Avenue Center in Portland.

14,695. Portland Neighborhood History Project
Oral history. Nd. Ca. 75 tapes.
Open. No guide.
Portland Neighborhood History Project.
Interviews containing reminiscences about Portland's neighborhoods in the late 19th century and the 20th century include interviews with women regarding their arrival and youth in a community and life in various neighborhoods. Contains an interview with Mildred Secrest, who discusses such facets of her WWII experiences as looking for housing, working in the shipyards, taking care of her children, and the day care provided at the Oregon Shipyards. The Project, which originated in 1975, has published "Voices of Portland," which contains quotations from the interviews.

14,696. Portland Police
Records. 1867-1957. Ca. 500 vols.
Open. Inventory.
Portland State University Library, Archives Collection.
Police arrest dockets, records of evidence, report books and logs of officers and detectives, correspondence, descriptions of paroled prisoners, municipal court records, and other records of the local police department. Women's names are contained in the arrest books, court records, and in other material, often with dates, offense or charge, state or county of birth, and fine or sentence.

14,697. Lovejoy, Esther (Clayson) Pohl
Papers. Ca. 1894-1967. Ca. 1 ft.
Open. No guide.
University of Oregon, Health Sciences Center Library.
Correspondence, photos, clippings, medals and awards, and ephemera of Lovejoy (1869-1967), a physician and author who was president of the American Medical Women's Association from 1932 to 1933 and chairman of the executive board of American Women's Hospitals from 1919 to the 1950s. Lovejoy graduated in 1894 from the University of Oregon Medical School and was the author of books about American Women's Hospitals, women physicians, and women's hospitals in general.

14,698. Pacific Northwest Biographies
Collection. Ca. 1860s-1970s. 6 drawers.
Open. No guide.
University of Oregon, Health Sciences Center Library.
Typescript biographies, photos, and clippings

regarding individuals in the medical field who were primarily connected with the University of Oregon Health Sciences Center or with medical history in Oregon. Contains material on prominent female physicians, hospital superintendents, and research scientists, including [Mrs.] Bethenia Angelina Owens-Adair, whose family settled in Oregon in 1843 and who received her MD from the University of Michigan in 1880; Mabel M. Akin, a psychiatrist who was active in civic work and was president of the Portland branch of the Medical Women's Association in 1936; Jessie L. Brodie, a specialist in adolescent gynecology and president of the American Medical Women's Association from 1959 to 1960 and executive director of the Planned Parenthood Association of Oregon from 1965 to 1967; and Amelia Ziegler, an 1895 graduate of Women's Medical College in Kansas City who worked exclusively with women and children. Also contains material regarding Bertha B. Hallman, librarian of the Health Sciences Center Library.

14,699. Women Graduates, University of Oregon Health Sciences Center
Papers. 1935. 4 in.
Open. No guide.
University of Oregon, Health Sciences Center Library.
Research notes, correspondence, questionnaires, and statistical data assembled by Lucy I. Davis, registrar of the Center, for a study on the 124 women who graduated from the Center from 1868 to 1934. Includes data on the states of residence, practices, and specialties of the graduates and correspondence from women physicians in response to the queries.

ROSEBURG

14,700. Casad Club, Smith River
Records. Ca. 1975. 3 pp.
Open. No guide.
Douglas County Museum.
Typescript history of this Douglas County, OR, women's social club, which originated in 1924 when women living in isolated homes along the Smith River began to gather regularly for potluck meals, picnics, and quilt-making. The women sewed for the American National Red Cross during WWII and provided layettes for new babies, remembrances for hospitalized members, food for needy families, and 4-H scholarships. Until the Civilian Conservation Corps built a road in 1936, the women commuted by boat to the gatherings. The Club remains extant.

14,701. George Starmer Auxiliary No. 18, United Spanish War Veterans
Records. Ca. 1938-71. Ca. 2 cu.ft.
Open. No guide.
Douglas County Museum.
Minute books, financial records, and correspondence of this Roseburg patriotic and social club. Includes correspondence with the state and national organizations regarding membership and dues.

14,702. Wells, Mary
Papers. 1893. 23-page vol.
Open. No guide.
Douglas County Museum.
Diary of [Miss] Wells (1863-1948), who lived with her parents on their Donation Land Claim ranch in Douglas County, concerns social activities, recreation, work, family, and a failed romance. A Donation Land Claim was free land given to Oregon settlers in exchange for which they were required to live on the land for a certain length of time. Prior to 1850, a husband and wife were each entitled to 320 acres, in their own names, totaling one square mile of land. From 1850 to 1855, settlers received half that amount.

SALEM

14,703. Duniway, Abigail Jane "Jennie" (Scott)
Papers. Ca. 1852-1915. 2 cu.ft.
Open. Inventory.
David C. Duniway (Personal Collection).
To promote women's education and property rights, [Mrs. Benjamin Charles] Duniway (1834-1915) supported woman suffrage through her *The New Northwest*, a Portland, OR, newspaper she edited from 1871 to 1886. In addition, she opposed prohibition, lectured widely in the Northwest, and was an author, teacher, and milliner. Family correspondence and correspondence about suffrage; poems, stories, and novels; journal of her 1852 overland trip to Oregon; business records; scrapbooks of suffrage and antiprohibition clippings; a family Bible with family records; and photos. Duniway wrote two published novels and several others that were serialized in newspapers as well as her published epic poem *David and Anna Mattson* and her autobiography *Pathbreaking*. A leading woman suffrage leader in the Northwest, Duniway also was active in the GFWC. Duniway was the grandmother of David C. Duniway.

14,704. Duniway, Alice (MacCormick)
Papers. Ca. 1892-1953. 1 cu.ft.
Open. No guide.
David C. Duniway (Personal Collection).
Correspondence, family papers, and clippings of [Mrs. Willis Scott] Duniway (1864-1953), a Portland, OR, philanthropist, contain information on Portland charities and Salem and Portland society as well as letters from Abigail (Scott) Duniway. Alice Duniway's husband was state printer of Oregon. She was the aunt of David C. Duniway.

14,705. Duniway, Caroline Moreland (Cushing)
Papers. Ca. 1890-1924. Ca. 2 cu.ft.
Open. Inventory.
David C. Duniway (Personal Collection).
Correspondence, manuscripts, and photos of Caroline "Carrie" Duniway (1871-1926), a public school teacher in San Luis Obispo and Oakland, CA, before she married Clyde Augustus Duniway in 1901. Thereafter she moved to Montana, Wyoming, Colorado, and Minnesota as her husband took positions as a professor or president of academic institutions in those states. Includes correspondence with her husband; her mother Anne M. (Kennedy) Cushing, who was active in California charities and in prison reform; and her mother-in-law Abigail (Scott) Duniway, an Oregon suffrage leader. Caroline Duniway's correspondence contains information about her activities with the GFWC and about women on college campuses. She was the mother of David C. Duniway.

14,706. Duniway, Clyde Augustus
Papers. Ca. 1890-1944. 18 cu.ft.
Open. Inventory.
David C. Duniway (Personal Collection).
Personal and professional papers of Duniway (1866-1944), a professor of history and college president, include correspondence with his wife Caroline (Cushing) Duniway, his mother Abigail (Scott) Duniway, and Myra R. Crandall, who was the blind wife of a Cornell University professor and Duniway's mentor. Also includes material concerning his work as tutor for the children of Henry Clay Frick and in many public activities. Duniway was a history professor at Stanford University and president of the universities of Montana and Wyoming and of Colorado College. He was the father of David C. Duniway.

14,707. Weinberg, Emily (Sievert)
Papers. Ca. 1905-58. 2 vols.
Open. No guide.
David C. Duniway (Personal Collection).
Correspondence, programs, photos, and clippings concerning the career of [Mrs. I. G.] Weinberg (1893-1958), a California and New Mexico painter. In 1905 Weinberg studied and exhibited at the Art Institute of Chicago; she was closely associated with the San Francisco Society of Women Artists and the Oakland Art Museum.

14,708. American Association of University Women
Records. 1923-56. Ca. 6 ft.
Open. Shelflist.
Oregon State Library.
Records of the Oregon state division of the AAUW include minutes, status of women committee records, correspondence, reports, scrapbooks, national AAUW material, programs, ephemera, and other records.

14,709. Bush Family
Papers. 1837-1950. 72 cu.ft.
Access restricted. Shelflist.
Oregon State Library.
Correspondence, diaries, literary manuscripts, financial and business records, photos, genealogies, and other papers of the Bush family, which was involved in banking in Oregon. Includes Eugenia Zieber Bush's correspondence and diary regarding her 1850 overland journey to Oregon and correspondence of Sally Bush, one of the first graduates of Smith College.

14,710. Goodin, Rebecca E. (MSS, EG-1)
Papers. 1952. 1 item.
Open. Shelflist.
Oregon State Library.
Letter Goodin wrote to the Oregon state archivist about the first public address of Abigail (Scott) Duniway, which was given at a barn raising in Washington County, OR.

14,711. Ladies Coffee Club (KL-1)
Records. 1882-85. 44-page vol.
Open. Shelflist.
Oregon State Library.
Minute book of this Salem social club.

14,712. Oregon Authors
Collection. Nd. 9 drawers.
Open. No guide.
Oregon State Library.
Clippings regarding such Oregon authors as Ursula Kroeber LeGuin, a science fiction writer; Evelyn (Sibley) Lampman, Marian Templeton Place, and Irene Brady Kistler, authors of children's literature; Margaret Jewett Bailey, Oregon's first novelist; Elizabeth Laura Horn, who wrote about wild flowers; and Montana H. R. Walking Bull, an Indian poet.

14,713. Oregon Vertical File
Collection. Nd. 38 drawers.
Open. No guide.
Oregon State Library.
Collection contains biographical material and clippings regarding Abigail (Scott) Duniway; Cornelia Marvin Pierce, a governor's wife who was active in library work; and Eleanor Sharpless Stephens; women in the Oregon legislature; the WCTU; women's clubs; and other topics.

14,714. Thompson, Claire Warner Churchill (56-10)
Papers. Ca. 1915-54. 3 ft.
Open. Shelflist.
Oregon State Library.
Correspondence, manuscripts, notes, scripts, photos of prisoner-of-war camps in Europe and Korea, scrapbooks, Hyland family papers, a Warner family genealogy, clippings, and other papers of Thompson, an Oregon writer. Includes material relating to her activities as director of the Federal Writers' Project in Oregon, as public relations

director for the Blue Cross hospital plan, and as a member of the WACs during WWII. Her writings include a book she wrote in 1936 about Sacajawea.

14,715. Whitman, Narcissa (Prentiss) (MSS, AW-2)
Papers. 1844-45. 2 items.
Open. Shelflist.
Oregon State Library.
Letters that [Mrs. Marcus] Whitman (1808-47), a pioneer missionary, wrote from Waiilatpu to Sarah Adelia Judson Olley [Mrs. David] Leslie.

PENNSYLVANIA

ALLENTOWN

14,716. College Archives
Records. 1867- . 110 ft., 6 drawers, and 17 boxes.
Open. Unpublished guide.
Cedar Crest College Library.
Minutes of faculty and committee meetings, policy papers, College catalogs, handbooks, publicity releases, alumnae journals, student newspapers, yearbooks, literary magazines, photos, and administrative papers documenting the educational philosophy, goals, and programs of Cedar Crest College, a women's college founded in 1867.

ALLISON PARK

14,717. Providence Heights Archives
Records. 1876- . 55 boxes, 2 files, 256 vols., 12 tapes, and 17 motion pictures.
Access restricted. Unpublished guide.
Sisters of Divine Providence, Provincial House.
The congregation, members of which are involved in teaching, nursing, and social work, was established in Dungannon, OH, in 1876 and in Pittsburgh in 1877. Constitutions, chronicles, circular letters, unpublished biographies of the founders, writings of the founders, audio-visual material, photos, scrapbooks, clippings, and memorabilia.

AMBRIDGE

14,718. Harmony Society
Records. 1780-1951. Ca. 350 cu.ft.
Access restricted. Published guide.
Pennsylvania Historical and Museum Commission, Old Economy Village.
Religious and business correspondence; invoices, bills of lading, and other business records; music manuscripts; and other material that constitutes the archives of Harmony, a religious community of German pietists. This communal Society was involved in agriculture; the manufacture of cloth, yarn, hats, shoes, and whiskey; and then in railroads, building the town of Beaver Falls, bridges, and the oil business. Includes correspondence with many communal and philanthropic groups and individuals, among them Robert Owen, Dorothea Dix, and the Shakers. See Richard D. Wetzel, *Frontier Music Makers* (Athens, OH: Ohio University Press, 1976) and Karl J. R. Arndt, *George Rapp's Harmony Society, 1785-1847* (Cranbury, NJ, 1972).

ASTON

14,719. Congregation Archives
Records. 1855- . 96 drawers, ca. 316 tapes, ca. 74 motion pictures, 1 blueprint cabinet, and 28 shelves.
Open. Unpublished guide.
Sisters of St. Francis of Philadelphia, Our Lady of Angels Convent.
Founded in Philadelphia in 1855 by Saint John Neumann and Mother Francis Bachmann, the order is involved in education on all levels, particularly the education of underprivileged blacks and Puerto Ricans, as well as in care of homeless children and senior citizens and health care through hospitals, mobile clinic vans, and home visitation. Correspondence, chronicles, photos, slides, tapes, ecclesiastical directives, reports, questionnaires, clippings, and other records relating to apostolic missions staffed by the Sisters.

BLOOMSBURG

14,720. Aristes Fire Company Ladies' Auxiliary
Records. 1925-32. 1 vol.
Open. No guide.
Columbia County Historical Society.
Minutes of the monthly meetings of the Auxiliary, which raised funds to support the fire company in a town of approximately 300 residents.

14,721. Barton, Malvina
Papers. 1860-77. 1 vol.
Open. No guide.
Columbia County Historical Society.
Daybook of Barton, a middle-class Bloomsburg housewife, contains detailed household accounts.

14,722. Bloomsburg Delta Club
Records. 1943-64. 3 vols.
Open. No guide.
Columbia County Historical Society.
Minutes of the Club, which held monthly meetings for the members' self-improvement. The members occasionally engaged in civic activities.

14,723. Bloomsburg Hospital Ladies' Auxiliary
Records. 1915-34. 2 vols.
Open. No guide.
Columbia County Historical Society.
Minutes of the Auxiliary, founded in 1915 to raise funds for the town hospital, include information on the members' activities, projects, and expenditures. The Auxiliary is still in existence.

14,724. Briarcreek Presbyterian Church Women's Foreign Missionary Society
Records. 1879-80. 1 vol.
Open. No guide.
Columbia County Historical Society.
Minutes of the fund-raising and related activities of this rural church group.

14,725. Ivy Club
Records. 1898-1971. 7 vols.
Open. No guide.
Columbia County Historical Society.
Minutes and scrapbooks of the Club, a civic and social group founded in 1898 to promote town improvement. The Club is still in existence.

14,726. John, Mary Alice
Papers. 1883-98. 1 vol.
Open. No guide.
Columbia County Historical Society.
Daybook of John, a middle-class resident of Bloomsburg, contains a record of household expenses by item and amount paid.

14,727. Mary Vance Auxiliary Society, First Presbyterian Church
Records. 1935-49. 5 vols.
Open. No guide.
Columbia County Historical Society.
Minutes and annual statements of the Auxiliary of this Bloomsburg church provide a formal record of the activities and funds of the organization.

14,728. Women's Suffrage
Collection. 1918-19. 1 box.
Open. No guide.
Columbia County Historical Society.
Correspondence and registers of potential voters provide fragmentary information on the activities of suffragists in Bloomsburg.

14,729. Young, S. Ella
Papers. 1911-48. 2 boxes.
Open. No guide.
Columbia County Historical Society.
Diaries of [Miss] Young (ca. 1895-1948), daughter of a Columbia County agriculturist and an active participant in the Grange, consist of records on her household, Grange, and social activities.

BRYN ATHYN

14,730. Beekman, Lillian Grace
Papers. 1899-1915. 3.5 ft.
Open. No guide.
Academy of the New Church Archives.
A teacher, lecturer, and writer, [Miss] Beekman (1857-1946) was the only woman to have taught theological students at the Academy of the New Church. Correspondence, manuscripts, a biography, and photos reveal her interest in physiology, anatomy, philosophy, cosmology, and the correlation between the scientific works and writings of Emanuel Swedenborg.

14,731. Cooper, Dorothy Pendleton
Papers. 1908-73. 1 ft.
Open. No guide.
Academy of the New Church Archives.
Cooper (1900-73) was a kindergarten teacher and teacher of children with learning disabilities. Correspondence, diaries, comparative studies of education in foreign countries, and other papers reflect Cooper's interest in early childhood training.

14,732. Grant, Alice Eliza
Papers. 1884-1946. 1.5 ft.
Open. No guide.
Academy of the New Church Archives.
A teacher in New Church elementary schools, Grant (1858-1930) became principal of the Academy of the New Church Girls' Seminary and then dean of women at the Academy of the New Church College. Correspondence, addresses, a family history, course outlines, and photos pertain to Grant's interest in such areas of education as nature, science, ethics, and kindergarten.

14,733. Hogan, Maria C.
Papers. 1878-1914. 6 in.
Open. No guide.
Academy of the New Church Archives.
Correspondence and photos of Hogan (1851-1926), niece of Andrew Carnegie, hostess for John Pitcairn, and governess for his children, indicate that she was influential in New Church social life.

14,734. Pendleton Sisters
Papers. 1880-1976. 2.5 ft.
Open. No guide.
Academy of the New Church Archives.
Correspondence, biographies, photos, and other papers of the nine daughters of William F. Pendleton, bishop of the General Church of the New Jerusalem. The sisters, Augusta, Luelle, Venita, Freda, Eleora, Constance, Amena, Wertha,

and Korene Pendleton, lived between 1873 and 1976; they were teachers, astronomers, housewives, and a librarian.

14,735. Theta Alpha
Records. 1904- . 3 ft.
Open. No guide.
Academy of the New Church Archives.
Minutes, correspondence, journals, and other records of Theta Alpha, the alumnae association of the Academy of the New Church, an organization founded in 1904 to support New Church education. Most of the material pertains to Theta Alpha meetings.

BRYN MAWR

14,736. Barnes, Margaret Ayer
Papers. 1927-67. 5 ft.
Open. Unpublished guide.
Bryn Mawr College Archives.
Correspondence, scrapbooks, and other papers of Barnes (1886-1967), an author and playwright. Contains manuscripts of her plays, including *Dishonest Lady* and *Johnny;* novels, including *Years of Grace;* and many of her short stories, including "Set a Thief" and "The Charmer." Bulk of the collection pertains to Barnes's long litigation with Metro-Goldwyn-Mayer concerning alleged infringement of copyright, with appeal briefs; legal opinions; extensive correspondence with the law firm O'Brien, Driscoll and Raftery; and other trial records. Collection also contains agreements between Barnes and Cornelia Otis Skinner, Edith Wharton, Charles Frohman, and RKO Pictures.

14,737. Bryn Mawr College
Records. 1884- . 334 ft. and ca. 15 microfilm reels.
Access restricted. Unpublished guide.
Bryn Mawr College Archives.
Founded in 1884, Bryn Mawr College was one of the pioneers in higher and graduate education for women; currently, this women's college also admits male graduate students. Minutes of the board of directors and of the faculty, treasurers' reports and other financial records, correspondence, College catalogs, complete sets of student literary publications and newspapers, and other records. Contains speeches, many of which pertain to the higher education of women, by [Miss] Martha Carey Thomas, College dean from 1884 to 1894 and president from 1894 to 1922; Marion Edwards Park, president from 1922 to 1942; and Katharine E. McBride, president from 1942 to 1970. Also includes correspondence (2 ft.) concerning the Bryn Mawr Summer School for Women Workers in Industry, a school for women industrial workers sponsored at Bryn Mawr between 1921 and 1939; correspondence with presidents and officials of other women's colleges and associations; and correspondence with Susan B. Anthony, Anna Howard Shaw, Carrie Chapman Catt, Emmeline Pankhurst, and other suffragists.

14,738. Bryn Mawr School
Records. 1885-ca. 1907. 6 ft.
Closed. Unpublished guide.
Bryn Mawr College Archives.
This girls' preparatory school was founded in 1885 to prepare women for colleges with high academic standards and difficult admissions requirements; the School is still operating in Baltimore. Although there was no formal connection between the School and Bryn Mawr College, College president Martha Carey Thomas was one of the School's founders. Correspondence; clippings about the School; catalogs describing the sculpture, paintings, and photos decorating the School; and other records. Includes correspondence of the founders Martha Carey Thomas, Mary Gwinn, Mary Elizabeth Garrett, Elizabeth King, and Julia Rogers with headmistresses of the School, including Edith Hamilton, on such matters as admissions, curriculum, financial affairs, and teacher applications and contracts. Collection will be available on microfilm in ca. 1980. The access restrictions are scheduled to expire in 1980.

14,739. Catt, Carrie Chapman
Papers. 1848-1925. 6 vols.
Open. No guide.
Bryn Mawr College Archives.
Photo albums of Catt (1859-1947), a suffrage leader, provide a history of the suffrage movement. Includes volumes on pioneers and leaders, publicity and pageants, and the state, national, and international movement.

14,740. Chapin, Helen
Papers. 1934-48. 1.5 ft.
Open. Unpublished guide.
Bryn Mawr College Archives.
An Orientalist, Chapin (1882-1950) was secretary to the American consul at Shanghai, English secretary to the Japanese National Research Council, and curator of the Japanese Collection at Swarthmore College. Bulk of the correspondence, notes, and photos pertains to Chapin's travels and research in the Orient. Includes correspondence with Ananda K. Coomaraswamy; notes on the architecture of buildings Chapin studied; information she collected on such subjects as poetry, novels, Taoism, jade, pottery, and prints; printed surveys and catalogs of historical places and cultural objects; and photos of places and things she encountered during her travels.

14,741. Hall, Margaret
Papers. 1918-19. 1 vol.
Open. No guide.
Bryn Mawr College Archives.
Hall (1899-1964) was a suffragist, philanthropist, and antiquarian. Volume contains copies of letters to her family, excerpts from her diary, and photos concerning her work as an American National Red Cross volunteer in the Cantine des Deux Drapeaux at Chalons-sur-Marne, an area that was close to the front and heavily bombarded. After the armistice she visited many of the battlefields and witnessed the victory celebration in Paris on July 14, 1919.

14,742. Kingsbury, Susan Myra
Papers. Ca. 1914-18. 5 in.
Open. No guide.
Bryn Mawr College Archives.
An educator, administrator, historian, and economist, Kingsbury (1870-1949) was the first director of the Bryn Mawr department of social economy and social research, which was the first graduate program in social work in the US. Notebooks contain research notes on women industrial workers in the US, Great Britain, France, Germany, and Italy, which Kingsbury copied by hand from such sources as government reports, newspapers, and studies and surveys made by the YWCA, the Society of Friends, and other religious organizations. The volumes pertain to women workers in the US, the problems of women workers in European war industries, the problems of motherhood and work, and the issue of providing social welfare services during war and other disasters.

14,743. Swindler, Mary Hamilton
Papers. 1911-67. 2 ft.
Open. Unpublished guide.
Bryn Mawr College Archives.
Personal papers of Swindler (1884-1967), an archaeologist, faculty member at Bryn Mawr College from 1912 to 1967, and editor of the *American Journal of Archaeology* for 14 years. Scrapbooks contain congratulatory letters and notes she received from noted academicians upon the publication of various books and articles and her receipt of scholarly honors. Also includes passports, address books, photos, and other items.

14,744. Taylor, Lily Ross
Papers. 1911-67. 2.5 ft.
Open. No guide.
Bryn Mawr College Archives.
The first woman appointed professor in charge of the School of Classical Studies of the American Academy in Rome, Taylor (1886-1970) was a classical scholar and faculty member at Bryn Mawr College from 1926 until her death. Half of the collection is composed of drafts and notes for her articles, lectures, and books on the Roman Senate. Also includes her official correspondence with such organizations and institutions as the American Academy in Rome, the Guggenheim Foundation, the American Philological Society, and *L'Année Philologique,* with letters from Juliette Ernst. Notes Taylor compiled on Horace, Caesar, the Republic, social life, and other aspects of ancient Roman history are also included.

14,745. Thomas, Martha Carey
Papers. 1817-1935. 117 ft.
Closed. No guide.
Bryn Mawr College Archives.
Personal and family papers of Thomas (1857-1935), dean from 1884 to 1894 and president from 1894 to 1922 of Bryn Mawr College, primarily consist of correspondence, but diaries, financial papers, scrapbooks, and photos are included as well. Much of the correspondence of her grandparents, parents, aunt and uncle Hannah and Robert Pearsall Smith, and other relatives and friends contains descriptions of Quaker life. Also contains documentation of Thomas's education in Baltimore Quaker schools, the Howland Institute, Cornell University, and the universities of Leipzig and Zurich. Her personal correspondence from the period of her involvement with the College reflects her attitude toward academic freedom, postgraduate education for women, faculty and student self-government, woman suffrage, the Bryn Mawr Summer School for Women Workers in Industry, the Carola Woerishoffer department of social economy and social research, and the Phebe Anna Thorne Open Air Model School. Thomas also discusses administration of the College; relations with faculty, trustees, and students; notable visitors to the College; and individuals she met. Correspondents include Thomas's friend and companion Mary Elizabeth Garrett, Ray Strachey, Alys and Bertrand Russell, Anna Howard Shaw, John D. Rockefeller, Lockwood de Forest, Mary (Putnam) Jacobi, William James, Simon Flexner, Bernard Berenson, and Lucy Martin Donnelly. Collection also contains information about Thomas's involvement in the American League to Enforce Peace and the League of Nations Non-Partisan Association as well as her personal life, travels, tastes, her health and that of her correspondents, contemporary medical practice and treatment, attitudes, cultural events, fashion, and moral standards.

In addition, the collection contains papers (21 ft.) of Mary Garrett, an heir to the B&O Railroad fortune, who was instrumental in the endowment campaign for the medical school of Johns Hopkins University and in the establishment and administration with Thomas and other women of the Bryn Mawr School in Baltimore. Garrett also was a supporter of the women's suffrage movement. Her papers reflect these activities and her personal life. Collection will be available on microfilm in ca. 1980. Access restrictions are scheduled to expire in that year.

CARLISLE

14,746. Carlisle Civic Club
Records. 1898-1972. 1 cu.ft.
Open. No guide.
Cumberland County Historical Society and Hamilton Library Association.
Minutes of the membership and of the executive committee and annual yearbooks of this women's service club, founded in 1898 to contribute to the improvement of the community. The Carlisle chapter of the American National Red Cross developed out of Red Cross work initiated by the Club. Similarly, the Club's sale of Christmas Seals led to the formation of the Cumberland County Tuberculosis Association. Other early Civic Club projects included support of the first hospital in Carlisle and the inauguration of street cleaning and sprinkling, public playgrounds, and school gardens.

14,747. Carlisle Fortnightly Club
Records. 1886- . 2 cu.ft.
Open. No guide.
Cumberland County Historical Society and Hamilton Library Association.
Constitutions and bylaws, minute books, correspondence, annual yearbooks, programs, and copies of papers presented to this literary club, founded in 1886 for "the pursuit of study as a means of mutual improvement and culture." One of the oldest women's discussion groups in the US, the Fortnightly Club, modeled after the Fortnightly Clubs of Denver and Chicago, became a member of the Pennsylvania Federation of Women's Clubs in 1897 but then resigned from the Federation in 1913. The Club has made contributions to such local organizations as the Bosler Free Library and the Hamilton Library Association.

14,748. Carlisle Indian School
Records. 1879-1918. 4 cu.ft. and 65 vols.
Open. No guide.
Cumberland County Historical Society and Hamilton Library Association.
Annual reports, correspondence, commencement programs, programs of special events, drawings by students, photos, clippings, newspapers, and guidebooks of the Indian School, founded in 1879 as an elementary and industrial school for Indian boys and girls from throughout the US. The program emphasized the study of the English language and the acquisition of such skills and trades as carpentry, masonry, and tailoring for boys and cooking, housekeeping, nursing, and dressmaking for girls.

Opening with 147 pupils from seven tribes, the Carlisle Indian School grew to over 1000 students from nearly every tribe in the US before 1918, when it was closed. Students, who could advance through the various grades at their own pace, spent half of each day in coeducational classes similar to those in public elementary schools; the classes were gradually extended to include instruction comparable to junior high school. Students spent the other half of the day learning vocational skills. In addition, students performed much of the work needed for the School's operation and maintenance. The School's program also included an "outing" system through which Indian students lived with families, attended public school, and earned wages for skills they had acquired at the School. Most of the girls who participated in this system were employed as domestics.

Collection includes 65 volumes of school newspapers, including the *School News, Indian Helper, Carlisle Arrow, Eadle Keatah Toh,* and *The Red Man,* as well as photographic portraits by Carlisle photographer John N. Choate of many of the Indian pupils, who were identified by name and tribe, and pictures of School classes and activities.

14,749. Female Benevolent Society of Carlisle
Records. 1884-1971. 0.5 cu.ft.
Open. No guide.
Cumberland County Historical Society and Hamilton Library Association.
Minute books, financial statements, correspondence, a history by Christine Stuart Ritter, and clippings of the Society, founded in 1828 to provide financial help and advice to needy persons; for many years it was the only organized nondenominational charity in Carlisle. The group raised funds for food and small pensions through church collections, door-to-door campaigns, emergency appeals, and occasional bequests.

In 1901 the Society took over operation of the Lydia Baird Home, which had been established several years earlier by Mary (Baird) Biddle of Philadelphia in memory of her sister Lydia Baird. Operating this residence for older women is now the Society's major project

14,750. American Association of University Women
Records. 1919-44. No size given.
Open. Published guide.
Dickinson College Library.
Material on the founding and early history of the Carlisle branch of the AAUW. Taken from Charles Coleman Sellers and Martha Calvert Slotten, comps., *Archives and Manuscript Collections of Dickinson College* (Carlisle, PA: Friends of the Dickinson College Library, 1972).

14,751. Besant, Annie
Papers. 1874-1932. 5 ft.
Open. Unpublished guide.
Dickinson College Library.
Correspondence, pamphlets, photos, and books of Besant (1847-1933), a British theosophist, author, and pamphleteer who founded the Hindu university in Benares, India. Correspondence primarily concerns theosophical matters and is addressed to theosophists in the US, England, and Holland. Other letters relate to her work in India, her championing of home rule there, and her work for other causes.

14,752. Coeducation
Collection. 1923. 1 box.
Open. Published guide.
Dickinson College Library.
Correspondence concerns efforts to expand coeducation at Dickinson College. Taken from Charles Coleman Sellers and Martha Calvert Slotten, comps., *Archives and Manuscript Collections of Dickinson College* (Carlisle, PA: Friends of the Dickinson College Library, 1972).

14,753. Fergusson, Elizabeth (Graeme)
Papers. 1787. 194-page vol.
Open. No guide.
Dickinson College Library.
Commonplace book that [Mrs. Hugh Henry] Fergusson (1737-1801), a poet and translator, addressed to Annis Boudinot Stockton. Volume contains correspondence and poems by Fergusson, poems of Francis Hopkinson and other friends, and autobiographical accounts in which Fergusson refers to her tragic marriage, her part in the Revolutionary War, and her friendship with prominent Philadelphians.

14,754. Fisher, Sarah Logan
Papers. 1823-50. 4 vols.
Open. Published guide.
Dickinson College Library.
Journal of a trip [Mrs. William Wister] Fisher (1806-91) took from Philadelphia to Boston in 1826 is included with her diary, a collection of her poems, and some accounts. Taken from Charles Coleman Sellers and Martha Calvert Slotten, comps., *Archives and Manuscript Collections of Dickinson College* (Carlisle, PA: Friends of the Dickinson College Library, 1972).

14,755. Fry, Elizabeth (Gurney)
Papers. 1836-41. 9 items.
Open. Published guide.
Dickinson College Library.
Correspondence of [Mrs. Joseph] Fry (1780-1845), a Quaker prison reformer. Taken from Charles Coleman Sellers and Martha Calvert Slotten, comps., *Archives and Manuscript Collections of Dickinson College* (Carlisle, PA: Friends of the Dickinson College Library, 1972).

14,756. Harman Literary Society
Records. 1900-35. 2 vols.
Open. Published guide.
Dickinson College Library.
Constitution and minutes of this women's literary group. Taken from Charles Coleman Sellers and Martha Calvert Slotten, comps., *Archives and Manuscript Collections of Dickinson College* (Carlisle, PA: Friends of the Dickinson College Library, 1972).

14,757. Independent Women
Records. 1924-55. 0.5 ft.
Open. Published guide.
Dickinson College Library.
Constitution; minutes, 1924-27 and 1951-55; treasurer's records, 1954-55; and correspondence of the Independent Women, a group of Dickinson College women students who chose not to join sororities. Taken from Charles Coleman Sellers and Martha Calvert Slotten, comps., *Archives and Manuscript Collections of Dickinson College* (Carlisle, PA: Friends of the Dickinson College Library, 1972).

14,758. Kingsbury, Susan Myra
Papers. 1902-06. 28 items.
Open. Published guide.
Dickinson College Library.
Papers of Kingsbury (1870-1949), an historian and social economist, pertain to her search for records of the Virginia Company of London. Correspondents include Worthington C. Ford, Herbert Levi Osgood, Herbert Putnam, and David Camp Rogers. Taken from Charles Coleman Sellers and Martha Calvert Slotten, comps., *Archives and Manuscript Collections of Dickinson College* (Carlisle, PA: Friends of the Dickinson College Library, 1972).

14,759. Meredith, Josephine (Brunyate)
Papers. 1919-48. 2 ft.
Open. Published guide.
Dickinson College Library.
Photo albums of [Mrs. Arthur J.] Meredith (1879-1965), a Dickinson College professor who served as dean of women from 1919 to 1945. Also includes administrative correspondence, rules, and regulations from her tenure as dean. Taken from Charles Coleman Sellers and Martha Calvert Slotten, comps., *Archives and Manuscript Collections of Dickinson College* (Carlisle, PA: Friends of the Dickinson College Library, 1972).

14,760. Metzger Institute
Records. Ca. 1798-1912. 3 ft.
Open. Published guide.
Dickinson College Library.
Records beginning in 1881 of this college for young ladies, founded in Carlisle under the terms of the will of George Metzger (1782-1879). Consists of student and general accounts, monthly reports of classwork and general average, examination records, grade books, a chapel attendance record, and records of library circulation. Also includes miscellaneous papers and a student notebook of George Metzger. Taken from Charles Coleman Sellers and Martha Calvert Slotten, comps., *Archives and Manuscript Collections of Dickinson College* (Carlisle, PA: Friends of the Dickinson College Library, 1972).

14,761. Moore, Marianne Craig
Papers. Nd. More than 75 items.
Access restricted. Unpublished guide.
Dickinson College Library.
Correspondence and books of [Miss] Moore (1887-1972), who received the Pulitzer Prize for poetry. She lived in Carlisle for about 20 years, attending the Metzger Institute and later teaching at the Carlisle Indian School. Dickinson College awarded her an honorary degree in 1952.

14,762. Sigoigne, Mrs. A.
Papers. 1837-55. 2 vols.
Open. Published guide.
Dickinson College Library.
Accounts Sigoigne had with pupils at her young ladies' academy in Washington Square, Philadelphia. Taken from Charles Coleman Sellers and Martha Calvert Slotten, comps., *Archives and Manuscript Collections of Dickinson College* (Carlisle, PA: Friends of the Dickinson College Library, 1972).

14,763. Straw, Zatae Longsdorff
Papers. 1874-1955. 3 ft.
Open. Published guide.
Dickinson College Library.
Photos, clippings, Indian artifacts, and memorabilia document the career of Straw (1866-1955), the first woman graduate of Dickinson and a physician and state legislator in New Hampshire. In 1890 she earned her MD at the Women's Medical College of Pennsylvania and then worked as a government physician for the Shoshoni Indians on the Fort Hall Reservation in Idaho. Thereafter, she and her husband Amos Gale Straw (1864-1926), who also was a physician, lived and practiced in Manchester, NH. See Charles Coleman Sellers and Martha Calvert Slotten, comps., *Archives and Manuscript Collections of Dickinson College* (Carlisle, PA: Friends of the Dickinson College Library, 1972).

14,764. Student Government
Records. 1919-45. 4 vol.
Open. Published guide.
Dickinson College Library.
Includes records of the Dickinson College Women's Student Senate, 1929-34; minutes of the Panhellenic Council, 1920-45; and the Women's Student Government Association, 1919-44. Taken from Charles Coleman Sellers and Martha Calvert Slotten, comps., *Archives and Manuscript Collections of Dickinson College* (Carlisle, PA: Friends of the Dickinson College Library, 1972).

14,765. Young Women's Christian Association
Records. 1902-32. 7 vols.
Open. Published guide.
Dickinson College Library.
Constitution, minutes of meetings of the membership and the cabinet, reports, treasurer's records, and other material concerning members of the Dickinson College branch of the YWCA. Taken from Charles Coleman Sellers and Martha Calvert Slotten, comps., *Archives and Manuscript Collections of Dickinson College* (Carlisle, PA: Friends of the Dickinson College Library, 1972).

CARLISLE BARRACKS

14,766. Archives
Records. 1600-1978. 8300 boxes and 3 microfilm reels.
Open. Published and unpublished guides.
United States Army Military History Institute.
Archives of the Institute contain personal and official correspondence, diaries, memoirs, reports and returns, scrapbooks, and annotated publications of Army officers and enlisted men, particularly those who served after 1860. Many of the collections refer to and occasionally contain letters from the mothers, sisters, grandmothers, aunts, female cousins, wives, and girl friends of the soldiers. Includes information on particular facets of military history, such as the role of Pennsylvania women during the Civil War. (The following 12 entries describe separate portions of the Archives.) See Richard J. Sommers, *Manuscript Holdings of the Military History Research Collection,* pt. I (Carlisle Barracks, PA: US Army Military History Institute, 1972); Richard J. Sommers, *Manuscript Holdings of the Military History Research Collection,* vol. II (Carlisle Barracks, PA: US Army Military History Institute, 1975).

14,767. Bradley, Luther P.
Papers. 1822-1950. 10 boxes.
Open. Unpublished guide.
United States Army Military History Institute.
Personal and official papers of Bradley, a lieutenant-colonel and colonel in the US Infantry and brigade commander of the Army of the Cumberland, contain memoirs of his wife Ione (Dewey) Bradley about her life as an Army wife in the West and South between 1868 and 1886, her reminiscence concerning garrison duty in New Orleans in 1880, and miscellaneous material concerning her career from 1857 to 1867 as an opera singer.

14,768. Burt, Reynolds J.
Papers. 1896-1935. 1 box.
Open. Published and unpublished guides.
United States Army Military History Institute.
Personal correspondence of Burt, a colonel in the 15th US Infantry Regiment, includes letters sent by his wife Lilian (Stewart) Burt to her mother about her experiences in China between 1932 and 1935 as the wife of the senior US Army officer stationed there. Most of her letters concern life in Tientsin and visits to Peking. See Richard J. Sommers, *Manuscript Holdings of the Military History Research Collection,* pt. I (Carlisle Barracks, PA: US Army Military History Institute, 1972).

14,769. Civil War Times Illustrated Collection: Garlach, Anna
Papers. 1863. 1 folder.
Open. Published and unpublished guides.
United States Army Military History Institute.
Recollections of Garlach's experiences as a child in the town of Gettysburg, PA, during military operations in the area during the battle of Gettysburg. One of her accounts concerns the refuge her family provided for Brigadier-General Alexander Schimmelpfennig during the battle and following the rout of his division July 1. See Richard J. Sommers, *Manuscript Holdings of the Military History Research Collection,* vol. II (Carlisle Barracks, PA: US Army Military History Institute, 1975).

14,770. Civil War Times Illustrated Collection: Hunt, Frances
Papers. 1865. 1 folder.
Open. Published and unpublished guides.
United States Army Military History Institute.
An account by Hunt, a 14-year-old girl, of the fall of Richmond, VA; the occupation of that city by Union forces; reactions to the assassination of Abraham Lincoln; and her family's move from the Confederate capital to the Union capital. See Richard J. Sommers, *Manuscript Holdings of the Military History Research Collection,* pt. I (Carlisle Barracks, PA: US Army Military History Institute, 1972).

14,771. Halstead and Maus
Papers. 1851-1939. 2 boxes.
Open. Published and unpublished guides.
United States Army Military History Institute.
Includes recollections by Anna (Russell) Maus of her childhood in Kentucky, her life as the wife of Colonel L. Mervin Maus during his long career in the US Army Medical Corps, and her retirement. Recollections contain information on her sharing her husband's experiences in the Indian wars, during the occupation of Havana after the Spanish-American War, and while he worked to solve health problems in Manila during the early years of American rule in the Philippines. See Richard J. Sommers, *Manuscript Holdings of the Military History Research Collection,* vol. II (Carlisle Barracks, PA: US Army Military History Institute, 1975).

14,772. McCann: Women in Uniform
Collection. 1938-44. 2 boxes.
Open. Published and unpublished guides.
United States Army Military History Institute.
Scrapbooks of clippings and government recruiting and information brochures and a letter from a WAC at the Daytona Beach Training Camp were compiled by members of the McCann family, particularly Dorothy McCann. The material concerns women in the armed forces during WWII; most of it relates to the WACs, WAVES, WAFs (Women in the Air Force), SPARS (Women's Coast Guard Reserves), the US Army Nurse Corps, and the US Marine Corps Women's Reserve. Also contains some material on comparable units in other countries, principally the United Kingdom. See Richard J. Sommers, *Manuscript Holdings of the Military History Research Collection,* vol. II (Carlisle Barracks, PA: US Army Military History Institute, 1975).

14,773. Morrow and Boniface
Papers. 1860-1957. 1 box.
Open. No guide.
United States Army Military History Institute.
Although most of the material pertains to Brevet Major-General Henry A. Morrow of the Union Army and the regular US Army, the collection also contains diaries of his daughter Isabella (Morrow) Boniface, who was the wife of Captain John J. Boniface. Her 1915 diary concerns Army life at Governor's Island in New York and at Schofield Barracks in Hawaii. Her 1935 and 1937 diaries contain descriptions of her activities as a civilian in Washington, DC.

14,774. Olson, Betty M.
Papers. 1942-45. 1 box.
Open. Unpublished guide.
United States Army Military History Institute.
Letters home and reminiscences of Olson, a WAC sergeant, concern her experiences at the Fort Des Moines Training Camp in Iowa, at the Hampton Roads Port of Embarkation in Virginia, and as a sergeant in the 29th WAC Traffic Regulating Company, principally in Paris, France. In the latter assignment, she served in the first WAC unit to enter France after D-Day. From 1944 to 1945 she also served as secretary to Major-General Frank S. Ross, chief of transportation of the European theater.

14,775. P. J. Hohlweck Collection: Stone, Callie M.
Papers. 1864. 1 folder.
Open. Published and unpublished guides.
United States Army Military History Institute.
Diary that [Miss] Stone kept while she was serving with the US Sanitary Commission as a teacher of Negro, German, and French recruits for Massachusetts regiments at the draft rendezvous in Boston harbor. See Richard J. Sommers, *Manuscript Holdings of the Military History Research Collection,* vol. II (Carlisle Barracks, PA: US Army Military History Institute, 1975).

14,776. Pardee and Robison
Papers. 1861-64. 1 box.
Open. Published and unpublished guides.
United States Army Military History Institute.
Correspondence of Brevet Brigadier-General Ariovistus Pardee and various of his relatives who served in or for the Union army includes letters reflecting the work of his aunts Bell and Jane

Robison, who were volunteer nurses in military hospitals in Washington, DC, and in Fredericksburg, Falls Church, and Belle Plain, VA. Following the battle of Gettysburg, Brigadier-General Solomon Meredith was one of Bell Robison's patients. See Richard J. Sommers, *Manuscript Holdings of the Military History Research Collection,* vol. II (Carlisle Barracks, PA: US Army Military History Institute, 1975).

14,777. Paulding, William, and Paulding, Grace
Papers. 1873-1956. 1 box.
Open. Published and unpublished guides.
United States Army Military History Institute.
Among the papers of Colonel William Paulding are recollections by his second wife Grace (Bunce) Paulding of her experiences between 1894 and 1913 as the wife of an Army officer. She met Geronimo at Fort Sill, OK; accompanied her husband during the occupation of Cuba and the suppression of the Philippine Insurrection; and was present when her husband commanded a Negro regiment at Madison Barracks in New York and a white regiment at Galveston, TX. See Richard J. Sommers, *Manuscript Holdings of the Military History Research Collection,* pt. I (Carlisle Barracks, PA: US Army Military History Institute, 1972).

14,778. World War I Survey: Army Nurse Corps
Records. 1918-19. 2 boxes.
Open. No guide.
United States Army Military History Institute.
Correspondence, questionnaires, scrapbooks, and official records concerning the Corps, which were donated by Grace (Williams) Major of Base Hospital No. 35, Emma (Blome) Peterson of Base Hospital No. 49, Annette L. Munro of Camp Hospital No. 43, Charlotte Grace (Light) Chilson of Base Hospital No. 36, Lydia (Oden) Linge of Base Hospital No. 66, and Marion V. (Dunn) Adams of Army Nurse Corps Unit No. 55.

CHAMBERSBURG

14,779. Bashkirtseff, Marie
Papers. 1860-1942. 9 ft.
Open. Unpublished guide.
Wilson College Library.
Correspondence, diaries, financial papers, scrapbooks, photos, and other papers of Bashkirtseff (1860-84), an artist and writer.

14,780. Wilsoniana
Records. 1869- . 1 cabinet and 17 cartons.
Open. Unpublished guide.
Wilson College Library.
Minutes, financial records, scrapbooks, photos, and other records of Wilson College, a liberal arts school for women founded in 1869.

CORNWELLS HEIGHTS

14,781. Archives
Records. 1858- . 172 boxes, 11 drawers, 55 shelves, 58 vols., and 30 microfilm reels.
Access restricted. Unpublished guide.
Sisters of the Blessed Sacrament, St. Elizabeth Convent.
This congregation of religious women was founded in 1891 to work among the "Indians and Colored People" of the US. Correspondence of superiors general, other superiors, and others associated with the congregation; letters from the missions to the Motherhouse; annals of the congregation, houses, and convents; photos of missions; booklets; clippings; and other records. Also includes correspondence, diaries, journals, photos, genealogies, and other papers of Mother Mary Katharine Drexel, foundress of the Sisters of the Blessed Sacrament; her younger sister Louise (Drexel) Morrell; and other members of the Drexel family.

DEVON

14,782. Archives
Records. 1955- . 1 folder and 2 boxes.
Access restricted. No guide.
Sisters of Jesus Crucified, American Novitiate.
Minutes of council meetings, financial records, correspondence, chronicle of the community, reports, photos, scrapbooks, and other records of this monastic contemplative community, which was founded in Devon in 1955 as Regina Mundi Priory. This was the first American foundation of the congregation of the Sisters of Jesus Crucified, which was founded in Paris, France, in 1930.

ELKINS PARK

14,783. Archives
Records. 1880- . No size given.
Partially restricted. Unpublished guide.
Dominican Convent of Our Lady of Prouille.
The congregation was founded in 1880 at Glen Falls, NY, primarily to conduct retreat work; its members later established schools for the religious instruction of children and homes for working girls and businesswomen. Financial records, correspondence, retreat notes, photos, scrapbooks, and other records of the congregation.

ELVERSON

14,784. Original Sources
Collection. 1784-1883. 80 vols. and 10,000 items.
Open. No guide.
Hopewell Village National Historic Site.
Correspondence, memoranda, bills, store records, typewritten interviews with Hopewell Village residents since the 1860s, and other items. Includes information on salaries paid to hired girls.

ELYSBURG

14,785. Archives
Records. 1953- . 3 boxes and 4 vols.
Access restricted. No guide.
Discalced Carmelite Nuns Monastery.
Correspondence regarding the foundation and building of the Monastery in 1953, photo albums, and scrapbooks of clippings of this community of cloistered contemplative nuns. Includes biographical information on the foundress Mother Marguerite Marie, born Marie Eugenie Melancon.

ERIE

14,786. Durkin Family
Papers. 1902-68. 1 Hollinger box and 2 tapes.
Open. Unpublished guide.
Mercyhurst College Archives/Center for Erie Studies.
Correspondence, programs, mass cards, and photos reflect the association of Mary Blaise (Walsh) [Mrs. Edmund J., Sr.] Durkin (1883-1968), a Cleveland housewife, and her family with the Sisters of Mercy and Mercyhurst College. Includes information on activities of the Sisters, events at Mercyhurst, and news of Titusville, PA.

14,787. Herrmann, Sister Carolyn
Papers. 1935-1972. 2 Hollinger boxes.
Open. Unpublished guide.
Mercyhurst College Archives/Center for Erie Studies.
Sister Carolyn, R.S.M. (ca. 1915-), was a teacher, administrator, and president of Mercyhurst College from 1963 to 1972. College publications, articles, speeches Sister Carolyn gave as Mercyhurst president, and 1940s photos of College students. Includes material on the construction and opening of new buildings and facilities during her administration, the admission of men to Mercyhurst, and the inauguration of intercollegiate sports.

14,788. Mercyhurst Alumnae
Records. 1951-59. Ca. 1 ft. and 2 vols.
Open. No guide.
Mercyhurst College Archives/Center for Erie Studies.
Letters sent to members, invitations, and clippings of the Alumnae Association of Mercyhurst College, a college for women which was founded in Erie in 1926 by the Sisters of Mercy of Titusville, PA.

14,789. Mercyhurst College
Records. 1926-76. Ca. 15 ft., 1 microfilm reel, and other items.
Partially restricted. Unpublished guide.
Mercyhurst College Archives/Center for Erie Studies.
Founded in 1926 by the Sisters of Mercy, Mercyhurst College admitted men after 1969. One reel of trustees' minutes, complete official programs of dramatic and musical performances, College newspapers and yearbooks, scrapbooks, photos and slides, and clippings on the activities of individual alumnae and official groups of alumnae. Most of the material concerns social events and student life.

14,790. Mercyhurst Memorabilia
Records. 1929-56. 1 Hollinger box and 16 items.
Open. Unpublished guide.
Mercyhurst College Archives/Center for Erie Studies.
Programs, a dance card, a class "last will and testament," and photos pertain to the activities of the class of 1931 and to the class's alumnae banquet in 1956.

14,791. Mercyhurst Photos
Records. 1929-72. 73 items.
Open. Unpublished guide.
Mercyhurst College Archives/Center for Erie Studies.
Photos of graduates of the class of 1929 with Mother Borgia, who founded the College; photos chronicling events during the College presidency of Sister Carolyn Herrmann, R.S.M.; a Pennsylvania Electric Company periodical showing Sister Carolyn with Company officials; photos of other graduating classes and of campus life; brochures describing the College; and an article discussing the cadet teaching program, which was established by the College in about 1955 to provide education majors with paid internships in parochial schools.

14,792. Stough, A. M.
Papers. 1876. 1 vol.
Open. Unpublished guide.
Mercyhurst College Archives/Center for Erie Studies.
Diary of Stough (ca. 1846-?), an Erie County, PA, housewife whose husband and infant had died shortly before the beginning of her narrative. She made almost daily notes about the weather and visits to friends and relatives. Diary also contains a pattern Stough wrote for knitting socks.

14,793. Strong, Caroline
Papers. 1901-03. 5 items (microfilm).
Open. Brief description.
Mercyhurst College Archives/Center for Erie Studies.
Letters in which Strong, apparently a housewife, discusses family matters, travel, and events in Erie County, PA.

14,794. Archives
Records. 1870- . 78 in., 12 files, 760 items, 82 tapes, 3 cabinets, and 1 cupboard.
Open. Unpublished guide.
Sisters of Mercy Archives.
Constitutions, minutes, financial records, correspondence, histories, diaries, surveys, tapes, photos, slides, scrapbooks, chronicles, yearbooks, newsletters, booklets, prayerbooks, liturgies and ceremonies, and other records of the congregation, which was founded in Titusville, PA, in 1870 to teach and to perform social services and nursing. Contains correspondence of the major superiors; biographical material about the sisters; proceedings of chapters, commissions, committees, and the Corporation of the Sisters of Mercy of Erie County, PA; and records relating to parochial schools served by the Sisters and institutions established by the Congregation, including St. Joseph Academy in Titusville, Mercyhurst College in Erie, Mercy Montessori School in Erie, Mercy Center of the Arts, and Du Bois Hospital in Du Bois, PA.

14,795. Archives
Records. 1650- . Ca. 69 ft., 4 files, 90 vols., 2 microfilm reels, and ca. 30 tapes.
Open. Card index.
Sisters of St. Joseph Motherhouse.
The order was founded in LePuy, France, in 1650. The Erie Diocese was established in 1860 in Pennsylvania. Constitutions, records of council meetings, financial records, accounts of various institutions, correspondence, papers of several mothers superior, photos, acts of profession, Holy Rules, biographies of superiors and sisters, scrapbooks, office books, liturgies, clippings, brochures, and other records of the congregation. Includes material relating to two hospitals, an orphanage, an academy, a college, parish schools, and catechetical centers with which the Sisters are involved.

GETTYSBURG

14,796. Albrecht, Amy (Sadtler)
Papers. 1889-1914. 267-page item.
Open. No guide.
Lutheran Theological Seminary Library.
Albrecht (1857-1942) was a Lutheran missionary who served in a Hindu girl's school in Guntur, India. Her husband, a German Lutheran missionary, also served in the Guntur district. Manuscript of an unpublished book written by Albrecht in the form of journal-style letters contains descriptions of customs of the Guntur area and of the lives of women in the area and gives a detailed account of pioneer mission work.

14,797. Markley, Mary Elizabeth
Papers. 1919-46. 3 ft.
Open. No guide.
Lutheran Theological Seminary Library.
Markley (?-1954) served from 1919 to 1946 as secretary to the board of education of the United Lutheran Church in America, the first woman to hold the position. Correspondence, reports, committee papers, papers relating to the Lutheran Nurses Guild, and articles and addresses on missions.

14,798. Paulsson, Bertha
Papers. 1946-63. 2.5 ft.
Open. No guide.
Lutheran Theological Seminary Library.
Paulsson (1891-1973), the first woman faculty member at any Lutheran seminary in the US, was a professor of Christian sociology and psychology at Lutheran Theological Seminary. Correspondence, notes, course outlines, and articles, including material in English and German used in teaching at the Seminary and in lectures at youth gatherings and retreats.

14,799. Sanford, Annie Evaline
Papers. 1896-1944. 5 in.
Open. No guide.
Lutheran Theological Seminary Library.
Sanford (1873-1961) was a Lutheran missionary in a Hindu girl's school in Guntur, India. She served for 50 years at Guntur as a missionary for the United Lutheran Church in America. Personal correspondence, photos, and journal-style letters that were sent home, typed by a receiver, and distributed include information on the social background of missionaries and on Indian women in an urban area.

GREENSBURG

14,800. Community Archives
Records. 1870- . 13 Paige boxes, 76 vols., 32 tapes, 6 cabinets, and 48 shelf files.
Open. No guide.
Sisters of Charity of Seton Hill.
The order of the Sisters of Charity was founded in 1809 in Emmitsburg, MD, by Mother Elizabeth Ann Seton, who was canonized in 1975. The Motherhouse of the Pittsburgh Diocese was established in 1870 in Altoona, PA, and moved to Greensburg in 1882. Constitution and rules; correspondence, journals, photos, scrapbooks, and other papers of mothers superior; personal files for living and deceased sisters from 1870 to the present; history of the community by Sister Electa Boyle, who holds a PhD and is head of the English department at Seton Hill College; papers relating to Mother Seton; community bulletins; and other records of this community of religious women devoted to teaching, health care, and social service.

HARRISBURG

14,801. Haldeman, Eliza E.
Papers. 1884-98. 8 folders.
Open. No guide.
Historical Society of Dauphin County.
Papers concerning settlement of the estate of [Mrs.] Haldeman (?-1884), a wealthy Harrisburg resident, include a copy of her will, inventories of her possessions, releases, bills, receipts, and family correspondence, which indicates there were tensions in the family.

14,802. Pennsylvania Female College
Records. 1854-ca. 1857. 4 folders.
Open. No guide.
Historical Society of Dauphin County.
Records of the College, which was founded in 1849 as the Harrisburg Female Seminary, contain a catalog listing instructors and students and describing the school and courses offered, 1857-58; a commencement program and address delivered at the first commencement, 1854; a grade book; and clippings. [Mrs.] Anna Leconte was an early principal of the school.

14,803. Anderson, John
Papers. 1864-1904. 14 cu.ft.
Open. Published guide and inventory.
Pennsylvania State Archives.
Papers of Anderson (1770-1840), a 1791 graduate of the University of Pennsylvania medical school, a physician, businessman, president of the Allegheny Bank of Pennsylvania, president of the Chambersburg and Bedford Turnpike Road Company, and developer of Bedford Mineral Springs. Also includes papers of George Woods, a surveyor and statesman who was the grandfather of Anderson's wife Mary (Espy) Anderson (1779-1815), and correspondence of her father David Espy, a lawyer; of Mary and John Anderson's son Espy L. Anderson; and of his son William Watson Anderson. Collection contains correspondence of or concerning Ann Jane Anderson (1811-18), Louisa Harrison Anderson (1850-1924), Louisa H. Watson Anderson (1817-84), Mary Espy Anderson (1846-90), Eliza Watson Anderson Beatty (1848-1904), Mary Woods Anderson Johnson (1813-72), and Ann Woods Ross (1771-1805). See Harry E. Whipkey, comp. and ed., *Guide to the Manuscript Groups in the Pennsylvania State Archives* (Harrisburg, PA: Pennsylvania Historical and Museum Commission, 1976).

14,804. Blatt, Genevieve
Papers. Ca. 1934-76. Ca. 40 cu.ft.
Open. Unpublished guide.
Pennsylvania State Archives.
A judge of the Commonwealth Court of Pennsylvania, [Miss] Blatt (1913-) was the first woman elected to state office in Pennsylvania. Correspondence, photos, scrapbooks, clippings, publications, memorabilia, and other offical and personal items. Includes files pertaining to her work as volunteer director of the Pennsylvania Intercollegiate Conference on Government and to her membership in various civic groups and on state and federal advisory committees, authorities, boards, and commissions. Blatt served as secretary of the Pittsburgh Civil Service Commission from 1938 to 1942, as assistant city solicitor in Pittsburgh from 1942 to 1945, and as deputy state treasurer from 1945 to 1949. She was elected secretary of internal affairs for the Commonwealth of Pennsylvania in 1954, 1958, and 1962; she was commissioned judge of the Commonwealth Court in 1972 and was elected to a full term in 1973.

14,805. Cope Family
Papers. 1793-1937. 3.5 cu.ft.
Open. Published guide and inventory.
Pennsylvania State Archives.
Consists primarily of correspondence of three generations of this Quaker family, which lived in Philadelphia and in Chester, Bucks, and Susquehanna counties, PA. Includes letters from Thomas P. Cope (1768-1854), a Philadelphia merchant and ship owner, and his wife Mary (Drinker) Cope to their son William Drinker Cope (1798-1870s) while he was a student at the Westtown School; correspondence of William Cope, who became a farmer, dairyman, and orchardist, with Susan L. Newbold during their courtship in the 1820s; and correspondence with their children, all of whom attended boarding schools, and with relatives and friends. Much of the latter material is from their daughters Clementine, Caroline, and Annette Cope. Family, religion, and education are the topics discussed most frequently. See Harry E. Whipkey, comp. and ed., *Guide to the Manuscript Groups in the Pennsylvania State Archives* (Harrisburg, PA: Pennsylvania Historical and Museum Commission, 1976).

14,806. Department of Public Welfare
Records. 1882-1967. 211 cu.ft.
Open. Unpublished guide.
Pennsylvania State Archives.
Included with records of the secretary of the Department is correspondence concerning birth control, 1958-59.

14,807. Department of State
Records. 1681-1971. 1036 cu.ft.
Open. Unpublished guide.
Pennsylvania State Archives.
Includes ships' lists of German passengers, 1727-1808; a clemency file, 1790-1873; pardon books, 1791-1877; records of births, marriages, and deaths, 1852-54; state employee lists, 1923-26; and registration records of charitable organizations involving women, 1924-61.

14,808. Ditmer and Lehmer Family
Papers. 1863-1914. 1 cu.ft.
Open. Published guide and inventory.
Pennsylvania State Archives.
Primarily diaries in which Jacob F. Lehmer (?-1914), a York County, PA, justice of the peace, surveyor, and farmer, writes about weather conditions, surveying and legal matters, visitors, travel, and his daily work and that of his wife Sarah A. (Ditmer) Lehmer. Also includes his correspondence with Sarah A. Liszman and correspondence of his wife's sister Lydia M. Ditmer with Susan Ditmer. See Harry E. Whipkey, comp. and ed., *Guide to the Manuscript Groups in the Pennsylvania State Archives* (Harrisburg, PA: Pennsylvania Historical and Museum Commission, 1976).

14,809. Dock Family
Papers. 1865-1951. 7.5 cu.ft.
Open. Published guide and inventory.
Pennsylvania State Archives.
Consists primarily of the papers of Mira Lloyd Dock (1853-1945), a lecturer and member of the State Forestry Reservation Commission from 1901 to 1913 and an advocate of forestry and community improvement in Pennsylvania and the US. Includes school notebooks and personal and professional diaries, 1869-1918; reports and speeches, 1902-13; photos of family, travel, and work-related scenes; family papers; and correspondence, 1878-1943, with such groups as the American Forestry Association, the Pennsylvania Department of Forestry, the Pennsylvania Forestry Association, the State Forestry Academy of Mount Alto, the Women's School of Horticulture at Ambler, the State Federation of Pennsylvania Women, and the GFWC. Correspondents include [Mrs.] Mary B. Colston, Florence Keen, Warren H. Manning, [Miss] F. R. Wilkinson, Henry W. Shoemaker, Gifford Pinchot, and Frederick Law Olmsted.

Collection also contains correspondence and travel and business papers of her grandfather William Dock (1793-1868); her father Gilliard Dock (1827-95), a machinist and mine superintendent; her uncle George Dock (1823-7?), a physician and professor of medicine at Jefferson Medical College; and her brother George Dock (1860-1951), a physician and professor of medicine. See Harry E. Whipkey, comp. and ed., *Guide to the Manuscript Groups in the Pennsylvania State Archives* (Harrisburg, PA: Pennsylvania Historical and Museum Commission, 1976).

14,810. Duff, James H.
Papers. 1943-51. 86.4 cu.ft.
Open. Published and unpublished guides.
Pennsylvania State Archives.
Papers relating primarily to the term of Duff (1883-1969), an attorney, as governor of Pennsylvania between 1947 and 1951. Includes correspondence from various women active in Pennsylvania politics. See Harry E. Whipkey, comp. and ed., *Guide to the Manuscript Groups in the Pennsylvania State Archives* (Harrisburg, PA: Pennsylvania Historical and Museum Commission, 1976).

14,811. Ethnic Studies Program, Oral History Projects.
Oral history. Ca. 1880-1970. 600 tapes.
Access restricted. Unpublished guide.
Pennsylvania State Archives.
Interviews of 250 working-class women concern their backgrounds and lives from ca. 1880 to 1970. The interviews are housed temporarily in the Pennsylvania Historical and Museum Commission division of history; they will be transferred to the division of archives and manuscripts.

14,812. Harris and Silverthorn Family
Papers. 1816-1924. 1 cu.ft.
Open. Published guide and inventory.
Pennsylvania State Archives.
Papers of the related Harris and Silverthorn families of Erie County, PA; Ohio; and Wisconsin. Contains letters about personal and family matters to [Mrs.] Priscilla Harris from her children and grandchildren, 1857-67; to [Mrs.] Rebecca Harris from her sister and children, 1860-92; to [Miss] Jane Harris from female cousins and friends, 1850-73; and to [Miss] Melissa Harris from relatives and friends, 1841-65. See Harry E. Whipkey, comp. and ed., *Guide to the Manuscript Groups in the Pennsylvania State Archives* (Harrisburg, PA: Pennsylvania Historical and Museum Commission, 1976).

14,813. Historical and Museum Commission
Records. 1903-76. 156 cu.ft.
Open. Unpublished guide.
Pennsylvania State Archives.
Records of the Commission and its predecessors include scattered correspondence relating to women involved in preserving the historical heritage of Pennsylvania as well as correspondence and files of [Miss] Frances Dorrance, Gertrude B. Fuller, Myrtle Keeny, Alice M. Kane, and [Mrs.] Mabel E. Bitner.

14,814. Howard, Liliane Stevens
Papers. 1915-59. 1 cu.ft.
Open. Published guide and inventory.
Pennsylvania State Archives.
Howard (1872-1958) was a suffragist and women's rights advocate who was active in the Pennsylvania County Woman Suffrage Society, the Pennsylvania Council of Republican Women, the Pennsylvania Woman Suffrage Association, and the National Woman's party. Correspondence; an autobiographical essay; a history she wrote of the Pennsylvania County Woman Suffrage Society; a 1945 annual report of a policewoman's unit; scrapbooks of clippings; reports on the International Woman Suffrage Conference held in Berlin, Germany, in 1904 and the Women's Centennial Congress held in New York City in 1940; and material on the Equal Rights Amendment. Also includes biographical essays Howard wrote on Ladson Hall, Harriet Annie Lucas, M. Estelle Russel, Suzanne Silvercruys, Mrs. Henry Hall Sinnamon, and Mary Walker, a physician. See Harry E. Whipkey, comp. and ed., *Guide to the Manuscript Groups in the Pennsylvania State Archives* (Harrisburg, PA: Pennsylvania Historical and Museum Commission, 1976).

14,815. Lawrence, David L.
Papers. 1959-66. 185 cu.ft.
Open. Published and unpublished guides.
Pennsylvania State Archives.
Correspondence and related papers of Lawrence (1889-1966), Democratic mayor of Pittsburgh and then governor of Pennsylvania from 1959 to 1963. Correspondents include Anne X. Alpern, Genevieve Blatt, Pearl S. Buck, and Emma (Guffey) Miller. See Harry E. Whipkey, comp. and ed., *Guide to the Manuscript Groups in the Pennsylvania State Archives* (Harrisburg, PA: Pennsylvania Historical and Museum Commission, 1976).

14,816. Lebanon County Historical Society Manuscript Collections
Collection. 1757-1940. 207 cu.ft.
Open. Published and unpublished guides.
Pennsylvania State Archives.
Included with collections pertaining to the history of Lebanon County, PA, is the Coleman collection, 1757-1940, primarily consisting of correspondence and business records of the Coleman family's iron furnaces and ore hills, which figured prominently in the 18th-and 19th-century iron industry in the US. Material, which dates primarily from 1850 to 1920, pertains to family members who owned an interest in the business, among them Anne C. Alden, Margaret C. Freeman, Sarah H. Coleman, Anne C. Coleman, Margaret C. Buckingham, and Isabel C. Freeman. See Harry E. Whipkey, comp. and ed., *Guide to the Manuscript Groups in the Pennsylvania State Archives* (Harrisburg, PA: Pennsylvania Historical and Museum Commission, 1976).

14,817. Logan, Algernon Sydney, and Logan, Robert Restalrig
Papers. Ca. 1680-1945. 2.5 cu.ft.
Open. Published guide and inventory.
Pennsylvania State Archives.
Papers of the Logan family, including James Logan (1674-1751), first provincial secretary of William Penn, and his father Patrick Logan, include an historical manuscript that Deborah (Norris) Logan (1761-1839), wife of physician George Logan, wrote beginning in 1815 about the Logan and Norris families. Also includes the journal, 1873-80, of Mary Wynne Wister Logan, who was the wife of author Algernon Logan; genealogical material; and family portraits and photos. See Harry E. Whipkey, comp. and ed., *Guide to the Manuscript Groups in the Pennsylvania State Archives* (Harrisburg, PA: Pennsylvania Historical and Museum Commission, 1976).

14,818. McCreath Family
Papers. 1836-92. 0.25 cu.ft.
Open. Published guide and inventory.
Pennsylvania State Archives.
This family collection primarily consists of the papers of Margaretha Flemming McCreath of Harrisburg. Includes her report books from the female seminary in Harrisburg, drafts of essays read before the Franklin Debating Society, and an 1841 annual report of the board of managers of the Young Men's and Young Ladies' Total Abstinence Society of Harrisburg. See Harry E. Whipkey, comp. and ed., *Guide to the Manuscript Groups in the Pennsylvania State Archives* (Harrisburg, PA: Pennsylvania Historical and Museum Commission, 1976).

14,819. McFarland, J. Horace
Papers. 1859-1951. 20 cu.ft.
Open. Published and unpublished guides.
Pennsylvania State Archives.
Papers of McFarland (1859-1948), a conservationist who conducted campaigns for the preservation of Niagara Falls and national parks, primarily relate to his work with the American Civic Association, the American Civic Association and National Conference on City Planning, and the American Planning and Civic Association. Correspondents include Mrs. Edward W. Biddle, Mira Lloyd Dock, Marie Mattingly Meloney, Mary (Roberts) Rinehart, Mrs. John Davison Rockefeller, Mrs. Franklin D. Roosevelt, Mrs. Russell Tyson, M. Frances Warren, and Julieta Lanteri Renshaw, a physician. See Harry E. Whipkey, comp. and ed., *Guide to the Manuscript Groups in the Pennsylvania State Archives* (Harrisburg, PA: Pennsylvania Historical and Museum Commission, 1976).

14,820. Martin, Edward
Papers. 1866-1967. 120 cu.ft.
Open. Published and unpublished guides.
Pennsylvania State Archives.
Bulk of the papers of Martin (1879-1967), a soldier, lawyer, and politician, relates to his term as governor of Pennsylvania from 1943 to 1947. Correspondents include Genevieve Blatt, Clare Boothe Luce, Mrs. Joseph R. McCarthy, Emma (Guffey) Miller, Mary Sachs, [Mrs.] Mary Worthington Scranton, and Margaret Chase Smith. See Harry E. Whipkey, comp. and ed., *Guide to the Manuscript Groups in the Pennsylvania State Archives* (Harrisburg, PA: Pennsylvania Historical and Museum Commission, 1976).

14,821. Meseroll, Sarah R.
Papers. 1733-1939. 1.5 cu.ft.
Open. Published guide and inventory.
Pennsylvania State Archives.
Papers relating to the Preston family of Bucks County, PA, contain material on family matters, education, women's rights, the Society of Friends, and other topics. Includes information about the education and teaching career of Mary Preston, who probably was the granddaughter of Paul Preston (1724-1806), a surveyor, tax collector, and clerk of the Buckingham Monthly Meeting of Friends. See Harry E. Whipkey, comp. and ed., *Guide to the Manuscript Groups in the Pennsylvania State Archives* (Harrisburg, PA: Pennsylvania Historical and Museum Commission, 1976).

14,822. Nauman, Gertrude Howard (Olmsted)
Papers. 1780-1972. 11 cu.ft.
Open. Published guide and inventory.
Pennsylvania State Archives.
Correspondence, genealogical data, family papers, reports, programs, campaign material, and photos of Nauman (1901-73), a politician, civic leader, and public official who was married to attorney Spencer G. Nauman. Involved in election campaigns for Dwight D. Eisenhower, Richard M. Nixon, Hugh Scott, and other Republicans, Gertrude Nauman also was a member of the Harrisburg Charter Commission, the Mayor's Advisory Council, the State Art Commission, and the national advisory council of the Girl Scouts of America; she also was a founder of the Harrisburg Area Community College. Her correspondents include Nixon, Scott, Milton Eisenhower, William Scranton, and Mr. and Mrs. Edward Martin.

Also contains political papers of her father Marlin E. Olmsted (1847-1913), a Republican congressman, and correspondence with his wife Gertrude (Howard) Olmsted McCormick (1874-1953), who was national vice-president of the Girl Scouts of America and an organizer of the Harrisburg Symphony and the Harrisburg Art Association. Includes her personal accounts and correspondence concerning family matters, the Girl Scouts, the Civic Club of Harrisburg, and the Colonial Dames of America. Among her correspondents are Mrs. Herbert Hoover, J. Horace McFarland, Mrs. Gifford Pinchot, Eleanor Roosevelt, John J. Pershing, and Margaretta "Happy" Rockefeller. See Harry E. Whipkey, comp. and ed., *Guide to the Manuscript Groups in the Pennsylvania State Archives* (Harrisburg, PA: Pennsylvania Historical and Museum Commission, 1976).

14,823. Office of the Governor
Records. 1917-66. 41 cu.ft.
Open. Inventory.
Pennsylvania State Archives.
Includes a one-volume awards book of the Distinguished Daughters of Pennsylvania, 1949-58.

14,824. Orbison Family
Papers. 1750-1902. 7 cu.ft.
Open. Published guide and inventory.
Pennsylvania State Archives.
Business and family papers of William Orbison (1777-1857), a Huntingdon, PA, lawyer, president of the Huntingdon Bank, and founder of the Huntingdon Academy. Includes letters from his sister Isabella (Orbison) Siemmons, correspondence of his wife Eleanor Elliott Orbison with friends and relatives, and related papers of Esther Cox Barton, 1808-41. Collection also contains personal correspondence of his daughter Ellen Matilda (Orbison) Harris (1816-1902), who was secretary of the Philadelphia Ladies' Aid Society, with friends, relatives, and, during the Civil war, with her husband John Harris, a physician who was writing from the battlefront. In addition, her papers also contain records of the Society, which was founded for the relief of soldiers during the war, 1861-65. Includes treasurer's accounts; secretary's reports; correspondence of [Mrs.] Margaret Bonsell, Dorothea Dix, Mrs. Joel Jones, and various surgeons and soldiers; an official statement of the Society; and printed circulars. See Harry E. Whipkey, comp. and ed., *Guide to the Manuscript Groups in the Pennsylvania State Archives* (Harrisburg, PA: Pennsylvania Historical and Museum Commission, 1976).

14,825. Pennsylvania Abortion Law Commission
Records. 1972. 4 cu.ft.
Open. Unpublished guide.
Pennsylvania State Archives.
Reports, testimony, correspondence, a reference file, and other records of the Commission's public hearings in Harrisburg, Philadelphia, Pittsburgh, and Erie, PA.

14,826. Pennsylvania Association of Women Deans and Counselors
Records. 1922-72. 1.5 cu.ft.
Open. Published guide and inventory.
Pennsylvania State Archives.
The Association was founded in 1921 to promote the counseling and administrative work of deans of women in Pennsylvania universities and colleges, state teachers colleges, and high schools. President's notebook, minutes, reports, programs of annual meetings, membership and registration lists, bulletins, and handbooks. See Harry E. Whipkey, comp. and ed., *Guide to the Manuscript Groups in the Pennsylvania State Archives* (Harrisburg, PA: Pennsylvania Historical and Museum Commission, 1976).

14,827. Pennsylvania Dietetic Association
Records. 1932-69. 1 cu.ft.
Open. Published and unpublished guides.
Pennsylvania State Archives.
Bylaws, minutes, reports, programs, bulletins, photos, and other records of this professional organization, the officers and members of which were primarily women. The Association was founded in 1932 to promote nutrition for human beings, advancement of the science of dietetics and nutrition, and education in fields related to dietetics. See Harry E. Whipkey, comp. and ed., *Guide to the Manuscript Groups in the Pennsylvania State Archives* (Harrisburg, PA: Pennsylvania Historical and Museum Commission, 1976).

14,828. Pennsylvania Writers
Collection. 1899-1970. 4 cu.ft.
Open. Published guide and inventory.
Pennsylvania State Archives.
Notes, drafts, and manuscripts of various Pennsylvania authors, composers, and poets, including Margaret Deland, Hildegarde Dolson, Grace (Livingston) Hill, Eunice Loncoske McCloskey, Helen (Reimensnyder) Martin, Katherine Mayo, Lois Miller, Mary (Roberts) Rinehart, Elsie Singmaster, Ida Tarbell, Cassandra Vivan, Neila Gardner White, Margeret Widdemer, and Homer Tope Rosenberger, who wrote *Harriet Lane, 1830-1903.* See Harry E. Whipkey, comp. and ed., *Guide to the Manuscript Groups in the Pennsylvania State Archives* (Harrisburg, PA: Pennsylvania Historical and Museum Commission, 1976).

14,829. Pennypacker, Samuel W.
Papers. 1703-1916. 48 cu.ft.
Open. Published and unpublished guides.
Pennsylvania State Archives.
Papers relating primarily to the term of Pennypacker (1843-1916), an attorney and judge, as governor of Pennsylvania from 1903 to 1907. Contains files on female suffrage, divorce legislation, the registration of graduate nurses, and other topics. Also includes correspondence with [Mrs.] Gertrude Gouverneur (Meredith) Biddle and Mira Lloyd Dock. See Harry E. Whipkey, comp. and ed., *Guide to the Manuscript Groups in the Pennsylvania State Archives* (Harrisburg, PA: Pennsylvania Historical and Museum Commission, 1976).

14,830. Reading Labor Advocate
Records. 1917-58. 1.5 cu.ft.
Open. Published and unpublished guides.
Pennsylvania State Archives.
Correspondence of the *Reading Labor Advocate,* which was the official organ of the Socialist party of Berks County, PA, includes letters pertaining to Sarah Limbach, executive secretary of the Socialist party of Pennsylvania. See Harry E. Whipkey, comp. and ed., *Guide to the Manuscript Groups in the Pennsylvania State Archives* (Harrisburg, PA: Pennsylvania Historical and Museum Commission, 1976).

14,831. Richmond Ladies Soldiers Aid Society
Records. 1861-65. 0.2 cu.ft.
Open. Published guide and inventory.
Pennsylvania State Archives.
Minute book, a report, lists of contributors, and correspondence of Society secretary Sarah E. Morris, who also was associate manager of the Women's Pennsylvania Branch of the US Sanitary Commission. Dorothea Dix was one of her correspondents. The Society was located in Mansfield, PA. See Harry E. Whipkey, comp. and ed., *Guide to the Manuscript Groups in the Pennsylvania State Archives* (Harrisburg, PA: Pennsylvania Historical and Museum Commission, 1976).

14,832. Supreme Court
Records. 1740-1965. 608 cu.ft.
Open. Unpublished guide.
Pennsylvania State Archives.
Court records include divorce papers, 1786-1815, and a divorce docket, 1800-05.

14,833. Swift, Mrs. Elisha D.
Papers. 1790-1917. 0.25 cu.ft.
Open. Published and unpublished guides.
Pennsylvania State Archives.
Collection primarily consists of correspondence of Swift, wife of the pastor of the First Presbyterian Church of Allegheny between 1835 and 1864, about the state of religion and the progress of missionary activity. See Harry E. Whipkey, comp. and ed., *Guide to the Manuscript Groups in the Pennsylvania State Archives* (Harrisburg, PA: Pennsylvania Historical and Museum Commission, 1976).

14,834. Tarnapowicz, Mrs. Francis P.
Papers. 1942-74. 5 folders.
Open. Unpublished guide.
Pennsylvania State Archives.
Correspondence, biographical material, news releases, photos, and clippings of Marie Tarnapowicz of Pittsburgh concern her activities during WWII as chairman of the nationality groups division, Fort Pitt Area, of the War Finance Committee for Pennsylvania.

14,835. Welles Family
Papers. 1805-98. 1.33 cu.ft.
Open. Published guide and inventory.
Pennsylvania State Archives.
Correspondence, accounts, and legal papers of Charles F. Welles (1789-1866), a Wyalusing, PA, farmer and businessman, and of his son George H. Welles of Dushore, PA. Personal correspondence of Charles Welles and his wife Ellen J. Welles with their sons and daughter concern family matters and student life at Vassar College and Princeton University. Also includes correspondence between George Welles and his wife. See Harry E. Whipkey, comp. and ed., *Guide to the Manuscript Groups in the Pennsylvania State Archives*

(Harrisburg, PA: Pennsylvania Historical and Museum Commission, 1976).

HAVERFORD

14,836. Allinson
Papers. 1710-1939. Ca. 2700 items.
Open. Unpublished guide.
Haverford College Library, Quaker Collection.
Collection of correspondence, journals and diaries, poetry, commonplace books, financial papers, scrapbooks, pictures, and silhouettes contains papers of Martha (Cooper) Allinson (1747-1823), Mary Allinson (1768-1859), Sarah Moore Grimké and others, as well as indentures and accounts concerning property owned by Sally Norris Dickinson (1774-1855). Also included are the papers of Rebecca Jones, a Quaker minister, with letters to friends describing her travels and religious experiences, a diary from on board *The Pigou* in 1788, a 1788-89 journal of religious musings, receipt book, almanac, memorandum books, and letterbooks.

14,837. Bettle
Papers. 1824-1911. Ca. 60 items.
Open. Unpublished guide.
Haverford College Library, Quaker Collection.
Journals that Jane (Temple) Bettle (ca. 1774-1840), the wife of Quaker minister Samuel Bettle, kept for 11 years are included with other material.

14,838. Charles Roberts Autograph Letters
Collection. Ca. 1400-1976. 22,000 items.
Open. Unpublished guide.
Haverford College Library, Quaker Collection.
One box and scattered material relates to wives and daughters of Presidents of the US, and to women artists, musicians, poets, novelists, scientists, educators, reformers, and members of European royal families.

14,839. Drinker
Papers. 1777-78. 72 items.
Open. Catalog cards.
Haverford College Library, Quaker Collection.
Diaries, financial documents, and correspondence of Henry Drinker and his wife Elizabeth (Sandwith) Drinker (1734-1807) pertain to life in Philadelphia during the Revolutionary War, including the winter when Elizabeth Drinker served as head of the household because her husband was absent, as well as to the period when Henry Drinker and other Friends were exiles in Winchester, VA.

14,840. Evans, Charles
Papers. Ca. 1681-1860. 750 items.
Open. Unpublished guide.
Haverford College Library, Quaker Collection.
Included with correspondence, memorials, and other papers are letters of Rebecca Jones, a Quaker minister, to Joseph Williams in Dublin concerning her orders and arrangements to pay for goods for her shop, as well as news of various Friends.

14,841. Female Society of Philadelphia for the Relief and Employment of the Poor
Records. 1795-1959. 75 vols.
Open. Unpublished guide.
Haverford College Library, Quaker Collection.
Minutes, treasurer's books, names of pupils, reports, and other records of the Society, founded in 1795.

14,842. Gummere, Amelia (Mott)
Papers. 1884-1937. 5 boxes (ca. 600 items).
Open. Unpublished guide.
Haverford College Library, Quaker Collection.
Correspondence, memoranda, biographical and genealogical sketches, and other material used by Gummere (1859-1937) for her various published writing, including *Journal of John Woolman,* and *The Quaker, a Study in Costume,* and 16 unpublished articles on Quaker and Pennsylvania history.

14,843. Haddon, Estaugh, and Hopkins
Papers. 1676-1841. 277 items.
Open. Unpublished guide.
Haverford College Library, Quaker Collection.
Correspondence and documents relating chiefly to the founding of Haddonfield, NJ, by Elizabeth Haddon, who in 1701 at the age of 19 came to West Jersey to assume control of her father's land; in 1702 she married John Estaugh, a young Quaker minister.

14,844. Hartshorne Family
Papers. 1797-1957. Ca. 3000 items.
Open. Unpublished guide.
Haverford College Library, Quaker Collection.
Included are ca. 50 letters in which Anna Cope Hartshorne (1860-1957) describes her studies at Bryn Mawr College, a trip to Europe, and missionary work in Japan.

14,845. Howland
Papers. 1700-1867. Ca. 1750 items.
Open. Unpublished guide.
Haverford College Library, Quaker Collection.
Correspondence, diaries, spiritual reflections and prophecies, poetry, genealogical notes, ships' logs, and other papers of Gulielma Maria (Hilles) Howland (1822-1907), wife of Charles Howland and daughter of the first superintendent of Haverford School, which became Haverford College. Included are items pertaining to James Logan's voyage to England in 1709 and other Logan family material; letters by Deborah (Norris) Logan; correspondence of Margaret H. Hilles concerning Quaker meetings, schools, travel, and family affairs between 1815 and 1832; letters in which Susanna Dillwyn Emlen describes the social scene in London and Burlington, NJ; and correspondence of Ann Cox and Margaret (Hill) Morris.

14,846. Jones Family
Papers. 1821-1918. 647 items.
Open. Unpublished guide.
Haverford College Library, Quaker Collection.
Papers of Eli and Sybil Jones, Friends ministers and missionaries, and correspondence to Charles and Ellen Jones from their family and friends while they managed the Eli and Sybil Jones Mission in Ramallah, Jerusalem. Correspondence, accounts of travels abroad, poetry, sketches, memorials, photos, maps, and albums.

14,847. Journals and Diaries
Collection. 1683-1954. Ca. 675 vols.
Open. Unpublished guide.
Haverford College Library, Quaker Collection.
Journals, diaries, collections of letters, account books, memorandum books, commonplace books, scrapbooks and other material. Includes the "Revolutionary Journal" of Margaret Hill Morris describing her experiences during the British occupation of Philadelphia, 1776-78; the diary of Sarah Cresson depicting her daily life and travels in the ministry, 1789-1829; the diary of Margaret Ellis detailing travels in the ministry in America and England, 1739-52; the diary of Mary Shackleton Leadbeater portraying her tour through the northern part of England in 1784; the journal kept by Martha Routh on her ocean voyage from London to America in 1794; Journals of Jane Maule, 1866-1939, with vivid recollections of family, Friends, and weather records; and diaries of Sybil Jones for ca. 1840 to 1869. Also included are a letterbook of Sarah Logan Fisher with many details of clothing, furnishings, and other aspects of living in a wealthy Quaker home between 1783 and ca. 1789; a poetry album of Mary Ann Newbold; and a commonplace book of Martha Allinson.

14,848. Lewis Family
Papers. 1853-1960. 207 items.
Open. Unpublished guide.
Haverford College Library, Quaker Collection.
Included are 88 letters in which Alice (Lewis) Pearson, teacher and principal of the Tokyo Friends Girls School, describes her youth in the US and later years in Japan, the fight against prostitution in Japan in 1916, the 1923 earthquake, and conditions during WWII.

14,849. Philadelphia Yearly Meeting, Marriage Council
Records. 1933-65. 2 boxes (315 items).
Open. Unpublished guide.
Haverford College Library, Quaker Collection.
The Council, founded in 1933, is comprised of an advisory board of professional and lay persons qualified by training and experience to counsel those members of the Philadelphia Yearly Meeting who wish advice on matters related to marriage and family life. Education and collection of data are other functions of the Council, which in 1945 became known as the Family Relations Committee. Statements of function and services, reports of the Committee, minutes, accounts, correspondence, speeches, and lists of members.

14,850. Quaker Miscellany
Collection. 1670-1937. 29 ms. boxes.
Open. Unpublished guide.
Haverford College Library, Quaker Collection.
Correspondence, journals and diaries, poems, accounts, wills, deeds, surveyors' maps, and other material. Includes letters in which Sarah Cadbury, writing from Slabtown, VA, in 1866 to her family in Germantown, PA, describes her experiences teaching in a Negro school operated by the Friends Freedmans Association. Also included are letters in which Rachel Scattergood (1832-1903) writes her mother and brother George about daily life at school, home, and while visiting friends.

14,851. Roberts Family
Papers. 1709-1937. 1 box (86 items).
Open. Unpublished guide.
Haverford College Library, Quaker Collection.
Collection of letters, diaries, genealogical material, and legal papers. Includes the diary for 1858 to 1880 in which Elizabeth (Hooton) Roberts describes the four years she and her husband Elisha were in charge of the farmhouse at Westtown School and later years during which they founded the Chalfonte Hotel in Atlantic City, NJ. Also included are a letterbook of Phebe Percival, 1832-33, and diaries and letters of other women in the family.

14,852. Shackleton Family
Papers. 1707-85. 82 items.
Open. Unpublished guide.
Haverford College Library, Quaker Collection.
In her correspondence with such relatives in Ireland and America as the Leadbeaters and Shackletons, Elizabeth (Carleton) Shackleton (1726-1804) mentioned the threat of the Revolutionary War and the departure of J. Woolman for England.

14,853. Sharpless Family
Papers. Ca. 1748-1875. Ca. 400 items.
Open. Unpublished guide.
Haverford College Library, Quaker Collection.
Correspondence, diaries, journals, and religious and biographical accounts, including ca. 200 letters of Mary Kite (1792-1861), a Quaker minister who in her work traveled through Virginia and North Carolina.

14,854. Smith, Edward Wanton
Papers. Ca. 1681-1967. 22 ms. boxes (ca. 3870 items).
Open. Unpublished guide.

Haverford College Library, Quaker Collection.
Correspondence, biographical accounts of Friends, genealogical material, essays, minutes, legal and financial papers, business accounts, deeds, notebooks, maps, pictures, and other papers of Smith's family. Included is a recipe book and 554 letters of Margaret (Hill) Morris (1736-1816) concerning medical and family matters, particularly during the 1793 yellow fever epidemic in Philadelphia. Also included are the diary and letters of Deborah Morris Smith Collins (1760-1822) as well as letters of other women Friends connected with the Smith family.

14,855. Spencer Family
Papers. 1728-1905. 476 items.
Open. Unpublished guide.
Haverford College Library, Quaker Collection.
Primarily family correspondence and commonplace books of Edith Spencer and Rachel Spencer with chief correspondents Rebecca Spencer (1794-1861), Amelia Spencer Jackson (1800s), Lydia Spencer Morris (ca. 1829-1903), and Anna Spencer (ca. 1832-1905). Material concerns most phases, including education at Westtown Boarding School, in the lives of various women in the family.

14,856. Strawbridge Family
Papers. 1776-1898. 17 items.
Open. Unpublished guide.
Haverford College Library, Quaker Collection.
Correspondence, journals, accounts of deceased Friends, and genealogical and other papers. Includes a 1793 will of Deborah Morris, an account book wherein Beulah Morris lists expenses incurred in 1830 assembling her trousseau, and a letter to Beulah M. Hacker from her sister describing a train ride in 1841.

14,857. Taylor Family
Papers. 1755-1930. 3265 items.
Open. Unpublished guide.
Haverford College Library, Quaker Collection.
Travel diaries and correspondence, including letters addressed in the late 1870s to Joseph W. Taylor, a medical doctor, from contractors, civil engineers, educators, and others concerning his preparations to found Bryn Mawr College.

14,858. Women Friends
Records. 1681-?. 1 box.
Open. Unpublished guide.
Haverford College Library, Quaker Collection.
Manuscripts of epistles and minutes of the Women Friends of New England Yearly Meeting beginning in 1843; of the Women Friends of Philadelphia Yearly Meeting beginning in 1861; of the Women Friends of London Yearly Meeting beginning in 1764; and of the Women Friends of Dublin Yearly Meeting beginning in 1809.

IMMACULATA

14,859. Archives
Records. 1840- . Ca. 150 cu.ft. and 3 microfilm reels.
Open. Unpublished guide.
Sisters, Servants of the Immaculate Heart of Mary.
Financial records, correspondence, chronicles, tapes, architectural drawings, photos, slides, scrapbooks, educational reports, and other records of this congregation, which was founded in 1845 in Monroe, MI. Members of the congregation are involved in teaching.

JOHNSTOWN

14,860. Barton, Clara
Papers. 1889-1924. 1 box.
Open. No guide.
Johnstown Flood Museum.
Correspondence and photos of Barton (1821-1912), founder and president of the American National Red Cross, concern Red Cross activities following the Johnstown flood of 1889. Includes letters to Mrs. E. L. Linton; a photo addressed to her husband, who was a prominent Johnstown physician; and letters to B. L. Yeagley, who was acting mayor of Johnstown in 1892.

14,861. Oral History Collection
Oral history. Nd. 20 tapes.
Open. No guide.
Johnstown Flood Museum.
Tapes of interviews with survivors of the Johnstown flood of 1889, including Jessie Canan, Ida Meyer, Amelia Devine, and Daisy Heslop. Also includes interviews with male survivors, who speak about the part women played in events surrounding the flood, and interviews by local high school students of their grandparents and other senior citizens about the role of women in society, current conditions, and other matters.

LANCASTER

14,862. Peart, Caroline
Papers. Ca. 1900. 2 vols.
Open. Catalog card.
Franklin and Marshall College Library.
Books of sketches drawn by Peart (1870-1963), a Philadelphia resident who attended the Academy of Fine Arts.

14,863. Reynolds Family
Papers. 1830-65. 3 ft.
Open. Catalog card.
Franklin and Marshall College Library.
Primarily papers of male members of this Lancaster family, including John Reynolds (?-1853), editor of the *Lancaster Journal,* and his sons William Reynolds (1815-79), an admiral, and John Fulton Reynolds (1820-63), a Union Army general who was killed at the Battle of Gettysburg. Also includes letters that Harriet Lane, niece of President James Buchanan, wrote to Lydia, Catharine, Mary, and Jane Reynolds; an 1849 diary of William Reynolds's wife Rebecca K. Reynolds; a scrapbook Ellie Reynolds compiled about the career of John Fulton Reynolds; clippings on notable Pennsylvania women; and miscellaneous calling cards, obituaries, and memorabilia.

14,864. Müller, Susanna Rohrer
Papers. 1791-1815. 1 vol.
Open. No guide.
Lancaster County Historical Society.
Journal Müller (1756-1815), a midwife, kept in German about babies she delivered in Lancaster County. She recorded the date, number of infants delivered, name of the family, payment for her work, and such family characteristics as "negro," unbeliever, or native German. The journal indicates that Müller delivered 22 sets of twins over the years. In the margins of the journal she added extracts from the Bible and hymns. The journal has been translated by the German American Historical Society in Philadelphia, *German American Annals,* 1, nos. 2 and 3 (Feb. and March 1903).

14,865. Nevin, Blanche
Papers. Ca. 1912-72. 1 folder.
Open. No guide.
Lancaster County Historical Society.
Poetry, family papers, photos, and clippings about the activities of Nevin, a sculptor.

14,866. Union Dorcas Society
Records. 1850-91. 2 vols.
Open. No guide.
Lancaster County Historical Society.
Minutes of this female charitable society contain information about the kinds of donations given to needy women.

14,867. Woman's Humane League
Records. 1917-34. 1 vol.
Open. No guide.
Lancaster County Historical Society.
The League was founded in 1917 to work for the prevention of cruelty to children, aged persons, and animals. Volume of proceedings contains minutes; records of cases the Society handled, with mistreated girls as a category separate from children; membership lists; and accounts.

14,868. Gauger, May S.
Papers. 1901-39. 0.33 cu.ft.
Open. No guide.
Lancaster Mennonite Conference Historical Society.
Papers of Gauger (1892-1949), a Mennonite mission worker, consist of notes on sermons and texts, Sunday school records, and records of the Mennonite Home Mission of Philadelphia, which was later known as the Norris Square Mennonite Church and currently as the Arca de Salvacion, in North Philadelphia.

14,869. Women's Missionary and Service Commission
Records. 1964- . 0.33 cu.ft.
Open. No guide.
Lancaster Mennonite Conference Historical Society.
Files of the *Threads of Truth,* a publication of this Lancaster Mennonite Conference commission, contain information on the Commission's activities, including its coordination of girls' activities, retirement home auxiliaries, literature distribution, sewing circles, nurses' activities, and retreats. Also includes information about Mennonite Central Committee projects for women and about the work of the Homebuilders, a subcommittee of the Women's Missionary and Service Commission that is devoted to home interest programs, to literature distribution to new mothers, and to related projects.

LANGHORNE

14,870. Archives
Records. 1910- . 1 trunk, 1 metal cabinet, and 1 shelf.
Closed. No guide.
Monastery of St. Clare.
Diary, retreat notes, photos, scrapbooks, and clippings of this contemplative Franciscan community, which was founded in Philadelphia in 1910 and moved to Langhorne in 1977.

LEWISBURG

14,871. Edgette, C. De Ette
Papers. 1870-1965. 1 box.
Open. No guide.
Union County Historical Society.
Papers of [Miss] Edgette (1895-1966), a physician and teacher, consist of essays and notes she used for several presentations about the history of medicine in Union County and clippings from local newspapers concerning medicine and physicians.

MEADVILLE

14,872. Tarbell, Ida Minerva
Papers. 1890-1944. Ca. 10,000 items.
Open. Unpublished guide.
Allegheny College Library.
Tarbell (1857-1944) was a journalist and author.

Correspondence, manuscripts of articles and books, and lecture notes. Also included are correspondence and working papers on Abraham Lincoln and miscellaneous material on Tarbell's published works about women.

MEDIA

14,873. Fussell and Lewis Family
Papers. 1830s-1900s. 8 boxes.
Access restricted. No guide.
Mrs. Charles R. Macaulay (Personal Collection).
Family papers include correspondence, a diary, and account books of Esther Fussell Lewis (1782-1848), a teacher and worker with the underground railroad whose husband John Lewis, Jr. (1781-1824), was a descendant of Thomas Lloyd, governor of Pennsylvania in 1684; correspondence and a diary of their daughter Rebecca (Lewis) [Mrs. Edwin] Fussell (1820-93), a temperance and underground railroad worker who was one of the first women to receive a medical education at the Women's Medical College in Philadelphia; genealogical material and other papers of their daughter Grace Anna Lewis (1821-1912), an abolitionist, ornithologist, and scientist whose work was shown at the centennial celebration in Philadelphia; correspondence and a diary of Esther Jane (Trimble) Lippincott (1838-88), an educator who was a niece of Esther Lewis; and material of Lydia Ada Fussell (1837-1900) and Susan Fussell (1832-89), both of whom were nieces of Esther Lewis and were teachers and administrators of schools and other institutions for the mentally retarded in Indiana.

MERION STATION

14,874. Convent Archives
Records. 1861- . 3 rooms.
Open. Unpublished guide.
Sisters of Mercy Convent.
Community files, financial records, correspondence, chapter records, annals, diaries, blueprints, ca. 100 tapes, survey results, pictures, slides, personal effects of Mother Mary Patricia Weldson, scrapbooks, samples of former habits, and memorabilia of church, civic, and community events. This religious order of women was founded in 1861 in Philadelphia.

PHILADELPHIA

14,875. Bache, Anna
Papers. 1833. 1 item.
Open. Published guide.
Academy of Natural Sciences.
A poem about shells, which Bache wrote in Pensacola, FL, had been tipped into Julia Planton's workbook on conchology but was later removed. Taken from Venia T. Phillips and Maurice E. Phillips, *Guide to the Manuscript Collections in The Academy of Natural Sciences* (Philadelphia: The Academy of Natural Sciences, 1963).

14,876. Calvert, Amelia Catherine (Smith)
Papers. 1909-10. 102 items.
Open. Published guide.
Academy of Natural Sciences.
A naturalist and zoologist, Calvert (1876-?) accompanied her husband Philip P. Calvert to Costa Rica in 1909, where she took photos the Calverts used in their book *A Year of Costa Rican Natural History*. Collection consists of photos, which were identified by Adolfo Tonduz, a botanist at the Museo Nacional in San José, and by Henry Francois Pittier. The photos were mounted on individual sheets with typewritten descriptions she wrote. Taken from Venia T. Phillips and Maurice E. Phillips, *Guide to the Manuscript Collections in The Academy of Natural Sciences* (Philadelphia: The Academy of Natural Sciences, 1963).

14,877. Fielde, Adele Marion
Papers. 1884-1919. 48 items.
Open. Published guide.
Academy of Natural Sciences.
Letters of [Miss] Fielde (1839-1916), a naturalist, missionary, lecturer, and suffragist, are primarily to Edward J. Nolan, a former librarian of the Academy of Natural Sciences; they contain information about the natural history of China and about the Academy, of which she was a member. Fielde worked at the Academy as a Jessup student in 1884 before going to work as a missionary in China, where she continued her studies in natural history. Upon returning to this country, Fielde spent summers at the Woods Hole Laboratory and by 1910 was attempting to earn a living as a lecturer in Seattle. Fielde specialized in the study of *Formicidae* and wrote many scientific papers on the subject. Near the end of her life, she became interested in mysticism. Collection also includes letters from Nolan and one from Fielde's friend and, later, biographer Helen N. Stevens of Seattle. Taken from Venia T. Phillips and Maurice E. Phillips, *Guide to the Manuscript Collections in The Academy of Natural Sciences* (Philadelphia: The Academy of Natural Sciences, 1963).

14,878. Lawson, Helen E.
Papers. 1842-57. 64 items.
Open. Published guide.
Academy of Natural Sciences.
Watercolors of shells, an etching, and an engraving of [Miss] Lawson, a natural history artist who was the daughter of Alexander Lawson, a noted Philadelphia engraver. In addition to making many drawings for her father's works, including S. S. Haldeman's *Freshwater Univalve Molluska of the United States* (1842) and Amos Binney's *Terrestrial Air-breathing Mollusks of the United States* (1857), Helen Lawson also hand colored many of her father's finished engravings. Collection also includes a lithograph of the illustration she made of the grounds of Haldeman's home. Taken from Venia T. Phillips and Maurice E. Phillips, *Guide to the Manuscript Collections in The Academy of Natural Sciences* (Philadelphia: The Academy of Natural Sciences, 1963).

14,879. Planton, Julia
Papers. 1920. 62-page vol.
Open. Published guide.
Academy of Natural Sciences.
A conchology workbook containing watercolor drawings, which came to the Academy of Natural Sciences from the estate of [Mrs.] Planton. Taken from Venia T. Phillips and Maurice E. Phillips, *Guide to the Manuscript Collections in The Academy of Natural Sciences* (Philadelphia: The Academy of Natural Sciences, 1963).

14,880. Say, Lucy Way (Sistare)
Papers. 1822-85. 79 items.
Open. Published guide.
Academy of Natural Sciences.
Correspondence, drawings, family papers, clippings, and memorabilia of Say (1800-86), the first woman to be elected a member of the Academy of Natural Sciences, a nature artist, and scientific collaborator with her husband Thomas Say. Includes drawings she made for his work *American Conchology* while they were living at the Owenite community of New Harmony, IN. Taken from Venia T. Phillips and Maurice E. Phillips, *Guide to the Manuscript Collections in The Academy of Natural Sciences* (Philadelphia: The Academy of Natural Sciences, 1963).

14,881. Aitken, Jane
Papers. 1801-14. 147 items.
Open. Published guide and table of contents.
American Philosophical Society.
[Miss] Aitken (1764-1832) was a Philadelphia printer and bookbinder. Correspondence, an inventory, and other papers concerning her printing business. The correspondence is chiefly with John Vaughan about the estate of her father Robert Aitken and her own financial difficulties. Also includes letters about her account with the Philosophical Society. See Whitfield J. Bell, Jr., and Murphy D. Smith, comps., *Guide to the Archives and Manuscript Collections of the American Philosophical Society* (Philadelphia: American Philosophical Society, 1966).

14,882. Andrews, Emma B.
Papers. 1889-1912. 2 vols.
Open. Published guide.
American Philosophical Society.
Journal of [Mrs.] Andrews (?-1922), apparently a trained archaeologist, concerns 17 trips she made up the Nile on archaeological expeditions with her relative Theodore M. David of New York and Newport, RI, who excavated the Valley of the Kings at Thebes. The journal is a daily account of her social and personal life during her travels. See Whitfield J. Bell, Jr., and Murphy D. Smith, comps., *Guide to the Archives and Manuscript Collections of the American Philosophical Society* (Philadelphia: American Philosophical Society, 1966).

14,883. Audubon, John James
Papers. 1821-45. 200 items.
Open. Published guide.
American Philosophical Society.
Correspondence of Audubon (1785-1851), an artist and naturalist, includes many letters he wrote his wife Lucy Bakewell Audubon (?-1874) during his trips to England and around the US. He talks about his work, the area he is visiting, and his desire to have her with him. Also includes correspondence with his son Victor, professional correspondence, papers on ornithology, and some of his publications. See Whitfield J. Bell, Jr., and Murphy D. Smith, comps., *Guide to the Archives and Manuscript Collections of the American Philosophical Society* (Philadelphia: American Philosophical Society, 1966).

14,884. Bache Family
Papers. 1768-1852. Ca. 265 items and 1 microfilm reel.
Open. Published guide.
American Philosophical Society.
Sarah (Franklin) Bache (1743-1808), the daughter of Benjamin Franklin, was a philanthropist who directed sewing and nursing activities in Philadelphia during the Revolutionary War. Her husband Richard Bache (1737-1811) was a Philadelphia merchant, life insurance salesman, and postmaster general between 1776 and 1782. Correspondence with her daughter-in-law Catharine Wistar [Mrs. William] Bache; her son Benjamin Franklin Bache (1769-98), a journalist; and with Mary Stevenson Hewson, Mary Eddy [Mrs. David] Hosack, Judith (Sargent) Murray, and Elizabeth (Graeme) Ferguson. Also includes Catharine Bache's correspondence with Mary Eddy Hosack, [Mrs.] Elizabeth Trist, Mary Jones, and others and Benjamin Bache's correspondence with his parents and his fiancée Margaret H. Markoe. See Whitfield J. Bell, Jr., and Murphy D. Smith, comps., *Guide to the Archives and Manuscript Collections of the American Philosophical Society* (Philadelphia: American Philosophical Society, 1966).

14,885. Bancker, Charles Nicoll
Papers. 1733-1912. Ca. 1000 items.
Open. Published guide and table of contents.

American Philosophical Society.
Papers of Bancker (1778?-1869), a merchant and financier, contain correspondence of female members of his family; wills of family women from 1802 and 1831; a receipt book, 1760-68, for the estate of Mary Alexander, a New York businesswoman; and a constitution for the Philadelphia Society for the Encouragement of Domestic Manufacturers, 1806. Includes letters from Anna de Peyster to [Mrs.] Maria de Peyster Bancker, 1733-34, and correspondence of Anne Taylor Bancker, Sarah N. Bancker, and Violetta T. Bancker Talbot. See Whitfield J. Bell, Jr., and Murphy D. Smith, comps., *Guide to the Archives and Manuscript Collections of the American Philosophical Society* (Philadelphia: American Philosophical Society, 1966).

14,886. Boas, Franz
Papers. 1862-1942. Ca. 10,000 items.
Open. Published guide and table of contents.
American Philosophical Society.
Family and professional correspondence, a diary, notes, and other papers of Boas (1858-1942), an anthropologist. Correspondence with his mother Marie Krackowizer Boas, his sister Helene (Boas) Yampolsky, anthropologist Amelia Louise Susman, and author Ruth (Fulton) Benedict and papers and correspondence with Ella Deloria concerning his work on Dakota Indian word lists. Also includes letters from Ruth Benedict to Margaret Mead concerning Boas's correspondence with Mead and Reo F. Fortune. See Whitfield J. Bell, Jr., and Murphy D. Smith, comps., *Guide to the Archives and Manuscript Collections of the American Philosophical Society* (Philadelphia: American Philosophical Society, 1966).

14,887. Coates, Margaret, and Others
Papers. 1770-73. 1 vol.
Open. Published guide.
American Philosophical Society.
Receipt book of Margaret Coates, Beulah Coates, and Alice Langdale, all of whom were executors of the estate of Mary Coates. See Whitfield J. Bell, Jr., and Murphy D. Smith, comps., *Guide to the Archives and Manuscript Collections of the American Philosophical Society* (Philadelphia: American Philosophical Society, 1966).

14,888. Duane Family
Papers. 1770-1933. Ca. 220 items.
Open. Published guide.
American Philosophical Society.
Papers of this prominent Philadelphia family include correspondence of Deborah (Bache) Duane, wife of lawyer and politician William John Duane (1780-1865) and daughter of Sarah (Franklin) Bache and Richard Bache; correspondence of Mrs. Russell Duane; and a will of Catharine Wistar Bache, 1820. See Whitfield J. Bell, Jr., and Murphy D. Smith, comps., *Guide to the Archives and Manuscript Collections of the American Philosophical Society* (Philadelphia: American Philosophical Society, 1966).

14,889. Flexner, Simon
Papers. 1891-1946. Ca. 200,000 items.
Partially restricted. Published guide and table of contents.
American Philosophical Society.
Papers of Flexner (1863-1946), a physician, pathologist, administrator, and professor at the University of Pennsylvania, contain information on medical science and on the social, cultural, and educational history of the period. Includes correspondence with such scientists and administrators as Anna von der Osten, Helen (Taft) Manning, Cornelia Otis Skinner, and Anna Robeson Burr and correspondence between the Flexner and Thomas families, including M. Carey Thomas, who was the dean and president of Bryn Mawr College and the sister of Flexner's wife Helen (Thomas) Flexner. Also includes college themes, calling cards, and papers on domestic matters by Helen Flexner. See Whitfield J. Bell, Jr., and Murphy D. Smith, comps., *Guide to the Archives and Manuscript Collections of the American Philosophical Society* (Philadelphia: American Philosophical Society, 1966).

14,890. Franklin, Benjamin
Papers. Nd. No size given.
Open. Published guide.
American Philosophical Society.
Papers of Franklin (1706-90), a printer, scientist, politician, diplomat, and philosopher, contain correspondence with his wife Deborah (Read) Franklin (ca. 1707-74), their daughter Sarah (Franklin) Bache, Mary Stevenson Hewson, Jane Mecom, Catharine Ray Greene, and others. See Whitfield J. Bell, Jr., and Murphy D. Smith, comps., *Guide to the Archives and Manuscript Collections of the American Philosophical Society* (Philadelphia: American Philosophical Society, 1966).

14,891. Kane, Elisha Kent
Papers. Nd. Ca. 220 items.
Open. Table of contents.
American Philosophical Society.
Papers of Kane (1820-57), an Arctic explorer, include correspondence with Lady Jane Franklin and Jane Duval (Leiper) Kane. Also includes correspondence of Margaret Fox, a young woman he loved and apparently educated at his own expense; a broadside for a ladies bazaar ball in 1845; and an advertisement for the Young Ladies Institute in Philadelphia.

14,892. LeConte Family
Papers. 1827-1901. 1 box.
Open. Published guide.
American Philosophical Society.
Family papers contain letters from John Lawrence LeConte (1825-83), an entomologist and physician, to [Mrs.] Matilda Jane Harden Stevens. Her other correspondents, writing on family matters, are [Mrs.] Jane LeConte Harden and [Mrs.] Ann LeConte Stevens. See Whitfield J. Bell, Jr., and Murphy D. Smith, comps., *Guide to the Archives and Manuscript Collections of the American Philosophical Society* (Philadelphia: American Philosophical Society, 1966).

14,893. Lesley, J. Peter
Papers. 1826-98. 29 boxes.
Open. Published guide.
American Philosophical Society.
Papers of Lesley (1819-1903), a geologist, and his wife Susan Lyman Lesley, a charity worker in Philadelphia and author of *Recollections of My Mother* (Boston, 1876), contain correspondence on scientific topics, abolition, educational reform, organized charity, and Unitarianism. Susan Lesley's correspondents include Lydia Maria Child, Jessie Perston, Rosa Hopper, Marie Bost, and Sarah Moore Grimké. See Whitfield J. Bell, Jr., and Murphy D. Smith, comps., *Guide to the Archives and Manuscript Collections of the American Philosophical Society* (Philadelphia: American Philosophical Society, 1966).

14,894. Mead, Margaret
Papers. Nd. 1 vol.
Open. Published guide.
American Philosophical Society.
Working draft of a book Ruth Benedict wrote about Mead (1901-1978), an anthropologist, which was published in 1959. Also includes correspondence of Benedict with Mead, Franz Boas, and Reo F. Fortune. See Whitfield J. Bell, Jr., and Murphy D. Smith, comps., *Guide to the Archives and Manuscript Collections of the American Philosophical Society* (Philadelphia: American Philosophical Society, 1966).

14,895. Mitchell, Maria, and Mitchell, William
Papers. Nd. 9 microfilm reels.
Open. Published guide.
American Philosophical Society.
Papers of Maria Mitchell (1818-89) and her father William Mitchell (1791-1869), both of whom were astronomers, include her correspondence with Dorothea Dix, Julia (Ward) Howe, Alexander Bache, Benjamin A. Gould, and others; diaries and accounts of her travels in the South and West, 1854-57, and in Europe, 1857-58; meteorological and astronomical observations and calculations; clippings; material on the woman's rights movement; and William Mitchell's autobiography. Originals of the papers are housed in the Maria Mitchell Science Library. See Whitfield J. Bell, Jr., and Murphy D. Smith, comps., *Guide to the Archives and Manuscript Collections of the American Philosophical Society* (Philadelphia: American Philosophical Society, 1966).

14,896. Montgomery Family
Papers. 1650-1900. 2 boxes.
Open. Published guide.
American Philosophical Society.
Papers of the family of William Montgomerie, a native of Brigend, Scotland, who emigrated to East Jersey in ca. 1701. Includes letters that John Burnet, a merchant of Edinburgh, London, and New York, and John Burnet, Jr., of Perth Amboy, NJ, wrote in 1755 to Elizabeth Forbes, who was their sister and aunt, respectively. See Whitfield J. Bell, Jr., and Murphy D. Smith, comps., *Guide to the Archives and Manuscript Collections of the American Philosophical Society* (Philadelphia: American Philosophical Society, 1966).

14,897. Parsons, Elsie Clews
Papers. 1835-1944. Ca. 77 vols. and 11,865 items.
Open. Published guide.
American Philosophical Society.
[Mrs. Herbert] Parsons (1875-1941) was an anthropologist and folklorist. Correspondence with Ruth Benedict, Franz Boas, Alfred V. Kidder, Leslie A. White, and others; notes and other papers relating to the tales, proverbs, and folklore of the West Indies; riddles, folk tales, and poems from York Village, ME; and manuscripts by Parsons on a Filipino village, sleep, a trip to Greece, and other subjects. Also includes miscellaneous material on birth control and on the Indians of the Southwest and of Central and South America, photos, and paintings of the Isleta pueblo of the Tewa Indians of New Mexico. See Whitfield J. Bell, Jr., and Murphy D. Smith, comps., *Guide to the Archives and Manuscript Collections of the American Philosophical Society* (Philadelphia: American Philosophical Society, 1966).

14,898. Patterson, Thomas Leiper
Papers. 1834-1964. 1 microfilm reel.
Open. Published guide and table of contents.
American Philosophical Society.
Personal and family correspondence of Patterson (1816-1905), a lawyer and engineer, including love letters between him and Louisa Patterson and correspondence of his sister Helen H. Patterson. Also includes notebooks and photos. See Whitfield J. Bell, Jr., and Murphy D. Smith, comps., *Guide to the Archives and Manuscript Collections of the American Philosophical Society* (Philadelphia: American Philosophical Society, 1966).

14,899. Peale, Mary Jane Patterson
Papers. 1844. 1 vol.
Open. Published guide.
American Philosophical Society.
Journal of Peale (1827-1902), a resident of Deer Park, PA, reflects her daily activities sewing, visiting, cooking, and going on outings. See Whitfield J. Bell, Jr., and Murphy D. Smith, comps., *Guide to the Archives and Manuscript Collections of the American Philosophical Society*

(Philadelphia: American Philosophical Society, 1966).

14,900. Sabin, Florence Rena
Papers. 1907-40. 20,000 items.
Open. Published guide.
American Philosophical Society.
Correspondence, notes, writings, research material, publications, and other papers of Sabin (1871-1953), an anatomist and physiologist. Correspondents include Carrie Chapman Catt, Dorothy Child, Women in Science, the Women's Medical Association, the AAUW, and the World Center for Women's Archives, Inc. Her professional correspondence relates to medical research on tuberculosis, cancer, the lymphatic system, and pernicious anemia. Also includes research notes and material she used to write a biography of Franklin Paine Mall in 1934. See Whitfield J. Bell, Jr., and Murphy D. Smith, comps., *Guide to the Archives and Manuscript Collections of the American Philosophical Society* (Philadelphia: American Philosophical Society, 1966).

14,901. Say, Thomas
Papers. 1819-83. Ca. 102 items.
Open. Published guide and table of contents.
American Philosophical Society.
Papers of Say (1787-1834), an entomologist and conchologist, and his wife Lucy Way (Sistare) Say (1800-86), an artist and naturalist, include her correspondence with Arthur F. Gray, unpublished drawings of shells and drawings and plates of shells used in *The Complete Writings of Thomas Say on the Conchology of the United States,* and Lucy Say's refutation of George Ord's memoir of her husband. See Whitfield J. Bell, Jr., and Murphy D. Smith, comps., *Guide to the Archives and Manuscript Collections of the American Philosophical Society* (Philadelphia: American Philosophical Society, 1966).

14,902. Sellers Family
Papers. 1675-1928. 6 vols. and ca. 1500 items.
Open. Published guide.
American Philosophical Society.
Correspondence of such Peale and Sellers family members as engineer Coleman Sellers (1781-1834), his wife Sophonisba Augusciola Peale Sellers (1786-1859), Ann Sellers (1785-?), Anna Sellers (1824-1908), Hannah Sellers, [Mrs.] Cornelia Wells Sellers (1831-1909), and [Mrs.] Elizabeth Coleman Sellers (1751-1832) on travel, household expenses, children, and social and cultural life in Philadelphia. Also includes account books of sums that Sophonisba Sellers's sons Charles and George Escol Sellers gave to her, 1834-36; a book of receipts for taxes, rents, groceries, interest, and other items relating to her administration of the estate of Coleman Sellers, 1834-35; and her record of expenses incurred while she was keeping house for her son-in-law Alfred Harrold, including wages, carriage fares, groceries, and "children's board," 1840-45. Collection also contains diaries in which Ann Sellers describes her trips from Philadelphia to the Catskill Mountains in 1828 and another to the Pocono Mountains and the Susquehanna River in 1830 and a diary in which Anna Sellers describes her life in Chattanooga, TN, visiting relatives and living in a boardinghouse, 1902-03. See Whitfield J. Bell, Jr., and Murphy D. Smith, comps., *Guide to the Archives and Manuscript Collections of the American Philosophical Society* (Philadelphia: American Philosophical Society, 1966).

14,903. Simpson, George Gaylord
Papers. 1918-62. 261 items.
Open. Published guide.
American Philosophical Society.
Letters in which Simpson (1902-), a paleontologist, tells his sister [Mrs.] Martha Lee (Simpson) Eastlake of his travels and experiences on scientific expeditions to New Mexico, Arizona, Argentina, and Chile. The letters also contain information on personal matters. See Whitfield J. Bell, Jr., and Murphy D. Smith, comps., *Guide to the Archives and Manuscript Collections of the American Philosophical Society* (Philadelphia: American Philosophical Society, 1966).

14,904. Vaughan, Benjamin
Papers. 1746-1900. 43 boxes.
Open. Published guide.
American Philosophical Society.
Papers of Vaughan (1751-1835), a diplomat, political economist, and agriculturist, contain correspondence of his mother Sarah Hallowell Vaughan (ca. 1727-?) and his wife Sarah Manning Vaughan (1754-1834) on the education of children, travel, social life, illnesses, and other family matters. Also includes letters to the Vaughan women from female friends and estate papers of Sarah Hallowell Vaughan, 1819. See Whitfield J. Bell, Jr., and Murphy D. Smith, comps., *Guide to the Archives and Manuscript Collections of the American Philosophical Society* (Philadelphia: American Philosophical Society, 1966).

14,905. Bremer, Fredrika
Papers. 1801-65. No size given.
Access restricted. No guide.
American Swedish Historical Museum.
Papers of Bremer (1801-65), a Swedish novelist and advocate of women's rights who traveled in the US from 1849 to 1851, are written primarily in Swedish and include correspondence, notes, the manuscript of Bremer's novel *Hertha,* photos, books, and artifacts. Her writings contain her views on the rights of women, education, and America.

14,906. Lind, Jenny
Papers. 1820-87. Ca. 170 items.
Access restricted. No guide.
American Swedish Historical Museum.
Correspondence, notes, photos and lithographs, sheet music of songs and arias, and memorabilia of Lind (1820-87), a Swedish singer who toured in the US.

14,907. Atiyeh, Wadeeha
Papers. 1931-72. 1 Hollinger box and other items.
Open. Unpublished guide.
Balch Institute.
Correspondence, writings, scripts and music from productions, programs, publicity announcements, reviews, photos, miscellaneous items, and published works of Atiyeh (1903-73), a Lebanese singer, dancer, actress, writer, and storyteller who came to the US as a child. After studying voice with Ruth Julia Hall, Atiyeh made her professional singing debut in Chicago in 1932; soon she added traditional dances and storytelling to her program, wrote her own scripts, adapted traditional lyrics and music to suit her routine, and designed her own costumes. Atiyeh also wrote autobiographical short stories, rewrote in English several traditional Middle Eastern tales, and compiled a Middle Eastern cookbook *Scheherezade Cooks!*

14,908. Bender, Rose I. (Magil)
Papers. 1929-46. 3 Hollinger boxes.
Open. Unpublished guide.
Balch Institute.
Correspondence, clippings, and miscellaneous items of Bender (1895-1964), daughter of Lithuanian immigrants and pioneer Zionists Joseph and Rachel Magil. Bender began her work for Zionism at an early age: while still in high school, she organized the club that developed into the first Young Judea club in the US. She joined Hadassah and was active in the group for many years; then, in 1945, she became executive director of the Philadelphia Zionist Organization of America, the only woman to hold such a high position in the organization at that time. Her papers relate to her activities in Hadassah, the Zionist Organization of America, the Allied Jewish Appeal, and such other Jewish concerns as the National Jewish Hospital, the American Palestine Music Association, and the Palestine Pavilion of the 1939 World's Fair in New York. Also includes notes and souvenirs of her attendance at Zionist congresses and other conventions.

14,909. Boyko, Anna Kobryn
Papers. 1910-73. 1 Hollinger box.
Open. Unpublished guide.
Balch Institute.
Papers of [Mrs.] Boyko (1889-1973), a Ukrainian immigrant who was instrumental in the establishment of the Protection of the Blessed Virgin Mary Ukrainian Catholic Church in Philadelphia, are mostly in Ukrainian. Includes correspondence, diaries, miscellaneous writings, an autobiography, tributes, obituaries, clippings, and other items. Boyko was also active in the Providence Association of Ukrainian Catholics in America, a fraternal insurance and benefit society, and she founded Daughters of Ukraine, a branch of the Ukrainian Women's Organization. Her diaries, 1910-64, contain short daily entries, essays on the founding of her parish, reminiscences of her childhood and early years in the US, accounts of church activities, minutes, and summaries of speeches delivered at meetings of church groups. A supporter of the Democratic party, she also wrote about the elections of Presidents Truman and Kennedy. Also includes a journal of the Council of Ukrainian Women in America and a short history of the Protection of the Blessed Virgin Church. Boyko married in 1907 and in 1913 immigrated with her daughter to America, where she joined her husband who had immigrated three years earlier.

14,910. Hintz Family
Papers. 1792-1894. 2 folders.
Open. Unpublished guide.
Balch Institute.
Bulk of the collection consists of correspondence between Friedrich Hintz, a carpenter who emigrated from Germany to the US in 1853, and his wife Maria, who with their three daughters joined him in Massachusetts in 1856. Their correspondence, most of which is written in German, concerns the problems he encountered in America. Also includes correspondence with Maria Hintz's sister and her family, who also immigrated to the US, and correspondence with relatives and friends in Europe; a few business letters; poems; an 1859 deed issued to Friedrich Hinz by the German Land Association of Minnesota for land in New Ulm; passports; birth, marriage, and baptismal certificates; greeting cards; clippings; and miscellaneous items. The family name is spelled variously Hintz or Hinz.

14,911. College Archives
Records. 1924- . 10 shelves.
Access restricted. No guide.
Chestnut Hill College Archives.
Chestnut Hill College was founded in 1924 by the Sisters of St. Joseph. Correspondence, College catalogs, admissions brochures, programs of College activities, alumnae bulletins and news sheets, scrapbooks, photos, and such student publications as the literary magazine, the College newspaper, yearbooks, and student teacher bulletins. Also includes material concerning the Sisters of St. Joseph, who came to the Chestnut Hill area during the 1840s.

14,912. Board and Bureau of Health (RG 76)
Records. 1855-1919. No size given.
Open. Published guide.
City Archives of Philadelphia.
Records include a nurses' register, 1896-98 (1 vol.), which gives the nurse's name, date of registration, and residence. Also included are marriage registers and returns, 1860-85 (30 cu.ft. and 23 vols.), which give date of marriage and registration; name, age,

race, place of birth and residence, and occupation; type of ceremony; and name of person performing the ceremony. See John Daly, *Descriptive Inventory of the Archives of the City and County of Philadelphia* (Philadelphia, PA, 1970).

14,913. Bureau of Charities (RG 65)
Records. Nd. No size given.
Open. Published guide.
City Archives of Philadelphia.
Contained in the records of the Bureau, which was formed in 1887 and became the Bureau of Charities and Correction in 1920, are Alms House hospital (later Philadelphia General Hospital) records, among them a record of admissions to the women's medical ward, 1894-98 (2 vols.), giving name, age, birthplace, habits, marital status, diagnosis, and treatment; a register for the women's eye ward, 1897-1905 (1 vol.), giving name, age, birthplace, habits, marital status, diagnosis, discharge, and remarks. Also includes a female register of admissions to the Alms House, 1888-1921 (13 vols.), giving date, name, race, age, birthplace, place of legal residence, occupation, marital status, and ward assigned; number of times admitted, with date of last previous admission and discharge or escape; date discharged, died, or escaped; and remarks, which often are the names and addresses of those to be notified concerning inmates. See John Daly, *Descriptive Inventory of the Archives of the City and County of Philadelphia* (Philadelphia, PA, 1970).

14,914. Clerk of the Court of Quarter Sessions and Oyer and Terminer (RG 21)
Records. Nd. No size given.
Open. Published guide.
City Archives of Philadelphia.
Records of the office of the Clerk, which was founded in 1682, include the domestic relations docket, 1922-38 (24 vols.), listing defendant, petition number and date, cause of action, and the ruling which often concerned child custody awards and support payments. Also contains municipal court support orders, 1911-13 (3 cu.ft.), with transcripts of the magistrate's hearing at which the charge was made; the transcripts list complainant, defendant, addresses, charge, bondsman, and witnesses. These records also contain a summary of the proceedings listing in detail the conditions, terms, and support payments to be made. The desertion docket, 1865-1914 (23 vols.), lists defendant, charge, judge's name, decision, date, terms of support ordered, and often the names of the wife and children. A miscellaneous desertion docket, 1879-1913 (8 vols.), lists defendants, judge, dates, and actions taken; the actions normally enforce support orders. See John Daly, *Descriptive Inventory of the Archives of the City and County of Philadelphia* (Philadelphia, PA, 1970).

14,915. Department of Public Health: Bureau of Hospitals (RG 80)
Records. Nd. No size given.
Open. Published guide.
City Archives of Philadelphia.
The Department was created in 1919 to succeed the Department of Public Health and Charities. Its records include a register of female patients at Pennsylvania General Hospital, 1921-46 (19 vols.), which gives the name, admission date, race, age, number of times admitted, dates of last former admission and discharge, birthplace, legal residence, date and manner of discharge or death, occupation, marital status, ward assigned, and remarks, which usually were the name and address of a relative or person to be notified concerning the patient. Beginning in 1934, the patient's religion and detainer notice by police or penal institutions are added. See John Daly, *Descriptive Inventory of the Archives of the City and County of Philadelphia* (Philadelphia, PA, 1970).

14,916. Guardians of the Poor (RG 35)
Records. Nd. No size given.
Open. Published guide.
City Archives of Philadelphia.
The Guardians of the Poor was established in 1788 and abolished in 1887 when its functions were transferred to the Bureau of Charities for the city of Philadelphia; the Guardians served Philadelphia and adjacent urbanized areas of the county. Includes extensive records of the Alms House and Alms House Hospital, including the Hospital receiving register, which covers portions of the 19th century; the female register, 1803-88; the women's receiving ward register, 1838-87; case records, 1815-86, including those of the nervous ward for 1883 to 1886; and the register of births, 1808-85. Alms House records include treasurer's ledgers, 1789-1887; minutes of the committee on support cases and collections, 1843-73; records of cases referred to the committee on bastardy, 1822-25; records of bonds for support of illegitimate children, 1853-58; a prostitutes' register, 1863; and a female vagrant register, 1874-77. See John Daly, *Descriptive Inventory of the Archives of the City and County of Philadelphia* (Philadelphia, PA, 1970).

14,917. House of Correction (RG 39)
Records. Nd. No size given.
Open. No guide.
City Archives of Philadelphia.
Includes a description docket, 1874-75 (1 vol.), giving name, age, race, sex, birthplace, physical description, education, marital status, occupation, charge, and remarks. See John Daly, *Descriptive Inventory of the Archives of the City and County of Philadelphia* (Philadelphia, PA, 1970).

14,918. Inspectors of the Jail and Penitentiary House: Inspectors of County Prisons (RG 38)
Records. Nd. No size given.
Open. Published guide.
City Archives of Philadelphia.
Records of the Inspectors, known from 1789 through 1835 as Inspectors of the Jail and Penitentiary House and from 1835 through 1951 as Inspectors of County Prisons, are primarily for the 19th century but also contain 20th-century prison records. Includes, for example, a female convicts docket, 1838-91 (3 vols.), with the prisoner's name, race, crime, sentence, and date of discharge; a petty criminal calendar, 1867-1900 (2 vols.), with the prisoner's name, race, crime, sentence, and date of discharge; a description docket for females, 1889-1917 (6 vols.), with the prisoner's name, age, physical description, birthplace, parental information, education, occupation, habits (such as intemperance), marital status, sentence, number of convictions, and date of discharge; matron's daily reports, 1929-32 (1 vol.), listing prisoner's illness, physician's treatments, and visitors; a prison births record, 1858-79 (1 vol.), giving the mother's name and the date of child's birth and its race and sex; a commutation docket for females, 1890-1951 (7 vols.), giving monthly listings of commutations with the prisoner's name, number, sentence, date, date of expiration of sentence by commutation, and discharge; a record of foreign-born female convicts, 1897-1905 (1 vol.), giving name, birthplace, whether an adult or minor, the number of years a resident, and state of residency; and a prison diary for the female department, 1850-1935 (6 vols.), which records punishments, prisoners received and discharged, and visits by inspectors. See John Daly, *Descriptive Inventory of the Archives of the City and County of Philadelphia* (Philadelphia, PA, 1970).

14,919. Office of the Mayor (RG 60)
Records. Nd. No size given.
Open. No guide.
City Archives of Philadelphia.
Includes the 1882 census of manufactures of Philadelphia (1 vol.) listing the types of manufactured products, names of firms, and numbers of women employed by entire trades. See John Daly, *Descriptive Inventory of the Archives of the City and County of Philadelphia* (Philadelphia, PA, 1970).

14,920. Private Associations (RG 226)
Records. Nd. No size given.
Open. Published guide.
City Archives of Philadelphia.
Included in the records of private associations are reports of the Pennsylvania Economy League-Bureau of Municipal Research, 1911-65 (48 vols.), including a 1933 report on unmarried mothers in municipal court. See John Daly, *Descriptive Inventory of the Archives of the City and County of Philadelphia* (Philadelphia, PA, 1970).

14,921. Prothonotary of the Court of Common Pleas (RG 20)
Records. Nd. No size given.
Open. Published guide.
City Archives of Philadelphia.
Records of the Prothonotary, which was founded in 1707 and which served what became the county of Philadelphia. Includes a midwife register for 1920 to 1934 (1 vol.), listing the midwife's name, birthplace, residence, and date of Pennsylvania certification as a midwife. Register entries are followed by the midwife's deposition to the truth of the facts, her signature, and the date of registry. Also contains the divorce docket for 1851 to 1874 (13 vols.), giving the names of the parties and their attorneys, a summary of the legal steps involved, and the final decree. See John Daly, *Descriptive Inventory of the Archives of the City and County of Philadelphia* (Philadelphia, PA, 1970).

14,922. Recorder of Deeds (RG 5)
Records. Nd. No size given.
Open. Published guide.
City Archives of Philadelphia.
The office of Recorder of Deeds was established in 1682 and abolished in 1951 when its functions were transferred to the Department of Records. Included among its records are femme sole petitions, 1878-1913 (2 vols.), listing the name of petitioner, address, husband's name, and the date of and purpose for petition. Also included are letters of attorney, 1791-1863 (31 vols.), listing the parties, their occupations and general places of residence, dates of making and recordings, and the specific function for which the power of attorney was granted. Femme sole petitions enable women to act independently of their husbands in business or trade. See John Daly, *Descriptive Inventory of the Archives of the City and County of Philadelphia* (Philadelphia, PA, 1970).

14,923. Sesquicentennial Exhibition Association (RG 232)
Records. 1920s. No size given.
Open. Published guide.
City Archives of Philadelphia.
Association records include papers and correspondence of the women's executive committee, correspondence concerning the women's department, and publications of the committee on historic areas in Philadelphia. See John Daly, *Descriptive Inventory of the Archives of the City and County of Philadelphia* (Philadelphia, PA, 1970).

14,924. United States Centennial Commission (RG 230)
Records. 1870s. No size given.
Open. Published guide.
City Archives of Philadelphia.
Contained in Commission records are annual reports of the women's centennial executive committee, 1875-77 (3 vols.), which include bylaws, published reports, and brief minutes. One

of the reports deals with charities conducted by women during the centennial celebration. See John Daly, *Descriptive Inventory of the Archives of the City and County of Philadelphia* (Philadelphia, PA, 1970).

14,925. Macfarlane, Catharine
Papers. Nd. 1 box.
Open. No guide.
College of Physicians of Philadelphia, Library.
Unpublished autobiography of Macfarlane (1877-1969), a physician.

14,926. Mudd, Emily Hartshorne
Oral history. 1974. 1 vol.
Open. No guide.
College of Physicians of Philadelphia, Library.
Interviews with Mudd (1898-), a physician, the originals of which are housed in the Schlesinger Library.

14,927. Sturgis, Katharine Rosenbaum Guest Boucot
Papers. Nd. 2 boxes.
Open. No guide.
College of Physicians of Philadelphia, Library.
Correspondence, diplomas, certificates, and other papers of Sturgis (1903-), a physician.

14,928. Sturgis, Margaret Castex
Papers. 1940-46. 2 vols.
Open. No guide.
College of Physicians of Philadelphia, Library.
Accounts of the patients of Sturgis (1885-1962), a physician.

14,929. Drexel Women's Club
Records. 1927-64. 4 ft.
Open. Unpublished guide.
Drexel University Libraries.
Financial records, files, and publications of this social organization of women members of the Drexel faculty and staff and wives of faculty members, founded in 1927. During WWII the Club was active keeping track of Drexel students and graduates in the armed services.

14,930. Graduate School of Library and Information Science
Records. 1892- . 4 ft.
Open. Unpublished guide.
Drexel University Libraries.
Annual reports, minutes of faculty meetings, alumni records, examinations, notebooks, and scrapbooks of one of the earliest library schools in the US. The School was opened in 1892 to train librarians; it closed in 1914 but was reopened in 1922.

14,931. Pennsylvania Library Club
Records. 1901-38. 1 ft.
Open. No guide.
Drexel University Libraries.
This association for Philadelphia area librarians was founded in 1891. Correspondence and records of [Mrs.] Martha Coplin Leister, Club secretary, primarily concern Club meetings.

14,932. Bureau of the Census (RG 29)
Records. 1790-1965. 8434 cu.ft. and 8564 microfilm reels.
Partially restricted. Unpublished guide.
Federal Archives and Records Center, Philadelphia Archives Branch.
The Bureau of the Census was established in 1790 to provide basic statistics about the people and economy of the nation in order to assist Congress, the Government, and the public in planning, implementing, and evaluating programs. Women were enumerated by name in all censuses from 1850 on; from 1790 to 1840 they were mentioned by name only if they were the heads of families. The later censuses give name, address, age, sex, and color; some provided information on occupation, place of birth of person and his or her parents, marital status, school attendance, and other items. Includes a soundex (phonetic) index to the 1880 census of Delaware. The microfilm reels are of census schedules for all states from 1790 to 1900.

14,933. Immigration and Naturalization Service (RG 85)
Records. 1787-1954. 1746 cu.ft. and 568 reels.
Partially restricted. Unpublished guide.
Federal Archives and Records Center, Philadelphia Archives Branch.
The Service, which was established in 1882, administers laws relating to admission, exclusion, deportation, and naturalization of aliens and investigates alleged violations of those laws; patrols US borders to prevent unlawful entry of aliens; and supervises naturalization work in designated courts and provides services that prepare candidates for naturalization. Includes departure records, 1907-53; Chinese cases, 1895-1923; aliens' applications to leave the US; and other administrative records (totaling more than 100 cu.ft.) for Philadelphia. Also contains on microfilm ships' passenger lists for Philadelphia, 1883-1945, which are restricted for 50 years; an index to Philadelphia, 1800-1906; a federal index for Baltimore, 1828-97; and a city index for Baltimore, 1833-66.

14,934. Internal Revenue Service (RG 58)
Records. 1791-1940. 2284 cu.ft. and 24 microfilm reels.
Open. Unpublished shelf list.
Federal Archives and Records Center, Philadelphia Archives Branch.
The IRS was established in 1791 to collect internal revenue taxes; it helped finance the Civil War, collected direct taxes from southern states, collected taxes on liquor and tobacco, and performed other revenue functions. Includes assessment lists (125 cu.ft.), 1874-1917, for Philadelphia, Pittsburgh, and Scranton, PA, and for Camden, NJ. Women appear on the assessment lists.

14,935. National Park Service (RG 79)
Records. 1785-1966. 3055 cu.ft.
Open. Unpublished shelf list.
Federal Archives and Records Center, Philadelphia Archives Branch.
Established in 1872, the Park Service promotes and regulates use of national parks, monuments, and similar areas in order to conserve scenery, natural and historical objects, and wildlife for the benefit of future generations. Consists of region 5 records, including correspondence and building reports providing information about women. The Dolley Todd Madison House, which is located in the region, is one of the buildings administered by the Service.

14,936. Office of Economic Opportunity (RG 381)
Records. 1964-72. 343 cu.ft.
Open. No guide.
Federal Archives and Records Center, Philadelphia Archives Branch.
The Office was established by the Economic Opportunity Act of 1964, which provided for a variety of programs to eliminate poverty "by opening to everyone the opportunity to live in decency and dignity." Includes community profiles reports (1 cu.ft.), 1967, which are termed "profiles of the poor" and which describe the population and geographic, social, and economic characteristics of each county and independent city in Pennsylvania and Delaware.

14,937. United States Courts of Appeals (RG 276)
Records. 1891-1951. 8087 cu.ft.
Open. Unpublished shelf list.
Federal Archives and Records Center, Philadelphia Archives Branch.
The Courts of Appeals are intermediate courts created by an act of 1891 to relieve the Supreme Court of considering appeals in cases originally decided by federal trial courts. Case files (2637 ft.), 1891-1951, many of which concern women, contain record copies of briefs of parties to the proceedings, with any supplements or appendices, and opinions of the Court.

14,938. United States District Courts (RG 21)
Records. 1789-1955. 89,929 cu.ft.
Open. Published guide and unpublished shelf list.
Federal Archives and Records Center, Philadelphia Archives Branch.
Circuit and district courts were created by the Judiciary Act of 1789, which gave them original jurisdiction in cases involving crimes, remedies of common law, and aliens suing for a tort. The circuit courts were abolished in 1911 and their jurisdiction was transferred to the district courts. Contains information on women scattered through equity, law, criminal, civil, admiralty, and bankruptcy cases. Includes naturalization records. See *Preliminary Inventory to Records of the U.S. District Court for the Eastern District of Pennsylvania, No. 124* (National Archives and Records Service, 1960).

14,939. Wage and Hour and Public Contracts Division (RG 155)
Records. 1938-52. 512 cu.ft.
Partially restricted. Unpublished shelf list.
Federal Archives and Records Center, Philadelphia Archives Branch.
The Division was established in 1938 to administer the wage and hour provisions of the 1938 Fair Labor Standards Act, which established minimum wage, overtime compensation, equal pay, and child labor standards for persons employed in interstate or foreign commerce and for certain other activities. Includes case files (64 cu.ft.), 1948-60, covering investigation of establishments for compliance with the Act. The cases, which provide information about women workers, are restricted until 30 years after the closing of the case.

14,940. Committee on Exhibitions
Records. 1824-1900. 14 ft.
Open. Unpublished guide.
The Franklin Institute.
To encourage artisans and manufacturers, The Franklin Institute sponsored exhibitions such as the International Electrical Exhibition in 1884, at which new inventions and processes were judged on their importance. Women were exhibitors of products and by 1854 were also serving as judges. The judges' reports may include opinions on the quality of work performed by women exhibitors lacking formal training and may contain suggestions that certain inventions were desirable because they could be used by females.

14,941. Committee on Instruction
Records. 1824-1923. 10 ft. and 16 vols.
Open. Unpublished guide.
The Franklin Institute.
The Committee on Instruction was responsible for The Franklin Institute's instruction program, which evolved from lecture series into formal schools. Institute lecture attendance reports, many of which cite the number of women attending. Beginning in the 1840s, women were accepted as students for the lecture series and the Drawing School, which was renamed the School of Mechanic Arts in 1910 to reflect the expansion of its curriculum from mechanical drawing and machine design to more technical kinds of engineering such as naval architecture and marine engine design. Between 1850 and 1853, at the urging of [Mrs.] Sarah Peters, the Institute developed the School of Design for Women, a predecessor of the Moore College of Art.

14,942. Committee on Science and the Arts
Records. 1824-1900. 75 ft.
Open. Published guide.
The Franklin Institute.
The Committee examined inventions and improvements in processes and equipment submitted to The Franklin Institute by the entrepreneurial community and, in addition, served as an advisory board for local, state, and federal government. Less than one percent of the case files show women as inventors, applicants, or members of the reviewing committee. Other reports prepared on items such as sewing machines reflect attitudes about women and women workers with comments on new machines which "children and Females" can operate or which ease "the burden of the fairer sex." Some advertisements may also be included. See *Technology in Industrial America: A Guide to the Records of the Committee on Science and the Arts* (Wilmington, DE: Scholarly Resources, Inc., 1977).

14,943. Scott, Julian P.
Papers. 1920-38. 2500 negatives.
Open. Unpublished guide.
The Franklin Institute.
At the Woods Hole Laboratory in Massachusetts, Scott photographed men and women scientists, including biochemist Ethel Ronzoni of the Washington University of St. Louis, anatomist Alice Brown of the Cornell Medical School, bacteriologist Julia Morgan Coffey of the New York state health department, zoologist Mildred Groscurth of the University of Oklahoma, public health physician Mary Greig of the American Museum of Natural History, and entomologist Elisabeth Skwarra of the education administration of Berlin, Germany.

14,944. Morris, Margaretta Hare
Papers. 1795-1915. 1 box.
Open. No guide.
Germantown Historical Society Library.
Scientific studies, articles, clippings, and other papers of [Miss] Margaretta Morris (1797-1867) and her sister [Miss] Elizabeth Carrington Morris (1775-1865), both of whom were botanists. Includes papers on insects that Margaretta Morris read before the American Philosophical Society and the Academy of Natural Sciences and clippings about her family's history. Particularly known for her work on the Hessian fly and locusts, Margaretta Morris was the second woman to be elected to the Academy.

14,945. Account Books
Collection. 1734-1936. 150 vols.
Open. Published guide.
Historical Society of Pennsylvania.
Business records and personal accounts of merchants, shopkeepers, real estate brokers, attorneys, innkeepers, and publishers include a receipt book, 1856-1920, and personal accounts and a ledger, 1873-90, of Mrs. E. C. Black and the Misses Black of Bryn Mawr, PA; personal receipt books of Mary Coates of Philadelphia, 1760-70; a cashbook and medicinal recipes of Mrs. Daniel W. Coxe, 1817-32; and a memorandum book of cases of a midwife, Mrs. Joseph Sarber of the Philadelphia area, 1814-31. See *Guide to the Manuscript Collections of the Historical Society of Pennsylvania,* 2nd ed. (Philadelphia: Historical Society of Pennsylvania, 1949).

14,946. Aero Club of Philadelphia
Records. 1908-53. 8 vols. and 300 items.
Open. Inventory.
Historical Society of Pennsylvania.
Established in 1908 and disbanded in 1953, the Philadelphia organization was the oldest Aero Club in continuous existence in the US; this social club of flying enthusiasts of any age, dedicated to promoting aeronautics and aviation, included women as board officers and equal members. Minutes, daily office reports for 1930 to 1932, correspondence, Club histories, speeches, notices, pamphlets, and scrapbooks. Included are clippings about the travels of Amelia Earhart; the 35 women members of the Club; the Betsey Ross Club, a group of women that owned and operated an airport for the exclusive use of women; Ruth Nichols, the first woman transport pilot in Pennsylvania; Myrtle Brown and Sylvia Nelson, the first female commercial pilots in the state; and [Miss] Eleanor Smith, who at the time was the world's record holder for flying altitude.

14,947. The Antediluvian, or, the Infants' Clothing Association
Records. 1813-1957. 50 items.
Open. Unpublished guide.
Historical Society of Pennsylvania.
Records of this women's charitable organization, which was founded in 1814, consist of a constitution, annual reports for the period 1901-41, minutes and cash and account books for most of the period, rules from 1826, scattered lists of members for 1881 to 1950, histories of the Association, and letters from 1813 to 1857 thanking the group for donations. The group was known both as the Antediluvian and as the Infants' Clothing Association.

14,948. Apprentices Library
Records. 1813-1945. 7 boxes and 23 vols.
Open. Published guide.
Historical Society of Pennsylvania.
Minute books, a record book for 1820 and 1821, cash ledgers for 1925 to 1935, book plates, and other business records of the first free circulating library in America, established in 1820. Includes minutes of the committee for a girls library, 1842-47; minutes of the board of managers and of the library committee for most of the period; minutes of the committee on attendance, 1830; and correspondence. See *Guide to the Manuscript Collections of the Historical Society of Pennsylvania,* 2nd ed. (Philadelphia: Historical Society of Pennsylvania, 1949).

14,949. Archambault, Anna Margaretta
Papers. 1876-1945. 3000 items.
Open. Published guide.
Historical Society of Pennsylvania.
Personal correspondence of Archambault, a portrait painter, miniaturist, author, and principal of the Seminary for Young Ladies and Children in ca. 1876, is included with sketches, photos, and correspondence concerning her work in miniatures. Also included are notes on *Guide Book of Art, Architecture, and Historic Interests in Pennsylvania* (Philadelphia, 1924), which was edited by Archambault and compiled by the art committee of the State Federation of Pennsylvania Women; histories of all the counties in Pennsylvania, written by various historians; a history of Philadelphia; and illustrations to accompany the histories. See *Guide to the Manuscript Collections of the Historical Society of Pennsylvania,* 2nd ed. (Philadelphia: Historical Society of Pennsylvania, 1949).

14,950. Armstrong, Emma Dean (Walker)
Papers. 1878. 3 vols.
Open. Published guide.
Historical Society of Pennsylvania.
Diaries of Armstrong (?-1878) of Hampton, VA, the wife of General S. C. Armstrong, contain her reminiscences as well as biographical sketches of her which were gathered for her daughters Louise and Edith Armstrong by their friend Mary Anna Longstreth. The diaries include many comments on Emma Armstrong's long illness and death. See *Guide to the Manuscript Collections of the Historical Society of Pennsylvania,* 2nd ed. (Philadelphia: Historical Society of Pennsylvania, 1949).

14,951. Ashton, Robert, and Roberts, Margaret (Ashton)
Papers. 1791-1841. 1 vol.
Open. Published guide.
Historical Society of Pennsylvania.
Family papers of Ashton (1726-1816), who probably was a farmer, and of his daughter Margaret Roberts (1761-1850) include Roberts's commonplace book for 1791 to 1841 containing genealogical notes, her certificate of marriage in 1791 to Nathan Roberts, and religious poems she wrote. See *Guide to the Manuscript Collections of the Historical Society of Pennsylvania,* 2nd ed. (Philadelphia: Historical Society of Pennsylvania, 1949).

14,952. Askew, Mary (Brown)
Papers. 1857-87. 8 vols.
Open. Unpublished guide.
Historical Society of Pennsylvania.
Diaries in which Askew (1796-?), a well-to-do resident of Burlington, NJ, and aunt of orator Henry Armitt Brown, writes of family and personal matters.

14,953. Associations, Clubs, and Societies
Collection. 1764-1937. 110 vols.
Open. Published guide.
Historical Society of Pennsylvania.
This collection of record books includes one or two volumes for the following organizations: minutes of the First Female Beneficial Society of Philadelphia, 1814-40; minutes of the Pennsylvania Society for the Encouragement of Manufactures and the Useful Arts, 1787-89; constitution, bylaws, and names of members of the Philadelphia Anti-Slavery Society, 1838; minutes of the Citizens Temperance Union, 1874-75; minutes of the Neighbors' Club, 1901-12; and minutes, resolutions, and reports of the Philadelphia Child Welfare Association, 1933-37. Also includes 19 volumes of minutes, financial accounts, and membership lists of the Pike Beneficial Society of Philadelphia, 1814-65, and three volumes of constitution, minutes, and other records of the Anti-Slavery Society of Pennsylvania, 1846-56. See *Guide to the Manuscript Collections of the Historical Society of Pennsylvania,* 2nd ed. (Philadelphia: Historical Society of Pennsylvania, 1949).

14,954. Baker, Ann G.
Papers. 1823-82. 1 vol.
Open. Published guide.
Historical Society of Pennsylvania.
The commonplace book of [Miss] Baker, who lived with her family, consists of poems, historical notes, essays, biographical sketches, and other compositions by Baker and by other members of her family, as well as copies of some of her favorite poems and Biblical verses. See *Guide to the Manuscript Collections of the Historical Society of Pennsylvania,* 2nd ed. (Philadelphia: Historical Society of Pennsylvania, 1949).

14,955. Ball
Papers. 1676-1850. Ca. 2200 items and 1 microfilm reel.
Open. Published guide.
Historical Society of Pennsylvania.
Bulk of the correspondence, receipt and account books, records of real estate transactions, and marine insurance policies relate to the estate of Joseph Ball (1752-1821), a merchant and real estate dealer. Also includes the letter book of Elizabeth (Byle) Ball, the wife of merchant William Ball, which contains letters from 1757 to 1783 to her female friends and relatives. See *Guide to the Manuscript Collections of the Historical Society of Pennsylvania,* 2nd ed. (Philadelphia: Historical Society of Pennsylvania, 1949).

14,956. Bartram
Papers. 1738-1893. 14 vols.
Open. Published guide.

Historical Society of Pennsylvania.
Correspondence, scientific papers, diaries and journals of expeditions, drawings, and family Bibles of John Bartram (1699-1777) and his son William Bartram (1739-1823), both of whom were naturalists. Correspondence includes letters from 1792 to 1805 between Isaac and Sarah Bartram; also included is an address which Caroline Bartram Kelly delivered at a Bartram family reunion in 1893 on the history of John Bartram and his family. See *Guide to the Manuscript Collections of the Historical Society of Pennsylvania,* 2nd ed. (Philadelphia: Historical Society of Pennsylvania, 1949).

14,957. Biddle and Craig
Papers. 1779-1837. 800 items.
Open. Published guide.
Historical Society of Pennsylvania.
Family correspondence, primarily of Mrs. John Craig, who was the mother-in-law of Nicholas Biddle (1786-1844), a litterateur, scholar, statesman, and financier, contains material on the Biddle and Craig families. Mrs. Craig's daughter was Jane (Craig) Biddle. See *Guide to the Manuscript Collections of the Historical Society of Pennsylvania,* 2nd ed. (Philadelphia: Historical Society of Pennsylvania, 1949).

14,958. Binney, Horace
Papers. 1836-68. 11 vols.
Open. Published guide.
Historical Society of Pennsylvania.
Binney (1780-1875) was a lawyer and a legal writer. Journals kept during a European trip from 1836 to 1837, an autobiography, essays, notes on Binney family genealogy, and a commonplace book which Binney wrote for his daughter Susan in 1858. See *Guide to the Manuscript Collections of the Historical Society of Pennsylvania,* 2nd ed. (Philadelphia: Historical Society of Pennsylvania, 1949).

14,959. Bogert, Judith
Papers. 1842-47. 1 vol.
Open. Published guide.
Historical Society of Pennsylvania.
Notebook in which [Miss] Bogert, apparently a landlady of substantial means, recorded her income and expenses. See *Guide to the Manuscript Collections of the Historical Society of Pennsylvania,* 2nd ed. (Philadelphia: Historical Society of Pennsylvania, 1949).

14,960. Borie Family
Papers. 1799-1886. 2500 items.
Open. Published guide.
Historical Society of Pennsylvania.
John Joseph Borie (1776-1834) was owner of a shipping firm; his wife was Sophie (Beauveau) Borie. Business correspondence, personal letters from both Bories, accounts and bills, material on the *Rogé vs. Borie* case, and other items, most of which are in French. See *Guide to the Manuscript Collections of the Historical Society of Pennsylvania,* 2nd ed. (Philadelphia: Historical Society of Pennsylvania, 1949).

14,961. Breck, Samuel
Papers. 1770s-1862. 15 vols.
Open. Unpublished guide.
Historical Society of Pennsylvania.
Diaries, journals, articles, reprints of speeches, memorabilia, clippings, and watercolor and charcoal sketches by Breck (1771-1862), a Philadelphia resident. His diaries contain information about social life in upper-class society in Boston during the Revolutionary War, in France during the 1780s, and in Philadelphia from the 1790s on; they also contain many references to the daily activities of Breck's wife Jean Ross Breck and their daughter Lucy. Also includes a journal Samuel Breck's sister Hannah (Breck) Lloyd wrote during a trip she took accompanied only by her niece to Batavia, NY, in 1828; she describes towns visited, mileage, local color, and accommodations.

14,962. Brewster, Anne Maria Hampton
Papers. 1845-92. Ca. 1000 items.
Open. Card catalog.
Historical Society of Pennsylvania.
Brewster (1819-92) was a novelist, journalist, and foreign correspondent. Correspondence; diaries; commonplace books; notebooks containing poetry; copybooks containing manuscript newspaper and magazine articles, 1870-88; drafts of stories; notes on life in Washington, DC, in 1846; autograph albums; and scrapbooks.

14,963. Bringhurst, Hannah, and Almy, Elizabeth
Papers. 1781-1810. 1 vol.
Open. Published guide.
Historical Society of Pennsylvania.
Quaker diaries consist of a contemplative journal of Hannah Bringhurst (ca. 1751-82), a Philadelphian, containing a preface by her husband James Bringhurst (?-1810); his account of the last days and death of his first wife Anna Bringhurst (?-1777); and a diary in which Almy (1770-1841) describes James Bringhurst's illness and subsequent death as well as her own life and illness. See *Guide to the Manuscript Collections of the Historical Society of Pennsylvania,* 2nd ed. (Philadelphia: Historical Society of Pennsylvania, 1949).

14,964. Brown, Charles Brockden
Papers. 1715-1827. 29 vols.
Open. Published guide.
Historical Society of Pennsylvania.
Journals, commonplace books, memorandum books, bankbook, obituary, and literary writings by Brown (1771-1810), a novelist and journalist. Includes a book in which his mother Mary Armitt Brown recorded domestic accounts, family births and deaths for the period 1804-11, and reflections on various family members. Also included are her 1760 book on the conversion, Christian experiences, and travels of Jane Hoskins; journals of Elijah Brown for the period 1811-27; and journals and papers for 1823 and 1824 of Maurice Lisle, which relate to domestic and commercial affairs in Philadelphia. See *Guide to the Manuscript Collections of the Historical Society of Pennsylvania,* 2nd ed. (Philadelphia: Historical Society of Pennsylvania, 1949).

14,965. Brown Family
Papers. 1788-1915. Ca. 3000 items.
Open. Unpublished guide.
Historical Society of Pennsylvania.
Correspondence, receipts, business papers, and commonplace books of the family of William Brown (1752-1834), a Quaker minister in Dover, NH. Includes correspondence from 1788 to 1807 in which William and Abigail Brown discuss the education of their children; correspondence and notes of Casper Wistar (1761-1818), a physician who was professor of anatomy, surgery, and midwifery at the University of Pennsylvania in 1792; financial, business, and personal correspondence from 1846 to 1880 of Elizabeth Waln Wistar with her sister Ellen and other relatives and friends; and letters Agnes Brown wrote her father J. Wistar Brown while traveling in Europe in 1908 and 1909.

14,966. Brown, Marjorie P. M.
Papers. 1763-1871. 2 Hollinger boxes.
Open. Unpublished guide.
Historical Society of Pennsylvania.
Material assembled by Brown includes correspondence between 1768 and 1771 of Margaret Emlen with her cousin Sarah Logan while both were teenagers, estate papers of Deborah Morris (?-1793), and miscellaneous correspondence of women in various generations of the Howell and Jones families.

14,967. Bryan, Hannah P.
Papers. Ca. 1829-31. 1 vol.
Open. Catalog card.
Historical Society of Pennsylvania.
Autograph book with poetic extracts written by friends of [Miss] Bryan.

14,968. Buchanan and Henry
Papers. 1770-1914. Ca. 100 items.
Open. Published guide.
Historical Society of Pennsylvania.
Family papers of James Buchanan (1791-1868), US President, contain correspondence and accounts of his mother Elizabeth Buchanan and of his sister Harriet (Buchanan) [Mrs. Robert] Henry. See *Guide to the Manuscript Collections of the Historical Society of Pennsylvania,* 2nd ed. (Philadelphia: Historical Society of Pennsylvania, 1949).

14,969. Bullock and Willets
Papers. 1820-63. 145 items.
Open. Inventory.
Historical Society of Pennsylvania.
Papers of [Miss] Edith Willets Bullock, a resident of Hanover, NJ, primarily consist of letters from family members describing such aspects of life as the year's crops, Indian handicrafts, the condition of schooling for females in 1846, death during the Civil War of the husband of one of Bullock's cousins, and the health and whereabouts of various relatives. Also includes a series of letters providing a graphic depiction of life in New York City during 1845, genealogical material, and a photo.

14,970. Burd, Shippen, and Hubley
Papers. 1749-1860. 1 vol. and 200 items.
Open. Unpublished guide.
Historical Society of Pennsylvania.
Correspondence of Margaret (Shippen) Arnold (1760-1804), Sarah (Shippen) Burd (1731-84), Margaret (Burd) Hubley (1761-?), Ann (Allen) Penn (?-1830), and other family members provides news of the family and comments on current events. Arnold's letters detail the years just prior to her death.

14,971. Centennial International Exposition Register of Visitors, Women's Department
Records. 1876. 1 vol.
Open. Published guide.
Historical Society of Pennsylvania.
Register book of visitors to the Women's Department of the International Exhibition, which was held during the centennial celebration in Philadelphia. See *Guide to the Manuscript Collections of the Historical Society of Pennsylvania,* 2nd ed. (Philadelphia: Historical Society of Pennsylvania, 1949).

14,972. Central Congregational Church
Records. 1864-1923. 1500 items.
Open. Unpublished guide.
Historical Society of Pennsylvania.
Constitution, bylaws, minutes for 1876 to 1900, correspondence, and rolls of the Ladies Aid Society of this Philadelphia church, a charitable group which was founded before 1876. Also included are financial records of the Church, 1880-1902; Church correspondence and certificates of recommendation and dismissal, 1864-1923; and minute books of the Central Congregational Society of Philadelphia, 1865-97.

14,973. Chambers and Folwell
Papers. 1768-1961. Ca. 875 items.
Open. Unpublished guide.
Historical Society of Pennsylvania.
Personal and business correspondence, diaries, estate papers, photos, and other papers of this West Grove, PA, family of merchants which dealt in

grain, feed, fertilizer, and salt. Included are diaries and copybooks of Mary Ballard Chambers for 1897 through 1904 and of Mary Chambers Folwell (1881-1966) for 1911 through 1957.

14,974. Chandler, Mary Ann
Papers. 1857-58. 1 vol.
Open. Published guide.
Historical Society of Pennsylvania.
Poetry, essays, and school notes of Chandler are included with a list of pupils and attendance records. See *Guide to the Manuscript Collections of the Historical Society of Pennsylvania,* 2nd ed. (Philadelphia: Historical Society of Pennsylvania, 1949).

14,975. Clark, Joseph Sill
Papers. 1947-68. 269 boxes, 94 vols., and 86 microfilm reels.
Access restricted. No guide.
Historical Society of Pennsylvania.
Campaign material of Clark, a US senator, includes material from the unsuccessful campaign of Genevieve Blatt for the US Senate in the 1963 Pennsylvania primary election.

14,976. Clayton, John
Papers. 1832-1940. 700 items.
Open. Unpublished guide.
Historical Society of Pennsylvania.
Correspondence and business papers of Clayton (1819-81), a Philadelphia attorney, include letters in which his wife Anna (Colton) Clayton (1820-?) describes social life in West Chester, PA, and Cape May, NJ, and letters in which John Clayton's mother Sarah (Medford) Clayton (1786-1849) discusses family matters.

14,977. Coates and Reynell
Papers. 1702-1843. 70 vols. and ca. 12,000 items.
Open. Published guide.
Historical Society of Pennsylvania.
Papers pertaining to the commercial interests of Samuel Coates (1748-1830) and of John Reynell, both of whom were Philadelphia businessmen, include some personal correspondence as well as correspondence of Sarah "Sally" Zane concerning the estate of Isaac Zane, for which Coates was executor, and Sally Zane's receipt book for 1796 to 1814. Also included are family estate papers from 1724 to 1793 of Anthony Morris, who was a Quaker statesman and wealthy Philadelphian; of his wife Pheobe Morris; and of his daughter Deborah Morris, whose papers are nearly complete. Morris family documents include correspondence relating to land transactions and social affairs, wills and inventories, accounts, bonds and agreements, and ledgers of Deborah Morris's brother Benjamin Morris, a physician. See *Guide to the Manuscript Collections of the Historical Society of Pennsylvania,* 2nd ed. (Philadelphia: Historical Society of Pennsylvania, 1949).

14,978. Coles, Lippincott, and Horstmann
Papers. 1775-1950. 13 boxes and 15 vols.
Open. No guide.
Historical Society of Pennsylvania.
Correspondence, diaries, business records, legal documents, manuscripts of books, and other papers of Bertha Horstmann (Lippincott) [Mrs. Stricker] Coles (1880-1963), an author who was honorary president of the US Service Club, primarily consist of papers of her grandfather Sigmund H. Horstmann, a manufacturer of army uniforms, insignia, and flags and of her father Walter Lippincott, a partner in the J. B. Lippincott Publishing Co. of Philadelphia. Correspondence, instructions to servants, inventories of personal belongings, Coles's writings and accounts of her activities for the Service Club during WWI and WWII, and clippings document the manner in which these members of the American business community lived.

14,979. Coombe
Papers. 1765-1803. 1 box.
Open. Unpublished guide.
Historical Society of Pennsylvania.
Correspondence and household accounts of Sarah Coombe Shields, including a letter she wrote her father, who was collector of the Port of Philadelphia between ca. 1770 and 1784, and a letter in which she describes the tyranny he exercised over his children.

14,980. Cornett, Jane
Papers. 1834-1904. 115 items.
Open. Unpublished guide.
Historical Society of Pennsylvania.
Correspondence, estate papers, and notices of Cornett, a resident of Phoenixville, PA. Contains many Civil War letters from her brother J. A. Cornett and others from her nieces and other relatives and friends.

14,981. Cox, Parrish, and Wharton
Papers. 1600-1900. Ca. 5000 items.
Open. Published guide.
Historical Society of Pennsylvania.
Correspondence, biographical sketches, receipt and account books, poetry, meeting reports, and broadsheets document the religious, social, and economic lives of a Quaker family. The bulk of the collection consists of letters from John Cox (1754-1847), a Burlington, NJ, farmer and Quaker leader, and his wife Ann Cox to their daughter Susannah (Cox) Parrish (1788-1851) and her husband Joseph Parrish (1779-1840), a Philadelphia physician. Also included are a volume of poems written to Susannah Parrish in 1820, letters of Hannah Lloyd and Dolley Madison, and a 1714 volume by Hannah Hill, which is entitled "Expressions of dying sayings." See *Guide to the Manuscript Collections of the Historical Society of Pennsylvania,* 2nd ed. (Philadelphia: Historical Society of Pennsylvania, 1949).

14,982. Dallas
Papers. 1791-1880. Ca. 1500 items.
Open. Published and unpublished guides.
Historical Society of Pennsylvania.
Correspondence of Alexander James Dallas (1759-1817), a lawyer and US secretary of the treasury, is included with his biography written by his son George Mifflin Dallas (1792-1864), a lawyer, diplomat, attorney general of Pennsylvania, and vice-president under President Polk. Also included is correspondence between George Dallas and his wife Sophia Chew (Nicklin) Dallas (1798-?), his children, and others, as well as invitations, notes, and other social correspondence addressed to George Dallas or to his daughter Susan Dallas. George Dallas's mother was Arabella Maria Dallas. See *Guide to the Manuscript Collections of the Historical Society of Pennsylvania,* 2nd ed. (Philadelphia: Historical Society of Pennsylvania, 1949).

14,983. Dallas, Constance H.
Papers. 1951-56. 35 boxes and 12 ft.
Open. Unpublished guide.
Historical Society of Pennsylvania.
[Mrs.] Dallas (1902-) was the first woman to serve on the Philadelphia City Council, where she was a member of its public welfare and public health committees. Personal and administrative correspondence, office files, published reports, and material pertaining to the Council's committees and to the Menninger Foundation.

14,984. Darlington, Georgine "Nina" Kelton (Murphy)
Papers. 1892-1937. 40 items.
Open. Unpublished guide.
Historical Society of Pennsylvania.
Manuscript of a book of poems entitled *Heart Songs* by Darlington (1866-?), a poet, is included with a copyright application, copyright renewals, and personal items.

14,985. Daughters of Africa Society
Records. 1822-38. 1 vol.
Open. Published guide.
Historical Society of Pennsylvania.
Located with the American Negro Historical Society records is a minute book of the Daughters of Africa Society, a beneficial association established in Philadelphia in 1821, which gives brief accounts of meetings and includes short financial notations. See *Guide to the Manuscript Collections of the Historical Society of Pennsylvania,* 2nd ed. (Philadelphia: Historical Society of Pennsylvania, 1949).

14,986. Daughters of the Founders and Patriots of America
Records. 1902-39. 70-page vol.
Open. Unpublished guide.
Historical Society of Pennsylvania.
Compiled by Mrs. J. Wistar Evans in 1939, this history of the Pennsylvania chapter of the Daughters, a club of women who were direct descendants of colonial and Revolutionary War patriots, contains speeches, excerpts from yearbooks, and lists of members of the Pennsylvania chapter as well as offices they held. Founded to preserve colonial and Revolutionary history, inculcate patriotism, and in time of war provide supplies for field hospitals, the club also sponsored lectures, social events, and charitable projects such as knitting socks for soldiers during WWII.

14,987. Day, Anna (Blakiston)
Papers. 1861-1932. 2000 items.
Open. Description.
Historical Society of Pennsylvania.
Day (1869-1952) was a Philadelphia clubwoman and reformer. Correspondence, bills and receipts, deeds, estate accounts, committee minutes and records, invitations, and anonymous diaries contain information on Day's activities with the Women's Committee for the City Party, the Women's League for Good Government, the Committee on the Cause and Cure of War, and the Franklin party, which was an independent political party in Philadelphia. Also included is material relating to Blakiston Publishing Co., the family business.

14,988. De Tilly, Maria Matilda Bingham
Papers. 1799. 1 vol.
Open. Published guide.
Historical Society of Pennsylvania.
Letters concerning the legal separation of de Tilly from James Alexander Comte de Tilly, most of which were written by their lawyers. Also included are copies of their marriage records and a description of the conditions Comte de Tilly demanded for a divorce. See *Guide to the Manuscript Collections of the Historical Society of Pennsylvania,* 2nd ed. (Philadelphia: Historical Society of Pennsylvania, 1949).

14,989. Dillwyn, William
Papers. 1770-1824. 846 items.
Open. Card catalog.
Historical Society of Pennsylvania.
A Philadelphia native, Dillwyn (1743-1824) was a Quaker merchant and member of the London Abolition Society. Correspondence with his daughter Susanna (Dillwyn) [Mrs. Samuel] Emlen (1769-1819) in Burlington and Philadelphia, while he was in London, concerns family matters, Philadelphia social life, politics, and current events.

14,990. Drink, Elizabeth (Sandwich)
Papers. 1758-1807. 33 vols.
Open. Unpublished guide.
Historical Society of Pennsylvania.
Journals in which [Mrs. Henry] Drinker (1734-1807), a Philadelphia Quaker, discusses

medical practices, a yellow fever epidemic, and the effect of the Revolutionary War on noncombatants. Portions of the journal were published and edited by Henry D. Biddle (Philadelphia, 1889).

14,991. Emlen Family
Papers. 1715-1885. 115 items.
Open. Published guide.
Historical Society of Pennsylvania.
Correspondence, legal documents, indentures, and other papers of various members of the Emlen and related families. Included are letters of Anne (Emlen) Mifflin from 1780 to 1814, many of which were written to her mother Anne Emlen in Philadelphia while she was traveling to preach at monthly meetings; copybooks of religious meditations and essays, most of which were Anne Mifflin's; a description of her husband Warner Mifflin (ca. 1745-98), an abolitionist, which was written by Anne Mifflin for their sons Samuel Emlen and Lemuel Mifflin; and a letter in which Joseph Galloway describes the unhappy marriage of his daughter. See *Guide to the Manuscript Collections of the Historical Society of Pennsylvania,* 2nd ed. (Philadelphia: Historical Society of Pennsylvania, 1949).

14,992. Emlen, Samuel
Papers. 1772-97. 1 vol.
Open. Unpublished guide.
Historical Society of Pennsylvania.
Correspondence, engraving, silhouettes, and map of Emlen (1730-99), a religious missionary to Europe. Includes letters he wrote describing his sermons and travels and exhorting the maintenance of piety to his wife Sarah Mott Emlen, their daughters Deborah and Elizabeth Emlen, and Samuel Emlen, Jr., who was his son by his first wife. In her letters Sarah Emlen describes her appreciation of the importance of her husband's mission and concern about her ability to manage her duties without his help.

14,993. Fahnestock, George Wolff, and Fahnestock, Anna Maria (Wolff)
Papers. 1863-73. 6 vols.
Open. Published guide.
Historical Society of Pennsylvania.
Included with the diaries of George Fahnestock (1823-68), a Philadelphia businessman, and of his mother Anna Fahnestock (1803-?) are notes on family history, a volume on the estate of George Fahnestock, and clippings about the 1868 collision of the steamboats *United States* and *America,* a disaster in which he and his daughter Grace Fahnestock were killed. See *Guide to the Manuscript Collections of the Historical Society of Pennsylvania,* 2nd ed. (Philadelphia: Historical Society of Pennsylvania, 1949).

14,994. Farmer, Eliza
Papers. 1774-89. 1 vol.
Open. Published guide.
Historical Society of Pennsylvania.
Addressed to her nephew Jack Halroyd, a clerk in the East India Company in London, the letters of Farmer, a Philadelphia resident, contain personal information as well as comments on the tea embargo, the nonimportation act, the secret session of Congress, and the state of military preparedness in Pennsylvania. See *Guide to the Manuscript Collections of the Historical Society of Pennsylvania,* 2nd ed. (Philadelphia: Historical Society of Pennsylvania, 1949).

14,995. Fels, Joseph
Papers. 1901-30. 17 boxes and 2 vols.
Open. Unpublished guide.
Historical Society of Pennsylvania.
Papers of Fels include correspondence, scrapbooks, and a manuscript of a book *Toward the Light, Joseph Fels—His Work* by his wife Mary Fels (1907-40), an author. Her letters reveal her interest in Palestine; many, addressed to Earl and Anna Barnes, concern her travels and companions such as Efrem Zimbalist. Also includes condolences on the death of her husband.

14,996. Female Tract Society
Records. 1816-34. 1 vol.
Open. Published guide.
Historical Society of Pennsylvania.
Minutes of this Episcopal women's group, which published tracts on home missionary work. See *Guide to the Manuscript Collections of the Historical Society of Pennsylvania,* 2nd ed. (Philadelphia: Historical Society of Pennsylvania, 1949).

14,997. Ferguson, Elizabeth (Graeme)
Papers. 1766-99. 2 vols.
Open. Published guide.
Historical Society of Pennsylvania.
Religious poetry and prose by [Mrs. Henry Hugh] Ferguson (1737-1801), a poet who was granddaughter of Sir William Keith. See *Guide to the Manuscript Collections of the Historical Society of Pennsylvania,* 2nd ed. (Philadelphia: Historical Society of Pennsylvania, 1949).

14,998. Ferguson, Elizabeth (Graeme)
Papers. 1762-97. Ca. 6 vols.
Open. Catalog card.
Historical Society of Pennsylvania.
Papers of [Mrs. Henry Hugh] Ferguson (1737-1801), a poet, include correspondence, poetry, prose, and memoranda about political, social, moral, religious, and economic subjects; "Telemachus," Ferguson's poetic translation of Fenelon's *Telemaque,* completed in 1769, with "translator's notes" added in subsequent years; and her poetic interpretation of the Book of Psalms, with her notations and an introductory letter addressed to Richard Peters.

14,999. Fields, Mrs.
Papers. Ca. 1880. 1 vol.
Open. Published guide.
Historical Society of Pennsylvania.
Manuscript cookbook of Fields, who probably was a housewife. See *Guide to the Manuscript Collections of the Historical Society of Pennsylvania,* 2nd ed. (Philadelphia: Historical Society of Pennsylvania, 1949).

15,000. Fisher, Samuel W.
Papers. 1762-1868. 100 items.
Open. Unpublished guide.
Historical Society of Pennsylvania.
Correspondence of Fisher (ca. 1765-1817), president of the Philadelphia Insurance Co., member of the Pennsylvania legislature, and president of the Philadelphia Select Council from 1811 to 1813, includes letters to Benjamin Morgan, Jr., an account with testimonies of a dispute in the legislature between Fisher and George Logan in 1800, and letters from Fisher's wife Elizabeth (Rhoads) Fisher (1770-96) and from his mother-in-law Sarah Pemberton Rhoads. Also included are daybooks of Rhoads and other material she collected for her daughter and granddaughter.

15,001. Fisher, Sarah (Logan)
Papers. 1771-96. 25 vols.
Open. Unpublished guide.
Historical Society of Pennsylvania.
Diaries of Fisher (1751-96), a housewife who was married to Thomas Fisher, a Philadelphia Quaker and merchant, contain personal information as well as some discussion of the Revolutionary War from the viewpoint of a British sympathizer. Extracts were published in *Pennsylvania Magazine of History and Biography,* Vol. 82 (October 1958).

15,002. Fisher, Sidney George
Papers. 1823-95. 5 boxes and 162 items.
Open. Unpublished guide.
Historical Society of Pennsylvania.
Correspondence of Fisher (1809-71), a Philadelphia lawyer and author, with his wife Elizabeth (Ingersoll) Fisher (1815-72) on family matters is included along with letters to her from her father Charles Jared Ingersoll (1782-1862) and others from other family members, some of which were written before her marriage. Also included are Elizabeth Fisher's diaries of daily activities for the period 1855-63, some childhood letters of Sidney and Elizabeth Fisher's son Sydney George Fisher, and an account book of Ann Eliza George Fisher for 1809 to 1815.

15,003. Franks, Rebecca
Papers. 1781. 1 item.
Open. Published guide.
Historical Society of Pennsylvania.
A letter in which Franks (ca. 1760-1823), writing from Flatbush, NY, gives an extensive description of New York society. See *Guide to the Manuscript Collections of the Historical Society of Pennsylvania,* 2nd ed. (Philadelphia: Historical Society of Pennsylvania, 1949).

15,004. Freeman and Frost
Papers. 1809-1929. 15 vols. and 1400 items.
Open. Unpublished guide.
Historical Society of Pennsylvania.
Papers of two Philadelphia families include business papers of Tristram William L. Freeman (?-ca. 1848), a businessman; diaries, account book, memorandum book, and scrapbooks of Isabel (Freeman) Frost (1849-1929), as well as her correspondence, some of which is from Matilda Coxe (Evans) Stevenson, an ethnologist; correspondence of Isabel Frost's daughter Augusta (Frost) Eisenbrey (1883-?); business records of the Frost Block Company from 1901 to 1903; and material on the city and state from a Philadelphia reform newspaper.

15,005. Freeman, Mrs. Walter Jackson
Papers. 1918-19. Ca. 2000 items.
Open. Published guide.
Historical Society of Pennsylvania.
Papers of Corinne (Keen) Freeman (1868-?), a Philadelphia civic leader who was chairman of the South Philadelphia Women's Liberty Loan Committee, consist primarily of correspondence, account books, name lists, reports, and other records of the Committee, a group of women who organized in order to sell Liberty Bonds during WWI. See *Guide to the Manuscript Collections of the Historical Society of Pennsylvania,* 2nd ed. (Philadelphia: Historical Society of Pennsylvania, 1949).

15,006. Friends
Papers. 1870-73. 30 items.
Open. Published guide.
Historical Society of Pennsylvania.
Correspondence in which William J. Buck, a Friend and researcher, recorded for John Jordan, Jr., of the Historical Society the births, deaths, and marriages of Quakers in Pennsylvania, Delaware, and New Jersey from both the orthodox and Hicksite branches of the church. Also included are Buck's description of the process by which he collected information and historical sketches of such persons as Ada Boone, a Quaker who was the grandmother of Abraham Lincoln. See *Guide to the Manuscript Collections of the Historical Society of Pennsylvania,* 2nd ed. (Philadelphia: Historical Society of Pennsylvania, 1949).

15,007. Galloway, Grace (Growdon)
Papers. 1778-81. 8 vols.
Open. Published guide.
Historical Society of Pennsylvania.
Originals and photocopies of correspondence, primarily to family members, and a diary for 1778 and 1779 of [Mrs. Joseph] Galloway (?-1782), wife of a Philadelphia lawyer, pertain to her remaining

in Philadelphia during the Revolutionary War and managing the family property while her Loyalist husband went to England. In her diary she discusses politics, war conditions, and her personal problems with her husband. See *Guide to the Manuscript Collections of the Historical Society of Pennsylvania,* 2nd ed. (Philadelphia: Historical Society of Pennsylvania, 1949).

15,008. Gibbons, John
Papers. 1866-84. 200 items.
Open. Unpublished guide.
Historical Society of Pennsylvania.
Correspondence, reminiscences, addresses, scrapbooks, photos, and clippings of Gibbons (1827-86), a US Military Academy graduate who served with the US Army and the US Volunteers during the Civil War and the Indian campaign in the 1870s and 1880s. Includes letters to his wife Frances North (Moale) Gibbons on domestic concerns and the course of the War.

15,009. Gillingham, Harrold E.
Papers. Ca. 1885-1954. 8 boxes and 1 vol.
Open. Unpublished guide.
Historical Society of Pennsylvania.
Correspondence, manuscripts, notes, and clippings of Gillingham (1864-1954) as well as the diary which his daughter Edith H. Gillingham wrote while serving as an American National Red Cross volunteer in France between 1917 and 1919; she provides detailed descriptions of her life and conditions in France.

15,010. Gratz
Papers. 1825-91. 50 items.
Open. Published guide.
Historical Society of Pennsylvania.
Estate and legal records pertaining to property owned by the family, including that of Louisa, Caroline, and Elizabeth Gratz, who were daughters of Simon Gratz (1840-1925), a Philadelphia lawyer and member of the Philadelphia Board of Education; and papers of Louisa Gratz containing information on her charitable activities in the city, her concern for Jews, and membership in the Mikveh Israel Synagogue. Includes correspondence, financial accounts, and legal documents. See *Guide to the Manuscript Collections of the Historical Society of Pennsylvania,* 2nd ed. (Philadelphia: Historical Society of Pennsylvania, 1949).

15,011. Greenfield, Albert Monroe
Papers. 1923-66. Ca. 400 ft.
Access restricted. Unpublished guide.
Historical Society of Pennsylvania.
Correspondence, financial records, drafts of speeches, pamphlets, and clippings of Greenfield (1887-1967), a Philadelphia banker, concern his business and philanthropic activities. Also contained are papers of his wife Edna Kraus Greenfield, a 1915 alumna of Bryn Mawr College and philanthropist who was involved in music and art functions in the area. Personal correspondence and correspondence with local businessmen about household and personal expenses is included with correspondence concerning the Philadelphia LWV chapter; the Jewish Hospital Association; Mercy Hospital, which was a medical facility for blacks in Philadelphia; the Girls High School of Philadelphia; Bryn Mawr College's Resident Summer School for Women Workers with which she was associated during 1927 and 1928; and College alumnae activities.

15,012. Gregg, Lizzie R.
Papers. 1873. 1 vol.
Open. Unpublished guide.
Historical Society of Pennsylvania.
School notebook of [Miss] Gregg (ca. 1861-?), a student at the Number One School in Cressona, PA, contains grammar and other exercises as well as original compositions on such subjects as Robinson Crusoe, gold, and the School, which reflect study of history, geography, science, the Bible, and proverbs. Entries have been corrected, presumably by Gregg's teacher, and also include penciled notes indicating the purpose of various of the exercises.

15,013. Griffitts, Hannah
Papers. 1711-1808. 2 boxes.
Open. Catalog card.
Historical Society of Pennsylvania.
Some of the poetry of [Miss] Griffitts (1727-1817), a poet, was published under the name "Fidelia" in Philadelphia newspapers. Correspondence, essays, and poems, many of which commemorate the deaths of her father, her sister Mary Griffitts, Eliza Norris, Mary Hamburg, and Mary Dickinson. Hannah Griffitts also wrote political poetry and notes about current events; during the Revolutionary War her sympathies were pro-Tory. Includes poems on Thomas Paine, social conditions during the late 18th century, and the "crisis" in 1777.

15,014. Grubb
Papers. Ca. 1730-1950. 6000 items.
Open. Unpublished guide.
Historical Society of Pennsylvania.
Business and social correspondence, legal records, and genealogical material of a family involved in manufacturing iron in Lancaster County, PA, relate mainly to family and social life. Included are items of Sarah (Grubb) Ogilvia (1818-83) and of Mary (Grubb) Parker (1816-1900), who were daughters of Henry Bates Grubb.

15,015. Gulager
Papers. 1813-1944. 1 box.
Open. Unpublished guide.
Historical Society of Pennsylvania.
Papers of this Philadelphia family consist of correspondence of Mary Gulager (1836-77) and of Catherine Gordon Gulager (1829-1910) on family matters, a receipt book of Mrs. William Gulager, Sr. (1760-1835), for 1813 to 1835, and photos.

15,016. Hand Family
Papers. 1823-1901. 78 items.
Open. Unpublished guide.
Historical Society of Pennsylvania.
Includes correspondence, 1823-24, between Cornelia Hand, a resident of Cape May, NJ, and her husband Captain Noah Hand.

15,017. Harris, George B.
Papers. 1750-1844. 525 items.
Open. Unpublished guide.
Historical Society of Pennsylvania.
Collection consists primarily of correspondence of Stephen Harris, a physician who worked in Chester County, PA, between ca. 1823 and 1839, and of his wife Mary Harris to friends and relatives about family matters. Also included are some business records and printed material relating to the medical profession.

15,018. Henderson and Wertmüller
Papers. 1779-1822. Ca. 150 items.
Open. Published guide.
Historical Society of Pennsylvania.
Most of the correspondence, accounts, and other papers of this Philadelphia family relate to property holdings and the settlement of various estates, including those of John Henderson (?-1792), a carpenter and painter, and of his sister Elizabeth (Henderson) Wertmüller (?-1812). Women were appointed administrators of several of these estates. Also included is correspondence of John Henderson's mother Lydia Henderson and of John Nicholson. See *Guide to the Manuscript Collections of the Historical Society of Pennsylvania,* 2nd ed. (Philadelphia: Historical Society of Pennsylvania, 1949).

15,019. Hildeburn, Charles R.
Papers. Ca. 1900. 1 package.
Open. Published guide.
Historical Society of Pennsylvania.
Manuscript of *A Trunkful of Old Letters from Loyalist Ladies in Revolutionary Times* (New York, 1900), which Hildeburn (1855-1901) edited and in which social life and Loyalist attitudes at the time of the American Revolution are discussed. See *Guide to the Manuscript Collections of the Historical Society of Pennsylvania,* 2nd ed. (Philadelphia: Historical Society of Pennsylvania, 1949).

15,020. Hopkinson
Papers. 1736-1944. 19 vols.
Open. Unpublished guide.
Historical Society of Pennsylvania.
Correspondence, documents, pamphlets, and other papers of this family include letters of Mary (Johnson) Hopkinson (1718-1804), who was wife of the colonial jurist Thomas Hopkinson; of Ann (Borden) Hopkinson, who was wife of jurist, author, and musician Francis Hopkinson (1737-91); and of Emily (Mifflin) Hopkinson, who was wife of congressman and federal judge Joseph Hopkinson (1770-1842).

15,021. Howell, Josephine R.
Papers. 1681-1886. 114 items.
Open. Published guide.
Historical Society of Pennsylvania.
Correspondence, poems, drawings, financial records, a marriage certificate, recipes, photos, and other 19th-century papers of the Gibbons, Howell, Richardson, and related families. Includes correspondence between Martha Gibbons and her sons and between Sarah Gibbons and her husband and her sister. Also includes a letter book of Rebecca Richardson of New York for 1680 and 1689 and her financial accounts for 1681. See *Guide to the Manuscript Collections of the Historical Society of Pennsylvania,* 2nd ed. (Philadelphia: Historical Society of Pennsylvania, 1949).

15,022. Indigent Widows and Single Women's Society of Philadelphia
Records. 1823-62. 400 items.
Open. Published guide.
Historical Society of Pennsylvania.
Correspondence and account books provide general information about this charitable Society, which offered assistance to poor women lacking families who could help them. See *Guide to the Manuscript Collections of the Historical Society of Pennsylvania,* 2nd ed. (Philadelphia: Historical Society of Pennsylvania, 1949).

15,023. Infant School Society of Philadelphia
Records. 1827-1940. 6 vols. and 45 items.
Open. Inventory.
Historical Society of Pennsylvania.
Annual reports, minutes, accounts, correspondence, and letter books for the entire history of the Society, a philanthropic club for women whose purpose was to provide schooling for underprivileged children in the city. The Society established the first public kindergarten in Philadelphia as well as schools for "coloured" children. The School, which trained approximately 70 girls and boys each year, later provided primarily for immigrants' children by attempting to turn them into "true" Americans before releasing them to public schools.

15,024. Jackson, Caroline (Hoopes)
Papers. 1824-51. 3 vols.
Open. Published guide.
Historical Society of Pennsylvania.
Memoir in which Jackson, a Quaker from West Chester, PA, who was the daughter of Thomas and Eliza Hoopes, discusses religion, economic and social standards, education, and daily life. See

Guide to the Manuscript Collections of the Historical Society of Pennsylvania, 2nd ed. (Philadelphia: Historical Society of Pennsylvania, 1949).

15,025. James, Dorothy Biddle
Papers. 1787-1871. 13 items.
Open. Unpublished guide.
Historical Society of Pennsylvania.
Family correspondence of Sally and Ann Biddle (1757-1807) with their father John Biddle is included with a personal receipt book of William Biddle for 1841 to 1871 and letters from 1797 and 1798 on Indians by General James Wilkinson, who married Ann Biddle.

15,026. Jefferson Committee
Records. 1826-28. 2 vols.
Open. Published guide.
Historical Society of Pennsylvania.
Subscriptions, financial accounts, and reports of the Jefferson Committee, which was organized by Philadelphia citizens to establish a fund for the relief of Thomas Jefferson. After Jefferson's death, the Committee decided to use the funds to help his daughter Martha (Jefferson) Randolph. See *Guide to the Manuscript Collections of the Historical Society of Pennsylvania,* 2nd ed. (Philadelphia: Historical Society of Pennsylvania, 1949).

15,027. Jefferson School
Records. 1864-1914. 15 vols.
Open. No guide.
Historical Society of Pennsylvania.
Pupil registers and minutes of the directors of a local school board in Philadelphia, which operated a grammar school for girls that was later combined with a boys school. Registers pertaining to the girls school and to the combined school contain information on date and place of birth of students, grade assignment, and parents' occupations.

15,028. Johnson, Anna G.
Papers. 1826-44. 1 vol.
Open. Published guide.
Historical Society of Pennsylvania.
The first part of the volume is an autograph album containing verse dedicated to Johnson; the second part is a diary, 1843-44, with personal entries and a description of a trip through Pennsylvania and New York. Johnson later married Ferdinand Hubble. See *Guide to the Manuscript Collections of the Historical Society of Pennsylvania,* 2nd ed. (Philadelphia: Historical Society of Pennsylvania, 1949).

15,029. Katzenstein, Caroline
Papers. 1910-63. 3 boxes.
Open. Unpublished guide.
Historical Society of Pennsylvania.
A leader in the national woman suffrage movement, Katzenstein (ca. 1888-1968) was executive secretary of the Pennsylvania Woman Suffrage Association. Correspondence, organizational records, programs, a copy of her leaflet "The Sporting Spirit" and her book *Lifting the Curtain,* photos of suffragists, and clippings. Includes reports of the executive secretary and of the corresponding secretary, addresses, programs, and leaflets of the Association and correspondence with the National Woman's party.

15,030. Kelley, William Darrah
Papers. 1837-1903. 600 items.
Open. Inventory.
Historical Society of Pennsylvania.
Family correspondence is included with political and business correspondence, telegrams, invitations, and clippings of Kelley (1814-90), a US congressman from Philadelphia from 1860 to 1890. Kelley's letters to his wife Caroline Bartram Kelley describe political and social events in Washington. Caroline Kelley's letters concern her efforts to manage a large house alone, to supervise the children who were often ill, and to deal with servants who frequently quit because they were overworked. Also included are letters from the children when they were young and later letters they wrote as adults to their mother to keep her informed about life in Philadelphia.

15,031. Kendall, Elizabeth
Papers. 1765. 1 vol.
Open. Published guide.
Historical Society of Pennsylvania.
Memorial volume for Elizabeth Kendall (ca. 1685-1765), an English Quaker minister, contains testimonials by Mary Bundock and the Mannington Monthly Meeting. Also includes a copy of Kendall's account of her religious experiences. See *Guide to the Manuscript Collections of the Historical Society of Pennsylvania,* 2nd ed. (Philadelphia: Historical Society of Pennsylvania, 1949).

15,032. Landon and Shattuck
Papers. 1849-90. 101 items.
Open. Published guide.
Historical Society of Pennsylvania.
Collection consists of correspondence, most of which was written between sisters, aunts and nieces, and friends of these families. Many letters are to or from Eliza (Hinckly) Landon (1819-?) and written from Philadelphia, Delaware, and Maine. See *Guide to the Manuscript Collections of the Historical Society of Pennsylvania,* 2nd ed. (Philadelphia: Historical Society of Pennsylvania, 1949).

15,033. League of Women Voters of Philadelphia
Records. 1920-61. 18 boxes.
Open. Unpublished guide.
Historical Society of Pennsylvania.
Bylaws; minutes and reports of the board of directors; auditor's statements; correspondence; reports of the nominating, advisory, budget, and publicity committees; and convention reports of the LWV chapter, most of which are from the 1940s and '50s.

15,034. Lee, William A.
Papers. 1822-48. 1 vol.
Open. Unpublished guide.
Historical Society of Pennsylvania.
Account book of Lee (1778-1848), a Pennsylvanian who established William A. Lee's Select Seminary in 1797, contains names of day scholars and their parents, fees, and attendance records. Most students only attended the Seminary for brief periods, and as many were female as male.

15,035. Levick
Papers. 1674-1782. Ca. 30 items and 1 microfilm reel.
Open. Published guide.
Historical Society of Pennsylvania.
Material on Welsh settlers in Pennsylvania includes correspondence of settlers, most of whom were men; letters of Katherine Roberts for the period 1683-1710; deeds and surveys for 1681 to 1695; and an account of the persecution of Quakers in England from 1681 to 1683. See *Guide to the Manuscript Collections of the Historical Society of Pennsylvania,* 2nd ed. (Philadelphia: Historical Society of Pennsylvania, 1949).

15,036. Lewes, Delaware
Collection. 1812-1936. 2 vols.
Open. Published guide.
Historical Society of Pennsylvania.
Correspondence, notes, photos, clippings, and other material pertaining to the town of Lewes include a daybook for 1812 and 1813 of a Lewes inn that was managed by Sarah Marriner. See *Guide to the Manuscript Collections of the Historical Society of Pennsylvania,* 2nd ed. (Philadelphia: Historical Society of Pennsylvania, 1949).

15,037. Lewis, Eleanor Parke (Custis)
Papers. 1794-1852. 2 vols.
Open. Unpublished guide.
Historical Society of Pennsylvania.
Correspondence in which [Mrs. Lawrence] Lewis (1779-1852), a granddaughter of George and Martha Washington, describes to Elizabeth Bordley [Mrs. James] Gibson of Philadelphia her early life at Mount Vernon and later southern family life.

15,038. Lewis, Emma
Papers. 1853-54. 1 vol.
Open. Published guide.
Historical Society of Pennsylvania.
Lyric and religious verse by Lewis. See *Guide to the Manuscript Collections of the Historical Society of Pennsylvania,* 2nd ed. (Philadelphia: Historical Society of Pennsylvania, 1949).

15,039. Logan
Papers. 1664-1890. 4 boxes, 2 vols., and ca. 12,000 items.
Open. Published guide.
Historical Society of Pennsylvania.
Business and personal correspondence, travel journals, financial accounts, legal documents, court records, estate papers, and other material of James Logan (1674-1751), who was a scholar, secretary to William Penn, clerk of the Provincial Council, and commissioner of property and receiver general for the province; of John Dickinson (1732-1808), a statesman who served as president of the Supreme Council of Delaware in 1781; and of the Logan, Dickinson, and Norris families. Included are official records of the Upland County Court from 1676 to 1681; appeals, petitions, and grievances presented to the Provincial Council between 1700 and 1713; and letters and pamphlets concerning Pennsylvania society, religion, and politics. Also included are correspondence and the marriage certificate of Mary Norris to John Dickinson and correspondence, an anatomy chart, and literary and biographical sketches by Deborah Norris Logan (1761-1839), a Philadelphian who was married to Thomas Jefferson's friend George Logan (1753-1821), a physician. See *Guide to the Manuscript Collections of the Historical Society of Pennsylvania,* 2nd ed. (Philadelphia: Historical Society of Pennsylvania, 1949).

15,040. Logan, Deborah (Norris)
Papers. 1821. 1 vol.
Open. Card catalog.
Historical Society of Pennsylvania.
Manuscript biography that Logan (1761-1839) wrote about her husband George Logan (1753-1821), a physician, farmer, and politician, after his death. A collector of historical records, she preserved the early correspondence of William Penn and of her husband's grandfather James Logan by copying it from deteriorating originals. The biography, which comments on her husband's life and character as well as on social and political events in Philadelphia, was published in 1899 by the Historical Society of Pennsylvania.

15,041. Logan, Deborah (Norris)
Papers. 1815-39. 17 vols.
Open. Published guide.
Historical Society of Pennsylvania.
Diaries of Logan (1761-1839), wife of George Logan, who was a Philadelphia physician, US senator, and friend of Thomas Jefferson, contain information on the social life of many prominent Philadelphia families and such topics as the Declaration of Independence, the Revolutionary War, cholera and yellow fever epidemics, slavery, conditions in Europe, travel and transportation facilities, natural phenomena and weather conditions, Friends meetings, and literature. Diaries also contain biographical notes on John Adams, Pierce Butler, John C. Calhoun, Benjamin Franklin, Jefferson, Henry Laurens, Francis Lightfoot Lee, Thomas Penn, George Washington,

and other notable men. Logan was author of *A Memoir of Dr. George Logan of Stenton;* she also collected papers of her family. See *Guide to the Manuscript Collections of the Historical Society of Pennsylvania,* 2nd ed. (Philadelphia: Historical Society of Pennsylvania, 1949).

15,042. Logan, Frances
Collection. 1684-1854. 1 box.
Open. Catalog card.
Historical Society of Pennsylvania.
Miscellaneous material collected by [Miss] Logan includes a religious account of Dorcas Lilly, a Quaker; records of the women Friends meeting in Philadelphia, 1793; a poem "To the Banished Society at Winchester" by Susan Hopkins, 1777; correspondence of Elizabeth Webb of Rhode Island, 1698-1712, including one letter to Anthony William Boehme, who was chaplain to George, prince of Denmark; correspondence of Mary Norris and of her daughter Deborah (Norris) Logan; an inventory of Mary (Parker) Norris, 1799; and a membership certificate of Sally A. Dickinson for her contribution to the House of Refuge in Philadelphia, 1829.

15,043. Loudon
Papers. 1760-1939. 85 boxes and 32 vols.
Open. Unpublished guide.
Historical Society of Pennsylvania.
Correspondence, household accounts, business records, legal documents, and photos of several generations of the residents of the Loudon mansion in Germantown, PA, which was built in 1801 by Thomas Armat, primarily concern domestic matters and property interests. Included are correspondence of Thomas Armat's fifth wife Ann Armat (?-1851), of her granddaughter Jane (Armat) [Mrs. William] Armat Skerrett (?-1856), of Jane Skerrett's daughters Ann Armat Logan (1820-95) and Frances Armat, and of Ann Logan's daughter Maria Dickinson Logan (1857-1939).

15,044. McCall
Papers. 1739-1889. 1500 items.
Open. Unpublished guide.
Historical Society of Pennsylvania.
Correspondence, commonplace book, and business and financial records of this family of a Philadelphia merchant. Includes extensive correspondence of George A. McCall (1802-68), a general in the US Army, with his wife Elizabeth McMurtrie McCall, much of which was written during the Civil War, and correspondence of George McCall with his sisters while he was traveling in Europe. Also includes some Cadwallader family correspondence and receipted bills.

15,045. McCall, Charlotte Manigault (Wilcocks)
Papers. 1842. 1 vol.
Open. Unpublished guide.
Historical Society of Pennsylvania.
Diary which this young Philadelphia woman kept during her courtship contains descriptions and discussion of personalities as well as detailed information about attitudes toward marriage.

15,046. McHenry, Margaret
Papers. 1929-49. 19 vols.
Open. Unpublished guide.
Historical Society of Pennsylvania.
Diaries in which McHenry (1904-), a teacher at Roxborough High School in Philadelphia, comments on daily events. After graduating with a BS from the University of Pennsylvania in 1925, she obtained an MA in 1927 and a PhD in education in 1931.

15,047. MacManus, Susan R. (Trautwine)
Papers. 1857-81. 14 vols.
Open. Unpublished guide.
Historical Society of Pennsylvania.
Diaries in which MacManus (1841-81?), a Philadelphia resident, comments on her personal activities and the Civil War.

15,048. Magdalen Society
Records. 1800-1921. 30 vols.
Open. Unpublished guide.
Historical Society of Pennsylvania.
Records of the Society, established in 1799 to aid "in restoring to the paths of virtue women who have been robbed of their innocence and are desirous of returning to a life of rectitude," and of the asylum the Society built in 1810 in Philadelphia. Consists of annual reports; minutes of the board of managers and of annual meetings; ledgers and register for most of the period; later minutes of the visiting committee; cashbooks, 1893-1917; records of admissions and releases, 1878-1917; a journal, 1917-21; and diaries, 1829-34 and 1878-1917, of daily events at the asylum, which were recorded by the matron. First president of the Society was William White, the Episcopal bishop of Philadelphia.

15,049. Marchand, Lizzie
Papers. 1864-99. 1 vol.
Open. Published guide.
Historical Society of Pennsylvania.
Diary which Marchand kept while she was at school is included with a diary kept by her daughter Susie Logan and clippings. See *Guide to the Manuscript Collections of the Historical Society of Pennsylvania,* 2nd ed. (Philadelphia: Historical Society of Pennsylvania, 1949).

15,050. Markoe
Papers. 1773-1939. Ca. 300 items.
Open. Inventory.
Historical Society of Pennsylvania.
Correspondence, diaries, financial records, scrapbooks, photos, and clippings of this Philadelphia family. Includes correspondence of Abraham Markoe, Jr. (ca. 1740-1808), to his mother about births, deaths, and the general health of family members. Also included are receipts, tax statements, wills, and other financial records of Markoe family women, which reveal their position in the family businesses.

15,051. Mary A. Longstreth School and Alumnae Association
Records. 1829-1942. Ca. 395 items.
Open. Published guide.
Historical Society of Pennsylvania.
Account books, pamphlets, and clippings of this private school for girls, which was operated between 1829 and ca. 1879 by Mary Anna Longstreth (1811-84), an educator. Also included are officers' books, treasurer's reports, minutes, correspondence, memoirs, and other records of the Association. See *Guide to the Manuscript Collections of the Historical Society of Pennsylvania,* 2nd ed. (Philadelphia: Historical Society of Pennsylvania, 1949).

15,052. Maxcy, Markoe, and Hughes
Papers. 1826-95. 84 items.
Open. Unpublished guide.
Historical Society of Pennsylvania.
Personal correspondence of Mrs. Virgil Maxcy and her daughters Sarah (Maxcy) Hughes and Mary Maxcy primarily concern domestic matters and their social life.

15,053. Mervine, William McKinley
Papers. 1685-1788. 25 items.
Open. Published guide.
Historical Society of Pennsylvania.
Records of the Chesterfield monthly meeting include minutes for 1685 to 1687; certificates of removal to the meeting for the Forman, Kelly, Van Horn, and Davies families; and scattered minutes of women's meetings during the period. See *Guide to the Manuscript Collections of the Historical Society of Pennsylvania,* 2nd ed. (Philadelphia: Historical Society of Pennsylvania, 1949).

15,054. Minford, William Alexander
Papers. 1923-46. 500 items.
Open. Unpublished guide.
Historical Society of Pennsylvania.
Personal correspondence; financial records; birth, marriage, and death notices; photos; memorabilia; and other family papers of Minford (1881-1946), an Irish immigrant accountant who formed his own corporation, invested heavily in the stock market in 1923, and then during the Depression worked as a kitchen helper and with the WPA. Effects of the Depression on a middle-class family of limited means are also reflected in the material concerning the property Minford's wife Sarah Patterson Minford lost in Wilkes-Barre, PA, and her attempts to sell her furniture and obtain a job.

15,055. Moore, Clara Sophia (Jessup)
Papers. 1890-97. 83 items.
Open. Unpublished guide.
Historical Society of Pennsylvania.
Correspondence of [Mrs. Bloomfield Haynes] Moore (1824-99), a Philadelphia poet and philanthropist, primarily concern her support of John Worrell Keely and his invention, the Keely motor. Other letters are by Keely or other friends and most of them are addressed to [Miss] Cornelia Frothingham of Philadelphia.

15,056. Morris, Deborah
Papers. 1759-86. 1 vol.
Open. Published guide.
Historical Society of Pennsylvania.
Account book of Morris pertains to the board, clothing, and schooling expenses of Sarah Powell. Also included are Morris's accounts as executrix of the estate of John Morris Potts. See *Guide to the Manuscript Collections of the Historical Society of Pennsylvania,* 2nd ed. (Philadelphia: Historical Society of Pennsylvania, 1949).

15,057. Morris, Lydia T., and Morris, John T.
Papers. 1889-1903. 8 vols.
Open. Unpublished guide.
Historical Society of Pennsylvania.
Descendants of Anthony Morris of Philadelphia, Lydia and John Morris were sister and brother who traveled together during their 20s and early 30s around the world, to Egypt, and to Europe three times. Post cards, menus, and diaries of Louise Kellner, a hired companion for Miss Morris, which contain detailed descriptions of lodgings, excursions, places visited, persons they met, and the "local peoples."

15,058. Morris, Susanna
Papers. 1729-54. 1 vol.
Open. Published guide.
Historical Society of Pennsylvania.
Journal comprises an account of the travels of Morris (1682-1755), a Quaker, in the American colonies. Contains descriptions of dangers encountered and a shipwreck; Friends meetings she visited in Virginia, the Carolinas, Maryland, Pennsylvania, New Jersey, Great Britain, Ireland, and the Netherlands; and a memorial testimony to Morris, which was written by members of the Society of Friends. See *Guide to the Manuscript Collections of the Historical Society of Pennsylvania,* 2nd ed. (Philadelphia: Historical Society of Pennsylvania, 1949).

15,059. Morris, Thomas Burnside
Papers. 1862-1923. 1176 items.
Open. Inventory.
Historical Society of Pennsylvania.
Business and personal correspondence, photos, and a Bible of Morris (1842-85), an engineer for the Union Pacific and Northern Pacific Railroads whose job entailed travel from Panama to

California to Minneapolis. In letters to his parents and to his future wife Sarah Andt Sletor, Morris vividly describes building of the railroad and family life on the West Coast during the 1870s and '80s as well as life among the Indians and among natives of South America. In addition to family news, he tells about the effects on women of moving from comfortable homes to the frontier where they led strenuous and isolated lives. Also included are letters his son Roland S. Morris wrote home while he was in boarding school, at Princeton, and in Japan as ambassador to that country under President Woodrow Wilson. Roland Morris's letters concern traditional Japanese society and the changing Japanese-American community in California.

15,060. Neall, Adelaide W.
Papers. 1908-47. 184 items.
Open. Unpublished guide.
Historical Society of Pennsylvania.
Correspondence and research material collected by Neall, an associate editor of the *Saturday Evening Post,* for her projected biography of George Horace Lorimer, *Post* editor. Includes letters by Mary Carolyn Davies, Margaretta (Wade) Deland, Corra May Harris, Rose (Wilder) Lane, and Agnes Repplier, as well as single letters by Katharine Brush, Pearl S. Buck, and Alice Duer Miller, which were written to Neall during her employment with the *Post* from 1909 to 1942. Also includes an album of photos of *Post* authors and editors.

15,061. Oberholtzer, Ellis Paxson
Papers. 1735-1931. Ca. 2500 items.
Open. Published guide.
Historical Society of Pennsylvania.
Correspondence, essays, deeds, inventories, minutes, poems, drawings, and posters of Oberholtzer (1868-1936), an historian who resided in Philadelphia, include material relating to his publications, lectures, and biographies he wrote. Also included are letters, poems, and essays of Sara Louise (Vickers) Oberholtzer (1841-1930), an humanitarian who was instrumental in establishing the thrift movement, school savings banks, and thrift savings banks and who was a speaker at the World's Congress of Representative Women held in 1893. Information on the Historical Pageant of Philadelphia in 1912 is also contained. See *Guide to the Manuscript Collections of the Historical Society of Pennsylvania,* 2nd ed. (Philadelphia: Historical Society of Pennsylvania, 1949).

15,062. Orphan Society of Philadelphia
Records. 1815-1963. Ca. 70 vols. and 1500 items.
Open. Inventory.
Historical Society of Pennsylvania.
A complete record of the activities of the Society, a charitable organization founded by women members of the Second Presbyterian Church to provide a home and education for orphan boys and girls, is contained in minutes, financial records, correspondence, publications, and clippings. Until 1945 membership in the Society was limited to women, who assumed complete management of the home housing approximately 70 children; most of the home's revenue came from gifts made by members. Contains marriage licenses of children's parents, information on fund raising and sermons delivered at the home, and detailed descriptions of the children's lives, education, menus, work details, and histories from before enrollment into the later life of each orphan. During the 19th century, a major concern of the Society was binding the children out to learn a trade.

15,063. Page, Anne F.
Papers. 1837. 1 vol.
Open. Published guide.
Historical Society of Pennsylvania.
Journal of Page, written in the form of a letter to her father and throughout which she refers to herself as Nancy, concerns her trip through France and Italy. She describes cities visited, historical monuments, and the manners and customs of the inhabitants. Page later married Joseph Pleasants. See *Guide to the Manuscript Collections of the Historical Society of Pennsylvania,* 2nd ed. (Philadelphia: Historical Society of Pennsylvania, 1949).

15,064. Paschall
Papers. 1734-1875. 50 items.
Open. Published guide.
Historical Society of Pennsylvania.
Correspondence, legal records, deeds, wills, and copybooks of the Paschall family. Includes letters for 1830 to 1832 from Jane Sellers to her sister Ann Sellers, a student at Westchester School; copybooks, poetry, historical essays, and other school material of Ann Sellers; and a ca. 1830 copybook of Mary Frances Paschall. See *Guide to the Manuscript Collections of the Historical Society of Pennsylvania,* 2nd ed. (Philadelphia: Historical Society of Pennsylvania, 1949).

15,065. Paschall, Sarah
Papers. 1786. 1 vol.
Open. Published guide.
Historical Society of Pennsylvania.
Autograph and commonplace book of [Miss] Paschall, a young resident of Philadelphia. See *Guide to the Manuscript Collections of the Historical Society of Pennsylvania,* 2nd ed. (Philadelphia: Historical Society of Pennsylvania, 1949).

15,066. Pearsall, Mary
Papers. 1873. 1 vol.
Open. Published guide.
Historical Society of Pennsylvania.
Journal in which Pearsall describes her trip from Philadelphia to Montreal, topography of the country, hotel accommodations, and means of travel. See *Guide to the Manuscript Collections of the Historical Society of Pennsylvania,* 2nd ed. (Philadelphia: Historical Society of Pennsylvania, 1949).

15,067. Pemberton
Papers. 1641-1900. Ca. 25,000 items.
Open. Published guide.
Historical Society of Pennsylvania.
Correspondence, diaries, biographical sketches, financial records, legal documents, estate papers, genealogical notes, photos, and other papers of an old Philadelphia family that was prominent in the colonial affairs of Pennsylvania. Includes extensive correspondence by female Pembertons with Quakers in America, England, and other parts of the world and the 1813 diary of Rebecca (Warner) Rawle [Mrs. Samuel] Shoemaker (?-1819) describing the weather, her health, excursions to county seats, and visits with friends. Also included are long, affectionate letters on family matters from Rebecca Clifford [Mrs. John] Pemberton (1792-1869) to her sons Israel Pemberton (1813-85), John Clifford Pemberton (1814-81), and Henry Pemberton (1826-1910), as well as letters of Anna Pemberton to her brothers, extensive correspondence between John C. Pemberton and his wife, and papers of Susan Lovering Pemberton, who was wife of Henry Pemberton, Jr. See *Guide to the Manuscript Collections of the Historical Society of Pennsylvania,* 2nd ed. (Philadelphia: Historical Society of Pennsylvania, 1949).

15,068. Pennsylvania Constitutional Convention
Records. 1872-73. 1 vol.
Open. Published guide.
Historical Society of Pennsylvania.
Minutes of the committee on suffrage, elections, and representation for the 1872-73 Convention. See *Guide to the Manuscript Collections of the Historical Society of Pennsylvania,* 2nd ed. (Philadelphia: Historical Society of Pennsylvania, 1949).

15,069. Pennsylvania Society for Promoting the Abolition of Slavery
Records. 1748-1916. Ca. 12,000 items (microfilm).
Open. Published guide.
Historical Society of Pennsylvania.
Records of the Society, which was founded in ca. 1780, consist of minutes of the acting committee, the electing committee, the committee on African slave trade, the committee for improving conditions for free Negroes, the committee on education, and the American Conventions between 1794 and 1809; membership lists; correspondence; and material on colonization projects, the formation of antislavery societies, and aid to Negroes. Also included are indenture books, manumission certificates, and other records concerning the manumission of male and female slaves; census books of the Negro population of Philadelphia during the 1840s; records of guardian schools, 1790-96; an entrance book for a Negro girls school, 1824-38; education and employment statistics, 1849-56; correspondence of the Female Anti-Slavery Society in Boston; and records of the Ladies First Union Association in Philadelphia. Collection also contains minutes, financial reports, correspondence with various abolitionists and antislavery societies, and clippings, 1833-53, of the Philadelphia Female Anti-Slavery Society, which was founded in 1833 and disbanded in 1870. See *Guide to the Manuscript Collections of the Historical Society of Pennsylvania,* 2nd ed. (Philadelphia: Historical Society of Pennsylvania, 1949).

15,070. Perot Malting Company
Records. 1819-1953. 80 vols. and 2000 items.
Open. No guide.
Historical Society of Pennsylvania.
Included with the business records of the Company, which was founded in 1687, are some personal papers of family members: estate papers of Elizabeth Marshall (1862-83) and Mary Ann Marshall (1881-1913), correspondence of Sarah T. Hallowell (?-1924), and correspondence in which her niece Harriet Hallowell (?-1943), a resident of France during WWI and WWII, comments on the wars.

15,071. Philadelphia Bicycle Club
Records. 1882-1902. 9 vols. and ca. 250 items.
Open. Unpublished guide.
Historical Society of Pennsylvania.
Financial records, minutes, and correspondence of the Club, a social group founded in 1882 to promote the "proper use" of the bicycle and bicycling for pleasure. Until 1898, female members of the Club belonged to the ladies division where they had fewer privileges and responsibilities; they always, however, took part in all Club social functions and races. In 1902 the Club was disbanded.

15,072. Philadelphia Catalogue of Contributors for Relief of the Poor
Records. 1766. 1 vol.
Open. Published guide.
Historical Society of Pennsylvania.
List of names of donors, dates, and amounts contributed to help Philadelphia's needy includes three women. See *Guide to the Manuscript Collections of the Historical Society of Pennsylvania,* 2nd ed. (Philadelphia: Historical Society of Pennsylvania, 1949).

15,073. Philadelphia Dancing Assembly
Records. 1749-1916. 4 vols.
Open. Published guide.
Historical Society of Pennsylvania.
Account book, subscription lists, rule books, menus, and clippings of the Assembly, founded in 1749 to provide musical entertainment. The Assembly

came to be a social affair for the elite, with dinner, dancing, a musical program, and a cotillion. Although women did not serve on Assembly boards, they managed the social activities. In one clipping the "Fancy Balls" are described as "unRepublican." See *Guide to the Manuscript Collections of the Historical Society of Pennsylvania,* 2nd ed. (Philadelphia: Historical Society of Pennsylvania, 1949).

15,074. Philadelphia Garden Club
Records. 1904-10. 5 vols.
Open. Published guide.
Historical Society of Pennsylvania.
Charter, reports of meetings, correspondence, and papers read before this women's club, founded to promote interest in gardens. See *Guide to the Manuscript Collections of the Historical Society of Pennsylvania,* 2nd ed. (Philadelphia: Historical Society of Pennsylvania, 1949).

15,075. Philadelphia General Hospital Women's Advisory Council
Records. 1915-57. 2500 items.
Open. Unpublished guide.
Historical Society of Pennsylvania.
Minutes, account books, bills and receipts, bank statements, correspondence, and Hospital shop reports of the Council, a volunteer group which advised the director of the city's Department of Health on conditions in the Hospital, and members of which were appointed by the director. Originally named the Women's Advisory Council of the Department of Health, the Council became active in promoting improved conditions at the Hospital. The organization was dissolved in 1957.

15,076. Philotacian Club
Records. 1914-17. 1 vol.
Open. Published guide.
Historical Society of Pennsylvania.
Minute book of the Club, an exclusive social group of Philadelphia women, contains names of officers and members and detailed descriptions of meetings and discussions on previously designated topics. See *Guide to the Manuscript Collections of the Historical Society of Pennsylvania,* 2nd ed. (Philadelphia: Historical Society of Pennsylvania, 1949).

15,077. Powel
Papers. 1700-1925. 50,000 items.
Open. Published guide.
Historical Society of Pennsylvania.
Personal papers, business records, and other material of related families: the Powels of Philadelphia, the Johnstons of Newport, RI, and the Johnstons, Taylors, and Coles of Jamaica. Included are pocket almanacs with diary entries, personal account books, receipt books, and correspondence of Elizabeth Willing Powel (1743-1830), wife of Samuel Powel (1738-93), who was elected mayor of Philadelphia in 1775; her correspondents include George Washington, Bishop William White, William Bingham, and clergyman Jacob Duché. Papers of Samuel Powel (1818-85), the son of her nephew and adopted son John Hare Powel, include correspondence with members of his family and letters to Dorothea Dix. Samuel Powel married Mary Johnston, who was born in Jamaica. Her family papers consist primarily of plantation records but also include diaries, ledgers, and medical records of Alexander Johnston (1739-87), a physician. Also contained are correspondence for 1883 to 1925, journals, notebooks, genealogical notes, and scrapbooks of Samuel and Mary Powel's daughter Mary Edith Powel (1846-1931). See *Guide to the Manuscript Collections of the Historical Society of Pennsylvania,* 2nd ed. (Philadelphia: Historical Society of Pennsylvania, 1949).

15,078. Purdon, James
Papers. 1839-41. 95 items.
Open. Unpublished guide.
Historical Society of Pennsylvania.
Correspondence of Purdon includes letters in which his sister Maria T. Purdon, while visiting in Easton, PA, describes local people and events.

15,079. Redwood, Mrs. Francis T.
Papers. 1762-1835. 69 items.
Open. Published guide.
Historical Society of Pennsylvania.
Family correspondence Redwood gathered is primarily between Mary (Johnson) Hopkinson (1718-1804) and her daughters Mary (Hopkinson) Morgan (1742-85), the wife of Dr. John Morgan of Philadelphia, who served as a physician to soldiers during the Revolutionary War; Elizabeth (Hopkinson) Duché (1738-?), wife of clergyman Jacob Duché; Jane Hopkinson; and Anne (Hopkinson) Coale (1745-1817) of Baltimore. In these affectionate letters which primarily concern family matters, the women, particularly Mary Morgan, often mention the War and its effect on their lives. Also included are copies of the wills of Mary Hopkinson and of Mary Morgan. See *Guide to the Manuscript Collections of the Historical Society of Pennsylvania,* 2nd ed. (Philadelphia: Historical Society of Pennsylvania, 1949).

15,080. Remey, George, and Remey, Mary
Papers. 1841-1928. 2 vols.
Open. Published guide.
Historical Society of Pennsylvania.
Genealogical data, travel and service records, photos, clippings, and coats of arms of George Collier Remey (1841-1928), a rear admiral in the US Navy. Includes reminiscences by his wife Mary Josephine (Mason) Remey (1845-1938) about social life and notable persons. See *Guide to the Manuscript Collections of the Historical Society of Pennsylvania,* 2nd ed. (Philadelphia: Historical Society of Pennsylvania, 1949).

15,081. Roberdeau, Buchanan
Papers. 1761-1831. 4 vols.
Open. Published guide.
Historical Society of Pennsylvania.
Correspondence, journal, and receipt book of General Daniel Roberdeau (1727-95), a merchant and Revolutionary War soldier. Includes a poetry album for 1829 to 1831 of Mary E. Roberdeau, which contains a poem written by John Quincy Adams and one signed by Abigail Adams. See *Guide to the Manuscript Collections of the Historical Society of Pennsylvania,* 2nd ed. (Philadelphia: Historical Society of Pennsylvania, 1949).

15,082. Rogers, Horace, and Rogers, Kate
Papers. 1849-82. 2 vols. and 248 items.
Open. Unpublished guide.
Historical Society of Pennsylvania.
Correspondence of Horace Rogers, a Philadelphia spiritualist, with his wife Kate Rogers and her letters to her cousin Carolyn Rogers and other family members primarily concern daily life.

15,083. Routh, Martha
Papers. 1794. 1 vol.
Open. Published guide.
Historical Society of Pennsylvania.
Journal in which Routh, a Quaker immigrant, describes her voyage from London to Boston, daily life, and her fears about safety and the adequacy of shipboard provisions. The journal was published in *The Friend* (January 5, 1888). See *Guide to the Manuscript Collections of the Historical Society of Pennsylvania,* 2nd ed. (Philadelphia: Historical Society of Pennsylvania, 1949).

15,084. Rush, Benjamin
Papers. Ca. 1761-1809. 2 vols.
Open. Catalog card.
Historical Society of Pennsylvania.
Papers of Rush (1745-1813), a physician and patriot, and of other family members include letters his wife Julia (Stockton) Rush (1759-1848) wrote to him while she was traveling in Canada in 1809, correspondence of their daughter Anne Emily (Rush) [Mrs. Ross] Cuthbert (1779-1850), and correspondence of Julia Rush's sister Mary Stockton (?-1846). Also includes bonds, indentures, bills, and receipts of Benjamin Rush's sister Rebecca (Rush) [Mrs. Thomas] Stamper (1743-93) and of his mother Susanna (Hall) [Mrs. Joseph] Harvey [Mrs. John] Rush [Mrs. Richard] Morris (1715?-95) as well as correspondence, poems, and literary extracts of Elizabeth Graeme Ferguson.

15,085. Sanitary Commission Great Central Fair
Records. 1864. 3 vols.
Open. Published guide.
Historical Society of Pennsylvania.
Memorandum book of the ladies' central committee and minutes of the wholesale dry goods department of the Fair. See *Guide to the Manuscript Collections of the Historical Society of Pennsylvania,* 2nd ed. (Philadelphia: Historical Society of Pennsylvania, 1949).

15,086. Scott, Hannah L.
Papers. 1903-09. Ca. 200 items.
Open. Published guide.
Historical Society of Pennsylvania.
Personal receipted bills of [Miss] Scott, who was a member of a prominent Philadelphia family. See *Guide to the Manuscript Collections of the Historical Society of Pennsylvania,* 2nd ed. (Philadelphia: Historical Society of Pennsylvania, 1949).

15,087. Shippen Family
Papers. 1701-1856. Ca. 10,000 items.
Open. Published guide.
Historical Society of Pennsylvania.
Family and business correspondence, journals, financial records, legal documents, estate and business papers, and scrapbooks of members of several generations of the Shippen and Burd families. Includes an 1824 album of Margaret Shippen, wife of physician Edward Shippen (1758-1809); a journal for 1847 to 1849, a bankbook, and a scrapbook of Sarah Burd; and correspondence from 1795 to 1818 between Anne Penn and John F. Mifflin. See *Guide to the Manuscript Collections of the Historical Society of Pennsylvania,* 2nd ed. (Philadelphia: Historical Society of Pennsylvania, 1949).

15,088. Shoemaker, Annie
Papers. 1891-97. 2 vols.
Open. Published guide.
Historical Society of Pennsylvania.
Letters of appreciation and tribute to Shoemaker, the principal of Friends Central School in Philadelphia, from her students and faculty concern her work in education from 1853 to 1897. See *Guide to the Manuscript Collections of the Historical Society of Pennsylvania,* 2nd ed. (Philadelphia: Historical Society of Pennsylvania, 1949).

15,089. Shoemaker, Samuel, and Shoemaker, Rebecca
Papers. 1780-86. 5 vols.
Open. Published guide.
Historical Society of Pennsylvania.
Diaries which Samuel Shoemaker (1724-1800), a Quaker, merchant, and statesman, wrote for his wife Rebecca (Warner) Rawle Shoemaker (?-1819) while he was a Loyalist refugee in London are included with diaries and correspondence of his wife and daughters Anna Rawle and Margaret Rawle. See *Guide to the Manuscript Collections of the Historical Society of Pennsylvania,* 2nd ed.

(Philadelphia: Historical Society of Pennsylvania, 1949).

15,090. Smiley, Sarah F.
Papers. 1868-69. 1 vol.
Open. Published guide.
Historical Society of Pennsylvania.
Journal of Smiley, written while she was en route to England on the steamer *Cuba,* contains details of her philanthropic interests, religious activities, sermons she heard, church meetings, and visits to schools and institutions. See *Guide to the Manuscript Collections of the Historical Society of Pennsylvania,* 2nd ed. (Philadelphia: Historical Society of Pennsylvania, 1949).

15,091. Smith, Mary Bainerd
Papers. 1894-1957. 64 vols.
Open. Unpublished guide.
Historical Society of Pennsylvania.
Diaries in which Smith, a Philadelphia resident, mentions family news, visits with friends, travel, and weather conditions.

15,092. Snowden, Louise Hortense
Papers. 1910-20. Ca. 200 items.
Open. Published guide.
Historical Society of Pennsylvania.
Notes of Snowden, a history professor at Wellesley College in ca. 1915, for lectures on the feudal system, church, and political organizations in medieval Europe; scientific notes; and drawings of specimens. See *Guide to the Manuscript Collections of the Historical Society of Pennsylvania,* 2nd ed. (Philadelphia: Historical Society of Pennsylvania, 1949).

15,093. South Carolina Photos
Collection. Ca. 1880. 20 items.
Open. Published guide.
Historical Society of Pennsylvania.
Photos taken by Laura H. Dade, some from great heights, depict her friends, the towns of Beaufort and Columbia, SC, and, frequently, the Baptist church in Columbia. The daughter of a physician, Dade appears to have enjoyed a life of privilege and leisure. See *Guide to the Manuscript Collections of the Historical Society of Pennsylvania,* 2nd ed. (Philadelphia: Historical Society of Pennsylvania, 1949).

15,094. Spring Garden Soup Society
Records. 1852-1929. 800 items.
Open. Unpublished guide.
Historical Society of Pennsylvania.
Records of the Society, a benevolent Philadelphia group founded in 1852, consist of minutes, a list of members, bills, receipts, coal orders, correspondence, and a receipt book of donations. Also included are registers of applicants for Society assistance from 1853 to 1929; name, occupation, residence, skin color, number of adults and children needing help, and name of reference are noted for each. Although the Society was not predominantly a women's group, women were members, contributors, and recipients of aid.

15,095. Stillwell, Mary H.
Papers. 1872-1933. 82 items.
Open. Published guide.
Historical Society of Pennsylvania.
A dentist who received her dental degree in 1888 from the University of Pennsylvania, Stillwell-Kuesel was the first president of the Women's Dental Association of the US, which was founded in 1892 and renamed the Federation of American Women Dentists in 1922. Includes correspondence, some of which was with Anna Howard Shaw and Carrie Chapman Catt; Association bylaws; lists of women dentists in Pennsylvania; editorials on the first women dental students at the University, 1872-74; memoirs of James Truman about the University's first women dental students; and clippings about women in dentistry. See *Guide to the Manuscript Collections of the Historical Society of Pennsylvania,* 2nd ed. (Philadelphia: Historical Society of Pennsylvania, 1949).

15,096. Stokes, Sallie M.
Papers. 1859-64. 1 vol.
Open. No guide.
Historical Society of Pennsylvania.
Diary in which Stokes, a young woman from Germantown, PA, comments on the Civil War and social life.

15,097. Sword Family
Papers. 1750-1863. Ca. 1000 items.
Open. No guide.
Historical Society of Pennsylvania.
Letters between Mary (Parry) Sword, who lived in Macao and Canton, China, and her family in Philadelphia contain information about social life and events in Philadelphia and about trade with China. Also contains other family correspondence.

15,098. Thomas, Lydia, and Thomas, Mary B.
Papers. 1826-32. 2 vols.
Open. Published guide.
Historical Society of Pennsylvania.
Autograph books of the Misses Thomas, who were sisters, contain poetry and watercolor sketches by friends. See *Guide to the Manuscript Collections of the Historical Society of Pennsylvania,* 2nd ed. (Philadelphia: Historical Society of Pennsylvania, 1949).

15,099. Thompson, Rebecca
Papers. 1827. 2 vols.
Open. Published guide.
Historical Society of Pennsylvania.
Lyrical compositions of Thompson were written both in prose and verse. See *Guide to the Manuscript Collections of the Historical Society of Pennsylvania,* 2nd ed. (Philadelphia: Historical Society of Pennsylvania, 1949).

15,100. Thompson, Sarah, and Robinson, Rebecca (Dunn)
Papers. 1782-1849. 1 vol.
Open. Published guide.
Historical Society of Pennsylvania.
Commonplace book of Thompson (1764-1821), a schoolgirl who later married Richard Dunn in 1787, contains genealogical notes by her daughter Rebecca Robinson. See *Guide to the Manuscript Collections of the Historical Society of Pennsylvania,* 2nd ed. (Philadelphia: Historical Society of Pennsylvania, 1949).

15,101. United Service Organization
Records. 1941-48. 78 vols. and 40,000 items.
Open. Unpublished guide.
Historical Society of Pennsylvania.
Minutes, financial records, and personnel records of the USO contain material of the Philadelphia USO, the South Broad Street USO Club, the USO Labor Plaza, and the Jewish Welfare Board. Also included are minutes, financial records, correspondence, reports, and a scrapbook of the USO women's committee and minutes, financial records, reports, membership lists, and a scrapbook of the USO Service Women's Club.

15,102. Van Varick, Margarita
Papers. 1695-96. 1 item.
Open. Published guide.
Historical Society of Pennsylvania.
Will and inventory of the estate of Van Varick, the widow of Rudolphus Van Varick of Flatbush, NY. See *Guide to the Manuscript Collections of the Historical Society of Pennsylvania,* 2nd ed. (Philadelphia: Historical Society of Pennsylvania, 1949).

15,103. War Relief, Pennsylvania Railroad Women's Division of
Records. 1916-19. 2 vols.
Open. Published guide.
Historical Society of Pennsylvania.
Accounts, correspondence, and other material concerning the activities of the Division. See *Guide to the Manuscript Collections of the Historical Society of Pennsylvania,* 2nd ed. (Philadelphia: Historical Society of Pennsylvania, 1949).

15,104. Warder, Ann
Papers. 1786-89. 14 vols.
Open. Published guide.
Historical Society of Pennsylvania.
Journals in which Warder, wife of Philadelphia merchant John Warder, writing to her sister Elizabeth Head in England, comments on travel, social customs, Quaker meetings, and prominent Philadelphians. She mentions the Waln, Emlen, Parke, Biddle, Owen, Vaux, and Morris families. See *Guide to the Manuscript Collections of the Historical Society of Pennsylvania,* 2nd ed. (Philadelphia: Historical Society of Pennsylvania, 1949).

15,105. Warder, E. H.
Papers. 1832. 1 vol.
Open. Published guide.
Historical Society of Pennsylvania.
Diary of [Miss] Warder in which she recorded her activities, chiefly sewing, visiting, and receiving guests, during a summer she spent near Germantown, PA. See *Guide to the Manuscript Collections of the Historical Society of Pennsylvania,* 2nd ed. (Philadelphia: Historical Society of Pennsylvania, 1949).

15,106. Warley Bascom's Sons
Records. 1881-1974. 2 boxes.
Open. Unpublished guide.
Historical Society of Pennsylvania.
Bills, receipts, estate documents, and other business records of this upholstery business, which was operated by a black family in Philadelphia between 1881 and 1974. Josephine Davis Bascom (?-1925) and her daughter Ethel (Bascom) Sarjeant (?-1974) managed the family company during separate periods in its history.

15,107. Watson, John Fanning
Papers. 1693-1855. 16 vols.
Open. Published guide.
Historical Society of Pennsylvania.
Papers of Watson (1779-1860), a Philadelphia historian, contain correspondence, manuscripts of his works, a journal, and research material. Included is Lucy Watson's 1762 account of settlers in western Pennsylvania. See *Guide to the Manuscript Collections of the Historical Society of Pennsylvania,* 2nd ed. (Philadelphia: Historical Society of Pennsylvania, 1949).

15,108. West Philadelphia Reading Society
Records. 1837-43. 1 vol.
Open. Inventory.
Historical Society of Pennsylvania.
Minutes of the Society, a social group of young men and women who met for their intellectual improvement and to provide aid to charitable institutions and poor persons in West Philadelphia. Meetings included readings by male Society members of the works of various authors. Women headed some of the committees, including the sewing group that made and distributed clothing to the needy.

15,109. Westcott, Esther Montgomery
Papers. Ca. 1812. 1 vol.
Open. Published guide.
Historical Society of Pennsylvania.
Poems by Westcott and others and clippings of poems. See *Guide to the Manuscript Collections*

of the Historical Society of Pennsylvania, 2nd ed. (Philadelphia: Historical Society of Pennsylvania, 1949).

15,110. Whales, Henry
Papers. 1830-1904. 50 items.
Open. Published guide.
Historical Society of Pennsylvania.
Account book of the pupils of Whales, a master of separate dancing classes for ladies and for gentlemen, contains blank pages on which Carroll Kleine drew pictures and wrote descriptions in 1904 of an attack on his grandmother by two Negroes. See *Guide to the Manuscript Collections of the Historical Society of Pennsylvania,* 2nd ed. (Philadelphia: Historical Society of Pennsylvania, 1949).

15,111. Wharton, Anne Hollingsworth
Papers. 1852-1926. 80,000 items.
Open. Published guide.
Historical Society of Pennsylvania.
Papers of Wharton (1845-1928), an author, consists of drafts of her writings, biographical data, historical notes, reproductions of portraits, and clippings on colonial persons and places. See *Guide to the Manuscript Collections of the Historical Society of Pennsylvania,* 2nd ed. (Philadelphia: Historical Society of Pennsylvania, 1949).

15,112. Wharton, Katherine Johnstone (Brinley)
Papers. 1856-1922. 11 vols. and 130 items.
Open. Unpublished guide.
Historical Society of Pennsylvania.
Diaries in which Wharton (?-1926), a Philadelphian, comments on current events and social life in Philadelphia and Newport, RI. Also included is correspondence, some of which contains descriptions of life in England during WWI.

15,113. Wilcocks, Harriet (Manigault)
Papers. 1813-16. 3 vols.
Open. Unpublished guide.
Historical Society of Pennsylvania.
Diaries in which [Mrs. Samuel] Wilcocks (1793-?) describes her life in Philadelphia before she married and her association with prominent people.

15,114. Williams, Annabelle
Papers. 1829-31. 3 vols.
Open. Published guide.
Historical Society of Pennsylvania.
Diary of a trip Williams took with her family from Philadelphia to Cleveland and back via Albany, Buffalo, and Pittsburgh. Also included are poems, financial accounts, and Williams's schoolbook containing poems and maps of various states along the East Coast. See *Guide to the Manuscript Collections of the Historical Society of Pennsylvania,* 2nd ed. (Philadelphia: Historical Society of Pennsylvania, 1949).

15,115. Wilson, James
Papers. 1718-1857. Ca. 1500 items.
Open. Published guide.
Historical Society of Pennsylvania.
Contains correspondence, journals, draft and corrected copies of the Constitution, treaties, maps, and other material relating to the business and professional activities of Wilson (1742-98), a congressman, jurist, businessman, and speculator. Included are letters of Mary Wilson Hollingsworth from 1801 to 1812. See *Guide to the Manuscript Collections of the Historical Society of Pennsylvania,* 2nd ed. (Philadelphia: Historical Society of Pennsylvania, 1949).

15,116. Wister Family
Papers. Ca. 1730-1940. 47 boxes.
Open. Description and shelflist.
Historical Society of Pennsylvania.
Correspondence, diaries, account books, genealogical items, photos, and other papers of Frances Anne (Kemble) Butler (1809-93), an English and American actress and author, and of her daughters Sarah (Butler) Wister (1835-1908) and Frances (Butler) Leigh (1838-1910), both of whom were active in social causes, document plantation administration, the Civil War, and family, business, and cultural life. Included is correspondence concerning the compilation of a volume of biographical sketches entitled *Worthy Women of Our First Century,* letters from the English feminist Frances Power Cobbe to Sarah Wister, and material of Sarah Yorke Stevenson, an archaeologist, columnist, and civic leader who was assistant curator of the Pennsylvania Museum in Philadelphia.

15,117. Wister, James W.
Papers. 1777-1889. Ca. 600 items.
Open. Published guide.
Historical Society of Pennsylvania.
Included with the correspondence, receipt books, estate papers, and other material of the family of Wister, a Philadelphia physician, are the receipt book of Sarah Whiteside for 1822 to 1841 and an 1833 "Germs of Thought" volume of contemplations written for Susan Wister. See *Guide to the Manuscript Collections of the Historical Society of Pennsylvania,* 2nd ed. (Philadelphia: Historical Society of Pennsylvania, 1949).

15,118. Wister, Sarah "Sally"
Papers. 1777-78. 1 vol.
Open. Published guide.
Historical Society of Pennsylvania.
Diary in which Wister (1761-1804), a Quaker, describes social life during the British occupation of Philadelphia. See *Guide to the Manuscript Collections of the Historical Society of Pennsylvania,* 2nd ed. (Philadelphia: Historical Society of Pennsylvania, 1949).

15,119. Women's Centennial Committee
Records. 1874-77. 2 vols.
Open. Published guide.
Historical Society of Pennsylvania.
Minutes; post card of the Women's Pavilion, which was erected as a result of the efforts of the Committee; and clippings, including an editorial by Mary Nolan, Missouri commissioner, about a controversial meeting the Committee held in November 1876. See *Guide to the Manuscript Collections of the Historical Society of Pennsylvania,* 2nd ed. (Philadelphia: Historical Society of Pennsylvania, 1949).

15,120. Women's Dental Association of the United States
Records. 1892-1921. 2 vols.
Open. Published guide.
Historical Society of Pennsylvania.
Minutes of meetings held between 1892 and 1906, committee reports, and lists of members of the Association, which was founded in 1892 to promote the interests of women dentists and to encourage their interaction. Also included are clippings on accidents from early x-ray use. See *Guide to the Manuscript Collections of the Historical Society of Pennsylvania,* 2nd ed. (Philadelphia: Historical Society of Pennsylvania, 1949).

15,121. World War II
Collection. 1939-45. 30,000 items.
Open. Published guide.
Historical Society of Pennsylvania.
Memoranda, reports, press releases, speeches, posters, and other material from such agencies as the Office of Price Administration, the Office of War Information, and the USO. Includes releases and reports on manufacturing requirements; hints on warmth; price information on women's clothing; and 1943 OWI releases to the editors of newspaper women's pages on food prices, encouraging one's children to purchase War Saving Stamps, and homemaking hints for working women. Also included is information on women in the work force; correspondence for 1940 and 1941, memoranda, and reports of the National Legion of Mothers of America, an organization opposed to American involvement in WWII; and material concerning the League for Human Rights and the Mothers of Pennsylvania. See *Guide to the Manuscript Collections of the Historical Society of Pennsylvania,* 2nd ed. (Philadelphia: Historical Society of Pennsylvania, 1949).

15,122. Youth's Missionary Society
Records. 1835-39. 1 vol.
Open. Published guide.
Historical Society of Pennsylvania.
Minutes of the Youth's Female Missionary Society, a girls' social organization of the First Independent Church in Philadelphia, which merged with the boys' Society in 1836. The Society, whose members were under the age of 18, was founded in 1737 and disbanded in 1847; it sent money to foreign and home missionaries, attempted to help start a Protestant church in Brussels, Belgium, and assumed the support and education of a "heathen" child who was to be called by the name Helen Chambers. In 1837 Chambers was made a member of the Society. See *Guide to the Manuscript Collections of the Historical Society of Pennsylvania,* 2nd ed. (Philadelphia: Historical Society of Pennsylvania, 1949).

15,123. Business Archives
Records. 1792- . 2500 ft., 395 vols., and microfilm.
Open. Unpublished guide.
INA Corporation.
The Insurance Company of North America (INA), founded in 1792, was the first marine insurance company in the US; it began to write marine insurance policies in 1794, and in 1967 it became the major subsidiary of INA Corporation, a holding company. Administrative and legal records; insurance blotters; loss books, 18th- and early 19th-century marine policies; perpetual fire insurance policies and surveys, 1841-1956; advertising and communications department material, with items concerning women from the 1940s to the present; microfilmed employee record cards for 1918 to 1944, with name, address, birth date, job title, and salary; and photos.

15,124. Archives
Records. 1950- . 12 drawers.
Open. No guide.
International Association for Personnel Women.
Records of the Association, founded in 1950 to advance the professional interests of women in personnel management and to provide a forum for the exchange of information and to serve as a medium for research into personnel problems. Consists of minutes, financial records, correspondence, administrative files, research papers, biographical data, pamphlets, and such professional publications as *The Personnel Woman,* the *IAPW Journal,* and the *Consultants Directory,* which listed IAPW members who were available to assist other personnel professionals. The *Directory* gave each woman's particular area of expertise.

15,125. American Medical Women's Association
Records. 20th century. Ca. 20 cu.ft.
Open. No guide.
Medical College of Pennsylvania, Archives and Special Collections.
Correspondence, personal papers, indexes, reprints, photos, and memorabilia of the AMWA, an organization of women physicians founded in 1915 by Bertha Van Hoosen. Collected by Van Hoosen, this material was intended to form the core of a collection on women in medicine. Administrative

records of the AMWA are held by Cornell University.

15,126. Bodley, Rachel Littler
Papers. 1856-91. 0.5 cu.ft.
Open. Unpublished guide.
Medical College of Pennsylvania, Archives and Special Collections.
Reports, bylaws, invoices, and reprints concern the work of [Miss] Bodley (1831-88), a physician, as professor and dean from 1874 to 1888 of the Woman's Medical College of Pennsylvania.

15,127. Broomall, Anna Elizabeth
Papers. 1890s. 10 cu.ft.
Open. Unpublished guide.
Medical College of Pennsylvania, Archives and Special Collections.
Memorabilia that [Miss] Broomall (1847-1931), a physician, collected during her travels around the world. Much of the material is from the Orient, and correspondence and clippings are included as well. Broomall was associated both with the Woman's Medical College of Pennsylvania and the Woman's Hospital of Philadelphia.

15,128. Hay
Papers. 1886-1940. 0.5 cu.ft.
Open. Unpublished guide.
Medical College of Pennsylvania, Archives and Special Collections.
Medical College faculty reports, exams, and drafts, many of which pertain to Clara Marshall and Martha Tracy.

15,129. Hurd-Mead, Kate Campbell
Papers. 1888-1949. 3 cu.ft.
Open. Unpublished guide.
Medical College of Pennsylvania, Archives and Special Collections.
Much of the correspondence, account book, manuscript, reviews, and photos of Hurd-Mead (1867-1941), a physician and historian, concern her garden club activities and work on her *History of Women in Medicine,* the first volume of which was published. She completed the manuscript for a second volume, but it was not published. Also includes notes and material she collected for a proposed third volume.

15,130. Macfarlane, Catharine
Papers. 20th century. Ca. 3 cu.ft.
Open. No guide.
Medical College of Pennsylvania, Archives and Special Collections.
Correspondence, reprints, photos, a film of a "This Is Your Life" television program, and memorabilia of Macfarlane (1877-1969), a physician and professor at the Woman's Medical College of Pennsylvania. She was noted for her work in founding a cancer detection clinic in Philadelphia.

15,131. Marshall, Clara
Papers. 1888-1920. 1 cu.ft.
Open. Unpublished guide.
Medical College of Pennsylvania, Archives and Special Collections.
Primarily correspondence concerning the career of Marshall (1847-1931), a physician, as dean of the Woman's Medical College of Pennsylvania from 1888 to 1917.

15,132. Medical College of Pennsylvania
Records. 1850- . 150 cu.ft.
Open. Unpublished guide.
Medical College of Pennsylvania, Archives and Special Collections.
Material relating to the history and activities of the College, founded in 1850 as the Female Medical College of Pennsylvania; to its hospital; and to students, faculty, and administrators involved with the institution. Includes minutes, financial and patient records, student theses, catalogs, bulletins, valedictory addresses, annual announcements, yearbooks, photos, slides, film, memorabilia, and other items. The name of the College was changed to Woman's Medical College of Pennsylvania in 1867. The first male students were admitted in 1969, and the name was changed to Medical College of Pennsylvania in 1970.

15,133. Northwestern University Woman's Medical School
Records. 1871-1901. 0.5 cu.ft.
Open. No guide.
Medical College of Pennsylvania, Archives and Special Collections.
Minutes reflect the organization and activities of the Woman's Medical School, founded in 1871 and discontinued in 1902. Also includes statistical information on the number of matriculants, correspondence, and a scrapbook.

15,134. Oral Histories of Women Physicians
Oral history. 1977- . 43 interviews.
Partially restricted. Unpublished guide.
Medical College of Pennsylvania, Archives and Special Collections.
In-depth interviews with women physicians, medical students, children of women physicians, a male medical student, and others, all of whom were selected to represent a wide range of ages, specialties, backgrounds, and life choices. Collection consists of tapes, transcripts, and collateral correspondence, manuscripts, reprints, and photos. Among those interviewed are physicians Alma Dea Morani, Natalie Shainess, Louise de Schweinitz, Marjorie Sirridge, Grace Holmes, Joni Magee, Doris Bartuska, Elizabeth McGrew, Maxine Bennett, Frances Conley, Gillian Karatinos, Dorothy Brown, Esther Bridgman Clark, Ida B. S. Scudder, and Rhonda Jeffries; medical students Vanessa Gamble, Catherine Scholl, and Fredericka Heller; and Florence Haseltine and Mary Howell, both of whom held PhD and MD degrees.

15,135. Photos
Collection. 19th and 20th centuries. More than 2000 items.
Open. Unpublished guide.
Medical College of Pennsylvania, Archives and Special Collections.
Photos, woodcuts, photoengravings, and glass slides of the College's buildings, anatomy laboratory and other classes, students, faculty, and many women in medicine.

15,136. Potter, Ellen Culver
Papers. 1903-54. 2 cu.ft.
Open. No guide.
Medical College of Pennsylvania, Archives and Special Collections.
Correspondence, telegrams, reprints, awards, photos, and clippings concern the life and work of Potter (1871-1958), a physician who specialized in preventive medicine.

15,137. Poynter, Lida
Papers. Nd. 14 ft.
Open. No guide.
Medical College of Pennsylvania, Archives and Special Collections.
Unpublished manuscript that Poynter (1832-1919), a physician, wrote about Mary Edwards Walker. Also includes notes, reprints, photos, and clippings she used in the preparation of the manuscript.

15,138. Reprints
Collection. 1750- . 25 cu.ft.
Open. Published and unpublished guides.
Medical College of Pennsylvania, Archives and Special Collections.
Articles, pamphlets, books, and other material written by or about women physicians. See Sandra L. Chaff, Ruth Haimbach, Carol Fenichel, and Nina B. Woodside, comps. and eds., *Women in Medicine: A Bibliography of the Literature on Women Physicians* (Metuchen, NJ: Scarecrow Press, Inc., 1977).

15,139. Selmon, Bertha Eugenia (Loveland)
Papers. 1940s. 1 cu.ft.
Open. No guide.
Medical College of Pennsylvania, Archives and Special Collections.
Selmon (1877-1949) was a physician, missionary, historian, and author. Bulk of the collection is typescripts of articles by and about women physicians. Also includes Selmon's correspondence, notes, biographical information on women physicians, manuscripts, photoengravings, and reprints.

15,140. Tracy, Martha
Papers. 1884-1934. 2.5 cu.ft.
Open. Unpublished guide.
Medical College of Pennsylvania, Archives and Special Collections.
Tracy (1876-1942), a physician, was dean of the Woman's Medical College of Pennsylvania from 1917 to 1940. Correspondence, minutes of the board of corporators, drafts, bulletins, and memorabilia primarily concern her work as dean.

15,141. Van Hoosen, Bertha
Papers. 20th century. 4 cu.ft.
Open. No guide.
Medical College of Pennsylvania, Archives and Special Collections.
Correspondence and reports relate to the American Medical Women's Association of which Van Hoosen (1863-1952), a physician, was founder and first president.

15,142. West Philadelphia Hospital for Women
Records. 1890s-1930s. 3 cu.ft.
Open. No guide.
Medical College of Pennsylvania, Archives and Special Collections.
The Hospital was founded in 1889 by physician Elizabeth Comly-Howell to provide medical care for women and a training school for nurses; in 1929 the Hospital was merged with Woman's Hospital of Philadelphia. Primarily minutes of executive committee meetings.

15,143. Woman's Medical College Students MD Theses
Records. 1851-1943. 24 cu.ft.
Open. Unpublished guide.
Medical College of Pennsylvania, Archives and Special Collections.
Papers on medical topics, which were written by students of the Female Medical College of Pennsylvania and Woman's Medical College of Pennsylvania in fulfillment of a graduation requirement.

15,144. Women Physicians
Collection. Late 19th century and 20th century. 3 cu.ft.
Open. No guide.
Medical College of Pennsylvania, Archives and Special Collections.
Correspondence, manuscripts, reprints, scrapbooks, photos, and other personal papers of such women physicians as Deliah Lynch, Ann Preston, Hannah Longshore, Elizabeth Blackwell, Rosina Wistein, Edith Millican, Margaret Cockett, and Nancy Gubisch. Also includes the manuscript of *The Doctors Jacobi* by Rhoda Truax.

15,145. Women's Medical Societies and Clubs
Collection. 20th century. 3.5 cu.ft.
Open. No guide.
Medical College of Pennsylvania, Archives and Special Collections.
Scattered bylaws, minutes, and account and record books of the Woman's Medical Society of Connecticut, 1930s-40s; the Broomall Club,

1909-60; and the Chicago Medical Women's Club, 1930s.

15,146. Keasey, Mother Boniface
Papers. 1968- . 13 drawers, 1200 items, and 250 tapes.
Access restricted. Unpublished guide.
Missionary Servants of the Most Blessed Trinity.
Research relating to the life and work of Mother Boniface (1885-1931), who was born Margaret Louise Keasey. The first reverend mother and cofounder with Father Thomas A. Judge of this American community of religious women, Mother Boniface also was active in planning the training of the men's community known as the Missionary Servants of the Most Holy Trinity and encouraged the development of lay apostles. Family history records of Mother Boniface, tapes of oral history interviews with persons who knew her, articles about her, slide presentations, photos, newsletters, magazines, obituaries of members of these religious communities and lay persons associated with the communities, research studies on the communities, and other papers relating to the Missionary Servants. Mother Boniface died of typhoid fever contracted while she was nursing others with the disease.

15,147. Archives
Records. 1904- . 3 boxes, 75 vols., and ca. 700 items.
Closed. No guide.
Monastery of the Visitation of Holy Mary.
Annual letters, ca. 700 circular letters, scrapbooks, and clippings of this community of Visitation Nuns, an order of contemplative women. This community of the Nuns was founded in Mexico in 1898; its members were given refuge in Philadelphia in 1926 after being exiled from Mexico.

15,148. Maternity Hospital
Records. 1872-1929. 7 vols. and other items.
Open. Unpublished guide.
Pennsylvania Hospital Archives.
Volumes of administrative records of the board of governors, of contributors, and of the treasurer of the Hospital, which was founded in 1872 as the State Hospital for Women and Infants. A lying-in hospital primarily for working-class women, many of them recent immigrants, the institution changed its name in 1883 and during the 1920s was absorbed by Pennsylvania Hospital. The collection also includes individual case histories containing personal information and medical data regarding the patient's labor. The volumes of administrative records are available on microfilm.

15,149. Pennsylvania Hospital Training School for Nurses
Records. 1875-1929. Ca. 1 box and 10 vols.
Open. Unpublished guide.
Pennsylvania Hospital Archives.
Founded in 1875, this training school for nurses functioned until 1974. Reports of the School's superintendent to the board of managers, records on individual students, and miscellaneous material on nurses corps in WWI. The Pennsylvania Hospital archives also houses minutes of the School's board of managers.

15,150. Philadelphia Lying-In Charity Hospital
Records. 1844-1929. 6 vols.
Open. Unpublished guide.
Pennsylvania Hospital Archives.
Administrative records of the Hospital, founded in 1844 as a lying-in facility principally for working-class women, many of whom were recent immigrants, consist of minutes of the board of managers, 1844-63; minutes of the executive committee, 1888-1905; minutes of the contributors, 1860-1929; and subscription books. The Hospital was absorbed by the Pennsylvania Hospital during the 1920s. Collection is also available on microfilm.

15,151. Preston Retreat
Records. 1836-98. 1 Hollinger box, 9 vols., and other items.
Open. Unpublished guide.
Pennsylvania Hospital Archives.
Administrative records concerning the operation of this lying-in hospital for working-class women, many of whom were recent immigrants, consist of minutes of the board of managers, 1836-64; minutes of the sub-visiting committee of women, 1866-98; miscellaneous volumes of the building committee, 1836-41; and other records, all of which are also available on microfilm. In addition, the collection contains registers of personal information as well as medical data concerning the labor of individual patients. The Retreat was founded in 1836 and absorbed by the Pennsylvania Hospital in ca. 1909.

15,152. Bishops and Archbishops of Philadelphia
Papers. 1808-1961. 15,117 items.
Access restricted. Unpublished guide.
Philadelphia Archdiocesan Archives.
Correspondence, diaries, and scrapbooks of the Diocese of Philadelphia, which was founded in 1808. Includes letters dealing with the apostolic works of religious women and letters of Mother Katharine Drexel, foundress of the Sisters of the Blessed Sacrament for Indians and Colored People.

15,153. Association for Jewish Children
Records. 1855-1974. 45 Hollinger boxes and 28 vols.
Open. Published guide.
Philadelphia Jewish Archives Center.
Records of this Philadelphia Jewish community child-care agency and its predecessors, including the Jewish Foster Home and Orphan Asylum, 1855-1929, and the Juvenile Aid Society, 1911-40.

The Jewish Foster Home and Orphan Asylum was an orphanage for Jewish children, which was founded by [Miss] Rebecca Gratz and other women in 1855 and which usually provided care for children until they were 14 years old, after which they were indentured into various occupations. Charter, annual reports, minutes, financial records, a history, a register, roll books, and reports contain data on female and male residents of the Home. [Miss] Anna Allen served as the Home's first directress, but after 1874 the role of women became less important; they became members of an associate board of directors, while men made up the regular board

The Juvenile Aid Society was founded by the Young Women's Union in 1901 to provide help for Jewish delinquent girls and boys; in 1911 the Society became an organization separate from the Union. Charter, bylaws, minutes of committee meetings, case histories, and court reports. Members of the Society accompanied children to court, urged the city to hire a Jewish parole officer, and gave educational and other kinds of help to their charges. See Lindsay B. Nauen, ed., *A Guide to the Philadelphia Jewish Archives Center* (Philadelphia: Philadelphia Jewish Archives Center, 1977).

15,154. Friends of the Deaf
Records. 1936-73. 4 Hollinger boxes.
Open. Published guide.
Philadelphia Jewish Archives Center.
The Friends, organized in 1936, provided a meeting place for social and educational activities for Jewish deaf people; [Mrs.] Rose Olanoff was one of the founders and is currently a director of the group. Minutes, correspondence, reports, a membership list, publicity, and yearbooks reflect Olanoff's role in the development and maintenance of the organization. Bulk of the collection is her correspondence. See Lindsay B. Nauen, ed., *A Guide to the Philadelphia Jewish Archives Center* (Philadelphia: Philadelphia Jewish Archives Center, 1977).

15,155. Hebrew Immigrant Aid Society
Records. 1884-1972. 1 folder and 45 vols.
Open. Published guide.
Philadelphia Jewish Archives Center.
The Society was founded in 1884 to provide financial and other aid to immigrants arriving at the Philadelphia port. Volumes of records, a 1970 fact sheet, and a history written in 1972. The volumes list demographic data on immigrants, with date of arrival, name of ship, and, for each family group, sex, age, occupation, place of birth, destination, and other information. See Lindsay B. Nauen, ed., *A Guide to the Philadelphia Jewish Archives Center* (Philadelphia: Philadelphia Jewish Archives Center, 1977).

15,156. Hebrew Sunday School Society
Records. 1838-1976. 14 Hollinger boxes.
Open. Published guide.
Philadelphia Jewish Archives Center.
Minute books, correspondence, reports, and photos of the Society, which was founded in 1838 by Rebecca Gratz to provide Jewish education one day per week to children of parents who were unaffiliated with a congregation. The Society's directors are all women, and, in its early years, all the teachers were women. The Society has a separate male advisory group. See Lindsay B. Nauen, ed., *A Guide to the Philadelphia Jewish Archives Center* (Philadelphia: Philadelphia Jewish Archives Center, 1977).

15,157. Jewish Sheltering Home for the Aged
Records. 1917-72. 1 folder.
Open. Published guide.
Philadelphia Jewish Archives Center.
Scattered constitutions, a history, and a clipping of this home for aged and infirm persons who could not afford to pay for their own support; the Home was established in 1890. The Home's directors and officers, who at first were all women, admitted men and women to the Home on the advice of a physician. Later boards of directors included both men and women. See Lindsay B. Nauen, ed., *A Guide to the Philadelphia Jewish Archives Center* (Philadelphia: Philadelphia Jewish Archives Center, 1977).

15,158. Lotman, Arline
Papers. 1971-74. 1 folder.
Open. Published guide.
Philadelphia Jewish Archives Center.
Clippings of newspaper columns that Lotman wrote for the *Jewish Exponent* describing Jewish life in Philadelphia during the 1940s. Also includes clippings concerning her appointment as executive director of the Commission on the Status of Women of the Commonwealth of Pennsylvania. See Lindsay B. Nauen, ed., *A Guide to the Philadelphia Jewish Archives Center* (Philadelphia: Philadelphia Jewish Archives Center, 1977).

15,159. Mogell, Claire
Oral history. 1976. 1 tape.
Open. Published guide.
Philadelphia Jewish Archives Center.
Interview in which [Mrs.] Mogell (1905-) describes her experiences in Poland and Germany during WWII, Nazi treatment of Polish Jews, her travels and hiding with her two daughters until Germany was liberated in 1945, and her immigration to the US in 1949. See Lindsay B. Nauen, ed., *A Guide to the Philadelphia Jewish Archives Center* (Philadelphia: Philadelphia Jewish Archives Center, 1977).

15,160. Neighborhood Centre
Records. Ca. 1901-67. Ca. 250 Hollinger boxes.
Access restricted. Unpublished guide.

Philadelphia Jewish Archives Center.
Minutes, financial records, correspondence, reports, case records, and other material of the Young Women's Union, founded in 1885 to provide a kindergarten and day nursery for the children of immigrant working mothers and recreational and social activities for persons of all ages. In 1918 the Union was renamed the Centre. Although the Union was run originally entirely by women, their role in the Centre gradually diminished over the years. Prior to 1943 several women served as executive director.

15,161. Newhoff, Sarah
Papers. 1915-58. 1 folder.
Open. Published guide.
Philadelphia Jewish Archives Center.
Papers of [Mrs. Lewis] Newhoff, a philanthropist, primarily relate to her activities on behalf of the Jewish Sheltering Home for the Aged, with a constitution, correspondence, promotional items, and a series of investigative requests made by the Society of Jewish Women of Philadelphia for Lodging the Homeless and Sheltering the Aged (Hachnasas Orchin Umoshav Z'keinim), the women's auxiliary of the Home. Also includes records from other groups in which Newhoff participated, including the Council of Social Agencies section for the care of the aged, the Home for the Jewish Aged, the Mount Sinai Hospital Auxiliary of the American National Red Cross, and the Down-Town Hebrew Day Nursery. See Lindsay B. Nauen, ed., *A Guide to the Philadelphia Jewish Archives Center* (Philadelphia: Philadelphia Jewish Archives Center, 1977).

15,162. Schleindlinger, Lena
Papers. 1937. 1 folder and 3 items.
Open. Published guide.
Philadelphia Jewish Archives Center.
Papers of Schleindlinger (ca. 1900-), the first woman customhouse broker in Philadelphia, consist of her broker license, a clipping about her accomplishments, and portrait photos. See Lindsay B. Nauen, ed., *A Guide to the Philadelphia Jewish Archives Center* (Philadelphia: Philadelphia Jewish Archives Center, 1977).

15,163. Schwartz, Lily (Garber)
Papers. 1967-76. 1 folder.
Open. Published guide.
Philadelphia Jewish Archives Center.
[Mrs. Ernest] Schwartz (1925-) is a secretary-receptionist. Correspondence she received in reply to letters she sent to US congressmen and government officials on topics relating to Israel and letters she wrote to the editors of various Philadelphia newspapers. See Lindsay B. Nauen, ed., *A Guide to the Philadelphia Jewish Archives Center* (Philadelphia: Philadelphia Jewish Archives Center, 1977).

15,164. Smilowitz, Anne
Papers. 1926-46. 1 folder.
Open. Published guide.
Philadelphia Jewish Archives Center.
[Miss] Smilowitz (1909-) is a retired school secretary. Consists of a 1926 Hebrew Sunday School Society diploma, certificates and a pin in recognition of her services with the USO during WWII, and an autographed program and photos pertaining to "A Romance of the People," a pageant depicting Jewish history that was performed for the purpose of raising money for the settlement of German-Jewish refugees in Palestine. Smilowitz was a dancer in the pageant. See Lindsay B. Nauen, ed., *A Guide to the Philadelphia Jewish Archives Center* (Philadelphia: Philadelphia Jewish Archives Center, 1977).

15,165. Society Esrath Nashim (Helping Women)
Records. 1887. 1 item.
Open. Published guide.
Philadelphia Jewish Archives Center.
Charter of this women's charitable organization, founded in 1873 to aid Jewish women during pregnancy. In 1891 the group changed its name to the Jewish Maternity Association and purchased a building that became the Jewish Maternity Home. See Lindsay B. Nauen, ed., *A Guide to the Philadelphia Jewish Archives Center* (Philadelphia: Philadelphia Jewish Archives Center, 1977).

15,166. Soffin, Estelle Marie
Papers. 1906-12. 1 folder and 3 items.
Open. Published guide.
Philadelphia Jewish Archives Center.
Contains a parody that Soffin (1902-) wrote at the age of 10 of Lincoln's Gettysburg Address, recounting the history of the women's suffrage movement, and photos of her, her sisters Rose and Lil, and Lena Soffin. See Lindsay B. Nauen, ed., *A Guide to the Philadelphia Jewish Archives Center* (Philadelphia: Philadelphia Jewish Archives Center, 1977).

15,167. Conner
Papers. 1816-56. 31 vols.
Open. No guide.
Philadelphia Maritime Museum.
Bulk of the collection consists of journals Susan Dillwyn (Physick) Conner (1803-56), daughter of Philadelphia physician Philip Physick, kept after her marriage to David Conner. Includes the journal she kept during her voyage with her husband, who was commander of the sloop-of-war *John Adams,* to the Mediterranean in 1834 and of her later life as a Philadelphia resident. Also includes a handwritten book of poems, an autobiography, a visiting book, accounts of her expenses for 1850 and 1851, and an 1816 scrapbook.

15,168. Hepburn
Papers. 1723-1876. 280 pp.
Open. Unpublished guide.
Philadelphia Maritime Museum.
Papers of the Barry, Hayes, Sommers, and Keen families include correspondence and receipts pertaining to the financial affairs of Sarah Austin Barry (1754-1831), wife of John Barry, who was a prominent naval officer, and correspondence, a daybook, and a journal of Elizabeth Keen Hayes (1764-1853), wife of Patrick Hayes, who was a nephew of John Barry. Her journal contains copies of poems and notes she made on the voyage of her husband from 1795 to 1798.

15,169. Dickinson, Emily
Papers. 1842-84. 33 items.
Open. Published and unpublished guides.
Philip H. & A. S. W. Rosenbach Foundation.
Letters from [Miss] Dickinson (1830-86), a poet, to Jane (Humphrey) Wilkinson, 1842-55, and to members of the Sweetser family, particularly Cornelia (Peck) Sweetser, 1868-84. See Thomas H. Johnson, ed., *The Letters of Emily Dickinson* (Cambridge, MA: The Belknap Press of Harvard University Press, 1958), which includes all of the letters.

15,170. Moore, Marianne
Papers. 1884- . Ca. 204 Hollinger boxes, 3 drawers, 2000 vols., and other items.
Open. No guide.
Philip H. & A. S. W. Rosenbach Foundation.
Correspondence, diaries, literary manuscripts, notebooks, financial papers, scrapbooks, photos, drawings, clippings, and other papers of Moore (1887-1972), a poet. The collection includes her personal library and her art collection. Correspondents include women prominent in the fields of literature, art, and fashion, such as Hilda Doolittle, Elizabeth Bishop, Sylvia Beach, Malvina Hoffman, Harriet Monroe, Louise Bogan, and Mary Butts.

15,171. Hawkes, Sarah Belknap "Belle" (Sherwood)
Papers. 1872-1919. 1 ft.
Open. Unpublished guide.
Presbyterian Historical Society.
[Mrs. James Woods] Hawkes (1854-1919) was a missionary for the Presbyterian Church in the U.S.A. in Hamadan, Persia, from 1883 until her death. Correspondence, scattered diaries dating from 1890 to 1919, condolence letters, biographical data, and photos.

15,172. Hill, Kate Alexander
Papers. 1896-1954. 2 ft.
Open. No guide.
Presbyterian Historical Society.
Hill (1873-1960) was a missionary and field secretary for the United Presbyterian Church of North America. Correspondence, notebook of a journey through Egypt in 1904, her speeches and articles, a daybook of Hill and of Nannie J. Spencer for 1898 and 1899, Sialkot Mission newsletters dating from 1910 to 1937, photos, scrapbooks, and miscellaneous material on WWII. Also contains a biography and correspondence pertaining to the missionary family of Andrew Gordon.

15,173. Presbyterian Church in the U.S.A., Woman's Board of Home Missions
Records. 1869-1948. 21 ft., 14 boxes, 49 vols., and ca. 72,600 items.
Partially restricted. Inventory and partial index.
Presbyterian Historical Society.
Commissioned by the General Assembly to provide financial, medical, and educational assistance for missions in the US, this central organization of local, presbyterial, and synodical societies of Presbyterian women was organized in 1879 as the Woman's Executive Committee of Home Missions. In 1897 its name was changed to the Woman's Board of Home Missions and in 1923, with several other boards, it was absorbed into the reorganized Board of National Missions. A woman's committee of the Board of National Missions was organized in the same year. Annual reports, 1925; minutes of various synodical societies' meetings; minutes and correspondence regarding the New Era Movement, 1918-21; cashbooks, ledgers, balance sheets, treasurer's accounts, and other financial records; correspondence; lists of members, officers, and teachers; a handbook for teachers and matrons in mission schools; school records; and a history of the Board, 1878-1906. Also includes material concerning the reorganization and incorporation of the Board and the controversy over the status of women in the Presbyterian Church, 1924-29; letters and reports from missionaries in the American West, 1879-83; information on the Board's work with Indians, Mormons, Mexicans, Orientals, Puerto Ricans, immigrants, and mountaineers; and general information on committees and projects in temperance, industrial work, and young people's work. Collection also contains material of Mary Katharine [Mrs. Fred S.] Bennett, who served as the Board's president from 1909 to 1923.

15,174. Presbyterian Historical Society Library
Records. Nd. No size given.
Open. Unpublished guide.
Presbyterian Historical Society.
The Society's Library includes correspondence files of the boards of foreign missions of the Presbyterian Church in the U.S.A. and of the United Presbyterian Church of North America, which contain letters and reports from overseas missionaries, many of them women; several thousand biographical and personnel files on individual women who served the church in missions, in the clergy, and in other leadership positions; diaries of women, including Mary E. (Wire) Ramsey, Lydia Belle (Walker) Good, Esther

Belle (McMillan) Hanna, and Mary (Laurie) Mattoon; and other material. The Presbyterian Church in the U.S.A., the largest of the American Presbyterian and Reformed denominations, traces its lineage from the first American presbytery, which was organized in 1705-06; it was established under the Presbyterian Church in the U.S.A. name in 1789. The United Presbyterian Church of North America was organized in 1858. The two groups united in 1958 to form the United Presbyterian Church in the U.S.A.

15,175. Thompson, Anna Young
Papers. 1871-1931. 1 ft., 1 box, 38 vols., and ca. 600 items.
Open. Unpublished guide.
Presbyterian Historical Society.
Thompson (1851-1932) was a Presbyterian missionary in Egypt. Correspondence, scattered diaries dating from 1872 to 1906, speeches, outlines, reports, notebooks, genealogical material, account books, an autograph album, photos, and a notebook, bulletins, and other papers relating to the WCTU, 1924-31. Also includes a 1918 memorial book of Jessie Harvey Robinson.

15,176. United Presbyterian Church in the U.S.A., Lois (Harkrider) Stair
Records. 1971-72. 4 ft.
Access restricted. Inventory.
Presbyterian Historical Society.
In 1971 [Mrs. Ralph Martin] Stair (1923-) became the first woman to serve as moderator of the UPCUSA's General Assembly. Correspondence and reports concern such topics as the Black Panthers, the elderly, homosexuality, planned parenthood, sexuality, the task force on women of United Presbyterian Women, and a grant to Angela Davis by the emergency fund for legal aid of the Council on Church and Race.

15,177. Province Archives
Records. 1911- . 59 boxes and 3 tapes.
Open. No guide.
Sisters of St. Basil the Great, Sacred Heart Province.
This religious order of women engaged in the care of orphans, ecclesiastical sewing, publication of religious works, catechetical work, and teaching was founded in Philadelphia in 1911. Business, statistical, and financial records; correspondence; manuscripts; oral history tapes; circulars and bulletins; photos; albums; programs; invitations; memorabilia; and publications of the Province, of benefactors and deceased members of the community, and of affiliated houses and schools.

15,178. Archives
Records. 1847- . 329 cu.ft.
Open. Unpublished guide.
Sisters of St. Joseph Motherhouse.
This religious congregation of women engaged primarily in teaching was established in Philadelphia in 1847. Financial records of convents, personnel records, correspondence, photos, scrapbooks, statistics on the growth of the community and its works, and translations of manuscripts and historical records pertaining to the Sisters in France before they came to America in 1836. The Sisters taught in elementary and secondary schools and in colleges.

15,179. Holy Family College for Women
Records. 1954-70. 4 cu.ft., 27 vols., and 1 microfilm reel.
Access restricted. Unpublished guide.
Sisters of the Holy Family of Nazareth Archives.
Founded in 1954 as Holy Family College for Women, the school began admitting male students in 1970 and changed its name to Holy Family College. The College offers undergraduate liberal arts, secondary and elementary teacher education, special education, nursing, prelegal, and premedical programs. Correspondence; College chronicles; a local history collection containing material on such women as Virginia Knauer; faculty papers and publications; tape recordings; photos; scrapbooks; lectures on women; outlines for courses on women in American history and women, marriage, and family; papers of prominent local persons that contain material on Marie Curie-Sklodowska, Marion Coleman, and [Mrs.] Helena Paderewski; alumnae files; clippings; College publications; and other records of the College.

15,180. Immaculate Conception Province Archives
Records. 1885- . 12 cu.ft. and 1 microfilm reel.
Access restricted. Unpublished guide.
Sisters of the Holy Family of Nazareth Archives.
The order was founded in Italy and established in the US in 1885. Its members teach in colleges, high schools, elementary parish schools, and nursing schools; work in nursing homes, hospitals, child care centers, and child education centers; and are involved in pastoral ministry and religious education. Records of the Province, which was founded in 1918, include annual reports, correspondence, retreat notes, annals of local houses, membership lists, circulars from provincial superiors and the superior general, photos, files pertaining to deceased members, files relating to the work of the Sisters, scrapbooks, newsletters, obituaries, and clippings.

15,181. Mother Mary of Jesus the Good Shepherd
Papers. 1873-1975. 3 cu.ft.
Access restricted. Unpublished guide.
Sisters of the Holy Family of Nazareth Archives.
Mother Mary (1842-1902), who was born Frances Siedliska, was the foundress and first superior general of the Sisters of the Holy Family of Nazareth. Correspondence, diary, autobiography, photos, conference proceedings, clippings containing biographical information and historical sketches of the congregation, studies of Mother Mary written by members of her congregation, and bibliographies of works by and about her. Photos show the different kinds of habits in use during Mother Mary's lifetime. Mother Mary founded an international Roman Catholic religious congregation for women in Rome, Italy, in 1875 and sailed in 1885 with 10 members to the US, where she became a citizen and founded Holy Family Academy and St. Mary's Hospital in Chicago and Holy Family Institute for orphaned children in Pittsburgh.

15,182. Carnell, Laura Horner
Papers. 1902-29. 6 ft.
Open. No guide.
Temple University Libraries, Conwellana-Templana Collection.
Correspondence, files, photos, programs, and clippings document the 35-year career of Carnell (1867-1929) as an educator and administrator of Temple University. The University was founded in 1887 by clergyman Russell Conwell, but because of his duties and frequent travels as a minister and as a lecturer on the Chautauqua circuit, Carnell assumed much of the responsibility for running the University after she was hired as principal of the women's department in 1893. She was acting dean from 1897 to 1905, dean from 1905 to 1925, and associate president of Temple from 1925 to 1929. The University awarded her an honorary doctor of literature degree in 1902. Correspondence and other papers contain information on relations with faculty, students, and trustees; the administration of buildings, schedules, curricula, and ceremonies; and the roles of women in WWI and the US Sesquicentennial Exhibition, held in Philadelphia in 1926.

15,183. College of Education
Records. 1916-73. 30 ft.
Partially restricted. Unpublished guide.
Temple University Libraries, Conwellana-Templana Collection.
This degree-granting college within Temple University was founded in 1916. Minutes, account books, correspondence, personnel files, reports, course outlines, and subject files of various of the College's administrators. Also includes programs, photos, and scrapbooks of the departments of home economics and music education. A high percentage of the College's faculty members and student body were women, particularly in its early years. Collection contains reports of department directors to the dean concerning kindergarten activities, early childhood education, physical education, home economics management, nursing education, music education, and the development of social work. Notable members of the College's faculty were Emma Johnson, who was involved in early childhood education; Grace Nadig, who was a faculty member in home economics; and Gertrude Peabody, who was dean of women.

15,184. Conwell, Russell H.
Papers. 1862-1972. 12 ft.
Open. Unpublished guide.
Temple University Libraries, Conwellana-Templana Collection.
Correspondence and manuscripts of Conwell (1843-1925), a Baptist clergyman, lecturer, author, and founder of Temple College, which was renamed Temple University in 1907. Includes letters from members of his congregation, his daughter Nima (Conwell) Tuttle (1868-1950), his niece Agnes Hayden, his first wife Jennie (Hayden) Conwell (1844-72), his second wife Sarah (Sanborn) Conwell (1842-1910), and his granddaughter Jane Conwell Tuttle concerning the church, fund raising for the church and the college, his lecture tours, the promotion of his books, and rural life in Massachusetts. Also includes a notebook on psychology that his daughter-in-law S. Harriette (Brewster) [Mrs. Leon M.] Conwell compiled and "Outline of the Book of Methods of the Baptist Temple," a manuscript book written in ca. 1920 by May Field McKean, who had been active in the church for an extended period.

15,185. De Frehn, Edna
Papers. 1953-54?. 2 in.
Open. No guide.
Temple University Libraries, Conwellana-Templana Collection.
Typed and illustrated notebooks contain detailed research by De Frehn on owls, their habits, breeding, and the role of owls in literature and mythology.

15,186. Dean of Students
Records. 1940-59. 6 ft.
Access restricted. Unpublished guide.
Temple University Libraries, Conwellana-Templana Collection.
Minutes, financial records, correspondence, notes, pamphlets, personnel records, flyers, and programs of the office that guided Temple University students in their extracurricular activities. The offices of dean of men and dean of women were created in 1930. In 1944 the dean of men became the dean of students and the dean of women became associate dean of students. In 1952 the earlier titles were restored, but in 1968 the duties of the two offices were again merged. Files of deans A. Blair Knapp and Gertrude Peabody contain information on the responsibilities and professional activities of the dean of women as well as information on sororities, women's athletics, the Miss America contest and other special events, family life education, student counseling, scholarships, and the handling of discrimination against black and Jewish students. Peabody's correspondence includes frequent exchanges with housemothers, the University Women's Club, the National Association of Deans of Women, and

other local, national, and international organizations.

15,187. Greatheart Society, Inc.
Records. 1930-41. 4 in.
Open. No guide.
Temple University Libraries, Conwellana-Templana Collection.
Minutes, programs, and souvenirs of the Society, founded in 1898 as the ladies auxiliary to the maternity department of the Samaritan Hospital, which was associated closely with Temple College. Members of the organization, who were from varied economic backgrounds, worked to improve the comfort and convenience of maternity patients and their newborn children. The group sponsored social gatherings, sewed, raised funds for the department, and provided substantial support for the Hospital. Blanche Whitecar, a Philadelphia philanthropist, was the most active Society officer. Many of the members belonged to the Grace Baptist Church and were supporters of its former pastor Russell Conwell.

15,188. Levin, Nora
Papers. 1964?-68. 5 in.
Open. Unpublished guide.
Temple University Libraries, Conwellana-Templana Collection.
Levin (1916-) was a librarian, Philadelphia high school teacher of history and English, and author of *The Holocaust* (Crowell, 1968). Working copy of the manuscript, published reviews, and critical articles about the book. Levin became a writer relatively late in life.

15,189. Scheuer, Lucile
Papers. 1950-76. 1.5 ft.
Access restricted. No guide.
Temple University Libraries, Conwellana-Templana Collection.
Official correspondence, reports, minutes, manuals, programs, photos, and souvenirs of Scheuer, who began work at Temple as dean of women in 1960; after the position of dean of women was abolished, she became assistant to the vice-president and worked primarily on the regulation of student affairs. In 1976 she retired from the University. Collection includes some of the files of her predecessor Dean Gertrude Peabody. It also contains information on the altered character of dormitory life during the 1960s and 1970s, changing codes of conduct, declining membership in sororities, and the greater participation of students in university governance.

15,190. Temple University Faculty Women's Club
Records. 1940- . 1 ft.
Open. No guide.
Temple University Libraries, Conwellana-Templana Collection.
Bylaws, minutes, financial records, correspondence, membership lists, photos, programs, and clippings of the Club, organized in 1940 to promote cohesion within the University, to help integrate new members into the staff and faculty, and to support philanthropic activities in the University's interest. Many of the Club's members are wives of University faculty and administrators. Club activities include meetings, educational forums, social events, and occasional fund raising.

15,191. Temple University Graduate English Office: Qualifying Papers for MA in English
Records. 1967-73. 3 ft.
Open. Unpublished guide.
Temple University Libraries, Conwellana-Templana Collection.
Approximately one-half of the research papers written by graduate students to qualify for the MA degree in English literature at Temple were written by women, although women comprised a small portion of the students in the graduate school. Papers deal chiefly with writers and themes in modern American and earlier British literature.

15,192. Temple University Hospital School of Nursing
Records. 1895-1971. 4 ft.
Access restricted. Partial unpublished guide.
Temple University Libraries, Conwellana-Templana Collection.
An archives of the School of Nursing, which was founded in 1893 and terminated in 1971, consisting of minutes, contracts and other legal documents, correspondence, student notebooks, lecture notes, notes of interviews, reports, charts, programs, pamphlets, photos, clippings, and textbooks. Contains a comprehensive record of work done by student nurses, their classroom training, hospital routine, social life and ceremonies, and activities of the faculty.

15,193. Temple University Theater Archives
Records. 1928- . 9 ft.
Open. No guide.
Temple University Libraries, Conwellana-Templana Collection.
Play programs, scrapbooks, and photos show that women students were involved as actresses and in other roles in the Theater, which was organized officially in 1930 when Paul Randall became director. Also includes scripts, a motion picture film, and promotional material pertaining to productions involving Temple students.

15,194. Temple University Women's Club
Records. 1909-58. 1.5 ft.
Open. No guide.
Temple University Libraries, Conwellana-Templana Collection.
Bylaws, minutes, financial records, correspondence, calendars, programs, and yearbooks of the Club, which was founded in 1909 as Women's Auxiliary of Temple University to develop moral and financial support for the University and its affiliated institutions, particularly the Samaritan Hospital. The Hospital, established in 1892, merged with Temple University in 1907; the institution's name was changed to Temple University Hospital in 1930. The Club was involved in philanthropy, public affairs, and self-improvement and held meetings on topics of literary, scientific, or general interest. Members of the Club also participated in the US Sesquicentennial celebration in Philadelphia.

15,195. Vice-President for University Relations: Files of Old University Events
Records. 1939-67. 4 ft.
Open. Unpublished guide.
Temple University Libraries, Conwellana-Templana Collection.
Financial records, correspondence, notes, vitae, lists of participants, photos, and award citations pertain to ceremonial and social occasions, both academic and extracurricular, planned by Temple University. Includes a file with lists and photos of the annual garden party held at the Stella Elkins Tyler School of Fine Arts to honor graduating Temple women from 1947 to 1960; Gertrude Peabody, dean of women, had the major responsibility for this function. The party was attended by graduates and their parents, women faculty, deans, wives of deans, nurses, women librarians, housemothers, female personnel of the student activities buildings, and, in the early period, the May Queen and her court. Also includes correspondence, descriptions, and lists of women faculty members and librarians who attended the annual tea given by the University president's wife in her role as honorary president of the Temple Faculty Women's Club. Held from 1947 to 1966, the teas honored new women faculty members and librarians in addition to the wives of new male faculty members and administrators. Also includes information about the annual tea held for senior women students from 1961 to 1963.

15,196. Wallace, Mary (Longstreet)
Papers. 1934-75. 1 ft.
Open. No guide.
Temple University Libraries, Conwellana-Templana Collection.
Correspondence, typescripts, galley and page proofs, and magazine tear sheets of Wallace (1906-), a novelist and short story writer whose works primarily concern the family life of Irish-Americans. Includes correspondence with Stuart Robertson, who was her English professor at Temple, and her literary agent Muriel Fuller as well as original and final versions of *Blue Meadow* and others of her works.

15,197. Women's Studies Lecture Series
Records. 1971-72. 2 folders and 8 tapes.
Access restricted. Unpublished guide.
Temple University Libraries, Conwellana-Templana Collection.
The Series, which dealt with women in American society, was organized in 1971 by Temple faculty and staff women. Collection consists of tapes of lectures, the question-and-answer period following, and discussions as well as papers from some of the speakers. National Organization for Women activist Warren Farrell spoke on "Male Attitudes Toward Females: The Politics of Women's Liberation"; black civil rights attorney Florynce Kennedy, "Institutional Oppression of Women"; Wesleyan University associate provost Sheila Tobias, "Sexual Politics in the Classroom"; sociologist Cynthia Fuchs Epstein, "Women and Professional Elites"; psychiatrist Natalie Shainess, "Toward a New Feminine Psychology"; historian Anne Firor Scott, "Making the Invisible Woman Visible"; humanities professor Florence Howe, "Feminism and Literature"; and journalist Caroline Bird, "After Liberation, What?"

15,198. Dragonette, Ree
Papers. 1958-68. 1 Hollinger box.
Open. Unpublished guide.
Temple University Libraries, Rare Book and Manuscript Collection.
Dragonette (1918-) is a New York metaphysical poet who was born in Philadelphia. Manuscripts of poetry, correspondence with other poets and editors, and printed matter. Correspondents include Jill Castro, Barbara Holland, Susan McMahon, Marianne Moore, Anaïs Nin, and Alice S. Morris of *Harper's Bazaar*. Dragonette has performed readings with the Eric Dolphy Quintet and the Ed Curran Quartet; she also has conducted the poetry workshop at the Greenwich House Music School.

15,199. Sargent, Pamela
Papers. 1969- . 5 in. and 18 items.
Open. Unpublished guide.
Temple University Libraries, Rare Book and Manuscript Collection.
Correspondence, manuscripts, periodicals, and books of [Miss] Sargent (1948-), a science fiction author who has published numerous short stories, juvenile stories, nonfiction articles, and novels in major science fiction magazines and anthologies. Active in the Science Fiction Writers of America, Sargent was assistant editor of the SFWA *Bulletin*. She also has edited an anthology of science fiction stories by women about women and has written on women in science fiction for a special issue of *Futures*. She has BA and MA degrees in philosophy and has taught college level philosophy courses.

15,200. Grossman, Mary Foley
Papers. 1934-69. 5 cu.ft.
Open. Unpublished guide.
Temple University Libraries, Urban Archives Center.
Correspondence, minutes, newsletters, and files relate to the official duties of [Mrs.] Grossman (ca. 1905-72) with the American Federation of Teachers, Local 192, from 1934 until 1941 when

this left-wing local was expelled from the AFT. Grossman was also active in the formation of the Teacher's Union of Philadelphia in 1941 and served as its president until 1942. She was national legislative representative of the AFT, vice-president for the metropolitan Philadelphia area, and president of the Local at the time of its expulsion.

15,201. Housing Association of Delaware Valley
Records. 1909-75. 188 cu.ft., ca. 15,780 items, and 22 microfilm reels.
Open. Published guide.
Temple University Libraries, Urban Archives Center.
The Association was organized in 1909 by the Octavia Hill Association to aid in the enforcement of existing housing and sanitary laws and in the development of wholesome living conditions. The Association was known as the Philadelphia Housing Commission from 1909 to 1916 and the Philadelphia Housing Association from 1916 to 1968. Annual reports, 1912-43 and 1966-72; minutes of the board of directors, 1909-73; correspondence; reports; financial records; budget files; staff records; yearly data on construction, demolitions, dwelling units, rents, public housing units, assessments, and vacancies; photos; maps; clippings; pamphlets; the publications *Memorandum* and *Infill;* files concerning the Health and Welfare Council and Community Chest-United Fund; and other records. The items reflect the participation of women in the Association's work; Dorothy Schoell Montgomery served as managing director from 1944 to the mid-1960s and Shirley Dennis assumed the post in 1971. See Sheryl Dams Pendzich, Fredric Miller, and Peter Silverman, *Housing Association of Delaware Valley: A Guide to the Collection* (Philadelphia: Temple University, 1976).

15,202. Houston Community Center
Records. 1904-70. 7 cu.ft.
Open. Published and unpublished guides.
Temple University Libraries, Urban Archives Center.
Annual reports, minutes of the board of directors, financial records, photos, and material on the membership, activities, and clubs of the Center, a settlement house founded in 1901 as St. Martha's House by Jean Colesbury, who served as the House's deaconess-in-charge until her resignation in 1930. Originally founded to "furnish a center of health, physical and spiritual improvement" and as a fieldwork center for young women training for church parish work, the settlement house changed its name in 1966 to honor Samuel F. Houston, who had proposed the House's establishment. Ties to the Episcopal church were strong at first, but lessened over time.
The House served local Jews, Italians, Poles, Lithuanians, and, later, blacks who moved into the area. Activities focused on improvement of homemaking skills, with classes in cooking, sewing, and gardening; a kindergarten, library, boys' gym, medical dispensary, dental clinic, milk station, and savings bank were established soon thereafter. After WWII St. Martha's House became more concerned with such community problems as urban renewal, the Delaware Expressway, race relations, welfare rights, and civil disorders. The House also worked with various neighborhood groups on job programs for youth. See *Guide to Philadelphia Social Service Collections at the Urban Archives Center, Temple University Libraries* (Philadelphia: Temple University, 1976).

15,203. Kirkbride, Elizabeth Butler
Papers. 1862-1903. 5 vols.
Open. Unpublished guide.
Temple University Libraries, Urban Archives Center.
Diaries, a notebook, and a ledger of Kirkbride (1836-1922), who was active in social welfare and educational organizations. An elementary school was named after her.

15,204. League of Women Voters of Swarthmore, PA
Records. 1925-72. 10 cu.ft.
Open. Unpublished guide.
Temple University Libraries, Urban Archives Center.
Records of this chapter of the LWV, organized in 1925, include minutes of annual meetings and of committees, correspondence, reports, office files, and program files, 1950s-69, concerning such local issues as planning, housing, zoning, recreation, law enforcement, and schools and such national issues as foreign aid and civil rights.

15,205. Octavia Hill Association, Inc.
Records. 1888-1941. 1 cu.ft.
Open. Published guide.
Temple University Libraries, Urban Archives Center.
Complete set of annual reports and of minutes of the board, correspondence, legislative files, publications, and other records of the Association, founded in 1896 to encourage home ownership among the poor by buying, renovating, renting, and managing low-cost housing. The Association's activities were modeled after the work in London of Octavia Hill, with whom Helen Parrish, one of the Association's founders, had studied. The founders wanted to manage clean, sanitary, safe houses for their black and immigrant tenants and to make a profit at the same time. By 1916 the Association owned or managed more than 400 houses. The Association used "friendly rent collectors" to insure regular payments, inspect the premises, and instruct tenants in cleanliness, sanitation, and good housekeeping. The Association's work also led to the establishment of new kindergartens and playgrounds in the area of its most intensive work. In addition, the Association worked with neighborhood agencies, lobbied in Harrisburg PA, for various housing bills, participated in drafting the Philadelphia Housing Code (passed in 1913), and in 1909 took the initiative in organizing the Philadelphia Housing Association, a private organization now known as the Housing Association of Delaware Valley.
Collection includes correspondence of Helen Parrish concerning management of the Association, child care, and housing problems; correspondence with Octavia Hill and others Parrish met in England about housing, the labor movement, and WWI; diaries of Parrish, which concern her original experimental work renting out properties to black tenants in Philadelphia in 1888; and notes and speeches, 1899-1927. Also includes material on Pennsylvania state housing ordinances and codes, pamphlets on housing and social conditions in Philadelphia and Washington, DC, and a photo archives, 1898-1929, which deals with housing, social conditions, and building renovation.
See *Guide to Philadelphia Social Service Collections at the Urban Archives Center, Temple University Libraries* (Philadelphia: Temple University, 1976).

15,206. Philadelphia Association of Day Nurseries
Records. 1909-36. 0.5 cu.ft.
Open. Published and unpublished guides.
Temple University Libraries, Urban Archives Center.
The Association was founded in 1898 by representatives of seven day nurseries to coordinate the activities, establish standards, and deal with the problems of child welfare in nurseries throughout Philadelphia. Annual reports, minutes, financial records, correspondence, and publications contain accounts of each member nursery, studies of conditions in nurseries, and recommendations for standards of the physical plant, staff, medical care, supervision, diet, and other matters. The Association added new member nurseries and helped create new nurseries in neighborhoods where they were needed. In 1928, with a membership of 21 nurseries, the Association became a section of the children's department of the Council of Social Agencies, which was a predecessor of the Health and Welfare Council, Inc., a local private organization. See *Guide to Philadelphia Social Service Collections at the Urban Archives Center, Temple University Libraries* (Philadelphia: Temple University, 1976).

15,207. Reed Street Neighborhood House
Records. 1915-65. 5.5 cu.ft.
Open. Published and unpublished guides.
Temple University Libraries, Urban Archives Center.
This settlement house, founded in 1913, served Jewish, Italian, and black immigrants, especially children and teenagers, in South Philadelphia. Minutes, financial records, reports, correspondence, group case records, youth workers' reports, and records of youth agencies. The Neighborhood House ran social, recreational, and educational clubs; it also operated an extensive gang work program, with youth workers attempting to direct neighborhood youth toward constructive activities and the settlement's counseling service. In 1970 the House affiliated with the Philadelphia YMCA and was renamed the Reed House Young Men's Christian Association. The Neighborhood House's predecessor was the St. James Industrial School for Girls and Women. See *Guide to Philadelphia Social Service Collections at the Urban Archives Center, Temple University Libraries* (Philadelphia: Temple University, 1976).

15,208. Settlement Music School
Records. 1910-66. 3 cu.ft.
Open. Published and unpublished guides.
Temple University Libraries, Urban Archives Center.
This music school was founded in 1908 by Jeanette Selig and Blanche Wolf, who worked at the College Settlement in Southwark, Philadelphia, to provide musical instruction for Philadelphia area children and adults, immigrants, and the indigent, regardless of their ability to pay. Minutes of board and executive meetings, financial records and statements, correspondence, material of the personal service committee, reports from the Kensington branch, programs, notebooks, scrapbooks, photos, and copies of the School's publication *Grace Notes.* By 1917 the School had expanded so much that it acquired its own building, and branches were established in Kensington at the Lighthouse Settlement and, in 1951, in Frankford and Germantown, PA. Instructors and volunteers were often obtained from the Philadelphia Orchestra. See *Guide to Philadelphia Social Service Collections at the Urban Archives Center, Temple University Libraries* (Philadelphia: Temple University, 1976).

15,209. Young Women's Christian Association of Philadelphia
Records. 1870-1969. 10 cu.ft.
Open. Published and unpublished guides.
Temple University Libraries, Urban Archives Center.
Annual reports, minutes of the board of directors and the executive committee, reports from YWCA branches, records of the consulting committee and the metropolitan planning committee, correspondence, financial and legal records, reports on fund raising, scrapbooks of clippings, publications, and publicity material. The Philadelphia YWCA was founded in 1870 as a boarding house for young women with small incomes and no homes in the city. In the next few years, services were expanded to include a dining room; an employment department; an industrial department, which provided instruction in the use of sewing machines; and a visiting committee, which attended inmates in hospitals and asylums. Later services included a lending library, a monthly magazine *Faith and Works,* and two seaside homes in New Jersey. YWCA branches were founded beginning in the late 1890s throughout the Philadelphia area and in Harvey Cedars, NJ.
During the 20th century the YWCA established classes for unemployed women, summer camps, religious services for members, and the International Institute (later known as the

Nationalities Service Center), to provide social, recreational, and educational facilities for immigrants and non-English speaking persons. Further program expansions involved the YWCA in volunteer work, day care, USO canteens, and various interfaith and interracial projects. Collection contains information on the YWCA's activities and includes a 1930 study of Philadelphia's ethnic population. See *Guide to Philadelphia Social Service Collections at the Urban Archives Center, Temple University Libraries* (Philadelphia: Temple University, 1976).

15,210. Young Women's Christian Association, Southwest-Belmont Branch
Records. 1923-67. 26 cu.ft.
Open. Published and unpublished guides.
Temple University Libraries, Urban Archives Center.
Annual reports, minutes, financial records, correspondence, department reports, membership records, and other material pertaining to this branch of the YWCA, which was formed in 1933 by the merger of several YWCA branches. The Southwest-Belmont Branch, formerly known as the Colored Branch, provided recreation, vocational education, emergency and holiday charity, fellowship, and shelter to a portion of Philadelphia's black population. Its programs included health education and operation of the Elizabeth Frye House, a residential facility. From the late 1930s the Branch became involved in the problems of discrimination, and after WWII providing services to teenagers became the Branch's highest priority. Collection contains material from the metropolitan and national YWCAs, staff reports, newsletters, and records of the Branch's committees, other Philadelphia agencies, the USO, and national black organizations. See *Guide to Philadelphia Social Service Collections at the Urban Archives Center, Temple University Libraries* (Philadelphia: Temple University, 1976).

PITTSBURGH

15,211. Archives
Records. 1870- . Ca. 105 boxes, 8 vols., and 8 tapes.
Access restricted. No guide.
Benedictine Sisters of Pittsburgh.
Histories of the priory and its missions, chronicles, records relating to deceased sisters and those who have left religious life, blueprints, community publications, and other records of the Sisters, who are involved in elementary and secondary education, gerontology, university student counseling and ministry, parish ministry, and other similar activities. The congregation was founded in 1870 in Carrolltown, PA. Members of the order established and operated Saint Benedict Academy, a school for girls.

15,212. College Archives
Records. 1929- . Ca. 50 boxes, 4 cabinets, 100 items, and 20 tapes.
Open. No guide.
Carlow College Archives.
Annual reports, minutes, correspondence, photos, clippings, and oral histories of Carlow College, a women's college founded in 1929 as Mount Mercy College; in 1969 the school adopted its current name. Collection contains material from the office of the president and from several departments as well as personal papers and writings of such faculty members as Sister Elizabeth Carroll, a professor of history who became the College's fifth president.

15,213. Cathcart, Ellen Weir
Papers. 1889-1902. Ca. 200 items.
Open. No guide.
Carnegie-Mellon University, Hunt Institute for Botanical Documentation.
Correspondence of [Miss] Cathcart, a scientific assistant in the US Department of Agriculture division of botany, concerns the exchange and determination of scientific cryptograms. Correspondents include botanist Elizabeth Britton. On deposit from the Smithsonian Institution Department of Botany.

15,214. Gates, Adelia
Papers. Ca. 1870-1913. 288 items.
Open. Description.
Carnegie-Mellon University, Hunt Institute for Botanical Documentation.
Watercolor drawings of flowers by [Miss] Gates (ca. 1817-80), a scientific illustrator, are included with a letter and a clipping about her. Born in New York state, Gates taught school when she was 16 years old, then worked in the Lowell cotton mills, apprenticed in a wire shop, and for two years attended Antioch College before ill health forced her to leave the school. At age 50 she learned to paint flowers in Switzerland. On deposit from the Smithsonian Institution Department of Botany.

15,215. Hitchcock, Albert Spear, and Chase, Mary "Agnes" (Merrill)
Papers. 1884-1963. 17.5 ft.
Open. List of correspondents.
Carnegie-Mellon University, Hunt Institute for Botanical Documentation.
Both Hitchcock (1865-1936) and [Mrs. William Ingraham] Chase (1869-1963), who was known as Agnes Chase, were agrostologists for the US Department of Agriculture. The correspondence and letter books of these coworkers relate to the determination and exchange of grasses; the grass collection at the US National Herbarium; Chase's work, after retiring from the USDA in 1939, as research associate in the division of plants of the US National Museum and as custodian of the grass collection; and publications and fieldwork collecting, particularly in South America, by themselves and their correspondents. On deposit from the Smithsonian Institution Department of Botany.

15,216. Langman, Ida (Kaplan)
Papers. 1917-75. Ca. 3 ft.
Open. No guide.
Carnegie-Mellon University, Hunt Institute for Botanical Documentation.
[Mrs. Oscar] Langman (1904-) was a public school teacher of the natural sciences and a botanical bibliographer who also taught in a Philadelphia museum. Notes from her high school and college science classes, correspondence, forms, and printed material. Included is information concerning Langman's work teaching, preparation and publication of her book *A Selected Guide to the Literature on the Flowering Plants of Mexico* (1964), activities in the Pan American Association of Philadelphia, and job hunting and grant applications.

15,217. Mathias, Mildred Esther
Papers. 1927-52. Ca. 673 items.
Open. List of correspondents.
Carnegie-Mellon University, Hunt Institute for Botanical Documentation.
Correspondence of Mathias (1906-), a taxonomist and professor of botany at the University of California, Los Angeles, includes reference to home life but focuses on Mathias's professional activities and those of her correspondents, particularly her determining specimens of the other work on the *Umbelliferae* family for a proposed book on North American flora, to be edited by Elmer D. Merrill and Henry A. Gleason of the New York Botanical Garden. Mathias was married to Gerald L. Hassler.

15,218. Swingle, Maude (Kellerman)
Oral history. 1971. 2 tapes.
Open. No guide.
Carnegie-Mellon University, Hunt Institute for Botanical Documentation.
[Mrs. Walter T.] Swingle (1888-) is a botanist who published her writings independently and in collaboration with her botanist husband Walter T. Swingle; she also is the daughter of mycologist William Ashbrook Kellerman and botanist Stella Victoria (Dennis) Kellerman. Swingle discusses the life and work of her father and her husband. She describes her early life; travels in Europe as a young unmarried woman; her job as a botanical translator for the US Department of Agriculture; moving to California where, at the age of 70, she applied for work as a volunteer at the California Historical Society; and helping her sister, who had a PhD in comparative philology, compile an Esperanto grammar in 1958. Swingle tells of taking a leave of absence from her USDA job in 1918 in order to accompany her husband to China for one year. Because she was married, however, she was not reinstated in her job and only returned to government service 20 years later.

15,219. College Archives
Records. 1869- . 15 drawers, 10 cartons, and 32 shelves.
Access restricted. Unpublished guide.
Chatham College Library.
Reports, catalogs, bulletins, pamphlets, monographs, scrapbooks, photos, newspapers, and memorabilia of this small, nonsectarian, liberal arts college for women, which was founded in 1869 by a group of Pittsburgh residents who believed that women deserved the same educational opportunities as men. Originally named the Pennsylvania Female College and then the Pennsylvania College for Women, the school was renamed Chatham College in 1955 to honor William Pitt, the first Earl of Chatham, for whom Pittsburgh was named.

15,220. Altrusa Club of Pittsburgh
Records. 1959-73. 2 boxes.
Access restricted. Catalog card.
Historical Society of Western Pennsylvania.
Records of the Pittsburgh chapter of the Club, a service organization founded in 1937, consist of minutes of meetings of the board and of members, committee reports, correspondence, and programs.

15,221. Denny and O'Hara Families
Papers. 1779-1889. 14 boxes.
Open. Published guide and inventory.
Historical Society of Western Pennsylvania.
Business and personal papers of James O'Hara (1754-1819), an ordnance general during the Revolutionary War, owner of the first glassworks in Pittsburgh, and president of the Pittsburgh branch of the Bank of Pennsylvania; of his son-in-law Ebenezer Denny (1761-1822), an agriculturist and Pittsburgh's first mayor; and of Denny's son Harmar Denny (1794-1852), a US congressman. Includes Denny family correspondence, DAR genealogical material, 1822-39 reports of the Female Bible Society, and an 1843 report of the Pittsburgh Select Female Seminary. Also includes correspondence of and reminiscences by O'Hara's granddaughter Mary Schenley (1826-1903) and correspondence between Anna Halsey and Charles Gardner Smith, 1823-30. See "The Manuscript and Miscellaneous Collections of the Historical Society of Western Pennsylvania, A Preliminary Guide," *Western Pennsylvania Historical Magazine,* vols. 49-55 (1966-72).

15,222. Jackson, John Beard
Papers. 1869-1909. 1 box.
Open. Inventory.
Historical Society of Western Pennsylvania.
Family correspondence of Jackson (1845-1908), a Pittsburgh resident who was president of the Fidelity Title and Trust Company and director of

the St. Clair Bridge Corporation. Also includes an 1879 obituary notice of his mother Mary Beard Jackson and letters from his granddaughter Mary Louise Jackson to various members of the family.

15,223. Knox, William Franciss
Papers. 1846-1920. 1 box.
Open. Published guide.
Historical Society of Western Pennsylvania.
Papers of Knox, a McKeesport, PA, physician, and his wife Elizabeth M. (Kidoo) Knox (1833-71) consist primarily of correspondence with members of their families. Also includes family bills and receipts, 1840s copybooks, and an 1880 exercise book of Jennie Knox. See "The Manuscript and Miscellaneous Collections of the Historical Society of Western Pennsylvania, A Preliminary Guide," *Western Pennsylvania Historical Magazine,* vols. 49-55 (1966-72).

15,224. Nurses' Association, Pennsylvania State
Records. Nd. 1 folder.
Open. Published guide.
Historical Society of Western Pennsylvania.
A roster of nurses in western Pennsylvania during WWI. See "The Manuscript and Miscellaneous Collections of the Historical Society of Western Pennsylvania, A Preliminary Guide," *Western Pennsylvania Historical Magazine,* vols. 49-55 (1966-72).

15,225. Pittsburgh Kindergarten Association
Records. 1903-59. 1 box.
Open. Inventory.
Historical Society of Western Pennsylvania.
In 1959 the Pittsburgh and Allegheny Free Kindergarten Association, founded in 1892 to promote the educational quality of Pittsburgh area kindergartens, adopted its current name. Bylaws, minutes, historical sketches and addresses, a petition, and material pertaining to Ellen Ruth Boyce. Also includes records of the Pittsburgh and Allegheny Kindergarten College, the kindergarten department of the Pittsburgh Training School for Teachers, and the Pittsburgh Public Schools kindergarten department as well as books used by Pittsburgh kindergartens.

15,226. Schenley, Mary (Croghan)
Papers. 1883-86. 1 folder.
Open. Published guide.
Historical Society of Western Pennsylvania.
A wealthy Pittsburgh resident, Schenley (1826-1903) owned sizable tracts of land, some of which she donated for Schenley Park, the West Penn Hospital, the Oakland Episcopal Church, the First United Presbyterian Church, and the Third Ward School. Correspondence concerning business and family matters is with Francis Torrence, the agent for her Pittsburgh estate; her attorney R. B. Carnahan; and others. See "The Manuscript and Miscellaneous Collections of the Historical Society of Western Pennsylvania, A Preliminary Guide," *Western Pennsylvania Historical Magazine,* vols. 49-55 (1966-72).

15,227. Smeltzer
Papers. 1914-62. 1 box.
Open. Published guide.
Historical Society of Western Pennsylvania.
Collection consists of records of the Women's Foreign Missionary Society, Pittsburgh Conference, with executive committee minutes, treasurer's reports, annual budgets, secretary's records of public meetings, pamphlets, and yearbooks. See "The Manuscript and Miscellaneous Collections of the Historical Society of Western Pennsylvania, A Preliminary Guide," *Western Pennsylvania Historical Magazine,* vols. 49-55 (1966-72).

15,228. Stuhldreher, Mary A. (McEnery)
Papers. 1921-74. 1 box.
Open. Inventory.
Historical Society of Western Pennsylvania.
Stuhldreher (1905-74) was a journalist; a lecturer at the Community College of Allegheny County, PA; director of the Trinity College alumni association; and dean of women at Duquesne University in Pittsburgh. Research notes and drafts of her articles and stories, which were published in such magazines as *McCall's, Sports Illustrated,* and *The Saturday Evening Post.* Includes information on Pittsburgh and *The Bulletin Index,* a magazine.

15,229. Swisshelm, Jane Grey (Cannon)
Papers. 1866-68. 1 folder.
Open. Published guide.
Historical Society of Western Pennsylvania.
[Mrs. James] Swisshelm (1815-84) was an abolitionist, women's rights advocate, and newspaper publisher. Consists of court records concerning the claim of James Ferguson to land owned by Swisshelm and her 1868 deed transferring one-third of that land to John P. Penny. See "The Manuscript and Miscellaneous Collections of the Historical Society of Western Pennsylvania, A Preliminary Guide," *Western Pennsylvania Historical Magazine,* vols. 49-55 (1966-72).

15,230. Watson, Ellen Murdoch
Papers. 1843-1914. 1 folder.
Open. Published guide.
Historical Society of Western Pennsylvania.
Family papers contain an 1843 school report of [Miss] Watson (?-1914), canceled checks, pamphlets, and a memorial booklet for her. Also contains papers of her mother Ellen Watson, including passes issued to Ellen Watson and Ellen Watson's father to nurse soldiers in the Army of the Potomac during the Civil War and a letter to her from Clara Barton about the Women's Home Missionary Society of the Pittsburgh Presbytery. See "The Manuscript and Miscellaneous Collections of the Historical Society of Western Pennsylvania, A Preliminary Guide," *Western Pennsylvania Historical Magazine,* vols. 49-55 (1966-72).

15,231. Woman's Club of the City of Pittsburgh
Records. 1887-1957. 5 boxes.
Open. Published guide.
Historical Society of Western Pennsylvania.
The Club, a social and charitable organization, was founded in 1875. Minutes for most of the period; roll books, 1924-35; yearbooks, 1905-57; a history, 1923; correspondence; a scrapbook; clippings; and a film of the anniversary pageant held in 1950. See "The Manuscript and Miscellaneous Collections of the Historical Society of Western Pennsylvania, A Preliminary Guide," *Western Pennsylvania Historical Magazine,* vols. 49-55 (1966-72).

15,232. Archives
Records. 1847-1977. Ca. 40 ft. and ca. 155 vols.
Partially restricted. Partial unpublished guide.
Mercy Hospital Archives.
Records of Mercy Hospital, founded in 1847 by seven Sisters of Mercy who emigrated from Ireland in 1843. The institution is the oldest hospital in western Pennsylvania. Minutes of the board of trustees, medical staff, Hospital departments, and related associations; financial records; correspondence; complete patient registers to 1890; in-house publications; brochures; historical sketches; photos; scrapbooks; and oral history interviews with doctors, Hospital employees, and Sister M. Ferdinand Clark, who retired in 1978 after serving as the Hospital's executive director for 25 years. Also includes papers of two Hospital administrators and one doctor as well as a journal kept by Sister M. Elizabeth Strange, one of the founding Sisters of Mercy.

15,233. Archives
Records. 1843- . 209 ft. and 53 drawers.
Open. Inventory and card catalog.
Sisters of Mercy of Allegheny County.
This religious order of women, the members of which are engaged in teaching, nursing, and social work, was founded in Ireland by Mother Catherine Mc Auley and established in the US in 1843 in Pittsburgh. Minutes of the Federation of the Sisters of Mercy of America, financial reports, correspondence, deeds, legal documents, diaries that sisters kept on the journey from Ireland, other journals, biographical information about sisters, a register of the founding group, a congregational history, annals, histories of the educational and social service work of the Sisters, photos, slides, scrapbooks, records of hospitals and schools with which the Sisters were affiliated, clippings, and necrology and other books.

15,234. Motherhouse Archives
Records. 1855- . 19 drawers, 30 boxes, 36 vols., 27 tapes, and 3 motion pictures.
Open. No guide.
Sisters of St. Francis of Millvale, Motherhouse.
The Pittsburgh branch of the Sisters of St. Francis was founded in 1871 and is involved in education, hospital work, social work, care of the aged, parish ministry, and religious education. Financial reports, correspondence, oral histories, histories of the community and of the founder St. John Neumann, a videotape, recording tapes, photos, scrapbooks, blueprints, and other records.

15,235. Archives
Records. 1922- . 120 boxes.
Access restricted. Inventory and index.
Sisters of St. Francis of the Providence of God.
The sisterhood was founded in 1922 in Pittsburgh; its members are engaged in teaching in parochial schools and nursing in hospitals. Financial records, correspondence, photos, circulars, annals, and other records pertaining to the early days of the sisterhood, its membership, activities, and government. The sisterhood was created in response to the need for bilingual teachers for Lithuanian children in parochial schools.

15,236. Advisory Council on Women's Opportunities
Records. 1963-74. 5 folders.
Open. Inventory.
University of Pittsburgh Archives.
Records of the Council, organized in 1970 to promote the status of women at the University, contain minutes, correspondence, reports on the equal opportunity affirmative action program, and 1970 reports on career opportunities for non-faculty women and on women in the school of medicine, the graduate school of public health, and the school of dental medicine. Also includes a 1971 chancellor's study of women in the University; material on the Women's Center, the 1970 Women's Rights Conference in Pittsburgh, and the women's studies department established at the University in 1971; and reports on graduate and professional education for women in 1963 and other background material that predates the founding of the Council.

15,237. Dean of Women
Records. 1922-47. 18 folders.
Open. Inventory.
University of Pittsburgh Archives.
Annual reports of the dean of women, whose office was established in 1919 to supervise women students' extracurricular activities, incorporated with the Office of Student Affairs in 1956, and abolished with the establishment of the office of the dean of student affairs in 1969. Also includes reports of the Women's Power Committee summarizing responses to a questionnaire on discrimination against women in the University; material on the Women's Self-Government Association, which in 1957 became the Associated Women Students; and information on Quo Vadis, a women's group.

15,238. Office of Student Activities
Records. 1962-76. 618 folders.
Open. Inventory.
University of Pittsburgh Archives.
Contains subject files on student organizations, programs, and such special events as homecoming and coffee houses. Material about women is included in files relating to the Women's Center, cultural festivals, the Women's Council, the Undergraduate Women's Union, and sororities.

15,239. Office of Student Affairs
Records. 1956-65. 428 folders.
Open. Inventory.
University of Pittsburgh Archives.
The Office was established in 1956 to supervise students' extracurricular activities. Subject files on student health, housing, religion, student aid, student organizations, admissions, commencement, the student union, and the cultural and educational exchange program. Also includes material of the dean of women; correspondence and memos of Dean Helen Rush, 1962-65; records of the women's organization Quo Vadis; a study guide for the class of 1961; a 1968 guide to apartment living; and items concerning the student hostess program and other women's activities.

15,240. Starrett, Agnes
Papers. Ca. 1937. 181 folders.
Open. Index.
University of Pittsburgh Archives.
Historical material gathered by Starrett for her book *Through 150 Years* (1937), a history of the University of Pittsburgh, includes information on the first women students at the Western University of Pennsylvania and other general material on University women.

15,241. Women
Collection. 1927- . 2 folders.
Open. Catalog cards.
University of Pittsburgh Archives.
Miscellaneous material concerning women students at the University includes a proposal by the University Committee for Women's Rights, the Council for Women's Rights, and the National Organization for Women to establish the Institute for Feminist Studies at the University. Also includes information on Annual Woman's Day, ca. 1928-35, and on women's opportunities in the health profession, 1970; a Mortar Board study of graduate educational opportunities for women at the University, 1970; and various pamphlets and notices.

15,242. Women at Pitt
Records. 1895-1947. 4 vols.
Open. Catalog card.
University of Pittsburgh Archives.
Consists of scrapbooks compiled by the alumnae association about women at the University of Pittsburgh.

15,243. Women's International Club
Records. 1939-49. 1 vol.
Open. Catalog card.
University of Pittsburgh Archives.
Records of this luncheon social club of the University, founded in 1939, consist of annual reports and minutes.

15,244. Congress of Women's Clubs of Western Pennsylvania
Records. 1908-63. 40 ft.
Open. Inventory.
University of Pittsburgh, Archives of Industrial Society.
A community service and social organization, the Congress was chartered in 1919; the organization had its origin in the Permanent Civic Committee of Women's Clubs of Western Pennsylvania, which was founded by [Miss] Kate Cassatt McKnight, an officer of the State Federation of Pennsylvania Women, and others in 1902. Minutes of the board of directors, the finance committee, and general meetings; correspondence; committee reports and other records; roll book of dancing classes sponsored by the Congress's department of recreation, 1926-29; a building fund team book; official directories; scrapbooks; and publications, including the official Congress monthly magazine *Congress Outlet* as well as *The Congress Lantern, The Clubwoman's Monthly News Magazine, Women's Club Life,* and *Magazine for Women's Clubs.*

15,245. Hadassah
Records. 1917-68. 1 ft.
Open. Inventory.
University of Pittsburgh, Archives of Industrial Society.
Records of the Pittsburgh chapter of this Jewish women's community service organization include constitution, correspondence, reports, ballots, membership cards, yearbooks, clippings, and copies of *Pittsburgh Hadassah News,* 1955-68. Also includes brochures, pamphlets, and a song of the national organization and material pertaining to national conventions.

15,246. Hoyt, Catherine (McCann)
Papers. 1907-51. 3 folders.
Open. Inventory.
University of Pittsburgh, Archives of Industrial Society.
Hoyt (1875?-1955), a social worker, was probation officer of the Allegheny County Juvenile Court from 1907 to 1918. Personal and business correspondence; a report on her probation work; studies of delinquency in the East End of Pittsburgh, one of which was conducted by a member of the Wellesley College Club under the direction of Hoyt; and her manuscripts and notes concerning the US Public Health Service, the Allegheny County Industrial and Training School for Boys, the home service of the American National Red Cross, the American National Red Cross hospital social service, and social work in the Veterans Bureau tuberculosis hospitals.

15,247. Italian Sons and Daughters of America
Records. 1929-70. Ca. 150 vols. and ca. 37,000 items.
Open. Inventory.
University of Pittsburgh, Archives of Industrial Society.
Records of the Pittsburgh chapter of the Italian Sons and Daughters, a service organization for Italian-Americans founded in ca. 1929, consist of applications for admission, some of which are in Italian; membership books arranged by lodge; applications for loans; and mortuary fund files. Contains information on name, date and place of birth, address, occupation, marital status, spouse, date and place of marriage, parents' names, medical examination, income, amount of loan requested, cosigner of loan, lodge and lodge number, initiation, assignment of death benefits, age and relationship of beneficiary, and amount of benefits. Also includes certificates of marriage and death, receipts for mortgage fund payments, and death notifications of spouses.

15,248. National Council of Jewish Women, Pittsburgh Section
Records. 1893-1967. 15 ft.
Open. Inventory.
University of Pittsburgh, Archives of Industrial Society.
Records of the Section of the National Council, a service organization founded in 1893, include constitutions, bylaws, annual reports, executive board minutes, financial records, presidents' and other correspondence, committee reports, membership lists, a history, case files of the student aid committee, scrapbooks, photos, and clippings. Also includes material concerning regional and national conventions; bylaws, resolutions, and correspondence of the New York Section; and material of the National Council.

15,249. National Organization for Women
Records. 1970- . 2 boxes.
Open. No guide.
University of Pittsburgh, Archives of Industrial Society.
Records of the Greater Pittsburgh Area chapter of NOW, founded in 1970, consist of bylaws with proposed revisions, minutes of general meetings, membership lists, releases, brochures, clippings, and such chapter publications as *McKeesport Feminist, Women Are People,* and *The Spokeswoman.*

15,250. Pittsburgh Conference of Jewish Women's Organizations
Records. 1923-63. 0.5 ft.
Open. Inventory.
University of Pittsburgh, Archives of Industrial Society.
The name of the Conference, a community service organization founded in 1923, was changed to the Federation of Jewish Women's Organizations in 1955, but it resumed its original name in 1959. Minutes of executive board, regular, and annual meetings; yearbooks; and a portfolio on Lillian Friedberg, a "distinguished daughter of Pennsylvania."

15,251. Rauh Family
Papers. 1903-51. 6 ft. and 4 vols.
Open. Inventory.
University of Pittsburgh, Archives of Industrial Society.
Family papers contain extensive material on Bertha (Floersheim) [Mrs. Enoch] Rauh (1865-1952), director of the city of Pittsburgh department of charities from 1920 until the 1930s and a philanthropist who was particularly concerned with immigrant Jewish women. Personal correspondence; general correspondence, 1920-41, concerning the reorganization of the charities department into the department of public welfare, social work with ex-servicemen, venereal disease, a mental hygiene survey, and other matters; and correspondence, 1903-30, about such subjects as birth control, the need for policewomen in Pittsburgh, the Allegheny County LWV, the Army Hostess Service, the Beulah Home for Babies, the Columbia Council of Jewish Women, the Family Welfare Association, the Girl Scouts, the Pennsylvania State Council of Republican Women, and the Women's Employment Service.

15,252. Roessing, Jennie Bradley
Papers. 1887-1961. 1.5 ft.
Open. Inventory.
University of Pittsburgh, Archives of Industrial Society.
A suffragist and clubwoman, [Mrs.] Roessing (ca. 1883-1963) was president of the Pennsylvania Woman Suffrage Association from 1912 to 1916. Correspondence, diaries, biographical data, pamphlets, photos, clippings, and other material, most of which concerns her suffrage and club activities between 1912 and 1961. Includes correspondence with and items about Sara M. Soffel, a common pleas judge in Pittsburgh, and Carrie Chapman Catt. Also includes information on feminism, the Women Leader's Conference with Industry, the Audubon Society, the First Unitarian Church of Pittsburgh, and the University of Pittsburgh.

15,253. Stasik, Margaret Darin
Papers. 1936-45. 0.5 ft.
Open. Inventory.
University of Pittsburgh, Archives of Industrial Society.
Secretary of Local 601 of the United Electrical and Radio Workers of America, an executive board member, and international trustee, Stasik (ca.

1907-) initiated the first UERWA women's conference. Her papers pertain to the union and to women's place in industry. Includes letters to the membership about wages and working conditions, union procedures and policies, and the improvement of local unions; correspondence concerning her work as a UERWA field organizer; speeches on the role of women in industry, ca. 1945; memoranda; subject files containing information on such union matters as picketing, grievances, contracts, locals, and Westinghouse Electric Corporation; constitution and bylaws; reference material; and publications.

15,254. Woman's Christian Temperance Union
Records. 1885-1955. 1.5 ft.
Open. Inventory.
University of Pittsburgh, Archives of Industrial Society.
Records of the Wilkinsburg, PA, chapter of the WCTU consist of constitution and bylaws, ca. 1935; minutes, 1885-1941; correspondence, 1924-41; reports; programs; checkbooks; receipt books; a membership roll book; a directory; state convention resolutions, 1917; a history of the Woman's Temperance Crusade and the Allegheny County WCTU, 1874-1930; and memorabilia.

15,255. Women's History
Collection. Nd. 124 items.
Open. Inventory.
University of Pittsburgh, Archives of Industrial Society.
Collected by several individuals at the University, these readings on the role of women in US history consist of manuscripts, poems, fables, songs, oral history transcripts, articles, pamphlets, periodicals, and newspapers. Women and work, immigrants, and blacks are topics emphasized in the collection.

15,256. Brackenridge, Henry Marie
Papers. 1816-70. 1 vol. and 195 items.
Open. Inventory.
University of Pittsburgh, Darlington Memorial Library.
Professional papers of Brackenridge (1786-1871), a lawyer, judge, and author, include correspondence with Andrew Jackson, Henry Clay, John Quincy Adams, and his sister Cornelia Brackenridge. Also includes many letters from Henry Brackenridge to his wife Caroline Marie Brackenridge and a few of her letters to friends.

15,257. Croghan and Schenley
Papers. 1813-42. 42 items.
Open. Checklist.
University of Pittsburgh, Darlington Memorial Library.
Correspondence of William Croghan (?-1850), a Pittsburgh businessman, includes letters concerning the elopement of his daughter Mary (1826-1903) with Captain Edward Schenley in 1842; she was a 14-year-old boarding school student on Staten Island at the time. These letters to Croghan are from his daughter, asking his understanding and forgiveness; from Edward Schenley; and from other family members and friends. Mary (Croghan) Schenley spent the majority of her married life in England, but she lived in Pittsburgh for a time and supported local philanthropic endeavors.

15,258. D'Happart, Joseph St. Leger
Papers. 1797-1815. 12 boxes.
Open. Checklist.
University of Pittsburgh, Darlington Memorial Library.
A French soldier and businessman, d'Happart immigrated to the US in 1794 during the French Revolution; in ca. 1800 he married Elizabeth Thompson, a resident of Connellsville, PA. Business and personal papers contain information on social conditions in western Pennsylvania. Includes correspondence between Joseph and Elizabeth d'Happart while he was on a business trip to France from 1803 to 1805, her correspondence with agents concerning her maintenance, and her financial accounts; Joseph d'Happart's correspondence in French with his niece Henriette de St. Leger concerning the maintenance of her child and herself, 1805-14; and correspondence relating to the estrangement of Joseph and Elizabeth d'Happart in 1812 and their divorce, which was granted by the Pennsylvania legislature in 1815. Collection also contains papers and correspondence of her mother Catherine Thompson and correspondence of Elizabeth d'Happart's sister Maria Read with her husband George Read.

15,259. Harmonia
Records. 1853-65. 2 ft.
Open. Checklist.
University of Pittsburgh, Darlington Memorial Library.
Settled in the valley of Kiantone Creek in New York and Pennsylvania, Harmonia was a utopian community founded on a philosophy combining socialism with spiritualism. Minutes, financial statements, correspondence, essays, and speeches, primarily by John Murray Spear, who was Harmonia's leader, and by Caroline Hinckley, who later married Spear. Also a leader of Harmonia, Hinckley was particularly concerned with marriage, birth, and the position of and education of women; she wrote that a child belonged only to its mother, who could shape the child's character spiritually. Harmonia's interests included abolition, education, marriage, and government. Its records include speeches on the equality of women, a Harmonia rule that "a just balance of the sexes should at all times be sought by the leading mind, in selections for committees or other positions," and material on the group's interest in promoting the development and sale of sewing machines. Also available on microfilm.

15,260. Knox, William Franciss
Papers. 1827-1915. 800 items.
Open. Checklist.
University of Pittsburgh, Darlington Memorial Library.
Family papers of Knox (1831-1915), a McKeesport, PA, physician, include correspondence of his wife Elizabeth M. (Kidoo) Knox (1833-71) and of female children and friends. Elizabeth Knox's correspondence primarily concerns family matters, but women's rights, slavery, and education are also discussed.

15,261. Lazenby, Mary Elinor
Papers. 1933-55. 21 items.
Open. Checklist.
University of Pittsburgh, Darlington Memorial Library.
Papers of Lazenby (1875-?), an author, consist of correspondence, transcripts, research material, clippings, and reviews of her book *Herman Husband, A Story of His Life* (1940).

15,262. Allen, Hervey
Papers. 1830s-ca. 1950. Ca. 50 ft. and 3 cabinets.
Partially closed. Index.
University of Pittsburgh Libraries, Special Collections.
Collection consists of the papers and library of Allen (1889-1949), a writer. Includes personal and business correspondence of Allen and his wife Ann Hyde Andrews Allen, financial papers, manuscripts of his books, clippings, and diaries of his grandfather and a diary and a scrapbook of his grandmother.

15,263. Rinehart, Mary (Roberts)
Papers. Ca. 1905-55. 41 ft.
Open. No guide.
University of Pittsburgh Libraries, Special Collections.
Rinehart (1876-1958) was a writer. Business correspondence, primarily with her publishers; unpublished manuscripts and drafts of her books; family photos; clippings; and first editions and originals of frontispieces of her books.

READING

15,264. Archives
Records. 1908- . No size given.
Closed. No guide.
Missionary Sisters of the Most Sacred Heart of Jesus, St. Michael Convent.
The order was founded in Germany in 1899 and established in the US in 1908. Financial records, deeds, correspondence, histories, photos, scrapbooks, and other records of the province. Includes correspondence of the founder; correspondence and chronicles of parochial schools for Slovak, German, and Hungarian ethnic groups; histories of the growth of community health care institutions in Pennsylvania and other states; and accounts of contributions in personnel, materials, and finance to domestic and foreign missions.

ROSEMONT

15,265. Archives
Records. 1862-1977. No size given.
Open. No guide.
Holy Child Jesus Convent.
The order was founded in England in 1846 by Cornelia Connelly, who was born in Philadelphia. Correspondence of Connelly, diaries kept by members of the convents and schools founded by the order, recollections by those who knew Connelly, photos, and oral history tapes. Members of the order were engaged in teaching.

SCRANTON

15,266. Archives
Records. 1845- . 159 vols.
Open. No guide.
Servants of the Immaculate Heart of Mary Generalate.
Founded in Monroe, MI, in 1845, this religious order of women, which engaged in teaching and health care, was separated from the Philadelphia missions and officially established in the Scranton area in 1871 after the Scranton diocese was organized. Financial records, letters from the foundress and other correspondence, a history, annals, notes on the congregation's history, photos, and volumes pertaining to superiors general and to each convent where the sisters maintain schools.

SHILLINGTON

15,267. American Province Archives
Records. 1925- . No size given.
Closed. No guide.
Missionary Sisters of the Precious Blood Convent.
Correspondence, yearly diaries, chronicles of events, personal papers, photos, and scrapbooks of this religious congregation of missionaries, which was founded in South Africa in 1885 and established in the US in 1925.

SWARTHMORE

15,268. Albums
Collection. 1729-1926. 22 document boxes.
Open. Inventory.
Swarthmore College, Friends Historical Library.
This collection of commonplace books, account books, copybooks, exercise books, autograph

albums, and scrapbooks contain volumes of ca. 89 women from throughout the period.

15,269. Biddle
Papers. 1711-1929. 8 boxes.
Open. Inventory.
Swarthmore College, Friends Historical Library.
Papers of this family include correspondence reflecting family life and social and cultural conditions between 1792 and 1860; marriage certificates, wills, and other legal documents; a ca. 1897 Swarthmore College scrapbook of Grace Brosius Biddle; and her papers concerning the family genealogy. Also include correspondence, 1915-22, of Lucy Biddle Lewis (1861-?), a peace advocate, concerning the International Congress of Women in the The Hague, 1915, and in Zurich, 1919; her association with Jane Addams, Emily Greene Balch, and Catherine Marshall; and the progress of her war relief work.

15,270. Bond, Elizabeth Powell
Papers. 1856-1958. 6 boxes.
Open. Inventory.
Swarthmore College, Friends Historical Library.
Bond (1841-1926) was an educator, author of *Words by the Way,* and dean of Swarthmore College. Correspondence with Ellen Russell Emerson, Hannah (Clothier) Hull, Louisa May Alcott, William Lloyd Garrison, and others; scattered diaries and journals, 1856-1925, in which she recorded her weekly talks and advice to Swarthmore women, books she read, visits and trips, and reminiscences of Garrison and of the Alcott and Emerson families; lists of her sources and amounts of income, contributions to organizations and institutions, subscriptions, account books, and other business papers; and photos of Bond, her family, and friends. Also includes 82 essays as well as speeches and articles she wrote, among them "Elements of Happiness," which she delivered in 1890 before the New York League of Unitarian Women; "The Scope of Motherhood," delivered in 1901 to the Mothers' Congress; "Reminiscences of the National Arbitration and Peace Congress," 1907; "Vassar, the Pioneer"; and a speech she delivered at a memorial meeting for Lucretia Mott and others.

15,271. Cadbury, Richard Tapper, Sr.
Papers. 1799-1924. 4 boxes.
Open. Inventory.
Swarthmore College, Friends Historical Library.
Cadbury (1853-1929) was a businessman, author, and art connoisseur. His family papers contain extensive correspondence of his wife Lydia Shinn Cadbury, 1858-76; of David Comfort and his wife Buelah Walton Comfort, 1818-40; of Lydia Comfort, 1820-65; of Martha (Patty) Comfort, 1840-85; of Thornton Comfort and his wife Joanna Comfort, 1827-80; of Elizabeth Shinn Haines, Henry Haines, and Fanny Hillborn, a young friend in whom the Haineses took a great interest, 1843-82; of Hannah Lloyd [Mrs. James] Neall, 1857-69; of Earl Shinn, Sr., and his wife Sarah Comfort Shinn, 1823-63; of Rebecca Shinn, 1866-78; and of Anna Shinn Shipley and her husband Samuel R. Shipley, 1850-87.

15,272. Central Employment Association
Records. 1840-1942. 2 boxes.
Open. Inventory.
Swarthmore College, Friends Historical Library.
Founded in 1840 to distribute food and clothing to the poor, the Northern Female Association for the Relief of the Sick and Infirm Poor changed its name to Central Employment Association in 1857 when it extended its functions to securing employment for the poor, usually by providing sewing for women to do in their homes. In 1940 the Association was dissolved. Constitution; bylaws; minutes, 1840-1940; correspondence of the secretary and treasurer, 1926-42, about state licenses, tax exemptions, orders for clothing, and the group's dissolution; 20th-century financial records, with lists of securities, contributions and subscriptions, and correspondence about mortgages; and work records, 1857-58 and 1934-40, the second volume of which cites work given out and clothing made and distributed.

15,273. Cleghorn, Sarah Norcliffe
Papers. Ca. 1917-55. 2 boxes.
Open. Inventory.
Swarthmore College, Friends Historical Library.
Cleghorn (1876-1959) was a Quaker journalist. Correspondence, much of which concerns the radio program "This I Believe"; manuscript essays and poems; biographical material; clippings; and memorabilia.

15,274. Coffin
Papers. 1797-1932. 3 boxes.
Access restricted. Inventory.
Swarthmore College, Friends Historical Library.
Family papers primarily relate to the work of clergyman Charles Fisher Coffin (1823-1916) and his wife Rhoda M. (Johnson) Coffin (1826-1909), both of whom were Quaker prison reformers, in founding the Indiana Reformatory Institute for Women and Girls. Correspondence, business papers, writings, addresses, biographical and genealogical material, photos, and memorabilia. Includes Rhoda Coffin's certificate of membership in the American Female Guardian Society, 1860; her certificate of appointment to the board of managers of the Reformatory for Women and Girls, 1877; and addresses and articles she wrote on the Reformatory, women's prisons, and the WCTU.

15,275. Eastburn
Papers. 1786-1951. 1 box.
Open. Inventory.
Swarthmore College, Friends Historical Library.
Family papers include correspondence of Margaret Roberts Eastburn (1880-1964), a teacher in various Quaker and public schools in Philadelphia and New Jersey.

15,276. Emlen
Papers. 1796-1866. 1 box.
Open. Inventory.
Swarthmore College, Friends Historical Library.
Family papers include piece books and letters. Sarah Foulke Farquhar Emlen (1787-1849), a Quaker minister, wrote primarily to her husband James Emlen while she was traveling in connection with her ministry in England, Ireland, Maryland, New England, Ohio, and other areas.

15,277. Female Association of Philadelphia
Records. 1829-1973. 7 boxes.
Open. Inventory.
Swarthmore College, Friends Historical Library.
The Association, a charitable society, was founded in 1829. Constitution and bylaws; annual reports, 1933-68; nearly complete minutes and membership lists; account books, donations, bills, investments, and other financial records; legal documents, 1925-49; correspondence, 1863-65; and accounts of goods given out to be made, lists of persons relieved, and an inventory of supplies, 1850-64.

15,278. Gillingham
Papers. 1849-1962. 7 boxes.
Access restricted. Inventory.
Swarthmore College, Friends Historical Library.
Family papers contain correspondence between Theodore T. Gillingham (1836-1923) and his wife Elizabeth A. Gillingham (1837-1929) as well as photos taken while Theodore Gillingham was an Indian agent in Iowa and Dakota from 1881 to 1889. Also includes correspondence of their daughter Anna Gillingham (1878-1964), a teacher at the Ethical Culture School in New York City, in Honolulu, and other places and cofounder of the Orton Society, a national organization promoting research and treatment of language disabilities. Her letters concern her college days at Swarthmore, travel, friends, and other matters.

15,279. Griscom, Anna Bassett
Papers. Ca. 1914-62. 3 boxes.
Open. Inventory.
Swarthmore College, Friends Historical Library.
Griscom, a Quaker leader who later married J. Passmore Elkinton, (1889-1974), was chairman of the Friends World Conference Committee from 1934 to 1937. Personal correspondence; writings on her personal philosophy, war and social idealism, and Lucretia Mott; and correspondence, speeches, and other material relating to Friends World Conferences, 1934-56.

15,280. Haines, Elizabeth Shinn
Papers. Ca. 1836-82. 1 box.
Open. Inventory.
Swarthmore College, Friends Historical Library.
Diaries for 1850 to 1881, autograph albums, and piece books of [Mrs. Henry] Haines (1823-83), a housewife.

15,281. Hancock
Papers. 1864-79. 1 box.
Open. Inventory.
Swarthmore College, Friends Historical Library.
Family correspondence and papers of Cornelia Hancock (1840-1926), a Quaker, educator, social reformer, and Civil War nurse. Letters she received during the War, letters concerning her experiences between 1865 and 1879 in South Carolina working with Negroes, and an account of her starting a school for Negro children in Mount Pleasant, SC, which became known as the Laing School.

15,282. Home for Destitute Colored Children
Records. 1855-1944. 4 boxes.
Open. Inventory.
Swarthmore College, Friends Historical Library.
Founded in 1855 by educator and social reformer Mary Jeanes (1804-89), the Home, which also functioned as a school, was located in West Philadelphia and accepted children of both sexes until 1919; in 1922 it was renamed the Sunnycrest Farm for Negro Boys and moved to Cheyney, PA. Nearly complete minutes of the board of trustees and of the committee on management; annual reports; a cashbook, 1922-31; and receipts and disbursements, 1925-37.

15,283. Howland Family
Papers. 1763-1929. 12 boxes and 1 package.
Open. Inventory.
Swarthmore College, Friends Historical Library.
Collection centers on Emily Howland (1827-1929), an educator, reformer, and philanthropist. Includes her correspondence with Alice Stone Blackwell, Agnes Tierney, Caroline F. Putnam, Pundita Ramabai, and others; scattered diaries, 1873-1929; lecture notes; writings; family papers; and photos of Susan B. Anthony, Lucretia Mott, the 1903 Lily Dale Woman's Week, the New York State Woman Suffrage Association, and suffragists.

15,284. Hunn, Lydia Jones Sharpless
Papers. 1881-1908. 3 boxes.
Open. Inventory.
Swarthmore College, Friends Historical Library.
Diaries of [Mrs. Ezekiel] Hunn, a Quaker, and her recollections in 1893 of her home and childhood.

15,285. Jennings
Papers. 1768-1871. 2 boxes.
Open. Inventory
Swarthmore College, Friends Historical Library.
Papers of this Quaker family include letters to Phebe Clark, 1805-07; Phebe Eldridge, 1808-17 and 1821-44; and Hannah A. (Clark) Jennings, 1807-52. Also includes meeting papers on the removal and disownment from various

Pennsylvania meetings of Phebe Clark, Phebe Eldridge, and Elizabeth Clark; marriage certificates; and the opening minutes and rules of the Female Association of Philadelphia, which was organized to promote the manufacture and use of cotton produced by free labor.

15,286. Johnson, Emily Cooper
Papers. 1884-1964. 1 box.
Open. Inventory.
Swarthmore College, Friends Historical Library.
[Mrs. Edwin James] Johnson (1885-1966) was a Quaker author and reformer. Correspondence concerning publication of *Dean Bond of Swarthmore: A Quaker Humanist* (1927) and *Under Quaker Appointment: The Life of Jane P. Rushmore* (1953); business and financial papers; family marriage certificates; reference material; photos; and clippings.

15,287. Johnson, Jane
Papers. 1701-1909. 1 box.
Open. Inventory.
Swarthmore College, Friends Historical Library.
Miscellaneous papers of Quakers, which Johnson collected, are included with her minutes of a reading circle, 1870-74, and letters to Ann G. Reeves. Also includes a 1701 certificate of removal for Letitia Penn and an account of a vision of Mary Levis and Joseph Hoag.

15,288. Ladies Art Association
Records. 1871-1914. 1 box.
Open. Inventory.
Swarthmore College, Friends Historical Library.
The Association was founded in 1867 to promote the interests of women artists; in 1872 it sponsored industrial art training for teachers, and in 1881 it established a studio for women. Constitution, correspondence, primarily of Association officer Alice Donlevy; a list of members; and publicity material. One letter gives a history of the Association and of the part Donlevy played in the society. Other officers, some of whom were Friends, include E. C. Fields, Gulielma Fields, Margarita Willets Harrison, and [Mrs.] Jane Russell.

15,289. Lightfoot
Papers. 1737-1899. 2 boxes.
Open. Inventory.
Swarthmore College, Friends Historical Library.
Papers of this family of Quakers and reformers include correspondence of Thomas Lightfoot (1865-96), an agent for the Great Nemaha Agency, and his wife Mary (Cadwallader) Lightfoot (1820-1907) with Philadelphia Friends about the welfare of the Iowa, Sacs, and Foxes Indian tribes of the Agency. Includes financial and other records of the Agency, censuses of Indian tribes, religious testimony in 1781 concerning Susanna Lightfoot, and genealogical material on Maiden Creek Friends Meeting members.

15,290. Manuscript Journals
Collection. 1712-1964. No size given.
Open. Inventory.
Swarthmore College, Friends Historical Library.
Journals and diaries of ca. 227 Friends, ca. 72 of whom were women. Although many of the volumes concern spiritual matters, some contain accounts of daily experiences. Includes diaries of Sarah (Foulke) [Mrs. William] Farquhar [Mrs. James] Emlen, 1807-44; Margaret Cook, 1734-1801; Jane Crosfield, 1760-61; Jane Fenn, 1727-29; Elizabeth Shinn Haines, 1850-81, 26 volumes; Emily Howland, 1873-1929; Lucretia Mott, 1840; Mary Pennington, 1680; and Margaret Ellis, 1752. Also includes the "War Journal of a Pacifist" by Sarah Norcliffe Cleghorn, 1917.

15,291. Mott
Papers. 1834-1949. 7 boxes.
Open. Inventory.
Swarthmore College, Friends Historical Library.
Lucretia (Coffin) Mott (1793-1880) was a Quaker minister, abolitionist, and women's rights advocate; her husband James Mott (1788-1868) was a teacher and businessman who dealt in foreign and domestic staples. Their correspondence with family members and reformers Joseph A. Dugdale, William Lloyd Garrison, Harriet Martineau, Elizabeth (Cady) Stanton, and Lucy Stone comprises the bulk of the collection. Also includes sermons, essays, antislavery documents, and Lucretia Mott's diary about attending the World Anti-Slavery Convention in 1840. Also includes notes on her by Margaret McHenry, 1947-49, and a scrapbook of obituary clippings.

15,292. Northern Association of the City and County of Philadelphia for the Relief and Employment of Poor Women
Records. 1841-1929. 2 boxes.
Open. Inventory.
Swarthmore College, Friends Historical Library.
At first the Association, founded in 1844 to aid poor women by giving them employment, rented rooms where women could come to sew; in 1849 it purchased a house to be used as a store and working area. Charter; constitutions; annual reports; financial records; deeds, mortgages, wills, searches, and other legal documents; inventories of nightgowns, aprons, wool, and other stock; and correspondence concerning financial matters and then the dissolution of the Association in 1926. Lucretia Mott was the group's first president; she served in that capacity until 1866.

15,293. Penn Sewing School
Records. 1868-1906. 1 box.
Open. Inventory.
Swarthmore College, Friends Historical Library.
Charters and trusts, minutes, reports, a history, and a rule book of the Friends Sewing School for girls, founded in 1868 in Philadelphia by Annie Caley and Augusta Taber. Its first-year class contained 79 black and white pupils; by 1875, 260 students had enrolled. The School was renamed Penn Sewing School and then, after establishing a separate sewing class for mothers, it was renamed the Friends Instruction Association. In 1898 the School was dissolved.

15,294. Rodman
Papers. 1775-1865. 1 box.
Open. Inventory.
Swarthmore College, Friends Historical Library.
Correspondence, Quaker testimonies and discourses, journals, and genealogical material of this Quaker Philadelphia family. Includes journals and correspondence of Elizabeth (Rodman) Rotch (1759-1828) and correspondence of Lydia (Rotch) Dean (1770-1822), Hannah (Rodman) Fisher (1764-1819), Mary (Rodman) Fisher (1781-1813), Anna (Rodman) Hazard (1761-1845), Anna (Rodman) Robeson (1787-1848), Mary (Borden) Rodman (1729-98), Sarah Rodman (1764-93), Charity (Rodman) Rotch (1766-1824), Elizabeth (Barker) Rotch (1764-1858), and [Miss] Mary Rotch (1777-1848). Elizabeth (Rodman) Rotch and Charity (Rodman) Rotch were sisters.

15,295. Sermons
Collection. 1680-1883. 1 box.
Open. Inventory.
Swarthmore College, Friends Historical Library.
Sermons delivered by various Quaker ministers, including Priscilla Cadwalader at Darby, PA, in 1831. Includes 12 sermons, 1849-70, by Lucretia (Coffin) Mott as well.

15,296. Shoemaker, Mary Williams, and Shoemaker, Thomas Howard
Papers. 1860-1957. 1 box.
Open. Inventory.
Swarthmore College, Friends Historical Library.
Papers of Mary Shoemaker (1861-1957), a Philadelphia philanthropist, consist of correspondence acknowledging her gifts to such organizations as the United Negro College Fund and the Women's Medical College of Pennsylvania, journals for 1934 to 1945, deeds and related correspondence concerning burials and cemetery plots, and photos of family members. Mary Shoemaker and Thomas Shoemaker (1851-?) were the children of Franklin and Mary Howard Shoemaker.

15,297. Walton, Margaretta (Walton)
Papers. 1812-1961. 4 boxes.
Open. Inventory.
Swarthmore College, Friends Historical Library.
Walton (1829-1904) was a Quaker minister. Her papers contain correspondence, primarily from family and friends; diaries, 1846-1902; her will and other business papers; four sermons she wrote; family photos; and memorabilia, including a copybook, 1841, and an autograph book, 1847. Also includes diaries of her husband Jessee Pusey Walton, 1855-58, and of her father Joseph S. Walton, 1836-53.

15,298. American Peace Society
Records. 1828-1947. 20 boxes.
Open. Inventory.
Swarthmore College Peace Collection.
Scattered records of the Society from its founding in 1828 until 1900. Consists of annual reports and pamphlets and personal papers of Benjamin Franklin Trueblood, an educator, pacifist, and general secretary of the Society between 1892 and 1915, and of his daughter Lyra (Trueblood) Wolkins, who acted as his secretary. Includes boxes of his correspondence with Priscilla H. Peckover, Lucia (Ames) Mead, Jane Addams, and Hannah J. Bailey; Lyra Wolkins's correspondence with and concerning Anna B. Eckstein; scrapbooks of the Boston Peace Congress in 1904 and during WWI; memorabilia; and other items. Collection also contains personal and family correspondence of Benjamin Trueblood; genealogical notes; articles and speeches; a draft of Charles E. Beal's *Prophet of Peace,* a biography of Trueblood; photos; periodicals; and memorabilia.

15,299. Art for World Friendship
Records. 1946-69. 26 boxes.
Open. Inventory.
Swarthmore College Peace Collection.
Founded in 1946 by Maud Muller of Media, PA, and local members of the Women's International League for Peace and Freedom, this Delaware County, PA, organization was the first to sponsor the exchange of children's art on an international level as an aid to international peace and understanding; the group was dissolved in 1970. Minutes, financial records, exhibit reports, correspondence, records of pictures received and sent, publicity, slides, articles, clippings, and other items. Also includes personal papers of Muller, including correspondence, manuscripts, scrapbooks, and other material concerning the League of American Pen Women and the WILPF.

15,300. Bailey, Hannah Clark (Johnston)
Papers. 1883-1923. 3 ft.
Open. Published guide and inventory.
Swarthmore College Peace Collection.
[Mrs. Moses] Bailey (1839-1923) was a Quaker reformer, peace worker, writer, superintendent of the department of peace and arbitration of the WCTU, and treasurer of the National Council of Women. Correspondence, diaries and guest books, manuscripts, reports, calendars, articles by and about her, scrapbooks, and photos of her. Also includes reports of the department, financial papers, programs, and literature of the WCTU as well as nearly complete files of *Pacific Banner,* 1890-95, and *Acorn,* 1889-1901, two peace periodicals of which Bailey was editor. Bailey served as a delegate to the 13th International Peace Congress

in Boston in 1904 and was twice appointed to represent Maine on the National Board of Charities and Correction. She was a member of the Universal Peace Union, the American Peace Society, and the National American Woman Suffrage Association. See Ellen Starr Brinton and Hiram Doty, comps., *Guide to the Swarthmore College Peace Collection, A Memorial to Jane Addams* (Swarthmore, PA: Swarthmore College, 1947).

15,301. Balch, Emily Greene
Papers. Ca. 1875-1955. 41 ft.
Open. Published guide and inventory.
Swarthmore College Peace Collection.
A peace worker and professor of economics at Wellesley College, [Miss] Balch (1867-1961) was asked to leave Wellesley when the US entered WWI; with Jane Addams she helped to found the Women's International League for Peace and Freedom and in 1946 was awarded the Nobel Peace Prize. Correspondence, diaries for 1889 to 1906, autobiographical notes, manuscripts, family papers, pamphlets, reference material, and clippings. Bulk of the collection is correspondence and manuscript articles and books she wrote on international peace work: the policies of the Woman's Peace party; the Women's Committee for Permanent Peace, The Hague; and the WILPF. Correspondents include Jane Addams, Hannah (Clothier) Hull, Dorothy Detzer, Anna Alice Thacher Post, Grace Abbott, Mercedes M. Randall, and Anna Melissa Graves. Also includes some correspondence from the period during which Balch was a professor at Wellesley. See Ellen Starr Brinton and Hiram Doty, comps., *Guide to the Swarthmore College Peace Collection, A Memorial to Jane Addams* (Swarthmore, PA: Swarthmore College, 1947).

15,302. Brinton, Ellen Starr
Papers. 1933-53. 2 boxes.
Open. Inventory.
Swarthmore College Peace Collection.
Brinton (1886-1954) was the first curator of the Swarthmore College Peace Collection; she also was an art historian and author of *Benjamin West's Painting of Penn's Treaty with the Indians* (1941). Correspondence, manuscripts, reference material, and journals concern her work as archivist and manuscript collector for the Collection; her notes on Jane Addams and her papers, which Brinton was instrumental in gathering and preserving, are included. Also contains Brinton's writings and research on peace, reform, the DAR, historical study of West's painting, Elihu Burritt, and the Universal Peace Union.

15,303. Detzer, Dorothy
Papers. 1893- . 4 boxes.
Open. Inventory.
Swarthmore College Peace Collection.
A lobbyist, peace worker, and writer, Detzer (1893-) was national secretary of the Women's International League for Peace and Freedom from 1924 to 1948 and author of *Appointment on the Hill* (1948). She was married to Ludwell Denny. Correspondence, manuscripts, biographical and publicity material, speeches and articles about her, and clippings document her most notable lobbying successes and her interest in Liberia in 1933 and 1934. Correspondents include Liberian secretary of state L. C. Grimes, Anna Melissa Graves, Emily Greene Balch, Roger Baldwin, Sumner Welles, W. E. B. DuBois, and Drew Pearson. Other material concerns civilian public service and conscription, 1942-44; the atomic bomb, 1945-46; and her congressional testimonies, 1935-46. Detzer was a resident of Hull-House from 1918 to 1920 and did relief work for the American Friends Service Committee in Austria and Russia from 1920 to 1923.

15,304. Forbes, Rose Dabney Malcolm
Papers. 1914-22. 2 boxes and 2 vols.
Open. Published guide and inventory.
Swarthmore College Peace Collection.
Correspondence, writings, reference material, scrapbooks, and memorabilia of [Mrs. J. Malcolm] Forbes, a reformer, peace worker, and chairman of the Massachusetts branch of the Woman's Peace party. Includes personal items and records of groups she worked with, among them the Peace party, the Massachusetts Peace Society, and the National Council for Prevention of War. Also includes information about Lucia (Ames) Mead, the Boston LWV, the International Conference of Women, the Women's Bureau, the Democratic National Convention, and the Women's National Committee for Law Enforcement. Scrapbooks contain clippings about WWI, cartoons, posters, and photos. See Ellen Starr Brinton and Hiram Doty, comps., *Guide to the Swarthmore College Peace Collection, A Memorial to Jane Addams* (Swarthmore, PA: Swarthmore College, 1947).

15,305. Graves, Anna Melissa
Papers. 1920-57. 15 ft.
Open. Published guide and inventory.
Swarthmore College Peace Collection.
Correspondence of [Miss] Graves (1875-1964), a reformer and peace worker, with people from around the world concerning various peace movements. Correspondents include Gertrude Baer, Angelica Balabanoff, Olga Tolstoy, Fanny (Garrison) Villard, Anna Louise Strong, Vida Scudder, Gabriela Mistral, Bertrand Russell, Emily Greene Balch, Jane Addams, Mary White Ovington, A. Maude Royden, Sarah Cleghorn, Pearl S. Buck, and Madeleine Rolland. Also includes a few photos. See Ellen Starr Brinton and Hiram Doty, comps., *Guide to the Swarthmore College Peace Collection, A Memorial to Jane Addams* (Swarthmore, PA: Swarthmore College, 1947).

15,306. Hull, Hannah (Clothier)
Papers. 1891-1958. 4 ft.
Open. Inventory.
Swarthmore College Peace Collection.
A peace worker and a Quaker, [Mrs. William Isaac] Hull (1872-1958) was president of the Women's International League for Peace and Freedom from 1924 to 1928 and from 1929 to 1939. The collection consists primarily of personal correspondence and correspondence concerning her work for peace, but it also contains manuscripts, family papers, photos, clippings, and other papers. Correspondents include Jane Addams, Emily Greene Balch, and Carrie Chapman Catt. Also includes material on her work for the WILPF education committee, labor committee, and women's committee for the recognition of Russia; woman suffrage; the Geneva Disarmament Conference in 1932; and trips to India in 1928 and to China in 1929.

15,307. Mead, Lucia True (Ames)
Papers. 1884-1936. 6 ft.
Open. Inventory.
Swarthmore College Peace Collection.
Peace worker, writer, and reformer, [Mrs. Edwin Doak] Mead (1856-1936) was president of the Massachusetts Woman Suffrage Association; vice-chairman of the National Council for Prevention of War; a delegate to the International Peace Congress, 1901, 1903, 1905, 1907, and 1908; and a member of the Women's International League for Peace and Freedom. Correspondence with David Starr Jordan, Vida D. Scudder, Dorothy Detzer, Adela Pankhurst, Carrie Chapman Catt, and others; diaries and notebooks, 1884-1934; manuscripts; pamphlets, clippings, and book reviews of her *Law or War;* editorials; publicity; photos of her and other peace leaders; cartoons; clippings; and other items.

15,308. National Council for Prevention of War
Records. 1921-71. 289 ft.
Access restricted. Inventory.
Swarthmore College Peace Collection.
Constitution and bylaws; minutes; financial records; correspondence; policy statements; programs of action; special projects and subject files; material on NCPW campaigns and on attacks on the organization; articles; books; and other NCPW literature.

Records of various NCPW departments and their officers contain correspondence, reports, writings, speeches, programs, pamphlets, publicity, and related documents for such departments as the education department, of which Florence (Brewer) Boeckel was director from 1921 to 1941; the speakers' bureau, secretaries of which were Mrs. Edward L. Hunt in 1921, Belle Rankin in 1922, and Gladys K. Gould Mackenzie from 1922 to 1954; the legislative department, directors of which included Laura (Puffer) Morgan from 1922 to 1938, and Jeannette Rankin from 1929 to 1940; and the rural life department, with Edna Southworth, associate director from 1928 to 1941.

Regional offices of the NCPW contain similar records and papers: the western office, of which Margaret McDiarmid was associate director from 1924 to 1944; the southern office, with Velma Land and Olga A. Tafel as associates from 1926 to 1930; the northwest office, with Mary Findlay, Mary Klemm, Dorothy Reed, and Emma Anderson as associate directors between 1929 and 1945; the New England office, with Cynthia H. Smith as associate from 1929 to 1954; and the midwest office, with [Mrs.] Hazel Richeson as associate from 1930 to 1938.

Also includes business and personal correspondence of such NCPW staff members as Mary Ida Winder, Carrie Wyckoff Ormsbeer, and Eleanor Brannan as well as records of the press and publicity, labor, and moving picture departments of the NCPW, including records of the Youth Movement for World Recovery.

Collection also contains papers of Frederick J. Libby, executive NCPW secretary from 1921 to 1954, including correspondence, writings, lectures, articles, notes, biographical sketches, clippings, and reference material. Contains material concerning his book *To End War* and extensive correspondence with his wife Faith Ward Libby.

15,309. O'Hare, Kate (Richards)
Papers. 1918-25. 19 folders.
Open. Inventory.
Swarthmore College Peace Collection.
Letters that O'Hare (1877-1948), a writer and lecturer on labor and socialism, international secretary of the Socialist party, and a prison reformer, wrote to her family during her imprisonment from April, 1919, to May, 1920, for violation of the Espionage Act. Her husband Francis "Frank" Patrick O'Hare duplicated these letters and mailed them, with bulletins about the case and appeal efforts, to friends and supporters. Collection also contains these bulletins. Kate O'Hare later married Charles C. Cunningham.

15,310. Peace and Disarmament Committee of the Women's International Organizations
Records. 1931-40. 1 box.
Open. Inventory.
Swarthmore College Peace Collection.
Composed of representatives from 14 women's international groups and located in Geneva, Switzerland, the Committee was founded in 1931 to influence public opinion in favor of the Conference for the Reduction and Limitation of Armaments held in Geneva in 1932. Constitution, annual reports, minutes, resolutions and releases, financial appeals, surveys and reports, and biographies of Committee officers Mary Dingham, Kathleen D. Courtney, L. Dreyfus Barney, and Rosa Manua. The group was known originally as

the Disarmament Committee of the Women's International Organizations.

15,311. People's Mandate to Governments to End War
Records. 1932-50. Ca. 21 ft.
Open. Inventory.
Swarthmore College Peace Collection.
Formed in 1935 by members of the Women's International League for Peace and Freedom, the Mandate was later disassociated from that group. Includes committee policies, history, correspondence, lists, reports, press releases, literature, and material concerning the Buenos Aires Peace Treaties in 1937. Correspondents include Hannah (Clothier) Hull; Mabel Vernon, the Mandate's first director; and Emily Greene Balch. Carrie Chapman Catt was honorary chairman of the executive committee of the People's Mandate Committee for the Western Hemisphere and the Far East; Mary Emma Woolley and Hull were chairmen; Grace Abbott, Ellen F. Pendleton, Dorothy (Canfield) Fisher, and Lillian D. Wald were vice-chairmen. In its early years the Mandate conducted an intensive campaign and collected two million signatures of people expressing opposition to war.

15,312. Spencer, Anna Carpenter (Garlin)
Papers. 1851-1931. 4 ft.
Open. Published guide and inventory.
Swarthmore College Peace Collection.
Correspondence, a diary, manuscripts, biographical material, family correspondence and genealogical data, articles, clippings, and printed matter of [Mrs. William Henry] Spencer (1851-1931), a social reformer, educator, minister, and lecturer. Spencer served as a Unitarian minister from 1891 to 1903, associate director of the New York School of Philanthropy, and a professor of sociology and ethics at the Meadville Theological School in Pennsylvania from 1913 to 1918; in addition, she taught courses for social workers at Columbia Teachers College. She also was an active member of the National American Woman Suffrage Association. Her correspondents include Lucy Stone, Susan B. Anthony, Edith Abbott, and Carrie Chapman Catt. See Ellen Starr Brinton and Hiram Doty, comps., *Guide to the Swarthmore College Peace Collection, A Memorial to Jane Addams* (Swarthmore, PA: Swarthmore College, 1947).

15,313. War Resisters' League
Records. 1923- . Ca. 64 boxes.
Open. Inventory.
Swarthmore College Peace Collection.
The League was founded in 1923 by Abraham Kaufman, Jessie Wallace Hughan, Tracy Mygatt, and Frances Witherspoon with the assistance of Frank Olmstead and Evan Thomas. Executive committee minutes and reports, reports of other committees, and correspondence, 1920s-70; a history, 1923-25; prison cases, briefs, and material on the Glendora strikers defense committee, 1942-46; and scrapbooks, manuscripts, photos, and copies of the periodical *The Conscientious Objector*. Also includes material about annual conferences, projects, and fieldwork; press releases; articles; book reviews; scattered material of Hughan; and records of the committee for nonviolent action and the war tax resistance campaign.

Consisting of representatives from various peace movements, the League met initially to establish a US section of the War Resisters' International. After this was accomplished, Hughan, the League's secretary, carried on much of the work by herself. In 1925 the League was organized as a unit separate from the International; it was then called the No More War Movement. In 1926 it resumed its former name and expanded to act as a pressure group against war, to provide nonmilitary services, and to emphasize war opposition based on nonreligious grounds.

15,314. Wentworth, Lydia G.
Papers. 1902-47. 4 ft.
Open. Inventory.
Swarthmore College Peace Collection.
Correspondence of and printed material about [Miss] Wentworth (1858-1947), a peace worker and writer who was confined to her bed by illness for more than 30 years. Her correspondents include Lucia (Ames) Mead, Emily Greene Balch, Belle Rankin, and Caroline Babcock.

15,315. Women's Committee to Oppose Conscription
Records. 1942-47. 9 ft.
Open. Inventory.
Swarthmore College Peace Collection.
Statements of purpose, minutes, correspondence, releases, literature, and clippings of the Committee, first called the Committee to Oppose the Conscription of Women and then the National Committee to Oppose the Conscription of Women, both in 1942, before it adopted its last name in 1944. Its names reflected its changing purposes: the Committee was first organized to protest the Austin-Wadsworth bills and similar measures designed to provide for the drafting of women in WWII; after drafting women was no longer a possibility, the Committee worked against conscription in general. Mildred (Scott) Olmsted was Committee director, A. J. Muste was treasurer, and Grace Rhoads was secretary. Katherine Pierce and Mrs. Allan Knight were also active in the Committee. Committee records contain material on the American Friends Service Committee, the national WCTU, the Women's League for Political Education, and the National Council Against Conscription as well as official correspondence of Olmsted.

15,316. Women's International League for Peace and Freedom
Records. 1915-ca. 1976. Ca. 234 ft.
Open. Published guide and detailed inventory.
Swarthmore College Peace Collection.
The WILPF grew from the International Women's Committee for Permanent Peace that met first at the International Congress of Women at The Hague in 1915; the Woman's Peace party participated in the Congress and became the US section of the WILPF in 1919.

Records of the international office of the WILPF, 1920-76, include minutes, correspondence, circular letters, press releases, resolutions, pamphlets, posters, periodicals, and other material concerning all congresses to 1965. Also includes records of the committee on the Americas, with material on the Inter-American Congress of Women, 1945-71, and correspondence of Heloise Brainerd, 1936-50.

Archives of the US section of the WILPF contain constitutions, annual reports, minutes, financial records, correspondence, resolutions, histories, biographies, reports, handbooks, press releases, newsletters, and reference and other material of the executive, lobbying, labor, nominating, conscientious objection, disarmament, refugee, civil rights, policy, and other committees. There are separate records of the New York and Pennsylvania state branches and selected material from the California, Colorado, Illinois, Maryland, Massachusetts, Michigan, Minnesota, Mississippi, and New Jersey state branches. Correspondents include Jane Addams, Emily Greene Balch, Hannah (Clothier) Hull, Lucy Carner, Mildred (Scott) Olmsted, Dorothy (Detzer) Denny, Lucy Biddle Lewis, Dorothy Medders Robinson, Heloise Brainerd, Dorothy Hutchinson, Emily (Parker) Simon, and Katherine L. Camp.

Collection also contains records, 1915-19, of the Woman's Peace party, which was founded in 1915 by Jane Addams, Carrie Chapman Catt, Fannie Fern (Phillips) Andrews, and others and was active throughout WWI. Minutes, financial records, correspondence, resolutions, membership files, reports, articles, clippings, and printed matter of the organizational conference in Washington, DC, in 1915; annual meetings; the executive council; the executive board; the legislative committee; state chairmen; and of the state branches, particularly the New York and Massachusetts branches. Also includes a history of the organization by Lucia (Ames) Mead and reports of the national office secretary. See Ellen Starr Brinton and Hiram Doty, comps., *Guide to the Swarthmore College Peace Collection, A Memorial to Jane Addams* (Swarthmore, PA: Swarthmore College, 1947).

15,317. Women's Peace Union
Records. 1921-41. 18 ft.
Open. Published guide and inventory.
Swarthmore College Peace Collection.
Founded in 1921, the Union agitated primarily for passage of a proposed constitutional amendment which would have abolished the government's war-making powers. Complete minutes, financial records, correspondence, reports, releases, literature, and clippings. Includes correspondence of Senator Lynn J. Frazier, an antiwar activist who introduced the constitutional amendment legislation; correspondence of Ruby Hughes; speeches of Jeannette Rankin; and material concerning Gertrude Baer, Frieda Langer Lazarus, Tracy D. Mygatt, and Caroline L. Babcock. See Ellen Starr Brinton and Hiram Doty, comps., *Guide to the Swarthmore College Peace Collection, A Memorial to Jane Addams* (Swarthmore, PA: Swarthmore College, 1947).

TITUSVILLE

15,318. Tarbell, Ida
Papers. 1878-1937. 10 Hollinger boxes.
Access restricted. Unpublished guide.
Drake Well Museum.
Correspondence, manuscripts, articles, a scrapbook, and other papers of Tarbell (1857-1944), a writer. Most of the material pertains to her writings on the petroleum industry and particularly her history of the Standard Oil Company.

TOWANDA

15,319. Murray, Elsie
Papers. 1903-64. 6 ft. and 583 vols.
Open. Unpublished guide.
French Azilum.
Murray (1878-1965) was a scientist at Cornell University and director of Tioga Point Museum in Athens, PA, and the French Azilum. Correspondence, diaries for 1911 to 1965, photos, lantern slides, and published books. Correspondents include French author Helene Foure, Pierre S. du Pont, author Helen Fuller Orton, writer and historian Elsie Singmaster, and author Lucille Wallower Van Horn. Murray earned a PhD.

UNIVERSITY PARK

15,320. All-American Girls' Baseball League
Records. 1943-54. 1 microfilm reel.
Open. Unpublished guide.
Pennsylvania State University Libraries, Pennsylvania Historical Collections and Labor Archives.
The League was founded in 1943 to promote and regulate women's baseball. Minutes of the board of directors, budget and playing statistics, rosters of players, rules and regulations, photos, and clippings.

15,321. Amalgamated Clothing Workers of America
Records. 1934-62. 106 items.
Open. Unpublished guide.

Pennsylvania State University Libraries, Pennsylvania Historical Collections and Labor Archives.
Minute books, correspondence, pamphlets, press releases, clippings, and other records of Local 118 of this labor union in Curwensville, PA, 1934-48; Local 628, Clearfield, PA, 1953-55; and Local 674, Philipsburg, PA, 1953-55. Also includes correspondence and other papers pertaining to the activities of Julia L. Maietta as an officer in Local 118, as ACWA representative in Local 674 and in the Puritan Sportswear company in Altoona, PA, as women's activities director for congressional district 20 of the Committee on Political Education from 1934 to 1962, and in organizing campaigns.

15,322. Aurandt, Margaret
Papers. 1860-75. 48 items.
Open. Unpublished guide.
Pennsylvania State University Libraries, Pennsylvania Historical Collections and Labor Archives.
Letters from Alfred Aurandt, a member of the Pennsylvania Volunteers, contain descriptions of Civil War battles and prisoners as well as later letters concerning rural family life and homesteading on the Kansas frontier.

15,323. Bernard, Jessie R.
Papers. 1932-76. 18 ft.
Open. Unpublished guide.
Pennsylvania State University Libraries, Pennsylvania Historical Collections and Labor Archives.
[Mrs. Luther Lee] Bernard (1903-) is a sociologist, professor, research scholar, and consultant to the Special Operations Research Organization. Correspondence with notable sociologists and others, typescripts of talks, and articles she wrote on women's roles in society, marriage, remarriage, sex roles, the family, and family planning, her areas of specialization.

15,324. Bernard, Luther Lee
Papers. 1899-1959. 61 ft.
Open. Unpublished guide.
Pennsylvania State University Libraries, Pennsylvania Historical Collections and Labor Archives.
Papers of Bernard (1888-1951), a sociologist, include biographies of 240 sociologists, histories of the development of sociology courses in ca. 85 institutions, and correspondence with his wife Jessie R. Bernard, who was a sociologist, and with his sister Helen Bernard.

15,325. Dickson, William B.
Papers. 1880-1940. No size given.
Open. Unpublished guide.
Pennsylvania State University Libraries, Pennsylvania Historical Collections and Labor Archives.
Includes 36 letters which Emma Dickson wrote while she worked in a YMCA canteen in France during WWI.

15,326. Dock, Mira Lloyd
Papers. 1900-45. 3 ft.
Open. Unpublished guide.
Pennsylvania State University Libraries, Pennsylvania Historical Collections and Labor Archives.
Papers of Dock (?-1945), a botanist, contain information on her career as commissioner of forestry on the Pennsylvania State Reservation Commission from 1901 to 1913. Photos and correspondence with Gifford Pinchot, Irvin Williams, J. T. Rothrock, Robert S. Conklin, William A. Buckhout, and state and national agencies.

15,327. Ellickson, Katherine Pollak
Papers. 1935-37. 3 microfilm reels.
Access restricted. Unpublished guide.
Pennsylvania State University Libraries, Pennsylvania Historical Collections and Labor Archives.
Files of Ellickson (1905-), assistant to Congress of Industrial Organizations (CIO) director John Brophy, contain correspondence, notes on meetings and conferences, speeches, field reports, articles, and other items.

15,328. Hale and Mull
Papers. 1850-1900. 27 ft.
Open. Unpublished guide.
Pennsylvania State University Libraries, Pennsylvania Historical Collections and Labor Archives.
Papers of the Hale family of Philipsburg, PA, include personal and business correspondence of female members of the family, material on the Parker Genealogical Society, church records, and scattered family and travel photos.

15,329. International Ladies' Garment Workers' Union
Records. 1956-72. 1.5 ft.
Open. Unpublished guide.
Pennsylvania State University Libraries, Pennsylvania Historical Collections and Labor Archives.
Records of this labor union, founded in 1900, include minutes of the Philadelphia joint board; proceedings; copies of the union journals *Justice, The Needle's Eye, Northeast News,* and *Garment Worker;* and booklets and photos from labor education institutes held at Penn State.

15,330. Jones, Mary (Harris) "Mother"
Papers. 1911, nd. 2 items.
Open. Unpublished guide.
Pennsylvania State University Libraries, Pennsylvania Historical Collections and Labor Archives.
Letters of Jones (1830-1930), an organizer for the United Mine Workers of America who worked on behalf of coal miners in western Pennsylvania, West Virginia, Colorado, and Arizona. In the first, she states that she witnessed a gathering of 12,000 persons and a four-mile-long parade against the courts in Denver; in the second, writing on the stationery of the Kofa, AZ, Miners' Union, no. 98, she gives encouragement to her correspondent.

15,331. McCloskey, Eunice M.
Papers. 1930-76. 18 ft.
Open. No guide.
Pennsylvania State University Libraries, Pennsylvania Historical Collections and Labor Archives.
Correspondence, poetry, scrapbooks, clippings, children's books, and a painting of McCloskey (1904-), a poet and painter. Correspondents include August Derleth, Faith Baldwin, Taylor Caldwell, Pearl Buck, and Charles McCabe.

15,332. Oral History Project
Oral history. 1968- . 209 tapes.
Access restricted. Published guide.
Pennsylvania State University Libraries, Pennsylvania Historical Collections and Labor Archives.
Tapes and transcripts of interviews with activists and leaders of the labor union movement, including Florence Clowes, Dorothy Paterson, Mrs. Stewart Miller, Mary Callahan, Sarah Fredgant, Julia L. Maietta, Bonnie Segal, Judy Mollinger, and others. Gloria Reehill, a member of Local 4889 of the United Steelworkers of America in Philadelphia, describes her experiences in factory work, sweeping, car blocking, operating a tractor, and driving a six-ton truck for the tin maintenance department, as well as the women's liberation movement, job discrimination, and ways of overcoming discrimination. Hilda Worthington Smith and Frank Fernbach, who were chairmen of the National Committee for the Extension of Labor Education, discuss the creation of the Committee in 1943, charges in the US House of Representatives against the Committee for radical activities, and the positive effects of legislative efforts to fund the Committee, even though they proved unsuccessful. Ernestine Friedmann, former director of the Barnard Labor Education Program and a member of the industrial department of the YWCA, describes her work in 1910 trying to interest girls in factories in the activities of the YWCA, her relationship with National Women's Trade Union League president Mrs. Raymond Robbins, and a women's meeting held in Washington, DC, with women from 15 countries participating; in 1921 Friedmann became involved in the Bryn Mawr Summer School for Women Workers.

Includes an interview in which Lee B. Stanley, former secretary to A. J. Muste at the Brookwood Labor College in Katonah, NY, discusses her experiences at the College, the school's administration, selection of students through their own unions, teachers, and the closing of Brookwood. In their interview, Helen Starr, who taught labor journalism at Brookwood Labor College from 1925 to 1935, and her husband Mark Starr, who joined the Brookwood faculty in 1928, describe the early history of the College; such faculty members as A. J. Muste, David Saposs, Julius Hochman, Arthur Calhoun, and Tucker Smith; the indictment of Brookwood as a communist organization and the financial problems that led to its closing in 1938; the way in which workers' education changed in the US as trade unions gained recognition; and the present and future economic needs which workers' education should serve.

Also includes an interview in which Ann Leifer, a social science teacher and member of Local 400, American Federation of Teachers in Pittsburgh, describes the formation of the Local and interviews with Rebecca Altschuler, a retired teacher from South Philadelphia High School and a former vice-president of the Philadelphia Federation of Teachers; Celia Pincus, a retired teacher and former president of the Philadelphia Federation; Margaret Root, a retired teacher from Olney High School and a consultant to and former president of the Philadelphia Federation; and Onah Weldon, grievance chairman and elementary representative of Local 3 of the Philadelphia Federation. Collection also contains an interview in which Sonya Richman, general vice-president of Local 3 of the Philadelphia Federation of Teachers, describes the poor conditions in many of the public schools in Philadelphia, the strike of 1972-73, and the personalities of such participants in strike negotiations as John Ryan and Frank Sullivan of the Teachers Union, Philadelphia mayor Frank Rizzo, Judge Donald Jamieson, Richardson Dilworth, and William Ross.

In addition, the collection contains the transcript of an interview, conducted at the Roosevelt Library, of Hilda Worthington Smith, who was former director of the Bryn Mawr Summer School for Women Workers and former director of WPA programs in workers' education. See Alice M. Hoffman et al., *Oral History Project* (College Park, PA: Pennsylvania State University, 1976).

15,333. Ruttenberg, Harold J.
Papers. 1933-67. 8 ft.
Open. Unpublished guide.
Pennsylvania State University Libraries, Pennsylvania Historical Collections and Labor Archives.
Correspondence, minutes, drafts of articles and books, pamphlets, bulletins, announcements, and clippings which Ruttenberg (1914-), an industrialist and research director of the Steel Workers Organizing Committee, collected while he was on the board of the Portsmouth Steel Company and a member of the US War Production Board. Includes information on general labor studies, Negroes in labor, steel negotiations, the CIO, the League of Women Shoppers, and other organizations.

15,334. Tapes
Collection. 1948-77. 1,300 tapes.
Open. Published guide.
Pennsylvania State University Libraries, Pennsylvania Historical Collections and Labor Archives.
Tapes of lectures, symposia, addresses, interviews, poetry readings, and other cultural activities, excepting for the most part musical events, at Penn

State. Speakers included Nikki Giovanni, Dorothy Roberts, Florynce Kennedy, Alice M. Hoffman, and Ellen Burstyn. See *A Catalog of Audio Tapes Recorded on the University Park Campus of Pennsylvania State University.*

15,335. Woman Suffrage
Collection. 1900-20. 0.5 ft.
Open. Unpublished guide.
Pennsylvania State University Libraries, Pennsylvania Historical Collections and Labor Archives.
Constitution and bylaws of the Pennsylvania Woman Suffrage Association, booklets and articles about woman suffrage, election maps, leaflets of the Pennsylvania Men's League for Woman Suffrage, cartoons, a declaration of the National Women's Trade Union League, and correspondence between Henry White and Emily Fogg of the United Garment Workers Union and the United Labor League of Philadelphia. Also includes pamphlets and leaflets from the Association Opposed to Woman Suffrage.

VILLA MARIA

15,336. Villa Maria Archives
Records. 1817- . 10 drawers and ca. 15 cartons.
Closed. No guide.
Sisters of the Humility of Mary, Villa Maria Community Center.
Founded in France in 1854, the entire Community came to the US in 1864. The activities of this religious order of women are primarily in the fields of education, health care, and social work. Minutes, financial reports, official and personal correspondence, annals, manuscripts, recollective writings, oral history tapes, scrapbooks, and other records of the Community pertain to its founding, emigration, and Americanization and to the establishment of its missions, schools, hospitals, and Community Center. Includes papers of general superiors and of Father John Joseph Begel, the founder of the order. Some members of the order traveled west from Villa Maria in 1870, eventually settling in Iowa with their motherhouse in Ottumwa.

VILLANOVA

15,337. Generalate Archives
Records. 1894- . 16 drawers and 1 cabinet.
Closed. No guide.
Bernardine Sisters, Generalate.
This religious order of women, founded in 1894 in Pennsylvania, is engaged primarily in teaching and nursing. Minutes, financial records, correspondence, history of the community, annals, biographies and records of deceased members, photos, slides, motion pictures, and other records of events and of the Generalate. Includes correspondence of mothers general and mothers provincial, brief histories of parish schools, information on the work of Mother Veronica Grzedowska and the Sisters among Polish immigrants in the late 19th and early 20th centuries, and record books listing important dates in the lives of members.

WEST CHESTER

15,338. Ashbridge Family
Papers. 1721-1893. Ca. 600 items.
Open. Card catalog.
Chester County Historical Society.
Papers of this family of Chester County residents concern family matters and local affairs. Includes correspondence of Rachel S. Ashbridge (1833-1920); Rachel V. Ashbridge, 1841-54; and Rebecca Ashbridge, 1835-50. Also includes an 1888 diary of Jeannette Ashbridge.

15,339. Brinton, Cassandra
Papers. 1840-66. 5 vols. and ca. 50 items.
Open. No guide.
Chester County Historical Society.
Piece books, autograph albums, and correspondence with friends of Brinton, a Chester County resident, concerning family matters and local events.

15,340. Chester County Federation of Women's Clubs
Records. 1934-64. 1 folder and 4 vols.
Open. Card catalog.
Chester County Historical Society.
The Federation was an organization of all the clubs in the county that performed services for the community and state. Bylaws; treasurer's reports, 1938-47; complete minutes for the period; brief reports of the home life, conservation and natural resources, international affairs, education, and fine arts committees; and a pamphlet.

15,341. Cope, Ellen
Papers. 1895-ca. 1965. 3 boxes and 3 vols.
Open. No guide.
Chester County Historical Society.
Correspondence, greeting cards, exercise books, and other papers pertain primarily to the education of [Miss] Cope (ca. 1885-), a Quaker resident of Chester County, who was a teacher at the Westtown School. She attended Wellesley College beginning in 1902, took two years off to earn money by teaching, and graduated in 1908; in 1910 she took a summer course in biology at Cornell University. Detailed college correspondence with her parents Anna Garrett Cope (1848-1918) and Gilbert Cope (1840-1928), a Quaker genealogist and local historian, concerns college life, family matters, and religion. Also includes correspondence with other family members and with friends, photos of classmates and activities at Wellesley, college examination books, pamphlets on student activities and commencement, and a diary that Ellen Cope kept during her childhood.

15,342. Daughters of the American Revolution
Records. 1894-1964. 1 folder and 16 vols.
Open. Card catalog.
Chester County Historical Society.
Complete minutes, 1894-1960, as well as applications for membership, registration books, and scrapbooks of this local chapter of the DAR, founded in 1894.

15,343. Diaries
Collection. 1735-1944. No size given.
Open. Card catalog.
Chester County Historical Society.
Diaries kept by 96 rural and small town residents, most of which date from the 19th century. The diaries of the rural women primarily concern family matters, health, weather conditions, and social events. Includes a composition book Olivia Work kept while she was a student at a young ladies' seminary in West Chester, 1844; diaries of Alice Long, 1882-1947, and of Elizabeth Passmore, 1891-1930; a diary of the child Esther Rachel Hayes, which her parents kept for her, 1897-1900; extracts from the diary of Hannah Greaves Peirce, 1771-81; and a copy of a diary of a religious tour of Mary Weston, 1750-51.

15,344. Home and School League of Chester County
Records. 1916-28. 1 vol.
Open. Card catalog.
Chester County Historical Society.
Minutes and financial records of the League, founded in 1916 to promote understanding and cooperation between parents and teachers. Women were prominent in the organization as officers, committee chairmen, and members. Issues such as teacher education, nutrition in schools, and library facilities were discussed during the group's meetings.

15,345. Recipes
Collection. 1702-1887. Ca. 75 items.
Open. Card catalog.
Chester County Historical Society.
Collection contains cookbooks, recipes for winemaking, dyes and whitewash recipes, sewing and knitting instructions, and a 1785 letter from Sarah Beale to Elizabeth Halley with medical recipes. Includes cures for cancer, colds, gout, titters, consumption, and pole evil.

15,346. WCTU of Chester County
Records. 1884-1943. 10 vols. and 8 items.
Open. Card catalog.
Chester County Historical Society.
Constitution and principles, complete minutes, treasurer's account books and ledgers, pamphlets, and other records of the Chester County chapter of the WCTU, founded in 1884. Also includes reports of annual conventions held in 1893, 1915, and 1921, and a 1943 scrapbook commemorating Frances Willard, with photos, articles, clippings, and reminiscences by Chester County residents of a speaking tour by Willard.

WESTTOWN

15,347. Girls' Merchandize
Records. 1832-1902. 8 vols.
Open. No guide.
Westtown School.
Account books kept by the Westtown School administration for each student's expenses contain listings and prices for books, school supplies and material for sewing class, and personal items.

15,348. Girls' Register
Records. 1799-1913. 4 vols.
Open. No guide.
Westtown School.
Ledger books list all women School students by date of admission with names, addresses, names of parents, dates of leaving the School, and remarks, including the name in which given accounts were kept.

15,349. Letters
Records. 1780-1977. 39 ms. boxes.
Open. Unpublished guide.
Westtown School.
Correspondence of women Westtown school students, teachers, and mothers, as well as of male students and teachers, fathers, alumni, and friends contains descriptions of life at Westtown, including lessons, activities, sports, dress, social life, and religion. The correspondence provides information on the role of Quaker women in the Society of Friends, at the School, and at home and on the philosophy of education for women.

15,350. Student Clubs and Committees
Records. 1836-1950. 20 vols.
Open. Unpublished guide.
Westtown School.
Minutes of literary clubs, student government, honorary societies, athletic clubs, and other Westtown School student groups document the roles women took as officers and members of campus organizations and the activities that interested women students.

15,351. The Westonian
Records. 1895- . 40 vols.
Open. No guide.
Westtown School.
Volumes of *The Westonian*, the journal of the Westtown alumni association, contain articles about the School, articles by alumnae, and information

about the activities of women students before and after graduation from the School.

15,352. Westtown Committee
Records. 1794-1963. 20 vols.
Open. Unpublished guide.
Westtown School.
Minutes of the Committee, which was founded in 1794 to oversee the administration of Westtown School, and of subcommittee meetings and reports to the Philadelphia Yearly Meeting of the Religious Society of Friends. Minutes contain reports on School life, individual students and teachers, admissions, finances, and other matters. Both women and men served on the Committee, which is still in existence.

WILKES-BARRE

15,353. Blumenfeld, Lillian (Rifkin)
Papers. 1937- . 1.5 ft.
Open. Unpublished guide.
King's College Library.
Correspondence, diaries, articles, scrapbooks, photos, clippings, tapes and transcript, and books of [Mrs. Gustav] Blumenfeld (1897-), an educator. After studying with John Dewey at Columbia University, Blumenfeld operated her own progressive school in Wilkes-Barre; she later taught at the Modern School in Stelton, NJ, and the Walden School in New York City, where she also directed the Tested Toy Laboratory, which tested toys for manufacturers, and created educational toys. Blumenfeld is now associate director of the Early Childhood Academy in Fort Myers, FL.

15,354. Wyoming Valley Artists
Collection. 1801- . 5 ft.
Open. Unpublished guide.
King's College Library.
Completed questionnaires, brochures, clippings, and other material contain biographical information about men and women artists who lived or painted in Pennsylvania's Wyoming Valley. Among the women represented are Elizabeth Denison (Lance) French, Alice (Welsh) Jenkins, Dorothy Rittenhouse Morgan, Rose O'Neill, and Edith Lindsley Reynolds.

15,355. Miscellaneous Women's Papers
Collection. Ca. 1864-1907. 8 items.
Open. No guide.
Wilkes College Library.
Includes a letter from Lydia Sigourney to a Mr. Butler of Wyoming; a statement by Lucretia Mott on women's rights, 1864; a letter from Harriet Beecher Stowe to an unidentified correspondent, 1882; a letter to a Mrs. Penrose from Ellen Wilson, wife of President Woodrow Wilson, 1907; a letter to Charles Penrose from Frances Cleveland, wife of President Grover Cleveland, 1907; and brief items by Lydia Maria Child and Emma Willard.

YARDLEY

15,356. Archives
Records. 1857- . No size given.
Open. No guide.
Grey Nuns of the Sacred Heart Motherhouse.
Correspondence, documents, tapes, photos, scrapbooks, and other records relating to the history of the Grey Nuns, especially the Congregation of the Grey Nuns of the Sacred Heart, which was established in Philadelphia in 1921. This religious order of women is engaged in education, health care, social work, and pastoral care in the US and foreign countries.

YORK

15,357. Delta, PA, Oral History Project
Oral history. 1976. 23 tapes.
Open. Unpublished guide.
Historical Society of York County.
The Project was conducted to obtain information about the history of Delta. Includes interviews with 11 women on such topics as farm life, the occupations of some women, and customs in Delta and Wales, PA.

15,358. Edwards and Chapin
Papers. Nd. No size given.
Open. Unpublished guide.
Historical Society of York County.
Papers of Jonathan Edwards, Jr. (1745-1801), a theologian; Calvin Chapin (1763-1851), a clergyman; and Edward Chapin, (1799-1868), an attorney and a member of the York County Bar Association. Includes 111 letters, 1837-50, to Edward Chapin from his sisters Jerusha Chapin and Eliza (Chapin) Robbins from Connecticut and New York City.

15,359. League of Women Voters of York County
Records. 1949-74. 1 ft. and 4 Hollinger boxes.
Open. No guide.
Historical Society of York County.
Records of this chapter of the LWV, founded in 1950, contain annual reports; minutes of the board of directors and of the membership; treasurer's monthly reports, bank statements, an audit, and other financial records; correspondence; scrapbooks; issues of the LWV *Bulletin* and *Leagueline;* and clippings.

15,360. Leifer, Mary E.
Papers. 1922-34. 0.4 ft.
Open. No guide.
Historical Society of York County.
Business records of Leifer, a dressmaker who operated a dressmaking establishment run by and for women. Her bookkeepers were Myrtle Duke and Mae Kindienst.

15,361. Pennsylvania Woman Suffrage Party, York County Committee
Records. 1913-19. 1 Hollinger box.
Open. No guide.
Historical Society of York County.
Correspondence from the parent organization, miscellaneous expense records, and clippings concerning woman suffrage and the Committee, which was founded by Anna Dill Gamble in 1913 to obtain votes for woman suffrage. Also includes letters to Gamble, who was Committee chairman, and a membership list of the York County Men's League for Woman Suffrage. Records document the activities of York County residents instituting campaigns, holding rallies, and engaging speakers to promote the cause of suffrage. An historian and author, Gamble was awarded the *Pro Ecclesia and Pontifice* by Pope Pius XII in 1942 for her work in promoting the welfare of the Catholic church.

15,362. Shrewsbury Temperance Society
Records. 1845-50. 0.1 ft.
Open. No guide.
Historical Society of York County.
Minutes of the Society, which was organized to "guard against a pernicious practice which is injurious to our health, standing, and families." Members, 50 percent of whom were women, pledged to abstain from "all ardent spirits, Malt Liquor, Wines, and fermented Cider."

15,363. Women's Auxiliary of the Historical Society of York County
Records. 1965-73. 1 Hollinger box.
Open. No guide.
Historical Society of York County.
Minutes of the Auxiliary, founded in 1965 to assist the Historical Society "in every possible way" in historical preservation, contain information on activities of the Auxiliary.

PUERTO RICO

SAN JUAN

15,364. Deliz, Monserrate
Papers. 1925-60. 3.6 cu.ft.
Open. Unpublished guide.
Archivo General de Puerto Rico.
A music teacher at the University of Puerto Rico, Deliz (1896-1968) cofounded the University's music department and the Pro-Arte Musical Association in San Juan; she also wrote music education books for children. Correspondence, financial records of music associations, concert programs, manuscript and printed music of various Puerto Rican composers, and clippings.

15,365. Departamento de Estado, Corporaciones Sin Fines de Lucro
Records. 1900-54. 26 file units.
Open. Unpublished guide.
Archivo General de Puerto Rico.
This series about nonprofit associations contains files on civic, social, educational, political, and feminist organizations incorporated by Puerto Rican women.

15,366. Departamento de Instrucción, Expedientes de Maestros
Records. Ca. 1920-40. Ca. 68 cu.ft.
Open. No guide.
Archivo General de Puerto Rico.
Department of education records contain information on women professors who taught at schools in Puerto Rico.

15,367. Távarez, Elisa
Papers. 1919-60. 1.2 cu.ft.
Open. Unpublished guide.
Archivo General de Puerto Rico.
Correspondence, concert programs, manuscript and printed music by 19th-century Puerto Rican composers, scrapbooks, and photos of [Mrs.] Távarez (1879-1960), a pianist and music teacher, provide information on her activities in and outside of Puerto Rico.

SANTURCE

15,368. Padilla de Sanz, Doña Trina
Papers. Nd. 8 items.
Open. Unpublished guide.
University of the Sacred Heart, Madre María Teresa Guevara Library.
Correspondence and poems by Padilla de Sanz (1864-1957), who was best known as Trina Padilla, a poet and journalist who used the pseudonym La Hija del Caribe, for her father Don José Gualberto Padilla (1829-96), a satiric Puerto Rican poet who used the pseudonym El Caribe. A piano teacher who founded a piano academy in Arecibo, PR, Trina Padilla also was honorary president of the Asociación Insular de Mujeres Votantes, which was founded to promote woman suffrage.

RHODE ISLAND

CUMBERLAND

15,369. Archives
Records. 1831- . 1265 ft., 20 drawers, 36 boxes, 6 cabinets, 10 shelves, and 70 tapes.
Open. Unpublished guide.
Sisters of Mercy Provincialate.
The order was founded in Ireland in 1831 and was established in the US by Mother Frances Xavier in 1845 in Pittsburgh and in 1851 in Rhode Island. Chronicles and histories of the Sisters and of individual convents; oral history tapes; records relating to education, ministries, foreign missions, and house meetings; scrapbooks; records of conferences, institutes, conventions, and workshops; studies regarding province-owned property, life styles, comparative ages in different ministries, and charisms of early sisters of the province; records relating to the government of the province; and annals and other books.

LITTLE COMPTON

15,370. Wilbor
Papers. 1860-90. 1 box and 7 vols.
Open. No guide.
Little Compton Historical Society.
Papers of Sarah Soule Wilbor (1804-90), a local historian, genealogist, and suffrage worker, include letters from members of her family who were living abroad and daily diaries, which contain information about her interest in politics, women's rights, and modern dress. Also includes an 1861 diary of Frances Gifford, a farm girl.

NEWPORT

15,371. Tennis Library
Collection. 1874- . 500 vols.
Open. Unpublished guide.
International Tennis Hall of Fame and Tennis Museum.
Diaries, scrapbooks, books, and other items document the participation of women in the game of tennis. Since 1955 at least 29 women have been elected to the Hall of Fame, including May Sutton Bundy, Sarah Palfrey Danzig, Margaret O. duPont, Eleonora Sears, Doris Hart, Suzanne Lenglen, and Helen Wills.

15,372. Archives
Records. 1807- . No size given.
Closed. No guide.
Sisters of St. Joseph Cluny Provincialate.
Constitutions, decrees and ordinances of general chapters, correspondence and biographies of the foundress and of several superiors general, bulletins of the congregation containing accounts of the apostolate and short biographies of deceased sisters, and other records of the congregation, which was founded in 1807 in Cluny, France.

PROVIDENCE

15,373. Altieri, Alice LaFond
Papers. 1903-77. 925 items.
Open. Unpublished guide.
Providence College Archives.
Correspondence, a scrapbook, clippings, and memorabilia of [Mrs.] Altieri (1894-1976), one of the first women to serve in the Rhode Island General Assembly and a member of the state's division of social security. She also was active in statewide civic and charitable endeavors.

15,374. Budenz, Louis F.
Papers. 1914-72. 52 Paige boxes.
Open. Unpublished guide.
Providence College Archives.
Papers of Budenz (1891-1972), editor of the Communist party organ *The Daily Worker,* contain material he collected on communism and women for numerous articles he wrote. A prominent Communist during the 1930s and 1940s, Budenz became an ardent anticommunist in 1945.

15,375. Providence College Archives
Records. 1911- . 375 ft. and 225 tapes.
Access restricted. Unpublished guide.
Providence College Archives.
Minutes, correspondence, faculty records, school publications, photos, clippings, tapes, and memorabilia of the College, founded in 1917. Although the School did not become fully coeducational until 1971, women were involved as summer, evening, and graduate students at the College. In addition, the collection contains four boxes of records of the Veridames, a women's auxiliary of the school, which consisted of wives and friends of faculty members and students.

15,376. Urban League of Rhode Island
Records. 1940-1976. 65,000 items and 8 microfilm reels.
Open. Unpublished guide.
Providence College Archives.
Financial records, correspondence, memoranda, reports, and clippings of the League, founded in 1939, pertain to the League's work for racial equality in the US and, specifically, in Rhode Island. Collection includes information on the role of black women in society, Rhode Island and national organizations, Rhode Island state government, the National Urban League, and the Newport and Providence Urban Leagues.

15,377. Bacon, Nathaniel Terry
Papers. Ca. 1780-1950. 50 cu.ft.
Open. Register.
Rhode Island College Library.
Family papers of Bacon (1857-1926), an industrialist, include correspondence of his wife Helen (Hazard) Bacon; his son Leonard Bacon, who won the Pulitzer Prize for poetry in 1940; and Nathaniel Bacon's sister-in-law [Miss] Caroline Hazard (1856-1945), a poet, philanthropist, and president of Wellesley College for more than a decade. Caroline Hazard's papers consist of poems, essays, speeches, and a partial autobiography as well as correspondence with her nephew Leonard Bacon and a few items of correspondence with such persons as Pearl S. Buck, author and philanthropist; J. W. Holley, president of the Georgia Normal and Agricultural College; Isabel (Fiske) Conant, a poet; F. D. Patterson, president of Tuskegee Institute; and Patience Adams, a friend of Hazard's.

15,378. Bray, Gertrude C.
Papers. 1918-68. 1 ft.
Open. No guide.
Rhode Island Historical Society Library.
[Miss] Bray (1888-1975) was a canteen worker with the 167th regiment of the 42nd (Rainbow) Division during WWI. Includes correspondence and a diary, 1918-19, in which she gives detailed accounts of her activities, experiences, and emotions.

15,379. Clark, John Innes.
Papers. 1783-1865. 4 ft.
Open. No guide.
Rhode Island Historical Society Library.
Papers of Clark consist almost entirely of letters to his wife Lydia (Bowen) Clark (ca. 1752-?), a housewife, from their daughters Harriet (Clark) Hare and Anne (Clark) Kane. In their letters they describe boarding school and later, after their marriages, their physical health and the problems of raising children and household management. Other letters are from Lydia Clark's father, brothers and sisters, grandchildren, and grand-nieces.

15,380. Daughters of Hope
Records. 1899-1935. 6 vols.
Open. No guide.
Rhode Island Historical Society Library.
Minutes, financial records, and correspondence of the Daughters of Hope, which existed from 1899 to 1935. Primarily a social organization connected with Saint Martin's Episcopal Church in Providence, the group occasionally made charitable contributions.

15,381. Eldridge, Mary Moffitt
Papers. 1912- . 1 ft.
Open. No guide.
Rhode Island Historical Society Library.
Correspondence, a genealogy, scrapbooks, photos, and other papers of Eldridge (1875-), an active participant in women's organizations, including the Rhode Island LWV; the WCTU, for which she served as president; and the Rhode Island Council of Women. Eldridge was born in Rhode Island and moved to Connecticut in 1947.

15,382. Gilman, Charlotte Anna (Perkins)
Papers. 1881-90. 32 items.
Open. No guide.
Rhode Island Historical Society Library.
Personal letters that [Mrs. Charles Walter] Stetson [Mrs. George Houghton] Gilman (1860-1935), an author and lecturer, wrote from Rhode Island and California to her sister [Mrs.] Martha Lane.

15,383. Girls City Club
Records. 1920-70. 15 ft.
Open. No guide.
Rhode Island Historical Society Library.
Annual reports, council meeting minutes, advisory board minutes, correspondence, president's file, records related to business meetings, programs, and fund-raising material of the Club, which provided recreational and educational activities for unmarried "girls" over 17 from 1920 to 1970. Members, who were primarily young working-class women, also engaged in volunteer work.

15,384. Kent County Female Anti-Slavery Society
Records. 1835-38. 1 vol.
Open. No guide.
Rhode Island Historical Society Library.
Contains minutes of this rural antislavery society, which was founded in 1835, as well as the names of subscribers.

15,385. Le Bien Etre du Blesse
Records. 1916-19. 1 box.
Open. No guide.
Rhode Island Historical Society Library.
Reports, bills, correspondence, and clippings of the Providence committee of this Franco-American society established in 1916 to supply supplementary foods to French military hospitals. Madame Marquise d'Andigne, formerly Madeleine Goddard, a daughter of Colonel Robert H. I. Goddard of Providence, was president. The Providence chapter was headed by Margaret Hazard Goddard, who was married to Robert H. I. Goddard, Jr. Letters, chiefly written from the group's headquarters in France and the American headquarters in New York to Margaret Goddard, concern the activities of the group and the need to raise money.

15,386. Local Council of Women
Records. 1894-1931. 5 vols.
Open. No guide.
Rhode Island Historical Society Library.
Minutes and other records of the Council, which was established in 1889 to provide a place where representatives from a variety of groups could gather to exchange information and promote action

on issues of mutual interest. Also includes scattered diaries dating from 1894 to 1922 and a scrapbook. Anna (Garlin) Spencer served as president from 1896 to 1903. The Council claimed to be the oldest organization of its type in the country.

15,387. Madeira, Jean
Papers. 1936-72. 25 ft.
Open. Unpublished guide.
Rhode Island Historical Society Library.
Correspondence, financial papers, scrapbooks, clippings, magazines, publicity material, programs, degrees, and awards of Madeira (1918-72), an international opera singer. Papers relate to arranging concerts and tours and her tenure at the Metropolitan Opera in New York from 1948 to 1971. Best known for her role as Carmen in Bizet's opera, Madeira's repertoire included the major contralto roles of operas performed throughout the US and abroad. Includes extensive fan mail.

15,388. Providence Female Charitable Society
Records. 1798-1934. 3 ft.
Open. No guide.
Rhode Island Historical Society Library.
Minutes dating from 1800 to 1934, financial records, correspondence, and applicant lists of the Society, a charitable organization founded in 1798 by prominent women in Providence. Records provide a picture of the changing philosophy and activities of the organization.

15,389. Providence Physiological Society
Records. 1850-62. 1 folder and 3 vols.
Open. No guide.
Rhode Island Historical Society Library.
Includes annual reports, meeting minutes, a membership list, a plea for funds, and broadsides of the Society, which existed from 1850 to ca. 1862 to promote interest in anatomy and physiology. Originally the Ladies Physiological Society, the group grew out of a series of lectures on anatomy and physiology delivered by Paulina Wright Davis, who helped form the organization and became its corresponding secretary. Monthly lectures, many of which were given by Davis, were delivered on subjects such as disease, the skin, and the eyes. Minutes note the resistance of the local male medical community to women acquiring medical information.

15,390. Providence Plantations Club
Records. 1916-35. 1 ft.
Open. No guide.
Rhode Island Historical Society Library.
Minutes of this women's club, which existed from 1916 to 1962, contain information about programs, lectures, and fund-raising activities. Includes a debate over opening a clubhouse. Also includes records of the monthly meeting, board of directors' and committee reports, lists of officers and committee chairmen, and yearbooks containing membership lists for some years. Originally intended to be a business and professional women's group, the Club's membership broadened to include non-working women. By 1919 the organization built its own clubhouse.

15,391. Quakers, New England
Records. 1657-1976. 110 ft., 90 boxes, and 14 vols.
Open. Partial unpublished guide and card catalog.
Rhode Island Historical Society Library.
Includes minutes of the yearly meeting of the Friends, 1657-1976; minutes of the women's business meetings, 1700-1890; a membership chart; and names of the clerks of yearly meetings from 1683. Also includes financial records, correspondence, diaries, scrapbooks, photos, and maps. Quaker women are ministers, clerks, and teachers. They also wrote spiritual journals, served on committees with men, and until 1890 had their own business meetings. Also includes records related to the Women's Foreign Missionary Society, which existed from 1873 to 1956. Minutes are also available on microfilm.

15,392. Root, Mary Elizabeth (Stafford)
Papers. 1892-1953. 3 ft.
Open. No guide.
Rhode Island Historical Society Library.
Root (1868-1953) was a children's librarian, lecturer, and author. Includes an autobiography she wrote in 1953 as well as correspondence, lectures, and clippings, which relate to her work as a children's librarian in Providence Public Library from 1900 to 1922. An early organizer of children's libraries in the US, she lectured and wrote articles on the subject. Also includes family letters, primarily to her daughters, in which she comments on her experiences with children and their reading.

15,393. Weaver
Papers. 1897-1913. 2 ft.
Open. No guide.
Rhode Island Historical Society Library.
Correspondence of George Norman Weaver (1851-1907), an investor in stocks, bonds, utilities, banks, and transportation, and of his wife Martha Dorman (Hubbard) Weaver, the administrator of his estate, both of whom were residents of Newport, RI. Letters relate to George Weaver's interests as an investor and are chiefly from Charles E. Cowan, a stockbroker and family friend, to Martha Weaver as the administrator of the estate. Correspondence relates primarily to investments, but it also contains some comments on the Weaver family.

15,394. Woman's Baptist Foreign Missionary Society of Rhode Island
Records. 1884-1911. 1 vol.
Open. No guide.
Rhode Island Historical Society Library.
Minutes of the Society, which functioned from 1884 to ca. 1930 to promote interest in foreign missions and to raise funds for missions.

15,395. Woman's Christian Temperance Union of Rhode Island
Records. 1880-1960. 12 ft.
Open. Register.
Rhode Island Historical Society Library.
Minutes, financial reports, correspondence, membership records, scrapbooks, histories, and printed items of the Rhode Island WCTU, which was organized in 1875 to promote temperance. Includes records of city and town unions as well as related organizations such as the Young Women's Christian Temperance Union and the Young People's branch.

15,396. Women's Baptist Home Missionary Society, Rhode Island Branch
Records. 1877-1916. 9 vols.
Open. No guide.
Rhode Island Historical Society Library.
Minutes of the Society, which existed from 1877 to 1916 to support missionary schools and fund field missionaries. Providence members appear to have been largely from the upper middle class.

15,397. Women's City Missionary Society
Records. 1867-1942. 1 box.
Open. No guide.
Rhode Island Historical Society Library.
Minute books, 1867-71 and 1927-41, and special reports of the Society, a benevolent society that existed from 1868 to 1942. One of the largest benevolent organizations in Providence, the Society provided relief both through direct grants and work programs. The group was actively involved in local efforts to systematize charity work.

15,398. Rhode Island Equal Suffrage Association
Records. 1860-1920. Ca. 10 vols.
Open. No guide.
Rhode Island State Archives.
Minutes, financial records, correspondence, and diaries of the Association.

WESTERLY

15,399. Brown, Margaret Wise
Papers. 1930s-52. 2 drawers.
Open. Unpublished guide.
Westerly Public Library.
Manuscripts and correspondence with editors and publishers of Brown (1910-52), an author of books for children of nursery school age.

SOUTH CAROLINA

BETHUNE

15,400. Bethune Chapter, South Carolina Division, United Daughters of the Confederacy
Records. 1928-41. Ca. 40 items.
Access restricted. No guide.
Lynches River Historical Society.
Minutes and a scrapbook of the local UDC chapter, which was founded in 1928 and disbanded in 1941. The chapter, which was composed of female descendants of Confederate veterans, sponsored civic functions, Confederate monuments, and other activities to perpetuate the memory of the Confederate States of America. The scrapbook contains first-hand accounts written by women who lived through the War Between the States as well as items documenting the chapter's civic activities.

15,401. Yarbrough, Tabitha A. E.
Papers. 1867-77. 9 items.
Access restricted. No guide.
Lynches River Historical Society.
Correspondence principally between Yarbrough (1848-1965), who managed a plantation near Lynchwood (now Bethune), SC, and her sister Martha Jane Yarbrough, who lived in Tennessee. The letters reflect conditions in the South during Reconstruction and describe the hardships the sisters faced. Tabitha, who married Captain Dave Seegars of the Confederate Army, tells her sister of agricultural and economic conditions. Her husband was disabled, and she continued to manage the plantation while operating a home school for her children and those of relatives and friends. She also worked to rid her community of carpetbagger rule. She sheltered in her home persons who launched ambushes against militiamen who patroled the area.

CHARLESTON

15,402. Alms House, Charleston
Records. 1801-1916. 37 vols.
Open. Card catalog and index.
Charleston City Archives.
Records of this social welfare institution of the city of Charleston include minutes, 1872-1911; financial records; hospital and death registers; letter and admission books; records of out-of-door pensioners; an index volume; and a volume about the transient sick and the city poor.

15,403. City Board of School Commissioners
Records. 1812-1913. 7 vols.
Open. Card catalog.
Charleston City Archives.
Records of this Charleston governmental agency include minute books of its predecessor, the Commission on Free Schools of the Parish of St. Philip's and St. Michael's. Over time increasing numbers of women were involved in the Board's management.

15,404. City Departments
Records. 1801-1938. 11 ft.
Access restricted. Card catalog.
Charleston City Archives.
Records of Charities Department units, including the Alms House, the William Enston Home for the Aged, and the Charleston Orphan House as well as of the City Board of School Commissioners.

15,405. Historical Commission
Records. Nd. No size given.
Open. Unpublished guide.
Charleston City Archives.
Items gathered by the Commission include records of the Ladies Memorial Association, 1935-39; the Rebecca Motte Chapter of the DAR, 1935-45; the Ladies' Hermitage Association, 1948 and 1956; and a tax book from the treasurer's office, 1864, pertaining to "free persons of color." Also includes correspondence of Anne K. Gregorie, 1935-43; Henrietta Johnston and Elizabeth Thurton, 1947-56; and Mary A. Sparkman, 1938-53.

15,406. Allen, M. M. S.
Papers. 1835-37. 700 pp.
Open. No guide.
Charleston Library Society.
Diary of Allen's tour of Europe and the Near East.

15,407. Burckmyer
Papers. 1863-65. 600 pp.
Open. No guide.
Charleston Library Society.
Correspondence between a husband and wife, Cornelius L. and C. R. Burckmyer, provides a picture of life in Charleston and in the Confederate colony in Europe. The letters were published as *The Burckmyer Letters, March, 1863-June, 1865* (Columbia, SC: The State Company, 1926).

15,408. Century Club
Records. 1937-70. 13 items.
Open. No guide.
Charleston Library Society.
Papers presented before this ongoing women's club include reports concerning the history of South Carolina, Charleston, religion, horse racing, and agriculture. The Club was formed in 1895.

15,409. Crigler, S. G.: "Education for Girls and Women in Upper South Carolina Prior to 1890"
Papers. 1956. 191 pp.
Open. No guide.
Charleston Library Society.
A thesis concerning the education of girls and women and related topics.

15,410. Crottet
Papers. Ca. 1578-1787. 3 vols.
Open. Card catalog.
Charleston Library Society.
Correspondence, church records, and ephemera of French Huguenots, many of whom settled in Charleston following the Edict of Nantes. Includes a manuscript concerning the Huguenots, with parish registers, correspondence, proceedings of consistories, and accounts of personal visits to Huguenot prisoners in the galleys.

15,411. Elliott Family
Papers. 1779-1869. 7 items.
Open. Card catalog.
Charleston Library Society.
Correspondence of a South Carolina planter family includes a letter dated 1829 that William Middleton wrote to Juliet Georgiana (Gibbes) Elliott in Charleston about his wish to marry her daughter. Apparently Elliott, speaking with "candor," had refused Middleton's request. Elliott was the widow of Barnard Elliott (?-1806). A letter dated 1869 by Frances (de Saussure) [Mrs. William Stuart] Gibbes concerns finances, family matters, and the hardship of the post-Civil War years.

15,412. Elliott, Juliet Georgiana
Papers. 1844-74. 1 vol.
Open. Card catalog.
Charleston Library Society.
Daily account book of Elliott, a member of an upper-class South Carolina family, includes expenses for wedding gifts, charitable contributions, and household and personal purchases. Examples of items listed include worked muslin, satin, corsets, lace, sewing implements, harp strings, gloves, and window screens. Elliott noted that she gave $8 to the Wilton Library for a two-year contribution, $5 to the Ashepoo Mission, $1.25 to St. Peter's School, and $5 to the missionary box. Her expenses totaled about $318 for 1844.

15,413. Gibbes, Mary Lee (Evans)
Papers. 1839-57. 12 items.
Open. Card catalog.
Charleston Library Society.
Correspondence of Gibbes (?-1888) and other members of a wealthy and politically powerful South Carolina family includes a letter of condolence and a document dated 1839, which indicates that Sarah and Mary Evans were to be the administrators of the estate of Mary Evans's father George Evans, a physician. After her father's death, Mary was considered "wholly an orphan"; by 1854, she was the wife of James Gibbes. Her letters deal with religious, social, and family matters.

15,414. Grimball Family
Papers. 1832-84. 3 vols.
Open. No guide.
Charleston Library Society.
Diary and journal of the family of John Berkeley Grimball (1800-93), a planter, and his wife Margaret Ann "Meta" (Morris) Grimball (1810-81) contain information about family and social life in South Carolina, plantation expenses, slavery, and the Civil War. Grimball's middle name was spelled Berkeley or Berkley.

15,415. Poetry Society of South Carolina, Group A
Records. 1922-24. 69 pp.
Open. No guide.
Charleston Library Society.
Minutes of the Society, which was formed in 1921 to promote southern poets and to help develop an appreciative audience for them.

15,416. Porcher, Ellen Barker
Papers. 1860-61. 5 items.
Open. No guide.
Charleston Library Society.
Correspondence provides a picture of plantation life.

15,417. Ross
Papers. 1793-1922. 146 items.
Open. Unpublished guide.
Charleston Library Society.
Correspondence, journals, and deeds of this family of merchants. Includes papers of [Miss] Mary Jane Ross (1835-1922), among them correspondence; journals of her travels from 1892 to 1901 to Europe, Africa, and the Near East; and deeds for property in Charleston and Philadelphia.

15,418. Smythe Family
Papers. Ca. 1808-1915. 111 items.
Open. Card catalog.
Charleston Library Society.
Correspondence of female members of this prominent South Carolina planter and commercial family includes letters of Margaret Hall Moffett Adger Smythe (1820-1915), Sarah Annie Smythe, Susan Dunlap Adger Symthe (1808-84), Jane Adger Smythe (1822-99), and Jane Ann Adger. Includes letters Sarah Annie Smythe wrote from Paris, Berlin, Amsterdam, and other points to her 20-year-old son in 1867 and 1868 with observations about life in Paris, visits to the Louvre, and family matters. Letters to a second son concern South Carolina business matters. Susan Smythe's letters were written from Rome, Venice, Lucerne, Frankfurt (Germany), Charleston, and other locations and concern events she observed and family matters.

15,419. South Carolina Newspapers
Collection. 1732-ca. 1873. No size given.
Open. No guide.
Charleston Library Society.
Originals and microfilm copies of such South Carolina newspapers as the *South-Carolina Gazette,* 1732-75; the *Gazette of the State of South Carolina,* 1777-80; the *South-Carolina Gazette and Country Journal,* 1765-75; the *Charlestown Gazette,* 1778-80; the *South-Carolina Weekly Gazette,* 1758-64; the *South-Carolina and American General Gazette,* 1764-81; the *Royal South-Carolina Gazette,* 1780-82; the *Royal Gazette,* 1781-82; *The Charleston Courier; The Charleston Daily Courier; The Charleston Mercury;* and *The Times* of Charleston.

15,420. Strobel Family
Papers. 1862-65. 10 items.
Open. No guide.
Charleston Library Society.
Correspondence of female family members concerns family life, Charleston, and the Civil War.

15,421. Study Club
Records. 1964. 1 item.
Open. No guide.
Charleston Library Society.
This women's group was interested in history. A paper on St. James and the scallop shell, which was read before the Club.

15,422. Thursday Club
Records. 1922. 3 items.
Open. No guide.
Charleston Library Society.
This women's club was organized before 1911 to promote the study of world and local history, culture, and other topics. Papers read before the group concern development of the interior of South Carolina, distinguished visitors in Charleston, and education in South Carolina. The Club is still in existence.

15,423. Windsor and Kensington Plantations
Records. 1840-88. 1 vol.
Open. Card catalog.
Charleston Library Society.
John Beaufain Irving, a physician, kept detailed notes about the slaves, planting, and crops on his rice plantations on the Cooper River in South Carolina; his notes contain information about the work of his wife, female slaves, and the high mortality rate of slave children. Irving took possession of Windsor in 1840 for $2000. He noted that he found the plantation in disarray. He said he was "aided by the characteristic energy of my wife, and her peculiar aptitude for management, which soon changed the aspect of the whole place. . ."

15,424. Smith, Alice Ravenel Huger
Papers. 1910-58. 3 boxes, 0.5 drawer, and 5 vols.
Open. No guide.
Gibbes Art Gallery.
Smith (1876-1956) was a Charleston artist who worked primarily in watercolors. Correspondence related to Gibbes Art Gallery, account book listing sale of her paintings, exhibition files, sketchbooks, scrapbooks containing photos of her works, clippings, and watercolors. Smith also wrote books about Charleston subjects.

15,425. Brown, Hannah Helen (Mendelsohn)
Papers. 1921. 1 vol.
Open. Card catalog.
Medical University of South Carolina.
[Mrs. Samuel] Brown (ca. 1901-), a student nurse who graduated in 1921, was president of the student body. A diary-yearbook volume in which she wrote about her struggles with her parents who had wanted her to be a musician. She wrote that she had been "afraid to assert myself, but God gave me courage. . . . I knew I had a calling . . . to serve humanity." Includes lists of teachers, courses, and pictures of buildings and students at Medical College of South Carolina and at Roper Hospital in Charleston.

15,426. College of Nursing
Records. 1883-1970. 9 drawers and 2 vols.
Open. No guide.
Medical University of South Carolina.
Manuscripts, documents, scrapbooks, and ephemera of the College, which was founded in 1883. Includes correspondence regarding the academic program, professional affiliations, and student applications; diaries of two students, dated 1906; correspondence, curriculum data, and clippings related to the Cadet Corps during WWII; records concerning accreditation; a booklet of rules adopted by the training committee in 1913; and material concerning students' backgrounds and credentials. The Medical University of South Carolina, of which the College is a part, was founded in 1824 as the Medical College of South Carolina. The school became the Medical College of the State of South Carolina in 1832 and retained that title until 1952 when the original name was reinstated. The present title was adopted in 1969.

15,427. Michel, Middleton
Papers. Ca. 1846-90. 1 Hollinger box.
Open. Card catalog.
Medical University of South Carolina.
Correspondence, business records, and coroner's reports of Michel (1822-94), a physician and coroner in Charleston. Includes coroner's reports listing the name, race, approximate age, apparent financial status, and cause of death of the individual. One of the reports describes Flora Campbell as "a colored person" of about 68 years, who died of "hypertrophy of the heart" after she was surprised by robbers. Another report stated that Margaret A. McLean died of "exhaustion and gastric hemorrhage," but there was "no derangement of uterus." Also contains essays about epidemic diseases in Charleston during the 1850s and 1870s; Negroid characteristics; children who were born with deformities, partially because of poor prenatal care; childbirth; and twins.

15,428. Plantation Prescription Book
Records. Ca. 1834. 1 vol.
Open. Index card.
Medical University of South Carolina.
Receipt book kept by Isabella (Peyre) Porcher (1803-90), who took charge of Sarrazin Plantation in Berkeley County, SC, after the death of her husband William Porcher (1800-33). Includes remedies Porcher used to treat slaves for such ailments as bowel complaints, rheumatism, "spasm in the stomach," dropsy, pleurisy, piles, and sores. Isabella Peyre, the granddaughter of botanist Thomas Walter, married William Porcher, a physician, in 1823. William and Isabella Porcher were the parents of Francis Peyre Porcher, a physician, medical school professor, and author.

15,429. South Carolina Women Doctors
Collection. 1890s-early 1940s. 5 folders.
Open. No guide.
Medical University of South Carolina.
Biographical material, photos, clippings, and ephemera about the state's women doctors, including Sarah C. Allen, a pioneer in psychiatry who graduated from the Women's Medical College of New York Infirmary in 1894; Hilla Sheriff, a specialist in pediatrics who was the first woman health officer in South Carolina; Jane Bruce Guignard; and Patricia A. Carter. An announcement was included in the 1894-95 catalog of the Medical College of the State of South Carolina that women would be admitted to the school. Correspondence indicates that the first women graduated from the College in 1901, but that the admission of women was not considered generally acceptable until 1921.

15,430. Wilson, Sophire W.
Papers. Nd. 37 items.
Open. Card catalog.
Medical University of South Carolina.
[Mrs.] Wilson, a former catalog librarian at the University, is a public school librarian in Charleston. Her 19-page paper concerning women in the medical profession in South Carolina includes biographical information on Sarah Campbell Allen, the state's first woman physician; Lucy Hughes Brown, the state's first black woman physician and, in 1896, the first woman physician in Charleston; Matilda A. Evans, a black physician in Columbia, SC, in 1898; Anna DeCosta Banks, a registered nurse who in 1898 became head nurse at the Hospital and Training School for Nurses in Charleston. Lucy Hughes Brown was instrumental in the establishment of the Hospital and Training School, one of the first US schools for the training of black nurses, and was associated with it until her death in 1911. Wilson presented the paper at South Carolina's First International Women's Year Conference in 1977. Also includes 36 slides she used to illustrate her presentation.

15,431. Women's Auxiliary to the South Carolina Medical Association
Records. 1923- . 12 folders and 40 vols.
Open. No guide.
Medical University of South Carolina.
Formed in 1923, the Auxiliary was composed of doctors' wives who wanted to promote public health, to recruit nurses, "to work diligently to maintain democratic ideals," and to "foster harmony" in the medical field. Constitution, bylaws, minutes, financial reports and investment records, correspondence, a history of the Auxiliary, photos of presidents, newsletters containing convention notes, bulletins, and ephemera. The history includes names of early officers. Contains correspondence with legislators concerning public health measures and public works.

15,432. Archives
Records. 1700-1950. 1 cabinet.
Open. No guide.
Protestant Episcopal Diocese of South Carolina Archives.
Vestry minutes and birth, death, and marriage registers of the diocese of South Carolina. Also contains minutes of subordinate bodies, including women's auxiliaries in local parishes, and accounts of annual meetings of churchwomen.

15,433. Archives
Records. 1829- . 10 drawers, 45 boxes, 3 vols., and ca. 48 tapes.
Access restricted. Unpublished guide.
Sisters of Charity of Our Lady of Mercy, Motherhouse.
Constitutions, minutes, financial records, property deeds, correspondence, diaries, annals, histories of the congregation, tapes of retreats, community register, blueprints of buildings owned by the congregation, photos, slides, scrapbooks, material pertaining to conferences and workshops, pamphlets, and other records of the congregation, which was founded in 1829 in Charleston. Includes correspondence and other papers of mothers superior and correspondence and other material relating to hospitals, an orphanage, and schools operated by the order. The Sisters are involved in education, health care, and social work.

15,434. Adger and Smyth
Papers. 1825-99. 14 vols. and 14 items.
Open. Card catalog.
South Carolina Historical Society.
Papers of James Adger (1777-?), an Ulster-born Charleston merchant; Sarah Elizabeth Ellison Adger, whom he married in 1806; his daughter Jane Ann Adger; and the family of Margaret Milligan (Adger) Smyth (1807-84) and her husband Thomas Smyth (1808-84), a local Presbyterian minister. Letters from James Adger to his wife and daughter; household and personal account books of Margaret Smyth, her daughter Sarah Ann Smyth (1846-1928), and Jane Ann Adger; and accounts of Margaret and Sarah Smyth and of Jane Ann Adger and Susan D. Adger with James Adger & Co. Some members of the Smyth family spelled the surname Smythe. Additional papers of the Smyth women can be found in the Historical Society's Smyth collection.

15,435. Adger, John B.
Papers. 1832-45. 17 items.
Open. Card catalog.
South Carolina Historical Society.
Correspondence of Adger, a minister, includes letters to Elizabeth K. Shewsbury, who became his wife.

15,436. Aldret, Mary
Papers. 1829-76. 1 vol.
Open. Card catalog.
South Carolina Historical Society.
Receipt book of [Mrs.] Aldret, a member of a planter family, includes receipts for rent, wages, doctors, and schooling. Two school mistresses are mentioned, E. Halliday in 1834 and Julia Norman in 1837. After 1868 the receipts are made out to [Miss] Anne S. Aldret.

15,437. All Saints Sunday School Society
Records. 1832-59. 1 vol.
Open. Card catalog.
South Carolina Historical Society.
Record book contains the constitution and journal, with entries dating from 1832 to 1838, of the Society. The record was written by Alexander Glennie, the Society's secretary and treasurer. The balance of the volume is the journal of Glennie, rector of All Saints Church from 1832 to 1866, listing the plantations he visited in the Waccamaw region of South Carolina and services he performed between 1852 and 1859.

15,438. Allder, Conrad
Papers. 1750. 2 pp.
Open. Card catalog.
South Carolina Historical Society.
Answer filed by Allder with the Court of Chancery to a petition by his wife Ann.

15,439. Allston, Pringle, and Hill
Papers. 1812-1929. 4393 items.
Access restricted. Card catalog and index.
South Carolina Historical Society.
Correspondence, diaries and financial records of Elizabeth Waties (Allston) Pringle (1845-1921), a rice planter, author, and wife of John Julius Pringle;

her sister Jane Louise (Allston) Hill (1850-1937), the wife of Charles A. Hill; and other members of these South Carolina planter families. Elizabeth Pringle's papers include diaries, time books, manuscripts of her books *A Woman Rice Planter* and *Chronicles of Chicora Wood,* and items related to the books' publication. These papers provide information about daily plantation life; the low-country Negro; and about the work of the National Society of Colonial Dames of America, the Huguenot Society of South Carolina, and the Mount Vernon Ladies Association.
Correspondence of Jane Hill describes social life in South Carolina, other parts of America, and England.

15,440. Allston, Robert Francis Withers
Papers. 1757-1929. 14 ft.
Open. Card catalog.
South Carolina Historical Society.
Allston (1801-64), a planter, civil engineer, legislator, and governor of South Carolina, was the father of Adele (Allston) [Mrs. Arnoldus] Vanderhorst (1842-1915), Elizabeth Waties (Allston) [Mrs. John Julius] Pringle (1845-1921), Jane Louise (Allston) [Mrs. Charles A.] Hill (1850-1937), and Benjamin and Charles Allston. Correspondence, diaries, plantation account books, estate records, muniments, and overseers' and factors' reports pertain largely to management of the Allston rice plantations and to inter-family relations, especially with the Petigru family. Included are papers of the five Allston children and records of the Chicora Wood, Nightengale Hall, Waterford, Exchange, Rose Bank, and Breakwater plantations. Many of the papers were published in J. H. Easterby, *The South Carolina Rice Plantation As Revealed in the Papers of R. F. W. Allston* (Chicago, 1945).

15,441. Bacot and Huger
Papers. 1754-1927. 14 Hollinger boxes and 2 vols.
Open. Card catalog and index.
South Carolina Historical Society.
Correspondence, financial papers, tax receipts, and plantation records of the families of Daniel Huger (1779-1858), a lawyer and South Carolina secretary of state in ca. 1814, and Thomas W. Bacot I (1765-1834), whose family was involved in the Bank of South Carolina, civic and Episcopal Church affairs, law firms, commission merchant trade, deep-sea fishing, and wholesale grocery. Includes a poetry album of Julia Huger; papers of Sarah H. Gibson; and material of Rebecca Motte (?-1825), a planter's widow, including an inventory of her estate. Also contains papers from the allied Cochran, DeSaussure, Lance, McCrady, and Wainwright families.

15,442. Ball, John: Clothing and Blanket Book
Papers. 1831-41. 1 vol.
Open. Card catalog and index.
South Carolina Historical Society.
Record book and accounts of the more than 600 slaves of John Ball, a South Carolina rice planter, including records from his Comingtee, Stoke, Kensington, and Midway plantations on the Cooper River. The records show that woolen material, greatcoats, caps, and blankets were distributed to the slaves in December and summer clothing in May. Accounts for 1840 list the Negroes by occupations, such as foreman, boatman, gardener, and hostler for men and cook, dairymaid, house servant, midwife, nurse, seamstress, and washers for women. Certain Negroes without designated duties are listed as "old."

15,443. Ball, Olivia Carolina
Papers. 1813. 8 vols.
Open. Card catalog.
South Carolina Historical Society.
Account books of Ball, a member of a planter's family.

15,444. Barbot, Blanche Hermine
Papers. 1875-1904. 1 vol.
Open. Card catalog.
South Carolina Historical Society.
[Madame] Barbot was involved in the Charleston Musical Association. Scrapbook containing material related to the Association dating from a concert at Hibernian Hall in 1875 to a sacred cantata at Pro-Cathedral in 1904. Material includes clippings, notes, and programs of operas, concerts, and other performances.

15,445. Bennett, John
Papers. 1900-57. 36 boxes and 6 vols.
Open. Card catalog.
South Carolina Historical Society.
Papers of Bennett (1865-1956), a Charleston author, illustrator, and lecturer, consist of correspondence; notes on local folklore, Negro music and dialects, and folksongs; and manuscripts. The papers contain many references to women. Notes on the origins of the South Carolina black "Gullah" dialect include copies of 18th-century shipping lists of slaves that reveal the slaves' origin. Also includes copies of lists of runaway slaves, many of them women, and notes on slave trade and superstitions of the blacks. Many of the special expressions of the Gullah dialect refer to women, family life, and children.

15,446. Bennett, Mrs. John
Papers. 1940-42. 1 folio.
Open. Card catalog.
South Carolina Historical Society.
Correspondence, bills, receipts, and instruction lists of Bennett relate to her work with the British War Relief Society, Inc., and to items made by the group.

15,447. Bowen and Cooke
Papers. 1772-1857. 421 items.
Open. Card catalog.
South Carolina Historical Society.
Correspondence and letter books of Penuel Bowen (?-1788), who worked as a Protestant Episcopal clergyman, include letters he wrote to his wife while he was in Charleston. After Bowen's death his widow's letters chiefly concern aid of the Society for the Relief of Widows and Orphans of the Protestant Episcopal Church. Also includes correspondence between Mrs. Bowen and her son Nathaniel Bowen (?-1838) and between Nathaniel Bowen and his sister Susan and correspondence of Nathaniel Bowen's wife Amanda Blake Bowen. Penuel Bowen was not an ordained minister.

15,448. Broughton
Papers. 1774-ca. 1825. 5 items.
Open. Card catalog.
South Carolina Historical Society.
Correspondence and wills of a family of Mulberry, SC, planters contain the wills of Daniel Ravenel, 1774; Thomas Broughton, 1808; Elizabeth Jane Ravenel, 1802; Philip Porcher Broughton, 1822; and Elizabeth Damaris Broughton, 1825.

15,449. Campbell: Bennett
Papers. 1824-1909. Ca. 60 items.
Open. Index.
South Carolina Historical Society.
Contained within the South Carolina Historical Society's Campbell collection are correspondence and legal documents of Mary Campbell, the sister of James Campbell; of Margaret Bennett Campbell, the wife of James Campbell; and of other members of this well-to-do Charleston family. Most of the early letters were from James Campbell to Mary and concern family matters, especially his apparently stormy courtship with Margaret Bennett in which he enlisted the aid of Daniel Webster. Also includes an 1862 letter from Mary Campbell to a niece in the North in which she speaks of the sorrows of separation caused by the war, but writes primarily of family and local news. Also includes copies of the wills of Mary Campbell and Helen L. Campbell.

15,450. Campbell, Mary Bennett
Papers. 1847. 138 pp.
Open. Card catalog.
South Carolina Historical Society.
[Miss] Campbell was a member of a plantation family. Receipt book includes receipts for bread, pudding, cordials, meats, oysters, vegetable dishes, preserves, brandied peaches, and cakes; also included is information on how to cure beef and tongue and how to wash blankets, gentlemen's clothes, and thread lace.

15,451. Charleston Civic Union
Records. 1941-43. 1 Hollinger box.
Open. Index.
South Carolina Historical Society.
Established in 1941, this local association sought to help legal authorities "establish and maintain an acceptable pattern of conduct in the community" during WWII. Clippings make up the bulk of the collection and provide information about the Union's activities and interests, which included local politics, vice, and corruption. Contains articles on the black community, the American National Red Cross, civil defense activities, and architecture and preservation in Charleston. Also includes the Union's constitution; reports on prostitution, gambling, and other illegal activities in Charleston; and a membership list. The Union, the membership of which was open to any adult white citizen, continued through 1943. Many of its members were women.

15,452. Charleston Female Seminary
Records. 1889-97. No size given.
Open. Calendar.
South Carolina Historical Society.
Operated by [Miss] Henrietta Aiken Kelley and commonly known as Miss Kelley's School, the Seminary was a local boarding and day school for girls. Annual reports of the alumnae association, printed courses of study for three of the Seminary's departments, invitations to literary evenings, and other material.

15,453. Charleston Independent or Congregational Church
Records. 1732-1912. 37 vols.
Open. Card catalog.
South Carolina Historical Society.
Minutes of the Clergy Society, the Charleston Benevolent Society, and other units of the Church; treasurers' accounts; registers; lists of interments, admissions, and marriages; rent lists of pews; legal conveyance of a lot to the Society for the Relief of Elderly and Disabled Ministers and of the Widows and Orphans of the Clergy of the Church; Sunday school records; and catalogs of the Bible school library. The Church's records are on deposit at the South Carolina Historical Society.

15,454. Charleston Protestant Episcopal Female Domestic Missionary Society
Records. 1857-63. 1 vol.
Open. Card catalog and index.
South Carolina Historical Society.
Account book and financial records include receipts for donations, subscribers, and bonds; notes of expenditures, chiefly for salaries of four clergymen and the sexton of St. John's Chapel in Charleston; and a checkbook.

15,455. Chesnut Family
Papers. 1790-1813. 10 items.
Open. Card catalog.
South Carolina Historical Society.
Correspondence and other family papers of Harriett Chesnut and other members of this South Carolina family.

15,456. Cheves Family
Papers. 1777-1938. 44 ft.
Open. Card catalog and calendar.
South Carolina Historical Society.
Papers of the Cheves and Middleton families, wealthy and politically active South Carolina planter families, include material of Eweretta Middleton (1840-99), Ann Middleton Izard, Sophia Lovell (Haskell) Cheves (1846-1922), and other women. Included is the 1799 diary of Anne Isabella (Cleland) Kinloch; letters from Ralph Izard to his mother [Mrs.] Alice De Lancey Izard of Charleston; letters of Elizabeth (Middleton) Izard (1787-1822), wife of Ralph Izard, to her mother-in-law; letters from Ann Middleton Izard, Ralph Izard's daughter, to her grandmother; and correspondence of Harriott and Susan Matilda Middleton, written in Charleston and in Flat Rock, NC, during the Civil War. The letters mention the death of Ralph Izard's first wife in 1822 and his remarriage in 1824 to Eliza Lucas Pinckney, daughter of General C. C. Pinckney.

15,457. Cheves-McCord-Miles
Papers. 1825-71. 69 items.
Open. Index.
South Carolina Historical Society.
Consists of affectionate letters of members of two generations of a South Carolina political family, including Mary Elizabeth Cheves, wife of Langdon Cheves; Mary Elizabeth McCord; William Porcher Miles; Anna E. Miles; Mary McCord; Mary Elizabeth Hampton, wife of Christopher Hampton; James Warley Miles; Louisa Susannah (Cheves) McCord (1810-79), wife of David James McCord; Langdon Cheves McCord; Louisa R. McCord; and Julia McCord.

15,458. Chicken, George
Papers. 1711-43. 13 items.
Open. Card catalog.
South Carolina Historical Society.
Manuscripts and legal documents of Chicken include a deed of settlement involving 300 acres of land, 18 Negroes, and 500 pounds in "money of the province," dating from his marriage to Lydia Child, the daughter of Isaac Child.

15,459. Childsbury, Chicken, and Childs
Papers. 1704-1800. 18 items.
Open. Card catalog.
South Carolina Historical Society.
Correspondence and legal documents of these planter families include an indenture, dated 1713, among James Childs, William Waites, and John Lawes, regarding Hester Hubbard, the widow of Thomas Hubbard; items containing discussion of a marriage arranged between James Childs and Hester Hubbard; will, dated 1738, of William Childs in which he leaves bequests to his mother, sisters, and niece; a memorial concerning several tracts belonging to Elias Ball and his wife Lydia of St. John's Parish; a petition for authority over the ferry on land belonging to Lydia Ball; Lydia Ball's will, dated 1765; and notes on the marriage of Isaac Childs and Margaret Tunsteed in 1763.

15,460. Coffin's Point
Records. 1800-21. 3 vols. and 2 items.
Open. Card catalog.
South Carolina Historical Society.
Notebooks contain information about the cotton plantation of Ebenezer Coffin (?-1816), including information about building a cotton house and a Negro house, supplies, medicine, clothing, blankets, tools, lists of workers and fields planted, and navigation directions. Also includes a daybook and notes on weekday talks, Sunday allowances, and the weather.

15,461. Community Club of Enlisted Men
Records. 1917-19. 186 items.
Open. Card catalog.
South Carolina Historical Society.
The Club was founded in 1917 in Charleston to operate the Enlisted Men's Club for WWI soldiers. Constitution, minutes, president's and treasurer's reports, correspondence, list of subscribers, and material about dissolution of the organization in 1919.

15,462. Confederate Home and College
Records. 1867-1904. 9 vols.
Open. Calendar.
South Carolina Historical Society.
The institution was established in 1867 in Charleston for mothers, widows, and daughters of Confederate soldiers. Minute and letter books, regulations, roll book, and pupil lists. Includes a constitution and rules for the cook, washerwomen, and others.

15,463. Conner, Julia Ann M.
Papers. 1827. 1 vol.
Open. Card catalog.
South Carolina Historical Society.
Conner, a young bride from Charleston, visited the Hermitage during a trip to Tennessee with her husband. Her journal includes her account of meetings with General and Mrs. Andrew Jackson and Sam Houston as well as her observations about towns visited along the way, food and accommodations, a visit to a Moravian school, a camp meeting, an elopement, and a wedding. On their way home, the Conners traveled through the Cherokee nation, staying with Indian families and visiting the Brainard Mission settlement and school for Indians.

15,464. Deas, Anne
Papers. Ca. 1900. 1 box.
Open. Card catalog.
South Carolina Historical Society.
[Miss] Deas, a relative of Colonel Alston Deas, was a member of a planter family. Her reminiscences about plantation life include discussions of planting and harvesting, winter clothes, the barnyard and threshing mill, weddings, medical receipts, and notes on superstitions.

15,465. Dehon Family
Papers. 1840-76. 23 items.
Open. Card catalog.
South Carolina Historical Society.
Correspondence, estate papers, and property records of William Dehon, an Episcopalian minister, and his wife Anne Middleton Dehon. Includes letters exchanged by the Dehons, William Dehon's estate papers dating from 1860 to 1864, letters to Anne Dehon from her son after her husband's death, and letters from William Dehon's mother. William Dehon, minister of the Parish of St. Stephens in Pineville, SC, was the son of Theodore Dehon who was bishop of the Episcopal Church in South Carolina from 1812 to 1817.

15,466. DeSaussure Family
Papers. 1519-1938. 3 ft.
Open. Card catalog.
South Carolina Historical Society.
Correspondence, memoirs, legal papers, and some literary items of this planter family, including literary works by a woman identified only as Belle. An aspiring essayist and poet, Belle wrote about such subjects as kindnesses to children. The bulk of the collection dates from the 17th through the 19th centuries and deals primarily with military experiences.

15,467. Dirlston Plantation
Records. 1859-66. 1 vol.
Open. Calendar.
South Carolina Historical Society.
Dirlston, originally a Heriot tract, became the property of James R. Sparkman (1815-97), a physician who married Mary Elizabeth Heriot. Memorandum book contains lists of Negroes and records of births and deaths, clothing received, receipts and expenditures, tax paid, and cattle taken by the military.

15,468. Edwards, Rebecca, and Edwards, Catherine
Papers. 1842. 4 pp.
Open. Card catalog.
South Carolina Historical Society.
Course of study and testimonial from S. Gilman for the Edwards sisters.

15,469. Elliott, Elizabeth B.
Papers. 1745. 1 item.
Open. Card catalog.
South Carolina Historical Society.
Deed of a gift of land for use by the church in Prince William Parish.

15,470. Emigrants for Liberia
Records. 1867. 1 box.
Open. Calendar.
South Carolina Historical Society.
Lists of some 235 persons who embarked on the *Golconda* at Charleston for passage to Bixley and Grand Cape Mount, Liberia. The lists, signed by William Coppinger of the American Colonization Society, contain names from Columbus and Macon, GA; Mars Bluff, SC; Philadelphia; and Dover Court House, TN.

15,471. Executive Relief Committee
Records. 1886-87. 300-page vol.
Open. Calendar.
South Carolina Historical Society.
Minutes and other records of the Committee, which was created to administer funds donated for victims of the Charleston earthquake of 1886. Includes reports of the four standing committees that focused on immediate relief, subsistence and shelter, building and repair, and finance and accounts; correspondence; lists of persons applying for aid and the amount granted to each; lists of donors; statements of receipts and expenditures; and clippings concerning the Committee's work.

15,472. Fielden and Smythe
Papers. 1851-1921. 3 vols. and 193 items.
Open. Card catalog and index.
South Carolina Historical Society.
Personal and family correspondence, scrapbook, and general orders of Julia (McCord) Fielden and her husband Henry Wemyss Fielden (?-1921), an officer in the British and American armies, Arctic explorer, and paymaster in the Boer War. Includes Julia Fielden's letters to friends and family and Civil War letters, many of them written by women. The largest single group of correspondence consists of Henry Fielden's letters to his wife's half-sister Mrs. Augustine T. Smythe, her daughter Mrs. Anton P. Wright, and her grandson David McCord Wright.

15,473. Gadsden, Jeanne
Papers. 1703-1950. 2 boxes and 1 vol.
Open. Card catalog.
South Carolina Historical Society.
Correspondence, receipts, and legal papers of [Miss] Gadsden, her family, and the related Boyle and Farr families. Includes letters of Gadsden, John Gadsden (1853-1902), and John B. Gadsden (1877-1924) as well as estate papers of Philip Gadsden (1864-95). The three families were plantation owners.

15,474. Gibbes and Gilchrist
Papers. 1769-1945. 3 Hollinger boxes and 1 vol.
Open. Index.
South Carolina Historical Society.
Family papers include letters from Ann Gibbes, wife of South Carolina planter Robert Gibbes (1732-94), to her son John at Princeton in 1783 and 1784. Her letters and others in the collection include descriptions of plantation life, low-country

sicknesses in Charleston and comments on plantations, problems with an Irish tutor, and Alexander Garden's courtship of Mary Ann Gibbes. Also includes a commonplace book of Maria H. Drayton Gibbes (1784-1826), a cookbook and household receipts, and clippings concerning the artistic career of Emma S. Gilchrist.

15,475. Gilman, Caroline (Howard)
Papers. 1810-80. 109 items.
Open. Card catalog.
South Carolina Historical Society.
Gilman (1794-1888), an author and editor, was the wife of Samuel Gilman, minister of Charleston's Unitarian Church from 1819 to 1858. Letters, the earliest of which Caroline Gilman wrote from Savannah, GA, to her sisters in Massachusetts concerning family matters. Letters written after 1819 relate to social and political events in Charleston and include accounts of events during the secession convention, the bombardment of Fort Sumter, and the fire of 1861. Letters written from Greenville, SC, in 1863 pertain to the war's hardships and a raid by Union soldiers under General Sherman. Some of the material has been published and was described in *South Carolina Historical and Genealogical Magazine,* vol. 46 (1945).

15,476. Good Hope Plantation
Records. 1835-59. 1 vol. and several items.
Open. Card catalog.
South Carolina Historical Society.
Cotton records; list of Negroes, their birth and death dates, and the causes of their deaths; business accounts; and other records for this St. Mark's Parish, SC, plantation, which was located near Orangeburg.

15,477. Haskell, Sophia Lovell
Papers. 1862-66. 1 vol.
Open. Calendar.
South Carolina Historical Society.
Haskell was a student at Miss de Choiseal's School at Flat Rock, NC. Her diary includes a list of family names beginning in 1693; the major part of the volume concerns books she read at school and at home and family incidents during the Civil War. Also includes poems on themes related to the Confederacy.

15,478. Hatten, Margaret
Papers. 1668. 1 item.
Open. Card catalog.
South Carolina Historical Society.
Probate of Hatten on Nicholas Bannistor's will.

15,479. Hering, Mary
Papers. 1800. 1 p.
Open. Card catalog.
South Carolina Historical Society.
Letter of [Mrs.] Hering of Bath contains references to her daughter's recent difficult voyage to Carolina, the "malignant fever," the insects, and the uncouth Sullivan islanders. Also includes mention of marriages of two Middleton sisters; weddings in Bath with descriptions of gowns, jewels, and coiffures; and her daughter's approaching confinement because of her pregnancy.

15,480. Heyward, DuBose
Papers. 1880-1940. 21 ft.
Open. Card catalog.
South Carolina Historical Society.
DuBose Heyward (1885-1940) was an author. Correspondence; literary manuscripts; drafts of Heyward's novels, poems, and screenplays; business and family papers; photos; and other items. Includes letters with references to the Poetry Society of South Carolina and to Charleston literary figures. Literary manuscripts include those of his mother Jane Screven Heyward (1864-1939) and of his wife Dorothy Hartzell (Kuhns) Heyward (1890-1961), with whom he collaborated on many of his writing projects.

15,481. Imer, Ann (Maurowmet)
Papers. 1765. 1 item.
Open. Card catalog.
South Carolina Historical Society.
Warrant of Imer as executrix to appraise the estate of John Maurowmet.

15,482. Inglesby
Papers. 1777-1865. 1 ft.
Open. Card catalog.
South Carolina Historical Society.
Personal and business papers, diaries, diplomas, and other material of John Inglesby, a planter, and his wife Hilda Inglesby include her correspondence with publishers and literary agents about a book by her husband. John Inglesby's diaries contain observations about family life and South Carolina families.

15,483. Izard, Ann, and Izard, Elizabeth C.
Papers. 1752-1812. 2 items.
Open. Card catalog.
South Carolina Historical Society.
A letter dated 1812, from Elizabeth C. [Mrs. George] Izard to Mrs. Ralph Izard, and an assignment of a mortgage of the Larwood estate to Richard Lubbock. Ann Middleton Izard, daughter of Ralph Izard, is listed as one of those incolved in the mortgage assignment.

15,484. Jervey, Mrs. Theodore Dehon
Papers. 1748-1914. 3 vols.
Open. Card catalog.
South Carolina Historical Society.
Jervey owned Rose Hill plantation and other estates on South Carolina's Ashley, Cooper, Cumbahee, and Peedee rivers. Records of Rose Hill include day and time books.

15,485. Johnson, Henrietta
Papers. Nd. No size given.
Open. Card catalog.
South Carolina Historical Society.
Johnson was an early 18th-century artist who painted portraits of Robert Johnson and Frances Lescott. Correspondence and 20th-century notes commenting about Johnson and her work.

15,486. Kershaw, Newman
Papers. 1830. 4 items.
Open. Card catalog.
South Carolina Historical Society.
Bills that Martha Miller filed in the chancery court against Kershaw to enjoin him from selling her two slaves, Phyllis and Jack.

15,487. Kinlock, Harriette
Papers. 1802. 2 items.
Open. Card catalog.
South Carolina Historical Society.
Kinlock was the wife of Cleland Kinlock, a planter. Writ of dedimus and renunciation of dower in payment of debt to Mary Shubrick. The Historical Society also holds the document by which Cleland Kinlock released a mortgage to Shubrick.

15,488. Koester, Antoinette
Papers. Nd. 3 vols. and 4 items.
Open. Card catalog.
South Carolina Historical Society.
Diaries, journals, school notes, and public school grade and behavior reports of Koester and May Taylor. Koester's papers include geography notes dating from the late 19th century. Taylor kept journals, signed by her parents, rating her behavior and learning at school in 1896. Her papers also include her school reports, which indicate she was an honor student at Memminger School in Charleston; a journal containing notes on English, geography, and philosophy; and a journal of history lessons.

15,489. Kruse, Kate
Papers. 1865. 1 vol.
Open. Card catalog.
South Carolina Historical Society.
Kruse (1853-1922), the daughter of Jacob and Christina Kurkop of Schleswig-Holstein, married Otto Muller, a Charleston professor. School compositions and exercises.

15,490. Ladies Benevolent Society
Records. 1915. 1 item.
Open. Card catalog.
South Carolina Historical Society.
Broadside report by Catherine Prioleau Ravenel, superintendent, regarding the group's 102nd anniversary.

15,491. Ladies Mutual Aid Association
Records. 1866-67. No size given.
Open. Card catalog.
South Carolina Historical Society.
Constitution, dated 1866, and reports that list the Association's officers.

15,492. Ladies' Ursuline Community
Records. Ca. 1884. 10 items.
Open. Card catalog.
South Carolina Historical Society.
Legal documents of this Catholic convent include a petition for renewal of a charter, plat, and title of property near Columbia, SC. Also includes bill to renew the charter.

15,493. LeJau, Huger, Downes, and Frost Families
Papers. 1800-21. 14 pp.
Open. Card catalog.
South Carolina Historical Society.
Birth records and family notes begin with Francis LeJau I and continue through Francis LeJau II, his daughter Ann who married Daniel Huger, her daughter Mary LeJau Huger who married Richard Downes, and later generations.

15,494. Lesesne, Anne Caroline
Papers. 1836. 1 vol.
Open. Card catalog.
South Carolina Historical Society.
Diary of Lesesne, a member of a planter family, principally concerns everyday life in Charleston. Also includes mention of the draft for the war against the Seminole Indians in Florida and the Society for the Advancement of Christianity in South Carolina, a group which advocated preaching Christianity among slaves.

15,495. Lord, Louisa
Papers. 1850-62. 29 items.
Open. Card catalog and calendar.
South Carolina Historical Society.
[Mrs. Samuel] Lord was in charge of Samuel Robertson, a slave and cobbler who was owned first by [Miss] Martha Winchester and later by her niece Martha Riggs, both of Prattville, AL. Letters written to Winchester, Riggs, and Martha Ann Parker [Mrs. George] Noble of Montgomery, AL, concern Robertson's wages and welfare and include news of St. John's Lutheran Church and the Boinest and Schirmer families of the Charleston area.

15,496. Macbeth, Malcolm
Papers. 1699-1854. 50 items.
Open. Card catalog.
South Carolina Historical Society.
Correspondence, plats, indentures, and other papers of the family of Macbeth, a Berkeley County, SC, planter during the 1820s and 1830s. Includes letters from the Robert Macbeth family, many referring to the settlement of estates, and letters from relatives in Scotland. Records of land transactions reflect the access of women family members to estate sharing.

15,497. Magrath
Papers. Ca. 1850-1949. 177 items.
Open. Calendar.
South Carolina Historical Society.
Sellina Bollin Magrath (ca. 1850-?) was the wife of William Joy Magrath, president of the South Carolina Railroad. Correspondence, a biographical sketch of William Magrath, notes on articles about railroads, and the transcripts of Sellina Magrath's recollections, one of the Ursuline Convent School in Columbia, SC, and the other concerning Columbia in general. Both of the reminiscences were written while Magrath was in her 80s.

15,498. Manigault
Papers. 1685-1873. 444 items.
Open. Card catalog.
South Carolina Historical Society.
Correspondence, journal extracts, business accounts, and other papers of four generations of this South Carolina planter family. Includes extracts from Ann Ashby Manigault's journal, 1754-81; correspondence, 1787-96, between Gabriel Manigault and his wife Margaret (Izard) Manigault and with their sons; and letters of Elizabeth Heyward Manigault, the wife of Charles Izard Manigault. Correspondents include Alice De Lancey [Mrs. Ralph] Izard, Henrietta Heyward, Emma Barnwell Heyward, and Anne Izard Deas. Also contains notes on art in South Carolina, household memoranda, receipts for cooking, school compositions, and clippings.

15,499. Marion, Esther
Papers. 1746-47. 2 pp.
Open. Card catalog.
South Carolina Historical Society.
Conveyance of the slaves of Esther Marion, which was signed in trust for Marion by Daniel Huger, John Cordes, William Keith, and Esther Cordes.

15,500. Middleton, Catherine
Papers. Ca. 1824. 1 vol.
Open. Card catalog.
South Carolina Historical Society.
Middleton (1812-94) was the daughter of Henry Middleton, a planter. Notebook of personal reminiscences and notes about plantation life and social events.

15,501. Middleton, Nathaniel Russell, Family
Papers. 1820-1937. 1257 items.
Open. Card catalog.
South Carolina Historical Society.
Correspondence, manuscripts, and typescripts of wills and other legal documents of the family of Middleton, a planter, and his wife Anna Elizabeth De Wolf Middleton. Includes the Middletons' correspondence before their marriage and their extensive correspondence during later periods of separation. Also includes correspondence of their children, copies of the will of Alicia Hopton (Russell) Middleton, and genealogical notes.

15,502. Miller, William C.
Papers. 1885-ca. 1920. 1 item and 156 pp.
Open. Calendar.
South Carolina Historical Society.
Miller, a Charleston attorney, was the father of Marguerite C. Miller, benefactress of many local organizations. Correspondence and speeches, most of them after-dinner speeches, responses to toasts, and presentations, and other talks by William Miller on such subjects as women, Mother Goose, politics, books, Charleston, and Robert E. Lee.

15,503. Misses Bates' Seminary
Records. Ca. 1853. 1 item.
Open. Calendar.
South Carolina Historical Society.
The Seminary was a Charleston school for young ladies. Folder describes the terms per quarter and the courses, which included English, Latin, Greek, modern languages, art, music, and wax flowers.

15,504. Motte, Isaac
Papers. 1780-83. 3 items.
Open. Card catalog.
South Carolina Historical Society.
Three wills of Motte, a planter, show changes he made in his bequests throughout the period. The last will provides for a division of his estate between his wife Mary and children Isaac and Anne; the document mentions specific Negroes and personal property.

15,505. Orphan House
Records. 1809-82. 18 vols.
Open. Card catalog.
South Carolina Historical Society.
Weekly reports of the House's steward list the number of children and servants, amounts and types of food, physicians' reports, and events. The events section included reports of admittances, deaths, funerals, children bound out, gifts, special occasions, repairs, clothing, employment of servants, and livestock and vegetable supplies. Other volumes give the name of the donor and condition of gifts presented to the asylum library.

15,506. Packard, Chilion
Papers. 1832-93. No size given.
Open. Card catalog.
South Carolina Historical Society.
Correspondence and other papers of Packard, a medical doctor, include letters to his wife Sarah Gordon Roulain Packard from her oldest son Charles concerning his studies at school, the beginning of the Civil War, and a battle with the Yankees; letters from Olive Packard to her brother; letters to Sarah [Mrs. A. J.] Davis from her niece Tallulah Roulain; a letter to Sarah Olive Packard Davis from her daughter Corinne; valentines; and a recipe for blackberry wine.

15,507. Pinckney Family
Papers. 1703-1856. 17 folders and several cases.
Open. Card catalog.
South Carolina Historical Society.
Correspondence, legal documents, and other family papers of the Pinckneys, rice and indigo planters in South Carolina. Includes letters of Eliza (Lucas) Pinckney (1722?-93), wife of Charles Pinckney, to her son concerning family news and letters to friends discussing children, crops, politics, and other topics. A letter to Eliza Pinckney from Sarah Rutledge discusses the family's health, the health of Negroes, and American independence. Material from 1863 includes a bond for $2500 to Benjamin Huger, executor of Eliza Pinckney's estate. Also included are a letter from Charles Pinckney regarding his mother's cancer and asking that leeches be sent to her; the will of Alexander Mackey bequeathing his entire estate to Elinor Mackey; a document that describes Colonel Lucas's Negroes at Garden Hill and lists 35 men, 16 women, 17 boys, and 11 girls; and a deed of gift of a slave girl from Daniel Horry to his daughter Harriott.

15,508. Pinckney, Maria Henrietta: Political Catechism
Papers. 1829-30. 14 pp.
Open. Card catalog.
South Carolina Historical Society.
Manuscript written by [Miss] Pinckney (ca. 1774-?), the eldest daughter of Charles Cotesworth Pinckney and Sarah Middleton Pinckney, was published as *The Quintessence of Long Speeches, arranged as a Political Catechism, by a Lady, for her God-daughter* (Charleston: A. E. Miller, 1830).

15,509. Poppenheim, Christopher Pritchard, and Poppenheim, Mary Elinor
Papers. 1860-65. 200 items.
Open. Calendar.
South Carolina Historical Society.
Correspondence between [Miss] Mary Elinor Bouknight of the Edgefield District of South Carolina and her cousin Sergeant Christopher Poppenheim, whom she married in 1864, includes his letters from Manassas, Yorktown, Fredericksburg, Richmond, and Petersburg in Virginia; Tennessee; and Charleston. After being wounded, Christopher Poppenheim was assigned to quartermaster duty in Charleston. Mary Bouknight's letters are primarily personal in nature, occasionally mentioning domestic life and war privations.

15,510. Porcher, Virginia Leigh
Papers. 1925-33. 1 folio.
Open. Card catalog.
South Carolina Historical Society.
[Miss] Porcher, a member of a prominent planter family, was active in the Mount Vernon Ladies Association. Notes, report to the Ladies Association's regents, paper about Ann Pamela Cunningham, photo of the regents taken at Mount Vernon in 1925, post card views of Mount Vernon, clipping about Rose Mont, and other material.

15,511. Quarterman, Chapman, and Bonneau
Papers. 1723. 1 p.
Access restricted. Card catalog.
South Carolina Historical Society.
Report of division and partition of certain South Carolina land among Mary Quarterman, William Parsons Chapman and his wife Rebecca, and Catherine Bonneau, pursuant to a writ in the Court of Common Pleas.

15,512. Quince
Papers. 1795-1818. 1 folio.
Open. Card catalog.
South Carolina Historical Society.
Correspondence and miscellaneous papers of the Quince family. Includes a letter concerning the financial settlement involved in the marriage of Mary Quince to Abraham Motte, correspondence and homilies of Mary's mother Susannah Quince, a visitor's book kept by Susannah Quince, her will, and a manuscript for a religious pamphlet.

15,513. Rutledge, Edward, and Rutledge, Sarah
Papers. 1793-99. 6 pp.
Open. Card catalog.
South Carolina Historical Society.
Letters from Edward Rutledge to his daughter Sarah Rutledge in which he discusses her education, including her studies in Paris, and warns her against vanity. Also includes mention of her cousin Emma's wedding.

15,514. St. David's Society
Records. 1777-1833. 1 folio.
Open. Card catalog.
South Carolina Historical Society.
Minutes of a school for poor Christian children, founded in 1770, include reports of monetary pledges, gifts of land, building construction, arrangements for financial control, the finding and hiring of women teachers, and school rules. The school was discontinued in 1833.

15,515. Salley, A. S., Jr.
Papers. 1898-1954. No size given.
Open. Calendar.
South Carolina Historical Society.
Memorabilia and records relate to Charleston social life and include material concerning the St. Cecilia Society, Cotillion Club, Wednesday Evening German Society, Spinsters of Charleston, Thailia Club, Ladies Benevolent Society, College of Charleston, and private parties and programs.

15,516. Sanders and Broughton
Papers. 1703-1836. 5 vols. and 43 items.
Open. Card catalog.
South Carolina Historical Society.
Correspondence, land grants, conveyances, wills, marriage settlements, account books, and

inventories of this planter family include frequent references to [Miss] Ann Broughton.

15,517. School Exercise Books
Papers. 1843-89. 4 vols.
Open. Card catalog.
South Carolina Historical Society.
School exercise books of Mary Julia Middleton (1829-1904), who later married Benjamin Huger Read; her sister Eleanor Maria Middleton, who married Benjamin Huger Rutledge; and Emily Read Fox. One of the books, kept by the Middleton sisters, includes maxims and notes on geography, mythology, and history. The volume was used first while the sisters were in school in Charleston and later at a school in England.

15,518. Simons, Harriet Stoney
Papers. 1963-69. 1 folio.
Open. Card catalog.
South Carolina Historical Society.
[Mrs. Albert] Simons (1896-1971) was an historic preservationist who with her husband co-authored a 1966 article "The William Burrows House." Correspondence and notes regarding the Simonses' article; restoration of the Robert Mills House in Columbia, SC; and Harriet Simons's article on the origin and history of bricks.

15,519. Sindrey, Elizabeth
Papers. 1705-21. 98-page vol.
Open. Card catalog.
South Carolina Historical Society.
Sindrey was the widow of planter Daniel Sindrey. Account book for her estate lists income from the estate and expenditures administered by Colonel William Rhet and his wife Sarah, including funeral expenses, repairs and estate property, and supportive expenses for Sindrey's survivors, among them a stepson and a daughter Sarah. The volume also lists the expenses for the wedding of Sarah to Joseph Blake in 1720. The record was discontinued after Sarah's wedding.

15,520. Society for the Relief of Orphans and Widows of the Clergy of the Protestant Episcopal Church
Records. 1762-1891. 5 vols.
Open. Card catalog.
South Carolina Historical Society.
Minute books, treasurer's book dating from 1829 to 1873, cash accounts, and 1879 membership list of this benevolent association, which was formed in 1762.

15,521. Society of the Bull Family of Ashley Hall
Records. 1737-1951. 1 Hollinger box.
Open. Card catalog.
South Carolina Historical Society.
Papers regarding the estates of Emma Anna Bull and Gracia Bull as well as correspondence, leases, and releases dating from 1737 to 1898. Also includes Bull family genealogical notes and other material.

15,522. South Carolina Clubs and Organizations
Records. 1784-1964. 17 ft.
Access restricted. Card catalog.
South Carolina Historical Society.
Minutes, treasurer's records, correspondence, reports, membership records, scrapbooks, clippings, and other records of South Carolina organizations, including the Charleston Chamber of Commerce; the Charleston Civic Club; the Charleston Preservation Society, fomerly the Society for Preservation of Old Dwellings; the Community Club of Charleston; the Ladies Benevolent Society, Charleston; the Ladies Memorial Association, formerly the Ladies Association of Charleston for Commemorating the Confederate Dead; St. David's Society; the New England Society of Charleston; St. David's Parish; and the South Carolina Society for Prevention of Cruelty to Animals.

15,523. South Carolina Low Country Land Records
Records. 1696-1854. 3 vols. and ca. 100 items.
Open. Card catalog.
South Carolina Historical Society.
Correspondence, conveyances, deeds, indentures, grants, surveys, plats, wills, and bills of sale for slaves. Includes documents, dating from 1696 to 1833, pertaining to Bull's Island; papers relating to James Child's attempt to found a town on the Cooper River in 1707; notes on the Child family; and land papers collected by Rees Fraser and Malcolm Macbeth.

15,524. Teague, B. H.
Papers. 1760-1894. 86 items.
Open. Card catalog.
South Carolina Historical Society.
Correspondence, business records, almanacs, and documents of the family of Teague, a planter, include a marriage settlement between L. Miles and Nancy Teague in Laurens District, SC; a deed of gift of a Negro boy, William, from Mary Reeder to Abner Griffin Teague in trust for Isaac Newton Teague; and a conveyance of land by William and Clary Dendy to William Carter.

15,525. Vanderhorst, Frances
Papers. 1736-1910. 4 ft.
Open. Card catalog.
South Carolina Historical Society.
Adele (Allston) Vanderhorst (1842-1915), the wife of Arnoldus Vanderhorst, was the daughter of Robert Francis Withers Allston (1801-64). Correspondence, primarily with Adele Vanderhorst's relatives; land conveyances; reports on sales of rice and cotton; and material relating to plantation life and social life in Charleston.

15,526. Vanderhorst, John; Mathews, Anthony; Peronneau, Alexander; and Lamboll, Thomas
Papers. 1733. 1 p.
Open. Card catalog.
South Carolina Historical Society.
Quadripartite indenture by Vanderhorst, Mathews, Peronneau, and Lamboll, trustees of a fund left by Sarah Fenwicke for the use of Protestant Dissenters.

15,527. Wayne, Maria L.
Papers. 1899-1951. 213 items.
Open. Calendar.
South Carolina Historical Society.
Family correspondence, legal papers, clippings, and ephemera of Wayne, a member of a prominent Charleston family. Includes a memory book from Wayne's birthday party in 1949; papers related to the estates of James P. Porcher, Arthur Trezevaut Wayne, and Maria Wayne; recipes; and booklets of clippings.

15,528. Webber, Mabel L.
Papers. Early 1900s. No size given.
Open. Card catalog.
South Carolina Historical Society.
Notes on Cherokee Indian tribes by Webber and others.

15,529. Weston, Paul
Papers. 1829-37. 1 folio.
Open. Card catalog.
South Carolina Historical Society.
Correspondence, accounts, and legal documents of Weston, a planter. Includes letters he wrote to his daughters while on a trip north with his wife and eldest daughter; a letter from Weston's wife Antonia; and a letter from Weston to his mother-in-law, a Mrs. Rently, in Scotland. The correspondence deals almost exclusively with travel schedules and family news.

15,530. White, Alonzo J.: List Book
Papers. 1853-63. 1 item.
Open. Card catalog and calendar.
South Carolina Historical Society.
Book listing Negroes sold by White includes the name, age, and job skill of each slave and identifies slave families, such as "Big Billy, aged 60, and his children, Moses, 20; Rhinah, 19; Kate, 18; Abraham, 12; and Davey, 10." Positions listed for female slaves included plantation cook; "half hand sickley"; "fine field hand"; cook, washer, and waiting maid; seamstress and waiting maid; and pastry cook. The book also catalogs physical problems of the particular slaves.

15,531. Wilkinson, Leila Fayssoux Davidson
Papers. 1920-50. 203 items.
Open. Card catalog.
South Carolina Historical Society.
[Mrs.] Wilkinson (1881-1970) was an American National Red Cross worker during WWI, a missionary in China during the 1920s, and a kindergarten and dancing teacher in Charleston and Charlotte, NC. Correspondence, much of it written from China and the Middle East; photos; school programs; clippings; and Lucy Chaplin Lee's *An American Sojourn in China,* which includes a chapter about Wilkinson.

15,532. Willis, Eola
Papers. 1919-56. 1 folio.
Open. Card catalog.
South Carolina Historical Society.
Correspondence and other papers of [Miss] Willis (1909-56), a member of a Charleston family that owned a cotton factorage, include notes about her artistic career, Charleston inns and taverns, wine and cookery, heraldry, and the theater. Also includes the invoice book of the cotton factorage, Chisolm and Willis.

15,533. Wilson, Robert
Papers. 1803-1924. 1 folio.
Open. Card catalog.
South Carolina Historical Society.
Diaries, manuscripts, and other papers of Wilson (1838-1924), a Confederate surgeon, minister, and writer. Includes Wilson's manuscripts on birds and other topics; sermons; an 1850 diary of John Knox, an Irish immigrant who settled in Charleston and married Elizabeth C. Wilson; tripartite marriage settlement, dated from 1845, between Catherine M. Wilson, her trustee James Wilson, and Samuel Crocker of Boston; and an indenture, dated 1803, between Margaret Nowell of Charleston and her factor John Cart for sale of a lot near Race Course.

15,534. Wragg, Samuel
Papers. 1784-87. 4 pp.
Open. Card catalog.
South Carolina Historical Society.
Will by which Wragg, a resident of South Carolina's Georgetown District, divided his estate among his sons Joseph and Samuel and daughters Ann, Judith, Elizabeth, and Henrietta. The will contained a special provision for building and furnishing an establishment for his unmarried daughters in Georgetown.

15,535. Yates Family
Papers. 1822-81. 198 items.
Open. Card catalog.
South Carolina Historical Society.
Correspondence and other papers of Joseph Yates, a Charleston cooper; his wife Elizabeth Ann (Saylor) Yates (1789-1868); and [Miss] Mary Amarinthia Yates (1819-98), who married William Snowden, a physician, in 1857. Most of the material concerns Elizabeth Yates, who from 1822 to 1825 lived as a widow in Philadelphia with her young children. Many of the letters were exchanged with her sons, the first of whom was reading law in a Charleston law office while the second was working in the family cooperage and

the third was in school in Scotland. Some of the letters concern her son's surgery in 1828 in New York for a "tumor of the clavicle." After 1837 the letters focus on Mary Yates. A biography describes her social service work during and after the Civil War and her role in establishment of the Confederate Home and College in Charleston.

COLUMBIA

15,536. Columbia College

Records. 1860- . 2 bookshelves.
Open. No guide.
Columbia College.
Columbia College, a Methodist liberal arts college with a current enrollment of about 900 women, was founded in 1854 as Columbia Female College. Trustee minutes, financial records, investment records, correspondence, yearbooks, college catalogs, literary magazines, and other records reflect the College's association with Wofford College and the school's closing by order of General Sherman for part of the Civil War. In 1866, Columbia College reported only 48 students; its size did not grow dramatically until the 1930s. Also contains minutes, financial and membership records, and other items of the school's alumni association, founded in 1886. Issues of the yearbook *The Columbian,* 1904- , contain information about the origin of the students, their patrons, College faculty, and trustees. Also includes issues of *The Criterion,* 1906- , a literary magazine containing student essays and poetry.

15,537. Child Constable

Records. 1868-1906. 3.5 cu.ft.
Open. Published guide.
South Carolina Department of Archives and History.
Includes a list of crimes committed (1 vol.), 1868-71. The list is arranged by county and gives the date, name of complainant, name of defendant, occupation, residence, type of offense, witnesses, court, judgment, bail, and miscellaneous remarks. Women appear frequently as complainants and witnesses for a variety of crimes, particularly those involving assault, and less frequently as defendants. In 1869 Hannah Garey accused Warren Donald of "assault with intent" and Adeline Leakes accused Fannie Kennedy of assault and battery. See Marion C. Chandler and Earl W. Wade, *The South Carolina Archives: A Temporary Summary Guide,* 2nd ed. (Columbia, SC: South Carolina Department of Archives and History, 1976).

15,538. Confederate Home Commission

Records. 1909-57. 15 cu.ft.
Open. Published guide.
South Carolina Department of Archives and History.
Includes records of the Confederate Home, a home for Confederate veterans and their wives, widows, daughters, and sisters. The Home records contain applications for admission, financial records, daily records, physicians' standing orders, narcotics records, medical records, and menus. The application petitions of the wives, widows, daughters, and sisters of the veterans provide specific information about the conditions of these women from 1925 to 1955. See Marion C. Chandler and Earl W. Wade, *The South Carolina Archives: A Temporary Summary Guide,* 2nd ed. (Columbia, SC: South Carolina Department of Archives and History, 1976).

15,539. County Boards of Education

Records. 19th and 20th centuries. No size given.
Open. Published guide.
South Carolina Department of Archives and History.
Included in the county and local records held by the State Archives are extensive records, dating from the late 19th century, of county boards of education. The records include minutes, teacher certification records, superintendent of education annual reports, general cashbooks, teachers' pay certificates, pay ledgers, and other records. Anderson County records, for example, include minutes of the board, 1891-1950; teacher certification records, 1872-1911; annual reports of the superintendent, 1912-30; general cashbooks, 1899-1911; and teachers' pay certificates, 1877-96. Records of Colleton County include minutes of the county board of examiners, 1891-96, as well as extensive financial records. See Marion C. Chandler and Earl W. Wade, *The South Carolina Archives: A Temporary Summary Guide,* 2nd ed. (Columbia, SC: South Carolina Department of Archives and History, 1976).

15,540. Department of Corrections: South Carolina Penitentiary/Central Correctional Institution

Records. Ca. 1866-1969. 70 cu.ft.
Open. Published guide.
South Carolina Department of Archives and History.
Includes central registers of prisoners (8 vols.), 1867-1930, which are rolls of convicts received at the South Carolina Penitentiary, Columbia. The registers give name, number, former occupation, age, sex, color, place of birth, height, hair, eyes, complexion, offense, court, admission date, term of imprisonment, sentence, judge, and remarks. Women appear infrequently but regularly in the records. Among them were Harriet Parker, a black nurse, who was convicted of robbery in 1877 at age 30 and was discharged after 18 months. See Marion C. Chandler and Earl W. Wade, *The South Carolina Archives: A Temporary Summary Guide,* 2nd ed. (Columbia, SC: South Carolina Department of Archives and History, 1976).

15,541. Department of Education

Records. Ca. 1868-1967. 50 cu.ft.
Open. Published guide.
South Carolina Department of Archives and History.
Includes records of the office of the superintendent, among them teachers monthly reports (1 cu.ft.), 1869-71, for schools in South Carolina. The reports provide the name and location of the school; the number of days in the month the school was open; and the race, sex, and regional identity of teachers. They also provide information about the average attendance; the age of students; whether the school was for white or colored children; the ownership, construction, and condition of the schoolhouse; and the number of scholars engaged in such skills as the alphabet, spelling, reading, writing, mental and written arithmetic, geography, English grammar, history, and "higher branches." In 1870 Augustus Howard, a Southern white male teacher, described the Liberty School in Greenville County. The school, which was enclosed inside a plantation, had 30 scholars between 6 and 16 years and seven who were more than 16 years old. Howard noted that the pupils, who were colored, attended regularly and punctually. See Marion C. Chandler and Earl W. Wade, *The South Carolina Archives: A Temporary Summary Guide,* 2nd ed. (Columbia, SC: South Carolina Department of Archives and History, 1976).

15,542. Fairfield County

Records. Ca. 1785-1970. 264 cu.ft.
Open. Published guide.
South Carolina Department of Archives and History.
Includes records of the ordinary/probate judge, which contain dower estates records (1 vol. and 1 reel), 1870-95. The records are of lawsuits made by widows claiming dower rights to estates against which claims had been levied at the deaths of husbands, many of whom had died intestate and in debt. The widows claimed one-third of the property, usually land, in their husbands' possession at death. Court settlements were made either in land or cash. Mary Poteet, Irma Parrott, and Meary Stokes, for example, claimed land because they had "never executed any relinquishment of right and claim of dower of, in, or to" the property. See Marion C. Chandler and Earl W. Wade, *The South Carolina Archives: A Temporary Summary Guide,* 2nd ed. (Columbia, SC: South Carolina Department of Archives and History, 1976).

15,543. General Assembly

Records. Ca. 1691-1974. 1800 cu.ft.
Open. Published and unpublished guides.
South Carolina Department of Archives and History.
Contains reports of committees of the General Assembly, among them reports on women's education. Included, for example, is a report of the Committee on Incorporation on the petition of David B. Rice and others of the Female Academy of Yorkville. Also contains resolutions made by the General Assembly, some of which pertain to specific women and widows, to free schools and women's education, and to restored estates.

Contains petitions by individuals, municipalities, and organizations to the Assembly, many by educational institutions seeking land, financial assistance, and the right to incorporate male and female academies. Other petitions concerned divorce, guardianship, and property.

Contains reports of free schools, which were sponsored by the state for the education of poor children. Reports provide information on salaries, land ownership and building ownership, and the number of pupils. Most of the free school teachers during the period were males. SeeMarion C. Chandler and Earl W. Wade, *The South Carolina Archives: A Temporary Summary Guide,* 2nd ed. (Columbia, SC: South Carolina Department of Archives and History, 1976).

15,544. Marlboro County

Records. Ca. 1785-1958. 131 cu.ft.
Open. Published guide.
South Carolina Department of Archives and History.
Contained in the records of Marlboro County are those of the board of education, including annual reports of the superintendent, 1939-50; minute books of the Teachers' Association, 1902-29, and of the Educational Society, 1907-52; and a register of teachers, 1918-58. Records of the Ordinary/Probate judge include a one-volume record of commitments of lunatics, 1888-94; most of those committed were women. They were committed for epilepsy, disturbing the domestic circle, pyromania, and paranoia. Symptoms, which included sleeplessness, wandering about, and melancholia, were linked to sexual disturbances, childbirth, and menstruation. Lina McNeil, for example, was committed at age 40 for insanity exhibited by "excessive profanity, vulgarity, destructiveness, and wandering over the country." See Marion C. Chandler and Earl W. Wade, *The South Carolina Archives: A Temporary Summary Guide,* 2nd ed. (Columbia, SC: South Carolina Department of Archives and History, 1976).

15,545. Office of the Governor

Records. Ca. 1798-1970. 800 cu.ft.
Open. Published guide.
South Carolina Department of Archives and History.
Includes pardons, paroles, and commutations; petitions for pardons; petitions for rewards; and letters received and sent. See Marion C. Chandler and Earl W. Wade, *The South Carolina Archives: A Temporary Summary Guide,* 2nd ed. (Columbia, SC: South Carolina Department of Archives and History, 1976).

15,546. Secretary of State

Records. Ca. 1671- . 1500 cu.ft.
Open. Published and unpublished guides.
South Carolina Department of Archives and History.
Consists of subgroups for recorded instruments, records deposited for security, fiscal and internal management records, corporation charter division records, securities division records, and records of the office of the surveyor general. In the records deposited for security are state census schedules,

1829-69. Contained in the recorded instruments subgroup are wills, 1732-76; inventories of estates, 1736-76; marriage settlements, 1785-1902; and pardons, 1866-1950.

Until ca. 1875 all wills for South Carolina were recorded in Charleston. Wills for settlers and their descendants, from the late seventeenth century through 1868, provide information about the extent to which women retained financial power after husbands' deaths, specifically about the inheritance of land and chattels, their rights to service of servants, and their powers as administrators of estates. SeeMarion C. Chandler and Earl W. Wade, *The South Carolina Archives: A Temporary Summary Guide,* 2nd ed. (Columbia, SC: South Carolina Department of Archives and History, 1976).

15,547. South Carolina Court of Appeals in Equity
Records. 1836-1959. 5 cu.ft.
Open. Published guide.
South Carolina Department of Archives and History.
Bound volumes containing summary case lists and minutes, amounts at risk, opinions, and dockets, as well as petitions to practice law in courts of equity jurisdiction. Women appear frequently as plaintiffs and defendants. Equity courts had original and appellate jurisdiction in matters pertaining to property, contract, and money. See Marion C. Chandler and Earl W. Wade, *The South Carolina Archives: A Temporary Summary Guide,* 2nd ed. (Columbia, SC: South Carolina Department of Archives and History, 1976).

15,548. South Carolina Court of Common Pleas
Records. 1703-90. 100 cu.ft.
Open. Published guide.
South Carolina Department of Archives and History.
Included in the records of the Court are renunciations of dower, 1726-75 (10 vols.). (By South Carolina law, before clear title to property could be obtained by a purchaser, the wife of the seller had to renounce her dower, or right to a portion of the property.) The renunciation was used to assign land and other dower possessions, such as buildings, slaves, and personal property, permanently to a third party. The woman usually appeared privately before the judge to acknowledge that she relinquished claims to her dower "freely and voluntarily without any manner of compulsion, dread, or fear from her said husband or any other person or persons whatsoever."

Also contained are judgment rolls (167 flat files and 4 oversize flat files), 1703-90, which are records related to placing suit, receiving testimony, and arriving at judgment. The index of judgment rolls indicates that women were active in contract and property litigation; women successfully sued for amounts owed an estate of which they were executrix or with husbands as co-executors for an estate. In 1786 Mary Elizabeth Droze, for example, successfully sued Thomas Abernathy for a sum owed her from an estate for which he was executor. In 1767 Sarah Ackerman, executrix for Albert Ackerman, successfully sued a planter, John Wright, for damages due to trespass. See Marion C. Chandler and Earl W. Wade, *The South Carolina Archives: A Temporary Summary Guide,* 2nd ed. (Columbia, SC: South Carolina Department of Archives and History, 1976).

15,549. South Carolina School for the Deaf and Blind
Records. 1849-79. 6.5 cu.ft.
Open. Published guide.
South Carolina Department of Archives and History.
The School, which was established in 1849, educated deaf, dumb, and blind Negro and white pupils. Contains minutes (2 vols.), 1879-1941, of the board of commissioners meetings. References to women occur in the early years, although men are more frequently cited as teachers and administrators. In 1879 Ada Walker was hired as teacher of the blind at a salary of $500 per year and Mrs. N. E. Walker was hired as matron at a salary of $300 per year. In 1880 new building plans were approved, and in 1881 the board moved to request legislative support to defray the expense of "colored pupils." A separate building was authorized for colored pupils, and a "colored department" was established. In 1886 Professor and Mrs. L. H. Comer were hired as teachers at salaries of $450 and $180 respectively. By 1893 the staff included 6 women and 3 men in the white department and 2 men assigned to the colored department.

Also contains records of teachers meetings, 1884-86 (1 vol.), held at 8 A.M. Saturday mornings, at which teachers discussed methods of teaching deaf mutes, child nature, correction (punishment), teaching arithmetic, and other topics. Among the faculty were Professor and Mrs. L. H. Comer, teachers in the blind department, and Bessy Eddy, who recorded minutes of the meetings and taught articulation. Blind girls were taught to knit lace, deaf girls learned "plain sewing," and suggestions were made that the girls be taught artificial flower making. See Marion C. Chandler and Earl W. Wade, *The South Carolina Archives: A Temporary Summary Guide,* 2nd ed. (Columbia, SC: South Carolina Department of Archives and History, 1976).

15,550. Adger, Smythe, and Flynn Family
Papers. 1830-1930. 635 items.
Open. Card catalog.
University of South Carolina, South Caroliniana Library.
Correspondence of these related families, the male members of which were Presbyterian missionaries and ministers, includes letters of John Bailey Adger, a missionary to Turkey; Hannah Longstreet; Mrs. Thomas Smyth; and Jane Ann Smyth. The correspondence principally deals with missionary work and funds for theological students, the work of Confederate chaplains during the Civil War, the 1865 fire in Columbia, and wartime hardships in Charleston, SC. Some members of the Smyth family spelled their surname Smythe.

15,551. Aichel Family
Papers. 1875-1913. 56 items.
Open. Card catalog.
University of South Carolina, South Caroliniana Library.
Correspondence includes a letter from Johanna Aichel in Brooklyn, NY, to her parents Mr. and Mrs. Oskar Aichel in Charleston regarding a visit with relatives and the 1876 centennial celebration in Philadelphia. In another letter to Oskar Aichel, E. A. Kelly outlines a course of education for girls and responds to Aichel's criticism of a recent school exercise, noting that "our pupils vacationed from July to Dec. This sent them back to us rather out of gear for intellectual work. . . ." Also includes a report from the Charleston Female Seminary concerning Alma Aichel.

15,552. Aiken Family
Papers. 1832-97. 88 items.
Open. Card catalog.
University of South Carolina, South Caroliniana Library.
Family correspondence and other papers contain an 1865 journal in which Mary Gayle Aiken recorded comments about the Civil War; a diary in which she chiefly wrote about weather conditions, but also mentioned family activities and the 1876 election; and a genealogical sketch of the family of David and Nancy Aiken.

15,553. Aimwell Presbyterian Church
Records. 1915. 1 item.
Open. Unpublished guide.
University of South Carolina, South Caroliniana Library.
Recollections of [Mrs.] Jane Roseborough Tucker concern the work of women in the Aimwell Presbyterian Church in Ridgeway, SC, and include mention of individuals and families.

15,554. Allston Family
Papers. 1847-1924. 3516 items.
Open. Card catalog.
University of South Carolina, South Caroliniana Library.
Family and business correspondence and plantation records of Robert Francis Withers Allston (1801-64), including an 1854 letter in which he defines to his wife Adele (Petigru) Allston his attitude toward her, his aims in life, and his accomplishments and bemoans her accusations that he was "selfish & illiberal"; an 1863 letter in which Adele Allston writes her son Charles Petigru Allston that she is leaving Charleston, SC, because of war developments and discusses the death of her brother James L. Petigru; a letter in which Adele Allston tells Charles of the death of his father; contracts dated 1869 and 1870 for Colonel Ben Allston and C. P. Allston, who were to be agents for Adele Allston; and a letter in which Elizabeth Waties (Allston) [Mrs. John Julius] Pringle (1845-1921) in Saratoga, NY, writes of attending a lecture by Thomas Edison, during which he demonstrated the telephone. Business records include bills for household and plantation supplies, medical bills for family and slaves, and receipts for subscriptions to national and foreign periodicals.

15,555. American Association of University Women, South Carolina Division
Records. 1924-63. 16 vols.
Open. Unpublished guide.
University of South Carolina, South Caroliniana Library.
Presidents' papers, including Division and committee reports, addresses, and national and state convention programs; secretary's records; branch surveys; and bulletins.

15,556. Anderson, Lily Strickland
Papers. 1920-47. 47 items.
Open. Unpublished guide.
University of South Carolina, South Caroliniana Library.
[Mrs. J. C.] Strickland (1887-1958) was a composer and author of poems and articles. Correspondence, poems, articles, and biographical and bibliographical information, including lists of her articles and musical compositions.

15,557. Arnold, Annie S.
Papers. 1881-86. 1 vol.
Open. Unpublished guide.
University of South Carolina, South Caroliniana Library.
Notebook of Arnold includes notes taken at the Teachers Institute of South Carolina College.

15,558. Associate Reformed Presbyterian Church, Hopewell
Records. 1876-1939. 1 vol.
Open. Unpublished guide.
University of South Carolina, South Caroliniana Library.
Minutes of the Church's women's missionary association.

15,559. Babcock, Katherine Guion
Papers. 1888-90. 2 vols.
Open. Unpublished guide.
University of South Carolina, South Caroliniana Library.
Notebooks that Babcock (1866-1943) kept while she was a student nurse at Massachusetts General Hospital and its affiliate, McLean Mental Hospital.

15,560. Bachman, Mrs. W. K.
Papers. 1865. 1 vol.
Open. Unpublished guide.
University of South Carolina, South Caroliniana Library.
Correspondence to Kate Bachman, including an account of the burning of Columbia.

15,561. Bacot, Ada
Papers. 1860-66. 7 vols. and 9 items.
Open. Unpublished guide.
University of South Carolina, South Caroliniana Library.
Correspondence and diaries of Bacot, a Civil War nurse at Monticello Hospital at Charlottesville, VA, include her record of work at the Charlottesville hospital and her life in Mars Bluff, SC. The correspondence includes reference to Bacot's marriage to a Mr. Clark.

15,562. Ball Family
Papers. 1696-1950. 947 items.
Open. Published and unpublished guides.
University of South Carolina, South Caroliniana Library.
Correspondence, business papers, and plantation records of this South Carolina planter family include papers of Jane Ball (1761-1804), the wife of John Ball, Sr.; Jane Ball (1823-?); Maria L. Gibbs Ball; and Mrs. S. C. Ball. Papers include information about plantation operations, slave mortality and fertility, and the lives of low-country gentry. See *South Carolina Historical Magazine,* vol. 65 (Jan. 1964), pp. 1-15.

15,563. Ball, Mrs. W. W.
Papers. 1888-90. 3 vols.
Open. Unpublished guide.
University of South Carolina, South Caroliniana Library.
Scrapbooks of clippings relating primarily to the political campaign of 1890, in which Benjamin Ryan Tillman was elected governor of South Carolina.

15,564. Billings, John Shaw
Papers. 1921-55. 4356 items.
Open. Unpublished guide.
University of South Carolina, South Caroliniana Library.
Billings (1898-1975), who began his career as a newspaper reporter, became managing editor of *Time* and *Life* and, later, editorial director of Time Incorporated publications. Correspondence, intra-office memoranda, and staff reports include correspondence with Clare (Boothe) Luce, Rebecca West, Winston Churchill, Dwight D. Eisenhower, Henry R. Luce, Douglas MacArthur, H. L. Mencken, John D. Rockefeller, Jr., Bertrand Russell, Harry S. Truman, and others.

15,565. Billings, John Shaw, and Billings, Frederica (Wade)
Papers. 1900-75. 11,615 items.
Open. Card catalog.
University of South Carolina, South Caroliniana Library.
John Billings (1898-1975) was editorial director of Time Incorporated publications; his wife Frederica Billings (1901-63) was the only daughter of Peyton Lisbey Wade, chief justice of the Georgia Court of Appeals. Frederica Billings's correspondence with relatives throughout the country constitutes the bulk of the collection. The Billingses' only child Frederica Wade Billings II died in childhood.

15,566. Billings, Katharine Hammond
Papers. 1880-97. 7 vols.
Open. Unpublished guide.
University of South Carolina, South Caroliniana Library.
Notebooks and exercise books of Billings (1867-1925), then Katharine Hammond, include penmanship exercises, lecture notes taken while she was a student nurse at Johns Hopkins Hospital, and an autograph album.

15,567. Blanding, William
Papers. 1807-50. 4 vols. and 129 items.
Open. Card catalog.
University of South Carolina, South Caroliniana Library.
Correspondence, a diary, and other papers of Blanding (1773-1857), a Camden, SC, physician whose family lived in Massachusetts; members of Blanding's family left the South because of their opposition to slavery. Includes an 1808 letter in which Susan Blanding in Camden writes Elizabeth Carpenter in Rehoboth, MA, about social events and says that it was a sacrifice to leave New England, "a land of liberty for a land of slavery"; an 1816 letter in which Rachel Blanding in Camden tells Hannah Lewis in Philadelphia about her family's decision to leave the South because they had "taken such a disgust to slavery"; and a journal kept by William Blanding's sister Lucy (Blanding) Carpenter during her trip from Massachusetts to South Carolina in 1848 and 1849.

15,568. Bleckley, Sylvester
Papers. 1845-1952. 286 items.
Open. Card catalog.
University of South Carolina, South Caroliniana Library.
Correspondence of Bleckley (1832-96), a merchant and banker, consists chiefly of business letters, Civil War letters to the brothers of Bleckley's wife Annie E. (Hammond) Bleckley, and family letters from points in South Carolina, Georgia, Florida, and Tennessee. Included is a 1906 letter in which Margaretta A. Harvey relates her experiences during the San Francisco earthquake to Annie Bleckley.

15,569. Blue Family
Papers. 1873-1955. 50 items.
Open. Card catalog.
University of South Carolina, South Caroliniana Library.
Family correspondence, biographical sketches of family members, and genealogical data of this South Carolina family. Includes correspondence of Kate Lilly Blue, a Democratic party worker who commented in a 1944 letter that she had taken politics seriously when women received the franchise, but as time passed she observed that women effected few changes. Includes letters in which Edward Blue Wheeler, writing Kate Blue from a British Red Cross Hospital in France in 1919, describes the horrors of a recent battle and a 1942 letter which John Stuart Blue wrote a week before he died when his ship sank at Guadalcanal.

15,570. Boyd, Rosamonde Ramsay
Papers. 1924-75. 3753 items.
Open. Card catalog.
University of South Carolina, South Caroliniana Library.
A professor at Converse College, Boyd (1900-) was an officer of the AAUW and the Association of Retired Persons; she also was active in groups concerned with the status, rights, and education of women. Correspondence, biographical data, photos, clippings, and published material include information on Boyd's activities in such groups as the International Federation of University Women, the South Carolina Conference of Social Work, the South Carolina Status of Women Commission, the South Carolina Women's Council for Common Good, the national advisory committee for the White House Conference on Aging, Japan International Christian University, and the National Traveler's Aid Association. Boyd earned a PhD degree at Duke University in 1945.

15,571. Brown, Mary Davis
Papers. 1854-1901. 9 vols.
Open. Card catalog.
University of South Carolina, South Caroliniana Library.
Diaries of Brown (1822-1903), a York County, SC, resident, principally include her record of family activities and her thoughts on religious subjects. Also contains information on births, marriages, and deaths in her family and the community; services attended at Bersheba Presbyterian Church; emigration to Mississippi and Arkansas; the Female College at Yorkville, SC; teachers and temperance meetings; the purchase and death of slaves; attending "a singing"; arrests and trials of members of the Ku Klux Klan; and earthquakes in 1886 and 1890.

15,572. Camden Female Institute
Records. 1870. 1 vol.
Open. Unpublished guide.
University of South Carolina, South Caroliniana Library.
Catalog lists activities, classes, and requirements of the institution.

15,573. Carson, Caroline Petigru
Papers. 1835-56. 2 vols.
Open. Catalog card.
University of South Carolina, South Caroliniana Library.
Poetry, including original verse and comments, of Carson (1820-92), a writer.

15,574. Cayce Family
Papers. 1869-1956. 49 items.
Open. Card catalog.
University of South Carolina, South Caroliniana Library.
Correspondence and other papers of this family of farmers include letters from [Mrs.] Jane C. Stingley in Mississippi to South Carolina relatives which reflect the depressed condition of agriculture and business during Reconstruction, removal of her family to Texas and Arkansas, and a legal dispute regarding ownership of the Cayce family's South Carolina home, Granby. Also contains legal papers of [Mrs.] Sue Elizabeth Cayce Traut and genealogical material.

15,575. Coles, Annie Cadwallader
Papers. 1902-65. 7 vols. and 109 items.
Open. Card catalog.
University of South Carolina, South Caroliniana Library.
Coles (1883-1969) was a Columbia-born artist. Correspondence, sketchbooks, a record of portrait orders, a photo album of her portraits, art exhibition catalogs, clippings, and other papers. Coles graduated from Converse College and attended art schools in New York, France, and England. She then opened a studio in Greenwich Village as a commercial artist and portraitist. During WWII she designed heat exchangers for the merchant marine, and after the war she returned to Columbia to concentrate on portraits.

15,576. Columbia Committee of the National Society of Colonial Dames of America
Records. 1925-62. 7 vols.
Open. Unpublished guide.
University of South Carolina, South Caroliniana Library.
Scrapbooks kept by Mrs. A. S. Salley, Mrs. Simpson Zimmerman, and Mrs. John A. Manning contain information regarding the group's activities; historic houses; marriages, deaths, and activities of prominent citizens; and such Columbia events as debutante balls and autograph parties.

15,577. Conner, Julia Margaret Courtney
Papers. 1827. 1 vol.
Open. Card catalog.
University of South Carolina, South Caroliniana Library.
Diary in which [Mrs. Henry W.] Conner describes her trip from Charleston, SC, to visit her husband's

family in Poplar Grove, NC, and finally to Nashville. Includes Conner's observations on camp meetings and descriptions of her social life in Nashville and of her meetings with Andrew Jackson and his wife and Sam Houston.

15,578. Cromer, Marie Samuella
Papers. 1910-12. 1 vol.
Open. Unpublished guide.
University of South Carolina, South Caroliniana Library.
Scrapbook contains correspondence and clippings regarding Cromer's organization of and work with the Girls' Tomato Clubs and the public schools.

15,579. Daughters of the American Colonists, Dr. Henry Woodward Chapter
Records. 1965-70. 2 vols.
Open. Unpublished guide.
University of South Carolina, South Caroliniana Library.
Scrapbooks of this women's historical society provide information about the Chapter and the South Carolina tricentennial.

15,580. Daughters of the American Colonists, South Carolina Society
Records. 1973-76. 1 vol.
Open. Unpublished guide.
University of South Carolina, South Caroliniana Library.
Scrapbook of this women's historical society includes information about the group's activities, particularly dedication ceremonies for historical markers and awards to American history students.

15,581. Daughters of the American Revolution, University of South Carolina Chapter
Records. 1970-76. 1 vol.
Open. Unpublished guide.
University of South Carolina, South Caroliniana Library.
Minutes and financial records.

15,582. Deas, Anne Simons
Papers. 1893-1910. 4 vols.
Open. Catalog card.
University of South Carolina, South Caroliniana Library.
Papers of Deas include a journal for the period 1893-97 with comments on family life, weather, and events in Summerville, SC, and a fictionalized account of life on Cedar Grove Plantation from about 1850 to 1880 with explanatory notes by Alston Deas.

15,583. Dial, Rebecca
Papers. 1922-62. 17 vols.
Partially restricted. Unpublished guide.
University of South Carolina, South Caroliniana Library.
A writer and operator of a Virginia resort home, Dial (1894-) is the daughter of US Senator Nathaniel Barksdale Dial. Dramatic scripts, radio and television programs, articles regarding speech fundamentals and women in war work, and reports on projects in sociodrama and courses in the teaching of reading. In addition to her literary and teaching careers, Dial was active in Washington, DC, social circles. In recent years she has published her autobiography and a biography of her father.

15,584. Dogwood Garden Club, Columbia
Records. 1935-47. 6 vols.
Open. Unpublished guide.
University of South Carolina, South Caroliniana Library.
Scrapbooks and a short history of this women's group.

15,585. DuBose, Louise (Jones)
Papers. 1918-75. 21 vols. and 632 items.
Open. Unpublished guide.
University of South Carolina, South Caroliniana Library.
An author and a poet, DuBose (1901-) began her career as a reporter for the *Columbus Enquirer Sun* in Columbus, GA, and later became director of the Federal Writers' Project in South Carolina, an instructor and assistant professor at the University of South Carolina, associate editor of *South Carolina Magazine* and, in 1950, director of the University of South Carolina Press. Correspondence, including letters from Pierre S. du Pont, J. G. de Roulhac Hamilton, DuBose Heyward, Francis B. Simkins, Katherine Drayton Mayrant Simons, and Elizabeth O'Neill Verner; DuBose's articles regarding Laura Beecher Comer, intelligence in black and white children, and other subjects; radio scripts concerning South Carolina counties and such other subjects as Aaron Burr, Jefferson Davis, Wade Hampton III, the Manigault family, S. F. B. Morse, Natalie Delage Sumter, Furman University, the Juvenile-Domestic Relations Court, and Winthrop College; biographical sketches; one-act plays regarding South Carolina subjects; background material for a study of labor in South Carolina; and other papers. DuBose's articles and poems were published in *The State Magazine* and other publications. She was active in the Poetry Society of South Carolina, the Southeastern Folklore Society, and the South Carolina Historical Society; she also was a charter member of the University South Caroliniana Society.

15,586. Duncan Memorial Methodist Episcopal Church
Records. 1811-46. 1 item.
Open. Card catalog.
University of South Carolina, South Caroliniana Library.
Register of marriages and baptisms of this Georgetown church.

15,587. Easterby, Hattie, and Easterby, Jessie
Papers. 1898-1901. 5 vols.
Open. Unpublished guide.
University of South Carolina, South Caroliniana Library.
Diaries in which these two sisters record their experiences as students at the South Carolina School for the Deaf and Blind at Cedar Spring, SC.

15,588. Easterling, Rebecca
Papers. 1851-76. 91 items.
Open. Card catalog.
University of South Carolina, South Caroliniana Library.
Correspondence of Easterling includes letters from Edward C. Easterling regarding the Cokesbury School, studies at the University of North Carolina, the lack of clothing and supplies during the Civil War, and other subjects; a letter from Agnes F. Oliver concerning the Carolina Female College; and letters to Easterling from Thorp Barton concerning his unsuccessful efforts at farming since a drought and the breaking of his engagement.

15,589. Edgefield Female Institute
Records. Ca. 1850. 1 item.
Open. Card catalog.
University of South Carolina, South Caroliniana Library.
Circular lists the Institute's course of study, terms, and instructors, with Robert H. Nickolls named as rector and general instructor.

15,590. Ellis, Emily Caroline
Papers. 1865. 1 vol.
Open. Card catalog.
University of South Carolina, South Caroliniana Library.
Diary in which [Mrs.] Ellis (1838-78) tells of her family's flight through Columbia as General Sherman's army approached.

15,591. English, Elisabeth Doby
Papers. 1959. 1 vol.
Open. Unpublished guide.
University of South Carolina, South Caroliniana Library.
Diary by English (1887-1978), a librarian, of a trip to Europe with post cards illustrating places she visited.

15,592. First Presbyterian Church
Records. 1900. 1 item.
Open. Unpublished guide.
University of South Carolina, South Caroliniana Library.
Constitution and bylaws of the Ella C. Davidson Auxiliary of this York, SC, church.

15,593. First Presbyterian Church Woman's Auxiliary
Records. 1925-26. 1 vol.
Open. Unpublished guide.
University of South Carolina, South Caroliniana Library.
Annual report written by Mrs. Henry C. Davis, who was president of the Auxiliary of Columbia's First Presbyterian Church.

15,594. Fouché Family
Papers. 1828-1953. 1037 items.
Open. Card catalog.
University of South Carolina, South Caroliniana Library.
Personal, business, and land papers of this South Carolina planter family include papers of Sallie Fouché, which reflect a southern farm woman's managerial role during the period 1890-1920. Included are records of goods bought by Fooshe & Sample, a cash and account book of Fouché & Duckett, constitution and general laws of the Knights of the Golden Rule, and a scrapbook of clippings. Civil War correspondence of James W. Fooshe includes a letter in which Melissa A. Fooshe wrote that some slaves in her area had put poison in their owners' food. Also contains the transcript of a trial by the military vigilance police of a person who had a seditious conversation with a slave.

15,595. Fripp Family
Papers. 1887-1903. 3 vols.
Open. Card catalog.
University of South Carolina, South Caroliniana Library.
Diary of Alice Louisa Fripp, a member of this Beaufort County, SC, planter family, includes her comments on family illnesses, deaths, marriages, social and religious activities, farm operations, community events, weather, a strike by Negroes in 1897 over the price for picking cotton, the sinking of the *Maine,* and the approaching war. An account book includes prices for products, wages, and memoranda with mention of the purchase of land for hunting clubs for northerners.

15,596. Geiger, Lizzie K.
Papers. 1858-97. 61 items.
Open. Catalog card.
University of South Carolina, South Caroliniana Library.
Consists primarily of letters Geiger exchanged with W. A. Leaphart during their courtship. Includes discussion of Grange activities, Wade Hampton's successful election campaign in 1876, and the reactions of Columbia and Orangeburg County residents to his victory.

15,597. Girls of the Sixties
Records. 1864-1974. 3 vols. and 3 items.
Open. Card catalog.
University of South Carolina, South Caroliniana Library.
Certificate of incorporation, correspondence, programs, and clippings concern this women's organization, which was founded in 1921 by Mrs.

Clark Waring and [Mrs.] Anna Goodwyn Legare of Columbia to "keep in memory the heroes of the War between the States and to assist in all patriotic and benevolent works." The records, which with one exception date from 1864 to 1929, include biographical sketches and notes about men and women of the Confederacy, a membership list, and a 1974 speech by Mrs. Horace T. Jacobs to the Columbia chapter of the United Daughters of the Confederacy. Also includes clippings concerning women's rights, Confederate heroes, the League of Nations, plantation recollections, the burning of Columbia, and activities of the Girls of the Sixties, the DAR, the United Daughters of the Confederacy, and the King's Daughters.

15,598. Greenville Ladies' Association
Records. 1861-65. 3 vols.
Open. Card catalog.
University of South Carolina, South Caroliniana Library.
The Association was founded in 1861 to help Confederate soldiers. Constitution, bylaws, minutes, correspondence, membership roll, lists of articles sent to hospitals and individuals, a petition for aid from the town council, and a notation dated 1865 stating that the Association was left without means for further operation because of the work of Yankee raiders.

15,599. Greer Presbyterian Church
Records. 1901-24. 2 vols.
Open. Unpublished guide.
University of South Carolina, South Caroliniana Library.
Minutes of this Greenville County, SC, church's Ladies Aid Society and of the church's sessions.

15,600. Hammond, Bryan, and Cumming Families
Papers. 1737-1976. 44 vols. and 7636 items.
Open. Card catalog.
University of South Carolina, South Caroliniana Library.
Correspondence, diary, account books, business papers, genealogical charts, scrapbooks, and other papers of these Georgia and South Carolina families joined in 1824 by the marriage of Henry Harford Cumming of Augusta, GA, and Julia Bryan of Mount Zion, GA, and the marriage in 1859 of their daughter Emily Cumming to Harry Hammond. The antebellum correspondence is primarily between Julia Cumming and her sister Maria Bryan and between Julia and her husband; the postwar correspondence chiefly consists of letters of Harry and Emily Hammond and three of their children, Katharine, Henry, and Julia. While the correspondence reflects the Civil War, conditions during Reconstruction, politics, and European travel, the emphasis of the letters is on family matters, personal and social relationships, illnesses, and religion. Included are scattered diaries of Julia Hammond and household expense records of Emily Hammond. In 1897 Katharine Hammond married John Sedgwick Billings, son of a US Army doctor and a founder of the New York Public Library.

15,601. Hampton, Sarah "Sally" Strong (Baxter)
Papers. 1853-97. 123 items.
Open. Card catalog.
University of South Carolina, South Caroliniana Library.
Sally Hampton (1833-62), the wife of General Wade Hampton's son Frank, was a member of a Boston family who chose to stay in South Carolina when the Civil War began. Her correspondence includes her letters to her family and letters from William Makepeace Thackeray. In a December 1860 letter to her family, Hampton speaks of her position as an outsider in South Carolina and criticizes abolitionist "fanaticism which has no foundation but fancy." A letter, written a month later by her husband, tells her family of her decision to remain in the South. Also includes a letter in which Thackeray wrote the Baxter family about his reaction to the news of Hampton's death. Other correspondence provides information about plantation society, Fredrika Bremer, slavery in Cuba, Civil War sentiments, and Henry Adams's opinions about history and the McKinley administration. Adams's letters were to his sister Lucy Baxter.

15,602. Harth, Mary Y.
Papers. 1851-1905. 199 items.
Open. Card catalog.
University of South Carolina, South Caroliniana Library.
Chiefly family correspondence of [Mrs. John] Harth (?-1898) concerning hardships during the Civil War and Reconstruction and the problems of education during the period. An 1860 letter congratulates Harth because she "got so good a price for Harriette and her children"; others provide information about secessionist sentiment in Texas, Sophie Sosnowski's school in Columbia, the fears of a mother whose son might go to war, and attitudes about marriage to a divorced man.

15,603. Heyward, Janie Screven
Papers. 1923-39. 3 vols.
Open. Unpublished guide.
University of South Carolina, South Caroliniana Library.
Notebooks contain writings and clippings of Heyward and DuBose Heyward, chiefly concerning the Gullah dialect and stories.

15,604. Heyward, Mrs. Albert Rhett
Papers. 1858-85. 36 items.
Open. Unpublished guide.
University of South Carolina, South Caroliniana Library.
Sallie Coles (Green) Heyward (1849-1929), the wife of Albert Rhett Heyward, was the daughter of Mr. and Mrs. Halcott Pride Green of Edgehill Plantation near Rock Hill, SC. Her correspondence provides information about the trials of a refugee family during the Civil War and difficulties of the planter class during Reconstruction. Letters written to her parents after her marriage in 1871 concern family matters and social activities.

15,605. Holmes, Eliza Ford (Gibbes)
Papers. 1859-1926. 52 items.
Open. Catalog card.
University of South Carolina, South Caroliniana Library.
Papers of Holmes (1808-75), a housewife, chiefly consist of her letters to her children.

15,606. Hort, Mary
Papers. 1830-71. 9 vols. and 1 item.
Open. Card catalog.
University of South Carolina, South Caroliniana Library.
Journals and correspondence of [Miss] Hort (1796-?), a schoolteacher, contain references to teaching school, her religious life, social and political affairs, and the Civil War, as well as extracts from correspondence of her friends and family in England. Her journals include comments on the difficulty of teaching at a school that included Negro children in 1859, the shelling of Fort Sumter, and movement of civilians by train during the War.

15,607. Huger, Harriet H.
Papers. 1874-87. 4 vols.
Open. Unpublished guide.
University of South Carolina, South Caroliniana Library.
Journal, notebooks, and scrapbook with notes on books and original compositions.

15,608. Huger, Mary Esther
Papers. 1890-92. 1 vol.
Open. Catalog card.
University of South Carolina, South Caroliniana Library.
Journal of Huger (1820-98), a planter's wife, includes reminiscences of her youth at Longhouse near Pendleton, SC, and descriptions of plantation life, Pendleton village, and meeting Robert E. Lee at West Point in 1837.

15,609. Illiteracy Commission of South Carolina
Records. 1915-35. 1 vol., 443 items, and 1 microfilm reel.
Open. Card catalog.
University of South Carolina, South Caroliniana Library.
The Commission was formed in about 1916 to promote the campaign against illiteracy in South Carolina. Correspondence, including letters from Wil Lou Gray, Mabel Montgomery, Mrs. J. L. Coker, and Mrs. Walter E. Duncan; Commission reports; and clippings about the agency's activities.

15,610. Janney and Leaphart Family
Papers. 1859-1918. 3 vols. and 557 items.
Open. Card catalog.
University of South Carolina, South Caroliniana Library.
Family correspondence includes letters of Elizabeth Frances (McCall) [Mrs. Benjamin Franklin] Perry, Hext M. Perry, and Ellen C. Janney, who operated a school in Columbia; it provides information about such subjects as the wartime destruction of Charleston, the trial of three Anderson, SC, men accused of murdering three northerners, postwar racial relations, economic hardships during Reconstruction, unionist sentiments among southerners, a female college in Greenville, SC, Furman University, and politics. Includes an 1875 letter to Ellen C. Janney in which Belle Boyd, a Confederate spy, was described as "passable in a large crowd (where she could not be seen)" and an 1895 letter in which Benjamin F. Perry Leaphart, who was in Saratoga Springs, NY, to attend the races, commented that he was disgusted with the familiarity between whites and blacks.

15,611. Jester, Annie Perry
Papers. 1896-1966. 129 items.
Open. Card catalog.
University of South Carolina, South Caroliniana Library.
[Mrs. J. R.] Jester (?-1970), who then was Annie Perry, attended Winthrop Normal and Industrial College in 1896 and 1897. Correspondence, including letters she wrote to her family about student life at the College and her visit to the state fair in 1896; programs; clippings regarding activities of the David Bancroft Johnson Chapter of the Winthrop Alumnae Association; and printed material.

15,612. Keith, Frances G. Gibbes
Papers. 1860-1946. 211 items.
Open. Card catalog.
University of South Carolina, South Caroliniana Library.
Keith (1880-1948) was a playwright and poet. Correspondence regarding her literary career and copies of her works, including *Dawn in Carolina, The Strange Woman,* and *Weapons,* all three-act plays, and *Lucy,* an autobiographical novel.

15,613. Keitt, Suzanne Mandeville Sparks
Papers. 1877-80. 89 items.
Open. Card catalog.
University of South Carolina, South Caroliniana Library.
[Mrs. Lawrence Massillon] Keitt (1834-1915) was a plantation manager. Papers consist chiefly of letters to William Andrew Carrigan, a merchant and cotton factor, regarding her efforts to pay debts

and retain her father's plantations. One of Keitt's letters states that she had worked hard and that she required certain privileges "whereby I will be enable[d] to do business with the advantages of a man."

15,614. Liberty Chapel Methodist Church
Records. 1867-97. 3 vols.
Open. Card catalog.
University of South Carolina, South Caroliniana Library.
Minutes and register of the Liberty Chapel Methodist Church of the Florence Circuit. Also includes the Church's Sunday school records, which contain names of classes, pupils, teachers, and officers.

15,615. Lynchburg Methodist Episcopal Church
Records. 1855-1938. 1 vol.
Open. Card catalog.
University of South Carolina, South Caroliniana Library.
Records of this Lee County, SC, church.

15,616. McAfee, John T.
Papers. 1867-68. 116 items.
Open. Card catalog.
University of South Carolina, South Caroliniana Library.
Correspondence, bills, receipts, promissory notes, and other business papers of McAfee (1830-79), a planter and businessman. Includes correspondence in which he advises his former wife Hannah Douglass McAfee about her property rights should she remarry, congratulates her on her new marriage, and requests payment of a note. Also includes biographical letters.

15,617. McAliley, Mary
Papers. 1848-1901. 49 items.
Open. Card catalog.
University of South Carolina, South Caroliniana Library.
Correspondence and personal memorabilia of [Mrs. Samuel L.] McAliley (1848-1901), a housewife and educator. Includes letters from school friends and items with discussion of work for the legislature in the 1850s. Also includes a letter from Sophie Reynolds regarding her marriage and life in Illinois. McAliley was involved with the South Carolina Female Collegiate Institute.

15,618. McBee, William Pinckney
Papers. 1819-1937. 105 items.
Open. Card catalog.
University of South Carolina, South Caroliniana Library.
Family correspondence of McBee, an engineer, includes a receipt for the sale of a Negro to his wife Harriet McBee and letters to Harriet McBee about conditions at engineers' camps in Newberry County, SC.

15,619. McBryde, Thomas Livingston
Papers. 1817-63. 2 items.
Open. Card catalog.
University of South Carolina, South Caroliniana Library.
McBryde (1817-63) was a missionary and the husband of Sarah C. McBryde. Correspondence includes a letter from Sarah B. Beck, which provides news of the Presbyterian Seminary in Columbia, South Carolina College, and various friends.

15,620. McCants Family
Papers. 1912-43. 10 items.
Open. Card catalog.
University of South Carolina, South Caroliniana Library.
Genealogical information compiled in connection with Buena Vista McCants Dixon's application for DAR membership.

15,621. McCrady Family
Papers. 1821-1907. 6 vols. and 199 items.
Open. Card catalog.
University of South Carolina, South Caroliniana Library.
Correspondence and account books of the family of Edward McCrady, Sr., an historian, and his wife Louisa Rebecca (Lane) McCrady, including letters from E. M. McCrady, Jr., to his wife Mary Fraser Davie McCrady, his mother, and others. The correspondence contains references to the Episcopal church, South Carolina politics, and food and prices during the Civil War.

15,622. McCrary, Robert
Papers. 1966. 1 vol.
Open. Card catalog.
University of South Carolina, South Caroliniana Library.
Genealogy compiled by Harriet Dickson Reynolds contains information dating from 1732 to 1804 concerning the McCrary, Collins, Culpepper, Edwards, and Morris families.

15,623. McCullough, Rosanna
Papers. 1832. 1 vol.
Open. Card catalog.
University of South Carolina, South Caroliniana Library.
A volume of arithmetic and poetry that McCullough, a student, compiled under the direction of George Smith, schoolmaster at Fishing Creek Church.

15,624. McDavid, Mrs. P. A.
Papers. 1905. 1 item.
Open. Card catalog.
University of South Carolina, South Caroliniana Library.
Recollections by McDavid of her experiences during the Civil War.

15,625. McDonald, Marie
Papers. 1898-1901. 1 vol.
Open. Card catalog.
University of South Carolina, South Caroliniana Library.
McDonald's diary includes entries regarding a trip to New York, life in Charleston, and some poetry.

15,626. McDowell, Davison
Papers. 1783-1966. 2 vols. and 59 items.
Open. Card catalog.
University of South Carolina, South Caroliniana Library.
Correspondence, journal excerpts, account books, a family history, obituaries, and other papers of McDowell (1784-1842), a planter and businessman. Includes correspondence he wrote his friend Agnes Kirkpatrick in Stateburg, SC, about his plans to bring her a piano, the indentures of Agnes Stitt, and conditions and clothing of Negroes. A family history, compiled by Mary James Richards in 1966, is also included.

15,627. McDowell, Sue
Papers. 1861. 1 vol.
Open. Card catalog.
University of South Carolina, South Caroliniana Library.
Private journal of McDowell includes her comments about social activities, secession, Fort Sumter, and the Kirkwood Rangers.

15,628. McDuffie, George
Papers. 1841. No size given.
Open. Card catalog.
University of South Carolina, South Caroliniana Library.
McDuffie (1790-1851) was a planter. His correspondence includes discussion of Mary McDuffie's education and a note that a check for 150 pounds was spent "to pay the half yearly advance for Mary's education."

15,629. McElhenney, Ada A.
Papers. 1841-64. 140 items.
Open. Card catalog.
University of South Carolina, South Caroliniana Library.
McElhenney (1836-74), a South Carolina businesswoman, later became Ada Clare. Correspondence and accounts from Charleston, New York, and Paris consist chiefly of business correspondence with Edward McCrady and Clarence Mitchell reflecting Ada McElhenney's business affairs and changing marital status. A letter to Mitchell states that she had assumed the name Ada Clare and that all transactions made under that name would be as valid as those under Ada McElhenney.

15,630. McIver, John J.
Papers. 1866. 1 item.
Open. Card catalog.
University of South Carolina, South Caroliniana Library.
Agreement signed in Darlington District, SC, between McIver and freedmen and women, as well as a list of subscribers.

15,631. McIver, Sarah Witherspoon Ervin
Papers. 1854-89. 1 vol.
Open. Card catalog.
University of South Carolina, South Caroliniana Library.
McIver (1826-97) was a planter's wife and churchwoman. Her diary includes remarks on family activities and plantation management at High Hill Creek, with special references to Black Creek Church, ministers, books read, children's education, earthquakes in 1886, the trustees of South Carolina College, and political remarks about the Civil War.

15,632. McKendree Methodist Episcopal Church
Records. 1852-90. 1 vol.
Open. Card catalog.
University of South Carolina, South Caroliniana Library.
Minutes of this church; a record of baptisms, marriages, and deaths; a membership list; and a list of the preachers in the Edgefield Circuit from 1820 to 1883.

15,633. MacKenzie Family
Papers. 1831-1945. 478 items.
Open. Card catalog.
University of South Carolina, South Caroliniana Library.
Correspondence, accounts, and estate records of this South Carolina family. Includes letters to Jemima MacKenzie and Elizabeth MacKenzie from friends and relatives in Scotland and letters in which Catherine Heriot laments to Louisa Heriot the death of a daughter in childbirth and warns that "the weight of petticoats worn round her waist would injure her frame internally." Catherine Heriot also inquires about Louisa Heriot's studies and urges her as a Southern girl to become a teacher. Also includes discussion of a girl's trip to Edinburgh for schooling, fear of Negroes, and the sale of a Negro woman declared physically unsound.

15,634. McKissick, James Rion
Papers. 1850-1944. 1903 items.
Open. Card catalog.
University of South Carolina, South Caroliniana Library.
Correspondence and miscellaneous papers of McKissick (1884-1944), an editor and publisher, educator, minister, and lawyer, include extensive correspondence with his mother and sister about such subjects as gifts, politics, the burning of Charleston, SC, the nature of education, the Palmetto Association, ministers, congressional elections, events in South Carolina cities, efforts to

control public drinking, secession, the need for clothing and food in the South, hospital facilities, and experiences with slaves and the Ku Klux Klan.

15,635. McLaurin, Catherine Louisa
Papers. 1859-75. 1 vol. and 1 item.
Open. Card catalog.
University of South Carolina, South Caroliniana Library.
Occasional diary of McLaurin, a well-educated plantation woman, includes her account of activities at Argyle Plantation and Harmony College, as well as poetry, lists of books read, professions of religious faith, and comments on such current events as Lincoln's election, South Carolina's secession convention, Negro vandalism in 1861, and the effects of the War on southerners and the North's laboring classes. Also includes her account of experiences during General Robert Potter's raid.

15,636. McLean Family and McLean, Ann
Papers. 1844-79. 30 items.
Open. Card catalog.
University of South Carolina, South Caroliniana Library.
Correspondence includes letters from Ann McLean describing conditions in the North, letters of consolation concerning her husband's death, and receipts for payment for female slaves. A letter to Hugh McLean asks that he purchase two Negro girls of a particular description for J. D. Gray.

15,637. McMaster, Fitz William, and McMaster, Mary Jane (Macfie)
Papers. 1811-1929. 1683 items.
Open. Card index.
University of South Carolina, South Caroliniana Library.
McMaster (1826-99) was an editor, businessman, and teacher; his wife Mary McMaster (1832-98) studied at South Carolina Female Collegiate Institute at Barhamville. Business and personal correspondence and legal papers include correspondence concerning agreements to purchase property from women, Macfie's school compositions, and records of the sale of Negroes.

15,638. McMaster, Helen G.
Papers. 1878-82. 1 vol.
Open. Card catalog.
University of South Carolina, South Caroliniana Library.
Poetry written in Columbia.

15,639. Magrath, Selina E. Bollin
Papers. 1929-33. 1 vol.
Open. Card index.
University of South Carolina, South Caroliniana Library.
Manuscripts include Magrath's narrative about the burning of the Ursuline Convent in 1865. The narrative, which was told to Magrath's daughter, describes life at the convent and tells of the girls who attended school there.

15,640. Mairs, Jane B.
Papers. 1874-89. 1 vol.
Open. Card catalog.
University of South Carolina, South Caroliniana Library.
Journal of Mairs, a Laurens County, SC, resident, records births, deaths, marriages, and visits made and received.

15,641. Marion, Esther
Papers. 1816. 1 item.
Open. Card catalog.
University of South Carolina, South Caroliniana Library.
Inventory and appraisal of the estate of Marion (?-1815) includes a list of claims by Francis Marion.

15,642. Mars Bluff Methodist Episcopal Church, Women's Missionary Society
Records. 1890-1915. 1 vol.
Open. Card catalog.
University of South Carolina, South Caroliniana Library.
Records of members, collections, and expenditures of the Women's Missionary Society of the Mars Bluff Methodist Episcopal Church in the Florence District. From 1908 to 1915 the Society was known as the Women's Foreign Missionary Society.

15,643. Marshall, Nancy
Papers. 1898-1909. 1 vol.
Open. Card catalog.
University of South Carolina, South Caroliniana Library.
Diary of Marshall, a student, includes a record of women she met at the Woman's College in Richmond, VA, and Greenville Female College at Greenville, SC.

15,644. Martin, Isabella Donaldson
Papers. 1876-89. 2 items.
Open. Card index.
University of South Carolina, South Caroliniana Library.
Martin (1839-1913) was a teacher. Roll of pupils and prospectus for her Columbia High School for Young Ladies and Little Girls, which was known as Miss Isabella's School.

15,645. Martin, Peter
Papers. 1795. 2 items.
Open. Card index.
University of South Carolina, South Caroliniana Library.
Deed and renunciation of dower for a lot in St. Michael's Parish in Charleston, SC.

15,646. Massey Family
Papers. 1788-1805. 3 items.
Open. Card catalog.
University of South Carolina, South Caroliniana Library.
Document in which Elizabeth Massey of Lancaster District, SC, conveys to James Massey 100 acres on the east side of the Catawba River.

15,647. Mathews, Ann
Papers. 1753-1902. 1 item.
Open. Card catalog.
University of South Carolina, South Caroliniana Library.
Memoir of Mathews (1753-1830) includes a sketch about the Caldwell family and information about Major Andrew Hamilton.

15,648. Mattison, Lina Wakefield
Papers. 1904-62. 1 vol.
Open. Card catalog.
University of South Carolina, South Caroliniana Library.
Scrapbook of Mattison concerns activities at the College for Women in Columbia and includes pictures of buildings and grounds, programs for social and dramatic events, a pamphlet for an arts and crafts exhibition in 1908 that contains biographical information on the artists, clippings, and information regarding organization of the alumnae.

15,649. Maverick and Van Wyck Families
Papers. 1772-1926. 200 items.
Open. Card catalog.
University of South Carolina, South Caroliniana Library.
Correspondence, reminiscences, land and genealogical records, and other papers of these families include correspondence from Oze Robert Broyles to his daughter Margaret Caroline Broyles concerning arrangements for her return from Miss Bates' School in Charleston, SC, in ca. 1852 and his objections to her becoming a teacher, because it would "make you the slave of a haughty community. . . ." Also includes a letter from Margaret C. (Broyles) Van Wyck in Washington, DC, to her mother describing the discomforts of travel and the mortification of having to ask her husband for money. Reminiscences of Sarah Broyles Williams are included as well.

15,650. Mazyck Family
Papers. 1748-1889. 97 items.
Open. Card catalog.
University of South Carolina, South Caroliniana Library.
Business papers, stock certificates, receipts, and invitations of William, Stephen, and Edmund Mazyck and of Elizabeth Porcher Mazyck, members of this South Carolina family.

15,651. Mazyck, Sarah Livingston
Papers. 1944. 1 item.
Open. Card catalog.
University of South Carolina, South Caroliniana Library.
Mazyck's manuscript "Some Memories of Our War" describes experiences of her family during the Civil War.

15,652. Means, Mary Hart
Papers. 1846-1911. 213 items.
Open. Card catalog.
University of South Carolina, South Caroliniana Library.
Means (1835-1916) was the daughter of Edward and Claudia Hart Means of South Carolina. Civil War and family correspondence and other papers include information about education and about the economic, social, and religious activities of the related Coalter, Davis, Bates, Means, and Poelnitz families.

15,653. Mellichamp, Saintlo
Papers. 1817. 1 item.
Open. Card catalog.
University of South Carolina, South Caroliniana Library.
Indenture between Saintlo Mellichamp, Sr., and Thomas Mellichamp, by means of which Thomas Mellichamp or his executors assume responsibility for emancipating the slave Maria and her four children.

15,654. Methodist Church, Winnsboro Circuit Missionary Society
Records. 1840-54. 1 vol.
Open. Card catalog.
University of South Carolina, South Caroliniana Library.
Records of the Society which held its meetings at the Mount Pleasant and New Hope churches and at the Mount Pleasant, Armenia, and Mount Prospect campgrounds. Also includes notes on sermons preached by Paul A. M. Williams.

15,655. Methodist Episcopal Church, Lynch's Creek Circuit
Records. 1787-1897. 1 vol.
Open. Card catalog.
University of South Carolina, South Caroliniana Library.
Records of this group of Darlington County, SC, churches.

15,656. Middleton Family
Papers. 1789-1921. 811 items.
Open. Card catalog.
University of South Carolina, South Caroliniana Library.
Family correspondence of Anne Manigault Middleton (1820-76), Alicia Hopton (Russell) [Mrs. Arthur] Middleton (?-1840), Maria Louisa Middleton (1844-?), Anna Elizabeth (De Wolf) Middleton (1815-?), Charlotte Middleton (1854-?), Edwardina "Edda" de Norman Middleton, and

Elizabeth Middleton (?-1784). Includes comments on business conditions, social life, and conditions following earthquakes in Charleston. Contains an 1817 letter in which Alicia Middleton chides her son Nathaniel in Bristol, RI, for not writing and calls his attention to the importance of social graces.

15,657. Middleton, Mrs. Arthur
Papers. 1835. 1 vol.
Open. Card catalog.
University of South Carolina, South Caroliniana Library.
Diary of Alicia Hopton (Russell) Middleton (?-1840) contains her record of a voyage from Charleston to Europe. Accompanied by her children Anne Manigault Middleton and Ralph Izard Middleton, Alicia Middleton traveled to Rouen, Nantes, Paris, Dijon, and Geneva. She speaks of South Carolinians she met in Europe and of reading Fannie Kemble's journal.

15,658. Middleton, Williams
Papers. 1847-88. 154 items.
Open. Card catalog.
University of South Carolina, South Caroliniana Library.
Family correspondence of Middleton (1809-83), a rice planter, and his wife Susan Middleton (?-1900) includes letters Middleton wrote to his wife describing his activities and those of his Negro crew in sandbagging military installations around Charleston harbor, letters from Middleton's overseer regarding operation of his plantation, and letters concerning various estates. The correspondence contains information about other family members, including Edda Middleton who was said to be living "scandalously" in New York. Also includes information about deaths and illnesses of slaves, insubordination of Negroes in South Carolina's low country, and Civil War conditions.

15,659. Miller, Eunice
Papers. 1900-05. 1 item.
Open. Card catalog.
University of South Carolina, South Caroliniana Library.
Recollections of Miller (1883-), who married E. Morgan Bailey, concerning her youth around Ellenton, SC, and her experiences as a student at South Carolina Coeducational Institute in Edgefield. Includes a list of Institute students and teachers for 1900 to 1901.

15,660. Millican, Arthenia Bates
Papers. 1976. 4 vols.
Open. Card catalog.
University of South Carolina, South Caroliniana Library.
Unpublished manuscripts by Millican, a writer, include drafts of "Where You Belong," which won the National Endowment of the Arts Award in 1976; "Journey to Somewhere," a novella; and "The Bottoms and Hills: Virginia Tales," a book of short stories, two of which have been published as "Homesick" and "Good Grazin."

15,661. Napier, Thomas
Papers. 1803-1947. 261 items.
Open. Card index.
University of South Carolina, South Caroliniana Library.
Correspondence and account records of Napier (1777-1860), a resident of Charleston. Letters from Napier to his daughter Rebecca concern her schooling. In letters to her father she relates her religious thoughts and activities, mentions several ministers, and requests golden spectacles. In 1856 a power of attorney was granted to Thomas Napier's wife Rebecca Napier to act as trustee for the estate of Revolutionary War soldier Simeon Theus. Other letters contain discussions of family illnesses, including yellow fever.

15,662. Neely, Jane E.
Papers. 1850-54. 1 vol.
Open. Card catalog.
University of South Carolina, South Caroliniana Library.
Journal of Neely concerns her life as a student at South Carolina Female Collegiate Institute in Barhamville, SC. Includes a list of the class of 1852.

15,663. Nelson, Annie Green
Papers. 1976. 1 vol.
Open. Unpublished guide.
University of South Carolina, South Caroliniana Library.
Unpublished typescript by Nelson, a writer, of "Letters to Paw with Love, An Autobiography."

15,664. New Century Club, Columbia
Records. 1901-56. 9 vols. and 2 items.
Open. Card index.
University of South Carolina, South Caroliniana Library.
The Club, which existed from 1901 to 1956, described its goal as "intellectual advancement and social development." Constitution, minutes, yearbooks, magazines, *Woman's Manual of Parliamentary Law*, and other records.

15,665. Noble Family
Papers. 1761-1879. 96 items.
Partially restricted. Card index.
University of South Carolina, South Caroliniana Library.
Correspondence and other papers of this planter and military family include letters of Elizabeth Noble Simons, the writ of petition for the marriage settlement of Kezia Ann Miles Pickens, and a scrapbook kept during the early 1800s by Eugenia Floride Noble. The scrapbook contains family records and statistics.

15,666. Norton, Cordelia
Papers. 1831. 1 item.
Open. Card index.
University of South Carolina, South Caroliniana Library.
Letter by Norton to her husband in Charleston, SC, contains family and community news, including descriptions of a local religious revival. She suggests that her husband leave Charleston and join her.

15,667. Pack Family
Papers. Nd. 1 item.
Open. Unpublished guide.
University of South Carolina, South Caroliniana Library.
Manuscript includes descriptions of Civil War and Reconstruction experiences of Eliza Walker Pack of Clarendon County, SC.

15,668. Palmer, Hattie Amelia
Papers. 1849-50. 1 vol.
Open. Unpublished guide.
University of South Carolina, South Caroliniana Library.
Poetry.

15,669. Parker, Henry Middleton, Jr.
Papers. 1859-1943. 66 items.
Open. Unpublished guide.
University of South Carolina, South Caroliniana Library.
Papers of Parker (1854-1926) consist chiefly of correspondence with his mother Marianna Rhett Parker about his experiences as a lay missionary in Africa.

15,670. Pendleton Female Academy, Anderson County, SC
Records. 1827-1904. 1 vol. and 196 items.
Open. Unpublished guide.
University of South Carolina, South Caroliniana Library.
Academy records principally consist of business papers, such as bills and receipts for supplies purchased, advertising in newspapers, and building repairs; teachers' reports that include the number of pupils and financial statements; applications for and resignations from teaching positions; and announcements by trustees listing teachers, courses of study, and tuition charges. A leaflet dated 1838 announces that Mary Bates, daughter of the president of Middlebury College in Vermont, was to be the Academy's principal, while her sister Ann Bates and [Miss] Laura Billings were to be her assistants.

15,671. Perry, Benjamin Franklin
Papers. 1760-1910. 98 items.
Open. Card catalog.
University of South Carolina, South Caroliniana Library.
Correspondence and legal papers of Perry (1805-86), a lawyer and legislator, and Elizabeth Frances (McCall) Perry, whom he married in 1837. The correspondence includes letters exchanged by the Perrys before and after their marriage, among them letters Elizabeth Perry wrote to her husband about campaign strategy and other matters while he was in Columbia for legislative sessions. She told Perry that she endured his absence for the "satisfaction it affords me to have you go to the Legislature."

15,672. Peterkin, Julia (Mood)
Papers. 1928-66. 42 items.
Open. Card catalog.
University of South Carolina, South Caroliniana Library.
Peterkin (1880-1961) was an author. Correspondence, much of it regarding her writing; a thesis about Peterkin; clippings about her life and literary work, including lists of poems, short stories, and a program for her performance in the title role of *Hedda Gabler;* and a first edition of her *Scarlet Sister Mary*. Peterkin's works also included *Green Thursday*.

15,673. Phillips Family
Papers. 1865-1916. 8 items.
Open. Unpublished guide.
University of South Carolina, South Caroliniana Library.
Land papers and reminiscences of this planter family include the Civil War reminiscences of [Mrs.] Elizabeth Phillips.

15,674. Pickens, Francis Wilkinson
Papers. 1834-1929. 108 items.
Open. Card catalog.
University of South Carolina, South Caroliniana Library.
Papers, chiefly correspondence, of Pickens (1805-69), a statesman, and his wife Lucy Petway (Holcombe) Pickens (1832-99) contain letters that Francis Pickens wrote in 1857 to Beverly Holcombe in Marshall, TX, announcing that Lucy had accepted his marriage proposal and letters that Lucy Pickens wrote from St. Petersburg in 1859 and 1860 while her husband was a diplomat in Russia. Also contains family correspondence, a notebook, business records, and other material, including an article entitled "Only Texas Girl Ever Pictured on Money" concerning Lucy and Francis Pickens and the Confederate $100 bill.

15,675. Pinckney, Charles Cotesworth, Jr.
Papers. 1860-69. 83 items.
Open. Card catalog.
University of South Carolina, South Caroliniana Library.
Papers of Pinckney (1839-1909), the son of a clergyman, consist chiefly of correspondence, much of it written to him while he was a student in Bonn. Includes letters from his mother Anne

Randolph McKenna Pinckney, grandmother Phoebe Caroline Pinckney, sisters Caroline and Mary Pinckney, and other relatives.

15,676. Pinckney, Elizabeth "Eliza" (Lucas)
Papers. 1773-83. 3 items.
Open. Card catalog.
University of South Carolina, South Caroliniana Library.
Correspondence of [Mrs. Charles] Pinckney (1722-93) includes letters to her children and others, with a mention of Rebecca Doyley's wedding and Pinckney's sympathy for the bride who was "not quite fourteen." Also includes comments about the selling of slaves.

15,677. Pinckney, Elizabeth Izard
Papers. 1859-60. Nd. 3 items.
Open. Card catalog.
University of South Carolina, South Caroliniana Library.
Correspondence of Pinckney (1784-1862), a planter, includes a letter in which she discusses her plan to bequeath her property to her daughters in the form of cash "so that there might be no money, or any other transactions between the Sisters." Also includes a letter in which she comments on Civil War events.

15,678. Pinckney, Harriott
Papers. 1854-61. 26 items.
Open. Card catalog.
University of South Carolina, South Caroliniana Library.
Pinckney (1776-1866) was a South Carolina planter. Correspondence, much of it with William Winningham regarding the operation of her Pinckney Island plantation; accounts; a list of clothing issued to the Negroes; comments on the cost of medical care and the ability of the drivers; and an account of the Pinckney family.

15,679. Pinckney, Josephine
Papers. 1931. 1 item.
Open. Catalog card.
University of South Carolina, South Caroliniana Library.
A letter in which Pinckney (1895-1957), a poet, writing to Herbert P. Small in Saranac Lake, NY, thanks him for his interest in her poetry and states her belief that "poetry is primarily a matter of feeling, not intellect" and that images created by words are more important than the meaning of words.

15,680. Pinckney, Rebecca R.
Papers. 1836-50. 1 vol.
Open. Unpublished guide.
University of South Carolina, South Caroliniana Library.
Account book indicates funds received and expended for Pinckney's granddaughters, who were the children of Richard Singleton Youngblood.

15,681. Pinckney, Thomas
Papers. 1776-1835. 63 items.
Open. Card catalog.
University of South Carolina, South Caroliniana Library.
Papers of Pinckney (1750-1828), a statesman, consist chiefly of correspondence, including letters to his sister Harriott (Pinckney) Horry (1748-1830) regarding family affairs and advice on planting and the use of her son's inheritance, to [Mrs.] Eliza (Lucas) Pinckney concerning the health of her family and Negroes and a doctor's success with smallpox inoculations, to his wife concerning family matters, and other letters relating to the War of 1812, agriculture, the death of George Washington, and other subjects. Includes a 1797 letter in which Harriott Lucas Pinckney describes to Mrs. Thomas Pinckney the social events surrounding the wedding of Maria Alston and Sir John Nisbet; she also mentions a disturbance among "french" Negroes in Charleston.

15,682. Porcher and Ford Families
Papers. 1845-1925. 401 items.
Open. Card catalog.
University of South Carolina, South Caroliniana Library.
Papers of these families of planters, writers, and merchants consist chiefly of correspondence, including letters written by Jane (Petigru) North to her sister Louise (Petigru) Porcher and letters in which Arthur Peronneau Ford in Atlanta comments to his wife in Aiken, SC, on his business situation, Atlanta society, and opening a furniture store in Aiken.

15,683. Porcher, Frederick Adolphus
Papers. 1862-1922. 62 items.
Open. Card catalog.
University of South Carolina, South Caroliniana Library.
Porcher (1809-88) was a professor of history and belles lettres at the College of Charleston; his wife served as organist at a Charleston church. Correspondence written by Porcher to his wife and daughters makes up the bulk of the collection and includes comments on family affairs, the Civil War, yellow fever, city politics and radical rule, trouble with Negroes, education, the College of Charleston, and the Fort Moultrie monument.

15,684. Pratt, Elizabeth
Papers. 1834-35. 1 vol.
Open. Unpublished guide.
University of South Carolina, South Caroliniana Library.
Letters that Pratt wrote regarding her life as a student.

15,685. Preston, [Mrs.] William Campbell
Papers. 1829-46. 2 vols.
Open. Unpublished guide.
University of South Carolina, South Caroliniana Library.
Diary kept by Preston (1807-53) while she lived in Columbia. Also includes a scrapbook of poems and clippings.

15,686. Pringle, John Julius
Papers. 1779-1825. 14 items.
Open. Card catalog.
University of South Carolina, South Caroliniana Library.
Correspondence of Pringle (1753-1845), a lawyer, includes a letter in which he instructs Charles Harris of Savannah, GA, to supply [Mrs.] Ann Timothy, the state printer, with certified copies of acts approved by the legislature.

15,687. Ramsay, Martha (Laurens)
Papers. 1785. 1 item.
Open. Unpublished guide.
University of South Carolina, South Caroliniana Library.
Letter in which [Mrs. David] Ramsay (1759-1811) reports to a doctor on her sister's condition and inquires about further treatment.

15,688. Ravenel, Harriott Horry (Rutledge)
Papers. 1871-1907. 7 items.
Open. Card catalog.
University of South Carolina, South Caroliniana Library.
Correspondence of Ravenel (1832-1912), an author, contains a letter to [Mrs.] Celina Eliza Means in Columbia regarding her completion of her book *Charleston, the Place and the People,* the marriage of a daughter, and other topics.

15,689. Ravenel, John
Papers. 1815-1915. 57 items.
Open. Card catalog.
University of South Carolina, South Caroliniana Library.
Correspondence makes up the bulk of the papers of Ravenel (1793-1862) and his wife Anna Elizabeth Ravenel. Includes his letters to his wife, dated 1830 and 1831, which discuss family matters and nullification and her replies, which concern family activities and events in Morristown, NJ. Also contains a romantic story about the family which was written in 1915 by Frances Emily Ford.

15,690. Ravenel, Rose Pringle
Papers. 1895-1923. 4 items.
Open. Unpublished guide.
University of South Carolina, South Caroliniana Library.
Articles by Ravenel (1850-1943).

15,691. Read Family
Papers. 1724-1843. 309 items.
Open. Unpublished guide.
University of South Carolina, South Caroliniana Library.
Correspondence of this planter family includes letters from Catherine Read, wife of Jacob Read, to her niece Polly Clarkson and her sister Elizabeth Ludlow regarding her social life, visitors at her home, and the education of her children.

15,692. Reid, William Moultrie
Papers. 1800-1916. 2022 items.
Open. Card catalog.
University of South Carolina, South Caroliniana Library.
Correspondence of the family of Reid (1798-1884), a Presbyterian minister, and his wife Margaret (Goulding) Reid provides information about the schooling of the Reids' daughter Mollie, "infant schools" in Charleston in 1829, the Civil War, and the Confederate Home School established by [Mrs.] Mary Amarinthia Snowden. Contains letters of William Reid's sister Ann Reid and Margaret Reid's father Thomas Goulding and a letter in which Mrs. E. K. Holmes comments to her daughter at Yorkville Academy on her problems as a schoolteacher.

15,693. Reynolds, John Schreiner, Jr.
Papers. 1888-1973. 296 items.
Open. Catalog card.
University of South Carolina, South Caroliniana Library.
Correspondence of Reynolds (1887-1918), a journalist and military officer who died in WWI, consists chiefly of his letters to Emily Simms Bellinger, who was his fiancée and later his wife, and letters of condolence written after his death. Includes material regarding Emily Reynolds' trip to France in 1932 as part of a government tour for Gold Star mothers and widows and information concerning the career of their daughter Joan (Reynolds) Faunt.

15,694. Richards, Julia Hammond
Papers. 1877-1935. 9 vols.
Open. Unpublished guide.
University of South Carolina, South Caroliniana Library.
Diaries and accounts of Richards (1860-1935), a planter, contain a record of her daily activities at Redcliffe Plantation; Beech Island, SC; and Augusta, GA. Also includes account books in which she listed sales of Redcliffe garden produce, grain, eggs, milk, and meat.

15,695. Richardson, John Smythe
Papers. 1845-90. 2338 items.
Open. Unpublished guide.
University of South Carolina, South Caroliniana Library.
Richardson (1828-94) was a newspaper editor, lawyer, Confederate soldier, South Carolina planter and legislator, and US congressman; his wife was Agnes Davison (McDowell) Richardson, the

daughter of a Georgetown District, SC, rice planter. Correspondence, diaries, legal notes, papers relating to John Richardson's service during the Civil War, and other items. Contains Agnes Richardson's correspondence with her family; letters she wrote to publishers, chiefly of Presbyterian magazines; a diary she kept during a trip to New York and Niagara Falls in 1859; and papers of her father Davison McDowell.

15,696. Ridley, Anna, and Ridley, Bettie
Papers. 1863-1963. 5 items.
Open. Card catalog.
University of South Carolina, South Caroliniana Library.
Anna Ridley (1849-1924) and Bettie Ridley (1846-1924) were sisters who were students at the Ursuline Convent in Columbia during 1863 and 1864. Their correspondence to their mother Mrs. Francis T. Ridley of Drewryville, VA, includes discussions of their schoolwork and activities, honors they received, and clothes they needed for special occasions. The two also describe Virginia soldiers who passed their school, the collection of $100 by the Convent girls for food for the soldiers, and their reaction to a Yankee raid in Virginia. Also includes a 1963 letter containing information about the Ridley family.

15,697. Rister Family
Papers. 1880-1909. 32 items.
Open. Unpublished guide.
University of South Carolina, South Caroliniana Library.
Correspondence in which Carolina Ward writes Martha Rister about family members who were in Canada and comments on crops, livestock, and prices.

15,698. Robertson, Alexander
Papers. 1863-65. 10 items.
Open. Card catalog.
University of South Carolina, South Caroliniana Library.
Correspondence of Robertson includes his letters to Mrs. M. A. Petigru of Abbeville District, SC, concerning his management of her business affairs. One letter concerns interest paid by Governor Robert F. W. Allston on a bond due to Petigru.

15,699. Robinson, Emmett E.
Papers. 1947-68. 4 vols.
Open. Catalog card.
University of South Carolina, South Caroliniana Library.
Plays of Robinson (1914-), an author, include *Dr. Jekyll and Mr. Hyde, A Christmas Carol, The Recruiting Officer,* and *Christmas Gift,* which he co-authored with his wife Patricia Colbert Robinson.

15,700. Robinson, Patricia Colbert
Papers. 1953-74. 7 vols.
Open. Catalog card.
University of South Carolina, South Caroliniana Library.
Plays by Robinson (1923-), an author, include *The Burning Tide; Jubalee; Hiddy-doddy; Syllabub; Sand Sprite,* which she wrote with Selma Tharin Furtwangler; and *Held in Splendor,* which she co-authored with Katherine Drayton Mayrant Simons.

15,701. Ronan, Henrietta
Papers. 1859. 1 item.
Open. Catalog card.
University of South Carolina, South Caroliniana Library.
Certificate issued to Ronan by the city schools female department to mark her good conduct, regular attendance, and academic proficiency.

15,702. Rose, Julia Rutledge
Papers. 1819-47. 7 items.
Open. Card catalog.
University of South Carolina, South Caroliniana Library.
Correspondence of Rose (?-1873) consists chiefly of family letters, among them letters from her husband James Rose discussing their son's encampment at West Point, NY, and their planned meeting in New York City.

15,703. Rutledge, Edward
Papers. 1789-1808. 55 items.
Open. Card catalog.
University of South Carolina, South Caroliniana Library.
Correspondence of Rutledge (1749-1800) includes a letter to Mrs. Nathanael Greene in which he discusses her financial situation and plans to persuade Congress to help her. He also mentions her intentions to introduce him to General George Washington and his wife. Also includes a letter that Rutledge wrote from Charleston, SC, to [Miss] Sarah Rutledge admonishing her to take advantage of opportunities for self-improvement.

15,704. St. John's Evangelical Lutheran Church, Ladies Aid Society
Records. 1888. 1 item.
Open. Unpublished guide.
University of South Carolina, South Caroliniana Library.
Sketch by Johanna Klinke concerning the history of the Society, which was founded in 1878.

15,705. St. Vincent's Female Orphan Society
Records. 1871-73. 3 items.
Open. Unpublished guide.
University of South Carolina, South Caroliniana Library.
Annual reports list officers, collectors, and those who contributed funds for care of Catholic orphans in the Charleston, SC, diocese.

15,706. Salley, Eulalie Chafee
Papers. 1914-22. 850 items.
Open. Card catalog.
University of South Carolina, South Caroliniana Library.
Correspondence and clippings of [Mrs. Julian B.] Salley (1883-1975), a realtor, concern her work as a leader in the South Carolina woman suffrage movement and the unsuccessful campaign in 1920 to win the state legislature's approval of the 19th Amendment. Includes letters from Anna Howard Shaw, [Mrs.] Carrie Chapman Catt, [Mrs.] Emma Anderson Dunnovant, Edna (Fischel) Gellhorn, Maud (Wood) Park, [Miss] Wil Lou Gray, and others which chronicle the women's efforts and their frustration at their defeat. The women held citizenship schools around the state in 1920 and prepared to celebrate the Amendment's ultimate victory. Salley organized the Aiken County Equal Suffrage League in 1916 and served as auditor, second vice-president, and president of the South Carolina Equal Suffrage Association. Salley later became a regional director of the LWV.

15,707. Sams Family
Papers. 1784-1934. 4257 items.
Open. Description.
University of South Carolina, South Caroliniana Library.
Correspondence and other papers of four generations of this South Carolina family, which acquired extensive plantation holdings during the antebellum period, saw its wealth diminished during the Civil War and Reconstruction, and later rebuilt its fortunes. The bulk of the collection consists of correspondence of Miles Brewton Sams (1811-94), who abandoned the study of medicine because of ill health and managed his father's plantation; Caroline "Carrie" Oswald Sams (1820-98), whom he married in 1837; and their six sons and four daughters, nine of whom lived to maturity. Of the daughters, Anna, Addie, and Carrie married, while the eldest Emmy remained with her parents and managed the family after her mother's death. The papers reflect the work of the eldest son Lewis "Luter," who apparently decided not to marry, amassed considerable land and business holdings, and bequeathed his money to the family. The letters reflect the family's anxiety when he died in 1892 without joining the church. The correspondence also speaks of the illnesses of other family members, their interest in education, and their religious beliefs as well as of the 1886 earthquake in South Carolina, the Spanish-American War, WWI, and the influenza epidemic of 1918.

15,708. Sams, Sarah Jane
Papers. 1865. 1 item.
Open. Unpublished guide.
University of South Carolina, South Caroliniana Library.
A letter in journal form that Sams (1835-1920) wrote to her husband relating her experiences during the Federal occupation of Barnwell, SC, and hardships resulting from fire and theft.

15,709. Sanders, Claudia Thomas
Papers. 1957-74. 5 items.
Open. Card catalog.
University of South Carolina, South Caroliniana Library.
The South Carolina home of Sanders and her husband James H. Sanders was bombed in 1957. Correspondence, published statement, and clippings relate to the bombing, which followed her statement in "South Carolinians Speak," published in *The Presbyterian Outlook.*

15,710. Screven, Edwards, Clarkson, and Heriot Families
Papers. 1794-1939. 65 items.
Open. Card catalog.
University of South Carolina, South Caroliniana Library.
Correspondence, including that of Sarah "Sallie" Screven Edwards and S. S. Edwards, and genealogical material.

15,711. Seabrook Family
Papers. 1838-1950. 678 items.
Open. Card catalog.
University of South Carolina, South Caroliniana Library.
Correspondence makes up the bulk of the papers of this South Carolina family and provides information about antebellum planter society, relationships among family members, the Civil War, society affairs during Reconstruction, governesses, and postwar relations between the family and its former slaves. Contains letters of C. Pinckney Seabrook at the University of Virginia, family letters regarding his death during the Civil War, and an 1897 letter in which Caroline Pinckney Mitchell sent Mary Seabrook her sympathy following a fire that destroyed the Seabrook home, Eldorado.

15,712. Shackelford, Sara C.
Papers. 1816. 1 item.
Open. Catalog card.
University of South Carolina, South Caroliniana Library.
A letter to [Mrs.] Mary Lupton Butler in Santee, SC, in which Shackelford requests that the Butlers send a cart for the Negroes, so that planting can begin.

15,713. Shaftsbury, Anthony Ashley Cooper, 1st Earl of
Papers. 1670-75. 2 items.
Open. Catalog card.

University of South Carolina, South Caroliniana Library.
Papers include a deed through which Shaftsbury (1621-83) received land from the Cusabo Indians for cloth, hatchets, and other goods. The deed bore the seals of four chiefs, 11 war captains, and 14 women captains.

15,714. Shand, Louly
Papers. 1874-1950. 2 vols.
Open. Catalog card.
University of South Carolina, South Caroliniana Library.
Scrapbooks of Shand (1870-1961), a schoolteacher, chiefly contain clippings of children's poems and articles and pictures regarding literary and theatrical figures, Civil War leaders, and the burning of Columbia. Also included are obituaries of family members and friends, charts showing the growth of the family's children from 1874 to 1876, and an album regarding children who attended her kindergarten from 1901 to 1950.

15,715. Shand, Mary Wright
Papers. 1894-1902. 1 vol.
Open. Catalog card.
University of South Carolina, South Caroliniana Library.
Scrapbook of Shand (1876-1953) contains a letter in which Wade Hampton appointed her sponsor of the Army of Northern Virginia Department at the 11th annual reunion of the United Confederate Veterans in Memphis, copies of poems, clippings, and other items.

15,716. Shinner, Charles
Papers. 1762-67. 5 items.
Open. Card catalog.
University of South Carolina, South Caroliniana Library.
Papers include writs of attachment against Mary Grange for debts due Thomas Middleton, Samuel Brailsford, and John Packrow and his wife. Also includes a writ ordering William Raven to appear in court to answer Rebecca Evance's plea for payment of a debt.

15,717. Shubrick, William Branford
Papers. 1853. 1 item.
Open. Unpublished guide.
University of South Carolina, South Caroliniana Library.
Letter in which Shubrick (1790-1874) mentions to Harriet Cordelia Shubrick that their daughter planned to go to the Senate with Mrs. Hamilton Fish and the James Fenimore Coopers.

15,718. Simons Family
Papers. 1798-1874. 62 items.
Open. Card catalog.
University of South Carolina, South Caroliniana Library.
Correspondence consists chiefly of letters of James Simons's descendants, with comments on weddings, funerals, religious activities, social events, and education. Contains letters of Harriet Hyrne Simons, Sarah H. Simons, Anna Waties, Maria Simons, and others. In a letter written in Columbia in 1811, Harriet Simons tells James Simons about the scarcity of vegetables in the town's market and says that Methodists and Baptists were in the majority in the area. A letter written by Waties in 1834 in Stateburg, SC, relates that attempts to establish a neighborhood Sunday school were abandoned because there were "no poor people." Also contains genealogical information.

15,719. Simons, Jane Kealhofer
Papers. 1940-44. 1 vol.
Open. Unpublished guide.
University of South Carolina, South Caroliniana Library.
Scrapbook of [Mrs. Arthur St. Julian] Simons contains Columbia Art Association programs and clippings regarding attempts to preserve the Hampton-Preston house and gardens.

15,720. Simons, Katherine Drayton Mayrant
Papers. 1941-66. 385 items.
Open. Unpublished guide.
University of South Carolina, South Caroliniana Library.
[Miss] Simons (1892-1968) was a novelist. Correspondence, reviews, press releases, photos, and other papers include accounts of interviews with Simons and items related to her novels, among them *Courage Is Not Given, Always A River, Lamp in Jerusalem,* and *A Sword From Galway,* and collections of poetry, *Silver Unicorn* and *White Horse Leaping.* Also contains manuscripts of her plays *Golden Slipper,* which she wrote with J. Whilden Blackwell; *Bewley's Bewitched; Held in Splendor,* which she co-authored with Patricia C. Robinson; and *Overheard in Hades.*

15,721. Simons, Mrs. H. H.
Papers. 1865. 1 vol.
Open. Unpublished guide.
University of South Carolina, South Caroliniana Library.
Account of the burning of Columbia.

15,722. Singleton and Deveaux Family
Papers. 1784-1931. 137 items.
Open. Calendar and catalog card.
University of South Carolina, South Caroliniana Library.
Correspondence of these South Carolina planter families contains information about the education of the Singleton girls and Mary McDuffie in Philadelphia and social life in South Carolina. Also contains letters by Angelica Singleton (1816-77) in Richmond, VA, describing social affairs and mention of a visit to the Singletons in 1842 by Martin Van Buren and James Kirk Paulding.

15,723. Singleton Family
Papers. 1750-1956. 732 items.
Open. Unpublished guide.
University of South Carolina, South Caroliniana Library.
Papers of Richard Singleton (1776-1852) and other members of this Sumter County, SC, family consist chiefly of material concerning horse breeding, cotton marketing, and land sales. Included are a few letters of Angelica Singleton (1816-77), who married President Martin Van Buren's eldest son Abram in 1838; Margaret Martin, a Columbia schoolmistress; and other women. Margaret Martin's letter to her husband William concerns her monotonous life and the need for improved school facilities. Nine letters of Angelica Van Buren tell of family matters and travel in Europe in 1854. Also contains genealogical information.

15,724. Smith, Annie Brunson
Papers. 1874-95. 1 vol.
Open. Unpublished guide.
University of South Carolina, South Caroliniana Library.
Diary and scrapbook from Charleston, SC.

15,725. Smith, Joseph P.
Papers. 1877. 1 item.
Open. Catalog card.
University of South Carolina, South Caroliniana Library.
Letter in which Smith explains to Edwards Pierrepont in London that his mother and sisters have been traveling in Europe for three years and have just arrived in London. He asks whether he may give Pierrepont their addresses so they could attend a reception for General and Mrs. U. S. Grant.

15,726. Smythe, Louisa McCord
Papers. 1928. 1 vol.
Open. Catalog card.
University of South Carolina, South Caroliniana Library.
Recollections of Smythe (1845-1928) include reminiscences about her life at Pendleton, Columbia, Charleston, and Lang Syne in South Carolina with anecdotes about the servants and comments on professors at the South Carolina College; summers at Naragansett, RI, and other resorts; a trip to Europe; secession; Civil War and women's aid; the burning of Columbia and its aftermath; her wedding; and Reconstruction. Also contains information about the Hayne, Cheves, Adger, and McCord families.

15,727. Snowden, Mary Amarinthia (Yates)
Papers. 1840-88. 636 items.
Open. Card catalog and index.
University of South Carolina, South Caroliniana Library.
Correspondence, scrapbooks, clippings, and other papers of Snowden (1819-98) include letters and clippings about the Confederate Home and College, the Ladies' Gunboat Fair, the Ladies' Mutual Aid Association, the Ladies' Mount Vernon Association, the Soldiers' Relief Association, Wayside Hospitals, and other organizations. The Ladies' Mutual Aid Association was established to help families of deceased soldiers. Also contains tributes to Snowden.

15,728. Social Survey Club, Columbia
Records. 1919-68. 5 vols.
Open. Unpublished guide.
University of South Carolina, South Caroliniana Library.
Scrapbooks containing minutes, programs, and yearbooks of the local organization.

15,729. Sosnowski and Schaller Family
Papers. 1828-62. 1259 items.
Open. Card catalog.
University of South Carolina, South Caroliniana Library.
Family and Civil War correspondence, business papers, and dental bills make up the bulk of the papers of these families; the material provides information about Sophie Sosnowski's work as a teacher at the DuPre School in Charleston, the South Carolina Female Collegiate Institute at Barhamville, and the Lucy Cobb Institute and Home School at Athens, GA, and about the career of Frank Schaller as a teacher at the Hillsborough Military Academy and the University of the South. Includes letters of Sosnowski and an account she wrote about the burning of Columbia.

15,730. South Carolina College for Women
Records. 1895. 1 item.
Open. Unpublished guide.
University of South Carolina, South Caroliniana Library.
Program of a benefit concert for the hospital fund at this Columbia school.

15,731. South Carolina Female Collegiate Institute
Records. 1828-1960. 1 vol. and 110 items.
Open. Unpublished guide.
University of South Carolina, South Caroliniana Library.
Correspondence by students at this Barhamville, SC, school to families and friends comprises the bulk of the collection. Includes an 1863 letter in which R. Acelie Togno tells school officials about his daughters' work habits, dispositions, and state of health because of proper diet and dress and a 1905 letter in which Mary Ancrum Shannon relates her memories of Barhamville, where she was a student during 1851 and 1852. Also contains a sketch by Sophie M. Reynolds concerning a southern school before the Civil War, student

reports and diplomas, a list of students, notes on courses, clippings, and a textbook.

15,732. South Carolina Industrial School for White Girls
Records. 1950-51. 1 vol.
Open. Unpublished guide.
University of South Carolina, South Caroliniana Library.
Monthly reports and financial statements.

15,733. South Carolina League of Women Voters
Records. 1909-52. 180 items.
Open. Card catalog.
University of South Carolina, South Caroliniana Library.
Correspondence of Emma Anderson Dunnovant, Eulalie Chafee Salley, Anna Howard Shaw, Harriet Powe Lynch, Benjamin R. Tillman, and others make up the bulk of the collection and provide information about voters' rights, the Equal Suffrage League, the 19th Amendment, and the LWV. Also includes minutes, pamphlets, a subscription list, and clippings concerning the activities of the South Carolina LWV and its leaders.

15,734. South Carolina Training School for Nurses
Records. 1883. 1 item.
Open. Unpublished guide.
University of South Carolina, South Caroliniana Library.
Circular letter from Robert A. Kinloch, president of the School's board of trustees, to A. S. Salley asking him to submit names of ladies in his area who might serve on the Board of Co-operating Lady Members. The letter mentions duties of women Board members.

15,735. Spann, James
Papers. 1810-64. 456 items.
Open. Card catalog.
University of South Carolina, South Caroliniana Library.
Correspondence, promissory notes, medical bills, account books, and other papers of Spann (ca. 1785-1838), a physician, contain material about his wife Elizabeth Spann's account with the Bank of Augusta and about her estate. Correspondence provides information about the sale of Negroes, military activities against the Seminoles, and life in Florida.

15,736. Spartanburg Female College
Records. 1859-62. 2 items.
Open. Unpublished guide.
University of South Carolina, South Caroliniana Library.
A circular listing the board of trustees, tuition rates, and system of instruction and an 1862 commencement broadside.

15,737. Springs Family
Papers. 1789-1932. 207 items.
Open. Card catalog.
University of South Carolina, South Caroliniana Library.
Correspondence and other family papers include letters of John Springs, Mary Springs, Richard Austin Springs, Leroy Springs, and Andrew Baxter Springs to Mary Laura Springs who studied during the 1820s and 1830s at Salem Academy in Salem, NC, and at Mrs. Sarazin's Seminary in Philadelphia; John and Richard Austin Springs argue in their letters that Mary's study of French "will be time lost." Also includes letters by Sophia C. Springs in Charleston, SC, discussing her studies at Madame Talvande's school.

15,738. Stanly, Mary E.
Papers. 1843. 1 item.
Open. Unpublished guide.
University of South Carolina, South Caroliniana Library.
Letter in which Stanly in Greenville, SC, discusses social affairs, news of friends, and the activities of an astronomy class at the female academy.

15,739. Stevens, Mary Ann Elizabeth
Papers. 1809-12. 3 items.
Open. Unpublished guide.
University of South Carolina, South Caroliniana Library.
Letters which Stevens wrote from Bristol, England, to Jervis Henry Stevens in Charleston, SC, about her mother in Jamaica, her concern about the War of 1812, and family matters.

15,740. Stoney, Sarah Barnwell
Papers. 1862. 1 item.
Open. Unpublished guide.
University of South Carolina, South Caroliniana Library.
Letter in which Stoney (?-1879) expresses her opinions about the Civil War, describes her family's situation, and remarks about the illness of a child, the prevalence of fever, and family news.

15,741. Strickland, Teresa Hammond
Papers. 1906-57. 4 items.
Open. Unpublished guide.
University of South Carolina, South Caroliniana Library.
Copy of Strickland's poem "A Legend of the Yellow Jasmine" and related correspondence.

15,742. Stuart, Mary M.
Papers. 1835. 1 item.
Open. Catalog card.
University of South Carolina, South Caroliniana Library.
Letter by Stuart in Beaufort, SC, to Mrs. Arthur S. Gibbes in Pendleton Village, SC, contains information about Stuart's upcoming move to a rental house and her uncle's decision to sell a slave called Little May who had been "behaving so intolerably . . . stealing constantly, and killing our neighbour's Cattle."

15,743. Sullivan Family
Papers. 1812-1925. 64 items.
Open. Card catalog.
University of South Carolina, South Caroliniana Library.
Correspondence and business papers include promissory notes and receipts of J. G. Sullivan & Co.; an 1892 diploma for Lidie May Miller from the Greenville, SC, city schools; and a letter from Valencia, Spain, in which Luiz Rubio, the husband of Mary Sullivan, tells William Dunklin Sullivan of his participation in the revolt against General Weyler in Cuba and of his imprisonment after his return to Spain. He asks Sullivan to look after his daughter.

15,744. Summers, Eliza A.
Papers. 1856-69. 47 items.
Open. Unpublished guide.
University of South Carolina, South Caroliniana Library.
A Woodbury, CT, native and schoolteacher, [Miss] Summers (1844-1900) taught freedmen at Hilton Head, SC, in 1867 and 1868. Her correspondence chronicles her year in South Carolina and includes later letters from blacks thanking her and another teacher for items sent to them, reporting on family and friends, and expressing regret that the teachers were no longer with them. Also includes letters in which Summers describes to her sister Sarah Maria Summers her voyage from New York to Charleston, SC, and her first impressions of Hilton Head. Her letters discuss the food and houses in the area as well as the freedmen, their children, and school officials with whom she worked.

15,745. Sumter and Delage Family
Papers. 1694-1936. 508 items.
Open. Card catalog.
University of South Carolina, South Caroliniana Library.
Natalie de Delage de Volude (1782-1841), a native of France, married Thomas Sumter, Jr., in ca. 1802. Family correspondence includes her letters to her relatives in France; letters from 1796 to 1801 in which Aaron Burr commented to Natalie on her improving English and her friendship with his daughter Theodosia; a letter in which Thomas Sumter asked Madame d'Amblimont, Natalie's grandmother, for her consent to their marriage; a letter in which Robert Livingston recommends to Madame Delage that Sumter would be a suitable husband for Natalie and comments that marriages in the US were not mercenary and were "always the choice of the parties"; and a letter from Sumter to Madame Delage discussing South Carolina laws dealing with the property rights of wives.

15,746. Sumter, Natalie Delage
Papers. 1840-41. 1 vol.
Open. Unpublished guide.
University of South Carolina, South Caroliniana Library.
Diary of Sumter (1782-1841) chronicles plantation life in Sumter District, SC.

15,747. Swearingen, John Eldred
Papers. 1772-1959. 1694 items.
Open. Unpublished guide.
University of South Carolina, South Caroliniana Library.
Correspondence and articles of Swearingen (1875-1957) and his wife Mary Hough Swearingen include information about the women's vote in 1922 and correspondence concerning Mary Swearingen's teaching career. Includes articles about Swearingen as "state mother" in 1962 and her immediate predecessor Mrs. P. Bradley Morrah, Sr. The South Caroliniana Library also holds an article by Mrs. Swearingen entitled "Blanding Street."

15,748. Taylor, Sally Elmore
Papers. 1909-10. 1 vol.
Open. Unpublished guide.
University of South Carolina, South Caroliniana Library.
Memoir that Taylor (1829-?) wrote at her nephew's request.

15,749. Tennent, Edward Smith
Papers. 1748-1915. 659 items.
Open. Unpublished guide.
University of South Carolina, South Caroliniana Library.
Tennent (1819-62), a physician, and Hattie Taylor (?-1905) of Wilmington, NC, were married in 1861 during the excitement over secession. Their correspondence contains references to the secession convention in Charleston, the bombardment of Fort Sumter, and the dislocation of the Tennent and Taylor families that was caused by the Civil War. Edward Tennent served with the Sumter Guards until he suffered a fatal wound in June 1862; his only furlough came in February 1862 for the birth of his son Edward II. Also included are letters of Ann Martha Smith Tennent, mother of the elder Edward Tennent; of Eliza Tennent, wife of Edward's brother William, who welcomed Hattie into the family and sought to allay the new bride's fears for her husband; and of Edward Tennent II while he was attending a Lenoir, NC, boarding school from 1876 to 1879. The younger Tennent decided not to attend college, went to work in Wilmington, and provided for his mother until her death.

15,750. Tennent Family
Papers. 1815-93. 25 items.
Open. Card catalog.

University of South Carolina, South Caroliniana Library.
Correspondence of this South Carolina planter family includes an 1815 letter in which John Charles Tennent comments to Susan [Mrs. William Mackey] Tennent that he and his wife have four children, "a pretty number & are not anxious to have it increased," and a post-Civil War letter from Mary Julia Tennent at the family's plantation near Charleston, SC, to Hattie [Mrs. Edward] Tennent in Wilmington, NC, describing difficulties her family faced.

15,751. Thomas, Anna Hasell
Papers. 1864-65. 1 vol.
Open. Catalog card.
University of South Carolina, South Caroliniana Library.
Diary in which Thomas (1828-1912) discusses the illness of her sister, their departure from New York for South Carolina, her sister's death during the voyage, the landing at Charleston, the trip through Columbia to Ridgeway, the burial of her sister, and her experiences at the hands of Union soldiers.

15,752. Thornton, Mrs. Phineas
Papers. 1856. 1 item.
Open. Unpublished guide.
University of South Carolina, South Caroliniana Library.
Reminiscences of Thornton, a Massachusetts native who moved to Camden, SC, in 1807.

15,753. Timrod, Henry
Papers. 1851-1937. 92 items.
Open. Card catalog.
University of South Carolina, South Caroliniana Library.
Correspondence and other papers of Timrod (1828-67), a poet, include a letter in which he tells his sister Emily (Timrod) Goodwin about the progress of the Civil War, Charlotte Bronte's *Villette,* and his dissatisfaction with teaching; a letter of condolence Henry Timrod wrote to Colonel Frank Schaller following the death of his wife Sophie Sosnowski Schaller; copies of Timrod's poems; clippings; and other papers.

15,754. Trinity Protestant Episcopal Church, Daughters of the Holy Cross
Records. 1936. 4 items.
Open. Unpublished guide.
University of South Carolina, South Caroliniana Library.
Records contain information about the Daughters' work to provide care for persons with tuberculosis, the Richland Anti-Tuberculosis Association, and the history of Ridgewood Camp. The Church was located in Columbia.

15,755. Tucker, Cornelia Dabney Ramseur
Papers. 1939-67. 634 items.
Open. Unpublished guide.
University of South Carolina, South Caroliniana Library.
Correspondence and other papers of [Mrs.] Tucker (1881-), a Charleston resident, provide information about her efforts to secure the secret ballot in South Carolina. Also includes information about antistrike legislation, civilian defense, stricter qualifications for US Supreme Court appointments, education for world peace, textbooks for South Carolina schools, the Anti-Communist League of America, efforts to expose communism in the National Council of Churches, and Tucker's work in patriotic and women's organizations. Includes her correspondence with state and national political, educational, and religious leaders, including John F. Kennedy, Lyndon B. Johnson, Hubert H. Humphrey, Strom Thurmond, Richard B. Russell, Sam Rayburn, L. Mendel Rivers, and 19 state governors.

15,756. United Daughters of the Confederacy, Marion Chapter
Records. 1896-1919. 2 vols.
Open. Unpublished guide.
University of South Carolina, South Caroliniana Library.
Record books.

15,757. United Daughters of the Confederacy, Secessionville Chapter, James Island
Records. 1906-27. 3 vols.
Open. Unpublished guide.
University of South Carolina, South Caroliniana Library.
Minutes, treasurer's book, and register.

15,758. United Daughters of the Confederacy, South Carolina Division
Records. 1927. 17 items.
Open. Unpublished guide.
University of South Carolina, South Caroliniana Library.
Circular letters signed by Mrs. Thomas J. Mauldin; she asks for donations for a statue of General Wade Hampton to be placed in Statuary Hall in Washington, DC.

15,759. Van Buren, Angelica (Singleton)
Papers. 1854-55. 2 vols.
Open. Unpublished guide.
University of South Carolina, South Caroliniana Library.
Diary of [Mrs. Abram] Van Buren (1816-77), daughter-in-law of President Martin Van Buren, includes an account of her trip to Europe with her family and niece Mary Singleton McDuffie.

15,760. Vernon, Ida
Papers. 1863. 1 vol.
Open. Unpublished guide.
University of South Carolina, South Caroliniana Library.
Notes on the study of minerals taken by Vernon while she was a student at Laurensville Female College in South Carolina.

15,761. Verstille, Tristram
Papers. 1811-60. 67 items.
Open. Calendar and catalog card.
University of South Carolina, South Caroliniana Library.
Correspondence of Verstille includes letters he wrote from Robertville, SC, and Savannah, GA, to his mother and sisters in New York and Connecticut concerning business, political, and family matters. Also includes letters from Charlotte Verstille to family members regarding educational, social, and religious affairs.

15,762. Wallace, Mrs. Robert M.
Papers. 1883. 1 vol.
Open. Card catalog.
University of South Carolina, South Caroliniana Library.
Diary of Wallace includes her account of a railroad trip from Charleston to San Francisco and Los Angeles by way of Atlanta, Chattanooga, TN, Cincinnati, St. Louis and Kansas City, Denver, Cheyenne, WY, Salt Lake City, Reno, NV, and Sacramento, CA. Includes detailed observations regarding cities and sites along the way, the mixing of northerners and southerners in Chattanooga, the prison at Ft. Leavenworth, KS, a lecture by Brigham Young, Jr., at the Mormon Tabernacle, and the industriousness, but lack of public spirit, of Chinese laborers.

15,763. Waring, Malvina Sarah Black
Papers. 1860-80. 2 vols.
Open. Card catalog.
University of South Carolina, South Caroliniana Library.
Diary of Waring (1842-1930) contains scattered entries including an eyewitness account of the secession convention, the outbreak of smallpox in Columbia, and celebration of the secession announcement. Also includes clippings of a story about Juliet Clayburn and a composition and exercise book.

15,764. Waties Family
Papers. 1844-1972. 24 items.
Open. Card catalog.
University of South Carolina, South Caroliniana Library.
Correspondence, genealogical information, and other papers consist chiefly of letters of John Waties; Thomas Waties; Mary Butler Waties, who became Mrs. Sebastian Sumter; and Anna Waties regarding the Civil War, family activities, and postwar conditions. Includes a letter in which Thomas Waties in Florida observes to Mary Butler Waties that there "has been a perfect mania for getting married. . . ."

15,765. Weyman Family
Papers. 1719-1934. 671 items.
Open. Card catalog.
University of South Carolina, South Caroliniana Library.
Papers of this merchant family with business interests in Columbia and Africa include correspondence, bills and receipts regarding household expenses, legal papers relating to settlement of Catherine Weyman's estate, items concerning Samuel Gale's involvement with the South Carolina factory at Rio Pongo in Africa, and papers documenting his claims following the destruction of the factory by British troops in ca. 1814. Includes letters from Catherine Weyman in Charleston, SC, to Edward Weyman in New York, which reflect changes in Charleston in ca. 1814 and her participation in family business affairs. Also includes letters to Mary Rosalie Weyman in Charleston and Lydia C. "Kate" Weyman.

15,766. Wilkes, Samuel Marion
Papers. 1851-1963. 79 items.
Open. Card catalog.
University of South Carolina, South Caroliniana Library.
Papers of Wilkes (?-1861), a South Carolina legislator and soldier, consist principally of correspondence with his wife Louisa Webb Wilkes during his service in the legislature and the Confederate army; his letters contain information on a secession meeting in 1851, legal cases, military life, the Confederate government, and the Civil War, while her letters concern domestic activities and social life in Anderson, SC. Also contains a letter to Marjorie W. Huntley regarding events in the life of her grandfather Samuel M. Wilkes and biographical information.

15,767. Williston Graded School
Records. 1902-03. 1 vol.
Open. Unpublished guide.
University of South Carolina, South Caroliniana Library.
Register kept by Ophelia Davidson, a teacher, for the first three grades includes records of attendance, deportment, and scholarship.

15,768. Wilson, Moultrie Reid
Papers. 1864-77. 20 items.
Open. Card catalog.
University of South Carolina, South Caroliniana Library.
Correspondence of Wilson (1839-1910), a soldier, includes love letters he exchanged with Sue Thermutis Montgomery during the Civil War. Her letters contain comments about civilians' reactions to the War and the mood of Mineral Spring, SC, residents as they awaited General Sherman's advancing army. Also includes a postwar letter which Elizabeth Stanley Hoole wrote Eveline Gertrude Brown Wilson mentioning her bankruptcy and lamenting the state of society.

15,769. Wingate Family
Papers. 1835-87. 188 items.
Open. Card catalog.
University of South Carolina, South Caroliniana Library.
Civil War letters of Willie Wingate, post-Civil War family correspondence, bills, receipts, and promissory notes make up the bulk of this South Carolina family's papers. Includes an extract from an 1835 Winnsboro, SC, town council meeting, which contains a reply to women who asked the council to refuse to issue licenses for the sale of alcohol. Also contains letters of Mrs. L. W. Waring, [Mrs.] Harriet E. Wingate, Mrs. E. V. Campbell, and other women. The correspondence provides information about sickness and casualties in the Confederate army, South Carolina's Reconstruction legislature, postwar race relations, Wade Hampton's election victory, and other topics.

15,770. Winthrop College
Records. 1917-63. 2 vols.
Open. Card catalog.
University of South Carolina, South Caroliniana Library.
Scrapbooks of this women's school, founded in ca. 1895, include clippings regarding student activities and alumnae association meetings as well as articles and editorials regarding the controversy over the Peabody Report.

15,771. Woman's Christian Temperance Union
Records. 1880-1939. 1 vol.
Open. Unpublished guide.
University of South Carolina, South Caroliniana Library.
History of the WCTU in South Carolina.

15,772. Woodward, Joanne
Papers. 1948-76. 30 items.
Open. Unpublished guide.
University of South Carolina, South Caroliniana Library.
Correspondence, scripts of plays, and scrapbooks of Woodward (1930-), an actress.

15,773. Yeargin, Mary Little
Papers. 1884-94. 148 items.
Open. Card catalog.
University of South Carolina, South Caroliniana Library.
Correspondence of Yeargin (1867-94) includes letters she wrote to her family and friends while she was studying law at Cornell University in Ithaca, NY, and teaching school in Leesville, SC. In one letter she wrote that she was to speak at a state WCTU meeting and comments that "temperance work has been on my heart and mind ever since 1886." Also includes condolence messages regarding her death and a biographical sketch.

15,774. Young Family
Papers. 1809-92. 94 items.
Open. Card catalog.
University of South Carolina, South Caroliniana Library.
Family correspondence includes an 1836 letter in which James A. Young in Paris comments to [Miss] Mary L. Young in Camden, SC, on the latest women's dress and hair fashions, activities in Paris, and attendance at a medical school; letters, dating from 1844 to 1851, from [Mrs.] Mary R. Young in Jackson County, FL, to Mary L. Young regarding the author's move to Florida and frontier conditions there; and Civil War letters, chiefly by George G. Young in Virginia and North Carolina. His letters note that the Sisters of Mercy sent the soldiers soap and hoppin john.

15,775. Young Ladies' Hospital Association, Columbia
Records. 1861-96. 1 vol.
Open. Unpublished guide.
University of South Carolina, South Caroliniana Library.
Records of the Association date from 1861 to 1864. Also includes records of the Columbia Memorial Association for the period 1866-96 and clippings concerning the observance of Memorial Day.

DARLINGTON

15,776. Darlington County Archives
Records. Ca. 1737- . 24 cabinets and 10 microfilm reels.
Open. Unpublished guide.
Darlington County Historical Commission.
Correspondence, diaries, ledgers, minute books, yearbooks, and other records and papers. Includes papers of Sarah E. Coker, the first Darlington County woman to become a physician, concerning her work with the Grenfell expedition in Labrador and later with Indian children in New Mexico.

DENMARK

15,777. Wright, Elizabeth Evelyn
Papers. 1876-1906. 10 folders.
Access restricted. Card catalog.
Voorhees College Archives.
Wright (1876-1906), a Negro educator, was founder of Denmark Industrial School, which now is Voorhees College. Correspondence, annual report of the School, photos and slides of her hometown in Georgia and of School activities, a biography, and other papers. Includes papers of Wright's assistant Jessie Dorsey and documents that relate to the growth of Voorhees College.

PENDLETON

15,778. Bowen, Clarissa Adger
Papers. 1854-1976. 2 vols.
Open. Unpublished guide.
Pendleton District Historical and Recreational Commission.
Diaries, photos, and biographical material of [Mrs.] Bowen (1837-1915). Her diaries concern her life on a plantation before and after the Civil War.

15,779. Calhoun, Floride (Colhoun)
Papers. ?-1975. 1 Hollinger box and 3 vols.
Open. Unpublished guide.
Pendleton District Historical and Recreational Commission.
Clippings, books, and other papers concerning the family of Calhoun (1782-1866), the wife of US Vice-President John C. Calhoun.

15,780. Clemson, Anna Maria (Calhoun)
Papers. 1817-1975. 1 archive box and 3 vols.
Open. Unpublished guide.
Pendleton District Historical and Recreational Commission.
Following the deaths of their children, Clemson (1817-75) and her husband Thomas Green Clemson gave their plantation land to the state of South Carolina for establishment of an agricultural college. Clemson wrote pamphlets and other items stressing the need for such an institution. Clippings, books, and other papers about the Clemson and Calhoun families. One of the Clemson children died in a railroad accident; the others died of natural causes.

15,781. Huger, Esther
Papers. ?-1974. 2 vols.
Open. Unpublished guide.
Pendleton District Historical and Recreational Commission.
Correspondence, a diary, and biographical material of Huger, who lived on a plantation. Includes comments by members of her family.

15,782. Hunter, Jane Edna
Papers. ?-1975. 1 archive box.
Open. Unpublished guide.
Pendleton District Historical and Recreational Commission.
Hunter (1882-1971), a nurse and author, was founder and director of the Phillis Wheatley Institute. Biographical and autobiographical material, an inventory of her estate, and clippings reflect the success of a black woman from rural Pendleton. She was the author of *A Nickel and a Prayer.*

15,783. Kennedy, Anne
Papers. ?-1976. 1 folder and 1 vol.
Open. Unpublished guide.
Pendleton District Historical and Recreational Commission.
Clippings, books, and other papers about Kennedy (1760-1836), a Revolutionary War heroine.

15,784. Pickens, Rebecca Calhoun
Papers. 1809-76. 1 Hollinger box and 5 vols.
Open. Unpublished guide.
Pendleton District Historical and Recreational Commission.
Pickens (1745-1814) lived in the wilderness with her husband Andrew Pickens and family, whose occupations were farming, trading, and military service. Family papers, clippings, and volumes about Andrew Pickens and his family.

ROCK HILL

15,785. Abortion Interest Movement
Records. Ca. 1969-75. Ca. 3 ft.
Open. No guide.
Winthrop College Archives.
This organization was formed in 1969 to promote liberalized abortion laws in South Carolina. Minutes, correspondence, resolutions, reference files on abortion, and clippings.

15,786. Amelia Pride Book Club of Rock Hill
Records. 1896-1973. 0.5 ft. and 1 vol.
Open. Unpublished guide.
Winthrop College Archives.
Founded in 1896, the Club is the oldest women's literary group in Rock Hill. Minutes, correspondence, historical file, a photo of the founder, scrapbook, program, yearbooks, college bulletins, and a clipping pertain to the Club's origin, growth, and activities.

15,787. American Association of University Women, Rock Hill Chapter
Records. 1925-75. 9 in.
Open. Unpublished guide.
Winthrop College Archives.
Women faculty members from Winthrop College constitute the majority in this local AAUW chapter, which was founded in 1925. Constitutions, bylaws, minutes, financial records, correspondence, reports, membership lists, and clippings provide information on the founding, development, and work of the chapter as it affected Winthrop College.

15,788. Boulware Family
Papers. 1850-1953. 2 vols. and 359 pp.
Open. Unpublished guide.
Winthrop College Archives.
This family resided in Chester County, SC. Includes a plantation journal containing references to the daily life of women on the plantation and a

genealogical history containing mention of women family members.

15,789. Bryant, Margaret Mae
Papers. 1934-75. 2 ft.
Open. Unpublished guide.
Winthrop College Archives.
Papers of Bryant (1900-), a linguist, author, and educator, include correspondence, minutes, speeches, program notes, brochures, photos, and clippings. Pertains primarily to Bryant's involvement with such professional groups as the National Council of Teachers of English, the American Name Society, and the New York branch of the AAUW.

15,790. Busbee, Thelma Ecord
Papers. 1950-73. 1.75 ft.
Open. Unpublished guide.
Winthrop College Archives.
[Mrs.] Busbee (1910-) is a clubwoman and civic leader. Principally contains organizational records, including constitutions, bylaws, financial records, correspondence, program notes, and clippings relating to Busbee's work in such women's groups as the South Carolina Federation of Women's Clubs, the South Carolina Status of Women's Clubs, the South Carolina Council for the Common Good, and the South Carolina Women's State Committee.

15,791. Castilian Club of Rock Hill
Records. 1901-73. 6 in.
Open. Unpublished guide.
Winthrop College Archives.
Minutes, correspondence, program notes, yearbooks, and clippings reflect the growth, development, and history of this women's literary group, which was founded in 1901.

15,792. Cochran, Mrs. W. Edward
Papers. Ca. 1936-76. Ca. 4 ft.
Open. Unpublished guide.
Winthrop College Archives.
Cochran (1908-) is a clubwoman. Correspondence, program notes, reports, short histories, photos, clippings, and other items concern the South Carolina Extension Homemakers' Council.

15,793. Delano, Lucile Kathryn
Papers. 1927-73. 9 in.
Open. Unpublished guide.
Winthrop College Archives.
Papers of Delano (1902-), an educator, principally consist of correspondence and diaries. Includes travel diaries in which she describes her impressions of the early days of the Spanish Civil War in 1936 and another in which she records her trip to Switzerland in 1950.

15,794. ERA South Carolina
Records. 1972-77. Ca. 1.5 ft.
Open. No guide.
Winthrop College Archives.
Financial records, correspondence, mailing lists, brochures, and related records of this political coalition formed in 1972 to seek the South Carolina legislature's ratification of the Equal Rights Amendment.

15,795. Frayser, Mary Elizabeth
Papers. 1841-1970. 9.5 ft.
Open. Unpublished guide.
Winthrop College Archives.
Frayser (1868-1968) was a home economist and clubwoman. Correspondence, speeches, organizational records, and clippings provide information about family, personal, professional, and organizational matters. Much of the material pertains to her activities in clubs, including the South Carolina Federation of Women's Clubs, the South Carolina Council for the Common Good, the South Carolina Status of Women's Conference, and the South Carolina Business and Professional Women's Clubs. Part of the material documents her role in the movement for tax-supported, free public libraries in the state, while a portion of the correspondence with Sarah Hughes concerns the creation of the Status of Women's Conference. Bulk of the material dates from 1930 to 1947.

15,796. Freeman, Grace Beacham
Papers. 1880-1977. 7 ft.
Open. Unpublished guide.
Winthrop College Archives.
Papers of Freeman (1916-), a South Carolina poet and writer, include family, personal, and professional correspondence; radio scripts; story drafts; poems; plays; reference files; and other papers relating to her work as a poet, scriptwriter, dramatist, and feature story writer. Also includes an 1880 diary in which Freeman's aunt, a 17-year-old deaf girl from Marion, AL, describes her life and thoughts.

15,797. Gates, Mary Johnston
Papers. Ca. 1914-71. Ca. 10 ft.
Open. Unpublished guide.
Winthrop College Archives.
[Mrs.] Gates (1920-) is a home extension worker. Correspondence, minutes, program notes, reports, short histories, photos, yearbooks, clippings, and other material relate to the Sumter County extension program, the South Carolina Extension Homemakers' Council, and to Gates's role in winning Congress's designation of the Bethel home demonstration club as the first club of its type in the world.

15,798. Gee, Christine South
Papers. 1902-71. 6 in.
Open. Unpublished guide.
Winthrop College Archives.
A home economist and clubwoman, [Mrs.] Gee (1884-) helped organize the South Carolina State Council of Farm Women in 1921. Principally consists of speeches, but also includes reports, genealogical records, photos, and clippings reflecting her work as a state home demonstration agent; her work with the Council on Women, now the South Carolina Extension Homemakers' Council; and her study in 1933 and 1934 of the home economics program for adult education.

15,799. Holler, Mary Louisa Oni Cornwell
Papers. 1885-1905. 260 pp.
Open. Unpublished guide.
Winthrop College Archives.
A housewife and mother in Rock Hill, [Mrs. Adlai Ellwood] Holler (1871-1951) was named State Mother of the Year in 1945. Correspondence makes up the bulk of the collection, which also includes biographical information about Holler and genealogical material on the Holler family. The correspondence concerns her social life and studies at Chester Female Institute in Chester, VA; her children; and her household duties after she was married.

15,800. Hutchison Family
Papers. 1785-1968. 1.25 ft.
Open. Unpublished guide.
Winthrop College Archives.
Correspondence, diaries, speeches, and genealogical records of this York County, SC, family include a diary in which Jennie Johnston Hutchison wrote from 1883 to 1887 about family affairs and farming in Rock Hill and one by Anne Claire Hutchison that includes entries from 1909 to 1930 and contains information about WWI's effect on Rock Hill.

15,801. Johnson, Elizabeth Frieuch
Papers. Ca. 1917-76. Ca. 1 ft.
Open. Unpublished guide.
Winthrop College Archives.
[Miss] Johnson (1890-), a Winthrop College faculty member who earned a PhD, was active in women's organizations, including the AAUW. Correspondence, diaries, speeches, unpublished essays and poems, membership lists, programs, photos, clippings, and other material concern her work at Winthrop and in women's groups as well as her interests in literature, horticulture, theology, and other subjects.

15,802. Laurence, Jessie Hughie
Papers. 1894-1967. 1 ft.
Open. Unpublished guide.
Winthrop College Archives.
Laurence (1886-1971) was an educator and a clubwoman. Correspondence, speeches, organizational records, photos, and clippings concern her efforts supporting improvements in education, health, planned parenthood, historic and wildlife preservation, and other conditions in South Carolina. Also includes information about her role in the South Carolina Federation of Women's Clubs from 1928 to 1937 and in the South Carolina Council for the Common Good from 1935 to 1937.

15,803. Liverance, Sara Vandiver
Papers. 1954-73. Ca. 25 ft.
Open. No guide.
Winthrop College Archives.
[Mrs.] Liverance (1914-), a journalist and clubwoman, was legislative chairman of the South Carolina Council for the Common Good. Correspondence, minutes, program notes, statements, and clippings pertain primarily to her Council work to persuade the state legislature to approve legislation that would allow women to serve on juries.

15,804. Lockwood, Mrs. J. Palmer
Papers. 1912-18. 80 pp.
Open. Unpublished guide.
Winthrop College Archives.
Journal which includes a brief history about how "Carolina" became the South Carolina state song and about Lockwood's work in popularizing the song.

15,805. McFadden, Robert Lawrence
Papers. 1960-76. 6.25 ft.
Open. Unpublished guide.
Winthrop College Archives.
McFadden (1929-) is a member of the South Carolina House of Representatives from York County; his papers reflect the legislature's consideration of the Equal Rights Amendment. Correspondence, minutes, financial reports, articles, and government publications. Contains correspondence, reports, petitions, clippings, and other papers concerning the efforts of individuals to influence McFadden's vote on ratification of the Amendment.

15,806. Massey, Mary Elizabeth
Papers. 1848-1974. 10 ft.
Open. Unpublished guide.
Winthrop College Archives.
Massey (1915-74) was a history professor at Winthrop College from 1952 until 1974. Correspondence, lecture and teaching notes, literary manuscripts, speeches, research notes, organizational records, clippings, and copies of historical manuscripts pertain to her work at Winthrop; to her publishing activities, especially regarding women in the Civil War; and to her role in the Southern Historical Association from 1953 to 1974 and in the Civil War Centennial Commission from 1957 to 1963.

15,807. Mr. USA Pageant
Records. 1977. 25 pp.
Open. Unpublished guide.
Winthrop College Archives.
Correspondence, news releases, photos, clippings, and memorabilia of the Pageant, which was held in

Charleston, SC, as an alternative to the Miss USA Pageant.

15,808. Neely, Juanita H.
Papers. 1926-70. 0.5 ft.
Open. Unpublished guide.
Winthrop College Archives.
Correspondence, speeches, genealogical records, photos, and clippings of Neely (1889-), a home economist, pertain primarily to her work in the state home economics extension program from 1946 to 1957.

15,809. Olsen, Lucy Hardee
Papers. 1941-45. 80 pp.
Open. Unpublished guide.
Winthrop College Archives.
Diary and a photo provide an account of the ordeal of [Mrs.] Olsen (1894-), a housewife who was held captive during Japan's occupation of the Philippines during WWII.

15,810. Over The Teacups
Records. 1896-1976. 1 ft.
Open. Unpublished guide.
Winthrop College Archives.
Minutes, financial records, correspondence, reports, membership lists, yearbooks, brochures, and memorabilia of this women's literary club, founded in 1896, document the group's involvement in civic projects.

15,811. Powell, Kathryn Summers
Papers. 1940-76. 2.75 ft.
Open. Unpublished guide.
Winthrop College Archives.
Powell (1920-) is a Winthrop College home economics professor, author, and specialist in family and child development. Correspondence, drafts and revisions of her speeches and dissertation, teaching notes, reference material, and biographical information primarily relate to her work at Winthrop and to her participation in such groups as the Christian Children's Fund and the Southeastern Council on Family Relations. Powell holds a PhD.

15,812. Rock Hill Jaycee-ettes
Records. 1953-71. 1 ft.
Open. Unpublished guide.
Winthrop College Archives.
Founded in 1952, this women's civic club supports various charitable projects and assists the local Jaycees. Correspondence, program notes, memoranda, newsletters, manuals, clippings, and other records.

15,813. Rock Hill Junior Welfare League
Records. 1938-72. 1.5 ft. and 6 vols.
Open. Unpublished guide.
Winthrop College Archives.
Organized in 1938, this group promoted Rock Hill area welfare, education, and cultural projects, including the establishment of the York County Children's Nature Museum. Minutes, financial records, correspondence, scrapbooks, yearbooks, newsletters, and photos.

15,814. Rock Hill Junior Woman's Club
Records. 1956-74. 5.75 ft.
Open. Unpublished guide.
Winthrop College Archives.
Correspondence, reports, brochures, yearbooks, and clippings of this women's civic organization, which was founded in 1955.

15,815. Rock Hill Music Club
Records. 1914-77. 3 in.
Open. Unpublished guide.
Winthrop College Archives.
Minutes, meeting programs, correspondence, membership records, historical sketches, scrapbooks, yearbooks, and clippings document the origin, growth, and activities of this women's group, which was founded in 1914. Bulk of the material dates from 1941 to 1977.

15,816. Russell, Leila A.
Papers. 1903. 65 pp. and 6 items.
Open. Unpublished guide.
Winthrop College Archives.
Journal and photos constitute a report by [Miss] Russell (1871-1963), an educator, to the Southern Education Board about the condition of Anderson County, SC, schoolhouses. Includes photos of schools Russell investigated.

15,817. Sadler, David Hope, Family
Papers. 1809-1941. 251 items.
Open. Unpublished guide.
Winthrop College Archives.
Principally correspondence of family members, most of whom lived in Rock Hill, includes items describing women's lives during and after the Civil War. Also contains wills, deeds, land grants, and clippings.

15,818. South Carolina Clergy Consultation Service on Problem Pregnancies
Records. Ca. 1970-73. Ca. 25 ft.
Open. No guide.
Winthrop College Archives.
Formed in 1970, the Service is primarily concerned with counseling and referring pregnant women to appropriate agencies. Correspondence, questionnaires, reference files on abortion, and clippings.

15,819. South Carolina Council for the Common Good
Records. Ca. 1960-77. 1 ft.
Open. Unpublished guide.
Winthrop College Archives.
The Council, which existed from 1935 until 1977, coordinated plans and policies of South Carolina women's groups that sought greater strength through united effort; the Council lobbied for jury service for women, equal pay, and the Equal Rights Amendment. Minutes, agenda and program notes, correspondence, reports, resolutions, and other records.

15,820. South Carolina Extension Homemakers' Council
Records. 1917-76. 1 ft.
Open. Unpublished guide.
Winthrop College Archives.
Founded in 1921 as the South Carolina Council of Farm Women, this group promotes the study of home economics and the work of the state's home economists. Minutes, financial records, correspondence, short histories, surveys, program notes, studies, and yearbooks.

15,821. South Carolina Federal Feminist Credit Union
Records. 1975-76. 23 pp.
Open. Unpublished guide.
Winthrop College Archives.
Women make up the majority of customers of this credit union, which was founded in 1975 as the first financial institution of its kind in the Southeast. Memoranda, statements, brochures, photos, and clippings.

15,822. South Carolina Food Service Association
Records. 1954-77. Ca. 8 ft.
Open. No guide.
Winthrop College Archives.
The Association was organized in 1954 to maintain and improve the health and education of South Carolina children through nutritionally adequate, nonprofit school food service programs. Minutes, financial records, correspondence, reports, pamphlets, brochures, photos, clippings, and related records document the group's effort to promote high standards for food service programs, legislation to foster adequate school food programs, and recruitment and training of food service personnel.

15,823. South Carolina Home Economics Association
Records. 1914-75. 4.25 ft.
Open. Unpublished guide.
Winthrop College Archives.
The Association was founded in 1914 as a professional organization for the state's home economists. Constitution, minutes, financial records, correspondence, membership lists, reports, newsletters, and handbooks.

15,824. Winthrop College Archives
Records. Nd. 260 ft., 827 vols., and 268 microfilm reels.
Open. Unpublished guide.
Winthrop College Archives.
A state-supported institution, Winthrop operated as a women's college from its founding in 1886 until 1973 when it became coeducational. Minutes, financial records, correspondence, reports, catalogs, yearbooks, photos, clippings, and other records document all aspects of the College's history, including student life and activities, offices and officers, departments, faculty, and alumnae and alumni.

15,825. York County Democratic Women's Club
Records. 1966-75. 194 items.
Open. Unpublished guide.
Winthrop College Archives.
The Club was organized by Democratic women in 1967 to encourage women to participate actively in the party's work. Minutes, correspondence, program notes, lists, reference material, and newsletters relate chiefly to the Club's organization, work, and relationship with local, state, and national branches of the Democratic party.

15,826. York County Friends of Food Stamp Applicants
Records. 1972-77. 145 pp.
Open. Unpublished guide.
Winthrop College Archives.
The organization, which existed from 1972 to 1974, helped persons complete food stamp applications and directed them to other social agencies for additional aid. Minutes, agenda notes, correspondence, historical statements, and other records.

15,827. York County League of Women Voters
Records. 1966-75. 6 in.
Open. Unpublished guide.
Winthrop College Archives.
Bylaws, minutes, correspondence, newsletters, bulletins, pamphlets, brochures, and other material concern the group's founding in 1966 and its activities.

ST. MATTHEWS

15,828. Banks
Papers. Ca. 1870-98. No size given.
Open. No guide.
Calhoun County Museum Archives.
Correspondence, diaries, documents concerning school tuitions, and other papers, including papers of Mrs. M. L. Banks.

15,829. Bible and Prayer Books
Papers. 1815-81. 16 vols. and microfiche.
Open. Name index.
Calhoun County Museum Archives.
Bible records include names and notes of Calhoun County families.

15,830. Cain, Lillian
Papers. Ca. 1735-1950. 2 boxes.
Open. No guide.
Calhoun County Museum Archives.
Correspondence, personal diaries, and research materials that Cain collected from 1918 to 1958.

15,831. Calhoun County Public Records
Records. 1907- . 10,000 items.
Access restricted. No guide.
Calhoun County Museum Archives.
Bills of sale, mortgages, divorce suits, and other public documents.

15,832. Crook
Papers. Nd. 107 items.
Open. Unpublished guides.
Calhoun County Museum Archives.
Correspondence, grants, plats, and family bills and receipts from Charleston, Columbia, and Orangeburg, SC.

15,833. Hennon
Papers. 1852-63. 32 items.
Open. Unpublished guide.
Calhoun County Museum Archives.
Correspondence and papers illustrate the work of women during the Civil War, particularly their efforts to carry supplies to family members involved in the war. Includes a burial bill.

15,834. Houser, David
Papers. 1735-ca. 1890. 4 folders.
Open. Index card.
Calhoun County Museum Archives.
Correspondence, accounting papers and other business records, estate papers, dental and medical receipts, and other papers of Houser, a planter and politician, and his wife Margaret Houser. Includes records of transactions involving female slaves; a document concerning the advance distribution in 1863 of $300 as an estate share to Sophia C. Dantzler; a list of personal financial accounts for Cornelia Dantzler; receipts for midwife fees in 1844; extensive records of tuition paid for a daughter's education at Columbia Female School; and lists of purchases and estate settlements. Provides information about the day-to-day participation of wives in the economic and social life of a plantation and about early partition of estates to sons and daughters with final settlements following the estate holder's death.

15,835. Keitt, Lawrence M.
Papers. 1851-59. 1 Hollinger box.
Open. No guide.
Calhoun County Museum Archives.
Correspondence, financial receipts, memorabilia, and other items of Keitt, a South Carolina politician; his fiancée and later wife Sue Sparks Keitt (1834-1915); and their daughters Stella Maria, who died at the age of 4, and Anna. Includes Anna Keitt's "Resolutions for 1893," a letter Lawrence Keitt wrote to Stella Maria for her second birthday, and memorabilia of the child. Sue Sparks Keitt, a member of a wealthy family, supported her husband's political career.

15,836. Thomson
Papers. 1732-1868. 1 box.
Open. Calendar.
Calhoun County Museum Archives.
Land grants, land plats, indentures, deeds of sale, and other documents, many of which were signed by women. Includes papers of Faith Joyner, the wife of Joseph Joyner.

SPARTANBURG

15,837. Wofford College Archives
Records. 1854- . No size given.
Open. Partial unpublished guide.
Wofford College Archives.
A Methodist-related women's college founded in 1854, Wofford became coeducational in 1976. Includes correspondence, a folder concerning coeducation at the College, individual folders about women graduates since the 1890s, scrapbooks, and clippings. Wofford College was founded with funds left by Benjamin Wofford, a Methodist minister and businessman.

15,838. Historical Society of the South Carolina Conference of the United Methodist Church
Records. 1856- . Ca. 2 ft.
Open. Partial unpublished guide.
Wofford College, Historical Society of the South Carolina Conference of the United Methodist Church.
Clippings and other records of the Historical Society, which was founded in 1856. Includes material concerning the Women's Missionary Society and a few individual Methodist women. The records pertain to units of the United Methodist Church and its predecessor denominations.

SOUTH DAKOTA

ABERDEEN

15,839. Church Histories
Collection. 1880-1970. Ca. 2 in.
Open. No guide.
Dacotah Prairie Museum.
Collection contains histories of Aberdeen churches, including St. Mary's Catholic Church, established in 1903; the First Presbyterian Church, 1881; Plymouth Congregational Church, 1890; the First Methodist Church, 1881; the First Evangelical Church, 1882; St. Paul's Evangelical Lutheran Church, 1888; and the Finnish Apostolic Lutheran Church, 1884. Also contains a history of St. Paul Lutheran Church, founded in 1923 in Fredrick, SD.

15,840. Mason, Meda
Papers. 1900-29. 21 vols.
Access restricted. No guide.
Dacotah Prairie Museum.
Diaries of Mason (1875-196?), a businesswoman who operated a tea room and sponsored dances, focuses on the social lives of individuals, boyfriends, business enterprises, and family matters.

15,841. Riggs, Williamson
Papers. 1860-1935. 3 ft.
Open. No guide.
Dacotah Prairie Museum.
Correspondence, financial records, and publications of educators, publishers, and Presbyterian missionaries to the Dakota Sioux. Includes extensive correspondence of missionaries with their wives in which local conditions and difficulties with mission work are discussed.

15,842. St. Luke's Hospital and School of Nursing
Records. Ca. 1954-74. Ca. 1 in.
Open. No guide.
Dacotah Prairie Museum.
The Hospital and School of Nursing were established in 1900-01 in Aberdeen by the Sisters of the Presentation of the Blessed Virgin Mary. A history of the Hospital, programs, bulletins, and clippings.

15,843. Woman's Christian Temperance Union of South Dakota
Records. 1934. 1 item.
Open. No guide.
Dacotah Prairie Museum.
Constitution, minutes, reports, and annual directory of the 46th annual WCTU state convention held in September 1934 in Yankton, SD.

15,844. Archives
Records. 1886- . No size given.
Open. No guide.
Presentation Sisters of the Blessed Virgin Mary.
This religious community of women was founded in 1880 at Wheeler, Dakota Territory. Correspondence, manuscripts by sisters containing accounts of the foundation and history of the community, papers of past leaders of the community, papers relating to the foundress and early superior generals, photos, scrapbooks, and histories of schools, hospitals, and nursing homes operated by the Sisters.

MARTY

15,845. Archives
Records. 1935- . No size given.
Closed. No guide.
Oblate Sisters of the Blessed Sacrament, St. Sylvester's Convent.
Financial records, correspondence, diaries, retreat notes, photos, scrapbooks, Convent newspapers, material about the missions, and other records of the Convent, which was founded in 1935 at St. Paul's Indian Mission in Marty. The Sisters work with the Indians.

MILBANK

15,846. Excelsior Study Club
Records. 1903-78. 2 ft.
Access restricted. No guide.
Grant County Public Library.
Established in 1903 to encourage mental development and to foster civic improvement, the Club opened membership to "any lady of suitable age, bearing a good reputation and of good moral character." Minutes, programs, membership lists, and memorabilia.

15,847. Makocha Study Club
Records. 1904-75. 3 in.
Access restricted. No guide.
Grant County Public Library.
Constitution and bylaws, minutes, programs, and a 1954 history of the Club, which was established in 1904 to promote the moral and intellectual development of its members and "to engender a spirit of harmony and mutual helpfulness."

PIERRE

15,848. Auxiliary of the United Spanish War Veterans
Records. 1912-40. 6 vols.
Open. No guide.
South Dakota State Historical Resource Center.
Constitution, rules and regulations, rituals, a book of ceremonies, and instruction pamphlets.

15,849. Babcock, Cora D.
Papers. 1880-85. 20-page item.
Open. Unpublished guide.
South Dakota State Historical Resource Center.
Reminiscences of Babcock (1855-?), a native New Yorker who homesteaded near Mitchell, SD, during the 1880s. Supporting herself during the winter by taking in laundry, she had some success with her crops before she gave up her claim and married. After her husband died in 1884, Babcock returned to New York with her infant daughter.

15,850. Borglum, Emma Vignal
Papers. 1899. 1 item.
Open. No guide.
South Dakota State Historical Resource Center.
Borglum accompanied her husband, French sculptor Solon Borglum, on a trip to Crow Creek Reservation, SD, to make studies of the Indians for a group portrait. Manuscript concerns her experiences at the Sioux reservation and the social life, customs, and religion of the Indian and white inhabitants.

15,851. Breeden, Jane Rooker (Smith)
Papers. 1886-1946. Ca. 1.5 ft. and 7 vols.
Open. No guide.
South Dakota State Historical Resource Center.
Breeden (1853-1955) was a leader in the South Dakota woman suffrage movement, president of the South Dakota Equal Suffrage Association, and an active member in the WCTU and other social and civic clubs. Correspondence with local newspapers regarding Breeden's articles on suffrage; annual reports of the national WCTU for 1887 and 1896; a scrapbook of clippings; yearbooks of the Illinois WCTU; publications of national, state, and local suffrage organizations, including "Objections Answered" by Alice Stone Blackwell; newsletters of the South Dakota Equal Suffrage Association; and an 1891 copy of *The Yellow Ribbon Speaker,* edited by Anna Howard Shaw, Alice S. Blackwell, and Lucy S. Anthony.

15,852. Corey, Elizabeth "Bess"
Papers. 1909-19. 1.5 ft.
Open. Unpublished guide.
South Dakota State Historical Resource Center.
In 1909 at the age of 22, Corey (1887-?) moved from Marne, IA, to a 160-acre homestead on the Bad River west of Fort Pierre, SD. Collection consists of approximately 100 letters from Corey to her family in Iowa detailing her day-to-day life, including descriptions of her teaching experiences, social life and customs, expenses, agricultural conditions, and family matters. Never marrying, Corey worked as a schoolteacher each winter and occasionally as a cook or housecleaner during the summers. Although often in debt, Corey earned enough money to finance improvement on her claim and eventually received her land patent and filed for an additional 40 acres. The letters are the primary source for an article, written by her younger brother Paul F. Corey, that appeared in *South Dakota Historical Collections* (1974).

15,853. Dakota Territorial Centennial Commission
Records. 1959-62. 3 ft.
Open. Unpublished guide.
South Dakota State Historical Resource Center.
Office files of the Commission, organized in 1959 to develop and coordinate activities for the celebration of the centennial of Dakota Territory. The Commission consisted of a 15-member board, appointed by the governor and the legislature, and a salaried director and supporting staff. The first director Merle A. Thiele was replaced in 1960 by Mary Loud Lund, who had originally been hired by the Commission as a secretary.

15,854. Irvine, Javan Bradley, Family
Papers. 1859-1902. Ca. 1.5 ft.
Open. Unpublished guide.
South Dakota State Historical Resource Center.
Irvine (1831-1904) served in the US Army during the Civil War and at various western forts until 1891. Correspondence between Irvine and his wife Margaret "Maggie" Louisa Irvine and from Maggie Irvine to others.

15,855. Lutheran Memorial Church
Records. 1883-1968. 33 vols. (microfilm).
Open. Unpublished guide.
South Dakota State Historical Resource Center.
Records of this local church contain minutes and financial accounts, 1896-1950, of the Ladies Aid Society, a social group founded in 1896 that still works to support the Church and its activities. Also included are minutes and financial accounts, 1926-68, of the Sunshine Circle, a social group organized in 1923 that still functions to support the Grace Evangelical Lutheran Church of Hayes, SD, and its activities.

15,856. M'Gillycuddy, Fanny
Papers. 1877-78. 1 item.
Open. No guide.
South Dakota State Historical Resource Center.
Diary written by M'Gillycuddy at Fort Robinson, SD, discussing such topics as the weather, social life and customs, Indian life, and the surrender, death, and burial of Crazy Horse.

15,857. National American Woman Suffrage Association
Records. 1897-98. 14 items.
Open. Unpublished guide.
South Dakota State Historical Resource Center.
Primarily letters from Carrie Chapman Catt, chairman of the committee on organization of the National American Woman Suffrage Association, to Jane Rooker (Smith) Breeden, a prominent South Dakota suffrage leader. The letters relate to problems in the South Dakota woman suffrage movement and a conflict between the suffrage movement and the WCTU.

15,858. Pioneer Daughters
Collection. Ca. 1850-1955. 4 drawers.
Open. No guide.
South Dakota State Historical Resource Center.
This collection, which was compiled by the South Dakota Federated Women's Clubs during the 1950s, consists of biographies of South Dakota women who helped settle the state and of children whose parents homesteaded in South Dakota.

15,859. Ringsrud, Olive A.
Papers. 1938-67. Ca. 1.5 ft. and 8 vols.
Open. No guide.
South Dakota State Historical Resource Center.
Ringsrud (1892-1971), a rural schoolteacher, was elected South Dakota secretary of state in 1938 and was the Republican nominee for the US Senate in 1940. Personal correspondence, journals, scrapbooks of original poetry, financial records, miscellaneous scrapbooks, and clippings.

15,860. Robinson, Doane
Papers. 1880-1946. 9 ft.
Open. Unpublished guide.
South Dakota State Historical Resource Center.
Papers of Robinson (1856-1946), an historian and director of the South Dakota State Historical Society, include correspondence with several state WCTU officials concerning funding of the memorial plaque to Mother Sherrard in the South Dakota state capitol, 1908-15; a letter in which he briefly sketched the history of the women's suffrage movement in South Dakota from 1872 to 1898; and "The Woman Power of South Dakota Through Registration," a manuscript he wrote in 1917.

15,861. Shakespeare and Art Club of Mitchell, SD
Records. 1916-71. Ca. 3 in.
Open. No guide.
South Dakota State Historical Resource Center.
Constitution, minutes, membership lists, history, and programs of this organization, established in 1916 for the mutual improvement of its members through the study of literature and art.

15,862. South Dakota League of Women Voters
Records. 1922-70. 1.5 ft. and 2 motion pictures.
Open. Unpublished guide.
South Dakota State Historical Resource Center.
Although the state LWV was not founded until 1955, the LWV has been active in South Dakota since 1920 when the Arlington League was organized. Within a few years Leagues were formed in Aberdeen, Brookings, Huron, Rapid City, Sioux Falls, and Vermillion; by 1967 membership in the local groups numbered 231. Minutes of state committees, state board reports, treasurer's reports, correspondence, position statements, motion pictures, announcements, convention programs, clippings, and publications, as well as annual reports of local chapters, a records book of the Arlington LWV, and a scrapbook of the Brookings LWV. Much of the material relates to 50th anniversary activities of the state and national Leagues.

15,863. Wegner, Nell (Norbeck), Family
Papers. 1921-66. Ca. 1 ft.
Access restricted. Unpublished guide.
South Dakota State Historical Resource Center.
A large part of the collection consists of family correspondence, including letters of Peter Norbeck (1870-1936), a South Dakota governor and US senator from 1921 to 1936; his wife Lydia Anderson Norbeck (1873-1961); and their daughter Nell (Norbeck) Wegner (1902-). Lydia Norbeck's correspondence contains letters to her daughter in Pierre and to her sisters in California as well as letters regarding life in Washington, DC, political developments in Washington and South Dakota, and Peter Norbeck's work.

15,864. Woman Suffrage Movement
Collection. 1889-1926. 1 ft. and 1 vol.
Open. Unpublished guide.
South Dakota State Historical Resource Center.
Constitution, bylaws, minutes, and correspondence of the Political Equality Club of Pierre, which became the Equal Suffrage Club of Pierre; correspondence of [Mrs.] Ruth B. Hipple, editor of the *South Dakota Messenger,* the official newspaper of the South Dakota Universal Franchise League; a history of the state's suffrage movement, written in 1920 by Hipple; petitions; pamphlets; leaflets; programs; government publications regarding woman suffrage; antisuffrage literature; and issues of the following newspapers: *The Woman's Column* from Boston; *The Woman's Tribune* from Washington, DC, edited by Clara Colby; *The Washington Woman* from Seattle, edited by Mrs. Homer Hill; *The Woman's Journal* from Boston, edited by Lucy Stone; *Woman's Standard* from Iowa; and *The South Dakota Anti-Suffragists.*

15,865. Woman's Relief Corps
Records. Ca. 1880-1920. 27 vols.
Open. No guide.
South Dakota State Historical Resource Center.
Financial records, correspondence, letter books, general orders, rosters, and programs of the Corp's South Dakota Department.

RAPID CITY

15,866. Archives
Records. 1889- . 4 drawers and 4 shelves.
Closed. No guide.
Benedictine Convent of St. Martin.
Financial records; legal papers; blueprints, plans, and contracts related to construction of community projects; correspondence; diaries of mothers superior; conferences written by mothers superior; photos; files on members; scrapbooks; and clippings of the Convent, which was founded in Sturgis, SD, in 1889.

ST. FRANCIS

15,867. Photo Archives
Collection. 1887- . Ca. 20,000 items.
Access restricted. No guide.
Buechel Memorial Lakota Museum.
Photo collection includes items depicting women.

VERMILLION

15,868. Pyle, Mrs. John
Papers. Ca. 1913-18. 10 boxes.
Open. No guide.
University of South Dakota, I. D. Weeks Library, Richardson Archives.
Correspondence of Mamie I. Shields Pyle (1866-1949), a leader in the woman suffrage movement and president of the South Dakota Franchise League, pertains to the suffrage campaign and field organization in South Dakota. Correspondents include Carrie Chapman Catt, Ruth B. Hipple, the LWV, the National Woman Suffrage Association, the South Dakota Equal Suffrage Association for Good Government, and the Leslie (SD) Woman Suffrage Commission.

15,869. South Dakota Oral History Project
Oral history. 1970- . No size given.
Open. Published guide.
University of South Dakota, I. D. Weeks Library, Richardson Archives.
Tapes and transcripts of ca. 1600 interviews with South Dakota residents cover the period from the 1860s to the present and include ca. 500 interviews with women. Interviewees discuss pioneering experiences of their parents, their own experiences homesteading, farming, cattle and sheep raising, the home life of settlers, social and cultural activities, religion and nonreligious life-styles, and politics. Most of those interviewed talk about their education; many are former schoolteachers. Also discussed are sicknesses, epidemics, and medical care; the weather, especially blizzards, tornadoes, floods (including the 1972 Rapid City, SD, disaster), and droughts; missionary work among the Indians; stories about local Indian tribes; relations with blacks, Ku Klux Klan activity, and anti-Semitism; relations among such immigrant groups as the Swedish, Norwegian, Danish, German, Russian, Dutch, Czech, French, Swiss, Lebanese, English, Polish, and Irish; class distinctions in early South Dakota towns; towns, cities, and their development; the depression; prohibition; businesses and employment; and travel by covered wagon, horseback, stagecoach, steamboat, and railroad. Women represented include Mrs. Harlan Bushfield, who succeeded her husband as US senator; [Miss] Kathryn Dewald, a homesteader; Nellie May Christensen, a teacher who describes her life as a single woman on a claim; Ruby Harmon Vance, who with her husband Howard Earl Vance recounts the early days of nursing in South Dakota; Gladys Pyle, a state legislator and US senator, who discusses women's suffrage and prohibition in South Dakota; [Miss] Meta Hellriegal, a businesswoman; Adeline Jenney, a poet, editor, and teacher; [Miss] Dana Harlow, an English and Spanish teacher, who wrote a history of Spink County pioneers; Irene Gerdes Treick, an employee and later president of Eureka National Bank; and Katherine Martha Soldat, a law secretary and court reporter during the 1920s, who later served as mayor of Sturgis, SD. Taken from *The South Dakota Experience: An Oral History Collection of Its People,* vols. 1-5 (Pierre and Vermillion, SD, 1972-1976).

YANKTON

15,870. Archives
Records. 1874- . 30 drawers.
Access restricted. No guide.
Benedictine Sisters of Sacred Heart Convent.
Property deeds, correspondence, files of members, retreat notes, chronicles, photos, blueprints, a manuscript history of the Catholic Church in South Dakota, and publications by the Sisters on the history of South Dakota and other subjects. The community was founded in 1874 in Maryville, MO, and is engaged in teaching, health care, and pastoral ministry.

TENNESSEE

CLARKSVILLE

15,871. Dix, Dorothy
Papers. Nd. No size given.
Open. No guide.
Austin Peay State University Library.
[Miss] Dix (1861-1951), a writer, was a newspaper and magazine columnist who lived in New Orleans. Family letters; six diaries in which she recorded trips taken to the Far East, Europe, and Africa from 1919 to 1931; Christmas cards; clippings by and about Dix; books; and other papers.

GREENEVILLE

15,872. Women's Literary Societies, Tusculum College
Records. 1884-1942. Ca. 1 cu.ft.
Open. Unpublished guide.
Tusculum College Archives.
The Clionian Society was formed in 1882 when only nine women were enrolled as students at Tusculum. The Alethean Society was established in 1902 after an increase in female enrollment. Secretary's minutes, treasurer's records, printed programs, and publications produced jointly in 1885 with a men's campus literary society. Minutes record debate questions, decisions, literary reviews, program participants, and selections. During the group's early years, Clionian women debated political, social, and philosophical topics. Both women's groups continued until ca. 1942.

15,873. Young Women's Christian Association
Records. 1884-1942. 1 folder and 5 vols.
Open. Unpublished guide.
Tusculum College Archives.
Constitution, secretary's minutes, treasurer's records, and receipts of the Tusculum College YWCA chapter, which was founded in 1884. Activities included missionary work and efforts to raise funds for the national YWCA.

KNOXVILLE

15,874. Moore, Grace
Papers. Ca. 1875-1953. More than 400 items.
Open. No guide.
University of Tennessee, Frank H. McClung Museum.
[Miss] Moore (1898-1947) was an operatic and film star. Personal and professional correspondence, photos, scrapbooks, invitations, articles, clippings, sheet music, music books, and other papers and memorabilia. Born Mary Willie Grace Moore, she married Valentin Parera.

15,875. Baker, Irene Bailey
Papers. 1964-65. 9 ft.
Access restricted. Unpublished guide.
University of Tennessee Library.
[Mrs. Howard H.] Baker (1901-) took her husband's seat in the US House of Representatives following his death. Correspondence, legislative files, speeches, photos, scrapbooks, clippings, and related material. Baker represented Tennessee's 2nd District.

15,876. Blanton, Margaret Gray
Papers. 1897-1972. 12 ft.
Open. Unpublished guide.
University of Tennessee Library.
Correspondence, manuscripts, research notes, short stories, poetry, essays, and memorabilia of Blanton (1887-1973), a novelist who worked with her husband Smiley Blanton, a psychoanalyst, on many of his writing projects. Includes Margaret Blanton's research material on Eliza (McCardle) [Mrs. Andrew] Johnson, Thomas à Becket, Dick Whittington, Bernadette of Lourdes, and other persons as well as manuscripts of her novel *The White Unicorn* and her unpublished manuscript "Flambeau." The Blantons lived in New York and Nashville.

15,877. Braden, Carl, and Braden, Anne
Papers. 1946-66. 9 ft. and 2 tapes.
Open. Unpublished guide.
University of Tennessee Library.
Carl Braden and his wife Anne (1924-), civil rights workers from Louisville, were involved in the Southern Conference Educational Fund. Correspondence, financial records, court records, newsletters, mailing lists, and clippings relate to their civil rights activities. Includes two tape recordings of proceedings of the Washington Conference on Voting Restrictions in 1960 and copies in Italian and Polish of Anne Braden's *The Wall Between.*

15,878. Dromgoole, Will Allen
Papers. 1831-1960. 3 ft.
Open. No guide.
University of Tennessee Library.
[Miss] Dromgoole (?-1934) was a Nashville journalist and author. Correspondence, journals, manuscripts of published and unpublished works, legal papers, family papers, photos, and clippings. Dromgoole was the author of at least 12 published novels, many of them for younger readers.

15,879. Justus, May
Papers. 1936- . 3 ft. and 1 tape.
Open. Unpublished guide.
University of Tennessee Library.
[Miss] Justus (1898-), a writer of children's stories, lives in Tracy City, TN. Correspondence, including letters exchanged with Jane Merchant, a Knoxville poet; manuscripts of Justus's books and stories; photos; and clippings of stories and songs. Also includes an interview with Justus taped in 1969.

15,880. Swisshelm, Dorothy
Papers. 1947-65. 1.5 ft.
Access restricted. Unpublished guide.
University of Tennessee Library.
Swisshelm was an author, social worker, and civil rights worker. Correspondence concerning Mississippi civil rights workers, Back Bay Mission, the Koinonia Farm, and professional social work; the manuscript of "Six Years Behind the Magnolia Curtain"; addresses; newsletters; clippings; and other papers, including material pertaining to civil rights organizations.

15,881. Temple, Mary Boyce
Papers. 1876-1920. 5 ft.
Open. Unpublished guide.
University of Tennessee Library.
Correspondence of [Miss] Temple (1856-1937), a

welfare worker, includes items related to the DAR and her work as vice-president general of that organization.

MEMPHIS

15,882. Banks, Lucille Webb
Papers. Ca. 1900-55. 13 ft. and 10 oversize items.
Open. Unpublished guide.
Memphis-Shelby County Public Library and Information Center, Memphis Room.
Banks (1874-1966) was a local historian and free-lance writer. Correspondence and clippings gathered by Banks for her research on the history of Memphis and the Midsouth region.

15,883. McIntyre, Florence
Papers. Ca. 1914-62. 36 ft.
Open. Unpublished guide.
Memphis-Shelby County Public Library and Information Center, Memphis Room.
McIntyre (1879-1963), an artist and art teacher, was founder in ca. 1914 of the Memphis Art Association, director of the James Lee Memorial Art Academy (now the Memphis Academy of Arts) from 1920 to 1937, and the first director of the Brooks Memorial Art Gallery. Correspondence, personal notes, and programs. Includes correspondence from a number of American artists. McIntyre was active in regional and national art associations and in the Tennessee Society for Preservation. Her autobiography is *Art and Life* (Memphis: Toof & Co., 1958).

15,884. Scruggs, Susanne Coulan
Papers. 1905-25. 18 ft.
Open. Unpublished guide.
Memphis-Shelby County Public Library and Information Center, Memphis Room.
Scruggs (1864-1945), the wife of Judge Thomas M. Scruggs of Memphis, promoted activities on behalf of local children, including the Memphis Playground Association, the Juvenile Court, and the PTA. Correspondence, photos, and clippings regarding child welfare activities in Memphis and Tennessee.

15,885. Allen, Louise
Oral history. 1970. 1 tape.
Open. Unpublished guide.
Memphis State University Library, Special Collections.
Interview in which Allen, secretary of the Tennessee Valley Authority, outlines the role of a woman executive in the TVA during the 1960s.

15,886. Bacon, Moriah K.
Papers. 1910. 1 vol.
Open. No guide.
Memphis State University Library, Special Collections.
[Mrs.] Bacon was a Memphis schoolteacher. Diary in which she records her activities and observations during a vacation in the northeastern US. Most of the notations refer to the historical significance of tourist attractions she visited in such cities as New York City, Philadelphia, and Pittsburgh. Also contains mention of subjects ranging from the dimensions of the Statue of Liberty to the 19th-century transcendentalist movement.

15,887. Burson, Mrs. Leo R.
Papers. 1967-70. 1 folder.
Open. No guide.
Memphis State University Library, Special Collections.
Copy of a scrapbook containing material about Josie Burson's work as commissioner of employment security during the administration of Tennessee governor Buford Ellington.

15,888. Chester Family
Papers. 1836-70. Ca. 4 in.
Open. No guide.
Memphis State University Library, Special Collections.
Correspondence and genealogical records of this family of Jackson, TN, settlers include letters about the lives of female family members, with references to upcoming parties, family illnesses, and schoolwork.

15,889. Church, Robert R., Family
Papers. 1859-1974. Ca. 10 cu.ft.
Open. No guide.
Memphis State University Library, Special Collections.
Correspondence, financial and legal records, photos, scrapbooks, items from *The Congressional Record,* articles, clippings, and ephemera of Robert R. Church, Sr. (1839-1912), a Memphis banker and philanthropist; his son Robert R. Church, Jr. (1885-1952), a Republican party leader and philanthropist; and Roberta Church (ca. 1915-), daughter of Robert Church, Jr., and a member of the National Advisory Council on Adult Education during the Eisenhower administration. Material concerns the business, family, and political activities of three generations of this prominent black Memphis family. Scrapbooks contain material concerning the founding in 1916 in Memphis of the Lincoln League, a black political action group; manuscripts reflect the family's NAACP activities.

15,890. Coe, Frances
Papers. 1940s-50s. 3 Hollinger boxes and 5 in.
Open. No guide.
Memphis State University Library, Special Collections.
Correspondence, pamphlets, and articles of Coe, a Democratic party worker in Tennessee. Includes material about local and national elections during the 1940s and 1950s.

15,891. Dukes, Laura
Oral history. 1967. 1 tape.
Open. Unpublished guide.
Memphis State University Library, Special Collections.
Interview in which Dukes (1907-) recounts her experiences as a blues singer with a group called the Beale Street Five.

15,892. Flowers, Paul
Papers. 1940s-60s. 2.5 in.
Open. No guide.
Memphis State University Library, Special Collections.
Correspondence, photos and clippings of Flowers, a writer and Memphis-area journalist. Includes letters from such writers as Catherine Drinker Bowen and Marjory S. Douglas.

15,893. Glaze, Eleanor
Papers. Nd. 15 in.
Open. No guide.
Memphis State University Library, Special Collections.
Manuscripts and rough drafts of the romantic novel *Fear and Tenderness* by Glaze, a novelist. Glaze was married to William Neal Ellis.

15,894. Glover, Lilly Mae
Oral history. 1967. 1 tape.
Open. Unpublished guide.
Memphis State University Library, Special Collections.
Interview in which Glover (1906-) recounts her life as a black jazz singer and comedienne from the 1920s to the 1960s.

15,895. Lumpkin, Martha Neville
Papers. 1861-71. 1 folder.
Open. No guide.
Memphis State University Library, Special Collections.
Correspondence and clippings of Lumpkin (1844-1915), a housewife. Includes letters from Cordelia Lewis Scales to Loulie W. Irby during and after the Civil War, giving news of the War and about her brother Dabney Scales, an officer on the Confederate sea raider *Shenandoah.* Many of the postwar letters tell of Dabney Scales's work as a University of Mississippi law student and of family illnesses and marriages.

15,896. McLaughlin, Harriet (McDill)
Papers. 1930s. 1 folder.
Open. No guide.
Memphis State University Library, Special Collections.
Manuscripts and an obituary of McLaughlin (1852-1937), a housewife and author, include her reminiscences about her parents Robert McDill and Nancy Wilson McDill. McLaughlin wrote of her mother's early life and schooling in South Carolina and of her parents' marriage in 1837. She also discusses her mother's proficiency in embroidery and the McDills' active role in the Winsboro, SC, church.

15,897. Memphis State University Archives
Records. 1912- . Ca. 54 ft.
Open. No guide.
Memphis State University Library, Special Collections.
Correspondence, memoranda, reports, newsletters, programs, photos, yearbooks, pamphlets, periodicals, clippings, and other records of Memphis State University, which was founded in 1912. The records reflect the role of women in the school's departments; the Columns Gallery; the University Wives Club; *Phoenix,* the English department's literary magazine; and other University activities.

15,898. Neilson, Caroline (McDougal)
Papers. 1830s-50s. 7.5 in.
Access restricted. Unpublished guide.
Memphis State University Library, Special Collections.
Correspondence of Neilson includes letters in which Andrew Jackson, writing his niece Mary (Donelson) Coffee and other Coffee family members, discusses his disappointment at being separated from his relatives and the appointment of Andrew J. Coffee to West Point. Other correspondence concerns Neilson and McDougal family matters, deaths, business dealings, and other subjects.

15,899. Oliver, Nola Nance
Papers. 1930s-40s. 1 box.
Open. No guide.
Memphis State University Library, Special Collections.
Correspondence, diaries, manuscripts, and family photos of Oliver, a writer primarily of short stories. Includes a draft of her book regarding Natchez, MS, articles she wrote for the Natchez *Times,* source notes for her stories, and manuscripts of her stories, poems, and novels. Many of the short stories that Oliver wrote during WWII reflect her interest in the US merchant marine.

15,900. Simon, Charlie May
Papers. 1940s-60s. 22.5 in.
Open. No guide.
Memphis State University Library, Special Collections.
Correspondence, royalty statements, and contracts of Simon, a writer and humanitarian who was the wife of John Donald Fletcher, a member of the Fugitive writer's circle. Includes letters from Albert Schweitzer, painter Thomas Hart Benton, and from writers Stephen Vincent Benét, T. S. Eliot, Conrad Aiken, Amy Bonner, Babette Deutsch, and Elizabeth Coatsworth. The letters

chiefly concern Simon's literary works and her activities in humanitarian and philanthropic endeavors.

15,901. Ward, Winifred
Oral history. 1967. 1 tape.
Open. Unpublished guide.
Memphis State University Library, Special Collections.
Interview in which Ward discusses her experiences as dramatics director of the Children's Theatre of Evanston, IL.

15,902. Winslow, Anne (Goodwin)
Papers. 1908-59. 75 in.
Open. Published guide.
Memphis State University Library, Special Collections.
Winslow (1875-1959) was a novelist, poet, and local historian. Correspondence, poetry notebook, unpublished poems, and fiction manuscripts constitute a complete collection of Winslow's works. See *Mississippi Valley Collection Bulletin,* No. 2 (Spring 1969).

15,903. Wurzburg, Jocelyn Maurie Dan
Papers. 1964-75. 1 box.
Open. Unpublished guide.
Memphis State University Library, Special Collections.
A political and social activist, Wurzburg (1940-) is a member of Tennessee's Republican party. Correspondence, newsletters, pamphlets, and brochures include information on women's, civil rights, and political groups in Memphis and Shelby County, TN.

NASHVILLE

15,904. Barclay, Julia Ann (Sowers)
Papers. 1855-77. 56 items.
Open. Unpublished guide.
Disciples of Christ Historical Society.
[Mrs. James Turner] Barclay (1813-1908) was an associate of many of the first-generation leaders of the Christian Church (Disciples of Christ). Consists of correspondence, chiefly letters from Mrs. S. H. Campbell, with Barclay family correspondence and letters from Mrs. M. G. Burnet included as well. Barclay's husband was a physician.

15,905. Bostick, Sarah Lue (Howard)
Papers. 1890-1950. 9 ft.
Open. No guide.
Disciples of Christ Historical Society.
Correspondence, minutes, photos, and pamphlets of [Mrs. Mancil Mathis] Bostick (1868-1948), a black home missionary in Arkansas.

15,906. Christian Women's Fellowship of Tennessee
Records. 1908-76. 7 ft.
Open. No guide.
Disciples of Christ Historical Society.
Minutes, financial records, correspondence, photos, and scrapbooks of the Fellowship, an organization of women in the Christian Church (Disciples of Christ) founded in 1908.

15,907. Irelan, Elma Clementine
Papers. 1905-49. 0.5 ft.
Open. No guide.
Disciples of Christ Historical Society.
Correspondence, memoirs, and photos of Irelan (1880-1956).

15,908. King, Jeanette Moore
Papers. 1911-48. 0.5 ft.
Open. No guide.
Disciples of Christ Historical Society.
Correspondence and photos.

15,909. McKeever, Jane (Campbell)
Papers. 1867-69. 9 items.
Open. No guide.
Disciples of Christ Historical Society.
Correspondence of [Mrs. Matthew] McKeever (1800-71).

15,910. Mathews, Nelle J.
Papers. 1941-65. 25 items.
Open. No guide.
Disciples of Christ Historical Society.
Letters from Mathews, a missionary in the Congo.

15,911. Wharton, Emma Virginia (Richardson)
Papers. 1908. 2 items.
Open. No guide.
Disciples of Christ Historical Society.
Letter and a manuscript in which [Mrs. Greene Lawrence] Wharton (?-1922) describes her personal feelings about life and church work.

15,912. Archives
Records. 1860- . Ca. 11 boxes and 15 vols.
Closed. Unpublished guide.
Dominican Sisters of St. Cecilia Congregation.
Financial records, correspondence, retreat notes, annals, photos, scrapbooks, and other records of the order, which was founded in 1860 by four sisters from Somerset, OH. Includes account books relating to the foundation in 1860 of an academy for girls, which is still operated by members of the community, and letters of several mothers general and bishops of Tennessee.

15,913. Anderson, Lizzie Crafton
Papers. 1972. 1 Hollinger box.
Open. No guide.
Fisk University Library, Special Collections.
Correspondence and biographical information about Anderson's father Laurine C. Anderson, a pioneer of Negro education in Texas and principal of Prairie View Normal and Industrial College in Texas from 1884 to 1897.

15,914. Brown, Dorothy
Papers. 1961- . 1 Hollinger box.
Open. No guide.
Fisk University Library, Special Collections.
Correspondence, speeches, and articles of Brown (1919-), a surgeon, member of the Tennessee legislature and the American Medical Association, and a Methodist churchwoman. Brown graduated from Bennett College in 1941 and Meharry Medical College in 1948.

15,915. Collins, Carrie B. H.
Papers. Nd. 1 Hollinger box.
Open. No guide.
Fisk University Library, Special Collections.
Sheet music of Collins, a music publisher and composer.

15,916. Egypt, Ophelia Settle
Papers. 1925- . 1 Hollinger box.
Open. No guide.
Fisk University Library, Special Collections.
Correspondence and writings of Egypt, a social worker and author of books for juveniles.

15,917. Gerda Lerner Collection on Black Women
Collection. 1972- . 1 folder.
Open. No guide.
Fisk University Library, Special Collections.
Speech by Lerner (1920-), an educator, writer, and professor at Sarah Lawrence College.

15,918. James, Grace
Papers. 1972. 1 Hollinger box.
Open. No guide.
Fisk University Library, Special Collections.
Speeches, biographical information, handbills, and other papers of James (1925-), a pediatrician who was the first black female lecturer at the University of Louisville medical school. James is also an active community worker.

15,919. Jefferson, Cecile Barefield
Papers. 1928-70. 17 Hollinger boxes.
Open. Unpublished guide.
Fisk University Library, Special Collections.
Jefferson (1883-1971) was the director of the Fisk University dining hall. Administrative, alumni, and personal correspondence; operational reports; biographical data; and other papers, including minutes, notebooks, photos, scrapbooks, handbooks, programs, and pamphlets.

15,920. Madgett, Naomi Cornelia Long
Papers. 1941-68. 1 Hollinger box.
Open. Unpublished guide.
Fisk University Library, Special Collections.
Letters to Ann Allen Shockley, work sheets, poems, clippings, and books of Madgett (1923-), a poet, educator, and publisher.

15,921. Meriwether, Louise
Papers. Nd. 1 Hollinger box.
Open. No guide.
Fisk University Library, Special Collections.
Correspondence of Meriwether, an author, and manuscripts of her *Daddy Was a Number Runner* and *The Freedom Ship of Robert Smalls.*

15,922. Simms, Margaret
Papers. 1952-70. 1 Hollinger box.
Closed. No guide.
Fisk University Library, Special Collections.
Photos, honorary degrees and awards, clippings, and other items of Simms (1903-74), a civic worker and assistant dean of women at Fisk.

15,923. Southern, Eileen
Papers. 1971- . 1 Hollinger box.
Open. No guide.
Fisk University Library, Special Collections.
Correspondence with colleges and universities, speeches, articles, and other writings by Southern (1920-), an ethnomusicologist, educator, author, and lecturer.

15,924. Spence, Mary
Papers. Nd. 5 cabinets.
Closed. No guide.
Fisk University Library, Special Collections.
Correspondence, primarily that of Spence with her father Adam K. Spence (1860-1902), a principal of Fisk Normal School and one of the first teachers at Fisk University.

15,925. Voorhees, Lillian
Papers. 1927-60. 7 Hollinger boxes.
Open. No guide.
Fisk University Library, Special Collections.
Voorhees was a professor of speech and drama at Fisk. Programs of educational, community, professional, and Fisk Stagecrafters theater productions.

15,926. Benedict, Anne (Scales)
Papers. 1923-51. 1 Hollinger box.
Open. Unpublished guide.
Joint University Libraries, Special Collections.
Benedict (1883-1958) and other Nashville women worked to persuade Vanderbilt University officials to hire a dean of women and to build a women's dormitory. She was involved in founding the Vanderbilt University Alumnae Council in 1923. Constitution of the Council, minutes, correspondence, fund-raising material, speeches, scrapbooks, pamphlets, and other items illustrate the women's efforts to attain greater administrative recognition and acceptance of women students at Vanderbilt.

15,927. Cheney, Brainard
Papers. 1932-70. 31 Hollinger boxes and 5 tapes.
Access restricted. Unpublished guide.

Joint University Libraries, Special Collections.
Cheney (1900-), a playwright and author of *River Rogue, Devil's Elbow,* and other books, has worked as a newspaper reporter and was a member of the Tennessee governor's public relations staff. Correspondence, manuscripts of novels, speeches, articles, short stories, tapes, and clippings. Includes letters from women authors, including Caroline Gordon, who was the wife of Fugitive poet Allen Tate; Flannery O'Connor; Katherine Anne Porter; Eudora Welty; and Mildred Haun.

15,928. Clark
Papers. 1816-99. 360 items.
Open. Unpublished guide.
Joint University Libraries, Special Collections.
Correspondence, business records, poems, a genealogy, and photos of members of the Clark family, settlers and farmers from Campbell County, VA. Originally Quakers, the family eventually joined other denominations. Part of the family migrated to Kentucky in 1832, while others remained in Virginia. Among the more frequent correspondents were Missouri P. W. Clark Ricks, who settled in Ohio in about 1843, and Julia A. B. Clark.

15,929. Davidson, Donald
Papers. 1917-68. 36 Hollinger boxes.
Open. Unpublished guide.
Joint University Libraries, Special Collections.
Correspondence, manuscripts, speeches and lectures, class material, research notes, student papers, photos, clippings, and other papers of Davidson (1893-1968), an author and educator. Includes letters from southern literary figures, including Caroline Gordon, Mildred Haun, Flannery O'Connor, Laura Riding, and Louise S. Cowan, author of *The Fugitive Group* and chairman of the University of Dallas English department. Davidson, the author of *Lee in the Mountains and Other Poems,* was an English professor at Vanderbilt University.

15,930. Dean for Student Services, Vanderbilt University
Records. 1938-74. 9 Paige boxes.
Open. Unpublished guide.
Joint University Libraries, Special Collections.
Financial reports, employment records, student organization and women's boards information, fraternity and sorority material, pamphlets, and other records of this office, formerly known as the dean of women's office. Includes handbooks for women students, which were issued by the Women's Advisory Council from 1946 to 1967.

15,931. Gault, Alma Elizabeth
Papers. 1925-68. 2 Hollinger boxes.
Open. Unpublished guide.
Joint University Libraries, Special Collections.
[Miss] Gault (1891-), a nurse, served as director of nursing schools in Illinois, at Meharry Medical College in Nashville, and at Vanderbilt University. Correspondence, speeches, articles, certificates, awards, and periodicals document Gault's participation in the development of nursing and education in the South. She headed the Vanderbilt nursing school from 1953 until 1967.

15,932. Harding, William Giles
Papers. 1827-72. 68 items.
Open. Unpublished guide.
Joint University Libraries, Special Collections.
Correspondence and photos of Harding (1808-86), a planter, race horse breeder, and Confederate officer, include letters that his wife Elizabeth McGavock Harding and his daughter Selene (Harding) Jackson wrote to him while he was held prisoner during the Civil War. Their letters contain descriptions of life at their Nashville plantation Belle Meade and descriptions of southern life during the war. Also includes a letter from one of the family servants, Susannah, to her "dear and honored master."

15,933. Haun, Mildred Eunice
Papers. 1927-66. 21 Hollinger boxes.
Open. Unpublished guide.
Joint University Libraries, Special Collections.
[Miss] Haun (1911-66), an educator, was an author of articles and books, including *The Hawk's Done Gone* (1940). Correspondence, diaries and personal records, research notes, manuscripts, financial records, holograph folk songs, photos, pamphlets, maps, clippings, and printed material include information she collected about Tennessee folklore, folk songs, and folk medicine. Also includes information about her life as a student in the 1930s at Vanderbilt University. Haun was an editor and writer for the US Air Force, the Department of Agriculture, and other government agencies.

15,934. Lytle, Andrew Nelson
Papers. 1868-1966. 5.04 ft.
Access restricted. Unpublished guide.
Joint University Libraries, Special Collections.
Lytle (1902-), a member of the Agrarian movement in Nashville during the 1930s, taught at Iowa State University; the University of the South, where he was editor of the *Sewanee Review;* and at other institutions. Correspondence, diaries, writings, biographical and genealogical data, research notes, land and estate records, photos, clippings, and other papers. Includes letters from Caroline Gordon; Katherine Anne Porter; Eudora Welty; Flannery O'Connor, who was Lytle's student; and other women involved in southern literature.

15,935. Rice, Grantland
Papers. 1905-54. 27 Hollinger boxes.
Open. Unpublished guide.
Joint University Libraries, Special Collections.
Rice (1880-1954) was a sportswriter and author of poetry, fiction, radio scripts, and plays. Correspondence, manuscripts, business and financial records, photos, sports guides and record books, clippings, and other papers. Includes photos of women sports figures of the 1920s, 1930s, and 1940s, among them golfer Virginia Van Wie, sharpshooter Annie Oakley, swimmers Gertrude Ederle and Helen Meany, track and field star Babe Didrickson, and tennis professionals Molla B. Mallory, Helen Wills Moody, Suzanne Lenglen, and Helen Jacobs.

15,936. Riding, Laura
Papers. 1923-33. 1 Hollinger box.
Open. Unpublished guide.
Joint University Libraries, Special Collections.
Riding (1901-), a poet, was the only woman elected to membership in the Fugitive writers group. Correspondence, poetry manuscripts, invoices and descriptions of poetry manuscripts, and lists of potential subscribers for the periodical *The Fugitive.* Educated at Cornell and the University of Illinois, Riding contributed poetry for *The Fugitive* and published a number of volumes of verse.

15,937. School of Nursing, Vanderbilt University
Records. 1912-69. 30 Paige boxes.
Open. Unpublished guide.
Joint University Libraries, Special Collections.
Committee minutes and reports, financial reports, memoranda, faculty and curriculum information, speeches, class lists, student records, photos, scrapbooks, pamphlets, clippings, and other records.

15,938. Wills, Jesse Ely
Papers. 1915-74. 3 Hollinger boxes.
Open. Unpublished guide.
Joint University Libraries, Special Collections.
Correspondence, manuscripts, literary society papers, tapes, and other papers of Wills (1900-), a poet and member of the Fugitive group who later headed the National Life and Accident Insurance Company. Includes letters from author Caroline Gordon.

15,939. Avery, Catherine Berry (Pilcher)
Papers. Ca. 1500-1971. 9.2 ft.
Open. Register.
Tennessee State Library and Archives.
Papers of Avery (1894-), historian, civic leader, and wife of Roy Avery, a physician, consist of correspondence, diaries, journals and reminiscences, biographical and genealogical data, estate papers, wills, land and farm records, accounts, Bible records, photos, clippings, and other papers. Includes a diary kept by Mary (Coburn) Dewees during a trip from Philadelphia to Lexington, KY, in 1787; another kept by Nancy (Barrow) Pilcher during a tour in 1845 by steamboat, stagecoach, canal boat, and railroad from Nashville to Boston and return to Louisville; and two kept by Catherine Avery during trips to western states in 1915 and 1917. Also includes more than 200 letters, 1938-70, from Margaret Dewees (Avery) Ritchie (1930-) to her parents Catherine and Roy Avery, the majority of which were written after her marriage in 1958. In the letters she describes daily activities in Atlanta.

15,940. Buford College
Records. 1903-07. Ca. 50 items.
Open.
Tennessee State Library and Archives.
Records of this boarding school for young ladies, established in Nashville in 1901 by Elizabeth Burgess Buford, consist of a 1903 souvenir catalog "The Mirror," which outlines the goals of the school; a catalog; photos of students; a list of the board of advisors, faculty, and servants; programs of exhibits, recitals, and other events; and six letters from alumnae who had been invited to a laying of the cornerstone of the West Building. The records were placed in the Building's cornerstone in 1907 and were discovered there when the Building was torn down. The school ceased operations in 1920.

15,941. Catt, Carrie Chapman
Papers. 1916-21. 1.6 ft.
Open. Register and card.
Tennessee State Library and Archives.
Correspondence, accounts, telegrams, clippings, and some writings of and about Catt, who was president of the National American Woman Suffrage Association. Contains information about the campaign for woman suffrage in Tennessee; the re-election of governor A. H. Roberts; writing the Tennessee chapter in the *History of Woman Suffrage,* which was edited by Ida Husted Harper; attitudes of journalists toward the suffrage campaign as depicted in clippings and cartoons; and woman suffrage planks for the 1920 Democratic and Republican party platforms.

15,942. Clift Family
Papers. Ca. 1820-1968. 150 items.
Open. Register.
Tennessee State Library and Archives.
Papers of the Clift family of Hamilton County, TN, center around Colonel William Clift (1794?-1886) of the 7th Tennessee Regiment of the US Army. Included with correspondence, historical and biographical sketches, Bible records, a deed, a will, and other papers are applications to the DAR and the Daughters of 1812 for his second wife Elizabeth Clift and genealogical data about the Brooks, Brothers, Clift, Doughty, Fowler, Hutcheson, Kearley, McDonald, Rawlings, and Rowland families.

15,943. Cody, Annie E.
Papers. 1927-57. 1.2 ft.
Open. Register.

Tennessee State Library and Archives.
Papers of Cody (1890-1957), an author and officer in the Felix K. Zollicoffer chapter of the Tennessee division of the United Daughters of the Confederacy, contain records of UDC chapters and conventions in Tennessee, including yearbooks, 1939-46; programs from conventions and conferences, 1933-55; and histories of UDC conventions, 1895-1952. Also includes minutes of the executive board of the Sam Davis Memorial Association, 1941-52; invitations and memorabilia; obituaries of prominent Tennesseans; and clippings about churches, schools, historic homes, early settlers, Confederate soldiers, and the UDC in Franklin and other parts of Williamson County, TN, and in Nashville.

15,944. Confederate Pension Board and Board of Pension Examiners
Records. 1905- . 28,161 folders.
Open. Published guide.
Tennessee State Library and Archives.
Includes 11,182 applications for pensions from Confederate veterans' widows. Applications give the names of the veteran and widow, dates and places of births and marriage, the unit in which the veteran served, the number of children, and the financial condition of the family. Supporting papers include affidavits and proof of marriage, correspondence with the Board of Pension Examiners, and, occasionally, notice of death. See *Index to Tennessee Confederate Pension Applications* (Nashville, TN: Tennessee State Library and Archives, 1964).

15,945. Correspondence by Subject: Tennessee Democratic Party
Papers. 1938. 60 items.
Open. Register.
Tennessee State Library and Archives.
Correspondence centers around the efforts of the women's division of the Democratic party to stimulate voter participation in the 1938 election. Includes correspondence of Bess Taylor [Mrs. Marc] Anthony, state chairman of the division, and lists of district, precinct and/or street chairmen and their assistants for the following Tennessee counties: Decatur, Gibson, Hardin, Haywood, Henry, Lauderdale, Loudon, McNairy, Madison, Pickett, Putnam, Rutherford, Smith, Tipton, Wayne, Weakley, Williamson, and Wilson.

15,946. Cox-McCormack, Nancy
Papers. 1911-65. 1.6 ft.
Open. Register.
Tennessee State Library and Archives.
Correspondence, photos, and memoirs of Nancy Cox-McCormack Cushman (1885-1967), a sculptor whose commissions included numerous prominent figures, among them Jane Addams. Much of the correspondence is with [Mrs.] Margaret Storrs Grierson, a professor of philosophy who became archivist at the Neilson Library at Smith College, and concerns the Sophia Smith Collection of papers of Smith College alumnae, which historian Mary (Ritter) Beard hoped would be the basis for a national women's archives in Washington, DC.

15,947. Daughters of the American Revolution, Tennessee
Collection. 1789-1952. 4.5 ft.
Open. Register.
Tennessee State Library and Archives.
Consists of records and papers donated by members of the Tennessee DAR. Contains records of the state division, including programs of state conferences, directory of committees, scrapbooks, chapter rolls of honor, and other records. Also contains records of individual chapters, including minutes of the Thomas McCrory chapter, 1932-39, and membership lists of the Wautauga chapter, 1894-1941. Also contains ca. 100 papers written by chapter members and placed in the DAR lending file.

15,948. Donelson, Bettie Mizell
Papers. 1787-1938. 2.9 ft.
Open. Register.
Tennessee State Library and Archives.
An early worker in the Tennessee suffrage movement, Donelson (1862-1939) was also a charter member and later regent of the Ladies Hermitage Association, a member of the women's department of the Tennessee Centennial Commission, and chairman of the Davidson County WCTU. Contains correspondence; land grants, powers of attorney, indentures, and other legal papers; photos of Rachel and Andrew Jackson, their home The Hermitage, Donelson, and other members of the Ladies Hermitage Association; and scrapbooks and clippings on the Jacksons, the assassination of her husband William Alexander Donelson, the WCTU and woman suffrage, the Ladies Hermitage Association, the Tennessee Centennial Exposition women's board, and other topics.

15,949. Elliott, Collins D.
Papers. 1816-1932. 2.1 ft.
Open. Register.
Tennessee State Library and Archives.
Elliott (1810-99) was a minister, teacher, and president of the Nashville Female Academy from 1840 to 1866. Contains family and other correspondence, biographical and genealogical data, sermon notes, lectures, and other papers, including woman suffrage and other material of Elliott's daughter Elizabeth "Lizzie" Porterfield Elliott (1860-1932) for the years 1860 to 1932. Also includes such records of the Academy as minutes of the board of trustees, material about the founding and history of the school, articles and papers about the controversy over dancing at the school, partial list of students, and statistics about the school during most of its existence.

15,950. Frank, Fedora (Small)
Papers. 1843-1964. 600 items.
Open. Register.
Tennessee State Library and Archives.
Papers of Frank, an author and historian who lives in Nashville. Her works include *Five Families and Eight Young Men* and *Nashville and Her Jewry, 1850-1961* (Nashville: Nashville Book Company, 1962). Includes correspondence; family records and essays; confirmation certificates; marriage, military, and cemetery records; speeches; historical sketches; naturalization papers; acts of incorporation; and other papers. The material depicts Nashville and its Jewish community; Jews in the Civil War, the Spanish-American War, and WWI; marriages, education, and land ownership; Jewish painters and paintings; religious and social activities; and deaths and burials.

15,951. Freeman, Mary Barry (Martin)
Papers. Ca. 1700-1962. 8.8 ft.
Open. Register.
Tennessee State Library and Archives.
Papers of Freeman (1882-1963), a genealogist, clubwoman, and wife of physician John Shaw Freeman of Robertson County, TN. Includes papers of the Freeman family, genealogical writings of and data gathered by Mary Freeman about 129 families from Robertson County or with Robertson County connections, and clippings concerning Robertson County history and personalities, the Civil War, national figures, and civil rights. Also includes records of state and local chapters of the American Legion Auxiliary, the DAR, the United Daughters of the Confederacy, Children of the Confederacy, and the National Society of the United States Daughters of 1812. The organization records include constitutions and bylaws, minutes, treasurers' reports, correspondence, yearbooks, membership lists, and other material.

15,952. French, Lucy Virginia (Smith)
Papers. 1860-65. 4 vols.
Open.
Tennessee State Library and Archives.
Civil War journals of French (1825-81), an author and poet who was the wife of Colonel John Hopkins French, a wealthy Tennessee stockman. The daughter of Mease W. and Elizabeth (Parker) Smith, Virginia French graduated from Mrs. Hannah's School at Washington, PA. She began her literary career as a contributor to the Louisville *Journal* under the nom de plume *L'Inconnue,* and in 1852, shortly before her marriage, she became editor of *The Southern Ladies' Book.* From 1856 to 1879 she was literary editor of such newspapers as the *Southern Homestead,* Nashville; *The Rural Sun, The Crusader,* and *The Ladies' Home,* Atlanta; and the *Southern Literary Messenger,* Richmond. She wrote poetry, including *Tecumseh's Foot, Wind Whispers,* and *Legends of the South* (1867); a five-act tragedy *Istalilxo, the Lady of Tula* (1856); and two novels *Darlington* (1870) and *My Roses* (1872). From the time of her marriage until her death she lived at Forest Home near McMinnville, TN.

French's journals describe war difficulties, among them raids by Union soldiers at the French plantation and at Beersheba Springs, where the French family went to live in 1863.

15,953. Howell, Alfred Elliott
Papers. 1842-1935. 1.6 ft.
Open. Register.
Tennessee State Library and Archives.
Family and other correspondence, diaries, memoirs, account books, autograph albums, and other papers of Howell (1863-1931), a manufacturer and musician. Includes correspondence of Howell with Jennie (Thompson) Howell before and after their marriage and letters of Jennie Howell's sisters Fanny and Mattie Thompson and Kate (Thompson) Weakley and of other family members. The correspondence covers the period 1880 to 1931 and provides information about the social history of Nashville. Also includes autograph albums of Jennie Thompson, her diaries for the period 1875 to 1919, and her last memoir "Family Talk," which was written from 1916 to 1926. Also contained are diaries by his daughter [Miss] Isabel Howell, 1920-23, while she attended Vanderbilt University and for a few months while she was in library school in New York City.

15,954. Ivie, Sallie (Lawing)
Papers. 1889. 3 vols.
Open. Register.
Tennessee State Library and Archives.
Scrapbooks compiled in 1889 by [Mrs. Thomas G.] Ivie (ca. 1845-ca. 1908) of Murfreesboro, TN, contain undated clippings about southern women in the Civil War and about Confederate veterans. Includes clippings about Nichola Marschall, designer of the Confederate flag and uniform.

15,955. Jones, Jane Margaret (Wood)
Papers. 1850-59. 3 vols. (microfilm).
Open.
Tennessee State Library and Archives.
Diaries kept by Jones (1832-63), the wife of Paul Tudor Jones (1828-1904) of Bolivar, TN, depict life on a farm near or in a small town. She kept diaries in 1850, 1857, and 1859.

15,956. Kemp, Augusta Thekla (Hasslock)
Papers. 1617-1967. 1 vol. and ca. 110 items.
Open. Register.
Tennessee State Library and Archives.
[Mrs. John F.] Kemp (1882-1963) was a geologist, paleontologist, and science teacher at Seymour, TX, from 1920 to 1943. Correspondence; genealogical data; manuscript of *Pegasus Limping,* a book of her poems, essays, and reminiscences; sketches; obituaries; and pamphlets and reprints of her articles. Includes two 1849 letters written by

Kemp's grandmother Thekla (Dombois) Hasslock describing her immigration with her husband Herman Wilhelm Hasslock to the US, the stay in New Orleans, the river trip to St. Louis, and their farm near there. Also includes genealogical data on the Hasslock and Dombois families, including birth, death, and marriage certificates from Germany covering the years 1689 to 1847, and historical sketches and other material relating to Kemp's ancestors in France and Germany. Kemp discovered a new fossil, which was named *Knightoceras kempae* in her honor.

15,957. Larew, Ada (Campbell)
Papers. Ca. 1925-63. 1.6 ft.
Open. Register.
Tennessee State Library and Archives.
Papers of [Mrs. Charles L.] Larew (1866-1963), a poet and author of historical sketches, drama, and short stories, include several of her poems and sketches; clippings of her writings over a 30-year period, which provide information about the history of Tennessee, its Indians and pioneers, the Civil War, and genealogical data; and photo albums. Also includes sketches by her husband.

15,958. Legislative Petitions
Records. 1799- . 51 Hollinger boxes.
Open. Unpublished subject index through 1865.
Tennessee State Library and Archives.
Includes many petitions written by women detailing the causes for bringing divorce proceedings, and justifications for tax relief and for "femme sole" status.

15,959. McEwen, Robert Houston
Papers. 1829-1908. 150 items.
Open. Register.
Tennessee State Library and Archives.
Papers of McEwen (1790-1868), a merchant in Kingsport, Fayetteville, and Nashville, TN; regimental quartermaster for Colonel John Brown's regiment in the War of 1812, and superintendent of common schools in Nashville. Includes a personal account book with prices of clothing and material for his wife Hetty (Kennedy) McEwen (1796-1881); letters from Robert McEwen to his daughter Kittie while she was on a trip abroad in 1859; a letter from Rutherford B. Hayes to Kittie McEwen; items regarding Mrs. M. A. Knox's school, the Nashville Ladies' College; and an 1846 act passed by the Tennessee legislature to incorporate the Nashville Protestant School of Industry for the Support and Education of Destitute Girls. Hetty McEwen attended Walladoid Academy prior to 1808.

15,960. Nashville College for Young Ladies
Records. 1881-99. Ca. 25 items.
Open.
Tennessee State Library and Archives.
Volume of minutes of the College, which was organized in 1881 as a Methodist school for girls, includes clippings, photos, and a sketch of the College written by Elizabeth Fraser Price, daughter of George Washington Fergus Price, head of the College.

15,961. Nashville Housewives League
Records. 1939-61. 1.2 ft.
Open. Register.
Tennessee State Library and Archives.
Founded in 1916, the League worked for improved canning and homemaking methods, clean-up drives, city beautification and anti-smoke campaigns, and aid to education. Contains minutes, 1948-61; treasurers' reports, 1949-61; League correspondence; and scrapbooks of clippings about League activities, 1939-42.

15,962. Nashville Woman Suffrage Association
Records. 1918-19. 1 vol.
Open. Card catalog.
Tennessee State Library and Archives.
Includes roll call and minutes of the Association, and a summary of the Association's 1919 convention.

15,963. Owen, Lou Cretia
Papers. 1918-19. 1 vol.
Open.
Tennessee State Library and Archives.
Diary kept by [Miss] Owen while she was a special service worker in the women's work department at Old Hickory Powder Plant, a Nashville explosives manufacturing firm. Provides details about her work with women at the plant.

15,964. Pearson, Josephine Anderson
Papers. Ca. 1860-1943. 7,100 items.
Open.
Tennessee State Library and Archives.
Correspondence, genealogical and biographical material, antisuffrage data, notebooks, school records, scrapbooks, photos, and clippings of Pearson (1868-1944), an educator and leader of antisuffrage associations. Pearson, the only child of the Reverend Philip Anderson Pearson and Amanda Caroline Roscoe Pearson, was born near Gallatin, TN. She attended Gallatin Female College, Gallatin, TN; Cumberland Female College, McMinnville, TN; and received a BA from Irving College, McMinnville, TN. She also studied at Vanderbilt University and the University of Missouri. Pearson was principal of McMinnville high school, 1890-94; principal of Nashville College for Young Ladies, 1895; member of the faculty of Winthrop State Normal and Industrial School, Rock Hill, SC; dean of Higbee Seminary in Memphis, 1902-08; dean and professor of philosophy and history at Woman's College, the University of Missouri at Columbia, 1909-14; dean and professor of philosophy at Southern Seminary in Buena Vista, VA, 1921-25; and in 1931 professor of English and philosophy at St. Agnes College in Memphis. Pearson served as president of the Tennessee State Association Opposed to Woman's Suffrage, 1916-20; president of the Auxiliary of the Dixie Highway on the Cumberland Divide, 1917-22; and president of the Southern Women's League for the Rejection of the Susan B. Anthony Amendment, 1920.

15,965. Query Club
Records. 1885-1968. 2.1 ft.
Open. Register.
Tennessee State Library and Archives.
Records of this Nashville women's literary club formed in 1885 include minutes, 1885-1941; treasurer's books, 1909-44; correspondence, 1891-1940; clippings; programs; membership lists; photos; resolutions; and 67 yearbooks, 1895-1962 and 1967-1968.

15,966. Rankin, Anne (Porterfield)
Papers. 1887-1941. 2.9 ft.
Open. Register.
Tennessee State Library and Archives.
Personal and business correspondence, manuscripts, poems, published articles, scrapbooks, and other papers and memorabilia of Rankin (1869-1942), an editor and newspaperwoman. In 1899 Rankin became literary editor of the *Nashville American* and from 1908 to 1920 served as editor of the *Southern Woman's Magazine.* From 1921 to 1927 she was movie critic and associate editor for the Nashville *Tennessean* and a columnist for the *Banner.* In 1927 she became editorial writer for the Knoxville *Journal* and began her "Rain Pool" column. The correspondence primarily concerns the *Southern Woman's Magazine* and WWI. Most of the manuscripts are feature articles and editorials for the *Southern Woman's Magazine,* the *Tennessean,* and the *Journal.*

15,967. Reeves, Henrietta (Kendrick)
Papers. 1860-1967. 5 vols.
Open. Register.
Tennessee State Library and Archives.
[Mrs. John H.] Reeves (1871-1968) was a poet, writer, and cultural and social leader in Nashville. Consists of her poems, short stories, and sketches, some of which were published, and a scrapbook that deals with the Centennial Club of Nashville and poets, writers, and artists who lectured to the Club. Includes letters to Reeves from Robert Frost, John Galsworthy, Amy Lowell, Algernon Blackwood, and others.

15,968. Smith, Mary Morriss
Papers. 1892. 1 vol.
Open.
Tennessee State Library and Archives.
Manuscript of the reminiscences of Smith (1802-95), a teacher, mother, and housewife, provide information about her childhood, her family's move from North Carolina to Tennessee in 1812, the local Methodist church, camp meetings, weddings, dyes women made from plants, and other women's roles.

15,969. Tennessee and North Carolina Land Grants
Records. 1777-1903. 260 vols.
Open. Unpublished name index.
Tennessee State Library and Archives.
Included in the land grants are the names of grantees, grant numbers, number of acres, the date of the grant, and the county. A few grants indicate that women held land before 1800. The collection is available on 203 rolls of microfilm.

15,970. Tennessee Equal Suffrage Association
Records. 1911-16. 2 vols. and ca. 25 items.
Open. Register.
Tennessee State Library and Archives.
Includes the original charter and bylaws from 1914, proceedings of the 1914 and 1915 conventions, minutes and reports for 1914, and clippings about the suffrage movement. Also includes minutes of the Nashville Equal Suffrage Association, 1911-14, and an address on female suffrage given by John J. Vertees.

15,971. Tennessee Federation of Business and Professional Women's Clubs, Inc.
Records. 1920- . 16 ft.
Open. Register.
Tennessee State Library and Archives.
Records of the Federation, which was organized in 1920 to promote the interests of women in business and the professions, include minutes, constitution and bylaws, a charter, lists of officers, reports, correspondence, biographical sketches of Tennessee women prominent in business and the professions, speeches, membership lists, proclamations, photos, club songs, and other records. Includes reports of the Governor's Commission on the Status of Women and a 1934 report regarding legislation on women, war, and work relief; material regarding school legislation, equal rights for women, and the equal rights amendment; a survey of women state officials in Tennessee; and material about the Southeast Region of the National Federation and of the International Federation of Business and Professional Women's Clubs.

15,972. Tennessee League for Nursing
Records. 1935-66. 2.4 ft.
Open. Register.
Tennessee State Library and Archives.
Records of the League, an organization of nurses and lay members that works to maintain or improve standards of nursing education and care of patients, include charter of incorporation, constitution and bylaws, annual reports, minutes and committee reports, convention programs, and publications or manuscripts dealing with the history of public health nursing, nursing resources, and

regulations for nursing homes in Tennessee. Includes records of the Tennessee League for Nursing Education, 1935-52, which was the predecessor of the League, and the Tennessee Council for Nursing, 1950-51. The League is the Tennessee branch of the National League for Nursing.

15,973. Ward-Belmont School
Records. 1900-57. 7 ft.
Open. Register.
Tennessee State Library and Archives.
Annuals, school directories, photos, literary magazines and other school publications, scrapbooks, programs, clippings, and other records relating to the Ward-Belmont School, a women's college formed in 1913 in Nashville by the merger of Ward Seminary, which had been established in 1865, and Belmont College, established in 1890.

15,974. Washington Family
Papers. 1796-1959. 67 vols. and 2000 items.
Open. Register and card catalog.
Tennessee State Library and Archives.
Correspondence, financial records, deeds, mortgages, farm and household account books, genealogy, telegrams, clippings, and other papers of tobacco planter Joseph Washington (1770-1848) and the Washington family at its home Wessyngton, which was built in 1819 near Cedar Hill, Robertson County, TN. Includes letters from Jane (Smith) Washington, 1856-66, to her husband George Augustine Washington in Louisville and New York City, where he had gone on business, revealing her responsibilities while he was away; letters from Jane Washington, 1865, to her children and mother-in-law Mary (Cheatham) Washington (1796-1865) at Wessyngton while she and her husband were trying to find a place to live in New York City so their children's education could be continued; and letters, 1865, from Mary Washington to her son and daughter-in-law in New York in which she describes the "uneasiness" of the period.

15,975. Wells, Emma (Middleton)
Papers. 1712-1945. 5 vols.
Open. Register.
Tennessee State Library and Archives.
A resident of Chattanooga, TN, [Mrs. Edward Oliver] Wells (1867-1945) was prominent in philanthropic and welfare work and the author of one volume of a history of Roane County, TN. Correspondence, including that with her husband before and after their marriage; memoirs; genealogical data of the Middleton, Anderson, and Montgomery families; manuscripts of her stories and sketches; a family Bible printed in 1712; obituaries; and scrapbooks. The papers document her activities in the United Daughters of the Confederacy, the Presbyterian church, and the Writers' Club.

15,976. Wilson, George
Papers. 1834-39. 84 items.
Open. Register.
Tennessee State Library and Archives.
George Wilson (1778-1848) was an editor and publisher of newspapers in Knoxville, TN, and Nashville and a state senator from 1811 to 1813. Correspondence, primarily that exchanged with his daughter Sarah Greer Wilson in 1838 and 1839 while she attended the Columbia Female Institute in Columbia, Maury County, TN. Also includes letters from Sarah Wilson to her sister Matilda Greer (Wilson) [Mrs. John King] Edmundson and her brother Wallace G. Wilson and from her friend Ann Winnick. The correspondence provides a detailed description of life at the Institute.

15,977. Zilphia Horton Folk Music Collection
Papers. 1935-56. 1,000 items.
Open. Register.
Tennessee State Library and Archives.
Correspondence, folk songs, labor union songbooks, picket line song sheets, musical tapes, notes, and published material of [Mrs. Myles] Horton (1910-56), director of music at Highlander Folk School, Grundy County, TN, from 1935 to 1956. The folk songs, songbooks, and song sheets were accumulated while Horton directed music at the Highlander School, which trained southern labor and civil rights leaders from 1932 to 1961. The bulk of the correspondence is that of Horton with folk singers, union leaders, and others interested in songs of social protest; also contains letters of condolence to Myles Horton after his wife's death. Includes material about the evolution of folk songs, especially songs of social protest, among them "We Shall Overcome," which evolved from the old hymn "We Will Overcome" and was revised at Highlander to become a pro-labor song. It was further revised in the 1950s to become the unofficial anthem of the civil rights movement. Horton was born in the Arkansas coal mining town of Sparda, and attended the College of the Ozarks, where she majored in music. She taught school and she collected labor songs for the United Textile Workers of America.

See *Zilphia Horton Folk Music Collection, Register No. 6* (Nashville, TN: Tennessee State Library and Archives, 1967).

PINEY FLATS

15,978. Patton, Mary (McKeehan)
Papers. 1770-?. 50 pp.
Open. No guide.
Rocky Mount Historical Association.
Reminiscences, court records, clippings, and other papers concern [Mrs. John] Patton (1751-1836), who made powder for soldiers during the American Revolution. She was particularly involved in the Battle of King's Mountain.

SEWANEE

15,979. Armes, Ethel
Papers. Ca. 1898-1945. 11 in.
Open. No guide.
University of the South Archives.
Correspondence, notes, manuscripts, photos, clippings, and other papers of [Miss] Armes (1880-1945), a newspaper reporter, writer, and editor who worked for the Washington *Post, Chicago Chronicle,* and *Birmingham Age.* She became editor of the magazine *Advance* in ca. 1906. During her work in Alabama she wrote *The Story of Coal and Iron in Alabama.* In 1913 she became active in efforts to improve conditions in Alabama coal mines; she sought unionization of coal mine workers and spoke before the United Mine Workers national convention in Indianapolis. Later she moved to New England where she continued her writing career. One of nine children, Armes was the daughter of Colonel George Augustus Armes, a Virginia resident who served in the Union Army.

15,980. Elliott, Sarah Barnwell
Papers. 1866-1928. Ca. 2 in.
Open. Unpublished guide.
University of the South Archives.
[Miss] Elliott (1848-1928) was an author and suffragist who served as president of the Tennessee Equal Suffrage Association from 1912 to 1914. Correspondence, including letters she wrote from Sewanee and New York to her brother Habersham Elliott; her poem "E. Q. B.," which includes reminiscences and sentiments about the E. Q. B. Club; manuscript of her unpublished "Sewanee Life"; a pamphlet she wrote to mark the semicentennial of the University of the South; a biographical paper about Elliott by [Miss] Louise Finley, the University librarian; newspaper reviews of Elliott's book *The Durket Sperret;* and an obituary. Elliott became active in the Tennessee woman suffrage movement after she returned to the state following the death of her sister in 1902. She raised her sister's three sons.

SIGNAL MOUNTAIN

15,981. Alexian Brothers Hospital
Records. 1940-70. 1.5 ft.
Open. Unpublished guide.
Alexian Brothers Congregation, Provincial Archives.
Minutes, correspondence, publicity material, and other records of the Woman's Board of the Alexian Brothers Hospital in Chicago, which later was known as the Woman's Board of the Alexian Brothers Hospital Foundation. The Board was founded in 1940 and was engaged primarily in fund-raising activities. Its records are intermingled with those of the Hospital Foundation because the two groups worked together. The Hospital first admitted women patients in 1963.

15,982. Alexian Brothers Hospital League
Records. 1963- . Ca. 6 in.
Open. Unpublished guide.
Alexian Brothers Congregation, Provincial Archives.
Bylaws, annual reports, minutes of board and general meetings, correspondence of presidents and the director of volunteers, membership rosters, news releases, issues of the newsletter "Alexiagram," and other records of the League, a women's organization established in 1963, the year in which the Alexian Brothers Hospital was built in San Jose, CA. Also includes bylaws and other records of League volunteers and junior volunteers.

15,983. Ladies Auxiliary, Alexian Brothers Hospital
Records. 1955- . 6 in.
Open. Unpublished guide.
Alexian Brothers Congregation, Provincial Archives.
Minutes, 1970-74; financial reports of the snack bar; and a scrapbook of the Auxiliary, which was founded in 1951. The Hospital, located in St. Louis, began admitting women patients in 1962.

15,984. Woman's Auxiliary, Alexian Brothers Rest Home
Records. 1950- . 6 in.
Open. Unpublished guide.
Alexian Brothers Congregation, Provincial Archives.
Bylaws, minutes of board meetings and general meetings, and lists of officers and membership of the Auxiliary. The Home, located in Signal Mountain, was founded in 1950 and was originally a home for retired persons; it now is an intermediate care health facility. The facility began admitting women patients in 1964.

TEXAS

ALPINE

15,985. Crosson Ranch
Records. 1861-1976. 4 ft. and 3 tapes.
Open. Unpublished guide.
Sul Ross State University, Archives of the Big Bend.
Elizabeth "Lizzie" Crosson (1844-1924) managed and expanded the Crosson Ranch after the death of George Crosson (1812-85), whom she had married in 1866. Correspondence, business papers, ledgers, oral history tapes, photos, legal documents, maps, and memorabilia. George and Lizzie Crosson established their cattle and sheep ranch in Brewster

County, TX, in the early 1880s. During the 1890s, Lizzie Crosson shifted from sheep to cattle raising and acquired more land. Under her direction, the ranch became one of the most successful ventures of its kind in the Big Bend region of Texas.

ARLINGTON

15,986. Allen, Ruth Alice
Papers. 1871-1963. 0.75 ft.
Open. Unpublished guide.
University of Texas at Arlington Library, Division of Special Collections.
A professor of economics at the University of Texas at Austin in the bureau of research in the social sciences before her retirement, Allen (1889-) is author of *The Great Southwest Strike* and *Chapters in the History of Organized Labor in Texas.* Research notes on labor history, photos, and clippings.

15,987. Amalgamated Clothing Workers of America, Farah Boycott Office
Records. 1964-74. 1.25 ft.
Open. Unpublished guide.
University of Texas at Arlington Library, Division of Special Collections.
The Dallas office coordinated the Dallas-Fort Worth portion of the boycott of products of Farah Manufacturing Company; women played a significant role in the Farah strike and the boycott. Correspondence, photos, and other material.

15,988. Andujar, Betty
Papers. 1973-75. 11.5 ft.
Open. Unpublished guide.
University of Texas at Arlington Library, Division of Special Collections.
Correspondence, memoranda, bills, clippings, and other papers of Andujar, a Texas state senator from Fort Worth, include material on pregnancy, abortion, and women's liberation.

15,989. Carter, Margaret
Papers. Ca. 1940-76. 18 ft.
Closed. No guide.
University of Texas at Arlington Library, Division of Special Collections.
[Mrs. Jack] Carter is a liberal leader in the Democratic party in Tarrant County, TX.

15,990. Committee on Political Education, AFL-CIO, Area 8
Records. 1963-65. 1.25 ft.
Open. Unpublished guide.
University of Texas at Arlington Library, Division of Special Collections.
Women take part in COPE through its Women's Activities Department. Correspondence of the area director, whose office is located in Dallas. Also includes field reports of state COPE directors; of Dorothy Hall, Oklahoma state director of the Women's Activities Department in 1963 and 1964; and of Hall's successor Fannie Webster, who held the post in 1964 and 1965. The Dallas COPE office carries on political activities in the AFL-CIO's Area 8, which includes Kansas, Missouri, New Mexico, and Texas.

15,991. Dallas Civil Liberties Union
Records. 1957-73. 1.5 ft.
Open. Unpublished guide.
University of Texas at Arlington Library, Division of Special Collections.
Women have been active leaders and members of this local branch of the American Civil Liberties Union. Constitutions, minutes of board of directors and membership meetings, correspondence, newsletters, records of the Texas Civil Liberties Union, ACLU newspapers, and clippings.

15,992. Graham, Charlotte
Oral history. 1973. 1 transcript and 1 tape.
Open. No guide.
University of Texas at Arlington Library, Division of Special Collections.
Interview of Graham (1914-), a former garment worker, includes her discussion of the Dallas garment workers' strike of 1933 in which she played a leading role.

15,993. Greater Fort Worth Civil Liberties Union
Records. 1957-74. 10.5 ft.
Open. Unpublished guide.
University of Texas at Arlington Library, Division of Special Collections.
Contains records of the GFWCLU, which is the Forth Worth, TX, chapter of the American Civil Liberties Union; of the national ACLU; and of other Texas chapters. ACLU records include information on such subjects as abortion, civil disobedience, discrimination, and the Vietnam War. Minutes of the board of directors, correspondence, and newsletters of the Texas Civil Liberties Union and the GFWCLU; court records of the GFWCLU; clippings of the state organization; miscellaneous records concerning the Forth Worth Independent School District, the Fort Worth Police Department, and other subjects; and records of the following Texas chapters: Brazos County, Central Texas, Corpus Christi, Dallas, Denton, El Paso, High Plains, Houston, Lubbock, San Antonio, the University of Texas at Arlington, and Waco.

15,994. International Association of Machinists, Ladies Auxiliary 490
Records. 1956-69. 1 ft.
Open. Unpublished guide.
University of Texas at Arlington Library, Division of Special Collections.
Minutes, financial records and correspondence of the union local's ladies' auxiliary in Brazosport, TX.

15,995. International Ladies' Garment Workers' Union, Local 180
Records. 1942-61. 0.75 ft.
Open. Unpublished guide.
University of Texas at Arlington Library, Division of Special Collections.
Financial records and correspondence of the San Antonio, TX, Local, which was composed chiefly of women. Includes records of the Local's strike in 1959 and 1960 against Tex-Son; the long strike was led by women.

15,996. International Ladies' Garment Workers' Union, Local 214
Records. 1947-63. 1 ft.
Open. Unpublished guide.
University of Texas at Arlington Library, Division of Special Collections.
Minutes, financial records, photos, and newsletters of the Houston Local. Most of the Local's members are women.

15,997. Lambert, George, and Lambert, Latane (Bartlett)
Papers. 1937-74. 15 ft.
Open. Inventory.
University of Texas at Arlington Library, Division of Special Collections.
Correspondence, financial records, union-organizing material, and photos of George Lambert (1913-74) and his wife Latane Lambert (1916-). Contains records of her work as a union organizer and as an activist in such groups as the Americans for Democratic Action, the LWV, the Texas Liberal Democrats, and the Democratic party.

15,998. Lambert, Latane (Bartlett)
Oral history. 1975. 1 transcript and 1 tape.
Open. No guide.
University of Texas at Arlington Library, Division of Special Collections.
Interview of [Mrs. George] Lambert (1916-), who is a former organizer for the UAW, the Amalgamated Clothing Workers of America, and the United Hatters, Cap and Millinery Workers. A former statistical analyst for the Dallas County Democratic Association, Lambert is an active member of the liberal wing of the Texas Democratic party. The interview concerns events dating from 1935 to 1975.

15,999. Leahy, Anna C.
Oral history. 1974. 1 transcript and 1 tape.
Open. No guide.
University of Texas at Arlington Library, Division of Special Collections.
Interview in which Leahy (1888-1977), a Fort Worth, TX, high school teacher and organizer of National Senior Citizens' Month, speaks of events dating from 1930 to 1974.

16,000. Leahy, Anna C.
Papers. 1954-72. 1.25 ft.
Open. Unpublished guide.
University of Texas at Arlington Library, Division of Special Collections.
Leahy (1888-1977) was a Fort Worth, TX, high school teacher, humanitarian, and organizer of National Senior Citizens' Month. Correspondence concerning Leahy's work with the program that sought designation of May as Senior Citizens' Month, photos and proclamations relating to the SCM program, and photos of public figures, including Presidents Kennedy, Johnson, and Nixon, and Texas governor Price Daniel.

16,001. Lucia, Carmen
Oral history. 1967. 1 transcript and 3 tapes.
Open. Unpublished guide.
University of Texas at Arlington Library, Division of Special Collections.
Interview of Lucia (1902-), an organizer and international officer of the United Hatters, Cap and Millinery Workers International Union, concerns events dating from 1904 to 1967.

16,002. McKnight, Reecy
Oral history. 1974. 1 transcript and 1 tape.
Open. Unpublished guide.
University of Texas at Arlington Library, Division of Special Collections.
Interview in which [Mrs. M. M.] McKnight (1907-), a businesswoman and former Fort Worth, TX, city councilwoman, discusses her political career from 1944 to 1963.

16,003. Mexican-American Farm Workers' Movement, Rio Grande Valley of Texas
Records. 1951-69. 5 ft.
Open. Unpublished guide.
University of Texas at Arlington Library, Division of Special Collections.
Correspondence, speeches, newsletters, articles, and clippings concerning formation of the United Farm Workers' Organizing Committee in Texas, the 1966-67 strike, migrant labor, Mexican-Americans, and the UFWOC in California. Women have been active participants in the movement.

16,004. Miller, Chris
Papers. Ca. 1972-76. No size given.
Closed. No guide.
University of Texas at Arlington Library, Division of Special Collections.
Miller, a Texas state representative from Fort Worth, was elected in 1972.

16,005. Office and Professional Employees International Union, Local 298
Records. 1952-69. 2 ft.
Open. Unpublished guide.

University of Texas at Arlington Library, Division of Special Collections.
Minutes and financial records of the Austin, TX, Local and its correspondence with the International Union. Also includes records from 1954 to 1963 of the OPEIU's predecessor, the Southwestern Organizational Conference of the Office Employees International Union. A large proportion of the Local's officers and members are women.

16,006. Raicoff, Anna (Duricy)
Oral history. 1975. 1 transcript and 1 tape.
Partially restricted. No guide.
University of Texas at Arlington Library, Division of Special Collections.
Interview in which [Mrs. James] Raicoff (1898-), a former milliner, supporter of organized labor, and grass roots political worker, discusses events spanning the period 1898-1975.

16,007. Texas AFL-CIO, Austin, TX
Records. 1928-73. 149.5 ft.
Open. Unpublished guide.
University of Texas at Arlington Library, Division of Special Collections.
Records of the Texas AFL-CIO, founded in 1957, include information on the group's female officers as well as women in Texas politics, women in industry, and women's activities in the liberal wing of the Texas Democratic party. Much of the material relating to women is included in executive board minutes, reports of vice-presidents, and correspondence and reading files of female officers. Other material is scattered throughout the collection's 27 series. The Texas AFL-CIO was formed by the merger of the Texas State Federation of Labor, founded in 1900, and the Texas State CIO Council, founded in 1937.

16,008. Twedell, Sam
Papers. 1945-61. 34 ft.
Open. Unpublished guide.
University of Texas at Arlington Library, Division of Special Collections.
Correspondence, organizers' reports, organizational material, photos, scrapbooks, and handbills of Twedell (1903-), a former district director for the Amalgamated Meat Cutters and Butcher Workmen of North America. Includes information about the Peyton strike from 1959 to 1961 in El Paso, TX, that involved many women as participants and leaders. Twedell was director from 1948 to 1968 for the Union's District 5, which included Texas, Oklahoma, Louisiana, Arkansas, New Mexico, and southern Kansas.

16,009. United Cannery, Agricultural, Packing, and Allied Workers of America, District 8, CIO
Records. 1938-47. 0.5 ft.
Open. Unpublished guide.
University of Texas at Arlington Library, Division of Special Collections.
Records of the union's District office include material on the pecan workers' strike of 1938 and 1939; the strike, led by a young Mexican-American Emma Tenayucca, involved many women. Correspondence concerns organizing efforts, financial problems of locals, strikes, the Pecan Workers' Union of San Antonio, and the pecan workers' strike. Also includes the board of arbitration decision in the pecan workers' strike, news releases, clippings, and copies of the proceedings of the first national convention of the UCAPAWA in 1937 in Denver.

16,010. United Farm Workers' Organizing Committee, Fort Worth Boycott
Records. 1968-72. 1.25 ft.
Open. Unpublished guide.
University of Texas at Arlington Library, Division of Special Collections.
Shirley Swallow was chairman of this Fort Worth, TX, group which organized to promote the grape boycott of the UFWOC in California. Correspondence, newsletters, leaflets, and clippings.

16,011. United Hatters, Cap and Millinery Workers International Union, Local 125
Records. 1958-66. 7 ft.
Open. Unpublished guide.
University of Texas at Arlington Library, Division of Special Collections.
Locals of the Union were composed chiefly of women and had female officers, among them Carmen Lucia, an International representative sent to help organize Texas workers. Minutes, financial records, and correspondence of Local 125 in Corsicana, TX, make up the bulk of the collection. Also includes miscellaneous records of Locals 126 in Dallas, 128 in Longview, TX, and 129 in Garland, TX, as well as correspondence of Lucia, Dennis Adams, John Kuliesh, and Carl Otto, all of whom were International officers and representatives who conducted organizing drives in Texas.

16,012. University Archives Oral History Project
Oral history. 1974-75. 8 transcripts and 8 tapes.
Open. No guide.
University of Texas at Arlington Library, Division of Special Collections.
Interviews in which eight women teachers and former teachers at the University of Texas at Arlington discuss their careers at the school. In another interview, the widow of a former teacher discusses her husband's work. The women reminisce about events that occurred between 1917 and 1974.

16,013. Vanderlee, John, and Vanderlee, Ann
Papers. 1950-74. 0.5 ft. and 1 tape.
Open. Unpublished guide.
University of Texas at Arlington Library, Division of Special Collections.
John Vanderlee is a pianist and student of classical ragtime; his late wife Ann Vanderlee studied ragtime and narrated his concerts. Scrapbook, entitled "John and Ann Vanderlee: Promoters and Preservers of Ragtime," and a tape recording of the Joplin Memorial Concert, a ragtime concert held in Texarkana, TX, in 1973.

AUSTIN

16,014. Fisher, Rebecca J.
Papers. 1847-1923. 1 document box.
Open. Unpublished guide.
Austin Public Library, Austin-Travis County Collection.
Rebecca Jane (Gilleland) [Mrs. Orceneth] Fisher (1831-1926), the wife of a Methodist minister, was a charter member and state president for 32 years of the Daughters of the Republic of Texas. Correspondence, a speech, pamphlets containing historical material about Texas and Fisher, tax receipts, membership certificates, clippings, and other items. Correspondents include Elisabet Ney, Mrs. Albert Sidney Johnston, Texas governor James E. Ferguson, and others.

16,015. McCallum
Papers. 1919-26. 15 document boxes.
Open. Unpublished guide.
Austin Public Library, Austin-Travis County Collection.
A leading figure in the Texas Woman Suffrage Association formed in 1915, [Mrs.] Jane (Yelvington) [Mrs. Arthur Newell] McCallum (1878-1957) was also the Texas secretary of state from 1927 to 1933. Correspondence, personal diaries, record books, photos, pamphlets, handbills, periodicals, and maps concern McCallum's work as secretary of state and the woman's suffrage movement in Texas. Some of the papers were collected by Minnie (Fisher) [Mrs. B. J.] Cunningham, a friend of McCallum and a woman's suffrage leader. Includes correspondence and printed material about the National American Woman Suffrage Association and the Texas LWV. The name of the Texas Woman Suffrage Association was changed to the Texas Equal Suffrage Association in 1916.

16,016. Pease, Graham, and Niles
Papers. 1829-1955. 141 document boxes and 156 vols.
Open. Unpublished guide.
Austin Public Library, Austin-Travis County Collection.
Correspondence, financial records, journals, photos, and printed items of the three families include the papers of Lucadia Niles Pease (1813-1905), the wife of Texas governor Elisha Marshall Pease, and [Miss] Julia Marie Pease (1853-1918), the second daughter of Elisha and Lucadia Pease. Lucadia Pease's papers include correspondence with her husband and her letters to her family in Connecticut describing her life as a bride in Brazoria, TX, in 1850 and as the wife of the state's governor in the 1850s in Austin; conditions in Austin during the Civil War are also described. Julia Pease was an Austin civic and social leader who reared the children of her deceased sister. She attended Hartford Female Seminary and received a BA from Vassar College in 1875. Her papers include personal letters; correspondence, course work, catalogs, social invitations, and other items relating to her years at Vassar; and correspondence, programs, clippings, and other papers collected in Austin.

16,017. Ladies of Charity of St. Vincent de Paul
Records. 1922-65. Ca. 1 Hollinger box.
Open. No guide.
Catholic Archives of Texas.
Certificate of incorporation, revised constitution of 1965, minute books, financial records, newsletters, and other records of this Austin organization, which existed from 1922 to 1975 and had as its purpose "performing works of charity and supporting charitable undertakings, by feeding and clothing the poor and aiding the sick and distressed."

16,018. Odin, Bishop
Papers. 1839-69. 136 folders and 604 items.
Open. Unpublished guide.
Catholic Archives of Texas.
Odin (1800-70) was an ecclesiastical administrator of the Catholic Church in Texas from 1841 to 1861 and was then elevated to the rank of archbishop of New Orleans. Correspondence between early Texas priests and bishops, letters from Odin to Archbishop Blanc of New Orleans concerning the difficulties of the large missionary territory of Texas, Odin's letters to Ursuline sisters concerning their arrival in Texas in 1847, administrative reports, and reports of trips to France seeking more priests and sisters. The letters are in French and some are also available on microfilm.

16,019. Ursuline Nuns
Records. 1847-1950. 14 folders.
Open. Unpublished guide.
Catholic Archives of Texas.
Correspondence, a history, and other records relating to foundations of Ursuline Nuns in Texas. The Nuns were involved in teaching. Includes an 1864 letter in which Sister St. Pierre of the Ursuline Convent in Galveston, TX, states, "At present we have only few boarders but a good number of Externes. Bad times and our exposed position to bombs and cannon balls are, I presume, the reasons why we have such a limited number." Some of the letters are on microfilm.

16,020. Women Religious
Collection. 1847-1975. 4 ft.
Open. Unpublished guide.
Catholic Archives of Texas.
Manuscripts, historical sketches, correspondence, statistics, pamphlets, photos, clippings, publications, and other items of each religious community or congregation of women in Texas. The women worked in such fields as teaching, nursing, and social work. Some of the papers are on microfilm.

16,021. Ney, Elisabet
Papers. 1870s-1907. Ca. 300 items.
Open. No guide.
Elisabet Ney Museum.
Correspondence, diaries, financial records, and photos of Ney (1833-1907), a sculptor who lived in Texas. Ney's work was exhibited in the US and abroad.

16,022. Bishop Tuttle School
Records. 1925-43. 1.5 ft.
Open. No guide.
Episcopal Church Archives and Historical Collections.
Founded in 1925, the School was also known as the National School for Training Colored Women as Church and Community Workers. Minutes, correspondence, reports, and publications. The School was associated with and located on the campus of St. Augustine's College in Raleigh, NC.

16,023. Corporation for the Relief of Widows and Children/Orphans of Clergymen of the Protestant Episcopal Church
Records. 1784-1975. 3 ft.
Open. Partial unpublished guide.
Episcopal Church Archives and Historical Collections.
Charters, minutes, financial records, and reports of this agency, which provided financial assistance for widows and orphans of Episcopal clergymen. The first of the corporations was founded in New York in 1769; similar groups were founded in the other colonies.

16,024. Domestic and Foreign Missionary Society
Records. 1820-1967. 463.5 ft.
Open. Description and finding aid.
Episcopal Church Archives and Historical Collections.
Missionary work of the Episcopal church was directed originally by the Domestic and Foreign Missionary Society, formed in 1820 or 1821. Minutes, financial records, correspondence, photos, and other records include information about women missionaries and women church workers and their evangelical, educational, and medical work. The National Council of the church later assumed direction of missionary activities; these responsibilities now rest with the church's Executive Council.

16,025. Girls' Friendly Society in the United States of America
Records. 1879-1970. 27 ft.
Closed. No guide.
Episcopal Church Archives and Historical Collections.
The Society, founded in the US in 1877, is an Episcopal organization that provides Christian education and service opportunities for young women ages 15 to 24. Annual reports, minutes, financial records, files, and publications.

16,026. Order of Holy Cross
Records. Nd. Ca. 90 ft.
Closed. No guide.
Episcopal Church Archives and Historical Collections.
Records of the Order of Holy Cross and the Order of St. Helena, two religious orders of the Episcopal church. The Order of Holy Cross, which is made up of men, was founded in 1884; the Order of St. Helena, an associate order comprised of women, was formed in 1945.

16,027. St. Margaret's House
Records. 1914-66. 2 ft.
Open. No guide.
Episcopal Church Archives and Historical Collections.
Incorporated in 1914, this institution houses the School for Christian Service and the Deaconess Training School of the Pacific. Minutes, reports, catalogs, and other publications.

16,028. Woman's Auxiliary
Records. 1872-1970. 36 ft.
Open. No guide.
Episcopal Church Archives and Historical Collections.
Annual reports and minutes of the national and diocesan levels of the Auxiliary, which was founded in 1871 to aid the Episcopal Domestic and Foreign Missionary Society in its missionary outreach programs. The group is known now as Episcopal Churchwomen.

16,029. Maxey, Samuel Bell
Papers. 1946-1966. Ca. 10,000 items.
Open. Published guide.
Texas State Archives.
Papers of Maxey (1825-95), an attorney, Confederate Army general, and US senator from Texas from 1875 to 1887, include those of his wife Marilda Cassa (Denton) Maxey (1833-1908), their adopted daughter Dora Rowell Maxey (1856-84), and other members of the Maxey and related families. Correspondence; financial, political, and legal papers; and memorabilia. Includes correspondence of Maxey and his wife, who was the daughter of a Baptist preacher and farmer from Overton County, TN; his letters to her written from 1875 to 1877 while Maxey was in Washington, DC record daily life there. Also contains family correspondence with Dora Maxey, who was legally adopted by the Maxeys in 1863 after her father Thomas Rowell died in the Civil War. Dora Maxey attended a girl's school in Danville, KY, from 1872 to 1874, and later married Judge Henry William Lightfoot (1846-1901), who was a law partner of Samuel Bell Maxey and later a Texas state senator and chief justice of the fifth supreme court of appeals at Dallas. See Louise Horton, *Samuel Bell Maxey Papers: An Inventory* (Austin, TX: Texas State Archives, 1969).

16,030. American War Mothers
Records. 1927-29. 13 items.
Open. Published guide.
University of Texas Archives.
Report, applications, petitions, bulletins, and pamphlets of the organization, which were collected by Violet A. Haynes, national historian of the AWM. Taken from Chester V. Kielman, comp. and ed., *The University of Texas Archives: A Guide to the Historical Manuscripts Collections in the University of Texas Library* (Austin, TX: University of Texas Press, 1967).

16,031. Andrews, Willie
Papers. Ca. 1872-1962. 9 in.
Open. Published guide.
University of Texas Archives.
Correspondence, telegrams, notes, memoranda, minutes, treasurers' reports, biographical sketches, lists, photos, tributes, memorials, broadsides, and clippings concerning the founding of the Andrews Pioneer Schools by Willie Andrews and her husband Whit Andrews. The Andrews schools, including Harris Chapel School, Nixon School, the Science Hall Institute, the Science Hall Home Institute, and Austin Home Institute, were pioneer coeducational boarding schools in the state; they preceded the establishment of a public school system in Texas in 1876. Collection also relates to local and state associations of Willie Andrews Pioneer Schools Ex-Students. Taken from Chester V. Kielman, comp. and ed., *The University of Texas Archives: A Guide to the Historical Manuscripts Collections in the University of Texas Library* (Austin, TX: University of Texas Press, 1967).

16,032. Atkinson, Mary Jourdan
Papers. 1930-40. 7 in.
Open. Published guide.
University of Texas Archives.
Correspondence, broadsides, pamphlets, and clippings of [Mrs.] Atkinson relate to the Civil War, WWI, early Texans, the University of Texas, Texas Memorial Museum, Elisabet Ney, the Central Christian Church in Austin, Indians of Texas, and family history. Taken from Chester V. Kielman, comp. and ed., *The University of Texas Archives: A Guide to the Historical Manuscripts Collections in the University of Texas Library* (Austin, TX: University of Texas Press, 1967).

16,033. Austin Women's Suffrage Association.
Records. 1906-14. 1 vol.
Open. Published guide.
University of Texas Archives.
Constitution, minutes of meetings, and list of charter members of the Association. Taken from Chester V. Kielman, comp. and ed., *The University of Texas Archives: A Guide to the Historical Manuscripts Collections in the University of Texas Library* (Austin, TX: University of Texas Press, 1967).

16,034. Barr, Agnes
Papers. 1818. 1 vol.
Open. Published guide.
University of Texas Archives.
Transcription of Barr's suit against Peter Samuel Davenport for the estate of her son William Barr. Taken from Chester V. Kielman, comp. and ed., *The University of Texas Archives: A Guide to the Historical Manuscripts Collections in the University of Texas Library* (Austin, TX: University of Texas Press, 1967).

16,035. Baylor, Mary
Papers. Nd. 1 vol.
Open. Published guide.
University of Texas Archives.
Baylor's recollections of early days in Texas cover the period 1827 to 1840 and include accounts of the Runaway Scrape and of prominent men and women who visited her family home. Taken from Chester V. Kielman, comp. and ed., *The University of Texas Archives: A Guide to the Historical Manuscripts Collections in the University of Texas Library* (Austin, TX: University of Texas Press, 1967).

16,036. Bell, Mrs. J. D.
Papers. Nd. 1 vol.
Open. Published guide.
University of Texas Archives.
Account of Bianca Babb Bell's capture by Comanche Indians. Taken from Chester V. Kielman, comp. and ed., *The University of Texas Archives: A Guide to the Historical Manuscripts Collections in the University of Texas Library* (Austin, TX: University of Texas Press, 1967).

16,037. Bewley, Lula Mary
Papers. 1859-1937. 16 items.
Open. Published guide.
University of Texas Archives.
Reminiscences, literary writings, and diplomas of Bewley, secretary to the University of Texas dean of women. Includes recollections of 30 years in a dean's office and a novel co-authored with Richard M. Swearingen. Taken from Chester V. Kielman, comp. and ed., *The University of Texas Archives: A Guide to the Historical Manuscripts Collections in the University of Texas Library* (Austin, TX: University of Texas Press, 1967).

16,038. Bonham, Dora Dieterich
Papers. Nd. 10 in.
Open. Published guide.

University of Texas Archives.
Correspondence, speeches, essays, literary writings, class notes, résumés, minutes, reports, legal documents, maps, drawings, photos, brochures, clippings, and other papers of Bonham (1902-), a businesswoman, historian, and writer. After attending Austin Senior High School and the University of Texas, Bonham worked as a secretary, statistician, and writer with the division of child health and public health nursing of the Texas State Department of Public Health. Papers relate to Dieterich and Fulkes family history; Elizabeth Houston Fulkes; Dora Bonham's marriage to Eugene Bonham and association with the Rauscher, Pierce Company; her service with the San Angelo Council of United Church Women, the United Council of Church Women of Texas, the San Angelo branch of the AAUW, and the Daughters of the Republic of Texas; and her historical research and writing, including a biographical study of Emma Kyle Burleson. Taken from Chester V. Kielman, comp. and ed., *The University of Texas Archives: A Guide to the Historical Manuscripts Collections in the University of Texas Library* (Austin, TX: University of Texas Press, 1967).

16,039. Borland, Margaret
Papers. 1858-79. 77 items.
Open. Published guide.
University of Texas Archives.
Memoranda, bills, powers of attorney, affidavits, lists of claims, promissory notes, receipts, bills of sale, deeds, and legal papers relating to the career of [Mrs.] Borland (?-1873), owner of one of the largest cattle herds in Texas and one of the first women to go up the trail to Kansas. Taken from Chester V. Kielman, comp. and ed., *The University of Texas Archives: A Guide to the Historical Manuscripts Collections in the University of Texas Library* (Austin, TX: University of Texas Press, 1967).

16,040. Brackenridge, Mary Eleanor
Papers. 1898. 44 items.
Open. Published guide.
University of Texas Archives.
Student notebooks, literary efforts, notes, calling cards, and maps of Brackenridge (1837-1924), a banker. Papers relate to the San Antonio de Béxar chapter of the DAR, the Texas Equal Franchise Society, the WCTU, and the Women Voters League. Taken from Chester V. Kielman, comp. and ed., *The University of Texas Archives: A Guide to the Historical Manuscripts Collections in the University of Texas Library* (Austin, TX: University of Texas Press, 1967).

16,041. Briscoe, Mary Jane Harris
Papers. Ca. 1886. 1 vol.
Open. Published guide.
University of Texas Archives.
Historical narrative and biography by Briscoe (1819-1903), an historian, concern Jane Long and the Civil War and the period 1815 to 1880. Taken from Chester V. Kielman, comp. and ed., *The University of Texas Archives: A Guide to the Historical Manuscripts Collections in the University of Texas Library* (Austin, TX: University of Texas Press, 1967).

16,042. Burleson, Adele Steiner
Papers. 1858-1944. 114 items.
Open. Published guide.
University of Texas Archives.
Correspondence, literary writings, scrapbooks, invitations, pamphlets, and broadsides relating to the career of Burleson, a writer. Taken from Chester V. Kielman, comp. and ed., *The University of Texas Archives: A Guide to the Historical Manuscripts Collections in the University of Texas Library* (Austin, TX: University of Texas Press, 1967).

16,043. Calohan, Mrs. W. L.
Papers. Ca. 1800-1931. 1 vol.
Open. Published guide.
University of Texas Archives.
Letters, reminiscences, and clippings concerning the career of Calohan (1847-?). Includes a brief summary of Calohan's life and a family history. Taken from Chester V. Kielman, comp. and ed., *The University of Texas Archives: A Guide to the Historical Manuscripts Collections in the University of Texas Library* (Austin, TX: University of Texas Press, 1967).

16,044. Cameron, Minnie B.
Papers. Ca. 1866-1924. 1 vol.
Open. Published guide.
University of Texas Archives.
Biographical sketches by Cameron of musicians, composers, painters, sculptors, and performing artists in Texas, including Elisabet Ney and Waldine Tauch. Taken from Chester V. Kielman, comp. and ed., *The University of Texas Archives: A Guide to the Historical Manuscripts Collections in the University of Texas Library* (Austin, TX: University of Texas Press, 1967).

16,045. Carter, Mary D.
Papers. Nd. 109 items.
Open. Published guide.
University of Texas Archives.
Letters, broadsides, clippings, and a magazine of Carter, president of the Virginia Historical Committee, concern the Civil War, Reconstruction, George Washington, and other subjects. Taken from Chester V. Kielman, comp. and ed., *The University of Texas Archives: A Guide to the Historical Manuscripts Collections in the University of Texas Library* (Austin, TX: University of Texas Press, 1967).

16,046. Cazneau, Jane McManus Storms
Papers. 1834-78. 1 vol.
Open. Published guide.
University of Texas Archives.
Correspondence, picture, and a will of [Mrs.] Cazneau (1807-78), a land speculator and writer, relate to her efforts to secure money to aid Texas in the fight against Mexico for independence and to her application for land in Matagorda. Taken from Chester V. Kielman, comp. and ed., *The University of Texas Archives: A Guide to the Historical Manuscripts Collections in the University of Texas Library* (Austin, TX: University of Texas Press, 1967).

16,047. Chandler, Alice Victoria
Papers. 1822-85. 1 in.
Open. Published guide.
University of Texas Archives.
Correspondence, literary efforts, an account book, legal documents, a deed, greeting cards, a genealogy, and other papers of Chandler (1867-?) relate to the Civil War, family matters, poetry, and songs. Taken from Chester V. Kielman, comp. and ed., *The University of Texas Archives: A Guide to the Historical Manuscripts Collections in the University of Texas Library* (Austin, TX: University of Texas Press, 1967).

16,048. Chappell Hill Female College
Records. 1911-12. 2 items.
Open. Published guide.
University of Texas Archives.
Collection contains a booklet describing social and academic conditions at the College and a poem about a brother who had fallen in battle. Taken from Chester V. Kielman, comp. and ed., *The University of Texas Archives: A Guide to the Historical Manuscripts Collections in the University of Texas Library* (Austin, TX: University of Texas Press, 1967).

16,049. Clow, Alice
Papers. 1846-1917. 1.5 in.
Open. Published guide.
University of Texas Archives.
Collection contains letters, poems, legal documents, account papers, pictures, and invitations of Clow. Also included are letters by Lizzie Adams and Robert J. Clow to Mary A. Maverick. Taken fromChester V. Kielman, comp. and ed., *The University of Texas Archives: A Guide to the Historical Manuscripts Collections in the University of Texas Library* (Austin, TX: University of Texas Press, 1967).

16,050. Coleman, Ann Raney Thomas
Papers. 1810-92. 3 vols.
Open. Published guide.
University of Texas Archives.
Letters and reminiscences of Coleman (1810-92) relate to life in England, a trip to America, life in the US, experiences in the Texas Revolution, the Runaway Scrape, the Civil War, and Reconstruction. Taken from Chester V. Kielman, comp. and ed., *The University of Texas Archives: A Guide to the Historical Manuscripts Collections in the University of Texas Library* (Austin, TX: University of Texas Press, 1967).

16,051. Colquitt, Alice F. Murrell
Papers. 1880-1916. 65 items.
Open. Published guide.
University of Texas Archives.
Correspondence, telegrams, minutes, financial papers, legal documents, a scrapbook, broadsides, pamphlets, clippings, and other papers of [Mrs.] Colquitt, director of the National Association for the Study and Prevention of Tuberculosis. Taken from Chester V. Kielman, comp. and ed., *The University of Texas Archives: A Guide to the Historical Manuscripts Collections in the University of Texas Library* (Austin, TX: University of Texas Press, 1967).

16,052. Coombs, Mrs. R. H.
Papers. 1862-1930. 1 vol.
Open. Published guide.
University of Texas Archives.
Recollections of life in New Orleans, Carthage, TX, Marshall, TX, and Nacogdoches, TX. Taken from Chester V. Kielman, comp. and ed., *The University of Texas Archives: A Guide to the Historical Manuscripts Collections in the University of Texas Library* (Austin, TX: University of Texas Press, 1967).

16,053. Cox, Nellie Stedman
Papers. 1843-1905. 1 in.
Open. Published guide.
University of Texas Archives.
Correspondence, literary efforts, photos, certificates of membership, clippings, and other papers of Cox (1855-1908), a teacher and newspaperwoman, relate to her literary writings, her membership in historical organizations, and the Civil War. Taken from Chester V. Kielman, comp. and ed., *The University of Texas Archives: A Guide to the Historical Manuscripts Collections in the University of Texas Library* (Austin, TX: University of Texas Press, 1967).

16,054. Crocheron, Helen
Papers. 1888-1940. 3.5 in.
Open. Published guide.
University of Texas Archives.
Correspondence and scrapbook relating to WWII, studies in Texas history, and geography. Taken from Chester V. Kielman, comp. and ed., *The University of Texas Archives: A Guide to the Historical Manuscripts Collections in the University of Texas Library* (Austin, TX: University of Texas Press, 1967).

16,055. Crockett, Fannie E.
Papers. Nd. 1 vol.
Open. Published guide.
University of Texas Archives.
Collection consists of an historical study by Crockett of Parson's Female Seminary and its transition into the Manor, TX, public schools. Taken from Chester V. Kielman, comp. and ed., *The University of Texas Archives: A Guide to the Historical Manuscripts Collections in the University of Texas Library* (Austin, TX: University of Texas Press, 1967).

16,056. Dabney, Lucy Jane
Papers. 1837-1934. 1 vol.
Open. Published guide.
University of Texas Archives.
Collection contains biographical and autobiographical narratives, photos, and clippings pertaining to the Walter Scates Dabney family and especially to Walter Dabney's daughter Lucy Jane Dabney (1880-), a teacher. Taken from Chester V. Kielman, comp. and ed., *The University of Texas Archives: A Guide to the Historical Manuscripts Collections in the University of Texas Library* (Austin, TX: University of Texas Press, 1967).

16,057. Davenport, Crittenden, and Harvey Families
Papers. 1806-94. 2 in.
Open. Published guide.
University of Texas Archives.
Letters, primarily by Nancy Davenport, Ann M. Crittenden, and Nancy Harvey, concern the personal and familial affairs of three generations of Davenport, Crittenden, and Harvey families, who were principally farmers, as they migrated gradually westward to Texas. Letters describe social and economic conditions in Alabama, Arkansas, Florida, Georgia, Tennessee, and Texas. Taken from Chester V. Kielman, comp. and ed., *The University of Texas Archives: A Guide to the Historical Manuscripts Collections in the University of Texas Library* (Austin, TX: University of Texas Press, 1967).

16,058. De Zavala, Adina Emilia
Papers. 1766-1955. 64.5 ft.
Open. Published guide.
University of Texas Archives.
Correspondence, notes, notebooks, account books, financial and legal papers, photos, albums, scrapbooks, broadsides, bulletins, clippings, and other papers of de Zavala (1861-1955), an historian, writer, collector, and clubwoman. Material relates to her interest in religious and patriotic societies, in the recognition and preservation of historical sites and buildings, and to the founding and affairs of the Daughters of the Republic of Texas, the Texas Historical and Landmarks Association, and the Texas State Historical Association. Also included are the papers of Manuel Lorenzo Justiniano de Zavala (1789-1836), governor of the state of México, vice-president of the Republic of Texas, congressman, and soldier. Taken from Chester V. Kielman, comp. and ed., *The University of Texas Archives: A Guide to the Historical Manuscripts Collections in the University of Texas Library* (Austin, TX: University of Texas Press, 1967).

16,059. Decherd, Mary
Papers. 1887-1946. 10 in.
Open. Published guide.
University of Texas Archives.
Collection contains correspondence, minutes, financial accounts, photos, pamphlets, and clippings pertaining to the work of Decherd, an educator, with the Methodist Episcopal church in Brazil and Austin, specifically with the Ladies Aid Society of the University Methodist Church and the Women's Missionary Society of Hotchkiss Memorial Church. Taken from Chester V. Kielman, comp. and ed., *The University of Texas Archives: A Guide to the Historical Manuscripts Collections in the University of Texas Library* (Austin, TX: University of Texas Press, 1967).

16,060. Diaries
Collections. 1730-1923. No size given.
Open. Published guide.
University of Texas Archives.
A number of diaries of pioneer women are included. Among them are an 1840 diary of Patricia Mercer and a daybook, 1851-53, of Annie Page Eanes Slaughter (1833-?) concerning a trip from Virginia to Texas, her marriage to A. B. Slaughter, and settling in Travis County, TX. Other diaries of the 1850s include one kept by Mrs. Charles Septimus Longscope during a two-month wedding journey from Texas to Virginia; daily observations of Abigail Baldwin, wife of a Congregational clergyman; a diary by Mary Ann Peebles concerning weather, sickness among family and friends, and a trip to Ohio; and one by Henrietta Embree (1834-61), wife of physician J. W. Embree, relating to hardships on the Texas frontier, problems with Indians, family news, and the deaths of her infant children. An 1860 diary of a trip to California by Mrs. Edward Dyer relates impressions of Indians and Mormons, while the diary of Lizzie H. Simons, wife of a Confederate soldier, recounts daily activities, prices of food and clothing, and current war news as supplied by letters and newspapers. Other material from the Civil War period includes a diary of Cornelia M. Noble pertaining to a journey from California to Hays County, TX, letters Noble received from her husband while he was away at the War, and letters and journals of [Mrs.] Tennessee Keys Embree. Diaries of Susan E. Newcomb (1848-?) and her husband Samuel P. Newcomb (1839-ca. 1869) relate to life at Fort Davis, TX, problems with Indians, buffalo hunting, a school begun by Samuel Newcomb, Susan Newcomb's life with her parents in Weatherford, TX, and her trip to Missouri after the death of her husband. Diaries of the 1870s include one by Margaret Armstrong Bowie telling of her life on a frontier farm, her marriage, and the birth of her son; one by Emily K. Andrews concerning a trip from Austin to Fort Davis; and a diary and account papers of Dorah Clegg concerning ranching transactions and a trip to Salado from Van Buren, AR. Mary Roselle Davis, a student at Vassar College, writes in 1876 about daily academic, religious, and social activities and her visit to the Centennial Exposition in Philadelphia while en route home to Texas. Notebooks of Mrs. Reeves Catt for the period 1887 to 1923, containing diary entries, poems, recipes, rosters, proverbs, and clippings, include notes on her trip to England and France in 1917 and items on Methodism in Texas and abroad. Journals of botanist Mary Sophie Young (1872-1919) contain notes relating to botanical explorations in the Trans-Pecos area as well as diary entries for 1914 to 1918. Also included are diaries of Margaret A. Mooar in the John Wright Mooar collection; diary and letters of Clara Brown Mitchel in the John Henry Brown collection; Sarah M. Peeble's diary and book of arithmetic and writing exercises in the Reuben G. White collection; an 1880s diary of Ella Cole; and an autobiographical narrative and travel journals of Mary Nicholson McDowall. In addition there is a diary of Margaret Lynn Lewis for 1730 to ca. 1800, which relates to early settlers in the Shenandoah Valley of Virginia. Taken from Chester V. Kielman, comp. and ed., *The University of Texas Archives: A Guide to the Historical Manuscripts Collections in the University of Texas Library* (Austin, TX: University of Texas Press, 1967).

16,061. Donelson, William A.
Papers. Ca. 1880-1937. 2 in.
Open. Published guide.
University of Texas Archives.
Letters, memoranda, photos, and clippings relate to social and genealogical interests of William A. Donelson and other descendants of Rachel Donelson Jackson. Included is material describing Bettie M. Donelson's activity in the Andrew Jackson Society, the Ladies' Hermitage Association, and the WCTU. Taken from Chester V. Kielman, comp. and ed., *The University of Texas Archives: A Guide to the Historical Manuscripts Collections in the University of Texas Library* (Austin, TX: University of Texas Press, 1967).

16,062. Dunn, Mary
Papers. 1910-46. 4.75 ft.
Open. Published guide.
University of Texas Archives.
Correspondence, memoranda, historical notes, a ledger, financial statements, a check register, programs, pamphlets, musical scores, and clippings of Dunn, a music educator and chairman of the applied music division of the Texas Department of Education. Dunn served as president of the Texas State Music Teachers Association and secretary of the South Plains Music Association. Material relates to the early history of music in Texas, Texas State Music Festivals, the Texas Federation of Music Clubs, the Texas Federation of Women's Clubs, and to Dunn's efforts to obtain accreditation in the state school system for music instruction given privately. Taken from Chester V. Kielman, comp. and ed., *The University of Texas Archives: A Guide to the Historical Manuscripts Collections in the University of Texas Library* (Austin, TX: University of Texas Press, 1967).

16,063. Dunn, Mary M.
Papers. 1845-1932. 1.67 ft.
Open. Published guide.
University of Texas Archives.
Correspondence, post cards, financial records, legal papers, a biographical sketch, poems, songs, photos, programs, pamphlets, clippings, and other papers of the family of Dunn, a physician. Included is the personal correspondence of Mary Marshall Dunn (1859?-ca. 1930) and of her sister Henrietta M. Dunn concerning health, religion, recreational and social functions, courtship, marriage, and the death of friends and relatives. Taken from Chester V. Kielman, comp. and ed., *The University of Texas Archives: A Guide to the Historical Manuscripts Collections in the University of Texas Library* (Austin, TX: University of Texas Press, 1967).

16,064. Earie, J. P.
Papers. 1900. 1 vol.
Open. Published guide.
University of Texas Archives.
Historical narrative of Clay County, TX, and the surrounding area in the period 1820 to 1900 concerns Indian raids, Cynthia Parker, Dot Babb, and stories of early settlers. Taken from Chester V. Kielman, comp. and ed., *The University of Texas Archives: A Guide to the Historical Manuscripts Collections in the University of Texas Library* (Austin, TX: University of Texas Press, 1967).

16,065. Edmond, Kate
Papers. 1866-1940. 1.56 in.
Open. Published guide.
University of Texas Archives.
Letters and notebooks of [Miss] Edmond (?-1940), a teacher at Dallas Academy in Selma, AL, relate to family matters and to chemistry, French, and cooking. Taken from Chester V. Kielman, comp. and ed., *The University of Texas Archives: A Guide to the Historical Manuscripts Collections in the University of Texas Library* (Austin, TX: University of Texas Press, 1967).

16,066. Eubanks, Mary
Papers. Ca. 1843-1931. 1 vol.
Open. Published guide.
University of Texas Archives.
Letters, a diary, and a genealogical chart of Eubanks relate to the history of the Eubanks family. Taken from Chester V. Kielman, comp. and ed., *The University of Texas Archives: A Guide to the Historical Manuscripts Collections in the University of Texas Library* (Austin, TX: University of Texas Press, 1967).

16,067. Flachmeier, Jeanette H.
Papers. 1948. 41 items.
Open. Published guide.
University of Texas Archives.
Correspondence and literary writings of [Mrs. W. A.] Flachmeier concern material collected for *The Handbook of Texas,* a book relating to early Texas pioneers and communities. Taken from Chester V. Kielman, comp. and ed., *The University of Texas Archives: A Guide to the Historical Manuscripts Collections in the University of Texas Library* (Austin, TX: University of Texas Press, 1967).

16,068. Gaines, Mrs. Reuben R.
Papers. 1882-1909. 1 in.
Open. Published guide.
University of Texas Archives.
Collection contains a letter, recipes, clippings, an Episcopal church hymnal, and a guest registry for the 50th wedding anniversary of Gaines, a housewife. Taken from Chester V. Kielman, comp. and ed., *The University of Texas Archives: A Guide to the Historical Manuscripts Collections in the University of Texas Library* (Austin, TX: University of Texas Press, 1967).

16,069. Gardner, Elizabeth F.
Papers. 1933-59. 1.25 ft.
Open. Published guide.
University of Texas Archives.
Correspondence, scrapbooks, pamphlets, and clippings of Gardner, a teacher, concern mental health in Texas and activities of the Hogg Foundation for Mental Health, the Texas Society for Mental Health, and the Texas Society for Mental Hygiene, of which Gardner was executive secretary. Taken from Chester V. Kielman, comp. and ed., *The University of Texas Archives: A Guide to the Historical Manuscripts Collections in the University of Texas Library* (Austin, TX: University of Texas Press, 1967).

16,070. Garrett, Mrs. C. C.
Papers. Ca. 1886-1917. 1 vol.
Open. Published guide.
University of Texas Archives.
Collection contains a pamphlet and clippings relating to the writings of Garrett. Taken from Chester V. Kielman, comp. and ed., *The University of Texas Archives: A Guide to the Historical Manuscripts Collections in the University of Texas Library* (Austin, TX: University of Texas Press, 1967).

16,071. Gerlach, Margaret Moody
Papers. 1863-1931. 1 vol.
Open. Published guide.
University of Texas Archives.
Collection consists of biographies and business accounts of Gerlach, a Texas pioneer, and biographies of George Gerlach and John Gerlach, the first merchants in Hemphill County, TX. Taken from Chester V. Kielman, comp. and ed., *The University of Texas Archives: A Guide to the Historical Manuscripts Collections in the University of Texas Library* (Austin, TX: University of Texas Press, 1967).

16,072. Given, Mrs. B. S.
Papers. 1850-1925. 28 items.
Open. Published guide.
University of Texas Archives.
Collection contains letters and biographical sketches of prominent Texans of the 19th and 20th centuries, including [Mrs.] Florence C. Floore, Mrs. William Clifton Martin, and Clara Driscoll Sevier. Taken from Chester V. Kielman, comp. and ed., *The University of Texas Archives: A Guide to the Historical Manuscripts Collections in the University of Texas Library* (Austin, TX: University of Texas Press, 1967).

16,073. Gordon, Mary Bouhanan
Papers. 1848-1932. 1 vol.
Open. Published guide.
University of Texas Archives.
Autobiography of [Mrs.] Gordon (1848-?) concerns her life in Alabama, moving to Texas, her education, teaching in Texas, married life, and her family. Taken from Chester V. Kielman, comp. and ed., *The University of Texas Archives: A Guide to the Historical Manuscripts Collections in the University of Texas Library* (Austin, TX: University of Texas Press, 1967).

16,074. Graham, Lucille Ross
Papers. 1954. 1 vol.
Open. Published guide.
University of Texas Archives.
Novel by Graham about the first Texas pioneers is entitled "These Are They." The novel was probably not published. Taken from Chester V. Kielman, comp. and ed., *The University of Texas Archives: A Guide to the Historical Manuscripts Collections in the University of Texas Library* (Austin, TX: University of Texas Press, 1967).

16,075. Graves, Ellen Armistead
Papers. Nd. 1 vol.
Open. Published guide.
University of Texas Archives.
Collection consists of a volume entitled "Old Plantation Days in Mississippi," which contains letters, reminiscences, a genealogical chart, and pictures concerning the life of Ellen Armistead. Taken from Chester V. Kielman, comp. and ed., *The University of Texas Archives: A Guide to the Historical Manuscripts Collections in the University of Texas Library* (Austin, TX: University of Texas Press, 1967).

16,076. Gray, Martha Nettie McFarlin
Papers. 1824-1924. 1 vol.
Open. Published guide.
University of Texas Archives.
Biography of John G. McFarlin, a Texas Ranger, Indian fighter, and pioneer of Llano County, TX, and an autobiography of Gray (1858-?), a pioneer woman. Taken from Chester V. Kielman, comp. and ed., *The University of Texas Archives: A Guide to the Historical Manuscripts Collections in the University of Texas Library* (Austin, TX: University of Texas Press, 1967).

16,077. Grimké, Sarah Moore
Papers. 1825-74. 30 items.
Open. Published guide.
University of Texas Archives.
Correspondence and reminiscences of Grimké (1792-1873), a plantation owner, relate to religion, abolition, and women's rights. Includes recollections of the Grimké sisters. Taken from Chester V. Kielman, comp. and ed., *The University of Texas Archives: A Guide to the Historical Manuscripts Collections in the University of Texas Library* (Austin, TX: University of Texas Press, 1967).

16,078. Hardy, Julia Wrenn
Papers. 1814-1912. 1 in.
Open. Published guide.
University of Texas Archives.
Correspondence, diaries for 1835 to 1865, account papers, legal papers, a scrapbook, genealogical material, and imprints of Hardy pertain to land transactions, crop production, business affairs, and family history. Taken from Chester V. Kielman, comp. and ed., *The University of Texas Archives: A Guide to the Historical Manuscripts Collections in the University of Texas Library* (Austin, TX: University of Texas Press, 1967).

16,079. Harris, Annie Pleasants Fisher Dallam
Papers. 1823-52. 1 vol.
Open. Published guide.
University of Texas Archives.
Memoirs of Harris (1823-?), a pioneer, concern her childhood, her family's move to Texas and settlement in Austin Colony, and her marriages to Wilbur Dallam and John W. Harris. Taken from Chester V. Kielman, comp. and ed., *The University of Texas Archives: A Guide to the Historical Manuscripts Collections in the University of Texas Library* (Austin, TX: University of Texas Press, 1967).

16,080. Harris, Jennie
Papers. 1871-1922. 1 vol.
Open. Published guide.
University of Texas Archives.
Correspondence and a biographical sketch of Harris (1871-1922), a teacher, writer, and artist, as well as poems, plays, stories, and essays. Includes material about her theories on education. Taken from Chester V. Kielman, comp. and ed., *The University of Texas Archives: A Guide to the Historical Manuscripts Collections in the University of Texas Library* (Austin, TX: University of Texas Press, 1967).

16,081. Harris, Rose
Papers. 1833-36. 1 vol.
Open. Published guide.
University of Texas Archives.
Literary writings of [Mrs. Dilue] Harris (1825-1914) concern early life in Texas. Taken from Chester V. Kielman, comp. and ed., *The University of Texas Archives: A Guide to the Historical Manuscripts Collections in the University of Texas Library* (Austin, TX: University of Texas Press, 1967).

16,082. Harrison, Nan Hillary
Papers. 1798-1880. 3 vols.
Open. Published guide.
University of Texas Archives.
Writings and photos of Harrison for a biography entitled "Jane Long: The Mother of Texas," which concerns Long's journey to and experiences in Texas. Taken from Chester V. Kielman, comp. and ed., *The University of Texas Archives: A Guide to the Historical Manuscripts Collections in the University of Texas Library* (Austin, TX: University of Texas Press, 1967).

16,083. Hatcher, Mattie Austin
Papers. 1715-1930. 1.88 ft.
Open. Published guide.
University of Texas Archives.
Correspondence, literary and historical writings, account papers, and a genealogy of Hatcher, an historian and archivist, relate to the Texas mission system, Napoleon, the revolutionary Spanish movement in Texas and Mexico, colonization contracts, and the Austin family. Taken from Chester V. Kielman, comp. and ed., *The University of Texas Archives: A Guide to the Historical Manuscripts Collections in the University of Texas Library* (Austin, TX: University of Texas Press, 1967).

16,084. Heartsill, Fannie A.
Papers. 1882-91. 4 items.
Open. Published guide.
University of Texas Archives.
Correspondence, minutes of meetings, and clippings relate to the Women's Missionary Society of the East Texas Conference of the Methodist Church. Taken from Chester V. Kielman, comp. and ed.,

The University of Texas Archives: A Guide to the Historical Manuscripts Collections in the University of Texas Library (Austin, TX: University of Texas Press, 1967).

16,085. Henderson, Samuel, and Henderson, Elizabeth
Papers. 1792-1894. 1 vol.
Open. Published guide.
University of Texas Archives.
Genealogical records and history, obituaries, clippings, and birth, marriage, and death registers pertain to the Carter, Henderson, Martin, Rodgers, and Williams families. Taken from Chester V. Kielman, comp. and ed., *The University of Texas Archives: A Guide to the Historical Manuscripts Collections in the University of Texas Library* (Austin, TX: University of Texas Press, 1967).

16,086. Hendricks, Pearl
Papers. 1819-1946. 2.08 ft.
Open. Published guide.
University of Texas Archives.
Collection contains correspondence, literary writings, and clippings collected by Hendricks, an historian and writer. Taken from Chester V. Kielman, comp. and ed., *The University of Texas Archives: A Guide to the Historical Manuscripts Collections in the University of Texas Library* (Austin, TX: University of Texas Press, 1967).

16,087. Hildebrand, Edith Fly
Papers. 1837-1952. 7.58 ft.
Open. Published guide.
University of Texas Archives.
Correspondence, diaries, literary writings, financial records, legal documents, photos, scrapbooks, drawings, and pamphlets relate to the personal, familial, and social activities of Hildebrand and her family. Material pertains to her interests in travel; religion; civic, social, and cultural affairs; genealogies and biographies of Fly-Hildebrand ancestors and prominent early Texans, including William Seat Fly; and to the medical career of her husband Walter Junius Hildebrand. Taken from Chester V. Kielman, comp. and ed., *The University of Texas Archives: A Guide to the Historical Manuscripts Collections in the University of Texas Library* (Austin, TX: University of Texas Press, 1967).

16,088. Holley, Mary Austin
Papers. 1808-46. 10 in.
Open. Published guide.
University of Texas Archives.
Correspondence, a diary, notes, and literary writings of [Mrs.] Holley (1784-1846), an historian and author of a biography of Stephen Fuller Austin. Includes notes on interviews with prominent Texans of the colonial period and letters to her daughter, other family members, and friends concerning personal and family matters, travel, conditions in Austin Colony and elsewhere in Texas, and her literary career. Taken from Chester V. Kielman, comp. and ed., *The University of Texas Archives: A Guide to the Historical Manuscripts Collections in the University of Texas Library* (Austin, TX: University of Texas Press, 1967).

16,089. Houston, Margaret Moffette (Lea)
Papers. 1840-67. 1 vol.
Open. Published guide.
University of Texas Archives.
Correspondence of Houston (1819-67) with her husband Sam Houston, her mother Nancy Moffette Lea, and her son Sam Houston, Jr. Taken from Chester V. Kielman, comp. and ed., *The University of Texas Archives: A Guide to the Historical Manuscripts Collections in the University of Texas Library* (Austin, TX: University of Texas Press, 1967).

16,090. International Ladies' Garment Workers' Union vs. Dorothy Frocks Company
Records. 1936. 1 vol.
Open. Published guide.
University of Texas Archives.
Collection contains petitions, briefs, appeals, and other documents which were used in the lawsuit of *International Ladies' Garment Workers' Local Union No. 123 et al. vs. Dorothy Frocks Company* of San Antonio, TX. Taken from Chester V. Kielman, comp. and ed., *The University of Texas Archives: A Guide to the Historical Manuscripts Collections in the University of Texas Library* (Austin, TX: University of Texas Press, 1967).

16,091. Jackson, Pearl Cashwell
Papers. 1883-1935. 8 in.
Open. Published guide.
University of Texas Archives.
Correspondence, post cards, literary writings, photos, broadsides, pamphlets, and clippings of [Mrs. J. A.] Jackson (1869-1928), president of the Texas Women's Press Association. Material relates to governors' wives and to travel in Europe, North Africa, the Near East, and the US. Taken from Chester V. Kielman, comp. and ed., *The University of Texas Archives: A Guide to the Historical Manuscripts Collections in the University of Texas Library* (Austin, TX: University of Texas Press, 1967).

16,092. Jones, Mary C.
Papers. 1846-1944. 4.5 ft.
Open. Published guide.
University of Texas Archives.
Correspondence, literary writings, reminiscences, minutes, proceedings, scrapbooks, a map, and clippings collected by Jones for a book on the history of Mitchell County, TX. Material pertains to family matters, reminiscences of old settlers, WWI and WWII, the American National Red Cross, Indians, hospitals and clinics, and agriculture, business, industry, and social activities in Mitchell County. Taken from Chester V. Kielman, comp. and ed., *The University of Texas Archives: A Guide to the Historical Manuscripts Collections in the University of Texas Library* (Austin, TX: University of Texas Press, 1967).

16,093. Lamar, Rebecca Ann
Papers. 1838-42. 1 in.
Open. Published guide.
University of Texas Archives.
Correspondence and a journal of Lamar relate to family matters, schooling, and a trip from Georgia to Texas. Taken from Chester V. Kielman, comp. and ed., *The University of Texas Archives: A Guide to the Historical Manuscripts Collections in the University of Texas Library* (Austin, TX: University of Texas Press, 1967).

16,094. Lavender, Eugenie Etiennette
Papers. 1817-97. 1 vol.
Open. Published guide.
University of Texas Archives.
Biography of Lavender (1817-98), an artist, describes her life in Paris, her marriage to Charles Lavender, her trip to America, and hardships she experienced in Texas. Taken from Chester V. Kielman, comp. and ed., *The University of Texas Archives: A Guide to the Historical Manuscripts Collections in the University of Texas Library* (Austin, TX: University of Texas Press, 1967).

16,095. Le Grand, Ann England
Papers. 1846-1924. 1.17 ft.
Open. Published guide.
University of Texas Archives.
Correspondence, account books, legal papers, receipts, brochures, and clippings concern the family of Le Grand, farm conditions, the Civil War, WWI, and the family of H. H. Fryer, a farmer, census enumerator, and member of the Anti-State Wide Prohibition Organization. Taken from Chester V. Kielman, comp. and ed., *The University of Texas Archives: A Guide to the Historical Manuscripts Collections in the University of Texas Library* (Austin, TX: University of Texas Press, 1967).

16,096. Ledbetter, Lena Dancy
Papers. 1830-1950. 1.25 ft.
Open. Published guide.
University of Texas Archives.
Correspondence, literary writings, reminiscences, memorabilia, pamphlets, clippings, and other papers of [Mrs.] Ledbetter, a housewife and civic leader, relate to her activities and to Texas history. Taken from Chester V. Kielman, comp. and ed., *The University of Texas Archives: A Guide to the Historical Manuscripts Collections in the University of Texas Library* (Austin, TX: University of Texas Press, 1967).

16,097. Letters
Collections. 1827- 1953. No size given.
Open. Published guide.
University of Texas Archives.
Correspondence by and about women includes a letter by [Mrs.] Harriet H. Schenck concerning family affairs and prayer meetings in Jacksonville, AL, in 1838; an 1846 letter concerning the purchase of Rosita Rodrigues from Comanche Indians; and letters and literary writings relating to the personal affairs of Mollie Vannemon for the period 1827 to 1864. Correspondence and literary writings by Laura M. Cole to Camilla S. Cheney concern daily life and the possibility of civil war. Letters Braxton Bragg's wife wrote him while he was serving as a Confederate general in the Civil War contain war and family news, while in another letter Mrs. E. A. Bowman expressed sympathy to Mrs. Bragg at the death of Mrs. Bragg's sister. Addie J. Simms wrote to her cousin Rufus K. Macomb about daily activities during a 14-month period of the Civil War in Gentry Station, a Harris County, TX, settlement. Mary J. Minor's letters relate to family affairs during the Civil War, while correspondence of novelist Amelia Barr (1831-1919) concerns her personal and professional activities and contains descriptions of events in Austin during 1861 and in Galveston, TX, during the Reconstruction period. A 1905 letter by Mrs. Moore Murdock relates to a Confederate reunion. Also included are letters of Harriet Virginia Scott (ca. 1824-1917) concerning a trip from New York to Houston, impressions of Texas, family matters, and her meeting with Sam Houston; personal correspondence of Sallie Neu with T. S. Trice; and correspondence of Bettie Beall with John F. Duke and Mattie A. Duke, Lucy Bridgwater, and Mollie Young about social affairs. Letters which Mrs. A. Bugbee (?-1898) wrote to her son Lester G. Bugbee, while he was at school and later a professor at the University of Texas, cover the period 1873 to 1898. An 1874 letter from [Mrs.] Lydia Van Wyke, a housewife, to Margaret Van Wyke describes San Antonio and the surrounding area. A letter by Agnes Sinclair in 1921 concerns her personal affairs, while letters and photos of the 1940s and 1950s relate to the Timmermann sisters, their friends, home, and church. Taken from Chester V. Kielman, comp. and ed., *The University of Texas Archives: A Guide to the Historical Manuscripts Collections in the University of Texas Library* (Austin, TX: University of Texas Press, 1967).

16,098. Lewis, Grace
Papers. Nd. 46 items.
Open. Published guide.
University of Texas Archives.
Correspondence, literary writings, and brochures of Lewis, an historian, relate to the history and development of Real County, TX. Taken from Chester V. Kielman, comp. and ed., *The University of Texas Archives: A Guide to the Historical*

Manuscripts Collections in the University of Texas Library (Austin, TX: University of Texas Press, 1967).

16,099. Lindley, Amanda
Papers. 1836-ca. 1890. 2 vols.
Open. Published guide.
University of Texas Archives.
Autobiography of Lindley (1836-ca. 1898), a housewife, concerns her early childhood, her marriage, and separation from her husband. Taken from Chester V. Kielman, comp. and ed., *The University of Texas Archives: A Guide to the Historical Manuscripts Collections in the University of Texas Library* (Austin, TX: University of Texas Press, 1967).

16,100. Locklin, Mary Fokes
Papers. 1834-44. 1 vol.
Open. Published guide.
University of Texas Archives.
Reminiscences of Locklin (1819-1902), a pioneer, about experiences of family and friends of Abigail McLennan Fokes, including hardships, Indian raids, and massacres in Milam and McLennan counties in Texas. Taken from Chester V. Kielman, comp. and ed., *The University of Texas Archives: A Guide to the Historical Manuscripts Collections in the University of Texas Library* (Austin, TX: University of Texas Press, 1967).

16,101. Long, Walter E.
Papers. 1964. 4 items.
Open. Published guide.
University of Texas Archives.
Memoirs of Fanny Andrews (1869-?), owner of Ye Qualitye Shoppe in Austin, and of her family, including her sister Jessie Andrews, who was the first female student to attend the University of Texas. Taken from Chester V. Kielman, comp. and ed., *The University of Texas Archives: A Guide to the Historical Manuscripts Collections in the University of Texas Library* (Austin, TX: University of Texas Press, 1967).

16,102. Looscan, Adele Lubbock Briscoe
Papers. 1828-1924. 1.5 in.
Open. Published guide.
University of Texas Archives.
Correspondence, literary writings, account papers, legal documents, biographical sketches, a genealogical sketch, and clippings of Looscan (1848-1935), a writer and president of the Texas State Historical Association from 1915 to 1925, relate primarily to prominent figures in Texas history. Taken from Chester V. Kielman, comp. and ed., *The University of Texas Archives: A Guide to the Historical Manuscripts Collections in the University of Texas Library* (Austin, TX: University of Texas Press, 1967).

16,103. McCallum, Jane Y.
Papers. 1836-1952. 2 in.
Open. Published guide.
University of Texas Archives.
Correspondence, telegrams, memoranda, photos, and a newspaper of McCallum, secretary of state of Texas, relate to the Texas Declaration of Independence. Taken from Chester V. Kielman, comp. and ed., *The University of Texas Archives: A Guide to the Historical Manuscripts Collections in the University of Texas Library* (Austin, TX: University of Texas Press, 1967).

16,104. Marshall, Mrs. Hudson Boatner
Papers. 1929. 1 vol.
Open. Published guide.
University of Texas Archives.
Collection contains anecdotes relating to the Hill Country section of Travis County, TX. Taken from Chester V. Kielman, comp. and ed., *The University of Texas Archives: A Guide to the Historical Manuscripts Collections in the University of Texas Library* (Austin, TX: University of Texas Press, 1967).

16,105. Minor, Mary J.
Papers. 1863-64. 1 vol.
Open. Published guide.
University of Texas Archives.
Letters of Minor concern family affairs during the Civil War. Taken from Chester V. Kielman, comp. and ed., *The University of Texas Archives: A Guide to the Historical Manuscripts Collections in the University of Texas Library* (Austin, TX: University of Texas Press, 1967).

16,106. Mohl, Aurelia Hadley
Papers. 1894. 1 vol.
Open. Published guide.
University of Texas Archives.
Biographical sketches of wives of 27 prominent pioneer Texans, including Mrs. James Bowie, Mrs. Sam Houston, Mrs. Mirabeau B. Lamar, and Mrs. James Long. Taken from Chester V. Kielman, comp. and ed., *The University of Texas Archives: A Guide to the Historical Manuscripts Collections in the University of Texas Library* (Austin, TX: University of Texas Press, 1967).

16,107. Mollenhauer, Margaret H.
Papers. 1894-1917. 2 items.
Open. Published guide.
University of Texas Archives.
Collection consists of letters relating to the history of San Antonio Female College. Taken from Chester V. Kielman, comp. and ed., *The University of Texas Archives: A Guide to the Historical Manuscripts Collections in the University of Texas Library* (Austin, TX: University of Texas Press, 1967).

16,108. Morgan, Ardita Berry
Papers. 1953. 1 vol.
Open. Published guide.
University of Texas Archives.
Narrative concerning the history of Chappell Hill Female College. Taken from Chester V. Kielman, comp. and ed., *The University of Texas Archives: A Guide to the Historical Manuscripts Collections in the University of Texas Library* (Austin, TX: University of Texas Press, 1967).

16,109. Neblett, Lizzie Scott
Papers. 1849-1928. 8.75 ft.
Open. Published guide.
University of Texas Archives.
Correspondence, a diary, notes, memoirs, literary writings, post cards, account papers, minutes, reports, legal documents, a biography, drawings, poems, photos, scrapbooks, programs, clippings, and other material relate to interests of the family of Neblett (1833-1917), a housewife. Taken from Chester V. Kielman, comp. and ed., *The University of Texas Archives: A Guide to the Historical Manuscripts Collections in the University of Texas Library* (Austin, TX: University of Texas Press, 1967).

16,110. Neeley, Elizabeth Montgomery
Papers. 1825-1937. 1 in.
Open. Published guide.
University of Texas Archives.
Autobiography and family history of Neeley. Taken from Chester V. Kielman, comp. and ed., *The University of Texas Archives: A Guide to the Historical Manuscripts Collections in the University of Texas Library* (Austin, TX: University of Texas Press, 1967).

16,111. Ney, Elisabet
Papers. 1859-1939. 1.17 ft.
Open. Published guide.
University of Texas Archives.
Correspondence, a diary, notes, a map, a broadside, clippings, and other papers of Ney (1833-1907), a sculptor, relate to her career, her son Lorne Ney Montgomery, her Austin studio, and her efforts to induce the Texas legislature to establish a state art academy. Taken from Chester V. Kielman, comp. and ed., *The University of Texas Archives: A Guide to the Historical Manuscripts Collections in the University of Texas Library* (Austin, TX: University of Texas Press, 1967).

16,112. North Texas Female College
Records. 1877-78. 1 item.
Open. Published guide.
University of Texas Archives.
Catalog of the College. Taken from Chester V. Kielman, comp. and ed., *The University of Texas Archives: A Guide to the Historical Manuscripts Collections in the University of Texas Library* (Austin, TX: University of Texas Press, 1967).

16,113. Paine Female Institute
Records. 1852-1933. 1 vol.
Open. Published guide.
University of Texas Archives.
Minutes and clipping relate to the board of trustees of Paine Female Institute, which was organized and operated by the West Texas Conference of the Methodist Church in Goliad, TX. Taken from Chester V. Kielman, comp. and ed., *The University of Texas Archives: A Guide to the Historical Manuscripts Collections in the University of Texas Library* (Austin, TX: University of Texas Press, 1967).

16,114. Pennington, May Williams
Papers. 1916. 1 vol.
Open. Published guide.
University of Texas Archives.
Correspondence, reminiscences, biographical sketches, and muster rolls of Texas infantry companies are included in the collection of [Mrs.] Pennington, who served as secretary of the Texas division of the United Daughters of the Confederacy. Also includes an essay by Pennington about Jefferson Davis and an essay by Mary C. Dixon entitled "Women of the Sixties." Taken from Chester V. Kielman, comp. and ed., *The University of Texas Archives: A Guide to the Historical Manuscripts Collections in the University of Texas Library* (Austin, TX: University of Texas Press, 1967).

16,115. Pennybacker, Mrs. Percy V.
Papers. 1878-1938. 53 ft.
Open. Published guide.
University of Texas Archives.
Correspondence, telegrams, invitations, receipts, canceled checks, photos, programs, pamphlets, clippings, and magazines of Pennybacker (1861-1938), a teacher and writer, relate to cultural and social affairs, education, the Texas Federation of Women's Clubs and the GFWC, the Chautauqua Institution, Chautauqua women's clubs, the National American Woman Suffrage Association, the Texas Teachers' Bureau, the Democratic National Committee, and other organizations. Taken from Chester V. Kielman, comp. and ed., *The University of Texas Archives: A Guide to the Historical Manuscripts Collections in the University of Texas Library* (Austin, TX: University of Texas Press, 1967).

16,116. Perry, Hally Ballinger (Bryan)
Papers. Ca. 1761-1958. Ca. 9.5 ft.
Open. Published guide.
University of Texas Archives.
Correspondence, literary writings, research notes, memoranda, narratives, legal and business papers and reports, photos, a scrapbook, programs, pamphlets, clippings, memorabilia, an autobiographical sketch by Perry, reminiscences about Perry by her friends, and other papers of Perry (1868-1955). Included are the constitution, bylaws, membership applications, and committee reports of the Daughters of the Republic of Texas, of which she was cofounder; material pertaining to

the founding of chapters of the Daughters of the Republic of Texas in Brazoria County and the Big Bend region; and material pertaining to the DAR, the Colonial Dames of America, and various organizations concerned with Texas history. Taken from Chester V. Kielman, comp. and ed., *The University of Texas Archives: A Guide to the Historical Manuscripts Collections in the University of Texas Library* (Austin, TX: University of Texas Press, 1967).

16,117. Pioneer Women
Collections. 1828-1933. No size given.
Open. Published guide.
University of Texas Archives.
Reminiscences of pioneer women include those of Elizabeth McAnulty Owens, who wrote of the McMullen-McGloin Colony in 1828, the Fannin massacre, a Comanche raid on Linnville and Victoria, TX, and business activities in Victoria before the Civil War; reminiscences of an anonymous female concerning her childhood during the 1830s in Washington County, TX, in the collection of James W. Oates; memoirs of Harriet A. Ames concerning the Texas Revolution and the Republic of Texas; and memoirs of Effie Graves, written in 1850. Mary Adams Maverick wrote about the Maverick family in Texas from 1838 to 1859, while Mrs. Richard Smith Morgan reminisced in 1848 about social and cultural conditions in Austin. [Mrs.] Francena Martin Sutton (ca. 1838-1914) described a journey she and seven others made from Fayetteville, AR, to Paris, TX, in 1864 and difficulties they experienced while traveling with small children through Indian territory. Autobiography of [Mrs.] Rosalie Bridget Hart Priour (1826-?), a schoolteacher, concerns her family's emigration to Texas in 1834, the passage, Gulf Coast diseases, and experiences with Mexicans, Indians, and Civil War troops. Martha Virginia Webster Strickland Simmons (1836-?) wrote of an attack and massacre by Comanche Indians on Brushy Creek, her capture, and her escape to San Antonio. Helen Beall Houston's memoirs concern family history, genealogy, and her youth up to about 1893, while the autobiography of Ella Bird-Dumont covers the period 1861 to 1927 and contains recollections of life on the western Texas frontier. Also included are reminiscences of Lizzie C. (Stillwell) Saunders (1860-1946). Taken from Chester V. Kielman, comp. and ed., *The University of Texas Archives: A Guide to the Historical Manuscripts Collections in the University of Texas Library* (Austin, TX: University of Texas Press, 1967).

16,118. Prairie Blume Literary Society
Records. 1857-1941. 2 in.
Open. Published guide.
University of Texas Archives.
Letters, literary writings, and a newspaper of Anna Romberg relate to the history of the Society and to programs presented at monthly meetings. Taken from Chester V. Kielman, comp. and ed., *The University of Texas Archives: A Guide to the Historical Manuscripts Collections in the University of Texas Library* (Austin, TX: University of Texas Press, 1967).

16,119. Queen City Chautauqua Circle
Records. 1883-1932. 0.5 in.
Open. Published guide.
University of Texas Archives.
Collection contains constitutions, bylaws, minutes, correspondence, a bulletin, an advertisement, a poem, and clippings of Virginia Crenshaw Harper Holland, who was president of the Queen City, MO, CLSC, which probably was the Queen City Chautauqua Literary and Scientific Circle, and Friends-in-Council. Also includes a record book relating to meetings of Springfield, MO, women's groups for historical, religious, political, economic, sociological, and literary studies. Taken from Chester V. Kielman, comp. and ed., *The University of Texas Archives: A Guide to the Historical Manuscripts Collections in the University of Texas Library* (Austin, TX: University of Texas Press, 1967).

16,120. Quillen, Jane Lowe
Papers. 1887-ca. 1906. 1 vol.
Open. Published guide.
University of Texas Archives.
Autobiography of Quillen concerns her life on the high plains in Hale County, TX, and Plainview, TX. Taken from Chester V. Kielman, comp. and ed., *The University of Texas Archives: A Guide to the Historical Manuscripts Collections in the University of Texas Library* (Austin, TX: University of Texas Press, 1967).

16,121. Rabb, Mary
Papers. 1823-1922. 3 vols.
Open. Published guide.
University of Texas Archives.
Correspondence, reminiscences, tax receipts, legal documents, a land grant, and clippings of the Rabb family relate to Civil War activities, early settlements in Texas, Spanish colonial Texas, and the history of Fayette County, TX. Taken from Chester V. Kielman, comp. and ed., *The University of Texas Archives: A Guide to the Historical Manuscripts Collections in the University of Texas Library* (Austin, TX: University of Texas Press, 1967).

16,122. Raphael, Alice Pearl
Papers. 1812-1960. 4 in.
Open. Published guide.
University of Texas Archives.
Correspondence, an invitation, literary writing, a marriage contract, a passport, photos, programs, pamphlets, broadsides, clippings, and other papers of [Mrs.] Raphael, a writer and translator. Included are memoirs concerning the history of the Raphael family in Canada, Europe, and the US and items relating to her translations, the Brownsville-Matamoros area, lawlessness and mob rule, and the Texas Rangers. Taken from Chester V. Kielman, comp. and ed., *The University of Texas Archives: A Guide to the Historical Manuscripts Collections in the University of Texas Library* (Austin, TX: University of Texas Press, 1967).

16,123. Ring, Elizabeth L.
Papers. 1920-30. 1.67 ft.
Open. Published guide.
University of Texas Archives.
Correspondence, memoranda, minutes, reports, petitions, bulletins, resolutions, broadsides, brochures, and pamphlets of [Mrs. Henry E.] Ring, a clubwoman, pertain to efforts of various women's organizations to effect prison reforms in Texas. Taken from Chester V. Kielman, comp. and ed., *The University of Texas Archives: A Guide to the Historical Manuscripts Collections in the University of Texas Library* (Austin, TX: University of Texas Press, 1967).

16,124. Roberts, Lou Conway
Papers. 1928. 1 vol.
Open. Published guide.
University of Texas Archives.
Reminiscences of [Mrs. Daniel Webster] Roberts about life in a Texas Ranger camp between 1875 and 1882 deal with amusements, living accommodations, travel, Indian raids, and a war in Mason County, TX. Taken from Chester V. Kielman, comp. and ed., *The University of Texas Archives: A Guide to the Historical Manuscripts Collections in the University of Texas Library* (Austin, TX: University of Texas Press, 1967).

16,125. Rosson, Mary Emma
Papers. 1939. 27 items.
Open. Published guide.
University of Texas Archives.
Letters, a literary writing, and a clipping of Rosson pertain to her master's thesis about Presbyterian-sponsored education for women in Texas. Includes inquiries to individuals who attended Texas Presbyterian College for Girls. Taken from Chester V. Kielman, comp. and ed., *The University of Texas Archives: A Guide to the Historical Manuscripts Collections in the University of Texas Library* (Austin, TX: University of Texas Press, 1967).

16,126. Salmon, George W.
Papers. 1872-1960. 2 items.
Open. Published guide.
University of Texas Archives.
Letter and an historical sketch of Oma Edna Spiva Chamblee (1894-?), a clubwoman, concern the history of Atlanta, TX, and the Atlanta Women's Thursday Study Club. Taken from Chester V. Kielman, comp. and ed., *The University of Texas Archives: A Guide to the Historical Manuscripts Collections in the University of Texas Library* (Austin, TX: University of Texas Press, 1967).

16,127. Scrapbooks
Collection. Nd. No size given.
Open. Published guide.
University of Texas Archives.
Scrapbooks compiled by or pertaining to women date from the 1830s to the 1950s. Among them are scrapbooks pertaining to the Better Babies Movement, the DAR, the Daughters of the Republic of Texas, the Texas Federation of Women's Clubs, the Texas WCTU, the United Daughters of the Confederacy, and the Woman's Liberty Loan Committee. Also included are scrapbooks of ca. 15 women. Taken from Chester V. Kielman, comp. and ed., *The University of Texas Archives: A Guide to the Historical Manuscripts Collections in the University of Texas Library* (Austin, TX: University of Texas Press, 1967).

16,128. Sharp, Estelle Boughton
Papers. 1899-1937. 3.33 ft.
Open. Published guide.
University of Texas Archives.
Correspondence, notes, receipts, legal papers, land papers, insurance policies, invitations, calling cards, photos, clippings, directories of women's organizations, and other papers relating to [Mrs. Walter B.] Sharp's activities as a member of the Texas Federation of Women's Clubs, the advisory board of the Volunteer Prison League, the Federal Food Administration executive committee, the War Work Council, the National League for Woman's Service, and the LWV. Included is printed material on social welfare, child guidance, the Democratic party, food rationing, agriculture, and education. Taken from Chester V. Kielman, comp. and ed., *The University of Texas Archives: A Guide to the Historical Manuscripts Collections in the University of Texas Library* (Austin, TX: University of Texas Press, 1967).

16,129. Sinks, Julia Lee
Papers. 1817-1904. 1 ft.
Open. Published guide.
University of Texas Archives.
Correspondence, historical sketches, literary writings, receipts, promissory notes, photos, clippings, and other papers of Sinks (1817-1904), an historian, relate to the history of Texas. Includes correspondence with prominent Texas figures of the Republic and early statehood periods. Taken from Chester V. Kielman, comp. and ed., *The University of Texas Archives: A Guide to the Historical Manuscripts Collections in the University of Texas Library* (Austin, TX: University of Texas Press, 1967).

16,130. Sparks, Lyra Haisley
Papers. 1896-1963. 8 in.
Open. Published guide.
University of Texas Archives.
Letters, diaries, literary articles, a speech, photos, recipes, and a brochure of Sparks, a writer. Included are Haisley family correspondence and correspondence of Sparks with George H. Paul pertaining to the history and promotion of real estate enterprises in the Coastal Bend area of Texas. Taken from Chester V. Kielman, comp. and ed., *The University of Texas Archives: A Guide to the Historical Manuscripts Collections in the University of Texas Library* (Austin, TX: University of Texas Press, 1967).

16,131. Spell, Lota Mae
Papers. 1923-35. 2.61 ft.
Open. Published guide.
University of Texas Archives.
Correspondence, notes, a university course program, photos, pamphlets, plays, music, clippings, and other papers of [Mrs. Jefferson Rea] Spell (1885-), an historian, relate to her activities as librarian of the University of Texas García Collection. Taken from Chester V. Kielman, comp. and ed., *The University of Texas Archives: A Guide to the Historical Manuscripts Collections in the University of Texas Library* (Austin, TX: University of Texas Press, 1967).

16,132. Teachers
Collections. 1750-1957. No size given.
Open. Published guide.
University of Texas Archives.
Papers of teachers include an 1835 letter of Elizabeth Hullock discussing the purchase of clothing, illness, her studies, religious training, and operation of a Greek grammar school; correspondence and a biographical sketch of [Mrs.] Laura Clarke Carpenter (1825-60) concerning her teaching career and a letter by her husband telling of her death; and a teacher's certificate and biographical sketch of Annie Josephine Wagner (1846-1950). Mattie Belle Anderson reminisced in 1883 about teaching at Fort Davis, TX. A letter, biographical data, periodicals, and clippings of [Mrs.] Maud Jeannie (Fuller) Young (1826-82), an author, teacher, and botanist, relate to Young's literary writings on the Civil War and to her work in botany, while correspondence, biographical sketches, and other papers of Bettie Scoggin Dalby (1850-1929) concern the Scoggin family's migration from Indiana and settlement in Ellis County, TX, in 1848, family affairs, and Bettie Dalby's study and teaching at McKenzie College. Also included are literary writings and a scrapbook of Florence Ralston Brooke (1858-1944); reminiscences, poetry, a will, a genealogy, and clippings of Emma Lapsley Wofford (1861-); in the Rosa Ingraham collection, certificates and examinations of elementary teachers of the Texas Summer Normal School in Nacogdoches, TX; and photos, certificates, and clippings relating to Minnie Dill's interest in the University of Texas and in education. Correspondence, literary writings, a memorandum, photos, and a clipping of Amanda Stoltzfus (?-1930) relate to her activities as a rural schoolteacher and as a lecturer to public schools on rural and vocational education for the University of Texas division of extension, while a 1924 report concerns teacher Maud E. Moody and her intelligence activities investigating the Katipunan Society in the Philippine Islands. Also included are autobiographical notes and addresses of Margie E. Neal (1875-?), a teacher, editor of the *East Texas Register,* and organizer of the Texas Society for Crippled Children, pertaining to her education, social and religious activities, and political associations. Taken from Chester V. Kielman, comp. and ed., *The University of Texas Archives: A Guide to the Historical Manuscripts Collections in the University of Texas Library* (Austin, TX: University of Texas Press, 1967).

16,133. Texarkana Pioneer Family Histories
Papers. 1961. 1 item.
Open. Published guide.
University of Texas Archives.
Texarkana Pioneer Family Histories (1961), a booklet by Nancy Mores Watts Jennings (1913-), secretary of the Texarkana Pioneer Association, covers the period 1873 to 1951. Taken from Chester V. Kielman, comp. and ed., *The University of Texas Archives: A Guide to the Historical Manuscripts Collections in the University of Texas Library* (Austin, TX: University of Texas Press, 1967).

16,134. Texas Association of Deans of Women and Deans of Girls
Records. 1922-24. 7 items.
Open. Published guide.
University of Texas Archives.
Minutes, announcements, and clippings relate to annual meetings of the Association in Dallas, Houston, and San Antonio. Taken from Chester V. Kielman, comp. and ed., *The University of Texas Archives: A Guide to the Historical Manuscripts Collections in the University of Texas Library* (Austin, TX: University of Texas Press, 1967).

16,135. Texas Composers
Collection. 1840-1950. 2 ft.
Open. Published guide.
University of Texas Archives.
Correspondence and music of Texas composers of classical, popular, band, and folk music. Taken from Chester V. Kielman, comp. and ed., *The University of Texas Archives: A Guide to the Historical Manuscripts Collections in the University of Texas Library* (Austin, TX: University of Texas Press, 1967).

16,136. Texas Federation of Music Clubs
Records. 1915-62. 12.83 ft.
Open. Published guide.
University of Texas Archives.
Minutes, correspondence, reports, scrapbooks, broadsides, clippings, and songbooks of the Federation. Taken from Chester V. Kielman, comp. and ed., *The University of Texas Archives: A Guide to the Historical Manuscripts Collections in the University of Texas Library* (Austin, TX: University of Texas Press, 1967).

16,137. Texas Poet Laureate Contest
Records. 1935. 1.5 in.
Open. Published guide.
University of Texas Archives.
Biographies and poetry entered in the official poet laureate of Texas contest, which was won by Grace Noll Crowell of Dallas. Includes the work of a number of women. Taken from Chester V. Kielman, comp. and ed., *The University of Texas Archives: A Guide to the Historical Manuscripts Collections in the University of Texas Library* (Austin, TX: University of Texas Press, 1967).

16,138. Texas State Senators' Wives Club
Records. 1927-57. 2 items.
Open. Published guide.
University of Texas Archives.
History of the social activities of the Club. Taken from Chester V. Kielman, comp. and ed., *The University of Texas Archives: A Guide to the Historical Manuscripts Collections in the University of Texas Library* (Austin, TX: University of Texas Press, 1967).

16,139. Texas Women's Press Association
Records. Ca. 1900-27. 4 in.
Open. Published guide.
University of Texas Archives.
Correspondence, literary writings, committee reports and programs, lists of members, scrapbooks, programs, broadsides, clippings, and printed material, including items published or written by or about members of the Association and items pertaining to convention planning and encouragement for a university journalism school. Taken from Chester V. Kielman, comp. and ed., *The University of Texas Archives: A Guide to the Historical Manuscripts Collections in the University of Texas Library* (Austin, TX: University of Texas Press, 1967).

16,140. United Daughters of the Confederacy
Records. 1904-14. 3 in.
Open. Published guide.
University of Texas Archives.
Records of the Albert Sidney Johnston chapter of the UDC in Austin. Taken from Chester V. Kielman, comp. and ed., *The University of Texas Archives: A Guide to the Historical Manuscripts Collections in the University of Texas Library* (Austin, TX: University of Texas Press, 1967).

16,141. Vernon, Ida Stevenson Weldon
Papers. 1944. 1 vol.
Open. Published guide.
University of Texas Archives.
Letters, memoirs, a family history, and a biography by [Mrs. W. C.] Vernon pertain to a history of the Seguins in Texas from 1782 to 1889. Taken from Chester V. Kielman, comp. and ed., *The University of Texas Archives: A Guide to the Historical Manuscripts Collections in the University of Texas Library* (Austin, TX: University of Texas Press, 1967).

16,142. Wade, Mrs. John W.
Papers. 1845-1932. 1 vol.
Open. Published guide.
University of Texas Archives.
Reminiscences of Wade (1844-?), a pioneer housewife, concern her childhood days on a Texas plantation. Taken from Chester V. Kielman, comp. and ed., *The University of Texas Archives: A Guide to the Historical Manuscripts Collections in the University of Texas Library* (Austin, TX: University of Texas Press, 1967).

16,143. Walter, Hulda Saenger
Papers. 1873-1943. 1.25 ft.
Open. Published guide.
University of Texas Archives.
Correspondence, a notebook, literary writings, a biographical sketch, a review, pamphlets, newspapers, and magazines concern the career of Walter (1867-1929), a poet. Taken from Chester V. Kielman, comp. and ed., *The University of Texas Archives: A Guide to the Historical Manuscripts Collections in the University of Texas Library* (Austin, TX: University of Texas Press, 1967).

16,144. Watson, Margaret L.
Papers. 1829-1920. 2 vols.
Open. Published guide.
University of Texas Archives.
Historical narratives by Watson include one on the life of Catherine Border Roberts, who was the widow of O. M. Roberts, and one on fortifications and activities on the Texas coast during the Civil War. Taken from Chester V. Kielman, comp. and ed., *The University of Texas Archives: A Guide to the Historical Manuscripts Collections in the University of Texas Library* (Austin, TX: University of Texas Press, 1967).

16,145. Watson, May Mathis Green
Papers. Ca. 1887-1959. 24 vols.
Open. Published guide.
University of Texas Archives.
Scrapbooks containing manuscripts, imprints, photos, and clippings of [Mrs.] Watson (1883-), an artist, writer, and housewife, relate to the social, economic, and cultural life of Corpus Christi, TX, and the Texas Gulf Coast and to activities of the Texas Federation of Women's Clubs. Taken from Chester V. Kielman, comp. and ed., *The University of Texas Archives: A Guide to the Historical*

Manuscripts Collections in the University of Texas Library (Austin, TX: University of Texas Press, 1967).

16,146. White, Mrs. Robert Leon
Papers. 1927-63. 8.5 in.
Open. Published guide.
University of Texas Archives.
Constitution, bylaws, minutes, invitations, reports, a press release, maps, programs, clippings, a newspaper, and other papers of White relate to dramatic, musical, and cultural performances and exhibits in Austin and elsewhere, to University of Texas general faculty meetings, and to various organizations including the Texas Prison Centralization Commission and the University Ladies' Club. Taken from Chester V. Kielman, comp. and ed., *The University of Texas Archives: A Guide to the Historical Manuscripts Collections in the University of Texas Library* (Austin, TX: University of Texas Press, 1967).

16,147. Wilson, M. A. C.
Papers. Nd. 1 vol.
Open. Published guide.
University of Texas Archives.
Letters, poems, certificates, badges, commissions, and clippings of Wilson, widow of William F. Wilson, who had been taken prisoner during the Mier Expedition of 1842-43, the last of the raiding expeditions into Mexico during the days of the Republic of Texas. Taken from Chester V. Kielman, comp. and ed., *The University of Texas Archives: A Guide to the Historical Manuscripts Collections in the University of Texas Library* (Austin, TX: University of Texas Press, 1967).

16,148. Wright, Josepha "Jodie"
Papers. 1845-84. 41 items.
Open. Published guide.
University of Texas Archives.
Letters, financial and legal documents, land papers, and a photo of Caledonia Wright Clapp (1830-70), a tutor, relate to social affairs, the education of children, legal guardianship of minor children, hiring of freedmen, purchase of slaves, the return of local men from Confederate armies, resentment of Reconstruction troops, religious activities, courtings, weddings, births, deaths, farming, land improvement, and land rental. Taken from Chester V. Kielman, comp. and ed., *The University of Texas Archives: A Guide to the Historical Manuscripts Collections in the University of Texas Library* (Austin, TX: University of Texas Press, 1967).

16,149. Albert Davis-Messmore Kendall: Biographic File
Collection. Ca. 1820-1950. No size given.
Open. Unpublished guide.
University of Texas at Austin, Humanities Research Center.
Correspondence, contracts, legal documents, motion pictures, photos, programs, playbills, advertisements, sheet music, articles, clippings, and other papers of Ethel Barrymore, Lotta Crabtree, [Mrs.] Minnie Maddern Fiske, Helen Hayes, Cornelia Otis Skinner, Cora Urquhart Potter, Geraldine Farrar, Lillian Russell, and many others who performed in theater, dance, minstrel shows, musical comedies, or opera.

16,150. Albert Davis-Messmore Kendall: Holographic File
Collection. Nd. No size given.
Open. Unpublished guide.
University of Texas at Austin, Humanities Research Center.
Letters, notes, and reminiscences by persons associated with the theater, including authors Rachel M. Field, Harriet Ford, and Olive Logan; dramatic performers Marie Burroughs, Rose Etyinge, Kathryn Kidder, Pauline Lord, May Robson, Genevieve Ward, and Helen Ware; and musical and variety performers Emma Calvé, Della Fox, Loie Fuller, Clara Louise Kellogg, Jenny Lind, Adelina Patti, and Adele Ritchie.

16,151. Atherton, Gertrude Franklin (Horn)
Papers. 1889-1947. 87 items.
Open. Unpublished guide.
University of Texas at Austin, Humanities Research Center.
Correspondence with R. L. Giffen, John Stuart Groves, and John Lane; manuscripts, including one written in 1917 about the war; photos; and clippings of Atherton (1857-1948), a novelist. Includes correspondence and a manuscript concerning an interview of Atherton by John Burton Davis in 1938.

16,152. Boyle, Kay
Papers. 1934-67. Ca. 215 items.
Open. Unpublished guide.
University of Texas at Austin, Humanities Research Center.
Papers of Boyle (1903-), a novelist and poet, include typescripts of poems and correspondence with Nancy Cunard, Edward Dahlberg, Katherine Anne Porter, Jerome Weidman, and William Carlos Williams.

16,153. Buck, Pearl (Sydenstricker)
Papers. 1932-50. 15 items.
Open. Unpublished guide.
University of Texas at Austin, Humanities Research Center.
Papers of Buck (1892-1973), a novelist, include letters she wrote to Philip Moeller, Christopher Morley, and Robert Payne; typescripts of her works; and clippings. Includes typescripts of her story "Shanghai Scene"; *East Wind: West Wind;* "American Woman," which was published as *The Exile;* and "Pilgrim's Pride." Also contains galley proofs for *Writing for Love or for Money* (1949), a collection of essays including one by Buck, reprinted from the *Saturday Review of Literature* and edited by Norman Cousins.

16,154. Cousins, Margaret
Papers. Nd. 8 cartons and 6 items.
Open. Partial unpublished guide.
University of Texas at Austin, Humanities Research Center.
Cousins (1905-) was managing editor of *Good Housekeeping* from 1945 to 1958 and of *McCalls* from 1958 to 1962. Correspondence with editors, writers, and illustrators; manuscripts of short stories, verse essays, and articles; notes; memoranda; reports; and other papers relating to her work. Also includes material about the anthology *Love and Marriage,* which she edited, and *Souvenir,* of which she was ghost writer. Correspondents include Margaret Truman, Samuel Behrman, J. Frank Dobie, and Harpers.

16,155. Fay, Sarah Elizabeth (Shields)
Papers. 1862-94. 1 vol. and 126 items.
Open. Unpublished guide.
University of Texas at Austin, Humanities Research Center.
Letters to Fay (?-1919) during the Civil War from her husband Edwin Hedge Fay, a Confederate soldier, and her journal covering the period 1862 to 1894.

16,156. Hellman, Lillian
Papers. 1931-70. Ca. 11 ft.
Open. Published guide.
University of Texas at Austin, Humanities Research Center.
Papers of [Miss] Hellman (1905-), a playwright, include correspondence with Maxwell Anderson, Jerome Weidman, and Dashiell Hammett; manuscripts of her plays, with up to 18 drafts for some works; and clippings. See Manfred Triesch, compiler, *The Lillian Hellman Collection at the University of Texas* (Austin: Humanities Research Center, 1966).

16,157. Hurst, Fannie
Papers. 1927-60. 102 ft. and 16 items.
Open. Partial unpublished guide.
University of Texas at Austin, Humanities Research Center.
Correspondence, typescripts of novels and articles, a reply to a questionnaire, photos, and clippings of Hurst (1889-1968), a novelist. Correspondents include Grace Lewis, Lillian Gish, Grace Gleaves Neuscheler [Mrs. Samuel] Gompers, Helen Keller, Blanche Knopf, Eleanor Roosevelt, Rebecca West, Harpers, and Knopf, Inc.

16,158. Kaup, Elizabeth Dewing
Papers. 1885-1966. 6 ft. and 1 vol.
Open. Unpublished guide.
University of Texas at Austin, Humanities Research Center.
Papers of Kaup (1885-1966), a novelist, include correspondence; diaries; typescripts of her works; birth, marriage, and divorce certificates; a memorandum concerning E. B. Dewing; a scrapbook; an obituary; and other papers.

16,159. Lasswell, Mary
Papers. Ca. 1944-62. 6 ft. and 4 items.
Open. Partial unpublished guide.
University of Texas at Austin, Humanities Research Center.
Papers of Lasswell (1905-), a Texas writer, include correspondence, notes, and manuscripts for various columns and books, including *Let's Go For Broke, Tio Pepe,* and *I'll Take Texas.* Includes letters to J. Frank Dobie.

16,160. McCarthy, Mary Therese
Papers. 1955-66. 3 boxes and 5 items.
Open. Unpublished guide.
University of Texas at Austin, Humanities Research Center.
Papers of McCarthy (1912-), a novelist, include correspondence with Charles Henri Ford, David Otis Kelley, Harpers, and others; a typescript of *A Tin Butterfly;* and a typescript, synopsis, and early versions of *The Group.*

16,161. McCullers, Carson
Papers. Ca. 1930-66. Ca. 20 ft. and 7 items.
Open. Unpublished guide.
University of Texas at Austin, Humanities Research Center.
Correspondence, manuscripts, financial records, galleys and page proofs, photos, and books of McCullers (1917-67), a novelist. Includes manuscripts of *The Member of the Wedding, Ballad of the Sad Cafe,* and *Clock without Hands.* Among her correspondents are her husband Reeves McCullers, Edward Albee, Margarita Smith, Marguerite Waters Smith, Mary Tucker, and Tennessee Williams. Collection also contains the manuscript of Oliver Evans's book *Carson McCullers: Her Life and Work,* his correspondence with McCullers and others, and research material he used in writing the book. Other material about McCullers is found in the Rita Smith collection at the Center.

16,162. Mitford, Jessica
Papers. Ca. 1963-73. 45 ft.
Open. No guide.
University of Texas at Austin, Humanities Research Center.
Correspondence, typescripts, notebooks, galleys, and scrapbooks of Mitford (1917-), a writer, relating to her books *The American Way of Death, The Trial of Dr. Spock,* and *Kind and Unusual Punishment.* Also includes files relating to the trial of the Chicago Seven.

16,163. Moore, Marianne
Papers. 1921-71. 410 items.
Open. Unpublished guide.
University of Texas at Austin, Humanities Research Center.
Papers of Moore (1887-1972), a poet, include correspondence with Merle Armitage, Cid Corman, E. E. Cummings, T. S. Eliot, Oliver Evans, Harpers, D. H. Lawrence, Christopher Morley, Dame Edith Sitwell, and others; typescripts of *The Absentee* and *O To Be A Dragon;* galley proofs of *Selected Poems;* and writings for the *Marianne Moore Festschrift.* Also includes letters to Thurairajah Tambimuttu from Peggy Bacon, Djuna Barnes, Louise Bogan, Jane Cooper, Babette Deutsch, Eleanor Edelstein, Jane Mayhall, and others.

16,164. Porter, Katherine Anne
Papers. 1943-67. 31 items.
Open. Unpublished guide.
University of Texas at Austin, Humanities Research Center.
Papers of Porter (1894?-), a novelist and short story writer, include correspondence with William J. Handy, Dame Edith Sitwell, Kay Boyle, Tennessee Williams, J. Frank Dobie, and Joseph Conrad; typescript of "The Fig Tree"; and galley proofs of *Collected Stories* and *Ship of Fools.* Also includes a 1953 master's thesis by Deirdre C. Handy of the University of Oklahoma, Norman, OK, concerning the family legend in the stories of Katherine Anne Porter.

16,165. Riding, Laura
Papers. 1923-55. Ca. 83 items.
Open. Unpublished guide.
University of Texas at Austin, Humanities Research Center.
Papers of Riding (1901-), a poet and critic, include correspondence with Ronald Bottrall, Herbert E. Palmer, R. D. Kilham, Idella Purnell Stone, John Lehmann, and William Butler Yeats; manuscripts of *What to Say When the Spider* (1930) and *When the Skies Part;* page proofs of *Love as Love, Death as Death* (1929); and an advance copy of *The Life of the Dead* (1933). Also includes a manuscript of *Laura Riding* by Martin Seymour-Smith.

16,166. Robins, Elizabeth
Papers. 1891-1940. 1 box and ca. 516 items.
Open. Unpublished guide.
University of Texas at Austin, Humanities Research Center.
Correspondence of Robins (1862-1952), an actress and writer, on various subjects, including woman suffrage and other political matters. Among the correspondents are J. L. Garvin, Marie Lowndes, George Bernard Shaw, John Galsworthy, Thomas Hardy, Henry James, H. G. Wells, Virginia Woolf, Mrs. Patrick Campbell, John Masefield, Emmeline and Christabel Pankhurst, Lady Sybil Smith, and Evelyn Sharp.

16,167. Ross, Nancy Wilson
Papers. 1940-73. 11 ft. and 19 items.
Open. Partial unpublished guide.
University of Texas at Austin, Humanities Research Center.
Papers of Ross (1905-), a novelist, include correspondence with Merle Armitage and Harpers; manuscripts of *The Left Hand Is the Dreamer, Westward the Women, The Return of Lady Brace, Nellie C. Cornish, Beloved Prophet, Three Ways of Asian Wisdom,* and *The World of Zen;* research material; articles; and clippings.

16,168. Scott, Evelyn
Papers. 1921-54. 1 box, 2 cartons, and 25 items.
Open. Unpublished guide.
University of Texas at Austin, Humanities Research Center.
Correspondence of Scott (1893-), a writer, with J. D. Adams, T. I. F. Armstrong, James Joyce, Sherwood Anderson, and Witter Bynner and manuscript novels, short stories, and verse. Includes typescripts of "Escape into Living," "The Gravestones Wept," "The Youngest Smiles," and "Before Cock Crow." Also includes correspondence and manuscripts of Owen Merton and Maud Dunn.

16,169. Stone, Idella Purnell
Papers. 1919-68. 4.4 ft.
Open. Unpublished guide.
University of Texas at Austin, Humanities Research Center.
Correspondence of Idella Purnell (1901-), a poet and critic who was married to Remington Stone, relates to *PALMS* magazine, manuscripts by various writers, drawings by Vachel Lindsay, cover designs by Purnell and D. H. Lawrence, photos, and clippings. Correspondents include Mark Van Doren, Vachel and Elizabeth Lindsay, Laura Riding, Harriet Monroe, Spud Johnson, Witter Bynner, Ezra Pound, and Frieda Lawrence. Purnell wrote under the name Ikey Stone as well as under her maiden and married names.

16,170. Story, Emelyn (Eldridge)
Papers. 1843-91. 2 vols. and 392 items.
Open. Unpublished guide.
University of Texas at Austin, Humanities Research Center.
Correspondence of Story (1821-94) with other Story family members, especially her husband William Wetmore Story and Thomas Waldo Story, and with Robert Browning and Elizabeth (Barrett) Browning, G. B. McClellan, Elizabeth C. Gaskell, and James Russell Lowell. Also includes a notebook and scrapbooks.

16,171. Story, Sarah Waldo (Wetmore)
Papers. 1816-45. 99 items.
Open. Unpublished guide.
University of Texas at Austin, Humanities Research Center.
Correspondence of Story, who was the wife of US representative and Supreme Court justice Joseph Story, includes letters to her husband, to William Wetmore Story, and to other members of the Story family and letters from Charles Sumner.

16,172. Welty, Eudora
Papers. 1947-64. 52 items.
Open. Unpublished guide.
University of Texas at Austin, Humanities Research Center.
Papers of Welty (1909-), a novelist, include correspondence with Elizabeth Bowen, John Lehmann, and Harpers; drafts of *The Bride of the Innisfallen;* and galley and page proofs of *The Ponder Heart* and several short works, including "The Burning," "Circe," "Going to Naples," "Kin," and "Ladies in the Spring."

16,173. Wharton, Edith Newbold (Jones)
Papers. 1917-36. 44 items.
Open. Unpublished guide.
University of Texas at Austin, Humanities Research Center.
Papers of Wharton (1862-1937), a novelist, include correspondence with [Mrs.] Marie Lowndes, Lady Ottoline Morrell, Grace Lewis, and William Gerhardi; manuscript of the essay "What America Is Fighting For" (1917); and a galley proof of *Writing for Love or for Money,* which was edited by Norman Cousins and contains a selection by Wharton.

16,174. Wilcox, Ella (Wheeler)
Papers. 1880-1917. 148 items and 512 pp.
Open. Partial unpublished guide.
University of Texas at Austin, Humanities Research Center.
Correspondence of Wilcox (1850-1919), a poet, with Eugene Field, Bessie Hatton, Richard Le Gallienne, Rothmell Wilson, and the American Press Association; poem fragments; manuscripts of her essays "As Seen by Herself" and "Do Men Like Flirts?"; manuscripts of "The Day We Celebrate," "Solitude," and other poems; and page proofs of her essay "Women of No Tact."

16,175. Files and Archives
Records. 1915- . 15 ft., 20 cabinets, and 41 tapes.
Open. No guide.
Women in Communications, Inc.
Founded in 1909 as Theta Sigma Phi, Women in Communications is an international, nonprofit professional organization for women in journalism and communications. Minutes, correspondence, administrative files, chapter files with annual reports, videotapes, photos, pamphlets, tape cassettes, clippings, publications, and other records. Includes information about the progress of women in communication, first amendment issues, freedom of information, and career information in journalism and communications. Also contains issues of the group's official publication *Matrix,* which was begun in 1915.

BASTROP

16,176. Women's History
Collection. 1800s- . No size given.
Access restricted. No guide.
Bastrop County Historical Society Museum and Archives.
Gathered by the Bastrop County Historical Society, this collection includes journals, ledgers, biographical information, scrapbooks, original art, and other papers by area women, including Margaret Barker [Mrs. Josiah Pugh] Wilbarger [Mrs. Thomas Washington] Chambers, Nina Craft, Tibbie Damon Friedburger, Mary Jane Gill, Mrs. J. A. Haralson, Margaret Bell Jones, Eva Hill LeSeuer Karling, Rubelle McMillan, Mrs. W. J. Miley, Sarah Jane Orgain, Lois Stoneham, and Kezia Payne. Also includes a manuscript of the reminiscences of Mary Ann McDowell, which was published as *Memoirs of Mollie McDowall* by the National Society of the Colonial Dames of America in the State of Texas, and family records. The Historical Society was founded in 1952; women make up the bulk of the membership and have been prominent in its work.

BEAUMONT

16,177. American Association of University Women
Records. 1937-74. 10 vols.
Open. No guide.
Tyrrell Historical Library.
Minutes of monthly meetings, monthly bulletins, membership booklets, photos, clippings, and other records of this local AAUW chapter. Includes descriptions of members' activities.

16,178. Women's Organizations
Records. Nd. 12 drawers.
Closed. No guide.
Tyrrell Historical Library.
Contains records of the local chapters of the United Daughters of the Confederacy and the Daughters of the Republic of Texas as well as of the Colonel George Moffett Chapter of the DAR, which also was located in Beaumont.

BELLAIRE

16,179. Convent Archives
Records. 1873- . 80 ft.
Open. No guide.

Sisters of the Incarnate Word and Blessed Sacrament. Financial records, property deeds, correspondence, diaries, retreat notes, blueprints, photos, scrapbooks, articles, publications by the Sisters, and books of the order, which was founded in Houston in 1873. Includes papers of mothers superior, a file on schools founded and administered by the Sisters, and information on the history of Houston.

BELTON

16,180. Sanctificationists
Collection. 1893-1974. 13 folders.
Open. No guide.
Belton City Library.
The Sanctificationists, who banded together in about 1879 under the leadership of Martha (White) [Mrs. George] McWhirter, were women who left their husbands because of their religious convictions and worked at various jobs for their mutual support. Personal reminiscences; court records; photos; articles; clippings, including an interview with McWhirter; and other material provide information about the group, the formal title of which was the Women's Commonwealth. Includes county court records from a divorce trial in which one of the Sanctificationists was named as a defendant. McWhirter and other members of the group testified, discussing their beliefs and practices. For a time the group owned a hotel and other businesses in Belton.

BIG BEND NATIONAL PARK

16,181. Oral History
Oral history. 1975. Ca. 120 tapes.
Access restricted. Unpublished guide.
Big Bend Natural History Association.
Interviews with long-time residents of the Big Bend country concern their experiences as settlers in the region. Events discussed date from about 1900 to the present. About one-fifth of the persons interviewed were women.

BURNET

16,182. Family History
Collection. Ca. 1850- . 50 folders and microfilm reels.
Access restricted. No guide.
Burnet County Historical Society.
Correspondence, biographical sketches, financial records, newspapers, and other papers concerning families in Burnet County and other county residents. Some of the biographical sketches were written by women. Includes a list of early Burnet County school teachers. Collection is housed at the Burnet County Library.

COLLEGE STATION

16,183. Amarillo A&M Mothers' Club
Records. 1949-60. 6 in.
Open. No guide.
Texas A&M University Library.
A&M Mothers' Clubs include women who have children who are present or past students at the University. The Amarillo chapter was founded in 1949. Minutes and scrapbooks of clippings and memorabilia about the Amarillo club's activities and about the University. The Mothers' Clubs plan social activities and fund-raising projects. Money raised by the Club is used to help the University, its programs, and its students.

16,184. American Association of University Women
Records. 1948-72. 1.5 ft.
Open. Unpublished guide.
Texas A&M University Library.
Minute books and newsletters of the Bryan-College Station AAUW branch, which was founded in 1948. Also includes issues of the *General Director's Letter,* the *AAUW Journal,* the *AAUW Journal Newspaper,* and other national AAUW publications.

16,185. Austin A&M Mothers' Club
Records. 1952-71. 2 ft.
Open. No guide.
Texas A&M University Library.
Minutes, officers' correspondence, scrapbooks of clippings and memorabilia, and yearbooks listing names of officers and members of this Austin, TX, organization, which was founded in 1952. Made up of women who have children who studied at the University, the Club conducts social activities and raises money for the benefit of the school and its programs.

16,186. Auxiliary to the Texas Student Chapter of the American Veterinary Medical Association
Records. 1955-68. 3 in.
Open. No guide.
Texas A&M University Library.
Founded in 1950 at Texas A&M, the Auxiliary plans social events and raises funds, a large portion of which are contributed to the University's medical sciences library. Scrapbook of clippings and memorabilia. The group is referred to frequently as the Vet Students Wives Auxiliary.

16,187. Baytown A&M Mothers' Club
Records. 1953-72. 2 in.
Open. No guide.
Texas A&M University Library.
Minutes, treasurers' records, receipt book, checkbook, and yearbooks listing officers and members of this Baytown, TX, group, which was founded in 1953 and includes mothers of present and past University students.

16,188. Bell County A&M Mothers' Club
Records. 1949-70. 1 in.
Open. No guide.
Texas A&M University Library.
Minutes of the Bell County Club, which was founded in 1949. Club members engage in social activities and plan fund-raising projects for the benefit of the University.

16,189. Brown County A&M Mothers' Club
Records. 1951-54. 3 in.
Open. No guide.
Texas A&M University Library.
Founded in 1951, this Brown County group is open to women who have children who are past or present students at Texas A&M. Scrapbook of clippings and memorabilia concerning the group's social activities and fund-raising projects.

16,190. Campus Study Club
Records. 1916-62. 3 ft.
Open. No guide.
Texas A&M University Library.
The Club was organized in 1916 by wives of faculty members and administrators of Texas A&M, then a small land grant men's college; early students were required to be members of the Cadet Corps. Minutes, reports, scrapbooks, yearbooks listing the officers and program activities, and award certificates. In 1916 most of the faculty and administrators lived on the University campus. Club members met for social activities and to hear speeches on various topics.

16,191. College Station League of Women Voters
Records. 1967-72. 2 in.
Open. No guide.
Texas A&M University Library.
Newsletters of the local LWV, which was founded in 1967; voter guides; and samples of other local LWV publications.

16,192. Dallas A&M Mothers' Club
Records. 1922-68. 5 ft.
Open. No guide.
Texas A&M University Library.
Minutes, treasurers' records, officers' correspondence, and scrapbooks of clippings and memorabilia of this Dallas organization, which was founded in 1922. Like all A&M Mothers' Clubs, the Dallas group includes women whose children have attended or are attending the University. The Club meets for social activities and to raise funds that are used for the benefit of Texas A&M.

16,193. Extension Service Wives Club
Records. 1919-72. 6 ft.
Open. No guide.
Texas A&M University Library.
The Club, founded in 1919, consists chiefly of wives of professional employees of the Texas Agricultural Extension Service and some female professional Extension Service employees. Minutes, treasurers' books, scrapbooks and pressbooks of memorabilia and clippings, and yearbooks listing officers and members. The Club is primarily a social group. The Extension Service has headquarters in College Station.

16,194. Federation of Texas A&M Mothers' Clubs
Records. 1928-76. 1.5 ft.
Open. No guide.
Texas A&M University Library.
Founded in 1928, the Federation suggests programs for and coordinates activities of local A&M Mothers' Clubs. Constitution, bylaws, minutes, treasurer's books, officers' correspondence, scrapbooks of clippings and memorabilia, and yearbooks listing Federation and local club officers. The Federation meets regularly with University administrators who tell members of the school's needs. The first local A&M Mothers' Clubs were organized in 1922.

16,195. Fine Arts Group of A&M Women's Social Club
Records. 1966-72. 6 in.
Open. No guide.
Texas A&M University Library.
A subsidiary of the Women's Social Club, the Group consists chiefly of wives of University faculty members and administrators who attend dramatic and musical performances and visit art exhibits. Minutes, officers' correspondence, and scrapbook of clippings and memorabilia. The section was organized in 1966 to foster an appreciation and understanding of the fine arts.

16,196. Fort Worth A&M Mothers' Club
Records. 1922-70. 2 ft.
Open. No guide.
Texas A&M University Library.
Minutes, treasurer's books, a brief Club history, and yearbooks listing officers and members of this Fort Worth, TX, organization, which was organized in 1922 by mothers of University students and mothers of University alumni. The Club sponsors social events and raises money for the University's benefit.

16,197. Hill, Ethel Osborn
Papers. 1925-73. 1 ft.
Open. No guide.
Texas A&M University Library.
[Mrs.] Hill (1880-), a newspaper columnist and conservationist, wrote for several different Texas

newspapers. Correspondence, clippings about her, and clippings of her articles about agriculture, Texas history and folklore, and conservation. Most of Hill's papers were destroyed by fire in the early 1970s.

16,198. Houston A&M Mothers' Club
Records. 1956-65. 6 in.
Open. No guide.
Texas A&M University Library.
Organized in 1927, the Houston Club includes women whose children are attending or have attended the University. Photos, scrapbook of clippings, programs, and other brochures. The Club raises money that is used to benefit the University, its programs, and its students.

16,199. Texas A&M University Newcomers Club
Records. 1956-70. 1 ft.
Open. No guide.
Texas A&M University Library.
A subsidiary of the Texas A&M University Women's Social Club, the group is made up of wives of new University faculty members and new female faculty members. Officers' annual reports, scrapbook of clippings and memorabilia, yearbooks listing officers and members, information books about Texas A&M, and guest books. Women may belong to the Club for two years; then they may transfer to the Social Club. The Newcomers Club was founded in 1956.

16,200. Texas A&M University Women's Social Club
Records. 1919-72. 1 ft.
Open. No guide.
Texas A&M University Library.
Organized at Texas A&M in 1919 when nearly all faculty members lived on the University campus, the Club allowed the wives of faculty members and administrators to become better acquainted with each other and the University. Minutes, treasurers' records, and scrapbook of memorabilia and clippings. The Club's current membership chiefly consists of wives of current or former A&M faculty members or administrators.

16,201. Wildlife Science Wives Club
Records. 1968-71. 3 in.
Open. No guide.
Texas A&M University Library.
Scrapbook of clippings and memorabilia of the Club, which was founded in about 1955 to promote social activities and fund-raising efforts. The Club consists principally of the wives of students registered in the wildlife and fisheries sciences department; faculty wives and single women students are also eligible for membership.

16,202. Williamson County A&M Mothers' Club
Records. 1949-70. 1 ft.
Open. No guide.
Texas A&M University Library.
Minutes, treasurers' books, officers' correspondence, yearbooks containing names of officers and members, and scrapbooks of clippings and memorabilia of the Williamson County group, which was organized in 1949 by the mothers of past and present Texas A&M students. Club members plan social activities and fund-raising projects.

COMANCHE

16,203. Comanche Study Club
Records. 1922-47. 3 vols.
Open. No guide.
Comanche Public Library.
Minutes document the interest of the Club, organized in 1911, in the development of the local school and public library. The group meets for educational and social programs.

COMMERCE

16,204. East Texas State University
Oral history. 1972-76. 12 vols. and 20 tapes.
Partially restricted. No guide.
East Texas State University Library, Special Collections and Archives.
Interviews in which men and women describe their experiences at East Texas State. The interviews provide a history of the school, which has existed under several names. Includes transcripts.

16,205. History of Blacks
Oral history. 1972-76. 10 vols. and 13 tapes.
Partially restricted. No guide.
East Texas State University Library, Special Collections and Archives.
Interviews concern experiences and changing attitudes of black men and women in the Commerce area. Includes transcripts.

16,206. Regional History
Oral history. 1970-76. 10 vols. and 10 tapes.
Partially restricted. No guide.
East Texas State University Library, Special Collections and Archives.
Interviews with women concerning various topics of local and regional interest. Includes transcripts.

CROSBYTON

16,207. Women of West Texas
Collection. 1876-1977. 20 ft.
Open. Unpublished guide.
Crosby County Pioneer Memorial.
Written and oral histories reflect the role of Crosby County women in this rural area's history.

DALLAS

16,208. Southern Methodist University Oral History Project
Oral history. Nd. 45 interviews.
Open. Unpublished guide.
Southern Methodist University, DeGolyer Institute.
Interviews with Rosemary Clooney, Imogene Coca, Ann B. Davis, Virginia Mayo, ballerinas Maria and Marjorie Tallchief, and exotic dancers Chastity Fox and Terre Tale are included among those of other persons involved in radio, television, motion pictures, dance, and the theater. Fifteen of those interviewed were women.

16,209. Methodist Church of the United States
Records. 1773- . Ca. 1000 ft.
Open. Card catalog and calendars.
Southern Methodist University Library, Methodist Historical Library.
Officially organized in 1773, the Methodist Church in the US split over the slavery issue in 1844. The resulting groups, the Methodist Episcopal Church and the Methodist Episcopal Church, South, joined with the Methodist Protestant Church in 1939 to form the Methodist Church. Records of the Board of Foreign Missionaries and the Council of Bishops, bishops' papers, minutes, records delineating Church ceremony and liturgy, General Conference and regional reports, photos, and other records. Contains annual reports and other records of Methodist women's missionary groups and societies, including some from the Methodist Episcopal Church, South; annual reports of the Women's Society of Christian Service of the North Texas Conference, South Central Jurisdiction; and data about women's participation in the United Methodist Church. The United Methodist Church was formed in 1968 through the merger of the Evangelical United Brethren and Methodist churches.

DENTON

16,210. Dallas Museum of Fashion
Collection. Nd. Ca. 3000 items.
Access restricted. Unpublished guide.
North Texas State University, Texas Center for Fashion Studies.
Museum collection includes information about and works by 200 designers, principally of the 20th century. Includes the Claudia deOsborne collection of Balenciaga garments and the collection of [Miss] Carrie Neiman, a founder of Neiman-Marcus, the Dallas-based specialty store. The bulk of Neiman's collection consists of 3500 garments and accessories, which provide an American fashion retrospective; also included are a record of fabric development, photos, drawings of apparel and accessories, and a library tracing the history of design.

EDINBURG

16,211. Edinburg Study Club
Records. 1925- . 3 ft.
Open. Unpublished guide.
Pan American University Library, Special Collections.
Minutes and yearbooks of this local club, which was established in 1925. The yearbooks include bylaws, annual reports, membership lists, names of officers and committees, and programs that illustrate the group's literary and cultural interests. The records reflect concerns and activities of Rio Grande Valley women.

EL PASO

16,212. Duke, Eleanor (Lyon)
Papers. 1950-72. 2 boxes.
Closed. No guide.
University of Texas at El Paso Library, Special Collections and Archives.
Correspondence and photos of Duke, a biology professor and president of the Texas Association of College Teachers. Duke began her association with the University as a student in about 1939. Her papers reflect the University's history and the formation of the faculty council and the biology department as well as her membership in the Texas Association of College Teachers.

16,213. Fox, Josephine (Clardy)
Papers. Ca. 1900-70. 53 boxes.
Open. Unpublished guide.
University of Texas at El Paso Library, Special Collections and Archives.
Fox (1881-1970) was a wealthy socialite and benefactor of the University. Correspondence, financial records, and photos concern her travels and her activities as an art and furniture collector, property owner, and housewife.

16,214. Isaacks, Maud
Papers. 1963-65. 1 box.
Open. No guide.
University of Texas at El Paso Library, Special Collections and Archives.
Papers relating to the political career of [Mrs.] Isaacks, a teacher and legislator.

FORT WORTH

16,215. Fort Worth Federal Archives and Records Center
Records. 1806-1974. 24,171 cu.ft. and 20,000 microfilm reels.
Open. No guide.
Federal Archives and Records Center, Fort Worth Archives Branch.
Administrative and fiscal records, correspondence, census records, and other records of federal agencies, primarily those of US district courts in Arkansas, Louisiana, Oklahoma, and Texas; the US Court of Appeals for the 5th Circuit; and field offices of the Bureau of Indian Affairs. Records of the district courts and circuit courts (RG 21) consist of judicial proceedings for criminal and civil cases, with indexes for some volumes, for Arkansas, 1866-1952; Louisiana, 1806-1952; Oklahoma, 1907-52; and Texas, 1866-1952. Records of the Bureau of Indian Affairs (RG 75), 1856-1952, contain records of Indian agencies, schools, and sanatoriums located in what is now the state of Oklahoma; includes school records, allotment files regarding land holdings of individuals and tribes, and census records, 1848-1940, relating to the Cherokee, Choctaw, Chickasaw, Creek, and Seminole Nations. War Manpower Commission records (RG 211), 1942-45, contain records for Texas, Louisiana, and New Mexico, and document the role women and women's clubs played in WWII. Material from the Office of Economic Opportunity, ca. 1960-70, contains community profiles, which are termed "profiles of the poor." These profiles report the population and the geographic, social, and economic characteristics of each county and independent city in Arkansas, Louisiana, New Mexico, Oklahoma, and Texas and provide comparisons for each. With the exception of 307 reels, the microfilmed records are copies made from originals held by the National Archives, Washington, DC.

GALVESTON

16,216. Galveston Chapter of the American National Red Cross
Records. 1916-65. 5.5 ft.
Open. Unpublished guide.
Rosenberg Library.
Founded in 1916, the local Red Cross provided assistance during WWI and WWII and helped establish a local public nursing service. Minutes of board meetings, correspondence, reports, orders, circulars, booklets, and other records. Includes material on the two world wars, fund raising, the Public Health Nursing Service, and the Family Service Board.

16,217. Galveston Chapter of the League of Women Voters
Records. 1936-58. 4 vols.
Open. No guide.
Rosenberg Library.
Scrapbooks containing photos and clippings of the Galveston LWV, which was founded in 1920.

16,218. Galveston Equal Suffrage Association
Records. 1912-13. 4 in.
Open. No guide.
Rosenberg Library.
Correspondence, pamphlets, broadsides, and clippings of the Association, founded in 1912 to work for passage of state laws that would give women the right to vote and for approval of the 19th Amendment. Association members attempted to make the suffrage position known both to men and women in Galveston.

16,219. Galveston Garden Club
Records. 1938-45. 4 in.
Open. Unpublished guide.
Rosenberg Library.
Organized in 1938, the Club promotes education and social growth through projects involving youth, schools, and hospitals. Minute books, treasurer's reports, membership lists, and scrapbooks.

16,220. Letitia Rosenberg Women's Home
Records. 1894-1971. 1.5 ft.
Open. Unpublished guide.
Rosenberg Library.
The Home was founded in 1896 "to serve as a permanent, benevolent, nonsectarian institution for the care of aged and deserving women unable to care for themselves." Minutes of board meetings, financial records, correspondence, and other records.

16,221. Thompson, Libbie (Moody)
Papers. 1943-76. 5 ft.
Open. Unpublished guide.
Rosenberg Library.
[Mrs. Clark W.] Thompson (1897-), a civic worker and mother, served as head of the Libbie Moody Thompson Foundation and as a member of the national board of the Woman's Medical College of Pennsylvania. Correspondence, diaries, photos, invitations, and clippings reflect her social, charitable, and philanthropic activities. Much of the material centers on her life from 1933 to 1966 in Washington, DC, while her husband was a member of the US House of Representatives. She was a member of the fine arts commission of the US state department, the advisory council of the University of Texas, and many other organizations.

16,222. Werlin, Rosella Horowitz
Papers. Ca. 1930-50. 1 ft.
Open. No guide.
Rosenberg Library.
Scrapbooks containing articles and clippings of [Mrs. Joseph S.] Werlin (ca. 1910-), publicity director of the Galveston Chamber of Commerce from 1937 to 1942 and a free-lance reporter for various newspapers and periodicals. Werlin also was a member of the Writers' War Board during WWII and publicity director for the Houston and Galveston chapters of the American Women's Voluntary Services.

16,223. Women's Choral Club
Records. 1923-25. 1 vol.
Open. No guide.
Rosenberg Library.
The Club was founded in 1923 to foster "a love of music in its members, to stimulate an interest in choral singing, and to add to the artistic life of our city." Scrapbook containing a constitution, minutes, correspondence, and a membership list.

16,224. Women's Civic League
Records. 1929-36. 4 in.
Open. Unpublished guide.
Rosenberg Library.
Correspondence of the corresponding secretaries of the League, which was organized in 1924 to promote civic improvement through better sanitation and landscaping.

16,225. Aynesworth, Kenneth Hazen
Papers. 1933-44. 6.25 ft.
Open. Unpublished guide.
University of Texas Medical Branch, Moody Medical Library.
Correspondence, minutes, photo, and clippings of Aynesworth (1873-1944), a Waco, TX, physician. Includes Aynesworth's correspondence with Marguerite [Mrs. I. D.] Fairchild of Lufkin, TX. Aynesworth and Fairchild served together on the University of Texas board of regents, and their correspondence concerns matters relating to the school. Fairchild's husband was a Lufkin businessman and a member of the Texas legislature.

16,226. Bonnet, Edith Marguerite
Papers. 1916-75. 5 in.
Open. Unpublished guide.
University of Texas Medical Branch, Moody Medical Library.
A San Antonio, TX, pediatrician, Bonnet (1897-) and four other doctors were the first female graduates of the University of Texas Medical Branch to serve internships at John Sealy Hospital in Galveston. They appealed to the University of Texas board of regents, charging that the hospital was guilty of sex discrimination. Correspondence, diary dating from 1916 to 1969, student notebooks, oral history tape, photos, and clippings concern Bonnet's career, family, and social activities. Bonnet had also applied to Harvard Medical School Children's Hospital for an internship, but was rejected because of her sex. She was elected a fellow of the American Academy of Pediatrics in 1959.

16,227. Galveston County Medical Assistants Society
Records. 1958-61. 2 vols.
Open. No guide.
University of Texas Medical Branch, Moody Medical Library.
Founded in 1958, the Society is composed mainly of women assistants in doctors' offices, hospitals, or clinics. Scrapbooks containing correspondence, photos, invitations, programs, and clippings reflect the activities of the group, which sought to provide educational opportunities through lectures, demonstrations, instructions, and study.

16,228. Short Hairs
Records. 1951-55. 1 vol.
Open. No guide.
University of Texas Medical Branch, Moody Medical Library.
Minute book of the Short Hairs, a social club the members of which were women associated with the University of Texas Medical Branch. There was a similar group for men called the Long Hairs.

16,229. University of Texas Medical Branch School of Nursing Alumnae Association
Records. 1895-1964. 1 vol.
Open. No guide.
University of Texas Medical Branch, Moody Medical Library.
In 1897 the University of Texas assumed control of the John Sealy Hospital Training School for Nurses, which was founded in 1890. Scrapbook containing photos of nursing classes, individual nurses, wards, hospital buildings, and operating rooms.

HELOTES

16,230. Archives
Records. 1866- . 11 drawers, ca. 250 tapes, and 50 motion pictures.
Open. Card catalog.
Sisters of Divine Providence, Generalate.
Minutes, financial records, chapter proceedings, correspondence, circular letters of mothers superior, biographies of sisters, manuscripts, histories of schools and convents operated by the Sisters, lectures, congregational newsletters, photos, scrapbooks on schools operated by the Sisters, clippings, other records, paintings, needlework, statues, and antiques. Records of Our Lady of the Lake University, which is owned by the congregation, include minutes of the board of trustees and council, a history, and other documents. The order was founded in 1762 in France and established in the US in 1866.

HOUSTON

16,231. Bailey, Kay
Papers. 1972-76. 22 ft.
Open. Unpublished guide.
Houston Public Library, Houston Metropolitan Research Center.
A Republican party activist, Bailey (1943-) represented Harris County in the Texas legislature from 1972 to 1976. Correspondence, committee notes, photos, and clippings relate to the 63rd and 64th sessions of the Texas legislature, with particular emphasis on women's rights, rape legislation, mass transit, and land-use planning.

16,232. Cherry, E. Richardson
Papers. 1894-1951. 3.5 ft.
Open. Unpublished guide.
Houston Public Library, Houston Metropolitan Research Center.
Cherry (1892-1953) was a Houston artist. Correspondence, photos, exhibit catalogs, articles, clippings, and other papers relate to Cherry's family history, travels, artistic achievements, and role in helping to found the Museum of Fine Arts in Houston.

16,233. City of Houston: Library Department
Records. 1878- . 60 ft.
Open. No guide.
Houston Public Library, Houston Metropolitan Research Center.
Annual reports, board minutes, financial records, correspondence, memos, photos, and scrapbooks provide a record of the operation of the Houston public library system. The system had women directors until 1967, and women have held most of the system's administrative and service positions.

16,234. Clipping Files
Collection. 1920s- . Ca. 15 ft.
Open. No guide.
Houston Public Library, Houston Metropolitan Research Center.
Articles and clippings contain biographical and general information about prominent Texas women, including Oveta (Culp) Hobby, Ima Hogg, and Barbara Jordan.

16,235. Cunningham, Minnie Fisher
Papers. 1915-44. 25 Hollinger boxes.
Open. Unpublished guide.
Houston Public Library, Houston Metropolitan Research Center.
A clubwoman, politician, and suffragist, [Mrs.] Cunningham helped organize the Texas LWV and the Texas Equal Suffrage Association and was a candidate for governor of Texas in 1944. Correspondence, speech manuscripts, press releases, newsletters, pamphlets, clippings, and campaign literature relate to her activities in the National American Woman Suffrage Association, the Texas Equal Suffrage Association, and the Texas anti-vice movement and to her gubernatorial candidacy.

16,236. Daily, Ray K.
Papers. 1912-75. 1.5 ft.
Open. Unpublished guide.
Houston Public Library, Houston Metropolitan Research Center.
Daily (1891-1975) was a physician, educator, and member of the board of the Houston Independent School District from 1928 to 1952. Correspondence, medical and educational articles written by Daily, speech manuscripts, photos, and clippings contain information about her medical research and career, her activities with Houston schools, the founding of the University of Houston, and the Houston Open Forum.

16,237. Gulf, Colorado, and Santa Fe Railroad
Records. 1897-1968. 370 ft.
Open. Unpublished guide.
Houston Public Library, Houston Metropolitan Research Center.
Correspondence, legal documents, memos, notes, and photos of the Railroad pertain to its operations in Louisiana and Texas and contain information about the Railroad's policy concerning women's wages and labor practices, the Louisiana Hour and Health Law for Female Workers, and the Louisiana Minimum Wage Law for Female Workers. Both Louisiana statutes were approved in 1938.

16,238. HMRC Oral History
Oral history. 1974-77. Ca. 50 tapes.
Access restricted. Unpublished guide.
Houston Public Library, Houston Metropolitan Research Center.
Taped interviews with prominent Houston women who were involved in such areas as culture, social welfare services, law enforcement, politics, and education. The interviews include discussion of events dating from 1926 to 1977.

16,239. Ideson, Julia
Papers. 1900-45. 2 Hollinger boxes and 1 vol.
Open. Unpublished guide.
Houston Public Library, Houston Metropolitan Research Center.
Ideson (1880-1945) was head librarian at the Houston Public Library from 1904 to 1945. Correspondence, speech and article manuscripts, photos, a scrapbook, clippings, and other papers pertain to library development, the Philosophic Society of Texas, the Texas LWV, and the Texas Commission on Interracial Cooperation, 1940-42.

16,240. Kennedy, Louise
Papers. 1952-74. 3 ft.
Open. Unpublished guide.
Houston Public Library, Houston Metropolitan Research Center.
Kennedy was an active member of the LWV and a precinct worker for the Democratic party. Political campaign material, LWV pamphlets, precinct mailing lists, and personal memorabilia relate to political campaigns in Houston.

16,241. Looscan, Adele Lubbock (Briscoe)
Papers. 1911-26. 1 Hollinger box and 4 vols.
Open. Unpublished guide.
Houston Public Library, Houston Metropolitan Research Center.
A civic, social, and literary leader in Houston, Looscan (1848-1935) was president of the Texas State Historical Association from 1915 to 1925. Correspondence, notes, photos, and clippings relate to her activities with the Historical Association and to her work with Texas history.

16,242. Tinsley, Eleanor
Papers. 1969-73. 3 ft.
Open. Unpublished guide.
Houston Public Library, Houston Metropolitan Research Center.
Tinsley was a member of the Houston Independent School District board from 1969 to 1973. Correspondence, School District records, research files, memos, and clippings document her activities as a board member. Includes information on desegregation, student unrest, school politics, drug abuse, Houston Community College, and vocational education.

16,243. Autry, James L.
Papers. 1834-1925. 20 ft.
Open. Unpublished guide.
Rice University Library.
Correspondence, diaries, photos, legal documents, and other papers of Autry (1859-1926), first general counsel for Texaco and president of Fidelity Trust Company. Includes correspondence of his grandmother, mother, and aunt, all of whom were widowed at an early age and left with young children to raise. Their correspondence reflects the difficulties of their situations. Autry's grandmother Martha W. Autry lost her husband in the war for Texas's independence from Mexico. Autry's mother Jeanie Valliant Brown lost her first husband, Autry's father, in the Civil War. The husband of Autry's aunt Mary Autry Greer also died in the Civil War.

16,244. Broun, Catherine Hopkins
Papers. 1854-89. 1 vol.
Open. Unpublished guide.
Rice University Library.
Diary and correspondence of Broun (ca. 1834-1903), a plantation owner's wife who lived in Middleburg, VA, primarily concern family events and the Civil War. The Civil War entries, which reflect her Confederate sympathies, contain descriptions of her fears during major battles near her home. She recounts how she fed and helped nurse Confederate soldiers and the hardships her family faced. She also discusses Yankee movements and the demands that northern troops made upon area residents. The latter portions of the diary contain information about the difficulties of plantation life, the problems of Reconstruction, and later family events.

16,245. Craw, Elizabeth
Papers. 1835-41. 1 vol.
Open. No guide.
Rice University Library.
Diary in which Craw (1819-ca. 1909) recorded her journey from her home in Ohio to see her fiancé in Texas. She traveled with her future in-laws down the Mississippi and Red rivers to northern Louisiana, then overland to San Antonio. The diary indicates that her fiancé Samuel Evans was killed at the Alamo shortly after her arrival in Texas. The diary entries stop with Evans's death but the volume includes later poems reflecting her despair and an account of an Indian raid in 1836. Craw returned to Ohio.

16,246. Depelchin, Kenzia Payne
Papers. 1878-79. 1 vol.
Open. No guide.
Rice University Library.
Letters Depelchin (1828-93), a nurse, wrote to her sister describing her work during a yellow fever epidemic in Memphis. Depelchin traveled to Tennessee from Texas as part of a volunteer group recruited from areas where the disease was prevalent.

16,247. Dillingham, Mary Pauline
Papers. Ca. 1863-1958. 2.5 ft.
Open. Unpublished guide.
Rice University Library.
[Miss] Dillingham (1875-1964) was the daughter of a prominent Houston banker and businessman. Correspondence, diaries, and journals reflect the life of a wealthy, single woman; the prejudice against the education of women during the early 20th century; and her boredom with her life. She became interested in the arts in Houston and New York.

16,248. Flint, Hallie Rienzi
Papers. 1883-1965. 1 ft.
Open. Unpublished guide.
Rice University Library.
Correspondence, columns, and clippings of Flint, a local newspaper columnist who wrote mostly for women. Includes a few family letters and mementos.

16,249. Muir, Andrew Forest
Papers. Ca. 1800-1969. Ca. 17 ft.
Open. Unpublished guide.
Rice University Library.
Papers of Muir (1916-69), a history professor at Rice, contain copies of correspondence and records of Queen Emma Kaleleoanlani of Hawaii. Her papers particularly document her work with the

Anglican church in Hawaii and her establishment of church-related schools there.

16,250. Women's Suffrage
Records. 1915. 30 items.
Open. No guide.
Rice University Library.
Correspondence received in response to questionnaires distributed by the publicity committee of the Men's League for Women's Suffrage. The questionnaires solicited information about the effects of women's suffrage in various states. The replies are chiefly from persons in the western states.

16,251. Villa de Matel Archives
Records. 1865- . Ca. 75 ft., 11 boxes, 5 file cabinets, and several motion pictures.
Open. Index.
Sisters of Charity of the Incarnate Word, Motherhouse.
This religious order of women, which was founded in 1866 in Galveston, TX, is engaged in health care. Minutes, financial records, deeds, correspondence, diaries, retreat notes, histories, annals, ledgers, acts of profession, hospital registers, photos, scrapbooks, newspapers, schools of nursing yearbooks, articles, pamphlets, and other records. Includes material relating to the hospitals, orphanages, schools, and geriatric centers operated by the Sisters.

16,252. Cunningham, Minnie Fisher
Papers. Nd. 43 containers.
Open. Container list.
University of Houston Archives, Special Collections.
Correspondence, organization records, scrapbooks, press releases, political campaign material, clippings, and other papers of [Mrs.] Cunningham, a suffragist. Includes records of the National American Woman Suffrage Association, the Texas Equal Suffrage Association, the Democratic National Committee, and woman suffrage organizations in Arkansas, Maryland, Massachusetts, Michigan, New York, Oklahoma, Pennsylvania, Virginia, West Virginia, Wisconsin, and in various cities. Correspondents include Carrie Chapman Catt, Maud (Wood) Park, Anna Howard Shaw, and various political figures. In addition to suffrage issues, the papers include discussion of the 1920 Democratic National Convention for which Cunningham was a delegate, Liberty Loans, the League of Nations, the Republican party, prison reform, prohibition, anti-vice campaigns, politics, prostitution, and other issues.

16,253. Darden, Ida
Papers. Nd. 7 archival boxes.
Open. Accession list.
University of Houston Archives, Special Collections.
[Mrs.] Darden, a political conservative, was a writer and an editor of the newspaper *Southern Conservative*. Personal correspondence and issues of the *Conservative* provide information about Darden's political opinions.

IRVING

16,254. Chronicles
Records. 1961- . 3 vols.
Access restricted. No guide.
School Sisters of Notre Dame, South-Central Province.
Historical record of the principal activities of the South-Central Province, financial records, biographies of deceased sisters, photos, clippings, and other records of this religious community of women involved in education.

KINGSVILLE

16,255. Women's Auxiliary of the Brotherhood of Locomotive Firemen and Engineers
Records. 1914-42. 28 vols.
Open. No guide.
Texas A&I University, John E. Conner Museum.
Charter, minutes, and rituals of the Auxiliary, a social and civic club formed in 1914 by wives of railroad workers in Kingsville. The railroad's arrival in the area in 1904 provided the impetus that led to construction of Kingsville. Women worked through the Auxiliary for improved education and other goals. The club was dissolved in 1942.

LEAGUE CITY

16,256. Ladies Auxiliary of the National Association of Conservation Districts
Records. Ca. 1950- . Ca. 4 ft.
Open. No guide.
Davis Conservation Library.
The Auxiliary was organized in 1950 to strengthen the efforts of the National Association of Conservation Districts and to promote public understanding of the need for conservation and development of the nation's natural resources. Constitution and bylaws, yearly reports given by the president at annual NACD conventions, minutes of officers' meetings, correspondence of officers, photos, scrapbooks, newsletters, and other records, including material of individual state auxiliaries. The records document the Auxiliary's activities, which have included placing conservation material in schools and public libraries, working to have conservation and environmental education included in all school curricula, organizing and conducting conservation workshops for teachers and students, and providing scholarships for study of conservation-related subjects.

LONGVIEW

16,257. LeTourneau, Robert Gilmore
Papers. 1915- . Ca. 200 archives boxes and other items.
Open. No guide.
LeTourneau College Library.
Papers of LeTourneau (1888-1969), an industrialist and businessman, include correspondence, photos, scrapbooks, news releases, yearbooks, annuals, clippings, mementos and other items of his wife Evelyn Peterson LeTourneau (1900-), who with her husband founded LeTourneau College and the LeTourneau Foundation. An author, speaker, and philanthropist, Evelyn LeTourneau was named National Mother of the Year in 1969. From 1938 to 1948 she operated a Christian summer camp for young people at Winona Lake, IN. For two years she conducted religion classes for more than 600 students at the county school at Toccoa, GA. She also established camps in Arkansas and Texas for disadvantaged boys. The LeTourneaus were married in 1917 and had six sons and one daughter. One son died in infancy.

LUBBOCK

16,258. American Association of University Women
Records. 1925-77. 3189 pp.
Open. Unpublished guide.
Texas Tech University, Southwest Collection.
Minutes, reports, scrapbooks, programs, periodicals, maps, and a history of the Lubbock AAUW branch for the period 1925-41.

16,259. Anderson, Betty
Papers. 1957-76. 4509 pp.
Open. Unpublished guide.
Texas Tech University, Southwest Collection.
[Mrs. John] Anderson, who participates in many civic activities, has served as president of the Texas LWV. Correspondence, minutes, agenda, financial material, audit proposal, committee reports, memoranda, surveys, petitions, ordinances, photos, clippings, and other material pertaining to the Citizen's Advisory Commission, which helped plan a rehabilitation program after Lubbock was struck by a tornado in 1970; Head Start; the Lubbock Area Advisory Committee to the Texas Constitutional Revision Commission; the Lubbock Planning and Zoning Commission; a rape crisis center; and an urban renewal agency.

16,260. Baggett, Halcyon
Papers. 1946-76. 2165 pp.
Open. Unpublished guide.
Texas Tech University, Southwest Collection.
A former president of the Texas LWV, [Mrs. Hill] Baggett participated in civic activities and was a write-in candidate for the Lubbock city council. Correspondence, financial and scrapbook material, photos, invitations, and printed matter provide information about Baggett's work in such Lubbock groups as The Salvation Army, the LWV, the Community Chest, the Chamber of Commerce, and the Athena Symposium.

16,261. Card, Lottie (Holman)
Papers. 1825-1964. 9160 pp.
Open. Unpublished guide.
Texas Tech University, Southwest Collection.
An artist and writer on historic Texas folklore, [Mrs. James R.] Card (1882-1964) was a member of the Daughters of the Confederacy and the Texas Genealogical Society. Correspondence, financial and legal documents, literary writings, research notes, genealogical and scrapbook material, photos, sketches, and drawings concerning the Card, Burnham, and Holman families during the Texas Republic, the Civil War, and WWI. Also contains information on the Negro in Comanche, TX, and in the state as a whole. Card was the paternal granddaughter of Nancy Burnham, the first white child born in the Stephen F. Austin Colony.

16,262. Catholic Church in West Texas
Records. 1854-1964. 30 ft. of microfilm.
Open. Unpublished guide.
Texas Tech University, Southwest Collection.
Correspondence and reports include material on the Sisters of Mercy of Amarillo.

16,263. Colorado City, TX: Clubs
Collection. 1882-1961. 1833 pp.
Open. Unpublished guide.
Texas Tech University, Southwest Collection.
Includes minutes, a ledger, correspondence, speeches, membership lists, a resolution, programs, a yearbook, and study material of the Colorado Club, 1905-06; the Kimona Club, 1904; the Ladies Park Association, 1896; the Shakespeare Club, 1947-61; and the Standard Club, 1896-1942.

16,264. Culver, Barbara G.
Papers. 1970-75. 9111 pp. and 1 tape.
Open. Unpublished guide.
Texas Tech University, Southwest Collection.
A Texas county judge, [Mrs. John R.] Culver served a three-year term on the National Advisory Council on the Education of Disadvantaged Children and was a delegate to the White House Conference on Children and Youth; she also was chairman of the local government subcommittee of the Texas Constitutional Revision Commission. Correspondence, literary writings, and conference, scrapbook, and printed matter concern Culver's career.

16,265. Dingus, Georgia (Wilson)
Papers. 1895-1977. 34,432 pp. and 3 tapes.
Open. Unpublished guide.
Texas Tech University, Southwest Collection.
A writer and retired teacher, [Mrs. William G.] Dingus (1886-) is a member of clubs, including the LWV, the DAR, and the Lubbock branch of the AAUW. Correspondence, memoranda, typescripts, scrapbooks, and religious and political material pertain to her association with the AAUW, the Methodist Church Woman's Society of Christian Service, the United Church Women, and the Texas Council of Church Women, and to her radio broadcasts concerning teaching and religion. Many of the later papers deal with her work on the Lubbock Council for the UN.

16,266. Dunn, Mary
Papers. 1923-69. 724 pp. and 1 tape.
Open. Unpublished guide.
Texas Tech University, Southwest Collection.
[Miss] Dunn (1888-) is a music teacher. Correspondence, scrapbooks, directories, yearbooks, and programs pertain to her career, to the South Plains Music Teachers Association, and to other music-related activities.

16,267. Godeke, Mrs. H. F.
Papers. 1940-61. 195 pp.
Open. Unpublished guide.
Texas Tech University, Southwest Collection.
Scrapbooks of Daisy Godeke concern the Texas Federation of Women's Clubs and Olton study clubs.

16,268. Gracy, Alice (Duggan)
Papers. 1845-1951. 361 pp. and 1 tape.
Open. Unpublished guide.
Texas Tech University, Southwest Collection.
[Mrs. David C.] Gracy was the daughter of West Texas pioneer A. P. Duggan, Sr., who settled in Littlefield, TX. Correspondence, literary writings, biographical data, legal documents, clippings, and printed matter concern the history of the Duggan family and Lamb County, TX.

16,269. Hart, Julia (Duggan)
Papers. 1837-1970. 6780 pp.
Open. Unpublished guide.
Texas Tech University, Southwest Collection.
[Mrs. Edward M.] Hart (1873-1970) was a musician and poet. Correspondence, financial and legal documents, photos, scrapbook material, clippings, and maps concern the Hart, Duggan, and Webb families of Texas. Also contains genealogical material about the Duggan, McKie, Malone, Rylander, Hunter, and Pitts families.

16,270. Hill, Ida Linda (Blasienz)
Papers. 1912-63. 9924 pp.
Open. Unpublished guide.
Texas Tech University, Southwest Collection.
[Mrs. Ernest C.] Hill (1895-) was an agent for the Texas Game and Fish Commission. Correspondence, financial and legal documents, scrapbook material, and lists primarily concern her work with the Commission.

16,271. Hill, Katie Adele
Papers. 1861-1970. 2988 pp. and 50 ft. of microfilm.
Open. Unpublished guide.
Texas Tech University, Southwest Collection.
An author and past chairman of the Texas Literacy Council, Hill (1900-) served for 38 years as a home demonstration agent for the Texas Agricultural Extension Service. Correspondence, literary writings, photos, scrapbooks, and printed matter document her career in home demonstration work and include material on ranchers in the Hill family. Hill earned a PhD at Texas Woman's University at Denton, TX.

16,272. Hill, Sarah Miltia, and Hill, Katherine
Papers. 1852-1977. 20,946 pp. and 2 tapes.
Open. Unpublished guide.
Texas Tech University, Southwest Collection.
Daughters of Daniel Chapman Hill, the Hills are former teachers; Sarah Hill (1895-) was head of the art department at Sul Ross State College in Alpine, TX. Correspondence, literary writings, financial and legal documents, genealogical data, photos, and scrapbook material primarily relate to the D. C. Hill family.

16,273. Justin, Enid
Papers. 1939-65. 3 tapes and 40 ft. of microfilm.
Open. Unpublished guide.
Texas Tech University, Southwest Collection.
[Miss] Justin is the president of the Nacona Boot Company and the daughter of the founder of the Justin Boot Company. Papers pertain to the family-owned company.

16,274. Kemp, Augusta Thekla (Hasslock)
Papers. 1896-1974. 1759 pp.
Open. Unpublished guide.
Texas Tech University, Southwest Collection.
[Mrs. John Franklin] Kemp (1882-1963) was a teacher, geologist, and author. Correspondence, legal documents, lists, certificates, photos, and printed matter concern the Hasslock family and Kemp's activities.

16,275. Kent, Leona (Gelin)
Papers. 1942-46. 1036 pp.
Open. Unpublished guide.
Texas Tech University, Southwest Collection.
[Mrs. William C.] Kent was director of the Lubbock USO, executive director of the Lubbock Symphony Orchestra, and director of the local YWCA. Correspondence, photos, scrapbooks, and visitor lists relating to the Lubbock USO from 1942 to 1952 and 1942-45 issues of the Lubbock Chamber of Commerce's *Daily Doings,* which concerned recreation.

16,276. League of Women Voters of Texas
Records. 1920-76. 265,258 pp.
Open. Unpublished guide.
Texas Tech University, Southwest Collection.
Records of the state LWV.

16,277. Lee, Amy Freeman
Papers. 1934-77. 8406 pp. and 181 tapes.
Open. Unpublished guide.
Texas Tech University, Southwest Collection.
A member of the Philosophical Society of Texas and recipient of seven Who's Who awards, Lee is an artist, author, speaker, and art critic. Correspondence, taped lectures, transcripts, scrapbook material, and wax recordings pertain to the radio program "Call Board" from 1947 to 1951 and Lee's art career. Lee received an honorary doctor of letters degree from Incarnate Word College in San Antonio, TX.

16,278. Lubbock, TX, Clubs
Collection. 1911-76. 5359 pp.
Open. Unpublished guide.
Texas Tech University, Southwest Collection.
Consists of material from the following Lubbock clubs: the Church Women's Federation of Lubbock, 1933-57, 861 pages; the United Church Women of Lubbock, 1957-65, 3072 pages; the Lubbock Needle Club, 1911-39, 66 pages; the Twentieth Century Club, 1928-61; the Lubbock Junior Garden Club, 1939-74, 667 pages; NOW, 1976 newsletters; and the Lubbock Garden Club, 1939-73, 565 pages. Also includes 128 pages of records of the Texas Tech Faculty Women's Club, 1957-67.

16,279. McKenzie, Mrs. T. H.
Papers. 1908-40. 220 pp.
Open. Unpublished guide.
Texas Tech University, Southwest Collection.
Material reflects work in the American National Red Cross, the Carson County Children's Council, and other Texas and Carson County clubs.

16,280. Mooar, Lydia Louise
Papers. 1876-1971. 1479 pp. and 1 tape.
Open. Unpublished guide.
Texas Tech University, Southwest Collection.
The daughter of John Wesley Mooar, Lydia Mooar was a retired public school teacher. Correspondence, literary writings, and printed material concerning club activities of Lydia Mooar's mother in Colorado City, TX, and other Mooar family members.

16,281. Olive, Jeannette Ramsey
Papers. 1906-70. 1342 pp.
Open. Unpublished guide.
Texas Tech University, Southwest Collection.
Correspondence, school workbooks, record books, scrapbooks, and legal documents concern [Mrs. W. E.] Olive's career as a music teacher.

16,282. Record, James R.: West Texas Pioneers
Papers. 1936-59. 4589 pp.
Open. Unpublished guide.
Texas Tech University, Southwest Collection.
Record's papers include those of Pauline [Mrs. John W.] Naylor, who worked with Record as a pioneer editor of the Fort Worth *Star Telegram.* Correspondence of women's clubs and cancer and tuberculosis associations, photos, and clippings reflect Naylor's personal activities.

16,283. Riordan, J. E., Family
Papers. 1834-1965. 12,189 pp.
Open. Unpublished guide.
Texas Tech University, Southwest Collection.
Correspondence, diaries, financial and legal documents, literary writings, receipts, awards, and school and printed material of this Colorado City, TX, family, which was prominent in the town's society and in the Presbyterian church. Includes papers of Josie [Mrs. J. E.] Riordan and of Nellie, Frances, Sallie, and Mary Riordan, which describe life in the town from the 1880s to 1965.

16,284. Roddy, Mrs. P. E.
Papers. 1900-65. 524 pp.
Open. Unpublished guide.
Texas Tech University, Southwest Collection.
Roddy was a member of the state board of directors of the Texas Association for Mental Health. Correspondence, memo books, a lease, legal documents, invitations, photos, and printed matter relate to the Graham family and Texas history. Roddy's maiden name was Graham.

16,285. Slaughter, Carrie Averill
Papers. 1862-1960. 1 microfilm reel.
Open. Unpublished guide.
Texas Tech University, Southwest Collection.
Genealogical material and scrapbooks relating to the family of Slaughter, who was the second wife of Dallas cattleman Colonel C. C. Slaughter.

16,286. Texas Home Economics Association
Records. 1909-75. 7518 pp.
Open. Unpublished guide.
Texas Tech University, Southwest Collection.
Constitution, minutes, committee reports, membership rolls, lists of officers, histories of the Association and of county units, an historical survey, programs of work, a photo, a scrapbook, and other material, including a list of all home economics graduates from 22 colleges and universities before 1940.

16,287. Texas Tech: Dean of Women
Records. 1928-68. 1768 pp.
Open. Unpublished guide.

Texas Tech University, Southwest Collection.
Report, scrapbooks, and printed matter concern women's social activities at this Lubbock institution.

16,288. Tinsley, Willa Vaughn
Papers. 1936-72. 5008 pp.
Open. Unpublished guide.
Texas Tech University, Southwest Collection.
Speeches, literary writings, and printed material of Tinsley, the dean of the Texas Tech University school of home economics. Primarily concerns her speeches and publications on nutrition, education, and the role of women. Tinsley earned a PhD at the University of Minnesota in 1947.

16,289. West, Elizabeth Howard
Papers. 1935-36. 2500 pp.
Open. Unpublished guide.
Texas Tech University, Southwest Collection.
[Miss] West (1873-1948) was Texas state chairwoman of the Southwestern Library Association. Correspondence, notes, regional reports, literary writings, scrapbook material, maps, and printed matter concern West's work with the Association.

16,290. Williams, Jeanne
Papers. 1952-77. 9338 pp.
Open. Unpublished guide.
Texas Tech University, Southwest Collection.
Correspondence, literary writings, galley proofs, notes, photos, scrapbook material, books, and other printed matter relate to Williams's career as a writer of western fiction.

16,291. Wilton, Anna E. (Keener)
Papers. 1913-75. 2983 pp. and 25 ft. of microfilm.
Open. Unpublished guide.
Texas Tech University, Southwest Collection.
[Mrs. Louis R.] Wilton (1895-) is an artist, art critic, and art teacher. Correspondence and scrapbook material reflect her career in New Mexico.

16,292. Women's Air Force Service Pilots
Records. 1943-75. 1 tape and 2 microfilm reels.
Open. Unpublished guide.
Texas Tech University, Southwest Collection.
Correspondence, photos, scrapbook material, and printed items relating to the WASPs, women who flew nomcombat military planes for the US Army from 1942 to 1944.

16,293. Women's Groups
Collection. 1931-77. 75,181 pp.
Open. Unpublished guide.
Texas Tech University, Southwest Collection.
Consists of records of the following groups: the LWV of Lubbock, 1946-77, 74,695 pages; the South Plains Music Teachers Association, 1931-36, 181 pages; the Caprock district of the Texas Federation of Women's Clubs, 1947-72, 305 pages.

NACOGDOCHES

16,294. American Association of University Women, Nacogdoches Chapter
Records. 1930- . 2 Hollinger boxes and 2 vols.
Open. Unpublished guide.
Stephen F. Austin State University, Ralph W. Steen Library, Special Collections.
Minutes, correspondence, yearbooks, scrapbooks, photos, and clippings of this AAUW chapter founded in 1930.

16,295. Baker, Karle (Wilson)
Papers. 1885-1960. 61 Hollinger boxes and 2 vols.
Open. Unpublished guide.
Stephen F. Austin State University, Ralph W. Steen Library, Special Collections.
[Mrs. Thomas E.] Baker (1878-1960), a poet, novelist, and college instructor of English, helped organize literary societies, including the Texas Institute of Letters. Manuscripts of books and poems, galley proofs, correspondence with publishers and readers, financial records of royalties, historical research notes, speeches, scrapbooks, photos, and other material.

16,296. Colonial Dames, James Haggard Chapter
Records. 1958- . 4 Hollinger boxes.
Open. No guide.
Stephen F. Austin State University, Ralph W. Steen Library, Special Collections.
Annual reports, correspondence, yearbooks, photos, and clippings of the Nacogdoches chapter of the Colonial Dames, which was founded to aid in the preservation of records and historic places in the US and to foster colonial research and education of young people.

16,297. Cum Concilio Club
Records. 1894- . 6 boxes and vols.
Open. No guide.
Stephen F. Austin State University, Ralph W. Steen Library, Special Collections.
Founded in 1894, the Club is a literary and historical women's group with interests in education, fine arts, civic affairs, philanthropy, public welfare, and spiritual values. Constitution and bylaws, minutes, account books, yearbooks, and scrapbooks of one of the oldest federated clubs in Texas.

16,298. Daughters of the American Revolution, Nacogdoches Chapter
Records. 1926- . 30 Hollinger boxes and vols.
Open. No guide.
Stephen F. Austin State University, Ralph W. Steen Library, Special Collections.
Bylaws, minutes, yearbooks, scrapbooks, photos, clippings, and other material pertaining to local activities of the chapter.

16,299. Daughters of the Republic of Texas, Stone Fort Chapter
Records. 1950- . 4 Hollinger boxes and vols.
Open. No guide.
Stephen F. Austin State University, Ralph W. Steen Library, Special Collections.
The Daughters of the Republic of Texas was organized to encourage research into early Texas records, to foster preservation of documents and relics of the state's past, and "to perpetuate the memory and spirit of men and women who achieved and maintained the independence of Texas." Constitution and bylaws, business records, yearbooks, written history, scrapbooks, and program material of the Nacogdoches chapter.

16,300. Lindsay, Emaline
Papers. 1900-47. 1 box.
Open. No guide.
Stephen F. Austin State University, Ralph W. Steen Library, Special Collections.
[Mrs. Robert] Lindsay was a Nacogdoches resident, housewife, and club woman. Diaries, poems, notes, scrapbooks, clippings, invitations, and photos reflect Lindsay's daily activities.

16,301. Montgomery, Charlotte (Baker)
Papers. Nd. 1 box.
Open. No guide.
Stephen F. Austin State University, Ralph W. Steen Library, Special Collections.
[Mrs. Roger] Montgomery (1910-), an author of children's books and illustrator of her own books, uses the name Charlotte Baker in her work. Manuscripts, pen and ink illustrations, and galley proofs. Montgomery is also active in the humane society.

16,302. Pochmann, Virginia Ruth (Fouts)
Papers. 1934-69. 1 Hollinger box.
Open. Unpublished guide.
Stephen F. Austin State University, Ralph W. Steen Library, Special Collections.
A teacher, author, and lecturer, [Mrs. Henry A.] Pochmann (1903-) is active in garden and civic clubs and is the widow of an English professor. Manuscript of the book "Triple Ridge Farm," correspondence with publishers, biographical information, and photo.

16,303. Price, Missoura
Papers. 1905-46. 3 Hollinger boxes.
Open. No guide.
Stephen F. Austin State University, Ralph W. Steen Library, Special Collections.
[Mrs. W. F.] Price was a Nacogdoches resident and club woman. Correspondence, including letters from her daughter in Mexico during the 1930s; club records; autobiographical, literary, and historical notes; household and personal account books; and photos.

16,304. Turner, Janet
Papers. 1940s-60s. 2 portfolios.
Open. No guide.
Stephen F. Austin State University, Ralph W. Steen Library, Special Collections.
Formerly professor of art at SFASU and Guggenheim Fellow, Turner is an award-winning block print and serigraph artist and an art professor at Chico State College in Chico, CA. Portfolio of prints of eastern Texas and western Louisiana birds and one of illustrations for Frank E. Smith's *The Yazoo.* Turner has exhibited her work throughout the US and abroad.

PANHANDLE

16,305. Early Settlers
Collection. 1887-1925. No size given.
Open. No guide.
Carson County Square House Museum.
Diaries and accounts by early settlers include a diary kept by five sisters in the Jabez Lill family, which was of English ancestry.

16,306. German Settlers
Collection. 1889-1908. Ca. 35 items.
Open. No guide.
Carson County Square House Museum.
Oral history material, documents, and other historical items concern German settlers in the communities of Groom and St. Francis in the Texas counties of Carson and Potter. The settlers were farmers and landowners. The German settlers at Groom came to the town individually in the late 1880s; the Germans at St. Francis followed a priest to the town in ca. 1908. The material has been published in *A Time to Purpose* (Hereford, TX: Pioneer Publishers).

16,307. Polish Settlers of Texas
Collection. Nd. Ca. 20 items.
Closed. No guide.
Carson County Square House Museum.
Histories, photos, one tape recording, and other items about Polish families who purchased land near White Deer, TX, from a British syndicate and formed a colony in 1906. Women members of the Sacred Heart Catholic Church in White Deer wrote the histories, which were published in *A Time to Purpose* (Hereford, TX: Pioneer Publishers).

PORTLAND

16,308. Bayview College
Collection. 1873-1916. No size given.
Open. No guide.

Bell Public Library.
A coeducational institution that was in operation from 1873 to 1916, the College was the only formal institution of higher education open to women in the area at the time. Seven oral history interviews, a College catalog, clippings, and a book about local pioneers.

16,309. Chatwork History
Records. 1921- . No size given.
Open. No guide.
Bell Public Library.
History book and clippings concerning Chatwork, an organization involved with the Portland library.

SAN ANTONIO

16,310. Bexar County Archives
Records. 1717-1974. Ca. 500 ft.
Open. Inventory and brief description.
Bexar County Archives.
Records date from the beginning of Spanish settlement in what is now Bexar County and document military, religious, and political aspects of life in the Spanish province of Texas, the Mexican state of Coahuila y Texas, and in Bexar County after Texas gained its independence. Municipal and county records include marriage licenses, 1837-99; Confederate pension applications, 1861-1927; declarations of intentions to become a US citizen, 1852-1906; lists of paupers in Bexar County, 1916-21; and naturalization records, 1853-1906. Also includes estate papers of Maria Josefa Navarro and her husband Juan Martin Veramendi; accounts of expeditions, trials, Indian raids, and the Mexican Revolution; and correspondence of citizens, soldiers, and clergymen.

16,311. Congregational Orders: Women
Records. 1886- . Ca. 8 ft.
Access restricted. No guide.
Catholic Archives at San Antonio.
Correspondence of pioneer sisters of various congregations with the archbishop of San Antonio regarding finances, personal health and problems, constitutions, appointments, and other matters. Also includes clippings, brochures, and other records.

16,312. Blocker, W. B.
Papers. 1880s-1956. 0.5 cu.ft.
Open. No guide.
Daughters of the Republic of Texas Library.
Correspondence of Blocker, his mother Annie (Lane) [Mrs. J. R.] Blocker, and other members of this family that dominated the Texas cattle industry during the 1880s and 1890s. A large portion of the letters were exchanged between Annie Blocker and her son. The letters provide a picture of a woman's role in a cattle ranching family.

16,313. Clippings
Collection. Ca. 1900- . Ca. 7 ft.
Open. No guide.
Daughters of the Republic of Texas Library.
Clippings and ephemera include information about individual women and women's groups, such as the Battle of Flowers Association and the Woman's Club of San Antonio. Women represented in the collection include Mary Eleanor Brackenridge, who worked to improve the status of women and children; Miriam Amanda "Ma" Ferguson, who served as governor of Texas after her husband Governor Jim Ferguson was impeached in 1917 because of alleged financial irregularities; and Lucy (Holcombe) Pickens, wife of US ambassador Francis Wilkinson Pickens. Brackenridge was founder and first president in 1898 of the Woman's Club of San Antonio, the first Texas woman's club to endorse suffrage. She was president of the Texas Woman Suffrage Association and founder of the San Antonio de Béxar Chapter of the DAR. Ma Ferguson was elected governor in 1924 and in 1932; she was defeated in the 1926 and 1930 elections. Her husband served as her advisor. Collection includes reprints of some of her speeches and editorials concerning her performance in office. Pickens traveled with her husband to Russia, where he served as ambassador from 1856 to 1860. She also supported his efforts as Confederate governor of South Carolina from 1860. Her picture was placed on the Confederate $100 bill.

16,314. Eager, Sarah Elizabeth (Riddle)
Papers. 1830s-1930s. 2 cu.ft.
Open. Card catalog.
Daughters of the Republic of Texas Library.
[Mrs. Robert] Eager (1842-1947), the first Anglo-American girl born in San Antonio, became custodian of the Alamo Shrine. Correspondence between Eager family members; correspondence concerning activities of the Daughters of the Republic of Texas; poetry, including Mabell Biggart's poem about the Battle of the Alamo; programs; magazines; and clippings. Includes a description of the Alamo in 1836 and a description of the Battle of the Alamo.

16,315. Maverick, Lucy
Papers. 1913-41. 1.5 in.
Open. No guide.
Daughters of the Republic of Texas Library.
Correspondence of [Miss] Maverick, a founder of the San Antonio Art League, includes letters from her mother Jane (Maury) [Mrs. Albert] Maverick concerning family matters, from Frederick C. Chabot regarding his life in Mexico, and from Henry Moody about his painting habits, art exhibits, and other subjects.

16,316. Quillin, Ellen Dorothy (Schulz)
Papers. Ca. 1920s. Ca. 1 cu.ft.
Open. No guide.
Daughters of the Republic of Texas Library.
[Mrs. Roy W.] Quillin, a botanist, was founder and director of the Witte Memorial Museum in San Antonio. Notebooks focusing on her professional work and manuscripts, including one about Texas trees and shrubs and one concerning 500 wild flowers in the San Antonio area. Quillin headed the science department at San Antonio's Main Avenue High School in the 1920s.

16,317. Smith, Julia
Papers. 1965-68. Ca. 3 in.
Open. No guide.
Daughters of the Republic of Texas Library.
[Miss] Smith, a composer, wrote the music played during the inauguration of President Lyndon Baines Johnson. Music scores, including the Johnson inaugural music; photos; and documents relating to the concert premiere of "Remember the Alamo."

16,318. St. Philip's College
Records. 1893-1943. 5 ft.
Open. No guide.
Episcopal Diocese of West Texas Archives.
Originally a church school established in 1898 for Negro girls and later a religious junior college, St. Philip's became a municipal coeducational junior college. Minutes, financial records, correspondence, photos, and other records relate to St. Philip's and to Artemesia Bowden, headmistress and later dean.

16,319. Archives
Records. 1880- . Ca. 50 boxes and ca. 50 tapes.
Closed. Unpublished guide.
Missionary Catechists of Divine Providence, St. Andrew's Convent.
This religious order of women was founded in 1930 in Houston. Correspondence, including letters of the founder; papers of the first administration; records of mission work; tapes and transcriptions of interviews with persons connected with the early days of the Catechists; photos; clippings; and a book of pious thoughts and reflections of the founder.

16,320. Battle of Flowers Association
Records. 1891-1958. 20 vols.
Open. No guide.
San Antonio Public Library.
The Association, a local woman's club founded in 1891, organizes an annual parade to commemorate the Battle of San Jacinto through which Texas gained its independence from Mexico. Scrapbooks record annual parade preparations.

16,321. Chrysanthemum Ball Association of San Antonio
Records. 1954-71. 15 vols.
Open. No guide.
San Antonio Public Library.
Scrapbooks of the Association, which was founded in 1954 as the Charity Ball Association and which assumed its current name in 1971. The Association seeks to provide financial help for other organizations. Its first ball, held in 1954, was a benefit for Boysville and for Sunshine Cottage, a school for deaf children. Scrapbooks include lists of members and committees, photos, clippings, and other material about preparations for the balls.

16,322. City Federation of Women's Clubs
Records. 1922-64. 3 ft.
Open. No guide.
San Antonio Public Library.
The Federation, a local group involved in social service and cultural activities, was founded in 1904 and joined the Texas Federation of Women's Clubs in 1911. Annual reports, minutes, and photos, including those of the group's founders and past presidents.

16,323. Military Civilian Club of San Antonio
Records. 1931-70. Ca. 8 in.
Open. No guide.
San Antonio Public Library.
Founded in 1921 as the Army Civilian Club and renamed the Military Civilian Club in 1951, the organization promotes social relations between military and civilian residents of San Antonio. Constitution, bylaws, and yearbooks, which list club officers, committee members, names and addresses of members, and names of deceased members. Many women belong to the organization.

WACO

16,324. Aars, Rosalie (Rueter)
Oral history. 1972. 1 tape and 1 transcript.
Open. Unpublished guide.
Baylor University, The Texas Collection.
Interview in which [Mrs. Calvert Pernell] Aars (1916-), a housewife, discusses the history from 1949 to 1971 and preparation of the annual smorgasbord sponsored by Our Savior's Lutheran Church in the Norwegian community of Norse in Bosque County, TX.

16,325. Allen, Gladys
Papers. 1823-1953. 2.5 in.
Open. Register.
Baylor University, The Texas Collection.
[Miss] Allen (1897-1953) was an educator, home manager, and trustee of Baylor University. Correspondence, journals, reports, and clippings provide information primarily about Allen family genealogy and Gladys Allen's service as a Baylor trustee. Includes replies she received to a survey she conducted in 1944 regarding faculty salary scales and retirement provisions at other universities and reports about Baylor's 1947 improvement program. Includes two journals kept from 1883 to 1893 by her grandfather A. L. Allen that provide information on weather and crops.

16,326. American Association of University Women, Waco Branch
Records. 1926-70. 2.5 ft.
Open. Preliminary inventory.
Baylor University, The Texas Collection.
Correspondence, reports, scrapbooks, yearbooks, newsletters, and clippings of this local AAUW branch, established in 1926. Correspondence of the mid-1920s to the 1940s primarily concerns Baylor University's involvement with the AAUW on local, state, and national levels. Contains newsletters, reports, and other publications of the state and national organizations.

16,327. Amsler, Margaret (Harris)
Oral history. 1972. 3 tapes and 1 transcript.
Open. Unpublished guide and transcript index.
Baylor University, The Texas Collection.
Interviews of [Mrs. Sam] Amsler (1908-), a lawyer and former law professor at the Baylor School of Law, concern her family and educational background, her political experience as a member of the Texas House of Representatives, her activities at the Baylor School of Law, and her work in revising Texas corporation laws. Her family reminiscences include references beginning with the 1880s.

16,328. Armstrong, Chloe
Papers. 1950-73. 7 in.
Open. Preliminary inventory.
Baylor University, The Texas Collection.
Armstrong was a professor of oral communication at Baylor University from 1948 to 1973. Correspondence, primarily letters from her publishers and from Democratic politicians such as Ralph Yarborough and Lyndon Baines Johnson; manuscripts of two of her books on oral interpretation; programs and newsletters from various speech associations; reports; and a few political items.

16,329. Barron, Bertie R.
Papers. 1897-1908. 2 in.
Open. Register.
Baylor University, The Texas Collection.
Correspondence in which Barron (ca. 1880-), a student, describes to her parents her studies, rules, and student life at Baylor Female College in Belton, TX. Contains a 1908 letter from her sister Ruby Barron, a student at Baylor University.

16,330. Baylor Round Table
Records. Nd. 3 ft.
Open. No guide.
Baylor University, The Texas Collection.
Limited to Baylor University faculty wives and women faculty members, this group was organized in 1904 to "develop both the social and cultural life of the University Circle." Constitution, bylaws, correspondence, programs, photos, scrapbooks, and yearbooks.

16,331. Baylor University: Dean of the Union Building
Records. 1948-57. 2.5 ft.
Access restricted. Preliminary listing.
Baylor University, The Texas Collection.
Correspondence, notes, calendars of events, programs, and clippings generated by Lily Russell during her work as dean of Baylor's Union Building. Contains material on the American Ideals Conference, special convocations, visitors, and lectures.

16,332. Baylor University: Dean of Women
Records. 1927-40s. 4 ft.
Access restricted. Preliminary listing.
Baylor University, The Texas Collection.
Form letters, photos, student handbooks, and programs of the Baylor dean of women's office include rules for boarding students and students employed in the University's offices and dining services during the 1920s and 1930s.

16,333. Baylor University: School of Nursing
Records. 1913-56. 3.5 ft.
Access restricted. No guide.
Baylor University, The Texas Collection.
Annual reports to the Baylor University board of trustees and to accreditation committees, Nursing School student council minutes, correspondence, manuscripts, student handbooks, newsletters, commencement programs, photos, and textbooks of the Baylor University School of Nursing, founded in 1903. Includes copies of *The Baylor Nurse* and *The Baylor Star.*

16,334. Benaszeski, Linda
Oral history. 1976. 1 tape and 1 transcript.
Open. Unpublished guide.
Baylor University, The Texas Collection.
Interview in which Benaszeski (1949-), a teacher in the Crystal City, TX, Independent School District, describes her experiences as a child of Polish ancestry growing up in a German community in Wisconsin, her early associations with Chicano migrant workers, her teaching career in Crystal City, the town's Chicano movement, and attempts to discourage Anglo-American administrators in the city's school system.

16,335. Black, James, and Black, Patience (Crain)
Papers. 1862-64. 23 items.
Open. Calendar.
Baylor University, The Texas Collection.
Civil War correspondence reflects James Black's homesickness and Patience Black's sadness at being separated from her husband. Her letters provide information about the daily routine of her home, family, and community.

16,336. Boyer, Alice (Davidson)
Papers. Nd. 10 in.
Open. No guide.
Baylor University, The Texas Collection.
Correspondence, minutes, scrapbooks, clippings, and autograph books of Boyer, a housewife. Primarily consists of genealogical material and records of women's organizations, including minutes of a public speaking class, the Ernest Endeavor Study Club, and the Century Club. Also contains a scrapbook and notes from a literature survey class.

16,337. Brooks, Samuel Palmer
Papers. 188?-1937. 19 ft.
Open. Register.
Baylor University, The Texas Collection.
Brooks (1863-1931), an educator, was president of Baylor University from 1902 to 1931. Correspondence and typescripts contain some personal political papers concerning prohibition, peace movements, and woman suffrage.

16,338. Campbell, Emma A.
Papers. 1882-83. 5 items.
Open. No guide.
Baylor University, The Texas Collection.
Three letters written in 1882 by Campbell (?-1883) while she was a boarding student at Waco University describe life on campus and in Waco. Also includes a letter of condolence and an incomplete set of resolutions adopted by her classmates following her death.

16,339. Castellaw, Janie (Pender)
Papers. Nd. 15 in.
Open. No guide.
Baylor University, The Texas Collection.
[Mrs.] Castellaw (?-1969), a housewife, provided funding in 1968 for the Castellaw Communications Center at Baylor University, which was named for her son Jack who was killed in 1927 during his senior year at Baylor. Correspondence, notebooks, minutes, photos, scrapbooks, and clippings. Included are compilations of poetry and prose, much of it written by Janie Castellaw; minutes of what apparently was a literature study club; and correspondence, photos, and clippings about her gift to Baylor.

16,340. Certificates and Diplomas
Collection. 1857-1953. 4 in.
Open. Listing.
Baylor University, The Texas Collection.
Certificates from fraternal and religious organizations and schools and diplomas from secondary schools and colleges. Those awarded to women indicate their fields of study and degree received, such as maid of arts and maid of philosophy degrees granted by Baylor and Waco universities.

16,341. Clayton, Mary
Papers. 1850-1975. No size given.
Open. No guide.
Baylor University, The Texas Collection.
[Miss] Clayton is a retired music teacher. Correspondence, manuscript notes, appointment books, club reports, scrapbooks, sheet music, diplomas, clippings, and other papers contain information about Clayton's interest in music and travel, the Malone and Clayton families, and Waco women's groups.

16,342. Conner, George Sherman, and Conner, Jeffie Obrea (Allen)
Papers. 1914-72. 8 ft.
Open. Register.
Baylor University, The Texas Collection.
[Mrs.] Conner (1895-1972) was a home demonstration agent for the US Department of Agriculture and a school supervisor in McLennan County, TX. Correspondence, memoranda, speeches, financial papers, Texas state documents, reports, programs, photos, clippings, and other papers. Included are more than 300 letters written by George Conner, a physician, to his wife between 1932 and 1939 that relate events in Waco's black community; Jeffie Conner's biographical and academic records; her BS and MS theses; genealogical material; and items concerning her involvement in such civic groups as the Waco Human Relations Commission, the Waco Model City Agency, the National Association of Colored Women's Clubs, and the YWCA, as well as in black colleges in Texas and the New Hope Baptist Church. Also contains material on her work with the extension service and from 1966 to 1969 with the Governor's Committee on Public School Education.

16,343. Cusimano, Sister Austin
Oral history. 1973-75. 2 tapes and 2 transcripts.
Open. Unpublished guide.
Baylor University, The Texas Collection.
Sister Austin (1918-), who in 1975 legally changed her name to Sister Josephine, is a member of the Daughters of Charity of Saint Vincent De Paul and from 1961 to 1975 was administrator of Waco's Providence Hospital. Interviews in which she discusses her academic preparation for her position as hospital administrator, her activities in the Hospital and the community, her earlier appointment from 1940 to 1948 at Providence Hospital, the Hospital's public services, her teaching experiences in California, the Catholic position on abortion, and the history and purpose of her order.

16,344. Dallas Indian Urbanization Project
Oral history. 1972. 9 tapes.
Open. Unpublished guide.
Baylor University, The Texas Collection.
Six of the series's 17 interviews are with women; those of Indian ancestry discuss their self-imposed isolation during the first years after they moved to Dallas and the gradual reduction of barriers between white and Indian cultures. Other women, who were involved in the League for Educational Advancement in Dallas and VISTA programs,

discuss economic and cultural problems experienced by Indians.

16,345. Denson, Olive McGehee
Papers. Nd. 20 in.
Open. No guide.
Baylor University, The Texas Collection.
Scrapbooks and clippings regarding the history of Texas and Baptist work in the state.

16,346. Dobie, Bertha (McKee)
Oral history. 1971. 1 tape and 1 transcript.
Open. Unpublished guide.
Baylor University, The Texas Collection.
A teacher, Dobie (1890-1974) was the wife of author and folklorist J. Frank Dobie. Interview in which she discusses her life, career, marriage, and her influence upon her husband's literary works.

16,347. Eby, Frederick
Papers. Nd. No size given.
Closed. No guide.
Baylor University, The Texas Collection.
Eby (1874-1967) was a professor of education at Baylor University and the University of Texas at Austin. Correspondence, manuscripts, page proofs, financial records, student theses, photos, teaching aids, periodicals, clippings, and other material primarily pertaining to the history and philosophy of education, the development of education in Texas, and to women educators in the state.

16,348. Edmond, Katherine "Kate" McKinnon
Papers. 1886-1962. 2.5 ft.
Open. Register.
Baylor University, The Texas Collection.
[Miss] Edmond (1880-1963) was a public school teacher and journalist. Correspondence, diaries, literary works, financial records, biographical material, photos, and clippings. Included are literary works of Edmond and others, clippings of her society column in the Waco *Tribune-Herald,* and material about the Edmond family.

16,349. Edwards, Margaret (Royalty)
Papers. 1871-1971. 12.5 ft.
Open. Register.
Baylor University, The Texas Collection.
A newspaper columnist and poet, [Mrs. Herbert R.] Edwards (1895-1969) was poet laureate of Texas from 1957 to 1959. Correspondence, a journal, manuscripts, notebooks, financial and legal records, scrapbooks, pamphlets, certificates, diplomas, photos, clippings, and other material concern Edwards's life as a student at Baylor University and her writing career.

16,350. Emerson Club
Records. 1909-73. 7 in.
Open. No guide.
Baylor University, The Texas Collection.
Minutes and yearbooks of this Waco group, which was founded in 1907 to promote the study of literature, music, and art.

16,351. Emmons, Martha Lena
Papers. 1870-1974. 2.5 ft.
Open. Register.
Baylor University, The Texas Collection.
Emmons (1894-) is a retired college English instructor and folklorist. Correspondence, manuscripts, grade books, photos, and clippings relate to her teaching career and to her activities as a Texas folklorist. Includes manuscripts on the Irish in Texas, the Goodnight family, and the Negro Texan.

16,352. Ensemble Club
Records. 1942-75. 8 in.
Open. No guide.
Baylor University, The Texas Collection.
Minutes, financial records, a scrapbook, and yearbooks of this Waco group, founded in 1920 to "afford a means of contact between music lovers of the city," to stimulate interest in ensemble performance, and to promote the interest of school-aged children in music. The group was discontinued in 1975.

16,353. Fitzhugh, Elizabeth Lee
Papers. 1914-66. 5 ft.
Open. No guide.
Baylor University, The Texas Collection.
Correspondence, manuscripts, financial records, and clippings of [Miss] Fitzhugh, a schoolteacher, chiefly concern her research and writings about bells in Texas. Also includes some other material on Texas history.

16,354. Friend, Kate Harrison
Papers. 1899-1951. 5 in.
Open. Register.
Baylor University, The Texas Collection.
Correspondence, scrapbooks, photos, and clippings of [Miss] Friend (1856-1949), a newspaper society editor, primarily relate to her activities with Shakespeare study clubs and women's groups. Much of the correspondence expresses appreciation of or congratulations on publication of her outline studies of Shakespeare's plays, her lectures, and newspaper articles.

16,355. Garrett Family
Oral history. 1971-72. 2 recording discs and other items.
Open. No guide.
Baylor University, The Texas Collection.
Recordings of interviews with Elsie Garrett Townes (1883-) and Veannis Maddox Pressler (1876-) depict life in Texas at the turn of the century and relate family history and anecdotes. Also contains genealogical charts.

16,356. Gibbons, Maggie (McLennan)
Oral history. 1968. 1 tape and 1 transcript.
Open. Unpublished guide.
Baylor University, The Texas Collection.
Interview in which Gibbons (1885-) reminisces about her father Dan McLennan, who was a slave freed by the Neil McLennan family, and about early area settlers. She talks about gatherings at which her father played his fiddle and about relations between black and white settlers. McLennan County, TX, was named after the Neil McLennan family.

16,357. Graves and Earle Family
Papers. 1848-1963. 5.5 ft.
Open. Register.
Baylor University, The Texas Collection.
Correspondence, journals, literary works, financial records, crop and climate reports, photos, sheet music, and printed matter of the family of Adaline (Graves) Earle (1835-1906), her husband Isham Harrison Earle of Waco, and their daughter Hallie Earle (1880-1963), a physician and farmer. Included are correspondence, patient diagnoses, promotional literature on medication and treatments, and reports from professional journals, which reflect Hallie Earle's medical career. Family correspondence includes letters that portray Adaline and I. H. Earle's courtship and others that reveal the newly married Mrs. Earle's homesickness for Bonham, TX. Later letters provide information about Hallie Earle's student life during the early 1900s at the Baylor Medical Department in Dallas. Also contains student compositions by Adaline and Hallie Earle; journals from 1917 to 1963 in which Hallie Earle writes of her patients, family members, the weather, and social events; religious meditations by Adaline Earle; statistics on McLennan County crops recorded from 1876 to 1900 by I. H. Earle for the US Department of Agriculture; and information on climatological conditions, primarily rainfall, kept by I. H. Earle and later by Hallie Earle as weather observer for the US Department of Commerce.

16,358. Grove, Roxy Harriette
Papers. 1907-52. 3.5 ft.
Open. Register.
Baylor University, The Texas Collection.
[Miss] Grove (1889-1952) was a professor of music at Baylor University. Correspondence, music scores, financial papers, scrapbook, programs, clippings, publications, and other papers. Includes correspondence with Edward MacDowell and Frank Reaugh, Grove's MA thesis, articles published in *Musical America* magazine, and material related to her career at Baylor. Also includes programs of Baylor music events, the Waco Symphony Orchestra, and publications of such music and professional organizations as the National Symphony Orchestra Association, the National Guild of Piano Teachers, the AAUP, the National Association of Schools of Music, the American Matthay Association, and the Matthay School.

16,359. Hackworthe, Johnnie Mae
Oral history. 1971. 4 tapes and 1 transcript.
Open. Unpublished guide.
Baylor University, The Texas Collection.
Interview in which Hackworthe (1904-), a politician and a minister, describes her family and educational background, her personal life, and her career in politics and religion. From 1932 to 1937 she served in positions such as secretary to the speaker of the Texas House of Representatives, calendar clerk of the House, and chief public stenographer. Following her marriage in 1937 to Edwin H. Shaufler, she renewed her church activities and was involved with churches in Amarillo, Independence, Brenham, and Chappell Hill, TX, serving as Sunday school teacher, girls' auxiliary leader, and unofficial pastor. Hackworthe also speaks during the interview of some of her charismatic experiences. In her work, Hackworthe continued to use her maiden name.

16,360. Hill, Kate Adele
Papers. 1967. 4 in.
Open. No guide.
Baylor University, The Texas Collection.
Manuscript, page proofs, and photos of Hill, a college professor who had a PhD in home economics, concern Hill's book about A. L. Ward, a Texan.

16,361. Hill, William J., and Hill, Hattie (Green)
Papers. 1888-98. 1 in.
Open. Register.
Baylor University, The Texas Collection.
Correspondence, financial records, and invitations of William Hill and his wife Hattie. Letters from friends and relatives who were students in girls schools during the period provide information about life in female colleges and institutes.

16,362. Hirsch, Lydia [Becker]
Oral history. 1972. 1 tape and 1 transcript.
Partially closed. Unpublished guide.
Baylor University, The Texas Collection.
Interview in which Hirsch discusses the career of her father August Becker, who served from 1896 to 1939 as missionary to and pastor of German Baptist churches in Texas.

16,363. Johnson, Mrs. C. M. Watkins
Oral history. 1972. 1 tape and 1 transcript.
Open. Unpublished guide.
Baylor University, The Texas Collection.
Johnson (1912-) is funeral director of King Tears Mortuary in Austin, TX. Interview in which she traces the history of the King Funeral Home from its founding in 1933 to 1972, including its consolidation in 1955 with Tears Mortuary; the organization and growth of the Independent Funeral Directors Association of Texas, Inc.; and changes in the funeral home business since WWII.

16,364. Jones, Cleta Mildred
Oral history. 1972-73. 4 tapes and 1 transcript.
Access restricted. Unpublished guide.
Baylor University, The Texas Collection.
[Miss] Jones (1927-) is a missionary for The Salvation Army and a public school teacher. Interview in which Jones discusses her personal life; her educational experiences, particularly at the Chicago Evangelical Institution and The Salvation Army School for Officers Training; and her career from 1952 to 1969 in The Salvation Army. She served as a missionary to Argentina from 1962 to 1967.

16,365. Kincannon, Alma (Ehrhorn)
Oral history. 1972. 1 tape and 1 transcript.
Open. Unpublished guide.
Baylor University, The Texas Collection.
Interview in which [Mrs. Claud] Kincannon (1906-), a housewife, discusses the career of her father Julius Ernest Ehrhorn, pastor of German Baptist churches in Illinois, Texas, Iowa, Georgia, and Oklahoma, and the development of the Cottonwood Baptist Church near Waco. She describes the effect of WWI on the German Baptist churches, recalling that pastors were not allowed to preach in German, and comments on the German Baptist Conference of North America, now known as the North American Baptist Conference.

16,366. King, Irene (Marschall)
Papers. 1967. 7 in.
Open. No guide.
Baylor University, The Texas Collection.
[Mrs.] King is retired dean of women of Baylor University. Uncorrected manuscript of her *John O. Meusebach, German Colonizer in Texas* (1967) and clippings relating to Meusebach.

16,367. Kittlitz, Margaret Emma
Oral history. 1973. 2 tapes and 1 transcript.
Open. Unpublished guide.
Baylor University, The Texas Collection.
Interview in which Kittlitz (1906-) describes her childhood in central Texas, her educational preparation for the nursing profession, additional training to be a medical missionary, and her work from 1944 to 1959 as a nurse and missionary in the Cameroons.

16,368. Langenegger, Joyce
Oral history. 1972. 2 tapes and 1 transcript.
Partially closed. Unpublished guide.
Baylor University, The Texas Collection.
Interview in which Langenegger, a lawyer and elementary school teacher in the Crystal City, TX, Independent School District, relates her impressions of the Chicano movement there and the influence of La Raza Unida party in the District.

16,369. Mary Hardin-Baylor College
Records. 1860-1951. 6 in.
Open. Register.
Baylor University, The Texas Collection.
Mary Hardin-Baylor College was founded in Independence, TX, in 1845 as the female department of Baylor University; it was moved in 1886 to Belton, TX, and renamed Baylor Female College. Correspondence, student academic reports, scrapbook, catalogs, brochures, invitations, clippings, and other material, including catalog supplements for the music department, publications concerning the school's centennial in 1945, alumnae association newsletters, endowment brochures, and issues of the campus newspaper *The Bells.*

16,370. Montgomery, Ruth (Shick)
Papers. Ca. 1914- . Ca. 17 ft.
Access restricted. Preliminary inventory.
Baylor University, The Texas Collection.
[Mrs. Robert H.] Montgomery (1912-) is a journalist and an author. Personal and professional correspondence; manuscripts, proofs, and published editions of her books; notes and memoranda collected for her works; clippings of columns written by Montgomery; biographical material and clippings; professional and personal photos; and sound recordings collected as data for her publications.

16,371. Montgomery, Ruth (Shick)
Oral history. 1978. 2 items and 4 tapes.
Open. Unpublished guide.
Baylor University, The Texas Collection.
Interviews with [Mrs. Robert H.] Montgomery (1912-), a journalist and author, cover her childhood, education, and career as a reporter and syndicated columnist in Waco, Detroit, Chicago, and Washington, DC; background data concerning publication of biographies of Mary McCarran, Jeanne Dixon, and Lady Bird Johnson and a book on personalities and events in Washington, DC, from 1943 to 1968; and the circumstances leading to publication of several books on psychic phenomena.

16,372. Ney, Elisabet, and Montgomery, Edmund
Papers. 1889-1913. 10 in.
Open. No guide.
Baylor University, The Texas Collection.
Papers of Ney (1833-1907), a sculptor, and her husband Edmund Montgomery include her journals, legal papers, and photos. Contains journals entitled "My time with the General Garibaldi, 1865" and "Our trip to Egypt," 1867; passports; a patent for an invention; and certificates.

16,373. O'Hair, Madalyn Murray
Oral history. 1971-72. 10 tapes.
Access restricted. Unpublished guide.
Baylor University, The Texas Collection.
[Mrs.] O'Hair (ca. 1919-) has promoted and obtained recognition for the civil rights of atheists. Interview and transcripts in which she discusses the Baltimore Public School System case, strikes she participated in while serving in the WACs, campaigns against the House Un-American Activities Committee and atomic testing, social work experiences, her removal as an attorney in the Social Security Administration following her efforts to unionize government workers, and conflicts with the American Civil Liberties Union in Maryland.

16,374. Oral History of the Women in Waco
Oral history. 1975- . 93 reels and 93 transcripts.
Partially restricted. Unpublished guide.
Baylor University, The Texas Collection.
Memoirs of 66 central Texas women who made contributions to the area's political, educational, cultural, social, religious, and economic development. The women were selected and interviewed by members of the Junior League of Waco as part of the Baylor University Program for Oral History. The local Junior League, founded in 1935, seeks to train its members for effective community participation through educational and volunteer service. Copies of the interview transcripts are also available in the Waco Public Library.

16,375. Pace, Lula
Papers. 1899-1904. 8 in.
Open. Register.
Baylor University, The Texas Collection.
Pace (1868-1925) was chairman of the department of botany and geology at Baylor University. Class material, including notes and laboratory experiment records she kept in botany, geology, and plant physiology classes while attending the University of Chicago, from which she received her PhD in 1907.

16,376. Perez, Rebecca
Oral history. 1972. 1 tape and 1 transcript.
Access restricted. Unpublished guide.
Baylor University, The Texas Collection.
[Mrs.] Perez was a teacher's aide in the Crystal City, TX, Independent School District. The interview, which focuses on the School District, contains information on the Chicano movement for equality with Anglo-Americans in Crystal City. Perez discusses language problems she and her children encountered and teachers' discrimination against her as a teacher's aide because of her support for La Raza Unida party.

16,377. Perry, Laura L.
Papers. 1851-91. 36 items.
Open. Calendar.
Baylor University, The Texas Collection.
Correspondence, primarily letters to [Mrs.] Perry, a homemaker in Madison, GA, from relatives in Texas discussing news of the area, family gossip, attitudes toward the Negro in Texas before and after the Civil War, and tenant farming.

16,378. Pier, Sarah C.
Papers. 1847-64. 5 in.
Open. Index.
Baylor University, The Texas Collection.
Correspondence, diary, and autograph book of Pier (1840-?) primarily pertain to her student years at Baylor University at Independence and to the Civil War period. Her journal, which she kept during 1863, provides information about daily activities at home, military engagements, and camp life.

16,379. Poage, Frances Cotton
Oral history. 1972. 1 tape and 1 transcript.
Open. Unpublished guide.
Baylor University, The Texas Collection.
Interview contains the reminiscences of Poage, a housewife, about her experiences as the wife of Congressman William Robert "Bob" Poage and life in Washington, DC, during WWII.

16,380. Posednik, Frances
Papers. 1969. 1 item.
Open. No guide.
Baylor University, The Texas Collection.
Posednik (1876-?) was a farmer's wife. Typescript in which she discusses political conditions in Moravia in about 1868 that led her parents to immigrate to the US and her experiences growing up in central and south Texas.

16,381. Powell, Corrie Lee Taylor
Papers. 1896-1914. 0.5 in.
Open. No guide.
Baylor University, The Texas Collection.
Correspondence, a diary, and programs of [Mrs.] Powell (?-1914), a music student, primarily concern the 1897-98 school year, which she spent at the Cincinnati Conservatory of Music. Includes a journal describing her activities and recital programs.

16,382. Russell, Lily (McIlroy)
Papers. 1920s-58. 5 ft.
Open. No guide.
Baylor University, The Texas Collection.
[Mrs. Junius B.] Russell (1887-1958) served as dean of women, director of public relations, and dean of the Student Union Building at Baylor University. Personal and professional correspondence, reports, programs, certificates, and photos. Includes material on the Texas Baptist Woman's Missionary Union and the Daughters of the Republic of Texas.

16,383. Sallee, Annie (Jenkins)
Papers. 1897-1967. 2 ft.
Open. Register.
Baylor University, The Texas Collection.
[Mrs. William] Sallee (1877-1967) was a Southern Baptist missionary in China from 1906 to 1930 and

from 1935 to 1943. Correspondence, diaries, biographical material, photos, and clippings primarily concern members of the Jenkins family and the missionary work of Sallee and her husband. Correspondence recounts activities of the family in the US and missionary experiences in China. Her diaries provide additional information on their work in China, where they were pioneer missionaries in the country's interior.

16,384. Scarborough, Emily Dorothy
Papers. 1878-1935. 19.5 ft.
Open. Register.
Baylor University, The Texas Collection.
[Miss] Scarborough (1878-1935) was a professor of English and a novelist. Personal and business correspondence, manuscripts, notebooks, research material for several of her books, newsletters, greeting cards, photos, clippings, and other papers. Includes research material and manuscripts of some of her novels, including *The Wind, Land of Cotton,* and *Can't Get a Redbird* and her music anthologies *On the Trail of Negro Folk Songs* and *A Song Catcher in Southern Mountains;* her journalism and English notebooks; lectures and addresses; short stories submitted to her by other writers; and letters and telegrams concerning her death and funeral.

16,385. Scott, Jane
Papers. 1860. 4 items.
Open. No guide.
Baylor University, The Texas Collection.
Correspondence in which Scott describes to her brother George in Columbia, TX, her teaching duties in the Female Department of Baylor University and her loneliness because of her separation from her family.

16,386. Shaufler and Hackworthe
Papers. 1893-1971. 7 ft.
Open. Register.
Baylor University, The Texas Collection.
Correspondence, diaries, financial and legal records, minutes, photos, and clippings of Johnnie Mae Hackworthe (1904-), a politician and minister, and her husband Edwin Henry Shaufler. Contains some of her correspondence, radio scripts, and diaries, which include material about her church, the new Jerusalem Fellowship, and her gubernatorial and presidential campaigns. Bulk of the collection relates to Shaufler's business and finances.

16,387. Shawver, Lona Thomason
Papers. 1918-57. 4 in.
Open. No guide.
Baylor University, The Texas Collection.
[Mrs.] Shawver was a feature writer and newspaper columnist. Correspondence, photos, clippings, and periodicals primarily concern Shawver's writings and her columns "Southwest in Print" from *The Amarillo Times* and "Texas Centennial" from *The Wichita Falls Daily Times.* Also contains background material for her book *Chuck Wagon Windies.*

16,388. Smith, Cornelia (Marschall)
Oral history. 1973. 1 tape and 1 transcript.
Open. Unpublished guide.
Baylor University, The Texas Collection.
[Mrs. Charles G.] Smith (1895-) is a retired professor of biology at Baylor University and a former director of the University's John K. Strecker Museum. Interview in which she describes her experiences with the Museum and its personnel, the Museum's acquisition policy, and its various locations on the school's campus. Smith holds a PhD.

16,389. Sorosis Club
Records. 1923-72. 1 ft.
Open. No guide.
Baylor University, The Texas Collection.
Minutes, study papers, and yearbooks of this Waco group, founded in 1921 to foster the intellectual growth of its members.

16,390. Stephens, Pauline (Foster)
Papers. 1907-52. 3 in.
Open. No guide.
Baylor University, The Texas Collection.
Correspondence, manuscripts, and photos relate to Stephens's student days at Chevy Chase College. Includes letters from her family and classmates, invitations from male acquaintances, and other material. Also contains letters from her son John Foster Stephens when he was at West Point Military Academy, from her daughter-in-law during her son's tours of duty, and from family acquaintances.

16,391. Temperance
Collection. Nd. 4 in.
Open. No guide.
Baylor University, The Texas Collection.
Correspondence, legal records, broadsides, brochures, and newspapers concern temperance and prohibition in Texas and include a file on the *Ferguson vs. Austin American and Webb* case and publications of the United Friends of Temperance.

16,392. Thompson, Frances Judith Somes (Trask)
Papers. 1835-37. 3 items.
Open. No guide.
Baylor University, The Texas Collection.
Thompson (1806-92), a teacher, established the first female school in Texas. Includes a letter in which Frances Trask describes to her father Israel Trask the economic and political conditions in Texas under Mexican occupation. She writes of the charges for boarding students, the cost of provisions, the wages of hired help, and her living and teaching quarters. Later letters provide general family information.

16,393. Waco Bawdy House License Register
Records. 1889-95. 1 in.
Open. No guide.
Baylor University, The Texas Collection.
Register of fees assessed quarterly by the City of Waco, $2.50 for a prostitute and $3.15 per room for a bawdy house license. Also includes a list of prostitutes.

16,394. Waco Environmental Task Force, "Beautify Waco" Committee
Records. 1973-74. 3 in.
Open. No guide.
Baylor University, The Texas Collection.
The bulk of the Task Force records are those of Mrs. Carroll W. Sturgis, chairperson of the Committee for the Lake Brazos Drive Median Strip Beautification Project in 1973 and 1974. Includes correspondence, material about Committee operations, Sturgis's speaking notes, and promotional material.

16,395. Waco Literary Club
Records. 1897-1961. 10 in.
Open. No guide.
Baylor University, The Texas Collection.
Minutes, financial records, correspondence, and yearbooks of this local group, founded in 1891 to seek "the mutual improvement of its members in literature, art, science, and the vital interests of the day."

16,396. Weddington, Sarah
Oral history. 1973. 1 tape and 1 transcript.
Open. Unpublished guide.
Baylor University, The Texas Collection.
Interview in which Weddington, a member of the Texas House of Representatives from Travis County, discusses her role as attorney for the plaintiff in *Roe vs. Wade* and her efforts to gain liberal abortion and sterilization laws in Texas.

16,397. Woman's Club of Waco
Records. 1892-1974. 20 in.
Open. Preliminary listing.
Baylor University, The Texas Collection.
Minutes and yearbooks of the Club, founded in 1892 for the mutual improvement of its members and to make possible "combined action . . . upon measures that all can endorse."

UTAH

CEDAR CITY

16,398. Adams, R. D.
Papers. Early 1900s. 3 ft.
Open. No guide.
Southern Utah State College, Special Collections Library.
Photographs and negatives by Adams, a photographer, include portraits of southern Utah women and local scenes picturing women.

16,399. Ahlstrom, June Claudia (Farrer)
Papers. 1898-1968. 1 in.
Open. No guide.
Southern Utah State College, Special Collections Library.
Ahlstrom is a Cedar City resident. Ledger book from 1898 of the Cedar City Opera House and a history of the Opera House written in 1968.

16,400. Armstrong, Belle
Papers. Nd. 0.75 ft.
Open. No guide.
Southern Utah State College, Special Collections Library.
Armstrong was a county historian for the Daughters of Utah Pioneers. Notes, manuscripts, and collected material which was incorporated into the writings of her successor Rhoda Matheson Wood.

16,401. Benson, Zoella (Palmer)
Papers. 1963-68. 1 in.
Open. No guide.
Southern Utah State College, Special Collections Library.
[Mrs. Lamont] Benson is a seamstress, church worker, housewife, and member of the Daughters of Utah Pioneers. Biographical sketch of Sarah Whittaker Chatterly and a history of the iron industry in early Utah.

16,402. Betenson, Annette (Webster)
Papers. Nd. 0.25 ft. and 1 box.
Open. No guide.
Southern Utah State College, Special Collections Library.
[Mrs. Leland Stanley] Betenson (?-1971) was a housewife, singer, and civic and church worker. Material on the Branch Normal School/Branch Agricultural College; biographical sketches of Henry Lunt and Mary Ann Lunt; a phonotape; programs; photos; clippings; memorabilia, including such items as a candle mold and pioneer costumes; and other material.

16,403. Bethers, Jean Orme, and Bethers, Pratt M.
Papers. Nd. 6 ft.
Open. No guide.
Southern Utah State College, Special Collections Library.
Jean Bethers was a journalist and housewife, while her husband Pratt Bethers was a teacher and writer of local histories; both were civic and church

workers. Historical sketches, manuscripts, notes on education and religion source material for news stories, interview notes, political stories, news releases, page layouts for magazines and brochures, information on Indians, photos, and other material. The collection, the bulk of which consists of Jean Bethers's files, covers events in southern Utah during the years she was a correspondent for the *Deseret News*.

16,404. Booth, Mattie (Hunter)
Papers. Ca. 1960. 2 folders.
Open. No guide.
Southern Utah State College, Special Collections Library.
[Mrs. John A.] Booth (1889-) was a schoolteacher. Notes of an interview with Booth, an autobiography, and a biographical sketch written by Myrtle Janson focusing on Booth's teaching abilities.

16,405. Canonza Ladies Chorus
Records. 1939-56. 2 in.
Open. No guide.
Southern Utah State College, Special Collections Library.
Clippings regarding the community performances of the Chorus, founded in 1939 and made up of students and community members.

16,406. Canonza Society
Records. Early 1900s. 1 ft.
Open. No guide.
Southern Utah State College, Special Collections Library.
Minutes and programs of this singing group.

16,407. Cedar City and Iron County History
Collection. Ca. 1851- . 12 ft.
Open. No guide.
Southern Utah State College, Special Collections Library.
Manuscripts of histories and biographies, an autobiography, microfilm, photos, clippings, published material, and memorabilia regarding the history of Cedar City and Iron County, both of which were established in 1851.

16,408. College Archives
Records. 1897- . 30 ft.
Open. No guide.
Southern Utah State College, Special Collections Library.
Minutes of the board of regents, student government, and student organizations; financial papers; record books; correspondence; files of faculty and administrators; oral history tapes; photos; scrapbooks; yearbooks; catalogs; student publications; clippings; and memorabilia of the College, founded in 1897.

16,409. Dalley, Margaret (Pryor)
Papers. 1939. 1 folder.
Open. No guide.
Southern Utah State College, Special Collections Library.
Biography of Dalley's mother Margaret Evans Pryor (1842-1937), who was born in South Wales and whose parents converted to Mormonism and emigrated to Utah in 1862. In 1897 Pryor became a nurse and worked in the community for over 30 years.

16,410. Dalton, Luella (Adams)
Papers. Nd. 1.75 ft.
Open. No guide.
Southern Utah State College, Special Collections Library.
[Mrs. Harley W.] Dalton was a housewife, amateur historian, and amateur actress. Manuscript notes for her book *A History of Iron County and Parowan, the Mother Town*.

16,411. Dame, William H.
Papers. 1855-84. 2 microfilm reels.
Open. No guide.
Southern Utah State College, Special Collections Library.
Correspondence, telegrams, certificates, invitations, and clippings of Dame (?-1884), a farmer, local church leader, justice of the peace, and surveyor. Includes a letter from Pluma (Plierna) Libby to Dame's wife Louinna Dame regarding the illness of Louinna Dame's mother, a letter to William Dame from his mother Susan Dame concerning the death of his father, five letters from William Dame to his wives, and an 1876 bill of divorcement for William Dame and Lydia A. Killiam.

16,412. Daughters of Utah Pioneers
Records. Ca. 1940-62. 2 ft.
Open. No guide.
Southern Utah State College, Special Collections Library.
Autobiographies and biographies of southern Utah pioneers; manuscript accounts of the founding of communities, the development of industries, and related topics; and publications of the state Daughters of Utah Pioneers, which seeks to study, collect, and preserve the history of the state.

16,413. Faculty Ladies Club
Records. Ca. 1944-63. 0.5 ft.
Open. No guide.
Southern Utah State College, Special Collections Library.
Minutes and annual programs of the Club, formerly known as the Women's Club, which consists of female faculty members and staff and wives of male faculty members and staff of Southern Utah State College. The group seeks to foster friendship among the women, provide social and educational functions for them, and grant an annual scholarship for a worthy and needy woman student.

16,414. Fifty Year Club
Records. 1897- . 1.5 ft.
Open. No guide.
Southern Utah State College, Special Collections Library.
Minutes, life sketches of some members, and photos of the Club whose members are men and women who graduated from Southern Utah State College fifty or more years ago. Organized in 1950, the Club not only holds annual reunions but also lends support to the College. Most of the life sketches are of women Club members who gained prominence in the teaching profession or other pursuits.

16,415. Gardner, Ann (Jones)
Papers. Nd. 3 ft.
Open. No guide.
Southern Utah State College, Special Collections Library.
[Mrs. Robert Snow] Gardner was a teacher, housewife, and church and civic worker. Papers and other student material, clippings, and books on western and Utah history.

16,416. Haight, Sherman
Papers. Ca. 1890-1910. 1 ft.
Open. No guide.
Southern Utah State College, Special Collections Library.
Correspondence, photos, and clippings of Haight, a farmer, include photos of ca. 25 women in southern Utah.

16,417. Hendrickson, Jean
Papers. Nd. 1 folder.
Open. No guide.
Southern Utah State College, Special Collections Library.
[Mrs. Max C.] Hendrickson is a schoolteacher in Parowan, UT. Biographical sketches written by her students about Parowan settlers. Includes sketches of Susanah Ward Lister regarding her care of an orphan girl; Juliette Cecelia Bayles Adams, an obstetrics nurse who was trained by Paulina Lyman in Salt Lake City; Sarah Chaffin, who developed an effective method of suturing; Elizabeth Edwards Hanks, concerning her wedding in 1864; Eliza Anderson Barton, a practitioner of obstetrics since 1867; Ellen Miller Davenport, an informally educated nurse; Eliza Catherine Finnock Hunter, an early resident of Cedar City; and Sarah Elizabeth Gurr, an emigrant from Australia.

16,418. Higbee, Florence (Spilsbury)
Papers. Nd. 0.5 ft.
Open. No guide.
Southern Utah State College, Special Collections Library.
Photos and manuscript material on southern Utah history of [Mrs. Myron] Higbee, a housewife and civic and church worker.

16,419. Home Economics Club
Records. Early 1900s. 1 ft.
Open. No guide.
Southern Utah State College, Special Collections Library.
Minutes, programs, and other records of this service group, which was the auxiliary of a forerunner of the Chamber of Commerce, the Commercial Club for men.

16,420. Isbell, Josephine (Walker)
Papers. Nd. 2.5 ft.
Open. No guide.
Southern Utah State College, Special Collections Library.
[Mrs. John C.] Isbell was a nurse, housewife, and amateur historian. Manuscripts on Cedar City history collected by Isbell; photos of Cedar City homes and other buildings; scrapbooks of clippings, including obituaries and local historical items; and a scrapbook on Indians.

16,421. Jones, Iva (Rich)
Papers. Nd. 1 ft.
Open. No guide.
Southern Utah State College, Special Collections Library.
Minutes, programs, clippings and budgets of various organizations with which [Mrs. Kumen] Jones, a housewife and civic and church worker, was associated.

16,422. League of Women Voters
Records. Ca. 1955-60. 1 ft.
Open. No guide.
Southern Utah State College, Special Collections Library.
Reports, brochures, booklets, and published material collected by the Cedar City LWV for their studies.

16,423. Leigh, Ada (Bryant)
Papers. Nd. 0.25 ft. and 2 tapes.
Open. No guide.
Southern Utah State College, Special Collections Library.
Oral history tapes, photos, and memorabilia of [Mrs. Francis Webster] Leigh, a housewife and descendant of Cedar City pioneers, contain information on early Cedar City. Also includes a tape regarding Leigh's father's contribution to the founding of a college.

16,424. Leigh, Ella (Berry)
Papers. 1970. 1 folder.
Open. No guide.
Southern Utah State College, Special Collections Library.
[Mrs. William H.] Leigh (1879-) was the first student and graduate of the Branch Normal School, which became Southern Utah State College. Reminiscences of Leigh regarding her graduation in 1900 and a biographical sketch of Leigh.

16,425. McConnell, Gladys
Papers. Ca. 1846-1960. 2.5 ft.
Open. No guide.
Southern Utah State College, Special Collections Library.
[Miss] McConnell was a Cedar City resident, pharmacist, amateur historian, and civic and church worker. Correspondence, diaries, McConnell's writings, scrapbooks, autograph and recipe books, 1846 marriage certificate, photos, clippings, and memorabilia. Includes her play *The Women;* her biographies of her grandfather Jehiel McConnell and his Cedar City contemporaries; her written account of the memories of an uncle Robert William Bullock, who was a founder of the Branch Normal School; and her historical papers on southern Utah. Also contains diaries of an uncle Joseph Wilkinson, the justice of the peace and water master in the early days of the Silver Reef mining community; her mother's recipe book; recipes used in the ice-cream parlor of McConnell's drugstore; and a scrapbook containing calling cards.

16,426. Mace, Blanche
Papers. Nd. 1 ft.
Open. No guide.
Southern Utah State College, Special Collections Library.
Manuscript material, photos, and other papers of [Mrs.] Mace, a librarian, principally contain information on the pioneer days of Kanab, UT.

16,427. McFarlane, Lillian (Higbee)
Papers. Nd. 0.5 ft.
Open. No guide.
Southern Utah State College, Special Collections Library.
[Mrs. Erastus "Rass"] McFarlane was a housewife, pianist, and civic and church worker. Pertaining mainly to Cedar City and Branch Normal School history, the collection contains some manuscript material, programs, photos, clippings, and memorabilia, including items such as square nails made with pioneer tools from local iron.

16,428. Matheson, Alice Maude (Lunt)
Papers. Nd. 1 folder.
Open. No guide.
Southern Utah State College, Special Collections Library.
[Mrs. Daniel] Matheson (1876-?) was an early telegraph operator in Cedar City, UT. Biographical sketch written by Matheson about her mother Mary Anne Wilson (1834-1909) recounts Wilson's conversion to the Mormon Church and her migration to Cedar City in 1851.

16,429. Matheson, Annie (Isom)
Papers. Nd. 0.25 ft.
Open. No guide.
Southern Utah State College, Special Collections Library.
[Mrs. Christen] Matheson was a housewife, amateur genealogist, and church and civic worker. Correspondence, record book, biographical manuscripts, photos, and material on Cedar City history and her genealogy and family history.

16,430. Matheson, Zella (Barnson), and Matheson, Simon Alva
Papers. 1969-73. 1.5 ft.
Open. No guide.
Southern Utah State College, Special Collections Library.
Correspondence, manuscripts, and photos of Zella Matheson, a Cedar City housewife, amateur historian, member of the Iron County Historical Society, and church and civic worker. In her work for the Daughters of Utah Pioneers, she wrote about local history and collected manuscripts by others. Includes correspondence with the LDS Church historian regarding the Cedar City Primary Organization, a children's auxiliary, and a biography of Utah pioneer Amanda Lucinda Pace Sorenson. The collection also contains an autobiography and historical sketches of Zella Matheson's husband Simon Matheson (1903-), a local historian, including reminiscences about southern Utah mills and an account of the massacre of the Flancher party at Mountain Meadow in Utah. Unprocessed mining records are also included.

16,431. Mormon History
Collection. 1830- . 20 ft. and 61 microfilm reels.
Open. No guide.
Southern Utah State College, Special Collections Library.
Microfilm, pamphlets, books, and manuscripts include material on the status of women in the home and in the church, which early recognized the equality of women. Material contains accounts of the accomplishments of outstanding Mormon women.

16,432. Music Arts
Records. Nd. 1.5 ft.
Open. No guide.
Southern Utah State College, Special Collections Library.
Minutes, programs, and clippings of this organization that brought programs in the performing arts to the Cedar City schools and public. The group's membership was drawn from both the college and city communities.

16,433. Pucell, Margaret Perren (Parrin)
Papers. 1964. 5-page item.
Open. No guide.
Southern Utah State College, Special Collections Library.
Biography written by Wealth Millett Reeves about Pucell (1802-56), an early English convert to the Mormon Church who emigrated in 1856 to Utah. She traveled with the Martin Handcart Company, which encountered early snows and lost many of its members.

16,434. Redd, Amasa Jay
Papers. Nd. 1.25 ft.
Open. No guide.
Southern Utah State College, Special Collections Library.
Redd was a rancher, amateur historian, and genealogist. Correspondence of Redd and manuscript notes and photos he collected for a book on his father Samuel Hardison Redd contain material on the history of Blanding, UT, and on the women in Samuel Redd's polygamous family. Also includes correspondence from women family members who contributed data for the book.

16,435. Ruth, Iva (Haight)
Papers. 1942-56. 3 in.
Open. No guide.
Southern Utah State College, Special Collections Library.
Ruth was a housewife and Cedar City community worker. Correspondence pertaining to Ruth's interest in town beautification, health and sanitation, recreation, and the needs of youth; adult education forms; and programs from community musicals, art exhibits, and other events.

16,436. Sargent, David L.
Papers. Nd. 0.5 ft. and 2 tapes.
Open. No guide.
Southern Utah State College, Special Collections Library.
Sargent was a teacher of agriculture at Southern Utah State College, a farmer, and dairyman. Reminiscences, tapes and transcripts, and material from his SUSC files include information about women's experiences in education and in Utah.

16,437. Sargent, Mildred
Papers. Nd. 0.25 ft.
Open. No guide.
Southern Utah State College, Special Collections Library.
Papers of [Mrs. David L.] Sargent, a teacher, housewife, and civic and church worker, primarily concern southern Utah history.

16,438. Seymour, John Laurence
Papers. Nd. Ca. 80 ft.
Partially restricted. No guide.
Southern Utah State College, Special Collections Library.
Seymour, who held a PhD, was a teacher, composer, author, lecturer, and producer-director with a special interest in drama and opera. Diaries, research notes, opera scores, posters, photos, clippings, and other material include information about women musicians and actresses; his diaries describe dealings with various women artists and patrons. Also included are published autobiographies, biographies, travel books, and reminiscences, all by and about women, as well as items concerning history, languages, and religions such as Catholicism, Christian Science, and Mormonism.

16,439. Southern Utah History
Collection. Nd. 10 ft., 50 tapes, and 18 microfilm reels.
Open. No guide.
Southern Utah State College, Special Collections Library.
Manuscript material, microfilm, oral history tapes, and published works.

16,440. Southwick, Elaine (Christianson)
Papers. Nd. 0.25 ft.
Open. No guide.
Southern Utah State College, Special Collections Library.
[Mrs. Edward H.] Southwick was a teacher, author and poet, housewife, and church and civic worker. Collection primarily consists of published material she used in her teaching.

16,441. Starr, Mary Ann (Adams)
Papers. 1961. 1 folder.
Open. No guide.
Southern Utah State College, Special Collections Library.
Reminiscences of [Mrs.] Maggie May Smith Bess regarding experiences in Cedar City, her neighbors, and other aspects of her life. The material was transcribed by [Mrs. Cecil Franklin] Starr, a Cedar City resident and member of the Daughters of Utah Pioneers.

16,442. Thurber, Phebe (Cox)
Papers. Nd. 2.25 ft.
Open. No guide.
Southern Utah State College, Special Collections Library.
Thurber was a housewife, amateur historian, and writer. Correspondence; manuscripts of her writings, including poems, essays, short stories, and novels; tapes of her reminiscences of southern Utah, Idaho, and Oregon; and historical sketches.

16,443. Thurman, Mary E. E.
Papers. 1856-60. 1 folder.
Open. No guide.
Southern Utah State College, Special Collections Library.
Courtship letters from Alexander Farnsley to "Miss Bettie," whose full name was Mary E. E. Thurman. Thurman was a Louisville, UT, resident.

16,444. Wakeling, Rhea (Higbee)
Papers. 1885-1957. 1 folder.
Open. No guide.
Southern Utah State College, Special Collections Library.
Autobiography of [Mrs. Thomas Alma] Wakeling (1886-), a biography written by Wakeling about her mother Lorine Isabell Lamb Higbee

(1862-1958), a list of officers of the Young Ladies Mutual Improvement Association of Toquerville Ward, UT, a history of Silver Reef, a religious play, and photos.

16,445. Webster, Ada (Wood)
Papers. Nd. 1 in.
Open. No guide.
Southern Utah State College, Special Collections Library.
[Mrs. Thomas W.] Webster (1869-1951) was a Cedar City resident, community leader, and first president of the local Daughters of Utah Pioneers. Poetry regarding the pioneers of Utah, funeral addresses given by Webster at various friends' funerals, and the address given at Webster's funeral.

16,446. Williams, Cynthia
Papers. 1962-65. 1 in.
Open. No guide.
Southern Utah State College, Special Collections Library.
[Miss] Williams is a Cedar City musician and vocalist. A graduate music research paper regarding William Hart Manning, a history of dramatic organizations in Cedar City, and a history of the Music Arts Association of Cedar City. Williams was married to James S. Dunaway.

16,447. Wood, Rhoda (Matheson)
Papers. Nd. 1.75 ft.
Open. No guide.
Southern Utah State College, Special Collections Library.
[Mrs. William Henry] Wood was a housewife, church worker, and county historian for the Daughters of Utah Pioneers. Manuscripts of Wood's histories of Cedar City, notes, historical photos, and published material.

16,448. Woolley, Caroline Keturah (Parry)
Papers. 1877-1967. 1.75 ft.
Open. No guide.
Southern Utah State College, Special Collections Library.
Correspondence, diaries, a manuscript, research notes, photos, clippings, and other papers of [Mrs. LeGrande] Woolley (1885-1967), an artist and amateur historian who taught at the University of Utah, Weber State College, Utah State College, Utah State University, and the State School for the Blind. Includes collected information and her manuscript on the founding of the Branch Normal School; material on her grandfather Issac C. Haight and on Iron County's iron industry; some of her sculptures, oil paintings, and ceramics; clothing she designed and made; and her doll and other memorabilia. Also contains papers of her father John Parry, Iron County's first representative in the Utah legislature, with information about his missionary experiences in England for the Church of Jesus Christ of Latter-Day Saints and the founding of the Branch Normal School.

16,449. Woolley, Edwin Dilworth
Papers. 1909-44. 6 ft.
Open. No guide.
Southern Utah State College, Special Collections Library.
Correspondence, telegrams, post cards, and certificates of Woolley, a livestock man and Cedar City businessman, relate to business matters. Also contains papers of Alice Snow Woolley, including a letter to her from Woolley's son Erastus Dilworth Woolley regarding elections and the trials of several Indian horse thieves, biographical sketch about Jemima Lossee Cox, and papers written by Alice Woolley concerning women in American history and ways in which men can help beautify the home. Edwin Woolley was married to Florence Snow Woolley.

16,450. Woolley, Erastus Dilworth, and Woolley, Edwin Dilworth
Papers. Nd. 6 ft. and 2 tapes.
Open. No guide.
Southern Utah State College, Special Collections Library.
A Kanab, UT, pioneer whose papers comprise the bulk of the collection, Edwin Woolley was an early livestock man, merchant, church leader, and civic worker; his son Erastus Dilworth Woolley, who grew up as a cowboy in southern Utah, was a lawyer, judge, executor of his father's estate, and community and church worker. Correspondence, tapes of reminiscences of Erastus Dilworth Woolley, business records, manuscript accounts of business enterprises and community histories, deeds, claim filings, tax notices, photos, and clippings. The papers of Edwin Dilworth Woolley, a polygamist, contain information on the experience of pioneer Mormon women in southern Utah.

LOGAN

16,451. Baer, Jennie Miller
Papers. Nd. 9 frames of microfilm.
Open. Published guide.
Utah State University, Special Collections.
Biographical sketches written by [Mrs.] Baer of Marinda Miller and her husband Lois Thomas Miller, who settled in Hyrum, UT, and of Elizabeth Bradshaw, who came to Hyrum with the Martin handcart company in 1856. See Mary Washington, *An Annotated Bibliography of Western Manuscripts in the Merrill Library at Utah State University, Logan, Utah* (Salt Lake City: Western Text Society, Utah State University Press, 1971).

16,452. Butts, Frances Amelia
Papers. 1866-68. 49-page item.
Open. Published guide.
Utah State University, Special Collections.
Journal of Butts (1834-84), who was born in Rome, NY; married George Edgar Butts in 1854; and moved to Colorado in 1866. She writes of bartering eggs for coffee and soda and her first Christmas away from her friends and traditions. See Mary Washington, *An Annotated Bibliography of Western Manuscripts in the Merrill Library at Utah State University, Logan, Utah* (Salt Lake City: Western Text Society, Utah State University Press, 1971).

16,453. Cache County Board of Education
Records. 1880-1908. 46 items.
Open. Published guide.
Utah State University, Special Collections.
Superintendent's account and receipt books, ledgers, and day book; trustees' account and minute books; treasurers' account book; assessment rolls; and land lease records for the Cache County schools prior to their consolidation in 1908. Also included are school registers used by Armenia Parry at Logan. See Mary Washington, *An Annotated Bibliography of Western Manuscripts in the Merrill Library at Utah State University, Logan, Utah* (Salt Lake City: Western Text Society, Utah State University Press, 1971).

16,454. Clark, Caroline Hopkins
Papers. 1866. 11 frames of microfilm.
Open. Published guide.
Utah State University, Special Collections.
Journal of [Mrs.] Clark regarding her journey by ship and covered wagon from Liverpool, England, to Salt Lake City. Also included are several letters to England. See Mary Washington, *An Annotated Bibliography of Western Manuscripts in the Merrill Library at Utah State University, Logan, Utah* (Salt Lake City: Western Text Society, Utah State University Press, 1971).

16,455. Coburn, Mary Hulet
Papers. Ca. 1956. 1 microfilm reel.
Open. No guide.
Utah State University, Special Collections.
Journals of Coburn (1882-1958), who was born in Snowflake, AZ, contain historical information about the Coburn and Hulet families and about Summitt, UT, and Teton Valley, ID, where she lived. Also includes reminiscences regarding her education, teachers, church activities, recreation, and local Indians.

16,456. Cox, Codelia (Morley)
Papers. Nd. 40-page vol.
Open. Card catalog.
Utah State University, Special Collections.
Typescript regarding hardships experienced by Cox (1823-1915), her parents Issac and Sucy Gunn Morley, and her husband as they moved with other Mormons from Missouri to Illinois and then to Utah. Cox was born in Kirtland, OH, and died in Manti, UT.

16,457. Crockett, Ruth Clarkson
Papers. 1913-34. 5 vols. (microfilm).
Open. Published guide.
Utah State University, Special Collections.
Journals of [Mrs.] Crockett regarding church work and community life in Preston, ID. See Mary Washington, *An Annotated Bibliography of Western Manuscripts in the Merrill Library at Utah State University, Logan, Utah* (Salt Lake City: Western Text Society, Utah State University Press, 1971).

16,458. Crookston, Alice Rice
Papers. 1961. 1 microfilm reel.
Open. No guide.
Utah State University, Special Collections.
Biographical sketch of Crookston (1860-1925), a Mormon, written by her daughter Lucille C. Peterson, a North Logan, UT, resident. Crookston moved to Cache Valley at the age of 3, became a schoolteacher, and held several Church positions. While she was away on vacation, Crookston's husband took a second wife.

16,459. Eliason Sisters
Records. 1916-17. 1 vol.
Open. Published guide.
Utah State University, Special Collections.
Accounts carried by the Eliason Sisters dress shop in Logan. See Mary Washington, *An Annotated Bibliography of Western Manuscripts in the Merrill Library at Utah State University, Logan, Utah* (Salt Lake City: Western Text Society, Utah State University Press, 1971).

16,460. Evans, Morgan S.
Papers. Nd. 1 microfilm reel.
Open. Published guide.
Utah State University, Special Collections.
Biographical notes, financial papers, legal documents, clippings, and other papers of Evans. Includes an account written by Evans in 1908 regarding Utah pioneers, their clothes, customs, and his work as a stonemason; a biographical sketch written by Mary and Afton Purdie in ca. 1940 regarding [Mrs.] Mary Rees Phillips Evans (1828-92), who was born in Wales; and a paper written by Mary E. Smith of the Relief Society, a women's organization of the Mormon Church, regarding the settling of Cache Valley, UT. See Mary Washington, *An Annotated Bibliography of Western Manuscripts in the Merrill Library at Utah State University, Logan, Utah* (Salt Lake City: Western Text Society, Utah State University Press, 1971).

16,461. Faculty Women's League
Records. 1902-73. 1 box.
Open. No guide.
Utah State University, Special Collections.
A history, programs, yearbooks, and other material

of the Utah State University League, including recollections of Mrs. David H. Burgoyne regarding the University.

16,462. Girls' State
Records. 1949-66. 1 box.
Open. No guide.
Utah State University, Special Collections.
Lists of officers, schedules, printed guides, handbook on parliamentary procedure, and publications about Utah's annual one-week educational program sponsored by the American Legion to instruct selected female high school seniors in the processes of state and local government.

16,463. Heywood, Martha (Spence)
Papers. 1850-56. 125-page vol.
Open. Published guide.
Utah State University, Special Collections.
Journal of Heywood, a British cap maker who converted to the Mormon Church, came to Utah in 1850, married Bishop Joseph L. Heywood, and settled in Nephi, UT, in 1851. Contains her description of bearing a child in a wagon, Chief Walker and conflicts with the Indians, and home remedies. See Mary Washington, *An Annotated Bibliography of Western Manuscripts in the Merrill Library at Utah State University, Logan, Utah* (Salt Lake City: Western Text Society, Utah State University Press, 1971).

16,464. Hunter, Rodello
Papers. Ca. 1960-74. 4 ft.
Open. Register.
Utah State University, Special Collections.
Papers of Hunter, an author, include manuscripts of *Wyoming Wife, A House of Many Rooms,* short stories, and other works as well as correspondence relating to her publications.

16,465. Hyrum, UT: Mutual Improvement Associations
Records. 1884-1953. 11 folders.
Open. Published guide.
Utah State University, Special Collections.
Collection includes manuscript newspapers of the Young Ladies Mutual Improvement Association and the Young Men's Mutual Improvement Association, 1885-1900. The newspapers contain jokes, poetry, and articles on modesty, simplicity, honesty, the Word of Wisdom (the Mormon health code), education, elections, and local activities. The newspapers were circulated in manuscript form to YLMIA and YMMIA members. Editors served one month each. See Mary Washington, *An Annotated Bibliography of Western Manuscripts in the Merrill Library at Utah State University, Logan, Utah* (Salt Lake City: Western Text Society, Utah State University Press, 1971).

16,466. Jensen, Abby Groesbeck
Papers. 1928-63. 8 vols.
Open. Published guide.
Utah State University, Special Collections.
Garden diary, journals, and household account book of Jensen (1875-1963), most of which were written in Bear River City. Jensen married in 1925; her husband died in 1939. In 1942 she moved to Logan, where she worked in the Mormon temple. In 1961 she moved to a nursing home, where she died. See Mary Washington, *An Annotated Bibliography of Western Manuscripts in the Merrill Library at Utah State University, Logan, Utah* (Salt Lake City: Western Text Society, Utah State University Press, 1971).

16,467. Keetch, Mercy Truth Barker
Papers. Nd. 1 microfilm reel.
Open. Published guide.
Utah State University, Special Collections.
Autobiography of [Mrs.] Keetch, a British convert to the Mormon church in 1854. She emigrated to Utah in 1860, crossing the plains with Joseph W. Young's company. Includes a description of her life in England and in Bear Lake, UT. See Mary Washington, *An Annotated Bibliography of Western Manuscripts in the Merrill Library at Utah State University, Logan, Utah* (Salt Lake City: Western Text Society, Utah State University Press, 1971).

16,468. Killian, Rachel Powell
Papers. Nd. 9-page item (microfilm).
Open. No guide.
Utah State University, Special Collections.
Biographical sketch of Killian (1851-?), a British convert to Mormonism in 1860, written by her daughter Marie Buchanan. Describes her conversion, emigration to Utah, marriage at age 15, move to San Pete County, children, and church activities.

16,469. Ladies Anti-Polygamy Society of Utah
Records. 1880-83. 3 vols. (microfilm).
Open. No guide.
Utah State University, Special Collections.
Newspaper published in Salt Lake City by the Society, which met once a month; the theme of the newspaper, as taken from the New Testament, was "Let every man have his own wife, and let every woman have her own husband."

16,470. London, Jack, and London, Charmian (Kittredge)
Papers. 1894-1953. 14 ft. and 6 microfilm reels.
Access restricted. No guide.
Utah State University, Special Collections.
Correspondence, manuscripts, and other papers of authors Jack London (1876-1916) and Charmian K. London (1883-1955). Includes Charmian London's correspondence with Ninetta Eames Payne and Eliza Shepard and her genealogy, articles, clippings, passports, and ephemera. Also included are copies of correspondence, some of which are from Jack London to the Macmillan Company. See *Register of the Jack and Charmian London Collection* (Utah State University, 1975).

16,471. MacDowell, Mrs. Edward
Papers. 1926-53. 1 microfilm reel.
Open. No guide.
Utah State University, Special Collections.
Correspondence of Marion MacDowell, widow of composer Edward MacDowell, regarding the establishment of the MacDowell Club, also known as the MacDowell Colony, a meeting place for creative artists on Marion MacDowell's estate at Peterborough, NH.

16,472. Maughan, Mary Ann Weston
Papers. 1894-97. 3 vols.
Open. Published guide.
Utah State University, Special Collections.
Journal and autobiography of Maughan, who left England for Nauvoo, IL, in 1841 and moved to Utah in 1850. In 1856 she came to Logan with her husband Peter Maughan. Contains description of Indian conflicts and of her life as a midwife. See Mary Washington, *An Annotated Bibliography of Western Manuscripts in the Merrill Library at Utah State University, Logan, Utah* (Salt Lake City: Western Text Society, Utah State University Press, 1971).

16,473. Mendenhall Family
Papers. Ca. 1860-1940. 6 vols. and 1 microfilm reel.
Open. No guide.
Utah State University, Special Collections.
Collection includes biographical sketch and diary notes of state senator Jane Johnson Mendenhall of Mapleton, UT, and a biographical sketch of Eliza T. Mendenhall of Springfield, UT. Both sketches describe domestic duties, women's clothing, education, courtship, and child rearing.

16,474. Naisbitt, Catherine Hagell
Papers. Nd. 10-page item (microfilm).
Open. No guide.
Utah State University, Special Collections.
Autobiographical sketch of Naisbitt (1850-?),a British convert to Mormonism, regarding her emigration to Utah in 1865.

16,475. Nuttall, Grace Greer
Papers. 1896-1961. 1 microfilm reel.
Open. Published guide.
Utah State University, Special Collections.
Journal of Nuttall (1880-), who was born in Wallsburg, UT, where her parents were shopkeepers. In 1899 she attended school in Provo, UT, and in 1904 she married William Nuttall. The Nuttalls operated a dairy after their marriage. Contains descriptions of farm work and Mormon Church activities. See Mary Washington, *An Annotated Bibliography of Western Manuscripts in the Merrill Library at Utah State University, Logan, Utah* (Salt Lake City: Western Text Society, Utah State University Press, 1971).

16,476. Penrod, Doris Bauer
Papers. 1951. 3-page item.
Open. Published guide.
Utah State University, Special Collections.
History written by [Mrs.] Penrod regarding Elberta, UT, which was settled in 1892 as a farming community that specialized in peaches and cherries. The project went into receivership and was purchased by the Mormon Church. See Mary Washington, *An Annotated Bibliography of Western Manuscripts in the Merrill Library at Utah State University, Logan, Utah* (Salt Lake City: Western Text Society, Utah State University Press, 1971).

16,477. Porter, Sarah Jane Clayton
Papers. Nd. 1 microfilm reel.
Open. Published guide.
Utah State University, Special Collections.
Genealogy of the Clayton family includes biographical notes on members of the Edward Clayton family. Contains information regarding Ellen Morrison Clayton (?-1911), wife of Edward Clayton (1840-1925) who emigrated from England to Utah in 1855. See Mary Washington, *An Annotated Bibliography of Western Manuscripts in the Merrill Library at Utah State University, Logan, Utah* (Salt Lake City: Western Text Society, Utah State University Press, 1971).

16,478. Ralph, Lovina Anderson
Papers. Nd. 6 frames of microfilm.
Open. Published guide.
Utah State University, Special Collections.
Papers of [Mrs.] Ralph consist of biographical notes on the Anderson family. Includes information on her mother Alice Brooks Anderson (?-1915), who came to Utah in 1856 with the Martin handcart company and later moved to Hyrum, UT, where she died. See Mary Washington, *An Annotated Bibliography of Western Manuscripts in the Merrill Library at Utah State University, Logan, Utah* (Salt Lake City: Western Text Society, Utah State University Press, 1971).

16,479. Snow, Eliza Roxcy
Papers. 1846-49. 1 microfilm reel.
Open. Published guide.
Utah State University, Special Collections.
Journals of Snow, who was born in Beckett, MA, describe her departure from Nauvoo, IL; crossing the Mississippi River with Heber C. Kimball's company in 1846; and their arrival in Council Bluffs six months later. In 1847 she left winter quarters with Jedediah M. Grant's company and arrived in Salt Lake Valley within four months. Contains Snow's songs and poems, many of which were dedicated to Brigham Young, whom she later married. Snow helped found the Relief Society of the Mormon Church. See Mary Washington, *An*

Annotated Bibliography of Western Manuscripts in the Merrill Library at Utah State University, Logan, Utah (Salt Lake City: Western Text Society, Utah State University Press, 1971).

16,480. Stewart, I. P.
Papers. Nd. 1 microfilm reel.
Open. Published guide.
Utah State University, Special Collections.
Biographical notes of the Stewart family include a biography by Jessie F. S. Reese of [Mrs.] Julia Ann Wadsworth Stewart (1854-1933), who was born in Draper, UT, and moved to Logan, where she died. See Mary Washington, *An Annotated Bibliography of Western Manuscripts in the Merrill Library at Utah State University, Logan, Utah* (Salt Lake City: Western Text Society, Utah State University Press, 1971).

16,481. Stewart, Rebecca Evans
Papers. Nd. 23-page item.
Open. Published guide.
Utah State University, Special Collections.
Papers of [Mrs.] Stewart consist of a biography of Johanna Lovisa Lofdahl Evans (1834-1912), who was born in Sweden, emigrated to Utah in 1863, and married Morgan Evans in 1864. Includes descriptions of such Swedish customs as the lighting of a Christmas candle. See Mary Washington, *An Annotated Bibliography of Western Manuscripts in the Merrill Library at Utah State University, Logan, Utah* (Salt Lake City: Western Text Society, Utah State University Press, 1971).

16,482. Tanner, Mary Jane (Mount)
Papers. 1837-85. 1 microfilm reel.
Open. No guide.
Utah State University, Special Collections.
Journal of Tanner (1837-90) portrays life in Salt Lake City and Provo, UT, and contains "Fugitive Poems" written by Tanner.

16,483. Thatcher, Sarah Catherine Hopkins
Papers. 1888-91. 1 vol. (microfilm).
Open. No guide.
Utah State University, Special Collections.
Diary of Thatcher regarding sewing, reading, visits to relatives, letters received and sent, and quotes from Longfellow and other poets.

16,484. Utah Extension Service
Records. Ca. 1910-71. 152 Hollinger boxes.
Open. No guide.
Utah State University, Special Collections.
Annual directors' reports; county records and reports; printed material from institutes, workshops, and short courses; University Extension newsletter; and other items of the Service, which specialized in agricultural assistance, domestic education, youth guidance, and other services. Includes descriptions of homes visited by extension service agents; the education level, diet, clothing, and health of women and children; and the Service's response to what were determined as needs.

16,485. Utah State University Oral History Project
Oral history. Ca. 1970-77. 5 ft.
Open. No guide.
Utah State University, Special Collections.
Tapes, with a few transcripts, of interviews with Utah women, among them Edna Robison (?-1976), a housewife and resident of Hanksville, UT, who describes the outlaws who stayed at her father's guest house and at Robbers Roost, a hideout for outlaws; with Josephine Fabian (1885-), who was born in Salt Lake City and who discusses her and her husband's work to preserve historic sites and wilderness areas such as Grand Teton National Park; with Mrs. Sherwin Maeser, wife of a local politician, who relates the difficulties of putting her husband through school and of public life; with Edith Shaw (1905-), professor emeritus in elementary education at Utah State University, who describes her life and professional accomplishments; and with [Mrs.] Lula Parker Betenson (ca. 1880-), the sister and biographer of the Utah outlaw Butch Cassidy, who recalls growing up with Cassidy. The collection also contains interviews with [Mrs.] Gertrude Christensen (1875-1976), an Idaho pioneer; Frank and Rodello Hunter Calkins, authors in Jackson Hole, WY; Vesta Lynn Jackson and Ida Lundy, residents of Jackson Hole and Wilson, WY; [Mrs.] Bertha Woodward (1882-) of Springfield, UT; [Mrs.] Verda Mann, an historian and collector; and Leora Thatcher (1894-), an actress.

16,486. Utah Writers Project
Collection. Ca. 1932-38. 106 folders.
Open. Published guide.
Utah State University, Special Collections.
Part of the WPA Federal Writers Project, the Utah Writers Project gathered information regarding Utah pioneers through interviews, through writings of the pioneers and their descendants, and occasionally through secondary sources. Of the 106 women represented, all of whom were Mormons, 41 had been interviewed. Nearly half of the women in the collection were immigrants; they came primarily from England but also from Switzerland, Denmark, Scotland, Sweden, Norway, Holland, Ireland, and Australia. The accounts contain information regarding living conditions, ranching, farming, the barter economy, irrigation, and the United Order. Also includes extensive material regarding various Indian tribes and Indian wars. Some of the pioneer women were involved in such occupations as doctor, midwife, dressmaker, hotel manager, painter, hymn writer, and keeper of bees and silkworms.

Among the items included are an account of [Mrs.] Rosina Beacham (1866-?) describing her family's conversion to the Mormon Church in Switzerland; their emigration to Utah in 1860; their dugout and adobe house in Santa Clara, UT; and the baking of bread in a rock oven. She relates that mountain rush was called Brigham tea by the pioneers. Also included are interviews with [Mrs.] Lydia Hamp Baker (1848-?), a resident of Logan who was born in England and came to the US in 1877, in which she describes the things she missed, such as furniture, good food, comfort, and culture; with Ellen George Bird (1858-?), who was born in Ogden, UT, and later moved to Kanosh, UT, in which she describes life in Kanosh, where her father operated a stage station, and relates stories about the Phavant Indians; and with [Mrs.] Isabel King Rodgers (1858-?), a resident of Fillmore, UT. Born in Utah Fort, now Provo, UT, Rodgers recalls the introduction of alfalfa into Utah and describes the United Order, wherein each man taught his profession to younger men. Also contains an interview with [Mrs.] Addie Taylor Maxwell (1866-?), who was born in Santaquin, UT, and whose father Norman Taylor had emigrated to Utah with Brigham Young. Maxwell moved to Moab where she operated the Maxwell House hotel. She also tells of the death of Billy McCarthy, a Delta bank robber.

Included also are biographical notes of [Mrs.] Alice Ann Langston Dalton (1865-?) regarding Indian marriage customs and the United Order in Rockville, UT, where she was born; of [Mrs.] Caroline Lambe Slack (1859-?), who lived in Virgin, UT, in 1861 and later in Toquerville, UT, regarding Brigham Young, the Piute and Navajo Indians, and Mountain Meadows; and of Elizabeth Jennett Smithson Smith (1861-?), who was born in Washington and moved with her family to Pahreah, UT, in 1877 where she married James Edward Smith. The Smiths moved to Henrieville, UT, in 1889 and later to Arizona to avoid arrest for polygamy. Also contained is a biographical note written by relatives of Helene Anderson Peterson Kjaer (1805-78), a resident of Huntsville, UT, who was born in Denmark and who divorced her husband in order to emigrate to Utah, where she married Jorgen Christian Swanner, and one written by Mae Spencer regarding Amy Carolina Davis Phillips (1851-1936), who was born in Spanish Fork, UT, and died in Paradise, UT. A sister of Phillips married Frank Warner, the son of the Indian chief Sagwick and a survivor of the battle of Battle Creek.

Also found in the collection are an excerpt from *Utah Pioneer* regarding Ellis R. Shipp, a medical doctor who attended Women's Medical College in Philadelphia from 1875 to 1878, which describes crossing the plains in 1852, and one from the *Deseret News* regarding Clarissa Hamilton (Young) Spencer (?-1939), the daughter of Brigham Young and the wife of John D. Spencer.

The collection is also available on microfilm. See *Name Index to Mormon Diaries* (Salt Lake City: Western Text Society, Utah State University Press, 1971).

16,487. Vance, Angus
Papers. Nd. 1 microfilm reel.
Open. Published guide.
Utah State University, Special Collections.
Biographical notes on the Vail family include biographies of Martha Bartholomew Vail (1803-91), who was born in Indiana, converted to the Mormon Church in 1842, emigrated to Utah in 1851, and died at Salt River, WY, and of Elvira Vail Nelson (1839-1932), who died in Riverdale, ID. See Mary Washington, *An Annotated Bibliography of Western Manuscripts in the Merrill Library at Utah State University, Logan, Utah* (Salt Lake City: Western Text Society, Utah State University Press, 1971).

16,488. Western Studies Oral History Project
Oral history. 1972- . No size given.
Open. No guide.
Utah State University, Special Collections.
Tapes and transcripts of ca. 102 interviews conducted through the Utah State University history department. Includes interviews with Beth Wyatt Winn, a Logan resident who recalls childhood experiences on the Wyatt farm, neighbors and friends, and her parents' beliefs concerning family life, religion, and education; with [Mrs.] Thelma Packer, who recounts life during the depression, homesteading in Idaho, being a dependent mother, and living in Brigham City, UT; with Wella Satterthwaite (1901-), life-long resident of Laketown, UT, who describes community life, church activities, Chief Washaki's Indian tribe, and a story regarding an Indian woman who was burned to death because two Indian men were in love with her; with Katherine J. Vilas (1919-), who describes the hardships her family encountered emigrating from Greece to Utah, among them the discrimination, cultural shock, and type of work they were required to do; and with Juanita Brooks, a Utah historian and writer, who discusses her life. The collection also contains interviews with Mary Lamphier (1893-), a Montana homesteader; Hattie Swenson (?-1973) and Eva Mae Issaelson, North Logan residents; [Mrs.] Emma Walker of Moab, UT; Eulella Bryne (1905-), a Roberts, ID, resident; Bernice Weston Sims of Rich County, UT; and [Mrs.] Phebe Smith (1889-), a Randolph, UT, resident.

16,489. Wilhelm, Clarissa
Papers. Nd. 12 pp.
Open. Published guide.
Utah State University, Special Collections.
Journal and autobiography of Wilhelm (1820-1901), who was born in New York, converted to the Mormon Church, and moved to Nauvoo, IL. After her husband died in 1851, she took her children to Utah. She moved to Toquerville, UT, where she lived under the United Order, a Mormon communal living program. She later moved to Orderville, UT, one of the last communities to practice the United Order. She died there. See

Mary Washington, *An Annotated Bibliography of Western Manuscripts in the Merrill Library at Utah State University, Logan, Utah* (Salt Lake City: Western Text Society, Utah State University Press, 1971).

16,490. Williams, Alice L. L.
Papers. Nd. 12 frames of microfilm.
Open. Published guide.
Utah State University, Special Collections.
Biographical sketches of the Hansen and Linjenquist families include sketches of Christiene Linjenquist (1822-1903), who was born in Denmark and died in Hyrum, UT, and Mary Cockshott Hansen (1835-1925), a British convert to the Mormon Church who emigrated to Utah and died in Hyrum. See Mary Washington, *An Annotated Bibliography of Western Manuscripts in the Merrill Library at Utah State University, Logan, Utah* (Salt Lake City: Western Text Society, Utah State University Press, 1971).

16,491. Wilson, Lucy Benson
Papers. Nd. 1 vol. (microfilm).
Open. Published guide.
Utah State University, Special Collections.
Autobiography of Wilson (1830-1914), who was born in Indiana; moved to Nauvoo, IL; emigrated to Utah in 1852; married John G. Wilson that same year; and moved to Hyrum in 1862. Describes her first furniture and her attempts to make baby clothes and contains her will. See Mary Washington, *An Annotated Bibliography of Western Manuscripts in the Merrill Library at Utah State University, Logan, Utah* (Salt Lake City: Western Text Society, Utah State University Press, 1971).

16,492. Woodland, Blanche Hatch
Papers. Nd. 15-page item.
Open. Published guide.
Utah State University, Special Collections.
Papers of [Mrs.] Woodland, a Logan resident, contain biographical sketches of family members, including Ruth Amorette Hatch Hale, Elizabeth Fox, and Annie Scarborough Hatch. See Mary Washington, *An Annotated Bibliography of Western Manuscripts in the Merrill Library at Utah State University, Logan, Utah* (Salt Lake City: Western Text Society, Utah State University Press, 1971).

PROVO

16,493. Adams, Dorothy
Oral history. Ca. 1972. 1 vol.
Open. Published guide.
Brigham Young University Library, Division of Archives and Manuscripts.
Reminiscences in which Adams describes the development of Monticello, UT, during the early 1900s. See *Women in History: A Guide to Selected Holdings of the Women's History Archives* (Provo, UT: Brigham Young University, Harold B. Lee Library, 1975).

16,494. American Association of University Women
Records. 1833-70. 5 vols.
Open. Published guide.
Brigham Young University Library, Division of Archives and Manuscripts.
Scrapbooks of the Provo branch of the AAUW contain minutes, correspondence, newsletters, clippings, bulletins, yearbooks, flyers, and programs. Also includes information on the Utah state division of the AAUW. See *Women in History: A Guide to Selected Holdings of the Women's History Archives* (Provo, UT: Brigham Young University, Harold B. Lee Library, 1975).

16,495. Anderson, Marybell (Harmon)
Papers. 1847-1967. 2 boxes.
Open. Published guide.
Brigham Young University Library, Division of Archives and Manuscripts.
Correspondence, typescripts, galley proofs, photos, and other papers relate to the publication of the diaries of Appleton Milo Harmon and other histories by Anderson, his granddaughter. Includes information on the Spilsbury and Harmon families. See *Women in History: A Guide to Selected Holdings of the Women's History Archives* (Provo, UT: Brigham Young University, Harold B. Lee Library, 1975).

16,496. Astor, Mary
Papers. 1940-42. 1 vol.
Open. Published guide.
Brigham Young University Library, Division of Archives and Manuscripts.
Scrapbook and photo of Astor (1906-), an actress, relate to her role in the motion picture *Brigham Young* and the publicity for the picture.

16,497. Ball, Eve
Papers. Nd. 2 cartons.
Open. Published guide.
Brigham Young University Library, Division of Archives and Manuscripts.
Correspondence, interview and research notes, and manuscripts of Ball, a southwestern author and expert on the Apaches, primarily concern her books *In the Days of Victorio, Ruidoso,* and *Ma'am Jones of the Pecos.* See *Women in History: A Guide to Selected Holdings of the Women's History Archives* (Provo, UT: Brigham Young University, Harold B. Lee Library, 1975).

16,498. Ballif, Algie
Papers. 1957-61. 2 folders.
Open. Published guide.
Brigham Young University Library, Division of Archives and Manuscripts.
Papers of Ballif, a member of the Utah House of Representatives, include correspondence from 1961, research notes, items concerning bills and special interest groups, and petitions. See *Women in History: A Guide to Selected Holdings of the Women's History Archives* (Provo, UT: Brigham Young University, Harold B. Lee Library, 1975).

16,499. Beatty, Sue (Smith)
Papers. 1905-18. 2 vols.
Open. Published guide.
Brigham Young University Library, Division of Archives and Manuscripts.
Album of Beatty contains post cards she collected. See *Women in History: A Guide to Selected Holdings of the Women's History Archives* (Provo, UT: Brigham Young University, Harold B. Lee Library, 1975).

16,500. Beaver Women's Suffrage Association
Records. 1892-95. 1 folder.
Open. Published guide.
Brigham Young University Library, Division of Archives and Manuscripts.
Includes bylaws and regulations; a minute book; a letter from Emmeline B. Wells, president of the Relief Society of the Latter-day Saints Church; handwritten newspapers entitled "Equal Rights Banner"; and a woman suffrage songbook of the Beaver County, UT, branch of the Association. See *Women in History: A Guide to Selected Holdings of the Women's History Archives* (Provo, UT: Brigham Young University, Harold B. Lee Library, 1975).

16,501. Brontë Society
Records. 1888-1937. 1 box.
Open. Published guide.
Brigham Young University Library, Division of Archives and Manuscripts.
Correspondence, addresses, writings, photos, and drawings concern the activities of the Society, which perpetuated the memory of Charlotte Brontë (1816-55) and Emily Brontë (1818-48) through lectures, meetings, and publications. Many prominent Victorians are represented among the correspondents. See *Women in History: A Guide to Selected Holdings of the Women's History Archives* (Provo, UT: Brigham Young University, Harold B. Lee Library, 1975).

16,502. Butt, Pearl (Bliss)
Oral history. Ca. 1972. 1 vol.
Open. Published guide.
Brigham Young University Library, Division of Archives and Manuscripts.
Interview with Butt (1894-), a former San Juan County clerk, concerns homesteading near Moab and Monticello, UT, during the early 1900s. Also includes information on the women's suffrage movement in Utah. See *Women in History: A Guide to Selected Holdings of the Women's History Archives* (Provo, UT: Brigham Young University, Harold B. Lee Library, 1975).

16,503. Carson, Elvira (Egbert)
Papers. 1901. 1 folder.
Open. Published guide.
Brigham Young University Library, Division of Archives and Manuscripts.
Reminiscences of Carson (1821-1908), an early member of the Latter-day Saints and Utah pioneer, as given to her grandson H. Carson Healy. See *Women in History: A Guide to Selected Holdings of the Women's History Archives* (Provo, UT: Brigham Young University, Harold B. Lee Library, 1975).

16,504. Clayton, Roberta (Flake)
Papers. Ca. 1969-74. 5 boxes.
Open. Published guide.
Brigham Young University Library, Division of Archives and Manuscripts.
Manuscripts of *Pioneers and Prominent Men of Arizona* (1974) and *Pioneer Women of Arizona* (1969) by Clayton (1877-) contain personal reminiscences of Mormon pioneers who were early settlers in Arizona. See *Women in History: A Guide to Selected Holdings of the Women's History Archives* (Provo, UT: Brigham Young University, Harold B. Lee Library, 1975).

16,505. Coray, Martha Jane (Knowlton)
Papers. 1855-78. 4 folders.
Open. Published guide.
Brigham Young University Library, Division of Archives and Manuscripts.
Diaries of Coray (1821-81), a schoolteacher, close friend to Joseph Smith and Hyrum Smith, and member of the board of trustees of Brigham Young Academy, contain information pertaining to the Academy, herbal remedies for sale, and farm activities. Also includes recorded sermons of Joseph Smith, Brigham Young, and others as well as a research paper by Robert Cooper on *The History of Joseph Smith by his Mother,* a book that Lucy Mack Smith dictated to Coray. See *Women in History: A Guide to Selected Holdings of the Women's History Archives* (Provo, UT: Brigham Young University, Harold B. Lee Library, 1975).

16,506. Cox, Martha (Cragun)
Papers. 1928. 1 folder.
Open. Published guide.
Brigham Young University Library, Division of Archives and Manuscripts.
Autobiographical account in which Cox (1852-?) describes living in early Salt Lake City and her life as a plural wife in Manti, UT. See *Women in History: A Guide to Selected Holdings of the Women's History Archives* (Provo, UT: Brigham Young University, Harold B. Lee Library, 1975).

16,507. Custer, Elizabeth (Bacon)
Papers. 1876-1927. 1 folder and 14 microfilm reels.
Open. Published guide.
Brigham Young University Library, Division of Archives and Manuscripts.
Correspondence, notes, manuscripts, photos, and clippings of Custer (1842-1933), an author, concern her literary and public career after the death of her husband General George Armstrong Custer (1839-76). See *Women in History: A Guide to Selected Holdings of the Women's History Archives* (Provo, UT: Brigham Young University, Harold B. Lee Library, 1975).

16,508. Dalton, Hannah Daphne (Smith)
Papers. 1897-1937. 1 folder.
Open. Published guide.
Brigham Young University Library, Division of Archives and Manuscripts.
Correspondence and a book of genealogical information that Dalton, a Latter-day Saints pioneer and homemaker, gave to her daughter Daphne in 1922. Also includes a tribute to Dalton, patriarchal blessings of her daughter, a photo, and clippings. See *Women in History: A Guide to Selected Holdings of the Women's History Archives* (Provo, UT: Brigham Young University, Harold B. Lee Library, 1975).

16,509. Dudley, Susan J.
Papers. 1844-96. 1 folder.
Open. Published guide.
Brigham Young University Library, Division of Archives and Manuscripts.
Letters written from Nauvoo, IL, Salt Lake City, and other places by Susan Dudley, Mary Ann Robinson, and other early Latter-day Saints Church members and Utah pioneers. See *Women in History: A Guide to Selected Holdings of the Women's History Archives* (Provo, UT: Brigham Young University, Harold B. Lee Library, 1975).

16,510. Erickson, Hilda
Papers. 1888-1924. 5 boxes.
Open. Published guide.
Brigham Young University Library, Division of Archives and Manuscripts.
Ledgers, daybooks, receipts, and bills of Erickson, a businesswoman and resident of Grantsville, UT, pertain to the family general store in Grantsville, the Federal Land Bank there, and other business activities she and her husband John A. Erickson conducted. See *Women in History: A Guide to Selected Holdings of the Women's History Archives* (Provo, UT: Brigham Young University, Harold B. Lee Library, 1975).

16,511. Female Relief Society
Records. 1854. 1 vol.
Open. Published guide.
Brigham Young University Library, Division of Archives and Manuscripts.
Minute book of this Great Salt Lake City, Utah Territory, organization, a predecessor to the Relief Society of the Church of Jesus Christ of Latter-day Saints, which Brigham Young organized in 1855. Louisa R. Taylor, the secretary, kept the book. See *Women in History: A Guide to Selected Holdings of the Women's History Archives* (Provo, UT: Brigham Young University, Harold B. Lee Library, 1975).

16,512. Flake, Lucy Hannah (White)
Papers. 1894-1900. 3 vols.
Open. Published guide.
Brigham Young University Library, Division of Archives and Manuscripts.
Autobiography and a diary of Flake (1842-1900), a Utah pioneer who joined the Mormon church in Nauvoo, IL, and later emigrated to Utah. Contains accounts of polygamy, the United Order, and other personal experiences. A resident of Lehi and Beaver, UT, Flake also participated in the colonization of the Snowflake, AZ, area. See *Women in History: A Guide to Selected Holdings of the Women's History Archives* (Provo, UT: Brigham Young University, Harold B. Lee Library, 1975).

16,513. Freeze, Mary Ann (Burnham)
Papers. 1875-99. 5 folders.
Open. Published guide.
Brigham Young University Library, Division of Archives and Manuscripts.
Diaries of Freeze (1845-1912), a Utah pioneer who was born in Nauvoo, IL, emigrated to Utah in 1852, and settled in Bountiful and later Salt Lake City. The diaries cover the period during which Freeze served as president of the 11th Ward Retrenchment Society and as president and general board member of the Young Women's Mutual Improvement Association of the Latter-day Saints Church. See *Women in History: A Guide to Selected Holdings of the Women's History Archives* (Provo, UT: Brigham Young University, Harold B. Lee Library, 1975).

16,514. Front, Maxine (Redd)
Oral history. Ca. 1972. 1 vol.
Open. Published guide.
Brigham Young University Library, Division of Archives and Manuscripts.
Reminiscences of Front concern her work as a secretary at the Farm Security Administration, a vanadium mill, and the Monticello, UT, school district during the mid-1900s. See *Women in History: A Guide to Selected Holdings of the Women's History Archives* (Provo, UT: Brigham Young University, Harold B. Lee Library, 1975).

16,515. Front, Thressa (Lewis)
Oral history. Nd. 1 vol.
Open. Published guide.
Brigham Young University Library, Division of Archives and Manuscripts.
Reminiscences of Front concern life in Monticello, UT, after 1913. See *Women in History: A Guide to Selected Holdings of the Women's History Archives* (Provo, UT: Brigham Young University, Harold B. Lee Library, 1975).

16,516. Hafen, Leroy R., and Hafen, Ann (Woodbury)
Papers. Ca. 1940-50. 10 boxes.
Open. Published guide.
Brigham Young University Library, Division of Archives and Manuscripts.
Manuscript of the 14-volume work *The Far West and the Rockies* (1954) by Leroy Hafen (1893-) and his wife Ann Hafen (1893-1970). See *Women in History: A Guide to Selected Holdings of the Women's History Archives* (Provo, UT: Brigham Young University, Harold B. Lee Library, 1975).

16,517. Hale, Nathan, and Hale, Ruth
Papers. Nd. 2 boxes.
Open. Published guide.
Brigham Young University Library, Division of Archives and Manuscripts.
Manuscripts of plays by Nathan Hale and his wife Ruth, Utah playwrights who began writing plays during the depression. Approximately half of the plays, which range from comedy to musicals, have been published. See *Women in History: A Guide to Selected Holdings of the Women's History Archives* (Provo, UT: Brigham Young University, Harold B. Lee Library, 1975).

16,518. Hales, Belle W.
Papers. 1941-62. 2 vols.
Open. Published guide.
Brigham Young University Library, Division of Archives and Manuscripts.
Diary and a journal of Hales, a civic leader, homemaker, and wife of Wayne B. Hales, the first dean of the general college at the University. See *Women in History: A Guide to Selected Holdings of the Women's History Archives* (Provo, UT: Brigham Young University, Harold B. Lee Library, 1975).

16,519. Harris, Beth Kay
Papers. Nd. 2 boxes.
Open. Published guide and register.
Brigham Young University Library, Division of Archives and Manuscripts.
Manuscripts of Harris's *Towns of Tintic* (1961), which was written for the Federal Writers Project, and *Soapy Smith, King of the Frontier Con Men* (1961), written in collaboration with Frank C. Robertson. See *Women in History: A Guide to Selected Holdings of the Women's History Archives* (Provo, UT: Brigham Young University, Harold B. Lee Library, 1975).

16,520. Hatch, Nelle (Spilsbury)
Papers. Nd. 2 boxes.
Open. Published guide.
Brigham Young University Library, Division of Archives and Manuscripts.
Manuscripts of Hatch's *Colonia Juarez* (1954), and correspondence, diary excerpts, notes, biographies, articles, photos, and maps relating to Mormon exploration, colonization, and missionary work in Mexico and the Juarez Latter-day Saints Stake; the Juarez Stake Academy; the Mexican revolution of 1910; the "punitive expedition"; and the exodus of Mormon settlers from Mexico in 1912 and 1914. See *Women in History: A Guide to Selected Holdings of the Women's History Archives* (Provo, UT: Brigham Young University, Harold B. Lee Library, 1975).

16,521. Hayes, Rose B.
Papers. 1888-1942. 3 vols.
Open. Published guide.
Brigham Young University Library, Division of Archives and Manuscripts.
Includes scrapbooks containing clippings concerning WWI victory loans, obituaries, pioneer and Utah history, and other items of Hayes (1861-?). See *Women in History: A Guide to Selected Holdings of the Women's History Archives* (Provo, UT: Brigham Young University, Harold B. Lee Library, 1975).

16,522. Henrie, Susan (Coleman)
Papers. 1934-70. 1 folder.
Open. Published guide.
Brigham Young University Library, Division of Archives and Manuscripts.
Correspondence pertaining to and a photo of Henrie (1839-?), a Utah pioneer and homemaker. See *Women in History: A Guide to Selected Holdings of the Women's History Archives* (Provo, UT: Brigham Young University, Harold B. Lee Library, 1975).

16,523. Henrie, Thea Annie (Lund)
Papers. Nd. 1 folder.
Open. Published guide.
Brigham Young University Library, Division of Archives and Manuscripts.
History about Henrie, an early resident of Manti, UT, and her family was written by her granddaughter Vivian Henrie Crawford. See *Women in History: A Guide to Selected Holdings of the Women's History Archives* (Provo, UT: Brigham Young University, Harold B. Lee Library, 1975).

16,524. Hess, Arlene
Papers. Nd. 11 folders.
Open. Published guide.
Brigham Young University Library, Division of Archives and Manuscripts.
Papers of Hess, a joint editor of the sesquicentennial publication "The History of Friendship, New York," include correspondence with George W. Robinson and Josephine "Jessie" Rigdon Secord; genealogical information on Sidney

Rigdon, Secord's grandfather and a resident of Friendship for 30 years; and biographical information on his descendants. See *Women in History: A Guide to Selected Holdings of the Women's History Archives* (Provo, UT: Brigham Young University, Harold B. Lee Library, 1975).

16,525. Hess, Margaret (Steed)
Collection. 1811-1944. 1 box.
Open. Published guide.
Brigham Young University Library, Division of Archives and Manuscripts.
Pioneer reminiscences collected by Hess (1884-), the historian of the Daughters of Utah Pioneers, pertain to early residents of Davis County, UT, and their descendants. Contains information on various subjects, including the lynching of Joseph Smith, the Mormon Battalion, handcart companies, conversion of Mormon pioneers, Mormon persecution, Mormon and Indian relations, and pioneer women. Excerpts from the reminiscences have been published in *Heart Throbs of the West* by Kate Carter and in similar works published by the Daughters of Utah Pioneers. See *Women in History: A Guide to Selected Holdings of the Women's History Archives* (Provo, UT: Brigham Young University, Harold B. Lee Library, 1975).

16,526. Johnson, Maria
Papers. 1903-65. 2 folders.
Open. Published guide.
Brigham Young University Library, Division of Archives and Manuscripts.
Correspondence, photos, clippings, and certificates of Johnson (1888-1974), who was a superintendent of nurses and director of the school of nursing at the Salt Lake LDS Hospital. See *Women in History: A Guide to Selected Holdings of the Women's History Archives* (Provo, UT: Brigham Young University, Harold B. Lee Library, 1975).

16,527. Kane, Sybil
Oral history. 1973- 74. 1 tape.
Open. Published guide.
Brigham Young University Library, Division of Archives and Manuscripts.
Interview with [Miss] Kane, a descendant of Colonel Thomas Kane, a prominent Pennsylvanian, Civil War officer, and friend to the Mormons, concerns Kane family incidents and Pennsylvania history. See *Women in History: A Guide to Selected Holdings of the Women's History Archives* (Provo, UT: Brigham Young University, Harold B. Lee Library, 1975).

16,528. Keele, Reba
Oral history. Ca. 1976. 1 tape.
Open. Published guide.
Brigham Young University Library, Division of Archives and Manuscripts.
Consists of interviews with various people regarding their memories of Alice Louise Reynolds. See *Women in History: A Guide to Selected Holdings of the Women's History Archives* (Provo, UT: Brigham Young University, Harold B. Lee Library, 1975).

16,529. Klasner, Lily
Papers. Ca. 1900-30. 9 cartons.
Open. Published guide.
Brigham Young University Library, Division of Archives and Manuscripts.
Correspondence, a diary, manuscripts, notes, financial records, and photos of Klasner (1862-1946), a southeastern New Mexico pioneer, rancher, teacher, historian, and participant in the Lincoln County war; she also was a close friend of cattle baron John Chisum. See *Women in History: A Guide to Selected Holdings of the Women's History Archives* (Provo, UT: Brigham Young University, Harold B. Lee Library, 1975).

16,530. Knight, Hattie (Madson)
Papers. 1975. 1 folder.
Open. Published guide.
Brigham Young University Library, Division of Archives and Manuscripts.
Reminiscences of Knight (1908-), a former member of the University staff and library school faculty, include her memories of growing up on an Idaho farm. See *Women in History: A Guide to Selected Holdings of the Women's History Archives* (Provo, UT: Brigham Young University, Harold B. Lee Library, 1975).

16,531. Knight, Lydia (Goldthwaite)
Papers. 1833-83. 5 in.
Open. Published guide.
Brigham Young University Library, Division of Archives and Manuscripts.
Correspondence and genealogical papers of Knight (1812-84) include information on some of the first Massachusetts families to join the Latter-day Saints Church, among them the Steed, Burt, Very, Holland, and Goldthwaite families. See *Women in History: A Guide to Selected Holdings of the Women's History Archives* (Provo, UT: Brigham Young University, Harold B. Lee Library, 1975).

16,532. Kopp, Barbara
Papers. 1885-1973. 1 folder.
Open. Published guide.
Brigham Young University Library, Division of Archives and Manuscripts.
Includes articles and information on Kopp (1836-1918), also known as Mother Marianne, and her work with the Sisters of St. Francis at the Kakaako and Molokai leper colonies in Hawaii. See *Women in History: A Guide to Selected Holdings of the Women's History Archives* (Provo, UT: Brigham Young University, Harold B. Lee Library, 1975).

16,533. Lightner, Mary Elizabeth (Rollins)
Papers. 1867-1914. 1 folder.
Open. Published guide.
Brigham Young University Library, Division of Archives and Manuscripts.
Correspondence, a recorded dream, a blessing, an article about the organization of the Relief Society, and an address by Lightner (1818-1913), a plural wife of prophet Joseph Smith. Also includes reminiscences about Joseph Smith and his plural wives, which were recorded in 1905. Correspondents include Brigham Young, John Taylor, Joseph F. Smith, and Wilford Woodruff, all of whom were presidents of the Mormon church. See *Women in History: A Guide to Selected Holdings of the Women's History Archives* (Provo, UT: Brigham Young University, Harold B. Lee Library, 1975).

16,534. Lott, Elsie (Moore)
Papers. 1869-94. 1 folder.
Open. Published guide.
Brigham Young University Library, Division of Archives and Manuscripts.
History in which Lott, the daughter of Stephen Bliss Moore, who was a developer of the Tintic mining district, gives an account of the discovery and development of the district as well as information about her father and herself. See *Women in History: A Guide to Selected Holdings of the Women's History Archives* (Provo, UT: Brigham Young University, Harold B. Lee Library, 1975).

16,535. Lund, Cornelia (Sorenson)
Papers. 1931-45. 2 boxes.
Open. Published guide and register.
Brigham Young University Library, Division of Archives and Manuscripts.
Lund (1882-1959) was a president of the Women's Chamber of Commerce in Salt Lake City, UT. Includes minutes of the Utah Smokeless Fuel Cooperative Association; correspondence, radio programs, and clippings relating to a smoke abatement campaign in Salt Lake City; legislation, reports, and historical sketches of the Salt Lake Women's Chamber of Commerce; early Utah land papers; and talks by A. C. Lund. See *Women in History: A Guide to Selected Holdings of the Women's History Archives* (Provo, UT: Brigham Young University, Harold B. Lee Library, 1975).

16,536. Lyman, Amy Cassandra (Brown)
Papers. 1888-1957. 12 boxes.
Open. Published guide.
Brigham Young University Library, Division of Archives and Manuscripts.
Correspondence, articles, photos, clippings, mementos, reports, and legislative bills of Lyman (1872-1959), a wife of Richard R. Lyman, a president of the Relief Society of the Latter-day Saints Church, an officer of national and international women's organizations, a legislator in the Utah House of Representatives, and a student and teacher at Brigham Young Academy. Includes items concerning the origin of the Relief Society, Nauvoo, IL; Richard Lyman; Joseph Smith; early Mormon pioneers; and the University Emeritus Club. Also includes biographical sketches of prominent Utah residents and notable women of the nation and the world as well as biographies of Amasa and Francis M. Lyman. See *Women in History: A Guide to Selected Holdings of the Women's History Archives* (Provo, UT: Brigham Young University, Harold B. Lee Library, 1975).

16,537. Lyman, Eliza Maria (Partridge)
Papers. 1846-85. 1 vol.
Open. Published guide.
Brigham Young University Library, Division of Archives and Manuscripts.
Lyman (1820-86), an early Mormon convert and Utah pioneer, was a plural wife of both Joseph Smith, the Mormon prophet, and Amasa M. Lyman, a member of the Council of the Twelve. Consists of a journal in which she describes her experiences during the exodus from Nauvoo, IL, and life on the plains and in Utah. The journal also includes an extensive discourse she delivered defending polygamy and protesting the Anti-Polygamous Ladies of Utah. See *Women in History: A Guide to Selected Holdings of the Women's History Archives* (Provo, UT: Brigham Young University, Harold B. Lee Library, 1975).

16,538. McFarlane, Viola (Pratt) Gillette
Papers. 1897-1951. 4 folders.
Open. Published guide.
Brigham Young University Library, Division of Archives and Manuscripts.
Biographical data, photos, clippings, programs, and mementos of McFarlane (1871-1956) pertain to her career as a Utah opera star and her travels throughout America. See *Women in History: A Guide to Selected Holdings of the Women's History Archives* (Provo, UT: Brigham Young University, Harold B. Lee Library, 1975).

16,539. Mack, Temperance
Papers. 1835-43. 1 folder.
Open. Published guide.
Brigham Young University Library, Division of Archives and Manuscripts.
Contains correspondence primarily between Mack (1771-1850) and her daughter Harriet Whittemore and other children. The letters concern family matters and events in early Latter-day Saints church history. Includes information on the death of her husband Colonel Stephen Mack. Temperance Mack's sister was Lucy (Mack) Smith, the mother of prophet Joseph Smith. See *Women in History: A Guide to Selected Holdings of the Women's History Archives* (Provo, UT: Brigham Young University, Harold B. Lee Library, 1975).

16,540. Marsh, Eudocia (Baldwin)
Papers. Nd. 1 microfilm reel.
Open. Published guide.
Brigham Young University Library, Division of Archives and Manuscripts.
Correspondence and legal documents of Marsh (1829-?), a non-Mormon who was the wife of a prominent Warsaw, IL, lawyer. Also includes an account she wrote concerning the Mormons in Hancock County, IL, and the lynching of Joseph and Hyrum Smith. See *Women in History: A Guide to Selected Holdings of the Women's History Archives* (Provo, UT: Brigham Young University, Harold B. Lee Library, 1975).

16,541. Marshall, Sarah (Goode)
Papers. 1856. 1 folder.
Open. Published guide.
Brigham Young University Library, Division of Archives and Manuscripts.
Diary and sketch of the life of Marshall (1822-?), a Mormon handcart pioneer, which she wrote during her journey across the plains. See *Women in History: A Guide to Selected Holdings of the Women's History Archives* (Provo, UT: Brigham Young University, Harold B. Lee Library, 1975).

16,542. Maw, Margaret (Petersen)
Papers. 1909-55. 8 boxes.
Open. Published guide and register.
Brigham Young University Library, Division of Archives and Manuscripts.
Papers of Maw (1874-1966), a writer, include manuscripts of books, short stories, and articles; records of the Provo and Utah Women's Clubs; a photo album of the Provo School of Beauty Culture, 1933-44; and mementos. See *Women in History: A Guide to Selected Holdings of the Women's History Archives* (Provo, UT: Brigham Young University, Harold B. Lee Library, 1975).

16,543. Morse, Eva S.
Papers. 1859. 1 folder.
Open. Published guide.
Brigham Young University Library, Division of Archives and Manuscripts.
Journal that Morse kept during an overland journey from Illinois to California contains her disparaging description of Mormon wagon trains. See *Women in History: A Guide to Selected Holdings of the Women's History Archives* (Provo, UT: Brigham Young University, Harold B. Lee Library, 1975).

16,544. Nielson, Emma (Waitsill) Mecham
Papers. 1887-1902. 1 vol.
Open. Published guide.
Brigham Young University Library, Division of Archives and Manuscripts.
Diary in which Nielson, a plural wife of Frihoff Godfred Nielson, recounts her experiences in St. George, UT, and New Mexico. See *Women in History: A Guide to Selected Holdings of the Women's History Archives* (Provo, UT: Brigham Young University, Harold B. Lee Library, 1975).

16,545. Norman, Mary
Papers. 1915. 1 folder.
Open. Published guide.
Brigham Young University Library, Division of Archives and Manuscripts.
Letter that Norman wrote from Idaho Falls, ID, to Sue Smith Beatty, her niece, reminiscing about Samuel H. Smith, who was the younger brother of prophet Joseph Smith. Samuel Smith was Mary Norman's father and Sue Beatty's grandfather. See *Women in History: A Guide to Selected Holdings of the Women's History Archives* (Provo, UT: Brigham Young University, Harold B. Lee Library, 1975).

16,546. Nuttall, Grace (Greer)
Papers. 1896-99. 4 vols.
Open. Published guide.
Brigham Young University Library, Division of Archives and Manuscripts.
Diaries that Nuttall kept concern her early childhood in Wallsburg, UT, and her experiences at Brigham Young Academy. Includes a theology notebook she used while she was a student at the University. See *Women in History: A Guide to Selected Holdings of the Women's History Archives* (Provo, UT: Brigham Young University, Harold B. Lee Library, 1975).

16,547. Oakley, Annie
Papers. 1886-1921. 1 folder.
Open. Published guide.
Brigham Young University Library, Division of Archives and Manuscripts.
Correspondence and photos of Oakley (1860-1926), a sharpshooter; of her husband; and of other members of Buffalo Bill's Wild West Show. See *Women in History: A Guide to Selected Holdings of the Women's History Archives* (Provo, UT: Brigham Young University, Harold B. Lee Library, 1975).

16,548. Palmer, Ada
Oral history. Nd. 1 vol.
Open. Published guide.
Brigham Young University Library, Division of Archives and Manuscripts.
Oral history in which Palmer, who was a schoolteacher in San Juan and Grand counties in Utah and a county clerk in Grand County, describes life in southern Utah from 1900 to 1950. See *Women in History: A Guide to Selected Holdings of the Women's History Archives* (Provo, UT: Brigham Young University, Harold B. Lee Library, 1975).

16,549. Peterson, Hermese
Papers. Nd. 1 folder.
Open. Published guide.
Brigham Young University Library, Division of Archives and Manuscripts.
Includes a life history of and tributes to Peterson (1879-1961), a teacher and principal of the Brigham Young University Training School. See *Women in History: A Guide to Selected Holdings of the Women's History Archives* (Provo, UT: Brigham Young University, Harold B. Lee Library, 1975).

16,550. Peterson, Zola
Papers. Ca. 1967. 1 folder.
Open. Published guide.
Brigham Young University Library, Division of Archives and Manuscripts.
Reminiscences in which Peterson (1889-1971), a prominent Utah citizen, describes her birth, childhood, experiences as a student at the University, and marriage; she also gives information about Monticello and Blanding, UT. See *Women in History: A Guide to Selected Holdings of the Women's History Archives* (Provo, UT: Brigham Young University, Harold B. Lee Library, 1975).

16,551. Phillips, Ann (Thomas)
Papers. Nd. 1 folder.
Open. Published guide.
Brigham Young University Library, Division of Archives and Manuscripts.
Consists of information about the life and family of Phillips (1839-1920), a Utah pioneer, which was compiled by her daughter Adah (Phillips) Jessee. See *Women in History: A Guide to Selected Holdings of the Women's History Archives* (Provo, UT: Brigham Young University, Harold B. Lee Library, 1975).

16,552. Pound, Louise
Papers. 1908-43. 4 boxes.
Open. Published guide and register.
Brigham Young University Library, Division of Archives and Manuscripts.
Pound (1872-1958) was an educator, author, and collector of folklore. Includes correspondence, writings in manuscript and published form, notes on Chaucer, examination and term papers from her classes, and an extensive collection of American folklore. See *Women in History: A Guide to Selected Holdings of the Women's History Archives* (Provo, UT: Brigham Young University, Harold B. Lee Library, 1975).

16,553. Price, Elizabeth Fraser
Oral history. Nd. 1 vol.
Open. Published guide.
Brigham Young University Library, Division of Archives and Manuscripts.
Reminiscences in which Price talks about her childhood; teaching in Murray, Salt Lake City, and Blanding, UT; teaching college in Hawaii and at Ricks College in Rexburg, ID; travel in Europe with a Brigham Young University tour group; and an insurrection in Guatemala. The events described took place between ca. 1900 and 1950. See *Women in History: A Guide to Selected Holdings of the Women's History Archives* (Provo, UT: Brigham Young University, Harold B. Lee Library, 1975).

16,554. Pulley, Mary
Oral history. Ca. 1972. 2 vols.
Open. Published guide.
Brigham Young University Library, Division of Archives and Manuscripts.
Interview in which Pulley (1900-), a prominent resident of Utah, describes her activities at the American Fork Training School, her education, time she spent as a Latter-day Saint missionary, and business in American Fork and Utah during WWI, the depression, and WWII. See *Women in History: A Guide to Selected Holdings of the Women's History Archives* (Provo, UT: Brigham Young University, Harold B. Lee Library, 1975).

16,555. Reynolds, Alice Louise
Papers. 1923-37. 10 vols.
Open. Published guide.
Brigham Young University Library, Division of Archives and Manuscripts.
Papers of Reynolds (1873-1938), a University professor, author, international traveler, member of the general board of the Relief Society of the Latter-day Saints Church and of the GFWC, editor of the *Relief Society Magazine,* and a speaker on woman suffrage. Includes correspondence, 1923-37; diaries for 1925 and 1932 to 1937; lecture notes on English literature and modern European history; a club minute book; and autobiographical notes. See *Women in History: A Guide to Selected Holdings of the Women's History Archives* (Provo, UT: Brigham Young University, Harold B. Lee Library, 1975).

16,556. Roberts, Josephine (Redd)
Oral history. Ca. 1972. 1 vol.
Open. Published guide.
Brigham Young University Library, Division of Archives and Manuscripts.
Reminiscences in which Roberts describes Blanding, UT, during the mid-1900s. See *Women in History: A Guide to Selected Holdings of the Women's History Archives* (Provo, UT: Brigham Young University, Harold B. Lee Library, 1975).

16,557. Smith, Bathsheba W.
Papers. 1822-1927. 1 folder.
Open. Published guide.
Brigham Young University Library, Division of Archives and Manuscripts.
Autobiography in which Smith (1822-1910), an early convert to Mormonism who became the fourth president of the Female Relief Society of the Latter-day Saints Church, recounts her conversion; her family's travels through Missouri during the persecution of the Mormons; their settlement in Nauvoo, IL; her marriage to George A. Smith, a cousin of Joseph Smith and an apostle of the LDS

Church; and her association with Joseph Smith and other ecclesiastical leaders. See *Women in History: A Guide to Selected Holdings of the Women's History Archives* (Provo, UT: Brigham Young University, Harold B. Lee Library, 1975).

16,558. Smith, Ruby K.
Papers. 1800-1966. 7 boxes.
Open. Published guide.
Brigham Young University Library, Division of Archives and Manuscripts.
Correspondence, diaries for 1921 to 1941, book manuscripts, pioneer and family biographies, scrapbooks, and photo albums of Smith, an author, home economics expert, and home demonstration agent for Utah, Uintah, and Tooele counties in Utah. See *Women in History: A Guide to Selected Holdings of the Women's History Archives* (Provo, UT: Brigham Young University, Harold B. Lee Library, 1975).

16,559. Smoot, Margaret (Thompson)
Papers. 1850-81. 3 folders and 1 microfilm reel.
Open. Published guide.
Brigham Young University Library, Division of Archives and Manuscripts.
Journal and daybook for 1850 to 1859, an autobiography, and a genealogy of [Mrs. Abraham O.] Smoot (1809-84), a prominent citizen of Utah Valley. Also includes a sketch of Smoot's life by Olive Smoot Bean and an article "Experience of a Mormon Wife," which documents Smoot's life. See *Women in History: A Guide to Selected Holdings of the Women's History Archives* (Provo, UT: Brigham Young University, Harold B. Lee Library, 1975).

16,560. Snow, Eliza Roxcy
Papers. 1846-49. 1 microfilm reel.
Open. Published guide.
Brigham Young University Library, Division of Archives and Manuscripts.
Journal of Snow (1804-87), a poet, author, early Utah pioneer, second president of the Relief Society of the Latter-day Saints Church, and plural wife of Joseph Smith and Brigham Young. Includes poetry and accounts of her experiences while she was crossing the plains and in Salt Lake City, UT, during the earliest years of its settlement. She used her maiden name Snow throughout her life. See *Women in History: A Guide to Selected Holdings of the Women's History Archives* (Provo, UT: Brigham Young University, Harold B. Lee Library, 1975).

16,561. Thurber, Laura Ann (Keeler)
Papers. 1817-1909. 1 vol.
Open. Published guide.
Brigham Young University Library, Division of Archives and Manuscripts.
Consists of a diary of Thurber (1859-1909), a resident of Greenwich in Piute County, UT. Extracts from the diary of her father James Keeler (1817-?) are included in the first part of the volume and cover the period from his birth to the family's settlement in Utah in 1855. Portions of the diary of Thurber's mother Eliza Keeler (1840-?) cover the period from Thurber's birth to her marriage in 1876 and include a record of her life as a plural wife in Richfield, UT. Thurber's account relates to her life in Greenwich as the plural wife of a farmer. Also includes a Keeler family genealogy. See *Women in History: A Guide to Selected Holdings of the Women's History Archives* (Provo, UT: Brigham Young University, Harold B. Lee Library, 1975).

16,562. Van Buren, Lotta
Papers. 1912-60. 5 boxes.
Open. Published guide and register.
Brigham Young University Library, Division of Archives and Manuscripts.
Van Buren (1877-1960) was a musician and a collector and restorer of old musical instruments. Includes an unpublished biography of Van Buren by her husband Henry Bizallion, notes on and photos of her instrument collection, a scrapbook, clippings, programs, sheet music, and a motion picture *What Do You Know About the Piano?*. See *Women in History: A Guide to Selected Holdings of the Women's History Archives* (Provo, UT: Brigham Young University, Harold B. Lee Library, 1975).

16,563. Verrill, Ruth
Papers. 1947-69. 4 boxes.
Open. Published guide.
Brigham Young University Library, Division of Archives and Manuscripts.
Correspondence, magazine articles, drafts, research notes, and photos of Verrill, an author and lecturer. Papers primarily relate to the archaeology and history of the American continent and the similarity of its culture, arts, and beliefs to those of ancient Europe and Asia. See *Women in History: A Guide to Selected Holdings of the Women's History Archives* (Provo, UT: Brigham Young University, Harold B. Lee Library, 1975).

16,564. Warnock, Irvin L., and Warnock, Lexia D.
Papers. Nd. 2 boxes.
Open. Published guide.
Brigham Young University Library, Division of Archives and Manuscripts.
Proofs that Irvin Warnock (1892-1974) and his wife Lexia Warnock (1890-), local historians and residents of Sevier County, UT, used in the preparation of *Our Own Sevier, A Comprehensive Centennial Volume* (1965). Includes many biographies and town histories of Sevier County. See *Women in History: A Guide to Selected Holdings of the Women's History Archives* (Provo, UT: Brigham Young University, Harold B. Lee Library, 1975).

16,565. Webster, Rose (Glen)
Papers. 1897-1904. 1 folder.
Open. Published guide.
Brigham Young University Library, Division of Archives and Manuscripts.
Papers of Webster, an anti-Mormon lecturer, include letters from *The Concord,* a Washington, DC, publication, offering congratulations on her correspondence on Mormonism as well as letters from elder W. H. Smith of Chattanooga, TN, in response to questions about the church. Also includes a handbill advertising a free lecture on Mormonism, which Webster was to deliver in Salt Lake City. See *Women in History: A Guide to Selected Holdings of the Women's History Archives* (Provo, UT: Brigham Young University, Harold B. Lee Library, 1975).

16,566. Wells, Emmeline Blanch (Woodward)
Papers. 1844-1920. 45 vols.
Open. Published guide.
Brigham Young University Library, Division of Archives and Manuscripts.
Diaries of Wells (1828-1921), a Mormon pioneer who served as general president of the Relief Society for 11 years and general secretary and editor of the *Woman's Exponent* for 38 years, date from 1844 to 1846 and from 1874 to 1920. The volumes include information on Latter-day Saints church history and her personal life; they also provide insight into polygamy. She was married successively to James Harris, Newel K. Whitney, and Daniel Hanmer Wells. She worked on behalf of women and women's suffrage, attended the Women's International Council and Congress in London in 1899, and served as chairman of the Utah Woman's Republican League, an officer in the Woman's National Council, poet laureate of Utah, a member of the National Woman's Suffrage Association, and an organizer of the Reaper's Club, the Utah Woman's Press Club, and numerous women's literary groups. See *Women in History: A Guide to Selected Holdings of the Women's History Archives* (Provo, UT: Brigham Young University, Harold B. Lee Library, 1975).

16,567. Wescott, Angeline
Oral history. Ca. 1972. 1 vol.
Open. Published guide.
Brigham Young University Library, Division of Archives and Manuscripts.
Reminiscences in which Wescott describes life in Monticello, UT, during the early and mid-1900s. See *Women in History: A Guide to Selected Holdings of the Women's History Archives* (Provo, UT: Brigham Young University, Harold B. Lee Library, 1975).

16,568. Wheeler, Florence Ida
Papers. 1920-21. 1 folder.
Open. Published guide.
Brigham Young University Library, Division of Archives and Manuscripts.
Correspondence between Wheeler and Gerald Niels Christiansen while he was serving in the Western States Mission. See *Women in History: A Guide to Selected Holdings of the Women's History Archives* (Provo, UT: Brigham Young University, Harold B. Lee Library, 1975).

16,569. Whipple, Marilyn
Papers. 1975. 1 folder.
Open. Published guide.
Brigham Young University Library, Division of Archives and Manuscripts.
Photos, clippings, and printed items of Whipple, a model; former fashion coordinator for ZCMI, which was originally known as Zion's Cooperative Mercantile Institution; lecturer for University education week and special courses; actress; and Latter-day Saint homemaker. ZCMI is a large Utah department store. See *Women in History: A Guide to Selected Holdings of the Women's History Archives* (Provo, UT: Brigham Young University, Harold B. Lee Library, 1975).

16,570. Wilcox, Ella (Wheeler)
Papers. 1869-1942. 1 box.
Open. Published guide.
Brigham Young University Library, Division of Archives and Manuscripts.
Correspondence, a photo, and clippings of [Mrs. Robert Marius] Wilcox (1850-1919), a poet and author of more than 40 volumes, including *Poems of Passion.* Includes letters to and items concerning poet Ethelyn Bryant Chapman. See *Women in History: A Guide to Selected Holdings of the Women's History Archives* (Provo, UT: Brigham Young University, Harold B. Lee Library, 1975).

16,571. Woodbury, Phoebe K. (Pratt)
Papers. 1851-67. 1 folder.
Open. Published guide.
Brigham Young University Library, Division of Archives and Manuscripts.
Letters in which Woodbury, an early settler in Salt Lake City, describes life in Utah to her family in the East. Also includes genealogical research material from the Latter-day Saints church historian's office and a record book containing a patriarchal blessing, a genealogy, poems, and other items. See *Women in History: A Guide to Selected Holdings of the Women's History Archives* (Provo, UT: Brigham Young University, Harold B. Lee Library, 1975).

16,572. Woolley, Florence "Flora" (Snow)
Papers. Ca. 1933. 1 folder.
Open. Published guide.
Brigham Young University Library, Division of Archives and Manuscripts.
Reminiscences in which Woolley (1857-?), a daughter of Erastus Snow and plural wife of Edwin Dilworth Woolley, describes her memories of colonizing St. George, UT, and living underground to escape persecution for polygamy. See *Women*

in History: A Guide to Selected Holdings of the Women's History Archives (Provo, UT: Brigham Young University, Harold B. Lee Library, 1975).

16,573. Yearsley, Mary Ann
Papers. 1871-1914. 1 folder.
Open. Published guide.
Brigham Young University Library, Division of Archives and Manuscripts.
Life history and diary of Yearsley (1811-1903), an early Latter-day Saints church member and Utah pioneer, concern a journey she took to Pennsylvania from Utah in 1871 and 1872. See *Women in History: A Guide to Selected Holdings of the Women's History Archives* (Provo, UT: Brigham Young University, Harold B. Lee Library, 1975).

16,574. Yesharah Society
Records. 1929-60. 5 in.
Open. Published guide.
Brigham Young University Library, Division of Archives and Manuscripts.
Minute books, 1929-60; an account book, 1935-51; financial reports; histories of members; a scrapbook; clippings; and items concerning the activities of the University chapter of the Society, an organization for women Latter-day Saints missionaries who had returned home. See *Women in History: A Guide to Selected Holdings of the Women's History Archives* (Provo, UT: Brigham Young University, Harold B. Lee Library, 1975).

16,575. Young, Dorothy (Weir)
Papers. 1798-1956. 30 boxes.
Access restricted. Published guide and register.
Brigham Young University Library, Division of Archives and Manuscripts.
Correspondence, government papers, certificates, and artworks of Young, an author and painter. Also includes manuscripts of *The Life and Letters of J. Alden Weir* (1960) by Young, along with papers of the Weir and Young families, which primarily relate to artist J. Alden Weir and artist and sculptor Mahonri Mackintosh Young. See *Women in History: A Guide to Selected Holdings of the Women's History Archives* (Provo, UT: Brigham Young University, Harold B. Lee Library, 1975).

SALT LAKE CITY

16,576. Boulter, Grace (Foutz)
Papers. Nd. 1 microfilm reel.
Open. Published guide.
Brigham Young University Library, Division of Archives and Manuscripts.
"History of Bishop Jacob Foutz, Sr., and family including a story of the Haun's Mill Massacre, religious and social," a manuscript by Boulter and Mary Foutz Corrigan. See *Women in History: A Guide to Selected Holdings of the Women's History Archives* (Provo, UT: Brigham Young University, Harold B. Lee Library, 1975).

16,577. Bowen, Emma Lucy (Gates)
Papers. 1892-1950. 16 boxes.
Open. Published guide.
Brigham Young University Library, Division of Archives and Manuscripts.
Bowen (1880-1951) was a Utah singer, violinist, pianist, actress, teacher, and the first Latter-day Saint woman to study music in Europe. Includes correspondence from the period between 1898 and 1914 when she was a student and opera singer in Germany, photos, libretti, and concert programs. Her chief correspondents were her husband Albert E. Bowen, her agent Catherine A. Bamman, and the members of the Gates family. Also includes material on the Lucy Gates Opera Company of Salt Lake City. See *Women in History: A Guide to Selected Holdings of the Women's History Archives* (Provo, UT: Brigham Young University, Harold B. Lee Library, 1975).

16,578. Adams, Colenda Chrilla (Rogers)
Papers. 1885-1923. 1 vol.
Open. Published guide.
LDS Church Archives.
Diary in which [Mrs. Joseph] Adams (1869-?) recorded family and community events in Pleasant Grove, UT. Taken from Christy Best, *Guide to Sources for Studies of Mormon Women in the Church Archives, The Church of Jesus Christ of Latter-day Saints* (Salt Lake City: Historical Department of The Church of Jesus Christ of Latter-day Saints, 1976).

16,579. Adams, Margaret (Webster)
Papers. 1858-59. 2 items.
Open. Published guide.
LDS Church Archives.
Correspondence in which [Mrs. Hugh] Adams (1831-62) writes about events connected with the Utah war and her beliefs as a Mormon. Taken from Christy Best, *Guide to Sources for Studies of Mormon Women in the Church Archives, The Church of Jesus Christ of Latter-day Saints* (Salt Lake City: Historical Department of The Church of Jesus Christ of Latter-day Saints, 1976).

16,580. Alder, Lydia (Dunford)
Papers. Ca. 1905. 4 items.
Open. Published guide.
LDS Church Archives.
Papers of [Mrs. George Alfred] Alder (1846-1923) include poetry concerning Mormon pioneers and religious subjects and a report about her activities as a guest of the German Council of Women during the quinquennial held in Berlin in 1904. Taken from Christy Best, *Guide to Sources for Studies of Mormon Women in the Church Archives, The Church of Jesus Christ of Latter-day Saints* (Salt Lake City: Historical Department of The Church of Jesus Christ of Latter-day Saints, 1976).

16,581. Andersen, Hazel
Papers. 1924. 6-page item.
Open. Unpublished guide.
LDS Church Archives.
Papers of Andersen in which she recounts the history of Joseph Smith and adds her testimony concerning why she believes him to be a true prophet of God.

16,582. Anderson, Amanda Wilhelmina
Papers. 1934. 2 items.
Open. Unpublished guide.
LDS Church Archives.
Account of [Miss] Anderson (1859-?) relates to her dreams concerning the Savior and the Church.

16,583. Andreasen, Anna Lena (Frandsen)
Papers. 1921. 6-page item.
Open. Published guide.
LDS Church Archives.
Brief history of [Mrs. Axel Ferdenand] Andreasen about the Vineyard Ward Relief Society in Orem, UT. Taken from Christy Best, *Guide to Sources for Studies of Mormon Women in the Church Archives, The Church of Jesus Christ of Latter-day Saints* (Salt Lake City: Historical Department of The Church of Jesus Christ of Latter-day Saints, 1976).

16,584. Ashby, Beth
Papers. 1934. 1 item.
Open. Unpublished guide.
LDS Church Archives.
Talk of Ashby (1914-) concerns the battle between the forces of good and evil throughout the ages.

16,585. Ashworth, Mary Elizabeth (Shepherd)
Papers. Nd. 21-page item.
Open. No guide.
LDS Church Archives.
Essay of [Mrs. William Booth] Ashworth (1854-1932) concerns land jumpers in Beaver and Cedar City, UT.

16,586. Austin, Octavia A. (Lane)
Papers. 1846. 4 pp.
Open. Published guide.
LDS Church Archives.
Letter from [Mrs. Julius Augustus Caesar] Austin (1814-63) in Honolulu to Ashbel Lane in Siffield, CT, in which she recounts her voyage on the ship *Brooklyn* with Church members led by Samual Brannan. Also includes genealogy of the Lane family. Taken from Christy Best, *Guide to Sources for Studies of Mormon Women in the Church Archives, The Church of Jesus Christ of Latter-day Saints* (Salt Lake City: Historical Department of The Church of Jesus Christ of Latter-day Saints, 1976).

16,587. Baird, Gertrude Luck
Papers. 1927-31. 3 vols.
Open. Unpublished guide.
LDS Church Archives.
Papers of Baird (1885-) include a notebook pertaining to genealogy; a history, written partly in German, of the first German genealogical society in Salt Lake City, including biographies of members and photos; and a scrapbook containing pictures of the employees of the Latter-day Saints Church Genealogical Society.

16,588. Baker, Elisabeth Annie (Nuttall)
Papers. Nd. 2-page item.
Open. Unpublished guide.
LDS Church Archives.
A story of [Mrs. John Daniel] Baker (1881-1968) about a Scandinavian woman who married an Indian in Provo, UT.

16,589. Baker, Jane Rio (Griffiths)
Papers. 1851-80. 1 vol.
Open. Published guide.
LDS Church Archives.
Diary of [Mrs. Henry] Baker (1810-83), 1851-52 and 1869-80, in which she records her journey from England to Salt Lake City, and her later move to California. Taken from Christy Best, *Guide to Sources for Studies of Mormon Women in the Church Archives, The Church of Jesus Christ of Latter-day Saints* (Salt Lake City: Historical Department of The Church of Jesus Christ of Latter-day Saints, 1976).

16,590. Barger, Fereba (Frost)
Papers. 1846. 1-page item.
Open. Published guide.
LDS Church Archives.
Letter of Barger (1818-1900) to her husband William H. Barger, who was with the Mormon Battalion during the Mexican War, concerns her family and life in Mount Pisgah, IA. The Battalion, composed of 500 Mormon men, marched to California. Fereba Barger later married John Eli Beatty. See Christy Best, *Guide to Sources for Studies of Mormon Women in the Church Archives, The Church of Jesus Christ of Latter-day Saints* (Salt Lake City: Historical Department of The Church of Jesus Christ of Latter-day Saints, 1976).

16,591. Barker, Nancy
Papers. 1924. 1 item.
Open. No guide.
LDS Church Archives.
A Latter-day Saints High School graduation diploma.

16,592. Barlow, Elizabeth (Haven)
Papers. 1839. 2 items.
Open. Published guide.
LDS Church Archives.
Letters of [Mrs. Israel] Barlow (1811-91) in which she describes the hardships of the Mormons in their exodus from Missouri. Taken from Christy Best, *Guide to Sources for Studies of Mormon Women in the Church Archives, The Church of Jesus Christ of Latter-day Saints* (Salt Lake City: Historical Department of The Church of Jesus Christ of Latter-day Saints, 1976).

16,593. Barney, Elvira (Stevens)
Papers. 1865. 12-page item.
Open. Published guide.
LDS Church Archives.
Account book of personal items of [Mrs. Royal] Barney (1832-1909). Prior to her marriage to Barney, she had been married to John S. Woodbury and then Oliver B. Huntington. See Christy Best, *Guide to Sources for Studies of Mormon Women in the Church Archives, The Church of Jesus Christ of Latter-day Saints* (Salt Lake City: Historical Department of The Church of Jesus Christ of Latter-day Saints, 1976).

16,594. Bay, Mary Eva (LeBaron)
Papers. 1879-1947. 1.25 ft.
Open. Published guide.
LDS Church Archives.
Letters of Bay (1867-1958), a resident of Junction, UT, and wife of James Willard Bay, Jr., are addressed primarily to her family. Also includes post cards, greeting cards, and ephemera. Taken from Christy Best, *Guide to Sources for Studies of Mormon Women in the Church Archives, The Church of Jesus Christ of Latter-day Saints* (Salt Lake City: Historical Department of The Church of Jesus Christ of Latter-day Saints, 1976).

16,595. Bean, Olive (Smoot)
Papers. Nd. 89-page item.
Open. Unpublished guide.
LDS Church Archives.
Biographical sketch by [Mrs. James W.] Bean (1860-1943) concerns Margaret Thompson Smoot. In the sketch, Bean describes life in the early days of the Church in Missouri and Utah, including a description of Relief Society Work.

16,596. Beeching, Jane
Papers. 1915-17. 1 vol.
Open. Published guide.
LDS Church Archives.
Daybook of [Miss] "Jennie" Beeching (1855-1926) in which she gives an account of a trip to San Francisco and her life in Salt Lake City. Taken from Christy Best, *Guide to Sources for Studies of Mormon Women in the Church Archives, The Church of Jesus Christ of Latter-day Saints* (Salt Lake City: Historical Department of The Church of Jesus Christ of Latter-day Saints, 1976).

16,597. Behunin, Caroline (Hill)
Papers. Nd. 11 pp.
Open. Published guide.
LDS Church Archives.
Reminiscences of Behunin (1854-1914), in which she recounts her experiences as a missionary to the Indians in southern Utah with her husband Mosiah Steven Behunin. Taken from Christy Best, *Guide to Sources for Studies of Mormon Women in the Church Archives, The Church of Jesus Christ of Latter-day Saints* (Salt Lake City: Historical Department of The Church of Jesus Christ of Latter-day Saints, 1976).

16,598. Belnap, Della Augusta
Papers. Nd. 8 folders.
Open. Published guide.
LDS Church Archives.
Papers of [Miss] Belnap (1907-?) contain correspondence of Martha (McBride) Knight, including one letter that tells of her experiences in Nauvoo, IL, after the main body of Mormons had left, and an affidavit of Almira Knight Hanscom stating that Joseph and Hyrum Smith taught plural marriage in Nauvoo. Taken from Christy Best, *Guide to Sources for Studies of Mormon Women in the Church Archives, The Church of Jesus Christ of Latter-day Saints* (Salt Lake City: Historical Department of The Church of Jesus Christ of Latter-day Saints, 1976).

16,599. Belnap, Flora
Papers. 1902-58. 2 ft.
Open. No guide.
LDS Church Archives.
Papers of [Miss] Belnap (1884-1955), a family genealogist, include correspondence, diaries, genealogical papers, and other items.

16,600. Bench, Nancy Elvira (Cox)
Papers. Ca. 1904. 2 vols.
Open. No guide.
LDS Church Archives.
Notebooks of Bench (1882-1964) contain school work for the elementary grades, including compositions.

16,601. Bennion, Desla Slade
Papers. 1942-44. 1 vol. and 23-page item.
Open. No guide.
LDS Church Archives.
Includes a journal of Bennion, a president of the Northwestern States Mission, in which he describes activities in the Mission, including detailed reports of meetings. Also contains a biography of Amelia Eliza (Slade) Bennion, a resident of Morgan, Salt Lake City, and Taylorsville, UT.

16,602. Bentley, Mary Ann (Mansfield)
Papers. Ca. 1933. 1 vol.
Open. Published guide.
LDS Church Archives.
Reminiscences of [Mrs. William Oscar] Bentley (1859-1949), in which she describes her family's settlement in St. George, UT, and her activities there. Includes an historical sketch of the family. Taken from Christy Best, *Guide to Sources for Studies of Mormon Women in the Church Archives, The Church of Jesus Christ of Latter-day Saints* (Salt Lake City: Historical Department of The Church of Jesus Christ of Latter-day Saints, 1976).

16,603. Bery, R. E.
Papers. 1917. 3-page item.
Open. No guide.
LDS Church Archives.
Letter the auxiliaries of the Church distributed to promote seminars on infant care within the stakes, which Bery, a man who was in St. Johns, AZ, forwarded to a Sister Swap.

16,604. Bethers, Almira (Tiffany)
Papers. Nd. 1 vol.
Open. Unpublished guide.
LDS Church Archives.
Biography of [Mrs. Albert Francis] Bethers (1888-1966) concerns Sarah Jane York Tiffany and tells of her experiences in Grafton, ID, and her experiences among the Indians in Arizona from 1884 to 1906.

16,605. Bickmore, Christina (Bagley)
Papers. 1853-56. 3 items.
Open. Published guide.
LDS Church Archives.
Letters of [Mrs. William] Bickmore (1809-80) to her sister Prudence Canfield who was a non-Mormon living in the East. Two of the letters are from San Bernardino, CA, and tell of her activities there. Taken from Christy Best, *Guide to Sources for Studies of Mormon Women in the Church Archives, The Church of Jesus Christ of Latter-day Saints* (Salt Lake City: Historical Department of The Church of Jesus Christ of Latter-day Saints, 1976).

16,606. Bird, Adele Antoinette Agnes (Aegerter)
Papers. Nd. 1 vol.
Open. Unpublished guide.
LDS Church Archives.
History of [Mrs. Arthur D.] Bird (1891-1970) pertains to the Salt Lake Mission Home from 1924 to 1962 and includes an account of its establishment, directors, and curriculum. Includes photos of Mission Home personnel.

16,607. Bishop, Ellen C.
Papers. 1854. 2-page item.
Open. Published guide.
LDS Church Archives.
Letter from Bishop, who was in New Haven, CT, to Lucretia, a friend who was leaving for Utah. In the letter, she describes her activities and mentions the Mormon Church and the problems of plural marriage. Taken from Christy Best, *Guide to Sources for Studies of Mormon Women in the Church Archives, The Church of Jesus Christ of Latter-day Saints* (Salt Lake City: Historical Department of The Church of Jesus Christ of Latter-day Saints, 1976).

16,608. Booth, Lillian (Clayson)
Papers. 1956. 13 pp.
Open. Published guide.
LDS Church Archives.
Research of [Mrs. Wayne Chipman] Booth (1894-) concerns the women who served as matron, dean of women, and counselor for women at Brigham Young University from 1879 to 1956. Taken from Christy Best, *Guide to Sources for Studies of Mormon Women in the Church Archives, The Church of Jesus Christ of Latter-day Saints* (Salt Lake City: Historical Department of The Church of Jesus Christ of Latter-day Saints, 1976).

16,609. Bradshaw, Harriet Olive (Ririe)
Oral history. 1973. 31-page item.
Open. Published guide.
LDS Church Archives.
Interview with [Mrs. Richard] Bradshaw (1892-) in which she describes her family's move from Utah to Magrath in Alberta, Canada, including information about life during the settlement of southern Alberta and her activities as a Church leader in the area. Taken from Christy Best, *Guide to Sources for Studies of Mormon Women in the Church Archives, The Church of Jesus Christ of Latter-day Saints* (Salt Lake City: Historical Department of The Church of Jesus Christ of Latter-day Saints, 1976).

16,610. Brewer, Nina (Brinkerhoff)
Papers. 1962-64. 4 folders.
Open. Published guide.
LDS Church Archives.
Papers of Brewer (1908-), who is married to Leslie Odell Brewer, Central American Mission president, include letters to her parents and a diary in which she describes the proselytizing activities of the Mission in Central and South America. Taken from Christy Best, *Guide to Sources for Studies of Mormon Women in the Church Archives, The Church of Jesus Christ of Latter-day Saints* (Salt Lake City: Historical Department of The Church of Jesus Christ of Latter-day Saints, 1976).

16,611. Brienholt, Maxine (Lund)
Papers. 1958-74. 3 microfilm reels and 55 ft. of microfilm.
Open. No guide.
LDS Church Archives.
Papers of [Mrs. Harvey Cowley] Breinholt (1926-) include a journal of the Mormons aboard the ship *Luca;* autobiographies of members of Wandamere camp of the Daughters of the Utah Pioneers;

biographies of early residents of Paragonah, UT, and other early pioneers; and histories dealing with Iron County, UT, and Holden, UT.

16,612. Brodie, Fawn (McKay)
Papers. 1946-47. 2 items.
Open. No guide.
LDS Church Archives.
Consists of letters from [Mrs. Richard] Brodie (1915-), who was in New Haven, CT, to Gordon Ray Young in Los Angeles concerning her writings and future projects and to Francis W. Kirkham in Salt Lake City concerning research she was doing about early Mormon history. She enclosed an article about Joseph Smith by William D. Purple and some biographical information concerning Purple.

16,613. Brown, Harriet S.
Papers. 1846. 2 items.
Open. Published guide.
LDS Church Archives.
Letters of Brown to her family concern her travels with the Mormon Battalion during the Mexican War and the detachment that traveled from Sante Fe, NM, to Pueblo, CO. Taken from Christy Best, *Guide to Sources for Studies of Mormon Women in the Church Archives, The Church of Jesus Christ of Latter-day Saints* (Salt Lake City: Historical Department of The Church of Jesus Christ of Latter-day Saints, 1976).

16,614. Burt, Jane (Rutherford)
Oral history. 1954. 15-page item.
Open. No guide.
LDS Church Archives.
Interview with Burt in which she gives an account of her early life in Scotland, the conversion of her family to Mormonism, emigration to Utah, and her Church activities in the 6th Ward, Salt Lake Stake. Includes comments on an experience she had with David O. McKay as well as comments by her husband John H. Burt and her daughter Agnes (Burt) Van Santan.

16,615. Callister, Helen Marr (Clark)
Papers. Ca. 1878. 2-page item.
Open. Published guide.
LDS Church Archives.
Address of [Mrs. Thomas] Callister (1829-1917) in which she defends the principle of plural marriage and tells of the harmonious relationship that existed between herself and her husband's first wife. Taken from Christy Best, *Guide to Sources for Studies of Mormon Women in the Church Archives, The Church of Jesus Christ of Latter-day Saints* (Salt Lake City: Historical Department of The Church of Jesus Christ of Latter-day Saints, 1976).

16,616. Campbell, Ella
Papers. 1914. 4 pp.
Open. No guide.
LDS Church Archives.
Papers of Campbell include items concerning the early settlers of Providence, UT. Gathered from oral sources, the papers contain information about the Martin Handcart Company provided by Jane Griffiths Fullmer, a member of the Company.

16,617. Cannon, Angus Munn
Papers. 1855-1915. 4 ft.
Open. Published guide.
LDS Church Archives.
Papers of Cannon, an LDS Church leader, contain letters from his wife Martha (Hughes) Cannon (1857-1932) while she was in exile in England and San Francisco for polygamy and letters to her from family members. Taken from Christy Best, *Guide to Sources for Studies of Mormon Women in the Church Archives, The Church of Jesus Christ of Latter-day Saints* (Salt Lake City: Historical Department of The Church of Jesus Christ of Latter-day Saints, 1976).

16,618. Cannon, Clara Cordelia (Moses)
Papers. Ca. 1891-1921. 6 folders.
Open. Published guide.
LDS Church Archives.
[Mrs. Angus Munn] Cannon (1839-1926) was a counselor in the general presidency of the Primary Association. Includes letters from family members, along with a note from Emmeline B. Wells and a letter from Mary Isabella Horne. Also contains diary entries in which Cannon describes her activities, particularly in the Primary; an appointment book; genealogy; clippings; and other papers. Taken from Christy Best, *Guide to Sources for Studies of Mormon Women in the Church Archives, The Church of Jesus Christ of Latter-day Saints* (Salt Lake City: Historical Department of The Church of Jesus Christ of Latter-day Saints, 1976).

16,619. Capener, Clara (Oyler), and Last, Hettie Mildred (Leavitt)
Papers. 1898-1942. 20 ft. of microfilm.
Open. Published guide.
LDS Church Archives.
Scrapbook of [Mrs. Samuel William] Capener (1891-) and [Mrs. Charles Henry] Last (1898-) contains a history of the Garland Ward Relief Society in Garland, UT. Taken from Christy Best, *Guide to Sources for Studies of Mormon Women in the Church Archives, The Church of Jesus Christ of Latter-day Saints* (Salt Lake City: Historical Department of The Church of Jesus Christ of Latter-day Saints, 1976).

16,620. Card, Zina Priscenda (Young)
Papers. 1876-1931. 1 folder and 4 items.
Open. Unpublished guide.
LDS Church Archives.
Papers of [Mrs. Charles Ora] Card (1850-1931), a daughter of Brigham Young, include letters to the First Presidency of the Mormon Church, concerning her activities in the Church; from [Mrs.] Emmeline B. Wells and [Mrs.] Zina Y. Williams to President Rutherford B. Hayes, concerning plural marriage in Utah and government actions against the Mormons; and to Karl G. Maeser, concerning material being prepared for the ladies department of the Church schools. Also includes a transcript of funeral services for Card, including talks by Susa Gates, George F. Richards, President Heber J. Grant, and others.

16,621. Chamberlain, Genevieve
Papers. Ca. 1924. 5-page item.
Open. No guide.
LDS Church Archives.
Papers of Chamberlain (1905-) consist of a summary of the life of her grandmother Kezia (Giles) Carroll (1840-1927), who was the wife of Charles N. Carroll.

16,622. Cheney, Alice (Cannon)
Papers. 1916-33. 3 items.
Open. No guide.
LDS Church Archives.
Correspondence of [Mrs. Joseph LeRoy] Cheney (1882-1967) includes letters from family members.

16,623. Clapp, Harriet Cecelia (Snow)
Papers. Ca. 1908-29. 2 folders.
Open. Published guide.
LDS Church Archives.
Papers of [Mrs. Elisha Drown] Clapp (1861-1937) include diaries in which she gives accounts of her travels and activities in Logan, UT, as well as a notebook containing family genealogy. Taken from Christy Best, *Guide to Sources for Studies of Mormon Women in the Church Archives, The Church of Jesus Christ of Latter-day Saints* (Salt Lake City: Historical Department of The Church of Jesus Christ of Latter-day Saints, 1976).

16,624. Clark, Joshua Reuben, and Clark, Mary Louisa (Woolley)
Papers. Nd. 1 vol.
Open. No guide.
LDS Church Archives.
Includes correspondence, diaries, and notes of the Clarks concerning their activities in Grantsville, UT.

16,625. Clawson, Margaret Gay (Judd)
Papers. 1904-11. 3 folders.
Open. Published guide.
LDS Church Archives.
Reminiscences of [Mrs. Hiram Bradley] Clawson (1831-1912), in which she describes her childhood in New York and Nauvoo, IL; emigration to Utah; her move south during the Utah war; family incidents in Salt Lake City; and other events. Also includes memoirs of her participation in dramatics productions and in the Society of Eighty-Eight, a social group. Taken from Christy Best, *Guide to Sources for Studies of Mormon Women in the Church Archives, The Church of Jesus Christ of Latter-day Saints* (Salt Lake City: Historical Department of The Church of Jesus Christ of Latter-day Saints, 1976).

16,626. Clayson, William Argent
Papers. 1899-1940. 1 ft. and 2 microfilm reels.
Open. Register.
LDS Church Archives.
Clayson (1873-1901), a Mormon missionary who died while working in the Eastern States Mission, was married to Annie Romney Clayson (1879-1955), who lived in the Mexican colonies. Includes correspondence between the Claysons; his diary, at the end of which Annie Clayson discusses her feelings about his death; and his notebook.

16,627. Clement, Loretta
Papers. 1844-46. 6 items.
Open. Published guide.
LDS Church Archives.
Letters from [Miss] Clement to her family in Nauvoo, IL, in which she gives information about their mutual friends in Dryden, NY. Taken from Christy Best, *Guide to Sources for Studies of Mormon Women in the Church Archives, The Church of Jesus Christ of Latter-day Saints* (Salt Lake City: Historical Department of The Church of Jesus Christ of Latter-day Saints, 1976).

16,628. Cluff, Sarah (Eggertsen)
Papers. 1893-1936. 1 vol.
Open. Published guide.
LDS Church Archives.
Notebook of [Mrs. Harvey Harris] Cluff (1858-1944) contains letters of condolence upon the death of her son, diary entries for 1893, an account of flax growing, items relating to family matters, and clippings. Taken from Christy Best, *Guide to Sources for Studies of Mormon Women in the Church Archives, The Church of Jesus Christ of Latter-day Saints* (Salt Lake City: Historical Department of The Church of Jesus Christ of Latter-day Saints, 1976).

16,629. Coles, Ida B.
Papers. 1914. 2-page item.
Open. Published guide.
LDS Church Archives.
Letter from Coles in Chautauqua, NY, to a Mrs. Marriott contains references to her defense of the Mormon Church while on the Chautauqua lecture circuit. Taken from Christy Best, *Guide to Sources for Studies of Mormon Women in the Church Archives, The Church of Jesus Christ of Latter-day Saints* (Salt Lake City: Historical Department of The Church of Jesus Christ of Latter-day Saints, 1976).

16,630. Collins, Hannah (Daggett)
Papers. 1872-75. 1 vol.
Open. Published guide.

LDS Church Archives.
Notebook of Collins (1802-?) contains correspondence with her sons, notes, original poetry, and biographical information. Taken from Christy Best, *Guide to Sources for Studies of Mormon Women in the Church Archives, The Church of Jesus Christ of Latter-day Saints* (Salt Lake City: Historical Department of The Church of Jesus Christ of Latter-day Saints, 1976).

16,631. Cook, Nancy Smith
Papers. 1936-37. 1 vol.
Open. Published guide.
LDS Church Archives.
Diary in which Cook describes her daily activities in Lovell, WY. Taken from Christy Best, *Guide to Sources for Studies of Mormon Women in the Church Archives, The Church of Jesus Christ of Latter-day Saints* (Salt Lake City: Historical Department of The Church of Jesus Christ of Latter-day Saints, 1976).

16,632. Coolbrith, Ina Donna
Papers. 1857-1927. 4 folders.
Open. Published guide.
LDS Church Archives.
Papers of Coolbrith (1841-1928) include correspondence with her cousin Church president Joseph F. Smith concerning family matters and Mormonism; poetry, much of it in her handwriting; and clippings of her published works. Taken from Christy Best, *Guide to Sources for Studies of Mormon Women in the Church Archives, The Church of Jesus Christ of Latter-day Saints* (Salt Lake City: Historical Department of The Church of Jesus Christ of Latter-day Saints, 1976).

16,633. Coombs, Isiah Moses
Papers. 1835-1938. 4 ft. and 6 microfilm reels.
Open. Register.
LDS Church Archives.
Coombs (1834-86) was a schoolteacher in Payson, UT. Includes correspondence; diaries in which he describes his proselytizing missions in the eastern states and Great Britain, his life in Salt Lake City and Payson, and his association with the Polysophical Society; addresses; accounts of Indian problems; poetry; notebooks; and clippings. Contains correspondence with his polygamous wives Sarah Agnes Turk Coombs, Fanny McLean Coombs, and Charlotte August Hardy Coombs, as well as with his sister Mary (Coombs) Pendleton.

16,634. Coombs, Sarah Ellis (Day)
Papers. 1960-68. 1 vol.
Open. Published guide.
LDS Church Archives.
Autobiography of [Mrs. Leslie McLean] Coombs (1883-), in which she gives an account of her early life in Sanpete County, UT, teaching in Utah schools, and her experiences in Alberta, Canada, and Colonia Juarez, Mexico. Taken from Christy Best, *Guide to Sources for Studies of Mormon Women in the Church Archives, The Church of Jesus Christ of Latter-day Saints* (Salt Lake City: Historical Department of The Church of Jesus Christ of Latter-day Saints, 1976).

16,635. Coray, Martha Jane (Knowlton)
Papers. 1873-78. 5 vols.
Open. Published guide.
LDS Church Archives.
[Mrs. Howard] Coray (1821-81) was a schoolteacher, a member of the board of directors at Brigham Young Academy, and an acquaintance of Joseph and Hyrum Smith. Consists of diaries in which she describes her activities while she was living on a farm near Provo, UT. Taken from Christy Best, *Guide to Sources for Studies of Mormon Women in the Church Archives, The Church of Jesus Christ of Latter-day Saints* (Salt Lake City: Historical Department of The Church of Jesus Christ of Latter-day Saints, 1976).

16,636. Covey, Almira (Mack)
Papers. 1835-44. 5 items.
Open. Published guide.
LDS Church Archives.
Correspondence of [Mrs. Benjamin] Covey (1805-86), a cousin of Joseph Smith, in which she recounts incidents related to the Church in Missouri, Illinois, and Iowa. One letter deals with Joseph Smith's death. Taken from Christy Best, *Guide to Sources for Studies of Mormon Women in the Church Archives, The Church of Jesus Christ of Latter-day Saints* (Salt Lake City: Historical Department of The Church of Jesus Christ of Latter-day Saints, 1976).

16,637. Cowdery, Patience (Simonds)
Papers. 1849-51. 1 vol.
Open. Published guide.
LDS Church Archives.
Diary in which [Mrs. Warren F.] Cowdery (1794-1862) describes her activities in Kirtland, OH. Taken from Christy Best, *Guide to Sources for Studies of Mormon Women in the Church Archives, The Church of Jesus Christ of Latter-day Saints* (Salt Lake City: Historical Department of The Church of Jesus Christ of Latter-day Saints, 1976).

16,638. Cowley, Abigail "Abbie" (Hyde)
Papers. Ca. 1874-1946. 4 folders.
Open. Published guide.
LDS Church Archives.
Papers of Cowley (1863-1931) include letters to her husband Church leader Matthias Foss Cowley and her son Moses F. Cowley as well as reminiscences and a diary in which she describes the lives of her mother and father, her marriage, and her family life. Also includes articles and certificates. Taken from Christy Best, *Guide to Sources for Studies of Mormon Women in the Church Archives, The Church of Jesus Christ of Latter-day Saints* (Salt Lake City: Historical Department of The Church of Jesus Christ of Latter-day Saints, 1976).

16,639. Cox, Martha (Cragun)
Papers. 1928-30. 1 vol.
Open. Published guide.
LDS Church Archives.
Papers of [Mrs. Isaiah] Cox (1852-?), an early teacher in Utah and Nevada, include correspondence; reminiscences of her life in southern Utah, the Muddy Valley, Nevada, and Mexico; accounts of Joseph Smith told to her by others; and family history. Taken from Christy Best, *Guide to Sources for Studies of Mormon Women in the Church Archives, The Church of Jesus Christ of Latter-day Saints* (Salt Lake City: Historical Department of The Church of Jesus Christ of Latter-day Saints, 1976).

16,640. Crandall, Eva (Maeser)
Oral history. 1964. 104-page transcript.
Open. Published guide.
LDS Church Archives.
Interview with [Mrs. Myron E.] Crandall (1876-1967), a daughter of educator Karl G. Maeser, concerns her father, the Brigham Young Academy, and teachers and students she remembered from the Academy. Taken from Christy Best, *Guide to Sources for Studies of Mormon Women in the Church Archives, The Church of Jesus Christ of Latter-day Saints* (Salt Lake City: Historical Department of The Church of Jesus Christ of Latter-day Saints, 1976).

16,641. Crawford, Vesta Maude (Pierce)
Papers. Nd. 3 microfilm reels.
Open. Published guide.
LDS Church Archives.
Papers of [Mrs. Arthur Lorenzo] Crawford (1899-) include correspondence; a rough draft of a biography; extracts from articles concerning polygamy, Nauvoo, IL, and Emma Smith, the wife of Church founder Joseph Smith; notes on Smith family members; and photos. Also includes a biography of Emma Smith's early life, which was compiled by Fay Ollerton. Taken from Christy Best, *Guide to Sources for Studies of Mormon Women in the Church Archives, The Church of Jesus Christ of Latter-day Saints* (Salt Lake City: Historical Department of The Church of Jesus Christ of Latter-day Saints, 1976).

16,642. Crockett, Ruth (Clarkson)
Papers. 1913-34. 40 ft. of microfilm.
Open. Unpublished guide.
LDS Church Archives.
Diaries of [Mrs. Ozro O.] Crockett (1857-1947) in which she describes her activities in Preston and Marsh Valley, ID.

16,643. Crosby, Caroline (Barnes)
Papers. 1851-82. 2 microfilm reels.
Open. Published guide.
LDS Church Archives.
Diary and memoirs of [Mrs. Jonathan] Crosby (1807-83) contain autobiographical notes, including mention of her life in Kirtland and Nauvoo, IL, as well as an account of her experiences with her husband in the Society Islands Mission, San Bernardino, CA, and San Francisco; their return to Utah; and her life there. Taken from Christy Best, *Guide to Sources for Studies of Mormon Women in the Church Archives, The Church of Jesus Christ of Latter-day Saints* (Salt Lake City: Historical Department of The Church of Jesus Christ of Latter-day Saints, 1976).

16,644. Crosby, Hannah Adelia (Bunker)
Papers. Nd. 1 vol.
Open. Published guide.
LDS Church Archives.
Reminiscences of [Mrs. Samuel Obed] Crosby (1853-1932), in which she gives an account of her activities in Toquerville, Santa Clara, and Panguitch, UT, and in Bunkerville, NV. Includes a tribute from her daughters. Taken from Christy Best, *Guide to Sources for Studies of Mormon Women in the Church Archives, The Church of Jesus Christ of Latter-day Saints* (Salt Lake City: Historical Department of The Church of Jesus Christ of Latter-day Saints, 1976).

16,645. Curtis, Bardella (Shipp)
Papers. Ca. 1942. 3 folders.
Open. Published guide.
LDS Church Archives.
Papers of [Mrs. Theodore E.] Curtis (1874-1957) include her autobiography and a manuscript for her book *Sacred Scriptures and Religious Philosophy.* Taken from Christy Best, *Guide to Sources for Studies of Mormon Women in the Church Archives, The Church of Jesus Christ of Latter-day Saints* (Salt Lake City: Historical Department of The Church of Jesus Christ of Latter-day Saints, 1976).

16,646. Curtis, Sarah Wells (Hartley)
Papers. Nd. 6-page item.
Open. No guide.
LDS Church Archives.
Account of the life of [Mrs. Lyman] Curtis (1836-1921), who was a handcart pioneer and early Utah resident. Before her marriage to Curtis, she was married to Richard Soper.

16,647. Dalton, Luella (Adams)
Papers. 1955. 11 pp.
Open. No guide.
LDS Church Archives.
Papers of [Mrs. Harley Warren] Dalton (1889-1967) concern pioneer life in Parowan, UT, and include information about social activities, the Sunday school, and education.

16,648. Daughters of the Utah Pioneers
Records. 1885-1967. 1 vol., 5 items, and 7 microfilm reels.
Open. No guide.
LDS Church Archives.
Includes correspondence, personal writings, financial and legal papers, clippings, and ephemera of Alice Ann Paxman McCune, a resident of Nephi, UT, and a member of the Daughters. Contains letters from her future husband about his mission in Samoa and letters from her daughter in the Eastern States Mission; biographies of Utah pioneers; a history the Daughters prepared about the founding and growth of Huntsville, UT, including a list of some of the town's early residents, 1933; a scrapbook of Myrtle R. Goff, chairman of the Battle Creek Monument Committee, which contains information on the Daughters' erection of the monument at Battle Creek, ID, 1926-32; a history of Camp G of the Daughters in Weber County, UT, by Clara Farr and Ella G. Shupe, 1935; a paper Josephine J. Miles read at a meeting of the St. George, UT, chapter of the Daughters, 1923; a history of Camp 10 of the Daughters by Ella Duncan Morris, which records the beginning of the organization and contains minutes, 1933; and papers of Alice Miller Pickering concerning the organization of Camp 10 of the Daughters and its subsequent history, 1923.

16,649. Davis, Jane (Brough)
Papers. 1853-1900. 4 items.
Open. Published guide.
LDS Church Archives.
Letters from [Mrs. William] Davis (1820-1908), a resident of Ogden, UT, to her family in England, in which she describes Utah, Mormonism, and her attitude toward plural marriage. Taken from Christy Best, *Guide to Sources for Studies of Mormon Women in the Church Archives, The Church of Jesus Christ of Latter-day Saints* (Salt Lake City: Historical Department of The Church of Jesus Christ of Latter-day Saints, 1976).

16,650. Day, Elvira Euphrasia (Cox)
Papers. 1889-1934. 15 ft. of microfilm.
Open. Published guide.
LDS Church Archives.
Diary of [Mrs. Eli Azariah] Day (1864-1944) concerns life in Fairview, UT. Also includes poetry and short stories written by Day. Taken from Christy Best, *Guide to Sources for Studies of Mormon Women in the Church Archives, The Church of Jesus Christ of Latter-day Saints* (Salt Lake City: Historical Department of The Church of Jesus Christ of Latter-day Saints, 1976).

16,651. Dillman, Mildred Myrtle (Miles)
Papers. 1947-56. 14 folders.
Open. Published guide.
LDS Church Archives.
Papers of Dillman (1893-), the wife of Ray Eugene Dillman, president of the Western States Mission and of the Hawaiian Temple, include correspondence, a diary of her activities in Hawaii, a journal concerning missionaries' experiences in the western states, notebooks, and a photo album. Taken from Christy Best, *Guide to Sources for Studies of Mormon Women in the Church Archives, The Church of Jesus Christ of Latter-day Saints* (Salt Lake City: Historical Department of The Church of Jesus Christ of Latter-day Saints, 1976).

16,652. Dorius, Anne Maria (Stalleson)
Papers. 1877-96. 6 items.
Open. No guide.
LDS Church Archives.
Correspondence of [Mrs. John F. F.] Dorius (1857-1939) includes letters from her husband, who was on a mission in Scandinavia, and from a friend concerning family news and genealogy.

16,653. Dowdle, John Clark
Papers. Ca. 1884-1920. 60 ft. of microfilm.
Open. No guide.
LDS Church Archives.
Autobiographies and diaries of Dowdle (1836-?) in which he recounts early experiences in the Church and activities in Willard and Millville, UT. Includes a sketch of his wife Mary Ann (Chandler) Dowdle (1847-1929) written by Hannah C. Dowdle in 1920.

16,654. Driggs, Alice Nevada (Watson)
Oral history. 1975. 38-page item.
Open. No guide.
LDS Church Archives.
Interview with [Mrs. Burton] Driggs (1891-1976) in which she describes her early life in a plural family, her marriage, and the work that she and her husband did in training the deaf in California, North Dakota, and Idaho.

16,655. Driggs, Olive Russell (Harrington)
Papers. 1884-93. 12-page item.
Open. Published guide.
LDS Church Archives.
Journal of [Mrs. Benjamin Woodbury] Driggs (1861-93) in which she describes her activities as a young mother in Pleasant Grove, UT. Taken from Christy Best, *Guide to Sources for Studies of Mormon Women in the Church Archives, The Church of Jesus Christ of Latter-day Saints* (Salt Lake City: Historical Department of The Church of Jesus Christ of Latter-day Saints, 1976).

16,656. Dusenberry, Harriet Knowlton Virginia (Coray)
Papers. 1863-64. 1 vol.
Open. Published guide.
LDS Church Archives.
Diary in which [Mrs. Wilson Howard] Dusenberry (1846-72) gives an account of her activities as a young woman in Provo, UT. Taken from Christy Best, *Guide to Sources for Studies of Mormon Women in the Church Archives, The Church of Jesus Christ of Latter-day Saints* (Salt Lake City: Historical Department of The Church of Jesus Christ of Latter-day Saints, 1976).

16,657. Eldredge, Leila (Moss)
Papers. 1958. 1 vol.
Open. Published guide.
LDS Church Archives.
Volume of [Mrs. Clarence] Eldredge (1895-1962) contains an account of the development of local relief societies in Bountiful, UT. The societies were made up of women who studied religion and gave aid to each other and to the poor. Before her marriage to Clarence Eldredge, Leila Eldredge had been married to Horace J. Grant and then to John E. Lee. See Christy Best, *Guide to Sources for Studies of Mormon Women in the Church Archives, The Church of Jesus Christ of Latter-day Saints* (Salt Lake City: Historical Department of The Church of Jesus Christ of Latter-day Saints, 1976).

16,658. Ellsworth, Emma Augusta (Anderson)
Papers. Nd. 1 microfilm reel.
Open. Published guide.
LDS Church Archives.
Papers of Ellsworth (1894-1969) include scrapbooks that outline her activities and those of her family. Also contains items concerning her husband German Edgar Ellsworth and the Northern States Mission as well as a collection of talks given by Church leaders. Taken from Christy Best, *Guide to Sources for Studies of Mormon Women in the Church Archives, The Church of Jesus Christ of Latter-day Saints* (Salt Lake City: Historical Department of The Church of Jesus Christ of Latter-day Saints, 1976).

16,659. Emmeline B. Wells Centennial Memorial Committee
Records. 1928. 1 folder.
Open. No guide.
LDS Church Archives.
Financial report and memorial programs of the Committee, of which Jane W. Skolfield was chairman.

16,660. Equal Rights Amendment
Collection. 1975. 1 tape.
Open. No guide.
LDS Church Archives.
Videotape of a television program in which four women Church members discuss their reasons for supporting or opposing the ERA.

16,661. Erickson, Hilda (Andersson)
Oral history. 1966. 46-page item.
Open. Published guide.
LDS Church Archives.
Interview with [Mrs. John A.] Erickson (1859-1968) in which she gives an account of her life in Tooele County, UT, including her activities at the Church Indian farm at Deep Creek and her memories of Brigham Young and her emigration to Utah. Taken from Christy Best, *Guide to Sources for Studies of Mormon Women in the Church Archives, The Church of Jesus Christ of Latter-day Saints* (Salt Lake City: Historical Department of The Church of Jesus Christ of Latter-day Saints, 1976).

16,662. Ertmann, Anna E.
Papers. Ca. 1936. 27-page item.
Open. Published guide.
LDS Church Archives.
An outline of the history of the Wilford Ward Primary in Wilford, UT, from 1900 to 1935. Taken from Christy Best, *Guide to Sources for Studies of Mormon Women in the Church Archives, The Church of Jesus Christ of Latter-day Saints* (Salt Lake City: Historical Department of The Church of Jesus Christ of Latter-day Saints, 1976).

16,663. Evans, Priscilla (Livingston)
Papers. 1945-49. 4 vols.
Open. Published guide.
LDS Church Archives.
Daybooks of [Mrs. Frank] Evans (1881-1957), a member of the Relief Society general board of the Church, include an account of her activities. Taken from Christy Best, *Guide to Sources for Studies of Mormon Women in the Church Archives, The Church of Jesus Christ of Latter-day Saints* (Salt Lake City: Historical Department of The Church of Jesus Christ of Latter-day Saints, 1976).

16,664. Evans, Priscilla (Merriman)
Papers. Ca. 1914. 25-page item.
Open. Published guide.
LDS Church Archives.
Autobiography of [Mrs. Thomas David] Evans (1835-1914) in which she describes her early life in Wales, emigration to Utah, settlement in Spanish Fork, and work with the Relief Society of the Church. Taken from Christy Best, *Guide to Sources for Studies of Mormon Women in the Church Archives, The Church of Jesus Christ of Latter-day Saints* (Salt Lake City: Historical Department of The Church of Jesus Christ of Latter-day Saints, 1976).

16,665. Farley, Angelina (Calkins)
Papers. 1846-88. 15 ft. of microfilm.
Open. Published guide.
LDS Church Archives.
Diaries of [Mrs. Winthrop] Farley (1818-1900) in which she describes her life in Illinois, her journey across the plains to Utah, and her unhappy experiences while living in plural marriage. Taken from Christy Best, *Guide to Sources for Studies of*

Mormon Women in the Church Archives, The Church of Jesus Christ of Latter-day Saints (Salt Lake City: Historical Department of The Church of Jesus Christ of Latter-day Saints, 1976).

16,666. Faust, Elsie Ann (Akerley)
Papers. 1871-73. 1 vol.
Open. Published guide.
LDS Church Archives.
Diary of [Mrs. Henry Jacob] Faust (1842-83) in which she gives an account of her trip to Europe with her husband. Taken from Christy Best, *Guide to Sources for Studies of Mormon Women in the Church Archives, The Church of Jesus Christ of Latter-day Saints* (Salt Lake City: Historical Department of The Church of Jesus Christ of Latter-day Saints, 1976).

16,667. Felt, Louie (Bouton)
Papers. Nd. 2-page item.
Open. Published guide.
LDS Church Archives.
Reminiscence of [Mrs. Joseph H.] Felt (1850-1928) concerns her call as general president of the Primary by Eliza R. Snow, Presendia Kimball, and Zina D. H. Young. Taken from Christy Best, *Guide to Sources for Studies of Mormon Women in the Church Archives, The Church of Jesus Christ of Latter-day Saints* (Salt Lake City: Historical Department of The Church of Jesus Christ of Latter-day Saints, 1976).

16,668. Field, Kate
Papers. 1886. 33-page item.
Open. Published guide.
LDS Church Archives.
Lecture [Miss] Field (1838-96), a non-Mormon, gave in Washington, DC, denouncing Mormonism and polygamy. Taken from Christy Best, *Guide to Sources for Studies of Mormon Women in the Church Archives, The Church of Jesus Christ of Latter-day Saints* (Salt Lake City: Historical Department of The Church of Jesus Christ of Latter-day Saints, 1976).

16,669. Flake, Lucy Hannah (White)
Papers. 1894-1900. 3 vols.
Open. Published guide.
LDS Church Archives.
Reminiscences and diaries of [Mrs. William Jordan] Flake (1842-1900) in which she describes her activities in Snowflake, AZ. Includes family genealogy and poetry. Taken from Christy Best, *Guide to Sources for Studies of Mormon Women in the Church Archives, The Church of Jesus Christ of Latter-day Saints* (Salt Lake City: Historical Department of The Church of Jesus Christ of Latter-day Saints, 1976).

16,670. Ford, Maria (Bidgood)
Papers. 1888-1919. 1 vol.
Open. Published guide.
LDS Church Archives.
Notebook of [Mrs. Robert Henry] Ford (1832-?), in which she gives an account of a journey to England in 1888, includes sporadic diary entries for 1891, 1892, and 1919. Also includes family genealogy, notes, and information about her first husband William Jarman, who was anti-Morman. Taken from Christy Best, *Guide to Sources for Studies of Mormon Women in the Church Archives, The Church of Jesus Christ of Latter-day Saints* (Salt Lake City: Historical Department of The Church of Jesus Christ of Latter-day Saints, 1976).

16,671. Fowler, Mary Susannah Sumner (Fackrell)
Papers. 1899-1900. 1 vol.
Open. Published guide.
LDS Church Archives.
Diary in which [Mrs. Henry Ammon] Fowler (1862-1920), a resident of Huntington, UT, describes her family, church, and community activities. Taken from Christy Best, *Guide to Sources for Studies of Mormon Women in the Church Archives, The Church of Jesus Christ of Latter-day Saints* (Salt Lake City: Historical Department of The Church of Jesus Christ of Latter-day Saints, 1976).

16,672. Fraser, Elizabeth (Ramsay)
Papers. 1887-95. 1 vol.
Open. Published guide.
LDS Church Archives.
Diary in which [Mrs. George] Fraser (1857-1924) gives an account of her daily life in Richfield, UT. Taken from Christy Best, *Guide to Sources for Studies of Mormon Women in the Church Archives, The Church of Jesus Christ of Latter-day Saints* (Salt Lake City: Historical Department of The Church of Jesus Christ of Latter-day Saints, 1976).

16,673. Freeze, Leila "Lillie" (Tuckett)
Papers. 1886-1928. 32 items.
Open. Published guide.
LDS Church Archives.
[Mrs. James Perry] Freeze (1855-1937) was a member of the general board of the Primary Association of the Church. Contains correspondence dealing with the Primary, including letters from Emmeline B. Wells and Louie B. Felt; personal writings; and mementos. Taken from Christy Best, *Guide to Sources for Studies of Mormon Women in the Church Archives, The Church of Jesus Christ of Latter-day Saints* (Salt Lake City: Historical Department of The Church of Jesus Christ of Latter-day Saints, 1976).

16,674. Fullmer, Desdemona Wadsworth
Papers. Ca. 1868-81. 2 folders.
Open. Published guide.
LDS Church Archives.
Papers of [Miss] Fullmer (1809-86) include an autobiography concerning her conversion to the Church and troubles in Kirtland, OH, and in Missouri as well as statements of her spiritual experiences. Taken from Christy Best, *Guide to Sources for Studies of Mormon Women in the Church Archives, The Church of Jesus Christ of Latter-day Saints* (Salt Lake City: Historical Department of The Church of Jesus Christ of Latter-day Saints, 1976).

16,675. Fullmer, Rhoda Ann (Marvin)
Papers. 1885. 1 vol.
Open. Published guide.
LDS Church Archives.
Reminiscences of [Mrs. David] Fullmer (1813-92) in which she describes her experiences in Missouri and in Nauvoo, IL; crossing the plains to Utah; and other events. Taken from Christy Best, *Guide to Sources for Studies of Mormon Women in the Church Archives, The Church of Jesus Christ of Latter-day Saints* (Salt Lake City: Historical Department of The Church of Jesus Christ of Latter-day Saints, 1976).

16,676. Funeral Services
Collection. 1915-70. 1 vol., 8 items, 2 tapes, and 8 recording discs.
Open. No guide.
LDS Church Archives.
Includes an account of the funeral service and life of Sister Margaret Storey; eulogies president Heber J. Grant and Susa (Young) Gates gave at the service for Sister Zina (Young) Card; eulogies George D. Pyper and George Q. Cannon gave at the service for Edna Wells Sloan, 1935; an account of the eulogies given at the funeral of Sister Gladys Nielsen Smith; an account of the eulogies given at the funeral of Zina Robison Kirkham, 1941; a transcript of the talks, prayers, and musical numbers at the funeral of Mary Field Garner; eulogies given at the services for Lillie Fagergren Kammerman; a recording of the services of Louise Yates Robison; a recording of the services for May Anderson; eulogies Harold W. Langton and George Albert Smith gave at the funeral of Josephine Groesbeck Smith, a wife of John Henry Smith; an address David O. McKay gave at the services for Ruth Middlemiss Peterson; a phonotape of the services for Emma Ray Riggs McKay; and a phonotape of the services for Jessie Evans Smith, 1971.

16,677. Gardner, Bernella Elizabeth (Snow)
Papers. Ca. 1882-1950. 6 folders.
Open. Published guide.
LDS Church Archives.
Papers of [Mrs. Robert Berry] Gardner (1866-1952) include reminiscences and diaries in which she outlines her family history, summarizes her early life, and describes her activities in southern Utah, particularly in Pine Valley. Includes notebooks containing theology notes and sewing instructions. Taken from Christy Best, *Guide to Sources for Studies of Mormon Women in the Church Archives, The Church of Jesus Christ of Latter-day Saints* (Salt Lake City: Historical Department of The Church of Jesus Christ of Latter-day Saints, 1976).

16,678. Gardner, Leonora (Cannon)
Papers. 1892-1924. 10 ft. of microfilm.
Open. Published guide.
LDS Church Archives.
Diary in which [Mrs. Robert] Gardner (1840-1924) describes her daily activities in southern Utah, especially in Pine Valley. Taken from Christy Best, *Guide to Sources for Studies of Mormon Women in the Church Archives, The Church of Jesus Christ of Latter-day Saints* (Salt Lake City: Historical Department of The Church of Jesus Christ of Latter-day Saints, 1976).

16,679. Garlick, Elizabeth Rebecca (Rawson)
Papers. 1933. 9-page item.
Open. Published guide.
LDS Church Archives.
Papers of [Mrs. Joseph Elsbury] Garlick (1873-1961) consist of a history of Farr West, UT, with notes on the organization of the West Harrisville Relief Society. Taken from Christy Best, *Guide to Sources for Studies of Mormon Women in the Church Archives, The Church of Jesus Christ of Latter-day Saints* (Salt Lake City: Historical Department of The Church of Jesus Christ of Latter-day Saints, 1976).

16,680. Garner, Mary (Field)
Papers. Nd. 5-page item.
Open. Published guide.
LDS Church Archives.
Writings of Garner (1836-1943) in which she recounts her early experiences in Nauvoo, IL. Garner was married to William Garner, Jr. Taken from Christy Best, *Guide to Sources for Studies of Mormon Women in the Church Archives, The Church of Jesus Christ of Latter-day Saints* (Salt Lake City: Historical Department of The Church of Jesus Christ of Latter-day Saints, 1976).

16,681. Gates, Susa Amelia (Young)
Papers. 1842-1929. 3.5 ft.
Open. Published guide.
LDS Church Archives.
Gates (1856-1933) was the daughter of Brigham Young. Includes correspondence, manuscripts, and printed matter dealing with her duties and interests in the Young Ladies Mutual Improvement Association, the Relief Society general board, the National Council of Women, and the Genealogical Society. Gates was married first to Alma Bailey Dunford and then to Jacob Forsberry Gates. See Christy Best, *Guide to Sources for Studies of Mormon Women in the Church Archives, The Church of Jesus Christ of Latter-day Saints* (Salt Lake City: Historical Department of The Church of Jesus Christ of Latter-day Saints, 1976).

16,682. Goddard, Elizabeth (Harrison)
Papers. Ca. 1879-81. 3 folders.
Open. Published guide.
LDS Church Archives.
Papers of [Mrs. George] Goddard (1815-1907) include an autobiography and a diary in which she gives an account of her experiences while crossing the plains and of her daily activities. Also includes an autograph book containing poetry and signatures. Taken from Christy Best, *Guide to Sources for Studies of Mormon Women in the Church Archives, The Church of Jesus Christ of Latter-day Saints* (Salt Lake City: Historical Department of The Church of Jesus Christ of Latter-day Saints, 1976).

16,683. Gold, Edith Annie (Benfell)
Papers. 1964-75. 22-page item.
Open. Published guide.
LDS Church Archives.
Autobiography of [Mrs. Cyrus Williams] Gold (1893-) in which she describes her early life in England and activities in Salt Lake City. Includes an appendix written in 1975. Taken from Christy Best, *Guide to Sources for Studies of Mormon Women in the Church Archives, The Church of Jesus Christ of Latter-day Saints* (Salt Lake City: Historical Department of The Church of Jesus Christ of Latter-day Saints, 1976).

16,684. Gordon, Margaret Elizabeth (Schutt)
Papers. 1954. 47-page item.
Open. Published guide.
LDS Church Archives.
Autobiographical account of [Mrs. James Frater] Gordon (1866-1966) concerns her life as a daughter of an Episcopal missionary, Mormon convert, pioneer in Canada, and genealogical worker in the California Mission. Taken from Christy Best, *Guide to Sources for Studies of Mormon Women in the Church Archives, The Church of Jesus Christ of Latter-day Saints* (Salt Lake City: Historical Department of The Church of Jesus Christ of Latter-day Saints, 1976).

16,685. Grant, Susan Fairchild (Noble)
Papers. 1886-96. 1 vol.
Open. Published guide.
LDS Church Archives.
Journal in which [Mrs. Jedediah Morgan] Grant (1832-1914) describes her activities as Relief Society president of the Davis Stake. Includes items concerning conferences and meetings she attended. The Davis Stake, like other similar stakes, was an ecclesiastical Mormon Church unit that included several congregations. See Christy Best, *Guide to Sources for Studies of Mormon Women in the Church Archives, The Church of Jesus Christ of Latter-day Saints* (Salt Lake City: Historical Department of The Church of Jesus Christ of Latter-day Saints, 1976).

16,686. Greenwood, Annie Pike
Papers. Ca. 1945. 1.5 ft.
Open. Published guide.
LDS Church Archives.
Greenwood (1880-1956) was a non-Mormon author. Contains the manuscript for her book *Too Many Wives,* which concerns the history of the Gardner and Snow families within the framework of Church history. Includes correspondence relating to research on the book, autobiographical information, and clippings. Taken from Christy Best, *Guide to Sources for Studies of Mormon Women in the Church Archives, The Church of Jesus Christ of Latter-day Saints* (Salt Lake City: Historical Department of The Church of Jesus Christ of Latter-day Saints, 1976).

16,687. Hale, Olive (Boynton)
Papers. 1841. 1 item.
Open. No guide.
LDS Church Archives.
Letter of Hale (1805-46), the wife of Bishop Jonathan Harriman Hale, written from New Liberty, IL, to Jonathan Hale's mother Martha Harriman Hale in Bradford, MA, in which she gives news of her household and mentions the condition of the Latter-day Saints in Missouri and Illinois.

16,688. Hanscom, Almira (Knight)
Papers. 1908. 1-page item.
Open. Unpublished guide.
LDS Church Archives.
Affidavit of Hanscom (1827-1912) states that Joseph and Hyrum Smith taught plural marriage in Nauvoo, IL, and that the Partridge sisters tried to convince her to accept the concept. She left the Church at that time. Before her marriage to George Hanscom, Almira Hanscom was married to Sylvester V. Stoddard.

16,689. Hansen, Mae
Papers. Nd. 2-page item.
Open. Published guide.
LDS Church Archives.
Consists of a history of the Evans Young Ladies Mutual Improvement Association, which was organized in 1923. Taken from Christy Best, *Guide to Sources for Studies of Mormon Women in the Church Archives, The Church of Jesus Christ of Latter-day Saints* (Salt Lake City: Historical Department of The Church of Jesus Christ of Latter-day Saints, 1976).

16,690. Harris, Eunice Polly (Stewart)
Papers. 1932. 1 vol.
Open. Published guide.
LDS Church Archives.
Autobiography of [Mrs. Dennison Emer] Harris (1860-1942) in which she recounts her childhood experiences and later activities in the Mexican colonies and in Cardston in Alberta, Canada. Includes family genealogy. Taken from Christy Best, *Guide to Sources for Studies of Mormon Women in the Church Archives, The Church of Jesus Christ of Latter-day Saints* (Salt Lake City: Historical Department of The Church of Jesus Christ of Latter-day Saints, 1976).

16,691. Hart, Emily (Ellingham)
Papers. 1856-86. 5 vols.
Open. Published guide.
LDS Church Archives.
Diaries of [Mrs. James Henry] Hart (1821-92) describe her life as a convert to Mormonism in St. Louis before crossing the plains as well as life in Salt Lake City and Provo, UT. She also discusses her relationship with her husband's second wife. Also includes clippings. Taken from Christy Best, *Guide to Sources for Studies of Mormon Women in the Church Archives, The Church of Jesus Christ of Latter-day Saints* (Salt Lake City: Historical Department of The Church of Jesus Christ of Latter-day Saints, 1976).

16,692. Hendricks, Drusilla Dorris
Papers. Ca. 1885. 1 vol.
Open. Published guide.
LDS Church Archives.
Reminiscences of [Mrs. James] Hendricks (1810-81) in which she gives an account of her conversion to the Church in Tennessee and her experiences in Missouri, Nauvoo, IL, and Utah. Includes genealogy of her descendants. Taken from Christy Best, *Guide to Sources for Studies of Mormon Women in the Church Archives, The Church of Jesus Christ of Latter-day Saints* (Salt Lake City: Historical Department of The Church of Jesus Christ of Latter-day Saints, 1976).

16,693. Heywood, Martha (Spence)
Papers. Ca. 1849-69. 5 folders and 1 vol.
Open. Published guide.
LDS Church Archives.
Papers of Heywood (1812-?) include letters from her husband Joseph L. Heywood, another of his wives Sarepta Heywood, other family members, and friends; the letters relate to events in Salt Lake City and family industries. Also includes reminiscences and a diary in which she describes her conversion and early experiences with the Church, emigration to Utah, marriage, and activities in Salt Lake City and Nephi, UT; an essay; and poetry, including a poem Eliza R. Snow wrote to console her after the death of her daughter. Taken from Christy Best, *Guide to Sources for Studies of Mormon Women in the Church Archives, The Church of Jesus Christ of Latter-day Saints* (Salt Lake City: Historical Department of The Church of Jesus Christ of Latter-day Saints, 1976).

16,694. Higbee, Emma Isabella (Carroll) Seegmiller
Papers. Ca. 1937. 134-page item.
Open. Published guide.
LDS Church Archives.
History by Higbee (1868-1954), who lived in Orderville, UT, as a young girl, pertains to her experiences there. Before her marriage to Myron D. Higbee, she was married to Daniel Seegmiller. See Christy Best, *Guide to Sources for Studies of Mormon Women in the Church Archives, The Church of Jesus Christ of Latter-day Saints* (Salt Lake City: Historical Department of The Church of Jesus Christ of Latter-day Saints, 1976).

16,695. Higgins, Nancy Meribah (Behunin)
Papers. 1872-1910. 1 vol.
Open. Published guide.
LDS Church Archives.
Notebook of [Mrs. Nelson] Higgins (1839-1910) includes autobiographical sketches, her poetry, financial accounts, genealogy, and patriarchal blessings. Taken from Christy Best, *Guide to Sources for Studies of Mormon Women in the Church Archives, The Church of Jesus Christ of Latter-day Saints* (Salt Lake City: Historical Department of The Church of Jesus Christ of Latter-day Saints, 1976).

16,696. Hindley, Jane Charters (Robinson)
Papers. 1855-1931. 7 vols.
Open. Published guide.
LDS Church Archives.
Reminiscences and diaries of [Mrs. John] Hindley (1828-1907) in which she describes her early life, emigration to Utah, activities there, and her feelings regarding polygamy. Taken from Christy Best, *Guide to Sources for Studies of Mormon Women in the Church Archives, The Church of Jesus Christ of Latter-day Saints* (Salt Lake City: Historical Department of The Church of Jesus Christ of Latter-day Saints, 1976).

16,697. Hodapp, Minnie Josephine (Iverson)
Papers. Nd. 1 vol.
Open. Published guide.
LDS Church Archives.
Reminiscences of [Mrs. Frederick] Hodapp (1889-?) in which she recounts her early childhood experiences, education, and teaching activities. Also includes biographical sketches of her parents Andrew and Julia Iverson and poetry she composed. Taken from Christy Best, *Guide to Sources for Studies of Mormon Women in the Church Archives, The Church of Jesus Christ of Latter-day Saints* (Salt Lake City: Historical Department of The Church of Jesus Christ of Latter-day Saints, 1976).

16,698. Hofheins, Amanda Lucretia (Braffett)
Papers. 1893. 2-page item.
Open. No guide.
LDS Church Archives.
Papers relate to a widow's pension given to Hofheins (1830-1910), who was married to Jacob Michael Hofheins, a member of the Mormon Battalion.

16,699. Hopfenbeck, Elizabeth Ann (White)
Papers. Nd. 5-page item.
Open. Published guide.
LDS Church Archives.
Papers of [Mrs. Alphonzo] Hopfenbeck (1866-1961) relate to silkworms her mother raised at the request of Zina D. H. Young. Taken from Christy Best, *Guide to Sources for Studies of Mormon Women in the Church Archives, The Church of Jesus Christ of Latter-day Saints* (Salt Lake City: Historical Department of The Church of Jesus Christ of Latter-day Saints, 1976).

16,700. Horne, Alice (Merrill)
Papers. Nd. 2 ft. of microfilm.
Open. Published guide.
LDS Church Archives.
Reminiscences of [Mrs. George Henry] Horne (1868-1948) in which she gives an account of her childhood memories of her grandmother Bathsheba W. Smith. Includes some poetry. Taken from Christy Best, *Guide to Sources for Studies of Mormon Women in the Church Archives, The Church of Jesus Christ of Latter-day Saints* (Salt Lake City: Historical Department of The Church of Jesus Christ of Latter-day Saints, 1976).

16,701. Horne, Flora B.
Papers. Ca. 1919. 1 item.
Open. No guide.
LDS Church Archives.
Photo of an 1847 engraving that includes Ellen Sanders Kimball, Harriett Decker Young, and Clara Decker Young, all of whom were Utah pioneer women.

16,702. Horne, Mary Isabella (Hales)
Papers. Nd. 4 pp.
Open. Published guide.
LDS Church Archives.
Account of Sister Horne (1818-1905), the wife of Joseph Horne, concerns her association with Joseph Smith and his teachings. Includes her testimony about plural marriage. Taken from Christy Best, *Guide to Sources for Studies of Mormon Women in the Church Archives, The Church of Jesus Christ of Latter-day Saints* (Salt Lake City: Historical Department of The Church of Jesus Christ of Latter-day Saints, 1976).

16,703. Hulet, Catherine (Stoker)
Papers. Nd. 3 frames of microfilm.
Open. No guide.
LDS Church Archives.
Sketch of the life of Hulet (1829-82) and her husband Sylvanus Cyrus Hulet.

16,704. Hunt, Celia (Mounts)
Papers. 1887. 6 items.
Open. No guide.
LDS Church Archives.
Papers of Hunt (1805-97), the wife of Jefferson Hunt, a captain in the Mormon Battalion during the Mexican War, relate to her claim of a Mexican War widow's pension, including affidavits of relationship, and to death.

16,705. Hunter, Susanna (Wann)
Papers. 1878-83. 4 items.
Open. Published guide.
LDS Church Archives.
Letters from Hunter (1825-85), who was married to Edward Hunter, presiding bishop of the Church, to her son Edward concern family matters. Taken from Christy Best, *Guide to Sources for Studies of Mormon Women in the Church Archives, The Church of Jesus Christ of Latter-day Saints* (Salt Lake City: Historical Department of The Church of Jesus Christ of Latter-day Saints, 1976).

16,706. Isom, Alice (Parker)
Papers. 1918-23. 1 vol.
Open. Published guide.
LDS Church Archives.
Reminiscences of Isom (1848-1924) concern her husband George Isom and family life in Salt Lake City and Virgin, UT. Taken from Christy Best, *Guide to Sources for Studies of Mormon Women in the Church Archives, The Church of Jesus Christ of Latter-day Saints* (Salt Lake City: Historical Department of The Church of Jesus Christ of Latter-day Saints, 1976).

16,707. Jackson, Victoria (Hancock)
Papers. 1918-54. 1 vol.
Open. Published guide.
LDS Church Archives.
Reminiscences and a diary of [Mrs. Jonathan] Jackson (1880-1967) contain her recollections of her childhood in a polygamous family, experiences in Woodruff, AZ, and activities in Provo, UT. Taken from Christy Best, *Guide to Sources for Studies of Mormon Women in the Church Archives, The Church of Jesus Christ of Latter-day Saints* (Salt Lake City: Historical Department of The Church of Jesus Christ of Latter-day Saints, 1976).

16,708. James, Jane Elizabeth (Manning)
Papers. 1893. 9-page item.
Open. Published guide.
LDS Church Archives.
Biography of [Mrs. Isaac] James (1813-1908), an early black member of the Church, describes her activities in Nauvoo, IL, and early Salt Lake City. Taken from Christy Best, *Guide to Sources for Studies of Mormon Women in the Church Archives, The Church of Jesus Christ of Latter-day Saints* (Salt Lake City: Historical Department of The Church of Jesus Christ of Latter-day Saints, 1976).

16,709. Jarvis, Janet
Papers. 1906. 1 vol.
Open. Published guide.
LDS Church Archives.
Diary in which Jarvis describes her daily activities as a young girl in Arizona. Taken from Christy Best, *Guide to Sources for Studies of Mormon Women in the Church Archives, The Church of Jesus Christ of Latter-day Saints* (Salt Lake City: Historical Department of The Church of Jesus Christ of Latter-day Saints, 1976).

16,710. Jarvis, Zora (Smith)
Papers. 1854. 2 items.
Open. Unpublished guide.
LDS Church Archives.
Includes a letter from [Mrs. Brigham] Jarvis (1881-1969), who was in St. George, UT, to a Church historian containing information about her grandfather George A. Smith and the naming of St. George, UT. Also includes a biography of Smith's wife Zilpha Stark Smith relating to her activities as a pioneer in Utah.

16,711. Jensen, Hattie (Critchlow)
Papers. Ca. 1929. 16-page item.
Open. Published guide.
LDS Church Archives.
Account of a trip [Mrs. Ephraim] Jensen (1864-1948) took to Europe, during which she visited Church missionaries and stayed at the mission homes. Taken from Christy Best, *Guide to Sources for Studies of Mormon Women in the Church Archives, The Church of Jesus Christ of Latter-day Saints* (Salt Lake City: Historical Department of The Church of Jesus Christ of Latter-day Saints, 1976).

16,712. Jenson, Emma (Howell)
Papers. 1885-96. 3 vols.
Open. Published guide.
LDS Church Archives.
Diaries in which Jenson (1862-1937), who was the wife of historian Andrew Jenson, gives an account of a trip from Liverpool, England, to Salt Lake City, from Salt Lake City to England, and from Copenhagen to Salt Lake City. Includes biographical information. Taken from Christy Best, *Guide to Sources for Studies of Mormon Women in the Church Archives, The Church of Jesus Christ of Latter-day Saints* (Salt Lake City: Historical Department of The Church of Jesus Christ of Latter-day Saints, 1976).

16,713. Jepson, Brenda (Angell)
Papers. Ca. 1939. 1 vol.
Open. No guide.
LDS Church Archives.
Papers of [Mrs. Jesse Nightingale] Jepson (1890-1954) concern the life of her mother Emma Frances (Hartley) [Mrs. Charles August] Angell (1868-?) and contain information relating to her mother's early life in Iowa, conversion to the Church, emigration to Utah, and family and Church activities in southern Utah.

16,714. Johnson, Anna
Papers. 1932-74. 1.5 ft.
Open. Published guide.
LDS Church Archives.
Papers of [Miss] Johnson (1892-) contain poetry, biographical information, and a scrapbook containing photos of Salt Lake City in ca. 1932. Taken from Christy Best, *Guide to Sources for Studies of Mormon Women in the Church Archives, The Church of Jesus Christ of Latter-day Saints* (Salt Lake City: Historical Department of The Church of Jesus Christ of Latter-day Saints, 1976).

16,715. Johnson, Susan Elvira (Martineau)
Papers. 1934. 4 ft. of microfilm.
Open. Published guide.
LDS Church Archives.
Autobiography of [Mrs. Benjamin Samuel] Johnson (1856-1942) in which she describes settlement in northern Arizona in 1876, particularly at Moencopi and Egar, and relations with the Indians there. Taken from Christy Best, *Guide to Sources for Studies of Mormon Women in the Church Archives, The Church of Jesus Christ of Latter-day Saints* (Salt Lake City: Historical Department of The Church of Jesus Christ of Latter-day Saints, 1976).

16,716. Jones, Ivie Maude (Huish)
Papers. 1943-51. 2 folders.
Open. Published guide.
LDS Church Archives.
Papers of Jones (1891-), the wife of Lorin Franklin Jones, president of the Spanish American Mission, relate to incidents that occurred at the Mission. Taken from Christy Best, *Guide to Sources for Studies of Mormon Women in the Church Archives, The Church of Jesus Christ of Latter-day Saints* (Salt Lake City: Historical Department of The Church of Jesus Christ of Latter-day Saints, 1976).

16,717. Jones, Margaret (Lee)
Papers. 1888-90. 5 ft. of microfilm.
Open. Published guide.
LDS Church Archives.
Diary in which [Mrs. John Pidding] Jones (1821-1900) describes her activities in Enoch, UT. Taken from Christy Best, *Guide to Sources for Studies of Mormon Women in the Church Archives, The Church of Jesus Christ of Latter-day Saints* (Salt Lake City: Historical Department of The Church of Jesus Christ of Latter-day Saints, 1976).

16,718. Jones, Mary Eliza (Brown)
Papers. Nd. 7-page item.
Open. Unpublished guide.
LDS Church Archives.
Recollections of Jones (1836-1916) in which she tells stories about Joseph Smith and persecutions in

Nauvoo, IL. Before her marriage to Nathaniel Vary Jones, she was married to James A. Brown.

16,719. Jones, May (Chadwick)
Oral history. 1975. 15-page item.
Open. No guide.
LDS Church Archives.
Interview with [Mrs. Charles] Jones (1884-) in which she gives an account of her early life in Idaho, including her Church and social activities and the early settlement of Rupert.

16,720. Jones, Sarah (Fletcher)
Oral history. 1965. 31-page item.
Open. Published guide.
LDS Church Archives.
Interview with [Mrs. Albert] Jones concerns her life as a student at the Brigham Young Academy and includes information concerning teachers and social events in Provo, UT. Taken from Christy Best, *Guide to Sources for Studies of Mormon Women in the Church Archives, The Church of Jesus Christ of Latter-day Saints* (Salt Lake City: Historical Department of The Church of Jesus Christ of Latter-day Saints, 1976).

16,721. Judd, Mary Minerva (Dart)
Papers. Nd. 33 frames of microfilm.
Open. No guide.
LDS Church Archives.
Sketch of the life of [Mrs. Zadok Knapp] Judd (1838-?), a resident of Parowan, UT.

16,722. Keeler, Eliza (Shelton)
Papers. Ca. 1886-1909. 82-page item.
Open. Published guide.
LDS Church Archives.
Autobiography and journal of [Mrs. James] Keeler (1840-1909) in which she gives an account of her life in Canada, emigration to Utah, life in Santaquin and Richfield, experience with plural marriage, and activities in the United Order. Taken from Christy Best, *Guide to Sources for Studies of Mormon Women in the Church Archives, The Church of Jesus Christ of Latter-day Saints* (Salt Lake City: Historical Department of The Church of Jesus Christ of Latter-day Saints, 1976).

16,723. Keetch, Mercy Truth (Barker)
Papers. 1902. 2 vols.
Open. No guide.
LDS Church Archives.
Reminiscences of [Mrs. Charles Greenwood] Keetch (1835-1922) in which she recounts her early life in England, conversion, labors in the Church, emigration to Utah, and activities in Grantsville and Bear Lake Valley. Includes a photo.

16,724. Kelsey, Bessie Catherine Smith (Cook)
Papers. 1969. 1 vol.
Open. Published guide.
LDS Church Archives.
Reminiscences of [Mrs. Leander] Kelsey (1902-) concern her life from 1902 to 1969. Taken from Christy Best, *Guide to Sources for Studies of Mormon Women in the Church Archives, The Church of Jesus Christ of Latter-day Saints* (Salt Lake City: Historical Department of The Church of Jesus Christ of Latter-day Saints, 1976).

16,725. Kent, Nancy (Young)
Papers. 1847-55. 1 vol.
Open. Published guide.
LDS Church Archives.
Diary in which [Mrs. Daniel] Kent (1786-1860), a sister of Brigham Young, describes her activities and makes reference to family members. Also includes a letter she wrote to her children in 1855. Taken from Christy Best, *Guide to Sources for Studies of Mormon Women in the Church Archives, The Church of Jesus Christ of Latter-day Saints* (Salt Lake City: Historical Department of The Church of Jesus Christ of Latter-day Saints, 1976).

16,726. Kerr, Marion Adaline (Belnap)
Papers. 1904-13. 4 vols.
Open. Published guide.
LDS Church Archives.
Notebooks of [Mrs. Walter Affleck] Kerr (1886-1972) contain notes on education and millinery classes and include fabric samples. Taken from Christy Best, *Guide to Sources for Studies of Mormon Women in the Church Archives, The Church of Jesus Christ of Latter-day Saints* (Salt Lake City: Historical Department of The Church of Jesus Christ of Latter-day Saints, 1976).

16,727. Kesler, Donette (Smith)
Papers. Ca. 1890-91. 1 vol. and 3-page item.
Open. Published guide.
LDS Church Archives.
[Mrs. Alonzo Pratt] Kesler (1872-1961) was the daughter of Church president Joseph F. Smith. Diary concerning family activities, minutes from a theological class, and a debate speech she gave at the Latter-day Saints college, in which she states that women are more intelligent than men. Taken from Christy Best, *Guide to Sources for Studies of Mormon Women in the Church Archives, The Church of Jesus Christ of Latter-day Saints* (Salt Lake City: Historical Department of The Church of Jesus Christ of Latter-day Saints, 1976).

16,728. Kimball, Laura Pitkin
Papers. 1858-60. 1 vol.
Open. Published guide.
LDS Church Archives.
Diary of Kimball, the wife of Church leader Heber Chase Kimball, in which she describes her activities in Salt Lake City. Taken from Christy Best, *Guide to Sources for Studies of Mormon Women in the Church Archives, The Church of Jesus Christ of Latter-day Saints* (Salt Lake City: Historical Department of The Church of Jesus Christ of Latter-day Saints, 1976).

16,729. Kimball, Lucy (Walker)
Papers. Ca. 1902. 4 folders.
Open. Published guide.
LDS Church Archives.
Papers of Kimball (1826-1910), a wife of Church leader Heber Chase Kimball, include biographical sketches that describe her early life and activities in the Church, including an account of her first marriage to Joseph Smith and of her feelings toward the other wives and children of Heber Kimball. Taken from Christy Best, *Guide to Sources for Studies of Mormon Women in the Church Archives, The Church of Jesus Christ of Latter-day Saints* (Salt Lake City: Historical Department of The Church of Jesus Christ of Latter-day Saints, 1976).

16,730. Kimball, Mary Ellen (Able)
Papers. 1857-95. 4 folders.
Open. Published guide.
LDS Church Archives.
Papers of Kimball (1818-1902), a wife of Church leader Heber Chase Kimball, contain a journal in which she describes her activities in the Kimball family and events in Salt Lake City and during the Utah war. Also includes a discourse on the history of the pioneers, her conversion to the Church, her move to Nauvoo, IL, her activities there, her marriage to Heber Kimball, and her emigration to Utah. Taken from Christy Best, *Guide to Sources for Studies of Mormon Women in the Church Archives, The Church of Jesus Christ of Latter-day Saints* (Salt Lake City: Historical Department of The Church of Jesus Christ of Latter-day Saints, 1976).

16,731. Kimball, Olive (Woolley)
Papers. 1884-1903. 7 vols.
Open. Published guide.
LDS Church Archives.
Journals in which [Mrs. Andrew] Kimball (1860-1906) describes the Church and her family life and daily activities in Salt Lake City and Thatcher, AZ, including Relief Society work and other activities in the St. Joseph Stake. Also includes an account of a trip to Independence, MO. Taken from Christy Best, *Guide to Sources for Studies of Mormon Women in the Church Archives, The Church of Jesus Christ of Latter-day Saints* (Salt Lake City: Historical Department of The Church of Jesus Christ of Latter-day Saints, 1976).

16,732. Kimball, Presendia Lathrop (Huntington)
Papers. 1881. 2 items.
Open. Published guide.
LDS Church Archives.
Reminiscences of Kimball (1810-92), a wife of Church leader Heber Chase Kimball, in which she gives a brief sketch of her activities in the Church and her first marriage to Joseph Smith. Taken from Christy Best, *Guide to Sources for Studies of Mormon Women in the Church Archives, The Church of Jesus Christ of Latter-day Saints* (Salt Lake City: Historical Department of The Church of Jesus Christ of Latter-day Saints, 1976).

16,733. Kimball, Sarah Melissa (Granger)
Papers. 1848-98. 1 vol. and 2 items.
Open. Published guide.
LDS Church Archives.
Papers of [Mrs. Hiram S.] Kimball (1818-98), a leader of the Mormon Suffrage Association, include correspondence and essays containing comments on the Women's Triennial Council as well as an autograph book containing poetry by friends and prominent Church leaders. Taken from Christy Best, *Guide to Sources for Studies of Mormon Women in the Church Archives, The Church of Jesus Christ of Latter-day Saints* (Salt Lake City: Historical Department of The Church of Jesus Christ of Latter-day Saints, 1976).

16,734. Kimball, Vilate (Murray)
Papers. 1843. 3-page item.
Open. Published guide.
LDS Church Archives.
Copy of a letter from Kimball (1806-67), a wife of Church leader Heber Chase Kimball, to her husband concerns her activities in Nauvoo, IL, and the principle of plural marriage. Taken from Christy Best, *Guide to Sources for Studies of Mormon Women in the Church Archives, The Church of Jesus Christ of Latter-day Saints* (Salt Lake City: Historical Department of The Church of Jesus Christ of Latter-day Saints, 1976).

16,735. King, Hannah (Tapfield)
Papers. 1860-78. 9 items.
Open. Published guide.
LDS Church Archives.
Papers of [Mrs. Thomas Owen] King (1807-86) include a compilation of earlier diary entries, 1842-57, in which she describes her early life and activities in England, conversion to the Church, and emigration to Utah. Also includes her poems, which deal with the Church. Taken from Christy Best, *Guide to Sources for Studies of Mormon Women in the Church Archives, The Church of Jesus Christ of Latter-day Saints* (Salt Lake City: Historical Department of The Church of Jesus Christ of Latter-day Saints, 1976).

16,736. Knight, Martha (McBride)
Papers. 1875-98. 8 items.
Open. Published guide.
LDS Church Archives.
Correspondence of [Mrs. Vinson] Knight (1805-1901) includes letters from her daughter Almira (Knight) Hanscom, in which she discusses family matters and criticizes polygamy. Taken from Christy Best, *Guide to Sources for Studies of*

Mormon Women in the Church Archives, The Church of Jesus Christ of Latter-day Saints (Salt Lake City: Historical Department of The Church of Jesus Christ of Latter-day Saints, 1976).

16,737. Knuteson, Annetta Verna Marie (Williams)
Oral history. 1975. 21-page item.
Open. No guide.
LDS Church Archives.
Interview with [Mrs. Albert] Knuteson (1913-) in which she describes her early life, Church and social activities, and buildings in the Holladay area of Salt Lake County.

16,738. Lambert, Mary Alice (Cannon)
Papers. 1905-18. 5 vols.
Open. Published guide.
LDS Church Archives.
Diaries in which [Mrs. Charles] Lambert (1828-?) describes her activities, which included trips to the Mexican colonies and England. Taken from Christy Best, *Guide to Sources for Studies of Mormon Women in the Church Archives, The Church of Jesus Christ of Latter-day Saints* (Salt Lake City: Historical Department of The Church of Jesus Christ of Latter-day Saints, 1976).

16,739. Larsen, Oluf
Papers. Nd. 4 frames of microfilm.
Open. No guide.
LDS Church Archives.
Biographical sketch of Larsen concerns the life of his mother Anne Marie (Pedersen) [Mrs. Oluf Christian] Larsen (1847-1916) during the settlement of Utah.

16,740. LeBaron, Ellice Marie (Bentley)
Oral history. 1973. 26-page item.
Open. Published guide.
LDS Church Archives.
Interview with [Mrs. William Farland] LeBaron (1887-) in which she gives an account of her early life in the Mexican colonies, her move with her husband to Alberta, Canada, and her Church and civic activities there. Includes information concerning her father's plural marriages. Taken from Christy Best, *Guide to Sources for Studies of Mormon Women in the Church Archives, The Church of Jesus Christ of Latter-day Saints* (Salt Lake City: Historical Department of The Church of Jesus Christ of Latter-day Saints, 1976).

16,741. Lee, Rachel Andora (Woolsey)
Papers. 1856-60. 1 vol.
Open. Published guide.
LDS Church Archives.
Diary in which Lee (1825-1912), who was married to Indian agent John Doyle Lee, describes the Church services held in Harmony, UT, meetings of the Indian missionaries, and daily events. Taken from Christy Best, *Guide to Sources for Studies of Mormon Women in the Church Archives, The Church of Jesus Christ of Latter-day Saints* (Salt Lake City: Historical Department of The Church of Jesus Christ of Latter-day Saints, 1976).

16,742. Leishman, Anne Eliza (Wyatt)
Oral history. Ca. 1973. 3 folders.
Open. Published guide.
LDS Church Archives.
Includes an interview with Leishman in which she discusses her life in Wellsville, UT. Also includes items she collected relating to the Mormons and Cache Valley. Before her marriage to Robert Adamson Leishman, she was married to Franklin L. Gunnell. See Christy Best, *Guide to Sources for Studies of Mormon Women in the Church Archives, The Church of Jesus Christ of Latter-day Saints* (Salt Lake City: Historical Department of The Church of Jesus Christ of Latter-day Saints, 1976).

16,743. Lowe, Mary Louise (Belnap)
Papers. 1941. 3-page item.
Open. Published guide.
LDS Church Archives.
Statement of [Mrs. Joseph] Lowe concerns her mother Adaline (Knight) Belnap, her grandmother Martha McBride Knight, the organization of the Relief Society in Nauvoo, IL, Joseph Smith's statements, and the watch he gave to Eliza R. Snow. Taken from Christy Best, *Guide to Sources for Studies of Mormon Women in the Church Archives, The Church of Jesus Christ of Latter-day Saints* (Salt Lake City: Historical Department of The Church of Jesus Christ of Latter-day Saints, 1976).

16,744. Lucy Mack Home for Girls
Records. 1914. 4 pp.
Open. Published guide.
LDS Church Archives.
Includes a financial report for the Home, which lists earnings, expenditures, liabilities, and salaries. Taken from Christy Best, *Guide to Sources for Studies of Mormon Women in the Church Archives, The Church of Jesus Christ of Latter-day Saints* (Salt Lake City: Historical Department of The Church of Jesus Christ of Latter-day Saints, 1976).

16,745. Lund, August William
Papers. 1906-70. 6 ft. and 11 microfilm reels.
Open. Register.
LDS Church Archives.
Family and general correspondence, diaries, speeches, financial papers, and other papers of Lund (1886-1971), an assistant LDS Church historian and British Mission president. Includes letters from the Lund children, between Lund and his wife, and to family members. Also contains papers of his mother Sarah Ann Peterson Lund.

16,746. Lund, Elizabeth Martha Ellis
Oral history. 1975. 69-page item.
Open. Published guide.
LDS Church Archives.
Oral dictation of [Mrs. Francis Marion] Lund (1887-), in which she gives an account of her early life in Bountiful, UT, including details concerning her social activities, duties in the home, and early married life. Also includes articles concerning her ancestors, among them Patty Bartlett Sessions. Taken from Christy Best, *Guide to Sources for Studies of Mormon Women in the Church Archives, The Church of Jesus Christ of Latter-day Saints* (Salt Lake City: Historical Department of The Church of Jesus Christ of Latter-day Saints, 1976).

16,747. Lunt, Henry
Papers. Nd. 1 vol.
Open. No guide.
LDS Church Archives.
Includes a history of Lunt, his activities in England and in Parowan and Cedar City, UT; sketches of his wives; and sketches of Thomas Jones and his wife Sage (Treaharne) Jones.

16,748. Lyman, Amy Cassandra Brown
Papers. 1888-1957. 1 box.
Open. Published guide.
LDS Church Archives.
[Mrs. Richard Roswell] Lyman (1872-1959) was general president of the Relief Society, an officer in national and international women's organizations, and a Utah legislator. Includes correspondence, addresses, articles, reports, items related to history, clippings, and mementos. Taken from Christy Best, *Guide to Sources for Studies of Mormon Women in the Church Archives, The Church of Jesus Christ of Latter-day Saints* (Salt Lake City: Historical Department of The Church of Jesus Christ of Latter-day Saints, 1976).

16,749. Lyman, Eliza Maria (Partridge)
Papers. 1846-85. 3 folders.
Open. Published guide.
LDS Church Archives.
Papers of Lyman (1820-86), a wife of Church leader Amasa Mason Lyman, contain correspondence dealing with family activities; reminiscences and a diary summarizing her early life in Missouri and Nauvoo, IL; a speech defending polygamy; and an account of her emigration to Utah and activities in Salt Lake City and Fillmore, UT. Prior to her marriage to Lyman, she was married to Joseph Smith. See Christy Best, *Guide to Sources for Studies of Mormon Women in the Church Archives, The Church of Jesus Christ of Latter-day Saints* (Salt Lake City: Historical Department of The Church of Jesus Christ of Latter-day Saints, 1976).

16,750. Lyman, Florence Vern (Nielson)
Oral history. 1974. 63-page item.
Open. No guide.
LDS Church Archives.
Interview with [Mrs. Callis] Lyman (1891-1976) in which she gives an account of her childhood in Oak City, UT; her early married life in Millard County, UT; her family's move to Sunset, UT; and her Church activities. Includes details of life in a small town as well as a biography her daughter Virginia (Lyman) Lovell wrote.

16,751. Lyman, Louisa Maria (Tanner)
Papers. 1847-72. 1 folder.
Open. Unpublished guide.
LDS Church Archives.
Letters from Lyman (1818-1906), a wife of Church leader Amasa Mason Lyman, to her husband; the letters concern family and personal activities and include notes from their children and information about pioneer life in San Bernardino, CA.

16,752. Lyman, Pauline Eliza (Phelps)
Papers. 1855-1903. 1 folder.
Open. Unpublished guide.
LDS Church Archives.
Letters from Lyman (1827-1912) to her husband Church leader Amasa Mason Lyman concern family matters, including the death of their son Oscar. Also includes a sworn statement that Joseph Smith blessed her to come to the Rocky Mountains.

16,753. Lynne Literary and Social Institute
Records. 1896-98. 2 folders.
Open. No guide.
LDS Church Archives.
Minutes of the Institute in Lynne, UT, include a constitution, bylaws, and an account of meetings held.

16,754. McCloud, Susan Evans
Papers. Nd. 5-page item.
Open. Published guide.
LDS Church Archives.
Papers of McCloud relate to her personal experiences with Jessie Evans Smith, a wife of Church president Joseph Fielding Smith. Taken from Christy Best, *Guide to Sources for Studies of Mormon Women in the Church Archives, The Church of Jesus Christ of Latter-day Saints* (Salt Lake City: Historical Department of The Church of Jesus Christ of Latter-day Saints, 1976).

16,755. McCune, Alice Ann (Paxman)
Papers. 1885-1967. 5 microfilm reels.
Open. Published guide.
LDS Church Archives.
[Mrs. George] McCune (1870-1972) was a resident of Nephi, UT, and a member of the Daughters of the Utah Pioneers. Contains correspondence, personal writings, financial and legal papers, clippings, and ephemera. Includes letters from her future husband while he was on a mission in Samoa and letters from her daughter in the Eastern States

Mission. Taken from Christy Best, *Guide to Sources for Studies of Mormon Women in the Church Archives, The Church of Jesus Christ of Latter-day Saints* (Salt Lake City: Historical Department of The Church of Jesus Christ of Latter-day Saints, 1976).

16,756. MacDonald, Elizabeth (Graham)
Papers. 1875. 46-page item.
Open. Published guide.
LDS Church Archives.
Autobiography of [Mrs. Alexander Findlay] MacDonald (1831-1917) in which she describes her activities as a convert to Mormonism in Scotland, her emigration to Utah, and her feelings concerning plural marriage. She also tells about the relationship of the federal soldiers with the Mormons in Utah County. Taken from Christy Best, *Guide to Sources for Studies of Mormon Women in the Church Archives, The Church of Jesus Christ of Latter-day Saints* (Salt Lake City: Historical Department of The Church of Jesus Christ of Latter-day Saints, 1976).

16,757. Mace, Rebecca Elizabeth (Howell)
Papers. 1865-1916. 17 folders.
Open. Published guide.
LDS Church Archives.
Correspondence, diaries, memoirs, letter books, and other papers of [Mrs. Wandle] Mace (1833-1917) in which she describes her life in Kanab, UT, and her Church activities. Taken from Christy Best, *Guide to Sources for Studies of Mormon Women in the Church Archives, The Church of Jesus Christ of Latter-day Saints* (Salt Lake City: Historical Department of The Church of Jesus Christ of Latter-day Saints, 1976).

16,758. McIntire, Cleopatra (Barzee)
Papers. Ca. 1962. 1 vol.
Open. Published guide.
LDS Church Archives.
A history of the Ontario, CA, Relief Society from 1923 to 1962, which was compiled by [Mrs. E. William] McIntire (1892-) from histories and reminiscences of the Society's members. Also includes family histories and a history of the San Bernardino (CA) Stake. Taken from Christy Best, *Guide to Sources for Studies of Mormon Women in the Church Archives, The Church of Jesus Christ of Latter-day Saints* (Salt Lake City: Historical Department of The Church of Jesus Christ of Latter-day Saints, 1976).

16,759. Mack, Temperance (Bond)
Papers. 1847. 1 item.
Open. Published guide.
LDS Church Archives.
Letter from [Mrs. Stephen] Mack (1771-?) who was in winter quarters in Nebraska to her children, in which she asks them for clothes, a wagon, and provisions for her journey to Utah, and expresses the hope that they will join her there. Taken from Christy Best, *Guide to Sources for Studies of Mormon Women in the Church Archives, The Church of Jesus Christ of Latter-day Saints* (Salt Lake City: Historical Department of The Church of Jesus Christ of Latter-day Saints, 1976).

16,760. McKay, Emma Ray (Riggs)
Papers. 1954. 3 items.
Open. Published guide.
LDS Church Archives.
Addresses McKay (1877-1970), who was married to Church president David Oman McKay, gave at the Argentina Mission Conference concern Relief Society work, setting a good example, and the Book of Mormon. Taken from Christy Best, *Guide to Sources for Studies of Mormon Women in the Church Archives, The Church of Jesus Christ of Latter-day Saints* (Salt Lake City: Historical Department of The Church of Jesus Christ of Latter-day Saints, 1976).

16,761. MacKenna, Irma Hortensia (Lazo) de
Oral history. 1973. 77-page item.
Open. No guide.
LDS Church Archives.
Interview with [Mrs. Haroldo Ruben] de MacKenna (1920-) concerns her early life in Chile, conversion to the Church in 1961, activities in the Quilpue branch, work as a Relief Society president, emigration to the US, and work with the Church translation department.

16,762. McMaster, Nabbie Howe Young (Clawson)
Oral history. 1975. 12-page item.
Open. No guide.
LDS Church Archives.
Oral dictation of [Mrs. Frank Athol] McMaster (1891-), a granddaughter of Brigham Young, in which she describes her early life in Salt Lake City, her schooling in New York City, her social life in Salt Lake City, and members of the Young family.

16,763. Margetts, Lucy Marie (Canfield)
Papers. 1862. 1 vol.
Open. Published guide.
LDS Church Archives.
Diary of Margetts (1846-1915) in which she describes her emigration to Utah. Includes a biographical sketch of Eliza R. Snow. Before her marriage to Phillip H. Margetts, Lucy Margetts was married to John W. Young and then Ara W. Sabin. Taken from Christy Best, *Guide to Sources for Studies of Mormon Women in the Church Archives, The Church of Jesus Christ of Latter-day Saints* (Salt Lake City: Historical Department of The Church of Jesus Christ of Latter-day Saints, 1976).

16,764. Mason, Veda Pauline (Barker)
Papers. Ca. 1921. 10-page item.
Open. Published guide.
LDS Church Archives.
Consists of a history by [Mrs. Mirl Reese] Mason (1898-) of the Willard Ward Young Ladies Mutual Improvement Association in Willard, UT. Includes a list of the Association's past presidents. Taken from Christy Best, *Guide to Sources for Studies of Mormon Women in the Church Archives, The Church of Jesus Christ of Latter-day Saints* (Salt Lake City: Historical Department of The Church of Jesus Christ of Latter-day Saints, 1976).

16,765. Meeting of Twelve Apostles
Records. 1873. 1-page item.
Open. Published guide.
LDS Church Archives.
Includes a list of women who were set apart by apostles Orson Pratt and George Q. Cannon to serve as midwives or nurses. Taken from Christy Best, *Guide to Sources for Studies of Mormon Women in the Church Archives, The Church of Jesus Christ of Latter-day Saints* (Salt Lake City: Historical Department of The Church of Jesus Christ of Latter-day Saints, 1976).

16,766. Mildon, Kay Jon
Papers. Nd. 3-page item.
Open. Published guide.
LDS Church Archives.
Paper of Mildon (1933-) deals with women's ideals she wanted to acquire. Taken from Christy Best, *Guide to Sources for Studies of Mormon Women in the Church Archives, The Church of Jesus Christ of Latter-day Saints* (Salt Lake City: Historical Department of The Church of Jesus Christ of Latter-day Saints, 1976).

16,767. Mitchell, Clara Edna Lockling Liley
Papers. 1936-74. 2 microfilm reels.
Open. Published guide.
LDS Church Archives.
Reminiscences and a diary of [Mrs. Frederick A. H. F.] Mitchell (1892-) in which she describes her early experiences, association with the Reorganized Church, and Mormon Church activities in Missouri. Includes poetry, family genealogy, and photos. Taken from Christy Best, *Guide to Sources for Studies of Mormon Women in the Church Archives, The Church of Jesus Christ of Latter-day Saints* (Salt Lake City: Historical Department of The Church of Jesus Christ of Latter-day Saints, 1976).

16,768. Morris, John
Papers. 1848-50. 2 ft. of microfilm.
Open. No guide.
LDS Church Archives.
Diary in which Morris describes his labors as a traveling elder in Wales. Includes reminiscences of his wife Mary (Ormond) George Morris (1821-92), who recounts the family's emigration to Utah and gives the genealogy of the Ormond and George families. Before her marriage to Morris, Mary Morris was married to William George.

16,769. Morris, Mary Lois (Walker)
Papers. 1879-1918. 5 microfilm reels.
Open. Published guide.
LDS Church Archives.
Diaries and reminiscences of [Mrs. Elias] Morris (1835-1919) relate to her early life in Scotland; her journey to Utah; reminiscences of her children, including Church leader George Q. Morris; and her activities, particularly in Salt Lake City with the Primary Association and in Colonia Juarez, Mexico. Also includes poetry. Taken from Christy Best, *Guide to Sources for Studies of Mormon Women in the Church Archives, The Church of Jesus Christ of Latter-day Saints* (Salt Lake City: Historical Department of The Church of Jesus Christ of Latter-day Saints, 1976).

16,770. Mountford, Lydia Mary Olive Von Finklestein Mamreov
Papers. 1906-10. 4 folders.
Open. Published guide.
LDS Church Archives.
Mountford (1848-1917) was a Mormon lecturer on the Holy Land and the Bible. Includes correspondence, financial papers, broadsides, and clippings. Taken from Christy Best, *Guide to Sources for Studies of Mormon Women in the Church Archives, The Church of Jesus Christ of Latter-day Saints* (Salt Lake City: Historical Department of The Church of Jesus Christ of Latter-day Saints, 1976).

16,771. Munson, Eliza Mariah (Allred)
Papers. Nd. 6-page item.
Open. No guide.
LDS Church Archives.
History by [Mrs. James Willard] Munson (1848-1939) in which she recounts the experiences of her grandparents James and Elizabeth Allred in Nauvoo, IL, and of her parents. She also describes emigration and settlement in Utah.

16,772. Murray, Fanny (Young)
Papers. 1846-51. 1 folder.
Open. Published guide.
LDS Church Archives.
Correspondence of [Mrs. Roswell] Murray (1787-1859), a sister of Brigham Young, concerns family and personal activities. Taken from Christy Best, *Guide to Sources for Studies of Mormon Women in the Church Archives, The Church of Jesus Christ of Latter-day Saints* (Salt Lake City: Historical Department of The Church of Jesus Christ of Latter-day Saints, 1976).

16,773. National Council of Women of the United States
Phonotape. Ca. 1960. 1 tape.
Open. No guide.
LDS Church Archives.
Panel discussion of the Council relates to women, "the nation's greatest untapped resource." Emily

Kimbrough moderated the discussion, which was introduced by Sophia Yarnell Jacobs.

16,774. National Woman's Christian Temperance Union
Records. Nd. 1 motion picture.
Open. No guide.
LDS Church Archives.
Motion picture of the WCTU concerns alcohol.

16,775. Nelson, Belle (Harris)
Papers. 1883. 69 pp.
Open. Published guide.
LDS Church Archives.
Includes correspondence of Nelson (1861-1938) as well as a diary she kept while she was imprisoned at the Utah Penitentiary because she refused to testify against her husband, who was a polygamist. Before her marriage to N. L. Nelson, she was married to Clarence Merrill. See Christy Best, *Guide to Sources for Studies of Mormon Women in the Church Archives, The Church of Jesus Christ of Latter-day Saints* (Salt Lake City: Historical Department of The Church of Jesus Christ of Latter-day Saints, 1976).

16,776. Nestler, Lina Selma (Stock)
Papers. 1909-66. 2.5 ft.
Open. Published guide.
LDS Church Archives.
Papers of [Mrs. Friedrich Herman] Nestler (1876-1967) include correspondence; autobiographical notes concerning her life in Germany, conversion to the Church, emigration to Utah, and experiences there; notebooks; poetry; prose; and clippings. Some papers are in German. Taken from Christy Best, *Guide to Sources for Studies of Mormon Women in the Church Archives, The Church of Jesus Christ of Latter-day Saints* (Salt Lake City: Historical Department of The Church of Jesus Christ of Latter-day Saints, 1976).

16,777. Nielson, Emma Waitstill (Mecham)
Papers. 1887-97. 1 vol.
Open. Published guide.
LDS Church Archives.
Diary in which Nielson (1858-1920), who was married to Frihoff Godfred Nielson, a Mormon colonizer in Arizona and New Mexico, gives an account of her Church and home activities in St. George, UT, and in Ramah, NM, including comments on her feelings toward polygamy and her husband's second wife. Taken from Christy Best, *Guide to Sources for Studies of Mormon Women in the Church Archives, The Church of Jesus Christ of Latter-day Saints* (Salt Lake City: Historical Department of The Church of Jesus Christ of Latter-day Saints, 1976).

16,778. Nuttall, Margaret Grace (Greer)
Papers. 1896-1962. 2 microfilm reels.
Open. Published guide.
LDS Church Archives.
Diaries of [Mrs. William Albert] Nuttall (1880-) in which she describes her experiences in Wallsburg and Provo, UT, her activities in the Texas-Louisiana Mission, and her travels. Includes autobiographies and family genealogy. Taken from Christy Best, *Guide to Sources for Studies of Mormon Women in the Church Archives, The Church of Jesus Christ of Latter-day Saints* (Salt Lake City: Historical Department of The Church of Jesus Christ of Latter-day Saints, 1976).

16,779. Omer, Leona (Sutherland)
Oral history. 1975. 26-page item.
Open. No guide.
LDS Church Archives.
Interview with [Mrs. August Gideon] Omer (1892-) in which she gives an account of her early life in the Holladay area of Salt Lake County and her Church and social activities there.

16,780. Oral History
Collection. 1972-74. No size given.
Open. Published guide.
LDS Church Archives.
Collection includes interviews with Annie Dexter Clayton concerning her association with Samuel Chambers and the Leggroan family, who were black members of the Church, as well as her family's emigration to Utah in 1904 and the William Clayton family into which she married; Flore Guillemine Catherine Lahon Chappuis concerning her activities as a Church member in Belgium, the hardships during the German occupation, the closing of the French Mission, emigration to Utah, and her work in the Church historian's office; Minnie Lee Prince Haynes regarding her association with her husband's grandfather Samuel Chambers, a black Mormon living in Salt Lake City, as well as early life in Mississippi as a black sharecropper and her feelings about race problems there; Afton Grant Affleck concerning her family and her activities as a temple worker, Relief Society president, member of the Young Women's Mutual Improvement Association general board, and organizer of the volunteer program at the Salt Lake County Detention Center; Maud Leone Openshaw [Mrs. Joseph] Jacobs concerning her husband's life as an Armenian in Syria, emigration to Utah, their return to work in the Palestine-Syria Mission, and her work on the Relief Society general board; Carol Jeanne Graff Gunn concerning her activities as a musician, composer, and ward choir director, as well as her association with LeRoy J. Robertson; Ann Amelia Chamberlain Esplin concerning her life in Orderville, UT, as a member of a polygamous family and in Cedar City as a Relief Society president during the depression; Sarah Langston Adams concerning her life in Rockville, Hinckley, Lynndyl, and Beaver, UT, and in the Mexican colonies as well as her mission in California; Annie Matilda Gerber Andersen concerning her life as a daughter in a polygamous family in the Taylorsville area; Maureen Ursenbach concerning her interest in Mormon architecture and historic preservation; Elizabeth (Fetzer) Bates concerning the architectural work of her father John Fetzer, as well as her work in writing and teaching music; Mary (Pratt) Parrish concerning her father Rey L. Pratt, his work as president of the Mexican mission, the family's activities in El Paso, TX, and her activities as a member of the Primary General Board and a resident of Centerville, UT, including an autobiography of her mother Mary Stark Pratt and remembrances of her sisters; Rose Marie Yancey Reid concerning her early life in Canada, her experiences as a designer and businesswoman, and her activities in teaching the gospel to Jewish people; Helen (Lee) Goates concerning the personal and family life of her father Harold B. Lee; and Bertha Julia Stone Richards concerning her early life in Ogden, UT, her activities when her husband was president of the New England Mission from 1941 to 1947, and her term as president of the Young Women's Mutual Improvement Association. Also contains an interview with Susanna Smart (Parkinson) Nielson concerning her father Samuel Parkinson, a civic and Church leader in Franklin, ID; life in a plural family; cultural and social life in a small Mormon community; and her brother-in-law Apostle Matthias Cowley. Also includes comments by her daughter LaRue (Nielson) Bates. See *Guide to the Oral History Program of the Historical Department, The Church of Jesus Christ of Latter-day Saints* (Salt Lake City: Historical Department of The Church of Jesus Christ of Latter-day Saints, 1975).

16,781. Pack, Alvin G.
Papers. Nd. 3 items.
Open. No guide.
LDS Church Archives.
Papers of Pack concern the lives of some of the women founders of the Church, among them Lucy Mack Smith, Emma Smith, Mary Ann Young, and Mary Fielding Smith.

16,782. Pearce, May Penrose
Papers. 1928-46. 7 folders.
Open. Published guide.
LDS Church Archives.
Papers of [Miss] Pearce (1855-1949) include correspondence, reminiscences and diaries in which she gives an account of her activities in New Zealand and Utah, and notes. The bulk of the papers pertains to her extensive genealogical work. Taken from Christy Best, *Guide to Sources for Studies of Mormon Women in the Church Archives, The Church of Jesus Christ of Latter-day Saints* (Salt Lake City: Historical Department of The Church of Jesus Christ of Latter-day Saints, 1976).

16,783. Pearson, Sarah E.
Papers. Ca. 1904. 1 vol.
Open. Published guide.
LDS Church Archives.
Notebook of Pearson in which she wrote about her feelings concerning plural marriage. Taken from Christy Best, *Guide to Sources for Studies of Mormon Women in the Church Archives, The Church of Jesus Christ of Latter-day Saints* (Salt Lake City: Historical Department of The Church of Jesus Christ of Latter-day Saints, 1976).

16,784. Peirson, Nancy (Richards)
Papers. 1837-51. 2 folders.
Open. Published guide.
LDS Church Archives.
Papers of Peirson (1792-1852) include correspondence; diaries in which she gives an account of her activities in Richmond, MA, with references to her family in Utah; and poetry. Taken from Christy Best, *Guide to Sources for Studies of Mormon Women in the Church Archives, The Church of Jesus Christ of Latter-day Saints* (Salt Lake City: Historical Department of The Church of Jesus Christ of Latter-day Saints, 1976).

16,785. Penrose, Charles W.
Papers. 1880-1922. 1 ft. and 1 microfilm reel.
Open. Register.
LDS Church Archives.
Penrose (1832-1925) was a Mormon general authority, a British missionary, an author, and a poet. Includes his writings and addresses on plural marriage and the adoption of an amendment concerning polygamy to the Utah constitution, poetry, papers of the Mammoth Coal Company, and ephemera.

16,786. Penrose, Esther Romania (Bunnell)
Papers. 1875-98. 2 vols. and 4 items.
Open. Published guide.
LDS Church Archives.
Penrose (1839-1932), one of the first women physicians in Utah, was married to Church leader Charles W. Penrose. Includes letters from her husband; a letter of appointment from the Relief Society to represent the organization in Washington, DC; a memoir of her life, including comments on her attitude toward plural marriage and her medical work; papers containing family dates and events; a blessing given by Joseph F. Smith pertaining to her medical career; and a class schedule from the Women's Medical College of Pennsylvania. Before her marriage to Penrose, she was married to Parley P. Pratt, Jr. See Christy Best, *Guide to Sources for Studies of Mormon Women in the Church Archives, The Church of Jesus Christ of Latter-day Saints* (Salt Lake City: Historical Department of The Church of Jesus Christ of Latter-day Saints, 1976).

16,787. Peterson, Canute
Papers. 1852-1901. 7 folders.
Open. No guide.
LDS Church Archives.
Letters Peterson (1824-1902) wrote to his family while he was on a mission in the Scandinavian countries pertain to his activities in Sanpete County. Also includes letters to his wife Sarah Ann Peterson from Zina D. H. Young, Mary Ann Hyde, Emmeline B. Wells, and Eliza R. Snow pertaining to her activities with the Relief Society.

16,788. Phillips, Harriet Byrle (Hamblin)
Papers. Nd. 4-page item.
Open. Unpublished guide.
LDS Church Archives.
Speech of [Mrs. Hugh J.] Phillips (1920-?) concerns incidents in her grandfather Jacob Hamblin's relations with the Indians.

16,789. Photos of Mormon Women
Collection. Ca. 1852- . 1000 items.
Open. No guide.
LDS Church Archives.
Photos include portraits of prominent Mormon women; women involved in the Relief Society of Cannonville, UT, ca. 1880; the Bingham Stake Relief Society sisters in Idaho Falls, ca. 1894; midwives in Salt Lake City, 1896; the graduating class of the Salt Lake Stake Relief Society Nurse School, 1898; a class of practical nurses at LDS Hospital, 1911; women temple workers, 1917; a group of nurses, ca. 1920; the victory convention of the National American Woman Suffrage Association and Congress of the LWV in Chicago, 1920; the convention and dinner for Women Lawyers of the US in Chicago, including Susa (Young) Gates, Donette (Smith) Kesler, and Carrie Chapman Catt, 1920; women who worked in the Endowment House; Emily Dow Young and her children; Zina D. H. Young, Bathsheba Smith, and Eliza R. Snow; five generations of Mormon women voters; prominent Church leaders; families; Indians; temples; the territorial penitentiary; and Salt Lake City.

16,790. Pickering, Alice (Miller)
Papers. 1923. 4-page item.
Open. Published guide.
LDS Church Archives.
Papers of [Mrs. John Edson] Pickering (1887-1951) relate to organization and history of camp 10 of the Daughters of the Utah Pioneers, a local unit of the organization. Taken from Christy Best, *Guide to Sources for Studies of Mormon Women in the Church Archives, The Church of Jesus Christ of Latter-day Saints* (Salt Lake City: Historical Department of The Church of Jesus Christ of Latter-day Saints, 1976).

16,791. Poelman, Eva Beatrice Swain (Squires)
Papers. 1972. 43-page item.
Open. Published guide.
LDS Church Archives.
Autobiography of [Mrs. Walter Jenkins] Poelman (1897-) in which she describes her childhood in Salt Lake City, marriage, and struggles during the depression. Taken from Christy Best, *Guide to Sources for Studies of Mormon Women in the Church Archives, The Church of Jesus Christ of Latter-day Saints* (Salt Lake City: Historical Department of The Church of Jesus Christ of Latter-day Saints, 1976).

16,792. Pratt, Ann Agatha (Walker)
Papers. 1907. 1 item.
Open. No guide.
LDS Church Archives.
Reminiscences of Pratt (1829-1908) contain recollections of her husband Parley Parker Pratt and copies of correspondence with him, 1847-57. Also contains information concerning his missionary work, his activities in California, and the relationship of his plural wives.

16,793. Pratt, Louisa (Barnes)
Papers. 1850-80. 1 microfilm reel.
Open. Published guide.
LDS Church Archives.
Journals and an autobiography of [Mrs. Addison] Pratt (1802-80) in which she describes her activities in the Society Island Mission in the South Pacific and in Nauvoo, IL; emigration to Utah; and settlement in San Bernardino, CA, and later in Cedar City and Beaver, UT. Taken from Christy Best, *Guide to Sources for Studies of Mormon Women in the Church Archives, The Church of Jesus Christ of Latter-day Saints* (Salt Lake City: Historical Department of The Church of Jesus Christ of Latter-day Saints, 1976).

16,794. Pratt, Sarah Marinda (Bates)
Papers. 1884. 7-page item.
Open. Published guide.
LDS Church Archives.
Papers of Pratt (1817-88), who was married to Church leader Orson Pratt, concern the beginning of polygamy in Nauvoo, IL. Taken from Christy Best, *Guide to Sources for Studies of Mormon Women in the Church Archives, The Church of Jesus Christ of Latter-day Saints* (Salt Lake City: Historical Department of The Church of Jesus Christ of Latter-day Saints, 1976).

16,795. Presiding Bishopric
Records. 1851- . 951.5 ft. and 2549 microfilm reels.
Partially restricted. Inventory.
LDS Church Archives.
Since 1847 the Church has had one presiding bishop and two counselors; these officials were general authorities, or officials for the entire Mormon Church, and were responsible for the temporal needs of the Church members. Their responsibilities now include the youth of the Church and administrative and welfare services. Includes annual reports, minutes, office journals, financial records, vital and social statistics, employee records, welfare assistance records, mortality lists, correspondence, membership records, and bulletins. Includes statistics on education, literacy, economic levels, cause of death, crime, and mental illness among the Mormons.

16,796. Primary Association
Records. 1881- . 15 ft. and 76 microfilm reels.
Open. Inventory.
LDS Church Archives.
Annual reports, general board minutes, financial records, correspondence, motion pictures, phonotapes, speeches, attendance statistics, and ephemera of the Association, which was created in 1878 as an auxiliary program of the Church to teach children from ages 3 to 12 about Church doctrines and principles. The Association has been directed by women since its beginning. Papers relating to the Association presidency may be found in the collections of Louie B. Felt, May Anderson, May Green Hinckley, Adele Cannon Howells, LaVern Watts Parmley, and Naomi M. Shumway.

16,797. Pye, Mary Emily Francis (Kelly)
Papers. 1920-40. 1 folder.
Open. No guide.
LDS Church Archives.
Poetry by [Mrs. Caleb Enoch] Pye (1867-1945), her stepdaughter Dorothy (Pye) Barrett, and others.

16,798. Randall, Sally (Carlisle)
Papers. 1843-52. 8 items.
Open. Published guide.
LDS Church Archives.
Letters that [Mrs. James] Randall (1805-?) wrote from Nauvoo, IL, and Iowa tell of her trip to Nauvoo, family happenings there, and Church doctrine. Includes accounts of the deaths of Joseph and Hyrum Smith and of a visit to Silver Creek, IA. Taken from Christy Best, *Guide to Sources for Studies of Mormon Women in the Church Archives, The Church of Jesus Christ of Latter-day Saints* (Salt Lake City: Historical Department of The Church of Jesus Christ of Latter-day Saints, 1976).

16,799. Reed, Mary (Curtis)
Papers. Ca. 1886. 1 vol.
Open. Published guide.
LDS Church Archives.
Papers of Reed (1821-88) contain extracts of the diaries of Alexander Clough and her husband Calvin Reed along with her reminiscences about their experiences in the Stephen Markham Company and about the Reed family's journey to Utah. Also includes a sketch of her early life and other family papers. Taken from Christy Best, *Guide to Sources for Studies of Mormon Women in the Church Archives, The Church of Jesus Christ of Latter-day Saints* (Salt Lake City: Historical Department of The Church of Jesus Christ of Latter-day Saints, 1976).

16,800. Relief Society
Records. 1842- . 25 ft. and 128 microfilm reels.
Access restricted. Inventory.
LDS Church Archives.
Founded in 1842, the Society is the adult women's auxiliary of the Mormon Church. Minutes; financial and statistical reports; correspondence; phonotapes of conference proceedings; motion pictures presenting historical information, objectives, and goals of the Society; instructions to local Society leaders; lesson plans; bulletins; circular letters; and printed material. The Society was founded in Nauvoo, IL, by Joseph Smith, founder of the Mormon Church, to assist the needy and provide spiritual, educational, and social improvement for the women of the Church. Presidents of the Society have included Emma (Hale) Smith, 1842-44; Zina Diantha Young, 1888-1901; Amy Brown Lyman, 1940-45; and Barbara B. Smith, 1974- .

16,801. Relief Society, Lewiston First Ward
Records. Nd. 1 vol.
Open. Published guide.
LDS Church Archives.
Records concern the history of the Lewiston, UT, First Ward Relief Society from 1908 to 1971. Taken from Christy Best, *Guide to Sources for Studies of Mormon Women in the Church Archives, The Church of Jesus Christ of Latter-day Saints* (Salt Lake City: Historical Department of The Church of Jesus Christ of Latter-day Saints, 1976).

16,802. Reynolds, Alice Louise
Papers. 1894-1938. 11 folders.
Open. Published guide.
LDS Church Archives.
Papers of [Miss] Reynolds (1873-1938) include correspondence; autobiographical notes and diaries containing an account of her experiences in the Relief Society, teaching at Brigham Young University, and travels; and notebooks. Taken from Christy Best, *Guide to Sources for Studies of Mormon Women in the Church Archives, The Church of Jesus Christ of Latter-day Saints* (Salt Lake City: Historical Department of The Church of Jesus Christ of Latter-day Saints, 1976).

16,803. Rich, Emmeline (Grover)
Papers. 1892-1912. 2 folders.
Open. Published guide.
LDS Church Archives.
Rich (1831-1917) was married to Church leader Charles Coulsen Rich. Includes a diary of her activities in Paris, ID, and Logan, UT, particularly as a midwife. Taken from Christy Best, *Guide to Sources for Studies of Mormon Women in the Church Archives, The Church of Jesus Christ of Latter-day Saints* (Salt Lake City: Historical

Department of The Church of Jesus Christ of Latter-day Saints, 1976).

16,804. Rich, Sarah Dearmon (Pea)
Papers. 1884-93. 4 folders.
Open. Published guide.
LDS Church Archives.
Papers of Rich (1814-93), a wife of Church leader Charles Coulsen Rich, include an autobiography in which she recounts her early life, experiences in Far West, MO, emigration to Utah, and later experiences. Also includes poetry, financial accounts, and family genealogy. Taken from Christy Best, *Guide to Sources for Studies of Mormon Women in the Church Archives, The Church of Jesus Christ of Latter-day Saints* (Salt Lake City: Historical Department of The Church of Jesus Christ of Latter-day Saints, 1976).

16,805. Richards, Louisa "Lula" (Greene)
Papers. 1867-1935. 7 folders.
Open. Published guide.
LDS Church Archives.
[Mrs. Levi Willard] Richards (1849-1944) was author and editor of the *Woman's Exponent.* Contains correspondence, including letters from Church leaders concerning her journalism activities; a diary of her experiences while she was teaching and attending school in Smithfield, UT, and Salt Lake City; articles; stories; and poetry. Taken from Christy Best, *Guide to Sources for Studies of Mormon Women in the Church Archives, The Church of Jesus Christ of Latter-day Saints* (Salt Lake City: Historical Department of The Church of Jesus Christ of Latter-day Saints, 1976).

16,806. Richards, Sarah Griffith
Papers. 1850-90. 3 items.
Open. Published guide.
LDS Church Archives.
Correspondence of Richards (1802-92) to Zina D. H. Young in which she reminisces about events surrounding the murder of Joseph Smith. Also includes a journal in which she describes a mission to England in the company of her husband Levi Richards. Taken from Christy Best, *Guide to Sources for Studies of Mormon Women in the Church Archives, The Church of Jesus Christ of Latter-day Saints* (Salt Lake City: Historical Department of The Church of Jesus Christ of Latter-day Saints, 1976).

16,807. Ricks, Mrs. Thomas
Papers. Ca. 1889. 6-page item.
Open. Published guide.
LDS Church Archives.
Papers concern a dream Ricks had in which her dissatisfaction with her marriage is resolved. Ricks's husband was a polygamist. Taken from Christy Best, *Guide to Sources for Studies of Mormon Women in the Church Archives, The Church of Jesus Christ of Latter-day Saints* (Salt Lake City: Historical Department of The Church of Jesus Christ of Latter-day Saints, 1976).

16,808. Robeson, Eva Jane
Papers. 1959-60. 26 items.
Open. No guide.
LDS Church Archives.
Papers of [Miss] Robeson (1937-) include correspondence and interviews with Church members who had lived in Mexico and left during the 1912 revolution. The correspondence contains information concerning their settlement in southern New Mexico.

16,809. Rogers, Aurelia (Spencer)
Papers. 1916-19. 3 items.
Open. Published guide.
LDS Church Archives.
[Mrs. Thomas] Rogers (1834-1922) was a founder of the Primary Association. Includes correspondence in which Rogers reminisces about Christmas in pioneer days and describes her activities in the Primary. Taken from Christy Best, *Guide to Sources for Studies of Mormon Women in the Church Archives, The Church of Jesus Christ of Latter-day Saints* (Salt Lake City: Historical Department of The Church of Jesus Christ of Latter-day Saints, 1976).

16,810. Rollins, Mary Emeline "Marie" (Hutchings)
Oral history. 1965. 1 vol.
Open. Published guide.
LDS Church Archives.
Interview with [Mrs. James Henry] Rollins (1881-) in which she describes her activities as a student at the Beaver branch of the Brigham Young University and later at the Murdock Academy in Beaver County, UT. Taken from Christy Best, *Guide to Sources for Studies of Mormon Women in the Church Archives, The Church of Jesus Christ of Latter-day Saints* (Salt Lake City: Historical Department of The Church of Jesus Christ of Latter-day Saints, 1976).

16,811. Romney, Amy Wilcken (Pratt)
Oral history. 1973. 61-page item.
Open. Published guide.
LDS Church Archives.
Interview with [Mrs. Gaskell] Romney (1890-1927) in which she gives an account of her family's activities in Mexico, including information concerning her father Helaman Pratt and her brothers Rey L. Pratt and Harold W. Pratt. She also talks about the Romney family, George W. Romney, and her work in the Liberty Stake Relief Society. Taken from Christy Best, *Guide to Sources for Studies of Mormon Women in the Church Archives, The Church of Jesus Christ of Latter-day Saints* (Salt Lake City: Historical Department of The Church of Jesus Christ of Latter-day Saints, 1976).

16,812. Roundy, Elizabeth Jeffords (Drake)
Papers. 1912. 3 items.
Open. Published guide.
LDS Church Archives.
Papers of Roundy (1830-1916) include a letter in which she protests against the jury called to hear a murder charge against president Brigham Young and others; a letter she wrote to Mrs. Rutherford B. Hayes urging her not to support an anti-polygamy petition, along with background information concerning the letter; statements regarding a petition she started in Washington, DC, to benefit families of soldiers; and an explanation of a letter she sent to George C. Bates, US prosecuting attorney for Utah Territory. Before her marriage to Jared Curtis Roundy, she was married to Daniel Davis. See Christy Best, *Guide to Sources for Studies of Mormon Women in the Church Archives, The Church of Jesus Christ of Latter-day Saints* (Salt Lake City: Historical Department of The Church of Jesus Christ of Latter-day Saints, 1976).

16,813. Sartwell, Wilbur K.
Papers. 1963. 4-page item.
Open. No guide.
LDS Church Archives.
Press release of Sartwell concerns the death of Mary Audentia (Smith) Anderson, an author and daughter of Reorganized Church president Joseph Smith, III. Includes biographical information.

16,814. Senior, Ellen (Hodgson)
Papers. 1887. 10-page item.
Open. No guide.
LDS Church Archives.
Diary of [Mrs. Joseph] Senior (1840-1917) concerns her trip to England, her family there, and her return with her mother.

16,815. Sessions, Patty (Bartlett)
Papers. 1846-80. 7 folders.
Open. Published guide.
LDS Church Archives.
[Mrs. David] Sessions (1795-1892) was a pioneer midwife. Contains diaries in which she describes her emigration to Utah and activities in Salt Lake City, an account book, a statement that she was sealed to Joseph Smith in 1842, and poetry written by Eliza R. Snow. Taken from Christy Best, *Guide to Sources for Studies of Mormon Women in the Church Archives, The Church of Jesus Christ of Latter-day Saints* (Salt Lake City: Historical Department of The Church of Jesus Christ of Latter-day Saints, 1976).

16,816. Sheets, Elijah F.
Papers. 1840-85. 5 in.
Open. Register.
LDS Church Archives.
Diaries of Sheets (1821-1904), a church leader among the local units of the Mormon Church, in which he describes his missionary experiences in England and Pennsylvania. Also includes a diary of his first wife Margaret Hutchinson Sheets, 1840-45, in which she describes her activities in England before her marriage.

16,817. Sheets, Margaret (Hutchinson)
Papers. 1833-37. 1 vol.
Open. Published guide.
LDS Church Archives.
Includes poetry of [Mrs. Elijah Funk] Sheets (1819-47) and financial accounts. Taken from Christy Best, *Guide to Sources for Studies of Mormon Women in the Church Archives, The Church of Jesus Christ of Latter-day Saints* (Salt Lake City: Historical Department of The Church of Jesus Christ of Latter-day Saints, 1976).

16,818. Shepard, Lulu Loveland
Papers. 1917-21. 1 vol.
Open. Published guide.
LDS Church Archives.
Notebook of Shepard, a WCTU lecturer, contains notes for talks in which she expresses a negative attitude toward Mormonism. Taken from Christy Best, *Guide to Sources for Studies of Mormon Women in the Church Archives, The Church of Jesus Christ of Latter-day Saints* (Salt Lake City: Historical Department of The Church of Jesus Christ of Latter-day Saints, 1976).

16,819. Smith, Amanda Barnes
Papers. 1854-58. 1 vol.
Open. Published guide.
LDS Church Archives.
Notebook of [Mrs. Warren] Smith (1809-86) contains Relief Society minutes, family genealogy, and autobiographical information. Taken from Christy Best, *Guide to Sources for Studies of Mormon Women in the Church Archives, The Church of Jesus Christ of Latter-day Saints* (Salt Lake City: Historical Department of The Church of Jesus Christ of Latter-day Saints, 1976).

16,820. Smith, Bathsheba Wilson (Bigler)
Papers. 1839-1907. 5 folders.
Open. Published guide.
LDS Church Archives.
Smith (1822-1910) was general president of the Relief Society and a plural wife of Church leader George A. Smith. Contains correspondence; an autobiography and journal in which she recounts her activities, particularly at winter quarters in Nebraska; affidavits affirming that Joseph Smith taught plural marriage; and a statement concerning her relationship with the other wives of George A. Smith. Taken from Christy Best, *Guide to Sources for Studies of Mormon Women in the Church Archives, The Church of Jesus Christ of Latter-day Saints* (Salt Lake City: Historical Department of The Church of Jesus Christ of Latter-day Saints, 1976).

16,821. Smith, Catherine Delphina "Della" (Fish)
Papers. Ca. 1928-33. 1 vol.
Open. No guide.
LDS Church Archives.
Reminiscences and diary of [Mrs. Joseph West] Smith (1864-1934) in which she recounts her childhood experiences in Parowan, UT, and activities in Snowflake, AZ. Includes minutes of the Snowflake Cooperative Tannery, 1882-91.

16,822. Smith, Emma (Hale)
Papers. Ca. 1842-45. 4 items.
Open. Published guide.
LDS Church Archives.
Smith (1804-79) was a wife of Joseph Smith, Jr. Includes a letter she wrote to Sidney Rigdon concerning the handling of her husband's papers at the post office in Nauvoo, IL. Also includes Rigdon's reply to her letter, a deed for land in Nauvoo, and a letter addressed to her that concerns an anti-Mormon writer. Taken from Christy Best, *Guide to Sources for Studies of Mormon Women in the Church Archives, The Church of Jesus Christ of Latter-day Saints* (Salt Lake City: Historical Department of The Church of Jesus Christ of Latter-day Saints, 1976).

16,823. Smith, Jessie Ella (Evans)
Papers. 1967-68. 2 items.
Open. Published guide.
LDS Church Archives.
Addresses of Smith (1902-71), a wife of Church president Joseph Fielding Smith, include a speech given before the Associated Women Students of Ricks College, concerning the characteristics of a righteous woman, and a speech she gave at the University 13th Ward in Salt Lake City, concerning the brotherhood of man. Taken from Christy Best, *Guide to Sources for Studies of Mormon Women in the Church Archives, The Church of Jesus Christ of Latter-day Saints* (Salt Lake City: Historical Department of The Church of Jesus Christ of Latter-day Saints, 1976).

16,824. Smith, Julina (Lambson)
Papers. 1870-1933. 7 items and 2 ft. of microfilm.
Open. Published guide.
LDS Church Archives.
Smith (1849-1936) was a wife of Church president Joseph F. Smith. Letters from Joseph Smith containing poetry, diaries she kept concerning her activities in Salt Lake City and the Laie Plantation in Hawaii, reminiscences of her childhood and marriage, and other papers. Taken from Christy Best, *Guide to Sources for Studies of Mormon Women in the Church Archives, The Church of Jesus Christ of Latter-day Saints* (Salt Lake City: Historical Department of The Church of Jesus Christ of Latter-day Saints, 1976).

16,825. Smith, Lucy Emily Woodruff
Papers. 1893-94. 1 vol.
Open. Published guide.
LDS Church Archives.
Diary in which Smith (1869-1937), a wife of Church president George Albert Smith, describes her activities while she was on a mission with her husband to the southern states. Taken from Christy Best, *Guide to Sources for Studies of Mormon Women in the Church Archives, The Church of Jesus Christ of Latter-day Saints* (Salt Lake City: Historical Department of The Church of Jesus Christ of Latter-day Saints, 1976).

16,826. Smith, Lucy Meserve (Smith)
Papers. 1886. 2-page item.
Open. Published guide.
LDS Church Archives.
Reminiscences of Smith (1817-92), a wife of Church leader George A. Smith. Taken from Christy Best, *Guide to Sources for Studies of Mormon Women in the Church Archives, The Church of Jesus Christ of Latter-day Saints* (Salt Lake City: Historical Department of The Church of Jesus Christ of Latter-day Saints, 1976).

16,827. Smith, Maria Elizabeth (Bushman)
Papers. 1937. 36-page item.
Open. No guide.
LDS Church Archives.
Sketch by [Mrs. Silas Derryfield] Smith (1869-?) relates to the life of her mother Lois Angeline (Smith) [Mrs. John] Bushman (1844-1921), a pioneer in Utah and Arizona.

16,828. Smith, Mary (Heathman)
Papers. 1878-95. 1 vol.
Open. Published guide.
LDS Church Archives.
Notebook of [Mrs. John A.] Smith (1816-95), a midwife in Huntsville, UT, in which she lists babies she delivered and money she received. Taken from Christy Best, *Guide to Sources for Studies of Mormon Women in the Church Archives, The Church of Jesus Christ of Latter-day Saints* (Salt Lake City: Historical Department of The Church of Jesus Christ of Latter-day Saints, 1976).

16,829. Smith, Winslow Whitney
Papers. 1839-1931. 2 ft.
Open. Register.
LDS Church Archives.
Contains correspondence, diaries, financial papers of Orson F. Whitney, an ancestor of Smith (1907-), who is a professor of bacteriology and public health at Utah State University. Includes correspondence between Whitney and Zina B. Smoot in 1879 as well as that between Whitney and his wife Zina S. Whitney, 1879-98. Also includes a letter to the Whitney family from Susa (Young) Gates, a daughter of Brigham Young, a leader among Mormon women, an author, and a suffrage worker.

16,830. Snow, Eliza Roxey
Papers. 1834-84. 5 folders, 4 items, and 13 ft. of microfilm.
Open. Published guide.
LDS Church Archives.
Snow (1804-87) was a general president of the Relief Society. Contains letters to women regarding the Society and temple ordinances, to the Welch family giving commendation and advice to Robert Welch and information concerning books for the Primary Association to Harriet Welch, and to Louisa "Lula" Greene Richards. Also includes a note to Martha Spence Heywood to accompany a gift of an apron and to tell her about General Conference; journals of Snow's emigration to Utah and settlement in Salt Lake City; a notebook containing diary entries for her activities in Nauvoo, IL; poetry; and an autograph book containing signatures of famous persons in the Church and nation. Snow was married to Joseph Smith and then to Brigham Young. Taken from Christy Best, *Guide to Sources for Studies of Mormon Women in the Church Archives, The Church of Jesus Christ of Latter-day Saints* (Salt Lake City: Historical Department of The Church of Jesus Christ of Latter-day Saints, 1976).

16,831. Steinacher, Marie Helen
Papers. Nd. 1 folder.
Open. No guide.
LDS Church Archives.
Scrapbook of Steinacher (1885-) contains photos of her family, particularly her father Rudolph Steinacher; her friends; and her homeland of Czechoslovakia. Steinacher married Benjamin F. LeBaron.

16,832. Stevenson, Emily Electra (Williams)
Papers. 1886-87. 1 vol.
Open. Published guide.
LDS Church Archives.
Diary of [Mrs. Edward] Stevenson (1841-1918) in which she describes her journey to the East with her husband. Includes a partial speech on women's suffrage, poetry she composed, and family genealogy. Also contains an autobiography of her mother Electra Williams in which she describes events in Nauvoo, IL, after the death of Joseph Smith. Taken from Christy Best, *Guide to Sources for Studies of Mormon Women in the Church Archives, The Church of Jesus Christ of Latter-day Saints* (Salt Lake City: Historical Department of The Church of Jesus Christ of Latter-day Saints, 1976).

16,833. Stirling, Florence Violet (Miles)
Papers. Nd. 4-page item.
Open. No guide.
LDS Church Archives.
Account by [Mrs. James Y.] Stirling (1880-) in which she describes her experiences while she was growing up in Salt Lake City. Also contains an account of her mother Jane Fox Stevenson [Mrs. William Hart] Miles (1842-1924) and her experiences working for the Utah Commission.

16,834. Taylor, Rachel (Smith)
Oral history. 1974. 4-page item.
Open. Published guide.
LDS Church Archives.
Interview with [Mrs. Albert LeRoy] Taylor (1890-) concerns her father Church president Joseph F. Smith. The interview was conducted by her daughter. Taken from Christy Best, *Guide to Sources for Studies of Mormon Women in the Church Archives, The Church of Jesus Christ of Latter-day Saints* (Salt Lake City: Historical Department of The Church of Jesus Christ of Latter-day Saints, 1976).

16,835. Thompson, Mercy Rachel (Fielding)
Papers. 1880. 6-page item.
Open. Published guide.
LDS Church Archives.
Autobiographical sketch of [Mrs. Robert Blashel] Thompson (1807-93), who became a plural wife of Hyrum Smith, in which she recounts her experiences with the early Church and the Nauvoo, IL, Temple as well as her association with Hyrum Smith. Taken from Christy Best, *Guide to Sources for Studies of Mormon Women in the Church Archives, The Church of Jesus Christ of Latter-day Saints* (Salt Lake City: Historical Department of The Church of Jesus Christ of Latter-day Saints, 1976).

16,836. Thurber, Laura Ann (Keeler)
Papers. 1887-1903. 1 vol.
Open. Published guide.
LDS Church Archives.
Reminiscences and a diary of [Mrs. Joseph Heber] Thurber (1859-1909) in which she recounts her activities, particularly as a plural wife. Includes autobiographical sketches of her parents James and Eliza S. Keeler, poetry, and family genealogy. Taken from Christy Best, *Guide to Sources for Studies of Mormon Women in the Church Archives, The Church of Jesus Christ of Latter-day Saints* (Salt Lake City: Historical Department of The Church of Jesus Christ of Latter-day Saints, 1976).

16,837. Van Noy, Elsie (Hogan)
Papers. Ca. 1957. 3 folders.
Open. Published guide.
LDS Church Archives.
Papers of [Mrs. William Ray] Van Noy, a general secretary of the Young Women's Mutual Improvement Association, contain items on the development of the Association and its programs, particularly during the presidency of Ruth May Fox. Also includes information on the 104th birthday celebration of Ruth Fox and the writing of the song "Carry On." Taken from Christy Best, *Guide to Sources for Studies of Mormon Women in the Church Archives, The Church of Jesus Christ of Latter-day Saints* (Salt Lake City:

Historical Department of The Church of Jesus Christ of Latter-day Saints, 1976).

16,838. Wade, Minerva
Papers. Ca. 1892-1900. 1 vol.
Open. Published guide.
LDS Church Archives.
Reminiscences of [Miss] Wade (1829-1918) in which she describes her family's conversion to the Church, activities with the Mormon Battalion, and journey to Utah. Also includes a record of children born to women for whom she acted as midwife in West Jordan Ward and North Ogden, UT, and family genealogy. Wade married William Adams Hickman, but the couple later separated and she resumed the use of her maiden name. See Christy Best, *Guide to Sources for Studies of Mormon Women in the Church Archives, The Church of Jesus Christ of Latter-day Saints* (Salt Lake City: Historical Department of The Church of Jesus Christ of Latter-day Saints, 1976).

16,839. Wells, Emmeline Blanche (Woodward)
Papers. Ca. 1855-1919. 3 folders and 3-page item.
Open. Published guide.
LDS Church Archives.
Wells (1828-1921) was a general president of the Relief Society and married to Church leader Daniel Hanmer Wells. Contains letters to other wives of Daniel Wells, a letter written to President Rutherford B. Hayes concerning plural marriage in Utah and government action against the Mormons, items dealing with the National Council of Women and the Relief Society, and a tribute to Romania B. Pratt Penrose, a physician, extolling her character and devotion to the medical profession. Wells had previously been married to James Harvey Harris and Newel Kimball Whitney. Taken from Christy Best, *Guide to Sources for Studies of Mormon Women in the Church Archives, The Church of Jesus Christ of Latter-day Saints* (Salt Lake City: Historical Department of The Church of Jesus Christ of Latter-day Saints, 1976).

16,840. Wells, Hannah Corrilla (Free)
Papers. Ca. 1856-85. 3 folders and 1 vol.
Open. Published guide.
LDS Church Archives.
Papers of Wells (1829-1913), a wife of Church leader Daniel H. Wells, include letters she wrote from Fillmore, UT, to the other wives of Daniel H. Wells, letters to her son Junius F. Wells while he was on a mission in England, and a diary in which she describes her activities in Salt Lake City. Taken from Christy Best, *Guide to Sources for Studies of Mormon Women in the Church Archives, The Church of Jesus Christ of Latter-day Saints* (Salt Lake City: Historical Department of The Church of Jesus Christ of Latter-day Saints, 1976).

16,841. Whitney, Helen Mar (Kimball)
Papers. 1881-90. 3 folders.
Open. Published guide.
LDS Church Archives.
Papers of [Mrs. Horace Kimball] Whitney (1828-96) include letters to her son Apostle Orson F. Whitney; an autobiography of her life and activities, particularly her marriage to Joseph Smith, Jr.; indentures; warranty deeds; and insurance policies. She was married to Smith and then to Horace Whitney. See Christy Best, *Guide to Sources for Studies of Mormon Women in the Church Archives, The Church of Jesus Christ of Latter-day Saints* (Salt Lake City: Historical Department of The Church of Jesus Christ of Latter-day Saints, 1976).

16,842. Whitney, Orson Ferguson
Papers. 1868-1931. 1 box.
Open. No guide.
LDS Church Archives.
Papers of Whitney (1855-1931), a member of the Council of the Twelve, consist of family correspondence, including letters to his wife Zina Whitney, his parents, Abraham O. Smoot, Heber M. Wells, Susa (Young) Gates, and A. Milton Musser.

16,843. Widtsoe, Leah Eudora (Dunford)
Oral history. 1965. 73-page item.
Open. Published guide.
LDS Church Archives.
Interview with Widtsoe (1874-1965) concerns her association with Brigham Young Academy as a student and as a teacher. Includes information concerning her mother Susa (Young) Gates (1856-1933) and her husband, Church leader John Andrew Widtsoe. Also includes a transcript of her funeral services. Taken from Christy Best, *Guide to Sources for Studies of Mormon Women in the Church Archives, The Church of Jesus Christ of Latter-day Saints* (Salt Lake City: Historical Department of The Church of Jesus Christ of Latter-day Saints, 1976).

16,844. Williams, Nancy Abigail (Clement)
Papers. Ca. 1872-1954. 7 folders.
Open. Published guide.
LDS Church Archives.
Papers of [Mrs. Frederick Granger] Williams (1872-1954) include correspondence between family members, diaries and notebooks in which she describes her life and the activities of the Mormon Church in Dublan, Mexico, and in Utah; poetry; blessings; a play; and miscellaneous notes. Taken from Christy Best, *Guide to Sources for Studies of Mormon Women in the Church Archives, The Church of Jesus Christ of Latter-day Saints* (Salt Lake City: Historical Department of The Church of Jesus Christ of Latter-day Saints, 1976).

16,845. Willis, Bertram Trowbridge
Papers. 1938. 2-page item.
Open. No guide.
LDS Church Archives.
Radio talk of Willis (1912-) concerns the effects of smoking on a girl.

16,846. Woodruff, Emma (Smith)
Papers. 1832-1919. 38 folders.
Open. Published guide.
LDS Church Archives.
Woodruff (1838-1912) was married to Church president Wilford Woodruff. Contains correspondence and items related to family matters. Taken from Christy Best, *Guide to Sources for Studies of Mormon Women in the Church Archives, The Church of Jesus Christ of Latter-day Saints* (Salt Lake City: Historical Department of The Church of Jesus Christ of Latter-day Saints, 1976).

16,847. Woodruff, Phebe Whittemore (Carter)
Papers. 1838-85. 2 folders and a 3-page item.
Open. Published guide.
LDS Church Archives.
Woodruff (1807-85) was married to Church president Wilford Woodruff. Includes a letter to her grandson concerning family matters and mentioning arrests for plural marriage, an autograph book containing verses and poetry by her husband and other Church leaders, and mementos of her daughter Beulah Augusta Beatie. Taken from Christy Best, *Guide to Sources for Studies of Mormon Women in the Church Archives, The Church of Jesus Christ of Latter-day Saints* (Salt Lake City: Historical Department of The Church of Jesus Christ of Latter-day Saints, 1976).

16,848. Woolley, Zina Olivia (Boothe)
Papers. 1896-99. 1 vol.
Open. Published guide.
LDS Church Archives.
Diary [Mrs. Dilworth] Woolley (1877-1901) kept concerns her activities as a young woman in Grantsville, UT. Also includes published poetry. Taken from Christy Best, *Guide to Sources for Studies of Mormon Women in the Church Archives, The Church of Jesus Christ of Latter-day Saints* (Salt Lake City: Historical Department of The Church of Jesus Christ of Latter-day Saints, 1976).

16,849. Young, Brigham
Papers. 1851-79. 104 microfilm reels.
Partially restricted. Inventory.
LDS Church Archives.
Young (1801-77) was the second president of the Mormon Church and a colonizer of the West. Includes family and other correspondence, letter books, journals, minutes, addresses, circular letters to Mormon officials, and governor's papers relating to political and Indian matters, marriage, and divorce. Includes correspondence of his wives Augusta Adams Young; Jemima Angel Young; Mary Ann Angel Young; Lucy Bigelow Young; Mary Bigelow Young; Eliza Burgess Young; Harriet E. Cook Young; Clarissa C. Decker Young; Lucy Ann Decker Young; Zina D. Huntington Young; Phebe Morton Young; Margaret Pierce Young; Eliza R. Snow, who retained her maiden name; and Mary Van Cott Young. Also includes letters from his daughters Alice Young, Clara F. Young, Luna Young, and Susan Y. Dunford and from his daughters-in-law Jane M. C. Young and Mary Ann Young. Also includes papers relating to personal family matters and divorces as well as recommendations for religious ordinances and marriages.

16,850. Young Ladies' Mutual Improvement Association, Brigham City, Second Ward
Records. Ca. 1926. 6-page item.
Open. No guide.
LDS Church Archives.
History of the Association of the 2nd Ward, Box Elder Stake of Zion, concerns the period from 1878 to 1926 and primarily contains lists of officers.

16,851. Young Ladies' Mutual Improvement Association, Mantua Ward
Records. Ca. 1918. 9-page item.
Open. No guide.
LDS Church Archives.
History of the Ward of the Association, founded in 1875, includes lists of the presidencies until 1918.

16,852. Young, Louisa (Beaman)
Papers. 1849. 3-page item.
Open. Published guide.
LDS Church Archives.
Letter from Young (1815-50), a wife of Brigham Young, from Salt Lake City to Marinda Hyde in Kanesville, IA, in which she describes life in early Utah and the death of her children. Before her marriage to Brigham Young, she was married to Joseph Smith. See Christy Best, *Guide to Sources for Studies of Mormon Women in the Church Archives, The Church of Jesus Christ of Latter-day Saints* (Salt Lake City: Historical Department of The Church of Jesus Christ of Latter-day Saints, 1976).

16,853. Young, Margaret (Pierce)
Papers. Ca. 1880. 15-page item.
Open. Published guide.
LDS Church Archives.
Autobiography of Young (1823-1907), a wife of Brigham Young, in which she gives an account of her early life, her family's conversion to the Church, her activities in Nauvoo, IL, and her emigration to Utah. Also includes an account of her marriage to Brigham Young and a poem by Eliza R. Snow. Before her marriage to Young, she was married to Morris Whitesides. See Christy Best, *Guide to Sources for Studies of Mormon Women in the Church Archives, The Church of Jesus Christ of Latter-day Saints* (Salt Lake City:

Historical Department of The Church of Jesus Christ of Latter-day Saints, 1976).

16,854. Young, Martha (Bowker)
Papers. 1852-71. 2 items.
Open. Published guide.
LDS Church Archives.
Letters from Young (1822-90), a wife of Brigham Young, to her sister in New Jersey. One letter tells of conditions in Salt Lake City and the outlying settlements. Taken from Christy Best, *Guide to Sources for Studies of Mormon Women in the Church Archives, The Church of Jesus Christ of Latter-day Saints* (Salt Lake City: Historical Department of The Church of Jesus Christ of Latter-day Saints, 1976).

16,855. Young, Mary Ann (Angel)
Papers. 1843. 3-page item.
Open. Published guide.
LDS Church Archives.
Letter of Young (1803-82), a wife of Brigham Young, to her husband concerns their children and family problems. Taken from Christy Best, *Guide to Sources for Studies of Mormon Women in the Church Archives, The Church of Jesus Christ of Latter-day Saints* (Salt Lake City: Historical Department of The Church of Jesus Christ of Latter-day Saints, 1976).

16,856. Young, Minerva (Richards)
Papers. 1882-83. 1 vol.
Open. Published guide.
LDS Church Archives.
Reminiscences and diary of Young (1862-1958) in which she describes her life before and during her marriage to Richard Willard Young. Includes diary entries for a brief period when she and her husband lived on Governor's Island in New York. Taken from Christy Best, *Guide to Sources for Studies of Mormon Women in the Church Archives, The Church of Jesus Christ of Latter-day Saints* (Salt Lake City: Historical Department of The Church of Jesus Christ of Latter-day Saints, 1976).

16,857. Young, Naamah Kendel Jenkins (Carter)
Papers. 1846-1901. 5 items.
Open. Published guide.
LDS Church Archives.
Letters from Young (1821-1909), a wife of Brigham Young, to her sister in Peterborough, NH, concern life with the Mormons. Before her marriage to Brigham Young, she was married to John Saunders Twiss. See Christy Best, *Guide to Sources for Studies of Mormon Women in the Church Archives, The Church of Jesus Christ of Latter-day Saints* (Salt Lake City: Historical Department of The Church of Jesus Christ of Latter-day Saints, 1976).

16,858. Young, Seymour Bicknell
Papers. 1857-1924. 7 ft.
Open. Register.
LDS Church Archives.
Journals, physician's logbook, notebooks, scrapbooks, and other papers of Young (1857-1924), a physician who practiced in Salt Lake City. Logbooks contain information on the treatment and care of patients. Young was a Mormon general authority, or a general officer of the Mormon Church.

16,859. Young Women's Mutual Improvement Association
Records. 1890- . 22 ft. and 64 microfilm reels.
Open. Inventory.
LDS Church Archives.
Annual reports, general board minutes, program reports for stakes and missions, correspondence, enrollment reports, circular letters, and printed items of the Association, which was created in 1869 by Brigham Young to reform young women's dress and social activities and to stimulate homemaking skills. Originally called the Young Ladies' Mutual Improvement Association, the organization has been led by women since its inception. Presidents have included Elmina Shephard Taylor, 1880-1904; Lucy Grant Cannon, 1937-48; and Florence S. Jacobsen, 1961-72.

16,860. Young, Zina Diantha (Huntington)
Oral history. Nd. 6-page item.
Open. Published guide.
LDS Church Archives.
Interview with Young (1821-1901), general president of the Relief Society, concerns her marriage to Joseph Smith, Jr. Before her marriage to Smith, she was married to Henry Bailey Jacobs. Brigham Young was her third husband. See Christy Best, *Guide to Sources for Studies of Mormon Women in the Church Archives, The Church of Jesus Christ of Latter-day Saints* (Salt Lake City: Historical Department of The Church of Jesus Christ of Latter-day Saints, 1976).

16,861. Adams, Barbara Ellen Matheson
Papers. 1973. 1 vol.
Open. Card index.
University of Utah, Special Collections.
Reminiscences and photos of Adams (1883-), a church and civic worker, relate to her experiences raising children and to social life in Iron County, UT.

16,862. Adams Family
Papers. 1817-1912. 5 in.
Open. Register.
University of Utah, Special Collections.
Biographies of William Henry Adams, Sr., and Matthew Caldwell and biographical sketches of Barzilla Guyman Caldwell; William Henry Adams, Jr.; and his wife Melissa Jane Caldwell Adams (1851-?). The sketch of Melissa Adams and her husband includes reminiscences of Melissa Adams regarding their early life together as settlers in Utah County, her father's second marriage to Maria Gelispe after the death of her mother in 1869, raising sheep and weaving wool into blankets and clothing, raising chickens and selling their eggs, logging, building, and local Indians.

16,863. American Indian Oral History Duke Collection: Apache
Oral history. 1968. 54 pp.
Access restricted. Unpublished guide.
University of Utah, Special Collections.
Interviews with Anna Early, who discusses education, welfare, population, alcohol, the Bureau of Indian Affairs, language, discrimination, and storytelling, and with Cecelia Panteloon Lambeth, who discusses her ancestry, background, marriage, plants, legends, arts and crafts, clothes, relations between whites and Indians, reservation and home life, children, religion, and language.

16,864. American Indian Oral History Duke Collection: Hopi
Oral history. 1967. 2 pp.
Access restricted. Unpublished guide.
University of Utah, Special Collections.
Interview with Gloria Quanimptewa, a Hopi Indian, who discusses farming, leaving the reservation, and relations between Quanimptewas and Tewas.

16,865. American Indian Oral History Duke Collection: Hualapai
Oral history. 1967-68. No size given.
Access restricted. Unpublished guide.
University of Utah, Special Collections.
Interviews with or concerning Hualapais include one with Mrs. Tim McGee, who discusses her childhood and education, language, a court battle with other Indians, starting a cattle herd, her ancestry, fighting between Hualapais and Apaches, a dispute over sending children to school, making utensils, trade, hunting, food preparation, shelters, marriage, medicine men, names and their meanings, procedures used during childbirth, means of child discipline, social laws, origins of the Hualapais, an army massacre of Apaches and Yavapais, and relations among Navajos, Hualapais, Apaches, Yavapais, and Hopis. Also includes interviews with Lillian Anderson, who talks about missionary life with the Hualapais, their religious customs, relations with the Mohaves and Apaches, removal of the Hualapais, and basketmaking, and with Helen Livingston Shawl, who speaks of recreation, medicine, and early Chloride, AZ.

16,866. American Indian Oral History Duke Collection: Isleta
Oral history. 1967. 4 pp.
Access restricted. Unpublished guide.
University of Utah, Special Collections.
Interview with Mrs. Louis Lente in which she gives an account of the establishment of the Laguna Colony in 1879 and discusses intermarriage, relations between the Catholic Church and the Isletas, and Father Frederick Statmueller, a Franciscan priest who served in the Colony from ca. 1960 to 1967 and was known as Father Fred.

16,867. American Indian Oral History Duke Collection: Kaibab Indians
Oral history. 1967. 29 pp.
Access restricted. Unpublished guide.
University of Utah, Special Collections.
Interview with Margaret C. Heaton, a non-Indian, who discusses farming in the early days at Moccasin, AZ, relations between Indians and whites, Indian agents and superintendents, Indian and Mormon relations, the United Order, an experiment in communitarianism among the Mormons, employment and teaching of Indians by Mormons, trade, land and water disputes, childbirth, and clothing.

16,868. American Indian Oral History Duke Collection: Laguna
Oral history. 1967. 76 pp.
Access restricted. Unpublished guide.
University of Utah, Special Collections.
Interviews with Vedna Hunt, a non-Indian; Susie Marmon; and Marie Paisano concerning the Laguna people. Paisano discusses early living conditions, early farming, and arts and crafts, while Hunt talks about rituals, religion, ancestors, intermarriage, epidemics, traders, the sacred Cha' kwena Order, Zuni voting, and relations of Lagunas with whites, Acomas, and Spanish-speaking persons. Marmon discusses her ancestry and her experiences at a mission school, religion, early settlers, the Lagunas' written constitution, the breakdown of communal work, self-government, the scalping custom, land controversies, the history of the Laguna village of Paguate, the founding of the village of Mesita, migration of the Laguna, and relations between the Lagunas and the Acomas, Apaches, Navajos, and Utes.

16,869. American Indian Oral History Duke Collection: Navajo
Oral history. 1968. 68 pp.
Access restricted. Unpublished guide.
University of Utah, Special Collections.
Interview with Sallie P. Harris, a non-Indian, in which she discusses place names, the language, ceremonialism, history, sacred places, legends, trails, and landmarks of the Navajos; Navajo-Mexican relations; and plants.

16,870. American Indian Oral History Duke Collection: Paiute
Oral history. 1967-68. No size given.
Access restricted. Unpublished guide.
University of Utah, Special Collections.
Mabel Dry, a Paiute, discusses relations with Mormons, whites, Navajos, and Utes; life in school; gathering and preparing wild plants; Paiute names for geographic locations in southern Utah; the creation story; dances; language problems; illness;

farming; medicines; housing; and trails into Southern Paiute territory. Also includes interviews with non-Indians Rhoda (Matheson) Wood, who discusses an incident between Indians and a pioneer housewife; Mildred Morrison, who talks about Paiute legends, marriage, family relationships, and relations of Indians with Mormons and other whites; and Alva Matheson, who talks about her childhood friends who were Indians, various legends of the Southern Paiutes, the origin of Indians, white influence, religion, hieroglyphics, the buying and trading of children, and her beliefs about past civilizations and their relationship to present-day Indians. In addition, there are interviews with Edna B. Patterson, Mr. and Mrs. Tony Smiraldo, and Zella Matheson.

16,871. American Indian Oral History Duke Collection: Santa Clara
Oral history. 1967. 11 pp.
Access restricted. Unpublished guide.
University of Utah, Special Collections.
Interview with Elaine Naranjo who discusses her personal background, her education, and living in a Santa Clara pueblo.

16,872. American Indian Oral History Duke Collection: Shoshoni
Oral history. 1967-68. 190 pp.
Access restricted. Unpublished guide.
University of Utah, Special Collections.
Includes interviews with Haddie Arriwite and Lucy Jones, who discuss Shoshoni legends; Doris Ponzo, who speaks of her father's experience in the army and after he left the army, her childhood, alcohol, the origin of Indian names, religion, philosophy, Shoshoni-Bannock relations, and Indian-white relations; and Edna B. Patterson, a non-Indian who discusses her information sources, Indian-Anglo relations, trade, and poverty. Also includes a master's thesis by Helen Clark Rountree concerning reservations, life at Skull Creek, a summer festival, education, marriage, children, health, employment, and old age among Shoshoni Indians.

16,873. American Indian Oral History Duke Collection: Taos
Oral history. 1967. 6 pp.
Access restricted. Unpublished guide.
University of Utah, Special Collections.
Interview with Wahleah Lugan, a Taos Indian, in which she discusses her experience as Miss Indian America, reservation and college life, and contemporary Indian problems.

16,874. American Indian Oral History Duke Collection: Tewa
Oral history. 1967. 11 pp.
Access restricted. Unpublished guide.
University of Utah, Special Collections.
Interview with Elaine Naranjo, who discusses her life in Utah, joining the Mormon Church, her move to Pueblo, her education, persecution of the Mormon Church, recreation, youth problems, life in a Santa Clara pueblo, and Brigham Young University.

16,875. American Indian Oral History Duke Collection: Thlingit
Oral history. 1967. 30 pp.
Access restricted. Unpublished guide.
University of Utah, Special Collections.
Interview with Elaine Erickson in which she discusses life in Alaska, Indian identity, religion, conceptions of time, relations between the federal government and Indians, alcohol, education, Fort Lewis College in Durango, CO, and reservations.

16,876. American Indian Oral History Duke Collection: Ute
Oral history. 1960-69. No size given.
Access restricted. Unpublished guide.
University of Utah, Special Collections.
Interviews with Utes or concerning Utes contain discussion of such topics as hunting and farming; food; education; recreation; gold; medicine; intermarriage; religion; employment; national awareness; voting; alcohol; Vietnam; legends; language; the bear dance, the sun dance, and the tea dance; the Ute-Navajo riot; relations between Utes, whites, and other Indian tribes; the Meeker Massacre; the kidnapping of Rose Daniels; differences between white and Indian culture; law; inter-band tribes; migrations; segregation; and Christian churches. Among those interviewed were Ina Lou Chapoose, Marietta Redd, Mentora Daniels Crumbo, Ethel Daniels Kolb, Anna Marie Ketchum Nat, Cuch Pawwannee, [Mrs.] Hazel Wardle, Sarah Van Hackford, Helen Knight, Gwen Mulder, Lena Sixkiller, Nellie Coston, Maude Darnell, and Elvira Pike.

Also includes interviews with Lydia Taylor Skewes, who discusses the settlement of Moab and the Pinhook War; Claude and Estella Taylor, who discuss Ute dress and hair, individual Indians, Ute residential areas, ceremonies, burial customs, trade, and white attitudes toward Indians; Pearl Watts Taylor, who speaks of Indian visitors and friends, a squaw giving birth, and migratory Indians; and Lulu Wash Chapoose Brock, who discusses her ancestors and childhood, her children, tribal affairs, her education, customs, Indian agents, Chief Ouray, and artisans.

Conner Chapoose discusses the role of women, pregnancy, childbirth, parent-child relationships, sexual behavior, menstruation, morals and virtues, bathing customs, marriage customs, polygamy, and justice for unfaithful spouses. Eva Hayes speaks of the Old West, Fort Lewis in Durango, CO, her impressions of Utes and Navajos, land claims, contacts between Indians and whites, the tourist trade, Mormons, and mining. Orville Day tells of Chief Walker courting a white girl and the custom of abandoning old women. Also includes interviews with Margaret Eberly, who speaks of her VISTA training, the contrast between Ouray, UT, and New York City, missionaries, discrimination, raising children, masculinity, and family problems; Bessie Owens Kohl, who speaks of water rights, influential Indians, and medical care; and Edith L. Richards, a registered nurse, who discusses her ancestry, her work on a reservation, and hospital conditions.

16,877. American Indian Oral History Duke Collection: Zuni
Oral history. 1967-68. No size given.
Access restricted. Unpublished guide.
University of Utah, Special Collections.
Interviews with or concerning Zuni Indians contain discussion of such topics as the origin of the Zunis, revelations about the white man, Zuni legends and stories, the scalp dance and other dances, the first missionaries in Zuni, NM, relations between Zunis and missionaries and between Zunis and anthropologists, witchcraft, a Negro medicine man, beliefs about lightning, tribal morals, rustlers, a smallpox epidemic, food, clothing, shelter, trade, farming, hunting, transportation, pueblo life, schools and education, recreation, the Bureau of Indian Affairs, marriage, child-adult relations, and relations between Zunis, Navajos, and Apaches. Among those interviewed were Patrick Bankatewa, Edna Danver, Clara Gonzales, Merle Sheka, Mrs. Nunuche Enote, Lonkeena, and Margaret Lewis, a Cherokee.

16,878. Bills, Ella Mae Donohoo
Papers. 1915. 25-page vol.
Open. Card index.
University of Utah, Special Collections.
Diary in which Bills (1896-) describes the beginning of the Donohoo family's move from their East Crescent farm to Lonetree, WY.

16,879. Blue Tea Literary Club of Salt Lake City
Records. 1877-83. 1 vol.
Open. Card index.
University of Utah, Special Collections.
Minutebook of this women's group, founded in 1877 for "the promotion of mental culture" and literary research, contains a constitution, minutes, and other items.

16,880. Bosone, Reva Beck
Papers. 1927-68. 18 ft.
Open. Published guide.
University of Utah, Special Collections.
Bosone (1895-) was a Utah state representative from 1933 to 1935, a Salt Lake City judge from 1936 to 1948, a US representative from 1949 to 1952, and a judicial officer and chairman of the contract board of appeals of the US Post Office in 1961. Correspondence, autobiography, speeches, photos, biographical material, scrapbooks, campaign material, clippings, and publications. See *Register of the Papers of Reva Beck Bosone (1895-), Register 20* (Salt Lake City: Special Collections Department, University of Utah Libraries, 1978).

16,881. Brodie, Fawn M.
Papers. 1943-78. 4 ft.
Open. Card index.
University of Utah, Special Collections.
Brodie (1915-) is an author and history professor at the University of California at Los Angeles. Correspondence with friends and with historian Dale L. Morgan from 1943 to 1972, manuscripts of her books on Thaddeus Stevens and Thomas Jefferson, speeches, biographical material, book reviews of *Thomas Jefferson: An Intimate History,* articles, and reprints.

16,882. Brooks, Juanita Leavitt
Papers. Nd. 4 in.
Open. Card index.
University of Utah, Special Collections.
Brooks (ca. 1900-) is an author and historian. Transcript of a 1973 interview with Brooks, correspondence with historian Dale L. Morgan from 1921 to 1953, research notes, copies of documents dating 1877, and clippings.

16,883. Bullock, Electa Wood
Papers. Nd. 4 pp.
Open. Register.
University of Utah, Special Collections.
Biographical sketch of Bullock (1834-1911), who assisted in managing the family hotel in Provo, UT, and was involved in the Latter-day Saints Church Relief Society and women's suffrage work.

16,884. Burt, Olive W.
Papers. Nd. 1 ft.
Open. Card index.
University of Utah, Special Collections.
Manuscripts of published ballads about murder written by Burt (1894-), an author.

16,885. Butler, Jane Elizabeth Lee
Papers. Nd. 1 folder.
Open. Card index.
University of Utah, Special Collections.
Autobiographical account of Butler (1875-1963), a resident of Panaca, NV, and a local historian and church and civic worker.

16,886. Campbell, Esther, and Campbell, Duward
Papers. 1969. 2 in.
Open. Card catalog.
University of Utah, Special Collections.
Interview with Esther Campbell and her husband Duward Campbell, who were residents of Brown's Hole, where numerous western outlaws took refuge.

16,887. Cannon, Sarah Maria Mousley
Papers. 1857. 15-page vol.
Open. Card index.
University of Utah, Special Collections.
Journal of Cannon, a Mormon pioneer, chronicles her journey across the plains to Utah.

16,888. Clawson, Hiram B., Family
Papers. 1847-99. 1 ft.
Open. Published guide.
University of Utah, Special Collections.
Collection consists primarily of correspondence of the family of Hiram B. Clawson (1826-1912), who was the manager of Brigham Young's private business, manager of the Salt Lake Theatre, first general superintendent of Zion's Cooperative Mercantile Institution, member of the Nauvoo Legion, and twelfth ward bishop of the Church of Jesus Christ of Latter-day Saints. Letters from 1847 to 1849 of Orson Spencer to his children in Council Bluffs and Salt Lake City while on his proselyting mission to the British Isles and letters from relatives of Catherine Curtis Spencer, who died during the 1846 exodus from Nauvoo, expressing concern for her children. Hiram Clawson's letters to Ellen Spencer Clawson from 1857 to 1894 concern his time with the Nauvoo Legion in Echo Canyon and at Fort Bridger observing the approaching army; business trips to the East for ZCMI; time spent in the territorial penitentiary from 1885 to 1886 for violation of the federal anticohabitation laws; his trip to Arizona to help establish friendly relations between Arizona and Utah territories; and his activities in Washington, DC, from 1892 to 1894. Correspondence between Ellen Spencer Clawson and Ellen Pratt McGary from 1857 to 1870 contains information on polygamy. See *Register of the Papers of Hiram B. Clawson (1826-1912), Register 1* (Salt Lake City: Western Americana Department, University of Utah Libraries, 1972).

16,889. Crawford, Vesta
Papers. Ca. 1917-71. 20 in.
Open. Card catalog.
University of Utah, Special Collections.
Papers of Crawford (1899-) include letters from Arlon Rowes during WWI; notebooks of poetry of Grace Inglis Frost; correspondence, research notes, and clippings that relate to a manuscript regarding the life of Emma Smith, who was the wife of Joseph Smith, organizer of the Mormon Church; and a biography of Olive Alger Truman written by Eva A. Paxman.

16,890. Davis Bitton Oral History
Oral history. 1971-75. 2 boxes.
Open. Card index.
University of Utah, Special Collections.
Tapes and transcripts of interviews conducted by history professor Davis Bitton's students, including interviews with Catherine Fratto regarding Italian folklore; Jessie Marguerite Pace Graham concerning her family's history in St. George, UT; Joy Hashimoto describing life in a Japanese relocation center at Granada, CO, from 1942 to 1945; Joyce Matsuno, a Japanese-American living in Salt Lake City; Dorothy G. Snow, a University of Utah English professor; Elizabeth Vance, field representative for the anti-discrimination division of the State Industrial Commission; Mary E. Webster, teacher of speech pathology and remedial reading in the 1920s; and Veronica Colby regarding bombing raids in England during WWII.

16,891. Fowler, Mary Susannah Sumner Fackrell
Papers. 1899-1900. 2 vols.
Open. Card catalog.
University of Utah, Special Collections.
Account of Fowler documents family, religious, and community activities in Huntington, UT, with mention made of Sunnyside, Castledale, Scofield, and Price, UT.

16,892. Hasler, Louisa (Thalman)
Papers. Nd. 1 folder.
Open. Register.
University of Utah, Special Collections.
Autobiographical account of Hasler (1843-97) describes her early years in Switzerland, conversion to the Mormon Church of herself and her husband John Hasler in 1869, their emigration to Utah, and their pioneering efforts in Mount Pleasant, UT.

16,893. Hayne, Julia Dean
Papers. 1865. 1 folder.
Open. Card index.
University of Utah, Special Collections.
Divorce proceedings of Hayne (1830-68), an early Utah resident and actress, and her husband Arthur P. Hayne in Salt Lake County probate court. Julia Hayne requested the divorce for reasons of incompatibility and because of her husband's intemperate habits.

16,894. Helwing, Anna
Papers. 1938-55. 1.5 ft.
Open. Card index.
University of Utah, Special Collections.
Anna Helwing (1893-1956) and her husband Sigmund Helwing were Jewish refugees from Nazi Germany who arrived in Utah in 1940. Contains Anna Helwing's autobiography; correspondence, photos, and a scrapbook of clippings pertaining to wartime efforts of the Salt Lake City Jewish community; and reminiscences of Anna Helwing regarding her life in Nazi Germany and in the US.

16,895. Heywood, Martha Spence
Papers. 1850-56. 1 vol.
Open. Card index.
University of Utah, Special Collections.
Diary, reminiscences, and a poem of Heywood (1812-?), a pioneer, regarding her conversion to the Mormon Church, experiences within the Church, emigration to Utah, marriage, and activities in Salt Lake City and Nephi, UT.

16,896. Hoffman, Naomi R.
Papers. 1914-19. 1 vol.
Open. Card index.
University of Utah, Special Collections.
Diary of Hoffman regarding domestic activities, friends, neighbors, and travels.

16,897. Jarvis, Ann Prior
Papers. Nd. 24-page item.
Open. Register.
University of Utah, Special Collections.
Autobiography of Jarvis (1830-85), a Mormon and early resident of southern Utah, describes the conversion to the Mormon Church of herself and her husband George Jarvis, their emigration to Utah, and their pioneering efforts in the Dixie Mission in 1861.

16,898. Jarvis, Eleanor C. W.
Papers. 1854-1923. 34 pp.
Open. Register.
University of Utah, Special Collections.
Two diaries of Jarvis, a Mormon, in which she describes family births and deaths, family visits, miraculous healings, and hardships her family experienced during periods while polygamists were hiding from federal marshals to avoid prosecution for violating anticohabitation laws. Born in Salt Lake City, Jarvis went at the age of 7 to the Dixie Cotton Mission, which was founded by Brigham Young at St. George, UT. She learned to spin wool and cotton and relates how she earned a calico dress and a pair of shoes by spinning for her relatives.

16,899. Junior League of Salt Lake City
Records. 1934-61. 4 ft.
Open. Card index.
University of Utah, Special Collections.
The League is a community service organization of young women who raise money and support for various projects. Scrapbooks of League ephemera, clippings, and copies of *Junior League Magazine.*

16,900. Leavitt, Sarah Studevant
Papers. Nd. 42-page vol.
Open. Card index.
University of Utah, Special Collections.
Biography of Leavitt (1798-), written by Juanita Leavitt Pulsipher Brooks, recounts Leavitt's witness to major events in the Mormon Church's history.

16,901. Lee, Amarilla (Hamblin)
Papers. 1970. 13-page vol.
Open. Card catalog.
University of Utah, Special Collections.
Interview in which Lee (1884-?), daughter of Utah pioneer Jacob Hamblin, recounts her early life in Alpine and Nutrioso, AZ. Her father died when she was 2 years old.

16,902. Lyman, Eliza Maria Partridge
Papers. Nd. 2 vols.
Open. Register.
University of Utah, Special Collections.
A Mormon pioneer in Utah, Lyman (1820-86) was a plural wife of Joseph Smith and, after Smith's death, a wife of Amasa M. Lyman, a member of the Council of Twelve Apostles who later apostatized from the Church. Journal in which Lyman describes the hardships of crossing the plains as a young wife and mother.

16,903. Mormon Settlements in Arizona
Collection. 1876-1972. 6.5 ft.
Open. Published guide.
University of Utah, Special Collections.
Correspondence, diaries, journals, autobiographies, biographies, and local histories regarding the early Mormon settlements of Brigham City, Joseph City, Obed, and Sunset in Arizona and current settlements. Includes autobiographies of Lucy Hannah White Flake and Ida Frances Hunt Udall, autobiography and diary of May Hunt Larsen from 1876 to 1878, and biographical sketch of Ida Udall written by Pauline Udall Smith. Also contains accounts of Indian and exploratory missions to Arizona. See *Register of the Records of Mormon Settlements in Arizona, Register 8* (Salt Lake City: Special Collections Department, University of Utah Libraries, 1974).

16,904. Morris, Josie
Papers. 1959. 60-page vol.
Open. Card index.
University of Utah, Special Collections.
Interview in which Morris describes life in Brown's Hole, outlaws, cattle rustling, and cattle ranching from 1874 to 1959.

16,905. Noall, Matthew, and Noall, Claire
Papers. Ca. 1845-1977. 8 ft.
Open. Card index.
University of Utah, Special Collections.
Correspondence, diaries, journals, manuscripts, court orders, legal documents, and other papers of the Richards, Noall, and Stevenson families. Includes a journal and diary from 1846 to 1850 of Nancy (Richards) Peirson (1792-1852), sister of Willard Richards, a medical doctor and Mormon general authority, regarding domestic activities and her longing to join her family in the Mormon Church and in the emigration to Utah; journals from 1886 to 1895 of Elizabeth "Libby" Laker Noall concerning her mission to Hawaii; diaries from 1898 to 1905 of Elizabeth Jane DuFresne Stevenson (1838-1906), wife of Edward Stevenson; and correspondence, poetry, manuscripts and research material for four published books, and articles of Claire Noall (1892-1971), a poet and author.

16,906. Pearce, Jean Rio
Papers. 1851-80. 65 pp.
Open. Register.
University of Utah, Special Collections.
Diary in which Pearce (1810-?), a native of England who joined the Mormon Church, describes her emigration from England to Salt Lake City in 1851, her years in Utah, and her move to California in 1877.

16,907. Potter, Olive Andelin
Papers. 1932. 8-page vol.
Open. Card index.
University of Utah, Special Collections.
Biography of Potter (1868-?), a Richfield, UT, resident, in which she recounts the hardships of her polygamous marriage.

16,908. Reid, Agnes Just
Papers. Nd. 5 in.
Open. Card catalog.
University of Utah, Special Collections.
Correspondence, autobiography, biographical sketches, photos, poetry, printed material, and other items of Reid (1886-1976), an author. Includes a biographical sketch, with photos, about Emma Thompson Just written by Agnes Reid and Marlene Stibal Reid and biographical sketches about Agnes Reid written by Marlene Stibal Reid and Ann Hansen Hayes.

16,909. Richards, Mary Haskin Parker
Papers. 1846-48. 69-page item.
Open. Register.
University of Utah, Special Collections.
Diary in which Richards (1825-60), a Mormon, describes life in Council Bluffs while she waited for her husband Samuel W. Richards to return from his mission to England.

16,910. Seegmiller, Mary Jane Orrock
Papers. 1954. 1 folder.
Open. Card index.
University of Utah, Special Collections.
A family history compiled by Seegmiller contains biographical information about her grandmother Mary Cumming Orrock (1819-?), a Scottish convert to the Mormon Church and resident of Richfield, UT.

16,911. Smith, George A., Family
Papers. 1731-1969. 85 ft.
Open. Published guide.
University of Utah, Special Collections.
Correspondence, journals, minutes, financial records, photos, scrapbooks, certificates, estate records, and other papers of the Smith family, whose members were active in the Mormon Church and in Utah business matters and politics. Contains material of Joseph Smith, Jr., founder of the Mormon Church; George A. Smith (1817-75) and John Henry Smith, apostles in the Church; and George Albert Smith, the Church's eighth president from 1945 to 1951. Papers of three of George A. Smith's wives include correspondence and an 1849 diary of Bathsheba W. Bigler Smith (1822-1910), regarding her journey across the plains to Utah, a biographical sketch of Susan Elizabeth West Smith (1833-1926), and material of Lucy S. Smith. Papers of John Henry Smith's wife Sarah Farr Smith (1849-1921) include correspondence and other items. Also found in the collection are a biographical sketch of Tirzah Wells Chase (1796-1867); correspondence and a history of the Relief Society written by Eliza R. Snow (1804-87); correspondence, poetry, patriarchal blessings, and other items of Lucy Messerve Smith (1817-92); a biographical sketch of Nancy B. Chase Farr (1823-92); a memorial of Tirzah Farr Gay (1852-1946); correspondence, diary, and reminiscences of Clara M. Woodruff Beebe (1868-?); correspondence, journals, personal documents, and other material of Lucy Emily Woodruff Smith (1869-1937); and personal and business correspondence and other items of Emily Smith Stewart (1895-1973), including material regarding the National Foundation for Infantile Paralysis, Beta Sigma Phi, the March of Dimes, the Utah Polio Emergency Committee, Vocational Rehabilitation, and UNESCO. See *Register of the Papers of the George A. Smith Family, 1731-1969, Register 9* (Salt Lake City: Special Collections Department, University of Utah Libraries, 1975).

16,912. Snow, Julia Josephine Spencer
Papers. 1957. 12-page vol.
Open. Card index.
University of Utah, Special Collections.
Biography of Snow (1837-1909), a southern Utah pioneer and fourth wife of Erastus Snow, a Mormon general authority. The biography was written by a relative of Snow.

16,913. Tanner, John
Papers. 1849-1974. 2.5 ft.
Open. Card index.
University of Utah, Special Collections.
Family papers of Tanner (1778-?), a Mormon pioneer, include diaries of Mary Jane Mount Tanner (1837-90), a poet and journalist, regarding community and family events.

16,914. Thatcher, Paul
Papers. 1815-1972. 1 box.
Open. Card index.
University of Utah, Special Collections.
Family papers of Thatcher include a diary kept by Sarah Maria Davis Thatcher from 1878 to 1887 regarding family and local Mormon Church activities; a biographical sketch of Margaret Thompson Smoot (1809-84), who was the first wife of Abraham O. Smoot, first mayor of Salt Lake City and a local Church official; a biography of Diana Eldredge Smoot (1837-1914), third wife of Abraham O. Smoot, describing crossing the plains to Utah; and correspondence, an autobiography, and reminiscences about life in Utah of Olive Smoot [Mrs. James William] Bean (1860-?).

16,915. Utah Humanities Research Foundation
Records. Nd. 5 ft.
Open. Published guide.
University of Utah, Special Collections.
Correspondence, diaries, journals, autobiographies, biographies, and documents of the Foundation, which was founded in 1944 to collect, preserve, and interpret cultural materials from the Utah region. Includes a diary and correspondence, 1882-1919, of Emily Stevens Dalton of Parowan in Iron County, UT; reminiscences of Julia Putman Foster describing life in Pine Valley in Washington County, UT; and a biographical sketch of Eliza Lewis Fish, wife of Joseph Fish and a southern Utah and Arizona pioneer, written in 1853 by Emma Ward. Also contains letters written from 1881 to 1887 to a missionary in New Zealand by his father, mother, wife, brothers, and sisters and from the missionary to his wife; the family was polygamous. See *Register of the Utah Humanities Research Foundation, Register 7* (Salt Lake City: Special Collections Division, University of Utah Libraries, 1973).

16,916. Van Striprian, Dorothy
Papers. 1868-1965. 2 in. and 1 microfilm reel.
Open. Card index.
University of Utah, Special Collections.
A Utah artist, Van Striprian wrote a biographical dictionary of other Utah artists. Biographical sketches of William N. B. Shepherd and other artists, several of whom are women; minutes of the Sugar House Relief Society in Salt Lake City, 1868-71; and minutes of the Salt Lake State Young Women's Mutual Improvement Association, 1879-96.

16,917. Young, Richard W.
Papers. 1876-1957. 2.5 ft.
Open. Published guide.
University of Utah, Special Collections.
Young (1858-1919) was a military officer, Mormon Church official, attorney, civil officer, author, and associate justice in the supreme court of the Philippines from 1898 to 1899. Correspondence, journals, publications, and other papers of Young, his wife Minerva Richards Young (1862-1958), and Richard W. Young, Jr. Includes Minerva Young's diary from 1882 to 1886 regarding her marriage and their four years on Governors Island in New York City, her reminiscences about trips abroad from 1911 to 1928, her autobiography, and correspondence primarily pertaining to her husband's activities. See *Register of Richard W. Young (1858-1919), Register 11* (Salt Lake City: Special Collections Department, 1976).

16,918. Allen, Florence E.
Papers. Nd. 10-page item.
Open. Card catalog.
Utah State Historical Society Library.
Speech of Allen, a women's rights worker, concerns the outlawing of war. She presented the speech at a Des Moines, IA, convention of an organization for the improvement of the status of women.

16,919. American Association of University Women
Records. 1969. Ca. 100 pp.
Open. Card catalog.
Utah State Historical Society Library.
Catalog of art held by 17 Salt Lake City institutions compiled by the AAUW special art committee, which was chaired by Jane K. Hearn.

16,920. The Beehive
Records. 1886-89. 1 folder.
Open. Unpublished guide.
Utah State Historical Society Library.
Twelve issues of this manuscript newspaper written by young women in St. George, UT, include stories, poems, proverbs, advice, and recipes.

16,921. Bills, Hattie M.
Papers. 1936-40. 365-page vol.
Open. Card catalog.
Utah State Historical Society Library.
Diary in which Bills describes family and domestic activities, visits with relatives, and her work in the Mormon Church.

16,922. Bowen, Lucy (Gates)
Papers. Ca. 1900-35. 2.5 ft.
Open. Published guide.
Utah State Historical Society Library.
Correspondence, notebooks, scrapbooks, programs, clippings, and other items of Bowen (1880-1951), an opera singer. Includes letters from her mother Susa Young Gates and her sister Leah D. Widtsoe. Bowen's full name was Emma Lucy (Gates) Bowen.

16,923. Brodie, Fawn (McKay)
Papers. Nd. 1 folder.
Open. Card catalog.
Utah State Historical Society Library.
Correspondence of Brodie (1915-), an author and professor of history at the University of California at Los Angeles, with the Utah State Historical Society regarding manuscripts and reviews she has submitted to the Society and her desire to write a biography of Brigham Young.

16,924. Brooks, Juanita
Papers. Ca. 1934-69. 1 Hollinger box.
Open. No guide.
Utah State Historical Society Library.
Correspondence, manuscripts, and other papers of Brooks (1900?-), a Utah historian and author. Includes correspondence concerning her publications and professional activities; drafts of articles on the Dixie cotton mission, the St.

George, UT, normal school, and the Mountain Meadow historic stopping place on the Spanish Trail; a history of the Green River; and material regarding her book about her husband Will Brooks.

16,925. Butterfield, Jacob K.
Papers. 1836-50. 1 folder.
Open. Card catalog.
Utah State Historical Society Library.
Letters that Butterfield, a convert to the Mormon Church, wrote from Ohio, Kansas, and Utah to his mother Persis Butterfield in East Wilton, ME, expressing affection and concern for her.

16,926. Butts, Frances Amelia (Buss)
Papers. 1866-68. 48-page vol.
Open. Card catalog.
Utah State Historical Society Library.
Diary of Butts (1834-84) regarding her family's journey from New York, where she had been born, to Fort Collins, CO, where she settled. Includes information about her sister, aunts, and other women and about her first year in Colorado. Butts died in Fort Collins.

16,927. Cannon, Sarah Maria (Mousley)
Papers. 1857. 15-page vol.
Open. Card catalog.
Utah State Historical Society Library.
Journal of [Mrs. Angus M.] Cannon, written prior to her marriage, regarding her journey across the plains to Utah.

16,928. Capitol Girls Club
Records. 1921-40. 1 folder.
Open. Card catalog.
Utah State Historical Society Library.
Constitution, bylaws, minutes, and programs of this social organization for women employed at the state capitol in Salt Lake City.

16,929. Chase, Alice
Papers. 1891. 4-page item.
Open. Card catalog.
Utah State Historical Society Library.
Letter of Chase to her mother Mrs. George O. Chase regarding school and family matters and domestic activities.

16,930. Church of Jesus Christ of Latter-day Saints, Laketown Relief Society
Records. 1878-1916. 1 vol.
Open. Card catalog.
Utah State Historical Society Library.
Volume containing minutes, attendance records, accounts, and receipts of this women's organization concerned with cultural refinement, education, and charity.

16,931. Clark, Lucy A. Rice
Papers. Ca. 1914-18. 1 folder.
Open. Card catalog.
Utah State Historical Society Library.
Clark was a Utah resident and songwriter who wrote "The American Army Song." Includes correspondence, story of the writing of the song, clippings, and other papers.

16,932. Cumming, Alfred
Papers. 1857-58. 1 folder.
Open. Card catalog.
Utah State Historical Society Library.
Correspondence of Cumming (1792-1889), Utah territorial governor, includes a letter from Rebecca Foster requesting assistance in re-claiming her children from her husband, whom she divorced after he converted to the Mormon Church. She had moved to Connecticut, and he came and took the children away to Utah.

16,933. Cumming, Elizabeth Wells (Randall)
Papers. 1857-58. 17 items.
Open. Card catalog.
Utah State Historical Society Library.
Correspondence of Cumming, wife of Alfred Cumming, Utah territorial governor, describes her journey with Johnston's army from St. Louis to Camp Scott; life in an army camp during the Utah war, which involved noncombat military action against the Mormons, who were alleged to be in rebellion; and the desertion of Salt Lake City in 1858.

16,934. Dallin, Victoria Colonna (Murray)
Papers. 1893-1947. 132-page item.
Open. Card catalog.
Utah State Historical Society Library.
Diary in which Dallin (1861-?), wife of sculptor Cyrus Edwin Dallin (1861-1944), describes family activities, her teaching career, and other positions she held in Boston.

16,935. Day, Eli Azariah
Papers. Ca. 1943. 63-page item.
Open. Card catalog.
Utah State Historical Society Library.
Reminiscences of Day (1856-?), a resident of Mount Pleasant in Sanpete County, UT, regarding his childhood experiences in a polygamous family. Includes descriptions of the wives in the family and the domestic duties of his sisters.

16,936. Dyer, Frank H.
Papers. 1890-1954. 2 in.
Open. Card catalog.
Utah State Historical Society Library.
Scrapbooks provide information on Ella B. DeVoto (1889-1929) and other Dyer family members, the Women's Industrial Home of Salt Lake City, Mormonism, polygamy, and Utah politics.

16,937. Eakle, Mary Alice, and Eakle, Arlene
Oral history. 1975. 11 tapes.
Open. No guide.
Utah State Historical Society Library.
Interviews regarding the burning in 1975 of a Mormon chapel in Bountiful, UT, include those with seven women. Arlene Eakle is the director of the Genealogical Institute in Salt Lake City and a graduate student at the University of Utah.

16,938. Eddington, Henry Charles
Papers. 1887-1901. 2 in.
Open. Card catalog.
Utah State Historical Society Library.
Letters from Eddington to his wife Sarah Eddington while he was working on railroad construction in New Mexico. He describes the intense persecution of polygamy in that area and expresses concern for his wives and children.

16,939. Ferris, Benjamin G.
Papers. 1853. 3-page item.
Open. Card catalog.
Utah State Historical Society Library.
Letter from Ferris in Salt Lake City to his cousin [Mrs.] May Hathaway reporting a pleasant winter among the Mormons. In the 1850s Ferris wrote a book condemning polygamy.

16,940. Field, Kate
Papers. 1885-87. 5 items.
Open. Card catalog.
Utah State Historical Society Library.
Letters from [Miss] Field, a non-Mormon who visited Salt Lake City, to friends in New York regarding her observations of Utah and the Mormons. Field later went on a lecture tour condemning polygamy.

16,941. Gates, Susa (Young)
Papers. Ca. 1865-1920. 11 ft.
Open. Published guide.
Utah State Historical Society Library.
Gates (1856-1933), the daughter of Brigham Young, was an author, editor, suffragist and women's rights leader, poet, musician, and mother of 13 children. Business and personal correspondence, manuscripts of her biography of Brigham Young and of her history of women, photos, biographical material, bibliography of her works, and mementos. See *Register of the Susa Young Gates Collection in the Library of the Utah State Historical Society* (Salt Lake City, 1976).

16,942. Japanese-American Oral History Project
Oral history. 1975-76. No size given.
Partially restricted. No guide.
Utah State Historical Society Library.
Interviews sponsored by the Utah State Historical Society and the Salt Lake City Japanese-American Association include interviews with 15 Japanese-American women. Among them are [Mrs.] Tokiko Tabari (1898-), regarding her immigration to the US, treatment of the Japanese during WWII, and life in the Topaz relocation camp; [Mrs.] Take Uchida (1890-), who was born near Kyoto, Japan, and immigrated to the US in 1914, regarding her travels and occupations in the US and Christianity among the Japanese; and [Mrs.] Suga Yano, concerning her life in Utah.

16,943. King, Hannah Tapfield
Papers. Ca. 1857. 145-page item.
Open. Card catalog.
Utah State Historical Society Library.
Autobiography of King (1807-86) documents her life in England, conversion to the Mormon Church, and emigration to Utah. Compiled from diary entries of 1842 to 1857.

16,944. Leatham, Margaret
Papers. 1893. 1 item.
Open. Card catalog.
Utah State Historical Society Library.
Medical license to practice obstetrics granted to Leatham by the Territory of Utah board of medical examiners.

16,945. Lyman, Eliza Maria (Partridge) Smith
Papers. 1846-85. 1 folder.
Open. Card catalog.
Utah State Historical Society Library.
Diaries and reminiscences of Lyman (1820-86), a plural wife of Amasa M. Lyman, an apostle of the Mormon Church, describe her early life in Missouri and Nauvoo, IL; her emigration to Utah; and activities in Salt Lake City and Fillmore. Includes a speech defending polygamy.

16,946. McCrimmon, Elizabeth (Cannon) Porter
Papers. Nd. 1 folder.
Open. Unpublished guide.
Utah State Historical Society Library.
Paper written by McCrimmon regarding Martha Hughes Cannon, who was born in Wales, emigrated to Salt Lake City in 1860, became a physician, married Angus M. Cannon as his fourth wife, operated a nursing school, participated in the suffrage movement, and in 1897 became the first woman in the US to be elected a state senator. Includes correspondence and photos.

16,947. Maughan, Mary Ann (Weston)
Papers. 1817-98. 3 vols.
Open. Unpublished guide.
Utah State Historical Society Library.
Journals of Maughan (1817-1901) document her life in England; conversion to the Mormon Church; emigration to Kirtland and Nauvoo; her journey in 1850 to Tooele, UT, and Logan, UT; and marriage to Peter Maughan. Includes genealogical material of the Weston family.

16,948. Mother of the Year
Records. 1949-71. 4.5 ft.
Open. Card catalog.
Utah State Historical Society Library.
Scrapbooks and other items of this Utah group,

which honors exemplary mothers and homemakers, include autobiographies of 124 contestants.

16,949. Musser Family
Papers. Ca. 1900-60. 10 ft.
Closed. Register.
Utah State Historical Society Library.
Correspondence, diaries, notebooks, poetry, military and missionary papers, photos, school records, biographical information, and other papers of the family of Joseph White Musser (1872-1954), the leader of a fundamentalist Mormon sect espousing polygamy, and his wife Ellis (Shipp) Musser, who worked in insurance. Ellis Musser's papers contain notebooks; material for a biography of her mother Ellis Reynolds Shipp, a medical doctor who graduated from Woman's Medical College of Pennsylvania in 1878; photos; miscellaneous items; and correspondence, some of which is written between Joseph and Ellis Musser documenting their courtship, their decision to enter into a secret polygamous marriage, and their married years. Collection also includes the papers of Joseph and Ellis Musser's daughters Lucile (Musser) Jackson, Ellis (Musser) Kirkham, and Josephine (Musser) Tillotson. Papers of Joseph and Ellis Musser's son Samuel Shipp Musser contain his correspondence with his father regarding polygamy.

16,950. Pack, John
Papers. 1847. 1 folder.
Open. Card catalog.
Utah State Historical Society Library.
Letters written by Pack to his wife Julia Pack while he was crossing the plains. He tells his family about the trip and exhorts them to be faithful to the Mormon Church.

16,951. Retrenchment Society
Records. 1975-76. 1 folder and 2 tapes.
Open. No guide.
Utah State Historical Society Library.
Tapes of guest lectures and question-and-answer sessions of the Society, which was founded in 1975 as a public forum on women's issues in Utah. The Society was funded through the State Endowment for the Humanities.

16,952. Richards, Jane (Snyder)
Papers. 1880. 2 folders.
Open. Card catalog.
Utah State Historical Society Library.
Interview in which Richards (1823-?), the first wife of Franklin D. Richards, a Mormon Church authority, discusses polygamy. Also contains her reminiscences, which relate that she was born in Canada, converted to the Mormon Church, moved to Nauvoo, IL, and crossed the plains to Salt Lake City, where she was involved in social and religious activities.

16,953. Richardson, Verna
Oral history. 1974. No size given.
Open. No guide.
Utah State Historical Society Library.
Transcripts of interviews conducted by Richardson, creator of the Grouse Creek oral history project and long-time resident of Grouse Creek in Box Elder County, UT. Also contains biographical sketches of those interviewed. Women interviewed include Bertha M. Kimball; Mary Hadfield Betteridge; Lillian Grace Chadwick Warburton (1901-), regarding the Grouse Creek elementary school and her teaching experiences; and Ellen Sarah Ballingham Betteridge (1882-), concerning her family's move to northwestern Utah. Betteridge's interview contains descriptions of community members.

16,954. Rowland Hall School
Records. 1867-1959. 2 ft.
Open. No guide.
Utah State Historical Society Library.
Correspondence, photos of students, alumnae material, commencement announcements, school catalogs, literary publications, school newspapers, and other items of this girls school founded in 1881 by the Episcopal Church in Salt Lake City.

16,955. Sessions, Patty (Bartlett)
Papers. 1846-80. 1 folder.
Open. Card catalog.
Utah State Historical Society Library.
Papers of Sessions (1795-1892), a pioneer midwife, contain diaries regarding her emigration to Utah and activities in Salt Lake City, statement declaring that Sessions was sealed to Joseph Smith in 1842, account book, and poetry written by Eliza R. Snow.

16,956. Shipp, Ellis Reynolds
Papers. Ca. 1864-1932. 3 ft.
Open. No guide.
Utah State Historical Society Library.
Family correspondence, diary, autobiography, notebooks, poems, clippings, and other papers of Shipp, a medical doctor in UT. Also contains manuscripts of lectures on women in medicine.

16,957. Smith, Bathsheba Wilson (Bigler)
Papers. 1849. 1 folder.
Open. Card catalog.
Utah State Historical Society Library.
Diary of Smith (1822-1910), general president of the Relief Society and plural wife of George A. Smith, an apostle of the Mormon Church. Concerns her journey from Carbonca, IA, to Salt Lake City.

16,958. Smith, Eliza Roxey (Snow)
Papers. Ca. 1839-70. 1 folder.
Open. Card catalog.
Utah State Historical Society Library.
Correspondence, journal excerpts, poetry, autograph book, and Snow family genealogy of [Mrs. Joseph] Smith (1804-87), general president of the Relief Society. Includes a letter written from Portage County, OH, to Isaac Streator.

16,959. Smith, Joseph, III
Papers. 1855-56. 1 folder.
Open. Unpublished guide.
Utah State Historical Society Library.
Correspondence of Smith, president of the Reorganized Church of Jesus Christ of Latter Day Saints and son of Joseph Smith, Jr., founder of the Mormon Church. Includes letters from Nauvoo, IL, to Emma Knight regarding family matters and spiritualism.

16,960. Spring City, UT, Oral History Project
Oral history. 1974. No size given.
Open. No guide.
Utah State Historical Society Library.
Interviews containing biographical information about 12 women, their family histories, reminiscences regarding Spring City, and descriptions of the customs and personalities of Danish immigrants who settled there.

16,961. Taylor, Jane (Ballantyne)
Papers. 1839-1963. 5 in.
Open. Card catalog and accession list.
Utah State Historical Society Library.
Correspondence, invitations, a certificate of proclamation of marriage, divorce papers, patriarchal blessings, and other papers of Taylor (1813-?), a plural wife of John Taylor, who was a president of the Mormon Church. The papers concern the Ballantyne, Taylor, and Hyde families.

16,962. Thompson, Ellen L. "Nellie" (Powell)
Papers. 1872. 46-page item.
Open. Card catalog.
Utah State Historical Society Library.
Diary of Thompson, who stayed in Kanab, UT, while her husband Almon H. Thompson and other members of the Powell expedition were surveying the country.

16,963. Utah Cowbelles
Records. 1942-71. 2 vols.
Open. No guide.
Utah State Historical Society Library.
Records of this women's auxiliary of the Utah Cattlemen's Association include scrapbooks containing records from local chapters, photos, programs, invitations, articles regarding the group, and clippings containing biographical information on members.

16,964. Utah Minute Women
Records. 1942-45. 1 folder.
Open. Card catalog.
Utah State Historical Society Library.
Collection includes minutes kept by secretary-treasurer Marion B. Kerr. This organization had 8000 members in Utah, 6000 of whom were volunteers. It conducted 35 war programs in addition to gathering fat, tin cans, rags, and paper salvage.

16,965. Utah State Historical Society Oral History
Oral history. 1953-76. Ca. 52 tapes and ca. 24 items.
Partially closed. No guide.
Utah State Historical Society Library.
Tapes and transcripts of 41 interviews with women, some of whom emigrated to Utah from England, Denmark, Sweden, and Finland. Contains interviews with pioneers, housewives, a telephone operator, a worker in the cotton mills, a licensed practical nurse, a records librarian for a Veterans Administration hospital, a local historian, an educator, and a journalist. Topics represented include polygamy, Brigham Young, the 1917 San Francisco World's Fair, the Utah Heritage Foundation, mining communities, skiing, diet, Butch Cassidy, the depression, and the Episcopal Church in Utah. Among those interviewed is [Mrs.] Jean M. Westwood, an aid to Congressman David S. King from Utah and national Democratic chairperson who worked for George McGovern, Terry Sanford, Lyndon B. Johnson, and Hubert H. Humphrey. She discusses other political figures and activities, her conflicts with Richard M. Nixon, and the Watergate scandal. Also includes interviews with Dorothy Jacobs Buchnan, who recounts her moving to Cardston in Alberta, Canada, as a child, the growth of the settlement, and community members; with Edith Melendez, vice-president of SOCIO, a minority assistance organization, who describes the progress of the Chicano movement in Utah; and with Lydia Peterson, daughter of Levi Savage, a settler of the Little Colorado River settlement in Utah. Peterson discusses the history of the area, the United Order, midwifery, responsibilities of the women, and ways in which the community was affected by the Woodruff Manifesto, the official statement ending polygamy among the Mormons. Also contains interviews with Mrs. John Wallace, community worker, patron of the arts, and founder and past president of the Utah Symphony Orchestra, who recounts the founding and sponsorship of the Orchestra and Ballet West and her memories of Salt Lake City, and with [Mrs.] Clara Kimball Ruggieri, a community worker who reminisces about life in Price, UT, the Ku Klux Klan in Utah, ethnic groups, Masonic lodges, various churches, marriage between a Mormon woman and an Italian Catholic man, and the Black Hand, an Italian criminal element reputedly guilty of extortion of northern Italian emigrants.

16,966. Utah Woman's Press Club
Records. 1894-95. 1 folder.
Open. Unpublished guide.

Utah State Historical Society Library.
Minute book and clippings of the Club, the members of which included Ellis Reynolds Shipp, Ruth May Fox, Romania Pratt, and Emmeline B. Wells.

16,967. Utah Women Autobiographies and Biographies

Collection. Nd. 76 folders.
Open. No guide.
Utah State Historical Society Library.
Primarily biographies and autobiographies of Utah women pioneers, this collection also contains several reminiscences, interviews, and family and local histories. Of the women represented, ca. 18 were immigrants, primarily from England but also from Ireland, Scotland, Denmark, and other Scandinavian countries. Besides being active in Mormon Church work, the women were actresses, musicians, midwives, teachers, historians, physicians, factory workers, and telegraph operators. Subjects discussed in the accounts include polygamy, Indians, Joseph Smith, the United Order, and the depression. Contains reminiscences of Clarissa (Harden) Lewis Terry Wilhelm, who was born in New York and emigrated to Utah, in which she describes life under the United Order in Orderville, UT, and hardships in Utah and Arizona, including raids carried out by US marshals against polygamists; a biography of Emma Rigby Jacobs Williams, who was born in Rigby, ID, regarding her travels, family life, church activities, and her association with women's rights worker Zina D. Young; and a biography of Jane Wilkie Manning Skolfield, a physician, educator, and civic worker, who lived in Salt Lake City, Ogden, and Provo, UT. The biography was written in 1951 by her daughter Jennie Manning Thomas.

Also includes a biography of [Mrs.] Ellen Pucell Unthank, who emigrated from England to Utah at the age of 9 as part of the Martin Handcart Company, which describes early snows that killed numerous members of the Company and necessitated the amputation of both of Unthank's legs at the knee. Unthank became a plural wife, bore six children, and supported her family. Also contained is an autobiographical sketch of Clara Jane (Sanford) Packard, who was born in Springville, UT, which describes her childhood, comfortable pioneer life, and civic and Church work, and a biographical sketch of Annie Rice Wilcox, a Bannock Indian baby found on a battlefield. Wilcox was raised among the whites in Ogden, UT; married Jonathan F. Wilcox, a veteran of the Civil War; and lived in Farmington, UT. The biographical sketch of Sarah Alydia Terry Winsor, a telegraph operator who was born in Salt Lake City, was written by Orilla W. Hafen and relates that Winsor's family was called by Brigham Young in 1863 to go to southern Utah. She married in 1877.

Some of these accounts were part of a WPA federal writers' project.

16,968. Utah Writers Project

Collection. Ca. 1932-38, nd. 113 folders.
Open. No guide.
Utah State Historical Society Library.
Part of the WPA Federal Writers Project, the Utah Writers Project gathered information regarding Utah pioneers through interviews; from autobiographies, diaries, and other writings of the pioneers; and from writings about them. Nearly a third of the 113 women represented were immigrants, primarily from England but also from Denmark, Sweden, Scotland, Wales, Ireland, and Switzerland. The women were involved in such occupations as housewife, midwife, practical nurse, doctor, dressmaker, corset maker, postmistress, schoolteacher, and welfare supervisor. The accounts contain information regarding polygamy; Indians; the railroad; the United Order; farming; social functions such as quilting and spinning bees, canning, wool picking, dances, and candy pulls; mining; divorce; theater; entertainment for children; courtship; relief societies; the selling of wine; lighting, fuel, and bedding; and conflicts between cattlemen and sheep ranchers. Includes material about Rhoda Luann B. (Smith) Allred, resident of Weber and Cache counties in Utah and of Idaho and California, regarding the hardships she encountered aiding her invalid husband and later raising and supporting her 11 children; of Pernilla Anderson, a housekeeper who emigrated from Sweden in 1863 and walked the entire journey westward, who recalls that women would walk ahead of the wagon train to avoid the dust and that her first home was a dugout in the ground; of Manomas Lavina (Gibson) Andrus, who came to Utah with Mormons from Mississippi and settled in Big Cottonwood, who describes pioneer life, her travels, clothing, and her life as a second wife in a plural marriage; and of Ellen (George) Bird, who was born in Ogden, UT, and was a housekeeper and a school trustee for 22 years. Bird relates that it was not fashionable to have children in the 1880s. Also included is material of Lucy (Walker) Smith Kimball, wife of Joseph Smith and later of Heber C. Kimball, regarding pioneer life, polygamy, and Vilate Kimball; of Mary Ophelia (Cooper) Myers, who was born in Salem, drove an oxteam to Panaca, NV, at the age of 9, married John Ephraim Myers, and settled in Panguitch; and of Naomi (Read) Cowan, who was born in Fort Bridger, WY, lived in Slaterville, UT, and moved to Franklin, ID, when Brigham Young asked for colonizers. Cowan describes conflicts with the Indians, water carrying, diet, and holidays and celebrations.

The collection also contains material of Mary Emma Ritchie, including a diary regarding her trip to England in 1868 and a letter from Abraham Lincoln; of Harriett (Weaver) Taylor, who was born in England, emigrated to Utah in 1869, settled in Ogden, UT, and married Henry Taylor, son of John Taylor, who was president of the Mormon Church; and of Mary (Nelson) Johnson Felshaw, who was born in Copenhagen, Denmark, and came to Corinne by railroad from St. Joseph, MO. Felshaw describes the Chinese living there, the 1872 diphtheria epidemic, her move in 1880 to Blackfoot, and her work with the Indians. She was president of the WCTU in Idaho. Other women represented include Mary Evans (Williams) Leatham and Emma Nettie (Kilgore) Montgomery. Leatham, who was born in South Wales, converted to the Mormon Church and came to Utah in 1862. She discusses her fear of the Indians and the 1869 grasshopper plague. She had 10 children, five of whom predeceased her. Montgomery, known as Mother Montgomery, was a resident of Ogden, UT, who helped prisoners, hobos, and the unemployed. She was a member of the WCTU and Industrial Workers of the World.

16,969. Wahlquist, P. E.

Papers. 1891. 1 folder.
Open. Card catalog.
Utah State Historical Society Library.
Love letters written by Wahlquist in Ophir, UT, to his fiancée Mary.

16,970. Ware, Florence

Papers. Ca. 1920-52. 1 ft.
Open. No guide.
Utah State Historical Society Library.
Scrapbooks containing primarily correspondence and clippings regarding the paintings of Ware, a WPA artist in Utah.

16,971. Warenski, Marilyn

Oral history. 1974-76. No size given.
Open. No guide.
Utah State Historical Society Library.
Interviews conducted by Warenski (1931-), a writer, interior designer, and schoolteacher, in preparation for her book concerning the opinions of notable women regarding the current role and status of women in the Mormon Church. Includes interviews with Juanita Brooks, a Utah historian and author; Chris Durham, an attorney and worker for the Equal Rights Amendment in Utah; Shauna Adix, director of the University of Utah's women's resource center; Phyllis Snow, Utah State University's dean of the college of family life; Alison (Cornish) Thorne, lecturer in Utah State University's family and child development department; Suzanne Bigelow; and Dixie Huefner. Also includes an interview with Warenski.

16,972. Whipple, Maurine

Papers. 1939-44. 1 folder.
Open. Card catalog.
Utah State Historical Society Library.
Correspondence between [Miss] Whipple, an author, and Marguerite Sinclair, primarily regarding background material for Whipple's book *The Giant Joshua*.

16,973. Widtsoe Family

Papers. Ca. 1850-1966. 7 ft.
Open. Published guide.
Utah State Historical Society Library.
Correspondence, journals, manuscripts, and biographical information of the Widtsoe family. Includes manuscripts of Leah Eudora Dunford Widtsoe (1874-1965), the daughter of Susa Young Gates and wife of John Andreas Widtsoe (1872-1965), a scientist and apostle in the Mormon Church. Leah Widtsoe wrote on nutrition and was active in the women's movement and the Church. Also contained in the collection are correspondence, journals, and biographical information of her daughter Anna (Widtsoe) Wallace (1899-). See *Register of the Widtsoe Family Collection in the Library of the Utah State Historical Society* (Salt Lake City, 1976).

16,974. William, Henry

Papers. Ca. 1870. 1 folder.
Open. Unpublished guide.
Utah State Historical Society Library.
Papers of William, an active Mormon Church member, include the journal of his wife Elmira Pond Miller (1811-?), who was born in Barlow, OH, converted to the Mormon Church in 1839, and moved to Nauvoo, IL. Her journal describes her Church work and her feelings about her husband's entering into plural marriage.

16,975. Women's Democratic Club of Salt Lake City

Records. 1913-69. 1 ft.
Open. No guide.
Utah State Historical Society Library.
Constitution, bylaws, minute book, account books, correspondence, roll books, programs, yearbooks, guide book for Democratic women's ward and precinct study groups, and other records of this Democratic women's organization founded ca. 1932.

16,976. Woolley, Maria Lucy (Dewey)

Papers. 1842-47. 1 folder.
Open. Card catalog.
Utah State Historical Society Library.
Fourteen letters by Woolley to her family, parents, and grandparents in Illinois and Massachusetts concern personal matters, Joseph Smith, and activities of the Mormon Church when it was located in Nauvoo, IL.

16,977. Young Ladies Diadem

Records. 1877-78. 1 folder.
Open. Card catalog.
Utah State Historical Society Library.
Six issues of a manuscript newspaper published in St. George, UT, include stories, poems, recipes, anecdotes, and feature articles.

VERMONT

ARLINGTON

16,978. Canfield, Flavia C.

Papers. 1890-?. No size given.
Access restricted. No guide.
Martha Canfield Memorial Free Library, Inc.
Correspondence, diaries, clippings, and other papers of Canfield, an artist who was married to James H. Canfield, a professor, chancellor of the University of Nebraska, and president of the University of Ohio. In her diaries she describes life in Lincoln, NE, as well as in Ohio, Vermont, and elsewhere. Canfield was also a founder of women's clubs and a sorority chapter.

16,979. Canfield, Martha

Papers. 1850-1915. No size given.
Access restricted. No guide.
Martha Canfield Memorial Free Library, Inc.
Correspondence, diaries, and clippings of [Miss] Canfield, who founded the Library and operated it in her own home. Involved in church and social activities, Canfield also took care of her elderly relatives.

16,980. Fisher, Dorothy (Canfield)

Papers. 1890-1960. No size given.
Access restricted. No guide.
Martha Canfield Memorial Free Library, Inc.
Primarily family papers of [Mrs. John] Fisher, a novelist and community and public service leader who worked in Paris during WWI. Includes correspondence, manuscripts, photos, clippings, pamphlets, and books.

16,981. Miscellany

Papers. 1840-1977. No size given.
Access restricted. Card index.
Martha Canfield Memorial Free Library, Inc.
Includes biographical articles, memorials, obituaries, and clippings of Vermont writers, poets, artists, teachers, and political and social leaders.

16,982. Prince, Lucy

Papers. 1768-?. No size given.
Access restricted. No guide.
Martha Canfield Memorial Free Library, Inc.
[Mrs. Abisah] Prince was an 18th-century self-educated Negro poet, settler, and supporter of Negro rights. Includes town and court records, clippings, and a fictionalized biography of Prince, Bernard Katz's *Black Woman*. Also includes letters from Katz concerning his research for the book. Prince had two children who lived and died in Sunderland Township, VT.

16,983. Thompson, Mary Wolfe

Papers. Nd. No size given.
Access restricted. No guide.
Martha Canfield Memorial Free Library, Inc.
Includes correspondence, manuscripts of books, autobiographical articles, biographical articles, clippings, and books of Thompson, a writer of juvenile fiction, career books, and historical novels who was married to Charles Thompson. Born in New Jersey, she moved to Vermont late in her life.

BELLOWS FALLS

16,984. Hayes, Lyman S.

Papers. Ca. 1885- . Ca. 7 ft.
Open. Card index.
Rockingham Free Public Library.
Correspondence, notes, genealogical material, financial and legal documents, transcripts, photos, and clippings of Hayes (1850-1934), a town clerk and historian of the Bellows Falls area. Includes information on such noteworthy women as Hetty Howland (Robinson) Green, an heiress whose fortune and eccentricities made national news, and on such local women's groups as the Woman's Club of Bellows Falls, which was founded in 1901 and known for its work to improve the health of townspeople through a visiting nurses program and special clinics.

16,985. Photos

Collection. Ca. 1860- . Ca. 1500 items.
Open. Card indexes.
Rockingham Free Public Library.
Prints of photos of Rockingham-Bellows Falls area sites, events, and people include pictures of women as parade participants, office workers, telephone operators, nurses, librarians, and schoolgirls. Usually there is identification of the site and persons included and the date the photo was taken.

BENNINGTON

16,986. College Personnel Inactive Folders

Records. 1932- . 5 drawers.
Closed. No guide.
Bennington College Archives.
Correspondence, financial records, and completed forms, most of which are primarily fiscal in nature, document the careers of faculty and other College employees.

16,987. Dance Division

Records. 1934- . 15 ft.
Open. No guide.
Bennington College Archives.
Included with administrative files, reports, correspondence, academic schedules, choreographic notes, news releases, clippings, and other records of the Division are numerous files containing biographical, educational, and professional information on each student, some of whom were male, attending the Bennington School of Dance between 1934 and 1942. Also included are items concerning College Dance Group Tours in 1949, 1953, and 1956.

16,988. Dean of Studies

Records. 1932-67. 10 ft.
Partially closed. No guide.
Bennington College Archives.
Reports, lists, statistical tables, and completed questionnaires include descriptions of courses; reports of student work; faculty schedules listing instructors, classes taught by each, names of students enrolled, and time and place of meeting; and data on the performance of College women on standardized national educational tests between 1934 and 1952.

16,989. Educational Counseling Committee

Records. 1954- . 21 vols.
Closed. No guide.
Bennington College Archives.
Minutes of the Committee that, before ratifying each student's choice of courses or recommending a different curriculum program, reviews reports on the student's work in classes and the assessment by the student's counselor, a faculty member appointed to advise each student on her or his program and to monitor the student's progress. The Committee may also suggest remedial action for students with academic difficulties.

16,990. Non-Current Student Personnel Folders

Records. 1932- . 135 drawers.
Closed. No guide.
Bennington College Archives.
Student files contain material from each student's application to Bennington, with letters of recommendation and high school transcripts; written reports from faculty assessing the student's performance in class; confidential reports from the student's advisor; recommendations from the educational counseling committee on the student's program; and data on financial aid, if awarded.

16,991. Office of Alumnae Services

Records. 1949- . 31 ft.
Access restricted. File lists.
Bennington College Archives.
Minutes, correspondence, reports, completed questionnaires, and printed publications from the main and regional offices of the Alumnae Association concern ski weekends, alumnae weekends, commencement, fund raising, and a 1967-69 survey of alumnae.

16,992. President's Office Administration

Records. 1923- . 40 drawers.
Access restricted. No guide.
Bennington College Archives.
Financial records, reports, minutes, correspondence, memoranda, and printed material of Bennington presidents, the first of whom was appointed in 1925 though students were not admitted to the women's College until 1932. Material details College administration, including personnel matters, policy formation, and student life. Organized by academic year and then by subject, the files provide information about the period 1923-32, when the decision to form the College was implemented; for the period 1932-69, when the school admitted only women; and for 1972 to 1976, when Gail Thain Parker was president.

16,993. President's Office Files

Records. 1923- . 22 ft.
Access restricted. Inventory.
Bennington College Archives.
Files include records of conferences, 1923-32, in which the nature and direction of the College was decided; reports to the president by administrative officers; proposals for new special studies programs and evaluations of existing ones; items pertaining to the inauguration of presidents; a file on commencements; documents relating to fund raising; and scholarly and administrative publications of the presidents.

16,994. Senior Theses

Collection. 1935- . 15 drawers and ca. 1800 microfiche.
Open. Card file.
Bennington College Archives.
Because Bennington requires each senior student in literature and the social sciences to write a scholarly thesis before receiving a bachelor's degree, original typescripts of these works provide an index of the direction of education at the College.

16,995. Students

Collection. 1932-61. 10 ft.
Open. No guide.
Bennington College Archives.
Minutes, reports, correspondence, and memoranda document those activities at Bennington which students organized, among them recreational programs, the store, and community chest fund raising, as well as the influence of students on College policy through student government, the educational committee, and the judicial committee, which enforced rules on student behavior.

16,996. Trustees

Records. 1928-57. Ca. 1 ft.
Access restricted. Inventory.
Bennington College Archives.
Records of College Trustees primarily consist of minutes of meetings of the Trustees' educational policy, executive, budget, nominating, building, dance school, and health services committees. Also included are early minutes of the organization committee, minutes of the ways and means committee on financial needs, correspondence, reports, and photos.

16,997. Moses, Grandma
Papers. 1940-73. 2 vols.
Open. No guide.
Bennington Museum.
Scrapbooks of Anna Mary Robertson [Mrs. Thomas Salmon] Moses (1860-1961), the artist known as Grandma Moses, contain correspondence, genealogical data, biographical articles, cards, photos, and clippings pertaining to her life and her painting career, which she did not begin until she was 78 years old. Some of the material also reflects her interest in the DAR.

BRATTLEBORO

16,998. Local History
Collection. 1700s- . Ca. 30 ft.
Open. No guide.
Brooks Memorial Library.
Material documenting the history of Brattleboro, which was chartered in 1753, consists of deeds and other legal documents, annual reports of the town government and of organizations, minutes, correspondence, biographies, historical pamphlets, programs, school yearbooks, maps, photos, scrapbooks, albums, clippings, newspapers, and artifacts. Includes information on women active in families, businesses, churches, educational activities, and social and intellectual clubs. Nearly complete records of the Brattleboro High School and of the Austine School for the Deaf, founded in 1912, where women served in teaching, financing, and administration; records of the Woman's Club, founded in 1896; and material on the Mutual Aid Association, an organization which was founded in 1907, managed mainly by women, and noted for its efforts to improve the health of older and poor local residents.

16,999. Photos
Collection. 1853- . Ca. 9 ft.
Access restricted. No guide.
Brooks Memorial Library.
Photos documenting local history include pictures of women as typists at a business school, telephone operators, makers of badges for the American National Red Cross, participants in Brattleboro's 1912 pageant, and schoolgirls. Also included are family scrapbooks of Leila Thompson, containing individual portraits of women in her family, and photos of such buildings as Glenwood Seminary, an educational institution. Many of the photos have been printed in Harold A. Barry et al., *Before Our Time: A Pictorial History of Brattleboro, Vermont from 1830 to 1930* (Brattleboro: Stephen Greene Press, 1974).

BURLINGTON

17,000. College of Education and Nursing
Records. 1922-58. 26 ft.
Access restricted. No guide.
University of Vermont Archives.
Office files of the dean of this College for all but the years 1945 through 1949.

17,001. Dean of Women
Records. 1939-72. 6.5 ft.
Access restricted. No guide.
University of Vermont Archives.
Office files of Mary Jean Simpson, who was dean of women from 1938 to 1954; of Anna Rankin Harris, dean from 1954 to 1966; and of Jackie Marie Gribbons, dean from 1966 to 1975, when the office was abolished.

17,002. Faculty Papers
Papers. 1905-74. 5 ft. and 6 vols.
Open. No guide.
University of Vermont Archives.
Papers of UV faculty members include correspondence from 1951 to 1974, lecture and research notes, unpublished writings, and examinations of Betty Bandel, professor of English from 1947 to 1975; diaries for 1936 to 1939 of Mary Bates, cataloging librarian in 1894; and correspondence for 1905 to 1913 and high school and college notes of Mary Jean Simpson, dean of women from 1938 to 1954. Also included are records of the Ladies of the Faculty, 1910-25; of the Faculty Wives, 1949; and of the Women's Faculty Club, 1931-48.

17,003. Records of Sororities
Records. 1930-70. Ca. 5 ft.
Open. No guide.
University of Vermont Archives.
Minutes, correspondence, manuals, a scrapbook, and songs of Kappa Delta, 1930-65; scrapbooks of Gamma Phi Beta, 1950-70; and record books and correspondence of Sigma Gamma, 1940-57.

17,004. Records of Student Activities
Records. 1921-70. No size given.
Open. No guide.
University of Vermont Archives.
Minutes and accounts from 1941 to 1947 of the Bluestockings, a literary society; records of the Women's Student Union, 1921-26; Lilac Day photos, 1924-28; minutes and handbooks of the Women's Student Government Association, 1950-70; and publications of the Women's Athletic Association.

17,005. School of Home Economics
Records. 1937-73. 16 ft.
Access restricted. Folder list.
University of Vermont Archives.
Records of the School, a department in the College of Arts and Sciences from 1909 to 1935 and then in the College of Agriculture and Home Economics from 1935 to 1973, are primarily from the years after 1956.

17,006. University Archives
Records. 1871- . No size given.
Partially restricted. No guide.
University of Vermont Archives.
Information on women is available from the following files of the University, which has been coeducational since 1871: files of the presidents since 1911, the dean of agriculture since 1920, the dean of arts since 1940, the dean of engineering since 1924, the dean of medicine since 1921, and the dean of students since 1938; files of deceased alumni; files of the library, which was headed by Emily Edith Clarke from 1898 to 1909 and by Helen B. Shattuck from 1909 to 1946; files of the registrar; public relations files; faculty personnel files; and performing arts files. Examples of material included are the scrapbook kept by Mary Newton Baldwin, class of 1924; lecture notes of May Olive Boynton, class of 1894; patient accounts from 1967 to 1970 of Barbara Beardslee, an obstetrician who graduated from UV in 1939; and negatives from the University photographic and the student photographic services.

EAST DOVER

17,007. Rice Family
Papers. 1820-50. 2 ft.
Open. No guide.
Dover Free Library.
Correspondence, a diary fragment, leases, accounts, receipts, bills, notes of indebtedness, and recipes of this family of farmers who lived in Somerset, VT. Includes correspondence from the 1840s in which Mary Rice describes to her father-in-law Hazelton Rice, Sr., her life as the wife of a farmer and her struggles to keep herself and her family in good health. Also included are detailed letters from Sarah "Sally" Rice (ca. 1820-?), who married James Alger in 1847, to her parents Rhoda Rice and Hazelton Rice, Sr.; she describes her life as a hired hand on a family farm in Union Village, NY, and elsewhere and work in a cotton textile factory in Thompson, CT, which she left because the job threatened her health. Sally Rice's letters have been published in Nell Kull, "I Can Never Be Happy There Among So Many Mountains," *Vermont History,* 38 (1970).

ISLE LA MOTTE

17,008. Isle La Motte Free Public Library
Records. 1895- . 1 folder.
Open. No guide.
Isle La Motte Historical Society.
The Library was founded in 1904 by seven women who raised money for the building by sponsoring social events. Includes a 1966 fund-raising letter, notes, and photos of the building.

MIDDLEBURY

17,009. Dorr, Julia Caroline (Ripley)
Papers. 1839-1924. 3 ft.
Open. Item list.
Middlebury College, Abernethy Collection of American Literature.
Dorr (1825-1913) was a poet and novelist. Literary manuscripts of *Expiation, Sybil Huntington* and some poems and short stories; biographical material; pamphlets; clippings; scrapbooks; and correspondence from Helena Rutherford Ely, Harriet L. Humphreys, Louise (Chandler) Moulton, Bliss Perry, Lydia Howard (Huntley) Sigourney, and Elizabeth Drew (Barstow) Stoddard.

17,010. Library Miscellany
Collection. 1800s- . 4 boxes.
Open. Card index.
Middlebury College, Abernethy Collection of American Literature.
Correspondence and drafts of literary writings include items, often just one letter, of such persons as Anne Charlotte (Lynch) Botta, Elizabeth Stuart (Phelps) Ward, Lilian Whiting, Adeline Dutton (Train) Whitney, Edith Matilda Thomas, Harriet Elizabeth Prescott Spofford, Edith Kermit (Carow) Roosevelt, Dora Read Goodale, Julia Magruder, Ella Wheeler Wilcox, Mary Elizabeth (Wilson) Sherwood, Sara Jane (Clarke) Lippincott, Sarah Chauncey Woolsey, Willa Sibert Cather, Edna St. Vincent Millay, Sara Teasdale, Clara Barrus, Mary Moody Emerson, Rose (Terry) Cooke, Emily Dickinson, Amelia Edith (Huddleston) Barr, Mary Eleanor (Wilkins) Freeman, Julia (Ward) Howe, Sarah Orne Jewett, Helen Keller, Lucy Larcom, Sarah Margaret (Fuller) Ossoli, Elizabeth Palmer Peabody, Alice (Freeman) Palmer, Agnes Repplier, Celia Thaxter, Una Hawthorne, Rose (Hawthorne) Lathrop, Sophia Amelia (Peabody) Hawthorne, Elizabeth Blackwell, Marianne (Dwight) Orvis, Elizabeth Drew (Barstow) Stoddard, Dorothy Frances (Canfield) Fisher, Sophia Thoreau, Hannah Flagg Gould, Lydia Howard (Huntley) Sigourney, Sarah Helen (Power) Whitman, Elizabeth Clementine (Dodge) Kinney, Zephine Humphrey, and Emily S. Willard.

Also includes a poem by Mary A. De Vere, an 1882 letter by Mary B. Merriam, a 1934 letter by Mae S. Walker, a 1922 historical essay by Mary Cady, an 1851 letter by Ellen Channing, an 1843 letter by Sophia Eastman, an 1847 letter by Lizzie Hoxie, an 1840s item of Boston reformer Anna Q. T. Parsons, an 1848 letter by Gertrude Sears, an 1847 letter by Mary Emerson, an 1878 letter by Maria Thoreau, an 1838 letter by Prudence Ward, and a 1930s item of Helen (Hartness) Flanders.

Collection also contains letters to Susan Brownell Anthony from Wendell Phillips and other letters to women.

17,011. White, Viola Chittenden
Papers. 1918-60. 6 boxes.
Open. List.
Middlebury College, Abernethy Collection of American Literature.
Diary volumes of White (1890-1977), a curator, poet, and nature writer, were the source for many of her writings; they also contain some correspondence, poems, and clippings.

17,012. White, Viola Chittenden
Papers. 1939-57. 64 items.
Open. No guide.
Middlebury College, Abernethy Collection of American Literature.
Correspondence of White (1890-1977), a poet and nature writer, with John Israel Smith about books and literary figures reflects in part her work as librarian of the Abernethy Collection between 1933 and 1957.

17,013. Wilkinson, Marguerite Ogden Bigelow
Papers. 1912-28. 2 boxes.
Open. Item list.
Middlebury College, Abernethy Collection of American Literature.
Correspondence of [Mrs. James G.] Wilkinson (1883-1928), a poet, relates to her work as an anthologist. Among the letters with approximately 130 poets and 60 publishers are items of Sarah Norcliffe Cleghorn, Amy Lowell, Edna St. Vincent Millay, Sara Teasdale, Elizabeth Conner Lindsay, Harriet Monroe, and Lizette Woodworth Reese.

MONTPELIER

17,014. Census
Records. 1860-80. 44 vols. and 5 items.
Open. Accessions record.
State of Vermont, Department of Libraries.
Federal census schedules, lists, and statistics for surveys taken in 1860, '70, and '80 contain information on women's contribution to farm production, among other data concerning residents of all the counties in Vermont. For example, collection includes Censuses on inhabitants, deaths, and agricultural production for 1860 in Chittenden County, which includes Burlington, and for 1870 in Caledonia County, which includes St. Johnsbury, and name, race, age, and sex of residents of Caledonia and Chittenden counties during 1880.

17,015. Board of Cosmetology
Records. 1938- . 23 microfilm reels.
Open. Catalog cards.
State of Vermont, Public Records Division.
Records of this state agency for a predominantly female occupation include minutes of meetings of the Board, applications for licenses to practice, scores on examinations for licenses, and correspondence and complaints concerning alleged misconduct by individual practitioners of cosmetology.

17,016. Courts
Records. 1788-1958. 42 cu.ft., 82 vols., and 5 microfilm reels.
Access restricted. Accessions records.
State of Vermont, Public Records Division.
Court records show women as émigrés seeking citizenship and as defendants and plaintiffs in civil actions. Collections consists of court naturalization records for Bennington County, 1842-1958; Windham County, 1851-1920; and the Chittenden municipal court, 1869-1906. Also included are Rutland city court civil and criminal dockets, 1873-1907; Winooski municipal court criminal and civil records and dockets, 1909-37; Chittenden County court dockets and judgments, 1788-1829; and Vermont Supreme Court dockets and files, 1794-1829.

17,017. Department of Education Teaching Training and Certification Program
Records. 1916-34. 16 in. and 3 microfilm reels.
Open. Accession record.
State of Vermont, Public Records Division.
Records concerning schoolteachers in Vermont, most of whom were women, consist of entrance and registration forms completed in conjunction with education classes at state secondary schools, normal schools, and the University of Vermont, accompanied by signed declarations wherein each student promised to teach in the state for at least as long a period as she had taken classes at these schools; cards on the certification of teachers and records of their experience; and cards on the certification status of those teachers born before 1895 who were inactive as teachers in 1934.

17,018. Eugenics Survey and Country Life Commission
Records. 1925-31. 60 ft.
Open. Accession record.
State of Vermont, Public Records Division.
The Survey and Commission were related government fact-finding agencies founded in 1925. Case studies of families; questionnaires; transcripts of interviews; statistical and topical reports; institutional reports; charts, biographic, geographic, and bibliographic card indexes, lists, and clippings. Material contains information about such Survey or Commission workers as [Miss] Harriet Abbott, a fieldworker from the Vermont Children's Aid Society, Frances E. Konkin, a statistical analyst from the Eugenics Record Office at Cold Spring Harbor, NY; [Mrs.] Martha Wadman, a fieldworker with experience in intelligence testing at the Riverside Reformatory for Women and other institutions; and [Miss] Elin L. Anderson, a graduate of the New England School of Social Work, whose *We Americans* (1937), a best-selling study of the assimilation of members of ethnic minorities in Burlington, VT, stemmed in part from her work with the Survey and Commission. Collection also reflects the lives of the Vermont women who were studied during the 1920s and the depression. Includes detailed information concerning poor, physically handicapped, rural, imprisoned, and mentally retarded women. As a result of the work of the Survey and Commission, Vermont reformed its marriage laws, improved the quality of medical exams given in its prisons, and passed a eugenics sterilization law in 1931.

17,019. Jail Registers
Records. 1877-1965. 2 vols.
Access restricted. Accessions record.
State of Vermont, Public Records Division.
Records for the jails in Grand Isle County and Rutland County provide names and descriptions of prisoners, some of whom were women; place of abode, and date and cause of committal.

17,020. Rutland Women Reformatory.
Records. 1921-67. 11 microfilm reels.
Access restricted. No guide.
State of Vermont, Public Records Division.
Case records of this women's prison, which was closed in 1967, contain documents providing name, number, history of previous commitments, physical description, residence, age, and marital status, as well as such information on conviction as place, date, crime, and sentence for each prisoner.

17,021. Social Welfare Department
Records. 1916-64. 2 microfilm reels.
Open. Card entry.
State of Vermont, Public Records Division.
Consists of proceedings of the Vermont Conference on Social Welfare from 1916 to 1956 and minutes of the Vermont chapter of the National Association of Social Workers from 1957 to 1964. Women were active in both groups.

17,022. Vermont State Board of Nursing
Records. 1911- . 36 microfilm reels.
Open. Card index of reel titles.
State of Vermont, Public Records Division.
Records of this state agency for a predominantly female occupation include treasurer's reports on the Board's expenses; minutes of Board meetings; rules and regulations promulgated by the Board for accreditation of nurses' training schools and other matters; applications for qualification as a Licensed Practical Nurse, with registration number, recommendations and endorsements, education information, and other data for each applicant; and case records on disputes and complaints involving nurses.

17,023. Brown, Helen Tyler (DOC-45 to 52, 77, and 78)
Papers. 1745-1932. 10 boxes.
Open. Calendar.
Vermont Historical Society.
Correspondence, historical and genealogical notes, drafts of publications, legal documents, reports, pamphlets, scrapbooks, maps, obituaries, clippings, newspapers, magazines, and books of Brown, a 20th-century author on American literature, were gathered by her primarily for her research on Royall Tyler.

Includes material about women in the Tyler and related families and information about Brown's personal life

17,024. Cabot, Mary R. (MSC-126 and 127)
Papers. 1789-1931. 2 boxes.
Open. Calendar.
Vermont Historical Society.
Notes, drafts, proofs, historical documents for research, clippings, and printed items of Cabot (1856-?), a local historian of Brattleboro, VT, relate to her *Annals of Brattleboro, 1681-1895* (Brattleboro: E. L. Hildreth, 1921-22). Includes a draft of an unpublished supplementary volume.

17,025. Canfield, Mary Grace (MSS-4)
Papers. 1888-1934. 1 box.
Open. Calendar.
Vermont Historical Society.
Papers of [Mrs.] Canfield, an author of historical works and a suffragist of Woodstock, VT, contain correspondence, book orders, reports, pamphlets, scrapbooks, posters, photos, and magazines, some of which relate to the Vermont Equal Suffrage Association and to other suffrage groups as well as to Canfield's publications.

17,026. Freeman, Mrs. Frederick (MS-110)
Papers. 1871-1909. 1 box.
Open. Calendar.
Vermont Historical Society.
Diaries in which Lucy (West) Freeman, a farmwife in South Royalton and Brookfield, VT, records family news. Also included is the 1893 diary of her daughter Laura A. Freeman, a schoolgirl.

17,027. Kent, Louise (Andrews) (DOC-165 and 166)
Papers. Ca. 1930-59. 2 boxes.
Open. Calendar.
Vermont Historical Society.
Literary notes, manuscripts, and recipes of Kent (1886-1969), an author, relate to her cookbooks and historical novels.

17,028. Landon (MSA-32)
Papers. 1917-26. 1 box.
Open. Calendar.
Vermont Historical Society.
Correspondence, post cards, notes, and poems of this Chester, VT, family. Primarily consists of correspondence between Alice E. Landon in Chester and her sister Flora Landon, a nurse who

served in Europe during WWI and then in the Near East before returning to Chester in 1926. Flora Landon's letters contain graphic descriptions of wartime conditions.

17,029. Miscellaneous Files
Collection. 1800s- . 16 drawers.
Open. Lists.
Vermont Historical Society.
Small groups of personal papers and business and town records, all pertaining to state and local history and biography, include papers of numerous women. Among them are letters of Fannie C. Adams, writing from London and Geneva in 1873; of Louise Jones about teaching school in East Bethel and North Pomfret, 1867-68; of Grace Coolidge on a monument in Vermont to her husband US President Calvin Coolidge, 1934; of Lucy Emerson of Barnard to her suitor, 1852; of Dorothea (Canfield) Fisher, 1915-55; of Mary O. Nutting on the Mount Holyoke Female Seminary, 1850-52; and of Sarah Town describing her trip to Illinois, 1849. Diaries include those of Abigail Baldwin, the wife of a Congregational minister, 1853-54; of [Mrs.] Aurelia Herrick of Montpelier, 1848; and of Lucy (Weston) Gibbs of Randolph, 1823-25, which is included along with Gibbs's commonplace book, a poem, and her sketchbook. Also found in the collection is material from 1914 and 1915 about Bettie Van Metre of Berryville, VA, who saved the life of Lt. Henry Bedell of Vermont during the Civil War; material of a Miss Marion Blake from the 1930s and 1940s on an historic records survey marker describing the history of Grand Isle as well as her notes on adult education in Vermont; items on the nomination of Laura Cowles as Vermont Mother of the Year, 1954; a 1959 news release about Sister St. Mary Magdalen, a black superior of a convent in St. Albans between 1903 and 1918; reminiscences of Bernice L. Wing on her life from ca. 1850 to 1900 in Proctor and Ferrisburg; and 1842 notes by Mary Walker of Springfield, VT, for calculating lunar eclipses. Also contains records of the Cabot Overseers of the Poor, 1844-1909, which provide data on poverty-stricken women of Cabot; 16 volumes of records of the DAR; and minutes of the Meeting of Women Friends of Grand Isle, 1801-22.

17,030. Nye, Mary (Greene) (MS-131)
Papers. 1889-1954. 1 box.
Open. Calendar.
Vermont Historical Society.
Correspondence, drafts of articles and lectures, reports, administrative material, lists, and photos of Nye, editor of *The State Papers of Vermont,* document her work on Vermont state history.

17,031. Reed, Hezekiah H. (MS-126)
Papers. 1823-1944. 1 box.
Open. Calendar.
Vermont Historical Society.
Correspondence, genealogical notes, financial accounts, and other papers and printed material of Reed, a Montpelier lawyer. Consists primarily of letters and other papers relating to the education of his daughters during the 1840s and 1850s at such schools as the Troy Female Seminary and Mount Holyoke Female Seminary.

17,032. Richardson, Nellie (Simpson) (DOC-149 and 150)
Papers. 1930-58. 2 boxes.
Open. Calendar.
Vermont Historical Society.
Correspondence, literary manuscripts, notes, and reviews of Richardson (1871-?), a poet, relate to her poetry. Some of the material was generated by her secretary Dorothy C. Walter.

17,033. Sabin Family (MS-25)
Papers. 1782-1893. 1 box.
Open. Calendar.
Vermont Historical Society.
Correspondence; diaries; account books; deeds, mortgages, leases, indentures, wills, and other legal documents; sermons; programs; and newspapers of this Windsor, VT, family. Included are family letters, 1829-63, of Louisa and Charlotte Sabin; account books of a Sabin woman, 1835-62; a diary of a Sabin housewife, 1870-78; and correspondence of Julia A. Sabine with her printer about her book *At the End of the Rainbow* (New York: T. Whittaker, 1892).

17,034. Sprague, Ascha (DOC-181)
Papers. 1845-64. 1 box.
Open. Calendar and unpublished essay.
Vermont Historical Society.
Invitations to lecture, family correspondence, reports and philosophical exchanges on spiritualism, sermons, poems, drafts of lectures, legal documents, bills, petitions, and recipes of Sprague document her work as a spiritualist, her travels, lectures, trances, publications, and advocacy of spiritualism, as well as her personal and family life and her defense of women's rights.

17,035. Stevens (DOC-30)
Papers. 1844-62. 8 boxes.
Open. Calendar.
Vermont Historical Society.
Correspondence, poems, essays, genealogical material, bills, and printed items of this Barnet, VT, family. Consists primarily of family letters to Henry Stevens, Sr., but also includes correspondence of Sophia Stevens, which details her experiences. After studying at St. Johnsbury Academy and the University of Vermont, Sophia Stevens served as president of the Orleans County Teachers Institute in 1848 and as a teacher at Hartford High School in Connecticut under Thomas Beecher from 1849 to 1850. In 1851 she married Stephen Hitchcock and ran a school in Middlebury, VT, with him until his death two years later. She then moved to Paris where she wrote for the *New York Tribune* and painted, then to Rome where she married William Page in 1857, and then to New York City in 1860 with Page, where she continued to write for newspapers. In 1862 she settled in Perth Amboy, NJ.

17,036. Townsend, William (MSC-133)
Papers. 1827-1909. 1 box.
Open. Calendar.
Vermont Historical Society.
Correspondence, draft of a biographical article, family papers, commencement programs, and other papers of Townsend (1814-64), a resident of Felchville, VT. Included is correspondence of such family members as Townsend's widow, who was a spiritualist from the South; Aurelia (Townsend) Herrick (1811-91), a New England schoolteacher who married clergyman Horace Herrick; Aurelia [Mrs. Alstyne] Townsend, a late 19th-century resident of Springfield, VT; and Isabella (Townsend) [Mrs. Henry] Waterman (1827-95), a farmwife in the Midwest. Their letters, which graphically portray life in their various regions of the country, were written for the benefit of family members who remained in Felchville.

17,037. Tyler, Royall (MSS-8 and 9)
Papers. 1773-1879. Ca. 5 ft.
Open. Calendar.
Vermont Historical Society.
Correspondence; diaries; autobiographies; drafts of plays, poems, and stories; autograph books; and newspapers of Tyler (1757-1826), a jurist and author, and of his family. Included are diaries for 1817 to 1840 of his wife Mary Hunt (Palmer) Tyler (1775-1866), an autograph book of her grandmother Amelia Hunt, the autobiography of Mary Tyler's mother Elizabeth (Hunt) Palmer, and correspondence from 1825 to 1861 of her daughter-in-law Mrs. Royall Tyler II. Letters contain frequent mentions and occasional correspondence of Mary Tyler's nieces Sophia Amelia (Peabody) [Mrs. Nathaniel] Hawthorne (1809-71), an author and artist, and Elizabeth Palmer Peabody (1804-94), a writer and educator.

17,038. Tyng, Harriet Morgan (MS-106)
Papers. 1939-53. 1 box.
Open. Calendar.
Vermont Historical Society.
Correspondence; drafts of poems, plays, and speeches; and printed booklets of poems of Tyng (?-1952), a poet, primarily relate to her poetry. Also included are descriptions of the Continent in diaries she kept while traveling during 1939 in Europe.

17,039. Vail and Congdon (MS-28)
Papers. 1819-89. 1 box.
Open. Calendar.
Vermont Historical Society.
Correspondence, drafts of poems, legal documents, and a few printed items of these Vermont families. Contains letters of family women about travels, education, and such personal matters as births, deaths, marriages, and illnesses. Included are letters documenting the medical training and practice of Mary (Vail) [Mrs. L. J.] Grinnell, who studied in Philadelphia before returning to Vermont to practice medicine, and letters to, from, and about Grinnell's mother Alvira (Allen) [Mrs. William] Vail of Danby, VT.

17,040. Vermont Department of Classroom Teachers (MSB-25)
Records. 1948-74. 1 box.
Open. Calendar.
Vermont Historical Society.
Constitution, minutes, committee reports, lists of members, newsletters, mimeographed material, and a history of this professional association of educators, in which women played prominent roles.

17,041. Vermont Federation of Women's Clubs (DOC-142)
Records. 1896-1959. 1 box.
Open. Calendar.
Vermont Historical Society.
Records of the secretary of the Federation, a consortium of women's organizations, are included with 50 draft histories of local social, educational, and charitable women's groups in various Vermont towns.

17,042. Vermont League of Women Voters (MSC-144, 145, and 146)
Records. 1883-1921. 3 boxes.
Open. Calendar.
Vermont Historical Society.
Record books, correspondence, notebooks, legal briefs, petitions, reports, membership lists, programs, news releases, broadsides, post cards, photos, and newspapers document the work of the LWV's forerunner, the Vermont Equal Suffrage Association, in gaining the vote for women in towns, the state, and the nation. Also included is some material of other local and national suffrage groups.

17,043. Willard, Charles Wesley (DOC 24 to 29)
Papers. 1810-1920. 5496 items.
Open. Calendar.
Vermont Historical Society.
Correspondence, speeches, cashbooks and other financial records, legal documents, and other papers of Willard (1827-80), a Montpelier lawyer, editor, and politician. Included is material on 19th-century Willard women and on women from the related Reed family, with correspondence of Martha (Barnard) [Mrs. Hezekiah H.] Reed and of her daughters Mary Reed and Emily Reed, and notes on courses and readings by another of her daughters, Cornelia Reed. Also included are letters from 1893 and 1894 by Eliza May Willard, writing

about her education at Smith College; letters of Mary Willard regarding her studies at school in Westfield, MA, during 1878; and correspondence from such women outside the family as Julia Caroline (Ripley) Dorr, a poet, and Isabella Beecher Hooker, a reformer.

NORTH BENNINGTON

17,044. Hall, Park, and McCullough Family
Papers. 1789-1925. 28 ft.
Open. Folder list.
Manuscript Library of the Park-McCullough House.
Correspondence, business papers, and legal documents of this Vermont family include material reflecting the lives of many of the family women. Details of the women's personal and social lives are contained in the correspondence of Thankful Morgan Pratt (?-1837); of her daughter Cynthia Pratt, who married Luther Park in 1816; of Laura van der Spiegel Hall (1828-75), who married Cynthia Park's son Trenor Park; of Laura Park's mother Dolly Tuttle Davis Hall (1792-1879); of Laura Park's sister Eliza Hall; and of Laura Park's daughter Lizzie McCullough (1848-1938).

17,045. McCullough, Edith Van Benthuysen
Papers. 1954. 111-page vol.
Open. No guide.
Manuscript Library of the Park-McCullough House.
Memoir in which McCullough (ca. 1880-1965), a resident of North Bennington and Albany, NY, recalls the history of the Van Benthuysen family in Albany, events in her own life and in those of her contemporaries, and her extensive travels in Europe. Includes a chapter on the founding of Bennington College, an institution in which McCullough took an interest.

17,046. McCullough, Eliza "Lizzie" Hall (Park)
Papers. 1870-1938. 71 vols.
Open. Inventory.
Manuscript Library of the Park-McCullough House.
A New York City and North Bennington resident, McCullough (1848-1938) was the wife of Vermont governor John Griffin McCullough (1835-1915). Diaries, notebooks, account books, address books, lists of Christmas presents given, and material pertaining to her work during WWI provide a detailed description of her management of a large household and her interest in such community affairs as the creation of a local library and the founding of Bennington College. Also includes a copy of her recollections of family history and her early life during the 1850s in northern California.

POULTNEY

17,047. College Archives
Records. 1834- . No size given.
Access restricted. No guide.
Green Mountain College Archives.
Annual reports, minutes, budget records, correspondence, studies, reports, curriculum materials, clippings, and faculty publications of the College, which was established in 1834 as Troy Conference Academy. The school went through various transitions, and the composition of its student body varied. In 1973 it became a four-year coeducational college.

SPRINGFIELD

17,048. Ellis, Mary
Papers. 1764-1971. Ca. 10 ft.
Open. No guide.
Springfield Town Library.
Papers of [Miss] Ellis (1875-1972) document her personal life and her work as an historian. Includes correspondence, historical and genealogical notes, texts of her radio broadcasts and articles, autograph and address books, health records, military documents, patents, theater programs, photos, clippings, almanacs, newspapers, magazines, and other material. Also included are items pertaining to the General Lewis Morris Chapter of the DAR, founded in Springfield in 1908; records of other local organizations; material on local private and public schools; ledgers of Springfield businesses from the 1830s to 1890s, which provide evidence of women's employment; and area weather records from 1848 to 1915.

VIRGINIA

ARLINGTON

17,049. Arlington Hall Junior College
Records. 1928-42. 2 ft.
Open. No guide.
Arlington County Department of Libraries, Central Library, Virginiana Collection.
Yearbooks, alumnae list, and a scrapbook of the institution, a finishing school for young ladies that offered a two-year college curriculum with a four-year high school department. The school was located in Arlington County, VA, until 1942 when the government took over use of its property.

17,050. Goss, Beulah S.
Papers. 1940s. 3 ft.
Open. No guide.
Arlington County Department of Libraries, Central Library, Virginiana Collection.
The owner of an Arlington real estate agency, [Mrs.] Goss (1898-1974) was active in the Civic Federation, the Arlington County Women's Democratic Club, the Iwo Jima statue committee, the March of Dimes, and a nursing homes committee. Correspondence, minutes, and scrapbooks. During WWII Goss was chairman of the price panel of the Arlington County Ration Board; after the war she served for 11 years on the organizations and procedures committee of the Arlington County Board.

17,051. Library-Zonta Oral History Project
Oral history. Nd. 50 interviews.
Open. Unpublished guide.
Arlington County Department of Libraries, Central Library, Virginiana Collection.
Interviews concern 20th-century events in Arlington County, VA. Twenty-two of the interviewees were women, among them housewives, former members of the county board, former teachers, and civic workers.

BRISTOW

17,052. Archives of the Benedictine Sisters of Virginia
Records. 1868- . 36 boxes and 10 vols.
Open. Unpublished guide.
St. Benedict Convent.
Corporation minutes, correspondence, diary, photos, scrapbooks, chronicles, biographies of bishops of the diocese, local Catholic newspapers, and a history of the religious community, which was founded in 1868 in Richmond, VA, and moved to Bristow in 1901. The Sisters are engaged in teaching, inner city work, and pastoral ministry. Includes material concerning a history of the diocese, individual parish development, and the Catholic department of education.

CHARLOTTESVILLE

17,053. Barrett, Clifton Waller
Collection. Ca. 1770- . Ca. 325 ft.
Open. Unpublished guides.
University of Virginia Library, Manuscripts Department.
Correspondence, literary manuscripts, photos, and other papers of major American authors, of which ca. 250 are women. Among the women represented by substantial holdings are Louisa May Alcott, Frances Eliza (Hodgson) Burnett, Willa Sibert Cather, Mary Eleanor (Wilkins) Freeman, Ellen Anderson Gholson Glasgow, Julia (Ward) Howe, Sarah Orne Jewett, Lucy Larcom, Amy Lowell, Edna St. Vincent Millay, Katherine Anne Porter, Lizette Woodworth Reese, Elizabeth Shepley Sergeant, Harriet Elizabeth (Beecher) Stowe, Elizabeth Stuart (Phelps) Ward, Edith Newbold (Jones) Wharton, Kate Douglas (Smith) Wiggin, and Elinor Morton (Hoyt) Wylie.

17,054. Charlottesville Business and Professional Women's Club
Records. 1951-76. 5 drawers, 2 Hollinger boxes, and 3 vols.
Access restricted. No guide.
University of Virginia Library, Manuscripts Department.
Correspondence, press books, and scrapbooks of the Club, the local chapter of the Virginia Federation of Business and Professional Women's Clubs.

17,055. Cocke
Papers. 1725-1953. 87 Hollinger boxes and 6 vols.
Open. Unpublished guide.
University of Virginia Library, Manuscripts Department.
Correspondence, diaries, speeches, essays, plantation account books, ledgers, remedy and recipe books, and other papers of the family of John Hartwell Cocke (1780-1866), a Virginia planter and experimental agriculturist who was active in the temperance movement and the recolonization of slaves to Africa. Includes correspondence, diaries, recipe books, copybooks, and essays of his wife Louisa Maxwell Holmes Cocke, Lucy Cocke, and other family women as well as more than 60 letters to his daughters from former male and female slaves whom he had taught to read and write, provided with training in trades, and sent back to Liberia.

17,056. Coolidge
Papers. 1789-1858. 3 Hollinger boxes and 1 oversize box.
Partially closed. Unpublished guide.
University of Virginia Library, Manuscripts Department.
Correspondence between Ellen Wayles (Randolph) Coolidge (1796-1879) and other family members, chiefly her mother Martha (Jefferson) [Mrs. Thomas Mann] Randolph (1772-1836) and her sisters. Coolidge was the wife of Joseph Coolidge, IV, and the granddaughter of Thomas Jefferson and Martha (Wayles) [Mrs. Bathurst] Skelton Jefferson (1748-82).

17,057. Daughters of the American Revolution
Records. 1891-1971. Ca. 40 vols. and other items.
Open. No guide.
University of Virginia Library, Manuscripts Department.
Records of the Albemarle County, Jack Jouette, and Point of Fork chapters of the DAR consist of membership lists, which include genealogical data; cemetery records; Albemarle County tombstone inscriptions; and scrapbooks.

17,058. Edgehill and Randolph
Papers. 1749-1942. Ca. 30 Hollinger boxes.
Open. Unpublished guide.
University of Virginia Library, Manuscripts Department.
Correspondence, legal documents, photos, and scrapbooks of this family of Virginia planters and professional men, who resided at their estate Edgehill. Much of the correspondence is between women family members and includes items concerning the female academy run by the Randolphs. The Randolphs were related to the Thomas Jefferson family.

17,059. Glasgow, Ellen Anderson Gholson
Papers. 1909-45. 30 boxes and 3 microfilm reels.
Open. Unpublished guide.
University of Virginia Library, Manuscripts Department.
Glasgow (1873-1945) was a novelist. Correspondence, including ca. 800 letters from Henry W. Anderson; manuscripts of *Phases of an Inferior Planet, Vein of Iron, A Certain Measure, In This Our Life,* and *The Woman Within;* articles and speeches; notebooks; photos; drawings; and miscellaneous papers.

17,060. Johnston, Mary
Papers. Ca. 1900-60. 10.3 ft.
Open. Unpublished guide.
University of Virginia Library, Manuscripts Department.
Johnston (1870-1936), a novelist, was active in the women's suffrage movement. Correspondence, diaries, manuscripts, speeches, notebooks, ledgers, and clippings reflect Johnston's interest in the suffrage movement and in Virginia history. Includes information about events in Virginia from about 1880 to 1930. During WWI Johnston worked to further the cause of pacifism.

17,061. League of Women Voters of Charlottesville and Albemarle
Records. 1942-70. 5 Hollinger boxes and 1 cabinet.
Access restricted. No guide.
University of Virginia Library, Manuscripts Department.
Bylaws, minutes, correspondence, reports, scrapbooks, pamphlets, and publications reflect national, state, and local issues with which the LWV was concerned.

17,062. Randolph and Meikleham
Papers. 1792-1954. 3 Hollinger boxes.
Open. Unpublished guide.
University of Virginia Library, Manuscripts Department.
Family papers include letters to Septimia Anne Cary (Randolph) Meikleham (1814-87) and papers of her husband David Scott Meikleham, a physician. Septimia Meikleham was the daughter of Martha (Jefferson) Randolph (1772-1836) and Thomas Mann Randolph and the granddaughter of Thomas Jefferson and Martha (Wayles) [Mrs. Bathurst] Skelton Jefferson (1748-82). Her letters are primarily from her brothers and sisters.

EMORY

17,063. Appalachian Oral History Project
Oral history. 1972- . Ca. 700 tapes.
Open. Published guide.
Emory and Henry College, Appalachian Oral History Project.
Collection contains interviews with 87 female residents of southwestern Virginia. The interviewees, including both black and white women, were principally from agricultural and mining counties. Most were homemakers, but some had careers in teaching or business. They reminisce about regional events dating from about 1900 to the present. The Emory and Henry College interviews are part of the overall Appalachian Oral History Project, which also is underway at Alice Lloyd College, Lees Junior College, and Appalachian State University. Transcripts of some Project interviews have been published, and some are available on microfiche. See *Appalachian Oral History Project Union Catalog* (Pippa Passes, KY: Appalachian Oral History Project, 1977).

FREDERICKSBURG

17,064. Kenmore Association
Records. Nd. 100 drawers and 1 microfilm reel.
Partially closed. No guide.
Kenmore Association, Inc.
Founded in 1922 under the leadership of [Mrs.] Vivian Minor Fleming and her daughter Annie Smith, the Association restored Kenmore, the home of George Washington's brother-in-law Fielding Lewis. Financial records, correspondence, photos, slides, and clippings of the Association describe how the house was saved from demolition or conversion into apartments. Also includes ca. 180 18th-century letters relating to the Lewis family. Members of the Association, many of them women, lead tours of the Lewis home.

LEXINGTON

17,065. Armstrong, Catherine
Papers. 1936-58. 51 items.
Open. Unpublished guide.
George C. Marshall Research Foundation.
Armstrong was a personal friend of George C. Marshall from early childhood days. Letters from Marshall to Armstrong and Nan Lindsay illustrate their friendship and contain information about Marshall's work during WWII as chief of staff of the US Army, as secretary of state from 1947 to 1949, and as secretary of defense in 1950 and 1951.

17,066. Bagby, Lelia Cocke
Papers. 1942-44. 100 items.
Open. No guide.
George C. Marshall Research Foundation.
A member of the first officer's candidate class to graduate following establishment of the Women's Army Auxiliary Corps, [Mrs.] Bagby (1915-) served as an officer in the WAACs and the WACs. Photos, magazines, and a scrapbook containing correspondence, cartoons, and clippings about her military service. Most of the material pertains to the WAAC officer training program and to the role of women officers in the military.

17,067. Fry, Mary Fourqurean
Papers. 1942-45. 200 items.
Open. Unpublished guide.
George C. Marshall Research Foundation.
Correspondence, photos, pamphlets, programs, and clippings document the career of [Mrs.] Mary Fry Fritch (1910-) as an officer in the Women's Army Auxiliary Corps and the WACs during WWII. Includes material concerning WAAC enlistment procedures; the WAAC officer training program at Des Moines, IA; WAC life at Camp Upton, NY; military service at Naples, Italy; and the V-E Day celebration in Italy. Also contains information about Fritch's retirement from the service and about the development of the WAC Mother's Club, of which Fritch's mother was a state leader.

17,068. McGee, Martha Rector
Papers. 1942-43. 20 items.
Open. No guide.
George C. Marshall Research Foundation.
An officer in the Women's Army Auxiliary Corps and the WACs, McGee was a member of the first WAAC officer's candidate class. Correspondence, photos, orders, and magazines pertain chiefly to the officer training program.

17,069. Marshall, Katherine Tupper
Papers. 1930-50. 4 ft.
Open. No guide.
George C. Marshall Research Foundation.
Marshall (1882-) was the wife of General George Catlett Marshall; her son Allen Brown was killed during WWII. Correspondence with friends and associates of the Marshalls; condolences on the death of her son; correspondence regarding *Together,* her book about her life with George Marshall; and bills and receipts.

17,070. Martin, Cecilia (Jackie)
Papers. 1952-54. 6 ft. and 4 motion pictures.
Open. Unpublished guide.
George C. Marshall Research Foundation.
A Washington photographer, newspaperwoman, and author, Martin (1904-69) was chief of the photo section of the European Cooperation Administration, Office of the Special Representative, US Information Agency, in Paris from 1952 to 1954. Correspondence, notebooks containing business records, financial records, press releases, photos, clippings, books, and other papers relate to her work in Paris and consist largely of records concerning photo section operations. Three of the motion pictures included in the collection were produced for use in Dutch schools. The correspondence concerns termination of her assignment. Martin was the first woman named photographic and art director of a major metropolitan newspaper, the Washington *Times-Herald;* she also was the first woman member of the White House News Photographers Association and a founder of the American Newspaper Women's Club.

17,071. Singer, Marie (Marshall)
Papers. 1834-1948. 1.5 ft.
Open. Unpublished guide.
George C. Marshall Research Foundation.
Correspondence; tax, lease, and rent receipts; a promissory note; a genealogy; photos and daguerrotypes; menus; itineraries; clippings; and other papers of Singer (1876-1962) chiefly concern the career of her brother George Catlett Marshall (1880-1959) as chief of staff of the US Army, secretary of state, and secretary of defense. Items particularly focus on Marshall's early career as an aide to General John J. Pershing and work during WWI.

LYNCHBURG

17,072. Red Cross Canteen
Records. 1917-27. 8 items.
Closed. No guide.
Lynchburg Museum System.
Photos, post cards, and a booklet concerning the local American National Red Cross Canteen, which provided refreshments for men on troop trains that passed through Lynchburg from 1917 to 1919.

MANASSAS

17,073. Ricketts, Fanny
Papers. 1861. 130-page vol.
Open. No guide.
Manassas National Battlefield Park.
Ricketts was the wife of Captain James Ricketts, a Union Army officer wounded in the first battle of Manassas. Her diary describes her experiences in traveling to join her husband and in nursing him before and after his transfer to Libby Prison in Richmond, VA. Includes descriptions of the care

of the wounded and of southerners' reactions to prisoners of war.

NORFOLK

17,074. MacArthur Memorial Archives and Library
Records. 1880-1964. Ca. 690 ft.
Open. Unpublished guide.
General Douglas MacArthur Memorial.
Correspondence, diaries, radio messages, reports, recording discs, motion picture reels, photos, scrapbooks, scrolls, artifacts, and other papers of MacArthur (1880-1964), a general of the US Army. Includes personal papers of MacArthur's wife Jean Marie (Faircloth) MacArthur. Also contains records of the general headquarters of the Supreme Commander for Allied Powers pertaining to women and women's organizations, 1945-51. Eleanor Hadley, Ethel Weed, Beata Sirota, and other women served on MacArthur's staff during the postwar occupation of Japan.

17,075. Norfolk Women's Oral History Project
Oral history. Nd. 19 interviews.
Open. Unpublished guide.
Old Dominion University, Archives and Manuscripts.
Primarily reminiscences of women about their lives in Norfolk during the depression. Society women, blacks, and working women were asked about their economic, religious, social, and educational backgrounds and other topics.

RICHMOND

17,076. Caperton, Helena Trench (Lefroy)
Papers. Ca. 1920-62. Ca. 3600 items.
Open. Unpublished guide.
Virginia Commonwealth University, James Branch Cabell Library.
The winner of the O. Henry Award in 1930 for "The Honest Wine Merchant," [Mrs. Clifford Randolph] Caperton (1878-1962) was a short story and nonfiction writer who wrote chiefly about life and culture in Richmond. Correspondence and drafts of her works. She contributed book reviews for the Richmond *Times Dispatch,* the Louisville *Courier-Journal,* and the Louisville *Times.*

17,077. Clark, Adele
Papers. Ca. 1909-39. Ca. 30 ft.
Open. Unpublished guide.
Virginia Commonwealth University, James Branch Cabell Library.
A Richmond artist and suffragist, [Miss] Clark (1884?-) was among the founders of the Virginia Equal Suffrage League in 1909 and became the first president of the Virginia LWV in 1920. Correspondence, memoranda and minutes, financial records, photos, scrapbooks, and pamphlets, including records of the Equal Suffrage League and of the state and national LWV.

17,078. Williams, Frances Leigh
Papers. Ca. 1950-76. Ca. 100 items.
Open. No guide.
Virginia Commonwealth University, James Branch Cabell Library.
[Miss] Williams (1909-) is a newspaper columnist and free-lance writer. Manuscripts and proofs of Williams's books and seven letters of Ellen Glasgow.

17,079. Cary, Harriette
Papers. 1862. 29 pp.
Open. Unpublished guide.
Virginia State Library.
[Miss] Cary (1838-post 1926) married William Christian of Craighton in Henrico County, VA, in 1868. Diary in which she describes her life in Williamsburg, VA, beginning with its occupation by the Union Army under General McClellan.

17,080. Chandler, Sarah Ann Quarles
Papers. Nd. 4 pp.
Open. Unpublished guide.
Virginia State Library.
Clipping contains [Mrs.] Chandler's diary account of a wagon trip by her family from Louisa County, VA, to Cooper County, MO.

17,081. Custis, Lee, and Mason
Papers. 1756-1863. 63 items.
Open. Unpublished guide.
Virginia State Library.
Principally letters to Mary Lee Fitzhugh Custis, the wife of George Washington Parke Custis, or to her daughter Mary Anna Randolph (Custis) Lee, the wife of Robert E. Lee, from relatives and friends; these letters provide vignettes of daily life in 19th-century plantation society. Also includes letters to G. W. Custis Lee concerning an incident in which he was involved as a student at West Point and letters pertaining to the dispute surrounding ownership of the Chew home, known as Cliveden, in Germantown, PA, and legal matters involving the estate of Benjamin Chew.

17,082. Davis, Catherine
Papers. ?-1822. 1 vol.
Open. Unpublished guide.
Virginia State Library.
Diary of Davis (1757-?), a Pennsylvania native, contains stories, songs, poems, genealogical information, and recipes.

17,083. Eppes, Martha Burke (Jones)
Papers. 1823-57. 55-page vol. and 3 items.
Open. Unpublished guide.
Virginia State Library.
In 1809 Eppes (1790-1863), the daughter of General Willie Jones, became the second wife of John Wayles Eppes (1772-1823), a US senator from Buckingham County, VA. Her notebook includes personal accounts, a record of the distribution of clothing and blankets to slaves, and recipes. Martha Eppes's father served as a representative in the Continental Congress and as governor; her husband's first wife was Mary "Maria" Jefferson, daughter of Thomas Jefferson.

17,084. Franklin, Edith A.
Papers. 1955. 108 pp.
Open. Unpublished guide.
Virginia State Library.
An account of the Virginia State Industrial Farm for Women at Goochland, VA, by Franklin, who served as matron, librarian, and religious director at the Farm from 1939 to 1955.

17,085. Gibbs, Jane
Papers. 1857-60. 117-page vol.
Open. No guide.
Virginia State Library.
Diary and records of [Miss] Gibbs, who apparently was a private tutor. The material was written at Green Pond School in Nelson County, VA.

17,086. Kern, Margaret Ethel Kelley
Papers. 1907-38. 326 items.
Open. Unpublished guide.
Virginia State Library.
[Mrs. G. T. W.] Kern (1874-1975) was an author and volunteer worker who was appointed information officer for the Virginia State Chamber of Commerce. Papers reflect her involvement with relief and volunteer work during WWI and with the Eightieth Division Veterans Association; the papers also contain information on such subjects as the forced retirement of General Adelbert Cronkhite, a pardon for William Robinson, and her Chamber of Commerce position. Includes photos and other research material for the second edition of her book *The Trail of the Three Notched Road* (Richmond: William Byrd Press, 1928).

17,087. League of Women Voters
Records. 1921-23. 125 items.
Open. Unpublished guide.
Virginia State Library.
Clippings concern the LWV, civic affairs in Richmond, and matters of particular interest to women.

17,088. League of Women Voters
Records. 1950-70. Ca. 2000 items.
Open. Unpublished guide.
Virginia State Library.
Annual reports, minutes of state and local LWV groups, financial papers, correspondence, and issue files. Includes the records of the Portsmouth, VA, League, which was disbanded in 1965. The National LWV was organized in 1920.

17,089. MacGill, Mary Bell (Peirce), Family
Papers. 1890-1910. Ca. 500 items.
Open. Unpublished guide.
Virginia State Library.
MacGill (?-1879) was the daughter of James N. and Ann Dabney Peirce; her mother was the sister of J. E. B. Stuart. Papers consist principally of correspondence with friends and family, particularly her sister Elizabeth Pannill (Peirce) Litchfield of Abingdon, VA, and her brother David Stuart Peirce of Wytheville, VA.

17,090. Moffett, Carrie Lena Crawford
Papers. 1871-98. 9 vols. (microfilm).
Open. Unpublished guide.
Virginia State Library.
Diaries of Moffett (?-1898) cover the period from her last year as a student at Louisville Female High School until her death; the last entry is written by another author. The diary includes Moffett's observations concerning her last year at school as well as play notices, marriage invitations, compositions, Sunday school class books, and clippings. Contains an account of her marriage in 1876 to A. L. Moffett, a minister. Places mentioned include Locust Hill in Virginia and Round Hill Manse.

17,091. Munford, Mary Cooke Branch
Papers. 1905-30. Ca. 15,000 items.
Open. No guide.
Virginia State Library.
[Mrs.] Munford (1865-1938) was active in reform and public service organizations, including the Richmond Women's Club, the Richmond Education Association, and the "May Campaign"; she also supported the opening of colleges and universities to women. Correspondence, reference files, and other papers include references to the Women's Club, the Education Association, and "May Campaign," as well as to the Urban League, the LWV, the National Council of Defense, and the Co-ordinate College League.

17,092. Pennybacker, Margaret Muse
Papers. Nd. 23-page item.
Open. No guide.
Virginia State Library.
Recollections by Pennybacker, who lived in Mount Jackson in Shenandoah County, VA, an area occupied by Union forces several times during the Civil War.

17,093. Pryor, Mrs. Archibald Campbell
Papers. Nd. 11 pp.
Open. Unpublished guide.
Virginia State Library.
Anne Augusta (Banister) Pryor, wife of Archibald Campbell Pryor, was the daughter of William C. Banister. Recollections of Anne Pryor include descriptions of hardships suffered by Petersburg, VA, residents during the closing months of the Civil War. Includes her report of the death of her

father, who died while defending against Kautz's Raiders.

17,094. Raine, Frances Bouldin
Papers. 1903. 14 pp.
Open. Unpublished guide.
Virginia State Library.
A Halifax County, VA, native and daughter of Thomas and Nancy Spragins, Raine (1816-?) lived in Kentucky, Alabama, and Texas and visited numerous other states. Reminiscences deal primarily with the period 1816-75. Raine moved to Oak Hill in Charlotte County, VA, during the 1840s after her marriage to her second husband Colonel Raine.

17,095. Randolph, Jane
Papers. 1743. 197-page vol.
Open. Unpublished guide.
Virginia State Library.
Medicinal and culinary recipes.

17,096. Reese, Lizette Woodworth
Papers. 1928-34. 16 items.
Open. Unpublished guide.
Virginia State Library.
Reese (1856-1935) was a Baltimore schoolteacher and poet. Letters, apparently to [Mrs.] Naomi Chappell, and clippings.

17,097. Rice, Mrs. Gordon Pryor
Papers. Ca. 1860-90. 24-page vol.
Open. Unpublished guide.
Virginia State Library.
Account of family and plantation life in Charlotte County, VA.

17,098. Seawell, Molly
Papers. 1888-1912. 10 items.
Open. Unpublished guide.
Virginia State Library.
[Miss] Seawell was a Gloucester County, VA, native who lived most of her life in Washington, DC. Correspondence to Seawell's literary agents concern the sale of *The Berkeleys and Their Neighbor,* "Lady Betty," *The House of Egremont,* and other stories.

17,099. Simpson, Mr. and Mrs. William S.
Papers. 1819-61. 10 vols.
Open. Unpublished guide.
Virginia State Library.
William Simpson (1795 or 1796-1868), a native of London, emigrated to Petersburg, VA, where he operated an insurance agency. Letterbook consisting mainly of Simpson's letters to his friends and relatives, diaries of Simpson and his wife, 1858-59, concerning observations in England and Wales; a volume containing descriptions of Simpson's Petersburg residence, St. Levens Lodge; catalogs of books; drawings; pictures; and other items. Includes letters written in Petersburg in 1865, one of which details the city's occupation by Union troops.

17,100. Sperry, Sarah Catherine "Kate" S.
Papers. 1861-1941. 634-page item and 7 booklets.
Open. Unpublished guide.
Virginia State Library.
Sperry was a Winchester, VA, girl during the Civil War. Her diary, begun shortly after the War's outbreak, gives an almost day-by-day account of activities by Confederate and Union forces in and around Winchester as well as a description of her daily life. The first typescript edition of the diary was produced in 1941 by her daughter Lenoir Hunt.

17,101. Stribling, Mary Cary Ambler
Papers. 1862. 2 vols.
Open. Unpublished guide.
Virginia State Library.
Diary of Stribling, the wife of Robert M. Stribling.

17,102. Sully, Julia
Papers. 1920-40. 2000 items.
Open. Unpublished guide.
Virginia State Library.
[Miss] Sully (?-1948), chairman of the Richmond branch of the Women's Organization for National Prohibition Reform, wrote weekly articles for the Richmond *News Leader* during the mid-1930s. Notes regarding artists and artwork relevant to Virginia, copies of Sully's lectures and of her *News Leader* articles, items pertaining to prohibition, and material reflecting the friction between officials and sculptor Gutzon Borglum, who was commissioned to carve the Stone Mountain Confederate Memorial near Atlanta. Sully was the great-great-niece of Thomas Sully and the granddaughter of Robert Sully, both of whom were artists.

17,103. Taliaferro, Mrs. William Booth
Papers. 1849-64. 177-page item.
Open. Unpublished guide.
Virginia State Library.
Diary kept by Sally Lyons Taliaferro, wife of Confederate brigadier general William Taliaferro, principally concerns family activities and the weather. Also includes a few comments on economic conditions and reports that circulated on the home front regarding battles and conditions in areas occupied by Federal troops.

17,104. Thompson, Ida M.: Virginia Woman Suffrage
Collection. 1910-25. 25,000 items.
Open. No guide.
Virginia State Library.
Correspondence, subject files, membership lists, clippings, and other records of the Equal Suffrage League of Virginia; a few items concern the Virginia LWV.

17,105. Varnier, Martha "Mattie"
Papers. 1859-61. 1 vol.
Open. Unpublished guide.
Virginia State Library.
Diary by Varnier contains information about the daily activities of a young lady in antebellum Virginia.

17,106. Weisiger, [Miss]
Papers. 1824-47. 197-page vol.
Open. Unpublished guide.
Virginia State Library.
Diary of Weisiger, the sister of Confederate general Daniel Weisiger, reflects the daily life of a young lady in the antebellum South, with emphasis on her activities in the Methodist church.

WILLIAMSBURG

17,107. Barnes Family
Papers. 1797-1926. 247 items.
Open. Unpublished guide.
College of William and Mary, Earl Gregg Swem Library.
Correspondence, financial papers, and clippings of Newman Williamson B. Barnes (?-1858) of Falmouth, Greenfield, and Richmond, VA; his wife Margaret W. Tomlin Barnes (?-1859); and their daughter Margaret W. Barnes. Correspondence, which makes up the bulk of the collection, includes social and family news chiefly from female members of the Braxton, Coalter, and Oliver families of Virginia.

17,108. Blair, Banister, Braxton, Horner, and Whiting
Papers. 1760-1890. 111 items.
Open. Unpublished guide.
College of William and Mary, Earl Gregg Swem Library.
Family correspondence and business records of John Blair (1732-1800), a Williamsburg jurist and associate justice of the supreme court, include correspondence of his daughter Mary (Blair) Braxton, Elizabeth Braxton Whiting of Enfield in Prince William County, VA, Anne Banister of Williamsburg, and [Mrs.] Mary Burwell. The letters date chiefly from the late 18th and early 19th centuries.

17,109. Brown, Coalter, and Tucker
Papers. 1780-1929. 3433 items.
Open. Unpublished guide.
College of William and Mary, Earl Gregg Swem Library.
Correspondence, business records, poems, photos, and clippings of John Coalter (1769-1838), judge of the Supreme Court of Appeals of Virginia, and John Thompson Brown (1802-36), a member of the Virginia House of Delegates. Contains correspondence of Frances Bland (Tucker) Coalter (1785-1813), wife of John Coalter; Elizabeth Tucker (Coalter) Bryan (1805-56), Coalter's daughter; Judith H. Tomlin Coalter (1809-59), Coalter's daughter-in-law, and Frances Bland Coalter Brown (1835-94), Coalter's granddaughter. Papers of the three families, who lived in Williamsburg, Staunton, Petersburg, Bedford, Gloucester, and Hanover counties, VA, concern family and social matters and date principally from the early to mid-19th century.

17,110. Chapman, Anne T.
Papers. 1884-1948. 18 boxes.
Open. No guide.
College of William and Mary, Earl Gregg Swem Library.
Chapman (1884-1954), a Williamsburg civic and social leader after 1901, helped found the Williamsburg Civic League, which started the Williamsburg Public Library in 1910. Correspondence, diaries, financial records, minutes, photos, clippings, publications, and other material. Chapman, who lived in Madison, WI, and attended the University of Wisconsin before moving to Williamsburg, was active in Williamsburg groups including the Garden Club, the public health program, and the Gamma Phi Beta chapter at the College of William and Mary. She served for many years as a voluntary librarian at the Williamsburg Public Library.

17,111. Christian Family
Papers. 1866-1910. 850 items.
Open. Unpublished guide.
College of William and Mary, Earl Gregg Swem Library.
Correspondence, a memorandum, accounts, and other business records of this Richmond, VA, family. Includes letters from family members who were students at Woodberry Forest, the University of Virginia, and Virginia Military Institute as well as business records of the Richmond Female Humane Association and the Richmond Woman's Christian Association.

17,112. Darling, Flora (Adams)
Papers. 1862-1908. 4536 items.
Open. Unpublished guide.
College of William and Mary, Earl Gregg Swem Library.
[Mrs. Edward Irving] Darling (1840-1910) was among the founders in 1890 of the DAR, in 1891 of the Daughters of the Revolution, and in 1892 of the Daughters of the US of the War of 1812. Correspondence, writings, scrapbooks, and printed matter chiefly relate to the founding of these three patriotic women's organizations.

17,113. King's Daughters, Kate Custis Memorial Circle
Records. 1893-1970. 4 boxes.
Open. Unpublished guide.

College of William and Mary, Earl Gregg Swem Library.
Founded in Williamsburg in 1888, this civic group provided assistance to the poor and participated in other projects. Minutes, financial records, correspondence, reports, photos, clippings, and memorabilia.

17,114. McCormick, Virginia Taylor
Papers. 1887-1953. 206 items.
Open. Unpublished guide.
College of William and Mary, Earl Gregg Swem Library.
McCormick (1873-1957) was a Norfolk, VA, poet, literary critic, essayist, lecturer, and editor of *The Lyric* from 1921 to 1929. Correspondence, diaries, writings, scrapbooks, and clippings relate to her literary activities and include letters from Gamaliel Bradford, Edwin Markham, Marjorie (Kinnan) Rawlings, Evelyn Norcross Sherrill, Ellen Glasgow, Amy Lowell, and Lizette Reese.

17,115. Page and Saunders
Papers. 1790-1932. 190 items.
Open. Unpublished guide.
College of William and Mary, Earl Gregg Swem Library.
Correspondence and other papers of these families from Rosewell in Gloucester County and Williamsburg include correspondence of Margaret (Lowther) Page, wife of Virginia governor John Page; her daughter Lucy Burwell (Page) Saunders (1807-?); and her son-in-law Robert Saunders (?-1868), a professor at the College of William and Mary. Also includes manuscript stories of Robert and Lucy Saunders' daughter Roberta Page Saunders (?-1894).

17,116. Page, Thomas Nelson
Papers. 1893-1953. 305 items.
Open. Unpublished guide.
College of William and Mary, Earl Gregg Swem Library.
An author and diplomat, Page (1853-1922) was US ambassador to Italy from 1913 to 1918. Correspondence and photos, including letters from his second wife Florence Lathrop Field (1858-1921) to her daughters Minna Burnaby (1882-) and Florence Lindsay and to other relatives. The majority of Field's letters were written from Rome between 1913 and 1919 and concern current events, WWI, family news, and women's volunteer work during the war.

17,117. Pollard, Violet McDougall
Papers. Ca. 1919-75. 5 cabinets.
Closed. No guide.
College of William and Mary, Earl Gregg Swem Library.
[Mrs. John Garland] Pollard (1889-1977), a Richmond, VA, civic leader, was executive secretary to governors of Virginia from 1918 to 1934, a member of the Democratic National Committee from 1940 to 1968, and associate director of the Virginia Museum of Fine Arts from 1940 to 1956. Correspondence, clippings, and printed material particularly reflect her activities in Richmond's civic life and in the Democratic party.

17,118. Riddle Family
Papers. 1812-1915. 927 items.
Open. Unpublished guide.
College of William and Mary, Earl Gregg Swem Library.
Horace R. Riddle, a Baltimore banker and businessman, was active during the last half of the 19th century. Correspondence, accounts, business and legal records, minutes, and clippings, including minutes, 1903-06, relating to the Harriet Lane Home for Invalid Children at Johns Hopkins Hospital. [Miss] Katherine Riddle was secretary of the Home's board of managers.

17,119. Ritchie and Harrison
Papers. 1807-1938. 856 items.
Open. Unpublished guide.
College of William and Mary, Earl Gregg Swem Library.
Correspondence, a diary, business records, and clippings of Thomas Ritchie (1778-1854), a journalist and politician who was editor of the *Richmond Enquirer* and Washington *Union,* including correspondence of his wife Isabella Foushee Ritchie and their 12 children, particularly Isabella H. (Ritchie) Harrison of Brandon in Charles City County, VA, concerning family and social news and including mention of many prominent 19th-century Virginians.

17,120. Seawell, Molly Elliot
Papers. 1900-14. 2 vols.
Open. No guide.
College of William and Mary, Earl Gregg Swem Library.
Diaries of Seawell (1860-1916), an author and antisuffragist.

17,121. Tucker and Coleman
Papers. 1675-1956. 30,000 items.
Open. Unpublished guide.
College of William and Mary, Earl Gregg Swem Library.
Correspondence, literary manuscripts, notebooks, financial records, photos, and legal documents of St. George Tucker (1752-1827), a Revolutionary War patriot, lawyer, professor of law, jurist, and poet, and of his son Nathaniel Beverley Tucker (1784-1851), a lawyer, law professor, and author. Includes correspondence of Nathaniel Tucker's wife Lucy Ann (Smith) Tucker (1812-67), daughter of Thomas Adams Smith (1781-1844), and correspondence and unpublished historical writings of Cynthia Beverley (Tucker) Coleman (1832-1908), daughter of Nathaniel and Lucy Tucker. Cynthia Coleman, a Williamsburg social and civic leader, was a founder of the Association for the Preservation of Virginia Antiquities and a charter member of the Society of Colonial Dames in Virginia. Her correspondence includes Civil War letters from her husband Charles Washington Coleman, a physician, and letters from other relatives concerning family and social news.

17,122. Van Lew, Elizabeth L.
Papers. 1836-1926. Ca. 200 items.
Open. Unpublished guide.
College of William and Mary, Earl Gregg Swem Library.
A Richmond, VA, resident, Van Lew (1818-1900) was a Union spy during the Civil War. Correspondence and a speech that John Albree of Boston wrote about Van Lew. Also includes photos, clippings, and other items Albree collected about Van Lew.

17,123. Whittle and Greene
Papers. 1855-1924. 398 items.
Open. No guide.
College of William and Mary, Earl Gregg Swem Library.
Diaries, photos, clippings, and printed matter of the family, including 60 diaries for 1861 to 1924 of Chloe Tyler (Whittle) Greene, wife of John Newport Greene, and a diary by her sister Grace Latimer Whittle, dated 1855. Both women were members of the upper class in Norfolk, VA.

17,124. Williamsburg Civic League
Records. 1907-36. 471 items.
Open. Unpublished guide.
College of William and Mary, Earl Gregg Swem Library.
Minutes, monthly and annual committee reports, and photos of the League, a civic improvement society founded in 1907 by local women.

17,125. Oral History
Oral history. 1952-76. Tapes and 32 transcripts.
Access restricted. Unpublished guide.
Colonial Williamsburg Foundation, Department of Archives and Records.
A nonprofit, educational institution, the Foundation and its predecessors date from 1926. Collection supplements the Foundation's written record through oral memoirs of employees and Williamsburg citizens, 14 of whom are women. Those identified as local citizens are Emma Louise Barlow, Mary H. B. [Mrs. George] Coleman, the Misses Morecock, and Miriam Tilledge. Foundation employees interviewed include Frances Burns, hotel administration; Helen D. Bullock and Mary Frances Goodwin, the research department; Elizabeth L. Henderson, hostess supervisor; Susan H. Nash, an interior design consultant; Alma Lee Rowe, public relations; and Mrs. Albert Sneed, hostess. Other women included are Virginia Blanchard, clerk of the Williamsburg-James City county court; Louise B. Fisher, Colonial Williamsburg hostess and author; and [Mrs.] Fannie Lou Stryker, Colonial Williamsburg hostess and wife of a former mayor.

17,126. Ambler, Eliza Jacquelin
Papers. 1780-1823. 24 items.
Open. Unpublished guide.
Colonial Williamsburg Foundation, Research Archives.
Correspondence of Ambler (1765-1847) with Mildred Smith Dudley and Ambler's letters to Frances Caines and Ann "Nancy" Ambler Fisher. Topics include the Amblers' difficulties during the Revolutionary War, the death of Ambler's first husband William Brent, and the life of one of her childhood friends, who had an affair with a French officer stationed in Williamsburg and later bore an illegitimate child.

17,127. Anderson, Robert
Papers. 1693-1877. 35 vols. and 4140 items.
Open. Unpublished guide.
Colonial Williamsburg Foundation, Research Archives.
Much of the family correspondence of Anderson (1781-1859), a merchant, is composed of letters from his nieces and other female relatives and correspondence, 1845-52, with his grandnephew Robert A. Ashburn, largely regarding Ashburn's relationship with a female member of the Anderson household. Collection, the bulk of which dates from 1787 to 1858, consists of correspondence, insurance and estate papers, business accounts, political papers, deeds, and other legal papers. Contains correspondence with Mary M. Peachy, Maria Crump, and other women and papers concerning the estates of several women, including Mary Williamson and Mary Charlton.

17,128. Galt Family
Papers. 1745-1899. 171 vols. and 5992 items.
Open. Unpublished guide.
Colonial Williamsburg Foundation, Research Archives.
Family papers of John M. Galt (1744-1808), an apothecary; his wife Judith C. Galt (ca. 1749-?); his son Alexander D. Galt (1771-1841) and grandson John M. Galt II (1819-62), superintendents of the Lunatic Hospital in Williamsburg; and his granddaughters Elizabeth (1816-54) and Sarah Maria Galt (1822-80). Correspondence, diaries, medical papers, account books, household accounts, memorandum books, essays, and poems. Papers of Alexander D. Galt, Jr.; John M. Galt II; and Elizabeth and Sarah Galt form the bulk of the collection. Includes Elizabeth Galt's drafts of letters, poetry, and essays; her memorandum book for 1842 to 1851 listing her activities; and Sarah Galt's letters, essays, and a scrapbook. Medical papers include correspondence with Dorothea Dix from 1848 to 1876.

17,129. Norton, John, and Sons
Papers. 1750-1902. 2294 items.
Open. Unpublished guide.

Colonial Williamsburg Foundation, Research Archives.
Family papers and business records of John Norton (1719-77) and John Hatley Norton (1745-97), merchants of London and Virginia. Included are letters, 1768-95, to John Hatley Norton in Virginia from his mother Cortenay Norton; his sisters Frances, Ann, and Caroline; and his aunt Susanna Turner in England. Business papers of the House of John Norton and Sons consist of accounts, bills, receipts, correspondence, and other material, primarily relating to the period 1766 to 1798. Letters regarding business and personal matters from John Norton in London to Martha Gooseley in York, VA, and from Mary Tucker of the Barbados to James Withers in London are included as are accounts and letters from women with whom Norton and Sons conducted business.

17,130. Walker, Robert: Clinical Cases
Papers. 1785-87. 138-page vol.
Open. Unpublished guide.
Colonial Williamsburg Foundation, Research Archives.
Volume of notes taken by Walker (?-ca. 1820), a Virginia physician, while he was a medical student at the University of Edinburgh. Notes pertain to clinical observation of female patients, their diseases, and treatments used at the Royal Infirmary, Edinburgh. Volume contains its own rough index.

WASHINGTON

BELLINGHAM

17,131. Higgenson, Ella
Papers. Ca. 1894-1949. Ca. 6 cu.ft.
Access restricted. No guide.
Bellingham Public Library.
Correspondence, manuscripts, proofs, movie scripts, photos, and scrapbooks of press notices of Higgenson, an author and poet in Bellingham. Includes correspondence with publishers and manuscripts of published and unpublished books and stories. Higgenson wrote under the pen names of Anne Lester and Ethelind Ray.

17,132. Bellingham Women's Music Club
Records. 1917-72. Ca. 3 cu.ft.
Open. No guide.
Western Washington University, Music Library.
Scrapbooks containing minutes, programs, yearbooks, and clippings of the Club, which was made up of socially prominent women. The bulk of the records pertains to programs presented by the Club and to persons who attended its meetings.

CHEHALIS

17,133. Banks
Papers. Ca. 1896-1909. Ca. 2 ft.
Access restricted. No guide.
Lewis County Historical Society.
Banks apparently was a teacher, principal, and physician. Family correspondence with children and friends include love letters written by Banks and his wife before and just after marriage. Centralia, WA, and Michigan and some Montana areas are mentioned.

17,134. Centralia Music Club
Records. 1919-68. Ca. 2 ft.
Access restricted. No guide.
Lewis County Historical Society.
The Club presented music programs and supported area music events. Minutes, programs, scrapbooks, convention attendance information, and material from the Washington State Federation of Music Clubs and the National Federation of Music Clubs. The Centralia Music Club was preceded by the music department of the Centralia Ladies Civic Club, which was founded in 1916.

17,135. Cory, Johanna
Papers. Ca. 1900-50. Ca. 4 ft.
Access restricted. No guide.
Lewis County Historical Society.
Cory (ca. 1880-1960), a member of the St. Helen's Club, was the wife of Arthur S. Cory, a local banker and state legislator. Diaries regarding travels with her husband to foreign missions, scrapbooks, 47 reels of home movies, magazines, and church and missionary items.

17,136. Daughters of Pioneers of Washington
Records. Ca. 1938-60. Ca. 2 ft.
Open. No guide.
Lewis County Historical Society.
Minutes, programs, receipts, and clippings of Lewis County chapter number 9, founded in 1939 to perpetuate the memory and spirit of the pioneers of Washington through preservation of historic sites and documents, promotion of historical research about the pioneers, and celebration of historic events relating to Washington state.

17,137. Garden Department of Women's Civic Club
Records. 1926-35. 1 vol.
Access restricted. No guide.
Lewis County Historical Society.
Garden Department minutes contain information about presentations on the care of flowers.

17,138. St. Helen's Club
Records. 1895- . Ca. 2 ft.
Access restricted. Unpublished guide.
Lewis County Historical Society.
Members of the Club, described as the oldest in the county, are wives of leading area business and professional men. Collection contains minutes describing early Club efforts for social and civic improvements, among them wooden sidewalks and a public ladies' lounge where farm wives could rest during their shopping and care for their infants. Scrapbooks and programs are also included.

17,139. Severson, Bessie
Papers. Ca. 1900-65. Ca. 1 ft.
Access restricted. No guide.
Lewis County Historical Society.
Severson and her husband, a mechanic, worked for the largest and oldest Ford automobile agency in Chehalis. Correspondence, ration books, Christmas cards, and other material that includes information regarding two Christmas bonuses the couple received.

17,140. Smith, Herndon
Papers. 1938-39. Ca. 3 ft.
Open. No guide.
Lewis County Historical Society.
Interviews, note cards, clippings, and drafts of stories for the proposed book "Centralia, First 50 Years" constitute the results of research done by high school students for an English class taught by Smith (?-).

CHENEY

17,141. Danskin Family
Papers. Ca. 1915-40. Ca. 1.5 cu.ft. and 1 microfilm reel.
Open. Inventory.
Eastern Washington University Library, Archives and Special Collections.
Family papers of Floyd B. Danskin, a Spokane politician and Washington state representative, and of his wife Hannah (Mitchell) Danskin, a journalist in New York and Kansas who, after her marriage in 1929, became a Republican party and civic worker in Washington. Includes letters from William Allen White, 1907-28, a progressive Kansas newspaperman, and letters in which he recommended Hannah Danskin as a journalist to prospective employers; in one he wrote, "she can handle any department around a newspaper that pertains to women." Includes scrapbooks containing clippings of articles she wrote for the *Kansas City Star,* the *New York Tribune,* and the *Scarsdale Inquirer* in New York, which she also edited, and correspondence concerning Republican party politics. A delegate to the 1936 Republican national convention, Hannah Danskin received a telegram in which national chairman Lilian D. Rock told her of rising sentiment for nominating a woman for vice-president. Collection also contains minutes, agenda, and ephemera of the National Federation of Women's Republican Clubs, 1938, and committee lists and budgets, membership and salary lists, mimeographed letters from the national organization, and ephemera of the YWCA of Spokane, 1930-36.

17,142. University Archives
Records. Ca. 1890- . No size given.
Open. Accession lists and transmittal forms.
Eastern Washington University Library, Archives and Special Collections.
Founded in 1881, Eastern Washington University was a normal school and later a college of education until the early 1960s. Records of the president, the provost for academic affairs, the registrar, and the personnel, housing, scholarship, financial aid, placement, and student government offices. Oral history interviews being conducted with graduates of 1890 to 1930 will be deposited in the Archives.

17,143. Adams, Spokane, and Franklin Counties
Records. Nd. No size given.
Open. Schedules.
Eastern Washington University Library, Regional Depository, Washington State Archives.
Adams County records include 218 cubic feet of trial records of civil cases, 1907-33; criminal cases, 1889-1957; and probate cases, 1885-1940. Also contains records of Spokane County, 1961-64, and of Franklin County, 1960-67. The records contain scattered references to women.

17,144. Cities of Spokane and Colville
Records. Nd. No size given.
Open. Schedules.
Eastern Washington University Library, Regional Depository, Washington State Archives.
Voter registration records, 1925-40, of Colville, WA, and 475 cubic feet of Spokane, WA, voter registration books and warrant and voucher registers, 1891-1975. The voter registration books include such data as dates of registration, dates voted, occupation, address, place of birth, time of residence in the state of Washington, and precinct.

EDMONDS

17,145. Archives
Records. 1889- . No size given.
Closed. No guide.
Dominican Sisters, Congregation of Holy Cross.
The Congregation was founded in 1890 in Aberdeen, WA, with Sister M. Anselm Weber as the first general superior. Financial records, annuals, correspondence, notebooks, manuscripts of theses and dissertations, tapes, photos, scrapbooks, clippings, and other records of the Congregation, whose members are active in the education of youth and care of the sick. The order was established in the US in 1853 in Brooklyn, NY, by Sister M. Augustine Neuhierl.

LA CONNER

17,146. Associated Garden Clubs of Skagit County
Records. 1955-62. Ca. 9 in.
Open. No guide.
Skagit County Historical Museum.
Typescripts, photos, scrapbooks, clippings, and memorabilia of this women's club concern the annual flower show at the county fair.

17,147. Burlington Garden Club
Records. 1938-74. Ca. 1 ft.
Open. No guide.
Skagit County Historical Museum.
Records of the Club, founded in 1938 to organize exhibits for county and state fairs, include minute books, annual summaries, correspondence with the Washington State Federation of Garden Clubs, calendars, membership lists, photos of garden exhibits, a history of the Club, clippings, and other records.

17,148. Clippings
Collection. Nd. Ca. 1 ft.
Open. No guide.
Skagit County Historical Museum.
Contains numerous historical articles concerning women.

17,149. Daughters of the Pioneers
Records. Ca. 1864-1956. 4 in.
Open. No guide.
Skagit County Historical Museum.
Photos, clippings, obituaries, ephemera, and memorabilia of Skagit chapter No. II of this organization that sought to perpetuate the memory and spirit of the pioneers of Washington. Concerns such aspects of pioneer life as traveling to the Northwest, settling, and work.

17,150. Funeral Eulogies by A. W. Wilson
Papers. Ca. 1938-56. 2 in.
Open. No guide.
Skagit County Historical Museum.
Eulogies for both men and women presented by Wilson, a clergyman. Also includes obituaries.

17,151. Interviews of Pioneers
Oral history. 1965-66. 45 tapes.
Open. No guide.
Skagit County Historical Museum.
Includes interviews with female pioneers of the Skagit Valley regarding various topics.

17,152. Letters
Collection. Ca. 1850-1960. 112 items.
Open. No guide.
Skagit County Historical Museum.
Letters donated to the Museum by local residents contain material by or about women on a variety of subjects.

17,153. Scrapbook
Collection. Ca. 1882-1975. 55 items.
Open. No guide.
Skagit County Historical Museum.
Scrapbooks regarding Skagit Valley history contain correspondence, reminiscences, clippings, obituaries, and other material.

17,154. Skagit County WCTU
Records. 1904-05. 1 in.
Open. No guide.
Skagit County Historical Museum.
Clippings of articles written by Harriet "Hattie" Ball Dunlap for an unknown newspaper regarding the national and local WCTU. Topics of speeches described in the articles include "civic uprightness," patriotism and home and school, and the influence of women. Collection also includes photos.

17,155. Skagit Garden Club
Records. 1939-70. Ca. 5 in.
Open. No guide.
Skagit County Historical Museum.
Minutes, photos, scrapbooks, yearbooks, and clippings of the Club, which was founded in 1939 to organize exhibits for county and state fairs.

17,156. Territorial Daughters of Washington, Chapter II
Records. Ca. 1947-73. Ca. 9 in.
Open. No guide.
Skagit County Historical Museum.
Memoirs, essays, scrapbooks of clippings, and obituaries of this organization of descendants of Washington pioneers.

NORTH BEND

17,157. Fall City Methodist Church
Records. 1898-1930. Ca. 1 in.
Open. No guide.
Snoqualmie Valley Historical Society Museum.
Minutes of the Church, which has been in operation from 1898 to the present, include references to female Sunday school teachers and the Ladies Aid, which sponsored socials, dances, and bake sales and sold jam and baked goods to miners and lumberjacks in the countryside.

17,158. Fall City Study Club
Records. 1914-48. 1 cu.ft.
Open. No guide.
Snoqualmie Valley Historical Society Museum.
Minute books, an annual chronicle, financial records, lectures, membership lists, scrapbooks, and clippings of the Club, which has been in operation from 1914 to the present. Includes lectures on such topics as whether a girl's education should proceed beyond high school, women after the war from 1918 to 1919, and housekeeping in Japan as well as a scrapbook regarding the 21st biennial convention of the GFWC held in Seattle in 1932. The Club was originally known as the North Bend Study Club.

17,159. Gardner Family
Papers. 1750-1968. 41 pp.
Open. No guide.
Snoqualmie Valley Historical Society Museum.
Memoirs, photos, and a family tree of the Gardner family, members of which emigrated from England and settled and farmed in Snoqualmie Valley. One of the female family members was a music teacher.

17,160. Hill, Ada E. S.
Papers. Nd. 1 in.
Open. No guide.
Snoqualmie Valley Historical Society Museum.
[Mrs.] Hill was a teacher and founder of the Snoqualmie Valley Historical Society, which houses material documenting the history of North Bend, Snoqualmie, and Fall City, WA. Memoirs, a scrapbook containing a handwritten history of the Snoqualmie Valley, and clippings include information regarding the first white woman in the Valley in the 1870s and the first Indian woman to marry a white settler. The collection contains papers regarding events of 1855.

17,161. North Bend Community Church
Records. 1897-1938. Ca. 2 in.
Open. No guide.
Snoqualmie Valley Historical Society Museum.
Minutes of the Church, which was founded in 1897 as a Baptist church and reorganized in the 1920s, include references to Sunday school teachers and the Ladies' Aid, which sponsored socials, dances, and bake sales and sold jam and baked goods to miners and lumberjacks in the countryside.

17,162. Scrapbooks
Collection. Nd. 6 in.
Open. No guide.
Snoqualmie Valley Historical Society Museum.
Scrapbooks of the Snoqualmie Valley Historical Society, founded in 1959, contain clippings regarding the first settler in Snoqualmie Valley in 1858, the marriage of an Indian woman to a white settler in 1876, the arrival of the first white woman, and the birth of the first white child in the Valley. Includes obituaries of pioneer women and articles regarding current events from ca. 1959 to the present.

OLYMPIA

17,163. Oral History Project
Oral history. 1974-76. Ca. 20 boxes.
Open. No guide.
Washington State Archives.
The Project was started in 1974 to collect oral histories in selected counties in the state. Consists of tape-recorded interviews, transcripts, and photos. Contains a series on women rural school teachers in Kittisas County, with information on where teachers lived, salaries, duties in and out of school, social life, community attitudes, and isolation; the series covers the years from ca. 1905 through the 1930s. Also includes information on a woman jazz singer in Whatcom County, 1920s; a German woman's experience in Pacific County during WWII; and black women in King County. Most of the interviewers were women.

17,164. Bates, Kate (Stevens)
Papers. Ca. 1878-1940. 5 ft.
Open. No guide.
Washington State Library, Washington-Northwest Room.
Correspondence, manuscripts, notes, scrapbooks, atlases, clippings, and other papers of Bates (1852-1941), a writer and traveler who was the daughter of Isaac Stevens, the first governor of Washington Territory, and wife of H. S. Bates, an engineer. Includes Bates' correspondence with historian Edmund S. Meany regarding her father's life, a request her mother made to Congress after Isaac Stevens's death for compensation for his service, and a letter to Bates that her brother Hazard Stevens wrote in 1905 demanding that she not marry beneath her station.

17,165. Brown Family
Papers. 1861-ca. 1886. 1 in.
Open. No guide.
Washington State Library, Washington-Northwest Room.
Correspondence, wills, and legal papers of the Brown family, including correspondence of Mary (Olney) [Mrs. Benjamin] Brown (1821-86) and Emily French in Washington Territory with their sister in the Midwest regarding daily life; correspondence of Catherine and George Franklin Lotz in Yelm, WA, with their son in Texas; and the wills of Mary and Benjamin Brown.

17,166. DeVoe, Emma (Smith)
Papers. 1880-1913. 5 ft.
Open. Inventory.
Washington State Library, Washington-Northwest Room.
Correspondence, notes, and scrapbooks of clippings, leaflets, and programs of DeVoe (1858-1927), president of the Washington Equal Suffrage Association. A professional organizer for woman suffrage, she was brought from Illinois to Washington to lead the successful campaign for the ballot in 1910 and 1911. Contains correspondence with local and national suffrage workers and leaders, including Carrie Chapman Catt, Abigail Scott Duniway, Susan B. Anthony, and Alice Stone Blackwell; the letters document the strategy of the

movement as well as its internal politics and conflicts.

17,167. Eells, Ida Myra
Papers. 1947. 78 pp.
Open. No guide.
Washington State Library, Washington-Northwest Room.
Biography that Eells, a teacher, wrote about her grandmother Myra (Fairbanks) "Mother" Eells (1805-78), a missionary and teacher who, with her husband Cushing Eells, established the Tshimakain mission near what is now Spokane, lived in the Willamette Valley from 1848 to 1866, and founded Whitman Seminary (now Whitman College) in Walla Walla in 1866. The account is based on Ida Eells's conversations with her grandfather, on family papers, and on Myra Eells's journal, which she kept in 1838 while crossing the Oregon Trail for the American Board of Commissioners for Foreign Missions.

17,168. Funk, Goldie R.
Papers. 1956. 14 pp.
Open. No guide.
Washington State Library, Washington-Northwest Room.
Typescript of a speech in which [Mrs. George H.] Funk reminisces about teaching school in Washington and other topics. She taught in the Midwest and in Olympia after moving there in 1889.

17,169. Haller, Constance (Reed)
Papers. 1866-1927. 5 in.
Open. No guide.
Washington State Library, Washington-Northwest Room.
Correspondence, manuscripts, clippings, memorabilia, and other papers of the McKenny and Reed families. Haller, the wife of businessman Theodore N. Haller, was a society woman of Alaska, Seattle, and San Francisco; she also was interested in the fine arts. She was the daughter of Thomas M. Reed, a Seattle attorney and US district judge in Alaska, and Ida McKenny Reed, a writer of historical short stories about Puget Sound. Includes some of Ida Reed's manuscripts and Haller's rewrite of one of Reed's stories.

17,170. Hilburger, Jessie (Cantwell)
Papers. Ca. 1887-1971. Ca. 3 ft.
Open. No guide.
Washington State Library, Washington-Northwest Room.
Correspondence, manuscripts, family papers, photos, biographical data, and clippings of Hilburger (1887-1971), a dressmaker, writer, and pioneer, who was born in Little Falls (now Vader), WA, to James C. and Catherine Simmons Cantwell, founders of the town. Includes manuscripts of articles she wrote regarding her grandparents' overland journey in 1844 and 1845 to what is now Washington, where they established the first American settlement, and correspondence pertaining to family matters, dances, and crops. She was active in the Daughters of the Pioneers and the DAR. She told fortunes in later life.

17,171. Hutton, May Arkwright
Papers. 1908-12. 1 in.
Open. No guide.
Washington State Library, Washington-Northwest Room.
Correspondence of Hutton (ca. 1860-1915), a woman suffrage leader, businesswoman, and philanthropist, regarding the suffrage campaign in Washington. Hutton was the leader of the campaign in eastern Washington, but she was in conflict with the Seattle headquarters and with the president of the Washington Equal Suffrage Association, Emma (Smith) DeVoe.

17,172. Miles, Luella
Papers. 1872. 11 pp.
Open. No guide.
Washington State Library, Washington-Northwest Room.
Diary in which Miles describes primarily the unpleasant conditions of her journey by train from Omaha to San Francisco and by steamship to Portland in 1872.

17,173. Pringle, Catherine Sager
Papers. 1908. 1 in.
Open. No guide.
Washington State Library, Washington-Northwest Room.
Pringle's account of her 1844 overland journey with her parents, both of whom died en route; the Whitman mission, where she was raised by the Whitmans; and the Whitman massacre of 1847 near Walla Walla, WA, of which she was one of the few survivors.

17,174. Putnam, Goldie Van Bibber
Papers. 1824-ca. 1935. 2 in.
Open. No guide.
Washington State Library, Washington-Northwest Room.
Papers of Putnam, a writer in Washington and Oregon, include correspondence dated 1824 of Samuel Putnam, an ancestor of her husband Charles Frederick Putnam III; autobiographical sketches regarding the years from 1896 to 1935 in Ferry County, WA, and Mitchell, OR; and articles.

17,175. Sale, Elizabeth
Papers. 1943-44. Ca. 5 in.
Open. No guide.
Washington State Library, Washington-Northwest Room.
Sale was an author. Manuscript of her *Recitation From Memory* (Dodd Mead and Company, 1943) regarding the Rand family in Tacoma from 1896 to 1900; the manuscript is 60,000 words longer than the published edition. Also includes the manuscript for the sequel *My Mother Bids Me Bind My Hair* (Dodd Mead and Company, 1944).

17,176. Sargent, Jennie (Smith)
Papers. 1879. 27 pp.
Open. No guide.
Washington State Library, Washington-Northwest Room.
Diary of Sargent (1860-1934) regarding her journey by wagon from Independence to Portland in 1879 with her parents Rowland and Margaret Smith and five siblings.

17,177. Seattle Business and Professional Women's Club
Records. 1926-67. Ca. 1.5 ft.
Open. No guide.
Washington State Library, Washington-Northwest Room.
Scrapbooks of clippings from Seattle newspapers and the newsletter of the Club, which was founded in 1926, primarily concern Club gatherings, speakers, topics covered at meetings, and electicns.

17,178. Washington State History
Collection. Nd. No size given.
Open. No guide.
Washington State Library, Washington-Northwest Room.
Collection of clippings contains one foot of material pertaining directly to women, including files on biographies of women, beauty queens, Mercer Girls, women's clubs, Pearl Wanamaker, and women in such fields as aeronautics, business, medicine, sports, trade, and journalism.

17,179. Wiggins, Myra Albert
Papers. Ca. 1900-56. 3 in.
Open. No guide.
Washington State Library, Washington-Northwest Room.
Christmas cards and messages, programs, lists of prizes, booklets, and clippings of [Mrs.] Wiggins (1876-1956), a photographer and painter who was a founder of Women Painters of Washington. Active in the National League of American Pen Women, she was named Pen Woman of the Year in 1954. In her Christmas messages she discussed her efforts to get showings for her work.

PORT TOWNSEND

17,180. Smith, May B.
Papers. Ca. 1930. 129-page item.
Open. No guide.
Jefferson County Historical Society.
A manuscript history of Port Townsend in which Smith (?-1941), who came to the city in 1888 as a young girl from San Francisco, reminisces about social life, businesses, and local residents.

PULLMAN

17,181. Abel-Henderson, Annie Heloise
Papers. 1860-1939. 8 ft.
Open. Unpublished guide.
Washington State University Library.
Correspondence, notes, manuscripts, clippings, and printed material collected and compiled by Abel-Henderson (1873-1947), an historian with a PhD, regarding policies of governments in English-speaking countries toward their native inhabitants, American and Russian history, and women's suffrage.

17,182. Audrain, F. L.
Papers. 1897-1917. 1 item.
Open. No guide.
Washington State University Library.
Scrapbook containing correspondence, photos, and clippings of Audrain, who was superintendent of schools in Kiona, WA, and a leader of boys and girls clubs in the state, particularly regarding Audrain's leadership in the Kiona-Benton City Canning Club from 1915 to 1916. Members of the Canning Club were predominantly female.

17,183. Avard, Stephen; Avard, Julia; and Avard, Charles
Papers. 1872-1956. Ca. 1200 items.
Open. Unpublished guide.
Washington State University Library.
Correspondence, reminiscences, business and legal papers, photos, genealogies, and other papers of Stephen Avard, his wife Julia Hamacker Eastman Avard (1881-1956), his brother Charles Avard, and related families documenting their early years in California, homesteading efforts on the Colville Indian Reservation, railroading in northern Idaho, and other aspects of frontier life. The Avards were farmers in Nespelem, WA.

17,184. Baird, Lenna E.
Papers. 1917-43. Ca. 825 items.
Open. No guide.
Washington State University Library.
Baird was the captain of the American National Red Cross Canteen in Spokane, WA, from 1917 to 1919. Correspondence, memoranda, photos, clippings, and other papers regarding soldier's relief.

17,185. Carpenter and Richardson Family
Papers. 1880-1972. 8 ft.
Open. Unpublished guide.
Washington State University Library.
Correspondence and other papers of Frank Carpenter, a Cle Elum, WA, banker; his wife Norah Carr Carpenter (ca. 1875-1962); their

daughter Margaret (Carpenter) Richardson (1910-73); and her husband John P. Richardson, a physician, regarding the family's move from Illinois to Washington, the operation of the Cle Elum State Bank, the education of Margaret Carpenter at Annie Wright Seminary and Sarah Lawrence College, John Richardson's medical practice, and personal relations among family members, with friends, and with Carr family members in Girard, IL.

17,186. Carr, Hamptonetta Burgess
Papers. 1881-1950. Ca. 200 items.
Open. No guide.
Washington State University Library.
Correspondence of [Miss] Carr and her sister [Miss] Catherine Burgess Carr with family and friends regarding Hamptonetta Carr's school days at Swarthmore, the sisters' move westward, Catherine Carr's commercial and business experiences in northern Idaho, and other topics.

17,187. Clark, Ella Elizabeth
Papers. 1944-77. Ca. 530 items.
Open. Unpublished guide.
Washington State University Library.
Correspondence, drafts, research notes, photos, articles, clippings, and printed material of Clark (1896-), a professor of English at Washington State University, primarily regarding the collection and publication of Indian legends and mythology, including those of the Indians of Canada and the northern Rocky Mountains.

17,188. Crandall, Lulu Donnell Brown
Papers. 1895-1929. 3.5 ft.
Open. Unpublished guide.
Washington State University Library.
Correspondence, drafts of articles and speeches, notes, photos, transcripts of documents, and clippings of Crandall (1854-1931), an historian, pertaining to her research on the history of the Pacific Northwest, particularly of The Dalles, OR. The papers primarily relate to the years from 1835 to 1870 and concern such topics as missionaries, early settlers, the Yakima War, transportation, and local historic sites.

17,189. Dana, Lucile Olive (Davis)
Papers. 1870-1974. 6.5 ft.
Open. Unpublished guide.
Washington State University Library.
Correspondence, drafts of essays, student notes, and photos of Dana (1891-1974), a teacher, amateur essayist, and housewife in Pullman, regarding her student experiences, her position as a faculty wife, and her interest in the DAR and the AAUW. Includes papers regarding her relationship with family members, primarily her father William H. Davis, an ordained United Brethren minister; her sister Grace Davis (ca. 1885-1953), a mission teacher in India; and her stepmother Martha Jenks Davis (1869-1955).

17,190. Decker, Hermine Duthie
Papers. Ca. 1941-69. Ca. 25 items.
Open. No guide.
Washington State University Library.
Correspondence, typescripts of plays, and photos of Decker (1908-), a dramatist.

17,191. Dreamer, Marion (Billbrough)
Papers. 1905-71. Ca. 110 items.
Open. No guide.
Washington State University Library.
Correspondence, journals, illustrated reminiscences, photos, scrapbooks, and printed material of Dreamer, an educator, primarily concerning her teaching experiences at various Sioux Indian reservations, Indian schools, and Job Corps camps. Also includes a journal Dreamer kept while she was a policewoman in Detroit in 1929.

17,192. Hawes, Evelyn Johnson
Papers. 1924-71. 12 ft.
Open. Unpublished guide.
Washington State University Library.
Personal and professional papers of Hawes (1915-), an author, including correspondence, manuscripts, drafts, notes, articles, and other papers.

17,193. Hult, Ruby El
Papers. 1924-71. 12 ft.
Open. Unpublished guide.
Washington State University Library.
Correspondence, taped interviews, drafts, notes, photos, and clippings of Hult (1912-), an author, pertaining to her research for her books and articles.

17,194. Hunt, Leila Wall
Papers. 1897-1966. Ca. 400 items.
Open. No guide.
Washington State University Library.
Hunt (?-1968) was a home economist and educator in Pullman. Articles regarding home economics, published and in typescript; student notebooks about sewing and meal planning from 1906 to 1907; photos; awards, certificates, and diplomas; clippings; and other papers.

17,195. James, Florida Virginia Hill
Papers. 1909-50. 2 ft.
Open. Unpublished guide.
Washington State University Library.
Correspondence, diaries, photos, and other papers of James (1896-) regarding her experiences as a student at the University of Oregon and the University of Southern California from 1918 to 1922, as a schoolteacher from 1923 to 1930, and as a rural housewife in Whitman County, WA. Also includes correspondence, legal and financial papers, photos, and memorabilia of other members of the Hill and James families.

17,196. Kennedy, Alice Carey (Traver) Libby
Papers. 1903-59. Ca. 2000 items.
Open. Unpublished guide.
Washington State University Library.
Correspondence, post cards, photos, and other papers of Kennedy (1874-1959), an employment counselor in Spokane, WA, and her sister Edith G. Traver (1881-), a Baptist missionary in China. Also includes scrapbooks regarding Kennedy's employment with Western Union from 1908 to 1912 and the Women's Free Employment Bureau in Spokane from 1912 to 1919 and clippings concerning the pioneers and history of eastern Washington and northern Idaho, an area known as the Inland Empire.

17,197. Kies, Paul Philemon
Papers. 1621-1970. 2 ft.
Open. Unpublished guide.
Washington State University Library.
Kies (1891-1971) was a scholar and educator who collected letters and autographs of American and European actors, composers, musicians and singers, statesmen, educators, writers, political figures, and civic leaders. Also includes Kies's drafts, research notes, translations, exhibit lists and notes, and other papers. Among the women represented are Mabel G. Bell; Sarah Bernhardt; Pearl (Sydenstricker) Buck; Emma Calvé; Charlotte Sophia, Queen of England; Eleanor, Empress of the Holy Roman Empire; Julia Ward Howe; Lillie Langtry; Amy Lawrence Lowell; Julia Marlowe; Christine Nilsson; Adelina Patti; Mrs. E. Charles Ringling; Anna Eleanor Roosevelt; Olga Samaroff Stokowski; and Ellen Alicia Terry.

17,198. McEwan, Inez Puckett
Papers. 1948-65. 6 ft.
Open. Unpublished guide.
Washington State University Library.
Correspondence, journals, manuscripts, photos, clippings, mementos, and other papers of McEwan (1904-), a northwestern author.

17,199. Martin, Mary Hetty (Bonar)
Papers. 1863-1918. Ca. 30 items.
Open. No guide.
Washington State University Library.
Papers of Martin (1860-?) include diaries regarding farm life in the Entiat Valley in Washington, 1885-1918, and clippings and other material. Also contains a ledger and portrait of her father J. C. Bonar.

17,200. May, Catherine Dean (Barnes)
Papers. 1958-71. 210 ft.
Open. Published guide.
Washington State University Library.
Papers of May (1914-), a US representative from Washington State from 1959 to 1971, include correspondence, notes, memoranda, press releases, radio broadcasts, reports, photos, newsletters, clippings, and other papers regarding government operations, legislation, committee work, voter questionnaires, and the National Commission on Food Marketing. May married a Mr. Bedell shortly after the end of her term. See *Catherine May: An Indexed Register of Her Congressional Papers, 1959-1970, in the Washington State University Library* (Pullman: Washington State University Library, 1972).

17,201. Myers, Florence W.
Papers. 1934-68. Ca. 50 items.
Open. No guide.
Washington State University Library.
Correspondence, addresses, and other papers of Myers, a Washington State representative.

17,202. Parrish, Emily E.
Papers. 1867-1932. Ca. 60 items.
Open. No guide.
Washington State University Library.
Correspondence, financial papers, deeds, mortgages, bills, and receipts of Parrish (1849-?) regarding farmland in Iowa, Wisconsin, Illinois, North Dakota, and Whitman County, WA.

17,203. Phillips, Velma
Papers. 1938-53. 54 ft.
Open. Unpublished guide.
Washington State University Library.
Correspondence and other papers of Phillips (1891-) regarding Washington State University's college of home economics of which she was dean from 1938 to 1961.

17,204. Price Family
Papers. 1840-1906. 12 items.
Open. Unpublished guide.
Washington State University Library.
Documents, certificates, and other papers of the Price family, including correspondence from the 1880s with Eliza Ballou Garfield and Lucretia (Rudolph) Garfield.

17,205. Putnam, Goldie Van Bibber
Papers. 1950-65. Ca. 50 items.
Open. No guide.
Washington State University Library.
Correspondence, research notes, and manuscripts of articles of Putnam (1885-1965) regarding ferries of the Pacific Northwest, Silver King Mine, Silver King Ferry, and the history of Stevens County, WA.

17,206. Raymond, Almira Adeline David
Papers. 1839. 1 vol.
Open. No guide.
Washington State University Library.
Diary of Raymond (1814-), a Methodist missionary, regarding her voyage on the *Lausanne* from New York to Oregon with a Methodist group; the diary relates to that part of the journey from New York to Rio de Janeiro. Also contains

information relating to her life before her marriage and her decision to go to Oregon.

17,207. Rebow, Mary Martin
Papers. 1767-79. 118 items.
Open. No guide.
Washington State University Library.
Correspondence of Rebow (1750?-1804), an English gentlewoman, in which she describes to her husband her social and domestic life. Includes letters written both prior to and following her marriage. The collection is described by Josephine Manning in "The Mary Martin Rebow Letters," *The Record* (Friends of the Library, Washington State University), vols. 32-33 (1971-72).

17,208. Robins, Elizabeth
Papers. 1851-1942. Ca. 60 items.
Open. Unpublished guide.
Washington State University Library.
Correspondence of Robins (1862-1952), an actress and author, with John Galsworthy, Somerset Maugham, William Archer, Charles Trevelyan, Isabelle Smith, and others. Also includes a Norwegian-English lexical notebook.

17,209. Tannatt Family
Papers. 1813-1919. 5.5 ft.
Open. Unpublished guide.
Washington State University Library.
Correspondence, diaries, drafts, photos, and certificates concerning the Civil War service and Colorado mining activities of General Thomas R. Tannatt, a representative of Villard railroad interests in Walla Walla, Washington State University regent, and Farmington orchardist; the activities of his wife Elizabeth Foster Tappan Tannatt (1837-?) as a student in Boston, army wife, historian, and essayist; and the experiences of their daughter Miriam Hooper (Tannatt) Merriam (1866-?) as a student in Walla Walla and a librarian at WSU.

17,210. Thomas, Edith Matilda
Papers. 1886-1911. 24 items.
Open. No guide.
Washington State University Library.
Letters and poems that Thomas (1854-1925), an American poet, sent to William Hayes Ward and other editors of the New York *Independent.*

17,211. Union Center Goodwill Club
Records. 1936-54. Ca. 350 items.
Open. No guide.
Washington State University Library.
Minutes, bills, receipts, correspondence, documents, and other records of this rural women's club in Whitman County, WA.

17,212. Walker, Elkanah, and Walker, Mary Richardson
Papers. 1821-1938. 4 ft.
Open. Published and unpublished guides.
Washington State University Library.
Correspondence, diaries, photos, and other papers of Elkanah Walker and his wife Mary Richardson Walker (1811-97), who were missionaries to the Spokan Indians. Mary Walker's papers concern country life in New England, her overland journey to Oregon in 1838, missionary work among the Spokan Indians at Tshimakain Mission, and educational and religious activities in the Willamette Valley. Correspondents include family members, the American Board of Commissioners for Foreign Missions, and other Oregon missionaries and settlers. See *Oregon Historical Quarterly* (1941) and *The Record* (1956), which was published by the Friends of the Library, Washington State University.

17,213. Whitman, Marcus, and Whitman, Narcissa (Prentiss)
Papers. 1823-1961. Ca. 200 items.
Open. Unpublished guide.
Washington State University Library.
Correspondence, journals, photos, church records, clippings, and other papers by and about Marcus Whitman and his wife Narcissa Whitman (1808-47), missionaries to the Cayuse Indians. Includes Narcissa Whitman's 1842 letter to Maria Pambrun, the papers of Jonathan Pratt from 1823 to 1830, the papers of S. W. Pratt, and biographical material about the Whitmans.

SEATTLE

17,214. Company Archives
Records. 1916- . No size given.
Open. Inventory.
The Boeing Company, Historical Services.
Financial and technical records, correspondence, reports, employee lists, advertising copy, booklets, and clippings of this airplane manufacturing company, which was founded in 1916. From its early years, Boeing employed women as secretaries and stenographers and for work in handling, shrinking, and sewing fabric for airplanes; the archives' industrial relations files contain accident records and other material that provides information on the number of women who worked for the Company up to 1937, their jobs, and their wages. During WWII, however, Boeing employed women in a variety of positions, including manual labor. Information on these workers is available in the personnel and collective bargaining sections of the industrial relations files, with reports and statistical data on women workers, advertising for women workers, material on the rationale behind that advertising, and information on the transition to peacetime production, at which point women workers were encouraged to leave the Company. Boeing's commercial passenger service also employed women nurses as flight attendants in 1930, but these records are housed in the United Airlines archives in Chicago.

17,215. Archives
Records. 1908- . 7 boxes and 13 vols.
Closed. No guide.
Discalced Carmelite Nuns Monastery.
Financial records, correspondence, photos, and other records of this religious order of women, which was founded in Baltimore. The Monastery was established in 1908.

17,216. Bureau of Indian Affairs (RG 75)
Records. 1854-1952. 5039 cu.ft.
Access partially restricted. Unpublished guides.
Federal Archives and Records Center, Seattle Archives Branch.
Consists of records of 23 northwestern Indian agencies which administered Indian treaties and reservations and promoted the general welfare of Indians. Agency records contain correspondence, school records, medical records (which are restricted), family census records, tribal council records, personnel records, and other material. Includes records documenting women's activities as field nurses and teachers on reservations, statistical and other data collected about Indian women and Indian life, and information about the introduction of white values in areas of Indian life such as marriage, divorce, and illegitimacy.

17,217. Office of the Governor of Alaska (RG 348)
Records. 1884-1958. 378 microfilm reels.
Access restricted. Unpublished preliminary inventory.
Federal Archives and Records Center, Seattle Archives Branch.
Includes a file on The Women of 1915 and other prominent Alaska women who worked for national defense and contributed funds to the Aero Club of America to purchase airplanes and land for airfields; a file on women's suffrage, which contains correspondence from 1915 of Alaska governor John F. A. Strong with the Men's League for Women's Suffrage of the State of New York, the "Votes for Women" Empire State Campaign Committee, the Equal Franchise Federation of Pittsburgh, and the National Council of Women Voters regarding Strong's opinion about woman suffrage and the 1913 enfranchisement of women in Alaska Territory; a file on the Alaska Dental Board, 1920, which documents Governor Strong's appointment of Leonie von M. Zesch to the Board and the objections of numerous dentists in Alaska; a file on the Pioneer's Home for Women, 1934-58, which contains correspondence and other papers concerning a survey of the territory made to determine the need for a home for aged women; and a file on the Alaska Native Brotherhood and Sisterhood, 1943-46, which concerns the organization's position on women's rights and its advocacy of equal pay for equal work, an equal rights amendment, revisions in the legal status of women, and the creation of a women's bureau. The original records are in the custody of the Alaska State Archives in Juneau. See Chris Ferrier, "Items of Possible Interest to a Study of Women's History Contained in the Seattle Archives Branch, Federal Archives and Records Center (1977)."

17,218. United States District Courts (RG 21)
Records. 1859-1956. 5665 cu.ft.
Open. Unpublished inventories.
Federal Archives and Records Center, Seattle Archives Branch.
Transcripts and exhibits of federal criminal and civil court cases, with indexes and dockets of most cases tried. Includes *USA versus Na Lay, Alias Annie Kum Chee* (No. 1075, Criminal, US District Court, Montana), an immigration case against a woman sold by her parents into prostitution in San Francisco and rehabilitated by the Presbyterian Home for the Chinese.

17,219. Wellcome, Sir Henry S. (RG 316)
Records. Ca. 1856-1936. 105 cu.ft.
Open. Published and unpublished guides.
Federal Archives and Records Center, Seattle Archives Branch.
Correspondence, reports, photos, and other papers concern the efforts of Wellcome (?-1936), a British scientist and philanthropist, to assist Father William Duncan in Duncan's efforts to retain control of the Metlakahtla mission on Annette Island, AK. As pastor, magistrate, and commercial leader on the Island, Duncan controlled the Metlakahtla community; when the US government took steps to provide education for a number of Metlakahtlans who had petitioned for a secular school, Duncan resisted. Papers document Duncan's efforts to establish a Victorian society among the Indians there and provide information about the role of women in that society.

17,220. Carkeek, Mrs. Morgan
Papers. Ca. 1910-26. No size given.
Open. No guide.
Seattle Historical Society.
Scrapbooks of Emily Carkeek, a socialite, leader in the Seattle Historical Society, and wife of Morgan Carkeek, include clippings from various Seattle newspapers regarding social welfare clubs and women's work in charities, relief, day nurseries, health, education, child welfare, and religion.

17,221. Denny, Emily Inez
Papers. Nd. Ca. 6 in.
Open. No guide.
Seattle Historical Society.
Reminiscences, manuscripts, poems, stories, and paintings of Denny (ca. 1860-1940), an amateur historian of Seattle, an author, and the daughter of David Denny, who was one of the founders of Seattle.

17,222. Guye, Elizabeth W. P.
Papers. 1908-14. Ca. 2 ft.
Open. Index.
Seattle Historical Society.
Twelve scrapbooks containing clippings from Seattle newspapers include information regarding the woman suffrage movement, women's clubs, influential women, socialites, charities, and women in such professions as medicine, hop buying, electrical engineering, and banking.

17,223. La Boheme Music Club
Records. 1921-39. Ca. 1 ft.
Open. No guide.
Seattle Historical Society.
Scrapbooks containing press notices, programs, and radio schedules of the Club, which studied and sponsored classical music.

17,224. Minor Hospital Alumnae
Records. Ca. 1910-53. 2 in.
Open. No guide.
Seattle Historical Society.
Records of the Minor Hospital nursing school alumnae association include a scrapbook containing photos, clippings, and accounts of the achievements of each class of alumnae after graduation.

17,225. Spinning, Elizabeth P.
Papers. 1887-89. 1 in.
Open. No guide.
Seattle Historical Society.
Diary in which Spinning, a housewife of Puyallup, WA, who later became a woman suffrage leader, describes everyday life in a rural western Washington town and efforts to achieve woman suffrage in Washington Territory. The efforts were successful before Washington became a state in 1889.

17,226. Woman Suffrage
Collection. 1888-ca. 1912. Ca. 1 in.
Open. No guide.
Seattle Historical Society.
Correspondence and speeches relating to woman suffrage include three letters that Lucy Stone of the Massachusetts Woman Suffrage Association, Abigail (Scott) Duniway of the Oregon Woman Suffrage Association, and Frances Willard, president of the National WCTU wrote congratulating Eugene Semple, territorial governor of Washington, for signing the suffrage bill of 1887; a letter from former territorial governor Elisha P. Ferry opposing the suffrage bill; and speeches from 1905 and 1907 written by Elizabeth P. Spinning on behalf of the suffrage movement.

17,227. Blaine, David E., and Blaine, Catherine V. (Paine)
Papers. Nd. 2 in.
Open. No guide.
Seattle Public Library.
Correspondence from 1849 to 1862 and other papers of David Blaine (1824-1900), a Methodist clergyman and missionary who established the first church in Seattle in 1853, and his wife Catherine Blaine (1829-1908), a schoolteacher and homemaker, who founded Seattle's first school. Catherine Blaine's correspondence from Seattle, where the Blaines stayed until 1856, pertains to homemaking in a pioneer town, social life, and Seattle's first five years. Also includes letters written by the Blaines in Oregon City and Lebanon in Oregon Territory.

17,228. Women's Democratic Club of King County
Records. 1913-36. No size given.
Open. No guide.
Seattle Public Library.
Eleven-page typescript by Alice V. Robinson and clippings regarding the history of the Club, which was in existence from 1913 to 1936 in Seattle, and the woman suffrage movement in Washington.

17,229. Province Archives
Records. 1856- . 2648 ft.
Open. Unpublished guide and inventories.
Sisters of Providence Archives, Sacred Heart Province.
The Sacred Heart Province was established in 1856 in Washington Territory; its members have founded and operated schools, hospitals, and Indian missions in Washington, Oregon, California, and Alaska, including one of the first schools in Washington Territory (1856) and the first hospital (1858). Administrative, religious, personnel, and historical records of the Province and of the hospitals, schools, missions, and other institutions founded by the Sisters include minutes, financial records, contracts, audiovisual materials such as tapes and films, correspondence, reports, theses, dissertations, chronicles, statistical data, photos, scrapbooks, clippings, publications, and artifacts. Also includes ca. 30 feet of papers of Mother Joseph, formerly Esther Pariseau, the foundress of the Province. Mother Joseph served as mother vicar for the West from 1856 to 1866 and as director of building construction from 1866 to 1902; she drew the plans and helped collect funds for 33 hospitals, academies, and orphanages in the Northwest. Biographical material on deceased sisters, handwritten chronicles, published and unpublished historical records, and business, educational, and medical records are also contained in the Archives.

17,230. Abernathy, Ruth
Papers. Ca. 1930-73. 6 ft.
Access restricted. Data sheet and container list.
University of Washington Libraries, Archives and Manuscripts Division.
Correspondence, notes, speeches and writings, financial records, legal documents, conference and convention material, and reprints of Abernathy, a professor of physical and health education for women at the University of Washington, chairwoman of the department from 1966 to 1972, and president of the American Association for Health, Physical Education and Recreation from 1954 to 1956. The material documents her career and contains information on various University committees and groups and on national professional organizations in which she participated. Correspondents include Catherine L. Allen, C. L. Brownell, E. Vickery Hubbard, Edward M. Kennedy, Minnie L. Lynn, Donna M. Miller, Delbert Oberteuffer, and Jesse F. Williams. Also included is material on the breach of contract suit that John "Jack" V. Scott brought against the University.

17,231. Abrams, Maria Frank
Oral history. Nd. 17-page item and 1 tape.
Open. Data sheet.
University of Washington Libraries, Archives and Manuscripts Division.
Interview and transcript in which Abrams, a Washington oil painter, reminisces about events from the 1940s to 1975, including her early years in Hungary, her art career beginning with her student days at the University of Washington, her ways of working, media, inspiration, her friendship with Mark Tobey, and her work in set design.

17,232. Afro-American Project
Oral history. Nd. Ca. 28 tapes.
Open. Data sheets.
University of Washington Libraries, Archives and Manuscripts Division.
Interviews and transcripts dealing with the social, economic, and political aspects of life of Afro-Americans in the Northwest from ca. 1888 to 1970. Ten black women interviewed primarily discuss personal experiences and family history. Those who were active in civil rights, politics, education, and civic groups also spoke about these activities. Interviewees include Virginia Gayton, wife of an early 20th-century black community leader in Seattle; Flo Ware; and [Mrs.] Beulah (Craven) Hart and [Mrs.] Liola (Craven) Woffort, daughters of a family who came to Roslyn, WA, in 1888 to break a coal strike, as did many early black families who settled in the Seattle area.

17,233. Aliesan, Jody
Papers. 1969-72. 1 ft.
Open. Inventory.
University of Washington Libraries, Archives and Manuscripts Division.
Correspondence, speeches and writings, financial records, clippings, magazines, and other material of Aliesan, who has been described as an activist in the feminist movement. She served as consultant to the University of Washington office of equal employment opportunity programs and as coordinator of the Associated Students of the UW's Women's Commission speaker's bureau; she was cowriter and coresearcher of the Associated Students' Women's Commission report on the status of women faculty and staff and in 1971 was appointed by the mayor to the Seattle Women's Commission. Material from the city commission documents the development of a conscious municipal policy toward women as employees and citizens; it also reveals Aliesan's frustrations, leading to her 1972 resignation, over the makeup of the Commission.

17,234. Asberry, Nettie J.
Papers. 1889-1966. 5 in.
Open. Data sheet.
University of Washington Libraries, Archives and Manuscripts Division.
A music teacher, civil rights activist, and wife of a prosperous businessman, Asberry (1865-?) was founder of the Tacoma, WA, chapter of the NAACP and president of the Colored Women's Federation of Washington and Jurisdiction. Correspondence, journal, biographical sketches, minutes, photos, clippings, reports, and certificates. Often called Dr. Asberry in her work as a music teacher, she gave up her profession in 1909 to organize the colored women of Tacoma and Pierce County. Collection also contains 17 biographical or autobiographical sketches of other black women with whom Asberry was associated.

17,235. Banks, Virginia
Oral history. Nd. 38-page item and 1 tape.
Access restricted. Data sheet.
University of Washington Libraries, Archives and Manuscripts Division.
Interview and transcript in which Banks, a Washington artist in oils and mixed media, discusses her career as a painter from 1945 to 1972 and comments upon the relationship between artists and museums and galleries of the Northwest, technical information, discussions of aesthetics, major art figures of the Northwest, and various other subjects related to art.

17,236. Bauer, Patti (Warashina)
Oral history. Nd. 14-page item and 1 tape.
Open. Work sheet.
University of Washington Libraries, Archives and Manuscripts Division.
Interview and transcript of Bauer, a potter and sculptor, who later obtained a divorce and legally reassumed her maiden name. The interview was conducted in connection with Survivors '72, an exhibition of women artists held at the University of Washington's Henry Gallery.

17,237. Beck, Eleanor Nordhoff
Papers. 1920-66. 7 ft.
Open. Data sheet.
University of Washington Libraries, Archives and Manuscripts Division.
Correspondence, theater and music programs, and clippings of [Mrs. Broussais C.] Beck (?-1966), a cultural and civic leader, show her interest in literary criticism, the theatre, and music.

17,238. Benson, Naomi Achenbach
Papers. 1897-1961. 21 ft.
Open. Inventory.
University of Washington Libraries, Archives and Manuscripts Division.
A teacher, Benson was also a political and community worker active in national and local Washington organizations such as the Democratic party, the Progressive party of 1948, the Mid-Century Conference for Peace, Everett Consumer's Co-op Association, the Snohomish County Legislative Council, the American Civil Liberties Union, Americans for Democratic Action, the American Friends Service Committee, and a women's group that supported Henry A. Wallace's 1948 Progressive party presidential candidacy. Correspondence, journals and notebooks, financial records, writings, campaign material, and clippings. Correspondence concerns subjects such as unpopular support for civil rights of radicals and racial minorities, auto clubs, and societies to aid the blind and to fight cancer. Correspondents include the Women's Committee for Equal Justice, the Women's International League for Peace and Freedom, and various state Democratic politicians.

17,239. Bringloe, Frances
Oral history. Nd. 17-page item and 1 tape.
Open. Work sheet.
University of Washington Libraries, Archives and Manuscripts Division.
Interview and transcript in which Bringloe, an historical doll maker, discusses her early training in the 1930s in costume design and art, her career in making historical figures of all cultures for schools and museums, problems of authenticity, materials and techniques, preparations of study guides, and doll collecting as a business. The discussion covers subjects dating to 1975.

17,240. Broer, Marion Ruth
Papers. 1936-71. Ca. 1.5 ft. and 8 tapes.
Open. Records transmittal form.
University of Washington Libraries, Archives and Manuscripts Division.
Broer (1910-) was a professor in the school of physical and health education at the University of Washington. Correspondence, notes, manuscripts, lectures, speeches, MA thesis, PhD dissertation, lesson plans, clippings, articles, books, ephemera, and other papers.

17,241. Burke, Caroline Ethel (McGilvra)
Papers. 1884-1934. 4 ft.
Open. Inventory and name index.
University of Washington Libraries, Archives and Manuscripts Division.
Burke (1858-1932) was a Seattle social leader, businesswoman, philanthropist, and world traveler. Correspondence, diaries, financial and medical records, cashbooks, genealogical data, legal documents, notes, photos, guest books, scrapbook, recipes, Indian baskets, and other material document Burke's social life, business activities, and work for public libraries, historical societies, the American Committee for Devastated France, and the Children's Orthopedic Hospital. Burke was the daughter of John McGilvra, Seattle attorney and landholder. From 1880 to 1925 she was married to Thomas Burke, an attorney, judge, and businessman.

17,242. Chambers, Andrew Jackson
Papers. Ca. 1853-1922. 2.5 ft.
Open. Inventory.
University of Washington Libraries, Archives and Manuscripts Division.
Correspondence, diary, reminiscences, financial miscellany, photos, and legal documents of the Chambers family, settlers in Washington's Pierce and Thurston counties. The correspondence, most of which is between Chambers's several daughters, provides information on daily activities and social life in Washington Territory.

17,243. Chase, Gail
Oral history. Nd. 15-page item and 1 tape.
Open. Data sheet.
University of Washington Libraries, Archives and Manuscripts Division.
Interview and transcript in which Chase discusses her activities and views as a Washington potter, art dealer, and gallery owner, and her thoughts on art of the 1970s.

17,244. Coney, Thelma
Papers. 1967-71. 1 ft.
Open. Inventory.
University of Washington Libraries, Archives and Manuscripts Division.
Correspondence, bylaws, minutes, financial records, legal documents, reports, and newsletters of Coney, a social worker and pacifist. Material primarily concerns the National Association of Social Workers and the Seattle Peace Information Center, with the University of Washington school of social work and the World Without War Council as major correspondents.

17,245. Cooper, Bella Taylor McKnight
Papers. 1943-68. 7 in.
Open. Inventory.
University of Washington Libraries, Archives and Manuscripts Division.
A Seattle civic leader, [Mrs. Felix] Cooper was a member of the Governor's Council on Aging, first vice-president and finance chairman of the Christian Friends of Racial Equality, and a board member of the Seattle-King County Mental Health Association and of the Seattle Civic Unity Committee, a civil rights group. Correspondence, speeches and writings, biographical and historical material, photos, reports, and clippings document Cooper's activities in Seattle and Washington. Earlier she was a professional sociologist for the Chicago YWCA, executive director of the Cleveland NAACP, and the first Negro to serve on the US Civil Service Commission. She was in charge of civilian naval appointments for the Commission's Sixth Region.

17,246. Cooper, Sue Hamilton
Papers. 1926-63. 6.5 ft.
Open. Inventory.
University of Washington Libraries, Archives and Manuscripts Division.
Cooper (1887-1968), who believed that women's organizations could provide the power base necessary for affecting social welfare and educational reform, served as president or chairperson of such organizations as the Seattle LWV, the Seattle Federation of Women's Clubs, the Washington State Federation of Women's Clubs, the American Association for the UN, and the Women's Society of the University Baptist Church. Personal papers and biographical material of Cooper as well as a substantial amount of material pertaining to the organizations she headed, including correspondence, minutes, financial records, reports, speeches and writings, notes, newsletters, scrapbooks, clippings, and other records.

17,247. Council of Jewish Women, Seattle Section
Records. 1914-68. 6.5 ft.
Open. Unpublished guide.
University of Washington Libraries, Archives and Manuscripts Division.
Minutes, financial records, correspondence, reports, and scrapbooks of this educational and welfare organization, founded in 1900 for the Seattle Jewish community. Includes records of the Section's settlement house, which became Neighborhood House in 1948.

17,248. Crisler, Lois Brown
Papers. 1941-58. 4 ft.
Open. Inventory.
University of Washington Libraries, Archives and Manuscripts Division.
[Mrs. Herb] Crisler (1897-1971) was a naturalist who concentrated on wildlife in Washington state, Colorado, and the Arctic region, as well as an author of books and articles, particularly about wolves. Literary manuscripts, some of which are fragmentary; correspondence; financial records; logbook; photos; clippings; and notes on wolves, Washington's Olympic Peninsula, and the Olympic elk. Her first book *Arctic Wild* was published in 1953 after she and her photographer husband returned from an assignment to Alaska for Walt Disney. *Captive Wild* is the most notable of books she wrote about her experience raising Alaskan wolves in captivity.

17,249. Crumbaker, Martha
Papers. 1877-1906. 11 items.
Open. Data sheet.
University of Washington Libraries, Archives and Manuscripts Division.
Letters in which Crumbaker, a settler in Carfield and Colfax in Washington Territory, writing to her family in Selma, IL, describes aspects of pioneer life, particularly farming, mining, and Indians.

17,250. Cunningham, Imogen
Oral history. Nd. 3 items and 3 tapes.
Open. Data sheet.
University of Washington Libraries, Archives and Manuscripts Division.
In a press conference and radio interviews and transcripts Cunningham (1883-1976), an internationally recognized photographer, discusses her career and life, her philosophy of photography, and her views on various subjects. Her career began in Seattle around the turn of the century and ended in San Francisco, where she died.

17,251. Double K Mountain Ranch
Records. 1959-69. 10 in.
Open. Inventory and name index.
University of Washington Libraries, Archives and Manuscripts Division.
Wilderness conservation is the aim of Isabelle Lynn and Katheryn Kershaw who own and operate the Ranch. Correspondence, speeches and writings, notes, reports, resolutions, bulletins, bibliography, mailing list, maps, and clippings document the women's activities and interest in the Cougar Lakes Wilderness Area east of Mt. Rainier Wilderness Park. Correspondents include the Wilderness Society, US Supreme Court Justice and wilderness advocate William O. Douglas, US Senator Henry M. Jackson of Washington, wilderness expert and author Harvey Manning, wilderness conservation policy makers, and other interested individuals and organizations.

17,252. Edel, May Mandelbaum
Papers. 1890-1939. 3 ft.
Open. Inventory.
University of Washington Libraries, Archives and Manuscripts Division.
Edel (1909-65) was an anthropological linguist who studied the Tillamook and Salish Indian languages. Manuscripts, vocabulary lists, field notes, and notebooks compiled in 1890 on the Tillamook language by Franz Boas, of whom Edel was a student.

17,253. Equal Rights Amendment, House Joint Resolution 61, Washington Campaign Committee
Records. 1972. 1.5 ft.
Open. Data sheet.
University of Washington Libraries, Archives and Manuscripts Division.
Correspondence, newsletters, fact sheets, statistics, lists, clippings, and ephemera of the Seattle office of this lobbyist group formed in 1972 for Washington ratification of the Equal Rights Amendment. Also included is material from the

Tri-Cities (Richland, Pasco, and Kenniwick) ERA campaign. The Committee disbanded in 1972 when the state ratified the ERA.

17,254. Farquharson, Mary
Papers. 1935-42. 1 ft.
Open. Inventory and name index.
University of Washington Libraries, Archives and Manuscripts Division.
A Washington state senator from 1935 to 1942, [Mrs. B. F.] Farquharson (1902-) is a Seattle civic leader who was active in the Women's International League for Peace and Freedom, the Seattle branch of the American Civil Liberties Union, and with her husband in political affairs for the Washington Commonwealth Federation during the 1930s and 1940s. Correspondence and clippings relating to her term as state senator make up the bulk of the collection; the rest is minutes and campaign material. Included is Farquharson's correspondence with Dorothy Ditzer, executive secretary of the WILPF's parent organization the National Council for Prevention of War; material Farquharson collected concerning the Communist party, Communist activities, Communist infiltration of the Olympia office of the WPA federal writers' project, and Anne Windhusen's leadership as state director of the project in 1939; and records of the Seattle Council Against War, of which B. F. Farquharson was president.

17,255. Farris, Linda
Oral history. Nd. 36-page item and 2 tapes.
Access restricted. Data sheet.
University of Washington Libraries, Archives and Manuscripts Division.
Interview and transcript in which Farris discusses her work during the 1970s as an art dealer and gallery owner, the role of the gallery, the difference between the Seattle and San Francisco art worlds, the One Percent for Art program of Seattle, women as artists, education, and conceptual art and the public.

17,256. Feminist Coordinating Council
Records. 1972-75. 5 in.
Open. Data sheet.
University of Washington Libraries, Archives and Manuscripts Division.
Agenda and minutes, correspondence, press releases, clippings, and ephemera of this organization of Seattle feminist groups. Minutes illuminate internal workings and conflicts of the Council, while correspondence and releases directed at local government reveal the group's political concerns. The Council was particularly interested in the establishment by city ordinance of a commission on crimes against women and a protection unit.

17,257. Fick, Nellie Mitchell
Papers. 1917-44. 7 in.
Open. Inventory.
University of Washington Libraries, Archives and Manuscripts Division.
Correspondence, two scrapbooks on woman suffrage, clippings, and theater programs of Fick, a Seattle suffrage leader. Includes material on woman suffrage and the LWV and correspondence from Bertha K. Landes, Seattle city councilwoman and mayor in the 1920s.

17,258. Firth, Lila Hannah
Papers. 1945. 35 pp.
Open. Data sheet.
University of Washington Libraries, Archives and Manuscripts Division.
Autobiography in which Firth, a settler on San Juan Island in Washington Territory, describes her life between 1865 and 1881.

17,259. Fisher, Anne
Papers. Ca. 1940-59. 3 ft.
Open. Inventory.
University of Washington Libraries, Archives and Manuscripts Division.
Correspondence, manuscripts, notes, and other papers of Fisher, a Washington state author, reporter, and civil rights activist. Most of the material deals with the evacuation in early 1942 of Japanese-Americans from the West Coast, their internment in camps, and their release in January 1945, which Fisher described in articles for the *Reporter* magazine as well as in her book *Exile of a Race.* Because of Earl Warren's role as California governor in the evacuation, she opposed his nomination to the Supreme Court; other papers reflect her position. Also included is material and notes from interviews about the founding in San Francisco of the UN, about which Fisher reported for the Socialist newspaper *CALL.*

17,260. Forbus, Lady Willie
Papers. 1945-63. 6 ft.
Open. Inventory.
University of Washington Libraries, Archives and Manuscripts Division.
A Seattle attorney, civic leader, and Democratic party politician, Forbus (1892-) held the offices of state assistant attorney general from 1940 to 1942 and state senator from 1942 to 1946. Correspondence, speeches, bylaws, minutes, financial reports, newsletters, clippings, and other papers, including campaign material from Forbus's unsuccessful 1946 and 1950 election campaigns and information about her post-1945 work with the Democratic party organizations of King County and Seattle's 36th District, the Seattle-King County Bar Association civil rights committee and fair housing activities, the American Civil Liberties Union, and the Magnolia Community Club.

17,261. Friedlander, Polly
Oral history. 1974. 10-page item and 1 tape.
Open. Work sheet.
University of Washington Libraries, Archives and Manuscripts Division.
During the interview taped in connection with a University of Washington women's art exhibition entitled "Survivors '72," Friedlander, a Washington art dealer, discusses operation of an art gallery, focusing on problems she and other female artists face as women.

17,262. Gage, Fern
Papers. 1933-67. 8 ft.
Open. Preliminary inventory.
University of Washington Libraries, Archives and Manuscripts Division.
Correspondence, scrapbooks, clippings, and newspapers of Gage (1893-1963), a church, civic, and civil rights leader in Oregon. Much of the material concerns her church activities including the Fellowship of Reconciliation, a group which focused on conscription and conscientious objection. Gage also was active in politics and worked in the Urban League of Portland, Portland's YWCA, the Oregon Prison Association, and various peace groups.

17,263. Garfield, Viola
Papers. 1928-64. 4 ft. and 3 tapes.
Open. Records transmittal form.
University of Washington Libraries, Archives and Manuscripts Division.
Correspondence, manuscripts of articles, writings, field notebooks, class notes, MA thesis, photos, clippings, and other papers of Garfield (1898-), a professor of anthropology at the University of Washington who is an expert on North American Indians, particularly those of Washington, British Columbia, and Alaska, and on primitive literature. Also included are tapes of interviews with Alaskan Indians about their art and history.

17,264. Gearhart, Lucy
Papers. Ca. 1880-1940. 3.5 ft.
Open. Data sheet.
University of Washington Libraries, Archives and Manuscripts Division.
[Mrs. John W.] Gearhart was a temperance and woman's suffrage worker in Washington state. Much of the correspondence, photos, books, and memorabilia (including a temperance china tea set) was gathered for a history of the temperance movement Gearhart intended to write. Primarily includes reminiscences on the woman suffrage and temperance movements as well as information about the WCTU, the International Order of Good Templars, and George Cotterill who was a Seattle mayor, Washington state representative and senator, and temperance leader.

17,265. Gordon, Wyona Eliza Surfus (Stahlnecker)
Papers. 1957-58. 102 pp.
Open. Data sheet.
University of Washington Libraries, Archives and Manuscripts Division.
Account of a five-month wagon trek from Kansas to Oregon made in 1883 by Gordon (1878?-?), a pioneer.

17,266. Gunther, Erna
Papers. Ca. 1950-61. 5 ft.
Open. Inventory.
University of Washington Libraries, Archives and Manuscripts Division.
Gunther (1896-) was a professor of anthropology at the University of Washington. Correspondence, Gunther's research notes and writings, field notes, manuscripts, minutes, membership lists, convention material, genealogies of Makah Indians, ordinances, clippings, and ephemera contain material on most of the following organizations which Gunther was a member of: the Washington Advisory Board on Historic Sites; the American Anthropology Association; the American Association of Museums, New Mexico; the Commission on Indian Affairs; the Committee on Northwest Indian Affairs; the Association on American Indian Affairs; the National Congress of American Indians; the Puget Sound Academy of Science; and the American Indian Charter Convention.

17,267. Haig, Emily H.
Papers. 1934-72. 27 ft.
Partially closed. Inventory.
University of Washington Libraries, Archives and Manuscripts Division.
[Mrs. Neil] Haig (1890-?) was a conservationist active in the Washington Environmental Council and the Sierra Club; she served as president of the Seattle Audubon Society from 1952 to 1956. She also was an author, president of the Seattle PTA, and during WWII an executive in the Seattle-King County chapter of the American National Red Cross. Correspondence, biographical information, speeches and writings, financial records, minutes, petitions, photos, maps, and other papers including copies of "Birds for Beginners," the column Haig wrote from 1965 to 1969 for the Seattle *Post-Intelligencer.* Also contains material on other organizations in which she served, such as the Federation of Western Outdoor Clubs, the Mountaineers, the North Cascades Conservation Council, the Girl Scouts of America, the North End Flower Club, the Seattle-Kobe (Japan) Affiliation Committee, and the Washington State Graduate Nurses Association.

17,268. Hansen, Julia Butler
Papers. 1948-70. Ca. 175 ft. and 3 microfilm reels.
Open. Inventory.
University of Washington Libraries, Archives and Manuscripts Division.
Legislative and personal correspondence and scrapbooks of Hansen (1907-), a Washington state representative between 1939 and 1960 who served as a US congresswoman from Clark and Cowlitz counties from 1960 to 1974. Hansen's professional

interests included highways, the Democratic Central Committee, and federal policy as it pertained to the western US.

17,269. Hanson, Isabel
Papers. 1955-73. 5 in.
Open. Inventory.
University of Washington Libraries, Archives and Manuscripts Division.
Hanson (1901-75) was a Washington oil painter and member of the American Pen Women. Correspondence, catalogs and notices of exhibitions, biography, awards, yearbooks, programs, and clippings, including correspondence with other northwestern artists and information on her works and shows. Also contains newsletters of the Pen Women and of Seattle Co-Arts.

17,270. Harris, Florence R.
Papers. 1941-71. 2 ft.
Open. Records transmittal form.
University of Washington Libraries, Archives and Manuscripts Division.
Harris was director of the Developmental Psychology Laboratory Preschool at the University of Washington. Manuscripts, clinical studies, administrative and teaching material, grant requests, course outlines, student evaluation sheets, and films deal with Harris's scholarly and administrative work in child development education, particularly concerning retarded children. Also includes information on Head Start and other local and national child development programs.

17,271. Hartman, Sarah McAllister
Papers. 1893. 55 pp.
Open. Data sheet.
University of Washington Libraries, Archives and Manuscripts Division.
Hartman was a pioneer in Newmarket, Washington Territory. Reminiscences in which she describes her life between 1843 and 1878, the Indian wars, and farming.

17,272. Hartshorn, Florence M.
Papers. 1909-34. 10 in.
Open. Data sheet.
University of Washington Libraries, Archives and Manuscripts Division.
Diaries, notes, and notebooks, typescripts, and clippings of Hartshorn (1869-1943), a writer of children's stories and articles about Alaska and Seattle, who was interested in the history and literature of the Northwest.

17,273. Hartsuck, Ann S. (Conner)
Papers. 1824-66. 10 items.
Open. Data sheet.
University of Washington Libraries, Archives and Manuscripts Division.
A teacher, pioneer, and settler in Washington Territory, [Mrs. Mark] Hartsuck (1826-1918) sailed from New York to Seattle in 1866 with other women school teachers. Diary in the form of a letter to a friend describes the voyage of the group known as the Mercer Girls but stops before Hartsuck, then [Miss] Conner, reached San Francisco. It also gives her views of some of her traveling companions and of Asa Mercer, who recruited the women. Documents and ephemera include Conner's ticket, her teacher's certificate, a contract with Mercer, and a letter from Mercer to Territorial Governor William Pickering on Conner's behalf.

17,274. Hartsuck, Mrs. Ben
Papers. Ca. 1905-19. 1 in.
Open. Data sheet.
University of Washington Libraries, Archives and Manuscripts Division.
Reminiscences of life and working conditions in logging communities in Oregon and Washington include mention of the Industrial Workers of the World.

17,275. Hayden, Mary Logan
Oral history. 1974. 1 tape.
Open. Data sheet.
University of Washington Libraries, Archives and Manuscripts Division.
Interview in which Hayden, a settler in the lower Methow Valley of eastern Washington Territory, describes pioneer life from 1890.

17,276. Hebrew Ladies Free Loan Society of Seattle
Records. 1948-73. 1.5 ft.
Access restricted. Data sheet.
University of Washington Libraries, Archives and Manuscripts Division.
Minutes, financial records, and membership lists of this independent, volunteer service organization which makes free loans to needy persons of the Jewish faith and to organizations. Founded in 1909, it is patterned after the traditional Gmilith Khesed organizations of small Eastern European Jewish towns.

17,277. Higginson, Ella Rhoades
Papers. 1924-39. Ca. 25 items.
Open. Data sheet.
University of Washington Libraries, Archives and Manuscripts Division.
Higginson (1862-1940) was a Bellingham, WA, poet and author. Poems, some of which are in manuscript form, and letters to Higginson's friend Mabel Zoe Wilson of Bellingham.

17,278. Hopkinson, Mary, and Hopkinson, Edwin William
Papers. 1923-64. 4.5 ft. and 1 microfilm reel.
Open. Data sheet.
University of Washington Libraries, Archives and Manuscripts Division.
Associated with the Communist party, Mary Hopkinson was an osteopathic physician while her husband Edwin was a chicken farmer, Industrial Workers of the World activist, and chairman of the Pierce County, WA, Communist party. Correspondence, minutes, and rosters reflect the Hopkinsons' activities with the Unemployed Citizens Council of Pierce County, the Washington Pension Union, the Washington Commonwealth Federation, and the Northwest Citizens' Defense Committee.

17,279. Horwood, Rosemary
Papers. 1966-73. 7 ft.
Open. Inventory.
University of Washington Libraries, Archives and Manuscripts Division.
Horwood, a section head in the Seattle Model Cities Program in 1970 and 1971, became a city planner in Seattle's Department of Community Development after 1971. Correspondence, financial records, notes, minutes and agendas, writings, proposals, reports, legal documents, environmental impact statements, maps, and charts. Horwood helped plan Interstate Highway 90 and other projects as part of her government work.

17,280. Hovda, Jane
Oral history. Nd. 1 tape.
Open. Work sheet.
University of Washington Libraries, Archives and Manuscripts Division.
Hovda was a painter and teacher from Bellingham, WA, who studied with northwestern artist Mark Tobey. During the interview she discusses those who influenced her in her career as a 20th-century artist as well as her techniques and the origin of a number of paintings.

17,281. James, Florence B.
Papers. 1918-72. 3 ft.
Open. Preliminary inventory.
University of Washington Libraries, Archives and Manuscripts Division.
Correspondence, speeches and writings, photos, clippings, and ephemera of James (1918-72), a Washington theater director and drama consultant, reflect her activities in Northwest drama with the Seattle Repertory Playhouse, the Cornish Theater, the US Federal Theater Project, and the Washington State Theater. Also includes material on the Canwell Committee, a Washington state legislative committee similar to the US House Un-American Activities Committee, which investigated the Seattle Repertory Playhouse for subversive activities. James's given name was Mary Florence Bean.

17,282. Jewish Archive Project
Collection. Ca. 1849-1975. No size given.
Open. Data sheets.
University of Washington Libraries, Archives and Manuscripts Division.
Collection includes organizational records, photos, and ephemera, but it consists principally of taped interviews on such subjects as Europe and Turkey, immigration, Jewish communities in Seattle and elsewhere in Washington state, business, family, Jewish organizations, WWII refugees, and Jewish education. Interviews with the following women primarily cover the first half of the 20th century: Sophie Altose, Libby Anches, Lydia Angel, Rose Arensberg, Laura Berch, Minnie Bernhard, Rosa Scharhon Berro, Helen (Birkman) Blumenthal, Ruth Kutoff Lukov Brenner, Sema Calvo, Jennie Caston, Betty Dreifus, Joanna Eckstein, Esther Friedman, Fannie Gens, Bernice (Degginger) Greengard, Esther Gross, Hannah Grunbaum, Rachel Cohen Israel, Rebecca Israel, Victoria Israel, Manya Lawson, Louisa F. Levy, Esther Lighter, Edith (Rosenberg) Lindenberger, Ada Loussac, Edith [Mrs. Meyer] Lurie, Rebecca (Morhaime) Mosheatel, Emma Ginsberg Nelson, Rose Ringold, Esther (Schreiber) Rogoway, Stella Sameth, Jennie Schermer, Anita Snyder, Emelie Steinbrecher, Mary Sussman, Perla Bensal Uziel, Ruby (Clein) Webber, and Gertrude (Pearl) Wolfe. Also interviewed were several women members of Seattle's Sephardic community which is comprised of Spanish-speaking Jews who had been exiled to Turkey and the Isle of Rhodes. Also included is limited material on the Jewish Consumptive Relief Society, Seattle Ladies Auxiliary; the Bikur Cholim Sisterhood; and the Seattle chapter of the Mizrachi Women's Organization of America.

17,283. Jones, Fay
Oral history. Nd. 25-page item and 1 tape.
Open. Work sheet.
University of Washington Libraries, Archives and Manuscripts Division.
Interview and transcript in which Jones, a Washington oil painter, talks about her work during the 1970s and gives opinions on other artists and their work.

17,284. Juvonen, Helmi
Oral history. 1930s-70. 44-page item and 2 tapes.
Closed. Data sheet.
University of Washington Libraries, Archives and Manuscripts Division.
Transcript of and interview with Juvonen, a Washington watercolor and oil painter, relate memories of her life as an artist and include mention of artist Mark Tobey, Jacob Elshin, gallery operator Zoe Dusanne, and Theodosia Young.

17,285. Katayama, May Herd
Papers. 1899-1964. 1 tape.
Open. Data sheet.
University of Washington Libraries, Archives and Manuscripts Division.
Katayama was a Baptist missionary among Japanese immigrants and Nisei at Seattle's Fugin Home from 1937 to 1942 and, again, beginning in 1948. In the taped interview, Katayama discusses

her work at Fugin Home, which included care of children of sick families; Florence Rumsey's work at the Home for Japanese; the federally ordered relocation in 1942 of Japanese-Americans into the US interior; and the Japanese Baptist Church in Seattle including the 1929 construction of the church. Katayama was relocated to Santa Anita, CA, and then to Jerome, AR, during WWII.

17,286. Kirk, Lucy, and Kirk, Blair
Oral history. Nd. 41-page item and 2 tapes.
Access restricted. Data sheet.
University of Washington Libraries, Archives and Manuscripts Division.
Interview and transcript in which the Kirks discuss the history of and motivation for their collecting art between 1933 and 1975 and their views on the contemporary art world.

17,287. Knight, Amelia
Papers. 1853. 0.5 in.
Open. Data sheet.
University of Washington Libraries, Archives and Manuscripts Division.
Journal of Knight, a pioneer and Oregon settler, includes an account of her 1853 journey across the continent and first impressions of Oregon. Material was published in *Transactions* (Oregon Historical Society, ca. 1928).

17,288. Lambda Rho
Phonotape. 1970s. 1 tape.
Open. Work sheet.
University of Washington Libraries, Archives and Manuscripts Division.
Lambda Rho is the women's art honorary society at the University of Washington. Panel discussion in which artists Leah Fish, Betty Hagen, Betty Gordon, Judy Kleinberg, and Elizabeth (Sandvig) Spafford talk about their work and how they, as women, fit their art careers into their personal lives. Ruth Pennington, faculty member for 20 years of the University of Washington's School of Art, answers questions from the audience.

17,289. Landes, Bertha Knight
Papers. 1921-32. 7 in.
Open. Data sheet.
University of Washington Libraries, Archives and Manuscripts Division.
Landes (1868-1943) was a civic leader and Seattle mayor and city councilwoman during the 1920s. Correspondence, reports, and clippings regarding politics and employment for women.

17,290. Larsen, Kirsten
Papers. Ca. 1870-1900. 1 in.
Open. Data sheet.
University of Washington Libraries, Archives and Manuscripts Division.
Reminiscences by Larsen, a Danish pioneer and settler in Washington's Skagit Valley.

17,291. Lawrence, Cora
Papers. 1884-1952. 7 in. and tapes.
Open. Inventory.
University of Washington Libraries, Archives and Manuscripts Division.
Lawrence was a Washington state educator and nurse. Taped interviews and transcripts, minutes, record books, and reports comprise material Lawrence gathered for her PhD dissertation on the history of nursing and nursing education in Washington. Included are 1923-27 minutes of the American Nurses' Association, 1884-1952 report memos, and interviews with Elizabeth Soule and Kathleen Leahy, respectively dean emeritus and professor emeritus of the University of Washington nursing school.

17,292. League of Women Voters
Records. 1954-73. 16 ft.
Open. Unpublished guide.
University of Washington Libraries, Archives and Manuscripts Division.
Minutes, financial records, correspondence, speeches and writings, reports, questionnaires, newsletters, maps, clippings, memorabilia, ephemera, and other records of local, Seattle, and Washington state LWV chapters.

17,293. Leary, Eliza (Ferry)
Papers. 1868-99. 1.5 ft.
Open. Inventory.
University of Washington Libraries, Archives and Manuscripts Division.
Leary (ca. 1851-1936) was a society leader; daughter of Elisha P. Ferry, governor of Washington Territory from 1870 to 1880 and first governor of Washington state from 1889 to 1893; and wife of John Leary, a Seattle businessman, owner of the Seattle *Post,* and during the 1880s mayor of Seattle. Correspondence, some of John Leary's business records, and memorabilia, including locks of hair, dance programs, calling cards, and menus. Her correspondence, principally with women friends in the Midwest, Northwest, and California, deals with subjects such as sickness, beaux, parties, engagements, marriages, and the weather. Also included are letters written while Leary attended a boarding school in Portland, OR. Founder of the local Children of the American Revolution chapter, Leary was also honorary vice-president general of the DAR, a member of the Mount Vernon Ladies Association of the Union, and an American National Red Cross worker. She also helped mark the old Oregon Trail.

17,294. Lehmann, Thelma
Oral history. Nd. 1 tape.
Open. Data sheet.
University of Washington Libraries, Archives and Manuscripts Division.
Interview in which Lehmann, a Washington oil painter and critic, discusses her work as a painter, women as artists, the art milieu in Seattle and the Northwest, her activities as a collector and dealer of African art, and the social-artistic aspects of African art. The discussions relate to the years from 1900 to 1975.

17,295. Levine, Naomi
Papers. 1967-70. 3 ft.
Open. Data sheet.
University of Washington Libraries, Archives and Manuscripts Division.
A geriatric social worker, Levine was active in the Puget Sound section of the National Association of Social Workers. Correspondence and notes reflect her career and research interests as well as her involvement in race relations and in the peace movement during the Vietnam War.

17,296. Lipetz, Lin
Oral history. Nd. 15-page item and 1 tape.
Access restricted. Data sheet.
University of Washington Libraries, Archives and Manuscripts Division.
Interview and transcript in which Lipetz, an artist and educator, discusses the status of women in the arts in 1972. The interview was conducted in conjunction with Survivors '72, an exhibition of women's art at the University of Washington's Henry Gallery.

17,297. Loughran, Henrietta Adams
Papers. Ca. 1930-44. 5 ft.
Open. Inventory.
University of Washington Libraries, Archives and Manuscripts Division.
Loughran was director of the University of Washington School of Nursing from 1937 to 1938 and dean of the University of Colorado College of Nursing from 1942 to 1965. Personal papers, correspondence, notes, minutes, financial reports, course and reference material, news releases, talks, clippings, journal publications, and other papers document Loughran's tenure at the University of Washington and contain material on local, state, and national nursing and nursing education organizations.

17,298. Maahi, Sugi
Papers. 1925-68. 3 vols. and 1 tape.
Open. Data sheet.
University of Washington Libraries, Archives and Manuscripts Division.
A prima donna in Japan, the US, and Italy, Maahi was a founder in 1932 of the Japanese Cultural Broadcasting Association, KRKD, in Los Angeles; a soprano, she performed with the Seattle Civic Opera Company and sang on Seattle radio stations from 1925 to 1928. Interview with Maahi concerns her career. Also includes scrapbooks containing photos, concert programs, and clippings on her career; notices from the world press; and material on the formation of the Japanese Cultural Broadcasting Association. Maahi's given name was Miyoshi Sugimachi and she was married to Goro Yorita.

17,299. McCabe, Eliza
Papers. 1909-66. 2 boxes.
Open. Data sheet.
University of Washington Libraries, Archives and Manuscripts Division.
Correspondence, journals, organizational material, reports, and magazines of McCabe, the president of the Washington Association of Colored Women. The WACW, the National Association of Colored Women, and the Washington Federation of Colored Women's Clubs are major correspondents.

17,300. McCaffree, Mary Ellen
Papers. 1968-74. 6 ft.
Open. Preliminary inventory.
University of Washington Libraries, Archives and Manuscripts Division.
McCaffree was a Washington state representative from 1962 to 1970, director of the Governor's Tax Advisory Council from 1974, and president of a local LWV chapter. Correspondence, notes, speeches, questionnaires, and reports chiefly relate to a comprehensive state tax policy.

17,301. McCullough, Esther Mary
Papers. 1936-ca. 1950. 1 ft.
Open. Data sheet.
University of Washington Libraries, Archives and Manuscripts Division.
McCullough was a missionary for the Women's American Baptist Home Missionary Society to the Japanese in Washington state. Scrapbooks, which contain photos, notes, postcards, and clippings, relate to McCullough's work in Seattle, Bellevue, and Bainbridge Island, WA, and to Japanese-American society, particularly the Japanese Baptists. McCullough was associated with the Fugin Home established in 1909 by Baptist missionaries to help Japanese in Seattle. Material on Florence Rumsey and May Katayama, two other missionaries, is also included.

17,302. McElroy Family
Papers. 1847-1927. 1.5 ft.
Open. Inventory.
University of Washington Libraries, Archives and Manuscripts Division.
Correspondence, financial miscellany, legal documents, photos, and clippings of the family of printer Thornton Fleming McElroy (1825-85) who in 1852 moved with his wife Sarah Collins McElroy (1827-94) to Olympia in Washington Territory. He was the first newspaper publisher north of the Columbia River and the seventh official printer for the Territory. Contains Sarah McElroy's letters to their son Harry Bates McElroy (1861-1928), which reflect social life and living conditions in the Puget Sound region.

17,303. McMahon, Teresa
Papers. Ca. 1929-60. 3 ft.
Open. Data sheet.
University of Washington Libraries, Archives and Manuscripts Division.
McMahon (1878-1960?) was an economics professor at the University of Washington and wife of Edward McMahon, who was a history professor at the University. Material relating to education and economics, including a manuscript autobiography which provides a history of the liberal movement at the University.

17,304. Marple, Lorna
Papers. 1936-61. 10 ft.
Open. Inventory.
University of Washington Libraries, Archives and Manuscripts Division.
[Mrs. Warren H.] Marple, an Oregon civic and civil rights leader, was influential in rebuilding the Democratic party in the late 1940s and early 1950s. Correspondence, speeches and writings, notes, biographical material, reports, reprints, and clippings primarily relate to Marple's work as president of the NAACP of Portland, OR, from 1955 to 1957, as a member of the state and national LWV, and as a Democratic party leader. Also contains material documenting Communist infiltration of civil rights groups, Democratic party groups, and of Henry Wallace's 1948 presidential campaign. Marple's papers include files on the American National Red Cross; the Portland Council of Churches, division of Christian life and work; the Portland Public Forum Association; the Patrons of Husbandry of the Oregon State Grange; the Democratic National Committee and the party's Multnomah, OR, County organization; the Urban League of Portland; and the LWV.

17,305. Marshall, Louise B.
Papers. 1965-71. 3 ft.
Open. Inventory.
University of Washington Libraries, Archives and Manuscripts Division.
Marshall is a conservationist, recreationist, editor and publisher of *Signpost,* and author of two guides to the backcountry entitled *100 Hikes* and *High Trails.* Most of the collection of correspondence, manuscript, notes, and clippings relate to publication of *Signpost,* an outdoor recreation newsletter that provides information on backcountry trails and hikes and advocates conservation of wilderness areas. Collection also provides insight into Marshall's involvement in the Mountaineers, the Washington Environmental Council, and the Alpine Lakes Protection Society.

17,306. Miller, Mary A.
Papers. 1942-45. 2 in.
Open. Data sheet.
University of Washington Libraries, Archives and Manuscripts Division.
Letters to a friend written while Miller, a nurse, was working at US Army camps in the US and England during WWII.

17,307. Minor, Louella
Papers. 1884-1935. 1 ft.
Open. Inventory.
University of Washington Libraries, Archives and Manuscripts Division.
A graduate of Oberlin College, Minor (1861-1935) was a missionary and educator in China from 1887 to 1935; in addition, she wrote *Two Heroes of Cathay* (1902) and *China's Book of Martyrs* as well as *Textbook of Theology* in Chinese. Correspondence, writings, photos, and clippings.

17,308. Moran, Mary Adelaide
Papers. Ca. 1942-51. 2 in.
Open. Data sheet.
University of Washington Libraries, Archives and Manuscripts Division.
Moran (1914-72) was a first sergeant in the WACs. Correspondence, photos, clippings, and memorabilia concern women in the armed forces during WWII.

17,309. Morse, Emily Hall
Oral history. Nd. 11-page item and 1 tape.
Open. Work sheet.
University of Washington Libraries, Archives and Manuscripts Division.
In the interview, Morse discusses her work during the 1960s and 1970s as a teacher and artist in oils and mixed media, as well as other current art subjects.

17,310. National League of American Pen Women, Seattle
Records. 1927-70. 4 ft.
Open. Data sheet.
University of Washington Libraries, Archives and Manuscripts Division.
Constitution and bylaws, minutes, membership rosters, correspondence, clippings, and scrapbooks of this local branch, founded in 1927, of a national organization of women in the creative arts, including artists, musicians, and writers.

17,311. National Organization for Women, Seattle Chapter
Records. 1971-72. 7 in.
Open. Data sheet.
University of Washington Libraries, Archives and Manuscripts Division.
Correspondence, reports, clippings, and ephemera of a major women's rights organization. Includes papers of Helen Sommers, Seattle NOW president who later became a state representative.

17,312. Nicholson, Patricia K.
Papers. 1923-73. 6 ft.
Open. Preliminary inventory.
University of Washington Libraries, Archives and Manuscripts Division.
Nicholson (1900-) is a Washington tempera and oil painter. Correspondence, diaries, notes, personal financial records, photos, clippings, biographical material, sketches, paintings, slides, and rare copies of *Poetry Magazine.* Includes correspondence with museums, galleries, artists, and patrons; speeches and writings on art and religion; and catalogs and notices of her shows in the Northwest and California.

17,313. Northwest Designer Craftsmen
Records. 1956-72. 1.67 ft.
Open. Data sheet.
University of Washington Libraries, Archives and Manuscripts Division.
Many women were active members and officers of this artists' and craftsmen's organization founded in 1956. Constitution, minutes, financial records, correspondence, biographical material on members, and photos.

17,314. Norwood, Jean Eileen
Papers. 1951-70. 10 ft.
Open. Preliminary inventory.
University of Washington Libraries, Archives and Manuscripts Division.
A civic leader, Norwood (1919-) was city councilwoman of Vancouver, WA, from 1960 to ca. 1967. Biographical data, chronological and subject files, agendas and minutes, budgets, and scrapbook. Norwood was active in the Vancouver PTA, the Washington Congress of Parents and Teachers, the Fort Vancouver Civic Club, the Washington State Federation of Garden Clubs, a regional library, Vancouver Operation CIVIC (a semi-official community action group), the Vancouver LWV, the United Fund of Clark County, the Columbia Region Association of Governments, and the Equal Opportunity Committee of Clark County.

17,315. Ober, Caroline Haven
Papers. 1887-1929. 9.5 ft.
Open. Inventory.
University of Washington Libraries, Archives and Manuscripts Division.
Ober (1866?-1929) was a teacher at a Nevada public school from 1886 to 1887 and at Montana's Bozeman Academy from 1887 to 1888, a student at Massachusetts Normal School in Salem from 1888 to 1889, regent and vice-directress of government normal schools of the Argentine Republic from 1889 to 1893, and professor of Romance languages at the University of Washington from 1897 to 1929. Correspondence, 57-volume diary, 1901 log book of a cruise to California, notes, speeches and writings, financial records, stock certificates, photos, greeting cards, clippings, and other papers. Ober's diary records her daily life and travels and includes photos, clippings, and memorabilia. Together with her correspondence, the diary documents her trips from about 1912 to 1916 to the Orient where she met Chinese students whom she brought back to study in the Northwest, particularly at the Vashon College and Academy. Also included are notes on trades she made with stamp collectors around the world; a file on Ober's sister Sarah Ober, which contains clippings recounting adventures as a missionary to the Indians; and correspondence and ephemera documenting the formative years of the University of Washington.

17,316. Pacific, Gertrude
Oral history. 1972. 18-page item and 1 tape.
Access restricted. Data sheet.
University of Washington Libraries, Archives and Manuscripts Division.
Interview and transcript in which Pacific, a Washington painter in oils and acrylic, discusses the status of women in the arts. The interview was conducted in connection with Survivors '72, an exhibition of women's art at the University of Washington's Henry Gallery.

17,317. Pailthorpe, Michele
Oral history. 1972. 1 tape.
Open. Data sheet.
University of Washington Libraries, Archives and Manuscripts Division.
Pailthorpe was executive director of the Washington Equal Rights Amendment campaign. Interview in which she discusses the problems, individuals, and organizations involved in the successful campaign for ERA ratification by the state legislature.

17,318. Parents and Teachers Association, Washington, and Washington Congress of Parents, Teachers and Students
Records. 1906-74. 25 ft.
Open. Inventory.
University of Washington Libraries, Archives and Manuscripts Division.
Minutes, financial records, journals, correspondence, committee papers, programs, and reports of the PTA and its successor the Washington Congress of Parents, Teachers and Students.

17,319. Parkhurst, Minnie
Papers. 1913-22. 7 in.
Open. Inventory.
University of Washington Libraries, Archives and Manuscripts Division.
Correspondence, trial transcripts, and clippings of Parkhurst (?-1971), a Washington state political activist who supported pacifist, feminist, socialist, and anarchist causes. Bulk of the collection concerns the sedition trial of Louise Olivereau and her imprisonment. Parkhurst and Olivereau became close friends and exchanged more than 200 letters from 1917 to 1920. Parkhurst was married to Ed Rimer but used her maiden name throughout her life.

17,320. Patha, Darlene Camille
Oral history. Nd. 25-page item and 1 tape.
Access restricted. Data sheet.
University of Washington Libraries, Archives and Manuscripts Division.
Interview and transcript in which Patha, a Washington painter in oils and acrylic, discusses the artist as teacher, the academic training for an artist, photo realism, her own work, her studio and work habits, women in art, the scale of her work, her inspiration, art criticism, dealers, shows, and art fairs. Her discussion covers the years 1965 to 1972.

17,321. Patterson, Viola
Oral history. Nd. 1 tape.
Access restricted. Data sheet.
University of Washington Libraries, Archives and Manuscripts Division.
Interview in which Patterson discusses the careers of herself and her husband Ambrose as artists in Seattle and abroad.

17,322. Payne, Blanche
Papers. 1951-64. 1 ft.
Open. Records transmittal form.
University of Washington Libraries, Archives and Manuscripts Division.
Payne was professor of home economics at the University of Washington, author of *History of Costume,* and member of the original board of the Costume/Textile Study Center established in 1958. Correspondence, writings, financial records, reports, clippings, and ephemera.

17,323. Pizzuto, Laura
Oral history. Nd. 28-page item and 1 tape.
Access restricted. Work sheet.
University of Washington Libraries, Archives and Manuscripts Division.
Interview and transcript in which Pizzuto, a Washington artist in oils and mixed media, discusses women as artists in the 1970s. The interview was conducted in connection with Survivors '72, an exhibition of women's art at the University of Washington's Henry Gallery.

17,324. Powell, Mildred
Papers. 1935-60. 1 ft.
Open. Data sheet.
University of Washington Libraries, Archives and Manuscripts Division.
Correspondence, diaries, speeches and writings, campaign material, photos, and clippings of Powell (1886-) regarding her political career as Seattle city councilwoman from 1935 to 1955 and candidate for Congress in 1950 as well as her activities for Moral Rearmament.

17,325. Powell, Rosalyn Gale
Oral history. Nd. 13-page item and 1 tape.
Access restricted. Data sheet.
University of Washington Libraries, Archives and Manuscripts Division.
Interview and transcript in which Powell, a Washington oil painter, discusses the act of painting, her motivations, results, and the viewer. The interview, which dealt with topics of the 1950s and 1960s, is from a radio series entitled "Conversation with an Artist."

17,326. Riley, Edith Dolan
Papers. 1909-64. 5 ft.
Open. Inventory.
University of Washington Libraries, Archives and Manuscripts Division.
Riley (1885-) was a Democratic party leader in Washington state from ca. 1922 to 1940 and in California from ca. 1945 to 1965; she served as chairman of the Spokane County Democratic party. Correspondence, speeches and writings, photos, clippings, and memorabilia primarily concern Riley's political activities. Also included is material on the LWV and the Federation of Motion Picture Councils.

17,327. Risberg, Gerda
Papers. 1932-63. 5 vols.
Open. Data sheet.
University of Washington Libraries, Archives and Manuscripts Division.
Scrapbooks in Swedish of Risberg, a Swedish-American poet and columnist who lived in California.

17,328. Roderick, Stella Virginia
Papers. 1921-47. 2 in.
Open. Inventory.
University of Washington Libraries, Archives and Manuscripts Division.
Roderick (ca. 1880-) was a magazine editor in New York and Illinois and a suffrage leader. Correspondence, speeches and writings, itineraries, photos, clippings, and League of Nations ephemera. Most of the material pertains to Roderick's friend Carrie Chapman Catt, who urged Roderick to edit a women's magazine.

17,329. Roeder, Elizabeth A.
Papers. 1854. 0.5 in.
Open. Data sheet.
University of Washington Libraries, Archives and Manuscripts Division.
[Mrs. Henry] Roeder was a pioneer and settler in Washington Territory. Diary includes an account of an 1854 overland journey and mentions the Ebey and Yantis families and Ezra Meeker.

17,330. Rudene, Elizabeth Cornelius
Papers. Nd. 3 pp.
Open. Data sheet.
University of Washington Libraries, Archives and Manuscripts Division.
[Mrs. J. O.] Rudene (1849-?) was a settler in Oregon and in Washington Territory. Typescript contains reminiscences of frontier life in the Skagit Valley and on Whidbey Island.

17,331. Salzer, Lisel
Oral history. Nd. 1 tape.
Access restricted. Data sheet.
University of Washington Libraries, Archives and Manuscripts Division.
Interview in which Salzer, a 20th-century enamelist and painter, discusses her early training, her move from Vienna to the US, her enamel and painting technique, and various contemporary art subjects.

17,332. Sano, Minna
Oral history. Nd. 21-page item and 1 tape.
Access restricted. Data sheet.
University of Washington Libraries, Archives and Manuscripts Division.
Interview and transcript in which Sano, a Washington painter in oils and acrylic, talks about problems faced by the female artist in today's society. The interview was conducted in connection with Survivors '72, an exhibition of women's art at the University of Washington's Henry Gallery.

17,333. Schultz, Cecilia (Augspurger)
Papers. 1928-66. 10 in.
Open. Data sheet.
University of Washington Libraries, Archives and Manuscripts Division.
Correspondence, theater programs, biographical material, photos, clippings, and memorabilia of Schultz, a Washington concert impresario and pianist.

17,334. Seattle Arts Commission
Records. 1970-75. 10 ft.
Open. Inventory.
University of Washington Libraries, Archives and Manuscripts Division.
Minutes; director's, administrative, and subject files; correspondence; manuscripts; and committee records of this city agency which provides public money to promote the arts. Women have been active in the Commission's administration; they have also provided and received funds under the agency's auspices.

17,335. Semple, Eugene
Papers. 1865-1908. 8 ft.
Open. Inventory.
University of Washington Libraries, Archives and Manuscripts Division.
Correspondence of Semple (1840-1908), a businessman who was governor when Washington Territory enacted woman suffrage in 1887. Ca. 100 letters on the suffrage bill are included.

17,336. Shephard, Esther (Lofstrand)
Papers. 1897-1972. 24.5 ft.
Open. Inventory.
University of Washington Libraries, Archives and Manuscripts Division.
Shephard (1891-1975) was a Washington author. Correspondence, working papers, drafts, and other material relating to her book *Paul Bunyan,* first published in 1924, and to her poetry, plays, and scholarly articles on Walt Whitman.

17,337. Smith, Alice Maude
Papers. 1910-36. 3.5 ft.
Open. Inventory.
University of Washington Libraries, Archives and Manuscripts Division.
General and business correspondence, diary, notes, prose and poetry manuscripts, scrapbooks, and other papers of Smith (1868-1938), a Washington physician who wrote several medical manuscripts.

17,338. Spafford, Elizabeth Sandvig
Oral history. Nd. 14-page item and 1 tape.
Access restricted. Work sheet.
University of Washington Libraries, Archives and Manuscripts Division.
Interview and transcript in which Spafford, a sculptor who works in the US, Mexico, and Italy, discusses plastic sculpture, women in art, and working in Mexico and Italy.

17,339. Sparkman, Ida Ross
Papers. 1938. 8 pp.
Open. Data sheet.
University of Washington Libraries, Archives and Manuscripts Division.
Sparkman's autobiography provides information on life in early Seattle.

17,340. Spear, Lillian Sylten
Papers. 1936-63. 5.5 ft.
Open. Inventory and name index.
University of Washington Libraries, Archives and Manuscripts Division.
Spear (1897-1963) was a teacher and a public utility advocate and official. Correspondence, notes, speeches and writings, biographical data, financial records, clippings, and other personal papers, the bulk of which concern groups and agencies with which Spear served, such as the Snohomish County Public Utility Association, the Public Utility District No. 1 (Snohomish County), and the Washington Public Ownership League. Also includes material on the Snohomish County Legislative Council, the Democratic party, and the Grange Cooperative Wholesale.

17,341. Stephens, Mary Catherine
Papers. 1951-69. 2 ft.
Open. Inventory.
University of Washington Libraries, Archives and Manuscripts Division.
An educator and civic and social welfare leader, Stephens (1919-) was president of the Seattle LWV, educational director of the Washington State Board Against Discrimination in 1959, and member of the King County Council on Aging.

Correspondence, notes, speeches and writings, reports, minutes, financial records, agendas, photos, newsletters, and clippings reflect these activities as well as Stephens's involvement with the Urban League, the Civic Unity Committee, and the Puget Sound Council of Social Studies.

17,342. Stern, Bernice
Papers. 1958-75. 10.5 ft.
Partially restricted. Inventory.
University of Washington Libraries, Archives and Manuscripts Division.
Correspondence, minutes, reports, speeches, and agenda reflect Stern's work as a councilwoman in King County, WA; an officer of the National Council of Jewish Women and of the Council of Jewish Women, Seattle Section; and a leader in other groups, including the Citizens' Committee for Voluntary School Transfer, Seattle, in 1966.

17,343. Strong, Anna Louise
Papers. 1885-1970. 15 ft. and 7 microfilm reels.
Partially closed. Inventory.
University of Washington Libraries, Archives and Manuscripts Division.
A journalist and author, Strong (1885-1970) supported labor and radical causes in Washington state before 1920, then spent much of the last 50 years of her life in the USSR and China where she was close to Mao Tse-tung, Chou En-lai, and other leaders. Correspondence, writings, speeches, notes, notebooks, account and address books, and photos. The daughter of a clergyman, Strong graduated from Oberlin at 19 and received her PhD from the University of Chicago at 23. She came to Seattle in 1916 where, working as a reporter for a socialist newspaper, she covered the Everett, WA, "Massacre" trial of Industrial Workers of the World members in 1917. She served on the Seattle school board from ca. 1918 to 1919 and led the Seattle general strike in 1919. She moved to Moscow in 1920, married Soviet agronomist Joel Shubin in 1932, and in 1949 was deported as a spy. After living in California for nine years, Strong left for China where she remained until her death.

17,344. Strong, Ruth Tracy
Papers. 1884-1903. 2 in.
Open. Data sheet.
University of Washington Libraries, Archives and Manuscripts Division.
[Mrs. Sidney Dix] Strong (1860-1903) was a Christian leader primarily active in the missionary movement in the US, Europe, and South Africa. Diaries of 1884 and 1903 concern missionary experiences. Account books, memorial service text, and obituaries are also included.

17,345. Sunborg, Vilma
Papers. 1900-40. 1.5 ft.
Open. Inventory.
University of Washington Libraries, Archives and Manuscripts Division.
Correspondence, literary manuscripts, poems, photos, scrapbook pertaining to her career, and clippings of Sunborg (?-1945), an actress in the Swedish-American theater.

17,346. Swift, Louise
Papers. 1863-69. 0.5 in.
Open. Data sheet.
University of Washington Libraries, Archives and Manuscripts Division.
Correspondence in which Swift, a settler in the Skagit Valley in Washington Territory, describes life in the region.

17,347. Testu, Jeanette
Papers. 1933-62. 4.5 ft.
Open. Inventory.
University of Washington Libraries, Archives and Manuscripts Division.
Testu (1898-1963), a Washington state legislator from 1942 to 1962, served as Democratic national committeewoman. Correspondence includes some items from state and national Democratic party officials and leaders and others that deal with legislative issues. Material concerning the 1956 Democratic Convention during which Testu was a platform committee member and 22 scrapbooks are also included.

17,348. Thomas, Joan
Papers. 1955-71. 10 ft.
Open. Unpublished guide.
University of Washington Libraries, Archives and Manuscripts Division.
Correspondence, speeches and writings, memoranda, reports, newsletters, and subject series of Thomas, president of the Seattle LWV from 1962 to 1963, member of the LWV state board in 1963, and president of the state LWV from 1967 to 1969. Thomas was also active in the state redistricting campaign.

17,349. Timpe, Joyce, and Wilson, J.
Papers. Nd. 1 tape and other items.
Open. Data sheet.
University of Washington Libraries, Archives and Manuscripts Division.
Interview and photos of Timpe and Wilson, settlers in King County, WA, concern the area's pioneer life from 1890 to 1940.

17,350. Tomkins, Margaret
Oral history. Nd. 14-page item and 1 tape.
Access restricted. Data sheet.
University of Washington Libraries, Archives and Manuscripts Division.
Interview and transcript in which Tomkins, a Washington oil painter, and her husband James Fitzgerald, a sculptor, discuss their recent trip to Europe, contrasting US and European ideas and activities in the respective art worlds. Specific topics include commissions, dealers, production, survival of the artist, inspiration, and support from the community. Interview is from the "Conversation with an Artist" radio series.

17,351. Triem, Eve
Papers. 1936-73. 4.5 ft.
Open. Inventory.
University of Washington Libraries, Archives and Manuscripts Division.
Triem (1902-) is a poet who has lived in Iowa, CA, and Washington state. Correspondence, writings, notes, photo, books, and miscellany. Includes personal letters, the majority of which are to her husband Paul Ellsworth Triem. Others are from noted American poets.

17,352. University of Washington Dean of Women
Records. 1932-70. Ca. 27 ft.
Open. Data sheet.
University of Washington Libraries, Archives and Manuscripts Division.
Minutes, financial records, correspondence, reports, and technical reference material as well as conference, convention, and committee records largely reflect the work of Dorothy R. Strawn, dean of women from 1960 to 1970 and director of the office of women's studies from 1970 to 1972. The dean's office was abolished in 1970 and its functions were shifted to the women's studies department of continuing education.

17,353. University of Washington School of Nursing
Records. Ca. 1930-70. Ca. 27 ft.
Open. Data sheet.
University of Washington Libraries, Archives and Manuscripts Division.
Constitution, minute book, cash and ledger books, notebook, correspondence, reports, curriculum and teaching material, and published matter. Includes records of student groups as well as records of the School.

17,354. University of Washington Women's Studies
Records. 1909-70. No size given.
Open. Records transmittal form.
University of Washington Libraries, Archives and Manuscripts Division.
Records from the University dean of women's office before it merged into women's studies include material on residence halls, student activities, professional associations, and the local and national Intercollegiate Association of Women Students, as well as Panhellenic records and handbooks and extensive records of the National Association of Women Deans and Counselors, 1947-57. The residence hall and Intercollegiate Students records reflect changing regulations and mores of university women, particularly in the 1960s; abolition of closing hours for women's residence halls was a major development of that decade.

17,355. Walsh, Helen Julia Mason, and Walsh, Edward F.
Papers. 1883-1928. 0.5 in.
Open. Data sheet.
University of Washington Libraries, Archives and Manuscripts Division.
Biographical material and miscellaneous items include [Mrs.] Walsh's account of her experiences in the 1878 Nez Percé war in eastern Washington.

17,356. Wanamaker, Pearl Anderson
Papers. 1925-27. 31 ft.
Open. Inventory.
University of Washington Libraries, Archives and Manuscripts Division.
Wanamaker (1899-) was a state representative in Washington from 1928 to 1930, a state senator from 1936 to 1940, state superintendent of public instruction from 1940 to 1956, and president of the National Education Association. Correspondence, personal files, financial records, notes, legislative files, political campaign material, clippings, memorabilia, and other papers relate to Wanamaker's career as well as her positions as a member of the US Education Mission to Japan, the Democratic party of Island County, WA, and the Island County Welfare Board.

17,357. Ware, Florentine
Papers. 1967-70. 1 microfilm reel.
Access restricted. Data sheet.
University of Washington Libraries, Archives and Manuscripts Division.
Ware (1915-) is a civil rights and community leader in Seattle who was a candidate for the US House of Representatives in 1968.
Correspondence, speeches and writings, reports, and miscellany reflect her work with a variety of agencies and projects including the 1967 Poor People's Campaign and the Seattle school board. Ware was also a member of the Seattle-King County Equal Opportunity Board executive committee from 1967, chairman of the Model City Citizen Health Advisory Board from 1969, executive secretary of the Seattle-King County Economic Opportunity board of trustees from 1970, and vice-chairman of the Central Seattle Community Council.

17,358. Washington Citizens for Abortion Reform
Records. 1968-70. 1.5 ft.
Open. Data sheet.
University of Washington Libraries, Archives and Manuscripts Division.
Minutes, financial records, correspondence, notes, and news releases of this organization which coordinated the successful initiative campaign to legalize abortion in Washington.

17,359. Washington State League for Nursing
Records. 1948-64. 3.5 ft.
Open. Data sheet.

University of Washington Libraries, Archives and Manuscripts Division.
Financial records, correspondence, registers, reports, manuals, newsletters, and ephemera of this professional organization for nurses that had an exclusively female membership.

17,360. Washington State Nurses Association
Records. 1911-60. 77.5 ft.
Open. Preliminary inventory.
University of Washington Libraries, Archives and Manuscripts Division.
A professional nurses' organization affiliated with the American Nurses Association, this group succeeded the Washington State Graduate Nursing Association, which existed from 1922 to 1935, and the Washington State Organization for Public Health Nursing of 1941 and 1942. Organizational papers, financial records, payroll memos, personnel records, correspondence, legal documents, committee papers, research studies, newsletters, questionnaires, clippings, and manuals of the three organizations.

17,361. Wehmeyer, Gladys
Oral history. Nd. 1 tape.
Open. Data sheet.
University of Washington Libraries, Archives and Manuscripts Division.
Interview of Wehmeyer, a settler in Winthrop in Okanogan County, WA, about 20th-century pioneer life.

17,362. Westcoast, Wanda
Oral history. Nd. 27-page item and 1 tape.
Open. Work sheet.
University of Washington Libraries, Archives and Manuscripts Division.
Interview and transcript in which Westcoast, an artist in oils and mixed media, talks about the difficulties of the woman artist and events of the 1970s in the women's art movement. The interview was conducted in connection with Survivors '72, an exhibition of women's art at the University of Washington's Henry Gallery.

17,363. White, Carrie M.
Papers. 1882-91. 1 in.
Open. Data sheet.
University of Washington Libraries, Archives and Manuscripts Division.
Correspondence and diary of White, a settler in Washington Territory, provide information on pioneer life in the Territory and early Prohibition movements.

17,364. Widditsch, Ann
Papers. 1964-73. Ca. 15 ft.
Open. Data sheet.
University of Washington Libraries, Archives and Manuscripts Division.
Correspondence, speeches and writings, notes, reports, resolutions, programs, calendars, lists, agendas, and clippings of Widditsch, a Seattle environmentalist, reflect her work on environmental issues with various organizations.

17,365. Windoffer, Melba
Papers. 1939-66. 1.5 ft.
Access restricted. Inventory.
University of Washington Libraries, Archives and Manuscripts Division.
Windoffer was a Socialist Workers party activist and feminist. Correspondence, party documents, pamphlets, and ephemera, including Civil Rights Defense Committee material and a letter from Mary Gibson.

17,366. Wright, Virginia
Oral history. Nd. 31-page item and 2 tapes.
Open. Data sheet.
University of Washington Libraries, Archives and Manuscripts Division.
Interview and transcript in which Wright, a Washington art benefactor, discusses topics such as her interest in contemporary art, her Seattle gallery, her collection, women in the arts, public art, Seattle's One Percent for the Arts project, the Virginia Wright Foundation, the functions of museums, and the art market. Discussion covers the years from 1950 to 1975.

17,367. Young Women's Christian Association, University Branch
Records. 1920-73. 27.5 ft.
Open. Preliminary inventory.
University of Washington Libraries, Archives and Manuscripts Division.
Minutes, financial records, reports, photos, scrapbooks, programs, clippings, newsletters, memorabilia, miscellany, and ephemera show the YWCA branch founded in Seattle in 1878 evolving from a primarily religious and social organization into a clearinghouse for the area's most radical feminists of the early 1970s. Includes extensive file on the YWCA's abortion reform committee of 1970, which was a leader of the successful initiative campaign for abortion reform in the state.

SPOKANE

17,368. Avery, Mary Williamson
Papers. Ca. 1950-75. Ca. 20 ft. and 187 tapes.
Open. No guide.
Eastern Washington State Historical Society Library.
An historian, archivist, teacher, and author, Avery taught at the University of Washington and was archivist at Washington State University. Notes, collected material, and manuscripts of her books regarding Washington history and government. Also included are lecture notes on Northwest history, transcripts of talks, maps, and tapes from "Northwest Archives," which was Avery's radio program for 1961 to 1975 for Washington State University, during which she read from manuscript and published sources on area history.

17,369. Boyd, Edith L.
Papers. Ca. 1918-67. Ca. 2 ft.
Open. Inventory.
Eastern Washington State Historical Society Library.
Boyd was an author and teacher in Spokane. Bulk of the collection consists of manuscripts of her published and unpublished books, short stories, poems, and plays, most of which were written for children and concern Spokane and eastern Washington history; *Ben Follows Old Trails* was one of Boyd's most popular books. Correspondence, notes, biographical data, photos, memorabilia, and ephemera, including correspondence with publishers (chiefly rejections) and with Spokane and other school districts regarding the use of her books in the classroom. Also contains material of the Spokane chapter of the AAUW, including lists of officers and outstanding events and a book sale notice.

17,370. Browne, J. J.
Papers. 1853-1963. 3 ft.
Open. Inventory.
Eastern Washington State Historical Society Library.
John J. Browne, known as J. J. Browne, was a lawyer and banker. Correspondence, diaries, financial records, a genealogical list, photos, clippings, and other papers of Browne and his family. Bulk of the collection is correspondence between Browne and his wife Anna and with their children, grandchildren, relatives, and friends.

17,371. D'Arcy
Papers. Ca. 1853-1933. Ca. 16 ft.
Open. Inventory.
Eastern Washington State Historical Society Library.
Correspondence, ledgers and accounts, legal papers, speeches, photos, clippings, and other papers of Peter D'Arcy, Sr., a lawyer in Salem, OR, and his family. While most of the material pertains to Peter D'Arcy's law practice, the collection also contains correspondence of his wife Barbara O'Neill D'Arcy (1823-1901) and their daughters Maria and Theresa. Barbara D'Arcy, who was active in the Catholic church, received letters from her nephews and from her nieces, two of whom were nuns. Maria D'Arcy received letters from school friends and relatives. Material of Theresa D'Arcy contains her will and other legal papers and correspondence with her cousins, a friend, and Sister M. Geraldine, her former teacher at a Catholic girls school. Sister Geraldine, who later became a school administrator, discusses such topics as her work, religious matters, and politics. One of Theresa's cousins and a friend were also nuns.

17,372. Dare, Hazel T.
Papers. Ca. 1900-60. 10 in.
Open. Inventory.
Eastern Washington State Historical Society Library.
Clippings, magazines, and pamphlets on the Spokane schools and PTA, early Spokane, and early homemaking, with sewing, cooking, and home management as subjects.

17,373. Drury, Clifford M.
Papers. 1833-1965. 11 ft.
Access restricted. Inventory.
Eastern Washington State Historical Society Library.
Drury (1897-) was an historian, author, Presbyterian clergyman, and professor of church history at San Francisco Theological Seminary. Correspondence, copies of typed manuscripts, research notes, copies of original documents, photos, and clippings relating to Drury's research and writing on Congregational and Presbyterian missionaries of the American Board of Commissioners for Foreign Missions. Includes the manuscript for Drury's book *First White Women Over the Rockies* (Glendale, CA: 1963), a narrative history of women missionaries, which contains edited accounts by the women themselves. Early women missionaries to the Pacific Northwest included in Drury's work are Narcissa (Prentiss) Whitman, Eliza (Hart) Spalding, Mary (Richardson) Walker, Myra (Fairbanks) Eells, Sarah Gilbert (White) Smith, Mary Augusta (Dix) Gray, and Lucy Abigail (Peet) Cowley.

17,374. Frazier, Neta Lohnes
Papers. Ca. 1950-64. Ca. 7.5 ft.
Open. Inventory.
Eastern Washington State Historical Society Library.
Frazier (1890-1959) was a Washington teacher, historian, and author of historical books for children. Copies of manuscripts, research notes, biographical material, photos, booklets, clippings, and memorabilia, the bulk of which are manuscripts of her published works, such as *Sacajawea, The Girl Nobody Knew.*

17,375. Hawkins, Sally
Papers. Ca. 1860-1960s. 5 in.
Open. Inventory.
Eastern Washington State Historical Society Library.
Family narrative history, handwritten girls' newsletter "The Spinsters' Gazette," clippings, and memorabilia of [Mrs. Mark] Hawkins, a society woman. Her family narrative contains reminiscences of courting, her husband's family, and life in turn-of-the-century Minneapolis and St. Paul, MN. Also included are clippings and ephemera of the University Club of Spokane and clippings on Spokane society, with marriage notices, dance reports, and ballet and theater articles.

17,376. Hay, Marion E.
Papers. 1909-16. 15 ft.
Open. Inventory and index.
Eastern Washington State Historical Society Library.
Correspondence, drafts and printed copies of

speeches, business records, official reports, biographical material, photos, scrapbooks, clippings, memorabilia, and other papers of Hay (1865-1933), governor of Washington state from 1909 to 1913. Among Hay's correspondents were suffrage leaders, women's clubs, the WCTU, the Women's Union Label League, and the YWCA. Included is correspondence concerning bills on the eight-hour workday for women and girls and on jury duty for women as well as items opposing a prize fight bill. A substantial amount of correspondence concerns the firing of [Mrs.] Blanch Mason, deputy labor commissioner. Letters from labor groups and women around the state plead for Mason's retention and discuss her work as inspector for industrial safety. Following Mason's dismissal, Hay received letters recommending women to succeed her.

17,377. Hutton, May Arkwright
Papers. Ca. 1910-24. Ca. 2 cu.ft.
Open. No guide.
Eastern Washington State Historical Society Library.
A Spokane philanthropist of working-class background, Hutton (?-1915) was a leading suffrage advocate in eastern Washington state; after failing to win control of the established state suffrage organization, she broke with the Seattle-based group and with its president, Emma Smith DeVoe. Scrapbooks of clippings on suffrage, prostitution, Democratic politics, and Hutton's activities; condolences to her husband Al Hutton following her death; photos; and records of entertainment given at the Hutton Settlement, an orphan home established by the Huttons, who has made their fortune by backing an Idaho silver miner.

17,378. Kizer, Benjamin H.
Papers. Nd. 1 in.
Open. Inventory.
Eastern Washington State Historical Society Library.
Writings, lectures, and biographical material of Kizer (1878-?), an attorney, civic leader, author, and amateur historian who wrote an essay regarding "Grandma Page," the daughter of an Indian woman and white army officer, and her two daughters Elizabeth Gale Poindexter and Isabel (Page) Rutter. The wife of Miles Poindexter, US senator from Washington during the 1910s and 1920s, Elizabeth Poindexter wrote a gossip column about Washington, DC, society for the Spokane press. Isabel Rutter, the central figure of Kizer's essay and wife of banker Robert Louis Rutter, fought against the double sexual standard in divorce proceedings brought first by her husband and later by her. Material for Kizer's essay grew out of his role as an attorney for Robert Rutter.

17,379. Oral History
Oral history. 1971-76. 193 tapes.
Open. Card catalog.
Eastern Washington State Historical Society Library.
Tapes and some transcripts include interviews with a wide variety of women. Among them is Margaret Bean, who for 34 years was a reporter for the Spokane *Spokesman-Review* and served with General Pershing's WWI American Expeditionary Force in Europe; her interview extends from her Spokane childhood in 1883 to 1976. Binna Mason Dummeier, a teacher and daughter of settlers outside Cheney, WA, discusses her experiences and her family's life between ca. 1860 and 1948. Also includes reminiscences from 1889 of Hattie Conley, the daughter of German immigrants who settled in the Cheney area, about such topics as the reception of German immigrants, domestic work on a farm without modern conveniences, schooling and childhood memories, social life, quilting bees, and sports.

17,380. Shrader, Pearl (Hutton)
Papers. Ca. 1905-49. 5 in.
Open. Inventory.
Eastern Washington State Historical Society Library.
Bulk of the correspondence, photos, scrapbooks, programs, notices, and clippings of [Mrs. Edwin] Shrader, an opera singer, socialite, and civic leader, pertains to her singing career. Also includes material on Spokane music clubs, Spokane College, and the Hutton Settlement for orphans, which was established by persons unrelated to Pearl Hutton.

17,381. Holy Names Sisters, Washington Province Archives
Records. 1880- . Ca. 60 ft.
Access restricted. No guide.
Holy Names Convent.
The order was founded in Montreal in 1843. A Northwest mission was begun in Portland, OR, in 1859 and established in Washington Territory in 1880. Members of the order are involved in parish ministry and in teaching elementary, secondary, and college students. Minutes, financial records, correspondence, convent chronicles, material on education conferences and habit changes, photos, scrapbooks, newsletters, programs, and other records of the Province. The Sisters established the first private normal schools in Washington in 1907 in Spokane and Seattle.

17,382. Clark, Mrs. E.
Papers. Late 1800s. 2 pp.
Open. No guide.
Spokane Public Library.
Letter from Clark, a young frontier mother, to [Mrs.] Abigail Smith concerns the effect that her child had had on her life. She states that her mind is distracted and that she is overwhelmed by her domestic chores.

17,383. Lloyd, Mary
Papers. Nd. 18-page item.
Open. No guide.
Spokane Public Library.
Autobiographical account of Lloyd, also known as Indian Mary, who was a leader of the Colville Tribe in Washington, president of the Eagle Feathers Club for Indian women, and member of the Northwest Indian Congress executive committee in the early 1920s. She writes of her mother's tragic life and of her own experiences. After being orphaned, Lloyd was raised by the Sisters of Charity at the Colville Mission; she attended the Mission's convent school for Indian girls for more than 11 years.

17,384. Voices of the Pioneers
Oral history. Nd. 54 tapes.
Open. List.
Spokane Public Library.
Collection contains interviews with ca. 14 women, among them [Mrs.] Kate F. Simpson regarding community activities, [Mrs.] Pearl Hutton Schrader regarding music in Spokane, and [Miss] Margaret Bean regarding theater and celebrities.

TACOMA

17,385. School of Nursing
Records. 1951-62. Ca. 18 in.
Open. No guide.
Pacific Lutheran University Archives.
Minutes, reports, budgets, correspondence, curriculum information, applications, grades, rejection slips, class lists, and conference material of the School, which was founded in 1951. Includes information concerning the establishment and operation of the School, hospital training, the faculty, and other topics.

17,386. Tacoma General Hospital, School of Nursing
Records. 1897- . Ca. 2 cu.ft.
Open. Inventory.
Tacoma General Hospital School of Nursing.
Historical information, notes, interviews with early graduates, photos, catalogs, clippings, artifacts, and other records of the oldest nursing school in Washington, which was founded in 1897 as the Fannie Paddock Hospital.

17,387. Anderson, Ada (Woodruff)
Papers. 1900-27. Ca. 4 ft.
Open. Inventory.
Tacoma Public Library.
Papers of [Mrs. Oliver Phelps] Anderson, a Washington author and novelist, include correspondence with publishers and Charles M. Buchannan of the Tulalip (WA) Indian Agency, articles written by Anderson, speeches and writings of others, photos, business records, biographical material, clippings, memorabilia, and other papers. Anderson wrote for *Century, Harper's Bazaar,* and other magazines.

17,388. Edelweiss Study Club
Records. 1925-60. 1 ft.
Open. Preliminary inventory.
Tacoma Public Library.
Minutes, scrapbooks, and membership lists of this lunch and lecture club for women.

17,389. Gilman, Estella Mae (Trowbridge)
Papers. 1864-1969. 3 ft.
Open. Preliminary inventory.
Tacoma Public Library.
Correspondence, some of which was written during the Civil War, and a genealogy of [Mrs. Henry Alfred] Gilman, a schoolteacher.

17,390. Kuhn, Soule, McMillan, and Patton
Papers. 1890-1940. 12 Hollinger boxes.
Open. Inventory.
Tacoma Public Library.
Correspondence, historical and travel accounts, business documents, photos, paintings, mining claims, deeds, clippings, and other material of these four families include papers of Sarah Soule, who was married to John G. McMillan, a mining and lumber businessman in Grays Harbor County, WA, and then to Henry W. Patton, a journalist and explorer of Grays Harbor County. Contains Soule's correspondence with her first husband, 1897-1900, and papers regarding her activities in such Gray Harbor County organizations as the DAR.

17,391. Loring, Elizabeth Elaine (Brodt)
Papers. 1909-76. 2 ft.
Open. Preliminary inventory.
Tacoma Public Library.
Papers of Loring, a Tacoma playwright, include correspondence with her parents and children regarding the theater; plays, scripts, and other literary works; and material regarding Tacoma summer theater.

17,392. National League for Woman's Service
Records. 1917-19. 2 ft.
Open. Preliminary inventory.
Tacoma Public Library.
Registration forms of more than 1000 women active in the Pierce County chapter of this volunteer patriotic organization during WWI include the following information: name, education, nationality of parents, age, experience, occupation, physical handicaps, vaccinations, and type of work for which they were best suited.

17,393. Nessenson, Elsa Behaim
Papers. 1903-69. Ca. 10 in.
Open. Preliminary inventory.
Tacoma Public Library.
Correspondence, writings, notes, plays, short stories, photos, biographical information, clippings, and other papers of [Miss] Nessenson (1877-1969), a playwright, actress, director, high school teacher, and a founder of the Tacoma Little Theater.

Includes material regarding the founding and operation of the Little Theater.

17,394. Noel, Jacqueline
Papers. 1906-46. Ca. 10 in.
Open. Inventory.
Tacoma Public Library.
Correspondence, notes, biographical data, minutes, reports, financial records, legal documents, personnel information, clippings, and other papers of Noel (1881-1964), city librarian for the Tacoma Public Library from 1924 to 1947. Includes material concerning her activities in the Washington Library Association, the American Library Association, the Pacific Northwest Library Association, the Washington State Federation of Women's Clubs, the DAR, the Huguenot Society of America, and other organizations. Noel was chairman of the literary department of the Washington State Federation of Women's Clubs.

17,395. Pierce County Library Service Committee
Records. 1920-40. 5 in.
Open. Inventory.
Tacoma Public Library.
Minutes, reports, financial records, correspondence, notes, biographical information, legislation, clippings, and other records of this women's organization that surveyed the library needs of the county and sent speakers to inform communities of the opportunities for library services under state laws. Includes material regarding Jacqueline Noel, librarian of the Tacoma Public Library. [Mrs.] Marion Cromwell was chairman of the Committee.

17,396. Snell, Bertha M. (Denton)
Papers. 1886-1957. 4 Hollinger boxes and 6 oversize boxes.
Open. Inventory.
Tacoma Public Library.
Correspondence, writings, notes, speeches, financial records, legal documents, biographical material, clippings, and other papers of Snell (1870-1957), the first female attorney in Washington, who joined the bar in 1899; she also was the wife of Marshall K. Snell, an attorney. The Snells practiced in Tacoma and specialized in land and water rights cases. They invested extensively in real estate and were active in founding the Washington State Historical Society. Besides law and history, Bertha Snell's interests included poetry, rare books, and genealogy.

17,397. Stanley and Mason
Papers. 1907-59. 21 Hollinger boxes and 2 oversize boxes.
Open. Inventory.
Tacoma Public Library.
[Miss] Beatrice Birmingham (1887-1972) moved from the East Coast to Alaska to work as house matron at Fort Yukon; she married Willoughby Mason (1871-1935), an Alaska wilderness settler, and later, Lewis V. Stanley (1876-1956), an Alaska gold dredger. Correspondence, diaries, manuscripts, photos, home movies taken in Alaska, reports, legal documents, clippings, and other papers contain Birmingham's family correspondence, diaries from 1907 to 1959, and a manuscript regarding her life in the wilderness with Mason from about 1926 to 1934. Also contains the "Blue Candle," the newsletter of Alaska Friends, a society to aid elderly Alaskans that was founded by Beatrice Stanley after she and Lewis Stanley retired to Seattle in 1941. She later donated her house in Seattle to Alaska Friends as a home for elderly women.

17,398. Tilley, Margaret P.
Papers. Late 1940s-ca. 1971. Ca. 3 cu.ft.
Open. No guide.
Tacoma Public Library.
Correspondence, yearbooks, and ephemera of [Miss] Tilley, a foreign service officer with the US State Department. Consists primarily of correspondence between Tilley and various foreign embassies. Tilley was the daughter of Erna Spannagel Tilley.

17,399. Aurora Club
Records. 1903-76. 1 box.
Open. Inventory.
Washington State Historical Society Library.
Yearbooks and programs of this Tacoma women's study club founded in 1903.

17,400. Baker, Gertrude
Papers. Early 1900s. 5 in.
Open. Inventory.
Washington State Historical Society Library.
Papers of Baker, a Portland, OR, author, composer, and inventor, include correspondence with publishers; manuscripts of unpublished stories, poems, and plays; original musical scores; a notebook entitled "Love Letters to Rookie-Budd"; artwork; scrapbooks; and a patent. Baker patented a design for a "saleswoman's pocket" in 1910.

17,401. Blackwell, Ruby Chapin
Papers. 1920s-50s. 2 boxes.
Open. Inventory.
Washington State Historical Society Library.
Papers of Blackwell (1876-), a Tacoma pioneer, author, and painter, include correspondence, a 1925 journal, a log of a West Coast cruise in 1926, notes on Tacoma history used for speeches, scrapbooks of photos and clippings regarding her artwork and exhibitions, a typescript pertaining to teaching in a one-room school, and other papers.

17,402. Brewer, Henry Bridgeman
Papers. 1813-86. Ca. 400 items.
Open. Inventory.
Washington State Historical Society Library.
Correspondence, diaries, and other papers of Brewer, an Oregon missionary and farmer, including letters from Brewer and his wife Laura Giddings Brewer to relatives and friends regarding their voyage from New York to Fort Vancouver, WA; missionary work in northern and central Oregon; and relations with the Indians. Also includes family correspondence and letters to Laura Brewer from Myra (Fairbanks) Eells.

17,403. Daughters of the American Revolution
Records. Ca. 1913-50. Ca. 14 cu.ft.
Open. No guide.
Washington State Historical Society Library.
Records of Tacoma's Mary Ball Chapter No. 29 of the DAR include minute books, correspondence, reports, genealogical records, yearbooks, war service records, scrapbooks, programs, clippings, and ephemera generated by the state and local DAR.

17,404. Eells, Edwin
Papers. 1862-1914. 130 items.
Open. Inventory.
Washington State Historical Society Library.
Correspondence, diaries, literary manuscripts, account books, photos, scrapbooks, reports, and clippings of Eells (1841-1917), a Washington Indian agent and son of Washington missionaries Cushing and Myra F. Eells, and of his sister Ida M. Eells. Ida Eells's papers include correspondence and manuscripts she wrote regarding her mother Myra (Fairbanks) Eells (1805-78) and sister Eva Alice Eells (1876-98). Collection also contains correspondence, a biographical sketch written by Ida Eells, and a teaching certificate of Edwin Eells's wife Abbie Foster Eells (1844-1922).

17,405. Entz
Papers. Ca. 1849-1904. 1.5 cu.ft.
Open. Inventory.
Washington State Historical Society Library.
Correspondence, photos, scrapbooks, clippings, memorabilia, and other papers of the Matthews family, particularly of Beulah Matthews, who was the daughter of Horace and Elizabeth (Dennis) Matthews. Includes courtship letters from 1849 written by Horace Matthews to his future wife Elizabeth Dennis and correspondence from the beginning and the end of the Civil War between Horace Matthews in Mississippi and his sisters Ann Matthews and Maryette (Matthews) Paine in Connecticut. The latter reveals how the War split families.

17,406. Fife and Coultas
Papers. 1862-1964. 27 ft.
Open. Inventory.
Washington State Historical Society Library.
Correspondence, diaries, family papers, financial records, photos, a business journal, minutes, scrapbooks, and other papers of William H. Fife, founder of the town of Fife, WA, and owner of Tacoma's Fife Hotel, and of Mary Fife Smith Coultas, an author. The bulk of the family papers was generated by Mary Fife Coultas and includes correspondence and diaries from 1936 to 1938.

17,407. Haffer, Virna
Papers. Ca. 1960-73. Ca. 700 items.
Open. Inventory.
Washington State Historical Society Library.
Photos; negatives; photograms, which are cameraless pictures created in the darkroom; and photography equipment of Haffer (1900-74), a photographer whose works are included in the permanent collections of the Museum of Modern Art and the Addison Gallery of American Art. Her married name was Virna M. Randall.

17,408. Overland Journeys to the Pacific
Collection. Ca. 1837-68. 49 items.
Open. Inventory.
Washington State Historical Society Library.
Diaries, correspondence, and 30 reminiscences of journeys across the continent, about 10 of which were written by women.

17,409. Peeler, Ruth
Papers. 1950-75. Ca. 50 items.
Open. Accession list.
Washington State Historical Society Library.
Correspondence, reports, speeches, legislation, clippings, and ephemera of [Mrs.] Peeler relate to her work as a member of the Washington State Parks and Recreation Commission from 1951 to 1952 and her later historic preservation efforts. Correspondents include Washington governor Arthur B. Langlie and Senator Henry M. Jackson.

17,410. Whitman, Narcissa (Prentiss)
Papers. 1836. No size given.
Open. No guide.
Washington State Historical Society Library.
[Mrs. Marcus] Whitman (1808-47), a missionary to the Indians near Walla Walla, WA, was said to be the first white woman to travel across the continent. Diary written by Whitman at Fort Vancouver from field notes taken on her overland journey. The diary has been published in Clifford M. Drury, *First Woman Over the Rockies,* vol. 1 (1936).

17,411. Woman Suffrage
Collection. 1878-89. 26 items.
Open. No guide.
Washington State Historical Society Library.
Correspondence between [Mrs.] Barbara J. Thompson, a Nebraska woman suffrage leader, and such suffragists as Susan B. Anthony, Ada M. (Cole) Bittenbender, Amelia (Jenks) Bloomer, Lucy Stone, Alice Stone Blackwell, and Elizabeth Cady Stanton. Thompson's correspondence is a part of the collection her son Walter J. Thompson housed at the library.

17,412. Women's Clubs
Collection. 1900s. 10 cartons.
Open. No guide.
Washington State Historical Society Library.
Minute books, membership lists, scrapbooks, clippings, and ephemera of various Tacoma women's clubs, including the Tacoma Women's Study Club, the Tacoma Women's Club, and the United Daughters of the Confederacy.

17,413. WPA Federal Writers' Project, Women in State Development and Folklore
Records. 1938. Ca. 15 in.
Open. No guide.
Washington State Historical Society Library.
Biographical sketches of hundreds of women of the Northwest, most of whom were pioneers. The biographies were grouped into such categories as women journalists of Seattle, women artists of Tacoma, and Indian women, among them Sacajawea.

VANCOUVER

17,414. Knight Family
Papers. 1853. No size given.
Open. Card catalog.
Clark County Historical Museum.
Diaries and other papers of a prominent Clark County family. Includes a diary of Amelia (Stewart) Knight, wife of Joel Knight (1808-67), an MD, regarding her journey from Van Buren County, IA, to Clark County; books brought in their ox-drawn wagon, including a Bible, the complete works of Shakespeare, and Joel Knight's medical books; clippings and articles written about and by them; and material regarding Amelia Knight's nine children, especially one son who died in a sanitarium in New York. Amelia Knight's diary has been published in the Portland *Oregon Journal* and other periodicals.

17,415. Mother Joseph, Sister of Charity of Providence, and Sisters of Providence
Records. 1823- . 12 in.
Open. No guide.
Clark County Historical Museum.
Mother Joseph (1823-1902) traveled with four other nuns in 1856 to Vancouver where she established hospitals, academies, Indian schools, orphanages, and care for the insane in the present states of Oregon, Washington, Montana, and Idaho and in the Canadian province of British Columbia. Books, clippings, and other material. Mother Joseph was born Esther Pariseau in a French-Canadian settlement in Quebec.

17,416. Short, Amos, and Short, Esther
Papers. 1845-?. No size given.
Open. No guide.
Clark County Historical Museum.
In 1846 Esther (1806-62) and Amos Short located a claim on land used by the Hudson's Bay Company at the Hudson's Bay Post in Vancouver. In an ensuing gun battle Amos Short killed two Company men but was vindicated and filed a donation claim in 1848. Legal records, including deeds to land, wills, and abstracts; a play written about Esther Short's adventures and stories about the Shorts; and material on the Hudson's Bay Company and the Roman Catholic Church.

WALLA WALLA

17,417. American Political Audiovisual Library
Collection. Nd. No size given.
Open. No guide.
American Political Items Collectors.
Photos, slides, films, videotapes, audio tapes, and other audiovisual material assembled by this group, which was founded in 1945 to study American presidential politics. Includes items about persons running for office and information about national political issues, among them women's suffrage and abortion.

17,418. Babb, Mrs. E. S.
Papers. 1942. 5 pp.
Open. No guide.
Whitman College Library, Eells Northwest Collection.
A memoir written by Babb, a pioneer, contains an account of her overland journey in 1864, Indians, making butter and washing clothes, settling at Walla Walla, and attending school. Fay M. Orton edited the memoir.

17,419. Baker, Sarah Ann (Miller)
Papers. Ca. 1938. 37 pp.
Open. No guide.
Whitman College Library, Eells Northwest Collection.
Memoirs in which [Mrs. Edwin Franklin] Baker (1853-1945), a pioneer who was born in Illinois, describes such childhood memories as school, grandparents, and the mumps; living in Kansas during the Civil War; traveling overland and settling in Walla Walla in 1868; and her teacher Cushing Eells, a pioneer missionary. The memoirs were edited and prefaced by Baker's daughter Helen Dorothy (Baker) Reynolds.

17,420. Collins, Lizzie
Papers. 1922. 12 pp.
Open. No guide.
Whitman College Library, Eells Northwest Collection.
Reminiscences of Collins (1839-?), a pioneer and settler in The Dalles, OR, concern her family's move from Missouri to Oregon in 1844, Indians, and settling. She was acquainted with the Indian wife of Philip Sheridan, who later became a general; Sheridan apparently treated his wife well in Oregon but left her there when he returned east.

17,421. Eells, Myron
Papers. Ca. 1830-1907. 3 drawers.
Open. No guide.
Whitman College Library, Eells Northwest Collection.
Correspondence, a diary, writings, and notes of Eells (1843-1907), a language student and missionary to the Indians in Mason County, WA. Includes several letters that his mother wrote between the 1830s and the 1870s. Eells, whose parents were coworkers of the Whitmans and Spaldings, was born on the Tshimakain Mission.

17,422. Sager
Papers. 1847- . 1 drawer.
Open. No guide.
Whitman College Library, Eells Northwest Collection.
Correspondence, memoirs, photos, lectures, scrapbooks, and clippings of the seven Sager children, who were orphaned on their overland journey to the West Coast and were adopted by Narcissa Whitman; four of the children survived the Whitman massacre of 1847. The collection, which primarily relates to crossing the plains, living at the Whitman mission, and the massacre, includes correspondence with missionary Henry Spalding and the Sagers' cousins in Ohio; a scrapbook of Catherine (Sager) Pringle containing her notes and historical articles regarding the Whitmans, Spaldings, Eells, the mission, and the massacre; and papers of Matilda Jane (Sager) Delaney, one of the Sager children, and of the Sagers' descendants. Also contains correspondence of Catherine Pringle's granddaughter Mrs. Harry Platz regarding fictionalized accounts produced about the Sager family.

17,423. Spalding
Papers. Ca. 1836-90. 2 drawers.
Open. Unpublished guides.
Whitman College Library, Eells Northwest Collection.
Correspondence, diaries, and clippings of Henry Harmon Spalding (1803-73) and his first wife Eliza (Hart) Spalding (1807-51), who were missionaries in Oregon for the American Board of Commissioners for Foreign Missions, and of his second wife Rachel Jahonnet (Smith) Spalding (1808-80), whom he married in 1853. Papers of Eliza Spalding, who was one of the first white women to cross the continent in 1836, include a diary from 1836 to 1840 regarding the births of a daughter and a son and other topics. Also contains correspondence of Eliza Spalding and Rachel Spalding concerning frontier life, Indians, domestic life, religious matters, disease, and the mission and correspondence of the daughters and granddaughters of the Spaldings regarding frontier life, missionary work, family news, schooling, and domestic life. Edited versions of some of Eliza Spalding's correspondence and diaries were published in Clifford M. Drury's *First White Women Over the Rockies.*

17,424. Walla Walla Park and Civic Arts Club
Records. 1907-74. Ca. 2 cu.ft.
Open. No guide.
Whitman College Library, Eells Northwest Collection.
Minutes and clippings of this women's service club founded in 1907.

17,425. Walla Walla Symphony Society
Records. 1907- . Ca. 25 in.
Open. No guide.
Whitman College Library, Eells Northwest Collection.
Minute books, reports, correspondence, scrapbooks, concert programs, and clippings of the Society, which has been in existence since the Walla Walla Symphony Orchestra's first concert in 1907; women have been involved in the Society's operation since its founding. Mrs. Edgar S. Ficher conducted the Orchestra from 1925 to 1932.

17,426. Walla Walla Women's Reading Club
Records. 1894-1956. Ca. 4 cu.ft.
Open. No guide.
Whitman College Library, Eells Northwest Collection.
Minutes and clippings of this literary club, which was organized in 1894.

17,427. Whitman
Papers. Ca. 1802- . 4 drawers.
Open. Unpublished guides.
Whitman College Library, Eells Northwest Collection.
Correspondence, journals, speeches, drawings, pamphlets, maps, clippings, and books of missionaries Marcus Whitman (1802-47), a physician, and his wife Narcissa (Prentiss) Whitman (1808-47), a teacher and one of the first white women to cross the continent; the couple were killed in an Indian attack on the Whitman mission near Walla Walla. Includes Narcissa Whitman's correspondence and a journal compiled from field notes of her overland journey in 1836. The Whitmans were missionaries for the American Board of Commissioners for Foreign Missions. Portions of the Whitman papers have been published in Clifford M. Drury's books on the Whitmans.

YAKIMA

17,428. Religious Women in the Diocese of Yakima
Records. 1951- . 2 ft.
Access restricted. No guide.
Catholic Diocese of Yakima.
Correspondence, publicity material, and other records relate to work done by these women in teaching, nursing, and social work.

17,429. Wiley, Martha
Papers. Ca. 1900-50. Ca. 2 cu.ft.
Open. No guide.
Yakima Valley Museum and Historical Association.
Papers of Wiley, a missionary to China for the

American Board of Commissioners for Foreign Missions, contain correspondence documenting her activities at the Foochow Mission from 1900 to 1948, correspondence regarding travels to Egypt, correspondence with former students in China, diaries from 1924 to 1925, an autobiographical account about her childhood from 1874 to 1884, an account of the founding of a mission at Kuliang, notes on idolatry that were taken from Chinese books, photos, minutes of the Foochow College faculty from 1900 to 1901, passports, and other papers.

WEST VIRGINIA

BETHANY

17,430. Archives
Records. 1840- . 450 ft.
Access restricted. Unpublished guide.
Bethany College Archives.
Bethany College is a private, church-related institution founded in 1841. Minutes, financial records, correspondence, oral history transcripts, personal papers, photos, scrapbooks, and other records reflect the role of female members of the school's board of trustees, faculty, administration, and student body and organizations. Includes papers of Pearl Mahaffey, a Bethany faculty member and trustee from 1906 to 1970. Upon her retirement, the College awarded Mahaffey an honorary doctorate.

BUCKHANNON

17,431. Buck, Pearl Comfort (Sydenstricker)
Papers. 1921-73. 25 ft.
Closed. Catalog.
West Virginia Wesleyan College Library.
Manuscripts of books, plays, short stories, articles, speeches, and book reviews by Buck (1892-1973), including several of her articles concerning women in American society.

HUNTINGTON

17,432. Aleshire Family
Papers. 1862-88. 3 boxes.
Open. Unpublished guide.
Marshall University Library, Special Collections.
Correspondence of this Gallipolis, OH, family includes letters in which Mary Aleshire tells her family about her life at Ohio Female Seminary in Cincinnati and, later, about taking care of her home. The Aleshires were grain dealers and soldiers.

17,433. American Association of University Women, West Virginia Division
Records. 1923- . 11 cu.ft.
Access restricted. No guide.
Marshall University Library, Special Collections.
Noncurrent minutes, financial records, reports, newsletters, and programs of the West Virginia AAUW, which was founded in 1923.

17,434. Biddle, Ora Patterson
Papers. 1928-59. 4 boxes.
Open. No guide.
Marshall University Library, Special Collections.
Biddle, a housewife from Point Pleasant, WV, was a member of the DAR. Correspondence, newsletters, programs, and clippings illustrate Biddle's interest in the DAR and in historical events.

17,435. Clendenning Family
Papers. 1850-1944. 2 boxes.
Open. No guide.
Marshall University Library, Special Collections.
Correspondence, photos, certificates, and clippings of the family. Includes letters Arminda Holliday Clendenning wrote to her sister Anne Winder. These letters, dated from 1850 to 1867, portray life in a small farming community in eastern Ohio. The Clendennings were merchants, civil servants, and soldiers from Harrison County, OH, and Wheeling, WV.

17,436. Enslow, Catherine Bliss
Papers. 1899-1973. 22.5 ft.
Open. Unpublished guide.
Marshall University Library, Special Collections.
Correspondence, photos, slides, and clippings of [Miss] Enslow pertain to her work as a journalist and society editor for the Huntington *Advertiser,* as a delegate to national Democratic party conventions, as an organizer of the local corps of the American Women's Voluntary Service during WWII, and as a community leader.

17,437. Enslow, Mary Constance
Papers. 1892-1962. 4.5 ft.
Open. Unpublished guide.
Marshall University Library, Special Collections.
Diaries, genealogical notes, photos, scrapbooks, articles, and clippings of [Miss] Enslow, a commercial artist and genealogist in Chicago. Primarily consists of genealogical notebooks and items related to Enslow's personal interests, particularly in the British royal family.

17,438. Filson, Bertha Steinbach
Papers. 1885-1976. 2 boxes.
Open. No guide.
Marshall University Library, Special Collections.
Correspondence, certificates, clippings, and plaques reflect [Mrs.] Filson's life as a teacher and active churchwoman in Point Pleasant, WV, and as an active alumna of Marshall University.

17,439. Gilchrist, Robert, Family
Papers. 1783-1957. 4.33 ft.
Open. Unpublished guide.
Marshall University Library, Special Collections.
Included with the correspondence, diaries, journals, scrapbooks, and clippings of this Lebanon, OH, family of merchants and politicians are papers of Mary Wilson Gilchrist. Her correspondence and diaries, dating from 1842 to 1866, contain family news, household information, and notes on her travels and studies at school.

17,440. Jenkins, Samuel R.
Papers. 1887-1941. 2.33 ft.
Open. Unpublished guide.
Marshall University Library, Special Collections.
Diaries, receipts, and clippings of Jenkins, a civil engineer and Grafton, WV, florist. Jenkins began his diaries at the age of 17; the diaries contain his observations about his sister Mary, her activities, and their relationship.

17,441. Simmons, Ethel P.
Papers. 1925-57. 1 box.
Open. No guide.
Marshall University Library, Special Collections.
[Mrs.] Simmons, a Point Pleasant, WV, housewife, was a member of the DAR. Correspondence, unpublished manuscripts, a compilation of county marriage records, and newsletters reflect Simmons's interest in local history and in promoting interest in history and patriotism through the DAR.

17,442. West Virginia Association of Colleges and Universities
Records. 1961-74. 23 cu.ft.
Open. Unpublished guide.
Marshall University Library, Special Collections.
Minutes, financial records, correspondence, studies, and scrapbooks of the Association, which coordinated activities of West Virginia's institutions of higher education and was particularly active in areas concerning state legislation. Includes correspondence of Elizabeth V. Hallanan, executive director of the Association.

17,443. White, L. Marie
Papers. 1937-76. 1 box.
Open. No guide.
Marshall University Library, Special Collections.
White was assistant registrar and assistant alumni officer at Marshall College, now Marshall University. Manuscripts of published and unpublished historical information about the University and photos. White was an alumna of the College.

MARTINSBURG

17,444. Bergen, Christine
Papers. 1950s-early 1970s. 17 half-size deed books.
Open. Unpublished guide.
Berkeley County Court House, Surveyor of Lands and County Clerk.
[Mrs.] Bergen (1900-73) was a genealogist. Volumes contain information she gathered about families in Berkeley County and elsewhere. The information concerns events dating from the 17th century to the 1970s.

MORGANTOWN

17,445. Albright, Erbie Claire
Papers. 1915-43. 1 ft.
Open. No guide.
West Virginia University, West Virginia Collection.
A home economics teacher at Morgantown High School and the supervisor of the Monongalia County school system home economics program, Albright (1895-1964) was a graduate of West Virginia University who attended the University of Chicago and Columbia University. Correspondence, business papers, and education records, including WWI letters commenting on conditions at Camp Taylor, KY, and Fort Lee, VA, and WWII material about civilian support activities. Also contains information on schools in West Virginia, Pennsylvania, Michigan, and New York; the West Virginia Home Economics Association; and the National Education Association department of home economics.

17,446. American Association of University Women, Morgantown Branch
Records. 1922-70. 3 ft.
Open. No guide.
West Virginia University, West Virginia Collection.
Minutes, financial records, correspondence, yearbooks, and clipping scrapbooks.

17,447. American Association of University Women, West Virginia Division
Records. 1955-58. 2 items.
Open. No guide.
West Virginia University, West Virginia Collection.
Yearly narrative reports of the historians of the 19 AAUW branches in West Virginia.

17,448. Arthurdale Homestead Project
Records. 1930s. 1 ft., 1 microfilm reel, and 3 motion picture reels.
Open. Unpublished guide.
West Virginia University, West Virginia Collection.
Initiated by Eleanor Roosevelt in 1934, the project sought to resettle and retrain unemployed miners and laborers for farm work. Correspondence, photos, clippings, and printed material concern the Project's beginning and development at Arthurdale

in Preston County, WV, and include lists of applicants, methods employed in screening applicants, and essays and other material on local and state self-help and rehabilitation projects. Eleanor Roosevelt is one of the correspondents.

17,449. Association of Women Students
Records. 1927-67. 12 vols.
Open. No guide.
West Virginia University, West Virginia Collection.
Founded in 1927, this West Virginia University organization sought to provide a single voice for women students, to promote special activities, and to make and enforce dormitory and sorority rules. Minute and record books of various Association boards and committees, including the judiciary council's volume, which contains information on the trials, convictions, and punishment of women who violated dormitory rules.

17,450. Bennett, Mrs. Louis
Papers. 1900-26. 3 ft.
Open. Unpublished guide.
West Virginia University, West Virginia Collection.
Sallie Maxwell Bennett was the wife of Louis Bennett of Weston, WV, the Democratic gubernatorial candidate in 1908. Personal correspondence, a diary, and legal and financial papers primarily concern the career of Sallie Bennett's son Louis, Jr., particularly his student days at Yale University, his attempt to organize an aviation group in the state, his service in the Royal Air Force, his death in WWI, and Sallie Bennett's efforts to memorialize him. Also contains information about other family news and a South American trip during the late 1920s.

17,451. Bonafield, Julia A.
Papers. 1888-1943. 4 items.
Open. No guide.
West Virginia University, West Virginia Collection.
Clippings concern the career of Bonafield (1863-1956), a Buckhannon, WV, native who served as a missionary to China and a teacher at the girls school in Foochow, China, from 1888 to 1943.

17,452. Brand Family
Papers. Ca. 1861-1924. 52 items.
Open. No guide.
West Virginia University, West Virginia Collection.
Business and official papers of Monongalia County, WV, sheriff John M. Brand and his deputy, William N. Brand; a letter from Elizabeth I. Moore of Woodburn Female Seminary; diaries which Willa Brand kept during her trips to Europe in 1913 and to the British Isles in 1924; and genealogical notes compiled by Frank M. Brand concerning the family of Samuel and Elizabeth Musgrave and the McDougal family.

17,453. Coal Strikes
Records. 1912-14. 1 ft. and 1 microfilm reel.
Open. No guide.
West Virginia University, West Virginia Collection.
Files of Colonel George S. Wallace, the acting judge advocate general, concern coal strikes in southern West Virginia and include a speech given by Mary "Mother" Jones in several towns; records of military commission hearings at Pratt, WV, containing testimony by and about Jones; and hearing documents of the US Senate committee on education and labor.

17,454. Dandridge, Danske
Papers. 1869-1913. 1 ft.
Open. Unpublished guide.
West Virginia University, West Virginia Collection.
Correspondence of Dandridge (1858-1914), a poet, is primarily from members of her family but also includes letters from magazine editors, G. P. Putnam's Sons, William Hayes Ward, H. C. Hopkins, and Washington Gladden.

17,455. Davis, John J.
Papers. 1848-61. 5 ft.
Open. Unpublished guide.
West Virginia University, West Virginia Collection.
Davis was a West Virginia congressman and father of presidential candidate John W. Davis. Papers include correspondence from his aunt commenting on teaching and society in antebellum Mississippi and Arkansas; correspondence from his granddaughter, author Julia Davis; and material concerning Woodburn Female Seminary in Morgantown.

17,456. Davis, Julia McDonald
Papers. 1866-1963. 2 ft.
Open. Unpublished guide.
West Virginia University, West Virginia Collection.
An author, Davis (1900-) is the daughter of presidential candidate John W. Davis. Correspondence, manuscripts, class notes, and other papers include a biographical sketch of her grandfather E. H. McDonald, Civil War reminiscences, memoirs of Colonel A. W. McDonald, and notes on trips by her father especially in 1924. Correspondents include her father, William L. Wilson, and Julia McDonald.

17,457. Dille, Thomas Ray
Papers. 1774-1939. 59 ft.
Open. Unpublished guide.
West Virginia University, West Virginia Collection.
Dille was a lawyer, genealogist, and amateur historian. Correspondence; office files; historical notes; lists of soldiers; copies of birth, death, and marriage records; cemetery readings; and other material, including ledger books and other records relating to Woodburn Female Seminary in Morgantown.

17,458. Easton-Avery Farm Woman's Club
Records. 1945-59. 2 vols.
Open. No guide.
West Virginia University, West Virginia Collection.
Minutes of the Club, a social and homemakers group organized in a rural community near Morgantown.

17,459. Fleming Family
Papers. 1810-1943. 6 ft.
Open. Unpublished guide.
West Virginia University, West Virginia Collection.
Benjamin Fleming (1806-91) and his son Thurston Worth Fleming (1846-?), both of Fairmont, WV, carried on a large trade in manufacturing and in importing and selling hats, furs, general merchandise, fertilizer, and hardware. Business and personal papers, genealogies, photos, pamphlets, and clippings. Includes correspondence reflecting Florence Fleming's interests in the West Virginia Humane Society and the placement of homeless children, letters from family members attending Morgantown schools from 1863 to 1865, letters and advertisements from eastern mercantile houses, and material showing the current prices of furs and skins.

17,460. Harmer, Harvey W.
Papers. 1942-61. 2 ft. and 2 tapes.
Open. Unpublished guide.
West Virginia University, West Virginia Collection.
Correspondence, speeches, essays, and clippings of Harmer (1865-1961), a lawyer, state senator, and local historian, include information on prohibition, the WCTU, and the women's suffrage movement.

17,461. Harold, Nan (Brooke)
Papers. 1859-1958. 1 ft. and 1 tape.
Open. Unpublished guide.
West Virginia University, West Virginia Collection.
Harold (ca. 1888-1958) was the daughter of St. George Tucker Brooke, a member of the West Virginia University law faculty. Correspondence, diaries, an interview, and other material pertain to university life and social activities in Morgantown as seen by a woman student.

17,462. Hatfield, Henry Drury
Papers. 1913-58. 9 ft.
Open. Unpublished guide.
West Virginia University, West Virginia Collection.
A medical doctor, Hatfield (1875-1962) was governor of West Virginia from 1913 to 1917 and a US senator from 1929 to 1935. Correspondence; speeches; farm, legal, and financial records; medical files; a biographical sketch; photos; and clippings. Some items relate to Mary "Mother" Jones. Hatfield was chief surgeon and founder of Huntington Memorial Hospital.

17,463. Holt, Helen
Papers. 1938-59. 8 ft.
Access restricted. Unpublished guide.
West Virginia University, West Virginia Collection.
[Mrs. Rush D.] Holt (ca. 1918-), a college teacher, served as a delegate in the West Virginia legislature in 1955 and 1956, West Virginia secretary of state from 1957 to 1959, and assistant commissioner of public institutions in 1959 and 1960. Correspondence, speeches, and clippings deal with such subjects as school appropriations, aid to the blind and mentally ill, reading improvement programs, the state business and occupation tax, salaries of public employees, Korean veterans' bonus bonds, workmen's compensation, handicapped children, the prisoners' aid movement, the West Virginia Training School at St. Marys, capital punishment, and juvenile delinquency.

17,464. Hough, Clara
Papers. 1877. 1 vol.
Open. No guide.
West Virginia University, West Virginia Collection.
Diary in which Hough (ca. 1857-?) relates daily experiences and social activities in the Morgantown area.

17,465. Jarvis, Anna
Papers. 1858-1958. 2 ft. and 1 microfilm reel.
Open. Unpublished guide.
West Virginia University, West Virginia Collection.
Correspondence, speeches, business and legal papers, photos, and clippings of [Miss] Jarvis (1864-1948), who was the founder of Mother's Day and who was involved with the library department of a Philadelphia insurance company. Includes papers of Jarvis's father Grandville E. Jarvis, notes and drafts of her book of recollections concerning her mother Ann M. Jarvis (1833-1905), papers of Fairmont, WV, songwriter William Lynett, and information about her efforts to institute Mother's Day on a state-by-state basis and her later protest against commercialization of the observance. Also includes information on the Jarvis coal and farm lands in Taylor County, WV, real estate holdings in Philadelphia, and her work with the insurance company. Correspondents include Mrs. W. R. Hearst, Spessard L. Holland, John T. McGraw, John W. Mason, Matthew M. Nealy, and Jennings Randolph.

17,466. Kee, James, and Kee, Elizabeth
Papers. 1963-66. 16 ft.
Open. No guide.
West Virginia University, West Virginia Collection.
Correspondence of Elizabeth Kee, who served in the US House of Representatives from 1951 to 1964, and her son James, who served from 1965 to 1972, deals primarily with social security, welfare cases, and veterans' problems.

17,467. Ladies of the Maccabees, Progressive Hive No. 8, Morgantown
Records. 1907-46. 60 items.
Open. No guide.
West Virginia University, West Virginia Collection.
Correspondence, reports, and a history of the Hive, a ladies auxiliary founded in about 1907 for the

Knights of the Maccabees, a fraternal order. Also includes material concerning the Woman's Benefit Association, which originally was named Ladies of the Maccabees.

17,468. Ladwig, Mrs. Otto Worthington
Papers. 1899-1943. 80 items.
Open. No guide.
West Virginia University, West Virginia Collection.
Ladwig (1882-) was president in 1931 and 1932 of the Clarksburg Women's Club in Clarksburg, WV. Correspondence includes material concerning the West Virginia Federation of Women's Clubs, the National Council of Women of the US, Inc., the George Washington Bicentennial Committee, the *Clubwoman,* the Federated Garden Clubs of West Virginia, the GFWC, the Chicago Exposition of 1933, the World Court, and the International Disarmament Conference of 1932.

17,469. Leonian, Nell (Lanham)
Papers. 1892-1967. 43-page item.
Open. No guide.
West Virginia University, West Virginia Collection.
Sketches by Leonian (1892-), a Morgantown resident and schoolteacher, include information about her early life, family history, teaching experiences in southern West Virginia, and life as a student and teacher at West Virginia University.

17,470. McKown, Sarah Morgan
Papers. 1860-99. 2 microfilm reels.
Open. No guide.
West Virginia University, West Virginia Collection.
Yearly diaries of McKown, a Berkeley County, WV, resident.

17,471. Miller, Clay V.
Papers. 1928-52. 200 items.
Open. No guide.
West Virginia University, West Virginia Collection.
Correspondence, clippings, and printed material collected by Miller, historian of Andrews Methodist Church in Grafton, WV, the "Mother's Day Church," include information about Anna Jarvis, the Mother's Day movement, and Methodism in Taylor County. Includes some letters of Jarvis and photos of Jarvis and her mother Ann M. Reeves Jarvis.

17,472. Miller, Izetta Jewell Brown
Papers. 1908-73. 40 items.
Open. No guide.
West Virginia University, West Virginia Collection.
Photos and clippings of Miller (1882-), an actress, farmer, and political activist who unsuccessfully sought the Democratic nomination for the US Senate from West Virginia in 1922 and 1924. She was among the first women to address a national political convention, giving seconding speeches for John W. Davis in 1920 and 1924. Miller's career included work in theater, radio, television, and the suffrage movement. Her first husband was William Gay Brown, Jr., a West Virginia congressman from Kingwood. Her second marriage was to Hugh Miller, a faculty member at George Washington University and later at Union College in Schenectady, NY.

17,473. Montague, Margaret Prescott
Papers. 1906-44. 6 ft.
Open. Unpublished guide.
West Virginia University, West Virginia Collection.
Montague (1878-1955) was a West Virginia essayist, short story writer, poet, and novelist. Correspondence, diaries, manuscripts, notes, notebooks, photos, clippings, and printed material. Includes letters from editors, publishers, agents, critics, readers, and family members; outlines, plots, and drafts; and diaries and notebooks primarily concerning religious meditation, Christian mysticism, and her concept of human ennoblement through suffering. Correspondents include Bernard Baruch, Russell Doubleday, Howard M. Gore, M. A. De Wolfe Howe, Vachel Lindsay, Christopher Morley, Philip Van Doren Stern, Joseph P. Tumulty, and Woodrow Wilson. Montague won the first O. Henry memorial prize in 1919 for her short story "England to America."

17,474. Moore, Elizabeth I.
Papers. Nd. 2-page item.
Open. No guide.
West Virginia University, West Virginia Collection.
Moore (1832-1930), an educator, was principal of Woodburn Female Seminary in Morgantown and founder of the Morgantown Female Seminary. Eulogy of Moore, written by Emma H. Clark.

17,475. Morgantown Service League
Records. 1935-74. 2 ft.
Open. No guide.
West Virginia University, West Virginia Collection.
The League, a women's voluntary civic and social welfare organization founded in 1935, sponsored benefit programs for school and public libraries and was involved in preservation of historic sites. Annual reports, scrapbooks of clippings, and programs of the annual "Service League Follies" and other events.

17,476. Morgantown Women's Home Defense Club
Records. 1915-60. 1 ft.
Open. No guide.
West Virginia University, West Virginia Collection.
President's records, minutes, and financial records of a PTA that changed its name to Home Defense Club after the beginning of WWI. The group existed from 1915 to 1960.

17,477. Phillips, Marcia Louise Sumner
Papers. 1861-63. 1 item.
Open. No guide.
West Virginia University, West Virginia Collection.
Manuscript journal of Phillips, a resident of French Creek and Buckhannon, WV, contains commentary on local and family affairs, the Civil War, and military operations in Western Virginia and in Virginia. Her husband, S. B. Phillips, was a captain of Company E, Third Virginia Volunteer Infantry. Journal contains descriptions and quoted conversations of Confederate and Union officers and mentions military camps and various military units. Also includes references to churches, travel, elections, holiday celebrations, and the 1863 statehood convention in Parkersburg.

17,478. Seckar, Alvena V.
Papers. 1940- . 4 ft.
Open. No guide.
West Virginia University, West Virginia Collection.
[Miss] Seckar (1916-) is an artist and author. Correspondence, class notes, course outlines, photos, scrapbooks, pamphlets, and clippings include information on Islamic, Arabic, and Near Eastern art and the work of Paul Hogarth. Also contains manuscripts of books for juveniles written and illustrated by Seckar, including *Zuska of the Burning Hills, Trapped in the Old Mine,* and *Mischko.* Correspondents include Rockwell Kent.

17,479. Watson, Martha Dent
Papers. 1865. 1 item.
Open. No guide.
West Virginia University, West Virginia Collection.
Diary of Watson (1837-1905), a Fairmont, WV, resident who was the daughter of Thomas and Rebecca Haymond Watson, includes comments on the Civil War, the southern cause, Lincoln and his assassination, and the attitudes of Fairmont residents toward Southern sympathizers and returning Confederate soldiers.

17,480. Welshans, Harriet
Papers. 1845-68. 1 vol.
Open. No guide.
West Virginia University, West Virginia Collection.
Sentiment book of Welshans, a Shepherdstown, WV, girl.

17,481. West Virginia 4-H Clubs
Records. Ca. 1922-69. 2 ft. and 1 vol.
Open. No guide.
West Virginia University, West Virginia Collection.
Correspondence, photos, scrapbooks, newsletters, manuals, handbooks, bulletins, and other records of the state-wide group, founded in about 1911.

17,482. West Virginia Mining Investigation Commission
Records. 1912-13. 1 ft.
Open. No guide.
West Virginia University, West Virginia Collection.
Typescripts of proceedings of the Mining Investigation Commission at Charleston, WV, and of the military commission at Pratt, WV. The commissions were appointed by Governor William E. Glasscock to investigate conditions in the Cabin Creek and Paint Creek coal fields. Includes five speeches of Mary "Mother" Jones, military commission orders, clippings from the Charleston *Labor Argus,* and names of persons appearing before the commissions.

17,483. West Virginia State Board of Control
Records. 1909-49. 102 ft. (139 microfilm reels).
Open. Unpublished guide.
West Virginia University, West Virginia Collection.
The Board was reponsible for all state correctional and educational institutions and hospitals from 1909 to 1949. Correspondence includes that relating to the Industrial Home for Girls, the Industrial Home for Colored Girls, and the West Virginia Prison for Women.

17,484. Women's Music Club of Morgantown
Records. 1938-65. 1 ft.
Open. No guide.
West Virginia University, West Virginia Collection.
Founded in 1938, the Club promotes the musical arts and raises money for scholarships at West Virginia University. Treasurers' reports, correspondence, membership lists, program books, and other material.

17,485. Woodburn Female Seminary, Morgantown
Records. 1939. 2-page item.
Open. No guide.
West Virginia University, West Virginia Collection.
A sketch, written by Susan Maxwell Moore, about the school, which was founded in 1852 and disbanded in 1870.

17,486. Yost, Lenna Lowe
Papers. 1919-70. 2 ft.
Open. Unpublished guide.
West Virginia University, West Virginia Collection.
A worker in the suffrage and temperance movements, [Mrs.] Yost (1878-1972) was a member of the West Virginia board of education from 1921 to 1933 and, in 1920 and 1921, the first woman to serve on the Republican state executive committee. She later became director of the women's division of the Republican National Committee. Correspondence, clippings, and other papers of Yost, who championed measures to improve the lives of women and children, including child labor laws and bills to establish juvenile courts and public libraries.

WHEELING

17,487. Archives
Records. 1853- . 12 boxes and 57 vols.
Open. No guide.
Sisters of St. Joseph of Wheeling, Mount St. Joseph.
Articles of incorporation, financial records,

correspondence, photos, scrapbooks of clippings, and other records of this motherhouse, which was founded in 1853 in Wheeling. The Sisters care for the sick and for orphans. Includes records of Wheeling Hospital, St. Francis Hospital, St. Joseph Hospital, and St. Mary Hospital, all of which are operated by members of the congregation.

WISCONSIN

BARABOO

17,488. Circus Lithographs
Collection. 1847-1978. 5400 items.
Open. Unpublished guide.
Circus World Museum Library.
Many of the color advertisements feature female circus performers.

17,489. Circus Photos and Negatives
Collection. 1890- . 32,000 items.
Open. Unpublished guide.
Circus World Museum Library.
The 12,000 negatives and 20,000 photos (all in black and white) include many of female circus performers.

17,490. Circus World Museum
Collection. 1793- . No size given.
Open. Unpublished guide.
Circus World Museum Library.
Files on circus personalities, color slides, more than 1000 handbills, 1400 program books, 8000 newspaper advertisements, circus music, original art, periodicals, books, and other material reflecting the history of the circus and its people.

17,491. Lind, Jenny
Papers. 1850s-?. 1 drawer.
Open. No guide.
Circus World Museum Library.
Booklets, song sheets, articles, photos, and other papers of Jenny Maria Lind-Goldschmidt, the Swedish singer known as Jenny Lind, who was associated with circus owner P. T. Barnum.

17,492. Ringling Bros. and Barnum & Bailey Circus
Records. 1919-67. 209 drawers and 305 vols.
Access restricted. Unpublished guide.
Circus World Museum Library.
Archives of the firm include personnel records reflecting the work of women performers and other employees of the world's largest circus.

BEAVER DAM

17,493. Outstanding Women of Dodge County, WI
Collection. 1843-1976. 1 box.
Open. No guide.
Dodge County Historical Society.
Biographies of Dodge County women compiled from correspondence, personal interviews with the women and their families, minutes, photos, scrapbooks, and other papers held at the Historical Society.

BELOIT

17,494. Dougan, Vera Wardner
Papers. 1930- . 30 items.
Access restricted. No guide.
Bartlett Memorial Historical Museum.
Photos, annotated biography, lists of honors and citations, list of positions held, and clippings of Dougan (1898-?), a Beloit musician, educator, cultural leader, and administrator. She served as president of the Beloit Federation of Women's Clubs and of the Wisconsin Federation of Music Clubs from 1944 to 1948, founded the Wisconsin Composers League in 1946, served as vice-president of the National Music Council after 1955, and held various offices in the National Federation of Music Clubs, ultimately serving as president from 1955 to 1959. She was married to Ronald Arthur Dougan.

17,495. McLenegan, Annie S.
Papers. 1895-1962. 4 vols. and other items.
Access restricted. No guide.
Bartlett Memorial Historical Museum.
Papers of [Miss] McLenegan (1875-1962), a teacher in Wisconsin schools from 1900 to 1925, a writer, and an historian, include a family genealogy, photos, a scrapbook she compiled while an undergraduate at the University of Wisconsin at Madison in the late 1890s, clippings, and her works "The Harvey Play" and "Life in the Fox River Valley."

17,496. Neese, Mrs. Albert H., Sr.
Papers. 1940-67. 1 vol., 16 items, and other items.
Access restricted. No guide.
Bartlett Memorial Historical Museum.
[Mrs.] Laura Aldrich Neese (1889-1967), an artist, was a philanthropist and a businesswoman who served on the board of directors of her father's Beloit corporation. Photos of her art work; a scrapbook containing photos, invitations to gallery shows, and clippings; and an annotated biography about her career. Neese usually painted oil portraits and watercolor scenes.

17,497. Skavlem and Odegaarden Family
Papers. 1839-1976. 15 items.
Access restricted. No guide.
Bartlett Memorial Historical Museum.
Papers document the family history of the descendants of Halvor Gullikson Skavlem and his wife Bergit Olsdatter Skavlem, who in ca. 1840 were among the first Norwegian settlers in southern Wisconsin. Includes genealogies published in 1915, a passenger ship list, photos, and rosemaled artifacts. Among women family members represented in the papers are Birgit Skavlem, Gunhild Skavlem, and Vera Gilbertson.

17,498. Women of Beloit
Collection. 1850- . 15 cu.ft.
Access restricted. No guide.
Bartlett Memorial Historical Museum.
Personal papers and correspondence, biographies, photos, scrapbooks, pamphlets, and clippings contain information about the women's clubs in Beloit as well as about such well-known local residents as [Mrs.] Mary Bauchle, an historian and reporter; Minnie (McIntyre) Wallace, an historian and columnist; [Miss] Borghild Boe, director of Family Services; Katherine Van Akin Gates, a missionary; Helen (Brace) Emerson, curator of the local art museum; Mary, Edith, and Etta Bartlett, physicians; Laura (Aldrich) Neese, a painter and humanitarian; and Buelah Jackson Charmley, Wisconsin poet laureate in 1938. The three Bartlett sisters graduated from Hahnemann Medical College in Chicago; Etta Bartlett later married a man named Vaughn.

BENET LAKE

17,499. Holy Family Convent, Motherhouse
Records. Nd. No size given.
Access restricted. No guide.
Benedictine Sisters of Pontifical Jurisdiction, Holy Family Convent.
Files contain a history of the Convent.

EAU CLAIRE

17,500. Archives
Records. 1948- . 15 boxes and 3 cabinets.
Open. No guide.
Benedictine Sisters of Pontifical Jurisdiction, St. Bede Priory.
Founded in 1948 in Eau Claire, the order is engaged in teaching, pastoral ministry, care for the sick and aged, catechetical work, and liturgical functions. Financial records, correspondence, histories and yearly chronicles of the Priory and convents, school registers and yearbooks, photos, oral history tapes, scrapbooks, sketches of sisters, religious magazines, and other records. Includes records relating to purchase of a hospital at Durand, WI, in 1948 and the building of a new hospital in 1952. Members of the order operated the hospital until 1970.

17,501. King, Rose
Papers. Ca. 1900-14. 2 vols. and several items.
Open. Unpublished guide.
Chippewa Valley Museum.
King (1884-1967), daughter of German immigrants who came to the US after the Civil War, had a long career that extended from acting on mining camp stages to Broadway theaters. Photos concerning her life and scrapbooks containing theater programs and clippings.

17,502. Moffat, Betsy (Barland)
Papers. 1858-87. 1 portfolio.
Closed. Unpublished guide.
Chippewa Valley Museum.
Born in Scotland, Moffat (1807-88) emigrated to the US after her marriage in 1834 to George Moffat. She became a governess for the Griffith family at their Natchez, MS, plantation La Grange after her marriage ended in divorce. Correspondence includes letters from her relatives and friends, among them Martha Tudor and Cora Ford, whom she met in the South. For a time, Moffat taught Negroes on the Griffith plantation to read the Bible. She also helped found the Episcopal church in Eau Claire.

17,503. Affirmative Action Plan
Records. 1973-76. 1 box.
Access restricted. Published guide.
University of Wisconsin-Eau Claire, Area Research Center and University Archives.
Committee minutes, correspondence, reports, guidelines, drafts, alternative plans, and supplements describe the history and development of the Plan, which was established at the University in 1973. See *Guide to Archives and Manuscripts in the Chippewa Valley Museum, Eau Claire Public Library, and University of Wisconsin-Eau Claire Area Research Center and Archives* (Madison, WI: State Historical Society of Wisconsin, 1977).

17,504. American Association of University Women
Records. 1970-75. 1 folder.
Open. Published guide.
University of Wisconsin-Eau Claire, Area Research Center and University Archives.
Minutes, yearbooks, newsletters, and standards for women in higher education as prescribed by the AAUW on the Eau Claire campus. See *Guide to Archives and Manuscripts in the Chippewa Valley Museum, Eau Claire Public Library, and University of Wisconsin-Eau Claire Area Research Center and Archives* (Madison, WI: State Historical Society of Wisconsin, 1977).

17,505. Association of Wisconsin Normal School Faculty
Records. 1922-28. 1 folder.
Open. Published guide.
University of Wisconsin-Eau Claire, Area Research Center and University Archives.
Records of this teachers' organization include conference programs and a pamphlet. See *Guide to Archives and Manuscripts in the Chippewa Valley Museum, Eau Claire Public Library, and University of Wisconsin-Eau Claire Area Research Center and Archives* (Madison, WI: State Historical Society of Wisconsin, 1977).

17,506. Barker, Herbert C.
Papers. 1872-1912. 1 microfilm reel.
Open. Published guide.
University of Wisconsin-Eau Claire, Area Research Center and University Archives.
Papers of Barker (1872-1912), his wife Clara Barker, and his parents Charles P. and Agnes Barker contain correspondence and legal and financial records pertaining to family timber holdings in Wisconsin, some of which were owned in partnership with R. M. Forsman and Co. of Williamsport, PA. See *Guide to Archives and Manuscripts in the Chippewa Valley Museum, Eau Claire Public Library, and University of Wisconsin-Eau Claire Area Research Center and Archives* (Madison, WI: State Historical Society of Wisconsin, 1977).

17,507. Board of Regents Hearings on Minority/Disadvantaged Students
Records. 1976. 3 vols.
Open. Published guide.
University of Wisconsin-Eau Claire, Area Research Center and University Archives.
Transcripts and a summary of the hearings, which were held in Madison, Whitewater, Milwaukee's Lincoln High School, and the Milwaukee and Eau Claire campuses of the University of Wisconsin. The transcripts contain detailed testimony by minority women. See *Guide to Archives and Manuscripts in the Chippewa Valley Museum, Eau Claire Public Library, and University of Wisconsin-Eau Claire Area Research Center and Archives* (Madison, WI: State Historical Society of Wisconsin, 1977).

17,508. Cloverleaf School, Towns of Grant and Grow, School District No. 3, Rusk County
Records. 1916-58. 1 box.
Open. Published guide.
University of Wisconsin-Eau Claire, Area Research Center and University Archives.
Consists of School District records, clerk's records, School registers, teacher's reports, and treasurer's records. School district material consists of School board minutes, annual auditors' reports and clerk's annual financial statements, accounts of receipts and disbursements, clerk's tax levy reports, and a register of School officers, 1916-58. Clerk's records include annual reports and those of teachers and the principal, notices from the County superintendent, supervising teachers' reports, School censuses, and textbook inventories, 1947-58. Teachers' reports to the superintendent contain daily School program information, monthly reports on pupils' grades and attendance, final reports, plant and equipment statistics, textbook and visitors records, and names of District School officers, 1946-54. School registers show enrollment and attendance records of students, reports on work accomplished, reports to the board on School needs, School visitor records, and comments about individual pupils, 1948-58. Treasurer's book contains receipts and disbursements with date, amount, source or recipient, and fund information, 1940-58. See *Guide to Archives and Manuscripts in the Chippewa Valley Museum, Eau Claire Public Library, and University of Wisconsin-Eau Claire Area Research Center and Archives* (Madison, WI: State Historical Society of Wisconsin, 1977).

17,509. Commissioner of the Poor, City of Eau Claire
Records. 1911-17. 1 vol.
Access restricted. Published guide.
University of Wisconsin-Eau Claire, Area Research Center and University Archives.
Record book of 73 cases handled by the Commissioner contains such client information as name of party seeking assistance, occupation, residential history, and family circumstances. Also includes notes on investigations made and actions taken by the Commissioner. Most cases relate to poverty and illness; actions taken include provision for hospitalization and medical care, admission to the poor farm, provision of such temporary aid as groceries and fuel, and, most frequently, arrangement for transportation out of the city. The commissioner was responsible for determining the legal residence of each applicant in order to charge costs back to the proper local government. See *Guide to Archives and Manuscripts in the Chippewa Valley Museum, Eau Claire Public Library, and University of Wisconsin-Eau Claire Area Research Center and Archives* (Madison, WI: State Historical Society of Wisconsin, 1977).

17,510. County Nurse, Price County Department of Public Welfare
Records. 1919-49. 3 folders.
Open. Published guide.
University of Wisconsin-Eau Claire, Area Research Center and University Archives.
Monthly reports of the County Nurse, filed with the County clerk from 1919 to 1924 and from 1947 to 1949, relate to school and home medical inspections; casework, including aid in admission of inmates to state medical and psychiatric institutions, maternity aid, and bedside care; and talks, demonstrations, group instruction, exhibits, and other publicity activities of the Nurse. Statistics are provided on illnesses and defects discovered during routine examinations of schoolchildren and on the Nurse's office work and expenses. Also includes a County Nurse contract and the County clerk's quarterly reports to the state board of health regarding expenditures for public health purposes, 1947 and 1949. See *Guide to Archives and Manuscripts in the Chippewa Valley Museum, Eau Claire Public Library, and University of Wisconsin-Eau Claire Area Research Center and Archives* (Madison, WI: State Historical Society of Wisconsin, 1977).

17,511. County Nurse, Price County Department of Public Welfare
Records. 1920-24. 3 boxes.
Access restricted. Published guide and inventory.
University of Wisconsin-Eau Claire, Area Research Center and University Archives.
Case files of the County Nurse, a position established by the County board in 1918, and which became operational one year later. As prescribed by Wisconsin law in 1919, the Nurse acted as health consultant and examiner for public schools; assisted the poor and indigent; investigated juvenile delinquency, dependency, and neglect; prevented, reported, and helped control tuberculosis; and acted as health instructor and visiting nurse for the County. Each Nurse case file usually contains a case history, investigation notes, and correspondence bearing on the case. Most cases concerned tubercular patients, unwed mothers, and illegitimate, neglected, or abused children; others pertained to the Nurse's routine duties. In 1924 the County Nurse position was abolished, but it was reestablished some years later. See *Guide to Archives and Manuscripts in the Chippewa Valley Museum, Eau Claire Public Library, and University of Wisconsin-Eau Claire Area Research Center and Archives* (Madison, WI: State Historical Society of Wisconsin, 1977).

17,512. County Superintendent of Schools, Chippewa County
Records. 1919-61. 1 box.
Open. Published guide.
University of Wisconsin-Eau Claire, Area Research Center and University Archives.
Annual reports of the Superintendent to the state superintendent of public instruction provide the names of towns, villages, and cities in the County and the number of school age children and teachers employed; total enrollment; and types of schools in each local unit. Also includes the Superintendent's annual financial statement and statistical tables regarding enrollment and attendance by sex, grade, and type of school; teachers' salaries, tenure, and experience; students' transportation and tuition; school library and textbook holdings; handicapped children unable to attend school, 1919-37; and school facilities, equipment, and services. See *Guide to Archives and Manuscripts in the Chippewa Valley Museum, Eau Claire Public Library, and University of Wisconsin-Eau Claire Area Research Center and Archives* (Madison, WI: State Historical Society of Wisconsin, 1977).

17,513. Director, Eau Claire County Relief Group
Records. 1933-36. 2 boxes.
Open. Published guide.
University of Wisconsin-Eau Claire, Area Research Center and University Archives.
The County Relief Group served cities, villages, and towns in the Eau Claire region excluding the city of Eau Claire, which administered its own relief program through a public relief department. Correspondence, memoranda, statistical reports, and other material of various local governments, the Wisconsin Emergency Relief Administration, and other state and federal government agencies relate to unemployment relief, rural rehabilitation, work relief, Civilian Conservation Corps programs, the Wisconsin Transient Bureau, and other relief efforts. Records chiefly concern the administration of relief programs but include some information on poverty problems and other local conditions. Also contains items pertaining to Women's Work Programs during 1934 and resident schools for unemployed needy women. See *Guide to Archives and Manuscripts in the Chippewa Valley Museum, Eau Claire Public Library, and University of Wisconsin-Eau Claire Area Research Center and Archives* (Madison, WI: State Historical Society of Wisconsin, 1977).

17,514. Eau Claire Circuit Court
Records. Ca. 1876-1942. 204 record cartons.
Open. Published guide and index.
University of Wisconsin-Eau Claire, Area Research Center and University Archives.
Case files of the Court, established in 1857, consist of papers filed in civil and criminal cases and other Court proceedings. Contents of the files vary with the length and complexity of each case but may include a summons, complaint, answer, judgment, stipulations, attorney's motions and briefs, dispositions and transcripts of testimony, judge's orders and charges, jury verdicts, and records of appeal. Includes information about divorce and other legal actions in which women were involved. See *Guide to Archives and Manuscripts in the Chippewa Valley Museum, Eau Claire Public Library, and University of Wisconsin-Eau Claire Area Research Center and Archives* (Madison, WI: State Historical Society of Wisconsin, 1977).

17,515. Eau Claire City and County Health Department
Records. 1947-54. 2 cu.ft. and 2 folders.
Open. Published guide.
University of Wisconsin-Eau Claire, Area Research Center and University Archives.
Annual reports of the Health Department contain the names of board of health members, names of Department personnel and their respective

positions, budget and expenditure data, vital statistics, reports of communicable diseases, and information about tuberculosis control, maternal and child health, school health programs, dental and sanitation reports, and nursing services. See *Guide to Archives and Manuscripts in the Chippewa Valley Museum, Eau Claire Public Library, and University of Wisconsin-Eau Claire Area Research Center and Archives* (Madison, WI: State Historical Society of Wisconsin, 1977).

17,516. Eau Claire County Superintendent of Schools
Records. 1892-1903. 1 vol.
Open. Published guide.
University of Wisconsin-Eau Claire, Area Research Center and University Archives.
Letter book of Superintendents Anna Smith, who served from 1892 to 1893, and E. A. Cleasby, who served from 1899 to 1903, consists of reports; lists of books and prices; recommendations on school buildings; remarks on teachers' ability; correspondence with the state superintendent of schools, including letters on school district problems and policies; and general correspondence. Records are missing for the period 1894 to 1898. See *Guide to Archives and Manuscripts in the Chippewa Valley Museum, Eau Claire Public Library, and University of Wisconsin-Eau Claire Area Research Center and Archives* (Madison, WI: State Historical Society of Wisconsin, 1977).

17,517. Eau Claire Health Council
Records. 1924-37. 1 folder.
Open. Published guide.
University of Wisconsin-Eau Claire, Area Research Center and University Archives.
The Council, which existed between 1924 and 1937, was made up of Eau Claire County health officers. Minutes contain descriptions of reports presented and lectures given by state health officials as well as discussions of such problems as milk pasteurization and regulation and quarantines and diseases affecting the local area. Information about the county nurse, health care education, and school child health programs established by the Council is also included; such programs were frequently administered by women. See *Guide to Archives and Manuscripts in the Chippewa Valley Museum, Eau Claire Public Library, and University of Wisconsin-Eau Claire Area Research Center and Archives* (Madison, WI: State Historical Society of Wisconsin, 1977).

17,518. Episcopal Diocese of Eau Claire
Records. 1877-1949. 1 box.
Open. Published guide and inventory.
University of Wisconsin-Eau Claire, Area Research Center and University Archives.
Scattered records of the Diocese include a parish register and reports and letters from St. Luke's Mission of Neillsville, WI, and service record books from churches in Owen, Medford, Westboro, Mellen, Park Falls, Lugerville, and Prentice. See *Guide to Archives and Manuscripts in the Chippewa Valley Museum, Eau Claire Public Library, and University of Wisconsin-Eau Claire Area Research Center and Archives* (Madison, WI: State Historical Society of Wisconsin, 1977).

17,519. Ermatinger, James
Papers. 1833-1968. 1 folder.
Open. Published guide.
University of Wisconsin-Eau Claire, Area Research Center and University Archives.
Papers of Ermatinger (?-1866), a fur trader who founded Jim Falls, WI, relate in part to fur trading but principally pertain to his parents George and Caroline Ermatinger and his wife Charlotte (Cadott) Ermatinger. Also includes letters from Ralph Ermatinger to his aunt Annie Ermatinger, an interview conducted in 1968 with Annie Ermatinger concerning her grandfather, and a family genealogy. See *Guide to Archives and Manuscripts in the Chippewa Valley Museum, Eau Claire Public Library, and University of Wisconsin-Eau Claire Area Research Center and Archives* (Madison, WI: State Historical Society of Wisconsin, 1977).

17,520. Faculty Publications and Information File
Records. Nd. No size given.
Open. Published guide.
University of Wisconsin-Eau Claire, Area Research Center and University Archives.
File contains University faculty publications with accompanying pertinent information about individual faculty members. See *Guide to Archives and Manuscripts in the Chippewa Valley Museum, Eau Claire Public Library, and University of Wisconsin-Eau Claire Area Research Center and Archives* (Madison, WI: State Historical Society of Wisconsin, 1977).

17,521. Federal Emergency Relief Administration-National Youth Administration
Records. 1934-39. 2 boxes and 4 record cartons.
Closed. Published guide.
University of Wisconsin-Eau Claire, Area Research Center and University Archives.
Applications, correspondence, bulletins, and student records of this financial assistance program, which existed between 1934 and 1939. See *Guide to Archives and Manuscripts in the Chippewa Valley Museum, Eau Claire Public Library, and University of Wisconsin-Eau Claire Area Research Center and Archives* (Madison, WI: State Historical Society of Wisconsin, 1977).

17,522. Hansen School, Town of Montana, School District No. 5, Buffalo County
Records. 1923-55. 3 folders.
Open. Published guide.
University of Wisconsin-Eau Claire, Area Research Center and University Archives.
School records consist of a minute book, clerk's papers, and a School register. Minutes of annual and special District meetings pertain to such matters as election of officers, School finances and equipment, purchase of textbooks, length of term, auditing of books, transportation of pupils, and School consolidation. Clerk's papers contain annual reports, letters from the County superintendent, a consolidation order, auditing committee reports, applications for state aid for transportation, and School census reports, 1941-55. The School register provides each pupil's name, birth date, sex, class, scholarship and attendance records, and disposition at the end of each term. Also includes reports of work accomplished, textbooks used, and a daily School program, 1939-40. See *Guide to Archives and Manuscripts in the Chippewa Valley Museum, Eau Claire Public Library, and University of Wisconsin-Eau Claire Area Research Center and Archives* (Madison, WI: State Historical Society of Wisconsin, 1977).

17,523. Jack Pine School, Towns of Tilden and Woodmohr, Joint School District No. 5, Chippewa County
Records. 1928-48. 2 folders.
Open. Published guide.
University of Wisconsin-Eau Claire, Area Research Center and University Archives.
School records include District material, which contains minutes of annual and special District meetings and annual financial reports of receipts and expenditures, and a treasurer's journal of receipts and disbursements, which shows date, amount, and source or recipient information, 1941-48. Also contains a record of bank deposits. See *Guide to Archives and Manuscripts in the Chippewa Valley Museum, Eau Claire Public Library, and University of Wisconsin-Eau Claire Area Research Center and Archives* (Madison, WI: State Historical Society of Wisconsin, 1977).

17,524. League of Women Voters, Eau Claire
Records. 1960-63. Ca. 4 items and 44 pp.
Open. Published guide.
University of Wisconsin-Eau Claire, Area Research Center and University Archives.
Minutes, an agenda, a statement, a book review, and clippings of this LWV group relate to county government and the problems of urban expansion. See *Guide to Archives and Manuscripts in the Chippewa Valley Museum, Eau Claire Public Library, and University of Wisconsin-Eau Claire Area Research Center and Archives* (Madison, WI: State Historical Society of Wisconsin, 1977).

17,525. Ling School, Town of Sampson, School District No. 8, Chippewa County
Records. 1906-45. 3 vols.
Open. Published guide.
University of Wisconsin-Eau Claire, Area Research Center and University Archives.
Consists of such School District records as annual minutes and financial reports, clerk's annual statistical reports, treasurer's expenditures and bonds, teachers' contracts, and School censuses. School registration records from 1932 to 1937 show each teacher's name, dates of term, School visitors, and each pupil's name, age, classification, grades, and attendance record. See *Guide to Archives and Manuscripts in the Chippewa Valley Museum, Eau Claire Public Library, and University of Wisconsin-Eau Claire Area Research Center and Archives* (Madison, WI: State Historical Society of Wisconsin, 1977).

17,526. McDonald School, Town of Tilden, School District No. 2, Chippewa County
Records. 1897-1948. 2 boxes.
Open. Published guide.
University of Wisconsin-Eau Claire, Area Research Center and University Archives.
Consists of District clerk's records, School registers, clerks' records, and a treasurer's journal. District clerk's records contain School District and board minutes, annual financial reports and officer lists of the District board, order registers, reports of taxes voted, teachers' contracts, and School censuses, 1903-48. School registers show reports of work accomplished and of parents' meetings, a record of visitors at the School, daily programs, and pupils' names, ages, sex, and attendance record, 1917-38. Clerks' records include annual reports and those of the teachers, School censuses, teachers' contracts, pupils' physical exam records for 1917 to 1918, pupils' scholastic records from 1930 to 1938, and correspondence. Treasurer's journal of receipts and disbursements provide date, amount, source or recipient, and account information, 1897-1948. See *Guide to Archives and Manuscripts in the Chippewa Valley Museum, Eau Claire Public Library, and University of Wisconsin-Eau Claire Area Research Center and Archives* (Madison, WI: State Historical Society of Wisconsin, 1977).

17,527. Martinson, Martha
Papers. Nd. 7 pp.
Open. Published guide.
University of Wisconsin-Eau Claire, Area Research Center and University Archives.
Essay in which Martinson describes Porter's Mills, a lumbering community that flourished between 1873 and 1903 in Eau Claire County. See *Guide to Archives and Manuscripts in the Chippewa Valley Museum, Eau Claire Public Library, and University of Wisconsin-Eau Claire Area Research Center and Archives* (Madison, WI: State Historical Society of Wisconsin, 1977).

17,528. Midwives' and Physicians' Reports, Price County
Records. 1888-1903. 1 folder.
Open. Published guide.

University of Wisconsin-Eau Claire, Area Research Center and University Archives.
Reports filed with the County register of deeds, as required by a 1909 Wisconsin law, provide the name of each reporting midwife or physician, the date reports were made, the number of birth and death certificates issued to each midwife or physician during reporting periods, and the amount of the register's fee for said certificates. Includes an alphabetical index listing of the names of midwives and physicians. See *Guide to Archives and Manuscripts in the Chippewa Valley Museum, Eau Claire Public Library, and University of Wisconsin-Eau Claire Area Research Center and Archives* (Madison, WI: State Historical Society of Wisconsin, 1977).

17,529. Northwestern Wisconsin Schoolmasters Club
Records. 1921-68. 1 folder.
Open. Published guide.
University of Wisconsin-Eau Claire, Area Research Center and University Archives.
Minute books of this professional organization for men and women teachers, founded in 1920, contain financial statements and membership lists. See *Guide to Archives and Manuscripts in the Chippewa Valley Museum, Eau Claire Public Library, and University of Wisconsin-Eau Claire Area Research Center and Archives* (Madison, WI: State Historical Society of Wisconsin, 1977).

17,530. Oral History Collection
Oral History. 1960-76. No size given.
Access restricted. Published guide.
University of Wisconsin-Eau Claire, Area Research Center and University Archives.
Taped interviews with University staff and faculty, including women, document the history and development of the University. Also contains information about the Eau Claire area. See *Guide to Archives and Manuscripts in the Chippewa Valley Museum, Eau Claire Public Library, and University of Wisconsin-Eau Claire Area Research Center and Archives* (Madison, WI: State Historical Society of Wisconsin, 1977).

17,531. Peterson Grocery Store
Records. 1881-1920. 38 boxes.
Open. Published guide.
University of Wisconsin-Eau Claire, Area Research Center and University Archives.
Records of the Store, which existed in Eau Claire between 1881 and 1920, contain financial records, including invoices of wholesale purchases and daily customer orders; personal and business correspondence in Danish and English; and what were referred to as "poor orders," or grocery orders filled for the city's poor residents, 1897-1905 and 1909. See *Guide to Archives and Manuscripts in the Chippewa Valley Museum, Eau Claire Public Library, and University of Wisconsin-Eau Claire Area Research Center and Archives* (Madison, WI: State Historical Society of Wisconsin, 1977).

17,532. Photographs
Collection. 1870s-1972. Ca. 10,000 items.
Open. Published guide.
University of Wisconsin-Eau Claire, Area Research Center and University Archives.
Proofs, negatives, and a partial index of photos taken by the media development center at the University between 1960 and 1972 depict campus events, activities, and people connected with the University; also included are photos dating from the earliest days of the Eau Claire campus. Other photos in the collection show 1870s lumbering operations at Kennedy and Winter in northern Wisconsin and at Eau Claire. Also contains photos of homes, prominent citizens, and scenes in Eau Claire and Chippewa counties. See *Guide to Archives and Manuscripts in the Chippewa Valley Museum, Eau Claire Public Library, and University of Wisconsin-Eau Claire Area Research Center and Archives* (Madison, WI: State Historical Society of Wisconsin, 1977).

17,533. Pleasant Valley School, Town of Sampson, School District No. 12, Chippewa County
Records. 1914-41. 3 folders.
Open. Published guide.
University of Wisconsin-Eau Claire, Area Research Center and University Archives.
School records consist of District material, which contains annual minutes and financial statements, treasurer's expenditures, and teachers' contracts, 1914-29, and School registers, which provide each teacher's name, dates of term, reading circle reports, and each pupil's name, age, attendance record, grades, and classification, 1919-20 and 1933-41. See *Guide to Archives and Manuscripts in the Chippewa Valley Museum, Eau Claire Public Library, and University of Wisconsin-Eau Claire Area Research Center and Archives* (Madison, WI: State Historical Society of Wisconsin, 1977).

17,534. Public Assistance Expenditures, Price County Department of Public Welfare
Records. 1941-59. 1 box.
Open. Published guide.
University of Wisconsin-Eau Claire, Area Research Center and University Archives.
Monthly statements of expenditures include those for Aid to Dependent Children, Old Age Assistance, Aid to the Disabled, and Aid to the Blind. The statements were submitted to the State Department of Public Welfare, division of public assistance, to obtain state and federal reimbursement for portions of the expenditures. See *Guide to Archives and Manuscripts in the Chippewa Valley Museum, Eau Claire Public Library, and University of Wisconsin-Eau Claire Area Research Center and Archives* (Madison, WI: State Historical Society of Wisconsin, 1977).

17,535. Randall, Adin
Papers. 1880-1945. 1 folder.
Open. Published guide.
University of Wisconsin-Eau Claire, Area Research Center and University Archives.
Included in papers of the family of Randall, an Eau Claire businessman, are letters from a brother and sister serving in Europe during WWI, correspondence with Randall's great-aunt Celia Babcock and her guardian Katherine Boyles, and genealogical information. See *Guide to Archives and Manuscripts in the Chippewa Valley Museum, Eau Claire Public Library, and University of Wisconsin-Eau Claire Area Research Center and Archives* (Madison, WI: State Historical Society of Wisconsin, 1977).

17,536. Red Cross, Owen, WI
Records. 1918-45. 1 folder.
Open. Published guide.
University of Wisconsin-Eau Claire, Area Research Center and University Archives.
Minutes, financial records, and correspondence of the Owen branch of the American National Red Cross. See *Guide to Archives and Manuscripts in the Chippewa Valley Museum, Eau Claire Public Library, and University of Wisconsin-Eau Claire Area Research Center and Archives* (Madison, WI: State Historical Society of Wisconsin, 1977).

17,537. School Directory
Records. 1928-37. 1 folder.
Open. Published guide.
University of Wisconsin-Eau Claire, Area Research Center and University Archives.
Directory of the Clark County, WI, superintendent of schools provides names and addresses of school officers, dates, school district number and name, expiration date of officers' terms, teachers' names, addresses, monthly salaries, length of school term, and enrollment. For consolidated grade and high school teachers, the Directory lists the grades or subjects each instructor taught as well as his or her type of teaching certificate. See *Guide to Archives and Manuscripts in the Chippewa Valley Museum, Eau Claire Public Library, and University of Wisconsin-Eau Claire Area Research Center and Archives* (Madison, WI: State Historical Society of Wisconsin, 1977).

17,538. School District No. 1, Town of Glencoe, Buffalo County
Records. 1892-98. 1 folder.
Open. Published guide.
University of Wisconsin-Eau Claire, Area Research Center and University Archives.
Records, including statistical information, of the School District consist of clerks' annual reports, minutes of annual and special School board meetings, annual financial reports of the District board, treasurers' bonds, a statement of taxes voted, teachers' contracts and certificates, a register of orders drawn, and the School census. See *Guide to Archives and Manuscripts in the Chippewa Valley Museum, Eau Claire Public Library, and University of Wisconsin-Eau Claire Area Research Center and Archives* (Madison, WI: State Historical Society of Wisconsin, 1977).

17,539. School of Nursing
Records. 1961-71. 1 box.
Open. Published guide.
University of Wisconsin-Eau Claire, Area Research Center and University Archives.
Annual reports, accreditation committee minutes, program brochures, and building dedication material of the School, founded in 1961 at the University. See *Guide to Archives and Manuscripts in the Chippewa Valley Museum, Eau Claire Public Library, and University of Wisconsin-Eau Claire Area Research Center and Archives* (Madison, WI: State Historical Society of Wisconsin, 1977).

17,540. Shepherd, George F.
Papers. 1857-1901. 1 microfilm reel.
Open. Published guide.
University of Wisconsin-Eau Claire, Area Research Center and University Archives.
A Wisconsin immigrant farmer, Shepherd (1835-65) also served as a Union soldier in Company F of the 25th Wisconsin Infantry Volunteers. Civil War correspondence between Shepherd and his wife; letters from her family in Guernsey, England; legal records; and biographical data. See *Guide to Archives and Manuscripts in the Chippewa Valley Museum, Eau Claire Public Library, and University of Wisconsin-Eau Claire Area Research Center and Archives* (Madison, WI: State Historical Society of Wisconsin, 1977).

17,541. Student Organizations
Records. 1916-76. 2 boxes.
Open. Published guide.
University of Wisconsin-Eau Claire, Area Research Center and University Archives.
Minutes and other items of religious, social, special interest, and honorary University student groups. Includes the records of the YWCA and Sigma Gamma Zeta, a women's organization. See *Guide to Archives and Manuscripts in the Chippewa Valley Museum, Eau Claire Public Library, and University of Wisconsin-Eau Claire Area Research Center and Archives* (Madison, WI: State Historical Society of Wisconsin, 1977).

17,542. Superintendent of Schools, Eau Claire County
Records. 1905-64. 0.2 cu.ft. and 3 folders.
Open. Published guide.
University of Wisconsin-Eau Claire, Area Research Center and University Archives.
Annual reports of the Superintendent to the state superintendent provide the name of each town, village, or city; the number of children ages 4 to 19 years living in the district; the number of children

attending school; the number of districts in which schoolhouses are located in town; the number of reporting districts; the number of schools by type; the number of teachers employed; the total enrollment and number of boys and girls; the number of children from other counties; and the numerical breakdown of children by age. See *Guide to Archives and Manuscripts in the Chippewa Valley Museum, Eau Claire Public Library, and University of Wisconsin-Eau Claire Area Research Center and Archives* (Madison, WI: State Historical Society of Wisconsin, 1977).

17,543. Superintendent of Schools, Eau Claire County
Records. 1912-54. 2 folders.
Open. Published guide.
University of Wisconsin-Eau Claire, Area Research Center and University Archives.
Reports and miscellaneous items of the Superintendent include a 1937 annual report to the County board; expense statements and an auditor's report; a census of schoolchildren, tax valuations, and library fund reports of districts that include areas in counties adjoining Eau Claire County; town clerk's annual reports for Clear Creek and Brunswick, 1912; information on school district indebtedness for 1935, high school graduates by age in 1941, and the town of Augusta's claim for aid; and annual reports for 1951 and 1954 on handicapped children. See *Guide to Archives and Manuscripts in the Chippewa Valley Museum, Eau Claire Public Library, and University of Wisconsin-Eau Claire Area Research Center and Archives* (Madison, WI: State Historical Society of Wisconsin, 1977).

17,544. Taylor, Minnie Jones
Papers. Ca. 1940. 28 pp.
Open. Published guide.
University of Wisconsin-Eau Claire, Area Research Center and University Archives.
A history of Black River Falls, WI, to 1940 was written by Taylor (1863-1960) and re-edited in 1968 by Lawrence Jones. See *Guide to Archives and Manuscripts in the Chippewa Valley Museum, Eau Claire Public Library, and University of Wisconsin-Eau Claire Area Research Center and Archives* (Madison, WI: State Historical Society of Wisconsin, 1977).

17,545. Teachers' Certificate Stub Books
Records. 1908-39. 16 vols.
Open. Published guide.
University of Wisconsin-Eau Claire, Area Research Center and University Archives.
Stub books of the Clark County, WI, superintendent of schools provide issue date, number, grade, and expiration date of each teacher's certificate; the teacher's name, age, and address; examination grades and teacher's attendance records at institutes and professional teaching schools; and information about teaching experience. See *Guide to Archives and Manuscripts in the Chippewa Valley Museum, Eau Claire Public Library, and University of Wisconsin-Eau Claire Area Research Center and Archives* (Madison, WI: State Historical Society of Wisconsin, 1977).

17,546. Teachers' Reading Circle
Records. 1922-42. 2 vols.
Open. Published guide.
University of Wisconsin-Eau Claire, Area Research Center and University Archives.
Reading Circle records of the Clark County, WI, superintendent of schools indicate names of teachers in the Circle, date, books read, and awards received. See *Guide to Archives and Manuscripts in the Chippewa Valley Museum, Eau Claire Public Library, and University of Wisconsin-Eau Claire Area Research Center and Archives* (Madison, WI: State Historical Society of Wisconsin, 1977).

17,547. Tilden School, Town of Tilden, School District No. 3, Chippewa County
Records. 1886-1948. 2 folders.
Open. Published guide.
University of Wisconsin-Eau Claire, Area Research Center and University Archives.
School records consist of clerk's minutes and journal, which contain annual School District minutes as well as receipt and disbursement records, 1924-48, and a treasurer's journal of receipts and disbursements, which shows date, amount, source or recipient, and purpose of transaction, 1886-1948. See *Guide to Archives and Manuscripts in the Chippewa Valley Museum, Eau Claire Public Library, and University of Wisconsin-Eau Claire Area Research Center and Archives* (Madison, WI: State Historical Society of Wisconsin, 1977).

17,548. University History Research
Records. 1916-75. 12 boxes.
Open. Published guide.
University of Wisconsin-Eau Claire, Area Research Center and University Archives.
Research files include notes, rough drafts, and subject material used in the research and writing of the book *University of Wisconsin-Eau Claire: A History, 1916-1976* by Hilda Carter and John Jenswold. Also includes a typescript of the book, unpublished statistics and information for possible appendixes, and the complete book index. See *Guide to Archives and Manuscripts in the Chippewa Valley Museum, Eau Claire Public Library, and University of Wisconsin-Eau Claire Area Research Center and Archives* (Madison, WI: State Historical Society of Wisconsin, 1977).

17,549. University Scrapbooks
Collection. 1918-75. 28 vols.
Open. Published guide.
University of Wisconsin-Eau Claire, Area Research Center and University Archives.
Scrapbooks kept from 1918 to 1923 and from 1948 to 1975 contain clippings about University-related activities, people, and events. The clippings are taken primarily from Wisconsin newspapers. See *Guide to Archives and Manuscripts in the Chippewa Valley Museum, Eau Claire Public Library, and University of Wisconsin-Eau Claire Area Research Center and Archives* (Madison, WI: State Historical Society of Wisconsin, 1977).

17,550. Women of the Ku Klux Klan, Klan 14
Records. 1926-31. 1 folder.
Open. Published guide.
University of Wisconsin-Eau Claire, Area Research Center and University Archives.
Minutes of the Chippewa Falls, WI, chapter of Women of the Klan, financial reports, communications from the Wisconsin Realm office and from Imperial Headquarters, and other items. See *Guide to Archives and Manuscripts in the Chippewa Valley Museum, Eau Claire Public Library, and University of Wisconsin-Eau Claire Area Research Center and Archives* (Madison, WI: State Historical Society of Wisconsin, 1977).

GREEN BAY

17,551. Diocesan Council of Catholic Women
Records. 1924- . No size given.
Access restricted. No guide.
Catholic Diocese of Green Bay Archives.
The Council, a member of the National Council of Catholic Women, was incorporated in 1934 to unite Catholic women in a program of prayer, study, and apostolic work. Articles of incorporation; minutes of board meetings, conventions, institutes, and workshops; photos; and clippings.

17,552. Archives
Records. 1869- . 4 file drawers.
Access restricted. No guide.
Sisters of St. Francis of the Holy Cross, Convent.
This religious community of women was founded in 1881 in Bay Settlement, which is now Green Bay. Financial records, original statutes, correspondence, manuscript history of the order by a founder, photos, scrapbooks, clippings, and other records of the Convent. Includes material relating to the Shrine of Our Lady at Robinsonville, which has been operated by the sisters as a boarding school, a home for crippled children, a private high school, and, currently, a house of prayer.

HURLEY

17,553. Banér, Skulda Vanadis
Papers. 1900-64. 3 ft.
Open. No guide.
Gogebic-Iron Historical Museum.
Private and business correspondence; articles, stories, and books she wrote; book reviews; photos; gifts and mail from fans; and announcements for books by Banér (ca. 1898-1964), an author who was born and educated in Ironwood, MI. Her father Johann Gustaf R. Banér, a poet and newspaper publisher, encouraged her to become a writer. After graduation from college she taught school in North Dakota and worked as a dressmaker and photographer's apprentice, but she also wrote advertising copy for newspapers and radio. Over the years she wrote more than 50 magazine articles and a half-dozen books, including *Latchstring Out, Voice of the Lute,* and *Adventures of Pims;* she also wrote children's books and stories. Although Banér lost her sight in 1939 because of glaucoma, she continued her writing career.

KENOSHA

17,554. Archives of the Congregation
Records. 1910- . No size given.
Access restricted. Inventory.
Sienadale Motherhouse Archives.
This religious order of women, which was founded in Lisbon, Portugal, in 1866 to operate hospitals and schools, was established in the US in 1910 in Ontario, OR. Financial records, deeds, correspondence, diaries, spiritual notes, biography of the foundress, canonical and historical material, registers, photos, prayer books, rule books, and records of religious persecution of the sisters in Portugal in 1910.

17,555. Beth Israel Sinai Congregation Sisterhood
Records. 1920-ca. 1965. 1 folder.
Open. Published guide.
University of Wisconsin-Parkside, Archives and Area Research Center.
Script from a dramatic program of the Racine, WI, Sisterhood outlines the history of the group, with emphasis on the accomplishments during each Sisterhood president's term. See Nicholas C. Burckel, comp., *Guide to Archives and Manuscripts in the University of Wisconsin-Parkside Area Research Center* (Madison, WI: State Historical Society of Wisconsin, 1977).

17,556. Bristol Sewing Society
Records. 1858-64. 1 vol.
Open. Published guide.
University of Wisconsin-Parkside, Archives and Area Research Center.
Constitution, minutes, and financial accounts of the Society in Kenosha County, WI. See Nicholas C. Burckel, comp., *Guide to Archives and*

Manuscripts in the University of Wisconsin-Parkside Area Research Center (Madison, WI: State Historical Society of Wisconsin, 1977).

17,557. College of Racine
Records. Ca. 1935-74. 90 cartons.
Open. Published guide.
University of Wisconsin-Parkside, Archives and Area Research Center.
Records of the College, which was founded in 1946 as the Dominican College for women. The school became coeducational in 1955, and in 1962 it received full accreditation from the North Central Association. An independent nondenominational board assumed management of the College in 1968; two years later that body took over and moved the programs of Mount St. Paul College in Waukesha, WI, to the Racine campus. In 1972 the name Dominican College was changed to College of Racine, but financial problems forced the closing of the institution in 1974. See Nicholas C. Burckel, comp., *Guide to Archives and Manuscripts in the University of Wisconsin-Parkside Area Research Center* (Madison, WI: State Historical Society of Wisconsin, 1977).

17,558. Ela, Ida L.
Papers. 1903. 1 vol.
Open. Published guide.
University of Wisconsin-Parkside, Archives and Area Research Center.
Reminiscences of Ela (1855-1934) provide information about the settlement of Rochester in Racine County, WI. See Nicholas C. Burckel, comp., *Guide to Archives and Manuscripts in the University of Wisconsin-Parkside Area Research Center* (Madison, WI: State Historical Society of Wisconsin, 1977).

17,559. Ellinger, Flora
Papers. Nd. 20 cu.ft.
Open. Published guide.
University of Wisconsin-Parkside, Archives and Area Research Center.
Personal papers of Ellinger (1862-1966) and material regarding Ellinger family business interests in Milwaukee, Racine, and Chicago reflect her business, social, and political activities. See John Jacob, ed., *The Papers of Albert J. and Flora Hofmeister Ellinger, 1850-1976, A Guide to the Collection* (Madison: State Historical Society of Wisconsin, 1978).

17,560. Kemper Hall
Records. Ca. 1888-1975. 18 cartons and 5 bundles.
Closed. Published guide.
University of Wisconsin-Parkside, Archives and Area Research Center.
Administrative and departmental records of Kemper Hall, a private Episcopalian girls school in Kenosha, including records of the board of trustees, the headmaster's office, admissions, public relations, and the principal's office as well as financial records consisting of budgets, statements, financial reports, tax records, and daybooks. See Nicholas C. Burckel, comp., *Guide to Archives and Manuscripts in the University of Wisconsin-Parkside Area Research Center* (Madison, WI: State Historical Society of Wisconsin, 1977).

17,561. Knutson, Myrtle Bergman
Papers. 1924-27. 1 folder.
Open. Published guide.
University of Wisconsin-Parkside, Archives and Area Research Center.
Nursing school records of [Mrs.] Knutson (1906-), a registered nurse who graduated from the Kenosha Hospital Training School in 1927, show which courses she took and the grades she received. Also includes summaries of cases she observed and her medical history. See Nicholas C. Burckel, comp., *Guide to Archives and Manuscripts in the University of Wisconsin-Parkside Area Research Center* (Madison, WI: State Historical Society of Wisconsin, 1977).

17,562. Ladies Hearse Society of Wilmont
Records. 1874-1935. 1 folder.
Open. Published guide.
University of Wisconsin-Parkside, Archives and Area Research Center.
Also known as the Ladies' Benevolent Sewing Society, this group was organized in 1874 to purchase and maintain a hearse for rental by area residents. Constitution, minutes, and accounts for the period since 1908. See Nicholas C. Burckel, comp., *Guide to Archives and Manuscripts in the University of Wisconsin-Parkside Area Research Center* (Madison, WI: State Historical Society of Wisconsin, 1977).

17,563. Liberty Congregational Church Ladies Aid Society
Records. 1910-13. 1 vol.
Open. Published guide.
University of Wisconsin-Parkside, Archives and Area Research Center.
Minutes of this Trevor, WI, Society. See Nicholas C. Burckel, comp., *Guide to Archives and Manuscripts in the University of Wisconsin-Parkside Area Research Center* (Madison, WI: State Historical Society of Wisconsin, 1977).

17,564. McEachron, Edith
Papers. Nd. 11 pp.
Open. Published guide.
University of Wisconsin-Parkside, Archives and Area Research Center.
A history of the Tucker School, located in Mount Pleasant, Racine County, WI, school district no. 11, was written by McEachron (1883-). Also includes a description of early County roads. See Nicholas C. Burckel, comp., *Guide to Archives and Manuscripts in the University of Wisconsin-Parkside Area Research Center* (Madison, WI: State Historical Society of Wisconsin, 1977).

17,565. Malsch, Rose
Papers. 1947. 1 p.
Open. Published guide.
University of Wisconsin-Parkside, Archives and Area Research Center.
Speech given at the 50th anniversary dinner of the Racine Public Library consists of reminiscences of [Miss] Malsch, a longtime Library patron. See Nicholas C. Burckel, comp., *Guide to Archives and Manuscripts in the University of Wisconsin-Parkside Area Research Center* (Madison, WI: State Historical Society of Wisconsin, 1977).

17,566. Nelson, Florence B.
Papers. Nd. 30-page vol.
Open. Published guide.
University of Wisconsin-Parkside, Archives and Area Research Center.
A history of aviation in Kenosha was prepared by Nelson for the Kenosha County Historical Society. See Nicholas C. Burckel, comp., *Guide to Archives and Manuscripts in the University of Wisconsin-Parkside Area Research Center* (Madison, WI: State Historical Society of Wisconsin, 1977).

17,567. Police Women's Daily Report
Records. 1954-58. 1 box.
Open. Published guide.
University of Wisconsin-Parkside, Archives and Area Research Center.
Log of policewomen's activities and cases involving juveniles, child neglect and abuse, women, family problems, and welfare cases. See Nicholas C. Burckel, comp., *Guide to Archives and Manuscripts in the University of Wisconsin-Parkside Area Research Center* (Madison, WI: State Historical Society of Wisconsin, 1977).

17,568. Saint Luke's School of Nursing
Records. 1915-71. 1 box.
Open. Published guide.
University of Wisconsin-Parkside, Archives and Area Research Center.
Early alumnae association minutes of the School in Racine, WI, and scattered minutes of the training school committee, the nursing council, and the student government, 1915-55; applications to the School; completed questionnaires from 1932 describing facilities and operations; and a newsletter for 1971. See Nicholas C. Burckel, comp., *Guide to Archives and Manuscripts in the University of Wisconsin-Parkside Area Research Center* (Madison, WI: State Historical Society of Wisconsin, 1977).

17,569. Saint Mary's Hospital
Records. 1910-33. 1 folder.
Open. Published guide.
University of Wisconsin-Parkside, Archives and Area Research Center.
Reminiscences about Saint Mary's Hospital Training School for nurses in Racine, WI, private duty nursing regulations, and the constitution, bylaws, and minutes for 1933 of Saint Mary's Nurses Alumnae Association. See Nicholas C. Burckel, comp., *Guide to Archives and Manuscripts in the University of Wisconsin-Parkside Area Research Center* (Madison, WI: State Historical Society of Wisconsin, 1977).

17,570. Stevens Family
Papers. 1829-1911. 1 box.
Open. Published guide.
University of Wisconsin-Parkside, Archives and Area Research Center.
Originally from Broome, Schoharie County, NY, the Stevens family came to Wisconsin in 1844 and settled near Bristol, Kenosha County, sometime before the Civil War. Family correspondence, financial records, legal papers, a diary, teaching certificates, genealogies, and a literary publication. See Nicholas C. Burckel, comp., *Guide to Archives and Manuscripts in the University of Wisconsin-Parkside Area Research Center* (Madison, WI: State Historical Society of Wisconsin, 1977).

17,571. Woman's Christian Temperance Union
Records. 1874-79. 1 vol.
Open. Published guide.
University of Wisconsin-Parkside, Archives and Area Research Center.
Secretary's book of the Kenosha chapter of the WCTU contains a constitution, bylaws, minutes, a membership list, dues records, the national pledge adopted in 1877, and a national recommendation for organizing Young Ladies' Leagues. See Nicholas C. Burckel, comp., *Guide to Archives and Manuscripts in the University of Wisconsin-Parkside Area Research Center* (Madison, WI: State Historical Society of Wisconsin, 1977).

LA CROSSE

17,572. Archives
Records. 1849- . Ca. 19 tapes and other items.
Access restricted. Index.
Franciscan Sisters of Perpetual Adoration, St. Rose Convent.
The Convent was established in 1849. Minutes of the general council and of the general administrative board, 1898 to date; financial records; deeds and abstracts of Convent property;

correspondence of mothers general and others associated with the Convent; diaries relating to the Convent and to parishes and schools conducted by its members; tapes of general assemblies, 1969-76; tapes of interviews with sisters; tapes made by Sister Mileta Ludwig, the Convent's historian; folders on each sister, which contain autobiographies and information relating to family history and background; a motion picture relating to the various ministries and life of the order; dowry and inheritance records of each member; photos; scrapbooks; and obituaries of sisters.

17,573. Associated Women Students
Records. Ca. 1930-70. 3 Hollinger boxes.
Open. No guide.
University of Wisconsin-La Crosse, Area Research Center.
Minutes, accounts, and other records of this student organization at the University of Wisconsin at La Crosse, which encourages active and responsible participation in academic and social life on campus. The organization was founded in ca. 1930.

17,574. Comstock Family
Papers. 1780-1950. 10 Hollinger boxes.
Open. Unpublished guide.
University of Wisconsin-La Crosse, Area Research Center.
Correspondence, diaries, and financial records of the Comstock family, residents of Trempealeau County, WI, include the papers of physician Elizabeth Comstock (1875-1972), who lived in Arcadia, WI.

17,575. Oral History Project
Oral history. 1966- . 100 tape reels.
Open. No guide.
University of Wisconsin-La Crosse, Area Research Center.
Taped interviews, most of which are transcribed, with women who live in the La Crosse area. Contains reminiscences dating back to ca. 1880 regarding their occupations, families and personal lives, social activities, schools, local matters, and other subjects.

17,576. Photos
Collection. 1880s-1940s. Ca. 200 items.
Open. No guide.
University of Wisconsin-La Crosse, Area Research Center.
Photos of women of the La Crosse area include items showing women at work in factories and in shops, women in their homes, women enjoying recreational activities, costumes, farm scenes, portraits of children, and backyards and home interiors. The collection is part of the University of Wisconsin at La Crosse's 10,000-item photo collection depicting local and area history.

17,577. University of Wisconsin at La Crosse Campus Dames
Records. 1925- . 2 Hollinger boxes and 1 vol.
Open. Unpublished guide.
University of Wisconsin-La Crosse, Area Research Center.
Correspondence, scrapbooks, newsletters, and other records of this largely social, quasi-official campus organization of faculty members' wives. The Campus Dames first assembled in 1925.

LADYSMITH

17,578. Archives
Records. Ca. 1912- . Boxes, drawers, and 2 files.
Access restricted. No guide.
Servants of Mary, Our Lady of Sorrows Convent.
Founded in 1912 in Ladysmith, this order of religious women has been involved in teaching, nursing, and operating a home for care of the elderly. Minutes; financial records; correspondence, including that of bishops of dioceses where members of the order have worked; chronicles; photos; memorabilia; and spiritual books. Contains some material about the missions the sisters served and about the college and hospital they once owned and operated.

MADISON

17,579. Woman's Relief Corps: Department of Wisconsin
Records. 1884-1938. 10 Hollinger boxes.
Open. Unpublished guide.
G. A. R. Memorial Hall Museum.
Records of the WRC's Wisconsin office, established in 1884 as an auxiliary body to the state's Grand Army of the Republic organization, contain cashbooks, ledgers, Department convention delegate registers and lists, registers of Wisconsin delegates to national WRC conventions, general orders and circulars, state and local officers' lists, quarterly reports of local WRC units to the state Department, and printed ritual and rules booklets from the national WRC office.

17,580. Woman's Relief Corps: Wisconsin Local Units
Records. 1887-1946. 6 Hollinger boxes.
Open. Unpublished guide.
G. A. R. Memorial Hall Museum.
Charters, minutes, financial records, reports to Grand Army of the Republic post commanders, and membership rolls of 13 local WRC units in Wisconsin; each unit was an auxiliary to the local GAR post. The bulk of the collection covers the period from 1910 to 1940. The WRC in Wisconsin was established in 1884.

17,581. Addams, Jane
Papers. 1893-1935. 1 microfilm reel.
Open. Card catalog.
State Historical Society of Wisconsin.
Correspondence, lectures, addresses, and programs of [Miss] Addams (1860-1935), a Chicago settlement worker, were microfilmed from portions of the Cyrus H. McCormick Collection.

17,582. Advertising Women of New York
Records. 1912-55. 1 box and 35 vols.
Open. Published guide.
State Historical Society of Wisconsin.
A history of the Advertising Women of New York, a professional and service organization founded in 1912 in New York City; surveys of job opportunities from 1942 to 1955 for women in advertising; records of the AWNY's national defense work during WWII; scrapbooks concerning club activities through 1949; books prepared for submission for advertising awards; and AWNY publications. See Josephine L. Harper, ed., *Guide to the Manuscripts of the State Historical Society of Wisconsin, Supplement 2* (Madison, WI: State Historical Society of Wisconsin, 1966).

17,583. Allen, Pamela P.
Papers. 1967-73. 5 boxes and 2 tapes.
Partially restricted. Register.
State Historical Society of Wisconsin.
Correspondence, writings, seminar and class outlines, conference agenda, tapes, newsletters, and clippings of Allen (1943-), a writer, lecturer, author, and activist in the women's liberation movement who was among the founders of Radical Women of New York City, one of the early feminist groups of the 1960s. Correspondence includes discussion of such topics as the Jeannette Rankin Brigade and the Miss America Pageant demonstration in 1968 but also mentions more general concerns regarding feminist organizational structure, development of small groups, and objectives of radical feminism. Later correspondence relates to Allen's teaching activities and writings, International Woman's Day, coordination of a national radical women's conference, and feminist activity in the San Francisco area. Also contains her pamphlet *Free Space: A Perspective on the Small Group in Women's Liberation* and other items pertaining to Sudsofloppen, a small feminist group, as well as a manuscript of *The Reluctant Reformers: The Impact of Racism and American Social Reform Movements* by her husband Robert L. Allen. Pamela Allen was his research assistant and collaborator for the book, and she wrote the fifth chapter "Women Suffrage: Woman's Rights and White Supremacy." Also contains material about the Breakaway Conferences, 1970-71; seminars on women and racism she conducted for the San Francisco area YWCAs; the First National Radical Women's Conference; and Women, Inc. Access to all of Allen's correspondence and the Sudsofloppen material is restricted.

17,584. Allison, Isidore Johnson
Papers. 1855-63. 18 pp.
Open. Published guide.
State Historical Society of Wisconsin.
Two historical sketches by [Mrs. Duncan C.] Allison contain her recollections of border incidents in Kansas, one of which occurred in 1855 and the other in August 1863 following a Confederate raid led by William C. Quantrill. See Josephine L. Harper, ed., *Guide to the Manuscripts of the State Historical Society of Wisconsin, Supplement 2* (Madison, WI: State Historical Society of Wisconsin, 1966).

17,585. American Association of University Women
Records. 1923-53. 1 box and 8 vols.
Open. Card catalog and register.
State Historical Society of Wisconsin.
Ledger of the Madison chapter of the AAUW containing entries for cash received and disbursed, treasury credits, membership dues, and cash gifts; chronologically arranged scrapbooks concerning activities and programs; and publicity material from 1942 to 1945. The chapter was also known as the College Women's Club.

17,586. American Association of University Women, Wisconsin Division
Records. 1927-72. 23 boxes.
Open. Card catalog and register.
State Historical Society of Wisconsin.
Wisconsin branches of the Association of Collegiate Alumnae combined to form a state AAUW unit in 1921, the same year the AAUW became a nationwide organization. Correspondence, officers' and committee reports, subject files, scrapbooks, directories, newsletters, other documentation of Division and branch activities, and material regarding Ellen Clara Sabin, president of Milwaukee-Downer College and an active AAUW participant. Subject files include minutes of area workshops and state board meetings, historians' reports, legislative and miscellaneous conference reports, Division publications and handbooks, convention and conference programs, and other material documenting the organization's growth and influence. Bulk of the material dates from 1952 to 1972.

17,587. American Forest History Foundation
Oral history. 1955. 87 pp.
Open. Published guide.
State Historical Society of Wisconsin.
Transcripts of interviews with [Mrs.] Maud Carlgren, [Mrs.] Hope Garlick Mineau, Wirt Mineau, [Mrs.] Maggie Orr O'Neill, and Hugo Schlenk concerning early lumbering in northern Minnesota and Wisconsin, particularly in the St. Croix Valley. Interviews were conducted and edited by Helen McCann White for the American Forest History Foundation. See Josephine L.

Harper, ed., *Guide to the Manuscripts of the State Historical Society of Wisconsin, Supplement 2* (Madison, WI: State Historical Society of Wisconsin, 1966).

17,588. American Labor Education Service
Records. 1921-51. 78 boxes and 5 vols.
Open. Register.
State Historical Society of Wisconsin.
Correspondence, records, and files of early experiments in workers' education at the Bryn Mawr Summer School for Women Workers in Industry, its successor the Hudson Shore Labor School, the Vineyard Shore Workers School, the Barnard Summer School for Workers, the Affiliated School for Workers, and the National Committee for the Extension of Labor Education. The first of the projects, the Bryn Mawr Summer School, was founded in 1921 following a decision by M. Carey Thomas, former president of Bryn Mawr, to create an educational program for women in industry by welcoming them to buildings normally empty during the summer. The project received aid from the National Women's Trade Union League, workers in YWCA industrial departments, officers in state and federal agencies dealing with women in industry, and others. An administrative committee was formed with half of its members representing Bryn Mawr and half the women workers. Eighty students attended the opening session in 1921, while 100 women enrolled for eight-week sessions in later years. Under the direction of Hilda W. Smith, former dean of Bryn Mawr, the instructors were interested in the female workers' place in the community and wanted to help them understand and take a larger part in the economic and social life around them. Half of the women at the sessions were union members.

17,589. Anneke, Fritz, and Anneke, Mathilde Franziska (Giesler)
Papers. 1791-1884. 8 boxes and 2 vols.
Open. Published guide.
State Historical Society of Wisconsin.
Fritz Anneke (1818-72), an exiled leader of the Rhine Revolution and a foreign correspondent, and his wife Mathilde Anneke (1817-84), an author, editor, lecturer, educator, and suffragist, lived in Milwaukee after 1849. Correspondence, the bulk of which is in German script; manuscripts of articles, plays, poems, and addresses; and a two-volume sketch about the Annekes prepared from material in the collection by Henriette M. Heinzen in collaboration with their daughter [Mrs.] Hertha (Anneke) Sanne.

Fritz Anneke was associated with reform newspapers in several American cities; he worked as a foreign correspondent during an Italian war in 1859 and served as a colonel in the American Civil War. Mathilde Anneke wrote poems, dramas, and short articles; she also edited a revolutionary newspaper in Germany and a woman's rights newspaper in America during the 1850s. In addition to directing a girls school in Milwaukee for 18 years, she was a state and national pioneer in the equal suffrage movement.

Much of the material is the Annekes' correspondence about the affairs of their family and friends in America, their literary pursuits, the progress of the revolutionary movement, and world events. Includes letters from Susan B. Anthony, Elizabeth Cady Stanton, Elizabeth (Smith) Miller, other leaders of the equal suffrage movement, and Mary Booth, and ca. 400 letters from [Miss] Cecilie Kapp, daughter of a Zurich professor who accompanied Mathilde Anneke to the US in 1865. Kapp founded the Milwaukee girls school that Mathilde Anneke directed but left to begin a long career as a professor of German at Vassar College. Booth's letters were written from 1863 to 1865 during trips to Europe and after her return to New York. Part of the collection is available on microfilm. See Alice E. Smith, ed., *Guide to the Manuscripts of the Wisconsin Historical Society* (Madison, WI: State Historical Society of Wisconsin, 1944).

17,590. Attic Angel Association
Records. 1898-1960. 4 boxes.
Open. Register.
State Historical Society of Wisconsin.
Founded in ca. 1889 in Madison, the Association was a philanthropic organization of young unmarried women who were admitted only through invitation and who were required to resign when they married; in 1912 an auxiliary of married women was formed, but later constitutional amendments provided for the inclusion of married women into the primary group. Annual reports, minutes, secretaries' files, treasurers' and other financial reports, short histories of the Association, membership lists, and scrapbooks and other material relating to the group's activities. The Association, which admitted only a few members at a time, made layettes for poor families and provided Christmas parties and toys for poor children. One of the women's first major projects was to raise $1000 for construction of Madison General Hospital. The Association then decided to limit the breadth of its activities. In 1908 the group decided to sponsor Madison's first visiting nurse, a project that became the Association's main concern for the next 40 years. The Association had expanded to employ three visiting nurses by 1926 when it was advised to incorporate as a non-stock corporation. The Visiting Nurse Service was incorporated separately in 1950. The Attic Angels also were active in public health projects and helped to sponsor child health centers and chest clinics. The Attic Angel Nursing Home was opened in 1953.

17,591. Bailey, Louise
Papers. 1893-1950. 42 vols.
Open. Published guide.
State Historical Society of Wisconsin.
Diaries of Bailey (1869-?), a resident of Prairie du Sac, WI, primarily concern her life as a student from 1898 to 1900 at Whitewater Normal School and her long career as a schoolteacher in Wisconsin and Minnesota. Part of the collection is available on microfilm. See Josephine L. Harper, ed., *Guide to the Manuscripts of the State Historical Society of Wisconsin, Supplement 2* (Madison, WI: State Historical Society of Wisconsin, 1966).

17,592. Bailey, Lucy Antoinette (Crippen)
Papers. 1895-1931. 1 microfilm reel.
Open. Published guide.
State Historical Society of Wisconsin.
Reminiscences of [Mrs. James Monroe] Bailey (1834-1931) of Prescott, WI, include a description of her family's trip in 1842 from Saratoga County, NY, to Rock County, WI. Collection also contains biographical and genealogical data. See Josephine L. Harper, ed., *Guide to the Manuscripts of the State Historical Society of Wisconsin, Supplement 2* (Madison, WI: State Historical Society of Wisconsin, 1966).

17,593. Baird, Henry Samuel
Papers. 1798-1937. 6 boxes.
Open. Register.
State Historical Society of Wisconsin.
Personal and business correspondence and financial records, scrapbooks, clippings, and other papers of Baird (1800-75), a Green Bay, WI, attorney and territorial political figure, and his wife Elizabeth Thérèse (Fisher) Baird (1810-90), who was of Indian ancestry. Includes letters the two exchanged before their marriage in 1824; letters by Elizabeth Baird, frequently written in French, which depict frontier life in Green Bay and other Wisconsin communities; and a series of reminiscences she wrote in 1886 and 1887 for the *Green Bay State Gazette.* Also includes papers of Louise Baird Favill, Therese S. Favill, and Anna Tenney. Elizabeth Baird served as an interpreter for her husband's French clients and helped him through her knowledge of the area. The Bairds had four children. See Josephine L. Harper and Sharon C. Smith, eds., *Guide to the Manuscripts of the State Historical Society of Wisconsin, Supplement 1* (Madison, WI: State Historical Society of Wisconsin, 1957).

17,594. Baldwin, William Henry
Papers. 1922-65. 16 boxes, 9 vols., 2 charts, and 1 package.
Open. Published guide.
State Historical Society of Wisconsin.
Baldwin (1891-) was a public relations specialist who dealt with such organizations as the American Museum of Immigration and the Youth Consultation Service. Correspondence, financial statements, client reports, programs, and other items related to Baldwin's business comprise about half of the collection. Other papers include a folder of correspondence of Baldwin's mother Ruth Standish (Bowles) Baldwin, principally with the staff of the Highlander Folk School in Monteagle, TN; William Baldwin's correspondence with his cousin Chester B. Bowles about the Springfield, MA, *Republican,* a Bowles-Baldwin family business; reminiscences of Fannie Baldwin; a Baldwin family genealogy; and speeches, articles, and other writings. See Josephine L. Harper, ed., *Guide to the Manuscripts of the State Historical Society of Wisconsin, Supplement 2* (Madison, WI: State Historical Society of Wisconsin, 1966).

17,595. Barstow, Helen Augusta
Papers. 1851-56. 1 vol.
Open. Published guide.
State Historical Society of Wisconsin.
Diary entries by Barstow (1831-1924), niece of Governor William A. Barstow, principally concern domestic, social, and local events in Waukesha, WI. Barstow later married Frank Whitney. Taken from Josephine L. Harper and Sharon C. Smith, eds., *Guide to the Manuscripts of the State Historical Society of Wisconsin, Supplement 1* (Madison, WI: State Historical Society of Wisconsin, 1957).

17,596. Barton, Clara
Papers. 1901-17. 6 items.
Open. Published guide.
State Historical Society of Wisconsin.
Letters from [Miss] Barton (1821-1912), a nurse and founder of the American National Red Cross, to Imogene S. Pierce concerning the Red Cross's development; letters concerning the proposed establishment of a Barton memorial; and a biographical sketch of Barton. Taken from Josephine L. Harper and Sharon C. Smith, eds., *Guide to the Manuscripts of the State Historical Society of Wisconsin, Supplement 1* (Madison, WI: State Historical Society of Wisconsin, 1957).

17,597. Bearings for Re-Establishment, Inc.
Records. 1966-73. 1 box, 24 cartons, and 2 tapes.
Partially closed. Inventory.
State Historical Society of Wisconsin.
Established in 1966 to assist Catholic priests and others from religious professions who wished to return to secular life, Bearings opened offices throughout the US to counsel individuals about job prospects; it also offered other types of personal assistance according to the needs of each applicant. From 15 to 30 percent of the clientele were Protestant ministers and Jewish rabbis. The bulk of the collection consists of client files from the Bearings New York office, but also contained are minutes, including those of the board of directors; financial records; correspondence; newsletters; and clippings. In 1970 the group incorporated Opportunities for Professional Transition to handle its employment and placement service without offering other forms of personal assistance to clients. Bearings continued to operate until 1974.

17,598. Beckman, Ann
Papers. 1972-73. 3 in.
Open. Catalog card.
State Historical Society of Wisconsin.
Correspondence, notes, reports and summaries, legal opinion, news release, and clippings of Beckman, a reporter for the Madison *Capital Times,* focus on the issue of whether women can change or retain their own surname after marriage. Includes printed summaries of Wisconsin laws that include differing provisions for men and women.

17,599. Belfrage, Sally
Papers. 1962-66. 2 microfilm reels.
Open. Register and card catalog.
State Historical Society of Wisconsin.
Belfrage (1936-) is an author and former civil rights worker who participated in Mississippi summer projects aimed at improving the status of the state's blacks. Manuscript and manuscript index of her book *Freedom Summer,* her diary and notes concerning experiences in Mississippi in 1964, voter registration reports and lists, a transcript of a 1966 radio program "This Little Light," location file for activities in Mississippi, and miscellaneous newsletters and ephemera of the Council of Federated Organizations and the Student Non-Violent Coordinating Committee. The Mississippi summer projects sought to help Mississippi blacks through voter registration, six-week freedom schools, operation of community center programs, and research in the state's law. Belfrage resumed her original name after using the name Sally Belfrage Pomerance for a time.

17,600. Bernard, Jacqueline
Papers. 1964-67. 1 box.
Open. Register and card catalog.
State Historical Society of Wisconsin.
[Mrs.] Bernard was a New York City resident who actively supported the civil rights movement in Clay County, MS. Correspondence and miscellaneous material, including minutes of a 1965 meeting of the Poor People's Corporation, reports, press releases, a brochure, and clippings. Includes letters from Bernard's son Joel, who worked for the Council of Federated Organizations in community-organizing activities in Clay County; his widely circulated letters contain descriptions of conditions in Mississippi and requests for financial assistance. Also includes letters from Clay County civil rights workers, from black Clay County residents, and from northern families who supported the movement. A letter by COFO volunteer Nancy Myron concerns white workers' reactions to efforts of the Student Non-Violent Coordinating Committee to build a black leadership organization.

Jacqueline Bernard supported a program in which northerners adopted a Clay County family and provided them with clothing and other necessities. Working for her local Democratic party organization in 1966, she chaired a "Blocks for Freedom" campaign that raised funds for cement blocks for a fireproof building for Clay County's Una Sweing Co-op.

17,601. Billings, Sara
Papers. 1864. 3 items.
Open. Published guide.
State Historical Society of Wisconsin.
Letters that Billings, a resident of Woodlawn, wrote to her brother Levi, a Civil War soldier, about life in Wisconsin during the War. See Josephine L. Harper, ed., *Guide to the Manuscripts of the State Historical Society of Wisconsin, Supplement 2* (Madison, WI: State Historical Society of Wisconsin, 1966).

17,602. Blaine, Anita (McCormick)
Papers. 1828-1958. 1117 boxes and 59 vols.
Access restricted. Published guide.
State Historical Society of Wisconsin.
The daughter of Cyrus Hall McCormick and Nettie Fowler McCormick, Blaine (1866-1954) was a philanthropist who was interested in education, improved social and economic conditions, international understanding, and world peace. Composed of five series, Blaine's collection includes personal letters, diaries, memoranda, speeches, writings, essays, poems, checkbook stubs, minutes, photos, and pamphlets; material relating to the operation of her household and office; and clippings concerning her public and private life. See Margaret R. Hafstad, ed., *Guide to the McCormick Collection of the State Historical Society of Wisconsin* (Madison, WI: State Historical Society of Wisconsin, 1973).

17,603. Blair, Emma Helen
Papers. 1809-1910. 1 box and 1 vol.
Open. Published guide.
State Historical Society of Wisconsin.
Principally personal and family correspondence of Blair (1851-1911), librarian at the State Historical Society of Wisconsin. Also includes a few records of the Milwaukee YWCA and other social service organizations. Her personal correspondence relates chiefly to her work at the Historical Society. See Alice E. Smith, ed., *Guide to the Manuscripts of the Wisconsin Historical Society* (Madison, WI: State Historical Society of Wisconsin, 1944).

17,604. Blanton, Margaret Gray
Papers. 1845-1972. 13 boxes, 1 tape, and 1 package.
Partially restricted. Inventory.
State Historical Society of Wisconsin.
Blanton (1887-1973), the wife of psychiatrist Smiley Jordan Blanton, was an author whose works included the biography *Bernadette of Lourdes* (1939) and a novel *The White Unicorn* (1961). Correspondence, diaries, biographical material, writings, genealogical notes and documents, and other items. Includes correspondence of the Blantons and of Margaret Blanton with other relatives. She studied speech and child psychology and, with her husband, wrote *Speech Training for Children* (1919), *Child Guidance* (1927), *Emotional Life of Children* (1934), and *For Stutterers* (1936).

17,605. Bliss Family
Papers. 1867-88. 10 vols.
Open. Published guide.
State Historical Society of Wisconsin.
Diaries kept by Bell Rundlett Bliss, her husband M. N. Bliss, and their daughter Ida, who lived in the Wisconsin towns of Janesville, Baraboo, and Madison. M. N. Bliss recorded his daily trips as a railroad engineer; Bell Bliss described her household tasks and activities in her hometown; and Ida wrote about her school and social life. Taken from Josephine L. Harper and Sharon C. Smith, eds., *Guide to the Manuscripts of the State Historical Society of Wisconsin, Supplement 1* (Madison, WI: State Historical Society of Wisconsin, 1957).

17,606. Bohn, Belle C.
Papers. 1944. 13 pp.
Open. Published guide.
State Historical Society of Wisconsin.
Recollections of [Mrs.] Bohn (1857-1948) include descriptions of her early days in Sauk County, WI, of teaching school, and of the hop crash in 1868 and its disastrous effects on the financial status of farmers. Bohn's account also reflects the life of the wife of a village postmaster and storekeeper. Taken from Josephine L. Harper and Sharon C. Smith, eds., *Guide to the Manuscripts of the State Historical Society of Wisconsin, Supplement 1* (Madison, WI: State Historical Society of Wisconsin, 1957).

17,607. Booth, Sherman M.
Papers. 1818-1908. 8 boxes and 1 microfilm reel.
Open. Published guide.
State Historical Society of Wisconsin.
Letters and other papers of Booth (1812-1904), an abolitionist, politician, lecturer, publisher, businessman, and government clerk, primarily consist of material relating to the family of his second wife Mary Humphrey (Corss) Booth. See Josephine L. Harper, ed., *Guide to the Manuscripts of the State Historical Society of Wisconsin, Supplement 2* (Madison, WI: State Historical Society of Wisconsin, 1966).

17,608. Braden, Carl, and Braden, Anne Gambrell (McCarty)
Papers. 1928-72. 17 ft., 97 boxes, 5 microfilm reels, 88 tapes, 2 recording discs, and 1 motion picture.
Access restricted. Register.
State Historical Society of Wisconsin.
Personal files of Carl Braden (1914-75) and Anne Braden (1924-), journalists and activists in campaigns for civil rights and civil liberties, and records of the Southern Conference Educational Fund (SCEF), the Southern Conference for Human Welfare, the Appalachian Economic and Political Action Conference, and the southern office of the National Committee to Abolish the House Un-American Activities Committee. Included are minutes, correspondence, speeches, press releases, newsletters, and other items as well as records of SCEF director James Dombrowski. For 15 years the Bradens worked as field organizers and then as executive directors of SCEF, a group that built white support for the antidiscrimination movement. They also opposed the war in Vietnam and organized the Southern Mountain Project to assist residents of Appalachia.

Born in Louisville, Anne McCarty moved with her family to Mississippi and to Anniston, AL, where she attended public schools. She graduated from Randolph-Macon Woman's College in Lynchburg, VA, in 1945 and returned to Alabama where she worked as a reporter in Anniston and Birmingham. She became education editor of the Louisville *Times* in 1947 and in 1948 married Carl Braden, a *Times* staff member. Anne Braden was jailed in Jackson, MS, in 1951 after she led a group of white women to the state governor's office to protest the execution of a black man charged with rape. In 1954 the Bradens were indicted on sedition charges in Louisville after a house they bought and then sold to Andrew Wade IV, a black man, was bombed. Charges against Anne Braden were dropped; her *The Wall Between* grew out of the Bradens' experiences in the Wade case. The Bradens became field organizers for the New Orleans-based SCEF in 1957; they edited the SCEF newspaper *The Southern Patriot* and from 1966 to 1972 served as the group's executive directors. In 1961 Anne Braden joined the Emergency Civil Liberties Committee and the National Committee to Abolish the House Un-American Activities Committee after her husband was cited for contempt of Congress for refusing to answer questions about the civil rights movement. He served nine months in prison in connection with the charges. Anne Braden's booklet "House Un-American Activities Committee: Bulwark of Segregation" was published in 1964. The Bradens were arrested in 1967 in eastern Kentucky, again on sedition charges, in connection with their Southern Mountain Project work.

17,609. Buck, Harriet D.
Papers. 1889-99. 40 pp.
Open. Published guide.
State Historical Society of Wisconsin.
Buck (1823-99?) was a pioneer in Washington County, WI. Reminiscences written in 1896 about experiences in Washington County in 1845, a diary for the summer of 1899, and a group of poems and prayers. See Josephine L. Harper, ed., *Guide to the Manuscripts of the State Historical Society of*

Wisconsin, Supplement 2 (Madison, WI: State Historical Society of Wisconsin, 1966).

17,610. Buck, Pearl (Sydenstricker)
Papers. 1951. 1 item.
Open. Published guide.
State Historical Society of Wisconsin.
Letter in which Buck (1892-1973), an author, stresses the dangers of universal military training for the US and urges support for the Women's International League for Peace and Freedom. Taken from Josephine L. Harper and Sharon C. Smith, eds., *Guide to the Manuscripts of the State Historical Society of Wisconsin, Supplement 1* (Madison, WI: State Historical Society of Wisconsin, 1957).

17,611. Business and Professional Women's Club
Records. 1919-57. 7 boxes and 5 vols.
Open. Published guide.
State Historical Society of Wisconsin.
Reports of the president and of committee chairmen, minutes, a nearly complete set of treasurers' reports, scrapbooks, yearbooks, and other material related to the history and activities of the Madison branch of this women's service organization. See Josephine L. Harper, ed., *Guide to the Manuscripts of the State Historical Society of Wisconsin, Supplement 2* (Madison, WI: State Historical Society of Wisconsin, 1966).

17,612. Catt, Carrie Chapman
Papers. 1911-12. 1 box.
Open. Published guide.
State Historical Society of Wisconsin.
Diaries that [Mrs. George William] Catt (1859-1947), a leader in the woman suffrage movement, kept during a trip around the world contain lengthy entries about her travels in Palestine, South Africa, Ceylon, India, the East Indies, China, Korea, and Japan. See Josephine L. Harper, ed., *Guide to the Manuscripts of the State Historical Society of Wisconsin, Supplement 2* (Madison, WI: State Historical Society of Wisconsin, 1966).

17,613. Chandler, Sarah Ann Quarles
Papers. 1836. 13-page item.
Open. Published guide.
State Historical Society of Wisconsin.
Diary of an autumn trip that [Mrs.] Chandler, a southern matron, made from Virginia to St. Louis, by way of Tennessee, Kentucky, Indiana, and Illinois. Includes her often critical comments about Western residents, settlements, and roads. See Alice E. Smith, ed., *Guide to the Manuscripts of the Wisconsin Historical Society* (Madison, WI: State Historical Society of Wisconsin, 1944).

17,614. Chapelle, Dickey
Papers. 1933-68. 20 boxes, 1 vol., and 5 tapes.
Open. Register.
State Historical Society of Wisconsin.
Correspondence, drafts for books, notebooks, resource files, biographical information, and articles of Chapelle (1918-65), a journalist killed by a mine explosion while working as a war correspondent in Vietnam. Born in Shorewood, a Milwaukee suburb, Georgette L. "Dickey" Meyer married photographer Tony Chapelle in 1940. She got a job as a war correspondent and traveled with him to the South Pacific where she went ashore with the marines on Okinawa and on Iwo Jima. She divorced Chapelle in 1956 and worked as a free-lance writer-photographer in Algeria, Hungary, Lebanon, and Cuba. She also worked as a free-lance writer for *Saturday Evening Post, Reader's Digest, National Geographic, Look,* and other magazines. Chapelle wrote several books, including an autobiography for which she received the George Polk Memorial Award in 1962. In addition to her free-lance and literary work, Chapelle served as a public relations consultant for the National Research Institute, a business advisory service in New York, and as an associate editor of *Seventeen* from 1945 to 1947. She was killed while reporting on marine operations near Chu Lai Air Base; she was the first newswoman and the fourth member of the American press corps killed during the Vietnam conflict.

17,615. Chynoweth, Edna E. Phillips
Papers. 1940. 5-page item.
Open. Published guide.
State Historical Society of Wisconsin.
Recollections of [Mrs.] Chynoweth (1852-1950) about student life during the late 1860s at the University of Wisconsin, then under the direction of President Paul Chadbourne. Taken from Josephine L. Harper and Sharon C. Smith, eds., *Guide to the Manuscripts of the State Historical Society of Wisconsin, Supplement 1* (Madison, WI: State Historical Society of Wisconsin, 1957).

17,616. Colby, Clara Dorothy (Bewick)
Papers. 1861-1957. 3 boxes.
Open. Register.
State Historical Society of Wisconsin.
Founder and editor from 1883 to 1909 of *The Woman's Tribune,* [Mrs. Leonard Wright] Colby (1846-1916) was president of the Nebraska Women's Suffrage Association for 16 years. Correspondence, a diary outlining her California lecture tour of 1909, lectures, writings, biographical material, and items regarding the Federal Suffrage Association and other women's groups. Her correspondents include Susan B. Anthony, May Wright Sewall, Carrie Chapman Catt, Olive Logan, Harriet (Taylor) Upton, the National American Woman Suffrage Association, the International Woman Suffrage Alliance, the International Council of Women, the Women's Freedom League, and various state and national legislators. Colby's *Tribune* was the recognized organ of the National Woman Suffrage Association from 1886 to 1889. Interested in religion and philosophy, she wrote and spoke on the spiritual basis of the woman's movement. She was an officer of the Federal Suffrage Association, a delegate to the International Congress of Women in London in 1899, and a participant in the Panama Pacific Exposition in San Francisco in 1915. Biographical information is contained in anecdotes written in 1957 by her niece Mary Bewick Matthes. Colby's writings include an unpublished manuscript "London: Past and Present" and material about the suffrage movement in England, Florence Nightingale, Emmeline Pethick-Lawrence, Margaret Fuller, women in war, women in literature, and other subjects.

17,617. Committee to Secure Justice for Morton Sobell
Records. 1946-69. 62 boxes, 28 microfilm reels, 85 tapes, 3 disc recordings, and 9 motion pictures.
Open. Published guide and register.
State Historical Society of Wisconsin.
Established in 1951 to secure clemency for Ethel and Julius Rosenberg, who were convicted of atomic espionage and eventually executed, the Committee later turned its attention to the related case of Morton Sobell and began to work for Sobell's transfer from Alcatraz prison. The national Committee, located in New York City, and numerous city and state groups publicized Sobell's case and raised money for his legal fees and other expenses. Payroll books, a 1953 audit of the national Committee, and other financial records; legal records relating to all aspects of the Rosenberg and Sobell cases; correspondence of Sobell and his wife Helen Sobell, who answered a large portion of the Committee's mail personally and was involved in fund raising, publicity, and legal actions taken in the case; circulars and statements; clippings; publications produced and distributed by the Committee regarding the Rosenberg and Sobell cases; and tapes, disc recordings, and films that include radio and television interviews with Helen Sobell and other Committee members, panel discussions, rallies and fund-raising events, and documentaries about the Rosenberg and Sobell cases. The Sobell correspondence includes letters exchanged between Morton and Helen Sobell; letters to their parents and their children; Helen Sobell's correspondence with lawyers, clergymen, writers, journalists, and others to win support for her husband's release and vindication; and Morton Sobell's correspondence with lawyers, scholarly journals, and various institutions. Collection is available on microfilm. See Susan Davis Sharlin, ed., *Guide to the Records of The Committee to Secure Justice for Morton Sobell* (Madison: State Historical Society of Wisconsin, 1976).

17,618. Comstock, Elizabeth
Papers. 1779-1970. 14 boxes.
Open. Catalog card.
State Historical Society of Wisconsin.
A physician who returned to her hometown of Arcadia, WI, in 1923 to begin a general practice, Comstock (1875-1972) received her medical degree from Women's Medical College of Pennsylvania, interned at the College's Maternity Hospital in 1901 and 1902, and studied and worked at the New York Infirmary from 1902 until 1923. Correspondence, diaries, daybooks, memoranda books, writings, financial receipts and records, scrapbooks, professional certificates, clippings, and classwork and records regarding her medical degree. Also contains papers of her father Noah D. Comstock (1832-90) and other relatives. From 1903 to 1907 Elizabeth Comstock did clinical work at the New York Infirmary assisting doctor Augusta Vedin; from 1907 to 1911 she assisted physician Marie Chard in the Infirmary's surgical clinic; and from 1907 until her return to Wisconsin, she was chief of the Infirmary's Tuesday, Thursday, and Saturday gynecology clinic.

17,619. Concilio Mujeres
Records. 1966-75. 4 boxes.
Access restricted. Register.
State Historical Society of Wisconsin.
Formed in 1970 by a group of Spanish-speaking women attending San Francisco State College, Concilio Mujeres is a task force that encourages Raza women, or women of mixed Spanish and Indian ancestry, to enter nontraditional professions and higher levels of education; it also provides psychological and sociological support for Raza women. Correspondence with community action groups in the San Francisco area about services provided by Concilio Mujeres, address lists, clippings about Mexican-Americans, and drafts and publications of the organization, including *La Razon Mestiza* and *La Razon Mestiza II,* a news magazine published for International Women's Year.

Also contains the papers of Dorinda Moreno, one of the founders of Concilio Mujeres, who edited and published *La Razon Mestiza II,* produced seven public service television programs entitled "Pa 'Delante Mujer," and directed the Raza women's theater group Las Cucarachas. Moreno also is the author of *La Mujer En Pie de Lucha* and *La Mujer es La Tierre,* a collection of poetry. Includes her personal correspondence between 1967 and 1972, legal and financial papers, manuscripts of her poetry book, issues of the community newspaper *El Tecolote,* and activity announcements of the Casa Hispanica de Bellas Artes. Also includes correspondence of the Las Cucarachas group with other theater groups regarding performance schedules and papers concerning affiliation with Teatro National de Aztlan (TENAZ)

17,620. Conover, Obadiah Milton
Papers. 1842-1924. 4 boxes and 1 vol.
Open. Register.

State Historical Society of Wisconsin.
Correspondence, diaries, speeches, a notebook, genealogical material, and other papers of Conover (1825-84), a University of Wisconsin professor who became an attorney and reporter for the state supreme court. Consists chiefly of correspondence with [Mrs.] Sarah Fairchild Dean, whom he married in 1882, and with his brother Wilbur Conover of Dayton, OH. Includes a few letters from Obadiah Conover's first wife Julia Darst Conover (?-1863) and from the children of his first marriage, Edith Williams Conover (1852-1931), Allan Darst Conover (1854-1929), and Frederic King Conover (1857-1919); correspondence related to the reorganization of the University of Wisconsin in 1858; and records of the Wisconsin State Colonization Society.

17,621. Crownhart, Charles H., Family
Papers. 1862-1943. 29 boxes.
Access restricted. Register.
State Historical Society of Wisconsin.
Personal, political, and professional correspondence and legal and financial records of Charles H. Crownhart, Sr., chief justice of the Wisconsin Supreme Court and member of the Industrial Commission; of his wife Jessie (Evans) Crownhart, Douglas County superintendent of schools and a member of the board of regents of the normal school; of their son Jesse George, first secretary of the state medical society; and of their son Charles, Jr., the medical society's second secretary and campaign manager for Fred Wylie and John Blaine. Most of the papers are those of Charles Crownhart, Sr., and Jessie (Evans) Crownhart.

17,622. Day Family
Papers. 1839-93. 56 items.
Open. Published guide.
State Historical Society of Wisconsin.
Letters that Day family members in Ohio, Illinois, and Indiana wrote to relatives who remained in Avon, ME, contain descriptions of the conditions in their new homes. Includes letters from [Mrs.] Susie L. Todd, a relative of Mary Lincoln; Civil War letters of family members; and diaries of George E. Day and Captain Lionel Warrington Day. See Alice E. Smith, ed., *Guide to the Manuscripts of the Wisconsin Historical Society* (Madison, WI: State Historical Society of Wisconsin, 1944).

17,623. Dignam, Dorothy
Papers. 1907-59. 1 box, 1 vol., and 3 packages.
Open. Register.
State Historical Society of Wisconsin.
Among the first women in advertising, Dignam (1896?-) specialized in advertising for women's products and in designing advertising campaigns directed toward women. Correspondence, samples of Dignam's work, scripts, biographical material, a scrapbook, reports, clippings, and miscellaneous papers. Beginning in ca. 1908, Dorothy Dignam wrote a children's column "Cousin Dorothy" for *Dignam's Magazine,* a fashion journal published by her father, Chicago advertising pioneer J. B. Dignam. She entered the advertising field after working for *The Women's Press* in 1917 and 1918 and for the Chicago *Herald.* She was employed for 10 years as a copywriter for Vanderhoof and Company and McJunkin Advertising Company, and in 1929 she joined the staff of N. W. Ayer in Philadelphia. She moved to Ayer's New York office in 1939. She developed the Ford Company's women's advertising during the 1930s, a decade in which significant numbers of women began to drive automobiles; one of the campaign's features was a driving manual for women. She specialized in advertising for products such as cosmetics, clothing, fabrics, home appliances, and food. In 1927 and 1928 she went to Europe to visit trade fairs and to survey the "household situation," the strength of home service organizations, and the potential market for American household goods. While in Europe, Dignam served as a correspondent for five American trade journals. In 1939 she and Blanche Clair published *Advertising Careers for Women,* the first book for women on the subject. She also wrote the career sections of *How To Be a Successful Advertising Woman* (McGraw-Hill, 1948). In 1949 Dignam collaborated with Mary Lewis on *The Marriage of Diamonds and Dolls.* She retired in 1962.

17,624. Draper Manuscripts
Collection. Ca. 1730-1891. 491 vols.
Open. Unpublished guides.
State Historical Society of Wisconsin.
Corresponding secretary of the Wisconsin Historical Society from 1854 to 1891, Lyman C. Draper (1815-91) traveled extensively and carried on a 50-year correspondence that reflects his interest in history and other subjects. Divided into 50 series, the collection principally consists of papers Draper gathered, including notes on interviews he conducted during his travels, reminiscences and letters he received, comments on his interpretations, and copies of original documents. About one-fourth of the collection consists of original letters; receipts; maps; surveyors' notes; militia muster rolls; payrolls; order books; a few family records of James Boone, Daniel Boone, and John E. Finley; and family letters. While the material reflects the presence of women on the frontier, their role is emphasized infrequently. Exceptions include military heroines such as Elizabeth Zane, who is said to have helped a beleaguered fort at Wheeling, VA, withstand an Indian attack in 1782. Many of the letters in Draper's collection are from women descendants of pioneers, and ca. 125 of the more than 600 persons he interviewed were women. Also available on microfilm. A guide to the Draper Manuscripts is scheduled for publication in 1979 or 1980.

17,625. Edgar, Mary L.
Papers. 1935. 1 vol.
Open. Published guide.
State Historical Society of Wisconsin.
[Miss] Edgar (1865-1955) was a Madison schoolteacher. Letters she received from former students when she retired after 50 years in education. See Josephine L. Harper, ed., *Guide to the Manuscripts of the State Historical Society of Wisconsin, Supplement 2* (Madison, WI: State Historical Society of Wisconsin, 1966).

17,626. Edwards, Martha Letitia
Papers. 1789-1870. 12 boxes.
Open. Published guide.
State Historical Society of Wisconsin.
Edwards (?-1926) was a member of the University of Wisconsin extension division faculty from 1920 to 1926. Copies of Edwards's master's thesis "Growth of the Roman Catholic Church in the United States from 1820 to 1840" and of her doctoral dissertation "Government Patronage of Indian Missions, 1789-1836"; card file boxes of research notes; a bibliography of material regarding Indian missions in the US; and some book reviews and miscellaneous notes. Also includes personal letters from 1842 to 1864 of Sarah J. Cleveland Edwards, which contain information on dress, fashions, weddings, travels, social customs, and pioneer experiences in California and Texas. See Alice E. Smith, ed., *Guide to the Manuscripts of the Wisconsin Historical Society* (Madison, WI: State Historical Society of Wisconsin, 1944).

17,627. Esch, John J.
Papers. 1891-1921. 62 boxes and 31 vols.
Open. Published guide.
State Historical Society of Wisconsin.
Esch (1861-1941) was a Republican congressman from 1899 to 1921. His correspondence and congressional and personal papers reflect activities of woman suffrage proponents between 1912 and 1919. Taken from Josephine L. Harper and Sharon C. Smith, eds., *Guide to the Manuscripts of the State Historical Society of Wisconsin, Supplement 1* (Madison, WI: State Historical Society of Wisconsin, 1957).

17,628. Faber, Judith Ann
Papers. 1964-68. 2 boxes.
Open. Register.
State Historical Society of Wisconsin.
Faber (1945-) was a University of Wisconsin student leader during the early 1960s. Her correspondence and papers relate to organizations to which she belonged, including the University of Wisconsin Young Republican Club, the Madison and Dane County Young Republicans, the University of Wisconsin Committee to Support the People of South Vietnam, the University of Wisconsin Conservative Club, the Wisconsin Student Association, and the Student Rights party.

17,629. Fairchild, Lucius
Papers. 1819-1923. 90 boxes and 45 vols.
Open. Published guide.
State Historical Society of Wisconsin.
Personal papers and records of Fairchild (1831-96), Republican governor of Wisconsin from 1866 to 1872 and US consular and diplomatic representative in Liverpool, Paris, and Madrid from 1872 to 1881, and of his sister Sarah Fairchild, later Mrs. Eliab B. Dean. Personal and business correspondence, diaries, family business records, household accounts, record books, fee books, speeches, invitations, and miscellaneous items. Sarah Fairchild's correspondence from 1846 to ca. 1871 provides information on the life of women in Madison and Superior, WI. See Alice E. Smith, ed., *Guide to the Manuscripts of the Wisconsin Historical Society* (Madison, WI: State Historical Society of Wisconsin, 1944).

17,630. Feingold, Miriam
Papers. 1960-67. 3 boxes and 4 tapes.
Open. Register.
State Historical Society of Wisconsin.
Correspondence of Feingold (1941-) and clippings and other material concerning her activities as a member of the Swarthmore Political Action Club, as a worker for the Congress of Racial Equality in Louisiana and Mississippi, and as a field collector for the State Historical Society of Wisconsin from 1961 to 1967. The material, which concerns events such as freedom rides, demonstrations, and arrests, provides information about the impact these events had on civil rights workers.

17,631. Fishburn, Mrs. M. P.
Papers. Nd. 3 items.
Open. Published guide.
State Historical Society of Wisconsin.
Fishburn's recollections of her childhood and her family's migration in ca. 1845 from Ohio to Iowa. Also includes a paper on her religious beliefs. Taken from Josephine L. Harper and Sharon C. Smith, eds., *Guide to the Manuscripts of the State Historical Society of Wisconsin, Supplement 1* (Madison, WI: State Historical Society of Wisconsin, 1957).

17,632. Fletcher, Emilie C.
Papers. 1943. 2 pp.
Open. Published guide.
State Historical Society of Wisconsin.
[Mrs.] Fletcher (1847-?) was the daughter of Peter Conrad, a Baptist home missionary. Fletcher's recollections of Indians, of pioneer life at Newport, WI, and of her childhood at Wisconsin Dells (Kilbourn), WI. Taken from Josephine L. Harper and Sharon C. Smith, eds., *Guide to the Manuscripts of the State Historical Society of Wisconsin, Supplement 1* (Madison, WI: State Historical Society of Wisconsin, 1957).

17,633. Flynn, Elizabeth Gurley
Papers. 1917-23. 1 box.
Open. Register.
State Historical Society of Wisconsin.
A prominent New York socialist, Flynn (1890-1964) was an author who served as an organizer for the Workers Defense Union, a group associated with the Industrial Workers of the World. Correspondence and other material relating to Flynn's activities for persons accused of political crimes, labor agitation, or subversion. Includes material regarding legal efforts to block deportation of aliens and to secure release from prison of persons accused of political crimes. Contains letters and petitions to Presidents Wilson and Harding, cabinet members, and other government officials, as well as letters from persons in federal prisons and those awaiting deportation at Ellis Island. Also available on microfilm.

17,634. Gale, Zona
Papers. 1838-1941. 32 boxes.
Open. Register.
State Historical Society of Wisconsin.
Gale (1874-1938) was a Wisconsin writer who won the Pulitzer Prize for drama in 1921 for her play based on her novel *Miss Lulu Bett.* Correspondence; manuscripts of stories, essays, poems, novels, and plays; poems and writings of her mother Eliza Beers Gale; genealogical material on the Gale family; and miscellaneous papers. Gale worked for Milwaukee newspapers after receiving her bachelor's and master's degrees in 1895 and 1899 from the University of Wisconsin. She went to New York in 1901 and was employed by newspapers there before publishing her first novel *Romance Island* in 1906. In 1911 she returned to her home in Portage, WI, after receiving a $2000 first prize in a short story contest conducted by the *Delineator.* In addition to her literary work, Gale also wrote in behalf of women's suffrage, pacifism, world peace, prohibition, civil liberties, and racial equality.

17,635. Gannett, Betty
Papers. 1929-70. 11 boxes and 1 tape.
Open. Register.
State Historical Society of Wisconsin.
A Marxist theoretician, writer, and teacher, Gannett (1906-70) was active in the US Communist party for more than 45 years. She was a member of the party's national committee and at the time of her death was editor of *Political Affairs,* the party's theoretical journal. Personal correspondence; letters of condolence on her death; papers regarding her experiences in prison; legal documents, some of which deal with the government's attempt to deport her; eulogies she wrote; and material relating to her Communist party work, including lectures, papers, notes, course outlines, bibliographies, bulletins, and printed matter.

Born in Poland, Gannett came to the US with her family in 1914. Her widowed mother worked as a cook and maid in New York City to support Gannett and her six brothers and sisters. Gannett's public school education ended at age 13 when she began a two-year commercial course and became a secretary in the office of the AFL United Garment Workers. Two of her sisters who worked in garment district sweatshops also became members of the union. Gannett's next job was in the office of the *Brotherhood of Locomotive Engineers Journal.* A student of Marxist literature, she joined the Young Communist League and the Communist party in 1923. In 1927 she accompanied the first delegation of rank-and-file American trade unionists on a visit to the Soviet Union where she entered the Lenin School in Moscow. After her return to the US in 1928, the YCL sent her to Cleveland where her work as an organizer led to her arrest on charges of criminal syndicalism. She was sentenced to 10 years in prison, but her conviction was reversed on appeal. During this period she took an active part in coal mine disputes in western Pennsylvania and Ohio and worked as the YCL's national education director. Gannett returned to New York in the early 1930s to serve as editor of *The Community,* a forerunner of *Political Affairs,* and of another party publication, the *Party Organizer.* In 1935 she was transferred to the West Coast where she served until 1941 as the first educational director of the Communist party in California and as a leader in the struggle to organize agricultural workers. While in California, she helped found *Western Worker,* a local party publication that became *People's World.* From 1941 to 1944 Gannett served as the party's Midwest regional coordinator. Shortly before the end of WWII, she returned to New York to become assistant national organizational secretary and in 1950, national educational director. In 1963 she was named executive editor of *Political Affairs,* and in 1966 she became the publication's editor. Also available on microfilm

17,636. Gattiker, Emma
Papers. 1848-79. 2 boxes.
Open. Published guide.
State Historical Society of Wisconsin.
Correspondence in German script of three generations of the Bosshard and Gattiker families, Swiss immigrants who settled in Wisconsin's Green, La Crosse, and Sauk counties. Includes correspondence of [Miss] Emma Gattiker (1860-?) while she was a student at the University of Wisconsin from 1875 to 1879 and an article she wrote about Sauk County's Swiss settlements. The family's correspondence includes discussions of personal matters, the growth of community life, farm conditions, Civil War experiences of a son who settled in Owatonna, MN, and the lives of relatives who returned to Switzerland and those who remained in Europe throughout the period. See Alice E. Smith, ed., *Guide to the Manuscripts of the Wisconsin Historical Society* (Madison, WI: State Historical Society of Wisconsin, 1944).

17,637. Gitlin, Todd Alan, and Hollander, Nanci
Papers. 1961-70. 2 boxes.
Open. Register.
State Historical Society of Wisconsin.
Todd Gitlin (1943-) was national president of the Students for a Democratic Society (SDS) during the 1960s; Nanci Hollander (1943?-) was involved in SDS, the University of Michigan Friends of SNCC (Student Non-Violent Coordinating Committee), and other local and national student activist groups. Correspondence; subject files relating to student activism at Harvard and at the University of Michigan, to peace and protest groups, and to the 1962 Massachusetts senatorial campaign of H. Stuart Hughes; and a manuscript of Gitlin and Hollander's book *Uptown: Poor Whites in Chicago.* Hollander was an undergraduate at the University of Michigan and a worker in the SDS national office in Ann Arbor, MI, in 1963 and 1964. She married Gitlin in 1964, and they moved to Chicago where they became active in JOIN, a community organization initiated by SDS. She made motion picture shorts for Newsreel, a Chicago film company, and helped write *Uptown,* a description of southern migrants and JOIN's efforts to organize them.

17,638. Gleiter, Lois Linse
Oral history. 1974. 2 tapes.
Open. Tape abstract and index.
State Historical Society of Wisconsin.
Interview with Gleiter (1929-), a Wisconsin resident, in which she discusses her childhood on a family farm, her involvement with the Wisconsin Farmers Union junior program, teaching for the 4-H in Chile, and her experiences as a fieldworker for the National Farmers Union in the Midwest, Colorado, Montana, and Virginia.

17,639. Gold Star Mothers of Wisconsin
Records. 1947-73. 3 in.
Open. Catalog card.
State Historical Society of Wisconsin.
Charter, articles of dissolution, a convention register, and annual convention proceedings of this social organization comprised of the natural mothers of men and women killed while serving in the armed forces during WWI or WWII.

17,640. Gordon, Elizabeth S.
Papers. 1817-62. 2 boxes.
Open. Published guide.
State Historical Society of Wisconsin.
Personal letters to [Miss] Gordon (1824-1900), a Cleveland resident, from relatives and friends contain information about the social history of the period. Letters from Madison women, including Sarah Fairchild and Harriet D. [Mrs. John W.] Sterling, provide descriptions of the city's early history and social life. See Alice E. Smith, ed., *Guide to the Manuscripts of the Wisconsin Historical Society* (Madison, WI: State Historical Society of Wisconsin, 1944).

17,641. Gorham, James W.
Papers. 1832-96. 2 boxes.
Open. Published guide.
State Historical Society of Wisconsin.
Personal papers and business records, including account books of a general store, of Gorham (1808-81), who was owner of Madison's old Spring Hotel. Includes school records and diaries kept by Gorham's daughter Annie (Gorham) Marston from 1885 to 1891, with descriptions of household life on a farm and Madison social events. (The spelling of the family name is variously Gorham and Gorum.) See Alice E. Smith, ed., *Guide to the Manuscripts of the Wisconsin Historical Society* (Madison, WI: State Historical Society of Wisconsin, 1944).

17,642. Gove, George W.; Gove, George R.; and Gove, Marguerite
Papers. 1833-1963. 6 boxes.
Open. Register.
State Historical Society of Wisconsin.
Papers of George W. Gove (1844-1930), a Civil War soldier from Massachusetts who later lived in Milwaukee; his son George R. Gove (1881-1968), who worked for New York state, the Metropolitan Life Insurance Company, and the Atomic Energy Commission overseeing housing matters; and Marguerite Gove (ca. 1880-1969), a film production editor during the early 1920s and wife of the younger Gove. Marguerite Gove's papers document her work and include letters from 1923 concerning the motion picture *The White Tiger;* film records such as correspondence, story ideas, a conference syllabus, a list of film agents, an educational film catalog, and a list of educational films; diaries that provide information about weather and social engagements; and miscellaneous notes. Also contains biographical material about George W. Gove and biographical information, business correspondence, and other papers of George R. Gove.

17,643. Gratiot, Susan (Hempstead)
Papers. 1833-35. 13 pp.
Open. Published guide.
State Historical Society of Wisconsin.
Five letters that Gratiot of Gratiot's Grove, WI, wrote to her brother William Hempstead of St. Louis about family matters, local schools, her husband's work at the mill, and the condition of the Rock River Indians. The letters form the basis of an article in *Wisconsin Magazine of History* (Dec. 1927). See Alice E. Smith, ed., *Guide to the Manuscripts of the Wisconsin Historical Society* (Madison, WI: State Historical Society of Wisconsin, 1944).

17,644. Greenman, Caroline (Goodrich)
Papers. 1847-54. 1 microfilm reel.
Open. Published guide.
State Historical Society of Wisconsin.
Two diaries written by Greenman (1826-?), the niece of Joseph Goodrich who built the Milton House in 1844, concern the daily life, work, and social activities of a single girl in Massachusetts as well as a trip west via the Erie Canal and lake steamer and settling with relatives in Milton, WI. See Josephine L. Harper, ed., *Guide to the Manuscripts of the State Historical Society of Wisconsin, Supplement 2* (Madison, WI: State Historical Society of Wisconsin, 1966).

17,645. Gunnison, Martha E.
Papers. 1879-1957. 3 boxes.
Open. Published guide.
State Historical Society of Wisconsin.
Diaries chronicling the life of [Mrs. Arthur G.] Gunnison (1865-1960), a housewife in Waupun, WI, until 1940 and a resident of Detroit from 1940 until her death. The collection is housed at the Society's Oshkosh Area Research Center. See Josephine L. Harper, ed., *Guide to the Manuscripts of the State Historical Society of Wisconsin, Supplement 2* (Madison, WI: State Historical Society of Wisconsin, 1966).

17,646. Hadassah, Fond du Lac Chapter
Records. 1940-54. 1 box.
Open. Published guide.
State Historical Society of Wisconsin.
Membership and financial records, correspondence, and programs of this Wisconsin chapter of Hadassah, an international Jewish women's Zionist organization. Also includes several regional notices and national publications. The Fond du Lac Chapter was founded in 1940. The collection is housed at the Historical Society's Oshkosh Area Research Center. Taken from Lindsay B. Nauen, ed., *Guide to the Wisconsin Jewish Archives at the State Historical Society of Wisconsin* (Madison, WI: State Historical Society of Wisconsin, 1974).

17,647. Hadassah, Rachel S. Jastrow Chapter
Records. 1919-70. 11 boxes.
Open. Published guide and register.
State Historical Society of Wisconsin.
Minute books, financial records, correspondence, clippings, and printed items of the Madison chapter of this Jewish women's philanthropic organization founded in 1919. Includes correspondence of chapter officers Cecile Schein and Fannie Mack regarding local and regional Hadassah activities. Printed items pertain to the Hadassah Medical Organization, the Jewish National Fund, Youth Aliyah, Junior Hadassah, and Young Judea. Taken from Lindsay B. Nauen, ed., *Guide to the Wisconsin Jewish Archives at the State Historical Society of Wisconsin* (Madison, WI: State Historical Society of Wisconsin, 1974).

17,648. Hamilton, J. Talmai
Papers. 1837-77. 2 items.
Open. Published guide.
State Historical Society of Wisconsin.
Book of family history in which Hamilton (1815-?), who moved to Whitewater, WI, in 1843, entered diaries and letters by himself and his wife. Included are comments on teaching school, farming operations, and religious and economic life in the community. See Alice E. Smith, ed., *Guide to the Manuscripts of the Wisconsin Historical Society* (Madison, WI: State Historical Society of Wisconsin, 1944).

17,649. Hamwee, Lillian
Papers. 1965-67. 1 folder.
Open. Card catalog.
State Historical Society of Wisconsin.
Correspondence, reports, newsletters, notes, and summary of the experiences in 1967 of Hamwee, a summer volunteer for the Student Non-Violent Coordinating Committee in Albany, GA. Material concerns her work in the Dougherty County, GA, tutorial program and as a freedom school teacher.

17,650. Hazard, Aline W.
Papers. 1938-65. 2 boxes.
Open. Register.
State Historical Society of Wisconsin.
Correspondence, biographical information, annual reports and minutes, program subject file, news releases, and *For the Love of Mike,* the published autobiography of [Mrs.] Hazard (1895-), an announcer and later director of the WHA radio show "The Homemaker's Program." Hazard also was director of the state radio FM network in Wisconsin and assistant professor of agricultural journalism and radio education at the University of Wisconsin. Correspondence is almost entirely incoming mail she received from radio listeners, praising her and her broadcasts and requesting the bulletins and circulars advertised on her program. Bulletins range from recipes and craft instructions to suggestions for household planning techniques. Hazard's program subject file consists largely of scripts and circulars illustrating the various types of broadcasting sponsored by "The Homemaker's Program."

17,651. Hazeltine, Olivia A. (Brown)
Papers. 1857-63. 10 items.
Open. Published guide.
State Historical Society of Wisconsin.
Letters that Hazeltine received from her brother F. Delos Brown of Ashville, NY, while she was attending the Cherry Valley Female Seminary in Cherry Valley, NY, and later letters from classmate Augusta Kidder concerning Eau Claire, WI, society and the activities of girls of the seminary. Taken from Alice E. Smith, ed., *Guide to the Manuscripts of the Wisconsin Historical Society* (Madison, WI: State Historical Society of Wisconsin, 1944).

17,652. Heller, Janet
Papers. 1970-74. 2 folders and 2 envelopes.
Open. Card catalog.
State Historical Society of Wisconsin.
Minutes, correspondence, leaflets, and other material gathered by Heller, an active participant in the Women's Action Movement, relate to the Madison Abortion Action Coalition, the Rape Crisis Center, and other feminist groups.

17,653. Hibbard, Carlisle V., Family
Papers. 1811-1954. 5 boxes.
Open. Register.
State Historical Society of Wisconsin.
Correspondence, family deeds and mortgages, and other papers of Hibbard (?-1954), who held various YMCA positions in the Orient, Europe, and the US from 1902 until 1953; of his wife Sue Eugenia Lowell Hibbard; of their daughter Esther L. Hibbard, a missionary and dean of Doshisha Women's College in Kyoto, Japan; and of other family members. Esther Hibbard's letters to her parents from 1920 to 1929 reflect her life as an undergraduate at Mount Holyoke College, as a graduate student at the University of Wisconsin and the University of Colorado, and as a visitor in Europe. Later items document her life as a missionary. She lived in Japan from 1929 to 1952, returning to the US only for furloughs and during WWII. She received a doctorate from the University of Michigan in 1944. Her letters are primarily personal, but they contain some information about the Japanese invasion of Manchuria and Japanese war preparations during the 1930s.

17,654. Hooper, Jessie Annette (Jack)
Papers. 1881-1935. 21 boxes and 5 vols.
Open. Published guide and catalog card.
State Historical Society of Wisconsin.
[Mrs. Ben C.] Hooper (1865-1935), a Democratic party leader and candidate for the US Senate, was a suffrage speaker and a worker for permanent peace. Correspondence, copies of her addresses and radio speeches, biographical material, records such as minutes of executive boards and reports of various organizations to which she belonged, scrapbooks of clippings, engagement books, and a biography of Hooper. Hooper served as the first president of the Wisconsin LWV until her senatorial campaign in 1922. After her election race against Senator Robert M. La Follette, she served as chairman of the state LWV's department of Indian affairs. Her papers reflect the state Democratic party's split over the prohibition issue, her work for other party candidates, and her cooperation with the Wisconsin State Conference of Social Work and other state and national social and peace organizations. Bulk of the correspondence pertains to her speaking tours and work as chairman of the GFWC's department of international relations from 1928 to 1932 and includes correspondence with national and state officials concerning the League of Nations, the World Court, the Kellogg Pact, the Pan-American Treaties of Arbitration, and proposals for a neutrality bill. Collection also contains information about the origin of the Conference on the Cause and Cure of War and on Hooper's work as recording secretary of the group's national committee and as chairman of the CCCW committee that took petitions to the World Disarmament Conference at Geneva in 1932. Correspondents include [Mrs.] Carrie Chapman Catt, [Mrs.] Minnie Fisher Cunningham, [Mrs.] Anna J. H. Pennybacker, [Mrs.] Laura McMullen, and men and women active in state and national Democratic party work. Taken from Alice E. Smith, ed., *Guide to the Manuscripts of the Wisconsin Historical Society* (Madison, WI: State Historical Society of Wisconsin, 1944).

17,655. Howie, Adda F.
Papers. 1904-26. 1 box.
Open. Inventory.
State Historical Society of Wisconsin.
The first woman appointed to the Wisconsin Board of Agriculture, Howie (1852-1936) was one of the first Wisconsin women recognized as a leader in cattle breeding and in the state's dairy industry. Correspondence concerning speaking invitations, her trips, and various honors as well as letters about her gifts of purebred calves. Stressing cleanliness and breeding, Howie built Sunny Peak Farm in Elm Grove into one of the state's most outstanding dairy farms. From 1900 to 1907 she was a speaker and member of the University of Wisconsin's Wisconsin Farmers' Institute. She also was a lecturer for International Harvester. Howie sold her dairy herd in 1916.

17,656. Hoxie, Vinnie Ream
Papers. 1864-1954. 1 box.
Open. Published guide.
State Historical Society of Wisconsin.
Hoxie (1847-1914) was a sculptor. Correspondence between Hoxie and her husband principally concerns her opposition to the impeachment of President Andrew Johnson. Also contains writings by Hoxie and research material compiled about her by Harold E. Miner. Also available on microfilm. Taken from Josephine L. Harper and Sharon C. Smith, eds., *Guide to the Manuscripts of the State Historical Society of Wisconsin, Supplement 1* (Madison, WI: State Historical Society of Wisconsin, 1957).

17,657. Isham, Ruth Eliza (Wales)
Papers. 1880-1900. 2 vols.
Open. Published guide.
State Historical Society of Wisconsin.
Letters that Isham (1849-1929), then [Miss] Wales, wrote to her family and friends in Elkhorn, WI, concern her four years as a schoolteacher in Argentina. Includes comments about educational institutions and methods in Rosario, Mendoza, and

San Juan, Argentina; about customs in native homes; about two trips by mule across the Andes Mountains to Chile; and about political upheavals. Also contains some later correspondence. Taken from Alice E. Smith, ed., *Guide to the Manuscripts of the Wisconsin Historical Society* (Madison, WI: State Historical Society of Wisconsin, 1944).

17,658. Jaeck, Emma G.
Papers. Ca. 1958. 15 pp.
Open. Published guide.
State Historical Society of Wisconsin.
Reminiscences of Jaeck (1875-1963) concern her education and work as a schoolteacher in the Wisconsin towns of Neenah, Oshkosh, and Madison and in Berlin, Germany. Includes observations about declining standards of public instruction. Collection is housed at the Society's Oshkosh Area Research Center. See Josephine L. Harper, ed., *Guide to the Manuscripts of the State Historical Society of Wisconsin, Supplement 2* (Madison, WI: State Historical Society of Wisconsin, 1966).

17,659. James, Ada Lois
Papers. 1816-1952. 37 boxes and 2 vols.
Open. Published guide and card catalog.
State Historical Society of Wisconsin.
James (1876-1952) was a social reformer, humanitarian, and pacifist who lived in Richland Center, WI. Personal and family correspondence, diaries, speeches, and papers of other family members, including her parents David G. James and Laura Briggs James. Ada James was president of the Political Equality League, a women's suffrage group in Wisconsin. Later she was active in the Woman's party and movements advocating prohibition and birth control. David James's material reflects his interest in employment for women, woman suffrage, spiritualism, birth control, and socialism. Laura James's papers include diaries of 1865 and 1882 to 1904 and proceedings of the Wisconsin Woman's Suffrage Association from 1885 to 1903. Taken from Josephine L. Harper and Sharon C. Smith, eds., *Guide to the Manuscripts of the State Historical Society of Wisconsin, Supplement 1* (Madison, WI: State Historical Society of Wisconsin, 1957).

17,660. Jennings, Ann A.
Papers. 1850-51. 1 vol.
Open. Published guide.
State Historical Society of Wisconsin.
Diary of a girl in Philadelphia. Taken from Josephine L. Harper and Sharon C. Smith, eds., *Guide to the Manuscripts of the State Historical Society of Wisconsin, Supplement 1* (Madison, WI: State Historical Society of Wisconsin, 1957).

17,661. Jones, Jane Lloyd, and Jones, Ellen C. Lloyd
Papers. 1899-1940. 1 box.
Open. Published guide.
State Historical Society of Wisconsin.
Principally correspondence of the two sisters Jane Jones (1848-1917) and Ellen Jones (?-1919) concerning difficulties these educators encountered in running the Hillside Home School in Wyoming in Iowa County, WI. Includes a statement prepared in 1912 by Frank Lloyd Wright emphasizing that his aunts should not be criticized for his own behavior. Also includes a Wright family genealogy. See Josephine L. Harper, ed., *Guide to the Manuscripts of the State Historical Society of Wisconsin, Supplement 2* (Madison, WI: State Historical Society of Wisconsin, 1966).

17,662. Jones, Nellie Kedzie
Papers. 1881-1950. 1 box.
Open. Published guide.
State Historical Society of Wisconsin.
Correspondence, speeches, and articles by and about Jones (1858-1956), a pioneer college home economics educator. Taken from Josephine L. Harper, ed., *Guide to the Manuscripts of the State Historical Society of Wisconsin, Supplement 2* (Madison, WI: State Historical Society of Wisconsin, 1966).

17,663. Jordan, Joan
Papers. 1860-1972. 2 boxes.
Open. Register.
State Historical Society of Wisconsin.
Jordan, an author whose pen name is Vilma Sanchez, was active from 1966 to 1972 in the women's movement in northern California. Correspondence; a publication folder containing several of Jordan's articles and a list of publications; miscellaneous notes, poems, and statistical charts; semantic differential tests that sample opinions on various women's attitudes; articles; leaflets; and clippings. Includes material about Jordan's activities, about racism, and about the Independent Campus Women at San Francisco State College. The bulk of correspondence is between Jordan and Pat Robinson, a prominent figure in the New York women's liberation movement, and concerns black women, birth control, and other subjects. The bulk of the collection dates from 1948, but an 1860 article on racism is also included. Jordan lobbied to improve women's status and taught a course on women, economics, and method at Breakaway, a San Francisco women's community college. She attended the 1971 Indo-Chinese Women's Conference in Vancouver, British Columbia. Jordan has published articles in *The Militant, The Guardian, The Daily Gator,* and *Radical America* and in the *Psychology of Women* by Karen E. Paige. Jordan was a member of the Independent Campus Women, which after its organization in 1969 became the largest single group in San Francisco's women's liberation movement. The group consisted of committees on child care centers, abortion and birth control, education and speakers bureau, women's studies, and job discrimination.

17,664. Kander, Lizzie (Black)
Papers. 1875-1960. 2 boxes.
Open. Register.
State Historical Society of Wisconsin.
Known as the Jane Addams of Milwaukee, Kander (1858-1940) was one of the first women to begin social work activities among Russian Jewish immigrants who began arriving in the Wisconsin city during the 1880s. Correspondence, diaries, writings, minutes of the Abraham Lincoln Settlement House, settlement house reports and brochures, recipes, clippings, and other material. The daughter of John and Mary Black, Jewish pioneer farmers from near Green Bay, WI, Lizzie Black was born in Milwaukee and attended public schools there, graduating in 1878 from East Side High School. In 1881 she married Simon Kander, a real estate and insurance agent. Fifteen years later she established the Milwaukee Jewish Mission in borrowed quarters in Temple B'ne Jeshurun and Temple Emanu-El; the organization, now known as the Jewish Community Center of Milwaukee, changed its name and location several times before moving in 1951 to its present site. Sales of the *Settlement Cook Book,* composed of recipes from Kander's cooking classes, helped fund her settlement houses and center buildings. The collection is available on microfilm.

17,665. Keeley, Carrie Wilhelmina
Papers. 1905-11. 20 items.
Open. Published guide.
State Historical Society of Wisconsin.
Correspondence of [Mrs.] Keeley (1859-1942) of Hudson, WI, includes a letter from Olympia Brown, a minister, concerning a suffragist meeting and letters from Mr. and Mrs. Safford M. Thatcher. The Thatcher letters, written chiefly from Kansas, concern their early lives and personal affairs. See Alice E. Smith, ed., *Guide to the Manuscripts of the Wisconsin Historical Society* (Madison, WI: State Historical Society of Wisconsin, 1944).

17,666. Keith, Alice
Papers. 1906-62. 3 boxes, 3 vols., and 1 package.
Open. Published guide.
State Historical Society of Wisconsin.
Keith (1890-1962) was a pioneer in educational broadcasting, a music teacher, and a founder and director of the National Academy of Broadcasting. Correspondence, addresses and articles dealing with education, scripts from CBS's "American School of the Air" and the NAOB's "Music in the Air," press releases and printed material concerning NAOB educational broadcasting, and memorabilia. Letters from the 1930s reflect her efforts to win recognition as the first educational broadcaster. Taken from Josephine L. Harper, ed., *Guide to the Manuscripts of the State Historical Society of Wisconsin, Supplement 2* (Madison, WI: State Historical Society of Wisconsin, 1966).

17,667. Kellogg, Louise Phelps
Papers. Ca. 1900-41. 43 boxes.
Open. Register.
State Historical Society of Wisconsin.
A member of the staff of the Wisconsin Historical Society for more than 40 years, [Miss] Kellogg (1862-1942) was an historical scholar, lecturer, and writer. Personal and professional correspondence, diaries, autobiographical data, articles and radio speeches, records of interviews, research notes, manuscripts of her books, an unpublished volume about Wisconsin, notes on Wisconsin landmarks, notes on the history of Wisconsin and the Northwest, and the pageant *Under Three Flags.* Kellogg earned her PhD in history from the University of Wisconsin in 1901. Three years later her thesis *The American Colonial Charter* won the Justin Winsor prize in history. A founder of the Mississippi Valley Historical Association, Kellogg served as the organization's president in 1930 and 1931, the only woman to hold the position.

17,668. Kelly, Jane Bewel
Papers. 1866-98. 1 box.
Open. Published guide.
State Historical Society of Wisconsin.
Diaries kept by [Mrs.] Kelly on a farm near Cottage Grove, WI, contain descriptions of the daily life of a mother and later grandmother of a large family in a religious rural community. She recorded household activities, births, marriages, deaths, meetings at the Methodist church, and the farm work of her husband and sons. Taken from Alice E. Smith, ed., *Guide to the Manuscripts of the Wisconsin Historical Society* (Madison, WI: State Historical Society of Wisconsin, 1944).

17,669. Knight, Susan (Clark)
Papers. 1859-64. 1 microfilm reel.
Open. Published guide.
State Historical Society of Wisconsin.
Diary kept by Knight, the wife of Union Army Captain John H. Knight, concerns her social life and other experiences. Taken from Josephine L. Harper, ed., *Guide to the Manuscripts of the State Historical Society of Wisconsin, Supplement 2* (Madison, WI: State Historical Society of Wisconsin, 1966).

17,670. La Follette, Philip Fox
Papers. 1876-1973. 168 boxes, 24 vols., 1 tape, 1 package, 1 card file, and 32 recording discs.
Open. Register.
State Historical Society of Wisconsin.
Family papers of La Follette (1897-1965), three-term Wisconsin governor and Progressive party leader, and of his wife Isabel Bacon La Follette. Personal and political correspondence, financial records, publications and speeches, scrapbooks, press releases, and papers of other family members. Isabel La Follette's papers

include correspondence, diaries, her unpublished memoirs, speeches, scrapbooks, articles, and clippings.

17,671. LaBudde, Wilhelmine D.
Papers. 1924-56. 14 boxes and 5 vols.
Open. Register.
State Historical Society of Wisconsin.
Correspondence, a diary, notes, articles and speeches, scrapbooks, reports, resolutions, publicity material, and miscellaneous printed matter of [Mrs.] LaBudde (1880-1955), a leader in conservation for the Milwaukee County Federation of Women's Clubs during the 1920s. In 1930 she became conservation chairman for the state Federation, a position she held for more than a decade. She instituted a conservation education program and in 1937 was appointed the first woman member in the Wisconsin Conservation Congress.

17,672. Ladies Benevolent Society of Oshkosh, WI
Records. 1890-1974. 5 microfilm reels.
Open. Register.
State Historical Society of Wisconsin.
Established in 1862 as the Ladies Aid Society to help Civil War soldiers and their families, the Society continued its charitable work after the war and in 1889 founded a home for needy elderly women in Oshkosh. The Society financed the home through residents' admission fees, joint savings accounts, and estates. Articles of incorporation and bylaws; annual reports; minutes of the executive board and of Society meetings; legal records; financial records consisting of daybooks, dues books, and ledgers; resident records, including applications for admission, resident case files and profiles, and lists of accepted and rejected applicants; correspondence; and clippings. Includes information about the Society's efforts to provide balanced diets for the residents, to arrange for medical care when needed, and to keep the building and grounds properly maintained. The Society still exists and is the oldest women's organization in Oshkosh.

17,673. Lee, Portia, and Lee, Cornelia
Papers. 1797. 6 items.
Open. Published guide.
State Historical Society of Wisconsin.
Letters to Mr. and Mrs. Richard Bland Lee of London, England, primarily deal with family matters. Taken from Josephine L. Harper and Sharon C. Smith, eds., *Guide to the Manuscripts of the State Historical Society of Wisconsin, Supplement 1* (Madison, WI: State Historical Society of Wisconsin, 1957).

17,674. Levy, Augusta
Papers. Nd. 86 pp.
Open. Published guide.
State Historical Society of Wisconsin.
Reminiscences of [Mrs. John M.] Levy of La Crosse concern her life from her arrival in the Wisconsin city in 1845 until about 1914 and include anecdotes about early settlers, Winnebago Indians, the fur trade, and the community's growth. A condensed form of Levy's narrative, with editorial notes by Albert H. Sanford, was printed in the Wisconsin Historical Society *Proceedings,* 1912. Collection is also available on microfilm. Taken from Alice E. Smith, ed., *Guide to the Manuscripts of the Wisconsin Historical Society* (Madison, WI: State Historical Society of Wisconsin, 1944).

17,675. Lincoln, Grace Garrison
Papers. Ca. 1899-1965. 1 box.
Open. Register.
State Historical Society of Wisconsin.
Lincoln (1871-1970), an educator and newspaper correspondent, was involved in woman suffrage and socialist movements. Correspondence, primarily letters from Social-Democratic party officials; Lincoln's writings on socialism, suffrage, temperance, and other topics; a draft of a ca. 1949 note to William Evjue of the Madison *Capital Times* concerning development of her socialist philosophy; music material; receipts for building supplies; and clippings. Also includes copies of "The Duties and Demands of the New Women." Born in Green County, WI, Lincoln graduated from the University of Wisconsin in 1899. She joined the Social-Democratic party in Milwaukee in 1908 and lectured on socialism in the Richland County area. She also served as local correspondent for the Madison *Capital Times.* Active in the Richland Center Federation of Clubs, Lincoln helped in local projects, among them the Carnegie Library. She married Pearl Lincoln, an attorney, in 1899.

17,676. Long, Jean Stillman
Oral history. 1974. 9 tapes.
Open. Tape abstract and index.
State Historical Society of Wisconsin.
Interviews with Long (1891-), a Wisconsin activist in rural affairs, contain information about her involvement with the Wisconsin Farmers Union and her fieldwork for the National Farmers Union. She also discusses her childhood in New York state and Wisconsin, teaching in Montana, her marriage to Clifford Y. Long, experiences as a youth leader for the Farmers Union, her work for the Central Cooperative Wholesale in northern Wisconsin, and the role of women in 20th-century farm life.

17,677. McCormick, Anne (O'Hare)
Papers. 1936-54. 4 microfilm reels.
Open. Published guide.
State Historical Society of Wisconsin.
Principally clippings of international news that McCormick (1882-1954), a foreign correspondent, wrote for *The New York Times.* See Josephine L. Harper, ed., *Guide to the Manuscripts of the State Historical Society of Wisconsin, Supplement 2* (Madison, WI: State Historical Society of Wisconsin, 1966).

17,678. McCormick, Mary Virginia
Papers. 1871-1923. 63 boxes.
Closed. Published guide.
State Historical Society of Wisconsin.
The eldest daughter of Cyrus Hall McCormick and Nettie (Fowler) McCormick, Virginia McCormick (1861-1941) became mentally incompetent at the age of 19. Correspondence; early diaries and school notebooks; reports from doctors, nurses, and companions; financial records; and legal documents. Includes medical case histories and diaries by doctors Alice Bennett and Sanger Brown and letters and reports by Grace T. Walker, who headed Virginia McCormick's household for 40 years. See Margaret R. Hafstad, ed., *Guide to the McCormick Collection of the State Historical Society of Wisconsin* (Madison, WI: State Historical Society of Wisconsin, 1973).

17,679. McCormick, Nancy "Nettie" Maria (Fowler)
Papers. 1775-1962. 451 boxes and 1 package.
Partially closed. Published guide.
State Historical Society of Wisconsin.
Philanthropist and wife of inventor Cyrus Hall McCormick, "Nettie" McCormick (1835-1923) directed affairs of the McCormick Harvesting Machine Company after her husband's illness in 1878 and his death in 1884. Correspondence, diaries, memoranda, legal documents, and scrapbooks. Also contains manuscripts of the Nettie Fowler McCormick Biographical Association, including recollections, interviews, correspondence, genealogical and biographical information, and clippings. Half of her correspondence relates to her interest in philanthropy; she aided the McCormick Theological Seminary as well as small schools, academies, and civic causes in Chicago. Her diaries and notebooks cover her school years, the period from 1856 through 1877, and a trip to Egypt in 1896. A native of New York state, Nettie Fowler and her brother Eldridge were orphaned at an early age and were reared by their grandmother Maria Fowler and an uncle Eldridge G. Merick. By age 21, Nettie had completed public school, attended girls' seminaries for three years, and taught school. While visiting in Chicago, she joined the Presbyterian church, and in 1858 she married McCormick, who already was a manufacturer of agricultural implements. She accompanied her husband on many trips, discussed problems, and wrote letters for him; after McCormick's death, she acted as president of the firm, although she never held the title. See Margaret R. Hafstad, ed., *Guide to the McCormick Collection of the State Historical Society of Wisconsin* (Madison, WI: State Historical Society of Wisconsin, 1973).

17,680. MacDougall, Priscilla Ruth
Papers. 1970-75. 4 in. and 2 tapes.
Access restricted. Catalog card.
State Historical Society of Wisconsin.
MacDougall specialized in women's rights, particularly legal name rights, when she served as assistant attorney general of Wisconsin. Included with articles she wrote, judicial decisions, clippings, and pamphlets are taped interviews in which she describes her role in Wisconsin and national feminism, her work as assistant attorney general, and her involvement with the Center for a Woman's Own Name.

17,681. McKinnon, Isabella
Papers. 1852. 1 vol. and 3 items.
Open. Published guide.
State Historical Society of Wisconsin.
Diary of McKinnon (1833-?) is primarily an account of the journey of her family from Findhorn, Scotland, to Otsego, WI, by way of New York City, Detroit, Chicago, and Milwaukee. A few McKinnon family genealogical records are also included. Taken from Josephine L. Harper, ed., *Guide to the Manuscripts of the State Historical Society of Wisconsin, Supplement 2* (Madison, WI: State Historical Society of Wisconsin, 1966).

17,682. Madison Civics Club
Records. 1916-73. 5 boxes.
Access restricted. Register.
State Historical Society of Wisconsin.
Minutes, financial and membership records, correspondence, reports, scrapbooks, and other material of the Club, which was formed following the failure of the state campaign for woman suffrage in 1912. Club members discussed city and state problems at luncheon meetings and asked politicans to present their positions to them. Until 1924 the Club had an average attendance of 235; membership grew until the average attendance was more than 450.

17,683. Madison Ladies Benevolent Society of Grace Episcopal Church
Records. 1846-56. 1 vol.
Open. Published guide.
State Historical Society of Wisconsin.
Minutes, treasurers' reports, and lists of members. Taken from Alice E. Smith, ed., *Guide to the Manuscripts of the Wisconsin Historical Society* (Madison, WI: State Historical Society of Wisconsin, 1944).

17,684. Madison Ladies' Union League
Records. 1862-64. 17 items.
Open. Published guide.
State Historical Society of Wisconsin.
Correspondence of an organization formed to help needy families of active soldiers. Taken from Alice E. Smith, ed., *Guide to the Manuscripts of the Wisconsin Historical Society* (Madison, WI: State Historical Society of Wisconsin, 1944).

17,685. Mariner, John W., Family
Papers. 1881-1946. 11 boxes, 8 vols., and 3 packages.
Open. Register.
State Historical Society of Wisconsin.
Included with business papers of Mariner, an 1891 Harvard graduate who established a real estate business with his father in Milwaukee in 1920, are the papers of his wife Mary Fargo Antisdel Mariner, who served as state chairman of the National League for Woman's Service, an unofficial patriotic group during WWI. Her papers, comprising more than half of the collection, consist of correspondence with the national office of the League, local chairmen, the Council of Defense, the Woman's Liberty Loan Committee, the War Savings Committee, and other state groups. Also includes minutes of the League, reports, speeches, Wisconsin League membership lists, committee files, and questionnaires.

17,686. Matthews, Stella S.
Papers. 1949. 4 items.
Open. Published guide.
State Historical Society of Wisconsin.
Correspondence of Matthews (1868-1948), a Milwaukee-trained American National Red Cross nurse and holder of the Florence Nightingale medal for meritorious nursing service. Taken from Josephine L. Harper and Sharon C. Smith, eds., *Guide to the Manuscripts of the State Historical Society of Wisconsin, Supplement 1* (Madison, WI: State Historical Society of Wisconsin, 1957).

17,687. Mears Family
Papers. 1857-1942. 1 box.
Open. Published guide.
State Historical Society of Wisconsin.
Primarily biographical material relating to Mary Elizabeth Farnsworth [Mrs. John Hall] Mears (1830-1907), a Wisconsin poet who used the pen name Nellie Wildwood, and her daughters Helen, a sculptor; Mary, a novelist; and Louise, an illustrator. Also includes reminiscences of the elder Mary Mears; copies of her play *Black Hawk,* which was produced in Madison in 1857, and sketches about family members that the younger Mary Mears wrote in 1942. Taken from Josephine L. Harper and Sharon C. Smith, eds., *Guide to the Manuscripts of the State Historical Society of Wisconsin, Supplement 1* (Madison, WI: State Historical Society of Wisconsin, 1957).

17,688. Merrill, Maria M.
Papers. 1890-99. 36 pp.
Open. Published guide.
State Historical Society of Wisconsin.
Diary kept by [Mrs.] Merrill (1832-1903) deals with family and household affairs and the operation of a farm at Sechlersville in Jackson County, WI. Taken from Alice E. Smith, ed., *Guide to the Manuscripts of the Wisconsin Historical Society* (Madison, WI: State Historical Society of Wisconsin, 1944).

17,689. Milwaukee-Downer College
Records. 1852-1964. 120 boxes, 48 vols., and 3 packages.
Open. Register.
State Historical Society of Wisconsin.
Milwaukee-Downer College was created in 1895 by the merger of two Wisconsin women's schools: Milwaukee College, which was founded in Milwaukee in 1849 as the Female Normal Institute and High School, and Downer College of Fox Lake, chartered in 1855. Files of the president, dean, trustees, registrar, business office, faculty, student activities, alumnae association, and public relations office; a history of the College; photos; and scrapbooks, including office files and personal papers of Ellen Clara Sabin, president of Milwaukee-Downer College from 1895 to 1921. Acting during a meeting organized in 1849 by Increase Lapham, Milwaukee citizens approved a woman's college plan proposed by [Miss] Catharine Esther Beecher. The school's name was changed to Milwaukee Female College in 1853 and to Milwaukee College in 1876. Downer College was chartered as the Wisconsin Female College, but the name was changed in 1886 following a bequest made in 1884 by Judge Jason Downer. Ellen Sabin's personal papers include correspondence, diaries, a notebook, a memoranda book, speech notes and drafts, photos, clippings, and ephemera.

17,690. Milwaukee Druggists Ladies Club
Records. 1911-48. 1 box.
Open. Published guide.
State Historical Society of Wisconsin.
Minutes, treasurers' reports, and membership lists of two women's social and service groups formed as auxiliaries of organizations of Milwaukee druggists. Also contains minutes of the Women's Organization of the Milwaukee chapter of the National Retail Druggists Association from 1916 to 1940. Taken from Josephine L. Harper, ed., *Guide to the Manuscripts of the State Historical Society of Wisconsin, Supplement 2* (Madison, WI: State Historical Society of Wisconsin, 1966).

17,691. Montgomery, Lucille
Papers. 1963-66. 3 microfilm reels.
Open. Register.
State Historical Society of Wisconsin.
Correspondence, notes, project plans and reports, circulars, and news releases of Montgomery, an activist in the civil rights movement. She was a case worker and county welfare administrator in North Carolina before moving to Washington, DC, in the early years of the depression. There she joined the League of Women Shoppers. Her interest in the problems of literacy and poverty led her into the civil rights movement, and she began her association with the Student Non-Violent Coordinating Committee (SNCC) in 1964. In cooperation with SNCC, Montgomery has directed or participated in freedom workshops and citizenship workshops in the South. In addition she has served on the board at the Highlander Education and Research Center in Knoxville, TN, and has helped train college volunteers for the Mississippi Summer Project. In the Chicago area where she now resides, Montgomery has served on the board of SANE: A Citizens' Organization for a Sane World, helped establish the Henry Horner nursery school, and was one of the founders of Women for Peace.

17,692. Moore, Aubertine Woodward
Papers. 1781-1928. 10 boxes and 5 vols.
Open. Published guide.
State Historical Society of Wisconsin.
[Mrs.] Moore (1841-1929) was an author, musician, and translator who used the pen name Auber Forestier. Correspondence; Moore's description of visits with Ralph Waldo Emerson and Walt Whitman; volumes of poems and notes; articles on music, biographies, translations, and poems; genealogical information; and reminiscences regarding Ole Bull by his son Alexander. Includes letters from Elizabeth P. Peabody concerning literary figures and educational schemes; [Mrs.] Jane Cunningham Croly, editor of *Demorest's* and other publications; Elizabeth Jordon, writer and grandniece of Moore's husband; and Mrs. Valborg Hovind Stub, who was Aubertine Moore's collaborator in publication of a Scandinavian album *Songs from the North.* Taken from Alice E. Smith, ed., *Guide to the Manuscripts of the Wisconsin Historical Society* (Madison, WI: State Historical Society of Wisconsin, 1944).

17,693. Murray, Daniel
Papers. 1881-1966. 27 microfilm reels.
Open. Published guide.
State Historical Society of Wisconsin.
An employee of the Library of Congress for 52 years, Murray (1852-1925) was a leading black bibliographer and historian whose life's work was the compilation of an unpublished encyclopedia of the black race. Bulk of the collection consists of drafts, notes, and other material pertaining to "Murray's Historical and Biographical Encyclopedia of the Colored Race," including considerable biographical data on black women from biblical times to ca. 1925 and information on white women whose actions significantly affected the black race. Also contains some papers of Murray's wife Anna Jane Evans Murray (1858-1955), reflecting her interests in early childhood education and various black women's organizations; Murray's correspondence file; personal and financial items; and miscellaneous family papers. See Jane Wolff and Eleanor McKay, eds., *The Papers of Daniel Murray: Guide to a Microfilm Edition* (Madison: State Historical Society of Wisconsin, 1977).

17,694. National Council of Administrative Women in Education, Wisconsin Branch
Records. 1923-42. 4 vols. and 22 items.
Open. Published guide.
State Historical Society of Wisconsin.
Minute book, an account book, bankbooks, a few letters, and membership records. Taken from Josephine L. Harper and Sharon C. Smith, eds., *Guide to the Manuscripts of the State Historical Society of Wisconsin, Supplement 1* (Madison, WI: State Historical Society of Wisconsin, 1957).

17,695. National Council of Jewish Women
Records. 1924-61. 1 microfilm reel.
Open. Published guide.
State Historical Society of Wisconsin.
Scrapbook concerning charitable and philanthropic activities of the Council's Madison chapter, including reports of the president and committee chairman, minutes, correspondence, surveys, programs, clippings, and copies of the *Council Bulletin.* Taken from Josephine L. Harper, ed., *Guide to the Manuscripts of the State Historical Society of Wisconsin, Supplement 2* (Madison, WI: State Historical Society of Wisconsin, 1966).

17,696. National League of American Pen Women
Records. 1930-66. 4 boxes.
Open. Register.
State Historical Society of Wisconsin.
Founded in 1931, the Madison branch of the League included professional women in the creative arts who wanted to further their literary and artistic work and to establish contacts with others in their field. Principally minute books and scrapbooks. The scrapbooks contain examples of members' work, biographies of members, clippings, brochures, and photos concerning social and professional activities of League members.

17,697. Neprud, Marion C.
Papers. 1914-66. 6 boxes.
Open. Register.
State Historical Society of Wisconsin.
Neprud (1897-1965) was an administrator and manager of federal public housing projects and coordinator of public and private agency programs, community services, and facilities for low-income families in public housing. Correspondence, notes, speeches, writings, minutes and agenda, membership lists, job bulletins and descriptions, press releases, pamphlets, publications, and other material.

17,698. New University Conference
Records. Ca. 1964-72. Ca. 11 ft.
Open. Card catalog.
State Historical Society of Wisconsin.
Correspondence, newsletters, and printed items of the NUC, a national organization of radical University of Wisconsin faculty members, graduate students, and staff whose comprehensive reform program included the encouragement of radical research and scholarship relating to public policy,

"the culture and needs of the resistance, and black and poor people's movements." Includes information on regional affiliates of the NUC and conferences it sponsored as well as records from 1970 and 1971 of the Women's Caucus of the NUC, which was formed to fight sex discrimination within both the NUC and the University community.

17,699. Newcomb, Kate Pelham
Papers. 1945-62. 1 box.
Open. Register.
State Historical Society of Wisconsin.
Newcomb (1886-1956) was a physician in the wilderness area near Crandon, WI, from 1931 to 1956. Correspondence, newsletters, miscellaneous papers, and records and publicity releases of Lakeland Memorial Hospital, which Newcomb helped organize and build. She also practiced at this hospital, located in the Arbor-Vitae-Woodruff area, after its completion in 1954. Newcomb's life was chronicled in Adele Comandine's book *Angel on Snowshoes* (1956).

17,700. Oakley, Frank W.
Papers. 1859-1921. 1 box.
Open. Published guide.
State Historical Society of Wisconsin.
Letters to relatives in Beloit, WI, that Cynthia Oakley, wife of Lieutenant Frank Oakley (1841-1925), wrote describing life in Washington, DC, and Paris, KY, where her husband was stationed during the Civil War. Also contains papers concerning marking the graves of Confederate soldiers who died at Camp Randall and were buried in Forest Hill Cemetery in Madison. Taken from Alice E. Smith, ed., *Guide to the Manuscripts of the Wisconsin Historical Society* (Madison, WI: State Historical Society of Wisconsin, 1944).

17,701. Odegard, Ethel J.
Papers. 1919-72. 1 ft. and 2 boxes.
Open. Register.
State Historical Society of Wisconsin.
[Miss] Odegard (1891-) was a professional nurse and teacher of nursing. Personal and professional correspondence, biographical data, articles concerning nursing education, and eight scrapbooks. The scrapbooks, which make up the bulk of the collection, contain correspondence, biographical sketches, clippings, obituaries, and printed material. Collection also contains files about the Milwaukee Central School of Nursing from 1927 to 1930, with correspondence, photos, clippings about nurses' schools, and memorabilia. Odegard taught science courses related to nursing and wrote articles on the problems and progress of nursing education. She worked to further the professionalization of nursing and to link hospital nursing schools with colleges and vocational institutions. Odegard retired in 1957.

17,702. Oshkosh, WI, League of Women Voters
Records. 1942-63. 3 ft. and 2 boxes.
Open. Register.
State Historical Society of Wisconsin.
Annual reports, minutes, financial records, membership lists, correspondence, publicity clippings, and bulletins of this local branch of the LWV, established in 1942.

17,703. Pascoe, Mary Elizabeth
Papers. 1871. 1 package.
Open. Published guide.
State Historical Society of Wisconsin.
Pocket diary kept by Pascoe (1855-1936), a 16-year-old girl, describing daily activities on a family farm north of Hazel Green, WI. Also includes background information about the family by Mary Pascoe's son Stephen D. Stephens. Taken from Josephine L. Harper, ed., *Guide to the Manuscripts of the State Historical Society of Wisconsin, Supplement 2* (Madison, WI: State Historical Society of Wisconsin, 1966).

17,704. Pfankuch, Marjorie
Papers. 1962-63. 1 microfilm reel.
Open. Published guide.
State Historical Society of Wisconsin.
Letters that Pfankuch (1936-), a Peace Corps member who worked in the Philippines as a teacher of high school and college English, wrote to her family in Menasha, WI. Taken from Josephine L. Harper, ed., *Guide to the Manuscripts of the State Historical Society of Wisconsin, Supplement 2* (Madison, WI: State Historical Society of Wisconsin, 1966).

17,705. Phillips, Irna
Papers. 1931-68. 68 boxes.
Partially restricted. Register.
State Historical Society of Wisconsin.
Phillips (1901-73) was the originator and writer of soap operas for more than 45 years. Correspondence, outlines, scripts, and a plot calendar pertain to the following radio and television soap operas: "Today's Children/Women in White," "Masquerade," "Road of Life," "The Guiding Light," "The Right to Happiness," "The Brighter Day," "Lonely Women/Today's Children," "Another World," "Love Is a Many Splendored Thing," and "Our Private World."

17,706. Porter, Ann Eliza Bacon
Papers. 1838-1965. 1 box.
Open. Register.
State Historical Society of Wisconsin.
Correspondence, diaries, farm and household account book, and poems of Porter (1821-90), a Boston native who, after her marriage to Joseph Porter, moved with him to the Wisconsin Territory to the area now known as Cooksville. Also contains a manuscript for the book *Choice Seed in the Wilderness* (1964), which was written by her grandson's wife Lillian Russell Porter and based on accounts in Ann Porter's diaries.

17,707. Prairie Village Female Moral Reform Society
Records. 1839-43. 10 pp.
Open. Published guide.
State Historical Society of Wisconsin.
Constitution, lists of charter members, and minutes of the Waukesha, WI, branch of the American Female Moral Reform Society. Taken from Josephine L. Harper and Sharon C. Smith, eds., *Guide to the Manuscripts of the State Historical Society of Wisconsin, Supplement 1* (Madison, WI: State Historical Society of Wisconsin, 1957).

17,708. Pratt, Sarah
Papers. 1844-47. 115 pp.
Open. Published guide.
State Historical Society of Wisconsin.
Diary in which Pratt (1819-47), a schoolteacher, describes the canal and lake trip from her home in Jefferson County, NY, to Rock County, WI, as well as social events, teaching experiences, illnesses, and personal and family events. Also includes entries made by her sister after Pratt's death and an introductory sketch written by Edith Hadley. Taken from Alice E. Smith, ed., *Guide to the Manuscripts of the Wisconsin Historical Society* (Madison, WI: State Historical Society of Wisconsin, 1944).

17,709. Quiner, Emilie C.
Papers. 1861-63. 1 vol.
Open. Published guide.
State Historical Society of Wisconsin.
Diary in which Quiner (1840?-?), daughter of Madison writer and journalist Edwin B. Quiner, describes her social, educational, religious, and temperance activities in Madison during her years as a student, teacher, and editorial assistant to her father. Also includes entries from the summer of 1863 when she was a nurse in a Union hospital in Memphis. Taken from Josephine L. Harper, ed., *Guide to the Manuscripts of the State Historical Society of Wisconsin, Supplement 2* (Madison, WI: State Historical Society of Wisconsin, 1966).

17,710. Reed, Evelyn
Papers. 1973. 1 tape.
Open. Catalog card.
State Historical Society of Wisconsin.
Speech given by Reed at the University of Wisconsin is entitled "Is Biology Women's Destiny?".

17,711. Reynolds, Barbara
Papers. 1954-60. 1 microfilm reel.
Open. Card catalog.
State Historical Society of Wisconsin.
Correspondence, clippings, and articles chiefly relate to the voyage of the Reynolds family into the US Pacific nuclear testing zone in 1958 in protest and in violation of an Atomic Energy Commission regulation.

17,712. Roberts, Joan
Papers. 1974. 1 tape.
Open. Catalog card.
State Historical Society of Wisconsin.
Speech of Roberts, a women studies professor in the University of Wisconsin's educational policy studies department, is entitled "On Building a Feminist Future in Our Time" and includes her comments on her effort to obtain tenure.

17,713. Robinson, Jane A.
Papers. 1845-47. 4 items.
Open. Published guide.
State Historical Society of Wisconsin.
Letters from [Miss] Robinson (1827?-?) to Rachel Wright in Vermont concern life in her home at Rochester in Racine County, WI. Taken from Josephine L. Harper and Sharon C. Smith, eds., *Guide to the Manuscripts of the State Historical Society of Wisconsin, Supplement 1* (Madison, WI: State Historical Society of Wisconsin, 1957).

17,714. Robinson, Jo Ann (Ooiman)
Papers. 1960-66. 2 boxes and 1 tape.
Open. Register.
State Historical Society of Wisconsin.
Correspondence, diaries, minutes, and reports of Robinson (1942-), who participated in the Mississippi Summer Project of 1964 to establish the civil rights of the state's Negroes. Assigned to Canton, MS, by the Council of Federated Organizations, [Miss] Ooiman spent most of the summer teaching in the freedom school in nearby Pleasant Green. During the fall, she worked on elections for the Agricultural Stabilization and Conservation Service, an agency responsible for administering federal agricultural programs at the county level, and on mobilizing support for the Freedom Democratic party's challenge of the Mississippi congressional elections.

17,715. Roe, Gwyneth King
Papers. 1880-1968. 9 boxes and 1 package.
Open. Inventory.
State Historical Society of Wisconsin.
Roe (1868-1968), wife of a former law partner of Robert M. La Follette, was a teacher with Emily Mulkin Bishop of the Delsarte system of physical education; Roe also was an advocate of woman suffrage, the Women's Peace party, and freedom of dress for women. Correspondence, diaries, notes and drafts of her writings and those of her husband, and family, business, and teaching records. The major portion of Roe's writings consists of notes and drafts of an autobiography on which she worked for 20 years. Also includes her notes for speeches in support of woman suffrage and the Peace party.

17,716. Ross, Madeline Dane
Papers. 1914-71. 5 boxes.
Open. Register.
State Historical Society of Wisconsin.
Personal and business correspondence, research material, travel notes, articles, reports, scrapbooks, publicity material, and clippings of Ross (1902-72), a journalist and public relations representative. She was service editor for *Delineator Magazine;* managing editor for the *Journal of the American Institute of Homeopathy;* executive secretary of the Hudson Guild, a settlement house; and founder and editor of *Team News,* a periodical for the United Nations Relief and Rehabilitation Administration. Ross was responsible for fund raising and publicity at Hudson House. Includes material on organizations with which she worked, including the Jewish Family Welfare Society, the Guidance Center, the Brussels World's Fair, and the Human Betterment Association of America. Also contains copies of publications she edited; issues of *The Monitor,* a school magazine featuring her childhood writings; a scrapbook of personal memorabilia primarily from her years at Cornell; credentials, including passports and press cards; recommendations and résumés; material relating to the Overseas Press Club; and other items.

17,717. Rowland, Margaret
Papers. 1917-18. 19 pp.
Open. Published guide.
State Historical Society of Wisconsin.
Letters from [Miss] Rowland, a Red Cross war nurse at a French hospital in Mesgringny, to her family in Racine, WI, contain descriptions of her work as an operating room assistant. Taken from Alice E. Smith, ed., *Guide to the Manuscripts of the Wisconsin Historical Society* (Madison, WI: State Historical Society of Wisconsin, 1944).

17,718. Ruddy, Ella (Giles)
Papers. 1861-1916. 2 boxes and 1 vol.
Open. Published guide.
State Historical Society of Wisconsin.
Ruddy (1851-1915) was a Wisconsin author of novels, a book of poetry, and magazine and newspaper articles. Correspondence with other authors, poems signed by Ella (Wheeler) Wilcox and others, and scrapbooks that contain articles and poems by Ruddy and other Wisconsin authors. A close friend of Wisconsin authors Hattie Tyng Gregory and Ella Wheeler Wilcox, Ruddy wrote three novels in the sentimental style: *Bachelor Ben, Maiden Rachel,* and *Out of the Shadows.* See Josephine L. Harper, ed., *Guide to the Manuscripts of the State Historical Society of Wisconsin, Supplement 2* (Madison, WI: State Historical Society of Wisconsin, 1966).

17,719. Sanders, Luida E., and Sanders, Lewis E.
Papers. 1941-52. 2 boxes.
Open. Register.
State Historical Society of Wisconsin.
Papers of Luida Sanders (1917-), an educator and director of health education for the Wisconsin Board of Health, and her brother Lewis Sanders (1919-68) primarily relate to their US Army service. Letters to their mother, other family members, and friends; Luida Sanders's diary for 1943 and 1944; and material related to her work as a WAC, including Army orders, duty notes, recruitment material, and gossip sheets she wrote. Luida Sanders served from 1943 to 1946 as a secretary and recruitment officer in a hospital for WAC detachments 1 and 3. After her military service, she studied at the University of Wisconsin and taught school. In 1950 she began work for the state health board and from 1956 to 1966 served as director of health education. From 1966 until her retirement in 1975, she was the department of public instruction's health supervisor.

17,720. Segerstrom, Margaret, and Segerstrom, Rangnar
Oral history. 1976. 6 tapes.
Open. Tape abstract and index.
State Historical Society of Wisconsin.
Interview with Margaret Segerstrom (1903-) and her husband Rangnar Segerstrom (1896-), both Wisconsin farmers, in which they discuss the transformation of farm life and operations since they began farming in 1922, their involvement with the Wisconsin Farmers Union beginning in the 1930s, and changes in the rural community since the 1920s.

17,721. Sharon Equal Suffrage League
Records. 1917-28. 1 vol.
Open. Published guide.
State Historical Society of Wisconsin.
Constitution and secretary's records from 1917 to 1920 for the Sharon, WI, League and for its successor organization the Citizenship Class. This collection is housed at the Society's Whitewater Area Research Center. Taken from Josephine L. Harper, ed., *Guide to the Manuscripts of the State Historical Society of Wisconsin, Supplement 2* (Madison, WI: State Historical Society of Wisconsin, 1966).

17,722. Simons, Algie M.
Papers. 1894-1951. 6 boxes.
Open. Published guide.
State Historical Society of Wisconsin.
Algie Simons (1870-1950) and his wife May (Wood) Simons (?-1948) were Wisconsin-born journalists, authors, and socialists. Correspondence; diaries of May Simons, consisting chiefly of entries about family activities; notes on political economy lectures given at the University of Wisconsin; a paper evaluating Algie Simons's socialist histories; and articles on medical economics. Includes letters exchanged by the Simonses during lecture tours and trips to socialist meetings in the US and abroad, particularly letters describing the 1910 International Socialist Congress in Copenhagen, Denmark, to which May Simons was a delegate. A few letters relate to their work from 1906 to 1910 on the Chicago *Daily Socialist* staff. Taken from Josephine L. Harper and Sharon C. Smith, eds., *Guide to the Manuscripts of the State Historical Society of Wisconsin, Supplement 1* (Madison, WI: State Historical Society of Wisconsin, 1957).

17,723. Slaughter, Gertrude Elizabeth (Taylor)
Papers. 1858-1963. 6 boxes and 1 microfilm reel.
Open. Register.
State Historical Society of Wisconsin.
Slaughter (1870-1963), an author and prominent Madison resident, was an 1893 graduate of Bryn Mawr College and wife of Moses Stephen Slaughter (1860-1923), a classics professor at the University of Wisconsin. Correspondence, travel and research notes, family papers, drafts of her writings, and articles by others. Her memoir *Only the Past Is Ours: The Life Story of Gertrude Slaughter* (Exposition Press, 1963) is available on microfilm. Includes letters from Anne "Nancy" Crosby Emery Allinson, who earned a PhD from Bryn Mawr in 1896 and served as the first dean of women at the University of Wisconsin. Also includes letters from other Bryn Mawr alumnae, drafts of alumnae notes, and items from an alumnae weekend in 1950. Slaughter's publications include *Two Children in Old Paris, From the Notes of a Journal by Their Mother* (Macmillan, 1918); *Shakespeare and the Heart of a Child* (Macmillan, 1922); *Heirs of Old Venice* (Yale University Press, 1927); *The Amazing Frederic* (Macmillan, 1937); *Calabria, the First Italy* (University of Wisconsin Press, 1939); and *Saladin, 1138-1193, A Biography* (Exposition Press, 1955).

17,724. Smith, John, and Smith, Louisa Sargent
Papers. 1675-1891. 1 microfilm reel.
Open. Register.
State Historical Society of Wisconsin.
The Smiths were farmers who in 1840 settled in Bradford near Clinton, WI, after moving from Cook County, IL. Correspondence containing details about their daily activities, problems, trips to New Hampshire to visit Louisa Smith's family, and their reactions to and their sons' experiences during the Civil War; receipts; deeds; and a will of William Sargent probated in 1675 in Salem, MA. Also includes a review of events in 1891 taken from the memory book of the Bradford Society and a clipping about and a history of Smithton School, which was located in Bradford.

17,725. Stewart, Isaac N., and Stewart, Mary E.
Papers. 1828-1928. 2 boxes.
Open. Published guide.
State Historical Society of Wisconsin.
Papers of Isaac Stewart (1838-1915), an educator in Waukesha County and Appleton, WI, and his sister Mary (1841-1931); both of the Stewarts worked as editorial writers for the Milwaukee *Journal.* Family letters, letters concerning life in ca. 1860 at the University of Wisconsin, Civil War correspondence, letters from May Eliza (Wright) Sewall before her marriage, and letters from journalists and publishers to Mary Stewart. Also includes Mary Stewart's records of her visits to expositions; articles containing reminiscences about early life in the Pewaukee, WI, region; and records from 1828 to 1842 of Christ Church in Pompey, NY, including minutes and a register of births, baptisms, marriages, and deaths. Taken from Alice E. Smith, ed., *Guide to the Manuscripts of the Wisconsin Historical Society* (Madison, WI: State Historical Society of Wisconsin, 1944).

17,726. Sutherland, Elizabeth
Papers. 1964-66. 5 boxes.
Open. Register.
State Historical Society of Wisconsin.
Sutherland (1925-) is an author and editor. Papers relate exclusively to her book *Letters from Mississippi* and include general correspondence, letters from civil rights volunteers, biographical information on approximately 40 volunteers, news releases, drafts, galleys, page proofs, and promotional material. Contains successive drafts of published chapters and three unpublished chapters. The letters from the volunteers and the book drafts have been edited extensively.

17,727. Szold, Adele
Papers. 1895-1901. 1 folder.
Open. Published guide.
State Historical Society of Wisconsin.
Correspondence written in 1895 and 1896 by Szold (1876-1940), a University of Wisconsin freshman to her parents and sisters Henrietta and Bertha "Betsey" Szold in Baltimore regarding student activities, faculty, and classes at the University. During the 1895-96 academic year, she lived with her sister Rachel and her brother-in-law Joseph Jastrow, a University psychology professor. Taken from Lindsay B. Nauen, ed., *Guide to the Wisconsin Jewish Archives at the State Historical Society of Wisconsin* (Madison, WI: State Historical Society of Wisconsin, 1974).

17,728. Tesmer, Louise M.
Papers. Ca. 1973-74. 2.25 ft.
Open. Catalog card.
State Historical Society of Wisconsin.
Letters from constituents, questionnaires on public issues, and reference material of Tesmer, a Wisconsin state representative from the 19th district.

17,729. Tuttle, Ada Alice
Papers. 1896-1935. 1 box.
Open. Published guide.
State Historical Society of Wisconsin.
Letters that [Miss] Tuttle (1886-1936) of Portland, OR, wrote to her aunt describing her musical activities. Also includes a copy of a speech and a few letters concerning Tuttle's service in 1918 and 1919 with the YMCA entertainment corps in France and Germany. Taken from Josephine L. Harper and Sharon C. Smith, eds., *Guide to the Manuscripts of the State Historical Society of Wisconsin, Supplement 1* (Madison, WI: State Historical Society of Wisconsin, 1957).

17,730. United Women's Club
Records. 1916-46. 1 box.
Open. Register.
State Historical Society of Wisconsin.
Organized in 1917 in Madison after a preliminary meeting in 1916, this local group studied current political questions and supported laws for the welfare of humanity. Revised copies of the constitution and bylaws, minute books and minutes, correspondence, and a membership book. During WWI and WWII the Club participated in war bond drives, supported rationing and conservation of fats, and worked to combat diseases such as tuberculosis and cancer.

17,731. Versace, Tere Rios
Papers. 1941-73. 6 boxes and 12 tapes.
Partially closed. Register.
State Historical Society of Wisconsin.
Correspondence, biographical sketches, manuscripts and research material, notebooks, clippings, textbooks, and other items of Versace (1917-), a writer of short stories and novels whose eldest son Rocky Versace, a military advisor in South Vietnam, was captured by Viet Cong insurgents in 1963. For the next 10 years the Versace family worked to obtain his release and to obtain information about him. Much of Tere Versace's correspondence pertains to family matters, her son's capture, and her book publishing negotiations. Among her writings in the collection are manuscripts of an autobiographical account "Embroglio," pieces on the problem of prisoners of war and servicemen missing in action during the Vietnam war, and poetry. Also contains research material, including tapes and clippings, and other papers related to her book *The Flying Nun* about aviator Sister Aquinas. Versace has also written *An Angel Grows Up, Brother Angel,* and *The Fifteenth Pelican.* After her son's capture she became a member of the National League of Families of American Prisoners and Missing in Southeast Asia. Presently she is working as a journalist for *Off Duty Magazine* in West Germany.

17,732. Vilas, William F.
Papers. 1827-1959. 80 boxes and 29 vols.
Open. Register.
State Historical Society of Wisconsin.
General and family correspondence, diaries, notebooks, legal documents and records, accounts, and dockets of Vilas (1840-1908), a lawyer and a US senator from Wisconsin from 1891 to 1897. Includes letters from his wife Anna M. Vilas to her daughter Mary Esther concerning social life in Washington.

17,733. Visiting Nurse Service
Records. 1924-60. 2 vols.
Open. Register.
State Historical Society of Wisconsin.
In 1908 the Attic Angel Association, a local private charitable organization, sponsored the first visiting nurse in Madison; the Service began keeping separate files in 1924 but remained part of the Association until 1950 when it incorporated as a separate unit. Minutes, nursing committee reports, an index of minutes and correspondence, and a separate section of letters and reports "with Particular Historical Significance."

17,734. Vorse, Mary (Heaton)
Papers. 1928-30. 2 microfilm reels.
Open. Register.
State Historical Society of Wisconsin.
Papers of Vorse (1881-1966), a labor activist, journalist, and author, relate almost exclusively to the textile workers strikes in Gastonia and Marion, NC, and in Elizabethton, TN, in 1929. Correspondence; notes taken in Gastonia; manuscripts for her novel *Strike—A Novel of Gastonia* (1930) and for her article on the Marion strike, "Waitin' with the Dead"; news dispatches; and clippings.

17,735. Wales, Julia Grace
Papers. 1914-17. 1 box and 1 vol.
Open. Published guide.
State Historical Society of Wisconsin.
Papers of [Miss] Wales (1881-), a University of Wisconsin faculty member, concern the plan for continuous mediation without armistice that she developed in 1914. Drafts of the plan; correspondence from peace movement leaders, including Jane Addams and Louis P. Lochner of the Chicago Peace Society; letters that Wales wrote from the Netherlands and Scandinavia; and an account of a 1915 interview by Lochner and David S. Jordan with President Woodrow Wilson. Material reflects efforts to publicize Wales's mediation plan and to have Wilson call a conference of neutral nations. Includes material on the International Conference of Women at the Hague in 1915, the Ford Peace Expedition of 1915, and the Neutral Conference for Continuous Mediation in Stockholm in 1916. Wales's letters from the Netherlands and Scandinavia provide information about conditions in those countries that were neutral during WWI. See Alice E. Smith, ed., *Guide to the Manuscripts of the Wisconsin Historical Society* (Madison, WI: State Historical Society of Wisconsin, 1944).

17,736. Wheeler, William F., Sacajaweah: An Historical Sketch
Papers. 1893. 1 vol.
Open. Published guide.
State Historical Society of Wisconsin.
Sketch about Sacajaweah, the Shoshone Indian woman who accompanied the Lewis and Clark Expedition, was based largely on expedition journals. Taken from Alice E. Smith, ed., *Guide to the Manuscripts of the Wisconsin Historical Society* (Madison, WI: State Historical Society of Wisconsin, 1944).

17,737. Whetten, Harriet Douglas
Papers. 1855-65. 1 box.
Open. Register.
State Historical Society of Wisconsin.
Whetten (pre-1822-?), the daughter of John and Harriet Douglas Whetten, served as a Civil War army nurse on hospital ships sailing from New York and Philadelphia; later she became superintendent of nurses at Carver Hospital in Washington, DC. After the war she married a Mr. Gamble and lived for a time in Intervale, NH. Correspondence, a diary she kept in 1862, and miscellaneous family papers.

17,738. Wickenden, Elizabeth
Papers. Ca. 1950-72. Ca. 20 ft.
Access restricted. Catalog card.
State Historical Society of Wisconsin.
Correspondence, notes, memos, speeches, articles, reports, statements, and clippings document the career of Wickenden, an author, social welfare consultant, and professor of urban studies at the City University of New York graduate center. In 1956 Wickenden became a part-time consultant to the National Social Welfare Assembly, later called the National Assembly for Social Policy and Development. She served as the group's technical consultant in public schools. She visited Iran from 1957 to 1958 and served on committees concerned with public welfare in 1959 and 1966. Material reflects her activities in various organizations and concerns federal policy and legislation.

17,739. Wilcox, Ella (Wheeler)
Papers. 1917-20. 73 items.
Open. Published guide.
State Historical Society of Wisconsin.
Letters that [Mrs. Robert Marius] Wilcox (1850-1919), an author, wrote from California, Connecticut, France, and England primarily to her brother Marcus P. Wheeler of Windsor, WI, describing her interest in theosophy, various psychic phenomena, her war work in France, and her writings. Taken from Alice E. Smith, ed., *Guide to the Manuscripts of the Wisconsin Historical Society* (Madison, WI: State Historical Society of Wisconsin, 1944).

17,740. Willard, Frances Elizabeth Caroline
Papers. 1858-96. 13 items.
Open. Published guide.
State Historical Society of Wisconsin.
Willard (1839-98) was a temperance reformer and WCTU leader. Letters from Willard to her girlhood friend Theodora Smith, who later became Mrs. Solon Marks of Milwaukee. Also includes other items concerning personal affairs. Taken from Alice E. Smith, ed., *Guide to the Manuscripts of the Wisconsin Historical Society* (Madison, WI: State Historical Society of Wisconsin, 1944).

17,741. Wisconsin Council of Catholic Women
Records. 1916-70. 11 boxes.
Open. Register.
State Historical Society of Wisconsin.
Constitution and bylaws, executive board minutes, president's general correspondence, annual conference material, a subject file, historical data, and clippings of the Council, which was founded in 1916. Divided into 10 districts with 60 affiliate organizations, the Council's nearly 75,000 women are guided by a board of directors. Records reflect the attitudes of Catholic women and the church hierarchy toward a variety of issues.

17,742. Wisconsin Federation of Business and Professional Women's Clubs
Records. 1921-54. 5 ft.
Open. Catalog card.
State Historical Society of Wisconsin.
General correspondence, reports, and proceedings of state and national conventions of the group, which was founded in 1919. The National BPW was formed earlier in the year at the call of the YWCA.

17,743. Wisconsin History Commission
Records. 1861-1918. 5 boxes.
Open. Published guide.
State Historical Society of Wisconsin.
Material relating to the role of Wisconsin residents in the Civil War. Correspondence, including letters gathered in 1910 by Ethel A. Hurn concerning Wisconsin women during the War; minutes; sketches about Wisconsin volunteers; and miscellaneous items. Taken from Alice E. Smith, ed., *Guide to the Manuscripts of the Wisconsin Historical Society* (Madison, WI: State Historical Society of Wisconsin, 1944).

17,744. Wisconsin Jewish Oral History Interview Project
Oral history. 1954-74. 10 tapes and 2 transcripts.
Open. Published guide.
State Historical Society of Wisconsin.
Interviews with Jewish residents of Wisconsin conducted under the auspices of the State Historical Society in Madison and its regional centers in Milwaukee, LaCrosse, Racine, Kenosha, and Green Bay include those with the following

women: Pela Rosen Alpert (1920-), a Holocaust survivor who immigrated to Green Bay in 1949; Ida Berkowitz (1892-), a Kenosha woman who emigrated from Poland with her parents in 1906 and whose father was a rabbi and religious teacher; Clara Brown, a Milwaukee resident who emigrated from Russia in 1882 and recalls life in the Jewish community in Russia as well as changes in the Jewish immigrant community in Milwaukee; Esther Shapiro Cohen (1895-), a Milwaukee resident whose father was active in the Labor Zionist movement in 1914 and whose husband worked as a structural engineer and then as an insurance salesman in Milwaukee; Esther (Levitan) Goldstine, daughter of Wisconsin state treasurer Solomon Levitan who emigrated from Russia in 1862, and wife of Madison banker and philanthropist Sidney Goldstine; Nellie Jacob, a LaCrosse resident who discusses tensions between Orthodox and Reform Jews in the community and other topics; Bertha Langer Raymond (ca. 1867-?), an emigrant from Prague, Czechoslovakia, who describes her life in the Chicago, Detroit, and Milwaukee Jewish communities; Rae Ruscha (1881-), a Marinette and later Milwaukee resident who reminisces about Lizzie Black Kander and discusses problems between the old German-Jewish community and the newer Russian-Jewish community in Milwaukee after 1900; and Nellie Bornstein Winter (1869-?), a Racine resident whose grandfather was one of the first Jews to settle in Boston. Winter comments on her German-Jewish ancestors and on Jewish organizations in Racine. Taken from Lindsay B. Nauen, ed., *Guide to the Wisconsin Jewish Archives at the State Historical Society of Wisconsin* (Madison, WI: State Historical Society of Wisconsin, 1974).

17,745. Wisconsin League of Women Voters
Records. 1920-68. 69 boxes.
Open. Register.
State Historical Society of Wisconsin.
The Wisconsin LWV, an affiliate of the national LWV, was organized during a mass meeting called in 1920 in Milwaukee by the Wisconsin Woman's Suffrage Association. Minutes, correspondence, reports, bulletins, press releases, pamphlets, clippings, and other printed material relating to LWV interests and activities.

17,746. Wisconsin Society for the Equal Rights Amendment
Records. 1945-62. 2 boxes.
Open. Inventory.
State Historical Society of Wisconsin.
Formed in 1947 under the leadership of [Miss] Mabel E. Griswold, the Society sought to improve women's status and promote adoption of a constitutional amendment guaranteeing equal rights to women. Constitution, secretary and treasurer records, correspondence, speeches, voting records, convention material, information sheets, press releases, and other items, including correspondence with leaders of the National Woman's party, of whose executive council Griswold was secretary. The Wisconsin Society was very active until her death in 1955. In 1962 the Society transferred its remaining funds to the National Woman's party.

17,747. Wisconsin State Federation of Women's Clubs
Records. 1899-1954. 5 boxes and 12 vols.
Open. Register.
State Historical Society of Wisconsin.
The state Federation was formed in 1896 during a meeting held in Milwaukee at the invitation of the Milwaukee Endowment Association and attended by 105 delegates from 63 clubs. Minutes of the executive board, board of directors, and annual conventions; audit and financial reports; correspondence; general reports; and a *History of the Wisconsin Federation of Women's Clubs.* Includes correspondence of Mrs. Henry Youmans, president of the Wisconsin Federation of Women's Clubs and secretary of the GFWC. The Federation helped establish libraries throughout the state, win approval of better laws for women and children, and gain improved educational facilities. The group has supported a conservation program, an educational loan fund, nurses' scholarships, and other projects.

17,748. Wisconsin State League of Nursing Education
Records. 1919-50. 7 boxes.
Open. Register and card catalog.
State Historical Society of Wisconsin.
Constitutions and bylaws, minutes, correspondence, committee and convention reports, and printed matter of the League, which sought to further uniform standards in nursing education.

17,749. Wisconsin Woman's Suffrage Association
Records. 1892-1925. 26 boxes and 1 vol.
Open. Published guide.
State Historical Society of Wisconsin.
Records trace the Association's history and its reorganization as the LWV. Contains papers of [Mrs.] Theodora W. Youmans, Association president from 1913 to 1920 and member of the national Republican party Committee of Policies and Platforms in 1920. Minutes, financial and legislative reports, correspondence kept by Youmans, press releases, and historic and biographical sketches of the organization and its leaders. Women represented in the correspondence include [Mrs.] Meta Berger; Olympia Brown, a minister; [Mrs.] Carrie Chapman Catt; [Mrs.] Antoinette Funk; Zona Gale; Ada Lois James; [Mrs.] Rachael S. Jastrow; [Mrs.] Belle (Case) La Follette; and [Mrs.] Jennie McMullin Turner. Also contains papers concerning Youman's work as chairman of the Republican State Central Committee woman's division and as a national policies committee member as well as material presented by the Suffrage Association's legislative chairman [Mrs.] Jessie J. Hooper, which includes correspondence of the Political Equality League of Wisconsin. The records provide information about the relationships of suffragists to political parties and other women's groups, their interest in progressive legislation, and their service during WWI. Taken from Alice E. Smith, ed., *Guide to the Manuscripts of the Wisconsin Historical Society* (Madison, WI: State Historical Society of Wisconsin, 1944).

17,750. Woman's Christian Temperance Union, Loyal Temperance Legion of Wisconsin
Records. 1890-1964. 2 boxes.
Open. Register.
State Historical Society of Wisconsin.
The Legion, formed in the late 1880s by [Miss] Annie J. Bradbury, was devoted to educating children from ages 6 to 12 about temperance. Correspondence; manuscripts of "Prohibition and the Child" (1910) and "Alcohol Education" (1934); printed material, including new bulletins of the national WCTU and the program for the 70th convention in 1944; and letters, post cards, convention programs, photos, and clippings that form a history of the Wisconsin Legion. The group sponsored day camps, essay contests, and annual conventions.

17,751. Woman's Relief Corps, Department of Potomac, Washington, DC
Records. 1917-22. 1 vol.
Open. Published guide.
State Historical Society of Wisconsin.
Principally correspondence of Department presidents with other Corps officers and with other patriotic and charitable organizations concerning elections, memorial services, meetings, resignations, and other matters. Taken from Alice E. Smith, ed., *Guide to the Manuscripts of the Wisconsin Historical Society* (Madison, WI: State Historical Society of Wisconsin, 1944).

17,752. Women of the Ku Klux Klan, Klan 14
Records. 1926-31. 1 folder.
Open. Card catalog.
State Historical Society of Wisconsin.
Records of the Chippewa Falls, WI, chapter of the Klan auxiliary organization consist of minutes, financial reports, communications from the Wisconsin Realm office and from Imperial Headquarters, and miscellaneous items.

17,753. Women's International League for Peace and Freedom, Madison
Records. 1924-65. 1 box.
Open. Register.
State Historical Society of Wisconsin.
Organized in 1922, the Madison branch was affiliated with the WILPF, which had its origin in an international women's congress in 1915. Assembled at The Hague to protest WWI, the delegates to the congress formed the Women's International Committee for Permanent Peace, renamed WILPF in 1919. Minutes, treasurer's reports, correspondence, articles, speeches, a 1965 membership list, clippings, and mimeographed material.

17,754. Women's National Abortion Action Coalition
Records. 1971-72. 8 cu.ft.
Open. Register.
State Historical Society of Wisconsin.
Founded in 1971, this organization seeks repeal of anti-abortion legislation and opposes forced sterilization and restrictive laws governing the age of persons purchasing contraceptives. Minutes; office and reference files, including those on legal actions, abortion in various states, and the medical, legal, and psychological aspects of abortion; news releases; and clippings. Also contains tape recordings, primarily of abortion-related conferences.

17,755. Women's Overseas Service League
Records. 1926-43. 2 boxes.
Open. Register.
State Historical Society of Wisconsin.
Formed in 1926 by [Mrs.] Maude Webster Middleton, the Madison unit was part of the national League, which was founded in 1921 to unite women who served overseas with the WWI American Expeditionary Force. Records of the local, regional, and national League include the national constitution, bylaws, minutes of the executive board, annual reports, letters from national committees to the Madison unit, and publicity material; agenda, correspondence, and conference announcements of the regional League area, which consisted of Illinois, Michigan, Missouri, and Wisconsin; and minutes, a secretary's book, correspondence, treasurer's and service reports, membership lists, and other records of the Madison unit.

17,756. Women's Trade Union League, Milwaukee Chapter
Records. 1948-56. 2 boxes.
Open. Register.
State Historical Society of Wisconsin.
The group, founded in 1949, actively promoted social reform during the first half of the 1950s, particularly in connection with local and national efforts to obtain a medical health plan and to secure equal rights for women in industry and government. Minutes of membership and executive board meetings, financial and membership records, general correspondence, bulletins, newsletters, and miscellaneous items of the League and other labor and social action organizations. The Chapter supported Milwaukee unions in strikes and other activities and provided a social organization for the city's working women.

17,757. Woodbury, Helen Sumner
Papers. 1896-1933. 10 boxes.
Open. Register.
State Historical Society of Wisconsin.
A student of John R. Commons and one of the early women labor economists, Woodbury (1876-1933) was an industrial expert in the US Department of Labor from 1913 to 1915 and assistant chief of the US Children's Bureau from 1915 to 1918. Correspondence pertaining to her career, writings, and interests in liberal and socialist causes; files from the Children's Bureau and reference files on organizations to which she belonged; drafts and notes from her publications; and clippings. Includes her correspondence with James MacKaye and items reflecting her contributions to the founding of the Institute of Political Engineering. Among her published works are *The White Slave* (1896); *Labor Problems: A Textbook* (1905), co-authored by Thomas Sewall Adams; *Equal Suffrage: The Results of an Investigation in Colorado Made for the Collegiate Equal Suffrage League of New York State* (1909); and *History of Women in Industry* (1911).

17,758. Wright, Elizabeth Steele
Papers. 1846-58. 1 microfilm reel.
Open. Published guide.
State Historical Society of Wisconsin.
Selections from five diaries by [Mrs.] Wright (1825-1913), who describes impressions she formed of the Midwest when she accompanied her husband on a lecture tour after their marriage in 1846. Also includes articles written by her daughter and granddaughter about her life during the 1840s and 1850s in Sauk City, WI, and Prairie du Sac, WI. See Josephine L. Harper, ed., *Guide to the Manuscripts of the State Historical Society of Wisconsin, Supplement 2* (Madison, WI: State Historical Society of Wisconsin, 1966).

17,759. Yost, Barbara
Papers. 1962-66. 6 in.
Access restricted. Catalog card.
State Historical Society of Wisconsin.
Yost was a Peace Corps worker in Costa Rica. Correspondence with her parents, clippings, and material about the Peace Corps, including a volunteer questionnaire, description of a placement test, and orientation and registration schedule.

17,760. Young, Frances Berkeley
Papers. 1912. 30 items.
Open. Published guide.
State Historical Society of Wisconsin.
Correspondence received by [Mrs. Karl] Young of Madison and notes, articles, and clippings collected or prepared by her for addresses and debates on woman suffrage. Taken from Alice E. Smith, ed., *Guide to the Manuscripts of the Wisconsin Historical Society* (Madison, WI: State Historical Society of Wisconsin, 1944).

17,761. Young, Mrs. Ludwick Craven
Papers. 1748-1933. 1 box.
Open. Register.
State Historical Society of Wisconsin.
Letters from Hattie Young of Frederick County, MD, chiefly to her daughter Matilda, who was apparently in Europe serving as secretary to Mrs. Cornelius Vanderbilt II; letters from other Young family members containing genealogical information about Young ancestors; and family wills and deeds, 1748-1814, copied from records in Washington County, MD. Correspondence contains many personal references to Senator Robert M. LaFollette, Jr., and his wife Rachel Wilson (Young) LaFollette, who was also a daughter of Mr. and Mrs. Ludwick Young.

17,762. Zotos, Helen (Mamas)
Papers. 1947-67. 6 boxes.
Open. Register.
State Historical Society of Wisconsin.
Zotos (1923-) is a news correspondent and writer known for her work covering the Greek civil war from 1946 to 1949. Correspondence, notebooks, articles and files on her work for the Associated Press and for Radio Free Europe, biographical material, and other items. Bulk of the collection pertains to her articles, particularly to a five-part series "Europe's Teenagers," written in 1958 for *American Weekly* magazine. Her notebooks contain daily observations about news events and reports written in preparation for her dispatches. From 1946 to 1949 Helen Mamas, a reporter for the Associated Press, was the only woman accredited to the Greek General Staff and the youngest US overseas correspondent. She married Stephano Zotos in 1948, but the marriage was annulled. Using the name Miss Helen Zotos, she then worked as a free-lance magazine writer. During the late 1960s Zotos was a public affairs officer for the US Department of Commerce and editor of the *Sunday Feature,* a publication concerning the Department's internal activities.

17,763. American Association of University Women
Records. 1916- . 0.33 cu.ft.
Open. No guide.
University of Wisconsin-Madison Archives.
Bulletins and other material pertain to the AAUW on campus.

17,764. Association of Faculty Women
Records. Nd. No size given.
Open. No guide.
University of Wisconsin-Madison Archives.
Miscellaneous printed matter of the Association.

17,765. Brandeis, Elizabeth
Papers. 1927-65. 0.3 cu.ft.
Open. Unpublished guide.
University of Wisconsin-Madison Archives.
Correspondence, reference cards, and economics examinations of Brandeis (1896-), a professor in the University school of economics, chiefly relate to economics course work and, especially, her research on labor relations. She is married to Paul Raushenbush.

17,766. Cooper, Signe S.
Papers. 1954-74. 11 cu.ft.
Open. Unpublished guide.
University of Wisconsin-Madison Archives.
Cooper was a registered nurse who chaired the University extension division's department of nursing. The collection consists primarily of her general subject files about course offerings but also includes correspondence, course material, and taped lectures.

17,767. Dean of Women
Records. 1920-68. 2 cu.ft.
Open. Unpublished guide.
University of Wisconsin-Madison Archives.
Reports, correspondence, and information files of the Dean relate to student affairs. Includes financial reports from cooperative housing units, housing applications, admission requirements and high school relations material, information about budgets, and items of the student personnel and intellectual enterprise committees.

17,768. Gerry, Eloise
Papers. 1910-33. 0.3 cu.ft.
Open. No guide.
University of Wisconsin-Madison Archives.
Reports, work notebooks, photos, and clippings of [Miss] Gerry, an early associate of the Forest Products Laboratory.

17,769. Governor's Commission on the Status of Women
Records. 1964-70. 2.6 cu.ft.
Open. Unpublished guide.
University of Wisconsin-Madison Archives.
Correspondence, Commission reports, and conference documents from the files of Commission chairwoman Kathryn F. Clarenbach contain material pertaining to national, midwestern, and statewide conferences; recommendations for legislation; family problems; and women's employment.

17,770. Hazeltine, Mary Emogene
Papers. 1921-39. 0.5 cu.ft.
Open. Unpublished guide.
University of Wisconsin-Madison Archives.
Personal correspondence and files of [Miss] Hazeltine (1868-1949), a University library school faculty member, and working notes for her book *100 Years of Wisconsin Authors.*

17,771. Histories and Biographies
Collection. 1849- . No size given.
Open. No guide.
University of Wisconsin-Madison Archives.
Among many histories, biographies, and autobiographies relating to women and University activities are Helen R. Olin's *The Women of a State University* (New York, 1909); Nancy D. Sachse's *A Thousand Ages* (1965); Susan Henkel's *A Tribute to Rachel Katherine Schenk* (1963); and Gertrude Slaughter's *Only the Past Is Ours: The Life Story of Gertrude Slaughter.*

17,772. Hornback, May
Papers. 1948-76. 6 cu.ft.
Open. Unpublished guide.
University of Wisconsin-Madison Archives.
Papers of [Mrs.] Hornback (?-1976), who chaired the University extension department of nursing, include her research and working files, departmental records, student papers, and material relating to professional organizations.

17,773. Murray, Christina
Papers. 1938-48. 0.3 cu.ft.
Open. Unpublished guide.
University of Wisconsin-Madison Archives.
Papers of Murray (1896-1948), who directed the University school of nursing, include administrative and personal correspondence, speeches and addresses, and memorial material relating to her death.

17,774. National Organization for Women
Records. 1967-72. 3 cu.ft.
Open. No guide.
University of Wisconsin-Madison Archives.
Board minutes, correspondence, statements, and newsletters of NOW were gathered by Kathryn F. Clarenbach, a NOW member, and include material about NOW's local chapters throughout the country and about its national conventions. Position papers focus on abortion, proposed legislation, and educational matters.

17,775. Oral History Project
Oral history. 1972- . Ca. 7 vols.
Open. Index.
University of Wisconsin-Madison Archives.
Tapes, transcripts, and printed volumes of University reminiscences include those of faculty members Anna Grant Birge, Elizabeth Brandeis, Ruth Henderson, Margaret Irwin, and Germaine Mercier and of Mrs. Harry Hayden Clark and Lillian Dykstra, who were administrators' wives. The interviews attempt to correlate academic concerns with the general social climate of Madison over the years.

17,776. Peterson, Martha E.
Papers. 1963-67. 25 cu.ft.
Open. Unpublished guide.
University of Wisconsin-Madison Archives.
Peterson was dean of women, a special assistant to University of Wisconsin president Fred Harvey Harrington, and dean of student affairs.

Administrative correspondence relating to her University positions and duties and material about high school relations, the Herfurth Award, and the 1963 Fulbright Conference.

17,777. Schenk, Rachel Katherine
Papers. 1949-64. 2.5 cu.ft.
Open. Unpublished guide.
University of Wisconsin-Madison Archives.
Papers of [Miss] Schenk, a University library school director, include letters relating to social events and employment for library graduates; general work files, with material on the evaluation of the Madison Veterans Administration library; and class syllabi.

17,778. Senior Swingout
Records. 1936-65. 0.3 cu.ft.
Open. No guide.
University of Wisconsin-Madison Archives.
Correspondence, skits and programs, and clippings from the dean of women's office pertain to a commencement ritual involving graduating senior women and junior class women.

17,779. Smith, Louise
Papers. 1961-75. 1.3 cu.ft.
Open. Unpublished guide.
University of Wisconsin-Madison Archives.
Correspondence, status reports and organizational charts of the University school of nursing, material about committee meetings, and research papers of Smith, a director of the school of nursing.

17,780. Student Family History Interviews
Collection. 1972-76. 0.3 cu.ft.
Open. No guide.
University of Wisconsin-Madison Archives.
Open letter interviews written by University history students, some of them women, contain descriptions of the students' home life as well as the social climate they encountered after moving to and living on campus.

17,781. Student Folders
Records. 1945- . 50 cu.ft.
Access restricted. Unpublished guide.
University of Wisconsin-Madison Archives.
Admissions records, grade reports, and other basic information on all University students since WWII.

17,782. Student Scrapbooks and Diaries
Collection. 1893-1960. No size given.
Open. Unpublished guide.
University of Wisconsin-Madison Archives.
Diaries and scrapbooks of women students contain photos, clippings, programs of social events, and invitations and provide an especially detailed view of University social activities, students' classes, and daily life in the early 1900s.

17,783. Troxell, Louise
Papers. 1940-56. 0.2 cu.ft.
Open. Unpublished guide.
University of Wisconsin-Madison Archives.
Correspondence and reports of Troxell (?-1974), who was dean of women, pertain to her administrative functions and her retirement.

17,784. United States Cadet Nurse Corps
Records. 1943-47. 3 cu.ft.
Open. Unpublished guide.
University of Wisconsin-Madison Archives.
Records of the Corps, which functioned as part of the Bureau of Public Health Services on the University campus, include correspondence, fiscal records, and requisitions.

17,785. University Education of Women
Records. 1944-45. 0.15 cu.ft.
Open. No guide.
University of Wisconsin-Madison Archives.
File contains reports about a University conference on women's job opportunities and a statement of aims and objectives contemplated by the dean of women.

17,786. University League
Records. 1901-71. 0.33 cu.ft.
Open. Unpublished guide.
University of Wisconsin-Madison Archives.
Founded in 1901, the League was a social group for faculty members' wives. Histories of the League, scrapbooks, and programs of social events.

17,787. University YWCA
Records. 1884-1972. 14 cu.ft.
Open. Unpublished guide.
University of Wisconsin-Madison Archives.
Constitution, bylaws, minutes, correspondence, financial records, histories, and programs of the YWCA on campus. Material after 1968 highlights such social issues as abortion, civil rights, and birth control.

17,788. White, Helen C.
Papers. 1917-65. 28 cu.ft. and 1 tape.
Partially restricted. Unpublished guide.
University of Wisconsin-Madison Archives.
Professional correspondence and academic recommendations of White (1896-1967), a professor in and chairman of the University department of English. Also includes White's personal correspondence with family members, manuscripts and other writings, index cards, a taped interview, and bibliographies.

17,789. Women's Education Programs
Records. 1962- . 0.15 cu.ft.
Open. No guide.
University of Wisconsin-Madison Archives.
Reports of seminars pertaining to women, held between 1962 and 1963 during the two-year programs at Wisconsin Center campuses, were assembled from the University extension informal instructional services files.

17,790. Women's Self-Government Association
Records. 1889-1966. 5 cu.ft.
Open. Unpublished guide.
University of Wisconsin-Madison Archives.
Constitution of the Association, correspondence, scrapbooks of Association members, bulletins, financial records, and reports of career conferences, which were designed to help women plan their education.

17,791. Adato, Perry Miller
Papers. Nd. No size given.
Open. Unpublished guide.
University of Wisconsin-Madison, Wisconsin Center for Film and Theater Research.
Motion picture film and audio tapes of Adato, a film producer, consist primarily of outtakes from her documentary on Dylan Thomas, *The World I Breathe* (1968), and her documentary on designer Charles Eames, *An Eames Celebration* (1974).

17,792. Biberman, Herbert, and Sondergaard, Gale
Papers. 1908-64. 104 boxes, 7 packages, and 1 microfilm reel.
Access restricted. Unpublished guide.
University of Wisconsin-Madison, Wisconsin Center for Film and Theater Research.
Included with the correspondence, essays, radio broadcasts, and clippings of Biberman (1900-), a blacklisted film director, are numerous plays and film scripts of Sondergaard (1901-), an Oscar-winning actress who also was investigated by the House Committee on Un-American Activities in 1951, and essays she wrote, a script for *As the Pines,* photos, and scrapbooks. Also contains legal documents pertaining to the court case involving an alleged conspiracy by such film companies as RKO and Loew's Inc. and the theatrical unions to prevent completion and distribution of a film produced by Independent Productions Corporation, a film company founded by Biberman in 1951 to utilize the talents of blacklisted Hollywood personnel. The IPC lost the case in 1964 because the conspiracy charge could not be proven.

17,793. Caspary, Vera
Papers. 1929-68. 33 boxes and 3 packages.
Open. Inventory.
University of Wisconsin-Madison, Wisconsin Center for Film and Theater Research.
Correspondence of Caspary (1904-68), a novelist, playwright, and screen story writer; notes, drafts, revisions, manuscripts, and copies of published and unpublished material; and scrapbooks. Includes information about such Caspary works as *Wedding in Paris,* a musical; *A Chosen Sparrow* (1964), *The Man Who Loved His Wife* (1966), and *The Rosecrest Cell* (1968), novels; *The Husband,* a play; and *Illicit,* a screenplay.

17,794. Clarke, Shirley
Papers. 1952-72. 11 boxes and 1 motion picture.
Access restricted. Inventory.
University of Wisconsin-Madison, Wisconsin Center for Film and Theater Research.
In addition to being a pioneering film maker in the New America Cinema, also known as the avant-garde or underground film movement, Clarke (1927-) was an experimenting video artist and dancer. Correspondence, personal notebooks, budget records, production files, scripts, photos, biographical material, film festival information, and a motion picture.

17,795. Ferber, Edna
Papers. 1913-63. 24 boxes and 4 recording discs.
Access restricted. Inventory.
University of Wisconsin-Madison, Wisconsin Center for Film and Theater Research.
Correspondence of Ferber (1887-1968), a novelist; research material; drafts relating to her novels; short stories; autobiographies; recording discs; and material pertaining to the theater production of *Show Boat* and the films *Cimarron* and *Nobody's in Town.*

17,796. Fitzgerald, Ella
Collection. Nd. 3 packages.
Open. Inventory.
University of Wisconsin-Madison, Wisconsin Center for Film and Theater Research.
Holograph orchestrations by Nelson Riddle of Ira Gershwin songs are each autographed by Riddle, Gershwin, and Fitzgerald (1918-), a black singer.

17,797. Frings, Katherine "Ketti"
Papers. 1921-62. 25 boxes, 14 vols., and 1 package.
Open. Inventory.
University of Wisconsin-Madison, Wisconsin Center for Film and Theater Research.
Frings (1921-62) was a playwright, novelist, and screenwriter. Correspondence, notes, drafts, scripts, biographical material, scrapbooks, and other items relate to her stage plays, screenplays, short stories, and novels. Among the plays she wrote or adapted, which are represented in the collection, are *Command Performance* and *Look Homeward Angel;* among the screenplays are *Come Back Little Sheba, The Shrike,* and *Guest in the House.*

17,798. Goetz, Ruth (Goodman)
Papers. 1916-59. 13 boxes, 19 vols., and 1 package.
Open. Inventory.
University of Wisconsin-Madison, Wisconsin Center for Film and Theater Research.
Included with the papers of her husband and collaborator Augustus Goetz and her father Philip Goodman, who was a publisher, writer, and producer, are papers of Ruth Goetz (1912-59), a playwright. Correspondence, personal financial records, plays and play fragments, short stories,

annotated novels, sketches, photos, and costume plates.

17,799. Goodrich, Frances, and Hackett, Albert
Papers. 1927-61. 13 boxes, 9 vols., and 3 packages.
Open. Inventory.
University of Wisconsin-Madison, Wisconsin Center for Film and Theater Research.
Goodrich and Hackett were playwrights who collaborated to write many motion picture scripts as well as several stage plays. Scripts, including those for *Ah, Wilderness; Father of the Bride;* and the motion picture series *The Thin Man,* and correspondence. Most of the material pertains to the 1956 Pulitzer Prize-winning play *The Diary of Anne Frank,* for which Goodrich and Hackett wrote both the stage and screen adaptations. Goodrich and Hackett were married.

17,800. Harris, Reneé
Papers. 1904-70. 1 box.
Open. Inventory.
University of Wisconsin-Madison, Wisconsin Center for Film and Theater Research.
New York's first woman theatrical producer, Harris (1876-1969) also co-owned the Hudson Theatre with her husband Henry Harris. Correspondence about the Theatre; poetry, short stories, and articles Harris wrote; biographical information; theater programs and legal documents; and material about the sinking of the *Titanic.*

17,801. Hart, Moss, and Carlisle, Kitty
Papers. 1922-67. 14 boxes, 56 vols., 4 tapes, and 2 motion pictures.
Open. Inventory.
University of Wisconsin-Madison, Wisconsin Center for Film and Theater Research.
Items of Hart, a playwright and director, are supplemented by correspondence, scrapbooks, and clippings of Carlisle, an actress, singer, and television personality.

17,802. Head, Edith
Papers. 1934-65. 23 boxes.
Open. Inventory.
University of Wisconsin-Madison, Wisconsin Center for Film and Theater Research.
Costume designs by Head (1899-), a prominent motion picture and theater costume designer; annotated sketches for 55 motion pictures, including her Academy Award-winning designs; material about Head's awards and appearances; and serialized portions of her first book *The Dress Doctor.* Among her motion picture costume sketches are those for *Breakfast at Tiffany's, The Ten Commandments,* and *To Catch a Thief.* The Head sketches are available on microfilm.

17,803. Isaacs, Edith J. R.
Papers. 1889-1963. 1 box and 1 microfilm reel.
Access restricted. Inventory.
University of Wisconsin-Madison, Wisconsin Center for Film and Theater Research.
Isaacs (1878-1956), a journalist, was the editor of *Theatre Arts* magazine. Correspondence between Isaacs and Thornton Wilder, Edith Hamilton, D. H. Lawrence, and Martha Graham; writings of Isaacs and members of her family; and typescripts of two early 20th-century operettas that she and her husband Lewis Isaacs wrote.

17,804. Jeakins, Dorothy
Papers. 1938-73. 9 boxes.
Open. Register.
University of Wisconsin-Madison, Wisconsin Center for Film and Theater Research.
Notes of Jeakins (1914-), a costume designer for motion pictures, theater, and television; workbooks with swatches of cloth attached; sketches, including some in color transparencies; and photos. Among the 18 motion pictures represented in her sketches are *Green Mansions, Hawaii, Oliver, The Sound of Music,* and *Catch 22.* Also includes costume sketches for four California and seven New York theater productions, among them *King Lear* and *Major Barbara,* and her sketches for three television programs.

17,805. Kerby, Elizabeth Poe
Papers. 1953-61. 1 folder.
Open. Unpublished guide.
University of Wisconsin-Madison, Wisconsin Center for Film and Theater Research.
Copies of four published articles written by Kerby, a reporter, pertain to the 1952-53 Hollywood blacklist. Also includes an unpublished summary of her findings, which was prepared for the Fund for the Republic.

17,806. Kerr, Walter, and Kerr, Jean (Collins)
Papers. 1929-69. 72 boxes, 59 vols., 15 tapes, 1 package, 1 container and 16 recording discs.
Open. Inventory.
University of Wisconsin-Madison, Wisconsin Center for Film and Theater Research.
Jean Kerr (1923-), a playwright and humorist, and her husband Walter Kerr, working individually and together, wrote essays, short stories, lyrics, books, plays, and adaptations for stage and television productions. Correspondence between the Kerrs and numerous well-known persons; correspondence and legal information for Jean Kerr's books *Please Don't Eat the Daisies, The Snake Has All the Lines,* and *Penny Candy;* financial statements; notes, typescripts, and reviews of their writings; photos; clippings; and awards.

17,807. Lewis, Isabella W.
Papers. 1878-1944. 1 box and 4 vols.
Open. Unpublished guide.
University of Wisconsin-Madison, Wisconsin Center for Film and Theater Research.
Scrapbooks contain theater and opera programs from productions in the New York City area.

17,808. Mary Tyler Moore Enterprises
Records. 1970-77. 20 boxes.
Open. Unpublished guide.
University of Wisconsin-Madison, Wisconsin Center for Film and Theater Research.
Scripts and variant material of all television shows produced by MTM Enterprises, founded by actress Mary Tyler Moore (1937-), and a sampling of films and prints from the first to the final season of "The Mary Tyler Moore Show." Among other MTM productions represented are "Rhoda," "Phyllis," and "The Bob Newhart Show."

17,809. Moorehead, Agnes
Papers. 1923-74. 159 boxes.
Open. Unpublished guide.
University of Wisconsin-Madison, Wisconsin Center for Film and Theater Research.
Papers of Moorehead (1901-74), an actress, include radio, motion picture, television, and theater scripts; 104 scrapbooks; correspondence; photos; clippings; and programs. Beginning her career in such early radio shows as the "Mercury Theatre of the Air" and "Suspense Theatre," Moorehead then starred in films, including *Citizen Kane, The Magnificent Ambersons,* and *Journey into Fear;* in theater; and in television, particularly in the series "Bewitched." An organizer and teacher at her own drama school in California, she also lectured and performed throughout the US in a one-woman show.

17,810. Phillips, Irna
Papers. 1931-68. 68 boxes.
Open. Inventory.
University of Wisconsin-Madison, Wisconsin Center for Film and Theater Research.
A radio and television writer, Phillips (1901-73) originated the daytime drama soap opera format. Correspondence, program outlines, drafts, and production scripts of many of her radio and television productions and records of Radio Scripts, Inc., for which Phillips served as consultant.

17,811. Roberts, Flora
Papers. 1963. 1 tape.
Open. Unpublished guide.
University of Wisconsin-Madison, Wisconsin Center for Film and Theater Research.
Lecture entitled "Broadway or Theater" was given by Roberts, a theatrical agent.

17,812. Rosenthal, Jean
Papers. 1941-66. 41 boxes, 1 oversize file, and 1 package.
Open. Inventory.
University of Wisconsin-Madison, Wisconsin Center for Film and Theater Research.
Rosenthal (1912-69) was a noted theatrical lighting director and technical consultant. Lighting notes and plans, stage designs, and light plots for numerous theater and dance productions.

17,813. Sanders, Marlene
Papers. 1969-73. 2 boxes.
Open. Unpublished guide.
University of Wisconsin-Madison, Wisconsin Center for Film and Theater Research.
A radio and television news correspondent, Sanders also writes and produces television documentaries. Correspondence, budget material, production records, and reviews pertain to her documentary *Population: Boom or Doom.*

17,814. Shawa, Nadonis
Papers. 1921-51. 1 folder.
Open. Unpublished guide.
University of Wisconsin-Madison, Wisconsin Center for Film and Theater Research.
Correspondence, playbills, brochures, and performance outlines of Shawa, an Ojibwe poet and performer who presented programs of and about Indian music and legends in the US.

17,815. Sherry, Laura Case
Papers. 1853-1947. 3 boxes and 7 vols.
Open. Register and inventory.
University of Wisconsin-Madison, Wisconsin Center for Film and Theater Research.
Correspondence, manuscripts of pantomime ballets, theater programs, and press books with clippings of Sherry (1876-1947), who, along with Zona Gale and University of Wisconsin professor Thomas H. Dickinson, organized the Wisconsin Dramatic Society, the first experimental theater group in the US, in 1909. Also contains a journal, kept by her father Lawrence Case, about a journey via Panama to San Francisco and back between 1853 and 1855; it also contains descriptions of his work as a merchant in San Francisco.

Laura Sherry attended the University of Wisconsin but graduated from the Northwestern University School of Speech and the Empire Theatre Dramatic School in New York. Her work in establishing the Wisconsin Dramatic Society in 1909 led to creation of the Wisconsin Players of Milwaukee, a small amateur theater company, of which Sherry was the chief financial backer. In 1918 and 1919 she acted in and directed plays for a YMCA-sponsored entertainment program for soldiers in France. Throughout the 1920s and 1930s she lectured frequently, wrote plays and pantomime ballets, and remained active in the Wisconsin Players. During WWII she worked in a canteen for merchant marines in New York City.

17,816. Spier, William, and Havoc, June
Papers. 1931-68. 38 boxes.
Open. Inventory.
University of Wisconsin-Madison, Wisconsin Center for Film and Theater Research.
Papers of Spier include limited material of Havoc (1916-), an actress, which highlights her

performances in the television show "Willy" and in the motion picture *Lady Possessed.*

17,817. Taylor, Fan T.
Papers. 1946-73. 11 boxes.
Access restricted. Unpublished guide.
University of Wisconsin-Madison, Wisconsin Center for Film and Theater Research.
Taylor was a university professor and administrator with the National Endowment for the Arts. NEA annual and staff reports and audience surveys; progress reports and financial information about the University of Wisconsin Union Theater, 1946-65; and correspondence with violinist Isaac Stern.

17,818. Temple, Shirley
Papers. 1957-58. 1 box.
Open. Catalog card.
University of Wisconsin-Madison, Wisconsin Center for Film and Theater Research.
Scripts from five episodes of actress Temple's television series "Shirley Temple's Storybook."

17,819. Webster, Margaret
Papers. 1940-41. 1 folder.
Open. Catalog card.
University of Wisconsin-Madison, Wisconsin Center for Film and Theater Research.
Prompting script of Webster (1905-72), a theatrical producer, for her production of *The Three Sisters,* which was presented by the Wisconsin Players in 1969.

MANITOWOC

17,820. Archives
Records. 1856- . 8 drawers and 2 cupboards.
Closed. No guide.
Franciscan Sisters of Christian Charity, Holy Family Convent.
The community was founded in 1869 at Manitowoc and joined with a group of German sisters in 1875. Minutes, financial records, correspondence, diaries, oral history tapes, correspondence and other papers of mothers general, photos, scrapbooks, and other records of the community and of the German sisters' community, which was founded in 1856 in Germany. Includes reports on the founding of Holy Family Hospital in Manitowoc; Good Samaritan Hospital in Zanesville, OH; St. Joseph Home for Aged in West Point, NE; Indian missions in Arizona; and schools in Hawaii as well as records on the development of Catholic education at all levels, the chief work of the community.

MENASHA

17,821. Altrusa Club of Neenah and Menasha, USA
Records. 1960- . 0.5 ft.
Open. Unpublished guide.
Elisha D. Smith Public Library.
Financial records, correspondence, yearbooks, and scrapbooks of the Club, a community service organization organized in 1960; members raise money to provide scholarships for local high school students, adult women needing vocational training to return to the labor market, and the deaf as well as grants for foreign students requiring additional funds to complete their education in the US. The Club also provides financial assistance to Operation Santa Claus, the Half Way House, The ABC House, the American National Red Cross, and the American Field Service.

17,822. American Association of University Women
Records. 1940- . 1.5 ft.
Open. Unpublished guide.
Elisha D. Smith Public Library.
Minutes, financial records, correspondence, yearbooks, photos, and scrapbooks of the Neenah-Menasha branch of the AAUW, which was formed in 1940. The organization conducts study groups on topics of current interest to women and plans fund-raising projects such as book sales, home tours, style shows, and art exhibits to finance scholarships and fellowship grants. The scholarships are given to local high school girls for college expenses; the fellowships, awarded each year in the name of one local woman who is thought to have contributed most to the community, provide funds to the national AAUW.

17,823. Neenah-Menasha Federated Woman's Club
Records. 1898- . 0.5 ft.
Open. Unpublished guide.
Elisha D. Smith Public Library.
Financial records, yearbooks, photos, and scrapbooks of the Club, which originated in 1898 as the Household Economics Club, was renamed the Economics Club in 1900, and one year later became the Federated Economics Club. In 1974 the group assumed its present name. In addition to studying modern literature, drama, art, music, health, and civics, the Club devotes time to and raises money for education, conservation, public and international affairs, arts, and home life. For example, they support CARE, local libraries, Trees for Tomorrow scholarships for teachers, and other projects. They also select one local woman each year for the Theodora Youmans Citizenship award.

17,824. Neenah-Menasha Music Club
Records. 1944- . 0.25 ft.
Open. Unpublished guide.
Elisha D. Smith Public Library.
Financial records, yearbooks, notebooks, photos, and scrapbooks of the Club, begun in 1944 as a music department within the Neenah-Menasha Federated Woman's Club. In 1965 the group assumed its present separate identity. The Club, whose members share their interest and talent in music, sponsors musical programs, the proceeds from which are used to provide such community services as music books for nursing homes and phonograph records for libraries. Individual members perform or lead sing-alongs at the Winnebago County Mental Health Hospital and at various nursing homes. Members also perform at Club meetings.

17,825. Twin Cities Business and Professional Women's Club
Records. 1928- . 0.25 ft.
Open. Unpublished guide.
Elisha D. Smith Public Library.
Correspondence, photos, scrapbooks, and clippings of the Club, a community service organization established in 1928, whose members manage Operation Santa Claus at Christmas and provide several scholarships to Neenah-Menasha area high school students each year. In addition, the Club annually selects a "Woman of the Year" from the local community and honors their most active member as "Club Sweetheart" each June.

17,826. Visiting Nurse Association
Records. 1908- . 0.25 ft.
Open. Unpublished guide.
Elisha D. Smith Public Library.
Financial records, notebooks, yearbooks, histories, photos, and scrapbooks of the Association, established in 1908 to protect and promote better community health. Association-sponsored community services, which are financed by private donations and an annual benefit dance, include nurse house calls, prenatal classes, a rural nursing program, physical therapy, and a Loan Closet where wheel chairs, crutches, and other items are available. The Association also has established a child health center and a children's dental clinic.

17,827. YWCA Community Center of Neenah-Menasha
Records. 1911- . 0.5 ft.
Open. Unpublished guide.
Elisha D. Smith Public Library.
Minutes, correspondence, photos, and scrapbooks of this local YWCA branch, established in 1911 as the Women's Tuesday Club with a young women's auxiliary; in 1914 the auxiliary became a separate unit and in 1929 affiliated with the national YWCA. The Community Center has swimming, sports, sauna, and health club facilities; it also sponsors a Y-Teens Club, a summer youth employment program, a world fellowship committee, Partners with Youth, and a Big Sisters program. Its activities are now open to men and boys.

MILWAUKEE

17,828. Baer, Myrtle
Papers. 1917-20. 5 folders.
Open. File card.
Milwaukee County Historical Society.
Baer was a housewife and suffragist. Correspondence, constitutions, financial records, and publications pertaining to the Milwaukee County Women's Suffrage Association.

17,829. Bullard, Lola
Papers. 1920-40. 0.5 cu.ft.
Open. File card.
Milwaukee County Historical Society.
Correspondence, photos, and clippings of Bullard, one of Milwaukee's first women reporters.

17,830. Emer, Margaret
Papers. 1875-1964. 2 cu.ft.
Open. File card.
Milwaukee County Historical Society.
Emer (1875-1964) was a housewife. Financial records, convention material, and handbooks of the National Women's Relief Corps of the Grand Army of the Republic.

17,831. Matthews, Stella S.
Papers. 1914-48. 2 cu.ft.
Open. Unpublished guide.
Milwaukee County Historical Society.
A nurse who founded the Visiting Nurses Association in Milwaukee, Matthews (1868-1948) served in France during WWI, helped organize children's hospitals in Poland and Greece after the war, and later administered a clinic in the Hawaiian Islands. Correspondence, diaries, service records, reports, photos, clippings, and medals.

17,832. Milwaukee-Downer College
Records. 1895-1965. 2 cu.ft.
Open. Unpublished guide.
Milwaukee County Historical Society.
Founded in 1895, this women's college was noted particularly for its degree program in occupational therapy. Correspondence, including that of Ellen Sabin, the school's first president; catalogs; yearbooks; commencement programs; and bulletins.

17,833. National Council of Jewish Women
Records. 1909-53. 6 vols.
Open. Unpublished guide.
Milwaukee County Historical Society.
The Milwaukee section of the Council, a charitable and patriotic group, was founded in 1909. Minutes of the local group and its executive committee.

17,834. Women's Conservation League
Records. 1939-65. 9 cu.ft.
Open. Unpublished guide.
Milwaukee County Historical Society.
The League, founded in 1941, supported preservation of wildlife and the environment.

Minutes, financial records, correspondence, photos, clippings, and published material.

17,835. Women's Industrial Exchange
Records. 1882-1965. 2 cu.ft. and 19 vols.
Open. Unpublished guide.
Milwaukee County Historical Society.
Founded in 1882 to help provide financial relief to women in reduced circumstances, the Exchange operated a shop that sold items manufactured by women in their homes. Minutes, financial reports, ledgers, and correspondence. A restaurant and bake shop were operated in conjunction with the Exchange.

17,836. Women's International League for Peace and Freedom, Milwaukee Chapter
Records. 1945-61. 1 cu.ft.
Open. Unpublished guide.
Milwaukee County Historical Society.
Minutes, correspondence, newsletters, and publications of what is said to be one of Milwaukee's most politically active women's organizations. The chapter was founded in 1945 to promote liberal causes.

17,837. World Woman's Christian Temperance Union
Records. 1885-1960. 1 cu.ft.
Open. Unpublished guide.
Milwaukee County Historical Society.
Minutes, secretarial books, correspondence, scrapbooks, and postcards of the Milwaukee chapter, founded in 1885.

17,838. Archives of the Congregation
Records. 1866- . Ca. 200 cu.ft.
Open. Inventory.
School Sisters of St. Francis Archives.
The Congregation was founded in 1874 in New Cassel (now Campbellsport), WI; its members are devoted to education, health care, and social justice. Financial and corporate records, legal documents, correspondence, theses and dissertations, personal records, tapes, photos, scrapbooks, periodicals, books, and other records of the Congregation pertain to the work of the Sisters in the US and in foreign countries.

17,839. Archives
Records. 1883- . More than 13 cabinets and 4 vols.
Access restricted. No guide.
Sisters of the Sorrowful Mother, Milwaukee Province.
The Sisters of the Sorrowful Mother were established in the US in 1889. Financial records, legal documents, correspondence, chronicles of individual houses, autobiographical writings, memoirs, papers of mothers superior, personal files of members, four volumes of oral history transcriptions of recollections of early members of the order, photos, and other records. Includes official records of various convents, hospitals, convalescent homes, orphanages, and schools established and operated by members of the order.

17,840. Baer, Myrtle
Papers. 1854-1963. 1 folder.
Open. Published guide.
University of Wisconsin-Milwaukee, Area Research Center.
Papers of [Miss] Baer (1880-), a Jewish woman, volunteer social worker in Milwaukee, and member of the editorial staff of the *Settlement Cook Book,* contain German passports and citizenship papers of her father William Baer, 1854-66; a marriage license and a clipping about her parents' wedding in 1867; correspondence between her parents and her mother's brother, 1867 and 1873; and an interview in which Baer discusses the Milwaukee Jewish community, the Milwaukee Children's Outing Association, the *Settlement Cook Book,* and her early social life and education. Taken from Lindsay B. Nauen, ed., *Guide to the Wisconsin Jewish Archives at the State Historical Society of Wisconsin* (Madison, WI: State Historical Society of Wisconsin, 1974).

17,841. Kander, Lizzie (Black)
Papers. 1875-1960. 2 boxes and 10 items.
Open. Published guide and register.
University of Wisconsin-Milwaukee, Area Research Center.
Correspondence, speeches, reports, and biographical material on Kander (1858-1940), a Milwaukee social worker, pertain to her activities on behalf of the Milwaukee Jewish Mission, the Settlement House, the Abraham Lincoln House, the Girls' Trade and Technical High School, and the Milwaukee Jewish Community Center. Included are personal letters she wrote to her husband Simon Kander and correspondence concerning publication and revision of the *Settlement Cook Book,* which she compiled. Taken from Lindsay B. Nauen, ed., *Guide to the Wisconsin Jewish Archives at the State Historical Society of Wisconsin* (Madison, WI: State Historical Society of Wisconsin, 1974).

17,842. LaBudde, Wilhelmine D.
Papers. 1924-56. 2 cu.ft.
Open. Unpublished guide.
University of Wisconsin-Milwaukee, Area Research Center.
Correspondence, a diary, speeches, reports, resolutions, articles, and five scrapbooks of [Mrs.] LaBudde (1880-1955), a clubwoman and conservationist who campaigned for the teaching of conservation in Milwaukee schools, the restoration of the Horicon Marsh, a resident fishing license bill, better preservation of forests by lumber companies, and reforestation and preservation of tracts of virgin timber.

17,843. Little Review
Records. 1914-29. 2 cu.ft.
Open. Unpublished guide.
University of Wisconsin-Milwaukee, Area Research Center.
The *Little Review,* an avant-garde experimental literary magazine founded in 1914 and edited by Margaret Anderson, published essays, poems, and articles by and about art and artists, music, freedoms for women, and other subjects. Collection contains 145 letters from Ezra Pound, who was foreign editor of *Little Review* for several years and also coeditor for some time; correspondence of and short stories by Ernest Hemingway; letters from James Joyce, William Yeats, and many other writers and artists of the 1920s; typescripts and manuscripts by contributors to the magazine; and photos of art objects and persons featured in *Little Review.* Editor Margaret Anderson, who promoted such causes as freedom of action for women, freedom for minorities, labor union activity, and birth control, was joined on the *Little Review* staff by Jane Heap; together they moved the magazine from Chicago to New York and finally to Paris in 1920. They published Joyce's *Ulysses* in installments for the first time in the US but were arrested and tried for publishing obscene literature. The *Little Review* ceased publication in 1929.

17,844. Milwaukee-Downer College
Records. 1852-1964. 40 cu.ft.
Open. Unpublished guide.
University of Wisconsin-Milwaukee, Area Research Center.
Records of this women's college, which existed between 1852 and 1964, consist of presidents' papers, records of the business office and alumnae association, correspondence, histories, student publications, and items about the library and the trustees. Ellen Sabin, Mary Mortimer, and Catharine Beecher were among those who served as administrators of the College.

17,845. Ogden, Marion G.
Papers. Ca. 1890-1970. 5 boxes and 1 package.
Open. Register.
University of Wisconsin-Milwaukee, Area Research Center.
[Miss] Ogden (1875-), a social worker and social activist, was a member of the Milwaukee Children's Betterment League executive committee. Correspondence, diaries, addresses and articles on topics related to child welfare, records of organizations, and other papers provide information about her investigations of juvenile delinquency. Also includes papers documenting Ogden's efforts to secure child welfare legislation in Wisconsin. The bulk of the papers date from 1900 to 1930.

17,846. Partridge, Charlotte
Papers. 1881-1975. 34 cu.ft.
Closed. No guide.
University of Wisconsin-Milwaukee, Area Research Center.
Correspondence, financial records, art photos, catalogs, and clipping files of Partridge (1881-1975) and Miriam Frink pertain to their work with the Layton Art School, the Layton Art Gallery, the WPA art program, and the Zonta apartments for the aged, all in Milwaukee.

17,847. Saint Mary's School of Nursing
Records. 1894-1969. 14 cu.ft.
Open. Unpublished guide.
University of Wisconsin-Milwaukee, Area Research Center.
Records concerning the administration, faculty, accreditation program, curriculum, students, and alumnae of the School of Nursing in Milwaukee, which was established in 1894 and closed in 1969. Includes photos, lantern slides, and clippings.

17,848. Saint Mary's School of Nursing
Records. 1894-1969. 42 boxes.
Open. Register.
University of Wisconsin-Milwaukee, Area Research Center.
Founded by the Sisters of Charity in Milwaukee in 1894, this training school initially had nine women students in a two-year program; by 1969, when it affiliated with the University of Wisconsin-Milwaukee's nursing degree program, 1913 professional nurses had graduated from the institution. Contains all existing School records, including material regarding administration, the faculty, accreditation, curriculum, students, alumnae, and the School's history as well as photos, clippings, and lantern slides. During the late 1960s the School became one of several Milwaukee hospitals serving as clinical laboratories for University of Wisconsin-Milwaukee nursing degree candidates.

17,849. Wisconsin Female College
Records. 1860-61. 1 vol.
Open. Published guide.
University of Wisconsin-Milwaukee, Area Research Center.
Manuscript poems, letters, news items, stories, and editorials submitted to the *Normal Advocate* and the *Students Review,* publications of the College, a predecessor of Milwaukee-Downer College located in Fox Lake, WI. Taken from Josephine L. Harper and Sharon C. Smith, eds., *Guide to the Manuscripts of the State Historical Society of Wisconsin, Supplement 1* (Madison, WI: State Historical Society of Wisconsin, 1957).

17,850. Women's League for Jewish Education
Records. 1939-44. 1 folder.
Open. Published guide.
University of Wisconsin-Milwaukee, Area Research Center.
Minutes, financial records, correspondence, and membership lists of this organization of Milwaukee women's groups, members of which raised money for local Jewish education chiefly by selling

secondhand items at a thrift shop. In 1944 the League disbanded, and operation of the thrift shop was taken over by the Milwaukee section of the National Council of Jewish Women. Taken from Lindsay B. Nauen, ed., *Guide to the Wisconsin Jewish Archives at the State Historical Society of Wisconsin* (Madison, WI: State Historical Society of Wisconsin, 1974).

17,851. Young Women's Christian Association
Records. 1892-1961. 4 cu.ft. and 2 microfilm reels.
Open. Unpublished guide.
University of Wisconsin-Milwaukee, Area Research Center.
Business records, correspondence, programs, pamphlets, and 15 scrapbooks of the YWCA in Milwaukee, which was founded in 1892 and continues to offer community services. Originally planned to aid working girls and provide housing for them, the YWCA later added gym, dance, charm school, bowling, and swimming programs for various age groups. The organization has also sponsored a summer camp for several years.

RACINE

17,852. Brown, Olympia
Papers. Nd. 3 folders and 1 vol.
Open. No guide.
Racine County Historical Museum Library.
Papers of Brown (1835-1926), pastor of Universalist Church of the Good Shepherd in Racine from 1879 to 1888 and a woman suffragist, include reminiscences of her daughter Gwendolyn Willis, an address by Corinna del Greco Lobner, church histories, clippings, and Brown's book *Acquaintances, Old and New, Among Reformers* (1911). Includes references to Susan B. Anthony, with whom she toured New York state, Kansas, and elsewhere on behalf of woman suffrage, and notes on Elizabeth Cady Stanton and Lucy Stone. Brown studied for the ministry at St. Lawrence University theological school in Canton, NY, and in 1863 became the first ordained woman minister in the US. She married John Henry Willis 10 years later in Bridgeport, CT, but retained her maiden name. An elementary school in Racine was named after her in 1975.

17,853. Davis, Marguerite
Papers. Nd. 3 folders.
Open. No guide.
Racine County Historical Museum Library.
Davis (1887-1967) was codiscoverer with Elmer V. McCollum of vitamins A and B at the University of Wisconsin in 1913; she also founded nutrition laboratories there and at Rutgers University. Personal correspondence, family data, a pamphlet she wrote, clippings, and other papers. Also includes information about the work of her father John Jefferson Davis, who was the first director of the University of Wisconsin herbarium.

17,854. Archives
Records. 1862- . 24 cabinets.
Access restricted. Unpublished guide.
Sisters of St. Dominic, Siena Center.
This religious community was founded in Racine in 1862 by Mother Benedicta Bauer; its members are engaged in education, social ministry, and in providing health care services. Accounts, correspondence, community chronicles, applications of sisters, registers, baptism and marriage records, histories of the community, manuscripts and theses by sisters, tapes and filmstrips, autobiographies of sisters, pictures, brochures, illuminated booklets, and books. Also contains circulars, catalogs, student accounts, educational material, and other records of secondary schools and colleges operated by the Sisters. Includes correspondence, personal notebooks, and writings by Mother Benedicta Bauer.

RIVER FALLS

17,855. Atwood, Elizabeth Garrett
Papers. 1816-64. 1 folder.
Open. Published guide.
University of Wisconsin-River Falls, Area Research Center.
Correspondence, diaries, and other papers of [Mrs. Edwin] Atwood (1800-33) and her daughter Elizabeth C. Atwood, residents of Nelson, OH, detail their daily activities. Taken from W. Massa et al., comps., *Guide to Archives and Manuscripts in the University of Wisconsin-River Falls Area Research Center* (Madison, WI: State Historical Society of Wisconsin, 1975).

17,856. Beldenville, WI, Community Sewing Circle
Records. Nd. No size given.
Open. Published guide.
University of Wisconsin-River Falls, Area Research Center.
Minute book, 1920-21, of the Sewing Circle and a membership list of the Beldenville chapter of the American National Red Cross. After WWI, the Red Cross chapter became the Sewing Circle, which in turn became the Hill and Valley Club. Taken from W. Massa et al., comps., *Guide to Archives and Manuscripts in the University of Wisconsin-River Falls Area Research Center* (Madison, WI: State Historical Society of Wisconsin, 1975).

17,857. Cairns, Gertrude M.
Papers. 1845-1956. 16 boxes.
Open. Published guide.
University of Wisconsin-River Falls, Area Research Center.
Cairns (1872-1959), an Ellsworth, WI, resident, kept diaries recording her personal activities and social and cultural life in Pierce County. Contains her diaries from 1903 to 1936 and family papers, including correspondence, legal and government records, and minutes of her father George W. Cairns (1826-1900) and his brother A. W. Cairns. Also contains diaries, 1855-61, which were apparently written by Abbie S. Leavitt, who married George W. Cairns in 1866. Gertrude Cairns's papers include diaries containing precise weather records and her observations of birds, wild flowers, and garden plants; they also include records of the Ellsworth Pioneer School Girls' Club, a group she served as secretary-treasurer and unofficial historian. Her father came to Dane County, WI, from New York state in 1849 and moved to Pierce County in 1853. He worked as schoolteacher, clerk of the River Falls Academy, hotel keeper, and land agent. He was town clerk in Middleton, justice of the peace, deputy clerk of the district court, and Pierce County register of deeds. His papers include minutes he kept of the Middleton Lyceum, the River Falls Lyceum, and the River Falls Academy. Diaries of Leavitt, a native of Maine, describe her trip in 1857 from New England across northern Illinois and up the Mississippi River to Prescott, WI, where she resumed a teaching career. Also contains correspondence from the mid-1880s to 1891 between the Cairns children, William, Rollo, and Gertrude, while they were attending high school at River Falls and the University of Wisconsin at Madison. Taken from Josephine L. Harper, ed., *Guide to the Manuscripts of the State Historical Society of Wisconsin, Supplement 2* (Madison, WI: State Historical Society of Wisconsin, 1966).

17,858. Cowperthwaite, Margaret
Papers. 1970. 3-page item.
Open. Published guide.
University of Wisconsin-River Falls, Area Research Center.
Letter by [Mrs. L. LeRoy] Cowperthwaite, who was the wife of the head of the school of speech at Kent State University in Kent, OH, in which she describes events subsequent to the killing of four Kent State students by national guardsmen during an antiwar demonstration. Taken from W. Massa et al., comps., *Guide to Archives and Manuscripts in the University of Wisconsin-River Falls Area Research Center* (Madison, WI: State Historical Society of Wisconsin, 1975).

17,859. Diaries
Collection. Nd. 3 folders and 2 boxes.
Open. Published guide.
University of Wisconsin-River Falls, Area Research Center.
Includes a diary and scrapbook pages kept by Catherine (Ronyak) Walter from 1922 to 1926 while she was a student at River Falls Normal School; diaries kept by Marion E. Hawkins, an English professor at the University of Wisconsin at River Falls, during her trips to the United Kingdom in 1969 and to Germany and Austria in 1971; and a diary kept by Ellen Gibson Andrews from 1896 to 1900, which is contained in the collection of James A. Andrews and John Comstock. See W. Massa et al., comps., *Guide to Archives and Manuscripts in the University of Wisconsin-River Falls Area Research Center* (Madison, WI: State Historical Society of Wisconsin, 1975).

17,860. Hale, Ruth P.
Papers. 1970-71. 1 folder.
Open. Published guide.
University of Wisconsin-River Falls, Area Research Center.
Letters and notes written by Hale, a geography professor at River Falls, while on a 10-week trip through Argentina, Bolivia, Brazil, Chile, Colombia, Ecuador, Paraguay, Peru, Uruguay, and Venezuela. Taken from W. Massa et al., comps., *Guide to Archives and Manuscripts in the University of Wisconsin-River Falls Area Research Center* (Madison, WI: State Historical Society of Wisconsin, 1975).

17,861. Old Academy Girls
Records. 1900-45. 2 vols.
Open. Published guide.
University of Wisconsin-River Falls, Area Research Center.
Minutes, membership lists, and an account of the founding of this social club, the members of which attended River Falls Academy between 1856 and 1878. Taken from Josephine L. Harper, ed., *Guide to the Manuscripts of the State Historical Society of Wisconsin, Supplement 2* (Madison, WI: State Historical Society of Wisconsin, 1966).

17,862. Reminiscences
Collection. Nd. 2 folders and ca. 8 items.
Open. Published guide.
University of Wisconsin-River Falls, Area Research Center.
Includes reminiscences by Antoinette (Crippen) [Mrs. James Monroe] Bailey (1834-1931) of Prescott, WI, who describes her family's trip from Saratoga County, NY, to Rock County, WI, in 1842; [Mrs.] Norah (Halverson) Howe, a resident of Evanston, IL, who relates her experiences at River Falls Normal School; Anna (Magnuson) Anderson, who recalls her childhood in Pierce County, WI, around the turn of the century; Nellie (Grant) Skidmore, a resident of Balsam Lake, WA, who writes about family history and events of her youth in Pierce County, WI; Nancy (Weberg) Younggren, a long-time resident of the Mann Valley near River Falls; and [Mrs.] Sadie (Peterson) Cresswell. Cresswell recalls her life in Clifton Hollow, WI, until 1907; her work as a schoolteacher in Midway, ND, until 1912; and her activities as a housekeeper-companion to a woman

in California in the 1950s. Sylvia (Havre) [Mrs. Paul H.] Raihle (1892-) discusses her family, her early life and education in La Crosse, WI, and Minneapolis, teaching in Minnesota and South Dakota, her work with the Department of War during WWI, and her four terms as a Wisconsin state assemblywoman from 1948 to 1956. In her autobiography, Anna Katherina (Bezler) Dicke (1832-1930) recalls her youth and schooling in Eschenbach, Germany; her immigration to America in 1949; her subsequent employment; and her marriage to Peter Heinrich Dicke, a minister. Also includes reminiscences of Deloris Buckley of Spring Green, WI, who describes her experiences as a US Army nurse during WWII on the Italian front, and of Ines (Haken) Schubert, who recalls her life in post-WWII Germany and the emigration of the Schubert family from Germany to the US in ca. 1951. See W. Massa et al., comps., *Guide to Archives and Manuscripts in the University of Wisconsin-River Falls Area Research Center* (Madison, WI: State Historical Society of Wisconsin, 1975).

17,863. River Falls Improvement League
Records. 1900-16. 1 box.
Open. Published guide.
University of Wisconsin-River Falls, Area Research Center.
Constitution, minutes, and other records of this organization of women who campaigned for sidewalk repairs, weed control, the creation of parks, and other projects for community beautification and betterment. Taken from W. Massa et al., comps., *Guide to Archives and Manuscripts in the University of Wisconsin-River Falls Area Research Center* (Madison, WI: State Historical Society of Wisconsin, 1975).

17,864. St. Croix-Pierce Counties Federated Women's Club
Records. Nd. No size given.
Open. Published guide.
University of Wisconsin-River Falls, Area Research Center.
Minutes; correspondence; a registration book; local club reports, 1951-72; programs, 1922-72; local Club yearbooks; and ephemera. Taken from W. Massa et al., comps., *Guide to Archives and Manuscripts in the University of Wisconsin-River Falls Area Research Center* (Madison, WI: State Historical Society of Wisconsin, 1975).

17,865. Taylor, Ella (Atwater)
Papers. Nd. 1 folder.
Open. Published guide.
University of Wisconsin-River Falls, Area Research Center.
Biography of Taylor (1868-?), a teacher, homesteader, and civic leader in River Falls, by her daughter Margaret (Taylor) Miller. Taken from W. Massa et al., comps., *Guide to Archives and Manuscripts in the University of Wisconsin-River Falls Area Research Center* (Madison, WI: State Historical Society of Wisconsin, 1975).

17,866. Whitney, Myrta V.
Papers. 1899-1906. 1 folder.
Open. Published guide.
University of Wisconsin-River Falls, Area Research Center.
Correspondence of Whitney, primarily concerning her teaching experiences at the Wisconsin state normal schools at River Falls in 1900 and at Platteville from 1900 to 1905. Taken from W. Massa et al., comps., *Guide to Archives and Manuscripts in the University of Wisconsin-River Falls Area Research Center* (Madison, WI: State Historical Society of Wisconsin, 1975).

17,867. Williams, Essie W.
Papers. 1911-58. 1 folder.
Open. Published guide.
University of Wisconsin-River Falls, Area Research Center.
Correspondence, legal papers, certificates, and other papers of Williams, a teacher and attorney who resided in St. Paul, MN, and Hudson, WI, relate to her education and teaching career, her legal practice, an income tax dispute, genealogy, and bird-watching and horticultural activities. Taken from W. Massa et al., comps., *Guide to Archives and Manuscripts in the University of Wisconsin-River Falls Area Research Center* (Madison, WI: State Historical Society of Wisconsin, 1975).

SINSINAWA

17,868. Sinsinawa Dominican Archives
Records. 1847- . Ca. 101 boxes and 383 tapes.
Access restricted. Unpublished guide.
Sinsinawa Dominican Congregation of the Most Holy Rosary Dominican Motherhouse.
The Congregation was founded in 1847 at Sinsinawa by Father Samuel Mazzuchelli, O.P., and is dedicated to the apostolate of Christian education and related ministries. Minutes, financial records, administrative papers of mothers general, historical and church records, annals of missions and ministries, correspondence, diaries, oral history interviews, personal manuscripts of sisters, master's and doctoral theses, tapes, slides, films, photos, scrapbooks, clippings, pamphlets, and books of the Congregation. Includes papers of Sister Mary Emily Power, the first mother general; of subsequent mothers general, Sister Mary Samuel Coughlin, Sister Evelyn Murphy, Sister Mary Benedicta Larkin, and Sister Marie Amanda Allard. Also contains papers of sisters who have made contributions in education, literature, art, and music, including Sister Rosemary Crepeau, a scholar, college teacher, author, and linguist; Sister Angelico Dolan, a painter; Sister Mary Eva McCarty, an historian and head of the Rosary College history department who wrote a history of the Congregation's second 50 years and, in 1963, contributed to the *New Catholic Encyclopedia;* Sister Mary Nona McGreal, an author and lecturer who has served as diocesan director of educational development in Madison, WI, and as president of Edgewood College in Madison and as vicaress general of the Congregation; Sister Mary Ellen O'Hanlon, a biological researcher, author, and professor at Rosary College; Sister Thomas Aquinas O'Neill, Thomistic philosopher at St. Clara College and president of Rosary College; Sister Imelda Therese Swift, who before her conversion to Catholicism was secretary to Eva Booth of The Salvation Army; and Sister Vincent Ferrer Bradford, a professor of economics and political science, lecturer, and vice-president of the Catholic Association of International Peace.

STEVENS POINT

17,869. Allen, Bessie May
Papers. Ca. 1893-1969. 3 cu.ft.
Open. Unpublished guide.
University of Wisconsin-Stevens Point Archives.
Professional and personal correspondence, family and travel photos, a research paper, course syllabi, grade transcripts, clippings, a biographical pamphlet, bulletins and other printed items, and memorabilia of Allen (1882-1969), a Stevens Point civic leader and local activist who for 39 years was director of home economics at Central State College, now the University of Wisconsin at Stevens Point, where she also taught home economics courses. In addition, she was the first woman to be elected chairman of the College faculty and was accorded emeritus status after her retirement in 1952. A campus residence center is named in her honor.

17,870. Parkhurst, Helen
Papers. 1916-72. 7.5 cu.ft.
Open. Unpublished guide.
University of Wisconsin-Stevens Point Archives.
Correspondence, notes from lectures by Maria Montessori, photos, recording discs, scrapbooks, books and pamphlets, and memorabilia of Parkhurst (1887-1973), an internationally known educator, writer, and humanitarian. Her plan for individualized education, the Dalton Plan, became a model for schools around the world; her philosophy was that "children learn more effectively in an environment which permits freedom of choice and allows them to progress at their own pace." Collection includes copies of Parkhurst's major works *Education on the Dalton Plan, Exploring the Child's World, Growing Pains,* and *Undertow.*

Parkhurst taught from 1912 to 1915 at Stevens Point Normal School (now the University of Wisconsin at Stevens Point) as director of the primary department, but she spent most of her career in the East where she worked with Maria Montessori and then developed her own plan for education

SUPERIOR

17,871. Archives
Records. 1907- . No size given.
Closed. No guide.
Sisters of St. Joseph Motherhouse.
Correspondence, photos, and scrapbooks of early sisters. The Motherhouse was founded in 1907 at Somerset, WI; its members are involved in teaching and nursing.

WAUKESHA

17,872. Rankin Family
Papers. 1880-1941. Ca. 15 ft.
Open. No guide.
Carroll College Library.
Walter L. Rankin (1841-1910) was president of Carroll College from 1866 to 1903 and his daughter May N. Rankin (1870-1931) was a professor of dramatics, oratory, and debate at the College from 1888 to 1930. Correspondence, including 150 letters May Rankin wrote to her sister C. Adela Rankin between 1894 and 1923 concerning family matters, students, courses, plays, and other college affairs; course notes; annotated texts of plays; photos; and theater programs and scrapbooks. Also contains a biography of May Rankin by C. Adela Rankin.

17,873. Barstow, Helen Augusta
Papers. 1851-56. 1 vol.
Open. Unpublished guide.
Waukesha County Historical Museum.
Diary in which Barstow (1831-1924), a Waukesha County pioneer, notes everyday experiences, customs, and activities. She married William F. Whitney in 1854.

17,874. Bell Family
Papers. 1837-1921. 6 items.
Open. Unpublished guide.
Waukesha County Historical Museum.
Correspondence of an early Waukesha County pioneer family includes two letters written by Sarah M. Bell, who discusses her career as a schoolteacher in Lisbon, WI, in the 1850s.

17,875. Dunlap, Mrs. Robert
Papers. 1876. 1 vol.
Open. Unpublished guide.

Waukesha County Historical Museum.
Diary of Sophia Mary (Chesley) Dunlap (1831-1905), the wife of a physician, contains her descriptions of the weather and pioneer life.

17,876. Morris, Alice Webber (Palmer)
Papers. 1905-44. 3 vols.
Open. Unpublished guide.
Waukesha County Historical Museum.
Diaries of [Mrs. Raymond] Morris (1890-?), an early Waukesha resident, contain scattered weather accounts and brief statements about her everyday activities. She was a 1913 graduate of Carroll College in Waukesha.

17,877. Palmer Family
Papers. 1844-75. 156 pp.
Open. Unpublished guide.
Waukesha County Historical Museum.
Correspondence of an early Waukesha pioneer family includes letters in which Mr. and Mrs. Rodman Palmer detail their life and customs in Waukesha.

17,878. Palmer, Harriet "Hattie" C.
Papers. Ca. 1844-89. 2 vols.
Open. Unpublished guide.
Waukesha County Historical Museum.
Consists of a diary in which Palmer (1854-ca. 1893) reports the temperature and weather conditions as well as her everyday experiences as a pioneer in Waukesha and a volume of typescript Palmer family correspondence, primarily that of Harriet Palmer.

17,879. Park, Maybelle M.
Papers. 1896-1916. 1 vol.
Open. Unpublished guide.
Waukesha County Historical Museum.
Diary of Park (1871-1946), a physician, includes her list of births and deaths in the community. Delivery records mention both parents' names and ages, birthplace, race, and sex; records of deaths include notations of names, date, and the cause of death.

17,880. Rankin Family
Papers. 1867-1933. 1 vol.
Open. Unpublished guide.
Waukesha County Historical Museum.
A history of the Rankin family in monograph form contains photos, articles, and ephemeral material about their role in Waukesha history. Walter Lowrie Rankin was president of Carroll College in Waukesha from 1866 to 1903. His wife Mary Jane (Nickell) Rankin was an early pioneer in the region, and their daughter May Nickell Rankin was active in theater at Carroll College.

17,881. Witte, Frances Margaret (Stewart)
Papers. 1863-96. 1 box.
Open. Unpublished guide.
Waukesha County Historical Museum.
Papers of [Mrs. Richard] Witte (1842-?) contain personal journals; extracts of her letters, which were published in the Waukesha *Freeman* in 1868; her poetry; and newspaper articles relating to her poetry. In her correspondence and in one of her journals she describes in great detail her voyage to and sojourn in Germany in 1865.

17,882. Women
Collection. 1890- . 3 files.
Open. Unpublished guide.
Waukesha County Historical Museum.
Vertical file collection of clippings and book catalogs pertain to the broad subject heading of women as well as to women in Waukesha County and woman suffrage.

WAUSAU

17,883. Business and Professional Women's Club of Wausau
Records. 1920-61. 4 vols.
Open. Unpublished guide.
Marathon County Historical Society.
Scrapbooks containing clippings, newsletters, and memorabilia of the Club, founded in 1919 to provide an atmosphere in which business and social contacts among local women could be strengthened and enlarged.

WYOMING

CHEYENNE

17,884. Albany County Clerk
Records. 1868-1914. 100 cu.ft.
Open. Register.
Wyoming State Archives and Historical Department.
Minutes, dockets, and other records of official County legal proceedings from 1868. One inch of these records pertains to the first women to serve jury duty in the US. The women, who were called on March 7, 1870, and served from 10 to 12 days each, were Amelia Hatcher, Jane Hilton, Mary Mackle, Anna Monnohan, Sarah W. Pease, and Elizabeth Stewart.

17,885. Anderson, Eunice G.
Papers. Nd. 1 folder.
Open. Card catalog.
Wyoming State Archives and Historical Department.
The Wyoming state historian from 1919 to 1923, Anderson (?-1964) was the founder of *Annals of Wyoming,* the state historical publication. Anderson's research project on the accomplishments of Wyoming women contains biographical sketches of Nellie Tayloe Ross, Grace Raymond Hebard, Esther Hobart Morris, and others.

17,886. Anesi, Janet
Papers. 1968. 1 folder.
Open. Card catalog.
Wyoming State Archives and Historical Department.
Research paper of Anesi (1954?-), a student, concerns the life of Dora Robertson, one of the oldest residents of Lander, WY. Includes descriptions of Robertson's family life, chores and responsibilities while she was young, and other experiences.

17,887. Baltzly, Mary Francis
Papers. 1861-1942. 1 folder.
Open. Card catalog.
Wyoming State Archives and Historical Department.
Autobiographical material of Baltzly (1861-?), a Wyoming schoolteacher and settler, includes descriptions of her teaching experiences, the family cattle ranching business, the coming of the railroad, homesteading, and her life in Illinois and South Dakota.

17,888. Beard, Mrs. Cyrus
Papers. 1930. 26 in.
Open. Card catalog.
Wyoming State Archives and Historical Department.
Frances (Birkhead) Beard (1859-1964), the Wyoming state historian from 1923 to 1933, was the author of a history of Wyoming from its territorial days. Correspondence, manuscripts, research notes, photos, a scrapbook, and other items provide information about Wyoming pioneer life, trails, Indian conflicts, trading posts, legends, and census taking in the 1880s. Includes her manuscripts on the Powder River and economic depressions in the US.

17,889. Bellamy, Mary (Godat)
Papers. 1911-52. 3 folders.
Open. Card catalog.
Wyoming State Archives and Historical Department.
Personal correspondence of and research manuscripts regarding the development of transportation by Bellamy (1861-1955), who in 1910 was the first woman elected to a state legislature. The first licensed engineer in Wyoming and the Johnson County, WY, superintendent of public education, she represented Wyoming women in 1917 in Washington, DC, during the national campaign for the Nineteenth Amendment, which granted woman suffrage. As a legislator she worked to improve conditions for women and children and introduced a bill to permit married women to administer estates.

17,890. Bernstein, Jeannette Warsharsky
Papers. 1954-75. 3 folders.
Open. Card catalog.
Wyoming State Archives and Historical Department.
Bernstein (1896?-) was a researcher and historian of the Wyoming Jewish community. Correspondence with Jews requesting data, manuscripts of research on the Cheyenne Jewish community, and oral history transcripts pertinent to Bernstein's research.

17,891. Blake, Sadie Evalena Hale
Papers. Ca. 1975. 1 folder and 1 tape.
Open. Card catalog.
Wyoming State Archives and Historical Department.
Interview in which Blake, a Wyoming settler, describes her life in Montana and Wyoming during the late 1800s, including such topics as social activities, Indian threats, hostilities precipitating the Wounded Knee Creek battle, and the life style of early western settlers.

17,892. Board of Charities and Reform
Records. 1873-1969. Ca. 10 cu.ft.
Open. Card catalog.
Wyoming State Archives and Historical Department.
The Board was created in 1890 to govern state charitable institutions, among them the Children's Home, State Penitentiary, State Mental Hospital, and State Tuberculosis Sanitorium. Minutes of Board meetings, correspondence, reports, and prison records. Women who have been Board administrators are Amy Abbott, 1929-31, and Leslie R. Brewer, 1939-40.

17,893. Brown, Susie
Papers. 1974. 11-page item.
Open. Card catalog.
Wyoming State Archives and Historical Department.
Biography of Brown (ca. 1895-1960?), an early Wyoming citizen, was written by Sylvia Irene Hansen and contains descriptions of Brown's experiences in Wyoming, including details about her social life and the difficulties of raising a family on a limited income.

17,894. Canterbury, Hazel
Papers. Nd. 14-page item.
Open. Card catalog.
Wyoming State Archives and Historical Department.
Biographical sketches written by Canterbury, a member of the History and Art Club of Buffalo, WY, include sketches of Elsa (Spear) Edwards Byron, [Mrs.] Ruth Joy Hopkins, Evelyn (Corthell) [Mrs. John] Hill, Mrs. Joe Breckens, Mrs. Thomas Carigen, and Mrs. Arthur Keyes, club members who were artists, writers, or historians. The sketches cover from ca. 1908 to 1931.

17,895. Central National Society for Women's Suffrage
Records. 1891. 1 item.
Open. Card catalog.

Wyoming State Archives and Historical Department. Certificate of congratulations sent from the 1891 Women's Suffrage Convention held in Washington, DC, to the women of Wyoming for being the first state to pass legislation permitting women to vote.

17,896. Clark, Edith K. O.
Papers. 1919-23. 1 folder.
Open. Card catalog.
Wyoming State Archives and Historical Department. A Wyoming educator, Clark (1881-1936) organized the first Sheridan County association of school district trustees, and in 1914 she was elected state superintendent of public instruction. In 1919 she worked with the YWCA in France to assist the US Army, and she continued to work for the YWCA in later years. Correspondence with family and friends regarding her overseas experiences and clippings praising her service.

17,897. Dobbins, Emma Jane
Papers. Ca. 1890-1931. 7 in.
Open. Card catalog.
Wyoming State Archives and Historical Department. Dobbins (1853-1932), a Cheyenne settler, was a compiler and editor of pioneer stories and accounts. Diaries and journals, four manuscripts written by Dobbins regarding pioneer life, photos of family members and Wyoming scenes, a scrapbook of clippings, and other clippings.

17,898. Dobbins, Gertrude Wyoming
Papers. 1864-1948. 1 ft.
Open. Card catalog.
Wyoming State Archives and Historical Department. Clippings, a scrapbook, and other items of Dobbins contain material on Wyoming women, including Helen Frances Warren, wife of General John J. Pershing; Esther Hobart Morris, Susan B. Anthony; Elizabeth (Cady) Stanton; and several Wyoming governors' wives.

17,899. Dominick, David
Papers. 1959. 1 folder.
Open. Card catalog.
Wyoming State Archives and Historical Department. Manuscript of Dominick (1937-), an attorney, regarding the life of Caroline Lockart, a journalist and author who worked for *The Boston Post, The Philadelphia Bulletin,* and *The Denver Post;* she also owned and edited *The Cody Enterprise.* She was the author of *The Man from the Bitter Roots, The Old West and the New, The Lady-Doc,* other books, and articles for pulp magazines.

17,900. Eder, Mrs. Ernest
Papers. 1975. 1 folder and 1 tape.
Open. List.
Wyoming State Archives and Historical Department. Interview in which Bessie N. Eder (1895?-), a homesteader in Johnson County, WY, from 1914 to 1924, describes harsh winters, reliance on neighbors, expenses, meeting government requirements in order to keep their land, transportation, the need for a school, and other homesteading experiences.

17,901. Education Department
Records. 1879-1976. Ca. 100 ft.
Open. Card catalog.
Wyoming State Archives and Historical Department. Records of the Department, which was created in 1869, document the state and county education systems and include financial records, minutes of county and state school board meetings, reports, curriculum schedules, certificates, teacher employee lists, and publications. The majority of employees of the Department have been women, and women served as county superintendents in Wyoming from 1882. Women who have served as superintendents of public instruction in the state are Minnie Slaughter, 1890; Estelle Reel, 1895-98; Edith K. O. Clark, 1915-19; Katherine A. Morton, 1919-35; Ester Anderson, 1933-46; Edna B. Stolt, 1946-54; and Velma Linford, 1954-63.

17,902. Ekstrom, Laura Allyn
Papers. 1922-64. 2 folders.
Open. Card catalog.
Wyoming State Archives and Historical Department. Ekstrom was a Cheyenne Baptist church worker and director of the Christian Americanization Program. Correspondence with members of the Program living in Japan, a journal relating to Program meetings and the activities of members, and photos of Program members. The Program in Cheyenne assisted its Japanese members in adjusting to their new life style; taught the women sewing, cooking, other domestic skills, and English; and provided recreation. Some Program members proselytized in Japan. Most of the Japanese members returned to Japan before 1941.

17,903. Erwin, Marie H.
Papers. 1868-1943. 2 ft.
Open. Card catalog.
Wyoming State Archives and Historical Department. Wyoming state historian from 1933 to 1938, Erwin was the author of the *Wyoming Blue Book,* a reference work pertaining to the state's government and public officials. Manuscripts and research notes for the *Wyoming Blue Book* and photos of early Wyoming communities, businesses, and residents.

17,904. Feldman, Mrs. Joe E.
Papers. 1975. 2 folders.
Open. Card catalog.
Wyoming State Archives and Historical Department. Dorothy Feldman (ca. 1950-), a student, pioneered efforts to survey Cheyenne church records and conducted research into the history of various local religious denominations; she helped locate records of women's auxiliaries organized by nearly every denomination in Cheyenne. Correspondence with units of local denominations, research notes, and her research paper.

17,905. Graf, Louise Spinner
Papers. Ca. 1975. 1 folder and 1 tape.
Open. Card catalog.
Wyoming State Archives and Historical Department. In 1950 Graf (1933-) was the first woman to serve as jury foreman in Wyoming and one of the first women to serve jury duty in the state. Interview in which Graf describes her childhood experiences, school, hometown, jury duty experiences, and her interest in writing and research.

17,906. Hebard, Grace Raymond
Papers. Ca. 1869-1918. 6 in.
Open. Card catalog.
Wyoming State Archives and Historical Department. Hebard (1861-1936) was a suffrage worker and professor of history and economics at the University of Wyoming. Correspondence regarding women's suffrage, the National American Woman's Suffrage Association, the National Council of Women Voters, and rebuttals to antisuffrage arguments; research manuscripts concerning woman suffrage in Wyoming and pioneer women; and clippings.

17,907. Holmberg, Lottie
Papers. Nd. 1 folder.
Open. Card catalog.
Wyoming State Archives and Historical Department. An article written by [Mrs.] Holmberg, an interviewer and writer for the WPA during the 1930s, about Laura Inghram Bragg, the widow of cattle rancher Fred Bragg. Includes Bragg's reminiscences regarding her move westward from Iowa, her fear of Indians, marriage to Fred Bragg, their cattle ranching business, and living conditions in Wyoming from ca. 1870 to 1880. Laura Bragg did not remarry.

17,908. Hooker, Mrs. S. I.
Papers. 1933. 1 folder.
Open. Card catalog.
Wyoming State Archives and Historical Department. Hooker was a poet and president of the Denver Women's Club in 1919, 1920, and 1933. Speech to the Club containing biographical sketches of Sacajawea; Narcissa (Prentiss) Whitman and Eliza Hart Spalding, missionaries to the Indians; Mary E. Homsley, a pioneer who died of measles; Esther Hobart Morris, a suffragist and first woman justice of the peace; Nellie Tayloe Ross, governor of Wyoming from 1925 to 1927, who later became director of the US Mint; Grace Raymond Hebard, an historian, professor, and suffrage worker; [Miss] Ruth Harrington, state librarian and historian ex-officio; Frances (Birkhead) [Mrs. Cyrus] Beard, second state historian and an author; Cora M. Beach, an author and historian; and June Downey, an author and University of Wyoming instructor.

17,909. Hurd, G. H.
Papers. 1880-1951. 5 in.
Open. Card catalog.
Wyoming State Archives and Historical Department. Correspondence and clippings of J. D. Hurd, the legislator who introduced the woman suffrage bill to the Wyoming legislature. Includes an 1893 letter from Clara (Bewick) Colby and a clipping that relates to the bill.

17,910. Justice of the Peace, Sweetwater County, Wyoming Territory
Records. 1870. 1 vol.
Open. Card catalog.
Wyoming State Archives and Historical Department. One handwritten docket book of cases heard before Esther Hobart Morris (1814-1902), who was the first female justice of the peace in the US and who was considered the mother of Wyoming's equal suffrage movement.

17,911. Linford, Velma
Papers. 1862-1963. 3 in.
Access restricted. Card catalog.
Wyoming State Archives and Historical Department. Correspondence, a manuscript, photos, and clippings of [Miss] Linford (1907-), superintendent of public schools in Wyoming from 1954 to 1963 and education consultant for overseas schools in 1962; she later worked for VISTA in Washington, DC. All the material pertains to Linford's research for her publication "Women at the Polls."

17,912. McCarthy, Clara Field
Papers. 1909-11. 1 folder.
Open. Card catalog.
Wyoming State Archives and Historical Department. Typescript and correspondence of McCarthy, a settler in the Big Horn River area of Wyoming, concern the hardships of raising a family in an unsettled area with inadequate provisions.

17,913. McCreery, Eleanor Alice (Richards)
Papers. 1887-1954. 7 in.
Open. Card catalog.
Wyoming State Archives and Historical Department. The daughter of William A. Richards, McCreery (1877-1967) served as Richards's private secretary while he was governor of Wyoming from 1894 to 1896 and US surveyor general. Correspondence, diaries, and clippings pertaining to the settlement of McCreery's family in Wyoming. The diaries relate to the period before her father became governor.

17,914. Meyer, Estelle Reel
Papers. 1883-1911. 5 ft.
Open. Card catalog.
Wyoming State Archives and Historical Department. Meyer (1862-1959), an educator, in 1894 became the first woman in the US to be elected to a state office, that of Wyoming superintendent of public education; she later became national superintendent

of Indian schools under President McKinley. Correspondence, photos, scrapbooks of clippings, an 1895 proposal to allow women to obtain life insurance, and other material.

17,915. Office of the Governor
Records. 1923-31. 15 in.
Open. Card catalog.
Wyoming State Archives and Historical Department.
Records of Nellie Tayloe Ross, governor of Wyoming from 1925 to 1927, include correspondence, minutes of meetings, financial records, certificates, and publications pertaining to her term of office.

17,916. Snow, Mrs. William C.
Papers. 1877-1939. 1 in.
Open. Card catalog.
Wyoming State Archives and Historical Department.
In 1939 Agnes K. Snow was chairman of the Wyoming Day Committee, which was concerned with the commemoration of the 70th anniversary of equal suffrage in Wyoming. Correspondence and clippings, including letters from Carrie Chapman Catt regarding an address of congratulation from the Central National Society for Women's Suffrage to the women of Wyoming, whose state was the first place in the world to establish woman suffrage, and a joint address of congratulation from women representing ca. 14 societies in Great Britain, including the Edinburgh Women's Suffrage Society, the British Women's Temperance Association, and the International Arbitration of Peace Society.

17,917. State Auditor
Records. 1869-1965. Ca. 10 ft.
Open. Card catalog.
Wyoming State Archives and Historical Department.
Financial records, ledgers, office journals, and correspondence generated in the office of the state auditor, which was created in 1869 to make formal examination of and verify financial accounts of the state. Includes records from the administration of Minnie A. Mitchell (1896-), who first ran for the position of auditor in 1954 after completing her late husband's term as state treasurer. She was the first woman to serve in either capacity. She served as state auditor for 12 years and served four additional years as treasurer before retiring in 1971.

17,918. State Historical Board
Records. 1919-50. 4.5 cu.ft.
Open. Card catalog.
Wyoming State Archives and Historical Department.
The Board was founded in 1895 to "illustrate the history of the state and the Northwest with its collections, secure pioneer narratives, investigate the history, progress, and decay of the state's Indian tribes, and to build its collections to encourage historical, scientific and antiquarian research." Minutes, correspondence, reports, legal documents, manuscripts, and publications of the Board. Women who served as state historian are Eunice G. Anderson, 1919-23; Mrs. Cyrus Beard, 1923-33; Margaret Burke, 1933-38; Marie H. Erwin, 1938-39 and 1943; Inex B. Taylor, 1939-41; and Lola M. Homsher, 1943 and 1953-65. State historians ex-officio, many of whom served concurrently as state librarian, were Ruth Harrington, 1933-34; Alice Lyman, 1934-37; Nina M. K. Moran, 1937-39; Gladys Riley, 1939-43; Mary A. McGrath, 1943-48; Ellen Crowley, 1948-51; and Lola Homsher, 1951-53.

17,919. State Library
Records. 1877-1972. Ca. 10 ft.
Open. Card catalog.
Wyoming State Archives and Historical Department.
The state library was created by the Wyoming state legislature in 1871 to document the history of Wyoming and of the Northwest and to encourage historical, scientific, and antiquarian research. It also serves as a reference library for the state supreme court and the governor. Includes correspondence, inventories of equipment, blueprints of buildings, and publications. Women who have served as state librarian are Minnie Slaughter, 1890-92; [Mrs.] Clara W. Bond, 1905-13; Agnes R. Wright, 1917-21; Genevra Brock, 1921-23; Flo Lachappelle, 1923-27; Clare E. Ausherman, 1927-33; Ruth Harrington, 1933-34; Alice Lyman, 1934-37; Nina M. K. Moran, 1937-39; Gladys F. Riley, 1939-43; Mary A. McGrath, 1943-48; Mary Ellen Crowley, 1949-51; [Mrs.] Eveline Smith, 1951; May Gillies, 1951-63; and Rosemary Martin, 1963 and 1969-70.

17,920. State Treasurer
Records. 1877-1971. 165 Hollinger boxes, 67 records center boxes, and 1085 microfilm reels.
Open. Card catalog.
Wyoming State Archives and Historical Department.
The office of treasurer was created in 1890 to record and report the use of state funds. Financial records, correspondence, reports, blueprints, ledgers, and publications. Includes records from the administration of Minnie A. Mitchell (1896-), who served as state treasurer when she was appointed in 1952 to complete her late husband's term. Unable to succeed herself, she ran for the state auditor's position in 1954 and served in that capacity until 1967 when she served a second term as treasurer. She retired in 1971. Mitchell was the first woman to hold either office.

17,921. Trenholm, Virginia Cole
Papers. 1839-1966. 3 in.
Open. Card catalog.
Wyoming State Archives and Historical Department.
Trenholm is an editor, author, and co-author with Maurine Carley of books about Indians of the West, including the Arapahoes and the Shoshonis. Photos, maps, and books relating to her research. Trenholm is a resident of Cheyenne.

17,922. University of Wyoming
Records. 1925-48. 1 in.
Open. Card catalog.
Wyoming State Archives and Historical Department.
Speeches by Nellie Tayloe Ross (1876-1977), governor of Wyoming from 1925 to 1927, regarding women's rights and suffrage. The collection was donated by the University of Wyoming, which was founded in 1887.

17,923. Whitman, Narcissa (Prentiss)
Papers. 1836-43. 1 folder.
Open. Card catalog.
Wyoming State Archives and Historical Department.
Whitman (1808-47) was a missonary to the Indians. Correspondence and a journal relate her missionary experiences, pioneering hardships, and customs of various Indian tribes. Whitman and her husband were killed by Indians in 1847.

17,924. Wright, Anne
Papers. Ca. 1956-59. 4 in.
Open. Card catalog.
Wyoming State Archives and Historical Department.
Wright (1876-1929) was a schoolteacher. Biographical sketches of Wyoming woman educators, including Christine Cassill, Bertha Van Devender, Mary Alice Davis, Annie Maud Smith Gudmundsen, and Minnie May Swain Logan. The sketches were written under the auspices of the Eta chapter of the Delta Kappa Gamma sorority for educators.

17,925. Wyman, W. A.
Papers. 1881-1920. 1 Hollinger box.
Open. Card catalog.
Wyoming State Archives and Historical Department.
Medical journals and records of appointments and treatments of Wyman, a physician and secretary of the Wyoming board of health from 1911 to 1917. Includes names and illnesses of his patients, many of whom were women.

17,926. Wyoming Cowbelles Association
Records. 1955-72. 1 ft.
Open. Card catalog.
Wyoming State Archives and Historical Department.
Minutes, correspondence, clippings, and other material of this women's auxiliary of the Stockgrowers Association.

17,927. Wyoming Extension Homemakers Council
Records. 1912-72. 2 ft.
Open. Card catalog.
Wyoming State Archives and Historical Department.
The Council was founded to provide information regarding home economics to citizens through lectures, home demonstrations, community programs, and publications. Scrapbooks of state activities, certificates indicating completion of courses, clippings, and publications of the Council.

17,928. Wyoming Federation of Women's Clubs
Records. 1902-76. 17 ft.
Open. Card catalog.
Wyoming State Archives and Historical Department.
Executive board minutes, photos, certificates, scrapbooks pertaining to organizations and activities sponsored by the Federation, clippings, and records of local chapters of women's clubs.

17,929. Wyoming Homemakers
Records. 1946-71. 6 in.
Open. Card catalog.
Wyoming State Archives and Historical Department.
Associated with the Wyoming Agricultural Extension Service, this organization instructed women in homemaking skills. Minutes; Mrs. Susan J. Quealy Award certificates, which were presented to women demonstrating leadership in the community and in the Extension Service's home demonstration programs; and publications of the Homemakers.

17,930. Wyoming Press Women
Records. 1955-59. 4 in.
Open. Unpublished guide.
Wyoming State Archives and Historical Department.
Scrapbook of this organization for women associated with publishing and the media documents its local activities and affiliation with the National Federation of Press Women.

17,931. Yoder, Myrtle
Papers. 1899-1941. 7 in.
Open. Card catalog.
Wyoming State Archives and Historical Department.
[Mrs.] Yoder's papers consist of the minutes of the Shakespeare Club, a women's group organized in 1899 to study American and European literature, poetry, and plays. It disbanded in 1941.

CODY

17,932. Oakley, Annie
Papers. 1870-1925. 9 vols. and 3 microfilm reels.
Open. No guide.
Buffalo Bill Historical Center.
Oakley (1860-1926) was a rifle and shotgun artist. Correspondence, photos, clippings, guns, and mementos primarily relate to the 17-year period during which she was a star in Buffalo Bill's Wild West Show.

GREEN RIVER

17,933. County Commissioners of Sweetwater County
Records. 1870-79. 1 vol.
Open. No guide.

Sweetwater County Historical Museum.
Minutes of the County Commissioners include records of the 1870 meeting during which the Commissioners decided to appoint [Mrs.] Esther Hobart Morris a justice of the peace. Morris later led the successful campaign for woman suffrage in Wyoming.

17,934. Graf, Louise S.
Papers. 1950. 1 folder.
Open. No guide.
Sweetwater County Historical Museum.
Papers of Graf (1904-), who in 1950 became the first woman in 80 years to serve on a jury in Wyoming, consist of a transcript of a speech she made about the trial for which she was jury foreman, a certificate of duty, and clippings about the case and the historical significance of her service.

LARAMIE

17,935. Alexander, Mary L.
Papers. Nd. 1 Hollinger box.
Open. Accession list.
University of Wyoming, American Heritage Center.
Two scrapbooks of Alexander, an aviator, contain clippings and photos regarding women aviators, including clippings about an organization of women pilots. Also includes an autographed photo of Amelia Earhart in her flight suit standing on the wing of her plane and pages from Alexander's logbook beginning in 1931 and listing hours logged as a student, solo flights, and flights she made after she became licensed.

17,936. American Association of University Women
Records. 1914-71. 10 ft.
Open. Accession list.
University of Wyoming, American Heritage Center.
Minutes, correspondence, reports, budget proposals, scrapbooks regarding activities, programs, clippings, branch publications, and other material of the Wyoming AAUW, founded in 1914. Contains information about state and local AAUW activities.

17,937. American National Cowbelles
Records. 1953-75. 54 Hollinger boxes.
Open. Accession list.
University of Wyoming, American Heritage Center.
Collection includes records of Mary Louise Lynam, administrator of the ANC; financial records; files from state and local chapters; correspondence with state and local chapter leaders regarding conventions, activities, and ANC membership; notebooks; scrapbooks containing photos, programs, and clippings; yearbooks; printed material produced by the ANC; and other material of the ANC.

17,938. Arnold, Maria
Papers. 1881. 2 Hollinger boxes.
Open. Accession list.
University of Wyoming, American Heritage Center.
Diaries of Arnold contain descriptions of home life, school, and customs in Germany; life in London and her impressions of England; her missionary work in Africa; and the culture shock she experienced after emigrating to the US.

17,939. Babcock, Caroline Lexow
Papers. Ca. 1924-61. 1 Hollinger box.
Open. Accession list.
University of Wyoming, American Heritage Center.
Printed material and books of [Mrs.] Babcock (1882-), a Blairstown, NJ, resident, regarding peace efforts. Includes material of the National Council Against Conscription, the War Resisters League, the Women's International League for Peace and Freedom, and the Absolutists War Objectors Association.

17,940. Bellamy, Mary (Godat)
Papers. 1868-1943. 1 Hollinger box.
Open. Accession list.
University of Wyoming, American Heritage Center.
Bellamy (1861-1955), a schoolteacher, was the first woman legislator in Wyoming. Correspondence concerning personal and family matters, scrapbooks of clippings regarding WWII and the Laramie Woman's Club, photos, maps, books, and other items contain information on Bellamy's travels to the Orient, community service, women's issues, prominent Wyoming women, and Carrie Chapman Catt.

17,941. Beach, Cora M.
Papers. 1923-28. 1 Hollinger box.
Open. Accession list.
University of Wyoming, American Heritage Center.
Correspondence, a book manuscript, and clippings of [Mrs.] Beach (1878-), author of *Women of Wyoming* (1927) and an active community member. Correspondence between Anne Parker Miner and professor Grace Raymond Hebard of the University of Wyoming, between Beach and Hebard, and between Beach and Wyoming governor Nellie Tayloe Ross pertains to biographical sketches and research for *Women of Wyoming.*

17,942. Bechko, Peggy Anne
Papers. 1973. 2 Hollinger boxes.
Open. Accession list.
University of Wyoming, American Heritage Center.
Papers of Bechko (1950-), a writer, include correspondence with publishers and editors and manuscripts of her *Gunman's Justice* and *Night of the Flaming Guns.*

17,943. Benzell, Mimi
Papers. Nd. 1200 ft. of tapes and 4 video tapes.
Open. Accession list.
University of Wyoming, American Heritage Center.
The sound library of Benzell (1924-70), an opera soprano who made a transition to musical comedy, night club entertainment, and radio broadcasting. Contains excerpts by Benzell; singer Kathryn Grayson; actresses Julie Christie, Martha Scott, Helen Hayes, and Janet Leigh; and Amy Vanderbilt. Also contains video tapes of Benzell on "The Mike Douglas Show."

17,944. Bergman, Marilyn (Keith), and Bergman, Alan
Papers. Ca. 1959-69. 2 Hollinger boxes.
Open. Accession list.
University of Wyoming, American Heritage Center.
Marilyn Bergman, wife of Alan Bergman (1925-), is an author and lyricist who composed revues and songs for night clubs, films, and theater; she received the Academy Award for best song in 1968. Lyrics for motion pictures and for songs performed by Bing Crosby, Louis Armstrong, the Doodletown Pipers, and Rosemary Clooney and material written for the Academy Award shows.

17,945. Blakely, Kate
Papers. 1953-62. 2 Hollinger boxes.
Open. Accession list.
University of Wyoming, American Heritage Center.
Blakely was a conservationist and environmentalist. Correspondence with friends and the federal government regarding environmental problems; publications written by Blakely; maps, charts, and graphs used in research; documents from the US House of Representatives pertaining to conservation and the environment; and leaflets promoting environmental consciousness.

17,946. Boice, Mrs. Fred
Papers. 1885-1947. 1 Hollinger box.
Open. Accession list.
University of Wyoming, American Heritage Center.
Margaret McIntosh Boice (1884-1967) was an author who also bought and sold pedigreed horses. Photos, certificates, ephemera from the Wyoming statehood celebration of 1890, and clippings, most of which relate to Boice's interest in horses. Boice wrote *The Kashmir Bridge-Woman* (1966).

17,947. Bombeck, Erma
Papers. Ca. 1967-71. 1 Hollinger box.
Open. Accession list.
University of Wyoming, American Heritage Center.
[Mrs. William] Bombeck (1927-), whose given name was Louise Fiste, is a syndicated newspaper columnist. Correspondence with publishers; notes; galley proofs; a *Life* magazine article about Bombeck entitled "Socrates of the Ironing Board"; copies of her books *Wit's End* (1967), *Just Wait Till You Have Children of Your Own,* and *Bill Keane;* and promotional ephemera about her column.

17,948. Brossman, Adeline H.
Papers. 1954. 1 folder.
Open. Accession list.
University of Wyoming, American Heritage Center.
Autobiography of Brossman, a Pinedale, WY, resident, regarding homesteading in Wyoming around 1900. Contains information on cattlemen, the scarcity of supplies, building a home, raising children on a homestead, and the dangers and harsh physical conditions she experienced.

17,949. Bunting, Pauline
Papers. Ca. 1890. 2 vols.
Open. Accession list.
University of Wyoming, American Heritage Center.
Photo albums of [Miss] Bunting, a teacher of the seventh and eighth grades. The albums depict southern Utah.

17,950. Burt, Olive W.
Papers. 1947-69. 14 Hollinger boxes.
Open. Accession list.
University of Wyoming, American Heritage Center.
Correspondence, book manuscripts, research notes, photos, articles, and clippings of Burt (1894-), an author and resident of Salt Lake City. Contains manuscripts for her books on salt; copper; teenagers and Negroes of the early West; the Ringling brothers; the first woman editor of *Godey's Lady's Book;* Brigham Young; Luther Burbank; James P. Beckworth, mulatto chief of the Crow Indians; and 23 others.

17,951. Byron, Elsa Spear
Papers. 1881-1968. Ca. 3 in.
Open. Accession list.
University of Wyoming, American Heritage Center.
Correspondence, photos, a scrapbook about the Johnson County war, and clippings of Byron (1897-), a Big Horn, WY, resident, civic leader, and local historian, pertain to material Byron collected to document the history of Big Horn.

17,952. Cather, Willa Sibert
Papers. Ca. 1906-37. 1 in.
Open. Accession list.
University of Wyoming, American Heritage Center.
Correspondence, a post card, and notes of [Miss] Cather (1873-1947), an author. Includes a letter to a friend that Cather wrote while she was abroad and an explanation of how to pronounce her last name.

17,953. Catt, Carrie Clinton (Lane) Chapman
Papers. 1925-47. 2 Hollinger boxes.
Open. Accession list
University of Wyoming, American Heritage Center.
Catt (1859-1947), a suffragist and peace leader, was the president of the National American Woman Suffrage Association from 1900 to 1904. Includes correspondence with Grace Raymond Hebard regarding women's suffrage, their respective work, and personal matters; a letter to [Miss] Alda H. Wilson, executor to the librarian of the University of Wyoming; letters from Catt to several Wyoming

women regarding suffrage efforts and personal matters; and clippings about Catt. She was first married to Leo Chapman, then to George William Catt.

17,954. Clapper, Olive Ewing
Papers. 1934-65. 2 Hollinger boxes.
Open. Accession list.
University of Wyoming, American Heritage Center.
Clapper (1896-1968), a radio commentator and contributing editor for *Look* magazine in the 1940s, was director of the Washington, DC, bureau of CARE from 1952 to 1962. She edited a collection of newspaper columns, written by her late husband Raymond Clapper, entitled *Watching the World* (1944), and she wrote *Washington Tapestry* (1946). Correspondence; speeches; two cablegrams, one from Adolph Hitler and the other from Joseph Stalin; a scrapbook of letters, photos, clippings, and cablegrams relating to the Clappers' trip to Europe; photos; broadcast transcripts; invitations; articles; clippings; and other papers.

17,955. Clark, Helen
Papers. 1946-76. Ca. 4 ft.
Open. Accession list.
University of Wyoming, American Heritage Center.
Clark is a Montana journalist. Correspondence, manuscripts of her writings, poetry and articles by Clark, photos, 20 awards from the Montana State Press Women and the National Federation of Press Women, periodicals, and books.

17,956. Clifford, Eth (Rosenberg)
Papers. 1957-67. Ca. 5 in.
Open. Accession list.
University of Wyoming, American Heritage Center.
Clifford was an author of children's books. Correspondence with friends and other authors; manuscripts for *Mommies Are for Loving, Red Is Never a Mouse, The Whistling Boy, Why Is an Elephant Called an Elephant?,* and other books; and her published works.

17,957. Cooper, Barbara
Papers. 1880. 1 folder.
Open. Accession list.
University of Wyoming, American Heritage Center.
Two letters donated by Barbara Cooper that Frank Cooper wrote to his mother and sister Ada in Laramie concern the scenery, family matters, and his activities while traveling in Colorado, Utah, and Wyoming.

17,958. Cooper, Maude (Doyle) Prickett
Papers. Ca. 1938-72. 3 Hollinger boxes.
Open. Accession list.
University of Wyoming, American Heritage Center.
A TV actress, Cooper (1914-76) played the role of Rosie in the "Hazel" series; she also appeared on "The Jack Benny Show," "The Red Skelton Show," "The Andy Griffith Show," "Fury," "Bewitched," "Get Smart," and others. Correspondence, 1948-61; family photos; a movie still of "Maudie" Prickett, 1944; scripts from stage productions; certificates; scrapbooks of clippings and *Playbill Magazine;* articles and books; and other papers.

17,959. Curry, Peggy Simson
Papers. Ca. 1956-59. 1 Hollinger box.
Open. Accession list.
University of Wyoming, American Heritage Center.
Curry (1911-) was a creative writing instructor, an author, and a lecturer at various colleges. Manuscripts for her books *So Far from Spring* (1956) and *The Oil Patch* (1959).

17,960. Dahlquist, John, and Dahlquist, Laura
Papers. 1878-1949. 1 Hollinger box.
Open. Accession list.
University of Wyoming, American Heritage Center.
Correspondence, business records, a registration and poll book of 1906 and 1926 elections, and photos of the Dahlquists, residents of Wyoming.

17,961. Darrow, Bob
Papers. 1965. 1 folder.
Open. Accession list.
University of Wyoming, American Heritage Center.
Darrow is a Lusk, WY, resident. Photos of the dedication of the Mother Featherlegs monument. "Old Mother Featherlegs," who operated a hangout for outlaws along the Cheyenne-Black Hill Trail, received her name because she wore red, ruffled pantalettes around her ankles, which fluttered in the breeze "like a feather-legged chicken" when she rode horseback. She was murdered by the outlaw "Dangerous Dick."

17,962. Daughters of the American Colonists
Records. 1866-1909. Ca. 1 ft. and 7.5 Hollinger boxes.
Open. Accession list.
University of Wyoming, American Heritage Center.
Correspondence and photos of members and activities of this group concerned with community service and personal betterment. Also contains Wyoming church records, including baptismal, marriage, and death records; mortality schedules; membership rolls; and a parish register of the Methodist and First Presbyterian churches in Cheyenne, WY, and of the First Baptist, Presbyterian, Methodist-Episcopal, St. Paul's Evangelical, and other churches in Laramie.

17,963. Dean of Women's Office, University of Wyoming
Records. 1921-58. 1 Hollinger box.
Access restricted. Accession list.
University of Wyoming, American Heritage Center.
Organized in ca. 1907 to encourage women to strengthen their domestic skills, the Office later supervised and coordinated women's campus activities. Panhellenic, social committee, and other minutes; a scrapbook and other material of the Associated Women Students; the University *Handbook;* and other items.

17,964. Eastman, Ida Rauh
Papers. 1905-67. 2 Hollinger boxes.
Open. Accession list.
University of Wyoming, American Heritage Center.
Best known as Ida Rauh, Eastman (1877-1970) was the founder of the Provincetown Players, a women's rights advocate, a poet, and a sculptor; she was also active in Margaret Sanger's campaigns for birth control. Correspondence with friends, manuscripts for stage productions of the Players, poems by Eastman, an article and a clipping about the Players, and greeting cards.

17,965. Fisher, Ruth Page
Papers. 1931-72. 1 Hollinger box.
Open. Accession list.
University of Wyoming, American Heritage Center.
Photos, publicity sheets, programs, articles, and clippings of Fisher (1900?-), a dancer and choreographer. Includes articles about Fisher and programs from the Chicago Opera Ballet, the International Ballet, and the Theatre de L'Empire in Paris.

17,966. Foote, Dorothy Cooper
Papers. 1951-69. 7 Hollinger boxes.
Open. Accession list.
University of Wyoming, American Heritage Center.
Foote (1911?-) was the writer of screenplays for such TV programs as "Father Knows Best" and "My Three Sons." Correspondence regarding her productions; manuscripts of some of her screenplays; photos; programs; an advertisement for the motion picture *The Lost Sunset,* for which Foote wrote the screenplay; periodicals; and clippings.

17,967. Foote, Mary Anna (Hallock)
Papers. 1955-56. 1 in.
Open. No guide.
University of Wyoming, American Heritage Center.
Correspondence of Mrs. Harold W. Benn, who wrote a thesis on [Mrs. Arthur Dewint] Foote (1847-1938), a novelist, with persons who had biographical data on Foote.

17,968. Girl's Cadet Corporation
Records. 1898-1906. 15 items.
Open. No guide.
University of Wyoming, American Heritage Center.
Photos of members of the Corp in uniform and in formation on the University of Wyoming campus. The Corp was founded in ca. 1898.

17,969. Gleason, Ida Riner
Papers. Ca. 1920-55. Ca. 10 in.
Open. Accession list.
University of Wyoming, American Heritage Center.
Born in Cheyenne, WY, [Mrs.] Gleason (1900?-) was a writer and author of *Boy from Nowhere.* Correspondence, photos, scrapbooks, and copies of most of Gleason's works, including plays, poems, stories, and clippings.

17,970. Gray, Annie Ruth
Papers. Ca. 1920-65. 1 Hollinger box.
Open. Accession list.
University of Wyoming, American Heritage Center.
Photo, musical scores, articles, and clippings of [Miss] Gray (1900?-), a theatrical performer, musician, and entertainer. Includes scores, among them "The Rocky Mountain Canary Speaks," "The Hermit Thrush," and "Smoke From My Chimney."

17,971. Gray, W. B. D., and Gray, Annette B.
Papers. 1906-51. 2 Hollinger boxes.
Open. Accession list.
University of Wyoming, American Heritage Center.
W. B. D. Gray (1846-1926) was superintendent of the Congregational mission of Wyoming until his retirement in 1918; Annette Gray, whom he married in 1902, was pastor of the South Congregational Church. Correspondence with community members and other Congregational church leaders, photos and slides, certificates, a scrapbook, and clippings.

17,972. Hanalis, Blanche
Papers. 1957-75. 4 Hollinger boxes.
Open. Accession list.
University of Wyoming, American Heritage Center.
Hanalis was a screenplay writer and actress. Correspondence regarding contracts and future professional plans; scripts for five motion pictures, three plays, and 14 television shows for which Hanalis wrote the screenplays; notes regarding productions in which she acted; news releases; and advertisements of motion pictures for which Hanalis wrote the screenplays, including *From the Mixed-Up Files of Mrs. Basil E. Frankweiler, Train for Tecumuh,* and *The Trouble With Angels.* Hanalis also wrote screenplays for *The Hideaways, A Tree Grows in Brooklyn,* and *The Case Against Colonel Sutton.*

17,973. Hearst, Phoebe (Apperson)
Papers. Ca. 1887-1907. 1 Hollinger box and 2 tapes.
Open. Accession list.
University of Wyoming, American Heritage Center.
Hearst (1842-1919), who was married in 1863 to George Hearst, a US senator and only son of William Randolph Hearst, cofounded the PTA with [Mrs.] Alice Birney, established the first kindergarten in the US, and was a major benefactor of the University of California, Berkeley. Correspondence with friends and relatives, poems, clippings, and tapes of Edward Hardy Clark's recollections of Hearst.

17,974. Hebard, Grace Raymond
Papers. Ca. 1882-1936. 37 Hollinger boxes.
Open. Accession list.

University of Wyoming, American Heritage Center. Correspondence, book manuscripts, research notes, speeches, certificates, scrapbooks, clippings, and other material of Hebard (1861-1936), an educator, historian, lawyer, and women's rights activist. Includes correspondence with notable Wyoming women and Carrie Chapman Catt. Hebard received her BS in civil engineering from the University of Iowa in 1882 and her PhD from Ohio Wesleyan University in 1893. In 1909 she was the first woman admitted to the Wyoming bar and permitted to practice law before the Wyoming Supreme Court. A professor at the University of Wyoming, where she taught several subjects, Hebard retired in 1919 to conduct historical research and to work for women's suffrage.

17,975. Hershman, Arlene
Papers. 1969-71. 3 Hollinger boxes.
Open. Accession list.
University of Wyoming, American Heritage Center. Hershman (1934-) was an editor in 1967 and senior editor in 1968 of *Dun's Review,* a member of the executive committee of the New York State New Democratic Coalition from 1971 to 1972, and chair of the Coalition's women's rights committee since 1970. Notebooks containing her research material regarding child care, prostitution, and legislation affecting women; literature from such feminist organizations as the Committee for a Women's National Abortion Coalition, Female Liberation, the International Socialist Women's Caucus, Media Woman, the National Organization for Women, the Congress to Unite Women, The Feminists, and the United Women's Contingent; clippings concerning abortion, sex discrimination, marriage, children, divorce, rape, and the women's movement; and other material.

17,976. Hodgson, Mrs. Colin
Papers. 1951. 1 Hollinger box.
Open. Accession list.
University of Wyoming, American Heritage Center. Research notes on the history and development of Carbon, WY, written by Mary E. [Mrs. Colin] Hodgson for the Wyoming State Archives Department.

17,977. Homsher, Lola M.
Papers. Ca. 1868-90. Ca. 7 in.
Open. Accession list.
University of Wyoming, American Heritage Center. An early resident of Wyoming, Homsher was state historian from 1941 to 1943 and ex-officio state historian from 1951 to 1953. Photos of Albany County residents, scenes, and businesses, which were used in a history of the County to 1880 that Homsher wrote.

17,978. Hornaday, Mary
Papers. 1921-65. 13 in.
Open. Accession list.
University of Wyoming, American Heritage Center. Hornaday (1906-) did volunteer work in Europe during WWII. Correspondence with her mother from the period when Hornaday was in Europe and letters from Eleanor Roosevelt from 1942 to 1946; photos; a commemorative medal certificate from the Assembly of Captive European Nations that was awarded to Hornaday in 1965 in recognition of her work for freedom in east-central Europe; invitations from President and Mrs. Coolidge, Mrs. Hoover, Mrs. Roosevelt, Mrs. Truman, Madame Chiang Kai-shek, and Indira Ghandi; scrapbooks of clippings regarding women's efforts during WWII; and other clippings.

17,979. Huxtable, Ada Louise
Papers. 1967-75. 12 Hollinger boxes.
Open. Accession list.
University of Wyoming, American Heritage Center. An architecture critic for *The New York Times,* Huxtable was the winner of the first Pulitzer Prize for distinguished criticism in 1970. Correspondence with family, friends, publishers, and associates; manuscripts of Huxtable's writings; her editorials; reports; photos; press releases; programs; newsletters; clippings; and other papers.

17,980. Ingersoll, Robert G.
Papers. 1862-1956. 2 Hollinger boxes.
Open. Accession list.
University of Wyoming, American Heritage Center. Ingersoll (1833-99) was an agnostic and freethinker. Correspondence with other agnostics and freethinkers and pamphlets, articles, and books written by Ingersoll. Also includes correspondence, 1908-15, of Ingersoll's wife Eva A. Parker Ingersoll (?-1915) regarding spiritualistic contacts she had made with her deceased husband and correspondence and files, 1940-56, of Eva (Ingersoll) Wakefield, daughter of Robert and Eva Ingersoll, concerning her work on the Robert G. Ingersoll Memorial.

17,981. Ivinson Memorial Hospital Ladies Auxiliary
Records. 1951-69. 1 Hollinger box.
Open. Accession list.
University of Wyoming, American Heritage Center. Bylaws, president's reports, minutes, correspondence, and committee reports of this Laramie group, founded in 1951 to assist the hospital's patients in a nonprofessional capacity and to raise funds for the institution.

17,982. James, Mrs. David C.
Papers. 1915. 1 folder.
Open. Accession list.
University of Wyoming, American Heritage Center. Journal kept by Linda McKinstry describing homesteading conditions in Jackson Hole, WY, isolation, harsh weather, and inadequate supplies Also includes a photo of the Jackson Hole mail stage.

17,983. Janis, Joan Gardner
Papers. Ca. 1949-71. 2 boxes.
Open. Accession list.
University of Wyoming, American Heritage Center. Janis (1926-) is an actress, author, screenwriter, composer, and two-time Emmy award winner for an animated cartoon character. Personal and business correspondence, 13 movie scripts, two musical scores, four audiovisual tapes from commercials in which Janis performed, photos of Janis, movie stills, broadside publicity sheets, and clippings about her performances and career.

17,984. Jordan, Constance B.
Papers. 1921-67. 1 Hollinger box.
Open. Accession list.
University of Wyoming, American Heritage Center. An American National Red Cross volunteer for 50 years, [Mrs. Eldridge] Jordan (1896?-1971) was one of the original Gray Ladies during WWI. Letter of congratulations and gratitude from the Department of the Navy in 1921, correspondence with the Red Cross regarding Jordan's volunteer record, a letter from Mamie Eisenhower thanking Jordan for writing a letter on behalf of the men at Walter Reed General Hospital wishing the President well in his recovery from an illness, and certificates from the Red Cross for 45 years of service and from Walter Reed Hospital for 35 years of service.

17,985. Keyes, Verna
Papers. 1917-25. 1 Hollinger box.
Open. Accession list.
University of Wyoming, American Heritage Center. Keyes (1893-?) was the designer of the Wyoming state flag. Correspondence with Grace Raymond Hebard regarding state activities, history, and personal matters; a letter from state historian Eunice G. Anderson concerning the design of the state flag; an outline of a buffalo for the flag; an article on the symbolism of the Wyoming state flag; and clippings.

17,986. LaMar, Estella
Papers. 1903-61. 2 in.
Open. Accession list.
University of Wyoming, American Heritage Center. Scrapbook of LaMar, a popular vocalist and pianist who resided in Houston, contains photos and letters about her concerts.

17,987. Laramie Woman's Club
Records. 1885-1956. 8 Hollinger boxes.
Access restricted. Accession list.
University of Wyoming, American Heritage Center. Minutes, legal documents, correspondence, reports, photos, scrapbooks, Club histories, yearbooks, clippings, pamphlets, and magazines of the Club, which was concerned with community service and the personal betterment of its members. The Club's constitution was written in 1885.

17,988. Laramie-WPA Nursery School
Records. 1936-43. Ca. 2 in.
Open. Accession list.
University of Wyoming, American Heritage Center. Bank statements, budget proposals, food guides with recipes, and clippings from the Laramie newspaper of this child-care center, which was founded in about 1938, conducted with the assistance of the University of Wyoming, and disbanded in about 1943. The staff was comprised solely of women.

17,989. Lennart, Isobel
Papers. 1942-69. 14 Hollinger boxes.
Open. Accession list.
University of Wyoming, American Heritage Center. Lennart (1915-71) was the award-winning writer of the book and screenplay for the Broadway musical and motion picture *Funny Girl.* Includes Lennart's scripts for the Broadway play *Funny Girl; East Side, West Side; Lost Angel;* and *The Sundowners.*

17,990. Lenski, Lois
Papers. Ca. 1932-72. 9 Hollinger boxes.
Open. Accession list.
University of Wyoming, American Heritage Center. Lenski (1893-1974), who was married to Arthur S. Covey, was an author and illustrator of children's books. Photo album, awards, brochures, pamphlets, and published books by Lenski pertain to the writing, publishing, and marketing of her books.

17,991. Lindsay, Patricia Coffin
Papers. 1953-74. 8 Hollinger boxes.
Open. Accession list.
University of Wyoming, American Heritage Center. Lindsay (?-1974) was a writer and editor for *Life* and *Look* magazines, a painter, and a poet. Correspondence with friends and colleagues, including Amy Vanderbilt and Barbara Walters; research notes for her book *One, Two, Three, Four, Five, Six* and for many of her articles, which deal with such topics as the American family, children, adoption, parent-child relations, communes, contract marriages, divorce, and unwed parents; photos for *Life* articles; memoranda; notebooks regarding specific articles; and other material.

17,992. Ludlow, Dunlop, and Chambers
Papers. 1821-99. Ca. 6 in.
Open. Accession list.
University of Wyoming, American Heritage Center. Correspondence, photos, and scrapbooks of the Ludlow, Dunlop, and Chambers families, which were prominent in New England and the Mid-Atlantic states. Contains correspondence of Sarabella (Chambers) Dunlop McAllister with her daughter Jane Catherine (Dunlop) Wever regarding family life in Cincinnati and with her granddaughter Catherine (Wever) Collins; of Jane Catherine (Dunlop) Wever with her husband Caspar W. Wever, her sister Josephine (Dunlop) Ludlow, her niece Catherine (Ludlow) Baker, and her sister Charlotte (Dunlop) Clarkson regarding the California gold rush; of Charlotte (Dunlop)

Clarkson with her niece Catherine (Wever) Collins and John McLean; of Josephine (Dunlop) Ludlow with her sister Rubamah Chambers Scott and her sister-in-law Susan (Middlecoff) Ludlow; of Catherine (Wever) Collins with Josephine (Dunlop) Ludlow and Ludlow's daughter Sarabella Ludlow; of Susan (Middlecoff) Ludlow with her brother Samuel Middlecoff in Pera (later Ludlow), IL, a town that he founded; of Susan (Middlecoff) Ludlow with Mary Grant Cramer, her sister-in-law Josephine Ludlow, and her husband James Dunlop Ludlow regarding a search for his brother Israel, who was missing behind Confederate lines; of Annie Rubamah (Ludlow) Hunt with Jefferson Davis, her sister Catherine (Ludlow) Whiteman, and her sister Charlotte (Ludlow) Jones while Hunt was in New Orleans, as well as with her husband Randell Hunt regarding the American party campaign in Louisiana, with her brother James Dunlop Ludlow in Cincinnati regarding his marriage to Susan Middlecoff, and with Nettie Chase Hoyt regarding Chase's half-sister Kate Chase Sprague; of Charlotte (Ludlow) Jones with her brother-in-law Salmon P. Chase, William Pitt Fessenden, and Sarabella McLean; of Jane Catherine Wever with James Chambers Ludlow; of Henry Clay; of James Ludlow's cousin William Scott; of Charles A. Jones; of Israel Ludlow; of Winfield Scott Hancock; and of Ferdinand V. Hayden. Also includes a genealogical table and R. Clapper's comment on an 1840 speech by James C. Ludlow, which was annotated by Rubamah (Ludlow) Hunt.

17,993. Matthews, Elsie Albert
Papers. 1913-74. 1 Hollinger box.
Open. Accession list.
University of Wyoming, American Heritage Center.
Correspondence, photos, articles, clippings, and other papers of Matthews, an actress. Includes correspondence with her family, friends, and fans; motion picture stills; and a poem Matthews wrote in memory of her son Lieutenant Harold Clarke Matthews, who died when his plane crashed in 1954.

17,994. Moudy, Alice M.
Papers. 1890-1972. 1 folder.
Open. Accession list.
University of Wyoming, American Heritage Center.
Moudy received a BA from the University of Wyoming in 1897, chaired the French department at Heidelburg College in Tiffin, OH, and later resided in Laramie. Correspondence with friends and colleagues; manuscripts by Moudy; travel notes; slides from her travels in Africa, Europe, Asia, and the South Pacific; photos, including one of the class of 1900 at the University of Wyoming; and clippings.

17,995. Moudy, Mable Cheney
Papers. 1890-1954. 1 Hollinger box.
Open. Accession list.
University of Wyoming, American Heritage Center.
Correspondence, an autobiography, photos, a scrapbook containing genealogical information, clippings, and other papers of Moudy (1878-1972), a schoolteacher, community worker, and resident of Laramie. Includes correspondence with Grace Raymond Hebard and other prominent Wyoming women and information about Laramie and Wyoming history.

17,996. Musical Arts Club
Records. 1930-65. 2 Hollinger boxes.
Open. Accession list.
University of Wyoming, American Heritage Center.
Founded in 1930 by women in Laramie, the Club sponsored concerts and entertainment and promoted social and cultural improvement. Bylaws, minutes, treasurer's reports, financial records, receipt books, membership records, and programs. The Club disbanded in 1965.

17,997. Mygatt, Emmie D.
Papers. 1889-1973. 8 Hollinger boxes.
Open. Accession list.
University of Wyoming, American Heritage Center.
Mygatt is a researcher and historian of the Indian in the western US. Correspondence with friends, researchers, and publishers, 1950-63; manuscripts of articles; manuscripts and galley proofs for *Prisoner in the Circle* and *Rim Rock;* galley proofs for *Search for the Hidden Places* and *Stand By for Danger;* drawings used in her writings; research material on the Northern Cheyenne, including letters and documents from 1892 to 1958; seven scrapbooks of clippings, 1951-73, regarding social problems of the Indians and their efforts to resolve them; federal documents pertaining to US policy on western Indians; pamphlets; periodicals; books; and other material.

17,998. Nicolay, Helen
Papers. 1871-1954. 1 Hollinger box.
Open. Accession list.
University of Wyoming, American Heritage Center.
A Washington, DC, resident, Nicolay (1866-1954?) was the daughter of John George Nicolay, secretary to President Abraham Lincoln. Correspondence with her mother, other family members, and friends regarding domestic interests, politics, community activities, and Nicolay's involvement with the Red Cross; photos; and clippings.

17,999. O'Hara, Mary
Papers. Ca. 1941-50. 6 Hollinger boxes.
Open. Accession list.
University of Wyoming, American Heritage Center.
Book manuscripts, photos, and published works of O'Hara (1885-), an author and composer, include manuscripts of her *My Friend Flicka* (1941), *Thunderhead* (1943), and *Green Grass of Wyoming* (1946). O'Hara was also known as Mary Alsop.

18,000. Phillips, Peggy
Papers. 1937-66. 4 Hollinger boxes.
Open. Accession list.
University of Wyoming, American Heritage Center.
Phillips was chief writer for the TV program "Days of Our Lives;" she also was story editor for "My Three Sons," "Lassie," "National Velvet," and "The Donna Reed Show." Scripts and manuscripts of books written by Phillips; her résumé; a scrapbook of clippings and photos from "Listen Professor!," "Hear That Trumpet Talk," and "Crimson Canary"; and other photos.

18,001. Powell, Eleanor
Collection. Nd. 127 vols.
Open. Accession list.
University of Wyoming, American Heritage Center.
Recording discs of Powell (1912-), an actress and singer, include selections by the Andrews Sisters, the Boswell Sisters, Connie Boswell, Ella Fitzgerald, and Dinah Shore.

18,002. Powell, Jane
Papers. 1944-69. 36 Hollinger boxes.
Open. Accession list.
University of Wyoming, American Heritage Center.
Powell (1929-), whose given name is Suzanne Burch, is an actress and singer. Correspondence; telegrams; galley proofs; movie scripts; contracts; photos; paintings, including an oil painting of Powell by Sherman Monahan; certificates; scrapbooks, some of which were compiled by Powell's fans; music books and scores; programs; clippings; costumes; and other papers.

18,003. Ralston, Esther
Papers. 1925-29. 2 vols.
Open. Accession list.
University of Wyoming, American Heritage Center.
Publicity scrapbooks of Ralston (1902-), an actress during the 1920s and 1930s, contain clippings regarding movies in which Ralston performed, including *Lucky Devil, A Kiss for Cinderella, Beggar on Horseback, Trouble with Wives, A Tale of the Alps,* and *Something Always Happens.*

18,004. Ritchie, Barbara
Papers. 1952-69. Ca. 10 in.
Open. Accession list.
University of Wyoming, American Heritage Center.
Ritchie (1943-) is an author. Correspondence with friends, other authors, and publishers; book manuscripts of *Ramon Makes a Trade, Who Will Buy My Mongoose?,* and *The Mind and Heart of Frederick Douglass;* stories, articles, and book reviews written by Ritchie; and clippings.

18,005. Ross, Nellie Tayloe
Papers. Ca. 1922-60. 8 Hollinger boxes and 8 vols.
Open. Accession list.
University of Wyoming, American Heritage Center.
Ross (1876-1977), a governor of Wyoming, became director of the US Mint. Correspondence from 1924 to 1926 regarding the Governor's Conference, the Women's World Fair, Ross's retirement, and personal matters; a diary; manuscripts concerning women's suffrage; speeches and other writings, press releases, and invitations produced during Ross's tenure as governor; scrapbooks containing personal notes and information on public duties, trips, and social functions; clippings; and other material.

18,006. Royle, Selena
Papers. 1930-73. 1 Hollinger box.
Open. Accession list.
University of Wyoming, American Heritage Center.
Royle was an author and theatrical and film personality until she retired to Mexico in the 1940s. Includes correspondence regarding her career, the American National Red Cross, and legal matters; letters from Eleanor Roosevelt in 1952 and from Archibald MacLeish; an award for service from the Red Cross camp fund campaign in 1948; a Veterans Administration certificate from 1952; copies of *A Gringa's Guide to Mexican Cooking* (1973) and *Guadalajara As I Know It. . . Live It. . . Love It. . .* (1969) by Royle; and clippings.

18,007. Schaedel, Grace Logan
Papers. 1937-76. 2 Hollinger boxes.
Open. Accession list.
University of Wyoming, American Heritage Center.
Correspondence, photos, and clippings pertain to Schaedel's publishing and selling efforts. Also includes a book manuscript for *The Lord Loveth a Cheerful Liar* and a copy of Ernest Alfred Logan's *The Biography of an Old Cowboy.*

18,008. Schemm, Mildred Walker
Papers. Ca. 1938-74. 5 Hollinger boxes.
Open. Accession list.
University of Wyoming, American Heritage Center.
Schemm (1905-), an author and professor of English literature at Wells College from 1955, was married to Ferdinand Ripley Schemm in 1927. Correspondence relating to Mildred Schemm's publications, correspondence with family and friends, book manuscripts, research notes, photos, articles, and clippings.

18,009. Shaw, Mildred Hart
Papers. Ca. 1957-67. 2 in.
Open. Accession list.
University of Wyoming, American Heritage Center.
[Mrs.] Shaw (1909-) was society editor and reporter from 1935 to 1940 and chief editorial writer from 1956 to 1972 for the *Daily Sentinel* in Grand Junction, CO. Correspondence, material from court cases, and articles regarding freedom of the press questions.

18,010. Spring, Agnes Wright
Papers. Ca. 1877-1972. 6 Hollinger boxes.
Access restricted. Accession list.

University of Wyoming, American Heritage Center. Spring (1894-) was Wyoming state librarian, a civic leader, and an author. Correspondence with family and friends regarding her research and personal matters, biographical manuscripts, research notes for her articles and books, legal documents, photos, scrapbooks, maps, clippings, and printed material. Also includes diaries, 1906-36, of Edith K. O. Clark, superintendent of schools in Sheridan, WY.

18,011. Stenberg, Molly Peacock
Papers. 1934-61. 5 Hollinger boxes.
Open. Accession list.
University of Wyoming, American Heritage Center. Stenberg was a writer, local historian, and resident of Laramie. Correspondence, some of which pertains to Stenberg's writing and research; manuscripts of Stenberg's "Theodore Winthrop, American Writer" and "The Peyote Cult Among Wyoming Indians"; 81 of her student papers; and yearbooks, pamphlets, reprints, and clippings.

18,012. Strayer, Martha
Papers. Ca. 1921-66. 10 Hollinger boxes.
Open. Accession list.
University of Wyoming, American Heritage Center. [Mrs.] Strayer was a journalist, free-lance writer, and author of *An Informed History of the DAR.* Correspondence, a manuscript of *Bucketful Full of Diamonds,* photos, certificates, a 1966 invitation to Strayer from the White House signed by Mrs. Johnson, pamphlets, and published works.

18,013. Suffrage Archives
Collection. Ca. 1850-1940. 2 ft.
Open. Accession list.
University of Wyoming, American Heritage Center. Minutes, printed material, clippings, and other items relating to women's suffrage in America. The material, which was collected by Edna Lamprey Stantial of Massachusetts, includes proceedings of the National American Woman Suffrage Association from 1893 to 1920 and minutes of the Association's jubilee convention in 1919; proceedings of the LWV for 1923; printed material regarding the Women's Centennial Congress in 1940; a 1930 survey of the legal status of women in the 48 states; biographical sketches of Frances E. Willard and Josephine Butler; addresses, broadsides, and pamphlets concerning women's suffrage; clippings regarding Elizabeth Blackwell, Alice Stone Blackwell, Lucy Stone, Carrie Chapman Catt, Henry B. Blackwell, and Anna Howard Shaw; a 1917 women's suffrage yearbook; US documents concerning suffrage legislation; and other material.

18,014. Susan J. Quealy Award
Records. 1946-76. 1 Hollinger box.
Open. Accession list.
University of Wyoming, American Heritage Center. In 1946 [Mrs.] Quealy, a resident of Kremmer, WY, donated $500 to the University of Wyoming extension service to establish an award for women exhibiting outstanding homemaking abilities. Nominations for the award, a list of those selected, and certificates of some women who received the award.

18,015. Todd, Della M.
Papers. 1911-12. 1 folder.
Open. Accession list.
University of Wyoming, American Heritage Center. Daily journal of Todd (1893-1967) documents ranch life on the Lower Piney Creek in northern Wyoming and the social, economic, and religious life of pioneers on the Tongue River, where her family later moved. The journal also contains photos.

18,016. Tuckey, Grace
Papers. Nd. 1 vol.
Open. Accession list.
University of Wyoming, American Heritage Center. Scrapbook of photos, clippings, and printed material of Tuckey, a child movie star in the late 1920s and early 1930s. Includes photos of Tuckey both in and outside her movie role as Baclanova, of her husbands, of her home, and of other subjects.

18,017. Urbanek, Mae (Bobb)
Papers. Ca. 1960. 1 Hollinger box.
Open. Accession list.
University of Wyoming, American Heritage Center. An author, free-lance writer, and resident of Lusk, WY, Urbanek (1903-) was president of Wyoming Press Women from 1963 to 1965. Book manuscript for *Wyoming Wonderful* and research notes for *Chief Washakie.*

18,018. Walker, Tacetta
Papers. 1937-48. 1 Hollinger box.
Open. Accession list.
University of Wyoming, American Heritage Center. Correspondence, book manuscripts, and clippings of [Mrs.] Walker, a Wyoming resident and local historian, contain information about Wyoming history.

18,019. Wergeland, Agnes Matilde
Papers. Nd. 1 in.
Open. Accession list.
University of Wyoming, American Heritage Center. Wergeland (1857-1914) received a PhD in 1890, and in 1902 she was appointed professor of history and French at the University of Wyoming at Laramie; she also was an advocate of universal suffrage. Notebook in Norwegian possibly containing Wergeland's research notes for her classes. Wergeland may have been the first Norwegian woman to receive a PhD.

18,020. Windsor, Marie
Papers. 1939-75. 1 Hollinger box.
Open. Accession list.
University of Wyoming, American Heritage Center. Windsor (1919-), whose given name was Emily Bertelsen Hupp, was an actress; she has worked with Metro-Goldwyn-Mayer since 1940 and wrote a television-movie column for a Los Angeles magazine from 1962 to 1966. Publicity photos, two television scripts for "Marcus Welby, M.D.," programs, newsletters, and clippings. All the material pertains to Windsor's acting career.

18,021. Winslow, Ann
Papers. 1930-66. 6 Hollinger boxes.
Open. Accession list.
University of Wyoming, American Heritage Center. A poet and teacher, Winslow (1894-1974) was a faculty member in the University of Wyoming's English department from 1936 to 1960, founder and executive secretary of the College Poetry Society of America, and editor of *College Verse* and a book of poems entitled *Trial Balances.* Correspondence, manuscripts of poems for "The Flicker and the Flame," manuscripts submitted to Winslow, files of the CPSA, photos, and volumes of *College Verse.* Includes correspondence with T. S. Eliot, Robert Frost, Stephen Vincent Benét, S. I. Hayakawa, Conrad Aiken, Theodore Roethke, Archibald MacLeish, Ezra Pound, Marianne Moore, J. W. Rankin, and Edna Ferber.

18,022. Women's History Research Center, Incorporated
Collection. Nd. Ca. 200 ft.
Open. Accession list.
University of Wyoming, American Heritage Center. A tax-exempt foundation located in Berkeley, CA, from 1968 to 1974, the Center collected material documenting the past and contemporary history of women and the women's movement. The University of Wyoming received the subject files from the collection. Contains personal correspondence, research papers, legal papers, graphics, pamphlets, leaflets, articles, clippings, publications of underground presses, and other items. Subjects include women in history, non-women's liberation groups, projects and services, protests and events, women's fiction and works, mass periodicals, women's newsletters, journals, bibliographies and syllabi, and other subjects. The material concerns various countries and time periods.

18,023. Wyoming Extension Homemakers Council
Records. 1939-58. 2 vols.
Open. Accession list.
University of Wyoming, American Heritage Center. Minutes of the Council.

18,024. Young, Mary
Papers. 1915-67. 13 Hollinger boxes.
Open. Accession list.
University of Wyoming, American Heritage Center. Young (1875-1965) was a stage and motion picture actress. Correspondence with friends, fans, and employers; motion picture contracts; photos; radio, stage, and motion picture scripts; musical scores; and clippings.

YELLOWSTONE NATIONAL PARK

18,025. Archive Tape Library
Collection. 1930- . Ca. 50 tapes.
Access restricted. Unpublished guide.
Yellowstone National Park Library and Archives. Recorded material on the Park's history includes a taped interview in which Bessie Haynes [Mrs. Fred] Arnold discusses daily life in Fort Yellowstone in ca. 1915 and a 17-page letter she wrote on the same topic; a diary of a visit Jane Clem made to the Park in 1911; an interview of Mrs. R. Cutler, an early Park employee; an interview of [Mrs.] Lena Potter, an early Gardiner, MT, resident, about early Park history; and an interview of [Mrs.] Edith Ritchie, another early resident of Gardiner.

18,026. Manuscripts
Collection. 1870- . 2 drawers.
Open. Card catalog.
Yellowstone National Park Library and Archives. Correspondence, journals, photos, and other material concerning the history of the Park, which was established by Congress in 1872, include letters written in 1899 by Lilla Cook and Mary Dexter about visits to the Park, reminiscences of visiting the Park in 1874 by Mabel Cross Osmond, a diary of a visit in 1897 by Caroline L. Paul, letters Flora Chase [Mrs. Charles E.] Pierce wrote from the Park in 1897, and an account by Lillian [Mrs. H. E.] Kirkemo of a trip she made to the Park in 1910 at the age of 11.

Directory of Contributing Repositories

Abbott-Northwestern Hospital Corporation, Sister Kenny Institute, Health Science Library, Chicago at 27 St., Minneapolis, MN 55407

Aberdeen-Matawan Public Library, 165 Main St., Matawan, NJ 07747

Abernethy Collection of American Literature. *See* Middlebury College, Abernethy Collection of American Literature

Academy of Natural Sciences. *See* Natural Sciences, The Academy of

Academy of the New Church Archives, 2815 Huntingdon Pike, Bryn Athyn, PA 19009

Adams County Historical Society. *See* Quincy and Adams County, Historical Society of

Adams County Historical Society, Box 102, Hastings, NE 68901

Adorers of the Blood of Christ, Province of Ruma, Rte. 1, Box 115, Red Bud, IL 62278

Adorers of the Blood of Christ, Provincial House, 1400 S. Sheridan, Wichita, KS 67213

Adrian Dominican Sisters, 1257 E. Siena Heights Dr., Adrian, MI 49221

Agnes Scott College, McCain Library, Decatur, GA 30030

Air Force Museum, Wright-Patterson A.F.B., OH 45433

Akron, University of, American History Research Center, Bierce Library, Akron, OH 44325

Akron, University of, Archives of the History of American Psychology, Akron, OH 44325

Alabama Civil Archives. *See* Alabama Department of Archives and History, Alabama Civil Archives

Alabama Department of Archives and History, Alabama Civil Archives, 624 Washington Ave., Montgomery, AL 36130

Alabama Department of Archives and History, Manuscripts Div., 624 Washington Ave., Montgomery, AL 36130

Alabama Historical Collection. *See* Alabama in Birmingham, University of, The Medical Center, Lister Hill Library of the Health Sciences, Alabama Historical Collection

Alabama in Birmingham, University of, The Medical Center, Lister Hill Library of the Health Sciences, Alabama Historical Collection, Birmingham, AL 35294

Alabama in Birmingham, University of, The Medical Center, Lister Hill Library of the Health Sciences, Reynolds Historical Library, Birmingham, AL 35294

Alabama State University Archives, Levi Watkins Learning Center, Montgomery, AL 36101

Alabama, The University of, W. S. Hoole Special Collections Library, Gorgas Library, University, AL 35476

Alaska Division of State Libraries and Museums, Alaska Historical Library, Pouch G, Juneau, AK 99811

Alaska Historical Library. *See* Alaska Division of State Libraries and Museums, Alaska Historical Library

Alaska, University of, Archives, Elmer E. Rasmuson Library, University of Alaska, Fairbanks, AK 99701

Albany Institute of History and Art, McKinney Library, 125 Washington Ave., Albany, NY 12210

Albert F. Simpson Historical Research Center, Maxwell A.F.B., AL 36112

Albuquerque, Museum of, Box 1293, Albuquerque, NM 87103

Albuquerque Public Library, Southwest Room, 501 Copper N.W., Albuquerque, NM 87102

Alden Historical Society Museum, 13213 Broadway, Alden, NY 14004

Alexian Brothers Congregation, Provincial Archives, 100 James Blvd., Signal Mountain, TN 37377

Alfred P. Sloan, Jr., Museum, 1221 E. Kearsley St., Flint, MI 48503

Alfred University, Herrick Memorial Library, Alfred, NY 14802

Alice Lloyd College, Appalachian Oral History Project, Pippa Passes, KY 41844

Allegheny College Library, Meadville, PA 16335

Alpha Kappa Alpha Sorority, 5211 S. Greenwood Ave., Chicago, IL 60615

Amalgamated Clothing and Textile Workers Union Archives, 15 Union Sq., New York, NY 10003

Amana Church Society, Amana, IA 52203

American Academy and Institute of Arts and Letters, Library, 633 W. 155 St., New York, NY 10032

American Antiquarian Society, 185 Salisbury St., Worcester, MA 01609

American Art, Archives of, Midwest Area Center, 5200 Woodward Ave., Detroit, MI 48202

American Art, Archives of, National Portrait Gallery, Rm. 331, Smithsonian Institution, Washington, DC 20560

American Art, Archives of, New England Area Center, 87 Mt. Vernon St., Boston, MA 02108

American Art, Archives of, New York Area Center, 41 E. 65 St., New York, NY 10021

American Art, Archives of, West Coast Area Center, M. H. de Young Museum, Golden Gate Pk., San Francisco, CA 94118

American Association of University Women Archives, 2401 Virginia Ave. N.W., Washington, DC 20037

American Baptist Historical Society, 1106 S. Goodman St., Rochester, NY 14620

The American Film Institute, Center for Advanced Film Studies, Charles K. Feldman Library, 501 Doheny Rd., Beverly Hills, CA 90210

American Foundation for the Blind, 15 W. 16 St., New York, NY 10011

American Heritage Center. *See* Wyoming, University of, Library, American Heritage Center

American History Research Center. *See* Akron, University of, American History Research Center, Bierce Library

American Indian, Library Museum of the, 9 Westchester Sq., Bronx, NY 10461

American Institute for Exploration, Bartlett Memorial Library on Exploration, 1809 Nichols Rd., Kalamazoo, MI 49007

American Institute of Physics, Niels Bohr Library, 335 E. 45 St., New York, NY 10017

American Jewish Archives, 3101 Clifton Ave., Cincinnati, OH 45220

American Jewish Committee, William E. Wiener Oral History Library, 165 E. 56 St., New York, NY 10022

American Jewish Historical Society, 2 Thornton Rd., Waltham, MA 02154

The American Lutheran Church Archives, 333 Wartburg Pl., Dubuque, IA 52001

American Lutheran Church, Archives of the, Luther Theological Seminary, 2375 Como Ave. W., St. Paul, MN 55108

American National Red Cross. *See* American Red Cross, National Headquarters Library and Archives

American Old Time Fiddlers Association, 6141 Morrill Ave., Lincoln, NE 68507

American Philosophical Society, 105 S. Fifth St., Philadelphia, PA 19106

American Political Items Collectors, 1008 Bonsella, Walla Walla, WA 99362

American Portraits, Catalog of, National Portrait Gallery, F St. at Eighth N.W., Washington, DC 20560

American Psychiatric Association, Library and Archives, 1700 18th St. N.W., Washington, DC 20009

American Red Cross, National Headquarters Library and Archives, Washington, DC 20006

American Society for Nursing Service Administrators, 840 N. Lake Shore Dr., Chicago, IL 60611

American Swedish Historical Museum, 1900 Pattison Ave., Philadelphia, PA 19145

American Woman's Society of Certified Public Accountants, Box 389, Marysville, OH 43040

Amherst College Library, Amherst, MA 01002

Amistad Research Center, Dillard University, 2600 Gentilly Blvd., New Orleans, LA 70122

Anchorage Historical and Fine Arts Museum Archives, 121 W. Seventh Ave., Anchorage, AK 99501

Anderson College, School of Theology Library, Anderson, IN 46011

Andover-Harvard Theological Library. *See* Harvard Divinity School, Andover-Harvard Theological Library

Andover Newton Theological School Library, Special Collections, Newton Centre, MA 02159

Anna Palmer Museum, York Community Center Bldg., 211 Seventh St. E., York, NE 68467

Annisquam Historical Society, Walnut St., Gloucester, MA 01930

Anoka County Historical Society, 1900 Third Ave. S., Anoka, MN 55303

Anson County Library, Wadesboro, NC 28170

Antioch College, Olive Kettering Library, Antiochiana, Yellow Springs, OH 45387

Appalachian Oral History Project. *See* Alice Lloyd College, Appalachian Oral History Project; *also* Emory and Henry College, Appalachian Oral History Project

Archives of . . . *See* other part of title, e.g., Mennonite Church, Archives of the

Archives of American Art. *See* American Art, Archives of

DIRECTORY OF CONTRIBUTING REPOSITORIES

Archives of the History of American Psychology. *See* Akron, University of, Archives of the History of American Psychology
Archivo General de Puerto Rico. *See* Puerto Rico, Archivo General de
Arizona Collection. *See* Arizona State University Library, Arizona Collection
Arizona Department of Library, Archives, and Public Records, 1700 W. Washington, Phoenix, AZ 85007
Arizona Historical Society Library, Tucson, AZ 85719
Arizona Historical Society, Phoenix Chapter and Museum, 1242 N. Central Ave., Phoenix, AZ 85004
Arizona State Library. *See* Arizona Department of Library, Archives, and Public Records
Arizona State Museum, University of Arizona, Tucson, AZ 85721
Arizona State University Archives, University Library, Tempe, AZ 85281
Arizona State University Library, Arizona Collection, Tempe, AZ 85281
Arizona, University of. *See also* Arizona State Museum, University of Arizona
Arizona, University of, Library, Special Collections Dept., Tucson, AZ 85721
Arkansas History Commission, 300 W. Markham St., Little Rock, AR 72201
Arkansas Territorial Restoration, Territorial Sq., Third & Scott, Little Rock, AR 72201
Arkansas, University of, Library, Special Collections, Fayetteville, AR 72701
Arlington County Department of Libraries, Virginiana Collection, 1015 N. Quincy St., Arlington, VA 22201
Armed Forces Institute of Pathology. *See* Armed Forces Medical Museum, Armed Forces Institute of Pathology
Armed Forces Medical Museum, Armed Forces Institute of Pathology, Washington, DC 20306
Art Institute of Chicago, Burnham Library, Michigan Blvd. at Adams, Chicago, IL 60603
Art Institute of Chicago, Ryerson Library, Michigan Blvd. at Adams, Chicago, IL 60603
Ashland Historical Society, Ashland, NH 03217
Association of (or for) . . . *See* other part of title, e.g., Operating Room Nurses, Association of
ATAS-UCLA Television Archives. *See* California, Los Angeles, University of, UCLA Film, Television, and Radio Archives
Atchison County Historical Society, Box 201, Atchison, KS 66002
Athens State College Library, Rare Book Room, Athens, AL 35611
Athol Historical Society, Inc., 1307 Main St., Athol, MA 01331
Atlanta Historical Society, Box 12423, Atlanta, GA 30355
Atlanta Public Library, Special Collections Dept., 10 Pryor St. S.W., Atlanta, GA 30303
Atlanta University, Trevor Arnett Library, Negro Collection, Atlanta, GA 30314
Atlantic County Historical Society, Box 301, Somers Point, NJ 08244
Auburn Public Library, Auburn, MA 01501
Auburn University Archives, Auburn, AL 36830
Augusta Regional Library, Oral History Project, Augusta, GA 30902
Augustana College Library, Special Collections, Rock Island, IL 61201
Aurora College, Charles B. Phillips Library, 347 Gladstone, Aurora, IL 60507
Aurora Colony Historical Society, Aurora, OR 97002
Austin Peay State University, Felix G. Woodward Library, Clarksville, TN 37040
Austin Public Library, Austin-Travis County Collection, Box 2287, Austin, TX 78767

Baker University Library, United Methodist Historical Collection and Library, Baldwin City, KS 66006
The Balch Institute, Research Library, 18 S. Seventh St., Philadelphia, PA 19106
Ball State University Library, Special Collections, Muncie, IN 47306
Baltimore Hebrew College Library, 5800 Park Heights Ave., Baltimore, MD 21215
The Baltimore Museum of Art, Art Museum Dr., Baltimore, MD 21218
Baltimore Region Institutional Studies Center. *See* Baltimore, University of, Baltimore Region Institutional Studies Center
Baltimore, University of, Baltimore Region Institutional Studies Center, 847 N. Howard St., Baltimore, MD 21201
The Bancroft Library. *See* California, Berkeley, University of, The Bancroft Library
Bangor Public Library, 145 Harlow St., Bangor, ME 04401
Bank of America Archives, Box 37000, San Francisco, CA 94137
Bank Street College of Education, Library, 610 W. 112 St., New York, NY 10025
Baptist General Conference Archives, Bethel Seminary Library, 3949 Bethel Dr., St. Paul, MN 55112
Barker Texas History Center. *See* Texas at Austin, University of, Archives, Barker Texas History Center
Barnard College Archives, Lehman Hall, Columbia University, New York, NY 10027
Barnard College Library, Columbia University, New York, NY 10027
Barre Historical Society, Inc., Common St., Barre, MA 01005
Bartlesville Public Library, History Room, Bartlesville, OK 74003
Bartlett Memorial Historical Museum, 2149 St. Lawrence Ave., Beloit, WI 53511
Bastrop County Historical Society Museum and Archives, Box 279, Bastrop, TX 78602
Batavia Historical Society, 11 Batavia Ave. N., Box 15, Batavia, IL 60510
Baxter Memorial Library, Gorham, ME 04038
Bayliss Public Library, Special Collections Room, Sault Ste. Marie, MI 49783
Baylor University Program for Oral History. *See* Baylor University, The Texas Collection
Baylor University, The Texas Collection, Box 6396, Waco, TX 76706
Bell Public Library, Eighth & Austin St., Portland, TX 78374
Bellingham Public Library, Bellingham, WA 98225
Bellport-Brookhaven Historical Society Museum, Box 6, Bellport, NY 11713
Beloit Historical Society. *See* Bartlett Memorial Historical Museum
Belton City Library, Box 89, Belton, TX 76513
Bemidji State University. *See also* North Central Minnesota Historical Center, Bemidji State University
Bemidji State University, A. C. Clark Library, Archives Collection, Bemidji, MN 56601
Benedictine Convent of Perpetual Adoration, 8300 Morganford Rd., St. Louis, MO 63123
Benedictine Convent of St. Martin, Rte. 4, Box 253, Rapid City, SD 57701
Benedictine Sisters of Florida, Holy Name Priory, Drawer H, St. Leo, FL 33574
Benedictine Sisters of Our Lady of Sorrows, 5900 W. 147 St., Oak Forest, IL 60452
Benedictine Sisters of Pittsburgh, Mt. St. Mary Priory, 4530 Perrysville Ave., Pittsburgh, PA 15229
Benedictine Sisters of Pontifical Jurisdiction, Holy Family Convent, Benet Lake, WI 53102
Benedictine Sisters of Pontifical Jurisdiction, St. Bede Priory, Priory Rd., Eau Claire, WI 54701
Benedictine Sisters of Sacred Heart Convent, 1101 W. Fifth, Yankton, SD 57078
Benedictine Sisters, Queen of Angels Priory, Mt. Angel, OR 97362
Benedictine Sisters, Sacred Heart Convent, Box 700, Cullman, AL 35055
Benedictine Sisters, Sacred Heart Priory, Richardton, ND 58652
Benedictine Sisters, St. Gertrude Priory, Ridgely, MD 21660
Benedictine Sisters, St. Joseph's Convent, 2200 S. Lewis, Tulsa, OK 74114
Benedictine Sisters, St. Scholastica Convent, Box 3489, Ft. Smith, AR 72913
Benedictine Sisters, St. Scholastica Priory, Box 1118, Covington, LA 70433
Bennett College, Thomas F. Holgate Library, Greensboro, NC 27420
Bennington College Archives, Rte. 67A, Bennington, VT 05201
Bennington Museum, Bennington, VT 05201
Bentley Historical Library. *See* Michigan, University of, Bentley Historical Library, Michigan Historical Collections
Berea College Library, Special Collections, Berea, KY 40404
Berkeley County Court House, Surveyor of Lands and County Clerk, Martinsburg, WV 25401
Berkshire Christian College, Dr. Linden J. Carter Library, 200 Stockbridge Rd., Lenox, MA 01240
Bernardine Sisters OSF, Generalate, Maryview, 647 Spring Mill Rd., Villanova, PA 19085
Bethany College Archives, T. W. Phillips Memorial Library, Bethany, WV 26032
Bethel College, Mennonite Library and Archives, North Newton, KS 67117
Bethel Historical Society, Bethel, ME 04217
Bethel Seminary Library. *See* Baptist General Conference Archives, Bethel Seminary Library
Beverly Historical Society, 117 Cabot St., Beverly, MA 01915
Bexar County Archives, Office of the County Clerk, Courthouse, San Antonio, TX 78285
Big Bend, Archives of the. *See* Sul Ross State University, Archives of the Big Bend
Big Bend Natural History Association, Big Bend National Park, TX 79834
Biloxi Public Library, 217 Lameuse St., Biloxi, MS 39533
Black Hawk College Library, 6600 34th Ave., Moline, IL 61265
Blessed Sacrament Monastery, 23 Park Ave., Yonkers, NY 10703
Bloomfield Public Library, 90 Broad St., Bloomfield, NJ 07003
Bloomington Historical Society, 10200 Penn Ave. S., Bloomington, MN 55431
Bloomington Public Library, 205 E. Olive St., Box 3308, Bloomington, IL 61701
Blue Earth County Historical Society Museum, 606 S. Broad St., Mankato, MN 56001
Blue Hill Public Library, Blue Hill, ME 04614
Blue Mountain College, May Gardner Black Alumnae Room, Blue Mountain, MS 38610
Bluffton College, Mennonite Historical Library, Bluffton, OH 45817
The Boeing Company, Historical Services, Mail Stop 11-24, Box 3707, Seattle, WA 98124
Boise State University Library, Special Collections, 1910 University Dr., Boise, ID 83725
Boone County Historical Society, c/o 1521 Carroll St., Boone, IA 50036
Boston Athenaeum, 10½ Beacon St., Boston, MA 02108
Boston Museum of Fine Arts. *See* Fine Arts, Museum of
Boston Public Library, Dept. of Rare Books & Manuscripts, Box 286, Boston, MA 02117
Boston State College Library, 625 Huntington Ave., Boston, MA 02115
Boston University, Mugar Memorial Library, Dept. of Special Collections, 771 Commonwealth Ave., Boston, MA 02215
Boston University, Mugar Memorial Library, Dept. of Special Collections, Nursing Archive, 771 Commonwealth Ave., Boston, MA 02215
Bowdoin College Library, Special Collections Dept., Brunswick, ME 04011

DIRECTORY OF CONTRIBUTING REPOSITORIES

Bowers Museum, 2002 N. Main St., Santa Ana, CA 92706

Bowling Green State University Archives, Center for Archival Collections, University Library, Bowling Green, OH 43403

Boxborough Library, Boxborough, MA 01720

Bradford College Library, Haverhill, MA 01830

Brescia College Archives, Owensboro, KY 42301

Brethren Room. *See* McPherson College Library, Brethren Room

Brewster Ladies Library, Brewster, MA 02631

Bridgeport Public Library, Historical Collections, 925 Broad St., Bridgeport, CT 06604

Bridgeport, University of, Fones School of Dental Hygiene, 30 Hazel St., Bridgeport, CT 06602

Brigham Young University, Harold B. Lee Library, Div. of Archives & Manuscripts, Women's History Archives, Provo, UT 84602

Broadcast Pioneers Library, NAB Building, 1771 N St. N.W., Washington, DC 20036

Bronx County Historical Society, Research Library, 3266 Bainbridge Ave., Bronx, NY 10467

Brookline Public Library, 361 Washington St., Brookline, MA 02146

Brooklyn College Library, Special Collections Div., Bedford Ave. & Avenue H, Brooklyn, NY 11210

Brooklyn Public Library, History Div., Brooklyn Collection, Grand Army Plaza, Brooklyn, NY 11238

Brooks Memorial Library, 224 Main St., Brattleboro, VT 05301

The Bryant Library, Local History Collection, Paper Mill Rd., Roslyn, NY 11576

Bryn Mawr College Archives, College Library, Bryn Mawr, PA 19010

Bucyrus Historical Society, S. Walnut St., Bucyrus, OH 44820

Buechel Memorial Lakota Museum, Little Sioux, St. Francis, SD 57572

Buena Vista College, Ballou Library, Storm Lake, IA 50588

Buffalo and Erie County Historical Society, 25 Nottingham Ct., Buffalo, NY 14216

Buffalo Bill Historical Center, Cody, WY 82414

Burlington Public Library, 501 N. Fourth St., Burlington, IA 52601

Burnet County Historical Society, Box 74, Burnet, TX 78611

Burnham Tavern Museum, 60 Court St., Machias, ME 04654

Burton Historical Collection. *See* Detroit Public Library, Burton Historical Collection

Business and Professional Women's Foundation, 2012 Massachusetts Ave. N.W., Washington, DC 20036

Butterick Fashion Marketing Company, Library, 161 Sixth Ave., New York, NY 10013

Calhoun County Historical Society, Rockwell City, IA 50579

Calhoun County Museum Archives, 303 Butler St., St. Matthews, SC 29135

California, Berkeley, University of, The Bancroft Library, Manuscripts Div., Berkeley, CA 94720

California, Berkeley, University of, The Bancroft Library, University Archives, Berkeley, CA 94720

California, Berkeley, University of, College of Environmental Design, Documents Collection, Berkeley, CA 94720

California, Berkeley, University of, Institute of Transportation and Traffic Engineering, Berkeley, CA 94720

California, Davis, University of, Shields Library, Dept. of Special Collections, Davis, CA 95616

California Historical Society, 2090 Jackson St., San Francisco, CA 94109

California Institute of Technology Archives, Pasadena, CA 91125

California, Los Angeles, University of, Biomedical Library, The Center for the Health Sciences, Los Angeles, CA 90024

California, Los Angeles, University of, Music Library, 405 Hilgard Ave., Los Angeles, CA 90024

California, Los Angeles, University of, UCLA Film, Television, and Radio Archives, Dept. of Theater Arts, Los Angeles, CA 90024

California, Los Angeles, University of, University Research Library, Dept. of Special Collections, Los Angeles, CA 90024

California, Los Angeles, University of, University Research Library, Public Affairs Service, Los Angeles, CA 90024

California, Riverside, University of. *See also* Riverside City Archives, General Library, University of California

California, Riverside, University of, Library, Special Collections, Box 5900, Riverside, CA 92507

California, San Diego, University of, Central University Library, Mandeville Dept. of Special Collections, La Jolla, CA 92093

California, San Francisco, University of, The Library, University Archives, San Francisco, CA 94143

California, Santa Barbara, University of, The Library, Dept. of Special Collections, Santa Barbara, CA 93106

California, Santa Cruz, University of, Lick Observatory Archives, McHenry Library, Santa Cruz, CA 95064

California State Archives, Office of the Secretary of State, 1020 O St., Sacramento, CA 95814

California State Library, Library-Courts Bldg., Box 2037, Sacramento, CA 95809

California State University, Chico, Library, Special Collections Dept., Chico, CA 95929

California State University, Hayward, Library, Special Collections, 25800 Hillary St., Hayward, CA 94542

California State University, Long Beach, Library, 1250 Bellflower Blvd., Long Beach, CA 90840

California State University, Sacramento, Archives, University Library, 6000 J St., Sacramento, CA 95819

California State University, Sonoma. *See* Sonoma State University

California, University of, San Francisco Medical Center. *See* California, San Francisco, University of, The Library, University Archives

Camden County Historical Society, Park Blvd. & Euclid Ave., Camden, NJ 08103

Canaan Historical Museum, Canaan, NH 03741

The Canal Museum, Weighlock Bldg., Erie Blvd. E., Syracuse, NY 13202

Canal Zone Library-Museum, Panama Collection, Balboa Heights, CZ

Carlow College Archives, 3333 Fifth Ave., Pittsburgh, PA 15213

Carlton County Historical Society, Carlton, MN 55718

Carmelite Monastery, R.R. 1, Eldridge, IA 52748

Carmelite Monastery, 1318 Dulaney Valley Rd., Baltimore, MD 21204

Carmelite Monastery, 68 Franklin Ave., Saranac Lake, NY 12983

Carmelite Sisters of St. Therese, Villa Theresa Convent, 1300 Classen Dr., Oklahoma City, OK 73103

Carnegie Library, 607 Broad St., Rome, GA 30161

Carnegie-Mellon University, Hunt Institute for Botanical Documentation, Pittsburgh, PA 15213

Caroline Martin-Mitchell Museum, Naperville Park District, 421 Martin Ave., Naperville, IL 60540

Carroll College Library, Waukesha, WI 53186

Carroll County, Historical Society of, 210 E. Main St., Westminister, MD 21157

Carson County Square House Museum, Box 276, Panhandle, TX 79068

Cary Library, Main St., Houlton, ME 04730

Case Western Reserve University, University Archives, Cleveland, OH 44106

Catalog of American Portraits. *See* American Portraits, Catalog of, National Portrait Gallery

Catawba County Historical Museum, Newton, NC 28658

Catholic Archdiocese of Omaha Archives, Chancery Office, 100 N. 62 Ave., Omaha, NE 68132

Catholic Archives at San Antonio, Box 32648, San Antonio, TX 78284

Catholic Archives of America. *See* Notre Dame, University of, Archives

Catholic Archives of Texas, Capitol Sta., Box 13327, Austin, TX 78711

Catholic Diocese of Green Bay, Archives, Box 66, Green Bay, WI 54305

Catholic Diocese of Yakima, Box 901, Yakima, WA 98907

Catholic University of America, Dept. of Archives and Manuscripts, Washington, DC 20064

Cayuga County Historical Research Center, County Office Bldg., Auburn, NY 13021

Cedar Crest College Library, Allentown, PA 18104

Centenary College of Louisiana. *See also* North Louisiana Historical Association Collection, Centenary College of Louisiana Library

Centenary College of Louisiana, Magale Library, Shreveport, LA 71104

Centenary College, Taylor Memorial Library, Hackettstown, NJ 07840

Center for Erie Studies. *See* Mercyhurst College Archives/Center for Erie Studies

Center for Migration Studies. *See* Migration Studies, Center for

Center for the History of Physics. *See* American Institute of Physics, Niels Bohr Library

Center for the Study of the Consumer Movement. *See* Consumers Union of the United States, Inc., Center for the Study of the Consumer Movement

Central Arkansas, University of, Torreyson Library, Conway, AR 72032

Central Methodist College, George M. Smiley Memorial Library, Fayette, MO 65248

Central Michigan University, Clarke Historical Library, Mt. Pleasant, MI 48859

Central Minnesota Historical Center, St. Cloud State University, St. Cloud, MN 56301

Chadron State College, Mari Sandoz Heritage Society, Chadron, NE 69337

Chandler Historical Museum, Box 926, 87 W. Chicago St., Chandler, AZ 85224

Charleston City Archives, 100 Broad St., Charleston, SC 29401

Charleston Library Society, 164 King St., Charleston, SC 29401

Chatham College Library, Woodland Rd., Pittsburgh, PA 15232

Chemung County Historical Society, 304 William St., Elmira, NY 14901

Chester County Historical Society, 225 High St. N., West Chester, PA 19380

Chesterwood, Archives, Box 248, Stockbridge, MA 01262

Chestnut Hill College Archives, Logue Library, Philadelphia, PA 19118

Chicago Art Institute. *See* Art Institute of Chicago

Chicago Board of Education Library, 228 N. LaSalle, Chicago, IL 60601

Chicago Conservatory College, Archives, 410 S. Michigan Ave., Chicago, IL 60605

Chicago Federal Archives and Records Center. *See* Federal Archives and Records Center, Chicago Archives Branch

Chicago Historical Society, North Ave. & Clark St., Chicago, IL 60614

Chicago Institute for Psychoanalysis, 180 N. Michigan Ave., Chicago, IL 60601

Chicago Jewish Archives. *See* Spertus College of Judaica, Chicago Jewish Archives

Chicago Poor Clares Monastery, 89 & Kean Ave., Hickory Hills, IL 60467

Chicago Public Library, Carter G. Woodsen Regional Library, 9525 S. Halsted St., Chicago, IL 60628

Chicago Public Library, Chicago Lawn Branch, 6120 S. Kedzie Ave., Chicago, IL 60629

Chicago Public Library, Hild Regional Library, 4544 N. Lincoln Ave., Chicago, IL 60625

DIRECTORY OF CONTRIBUTING REPOSITORIES

Chicago Public Library, Kelly Branch, 6151 S. Normal Blvd., Chicago, IL 60621
Chicago Public Library, Pullman Branch, 11001 S. Indiana Ave., Chicago, IL 60628
Chicago Public Library, South Shore Branch, 2505 E. 73 Pl., Chicago, IL 60649
Chicago Public Library, Special Collections Div., 78 E. Washington, Chicago, IL 60602
Chicago Public Library, Toman Branch, 4005 W. 27 St., Chicago, IL 60623
Chicago Public Library, Walker Branch, 11071 S. Hoyne Ave., Chicago, IL 60643
Chicago Public Library, Woodlawn Branch, 6247 S. Kimbark, Chicago, IL 60637
Chicago, University of. *See* Oriental Institute of the University of Chicago
Childhood Education International, Association for, 3615 Wisconsin Ave. N.W., Washington, DC 20016
Children's Literature Research Collections. *See* Minnesota, University of, Children's Literature Research Collections
Children's Memorial Hospital Historical Files, 2300 Children's Plaza, Chicago, IL 60614
Chippewa Valley Museum, Box 1204, Eau Claire, WI 54701
Christian Science Monitor Library, One Norway St., Boston, MA 02115
Christian Theological Seminary, Manuscript Collection, 1000 W. 42 St., Indianapolis, IN 46208
Church of Jesus Christ of Latter-day Saints. *See* Jesus Christ of Latter-day Saints, Church of, Historical Dept.
Cincinnati Art Museum Library, Cincinnati, OH 45202
Cincinnati Historical Society, Eden Park, Cincinnati, OH 45202
Cincinnati, University of, Library, Special Collections Dept., Cincinnati, OH 45221
Circus World Museum Library, Baraboo, WI 53913
Citizens Savings Athletic Foundation, Sports Library, 9800 S. Sepulveda Blvd., Los Angeles, CA 90045
City Archives of Philadelphia. *See* Philadelphia, City Archives of
City University of New York. *See* Hunter College of the City University of New York, Archives
Claremont Historical Society, Clay Hill Rd., Claremont, NH 03743
Clark County Historical Museum, 1511 Main St., Vancouver, WA 98660
Clark University Archives, Robert Hutchings Goddard Library, Worcester, MA 01610
Clark University, Robert Hutchings Goddard Library, Dept. of Rare Books and Special Collections, Worcester, MA 01610
Clements Library. *See* Michigan, University of, William L. Clements Library
Cleveland Landmarks Commission, 28 City Hall, Cleveland, OH 44114
Cleveland *Plain Dealer*. *See* The *Plain Dealer*, Newspaper Library
Cloistered Dominican Nuns of Perpetual Adoration, Monastery of the Angels, 1977 Carmen Ave., Los Angeles, CA 90068
Coastal Georgia Historical Society, Box 1151, St. Simons Island, GA 31522
Colby College Library, Special Collections, Waterville, ME 04901
College of . . . *See* other part of title, e.g., St. Catherine, College of, Library
The Colonial Williamsburg Foundation, Drawer C, Williamsburg, VA 23185
Colorado College Library, Special Collections, Colorado Springs, CO 80903
Colorado Historical Society, 1300 Broadway, Denver, CO 80203
Colorado State Archives, 1313 Sherman, Denver, CO 80203
Colorado State University Library, Special Collections, Ft. Collins, CO 80521
Colorado, University of, Libraries, Western Historical Collections, Boulder, CO 80309
Colorado Women's College, Porter Library, 7055 E. 18 Ave., Denver, CO 80220
Columbia College, 1300 Columbia College Rd., Columbia, SC 29203
Columbia College, Kirtley Library, Eighth & Rogers, Columbia, MO 65216
Columbia County Historical Society, 105 Bakeless Center for the Humanities, Bloomsburg State College, Bloomsburg, PA 17815
Columbia University. *See also* Barnard College Archives, Lehman Hall, Columbia University; Barnard College Library, Columbia University
Columbia University, Avery Architectural Library, New York, NY 10027
Columbia University, Columbiana Library, 210 Low Memorial Library, New York, NY 10027
Columbia University, Herbert H. Lehman Papers, 405 School of International Affairs Bldg., New York, NY 10027
Columbia University, Oral History Research Office, Box 20, Butler Library, New York, NY 10027
Columbia University, Rare Book and Manuscript Library, 801 Butler Library, New York, NY 10027
Columbia University, School of International Affairs, Herbert Lehman Papers. *See* Columbia University, Herbert H. Lehman Papers
Columbia University, Teachers College Library, Dept. of Archives and TCana, Box 307, New York, NY 10027
Columbus and Franklin County, Public Library of, Columbus and Ohio Div., 96 S. Grant St., Columbus, OH 43215
Comanche Public Library, Box 411, Comanche, TX 76442
Community Service Society, 105 E. 22 St., New York, NY 10010
Concordia Historical Institute, Dept. of Archives & History, 801 DeMun Ave., St. Louis, MO 63105
Congregation of . . . *See* other part of title, e.g., Our Lady of the Retreat in the Cenacle, Congregation of, Cenacle Retreat House
Congregational Library, 14 Beacon St., Boston, MA 02138
Connecticut Historical Society, One Elizabeth St., Hartford, CT 06105
Connecticut State Library, Archives, History, and Genealogy Unit, 231 Capitol Ave., Hartford, CT 06115
Constitution Island Association, Inc., Box 41, West Point, NY 10996
Consumers Union of the United States, Inc., Center for the Study of the Consumer Movement, 256 Washington St., Mount Vernon, NY 10550
Conwellana-Templana Collection. *See* Temple University Libraries, Conwellana-Templana Collection
Cook Inlet Historical Society Archives. *See* Anchorage Historical and Fine Arts Museum Archives
Corcoran Gallery of Art, Curatorial Library, 17 St. & New York Ave. N.W., Washington, DC 20006
Cornell College Archives, College Library, Mount Vernon, IA 52314
Cornell Medical Center. *See* The New York Hospital-Cornell Medical Center, Medical Archives
Cornell University, Dept. of Manuscripts and University Archives, John M. Olin Library, Ithaca, NY 14853
Cornell University, New York State School of Industrial and Labor Relations, Labor-Management Documentation Center, Ithaca, NY 14850
Corning Clionian Circle Archives, c/o Helen Peterson, 146 Cayuga St., Corning, NY 14830
Corning Community College, Arthur A. Houghton, Jr., Library, Corning, NY 14830
Corning Glass Works, The Archives, MP-CH 2, Corning, NY 14830
Cornwall Historical Society, Cornwall, CT 06753
Corpus Christi Monastery of Poor Clares, 2111 S. Main St., Rockford, IL 61102
Cortland County Historical Society, 25 Homer Ave., Cortland, NY 13045
Cottey College Archives, Nevada, MO 64772
Cottonwood County Historical Society, 812 Fourth Ave., Windom, MN 56101
Council Bluffs Free Public Library, 200 Pearl St., Council Bluffs, IA 51501
County Center Historical Society Museum, Wabasso, MN 56293
Crosby County Pioneer Memorial Museum, Box 386, Crosbyton, TX 79322
Cumberland County Historical Society and the Hamilton Library Association, Box 626, Carlisle, PA 17013
Cumberland Historical Society, Prince Memorial Library, Cumberland, ME 04021

Dacotah Prairie Museum, Box 395, Aberdeen, SD 57401
Danvers Archival Center, 13 Page St., Danvers, MA 01923
Darke County Historical Society, 205 N. Broadway, St. Rte. 118, Greenville, OH 45331
Darlington County Historical Commission, Courthouse, Rm. 307, Darlington, SC 29532
Dartmouth College Library, Special Collections, Hanover, NH 03775
Daughters of Charity of St. Vincent de Paul, Marillac Provincial House, 7800 Natural Bridge Rd., St. Louis, MO 63121
Daughters of Charity of St. Vincent de Paul, Mater Dei Provincial House, 9400 New Harmony Rd., Evansville, IN 47712
Daughters of Charity of St. Vincent de Paul, St. Joseph's Provincial House, Emmitsburg, MD 21727
Daughters of Charity of St. Vincent de Paul, Seton Provincialate, 26000 Altamont Rd., Los Altos Hills, CA 94022
Daughters of the Republic of Texas, Texas History Research Library, Box 2599, San Antonio, TX 78299
Dauphin County, Historical Society of, 219 S. Front St., Harrisburg, PA 17104
Davis Conservation Library, 408 E. Main St., League City, TX 77573
Dayton and Montgomery County Public Library, 215 E. Third St., Dayton, OH 45402
Dearborn Historical Museum, 915 Brady St., Dearborn, MI 48124
Deer Isle-Stonington Historical Society, Deer Isle, ME 04627
Delaware, Historical Society of, 505 Market St., Wilmington, DE 19801
Delta State University, W. B. Roberts Library, Cleveland, MS 38732
Dennis Historical Society, Box 607, South Dennis, MA 02660
Denver Federal Archives and Records Center. *See* Federal Archives and Records Center, Denver Archives Branch
Denver Public Library, Western History Dept., 1357 Broadway, Denver, CO 80203
DePauw University, Archives of DePauw University and Indiana United Methodism, Roy O. West Library, Greencastle, IN 46135
Des Plaines Historical Society, Box 225, Des Plaines, IL 60017
Detroit Public Library, Burton Historical Collection, 5201 Woodward Ave., Detroit, MI 48202
DeWitt Historical Society of Tompkins County, The Clinton House, 116 N. Cayuga St., Ithaca, NY 14850
Dickinson College Library, Special Collections, Carlisle, PA 17013
Dickinson County Historical Society, Box 506, Abilene, KS 67410
Dickinson County Museum, Spirit Lake, IA 51360
Dighton Historical Society, 1217 Williams St., Dighton, MA 02715
Dillard University. *See* Amistad Research Center, Dillard University
Discalced Carmelite Nuns Monastery, 2215 N.E. 147, Seattle, WA 98155
Discalced Carmelite Nuns Monastery, Thornbrow, Elysburg, PA 17824

Disciples of Christ Historical Society, 1101 19th Ave. S., Nashville, TN 37212
Division of Historical Services-New York State Museum, Cultural Education Center, Empire State Plaza, Albany, NY 12230
Dodge County Historical Society, Beaver Dam, WI 53916
Dominican Convent of Our Lady of Prouille, Elkins Park, PA 19117
Dominican Convent of Our Lady of the Rosary, Sparkill, NY 10976
Dominican Convent of San Rafael, Archives, San Rafael, CA 94901
Dominican Nuns of Perpetual Adoration, Corpus Christi Monastery, 215 Oak Grove Ave., Menlo Park, CA 94025
Dominican Nuns of Perpetual Adoration, Corpus Christi Monastery, 1230 Lafayette Ave., Bronx, NY 10474
Dominican Sisters, Congregation of Holy Cross, Rosary Heights, Box 280, Edmonds, WA 98020
Dominican Sisters, Congregation of the Most Holy Rosary, Mt. St. Mary, Newburgh, NY 12550
Dominican Sisters of St. Catharine of Siena, St. Catharine, KY 40061
Dominican Sisters of St. Cecilia Congregation, St. Cecilia Convent, Nashville, TN 37208
Dominican Sisters of Springfield, Sacred Heart Convent, 1237 W. Monroe St., Springfield, IL 62704
Dominican Sisters of the Sick Poor, Center House, Mariandale, Ossining, NY 10562
Dominican Sisters, St. Mary of the Springs Motherhouse, Columbus, OH 43219
Dorchester Historical Society, 195 Boston St., Dorchester, MA 02125
Douglas County Museum, Roseburg, OR 97470
Douglass College Library. *See* Rutgers University, Douglass College Library
Dover Free Library, East Dover, VT 05341
Dover Public Library, 73 Locust St., Dover, NH 03820
Downers Grove Historical Society and Museum, 831 Maple, Downers Grove, IL 60515
Downey Historical Society, Box 554, Downey, CA 90241
Drake Well Museum, Titusville, PA 16354
Drew University Library, Madison, NJ 07940
Drexel University Libraries, 32 & Chestnut Sts., Philadelphia, PA 19104
Du Sable Museum of African American History, 740 E. 56 Pl., Chicago, IL 60637
Duke University Archives, 341 Perkins Library, Durham, NC 27706
Duke University, William R. Perkins Library, Manuscript Dept., Durham, NC 27706
Dukes County Historical Society, Box 827, Edgartown, MA 02539
Dundee Township Historical Society, Inc., Dundee, IL 60118
Duniway, Mr. David C., 1365 John St. S., Salem, OR 97302
Durham Center Museum, Inc., East Durham, NY 12423
Durham Historic Association Museum, Old Landing Rd., Durham, NH 03824
Dutch Heritage Collection. *See* Northwestern College, Ramaker Library, Dutch Heritage Collection
Dwight D. Eisenhower Library, Abilene, KS 67410
Dyer-York Library, Museum, 371 Main St., Saco, ME 04072

Eagle Historical Society, Eagle, AK 99738
Earlham College Archives, Richmond, IN 47374
Earlham College, Lilly Library, Richmond, IN 47374
Early Southern Decorative Arts, Museum of, Salem Sta., Winston-Salem, NC 27108
East Aurora Town Hall, Town Historian, 5 S. Grove St., East Aurora, NY 14052
East Aurora Village Hall, Elbert Hubbard Library Museum, Main St., East Aurora, NY 14052
East Carolina University, Joyner Library, East Carolina Manuscript Collection, Greenville, NC 27834
East Hartford Public Library, 840 Main St., East Hartford, CT 06108
East Texas State University, James G. Gee Library, Special Collections and Archives, Commerce, TX 75428
Eastern Kentucky University, Crabbe Library, Townsend Room, Richmond, KY 40475
Eastern Montana College Library, Special Collections, Billings, MT 59101
Eastern Washington State Historical Society, Library, 2316 First Ave. W., Spokane, WA 99204
Eastern Washington University, Kennedy Memorial Library, Archives and Special Collections, Cheney, WA 99004
Eastern Washington University, Kennedy Memorial Library, Regional Depository, Washington State Archives, Cheney, WA 99004
Eastham Historical Society, Inc., Eastham, MA 02642
Ecumenism Research Agency, 10201 99th Ave., #61, Peoria, AZ 84345
Eden Archives and Library, Eden Theological Seminary, 475 E. Lockwood Ave., Webster Groves, MO 63119
Eden Historical Society, Office of the Town Historian, 2795 E. Church St., Eden, NY 14057
Eden Theological Seminary. *See* Eden Archives and Library, Eden Theological Seminary
Edina Historical Society, 4801 W. 50 St., Edina, MN 55424
Educational Testing Service, Archives, B-008, Princeton, NJ 08540
Eisenhower Library. *See* Dwight D. Eisenhower Library
Eleutherian Mills Historical Library, Greenville, DE 19807
Elisabet Ney Museum, 304 E. 44 St., Austin, TX 78751
Elisha D. Smith Public Library, 440 First St., Menasha, WI 54952
Elizabeth Free Public Library, 11 S. Broad St., Elizabeth, NJ 07202
Ella Sharp Museum, 3225 Fourth St., Jackson, MI 49203
Ellen G. White Estate, Inc., General Conference of Seventh-day Adventists, 6840 Eastern Ave. N.W., Washington, DC 20012
Elmhurst Historical Museum, 120 E. Park Ave., Box 84, Elmhurst, IL 60126
Elmira College Archives, Gannett-Tripp Learning Center, Elmira, NY 14901
Emma Willard School, Troy, NY 12181
Emory and Henry College, Appalachian Oral History Project, Emory, VA 24327
Emory University, Pitts Theology Library, Atlanta, GA 30322
Emory University, Robert W. Woodruff Library, Special Collections Dept., Atlanta, GA 30322
Enoch Pratt Free Library, George Peabody Dept., 17 E. Mt. Vernon Pl., Baltimore, MD 21202
Episcopal Church Archives and Historical Collections, Historical Society of the Episcopal Church, Box 2247, Austin, TX 78767
Episcopal Church, Historical Society of. *See* Episcopal Church Archives and Historical Collections, Historical Society of the Episcopal Church
Episcopal Diocese of Chicago, Archives and Historical Collections, 65 E. Huron St., Chicago, IL 60611
Episcopal Diocese of Connecticut Archives, Diocesan House, 1335 Asylum Ave., Hartford, CT 06105
Episcopal Diocese of Kansas Archives, Bethany Pl., Topeka, KS 66612
Episcopal Diocese of Massachusetts, Diocesan Library and Archives, One Joy St., Boston, MA 02108
Episcopal Diocese of Missouri, Archives, 1210 Locust St., St. Louis, MO 63103
Episcopal Diocese of New York, Archives, 1047 Amsterdam Ave., New York, NY 10025
Episcopal Diocese of South Carolina. *See* Protestant Episcopal Diocese of South Carolina Archives
Episcopal Diocese of West Texas, Archives, Cathedral House, Box 6885, San Antonio, TX 78209
Erie Studies, Center for. *See* Mercyhurst College Archives/Center for Erie Studies
Essex Institute, James Duncan Phillips Library, 132 Essex St., Salem, MA 01970
Eugene Field House and Toy Museum, 634 S. Broadway, St. Louis, MO 63102
Eugene V. Debs House, Eugene V. Debs Foundation, Box 843, Terre Haute, IN 47808
Evangelical Covenant Church of America Archives, North Park College and Theological Seminary, 5125 N. Spaulding Ave., Chicago, IL 60625
Evans Memorial Library, Aberdeen, MS 39730
Evanston Historical Society, 225 Greenwood St., Evanston, IL 60201
Evansville, University of, Archives, Box 329, Evansville, IN 47702

Fairfield Public Library, Fairfield, IA 52556
Fall River Historical Society, 451 Rock St., Fall River, MA 02720
Faribault County Historical Society, Wakefield House Museum, 405 E. Sixth St., Blue Earth, MN 56013
The Fashion Group, Inc., 9 Rockefeller Plaza, New York, NY 10020
Federal Archives and Records Center, Chicago Archives Branch, 7358 S. Pulaski Rd., Chicago, IL 60629
Federal Archives and Records Center, Denver Archives Branch, Bldg. 48, Denver Federal Center, Denver, CO 80225
Federal Archives and Records Center, Fort Worth Archives Branch, Box 6216, Ft. Worth, TX 76115
Federal Archives and Records Center, Kansas City Archives Branch, 2306 E. Bannister Rd., Kansas City, MO 64131
Federal Archives and Records Center, Los Angeles Archives Branch, 24000 Avila Rd., Laguna Niguel, CA 92677
Federal Archives and Records Center, Philadelphia Archives Branch, 5000 Wissahickon Ave., Philadelphia, PA 19144
Federal Archives and Records Center, San Francisco Archives Branch, 1000 Commodore Dr., San Bruno, CA 94066
Federal Archives and Records Center, Seattle Archives Branch, 6125 Sand Point Way N.E., Seattle, WA 98115
Felician Sisters, Assumption of Our Lady Provincial House, 4210 Meadowlark La., Rio Rancho, NM 87174
Feminist History Research Project, Box 1156, Topanga, CA 90290
Field Museum of Natural History, Dept. of Anthropology, East Roosevelt Rd., Chicago, IL 60605
Field Museum of Natural History, Div. of Planning and Development, East Roosevelt Rd., Chicago, IL 60605
Field Museum of Natural History, Registrar, East Roosevelt Rd., Chicago, IL 60605
Fillmore Museum, 24 Shearer Ave., East Aurora, NY 14052
The Filson Club, 118 W. Breckinridge St., Louisville, KY 40203
Fine Arts, Museum of, 465 Huntington Ave., Boston, MA 02115
Finney County Historical Museum, c/o Mike Etrick, 815 N. First, Garden City, KS 67846
Finney County Historical Society Research Library, Garden City Community College Library, Garden City, KS 67846
Finnish American Historical Archives. *See* Suomi College, Finnish American Historical Archives
The First Church of Christ, Scientist, Archives and Library, Christian Science Center, Boston, MA 02115

DIRECTORY OF CONTRIBUTING REPOSITORIES

First Unitarian Church of San Francisco, 1187 Franklin St., San Francisco, CA 94109
Fisk University Library, Special Collections, Nashville, TN 37203
Florida Historical Society, University of South Florida, Library, Tampa, FL 33620
Florida State Archives, Dept. of State, The Capitol, Tallahassee, FL 32304
Florida State Photographic Archives. *See* Florida State University, Strozier Library, State Photographic Archives
Florida State University, Project in Oral History, 419 Bellamy Bldg., Tallahassee, FL 32306
Florida State University, Strozier Library, Special Collections, Tallahassee, FL 32306
Florida State University, Strozier Library, State Photographic Archives, Tallahassee, FL 32306
Florida, University of, Libraries, Rare Books and Manuscripts Dept., Gainesville, FL 32611
Florida, University of, Oral History Project, 114 Florida State Museum, Gainesville, FL 32611
Florida, University of, P. K. Yonge Library of Florida History, Gainesville, FL 32611
Forbes Library, 20 West St., Northampton, MA 01060
Fort Dodge Historical Museum, Box U, Fort Dodge, IA 50501
Fort Hays Kansas State College Archives, Forsythe Library, Hays, KS 67601
Fort Plain Museum, Box 324, Canal St., Fort Plain, NY 13339
Fort Worth Federal Archives and Records Center. *See* Federal Archives and Records Center, Fort Worth Archives Branch
Framingham Public Library, Framingham, MA 01701
Franciscan Missionary Sisters of the Divine Child, Motherhouse, 6380 Main St., Williamsville, NY 14221
Franciscan Missionary Sisters of the Sacred Heart, Mt. St. Francis, 250 South St., Peekskill, NY 10566
Franciscan Sisters of Allegany, New York, St. Elizabeth Motherhouse, Allegany, NY 14706
Franciscan Sisters of Chicago, 1220 Main St., Lemont, IL 60439
Franciscan Sisters of Christian Charity, Holy Family Convent, 2409 S. Alverno Rd., Manitowoc, WI 54220
Franciscan Sisters of Little Falls, Eighth Ave. & Second St. S.E., Little Falls, MN 56345
Franciscan Sisters of Perpetual Adoration, St. Rose Convent, 912 Market St., La Crosse, WI 54601
Franciscan Sisters of St. Joseph, Immaculate Conception Convent, 5286 S. Park Ave., Hamburg, NY 14075
Franciscan Sisters of the Atonement, St. Francis Convent, Graymoor, Garrison, NY 10524
Franciscan Sisters of the Poor, Community Service Center, 23 Middagh St., Brooklyn, NY 11201
Franciscan Sisters of the Sacred Heart, Secretary General, St. Francis Woods, Mokena, IL 60448
Franciscan Sisters, Our Lady of the Angels Convent, Box 667, Wheaton, IL 60187
Frank H. McClung Museum. *See* Tennessee, University of, Frank H. McClung Museum
Franklin and Marshall College, Fackenthal Library, Lancaster, PA 17604
Franklin College Library, Franklin, IN 46131
Franklin D. Roosevelt Library, Hyde Park, NY 12538
The Franklin Institute, 20 & Parkway, Philadelphia, PA 19103
Free Public Library of Livingston. *See* Livingston Free Public Library
Free Public Library of the City of Trenton. *See* Trenton, Free Public Library of the City of
French Azilum, R.D. 2, Box 266, Towanda, PA 18848
Fresno City and County Historical Society, 7160 W. Kearney Blvd., Fresno, CA 93706
Friends Historical Library. *See* Swarthmore College, Friends Historical Library

Fruitlands Museums, Prospect Hill, Harvard, MA 01451
Fulton County Historical Society, Seventh & Pontiac Sts., Rochester, IN 46975

Galena Public Library, Historical Collection, Galena, IL 61036
Gallatin County Historical Society, Rte. 1, Ridgway, IL 62979
Gallaudet College Archives, Edward Miner Gallaudet Memorial Library, Kendall Green, Washington, DC 20002
G. A. R. Memorial Hall Museum, Capitol 419 N., Madison, WI 53702
Gardner Museum. *See* Isabella Stewart Gardner Museum
Garrett-Evangelical Theological Seminary Library, 2121 Sheridan Rd., Evanston, IL 60201
General Conference of Seventh-day Adventists Archives. *See* Seventh-day Adventists, General Conference Archives
General Douglas MacArthur Memorial, MacArthur Sq., Norfolk, VA 23510
General Federation of Women's Clubs, 1734 N St. N.W., Washington, DC 20036
General Theological Seminary, St. Mark's Library, 175 Ninth Ave., New York, NY 10011
Geneva Historical Society, Wheeler Pk., Geneva, IL 60134
George C. Marshall Research Foundation, Drawer 920, Lexington, VA 24450
George Eastman House. *See* International Museum of Photography at George Eastman House
Georgetown University Library, Special Collections Div., Washington, DC 20057
Georgetown Visitation Convent and Preparatory School, 1500 35th St. N.W., Washington, DC 20007
Georgia Baptist Historical Society. *See* Mercer University, Stetson Memorial Library, Georgia Baptist Historical Society
Georgia College, Ina Dillard Russell Library, Milledgeville, GA 31061
Georgia College, Museum and Archives of Georgia Education, Milledgeville, GA 31061
Georgia Department of Archives and History, c/o Office of the Secretary of State, Atlanta, GA 30334
Georgia Department of Natural Resources, Historic Preservation Section, 270 Washington St. S.W., Atlanta, GA 30334
Georgia Historical Society, 501 Whitaker St., Savannah, GA 31401
Georgia-Pacific Historical Museum, 900 S.W. Fifth Ave., Portland, OR 97204
Georgia Southern College Library, Landrum Box 8074, Statesboro, GA 30458
Georgia State University, Southern Labor Archives, University Plaza, Atlanta, GA 30303
Georgia, University of, Archives. *See* Georgia, University of, Library, Special Collections Dept.
Georgia, University of, Library, Special Collections Dept., Athens, GA 30602
Germantown Historical Society Library, 5208 Germantown Ave., Philadelphia, PA 19144
Gibbes Art Gallery, 135 Meeting St., Charleston, SC 29401
Gilbertsville Free Library, Committee for the Historic Preservation of Gilbertsville, Gilbertsville, NY 13776
Girl Scout Executive Staff, Association of, One State St., New Haven, CT 06511
Girl Scout National Center. *See* Juliette Gordon Low Girl Scout National Center
Girl Scouts of the USA Library and Archives, 830 Third Ave., New York, NY 10022
Gloucester County Historical Society Library, Box 409, Woodbury, NJ 08096
Gogebic-Iron Historical Museum, Hurley, WI 54534
Good Shepherd Provincial Convent, 9517 Leebrook Dr., Cincinnati, OH 45231
Good Shepherd Sisters of Quebec. *See* Servants of the Immaculate Heart of Mary, Provincial Residence

Goodhue County Historical Society, 1166 Oak St., Red Wing, MN 55066
Goucher College, Julia Rogers Library, Towson, MD 21204
Graduate Theological Union Library, 2451 Ridge Rd., Berkeley, CA 94709
Graham Historical Society, Inc., Graham, MO 64455
Grand Army of the Republic Memorial Hall Museum. *See* G. A. R. Memorial Hall Museum
Grand Prairie Historical Society, Box 122, Gillett, AR 72055
Grant County Museum, Box 127, Medford, OK 73759
Grant County Public Library, Box 109, Milbank, SD 57252
Graphic Arts International Union, 1900 L St. N.W., Washington, DC 20036
Grass Valley Library, 207 Mill St., Grass Valley, CA 95945
Great Plains, Museum of the, Box 68, Lawton, OK 73501
Greater Lawrence YWCA, 38 Lawrence St., Lawrence, MA 01840
Green Mountain College Archives, Poultney, VT 05764
Greene County District Library, Local History Dept., 76 E. Market St., Xenia, OH 45385
Greene County Historical Society, 106 E. State St., Jefferson, IA 50129
Greene County Historical Society, Vedder Memorial Library, Rte. US 9W, Coxsackie, NY 12051
Greensboro Public Library, Drawer X-4, Greensboro, NC 27405
Greenwich Library, 101 W. Putnam Ave., Greenwich, CT 06830
Grey Nuns of the Sacred Heart, Quarry Rd., Yardley, PA 19067
Grinnell College Archives, Burling Library, Grinnell, IA 50112
Guilford College Library, Quaker Collection, Greensboro, NC 27410
Gustavus Adolphus College. *See* Lutheran Church in America, Minnesota Synod Archives, Gustavus Adolphus College

Hackley Public Library, 316 W. Webster Ave., Muskegon, MI 49440
Hadassah, The Women's Zionist Organization of America, 50 W. 58 St., New York, NY 10019
Hamilton Library Association. *See* Cumberland County Historical Society and the Hamilton Library Association
Hancock Shaker Village Library, Shaker Community, Inc., Box 898, Pittsfield, MA 01201
Harlan-Lincoln Home, Mt. Pleasant, IA 52641
Harris-Stowe College Library, 3026 Laclede Ave., St. Louis, MO 63103
Harrodsburg Historical Society Library, 220 S. Chiles St., Harrodsburg, KY 40330
Harry S. Truman Library, Independence, MO 64050
Hart County Historical Society, Munfordville, KY 42765
Hartford Seminary Foundation Archives, Case Memorial Library, 55 Elizabeth St., Hartford, CT 06105
Hartwick College, Archives, Oneonta, NY 13820
Harvard College Library, Harvard Theatre Collection, Cambridge, MA 02138
Harvard College Observatory, Cambridge, MA 02138
Harvard Divinity School, Andover-Harvard Theological Library, 45 Francis Ave., Cambridge, MA 02138
Harvard Law School Library, Manuscript Div., Langdell Hall, Cambridge, MA 02138
Harvard Theatre Collection. *See* Harvard College Library, Harvard Theatre Collection
Harvard University Archives, Nathan Marsh Pusey Library, Cambridge, MA 02138
Harvard University, Baker Library. *See* Harvard University, Graduate School of Business Administration, Baker Library

Harvard University, Farlow Library, 20 Divinity Ave., Cambridge, MA 02138

Harvard University, Francis A. Countway Library of Medicine, 10 Shattuck St., Boston, MA 02115

Harvard University, Graduate School of Business Administration, Baker Library, Boston, MA 02163

Harvard University, Gray Herbarium Library, 22 Divinity Ave., Cambridge, MA 02138

Harvard University, Harvard College Observatory. *See* Harvard College Observatory

Harvard University, The Houghton Library, Cambridge, MA 02138

Harvard University, Littauer Library, Industrial Relations and Manpower Collection, Cambridge, MA 02138

Harvard University, Museum of Comparative Zoology, Cambridge, MA 02138

Harvard University, Peabody Museum of Archaeology and Ethnology, 11 Divinity Ave., Cambridge, MA 02138

Haverford College Library, Quaker Collection, Haverford, PA 19041

Hawaii at Manoa, University of, Archives, Sinclair Library, 2425 Campus Rd., Honolulu, HI 96822

Hawaii at Manoa, University of, Hamilton Library, Hawaiiana Collection, 2550 The Mall, Honolulu, HI 96822

Hawaii at Manoa, University of, Sinclair Library, Hawaii War Records Depository, 2425 Campus Rd., Honolulu, HI 96822

Hawaii Department of Accounting and General Services, Public Archives, Iolani Palace Grounds, Honolulu, HI 96813

Hawaii State Archives. *See* Hawaii Department of Accounting and General Services, Public Archives

Hawaii War Records Depository. *See* Hawaii at Manoa, University of, Sinclair Library, Hawaii War Records Depository

Hawaiian Mission Children's Society Library, 553 S. King St., Honolulu, HI 96813

Hawaiiana Collection. *See* Hawaii at Manoa, University of, Hamilton Library, Hawaiiana Collection

Hayward Area Historical Society Museum, Box 555, Hayward, CA 94543

Health and Hospitals Governing Commission of Cook County, Libraries, Archives, and Administrative Records Center, 1900 W. Polk St., Chicago, IL 60612

Helen Keller Archives. *See* American Foundation for the Blind

Henry County Historical Society, Mt. Pleasant, IA 52641

The Henry E. Huntington Library and Art Gallery, 1151 Oxford Rd., San Marino, CA 91108

Herbert H. Lehman Papers. *See* Columbia University, Herbert H. Lehman Papers

Herbert Hoover Presidential Library, West Branch, IA 52358

Herrick Public Library, 300 River Ave., Holland, MI 49423

High Point Museum, High Point Historical Society, 1805 E. Lexington Ave., High Point, NC 27262

Highland Park Historical Museum, 326 Central, Highland Pk., IL 60035

Hinsdale Public Library, 20 E. Maple, Hinsdale, IL 60521

Historic Landmark Society of Montana, Virginia City, MT 59755

The Historic New Orleans Collection, 533 Royal St., New Orleans, LA 70130

Historic Pullman Foundation, 11111 S. Forrestville, Chicago, IL 60628

Historical Society of . . . *See* other part of title, e.g., Delaware, Historical Society of

Hobart and William Smith Colleges, Warren Hunting Smith Library, Geneva, NY 14456

Hobart Historical Society, Pleak Library, Hobart, IN 46342

Holy Child Jesus Convent, Rosemont, PA 19010

Holy Cross, College of the, Dinand Library, Special Collections, Worcester, MA 01610

Holy Name College Archives. *See* Sisters of the Holy Family of Nazareth Archives

Holy Name Sisters, Oregon Province Archives, Marylhurst, OR 97036

Holy Names Convent, W. 2911 Ft. Wright Dr., Spokane, WA 99204

Hoosac Valley Collection for Local History. *See* North Adams State College, Freel Library

Hoover Institution on War, Revolution and Peace. *See* Stanford University, Hoover Institution on War, Revolution and Peace

Hoover Presidential Library. *See* Herbert Hoover Presidential Library

Hope College Archives, Holland, MI 49423

Hopewell Village National Historic Site, R.D. #1, Box 345, Elverson, PA 19520

Hopkins Historical Society, 1010 First St. S., Hopkins, MN 55343

Hotel Dieu Hospital Library, Box 61262, New Orleans, LA 70161

Houghton Library. *See* Harvard University, The Houghton Library

Houston Metropolitan Research Center. *See* Houston Public Library, Houston Metropolitan Research Center

Houston Public Library, Houston Metropolitan Research Center, 500 McKinney Ave., Houston, TX 77002

Houston, University of, Archives, University Libraries, Houston, TX 77004

Howard University, Moorland-Spingarn Research Center, Washington, DC 20059

Hudson Historical Society, Inc., Historical and Cultural Center, Derry Rd., Hudson, NH 03051

The Huguenot Society of America Library, 112 E. 58 St., New York, NY 10022

Humanities Research Center. *See* Texas at Austin, University of, The Humanities Research Center

Humility of Mary Convent, Ottumwa Heights Center, Ottumwa, IA 52501

Hunt Botanical Library. *See* Carnegie-Mellon University, Hunt Institute for Botanical Documentation

Hunt Institute for Botanical Documentation. *See* Carnegie-Mellon University, Hunt Institute for Botanical Documentation

Hunter College of the City University of New York, Archives, Box 36, 695 Park Ave., New York, NY 10021

Huntington College Library, Historical Collection, Huntington, IN 46750

The Huntington Library. *See* The Henry E. Huntington Library and Art Gallery

Hyde Park Historical Society, 9 Lochland Rd., Hyde Park, MA 02136

Idaho State Historical Society, 610 N. Julia Davis Dr., Boise, ID 83706

Idaho, University of, Library, Special Collections and Archives, Moscow, ID 83843

Iliff School of Theology, Ira J. Taylor Library, Archives of the Rocky Mountain Conference of the United Methodist Church, 2233 S. University Blvd., Denver, CO 80210

Illinois at Chicago Circle, University of, Archives, The Library, Box 8198, Chicago, IL 60680

Illinois at Chicago Circle, University of, Library, Manuscript Collection, The Library, Box 8198, Chicago, IL 60680

Illinois Historical Survey. *See* Illinois, University of, Illinois Historical Survey, Main Library

Illinois Office of the Secretary of State, State Archives Div., Archives Bldg., Springfield, IL 62756

Illinois State Archives. *See* Illinois Office of the Secretary of State, State Archives Div.

Illinois State Historical Library, Old State Capitol, Springfield, IL 62706

Illinois State University Archives, Milner Library, Normal, IL 61761

Illinois, University of, Archives, 19 Library, Urbana, IL 61801

Illinois, University of, Illinois Historical Survey, Main Library, Urbana, IL 61801

Illinois Wesleyan University Library, Archives Section, Bloomington, IL 61701

Immaculate Heart College Library, 2021 North Western Ave., Los Angeles, CA 90027

Immigration History Research Center. *See* Minnesota, University of, Libraries, Immigration History Research Center

INA Corporation Archives, 1600 Arch St., Box 7728, Philadelphia, PA 19109

Indiana Historical Society Library, 315 W. Ohio St., Indianapolis, IN 46202

Indiana Jewish Historical Society, 215 E. Berry St., Ft. Wayne, IN 46802

Indiana State Library, Indiana Div., 140 N. Senate Ave., Indianapolis, IN 46204

Indiana State University, Evansville Campus Library, Special Collections and University Archives, 8600 University Blvd., Evansville, IN 47712

Indiana United Methodist Archives. *See* DePauw University, Archives of DePauw University and Indiana United Methodism, Roy O. West Library

Indiana University, Lilly Library, Manuscripts Dept., Bloomington, IN 47401

Indiana University Oral History Research Project, Dept. of History, 112 N. Bryan St., Bloomington, IN 47401

Indianapolis-Marion County Public Library, 40 St. Clair St. E., Indianapolis, IN 46204

Indianola Public Library, Indianola, IA 50125

Industrial Relations and Manpower Collection. *See* Harvard University, Littauer Library, Industrial Relations and Manpower Collection

Industrial Society, Archives of. *See* Pittsburgh, University of, Hillman Library, Archives of Industrial Society

Inter-Tribal Indian Ceremonial Association, Box 1, Church Rock, NM 87311

International Association for Personnel Women, 2017 Walnut St., Philadelphia, PA 19103

International Harvester Corporate Archives, 401 N. Michigan Ave., Chicago, IL 60611

International Museum of Photography at George Eastman House, 900 East Ave., Rochester, NY 14607

International Tennis Hall of Fame and Tennis Museum, 194 Bellevue Ave., Newport, RI 02840

Iowa Masonic Library, Box 279, Cedar Rapids, IA 52406

Iowa Mennonite Museum and Archives, Box 576, Kalona, IA 52247

Iowa State Historical Department, Div. of Historical Museum and Archives, Historical Library, Des Moines, IA 50319

Iowa State Historical Department, Div. of the State Historical Society, 402 Iowa Ave., Iowa City, IA 52240

Iowa State Historical Library. *See* Iowa State Historical Department, Div. of Historical Museum and Archives, Historical Library

Iowa State Historical Society. *See* Iowa State Historical Department, Div. of the State Historical Society

Iowa, State Library Commission of, Historical Bldg., Des Moines, IA 50319

Iowa State University Library, Dept. of Special Collections, Ames, IA 50011

Iowa, University of, Libraries, Special Collections Dept., Iowa City, IA 52242

Iowa Wesleyan College Archives, Mt. Pleasant, IA 52641

Ipswich Public Library, Ipswich Historical Society Manuscript Collection, 25 N. Main St., Ipswich, MA 01938

Iron Work Farm in Acton, Inc., Box 11, Acton, MA 01720

Ironwood Historical Museum. *See* Gogebic-Iron Historical Museum

Iroquois County Genealogical Society, Old Courthouse Museum, 103 W. Cherry St., Watseka, IL 60970

DIRECTORY OF CONTRIBUTING REPOSITORIES

Isabella Stewart Gardner Museum, 2 Palace Rd., Boston, MA 02115
Isanti County Historical Society, Box 525, Cambridge, MN 55008
Isle La Motte Historical Society, Isle La Motte, VT 05463
Ithaca College Library, Ithaca, NY 14850

Jackson County Historical Society, Archives, Jackson Sq. Courthouse, Rm. 103, 115 W. Maple Ave., Independence, MO 64050
Jackson State University Library, Special Collections, Sta. C., Jackson, MS 39217
Jacksonville Museum. *See* Southern Oregon Historical Society
Jacob Edwards Memorial Library, 236 Main St., Southbridge, MA 01550
Janet Lehr, Inc., Box 617, New York, NY 10028
Jazz Archive. *See* Tulane University, William Ransom Hogan Jazz Archive, Special Collections Div., Howard-Tilton Memorial Library
Jazz Oral History Project. *See* National Endowment for the Arts Jazz Oral History Project, Div. of Performing Arts, Smithsonian Institution
Jefferson County Historical Society, City Hall, Madison St., Port Townsend, WA 98368
Jesus Christ of Latter-day Saints, Church of, Historical Dept., 50 E. North Temple, Salt Lake City, UT 84150
The Jewish Community Federation of Cleveland, 1750 Euclid Ave., Cleveland, OH 44115
Jewish Community Library, 6505 Wilshire Blvd., Los Angeles, CA 90048
John Jay Homestead, Box AH, Katonah, NY 10536
The Johns Hopkins University, Johns Hopkins Medical Archives, Turner Bldg., Baltimore, MD 21205
The Johns Hopkins University Medical Archives. *See* The Johns Hopkins University, Johns Hopkins Medical Archives
The Johns Hopkins University, Milton S. Eisenhower Library, Special Collections, Baltimore, MD 21218
The Johns Hopkins University, Welch Medical Library, 1900 E. Monument St., Baltimore, MD 21205
Johnson County Historical Society, The Heritage Library, 135 E. Pine St., Warrensburg, MO 64093
Johnstown Flood Museum, 304 Washington St., Johnstown, PA 15901
Joint University Libraries, Special Collections Dept., Nashville, TN 37203
Joslyn Art Museum Library, 2200 Dodge St., Omaha, NE 68102
Judah L. Magnes Memorial Museum. *See* Western Jewish History Center, Judah L. Magnes Memorial Museum
Judson College Library, Marion, AL 36756
The Juilliard School, Lila Acheson Wallace Library, Lincoln Center, New York, NY 10023
Juliette Gordon Low Girl Scout National Center, 11 York La. E., Savannah, GA 31401

Kandiyohi County Historical Society, Willmar, MN 56201
Kansas City Federal Archives and Records Center. *See* Federal Archives and Records Center, Kansas City Archives Branch
Kansas City Museum of History and Science, 3218 Gladstone Blvd., Kansas City, MO 64123
Kansas City Public Library, Missouri Valley Room, 311 12th St. E., Kansas City, MO 64106
Kansas City Public Library, West Branch, Mexican American Archives, 1936 Summit, Kansas City, MO 64108
Kansas State College of Pittsburg Library, Kansas Collection, Pittsburg, KS 66762
Kansas State Historical Society, Memorial Bldg., 120 W. Tenth, Topeka, KS 66612
Kansas State University Library, Special Collections Dept., Manhattan, KS 66506
Kansas Wesleyan University Library, Salina, KS 67401
Kansas West Conference of the United Methodist Church, Commission on History and Archives, Southwestern College, Winfield, KS 67156
Kendall Whaling Museum, Box 297, Sharon, MA 02067
Kendall Young Library, 1201 Willson Ave., Webster City, IA 50595
Kenmore Association, Inc., 1201 Washington Ave., Fredericksburg, VA 22401
Kennebunk Free Library, Kennebunk, ME 04043
Kent State University Archives, University Library, Kent, OH 44242
Kent State University Library, American History Research Center, Kent, OH 44242
Kentucky Division of Archives and Records Management, Dept. of Library and Archives, Box 537, Frankfort, KY 40602
Kentucky Historical Society, Old State House, Frankfort, KY 40602
Kentucky Library. *See* Western Kentucky University, Kentucky Library, Manuscript Div.
Kentucky State Archives. *See* Kentucky Division of Archives and Records Management, Dept. of Library and Archives
Kentucky United Methodist Heritage Center. *See* Kentucky Wesleyan College, Kentucky United Methodist Heritage Center
Kentucky, University of, Archives, Margaret King Library, Lexington, KY 40506
Kentucky Wesleyan College, Kentucky United Methodist Heritage Center, 3000 Frederica St., Owensboro, KY 42301
Kerlan Collection. *See* Minnesota, University of, Children's Literature Research Collections
King City Public Library, 212 S. Vanderhurst Ave., King City, CA 93930
King's College, D. Leonard Corgan Library, Wilkes-Barre, PA 18711
Knox College Archives, Galesburg, IL 61401
Koochiching County Historical Society Museum, Box 1147, International Falls, MN 56649

La Purisima Mission State Historic Park Archives, R.F.D. 102, Lompoc, CA 93436
La Salle County Historical Society Museum, Box 577, Ottawa, IL 61350
Labor and Urban Affairs, Archives of. *See* Wayne State University, Archives of Labor and Urban Affairs, Walter P. Reuther Library
Labor-Management Documentation Center. *See* Cornell University, New York State School of Industrial and Labor Relations, Labor-Management Documentation Center
Lake County Museum, Lakewood Forest Preserve, Wauconda, IL 60084
Lancaster County Historical Society, 230 President Ave. N., Lancaster, PA 17603
Lancaster Current Topics Club, Lancaster, MA 01523
Lancaster Historical Commission, Town Hall, Lancaster, MA 01523
Lancaster Mennonite Conference Historical Society, 2215 Mill Stream Rd., Lancaster, PA 17602
Lancaster Town Library, Thayer Dr., Lancaster, MA 01523
Lane County Museum, 740 W. 13 Ave., Eugene, OR 97402
LARITA. *See* Lewis Audiovisual Research Institute and Teaching Archive
Latter-day Saints, Church of Jesus Christ of. *See* Jesus Christ of Latter-day Saints, Church of, Historical Dept.
LDS Church Archives. *See* Jesus Christ of Latter-day Saints, Church of, Historical Dept.
Lebanon Historical Society, 40 Mascoma St., Lebanon, NH 03766
Legal Change Collection. *See* Wesleyan University, Collection on Legal Change
Lenawee County Historical Society Museum, Box 511, Adrian, MI 49221
Lenox Library Association, 18 Main St., Lenox, MA 01240
LeSueur County Historical Society Museum, Box 557, Elysian, MN 56028
LeTourneau College, Margaret Estes Library, Box 7001, Longview, TX 75602
Lewis Audiovisual Research Institute and Teaching Archive, 4350 N. Radin, Tucson, AZ 85705
Lewis County Historical Society, 78 N.E. Washington Ave., Chehalis, WA 98532
Lewiston Public Library, 105 Park St., Lewiston, ME 04240
Lexington Theological Seminary, Bosworth Memorial Library, 631 S. Limestone St., Lexington, KY 40508
Libertyville-Mundelein Historical Society, Inc., 413 N. Milwaukee Ave., Libertyville, IL 60048
Library Company of Philadelphia. *See* Pennsylvania, Historical Society of
Library Museum of the American Indian. *See* American Indian, Library Museum of the
Library of Congress, Manuscript Div., Washington, DC 20540
Library of Congress, Music Div., Washington, DC 20540
Lick Observatory Archives. *See* California, Santa Cruz, University of, Lick Observatory Archives, McHenry Library
Lincoln Library and Museum. *See* The Louis A. Warren Lincoln Library and Museum
Lincoln University, Page Library, Jefferson City, MO 65101
Lister Hill Library of the Health Sciences. *See* Alabama in Birmingham, University of, The Medical Center, Lister Hill Library of the Health Sciences
Litchfield Historical Society, Inc., Ingraham Memorial Library, Litchfield, CT 06759
Little Compton Historical Society, West Rd., Little Compton, RI 02837
Littleton Historical Museum, 6028 S. Gallup, Littleton, CO 80120
Livingston Free Public Library, Memorial Pk., Livingston, NJ 07039
Livonia Historical Village at Greenmead, 33024 Grennada, Livonia, MI 48150
Lombard Historical Society, 23 W. Maple, Lombard, IL 60148
Long Beach Public Library, Long Beach, CA 90802
Long Island Historical Society, 128 Pierrepont St., Brooklyn, NY 11201
Long Island University-Brooklyn Center Libraries, University Plaza, Brooklyn, NY 11201
Longfellow National Historic Site, 105 Brattle St., Cambridge, MA 02138
Los Angeles County Museum of Natural History, 900 Exposition Blvd., Los Angeles, CA 90007
Los Angeles Federal Archives and Records Center. *See* Federal Archives and Records Center, Los Angeles Archives Branch
Los Banos Historical Museum. *See* Milliken Museum
The Louis A. Warren Lincoln Library and Museum, 1300 S. Clinton St., Fort Wayne, IN 46801
Louisiana Archives and Records Division. *See* Louisiana Secretary of State, Archives and Records Div.
Louisiana Secretary of State, Archives and Records Div., 1515 Choctaw Drive, Baton Rouge, LA 70804
Louisiana State Library, Louisiana Section, Box 131, Baton Rouge, LA 70821
Louisiana State Museum, 751 Chartres St., New Orleans, LA 70116
Louisiana State University, Dept. of Archives & Manuscripts, Baton Rouge, LA 70803
Louisville Presbyterian Theological Seminary, Library, 1044 Alta Vista Rd., Louisville, KY 40205
Louisville, University of, Dwight Anderson Memorial Music Library, 9001 Shelbyville Rd., Louisville, KY 40222
Louisville, University of, Library, Rare Book Room, 2301 S. Third St., Louisville, KY 40208

Louisville, University of, Oral History Center, Dept. of History, Belknap Campus, Louisville, KY 40208
Lowell, University of, Alumni-Lydon Library, Special Collections, Lowell, MA 01854
Lowell, University of, O'Leary Library, Lowell, MA 01854
Luther College Library, Decorah, IA 52101
Luther Theological Seminary. *See* American Lutheran Church, Archives of the, Luther Theological Seminary
Lutheran Church in America Archives, Lutheran School of Theology, 1100 E. 55 St., Chicago, IL 60615
Lutheran Church in America, Minnesota Synod Archives, Gustavus Adolphus College, St. Peter, MN 56082
Lutheran Church—Missouri Synod, Kansas District Office Bldg., Tenth & Wayne, Topeka, KS 66604
Lutheran Church—Missouri Synod, Northwest District Archives, 1700 N.E. Knott St., Portland, OR 97212
Lutheran School of Theology. *See* Lutheran Church in America Archives, Lutheran School of Theology
Lutheran Theological Seminary, A. R. Wentz Library, Gettysburg, PA 17325
Lynchburg Museum System, Box 60, Lynchburg, VA 24505
Lynches River Historical Society, Box 26, Bethune, SC 29009
Lynn Historical Society, Inc., 125 Green St., Lynn, MA 01902

MacArthur Memorial. *See* General Douglas MacArthur Memorial
McArthur Public Library, 270 Main St., Box 346, Biddeford, ME 04005
Macaulay, Mrs. Charles R., 454 Kirk La., Media, PA 19063
McKendree College, Holman Library, Lebanon, IL 62254
McLean County Historical Society, 201 E. Grove, Bloomington, IL 61701
MacMurray College Archives, Henry Pfeiffer Library, Jacksonville, IL 62650
McPherson College Library, Brethren Room, McPherson, KS 67460
Madison County Historical Society, 435 Main St., Oneida, NY 13421
Madison Historical Society, Box 148, Madison, NJ 07940
Madison Township Historical Museum, c/o A. D. Martin, R.D. 1, Box 150, Matawan, NJ 07747
Mahoning Valley Historical Society, The Arms Museum, 648 Wick Ave., Youngstown, OH 44502
Maine at Orono, University of, Northeast Archives of Folklore and Oral History, Rm. B, S. Stevens Hall, Orono, ME 04473
Maine at Orono, University of, Raymond H. Fogler Library, Special Collections Dept., Orono, ME 04473
Maine Historical Society, 485 Congress St., Portland, ME 04111
Maine State Archives, State Capitol, Augusta, ME 04333
Maine State Library, Dept. of Educational and Cultural Services, Cultural Bldg., Augusta, ME 04330
Maine State Museum, State House, Augusta, ME 04333
Maine, University of. *See* Maine at Orono
Maine Women Writers Collection. *See* Westbrook College, Maine Women Writers Collection
Malden Public Library, Old and New of Malden, Malden, MA 10176
Manassas National Battlefield Park, Box 1830, Manassas, VA 22110
Manchester College, Funderburg Library, North Manchester, IN 46962
Manchester Historical Society, 10 Union St., Manchester, MA 01944
Mankato State University. *See* Southern Minnesota Historical Center, Mankato State University
Manuscript Library of the Park-McCullough House. *See* Park-McCullough House Manuscript Library
Marathon County Historical Society, 403 McIndoe St., Wausau, WI 54401
Marblehead Historical Society, Jeremiah Lee Mansion, 161 Washington St., Marblehead, MA 01945
Mari Sandoz Heritage Society. *See* Chadron State College, Mari Sandoz Heritage Society
Maria Mitchell Science Library, Vestal St., Nantucket, MA 02554
Marian College Archives, Indianapolis, IN 46222
Marian Sisters, Marycrest Motherhouse, Box 250, Waverly, NE 68462
Marietta College, Dawes Memorial Library, Marietta, OH 45750
Mark Twain Research Foundation, Inc., Perry, MO 63462
Marlboro Public Library, Marlboro, MA 01752
Mars Hill College Library, Special Collections, Appalachian Room, Mars Hill, NC 28754
Marshall County Historical Society, Box 806, Holly Springs, MS 38635
Marshall University, James E. Morrow Library, Special Collections, Huntington, WV 25701
Martha Canfield Memorial Free Library, Inc., Russell Vermontiana Collection, Arlington, VT 05250
Martin and Osa Johnson Safari Museum, 16 S. Grant Ave., Chanute, KS 66720
Martins Ferry Public Library, 20 S. Fifth St., Box 130, Martins Ferry, OH 43935
Mary Thompson Hospital, 140 N. Ashland Blvd., Chicago, IL 60607
Marycrest College, Cone Library, Davenport, IA 52804
Maryknoll Sisters Center, Maryknoll, NY 10545
Maryland Diocesan Archives, Maryland Historical Society, 201 W. Monument St., Baltimore, MD 21201
Maryland Historical Society. *See also* Maryland Diocesan Archives
Maryland Historical Society, Manuscripts Div., 201 W. Monument St., Baltimore, MD 21201
Maryland Historical Society, Oral History Office, 201 W. Monument St., Baltimore, MD 21201
Maryland, University of, McKeldin Library, Archives and Manuscripts, College Park, MD 20742
Marymount College Archives, Tarrytown, NY 10591
Massachusetts Diocesan Library. *See* Episcopal Diocese of Massachusetts, Diocesan Library and Archives
Massachusetts Institute of Technology, Historical Collections, N52-260, Cambridge, MA 02139
Massachusetts Institute of Technology, Institute Archives and Special Collections, Bldg. 14N-118, Cambridge, MA 02139
Massachusetts, University of, University Library, Amherst, MA 01002
Massillon Museum, 212 Lincoln Way E., Massillon, OH 44646
The Medical College of Pennsylvania, Archives and Special Collections on Women in Medicine, Florence A. Moore Library of Medicine, 3300 Henry Ave., Philadelphia, PA 19129
Medical College of South Carolina. *See* Medical University of South Carolina
Medical University of South Carolina, Waring Historical Library, 171 Ashley Ave., Charleston, SC 29403
Meiklejohn Civil Liberties Institute, 1715 Francisco St., Berkeley, CA 94703
Memorial Hall Library, Elm Sq., Andover, MA 01810
Memphis-Shelby County Public Library and Information Center, Memphis Room, 1850 Peabody Ave., Memphis, TN 38104
Memphis State University Libraries, Special Collections, Memphis, TN 38152
Mendocino Historical Research, Inc., Box 922, Mendocino, CA 95460
Menninger Foundation, Museum & Archives Div., Box 829, Topeka, KS 66601
Mennonite Church, Archives of the, 1700 S. Main St., Goshen, IN 46526
Mennonite Historical Library. *See* Bluffton College, Mennonite Historical Library
Mennonite Library and Archives. *See* Bethel College, Mennonite Library and Archives
Mercer University, Stetson Memorial Library, Georgia Baptist Historical Society, Macon, GA 31207
Mercy Hospital Archives, Pride & Locust Sts., Pittsburgh, PA 15219
Mercyhurst College Archives/Center for Erie Studies, 501 E. 38 St., Erie, PA 16501
Merrimack Valley Textile Museum, 800 Massachusetts Ave., North Andover, MA 01845
Methodist Historical Library. *See* Southern Methodist University Library, Methodist Historical Library
The Methodist Museum, Epworth-by-the-Sea, St. Simon's Island, GA 31520
Metropolitan Opera Association Archives, Metropolitan Opera House, Lincoln Center Plaza, New York, NY 10023
Metuchen Public Library, 480 Middlesex Ave., Metuchen, NJ 08840
Mexican American Archives. *See* Kansas City Public Library, West Branch, Mexican American Archives
Mexican American Women's National Association, L'Enfant Plaza Sta. S.W., Washington, DC 20024
Michael Reese Hospital and Medical Center, Dept. of Public Affairs, 29 St. & Ellis Ave., Chicago, IL 60616
Michigan Department of Education, State Library Services, Michigan Unit, 735 E. Michigan Ave., Box 30007, Lansing, MI 48909
Michigan Department of State, Michigan History Div., State Archives Unit, 3405 N. Logan St., Lansing, MI 48918
Michigan Historical Collections. *See* Michigan, University of, Bentley Historical Library, Michigan Historical Collections
Michigan State Archives. *See* Michigan Department of State, Michigan History Div., State Archives Unit
Michigan State Library. *See* Michigan Department of Education, State Library Services, Michigan Unit
Michigan State University, University Archives and Historical Collections, East Lansing, MI 48824
Michigan, University of, Bentley Historical Library, Michigan Historical Collections, 1150 Beal Ave., Ann Arbor, MI 48109
Michigan, University of, Library, Dept. of Rare Books and Special Collections, Ann Arbor, MI 48109
Michigan, University of, William L. Clements Library, Ann Arbor, MI 48109
Middlebury College, Abernethy Collection of American Literature, Middlebury, VT 05753
Middlesex County Historical Society, Middletown, CT 06457
Middleton Historical Society, 118 River St., Middleton, MA 01949
Midway College Library, Midway, KY 40347
Midwest China Oral History and Archives Collection, Gullixson Hall, 2375 Como Ave. W., St. Paul, MN 55108
Migration Studies, Center for, 209 Flagg Pl., Staten Island, NY 10304
Mill Valley Public Library, 375 Throckmorton Ave., Mill Valley, CA 94941
Milliken Museum, Los Banos, CA 93635
Mills College Library, Manuscript Collections, Oakland, CA 94613
Milwaukee County Historical Society, 910 N. Third St., Milwaukee, WI 53203
Minneapolis Public Library and Information Center, 300 Nicollet Mall, Minneapolis, MN 55401

Minnesota Conference of the United Methodist Church, Commission on Archives and History, 122 W. Franklin Ave., Minneapolis, MN 55404
Minnesota-Duluth, University of. *See* Northeast Minnesota Historical Center, University of Minnesota-Duluth
Minnesota Historical Society, Audio-Visual Library, 690 Cedar St., St. Paul, MN 55101
Minnesota Historical Society, Div. of Archives and Manuscripts, 1500 Mississippi St., St. Paul, MN 55101
Minnesota Historical Society, State Archives. *See* Minnesota Historical Society, Div. of Archives and Manuscripts
Minnesota-Morris, University of. *See* West Central Minnesota Historical Center, Briggs Library, University of Minnesota-Morris
Minnesota Mutual Life Insurance Company, 345 Cedar St., St. Paul, MN 55101
Minnesota State Archives. *See* Minnesota Historical Society, Div. of Archives and Manuscripts
Minnesota, University of, Andersen Horticultural Library, 3675 Arboretum Dr., Chaska, MN 55318
Minnesota, University of, Children's Literature Research Collections, 109 Walter Library, Minneapolis, MN 55455
Minnesota, University of, Libraries, Immigration History Research Center, Minneapolis, MN 55455
Minnesota, University of, Libraries, Social Welfare History Archives, Minneapolis, MN 55455
Minnesota, University of, University Archives, 10 Walter Library, Minneapolis, MN 55455
Miss Porter's School Archives, Farmington, CT 06032
Mission Helpers of the Sacred Heart, 1001 W. Joppa Rd., Baltimore, MD 21204
Missionary Benedictine Sisters, Immaculata Convent, 300 N. 18 St., Norfolk, NE 68701
Missionary Catechists of Divine Providence, St. Andrew's Convent, 2318 Castroville Rd., San Antonio, TX 78237
Missionary Servants of the Most Blessed Trinity, Office of Research & Development, 3501 Solly Ave., Philadelphia, PA 19136
Missionary Sisters of the Catholic Apostolate, Society of the, Pallottine Provincialate, Rte. 2, 15270 Old Hulls Ferry Rd., Florissant, MO 63034
Missionary Sisters of the Immaculate Conception Archives, Box 3026, Paterson, NJ 07509
Missionary Sisters of the Most Sacred Heart of Jesus, St. Michael Convent, Hyde Pk., Reading, PA 19605
Missionary Sisters of the Precious Blood, Precious Blood Convent, Box 97, Shillington, PA 19607
Mississippi Baptist Historical Commission, Mississippi College Library, Clinton, MS 39056
Mississippi Collection. *See* Mississippi, University of, Library, Archives and Special Collections
Mississippi College. *See* Mississippi Baptist Historical Commission
Mississippi Department of Archives and History, Box 571, Jackson, MS 39205
Mississippi State University, Mitchell Memorial Library, Box 5408, Mississippi State, MS 39762
Mississippi University for Women, Library, Special Collections, Columbus, MS 39701
Mississippi, University of, Library, Archives and Special Collections, University, MS 38677
Mississippi Valley Collection. *See* Memphis State University Libraries, Special Collections
Missouri Botanical Garden, 2345 Tower Grove Ave., St. Louis, MO 63110
Missouri Historical Society, Jefferson Memorial Bldg., St. Louis, MO 63112
Missouri-Kansas City, University of, Conservatory Library, 4420 Warwick Blvd., Kansas City, MO 64111
Missouri-St. Louis, University of, Archives, Thomas Jefferson Library, 8001 Natural Bridge Rd., St. Louis, MO 63121
Missouri-St. Louis, University of, Western Historical Manuscript Collection-St. Louis, 8001 Natural Bridge Rd., St. Louis, MO 63121
Missouri State Archives, Records Management & Archives Services, Box 778, Jefferson City, MO 65101
Missouri, State Historical Society of. *See* Missouri, University of, Library, Western Historical Manuscripts Collection, State Historical Society Manuscripts
Missouri, University of, Archives, 701 Lewis Hall, Columbia, MO 65201
Missouri, University of, Library, Western Historical Manuscripts Collection, State Historical Society Manuscripts, Columbia, MO 65201
Missouri Valley Room. *See* Kansas City Public Library, Missouri Valley Room
Missouriana Room. *See* Northwest Missouri State University, Missouriana Room
Mittleman Jewish Community Center, 6651 S.W. Capital Hwy., Portland, OR 97219
Mobile, Museums of the City of, 355 Government St., Mobile, AL 36602
Modern Art, The Museum of, Dept. of Photography, 11 W. 53 St., New York, NY 10019
Monastery of . . . *See* other part of title, e.g., Visitation, Monastery of the
Monmouth County Historical Association, 70 Court St., Freehold, NJ 07728
Monroe County Historian's Office, 115 South Ave., Rochester, NY 14604
Montague Museum and Historical Association, 4975 Stanton Blvd., Montague, MI 49437
Montana Historical Society, 225 N. Roberts, Helena, MT 59601
Montana State University Archives, MSU Library, Bozeman, MT 59717
Montana State University Library, Special Collections, Bozeman, MT 59715
Montana, University of, Library, Missoula, MT 59801
Montclair Public Library, 50 S. Fullerton Ave., Montclair, NJ 07042
Montgomery County Historical Society, Box 461, Dayton, OH 45402
Moody Bible Institute Library, 820 N. LaSalle, Chicago, IL 60610
Moorhead State University. *See* Northwest Minnesota Historical Center, Moorhead State University
Moorland-Spingarn Research Center. *See* Howard University, Moorland-Spingarn Research Center
Morningside College, Petersmeyer Library, Sioux City, IA 51106
Morton Arboretum, Sterling Morton Library, Lisle, IL 60532
Mount Carmel Generalate, Box 476, Lacombe, LA 70445
Mount Carmel Public Library, 727 Mulberry St., Mt. Carmel, IL 62863
Mount Holyoke College, Williston Memorial Library, South Hadley, MA 01075
Mount St. Joseph Ursuline Motherhouse, Maple Mount, KY 42356
Mount St. Mary's College, 12001 Chalon Rd., Los Angeles, CA 90049
Mount St. Scholastica Convent, Atchison, KS 66002
Mundelein College Archives, Learning Resource Center, 6339 Sheridan Rd., Chicago, IL 60660
Murray State University, Forrest C. Pogue Special Collections Library, Murray, KY 42071
Muscatine Community College Library, 152 Colorado St., Muscatine, IA 52761
Museum of . . . *See* other part of title, e.g., Albuquerque, Museum of
Muskingum College Archives, New Concord, OH 43762
Musser Public Library, 304 Iowa Ave., Muscatine, IA 52761
Mystic Seaport, Inc., G. W. Blunt White Library, Mystic, CT 06355

Nasson College Library, Springvale, ME 04083
The Natchez Garden Club Archives, Connelly's Tavern, Box 537, Natchez, MS 39120
National Academy of Design, 1083 Fifth Ave., New York, NY 10028
National Academy of Sciences, Archives, Rm. 234, 2101 Constitution Ave. N.W., Washington, DC 20418
National Anthropological Archives, National Museum of Natural History, Smithsonian Institution, Washington, DC 20560
National Archives. *See* National Archives and Records Service, Office of the National Archives
National Archives and Records Service. *See also* Federal Archives and Records Center
National Archives and Records Service, Office of the National Archives, Eighth St. & Pennsylvania Ave. N.W., Washington, DC 20408
National Baseball Hall of Fame and Museum, Cooperstown, NY 13326
National Board of Young Men's Christian Associations, Bowne Historical Library, 291 Broadway, New York, NY 10007
National Civil Rights Library. *See* United States Commission on Civil Rights, National Civil Rights Library
National Collection of Fine Arts, Smithsonian Institution, Washington, DC 20560
National College of Education, Chicago Campus, Herman H. Hegner Library, 18 S. Michigan Ave., Chicago, IL 60601
National College of Education, N. Dwight Harris Library, 2840 Sheridan Rd., Evanston, IL 60201
National Endowment for the Arts Jazz Oral History Project, Div. of Performing Arts, Smithsonian Institution, Washington, DC 20560
National Federation of Business and Professional Women's Clubs, Inc., 2012 Massachusetts Ave. N.W., Washington, DC 20036
National Federation of Press Women, Inc., 1105 Main St., Blue Springs, MO 64015
National League for Nursing, 10 Columbus Circle, New York, NY 10019
National Library of Medicine, History of Medicine Div., Bethesda, MD 20014
National Museum of History and Technology, Div. of Mechanisms, Smithsonian Institution, Washington, DC 20560
National Museum of History and Technology, Div. of Political History, Smithsonian Institution, Washington, DC 20560
National Opinion Research Center, Data Library, 6030 S. Ellis Ave., Chicago, IL 60637
National Portrait Gallery. *See* American Portraits, Catalog of, National Portrait Gallery
National Research Council. *See* National Academy of Sciences, Archives
National Safety Council Library, 444 N. Michigan Ave., Chicago, IL 60601
National Women's Association of Allied Beverage Industries, Inc., 425 13th St. N.W., Suite 1300, Washington, DC 20004
Natural Sciences, The Academy of, 19 & Parkway, Philadelphia, PA 19103
Nauvoo Public Library, Nauvoo, IL 62354
Naval Historical Center, Operational Archives, Washington Navy Yard, Bldg. 210, Washington, DC 20374
Naval History Division. *See* Naval Historical Center, Operational Archives
Nebraska-Lincoln, University of, Archives, Rm. 303, Love Library, Lincoln, NE 68588
Nebraska State Historical Society, 1500 R St., Lincoln, NE 68508
Nebraska, University of, Medical Center, Library of Medicine, 42 St. & Dewey Ave., Omaha, NE 68105
Nebraska Wesleyan University. *See* United Methodist Historical Center, Lucas Bldg., Nebraska Wesleyan University
Negro Collection. *See* Atlanta University, Trevor Arnett Library, Negro Collection; *also* Howard University, Moorland-Spingarn Research Center

Neptune Historical Museum, 25 Neptune Blvd., Neptune, NJ 07753
Netherlands Museum, City Hall, Holland, MI 49423
Nevada City Library, N. Pine St., Nevada City, CA 95959
Nevada County Library. *See* Grass Valley Library
Nevada Historical Society, 1650 N. Virginia St., Reno, NV 89503
Nevada, Reno, University of, University Library, Special Collections Dept., Reno, NV 89557
Nevada, Reno, University of, University Library, Special Collections Dept., Oral History Project, Reno, NV 89557
Nevada State, County, and Municipal Archives, Secretary of State, Capitol Complex, Carson City, NV 89710
New Almaden Museum, Box 1, New Almaden, CA 95042
New Brunswick Public Library, New Brunswick, NJ 08901
New Brunswick Theological Seminary. *See* Reformed Church in America, Archives of the, New Brunswick Theological Seminary, Gardner Sage Library
New England Historic Genealogical Society, 101 Newbury St., Boston, MA 02116
New Hampshire Antiquarian Society, Hopkinton, Rte. 1, Concord, NH 03301
New Hampshire Historical Society, 30 Park St., Concord, NH 03301
New Hampshire State Library, Box 189, Concord, NH 03301
New Hampshire, University of, Library, Special Collections, Durham, NH 03824
New Hanover County Museum, 814 Market St., Wilmington, NC 28401
New Haven Colony Historical Society, Library, 114 Whitney Ave., New Haven, CT 06510
New Jersey Department of Environmental Protection, Office of Historic Preservation, 109 W. State St., Trenton, NJ 08625
The New Jersey Historical Society, 230 Broadway, Newark, NJ 07104
New Jersey State Library, Bureau of Archives & History, Box 1898, Trenton, NJ 08625
New Market Historical Society, Stone School Museum, Newmarket, NH 03857
New Mexico Federation of Women's Clubs, 101 Barranca Rd., Santa Fe, NM 87501
New Mexico, Museum of, Box 2087, Santa Fe, NM 87503
New Mexico State Records Center and Archives, 404 Montezuma, Santa Fe, NM 87501
New Mexico, University of, Fine Arts Library, Albuquerque, NM 87131
New Mexico, University of, General Library, Special Collections, Albuquerque, NM 87131
New Mexico, University of, Jonson Gallery, 1909 Las Lomas Rd. N.E., Albuquerque, NM 87106
New Milford Historical Society, Box 566, New Milford, CT 06776
New Orleans Public Library, Louisiana Div., 219 Loyola Ave., New Orleans, LA 70140
New Orleans, University of, Earl K. Long Library, Archives and Manuscripts Dept., Lakefront, New Orleans, LA 70122
New Providence Historical Society, c/o D. Knox, Borough Hall, Springfield Ave., New Providence, NJ 07974
New Rochelle, College of, Archives, New Rochelle, NY 10801
New York Academy of Medicine, Malloch Rare Book and History Room, 2 E. 103 St., New York, NY 10029
New York Botanical Garden, Library, Bronx, NY 10458
New York City Municipal Archives, Dept. of Records & Information Services, 23 Park Row, New York, NY 10038
New-York Historical Society, Manuscript Dept., 170 Central Park W., New York, NY 10024
The New York Hospital-Cornell Medical Center, Medical Archives, 1300 York Ave., New York, NY 10021
New York, Museum of the City of, Manuscript Collection, Fifth Ave. at 103 St., New York, NY 10029
New York Public Library at Lincoln Center, Performing Arts Research Center, Dance Collection, 111 Amsterdam Ave., New York, NY 10023
New York Public Library at Lincoln Center, Performing Arts Research Center, Theatre Collection, 111 Amsterdam Ave., New York, NY 10023
New York Public Library, Manuscripts and Archives Div., 476 Fifth Ave., New York, NY 10018
New York Public Library, Schomburg Center for Research in Black Culture, 103 W. 135 St., New York, NY 10030
New York Society Library, 53 E. 79 St., New York, NY 10021
New York State Archives. *See* New York State Education Department, New York State Archives, Cultural Education Center
New York State Education Department, New York State Archives, Cultural Education Center, Empire State Plaza, Albany, NY 12230
New York State Library, Manuscripts and Special Collections, State Education Bldg., Albany, NY 12234
New York State Museum. *See* Division of Historical Services-New York State Museum, Cultural Education Center
New York State School of Industrial and Labor Relations. *See* Cornell University, New York State School of Industrial and Labor Relations, Labor-Management Documentation Center
New York, State University of. *See* State University of New York
New York University, Fales Library, Elmer Holmes Bobst Library, 70 Washington Sq. S., New York, NY 10012
New York University, Papers of William Livingston, Dept. of History, 19 University Pl., New York, NY 10003
New York University, Tamiment Library, 70 Washington Sq. S., New York, NY 10012
Newark Public Library, Art and Music Dept., 5 Washington St., Newark, NJ 07101
The Newberry Library, 60 W. Walton Pl., Chicago, IL 60610
Newton Free Library, 414 Centre St., Newton, MA 02158
Niagara County Historian, Court House, Lockport, NY 14094
Niagara Falls Public Library, Local History Dept., 1425 Main St., Niagara Falls, NY 14305
Niels Bohr Library. *See* American Institute of Physics, Niels Bohr Library
Niles Community Library, 620 E. Main St., Niles, MI 49120
No Man's Land Historical Museum, Panhandle State University, Goodwell, OK 73939
Nook Farm Research Library. *See* The Stowe-Day Foundation, Stowe-Day Library
North Adams State College, Freel Library, North Adams, MA 01247
North Alabama, University of, Wesleyan Archives and Museum, Box 5206, Florence, AL 35630
North Carolina at Charlotte, University of, Atkins Library, Charlotte, NC 28223
North Carolina at Greensboro, University of, Walter Clinton Jackson Library, Archives and Special Collections, Greensboro, NC 27412
North Carolina Baptist Historical Collection. *See* Wake Forest University, Z. Smith Reynolds Library, North Carolina Baptist Historical Collection
North Carolina Department of Cultural Resources, Div. of Archives and History, 109 E. Jones St., Raleigh, NC 27611
North Carolina Division of Archives and History. *See* North Carolina Department of Cultural Resources, Div. of Archives and History
North Carolina State Archives. *See* North Carolina Department of Cultural Resources, Div. of Archives and History
North Carolina State University Archives, D. H. Hill Library, Raleigh, NC 27650
North Carolina, University of, Library, Southern Historical Collection, Wilson Library 024-A, Chapel Hill, NC 27514
North Carolina, University of, Southern Oral History Program, 406 Hamilton Hall, Chapel Hill, NC 27514
North Central Minnesota Historical Center, Bemidji State University, Bemidji, MN 56601
North Country History Center. *See* State University College of Arts and Science, North Country History Center
North Dakota Institute for Regional Studies. *See* North Dakota State University, North Dakota Institute for Regional Studies
North Dakota, State Historical Society of, Liberty Memorial Bldg., Bismarck, ND 58505
North Dakota State University, North Dakota Institute for Regional Studies, Fargo, ND 58102
North Dakota, University of, Orin G. Libby Manuscript Collection, Chester Fritz Library, Grand Forks, ND 58202
North Louisiana Historical Association Collection, Centenary College of Louisiana Library, Shreveport, LA 71104
North Texas State University, Texas Center for Fashion Studies, Industrial Training Laboratory, Box 13336, Denton, TX 76203
Northampton Historical Society, 58 Bridge St., Northampton, MA 01060
Northeast Archives of Folklore and Oral History. *See* Maine at Orono, University of, Northeast Archives of Folklore and Oral History
Northeast Minnesota Historical Center, University of Minnesota-Duluth, Duluth, MN 55812
Northeastern Illinois University Library, University Archives, Bryn Mawr at St. Louis Ave., Chicago, IL 60625
Northeastern Nevada Museum, Box 503, Elko, NV 89801
Northern Arizona University Library, Special Collections, C.U. Box 6022, Flagstaff, AZ 86011
Northern Colorado, University of, James Michener Library, Greeley, CO 80631
Northern Illinois Regional History Center, Northern Illinois University, Swen Parson Library, DeKalb, IL 60115
Northern Indiana Historical Society, 112 S. Lafayette Blvd., South Bend, IN 46601
Northfield Public Library, Division at Third St., Northfield, MN 55057
Northwest Minnesota Historical Center, Moorhead State University, Moorhead, MN 56560
Northwest Missouri State University Library, Missouriana Room, Maryville, MO 64468
Northwest Oakland County Historical Society, 403 East Rd., Holly, MI 48442
Northwestern College, Ramaker Library, Dutch Heritage Collection, Orange City, IA 51041
Northwestern Memorial Hospital Archives, Superior St. & Fairbanks Ct., Chicago, IL 60611
Northwestern State University of Louisiana, Archives Div., Natchitoches, LA 71457
Northwestern University Archives, Northwestern University Library, Evanston, IL 60201
Northwestern University Library, Special Collections Dept., Evanston, IL 60201
Northwestern University, Music Library, Evanston, IL 60201
Norwegian-American Historical Association, St. Olaf College, Northfield, MN 55057
Notre Dame Educational Center, 13000 Auburn Rd., Chardon, OH 44024
Notre Dame, University of, Archives, Box 513, Notre Dame, IN 46556

Oak Park and River Forest, Historical Society of, Box 771, Oak Park, IL 60301
Oakland Public Library, California Room, 124 14th St., Oakland, CA 94612

Oberlin College Archives, Oberlin, OH 44074
Oblate Sisters of Providence, Our Lady of Mount Providence Convent, 701 Gun Rd., Baltimore, MD 21227
Oblate Sisters of the Blessed Sacrament, St. Sylvester's Convent, Marty, SD 57361
Ogunquit Free Library, Ogunquit, ME 03907
Ohio Agricultural Research and Development Center Library, Wooster, OH 44691
Ohio, Historical and Philosophical Society of. *See* Cincinnati Historical Society
The Ohio Historical Society, Archives & Manuscripts Div., Interstate 71 & 17 Ave., Columbus, OH 43211
Ohio State University Archives, Hitchcock Hall, 2070 Neil Ave., Columbus, OH 43210
Ohio University Archives. *See* Ohio University Library, Special Collections Div.
Ohio University Library, Special Collections Div., Athens, OH 45701
Ohioana Library Association, 1105 Ohio Depts. Bldg., 65 S. Front St., Columbus, OH 43215
Oklahoma Christian College, Oklahoma Living Legends, North Eastern & Memorial, Oklahoma City, OK 73111
Oklahoma City University Library, 2501 N. Blackwelder, Oklahoma City, OK 73106
Oklahoma Department of Libraries, Oklahoma State Archives, 200 N.E. 18 St., Oklahoma City, OK 73105
Oklahoma Heritage Association, Heritage House, 201 N.W. 14 St., Oklahoma City, OK 73103
Oklahoma Historical Society, Historical Bldg., Oklahoma City, OK 73105
Oklahoma Living Legends. *See* Oklahoma Christian College, Oklahoma Living Legends
Oklahoma State Archives. *See* Oklahoma Department of Libraries, Oklahoma State Archives
Oklahoma State University, Edmon Low Library, Special Collections, Stillwater, OK 74074
Oklahoma, University of Science and Arts of, Nash Library, Chickasha, OK 73018
Oklahoma, University of, Western History Collections, Rm. 452, Monnet Hall, 630 Parrington Oval, Norman, OK 73019
Old Dominion University, Dept. of Archives & Manuscripts, Box 6173, Norfolk, VA 23508
Old Economy Village, Pennsylvania Historical and Museum Commission, Great House Sq., Ambridge, PA 15003
Old Lyme—Phoebe Griffin Noyes Library, 2 Library La., Old Lyme, CT 06371
Old Orchard Beach Historical Society, Old Orchard Beach, ME 04064
Old Sturbridge Village Research Library, Sturbridge, MA 01566
Old Yarmouth, Historical Society of, Yarmouth, MA 02675
Olivet College Archives, Burrage Library, Olivet, MI 49076
Olivetan Benedictine Sisters, Holy Angels Convent, Drawer 130, Jonesboro, AR 72401
Olmsted County Historical Society, Box 6411, County Rd. 122 S.W., Rochester, MN 55901
Ontario City Library, 215 E. C St., Ontario, CA 91764
Operating Room Nurses, Association of, 10170 E. Mississippi Ave., Denver, CO 80231
Oregon Historical Society, 1230 S.W. Park Ave., Portland, OR 97205
Oregon State Library, State Library Bldg., Salem, OR 97310
Oregon State University Archives, Administrative Services Bldg., Corvallis, OR 97331
Oregon, University of, Health Sciences Center Library, Box 573, Portland, OR 97207
Oregon, University of, Library, Special Collections, Eugene, OR 97403
Oriental Institute of the University of Chicago, 1155 E. 58 St., Chicago, IL 60637
Ossining Historical Society Museum, 196 Croton Ave., Ossining, NY 10562
Oswego County Historical Society, 135 E. Third St., Oswego, NY 13126
Ottawa University, Myers Library, Tenth & Cedar Sts., Ottawa, KS 66067
Otter Tail County Historical Society, 1110 Lincoln Ave. W., Fergus Falls, MN 56537
Otterbein College Library, Westerville, OH 43081
Ottumwa Public Library, 129 N. Court St., Ottumwa, IA 52501
Our Lady of Holy Cross, Marianite Provincial House, 4123 Woodland Dr., New Orleans, LA 70114
Our Lady of Mercy, Russell Library, 535 Sacramento St., Auburn, CA 95603
Our Lady of the Mississippi Abbey, Dubuque, IA 52001
Our Lady of the Retreat in the Cenacle, Congregation of, Cenacle Retreat House, 513 Fullerton Pkway., Chicago, IL 60614
Our Lady of Victory Missionary Sisters, Victory Noll, Box 109, Huntington, IN 46750
Ozarks, The School of the. *See* Ralph Foster Museum, The School of the Ozarks

Pacific Center for Western Studies. *See* Pacific, University of the, The Pacific Center for Western Studies
Pacific Grove Public Library, 550 Central Ave., Pacific Grove, CA 93950
Pacific Lutheran University Archives, Tacoma, WA 98447
Pacific University, Harvey Whitfield Scott Library, Rare Book Room, Forest Grove, OR 97116
Pacific, University of the, The Pacific Center for Western Studies, Stockton, CA 95211
Palmer College Library, 1000 Brady St., Davenport, IA 42803
Pan American University Library, Special Collections, Edinburg, TX 78539
Panhandle State University. *See* No Man's Land Historical Museum, Panhandle State University
Park-McCullough House Manuscript Library, West St. at Park St., North Bennington, VT 05257
Pasadena Historical Society Museum, 470 W. Walnut St., Pasadena, CA 91103
Paterson Public Library, 250 Broadway, Paterson, NJ 07501
Peabody Museum of Salem, Phillips Library, East India Sq., Salem, MA 01970
Peace Collection. *See* Swarthmore College Peace Collection
Peace College, Raleigh, NC 27604
Pendleton District Historical and Recreational Commission, Box 234, Pendleton, SC 29670
Pendleton, Mr. William H., Searsport, ME 04974
Pennsylvania Historical and Museum Commission. *See also* Old Economy Village, Pennsylvania Historical and Museum Commission
Pennsylvania Historical and Museum Commission, Div. of Archives & Manuscripts (State Archives), William Penn Memorial Museum & Archives Bldg., Box 1026, Harrisburg, PA 17120
Pennsylvania Historical Collections and Labor Archives. *See* Pennsylvania State University, Pattee Library, Pennsylvania Historical Collections and Labor Archives
Pennsylvania, Historical Society of, 1300 Locust St., Philadelphia, PA 19107
Pennsylvania Hospital Archives, Medical Library, Eighth & Spruce Sts., Philadelphia, PA 19107
Pennsylvania, The Medical College of. *See* The Medical College of Pennsylvania, Archives and Special Collections on Women in Medicine, Florence A. Moore Library of Medicine
Pennsylvania State Archives. *See* Pennsylvania Historical and Museum Commission, Div. of Archives and Manuscripts (State Archives)
Pennsylvania State University, Pattee Library, Pennsylvania Historical Collections and Labor Archives, University Park, PA 16802
Penrose Public Library. *See* Pikes Peak Regional Library District, Local History Librarian
Pensacola Historical Museum, Lelia Abercrombie Historical Library, 405 S. Adams St., Pensacola, FL 32501
Peoria Historical Society, 942 Glen Oak Ave., Peoria, IL 61603
Performing Arts Research Center. *See* New York Public Library at Lincoln Center, Performing Arts Research Center
Perkins School for the Blind, Samuel P. Hayes Research Library, 175 N. Beacon St., Watertown, MA 02172
Petersham Historical Society, N. Main St., Petersham, MA 01366
Philadelphia Archdiocesan Archives, 222 N. 17 St., Philadelphia, PA 19103
Philadelphia, Archives of the City and County of. *See* Philadelphia, City Archives of
Philadelphia, City Archives of, c/o Dept. of Records, 156 City Hall, Philadelphia, PA 19107
Philadelphia Federal Archives and Records Center. *See* Federal Archives and Records Center, Philadelphia Archives Branch
Philadelphia Jewish Archives Center, Curtis Bldg., 625 Walnut St., Philadelphia, PA 19107
Philadelphia, Library Company of. *See* Pennsylvania, Historical Society of
Philadelphia Maritime Museum, 321 Chestnut St., Philadelphia, PA 19106
The Philip H. & A. S. W. Rosenbach Foundation, 2010 Delancey Pl., Philadelphia, PA 19103
Phillips Academy, Oliver Wendell Holmes Library, Andover, MA 01810
Phoebe Apperson Hearst Historical Society, Inc., c/o Mrs. Mabel Reed, Box 1842, St. Clair, MO 63077
Phoenix Historical Society and Museum. *See* Arizona Historical Society, Phoenix Chapter and Museum
Physicians of Philadelphia, College of, Library, Historical Collections, 19 S. 22 St., Philadelphia, PA 19103
Physics, American Institute of. *See* American Institute of Physics, Niels Bohr Library
Pi Beta Phi Fraternity, Central Office, 7730 Carondelet, Suite 333, St. Louis, MO 63105
Pikes Peak Regional Library District, Local History Librarian, Box 1579, Colorado Springs, CO 80901
Pioneer Museum and Haggin Galleries, Almeda May Petzinger Library, 1201 N. Pershing Ave., Stockton, CA 95203
Pittsburg State College Library. *See* Kansas State College of Pittsburg Library, Kansas Collection
Pittsburgh, University of, Darlington Memorial Library, 601 Cathedral of Learning, Pittsburgh, PA 15260
Pittsburgh, University of, Hillman Library, Archives of Industrial Society, Pittsburgh, PA 15260
Pittsburgh, University of, Hillman Library, Special Collections Dept., Pittsburgh, PA 15260
Pittsburgh, University of, University Archives, Hillman Library, Pittsburgh, PA 15260
The *Plain Dealer,* Newspaper Library, 1801 Superior Ave., Cleveland, OH 44114
Plainfield Public Library, 1120 Stafford Rd., Plainfield, IN 46168
Pocumtuck Valley Memorial Association Library, Box 53, Deerfield, MA 01342
Polk County Historical Commission, 511 Court House, Bartow, FL 33830
Pomona Public Library, Special Collections, Box 2271, Pomona, CA 91766
Poor Clare Nuns, Christ the King Monastery, 4000 Sherwood Blvd., Delray Beach, FL 33445
Poor Clares, Monastery of, 3501 Rocky River Dr., Cleveland, OH 44111
Portland Neighborhood History Project, 2200 N.E. 24, Portland, OR 97212
Portland State University Library, Archives Collection, Portland, OR 97207
Pratt Institute Archives, The Library, Brooklyn, NY 11205
Presbyterian Historical Society, 425 Lombard St., Philadelphia, PA 19147

Presentation Sisters of the Blessed Virgin Mary, Presentation Heights, 1500 N. Main St., Aberdeen, SD 57401
President Benjamin Harrison Memorial Home, 1230 N. Delaware St., Indianapolis, IN 46202
Princeton University Archives, Seeley G. Mudd Library, Olden St., Princeton, NJ 08540
Princeton University Library, Dept. of Rare Books and Special Collections, Princeton, NJ 08540
Princeton University Library, Manuscript Div. *See* Princeton University Library, Dept. of Rare Books and Special Collections
Princeton University, Seeley G. Mudd Manuscript Library. *See* Princeton University Library, Dept. of Rare Books and Special Collections
Principia College Library, Elsah, IL 62028
The Principia Corporation Archives, Principia College, Elsah, IL 62028
Priory of . . . *See* other part of title, e.g., St. Gertrude, Priory of
Protestant Episcopal Diocese of South Carolina Archives, Box 2127, Charleston, SC 29403
Providence College Archives, Providence, RI 02918
Psychology, Archives of the History of American. *See* Akron, University of, Archives of the History of American Psychology
Public Library of . . . *See* other part of title, e.g., Columbus and Franklin County, Public Library of, Columbus and Ohio Div.
Puerto Rico, Archivo General de, Instituto de Cultura Puertorriqueña, Apartado 4184, San Juan, PR 00905
Purdue University Archives. *See* Purdue University Libraries, Special Collections and Archives
Purdue University Libraries, Special Collections and Archives, West Lafayette, IN 47907
Putnam County Historical Society, Roy O. West Library, DePauw University, Greencastle, IN 46135

Quaker Collection. *See* Guilford College Library, Quaker Collection; *also* Haverford College Library, Quaker Collection
Queens Borough Public Library, Long Island Div., 89-11 Merrick Blvd., Jamaica, NY 11432
Queens College, Everett Library, Charlotte, NC 28274
Queens College, Paul Klapper Library, Historical Documents Collection, Flushing, NY 11367
Quincy and Adams County, Historical Society of, 425 S. 12 St., Quincy, IL 62301

Racine County Historical Museum Library, 701 Main St., Racine, WI 53403
Radcliffe College Archives, 10 Garden St., Cambridge, MA 02138
Radcliffe College, The Arthur and Elizabeth Schlesinger Library on the History of Women in America, 3 James St., Cambridge, MA 02138
Ralph Foster Museum, The School of the Ozarks, Point Lookout, MO 65726
Red Cross. *See* American Red Cross, National Headquarters Library and Archives
Redemptoristine Nuns, Mother of Perpetual Help Monastery, Esopus, NY 12429
Redlands, University of, Armacost Library, Special Collections, 1200 E. Colton Ave., Redlands, CA 92373
Redwood City Public Library, 881 Jefferson Ave., Redwood City, CA 94063
Reformed Church in America, Archives of the, New Brunswick Theological Seminary, Gardner Sage Library, New Brunswick, NJ 08901
Reisterstown Public Library, Reisterstown Room, Reisterstown, MD 21136
Renville County Historical Society, Buffalo Lake, MN 55314
Reorganized Church of Jesus Chirst of Latter Day Saints, Library-Archives, The Auditorium, Box 1059, Independence, MO 64051
Retail Clerks International Union, Suffridge Bldg., Washington, DC 20006
Reuther Library of Labor and Urban Affairs. *See* Wayne State University, Archives of Labor and Urban Affairs, Walter P. Reuther Library
Rhode Island College, James P. Adams Library, Special Collections, Providence, RI 02908
The Rhode Island Historical Society Library, 121 Hope St., Providence, RI 02906
Rhode Island State Archives, Rm. 43 State House, Providence, RI 02903
Rice University, Fondren Library, Box 1892, Houston, TX 77001
Richardson Archives. *See* South Dakota, University of, I. D. Weeks Library, Richardson Archives
Ricks College Archives, Rexburg, ID 83440
Riley County Historical Society and Museum, 2309 Claflin Rd., Manhattan, KS 66502
Riverside City Archives, General Library, University of California, Riverside, CA 92521
Riverside Municipal Museum, 3720 Orange St., Riverside, CA 92501
Riverside *Press-Enterprise* Library, 3512 14th St., Riverside, CA 92501
Riverside Public Library, One Burling Rd., Riverside, IL 60546
Robert Abbe Museum of Stone Antiquities, Bar Harbor, ME 04609
Rochester Museum and Science Center Library, 657 East Ave., Box 1480, Rochester, NY 14603
Rochester Public Library, Rochester, NH 03867
Rochester Public Library, Local History Div., 115 South Ave., Rochester, NY 14604
Rochester, University of, Library, Dept. of Rare Books, Manuscripts, & Archives, Rochester, NY 14627
Rochester, University of, School of Medicine and Dentistry, Edward G. Miner Library, History of Medicine Section, 601 Elmwood Ave., Rochester, NY 14642
Rockaways Historical Society, Box 100, Hibernia, NJ 07842
Rockefeller Archive Center, Rockefeller University, Hillcrest, Pocantico Hills, North Tarrytown, NY 10591
Rockefeller University. *See* Rockefeller Archive Center, Rockefeller University
Rockford College, Howard Colman Library, 5050 E. State St., Rockford, IL 61101
Rockford Public Library, Local History and Genealogy Div., 215 N. Wyman St., Rockford, IL 61101
Rockingham Free Public Library, Bellows Falls, VT 05101
Rocky Hill Historical Society, Inc., Box 185, Rocky Hill, CT 06067
Rocky Mount Historical Association, Rte. 2, Box 70, Piney Flats, TN 87686
Roosevelt Library. *See* Franklin D. Roosevelt Library
Roosevelt University Archives, 430 S. Michigan Ave., Chicago, IL 60605
Roosevelt University Library, Oral History Project in Labor History, 430 S. Michigan Ave., Chicago, IL 60605
Roper Public Opinion Research Center. *See* Williams College, Roper Public Opinion Research Center
Rosary College Archives, 7900 W. Division St., River Forest, IL 60305
Rosenberg Library, Special Collections, Galveston, TX 77550
Round Lake, Village of, Burlington Ave., Box 85, Round Lake, NY 12151
Roxbury Public Library, 103 Main St., Succasunna, NJ 07876
Rutgers University, Archibald Stevens Alexander Library, Special Collections Dept., New Brunswick, NJ 08901
Rutgers University Archives, Library, New Brunswick, NJ 08903
Rutgers University, Douglass College Library, New Brunswick, NJ 08903
Rutgers University Libraries, Special Collections. *See* Rutgers University, Archibald Stevens Alexander Library, Special Collections Dept.
Rutherford B. Hayes Library, 1337 Hayes Ave., Fremont, OH 43420

Sacramento Union, Editorial Library, 301 Capitol Mall, Sacramento, CA 95812
Sacred Heart Convent, Provincial House, One Main St., Groton, MA 01450
Sacred Heart, Society of the, Chicago Province, 2047 W. Fargo, Chicago, IL 60645
Sacred Heart, Society of the, Provincial Archives, 150 Valparaiso Ave., Menlo Park, CA 94025
Sacred Heart, University of the, Madre Maria Teresa Guevara Library, Apartado 12383, Correo Calle Lioza, Santurce, PR 00914
St. Benedict Convent Archives, 9535 Linton Hall Rd., Bristow, VA 22013
St. Benedict's Convent, St. Joseph, MN 56374
St. Catherine, College of, Library, 2004 Randolph Ave., St. Paul, MN 55105
St. Charles County Historical Society, Box 455, St. Charles, MO 63301
St. Clare, Monastery of, 509 S. Kentucky Ave., Evansville, IN 47714
St. Clare, Monastery of, 8650 Russell Ave. S., Bloomington, MN 55431
St. Clare, Monastery of, 3626 N. 65 Ave., Omaha, NE 68104
St. Clare, Monastery of, 1271 Langhorne-Newtown Rd., Langhorne, PA 19047
St. Cloud State University. *See also* Central Minnesota Historical Center, St. Cloud State University
St. Cloud State University, Learning Resources Center, Special Collections, St. Cloud, MN 56301
St. Dominic, Monastery of, 13 Ave. & S. Tenth St., Newark, NJ 07103
St. Elizabeth, College of, Archives, Convent Station, NJ 07961
St. Gertrude, Priory of, Box 107, Cottonwood, ID 83522
St. John's Seminary, Edward L. Doheny Memorial Library, Camarillo, CA 93010
St. Lawrence University Archives, Canton, NY 13617
St. Louis County Historical Society. *See* Northeast Minnesota Historical Center, University of Minnesota-Duluth
St. Mark's Lutheran Church, 1111 O'Farrell St., San Francisco, CA 94109
St. Mary's College Archives, Notre Dame, IN 46556
St. Mary's College, Sarah Graham Kenan Library, Raleigh, NC 27611
St. Mary's Hospital, 235 W. Sixth St., Reno, NV 89503
St. Mary's Hospital, Staff Library, 2414 S. Seventh St., Minneapolis, MN 55454
St. Olaf College. *See also* Norwegian-American Historical Association
St. Olaf College Archives, Rölvaag Memorial Library, Northfield, MN 55057
St. Paul's Priory, 2675 Larpenteur Ave. E., St. Paul, MN 55109
St. Petersburg Historical Society, 335 Second Ave. N.E., St. Petersburg, FL 33701
St. Rose, College of, Archives, 432 Western Ave., Albany, NY 12203
St. Teresa, College of, Archives, Winona, MN 55987
St. Teresa's Motherhouse and Novitiate, Avila on Hudson, Germantown, NY 12526
St. Ursula Convent and Academy, 1339 E. McMillan St., Cincinnati, OH 45206
St. Vincent Sisters, Daughters of the Cross Convent, 1000 Fairview, Shreveport, LA 71104
Salem College, Siewers Room, Winston-Salem, NC 27108
Saline County Historical Society, Inc., Dorchester, NE 68343
The Salvation Army Archives and Research Center, 120 W. 14 St., New York, NY 10011
Samford University Library, Special Collection Dept., 800 Lakeshore Dr., Birmingham, AL 35209

San Antonio Archdiocese Archives. *See* Catholic Archives at San Antonio
San Antonio Public Library, History Section, 203 S. St. Mary's St., San Antonio, TX 78205
San Bernardino County Museum, 2024 Orange Tree La., Redlands, CA 92373
San Diego County Law Library, 1105 Front St., San Diego, CA 92101
San Diego Historical Society, Library and Manuscripts Collection, Presidio Pk., Box 81825, San Diego, CA 92138
San Diego Public Library, California Room, 820 E St., San Diego, CA 92101
San Francisco Federal Archives and Records Center. *See* Federal Archives and Records Center, San Francisco Archives Branch
San Francisco Public Library, San Francisco History Room & Archives, Civic Center, San Francisco, CA 94102
San Francisco Theological Seminary Library, San Anselmo, CA 94960
San Gabriel Mission, 537 W. Mission Dr., San Gabriel, CA 91776
San Leandro Community Library, California Room, 300 Estudillo Ave., San Leandro, CA 94577
Sandwich Historical Commission, Box 490, Sandwich, MA 02563
Sandy Bay Historical Society and Museum, 40 King St., Rockport, MA 01966
Sanford Museum and Planetarium, 117 E. Willow, Cherokee, IA 51012
Santa Barbara Public Library, 40 Anapamu St., Santa Barbara, CA 93101
Santa Clara City Library, 2635 Homestead Rd., Santa Clara, CA 95051
Santa Clara Public Library. *See* Santa Clara City Library
Santa Rosa Junior College Archives, Mendocino Ave., Santa Rosa, CA 95402
Sarah Lawrence College Archives, Bronxville, NY 10708
Sarah Lawrence College Library, Bronxville, NY 10708
Sarasota Historical Commission, Courthouse, Sarasota, FL 33577
Saratoga County Historian's Office, 31 Woodlawn Ave., Saratoga Springs, NY 12866
Saratoga Springs City Archives, 297 Broadway, Saratoga Springs, NY 12866
Saratoga Springs City Historian, 297 Broadway, Saratoga Springs, NY 12866
Saratoga Springs, Historical Society of, Museum, Box 216, Saratoga Springs, NY 12866
Saratoga Springs Public Library, Broadway, Saratoga Springs, NY 12866
Schlesinger Library. *See* Radcliffe College, The Arthur and Elizabeth Schlesinger Library on the History of Women in America
Schomburg Center for Research in Black Culture. *See* New York Public Library, Schomburg Center for Research in Black Culture
School Sisters of Notre Dame, Rte. 2, Box 4, Irving, TX 75062
School Sisters of Notre Dame, Our Lady of Good Counsel Convent, Mankato, MN 56001
School Sisters of Notre Dame Provincial House, 6401 N. Charles St., Baltimore, MD 21222
School Sisters of St. Francis Archives, International Office, 1501 S. Layton Blvd., Milwaukee, WI 53215
Searls Historical Library, 214 Church St., Nevada City, CA 95959
Sears, Roebuck and Company Archives, Dept. 703, Sears Tower 40-10, Chicago, IL 60684
Seattle Federal Archives and Records Center. *See* Federal Archives and Records Center, Seattle Archives Branch
Seattle Historical Society, Sophie Frye Bass Memorial Library, 2161 E. Hamlin St., Seattle, WA 98112
Seattle Public Library, History-Government-Biography Dept., 1000 Fourth Ave., Seattle, WA 98104
Seneca Falls Historical Society, 55 Cayuga St., Seneca Falls, NY 13148
Servants of Mary Motherhouse, 7400 Military Ave., Omaha, NE 68134
Servants of Mary, Our Lady of Sorrows Convent, Ladysmith, WI 54848
Servants of the Blessed Sacrament, 2116 Oakland, Pueblo, CO 81004
Servants of the Holy Heart of Mary, Provincial House, 145 S. Fourth Ave., Kankakee, IL 60901
Servants of the Immaculate Heart of Mary, Provincial Residence, Saco, ME 04072
Servants of the Immaculate Heart of Mary, Scranton, Generalate—Marywood, Scranton, PA 18509
Seventh-day Adventists, General Conference. *See also* Ellen G. White Estate, Inc., General Conference of Seventh-day Adventists
Seventh-day Adventists, General Conference Archives, 6840 Eastern Ave. N.W., Washington, DC 20012
Shaker Community, Inc. *See* Hancock Shaker Village Library, Shaker Community, Inc.
Sharlot Hall Museum, 415 W. Gurley St., Prescott, AZ 86301
Shasta State Historic Park, Courthouse Museum, Box 507, Shasta, CA 96087
Shelby County Historical and Genealogical Society, Box 287, 303 N. Morgan St., Shelbyville, IL 62565
Sheldon Museum, Box 236, Haines, AK 99827
Shimer College Archives, c/o Business Manager, Mt. Carroll, IL 61053
Sienadale Motherhouse Archives, 4600 93rd St., Kenosha, WI 53140
Silverado Museum, Box 409, St. Helena, CA 94574
Simmons College Archives, 300 The Fenway, Boston, MA 02115
Sinsinawa Dominican Sisters, Congregation of the Most Holy Rosary, Dominican Motherhouse, Sinsinawa, WI 53824
Sioux City Public Museum, 2901 Jackson St., Sioux City, IA 51104
Siskiyou County Public Library, 719 Fourth St., Yreka, CA 96097
Sister Kenny Institute. *See* Abbott-Northwestern Hospital Corporation, Sister Kenny Institute, Health Science Library
Sisters of Charity (Grey Nuns of Montreal), St. Joseph Province Archives, 10 Pelham Rd., Lexington, MA 02173
Sisters of Charity of Cincinnati, Motherhouse, Mt. St. Joseph, OH 45051
Sisters of Charity of Leavenworth, Mother House, Leavenworth, KS 66048
Sisters of Charity of Nazareth, Mother House Archival Center, Nazareth, KY 40048
Sisters of Charity of New York, Mt. St. Vincent-on-Hudson, Bronx, NY 10471
Sisters of Charity of Our Lady of Mercy, May Forest, Box 12410, Charleston, SC 29412
Sisters of Charity of St. Augustine, 5232 Broadview Rd., Richfield, OH 44286
Sisters of Charity of Seton Hill, Community Archives, Greensburg, PA 15601
Sisters of Charity of the Blessed Virgin Mary, BVM Center, 1100 Carmel Dr., Dubuque, IA 52001
Sisters of Charity of the Incarnate Word, 6510 Lawndale, Houston, TX 77023
Sisters of Christian Charity, Eastern Province, Mallinckrodt Convent, Mendham, NJ 07945
Sisters of Divine Providence, Box 197, Helotes, TX 78023
Sisters of Divine Providence, Provincial House, 9000 Babcock Blvd., Allison Park, PA 15101
Sisters of Divine Providence, St. Anne Convent, Melbourne, KY 41059
Sisters of Jesus Crucified, American Novitiate. *See* Sisters of Jesus Crucified, Regina Mundy Priory
Sisters of Jesus Crucified, Regina Mundi Priory, Devon, PA 19333
Sisters of Mercy Archives, 444 E. Grandview Blvd., Erie, PA 16504
Sisters of Mercy Convent, 515 Montgomery Ave., Merion Station, PA 19066
Sisters of Mercy Motherhouse, 21 Searles Rd., Windham, NH 03087
Sisters of Mercy Motherhouse, 1437 Blossom Rd., Rochester, NY 14610
Sisters of Mercy of Allegheny County, 3333 Fifth Ave., Pittsburgh, PA 15213
Sisters of Mercy of Connecticut, Convent of Mercy, 249 Steele Rd., West Hartford, CT 06117
Sisters of Mercy of the Union, Province of New York, 541 Broadway, Dobbs Ferry, NY 10522
Sisters of Mercy, Province of Chicago, 10024 S. Central Park Ave., Chicago, IL 60642
Sisters of Mercy, Province of Detroit, 29000 Eleven Mile Rd., Farmington Hills, MI 48024
Sisters of Mercy Provincialate, 2039 N. Geyer Rd., St. Louis, MO 63131
Sisters of Mercy Provincialate, R.D. #3, Cumberland, RI 02864
Sisters of Mercy Provincialate, Omaha Province, 1801 S. 72 St., Omaha, NE 68124
Sisters of Notre Dame Convent, 1776 Hendrix Ave., Thousand Oaks, CA 91360
Sisters of Notre Dame de Namur, California Province Archives, College of Notre Dame, Belmont, CA 94002
Sisters of Notre Dame de Namur, Maryland Provincial House, Ilchester, MD 21083
Sisters of Notre Dame de Namur, Ohio Province Archives, 701 E. Columbia Ave., Cincinnati, OH 45215
Sisters of Our Lady of Charity, 3800 Howard Rd., Hamburg, NY 14075
Sisters of Our Lady of Christian Doctrine, Marydell Convent, Montebello Rd., Suffern, NY 10901
Sisters of Our Lady of Mt. Carmel, Carmelite Monastery, 2500 Cold Spring Rd., Indianapolis, IN 46222
Sisters of Providence Archives, Sacred Heart Province, 4800 37th Ave. S.W., Seattle, WA 98126
Sisters of Providence of Holyoke, Mother House, Holyoke, MA 01040
Sisters of St. Basil the Great, Sacred Heart Province, 710 Fox Chase Rd., Philadelphia, PA 19111
Sisters of St. Benedict, Convent Immaculate Conception, Ferdinand, IN 47532
Sisters of St. Benedict, Our Lady of Grace Convent, 1402 Southern Ave., Beech Grove, IN 46107
Sisters of St. Benedict, St. Mary Priory, Nauvoo, IL 62354
Sisters of St. Dominic, Immaculate Conception Convent, 3600 Broadway, Great Bend, KS 67530
Sisters of St. Dominic, Mt. St. Dominic, Caldwell, NJ 07006
Sisters of St. Dominic, Our Lady of the Elms Convent, 1230 W. Market St., Akron, OH 44313
Sisters of St. Dominic, Siena Center, 5635 Erie St., Racine, WI 53402
Sisters of St. Francis, Congregation of Our Lady of Lourdes, Assisi Heights, Rochester, MN 55901
Sisters of St. Francis Convent, 200 St. Francis Ave., Tiffin, OH 44883
Sisters of St. Francis Convent Archives, Oldenburg, IN 47036
Sisters of St. Francis Motherhouse, Mt. St. Francis, Box 1060, Colorado Springs, CO 80901
Sisters of St. Francis of Mary Immaculate, 520 Plainfield Ave., Joliet, IL 60435
Sisters of St. Francis of Millvale, Motherhouse, 146 Hawthorne Rd., Pittsburgh, PA 15209
Sisters of St. Francis of Penance and Christian Charity, Mt. Alverno Convent, Box 1028, Redwood City, CA 94064
Sisters of St. Francis of Penance and Christian Charity, Provincialate, 4421 Lower River Rd., Stella Niagara, NY 14144
Sisters of St. Francis of Philadelphia, Our Lady of Angels Convent, Glen Riddle, Aston, PA 19014
Sisters of St. Francis of the Holy Cross, 3025 Bay Settlement Rd., Rte. 1, Green Bay, WI 54301

Sisters of St. Francis of the Holy Family, Mt. St. Francis, 3390 Windsor Ave., Dubuque, IA 52001
Sisters of St. Francis of the Providence of God, Mt. Providence, Grove & McRoberts Roads, Pittsburgh, PA 15234
Sisters of St. Joseph Cluny Provincialate, Brenton Rd., Newport, RI 02840
Sisters of St. Joseph Convent, Nazareth History Room, Nazareth, MI 49074
Sisters of St. Joseph Generalate, One Agassiz Circle, Buffalo, NY 14214
Sisters of St. Joseph, Marymount Provincial Home, 12215 Granger Rd., Garfield Heights, OH 44125
Sisters of St. Joseph Motherhouse, 4095 East Ave., Rochester, NY 14610
Sisters of St. Joseph Motherhouse, 3430 Rocky River Dr., Cleveland, OH 44111
Sisters of St. Joseph Motherhouse, 819 W. Eighth St., Erie, PA 16502
Sisters of St. Joseph Motherhouse, Mt. St. Joseph Convent, Chestnut Hill, Philadelphia, PA 19118
Sisters of St. Joseph Motherhouse, 1412 E. Second St., Superior, WI 54880
Sisters of St. Joseph, Nazareth Motherhouse and Novitiate, Concordia, KS 66901
Sisters of St. Joseph of Boston, 637 Cambridge St., Brighton, MA 02135
Sisters of St. Joseph of Carondelet, Albany, New York, Province Archives, Watervliet-Shaker Rd., Latham, NY 12110
Sisters of St. Joseph of Carondelet, Generalate Archives, 2307 S. Lindbergh Blvd., St. Louis, MO 63131
Sisters of St. Joseph of Carondelet, St. Louis Province, Archives Office, 6400 Minnesota Ave., St. Louis, MO 63111
Sisters of St. Joseph of Carondelet, St. Mary's Provincialate, 11999 Chalon Rd., Los Angeles, CA 90049
Sisters of St. Joseph of Carondelet, St. Paul Province, 1884 Randolph Ave., St. Paul, MN 55105
Sisters of St. Joseph of La Grange, 1515 W. Ogden Ave., La Grange Park, IL 60525
Sisters of St. Joseph of Orange, 480 S. Batavia St., Orange, CA 92668
Sisters of St. Joseph of St. Augustine, Box 1570, St. Augustine, FL 32084
Sisters of St. Joseph of Wheeling, Mt. St. Joseph, Pogue Run Rd., Wheeling, WV 26003
Sisters of St. Joseph, St. Joseph's Provincial House, Crookston, MN 56716
Sisters of St. Mary of Oregon Motherhouse, St. Mary of the Valley, 4440 S.W. 148 Ave., Beaverton, OR 97005
Sisters of St. Mary of the Third Order of St. Francis, 1100 Bellevue Ave., St. Louis, MO 63117
Sisters of Social Service of Los Angeles Motherhouse, 1120 Westchester Pl., Los Angeles, CA 90019
Sisters of the Blessed Scarament, St. Elizabeth Convent, 1663 Bristol Pike, Cornwells Heights, PA 19020
Sisters of the Divine Compassion, Good Counsel Convent, 52 N. Broadway, White Plains, NY 10603
Sisters of the Good Shepherd, St. Paul Provincialate, 389 N. Oxford St., St. Paul, MN 55104
Sisters of the Holy Family of Nazareth Archives, Grant & Frankford Aves., Torresdale, Philadelphia, PA 19114
Sisters of the Holy Family of Nazareth, Immaculate Heart of Mary Provincialate, 1428 Monroe Tpke., Monroe, CT 06468
Sisters of the Humility of Mary, Villa Maria Community Center, Villa Maria, PA 16155
Sisters of the Immaculate Heart of Mary, Villa San Giuseppe, 3431 Waverly Dr., Los Angeles, CA 90027
Sisters of the Incarnate Word and Blessed Sacrament, 4600 Bissonnet St., Bellaire, TX 77401
Sisters of the Lamb of God, Our Lady of Hope Convent, 1516 Parrish Ave., Owensboro, KY 42301
Sisters of the Most Precious Blood Convent, 204 N. Main St., O'Fallon, MO 63366
Sisters of the Order of St. Dominic, Queen of the Rosary Motherhouse, Albany Ave., Amityville, NY 11701
Sisters of the Precious Blood, Salem Heights Archives, 4830 Salem Ave., Dayton, OH 45416
Sisters of the Presentation, 2340 Turk Blvd., San Francisco, CA 94118
Sisters of the Presentation, Mt. Loretto, 2360 Carter Rd., Dubuque, IA 52001
Sisters of the Presentation of Mary, Provincial House, 495 Mammoth Rd., Manchester, NH 03104
Sisters of the Resurrection of Our Lord Jesus Christ, St. Joseph Province, Mt. St. Joseph, Castleton-on-Hudson, NY 12033
Sisters of the Sorrowful Mother, Mother of Sorrows Convent, 6618 N. Teutonia Ave., Milwaukee, WI 53209
Sisters of the Sorrowful Mother, Our Lady of Sorrows Convent, 9 Pocono Rd., Denville, NJ 07834
Sisters of the Visitation, Villa de Chantal, 2000 16th Ave., Rock Island, IL 61201
Sisters, Servants of the Immaculate Heart of Mary Archives, St. Mary Convent, 610 W. Elm, Monroe, MI 48161
Sisters, Servants of the Immaculate Heart of Mary, Villa Maria House of Studies, Immaculata, PA 19345
Skagit County Historical Museum, Box 32, LaConner, WA 98257
Smith College Archives, Northampton, MA 01063
Smith College, Neilson Library, Rare Book Room, Northampton, MA 01063
Smith College, Sophia Smith Collection, Northampton, MA 01063
Smithsonian Institution. *See also* American Art, Archives of, National Portrait Gallery; American Portraits, Catalog of, National Portrait Gallery; National Anthropological Archives, National Museum of Natural History; National Collection of Fine Arts; National Endowment for the Arts Jazz Oral History Project, Div. of Performing Arts; National Museum of History and Technology, Div. of Mechanisms; National Museum of History and Technology, Div. of Political History
Smithsonian Institution Archives, Washington, DC 20560
Smoki Museum, Box 123, Prescott, AZ 86301
Snoqualmie Valley Historical Society Museum, Box 179, North Bend, WA 98045
Social Welfare History Archives. *See* Minnesota, University of, Libraries, Social Welfare History Archives
Society of . . . *See* other part of title, e.g., Woman Geographers, Society of
Somers Historical Society, Elephant Hotel, Somers, NY 10589
Sonoma State University Library, 1801 E. Cotati Ave., Rohnert Park, CA 94928
Sonoma State University, Women's Studies Program Office, 1801 E. Cotati Ave., Rohnert Park, CA 94928
Sophia Smith Collection. *See* Smith College, Sophia Smith Collection
South Carolina Conference of the United Methodist Church, Historical Society of the, Wofford College, Spartanburg, SC 29301
South Carolina Department of Archives and History, Box 11699, Capitol Sta., Columbia, SC 29211
South Carolina Historical Society, Fireproof Bldg., Charleston, SC 29401
South Carolina, Medical University of. *See* Medical University of South Carolina, Waring Historical Library
South Carolina, University of, South Caroliniana Library, Columbia, SC 29208
South Caroliniana Library. *See* South Carolina, University of, South Caroliniana Library
South Dakota Department of History. *See* South Dakota State Historical Resource Center
South Dakota State Historical Resource Center, Memorial Bldg., Pierre, SD 57501
South Dakota State Historical Society. *See* South Dakota State Historical Resource Center
South Dakota, University of, I. D. Weeks Library, Richardson Archives, Vermillion, SD 57069
South Florida, University of. *See also* Florida Historical Society, University of South Florida, Library
South Florida, University of, Library, Special Collections Dept., Tampa, FL 33620
South Georgia Regional Library, 300 Woodrow Wilson Dr., Valdosta, GA 31601
South, University of the, Archives, Jessie Ball duPont Library, Sewanee, TN 37375
Southeast Minnesota Historical Center, Winona State University, Winona, MN 55987
Southern Baptist Theological Seminary Library, 2825 Lexington Rd., Louisville, KY 40206
Southern California Library for Social Studies and Research, 6120 S. Vermont Ave., Los Angeles, CA 90044
Southern California, University of, Library, Dept. of Special Collections, University Pk., Los Angeles, CA 90007
Southern California, University of, School of Dentistry Library, 925 W. 34 St., Los Angeles, CA 90007
Southern Historical Collection. *See* North Carolina, University of, Library, Southern Historical Collection
Southern Illinois University Archives, Morris Library, Special Collections, Carbondale, IL 62901
Southern Labor Archives. *See* Georgia State University, Southern Labor Archives
Southern Methodist University, DeGolyer Institute, Dallas, TX 75275
Southern Methodist University Library, Methodist Historical Library, Dallas, TX 75275
Southern Minnesota Historical Center, Mankato State University, Mankato, MN 56001
Southern Mississippi, University of, William David McCain Graduate Library, Box 5148, Southern Sta., Hattiesburg, MS 39401
Southern Oral History Program. *See* North Carolina, University of, Southern Oral History Program
Southern Oregon Historical Society, Box 480, Jacksonville, OR 97530
Southern Utah State College, Special Collections Library, Cedar City, UT 84720
Southwest Collection. *See* Texas Tech University, Southwest Collection
Southwest Minnesota Historical Center, Southwest State University, Marshall, MN 56258
Southwest Museum Research Library, Box 128, Highland Pk., Los Angeles, CA 90042
Southwest State University. *See* Southwest Minnesota Historical Center, Southwest State University
Southwestern Archives and Manuscripts Collection. *See* Southwestern Louisiana, University of, Southwestern Archives and Manuscripts Collection
Southwestern College. *See* Kansas West Conference of the United Methodist Church, Commission on History and Archives, Southwestern College
Southwestern Louisiana, University of, Southwestern Archives and Manuscripts Collection, Box 40831, Lafayette, LA 70504
Southwestern Oregon Community College, Learning Resources Center, Coos Bay, OR 97420
Spalding College Archives, 851 S. Fourth St., Louisville, KY 40203
The Speedwell Village, 333 Speedwell Ave., Morristown, NJ 07960
Spertus College of Judaica, Chicago Jewish Archives, 618 S. Michigan Ave., Chicago, IL 60605

DIRECTORY OF CONTRIBUTING REPOSITORIES

Spokane Public Library, 906 Main Ave. W., Spokane, WA 99201
Springfield Town Library, 43 Main St., Springfield, VT 05156
Stanford University Archives, University Libraries, Stanford, CA 94305
Stanford University, Hoover Institution on War, Revolution and Peace, Stanford, CA 94305
Stanford University Libraries, Dept. of Special Collections, Manuscripts Div., Stanford, CA 94305
Stanford University Medical Center, Lane Medical Library, Stanford, CA 94305
State Historical Society of . . . *See* other part of title, e.g., North Dakota, State Historical Society of
State Historical Society of Missouri. *See* Missouri, University of, Library, Western Historical Manuscripts Collection, State Historical Society Manuscripts
State Library Commission of Iowa. *See* Iowa, State Library Commission of
State of . . . *See* other part of title, e.g., Vermont, State of, Dept. of Libraries
State University College at Buffalo, E. H. Butler Library, Special Collections, 1300 Elmwood Ave., Buffalo, NY 14222
State University College at Geneseo, Milne Library, Geneseo, NY 14454
State University College at Oswego, Penfield Library, Special Collections, Oswego, NY 13126
State University College of Arts and Science, North Country History Center, Plattsburgh, NY 12901
State University of New York at Albany, University Archives, UL B-43, 1400 Washington Ave., Albany, New York 12222
State University of New York at Binghamton, Glenn G. Bartle Library, Special Collections, Binghamton, NY 13901
State University of New York at Buffalo, University Archives, 420 Capen Hall, Amherst, NY 14260
State University of New York at Stony Brook Library, Dept. of Special Collections, Stony Brook, NY 11794
State University of New York College at Brockport, Drake Memorial Library, Brockport, NY 14420
State University of New York College at Potsdam Archives, F. W. Crumb Memorial Library, Potsdam, NY 13676
Staten Island Institute of Arts and Sciences Library, 75 Stuyvesant Pl., Staten Island, NY 10301
Steele County Historical Society, Hope, ND 58046
Stephen F. Austin State University, Ralph W. Steen Library, Special Collections Dept., Box 3055, Nacogdoches, TX 75962
Stephens College, Hugh Stephens Library, Columbia, MO 65215
Stevens Memorial Library, North Andover, MA 01845
Stillman College, William H. Sheppard Library, Tuscaloosa, AL 35401
Stillwater Town Historian, Stillwater, NY 12170
Stockbridge Library Association, Historical Room, Stockbridge, MA 01262
Stockton-San Joaquin County Public Library, 605 N. El Dorado St., Stockton, CA 95202
The Stowe-Day Foundation, Stowe-Day Library, 77 Forest St., Hartford, CT 06105
Stuhr Museum of the Prairie Pioneer, Rte. 2, Box 24, Grand Island, NE 68801
Suffolk County Historical Society, Library & Archives, 300 W. Main St., Riverhead, NY 11901
Suffolk Marine Museum, Montauk Hwy., W. Sayville. Long Island, NY 11796
Sul Ross State University, Archives of the Big Bend, Alpine, TX 79830
Sunnyvale Historical Society and Museum Association, Box 61301, Sunnyvale, CA 94088
SUNY. *See* State University of New York
Suomi College, Finnish American Historical Archives, Hancock, MI 49930
Swan Library Local History Archives, 4 N. Main St., Albion, NY 14411
Swarthmore College, Friends Historical Library, Swarthmore, PA 19081
Swarthmore College Peace Collection, Swarthmore, PA 19081
Sweetwater County Historical Museum, Sweetwater County Courthouse, Box 25, Green River, WY 82935
Syracuse University, George Arents Research Library, University Archives and Manuscripts Collections, Syracuse, NY 13210

Tacoma General Hospital School of Nursing, 314 S. Kay St., Tacoma, WA 98405
Tacoma Public Library, 1102 Tacoma Ave. S., Tacoma, WA 98402
Talladega College Historical Collections, Savery Library, Talladega, AL 35160
Tama County Historical Society Museum, N. Broadway, Toledo, IA 52342
Temple University Libraries, Conwellana-Templana Collection, Philadelphia, PA 19122
Temple University Libraries, Rare Book and Manuscript Collection, Philadelphia, PA 19122
Temple University Libraries, Urban Archives Center, Philadelphia, PA 19122
Tennessee State Library and Archives, Archives and Manuscripts Section, 403 Seventh Ave. N., Nashville, TN 37219
Tennessee, University of, Frank H. McClung Museum, Knoxville, TN 37916
Tennessee, University of, Library, Special Collections, Knoxville, TN 37916
Texas A&I University, John E. Conner Museum, Kingsville, TX 78363
Texas A&M University Library, College Station, TX 77843
Texas at Arlington, University of, Library, Div. of Special Collections, Box 19497, Arlington, TX 76019
Texas at Austin, University of, Archives, Barker Texas History Center, Austin, TX 78712
Texas at Austin, University of, The Humanities Research Center, Box 7219, Austin, TX 78712
Texas at El Paso, University of, Library, Special Collections and Archives, El Paso, TX 79968
Texas Center for Fashion Studies. *See* North Texas State University, Texas Center for Fashion Studies, Industrial Training Laboratory
The Texas Collection. *See* Baylor University, The Texas Collection
Texas History Research Library. *See* Daughters of the Republic of Texas, Texas History Research Library
Texas Labor Archives. *See* Texas at Arlington, University of, Library, Div. of Special Collectons
Texas Political History Collection. *See* Texas at Arlington, University of, Library, Div. of Special Collections
Texas State Archives. *See* Texas State Library, Archives Div.
Texas State Library, Archives Div., Box 12927, Capitol Sta., Austin, TX 78711
Texas Tech University, Southwest Collection, Box 4090, Lubbock, TX 79409
Texas, University of, Archives. *See* Texas at Austin, University of, Archives, Barker Texas History Center
Texas, University of, Medical Branch, Moody Medical Library, Galveston, TX 77550
Tioga County Historical Society Museum, 110 Front St., Owego, NY 13827
Tippecanoe County Historical Association, 909 South St., Lafayette, IN 47901
Toledo-Lucas County Public Library, 325 Michigan St., Toledo, OH 43624
Towson State University Archives, Baltimore, MD 21204
Trenton, Free Public Library of the City of, 120 Academy St., Trenton, NJ 08607
Trinity College Archives, Library, Hartford, CT 06106
Trinity College Archives, Michigan Ave. & Franklin Sts. N.E., Washington, DC 20017
Trinity College, Watkinson Library, Hartford, CT 06106
Trinity Episcopal Church, 1668 Bush St., San Francisco, CA 94109
Troy-Miami County Local History Room, 301 W. Main St., Troy, OH 45373
Truman Library. *See* Harry S. Truman Library
Tulane University Archives, Special Collections Div., Howard-Tilton Memorial Library, New Orleans, LA 70118
Tulane University, Special Collections Div., Howard-Tilton Memorial Library, New Orleans, LA 70118
Tulane University, William Ransom Hogan Jazz Archive, Special Collections Div., Howard-Tilton Memorial Library, New Orleans, LA 70118
Tulsa County Historical Society, 400 Civic Center, Tulsa, OK 74103
Tusculum College Archives, Greeneville, TN 37743
Tuskegee Institute Archives, Hollis Burke Frissell Library, Tuskegee Institute, AL 36088
Tyrrell Historical Library, Box 3827, Beaumont, TX 77704

UCLA. *See* California, Los Angeles, University of
UCLA Film Archives. *See* California, Los Angeles, University of, UCLA Film, Television, and Radio Archives, Dept. of Theater Arts
UCLA Radio Archives. *See* California, Los Angeles, University of, UCLA Film, Television, and Radio Archives, Dept. of Theater Arts
Union College Library, Lincoln, NE 68506
Union County Historical Society, Court House, Lewisburg, PA 17837
United Brethren Church Archives, 302 Lake St., Box 650, Huntington, IN 46750
United Church of Christ, Connecticut Conference Office, 125 Sherman St., Hartford, CT 06105
United Methodist Central Illinois Conference Commission on Archives and History, 1211 N. Park St., Box 2050, Bloomington, IL 61701
United Methodist Church Archives, Iowa Wesleyan College Archives, Mt. Pleasant, IA 52641
The United Methodist Church, Commission on Archives and History, Box 488, Lake Junaluska, NC 28745
United Methodist Church, Louisiana Conference Archives. *See* Centenary College of Louisiana, Magale Library
United Methodist Church, Rocky Mountain Conference Archives. *See* Iliff School of Theology, Ira J. Taylor Library, Archives of the Rocky Mountain Conference of the United Methodist Church
United Methodist Historical Center, Lucas Bldg., Nebraska Wesleyan University, Lincoln, NE 68504
United Methodist Historical Collection and Library. *See* Baker University Library, United Methodist Historical Collection and Library
United Nations Archives, Rm. Q-302A, New York, NY 10017
United Negro College Fund Archives, 500 E. 62 St., New York, NY 10021
United States Air Force Historical Repository. *See* Albert F. Simpson Historical Research Center
United States Army Aviation Museum, Bldg. 6007, Ft. Rucker, AL 36362
United States Army Military History Institute, Carlisle Barracks, PA 17013
United States Army War College. *See* United States Army Military History Institute
United States Commission on Civil Rights, National Civil Rights Library, 1121 Vermont Ave. N.W., #709, Washington, DC 20037
United States Marine Corps, Headquarters, History and Museums Div. (Code HD), Washington, DC 20380
United States Naval Academy Museum, Annapolis, MD 21402
United States Naval Institute, Oral History Program, Annapolis, MD 21402
University of . . . *See* other part of title, e.g., Wisconsin-Madison, University of
Urban Archives Center. *See* Temple University Libraries, Urban Archives Center

Ursuline Convent of the Sacred Heart, 2413 Collingwood Blvd., Toledo, OH 43620
Ursuline Sisters, 1026 N. Douglas, Belleville, IL 62221
Ursuline Sisters Convent, Ursuline Academy, Paola, KS 66071
Ursuline Sisters of the Immaculate Conception, Archives, 3105 Lexington Rd., Louisville, KY 40206
Utah State Historical Society, 307 W. Second S., Suite 1000, Salt Lake City, UT 84101
Utah State University, Merrill Library, Special Collections, UMC 30, Logan, UT 84322
Utah, University of, Marriott Library, Special Collections, Salt Lake City, UT 84112

Van Buren County Historical Society Museum, Hartford, MI 49045
Vandalia Historical Society, 307 N. Sixth St., Vandalia, IL 62471
Vanderbilt University Archives. *See* Joint University Libraries, Special Collections Dept.
Vermont Historical Society, 109 State St., Pavilion Bldg., Montpelier, VT 05602
Vermont, State of, Agency of Administration, Public Records Div., 133 State St., Montpelier, VT 05602
Vermont, State of, Dept. of Libraries, 111 State St., Montpelier, VT 05602
Vermont, University of, Archives, Rm. 427, Waterman Bldg., Burlington, VT 05401
Victorian Society of Maine Women, Morse-Libby-Holmes Mansion, 109 Danforth St., Portland, ME 04101
Vigo County Public Library, Special Collections, 222 Seventh St. N., Terre Haute, IN 47807
Village of . . . *See* other part of title, e.g., Round Lake, Village of
Vincennes University, Byron R. Lewis Historical Collections Library, Vincennes, IN 47591
Virginia Commonwealth University, James Branch Cabell Library, Special Collections Dept., 901 W. Franklin St., Richmond, VA 23284
Virginia State Library, Richmond, VA 23219
Virginia, University of, Library, Manuscript Dept., Charlottesville, VA 22901
Virginiana Collection. *See* Arlington County Department of Libraries, Virginiana Collection
Visitation Convent, 900 Alta Vista, Dubuque, IA 52001
Visitation, Monastery of the, 2055 Ridgedale Dr., Snellville, GA 30278
Visitation of Holy Mary, Monastery of the, 5820 City Ave., Philadelphia, PA 19131
Visual Studies Workshop Research Center, 31 Prince St., Rochester, NY 14607
Voorhees College Archives, Denmark, SC 29042

Wabash College, Lilly Library, Crawfordsville, IN 47933
Wake Forest University, Z. Smith Reynolds Library, North Carolina Baptist Historical Collection, Box 7777, Reynolda Sta., Winston-Salem, NC 27109
Wapello County Historical Society, 402 Chester Ave., Ottumwa, IA 52501
Washburn University, Mabee Library, Archives, Topeka, KS 66621
Washington Memorial Library, Genealogical and Historical Room, 1180 Washington Ave., Macon, GA 31201
Washington State Archives, Dept. of General Administration, Olympia, WA 98502
Washington State Historical Society, 315 N. Stadium Way, Tacoma, WA 98403
Washington State Library, Washington-Northwest Room, Olympia, WA 98504
Washington State Regional Archives. *See* Eastern Washington University, Kennedy Memorial Library, Regional Depository, Washington State Archives
Washington State University Libraries, Manuscripts, Archives, & Special Collections, Pullman, WA 99163
Washington, University of, Libraries, FM-25, University Archives and Manuscripts Div., Seattle, WA 98195
Washington University, School of Medicine Library Archives, 4850 Scott Ave., St. Louis, MO 63110
Waterloo Library and Historical Society, Waterloo, NY 13165
Waterville Historical Society, 64 Silver St., Waterville, ME 04901
Watkins Mill Historic Site, Rte. 2, Box 270, Lawson, MO 64062
Waukegan Historical Society, 1917 N. Sheridan Rd., Waukegan, IL 60085
Waukesha County Historical Museum, Court House Annex, 101 W. Main St., Waukesha, WI 53186
Wayland Historical Society, 12 Cochituate Rd., Wayland, MA 01778
Wayne Historical Commission, One Town Sq., Wayne, MI 48184
Wayne State University, Archives of Labor and Urban Affairs, Walter P. Reuther Library, Detroit, MI 48202
Wayne State University Archives, Walter P. Reuther Library, Detroit, MI 48202
Weaverville Free Library, Weaverville, CA 96093
Wellesley College Archives, Margaret Clapp Library, Wellesley, MA 02181
Wells College Archives, Long Library, Aurora, NY 13026
Wenham Historical Association, Timothy Pickering Library, 132 Main St., Wenham, MA 01984
Wesleyan Archives and Museum. *See* North Alabama, University of, Wesleyan Archives and Museum
Wesleyan College, Candler Alumnae Center, Macon, GA 31201
Wesleyan University Archives. *See* Wesleyan University, Olin Library
Wesleyan University, Collection on Legal Change, Middletown, CT 06457
Wesleyan University, Olin Library, Middletown, CT 06457
West Central Minnesota Historical Center, Briggs Library, University of Minnesota-Morris, Morris, MN 56267
West Florida, University of, John C. Pace Library, Special Collections, Pensacola, FL 32504
West Virginia Collection. *See* West Virginia University Library, West Virginia Collection
West Virginia University Library, West Virginia Collection, Morgantown, WV 26505
West Virginia Wesleyan College, A. M. Pfeiffer Library, Buckhannon, WV 26201
Westbrook College, Maine Women Writers Collection, Portland, ME 04103
Westerly Public Library, Westerly, RI 02891
Western Historical Collections. *See* Colorado, University of, Libraries, Western Historical Collections
Western Historical Manuscript Collection-St. Louis. *See* Missouri-St. Louis, University of, Western Historical Manuscript Collection-St. Louis
Western Historical Manuscripts Collection. *See* Missouri, University of, Library, Western Historical Manuscripts Collection, State Historical Society Manuscripts
Western History Collections. *See* Oklahoma, University of, Western History Collections
Western History Department. *See* Denver Public Library, Western History Dept.
Western Illinois University Libraries, Archives and Special Collections, Macomb, IL 61455
Western Jewish History Center, Judah L. Magnes Memorial Museum, 2911 Russell St., Berkeley, CA 94705
Western Kentucky University, Kentucky Library, Manuscript Div., Bowling Green, KY 42101
Western Maryland College Archives, College Library, Westminster, MD 21157
Western Michigan University, Archives & Regional History Collections, Kalamazoo, MI 49008
Western New York Conference of the United Methodist Church, Archives & Library, Box 156, Lyndonville, NY 14098
Western Pennsylvania, Historical Society of, 4338 Bigelow Blvd., Pittsburgh, PA 15213
The Western Reserve Historical Society, 10825 East Blvd., Cleveland, OH 44106
Western Theological Seminary of the Reformed Church in America, Beardslee Library, Holland, MI 49423
Western Washington University, Music Library, Bellingham, WA 98225
Westtown School, Alumni Association, Westtown, PA 19395
Westwood Public Library, Westwood, MA 02090
Wheaton College Archives, Norton, MA 02766
White-Westinghouse Appliance Company, 930 Ft. Duquesne Blvd., Pittsburgh, PA 15230
Whiting Historical Studies, Stiles Archives, 338 Fountain St., Cherokee, IA 51012
Whitman College, Penrose Memorial Library, Eells Northwest Collection, Walla Walla, WA 99362
Whitney Museum of American Art Library, 945 Madison Ave., New York, NY 10021
Wichita Historical Museum, 3751 E. Douglas, Wichita, KS 67218
Wichita Public Library, 223 S. Main St., Wichita, KS 67202
Wichita State University, Ablah Library, Dept. of Special Collections, Wichita, KS 67208
Wilkes College, Eugene Shedden Farley Library, Willkes-Barre, PA 18703
Willa Cather Historical Center, Red Cloud, NE 68970
Willard Library, 7 W. Van Buren St., Battle Creek, MI 49016
Willard Library of Evansville, 21 First Ave., Evansville, IN 47710
William and Mary, College of, Earl Gregg Swem Library, Manuscripts Dept., Williamsburg, VA 23185
William E. Wiener Oral History Library. *See* American Jewish Committee, William E. Wiener Oral History Library
William Livingston, Papers of. *See* New York University, Papers of William Livingston
William Ransom Hogan Jazz Archive. *See* Tulane University, William Ransom Hogan Jazz Archive, Special Collections Div., Howard-Tilton Memorial Library
Williams College Library, Williamsiana Collection, Williamstown, MA 01267
Williams College, Roper Public Opinion Research Center, Box 624, Williamstown, MA 01267
Williamstown Public Library, House of Local History, Rte. 2, Williamstown, MA 01267
Wilmette Historical Museum, 565 Hunter Rd., Wilmette, IL 60091
Wilson College Library, Chambersburg, PA 17201
Winchendon Historical Society, 50 Pleasant St., Winchendon, MA 01475
Winneshiek County Historical Society Archives. *See* Luther College Library
Winona County Historical Society, 160 Johnson St., Winona, MN 55987
Winona State University. *See* Southeast Minnesota Historical Center, Winona State University
Winthrop College Archives, Dacus Library, Rock Hill, SC 29733
Wisconsin Center for Film and Theater Research. *See* Wisconsin-Madison, University of, Wisconsin Center for Film and Theater Research
Wisconsin-Eau Claire, University of, Area Research Center and University Archives, William D. McIntyre Library, Eau Claire, WI 54701
Wisconsin-La Crosse, University of, Area Research Center, Murphy Library, La Crosse, WI 54601
Wisconsin-Madison, University of, Archives, Rm. 443F, Memorial Library, Madison, WI 53706
Wisconsin-Madison, University of, Wisconsin Center for Film and Theater Research, 6039 Vilas Communication Hall, Madison WI 53706
Wisconsin-Milwaukee, University of, Area Research Center, The Library, Milwaukee, WI 53201
Wisconsin-Parkside, University of, University Archives and Area Research Center, Kenosha, WI 53141

DIRECTORY OF CONTRIBUTING REPOSITORIES

Wisconsin-River Falls, University of, Area Research Center, River Falls, WI 54022
Wisconsin, State Historical Society of, Archives Div., 816 State St., Madison, WI 53706
Wisconsin-Stevens Point, University of, University Archives, Stevens Point, WI 54481
Wofford College. *See also* South Carolina Conference of the United Methodist Church, Historical Society of the, Wofford College
Wofford College Archives, Spartanburg, SC 29301
Woman Geographers, Society of, 1619 New Hampshire Ave. N.W., Washington, DC 20009
Woman's Christian Temperance Union National Headquarters, Frances Willard Memorial Library, 1730 Chicago Ave., Evanston, IL 60201
Women in Communications, Inc., Box 9561, Austin, TX 78766
Women Library Workers, Box 9052, Berkeley, CA 94709
Women's Clubs, General Federation of. *See* General Federation of Women's Clubs
Women's Council of Realtors® of the National Association of Realtors®, 430 N. Michigan Ave., Chicago, IL 60611
Women's History Archives. *See* Brigham Young University, Harold B. Young Library, Div. of Archives and Manuscripts, Women's History Archives
Worcester Historical Society, 39 Salisbury St., Worcester, MA 01608
Workingmen's Institute Library, Box 368, New Harmony, IN 47631
Wright State University Library, Archives and Special Collections, 7751 Colonel Glenn Hwy., Dayton, OH 45431
Wyandotte County Historical Society, 631 N. 126 St., Bonner Springs, KS 66012
Wyoming State Archives and Historical Department, State Office Bldg., Cheyenne, WY 82002
Wyoming, University of, Library, American Heritage Center, Laramie, WY 82071

Yakima Valley Museum and Historical Association, 2105 Tieton Dr., Yakima, WA 98902
Yale Divinity School Library, 409 Prospect St., New Haven, CT 06510
Yale University, John Herrick Jackson Music Library, 98 Wall St., New Haven, CT 06520
Yates County Genealogical and Historical Society, 200 Main St., Penn Yan, NY 14527
Yellowstone National Park Library and Archives, Mammoth Hot Springs Museum, Yellowstone National Park, WY 82190
YMCA. *See* National Board of Young Men's Christian Associations, Bowne Historical Library
York County Historical Association, York, NE 68467
York County Historical Society, 250 E. Market St., York, PA 17403
Young Men's Christian Associations. *See* National Board of Young Men's Christian Associations, Bowne Historical Library
Young Women's Christian Association, Archives of the National Board, 600 Lexington Ave., New York, NY 10022
Yuma Territorial Prison State Historic Park, Box 792, Yuma, AZ 85364
YWCA. *See* Young Women's Christian Association, Archives of the National Board

Zion Historical Society, 1300 Shiloh, Zion, IL 60099